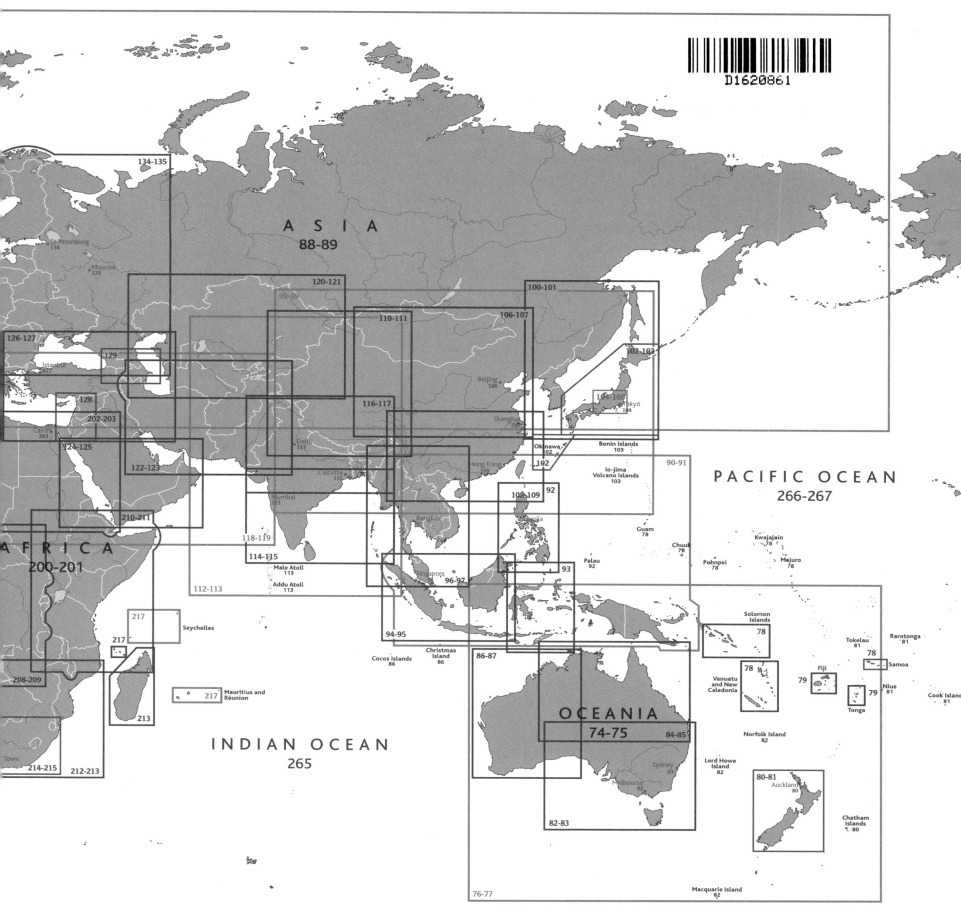

ARCTIC OCEAN
268

D1620861

ASIA
88-89

St. Petersburg
134

Moscow
139

134-135

126-127

129

128

202-203

124-125

122-123

210-211

AFRICA
200-201

208-209

217

217

Seychelles

217

Mauritius and
Réunion

213

120-121

98-99

110-111

106-107

100-101

102-103

104-105
Tōkyō
104

Beijing
106

Shanghai
107

116-117

Delhi
117

Calcutta
115

Mumbai
115

Bangkok

Okinawa
102

102

Hong Kong
109

108-109

92

Io-jima
Volcano Islands
103

Bonin Islands
103

90-91

PACIFIC OCEAN
266-267

118-119

114-115

Male Atoll
113

Addu Atoll
113

112-113

94-95

Cocos Islands
86

Christmas
Island
86

Singapore

96-97

93

86-87

Guam
78

Palau
92

Manila

Chuuk
78

Pohnpei
78

Kwajalein
78

Majuro
78

Solomon
Islands
78

Vanuatu
and New
Caledonia

78

79

Fiji

Norfolk Island
82

Lord Howe
Island
82

Tokelau
81

Rarotonga
81

Samoa

Niue
81

Tonga

Cook Islands
81

INDIAN OCEAN
265

OCEANIA
74-75

84-85

Sydney
83

Melbourne
82

80-81

Auckland
80

Chatham
Islands
80

82-83

76-77

Macquarie Island
82

KEY TO MAP PAGES

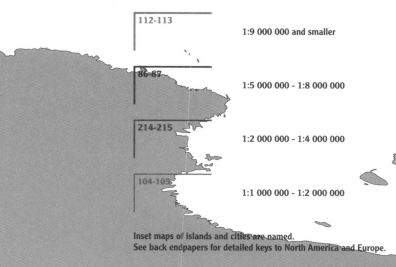

112-113	1:9 000 000 and smaller
86-87	1:5 000 000 – 1:8 000 000
214-215	1:2 000 000 – 1:4 000 000
104-105	1:1 000 000 – 1:2 000 000

ANTARCTICA
262-263

Inset maps of islands and cities are named.
See back endpapers for detailed keys to North America and Europe.

THE TIMES

CONCISE
ATLAS
OF THE
WORLD

Times Books, 77-85 Fulham Palace Road, London W6 8JB

First Edition 1972
Second Edition 1975
Third Edition 1978
Fourth Edition 1980
Fifth Edition 1986
Sixth Edition 1992
Seventh Edition 1995
Eighth Edition 2000
Ninth Edition 2004

Tenth Edition 2006

This edition produced for The Book People Ltd,
Hall Wood Avenue, Haydock, St Helens WA11 9UL

Copyright © Times Books Group Ltd 2006

Maps © Collins Bartholomew Ltd 2006

The Times is a registered trademark of Times Newspapers Ltd

Printed and bound in Thailand

British Library Cataloguing in Publication Data
A catalogue record for this book is available from the British Library

ISBN-13 978-0-00-777965-9
ISBN-10 0-00-777965-8

All mapping in this atlas is generated from Collins Bartholomew digital
databases. Collins Bartholomew, the UK's leading independent
geographical information supplier, can provide a digital, custom, and
premium mapping service to a variety of markets. For further information:
Tel: +44 (0) 141 306 3752
e-mail: collinsbartholomew@harpercollins.co.uk

www.harpercollins.co.uk
Visit the book lover's website

THE TIMES

CONCISE

ATLAS
OF THE
WORLD

TED SMART

THE WORLD TODAY

GEOGRAPHICAL INFORMATION

ATLAS OF THE WORLD

AFRICA

Pages	Title	Scale

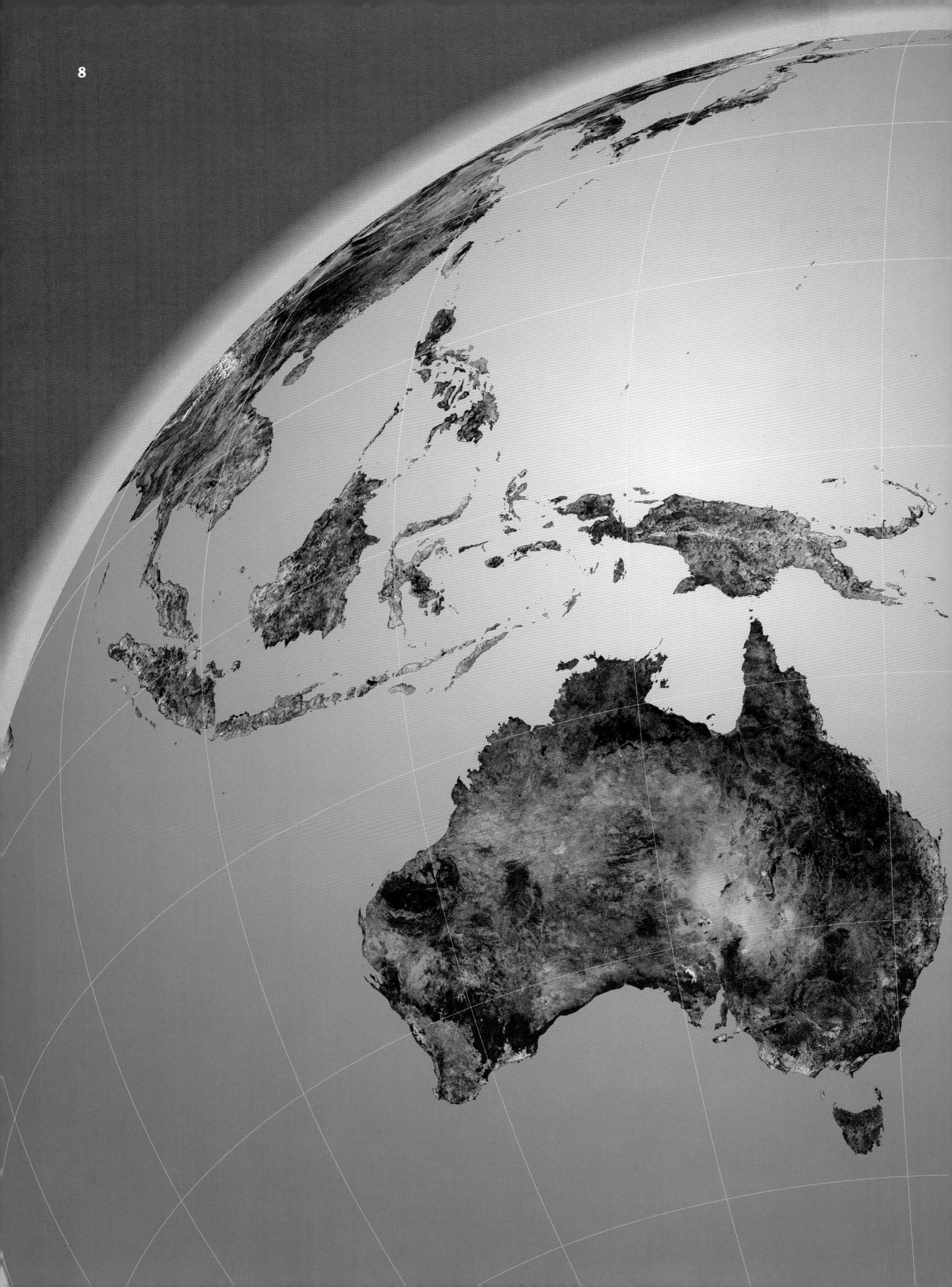

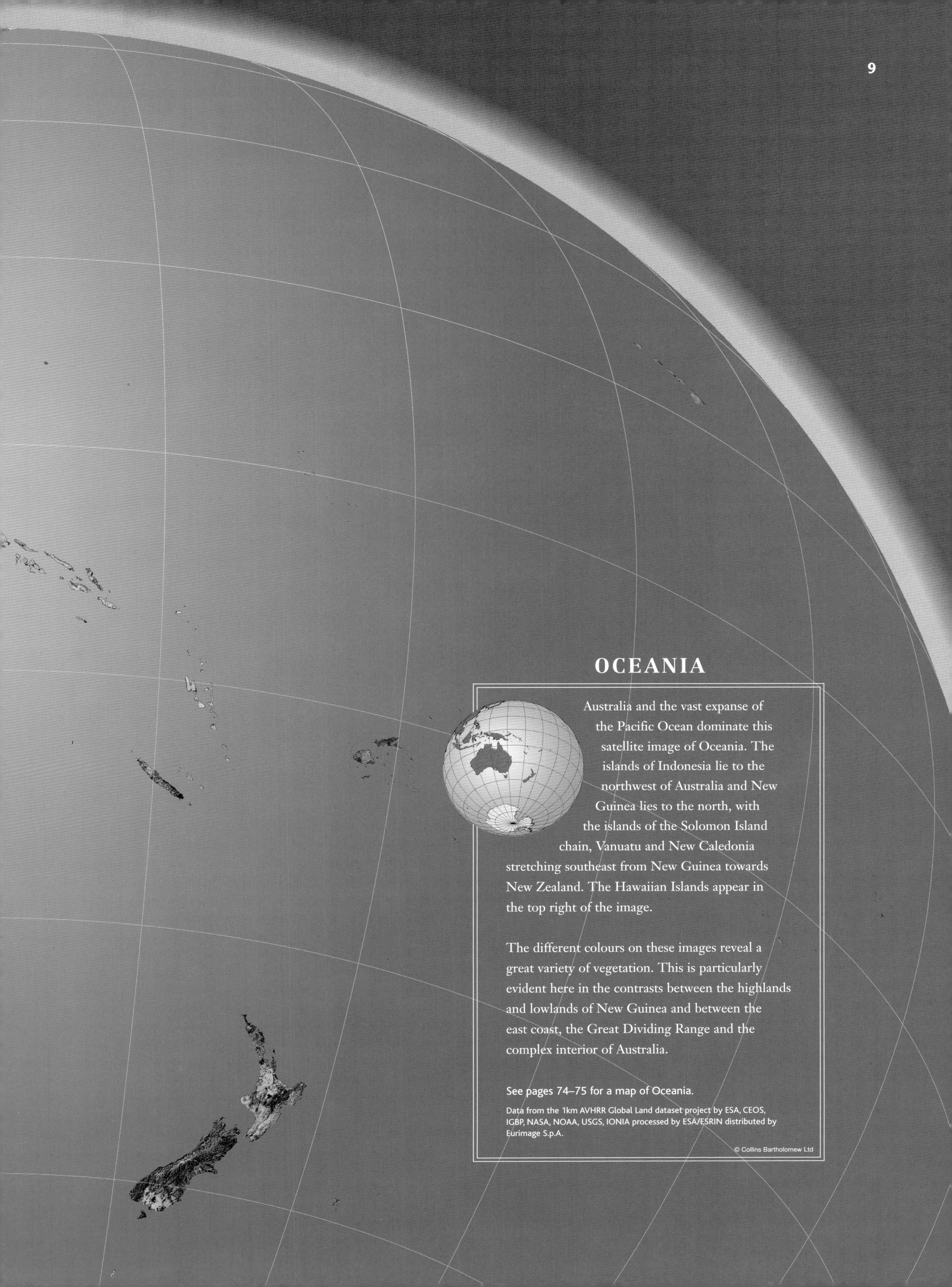

OCEANIA

Australia and the vast expanse of
the Pacific Ocean dominate this
satellite image of Oceania. The
islands of Indonesia lie to the
northwest of Australia and New
Guinea lies to the north, with
the islands of the Solomon Island
chain, Vanuatu and New Caledonia
stretching southeast from New Guinea towards
New Zealand. The Hawaiian Islands appear in
the top right of the image.

The different colours on these images reveal a
great variety of vegetation. This is particularly
evident here in the contrasts between the highlands
and lowlands of New Guinea and between the
east coast, the Great Dividing Range and the
complex interior of Australia.

See pages 74–75 for a map of Oceania.

Data from the 1km AVHRR Global Land dataset project by ESA, CEOS,
IGBP, NASA, NOAA, USGS, IONIA processed by ESA/ESRIN distributed by
Eurimage S.p.A.

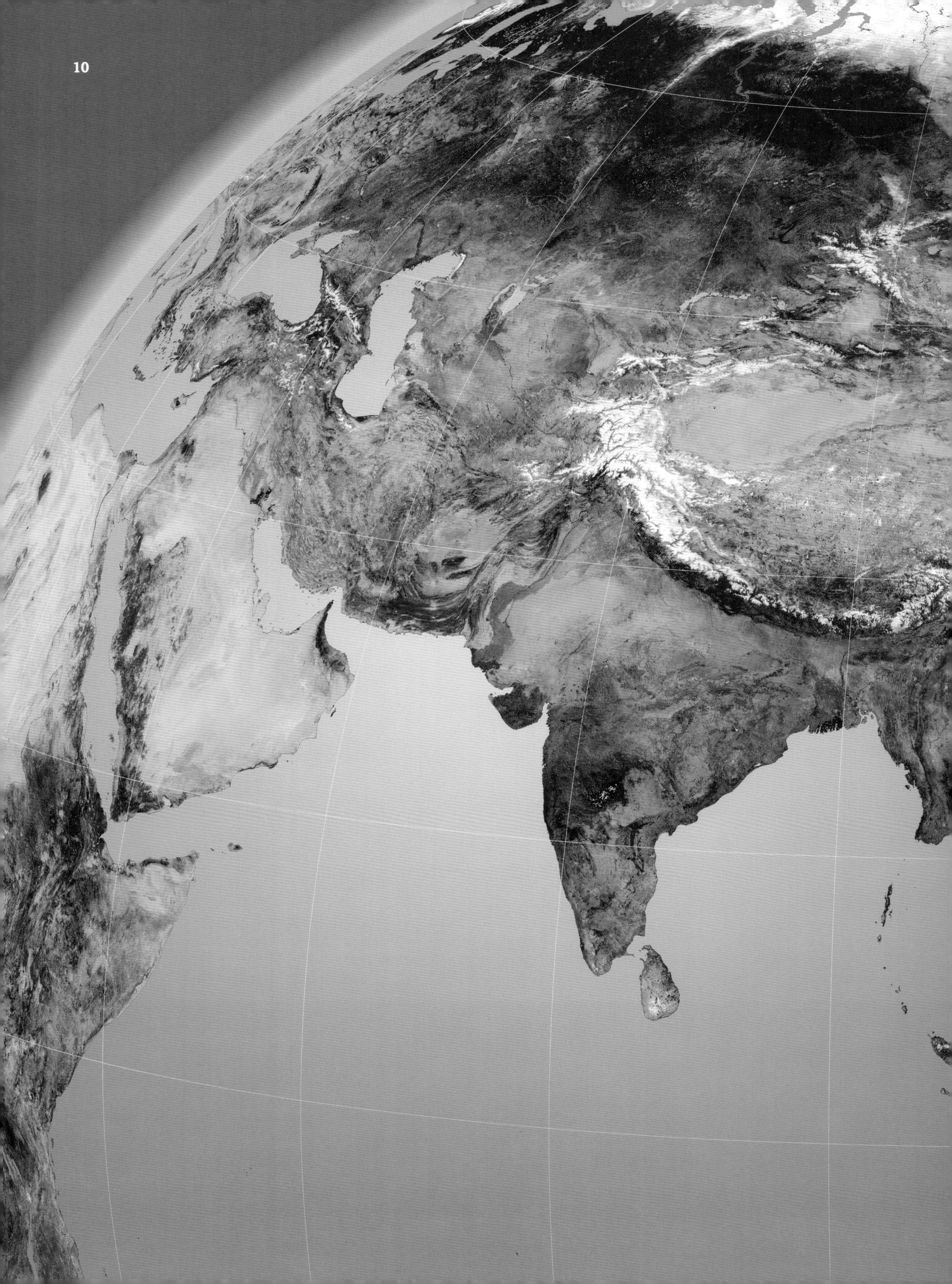

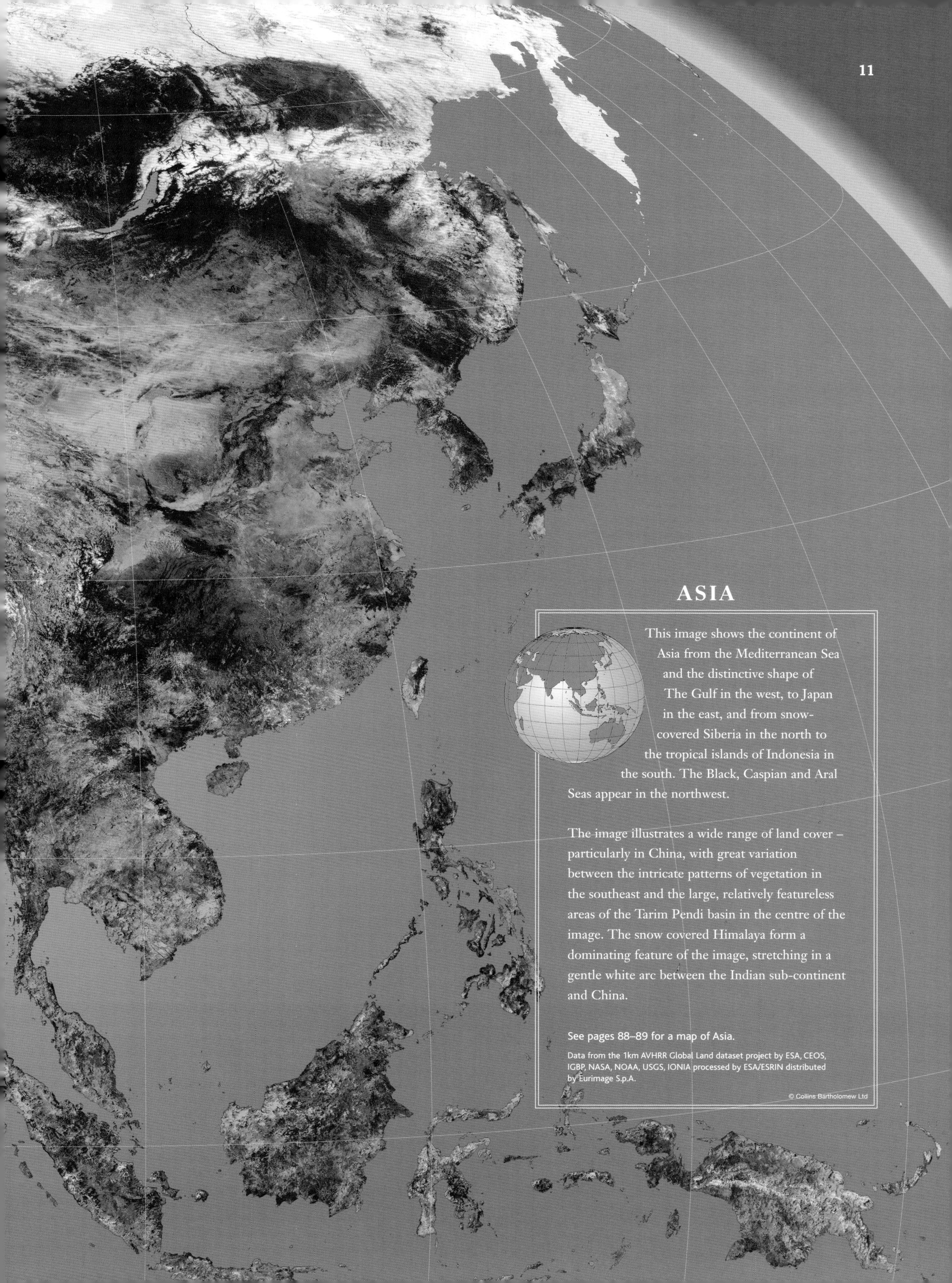

ASIA

This image shows the continent of
Asia from the Mediterranean Sea
and the distinctive shape of
The Gulf in the west, to Japan
in the east, and from snow-
covered Siberia in the north to
the tropical islands of Indonesia in
the south. The Black, Caspian and Aral
Seas appear in the northwest.

The image illustrates a wide range of land cover –
particularly in China, with great variation
between the intricate patterns of vegetation in
the southeast and the large, relatively featureless
areas of the Tarim Pendi basin in the centre of the
image. The snow covered Himalaya form a
dominating feature of the image, stretching in a
gentle white arc between the Indian sub-continent
and China.

See pages 88–89 for a map of Asia.

Data from the 1km AVHRR Global Land dataset project by ESA, CEOS,
IGBP, NASA, NOAA, USGS, IONIA processed by ESA/ESRIN distributed
by Eurimage S.p.A.

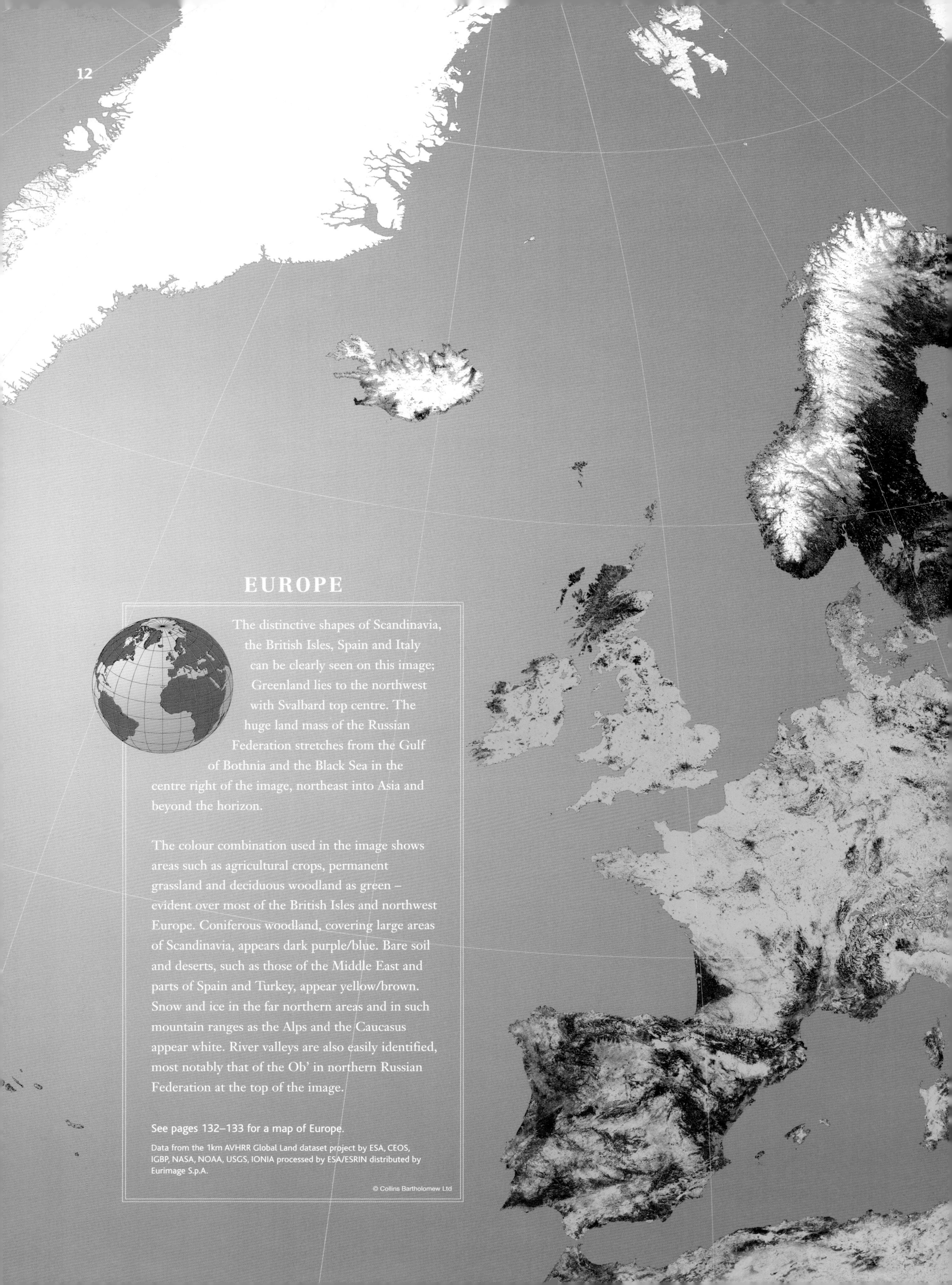

EUROPE

The distinctive shapes of Scandinavia, the British Isles, Spain and Italy can be clearly seen on this image; Greenland lies to the northwest with Svalbard top centre. The huge land mass of the Russian Federation stretches from the Gulf of Bothnia and the Black Sea in the centre right of the image, northeast into Asia and beyond the horizon.

The colour combination used in the image shows areas such as agricultural crops, permanent grassland and deciduous woodland as green – evident over most of the British Isles and northwest Europe. Coniferous woodland, covering large areas of Scandinavia, appears dark purple/blue. Bare soil and deserts, such as those of the Middle East and parts of Spain and Turkey, appear yellow/brown. Snow and ice in the far northern areas and in such mountain ranges as the Alps and the Caucasus appear white. River valleys are also easily identified, most notably that of the Ob' in northern Russian Federation at the top of the image.

See pages 132–133 for a map of Europe.

Data from the 1km AVHRR Global Land dataset project by ESA, CEOS, IGBP, NASA, NOAA, USGS, IONIA processed by ESA/ESRIN distributed by Eurimage S.p.A.

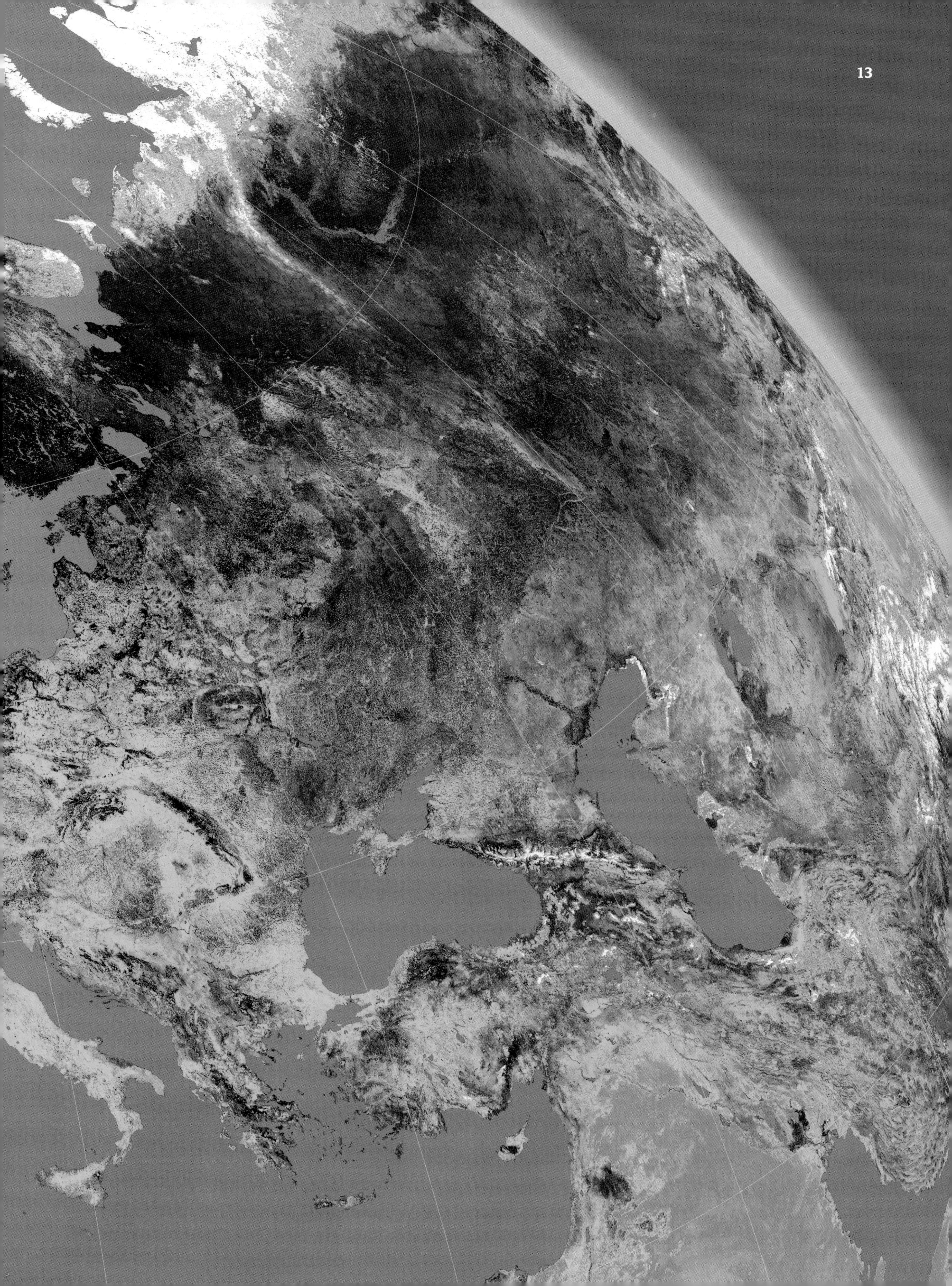

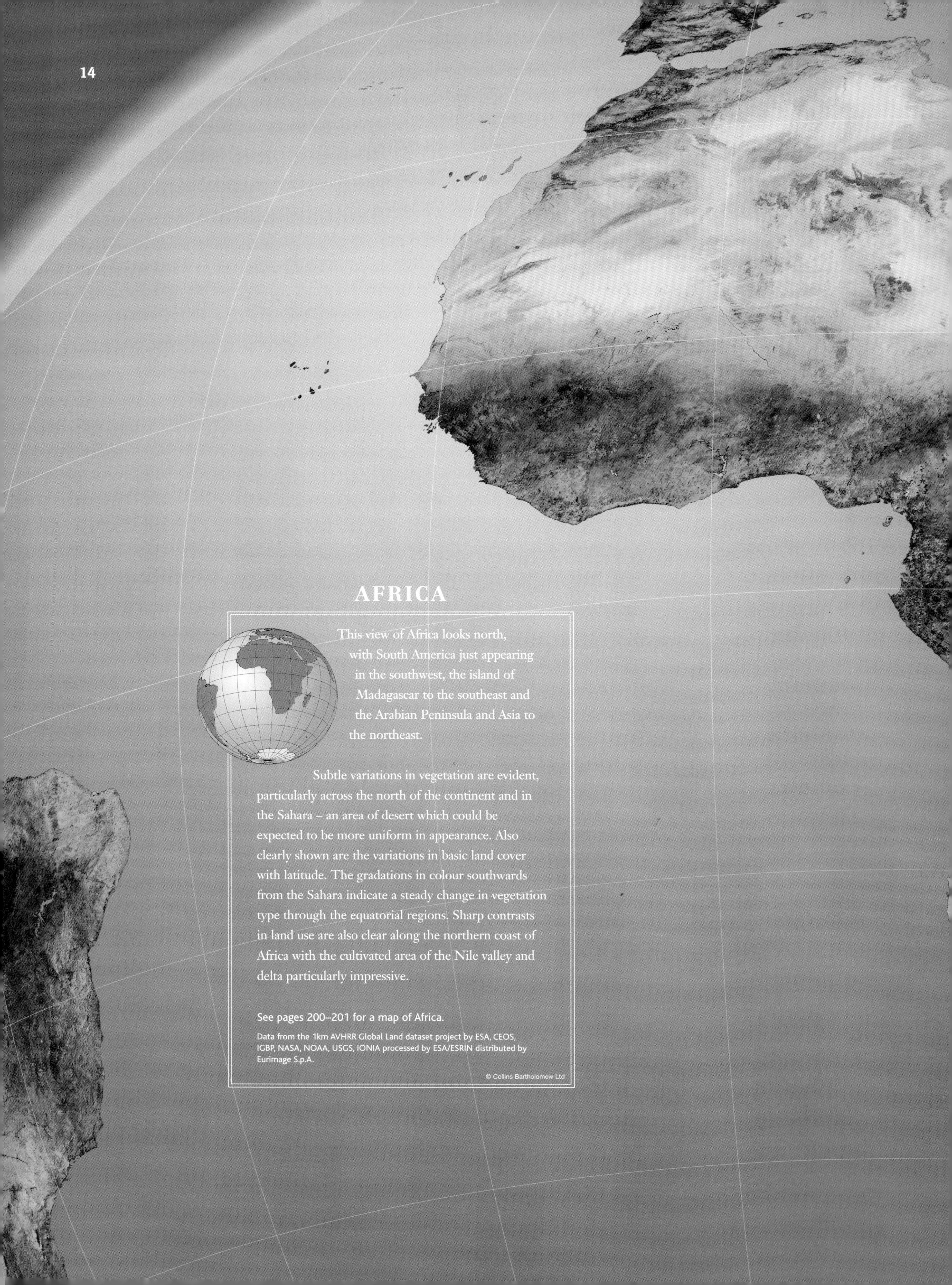

AFRICA

This view of Africa looks north, with South America just appearing in the southwest, the island of Madagascar to the southeast and the Arabian Peninsula and Asia to the northeast.

Subtle variations in vegetation are evident, particularly across the north of the continent and in the Sahara – an area of desert which could be expected to be more uniform in appearance. Also clearly shown are the variations in basic land cover with latitude. The gradations in colour southwards from the Sahara indicate a steady change in vegetation type through the equatorial regions. Sharp contrasts in land use are also clear along the northern coast of Africa with the cultivated area of the Nile valley and delta particularly impressive.

See pages 200–201 for a map of Africa.

Data from the 1km AVHRR Global Land dataset project by ESA, CEOS, IGBP, NASA, NOAA, USGS, IONIA processed by ESA/ESRIN distributed by Eurimage S.p.A.

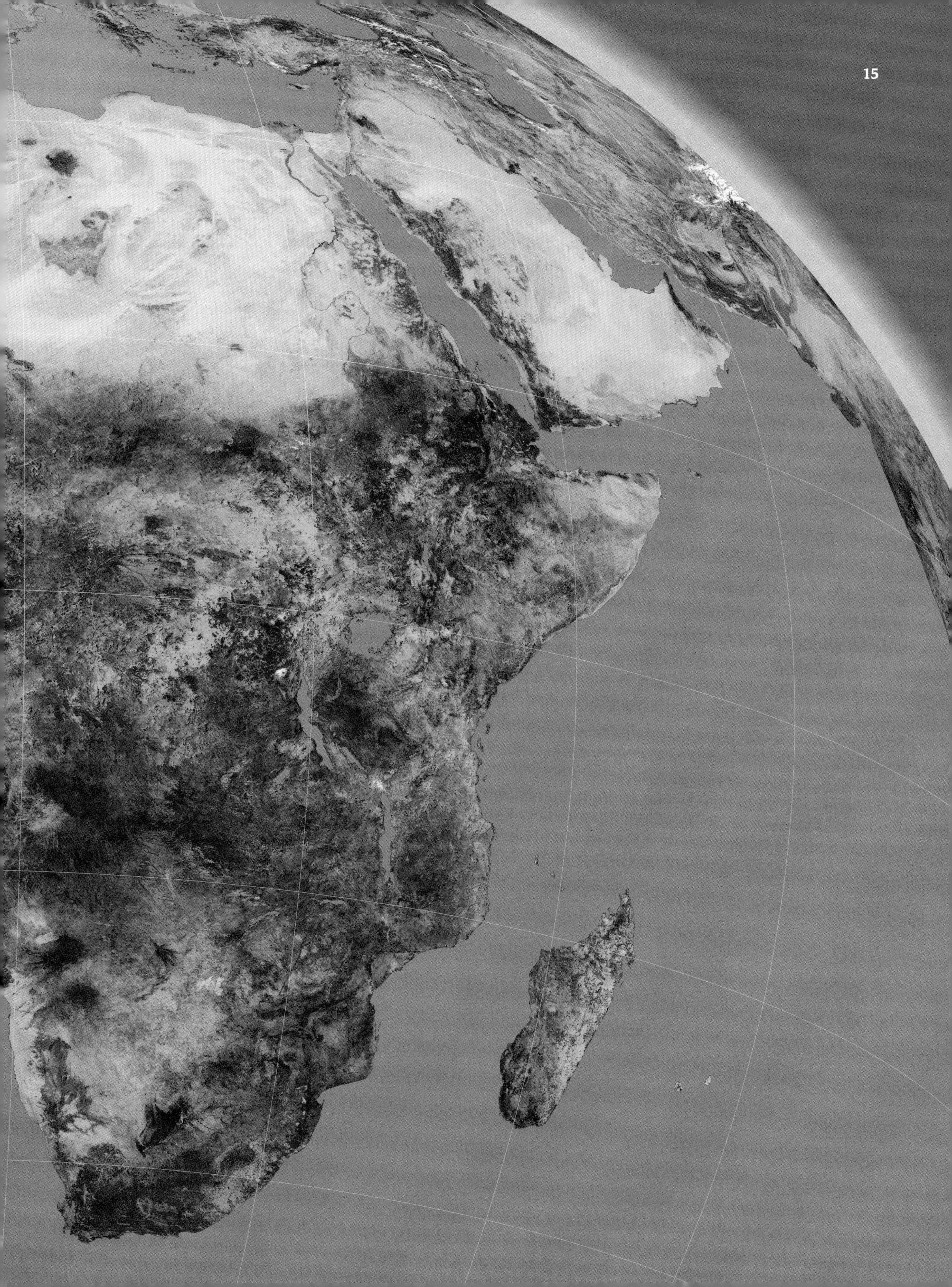

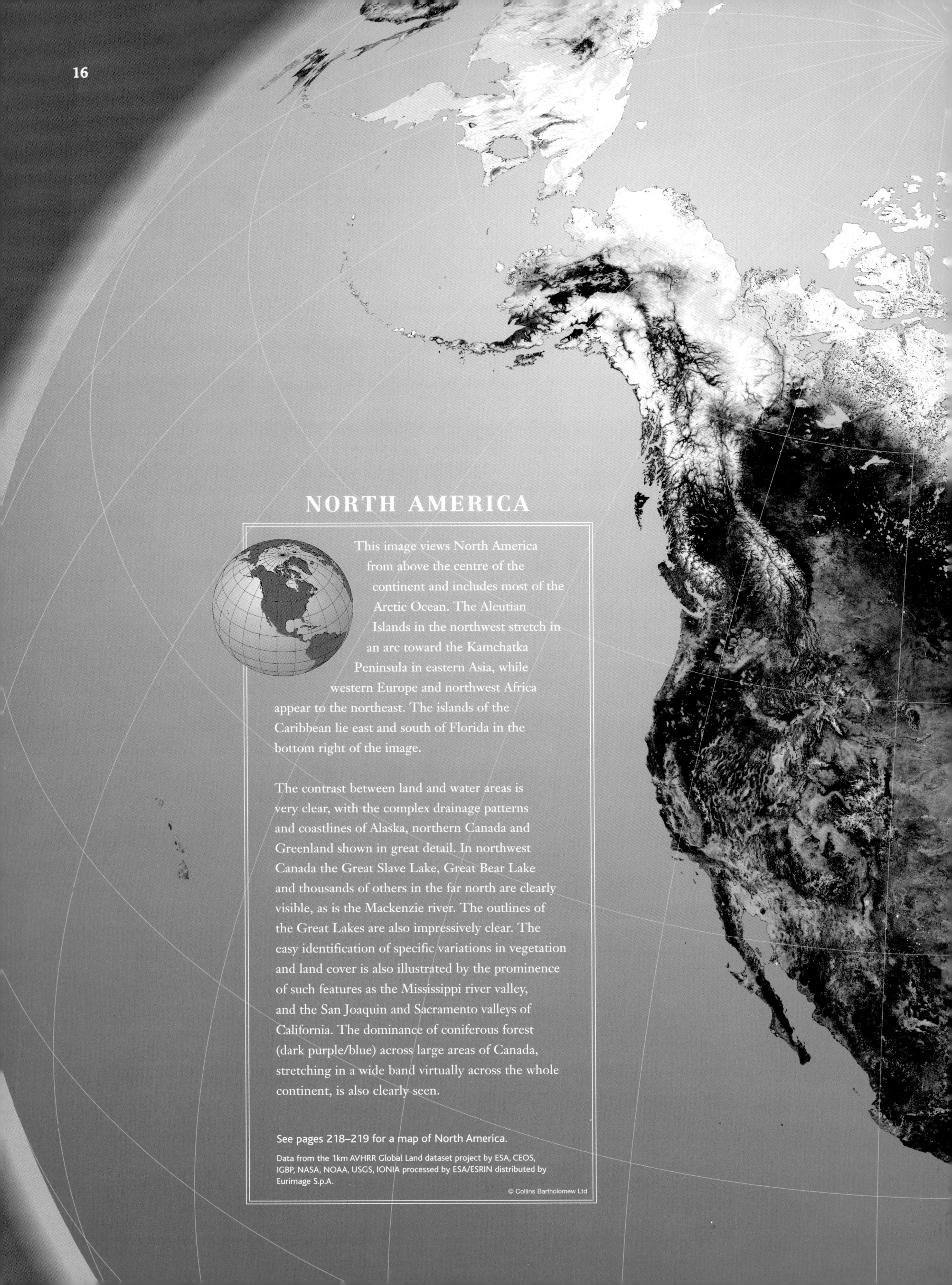

NORTH AMERICA

This image views North America from above the centre of the continent and includes most of the Arctic Ocean. The Aleutian Islands in the northwest stretch in an arc toward the Kamchatka Peninsula in eastern Asia, while western Europe and northwest Africa appear to the northeast. The islands of the Caribbean lie east and south of Florida in the bottom right of the image.

The contrast between land and water areas is very clear, with the complex drainage patterns and coastlines of Alaska, northern Canada and Greenland shown in great detail. In northwest Canada the Great Slave Lake, Great Bear Lake and thousands of others in the far north are clearly visible, as is the Mackenzie river. The outlines of the Great Lakes are also impressively clear. The easy identification of specific variations in vegetation and land cover is also illustrated by the prominence of such features as the Mississippi river valley, and the San Joaquin and Sacramento valleys of California. The dominance of coniferous forest (dark purple/blue) across large areas of Canada, stretching in a wide band virtually across the whole continent, is also clearly seen.

See pages 218–219 for a map of North America.

Data from the 1km AVHRR Global Land dataset project by ESA, CEOS, IGBP, NASA, NOAA, USGS, IONIA processed by ESA/ESRIN distributed by Eurimage S.p.A.

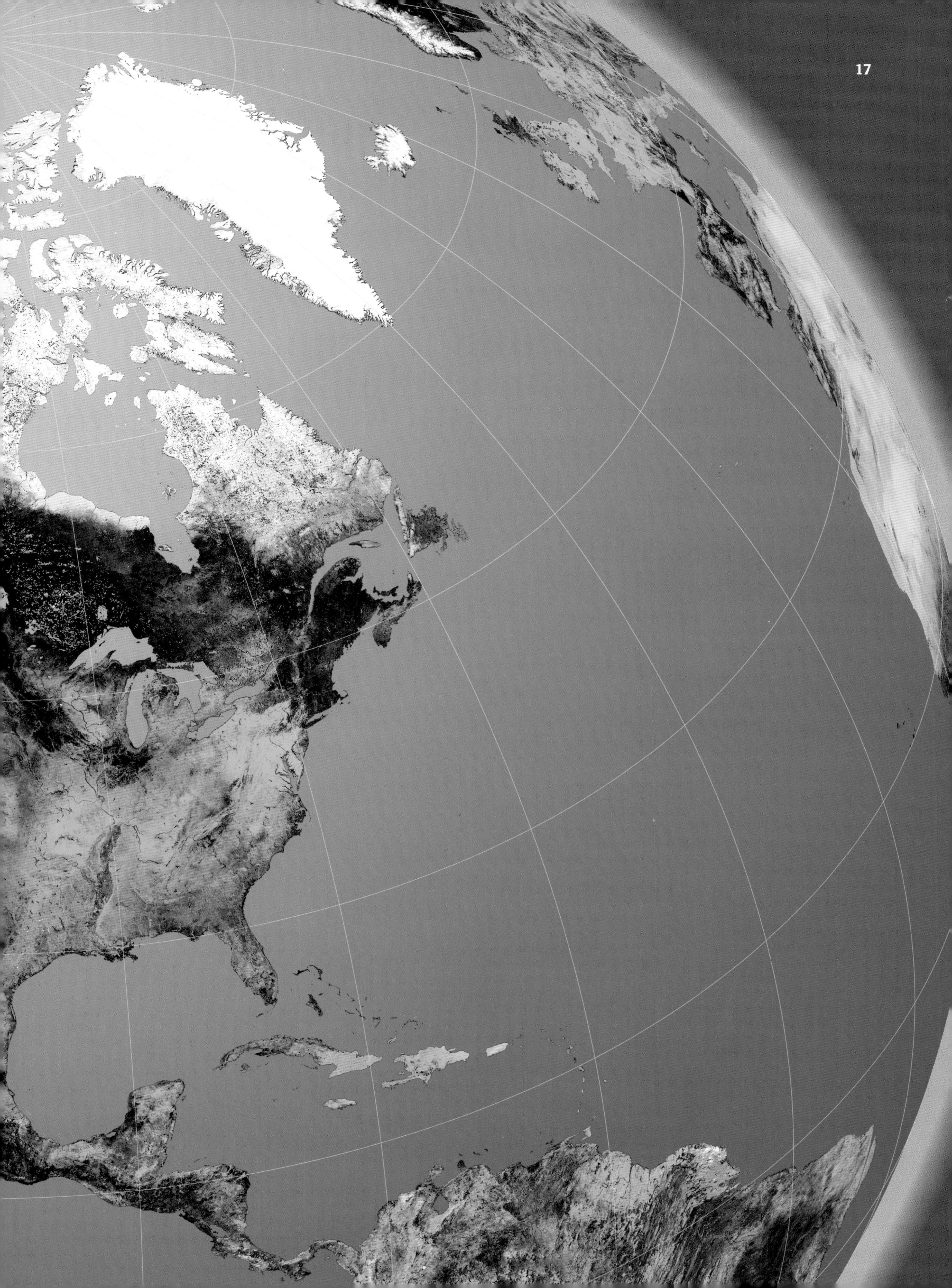

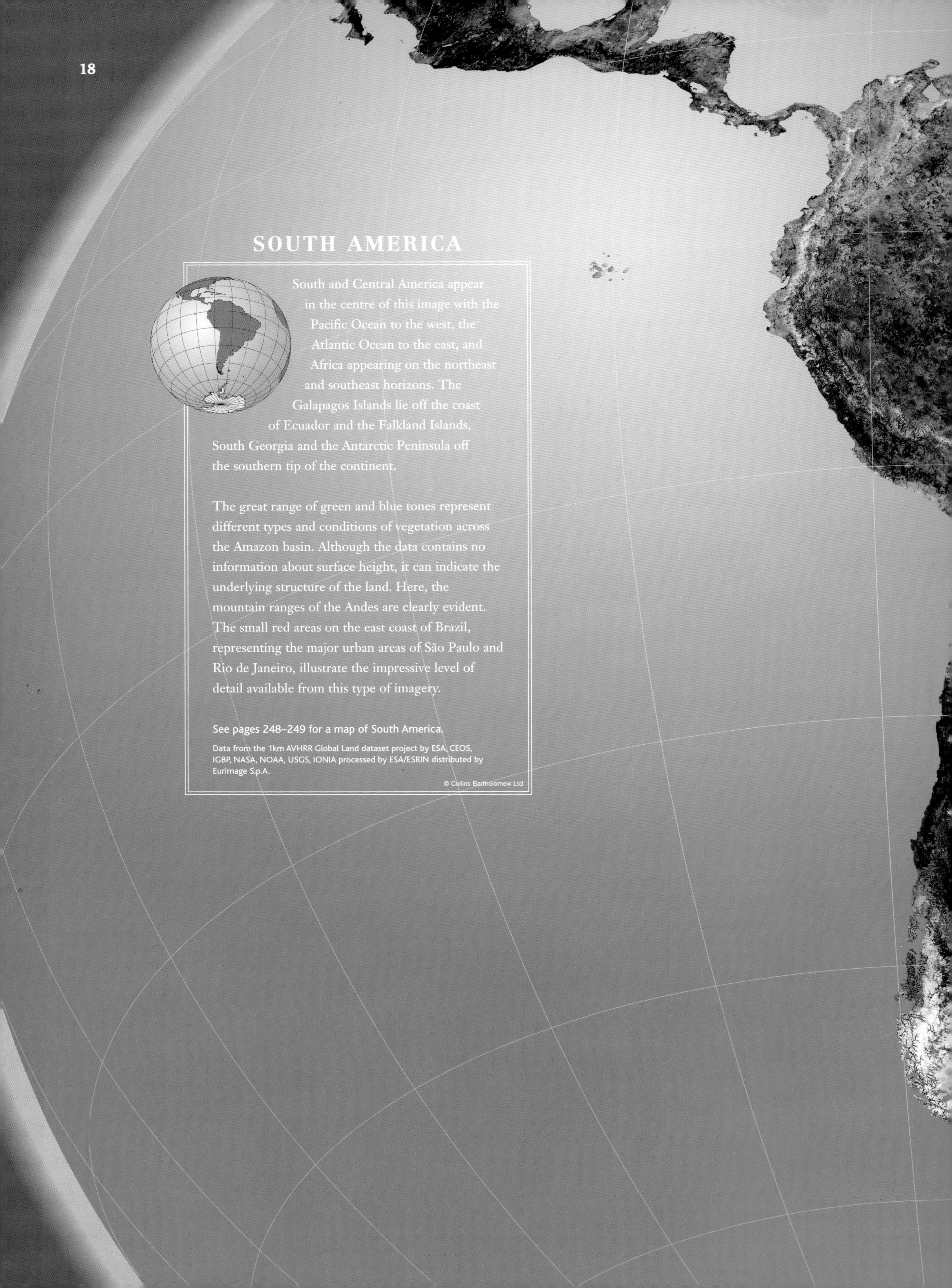

SOUTH AMERICA

South and Central America appear in the centre of this image with the Pacific Ocean to the west, the Atlantic Ocean to the east, and Africa appearing on the northeast and southeast horizons. The Galapagos Islands lie off the coast of Ecuador and the Falkland Islands, South Georgia and the Antarctic Peninsula off the southern tip of the continent.

The great range of green and blue tones represent different types and conditions of vegetation across the Amazon basin. Although the data contains no information about surface height, it can indicate the underlying structure of the land. Here, the mountain ranges of the Andes are clearly evident. The small red areas on the east coast of Brazil, representing the major urban areas of São Paulo and Rio de Janeiro, illustrate the impressive level of detail available from this type of imagery.

See pages 248–249 for a map of South America.

Data from the 1km AVHRR Global Land dataset project by ESA, CEOS, IGBP, NASA, NOAA, USGS, IONIA processed by ESA/ESRIN distributed by Eurimage S.p.A.

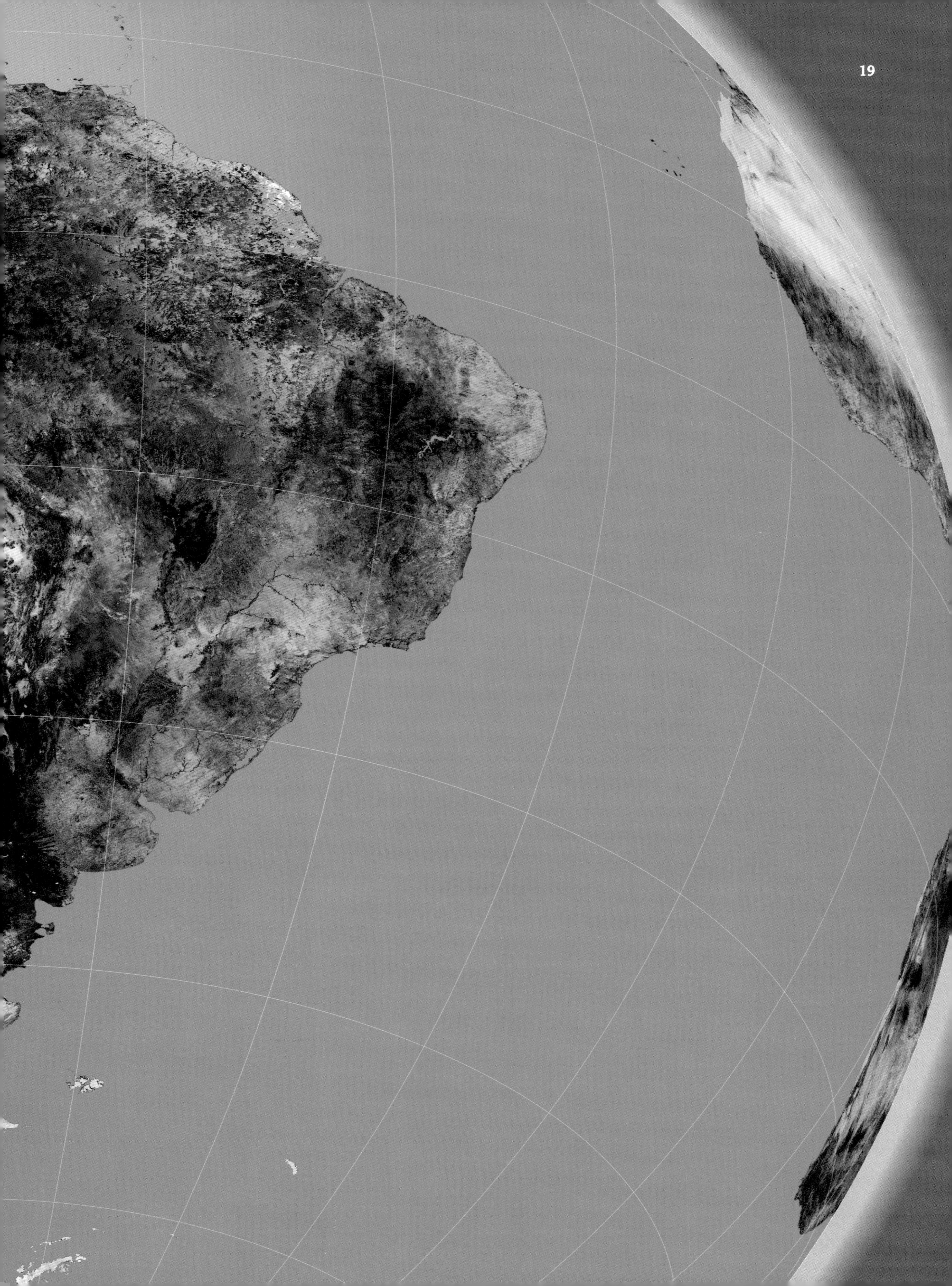

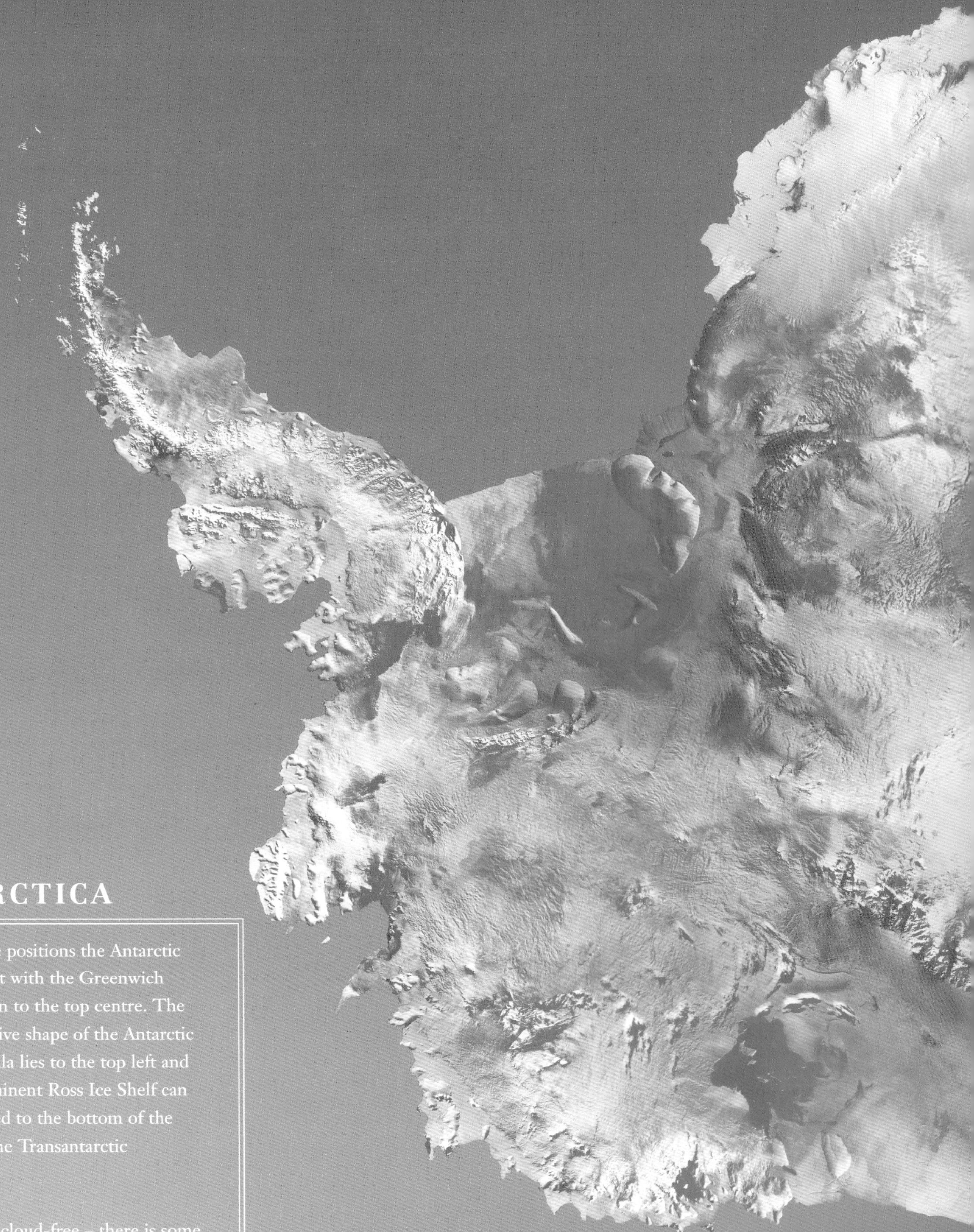

ANTARCTICA

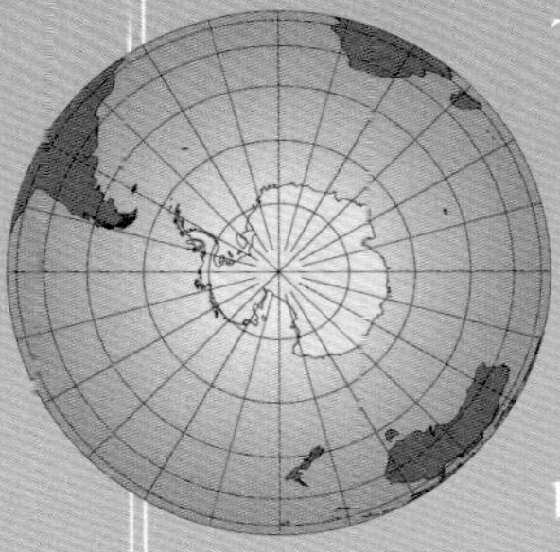

This image positions the Antarctic continent with the Greenwich meridian to the top centre. The distinctive shape of the Antarctic Peninsula lies to the top left and the prominent Ross Ice Shelf can be identified to the bottom of the image, below the Transantarctic Mountains range.

Although not completely cloud-free – there is some cloud cover in the eastern area to the right of the image – the view is impressive in its depiction of the physical features of the continent. The Ronne Ice Shelf, including Berkner Island, and the Transantarctic Mountains are particularly spectacular. Floating ice is excluded from the image, resulting in a clear definition of the extent of the continental ice sheet in an austral summer.

See pages 262–263 for a continental map of Antarctica.

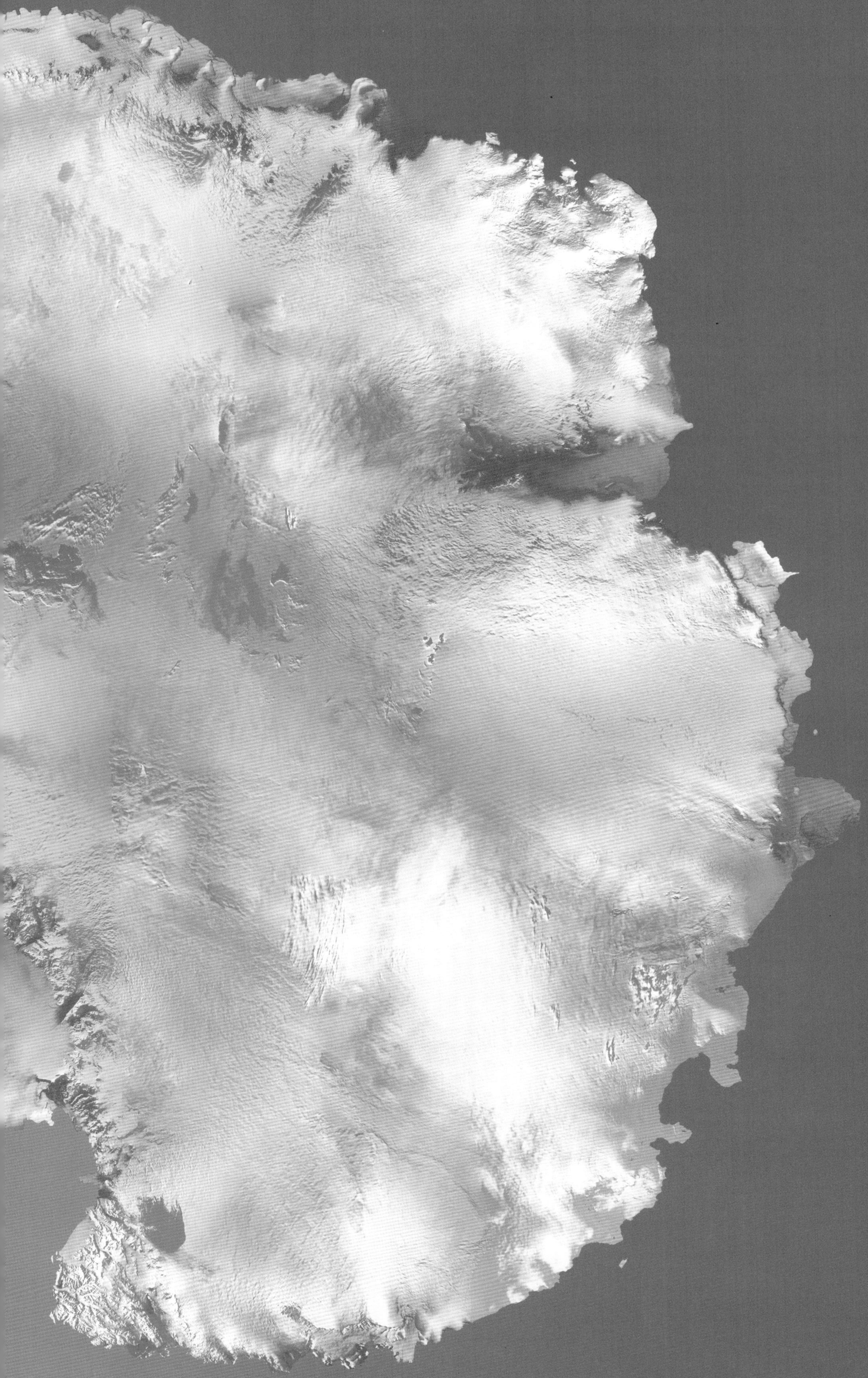

NEPTUNE

ORIGINS OF THE SOLAR SYSTEM

The nature and origin of our Solar System has been a subject of much debate. Early ideas of an Earth-centred system took many hundreds of years to be discarded in favour of Copernicus' heliocentric, or sun-centred model. More refined theories followed with Kepler's laws of orbital motion, and Newton's laws of gravity. The question of origin remained unanswered, and was regarded more as a philosophical matter.

The fact that the Sun and the planets rotate in a similar direction suggests a common formation mechanism - that of a large collapsing cloud or nebula. It is now believed that this did happen, about 4 600 million years ago. The nebula consisted of predominantly hydrogen and helium, but with a small amount of heavier elements. Over time, the cloud collapsed to form a rotating disk around a dense core. As core collapse continued and pressure in the core increased, material was heated enough to allow the nuclear fusion of hydrogen. Meanwhile as the disk cooled, the heavier elements began to condense and agglomerate. Larger bodies grew rapidly by sweeping up much of the remaining smaller material. As the core began to shine, its radiation pushed back much of the nearby volatile disk material into the outer Solar System, where it condensed and accumulated on the more distant planetary cores. This left the Inner Planets as small rocky bodies, and produced the Gas Giants of the outer system. Bombardment of the planets by a decreasing number of small bodies continued for several hundred million years, causing the craters now seen on many of the planets and moons.

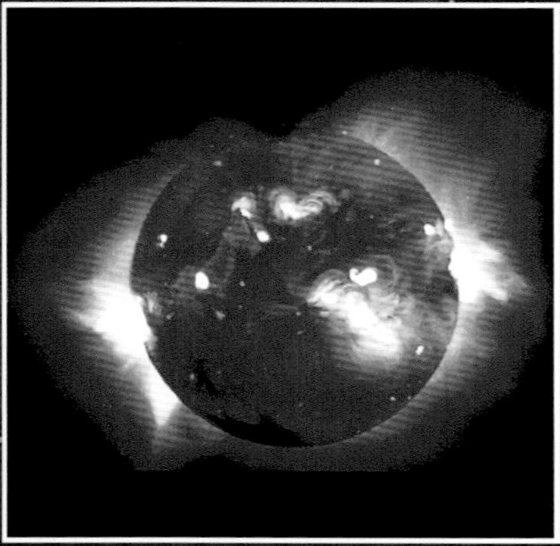

The Sun

The Sun is a typical star. It accounts for 99.85 per cent of the total mass contained within the Solar System, ensuring that it provides a dominating gravitational hold on its orbiting planets. The tremendous amount of heat and light produced by the Sun is the result of nuclear fusion reactions which occur in its core. In this process, hydrogen is converted into helium to produce a core temperature of roughly 15 million°C. Intense magnetic fields can induce cooling zones seen as dark sun spots on the Sun's surface. The Sun constantly emits a stream of charged particles which form the solar wind and cause auroral activity which can be seen on Earth.

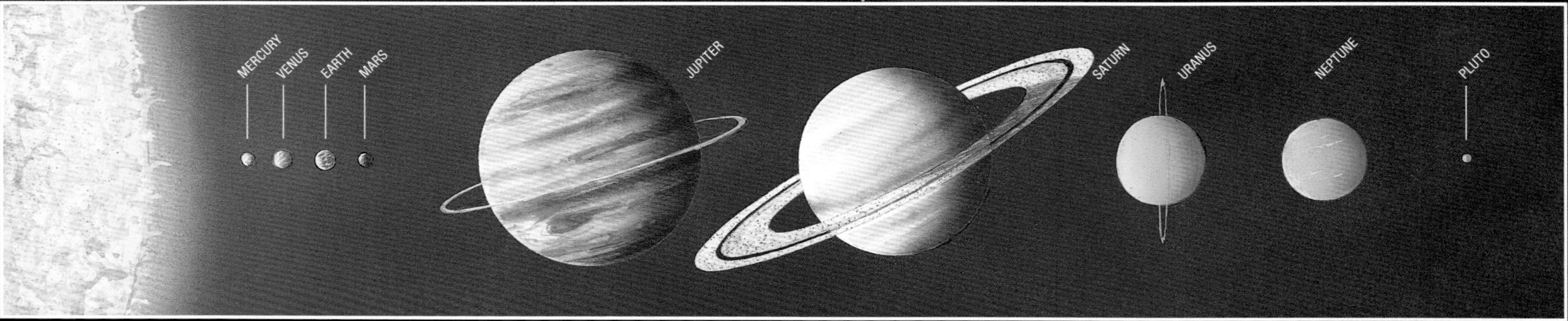

	Sun	Mercury	Venus	Earth	Mars	Jupiter	Saturn	Uranus	Neptune	Pluto
Mass (Earth=1)	332 830	0.055	0.815	1 (6 x 10²⁴)	0.107	317.82	95.161	14.371	17.147	0.002
Volume (Earth=1)	1 306 000	0.05	0.88	1	0.15	1 316	755	52	44	0.01
Density (Water=1)	1.41	5.43	5.24	5.52	3.94	1.33	0.70	1.30	1.76	1.10
Equatorial diameter (km)	1 392 000	4 879.4	12 103.6	12 756.3	6 794	142 984	120 536	51 118	49 528	2 390
Polar flattening	0	0	0	0.003	0.007	0.065	0.098	0.023	0.017	0
Surface gravity (Earth=1)	27.5	0.38	0.91	1	0.38	2.53	1.07	0.90	1.14	0.06
Number of satellites > 100 km	-	0	0	1	0	7	13	8	6	1
Total number of satellites	-	0	0	1	2	63	47	27	13	3
Rotation period (Earth days)	25–36	58.65	-243	23hr 56m 4s	1.03	0.41	0.44	-0.72	0.67	-6.39
Year (Earth days/years)	-	88 days	224.7 days	365.24 days	687 days	11.86 years	29.42 years	83.8 years	163.8 years	248 years
Mean orbital distance (million km)	-	57.9	108.2	149.6	227.9	778.4	1 426.7	2 871.0	4 498.3	5 906.4
Orbital eccentricity	-	0.2056	0.0068	0.0167	0.0934	0.0484	0.0542	0.0472	0.0086	0.2488
Mean orbital velocity (km/s)	-	47.87	35.02	29.79	24.13	13.07	9.67	6.84	5.48	4.75
Inclination of equator to orbit (deg.)	7.25	0	177.3	23.45	25.19	3.12	26.73	97.86	29.58	119.61
Orbital inclination (w.r.t. ecliptic)	-	7.005	3.395	0.00005	1.851	1.305	2.485	0.770	1.769	17.142
Mean surface temperature (°C)	5 700	167	457	15–20	-90– -5	-108	-139	-197	-200	-215.2
Atmospheric pressure (bars)	-	-	90	1	0.007–0.010	0.3	0.4	-	-	8x10⁻⁵
Atmospheric composition (selected gas components)	H_2 92.1% He 7.8% O_2 0.061%	-	CO_2 96% N_2 3%	N_2 77% O_2 21% Ar 1.6%	CO_2 95.3% N_2 2.7%	H_2 90% He 10%	H_2 97% He 3%	H_2 83% He 15% CH_4 2%	H_2 85% He 13% CH_4 2%	N_2 CO CH_4

MERCURY VENUS EARTH MARS JUPITER SATURN URANUS NEPTUNE PLUTO

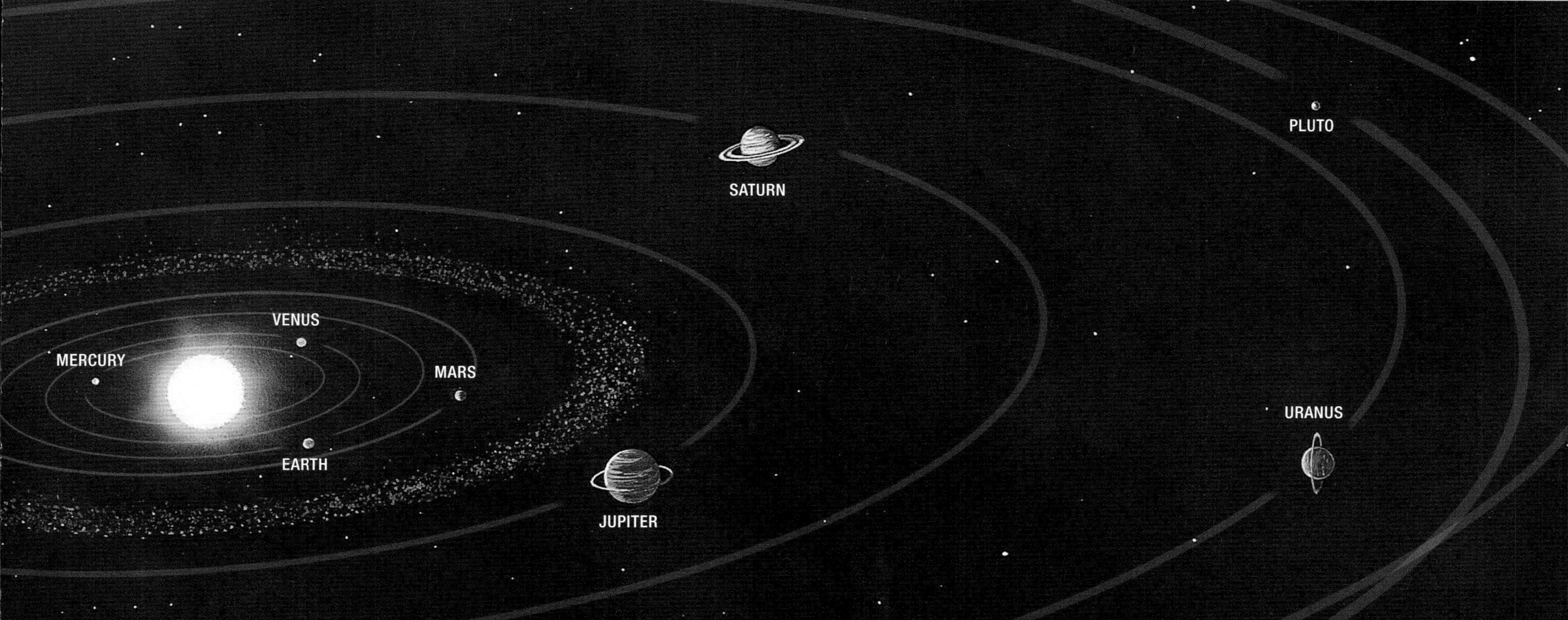

PLUTO

SATURN

VENUS

MERCURY

MARS

EARTH

URANUS

JUPITER

Mercury

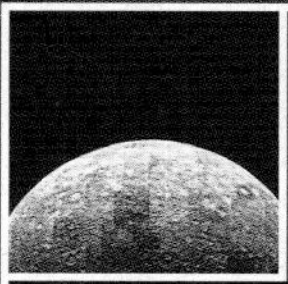

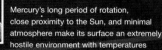

Mercury's long period of rotation, close proximity to the Sun, and minimal atmosphere make its surface an extremely hostile environment with temperatures ranging from 427 to minus 173°C between its day and night side. Mercury is similar to Earth's Moon in size and appearance; its cratered surface was first photographed in detail in the mid-1970s by the Mariner 10 space probe. However the internal structure differs from the Moon; analysis of its magnetic field suggests that the core consists of molten iron, believed to be 40 per cent of the planet's volume. Mercury has a very eccentric orbit with its orbital distance varying from 46 to 70 million km.

Venus

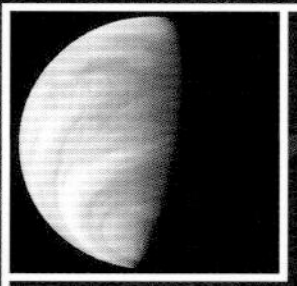

Venus' thick atmosphere of carbon dioxide and nitrogen creates not only a huge surface pressure of ninety times that on Earth but also a greenhouse effect producing temperatures in excess of 450°C. Traces of sulphur dioxide and water vapour form clouds of dilute sulphuric acid, making the atmosphere extremely corrosive. This atmosphere reflects almost all incident visible radiation and prevents direct observation of surface features. In 1990 use of radar imaging enabled the Magellan space probe to see through the cloud. Magellan mapped 98 per cent of the planet during three years to find a surface covered in craters, volcanoes, mountains and solidified lava flows. Venus is the brightest object in the sky after the Sun and Moon and is unusual in that its year is less than its rotation period.

Earth

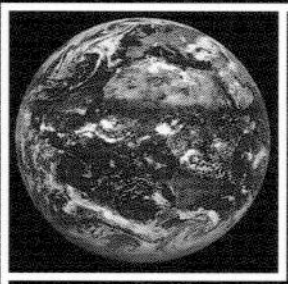

Earth is the largest and densest of the Inner Planets. Created some 4 500 million years ago, the core, rocky mantle and crust are similar in structure to Venus. The Earth's core is composed almost entirely of iron and oxygen compounds which exist in a molten state at temperatures of around 5 000°C. Earth is the only planet with vast quantities of life-sustaining water, with the oceans covering 70.8 per cent of its surface. The action of plate tectonics has created vast mountain ranges and is responsible for volcanic activity. The Moon is Earth's only natural satellite and with a diameter of over one quarter that of the Earth's, makes the Earth-Moon system a near double-planet.

Mars

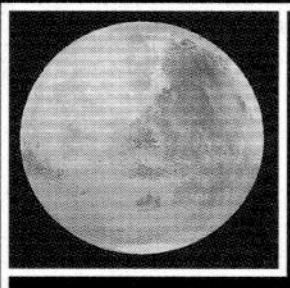

Named after the Roman god of war because of its blood-red appearance, Mars is the last of the Inner Planets. The red colour comes from the high concentration of iron oxides on its surface. Mars has impressive surface features, including the highest known peak in the Solar System, Olympus Mons, an inactive volcano reaching a height of 23 km above the surrounding plains, and Marineris, a 2 500 km long canyon four times as deep as the Grand Canyon. The Pathfinder mission in 1997 has shown that much of the Martian surface is shaped by intense dust storms which often engulf the entire planet. Mars has polar caps composed of water and carbon dioxide ice which partially evaporate during its summer.

Jupiter

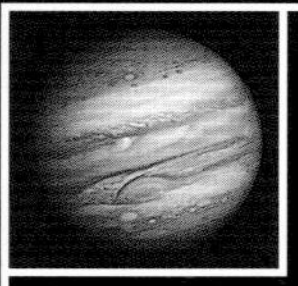

Jupiter is by far the most massive of all the planets and is the dominant body in the Solar System after the Sun. It is the innermost of the Gas Giants. The dense surface atmosphere is predominantly hydrogen, with helium, water vapour, and methane. Below this is a layer of liquid hydrogen, then an even deeper layer of metallic hydrogen. Unlike solid bodies, Jupiter's rotation period is somewhat ill-defined, with equatorial regions rotating faster than the polar regions; this, combined with convection currents in lower layers, causes intense magnetic fields and rapidly varying surface features. Most notable of these is the Great Red Spot, a giant circular storm visible since the first observations of Jupiter's surface, which shows no signs of abating.

Saturn

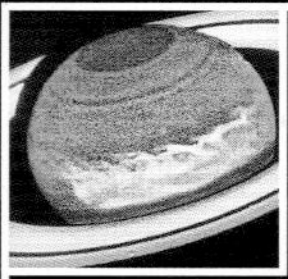

Although only slightly smaller that Jupiter, Saturn is a mere one-third of Jupiter's mass, and the least dense of all the planets - less dense than water. The low mass, combined with a fast rotation rate, leads to the planet's significant polar flattening. Saturn exhibits a striking ring system, more than twice the diameter of the planet; the rings consist of countless small rock and ice clumps which vary in size from a grain of sand to tens of metres in diameter. It is believed that the rings were formed from a stray moon coming too close to Saturn, and being ripped apart by it. Distinct bands and gaps in the rings are the result of complex interactions between the planet and its closer moons. Recent rare opportunities to view Saturn's rings edgeways have yielded the discovery of at least two other moons.

Uranus

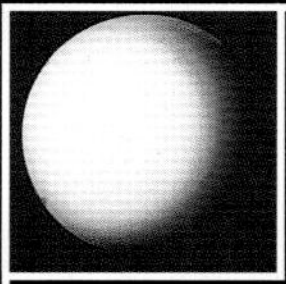

Uranus has many surprising features; the most prominent of these is the tilt of its rotation axis by over 90 degrees caused by a series of large collisions in its early history. Like the other Gas Giants, Uranus is predominantly hydrogen and helium with a small proportion of methane and other gases. However, because Uranus is colder than Jupiter and Saturn, the methane forms ice crystals which give Uranus a featureless blue-green colour. The interior is also different from that expected. Instead of having a gaseous atmosphere above liquid and metallic hydrogen layers, Uranus has a super-dense gaseous atmosphere extending down to its core. Uranus' magnetic field is inclined at 60 degrees to the rotation axis, and is off centre by one third of the planet's radius, which suggests that it is not generated by the core. The system of eleven narrow rings around Uranus is prevented from spreading by the interaction of nearby 'shepherd' moons. Two new moons, Caliban and Sycorax, were discovered in 1997 although their large orbits indicate they are probably captured asteroids.

Neptune

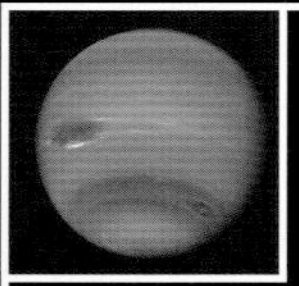

Neptune has always been associated with Uranus because of its similar size, composition and appearance, but, unexpectedly, Neptune's atmosphere is more active than that of Uranus. This was shown by Voyager 2 in 1989 with the observation of the Great Dark Spot, Neptune's equivalent to Jupiter's Great Red Spot. Voyager 2 recorded the fastest winds ever seen in the Solar System, 2 000 km per hour, around the Dark Spot. This feature disappeared in 1994, but has been replaced by a similar storm in the northern polar cap. Like Uranus, Neptune has a magnetic field highly inclined to the planet's axis of rotation and off-centre by more than half of the planet's radius. The cause of this magnetic field is convection currents in conducting fluid layers outside the core. Neptune's largest moon, Triton, is in an inclined retrograde orbit, indicating that it was captured by Neptune rather than formed alongside it. The slowly decaying orbit will one day bring Triton too close to Neptune, and it will be torn apart forming a spectacular ring.

Pluto

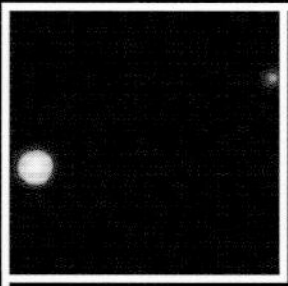

Pluto's existence was predicted before its discovery in 1930 from studies of the motions of Neptune and Uranus. Its orbit is highly tilted with respect to the orbits of the other planets and is so eccentric that it occasionally comes inside Neptune's orbit. Its only moon, Charon, is unusually large. Unusually, minerals make up about 70 per cent of its total mass, with the rest being ice. Pluto, unlike Charon, has methane ice on its surface and this forms a tenuous yet deep atmosphere when Pluto is closest to the Sun. These anomalies and, since 1992, the discovery of hundreds of other distant icy worlds, have often called Pluto's status as a planet into question. Astronomers now believe there are thousands of these icy mini-planets, many similar in size to Pluto and Charon. Most of them orbit in the Edgeworth-Kuiper belt which stretches from Neptune's orbit to about 7 500 million km from the Sun. A few objects travel even further away on very eccentric orbits. Beyond them lies only the Oort cloud of comets and the distant stars.

THE EARTH'S STRUCTURE

The interior of the Earth can be divided into three principal regions (see 1). The outermost region is known as the crust, which is extremely thin compared to the Earth as a whole. Under the continents the crust is about 33 km thick on average, only 0.5 per cent of the total radius of the Earth (6 370 km). Under the oceans the crust is even thinner: perhaps a third of its continental thickness. Over the course of geological time the Earth's crust has broken up into large fragments, which are known as lithospheric plates. These plates are slowly moving relative to one another at rates of a few centimetres per year – a process know as continental drift.

The next layer down is known as the mantle which is about 2 850 km thick. The distinction between the mantle and crust is made on the basis of composition and strength. There is a zone of the upper mantle, at depths between about 100 and 700 km, which behaves like a fluid when under stress. This weak zone is called the asthenosphere. The outermost 70 km or so of the mantle, together with the crust, is known as the lithosphere and is much stronger. The transition between the lithosphere and asthenosphere is due to variation in temperature, and is therefore gradual rather than being a distinct boundary.

Below the mantle is the Earth's core, which is about 3 470 km in radius, and is mainly made up of iron. The greater part of the core is completely liquid; however, there is a solid inner core, about 1 220 km in radius.

It is the dynamic processes operating in the upper parts of the Earth's interior which give rise to very dramatic and violent expressions of the huge energies involved: earthquakes and volcanoes. Both of these can be very destructive, even disastrous, in terms of both loss of life and economic impact. Consequently, study of these phenomena is very important if the natural disasters arising from them are to be mitigated.

	Crust
	Mantle
	Outer Core
	Inner Core

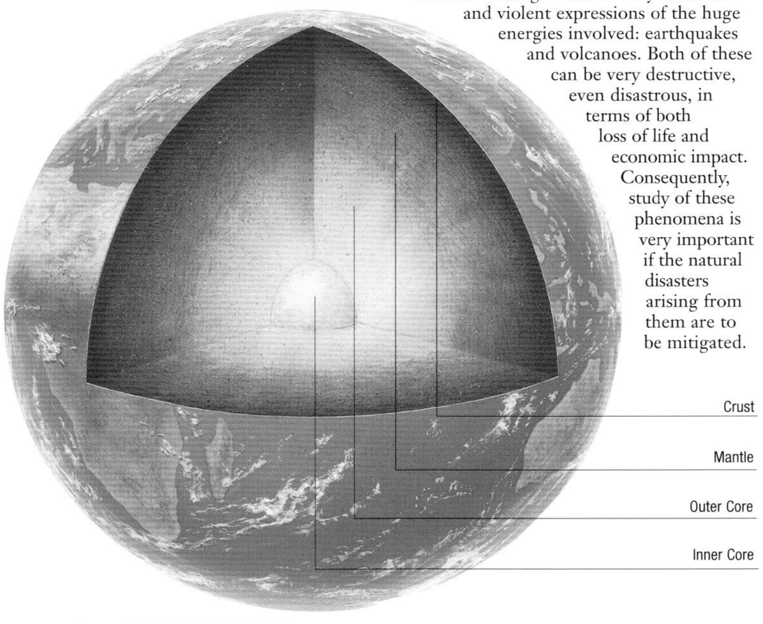

1. THE EARTH'S INTERIOR

DISTRIBUTION OF EARTHQUAKES AND VOLCANOES

Any map showing the distribution of earthquakes and volcanoes (see 2) will inevitably look very similar to a map showing the boundaries of the tectonic plates (see 3). This is because both phenomena are largely controlled by the processes of plate tectonics. The vast majority of the world's earthquakes occur at plate boundaries as a result of one plate pushing past another along what is known as a constructive boundary, or under another at a destructive boundary, creating a subduction zone. Even those earthquakes which occur away from plate margins (intraplate earthquakes) are still mostly due to stresses in the rocks that result indirectly from plate movements.

Most major volcanoes occur along lines parallel to subduction zones, as for example, in the Andes. Other volcanoes can form along mid-ocean ridges where the asthenosphere is close to the surface; such volcanoes can produce what are known as fissure eruptions, where vast amounts of basaltic lava suddenly erupt on the surface, inundating huge areas.

3. TECTONIC PLATE BOUNDARIES

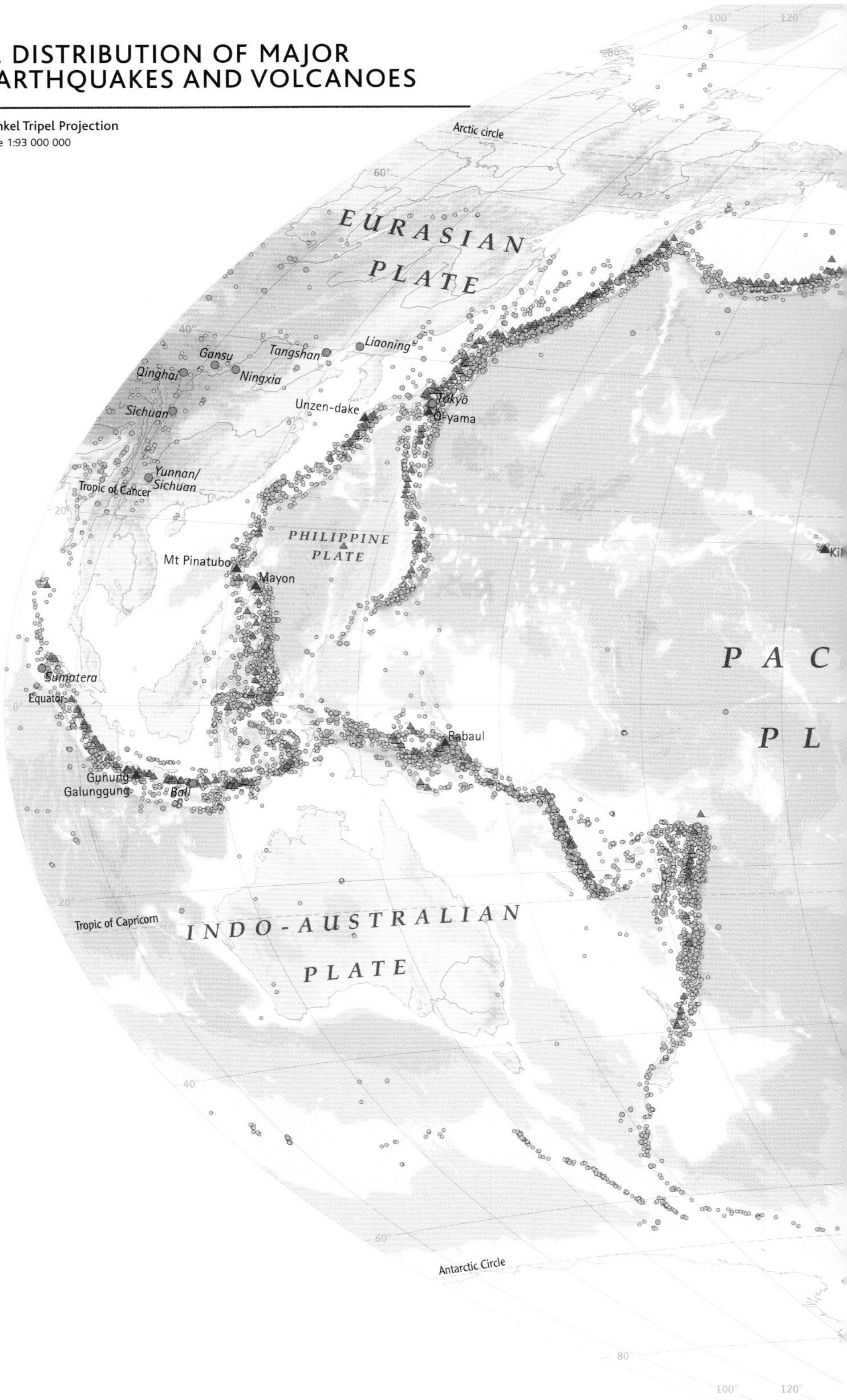

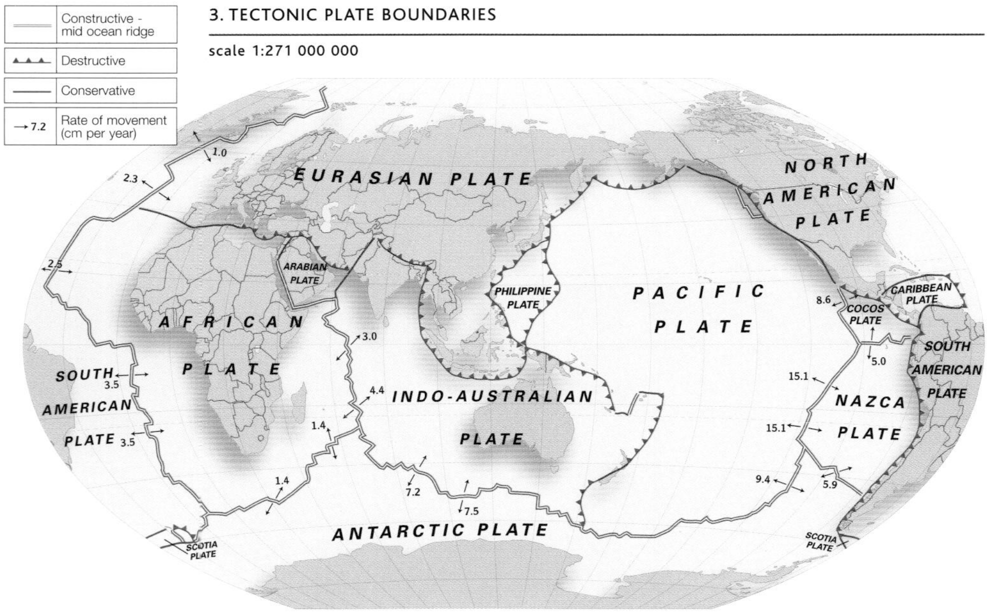

	Constructive - mid ocean ridge
▲▲▲	Destructive
	Conservative
→ 7.2	Rate of movement (cm per year)

scale 1:271 000 000

2. DISTRIBUTION OF MAJOR EARTHQUAKES AND VOLCANOES

Winkel Tripel Projection
scale 1:93 000 000

VOLCANOES

In the simplest terms, a volcano is a vent at the surface of the Earth where molten rock (magma) from the interior can reach the surface. The magma originates in the Earth's mantle. It then erupts either as a stream of liquid rock (called lava when it appears at the surface) or as fine particles of ash or cinder. The erupted material builds up over time into a mountain, typically conical in shape. The exact shape of the volcano is controlled by the type of material erupted.

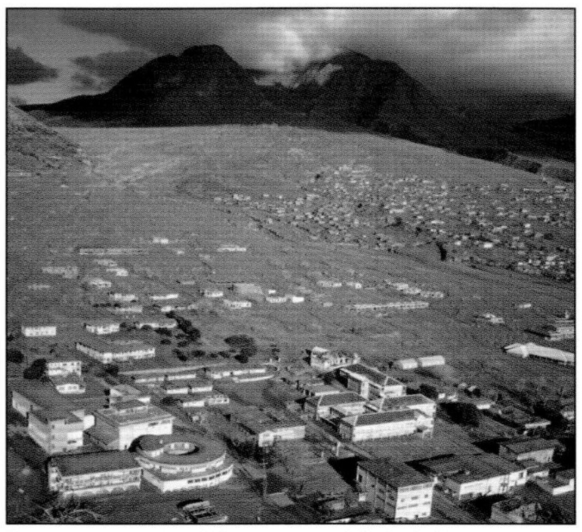

Plymouth, the capital of Montserrat, partially buried by volcanic ash after the eruption of Soufrière Hills in August 1997.

Volcanoes in oceanic locations (such as Hawaii) tend to erupt very basic (non-acidic) lava which flows relatively easily. Because it can run quite far before cooling, this produces a very flat volcano with gentle slopes, known as a shield volcano. Continental volcanoes produce more acidic lava which flows more slowly, and they produce more ash, and therefore have steeper-sided cones. Such volcanoes also tend to erupt more explosively, because of the greater amount of steam or gas in the lava, and are generally more dangerous. They can produce what is know as a pyroclastic flow, a fast-moving cloud of super-heated ash and gases, which is what destroyed Pompeii in AD79.

Volcanoes can also be classified according to their eruptive history. Active volcanoes are those that are currently erupting; an eruption can go on intermittently for years, and some volcanoes, such as Stromboli in Italy, are almost permanently active. However, most volcanoes erupt much less frequently, and those that have not erupted for tens or hundreds of years, but may be expected to erupt again, are said to be dormant. Volcanoes which were once active in response to the tectonic situation as it was millions of years ago, and which cannot possibly erupt again today, are said to be extinct.

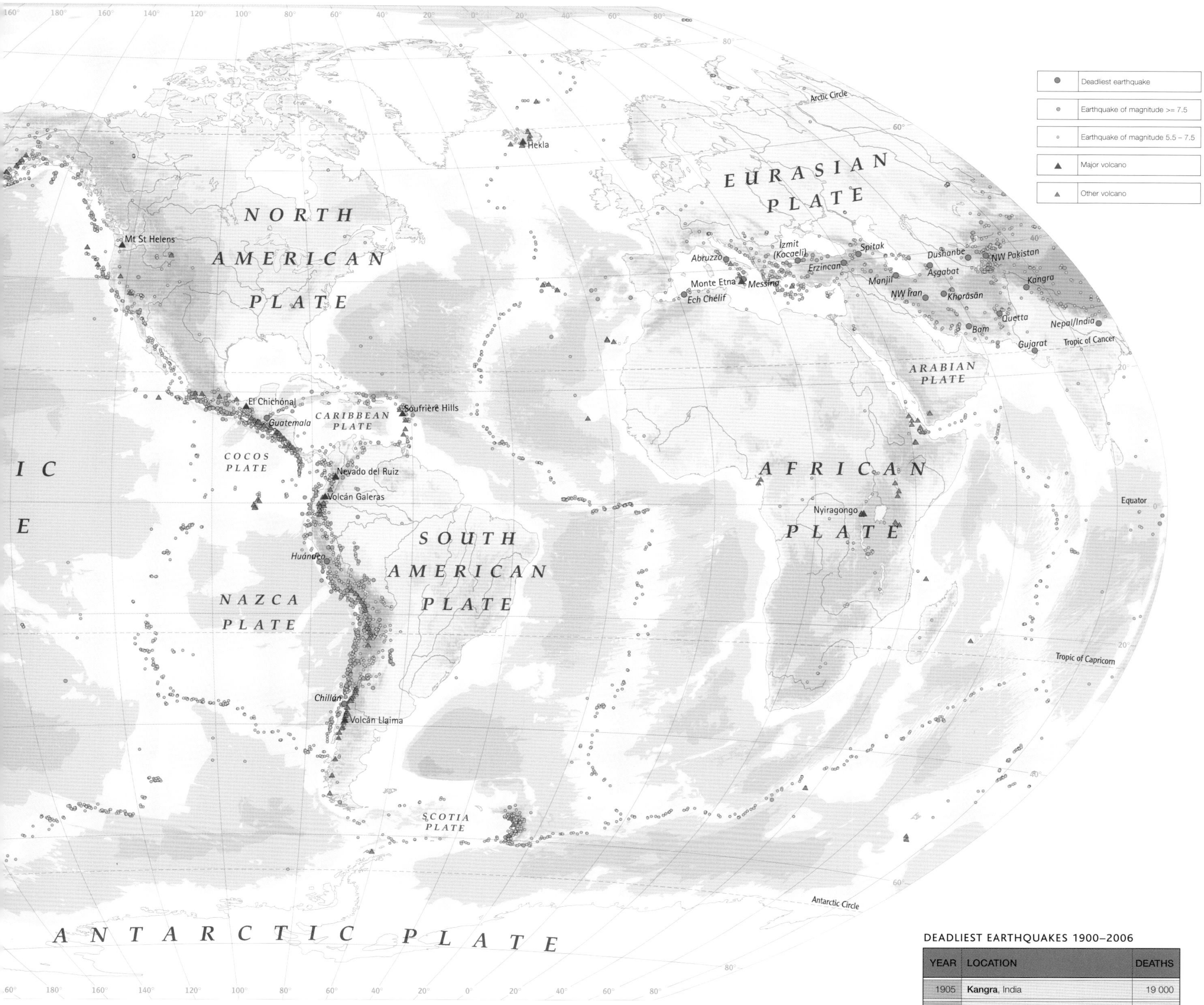

© Collins Bartholomew Ltd

MAJOR VOLCANIC ERUPTIONS 1980–2006

YEAR	VOLCANO	COUNTRY
1980	Mt St Helens	USA
1982	El Chichónal	Mexico
1982	Gunung Galunggung	Indonesia
1983	Kilauea	Hawaii
1983	Ō-yama	Japan
1985	Nevado del Ruiz	Colombia
1991	Mt Pinatubo	Philippines
1991	Unzen-dake	Japan
1993	Mayon	Philippines
1993	Volcán Galeras	Colombia
1994	Volcán Llaima	Chile
1994	Rabaul	Papua New Guinea
1997	Soufrière Hills	Montserrat
2000	Hekla	Iceland
2001	Monte Etna	Italy
2002	Nyiragongo	Democratic Republic of the Congo

EARTHQUAKES

An earthquake is produced by a sudden breaking of rock in the Earth's crust as the stresses become too great for the strength of the rock to withstand. Naturally, this is most likely to happen where the rock is weakest. Where the rock breaks, a fracture line, known as a fault is left, and because there is now a break, future movements are likely to happen along the same weakness. The forces involved derive mostly from the movements of the tectonic plates; for example, between the upper surface of a subducting plate and the lower surface of the plate under which it is sliding – conditions which have caused some of the world's largest earthquakes.

The force with which the rock breaks releases a large amount of energy in the form of waves that travel through the Earth. These radiate outwards from where the fault has ruptured. The point on the fault at which the rupture begins is known as the hypocentre; this is usually at a depth of 10 to 30 km for shallow earthquakes; earthquakes in subduction zones can be as deep as 600 km below the Earth's surface. The point on the Earth's surface directly above the hypocentre is called the epicentre; this is what is usually shown on a map. The magnitude of an earthquake, the so-called Richter scale, is a logarithmic approximation of the total amount of energy released. A large earthquake which may be severely damaging at the epicentre, is less strongly felt by people at greater distances. The strength of shaking at any point is known as the intensity, and this decreases with distance from the epicentre.

The tsunami of December 2004 originated from a major earthquake of magnitude 9.0 off the coast of Sumatera. It caused over 225 000 deaths and widespread destruction in eleven countries around the Indian Ocean.

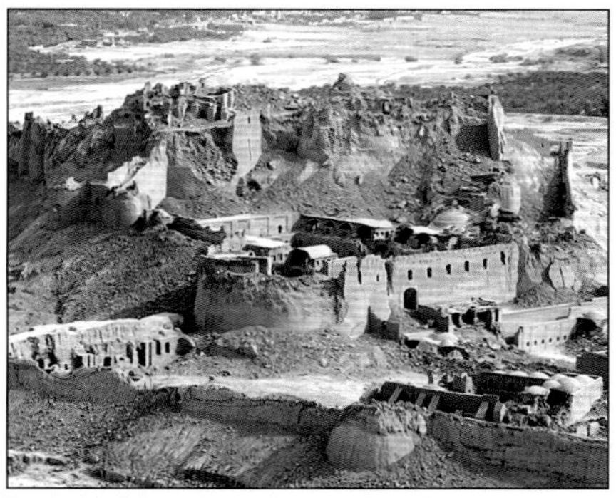

The citadel of the ancient Iranian city of Bam, devastated by a major earthquake in December 2003.

DEADLIEST EARTHQUAKES 1900–2006

YEAR	LOCATION	DEATHS
1905	**Kangra**, India	19 000
1908	**Messina**, Italy	110 000
1917	**Bali**, Indonesia	15 000
1920	**Ningxia Province**, China	200 000
1923	**Tōkyō**, Japan	142 807
1927	**Qinghai Province**, China	200 000
1932	**Gansu Province**, China	70 000
1935	**Quetta**, Pakistan	30 000
1939	**Chillán**, Chile	28 000
1939	**Erzincan**, Turkey	32 700
1948	**Aşgabat**, Turkmenistan	19 800
1970	**Huánuco Province**, Peru	66 794
1974	**Yunnan and Sichuan Provinces**, China	20 000
1976	central **Guatemala**	22 778
1976	**Tangshan**, Hebei Province, China	255 000
1978	**Khorāsān Province**, Iran	20 000
1988	**Spitak**, Armenia	25 000
1990	**Manjil**, Iran	50 000
1999	**İzmit (Kocaeli)**, Turkey	17 000
2001	**Gujarat**, India	20 000
2003	**Bam**, Iran	26 271
2004	**Sumatera**, Indonesia/Indian Ocean	>225 000
2005	**Northwest Pakistan**	87 000

OBSERVING THE OCEANS

The oceans cover 70.8 per cent of the surface of the Earth and exert an extraordinary influence on the physical processes of the Earth and its atmosphere. The circulation of water throughout the oceans is critical to world climate and climate change. Any study of these relationships relies upon a clear understanding of the role of the oceans and of the complex processes within them. Methods of direct and indirect observation of the oceans, particularly by sampling and through the application of satellite remote sensing, have developed enormously over the last forty years and continue to provide the data required to develop this understanding.

Until the advent of Earth-observation satellites in the late 1970s all ocean observations were made from ships. The first global survey of the oceans, their bathymetry and their physical and biological characteristics, was made by HMS Challenger between 1872 and 1876. Throughout the 20th century, comprehensive descriptions of the distributions of temperature and salinity were made through numerous regional and global expeditions. Analysis of the temperature and salinity characteristics of a water sample allowed its origins to be determined, and enabled overall patterns of water circulation to be deduced.

Until the 1960s there was no means of directly measuring currents below the ocean surface. Parallel developments produced two solutions to this problem. In the USA, current-recording meters were designed which returned records of current speed and direction, and water temperature. In the UK, devices were produced which could be made to drift with the currents at a predetermined depth and which could be tracked from an attendant ship. Such floats can now be used globally, independent of ships.

Earth observation satellites have become increasingly important in observing the oceans. Radiometers allow sea surface temperatures to be monitored and radar altimeters permit ocean surface currents to be inferred from measurements of sea surface height. Such developments meant that by the early 1990s routine monitoring of ocean surface currents was possible. The combination of satellite altimetry and other observation methods has also allowed a detailed picture of the ocean floor to be established (*see 1*).

1. GLOBAL SEAFLOOR TOPOGRAPHY

This image has been produced from a combination of shipboard depth soundings and gravity data derived from satellite altimetry from the ERS-1 and Geosat satellites. The range of colours represents different depths of the ocean – from orange and yellow on the shallow continental shelves to dark blues in the deepest ocean trenches. The heavily fractured mid-ocean ridges (ranging from green to yellow) are particularly prominent.

OCEAN CIRCULATION

Most of the Earth's incoming solar radiation is absorbed in the top few tens of metres of the ocean. Thus the upper ocean is warmed, the warming being greatest around the equator. Sea water has a high thermal capacity in comparison with the atmosphere or lithosphere and as a consequence, the ocean is an extremely effective store of thermal energy. Slow ocean currents play a major role in redistributing this heat around the globe and the oceans and their circulation are thus key elements in the climate system.

Estimates of the global transport of heat by the oceans (*see 2*) show a pattern of heat flow in the Indian and North Pacific Oceans away from the equator and towards the poles. However, the Atlantic Ocean has a clear northward flow throughout, decreasing from a maximum value of 1.4 petawatts (PW) at 24°N to effectively zero in the Arctic Ocean. This decrease is indicative of the heat loss to the atmosphere which is responsible for the temperate climate of western Europe.

Ocean currents are influenced by winds, by density gradients and by the Earth's rotation. They are also constrained by the topography of the seafloor. Surface currents are usually strong, narrow, western-boundary currents flowing towards the poles. Some of these are well known, for example the Gulf Stream in the North Atlantic Ocean, the Kuroshio Current in the northwest Pacific, and the Brazil Current (*see 3*). These poleward flows are returned towards the equator in broad, slow, interior flows which complete a gyre in each hemisphere basin. Sea surface circulation is reflected in variations in sea surface height which can vary greatly across currents (*see 4*). For example, differences in sea surface height of over 1m are evident across the Kuroshio Current. At high latitudes, winter cooling produces high density water which sinks towards the ocean floor and flows towards the equator, being constrained by the sea floor topography (*see 5*). This fills the deep ocean basins with water at temperatures close to 0°C.

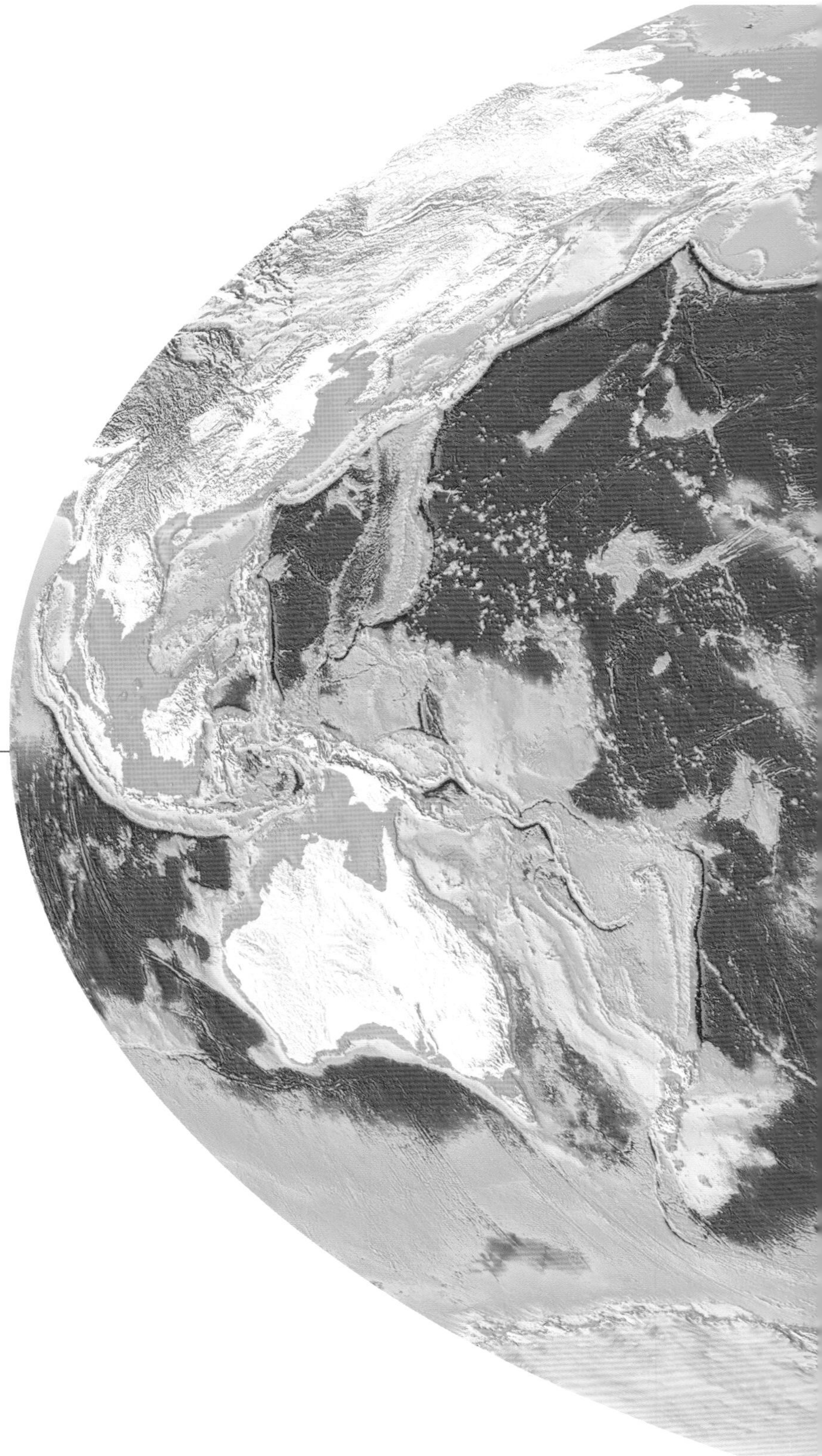

2. OCEAN TRANSPORT OF HEAT

In petawatts (PW) (10^{15} watts). 1 PW is about sixty times the global consumption of energy.

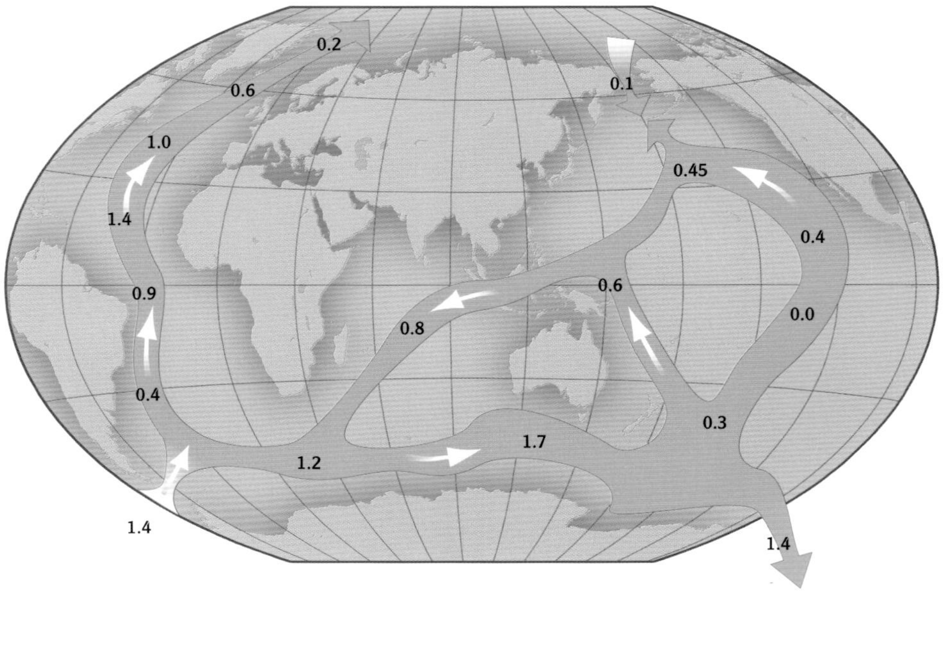

3. OCEAN SURFACE CURRENTS

scale 1 : 200 000 000

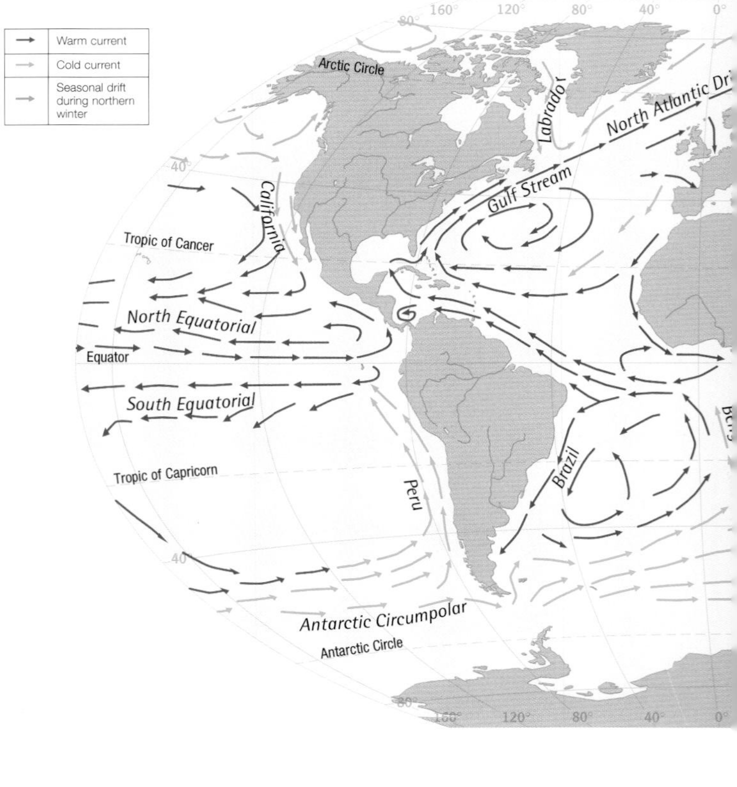

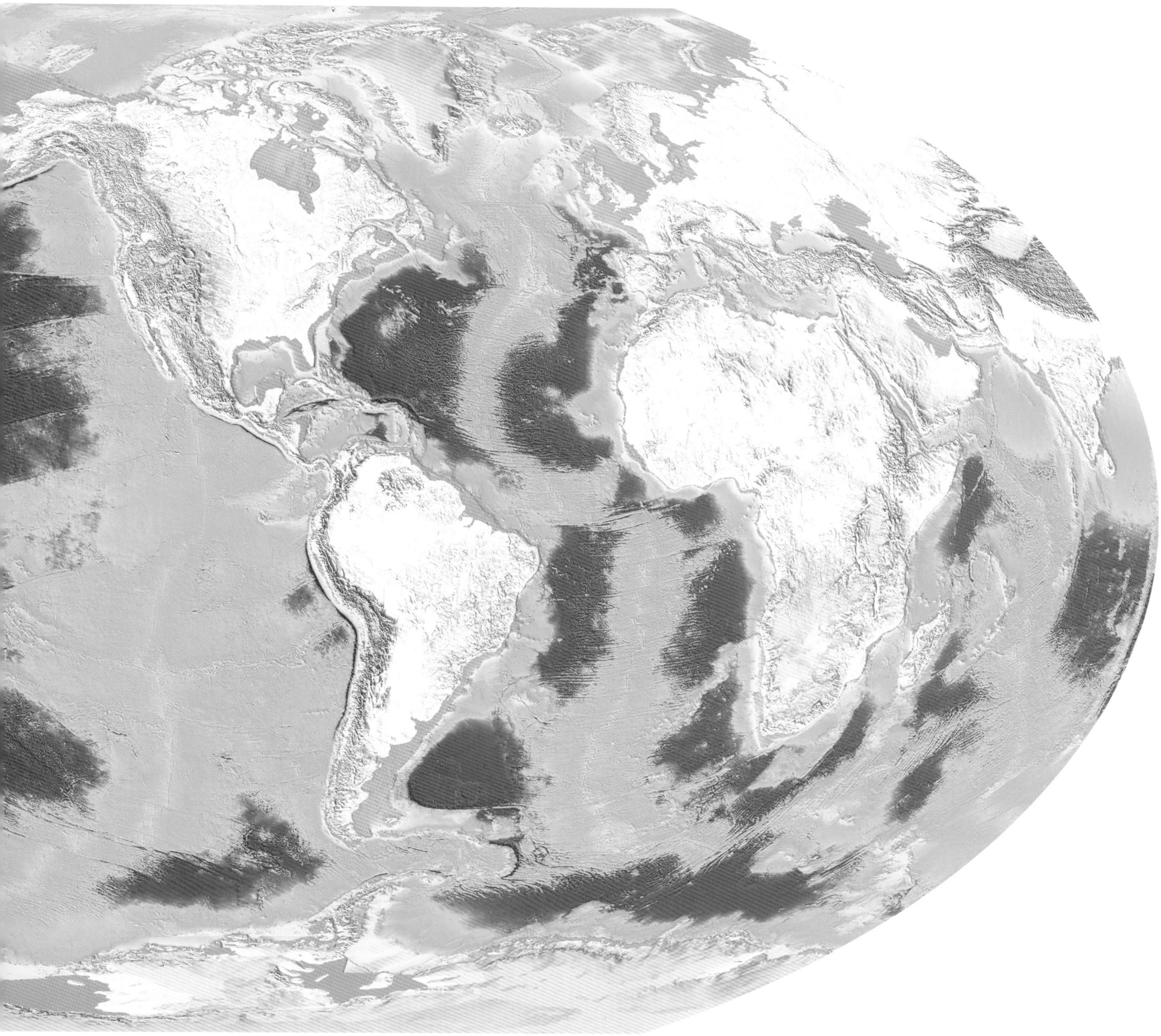

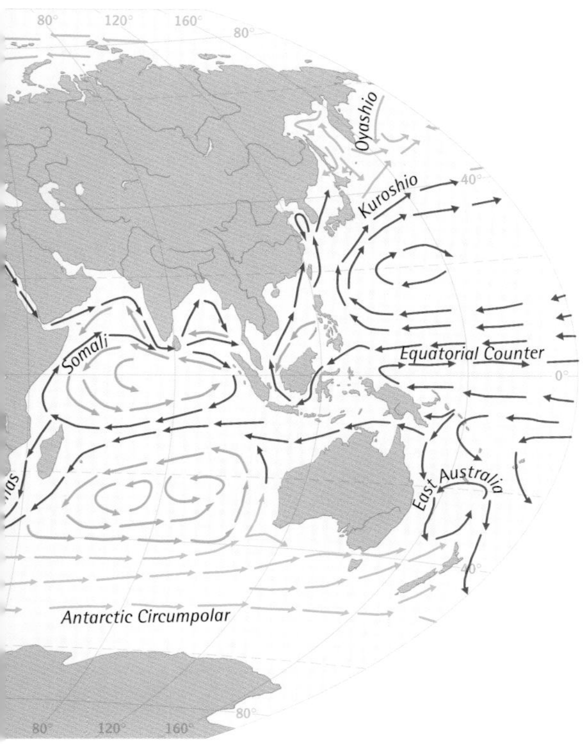

4. SEA SURFACE HEIGHT

From the TOPEX/POSEIDON satellite.
Currents flow along the slopes and are
strongest where the slopes are greatest.

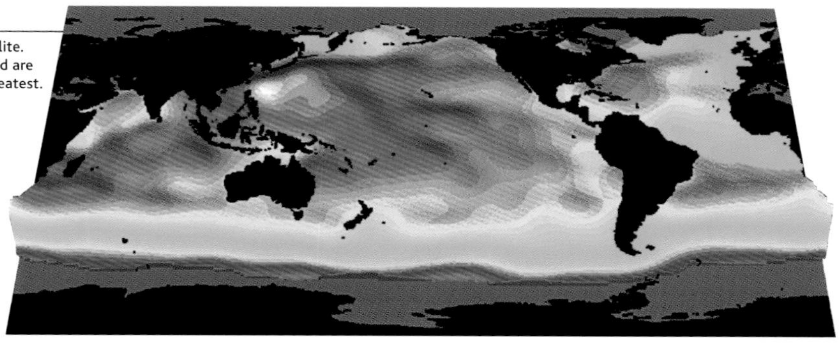

5. CROSS-SECTION OF SALINITY AND THE OCEAN FLOOR

Stretching 12 000 km across the Pacific Ocean from Antarctica (left) to Alaska (right) approximately along longitude 150°W. It shows water modified in the
Antarctic descending to the ocean floor and into the ocean interior.

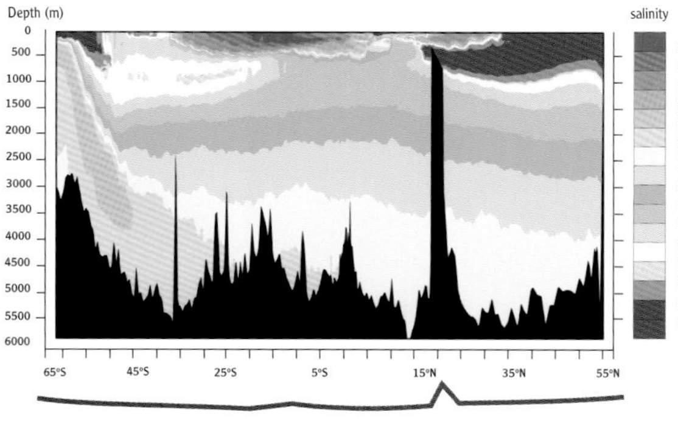

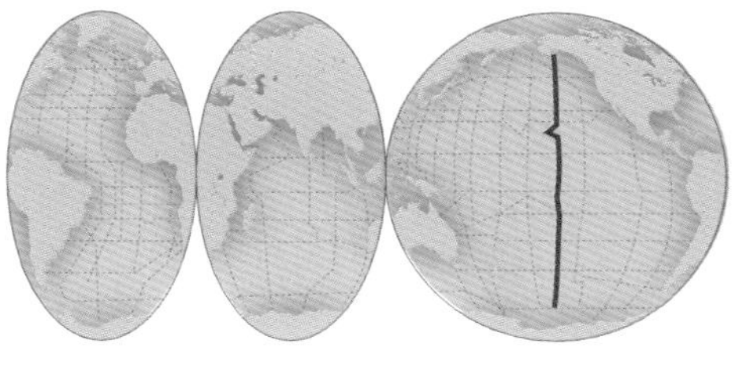

THE CLIMATE SYSTEM

The Earth's climate system is a highly complex interactive system involving the atmosphere, hydrosphere (oceans, lakes and rivers), biosphere (the Earth's living resources), cryosphere (particularly sea ice and polar ice caps) and lithosphere (the Earth's crust and upper mantle). This results in a great variety of climate types (*see 1*). Man's activities are affecting this system, and the monitoring of climate change, and of human influences upon it, is now a major issue.

Greenhouse gases such as carbon dioxide, methane and chlorofluorocarbons (CFCs) act to trap outgoing long-wave radiation, keeping the Earth's surface and lower atmosphere warmer than it would be otherwise. This is the phenomenon usually referred to as the greenhouse effect. Human activity has increased the atmospheric concentration of some of these gases and has therefore contributed to the effect. As a result of this, the world is about 0.6°C warmer than it was a hundred years ago with the three warmest years globally (in decreasing order) being 1998, 2002 and 2001 (*see 2*).

CLIMATE GRAPHS

These graphs relate by number, name and colour to the selected stations on the map and present mean temperature and precipitation values for each month. Red bars show average daily maximum and minimum temperatures for each month in degrees centigrade and fahrenheit. Vertical blue columns depict precipitation in millimetres and inches, with the total mean annual precipitation shown under the graph. The altitude of each station above sea level is given in metres and feet.

1. MAJOR CLIMATIC REGIONS AND SUB-TYPES

Köppen classification system
Winkel Tripel Projection
scale 1:110 000 000

•	Climate graph location	○	Weather extreme location

Polar
- EF Ice cap
- ET Tundra

Cooler humid
- Dc Dd Subarctic
- Db Continental cool summer
- Da Continental warm summer

Warmer humid
- Cb Cc Temperate
- Ca Humid subtropical
- Cs Mediterranean

Dry
- BS Steppe
- BW Desert

Tropical humid
- Aw As Savanna
- Af Am Rain forest

A   Rainy climate with no winter: coolest month above 18°C (64.4°F).

B   Dry climates; limits are defined by formulae based on rainfall effectiveness:
BS Steppe or semi-arid climate.
BW Desert or arid climate.

*C   Rainy climates with mild winters: coolest month above 0°C (32°F), but below 18°C (64.4°F); warmest month above 10°C (50°F).

*D   Rainy climates with severe winters: coldest month below 0°C (32°F); warmest month above 10°C (50°F).

E   Polar climates with no warm season: warmest month below 10°C (50°F).
ET Tundra climate: warmest month below 10°C (50°F) but above 0°C (32°F).
EF Perpetual frost: all months below 0°C (32°F).

* Modification of Köppen definition

a   Warmest month above 22°C (71.6°F).

b   Warmest month below 22°C (71.6°F).

c   Less than four months over 10°C (50°F).

d   As 'c', but with severe cold: coldest month below -38°C (-36.4°F).

f   Constantly moist rainfall throughout the year.

*h   Warmer dry: all months above 0°C (32°F).

*k   Cooler dry: at least one month below 0°C (32°F).

m   Monsoon rain: short dry season, but is compensated by heavy rains during rest of the year.

n   Frequent fog.

s   Dry season in summer.

w   Dry season in winter.

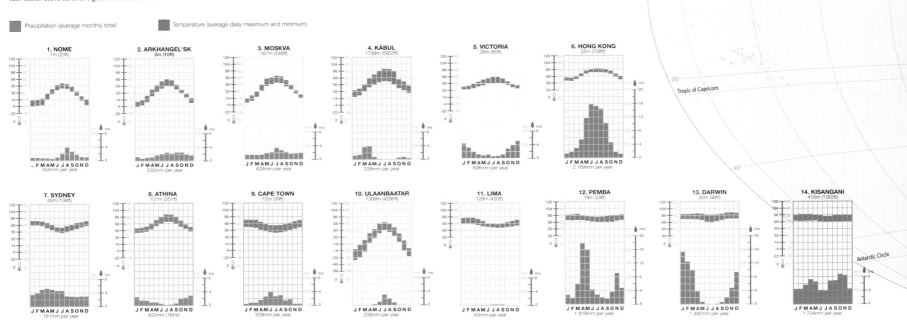

- Precipitation (average monthly total)
- Temperature (average daily maximum and minimum)

1. NOME — 7m (23ft) — 454mm per year
2. ARKHANGEL'SK — 3m (10ft) — 530mm per year
3. MOSKVA — 167m (548ft) — 624mm per year
4. KĀBUL — 1799m (5902ft) — 339mm per year
5. VICTORIA — 26m (85ft) — 696mm per year
6. HONG KONG — 33m (108ft) — 2 169mm per year
7. SYDNEY — 42m (138ft) — 1 181mm per year
8. ATHINA — 107m (351ft) — 402mm (16ins)
9. CAPE TOWN — 12m (39ft) — 509mm per year
10. ULAANBAATAR — 1309m (4295ft) — 209mm per year
11. LIMA — 128m (420ft) — 43mm per year
12. PEMBA — 18m (59ft) — 1 819mm per year
13. DARWIN — 30m (98ft) — 1 492mm per year
14. KISANGANI — 415m (1362ft) — 1 704mm per year

CLIMATE CHANGE

Future climate change depends on how quickly and to what extent the concentration of greenhouse gases and aerosols in the atmosphere increases. If we assume that no action is taken to limit future greenhouse gas emissions, then a warming during the 21st century of 0.2 to 0.3°C per decade is likely. Such a rate of warming would be greater than anything that has occurred over the last 10 000 years.

The detailed climatic response to the increase in carbon dioxide and other greenhouse gases is predicted using complex mathematical models of the climate. One of

the most advanced climate models in the world is that produced by the Hadley Centre of the UK Meteorological Office. This model has produced predictions of climatic change, including changes in temperature and precipitation (*see 3 and 4*). According to this model, some regions of the world will warm more quickly than others and precipitation will increase in some areas and decrease in others. Such changes are likely to have significant impacts on sea-level which could rise by as much as 50 cm over the next century. Human impacts would also be through the effects on water resources, food production and health.

3. TEMPERATURE IN THE 2080s

Predicted annual mean temperature change

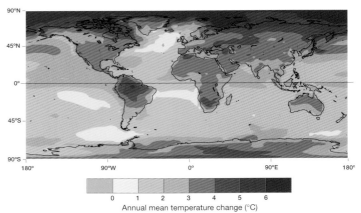

0	1	2	3	4	5	6

Annual mean temperature change (°C)

2. COMBINED GLOBAL LAND, AIR AND SEA SURFACE TEMPERATURES 1860–2004

Relative to 1961–1990 average. The purple line is a smoothing of the annual values to suppress sub-decadal time-scale variations.

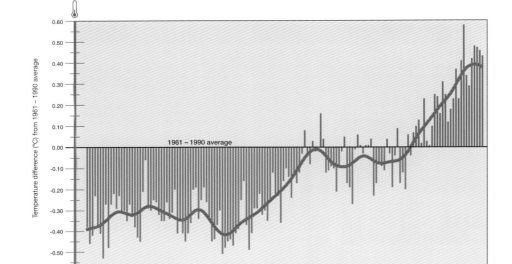

1961 – 1990 average

4. PRECIPITATION IN THE 2080s

Predicted average precipitation change

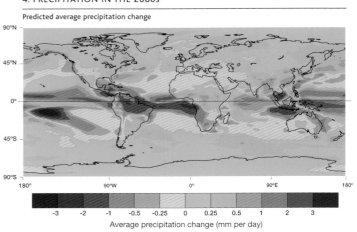

-3	-2	-1	-0.5	-0.25	0.25	0.5	1	2	3

Average precipitation change (mm per day)

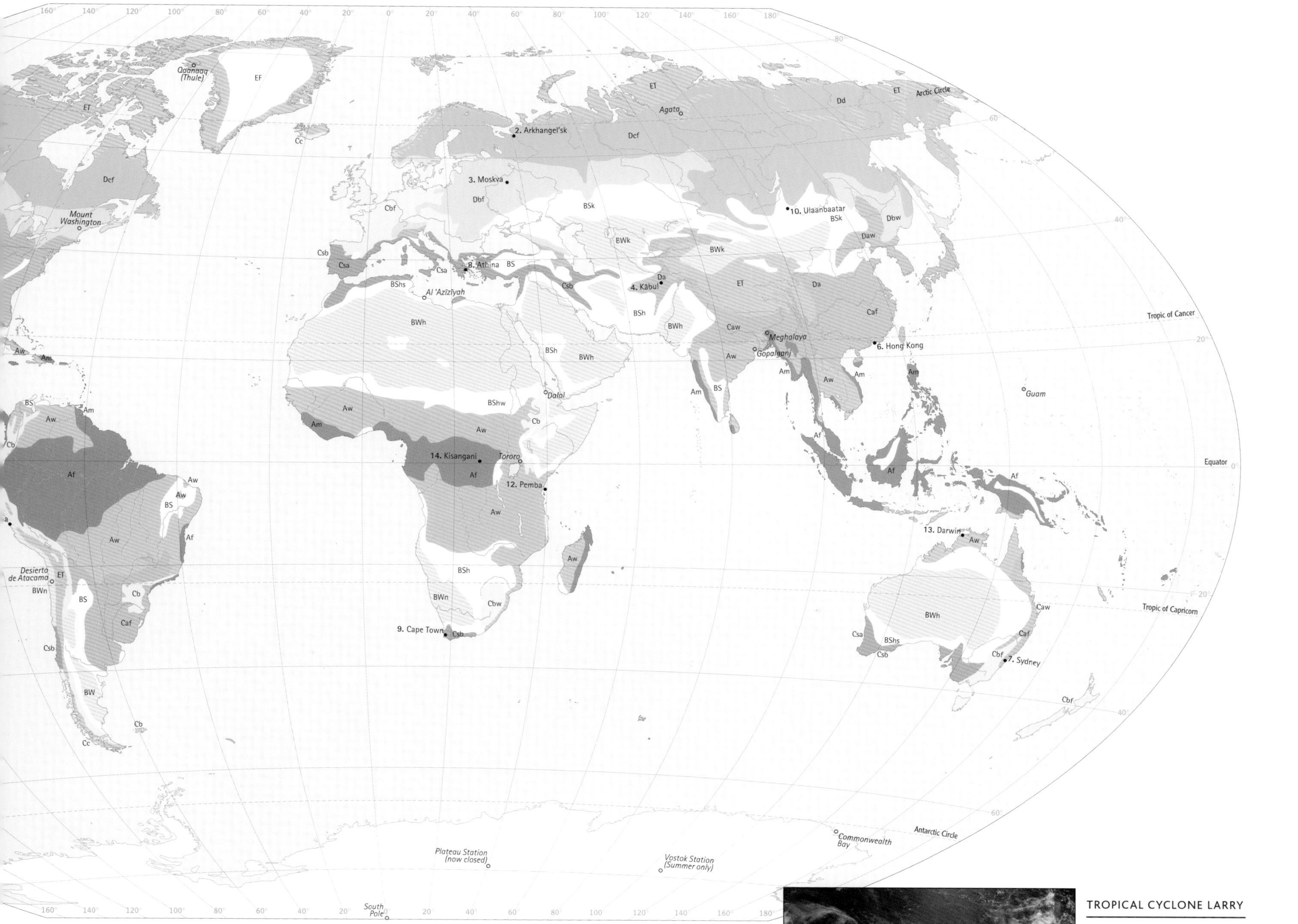

TROPICAL STORMS

Tropical storms develop, and have different names, in different parts of the world: hurricanes in the north Atlantic and east Pacific; typhoons in the northwest Pacific; and cyclones in the Indian Ocean region. There are also many local names for these events – those affecting the northern coast of Australia are known colloquially as the 'Willy-willies' (*see 5*).

Tropical storms are among the most powerful and destructive weather systems on Earth. Of the eighty to one hundred which develop annually over the tropical oceans, many make landfall and cause considerable damage to property and loss of life as a result of high winds and heavy rain.

The majority of tropical storms originate in the northwest Pacific, where as typhoons they commonly affect areas from

the Philippines through to China and Japan. They are also found as cyclones in the Bay of Bengal, either developing locally or on occasion being the remnants of typhoons which have moved westwards across Thailand. These storms bring heavy rains to eastern India or to the Ganges Delta in Bangladesh. In these places the land is so close to sea level that the rise in water levels has great potential for heavy loss of life.

The conditions required for the development of tropical storms – warm (over 26.5°C) ocean waters to a depth of at least 50 m; pre-existing cyclonic (low pressure) systems; thunderstorm activity; and moist layers of air in the mid-troposphere (around 5 km above the Earth's surface) – mean that most occur in mid- to late-summer in the areas concerned.

TROPICAL CYCLONE LARRY

Tropical cyclone Larry developed off northeast Australia on 18 March 2006. It reached maximum intensity on 20 March with gusts of wind reaching 290 km per hour, causing considerable damage to coastal towns and sugar cane fields. Most of the Australian banana crop was lost and the indusrty may take years to recover.

5. TRACKS OF TROPICAL STORMS

Wind speeds often over 160 km per hour
scale 1:295 000 000

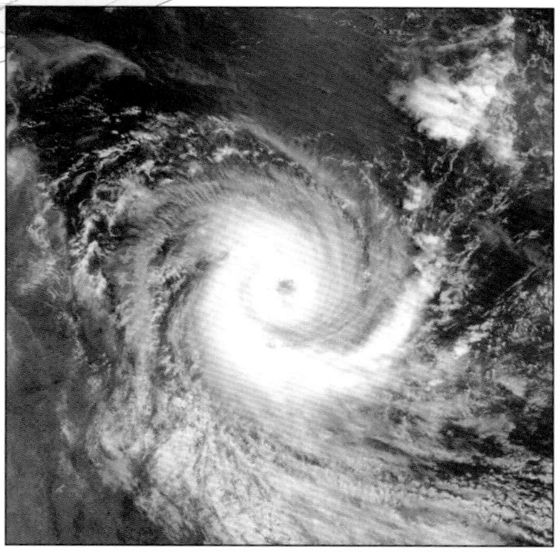

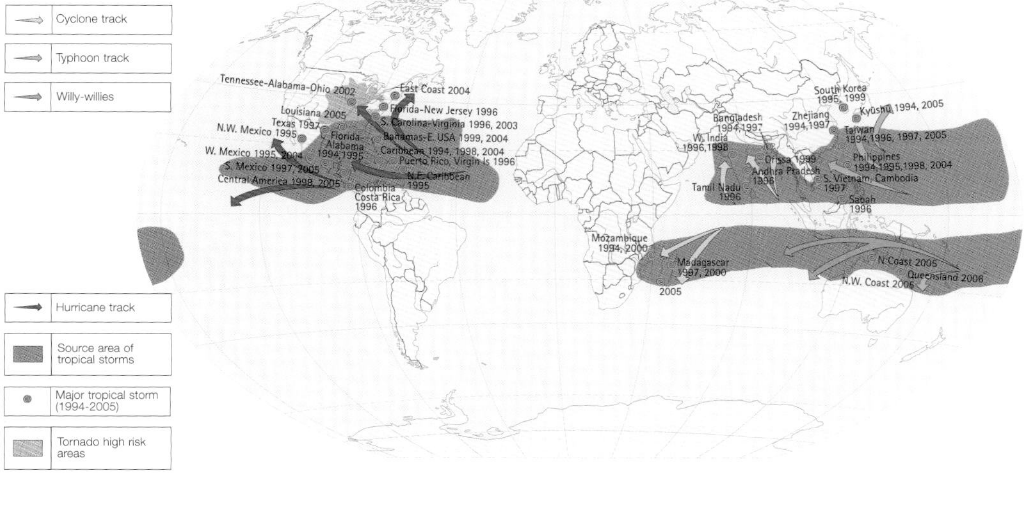

⟶	Cyclone track
⟶	Typhoon track
⟶	Willy-willies

→	Hurricane track
▬	Source area of tropical storms
•	Major tropical storm (1994-2005)
▨	Tornado high risk areas

WORLD WEATHER EXTREMES

Highest shade temperature	57.8°C/136°F Al 'Azīzīyah, Libya (13th September 1922)
Hottest place — Annual mean	34.4°C/93.9°F Dalol, Ethiopia
Driest place — Annual mean	0.1 mm/0.004 inches Desierto de Atacama, Chile
Most sunshine — Annual mean	90% Yuma, Arizona, USA (over 4 000 hours)
Least sunshine	Nil for 182 days each year, South Pole
Lowest screen temperature	89.2°C/-128.6°F Vostok Station, Antarctica (21st July 1983)
Coldest place — Annual mean	-56.6°C/-69.9°F Plateau Station, Antarctica
Wettest place — Annual mean	11 873 mm/467.4 inches Meghalaya, India
Most rainy days	Up to 350 per year Mount Waialeale, Hawaii, USA
Windiest place	322 km per hour/200 miles per hour in gales, Commonwealth Bay, Antarctica
Highest surface wind speed — High altitude	372 km per hour/231 miles per hour Mount Washington, New Hampshire, USA (12th April 1934)
Low altitude	333 km per hour/207 miles per hour Qaanaaq (Thule), Greenland 8th March 1972
Tornado	512 km per hour/318 miles per hour Oklahoma City, Oklahoma, USA (3rd May 1999)
Greatest snowfall	31 102 mm/1 224.5 inches Mount Rainier, Washington, USA (19th February 1971 — 18th February 1972)
Heaviest hailstones	1 kg/2.21 lb Gopalganj, Bangladesh (14th April 1986)
Thunder-days Average	251 days per year Tororo, Uganda
Highest barometric pressure	1 083.8 mb Agata, Siberia, Russian Federation (31st December 1968)
Lowest barometric pressure	870 mb 483 km/300 miles west of Guam, Pacific Ocean (12th October 1979)

GLOBAL LAND COVER

Many existing global land cover maps show only a general idea of the actual conditions on the Earth's surface. In 1999, a partnership led by the European Commission's Joint Research Centre (JRC) started the preparation of a new database to document the state of the world's land cover at the turn of the Millennium – the Global Land Cover 2000 project (GLC2000). The resulting land cover map as shown here was completed in March 2003 and shows the Earth's land cover as it was in 2000 at a ground resolution of 1km. The high resolution of the imagery used to compile the data set and map allows detailed interpretation of land cover patterns across the world. An additional benefit of holding the data in digital form is the ease with which information on land cover on world and continental scales can be extracted and analysed (see 2 and 3).

The scarcity of wetland habitats show just how rare these precious, fragile ecosystems are. Only small, regularly flooded shrublands of Siberia and areas of tree cover liable to inundation in South America and central Africa are really evident on the global scale. In contrast, the concentration of the world's cultivated land in the northern hemisphere is obvious with the cereal belt in North America clearly visible. This contrasts with western Europe where the smaller field sizes and more common mixed farming lead to much of this region being classified as cropland/natural vegetation mosaics. The cereal belts of eastern Europe show the transition once again to extensive agriculture. One of the most striking features are the belts of herbaceous cover and grassland/shrubland south of the Sahara desert. This clearly shows the area which is most at risk from desertification as the Sahara encroaches southward. Humankind's influence on the Earth's land cover is apparent throughout the map. This is evident from the major cities (in red) most prominent in northern India, eastern China and eastern United States of America.

Tropical forest cover is far from the uniform, unbroken swath so often depicted on world vegetation maps. In all areas of the world the tropical forest margins show encroachment of cultivated or grassland in the wake of human activity (see 4), although parts of their interiors still remain largely untouched. In the light of such patterns, the global figures for tropical deforestation rates (typically around 0.5–1 per cent per year) become even more alarming. Deforestation is not uniform, so such figures hide far more rapid rates of loss in the forest margins.

2. GLOBAL LAND COVER COMPOSITION

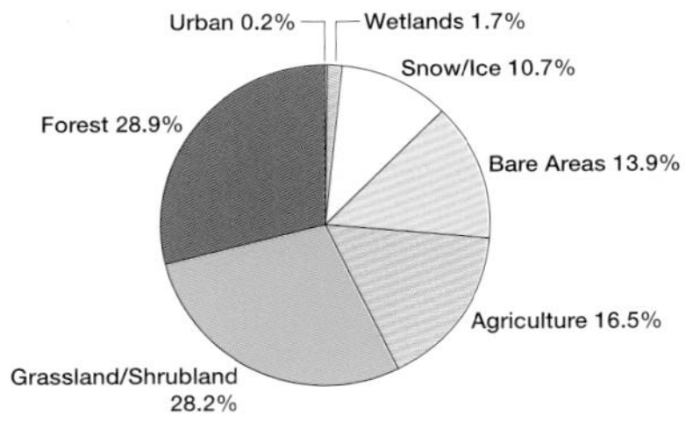

Urban 0.2% — Wetlands 1.7%
Snow/Ice 10.7%
Forest 28.9%
Bare Areas 13.9%
Agriculture 16.5%
Grassland/Shrubland 28.2%

3. CONTINENTAL LAND COVER COMPOSITION

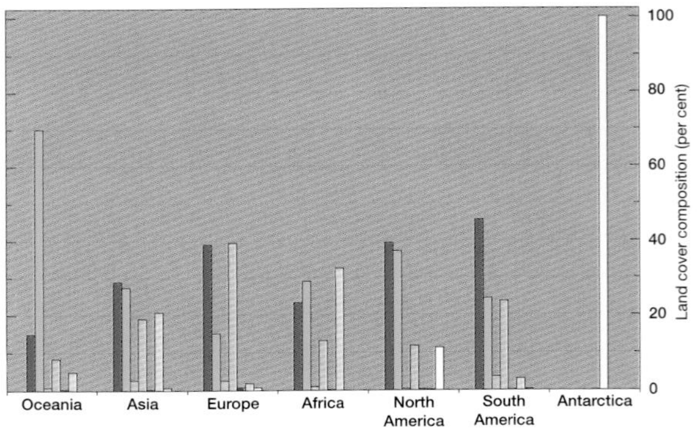

Oceania   Asia   Europe   Africa   North America   South America   Antarctica

Land cover composition (per cent)

1. WORLD LAND COVER

Winkel Tripel Projection
scale 1:85 000 000

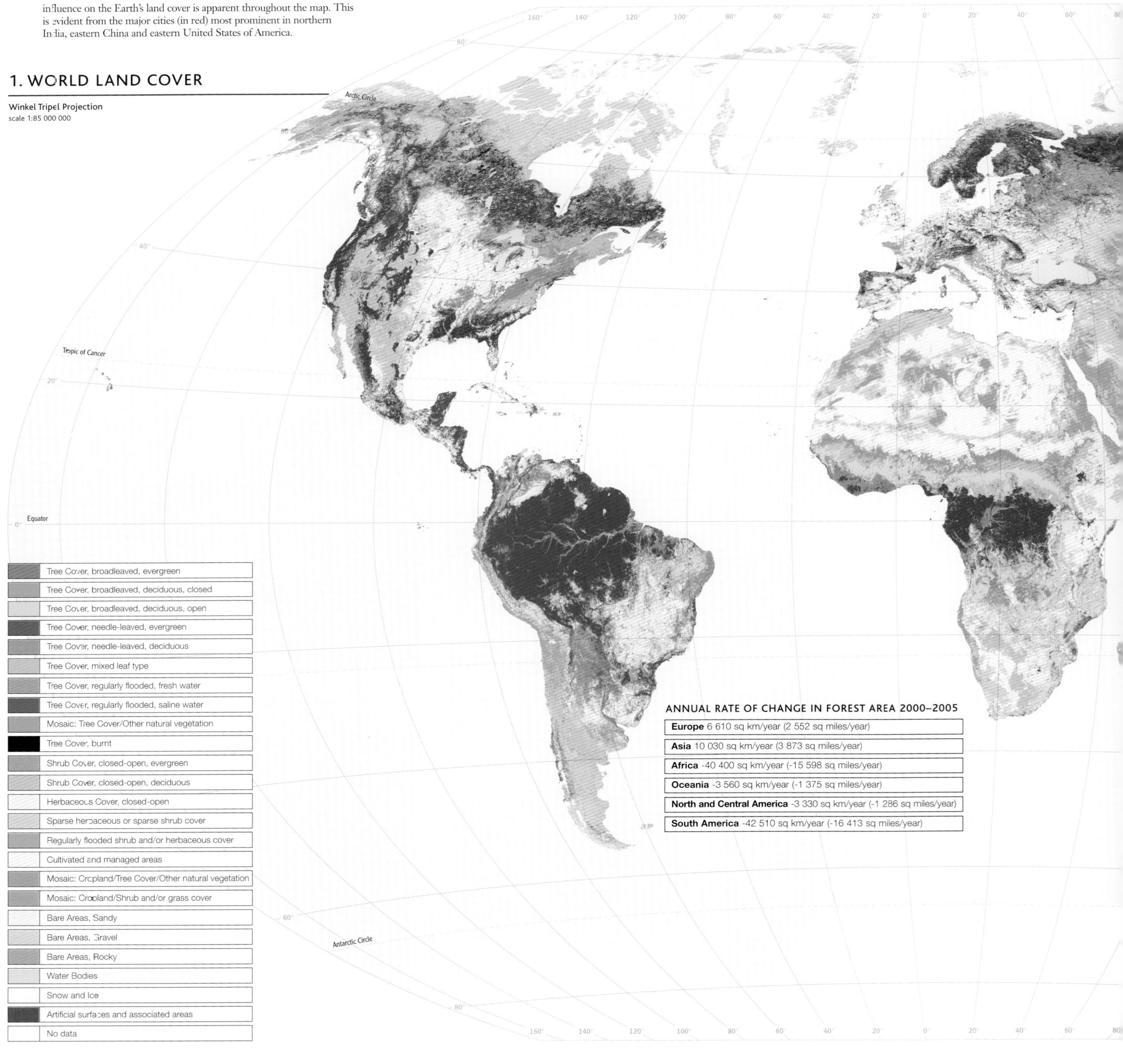

Land cover legend
Tree Cover, broadleaved, evergreen
Tree Cover, broadleaved, deciduous, closed
Tree Cover, broadleaved, deciduous, open
Tree Cover, needle-leaved, evergreen
Tree Cover, needle-leaved, deciduous
Tree Cover, mixed leaf type
Tree Cover, regularly flooded, fresh water
Tree Cover, regularly flooded, saline water
Mosaic: Tree Cover/Other natural vegetation
Tree Cover, burnt
Shrub Cover, closed-open, evergreen
Shrub Cover, closed-open, deciduous
Herbaceous Cover, closed-open
Sparse herbaceous or sparse shrub cover
Regularly flooded shrub and/or herbaceous cover
Cultivated and managed areas
Mosaic: Cropland/Tree Cover/Other natural vegetation
Mosaic: Cropland/Shrub and/or grass cover
Bare Areas, Sandy
Bare Areas, Gravel
Bare Areas, Rocky
Water Bodies
Snow and Ice
Artificial surfaces and associated areas
No data

ANNUAL RATE OF CHANGE IN FOREST AREA 2000–2005

Region	Rate
Europe	6 610 sq km/year (2 552 sq miles/year)
Asia	10 030 sq km/year (3 873 sq miles/year)
Africa	-40 400 sq km/year (-15 598 sq miles/year)
Oceania	-3 560 sq km/year (-1 375 sq miles/year)
North and Central America	-3 330 sq km/year (-1 286 sq miles/year)
South America	-42 510 sq km/year (-16 413 sq miles/year)

LAND COVER GRAPHS - CLASSIFICATION AND KEY

Class description	Global Land Cover class
Forest	Tree Cover, broadleaved, evergreen
	Tree Cover, broadleaved, deciduous, closed
	Tree Cover, broadleaved, deciduous, open
	Tree Cover, needle-leaved, evergreen
	Tree Cover, needle-leaved, deciduous
	Tree Cover, mixed leaf type
	Mosaic: Tree Cover/Other natural vegetation
	Tree Cover, burnt
Grass/Shrubland	Shrub Cover, closed-open, evergreen
	Shrub Cover, closed-open, deciduous
	Herbaceous Cover, closed-open
	Sparse herbaceous or sparse shrub cover
Wetlands	Tree Cover, regularly flooded, fresh water
	Tree Cover, regularly flooded, saline water
	Regularly flooded shrub and/or herbaceous cover
Agriculture	Cultivated and managed areas
	Mosaic: Cropland/Tree Cover/other natural vegetation
	Mosaic: Cropland/Shrub and/or grass cover
Urban	Artificial surfaces and associated areas
Snow/Ice	Water Bodies
	Snow and Ice
Bare Areas	Bare Areas

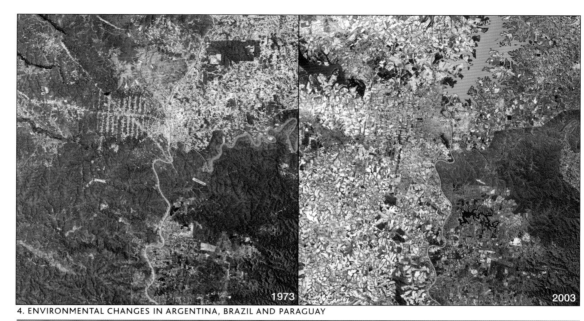

4. ENVIRONMENTAL CHANGES IN ARGENTINA, BRAZIL AND PARAGUAY

These two Landsat satellite images centre on the confluence of the Iguaçu and Paraná rivers in South America. Over the thirty-year time gap the Itaipu Dam was completed and the tremendous development in the area makes the Iguaçu National Park stand out clearly as an area where the native forest is being preserved.

ENVIRONMENTAL CHANGE AND CONSERVATION

The earth has a rich and diverse environment. Forests and woodland form the predominant natural land cover with tropical rain forests believed to be home to the majority of animal and plant species. Grassland and scrub tend to have a lower natural species diversity but has suffered the most impact from man's intervention through conversion to agriculture, burning and the introduction of livestock. Wherever man interferes with existing biological and environmental processes, degradation of that environment occurs, to varying degrees. This interference also affects inland water and oceans where pollution, over-exploitation of marine resources and the need for fresh water has had major consequences for land and sea environments.

Almost half of the world's post-glacial forest has been cleared or degraded and old-growth forest continues to decline. Often it is only in protected areas (*see 4*) that the natural forest remains untouched. In other areas the use of water for agriculture can upset the natural cycle of events causing significant changes. Lake Chad is currently much reduced in size from thirty years ago (*see 5*). In other places man has built dams, created reservoirs and significantly changed the landscape by irrigation.

Natural changes to the planet's equilibrium can occur which can impact on the surrounding environment and on man's use of the land. For example, the eruption of Mt St Helens in 1980 left a deep layer of ash and pumice covering the area up to eight kilometres away as well as felling woodland as a result of the blast, leaving a barren wasteland. Dust storms can travel great distances, polluting the atmosphere while the failure of seasonal rains or the sudden excess of water can devastate a year's food resources for man and nature.

UNESCO adopted an international treaty in 1972 to recognize sites, both cultural and natural, of universal significance. Such places are unique, irreplaceable sites of inspiration of man's achievement or nature's creation. Presently there are 788 official sites, 154 natural and 23 mixed, but 35 of the 788 are cited as 'in danger' either due to civil conflicts or war, such as those in the Democratic Republic of the Congo or through pressure from agriculture and logging, as in Honduras.

AREA THREATENED BY DESERTIFICATION

Europe (including Russian Federation) 21%	
Asia (excluding Russian Federation) 46%	
Africa 46%	
Oceania 86%	
North and South America 27%	

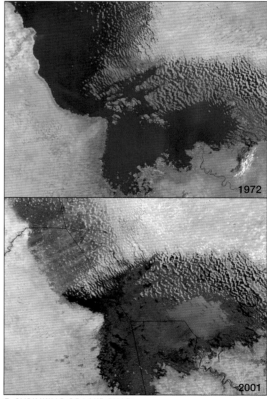

5. SHRINKING OF LAKE CHAD

Lake Chad is very shallow and the lake level has varied tremendously over time. During the past thirty-five years the climate has been dry and this coincided with increased human demand for water. The lake has shrunk dramatically as a result.

POPULATION DISTRIBUTION AND GROWTH

People are distributed very unevenly over the face of the planet. As shown on the main map (see 1), over a quarter of the land area is uninhabited or has extremely low population density. Approximately a quarter of the land area is occupied at densities of 25 or more persons per square km, with the three largest concentrations of east Asia, the Indian subcontinent and Europe accounting for over half the world total. China and India dominate the scene, together accounting for nearly two-fifths of world population (see 2).

Over the past half century world population has been growing faster than it has ever done before. Whereas world population did not pass the one billion mark until 1804 and took another 123 years to reach two billion in 1927, it then added the third billion in 33 years, the fourth in 14 years and the fifth in 13 years, with the 6 billion mark being passed only 12 years after this in 1999. It is expected that another three billion people will have been added to the world's population by 2050 (see 3). Recent projections looking even further into the future estimate that the total will have risen to around 9 billion by 2300.

Population growth since 1950 has been spread very unevenly between the continents. While overall numbers have been growing extremely rapidly since 1950, a massive 89 per cent increase has taken place in the less developed regions, especially southern and eastern Asia, while Europe's population is now stationary and ageing rapidly. Africa was the second largest contributor and represents by far the highest growth rate of all the continents. The latest trends in population growth at country level (see 4) emphasize the continuing contrast between the more and less developed regions. Annual growth rates of 1.1 per cent or more are very common in Latin America, Africa and the southern half of Asia. A number of countries have rates in excess of 2.8 per cent, which if continued would lead to the doubling of their populations in 25 years or less.

2. TOP TEN COUNTRIES BY POPULATION AND POPULATION DENSITY

TOTAL POPULATION 2005	COUNTRY	RANK	COUNTRY	POPULATION DENSITY 2005	
				per sq mile	per sq km
1 323 345 000	China	1	Monaco	35 000	17 500
1 103 371 000	India	2	Singapore	17 514	6 770
298 213 000	USA	3	Malta	3 295	1 272
222 781 000	Indonesia	4	Maldives	2 861	1 104
186 405 000	Brazil	5	Vatican City	2 760	1 104
157 935 000	Pakistan	6	Bahrain	2 723	1 052
143 202 000	Russian Federation	7	Bangladesh	2 551	985
141 822 000	Bangladesh	8	Nauru	1 750	667
131 530 000	Nigeria	9	Taiwan	1 636	632
128 085 000	Japan	10	Barbados	1 627	628

3. WORLD POPULATION GROWTH BY CONTINENT 1750–2050

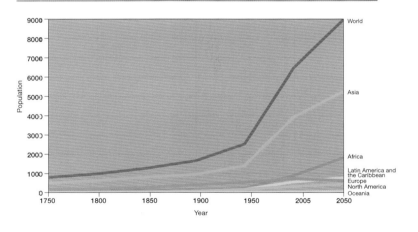

1. WORLD POPULATION DISTRIBUTION

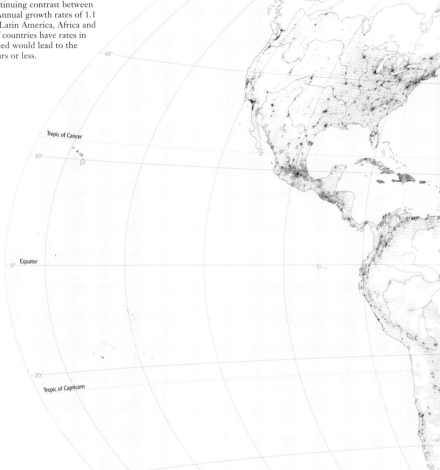

Winkel Tripel Projection
scale 1:93 000 000

Population density

inhabitants per sq mile
2 500   1 250   625   250   125   62.5   12.5   2.5   0   Uninhabited

1 000   500   250   100   50   25   5   1   0
inhabitants per sq km

4. POPULATION CHANGE 2000–2005

Average annual rate of population change (per cent) and the top ten contributors to world population growth (net annual addition).
scale 1:255 000 000

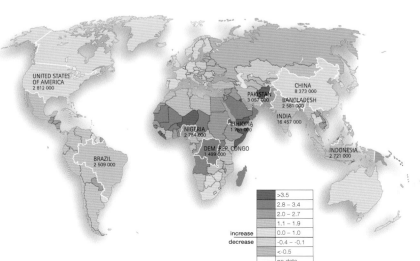

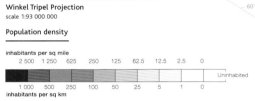

	>3.5
	2.8 – 3.4
	2.0 – 2.7
	1.1 – 1.9
increase	0.0 – 1.0
decrease	-0.4 – -0.1
	<-0.5
	no data

5. KEY POPULATION STATISTICS FOR MAJOR REGIONS

	Population 2005 (millions)	Growth (per cent)	Infant mortality rate	Total fertility rate	Life expectancy (years)	% aged 60 and over	
						2005	2050
World	6 453	1.21	57	2.65	65.4	10	22
More developed regions[1]	1 209	0.30	8	1.56	75.6	20	32
Less developed regions[2]	5 243	1.43	62	2.9	63.4	8	20
Africa	887	2.18	94	4.97	49.1	5	10
Asia	3 917	1.21	54	2.47	67.3	9	24
Europe[3]	725	0.00	9	1.4	73.7	21	35
Latin America and the Caribbean[4]	558	1.42	26	2.55	71.5	9	24
North America	332	0.97	7	1.99	77.6	17	27
Oceania	33	1.32	29	2.32	74	14	25

Except for population (2005), and % aged 60 and over figures, the data are annual averages projected for the period 2000–2005.
1. Europe, North America, Australia, New Zealand and Japan.
2. Africa, Asia (excluding Japan), Latin America and the Caribbean, and Oceania (excluding Australia and New Zealand).
3. Includes Russian Federation.
4. South America, Central America (including Mexico) and all Carribean Islands.

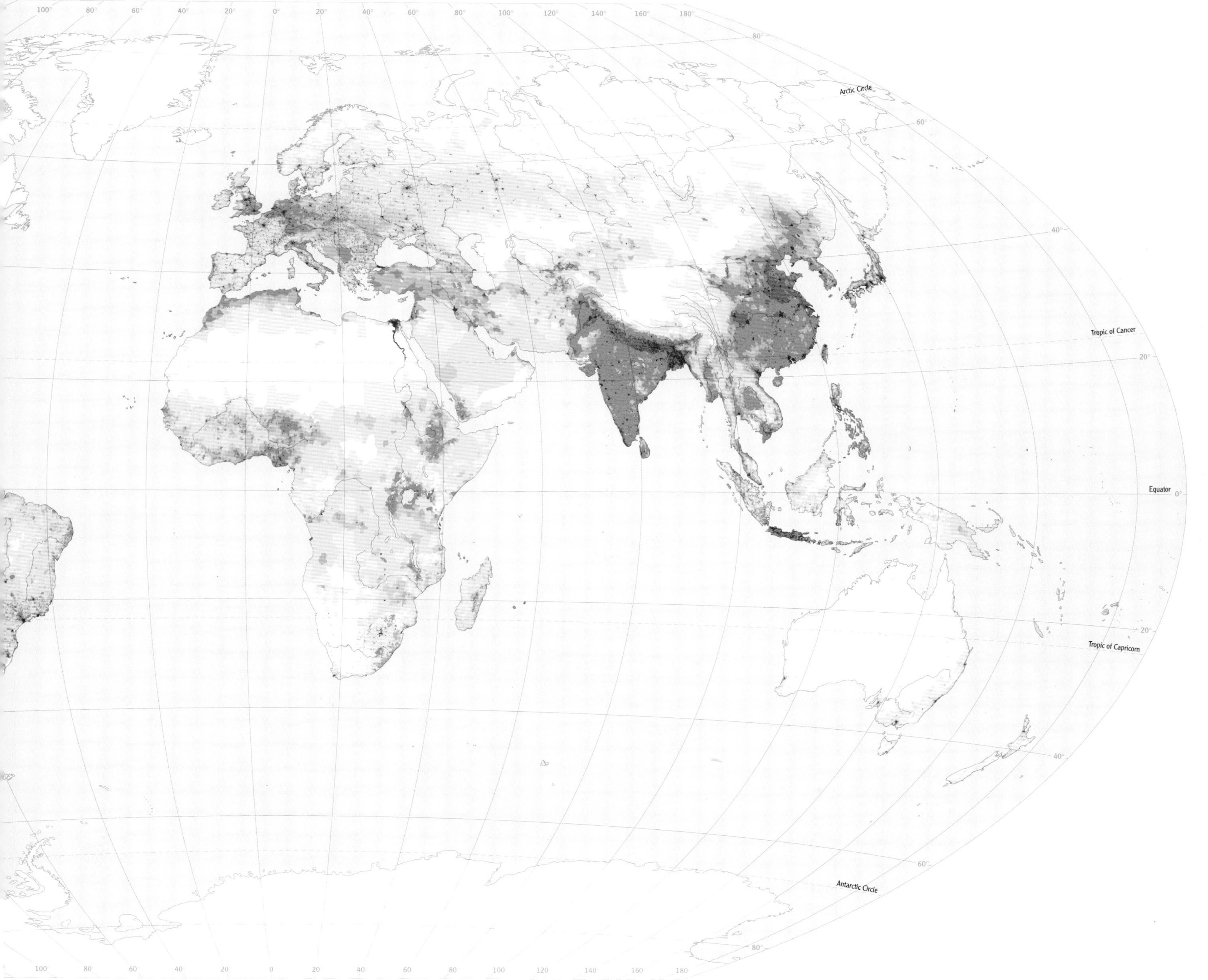

DEMOGRAPHIC TRANSITION

Behind patterns of population growth lies the 'demographic transition' process, where countries pass through a phase of falling death rates and then a phase of falling fertility. Most parts of the world have passed through the first phase, with the average life expectancy of 63.4 years in the less developed world now not far behind that of 75.6 years in the more developed regions (*see 5*). Even so, infant mortality – a very good indicator of human development levels –

remains a major challenge in the less developed regions (*see 6*). Here, an average of sixty-two out of every one thousand babies die before their first birthday, compared to only eight out of every one thousand in the more developed regions. Sub-Saharan Africa started this transitional phase later than most other parts of the world and has so far seen life expectancy rise to only 45.7 years, with progress being hampered by continuing high levels of infant

mortality and by rising numbers of AIDS-related deaths.

Reductions in fertility rate (*see 7*) hold the key to the successful completion of the transition and the future stabilization of population growth. Much of the more developed world is well advanced in this process. In particular, Europe's total fertility rate (broadly the average number of babies born to each woman) is now

down to 1.4 – well below the 'replacement rate' of 2.1 needed to give a constant population in the long term. Predictions indicate that there will be a major increase in the number of older people throughout the world especially in less developed regions (*see 5*). Europe's proportion of people aged 60 and over will rise from one-fifth to one-third whereas Latin America's will almost treble from 9 to 24 per cent.

6. INFANT MORTALITY RATE 2000–2005

Deaths of infants less than one year old per 1000 live births.
scale 1:315 000 000

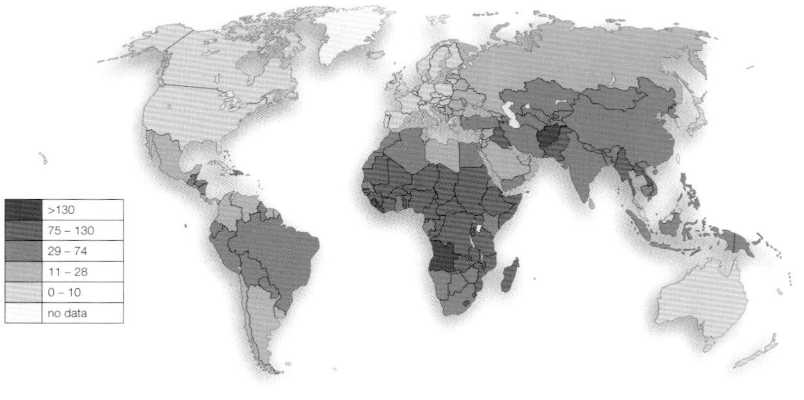

	>130
	75 – 130
	29 – 74
	11 – 28
	0 – 10
	no data

7. TOTAL FERTILITY RATE 2000–2005

Estimate of the number of children a woman will bear during her child-bearing years.
scale 1:315 000 000

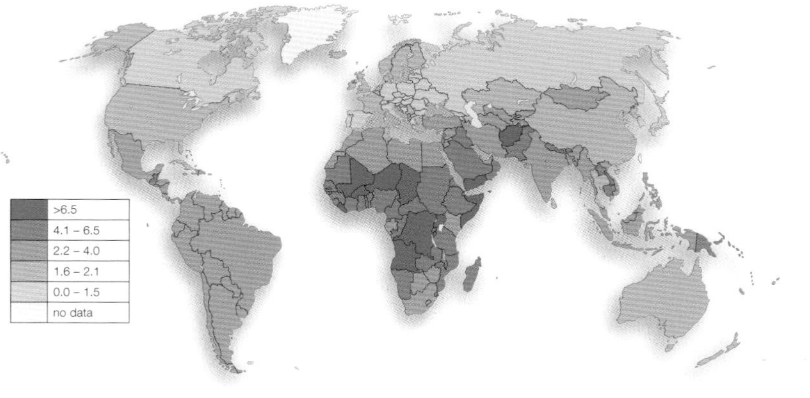

	>6.5
	4.1 – 6.5
	2.2 – 4.0
	1.6 – 2.1
	0.0 – 1.5
	no data

TOWARDS AN URBANIZED WORLD

World population is urbanizing rapidly but the current level of urbanization – the proportion of the population living in urban conditions – varies greatly across the world, as does its rate of increase. In the hundred years up to 1950 the greatest changes in urban population patterns took place in Europe and North America. Relatively few large cities developed elsewhere and most of these were in coastal locations with good trading connections with the imperial and industrial nations. This legacy is still highly visible on the world map of major cities (*see 1*). The main feature of the past half century has been the massive growth in the numbers of urban dwellers in the less developed regions. This process is still accelerating, posing an even greater logistical challenge during the next few decades than it did in the closing decades of the twentieth century.

The year 2007 is likely to be a momentous point in world history, when for the first time urban dwellers will outnumber those living in traditionally rural areas, according to UN projections. The annual rise in the percentage of the world's population living in cities has been accelerating steadily since the 1970s and will be running at unprecedentedly high levels until at least 2030. As a result, by then, 60.8 per cent of the world's population will be urbanites compared to 37.3 per cent in 1975 and 49.2 per cent in 2005 (*see 2*). In absolute terms, the global urban population more than doubled between 1970 and 2000 and is expected to grow by a further 2.1 billion by 2030 (*see 3*).

2. LEVEL OF URBANIZATION BY MAJOR REGION 1975–2030

Urban population as a percentage of total population

	1975	2005	2030
World	37.3	49.2	60.8
More developed regions[1]	67.2	74.9	81.7
Less developed regions[2]	26.9	43.2	57.1
Africa	25.3	39.7	53.5
Asia	24.0	39.9	54.5
Europe[3]	66.0	73.3	79.6
Latin America and the Caribbean[4]	61.2	77.6	84.6
North America	73.8	80.8	86.9
Oceania	71.7	73.3	74.9

1. Europe, North America, Australia, New Zealand and Japan.
2. Africa, Asia (excluding Japan), Latin America and the Caribbean, and Oceania (excluding Australia and New Zealand).
3. Includes Russian Federation.
4. South America, Central America (including Mexico) and all Caribbean Islands.

1. THE WORLD'S MAJOR CITIES

Urban agglomerations with over 1 million inhabitants
Winkel Tripel Projection
scale 1:111 000 000

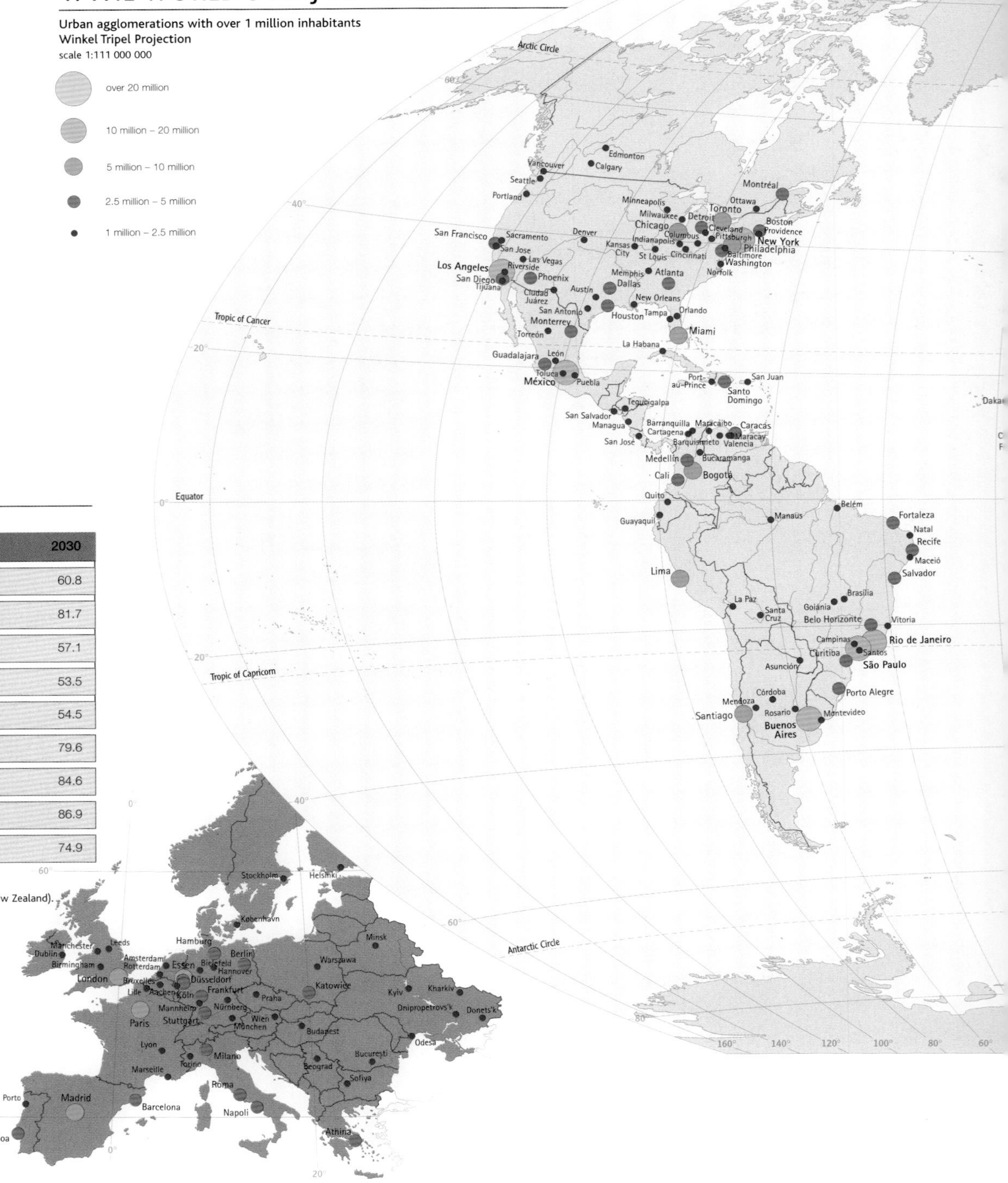

- over 20 million
- 10 million – 20 million
- 5 million – 10 million
- 2.5 million – 5 million
- 1 million – 2.5 million

3. TOTAL URBAN POPULATION OF MAJOR REGIONS 1950–2030

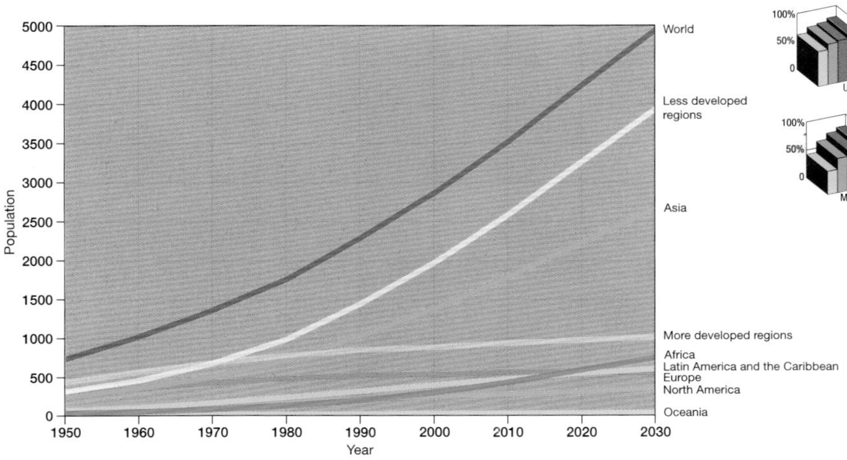

4. LEVEL OF URBANIZATION

Percentage of total population living in urban areas 2005 and growth in urbanization 1950–2025 (selected countries)
scale 1:280 000 000

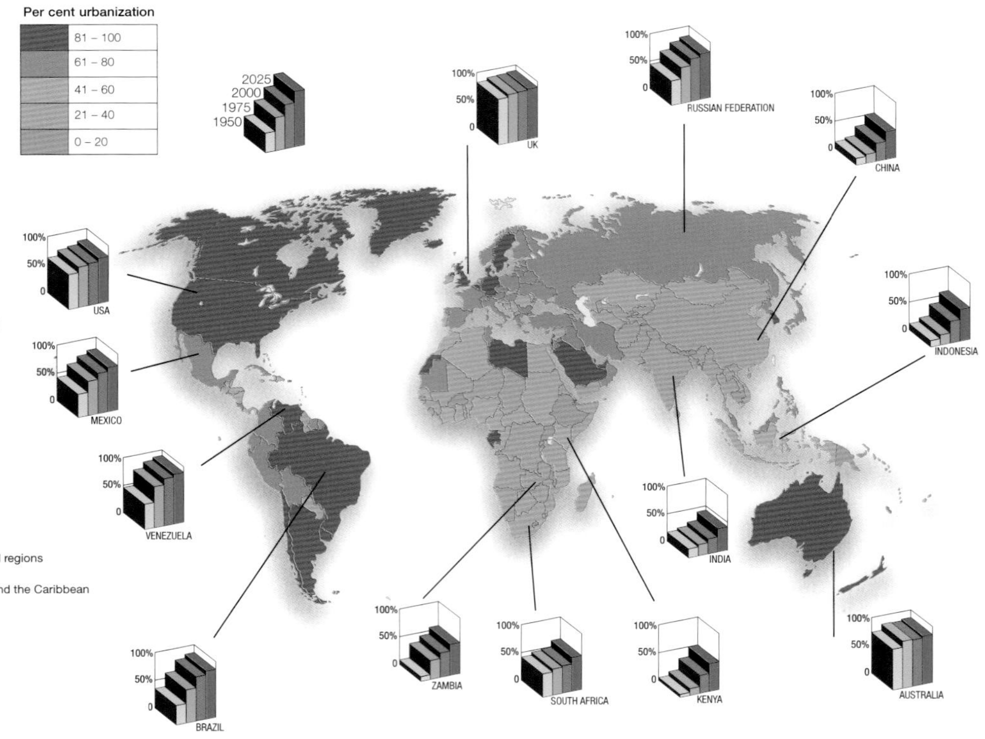

Per cent urbanization

- 81 – 100
- 61 – 80
- 41 – 60
- 21 – 40
- 0 – 20

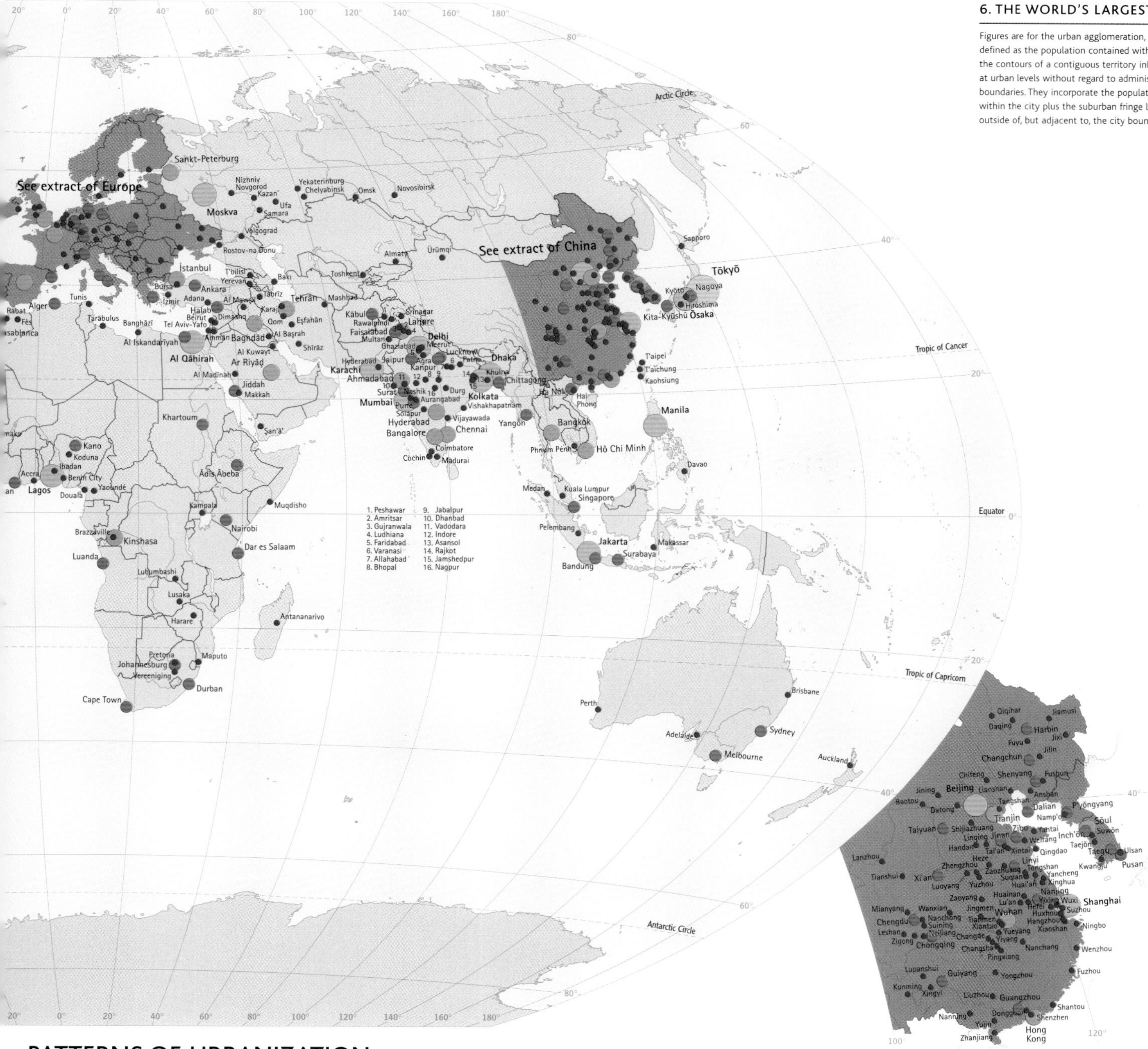

6. THE WORLD'S LARGEST CITIES 2005

Figures are for the urban agglomeration, defined as the population contained within the contours of a contiguous territory inhabited at urban levels without regard to administrative boundaries. They incorporate the population within the city plus the suburban fringe lying outside of, but adjacent to, the city boundaries.

City	Population
Cities >10 000 000 inhabitants	
Tōkyō Japan	35 327 000
México Mexico	19 013 000
New York USA	18 498 000
Mumbai India	18 336 000
São Paulo Brazil	18 333 000
Delhi India	15 334 000
Kolkata India	14 299 000
Buenos Aires Argentina	13 349 000
Jakarta Indonesia	13 194 000
Shanghai China	12 665 000
Dhaka Bangladesh	12 560 000
Los Angeles USA	12 146 000
Karachi Pakistan	11 819 000
Rio de Janeiro Brazil	11 469 000
Ōsaka Japan	11 286 000
Al Qāhirah Egypt	11 146 000
Lagos Nigeria	11 135 000
Beijing China	10 849 000
Manila Philippines	10 677 000
Moskva Russian Federation	10 672 000
Cities 5 000 000 – 10 000 000 inhabitants	
Paris France	9 854 000
İstanbul Turkey	9 760 000
Sŏul South Korea	9 592 000
Tianjin China	9 346 000
Chicago USA	8 711 000
Lima Peru	8 180 000
London United Kingdom	7 615 000
Bogotá Colombia	7 594 000
Tehrān Iran	7 352 000
Hong Kong China	7 182 000
Chennai India	6 915 000
Bangkok Thailand	6 604 000
Essen Germany	6 566 000
Bangalore India	6 532 000
Lahore Pakistan	6 373 000
Hyderabad India	6 145 000
Wuhan China	6 003 000
Baghdād Iraq	5 910 000
Kinshasa Democratic Rep. of the Congo	5 717 000
Santiago Chile	5 623 000
Ar Riyāḍ Saudi Arabia	5 514 000
Miami USA	5 380 000
Philadelphia USA	5 325 000
Sankt-Peterburg Russian Federation	5 315 000
Belo Horizonte Brazil	5 304 000
Ahmadabad India	5 171 000
Madrid Spain	5 145 000
Toronto Canada	5 060 000
Hô Chi Minh Vietnam	5 030 000
Cities 2 500 000 – 5 000 000 inhabitants	
Chongqing China	4 975 000
Shenyang China	4 916 000
Dallas USA	4 612 000
Khartoum Sudan	4 495 000
Pune India	4 485 000
Barcelona Spain	4 424 000
Sydney Australia	4 388 000
Singapore Singapore	4 372 000
Boston USA	4 313 000
Atlanta USA	4 284 000
Houston USA	4 283 000
Washington USA	4 190 000
Chittagong Bangladesh	4 171 000
Ha Nôi Vietnam	4 147 000
Yangôn Myanmar	4 082 000
Bandung Indonesia	4 020 000
Milano Italy	4 007 000
Detroit USA	3 980 000
Guadalajara Mexico	3 905 000
Guangzhou China	3 881 000
Jiddah Saudi Arabia	3 807 000
Porto Alegre Brazil	3 795 000
Al Iskandarīyah Egypt	3 760 000
Casablanca Morocco	3 743 000
Frankfurt am Main Germany	3 721 000
Surat India	3 671 000
Melbourne Australia	3 663 000
Ankara Turkey	3 593 000
Recife Brazil	3 527 000
Pusan South Korea	3 527 000
Monterrey Mexico	3 517 000
Abidjan Cote d'Ivoire	3 516 000
Montréal Canada	3 511 000
Chengdu China	3 478 000
Phoenix USA	3 393 000
San Francisco USA	3 342 000
Brasília Brazil	3 341 000
Salvador Brazil	3 331 000
Berlin Germany	3 328 000
Düsseldorf Germany	3 325 000
Johannesburg South Africa	3 288 000
Kābul Afghanistan	3 288 000
P'yŏngyang North Korea	3 284 000
Caracas Venezuela	3 276 000
Fortaleza Brazil	3 261 000
Alger Algeria	3 260 000
Xi'an China	3 256 000
Athina Greece	3 238 000
Medellín Colombia	3 236 000
Nagoya Japan	3 189 000
Cape Town South Africa	3 103 000
Changchun China	3 092 000
Köln Germany	3 084 000
Kanpur India	3 040 000
Tel Aviv-Yafo Israel	3 025 000
Seattle USA	2 959 000
Katowice Poland	2 914 000
Napoli Italy	2 905 000
Ādīs Ābeba Ethiopia	2 899 000
Harbin China	2 898 000
Kano Nigeria	2 884 000
Curitiba Brazil	2 871 000
Luanda Angola	2 839 000
San Diego USA	2 818 000
Nairobi Kenya	2 818 000
Kita-Kyūshū Japan	2 815 000
Nanjing China	2 806 000
Jaipur India	2 796 000
Zibo China	2 775 000
Surabaya Indonesia	2 735 000
Dalian China	2 709 000
Stuttgart Germany	2 705 000
Hamburg Germany	2 686 000
Dar es Salaam Tanzania	2 683 000
Jinan China	2 654 000
Durban South Africa	2 643 000
Inch'ŏn South Korea	2 642 000
Campinas Brazil	2 640 000
Roma Italy	2 628 000
Kyiv Ukraine	2 623 000
Lucknow India	2 589 000
Cali Colombia	2 583 000
Faisalabad Pakistan	2 533 000
Taiyuan China	2 516 000
Taegu South Korea	2 510 000
Halab Syria	2 505 000
İzmir Turkey	2 500 000

PATTERNS OF URBANIZATION

There is a broad contrast in the levels of urbanization between the more and less developed regions (*see 4*). In the more developed regions as a whole, three-quarters of the population now live in urban places. Excluding the smallest countries, levels range from 97 per cent for Belgium to under 50 per cent for Albania, Bosnia, Moldova and Slovenia. Many countries have seen very little increase in their level of urbanization over several decades, with some reporting renewed population growth in rural areas. Only 42.1 per cent of the population in the less developed regions are urbanites, but this represents a big jump from the 26.9 per cent figure for 1975. Africa and Asia both currently average less than this, but will be seeing the greatest changes in the future, with their urban proportions likely to pass the 50 per cent mark by 2025. Between 2000 and 2030, Africa and Asia are expected to account for 5 out of every 6 extra urbanites or around 453 and 1 300 million people in absolute terms.

Alongside the rise in the world's urban population has occurred a massive increase in the number and size of cities, especially of the very large cities or 'megacities'. In 1950, New York was the only agglomeration with over 10 million inhabitants, but the number of such cities had grown to six by 1980 and to twenty-one by 2000. There are expected to be twenty-five by 2015, according to United Nations figures (*see 5*). This increase has been principally an Asian phenomenon, as the additional four megacities are all in Asia. By 2000 North America's tally had risen to only two, and Latin America possessed four, but Asia had acquired twelve. This marked growth in the number of megacities in recent years is due to a combination of in-migration and natural increase, together with the physical outward expansion of their built-up areas and the incorporation of nearby settlements.

5. 10 MILLION CITIES

Dates by which cities attain 10 million population 1950–2015

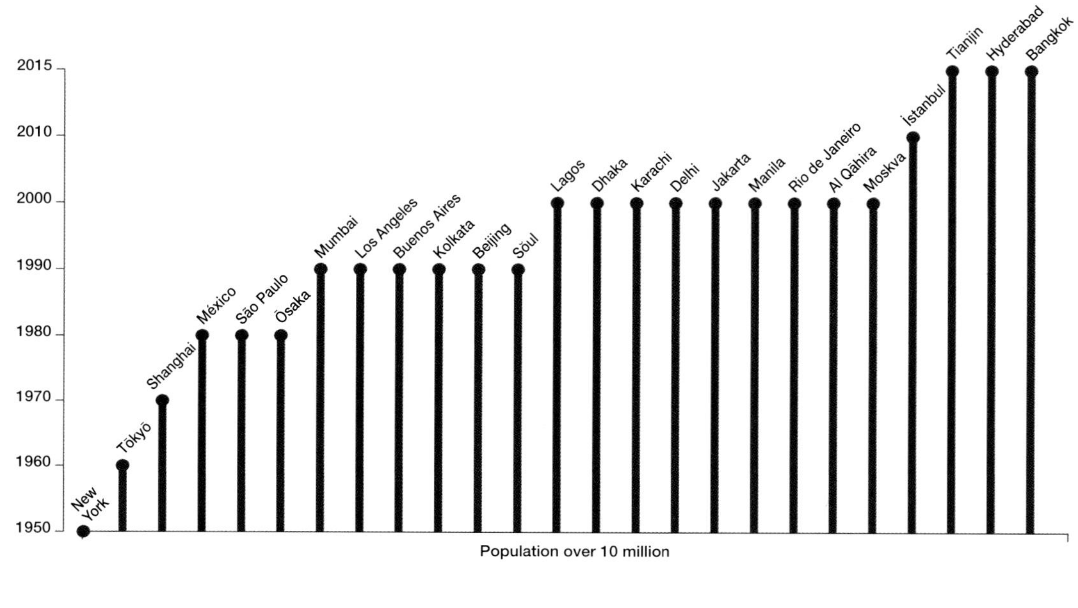

Population over 10 million

THE DISTRIBUTION OF MINERALS

Geological processes have determined the distribution of mineral resources but the location of productive mines is the result of geological, economic and political factors. The map *(see 1)* shows the locations of the most important mines producing industrial and metallic minerals. The bulk of world reserves – those resources which can be extracted economically at a particular time – are located at the mines shown.

Many aspects of the distribution of mineral resources are related to the Earth's tectonic structure. For example, the numerous large copper mines around parts of the Pacific rim are related to the destructive plate margins in these areas *(see pages 24–25)*. Most iron ore now comes from giant sedimentary deposits which have been naturally enriched by near-surface processes. These occur in ancient 'cratons' which are areas of the crust which have been internally stable for more than half a billion years and are typified by western Australia, eastern Brazil and the Canadian and Eurasian 'shields'. Output from the main iron ore producers has varied over time, with China becoming the leading world producer in the 1990s *(see 2)*.

Another striking relationship of mineral resources to geography and climate is provided by the distribution of bauxite, the main ore of aluminium. With few exceptions, major bauxite deposits are situated in the tropics, because bauxite is formed by the weathering of rocks at the Earth's surface under tropical climatic conditions *(see 3)*.

1. LOCATION OF SIGNIFICANT MINES

Producing mines or major deposits in active development, 2002
See table below for index to sites
Winkel Tripel Projection
scale 1:100 000 000

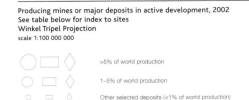

>5% of world production
1–5% of world production
Other selected deposits (<1% of world production)

METALLIC MINERALS

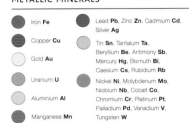

Iron **Fe**
Copper **Cu**
Gold **Au**
Uranium **U**
Aluminium **Al**
Manganese **Mn**
Lead **Pb**, Zinc **Zn**, Cadmium **Cd**, Silver **Ag**
Tin **Sn**, Tantalum **Ta**, Beryllium **Be**, Antimony **Sb**, Mercury **Hg**, Bismuth **Bi**, Caesium **Cs**, Rubidium **Rb**
Nickel **Ni**, Molybdenum **Mo**, Niobium **Nb**, Cobalt **Co**, Chromium **Cr**, Platinum **Pt**, Palladium **Pd**, Vanadium **V**, Tungsten **W**

INDUSTRIAL (NON METALLIC) MINERALS

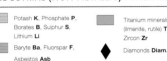

Potash **K**, Phosphate **P**, Borates **B**, Sulphur **S**, Lithium **Li**
Baryte **Ba**, Fluorspar **F**, Asbestos **Asb**
Titanium minerals (ilmenite, rutile) **Ti**, Zircon **Zr**
Diamonds **Diam.**

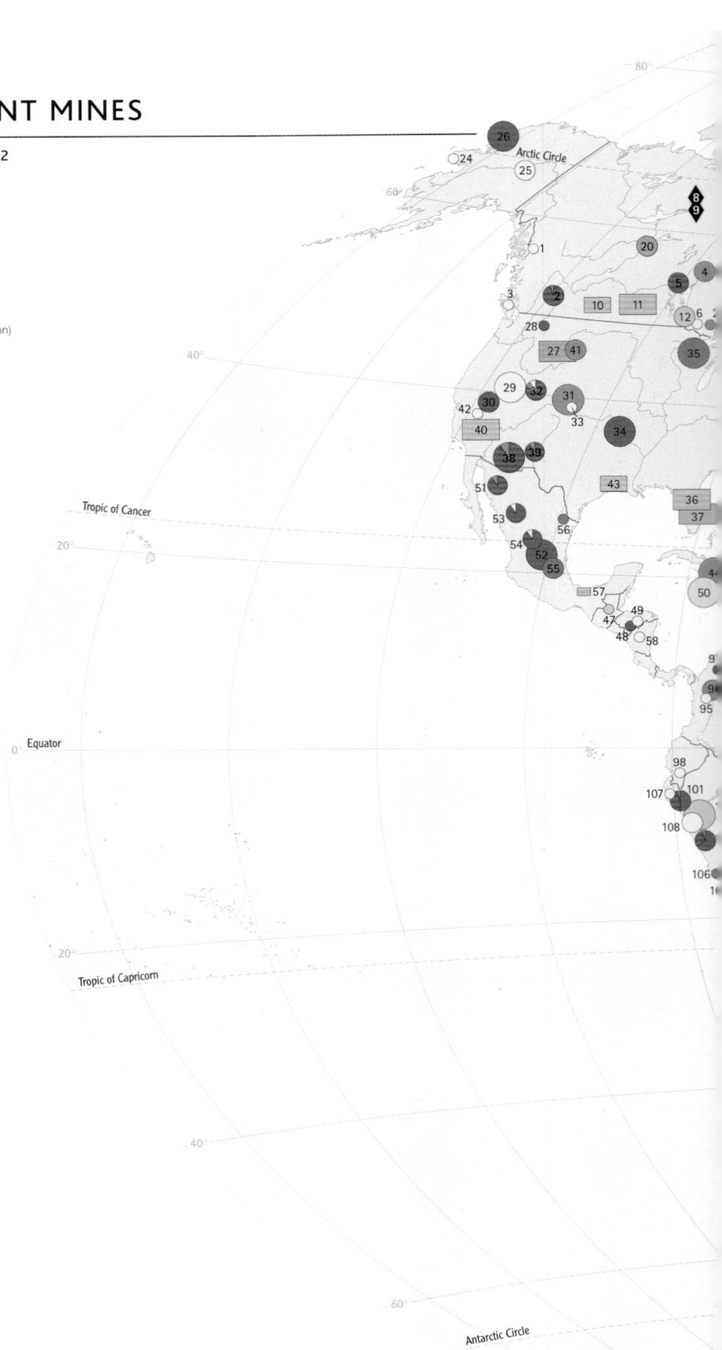

Arctic Circle
Tropic of Cancer
Equator
Tropic of Capricorn
Antarctic Circle

TYPES OF MINERALS

Minerals are usually grouped into four classes defined chiefly by their use:

Industrial minerals are minerals such as salt, fluorspar, barytes and sulphur, which are used in their natural state in industrial processes, and phosphate rock and potash which are vital constituents of fertilizers in addition to other uses. Gemstones are a special case in that, with the exception of industrial diamonds which are used as an abrasive, they are valued only for their aesthetic appearance.

Metallic minerals are mined to extract the metals they contain. Deposits of metallic minerals are evaluated chiefly on the costs of mining the ore and of extracting the metal from it.

Construction minerals such as sand, gravel, clay and gypsum, are used to make building materials. Their production costs are relatively low, but because their transport costs are high, they are normally used close to where they are produced. They are produced in most countries and are not shown on the map.

Energy minerals comprise coal, oil and natural gas, collectively known as 'fossil fuels', and uranium, the raw material for nuclear power. In terms of mass they are the most important traded minerals. Uranium is shown on the map; the others are shown on pages 38–39.

MINERAL PRODUCTION

Economies of scale have always been a strong influence on the geographic patterns of mineral production: a very large orebody is able to supply a significant proportion of world demand and can often be worked at a lower unit cost than a smaller deposit. Thus, for example, only a handful of giant mines in the Americas dominate the world supply of copper *(see 4)*. Similar geographical concentration of supply are marked also in other minerals, including chromium and nickel *(see 5 and 6)*. Production of gold *(see 7)* and diamonds was until fairly recently dominated by southern African countries but advances in exploration and processing technology have led to many new discoveries of both of these commodities in other continents, notably Australia and North America. China is the dominant producer of tungsten, antimony, tin, zinc and fluorspar *(see 8)*, having a large number of small to medium sized mines. The absence of mines of these materials elsewhere indicates not a lack of resources, but a lack of economic reserves.

2. IRON ORE PRODUCERS 1972–2005

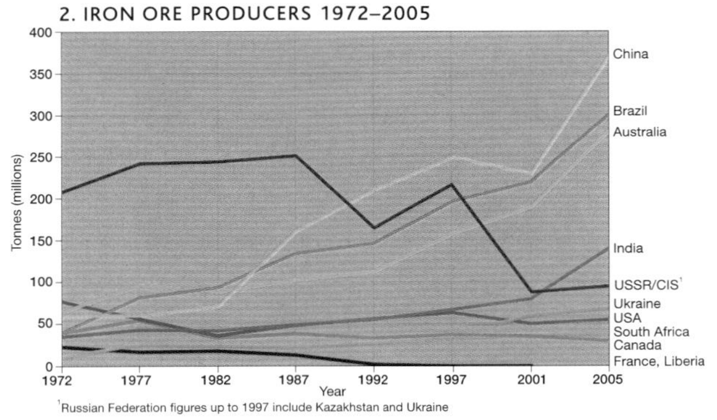

Tonnes (millions)
400
350
300
250
200
150
100
50
0
1972
1977
1982
1987
1992
1997
2001
2005
Year
China
Brazil
Australia
India
USSR/CIS[1]
Ukraine
USA
South Africa
Canada
France, Liberia

[1] Russian Federation figures up to 1997 include Kazakhstan and Ukraine

3. BAUXITE PRODUCTION 2005

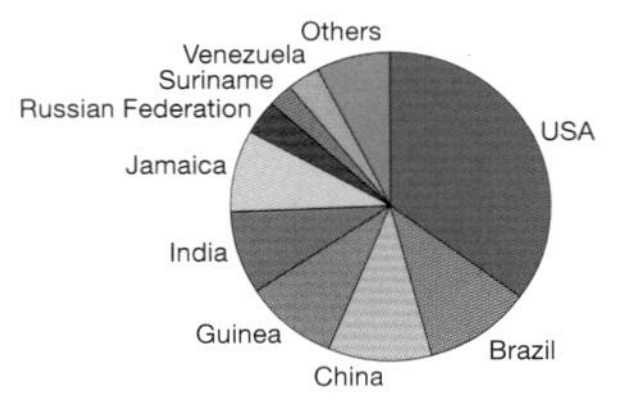

Others
Venezuela
Suriname
Russian Federation
Jamaica
India
Guinea
China
Brazil
USA

4. COPPER PRODUCTION 2005

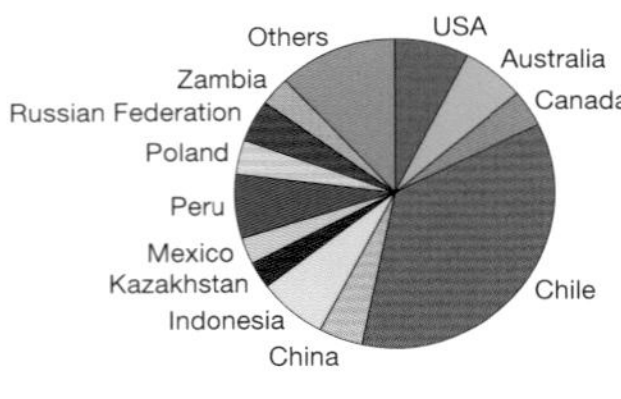

Others
USA
Australia
Canada
Zambia
Russian Federation
Poland
Peru
Mexico
Kazakhstan
Indonesia
China
Chile

INDEX TO SITES ON THE MAP

Key: Site number, Mine/*Province*/*District*/*Area*, **Minerals**

NORTH AMERICA

Canada
1 Eskay Creek, **Au, Ag**
2 Highland Valley, **Cu, Mo**
3 Myra Falls, **Au**
4 Thompson, **Ni**
5 Flin Flon, **Cu, Zn, Ag**
6 Red Lake, **Au**
7 *Marathon*, **Au**
8 Ekati (*Lac de Gras*), **Diam.**
9 Diavik, **Diam.**
10 Alberta, **S**
11 Saskatchewan, **K**
12 Bernic Lake, **Ta, Li, Cs, Rb**
13 *Sudbury*, **Ni, Cu, Co, Pt**
14 *Timmins, Noranda*, **Cu, Pb, Zn, Au**
15 *Asbestos*, **Asb**
16 Niobec, **Nb**
17 Brunswick, **Zn, Pb, Cu, Ag**
18 Lac Allard, **Ti**
19 *Northern Québec and Labrador*, **Fe**
20 *Athabasca Basin*, **U**
21 Lac des Iles, **Pd, Pt**
22 Raglan, **Ni, Cu, Co, Pt**

Greenland
23 Nalunaq, **Au**

USA
24 *Nome*, **Au**
25 *Fairbanks*, **Au**
26 Red Dog, **Zn, Pb, Ag**
27 Ruby Mountains, **Talc**
28 *Coeur d'Alene, Idaho* **Pb, Zn, Ag**
29 *Carlin, Nevada*, **Au**
30 *Nevada*, **Ag**
31 Henderson, **Mo, W**
32 Bingham Canyon, **Cu, Mo, Au**
33 Cresson (*Cripple Creek*), **Au**
34 *Viburnum Trend*, **Pb, Zn, Ag**
35 *Lake Superior, Minnesota*, **Fe**
36 *Florida*, **P**
37 *Florida, E Coast*, **Ti, Zr**
38 *Arizona*, **Cu, Mo**
39 *New Mexico*, **Cu, Mo**
40 Boron, Searles Lake, **B**
41 Stillwater, **Pt, Pd**
42 Briggs, **Au**
43 *Texas, Louisiana*, **S**

CENTRAL AMERICA

Cuba
44 *Eastern Cuba*, **Ni, Co**

Dominican Republic
45 Pueblo Viejo, **Au**
46 Falconado, **Ni**

Guatemala
47 *Ixtahuacan*, **Sb**

Honduras
48 El Mochito, **Zn, Pb, Ag**
49 Central Honduras, **Au**

Jamaica
50 *Jamaica*, **Al**

Mexico
51 *Sonora*, **Cu, Mo**
52 *San Luis Potosí*, **Pb, Zn, Ag, Sb**
53 *Chihuahua, Northern Durango*, **Pb, Zn, Ag,Cu, Au**
54 *Zacatecas*, **Pb, Zn, Ag, Cu, Au**
55 *Hidalgo*, **Mn**
56 Hercules, **Fe**
57 Coatzacoalcos, **S**

Nicaragua
58 El Limon, **Au**

SOUTH AMERICA

Argentina
59 Aguilar, **Pb, Zn, Ag**
60 Bajo de la Alumbrera, **Cu, Mo, Au**
61 El Pachon, **Cu, Mo, Au**
62 *Northern Provinces*, **B**
63 *Chubat Province*, **Cu, Au**
64 Martha Mine, **Au, Ag**

Bolivia
65 *Potosí, Oruro*, **Sn, Sb, Pb, Zn, Ag, W**
66 Kori Kollo Mine, **Au**

Brazil
67 Trombetas, **Al**
68 *Rondônia*, **Sn**
69 Carajás, **Fe**
70 Igarape Azul, *Carajás*, **Mn**
71 Caraiba, **Cu**
72 Campo Formoso, **Cr**
73 Cana Brava, **Asb**
74 Niquelândia, **Ni**
75 Morro do Niquel, **Ni**
76 Tocantins, **Ni**
77 Urucum, **Mn, Fe**
78 Vazantes, **Pb, Zn**
79 Boquira, **Pb, Zn**
80 Jequitinhonha, **Diam.**
81 *Araxá*, **Nb, P**
82 Morro Velho, **Au**
83 *Iron Quadrilateral*, **Fe**
84 Morro da Fumaça, **F**
85 *Roraima*, **Diam.**
86 *Tapera*, **P**

Chile
87 Chuquicamata, El Abra, **Cu, Mo**
88 Escondida, El Salvador, **Cu, Mo, Au**
89 Disputada, Andina, Pelambres, **Cu, Mo**
90 El Teniente, **Cu, Mo**
91 Cerro Colorado, Quebrada Blanca, **Cu, Mo**
92 La Candelaria, **Cu, Mo, Au**
93 *Atacama*, **Fe**
94 *El Tesoro*, **Au**

Colombia
95 Titiribi, **Au**
96 Cerro Matoso, **Ni**
97 *Angostura*, **Ag**

Ecuador
98 Portovelo, **Au**

Guyana
99 *Guyana*, **Al**
100 Omai, **Au**

Peru
101 *Northern Peru*, **Pb, Zn, Ag, Cu, Mo**
102 Paragsha, **Pb, Zn, Ag, Cu, Mo**
103 Cuajone, Toquepala, **Cu, Mo**
104 Tintaya, **Cu, Mo**
105 Cerro Verde, **Cu, Mo**
106 Marcona, **Fe**
107 Yanacocha, **Au**
108 Pierina Mine, **Au**
109 San Rafael, **Sn**

Suriname
110 *Suriname*, **Al**

Uruguay
111 San Jose goldfield, **Au**

Venezuela
112 Cedeno, **Al**
113 Cerro Bolivar, San Isidro, **Fe**
114 Cristinas, **Au, Cu**
115 La Camorra, **Au**
116 Loma de Niquel, **Ni**

EUROPE

Albania
1 *Kukës*, **Cr**

Austria
2 Mittersill, **W**

Belarus
3 Starobinsk, **K**

Belgium
4 Fleurus, **Ba**

Bulgaria
5 *Panagjurishte*, **Cu, Au**
6 Rhodope Mts, **Zn, Pb, F**

Czech Republic
7 Erzgebirge, **U**

Finland
8 Kemi, **Cr**
9 Orivesi, **Au**
10 Pyhasalmi, **Cu, Zn, S**
11 *Outokumpu area*, **Talc**

France
12 Chaillac, **Ba, F**
13 *South of Massif Central*, **F**
14 Lodève, **U**
15 Lacq, **S**
16 *Alsace*, **K**

Germany
17 *Stassfurt*, **K**
18 *Mechernich*, **Ba**
19 *Clara Mine*, **F**

Greece
20 Parnasse, **Al**
21 Euboea, **Ni**

Hungary
22 *Danube Region*, **Al**

Ireland
23 Navan, Lisheen, Galmoy, **Zn, Pb, Ag**

Italy
24 Iglesiente, **Pb, Zn, Ag, Ba, F**
25 Furtei, Sardinia, **Au**
26 Pinerelo, **Talc**
27 Sardegna mines, **F**

Norway
28 Tellnes, **Ti**
29 Middle Norway, Joma, **Pb, Zn**

Poland
30 *Lubin Region*, **Cu, Ag, Au**
31 *Upper Silesia* (*Kraków*), **Pb, Zn, Ag**
32 Tarnobrzeg, **S**

Portugal
33 Neves Corvo, **Cu, Sn, Zn**
34 *Iberian Pyrite Belt*, **Cu, Ag, Pb, Zn, S**
35 *Panasqueira, Northern Portugal*, **W, Cu, Sn**

Romania
36 *Apuseni Mountains*, **Au, Zn, Pb, Ag**

Russian Federation
37 Pechenga, **Ni, Cu, Pt, Co**
38 Monchegorsk, **Ni, Cu, Pt, Co**
39 Lovozero, Khibiny, **P, Nb**
40 Berezniki, Solikamsk, **K**
41 Kotshkanav, **Cr, Pt**
42 *Kursk*, **Fe**
43 Tyrny Auz, **W, Mo**
44 Sadan, **Pb, Zn, Ag**

Spain
45 *Iberian Pyrite Belt*, **Cu, Ag, Pb, Zn, S**
46 El Valle (Río Narcea), **Au**
47 Almaden, **Hg**
48 Reocin, **Zn, Pb, Ag**
49 La Collada, **F**

Sweden
50 Kiruna, **Fe**
51 *Skellefteå*, **Cu, Zn, Pb, Au, Ag**
52 Aitik, **Cu, Ag, Au**
53 Bjorkdal, **Au**
54 Laisvall, **Pb, Zn, Ag**
55 Falun, **Pb, Zn, Ag, Cu**
56 Zinkgruvan, **Zn, Pb, Ag**
57 Grängesberg, **Fe**
58 Malmberget, **Fe**

Ukraine
59 Kalush, **K**
60 *Krivoy Rog*, **Fe**
61 Nikopol, **Mn**

United Kingdom
62 Boulby, **K**
63 Foss, **Ba**
64 *Southern Pennines*, **F, Ba**

Serbia
65 Bor, **Cu, Au**

AFRICA

Algeria
1 *Djebel Onk and Gafsa Region*, **P**
2 Amesmessa, **Au**

Angola
3 *Lunda Norte*, **Diam.**

Botswana
4 Orapa & Damtshaa, **Diam.**
5 Jwaneng, **Diam.**
6 Selebi-Phikwe, **Ni, Cu**

Central African Republic
7 Berbérati, **Diam.**
8 Kotto, **Diam.**

Chad
9 Pala, **Au**

Democratic Republic of the
10 Kasai, **Diam.**
11 Bakwanga, **Diam.**
12 *Copperbelt*, **Cu, Co**

Egypt
13 *Egypt*, **P**

Ethiopia
14 Adola, **Au**

Gabon
15 Moanda, **Mn**

Ghana
16 Nsuta, **Mn**
17 *Ashanti, Obuasi, Tarkwa*, **Au**
18 Birim, **Diam.**

Guinea
19 Boké, Kindia, **Al**
20 *Kono, Sanniquellie, Macenta*, **Diam.**
21 *Siguiri*, **Au**

Ivory Coast (Côte d'Ivoire)
22 *Tortiya Segala*, **Diam.**
23 Ity, **Au**

Kenya
24 *Kerio Valley*, **F**

Liberia
25 *Kono, Sanniquellie, Macenta*, **Diam.**

Madagascar
26 Andriamena, **Cr**

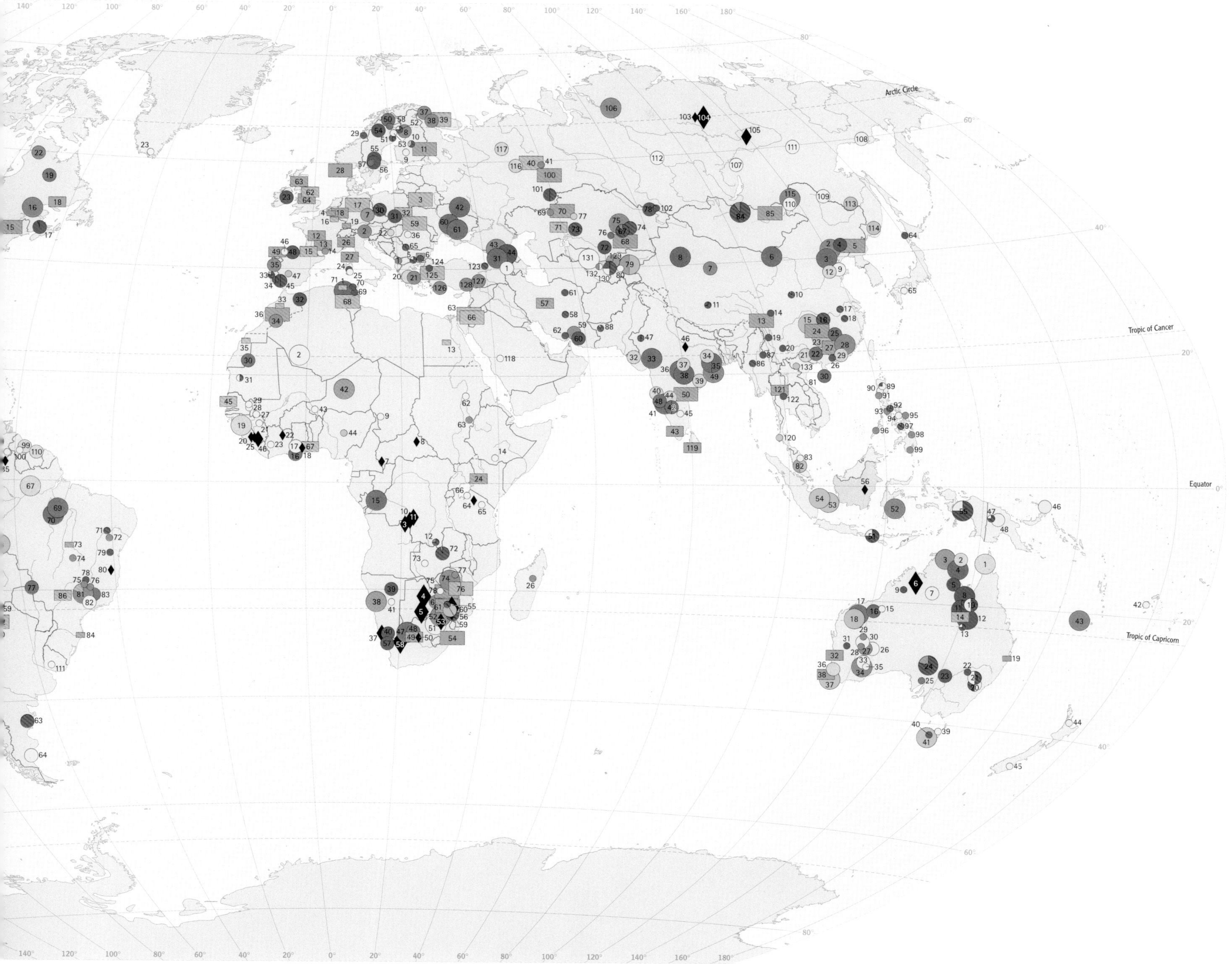

5. CHROMIUM PRODUCTION 2005

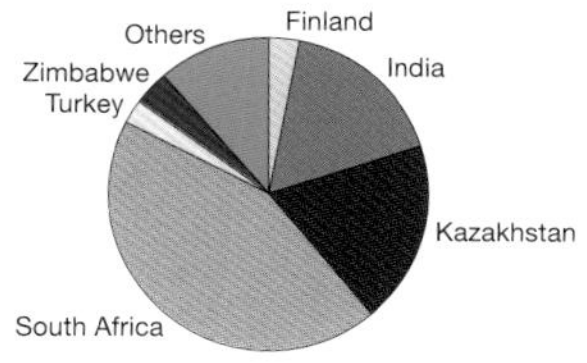

Others, Finland, India, Kazakhstan, South Africa, Turkey, Zimbabwe

6. NICKEL PRODUCTION 2005

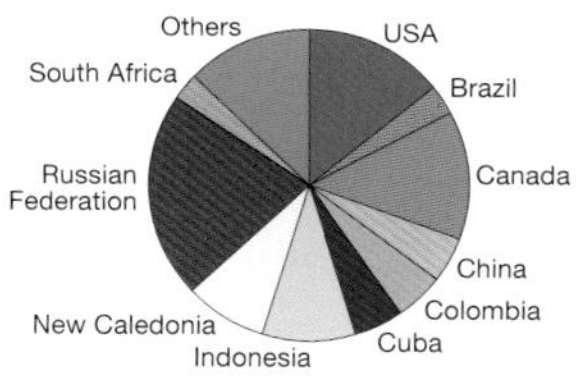

Others, USA, Brazil, Canada, China, Colombia, Cuba, Indonesia, New Caledonia, Russian Federation, South Africa

7. GOLD PRODUCTION 2005

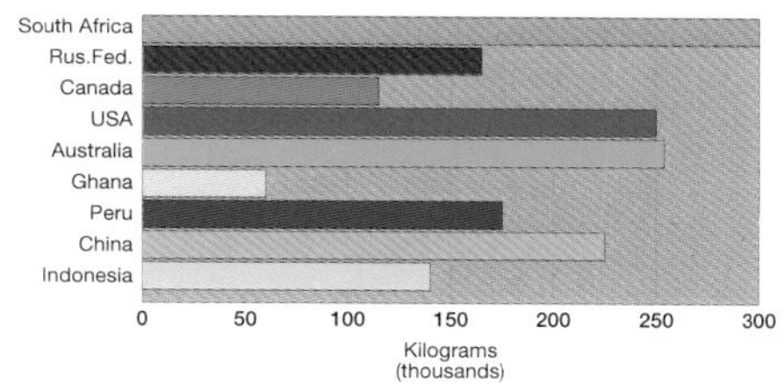

South Africa, Rus.Fed., Canada, USA, Australia, Ghana, Peru, China, Indonesia

Kilograms (thousands)
0 50 100 150 200 250 300

8. FLUORSPAR PRODUCTION 2005

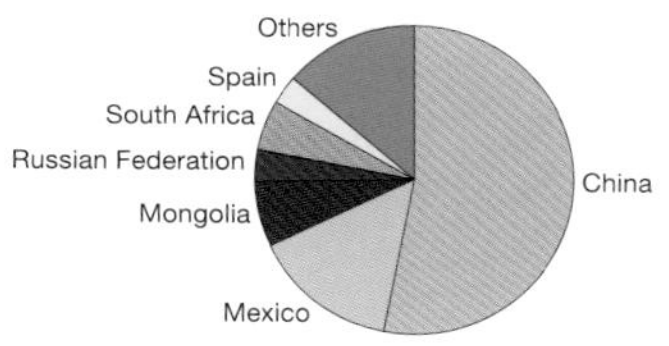

Others, Spain, South Africa, Russian Federation, Mongolia, Mexico, China

---

Mali
50 Kimberley, **Diam.**
orila, **Au**
51 Witwatersrand, **Au, U**
adiola, **Au**
52 Bushveld, **Cr, Pt, Ni, V, F**
atela, **Au**
53 Premier Mine, **Diam.**
54 Richards Bay, **Ti, Zr**
55 Murchison Range, **Sb**
dérik (Fort-Gouraud), **Fe**
56 Phalarborwa, **Cu, P**
uelb Moghrein, **Cu, Au**
57 Broken Hill, **Pb, Zn, Ag**
58 Finsch, **Diam.**
Morocco
59 Messina, **Cu**
ouissit, Boubeker, **Pb, Zn, Ag**
60 Venetia, **Diam.**
ou Azzer, **Co**
61 Vergenoeg, **F**
central Morocco, **P**
oukra, **P**
Sudan
bel Irhoud, Jebel Zelmou,
62 Hassai, **Au**
a, **F**
63 Ingessana Hills, **Cr**

Namibia
Tanzania
ranjemund, **Diam.**
64 Northern Tanzania, **Diam.**
ossing, **U**
65 Golden Pride, **Au**
ombat, **Pb, Zn, Ag**
66 Victoria Goldfields, **Au**
korpion, **Zn**
avachab, **Au**
Togo
67 Hahotoé, Akoumapé, **P**

iger
Tunisia
agadez Basin, **U**
68 Djebel Onk and Gafsa Region, **P**
amira, **U**
69 Northern Tunisia, **P**
70 Bou Grine, **Zn, Pb**
igeria
71 Djerissa, **Fe**
os, **Sn**

enegal
Zambia
72 Copperbelt, **Cu, Co**
73 Dunrobin, **Au**
ierra Leone
ono, Sanniquellie, Macenta,
Zimbabwe
iam.
74 Great Dyke, **Cr, Pt, Pd**
75 Zvishavane, **Asb**
outh Africa, Republic of
76 Bikita, **Li, Be, Sn**
orthern Cape, **Mn, Cu**
77 Bindura, **Ni, Cu**
ashen, **Fe**
78 Bulawayo, **Au**
riqualand, **Asb**

ASIA

Armenia
1 Armenia, **Cu, Mo, Au**

China
2 Jinzhou, **Mo**
3 Shijiaying, Shuicheng, **Fe**
4 Chengchengtsu, **Pb, Zn**
5 Liaoning & Shandong, **Talc**
6 Bayan Obo, **Fe**
7 Jinchuan, **Ni, Cu**
8 Xinjiang Uygur Zizhiqu (Sinkiang), **Au**
9 Penglai, **Au**
10 Changduicheng, **Cu, Mo**
11 Xiaotieshan / Zheyaoshan, **Cu, Zn, Pb, Ag**
12 Zibo, **Al**
13 Sichuan, **Asb**
14 Cheng Xian, **Pb, Zn**
15 Hunan-Sichuan, **Hg, Sb**
16 Dexing, **Cu, Ag, Au**
17 Shinchao, **Cu**
18 Tongshankou, **Cu**
19 Lanping, **Pb, Zn**
20 Zhehai, **Pb, Zn**
21 Pingguo, **Al**
22 Mugui, **Mn**
23 Hunan-Guangxi, **Sn, W**
24 Gongxi (Xinhuang), **Ba**
25 Qidong, **Mn**
26 Fankou, **Pb, Zn**
27 South China, **Ba, F**
28 South Jiangxi, Guangdong, **W**
29 Guizhou, **Al**
30 Hainan, **Fe, Ti**

Georgia
31 Chiatura, **Mn**

India
32 Bhuj, **Al**
33 Panch Mahals, **Mn**
34 Ranchi, **Al**
35 Bihar, Orissa, **Fe, Mn**
36 Nagpur, Balaghat, **Mn**
37 Madhya Pradesh, **Al**
38 Rowghat, Bailadila, **Fe**
39 Koraput, **Al**
40 Maharashtra, **Al**
41 Supa, **Mn**
42 Karnataka, **Fe, Mn**
43 Southeast Kerala (Travancore), **Ti, Zr**
44 Hutti, **Au**
45 Kolar, **Au**
46 Majhgawan, **Diam.**
47 Rajasthan, **Cu, Zn, Pb, Ag**
48 Goa, **Fe**
49 Cuttack, **Cr**
50 Mangampet, **Ba**

Indonesia
51 Batu Hijau, **Cu, Au**
52 Pomalaa, **Ni**
53 Belitung (Billiton), **Sn**
54 Bangka, **Sn**
55 Grasberg, **Cu, Au**
56 Penjom, **Au**

Iran
57 Iran, **Ba**
58 Sar Cheshmeh, **Cu, Ag, Au, Mo**
59 Faryab Area, **Cr**
60 Angorhan, **Pb, Zn, Ag**
61 Nakhlak, **Pb, Zn, Ag**
62 Anguran, **Zn, Pb**

Israel
63 Dead Sea Region, **K, P**

Japan
64 Toyoha, **Pb, Zn, Ag**
65 Hishikari, **Au, Ag**

Jordan
66 Dead Sea Region, **K, P**

Kazakhstan
67 Balkhash, **Cu, Mo**
68 Kargayly, Zhayrem, **Ba**
69 Donskoy, **Cr**
70 Dzhetygara, **Asb**
71 Kara Tau, **P**
72 Dzhezkazgan, **Cu, Ag**
73 Kounrad, **Cu, Mo**
74 Akchatau, **W, Mo**
75 Atasurda, **Mn**
76 Turgay, Krasnooktyabr, **Al**
77 Leninogorsk, **Zn, Pb**

Kyrgystan
79 Kyrgyzstan, **Hg, Sb, U**
80 Kumtor, **Au, Ag, Te, W**

Laos
81 Sepon, **Au, Ag**

Malaysia
82 Malaya, **Sn, Ti**
83 Penjom, **Au**

Mongolia
84 Erdenet, **Cu, Mo**
85 Hentiy Province, **F**

Myanmar
86 Monywa, **Cu**
87 Bawdwin, **Pb, Zn, Ag**

Pakistan
88 Saindak, **Cu, Au**

Philippines
89 Luzon, **Au, Cu**
90 Victoria, **Au**
91 Zambales Mountains, **Cr**
92 Marinduque, **Cu, Mo, Au**
93 Mindoro, **Ni, Co**
94 Masbate, **Au**
95 Samar, **Cr**
96 Palawan, **Ni, Co**
97 Cebu, **Cu, Mo, Au**
98 Northern Mindanao, **Ni, Co**
99 Southern Mindanao, **Ni, Co**

Russian Federation
100 Bazhenovskoye, **Asb**
101 Central Urals, **Cu, Zn, Au**
102 Altay, **Pb, Zn, Au, Cu**
103 Alakit, **Diam.**
104 Daldyn, **Diam.**
105 Malaya Botuobiya, **Diam.**
106 Noril'sk, **Ni, Cu, Pt, Co**
107 Lena, Vitim, **Au**
108 Magadan Region, **Au**
109 Amur, **Au**
110 Zabaykal'sk, **Au**
111 Yakutsk, **Au**
112 Yenisey, **Au**
113 Birobidzhan, **Sn**
114 Primorskiy Kray, **Sn, W**
115 Chitinskaya, **W, Sn**
116 North-Ural Bauxite, **Al**
117 Timan Bauxite, **Al**

Saudi Arabia
118 Madh adh Dabh, **Au, Ag, Cu, Zn**

Sri Lanka
119 Southern Sri Lanka, **Ti, Zr**

Thailand
120 Southern Thailand, Phuket, **Sn, W**
121 Northern Thailand, **Ba, F**
122 Mae Sod, **Zn, Cd**

Turkey
123 Murgul, **Cu**
124 Biga Region, **Pb, Zn, Ag, Ba**
125 Balikesir, **Emet, B**
126 Fethiye-Köyceğiz, **Cr**
127 Gulema-Elazığ, **Cr, Fe**
128 Karsanti, **Cr**

Uzbekistan/Tajikistan
129 Almalyk, **U, F**
130 Southeast Uzbekistan/Tajikistan, **Cu, Au, Pb, Zn, Ag**
131 Muruntau, Zarafshan, **Au**
132 Zarmitan, **Au, W**

Vietnam
133 Vietnam, **Sn**

OCEANIA

Australia
1 Weipa, **Al**
2 Gove, **Al**
3 Ranger, **U**
4 Groote Eylandt, **Mn**
5 McArthur River, **Pb, Zn, Ag**
6 Argyll, **Diam.**
7 The Granites / Tanami, **Au**
8 Century, **Zn, Pb, Ag**
9 Lennard Shelf, **Zn, Pb, Ag**
10 Ernest Henry, **Cu, Au**
11 Mount Isa Region, **Cu, Pb, Zn, Ag**
12 Cannington, **Pb, Zn**
13 Osborne, **Cu, Au**
14 Phosphate Hill, **P**
15 Telfer, **Au**
16 Woodie Woodie, **Mn**
17 Hamersley Range, **Fe**
18 Wodgina, **Ta, Sn**
19 Sydney, Brisbane, **Ti, Zr**
20 Cadia, **Au, Cu**
21 North Parkes, **Cu, Au, Ag**
22 Elura, **Zn, Pb**
23 Broken Hill, **Pb, Zn, Ag**
24 Olympic Dam, **Cu, U**
25 Granny Smith / Wallaby, **Au**
26 Murrin Murrin, **Ni, Co**
27 Leinster, **Ni, Cu**
28 Mount Keith, **Ni, Cu**
29 Agnew, **Au**
30 Golden Grove, **Zn, Ag, Au, Cu**
31 Eneabba, **Ti, Zr**
32 Kalgoorlie Region, **Au, Ag**
33 Kambalda, **Ni, Co**
34 Greenbushes, **Ta, Li**
35 St Ives, **Au**
36 Darling Ranges, **Al**
37 Greenbushes, **Ta, Li**
38 Capel, **Ti, Zr**
39 Beaconsfield, **Au**
40 Rosebery, **Zn, Pb, Ag**
41 Renison Bell, **Sn**

Fiji
42 Viti Levu, Emperor, **Au**

New Caledonia
43 New Caledonia, **Ni, Co**

New Zealand
44 Martha Hill, **Au, Ag**
45 Macraes, **Au, Ag**

Papua New Guinea
46 Lihir, **Au**
47 Ok Tedi, **Cu, Au**
48 Porgera, **Au**

© Collins Bartholomew Ltd

ENERGY PRODUCTION AND CONSUMPTION

The world's energy resources are unevenly distributed (*see 1*). Similarly, the geography of energy production and consumption is highly uneven, with three countries, the USA, the Russian Federation and China, dominating both the energy production and consumption of energy (*see 2 and 3*). Some countries – typically the oil-exporting states, such as Saudi Arabia, Iran and Nigeria – produce much more than they consume, but many of the most advanced industrial economies, such as the USA and Japan, as well as relatively newly industrialized countries such as South Korea and Taiwan, are net consumers. Peripheral countries, including Burkina, Chad and The Gambia, and some of the richest countries including Singapore are energy 'paupers' which produce no energy and are wholly reliant upon imports.

The USA is the largest primary energy consumer and, despite having only 5 per cent of the world's population, it consumes over a quarter of the world's energy. Together with Canada and Mexico, the USA's primary energy consumption increased by 15 per cent between 1992–2004, while the Middle East, South and Central America and Africa experienced higher growth rates from much lower base levels. Highest per capita energy consumption occurs in countries including Australia, Belgium and Canada as well as the USA. Lowest per capita energy consumption occurs in the world's poorest countries, including Benin, Burkina and Burundi. Uneven production and consumption mean that energy sources are the largest single items in international trade. Mexico and South and Central America, the Middle East, West and North Africa, Former Soviet Union and Canada are net oil exporters (*see 4*). The USA, Europe, eastern and South Africa, Australasia, China and Japan are net oil importers and generate wealth elsewhere to be able to pay for their imports.

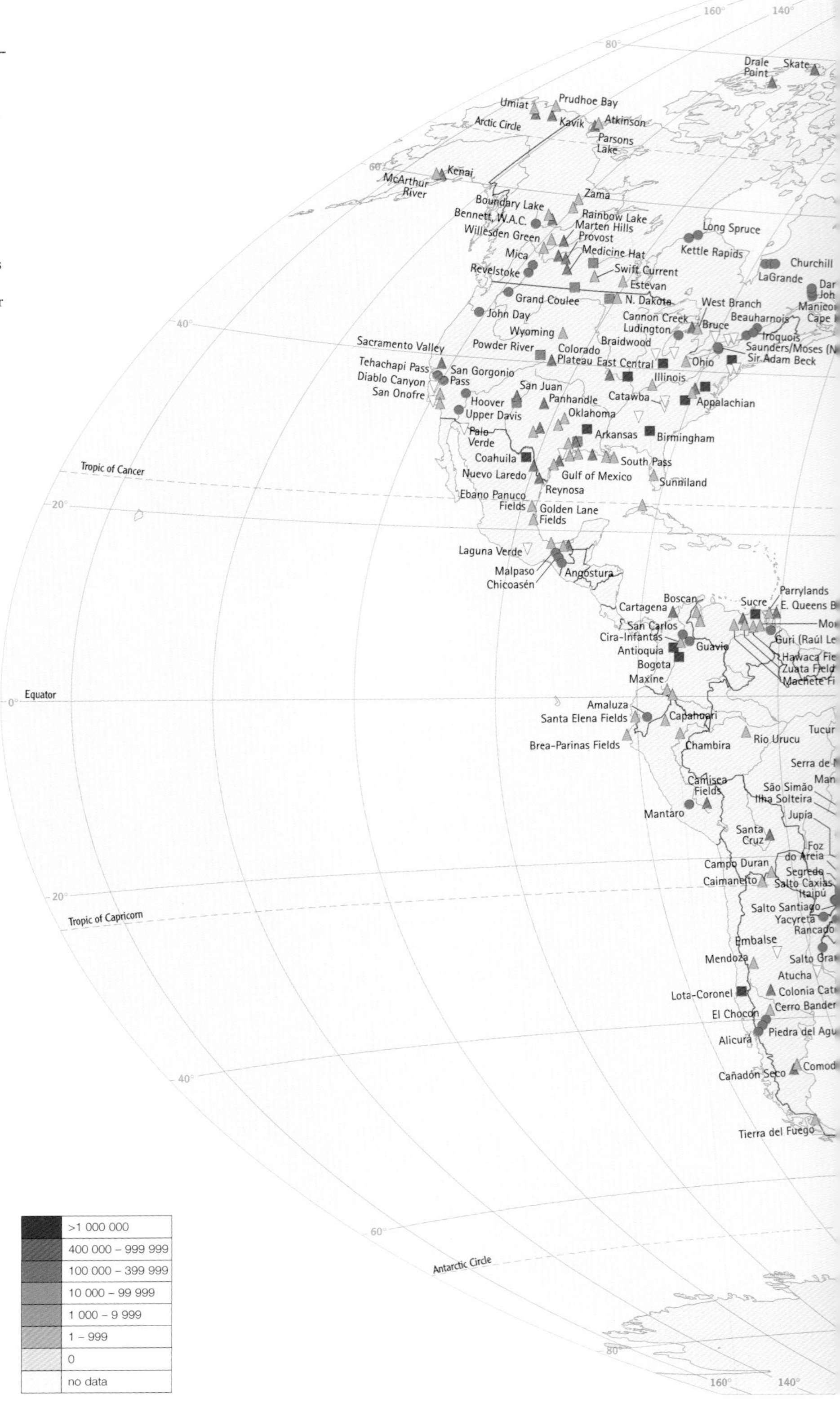

2. ENERGY PRODUCTION

Thousand tonnes of oil equivalent

scale 1:295 000 000

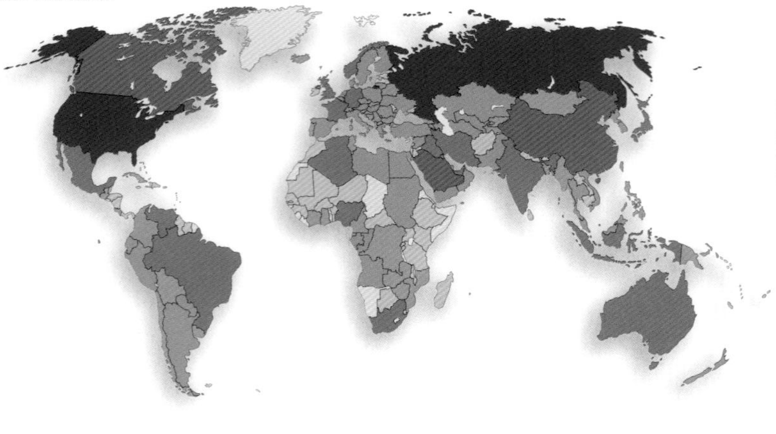

3. ENERGY CONSUMPTION

Thousand tonnes of oil equivalent

scale 1:295 000 000

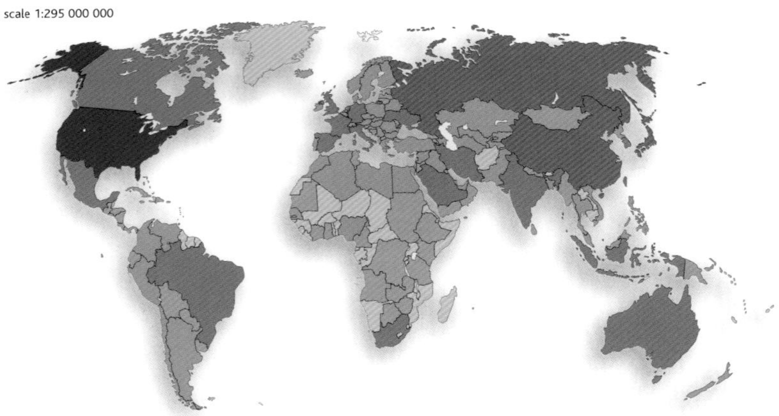

▓	>1 000 000
▓	400 000 – 999 999
▓	100 000 – 399 999
▓	10 000 – 99 999
▓	1 000 – 9 999
▓	1 – 999
▓	0
□	no data

ENERGY RESERVES AND RATES OF CONSUMPTION

Proven energy reserves are also unevenly distributed (*see 5*). Nearly two-thirds of proven oil reserves are concentrated in the Middle East. Reserves in the USA and Russian Federation have declined and Europe's reserves are expected to dry up early this century. Central America and Africa are expected to cease oil exports around 2025. Major import-dependent regions will be reliant upon the Middle East, underlining issues of security of supply in the context of global geopolitical instability. Proven reserves of natural gas are dominated by the Former Soviet Union and the Middle East while coal reserves are more evenly distributed between the Asia-Pacific region, North America and the Former Soviet Union.

Global energy use has grown historically and further growth is expected due to developing world industrialization. Between 1992 and 2004, global primary energy consumption increased by 20 per cent (*see 6*), led by the Middle East with a 42 per cent increase. Elsewhere, relatively costly energy in Europe depressed consumption to the relatively low level of 8 per cent while the dissolution of the Soviet Union led to the collapse in consumption which is slowly recovering. If rates of energy consumption were to remain constant then it has been estimated that the proven oil reserves would last forty years, natural gas sixty years and coal three hundred years. However, energy consumption rates are increasing and these estimates need regular revision.

4. OIL IMPORTS AND EXPORTS 2004

Movements within the regions indicated are not included in the figures.

	Crude Exports (million tonnes)	Crude Imports (million tonnes)	Balance of Trade (million tonnes)
USA	1.9	501.2	-499.3
Canada	80.5	46.6	33.9
Mexico	99.9	0	99.9
South and Central America	106.7	37.8	68.9
Western Europe	45.6	507.8	-462.2
Former Soviet Union[1]	254.3	0.3	254
Middle East	853.8	9.2	844.6
North Africa	115.8	8.7	107.1
West Africa	196.7	2.7	194
Eastern and Southern Africa	11.5	25.4	-13.9
Australasia	7.8	23.5	-15.7
China	5.7	122.7	-117
Japan	0	208.9	-208.9
Other Asia-Pacific	48.7	360.1	-311.4
Unidentified	26	0	26
Total World	1855	1855	0

1. Comprises: Russian Federation, Estonia, Latvia, Lithuania, Belarus, Ukraine, Moldova, Georgia, Armenia, Azerbaijan, Kazakhstan, Uzbekistan, Turkmenistan, Tajikistan and Kyrgyzstan.

5. PROVEN ENERGY RESERVES 2004

	💧	%	⚑	%	◗	%
North America[1]	61.0	5.1	7.32	4.1	254 432	28.0
South and Central America	101.2	8.5	7.10	4.0	19 893	2.2
Europe	18.4	1.6	6.60	3.6	59 841	8.1
Former Soviet Union[2]	120.8	10.2	57.41	32.0	227 254	23.4
Middle East	733.9	61.7	72.83	40.6	419	-
Africa	112.2	9.4	14.06	7.8	50 336	5.6
Asia Pacific	41.1	3.5	14.21	7.9	296 889	32.7
World	1188.6	100	179.53	100	909 064	100

1. Canada, USA and Mexico.
2. See footnote for table 4.

💧 Oil (thousand million barrels)   ⚑ Natural Gas (trillion cubic metres)   ◗ Coal (million tonnes)

1. DISTRIBUTION OF RESOURCES

Winkel Tripel Projection
scale 1:94 000 000

△	Major oil fields
▲	Major gas fields
■	Major coal deposits
◼	Major lignite deposits
▽	Major nuclear reactors
●	Major hydro plants
●	Major wind farm

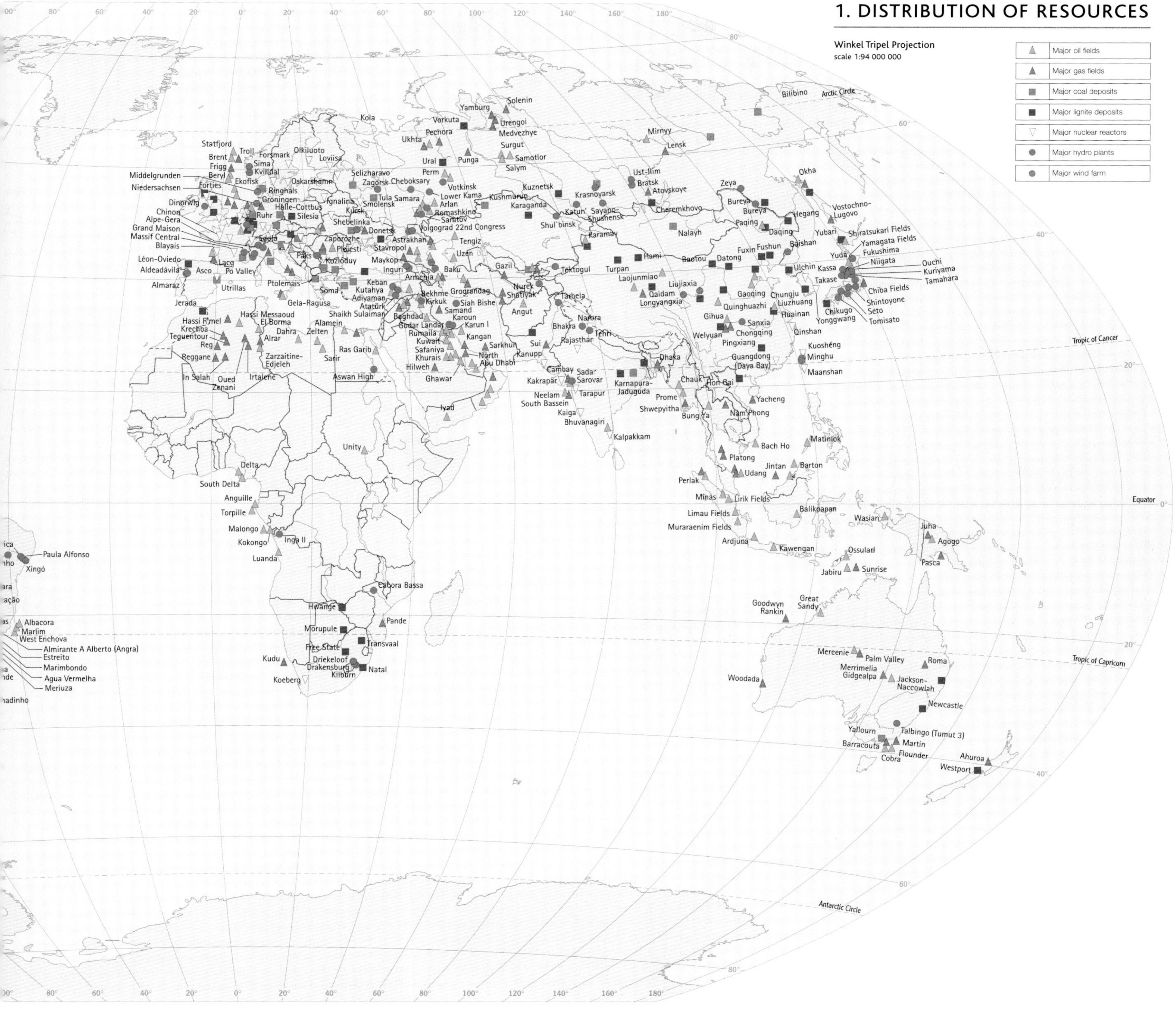

CONSERVATION AND RENEWABLE RESOURCES

Sustainability has underpinned the search for renewable energy sources that are less detrimental to environmental quality. Energy conservation aims to extend the life of non-renewable resources, reducing their environmental damage and increasing energy efficiency. Renewable energy sources may be another solution, although they currently only represent 11 per cent of world total primary energy supply (see 8).

Problems of cost and technical inefficiency are being addressed through technological advances and supportive government policy and growth is expected due to the longer-term constraints upon primary and non-renewable sources.

Biomass (wood and organic wastes) is prevalent in developing countries. Geothermal power is generated from underground water heated by the Earth's molten core. New Zealand utilizes this obtaining 10 per cent of its electricity from geothermal sources. Energy derived from water – hydroelectric power – is another renewable energy source. World hydroelectricity consumption has risen over 25 per cent between 1992 and 2004 (see 9). Solar energy has the benefit of being renewable on a daily basis and being available globally,

although it varies by season and latitude. Currently Japan, the USA and Germany account for 80 per cent of installed generation capacity. Wind power requires the right conditions in terms of terrain and weather to be commercially viable. Installed generation capacity has increased more than tenfold in the last decade, concentrated in Germany, the USA, Spain and Denmark.

6. PRIMARY ENERGY CONSUMPTION

Million tonnes of oil equivalent.

* Canada, USA and Mexico
** See footnote for table 4

7. NUCLEAR ENERGY CONSUMPTION

Million tonnes of oil equivalent.

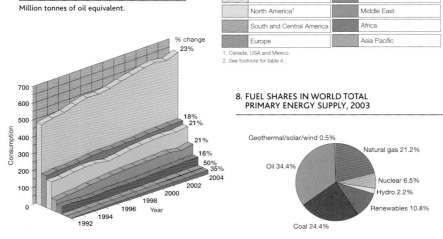

	World		Former Soviet Union[2]
	North America[1]		Middle East
	South and Central America		Africa
	Europe		Asia Pacific

1. Canada, USA and Mexico.
2. See footnote for table 4.

8. FUEL SHARES IN WORLD TOTAL PRIMARY ENERGY SUPPLY, 2003

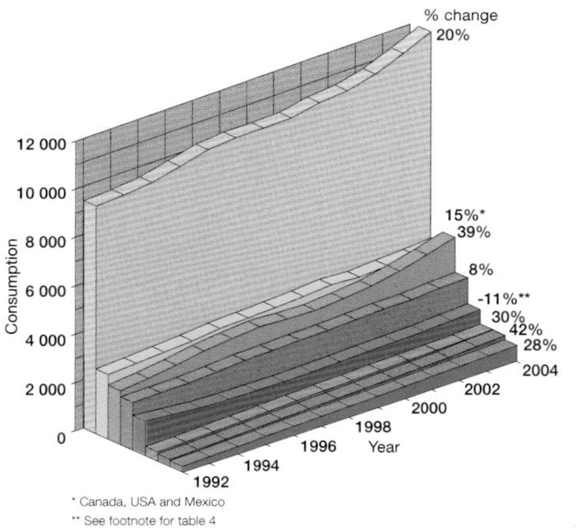

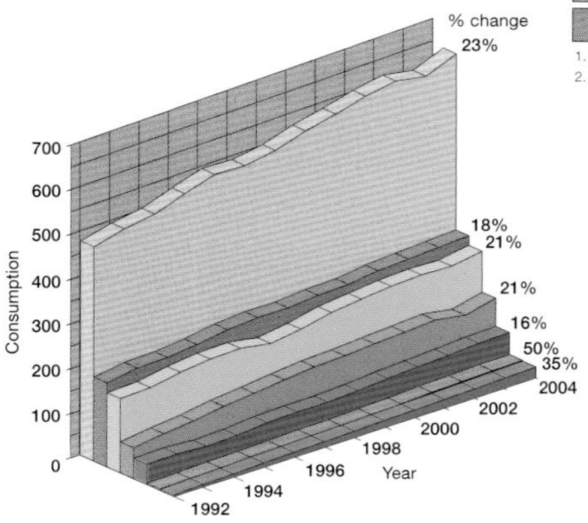

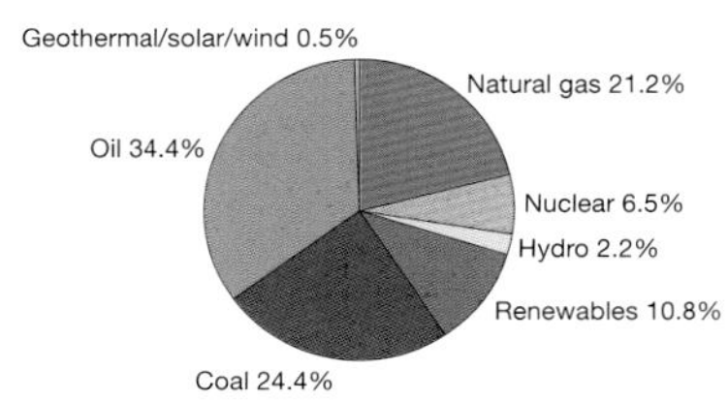

Geothermal/solar/wind 0.5%
Natural gas 21.2%
Oil 34.4%
Nuclear 6.5%
Hydro 2.2%
Renewables 10.8%
Coal 24.4%

9. HYDROELECTRICITY CONSUMPTION

Million tonnes of oil equivalent.

* Canada, USA and Mexico
** See footnote for table 4

© Collins Bartholomew Ltd

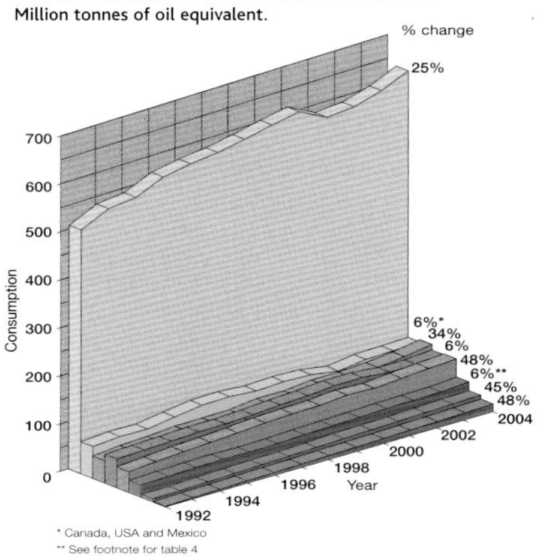

INTERNATIONAL TELECOMMUNICATIONS

Increased availability and ownership of telecommunications equipment over the last thirty years has aided the globalization of the world economy. Over half of the world's fixed telephone lines have been installed since 1987, and the majority of the world's Internet hosts (computers on which World Wide Web sites are stored) have come on-line since 1997 (*see 1*). Network access is uneven, however. Nearly half of existing telephone lines and cellular phones are in North America and Europe. Internet users in Asia, North America and Europe make up over 88 per cent of the world total (*see 2*).

This means that there is strong competition in the traditional telephone market in many parts of the world. In North America and Europe consumers have a wide choice available to them. This is not the case everywhere. For example, in many African countries there is little or no competition and consumers have little choice in the service they subscribe to. This is also affecting the development of broadband internet access (*see 4*).

One measure of the perceived 'death of distance' is the steady rise in international telephone calls, which has increased by 381 per cent since 1991. The map (*see 3*) shows accessibility to telephone lines and telephone traffic between countries in different continents for routes using at least 100 million minutes of telecommunications time in 2004. In that year, these streams totalled 77 billion minutes, 39 per cent of global international traffic.

Changes are taking place in the international telephone market. Many people now access low cost or free international calls through the internet by means of specialist software. Others make use of satellite or cellular phones to make their international calls, or they send a text message or use electronic mail.

1. WORLD COMMUNICATIONS EQUIPMENT 1976–2004

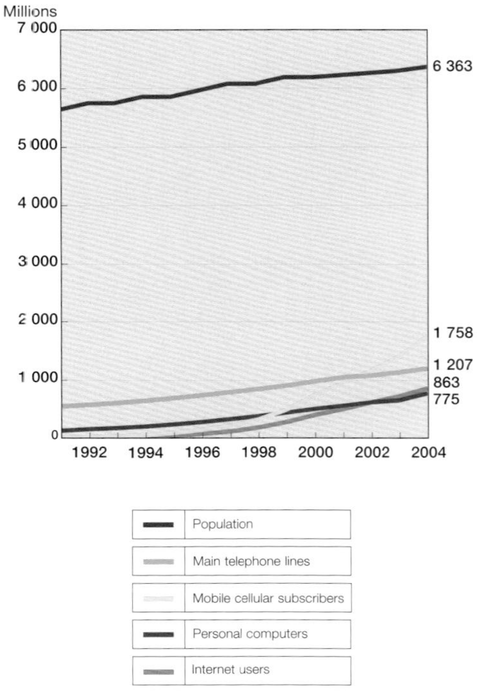

2. INTERNATIONAL TELECOMMUNICATIONS INDICATORS BY REGION 2004

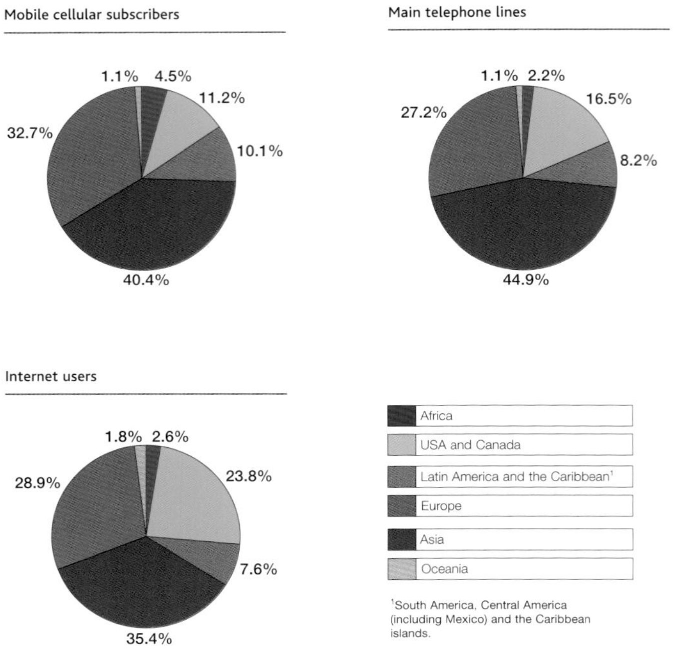

Mobile cellular subscribers

Main telephone lines

Internet users

- Africa
- USA and Canada
- Latin America and the Caribbean[1]
- Europe
- Asia
- Oceania

[1]South America, Central America (including Mexico) and the Caribbean islands.

4. TOP BROADBAND ECONOMIES 2004

Countries with the highest broadband penetration rate – subscribers per 100 inhabitants

	Top Economies	Rate
1	South Korea	24.8
2	Hong Kong, China	22.0
3	Netherlands	19.8
4	Denmark	19.1
5	Iceland	18.8
6	Canada	17.0
7	Taiwan	16.5
8	Switzerland	16.4
9	Belgium	15.6
10	Finland	15.3
11	Japan	15.3
12	Norway	14.9
13	Israel	14.0
14	Sweden	13.7
15	Liechtenstein	13.7
16	USA	12.9
17	United Kingdom	11.9
18	Singapore	11.9
19	France	11.2
20	Austria	10.0

3. INTERNATIONAL TELECOMMUNICATIONS TRAFFIC 2004

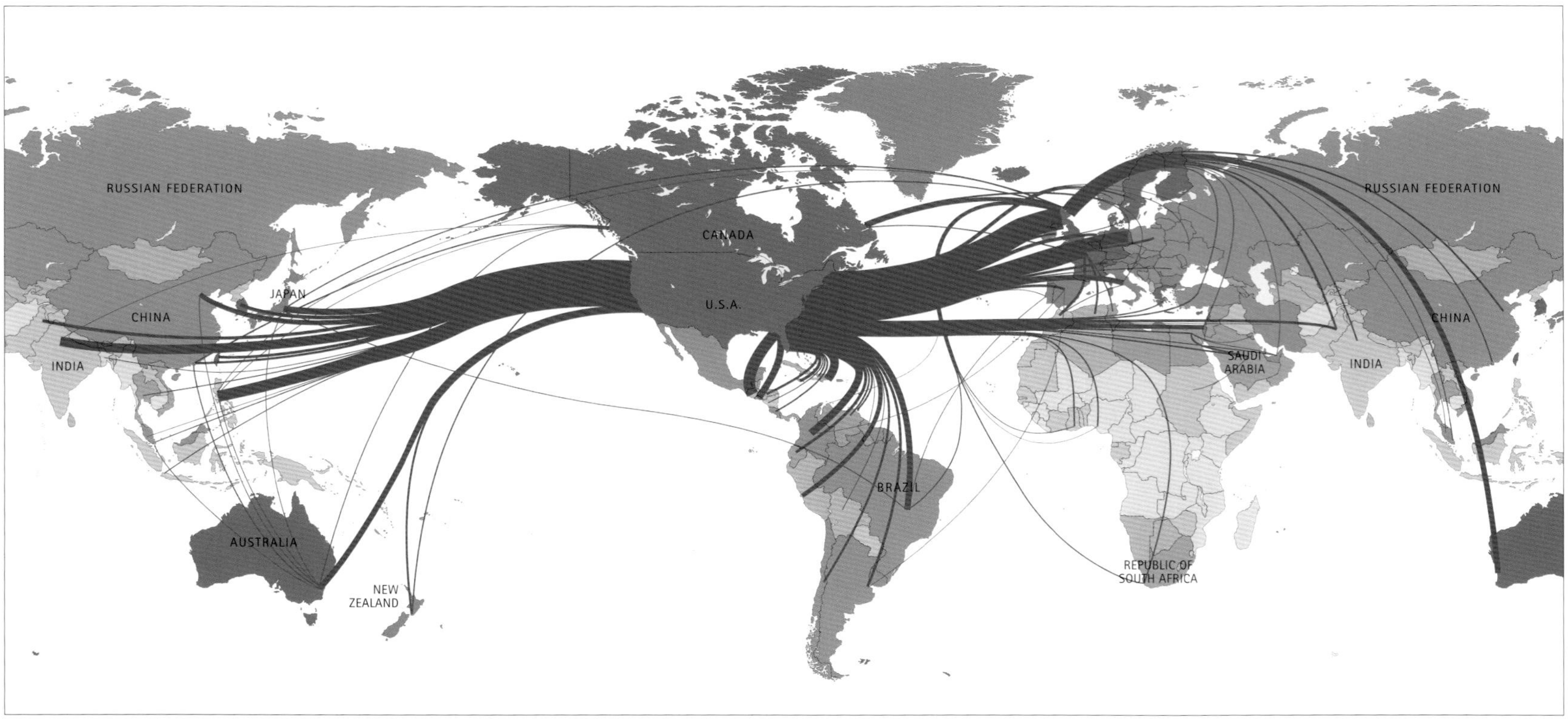

© Primetrica, Inc. Washington D.C. www.telegeography.com and www.primetrica.com

Million minutes of telecommunications traffic

5 000   2 500   1 000   100

Each band is proportional to the total annual traffic on the public network in both directions between each pair of countries.

Telephone lines per 100 inhabitants

over 50.0	15.0 – 34.9	5.0 – 9.9	0 – 0.9
35.0 – 50.0	10.0 – 14.9	1.0 – 4.9	no data

SATELLITE AND INTERNET COMMUNICATIONS

International telecommunications use either fibre-optic cables or satellites as transmission media. Although cables carry the vast majority of traffic around the world, communications satellites are important for person-to-person communication, including cellular telephones, and for broadcasting. Growing volumes of data traffic, particularly from the Internet (*see 5*), have boosted demand for international transmission capacity. Most traffic is routed over fibre-optic cables. In 1999, the world's trans-oceanic cables could carry approximately 250 gigabits per second (Gbps), which is equivalent to 17.5 million simultaneous phone calls. By 2003, international cable capacity had grown seventeen-fold and it continues to increase.

Unlike submarine cables, which must connect at fixed points, satellites can transmit information between Earth stations located anywhere within a satellite's radio beam, or 'footprint'. Geostationary satellites, which orbit at 36 000 kilometres above the Earth (*see 6*), may have footprints spanning over 1000 kilometres, thus providing a broad service area for point to multi-point voice, video and data communications. The positions of communications satellites are critical to their use, and reflect the demand for such communications in each part of the world. The satellites which are placed in 'geostationary' orbit sit above the equator. This means that they move at the same speed as the earth and remain fixed above a single point on the Earth's surface.

5. INTERNET USERS AND MAJOR INTERNET ROUTES

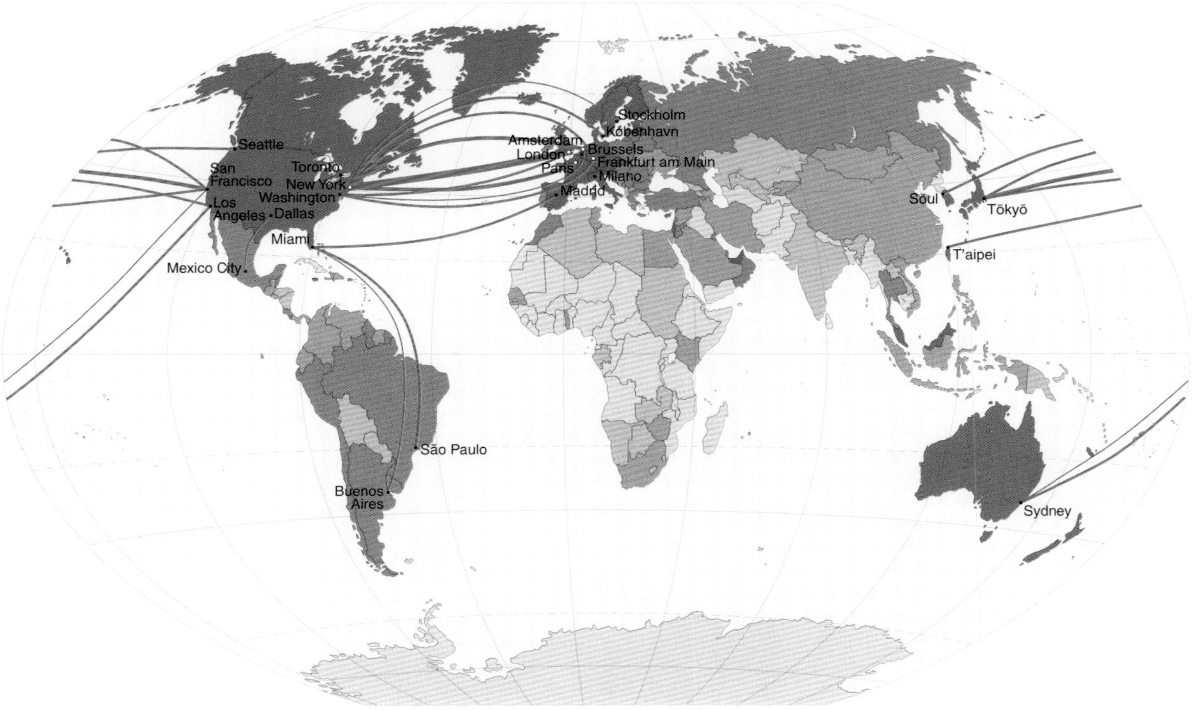

Internet users per 10 000 inhabitants 2004

	3 000–8 000
	1 000–2 999
	400–999
	200–399
	0–199
	no data

Major interregional internet routes

	0.0–0.9
	1.0–4.9
	5.0–24.9
	25.0–125.0

Internet hub cities

○	London

6. GEOSTATIONARY COMMUNICATIONS SATELLITES AND CELLULAR MOBILE SUBSCRIBERS

Cellular mobile subscribers per 100 inhabitants 2004

	over 100
	80–100
	60–79.9
	40–59.9
	20–39.9
	0–19.9
	no data

Geostationary communications satellites

◉	In service
●	Inclined orbit
○	Planned

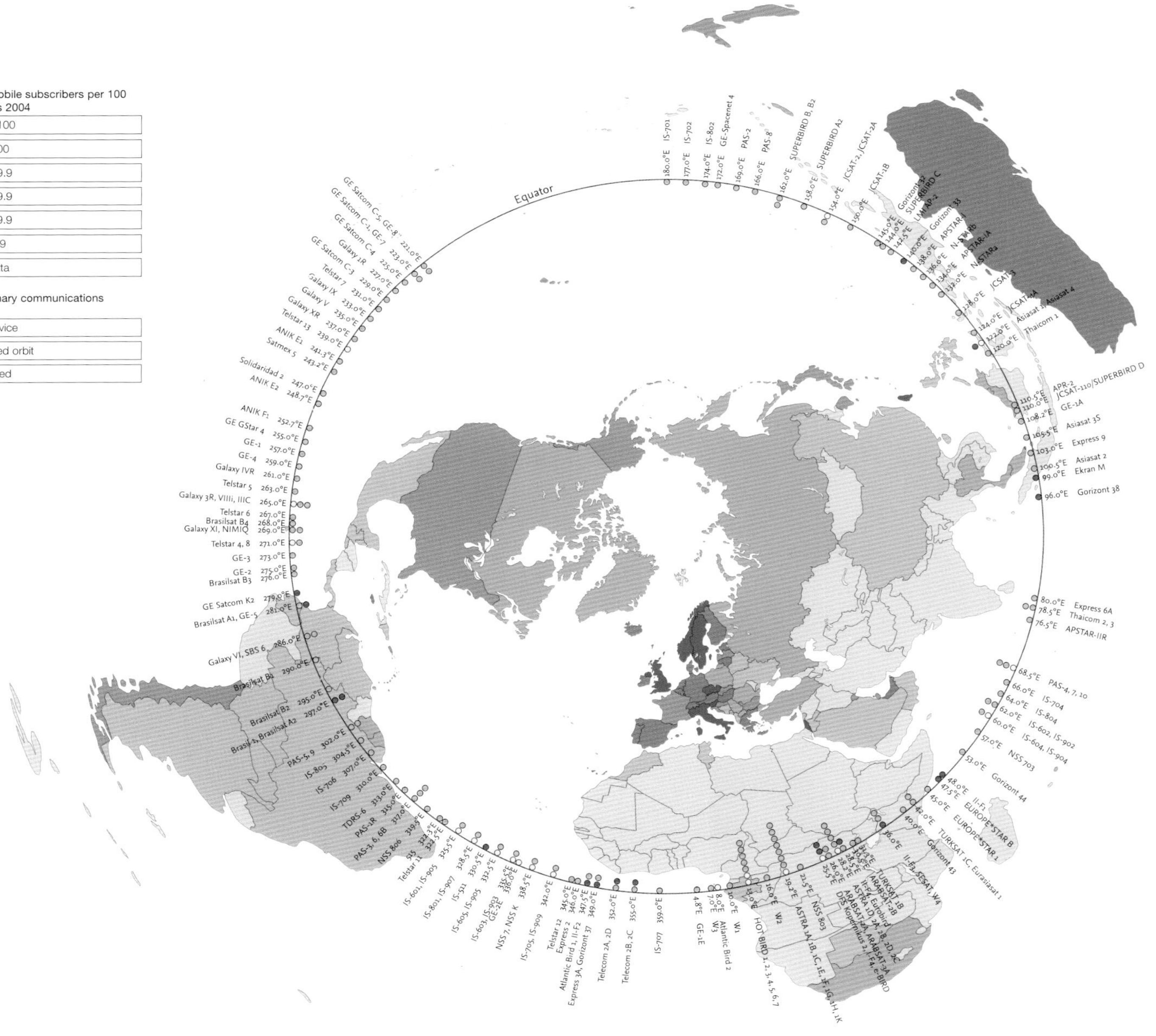

PREHISTORIC AND CLASSICAL CARTOGRAPHY (500 BC – AD 500)

The evolution of mapping has been inextricably linked to people's knowledge of the world and to related scientific and technological developments. Mapping skills have been influenced by factors such as way of life and the nature of the physical environment, and maps can therefore provide an excellent insight into cultures and civilizations. Surviving examples of ancient maps are rare. Their limits of coverage tended to be the extent of the producers' accurate geographical knowledge. Beyond the local area, maps appeared to reflect a speculative or cosmological approach (see 1).

The most significant contribution of the Greeks to cartography was theoretical rather than practical. It is primarily the work of Claudius Ptolemy, a Greek mathematician, astronomer and geographer living in the 2nd century AD, which provides us with information about the level of geographical knowledge at this time. Ptolemy's work *Geographia* included theoretical principles of cartography, lists of place names and computed co-ordinates. Later maps, based on this work, show how he believed the world to look at that time (see 2).

1. MAP OF THE WORLD

Carved on a Babylonian clay tablet, c. 600 BC. Babylon is shown as a rectangle intersected by vertical lines representing the Euphrates river. Small circles show other cities and countries, and the world is encircled by an ocean – the 'Bitter River'. British Museum, Department of Western Asiatic Antiquities, London, UK.

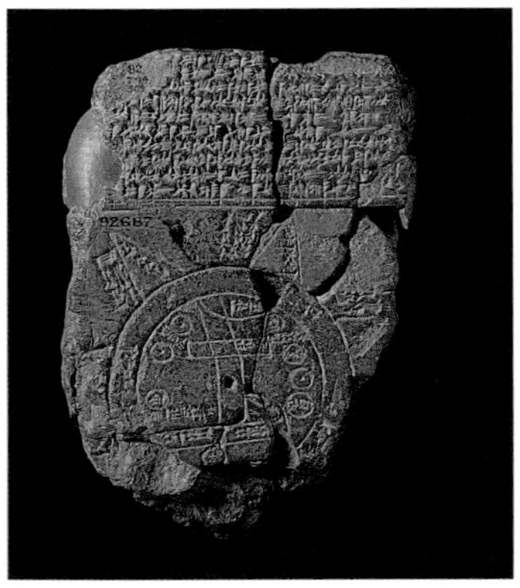

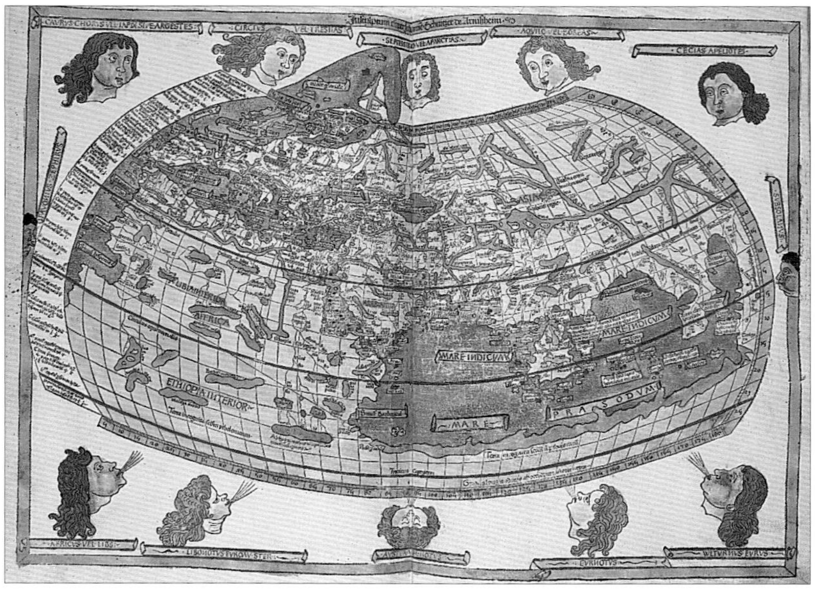

2. PTOLEMAIC WORLD MAP

Based on the work of Claudius Ptolemy, produced by Donis Nicolaus in Ulm, Germany, 1630. The map includes lines of latitude and longitude which give a sense of accuracy. The figures represent different wind directions. British Library, London, UK.

AD 500–1600

Religious beliefs played an important part in the cartography of this period. One particularly significant product was the Madaba map (c. AD 550) – a Christian map in the form of a floor mosaic discovered in a church in Madaba, Jordan, depicting biblical Palestine (see 3). Also during this period, maps originating in the classical tradition were overlain with later Christian elements. Such maps were usually oval or circular in shape, schematic in content, and centred on Jerusalem. These world maps (*mappæmundi*) conveyed a Christian perspective of the world, and their detail ranged from the virtually diagrammatic to the highly complex (see 4).

Maps from the later medieval period include sea charts, town plans and local, district and route maps. Of these, portolan charts – sea charts designed primarily for navigation – were by far the most significant and provided impressively detailed and accurate information on coastlines, harbours and related navigational matters. Route maps, for the use of pilgrims and merchants travelling overland, also developed over this period, as exemplified by Matthew Paris' map of the route from London to Otranto, Italy produced around AD 1250 (see 5).

The 15th and 16th centuries were essentially the age of exploration and discovery, a period which witnessed an explosion of global knowledge and a veritable renaissance in cartography. The period saw a great development of world maps, many of which began to include the coastal detail of the earlier portolan charts and to show the latest geographical information resulting from the voyages of discovery. Rome and Venice dominated European map production from 1550 to 1570, but later in the period dominance in mapmaking passed to the Low Countries. This 'Golden Age' of Dutch cartography is exemplified by the first printed 'atlas' of map sheets by Abraham Ortelius in 1570 – the *Theatrum Orbis Terrarum*. The term 'atlas' was coined by Gerard Mercator the Flemish cartographer – perhaps the most widely known figure in the history of cartography. His work, in particular his map projection published in 1569, makes him the geographical colossus of the period.

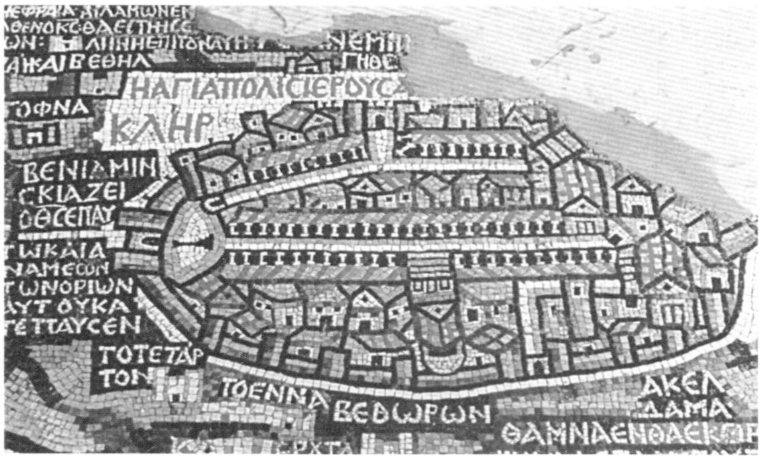

3. THE MADABA MOSAIC MAP

Detail from the Madaba map (c. AD 550) showing the walled city of Jerusalem and the surrounding area. Approximately a quarter of the original map, which covered 94 square metres of floor, is still intact.

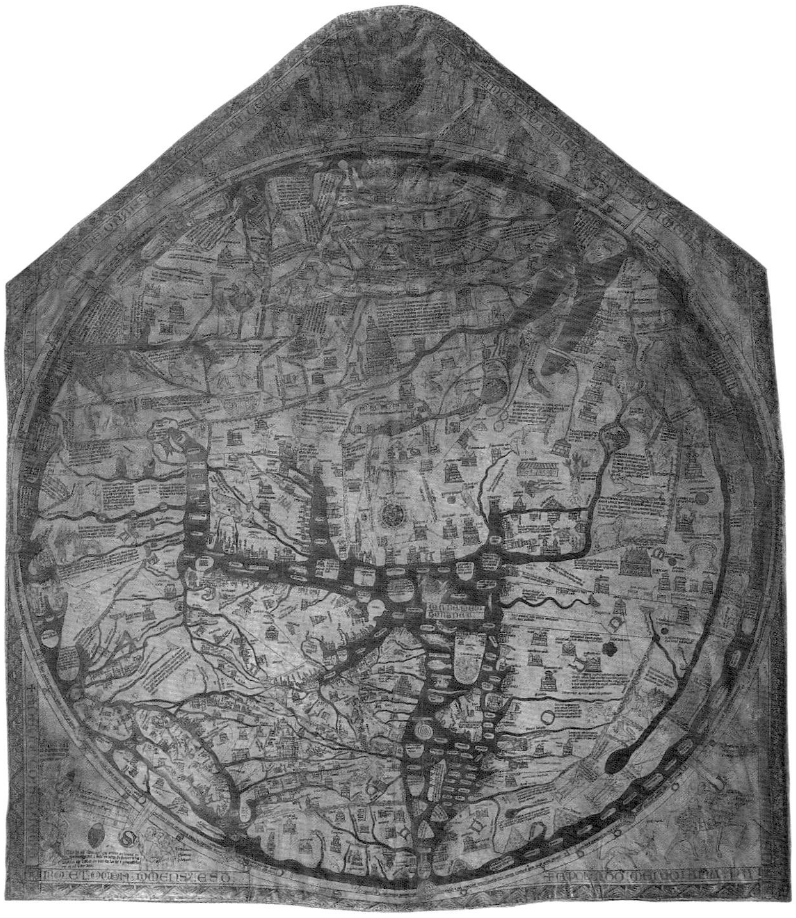

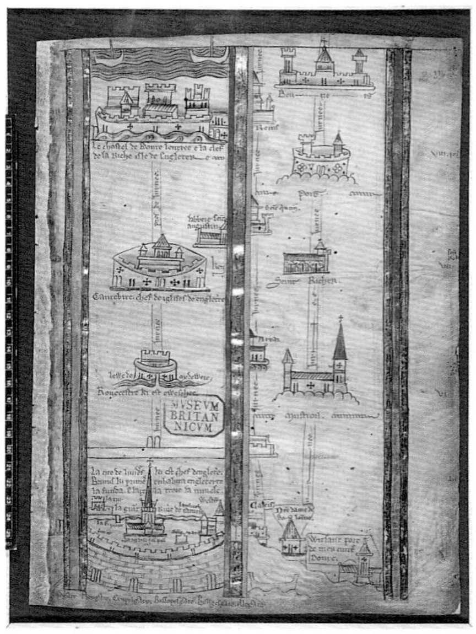

5. ITINERARY MAP OF A ROUTE FROM LONDON TO ITALY

Produced by Matthew Paris, c. 1250. This is a fine, early example of a road map in strip form. This extract includes Rochester, Canterbury and Dover. British Library, London, UK.

4. THE HEREFORD MAPPAMUNDI

Produced on vellum, and attributed to Richard of Haldingham and Lafford, c. 1290. The map follows the form of a T-O map, centred on Jerusalem, with east to the top. The continents of Asia (top), Africa (lower right) and Europe (lower left) are separated by the Mediterranean Sea and the Nile and Don rivers. Hereford Cathedral, Hereford, UK.

1600–1900

Cartography in the earlier years of the 17th century was dominated by the Low Countries, epitomized by the Blaeu publishing house (see 6) but, by the late 17th century, the world centre for cartographic production had shifted from Amsterdam to Paris. France was one of the first countries to recognize the importance of establishing a national survey and mapping programme. There, the Cassini family established the national survey of France well ahead of other such surveys in western Europe (see 7).

The colonial scramble for North America, and the American War of Independence (1775–1783), drove the development of cartography in North America, and it was an age, too, when the exploration of Australia, Tasmania and New Zealand resulted in their appearance on world maps. Such exploration was aided by great developments in navigation and particularly the ability to establish longitude more precisely.

During the 19th century special maps appeared in greater numbers reflecting scientific and social observation and analysis. One significant example of this development of thematic mapping was the *Physikalischer Atlas* of Heinrich Berghaus, published in two volumes in 1845 and 1848 (see 8). Lithographic printing of maps was developed in the early years of the century allowing the production of multiple copies of maps very much more cheaply, stimulating a proliferation of maps for mass consumption and for educational purposes.

As the 19th century progressed, factors such as exploration and emigration were reflected in extended world coverage of maps and charts. Work on national surveys proceeded, one particularly notable national cartographic achievement being the Great Trigonometrical Survey (GTS) of India which facilitated the creation of extensive and detailed topographic maps of the sub-continent.

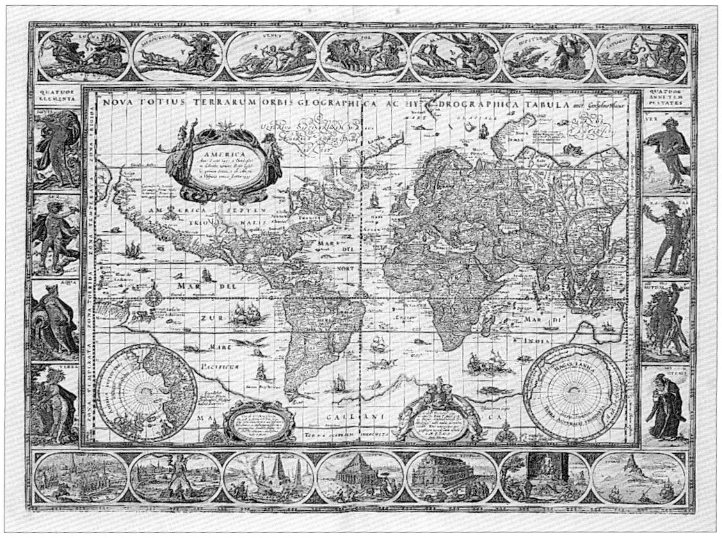

6. WORLD MAP

Produced in Amsterdam by Willem Blaeu, 1630. This is one of the finest examples of early maps on Mercator's projection. British Library, London, UK.

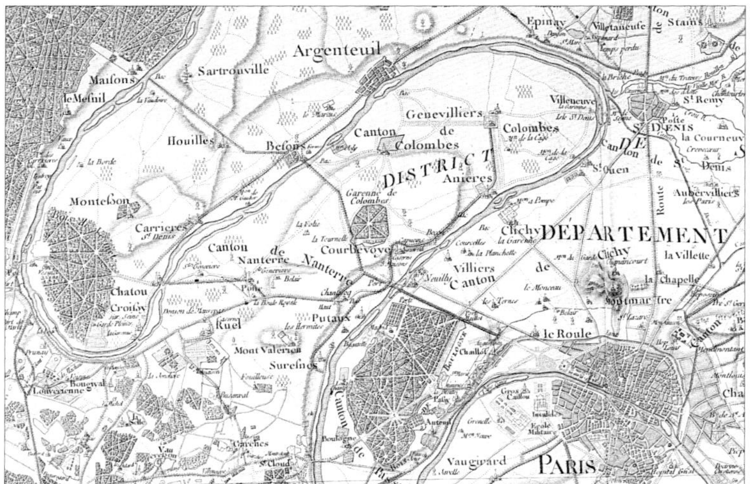

7. CARTE DE FRANCE

Detail from the first sheet – Sheet No. 1 Paris – by Cassini de Thury, 1736. Original scale 1:86 400.
National Library of Scotland, Edinburgh, UK.

20TH CENTURY

War, politics and technological development were instrumental in prompting the expansion of map and chart coverage throughout the 20th century. The development of aviation and, in turn, space exploration, and photography and imagery possible through them, have been particularly significant in recent developments in cartography and have spawned a new age in map making. The development of the computer has led to the production of digital maps and the consequent development of Geographical Information Systems (GIS). New digital cartographic techniques allow users to combine and manipulate geographical data sets, and also support new forms of output and visualization (see 9).

There has been a significant increase in map coverage throughout the world, and yet the fact that comprehensive national topographic mapping has been produced does not mean that it is readily available to the public. Many countries, particularly in Africa and Asia, impose strict restrictions on the release of their mapping. The question of national map coverage and availability is complicated by the activities of external mapping organizations. The former USSR had extensive programmes producing topographic mapping of countries throughout the world (see 10). Easy access to this previously classified military mapping has recently served to extend map availability.

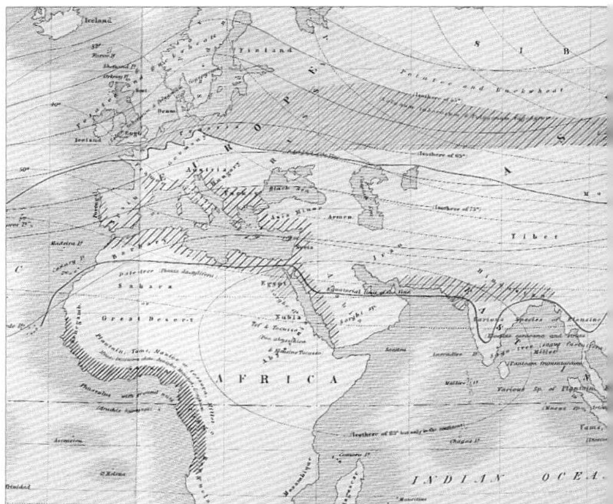

8. THEMATIC ATLAS MAP

Extract from a map of the *Survey of the geographical distribution and cultivation of the most important plants which are used as food for man: with indications of the isotheres and isokhimenes*, 1842. Published in the *Physikalischer Atlas* by Heinrich Berghaus,1845 and 1848. This English language version appeared as Plate 44 in W & A K Johnston's *National Atlas of Historical, Commercial and Political Geography*, 1847.
National Library of Scotland, Edinburgh, UK.

10. GROZNYY, RUSSIAN FEDERATION

Extract from a Russian military topographic map 1:500 000, 1988.

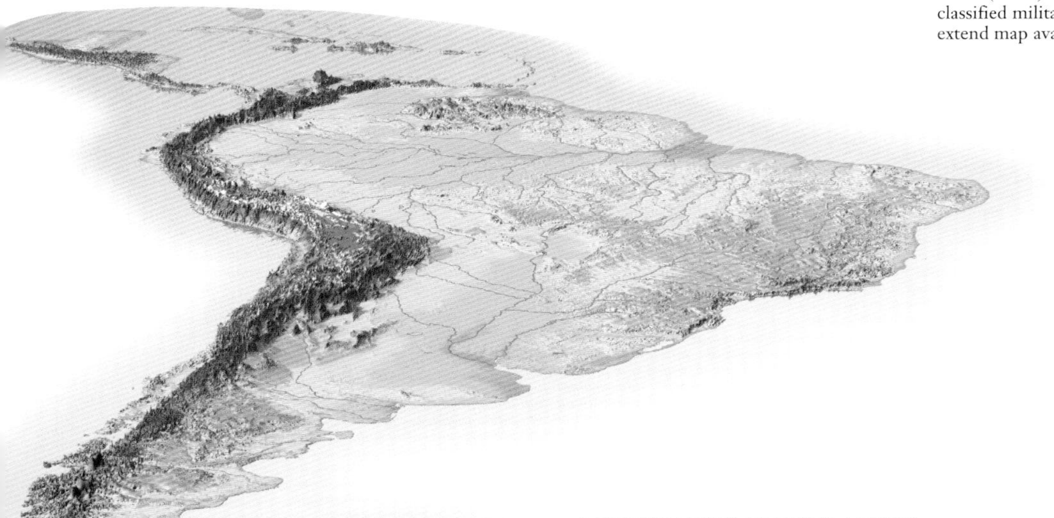

9. TERRAIN MODEL OF SOUTH AMERICA

A 3-D relief view of South America generated from a 1 km resolution digital elevation – or terrain – model.

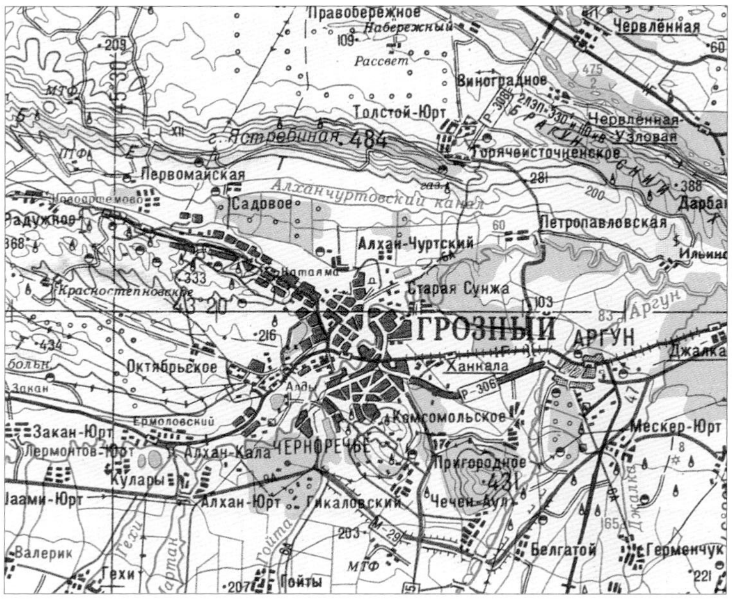

THE EARTH AND ITS REFERENCE SYSTEM

The earth was once believed to be stationary, flat, surrounded by water, and even the centre of the Universe. Belief in its spherical form arose from the ideas of the Greek philosopher Pythagoras (6th century BC) and, two centuries later, Aristotle's observations of how ships disappeared over the horizon. Important supporting evidence was also provided by astronomers noting the curved shadow cast by the Earth onto the Moon during an eclipse and by mariners' observations of stars rising and setting as they sailed their trade routes. The circumference of the globe was later determined in Alexandria by Eratosthenes (c. 250 BC), to within 1% of its true value.

Once knowledge of the Earth as a globe was established, there was a requirement for a reference system to permit the determination of geographical location. A graticule of meridians of longitude (stretching from pole to pole) and parallels of latitude (lines parallel to the Equator) is known to have existed in the 4th century BC. Early astronomers devised instruments to determine latitude on land and later the sextant was developed for use at sea. Determination of

longitude proved more difficult. Techniques employed into the 18th century included using the eclipses of the sun and moon and of Jupiter's moons. But as longitude's angular value is directly related to the rotation of the earth, a precise way of measuring time was the key to solving this problem. John Harrison, an English inventor and horologist, made the crucial breakthrough in the mid-18th century with his H4 chronometer which was not only extremely accurate but also reliable at sea.

With the Equator as the reference for lines of latitude, a longitudinal standard was required. Such a prime meridian could in theory be placed anywhere, and in the past many cities, including London, Paris, Cadiz and Stockholm had their own national reference. Not until the International Meridian Conference in Washington, DC in 1884, was the Greenwich Meridian established as the world-wide reference (see 1).

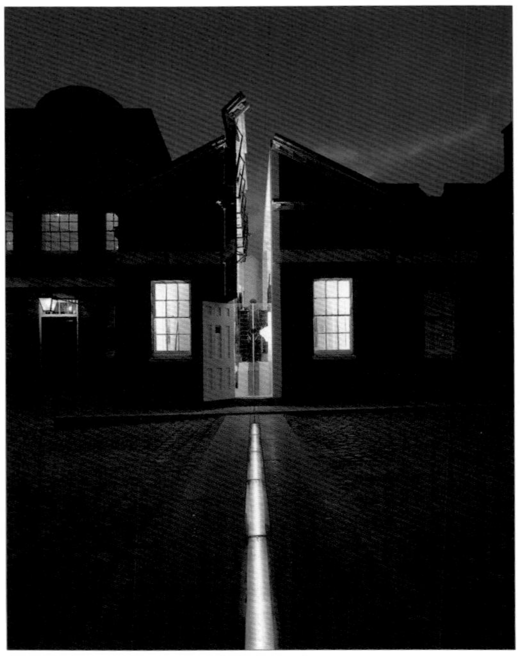

1. THE GREENWICH MERIDIAN

The Greenwich Meridian line at the Royal Observatory, Greenwich, London illuminated at night. This is the universally recognized 'prime meridian' marking the position of 0° longitude and the basis of Greenwich Mean Time.

MAP PROJECTIONS

One of the main challenges of cartography is how to depict a sphere on a plane surface. It is impossible to do this while preserving correct shapes and areas and compromises have to be reached. Transformations of the globe onto a flat surface are referred to as projections. The earliest examples (6th – 1st centuries BC) were vaguely 'cylindrical' (i.e. constructed as if the Earth's graticule is projected onto a cylinder of paper wrapped around the globe). These produce a rectangular pattern of lines of latitude and longitude. Ptolemy's written work of the 2nd century AD contained some of the most detailed cartographic instructions and in his Geography he also describes simple conic projections (produced as if projected onto a cone). The other main type of projection is azimuthal, with the graticule 'projected' onto a flat piece of paper in contact with, or cutting through the globe. Perhaps the most famous projection of all time is that of Mercator. Cylindrical in form, the lines of latitude are spaced to allow loxodromes (lines of constant compass bearing) to appear as straight lines to satisfy the convenience of the mariner who navigates by compass. This projection and variations of it are still used today for detailed topographic mapping. Although the projection does preserve shape around each point, areas, especially in high latitudes, are very distorted. Thus when the whole world is depicted, a hectare of forest in northern Canada would appear over 1000% larger than the equivalent ground area in central Africa. For this reason its use in an atlas to depict the world distribution of forest cover, for example, could be justly criticized. Today there are numerous map projections to choose from (see 2), many of which are appropriate for small-scale world maps.

2. WORLD MAP PROJECTIONS

Goode's Homolosine Projection

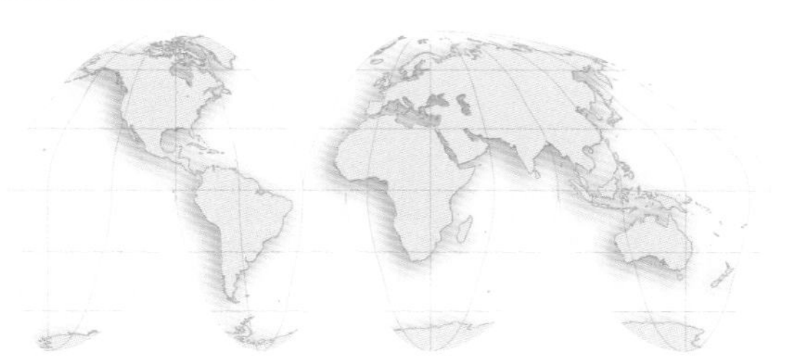

Winkel Tripel Projection

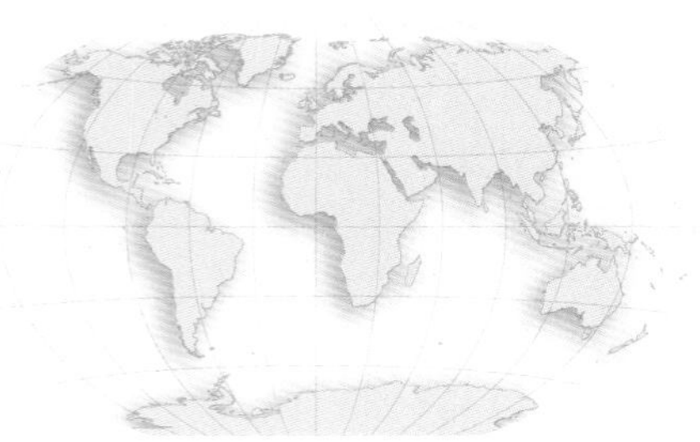

Mercator Projection

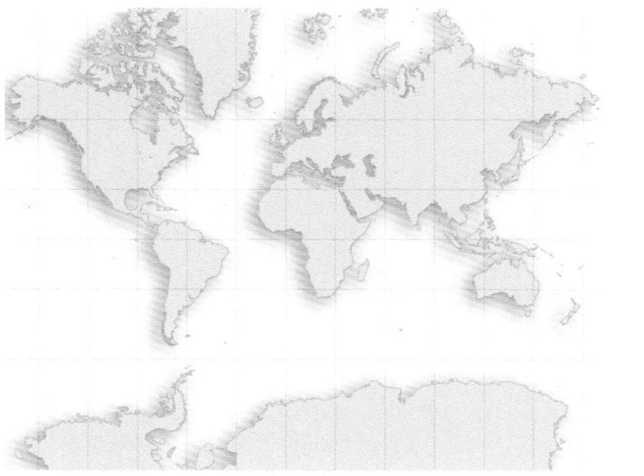

Briesemeister Projection

CARTOGRAPHIC DATA

Following the Dark Ages (AD 500–1300) mapping expanded both within Europe and globally with the growth of colonialism and world trade. The development of printing in the 15th century increased the demand from mariners for sea charts, and from the military for topographic maps of the land. Survey accuracy, an essential characteristic of such products, requires the measurement procedure of working from the whole (control frameworks at global and regional scales) to the part (detailed mapping at local level). With horizontal and vertical control in place, mapping progressed, initially with ground surveying techniques but later using aerial photography and photogrammetry (taking measurements from stereographic aerial photographs). New technologies such as satellite Global Positioning Systems (GPS), originally developed in the USA for military use, are now employed for navigation, establishing control and for detailed survey work. While topographic base maps are essential for many purposes, the growing

need to map and monitor global issues has led to the employment of advanced techniques including radar imagery and satellite imaging systems (see 3). Recent high-resolution (sub-metre) scanners on the Quick Bird and IKONOS satellites (see 4) are even adding fine metric data and permitting these images to act directly as map substitutes for some tasks. With the development of digital systems in recent decades the storage, manipulation, transmission and visualization of all this data are becoming much simpler and more routine. Such data, essential for producing accurate maps, are therefore much in demand by environmental scientists and planners.

Recently these high resolution images have become more accessible to the general public via the internet permitting the user to view high resolution satellite images of many major towns and cities throughout the world.

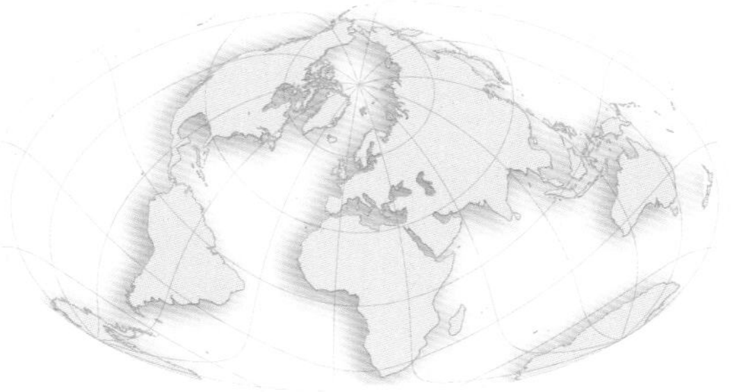

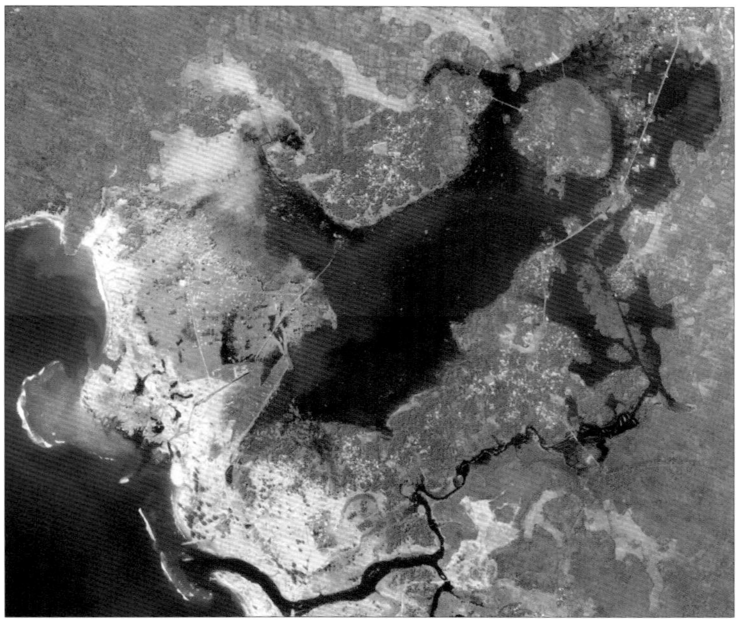

3. SATELLITE IMAGE OF SUMATRA

This satellite image taken on 29 December 2004, shows some of the damage done by the tsunami of 26 December 2004. The coastal area has been stripped of vegetation and buildings except for the mosque. Low-lying areas inland are flooded with salty water. Such imagery is an invaluable tool for assessing and mapping geological and environmental phenomena.

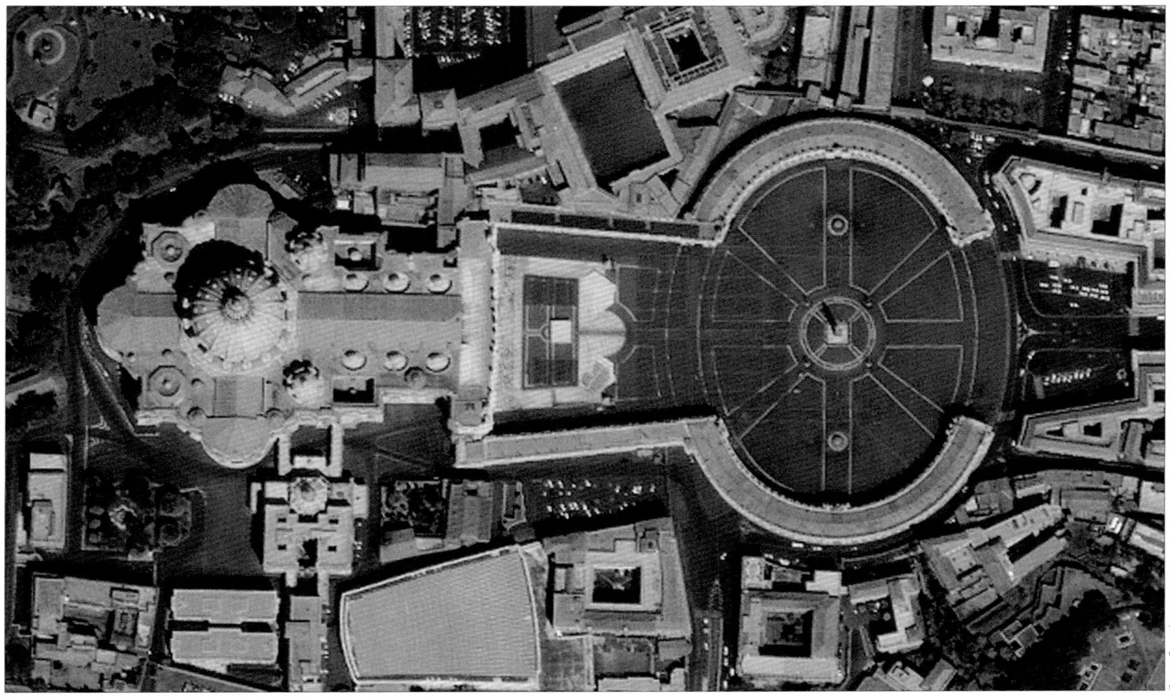

4. SATELLITE IMAGE OF VATICAN CITY

High resolution satellite images such as this one of Vatican City can provide huge amounts of data for cartographers and urban planners. They can serve as source material for the compilation of large-scale maps, or may sometimes be used directly as a map base.

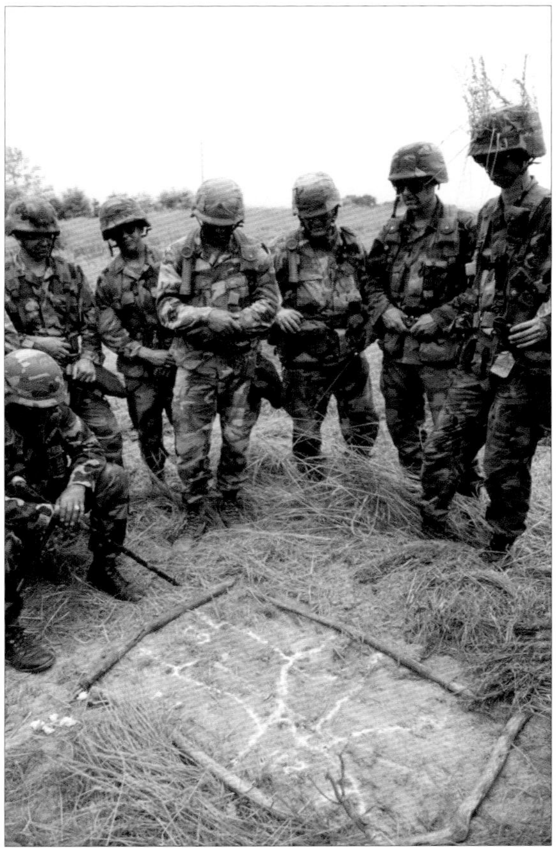

5. SAND MAP

Members of the US Pennsylvania National Guard examine a rudimentary map drawn in sand before an exercise. Maps can be 'externalized' in many ways using the most convenient and readily available media.

INTERACTING WITH GEOGRAPHIC INFORMATION

Spatial knowledge of the environment, structured as cognitive (mental) maps, is essential for human survival and routine activities. Although some people can retain complex geographies in their minds, most require external (for example, printed) maps for them to examine their surroundings and consider spatial problems or tasks in more detail. Cognitive maps can be externalized in several ways, for example verbally, through hand gestures (such as pointing) or through sketch maps, whether on paper or in sand (see 5). The last of these provide continuity between our instinctive abilities to make and use maps and what has become the professional discipline of cartography.

In the past, maps were used for both data storage and visualization. Once compiled, designed and printed they were normally sold and archived. However, because of the time-lapse introduced by these processes, maps can often be out of date or may not contain exactly the information required. Fundamental changes have followed the introduction of computers. Maps and geographic information are now stored in digital databases which can be constantly maintained, with direct updating possible from survey and satellite data. This procedure is increasingly being employed by national and commercial mapping agencies where maps, particularly at large scales, are compiled digitally and printed on demand rather than as part of a publishing programme or printed series. This means that choices are now available for the provision of geographic or cartographic information – through printing or via computer-based mapping systems on CD-ROM or the Internet.

The latter may carry some disadvantages (such as the need for the latest hardware, and the restricted view of a monitor screen) but these systems can also offer revolutionary advantages for the viewer. Not only can geographic information be selected and combined at will but the user may also have interactive control over the design and content of the image (see 6). Animation may also be provided as well as hyper-links to other parts of the database for images, video-clips or sounds.

Geographic information systems (GIS) – combining software and hardware for the manipulation and analysis of spatial data – develop these ideas much farther and are now used extensively within government, industry and commerce. Digital geographic data and cartographic facilities are now also being employed in what are often referred to as location-based services (LBS), including in-car navigation systems (see 7), mobile phones and personal digital assistants. These can incorporate GPS receivers and respond to geographic triggers such as the input of a town name, street name or postcode. The precise position of the user can then be identified and route guidance and local information provided directly. However, new technology need not change completely how we access and use maps. We still travel on foot, by bicycle, motorcar or aircraft as circumstances demand. Thus the future can be interpreted as offering a wider spectrum of cartographic sources and facilities for different uses – from high quality publications produced by cartographic specialists, to personal interactive experiences.

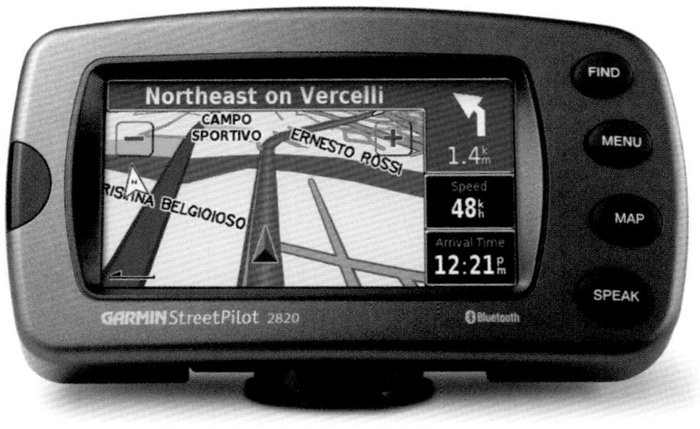

7. MOBILE MAPPING

The Garmin iQue was the first personal digital assistant (PDA) to include Global Positioning System (GPS) technology and carried map data and mapping software. It was capable of automatic route calculation and turn-by-turn voice guidance. The latest in-car systems use Bluetooth technology to facilitate 'hands-free' navigation, and real-time traffic information is also now available. This permits routes to be calculated around traffic bottlenecks, and road incidents affecting traffic are graphically represented on-screen as icons on the navigation map. It is also possible for the user to load customized points of interest (POIs) such as speed cameras to add to a pre-loaded POI database.

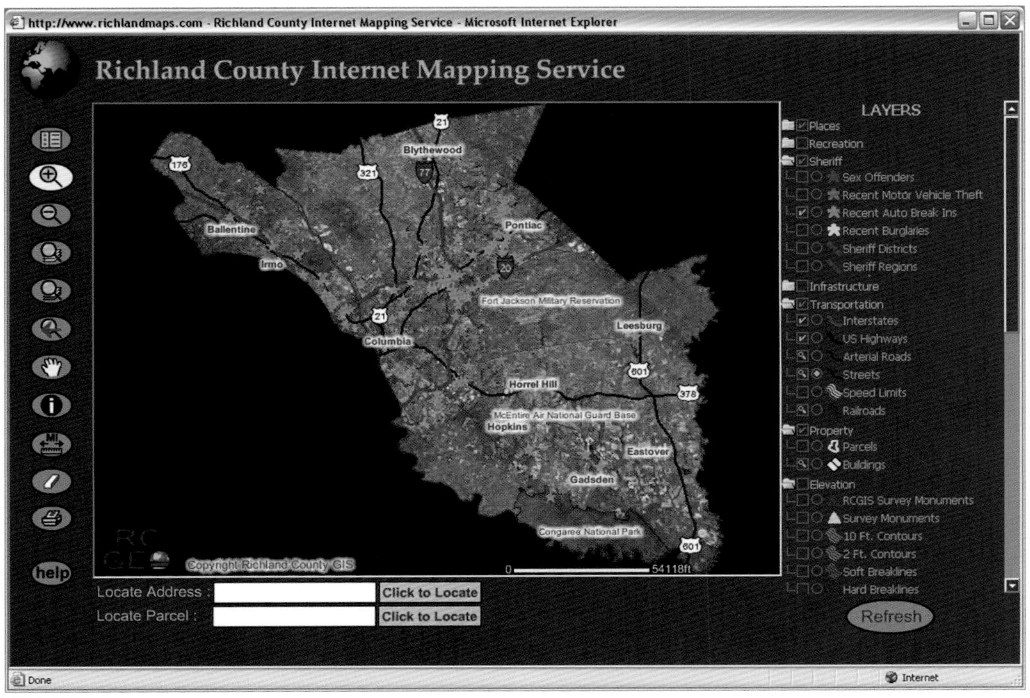

6. INTERACTIVE WEB MAPPING

Richland County Geographic Information Systems (RC GEO), South Carolina, use data from across several departments to develop spatial databases and mapping services for use by local government, the general public and businesses. Integration of the data within a geographic information system (GIS) allows each point on a map to become an index to cultural, environmental, demographic and political information about that location, and allows users to manipulate and output maps for their specific needs.

AUSTRALASIA Total Land Area 8 844 516 sq km / 3 414 887 sq miles (includes New Guinea and Pacific Island nations)

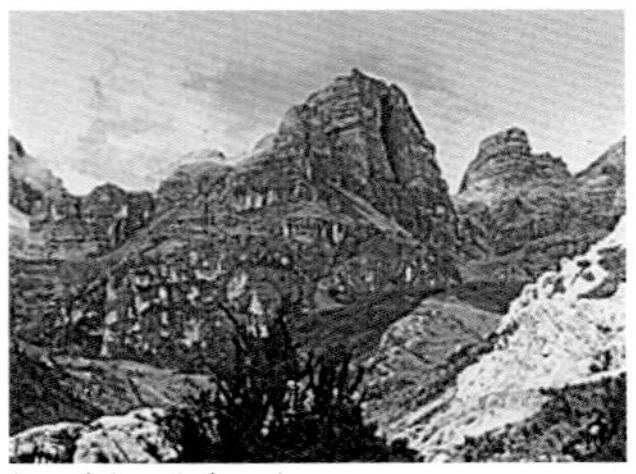

Puncak Jaya, Indonesia

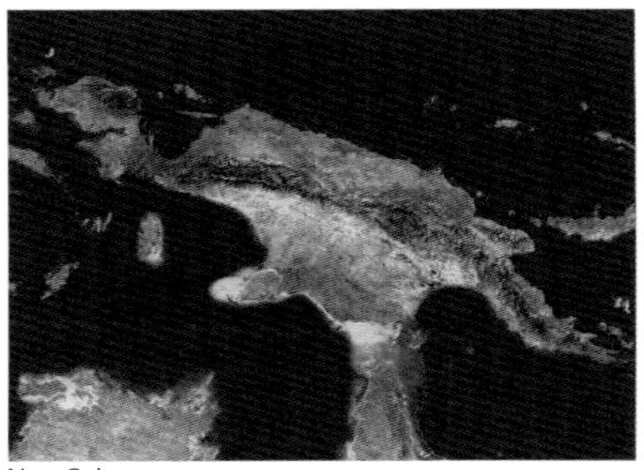

New Guinea

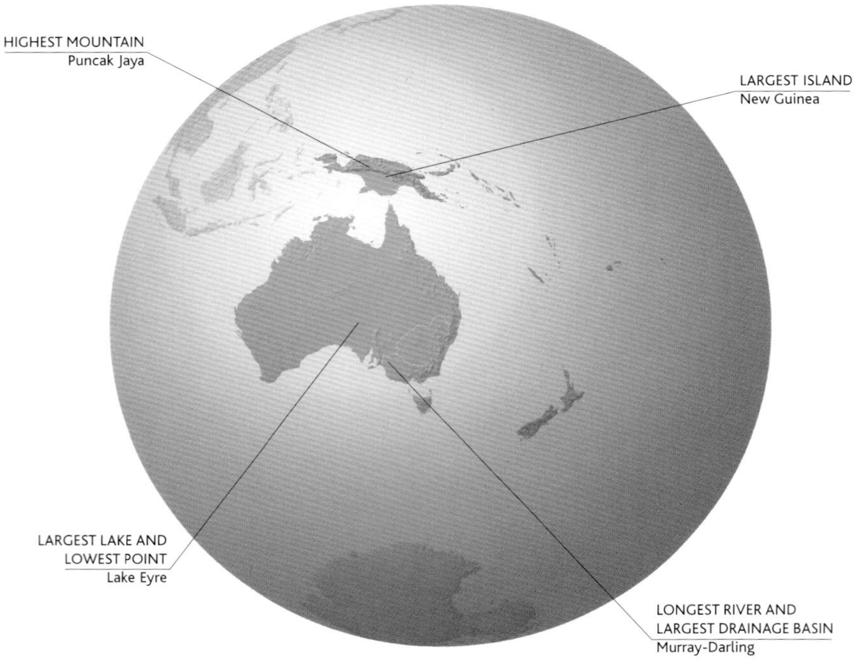

HIGHEST MOUNTAIN
Puncak Jaya

LARGEST ISLAND
New Guinea

LARGEST LAKE AND
LOWEST POINT
Lake Eyre

LONGEST RIVER AND
LARGEST DRAINAGE BASIN
Murray-Darling

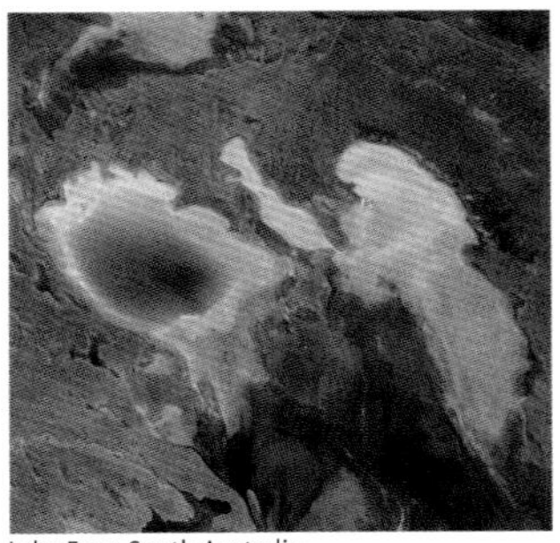

Lake Eyre, South Australia

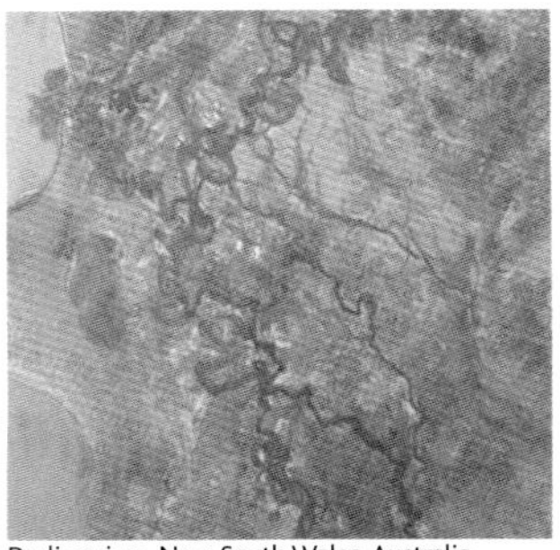

Darling river, New South Wales, Australia

HIGHEST MOUNTAINS	metres	feet	Location
Puncak Jaya	5 030	16 502	Indonesia
Puncak Trikora	4 730	15 518	Indonesia
Puncak Mandala	4 700	15 420	Indonesia
Puncak Yamin	4 595	15 075	Indonesia
Mt Wilhelm	4 509	14 793	Papua New Guinea
Mt Kubor	4 359	14 301	Papua New Guinea

LARGEST ISLANDS	sq km	sq miles
New Guinea	808 510	312 167
South Island, New Zealand	151 215	58 384
North Island, New Zealand	115 777	44 702
Tasmania	67 800	26 178

LONGEST RIVERS	km	miles
Murray-Darling	3 750	2 330
Darling	2 739	1 702
Murray	2 589	1 608
Murrumbidgee	1 690	1 050
Lachlan	1 480	919
Macquarie	950	590

LARGEST LAKES	sq km	sq miles
Lake Eyre	0–8 900	0–3 436
Lake Torrens	0–5 780	0–2 232

ASIA Total Land Area 45 036 492 sq km / 17 388 686 sq miles

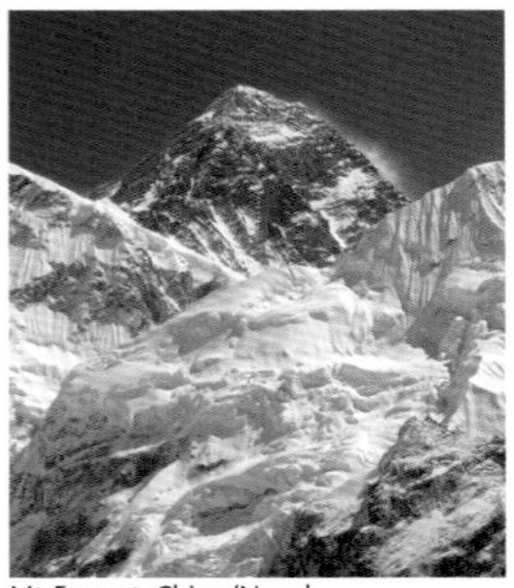

Mt Everest, China/Nepal

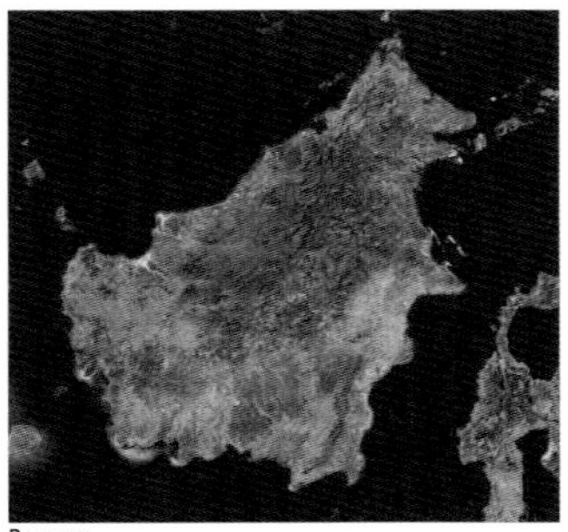

Borneo

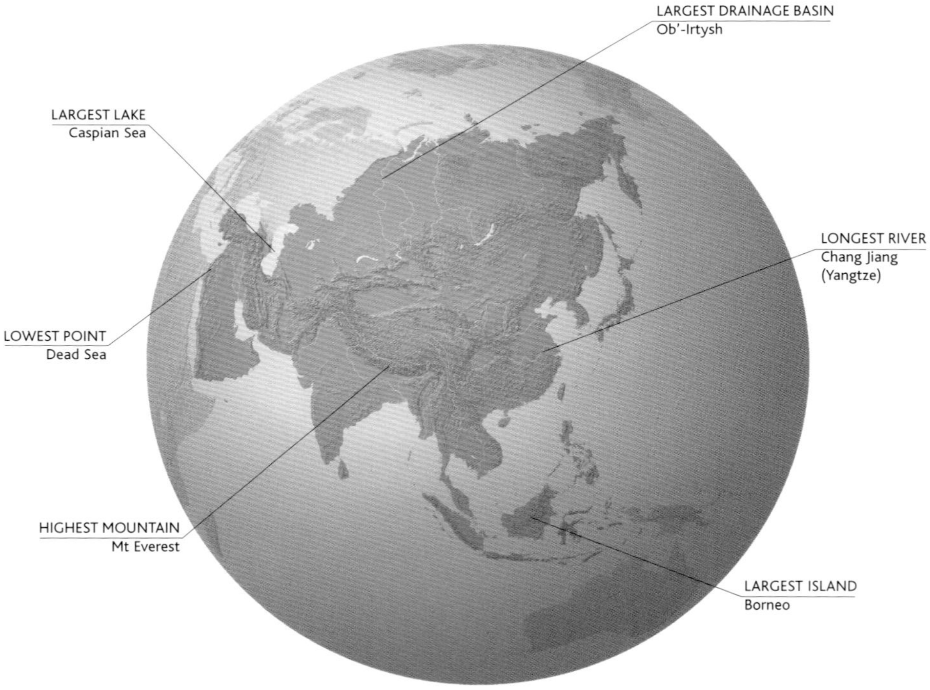

LARGEST DRAINAGE BASIN
Ob'-Irtysh

LARGEST LAKE
Caspian Sea

LONGEST RIVER
Chang Jiang
(Yangtze)

LOWEST POINT
Dead Sea

HIGHEST MOUNTAIN
Mt Everest

LARGEST ISLAND
Borneo

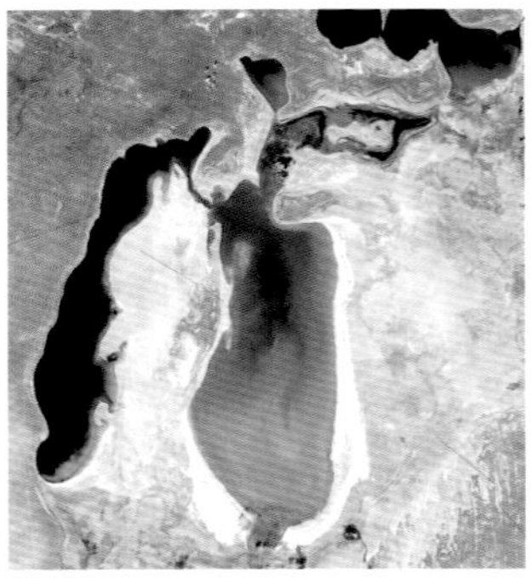

Aral Sea

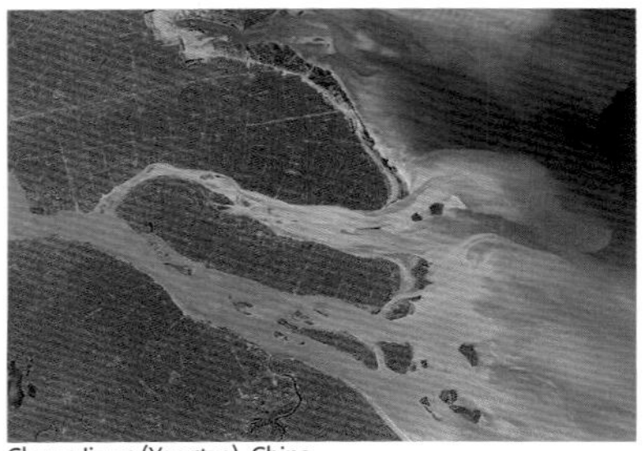

Chang Jiang (Yangtze), China

HIGHEST MOUNTAINS	metres	feet	Location
Mt Everest (Sagarmatha/ Qomolangma Feng)	8 848	29 028	China/Nepal
K2 (Qogir Feng)	8 611	28 251	China/Jammu and Kashmir
Kangchenjunga	8 586	28 169	India/Nepal
Lhotse	8 516	27 939	China/Nepal
Makalu	8 463	27 765	China/Nepal
Cho Oyu	8 201	26 906	China/Nepal

LARGEST ISLANDS	sq km	sq miles
Borneo	745 561	287 863
Sumatera (Sumatra)	473 606	182 860
Honshū	227 414	87 805
Sulawesi (Celebes)	189 216	73 057
Jawa (Java)	132 188	51 038
Luzon	104 690	40 421

LONGEST RIVERS	km	miles
Chang Jiang (Yangtze)	6 380	3 965
Ob'-Irtysh	5 568	3 460
Yenisey-Angara-Selenga	5 550	3 448
Huang He (Yellow River)	5 464	3 395
Irtysh	4 440	2 759
Mekong	4 425	2 749

LARGEST LAKES	sq km	sq miles
Caspian Sea	371 000	143 244
Ozero Baykal (Lake Baikal)	30 500	11 776
Ozero Balkhash	17 400	6 718
Aral Sea (Aral'skoye More)	17 158	6 625
Ysyk-Köl	6 200	2 393

EUROPE Total Land Area 9 908 599 sq km / 3 825 731 sq miles

El'brus, Russian Federation

Great Britain

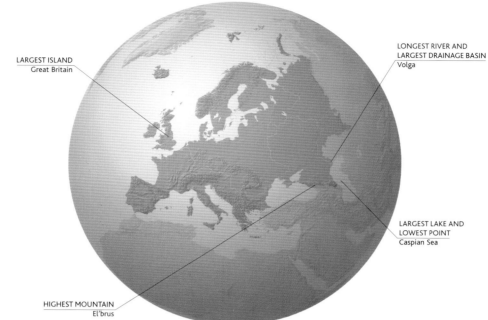

LARGEST ISLAND
Great Britain

LONGEST RIVER AND
LARGEST DRAINAGE BASIN
Volga

LARGEST LAKE AND
LOWEST POINT
Caspian Sea

HIGHEST MOUNTAIN
El'brus

Caspian Sea

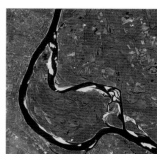

Volga, Russian Federation

HIGHEST MOUNTAINS	metres	feet	Location
El'brus	5 642	18 510	Russian Federation
Gora Dykh-Tau	5 204	17 073	Russian Federation
Shkhara	5 201	17 063	Georgia/Russian Federation
Kazbek	5 047	16 558	Georgia/Russian Federation
Mont Blanc	4 808	15 774	France/Italy
Dufourspitze	4 634	15 203	Italy/Switzerland

LARGEST ISLANDS	sq km	sq miles
Great Britain	218 476	84 354
Iceland	102 820	39 699
Novaya Zemlya	90 650	35 000
Ireland	83 045	32 064
Spitsbergen	37 814	14 600
Sicilia (Sicily)	25 426	9 817

LONGEST RIVERS	km	miles
Volga	3 688	2 291
Danube	2 850	1 770
Dnieper	2 285	1 419
Kama	2 028	1 260
Don	1 931	1 199
Pechora	1 802	1 119

LARGEST LAKES	sq km	sq miles
Caspian Sea	371 000	143 243
Ladozhskoye Ozero (Lake Ladoga)	18 390	7 100
Onezhskoye Ozero (Lake Onega)	9 600	3 706
Vänern	5 585	2 156
Rybinskoye Vodokhranilishche	5 180	2 000

AFRICA Total Land Area 30 343 578 sq km / 11 715 721 sq miles

Kilimanjaro, Tanzania

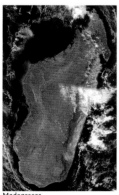

Madagascar

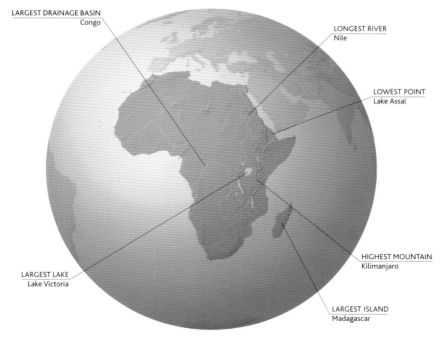

LARGEST DRAINAGE BASIN
Congo

LONGEST RIVER
Nile

LOWEST POINT
Lake Assal

HIGHEST MOUNTAIN
Kilimanjaro

LARGEST ISLAND
Madagascar

LARGEST LAKE
Lake Victoria

Lake Victoria, Kenya/Tanzania/Jganda

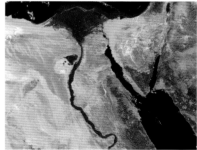

Nile, Egypt/Sudan

HIGHEST MOUNTAINS	metres	feet	Location
Kilimanjaro	5 892	19 331	Tanzania
Kirinyaga (Mt Kenya)	5 199	17 057	Kenya
Margherita Peak (Mt Stanley)	5 110	16 765	Democratic Republic of the Congo/Uganda
Meru	4 565	14 977	Tanzania
Ras Dejen	4 533	14 872	Ethiopia
Mt Karisimbi	4 510	14 796	Rwanda

LARGEST ISLANDS	sq km	sq miles
Madagascar	587 040	226 657

LONGEST RIVERS	km	miles
Nile	6 695	4 160
Congo	4 667	2 900
Niger	4 184	2 599
Zambezi (Zambeze)	2 736	1 700
Webi Shabeelle	2 490	1 547
Ubangi	2 250	1 398

LARGEST LAKES	sq km	sq miles
Lake Victoria	68 800	26 564
Lake Tanganyika	32 900	12 702
Lake Nyasa (Lake Malawi)	30 044	11 600
Lake Volta	8 485	3 276
Lake Turkana	6 475	2 500
Lake Albert	5 600	2 162

NORTH AMERICA   Total Land Area 24 680 331 sq km / 9 529 129 sq miles (including Hawaiian Islands)

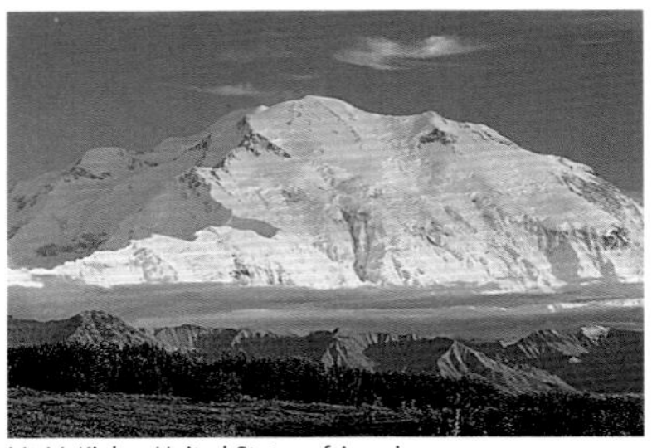

Mt McKinley, United States of America

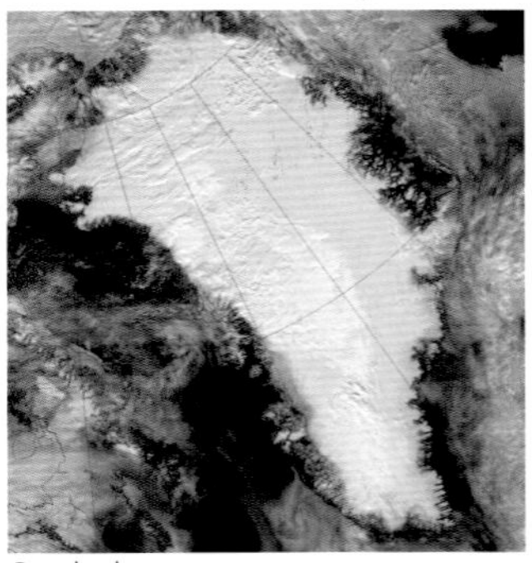

Greenland

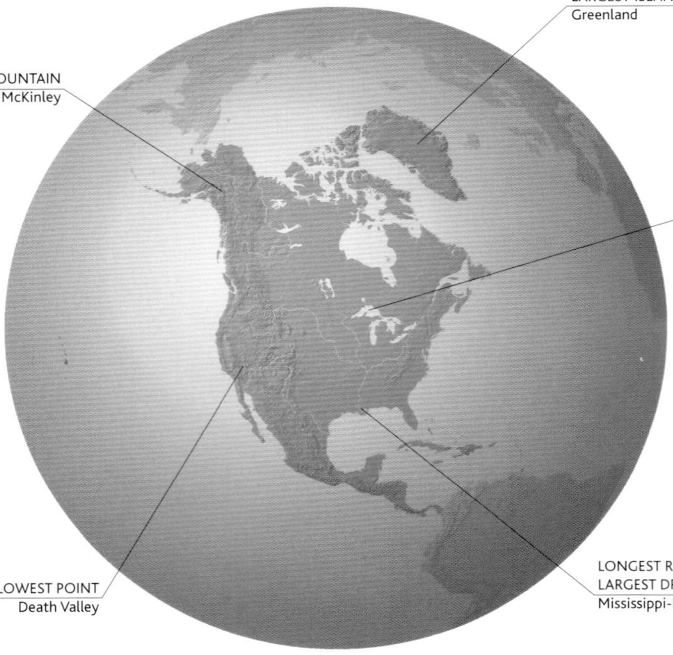

HIGHEST MOUNTAIN
Mt McKinley

LARGEST ISLAND
Greenland

LARGEST LAKE
Lake Superior

LOWEST POINT
Death Valley

LONGEST RIVER AND
LARGEST DRAINAGE BASIN
Mississippi-Missouri

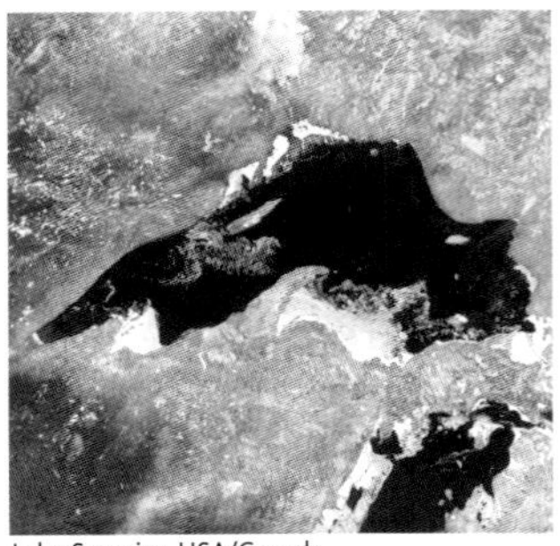

Lake Superior, USA/Canada

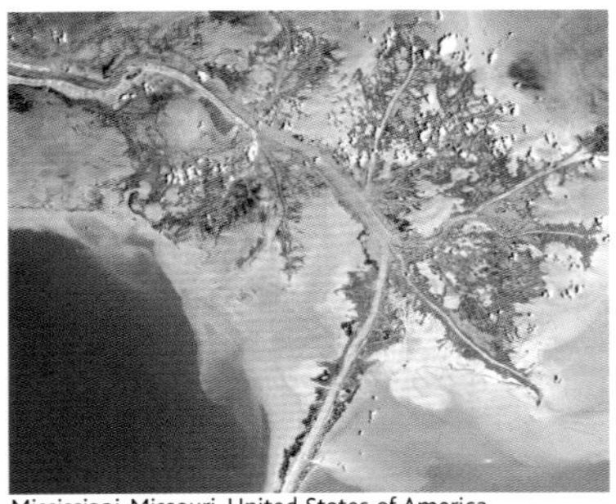

Mississippi-Missouri, United States of America

HIGHEST MOUNTAINS	metres	feet	Location
Mt McKinley	6 194	20 321	USA
Mt Logan	5 959	19 550	Canada
Pico de Orizaba	5 747	18 855	Mexico
Mt St Elias	5 489	18 008	USA
Volcan Popocatépetl	5 452	17 887	Mexico
Mt Foraker	5 303	17 398	USA

LARGEST ISLANDS	sq km	sq miles
Greenland	2 175 600	840 004
Baffin Island	507 451	195 928
Victoria Island	217 291	83 897
Ellesmere Island	196 236	75 767
Cuba	110 860	42 803
Newfoundland	108 860	42 031
Hispaniola	76 192	29 418

LONGEST RIVERS	km	miles
Mississippi-Missouri	5 969	3 709
Mackenzie-Peace-Finlay	4 241	2 635
Missouri	4 086	2 539
Mississippi	3 765	2 339
Yukon	3 185	1 979
Rio Grande (Rio Bravo del Norte)	3 057	1 899

LARGEST LAKES	sq km	sq miles
Lake Superior	82 100	31 699
Lake Huron	59 600	23 012
Lake Michigan	57 800	22 317
Great Bear Lake	31 328	12 095
Great Slave Lake	28 568	11 030
Lake Erie	25 700	9 922
Lake Winnipeg	24 387	9 415
Lake Ontario	18 960	7 320

SOUTH AMERICA   Total Land Area 17 815 420 sq km / 6 878 572 sq miles

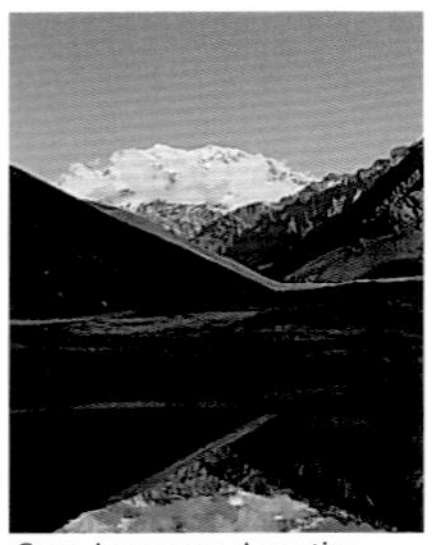

Cerro Aconcagua, Argentina

LONGEST RIVER AND
LARGEST DRAINAGE BASIN
Amazonas

LARGEST LAKE
Lago Titicaca

LOWEST POINT
Peninsula Valdés

HIGHEST MOUNTAIN
Cerro Aconcagua

LARGEST ISLAND
Isla Grande de Tierra del Fuego

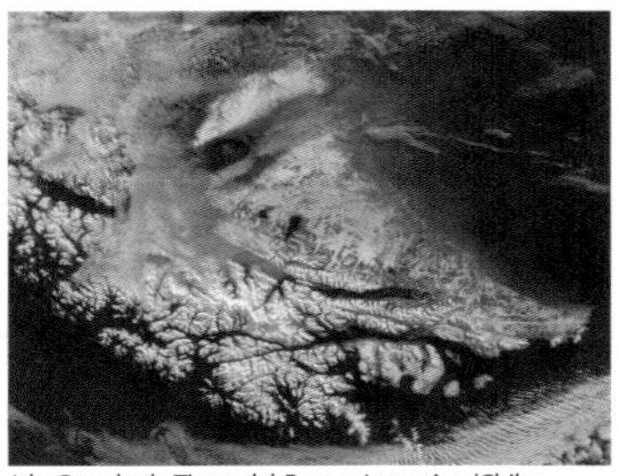

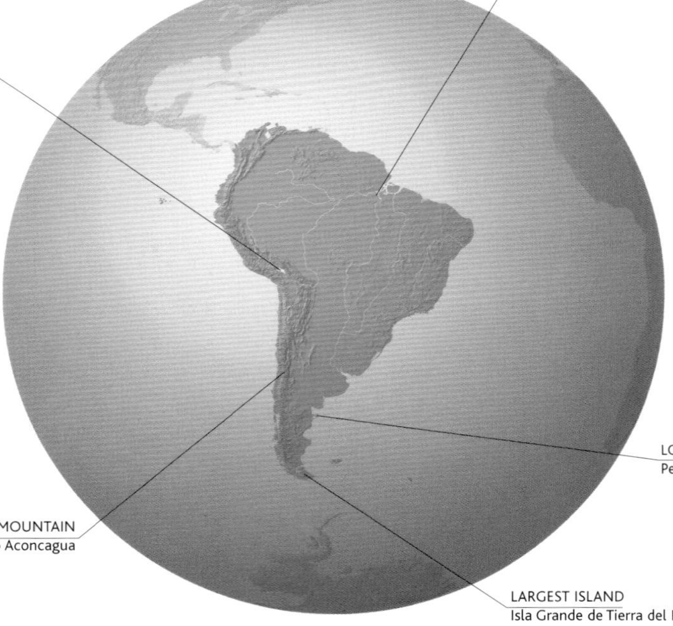

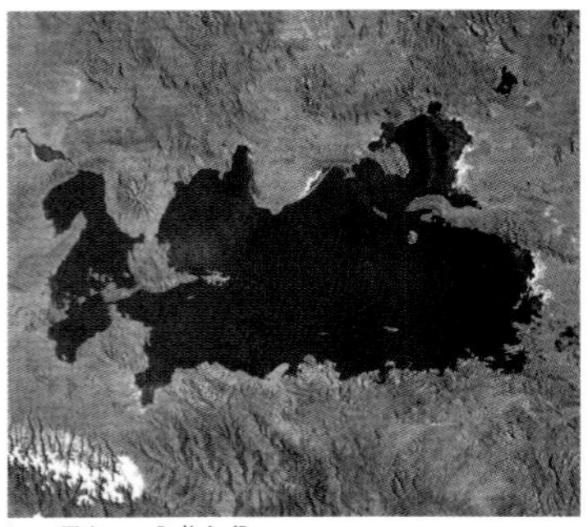

Lago Titicaca, Bolivia/Peru

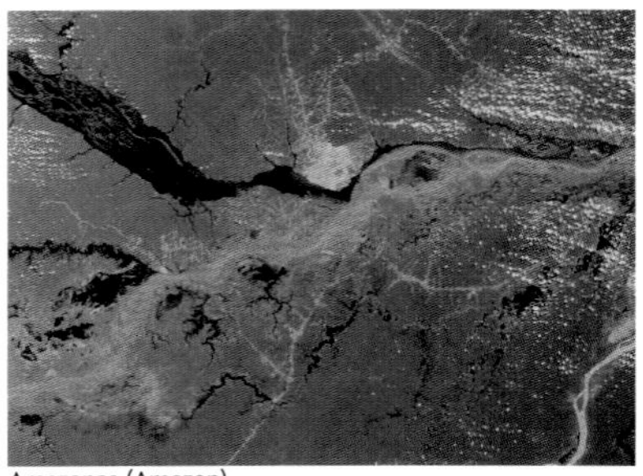

Amazonas (Amazon)

Isla Grande de Tierra del Fuego, Argentina/Chile

HIGHEST MOUNTAINS	metres	feet	Location
Cerro Aconcagua	6 959	22 831	Argentina
Nevado Ojos del Salado	6 908	22 664	Argentina/Chile
Cerro Bonete	6 872	22 546	Argentina
Cerro Pissis	6 858	22 500	Argentina
Cerro Tupungato	6 800	22 309	Argentina/Chile
Cerro Mercedario	6 770	22 211	Argentina

LARGEST ISLANDS	sq km	sq miles
Isla Grande de Tierra del Fuego	47 000	18 147
Isla de Chiloé	8 394	3 240
East Falkland	6 760	2 610
West Falkland	5 413	2 090

LONGEST RIVERS	km	miles
Amazonas (Amazon)	6 516	4 049
Rio de la Plata-Paraná	4 500	2 796
Purus	3 218	1 999
Madeira	3 200	1 988
São Francisco	2 900	1 802
Tocantins	2 750	1 708

LARGEST LAKES	sq km	sq miles
Lago Titicaca	8 340	3 220

OCEANS AND POLES

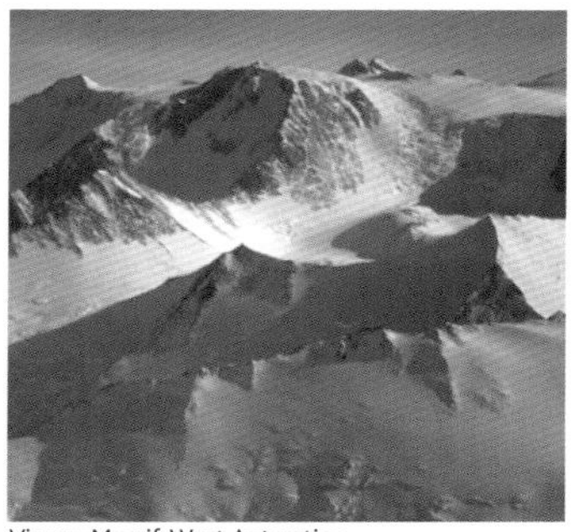

Vinson Massif, West Antarctica

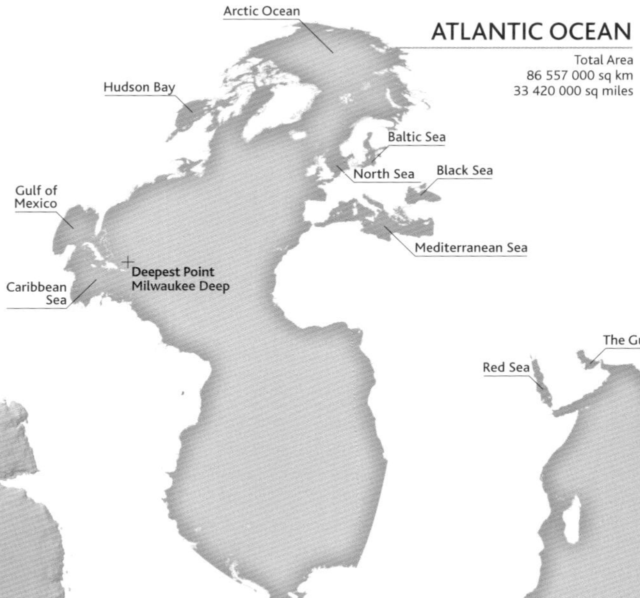

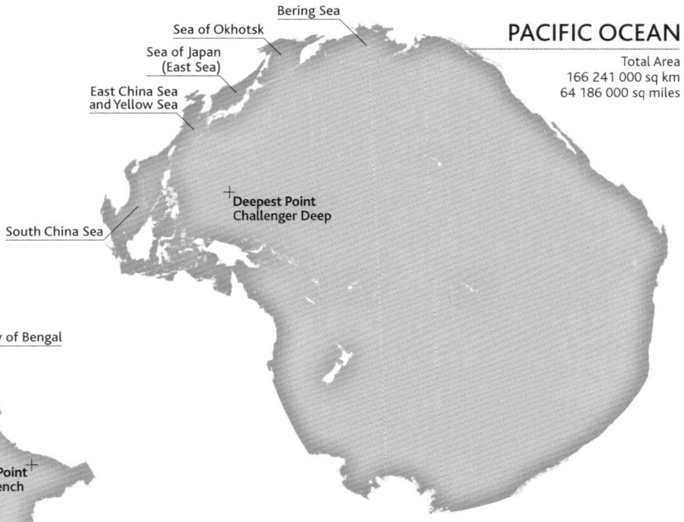

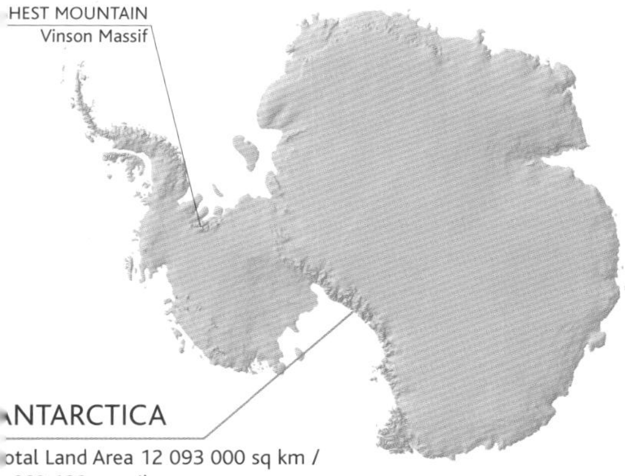

HEST MOUNTAIN
Vinson Massif

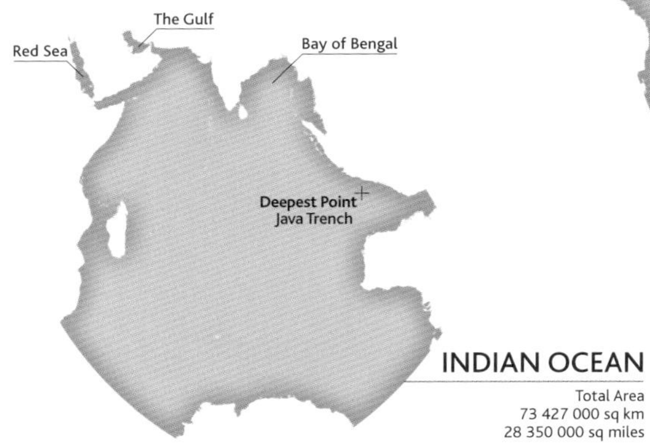

ANTARCTICA

Total Land Area 12 093 000 sq km / 4 669 133 sq miles (excluding ice shelves)

HIGHEST MOUNTAINS	metres	feet
Vinson Massif	4 897	16 066
Mt Tyree	4 852	15 918
Mt Kirkpatrick	4 528	14 855
Mt Markham	4 351	14 275
Mt Jackson	4 190	13 747
Mt Sidley	4 181	13 717

ATLANTIC OCEAN
Total Area
86 557 000 sq km
33 420 000 sq miles

Deepest Point
Milwaukee Deep

PACIFIC OCEAN
Total Area
166 241 000 sq km
64 186 000 sq miles

Deepest Point
Challenger Deep

INDIAN OCEAN
Total Area
73 427 000 sq km
28 350 000 sq miles

Deepest Point
Java Trench

ATLANTIC OCEAN	Area sq km	sq miles	Deepest Point metres	feet
Extent	86 557 000	33 420 000	8 605	28 231
Arctic Ocean	9 485 000	3 662 000	5 450	17 880
Caribbean Sea	2 512 000	970 000	7 680	25 196
Mediterranean Sea	2 510 000	969 000	5 121	16 800
Gulf of Mexico	1 544 000	596 000	3 504	11 495
Hudson Bay	1 233 000	476 000	259	849
North Sea	575 000	222 000	661	2 168
Black Sea	508 000	196 000	2 245	7 365
Baltic Sea	382 000	147 000	460	1 509

INDIAN OCEAN	Area sq km	sq miles	Deepest Point metres	feet
Extent	73 427 000	28 350 000	7 125	23 376
Bay of Bengal	2 172 000	839 000	4 500	14 763
Red Sea	453 000	175 000	3 040	9 973
The Gulf	238 000	92 000	73	239

PACIFIC OCEAN	Area sq km	sq miles	Deepest Point metres	feet
Extent	166 241 000	64 186 000	10 920	35 826
South China Sea	2 590 000	1 000 000	5 514	18 090
Bering Sea	2 261 000	873 000	4 150	13 615
Sea of Okhotsk	1 392 000	537 000	3 363	11 033
Sea of Japan (East Sea)	1 013 000	391 000	3 743	12 280
East China Sea and Yellow Sea	1 202 000	464 000	2 717	8 913

WORLD

HIGHEST MOUNTAINS	metres	feet	Location
Mt Everest	8 848	29 028	China/Nepal
K2	8 611	28 251	China/Jammu and Kashmir
Kangchenjunga	8 586	28 169	India/Nepal
Lhotse	8 516	27 939	China/Nepal
Makalu	8 463	27 765	China/Nepal
Cho Oyu	8 201	26 906	China/Nepal
Dhaulagiri	8 167	26 794	Nepal
Manaslu	8 163	26 781	Nepal
Nanga Parbat	8 126	26 660	Jammu and Kashmir
Annapurna I	8 091	26 545	Nepal
Gasherbrum I	8 068	26 469	China/Jammu and Kashmir
Broad Peak	8 047	26 401	China/Jammu and Kashmir
Gasherbrum II	8 035	26 361	China/Jammu and Kashmir
Xixabangma Feng	8 012	26 286	China
Annapurna II	7 937	26 040	Nepal
Nuptse	7 885	25 869	Nepal
Himalchul	7 864	25 800	Nepal
Masherbrum	7 821	25 659	Jammu and Kashmir
Nandi Devi	7 816	25 643	India
Rakaposhi	7 788	25 551	Jammu and Kashmir

LARGEST ISLANDS	sq km	sq miles	Continent
Greenland	2 175 600	840 004	North America
New Guinea	808 510	312 167	Australasia
Borneo	745 561	287 863	Asia
Madagascar	587 040	266 657	Africa
Baffin Island	507 451	195 928	North America
Sumatera	473 606	182 860	Asia
Honshū	227 414	87 805	Asia
Great Britain	218 476	84 354	Europe
Victoria Island	217 291	83 897	North America
Ellesmere Island	196 236	75 767	North America
Sulawesi (Celebes)	189 216	73 057	Asia
South Island, New Zealand	151 215	58 384	Australasia
Jawa (Java)	132 188	51 038	Asia
North Island, New Zealand	115 777	44 702	Australasia
Cuba	110 860	42 803	North America
Newfoundland	108 860	42 031	North America
Luzon	104 690	40 421	Asia
Iceland	102 820	39 699	Europe
Mindanao	94 630	36 537	Asia
Novaya Zemlya	90 650	35 000	Europe

LONGEST RIVERS	km	miles	Continent
Nile	6 695	4 160	Africa
Amazonas (Amazon)	6 516	4 049	South America
Chang Jiang (Yangtze)	6 380	3 965	Asia
Mississippi-Missouri	5 969	3 709	North America
Ob'-Irtysh	5 568	3 460	Asia
Yenisey-Angara-Selenga	5 550	3 449	Asia
Huang He (Yellow River)	5 464	3 395	Asia
Congo	4 667	2 900	Africa
Rio de la Plata-Paraná	4 500	2 796	South America
Irtysh	4 440	2 759	Asia
Mekong	4 425	2 750	Asia
Heilong Jiang (Amur)-Argun'	4 416	2 744	Asia
Lena-Kirenga	4 400	2 734	Asia
MacKenzie-Peace-Finlay	4 241	2 635	North America
Niger	4 184	2 600	Africa
Yenisey	4 090	2 542	Asia
Missouri	4 086	2 539	North America
Mississippi	3 765	2 340	North America
Murray-Darling	3 750	2 330	Australasia
Ob'	3 701	2 300	Asia

LARGEST DRAINAGE BASINS	sq km	sq miles	Continent
Amazonas (Amazon)	7 050 000	2 722 000	South America
Congo	3 700 000	1 429 000	Africa
Nile	3 349 000	1 293 000	Africa
Mississippi-Missouri	3 250 000	1 255 000	North America
Río de la Plata-Paraná	3 100 000	1 197 000	South America
Ob'-Irtysh	2 990 000	1 154 000	Asia
Yenisey-Angara-Selenga	2 580 000	996 000	Asia
Lena-Kirenga	2 490 000	961 000	Asia
Chang Jiang (Yangtze)	1 959 000	756 000	Asia
Niger	1 890 000	730 000	Africa
Heilong Jiang (Amur)-Argun'	1 855 000	716 000	Asia
Mackenzie-Peace-Finlay	1 805 000	697 000	North America
Ganga (Ganges)-Brahmaputra	1 621 000	626 000	Asia
St Lawrence-St Louis	1 463 000	565 000	North America
Volga	1 380 000	533 000	Europe
Zambezi (Zambeze)	1 330 000	514 000	Africa
Indus	1 166 000	450 000	Asia
Nelson-Saskatchewan	1 150 000	444 000	North America
Shatt al'Arab	1 114 000	430 000	Asia
Murray-Darling	1 058 000	408 000	Australasia

LARGEST LAKES	sq km	sq miles	Continent
Caspian Sea	371 000	143 244	Asia/Europe
Lake Superior	82 100	31 699	North America
Lake Victoria	68 800	26 564	Africa
Lake Huron	59 600	23 012	North America
Lake Michigan	57 800	22 317	North America
Lake Tanganyika	32 900	12 702	Africa
Great Bear Lake	31 328	12 095	North America
Ozero Baykal (Lake Baikal)	30 500	11 776	Asia
Lake Nyasa (Lake Malawi)	30 044	11 600	Africa
Great Slave Lake	28 568	11 030	North America
Lake Erie	25 700	9 922	North America
Lake Winnipeg	24 387	9 415	North America
Lake Ontario	18 960	7 320	North America
Ladozhskoye Ozero (Lake Ladoga)	18 390	7 100	Europe
Ozero Balkhash	17 400	6 718	Asia
Aral Sea (Aral'skoye More)	17 158	6 625	Asia
Onezhskoye Ozero (Lake Onega)	9 600	3 706	Europe
Lake Volta	8 485	3 276	Africa
Lake Titicaca	8 340	3 220	South America
Lago de Nicaragua	8 150	3 147	North America

EARTH'S DIMENSIONS	
Mass	5.974 X 10²¹ tonnes
Total area	509 450 000 sq km / 196 672 000 sq miles
Land area	149 450 000 sq km / 57 688 000 sq miles
Water area	360 000 000 sq km / 138 984 000 sq miles
Volume	1 083 207 x 10⁶ cubic km / 259 875 x 10⁶ cubic miles
Equatorial diameter	12 756 km / 7 926 miles
Polar diameter	12 714 km / 7 900 miles
Equatorial circumference	40 075 km / 24 903 miles
Meridional circumference	40 008 km / 24 861 miles

All 194 independent countries and all populated dependent and disputed territories are included in this list of the states and territories of the world; the list is arranged in alphabetical order by the conventional name form. For independent states, the full name is given below the conventional name, if this is different; for territories, the status is given. The capital city name is given in the local form as shown on the reference maps.

Area and population statistics are the latest available and include estimates. The information on languages and religions is based on the latest information on 'de facto' speakers of the language or 'de facto' adherents of the religion. This varies greatly from country to country because some countries include questions in censuses while others do not, in which case best estimates are used. The order of the languages and religions reflects their relative importance within the country; generally, languages or religions are included when more than one per cent of the population are estimated to be speakers or adherents.

Membership of selected international organizations is shown by the abbreviations below; dependent territories do not normally have separate memberships of these organizations.

APEC	Asia-Pacific Economic Cooperation
ASEAN	Association of Southeast Asian Nations
CARICOM	Caribbean Community
CIS	Commonwealth of Independent States
Comm.	The Commonwealth
EU	European Union
NATO	North Atlantic Treaty Organization
OECD	Organisation for Economic Co-operation and Development
OPEC	Organization of Petroleum Exporting Countries
SADC	Southern African Development Community
UN	United Nations

AFGHANISTAN
Islamic State of Afghanistan

Area Sq Km 652 225	**Currency** Afghani
Area Sq Miles 251 825	**Languages** Dari, Pushtu, Uzbek, Turkmen
Population 29 863 000	**Religions** Sunni Muslim, Shi'a Muslim
Capital Kābul	**Organizations** UN

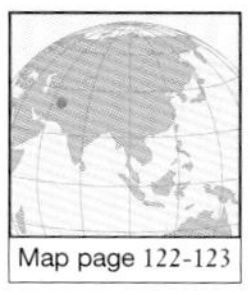
Map page 122-123

A landlocked country in central Asia with central highlands bordered by plains in the north and southwest, and by the Hindu Kush mountains in the northeast. The climate is dry continental. Over the last thirty years war has disrupted the economy, which is highly dependent on farming and livestock rearing. Most trade is with the former USSR, Pakistan and Iran.

ALBANIA
Republic of Albania

Area Sq Km 28 748	**Currency** Lek
Area Sq Miles 11 100	**Languages** Albanian, Greek
Population 3 130 000	**Religions** Sunni Muslim, Orthodox, Roman Catholic
Capital Tiranë	**Organizations** UN

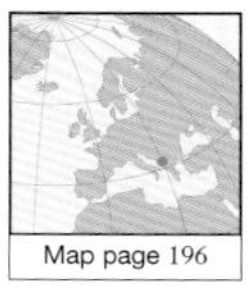
Map page 196

Albania lies in the western Balkan Mountains in southeastern Europe, bordering the Adriatic Sea. It is mountainous, with coastal plains where half the population lives. The economy is based on agriculture and mining. Albania is one of the poorest countries in Europe and relies heavily on foreign aid.

ALGERIA
People's Democratic Republic of Algeria

Area Sq Km 2 381 741	**Currency** Algerian dinar
Area Sq Miles 919 595	**Languages** Arabic, French, Berber
Population 32 854 000	**Religions** Sunni Muslim
Capital Alger (Algiers)	**Organizations** OPEC, UN

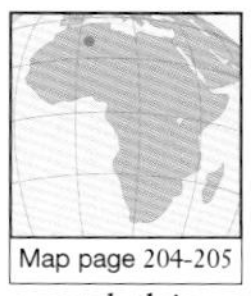
Map page 204-205

Algeria, the second largest country in Africa, lies on the Mediterranean coast of northwest Africa and extends southwards to the Atlas Mountains and the dry sandstone plateau and desert of the Sahara. The climate ranges from Mediterranean on the coast to semi-arid and arid inland. The most populated areas are the coastal plains and the fertile northern slopes of the Atlas Mountains. Oil, natural gas and related products account for over ninety-five per cent of export earnings. Agriculture employs about a quarter of the workforce, producing mainly food crops. Algeria's main trading partners are Italy, France and the USA.

American Samoa
United States Unincorporated Territory

Area Sq Km 197	**Currency** United States dollar
Area Sq Miles 76	**Languages** Samoan, English
Population 65 000	**Religions** Protestant, Roman Catholic
Capital Fagatogo	

Lying in the south Pacific Ocean, American Samoa consists of five main islands and two coral atolls. The largest island is Tutuila. Tuna and tuna products are the main exports, and the main trading partner is the USA.

Map page 78

ANDORRA
Principality of Andorra

Area Sq Km 465	**Currency** Euro
Area Sq Miles 180	**Languages** Spanish, Catalan, French
Population 67 000	**Religions** Roman Catholic
Capital Andorra la Vella	**Organizations** UN

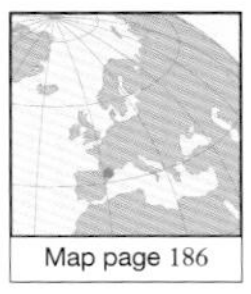
Map page 186

A landlocked state in southwest Europe, Andorra lies in the Pyrenees mountain range between France and Spain. It consists of deep valleys and gorges, surrounded by mountains. Tourism, encouraged by the development of ski resorts, is the mainstay of the economy. Banking is also an important economic activity.

ANGOLA
Republic of Angola

Area Sq Km 1 246 700	**Currency** Kwanza
Area Sq Miles 481 354	**Languages** Portuguese, Bantu, local languages
Population 15 941 000	**Religions** Roman Catholic, Protestant, traditional beliefs
Capital Luanda	**Organizations** SADC, UN

Angola lies on the Atlantic coast of south central Africa. Its small northern province, Cabinda, is separated from the rest of the country by part of the Democratic Republic of the Congo. Much of Angola is high plateau. In the west is a narrow coastal plain and in the southwest is desert. The climate is equatorial in the north but desert in the south. Over eighty per cent of the population relies on subsistence agriculture. Angola is rich in minerals (particularly diamonds), and oil accounts for approximately ninety per cent of export earnings. The USA, South Korea and Portugal are its main trading partners.

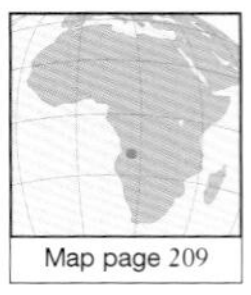
Map page 209

Anguilla
United Kingdom Overseas Territory

Area Sq Km 155	**Currency** East Caribbean dollar
Area Sq Miles 60	**Languages** English
Population 12 000	**Religions** Protestant, Roman Catholic
Capital The Valley	

Anguilla lies at the northern end of the Leeward Islands in the eastern Caribbean. Tourism and fishing form the basis of the economy.

Map page 247

ANTIGUA AND BARBUDA

Area Sq Km 442	**Currency** East Caribbean dollar
Area Sq Miles 171	**Languages** English, creole
Population 81 000	**Religions** Protestant, Roman Catholic
Capital St John's	**Organizations** CARICOM, Comm., UN

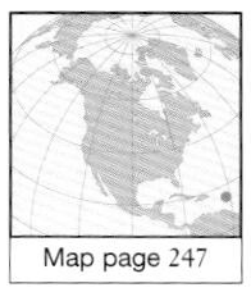
Map page 247

The state comprises the islands of Antigua, Barbuda and the tiny rocky outcrop of Redonda, in the Leeward Islands in the eastern Caribbean. Antigua, the largest and most populous island, is mainly hilly scrubland, with many beaches. The climate is tropical, and the economy relies heavily on tourism. Most trade is with other eastern Caribbean states and the USA.

ARGENTINA
Argentine Republic

Area Sq Km 2 766 889	**Currency** Argentinian peso
Area Sq Miles 1 068 302	**Languages** Spanish, Italian, Amerindian languages
Population 38 747 000	**Religions** Roman Catholic, Protestant
Capital Buenos Aires	**Organizations** UN

Argentina, the second largest state in South America, extends from Bolivia to Cape Horn and from the Andes mountains to the Atlantic Ocean. It has four geographical regions: subtropical forests and swampland in the northeast; temperate fertile plains or Pampas in the centre; the wooded foothills and valleys of the Andes in the west; and the cold, semi-arid plateaus of Patagonia in the south. The highest mountain in South America, Cerro Aconcagua, is in Argentina. Nearly ninety per cent of the population lives in towns and cities. The country is rich in natural resources including petroleum, natural gas, ores and precious metals. Agricultural products dominate exports, which also include motor vehicles and crude oil. Most trade is with Brazil and the USA.

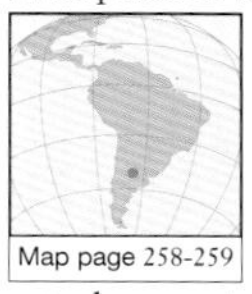
Map page 258-259

ARMENIA
Republic of Armenia

Area Sq Km 29 800	**Currency** Dram
Area Sq Miles 11 506	**Languages** Armenian, Azeri
Population 3 016 000	**Religions** Armenian Orthodox
Capital Yerevan (Erevan)	**Organizations** CIS, UN

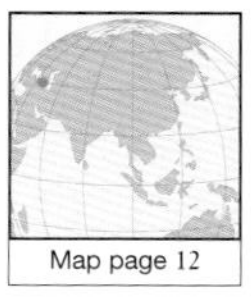
Map page 12

A landlocked state in southwest Asia, Armenia lies in the south of the Lesser Caucasus mountains. It is a mountainous country with a continental climate. One-third of the population lives in the capital, Yerevan. Exports include diamonds, scrap metal and machinery. Many Armenians depend on remittances from abroad.

Aruba
Self-governing Netherlands Territory

Area Sq Km 193	**Currency** Aruban florin
Area Sq Miles 75	**Languages** Papiamento, Dutch, English
Population 99 000	**Religions** Roman Catholic, Protestant
Capital Oranjestad	

The most southwesterly of the islands in the Lesser Antilles in the Caribbean, Aruba lies just off the coast of Venezuela. Tourism, offshore finance and oil refining are the most important sectors of the economy. The USA is the main trading partner.

Map page 247

Ascension Dependency of St Helena

Area Sq Km (Miles) 88 (34) **Population** 1 122 **Capital** Georgetown

A volcanic island in the south Atlantic Ocean about 1 300 kilometres (800 miles) northwest of St Helena.

Map page 216

AUSTRALIA
Commonwealth of Australia

Area Sq Km 7 692 024	**Currency** Australian dollar
Area Sq Miles 2 969 907	**Languages** English, Italian, Greek
Population 20 155 000	**Religions** Protestant, Roman Catholic, Orthodox
Capital Canberra	**Organizations** APEC, Comm., OECD, UN

Australia, the world's sixth largest country, occupies the smallest, flattest and driest continent. The western half of the continent is mostly arid plateaus, ridges and vast deserts. The central eastern area comprises the lowlands of river systems draining into Lake Eyre, while to the east is the Great Dividing Range, a belt of ridges and plateaus running from Queensland to Tasmania. Climatically, more than two-thirds of the country is arid or semi-arid. The north is tropical monsoon, the east subtropical, and the southwest and southeast temperate. The majority of Australia's highly urbanized population lives along the east, southeast and southwest coasts. Australia has vast mineral deposits and various sources of energy. It is among the world's leading producers of iron ore, bauxite, nickel, copper and uranium. It is a major producer of coal, and oil and natural gas are also being exploited. Although accounting for only five per cent of the workforce, agriculture continues to be an important sector of the economy, with food and agricultural raw materials making up most of Australia's export earnings. Fuel, ores and metals, and manufactured goods, account for the remainder of exports. Japan and the USA are Australia's main trading partners.

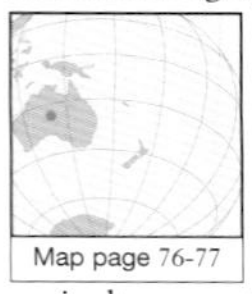
Map page 76-77

Australian Capital Territory (Federal territory)		
Area Sq Km (Miles) 2 358 (910)	**Population** 321 680	**Capital** Canberra
Jervis Bay Territory (Territory)		
Area Sq Km (Miles) 73 (28)	**Population** 611	**Capital**
New South Wales (State)		
Area Sq Km (Miles) 800 642 (309 130)	**Population** 6 609 304	**Capital** Sydney
Northern Territory (Territory)		
Area Sq Km (Miles) 1 349 129 (520 902)	**Population** 200 019	**Capital** Darwin
Queensland (State)		
Area Sq Km (Miles) 1 730 648 (668 207)	**Population** 3 635 121	**Capital** Brisbane
South Australia (State)		
Area Sq Km (Miles) 983 482 (379 725)	**Population** 1 514 854	**Capital** Adelaide
Tasmania (State)		
Area Sq Km (Miles) 68 401 (26 410)	**Population** 472 931	**Capital** Hobart
Victoria (State)		
Area Sq Km (Miles) 227 416 (87 806)	**Population** 4 822 663	**Capital** Melbourne
Western Australia (State)		
Area Sq Km (Miles) 2 529 875 (976 790)	**Population** 1 906 114	**Capital** Perth

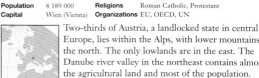

AUSTRIA
Republic of Austria

Area Sq Km 83 855	**Currency** Euro
Area Sq Miles 32 377	**Languages** German, Croatian, Turkish
Population 8 189 000	**Religions** Roman Catholic, Protestant
Capital Wien (Vienna)	**Organizations** EU, OECD, UN

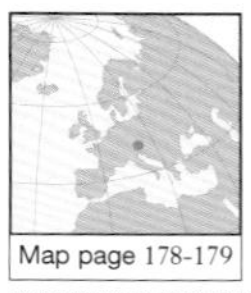
Map page 178-179

Two-thirds of Austria, a landlocked state in central Europe, lies within the Alps, with lower mountains to the north. The only lowlands are in the east. The Danube river valley in the northeast contains almost all the agricultural land and most of the population. Although the climate varies with altitude, in general summers are warm and winters cold with heavy snowfalls. Manufacturing industry and tourism are the most important sectors of the economy. Exports are dominated by manufactured goods. Germany is Austria's main trading partner.

AZERBAIJAN
Republic of Azerbaijan

Area Sq Km 86 600	**Currency** Azerbaijani manat
Area Sq Miles 33 436	**Languages** Azeri, Armenian, Russian, Lezgian
Population 8 411 000	**Religions** Shi'a Muslim, Sunni Muslim, Orthodox
Capital Bakı (Baku)	**Organizations** CIS, UN

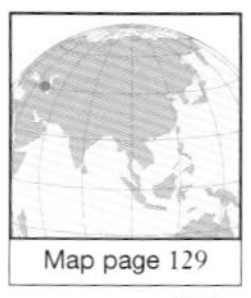
Map page 129

Azerbaijan lies to the southeast of the Caucasus mountains, on the Caspian Sea. Its region of Naxçivan is separated from the rest of the country by part of Armenia. It has mountains in the northeast and west, valleys in the centre, and a low coastal plain. The climate is continental. It is rich in energy and mineral resources. Oil production, onshore and offshore, is the main industry and the basis of heavy industries. Agriculture is important, with cotton and tobacco the main cash crops.

THE BAHAMAS
Commonwealth of the Bahamas

Area Sq Km 13 939	**Currency** Bahamian dollar
Area Sq Miles 5 382	**Languages** English, creole
Population 323 000	**Religions** Protestant, Roman Catholic
Capital Nassau	**Organizations** CARICOM, Comm., UN

The Bahamas, an archipelago made up of approximately seven hundred islands and over two thousand cays, lies to the northeast of Cuba and east of the Florida coast of the USA. Twenty-two islands are inhabited, and two-thirds of the population lives on the main island of

New Providence. The climate is warm for much of the year, with heavy rainfall in the summer. Tourism is the islands' main industry. Offshore banking, insurance and ship registration are also major foreign exchange earners.

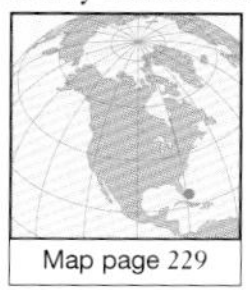
Map page 229

BAHRAIN
Kingdom of Bahrain

Area Sq Km	691	**Currency**	Bahraini dinar
Area Sq Miles	267	**Languages**	Arabic, English
Population	727 000	**Religions**	Shi'a Muslim, Sunni Muslim, Christian
Capital	Al Manāmah (Manama)	**Organizations**	UN

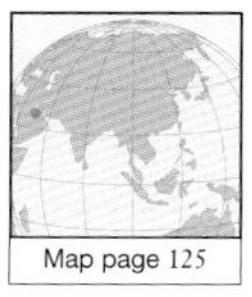
Map page 125

Bahrain consists of more than thirty islands lying in a bay in The Gulf, off the coasts of Saudi Arabia and Qatar. Bahrain Island, the largest island, is connected to other islands and to the mainland of Arabia by causeways. Oil production and processing are the main sectors of the economy.

BANGLADESH
People's Republic of Bangladesh

Area Sq Km	143 998	**Currency**	Taka
Area Sq Miles	55 598	**Languages**	Bengali, English
Population	141 822 000	**Religions**	Sunni Muslim, Hindu
Capital	Dhaka	**Organizations**	Comm., UN

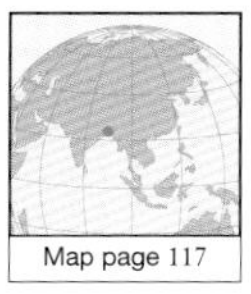
Map page 117

The south Asian state of Bangladesh is in the northeast of the Indian subcontinent, on the Bay of Bengal. It consists almost entirely of the low-lying alluvial plains and deltas of the Ganges and Brahmaputra rivers. The southwest is swampy, with mangrove forests in the delta area. The north, northeast and southeast have low forested hills. Bangladesh is one of the world's most densely populated and least developed countries. The economy is based on agriculture, though the garment industry is the main export sector. Floods and cyclones during the summer monsoon season often cause devastating flooding and crop destruction. The country relies on large-scale foreign aid and remittances from workers abroad.

BARBADOS

Area Sq Km	430	**Currency**	Barbados dollar
Area Sq Miles	166	**Languages**	English, creole
Population	270 000	**Religions**	Protestant, Roman Catholic
Capital	Bridgetown	**Organizations**	CARICOM, Comm, UN

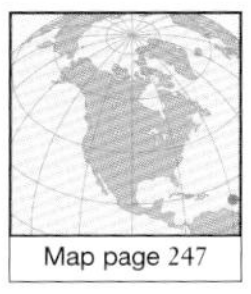
Map page 247

The most easterly of the Caribbean islands, Barbados is small and densely populated. It has a tropical climate and is subject to hurricanes. The economy is based on tourism, financial services, light industries and sugar production.

BELARUS
Republic of Belarus

Area Sq Km	207 600	**Currency**	Belarus rouble
Area Sq Miles	80 155	**Languages**	Belorussian, Russian
Population	9 755 000	**Religions**	Belorussian Orthodox, Roman Catholic
Capital	Minsk	**Organizations**	CIS, UN

Belarus, a landlocked state in eastern Europe, consists of low hills and plains, with many lakes, rivers and, in the south, extensive marshes. Forests cover approximately one-third of the country. It has a continental climate. Agriculture contributes one-third of national income, with beef cattle and grains as the major products. Manufacturing industries produce a range of items, from construction equipment to textiles. The Russian Federation and Ukraine are the main trading partners.

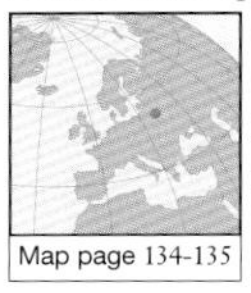
Map page 134–135

BELGIUM
Kingdom of Belgium

Area Sq Km	30 520	**Currency**	Euro
Area Sq Miles	11 784	**Languages**	Dutch (Flemish), French (Walloon), German
Population	10 419 000	**Religions**	Roman Catholic, Protestant
Capital	Bruxelles/Brussel (Brussels)	**Organizations**	EU, NATO, OECD, UN

Belgium lies on the North Sea coast of western Europe. Beyond low sand dunes and a narrow belt of reclaimed land, fertile plains extend to the Sambre-Meuse river valley. The land rises to the forested Ardennes plateau in the southeast. Belgium has mild winters and cool summers. It is densely populated and has a highly urbanized population. With few mineral resources, Belgium imports raw materials for processing and manufacture. The agricultural sector is small, but provides for most food needs. A large services sector reflects Belgium's position as the home base for over eight hundred international institutions. The headquarters of the European Union are in the capital, Brussels.

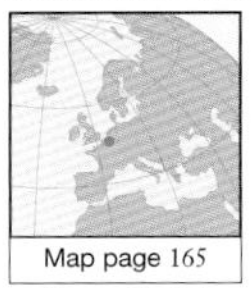
Map page 165

BELIZE

Area Sq Km	22 965	**Currency**	Belize dollar
Area Sq Miles	8 867	**Languages**	English, Spanish, Mayan, creole
Population	270 000	**Religions**	Roman Catholic, Protestant
Capital	Belmopan	**Organizations**	CARICOM, Comm., UN

Belize lies on the Caribbean coast of central America and includes numerous cays and a large barrier reef offshore. The coastal areas are flat and swampy. To the southwest are the Maya Mountains. Tropical jungle covers much of the country and the climate is humid tropical, but tempered by sea breezes. A third of the population lives in the capital. The economy is based primarily on agriculture, forestry and fishing, and exports include raw sugar, orange concentrate and bananas.

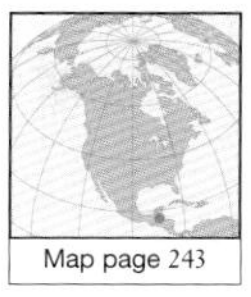
Map page 243

BENIN
Republic of Benin

Area Sq Km	112 620	**Currency**	CFA franc
Area Sq Miles	43 483	**Languages**	French, Fon, Yoruba, Adja, local languages
Population	8 439 000	**Religions**	Traditional beliefs, Roman Catholic, Sunni Muslim
Capital	Porto-Novo	**Organizations**	UN

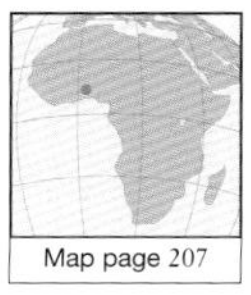
Map page 207

Benin is in west Africa, on the Gulf of Guinea. The climate is tropical in the north, equatorial in the south. The economy is based mainly on agriculture and transit trade. Agricultural products account for two-thirds of export earnings. Oil, produced offshore, is also a major export.

Bermuda
United Kingdom Overseas Territory

Area Sq Km	54	**Currency**	Bermuda dollar
Area Sq Miles	21	**Languages**	English
Population	64 000	**Religions**	Protestant, Roman Catholic
Capital	Hamilton		

In the Atlantic Ocean to the east of the USA, Bermuda comprises a group of small islands with a warm and humid climate. The economy is based on tourism, insurance and shipping.

Map page 231

BHUTAN
Kingdom of Bhutan

Area Sq Km	46 620	**Currency**	Ngultrum, Indian rupee
Area Sq Miles	18 000	**Languages**	Dzongkha, Nepali, Assamese
Population	2 163 000	**Religions**	Buddhist, Hindu
Capital	Thimphu	**Organizations**	UN

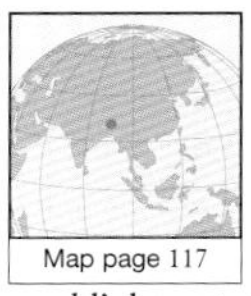
Map page 117

Bhutan lies in the eastern Himalaya mountains, between China and India. It is mountainous in the north, with fertile valleys. The climate ranges between permanently cold in the far north and subtropical in the south. Most of the population is involved in livestock rearing and subsistence farming. Bhutan is the world's largest producer of cardamom. Tourism is an increasingly important foreign currency earner.

BOLIVIA
Republic of Bolivia

Area Sq Km	1 098 581	**Currency**	Boliviano
Area Sq Miles	424 164	**Languages**	Spanish, Quechua, Aymara
Population	9 182 000	**Religions**	Roman Catholic, Protestant, Baha'i
Capital	La Paz/Sucre	**Organizations**	UN

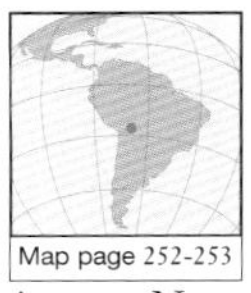
Map page 252–253

Bolivia is a landlocked state in central South America. Most Bolivians live on the high plateau within the Andes mountains. The lowlands range between dense rainforest in the northeast and semi-arid grasslands in the southeast. Bolivia is rich in minerals (zinc, tin and gold), and sales generate approximately half of export income. Natural gas, timber and soya beans are also exported. The USA is the main trading partner.

Bonaire part of Netherlands Antilles

Area Sq Km (Miles) 288 (111) **Population** 10 114 **Capital** Kralendijk

An island in the Caribbean Sea off the north coast of Venezuela, known for its fine beaches; tourism is the mainstay of the economy.

Map page 247

BOSNIA-HERZEGOVINA
Republic of Bosnia and Herzegovina

Area Sq Km	51 130	**Currency**	Marka
Area Sq Miles	19 741	**Languages**	Bosnian, Serbian, Croatian
Population	3 907 000	**Religions**	Sunni Muslim, Orthodox, Roman Catholic, Protestant
Capital	Sarajevo	**Organizations**	UN

Bosnia-Herzegovina lies in the western Balkan Mountains of southern Europe, on the Adriatic Sea. It is mountainous, with ridges running northwest–southeast. The main lowlands are around the Sava valley in the north. Summers are warm, but winters can be very cold. The economy relies heavily on overseas aid.

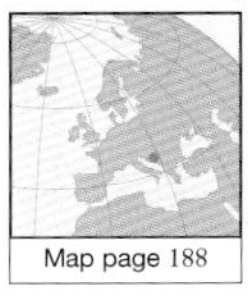
Map page 188

BOTSWANA
Republic of Botswana

Area Sq Km	581 370	**Currency**	Pula
Area Sq Miles	224 468	**Languages**	English, Setswana, Shona, local languages
Population	1 765 000	**Religions**	Traditional beliefs, Protestant, Roman Catholic
Capital	Gaborone	**Organizations**	Comm., SADC, UN

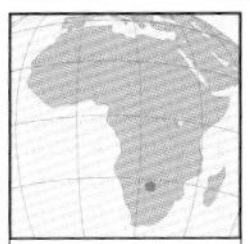
Map page 212–213

Botswana is a landlocked state in southern Africa. Over half of the country lies within the Kalahari Desert, with swamps to the north and salt-pans to the northeast. Most of the population lives near the eastern border. The climate is subtropical, but drought-prone. The economy was founded on cattle rearing, and although beef remains an important export, the economy is now based on mining. Diamonds account for seventy per cent of export earnings. Copper-nickel matte is also exported. Most trade is with members of the South African Customs Union.

BRAZIL
Federative Republic of Brazil

Area Sq Km	8 514 879	**Currency**	Real
Area Sq Miles	3 287 613	**Languages**	Portuguese
Population	186 405 000	**Religions**	Roman Catholic, Protestant
Capital	Brasília	**Organizations**	UN

Brazil, in eastern South America, covers almost half of the continent, and is the world's fifth largest country. The northwest contains the vast basin of the Amazon, while the centre-west is largely a vast plateau of savanna and rock escarpments. The northeast is mostly semi-arid plateaus, while to the east and south are rugged mountains, fertile valleys and narrow, fertile coastal plains. The Amazon basin is hot, humid and wet; the rest of the country is cooler and drier, with seasonal variations. The northeast is drought-prone. Most Brazilians live in urban areas along the coast and on the central plateau. Brazil has well-developed agricultural, mining, and service sectors, and the economy is larger than that of all other South American countries combined. Brazil is the world's biggest producer of coffee, and other agricultural crops include grains and sugar cane. Mineral production includes iron, aluminium and gold. Manufactured goods include food products, transport equipment, machinery and industrial chemicals. The main trading partners are the USA and Argentina. Despite its natural wealth, Brazil has a large external debt and a growing poverty gap.

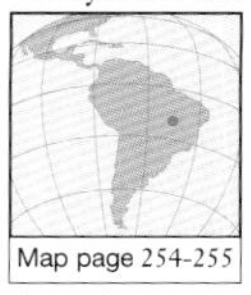
Map page 254–255

British Indian Ocean Territory
United Kingdom Overseas Territory

Area Sq Km (Miles) 60 (23) **Population** uninhabited

The territory consists of the Chagos Archipelago in the central Indian Ocean. The islands are uninhabited apart from the joint British-US military base on Diego Garcia.

Map page 88

BRUNEI
Brunei Darussalam

Area Sq Km	5 765	**Currency**	Brunei dollar
Area Sq Miles	2 226	**Languages**	Malay, English, Chinese
Population	374 000	**Religions**	Sunni Muslim, Buddhist, Christian
Capital	Bandar Seri Begawan	**Organizations**	APEC, ASEAN, Comm., UN

The Southeast Asian oil-rich state of Brunei lies on the northwest coast of the island of Borneo, on the South China Sea. Its two enclaves are surrounded by the Malaysian state of Sarawak. Tropical rainforest covers over two-thirds of the country. The economy is dominated by the oil and gas industries.

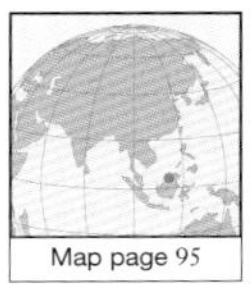
Map page 95

BULGARIA
Republic of Bulgaria

Area Sq Km	110 994	**Currency**	Lev
Area Sq Miles	42 855	**Languages**	Bulgarian, Turkish, Romany, Macedonian
Population	7 726 000	**Religions**	Bulgarian Orthodox, Sunni Muslim
Capital	Sofiya (Sofia)	**Organizations**	NATO, UN

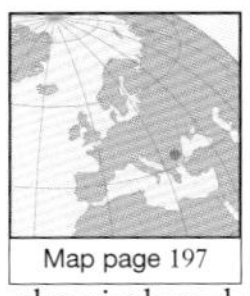
Map page 197

Bulgaria, in southern Europe, borders the western shore of the Black Sea. The Balkan Mountains separate the Danube plains in the north from the Rhodope Mountains and the lowlands in the south. The economy has a strong agricultural base. Manufacturing industries include machinery, consumer goods, chemicals and metals. Most trade is with the Russian Federation, Italy and Germany.

BURKINA
Democratic Republic of Burkina Faso

Area Sq Km	274 200	**Currency**	CFA franc
Area Sq Miles	105 869	**Languages**	French, Moore (Mossi), Fulani, local languages
Population	13 228 000	**Religions**	Sunni Muslim, traditional beliefs, Roman Catholic
Capital	Ouagadougou	**Organizations**	UN

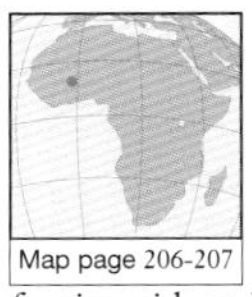
Map page 206–207

Burkina, a landlocked country in west Africa, lies within the Sahara desert to the north and semi-arid savanna to the south. Rainfall is erratic, and droughts are common. Livestock rearing and farming are the main activities, and cotton, livestock, groundnuts and some minerals are exported. Burkina relies heavily on foreign aid, and is one of the poorest and least developed countries in the world.

BURUNDI
Republic of Burundi

Area Sq Km	27 835	**Currency**	Burundian franc
Area Sq Miles	10 747	**Languages**	Kirundi (Hutu, Tutsi), French
Population	7 548 000	**Religions**	Roman Catholic, traditional beliefs, Protestant
Capital	Bujumbura	**Organizations**	UN

The densely populated east African state of Burundi consists of high plateaus rising from the shores of Lake Tanganyika in the southwest. It has a tropical climate and depends on subsistence farming. Coffee is its main export, and its main trading partners are Germany and Belgium. The country has been badly affected by internal conflict since the early 1990s.

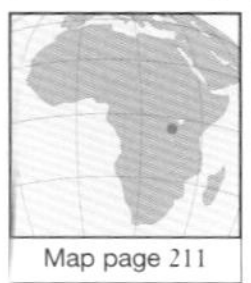

Map page 211

CAMBODIA
Kingdom of Cambodia

Area Sq Km	181 000	**Currency**	Riel
Area Sq Miles	69 884	**Languages**	Khmer, Vietnamese
Population	14 071 000	**Religions**	Buddhist, Roman Catholic, Sunni Muslim
Capital	Phnum Pénh	**Organizations**	ASEAN, UN

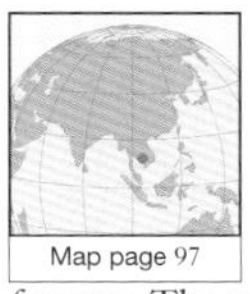

Map page 97

Cambodia lies in Southeast Asia on the Gulf of Thailand, and occupies the Mekong river basin, with the Tônlé Sap (Great Lake) at its centre. The climate is tropical monsoon. Forests cover half the country. Most of the population lives on the plains and is engaged in farming (chiefly rice growing), fishing and forestry. The economy is recovering slowly following the devastation of civil war in the 1970s.

CAMEROON
Republic of Cameroon

Area Sq Km	475 442	**Currency**	CFA franc
Area Sq Miles	183 569	**Languages**	French, English, Fang, Bamileke, local languages
Population	16 322 000	**Religions**	Roman Catholic, traditional beliefs, Sunni Muslim, Protestant
Capital	Yaoundé		
		Organizations	Comm., UN

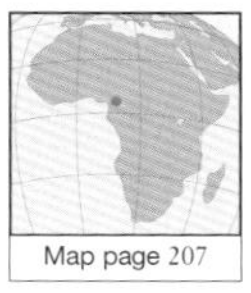

Map page 207

Cameroon is in west Africa, on the Gulf of Guinea. The coastal plains and southern and central plateaus are covered with tropical forest. Despite oil resources and favourable agricultural conditions Cameroon still faces problems of underdevelopment. Oil, timber and cocoa are the main exports. France is the main trading partner.

CANADA

Area Sq Km	9 984 670	**Currency**	Canadian dollar
Area Sq Miles	3 855 103	**Languages**	English, French, local languages
Population	32 268 000	**Religions**	Roman Catholic, Protestant, Orthodox, Jewish
Capital	Ottawa	**Organizations**	APEC, Comm., NATO, OECD, UN

The world's second largest country, Canada covers the northern two-fifths of North America and has coastlines on the Atlantic, Arctic and Pacific Oceans. In the west are the Coast Mountains, the Rocky Mountains and interior plateaus. In the centre lie the fertile Prairies. Further east, covering about half the total land area, is the Canadian Shield, a relatively flat area of infertile lowlands around Hudson Bay, extending to Labrador on the east coast. The Shield is bordered to the south by the fertile Great Lakes-St Lawrence lowlands. In the far north climatic conditions are polar, while the rest has a continental climate. Most Canadians live in the urban areas of the Great Lakes-St Lawrence basin. Canada is rich in mineral and energy resources. Only five per cent of land is arable . Canada is among the world's leading producers of wheat, of wood from its vast coniferous forests, and of fish and seafood from its Atlantic and Pacific fishing grounds. It is a major producer of nickel, uranium, copper, iron ore, zinc and other minerals, as well as oil and natural gas. Its abundant raw materials are the basis for many manufacturing industries. Main exports are machinery, motor vehicles, oil, timber, newsprint and paper, wood pulp and wheat. Since the 1989 free trade agreement with the USA and the 1994 North America Free Trade Agreement, trade with the USA has grown and now accounts for around seventy-five per cent of imports and around eighty-five per cent of exports.

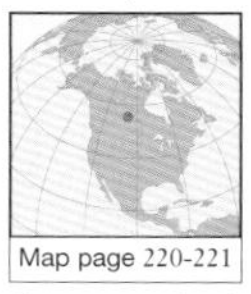

Map page 220-221

Alberta (Province)
Area Sq Km (Miles) 661 848 (255 541) **Population** 3 113 600 **Capital** Edmonton

British Columbia (Province)
Area Sq Km (Miles) 944 735 (364 764) **Population** 4 141 300 **Capital** Victoria

Manitoba (Province)
Area Sq Km (Miles) 647 797 (250 116) **Population** 1 150 800 **Capital** Winnipeg

New Brunswick (Province)
Area Sq Km (Miles) 72 908 (28 150) **Population** 756 700 **Capital** Fredericton

Newfoundland and Labrador (Province)
Area Sq Km (Miles) 405 212 (156 453) **Population** 531 600 **Capital** St John's

Northwest Territories (Province)
Area Sq Km (Miles) 1 346 106 (519 734) **Population** 41 400 **Capital** Yellowknife

Nova Scotia (Province)
Area Sq Km (Miles) 55 284 (21 345) **Population** 944 800 **Capital** Halifax

Nunavut (Territory)
Area Sq Km (Miles) 2 093 190 (808 185) **Population** 28 700 **Capital** Iqaluit

Ontario (Province)
Area Sq Km (Miles) 1 076 395 (415 598) **Population** 12 068 300 **Capital** Toronto

Prince Edward Island (Province)
Area Sq Km (Miles) 5 660 (2 185) **Population** 139 900 **Capital** Charlottetown

Québec (Province)
Area Sq Km (Miles) 1 542 056 (595 391) **Population** 7 455 200 **Capital** Québec

Saskatchewan (Province)
Area Sq Km (Miles) 651 036 (251 366) **Population** 1 011 800 **Capital** Regina

Yukon Territory (Territory)
Area Sq Km (Miles) 482 443 (186 272) **Population** 29 900 **Capital** Whitehorse

CAPE VERDE
Republic of Cape Verde

Area Sq Km	4 033	**Currency**	Cape Verde escudo
Area Sq Miles	1 557	**Languages**	Portuguese, creole
Population	507 000	**Religions**	Roman Catholic, Protestant
Capital	Praia	**Organizations**	UN

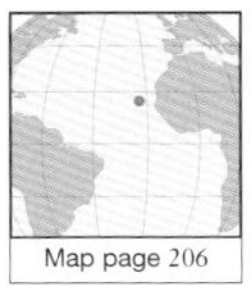

Map page 206

Cape Verde is a group of semi-arid volcanic islands lying off the coast of west Africa. The economy is based on fishing and subsistence farming but relies on emigrant workers' remittances and foreign aid.

Cayman Islands
United Kingdom Overseas Territory

Area Sq Km	259	**Currency**	Cayman Islands dollar
Area Sq Miles	100	**Languages**	English
Population	45 000	**Religions**	Roman Catholic, Protestant
Capital	George Town	**Organizations**	UN

A group of islands in the Caribbean, northwest of Jamaica. There are three main islands: Grand Cayman, Little Cayman and Cayman Brac. The Cayman Islands are one of the world's major offshore financial centres. Tourism is also important to the economy.

Map page 246

CENTRAL AFRICAN REPUBLIC

Area Sq Km	622 436	**Currency**	CFA franc
Area Sq Miles	240 324	**Languages**	French, Sango, Banda, Baya, local languages
Population	4 038 000	**Religions**	Protestant, Roman Catholic, trad. beliefs, Muslim
Capital	Bangui	**Organizations**	UN

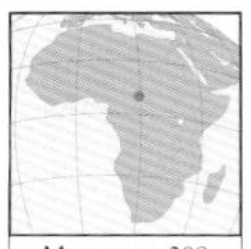

Map page 208

A landlocked country in central Africa, the Central African Republic is mainly savanna plateau, drained by the Ubangi and Chari river systems, with mountains to the east and west. The climate is tropical, with high rainfall. Most of the population lives in the south and west, and a majority of the workforce is involved in subsistence farming. Some cotton, coffee, tobacco and timber are exported, but diamonds account for around half of export earnings.

CHAD
Republic of Chad

Area Sq Km	1 284 000	**Currency**	CFA franc
Area Sq Miles	495 755	**Languages**	Arabic, French, Sara, local languages
Population	9 749 000	**Religions**	Sunni Muslim, Roman Catholic, Protestant
Capital	Ndjamena	**Organizations**	UN

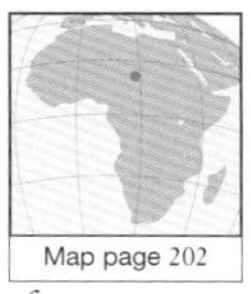

Map page 202

Chad is a landlocked state of north-central Africa. It consists of plateaus, the Tibesti mountains in the north and the Lake Chad basin in the west. Climatic conditions range between desert in the north and tropical forest in the southwest. With few natural resources, Chad relies on subsistence farming, exports of raw cotton, and foreign aid. The main trading partners are France, Portugal and Cameroon.

CHILE
Republic of Chile

Area Sq Km	756 945	**Currency**	Chilean peso
Area Sq Miles	292 258	**Languages**	Spanish, Amerindian languages
Population	16 295 000	**Religions**	Roman Catholic, Protestant
Capital	Santiago	**Organizations**	APEC, UN

Chile lies along the Pacific coast of the southern half of South America. Between the Andes in the east and the lower coastal ranges is a central valley, with a mild climate, where most Chileans live. To the north is the arid Atacama Desert and to the south is cold, wet forested grassland. Chile has considerable mineral resources and is the world's leading exporter of copper. Nitrates, molybdenum, gold and iron ore are also mined. Agriculture (particularly viticulture), forestry and fishing are also important to the economy.

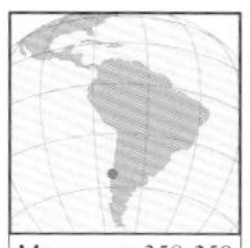

Map page 258-259

CHINA
People's Republic of China

Area Sq Km	9 584 492	**Currency**	Yuan, Hong Kong dollar, Macao pataca
Area Sq Miles	3 700 593	**Languages**	Mandarin, Wu, Cantonese, Hsiang, regional languages
Population	1 323 345 000		
Capital	Beijing	**Religions**	Confucian, Taoist, Buddhist, Christian, Muslim
		Organizations	APEC, UN

China, the world's most populous and fourth largest country, occupies a large part of east Asia, borders fourteen states and has coastlines on the Yellow, East China and South China Seas. It has a huge variety of landscapes. The southwest contains the high Plateau of Tibet, flanked by the Himalaya and Kunlun Shan mountains. The north is mountainous with arid basins and extends from the Tien Shan and Altai Mountains and the vast Taklimakan Desert in the west to the plateau and Gobi Desert in the centre-east. Eastern China is predominantly lowland and is divided broadly into the basins of the Huang He (Yellow River) in the north, the Chang Jiang (Yangtze) in the centre and the Xi Jiang (Pearl River) in the southeast. Climatic conditions and vegetation are as diverse as the topography: much of the country experiences temperate conditions, while the southwest has an extreme mountain climate and the southeast enjoys a moist, warm subtropical climate. Nearly seventy per cent of China's huge population lives in rural areas, and agriculture employs around half of the working population. The main crops are rice, wheat, soya beans, peanuts, cotton, tobacco and hemp. China is rich in coal, oil and natural gas and has the world's largest potential in hydroelectric power. It is a major world producer of iron ore, molybdenum, copper, asbestos and gold. Economic reforms from the early 1980s led to an explosion in manufacturing development concentrated on the 'coastal economic open region'. The main exports are machinery, textiles, footwear, toys and sports goods. Japan and the USA are China's main trading partners.

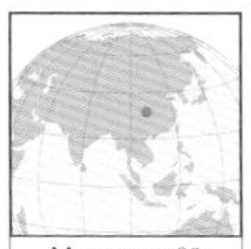

Map page 98

Anhui (Province)
Area Sq Km (Miles) 139 000 (53 668) **Population** 59 860 000 **Capital** Hefei

Beijing (Municipality)
Area Sq Km (Miles) 16 800 (6 487) **Population** 13 820 000 **Capital** Beijing

Chongqing (Municipality)
Area Sq Km (Miles) 23 000 (8 880) **Population** 30 900 000 **Capital** Chongqing

Fujian (Province)
Area Sq Km (Miles) 121 400 (46 873) **Population** 34 710 000 **Capital** Fuzhou

Gansu (Province)
Area Sq Km (Miles) 453 700 (175 175) **Population** 25 620 000 **Capital** Lanzhou

Guangdong (Province)
Area Sq Km (Miles) 178 000 (68 726) **Population** 86 420 000 **Capital** Guangzhou

Guangxi Zhuangzu Zizhiqu (Autonomous Region)
Area Sq Km (Miles) 236 000 (91 120) **Population** 44 890 000 **Capital** Nanning

Guizhou (Province)
Area Sq Km (Miles) 176 000 (67 954) **Population** 35 250 000 **Capital** Guiyang

Hainan (Province)
Area Sq Km (Miles) 34 000 (13 127) **Population** 7 870 000 **Capital** Haikou

Hebei (Province)
Area Sq Km (Miles) 187 700 (72 471) **Population** 67 440 000 **Capital** Shijiazhuang

Heilongjiang (Province)
Area Sq Km (Miles) 454 600 (175 522) **Population** 36 890 000 **Capital** Harbin

Henan (Province)
Area Sq Km (Miles) 167 000 (64 479) **Population** 92 560 000 **Capital** Zhengzhou

Hong Kong (Special Administrative Region)
Area Sq Km (Miles) 1 075 (415) **Population** 6 780 000 **Capital** Hong Kong

Hubei (Province)
Area Sq Km (Miles) 185 900 (71 776) **Population** 60 280 000 **Capital** Wuhan

Hunan (Province)
Area Sq Km (Miles) 210 000 (81 081) **Population** 64 400 000 **Capital** Changsha

Jiangsu (Province)
Area Sq Km (Miles) 102 600 (39 614) **Population** 74 380 000 **Capital** Nanjing

Jiangxi (Province)
Area Sq Km (Miles) 166 900 (64 440) **Population** 41 400 000 **Capital** Nanchang

Jilin (Province)
Area Sq Km (Miles) 187 000 (72 201) **Population** 27 280 000 **Capital** Changchun

Liaoning (Province)
Area Sq Km (Miles) 147 400 (56 911) **Population** 42 380 000 **Capital** Shenyang

Macao (Special Administrative Region)
Area Sq Km (Miles) 17 (7) **Population** 440 000 **Capital** Macao

Nei Mongol Zizhiqu (Inner Mongolia) (Autonomous Region)
Area Sq Km (Miles) 1 183 000 (456 759) **Population** 23 760 000 **Capital** Huhhot

Ningxia Huizu Zizhiqu (Autonomous Region)
Area Sq Km (Miles) 66 400 (25 637) **Population** 5 620 000 **Capital** Yinchuan

Qinghai (Province)
Area Sq Km (Miles) 721 000 (278 380) **Population** 5 180 000 **Capital** Xining

Shaanxi (Province)
Area Sq Km (Miles) 205 600 (79 383) **Population** 36 050 000 **Capital** Xi'an

Shandong (Province)
Area Sq Km (Miles) 153 300 (59 189) **Population** 90 790 000 **Capital** Jinan

Shanghai (Municipality)
Area Sq Km (Miles) 6 300 (2 432) **Population** 16 740 000 **Capital** Shanghai

Shanxi (Province)
Area Sq Km (Miles)156 300 (60 348) **Population** 32 970 000 **Capital** Taiyuan

Sichaun (Province)
Area Sq Km (Miles) 569 000 (219 692) **Population** 83 290 000 **Capital** Chengdu

Tianjin (Municipality)
Area Sq Km (Miles) 11 300 (4 363) **Population** 10 010 000 **Capital** Tianjin

Xinjiang Uygur Zizhiqu (Sinkiang) (Autonomous Region)
Area Sq Km (Miles) 1 600 000 (617 763) **Population** 19 250 000 **Capital** Ürümqi

Xizang Zizhiqu (Tibet) (Autonomous Region)
Area Sq Km (Miles) 1 228 400 (474 288) **Population** 2 620 000 **Capital** Lhasa

Yunnan (Province)
Area Sq Km (Miles) 394 000 (152 124) **Population** 42 880 000 **Capital** Kunming

Zhejiang (Province)
Area Sq Km (Miles) 101 800 (39 305) **Population** 46 770 000 **Capital** Hangzhou

Christmas Island
Australian External Territory

Area Sq Km	135	**Currency**	Australian dollar
Area Sq Miles	52	**Languages**	English
Population	1 508	**Religions**	Buddhist, Sunni Muslim, Protestant, Roman Catholic
Capital	The Settlement		

The island is situated in the east of the Indian Ocean, to the south of Indonesia. The economy was formerly based on phosphate extraction, although reserves are now nearly depleted. Tourism is developing and is a major employer.

Map page 86

Cocos Islands (Keeling Islands)
Australian External Territory

Area Sq Km	14	**Currency**	Australian dollar
Area Sq Miles	5	**Languages**	English
Population	621	**Religions**	Sunni Muslim, Christian
Capital	West Island		

The Cocos Islands consist of numerous islands on two coral atolls in the eastern Indian Ocean between Sri Lanka and Australia. Most of the population lives on West Island or Home Island. Coconuts are the only cash crop, and the main export.

Map page 86

COLOMBIA
Republic of Colombia

Area Sq Km	1 141 748	**Currency**	Colombian peso
Area Sq Miles	440 831	**Languages**	Spanish, Amerindian languages
Population	45 600 000	**Religions**	Roman Catholic, Protestant
Capital	Bogotá	**Organizations**	APEC, UN

A state in northwest South America, Colombia has coastlines on the Pacific Ocean and the Caribbean Sea. Behind coastal plains lie three ranges of the Andes mountains, separated by high valleys and plateaus where most Colombians live. To the southeast are grasslands and the forests of the Amazon. The climate is tropical, although temperatures vary with altitude. Only five per cent of land is cultivable. Coffee (Colombia is the world's second largest producer), sugar, bananas, cotton and flowers are exported. Coal, nickel, gold, silver, platinum and emeralds (Colombia is the world's largest producer) are mined. Oil and its products are the main export. Industries include the processing of minerals and crops. The main trade partner is the USA. Internal violence – both politically motivated and relating to Colombia's leading role in the international trade in illegal drugs – continues to hinder development.

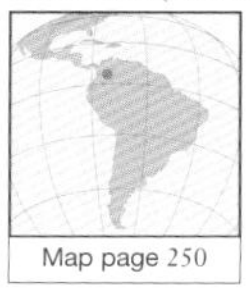
Map page 250

COMOROS
Union of the Comoros

Area Sq Km	1 862	**Currency**	Comoros franc
Area Sq Miles	719	**Languages**	Comorian, French, Arabic
Population	798 000	**Religions**	Sunni Muslim, Roman Catholic
Capital	Moroni	**Organizations**	UN

This state, in the Indian Ocean off the east African coast, comprises three volcanic islands of Njazidja, Nzwani and Mwali, and some coral atolls. These tropical islands are mountainous, with poor soil and few natural resources. Subsistence farming predominates. Vanilla, cloves and ylang-ylang (an essential oil) are exported, and the economy relies heavily on workers' remittances from abroad.

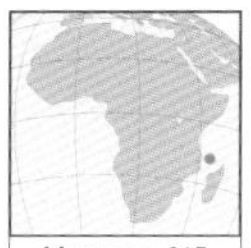
Map page 217

CONGO
Republic of the Congo

Area Sq Km	342 000	**Currency**	CFA franc
Area Sq Miles	132 047	**Languages**	French, Kongo, Monokutuba, local languages
Population	3 999 000	**Religions**	Roman Catholic, Protestant, trad. beliefs, Muslim
Capital	Brazzaville	**Organizations**	UN

Congo, in central Africa, is mostly a forest or savanna-covered plateau drained by the Ubangi-Congo river systems. Sand dunes and lagoons line the short Atlantic coast. The climate is hot and tropical. Most Congolese live in the southern third of the country. Half of the workforce are farmers, growing food and cash crops including sugar, coffee, cocoa and oil palms. Oil and timber are the mainstays of the economy, and oil generates over fifty per cent of export revenues.

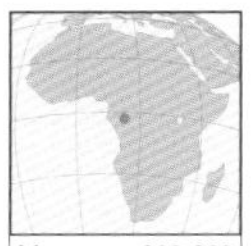
Map page 208-209

CONGO, DEMOCRATIC REPUBLIC OF THE

Area Sq Km	2 345 410	**Currency**	Congolese franc
Area Sq Miles	905 568	**Languages**	French, Lingala, Swahili, Kongo, local languages
Population	52 549 000	**Religions**	Christian, Sunni Muslim
Capital	Kinshasa	**Organizations**	SADC, UN

This central African state, formerly Zaire, consists of the basin of the Congo river flanked by plateaus, with high mountain ranges to the east and a short Atlantic coastline to the west. The climate is tropical, with rainforest close to the Equator and savanna to the north and south. Fertile land allows a range of food and cash crops to be grown, chiefly coffee. The country has vast mineral resources, with copper, cobalt and diamonds being the most important.

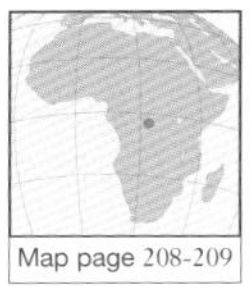
Map page 208-209

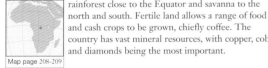

Cook Islands
New Zealand Overseas Territory

Area Sq Km	293	**Currency**	New Zealand dollar
Area Sq Miles	113	**Languages**	English, Maori
Population	18 000	**Religions**	Protestant, Roman Catholic
Capital	Avarua		

These consist of groups of coral atolls and volcanic islands in the southwest Pacific Ocean. The main island is Rarotonga. Distance from foreign markets and restricted natural resources hinder development.

Map page 81

COSTA RICA
Republic of Costa Rica

Area Sq Km	51 100	**Currency**	Costa Rican colón
Area Sq Miles	19 730	**Languages**	Spanish
Population	4 327 000	**Religions**	Roman Catholic, Protestant
Capital	San José	**Organizations**	UN

Costa Rica, in central America, has coastlines on the Caribbean Sea and Pacific Ocean. From tropical coastal plains, the land rises to mountains and a temperate central plateau, where most of the population lives. The economy depends on agriculture and tourism, with ecotourism becoming increasingly important. Main exports are textiles, coffee and bananas, and almost half of all trade is with the USA.

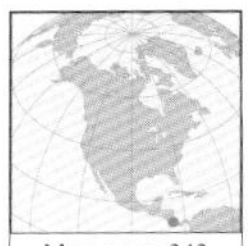
Map page 242

CÔTE D'IVOIRE (Ivory Coast)
Republic of Côte d'Ivoire

Area Sq Km	322 463	**Currency**	CFA franc
Area Sq Miles	124 504	**Languages**	French, creole, Akan, local languages
Population	18 154 000	**Religions**	Muslim, Roman Catholic, trad. beliefs, Protestant
Capital	Yamoussoukro	**Organizations**	UN

Côte d'Ivoire (Ivory Coast) is in west Africa, on the Gulf of Guinea. In the north are plateaus and savanna; in the south are low undulating plains and rainforest, with sand-bars and lagoons on the coast. Temperatures are warm, and rainfall is heavier in the south. Most of the workforce is engaged in farming. Côte d'Ivoire is a major producer of cocoa and coffee, and agricultural products (also including cotton and timber) are the main exports. Oil and gas have begun to be exploited.

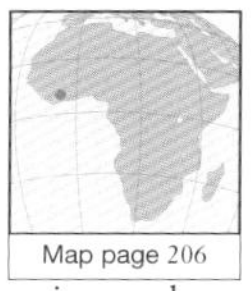
Map page 206

CROATIA
Republic of Croatia

Area Sq Km	56 538	**Currency**	Kuna
Area Sq Miles	21 829	**Languages**	Croatian, Serbian
Population	4 551 000	**Religions**	Roman Catholic, Serbian Orthodox, Sunni Muslim
Capital	Zagreb	**Organizations**	UN

The southern European state of Croatia has a long coastline on the Adriatic Sea, with many offshore islands. Coastal areas have a Mediterranean climate; inland is cooler and wetter. Croatia was once strong agriculturally and industrially, but conflict in the early 1990s, and associated loss of markets and a fall in tourist revenue, caused economic difficulties from which recovery has been slow.

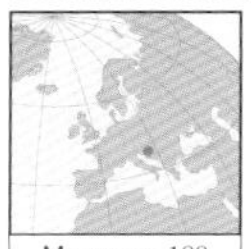
Map page 188

CUBA
Republic of Cuba

Area Sq Km	110 860	**Currency**	Cuban peso
Area Sq Miles	42 803	**Languages**	Spanish
Population	11 269 000	**Religions**	Roman Catholic, Protestant
Capital	La Habana (Havana)	**Organizations**	UN

The country comprises the island of Cuba (the largest island in the Caribbean), and many islets and cays. A fifth of Cubans live in and around Havana. Cuba is slowly recovering from the withdrawal of aid and subsidies from the former USSR. Sugar remains the basis of the economy, although tourism is developing and is, together with remittances from workers abroad, an important source of revenue.

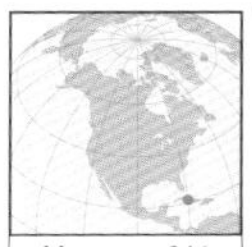
Map page 246

Curaçao part of Netherlands Antilles

Area Sq Km (Miles) 444 (171) **Population** 126 816 **Capital** Willemstad

An island in the Caribbean Sea off the north coast of Venezuela, it is the largest and most populous island of the Netherlands Antilles. Oil refining and tourism form the basis of the economy.

Map page 247

CYPRUS
Republic of Cyprus

Area Sq Km	9 251	**Currency**	Cyprus pound
Area Sq Miles	3 572	**Languages**	Greek, Turkish, English
Population	835 000	**Religions**	Greek Orthodox, Sunni Muslim
Capital	Lefkosia (Nicosia)	**Organizations**	Comm., EU, UN

The eastern Mediterranean island of Cyprus has hot dry summers and mild winters. The economy of the Greek south is based mainly on specialist agriculture and tourism, though shipping and offshore banking are also major sources of income. The Turkish north depends on agriculture, tourism and aid from Turkey. Cyprus joined the European Union in May 2004.

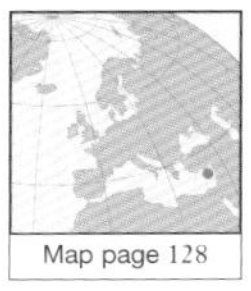
Map page 128

CZECH REPUBLIC

Area Sq Km	78 864	**Currency**	Czech koruna
Area Sq Miles	30 450	**Languages**	Czech, Moravian, Slovakian
Population	10 220 000	**Religions**	Roman Catholic, Protestant
Capital	Praha (Prague)	**Organizations**	EU, NATO, UN

The landlocked Czech Republic in central Europe consists of rolling countryside, wooded hills and fertile valleys. The climate is continental. The country has substantial reserves of coal and lignite, timber and some minerals, chiefly iron ore. It is highly industrialized, and major manufactured goods include industrial machinery, consumer goods, cars, iron and steel, chemicals and glass. Germany is the main trading partner. The Czech Republic joined the European Union in May 2004.

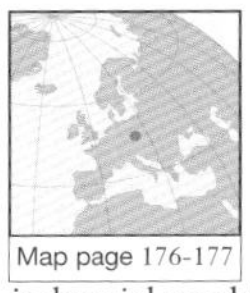
Map page 176-177

DENMARK
Kingdom of Denmark

Area Sq Km	43 075	**Currency**	Danish krone
Area Sq Miles	16 631	**Languages**	Danish
Population	5 431 000	**Religions**	Protestant
Capital	København (Copenhagen)	**Organizations**	EU, NATO, OECD, UN

In northern Europe, Denmark occupies the Jutland (Jylland) peninsula and nearly five hundred islands in and between the North and Baltic Seas. The country is low-lying, with long, indented coastlines. The climate is cool and temperate, with rainfall throughout the year. A fifth of the population lives in and around the capital, Copenhagen (København), on the largest of the islands, Zealand (Sjælland). The country's main natural resource is its agricultural potential: two-thirds of the total area is fertile farmland or pasture. Agriculture is high-tech, and with forestry and fishing employs only around six per cent of the workforce. Denmark is self-sufficient in oil and natural gas, produced from fields in the North Sea. Manufacturing, largely based on imported raw materials, accounts for over half of all exports, which include machinery, food, furniture, and pharmaceuticals. The main trading partners are Germany and Sweden.

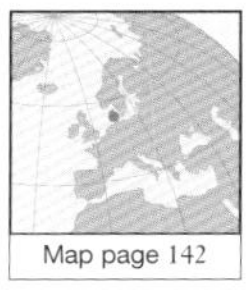
Map page 142

DJIBOUTI
Republic of Djibouti

Area Sq Km	23 200	**Currency**	Djibouti franc
Area Sq Miles	8 958	**Languages**	Somali, Afar, French, Arabic
Population	793 000	**Religions**	Sunni Muslim, Christian
Capital	Djibouti	**Organizations**	UN

Djibouti lies in northeast Africa, on the Gulf of Aden at the entrance to the Red Sea. Most of the country is semi-arid desert with high temperatures and low rainfall. More than two-thirds of the population lives in the capital. There is some camel, sheep and goat herding, but with few natural resources the economy is based on services and trade. Djibouti serves as a free trade zone for northern Africa, and the capital's port is a major transhipment and refuelling destination. It is linked by rail to Addis Ababa in Ethiopia.

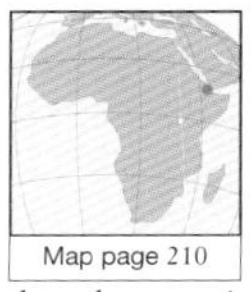
Map page 210

DOMINICA
Commonwealth of Dominica

Area Sq Km	750	**Currency**	East Caribbean dollar
Area Sq Miles	290	**Languages**	English, creole
Population	79 000	**Religions**	Roman Catholic, Protestant
Capital	Roseau	**Organizations**	CARICOM, Comm., UN

Dominica is the most northerly of the Windward Islands, in the eastern Caribbean. It is very mountainous and forested, with a coastline of steep cliffs. The climate is tropical and rainfall is abundant. Approximately a quarter of Dominicans live in the capital. The economy is based on agriculture, with bananas (the major export), coconuts and citrus fruits the most important crops. Tourism is a developing industry.

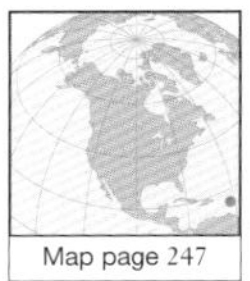
Map page 247

DOMINICAN REPUBLIC

Area Sq Km	48 442	**Currency**	Dominican peso
Area Sq Miles	18 704	**Languages**	Spanish, creole
Population	8 895 000	**Religions**	Roman Catholic, Protestant
Capital	Santo Domingo	**Organizations**	UN

The state occupies the eastern two-thirds of the Caribbean island of Hispaniola (the western third is Haiti). It has a series of mountain ranges, fertile valleys and a large coastal plain in the east. The climate is hot tropical, with heavy rainfall. Sugar, coffee and cocoa are the main cash crops. Nickel (the main export), and gold are mined, and there is some light industry. The USA is the main trading partner. Tourism is the main foreign exchange earner.

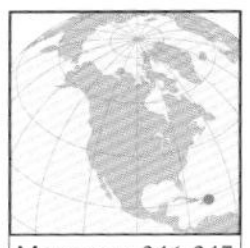
Map page 246-247

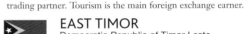

EAST TIMOR
Democratic Republic of Timor-Leste

Area Sq Km	14 874	**Currency**	United States dollar
Area Sq Miles	5 743	**Languages**	Portuguese, Tetun, English
Population	947 000	**Religions**	Roman Catholic
Capital	Dili	**Organizations**	UN

The island of Timor is part of the Indonesian archipelago, to the north of Western Australia. East Timor occupies the eastern section of the island, and a small coastal enclave (Ocussi) to the west. A referendum in 1999 ended Indonesia's occupation, after which the country was under UN transitional administration until full independence was achieved in 2002. The economy is in a poor state and East Timor is heavily dependent on foreign aid.

Map page 93

ECUADOR
Republic of Ecuador

Area Sq Km	272 045	**Currency**	United States dollar
Area Sq Miles	105 037	**Languages**	Spanish, Quechua, and other Amerindian languages
Population	13 228 000	**Religions**	Roman Catholic
Capital	Quito	**Organizations**	APEC, UN

Ecuador is in northwest South America, on the Pacific coast. It consists of a broad coastal plain, high mountain ranges in the Andes, and part of the forested upper Amazon basin to the east. The climate is tropical, moderated by altitude. Most people live on the coast or in the mountain valleys. Ecuador is one of South America's main oil producers, and mineral reserves include gold. Most of the workforce depends on agriculture. Petroleum, bananas, shrimps, coffee and cocoa are exported. The USA is the main trading partner.

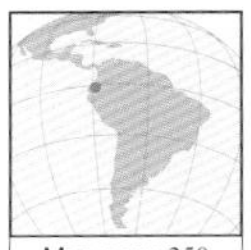
Map page 250

EGYPT
Arab Republic of Egypt

Area Sq Km	1 000 250	**Currency**	Egyptian pound
Area Sq Miles	386 199	**Languages**	Arabic
Population	74 033 000	**Religions**	Sunni Muslim, Coptic Christian
Capital	Al Qāhirah (Cairo)	**Organizations**	UN

Egypt, on the eastern Mediterranean coast of north Africa, is low-lying, with areas below sea level in the Qattara depression. It is a land of desert and semi-desert, except for the Nile valley, where ninety-nine per cent of Egyptians live. The Sinai peninsula in the northeast of the country forms the only land bridge between Africa and Asia. The summers are hot, the winters mild and rainfall is negligible. Less than four per cent of land (chiefly around the Nile floodplain and delta) is cultivated. Farming employs about one-third of the workforce; cotton is the main cash crop. Egypt imports over half its food needs. There are oil and natural gas reserves, although nearly a

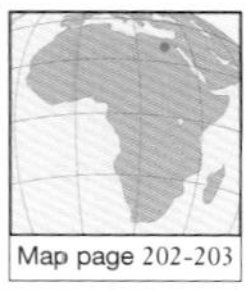

quarter of electricity comes from hydroelectric power. Main exports are oil and oil products, cotton, textiles and clothing.

Map page 202-203

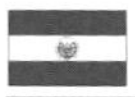

EL SALVADOR
Republic of El Salvador

Area Sq Km	21 041	Currency	El Salvador colón, United States dollar
Area Sq Miles	8 124	Languages	Spanish
Population	6 881 000	Religions	Roman Catholic, Protestant
Capital	San Salvador	Organizations	UN

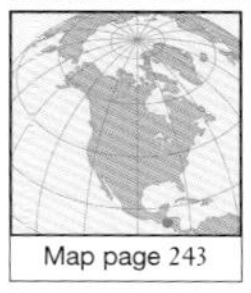

Located on the Pacific coast of central America, El Salvador consists of a coastal plain and volcanic mountain ranges which enclose a densely populated plateau area. The coast is hot, with heavy summer rainfall; the highlands are cooler. Coffee (the chief export), sugar and cotton are the main cash crops. The main trading partners are the USA and Guatemala.

Map page 243

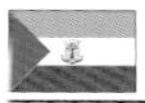

EQUATORIAL GUINEA
Republic of Equatorial Guinea

Area Sq Km	28 051	Currency	CFA franc
Area Sq Miles	10 831	Languages	Spanish, French, Fang
Population	504 000	Religions	Roman Catholic, traditional beliefs
Capital	Malabo	Organizations	UN

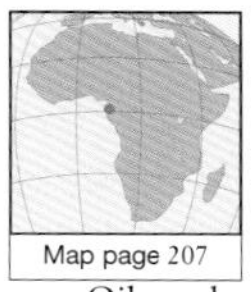

The state consists of Rio Muni, an enclave on the Atlantic coast of central Africa, and the islands of Bioco, Annobón and the Corisco group. Most of the population lives on the coastal plain and upland plateau of Rio Muni. The capital city, Malabo, is on the fertile volcanic island of Bioco. The climate is hot, humid and wet. Oil production started in 1992, and oil is now the main export, along with timber. The economy depends heavily on foreign aid.

Map page 207

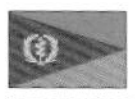

ERITREA
State of Eritrea

Area Sq Km	117 400	Currency	Nakfa
Area Sq Miles	45 328	Languages	Tigrinya, Tigre
Population	4 401 000	Religions	Sunni Muslim, Coptic Christian
Capital	Asmara	Organizations	UN

Eritrea, on the Red Sea coast of northeast Africa, consists of a high plateau in the north with a coastal plain which widens to the south. The coast is hot; inland is cooler. Rainfall is unreliable. The agriculture-based economy has suffered from over thirty years of war and occasional poor rains. Eritrea is one of the least developed countries in the world.

Map page 203

ESTONIA
Republic of Estonia

Area Sq Km	45 200	Currency	Kroon
Area Sq Miles	17 452	Languages	Estonian, Russian
Population	1 330 000	Religions	Protestant, Estonian and Russian Orthodox
Capital	Tallinn	Organizations	EU, NATO, UN

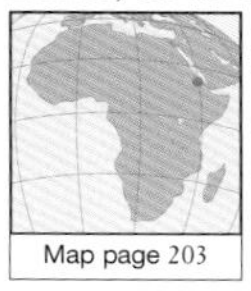

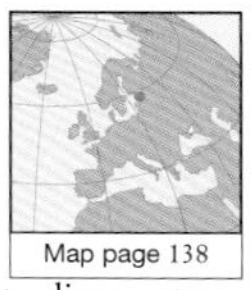

Estonia is in northern Europe, on the Gulf of Finland and the Baltic Sea. The land, over one-third of which is forested, is generally low-lying with many lakes. Approximately one-third of Estonians live in the capital, Tallinn. Exported goods include machinery, wood products, textiles and food products. The main trading partners are the Russian Federation, Finland and Sweden. Estonia joined the European Union in May 2004.

Map page 138

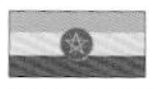

ETHIOPIA
Federal Democratic Republic of Ethiopia

Area Sq Km	1 133 880	Currency	Birr
Area Sq Miles	437 794	Languages	Oromo, Amharic, Tigrinya, local languages
Population	77 431 000	Religions	Ethiopian Orthodox, Muslim, trad. beliefs
Capital	Ādīs Ābeba	Organizations	UN

A landlocked country in northeast Africa, Ethiopia comprises a mountainous region in the west which is traversed by the Great Rift Valley. The east is mostly arid plateau land. The highlands are warm with summer rainfall. Most people live in the central–northern area. In recent years civil war, conflict with Eritrea and poor infrastructure have hampered economic development. Subsistence farming is the main activity, although droughts have led to frequent famines. Coffee is the main export and there is some light industry. Ethiopia is one of the least developed countries in the world.

Map page 210

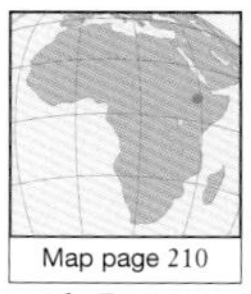

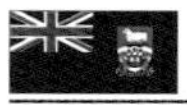

Falkland Islands
United Kingdom Overseas Territory

Area Sq Km	12 170	Currency	Falkland Islands pound
Area Sq Miles	4 699	Languages	English
Population	3 000	Religions	Protestant, Roman Catholic
Capital	Stanley		

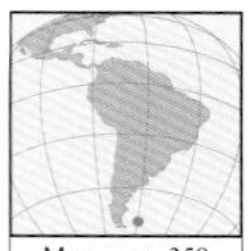

Lying in the southwest Atlantic Ocean, northeast of Cape Horn, two main islands, West Falkland and East Falkland and many smaller islands, form the territory of the Falkland Islands. The economy is based on sheep farming and the sale of fishing licences.

Map page 259

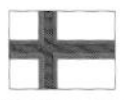

Faroe Islands
Self-governing Danish Territory

Area Sq Km	1 399	Currency	Danish krone
Area Sq Miles	540	Languages	Faroese, Danish
Population	47 000	Religions	Protestant
Capital	Tórshavn	Organizations	UN

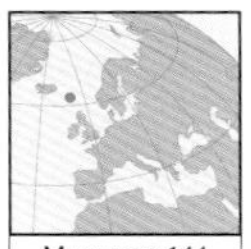

A self-governing territory, the Faroe Islands lie in the north Atlantic Ocean between the UK and Iceland. The islands benefit from the North Atlantic Drift, which has a moderating effect on the climate. The economy is based on deep-sea fishing.

Map page 144

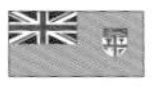

FIJI
Republic of the Fiji Islands

Area Sq Km	18 330	Currency	Fiji dollar
Area Sq Miles	7 077	Languages	English, Fijian, Hindi
Population	848 000	Religions	Christian, Hindu, Sunni Muslim
Capital	Suva	Organizations	Comm., UN

The southwest Pacific republic of Fiji comprises two mountainous and volcanic islands, Vanua Levu and Viti Levu, and over three hundred smaller islands. The climate is tropical and the economy is based on agriculture (chiefly sugar, the main export), fishing, forestry, gold mining and tourism.

Map page 79

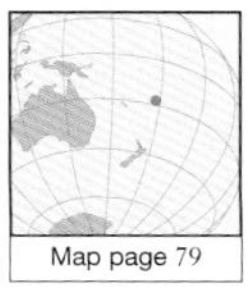

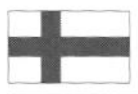

FINLAND
Republic of Finland

Area Sq Km	338 145	Currency	Euro
Area Sq Miles	130 559	Languages	Finnish, Swedish
Population	5 249 000	Religions	Protestant, Greek Orthodox
Capital	Helsinki	Organizations	EU, OECD, UN

Finland is in northern Europe, and nearly one-third of the country lies north of the Arctic Circle. Forests cover over seventy per cent of the land area, and ten per cent is covered by lakes. Summers are short and warm, and winters are long and severe, particularly in the north. Most of the population lives in the southern third of the country, along the coast or near the lakes. Timber is a major resource and there are important minerals, chiefly chromium. Main industries include metal working, electronics, paper and paper products, and chemicals. The main trading partners are Germany, Sweden and the UK.

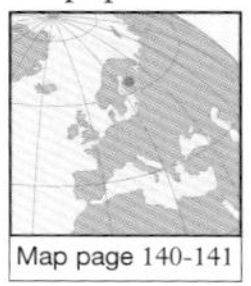

Map page 140-141

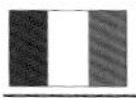

FRANCE
French Republic

Area Sq Km	543 965	Currency	Euro
Area Sq Miles	210 026	Languages	French, Arabic
Population	60 496 000	Religions	Roman Catholic, Protestant, Sunni Muslim
Capital	Paris	Organizations	EU, NATO, OECD, UN

France lies in western Europe and has coastlines on the Atlantic Ocean and the Mediterranean Sea. It includes the Mediterranean island of Corsica. Northern and western regions consist mostly of flat or rolling countryside, and include the major lowlands of the Paris basin, the Loire valley and the Aquitaine basin, drained by the Seine, Loire and Garonne river systems respectively. The centre-south is dominated by the hill region of the Massif Central. To the east are the Vosges and Jura mountains and the Alps. In the southwest, the Pyrenees form a natural border with Spain. The climate is temperate with warm summers and cool winters, although the Mediterranean coast has hot, dry summers and mild winters. Over seventy per cent of the population lives in towns, with almost a sixth of the population living in the Paris area. The French economy has a substantial and varied agricultural base. It is a major producer of both fresh and processed food. There are relatively few mineral resources; it has coal reserves, and some oil and natural gas, but it relies heavily on nuclear and hydroelectric power and imported fuels. France is one of the world's major industrial countries. Main industries include food processing, iron, steel and aluminium production, chemicals, cars, electronics and oil refining. The main exports are transport equipment, plastics and chemicals. Tourism is a major source of revenue and employment. Trade is predominantly with other European Union countries.

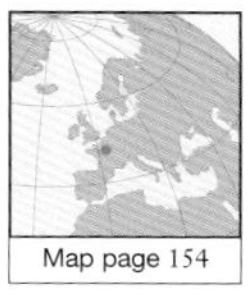

Map page 154

French Guiana
French Overseas Department

Area Sq Km	90 000	Currency	Euro
Area Sq Miles	34 749	Languages	French, creole
Population	187 000	Religions	Roman Catholic
Capital	Cayenne		

French Guiana, on the north coast of South America, is densely forested. The climate is tropical, with high rainfall. Most people live in the coastal strip, and agriculture is mostly subsistence farming. Forestry and fishing are important, but mineral resources are largely unexploited and industry is limited. French Guiana depends on French aid. The main trading partners are France and the USA.

Map page 251

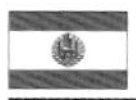

FRENCH POLYNESIA
French Overseas Country

Area Sq Km	3 265	Currency	CFP franc
Area Sq Miles	1 261	Languages	French, Tahitian, Polynesian languages
Population	257 000	Religions	Protestant, Roman Catholic
Capital	Papeete		

Extending over a vast area of the southeast Pacific Ocean, French Polynesia comprises more than one hundred and thirty islands and coral atolls. The main island groups are the Marquesas Islands, the Tuamotu Archipelago and the Society Islands. The capital, Papeete, is on Tahiti in the Society Islands. The climate is subtropical, and the economy is based on tourism. The main export is cultured pearls.

Map page 79

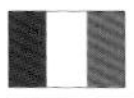

French Southern and Antarctic Lands
French Overseas Territory

Area Sq Km (Miles)	439 580 (169 723)	Population	uninhabited

This territory includes the Crozet Islands, Kerguelen, Amsterdam Island and St Paul Island. All are uninhabited apart from scientific research staff. In accordance with the Antarctic Treaty, French (and all other) territorial claims in Antarctica have been suspended.

Map page 73

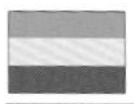

GABON
Gabonese Republic

Area Sq Km	267 667	Currency	CFA franc
Area Sq Miles	103 347	Languages	French, Fang, local languages
Population	1 384 000	Religions	Roman Catholic, Protestant, traditional beliefs
Capital	Libreville	Organizations	UN

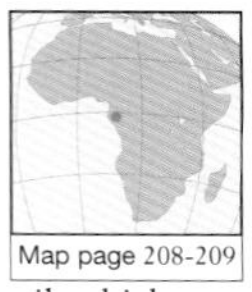

Gabon, on the Atlantic coast of central Africa, consists of low plateaus and a coastal plain lined by lagoons and mangrove swamps. The climate is tropical and rainforests cover over three-quarters of the land area. Over seventy per cent of the population lives in towns. The economy is heavily dependent on oil, which accounts for around seventy-five per cent of exports; manganese, uranium and timber are the other main exports. Agriculture is mainly at subsistence level.

Map page 208-209

THE GAMBIA
Republic of The Gambia

Area Sq Km	11 295	Currency	Dalasi
Area Sq Miles	4 361	Languages	English, Malinke, Fulani, Wolof
Population	1 517 000	Religions	Sunni Muslim, Protestant
Capital	Banjul	Organizations	Comm., UN

The Gambia, on the coast of west Africa, occupies a strip of land along the lower Gambia river. Sandy beaches are backed by mangrove swamps, beyond which is savanna. The climate is tropical, with most rainfall in the summer. Over seventy per cent of Gambians are farmers, growing chiefly groundnuts (the main export), cotton, oil palms and food crops. Livestock rearing and fishing are important, while manufacturing is limited. Re-exports, mainly from Senegal, and tourism are major sources of income.

Map page 206

Gaza Semi-autonomous region

Area Sq Km	363	Currency	Israeli shekel
Area Sq Miles	140	Languages	Arabic
Population	1 406 423	Religions	Sunni Muslim, Shi'a Muslim
Capital	Gaza		

Gaza is a narrow strip of land on the southeast corner of the Mediterranean Sea, between Egypt and Israel. This Palestinian territory has internal autonomy, but Israel exerts full control over its border with Israel. All Israeli settlers were evacuated in 2005. Hostilities between the two parties continue to restrict its economic development.

Map page 128

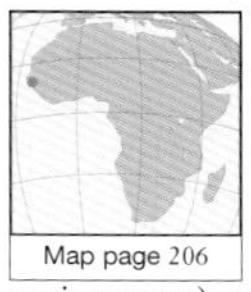

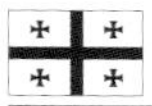

GEORGIA
Republic of Georgia

Area Sq Km	69 700	Currency	Lari
Area Sq Miles	26 911	Languages	Georgian, Russian, Armenian, Azeri, Ossetian, Abkhaz
Population	4 474 000	Religions	Georgian Orthodox, Russian Orthodox, Sunni Muslim
Capital	T'bilisi	Organizations	CIS, UN

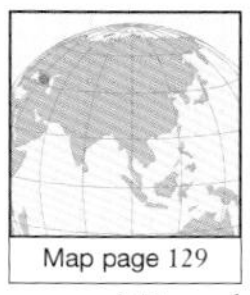

Georgia is in the northwest Caucasus area of southwest Asia, on the eastern coast of the Black Sea. Mountain ranges in the north and south flank the Kura and Rioni valleys. The climate is generally mild, and along the coast it is subtropical. Agriculture is important, with tea, grapes, and citrus fruits the main crops. Mineral resources include manganese ore and oil, and the main industries are steel, oil refining and machine building. The main trading partners are the Russian Federation and Turkey.

Map page 129

GERMANY
Federal Republic of Germany

Area Sq Km	357 022	Currency	Euro
Area Sq Miles	137 847	Languages	German, Turkish
Population	82 689 000	Religions	Protestant, Roman Catholic
Capital	Berlin	Organizations	EU, NATO, OECD, UN

The central European state of Germany borders nine countries and has coastlines on the North and Baltic Seas. Behind the indented coastline, and covering about one-third of the country, is the north German plain, a region of fertile farmland and sandy heaths drained by the country's major rivers. The central highlands are a belt of forested hills and plateaus which stretch from the Eifel region in the west to the mountains of the Erzgebirge along the border with the Czech Republic. Farther south the land rises to the Swabian Alps (Schwäbische Alb), with the high rugged and forested Black Forest (Schwarzwald) in the southwest. In the far south the Bavarian Alps form the border with Austria. The climate is temperate, with continental conditions in eastern areas. The population is highly

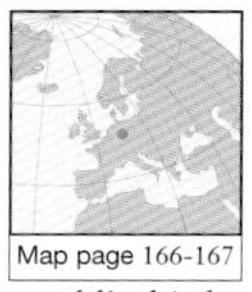
Map page 166-167

urbanized, with over eighty-five per cent living in cities and towns. With the exception of coal, lignite, potash and baryte, Germany lacks minerals and other industrial raw materials. It has a small agricultural base, although a few products (chiefly wines and beers) enjoy an international reputation. Germany is the world's third ranking economy after the USA and Japan. Its industries are amongst the world's most technologically advanced. Exports include machinery, vehicles and chemicals. The majority of trade is with other countries in the European Union, the USA and Japan.

Baden-Württemberg (State)
Area Sq Km (Miles) 35 752 (13 804) **Population** 10 601 000 **Capital** Stuttgart

Bayern (State)
Area Sq Km (Miles) 70 550 (27 240) **Population** 12 330 000 **Capital** München

Berlin (State)
Area Sq Km (Miles) 892 (344) **Population** 3 388 000 **Capital** Berlin

Brandenburg (State)
Area Sq Km (Miles) 29 476 (11 381) **Population** 2 593 000 **Capital** Potsdam

Bremen (State)
Area Sq Km (Miles) 404 (156) **Population** 660 000 **Capital** Bremen

Hamburg (State)
Area Sq Km (Miles) 755 (292) **Population** 1 726 000 **Capital** Hamburg

Hessen (State)
Area Sq Km (Miles) 21 114 (8 152) **Population** 6 078 000 **Capital** Wiesbaden

Mecklenburg-Vorpommern (State)
Area Sq Km (Miles) 23 173 (8 947) **Population** 1 760 000 **Capital** Schwerin

Niedersachsen (State)
Area Sq Km (Miles) 47 616 (18 385) **Population** 7 956 000 **Capital** Hannover

Nordrhein-Westfalen (State)
Area Sq Km (Miles) 34 082 (13 159) **Population** 18 052 000 **Capital** Düsseldorf

Rheinland-Pfalz (State)
Area Sq Km (Miles) 19 847 (7 663) **Population** 4 049 000 **Capital** Mainz

Saarland (State)
Area Sq Km (Miles) 2 568 (992) **Population** 1 066 000 **Capital** Saarbrücken

Sachsen (State)
Area Sq Km (Miles) 18 413 (7 109) **Population** 4 384 000 **Capital** Dresden

Sachsen-Anhalt (State)
Area Sq Km (Miles) 20 447 (7 895) **Population** 2 581 000 **Capital** Magdeburg

Schleswig-Holstein (State)
Area Sq Km (Miles) 15 761 (6 085) **Population** 2 804 000 **Capital** Kiel

Thüringen (State)
Area Sq Km (Miles) 16 172 (6 244) **Population** 2 411 000 **Capital** Erfurt

GHANA
Republic of Ghana

Area Sq Km	238 537	**Currency**	Cedi
Area Sq Miles	92 100	**Languages**	English, Hausa, Akan, local languages
Population	22 113 000	**Religions**	Christian, Sunni Muslim, traditional beliefs
Capital	Accra	**Organizations**	Comm., UN

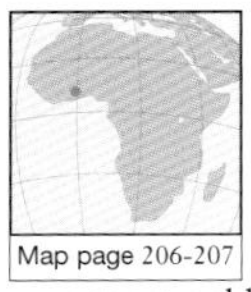
Map page 206-207

A west African state on the Gulf of Guinea, Ghana is a land of plains and low plateaus covered with savanna and rainforest. In the east is the Volta basin and Lake Volta. The climate is tropical, with the highest rainfall in the south, where most of the population lives. Agriculture employs around sixty per cent of the workforce. Main exports are gold, timber, cocoa, bauxite and manganese ore.

Gibraltar
United Kingdom Overseas Territory

Area Sq Km	7	**Currency**	Gibraltar pound
Area Sq Miles	3	**Languages**	English, Spanish
Population	28 000	**Religions**	Roman Catholic, Protestant, Sunni Muslim
Capital	Gibraltar		

Gibraltar lies on the south coast of Spain at the western entrance to the Mediterranean Sea. The economy depends on tourism, offshore banking and shipping services.

Map page 185

GREECE
Hellenic Republic

Area Sq Km	131 957	**Currency**	Euro
Area Sq Miles	50 949	**Languages**	Greek
Population	11 120 000	**Religions**	Greek Orthodox, Sunni Muslim
Capital	Athina (Athens)	**Organizations**	EU, NATO, OECD, UN

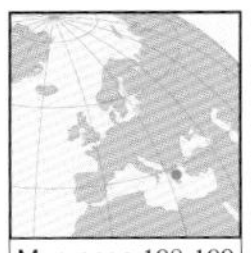
Map page 198-199

Greece comprises a mountainous peninsula in the Balkan region of southeastern Europe and many islands in the Ionian, Aegean and Mediterranean Seas. The islands make up over one-fifth of its area. Mountains and hills cover much of the country. The main lowland areas are the plains of Thessaly in the centre and around Thessaloniki in the northeast. Summers are hot and dry while winters are mild and wet, but colder in the north with heavy snowfalls in the mountains. One-third of Greeks live in the Athens area. Employment in agriculture accounts for approximately twenty per cent of the workforce, and exports include citrus fruits, raisins, wine, olives and olive oil. Aluminium and nickel are mined and a wide range of manufactures are produced, including food products and tobacco, textiles, clothing, and chemicals. Tourism is an important industry and there is a large services sector. Most trade is with other European Union countries.

GREENLAND
Self-governing Danish Territory

Area Sq Km	2 175 600	**Currency**	Danish krone
Area Sq Miles	840 004	**Languages**	Greenlandic, Danish
Population	57 000	**Religions**	Protestant
Capital	Nuuk (Godthåb)		

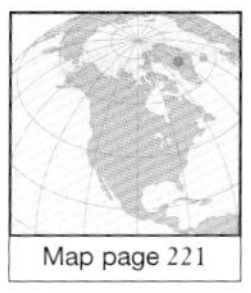
Map page 221

Situated to the northeast of North America between the Atlantic and Arctic Oceans, Greenland is the largest island in the world. It has a polar climate and over eighty per cent of the land area is covered by permanent ice cap. The economy is based on fishing and fish processing.

GRENADA

Area Sq Km	378	**Currency**	East Caribbean dollar
Area Sq Miles	146	**Languages**	English, creole
Population	103 000	**Religions**	Roman Catholic, Protestant
Capital	St George's	**Organizations**	CARICOM, Comm., UN

The Caribbean state comprises Grenada, the most southerly of the Windward Islands, and the southern islands of the Grenadines. Grenada has wooded hills, with beaches in the southwest. The climate is warm and wet. Agriculture is the main activity, with bananas, nutmeg and cocoa the main exports. Tourism is the main foreign exchange earner.

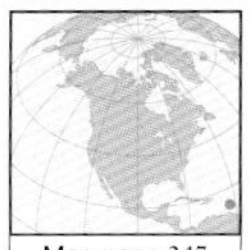
Map page 247

Guadeloupe
French Overseas Department

Area Sq Km	1 780	**Currency**	Euro
Area Sq Miles	687	**Languages**	French, creole
Population	448 000	**Religions**	Roman Catholic
Capital	Basse-Terre		

Guadeloupe, in the Leeward Islands in the Caribbean, consists of two main islands (Basse-Terre and Grande-Terre, connected by a bridge), Marie-Galante, and a few outer islands. The climate is tropical, but moderated by trade winds. Bananas, sugar and rum are the main exports and tourism is a major source of income.

Map page 247

Guam
United States Unincorporated Territory

Area Sq Km	541	**Currency**	United States dollar
Area Sq Miles	209	**Languages**	Chamorro, English, Tagalog
Population	170 000	**Religions**	Roman Catholic
Capital	Hagåtña (Agana)		

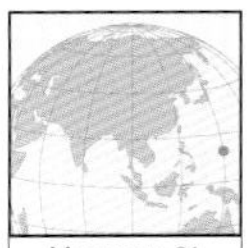
Map page 91

Lying at the south end of the Northern Mariana Islands in the western Pacific Ocean, Guam has a humid tropical climate. The island has a large US military base and the economy relies on that and on tourism, which has grown rapidly.

GUATEMALA
Republic of Guatemala

Area Sq Km	108 890	**Currency**	Quetzal, United States dollar
Area Sq Miles	42 043	**Languages**	Spanish, Mayan languages
Population	12 599 000	**Religions**	Roman Catholic, Protestant
Capital	Guatemala	**Organizations**	UN

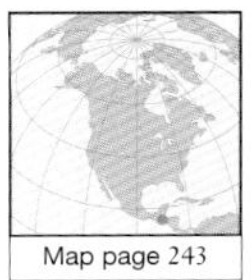
Map page 243

The most populous country in Central America after Mexico, Guatemala has long Pacific and short Caribbean coasts separated by a mountain chain which includes several active volcanoes. The climate is hot tropical in the lowlands and cooler in the highlands, where most of the population lives. Farming is the main activity and coffee, sugar and bananas are the main exports. There is some manufacturing of clothing and textiles. The main trading partner is the USA.

Guernsey
United Kingdom Crown Dependency

Area Sq Km	78	**Currency**	Pound sterling
Area Sq Miles	30	**Languages**	English, French
Population	62 692	**Religions**	Protestant, Roman Catholic
Capital	St Peter Port		

Guernsey is one of the Channel Islands, lying off northern France. The dependency also includes the nearby islands of Alderney, Sark and Herm. Financial services are an important part of the island's economy.

Map page 158

GUINEA
Republic of Guinea

Area Sq Km	245 857	**Currency**	Guinea franc
Area Sq Miles	94 926	**Languages**	French, Fulani, Malinke, local languages
Population	9 402 000	**Religions**	Sunni Muslim, traditional beliefs, Christian
Capital	Conakry	**Organizations**	UN

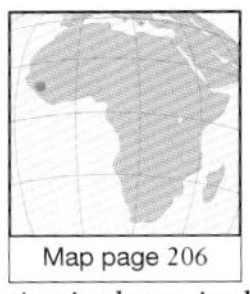
Map page 206

Guinea is in west Africa, on the Atlantic Ocean. There are mangrove swamps along the coast, while inland are lowlands and the Fouta Djallon mountains and plateaus. To the east are savanna plains drained by the upper Niger river system. The southeast is hilly. The climate is tropical, with high coastal rainfall. Agriculture is the main activity, employing nearly eighty per cent of the workforce, with coffee, bananas and pineapples the chief cash crops. There are huge reserves of bauxite, which accounts for more than seventy per cent of exports. Other exports include aluminium oxide, gold, coffee and diamonds.

GUINEA-BISSAU
Republic of Guinea-Bissau

Area Sq Km	36 125	**Currency**	CFA franc
Area Sq Miles	13 948	**Languages**	Portuguese, crioulo, local languages
Population	1 586 000	**Religions**	Traditional beliefs, Sunni Muslim, Christian
Capital	Bissau	**Organizations**	UN

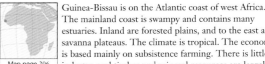

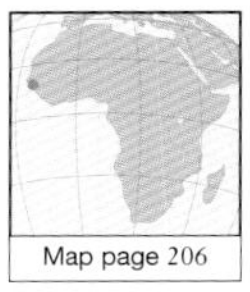
Map page 206

Guinea-Bissau is on the Atlantic coast of west Africa. The mainland coast is swampy and contains many estuaries. Inland are forested plains, and to the east are savanna plateaus. The climate is tropical. The economy is based mainly on subsistence farming. There is little industry, and timber and mineral resources are largely unexploited. Cashews account for seventy per cent of exports. Guinea-Bissau is one of the least developed countries in the world.

GUYANA
Co-operative Republic of Guyana

Area Sq Km	214 969	**Currency**	Guyana dollar
Area Sq Miles	83 000	**Languages**	English, creole, Amerindian languages
Population	751 000	**Religions**	Protestant, Hindu, Roman Catholic, Sunni Muslim
Capital	Georgetown	**Organizations**	CARICOM, Comm., UN

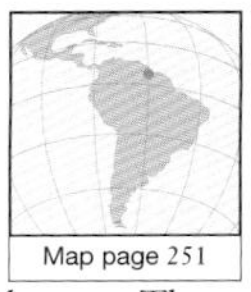
Map page 251

Guyana, on the northeast coast of South America, consists of highlands in the west and savanna uplands in the southwest. Most of the country is densely forested. A lowland coastal belt supports crops and most of the population. The generally hot, humid and wet conditions are modified along the coast by sea breezes. The economy is based on agriculture, bauxite, and forestry. Sugar, bauxite, gold, rice and timber are the main exports.

HAITI
Republic of Haiti

Area Sq Km	27 750	**Currency**	Gourde
Area Sq Miles	10 714	**Languages**	French, creole
Population	8 528 000	**Religions**	Roman Catholic, Protestant, Voodoo
Capital	Port-au-Prince	**Organizations**	CARICOM, UN

Haiti, occupying the western third of the Caribbean island of Hispaniola, is a mountainous state with small coastal plains and a central valley. The Dominican Republic occupies the rest of the island. The climate is tropical, and is hottest in coastal areas. Haiti has few natural resources, is densely populated and relies on exports of local crafts and coffee, and remittances from workers abroad.

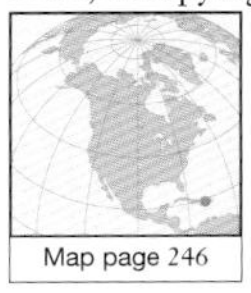
Map page 246

HONDURAS
Republic of Honduras

Area Sq Km	112 088	**Currency**	Lempira
Area Sq Miles	43 277	**Languages**	Spanish, Amerindian languages
Population	7 205 000	**Religions**	Roman Catholic, Protestant
Capital	Tegucigalpa	**Organizations**	UN

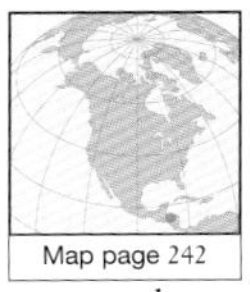
Map page 242

Honduras, in central America, is a mountainous and forested country with lowland areas along its long Caribbean and short Pacific coasts. Coastal areas are hot and humid with heavy summer rainfall; inland is cooler and drier. Most of the population lives in the central valleys. Coffee and bananas are the main exports, along with shellfish and zinc. Industry involves mainly agricultural processing.

HUNGARY
Republic of Hungary

Area Sq Km	93 030	**Currency**	Forint
Area Sq Miles	35 919	**Languages**	Hungarian
Population	10 098 000	**Religions**	Roman Catholic, Protestant
Capital	Budapest	**Organizations**	EU, NATO, OECD, UN

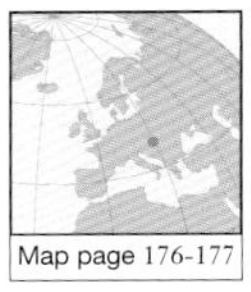
Map page 176-177

The Danube river flows north-south through central Hungary, a landlocked country in eastern Europe. In the east lies a great plain, flanked by highlands in the north. In the west low mountains and Lake Balaton separate a smaller plain and southern uplands. The climate is continental. Sixty per cent of the population lives in urban areas, and one-fifth lives in the capital, Budapest. Some minerals and energy resources are exploited, chiefly bauxite, coal and natural gas. Hungary has an industrial economy based on metals, machinery, transport equipment, chemicals and food products. The main trading partners are Germany and Austria. Hungary joined the European Union in May 2004.

ICELAND
Republic of Iceland

Area Sq Km	102 820	**Currency**	Icelandic króna
Area Sq Miles	39 699	**Languages**	Icelandic
Population	295 000	**Religions**	Protestant
Capital	Reykjavík	**Organizations**	NATO, OECD, UN

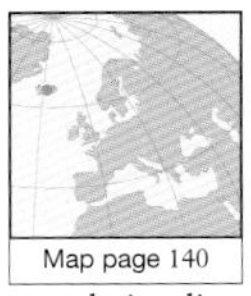
Map page 140

Iceland lies in the north Atlantic Ocean near the Arctic Circle, to the northwest of Scandinavia. The landscape is volcanic, with numerous hot springs, geysers, and approximately two hundred volcanoes. One-tenth of the country is covered by ice caps. Only coastal lowlands are cultivated and settled, and over half the population lives in the Reykjavik area. The climate is mild, moderated by the North Atlantic Drift ocean current and by southwesterly winds. The mainstays of the economy are fishing and fish processing, which account for seventy per cent of exports. Agriculture involves mainly sheep and dairy farming. Hydroelectric and geothermal energy resources are considerable. The main industries produce aluminium, ferro-silicon and fertilizers. Tourism, including ecotourism, is growing in importance.

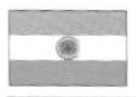

INDIA
Republic of India

Area Sq Km	3 064 898	**Currency**	Indian rupee
Area Sq Miles	1 183 364	**Languages**	Hindi, English, many regional languages
Population	1 103 371 000	**Religions**	Hindu, Sunni Muslim, Shi'a Muslim, Sikh, Christian
Capital	New Delhi	**Organizations**	Comm., UN

The south Asian country of India occupies a peninsula that juts out into the Indian Ocean between the Arabian Sea and Bay of Bengal. The heart of the peninsula is the Deccan plateau, bordered on either side by ranges of hills, the Western Ghats and the lower Eastern Ghats, which fall away to narrow coastal plains. To the north is a broad plain, drained by the Indus, Ganges and Brahmaputra rivers and their tributaries. The plain is intensively farmed and is the most populous region. In the west is the Thar Desert. The mountains of the Himalaya form India's northern border, together with parts of the Karakoram and Hindu Kush ranges in the northwest. The climate shows marked seasonal variation: a hot season from March to June; a monsoon season from June to October; and a cold season from November to February.

Map page 112-113

Rainfall ranges between very high in the northeast Assam region to negligible in the Thar Desert. Temperatures range from very cold in the Himalaya to tropical heat over much of the south. Over seventy per cent of the huge population – the second largest in the world. In the west is rural, although Delhi, Mumbai (Bombay) and Kolkata (Calcutta) all rank among the ten largest cities in the world. Agriculture, forestry and fishing account for a quarter of national output and two-thirds of employment. Much of the farming is on a subsistence basis and involves mainly rice and wheat. India is a major world producer of tea, sugar, jute, cotton and tobacco. Livestock is reared mainly for dairy products and hides. There are major reserves of coal, reserves of oil and natural gas, and many minerals, including iron, manganese, bauxite, diamonds and gold. The manufacturing sector is large and diverse – mainly chemicals and chemical products, textiles, iron and steel, food products, electrical goods and transport equipment; software and pharmaceuticals are also important. All the main manufactured products are exported, together with diamonds and jewellery. The USA, Germany, Japan and the UK are the main trading partners.

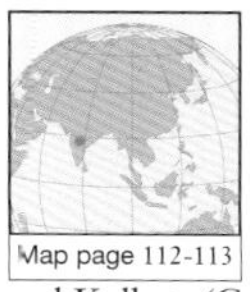

INDONESIA
Republic of Indonesia

Area Sq Km	1 919 445	**Currency**	Rupiah
Area Sq Miles	741 102	**Languages**	Indonesian, local languages
Population	222 781 000	**Religions**	Sunni Muslim, Protestant, Roman Catholic
Capital	Jakarta	**Organizations**	APEC, ASEAN, OPEC, UN

Map page 90-91

Indonesia, the largest and most populous country in Southeast Asia, consists of over thirteen thousand islands extending between the Pacific and Indian Oceans. Sumatra, Java, Sulawesi, Kalimantan (two-thirds of Borneo) and Papua (formerly Irian Jaya, western New Guinea) make up ninety per cent of the land area. Most of Indonesia is mountainous and covered with rainforest or mangrove swamps, and there are over three hundred volcanoes, many active. Two-thirds of the population lives in the lowland areas of the islands of Java and Madura. The climate is tropical monsoon. Agriculture is the largest sector of the economy and Indonesia is among the world's top producers of rice, palm oil, tea, coffee, rubber and tobacco. Many goods are produced, including textiles, clothing, cement, tin, fertilizers and vehicles. Main exports are oil, natural gas, timber products and clothing. Main trading partners are Japan, the USA and Singapore. Indonesia is a relatively poor country, and ethnic tensions and civil unrest often hinder economic development.

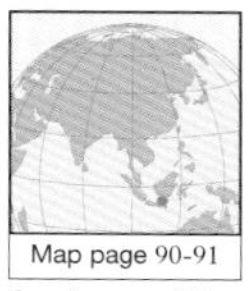

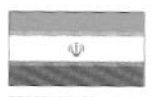

IRAN
Islamic Republic of Iran

Area Sq Km	1 648 000	**Currency**	Iranian rial
Area Sq Miles	636 296	**Languages**	Farsi, Azeri, Kurdish, regional languages
Population	69 515 000	**Religions**	Shi'a Muslim, Sunni Muslim
Capital	Tehrān	**Organizations**	OPEC, UN

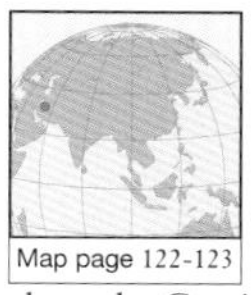

Map page 122-123

Iran is in southwest Asia, and has coasts on The Gulf, the Caspian Sea and the Gulf of Oman. In the east is a high plateau, with large salt pans and a vast sand desert. In the west the Zagros Mountains form a series of ridges, and to the north lie the Elburz Mountains. Most farming and settlement is on the narrow plain along the Caspian Sea and in the foothills of the north and west. The climate is one of extremes, with hot summers and very cold winters. Most of the light rainfall is in the winter months. Agriculture involves approximately one-third of the workforce. Wheat is the main crop, but fruit (especially dates) and pistachio nuts are grown for export. Petroleum (the main export) and natural gas are Iran's leading natural resources. Manufactured goods include carpets, clothing, food products and construction materials.

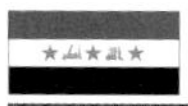

IRAQ
Republic of Iraq

Area Sq Km	438 317	**Currency**	Iraqi dinar
Area Sq Miles	169 235	**Languages**	Arabic, Kurdish, Turkmen
Population	28 807 000	**Religions**	Shi'a Muslim, Sunni Muslim, Christian
Capital	Baghdād	**Organizations**	OPEC, UN

Iraq, in southwest Asia, has at its heart the lowland valley of the Tigris and Euphrates rivers. In the southeast, where the two rivers join, are the Mesopotamian marshes and the Shaṭṭ al 'Arab waterway. Northern Iraq is hilly, while western Iraq is desert. Summers are hot and dry, while winters are mild with light, unreliable rainfall. One in five of the population lives in the capital, Baghdād. The economy has

Map page 127

suffered following the 1991 Gulf War and the invasion of US-led coalition forces in 2005. The latter resulted in the overthrow of the dictator Saddam Hussein, but there is continuing internal instability. Oil is normally the main export.

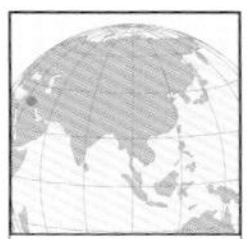

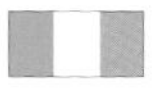

IRELAND

Area Sq Km	70 282	**Currency**	Euro
Area Sq Miles	27 136	**Languages**	English, Irish
Population	4 148 000	**Religions**	Roman Catholic, Protestant
Capital	Dublin	**Organizations**	EU, OECD, UN

Map page 147

The Irish Republic occupies some eighty per cent of the island of Ireland, in northwest Europe. It is a lowland country of wide valleys, lakes and peat bogs, with isolated mountain ranges around the coast. The west coast is rugged and indented with many bays. The climate is mild due to the modifying effect of the North Atlantic Drift ocean current and rainfall is plentiful, although highest in the west. Nearly sixty per cent of the population lives in urban areas, Dublin and Cork being the main cities. Resources include natural gas, peat, lead and zinc. Agriculture, the traditional mainstay, now employs less than ten per cent of the workforce, while industry employs nearly thirty per cent. The main industries are electronics, pharmaceuticals and engineering as well as food processing, brewing and textiles. Service industries are expanding, with tourism a major earner. The UK is the main trading partner.

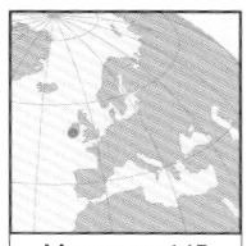

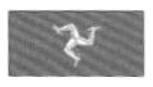

Isle of Man
United Kingdom Crown Dependency

Area Sq Km	572	**Currency**	Pound sterling
Area Sq Miles	221	**Languages**	English
Population	77 000	**Religions**	Protestant, Roman Catholic
Capital	Douglas		

The Isle of Man lies in the Irish Sea between England and Northern Ireland. The island is self-governing, although the UK is responsible for its defence and foreign affairs. It is not part of the European Union, but has a special relationship with the EU which allows for free trade. Eighty per cent of the economy is based on the service sector, particularly financial services.

Map page 148

ISRAEL
State of Israel

Area Sq Km	20 770	**Currency**	Shekel
Area Sq Miles	8 019	**Languages**	Hebrew, Arabic
Population	6 725 000	**Religions**	Jewish, Sunni Muslim, Christian, Druze
Capital	Jerusalem (Yerushalayim) (El Quds) De facto capital. Disputed	**Organizations**	UN

Map page 128

Israel lies on the Mediterranean coast of southwest Asia. Beyond the coastal Plain of Sharon are the hills and valleys of Samaria, with the Galilee highlands to the north. In the east is a rift valley, which extends from Lake Tiberias (Sea of Galilee) to the Gulf of Aqaba and contains the Jordan river and the Dead Sea. In the south is the Negev, a triangular semi-desert plateau. Most of the population lives on the coastal plain or in northern and central areas. Much of Israel has warm summers and mild, wet winters. The south is hot and dry. Agricultural production was boosted by the occupation of the West Bank in 1967. Manufacturing makes the largest contribution to the economy, and tourism is also important. Israel's main exports are machinery and transport equipment, software, diamonds, clothing, fruit and vegetables. The country relies heavily on foreign aid. Security issues relating to the West Bank and Gaza have still to be resolved.

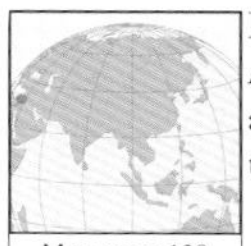

ITALY
Italian Republic

Area Sq Km	301 245	**Currency**	Euro
Area Sq Miles	116 311	**Languages**	Italian
Population	58 093 000	**Religions**	Roman Catholic
Capital	Roma (Rome)	**Organizations**	EU, NATO, OECD, UN

Most of the southern European state of Italy occupies a peninsula that juts out into the Mediterranean Sea. It includes the islands of Sicily and Sardinia and approximately seventy much smaller islands in the surrounding seas. Italy is mountainous, dominated by the Alps, which form its northern border, and the various ranges of the Apennines, which run almost the full length of the peninsula. Many of Italy's mountains are of volcanic origin, and its active volcanoes are

Map page 188-189

Vesuvius, near Naples, Etna and Stromboli. The main lowland area, the Po river valley in the northeast, is the main agricultural and industrial area and is the most populous region. Italy has a Mediterranean climate, although the north experiences colder, wetter winters, with heavy snow in the Alps. Natural resources are limited, and only about twenty per cent of the land is suitable for cultivation. The economy is fairly diversified. Some oil, natural gas and coal are produced, but most fuels and minerals used by industry are imported. Agriculture is important, with cereals, vines, fruit and vegetables the main crops. Italy is the world's largest wine producer. The north is the centre of Italian industry, especially around Turin, Milan and Genoa. Leading manufactures include industrial and office equipment, domestic appliances, cars, textiles, clothing, leather goods, chemicals and metal products. There is a strong service sector, and with over twenty-five million visitors a year, tourism is a major employer and accounts for five per cent of the national income. Finance and banking are also important. Most trade is with other European Union countries.

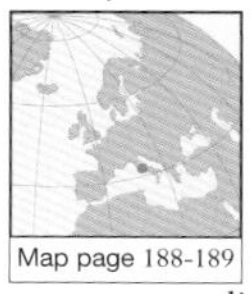

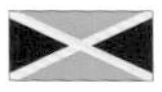

JAMAICA

Area Sq Km	10 991	**Currency**	Jamaican dollar
Area Sq Miles	4 244	**Languages**	English, creole
Population	2 651 000	**Religions**	Protestant, Roman Catholic
Capital	Kingston	**Organizations**	CARICOM, Comm., UN

Map page 246

Jamaica, the third largest Caribbean island, has beaches and densely populated coastal plains traversed by hills and plateaus rising to the forested Blue Mountains in the east. The climate is tropical, but cooler and wetter on high ground. The economy is based on tourism, agriculture, mining and light manufacturing. Bauxite, aluminium oxide, sugar and bananas are the main exports. The USA is the main trading partner. Foreign aid is also significant.

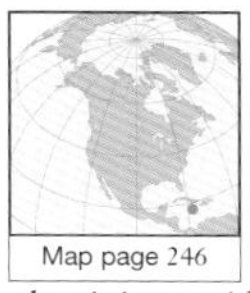

Jammu and Kashmir
Disputed territory (India, Pakistan, China)

Area Sq Km (Miles)	222 236 (85 806)	**Population**	13 000 000	**Capital**	Srinagar

A disputed region in the north of the Indian subcontinent, to the west of the Karakoram and Himalaya mountains. The 'Line of Control' separates the northwestern, Pakistani-controlled area and the southeastern, Indian-controlled area. China occupies the Himalayan section known as the Aksai Chin, which is also claimed by India.

Map page 116

JAPAN

Area Sq Km	377 727	**Currency**	Yen
Area Sq Miles	145 841	**Languages**	Japanese
Population	128 085 000	**Religions**	Shintoist, Buddhist, Christian
Capital	Tōkyō	**Organizations**	APEC, OECD, UN

Japan lies in the Pacific Ocean off the coast of eastern Asia and consists of four main islands – Hokkaidō, Honshū, Shikoku and Kyūshū – and more than three thousand smaller islands in the surrounding Sea of

Map page 102-103

Japan, East China Sea and Pacific Ocean. The central island of Honshū accounts for sixty per cent of the total land area and contains eighty per cent of the population. Behind the long and deeply indented coastline, nearly three-quarters of the country is mountainous and heavily forested. Japan has over sixty active volcanoes, and is subject to frequent earthquakes and typhoons. The climate is generally temperate maritime, with warm summers and mild winters, except in western Hokkaidō and northwest Honshū, where the winters are very cold with heavy snow. Only fourteen per cent of the land area is suitable for cultivation, and its few raw materials (coal, oil, natural gas, lead, zinc and copper) are insufficient for its industry. Most materials must be imported, including about ninety per cent of energy requirements. Yet Japan has the world's second largest industrial economy, with a range of modern heavy and light industries centred mainly around the major ports of Yokohama, Ōsaka and Tōkyō. It is the world's largest manufacturer of cars, motorcycles and merchant ships, and a major producer of steel, textiles, chemicals and cement. It is also a leading producer of many consumer durables, such as washing machines, and electronic equipment, chiefly office equipment and computers. Japan has a strong service sector, banking and finance being particularly important, and Tōkyō has one of the world's major stock exchanges. Owing to intensive agricultural production, Japan is seventy per cent self-sufficient in food. The main food crops are rice, barley, fruit, wheat and soya beans. Livestock rearing (chiefly cattle, pigs and chickens) and fishing are also important, and Japan has one of the largest fishing fleets in the world. A major trading nation, Japan has trade links with many countries in Southeast Asia and in Europe, although its main trading partner is the USA.

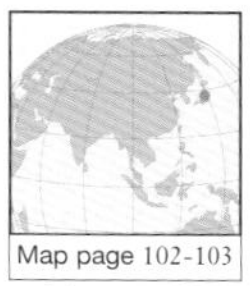

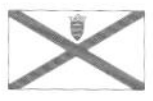

Jersey
United Kingdom Crown Dependency

Area Sq Km	116	**Currency**	Pound sterling
Area Sq Miles	45	**Languages**	English, French
Population	87 500	**Religions**	Protestant, Roman Catholic
Capital	St Helier		

One of the Channel Islands lying off the west coast of the Cherbourg peninsula in northern France. Financial services are the most important part of the economy.

Map page 148

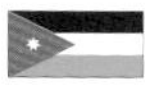

JORDAN
Hashemite Kingdom of Jordan

Area Sq Km	89 206	**Currency**	Jordanian dinar
Area Sq Miles	34 443	**Languages**	Arabic
Population	5 703 000	**Religions**	Sunni Muslim, Christian
Capital	'Ammān	**Organizations**	UN

Map page 128

Jordan, in southwest Asia, is landlocked apart from a short coastline on the Gulf of Aqaba. Much of the country is rocky desert plateau. To the west of the mountains, the land falls below sea level to the Dead Sea and the Jordan river. The climate is hot and dry. Most people live in the northwest. Phosphates, potash, pharmaceuticals, fruit and vegetables are the main exports. The tourist industry is important, and the economy relies on workers' remittances from abroad and foreign aid.

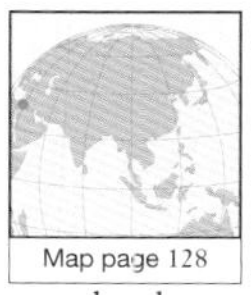

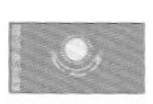

KAZAKHSTAN
Republic of Kazakhstan

Area Sq Km	2 717 300	**Currency**	Tenge
Area Sq Miles	1 049 155	**Languages**	Kazakh, Russian, Ukrainian, German, Uzbek, Tatar
Population	14 825 000	**Religions**	Sunni Muslim, Russian Orthodox, Protestant
Capital	Astana (Akmola)	**Organizations**	CIS, UN

Stretching across central Asia, Kazakhstan covers a vast area of steppe land and semi-desert. The land is flat in the west, with large lowlands

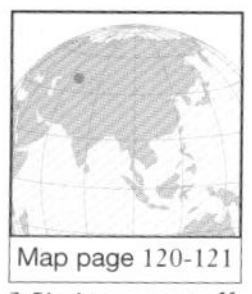
Map page 120-121

around the Caspian Sea, rising to mountains in the southeast. The climate is continental. Agriculture and livestock rearing are important, and cotton and tobacco are the main cash crops. Kazakhstan is very rich in minerals, including coal, chromium, gold, molybdenum, lead and zinc, and has substantial reserves of oil and gas. Mining, metallurgy, machine building and food processing are major industries. Oil, gas and minerals are the main exports, and the Russian Federation is the dominant trading partner.

KENYA
Republic of Kenya

Area Sq Km	582 646	**Currency**	Kenyan shilling
Area Sq Miles	224 961	**Languages**	Swahili, English, local languages
Population	34 256 000	**Religions**	Christian, traditional beliefs
Capital	Nairobi	**Organizations**	Comm., UN

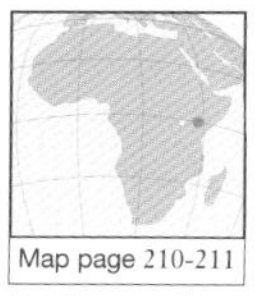
Map page 210-211

Kenya is in east Africa, on the Indian Ocean. Inland beyond the coastal plains the land rises to plateaus interrupted by volcanic mountains. The Great Rift Valley runs north-south to the west of the capital, Nairobi. Most of the population lives in the central area. Conditions are tropical on the coast, semi-desert in the north and savanna in the south. Hydroelectric power from the Upper Tana river provides most of the country's electricity. Agricultural products, mainly tea, coffee, fruit and vegetables, are the main exports. Light industry is important, and tourism, oil refining and re-exports for landlocked neighbours are major foreign exchange earners.

KIRIBATI
Republic of Kiribati

Area Sq Km	717	**Currency**	Australian dollar
Area Sq Miles	277	**Languages**	Gilbertese, English
Population	99 000	**Religions**	Roman Catholic, Protestant
Capital	Bairiki	**Organizations**	Comm., UN

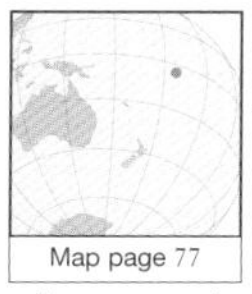
Map page 77

Kiribati, in the Pacific Ocean, straddles the Equator and comprises coral islands in the Gilbert, Phoenix and Line Island groups and the volcanic island of Banaba. Most people live on the Gilbert Islands, and the capital, Bairiki, is on Tarawa island in this group. The climate is hot, and wetter in the north. Copra and fish are exported. Kiribati relies on remittances from workers abroad and foreign aid.

KUWAIT
State of Kuwait

Area Sq Km	17 818	**Currency**	Kuwaiti dinar
Area Sq Miles	6 880	**Languages**	Arabic
Population	2 687 000	**Religions**	Sunni Muslim, Shi'a Muslim, Christian, Hindu
Capital	Al Kuwayt (Kuwait)	**Organizations**	OPEC, UN

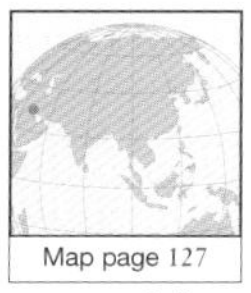
Map page 127

Kuwait lies on the northwest shores of The Gulf in southwest Asia. It is mainly low-lying desert, with irrigated areas along the bay, Kuwait Jun, where most people live. Summers are hot and dry, and winters are cool with some rainfall. The oil industry, which accounts for eighty per cent of exports, has largely recovered from the damage caused by the Gulf War in 1991. Income is also derived from extensive overseas investments. Japan and the USA are the main trading partners.

KYRGYZSTAN
Kyrgyz Republic

Area Sq Km	198 500	**Currency**	Kyrgyz som
Area Sq Miles	76 641	**Languages**	Kyrgyz, Russian, Uzbek
Population	5 264 000	**Religions**	Sunni Muslim, Russian Orthodox
Capital	Bishkek (Frunze)	**Organizations**	CIS, UN

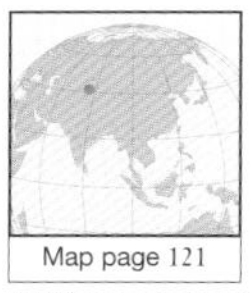
Map page 121

A landlocked central Asian state, Kyrgyzstan is rugged and mountainous, lying to the west of the Tien Shan mountain range. Most of the population lives in the valleys of the north and west. Summers are hot and winters cold. Agriculture (chiefly livestock farming) is the main activity. Some oil and gas, coal, gold, antimony and mercury are produced. Manufactured goods include machinery, metals and metal products, which are the main exports. Most trade is with Germany, the Russian Federation, Kazakhstan and Uzbekistan.

LAOS
Lao People's Democratic Republic

Area Sq Km	236 800	**Currency**	Kip
Area Sq Miles	91 429	**Languages**	Lao, local languages
Population	5 924 000	**Religions**	Buddhist, traditional beliefs
Capital	Viangchan (Vientiane)	**Organizations**	ASEAN, UN

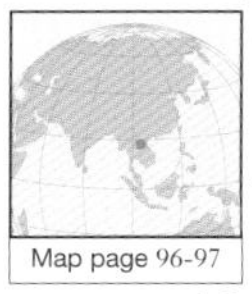
Map page 96-97

A landlocked country in Southeast Asia, Laos is a land of mostly forested mountains and plateaus. The climate is tropical monsoon. Most of the population lives in the Mekong valley and the low plateau in the south, where food crops, chiefly rice, are grown. Hydroelectricity from a plant on the Mekong river, timber, coffee and tin are exported. Laos relies heavily on foreign aid.

LATVIA
Republic of Latvia

Area Sq Km	63 700	**Currency**	Lats
Area Sq Miles	24 595	**Languages**	Latvian, Russian
Population	2 307 000	**Religions**	Protestant, Roman Catholic, Russian Orthodox
Capital	Riga	**Organizations**	EU, NATO, UN

Latvia is in northern Europe, on the Baltic Sea and the Gulf of Riga. The land is flat near the coast but hilly with woods and lakes inland. The country has a modified continental climate. One-third of the people live in the capital, Rīga. Crop and livestock farming are important. There are few natural resources. Industries and main exports include food products, transport equipment, wood and wood products and textiles. The main trading partners are the Russian Federation and Germany. Latvia joined the European Union in May 2004.

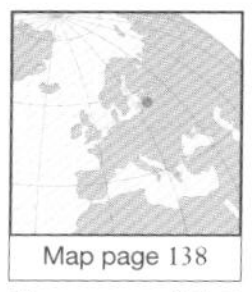
Map page 138

LEBANON
Republic of Lebanon

Area Sq Km	10 452	**Currency**	Lebanese pound
Area Sq Miles	4 036	**Languages**	Arabic, Armenian, French
Population	3 577 000	**Religions**	Shi'a Muslim, Sunni Muslim, Christian
Capital	Beirut	**Organizations**	UN

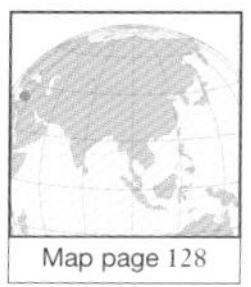
Map page 128

Lebanon lies on the Mediterranean coast of southwest Asia. Beyond the coastal strip, where most of the population lives, are two parallel mountain ranges, separated by the Bekaa Valley (El Beq'a). The economy and infrastructure have been recovering since the 1975-1991 civil war crippled the traditional sectors of financial services and tourism. Italy, France and the UAE are the main trading partners.

LESOTHO
Kingdom of Lesotho

Area Sq Km	30 355	**Currency**	Loti, South African rand
Area Sq Miles	11 720	**Languages**	Sesotho, English, Zulu
Population	1 795 000	**Religions**	Christian, traditional beliefs
Capital	Maseru	**Organizations**	Comm., SADC, UN

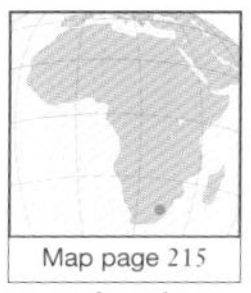
Map page 215

Lesotho is a landlocked state surrounded by the Republic of South Africa. It is a mountainous country lying within the Drakensberg mountain range. Farming and herding are the main activities. The economy depends heavily on South Africa for transport links and employment. A major hydroelectric plant completed in 1998 allows the sale of water to South Africa. Exports include manufactured goods (mainly clothing and road vehicles), food, live animals, wool and mohair.

LIBERIA
Republic of Liberia

Area Sq Km	111 369	**Currency**	Liberian dollar
Area Sq Miles	43 000	**Languages**	English, creole, local languages
Population	3 283 000	**Religions**	Traditional beliefs, Christian, Sunni Muslim
Capital	Monrovia	**Organizations**	UN

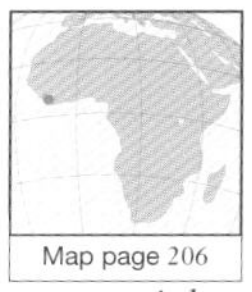
Map page 206

Liberia is on the Atlantic coast of west Africa. Beyond the coastal belt of sandy beaches and mangrove swamps the land rises to a forested plateau and highlands along the Guinea border. A quarter of the population lives along the coast. The climate is hot with heavy rainfall. Liberia is rich in mineral resources and forests. The economy is based on the production and export of basic products. Exports include diamonds, iron ore, rubber and timber. Liberia has a huge international debt and relies heavily on foreign aid.

LIBYA
Great Socialist People's Libyan Arab Jamahiriya

Area Sq Km	1 759 540	**Currency**	Libyan dinar
Area Sq Miles	679 362	**Languages**	Arabic, Berber
Population	5 853 000	**Religions**	Sunni Muslim
Capital	Ṭarābulus (Tripoli)	**Organizations**	OPEC, UN

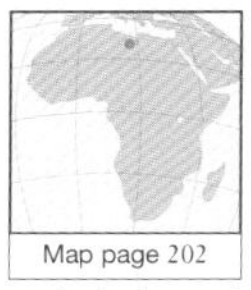
Map page 202

Libya lies on the Mediterranean coast of north Africa. The desert plains and hills of the Sahara dominate the landscape and the climate is hot and dry. Most of the population lives in cities near the coast, where the climate is cooler with moderate rainfall. Farming and herding, chiefly in the northwest, are important but the main industry is oil. Libya is a major producer, and oil accounts for virtually all of its export earnings. Italy and Germany are the main trading partners.

LIECHTENSTEIN
Principality of Liechtenstein

Area Sq Km	160	**Currency**	Swiss franc
Area Sq Miles	62	**Languages**	German
Population	35 000	**Religions**	Roman Catholic, Protestant
Capital	Vaduz	**Organizations**	UN

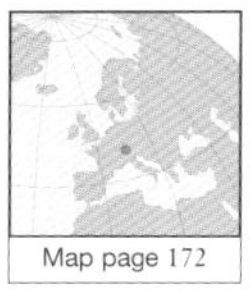
Map page 172

A landlocked state between Switzerland and Austria, Liechtenstein has an industrialized, free-enterprise economy. Low business taxes have attracted companies to establish offices which provide approximately one-third of state revenues. Banking is also important. Major products include precision instruments, ceramics and textiles.

LITHUANIA
Republic of Lithuania

Area Sq Km	65 200	**Currency**	Litas
Area Sq Miles	25 174	**Languages**	Lithuanian, Russian, Polish
Population	3 431 000	**Religions**	Roman Catholic, Protestant, Russian Orthodox
Capital	Vilnius	**Organizations**	EU, NATO, UN

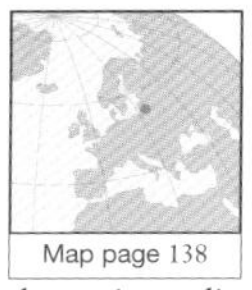
Map page 138

Lithuania is in northern Europe on the eastern shores of the Baltic Sea. It is mainly lowland with many lakes, rivers and marshes. Agriculture, fishing and forestry are important, but manufacturing dominates the economy. The main exports are machinery, mineral products and chemicals. The Russian Federation and Germany are the main trading partners. Lithuania joined the European Union in May 2004.

LUXEMBOURG
Grand Duchy of Luxembourg

Area Sq Km	2 586	**Currency**	Euro
Area Sq Miles	998	**Languages**	Letzeburgish, German, French
Population	465 000	**Religions**	Roman Catholic
Capital	Luxembourg	**Organizations**	EU, NATO, OECD, UN

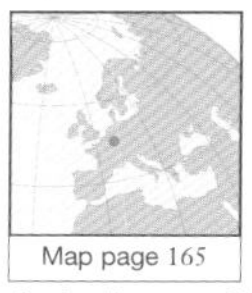
Map page 165

Luxembourg, a small landlocked country in western Europe, borders Belgium, France and Germany. The hills and forests of the Ardennes dominate the north, with rolling pasture to the south, where the main towns, farms and industries are found. The iron and steel industry is still important, but light industries (including textiles, chemicals and food products) are growing. Luxembourg is a major banking centre. Main trading partners are Belgium, Germany and France.

MACEDONIA (F.Y.R.O.M.)
Republic of Macedonia

Area Sq Km	25 713	**Currency**	Macedonian denar
Area Sq Miles	9 928	**Languages**	Macedonian, Albanian, Turkish
Population	2 034 000	**Religions**	Macedonian Orthodox, Sunni Muslim
Capital	Skopje	**Organizations**	UN

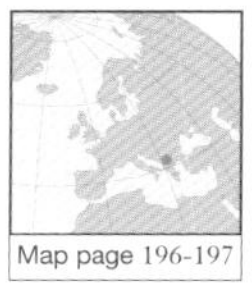
Map page 196-197

The Former Yugoslav Republic of Macedonia is a landlocked state in southern Europe. Lying within the southern Balkan Mountains, it is traversed northwest-southeast by the Vardar valley. The climate is continental. The economy is based on industry, mining and agriculture, but conflicts in the region have reduced trade and caused economic difficulties. Foreign aid and loans are now assisting in modernization and development of the country.

MADAGASCAR
Republic of Madagascar

Area Sq Km	587 041	**Currency**	Malagasy ariary, Malagasy franc
Area Sq Miles	226 658	**Languages**	Malagasy, French
Population	18 606 000	**Religions**	Traditional beliefs, Christian, Sunni Muslim
Capital	Antananarivo	**Organizations**	SADC, UN

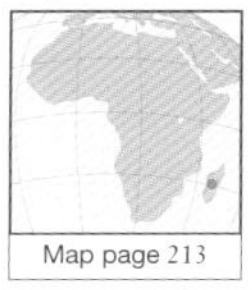
Map page 213

Madagascar lies off the east coast of southern Africa. The world's fourth largest island, it is mainly a high plateau, with a coastal strip to the east and scrubby plain to the west. The climate is tropical, with heavy rainfall in the north and east. Most of the population lives on the plateau. Although the amount of arable land is limited, the economy is based on agriculture. The main industries are agricultural processing, textile manufacturing and oil refining. Foreign aid is important. Exports include coffee, vanilla, cotton cloth, sugar and shrimps. France is the main trading partner.

MALAWI
Republic of Malawi

Area Sq Km	118 484	**Currency**	Malawian kwacha
Area Sq Miles	45 747	**Languages**	Chichewa, English, local languages
Population	12 884 000	**Religions**	Christian, traditional beliefs, Sunni Muslim
Capital	Lilongwe	**Organizations**	Comm., SADC, UN

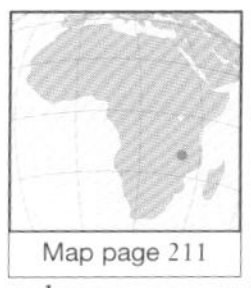
Map page 211

Landlocked Malawi in central Africa is a narrow hilly country at the southern end of the Great Rift Valley. One-fifth is covered by Lake Nyasa. Most of the population lives in rural areas in the southern regions. The climate is mainly subtropical, with varying rainfall. The economy is predominantly agricultural, with tobacco, tea and sugar the main exports. Malawi is one of the world's least developed countries and relies heavily on foreign aid. South Africa is the main trading partner.

MALAYSIA
Federation of Malaysia

Area Sq Km	332 965	**Currency**	Ringgit
Area Sq Miles	128 559	**Languages**	Malay, English, Chinese, Tamil, local languages
Population	25 347 000	**Religions**	Sunni Muslim, Buddhist, Hindu, Christian
Capital	Kuala Lumpur (Putrajaya)	**Organizations**	APEC, ASEAN, Comm., UN

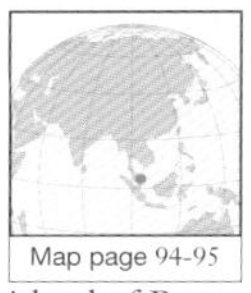
Map page 94-95

Malaysia, in Southeast Asia, comprises two regions, separated by the South China Sea. The western region occupies the southern Malay Peninsula, which has a chain of mountains dividing the eastern coastal strip from wider plains to the west. East Malaysia, consisting of the states of Sabah and Sarawak in the north of the island of Borneo, is mainly rainforest-covered hills and mountains with mangrove swamps along the coast. Both regions have a tropical climate with heavy rainfall. About eighty per cent of the population lives in Peninsular Malaysia. The country is rich in natural resources and has reserves of minerals and fuels. It is an important producer of tin, oil, natural gas and tropical hardwoods. Agriculture remains a substantial part of the economy, but industry is the most important sector. The main exports are transport and electronic equipment, oil, chemicals, palm oil, wood and rubber. The main trading partners are Japan, the USA and Singapore.

MALDIVES
Republic of the Maldives

Area Sq Km	298	**Currency**	Rufiyaa
Area Sq Miles	115	**Languages**	Divehi (Maldivian)
Population	329 000	**Religions**	Sunni Muslim
Capital	Male	**Organizations**	Comm., UN

The Maldive archipelago comprises over a thousand coral atolls (around two hundred of which are inhabited), in the Indian Ocean, southwest of India. Over eighty per cent of the land area is less than one metre above sea level. The main atolls are North and South Male

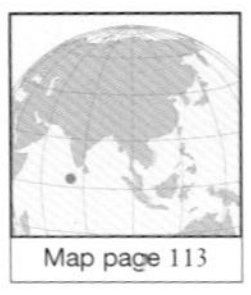
Map page 113

and Addu. The climate is hot, humid and monsoonal. There is little cultivation and almost all food is imported. Tourism has expanded rapidly and is the most important sector of the economy.

MALI
Republic of Mali

Area Sq Km	1 240 140	**Currency**	CFA franc
Area Sq Miles	478 821	**Languages**	French, Bambara, local languages
Population	13 518 000	**Religions**	Sunni Muslim, traditional beliefs, Christian
Capital	Bamako	**Organizations**	UN

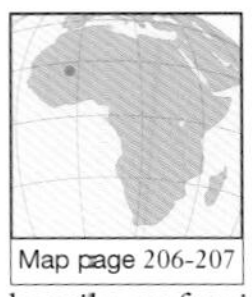
Map page 206-207

A landlocked state in west Africa, Mali is generally low-lying. Northern regions lie within the Sahara desert. To the south are marshes and savanna grassland. Rainfall is unreliable. Most of the population lives along the Niger and Falémé rivers. Exports include cotton, livestock and gold. Mali relies heavily on foreign aid.

MALTA
Republic of Malta

Area Sq Km	316	**Currency**	Maltese lira
Area Sq Miles	122	**Languages**	Maltese, English
Population	402 000	**Religions**	Roman Catholic
Capital	Valletta	**Organizations**	Comm., EU, UN

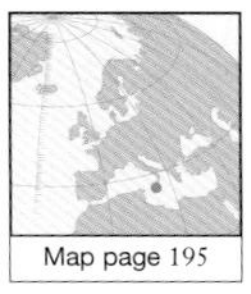
Map page 195

The islands of Malta and Gozo lie in the Mediterranean Sea, off the coast of southern Italy. The islands have hot, dry summers and mild winters. The economy depends on foreign trade, tourism and the manufacture of electronics and textiles. Main trading partners are the USA, France and Italy. Malta joined the European Union in May 2004.

MARSHALL ISLANDS
Republic of the Marshall Islands

Area Sq Km	181	**Currency**	United States dollar
Area Sq Miles	70	**Languages**	English, Marshallese
Population	62 000	**Religions**	Protestant, Roman Catholic
Capital	Delap-Uliga-Djarrit	**Organizations**	UN

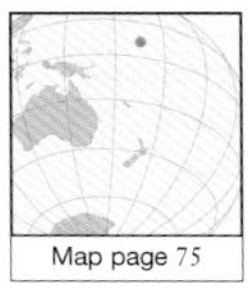
Map page 75

The Marshall Islands consist of over a thousand atolls and islands in the north Pacific Ocean. The main atolls are Majuro (home to half the population), Kwajalein, Jaluit, Enewetak and Bikini. The climate is tropical. About half the workforce is employed in farming or fishing. Tourism is a small source of foreign exchange and the islands depend heavily on aid from the USA.

Martinique
French Overseas Department

Area Sq Km	1 079	**Currency**	Euro
Area Sq Miles	417	**Languages**	French, creole
Population	396 000	**Religions**	Roman Catholic, traditional beliefs
Capital	Fort-de-France		

Martinique, one of the Caribbean Windward Islands, has volcanic peaks in the north, a populous central plain, and hills and beaches in the south. Tourism is a major source of income, and substantial aid comes from France. The main trading partners are France and Guadeloupe.

Map page 247

MAURITANIA
Islamic Arab and African Republic of Mauritania

Area Sq Km	1 030 700	**Currency**	Ouguiya
Area Sq Miles	397 955	**Languages**	Arabic, French, local languages
Population	3 069 000	**Religions**	Sunni Muslim
Capital	Nouakchott	**Organizations**	UN

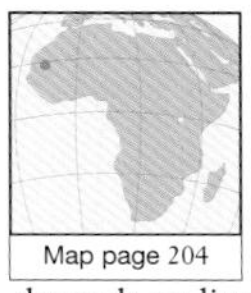
Map page 204

Mauritania is on the Atlantic coast of northwest Africa and lies almost entirely within the Sahara desert. Oases and a fertile strip along the Senegal river to the south are the only areas suitable for cultivation. The climate is generally hot and dry. About a quarter of Mauritanians live in the capital, Nouakchott. Most of the workforce depends on livestock rearing and subsistence farming. There are large deposits of iron ore which account for more than half of total exports. Mauritania's coastal waters are among the richest fishing grounds in the world. The main trading partners are France, Japan and Italy.

MAURITIUS
Republic of Mauritius

Area Sq Km	2 040	**Currency**	Mauritius rupee
Area Sq Miles	788	**Languages**	English, creole, Hindi, Bhojpuri, French
Population	1 245 000	**Religions**	Hindu, Roman Catholic, Sunni Muslim
Capital	Port Louis	**Organizations**	Comm., SADC, UN

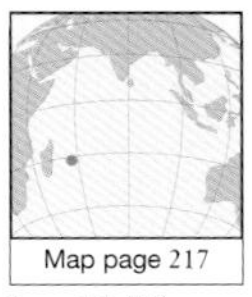
Map page 217

The state comprises Mauritius, Rodrigues and some twenty small islands in the Indian Ocean, east of Madagascar. The main island of Mauritius is volcanic in origin and has a coral coast, rising to a central plateau. Most of the population lives on the north and west sides of the island. The climate is warm and humid. The economy is based on sugar production, light manufacturing (chiefly clothing) and tourism.

Mayotte
French Departmental Collectivity

Area Sq Km	373	**Currency**	Euro
Area Sq Miles	144	**Languages**	French, Mahorian
Population	186 026	**Religions**	Sunni Muslim, Christian
Capital	Dzaoudzi		

Lying in the Indian Ocean off the east coast of central Africa, Mayotte is geographically part of the Comoro archipelago. The economy is based on agriculture, but Mayotte depends heavily on aid from France.

Map page 217

MEXICO
United Mexican States

Area Sq Km	1 972 545	**Currency**	Mexican peso
Area Sq Miles	761 604	**Languages**	Spanish, Amerindian languages
Population	107 029 000	**Religions**	Roman Catholic, Protestant
Capital	México	**Organizations**	APEC, OECD, UN

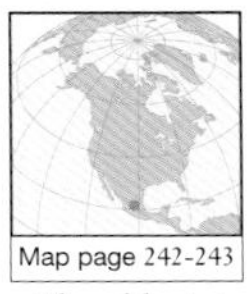
Map page 242-243

The largest country in Central America, Mexico extends south from the USA to Guatemala and Belize. Most of the country is high plateau flanked by the Sierra Madre mountains. The principal lowland is the Yucatán peninsula in the southeast. The climate is hot and humid in the lowlands, warm on the plateau and cool with cold winters in the mountains. The north is arid, while the far south has heavy rainfall. Mexico City is the second largest conurbation in the world and the country's economic centre. Agriculture involves a fifth of the workforce; crops include grains, coffee, cotton and vegetables. Mexico is rich in minerals, including copper, zinc, lead, tin, sulphur, and silver. It is one of the world's largest producers of oil, from vast reserves in the Gulf of Mexico. The oil and petrochemical industries still dominate the economy, but a variety of goods are produced, including iron and steel, motor vehicles, textiles, chemicals and food and tobacco products. Over three-quarters of all trade is with the USA.

MICRONESIA, FEDERATED STATES OF

Area Sq Km	701	**Currency**	United States dollar
Area Sq Miles	271	**Languages**	English, Chuukese, Pohnpeian, local languages
Population	110 000	**Religions**	Roman Catholic, Protestant
Capital	Palikir	**Organizations**	UN

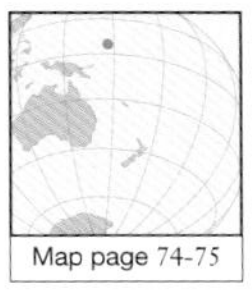
Map page 74-75

Micronesia comprises over six hundred atolls and islands of the Caroline Islands in the north Pacific Ocean. A third of the population lives on Pohnpei. The climate is tropical, with heavy rainfall. Fishing and subsistence farming are the main activities. Fish, garments and bananas are the main exports. Income is also derived from tourism and the licensing of foreign fishing fleets. The islands depend heavily on aid from the USA.

MOLDOVA
Republic of Moldova

Area Sq Km	33 700	**Currency**	Moldovan leu
Area Sq Miles	13 012	**Languages**	Romanian, Ukrainian, Gagauz, Russian
Population	4 206 000	**Religions**	Romanian Orthodox, Russian Orthodox
Capital	Chișinău	**Organizations**	CIS, UN

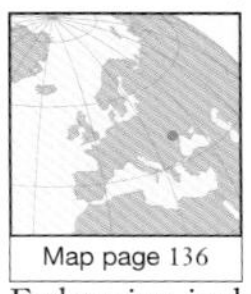
Map page 136

Moldova lies between Romania and Ukraine in eastern Europe. It consists of hilly steppe land, drained by the Prut and Dniester rivers. The economy is mainly agricultural, with sugar beet, tobacco, wine and fruit the chief products. Food processing, machinery and textiles are the main industries. The Russian Federation is the main trading partner.

MONACO
Principality of Monaco

Area Sq Km	2	**Currency**	Euro
Area Sq Miles	1	**Languages**	French, Monégasque, Italian
Population	35 000	**Religions**	Roman Catholic
Capital	Monaco-Ville	**Organizations**	UN

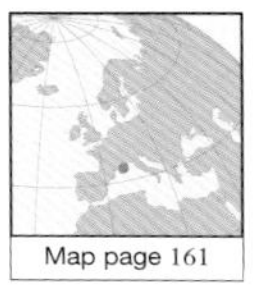
Map page 161

The principality occupies a rocky peninsula and a strip of land on France's Mediterranean coast. Monaco's economy depends on service industries (chiefly tourism, banking and finance) and light industry.

MONGOLIA

Area Sq Km	1 565 000	**Currency**	Tugrik (tögrög)
Area Sq Miles	604 250	**Languages**	Khalka (Mongolian), Kazakh, local languages
Population	2 646 000	**Religions**	Buddhist, Sunni Muslim
Capital	Ulaanbaatar	**Organizations**	UN

Mongolia is a landlocked country in eastern Asia between the Russian Federation and China. Much of it is high steppe land, with mountains and lakes in the west and north. In the south is the Gobi desert. Mongolia has long, cold winters and short, mild summers. A quarter of the population lives in the capital, Ulaanbaatar. Livestock breeding and agricultural processing are important. There are substantial mineral resources. Copper and textiles are the main exports.

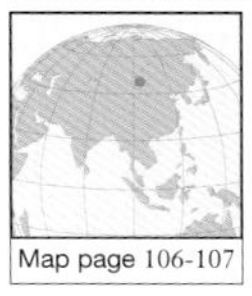
Map page 106-107

MONTENEGRO
Republic of Montenegro

Area Sq Km	13 812	**Currency**	Euro
Area Sq Miles	5 333	**Languages**	Serbian (Montenegrin), Albanian
Population	620 145	**Religions**	Montenegrin Orthodox, Sunni Muslim
Capital	Podgorica		

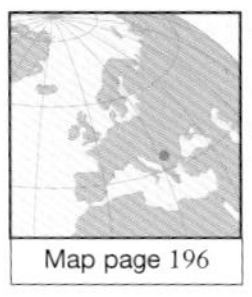
Map page 196

Montenegro was the last constituent republic of the former Yugoslavia to become an independent nation, in June 2006. At that time it opted to split from the state union of Serbia and Montenegro. Montenegro separates the much larger Serbia from the Adriatic coast.

Montserrat
United Kingdom Overseas Territory

Area Sq Km	100	**Currency**	East Caribbean dollar
Area Sq Miles	39	**Languages**	English
Population	4 000	**Religions**	Protestant, Roman Catholic
Capital	Plymouth	**Organizations**	CARICOM

An island in the Leeward Islands group in the Lesser Antilles, in the Caribbean. From 1995 to 1997 the volcanoes in the Soufrière Hills erupted for the first time since 1630. Over sixty per cent of the island was covered in volcanic ash and the capital was virtually destroyed. Many people emigrated, and the remaining population moved to the north of the island. Reconstruction is being funded by aid from the UK.

Map page 247

MOROCCO
Kingdom of Morocco

Area Sq Km	446 550	**Currency**	Moroccan dirham
Area Sq Miles	172 414	**Languages**	Arabic, Berber, French
Population	31 478 000	**Religions**	Sunni Muslim
Capital	Rabat	**Organizations**	UN

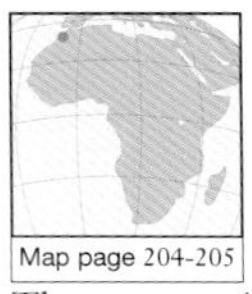
Map page 204-205

Lying in the northwest corner of Africa, Morocco has both Atlantic and Mediterranean coasts. The Atlas Mountains separate the arid south and disputed region of Western Sahara from the fertile regions of the west and north, which have a milder climate. Most Moroccans live on the Atlantic coastal plain. The economy is based on agriculture, phosphate mining and tourism; the most important industries are food processing, textiles and chemicals. France is the main trading partner.

MOZAMBIQUE
Republic of Mozambique

Area Sq Km	799 380	**Currency**	Metical
Area Sq Miles	308 642	**Languages**	Portuguese, Makua, Tsonga, local languages
Population	19 792 000	**Religions**	Traditional beliefs, Roman Catholic, Sunni Muslim
Capital	Maputo	**Organizations**	Comm., SADC, UN

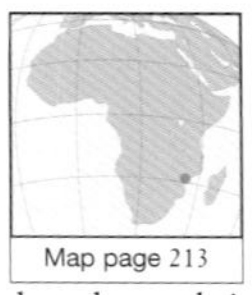
Map page 213

Mozambique lies on the east coast of southern Africa. The land is mainly a savanna plateau drained by the Zambezi and Limpopo rivers, with highlands to the north. Most of the population lives on the coast or in the river valleys. In general the climate is tropical with winter rainfall, but droughts occur. The economy is based on subsistence agriculture. Exports include shrimps, cashews, cotton and sugar, but Mozambique relies heavily on aid, and remains one of the least developed countries in the world.

MYANMAR (Burma)
Union of Myanmar

Area Sq Km	676 577	**Currency**	Kyat
Area Sq Miles	261 228	**Languages**	Burmese, Shan, Karen, local languages
Population	50 519 000	**Religions**	Buddhist, Christian, Sunni Muslim
Capital	Naypyidaw/Yangôn (Rangoon)	**Organizations**	ASEAN, UN

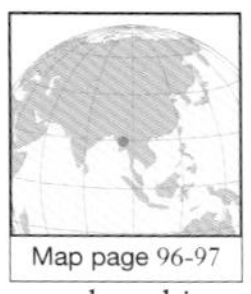
Map page 96-97

Myanmar (Burma) is in Southeast Asia, bordering the Bay of Bengal and the Andaman Sea. Most of the population lives in the valley and delta of the Irrawaddy river, which is flanked by mountains and high plateaus. The climate is hot and monsoonal, and rainforest covers much of the land. Most of the workforce is employed in agriculture. Myanmar is rich in minerals, including zinc, lead, copper and silver. Political and social unrest and lack of foreign investment have affected economic development.

NAMIBIA
Republic of Namibia

Area Sq Km	824 292	**Currency**	Namibian dollar
Area Sq Miles	318 261	**Languages**	English, Afrikaans, German, Ovambo, local languages
Population	2 031 000	**Religions**	Protestant, Roman Catholic
Capital	Windhoek	**Organizations**	Comm., SADC, UN

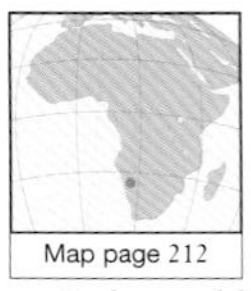
Map page 212

Namibia lies on the Atlantic coast of southern Africa. Mountain ranges separate the coastal Namib Desert from the interior plateau, bordered to the south and east by the Kalahari Desert. The country is hot and dry, but some summer rain in the north supports crops and livestock. Most of the workforce is employed in agriculture, although the economy is based on mineral extraction –predominantly diamonds, but also uranium, lead, zinc and silver. Fishing is increasingly important. The economy is closely linked to that of the Republic of South Africa.

NAURU
Republic of Nauru

Area Sq Km	21	**Currency**	Australian dollar
Area Sq Miles	8	**Languages**	Nauruan, English
Population	14 000	**Religions**	Protestant, Roman Catholic
Capital	Yaren	**Organizations**	Comm., UN

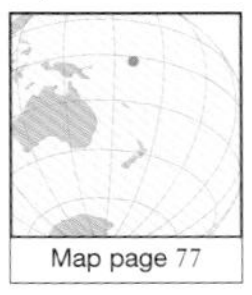
Map page 77

Nauru is a coral island near the Equator in the Pacific Ocean. It has a fertile coastal strip and a barren central plateau. The climate is tropical. The economy is based on phosphate mining, but reserves are near exhaustion and replacement of this income is a serious long-term problem.

NEPAL
Kingdom of Nepal

Area Sq Km	147 181	**Currency**	Nepalese rupee
Area Sq Miles	56 827	**Languages**	Nepali, Maithili, Bhojpuri, English, local languages
Population	27 133 000	**Religions**	Hindu, Buddhist, Sunni Muslim
Capital	Kathmandu	**Organizations**	UN

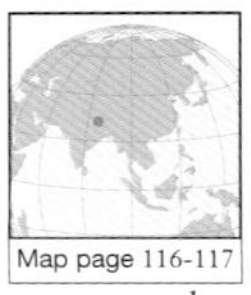
Map page 116-117

Nepal lies in the eastern Himalaya mountains between India and China. High mountains (including Everest) dominate the north. Most people live in the temperate central valleys and subtropical southern plains. The economy is based largely on agriculture and forestry. There is some manufacturing, chiefly of textiles and carpets, and tourism is important. Nepal relies heavily on foreign aid.

NETHERLANDS
Kingdom of the Netherlands

Area Sq Km	41 526	**Currency**	Euro
Area Sq Miles	16 033	**Languages**	Dutch, Frisian
Population	16 299 000	**Religions**	Roman Catholic, Protestant, Sunni Muslim
Capital	Amsterdam/ 's-Gravenhage (The Hague)	**Organizations**	EU, NATO, OECD, UN

The Netherlands lies on the North Sea coast of western Europe. Apart from low hills in the far southeast, the land is flat and low-lying, much of it below sea level. The coastal region includes the delta of five rivers and polders (reclaimed land), protected by sand dunes, dykes and canals. The climate is temperate, with cool summers and mild winters. Rainfall is spread evenly throughout the year. The Netherlands is a densely populated and highly urbanized country, with the majority of the population living in the cities of Amsterdam, Rotterdam and The Hague. Horticulture and dairy farming are important activities, although they employ less than four per cent of the workforce. The Netherlands ranks as the world's third agricultural exporter, and is a leading producer and exporter of natural gas from reserves in the North Sea. The economy is based mainly on international trade and manufacturing industry. The main industries produce food products, chemicals, machinery, electrical and electronic goods and transport equipment. Germany is the main trading partner, followed by other European Union countries.

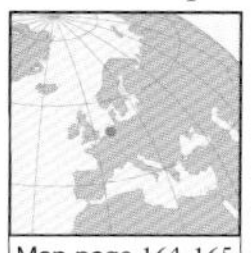
Map page 164-165

Netherlands Antilles
Self-governing NetherlandsTerritory

Area Sq Km	800	**Currency**	Netherlands Antilles guilder
Area Sq Miles	309	**Languages**	Dutch, Papiamento, English
Population	183 000	**Religions**	Roman Catholic, Protestant
Capital	Willemstad		

The territory comprises two separate island groups: Curaçao and Bonaire off the northern coast of Venezuela, and Saba, Sint Eustatius and the southern part of St-Martin (Sint Maarten) in the Lesser Antilles. Tourism, oil refining and offshore finance are the mainstays of the economy. The main trading partners are the USA, Venezuela and Mexico.

Map page 247

New Caledonia
French Overseas Country

Area Sq Km	19 058	**Currency**	CFP franc
Area Sq Miles	7 358	**Languages**	French, local languages
Population	237 000	**Religions**	Roman Catholic, Protestant, Sunni Muslim
Capital	Nouméa		

An island group lying in the southwest Pacific, with a sub-tropical climate. New Caledonia has over one-fifth of the world's nickel reserves, and the main economic activity is metal mining. Tourism is also important. New Caledonia relies on aid from France.

Map page 78

NEW ZEALAND

Area Sq Km	270 534	**Currency**	New Zealand dollar
Area Sq Miles	104 454	**Languages**	English, Maori
Population	4 028 000	**Religions**	Protestant, Roman Catholic
Capital	Wellington	**Organizations**	APEC, Comm., OECD, UN

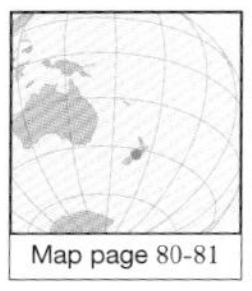
Map page 80-81

New Zealand comprises two main islands separated by the narrow Cook Strait, and a number of smaller islands. North Island, where three-quarters of the population lives, has mountain ranges, broad fertile valleys and a central plateau with hot springs and active volcanoes. South Island is also mountainous, with the Southern Alps running its entire length. The only major lowland area is the Canterbury Plains in the centre-east. The climate is generally temperate, although South Island has colder winters. Farming is the mainstay of the economy. New Zealand is one of the world's leading producers of meat (beef, lamb and mutton), wool and dairy products; fruit and fish are also important. Hydroelectric and geothermal power provide much of the country's energy needs. Other industries produce timber, wood pulp, iron, aluminium, machinery and chemicals. Tourism is the fastest growing sector of the economy. The main trading partners are Australia, the USA and Japan.

NICARAGUA
Republic of Nicaragua

Area Sq Km	130 000	**Currency**	Córdoba
Area Sq Miles	50 193	**Languages**	Spanish, Amerindian languages
Population	5 487 000	**Religions**	Roman Catholic, Protestant
Capital	Managua	**Organizations**	UN

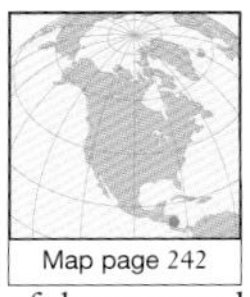
Map page 242

Nicaragua lies at the heart of Central America, with both Pacific and Caribbean coasts. Mountain ranges separate the east, which is largely rainforest, from the more developed western regions, which include Lake Nicaragua and some active volcanoes. The highest land is in the north. The climate is tropical. Nicaragua is one of the western hemisphere's poorest countries, and the economy is largely agricultural. Exports include coffee, seafood, cotton and bananas. The USA is the main trading partner. Nicaragua has a huge national debt, and relies heavily on foreign aid.

NIGER
Republic of Niger

Area Sq Km	1 267 000	**Currency**	CFA franc
Area Sq Miles	489 191	**Languages**	French, Hausa, Fulani, local languages
Population	13 957 000	**Religions**	Sunni Muslim, traditional beliefs
Capital	Niamey	**Organizations**	UN

A landlocked state of west Africa, Niger lies mostly within the Sahara desert, but with savanna in the south and in the Niger valley area. The mountains of the Massif de l'Aïr dominate central regions. Much of the country is hot and dry. The south has some summer rainfall, although droughts occur. The economy depends on subsistence farming and herding, and uranium exports, but Niger is one of the world's least developed countries and relies heavily on foreign aid. France is the main trading partner.

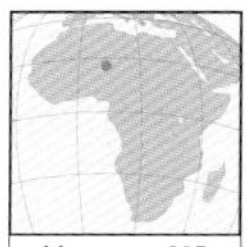
Map page 207

NIGERIA
Federal Republic of Nigeria

Area Sq Km	923 768	**Currency**	Naira
Area Sq Miles	356 669	**Languages**	English, Hausa, Yoruba, Ibo, Fulani, local languages
Population	131 530 000	**Religions**	Sunni Muslim, Christian, traditional beliefs
Capital	Abuja	**Organizations**	Comm., OPEC, UN

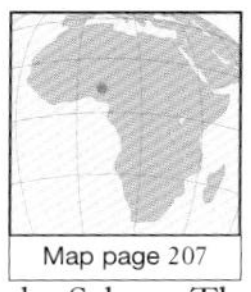
Map page 207

Nigeria is in west Africa, on the Gulf of Guinea, and is the most populous country in Africa. The Niger delta dominates coastal areas, fringed with sandy beaches, mangrove swamps and lagoons. Inland is a belt of rainforest which gives way to woodland or savanna on high plateaus. The far north is the semi-desert edge of the Sahara. The climate is tropical, with heavy summer rainfall in the south but low rainfall in the north. Most of the population lives in the coastal lowlands or in the west. About half the workforce is involved in agriculture, mainly growing subsistence crops. Agricultural production, however, has failed to keep up with demand, and Nigeria is now a net importer of food. Cocoa and rubber are the only significant export crops. The economy is heavily dependent on vast oil resources in the Niger delta and in shallow offshore waters, and oil accounts for over ninety per cent of export earnings. Nigeria also has natural gas reserves and some mineral deposits, but these are largely undeveloped. Industry involves mainly oil refining, chemicals (chiefly fertilizers), agricultural processing, textiles, steel manufacture and vehicle assembly. Political instability in the past has left Nigeria with heavy debts, poverty and unemployment.

Niue
Self-governing New Zealand Overseas Territory

Area Sq Km	258	**Currency**	New Zealand dollar
Area Sq Miles	100	**Languages**	English, Niuean
Population	1 000	**Religions**	Christian
Capital	Alofi		

Niue, one of the largest coral islands in the world, lies in the south Pacific Ocean about 500 kilometres (300 miles) east of Tonga. The economy depends on aid and remittances from New Zealand. The population is declining because of migration to New Zealand.

Map page 81

Norfolk Island
Australian External Territory

Area Sq Km	35	**Currency**	Australian dollar
Area Sq Miles	14	**Languages**	English
Population	2 601	**Religions**	Protestant, Roman Catholic
Capital	Kingston		

In the south Pacific Ocean, Norfolk Island lies between Vanuatu and New Zealand. Tourism has increased steadily and is the mainstay of the economy and provides revenues for agricultural development.

Map page 82

Northern Mariana Islands
United States Commonwealth

Area Sq Km	477	**Currency**	United States dollar
Area Sq Miles	184	**Languages**	English, Chamorro, local languages
Population	81 000	**Religions**	Roman Catholic
Capital	Capitol Hill		

A chain of islands in the northwest Pacific Ocean, extending over 550 kilometres (350 miles) north to south. The main island is Saipan. Tourism is a major industry, employing approximately half the workforce.

Map page 74

NORTH KOREA
People's Democratic Republic of Korea

Area Sq Km	120 538	**Currency**	North Korean won
Area Sq Miles	46 540	**Languages**	Korean
Population	22 488 000	**Religions**	Traditional beliefs, Chondoist, Buddhist
Capital	P'yŏngyang	**Organizations**	UN

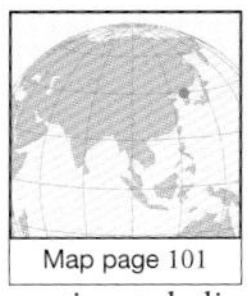
Map page 101

Occupying the northern half of the Korean peninsula in eastern Asia, North Korea is a rugged and mountainous country. The principal lowlands and the main agricultural areas are the plains in the southwest. More than half the population lives in urban areas, mainly on the coastal plains. North Korea has a continental climate, with cold, dry winters and hot, wet summers. Approximately one-third of the workforce is involved in agriculture, mainly growing food crops on cooperative farms. Various minerals, notably iron ore, are mined and are the basis of the country's heavy industries. Exports include minerals (lead, magnesite and zinc) and metal products (chiefly iron and steel). The economy declined after 1991, when ties to the former USSR and eastern bloc collapsed, and there have been serious food shortages.

NORWAY
Kingdom of Norway

Area Sq Km	323 878	**Currency**	Norwegian krone
Area Sq Miles	125 050	**Languages**	Norwegian
Population	4 620 000	**Religions**	Protestant, Roman Catholic
Capital	Oslo	**Organizations**	NATO, OECD, UN

Norway stretches along the north and west coasts of Scandinavia, from the Arctic Ocean to the North Sea. Its extensive coastline is indented with fjords and fringed with many islands. Inland, the terrain is mountainous, with coniferous forests and lakes in the south. The only major lowland areas are along the southern North Sea and Skagerrak coasts, where most of the population lives. The climate is modified by the effect of the North Atlantic Drift ocean current. Norway has vast petroleum and natural gas resources in the North Sea. It is one of western Europe's leading producers of oil and gas, and exports of oil account for approximately half of total export earnings. Related industries include engineering (oil and gas platforms) and petrochemicals. More traditional industries process local raw materials, particularly fish, timber and minerals. Agriculture is limited, but fishing and fish farming are important. Norway is the world's leading exporter of farmed salmon. Merchant shipping and tourism are major sources of foreign exchange.

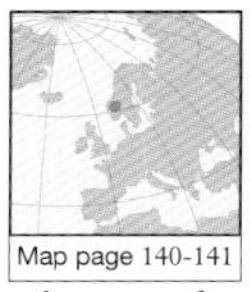
Map page 140-141

OMAN
Sultanate of Oman

Area Sq Km	309 500	**Currency**	Omani riyal
Area Sq Miles	119 499	**Languages**	Arabic, Baluchi, Indian languages
Population	2 567 000	**Religions**	Ibadhi Muslim, Sunni Muslim
Capital	Masqaţ (Muscat)	**Organizations**	UN

In southwest Asia, Oman occupies the east and southeast coasts of the Arabian Peninsula and an enclave north of the United Arab Emirates. Most of the land is desert, with mountains in the north and south. The climate is hot and mainly dry. Most of the population lives on the coastal strip on the Gulf of Oman. The majority depend on farming and fishing, but the oil and gas industries dominate the economy with around eighty per cent of export revenues coming from oil.

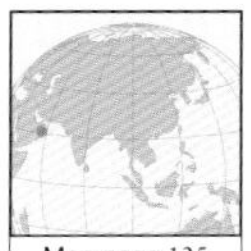
Map page 125

PAKISTAN
Islamic Republic of Pakistan

Area Sq Km	803 940	**Currency**	Pakistani rupee
Area Sq Miles	310 403	**Languages**	Urdu, Punjabi, Sindhi, Pushtu, English
Population	157 935 000	**Religions**	Sunni Muslim, Shi'a Muslim, Christian, Hindu
Capital	Islamabad	**Organizations**	Comm., UN

Pakistan is in the northwest part of the Indian subcontinent in south Asia, on the Arabian Sea. The east and south are dominated by the great basin of the Indus river system. This is the main agricultural area and contains most of the predominantly rural population. To the north the land rises to the mountains of the Karakoram, Hindu Kush and Himalaya mountains. The west is semi-desert plateaus and mountain ranges. The climate ranges between dry desert, and arctic tundra on the mountain tops. Temperatures are generally warm and rainfall is monsoonal. Agriculture is the main sector of the economy, employing approximately half of the workforce, and is based on extensive irrigation schemes. Pakistan is one of the world's leading producers of cotton and a major exporter of rice. Pakistan produces natural gas and has a variety of mineral deposits including coal and gold, but they are little developed. The main industries are textiles and clothing manufacture and food processing, with fabrics and ready-made clothing the leading exports. Pakistan also produces leather goods, fertilizers, chemicals, paper and precision instruments. The country depends heavily on foreign aid and remittances from workers abroad.

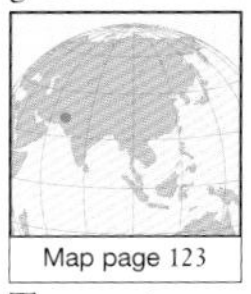
Map page 123

PALAU
Republic of Palau

Area Sq Km	497	**Currency**	United States dollar
Area Sq Miles	192	**Languages**	Palauan, English
Population	20 000	**Religions**	Roman Catholic, Protestant, traditional beliefs
Capital	Koror	**Organizations**	UN

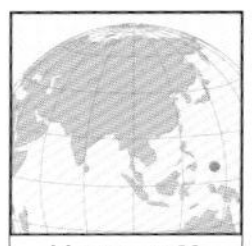
Map page 92

Palau comprises over three hundred islands in the western Caroline Islands, in the west Pacific Ocean. The climate is tropical. The economy is based on farming, fishing and tourism, but Palau is heavily dependent on aid from the USA.

PANAMA
Republic of Panama

Area Sq Km	77 082	**Currency**	Balboa
Area Sq Miles	29 762	**Languages**	Spanish, English, Amerindian languages
Population	3 232 000	**Religions**	Roman Catholic, Protestant, Sunni Muslim
Capital	Panamá	**Organizations**	UN

Panama is the most southerly state in central America and has Pacific and Caribbean coasts. It is hilly, with mountains in the west and jungle near the Colombian border. The climate is tropical. Most of the population lives on the drier Pacific side. The economy is based mainly on services related to the Panama Canal: shipping, banking and tourism. Exports include bananas, shrimps, coffee, clothing and fish products. The USA is the main trading partner.

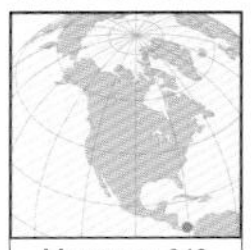
Map page 242

PAPUA NEW GUINEA
Independent State of Papua New Guinea

Area Sq Km	462 840	**Currency**	Kina
Area Sq Miles	178 704	**Languages**	English, Tok Pisin (creole), local languages
Population	5 887 000	**Religions**	Protestant, Roman Catholic, traditional beliefs
Capital	Port Moresby	**Organizations**	Comm., UN

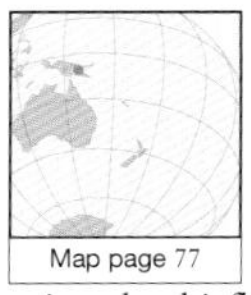
Map page 77

Papua New Guinea occupies the eastern half of the island of New Guinea and includes many island groups. It has a forested and mountainous interior, bordered by swampy plains, and a tropical monsoon climate. Most of the workforce are farmers. Timber, copra, coffee and cocoa are important, but exports are dominated by minerals, chiefly gold and copper. The country depends on foreign aid. Australia, Japan and Singapore are the main trading partners.

PARAGUAY
Republic of Paraguay

Area Sq Km	406 752	**Currency**	Guaraní
Area Sq Miles	157 048	**Languages**	Spanish, Guaraní
Population	6 158 000	**Religions**	Roman Catholic, Protestant
Capital	Asunción	**Organizations**	UN

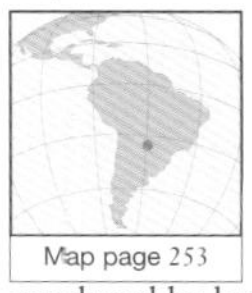
Map page 253

Paraguay is a landlocked country in central South America, bordering Bolivia, Brazil and Argentina. The Paraguay river separates a sparsely populated western zone of marsh and flat alluvial plains from a more developed, hilly and forested region to the east and south. The climate is subtropical. Virtually all electricity is produced by hydroelectric plants, and surplus power is exported to Brazil and Argentina. The hydroelectric dam at Itaipú is one of the largest in the world. The mainstay of the economy is agriculture and related industries. Exports include cotton, soya bean and edible oil products, timber and meat. Brazil and Argentina are the main trading partners.

PERU
Republic of Peru

Area Sq Km	1 285 216	**Currency**	Sol
Area Sq Miles	496 225	**Languages**	Spanish, Quechua, Aymara
Population	27 968 000	**Religions**	Roman Catholic, Protestant
Capital	Lima	**Organizations**	APEC, UN

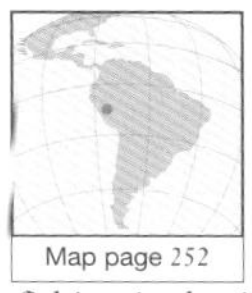
Map page 252

Peru lies on the Pacific coast of South America. Most Peruvians live on the coastal strip and on the plateaus of the high Andes mountains. East of the Andes is the Amazon rainforest. The coast is temperate with low rainfall while the east is hot, humid and wet. Agriculture involves one-third of the workforce and fishing is also important. Agriculture and fishing have both been disrupted by the El Niño climatic effect in recent years. Sugar, cotton, coffee and, illegally, coca are the main cash crops. Copper and copper products, fishmeal, zinc products, coffee, petroleum and its products, and textiles are the main exports. The USA and the European Union are the main trading partners.

PHILIPPINES
Republic of the Philippines

Area Sq Km	300 000	**Currency**	Philippine peso
Area Sq Miles	115 831	**Languages**	English, Filipino, Tagalog, Cebuano, local languages
Population	83 054 000	**Religions**	Roman Catholic, Protestant, Sunni Muslim
Capital	Manila	**Organizations**	APEC, ASEAN, UN

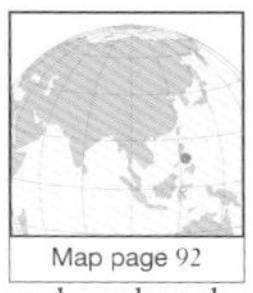
Map page 92

The Philippines, in Southeast Asia, consists of over seven thousand islands and atolls lying between the South China Sea and the Pacific Ocean. The islands of Luzon and Mindanao account for two-thirds of the land area. They and nine other fairly large islands are mountainous and forested. There are active volcanoes, and earthquakes and tropical storms are common. Most of the population lives in the plains on the larger islands or on the coastal strips. The climate is hot and humid with heavy monsoonal rainfall. Rice, coconuts, sugar cane, pineapples and bananas are the main agricultural crops, and fishing is also important. Main exports are electronic equipment, machinery and transport equipment, garments and coconut products. Foreign aid and remittances from workers abroad are important to the economy, which faces problems of high population growth rate and high unemployment. The USA and Japan are the main trading partners.

Pitcairn Islands
United Kingdom Overseas Territory

Area Sq Km	45	**Currency**	New Zealand dollar
Area Sq Miles	17	**Languages**	English
Population	47	**Religions**	Protestant
Capital	Adamstown		

An island group in the southeast Pacific Ocean consisting of Pitcairn Island and three uninhabited islands. It was originally settled by mutineers from *HMS Bounty* in 1790.

Map page 75

POLAND
Polish Republic

Area Sq Km	312 683	**Currency**	Złoty
Area Sq Miles	120 728	**Languages**	Polish, German
Population	38 530 000	**Religions**	Roman Catholic, Polish Orthodox
Capital	Warszawa (Warsaw)	**Organizations**	EU, NATO, OECD, UN

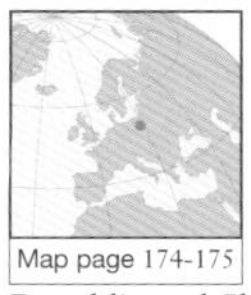
Map page 174–175

Poland lies on the Baltic coast of eastern Europe. The Oder (Odra) and Vistula (Wisła) river deltas dominate the coast. Inland, much of the country is low-lying, with woods and lakes. In the south the land rises to the Sudeten Mountains and the western part of the Carpathian Mountains, which form the borders with the Czech Republic and Slovakia respectively. The climate is continental. Around a quarter of the workforce is involved in agriculture, and exports include livestock products and sugar. The economy is heavily industrialized, with mining and manufacturing accounting for forty per cent of national income. Poland is one of the world's major producers of coal, and also produces copper, zinc, lead, sulphur and natural gas. The main industries are machinery and transport equipment, shipbuilding, and metal and chemical production. Exports include machinery and transport equipment, manufactured goods, food and live animals. Germany is the main trading partner. Poland joined the European Union in May 2004.

PORTUGAL
Portuguese Republic

Area Sq Km	88 940	**Currency**	Euro
Area Sq Miles	34 340	**Languages**	Portuguese
Population	10 495 000	**Religions**	Roman Catholic, Protestant
Capital	Lisboa (Lisbon)	**Organizations**	EU, NATO, OECD, UN

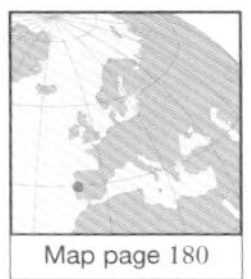
Map page 180

Portugal lies in the western part of the Iberian peninsula in southwest Europe, has an Atlantic coastline and is bordered by Spain to the north and east. The island groups of the Azores and Madeira are parts of Portugal. On the mainland, the land north of the river Tagus (Tejo) is mostly highland, with extensive forests of pine and cork. South of the river is undulating lowland. The climate in the north is cool and moist; the south is warmer, with dry, mild winters. Most Portuguese live near the coast, and more than one-third of the total population lives around the capital, Lisbon (Lisboa). Agriculture, fishing and forestry involve approximately ten per cent of the workforce. Mining and manufacturing are the main sectors of the economy. Portugal produces kaolin, copper, tin, zinc, tungsten and salt. Exports include textiles, clothing and footwear, electrical machinery and transport equipment, cork and wood products, and chemicals. Service industries, chiefly tourism and banking, are important to the economy, as are remittances from workers abroad. Most trade is with other European Union countries.

PUERTO RICO
United States Commonwealth

Area Sq Km	9 104	**Currency**	United States dollar
Area Sq Miles	3 515	**Languages**	Spanish, English
Population	3 955 000	**Religions**	Roman Catholic, Protestant
Capital	San Juan		

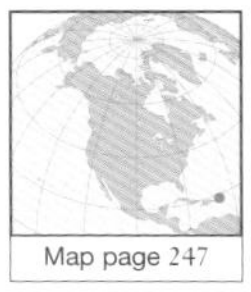
Map page 247

The Caribbean island of Puerto Rico has a forested, hilly interior, coastal plains and a tropical climate. Half of the population lives in the San Juan area. The economy is based on manufacturing (chiefly chemicals, electronics and food), tourism and agriculture. The USA is the main trading partner.

QATAR
State of Qatar

Area Sq Km	11 437	**Currency**	Qatari riyal
Area Sq Miles	4 416	**Languages**	Arabic
Population	813 000	**Religions**	Sunni Muslim
Capital	Ad Dawḩah (Doha)	**Organizations**	OPEC, UN

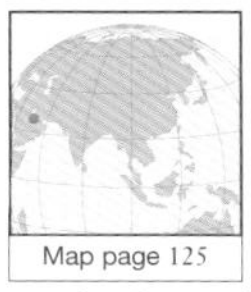
Map page 125

Qatar occupies a peninsula in southwest Asia that extends northwards from east-central Saudi Arabia into The Gulf. The land is flat and barren with sand dunes and salt pans. The climate is hot and mainly dry. Most people live in the area of the capital, Doha. The economy is heavily dependent on oil and natural gas production and the oil-refining industry. Income also comes from overseas investment. Japan is the largest trading partner.

Réunion
French Overseas Department

Area Sq Km	2 551	**Currency**	Euro
Area Sq Miles	985	**Languages**	French, creole
Population	785 000	**Religions**	Roman Catholic
Capital	St-Denis		

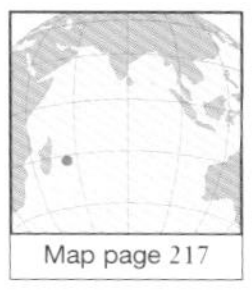
Map page 217

The Indian Ocean island of Réunion is mountainous, with coastal lowlands and a warm climate. The economy depends on tourism, French aid, and exports of sugar. Several widely-dispersed and uninhabited islets to the west are administered from Réunion.

ROMANIA

Area Sq Km	237 500	**Currency**	Romanian leu
Area Sq Miles	91 699	**Languages**	Romanian, Hungarian
Population	21 711 000	**Religions**	Romanian Orthodox, Protestant, Roman Catholic
Capital	București (Bucharest)	**Organizations**	NATO, UN

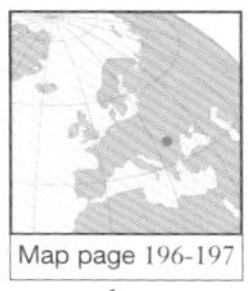
Map page 196–197

Romania lies in eastern Europe, on the northwest coast of the Black Sea. Mountains separate the Transylvanian Basin in the centre of the country from the populous plains of the east and south and from the Danube delta. The climate is continental. Romania has mineral resources (zinc, lead, silver and gold) and oil and natural gas reserves. Economic development has been slow and sporadic, but measures to accelerate change were introduced in 1999. Agriculture employs over one-third of the workforce. The main exports are textiles, mineral products, chemicals, machinery and footwear. The main trading partners are Germany and Italy.

RUSSIAN FEDERATION

Area Sq Km	17 075 400	**Currency**	Russian rouble
Area Sq Miles	6 592 849	**Languages**	Russian, Tatar, Ukrainian, local languages
Population	143 202 000	**Religions**	Russian Orthodox, Sunni Muslim, Protestant
Capital	Moskva (Moscow)	**Organizations**	APEC, CIS, UN

The Russian Federation occupies much of eastern Europe and all of northern Asia, and is the world's largest country. It borders fourteen countries to the west and south and has long coastlines on the Arctic and Pacific Oceans to the north and east. European Russia lies west of the Ural Mountains. To the south the land rises to uplands and the Caucasus mountains on the border with Georgia and Azerbaijan. East of the Urals lies the flat West Siberian Plain and the Central Siberian Plateau. In the south-east is Lake Baikal, the world's deepest lake, and the Sayan ranges on the border with Kazakhstan and Mongolia. Eastern Siberia is rugged and mountainous, with many active volcanoes in the Kamchatka Peninsula. The country's major rivers are the Volga in the west and the Ob', Irtysh, Yenisey, Lena and Amur in Siberia. The climate and

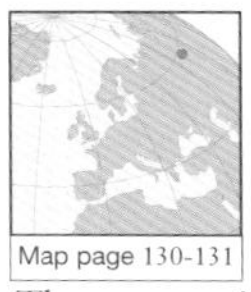
Map page 130–131

vegetation range between arctic tundra in the north and semi-arid steppe towards the Black and Caspian Sea coasts in the south. In general, the climate is continental with extreme temperatures. The majority of the population (the eighth largest in the world), and industry and agriculture are concentrated in European Russia. The economy is dependent on exploitation of raw materials and on heavy industry. Russia has a wealth of mineral resources, although they are often difficult to exploit because of climate and remote locations. It is one of the world's leading producers of petroleum, natural gas and coal as well as iron ore, nickel, copper, bauxite, and many precious and rare metals. Forests cover over forty per cent of the land area and supply an important timber, paper and pulp industry. Approximately eight per cent of the land is suitable for cultivation, but farming is generally inefficient and food, especially grains, must be imported. Fishing is important and Russia has a large fleet operating around the world. The transition to a market economy has been slow and difficult, with considerable underemployment. As well as mining and extractive industries there is a wide range of manufacturing industry, from steel mills to aircraft and space vehicles, shipbuilding, synthetic fabrics, plastics, cotton fabrics, consumer durables, chemicals and fertilizers. Exports include fuels, metals, machinery, chemicals and forest products. The most important trading partners include Germany, the USA and Belarus.

RWANDA
Republic of Rwanda

Area Sq Km	26 338	**Currency**	Rwandan franc
Area Sq Miles	10 169	**Languages**	Kinyarwanda, French, English
Population	9 038 000	**Religions**	Roman Catholic, traditional beliefs, Protestant
Capital	Kigali	**Organizations**	UN

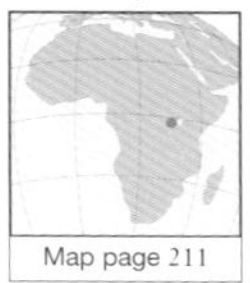
Map page 211

Rwanda, the most densely populated country in Africa, is situated in the mountains and plateaus to the east of the western branch of the Great Rift Valley in east Africa. The climate is warm with a summer dry season. Rwanda depends on subsistence farming, coffee and tea exports, light industry and foreign aid. The country is slowly recovering from serious internal conflict which caused devastation in the early 1990s.

Saba part of Netherlands Antilles

Area Sq Km (Miles) 13 (5) **Population** 1 387 **Capital** Bottom

An island in the Leeward Islands in the Lesser Antilles, in the Caribbean to the south of St-Martin.

Map page 247

St-Barthélemy Dependency of Guadeloupe (France)

Area Sq Km (Miles) 21 (8) **Population** 6 852 **Capital** Gustavia

An island in the Leeward Islands in the Lesser Antilles, in the Caribbean south of St-Martin. Tourism is the main economic activity.

Map page 247

St Helena
United Kingdom Overseas Territory

Area Sq Km	121	**Currency**	St Helena pound
Area Sq Miles	47	**Languages**	English
Population	5 000	**Religions**	Protestant, Roman Catholic
Capital	Jamestown		

St Helena and its dependencies Ascension and Tristan da Cunha are isolated island groups lying in the south Atlantic Ocean. St Helena is a rugged island of volcanic origin. The main activity is fishing, but the economy relies on financial aid from the UK. Main trading partners are the UK and South Africa.

Map page 216

ST KITTS AND NEVIS
Federation of St Kitts and Nevis

Area Sq Km	261	**Currency**	East Caribbean dollar
Area Sq Miles	101	**Languages**	English, creole
Population	43 000	**Religions**	Protestant, Roman Catholic
Capital	Basseterre	**Organizations**	CARICOM, Comm., UN

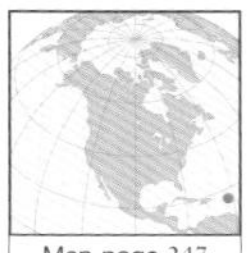
Map page 247

St Kitts and Nevis are in the Leeward Islands, in the Caribbean. Both volcanic islands are mountainous and forested, with sandy beaches and a warm, wet climate. About three-quarters of the population lives on St Kitts. Agriculture is the main activity, with sugar the main product. Tourism and manufacturing (chiefly garments and electronic components) and offshore banking are important activities.

ST LUCIA

Area Sq Km	616	**Currency**	East Caribbean dollar
Area Sq Miles	238	**Languages**	English, creole
Population	161 000	**Religions**	Roman Catholic, Protestant
Capital	Castries	**Organizations**	CARICOM, Comm., UN

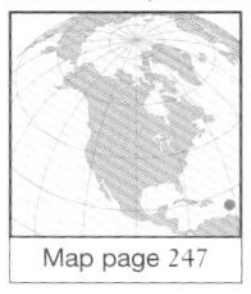
Map page 247

St Lucia, one of the Windward Islands in the Caribbean Sea, is a volcanic island with forested mountains, hot springs, sandy beaches and a wet tropical climate. Agriculture is the main activity, with bananas accounting for approximately forty per cent of export earnings. Tourism, agricultural processing and light manufacturing are increasingly important.

St-Martin Dependency of Guadeloupe (France)

Area Sq Km (Miles) 54 (21) **Population** 29 078 **Capital** Marigot

The northern part of one of the Leeward Islands, in the Caribbean. The other part of the island is part of the Netherlands Antilles (Sint Maarten). Tourism is the main source of income.

Map page 247

St Pierre and Miquelon
French Territorial Collectivity

Area Sq Km	242	**Currency**	Euro
Area Sq Miles	93	**Languages**	French
Population	6 000	**Religions**	Roman Catholic
Capital	St-Pierre		

A group of islands off the south coast of Newfoundland in eastern Canada. The islands are largely unsuitable for agriculture, and fishing and fish processing are the most important activities. The islands rely heavily on financial assistance from France.

Map page 225

ST VINCENT AND THE GRENADINES

Area Sq Km	389	**Currency**	East Caribbean dollar
Area Sq Miles	150	**Languages**	English, creole
Population	119 000	**Religions**	Protestant, Roman Catholic
Capital	Kingstown	**Organizations**	CARICOM, Comm., UN

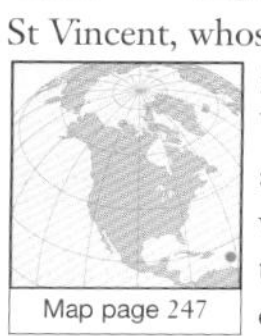
Map page 247

St Vincent, whose territory includes islets and cays in the Grenadines, is in the Windward Islands, in the Caribbean. St Vincent itself is forested and mountainous, with an active volcano, Soufrière. The climate is tropical and wet. The economy is based mainly on agriculture and tourism. Bananas account for approximately one-third of export earnings and arrowroot is also important. Most trade is with the USA and other CARICOM countries.

SAMOA
Independent State of Samoa

Area Sq Km	2 831	**Currency**	Tala
Area Sq Miles	1 093	**Languages**	Samoan, English
Population	185 000	**Religions**	Protestant, Roman Catholic
Capital	Apia	**Organizations**	Comm., UN

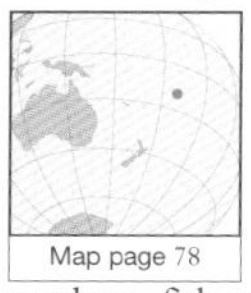
Map page 78

Samoa consists of two larger mountainous and forested islands, Savai'i and Upolu, and seven smaller islands, in the south Pacific Ocean. Over half the population lives on Upolu. The climate is tropical. The economy is based on agriculture, with some fishing and light manufacturing. Traditional exports are coconut products, fish and beer. Tourism is increasing, but the islands depend on workers' remittances and foreign aid.

SAN MARINO
Republic of San Marino

Area Sq Km	61	**Currency**	Euro
Area Sq Miles	24	**Languages**	Italian
Population	28 000	**Religions**	Roman Catholic
Capital	San Marino	**Organizations**	UN

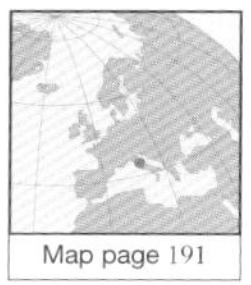
Map page 191

Landlocked San Marino lies in northeast Italy. A third of the people live in the capital. There is some agriculture and light industry, but most income comes from tourism. Italy is the main trading partner.

SÃO TOMÉ AND PRÍNCIPE
Democratic Republic of São Tomé and Príncipe

Area Sq Km	964	**Currency**	Dobra
Area Sq Miles	372	**Languages**	Portuguese, creole
Population	157 000	**Religions**	Roman Catholic, Protestant
Capital	São Tomé	**Organizations**	UN

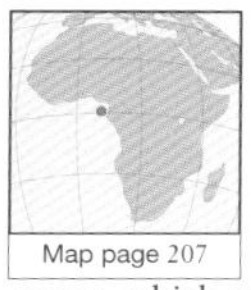
Map page 207

The two main islands and adjacent islets lie off the coast of west Africa in the Gulf of Guinea. São Tomé is the larger island, with over ninety per cent of the population. Both São Tomé and Príncipe are mountainous and tree-covered, and have a hot and humid climate. The economy is heavily dependent on cocoa, which accounts for around ninety per cent of export earnings.

SAUDI ARABIA
Kingdom of Saudi Arabia

Area Sq Km	2 200 000	**Currency**	Saudi Arabian riyal
Area Sq Miles	849 425	**Languages**	Arabic
Population	24 573 000	**Religions**	Sunni Muslim, Shi'a Muslim
Capital	Ar Riyāḍ (Riyadh)	**Organizations**	OPEC, UN

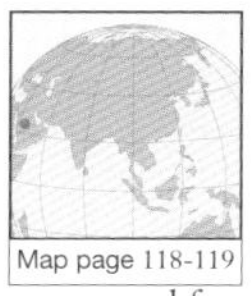
Map page 118-119

Saudi Arabia occupies most of the Arabian Peninsula in southwest Asia. The terrain is desert or semi-desert plateaus, which rise to mountains running parallel to the Red Sea in the west and slope down to plains in the southeast and along The Gulf in the east. Over eighty per cent of the population lives in urban areas. There are around four million foreign workers in Saudi Arabia, employed mainly in the oil and service industries. Summers are hot, winters are warm and rainfall is low. Saudi Arabia has the world's largest reserves of oil and significant natural gas reserves, both onshore and in The Gulf. Crude oil and refined products account for over ninety per cent of export earnings. Other industries and irrigated agriculture are being encouraged, but most food and raw materials are imported. Saudi Arabia has important banking and commercial interests. Japan and the USA are the main trading partners.

SENEGAL
Republic of Senegal

Area Sq Km	196 720	**Currency**	CFA franc
Area Sq Miles	75 954	**Languages**	French, Wolof, Fulani, local languages
Population	11 658 000	**Religions**	Sunni Muslim, Roman Catholic, traditional beliefs
Capital	Dakar	**Organizations**	UN

Senegal lies on the Atlantic coast of west Africa. The north is arid semi-desert, while the south is mainly fertile savanna bushland. The climate is tropical with summer rains, although droughts occur. One-fifth of the population lives in and around Dakar, the capital and main port. Fish, groundnuts and phosphates are the main exports. France is the main trading partner.

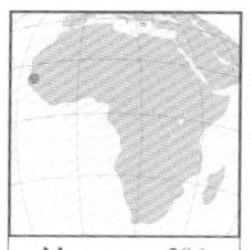
Map page 206

SERBIA
Republic of Serbia

Area Sq Km	88 361	**Currency**	Serbian dinar, euro
Area Sq Miles	34 116	**Languages**	Serbian, Albanian, Hungarian
Population	9 379 437	**Religions**	Serbian Orthodox, Sunni Muslim
Capital	Beograd (Belgrade)	**Organizations**	UN

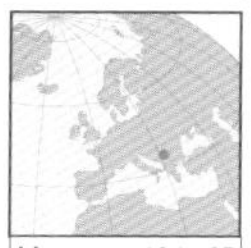
Map page 196-197

The southern European republic of Serbia was separated in 2006 from its neighbour, Montenegro – the two becoming independent countries. The state union of Serbia and Montenegro had retained the name Yugoslavia until 2003. The southern province of Kosovo, is under UN administration. After 1991 the economy was seriously affected by civil war and economic sanctions. The landscape is for the most part rugged, mountainous and forested. Northern Serbia is low-lying and is drained by the Danube river system.

SEYCHELLES
Republic of the Seychelles

Area Sq Km	455	**Currency**	Seychelles rupee
Area Sq Miles	176	**Languages**	English, French, creole
Population	81 000	**Religions**	Roman Catholic, Protestant
Capital	Victoria	**Organizations**	Comm., UN

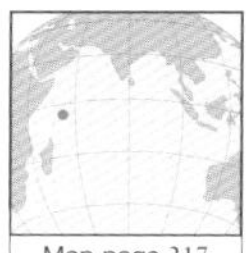
Map page 217

The Seychelles comprises an archipelago of over one hundred granitic and coral islands in the western Indian Ocean. Over ninety per cent of the population lives on the main island, Mahé. The climate is hot and humid with heavy rainfall. The economy is based mainly on tourism, fishing and light manufacturing.

SIERRA LEONE
Republic of Sierra Leone

Area Sq Km	71 740	**Currency**	Leone
Area Sq Miles	27 699	**Languages**	English, creole, Mende, Temne, local languages
Population	5 525 000	**Religions**	Sunni Muslim, traditional beliefs
Capital	Freetown	**Organizations**	Comm., UN

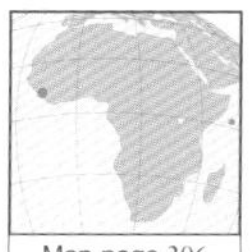
Map page 206

Sierra Leone lies on the Atlantic coast of west Africa. Its coastline is heavily indented and is lined with mangrove swamps. Inland is a forested area rising to savanna plateaus, with mountains to the northeast. The climate is tropical and rainfall is heavy. Most of the workforce is involved in subsistence farming. Cocoa and coffee are the main cash crops. Diamonds and rutile (titanium ore) are the main exports. Sierra Leone is one of the world's poorest countries, and the economy relies on substantial foreign aid.

SINGAPORE
Republic of Singapore

Area Sq Km	639	**Currency**	Singapore dollar
Area Sq Miles	247	**Languages**	Chinese, English, Malay, Tamil
Population	4 326 000	**Religions**	Buddhist, Taoist, Sunni Muslim, Christian, Hindu
Capital	Singapore	**Organizations**	APEC, ASEAN, Comm., UN

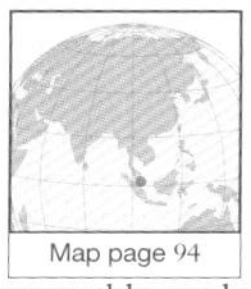
Map page 94

The state comprises the main island of Singapore and over fifty other islands, lying off the southern tip of the Malay Peninsula in Southeast Asia. Singapore is generally low-lying and includes land reclaimed from swamps and the sea. It is hot and humid, with heavy rainfall throughout the year. There are fish farms and vegetable gardens in the north and east of the island, but most food is imported. Singapore also lacks mineral and energy resources. Manufacturing industries and services are the main sectors of the economy. Their rapid development has fuelled the nation's impressive economic growth during recent decades. Main industries include electronics, oil refining, chemicals, pharmaceuticals, ship repair, food processing and textiles. Singapore is also a major financial centre. Its port is one of the world's largest and busiest and acts as an entrepôt for neighbouring states. Tourism is also important. Japan, the USA and Malaysia are the main trading partners.

Sint Eustatius part of Netherlands Antilles

Area Sq Km (Miles)	21 (8)	**Population**	2 829	**Capital**	Oranjestad

An island in the Leeward Islands, in the Caribbean south of St-Martin (Sint Maarten). It has a developing tourism industry.

Map page 247

Sint Maarten part of Netherlands Antilles

Area Sq Km (Miles)	34 (13)	**Population**	31 882	**Capital**	Philipsburg

The southern part of one of the Leeward Islands, in the Caribbean; the other part of the island is a dependency of France. Tourism and fishing are the most important industries.

Map page 247

SLOVAKIA
Slovak Republic

Area Sq Km	49 035	**Currency**	Slovakian koruna
Area Sq Miles	18 933	**Languages**	Slovakian, Hungarian, Czech
Population	5 401 000	**Religions**	Roman Catholic, Protestant, Orthodox
Capital	Bratislava	**Organizations**	EU, NATO, OECD, UN

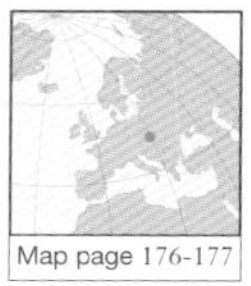
Map page 176-177

A landlocked country in central Europe, Slovakia is mountainous in the north, but low-lying in the southwest. The climate is continental. There is a range of manufacturing industries, and the main exports are machinery and transport equipment, but in recent years there have been economic difficulties and growth has been slow. Slovakia joined the European Union in May 2004. Most trade is with other EU countries, especially the Czech Republic.

SLOVENIA
Republic of Slovenia

Area Sq Km	20 251	**Currency**	Tólar
Area Sq Miles	7 819	**Languages**	Slovenian, Croatian, Serbian
Population	1 967 000	**Religions**	Roman Catholic, Protestant
Capital	Ljubljana	**Organizations**	EU, NATO, UN

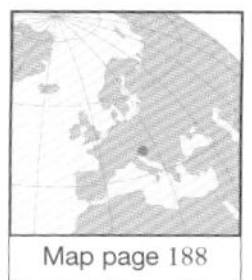
Map page 188

Slovenia lies in the northwest Balkan Mountains of southern Europe and has a short coastline on the Adriatic Sea. It is mountainous and hilly, with lowlands on the coast and in the Sava and Drava river valleys. The climate is generally continental inland and Mediterranean nearer the coast. The main agricultural products are potatoes, grain and sugar beet; the main industries include metal processing, electronics and consumer goods. Trade has been re-orientated towards western markets and the main trading partners are Germany and Italy. Slovenia joined the European Union in May 2004.

SOLOMON ISLANDS

Area Sq Km	28 370	**Currency**	Solomon Islands dollar
Area Sq Miles	10 954	**Languages**	English, creole, local languages
Population	478 000	**Religions**	Protestant, Roman Catholic
Capital	Honiara	**Organizations**	Comm., UN

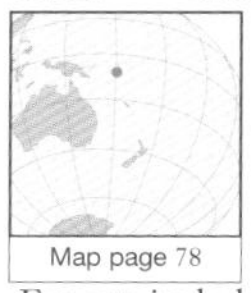
Map page 78

The state consists of the Solomon, Santa Cruz and Shortland Islands in the southwest Pacific Ocean. The six main islands are volcanic, mountainous and forested, although Guadalcanal, the most populous, has a large lowland area. The climate is generally hot and humid. Subsistence farming, forestry and fishing predominate. Exports include timber products, fish, copra and palm oil. The islands depend on foreign aid.

SOMALIA
Somali Democratic Republic

Area Sq Km	637 657	**Currency**	Somali shilling
Area Sq Miles	246 201	**Languages**	Somali, Arabic
Population	8 228 000	**Religions**	Sunni Muslim
Capital	Muqdisho (Mogadishu)	**Organizations**	UN

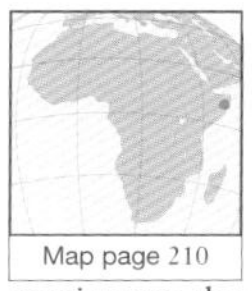
Map page 210

Somalia is in northeast Africa, on the Gulf of Aden and Indian Ocean. It consists of a dry scrubby plateau, rising to highlands in the north. The climate is hot and dry, but coastal areas and the Jubba and Webi Shabeelle river valleys support crops and most of the population. Subsistence farming and livestock rearing are the main activities. Exports include livestock and bananas. Frequent drought and civil war have prevented economic development. Somalia is one of the poorest, most unstable and least developed countries in the world.

SOUTH AFRICA, REPUBLIC OF

Area Sq Km	1 219 090	**Currency**	Rand
Area Sq Miles	470 689	**Languages**	Afrikaans, English, nine other official languages
Population	47 432 000	**Religions**	Protestant, Roman Catholic, Sunni Muslim, Hindu
Capital	Pretoria/ Cape Town	**Organizations**	Comm., SADC, UN

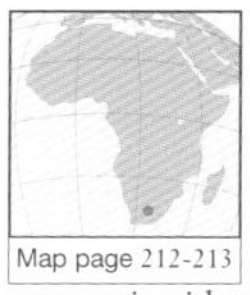
Map page 212-213

The Republic of South Africa occupies most of the southern part of Africa. It surrounds Lesotho and has a long coastline on the Atlantic and Indian Oceans. Much of the land is a vast plateau, covered with grassland or bush and drained by the Orange and Limpopo river systems. A fertile coastal plain rises to mountain ridges in the south and east, including Table Mountain near Cape Town and the Drakensberg range in the east. Gauteng is the most populous province, with Johannesburg and Pretoria its main cities. South Africa has warm summers and mild winters. Most of the country has the majority of its rainfall in summer, but the coast around Cape Town has winter rains. South Africa has the largest economy in Africa, although wealth is unevenly distributed and unemployment is very high. Agriculture employs approximately one-third of the workforce, and crops include fruit, wine, wool and maize. The country is the world's leading producer of gold and chromium and an important producer of diamonds. Many other minerals are also mined. The main industries are mineral and food processing, chemicals, electrical equipment, textiles and motor vehicles. Financial services are also important.

SOUTH KOREA
Republic of Korea

Area Sq Km	99 274	**Currency**	South Korean won
Area Sq Miles	38 330	**Languages**	Korean
Population	47 817 000	**Religions**	Buddhist, Protestant, Roman Catholic
Capital	Sŏul (Seoul)	**Organizations**	APEC, UN

The state consists of the southern half of the Korean Peninsula in eastern Asia and many islands lying off the western and southern coasts in the Yellow Sea. The terrain is mountainous, although less

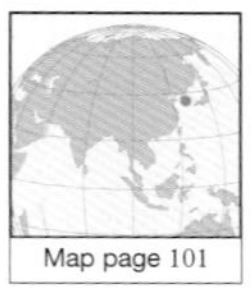
Map page 101

rugged than that of North Korea. Population density is high and the country is highly urbanized; most of the population lives on the western coastal plains and in the river basins of the Han-gang in the northwest and the Naktong-gang in the southeast. The climate is continental, with hot, wet summers and dry, cold winters. Arable land is limited by the mountainous terrain, but because of intensive farming South Korea is nearly self-sufficient in food. Sericulture (silk) is important, as is fishing, which contributes to exports. South Korea has few mineral resources, except for coal and tungsten. It has achieved high economic growth based mainly on export manufacturing. The main manufactured goods are cars, electronic and electrical goods, ships, steel, chemicals and toys, as well as textiles, clothing, footwear and food products. The USA and Japan are the main trading partners.

SPAIN
Kingdom of Spain

Area Sq Km	504 782	**Currency**	Euro
Area Sq Miles	194 897	**Languages**	Spanish, Catalan, Galician, Basque
Population	43 064 000	**Religions**	Roman Catholic
Capital	Madrid	**Organizations**	EU, NATO, OECD, UN

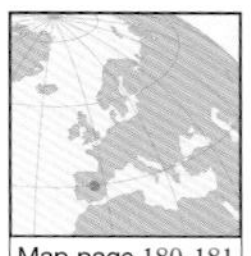
Map page 180-181

Spain occupies the greater part of the Iberian peninsula in southwest Europe, with coastlines on the Atlantic Ocean and Mediterranean Sea. It includes the Balearic Islands in the Mediterranean, the Canary Islands in the Atlantic, and two enclaves in north Africa (Ceuta and Melilla). Much of the mainland is a high plateau drained by the Douro (Duero), Tagus (Tajo) and Guadiana rivers. The plateau is interrupted by a low mountain range and bounded to the east and north also by mountains, including the Pyrenees, which form the border with France and Andorra. The main lowland areas are the Ebro basin in the northeast, the eastern coastal plains and the Guadalquivir basin in the southwest. Over three-quarters of the population lives in urban areas. The plateau experiences hot summers and cold winters. Conditions are cooler and wetter to the north, and warmer and drier to the south. Agriculture involves about ten per cent of the workforce, and fruit, vegetables and wine are exported. Fishing is an important industry, and Spain has a large fishing fleet. Mineral resources include lead, copper, mercury and fluorspar. Some oil is produced, but Spain has to import most energy needs. The economy is based mainly on manufacturing and services. The principal products are machinery, transport equipment, motor vehicles and food products, with a wide variety of other manufactured goods. With approximately fifty million visitors a year, tourism is a major industry. Banking and commerce are also important. Approximately seventy per cent of trade is with other European Union countries.

SRI LANKA
Democratic Socialist Republic of Sri Lanka

Area Sq Km	65 610	**Currency**	Sri Lankan rupee
Area Sq Miles	25 332	**Languages**	Sinhalese, Tamil, English
Population	20 743 000	**Religions**	Buddhist, Hindu, Sunni Muslim, Roman Catholic
Capital	Sri Jayewardenepura Kotte	**Organizations**	Comm., UN

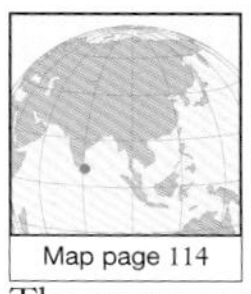
Map page 114

Sri Lanka lies in the Indian Ocean off the southeast coast of India in south Asia. It has rolling coastal plains, with mountains in the centre-south. The climate is hot and monsoonal. Most people live on the west coast. Manufactures (chiefly textiles and clothing), tea, rubber, copra and gems are exported. The economy relies on foreign aid and workers' remittances. The USA and the UK are the main trading partners.

SUDAN
Republic of the Sudan

Area Sq Km	2 505 813	**Currency**	Sudanese dinar
Area Sq Miles	967 500	**Languages**	Arabic, Dinka, Nubian, Beja, Nuer, local languages
Population	36 233 000	**Religions**	Sunni Muslim, traditional beliefs, Christian
Capital	Khartoum	**Organizations**	UN

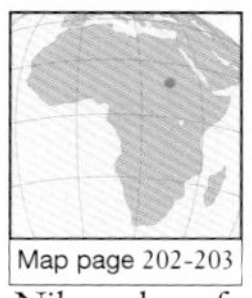
Map page 202-203

Africa's largest country, the Sudan is in the northeast of the continent, on the Red Sea. It lies within the upper Nile basin, much of which is arid plain but with swamps to the south. Mountains lie to the northeast, west and south. The climate is hot and arid with light summer rainfall, and droughts occur. Most people live along the Nile and are farmers and herders. Cotton, gum arabic, livestock and other agricultural products are exported. The government is working with foreign investors to develop oil resources, but civil war in the south continues to restrict the growth of the economy. Main trading partners are Saudi Arabia, China and Libya.

SURINAME
Republic of Suriname

Area Sq Km	163 820	**Currency**	Suriname guilder
Area Sq Miles	63 251	**Languages**	Dutch, Surinamese, English, Hindi
Population	449 000	**Religions**	Hindu, Roman Catholic, Protestant, Sunni Muslim
Capital	Paramaribo	**Organizations**	CARICOM, UN

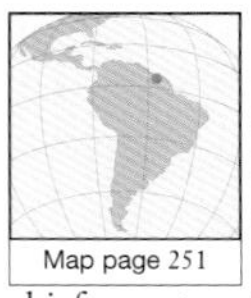
Map page 251

Suriname, on the Atlantic coast of northern South America, consists of a swampy coastal plain (where most of the population lives), central plateaus, and highlands in the south. The climate is tropical, and rainforest covers much of the land. Bauxite mining is the main industry, and alumina and aluminium are the chief exports, with shrimps, rice, bananas and timber also exported. The main trading partners are the Netherlands, Norway and the USA.

SWAZILAND
Kingdom of Swaziland

Area Sq Km	17 364	**Currency**	Emalangeni, South African rand
Area Sq Miles	6 704	**Languages**	Swazi, English
Population	1 032 000	**Religions**	Christian, traditional beliefs
Capital	Mbabane	**Organizations**	Comm., SADC, UN

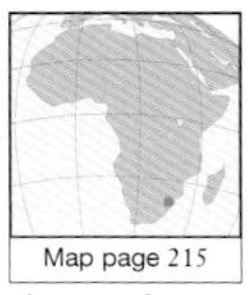
Map page 215

Landlocked Swaziland in southern Africa lies between Mozambique and the Republic of South Africa. Savanna plateaus descend from mountains in the west towards hill country in the east. The climate is subtropical, but temperate in the mountains. Subsistence farming predominates. Asbestos and diamonds are mined. Exports include sugar, fruit and wood pulp. Tourism and workers' remittances are important to the economy. Most trade is with South Africa.

SWEDEN
Kingdom of Sweden

Area Sq Km	449 964	**Currency**	Swedish krona
Area Sq Miles	173 732	**Languages**	Swedish
Population	9 041 000	**Religions**	Protestant, Roman Catholic
Capital	Stockholm	**Organizations**	EU, OECD, UN

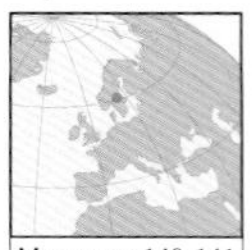
Map page 140-141

Sweden occupies the eastern part of the Scandinavian peninsula in northern Europe and borders the Baltic Sea, the Gulf of Bothnia, and the Kattegat and Skagerrak, connecting with the North Sea. Forested mountains cover the northern half, part of which lies within the Arctic Circle. The southern part of the country is a lowland lake region where most of the population lives. Sweden has warm summers and cold winters, which are more severe in the north. Natural resources include coniferous forests, mineral deposits and water resources. Some dairy products, meat, cereals and vegetables are produced in the south. The forests supply timber for export and for the important pulp, paper and furniture industries. Sweden is an important producer of iron ore and copper. Zinc, lead, silver and gold are also mined. Machinery and transport equipment, chemicals, pulp and wood, and telecommunications equipment are the main exports. The majority of trade is with other European Union countries.

SWITZERLAND
Swiss Confederation

Area Sq Km	41 293	**Currency**	Swiss franc
Area Sq Miles	15 943	**Languages**	German, French, Italian, Romansch
Population	7 252 000	**Religions**	Roman Catholic, Protestant
Capital	Bern	**Organizations**	OECD, UN

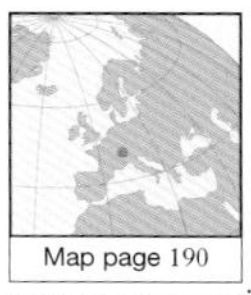
Map page 190

Switzerland is a mountainous landlocked country in west central Europe. The southern regions lie within the Alps, while the northwest is dominated by the Jura mountains. The rest of the land is a high plateau, where most of the population lives. The climate varies greatly, depending on altitude and relief, but in general summers are mild and winters are cold with heavy snowfalls. Switzerland has one of the highest standards of living in the world, yet it has few mineral resources, and most food and industrial raw materials are imported. Manufacturing makes the largest contribution to the economy. Engineering is the most important industry, producing precision instruments and heavy machinery. Other important industries are chemicals and pharmaceuticals. Banking and financial services are very important, and Zürich is one of the world's leading banking cities. Tourism, and international organizations based in Switzerland, are also major foreign currency earners. Germany is the main trading partner.

SYRIA
Syrian Arab Republic

Area Sq Km	185 180	**Currency**	Syrian pound
Area Sq Miles	71 498	**Languages**	Arabic, Kurdish, Armenian
Population	19 043 000	**Religions**	Sunni Muslim, Shi'a Muslim, Christian
Capital	Dimashq (Damascus)	**Organizations**	UN

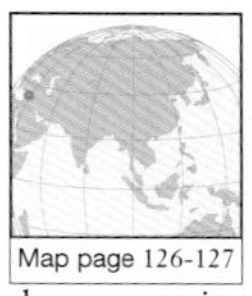
Map page 126-127

Syria is in southwest Asia, has a short coastline on the Mediterranean Sea, and stretches inland to a plateau traversed northwest-southeast by the Euphrates river. Mountains flank the southwest borders with Lebanon and Israel. The climate is Mediterranean in coastal regions, hotter and drier inland. Most Syrians live on the coast or in the river valleys. Cotton, cereals and fruit are important products, but the main exports are petroleum and related products, and textiles.

TAIWAN

Area Sq Km	36 179	**Currency**	Taiwan dollar
Area Sq Miles	13 969	**Languages**	Mandarin, Min, Hakka, local languages
Population	22 858 000	**Religions**	Buddhist, Taoist, Confucian, Christian
Capital	T'aipei	**Organizations**	APEC

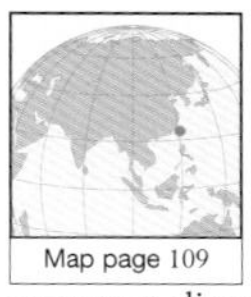
Map page 109

The east Asian state consists of the island of Taiwan, separated from mainland China by the Taiwan Strait, and several much smaller islands. Much of Taiwan is mountainous and forested. Densely populated coastal plains in the west contain the bulk of the population and most economic activity. Taiwan has a tropical monsoon climate, with warm, wet summers and mild winters. Agriculture is highly productive. The country is virtually self-sufficient in food and exports some products. Coal, oil and natural gas are produced and a few minerals are mined, but none of them are of great significance to the economy. Taiwan depends heavily on imports of raw materials and exports of manufactured goods. The main manufactures are electrical and electronic goods, including television sets, personal computers and calculators, textiles, fertilizers, clothing, footwear and toys. The main trading partners are the USA, Japan and Germany.

TAJIKISTAN
Republic of Tajikistan

Area Sq Km	143 100	**Currency**	Somoni
Area Sq Miles	55 251	**Languages**	Tajik, Uzbek, Russian
Population	6 507 000	**Religions**	Sunni Muslim
Capital	Dushanbe	**Organizations**	CIS, UN

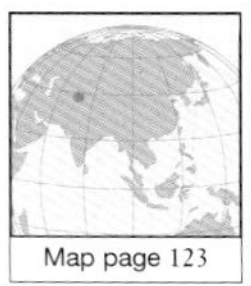
Map page 123

Landlocked Tajikistan in central Asia is a mountainous country, dominated by the mountains of the Alai Range and the Pamir. In the less mountainous western areas summers are warm, although winters are cold. Agriculture is the main sector of the economy, chiefly cotton growing and cattle breeding. Mineral deposits include lead, zinc, and uranium. Metal processing, textiles and clothing are the main manufactured goods; the main exports are aluminium and cotton. Uzbekistan, Kazakhstan and the Russian Federation are the main trading partners.

TANZANIA
United Republic of Tanzania

Area Sq Km	945 087	**Currency**	Tanzanian shilling
Area Sq Miles	364 900	**Languages**	Swahili, English, Nyamwezi, local languages
Population	38 329 000	**Religions**	Muslim, traditional beliefs, Christian
Capital	Dodoma	**Organizations**	Comm., SADC, UN

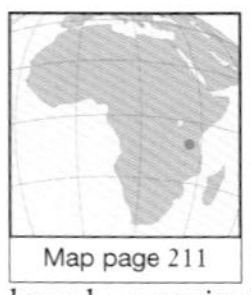
Map page 211

Tanzania lies on the coast of east Africa and includes the island of Zanzibar in the Indian Ocean. Most of the mainland is a savanna plateau lying east of the Great Rift Valley. In the north, near the border with Kenya, is Kilimanjaro, the highest mountain in Africa. The climate is tropical. The economy is predominantly based on agriculture, which employs an estimated ninety per cent of the workforce. Agricultural processing and gold and diamond mining are the main industries, although tourism is growing. Coffee, cotton, cashew nuts and tobacco are the main exports, with cloves from Zanzibar. Most export trade is with India and the UK. Tanzania depends heavily on foreign aid.

THAILAND
Kingdom of Thailand

Area Sq Km	513 115	**Currency**	Baht
Area Sq Miles	198 115	**Languages**	Thai, Lao, Chinese, Malay, Mon-Khmer languages
Population	64 233 000	**Religions**	Buddhist, Sunni Muslim
Capital	Bangkok	**Organizations**	APEC, ASEAN, UN

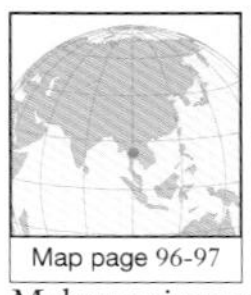
Map page 96-97

The largest country in the Indo-China peninsula, Thailand has coastlines on the Gulf of Thailand and Andaman Sea. Central Thailand is dominated by the Chao Phraya river basin, which contains Bangkok, the capital city and centre of most economic activity. To the east is a dry plateau drained by tributaries of the Mekong river, while to the north, west and south, extending down most of the Malay peninsula, are forested hills and mountains. Many small islands line the coast. The climate is hot, humid and monsoonal. About half the workforce is involved in agriculture. Fishing and fish processing are important. Thailand produces natural gas, some oil and lignite, minerals (chiefly tin, tungsten and baryte) and gemstones. Manufacturing is the largest contributor to national income, with electronics, textiles, clothing and footwear, and food processing the main industries. With around seven million visitors a year, tourism is the major source of foreign exchange. Thailand is one of the world's leading exporters of rice and rubber, and a major exporter of maize and tapioca. Japan and the USA are the main trading partners.

TOGO
Republic of Togo

Area Sq Km	56 785	**Currency**	CFA franc
Area Sq Miles	21 925	**Languages**	French, Ewe, Kabre, local languages
Population	6 145 000	**Religions**	Traditional beliefs, Christian, Sunni Muslim
Capital	Lomé	**Organizations**	UN

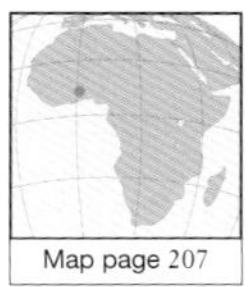
Map page 207

Togo is a long narrow country in west Africa with a short coastline on the Gulf of Guinea. The interior consists of plateaus rising to mountainous areas. The climate is tropical, and is drier inland. Agriculture is the mainstay of the economy. Phosphate mining and food processing are the main industries. Cotton, phosphates, coffee and cocoa are the main exports. Lomé, the capital, is an entrepôt trade centre.

Tokelau New Zealand Overseas Territory

Area Sq Km (Miles) 10 (4) **Population** 1 000

Tokelau consists of three atolls, Atafu, Nukunonu and Fakaofa, lying in the Pacific Ocean north of Samoa. Subsistence agriculture is the main activity, and the islands rely on aid from New Zealand and remittances from workers overseas.

Map page 81

TONGA
Kingdom of Tonga

Area Sq Km	748	**Currency**	Pa'anga
Area Sq Miles	289	**Languages**	Tongan, English
Population	102 000	**Religions**	Protestant, Roman Catholic
Capital	Nuku'alofa	**Organizations**	Comm., UN

Tonga comprises some one hundred and seventy islands in the south Pacific Ocean, northeast of New Zealand. The three main groups are Tongatapu (where sixty per cent of Tongans live), Ha'apai and Vava'u.

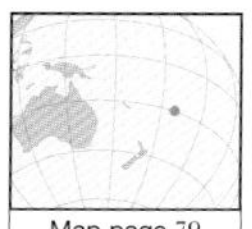
Map page 79

The climate is warm and wet, and the economy relies heavily on agriculture. Tourism and light industry are also important to the economy. Exports include squash, fish, vanilla beans and root crops. Most trade is with New Zealand, Japan and Australia.

TRINIDAD AND TOBAGO
Republic of Trinidad and Tobago

Area Sq Km	5 130	**Currency**	Trinidad and Tobago dollar
Area Sq Miles	1 981	**Languages**	English, creole, Hindi
Population	1 305 000	**Religions**	Roman Catholic, Hindu, Protestant, Sunni Muslim
Capital	Port of Spain	**Organizations**	CARICOM, Comm., UN

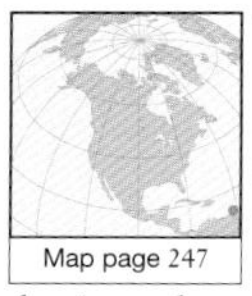
Map page 247

Trinidad, the most southerly Caribbean island, lies off the Venezuelan coast. It is hilly in the north, with a central plain. Tobago, to the northeast, is smaller, more mountainous and less developed. The climate is tropical. The main crops are cocoa, sugar cane, coffee, fruit and vegetables. Oil and petrochemical industries dominate the economy. Tourism is also important. The USA is the main trading partner.

Tristan da Cunha Dependency of St Helena

Area Sq Km (Miles) 98 (38) **Population** 284 **Capital** Settlement of Edinburgh

A group of volcanic islands in the south Atlantic Ocean: the other main islands in the group are Nightingale Island and Inaccessible Island. The group is over 2 000 kilometres (1 250 miles) south of St Helena. The economy is based on fishing, fish processing and agriculture. Ecotourism is increasingly important.

Map page 216

TUNISIA
Tunisian Republic

Area Sq Km	164 150	**Currency**	Tunisian dinar
Area Sq Miles	63 379	**Languages**	Arabic, French
Population	10 102 000	**Religions**	Sunni Muslim
Capital	Tunis	**Organizations**	UN

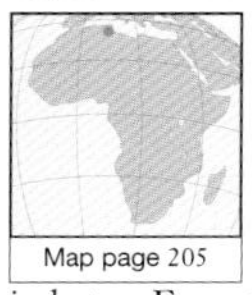
Map page 205

Tunisia is on the Mediterranean coast of north Africa. The north is mountainous with valleys and coastal plains, has a Mediterranean climate and is the most populous area. The south is hot and arid. Oil and phosphates are the main resources, and the main crops are olives and citrus fruit. Tourism is an important industry. Exports include petroleum products, textiles, fruit and phosphorus. Most trade is with European Union countries.

TURKEY
Republic of Turkey

Area Sq Km	779 452	**Currency**	Turkish lira
Area Sq Miles	300 948	**Languages**	Turkish, Kurdish
Population	73 193 000	**Religions**	Sunni Muslim, Shi'a Muslim
Capital	Ankara	**Organizations**	NATO, OECD, UN

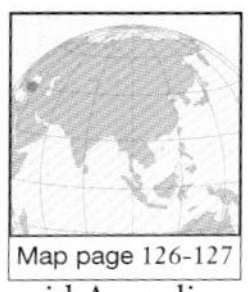
Map page 126-127

Turkey occupies a large peninsula of southwest Asia and has coastlines on the Black, Mediterranean and Aegean Seas. It includes eastern Thrace, which is in southeastern Europe and separated from the rest of the country by the Bosporus, the Sea of Marmara and the Dardanelles. The Asian mainland consists of the semi-arid Anatolian plateau, flanked to the north, south and east by mountains. Over forty per cent of Turks live in central Anatolia and on the Marmara and Aegean coastal plains. The coast has a Mediterranean climate, but inland conditions are more extreme with hot, dry summers and cold, snowy winters. Agriculture involves about forty per cent of the workforce, and products include cotton, grain, tobacco, fruit, nuts and livestock. Turkey is a leading producer of chromium, iron ore, lead, tin, borate, and baryte. Coal is also mined. The main manufactured goods are clothing, textiles, food products, steel and vehicles. Tourism is a major industry, with nine million visitors a year. Germany and the USA are the main trading partners. Remittances from workers abroad are important to the economy.

TURKMENISTAN
Republic of Turkmenistan

Area Sq Km	488 100	**Currency**	Turkmen manat
Area Sq Miles	188 456	**Languages**	Turkmen, Uzbek, Russian
Population	4 833 000	**Religions**	Sunni Muslim, Russian Orthodox
Capital	Aşgabat	**Organizations**	CIS, UN

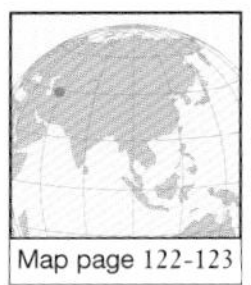
Map page 122-123

Turkmenistan, in central Asia, comprises the plains of the Karakum Desert, the foothills of the Kopet Dag mountains in the south, the Amudar'ya valley in the north and the Caspian Sea plains in the west. The climate is dry, with extreme temperatures. The economy is based mainly on irrigated agriculture (chiefly cotton growing), and natural gas and oil. Main exports are natural gas, oil and cotton fibre. Ukraine, Iran, Turkey and the Russian Federation are the main trading partners.

Turks and Caicos Islands
United Kingdom Overseas Territory

Area Sq Km (Miles) 430 (166) **Population** 26 000 **Capital** Grand Turk

The state consists of over forty low-lying islands and cays in the northern Caribbean. Only eight islands are inhabited, and two-fifths of the people live on Grand Turk and Salt Cay. The climate is tropical, and the economy is based on tourism, fishing and offshore banking.

Map page 246

TUVALU

Area Sq Km	25	**Currency**	Australian dollar
Area Sq Miles	10	**Languages**	Tuvaluan, English
Population	10 000	**Religions**	Protestant
Capital	Vaiaku	**Organizations**	Comm., UN

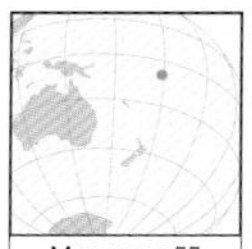
Map page 77

Tuvalu comprises nine low-lying coral atolls in the south Pacific Ocean. One-third of the population lives on Funafuti, and most people depend on subsistence farming and fishing. The islands export copra, stamps and clothing, but rely heavily on foreign aid. Most trade is with Fiji, Australia and New Zealand.

UGANDA
Republic of Uganda

Area Sq Km	241 038	**Currency**	Ugandan shilling
Area Sq Miles	93 065	**Languages**	English, Swahili, Luganda, local languages
Population	28 816 000	**Religions**	Roman Catholic, Protestant, Muslim, trad. beliefs
Capital	Kampala	**Organizations**	Comm., UN

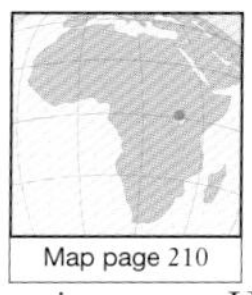
Map page 210

A landlocked country in east Africa, Uganda consists of a savanna plateau with mountains and lakes. The climate is warm and wet. Most people live in the southern half of the country. Agriculture employs around eighty per cent of the workforce and dominates the economy. Coffee, tea, fish and fish products are the main exports. Uganda relies heavily on aid.

UKRAINE

Area Sq Km	603 700	**Currency**	Hryvnia
Area Sq Miles	233 090	**Languages**	Ukrainian, Russian
Population	46 481 000	**Religions**	Orthodox, Ukrainian Catholic, Roman Catholic
Capital	Kyiv (Kiev)	**Organizations**	CIS, UN

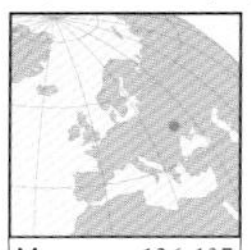
Map page 136-137

The country lies on the Black Sea coast of eastern Europe. Much of the land is steppe, generally flat and treeless, but with rich black soil, and it is drained by the river Dnieper. Along the border with Belarus are forested, marshy plains. The only uplands are the Carpathian Mountains in the west and smaller ranges on the Crimean peninsula. Summers are warm and winters are cold, with milder conditions in the Crimea. About a quarter of the population lives in the mainly industrial areas around Donets'k, Kiev and Dnipropetrovs'k. The Ukraine is rich in natural resources: fertile soil, substantial mineral and natural gas deposits, and forests. Agriculture and livestock rearing are important, but mining and manufacturing are the dominant sectors of the economy. Coal, iron and manganese mining, steel and metal production, machinery, chemicals and food processing are the main industries. The Russian Federation is the main trading partner.

UNITED ARAB EMIRATES
Federation of Emirates

Area Sq Km	77 700	**Currency**	United Arab Emirates dirham
Area Sq Miles	30 000	**Languages**	Arabic,English
Population	4 496 000	**Religions**	Sunni Muslim, Shi'a Muslim
Capital	Abū Ẓabī (Abu Dhabi)	**Organizations**	OPEC, UN

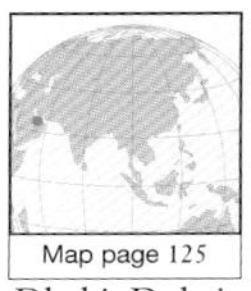
Map page 125

The UAE lies on the Gulf coast of the Arabian Peninsula. Six emirates are on The Gulf, while the seventh, Fujairah, is on the Gulf of Oman. Most of the land is flat desert with sand dunes and salt pans. The only hilly area is in the northeast. Over eighty per cent of the population lives in three of the emirates - Abu Dhabi, Dubai and Sharjah. Summers are hot and winters are mild, with occasional rainfall in coastal areas. Fruit and vegetables are grown in oases and irrigated areas, but the Emirates' wealth is based on hydrocarbons found in Abu Dhabi, Dubai, Sharjah and Ras al Khaimah. The UAE is one of the major oil producers in the Middle East. Dubai is an important entrepôt trade centre. The main trading partner is Japan.

Abū Ẓabī (Abu Dhabi) (Emirate)
Area Sq Km (Miles) 67 340 (26 000) **Population** 1 248 000 **Capital** Abu Dhabi

'Ajman (Emirate)
Area Sq Km (Miles) 259 (100) **Population** 189 000 **Capital** Ajman

Dubayy (Dubai) (Emirate)
Area Sq Km (Miles) 3 885 (1 500) **Population** 971 000 **Capital** Dubai

Al Fujayrah (Emirate)
Area Sq Km (Miles) 1 165 (450) **Population** 103 000 **Capital** Al Fujayrah

Ra's al Khaymah (Emirate)
Area Sq Km (Miles) 1 684 (650) **Population** 179 000 **Capital** Ras al Khaymah

Ash Shāriqah (Sharjah) (Emirate)
Area Sq Km (Miles) 2 590 (1 000) **Population** 551 000 **Capital** Sharjah

Umm al Qaywayn (Emirate)
Area Sq Km (Miles) 777 (300) **Population** 49 000 **Capital** Umm al Qaywayn

UNITED KINGDOM
United Kingdom of Great Britain and Northern Ireland

Area Sq Km	243 609	**Currency**	Pound sterling
Area Sq Miles	94 058	**Languages**	English, Welsh, Gaelic
Population	59 668 000	**Religions**	Protestant, Roman Catholic, Muslim
Capital	London	**Organizations**	Comm., EU, NATO, OECD, UN

The United Kingdom, in northwest Europe, occupies the island of Great Britain, part of Ireland, and many small adjacent islands. Great Britain comprises England, Scotland and Wales. England covers over half the land area and supports over four-fifths of the population, at its densest in the southeast. The English landscape is flat or rolling with some uplands, notably the Cheviot Hills on the Scottish border, the Pennines in the centre-north, and the hills of the Lake District in the northwest. Scotland consists of southern uplands, central lowlands, the Highlands (which include the UK's highest peak) and many islands. Wales is a land of hills, mountains and river valleys. Northern Ireland contains uplands, plains and the UK's largest lake, Lough Neagh. The climate of the UK is mild, wet and variable. There are few mineral deposits, but important energy resources. Agricultural activities involve sheep and cattle rearing, dairy farming, and crop and fruit growing in the east and southeast. Productivity is high, but approximately one-third of food is imported. The UK produces petroleum and natural gas from reserves in the North Sea and is self-sufficient in energy in net terms. Major manufactures are food and drinks, motor vehicles and parts, aerospace equipment, machinery, electronic and electrical equipment, and chemicals and chemical products. However, the economy is dominated by service industries, including banking, insurance, finance and business services. London, the capital, is one of the world's major financial centres. Tourism is also a major industry, with approximately twenty-five million visitors a year. International trade is also important, equivalent to one-third of national income. Over half of the UK's trade is with other European Union countries.

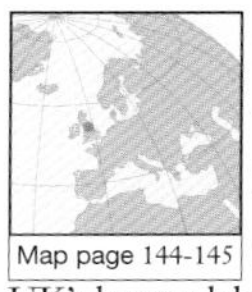
Map page 144-145

England (Constituent country)
Area Sq Km (Miles) 130 433 (50 360) **Population** 49 138 831 **Capital** London

Northern Ireland (Province)
Area Sq Km (Miles) 13 576 (5 242) **Population** 1 685 267 **Capital** Belfast

Scotland (Constituent country)
Area Sq Km (Miles) 78 822 (30 433) **Population** 5 062 011 **Capital** Edinburgh

Wales (Principality)
Area Sq Km (Miles) 20 778 (8 022) **Population** 2 903 085 **Capital** Cardiff

UNITED STATES OF AMERICA
Federal Republic

Area Sq Km	9 826 635	**Currency**	United States dollar
Area Sq Miles	3 794 085	**Languages**	English, Spanish
Population	298 213 000	**Religions**	Protestant, Roman Catholic, Sunni Muslim, Jewish
Capital	Washington D.C.	**Organizations**	APEC, NATO, OECD, UN

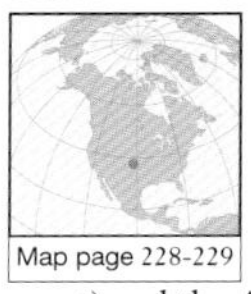
Map page 228-229

The USA comprises forty-eight contiguous states in North America, bounded by Canada and Mexico, plus the states of Alaska, to the northwest of Canada, and Hawaii, in the north Pacific Ocean. The populous eastern states cover the Atlantic coastal plain (which includes the Florida peninsula and the Gulf of Mexico coast) and the Appalachian Mountains. The central states occupy a vast interior plain drained by the Mississippi-Missouri river system. To the west lie the Rocky Mountains, separated from the Pacific coastal ranges by intermontane plateaus. The Pacific coastal zone is also mountainous, and prone to earthquakes. Hawaii is a group of some twenty volcanic islands. Climatic conditions range between arctic in Alaska to desert in the intermontane plateaus. Most of the USA has a temperate climate, although the interior has continental conditions. There are abundant natural resources, including major reserves of minerals and energy resources. The USA has the largest and most technologically advanced economy in the world, based on manufacturing and services. Although agriculture accounts for approximately two per cent of national income, productivity is high and the USA is a net exporter of food, chiefly grains and fruit. Cotton is the major industrial crop. The USA produces iron ore, copper, lead, zinc, and many other minerals. It is a major producer of coal, petroleum and natural gas, although being the world's biggest energy user it imports significant quantities of petroleum and its products. Manufacturing is diverse. The main industries are petroleum, steel, motor vehicles, aerospace, telecommunications, electronics, food processing, chemicals and consumer goods. Tourism is a major foreign currency earner, with approximately forty-five million visitors a year. Other important service industries are banking and finance, Wall Street in New York being one of the world's major stock exchanges. Canada and Mexico are the main trading partners.

Alabama (State)
Area Sq Km (Miles) 135 765 (52 419) **Population** 4 486 508 **Capital** Montgomery

Alaska (State)
Area Sq Km (Miles) 1 717 854 (663 267) **Population** 643 786 **Capital** Juneau

Arizona (State)
Area Sq Km (Miles) 295 253 (113 998) **Population** 5 456 453 **Capital** Phoenix

Arkansas (State)
Area Sq Km (Miles) 137 733 (53 179) **Population** 2 710 079 **Capital** Little Rock

California (State)
Area Sq Km (Miles) 423 971 (163 696) **Population** 35 116 033 **Capital** Sacramento

Colorado (State)
Area Sq Km (Miles) 269 602 (104 094) **Population** 4 506 542 **Capital** Denver

Connecticut (State)
Area Sq Km (Miles) 14 356 (5 543) **Population** 3 460 503 **Capital** Hartford

Delaware (State)
Area Sq Km (Miles) 6 446 (2 489) **Population** 807 385 **Capital** Dover

District of Columbia (District)
Area Sq Km (Miles) 176 (68) **Population** 570 898 **Capital** Washington

Florida (State)
Area Sq Km (Miles) 170 305 (65 755) **Population** 16 713 149 **Capital** Tallahassee

Georgia (State)
Area Sq Km (Miles) 153 910 (59 425) **Population** 8 560 310 **Capital** Atlanta

Hawaii (State)
Area Sq Km (Miles) 28 311 (10 931) **Population** 1 244 898 **Capital** Honolulu

Idaho (State)
Area Sq Km (Miles) 216 445 (83 570) **Population** 1 341 131 **Capital** Boise

Illinois (State)
Area Sq Km (Miles) 149 997 (57 914) **Population** 12 600 620 **Capital** Springfield

Indiana (State)
Area Sq Km (Miles) 94 322 (36 418) **Population** 6 159 068 **Capital** Indianapolis

Iowa (State)
Area Sq Km (Miles) 145 744 (56 272) **Population** 2 936 760 **Capital** Des Moines

Kansas (State)
Area Sq Km (Miles) 213 096 (82 277) **Population** 2 715 884 **Capital** Topeka

Kentucky (State)
Area Sq Km (Miles) 104 659 (40 409) **Population** 4 092 891 **Capital** Frankfort

Louisiana (State)
Area Sq Km (Miles) 134 265 (51 840) **Population** 4 482 646 **Capital** Baton Rouge

Maine (State)
Area Sq Km (Miles) 91 647 (35 385) **Population** 1 294 464 **Capital** Augusta

Maryland (State)
Area Sq Km (Miles) 32 134 (12 407) **Population** 5 458 137 **Capital** Annapolis

Massachusetts (State)
Area Sq Km (Miles) 27 337 (10 555) **Population** 6 427 801 **Capital** Boston

Michigan (State)
Area Sq Km (Miles) 250 493 (96 716) **Population** 10 050 446 **Capital** Lansing

Minnesota (State)
Area Sq Km (Miles) 225 171 (86 939) **Population** 5 019 720 **Capital** St Paul

Mississippi (State)
Area Sq Km (Miles) 125 433 (48 430) **Population** 2 871 782 **Capital** Jackson

Missouri (State)
Area Sq Km (Miles) 180 533 (69 704) **Population** 5 672 579 **Capital** Jefferson City

Montana (State)
Area Sq Km (Miles) 380 837 (147 042) **Population** 909 453 **Capital** Helena

Nebraska (State)
Area Sq Km (Miles) 200 346 (77 354) **Population** 1 729 180 **Capital** Lincoln

Nevada (State)
Area Sq Km (Miles) 286 352 (110 561) **Population** 2 173 491 **Capital** Carson City

New Hampshire (State)
Area Sq Km (Miles) 24 216 (9 350) **Population** 1 275 056 **Capital** Concord

New Jersey (State)
Area Sq Km (Miles) 22 587 (8 721) **Population** 8 590 300 **Capital** Trenton

New Mexico (State)
Area Sq Km (Miles) 314 914 (121 589) **Population** 1 855 059 **Capital** Santa Fe

New York (State)
Area Sq Km (Miles) 141 299 (54 556) **Population** 19 157 532 **Capital** Albany

North Carolina (State)
Area Sq Km (Miles) 139 391 (53 819) **Population** 8 320 146 **Capital** Raleigh

North Dakota (State)
Area Sq Km (Miles) 183 112 (70 700) **Population** 634 110 **Capital** Bismarck

Ohio (State)
Area Sq Km (Miles) 116 096 (44 825) **Population** 11 421 267 **Capital** Columbus

Oklahoma (State)
Area Sq Km (Miles) 181 035 (69 898) **Population** 3 493 714 **Capital** Oklahoma City

Oregon (State)
Area Sq Km (Miles) 254 806 (98 381) **Population** 3 521 515 **Capital** Salem

Pennsylvania (State)
Area Sq Km (Miles) 119 282 (46 055) **Population** 12 335 091 **Capital** Harrisburg

Rhode Island (State)
Area Sq Km (Miles) 4 002 (1 545) **Population** 1 069 725 **Capital** Providence

South Carolina (State)
Area Sq Km (Miles) 82 931 (32 020) **Population** 4 107 183 **Capital** Columbia

South Dakota (State)
Area Sq Km (Miles) 199 730 (77 116) **Population** 761 063 **Capital** Pierre

Tennessee (State)
Area Sq Km (Miles) 109 150 (42 143) **Population** 5 797 289 **Capital** Nashville

Texas (State)
Area Sq Km (Miles) 695 622 (268 581) **Population** 21 779 893 **Capital** Austin

Utah (State)
Area Sq Km (Miles) 219 887 (84 899) **Population** 2 316 256 **Capital** Salt Lake City

Vermont (State)
Area Sq Km (Miles) 24 900 (9 614) **Population** 616 592 **Capital** Montpelier

Virginia (State)
Area Sq Km (Miles) 110 784 (42 774) **Population** 7 293 542 **Capital** Richmond

Washington (State)
Area Sq Km (Miles) 184 666 (71 300) **Population** 6 068 996 **Capital** Olympia

West Virginia (State)
Area Sq Km (Miles) 62 755 (24 230) **Population** 1 801 873 **Capital** Charleston

Wisconsin (State)
Area Sq Km (Miles) 169 639 (65 498) **Population** 5 441 196 **Capital** Madison

Wyoming (State)
Area Sq Km (Miles) 253 337 (97 814) **Population** 498 703 **Capital** Cheyenne

URUGUAY
Oriental Republic of Uruguay

Area Sq Km	176 215	**Currency**	Uruguayan peso
Area Sq Miles	68 037	**Languages**	Spanish
Population	3 463 000	**Religions**	Roman Catholic, Protestant, Jewish
Capital	Montevideo	**Organizations**	UN

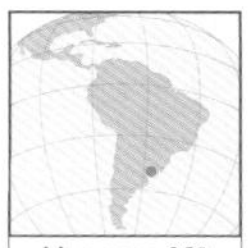
Map page 258

Uruguay, on the Atlantic coast of central South America, is a low-lying land of prairies. The coast and the River Plate estuary in the south are fringed with lagoons and sand dunes. Almost half the population lives in the capital, Montevideo. Uruguay has warm summers and mild winters. The economy is based on cattle and sheep ranching, and the main industries produce food products, textiles, and petroleum products. Meat, wool, hides, textiles and agricultural products are the main exports. Brazil and Argentina are the main trading partners.

UZBEKISTAN
Republic of Uzbekistan

Area Sq Km	447 400	**Currency**	Uzbek som
Area Sq Miles	172 742	**Languages**	Uzbek, Russian, Tajik, Kazakh
Population	26 593 000	**Religions**	Sunni Muslim, Russian Orthodox
Capital	Toshkent	**Organizations**	CIS, UN

A landlocked country of central Asia, Uzbekistan consists mainly of the flat Kyzylkum Desert. High mountains and valleys are found towards the southeast borders with Kyrgyzstan and Tajikistan. Most settlement is in the Fergana basin. The climate is hot and dry. The economy is based mainly on irrigated agriculture, chiefly cotton production.

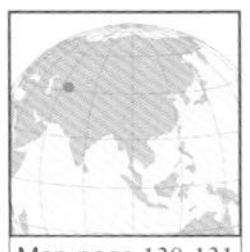
Map page 120-121

Uzbekistan is rich in minerals, including gold, copper, lead, zinc and uranium, and it has one of the largest gold mines in the world. Industry specializes in fertilizers and machinery for cotton harvesting and textile manufacture. The Russian Federation is the main trading partner.

VANUATU
Republic of Vanuatu

Area Sq Km	12 190	**Currency**	Vatu
Area Sq Miles	4 707	**Languages**	English, Bislama (creole), French
Population	211 000	**Religions**	Protestant, Roman Catholic, traditional beliefs
Capital	Port Vila	**Organizations**	Comm., UN

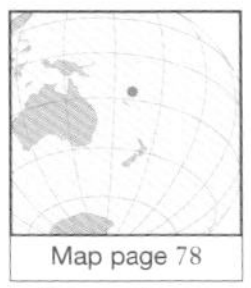
Map page 78

Vanuatu occupies an archipelago of approximately eighty islands in the southwest Pacific. Many of the islands are mountainous, of volcanic origin and densely forested. The climate is tropical, with heavy rainfall. Half of the population lives on the main islands of Éfaté and Espíritu Santo, and the majority of people are employed in agriculture. Copra, beef, timber, vegetables, and cocoa are the main exports. Tourism is becoming important to the economy. Australia, Japan and Germany are the main trading partners.

VATICAN CITY
Vatican City State or Holy See

Area Sq Km	0.5	**Currency**	Euro
Area Sq Miles	0.2	**Languages**	Italian
Population	552	**Religions**	Roman Catholic
Capital	Vatican City		

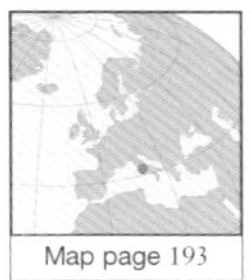
Map page 193

The world's smallest sovereign state, the Vatican City occupies a hill to the west of the river Tiber within the Italian capital, Rome. It is the headquarters of the Roman Catholic church, and income comes from investments, voluntary contributions and tourism.

VENEZUELA
Republic of Venezuela

Area Sq Km	912 050	**Currency**	Bolívar
Area Sq Miles	352 144	**Languages**	Spanish, Amerindian languages
Population	26 749 000	**Religions**	Roman Catholic, Protestant
Capital	Caracas	**Organizations**	OPEC, UN

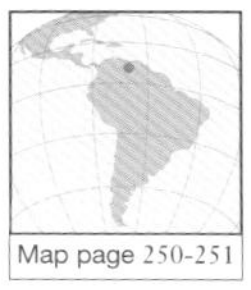
Map page 250-251

Venezuela is in northern South America, on the Caribbean. Its coast is much indented, with the oil-rich area of Lake Maracaibo at the western end, and the swampy Orinoco Delta to the east. Mountain ranges run parallel to the coast, and turn southwestwards to form a northern extension of the Andes. Central Venezuela is an area of lowland grasslands drained by the Orinoco river system. To the south are the Guiana Highlands, which contain the Angel Falls, the world's highest waterfall. Almost ninety per cent of the population lives in towns, mostly in the coastal mountain areas. The climate is tropical, with most rainfall in summer. Farming is important, particularly cattle ranching and dairy farming; coffee, maize, rice and sugar cane are the main crops. Venezuela is a major oil producer, and oil accounts for about seventy-five per cent of export earnings. Aluminium, iron ore, copper and gold are also mined, and manufactures include petrochemicals, aluminium, steel, textiles and food products. The USA and Puerto Rico are the main trading partners.

VIETNAM
Socialist Republic of Vietnam

Area Sq Km	329 565	**Currency**	Dong
Area Sq Miles	127 246	**Languages**	Vietnamese, Thai, Khmer, Chinese, local languages
Population	84 238 000	**Religions**	Buddhist, Taoist, Roman Catholic, Cao Dai, Hoa Hao
Capital	Ha Nôi	**Organizations**	APEC, ASEAN, UN

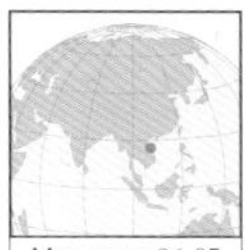
Map page 96-97

Vietnam lies in Southeast Asia on the west coast of the South China Sea. The Red River delta lowlands in the north are separated from the huge Mekong delta in the south by long, narrow coastal plains backed by the mountainous and forested terrain of the Annam Highlands. Most of the population lives in the river deltas. The climate is tropical, with summer monsoon rains. Over three-quarters of the workforce is involved in agriculture, forestry and fishing. Coffee, tea and rubber are important cash crops, but Vietnam is the world's second largest rice exporter. Oil, coal and copper are produced, and other main industries are food processing, clothing and footwear, cement and fertilizers. Exports include oil, coffee, rice, clothing, fish and fish products. Japan and Singapore are the main trading partners.

Virgin Islands (U.K.)
United Kingdom Overseas Territory

Area Sq Km	153	**Currency**	United States dollar
Area Sq Miles	59	**Languages**	English
Population	22 000	**Religions**	Protestant, Roman Catholic
Capital	Road Town		

The Caribbean territory comprises four main islands and over thirty islets at the eastern end of the Virgin Islands group. Apart from the flat coral atoll of Anegada, the islands are volcanic in origin and hilly. The climate is subtropical, and tourism is the main industry.

Map page 247

Virgin Islands (U.S.A.)
United States Unincorporated Territory

Area Sq Km	352	**Currency**	United States dollar
Area Sq Miles	136	**Languages**	English, Spanish
Population	112 000	**Religions**	Protestant, Roman Catholic
Capital	Charlotte Amalie		

The territory consists of three main islands and over fifty islets in the Caribbean's western Virgin Islands. The islands are hilly, of volcanic origin, and the climate is subtropical. The economy is based on tourism, with some manufacturing, including a major oil refinery on St Croix.

Map page 247

Wallis and Futuna Islands
French Overseas Territory

Area Sq Km	274	**Currency**	CFP franc
Area Sq Miles	106	**Languages**	French, Wallisian, Futunian
Population	15 000	**Religions**	Roman Catholic
Capital	Matā'utu		

The south Pacific territory comprises the volcanic islands of the Wallis archipelago and the Hoorn Islands. The climate is tropical. The islands depend on subsistence farming, the sale of licences to foreign fishing fleets, workers' remittances from abroad and French aid.

Map page 75

West Bank
Disputed Territory

Area Sq Km	5 860	**Currency**	Jordanian dinar, Israeli shekel
Area Sq Miles	2 263	**Languages**	Arabic, Hebrew
Population	2 421 491	**Religions**	Sunni Muslim, Jewish, Shi'a Muslim, Christian

The territory consists of the west bank of the river Jordan and parts of Judea and Samaria. The land was annexed by Israel in 1967, but some areas have been granted autonomy under agreements between Israel and the Palestinian Authority. Conflict between the Israelis and the Palestinians continues to restrict economic development.

Map page 128

Western Sahara
Disputed Territory (Morocco)

Area Sq Km	266 000	**Currency**	Moroccan dirhamr
Area Sq Miles	102 703	**Languages**	Arabic
Population	341 000	**Religions**	Sunni Muslim
Capital	Laâyoune		

Situated on the northwest coast of Africa, the territory of the Western

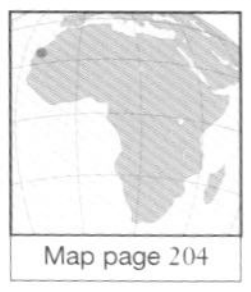
Map page 204

Sahara is now effectively controlled by Morocco. The land is low, flat desert with higher land in the northeast. There is little cultivation and only about twenty per cent of the land is pasture. Livestock herding, fishing and phosphate mining are the main activities. All trade is controlled by Morocco.

YEMEN
Republic of Yemen

Area Sq Km	527 968	**Currency**	Yemeni riyal
Area Sq Miles	203 850	**Languages**	Arabic
Population	20 975 000	**Religions**	Sunni Muslim, Shi'a Muslim
Capital	Şan'ā'	**Organizations**	UN

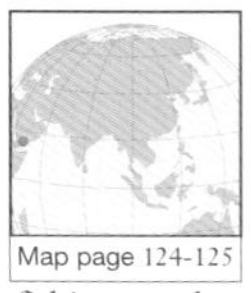
Map page 124-125

Yemen occupies the southwestern part of the Arabian Peninsula, on the Red Sea and the Gulf of Aden. Beyond the Red Sea coastal plain the land rises to a mountain range and then descends to desert plateaus. Much of the country is hot and arid, but there is more rainfall in the west, where most of the population lives. Farming and fishing are the main activities, with cotton the main cash crop. The main exports are crude oil, fish, coffee and dried fruit. Despite some oil resources Yemen is one of the poorest countries in the Arab world. Main trading partners are Thailand, China, South Korea and Saudi Arabia.

ZAMBIA
Republic of Zambia

Area Sq Km	752 614	**Currency**	Zambian kwacha
Area Sq Miles	290 586	**Languages**	English, Bemba, Nyanja, Tonga, local languages
Population	11 668 000	**Religions**	Christian, traditional beliefs
Capital	Lusaka	**Organizations**	Comm., SADC, UN

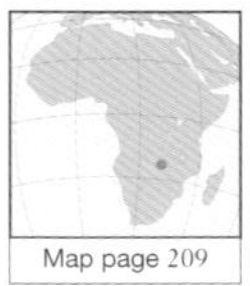
Map page 209

A landlocked state in south central Africa, Zambia consists principally of high savanna plateaus and is bordered by the Zambezi river in the south. Most people live in the Copperbelt area in the centre-north. The climate is tropical, with a rainy season from November to May. Agriculture employs approximately eighty per cent of the workforce, but is mainly at subsistence level. Copper mining is the mainstay of the economy, although reserves are declining. Copper and cobalt are the main exports. Most trade is with South Africa.

ZIMBABWE
Republic of Zimbabwe

Area Sq Km	390 759	**Currency**	Zimbabwean dollar
Area Sq Miles	150 873	**Languages**	English, Shona, Ndebele
Population	13 010 000	**Religions**	Christian, traditional beliefs
Capital	Harare	**Organizations**	SADC, UN

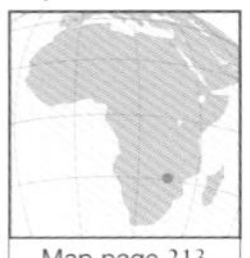
Map page 213

Zimbabwe, a landlocked state in south-central Africa, consists of high plateaus flanked by the Zambezi river valley and Lake Kariba in the north and the Limpopo river in the south. Most of the population lives in the centre of the country. There are significant mineral resources, including gold, nickel, copper, asbestos, platinum and chromium. Agriculture is a major sector of the economy, with crops including tobacco, maize, sugar cane and cotton. Beef cattle are also important. Exports include tobacco, gold, ferroalloys, nickel and cotton. South Africa is the main trading partner. The economy has suffered recently through significant political unrest and instability.

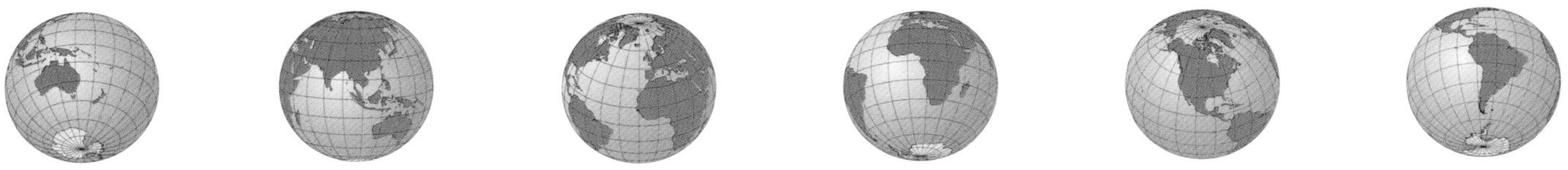

ATLAS OF THE WORLD

ATLAS MAPPING

The Atlas of the World includes a variety of styles and scales of mapping which together provide comprehensive coverage of all parts of the world; the map styles and editorial policies followed are introduced here. The area covered by each map is shown on the front and back endpapers.

Each continent is introduced by a politically coloured map followed by reference maps of sub-continental regions and then more detailed reference mapping of regions and individual countries. Scales for continental maps (*see 1*) range between 1:15 000 000 and 1:27 000 000 and regional maps (*see 2*) are in the range 1:11 000 000 to 1:13 000 000. Mapping for most countries is at scales between 1:3 000 000 and 1:7 500 000 (*see 3*) although selected, more densely populated areas of Europe, North America

and Asia are mapped at larger scales, up to 1:1 000 000 (*see 4*). Large-scale city plans of a selection of the world's major cities (*see 5*), are included on the appropriate map pages. A suite of maps covering the world's oceans and poles (*see 6*) at a variety of scales, concludes the main reference map section.

The symbols and place name abbreviations used on the maps are fully explained on pages 68–69 and a glossary of geographical terms is included at the back of the atlas on pages 269–272. The alphanumeric reference system used in the index is based on latitude and longitude, and the number and letter for each graticule square are shown within each map frame, in red. The numbers of adjoining or overlapping pages are shown by arrows in the page frame and accompanying numbers in the margin.

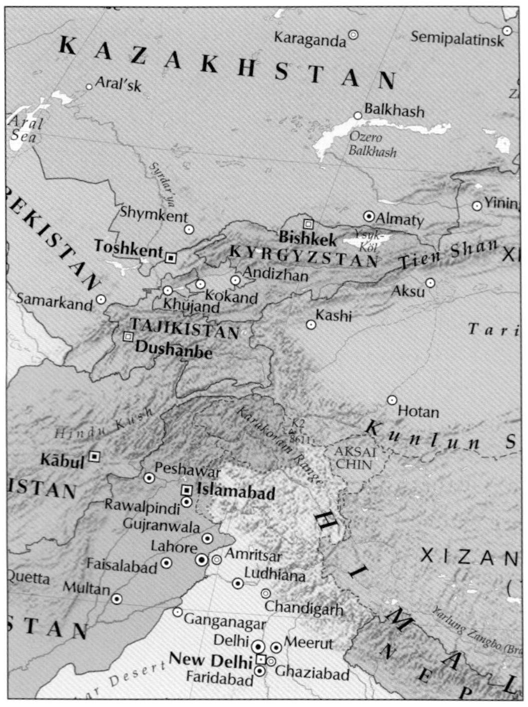

1. CONTINENTAL MAP OF ASIA (extract from pages 88–89)

BOUNDARIES

The status, names and boundaries of nations are shown in this atlas as they are at the time of going to press, as far as can be ascertained. Where an international boundary symbol appears in the sea or ocean it does not necessarily infer a legal maritime boundary, but shows which off-shore islands belong to which country.

Where international boundaries are the subject of dispute it may be that no portrayal of them will meet with the approval of any of the countries involved, but it is not seen as the function of this atlas to try to adjudicate between the rights and wrongs of political issues. The atlas aims to take a neutral viewpoint of all such cases. Although reference mapping at atlas scales is not the ideal medium for indicating territorial claims, every reasonable attempt is made to show where an active territorial dispute exists, and where there is an important difference between 'de facto' (existing in fact, on the ground) and 'de jure' (according to law) boundaries. This is done by the use of a different symbol where international boundaries are disputed, or where the alignment is unconfirmed, to that used for settled international boundaries. Cease-fire lines are also shown by a separate symbol. For clarity, disputed boundaries and areas are annotated where this is considered necessary but it is impossible to represent all the complexities of territorial disputes on maps at atlas scales.

The latest internal administrative division boundaries are shown on the maps for selected countries where the combination of map scale and the number of divisions permits, with recent changes to local government systems being taken into account as far as possible. Towns which are first-order and second-order administrative centres are also symbolized where scale permits.

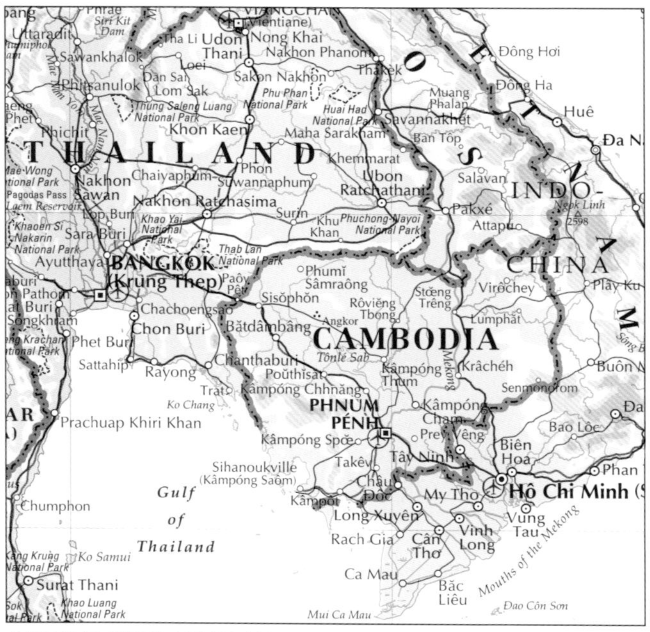

2. SOUTHEAST ASIA 1:13 000 000 (extract from pages 90–91)

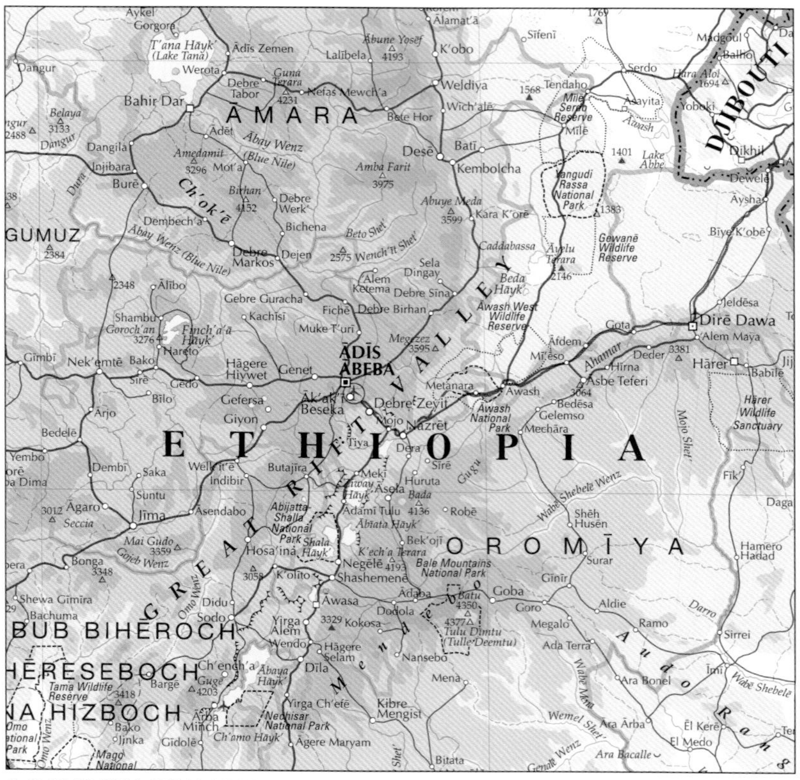

3. EAST CENTRAL AFRICA 1:7 500 000 (extract from pages 210–211)

PLACE NAMES

NAME FORM POLICY
The spelling of place names on maps has always been a matter of great complexity, because of the variety of the world's languages and the systems used to write them down. There is no standard way of spelling names or of converting them from one alphabet, or symbol set, to another. Instead, conventional ways of spelling have evolved in each of the world's major languages, and the results often differ significantly from the name as it is spelled in the original language. Familiar examples of English conventional names include Munich (München), Florence (Firenze) and Moscow (from the transliterated form, Moskva).

In this atlas, local name forms are used where they are in the Roman alphabet. These local forms are those which are recognized by the government of the country concerned, usually as represented by its official mapping agency. This is a basic principle laid down by the United Kingdom government's Permanent Committee on Geographical Names for British Official Use (PCGN).

For languages in non-Roman alphabets or symbol sets, names need to be 'Romanized' through a process of transliteration (the conversion of characters or symbols from one alphabet into another) or transcription (conversion of names based on pronunciation). Different systems often exist for this process, but

PCGN and its United States counterpart, the Board on Geographic Names (BGN), usually follow the same Romanization principles, and the general policy for this atlas is to follow their lead. One notable change in this edition is that PCGN and BGN principles are now followed for Arabic names in Egypt ('Al' style – for example Al Qāhirah for Cairo), where previous editions followed PCGN's former policy of using a local Survey of Egypt system ('El' style – El Qâhira).

Local name form mapping is the nearest that the cartographer can achieve to an international standard. It is in fact impossible, and perhaps unnecessary, to provide English names for the majority of mapped features, and translating names into English is fraught with linguistic hazards. Consequently, a local name form map is more internally consistent than a partly-anglicized one.

Although local forms in this atlas are given precedence, prominent English-language conventional names and historic names are not neglected. The names of countries, continents, oceans, seas and underwater features in international waters appear in English throughout the atlas, as do those of other international features where such an English form exists. Significant superseded names and other alternative spellings are included in brackets on the maps where space permits, and variants and former names are cross-referenced in the index.

NAME CHANGES
Continuing changes in official languages, in writing systems and in Romanization methods, have to be taken into account by cartographers. In many countries different languages are in use in different regions or side-by-side in the same region, and there is potential for widely varying name forms even within a single country. A worldwide trend towards national, regional and ethnic self-determination is operating at the same time as pressure towards increased international standardization.

Place names are, to an extent, a mirror for the changes that continue to transform the political world. Changes of territorial control may have a significant effect on name forms. Yet even in countries where name forms could be expected to have long been largely standardized, there are sometimes continuing issues for the cartographer to address. In the UK, for example, there is a trend for more Gaelic and Welsh-language names to be given official recognition. Similarly, there has been an increase in the official recognition and use of indigenous name forms in for instance New Zealand (Maori) and Canada (Inuit and Indian names). Name spelling issues are, in fact, likely to emerge in almost any part of the world.

Reflecting trends across the world, systematic alterations affecting various countries are reflected in this atlas. The dissolution of the

MAP PROJECTIONS

The creation of computer-generated maps presents the opportunity to select projections specifically for the area and scale of each map. As the only way to show the Earth with absolute accuracy is on a globe, all map projections are compromises. Some projections seek to maintain correct area relationships (equal area projections), true distances and bearings from a point (equidistant projections) or correct angles and shapes (conformal projections); others attempt to achieve a balance between these properties. The choice of projections used in this atlas has been made on an individual continental and regional basis. Projections used, and their individual parameters, have been defined to minimize distortion and to reduce scale errors (shown as percentage figures in the accompanying diagrams) as much as possible.

For world maps, the Bartholomew version of the Winkel Tripel Projection is used. This projection combines elements of conformality with that of equal area, and shows, over the world as a whole, relatively true shapes and reasonably equal areas. The Mercator Projection (see 7) has been selected for the regional maps of southeast Asia along the Equator , while in higher latitudes, particularly in Europe and to some extent in North America, the Conic Equidistant Projection (see 8) has been used extensively for regional mapping. The Lambert Azimuthal Equal Area Projection (see 9) has been employed in both South America and Australia.

7. MERCATOR PROJECTION

This rectangular or cylindrical projection is constructed on the basis of a cylinder in contact with the globe, in this case around the Equator. Scale is correct along the Equator and distortion increases away from it in both directions.

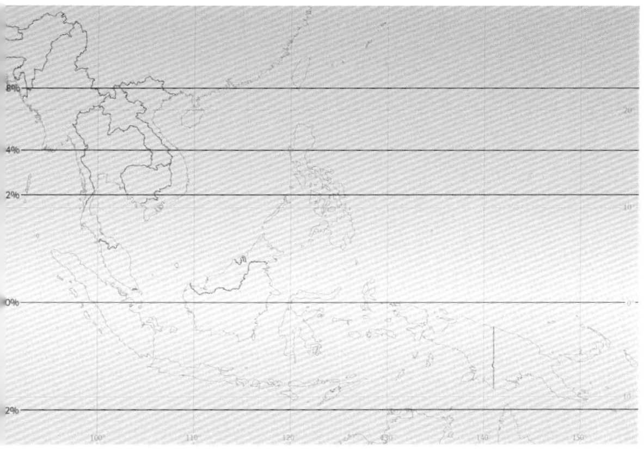

8. CONIC EQUIDISTANT PROJECTION

Constructed on the basis of a cone intersecting the globe along two standard parallels (55°N and 75°N in this illustration), along both of which scale is correct. Lines of equal scale error are parallel to the standard lines, with distortion increasing away from each.

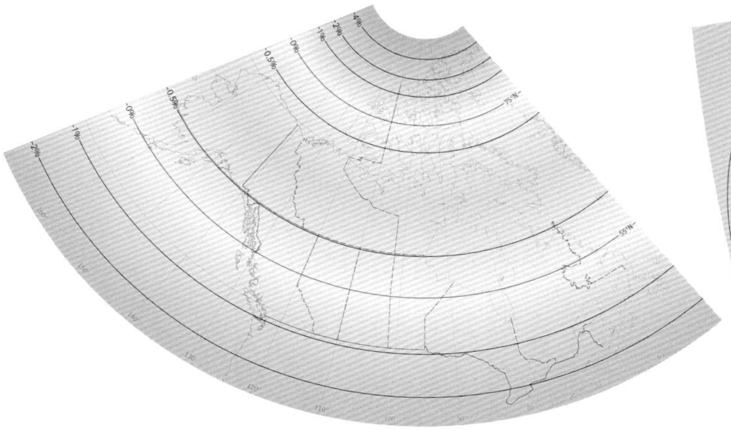

9. LAMBERT AZIMUTHAL EQUAL AREA PROJECTION

Points are projected onto a plane in contact with the globe at the centre point (25°S, 135°E in this illustration). Scale is correct at the centre, and scale errors increase in concentric circles away from it. Areas are true in relation to the corresponding areas on the globe.

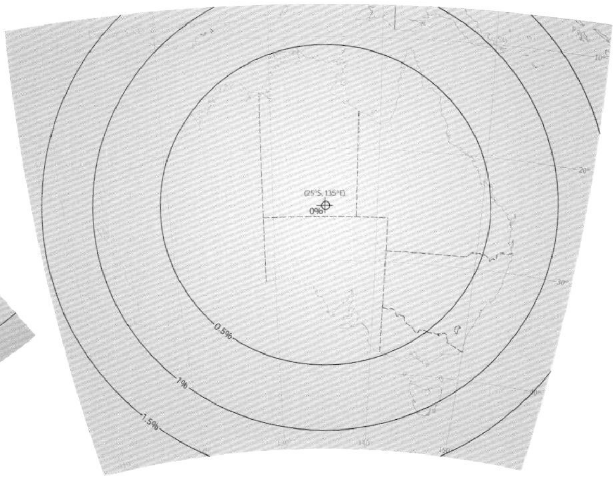

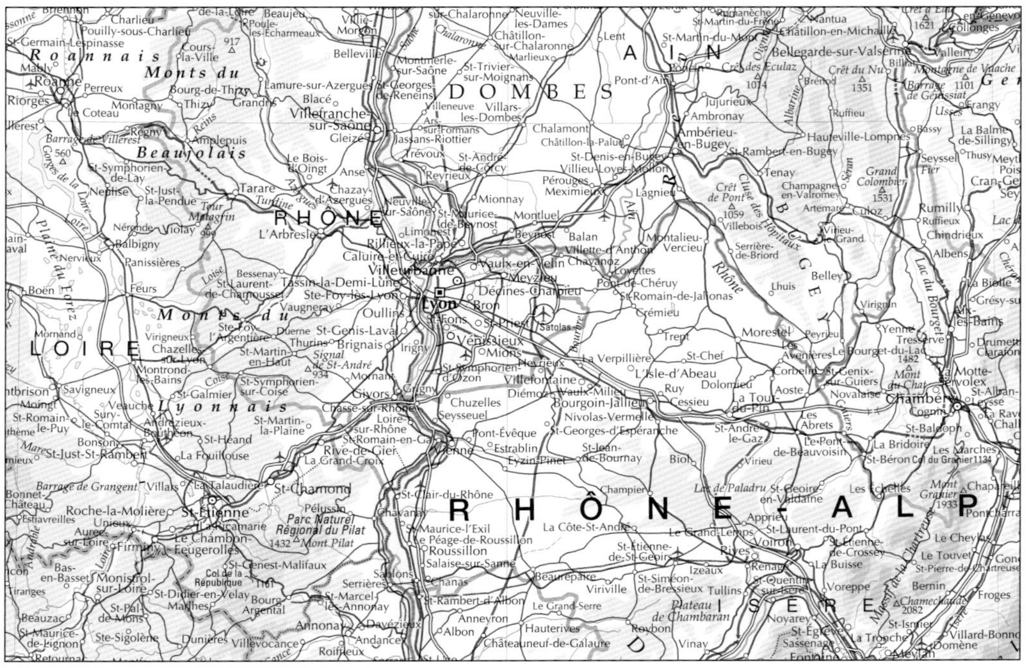

4. SOUTHEAST FRANCE 1:1 200 000 (extract from pages 160–161)

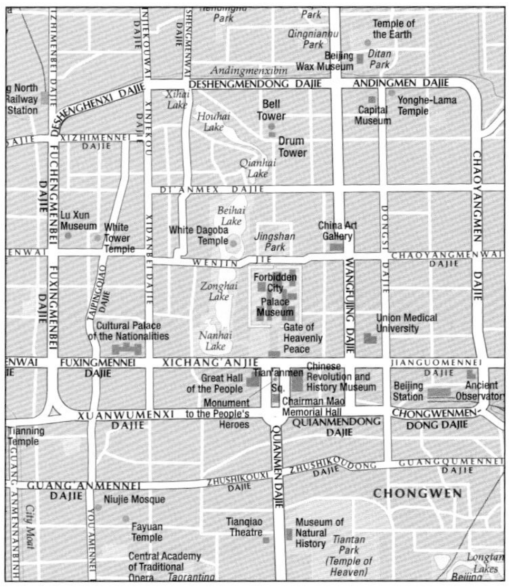

5. BEIJING CITY PLAN (extract from page 106)

former USSR has given rise to the greatest changes in recent years, and this atlas continues the policy established in the previous edition of names being converted from Russian to the main national language in Belarus, Ukraine, Moldova, Armenia, Georgia, Azerbaijan, Kyrgyzstan and Tajikistan. Uzbekistan is the latest to have been converted in this way, using the new Uzbek Roman alphabet. Russian naturally continues to be used as the main form in the Russian Federation and also continues to be used as the prime language on maps of Kazakhstan. Here, local-language name forms (derived from Kazakh Cyrillic) are included for main place names where space permits on the maps, with additional alternatives in the index. In Turkmenistan, main Turkmen Cyrillic-derived names are similarly covered, but native sources are starting to apply a finalized Roman alphabet, pointing the way to a future in which Cyrillic names will be dropped entirely. Main examples of new Turkmen forms are included as cross-references in the index.

In Spain, account is taken of the official prominence now given to Catalan, Galician and some Basque spellings, which results in name forms such as Eivissa for Ibiza and A Coruña for La Coruña. Reflecting these changes, many names are now represented in dual form on official Spanish mapping. Depending on their specific treatment on local mapping, some of these are shown in this atlas as hyphenated (for example Donostia-San Sebastián, Gijón-Xixón,

Elche-Elx) while others include the second forms as alternative names.

Chinese name forms, which were fully converted to the official Pinyin Romanization system some years ago in earlier editions of this atlas, continue to change. Name forms have been brought into line with the latest official sources, continuing to follow the principle whereby numerous towns which are the centres of administrative units such as the county or 'xian' officially take the name of the county itself. The alternative place name in common local use is shown in brackets on the map. The index also includes numerous cross-references for Chinese name forms as they were before the introduction of Pinyin – taking account of the main so-called 'Post Office' spellings such as Tientsin (now Tianjin), and more particularly of the long-familiar Wade-Giles Romanization, which gives, for instance, Pei-ching as against the Pinyin form Beijing.

As well as systematic changes in name forms such as those outlined above, occasionally places are given entirely new names for a variety of reasons. This atlas accounts for any such recent changes. One significant example is the official renaming of Calcutta as Kolkata, following earlier changes by the Indian authorities to Bombay (now Mumbai) and Madras (now Chennai).

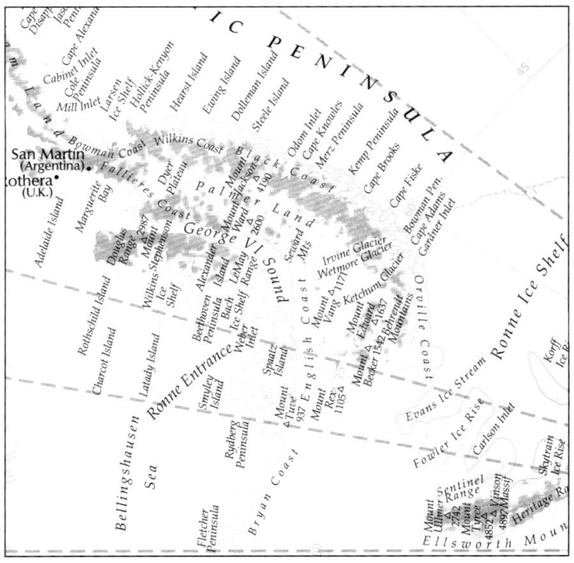

6. ANTARCTICA 1:18 000 000 (extract from pages 262–263)

REFERENCE MAPS

CITIES AND TOWNS

Population	National Capital	Administrative Capital Shown for selected countries only.		Other City or Town
		First order	Second order Scales larger than 1:9 000 000.	
over 10 million	**TŌKYŌ** ▣	**Karachi** ▣	**Los Angeles** ◉	**New York** ◉
5 million to 10 million	**SANTIAGO** ▣	**Tianjin** ▣	**Chicago** ◉	**Hong Kong** ◉
1 million to 5 million	**KĀBUL** ▣	**Sydney** ▣	**Tangshan** ◉	**Kaohsiung** ◉
500 000 to 1 million	BANGUI ▣	Trujillo ▣	Agra ◉	Jiddah ◉
100 000 to 500 000	WELLINGTON ▣	Mansa ▣	Naogaon ◉	Apucarana ◉
50 000 to 100 000	PORT OF SPAIN ▢	Potenza ▢	Trier ○	Arecibo ○
10 000 to 50 000	MALABO ▢	Chinhoyi ▢	Willimantic ○	Ceres ○
1 000 to 10 000	VALLETTA ▫	Ati ▫	Nepalganj ○	Abla ○
under 1000 Scales 1: 4 000 000 and larger		Chhukha ▫	Carmel ○	Lopigna ○

⬭ Built-up area

MISCELLANEOUS FEATURES

---------- National park   ·············· Regional park   ············· Reserve or special land area   ∴ Site of specific interest   ⌒⌒⌒⌒⌒ Wall

RELIEF

Contour intervals used in layer-colouring for land height and sea depth

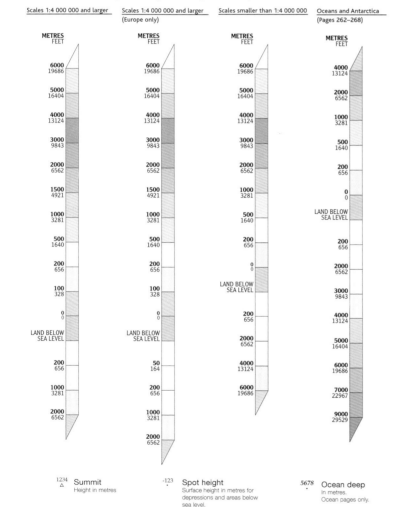

Scales 1:4 000 000 and larger METRES / FEET	Scales 1:4 000 000 and larger (Europe only) METRES / FEET	Scales smaller than 1:4 000 000 METRES / FEET	Oceans and Antarctica (Pages 262–268) METRES / FEET
6000 / 19686	6000 / 19686	6000 / 19686	4000 / 13124
5000 / 16404	5000 / 16404	5000 / 16404	2000 / 6562
4000 / 13124	4000 / 13124	4000 / 13124	1000 / 3281
3000 / 9843	3000 / 9843	3000 / 9843	500 / 1640
2000 / 6562	2000 / 6562	2000 / 6562	200 / 656
1500 / 4921	1500 / 4921	1000 / 3281	0 / 0
1000 / 3281	1000 / 3281	500 / 1640	LAND BELOW SEA LEVEL
500 / 1640	500 / 1640	200 / 656	200 / 656
200 / 656	200 / 656	0 / 0	2000 / 6562
100 / 328	100 / 328	LAND BELOW SEA LEVEL	3000 / 9843
0 / 0	0 / 0	200 / 656	4000 / 13124
LAND BELOW SEA LEVEL	LAND BELOW SEA LEVEL	2000 / 6562	5000 / 16404
200 / 656	50 / 164	4000 / 13124	6000 / 19686
1000 / 3281	200 / 656	6000 / 19686	7000 / 22967
2000 / 6562	1000 / 3281		9000 / 29529
	2000 / 6562		

△ 12̄3̄4̄ Summit
Height in metres.   ·-123 Spot height
Surface height in metres for depressions and areas below sea level.   ·5678 Ocean deep
In metres.
Ocean pages only.

LAND AND SEA FEATURES

	Rock desert
	Sand desert / Dunes
⌣	Oasis
	Lava field
▲ 1234	Volcano Height in metres.
	Marsh
	Ice cap / Glacier
	Nunatak
	Coral reef
··············	Escarpment
·············	Flood dyke
](123	Pass Height in metres.
	Ice shelf

LAKES AND RIVERS

	Lake
	Impermanent lake
	Salt lake or lagoon
	Impermanent salt lake
	Dry salt lake or salt pan
123	Lake height Surface height above sea level, in metres.
——	River
--------	Impermanent river
	Wadi or watercourse
	Waterfall
		Dam
	Barrage

BOUNDARIES

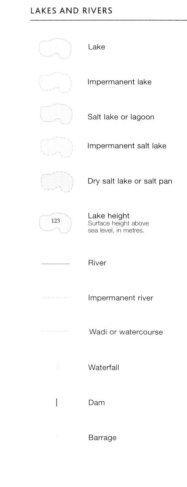

▪—·—▪	International boundary
▪ ▪ ▪ ▪	Disputed international boundary or alignment unconfirmed
◣	Undefined international boundary in the sea. All land within this boundary is part of state or territory named.
▪—▪—▪	Administrative boundary, first order internal division. Scales 1:4 000 000 and larger. Shown for selected countries only.
——	Administrative boundary, first order internal division. Scales smaller than 1:4 000 000. Shown for selected countries only.
——	Administrative boundary, second order internal division. Scales 1:4 000 000 and larger. Shown for selected countries only.
▪◄ ►▪	Disputed administrative boundary Scales 1:4 000 000 and larger. Shown for selected countries only.
● ● ● ● ● ●	Ceasefire line or other boundary described on the map

STYLES OF LETTERING

Cities and towns are explained separately

		Physical features	
Country	**FRANCE**		
Overseas Territory/Dependency	**Guadeloupe**	Island	*Gran Canaria*
Disputed Territory	AKSAI CHIN	Lake	*LAKE ERIE*
Administrative name, first order internal division Shown for selected countries only.	**SCOTLAND**	Mountain	*Mt Blanc*
Administrative name, second order internal division Scales 1:4 000 000 and larger. Shown for selected countries only.	MANCHE	River	*Thames*
Area name	ARTOIS	Region	*PAMPAS*

TRANSPORT

═══ ▪▪▪ under construction	Motorway Scales 1:4 000 000 and larger.	—— under construction	Main railway
—— under construction	Main road	—— under construction	Secondary railway
—— under construction	Secondary road	▪▪▪▪ under construction	Railway tunnel
═▪═	Motorway tunnel	——	Canal
—▪—	Road tunnel	——	Minor canal
-----	Track	⊕	Main airport
		✈	Regional airport

CITY PLANS

Symbol	Description
	Built-up area
	Cemetery
	Park
	Place of worship
	General place of interest
	Transport location
	Academic / municipal building

CONTINENTAL MAPS

BOUNDARIES

Symbol	Description
———	International boundary
-------	Disputed international boundary or alignment unconfirmed
	Undefined international boundary in the sea. All land within this boundary is part of state or territory named.
••••••••	Ceasefire line
- - - - -	Administrative boundary Shown for selected countries only.

CITIES AND TOWNS

Population	National Capital	Other City or Town
over 10 million	**México** ■	Mumbai ◉
5 million to 10 million	**London** ■	Belo Horizonte ◉
1 million to 5 million	**Kābul** ■	Kaohsiung ◉
500 000 to 1 million	**Bangui** ▣	Khulna ◎
100 000 to 500 000	**Wellington** ▣	Iquitos ⊙
50 000 to 100 000	**Port of Spain** ▢	Naga ○
10 000 to 50 000	**Malabo** ▢	Ushuaia ○
under 10 000	**Valletta** ▫	Arviat ○

ABBREVIATIONS

Abbr.	Term	Language	Meaning
A.C.T.	Australian Capital Territory		
Arch.	Archipelago		
	Archipiélago	Spanish	archipelago
B.	Bay		
	Bahia, Baía	Portuguese	bay
	Bahía	Spanish	bay
	Baie	French	bay
Bol.	Bol'shaya, Bol'shoy, Bol'shoye	Russian	big
C.	Cape		
	Cabo	Portuguese, Spanish	cape, headland
	Cap	Catalan, French	cape, headland
Cach.	Cachoeira	Portuguese	waterfall, rapids
Can.	Canal	French, Portuguese, Spanish	canal, channel
Cd	Ciudad	Spanish	city, town
Chan.	Channel		
Co	Cerro	Spanish	hill, mountain, peak
Cord.	Cordillera	Spanish	mountain range
Cr.	Creek		
Cuch.	Cuchilla	Spanish	hills, mountain range
D.	Dağ, Dağı	Turkish	mountain
	Dāgh	Farsi	mountain, mountains
	Dağları	Turkish	mountain range
	Danau	Indonesian, Malay	lake
Div.	Division		
Dr	Doctor		
E.	East, Eastern		
Emb.	Embalse	Spanish	reservoir
Est.	Estero	Spanish	estuary, inlet
	Estrecho	Spanish	strait
Fj.	Fjörður	Icelandic	fjord, inlet
Ft	Fort		
G.	Gebel	Arabic	hill, mountain
	Golfo	Italian, Spanish	gulf, bay
	Gora	Russian	mountain
	Gunung	Indonesian, Malay	hill, mountain
Gd	Grand	French	big
Gde	Grande	French, Italian, Portuguese, Spanish	big
Geb.	Gebergte	Afrikaans, Dutch	mountain range
Gen.	General		
Gl.	Glacier		
Gp	Group		
Gt	Great		
Harb.	Harbour		
Hd	Head		
I.	Island, Isle		
	Ilha	Portuguese	island
	Isla	Spanish	island
Î.	Île	French	island
im.	imeni	Russian	'in the name of'
Ind. Res.	Indian Reservation		
Ing.	Ingeniero	Spanish	engineer
Is	Islands, Isles		
	Islas	Spanish	islands
Îs	Îles	French	islands
J.	Jabal, Jebel	Arabic	mountain, mountains
Kep.	Kepulauan	Indonesian, Malay	archipelago, islands
Khr.	Khrebet	Russian	mountain range
L.	Lake		
	Loch	(Scotland)	lake
	Lough	(Ireland)	lake
	Lac	French	lake
	Lago	Portuguese, Spanish	lake
Lag.	Laguna	Spanish	lagoon
M.	Mys	Russian	cape, point
Mt	Mount		
	Mont	French	hill, mountain
Mt.	Mountain		
Mte	Monte	Portuguese, Spanish	hill, mountain

Abbr.	Term	Language	Meaning
Mts	Mountains		
	Monts	French	hills, mountains
N.	North, Northern		
Nev.	Nevado	Spanish	peak
Nat.	National		
Nat. Park	National Park		
Nat. Res.	Nature Reserve		
Nizh.	Nizhniy, Nizhnyaya	Russian	lower
N.E.	Northeast, Northeastern		
N.H.S.	National Heritage Site		
N.W.	Northwest, Northwestern		
O.	Ostrov	Russian	island
O-va	Ostrova	Russian	islands
Oz.	Ozero	Russian, Ukrainian	lake
P.	Paso	Spanish	pass
	Pulau	Indonesian, Malay	island
Pass.	Passage		
Peg.	Pegunungan	Indonesian, Malay	mountain range
Pen.	Peninsula		
	Península	Spanish	peninsula
Pk	Peak		
	Puncak	Indonesian	mountain, peak
P-ov	Poluostrov	Russian	peninsula
P. P.	Pulau-pulau	Indonesian	islands
Psa	Presa	Spanish	reservoir
Pt	Point		
Pta	Punta	Italian, Spanish	cape, point
Pte	Pointe	French	cape, point
Pto	Porto	Portuguese	harbour, port
	Puerto	Spanish	harbour, port
R.	River		
	Rio	Portuguese	river
	Río	Spanish	river
	Rivière	French	river
	Rūd	Farsi	river
Ra.	Range		
Rec.	Recreation		
Res.	Reservation, Reserve		
Resr	Reservoir		
S.	South, Southern		
	Salar, Salina, Salinas	Spanish	salt pan, salt pans
Sa	Serra	Portuguese	mountain range
	Sierra	Spanish	mountain range
Sd	Sound		
S.E.	Southeast, Southeastern		
Serr.	Serranía	Spanish	mountain range
Sk.	Shuiku	Chinese	reservoir
Sr.	Sredniy, Srednyaya	Russian	middle, central
St	Saint		
	Sankt	German, Russian	saint
	Sint	Dutch	saint
Sta	Santa	Italian, Portuguese, Spanish	saint
Ste	Sainte	French	saint
Sto	Santo	Italian, Portuguese, Spanish	saint
Str.	Strait		
S.W.	Southwest, Southwestern		
Tg	Tanjong, Tanjung	Indonesian, Malay	cape, point
Tk	Teluk, Telukan	Indonesian, Malay	bay, gulf
Tte	Teniente	Spanish	lieutenant
Va	Villa	Spanish	town
Vdkhr.	Vodokhranilishche	Russian	reservoir
Verkh.	Verkhniy, Verkhnyaya	Russian	upper
Vol.	Volcano		
	Volcan	French	volcano
	Volcán	Spanish	volcano
Vozv.	Vozvyshennost'	Russian	hills, upland
W.	West, Western		
	Wadi, Wâdi, Wādī	Arabic	watercourse

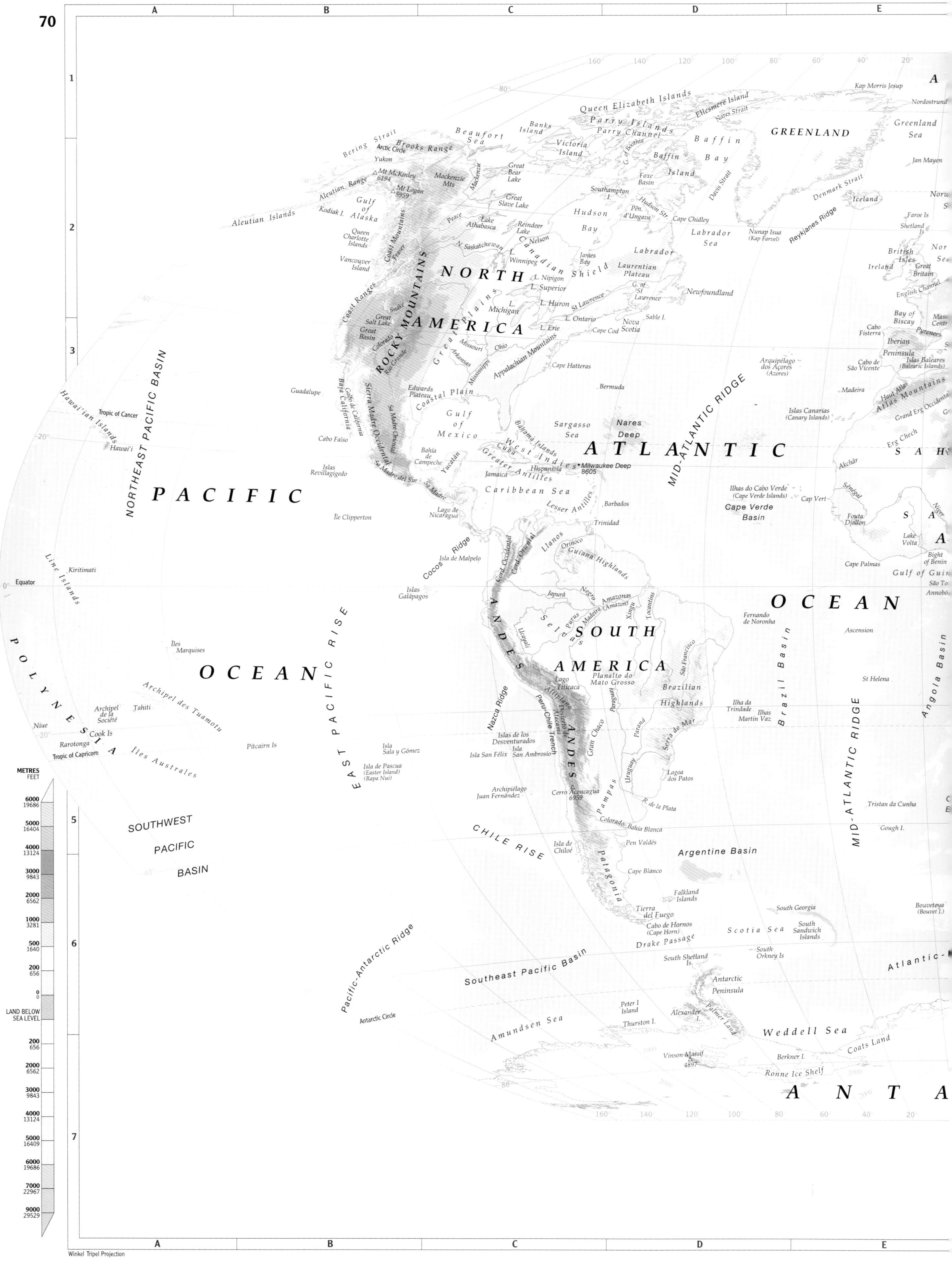

METRES
FEET

6000
19686

5000
16404

4000
13124

3000
9843

2000
6562

1000
3281

500
1640

200
656

0
0

LAND BELOW
SEA LEVEL

200
656

2000
6562

3000
9843

4000
13124

5000
16409

6000
19686

7000
22967

9000
29529

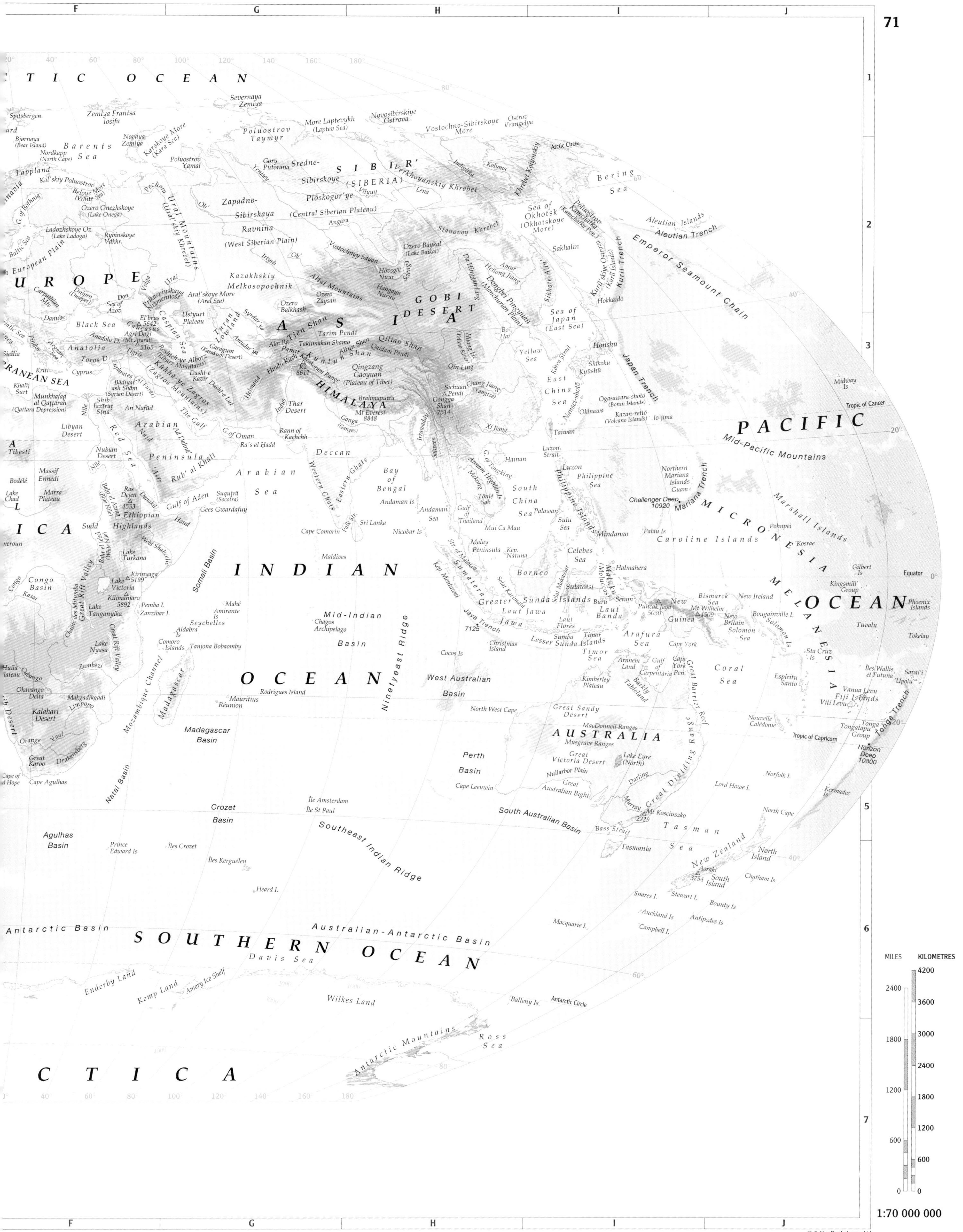

© Collins Bartholomew Ltd

F
G
J
1
2
3
4
5
6
7
T I C O C E A N
Severnaya Zemlya
Spitsbergen
Zemlya Frantsa Iosifa
Bjørnøya (Bear Island)
Barents Sea
Nordkapp (North Cape)
Novaya Zemlya
Karskoye More (Kara Sea)
Poluostrov Taymyr
More Laptevykh (Laptev Sea)
Novosibirskiye Ostrova
Vostochno-Sibirskoye More
Ostrov Vrangelya
Arctic Circle
Lappland
Kol'skiy Poluostrov
Beloye More (White Sea)
G. of Bothnia
Ozero Onezhskoye (Lake Onega)
Ladozhskoye Oz. (Lake Ladoga)
Baltic Sea
Rybinskoye Vdkhr.
European Plain
Pechora
Ural Mountains (Ural'skiy Khrebet)
Poluostrov Yamal
Gory Putorana
Sredne-Sibirskoye Ploskogor'ye (Central Siberian Plateau)
S I B I R' (SIBERIA)
Verkhoyanskiy Khrebet
Indigirka
Kolyma
Khrebet Kolymskiy
Lena
Vilyuy
Yenisey
Ob'
Zapadno-Sibirskaya Ravnina (West Siberian Plain)
Angara
Stanovoy Khrebet
Sea of Okhotsk (Okhotskoye More)
Poluostrov Kamchatka (Kamchatka Pen.)
Bering Sea
Aleutian Islands
Aleutian Trench
Emperor Seamount Chain
Sakhalin
Kuril'skiye Ostrova (Kuril Islands)
Kuril Trench
Hokkaidō
Irtysh
Vostochnyy Sayan
Ozero Baykal (Lake Baikal)
Amur
Heilong Jiang
Da Hinggan Ling
Dongbei Pingyuan (Manchurian Plain)
Sikhote-Alin'
Hövsgöl Nuur
Hangayn Nuruu
Altai Mountains
Ozero Zaysan
G O B I D E S E R T
U R O P E
Carpathian Mts
Dnipro (Dnieper)
Volga
Ural
Don
Sea of Azov
Prikaspiyskaya Nizmennost'
Kazakhskiy Melkosopochnik
Aral'skoye More (Aral Sea)
Ozero Balkhash
Danube
Black Sea
El'brus 5642
Caucasus
Ustyurt Plateau
Turan Lowland
Syrdar'ya
Caspian Sea
A S I A
Tien Shan
Tarim Pendi
Taklimakan Shamo
Altun Shan
Qilian Shan
Qaidam Pendi
Kunlun Shan
Bo Hai
Huang He (Yellow River)
Sea of Japan (East Sea)
Honshū
Yellow Sea
Korea Strait
Shikoku
Kyūshū
Japan Trench
Anatolia
Agri Dagi (Mt Ararat) 5165
Tigris
Garagum (Karakum Desert)
Amudar'ya
Alai Ra.
Pamir
Hindu Kush
Karakoram Range
K2 8611
Qingzang Gaoyuan (Plateau of Tibet)
Qin Ling
East China Sea
Nansei-shotō
Ogasawara-shotō (Bonin Islands)
Okinawa
Kazan-rettō (Volcano Islands)
Iō-jima
Midway Is
Tropic of Cancer
Sicilia
Pindus
Aegean Sea
Toros D.
Kriti
Cyprus
MEDITERRANEAN SEA
Euphrates
Reshteh-ye Alborz (Elburz Mountains)
Dasht-e Kavir
Kūhhā-ye Zagros (Zagros Mountains)
Dasht-e Lut
Helmand
Indus
Thar Desert
HIMALAYA
Brahmaputra
Mt Everest 8848
Ganga (Ganges)
Sichuan Pendi
Gongga Shan 7514
Chang Jiang (Yangtze)
Xi Jiang
Taiwan
P A C I F I C
Mid-Pacific Mountains
Bādiyat ash Shām (Syrian Desert)
An Nafūd
Khalīj Surt
Munkhafaḑ al Qaţţārah (Qattara Depression)
Nile
Shib Jazīrat Sīnā'
Libyan Desert
Arabian Peninsula
Najd
Ad Dahnā'
The Gulf
G. of Oman
Ra's al Ḩadd
Rann of Kachchh
Deccan
Irrawaddy
Salween
Tibesti
Nubian Desert
Red Sea
Rub' al Khālī
Asīr
Arabian Sea
Western Ghats
Eastern Ghats
Bay of Bengal
Hainan
G. of Tongking
Annam Highlands
Mekong
Luzon Strait
Luzon
Philippine Sea
Northern Mariana Islands
Guam
Mariana Trench
Massif Ennedi
Bodélé
Lake Chad
Marra Plateau
Bahr el Azraq (Blue Nile)
Ras Dejen 4533
Denakil
Gulf of Aden
Suquṭrā (Socotra)
Gees Gwardafuy
Haud
Ethiopian Highlands
Andaman Is
Andaman Sea
Gulf of Thailand
Tônlé Sab
South China Sea
Palawan
Philippine Islands
Sulu Sea
Challenger Deep 10920
M I C R O N E S I A
Marshall Islands
Pohnpei
Sri Lanka
Palk Str.
Cape Comorin
Nicobar Is
Mui Ca Mau
Mindanao
Palau Is
Caroline Islands
Kosrae
Sudd
Bahr el Jebel (White Nile)
Weti Shabelle
Lake Turkana
Maldives
Malay Peninsula
Str. of Malacca
Kep. Natuna
Celebes Sea
Halmahera
Gilbert Is
Equator
Kingsmill Group
I N D I A N
Somali Basin
Borneo
Selat Makassar
Maluku (Moluccas)
Congo
Congo Basin
Kasai
Kirinyaga 5199
Lake Victoria
Kilimanjaro 5892
Lake Tanganyika
Great Rift Valley
Pemba I.
Zanzibar I.
Mahé
Amirante Is
Seychelles
Chagos Archipelago
Mid-Indian Basin
Ninetyeast Ridge
Kep. Mentawai
Sumatera
Selat Karimata
Greater Sunda Islands
Sulawesi
Buru
Seram
Puncak Jaya 5030
New Guinea
Mt Wilhelm 4509
Bismarck Sea
New Ireland
New Britain
Bougainville I.
Solomon Is
Solomon Sea
M E L A N E S I A
O C E A N
Phoenix Islands
Tuvalu
Tokelau
Laut Jawa
Jawa
Java Trench 7125
Laut Flores
Laut Banda
Timor
Lesser Sunda Islands
Sumba
Timor Sea
Arafura Sea
Aldabra Is
Comoro Islands
Tanjona Bobaomby
Lake Nyasa
Zambezi
Christmas Island
Cocos Is
Cape York
Cape York Pen.
Gulf of Carpentaria
Arnhem Land
Kimberley Plateau
Barkly Tableland
Coral Sea
Sta Cruz Is
Espiritu Santo
Îles Wallis et Futuna
Savai'i
'Upolu
Vanua Levu
Fiji Islands
Viti Levu
Huíla Plateau
Cubango
Okavango Delta
Makgadikgadi
Limpopo
Kalahari Desert
Mozambique Channel
Madagascar
O C E A N
Mauritius
Réunion
Rodrigues Island
West Australian Basin
North West Cape
Great Sandy Desert
Great Barrier Reef
Great Dividing Range
MacDonnell Ranges
A U S T R A L I A
Musgrave Ranges
Nouvelle Calédonie
Tonga
Tongatapu Group
Tonga Trench
Tropic of Capricorn
Orange
Vaal
Drakensberg
Great Karoo
Cape of Good Hope
Cape Agulhas
Madagascar Basin
Natal Basin
Perth Basin
Cape Leeuwin
Great Victoria Desert
Lake Eyre (North)
Nullarbor Plain
Great Australian Bight
Darling
Murray
Horizon Deep 10800
Norfolk I.
Lord Howe I.
Kermadec Is
Île Amsterdam
Île St Paul
Crozet Basin
South Australian Basin
Mt Kosciuszko 2229
Bass Strait
Tasmania
Tasman Sea
North Cape
North Island
New Zealand
Agulhas Basin
Prince Edward Is
Îles Crozet
Southeast Indian Ridge
Îles Kerguélen
Heard I.
Aoraki 3754
South Island
Chatham Is
Snares I.
Stewart I.
Bounty Is
Auckland Is
Antipodes Is
Campbell I.
Macquarie I.
Antarctic Basin
Australian-Antarctic Basin
S O U T H E R N O C E A N
Davis Sea
Enderby Land
Kemp Land
Amery Ice Shelf
Wilkes Land
Balleny Is.
Antarctic Circle
Antarctic Mountains
Ross Sea
C T I C A
MILES
KILOMETRES
2400
1800
1200
600
0
4200
3600
3000
2400
1800
1200
600
0
1:70 000 000

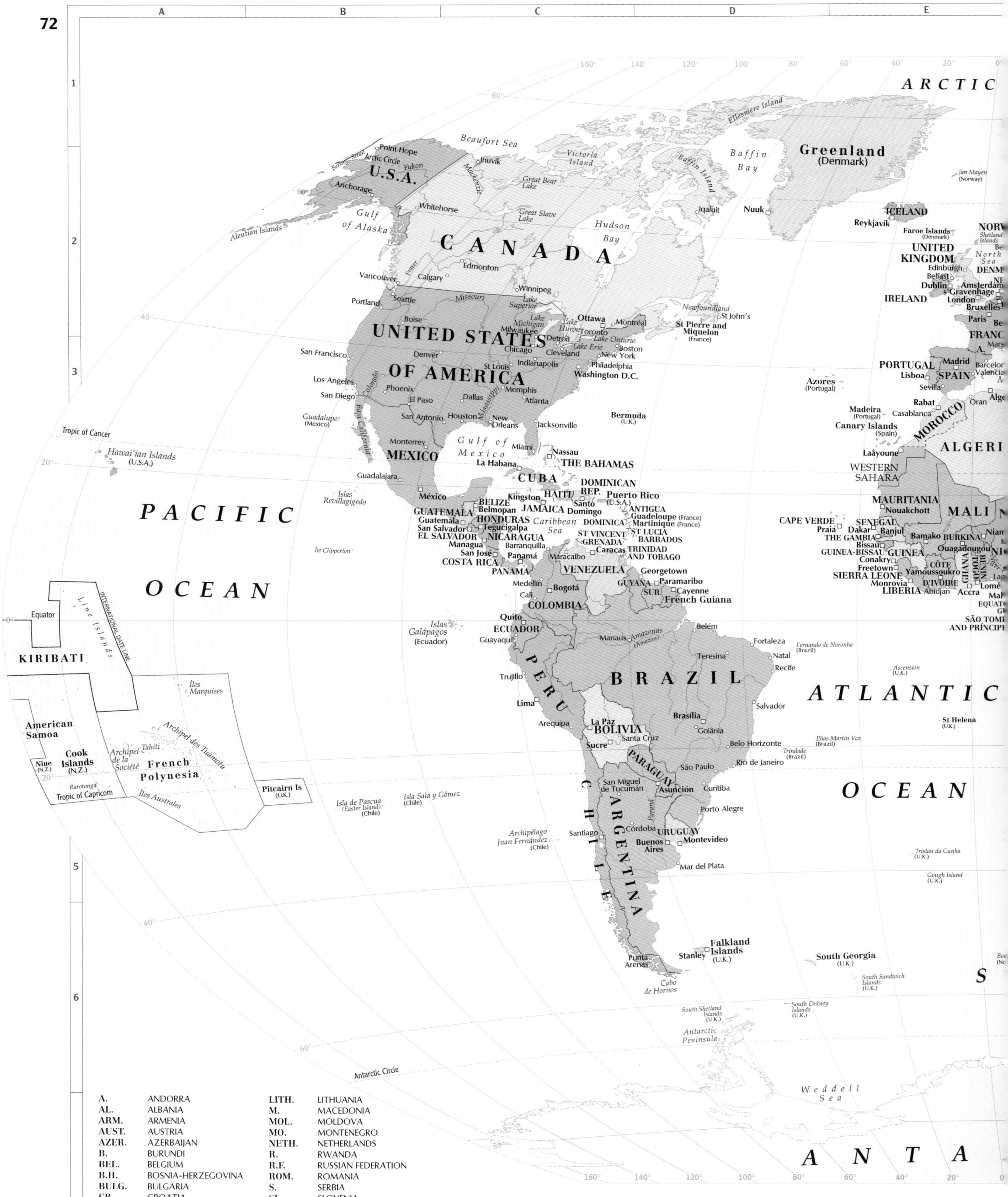

ARCTIC

Greenland
(Denmark)

Jan Mayen
(Norway)

Beaufort Sea

Victoria
Island

Baffin
Bay

Ellesmere Island

Bering Strait •Point Hope
Arctic Circle
Inuvik
Anchorage •Whitehorse
Yukon

U.S.A.

Gulf
of Alaska

Aleutian Islands

Mackenzie

Great Bear
Lake

Great Slave
Lake

Hudson
Bay

Iqaluit   Nuuk

ICELAND
Reykjavik   Faroe Islands
(Denmark)   *Shetland*
NORW
Islands Be
North
UNITED   *Sea*
KINGDOM DENM
Edinburgh
Belfast
Dublin   Amsterdam
IRELAND   London Gravenhage
Bruxelles
Paris   FRANC
Mars

CANADA

Vancouver   Edmonton
Calgary
Fraser
Seattle   *Missouri*
Portland Boise

UNITED STATES
OF AMERICA

Newfoundland
St John's
St Pierre and
Miquelon
(France)

Lake
Superior
Winnipeg
Milwaukee
Chicago
Detroit
Cleveland
Lake Erie

Ottawa Montréal
Toronto
Lake Ontario
Boston
New York
Philadelphia
Washington D.C.

Bermuda
(U.K.)

PORTUGAL Madrid
Lisboa   SPAIN
Barcelona
Valencia
M
Azores
(Portugal)
Sevilla
Madeira   Rabat
(Portugal) Casablanca MOROCCO
Canary Islands
(Spain)   Alge

Laâyoune   ALGERI

San Francisco
Denver
St Louis Indianapolis
Los Angeles
Phoenix   Memphis
San Diego   Dallas Atlanta
El Paso   Jacksonville
San Antonio Houston New
Colorado   Orleans
Guadalupe   *Mississippi*
(Mexico)
Baja California
Monterrey Gulf of
Mexico
Guadalajara
MEXICO
Nassau
La Habana
México   CUBA THE BAHAMAS
GUATEMALA BELIZE Kingston DOMINICAN
Belmopan JAMAICA Santo REP.
Guatemala HONDURAS Domingo
San Salvador Tegucigalpa DOMINICA
EL SALVADOR NICARAGUA ST LUCIA
Managua   GRENADA
San José   TRINIDAD
COSTA RICA Panamá AND TOBAGO
PANAMA   Maracaibo
VENEZUELA Georgetown
Medellín   Bogotá GUYANA Paramaribo
Cali   SUR. Cayenne
COLOMBIA   French Guiana

HAITI Puerto Rico
(U.S.A.)
ANTIGUA
Guadeloupe (France)
Martinique (France)
BARBADOS
ST VINCENT
Caribbean
Sea
Barranquilla
Caracas

Islas
Revillagigedo

Tropic of Cancer

Hawai'ian Islands
(U.S.A.)

PACIFIC

OCEAN

Île Clipperton

KIRIBATI

Line Islands
INTERNATIONAL DATE LINE

Equator

American
Samoa
Niue   Cook
(N.Z.) Islands
(N.Z.)
Rarotonga
Tropic of Capricorn

Îles
Marquises

Archipel des Tuamotu
Tahiti
Archipel
de la
Société French
Polynesia
Îles Australes

Pitcairn Is
(U.K.)

Isla de Pascua
(Easter Island)
(Chile)

Isla Sala y Gómez
(Chile)

WESTERN
SAHARA

MAURITANIA
Nouakchott
CAPE VERDE SENEGAL MALI
Praia Dakar   Banjul
THE GAMBIA   Bamako BURKINA
Bissau   Ouagadougou NI
GUINEA-BISSAU GUINEA
Conakry   CÔTE
Freetown   Yamoussoukro
SIERRA LEONE D'IVOIRE TOGO
Monrovia   Accra
LIBERIA Abidjan

EQUAT
SÃO TOMÉ
AND PRÍNCIPE

Quito
ECUADOR
Guayaquil

Galápagos
(Ecuador)

Belém
Manaus *Amazonas*
(Amazon)

Fortaleza

Fernando de Noronha
(Brazil)

PERU

Trujillo

Lima

Teresina Natal
Recife

Ascension
(U.K.)

ATLANTIC

St Helena
(U.K.)

Arequipa
La Paz
BOLIVIA Santa Cruz
Sucre

BRAZIL

Brasília
Goiânia

Salvador

Belo Horizonte
São Paulo
Rio de Janeiro

Ilhas Martin Vaz
(Brazil)

Trindade
(Brazil)

PARAGUAY
San Miguel
de Tucumán Asunción Curitiba
Córdoba URUGUAY Porto Alegre
ARGENTINA *Paraná*
Santiago Buenos Montevideo
Aires
Mar del Plata

CHILE

OCEAN

Tristan da Cunha
(U.K.)

Gough Island
(U.K.)

Falkland
Islands
(U.K.)
Punta Stanley
Arenas
Cabo
de Hornos

South Georgia
(U.K.)

South Sandwich
Islands
(U.K.)

S

Bo
(N

South Orkney
Islands
(U.K.)

South Shetland
Islands
(U.K.)

Antarctic
Peninsula

Weddell
Sea

ANTA

Antarctic Circle

ANTA

A.	ANDORRA	LITH.	LITHUANIA
AL.	ALBANIA	M.	MACEDONIA
ARM.	ARMENIA	MOL.	MOLDOVA
AUST.	AUSTRIA	MO.	MONTENEGRO
AZER.	AZERBAIJAN	NETH.	NETHERLANDS
B.	BURUNDI	R.	RWANDA
BEL.	BELGIUM	R.F.	RUSSIAN FEDERATION
B.H.	BOSNIA-HERZEGOVINA	ROM.	ROMANIA
BULG.	BULGARIA	S.	SERBIA
CR.	CROATIA	SL.	SLOVENIA
CZ.R.	CZECH REPUBLIC	SLA.	SLOVAKIA
EST.	ESTONIA	SUR.	SURINAME
GEOR.	GEORGIA	SW.	SWITZERLAND
HUN.	HUNGARY	TAJIK.	TAJIKISTAN
ISR.	ISRAEL	TURKM.	TURKMENISTAN
JOR.	JORDAN	U.A.E.	UNITED ARAB EMIRATES
L.	LUXEMBOURG	U.S.A.	UNITED STATES OF AMERICA
LAT.	LATVIA	UZBEK.	UZBEKISTAN
LEB.	LEBANON		

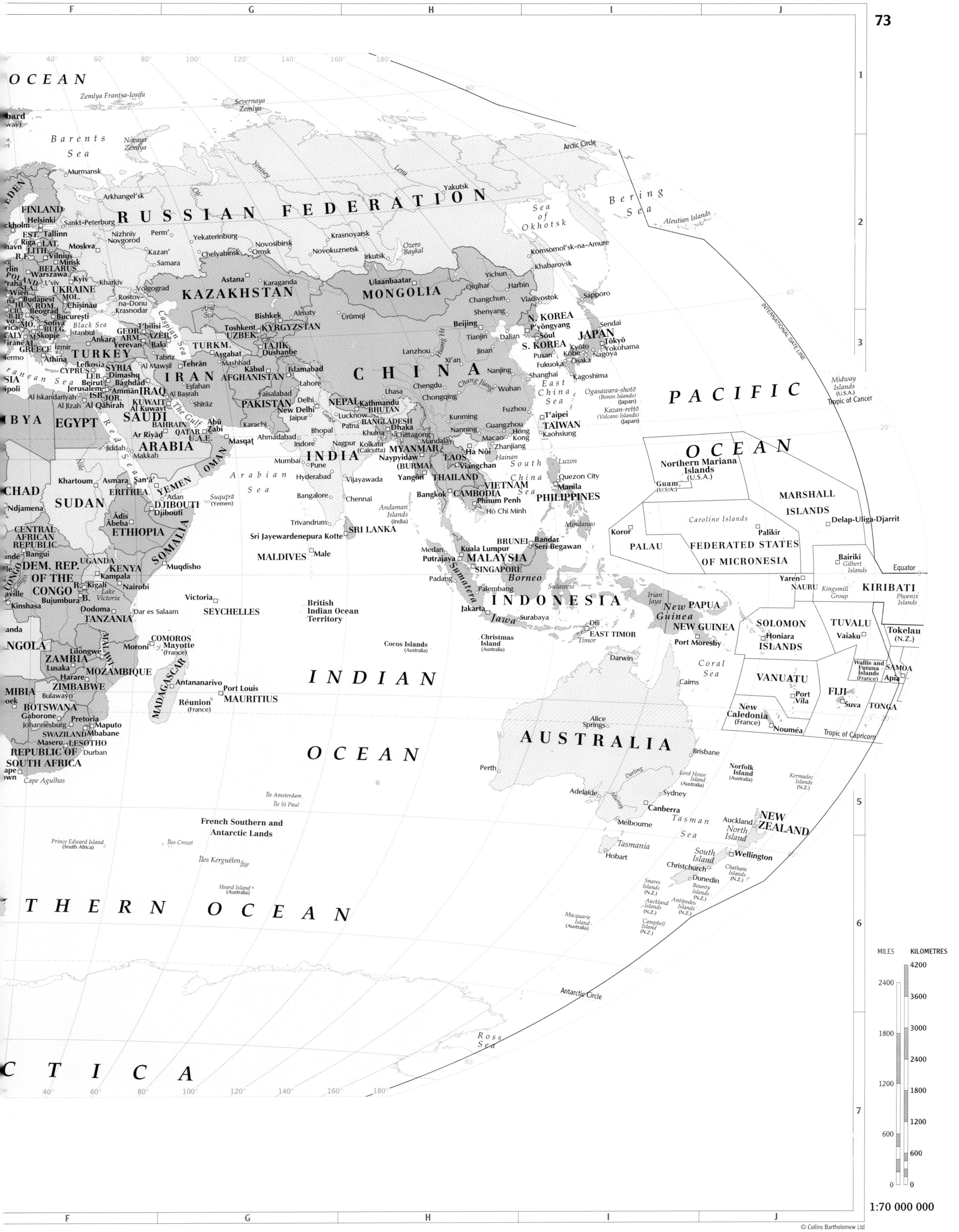

F G H I J

OCEAN

Zemlya Frantsa-Iosifa

Severnaya
Zemlya

Barents
Sea

Murmansk

Novaya
Zemlya

Arkhangel'sk

RUSSIAN FEDERATION

Yakutsk

Bering
Sea

Arctic Circle

Aleutian Islands

2

FINLAND
Helsinki
EST. Tallinn
LAT.
Riga
LITH.
Vilnius
BELARUS
Warszawa
POL.
Praha
UKRAINE
HUN. ROM.
Chişinău
BULG.
Beograd
Sofiya
MO.
Skopje
GREECE
Athína
CYPRUS
Lefkosia
SYRIA
Beirut
Dimashq
Jerusalem
ISR. JOR.
Al Iskandariyah
Al Qāhirah

Sankt-Peterburg
Moskva
Nizhniy
Novgorod
Minsk
Kyiv
Budapest
Bucureşti
İstanbul
Ankara
TURKEY
İzmir
T'bilisi
GEOR.
ARM.
AZER.
Yerevan
Baki
IRAN
Tabriz
Tehrān
Mashhad
Al Mawşil
Baghdad
IRAQ
Al Başrah
KUWAIT
Al Kuwayt
Ar Riyāḍ

Perm'
Yekaterinburg
Kazan'
Samara
Volgograd
Rostov-
na-Donu
Krasnodar
Black Sea
Caspian Sea
Kābul
AFGHANISTAN
Eşfahān
Shīrāz
BAHRAIN
QATAR
Abū Zabi
U.A.E.
Masqaţ
OMAN

Chelyabinsk
Omsk
Novosibirsk
Novokuznetsk
Astana
Karaganda
KAZAKHSTAN
Aral
Sea
Toshkent
Bishkek
Almaty
UZBEK.
TURKM.
Aşgabat
TAJIK.
Dushanbe
Islamabad
Lahore
PAKISTAN
Faisalabad
Karachi
Delhi
New Delhi

Krasnoyarsk
Irkutsk
Ozero
Baykal
Ūrümqi
Ulaanbaatar
MONGOLIA
Lhasa
NEPAL
Kathmandu
BHUTAN
Jaipur
Lucknow
Patna

Komsomol'sk-na-Amure
Khabarovsk
Yichun
Qiqihar
Harbin
Changchun
Shenyang
CHINA
Lanzhou
Huang He
Chengdu
Chongqing
Chang Jiang
Wuhan

Vladivostok
N. KOREA
P'yŏngyang
S. KOREA
Sŏul
Beijing
Tianjin
Dalian
Jinan
Nanjing
Shanghai
Fuzhou
Nanchang

Sapporo
JAPAN
Sendai
Tōkyō
Yokohama
Kyōto
Kōbe
Nagoya
Ōsaka
Fukuoka
Pusan
Kagoshima

East
China
Sea

Ogasawara-shotō
(Bonin Islands)
(Japan)

Kazan-rettō
(Volcano Islands)
(Japan)

PACIFIC

Midway
Islands
(U.S.A.)

Tropic of Cancer

3

INTERNATIONAL DATE LINE

CHAD
Ndjamena
SUDAN
CENTRAL
AFRICAN
REPUBLIC
Bangui
DEM. REP.
OF THE
CONGO
Kinshasa
NGOLA

Khartoum
Asmara
ERITREA
Ādīs
Ābeba
ETHIOPIA
UGANDA
Kampala
KENYA
Kigali
R.
B.
Bujumbura
Dodoma
TANZANIA

EGYPT
Red Sea
Nile
SAUDI
ARABIA
Makkah
Jiddah
YEMEN
Aden
DJIBOUTI
Djibouti
SOMALIA
Muqdisho
Nairobi
Lake
Victoria
Dar es Salaam

Arabian
Sea
Suquţrā
(Yemen)
SEYCHELLES
Victoria

Ahmadabad
Mumbai
Pune
INDIA
Hyderabad
Bangalore
Chennai
Trivandrum
Sri Jayewardenepura Kotte
MALDIVES
Male

Bhopal
Indore
Nagpur
Vijayawada
Andaman
Islands
(India)
SRI LANKA

Kolkata
(Calcutta)
BANGLADESH
Dhaka
Khulna
Chittagong
MYANMAR
(BURMA)
Mandalay
Naypyidaw
Yangôn
THAILAND
Bangkok

Kunming
Nanning
Guangzhou
Macao
Hong Kong
Zhanjiang
Hainan
Ha Nôi
LAOS
Viangchan
CAMBODIA
Phnum Penh
Hô Chi Minh
VIETNAM

T'aipei
TAIWAN
Kaohsiung
South
China
Sea
Luzon
Manila
Quezon City
PHILIPPINES
Mindanao

Northern Mariana
Islands
(U.S.A.)
Guam
(U.S.A.)

MARSHALL
ISLANDS
Delap-Uliga-Djarrit

OCEAN

Caroline Islands

Koror
PALAU
Palikir
FEDERATED STATES
OF MICRONESIA
Yaren

Bairiki
Gilbert
Islands
Equator
NAURU
KIRIBATI
Phoenix
Islands

British
Indian Ocean
Territory

Christmas
Island
(Australia)

Medan
Kuala Lumpur
MALAYSIA
BRUNEI
Bandar
Seri Begawan
SINGAPORE
Putrajaya
Padang
Borneo
Sumatera
Sulawesi
Jakarta
Jawa
Surabaya
Palembang
INDONESIA

Irian
Jaya
New
Guinea
Dili
EAST TIMOR
Timor
PAPUA
NEW GUINEA
Port Moresby

SOLOMON
ISLANDS
Honiara

TUVALU
Vaiaku

Kingsmill
Group

Wallis and
Futuna
Islands
(France)

Tokelau
(N.Z.)

SAMOA
Apia

4

COMOROS
Moroni
Mayotte
(France)
MALAWI
Lilongwe
ZAMBIA
Lusaka
MOZAMBIQUE
ZIMBABWE
Harare
Bulawayo
BOTSWANA
Gaborone
Johannesburg
Pretoria
Maputo
SWAZILAND Mbabane
Maseru LESOTHO
REPUBLIC OF
SOUTH AFRICA
Durban
Cape Agulhas

Antananarivo
MADAGASCAR
Réunion
(France)
Port Louis
MAURITIUS

INDIAN

OCEAN

Cocos Islands
(Australia)

Darwin
Cairns
Coral
Sea
Alice
Springs
AUSTRALIA
Brisbane
Perth
Darling
Adelaide
Murray
Sydney
Canberra
Melbourne
Tasman
Sea
Tasmania
Hobart

VANUATU
Port
Vila
New
Caledonia
(France)
Nouméa
FIJI
Suva
TONGA
Tropic of Capricorn

Norfolk
Island
(Australia)
Lord Howe
Island
(Australia)
Kermadec
Islands
(N.Z.)

Auckland
North
Island
NEW
ZEALAND
Christchurch
South
Island
Dunedin
Wellington
Chatham
Islands
(N.Z.)

5

Prince Edward Island
(South Africa)
Île Amsterdam
Île St Paul
French Southern and
Antarctic Lands
Îles Crozet
Îles Kerguélen
Heard Island
(Australia)

Snares
Islands
(N.Z.)
Bounty
Islands
(N.Z.)
Auckland
Islands
(N.Z.)
Antipodes
Islands
(N.Z.)
Campbell
Island
(N.Z.)
Macquarie
Island
(Australia)

THERN OCEAN

CTICA

Ross
Sea

Antarctic Circle

6

7

MILES KILOMETRES

4200
2400
3600
3000
1800
2400
1800
1200
1200
600
600
0 0

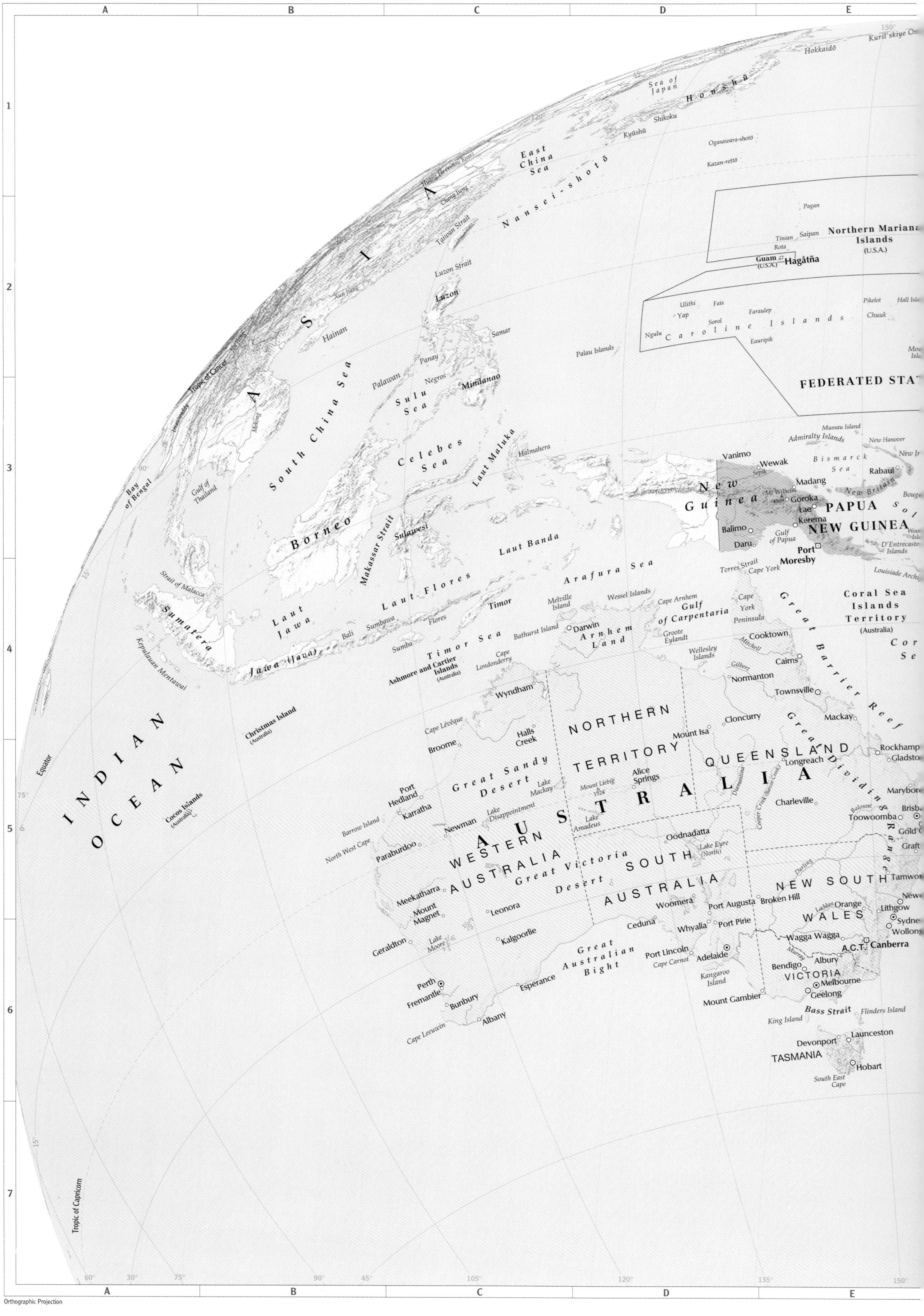
A
B
C
D
E
1
2
3
4
5
6
7
Kuril'skiye Os
Hokkaidō
Sea of Japan
Honshū
Shikoku
Kyūshū
Ogasawara-shotō
Kazan-rettō
East China Sea
Nansei-shotō
Huang He (Yellow River)
Chang Jiang
Taiwan Strait
A S I A
Pagan
Tinian
Saipan
Rota
Northern Mariana Islands
(U.S.A.)
Guam
(U.S.A.)
Hagåtña
Luzon Strait
Xun Jiang
Luzon
Ulithi
Fais
Yap
Sorol
Faraulep
Caroline Islands
Eauripik
Ngulu
Pikelot
Chuuk
Hall Isl
Hainan
Samar
Palau Islands
Panay
Palawan
Negros
Mindanao
Sulu Sea
South China Sea
FEDERATED STAT
Tropic of Cancer
Irrawaddy
Mekong
Mussau Island
Admiralty Islands
New Hanover
Bismarck Sea
New Ir
Halmahera
Laut Maluku
Celebes Sea
Vanimo
Wewak
Sepik
Madang
Rabaul
New Britain
Mt Wilhelm
4509
Goroka
Lae
PAPUA
NEW GUINEA
Kerema
Balimo
Gulf of Papua
Daru
Port Moresby
D'Entrecaste Islands
Louisiade Archi
Bay of Bengal
Gulf of Thailand
New Guinea
Borneo
Makassar Strait
Sulawesi
Laut Banda
Arafura Sea
Torres Strait
Cape York
Strait of Malacca
Sumatera
Laut Jawa
Laut Flores
Timor
Melville Island
Wessel Islands
Cape Arnhem
Gulf of Carpentaria
Cape York Peninsula
Coral Sea Islands Territory
(Australia)
Coral Sea
Kepulauan Mentawai
Bali
Sumbawa
Flores
Sumba
Jawa (Java)
Timor Sea
Bathurst Island
Darwin
Arnhem Land
Groote Eylandt
Cooktown
Mitchell
Wellesley Islands
Cairns
Great Barrier Reef
Ashmore and Cartier Islands
(Australia)
Cape Londonderry
Gilbert
Normanton
Wyndham
Townsville
Christmas Island
(Australia)
NORTHERN TERRITORY
Mount Isa
Cloncurry
Mackay
Cape Lévêque
Halls Creek
Broome
QUEENSLAND
Great Dividing Range
Rockhamp
Gladsto
Longreach
INDIAN OCEAN
Equator
Great Sandy Desert
Alice Springs
Mount Liebig
1524
Lake Mackay
Diamantina
Cooper Creek (Barcoo Creek)
Charleville
Maryboro
Port Hedland
Karratha
AUSTRALIA
Brisb
Toowoomba
Gold C
Cocos Islands
(Australia)
Barrow Island
Newman
Lake Disappointment
Lake Amadeus
Oodnadatta
Lake Eyre (North)
Balonne
North West Cape
Paraburdoo
WESTERN AUSTRALIA
Great Victoria Desert
SOUTH AUSTRALIA
Darling
NEW SOUTH WALES
Graft
Tamwo
Meekatharra
Mount Magnet
Leonora
Woomera
Port Augusta
Broken Hill
Lachlan
Orange
Lithgow
Newc
Sydne
Wollon
Ceduna
Whyalla
Port Pirie
Geraldton
Lake Moore
Kalgoorlie
Wagga Wagga
A.C.T.
Canberra
Great Australian Bight
Port Lincoln
Cape Carnot
Adelaide
Murray
Albury
Bendigo
VICTORIA
Melbourne
Geelong
Perth
Fremantle
Esperance
Kangaroo Island
Mount Gambier
Bunbury
Albany
Cape Leeuwin
Bass Strait
Flinders Island
King Island
Devonport
Launceston
TASMANIA
Hobart
South East Cape
Tropic of Capricorn
150°
120°
90°
75°
60°
30°
45°
105°
135°
15°
0°

Orthographic Projection

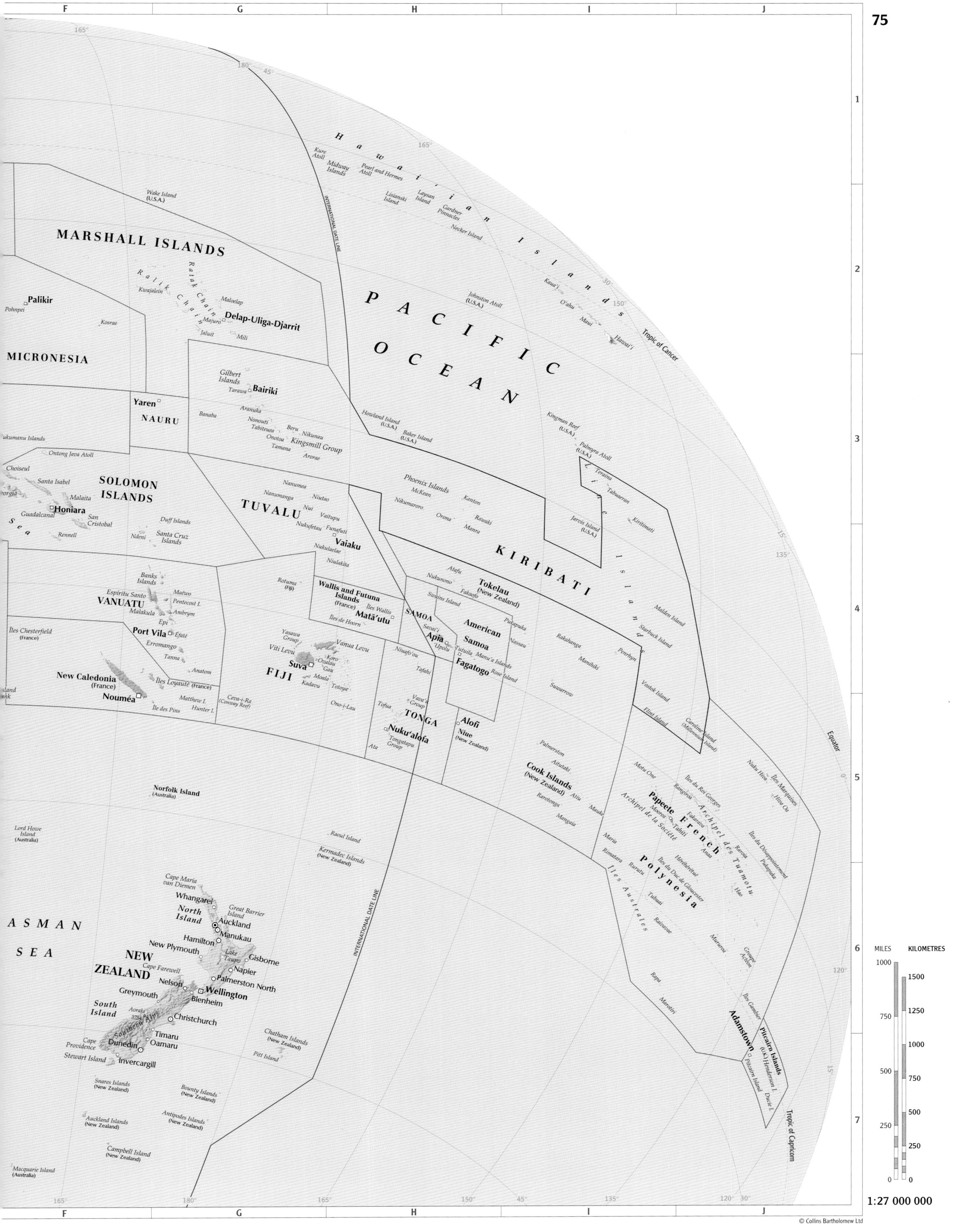

F G H I J

1

Hawaiian Islands

Kure Atoll
Midway Islands
Pearl and Hermes Atoll
Laysan Island
Lisianski Island
Gardner Pinnacles
Necker Island
Wake Island (U.S.A.)

2

MARSHALL ISLANDS

Ralik Chain
Ratak Chain
Kwajalein
Maloelap
Majuro
Delap-Uliga-Djarrit

Palikir
Pohnpei
Kosrae
Jaluit
Mili

MICRONESIA

Yaren □
NAURU

P A C I F I C

O C E A N

Johnston Atoll (U.S.A.)

Kaua'i
O'ahu
150°
Maui
Hawai'i
Tropic of Cancer

Gilbert Islands
Tarawa **Bairiki**
Banaba
Aranuka
Nonouti
Tabiteuea
Beru Nikunau
Onotoa
Tamana
Arorae
Kingsmill Group

Howland Island (U.S.A.)
Baker Island (U.S.A.)

Kingman Reef (U.S.A.)
Palmyra Atoll (U.S.A.)

3

Fukumanu Islands
Ontong Java Atoll

Choiseul
Santa Isabel
Georgia
Malaita
Guadalcanal **Honiara** ■
San Cristobal
Rennell

SOLOMON ISLANDS

Sea

Nandi
Santa Cruz Islands
Duff Islands

Nanumea
Nanumanga
Niutao
Nui
Vaitupu
Nukufetau Funafuti
Vaiaku □
TUVALU

Phoenix Islands
McKean
Nikumaroro
Kanton
Rawaki
Orona Manra

Teraina
Tabuaeran

Jarvis Island (U.S.A.)
Kiritimati

K I R I B A T I

Line Islands

4

Banks Islands
Espíritu Santo
Maéwo
Pentecost I.
Malakula
Epi
Ambrym
VANUATU

Rotuma (Fiji)

Nukulaelae
Niulakita

Wallis and Futuna Islands (France)
Îles Wallis
Îles de Hoorn
Matá'utu □

Nukunono
Fakaofo
Swains Island

Tokelau (New Zealand)

Pukapuka
Nassau

Maldèn Island
Starbuck Island

Vostok Island

Îles Chesterfield (France)

Yasawa Group
Viti Levu
Vanua Levu
Koro
Ovalau Gau
Suva □
Moala
Kadavu
FIJI
Totoyar

Niuafo'ou
Tafahi
Niuafo'ou
Apia □
SAMOA
Savai'i Upolu
Tutuila Manu'a Islands
Rose Island
Fagatogo □
American Samoa

Swarrow

Rakahanga
Manihiki
Penrhyn

Flint Island

Port Vila □
Efaté
Erromango
Tanna
Anatom

New Caledonia (France)
Îles Loyauté (France)
Nouméa ■
Île des Pins
Matthew I.
Hunter I.

Ceva-i-Ra (Conway Reef)
Ono-i-Lau

Vava'u Group
Tofua
TONGA
Nuku'alofa □
Tongatapu Group
Ata

Alofi □
Niue (New Zealand)

Cook Islands (New Zealand)
Palmerston
Aitutaki
Atiu
Rarotonga
Mangaia

5

Norfolk Island (Australia)

Lord Howe Island (Australia)

Raoul Island

Kermadec Islands (New Zealand)

Motu One
Maupiti
Îles du Roi Georges
Rangiroa
Tahiti
Papeete French
Moorea
Anaa
Archipel des Tuamotu
Archipel de la Société

Nuku Hiva
Îles Marquises
Hiva Oa

Îles du Désappointement
Puka puka

Hereheretue
Îles du Duc de Gloucester

Rimatara
Rurutu
Tubuai
Îles Australes
Maria
Polynesia

6

Cape Maria van Diemen
Whangarei
North Island
Great Barrier Island
Auckland ◎
Manukau ○
Hamilton ○
New Plymouth ○
Lake Taupo
Gisborne ○
Napier ○
Palmerston North ○
NEW ZEALAND
Cape Farewell
Nelson ○
Wellington □
Greymouth ○
Blenheim ○

INTERNATIONAL DATE LINE

Raivavae
Rapa
Marotiri

Mangareva
Gambier Islands

7

ASMAN
SEA

South Island
Aoraki
Southern Alps
Christchurch ○
Timaru ○
Oamaru ○
Cape Providence
Dunedin ◎
Stewart Island
Invercargill ○

Chatham Islands (New Zealand)
Pitt Island

Adamstown ○
Pitcairn Islands (U.K.) Henderson I.
Ducie I.
Pitcairn Island

Tropic of Capricorn

Snares Islands (New Zealand)
Bounty Islands (New Zealand)
Auckland Islands (New Zealand)
Antipodes Islands (New Zealand)

Campbell Island (New Zealand)

Macquarie Island (Australia)

MILES KILOMETRES
1000 1500
750 1250
1000
500 750
500
250 250
0 0

1:27 000 000

© Collins Bartholomew Ltd

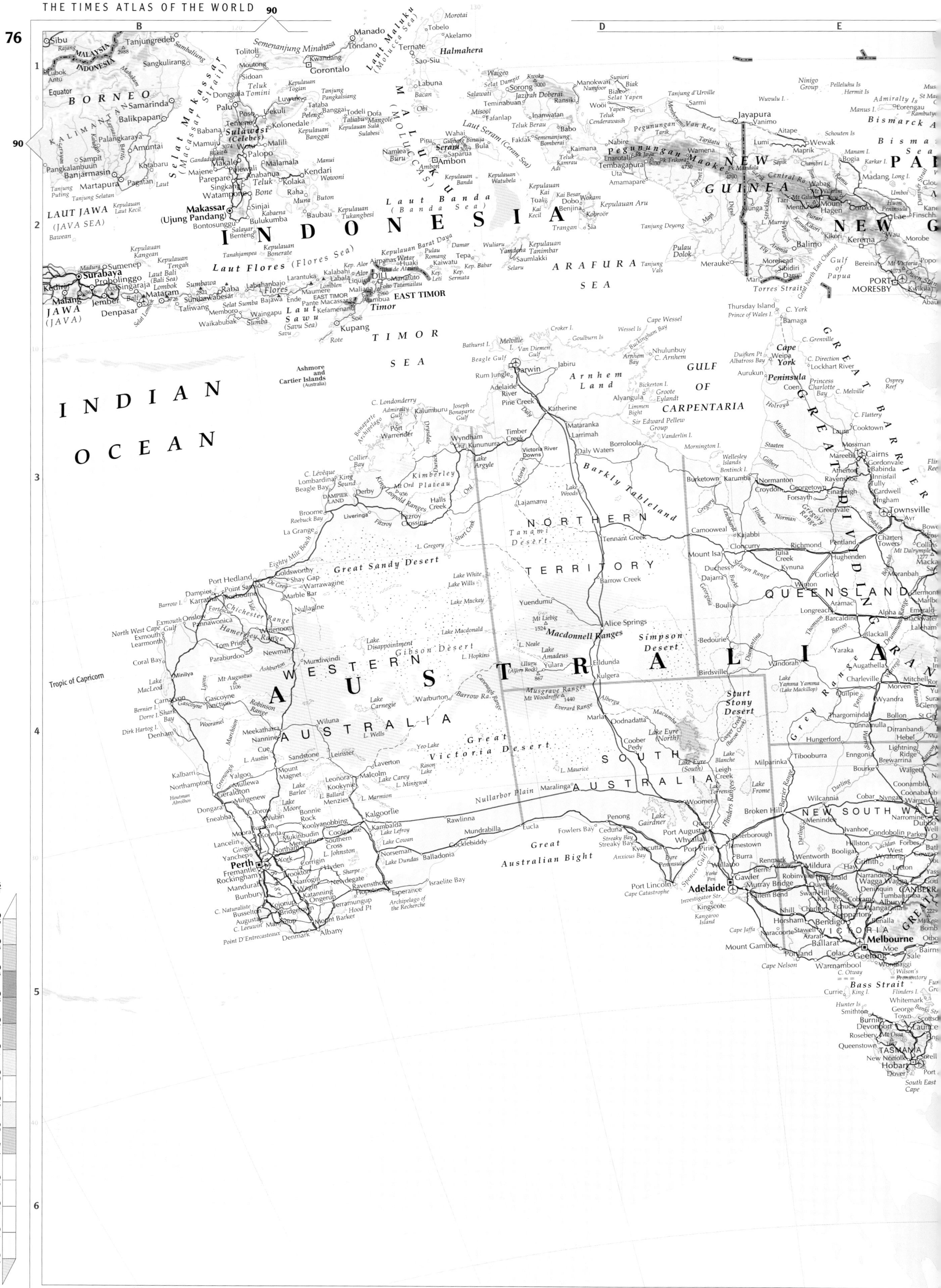

Indonesia / Australia Map

BORNEO

KALIMANTAN

Sibu
MALAYSIA
INDONESIA
Lubok
Antu
Equator

Tanjungredeb
Samballung
Sangkulirang
Samarinda
Balikpapan
Muara

Palu
Poso
Tentena
Kolonedale
Donggala
Toli-Toli
Moutong
Sidoan
Gorontalo
Kwandang
Tolitoli
Tondano
Manado
Semenanjung Minahasa
Laut Maluku
(Molucca Sea)
Ternate
Sao-Siu
Halmahera
Tobelo
Akelamo
Morotai

Sulawesi
(Celebes)
Malili
Malala
Palopo
Malamala
Kendari
Manui
Wowoni
Raha
Muna
Buton
Baubau
Bonerate

Pangkalsiang
Tanjung
Togian
Kepulauan
Togian
Tataba
Peleng
Banggai
Luwuku
Banggai
Taliabu
Sula
Sulabesi
Mangole

Waigeo
Sorong
Salawati
Misool
Wahai
Buru
Namlea
Pitu
Seram
Ambon
Laut Seram (Ceram Sea)
Kaimana
Fakfak
Babo
Teluk Berau
Jazirah Doberai

Manokwari
Numfoor
Biak
Supiori
Ransiki
Yapen
Serui
Wooi
Inanwatan

NEW GUINEA

Jayapura
Vanimo
Aitape
Wewak
Maprik
Sepik

Makassar
(Ujung Pandang)
Bulukumba
Sinjai
Bontosunggu
Selayar
Benteng

LAUT JAWA
(JAVA SEA)
Bawean

Surabaya
Probolinggo
Malang
Jember
Bali
JAWA
(JAVA)
Denpasar
Mataram
Lombok
Sumbawabesar
Taliwang
Waingapu
Sumba
Waikabubak

Madura
Sumenep
Kepulauan
Kangean
Kepulauan
Tengah

Laut Bali
(Bali Sea)
Bajawa
Ende
Flores
Maumere
Larantuka
Labuhanbajo

Laut Flores (Flores Sea)

Kepulauan
Tanahjampea
Bonerate

Kalabahi
Alor
Kep. Alor
Atapupu
Kupang
Rote
Savu
Laut Sawu
(Savu Sea)

Atambua
EAST TIMOR
Timor
Soé
Kelamenanu

TIMOR
SEA

ARAFURA
SEA

Kepulauan Aru
Dobo
Benjina
Kobroör
Trangan

Kepulauan
Kai
Tual
Kepulauan
Tanimbar
Saumlakki
Selaru

Damar
Wetar
Romang
Kisar
Kep. Babar
Kep. Leti
Kep. Sermata

Merauke

Port
MORESBY

Gulf of
Papua

Thursday Island
Prince of Wales I.
Bamaga
C. York

INDIAN

OCEAN

Ashmore
and
Cartier Islands
(Australia)

Melville
Bathurst I.
Beagle Gulf
Darwin
Adelaide River
Jabiru
Pine Creek
Katherine
Arnhem
Land
Van Diemen Gulf
Croker I.
Goulburn Is
Wessel Is

GULF
OF
CARPENTARIA

GREAT
DIVIDING
RANGE

Cape
York
Peninsula
Weipa
Aurukun
Coen

Cooktown
Mossman
Cairns
Gordonvale
Innisfail
Tully
Cardwell
Ingham
Townsville
Ayr

Broome
Derby
Halls Creek
Kimberley
Wyndham
Kununurra
Timber Creek
Victoria River Downs
Daly Waters
Borroloola
Camooweal
Mount Isa
Cloncurry
Richmond
Hughenden
Charters Towers

NORTHERN
TERRITORY

Tanami Desert
Tennant Creek
Barrow Creek

Yuendumu
Alice Springs
Macdonnell Ranges
QUEENSLAND
Boulia
Bedourie
Birdsville
Longreach
Barcaldine
Blackall

Port Hedland
Goldsworthy
Marble Bar
Nullagine
Great Sandy Desert
Lake White
Lake Wills
Lake Mackay

Dampier
Karratha
Onslow
Exmouth
Learmonth
Pannawonica
Tom Price
Newman
Paraburdoo

WESTERN
AUSTRALIA

Gibson Desert
Warburton
Lake Disappointment
Lake Carnegie

Simpson
Desert
Uluru
(Ayers Rock)
Yulara
Kulgera
Eringa
Oodnadatta
Coober Pedy
Lake Eyre
(North)

Sturt
Stony
Desert

Windorah
Charleville
Quilpie
Thargomindah
Cunnamulla
Bollon

AUSTRALIA

Tropic of Capricorn

Musgrave Ranges
Everard Range

SOUTH
AUSTRALIA
Lake Eyre
(South)
Lake Torrens
Lake Gairdner

Lake Frome
Lake Blanche

Broken Hill
Wilcannia
Cobar
Bourke

NEW SOUTH WALES

Great
Victoria Desert

Nullarbor Plain
Maralinga
Eucla
Cocklebiddy
Madura

Ceduna
Streaky Bay
Port Augusta
Whyalla
Port Pirie
Port Lincoln

Woomera
Pimba

Great
Australian Bight

Kalgoorlie
Coolgardie
Norseman
Esperance
Israelite Bay

Kambalda
Lake Lefroy
Balladonia
Rawlinna

Geraldton
Northampton
Dongara
Eneabba

Morawa
Mullewa
Yalgoo
Mount Magnet
Sandstone
Leonora
Laverton
Leinster
Wiluna

Perth
Fremantle
Rockingham
Mandurah
Bunbury
Busselton
Augusta
Albany
Denmark

York
Northam
Narrogin
Katanning
Mount Barker

ADELAIDE
Murray Bridge
Gawler
Renmark
Mildura

CANBERRA
Wagga Wagga
Albury

Melbourne
Geelong
Ballarat
Bendigo
VICTORIA
Warrnambool
Mount Gambier
Portland

Bass Strait

TASMANIA
Burnie
Devonport
Launceston
Queenstown
Hobart

INDIAN
OCEAN

METRES / FEET

METRES	FEET
6000	19686
5000	16404
4000	13124
3000	9843
2000	6562
1000	3281
500	1640
200	656
0	0

LAND BELOW SEA LEVEL

200	656
2000	6562
4000	13124
6000	19686

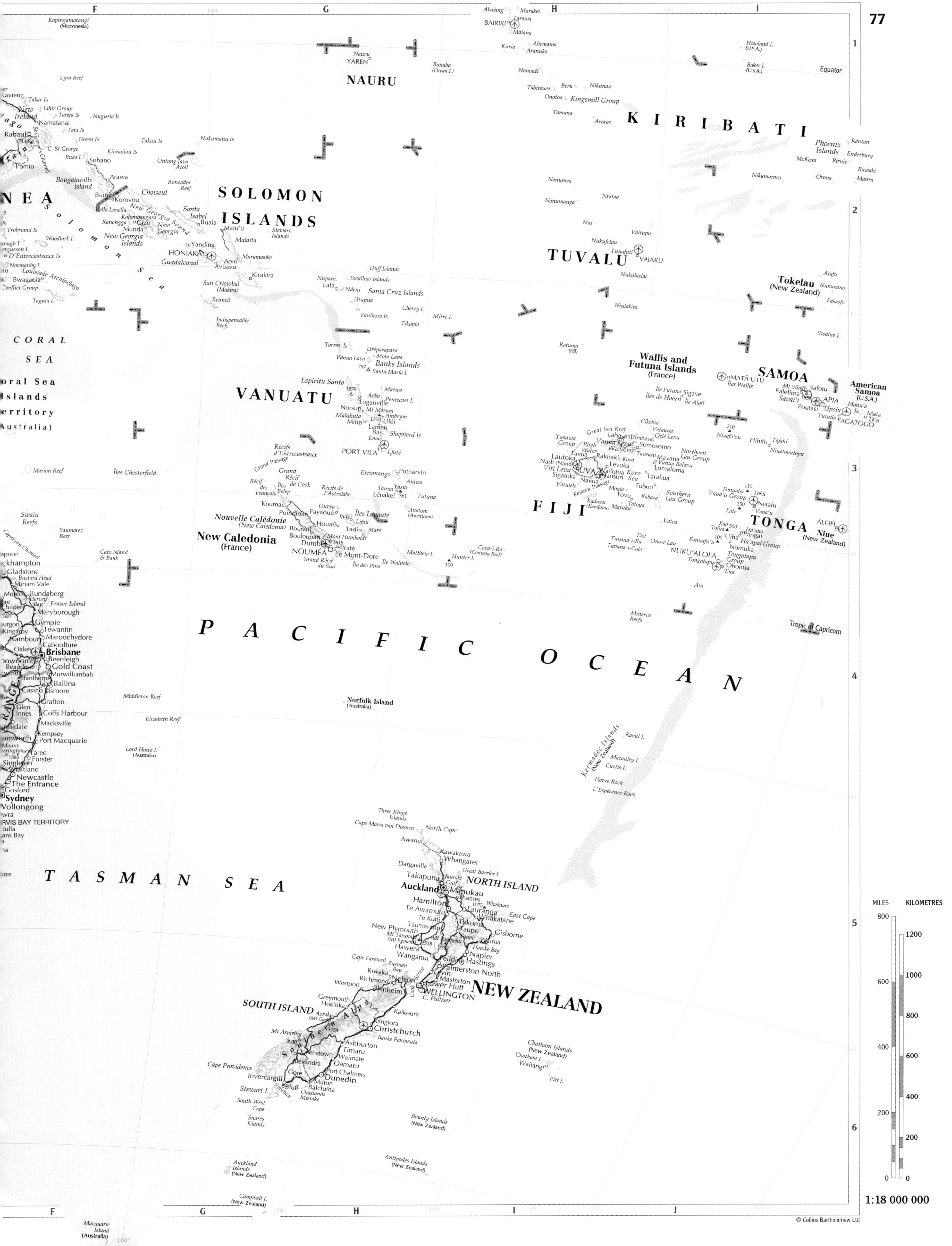
F
G
H
I
J
1
2
3
4
5
6
Kapingamarangi (Micronesia)
Abaiang
Marakei
BAIRIKI
Tarawa
Maiana
Kuria
Abemama
Aranuka
Nauru
YAREN
NAURU
Banaba (Ocean I.)
Nonouti
Howland I. (U.S.A.)
Baker I. (U.S.A.)
Equator
Tabiteuea
Beru
Nikunau
Onotoa
Kingsmill Group
Tamana
Arorae
KIRIBATI
Phoenix Islands
Kanton
Enderbury
McKean
Birnie
Rawaki
Nikumaroro
Orona
Manra
Lyra Reef
Kavieng
Tabar Is
Lihir Group
New Ireland
Tanga Is
Nuguria Is
Namatanai
Feni Is
Rabaul
Green Is
C. St George
Kilinailau Is
Takuu Is
Nukumanu Is
Buka I.
Sohano
Ontong Java Atoll
Pomio
Bougainville Island
Arawa
Roncador Reef
SOLOMON ISLANDS
Buin
Korovou
Choiseul
Vella Lavella
New Georgia Sound
Santa Isabel
Buala
Kolombangara
Ranongga
Gizo
New Georgia
Munda
New Georgia Islands
Malu'u
Malaita
Stewart Islands
Solomon Sea
Trobriand Is
Woodlark I.
Yandina
HONIARA
Guadalcanal
Maramasike
Apio
Avuavu
D'Entrecasteaux Is
Normanby I.
Louisiade Archipelago
Bwagaoia
Conflict Group
Tagula I.
Kirakira
San Cristobal (Makira)
Rennell
Indispensable Reefs
Duff Islands
Nupani
Lata
Swallow Islands
Ndeni
Santa Cruz Islands
Utupua
Vanikoro Is
Cherry I.
Tikopia
Mitre I.
Nanumea
Niutao
Nanumanga
Nui
Vaitupu
Nukufetau
Funafuti
VAIAKU
TUVALU
Nukulaelae
Niulakita
Atafu
Tokelau (New Zealand)
Nukunono
Fakaofo
Swains I.
CORAL SEA
Coral Sea Islands Territory (Australia)
Torres Is
Ureparapara
Vanua Lava
Mota Lava
Banks Islands
Santa Maria I.
Espíritu Santo
VANUATU
Maéwo
Aoba
Pentecost I.
Luganville
Norsup
Mt Marum
Malakula
Ambrym
Milip
Uléi
Lamen Bay
Émaé
Shepherd Is
PORT VILA
Éfaté
Rotuma (Fiji)
Wallis and Futuna Islands (France)
MATĀ'UTU
Îles Wallis
Île Futuna
Sigave
Îles de Hoorn
Île Alofi
SAMOA
Mt Silisili
Safotu
Falelima
Savai'i
APIA
Poutasi
Upolu
American Samoa (U.S.A.)
Tutuila
FAGATOGO
Manu'a Is
Ta'u
Cikobia
Great Sea Reef
Labasa
Vetauua
Qele Levu
Vanua Levu
Yasawa Group
Bligh Water
Waiyevo
Somosomo
Taveuni
Northern Lau Group
Mavana
Vanua Balavu
Lautoka
Rakiraki
Koro
Lomaloma
Nadi
Viti Levu
Levuka
Sigatoka
SUVA
Nausori
Koro Sea
Tarakua
Vatulele
Navua
Kadavu Passage
Moala
Tubou
Kadavu (Kandavu)
Matuku
Totoya
Kabara
Southern Lau Group
Tovu
FIJI
Niuafo'ou
Hihifo
Tafahi
Niuatoputapu
Marion Reef
Îles Chesterfield
Récifs d'Entrecasteaux
Grand Passage
Grand Récif de Cook
Récif des Français
Îles Belep
Récifs de l'Astrolabe
Erromango
Potnarvin
Aniwa
Tanna
Yasur
Lénakel
Futuna
Anatom (Aneityum)
Koumac
Poindimié
Ouvéa
Fayaoué
Wé
Îles Loyauté
Lifou
Houaïlu
Tadin
Maré
Nouvelle Calédonie (New Caledonia)
New Caledonia (France)
Bourail
Bouloupari
Mont Humboldt
Dumbéa
NOUMÉA
Yaté
Le Mont-Dore
Grand Récif du Sud
Île des Pins
Île Walpole
Matthew I.
Hunter I.
Ceva-i-Ra (Conway Reef)
Vatoa
Doi
Tuvana-i-Ra
Ono-i-Lau
Tuvana-i-Colo
Fonualei
Toku
Vava'u Group
Neiafu
Vava'u
Late
Kao
Tofua
Ha'ano
Pangai
Ha'apai Group
'Uiha
Fonuafo'ou
Nomuka
TONGA
ALOFI
Niue (New Zealand)
NUKU'ALOFA
Tongatapu Group
Tongatapu
'Ohonua
'Eua
Ata
Minerva Reefs
Tropic of Capricorn
Swain Reefs
Saumarez Reef
Capricorn Channel
Cato Island & Bank
Rockhampton
Gladstone
Bustard Head
Miriam Vale
Monto
Bundaberg
Hervey Bay
Fraser Island
Maryborough
Gympie
Tewantin
Nambour
Maroochydore
Caboolture
Oakey
Brisbane
Beenleigh
Gold Coast
Murwillumbah
Stanthorpe
Ballina
Casino
Lismore
Grafton
Glen Innes
Coffs Harbour
Macksville
Kempsey
Port Macquarie
Armidale
Tamworth
Taree
Forster
Singleton
Maitland
Newcastle
The Entrance
Gosford
Sydney
Wollongong
JERVIS BAY TERRITORY
Middleton Reef
Elizabeth Reef
Lord Howe I. (Australia)
PACIFIC OCEAN
Norfolk Island (Australia)
Kermadec Islands (New Zealand)
Raoul I.
Macauley I.
Curtis I.
Havre Rock
L'Espérance Rock
TASMAN SEA
Three Kings Islands
Cape Maria van Diemen
North Cape
Awanui
Kawakawa
Whangarei
Dargaville
Great Barrier I.
Takapuna
Hauraki Gulf
NORTH ISLAND
Auckland
Manukau
Thames
Whakaari
Hamilton
Tauranga
Te Awamutu
Whakatane
East Cape
Te Kuiti
Rotorua
New Plymouth
Taumarunui
Taupo
Gisborne
Mt Taranaki (Mt Egmont)
Mt Ruapehu
Wairoa
Hawera
Hawke Bay
Wanganui
Napier
Hastings
Feilding
Palmerston North
Cape Farewell
Tasman Bay
Riwaka
Richmond
Nelson
Levin
Masterton
Westport
Lower Hutt
Blenheim
Cook Strait
WELLINGTON
C. Palliser
NEW ZEALAND
Greymouth
Hokitika
SOUTH ISLAND
Aoraki (Mt Cook)
Southern Alps
Kaikoura
Rangiora
Christchurch
Mt Aspiring
Banks Peninsula
Ashburton
Queenstown
Timaru
Waimate
Alexandra
Oamaru
Cape Providence
Port Chalmers
Dunedin
Invercargill
Gore
Milton
Balclutha
Bluff
Foveaux Strait
Chaslands Mistake
Stewart I.
South West Cape
Snares Islands
Chatham Islands (New Zealand)
Chatham I.
Waitangi
Pitt I.
Bounty Islands (New Zealand)
Antipodes Islands (New Zealand)
Auckland Islands (New Zealand)
Campbell I. (New Zealand)
Macquarie Island (Australia)
MILES
KILOMETRES
1:18 000 000
© Collins Bartholomew Ltd

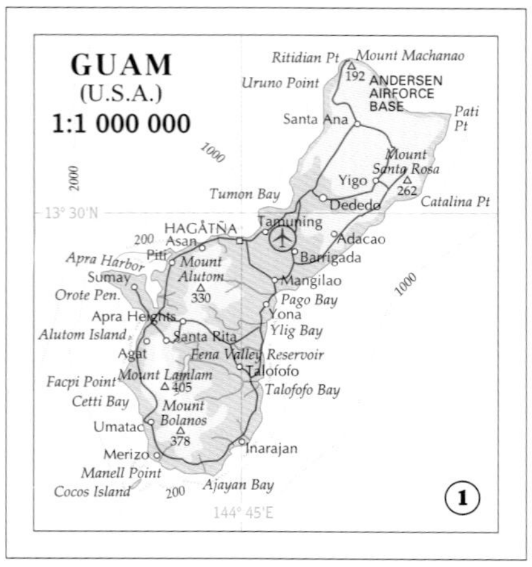

GUAM
(U.S.A.)
1:1 000 000

①

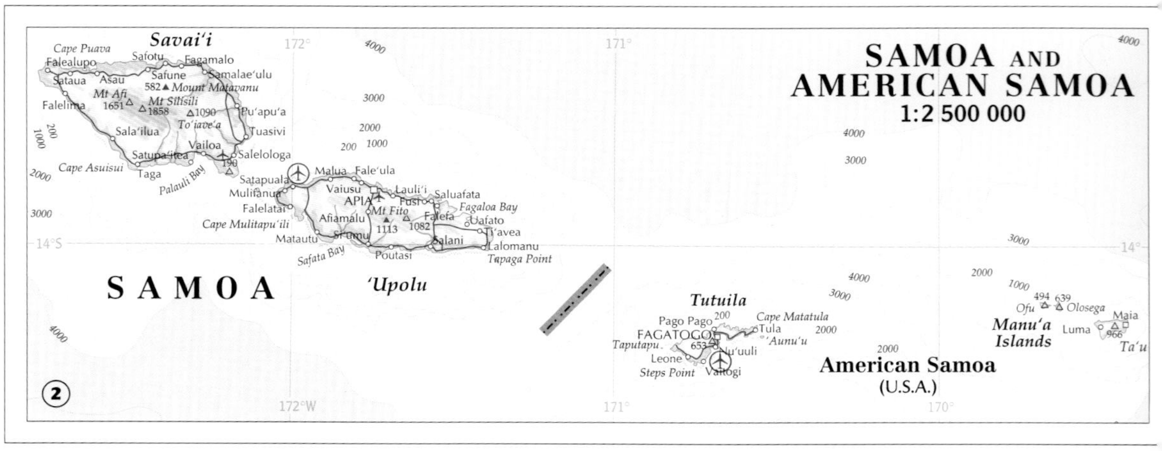

SAMOA AND
AMERICAN SAMOA
1:2 500 000

SAMOA

'Upolu

Tutuila

Manu'a
Islands

AMERICAN SAMOA
(U.S.A.)

②

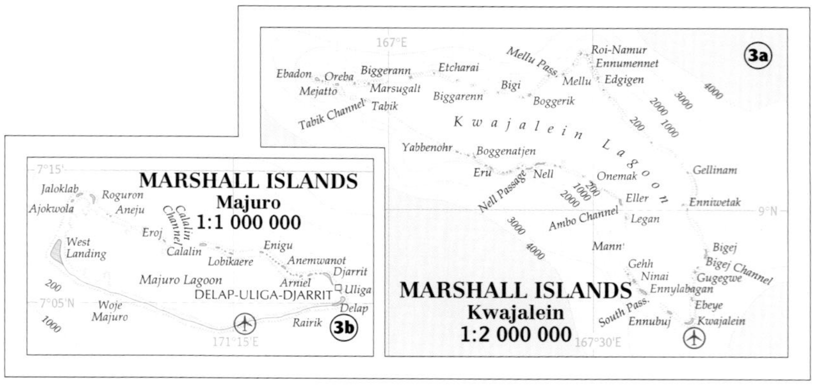

MARSHALL ISLANDS
Majuro
1:1 000 000

MARSHALL ISLANDS
Kwajalein
1:2 000 000

③a

③b

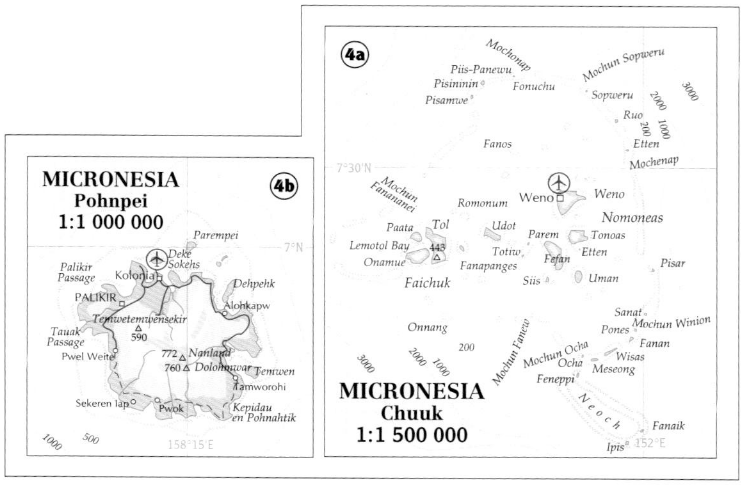

MICRONESIA
Pohnpei
1:1 000 000

④a

④b

MICRONESIA
Chuuk
1:1 500 000

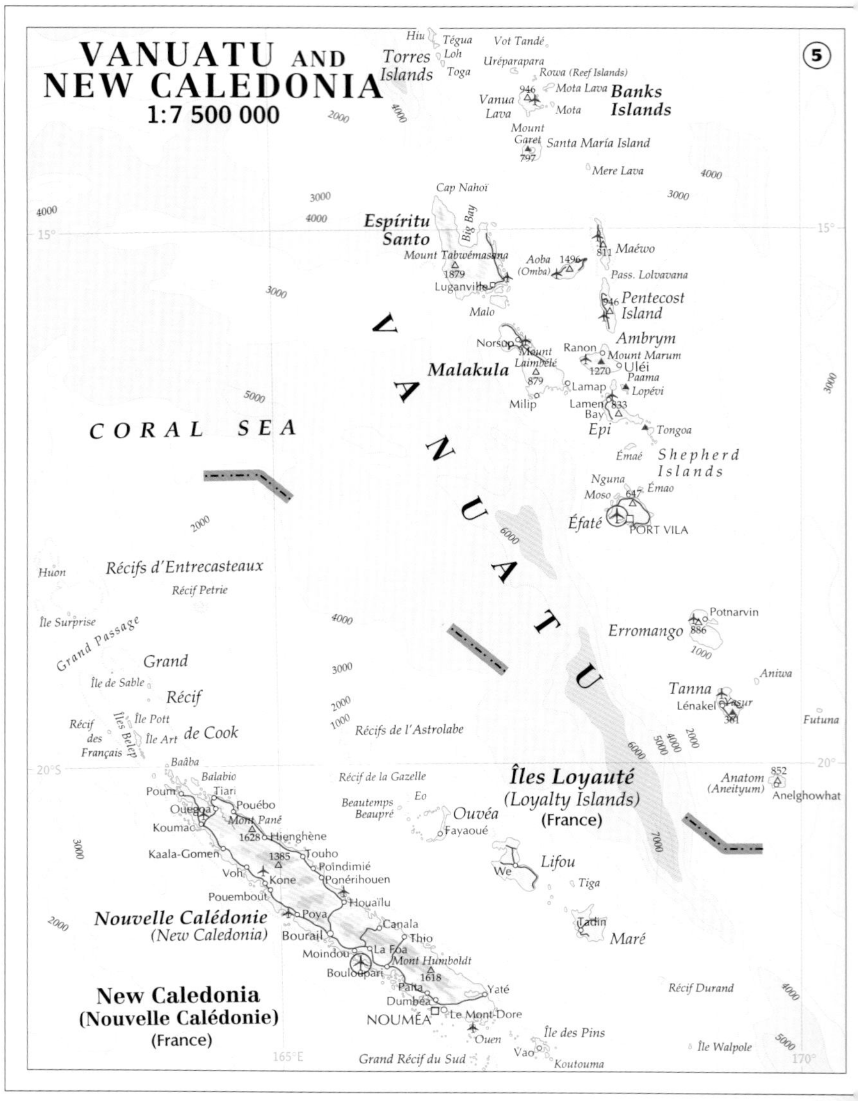

VANUATU AND
NEW CALEDONIA
1:7 500 000

Torres
Islands

Banks
Islands

Espíritu
Santo

Malakula

CORAL SEA

VANUATU

Ambrym

Epi

Shepherd
Islands

Éfaté
PORT VILA

Erromango

Tanna

Îles Loyauté
(Loyalty Islands)
(France)

Nouvelle Calédonie
(New Caledonia)

New Caledonia
(Nouvelle Calédonie)
(France)

NOUMÉA

⑤

**PAPUA
NEW GUINEA**

Bougainville
Island

Shortland
Island

Treasury
Islands

New Georgia
Islands

New
Georgia

Santa
Isabel

Russell
Islands

HONIARA

Guadalcanal

Solomon
Sea

Malaita

S O L O M O N

I S L A N D S

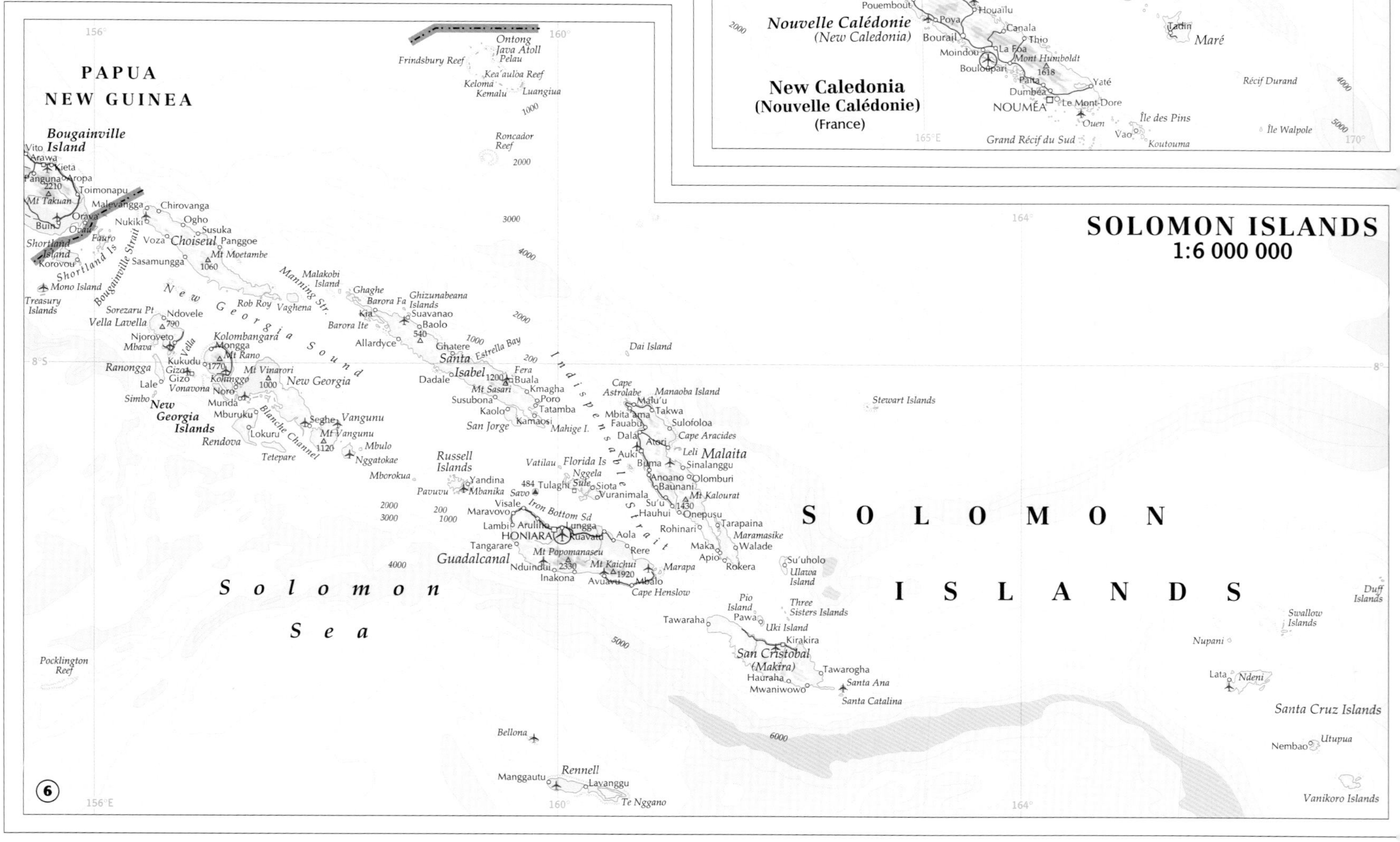

SOLOMON ISLANDS
1:6 000 000

San Cristobal
(Makira)

Santa Cruz Islands

Vanikoro Islands

⑥

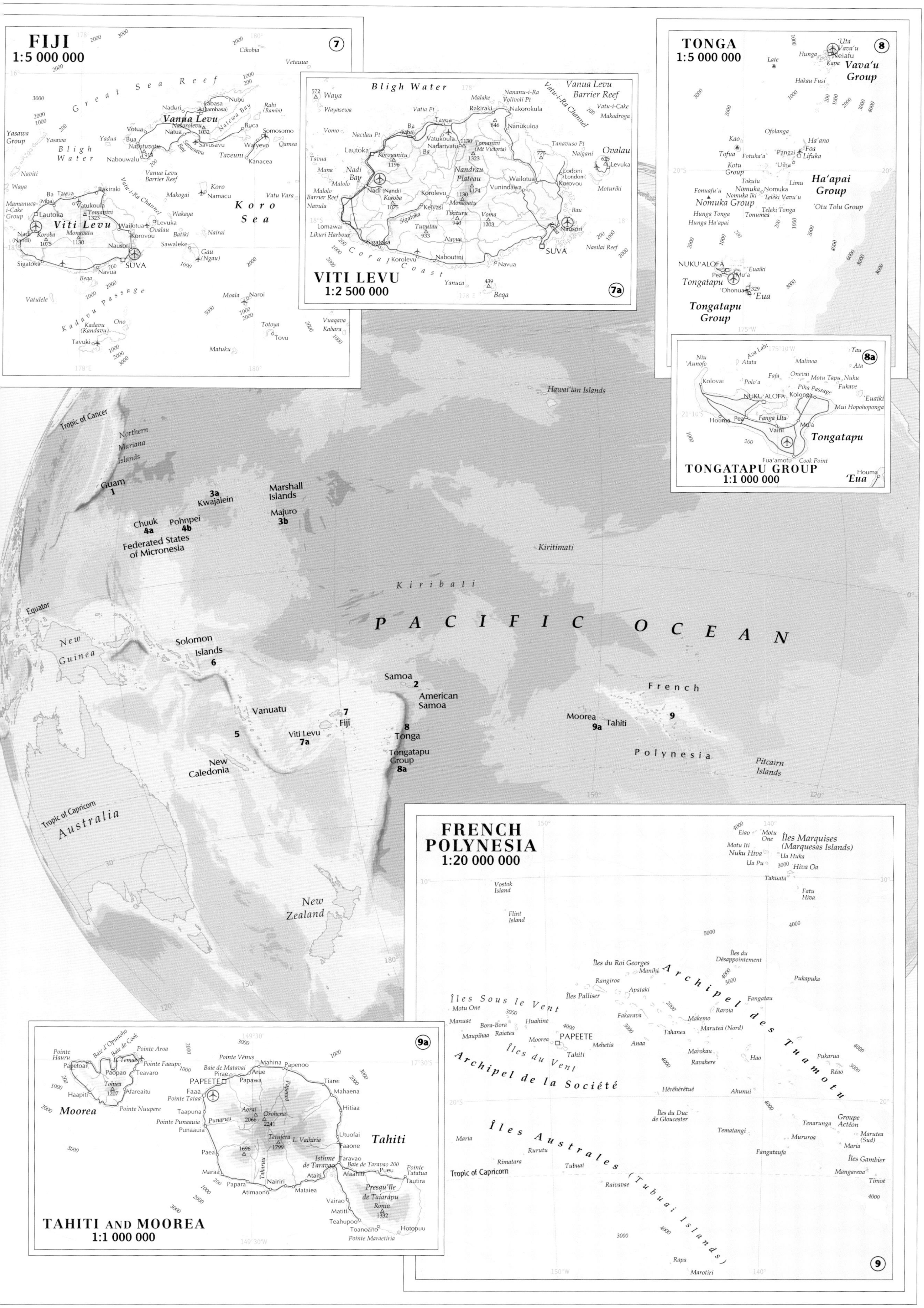

FIJI
1:5 000 000

7

Great Sea Reef

Cikobia

Vetauua

Vanua Levu

Koro Sea

Yasawa Group

Bligh Water

Viti Levu

SUVA

Kadavu Passage

Kadavu (Kandavu)

VITI LEVU
1:2 500 000

7a

Bligh Water

Vanua Levu Barrier Reef

Vatu-i-Ra Channel

Ovalau

Nandrau Plateau

Tomanivi (Mt Victoria) 1323

SUVA

Coral Coast

TONGA
1:5 000 000

8

'Uta Vava'u

Vava'u Group

Ha'ano

Ha'apai Group

Kotu Group

Nomuka Group

'Otu Tolu Group

NUKU'ALOFA

Tongatapu

'Eua

Tongatapu Group

TONGATAPU GROUP
1:1 000 000

8a

NUKU'ALOFA

Tongatapu

'Eua

PACIFIC OCEAN

Tropic of Cancer

Northern Mariana Islands

Guam
1

3a
Kwajalein

Marshall Islands

Chuuk
4a
Pohnpei
4b

Majuro
3b

Federated States of Micronesia

Kiritimati

Kiribati

New Guinea

Solomon Islands
6

Equator

Samoa
2

American Samoa

French

Moorea **9a** Tahiti **9**

Vanuatu

7
Fiji

5

Viti Levu
7a

8
Tonga

Tongatapu Group
8a

Polynesia

Pitcairn Islands

New Caledonia

Tropic of Capricorn

Australia

New Zealand

FRENCH POLYNESIA
1:20 000 000

Îles Marquises (Marquesas Islands)

Eiao Motu One

Motu Iti Nuku Hiva

Ua Huka

Hiva Oa

Tahuata

Fatu Hiva

Vostok Island

Flint Island

Îles du Roi Georges

Manihi

Rangiroa

Apataki

Îles du Désappointement

Pukapuka

Îles Sous le Vent

Motu One

Îles Palliser

Fangatau

Manuae

Bora-Bora

Huahine

Fakarava

Raroia

Maupihaa Raiatea

Moorea

PAPEETE

Tahiti

Mehetia

Anaa

Makemo

Marutea (Nord)

Marokau

Hao

Pukarua

Réao

Îles du Vent

Ravahere

Archipel de la Société

Hérehéretué

Ahunui

Archipel des Tuamotu

Îles du Duc de Gloucester

Maria

Groupe Actéon

Tematangi

Tenarunga

Marutea (Sud)

Fangataufa

Îles Gambier

Îles Australes (Tubuai Islands)

Rimatara

Rurutu

Tubuai

Timoé

Mangareva

Tropic of Capricorn

Raivavae

Rapa

Marotiri

9

TAHITI AND MOOREA
1:1 000 000

9a

Baie d'Opunohu

Baie de Cook

Pointe Aroa

Moorea

PAPEETE

Mahina

Papenoo

Arue

Papawa

Tiarei

FAAA

Mahaena

Aorai 2066

Orohena 2241

Hitiaa

Punaauia

Tetufera 1696

L. Vaihiria

Utuofai

Faaone

Tahiti

Paea

Taravao

Papara

Presqu'île de Taiarapu

Atimaono

Mataiea

Vairao

Teahupoo

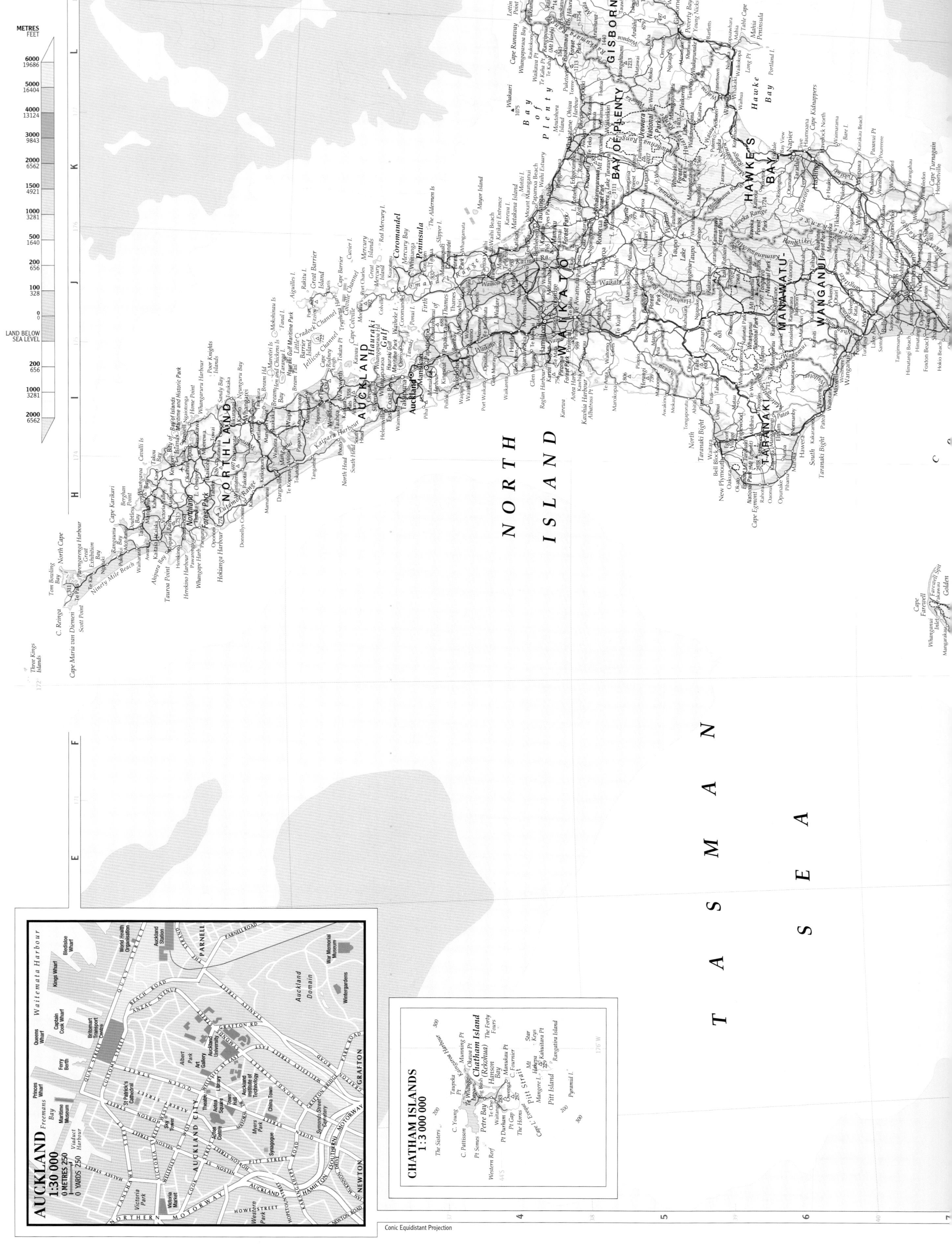
METRES
FEET
6000
19686
5000
16404
4000
13124
3000
9843
2000
6562
1500
4921
1000
3281
500
1640
200
656
100
328
0
0
LAND BELOW SEA LEVEL
200
656
1000
3281
2000
6562
NORTH ISLAND
TASMAN SEA
NORTHLAND
AUCKLAND
WAIKATO
BAY OF PLENTY
GISBORNE
HAWKE'S BAY
TARANAKI
MANAWATU-WANGANUI
Bay of Plenty
Hawke Bay
Hauraki Gulf
Coromandel Peninsula
North Taranaki Bight
South Taranaki Bight
Auckland
Hamilton
Napier
Hastings
Gisborne
New Plymouth
Wanganui
Lake Taupo
Ninety Mile Beach
Cape Reinga
North Cape
Three Kings Islands
Cape Egmont
East Cape
AUCKLAND
1:30 000
0 METRES 250
0 YARDS 250
Waitemata Harbour
Auckland Domain
CHATHAM ISLANDS
1:3 000 000
Chatham Island (Rekohua)
Pitt Island

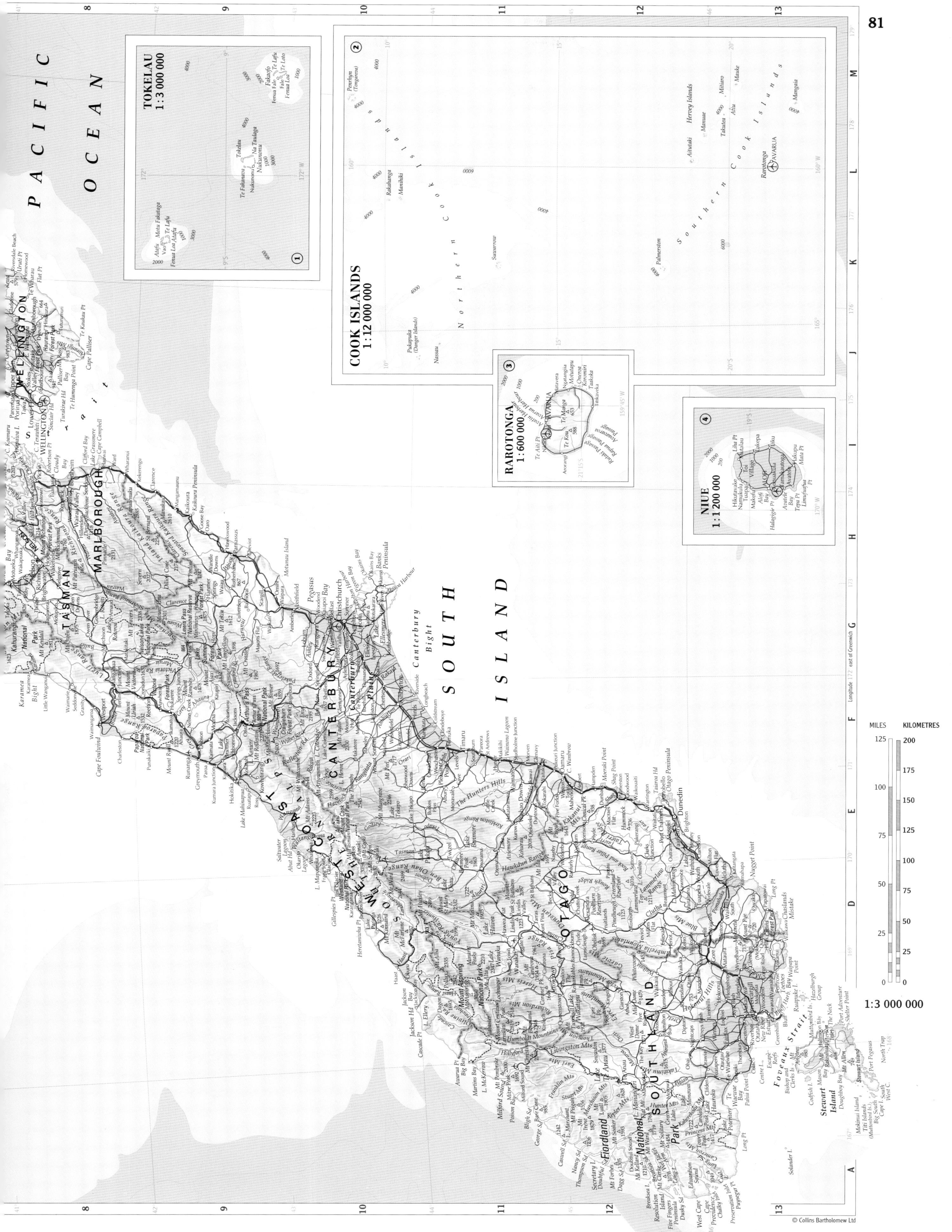

PACIFIC OCEAN

TOKELAU
1:3 000 000

Atafu
Motu Falega
Vaoto
Te Lafu
Femua Loa Atafu

Nukumatau
Na Taulaga
Nukunonu

Tokelau

Te Fakanava

Fenua Fala
Fale
Te Lafu
Te Loto
Fenua Loa
Fakaofo

COOK ISLANDS
1:12 000 000

Northern Cook Islands

Penrhyn
(Tongareva)

Rakahanga
Manihiki

Pukapuka
(Danger Islands)

Nassau

Suwarrow

Palmerston

Southern Cook Islands

Aitutaki
Manuae
Takutea
Atiu
Mitiaro
Mauke

Hervey Islands

Rarotonga
AVARUA
Mangaia

RAROTONGA
1:600 000

Matavera
Ngatangiia
Motutapu
Oneroa
Avarua
Takitumu

Te Atui Pt
Te Koau
Te Manga
653
Avarangi
Titikaveka

NIUE
1:1 200 000

Hikutavake
Namukulu
Makefu
Toi
Village
Alofi
Bay
ALOFI

Liku Pt
Mutalau
Lakepa

Hakupu
Anamataa
Avatele
Bay
Hakupu
Vaiea
Mata Pt

Halagigie Pt
Avatele
Tepa Pt
Limu Fuafua Pt

WELLINGTON

MARLBOROUGH

TASMAN

South Island

SOUTH ISLAND

CANTERBURY

Christchurch

Canterbury Bight

WEST COAST

OTAGO

Dunedin

SOUTHLAND

Foveaux Strait

Stewart Island

1:3 000 000

MILES   KILOMETRES
125   200
           175
100   150
           125
75   100
           75
50
           50
25   25
0   0

© Collins Bartholomew Ltd

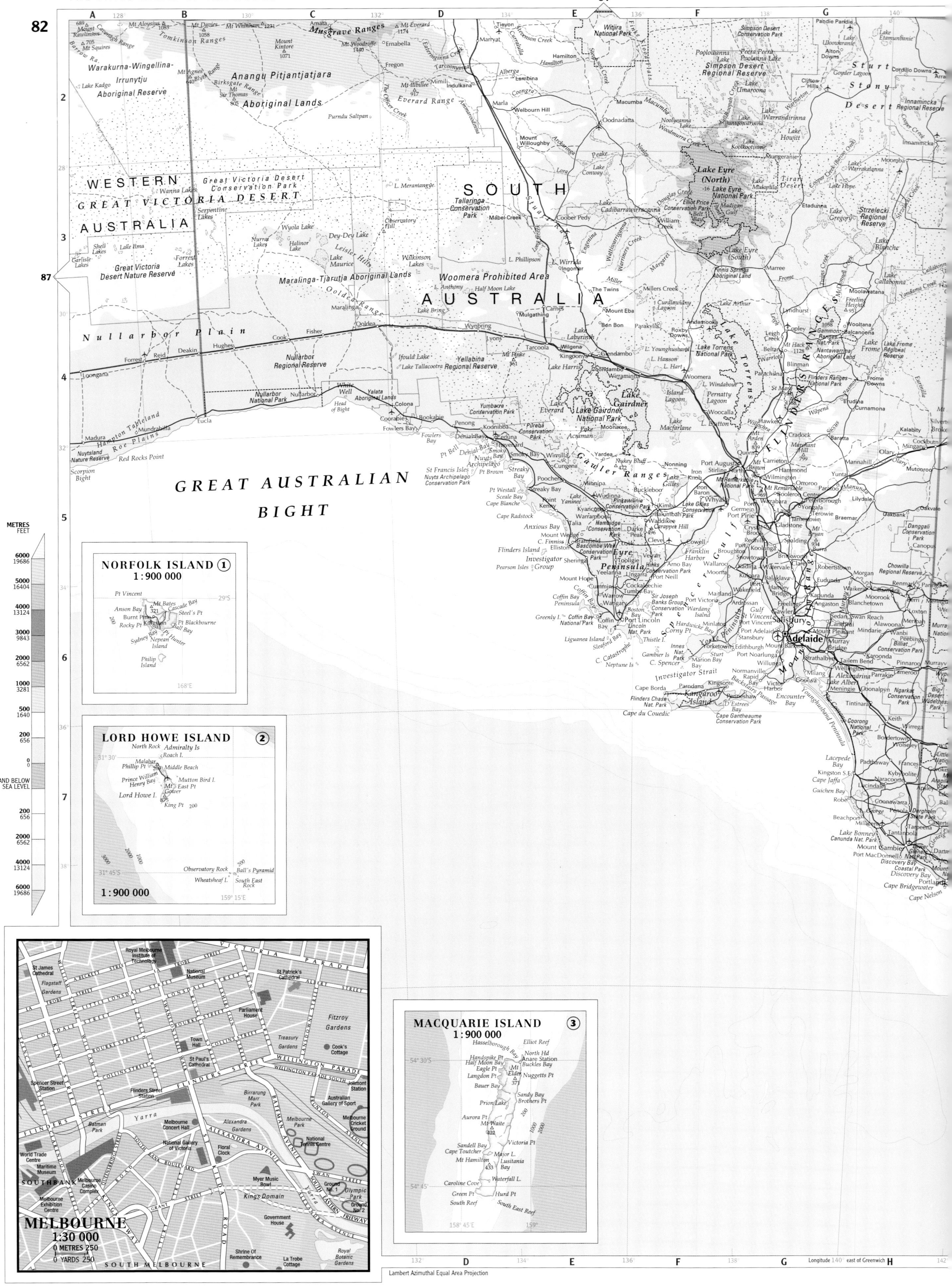

GREAT AUSTRALIAN
BIGHT

WESTERN
GREAT VICTORIA DESERT
AUSTRALIA

SOUTH
AUSTRALIA

Musgrave Ranges
Tomkinson Ranges
Anangu Pitjantjatjara
Aboriginal Lands

Warakurna-Wingellina-
Irrunytju
Aboriginal Reserve

Great Victoria Desert
Conservation Park

Great Victoria
Desert Nature Reserve

Nullarbor Plain

Maralinga-Tjarutja Aboriginal Lands

Woomera Prohibited Area

Nullarbor
National Park

Nullarbor
Regional Reserve

Lake Eyre
(North)

Lake Eyre
National Park

Simpson Desert
Regional Reserve

Simpson Desert
Conservation Park

Sturt
Stony
Desert

Strzelecki
Regional
Reserve

Lake Eyre
(South)

Lake Gairdner
National Park

Lake Torrens
National Park

Flinders Ranges
National Park

Eyre
Peninsula

Yorke
Peninsula

Spencer
Gulf

Gulf
St Vincent

Adelaide

Salisbury

Port Lincoln

Port Augusta

Port Pirie

Kangaroo
Island

Investigator Strait

Encounter
Bay

Coorong
National
Park

Mount Gambier

Coffin Bay
National Park

NORFOLK ISLAND ①
1 : 900 000

Pt Vincent
Anson Bay
Burnt Pine
Mt Bates
321
Cascade Bay
Steel's Pt
Pt Blackbourne
Rocky Pt
Kingston
Slaughter Bay
Sydney
Nepean
Island
Hunter
Island
Philip
Island

29°S
168°E

LORD HOWE ISLAND ②
1 : 900 000

North Rock
Admiralty Is
Roach I.
Malabar
Phillip Pt
Middle Beach
Prince William
Henry Bay
Mt East Pt
Gower
Mutton Bird I.
Lord Howe I.
King Pt

Observatory Rock
Ball's Pyramid
Wheatsheaf I.
South East
Rock

31°30'
31°45'S
159°15'E

MACQUARIE ISLAND ③
1 : 900 000

Hasselborough Bay
Elliot Reef
North Hd
Handspike Pt
Anare Station
Half Moon Bay
Buckles Bay
Eagle Pt
Nuggets Pt
Langdon Pt
Mt
Elder
Bauer Bay
Sandy Bay
Brothers Pt
Aurora Pt
Mt
Waite
822
Victoria Pt
Prion Lake
Sandell Bay
Cape Toutcher
Mt Hamilton
433
Lusitania
Bay
Caroline Cove
Waterfall L.
Green Pt
Hurd Pt
South Reef
South East Reef

54°30'S
54°45'S
158°45'E
159°

MELBOURNE
1:30 000
0 METRES 250
0 YARDS 250

VICTORIA PARADE
St James Cathedral
Flagstaff
Gardens
Royal Melbourne
Institute of
Technology
National
Museum
St Patrick's
Cathedral
Parliament
House
Fitzroy
Gardens
Treasury
Gardens
Town
Hall
Cook's
Cottage
St Paul's
Cathedral
Spencer Street
Station
Flinders Street
Station
WELLINGTON PARADE
Jolimont
Station
Birrarung
Marr
Park
Australian
Gallery of Sport
Yarra
Batman
Park
World Trade
Centre
Maritime
Museum
SOUTHBANK
Melbourne
Casino
Complex
Melbourne
Exhibition
Centre
National Gallery
of Victoria
Melbourne
Concert Hall
Alexandra
Gardens
Floral
Clock
Melbourne
Park
National
Tennis Centre
Melbourne
Cricket
Ground
Kings Domain
Myer Music
Bowl
Olympic
Park
Ground
No 1
Ground
No 2
Government
House
Shrine Of
Remembrance
Royal
Botanic
Gardens
La Trobe
Cottage
SOUTH MELBOURNE

METRES / FEET
6000 / 19686
5000 / 16404
4000 / 13124
3000 / 9843
2000 / 6562
1000 / 3281
500 / 1640
200 / 656
0 / 0
LAND BELOW
SEA LEVEL
200 / 656
2000 / 6562
4000 / 13124
6000 / 19686

Lambert Azimuthal Equal Area Projection

Longitude 140° east of Greenwich

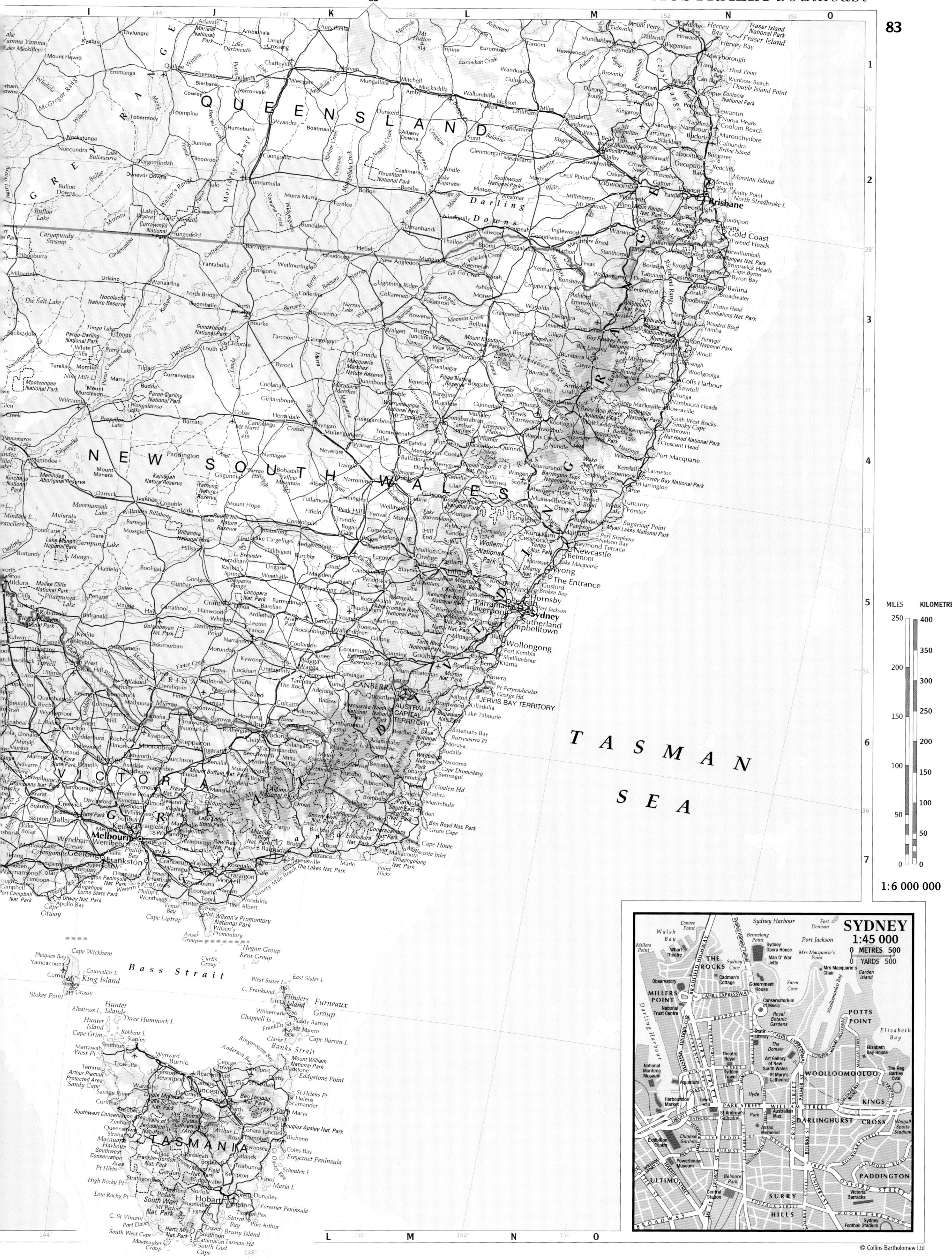

85

QUEENSLAND

NEW SOUTH WALES

VICTORIA

TASMANIA

Brisbane
Gold Coast
Tweed Heads
Newcastle
Sydney
Parramatta
Liverpool
Wollongong
Port Kembla
CANBERRA
AUSTRALIAN CAPITAL TERRITORY
JERVIS BAY TERRITORY
Melbourne
Geelong
Ballarat
Frankston
Hobart
Launceston
Devonport
Burnie

G R E A T   D I V I D I N G   R A N G E

GREY RANGE

Darling Downs

TASMAN SEA

Bass Strait

Furneaux Group
Flinders Island
King Island

Wilson's Promontory National Park
Cape Howe

MILES / KILOMETRES
250 / 400
350
200 / 300
250
150 / 200
100 / 150
100
50 / 50
0 / 0

1:6 000 000

© Collins Bartholomew Ltd

SYDNEY
1:45 000

0 METRES 500
0 YARDS 500

Sydney Harbour
Port Jackson
Sydney Opera House
THE ROCKS
MILLERS POINT
POTTS POINT
WOOLLOOMOOLOO
DARLINGHURST
KINGS CROSS
PADDINGTON
SURRY HILLS
ULTIMO
Royal Botanic Gardens
The Domain
Central Station
Darling Harbour

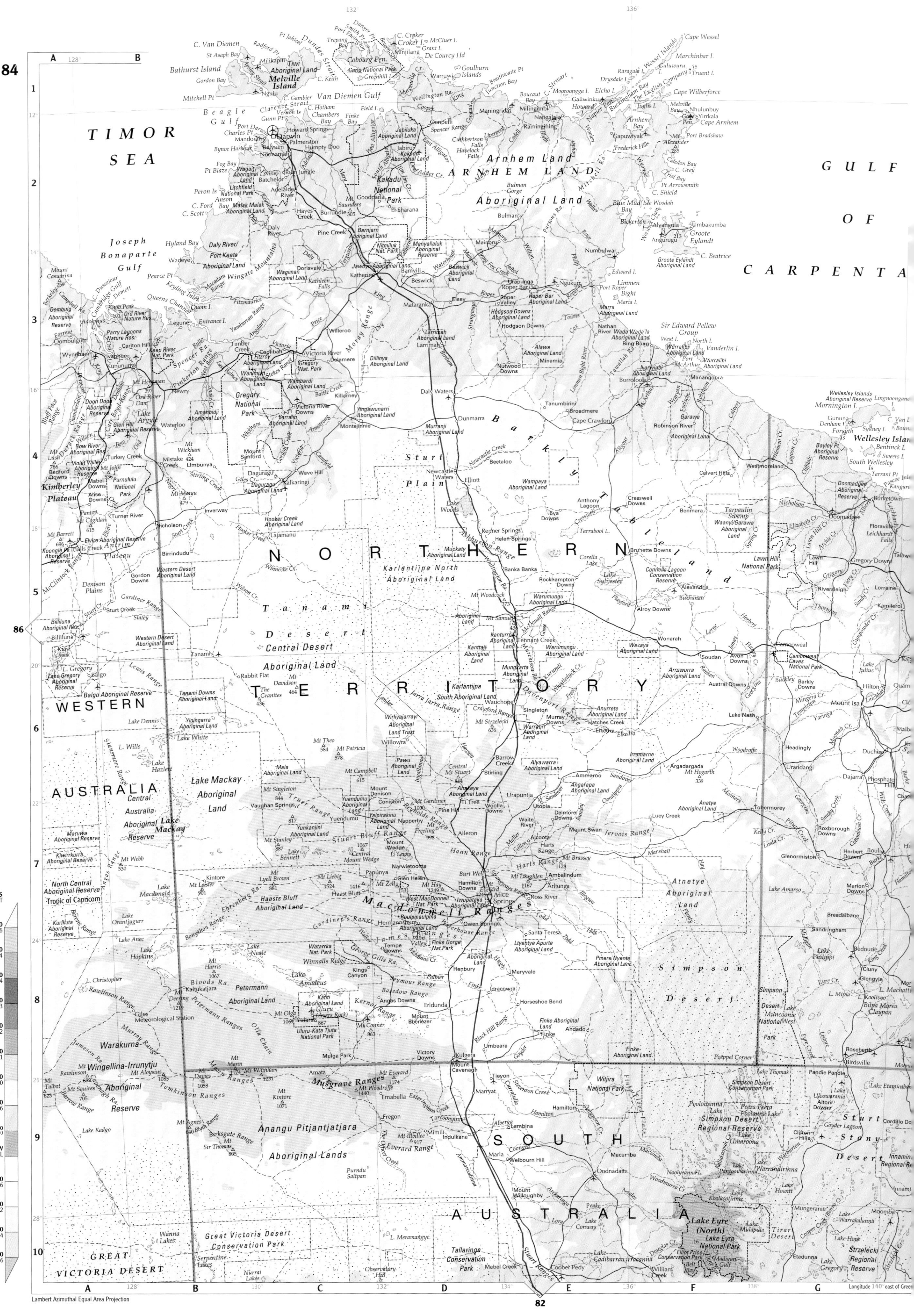

TIMOR SEA

Beagle Gulf

Van Diemen Gulf

Joseph Bonaparte Gulf

C. Van Diemen
Bathurst Island
Melville Island
Tiwi Aboriginal Land

Darwin
Palmerston
Humpty Doo

Kakadu National Park

Arnhem Land
ARNHEM LAND
Aboriginal Land

GULF OF CARPENTARIA

Groote Eylandt
Groote Eylandt Aboriginal Land

Cape Wessel
Wessel Islands

Nhulunbuy
Yirrkala
Arnhem Bay

Daly River/Port Keats Aboriginal Land

Pine Creek
Katherine
Nitmiluk Nat. Park
Mataranka

WESTERN AUSTRALIA

Kimberley Plateau

Lake Argyle
Purnululu National Park

Kununurra

Keep River Nat. Park
Gregory National Park
Victoria River

Daly Waters
Sturt Plain
Lake Woods
Elliott

Barkly Tableland

NORTHERN

Tanami Desert

Central Desert Aboriginal Land

Tennant Creek

TERRITORY

Western Desert Aboriginal Land

Lake Mackay

Central Australia Aboriginal Reserve

Lake Mackay Aboriginal Land

Tropic of Capricorn

Haasts Bluff Aboriginal Land

Macdonnell Ranges

Alice Springs

Simpson Desert

Petermann Aboriginal Land

Uluru-Kata Tjuta National Park
Uluru (Ayers Rock)
Mt Olga

Anangu Pitjantjatjara Aboriginal Lands

Musgrave Ranges

Great Victoria Desert

SOUTH AUSTRALIA

Lake Eyre (North)
Lake Eyre National Park

Simpson Desert Regional Reserve

Coober Pedy

GREAT VICTORIA DESERT

Great Victoria Desert Conservation Park

Simpson Desert Conservation Park

Sturt Stony Desert

METRES / FEET
6000 / 19686
5000 / 16404
4000 / 13124
3000 / 9843
2000 / 6562
1000 / 3281
500 / 1640
200 / 656
0
LAND BELOW SEA LEVEL
200 / 656
2000 / 6562
4000 / 13124
6000 / 19686

Lambert Azimuthal Equal Area Projection

Longitude 140° east of Greenwich

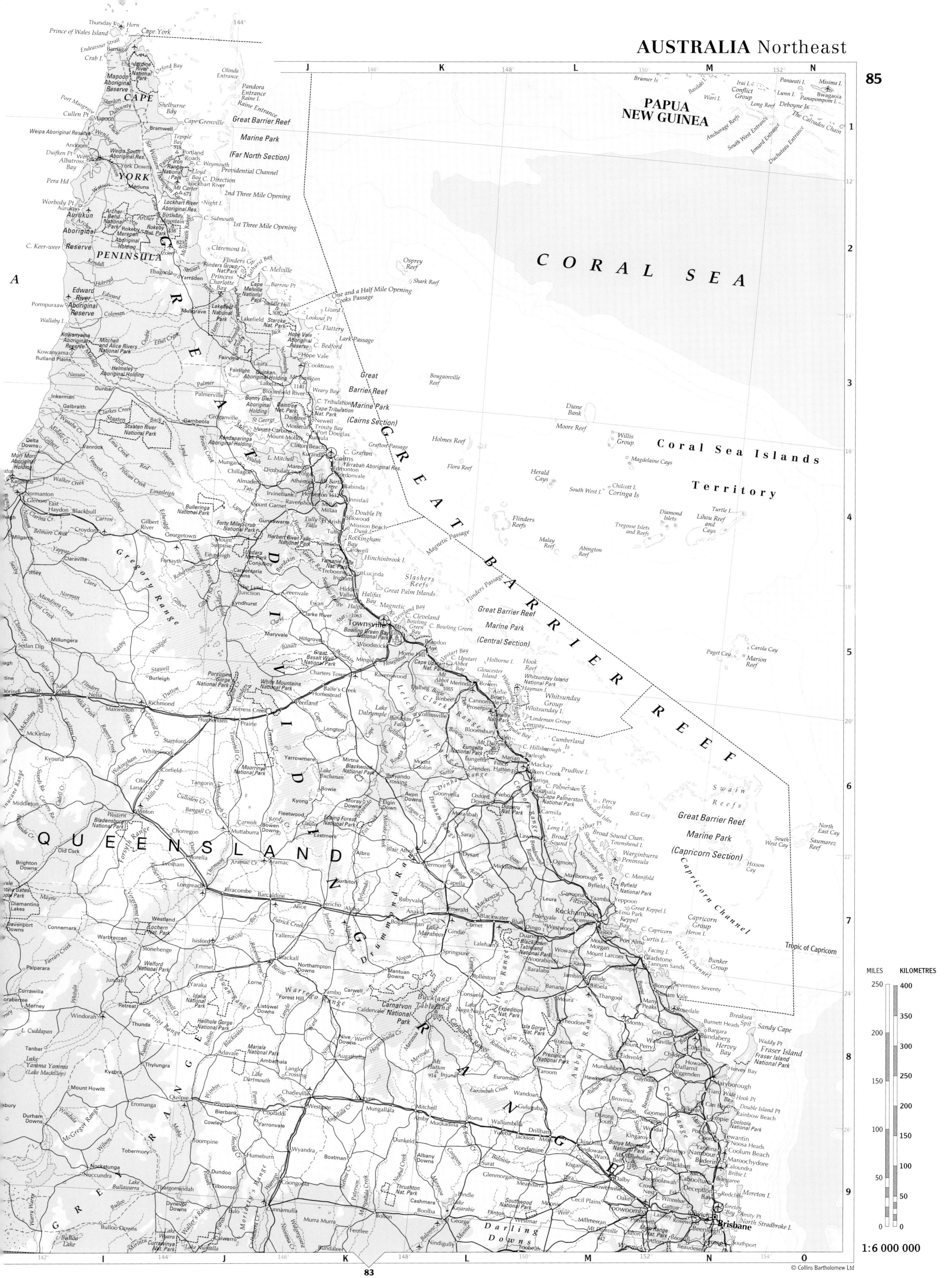

PAPUA NEW GUINEA

C O R A L   S E A

Coral Sea Islands

Territory

CAPE

YORK

PENINSULA

G R E A T   D I V I D I N G   R A N G E

Q U E E N S L A N D

Great Barrier Reef Marine Park (Far North Section)

Great Barrier Reef Marine Park (Cairns Section)

Great Barrier Reef Marine Park (Central Section)

Great Barrier Reef Marine Park (Capricorn Section)

G R E A T   B A R R I E R   R E E F

Cairns

Townsville

Mackay

Rockhampton

Gladstone

Bundaberg

Maryborough

Toowoomba

Brisbane

Tropic of Capricorn

Fraser Island National Park

MILES   KILOMETRES

250   400

200   350

300

150   250

200

100   150

100

50   50

0   0

1:6 000 000

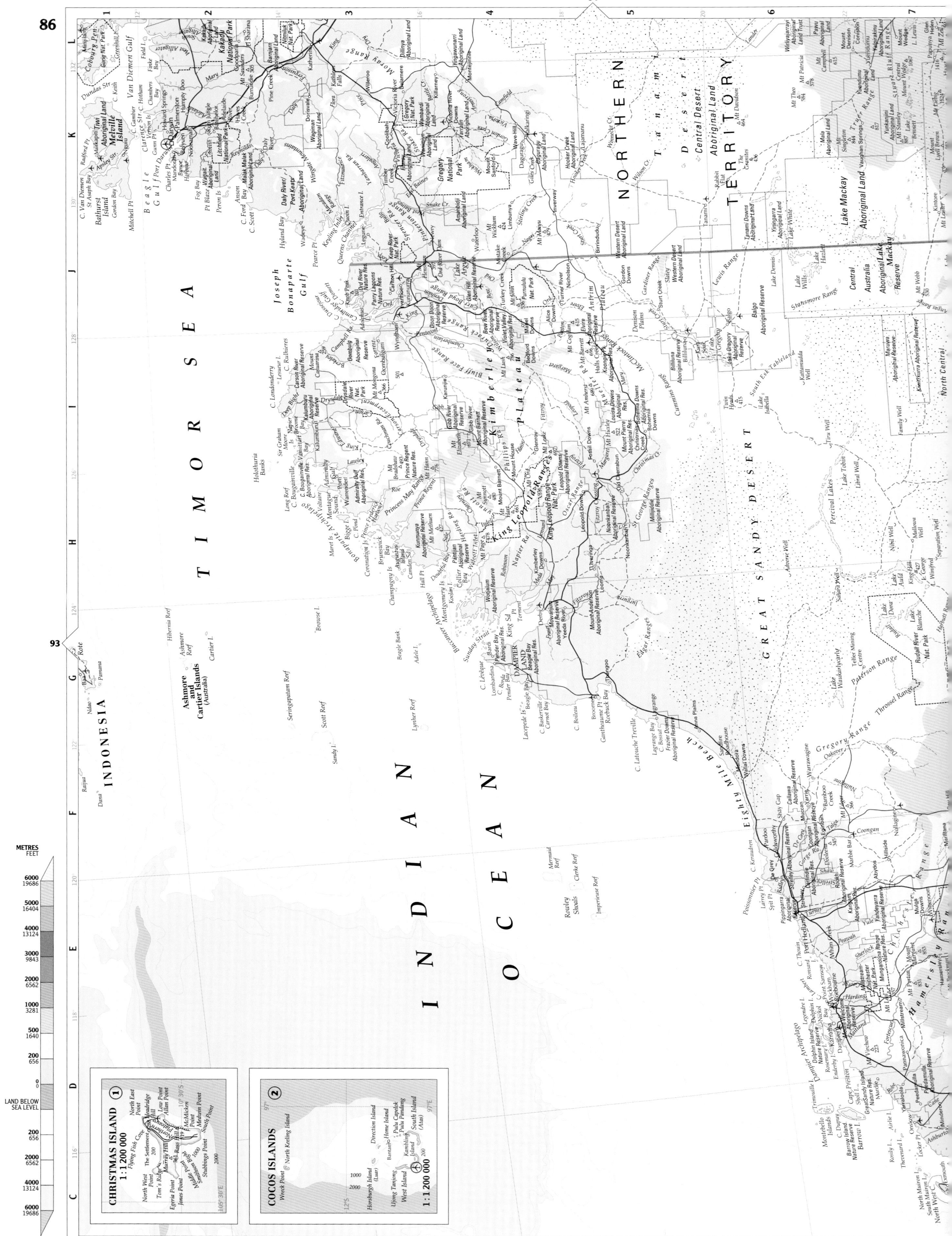

INDIAN OCEAN

TIMOR SEA

INDONESIA

NORTHERN TERRITORY

Tanami Desert

Central Desert Aboriginal Land

Lake Mackay

GREAT SANDY DESERT

Kimberley Plateau

King Leopold Ranges

Joseph Bonaparte Gulf

Beagle Gulf

Van Diemen Gulf

Melville Island

Bathurst Island

Kakadu Nat. Park

Darwin

Ashmore and Cartier Islands (Australia)

Eighty Mile Beach

Hamersley Range

Gregory Range

CHRISTMAS ISLAND (1)
1:1 200 000

COCOS ISLANDS (2)
1:1 200 000

METRES / FEET

6000 / 19686
5000 / 16404
4000 / 13124
3000 / 9843
2000 / 6562
1000 / 3281
500 / 1640
200 / 656
0 / 0

LAND BELOW SEA LEVEL

200 / 656
2000 / 6562
4000 / 13124
6000 / 19686

Lambert Azimuthal Equal Area Projection

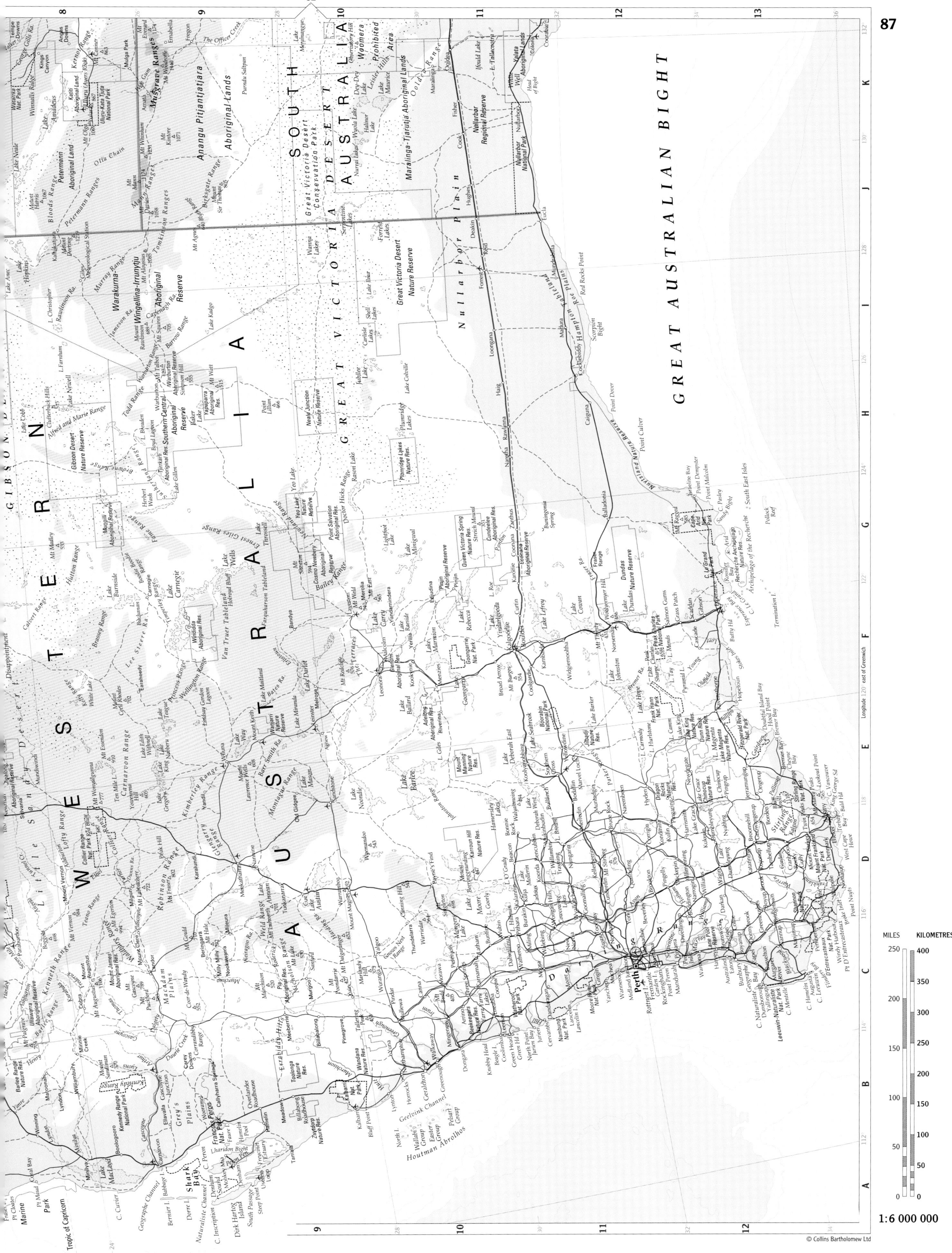

82

SOUTH AUSTRALIA

WESTERN AUSTRALIA

GREAT AUSTRALIAN BIGHT

GREAT VICTORIA DESERT

Great Victoria Desert Conservation Park

Great Victoria Desert Nature Reserve

Anangu Pitjantjatjara Aboriginal Lands

Maralinga-Tjarutja Aboriginal Lands

Musgrave Ranges

Nullarbor Plain

Nullarbor Regional Reserve

Nullarbor National Park

Woomera Prohibited Area

GIBSON DESERT

Gibson Desert Nature Reserve

LITTLE SANDY DESERT

Perth

Shark Bay

Tropic of Capricorn

Longitude 120 east of Greenwich

© Collins Bartholomew Ltd

1:6 000 000

MILES	KILOMETRES
250	400
200	350
	300
150	250
	200
100	150
	100
50	50
0	0

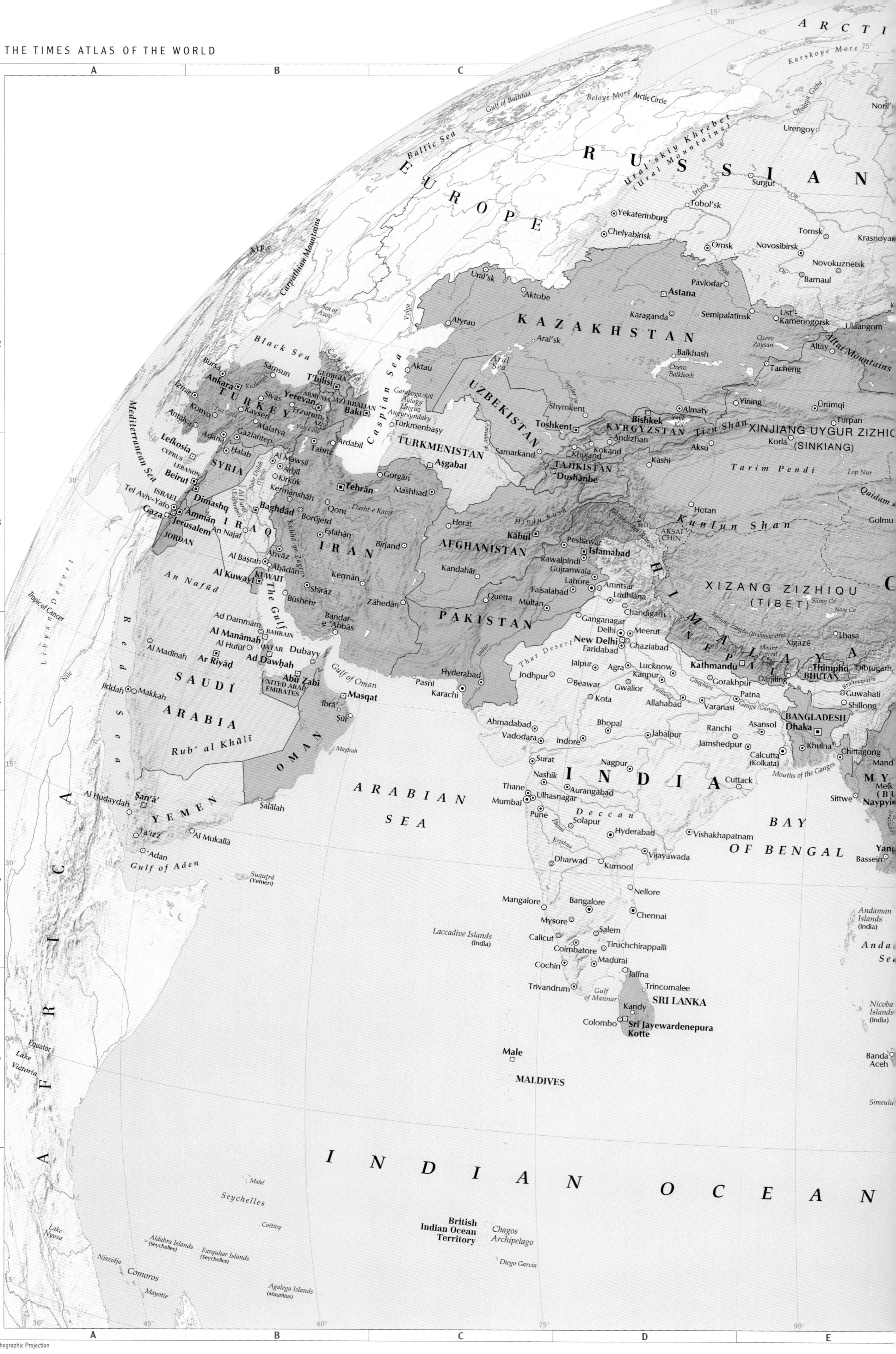

A B C D E

ARCTI

Karskoye More

EUROPE

RUSSIAN

Beloye More Arctic Circle

Gulf of Bothnia

Baltic Sea

Urengoy

Noril'

Ob'

Ural'skiy Khrebet (Ural Mountains)

Surgut

Yekaterinburg

Tobol'sk

Chelyabinsk

Omsk

Tomsk

Novosibirsk

Krasnoya

Irtysh

Pavlodar

Novokuznetsk

Astana

Aktobe

Karaganda

Semipalatinsk

Ust'-

Kamenogorsk

Ulaangom

Ural'sk

KAZAKHSTAN

Balkhash

Ozero Zaysan

Altay

Altai Mountains

Tacheng

Atyrau

Volga

Aral'sk

Aral Sea

Aktau

Ozero Balkhash

Black Sea

Sea of Azov

Bursa

Samsun

GEORGIA

T'bilisi

Kral

Caspian Sea

Garabogazköl Aylagy

Shymkent

UZBEKISTAN

Balkhash

Yining

Ürümqi

ARMENIA AZERBAIJAN

Toshkent

Almaty

Turpan

Ankara

Yerevan

Bakı

Bishkek

KYRGYZSTAN

Tien Shan

Korla

XINJIANG UYGUR ZIZHIQ

İzmir

Angursyndaky

Samarkand

Andizhan

(SINKIANG)

Konya

Kayseri

Erzurum

TURKEY

TURKMENISTAN

Türkmenbaşy

Kokand

Aksu

Sivas

Malatya

Lake Van

Tabrīz

Ardabil

Khujand

Kashi

Tarim Pendi

Lop Nur

Qaidam

Antalya

Adana

Gaziantep

Halab

Al Mawşil

Aşgabat

TAJIKISTAN

Lefkoşia

Gorgān

Dushanbe

Kunlun Shan

Hotan

Golmu

CYPRUS

SYRIA

Arbil

Tehrān

Mashhad

Himalaya

Kirkūk

AKSAI

CHIN

LEBANON

Beirut

Kermānshāh

Herāt

Kābul

Peshawar

Islāmābad

XIZANG ZIZHIQU

Siling Co

Dimashq

Baghdād

Qom

Rawalpindi

HIMALAYA

(TIBET)

Nam Co

Tel Aviv-Yafo

ISRAEL

Borūjerd

Eşfahān

AFGHANISTAN

Gujranwala

Lahore

Lhasa

Gaza

Amman

IRAQ

An Najaf

Dasht-e Kavir

Birjand

IRAN

Kandahar

Faisalabad

Amritsar

Ludhiāna

Xigazê

Jerusalem

JORDAN

Ahvāz

Ābādān

Kermān

Quetta

Multan

Chandigarh

Mount Everest

Darjiling

Dibrugarh

Al Başrah

PAKISTAN

Ganganagar

Delhi

Meerut

Lhasa

BHUTAN

Thimphu

Al Kuwayt

KUWAIT

Shīrāz

Brahmaputra

Guwahati

An Nafūd

The Gulf

Būshehr

Zāhedān

New Delhi

Ghaziabad

Kathmandu

Shillong

Bandar-e 'Abbās

Faridabad

Gorakhpur

Ad Dammām

BAHRAIN

Jaipur

Agra

Lucknow

Patna

Al Manāmah

QATAR

Dubayy

Pasni

Hyderabad

Jodhpur

Kanpur

Ganga (Ganges)

BANGLADESH

Al Hufūf

Ad Dawḩah

Gulf of Oman

Thar Desert

Kota

Gwalior

Allahabad

Varanasi

Dhaka

Al Madīnah

Ar Riyāḑ

Karachi

Beawar

Asansol

Khulna

Abū Ẕabī

UNITED ARAB

EMIRATES

Masqat

Ibrā

Şūr

Ahmadabad

Bhopal

Jabalpur

Ranchi

Chittagong

Jiddah

Makkah

SAUDI

Vadodara

Indore

Jamshedpur

Mand

ARABIA

OMAN

Maşīrah

Surat

Nagpur

Cuttack

M Y

(BU

Al Hudaydah

Ṣan'ā'

Rub' al Khālī

Nashik

INDIA

Metk

Sittwe

Naypyi

Thane

Aurangabad

Deccan

Şalālah

Mumbai

Ulhasnagar

Solapur

Hyderabad

Gulf of Aden

Ta'izz

YEMEN

Al Mukallā

Pune

Krishna

Vishakhapatnam

BAY

'Adan

Dharwad

Kurnool

Vijayawada

OF BENGAL

Yang

Suquţrá (Yemen)

Nellore

Bassein

ARABIAN

SEA

Mangalore

Bangalore

Salem

Chennai

Andaman Islands (India)

Mysore

And

Se

Calicut

Tiruchchirappalli

Coimbatore

Laccadive Islands (India)

Cochin

Madurai

Jaffna

Trivandrum

Gulf of Mannar

Trincomalee

Nicoba

Islands (India)

SRI LANKA

Kandy

Colombo

Sri Jayewardenepura

Kotte

Male

Banda

Aceh

MALDIVES

Simeulu

Equator

Lake Victoria

AFRICA

INDIAN OCEAN

Mahé

Seychelles

Coëtivy

British Indian Ocean Territory

Chagos Archipelago

Banda

Lake Nyasa

Aldabra Islands (Seychelles)

Farquhar Islands (Seychelles)

Diego Garcia

Njazidja

Comoros

Mayotte

Agalega Islands (Mauritius)

A B C D E

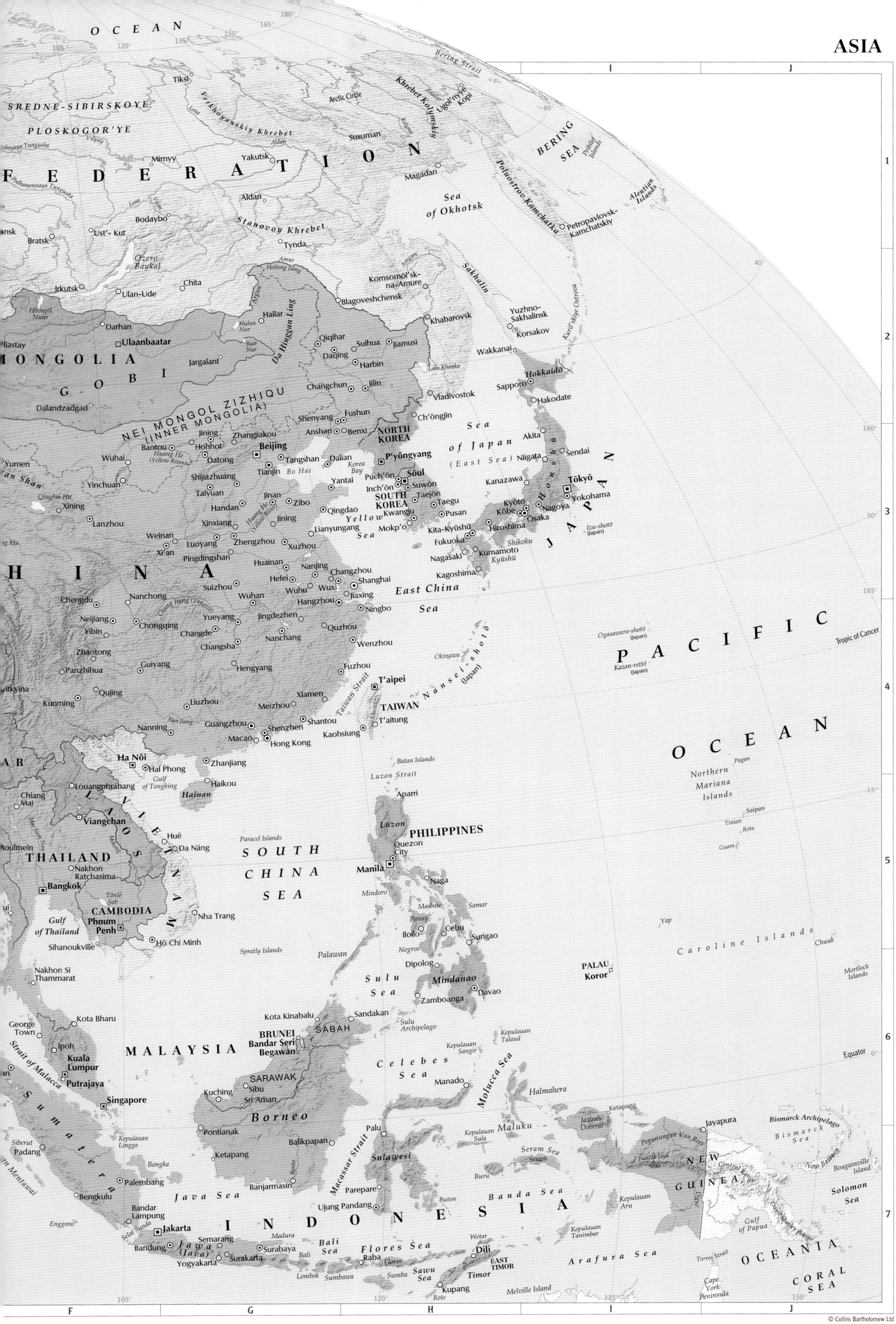

OCEAN

SREDNE - SIBIRSKOYE

PLOSKOGOR'YE

FEDERATION

Yenisey Tunguska

Kamennaya Tunguska

Tiksi

Arctic Circle

Khrebet Kolymskiy

Verkhoyanskiy Khrebet

Lena

BERING STRAIT

Ugol'nyye Kopi

Lena

Vilyuy

Aldan

Mirnyy

Yakutsk

Susuman

Magadan

BERING SEA

Pribilof Islands

60

Poluostrov Kamchatka

Bratsk

Ust'-Kut

Bodaybo

Ozero Baykal

Irkutsk

Ulan-Ude

Chita

Stanovoy Khrebet

Tynda

Amur

Heilong Jiang

Komsomol'sk-na-Amure

Blagoveshchensk

Khabarovsk

Amur

Sakhalin

45

Petropavlovsk-Kamchatskiy

Aleutian Islands

Hoosgol Nuur

Darhan

Hailar

Da Hinggan Ling

Qiqihar

Suihua

Jiamusi

Sea of Okhotsk

Yuzhno-Sakhalinsk

Korsakov

Kuril'skiye Ostrova

MONGOLIA

Ulaanbaatar

Jargalant

Hulun Nur

Buir Nur

Daqing

Harbin

Lake Khanka

Vladivostok

Wakkanai

Hokkaidō

180

GOBI

Dalandzadgad

NEI MONGOL ZIZHIQU (INNER MONGOLIA)

Changchun

Jilin

Shenyang

Fushun

NORTH KOREA

Ch'ŏngjin

Sapporo

Hakodate

Liaocheng

Jining

Zhangjiakou

Anshan

Benxi

P'yŏngyang

Sea of Japan (East Sea)

Niigata

Akita

Sendai

Baotou

Hohhot

Datong

Tangshan

Dalian

Inch'ŏn

Sŏul

Suwŏn

Kanazawa

Kōbe

Tōkyō

Yokohama

Wuhai

Beijing

Huang He (Yellow River)

Tianjin

Bo Hai

Korea Bay

Puch'ŏn

SOUTH KOREA

Taejŏn

Kyōto

Nagoya

30

Yumen

Yinchuan

Shijiazhuang

Yantai

Taegu

Osaka

JAPAN

Tian Shan

Xining

Taiyuan

Handan

Jinan

Zibo

Qingdao

Kwangju

Pusan

Hiroshima

Kita-Kyūshū

Izu-shotō (Japan)

Qinghai Hu

Lanzhou

Xinxiang

Jining

Lianyungang

Yellow Sea

Mokp'o

Fukuoka

Kumamoto

Kyūshū

Weinan

Luoyang

Zhengzhou

Xuzhou

Nagasaki

Kagoshima

165

Xi'an

Pingdingshan

CHINA

Huainan

Nanjing

Changzhou

Shanghai

Chengdu

Nanchong

Chang Jiang (Yangtze)

Suizhou

Hefei

Wuhu

Wuxi

Jiaxing

East China Sea

Nanjing

Wuhan

Hangzhou

Ningbo

Ogasawara-shotō (Japan)

PACIFIC

Neijiang

Chongqing

Changde

Yueyang

Jingdezhen

Quzhou

Wenzhou

Tropic of Cancer

Yibin

Zhaotong

Changsha

Nanchang

Kazan-rettō (Japan)

Panzhihua

Guiyang

Hengyang

Fuzhou

Kunming

Qujing

Liuzhou

Xiamen

T'aipei

TAIWAN

OCEAN

Nansei-shotō (Japan)

Meizhou

Okinawa

15

Nanning

Xun Jiang

Guangzhou

Shenzhen

Shantou

Kaohsiung

T'aitung

Taiwan Strait

AR

Macao

Hong Kong

Ha Nôi

Hai Phong

Zhanjiang

Haikou

Batan Islands

Luzon Strait

Pagan

Northern Mariana Islands

Louangphrabang

Gulf of Tongking

Hainan

Aparri

Saipan

Tinian

Chiang Mai

LAOS

VIETNAM

Huê

Da Năng

Paracel Islands

Luzon

PHILIPPINES

Quezon City

Rota

Guam

Viangchan

THAILAND

Nakhon Ratchasima

Bangkok

Tônlé Sap

Mekong

CAMBODIA

Phnum Penh

Nha Trang

Hô Chi Minh

SOUTH CHINA SEA

Manila

Naga

Mindoro

Masbate

Samar

Yap

Caroline Islands

Chuuk

Gulf of Thailand

Sihanoukville

Spratly Islands

Palawan

Iloilo

Panay

Cebu

Surigao

Nakhon Si Thammarat

Negros

PALAU

Koror

Mortlock Islands

George Town

Kota Bharu

Sulu Sea

Dipolog

Mindanao

Davao

Ipoh

MALAYSIA

Kota Kinabalu

Sandakan

Sulu Archipelago

Zamboanga

Kepulauan Talaud

Kuala Lumpur

Putrajaya

BRUNEI

Bandar Seri Begawan

SABAH

Sulu Archipelago

Kepulauan Sangir

Celebes Sea

Singapore

SARAWAK

Kuching

Sibu

Sri Aman

Manado

Halmahera

Molucca Sea

Ketapang

Bismarck Archipelago

Strait of Malacca

Borneo

Pontianak

Balikpapan

Palu

Kepulauan Maluku

Kepulauan Sula

Jazirah Doberai

Jayapura

Bismarck Sea

New Britain

Siberut

Padang

Kepulauan Lingga

Bangka

Sumatera

Ketapang

Sulawesi

Parepare

Seram Sea

Seram

Buru

Pegunungan Van Rees

Puncak Jaya

NEW GUINEA

Sepik

Bougainville Island

Solomon Sea

Palembang

Bengkulu

Banjarmasin

Ujung Pandang

Banda Sea

Kepulauan Aru

Central Range

Enggano

Bandar Lampung

Jakarta

Java Sea

INDONESIA

Buton

Kepulauan Tanimbar

Gulf of Papua

Torres Strait

Mentawai

Bandung

Semarang

Surabaya

Bali

Flores Sea

Wetar

Dili

EAST TIMOR

Arafura Sea

OCEANIA

Yogyakarta

Surakarta

Madura

Bali

Bali Sea

Raba

Flores

Sumba

Sawu Sea

Timor

Kupang

Melville Island

Cape York Peninsula

CORAL SEA

Lombok

Sumbawa

Rote

120

150

MILES   KILOMETRES

1000

1500

750

1250

1000

500

750

250

500

Equator

250

0

1:24 000 000

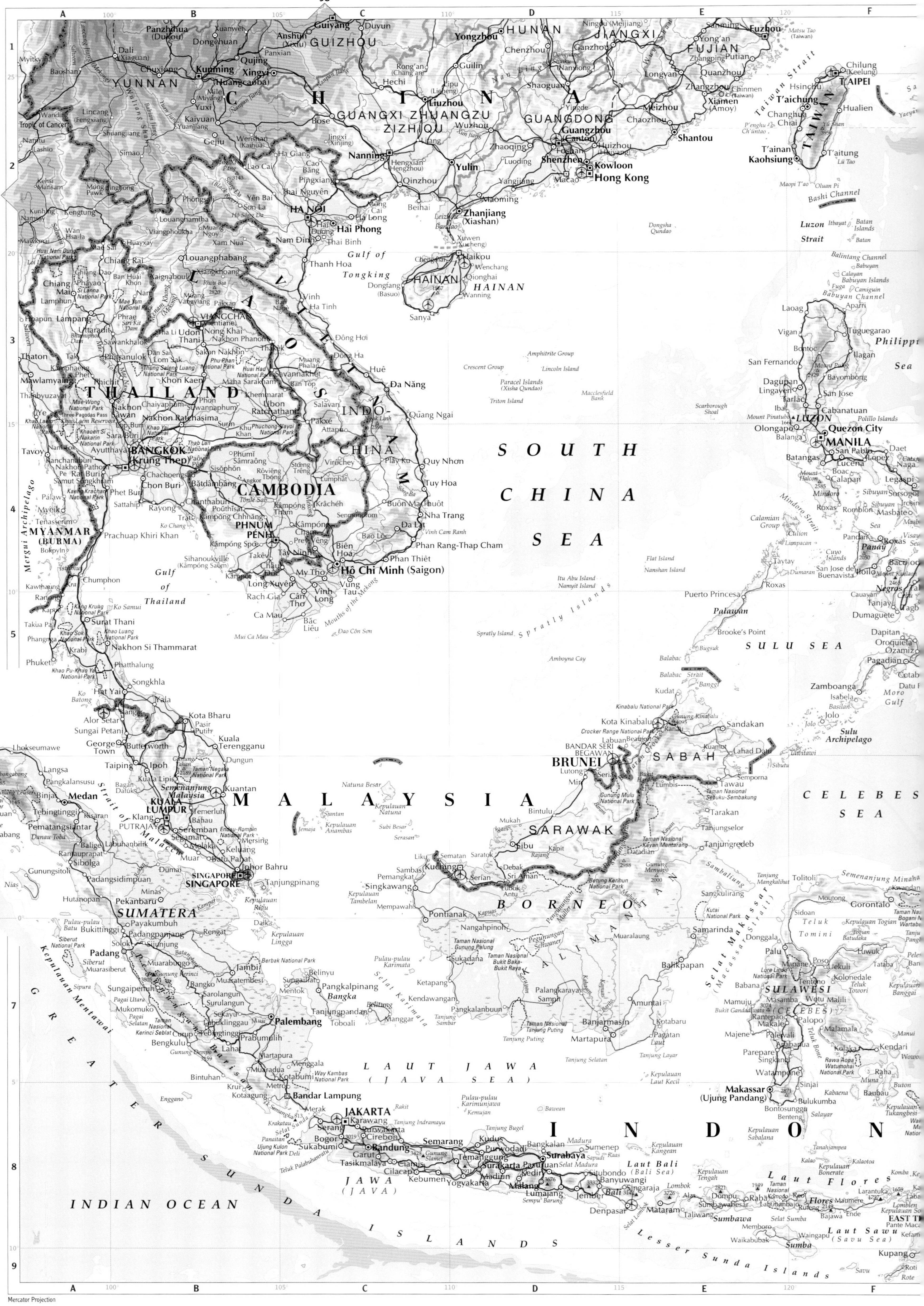

98

112

METRES
FEET

6000
19686

5000
16404

4000
13124

3000
9843

2000
6562

1000
3281

500
1640

200
656

0

LAND BELOW
SEA LEVEL

200
656

2000
6562

4000
13124

6000
19686

Myitkyina
Dali
(Xiaguan)
Panzhihua
(Dukou)
Xuanwei
Dongchuan
Anshun
(Xiau)
GUIZHOU
Duyun
Guiyang
Yongzhou
HUNAN
Chenzhou
JIANGXI
Ganzhou
Yong'an
FUJIAN
Zhangping
Putian
Fuzhou
Matsu Tao
(Taiwan)

Baoshan
Chuxiong
Kunming
Xingyi
Qujing
Panxian
Rong'an
(Chang'an)
Guilin
Shaoguan
Longyan
Quanzhou
Chilung
(Keelung)

YUNNAN
Kaiyuan
(Kaihua)
Milu
Miyang)
Liuzhou
Hechi
Liuzhou
Lipo
(Licheng)
Yingde
Meizhou
Zhangzhou
Xiamen
(Amoy)
Chinmen
T'aipei

Wanding
Lincang
(Fengqing)
Simao
Yuxi
Yuanjiang
GUANGXI ZHUANGZU
ZIZHIQU
Bose
Wuzhou
GUANGDONG
Chaozhou
T'aichung
Hsinchu
T'ainan
Kaohsiung
T'aitung

Namtu
Lashio
Shuangjiang
Wenshan
(Kaihua)
Nanning
Hengxian
(Hengzhou)
Guangzhou
Canton
Huizhou
Shenzhen
Shantou

Kok. Mansam
Mong Hkinglong
Pawk
Lao Cai
Qinzhou
Yulin
Yangjiang
Kowloon
Hong Kong
Macao

Namsam
Kunlong
Ha Giang
Cao Bang
Pingxiang
Thai Nguyen
HANOI
Ha Long
Beihai
Zhanjiang
(Xiashan)
Maoming

Kengtung
Yen Bai
Son La
Nam Dinh
Hai Phong
Thai Binh
Xuwen
Xincheng
Haikou
Wenchang

Wan Hsa-la
Viangphoukha
Muang
Ngoy
Xam Nua
Gulf of
Tongking
HAINAN
Qionghai

Chiang Rai
Louangphabang
Xiangkhoang
Thanh Hoa
Dongfang
(Basuo)
HAINAN
Wanning

LAOS
Wanning
Sanya

Chiang
Mai
Lampang
Nan
VIANGCHAN
(Vientiane)
Nong Khai
Nakhon Phanom
Vinh
Ha Tinh
Dong Hoi

THAILAND
Khon Kaen
Maha Sarakham
Hue
Da Nang

Mawlamyaing
Phichit
Phitsanulok
Nakhon Ratchasima
Ubon
Ratchathani
Pakxe
Quang Ngai

INDO-
CHINA
Kon Tum
Play Ku
Quy Nhon

BANGKOK
Krung Thep
Chachoengsao
Sisophon
Phumi
Samraong
Stoeng Treng
Virochey
Tuy Hoa

CAMBODIA
Battambang
Tonle Sap
Kampong Thum
Kampong Cham
Buon Ma Thuot
Nha Trang

Myeik
MYANMAR
(BURMA)
PHNUM
PENH
Kampong Spoe
Da Lat
Phan Rang-Thap Cham

Takua Pa
Phnum
Long Xuyen
Ho Chi Minh (Saigon)
Vung
Tau

Surat Thani
Nakhon Si Thammarat
Rach Gia
Can
Tho
Vinh
Long

Phuket
Phatthalung
Ca Mau
Bac
Lieu
Dao Con Son

Hat Yai
Yala
Kota Bharu
SULU SEA

Banda Aceh
Alor Setar
George
Town
Butterworth
Kuala
Terengganu
Kota Kinabalu
Sandakan

Langsa
Taiping
Ipoh
Kuantan
BANDAR SERI
BEGAWAN
SABAH
Lahad Datu

Medan
KUALA
LUMPUR
MALAYSIA
BRUNEI
Miri
SARAWAK
Tawau

Pematangsiantar
PUTRAJAYA
Seremban
Melaka
Sibu
Kuching
Tarakan
CELEBES
SEA

SINGAPORE
SINGAPORE
Johor Bahru
BORNEO
Pontianak
Samarinda

Padang
SUMATERA
Palembang
KALIMANTAN
Balikpapan
SULAWESI
(CELEBES)
Makassar
(Ujung Pandang)

SOUTH
CHINA
SEA

Paracel Islands
(Xisha Qundao)

Spratly Islands

LUZON
Quezon City
MANILA
Philippine
Sea

Laoag
Tuguegarao
San Fernando
Dagupan

Olongapo
San Pablo
Lucena
Legaspi

Puerto Princesa
Palawan
Roxas
Iloilo

Zamboanga
Jolo
Sulu
Archipelago

INDIAN OCEAN

JAKARTA
Bogor
Bandung
Semarang
Surabaya
JAWA
(JAVA)
LAUT JAWA
(JAVA SEA)
Bali
Denpasar
Mataram
Sumbawa
LESSER SUNDA ISLANDS

INDON

Mercator Projection

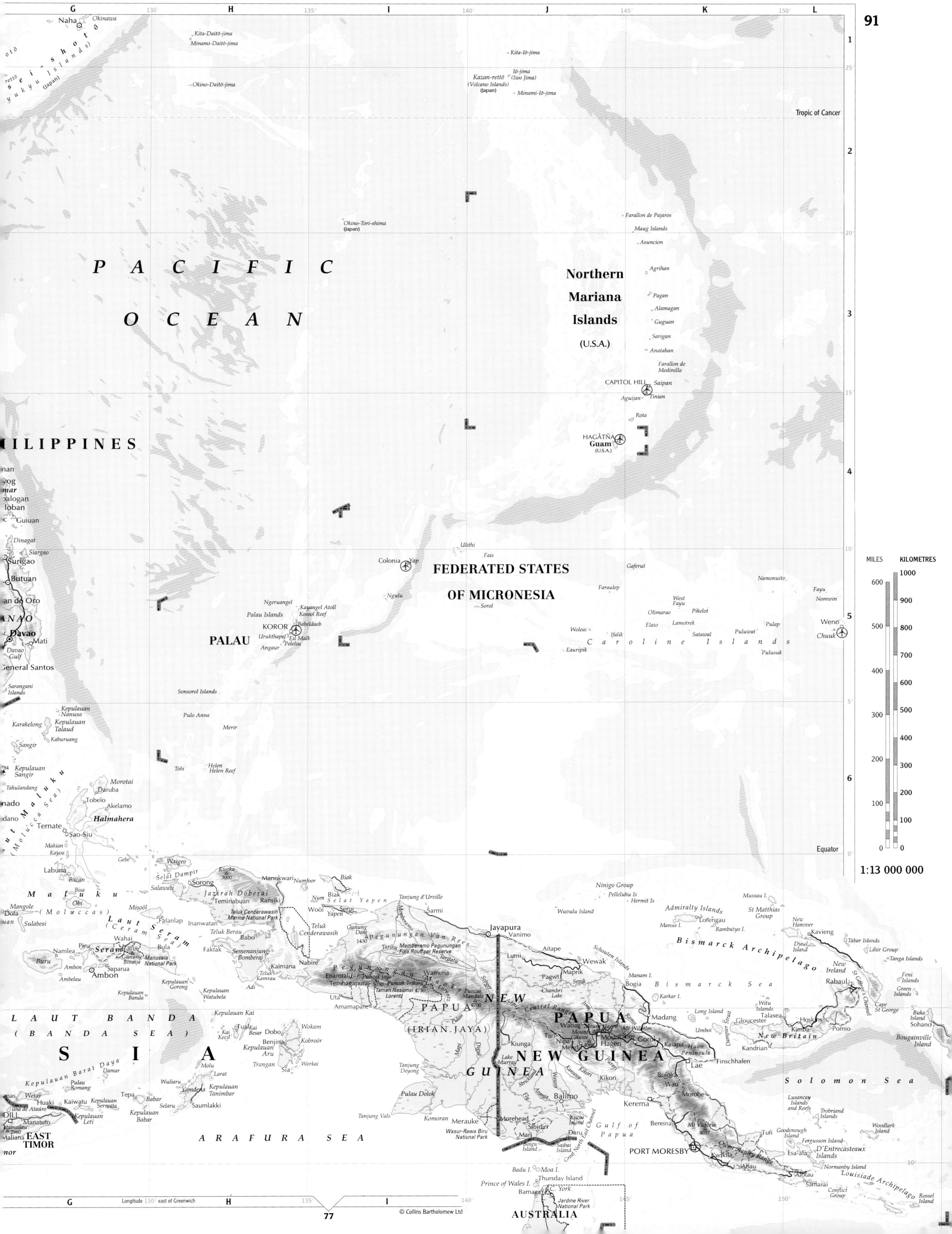
G
H
I
J
K
L
130°
135°
140°
145°
150°
1
2
3
4
5
6
25°
20°
15°
10°
5°
0°
Naha
Okinawa
Kita-Daitō-jima
Minami-Daitō-jima
Oki-Daitō-jima
Kita-Iō-jima
Iō-jima
(Iwo Jima)
Kazan-rettō
(Volcano Islands)
(Japan)
Minami-Iō-jima
Tropic of Cancer
Okino-Tori-shima
(Japan)
Farallon de Pajaros
Maug Islands
Asuncion
Agrihan
Pagan
Alamagan
Guguan
Sarigan
Anatahan
Farallon de Medinilla
CAPITOL HILL
Saipan
Aguijan
Tinian
Rota
HAGÅTÑA
Guam
(U.S.A.)
P A C I F I C
O C E A N
Northern
Mariana
Islands
(U.S.A.)
PHILIPPINES
Ulithi
Fais
Colonia
Yap
Ngulu
FEDERATED STATES
OF MICRONESIA
Sorol
Gaferut
Faraulep
Namonuito
Fayu
Nomwin
Weno
Chuuk
West Fayu
Pikelot
Olimarao
Elato
Lamotrek
Satawal
Puluwat
Pulap
Pulusuk
Woleai
Ifalik
Eauripik
C a r o l i n e   I s l a n d s
Ngeruangel
Kayangel Atoll
Kossol Reef
Palau Islands
KOROR
Babeldaob
Urukthapel
Eil Malk
Peleliu
Angaur
PALAU
Sonsorol Islands
Pulo Anna
Merir
Tobi
Helen
Helen Reef
Surigao
Siargao
Dinagat
Butuan
Guiuan
Davao
Mati
Davao Gulf
General Santos
Sarangani Islands
Kepulauan Nanusa
Kepulauan Talaud
Karakelong
Kaburuang
Sangir
Kepulauan Sangir
Tahulandang
Morotai
Daruba
Tobelo
Akelamo
Halmahera
Ternate
Sao-Siu
Makian
Kayoa
Laut Maluku
(Molucca Sea)
Equator
MILES
KILOMETRES
0
100
200
300
400
500
600
700
800
900
1000
1:13 000 000
Gebe
Waigeo
Selat Dampir
Sorong
Kofiau
Salawati
Labuha
Bacan
Bisa
Obi
Maluku
(Moluccas)
Mangole
Sulabesi
Misoöl
Laut Seram
(Ceram Sea)
Seram
Fakfak
Pafanlap
Inanwatan
Teminabuan
Ransiki
Manokwari
Numfoor
Biak
Num
Selat Yapen
Yapen
Serui
Teluk Cenderawasih Marine National Park
Teluk Cenderawasih
Teluk Berau
Babo
Bula
Wahai
Namlea
Piru
Buru
Binaija
Manusela National Park
Saparua
Ambon
Ambelau
Semenanjung Bomberai
Kaimana
Nabire
Teluk Kamrau
Adi
Kepulauan Gorong
Kepulauan Watubela
Kepulauan Banda
Kepulauan Kai
Tual
Kai Besar
Kai Kecil
Dobo
Wokam
Kobroor
Benjina
Kepulauan Aru
Workai
Trangan
LAUT BANDA
(BANDA SEA)
ASIA
Molu
Larat
Kepulauan Barat Daya
Damar
Pulau Romang
Wuliaru
Yamdena
Kepulauan Tanimbar
Saumlakki
Selaru
Wetar
Huaki
Kaiwatu
Kepulauan Sermata
Tepa
Babar
Kepulauan Babar
Kepulauan Leti
Manatuto
DILI
EAST TIMOR
ARAFURA SEA
Jayapura
Vanimo
Sarmi
Tanjung d'Urville
Memberamo
Pegunungan Van Rees
Memberamo Foja-Rouffaer Reserve
Enarotali
Puncak Jaya
Tembagapura
Puncak Trikora
Wamena
Taman Nasional Lorentz
Puncak Mandala
Uta
Amamapare
PAPUA
(IRIAN JAYA)
Tanjung Deyong
Pulau Dolok
Tanjung Vals
Komoran
Merauke
Wasur-Rawa Biru National Park
Morehead
Sibidiri
Mari
Bugu Island
Daru
Saibai Island
Kiunga
Lake Murray
NEW GUINEA
PAPUA NEW GUINEA
Lumi
Aitape
Wewak
Maprik
Schouten Islands
Manam I.
Bogia
Pagwi
Chambri Lake
Central Range
Wabag
Mount Hagen
Mt Wilhelm
Mount Giluwe
Tari
Nipa
Mendi
Hagen
Goroka
Kainantu
Madang
Karkar I.
Long Island
Huon Peninsula
Lae
Finschhafen
Bulolo
Wau
Kikori
Kerema
Balimo
Morobe
Bereina
Gulf of Papua
PORT MORESBY
Kwikila
Owen Stanley Range
Mt Victoria
Abau
Tufi
Great North East Channel
Kuoi Island
Badu I.
Moa I.
Thursday Island
Prince of Wales I.
Bamaga
C. York
Jardine River National Park
AUSTRALIA
Ninigo Group
Pelleluhu Is
Hermit Is
Wuvulu Island
Admiralty Islands
Lorengau
Manus I.
Rambutyo I.
Mussau I.
St Matthias Group
New Hanover
Kavieng
Tabar Islands
Lihir Group
Tanga Islands
Djaul Island
Bismarck Archipelago
Bismarck Sea
New Ireland
Rabaul
St George's Channel
Feni Islands
Green Islands
Cape St George
Witu Islands
Talasea
Gloucester
Umboi
Dampier Strait
New Britain
Hoskins
Kimbe
Pomio
Kandrian
Buka Island
Sohano
Bougainville Island
Solomon Sea
Lusancay Islands and Reefs
Trobriand Islands
Goodenough Island
Fergusson Island
D'Entrecasteaux Islands
Woodlark Island
Esa-ala
Normanby Island
Louisiade Archipelago
Alotau
Samarai
Conflict Group
Rossel Island
Longitude 130° east of Greenwich

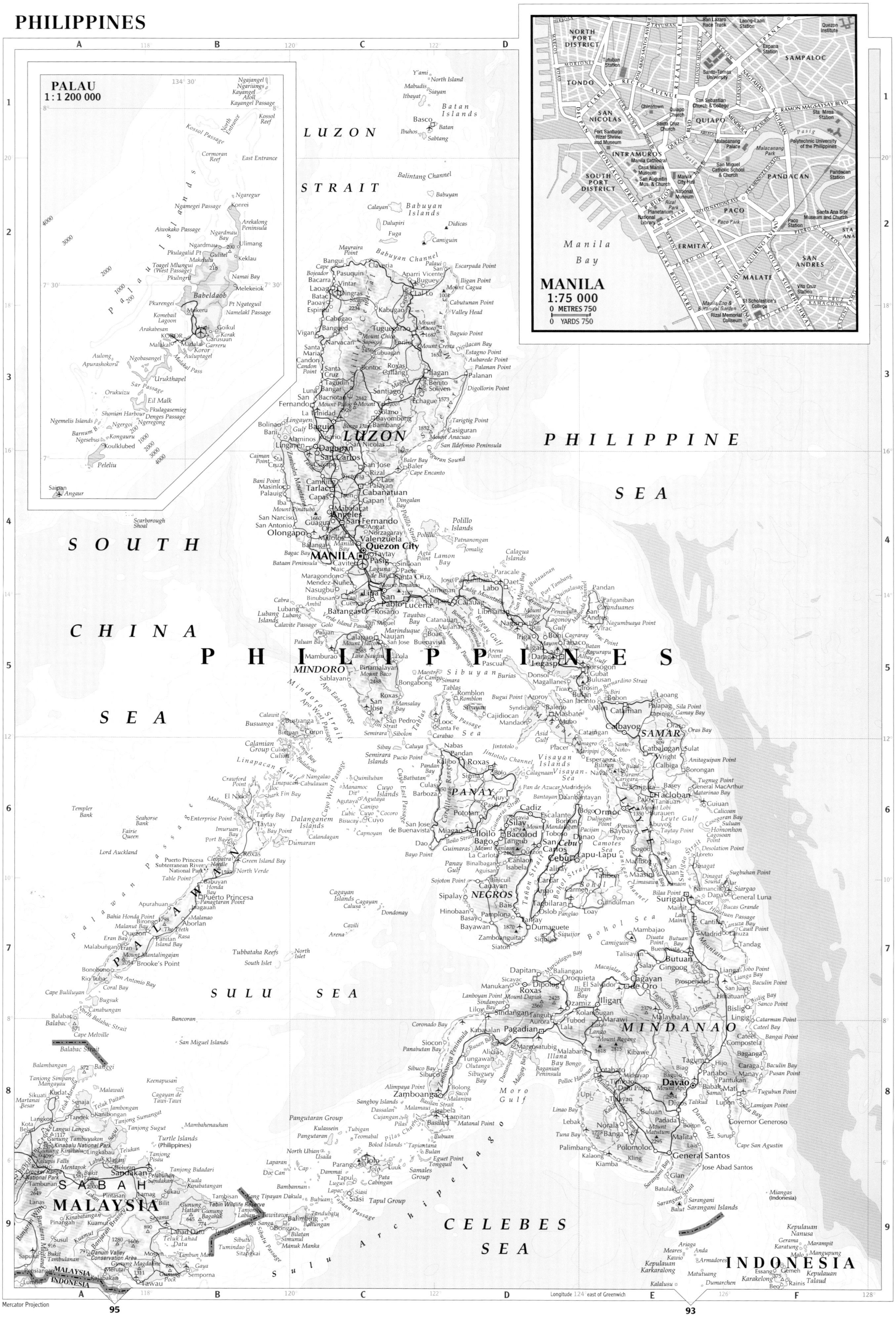

PALAU
1 : 1 200 000

MANILA
1 : 75 000
0 METRES 750
0 YARDS 750

LUZON STRAIT

PHILIPPINE SEA

SOUTH CHINA SEA

PHILIPPINES

MINDORO

PALAWAN SEA

SULU SEA

PANAY

NEGROS

SAMAR

MINDANAO

CELEBES SEA

SABAH
MALAYSIA

INDONESIA

MANILA

QUEZON CITY

Davao

General Santos

Zamboanga

Puerto Princesa

METRES / FEET
6000 19686
5000 16404
4000 13124
3000 9843
2000 6562
1000 3281
500 1640
200 656
0
LAND BELOW SEA LEVEL
200 656
2000 6562
4000 13124
6000 19686

Mercator Projection

Longitude 124 east of Greenwich

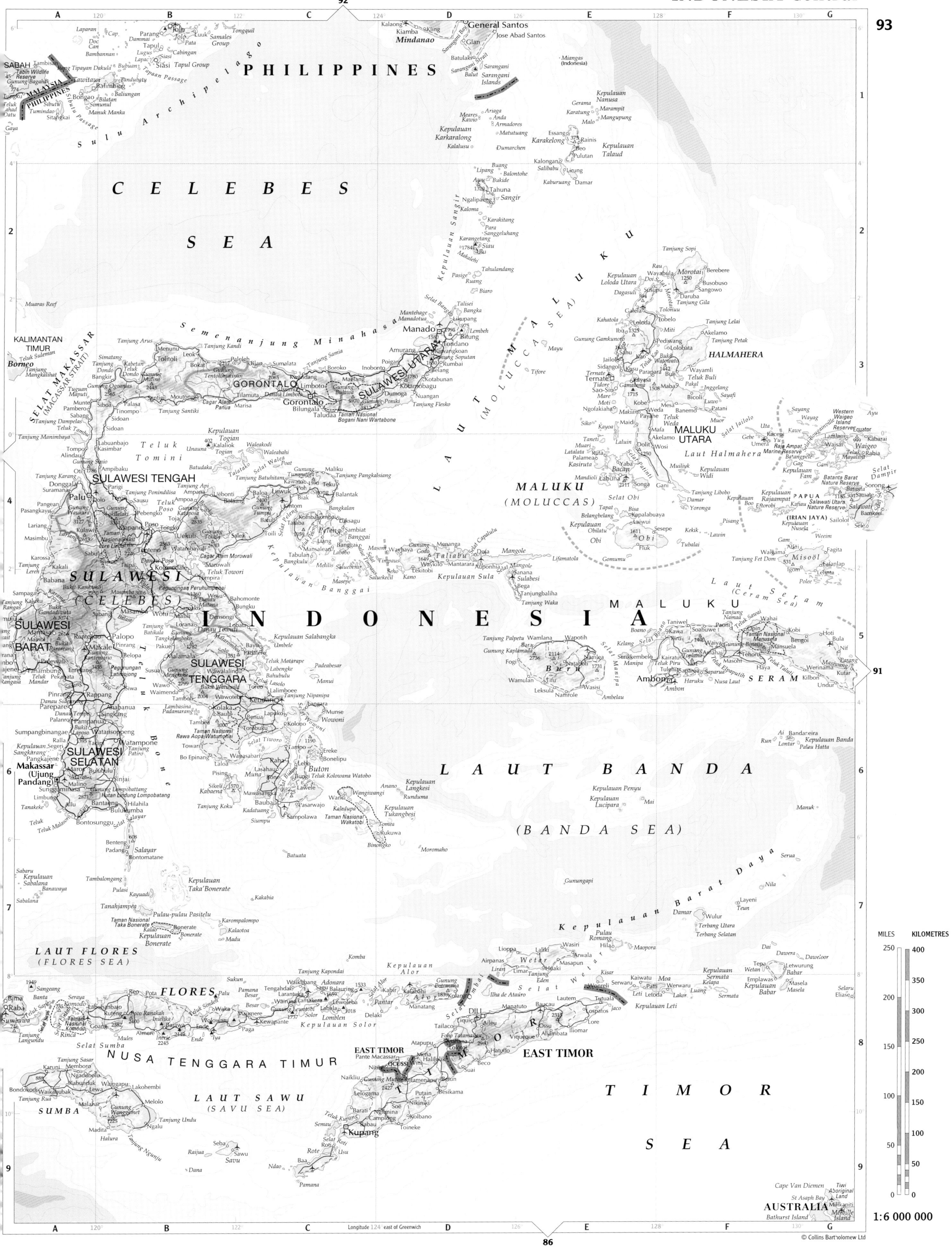
PHILIPPINES
Mindanao
General Santos
Sulu Archipelago
CELEBES SEA
Semenanjung Minahasa
Manado
SULAWESI UTARA
GORONTALO
Gorontalo
Teluk Tomini
SULAWESI TENGAH
Palu
SULAWESI (CELEBES)
SULAWESI BARAT
SULAWESI TENGGARA
Kendari
SULAWESI SELATAN
Makassar (Ujung Pandang)
Teluk Bone
Kepulauan Banggai
Kepulauan Sula
Kepulauan Talaud
Kepulauan Sangir
Morotai
HALMAHERA
Ternate
MALUKU UTARA
Laut Halmahera
LAUT MALUKU (MOLUCCA SEA)
MALUKU (MOLUCCAS)
Obi
Buru
SERAM
Ambon
Laut Seram (Ceram Sea)
MALUKU
INDONESIA
LAUT BANDA (BANDA SEA)
Kepulauan Banda
Buton
Kepulauan Tukangbesi
Kepulauan Barat Daya
Wetar
Kepulauan Alor
FLORES
LAUT FLORES (FLORES SEA)
Kepulauan Solor
NUSA TENGGARA TIMUR
SUMBA
LAUT SAWU (SAVU SEA)
Savu
TIMOR
DILI
EAST TIMOR
Kupang
Rote
TIMOR SEA
AUSTRALIA
PAPUA (IRIAN JAYA)
SABAH
KALIMANTAN TIMUR
Borneo
SELAT MAKASSAR (MACASSAR STRAIT)
MILES
KILOMETRES
1:6 000 000
Longitude 124° east of Greenwich

ANDAMAN

SEA

S O U T H

THAILAND

KEDAH

PERAK

KELANTAN

TERENGGANU

Kota Bharu

Kuala Terengganu

PINANG
George Town
Butterworth

Taiping

MALAYSIA

PAHANG

Kuantan

ACEH

SELANGOR

KUALA
LUMPUR

PUTRAJAYA

NEGERI
SEMBILAN

SEMANJUNG

MALAYSIA

MELAKA

Medan

S
U
M
A
T
E
R
A

SUMATERA UTARA

JOHOR

Johor Bahru
SINGAPORE

Strait of Singapore

KEPULAUAN RIAU

Pekanbaru

RIAU

Equator

Padang

SUMATERA
BARAT

JAMBI

I N D O

Palembang

Bangka

BANG

SUMATERA
SELATAN

BENGKULU

I N D I A N

O C E A N

Nias

Bengkulu

Kepulauan Mentawai

LAMPUNG

Bandar Lampung

JAKA

BANTEN

METRES
FEET

6000
19686

5000
16404

4000
13124

3000
9843

2000
6562

1000
3281

500
1640

200
656

0

LAND BELOW
SEA LEVEL

200
656

2000
6562

4000
13124

6000
19686

SINGAPORE
1:300 000

Johor Bahru

MALAYSIA

SEMBAWANG

WOODLANDS

NISHUN

Selat Johor

Sungai Johor

Kranji
Reservoir

MANDAI

Seletar
Reservoir

JALAN
KAYU

Pulau Ubin

PUNGGOL

SELETAR

Serangoon
Harbour

Lower Peirce
Reservoir

ANG MO

HOUGANG

CHANGI

Upper Peirce
Reservoir

Bedok
Reservoir

TAMPINES

Murai Reservoir

Lim Chu Kang

BUKIT BATOK

BUKIT
TIMAH

MacRitchie
Reservoir

TOA
PAYOH

BEDOK

Tengeh Reservoir

JURONG

ULU PANDAN

CLEMENTI

TANGLIN

GEYLANG

KATONG

SIGLAP

QUEENSTOWN

PASIR
PANJANG

SINGAPORE

Jurong Island

Selat Pandan

Sentosa

Strait of Singapore

Christmas Island
(Australia)

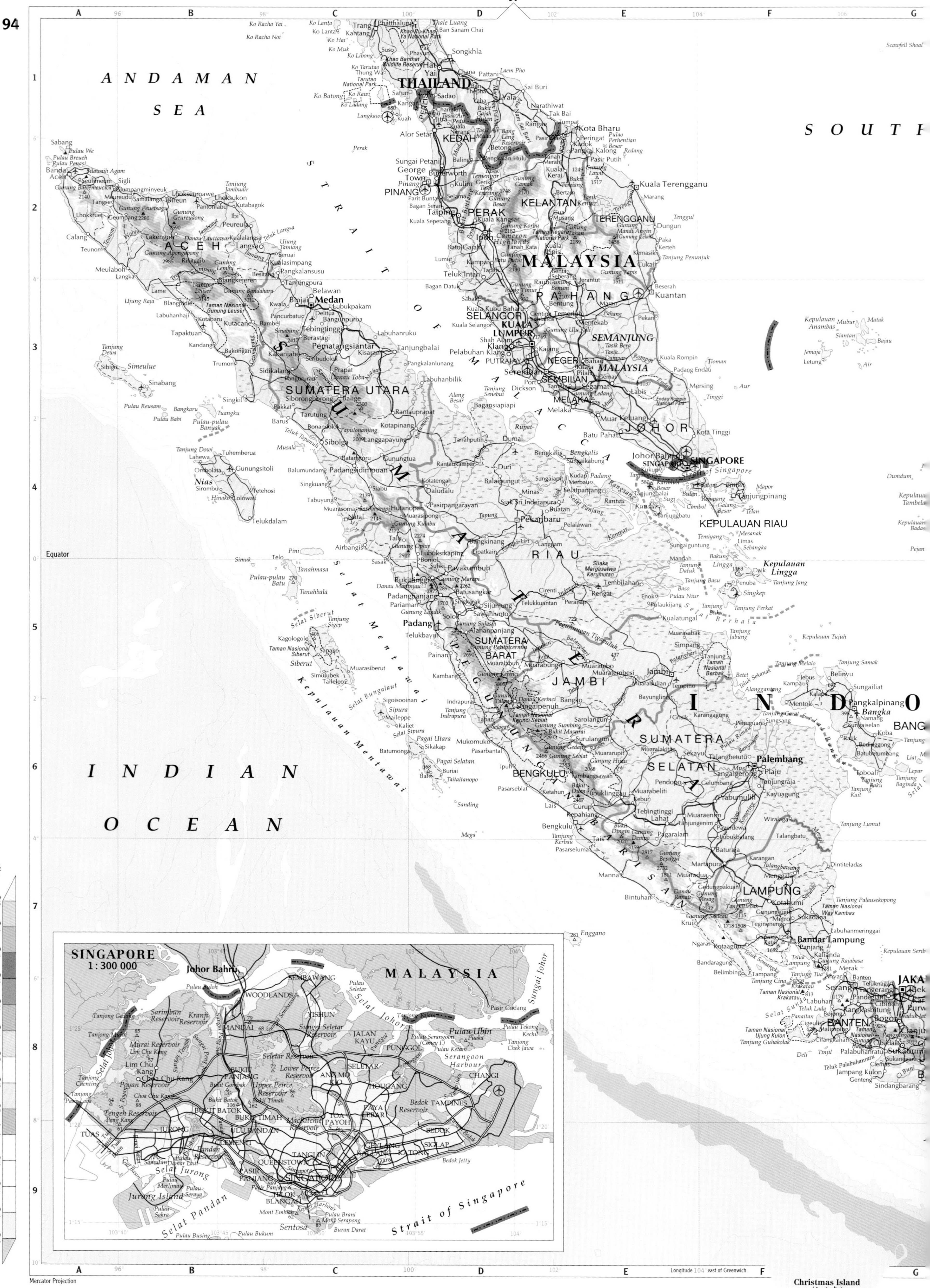

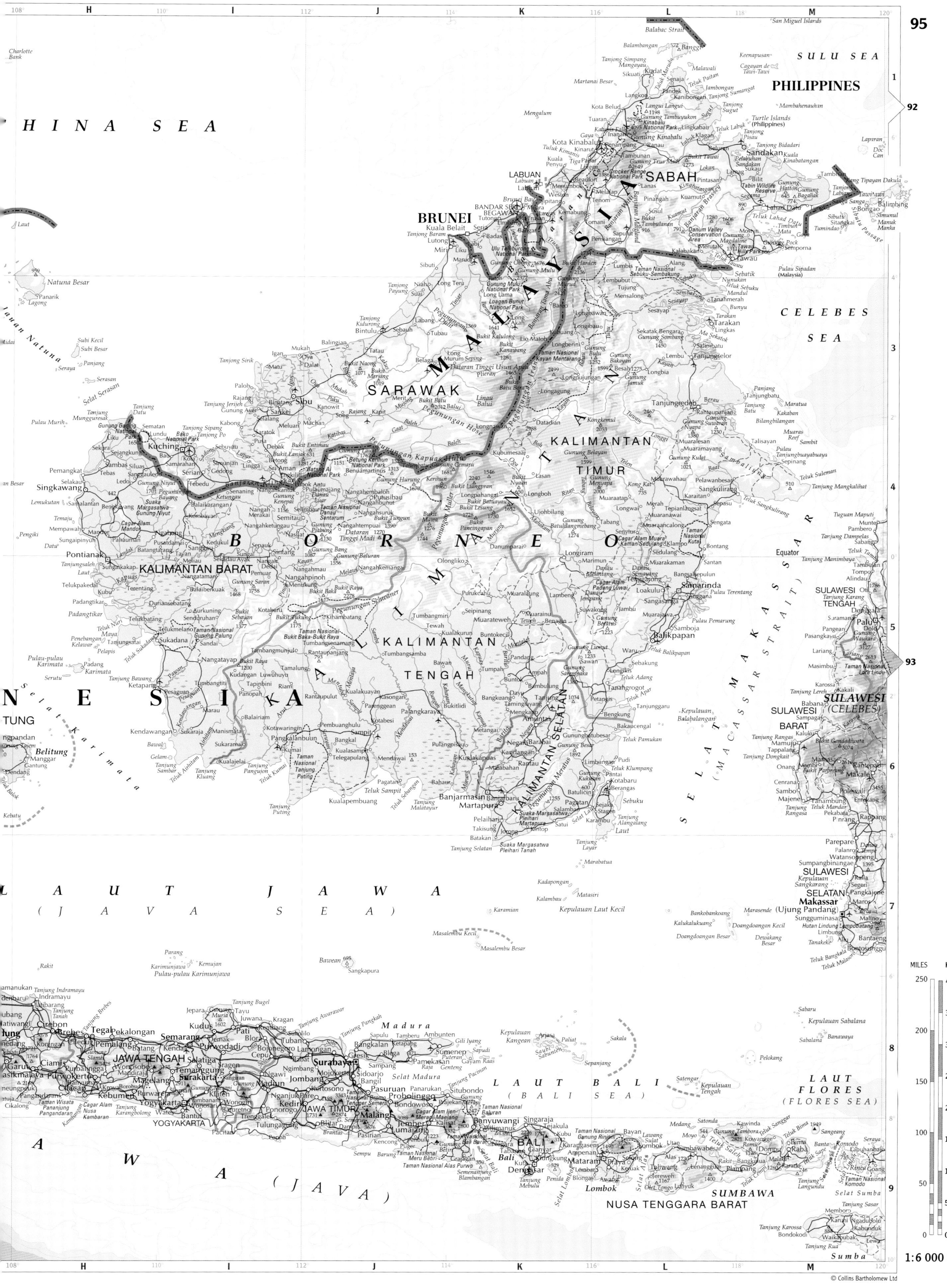

1:6 000 000

© Collins Bartholomew Ltd

CHINA SEA
PHILIPPINES
SULU SEA
CELEBES SEA
BRUNEI
SABAH
SARAWAK
MALAYSIA
BORNEO
KALIMANTAN
KALIMANTAN BARAT
KALIMANTAN TENGAH
KALIMANTAN TIMUR
KALIMANTAN SELATAN
SELAT MAKASSAR
(MACASSAR STRAIT)
SULAWESI
(CELEBES)
SULAWESI BARAT
SULAWESI TENGAH
SULAWESI SELATAN
LAUT JAWA
(JAVA SEA)
LAUT BALI
(BALI SEA)
LAUT FLORES
(FLORES SEA)
JAWA TENGAH
JAWA TIMUR
YOGYAKARTA
BALI
Lombok
SUMBAWA
NUSA TENGGARA BARAT
Madura
Kota Kinabalu
Sandakan
Tawau
Kuching
Sibu
Miri
Bintulu
Pontianak
Singkawang
Samarinda
Balikpapan
Banjarmasin
Palangkaraya
Tarakan
Makassar
(Ujung Pandang)
Palu
Surabaya
Semarang
Malang
Denpasar
Mataram
Equator
MILES
KILOMETRES

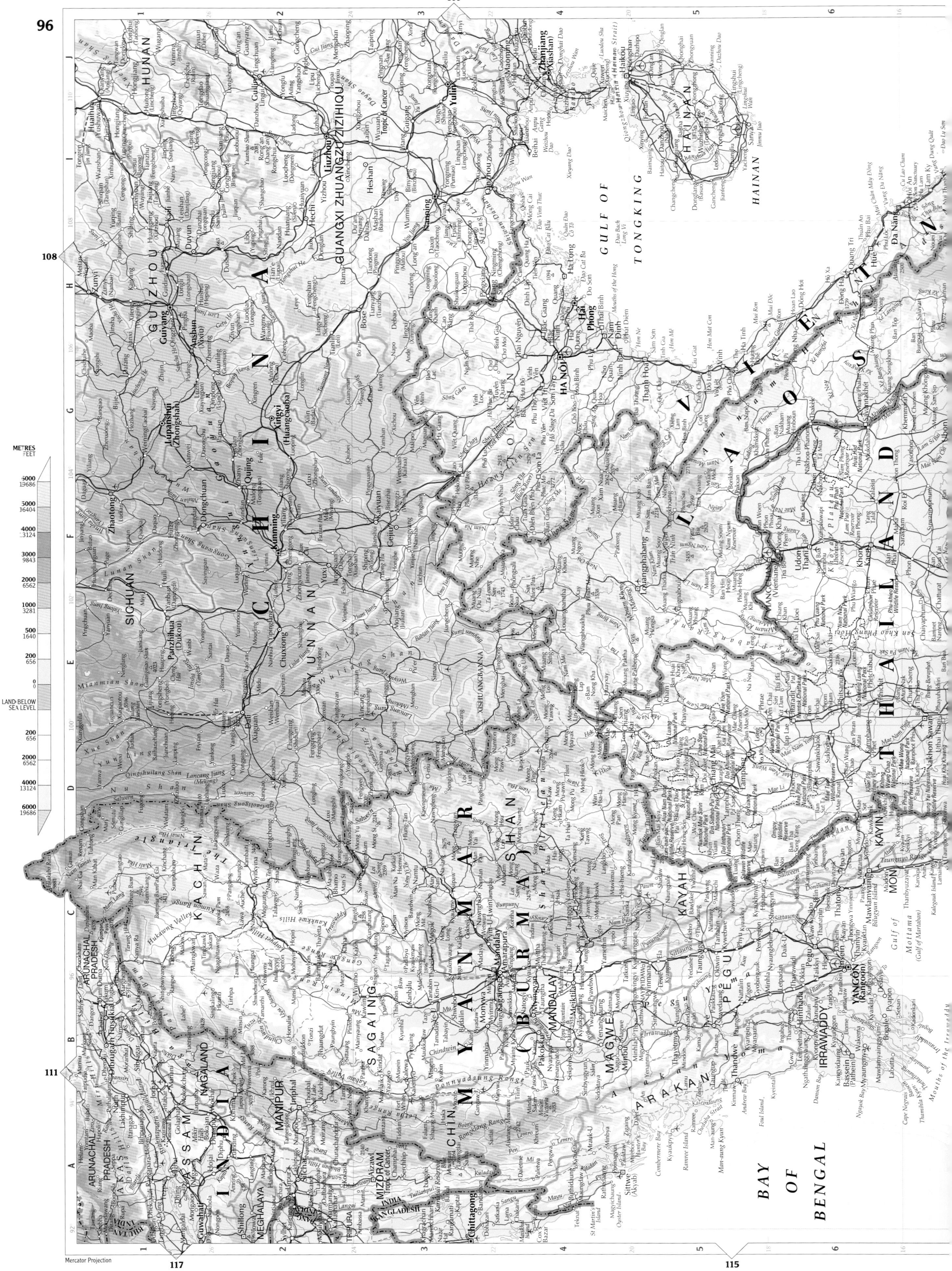

METRES
FEET

5000
19686

5000
16404

4000
13124

3000
9843

2000
6562

1000
3281

500
1640

200
656

0

LAND BELOW
SEA LEVEL

200
656

2000
6562

4000
13124

6000
19686

CHINA

HUNAN

GUIZHOU

GUANGXI ZHUANGZU ZIZHIQU

YUNNAN

SICHUAN

Guiyang

Kunming

Qujing

Panzhihua (Dukou)

Chuxiong

Dali

Yuxi

INDIA

ARUNACHAL PRADESH

ASSAM

NAGALAND

MANIPUR

MIZORAM

MEGHALAYA

TRIPURA

BHUTAN

BANGLADESH

Chittagong

MYANMAR
(BURMA)

KACHIN

SAGAING

CHIN

MANDALAY

Mandalay

MAGWE

PEGU

ARAKAN

IRRAWADDY

YANGON (Rangoon)

MON

KAYIN

KAYAH

RAKHINE

THAILAND

BANGKOK (Krung Thep)

Chiang Mai

LAOS

VIENTIANE (Viangchan)

VIETNAM

HANOI

Hai Phong

TONKIN

GULF OF TONGKING

HAINAN

Haikou

Zhanjiang (Xiashan)

Liuzhou

Yulin

BAY

OF

BENGAL

Gulf of Mottama (Gulf of Martaban)

Mouths of the Irrawaddy

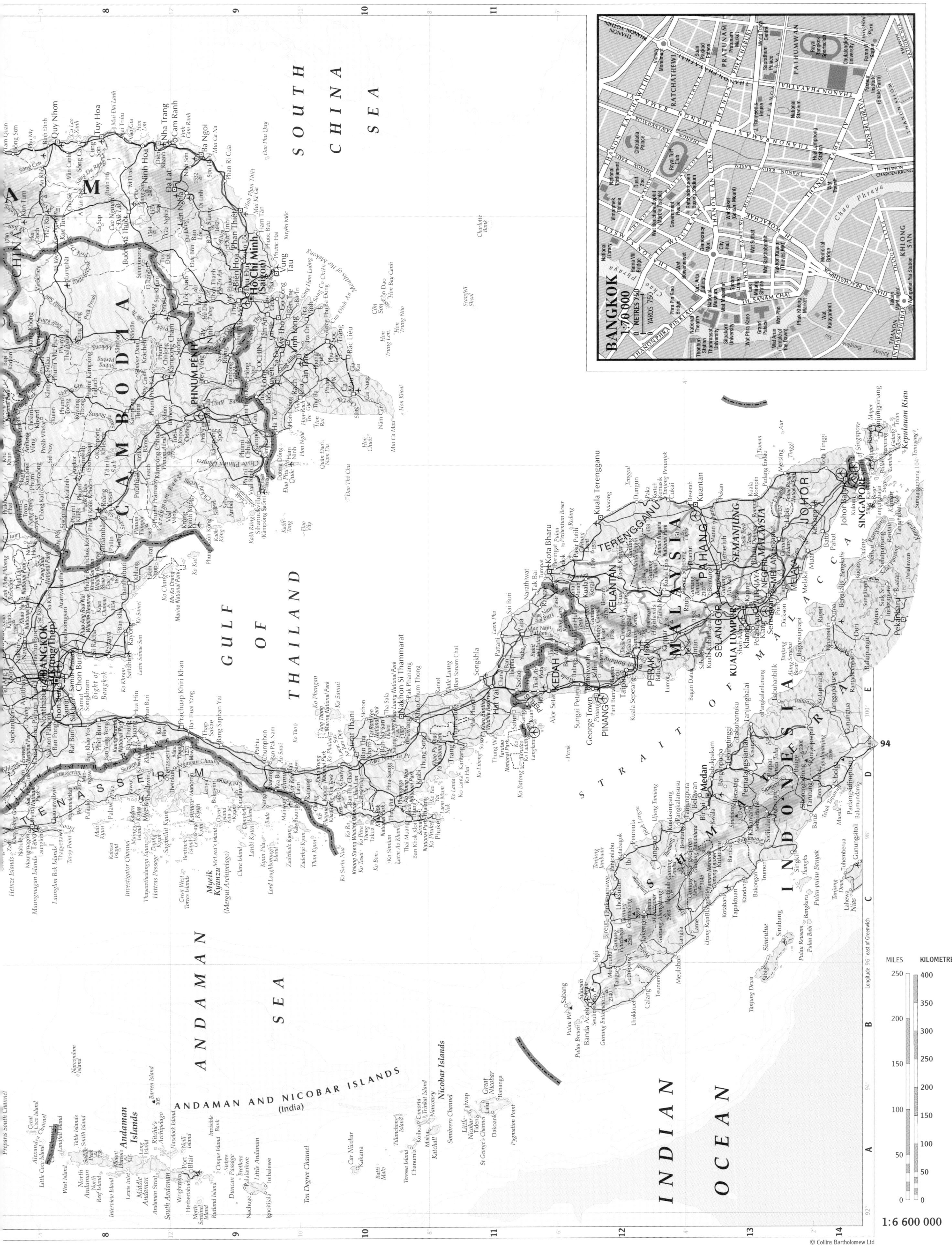
SOUTH CHINA SEA
GULF OF THAILAND
ANDAMAN SEA
INDIAN OCEAN
STRAIT OF MALACCA
ANDAMAN AND NICOBAR ISLANDS
(India)
CAMBODIA
MALAYSIA
INDONESIA
SUMATERA
BANGKOK
1:70 000
Phnum Penh
Hô Chi Minh (Saigon)
Kuala Lumpur
Singapore
Medan
George Town
Nicobar Islands
Andaman Islands
MILES
KILOMETRES
1:6 600 000

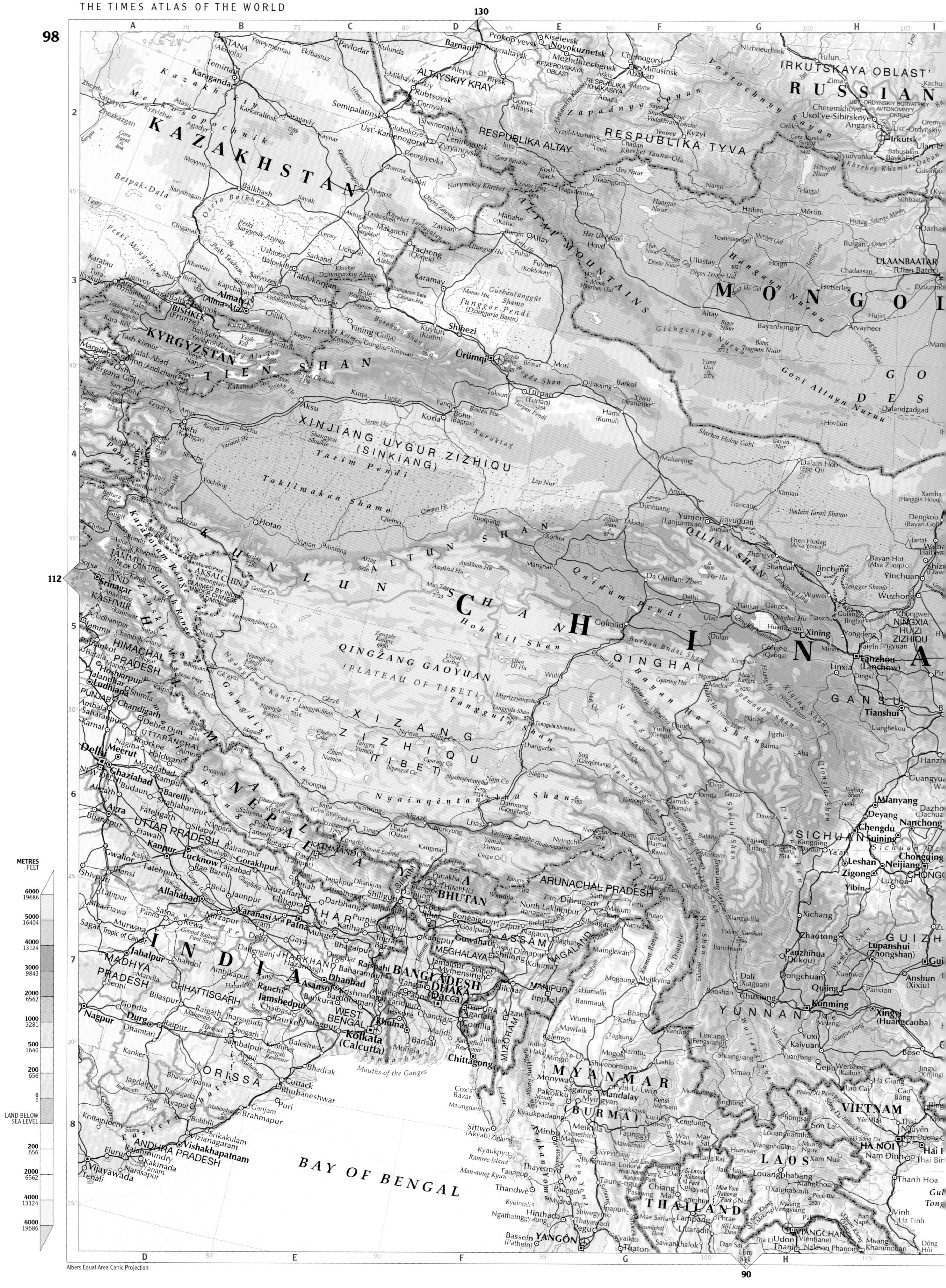

130

A 70 B 75 C 80 D 85 E 90 F 95 G 100 H 105 I

KAZAKHSTAN

RUSSIAN

IRKUTSKAYA OBLAST'

Astana (Akmola)

Pavlodar

Barnaul

Prokop'yevsk

Kiselevsk

Novokuznetsk

Chernogorsk

Minusinsk

Nizhneudinsk

Tulun

Irkutsk

ALTAYSKIY KRAY

RESPUBLIKA ALTAY

RESPUBLIKA TYVA

KEMEROVSKAYA OBLAST'

RESPUBLIKA KHAKASIYA

M O N G O L I A

ULAANBAATAR (Ulan Bator)

Karaganda

Temirtau

Semipalatinsk

Ust'-Kamenogorsk

Balkhash

KYRGYZSTAN

BISHKEK (Frunze)

TIEN SHAN

Almaty (Alma-Ata)

Ürümqi

ALTAI MOUNTAINS

G O B I

D E S

XINJIANG UYGUR ZIZHIQU (SINKIANG)

Taklimakan Shamo

Tarim Pendi

Lop Nur

QILIAN SHAN

QINGHAI

Hotan

Kashi (Kashgar)

K U N L U N S H A N

ALTUN SHAN

Hoh Xil Shan

C H I N A

Golmud

Xining

Lanzhou (Lanchow)

GANSU

JAMMU AND KASHMIR

Srinagar

QINGZANG GAOYUAN
(PLATEAU OF TIBET)

XIZANG ZIZHIQU (TIBET)

Tanggula Shan

Tianshui

HIMACHAL PRADESH

PUNJAB

Ludhiana

Chandigarh

NEPAL

Lhasa

SICHUAN

Chengdu

Chongqing

Delhi

NEW DELHI

Meerut

Agra

UTTAR PRADESH

Kanpur

Lucknow

KATHMANDU

BHUTAN

THIMPHU

Mount Everest

ARUNACHAL PRADESH

Guangyuan

Nanchong

Kunming

YUNNAN

GUIZHOU

Allahabad

Varanasi

Patna

BIHAR

SIKKIM

ASSAM

NAGALAND

MEGHALAYA

MANIPUR

Xichang

Zhaotong

I N D I A

MADHYA PRADESH

CHHATTISGARH

JHARKHAND

WEST BENGAL

BANGLADESH

DHAKA (Dacca)

TRIPURA

MIZORAM

Imphal

Panzhihua (Dukou)

Jabalpur

Nagpur

Jamshedpur

Asansol

Dhanbad

Kolkata (Calcutta)

Khulna

Chittagong

M Y A N M A R (B U R M A)

Mandalay

Dali (Xiaguan)

ORISSA

ANDHRA PRADESH

Vishakhapatnam

Bhubaneshwar

Mouths of the Ganges

Cox's Bazar

NAYPYIDAW

LAOS

HANOI

VIETNAM

Vijayawada

B A Y   O F   B E N G A L

YANGON (Rangoon)

THAILAND

VIENTIANE

METRES / FEET

6000 / 19686
5000 / 16404
4000 / 13124
3000 / 9843
2000 / 6562
1000 / 3281
500 / 1640
200 / 656
0 / 0
LAND BELOW SEA LEVEL
200 / 656
2000 / 6562
4000 / 13124
6000 / 19686

Albers Equal Area Conic Projection

D 85 E 90 F 95 G 100 H 105

90

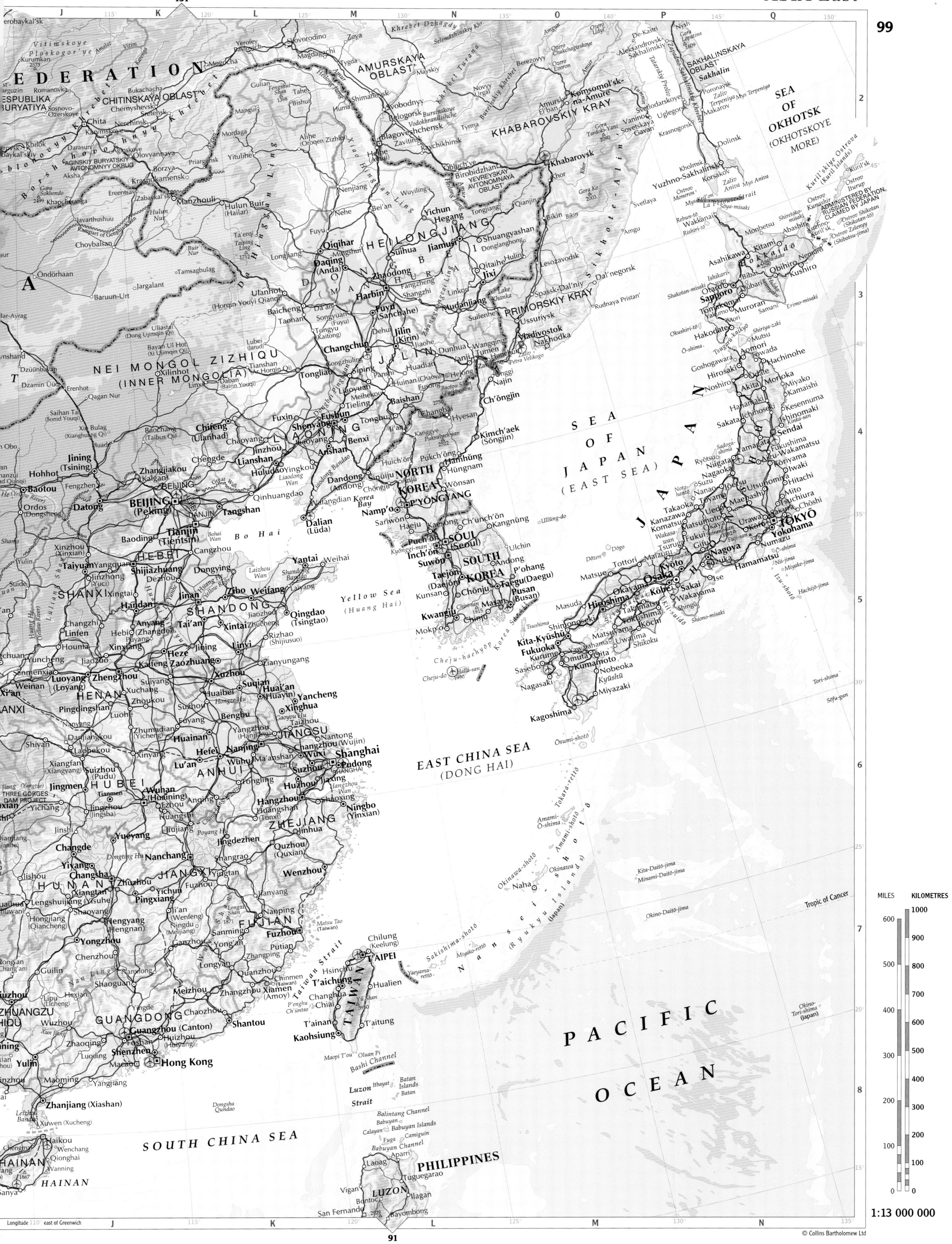

1:13 000 000

© Collins Bartholomew Ltd

131
FEDERATION
SEA OF OKHOTSK (OKHOTSKOYE MORE)
AMURSKAYA OBLAST'
CHITINSKAYA OBLAST'
RESPUBLIKA BURYATIYA
KHABAROVSKIY KRAY
SAKHALINSKAYA OBLAST'
Sakhalin
YEVREYSKAYA AVTONOMNAYA OBLAST
AGINSKIY BURYATSKIY AVTONOMNYY OKRUG
PRIMORSKIY KRAY
Khabarovsk
Komsomol'sk-na-Amure
Blagoveshchensk
Vladivostok
Yuzhno-Sakhalinsk
La Pérouse Strait
ADMINISTERED BY RUSSIAN FEDERATION, CLAIMED BY JAPAN
Kuril'skiye Ostrova (Kuril Islands)
HEILONGJIANG
Harbin
Qiqihar
Daqing (Anda)
JILIN
Changchun
Jilin (Kirin)
NEI MONGOL ZIZHIQU (INNER MONGOLIA)
LIAONING
Shenyang
Dalian (Lüda)
BEIJING (Peking)
Tianjin (Tientsin)
HEBEI
Shijiazhuang
SHANXI
Taiyuan
SHANDONG
Jinan
Qingdao (Tsingtao)
HENAN
Zhengzhou
JIANGSU
Nanjing
Shanghai
ANHUI
Hefei
HUBEI
Wuhan
THREE GORGES DAM PROJECT
ZHEJIANG
Hangzhou
JIANGXI
Nanchang
HUNAN
Changsha
FUJIAN
Fuzhou
Xiamen (Amoy)
GUANGDONG
Guangzhou (Canton)
Shenzhen
Hong Kong
Macao
HAINAN
Haikou
Bo Hai
Yellow Sea (Huang Hai)
Korea Bay
NORTH KOREA
P'YONGYANG
SOUTH KOREA
SŎUL (Seoul)
Inch'ŏn
Pusan (Busan)
Taegu (Daegu)
SEA OF JAPAN (EAST SEA)
JAPAN
Hokkaidō
Sapporo
Sendai
TŌKYŌ
Yokohama
Nagoya
Kyōto
Ōsaka
Kōbe
Hiroshima
Kita-Kyūshū
Fukuoka
Kagoshima
Shikoku
Kyūshū
Naha
Okinawa
Nansei-shotō (Ryukyu Islands) (Japan)
EAST CHINA SEA (DONG HAI)
TAIWAN
T'AIPEI
Kaohsiung
Taiwan Strait
Bashi Channel
Luzon Strait
Tropic of Cancer
PACIFIC OCEAN
SOUTH CHINA SEA
PHILIPPINES
LUZON
Longitude 110° east of Greenwich
91
MILES
KILOMETRES
600
500
400
200
100
1000
900
800
700
600
500
400
200
100

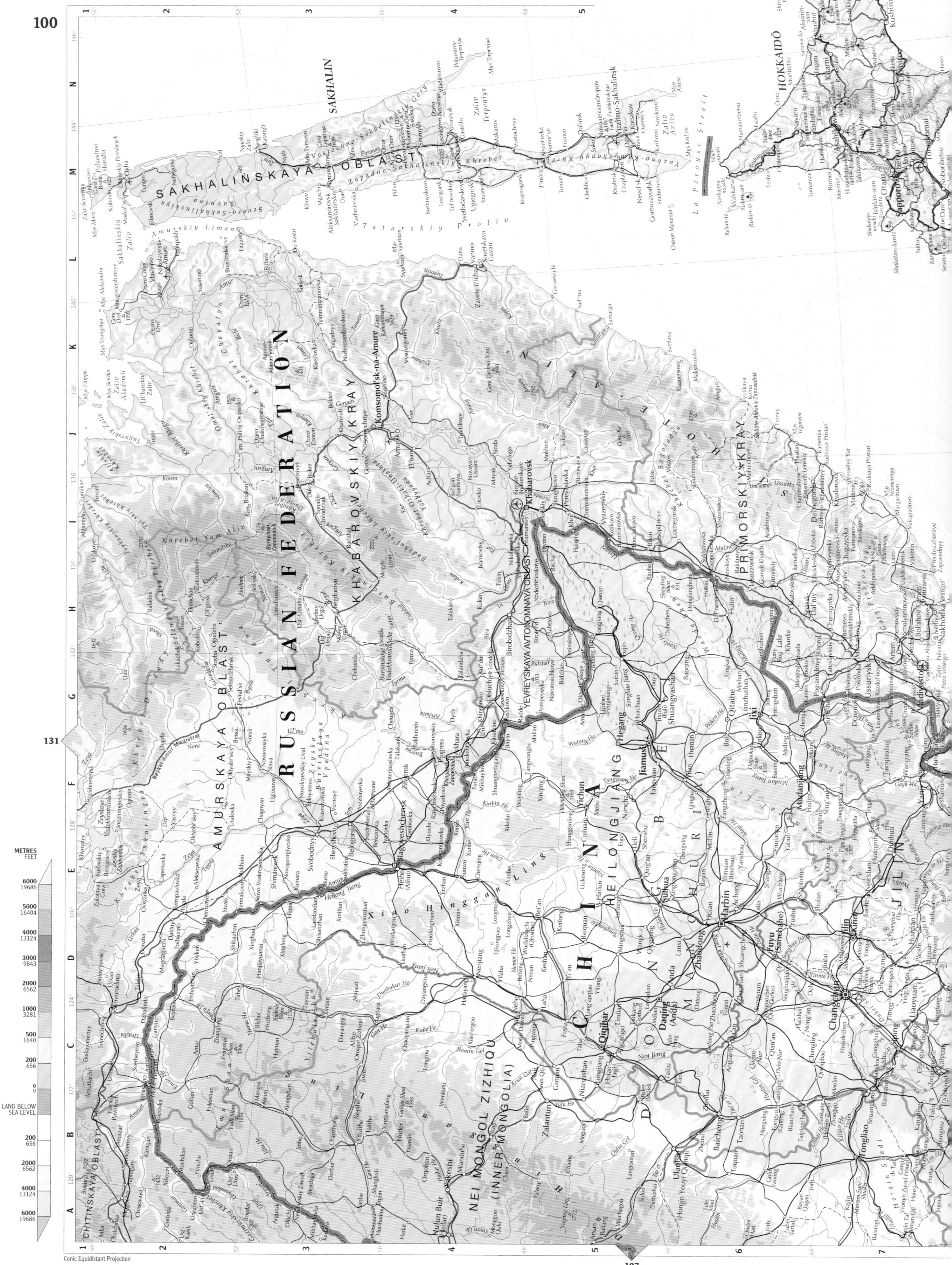

METRES
FEET

6000
19686

5000
16404

4000
13124

3000
9843

2000
6562

1000
3281

500
1640

200
656

0

LAND BELOW
SEA LEVEL

200
656

2000
6562

4000
13124

6000
19686

131

Conic Equidistant Projection

P A C I F I C   O C E A N

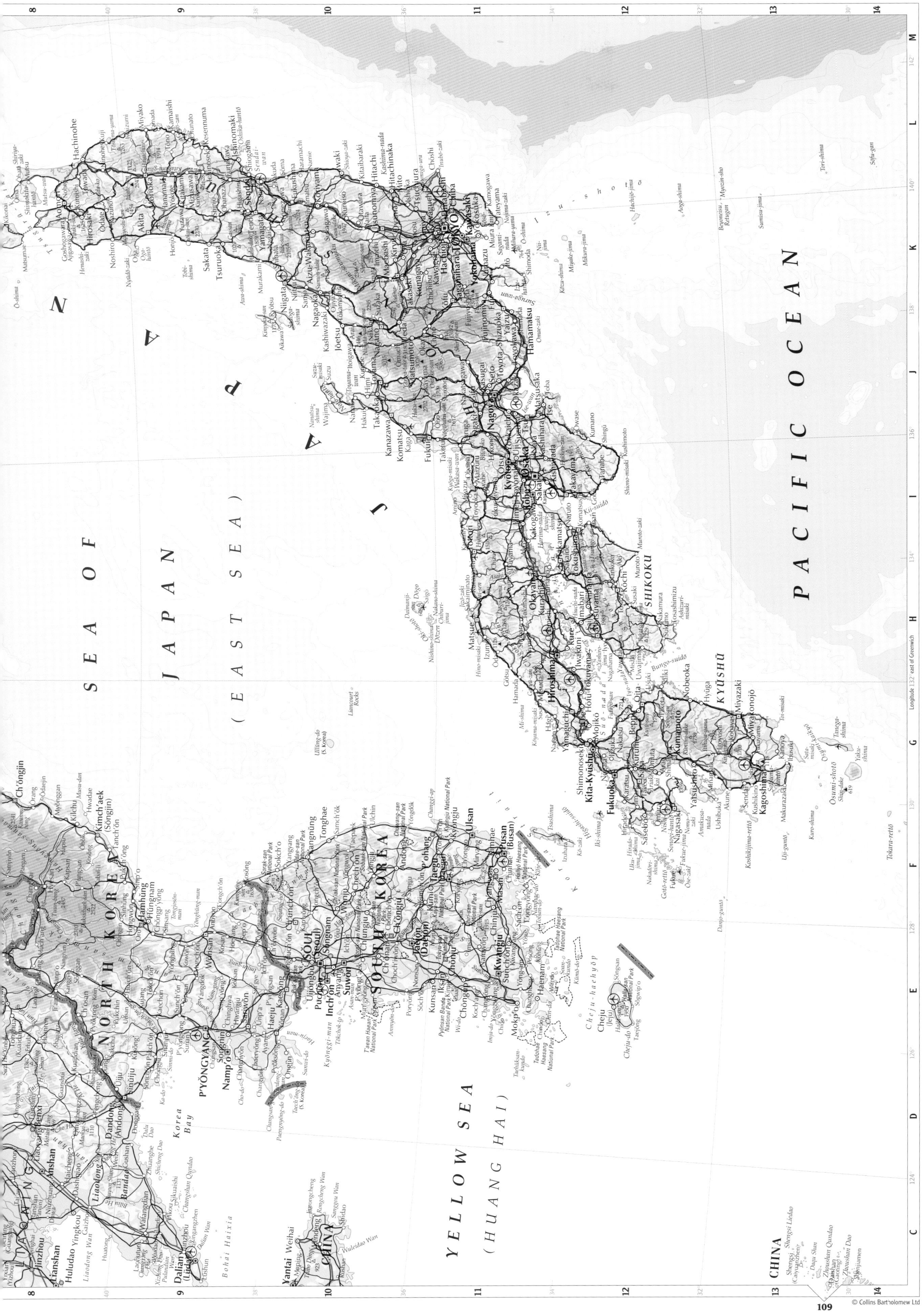

S E A   O F   J A P A N   (E A S T   S E A)

YELLOW SEA
(HUANG HAI)

NORTH KOREA

SOUTH KOREA

CHINA

PYONGYANG

SEOUL

TŌKYŌ

Pusan (Busan)

SHIKOKU

KYŪSHŪ

Korea Bay

Bohai Haixia

Liaodong Wan

Longitude 132° east of Greenwich

MILES	KILOMETRES
250	400
200	350
	300
150	250
	200
100	150
	100
50	50
0	0

1:6 000 000

© Collins Bartholomew Ltd

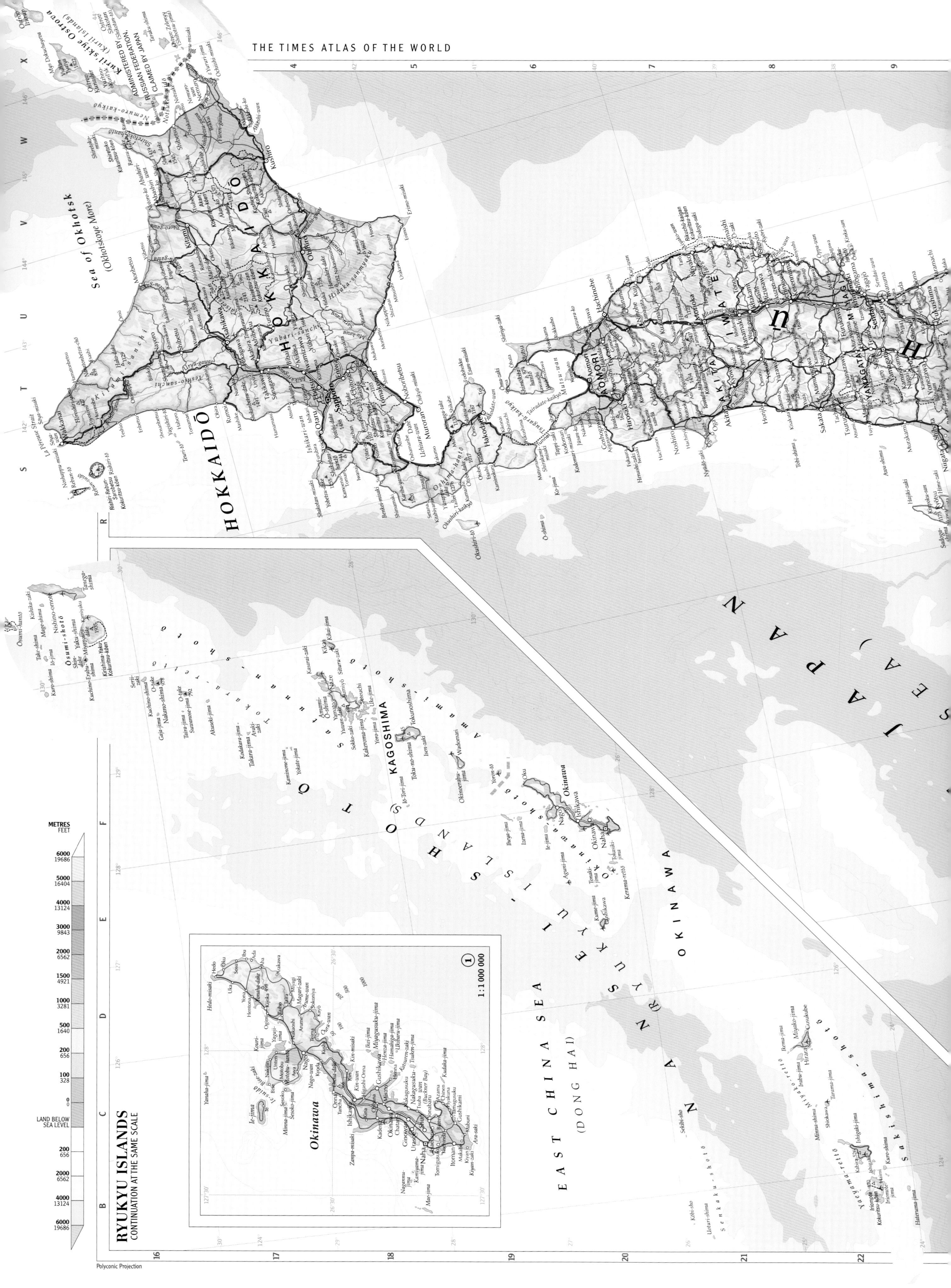

Sea of Okhotsk
(Okhotskoye More)

KURIL'SKIYE OSTROVA (Kuril Islands)

ADMINISTERED BY RUSSIAN FEDERATION, CLAIMED BY JAPAN

HOKKAIDŌ

Sapporo

La Pérouse Strait

HOKKAIDŌ

Hakodate

AOMORI

AKITA

IWATE

YAMAGATA

J A P A N

S E A

HONSHŪ

RYUKYU ISLANDS
CONTINUATION AT THE SAME SCALE

Polyconic Projection

KAGOSHIMA

Ōsumi-shotō

Tanega-shima

Yaku-shima

Amami-ō-shima

Tokunoshima

Okinawa

Naha

R Y Ū K Y Ū   I S L A N D S   (R Y U K Y U   S H O T Ō)

OKINAWA

E A S T   C H I N A   S E A
(D O N G   H A I)

Nansei-shotō

Miyako-jima

Ishigaki-jima

Iriomote-jima

Yaeyama-rettō

Senkaku-shotō

Okinawa

Naha

Itoman

Ishikawa

1 : 1 000 000

①

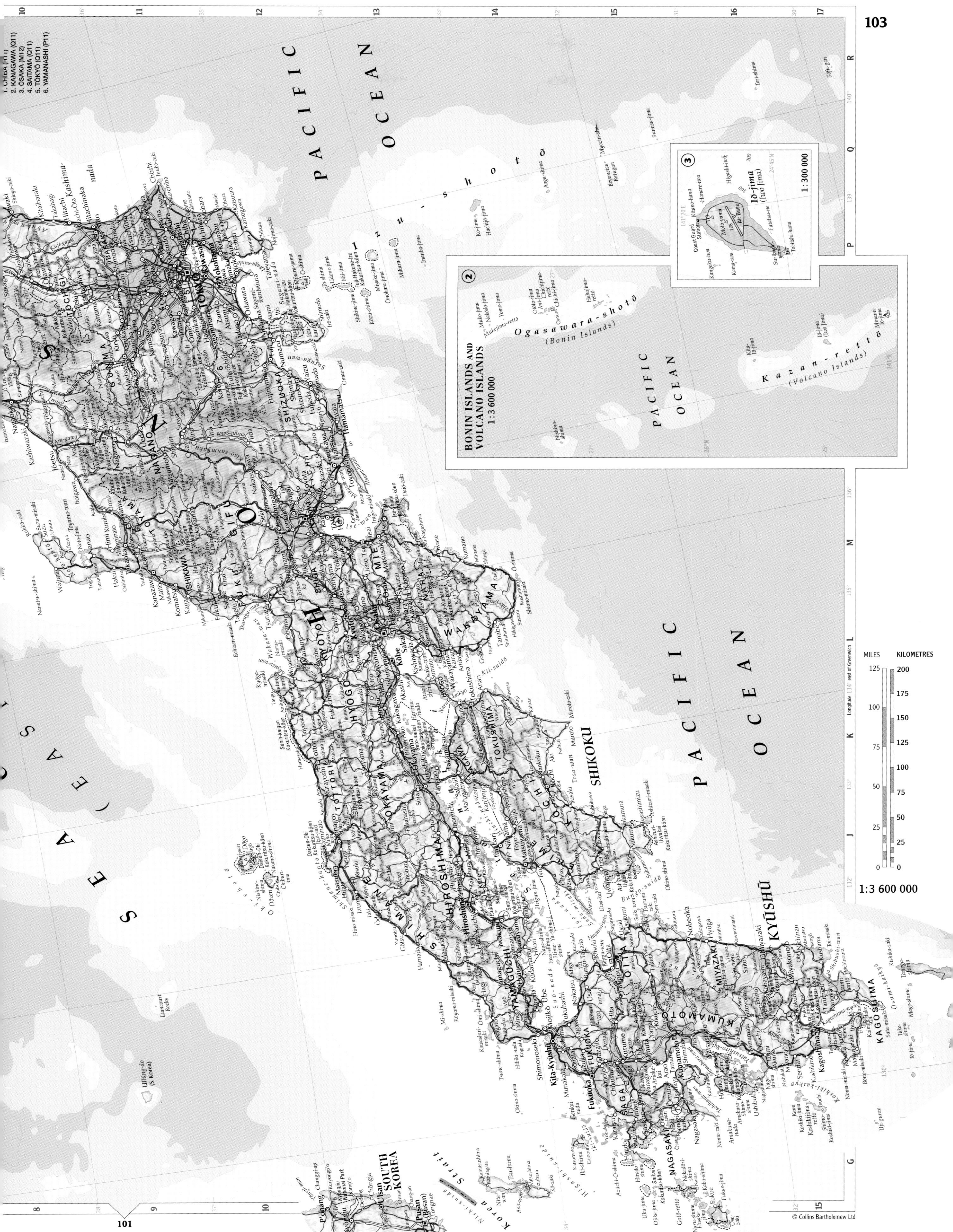

1. CHIBA (R11)
2. KANAGAWA (Q11)
3. OSAKA (M12)
4. SAITAMA (Q11)
5. TŌKYŌ (Q11)
6. YAMANASHI (P11)

PACIFIC OCEAN

Izu-shotō

BONIN ISLANDS AND
VOLCANO ISLANDS
1:3 600 000

Ogasawara-shotō
(Bonin Islands)

PACIFIC OCEAN

Kazan-rettō
(Volcano Islands)

Iō-jima (Iwo jima)
1:300 000

SEA OF JAPAN (EAST SEA)

SOUTH KOREA

KYŪSHŪ

SHIKOKU

PACIFIC OCEAN

MILES   KILOMETRES

125   200
         175
100   150
         125
75   100
50   75
         50
25   25
0   0

1:3 600 000

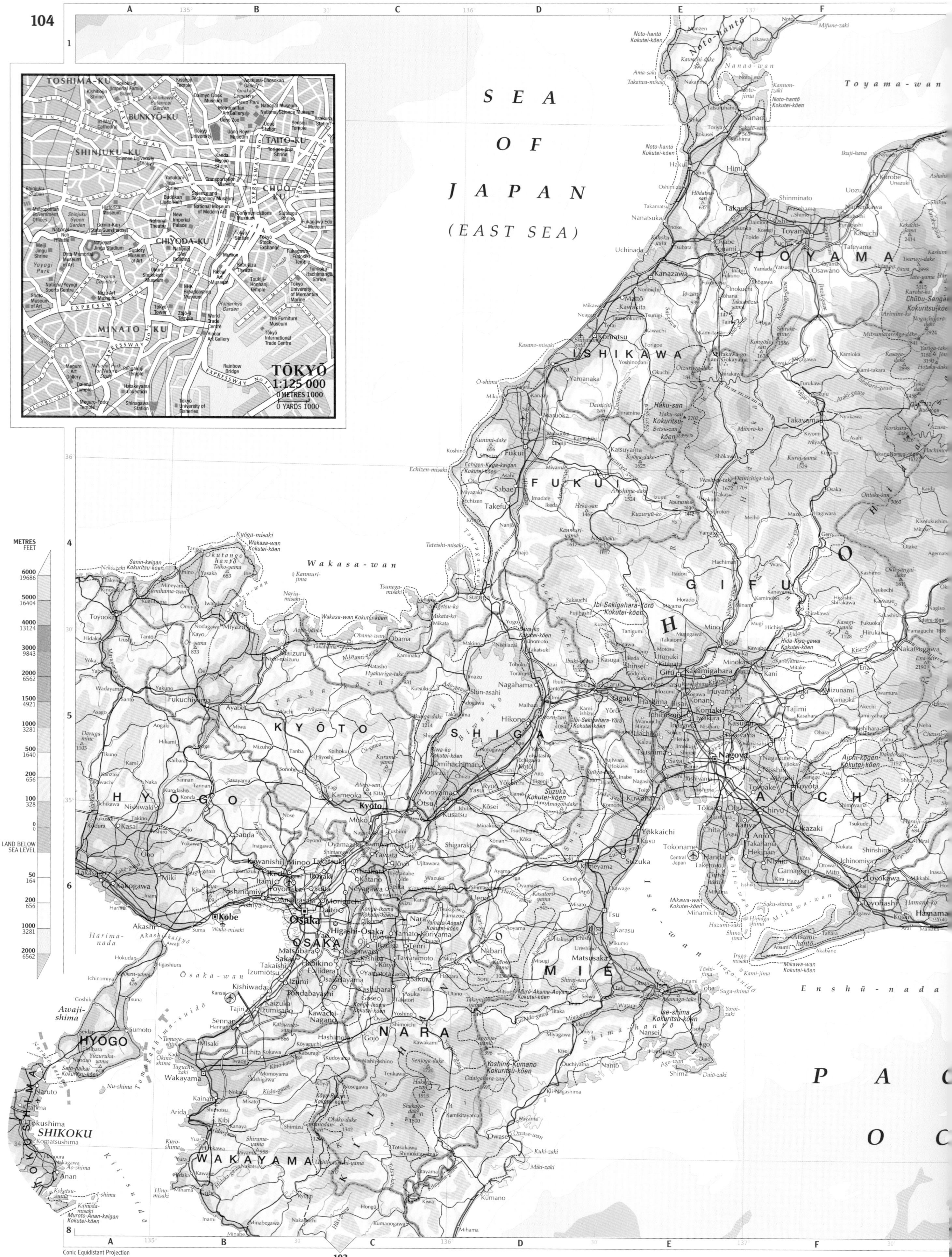

S E A
O F
J A P A N
(EAST SEA)

TŌKYŌ
1:125 000
0 METRES 1000
0 YARDS 1000

TOSHIMA-KU
BUNKYŌ-KU
SHINJUKU-KU
TAITŌ-KU
CHŪŌ-KU
CHIYODA-KU
MINATO-KU

METRES
FEET
6000
19686
5000
16404
4000
13124
3000
9843
2000
6562
1500
4921
1000
3281
500
1640
200
656
100
328
0
LAND BELOW
SEA LEVEL
50
164
200
656
1000
3281
2000
6562

TOYAMA
ISHIKAWA
FUKUI
GIFU
AICHI
SHIGA
KYŌTO
HYŌGO
MIE
NARA
WAKAYAMA
SHIKOKU
HYŌGO

Kanazawa
Komatsu
Fukui
Sabae
Takefu
Takayama
Nagoya
Gifu
Ōgaki
Toyota
Okazaki
Yokkaichi
Tsu
Matsusaka
Kyōto
Ōtsu
Osaka
OSAKA
Kobe
Sakai
Nara
Wakayama

P A C
O C

Conic Equidistant Projection

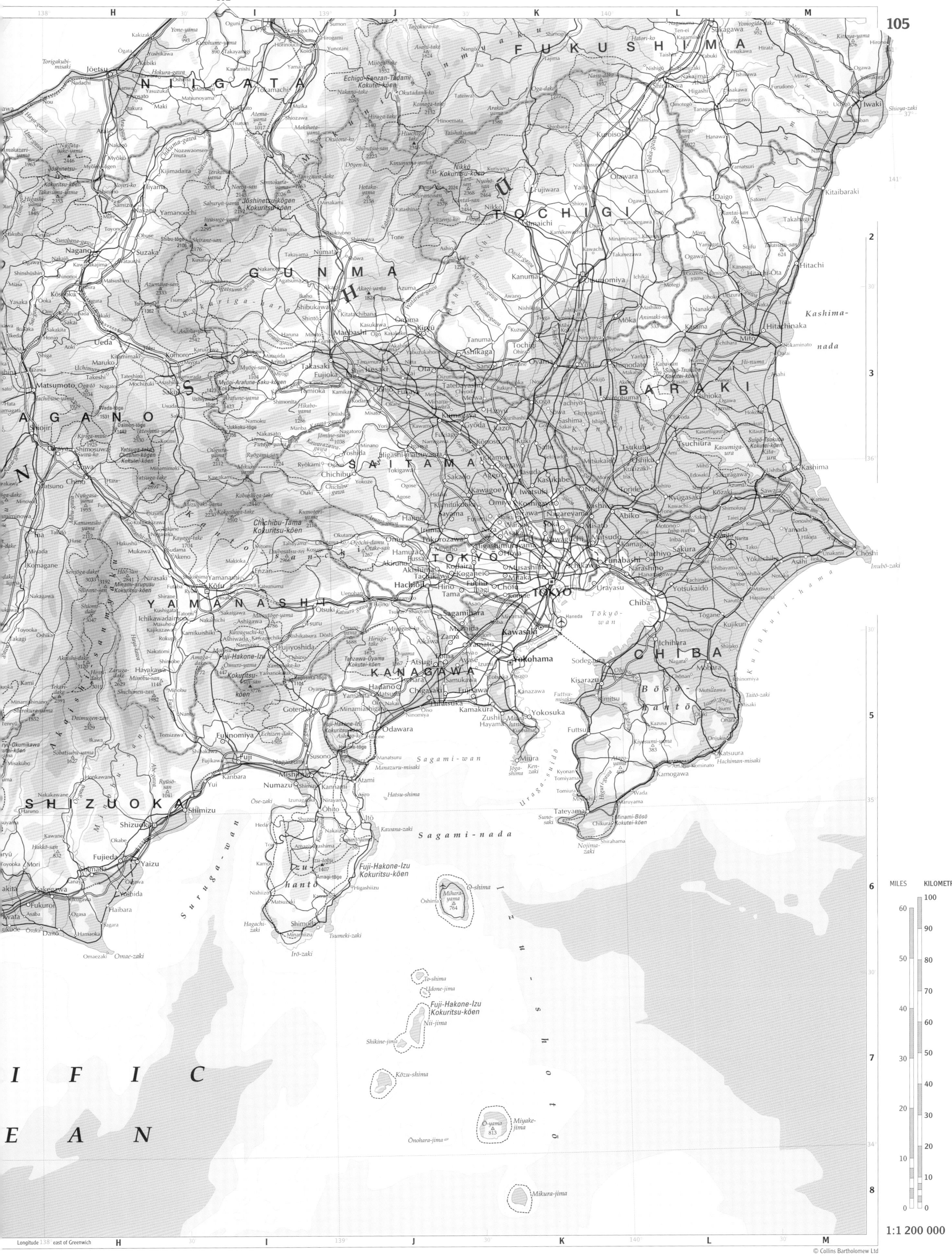

NIIGATA

FUKUSHIMA

TOCHIGI

GUNMA

IBARAKI

NAGANO

SAITAMA

YAMANASHI

TOKYO

CHIBA

KANAGAWA

SHIZUOKA

Nagano
Matsumoto
Ueda
Takasaki
Maebashi
Utsunomiya
Mito
Hitachi
Hitachinaka
Iwaki
Kōfu
Fujiyoshida
Tokyo
Hachiōji
Tachikawa
Kawagoe
Ōmiya
Kasukabe
Tsuchiura
Tsukuba
Kawaguchi
Matsudo
Funabashi
Chiba
Ichihara
Kisarazu
Kawasaki
Yokohama
Yokosuka
Kamakura
Odawara
Atami
Mishima
Numazu
Fuji
Shimizu
Shizuoka
Fujieda
Yaizu
Gotemba
Atsugi
Hiratsuka
Chigasaki
Fujisawa
Narita
Chōshi
Sakura
Togane
Mobara
Tateyama
Kamogawa

Tōkyō-wan

Sagami-wan

Sagami-nada

Suruga-wan

Bōsō-hantō

Izu-hantō

Ō-shima
Mihara-yama 764

Miyake-jima
Ō-yama 813

To-shima
Udone-jima
Nii-jima
Shikine-jima
Kōzu-shima
Mikura-jima
Ōnohara-jima

Fuji-Hakone-Izu Kokuritsu-kōen

Nikkō Kokuritsu-kōen

Chichibu-Tama Kokuritsu-kōen

Jōshinetsu-kōgen Kokuritsu-kōen

PACIFIC OCEAN

Kashima-nada

Uraga-suidō

Kujūkuri-hama

MILES   KILOMETRES
60   100
         90
50   80
         70
40   60
         50
30   40
20   30
         20
10
         10
0   0

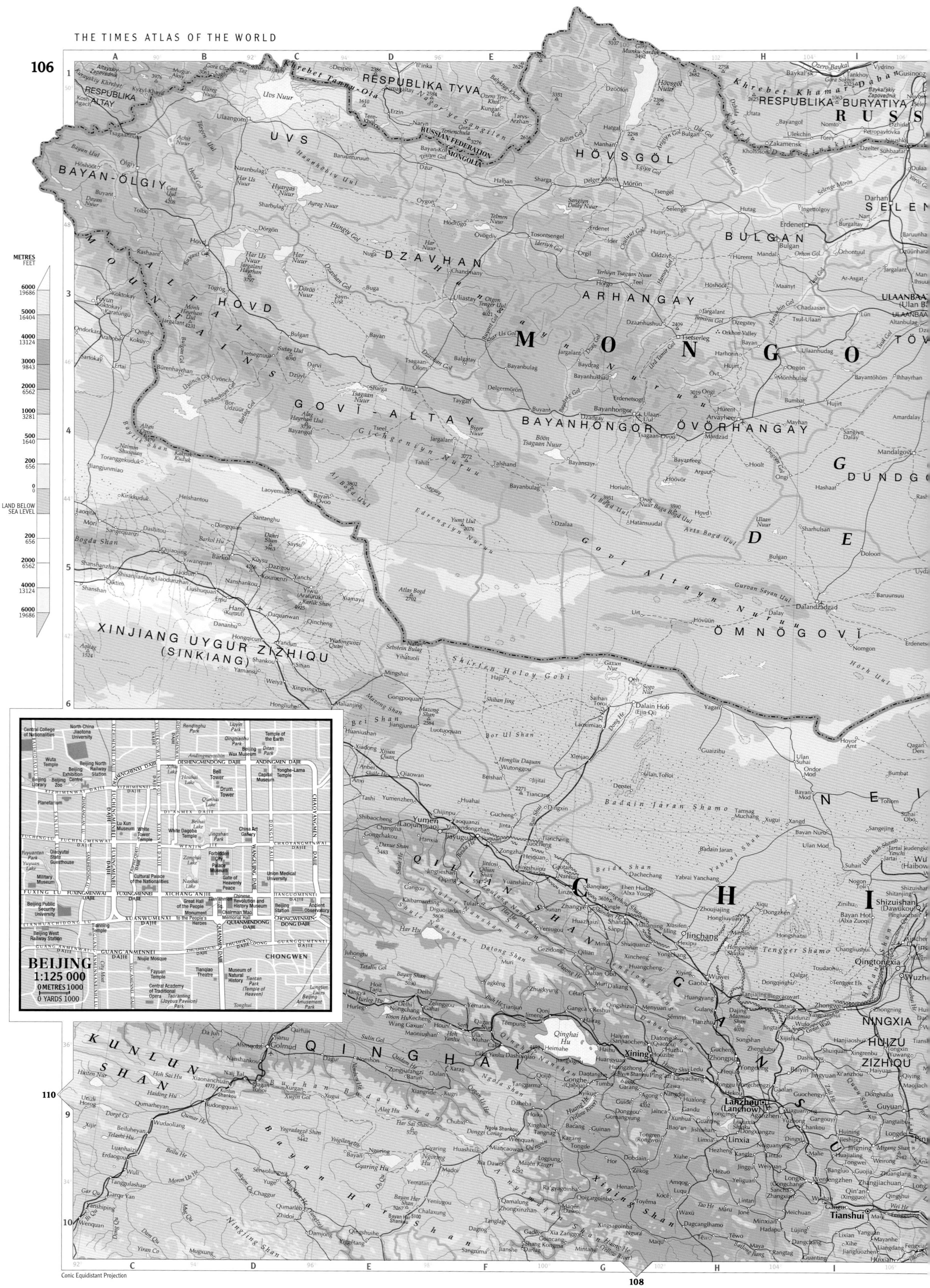
RESPUBLIKA TYVA
RESPUBLIKA ALTAY
RESPUBLIKA BURYATIYA
RUSSIAN FEDERATION
MONGOLIA
UVS
HÖVSGÖL
BAYAN-ÖLGIY
DZAVHAN
HOVD
ARHANGAY
BULGAN
MONGOLIA
GOVĬ-ALTAY
BAYANHONGOR
ÖVÖRHANGAY
DUNDGOVĬ
ÖMNÖGOVĬ
XINJIANG UYGUR ZIZHIQU
(SINKIANG)
QINGHAI
GANSU
NINGXIA HUIZU ZIZHIQU
KUNLUN SHAN
QILIAN SHAN
Uvs Nuur
Hövsgöl Nuur
Ozero Baykal
ULAANBAATAR
Lanzhou (Lanchow)
Xining
Golmud
Qinghai Hu
Badain Jaran Shamo
Tengger Shamo
Gobi
METRES
FEET
6000 19686
5000 16404
4000 13124
3000 9843
2000 6562
1000 3281
500 1640
200 656
0 0
LAND BELOW SEA LEVEL
200 656
2000 6562
4000 13124
6000 19686
BEIJING
1:125 000
0 METRES 1000
0 YARDS 1000

Conic Equidistant Projection

108

110

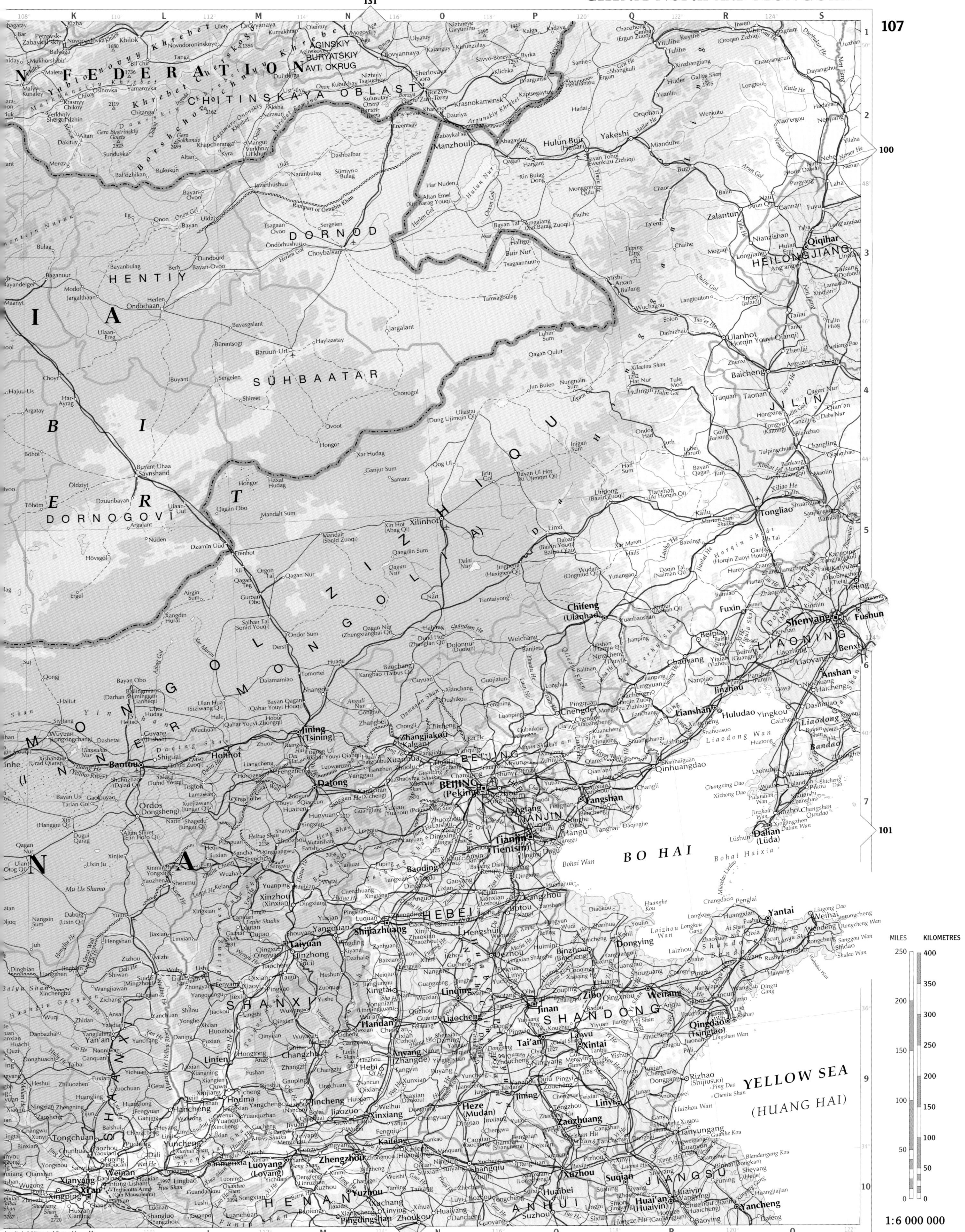

Major regions and labels

RUSSIAN FEDERATION

CHITINSKAYA OBLAST'

AGINSKIY BURYATSKIY AVT. OKRUG

HENTIY

DORNOD

SÜHBAATAR

DORNOGOVI

DZAMYN ÜÜD

NEI MONGOL ZIZHIQU (INNER MONGOLIA)

HEILONGJIANG

JILIN

LIAONING

HEBEI

SHANXI

SHAANXI

SHANDONG

HENAN

ANHUI

JIANGSU

Cities

Manzhouli · Hulun Buir (Hailar) · Yakeshi · Qiqihar · Zalantun · Nianzishan · Baicheng · Tongliao · Shenyang · Fushun · Benxi · Anshan · Haicheng · Jinzhou · Huludao · Yingkou · Dalian (Lüda) · Dandong

Chifeng (Ulanhad) · Fuxin · Beipiao · Chengde · Tianshan · Zhangjiakou · Kalgan · Hohhot · Baotou · Ordos (Dongsheng) · Datong · Jining (Tsining)

BEIJING (Peking) · Tianjin (Tientsin) · Tangshan · Qinhuangdao · Baoding · Cangzhou · Shijiazhuang · Hengshui · Dezhou · Binzhou · Dongying · Yantai · Weihai · Qingdao (Tsingtao) · Weifang · Zibo · Jinan · Tai'an · Xintai · Linyi · Rizhao (Shijiusuo)

Taiyuan · Yangquan · Linfen · Yuncheng · Handan · Anyang (Zhangde) · Hebi · Xinxiang · Jiaozuo · Zhengzhou · Kaifeng · Luoyang (Loyang) · Sanmenxia · Heze (Mudan) · Zaozhuang · Xuzhou · Suqian · Huai'an (Huaiyin) · Huaiyin · Yancheng · Lianyungang · Huaibei · Pingdingshan · Zhoukou · Xi'an · Xianyang · Xingping · Weinan · Tongchuan · Yan'an

Water bodies

BO HAI · Bohai Wan · Liaodong Wan · Laizhou Wan · YELLOW SEA (HUANG HAI) · Huang He (Yellow River) · Buir Nur · Hulun Nur · Dalai Nur · Qagan Nur

Scale

MILES · KILOMETRES

250 · 400
200 · 350
· 300
150 · 250
· 200
100 · 150
50 · 100
· 50
0 · 0

1:6 000 000

© Collins Bartholomew Ltd

Longitude 108° east of Greenwich

100
101

131

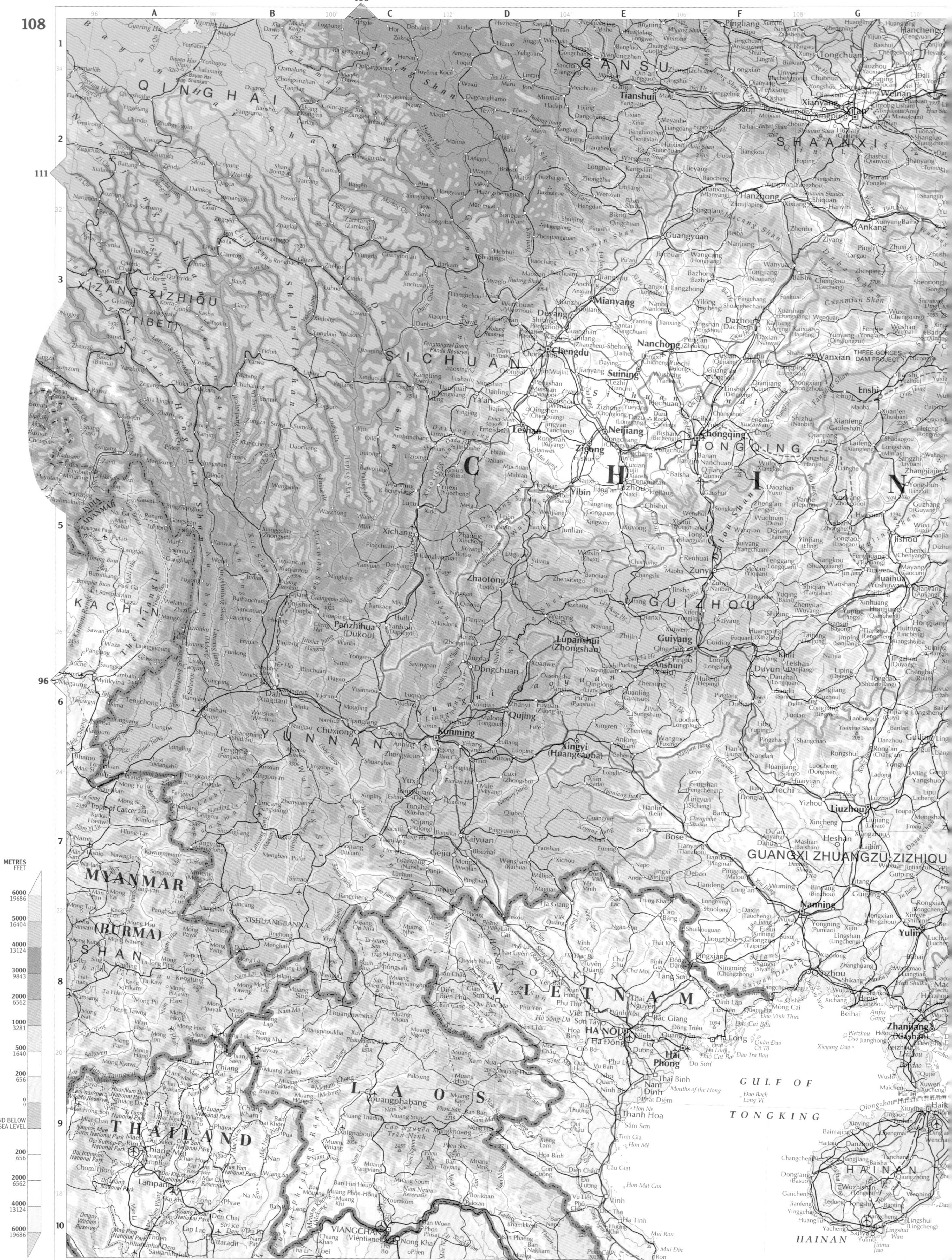

106

96

QINGHAI

GANSU

SHAANXI

XIZANG ZIZHIQU (TIBET)

SICHUAN

C H I N A

Chengdu

Mianyang

Deyang

Nanchong

Suining

Neijiang

Leshan

Zigong

Chongqing

CHONGQING

Wanxian

THREE GORGES DAM PROJECT

Enshi

Yibin

Zhaotong

GUIZHOU

Zunyi

Guiyang

Lupanshui (Zhongshan)

Anshun

Duyun

Kaili

Liuzhou

Xichang

Panzhihua (Dukou)

Dali (Xiaguan)

YUNNAN

Chuxiong

Kunming

Qujing

Yuxi

Xingyi (Huangcaoba)

Dongchuan

Gejiu

Kaiyuan

Wenshan (Kaihua)

Simao

GUANGXI ZHUANGZU ZIZHIQU

Nanning

Yulin

Qinzhou

Beihai

Zhanjiang (Xiashan)

MYANMAR (BURMA)

KACHIN

SHAN

Myitkyina

Bhamo

Lashio

Tengchong

Lancang

Jinghong

XISHUANGBANNA

V I E T N A M

Hà Giang

Cao Bằng

Lạng Sơn

Điện Biên Phủ

HANOI

Ha Đông

Hải Phòng

Nam Định

Thái Bình

Thanh Hoá

Vinh

TONKIN

L A O S

Louangphabang

Viangchan (Vientiane)

THAILAND

Chiang Mai

Lampang

Chiang Rai

GULF OF TONGKING

HAINAN

Haikou

Mouths of the Hong

Tropic of Cancer

Conic Equidistant Projection

METRES / FEET
6000 / 19686
5000 / 16404
4000 / 13124
3000 / 9843
2000 / 6562
1000 / 3281
500 / 1640
200 / 656
0
LAND BELOW SEA LEVEL
200 / 656
2000 / 6562
4000 / 13124
6000 / 19686

111

96

A   B   C   D   E   F   G

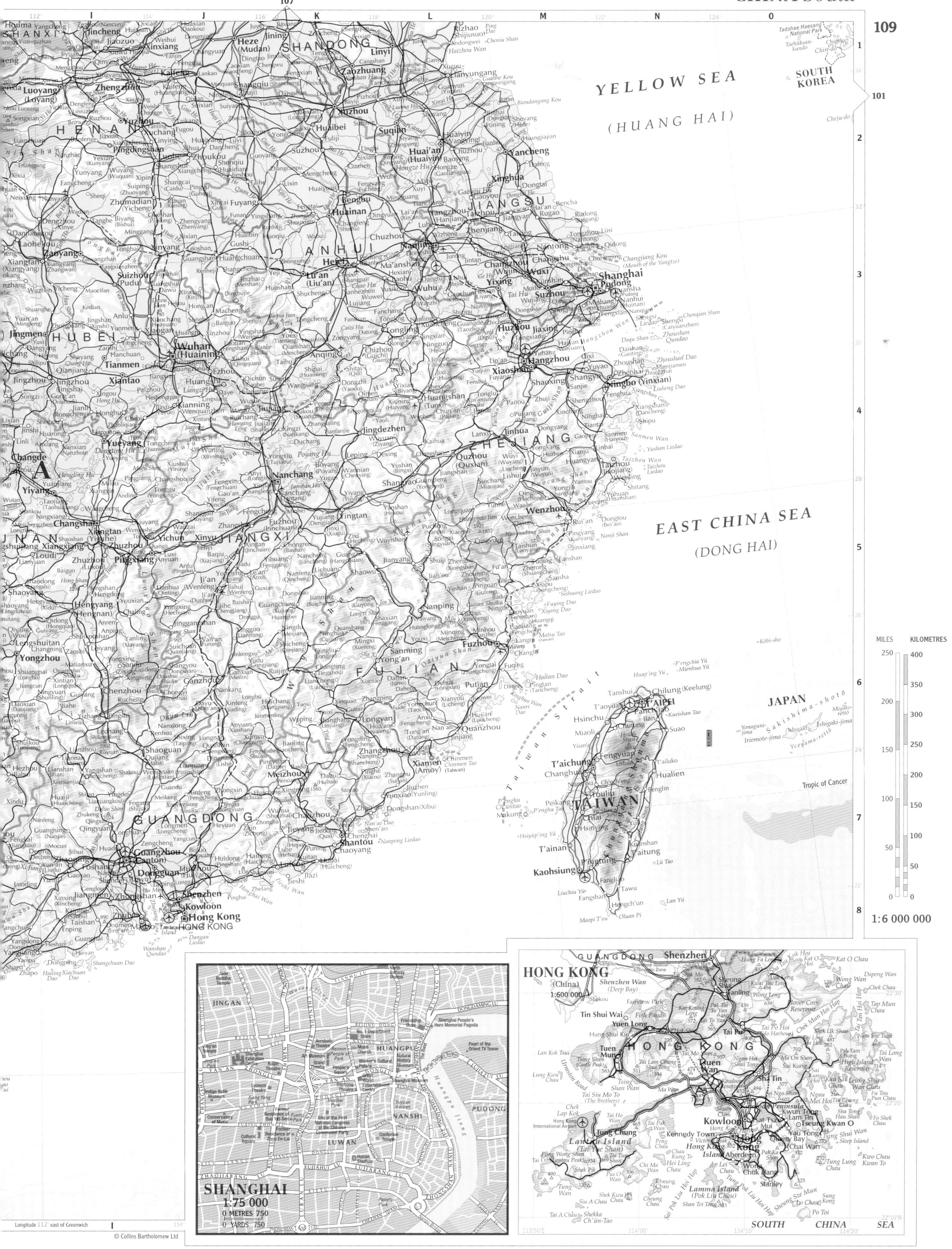
YELLOW SEA
(HUANG HAI)
EAST CHINA SEA
(DONG HAI)
SOUTH KOREA
JAPAN
SHANDONG
JIANGSU
ANHUI
HENAN
HUBEI
ZHEJIANG
JIANGXI
FUJIAN
GUANGDONG
TAIWAN
Taiwan Strait
Tropic of Cancer
Shanghai
Nanjing
Hangzhou
Wuhan
Nanchang
Fuzhou
Guangzhou (Canton)
Hong Kong
T'aipei
1:6 000 000
MILES
KILOMETRES
SHANGHAI
1:75 000
HONG KONG (China)
1:600 000
SOUTH CHINA SEA
Longitude 112 east of Greenwich

106

121

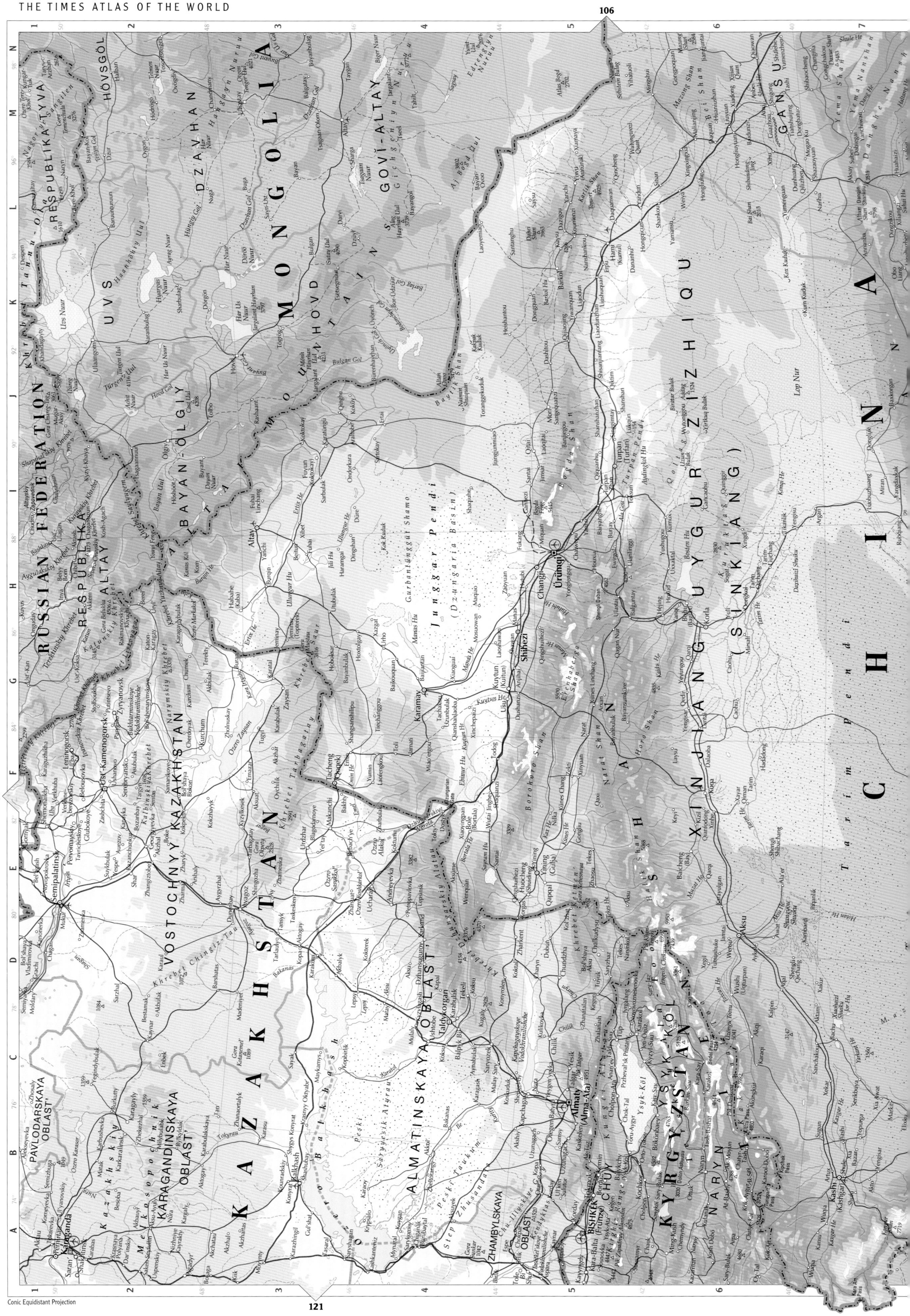

RUSSIAN FEDERATION

RESPUBLIKA-TYVA

HÖVSGÖL

DZAVHAN

MONGOLIA

UVS

GOVĬ-ALTAY

HOVD

BAYAN-ÖLGIY

ALTAY

RESPUBLIKA

KAZAKHSTAN

VOSTOCHNYY KAZAKHSTAN

PAVLODARSKAYA OBLAST'

KARAGANDINSKAYA OBLAST'

ALMATINSKAYA OBLAST'

ZHAMBYLSKAYA OBLAST'

KYRGYZSTAN

NARYN

CHUY

YSYK-KÖL

BISHKEK (Frunze)

Almaty (Alma-Ata)

Ürümqi

Shihezi

Changji

Karamay

XINJIANG UYGUR (SINKIANG) ZIZHIQU

GANSU

CHINA

Junggar Pendi (Dzungaria Basin)

Tarim Pendi

Gurbantünggüt Shamo

Lop Nur

Aksu

Kashi (Kashgar)

Semipalatinsk

Ust'-Kamenogorsk

Leninogorsk

Karaganda

Balkhash

Ozero Balkhash

Ozero Zaysan

Ozero Alakol'

Ozero Seletên

METRES / FEET

6000	19686
5000	16404
4000	13124
3000	9843
2000	6562
1000	3281
500	1640
200	656
0	0

LAND BELOW SEA LEVEL

200	656
2000	6562
4000	13124
6000	19686

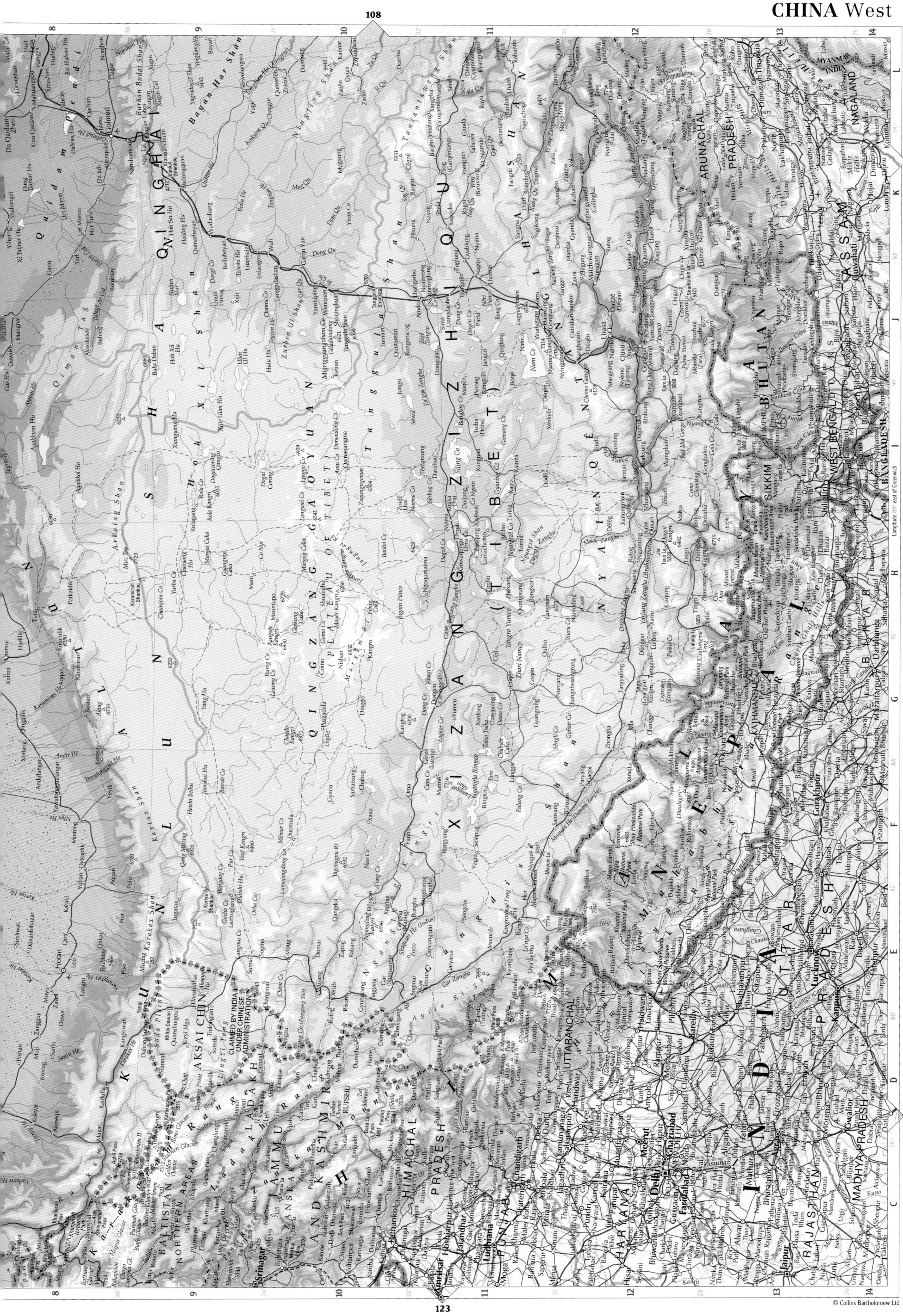

1:6 000 000

© Collins Bartholomew Ltd

108
117
116
123
QINGHAI
XIZANG ZIZHIQU (TIBET)
QINGZANG GAOYUAN (PLATEAU OF TIBET)
K U N L U N   S H A N
ARUNACHAL PRADESH
ASSAM
NAGALAND
BHUTAN
SIKKIM
WEST BENGAL
BANGLADESH
NEPAL
KATHMANDU
Lhasa
UTTAR PRADESH
UTTARANCHAL
HIMACHAL PRADESH
JAMMU AND KASHMIR
AKSAI CHIN
HARYANA
PUNJAB
RAJASTHAN
MADHYA PRADESH
INDIA
Delhi
Srinagar
Golmud
Hotan
MILES KILOMETRES

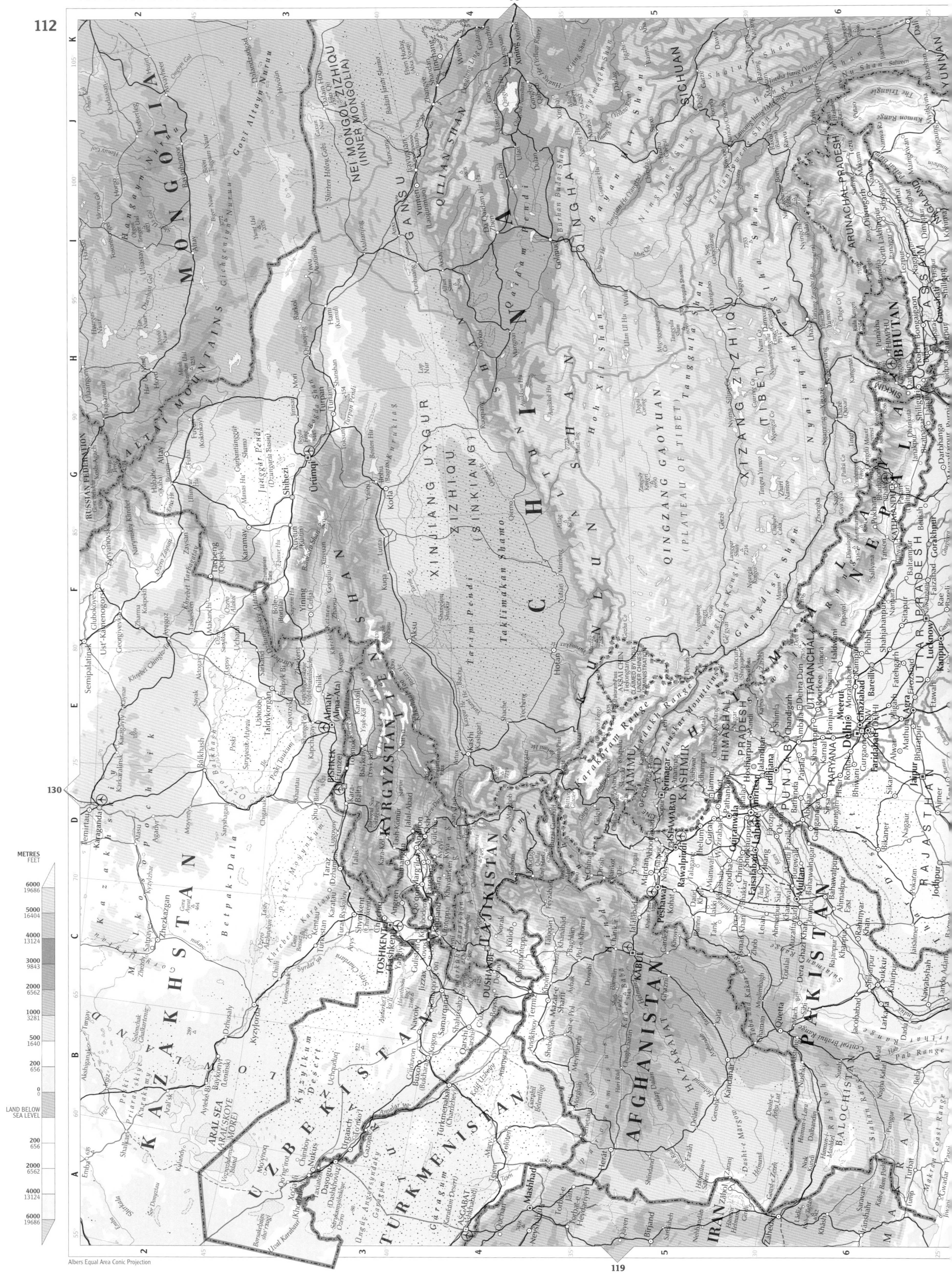

METRES
FEET

6000	19686
5000	16404
4000	13124
3000	9843
2000	6562
1000	3281
500	1640
200	656
0	0

LAND BELOW
SEA LEVEL

200	656
2000	6562
4000	13124
6000	19686

Albers Equal Area Conic Projection

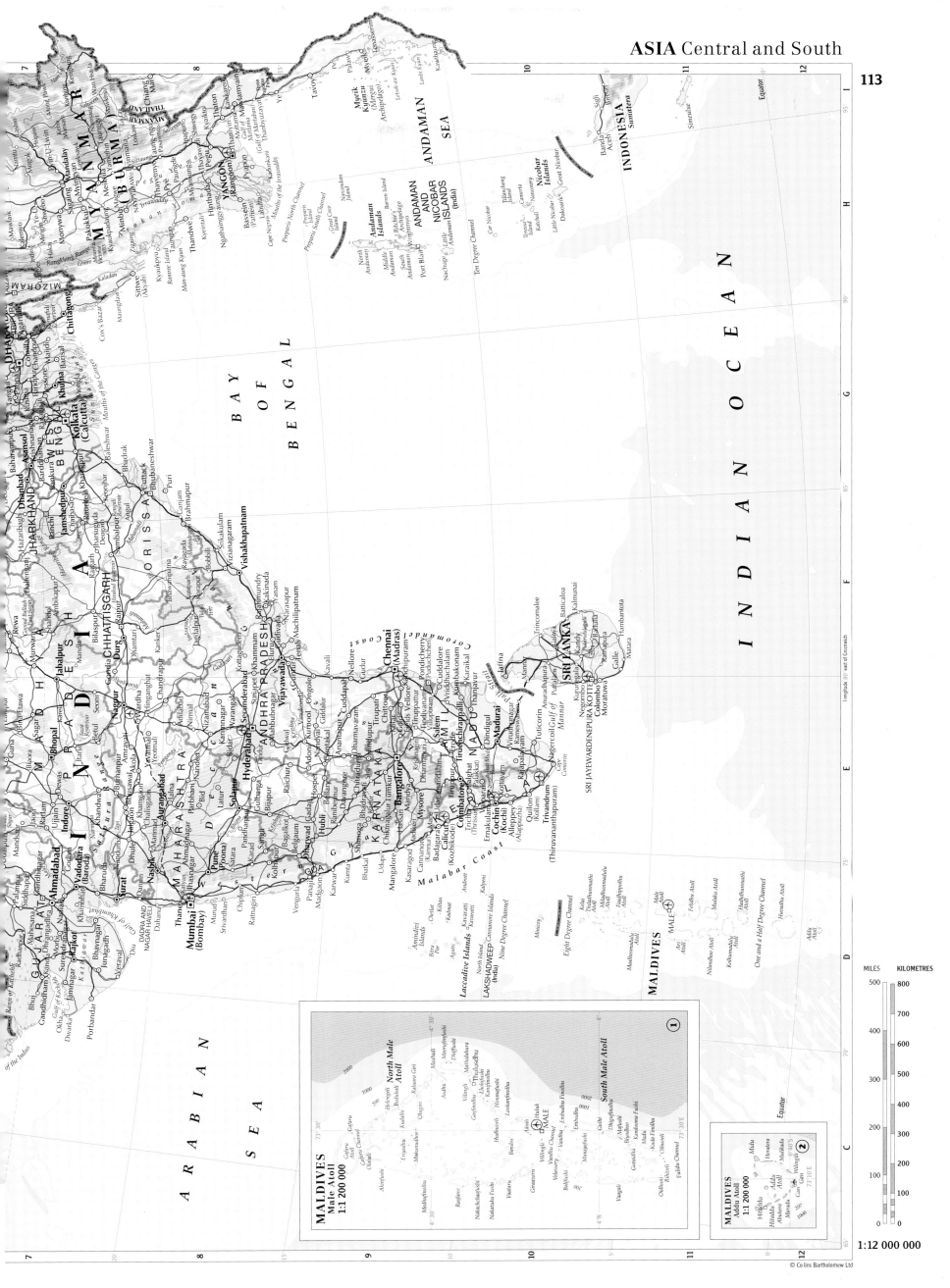
ARABIAN SEA
BAY OF BENGAL
INDIAN OCEAN
ANDAMAN SEA
MYANMAR (BURMA)
INDIA
SRI LANKA
MALDIVES
INDONESIA
ANDAMAN AND NICOBAR ISLANDS (India)
LAKSHADWEEP (India)
Mumbai (Bombay)
Kolkata (Calcutta)
Chennai (Madras)
Hyderabad
Bangalore
YANGON (Rangoon)
SRI JAYEWARDENEPURA KOTTE
Colombo
MALE
Equator
MALDIVES Male Atoll 1:1 200 000
North Male Atoll
South Male Atoll
MALDIVES Addu Atoll 1:1 200 000
MILES
KILOMETRES

1:12 000 000

INDIA

MADHYA PRADESH

Bhopal

Jabalpur

CHHATTIS...

Ahmadabad

Indore

GUJARAT

Rajkot

Vadodara
Baroda

Surat

Nagpur

MAHARASHTRA

Nashik

Aurangabad

Mumbai
(Bombay)

Navi Mumbai

Thane

Pune
Poona

Solapur

DECCAN

Hyderabad

Secunderabad

Gulbarga

ANDHRA PRADESH

Vijayawada

Guntur

Machilipatnam

Kolhapur

Ichalkaranji

Sangli

Belgaum

Dharwad

Hubli

Bijapur

Raichur

Kurnool

GOA

Panaji

KARNATAKA

Bellary

Ongole

Nellore

Hospet

Anantapur

Cuddapah

Tirupati

Tumkur

Bangalore

Chennai
(Madras)

Mangalore

Mysore

Salem

Coimbatore

TAMIL NADU

Tiruchchirappalli

Calicut
(Kozhikode)

KERALA

LAKSHADWEEP
(India)

Laccadive
Islands

Aminidivi Islands

Cannanore Islands

Cochin
(Kochi)

Madurai

Alleppey
(Alappuzha)

Quilon
(Kollam)

Trivandrum
(Thiruvananthapuram)

Nagercoil

Cape
Comorin

ARABIAN
SEA

Gulf of
Mannar

Jaffna

SRI LANKA

SRI JAYEWARDENEPURA KOTTE

Colombo

Moratuwa

MALDIVES

Nine Degree Channel

Eight Degree Channel

Coromandel Coast

Pondicherry
(Puducheri)

Conic Equidistant Projection

METRES / FEET
6000 / 19686
5000 / 16404
4000 / 13124
3000 / 9843
2000 / 6562
1000 / 3281
500 / 1640
200 / 656
0 / 0
LAND BELOW
SEA LEVEL
200 / 656
2000 / 6562
4000 / 13124
6000 / 19686

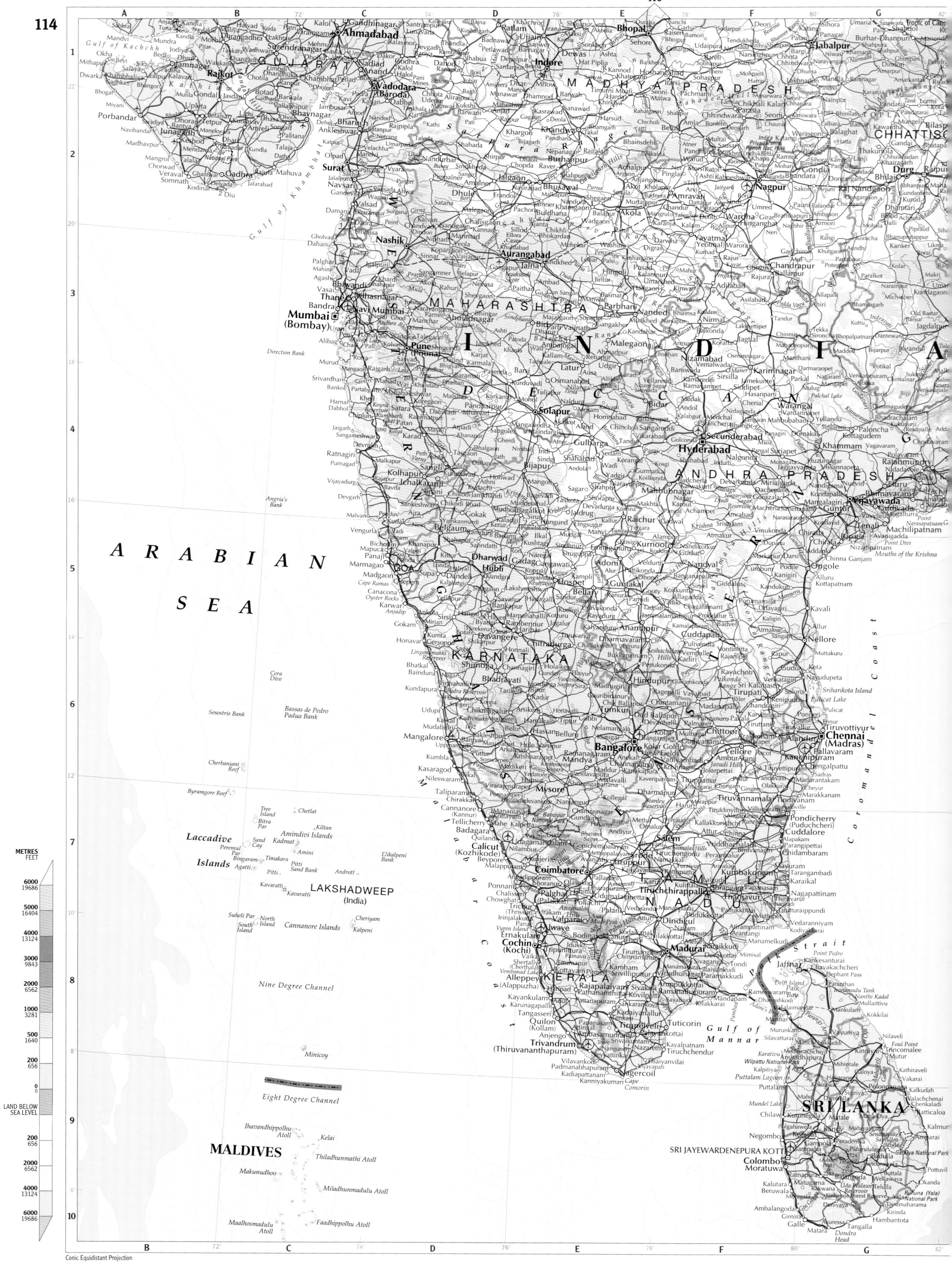

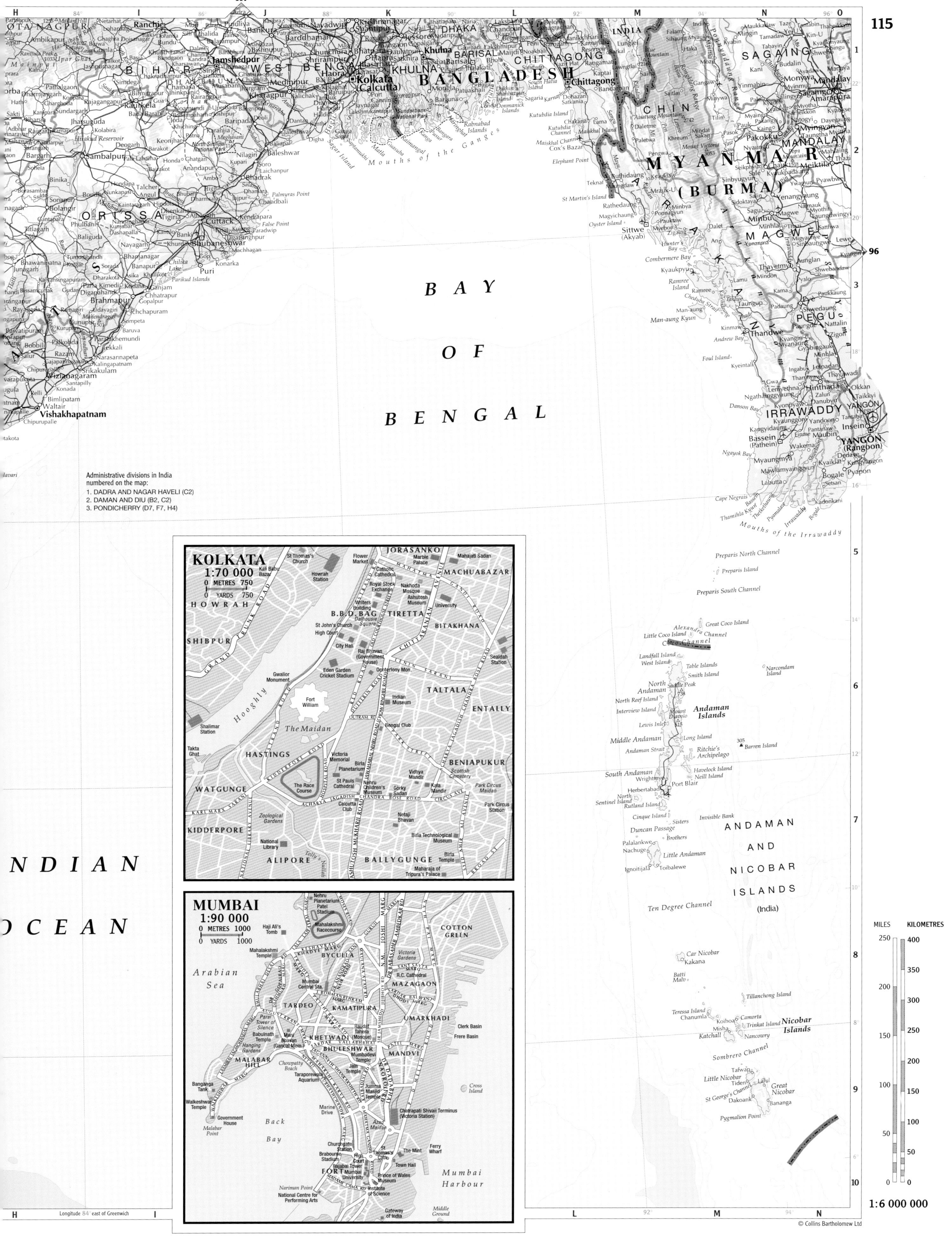

BAY

OF

BENGAL

MYANMAR
(BURMA)

Administrative divisions in India
numbered on the map:
1. DADRA AND NAGAR HAVELI (C2)
2. DAMAN AND DIU (B2, C2)
3. PONDICHERRY (D7, F7, H4)

KOLKATA
1:70 000
0 METRES 750
0 YARDS 750

MUMBAI
1:90 000
0 METRES 1000
0 YARDS 1000

ANDAMAN

AND

NICOBAR

ISLANDS

(India)

Nicobar
Islands

MILES   KILOMETRES

1:6 000 000

© Collins Bartholomew Ltd

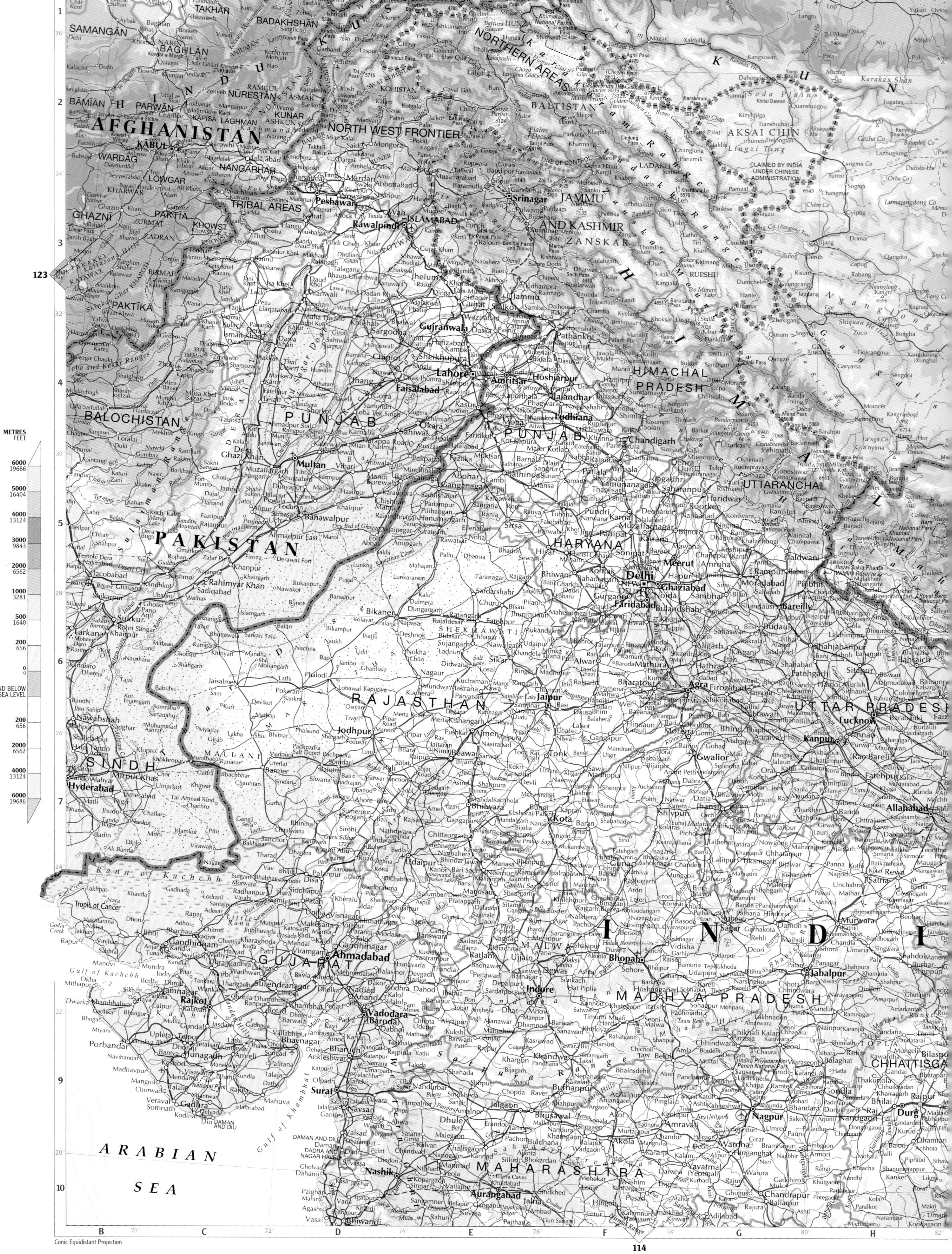
AFGHANISTAN
PAKISTAN
INDIA
ARABIAN SEA
HINDU KUSH
NORTHERN AREAS
NORTH WEST FRONTIER
TRIBAL AREAS
JAMMU AND KASHMIR
BALOCHISTAN
PUNJAB
SINDH
HIMACHAL PRADESH
UTTARANCHAL
HARYANA
RAJASTHAN
UTTAR PRADESH
GUJARAT
MADHYA PRADESH
MAHARASHTRA
CHHATTISGARH
AKSAI CHIN
CLAIMED BY INDIA UNDER CHINESE ADMINISTRATION
LINE OF CONTROL
Tropic of Cancer
Rann of Kachchh
Gulf of Kachchh
Gulf of Khambhat
DAMAN AND DIU
DADRA AND NAGAR HAVELI
METRES
FEET
6000 19686
5000 16404
4000 13124
3000 9843
2000 6562
1000 3281
500 1640
200 656
0
LAND BELOW SEA LEVEL
200 656
2000 6562
4000 13124
6000 19686
121
123
114

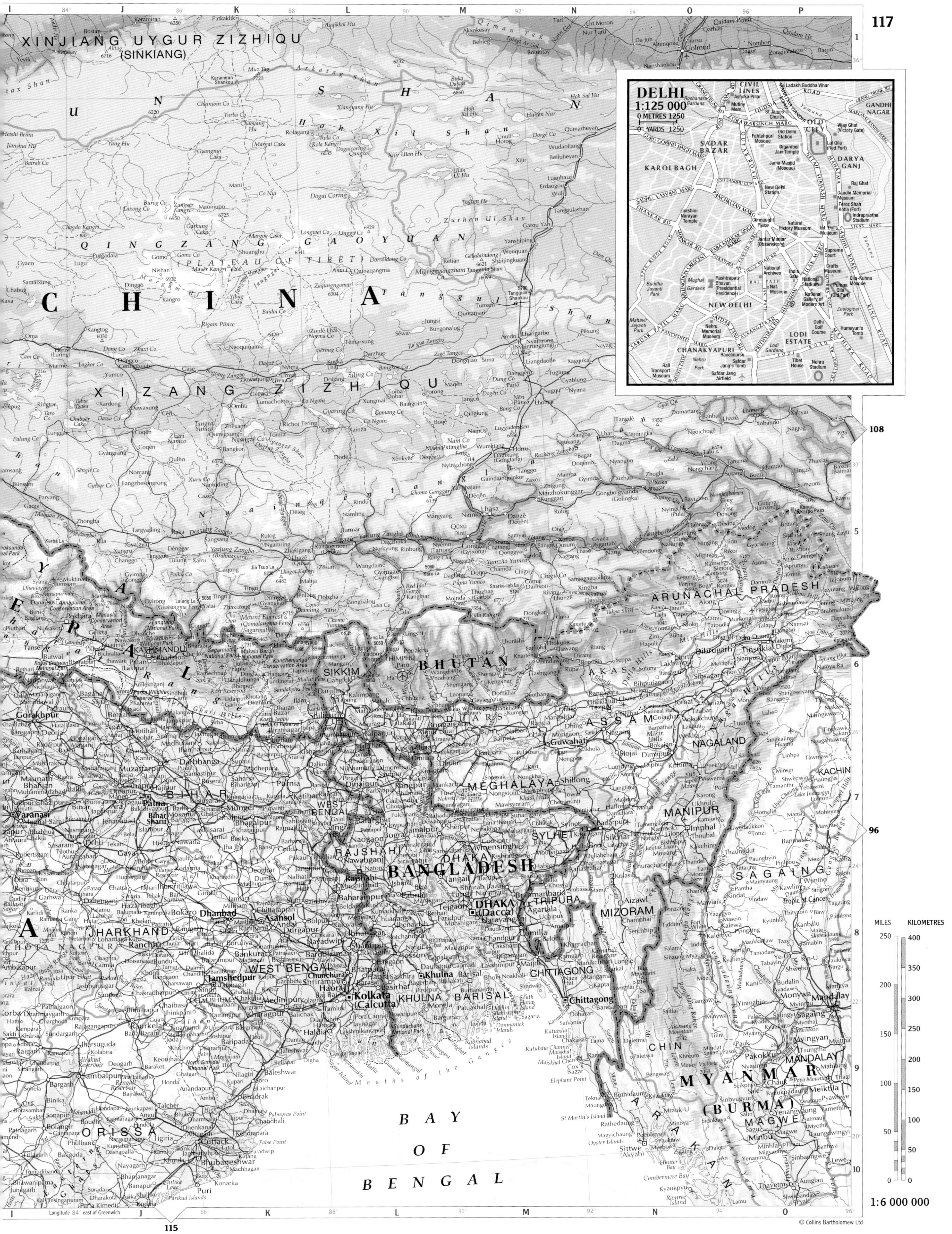
XINJIANG UYGUR ZIZHIQU
(SINKIANG)
QINGZANG GAOYUAN
(PLATEAU OF TIBET)
CHINA
XIZANG ZIZHIQU
DELHI
1:125 000
0 METRES 1250
0 YARDS 1250
OLD CITY
NEW DELHI
KAROL BAGH
SADAR BAZAR
CIVIL LINES
DARYA GANJ
GANDHI NAGAR
CHANAKYAPURI
LODI ESTATE
NEPAL
BHUTAN
SIKKIM
ARUNACHAL PRADESH
ASSAM
NAGALAND
MEGHALAYA
MANIPUR
MIZORAM
TRIPURA
BIHAR
JHARKHAND
WEST BENGAL
ORISSA
BANGLADESH
RAJSHAHI
DHAKA
SYLHET
KHULNA
BARISAL
CHITTAGONG
MYANMAR
(BURMA)
SAGAING
MANDALAY
MAGWE
KACHIN
CHIN
ARAKAN
BAY OF BENGAL
Kathmandu
Thimphu
Lhasa
Patna
Varanasi
Guwahati
Shillong
Imphal
Aizawl
Kolkata (Calcutta)
Dhaka (Dacca)
Chittagong
Khulna
Ranchi
Jamshedpur
Bhubaneshwar
Cuttack
Sittwe (Akyab)
Mandalay
Mount Everest (Qomolangma Feng) 8848
Tropic of Cancer
Mouths of the Ganges
MILES
KILOMETRES
1:6 000 000
108
96
Longitude 84° east of Greenwich

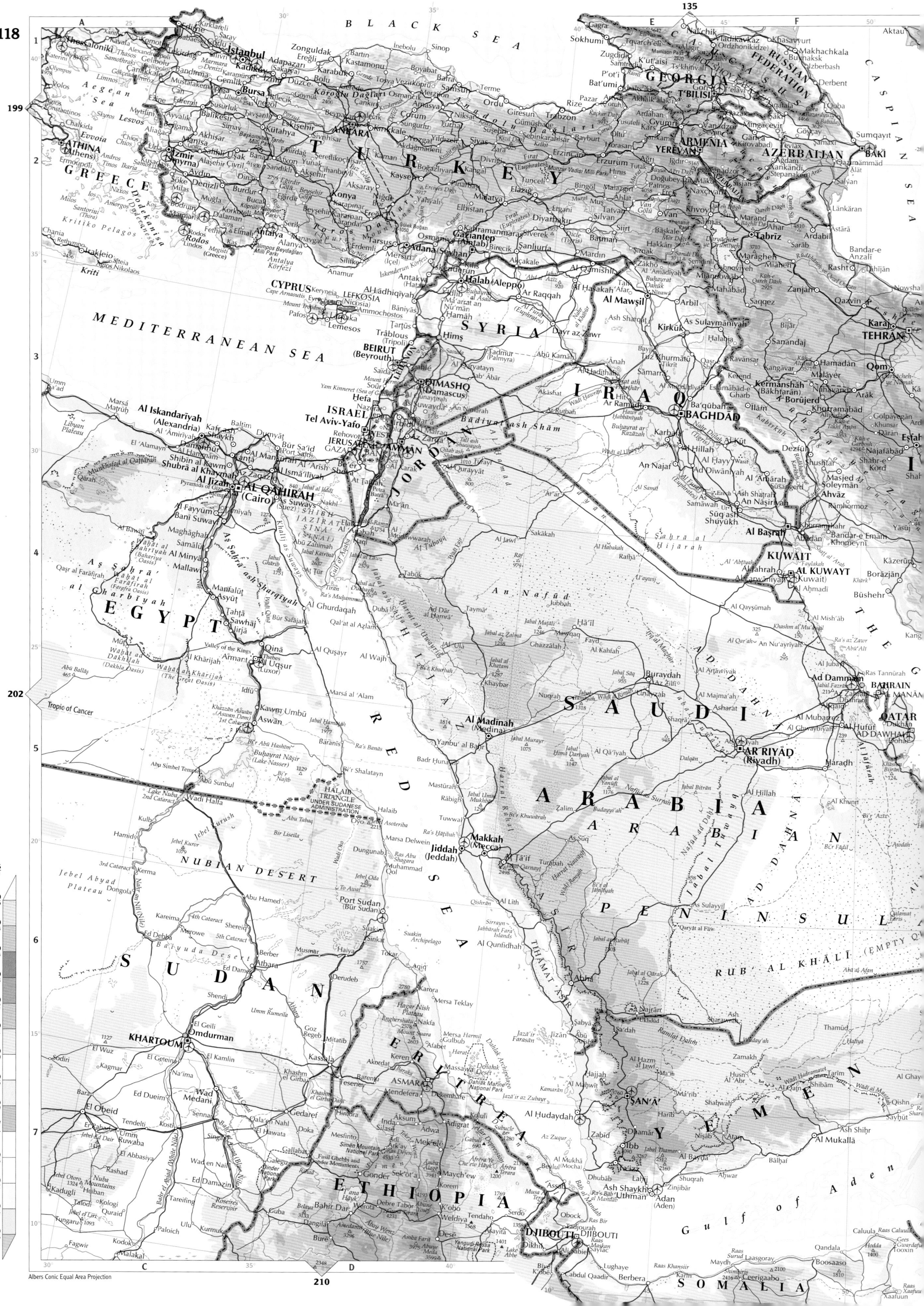

199

202

210

135

BLACK SEA

GEORGIA T'BILISI
ARMENIA YEREVAN
AZERBAIJAN BAKI
RUSSIAN FEDERATION
Makhachkala

TURKEY
Istanbul
Kadıköy
Bursa
ANKARA
İzmir (Smyrna)
Konya
Adana
Gaziantep
Tabriz

GREECE
THESSALONIKI
ATHINA (Athens)
Aegean Sea

Kriti

MEDITERRANEAN SEA

CYPRUS LEFKOSIA (Nicosia)

SYRIA
Halab (Aleppo)
Hims
DIMASHQ (Damascus)
Dayr az Zawr

LEBANON
BEIRUT (Beyrouth)

ISRAEL
Tel Aviv-Yafo
JERUSALEM
Hefa (Haifa)

IRAQ
Al Mawsil
Kirkūk
BAGHDAD
An Najaf
Al Başrah
Karbalā'

IRAN
TEHRĀN
Qom
Esfahān
Ahvāz

JORDAN
AMMAN

KUWAIT
AL KUWAYT (Kuwait)

BAHRAIN AL MANĀMAH
QATAR AD-DAWHAH (Doha)

EGYPT
AL QĀHIRAH (Cairo)
Al Iskandarīyah (Alexandria)
Al Jīzah
As Suways (Suez)
Asyūţ
Aswān
Al Uqşur (Luxor)
Port Said (Būr Sa'īd)

SINAI (JAZĪRAT SĪNĀ')

Tropic of Cancer

RED SEA

SAUDI ARABIA
AR RIYĀD (Riyadh)
Makkah (Mecca)
Jiddah (Jeddah)
Al Madīnah (Medina)
Ad Dammām
Al Hufūf

ARABIAN PENINSULA

RUB' AL KHĀLĪ (EMPTY QUARTER)

NUBIAN DESERT

SUDAN
KHARTOUM
Omdurman
Port Sudan (Būr Sūdān)
Atbara
Wad Medani
Kassala
El Obeid

ERITREA
ASMARA

ETHIOPIA
Gonder
Mek'elē

YEMEN
ŞAN'Ā'
Al Hudaydah
Ta'izz
Al Mukallā
Aden ('Adan)

DJIBOUTI DJIBOUTI

SOMALIA

Gulf of Aden

METRES / FEET
6000 / 19686
5000 / 16404
4000 / 13124
3000 / 9843
2000 / 6562
1000 / 3281
500 / 1640
200 / 656
0 / 0
LAND BELOW SEA LEVEL
200 / 656
2000 / 6562
4000 / 13124
6000 / 19686

Albers Conic Equal Area Projection

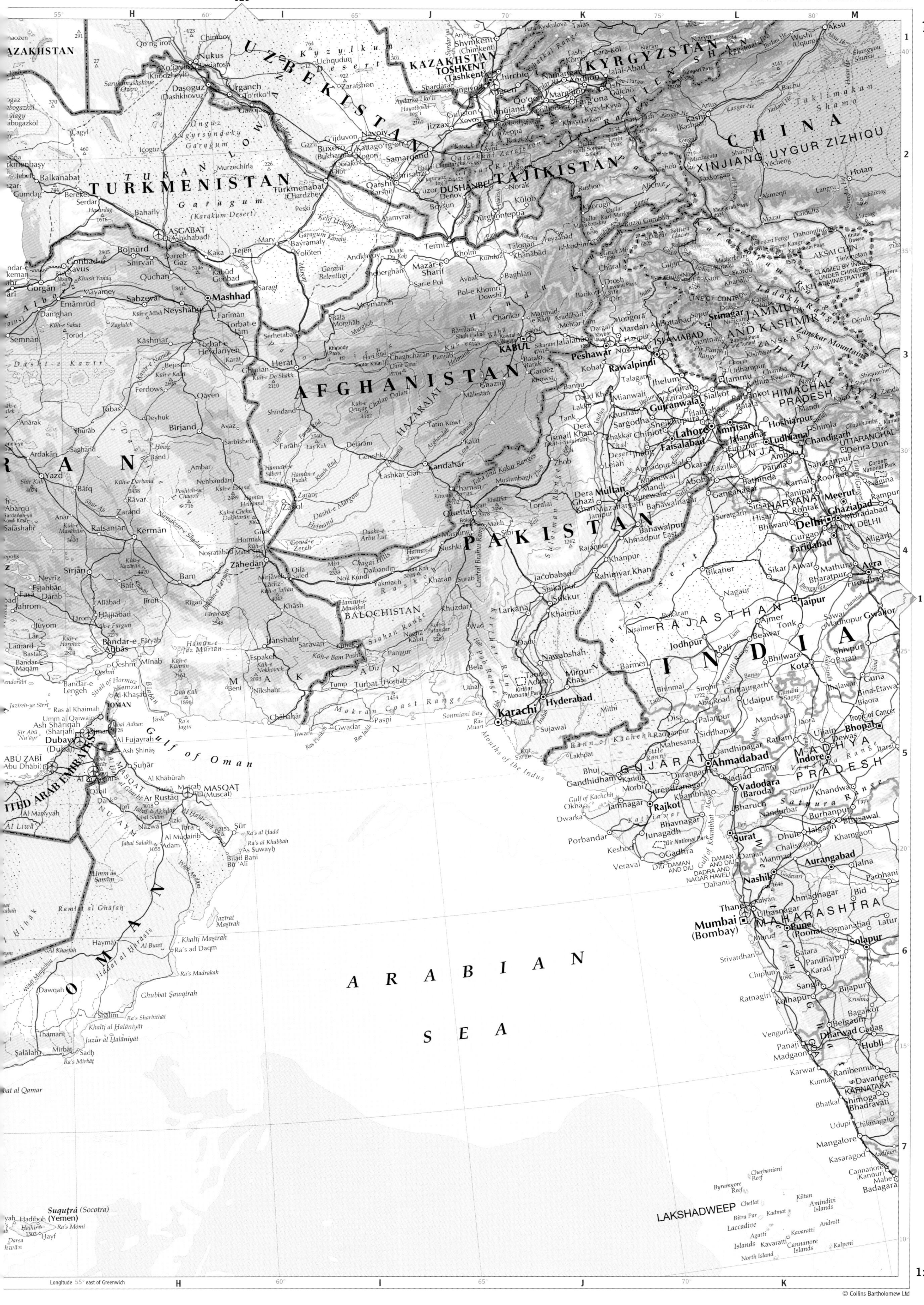

120

H   I   J   K   L   M

KAZAKHSTAN

UZBEKISTAN

KAZAKHSTAN

KYRGYZSTAN

TIEN SHAN

CHINA

XINJIANG UYGUR ZIZHIQU

Taklimakan Shamo

Nukus
Qo'ng'irot
Urganch
Dasoguz (Dashkhovuz)
Toshkent (Tashkent)
Chirchiq
Andijon
Kashi (Kashgar)
Aksu
Hotan
Yecheng

TURKMENISTAN

Garagum (Karakum Desert)

Buxoro (Bukhara)
Samarqand
Qarshi
DUSHANBE
TAJIKISTAN

ASGABAT (Ashkhabad)

Mary
Termiz
Mazar-e Sharif
Kunduz
Baghlan

Balkanabat

Serdar

Mashhad

Neyshabur

HINDU KUSH

Srinagar
JAMMU AND KASHMIR

AKSAI CHIN
CLAIMED BY INDIA
UNDER CHINESE
ADMINISTRATION

LINE OF CONTROL

Herat

AFGHANISTAN

KABUL
Charikar
Jalalabad
Mardan
ISLAMABAD
Peshawar
Rawalpindi
HIMACHAL
PRADESH

HAZARAJAT

Ghazni

Gardez
Khost

Gujranwala
Lahore
Amritsar
Jalandhar
Ludhiana
Chandigarh
UTTARANCHAL
Dehra Dun

IRAN

Kandahar

Quetta

PUNJAB
Faisalabad

PAKISTAN

Multan

HARYANA

Meerut
Ghaziabad
Delhi
NEW DELHI
Faridabad

Zahedan

BALOCHISTAN

Sukkur

Jaipur
RAJASTHAN

Agra
Bharatpur
Gwalior

112

Bandar-e Abbas

Qeshm
Strait of Hormuz

MAKRAN

Turbat

Karachi
Hyderabad

Jodhpur

Ajmer
Kota

INDIA

OMAN

Gulf of Oman

Mouths of the Indus

GUJARAT
Ahmadabad
Gandhinagar

MADHYA
PRADESH
Indore
Bhopal

Dubayy (Dubai)
Abu Dhabi
UNITED ARAB EMIRATES

MASQAT (Muscat)

Bhuj

Rajkot
Vadodara (Baroda)

Surat
Nashik

Gulf of Kachchh

MAHARASHTRA
Mumbai (Bombay)
Pune
Solapur

Aurangabad

ARABIAN

SEA

Kolhapur

Salalah

KARNATAKA
Hubli
Dharwad

Mangalore

LAKSHADWEEP

Laccadive Islands

Amindivi Islands

Longitude 55° east of Greenwich

MILES   KILOMETRES
400   700
  600
300   500
  400
200   300
  200
100
  100
0   0

1:11 000 000

© Collins Bartholomew Ltd

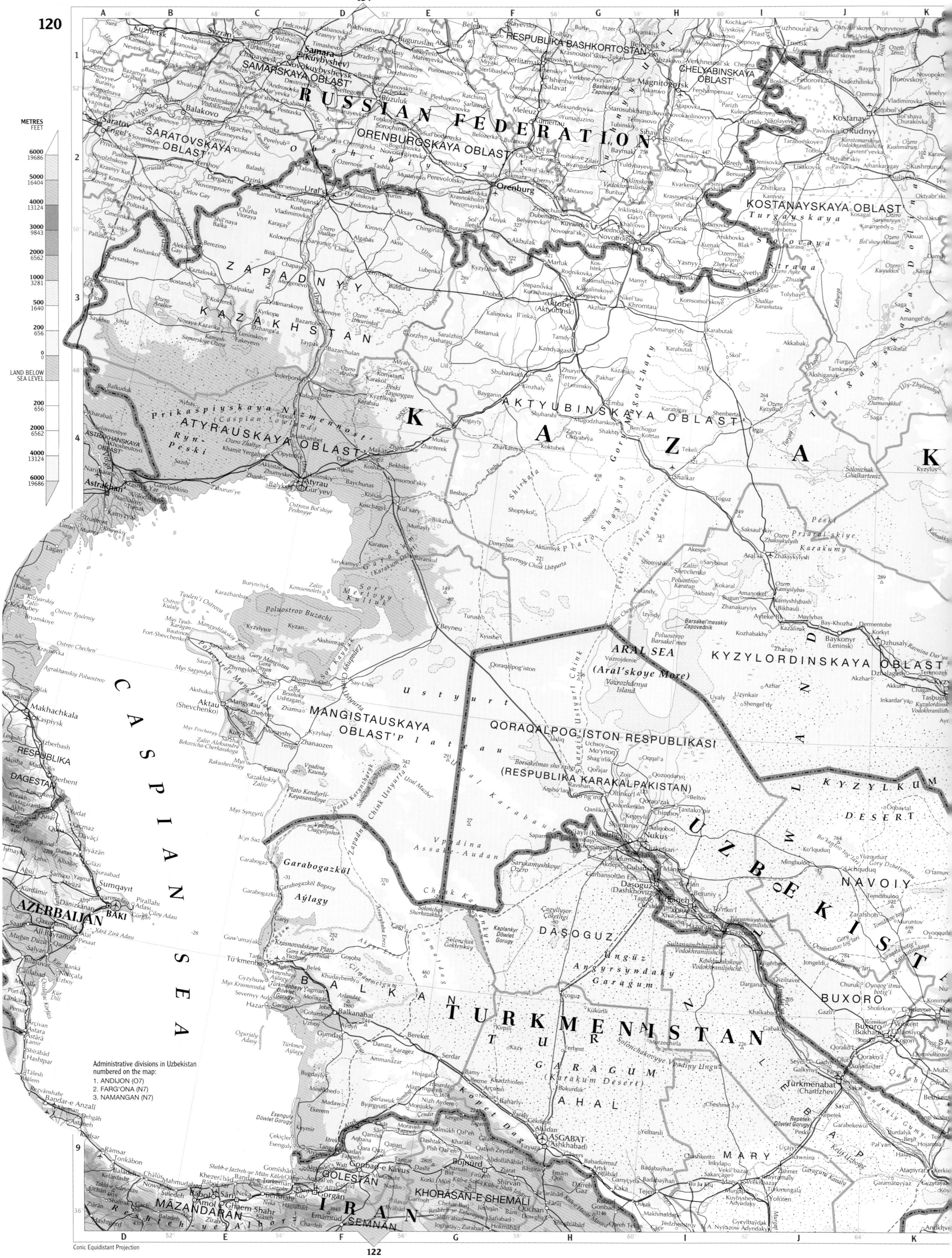

METRES
FEET

6000
19686

5000
16404

4000
13124

3000
9843

1000
3281

500
1640

200
656

0

LAND BELOW
SEA LEVEL

200
656

2000
6562

4000
13124

6000
19686

Administrative divisions in Uzbekistan
numbered on the map:
1. ANDIJON (O7)
2. FARG'ONA (N7)
3. NAMANGAN (N7)

Conic Equidistant Projection

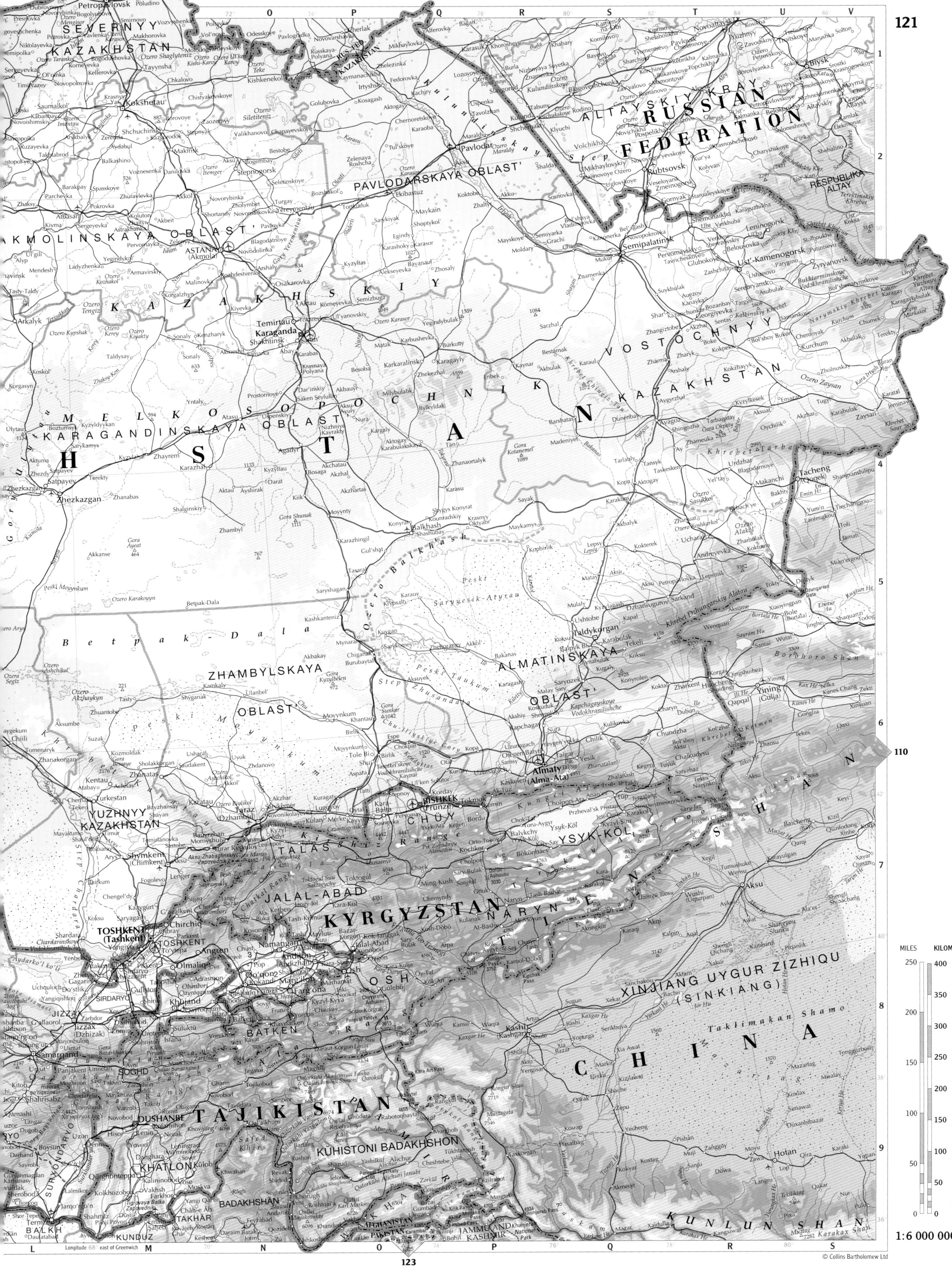

RUSSIAN FEDERATION

RESPUBLIKA ALTAY

SEVERNYY KAZAKHSTAN

AKMOLINSKAYA OBLAST'

ASTANA (Akmola)

K A Z A K H S K I Y

VOSTOCHNYY KAZAKHSTAN

PAVLODARSKAYA OBLAST'

Pavlodar

Semipalatinsk

Ust'-Kamenogorsk

Temirtau
Karaganda

KARAGANDINSKAYA OBLAST'

H S T A N

MELKOSOPOCHNIK

Zhezkazgan

Betpak-Dala

Balkhash

Ozero Balkhash

ZHAMBYLSKAYA

OBLAST'

ALMATINSKAYA

OBLAST'

Peski Moyynkum

T I E N

YUZHNYY KAZAKHSTAN

Almaty (Alma-Ata)

BISHKEK

Shymkent (Chimkent)

CHÜY

YSYK-KÖL

S H A N

TOSHKENT (Tashkent)

TALAS

TOSHKENT

JALAL-ABAD

KYRGYZSTAN

NARYN

SIRDARYO

JIZZAX

OSH

XINJIANG UYGUR ZIZHIQU (SINKIANG)

BATKEN

CHINA

Taklimakan Shamo

SOGHD

Samarqand

TAJIKISTAN

DUSHANBE

KUHISTONI BADAKHSHON

BADAKHSHAN

KHATLON

Kashi (Kashgar)

KUNLUN SHAN

Hotan

BALKH

TAKHÄR

KUNDUZ

AFGHANISTAN

PAKISTAN

JAMMU AND KASHMIR

MILES KILOMETRES

250 400
350
200 300
150 250
200
100 150
100
50 50
0 0

1:6 000 000

© Collins Bartholomew Ltd

Longitude 68 east of Greenwich

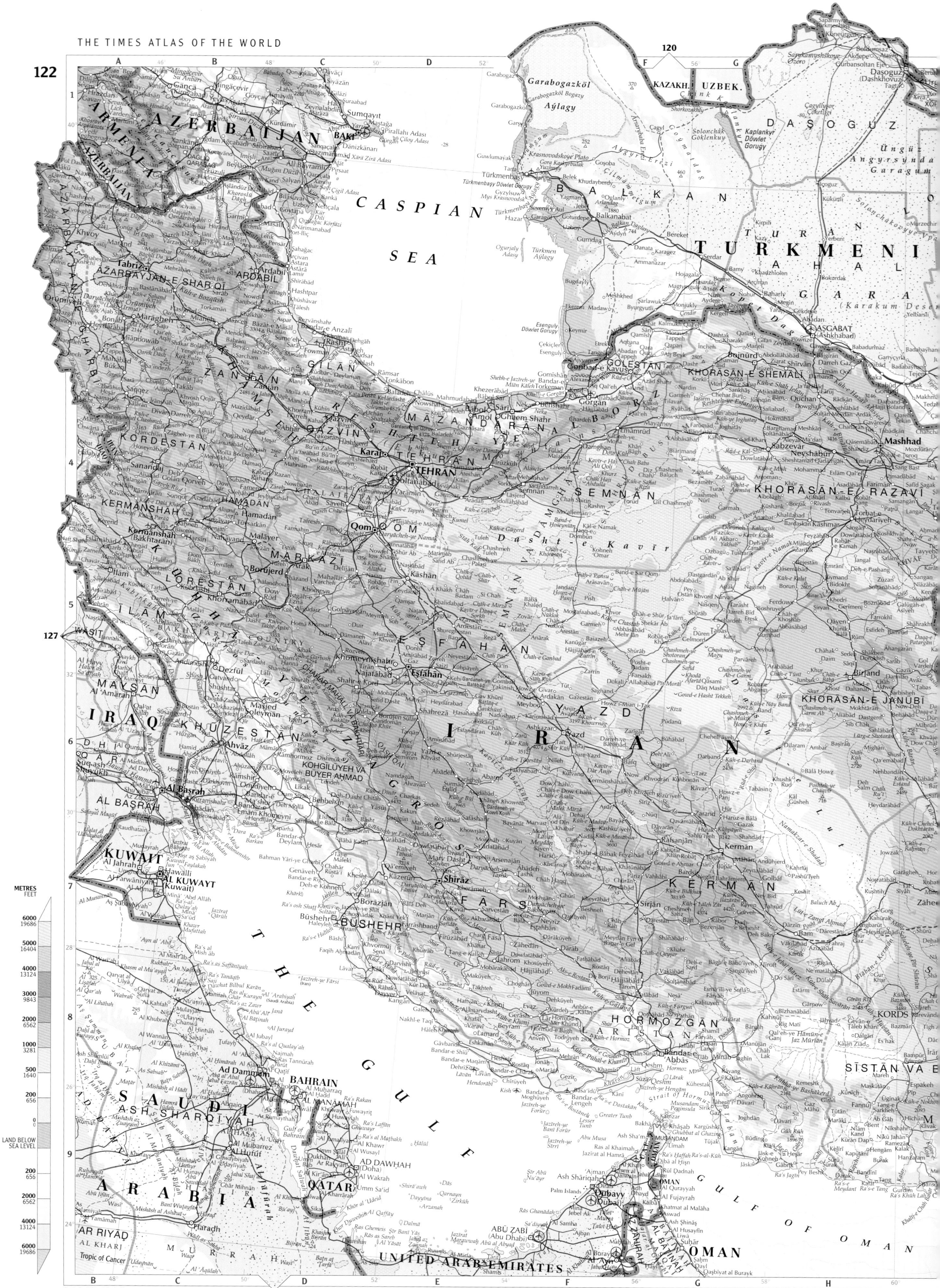

120

CASPIAN SEA

AZERBAIJAN
ARMENIA

KAZAKH. UZBEK.

DAŞOGUZ

TURKMENI
BALKAN
GARA
(Karakum Desert)

ASGABAT
Ashkhabad

KHORĀSĀN-E SHEMĀLĪ

KHORĀSĀN-E RAZAVĪ

Mashhad

Tabrīz
ĀZARBĀYJĀN-E SHARQĪ
ARDABĪL

GĪLĀN
MĀZANDARĀN
GOLESTĀN
Gorgān

ZANJĀN
QAZVĪN
Karaj
TEHRĀN
SEMNĀN

KORDESTĀN
HAMADĀN
Qom
QOM

IRAN

KERMĀNSHĀH
MARKAZĪ

LORESTĀN
ILĀM

KHŪZESTĀN
Ahvāz

IRAQ

Eşfahān
ESFAHĀN

YAZD
Yazd

KHORĀSĀN-E JANUBĪ

Al Başrah
AL BAŞRAH

KUWAIT
AL KUWAYT
Kuwait

FĀRS
Shīrāz

KERMĀN
Kermān
Sīrjān

HORMOZGĀN
Bandar-e Abbās

SĪSTĀN VA

SAUDI ARABIA
AR RIYĀD

BAHRAIN
AL MANĀMAH

AD DAMMĀM

QATAR

Būshehr
BUSHEHR

THE GULF

AD DAWHAH
(Doha)

UNITED ARAB EMIRATES

ABŪ ZABĪ
Abu Dhabi

Dubayy
Dubai

OMAN

GULF OF OMAN

Strait of Hormuz

Tropic of Cancer

METRES FEET
6000 19686
5000 16404
4000 13124
3000 9843
2000 6562
1000 3281
500 1640
200 656
0
LAND BELOW SEA LEVEL
200 656
2000 6562
4000 13124
6000 19686

127

Conic Equidistant Projection

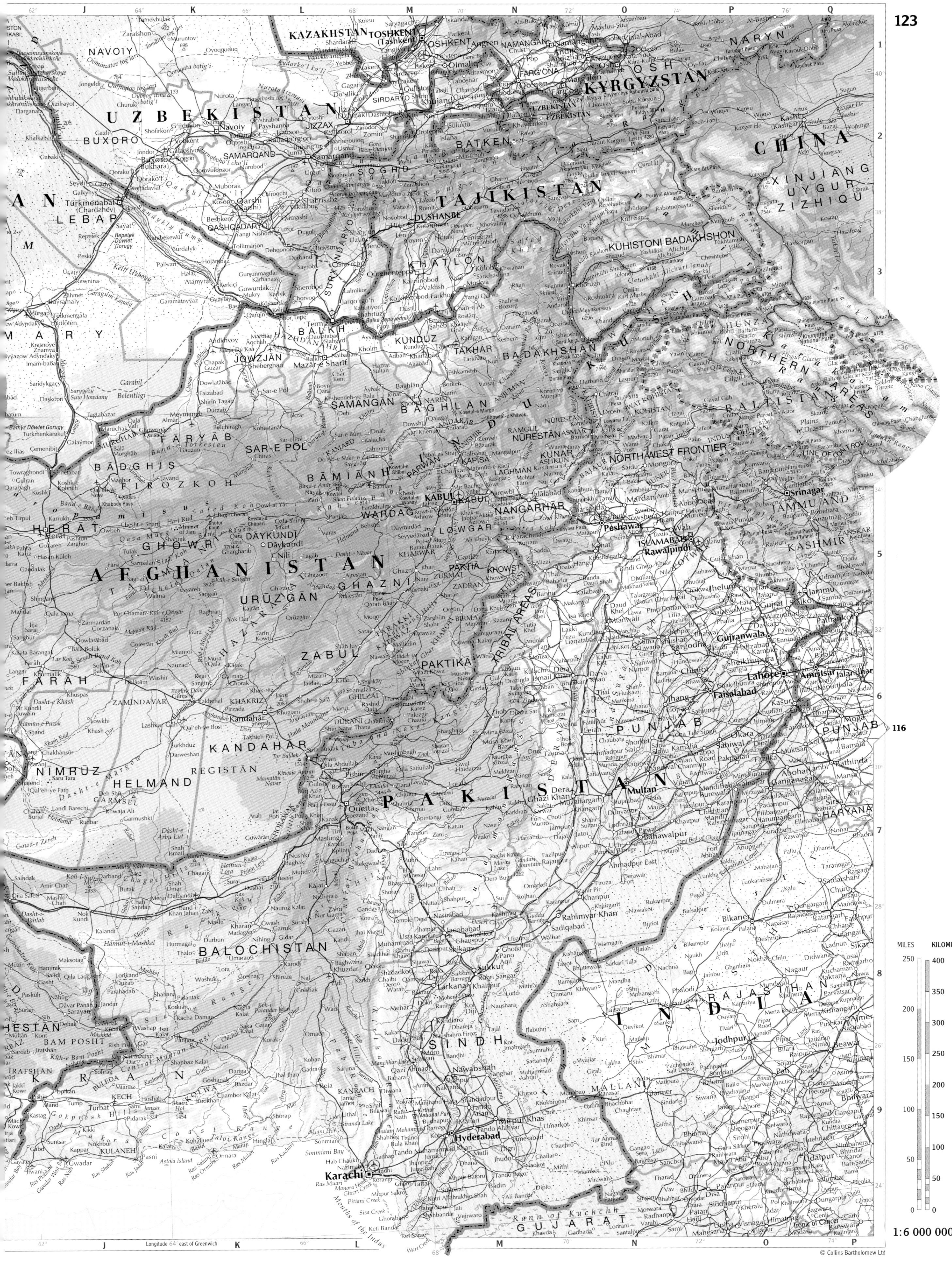

116

MILES   KILOMETRES

250 — 400
     — 350
200 — 300
     — 250
150 — 200
100 — 150
     — 100
50 — 50
0 — 0

1:6 000 000

© Collins Bartholomew Ltd

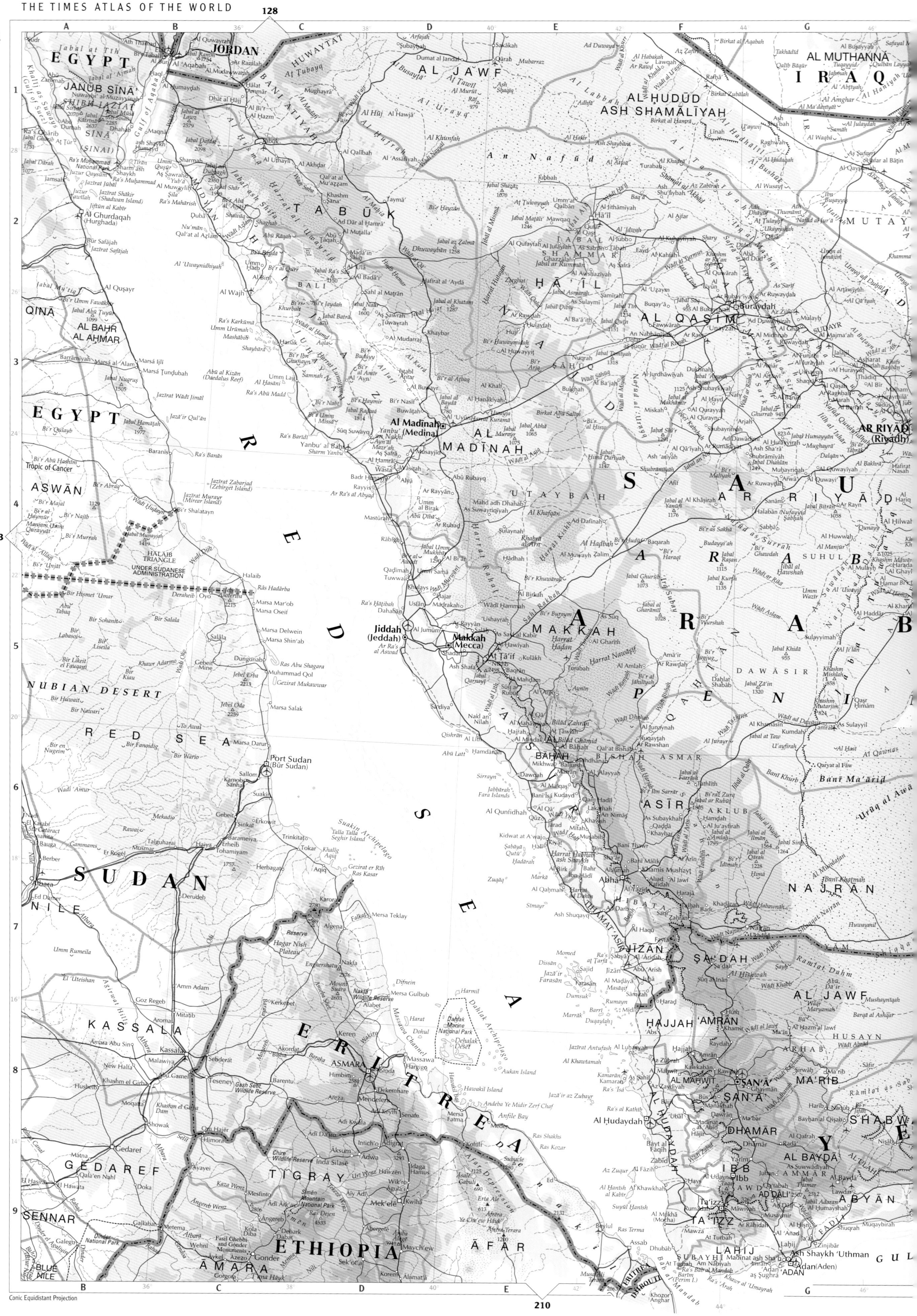

EGYPT
JORDAN
JANŪB SĪNĀʾ
SINAI
QINĀ
AL BAHR AL AHMAR
EGYPT
ASWĀN
Tropic of Cancer
HALAIB TRIANGLE
UNDER SUDANESE ADMINISTRATION
NUBIAN DESERT
RED SEA
SUDAN
NILE
KASSALA
ERITREA
GEDAREF
SENNAR
BLUE NILE
TIGRAY
ĀMARA
ETHIOPIA
ĀFAR

TABŪK
AL JAWF
AL HUDŪD ASH SHAMĀLĪYAH
IRAQ
AL MUTHANNĀ
An Nafūd
ḤĀʾIL
JABAL SHAMMAR
AL QAṢĪM
Buraydah
MUTAYR
AL MADĪNAH
Al Madīnah (Medina)
Yanbuʿ al Baḥr
AR RIYĀḌ (Riyadh)
S A U D I   A R A B I A
UTAYBAH
Jiddah (Jeddah)
Makkah (Mecca)
MAKKAH
Aṭ Ṭāʾif
DAWĀSIR
BĀHAH
BISHAH
ASĪR
Abhā
NAJRĀN
Jīzān
SAʿDAH
AL JAWF
HAJJAH
ʿAMRAN
Ṣanʿāʾ
SANʿĀʾ
MAʾRIB
AL MAHWĪT
AL ḤUDAYDAH
DHAMĀR
IBB
TAʿIZZ
LAHIJ
ADD ĀLIʿ
ABYĀN
SHABW
YE
ADAN (Aden)

R E D   S E A

Port Sudan (Bür Sudan)

Conic Equidistant Projection

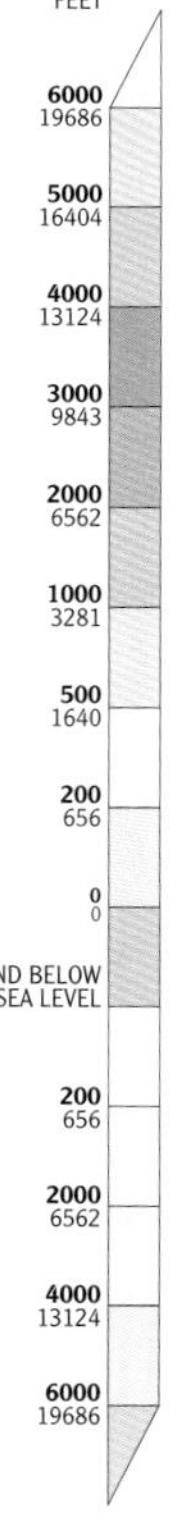

METRES FEET
6000 19686
5000 16404
4000 13124
3000 9843
2000 6562
1000 3281
500 1640
200 656
0
LAND BELOW SEA LEVEL
200 656
2000 6562
4000 13124
6000 19686

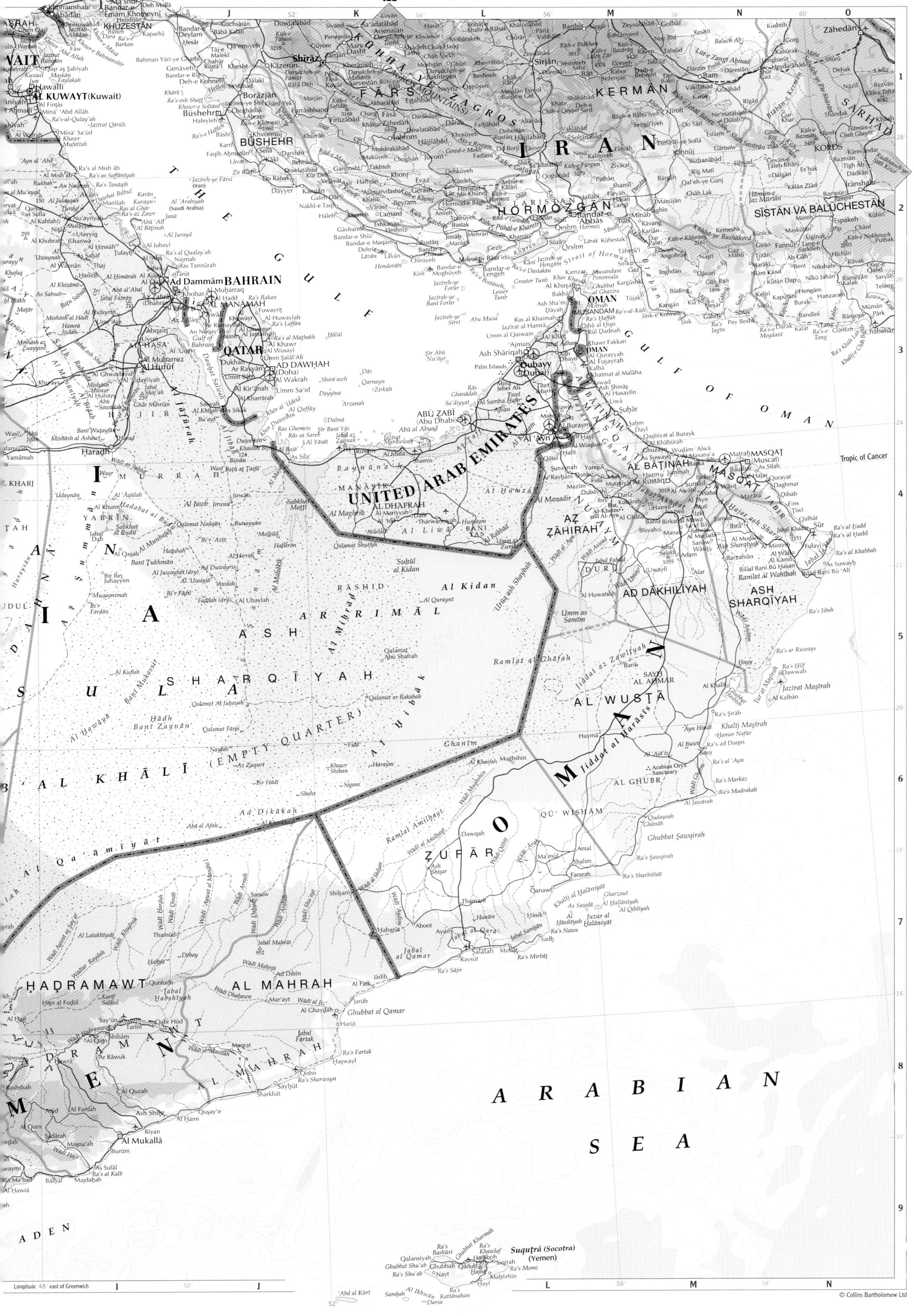
122
IRAN
FARS
KERMAN
HORMOZGAN
SISTAN VA BALUCHESTAN
KHUZESTAN
BUSHEHR
Shiraz
Bandar-e Abbas
Strait of Hormuz
THE GULF
GULF OF OMAN
BAHRAIN
AL MANAMAH
QATAR
AD DAWHAH (Doha)
AL KUWAYT (Kuwait)
Ad Dammam
UNITED ARAB EMIRATES
ABU ZABI (Abu Dhabi)
Dubayy (Dubai)
OMAN
MUSANDAM
MASQAT (Muscat)
AL BATINAH
AD DAKHILIYAH
ASH SHARQIYAH
AZ ZAHIRAH
AL WUSTA
ZUFAR
Salalah
Tropic of Cancer
AR RUB' AL KHALI (EMPTY QUARTER)
HADRAMAWT
AL MAHRAH
YEMEN
Al Mukalla
ARABIAN SEA
ADEN
Suqutra (Socotra) (Yemen)
Jazirat Masirah
Longitude 48° east of Greenwich

MILES | KILOMETRES

1:6 000 000

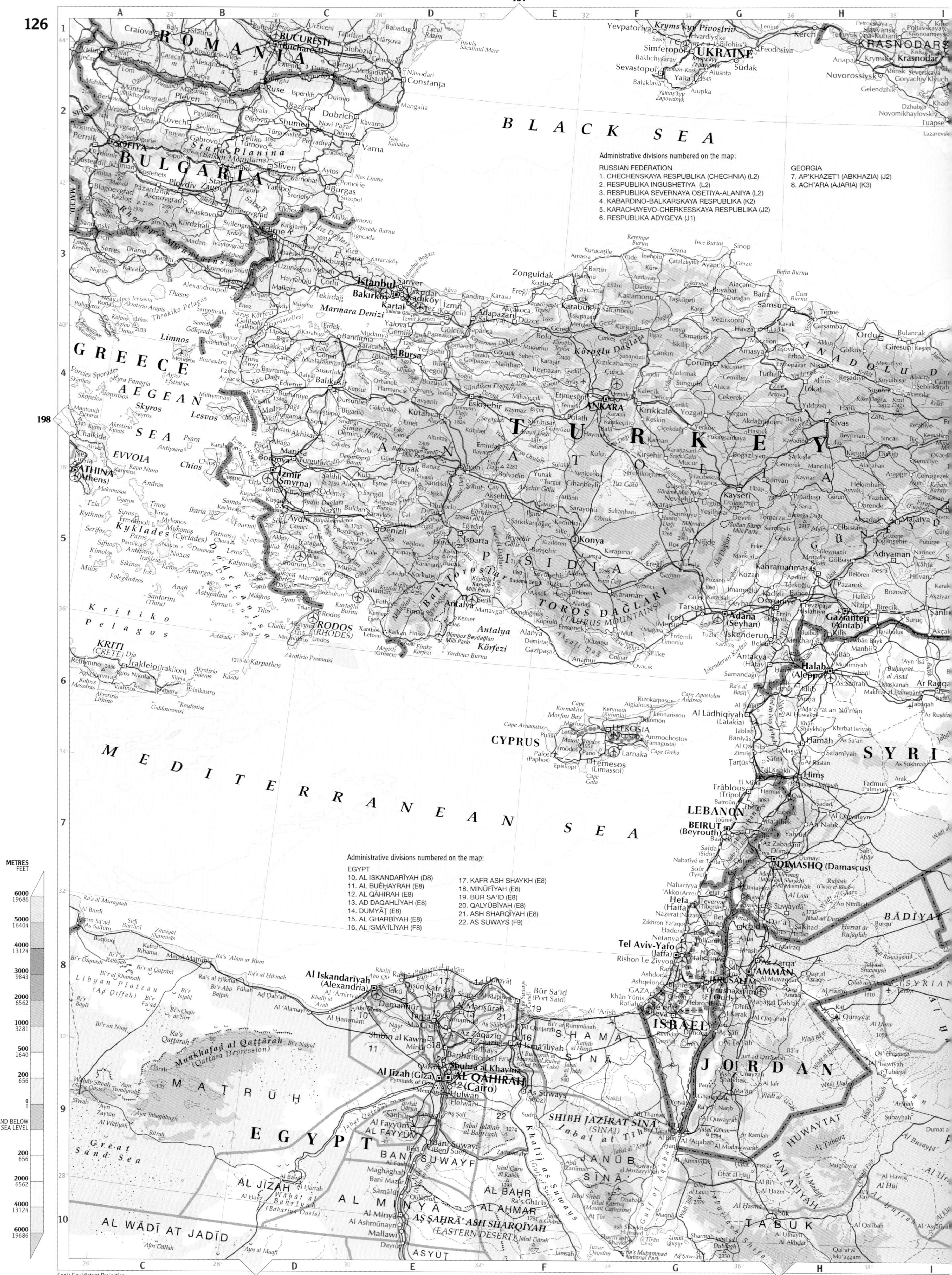

Major labels

ROMANIA
BULGARIA
GREECE
AEGEAN SEA
TURKEY
ANATOLIA
UKRAINE
KRASNODAR
BLACK SEA
CYPRUS
SYRIA
LEBANON
ISRAEL
JORDAN
EGYPT
MEDITERRANEAN SEA

BUCUREŞTI
SOFIA
İstanbul
ANKARA
İzmir (Smyrna)
Konya
Adana (Seyhan)
Gaziantep (Aintab)
Halab (Aleppo)
Ḥimş
DIMASHQ (Damascus)
BEIRUT (Beyrouth)
Hefa (Haifa)
Tel Aviv-Yafo (Jaffa)
JERUSALEM (Yerushalayim) (El Quds)
AMMAN
Al Iskandarīyah (Alexandria)
AL QĀHIRAH (Cairo)
Al Jīzah (Giza)

Administrative divisions numbered on the map:

RUSSIAN FEDERATION
1. CHECHENSKAYA RESPUBLIKA (CHECHNIA) (L2)
2. RESPUBLIKA INGUSHETIYA (L2)
3. RESPUBLIKA SEVERNAYA OSETIYA-ALANIYA (L2)
4. KABARDINO-BALKARSKAYA RESPUBLIKA (K2)
5. KARACHAYEVO-CHERKESSKAYA RESPUBLIKA (J2)
6. RESPUBLIKA ADYGEYA (J1)

GEORGIA
7. AP'KHAZET'I (ABKHAZIA) (J2)
8. ACH'ARA (AJARIA) (K3)

Administrative divisions numbered on the map:

EGYPT
10. AL ISKANDARĪYAH (D8)
11. AL BUḤAYRAH (E8)
12. AL QĀHIRAH (E8)
13. AD DAQAHLĪYAH (E8)
14. DUMYĀŢ (E8)
15. AL GHARBĪYAH (E8)
16. AL ISMĀ'ĪLĪYAH (F8)
17. KAFR ASH SHAYKH (E8)
18. MINŪFĪYAH (E8)
19. BŪR SA'ĪD (E8)
20. QALYŪBĪYAH (E8)
21. ASH SHARQĪYAH (E8)
22. AS SUWAYS (F9)

Scale bar

METRES / FEET
6000 / 19686
5000 / 16404
4000 / 13124
3000 / 9843
2000 / 6562
1000 / 3281
500 / 1640
200 / 656
0 / 0
LAND BELOW SEA LEVEL
200 / 656
2000 / 6562
4000 / 13124
6000 / 19686

Conic Equidistant Projection

198

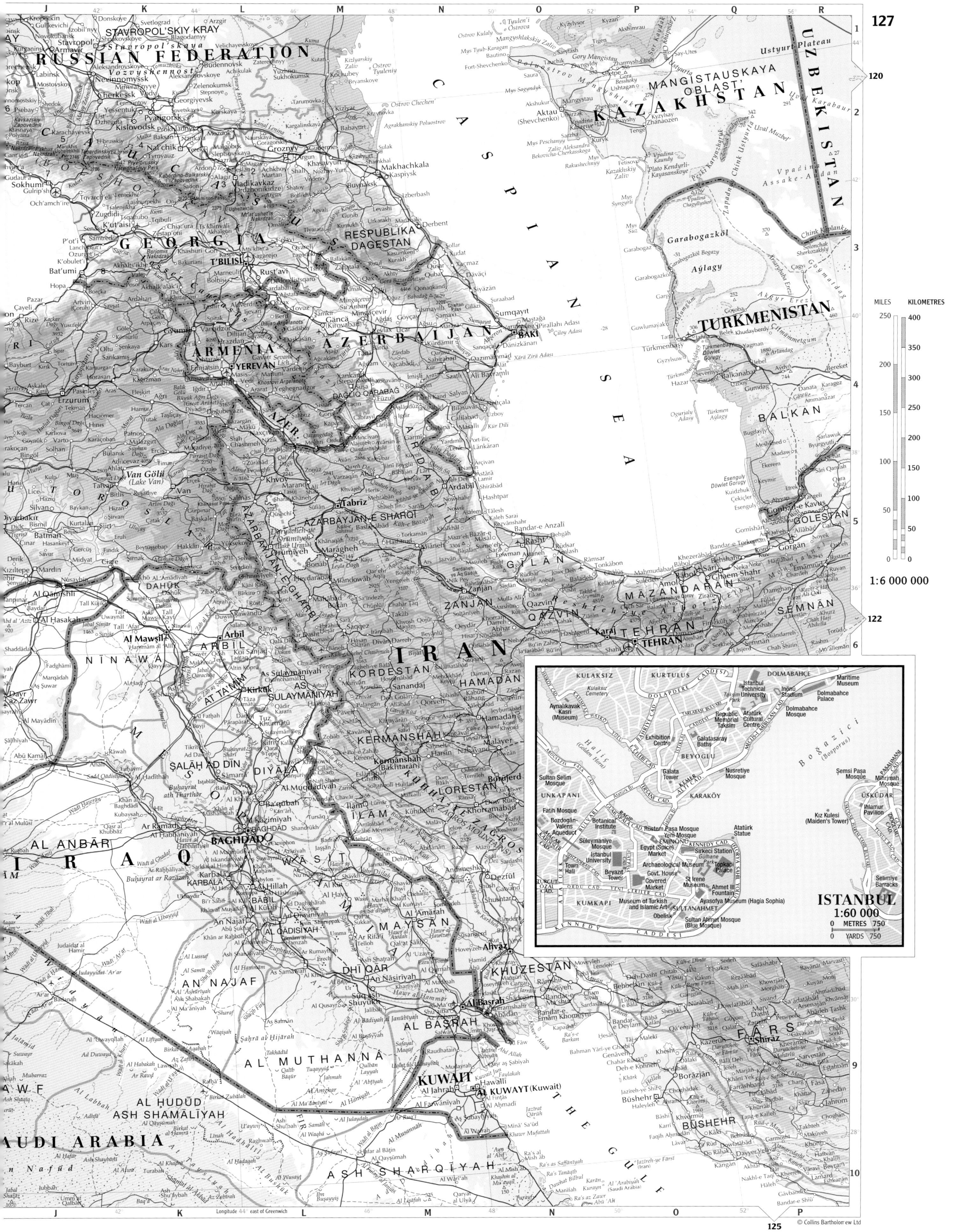

ISTANBUL
1:60 000

0 METRES 750
0 YARDS 750

1:6 000 000

MILES   KILOMETRES
250   400
        350
200   300
        250
150   200
100   150
        100
50   50
0   0

MEDITERRANEAN SEA

TURKEY

KARAMAN
MERSIN
ANTALYA
ADANA
HATAY
KILIS
GAZIANTEP
ŞANLIURFA
AR RAQQAH

CYPRUS
LEFKOŞA (Nicosia)
Dhekelia Sovereign Base Area (U.K.)
Akrotiri Sovereign Base Area (U.K.)

SYRIA
HALAB
Halab (Aleppo)
IDLIB
AL LĀDHIQĪYAH
Al Lādhiqīyah (Latakia)
HAMĀH
HIMȘ
Himș
DIMASHQ
Dimashq (Damascus)

LEBANON
BEIRUT (Beyrouth)
TARȚŪS

ISRAEL
Tel Aviv-Yafo
Hefa (Haifa)
JERUSALEM (El Quds / Yerushalayim)
GAZA

CEASE-FIRE LINES 1974

WEST BANK

DAR'Ā
AS SUWAYDĀ'

IRAQ

BADIYAT ASH SHĀM
(SYRIAN DESERT)

JORDAN
AMMAN

AL HUDŪD ASH SHAMĀLIYAH

EGYPT
AL ISMĀ'ĪLIYAH
AS SUWAYS
SHAMĀL SĪNĀ'
JANŪB SĪNĀ'
AL BAḤR AL AḤMAR

SAUDI ARABIA
AL JAWF
TABŪK

1:3 000 000

Conic Equidistant Projection

© Collins Bartholomew Ltd

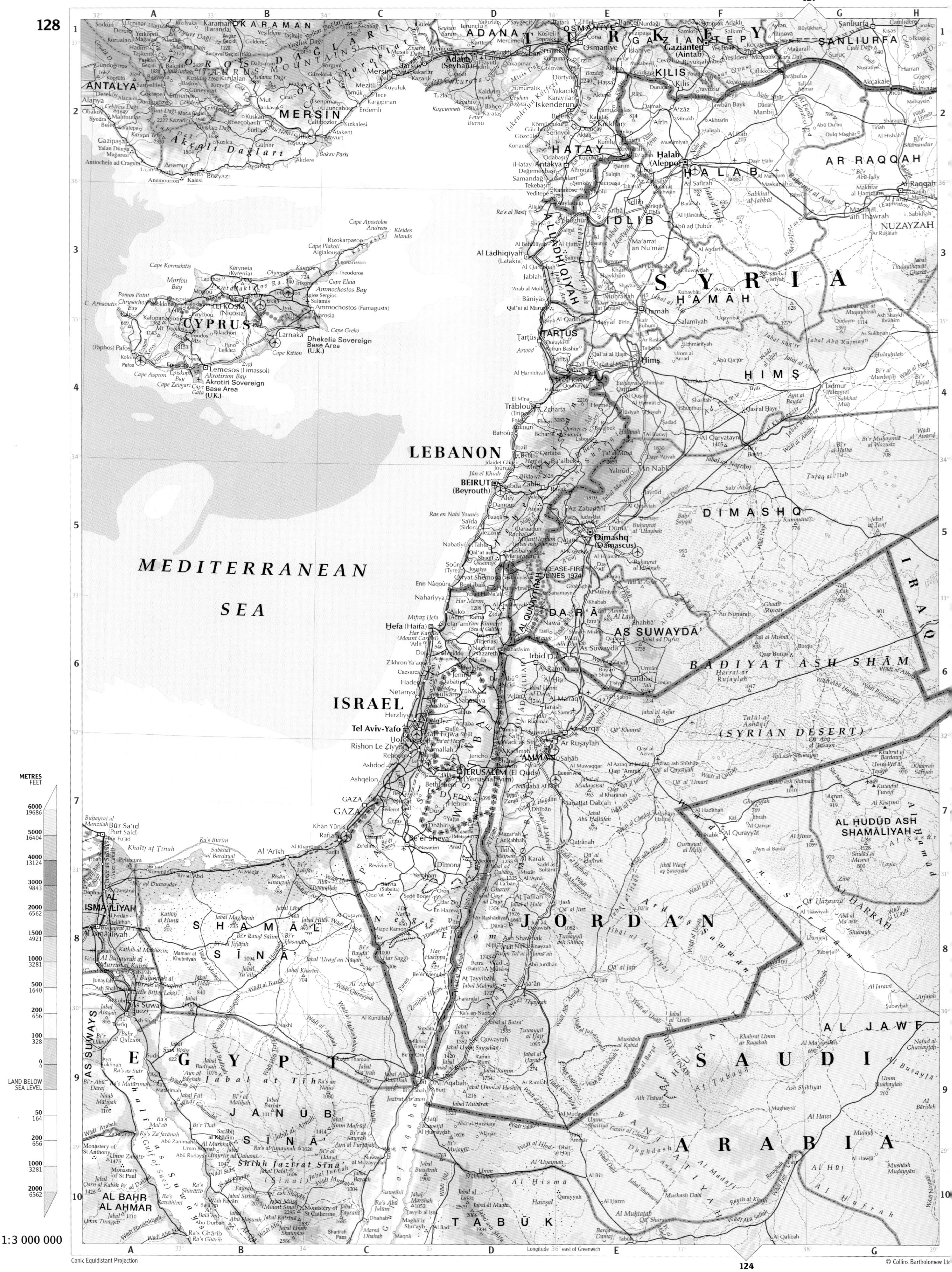

METRES / FEET
6000 / 19686
5000 / 16404
4000 / 13124
3000 / 9843
2000 / 6562
1500 / 4921
1000 / 3281
500 / 1640
200 / 656
100 / 328
0
LAND BELOW SEA LEVEL
50 / 164
200 / 656
1000 / 3281
2000 / 6562

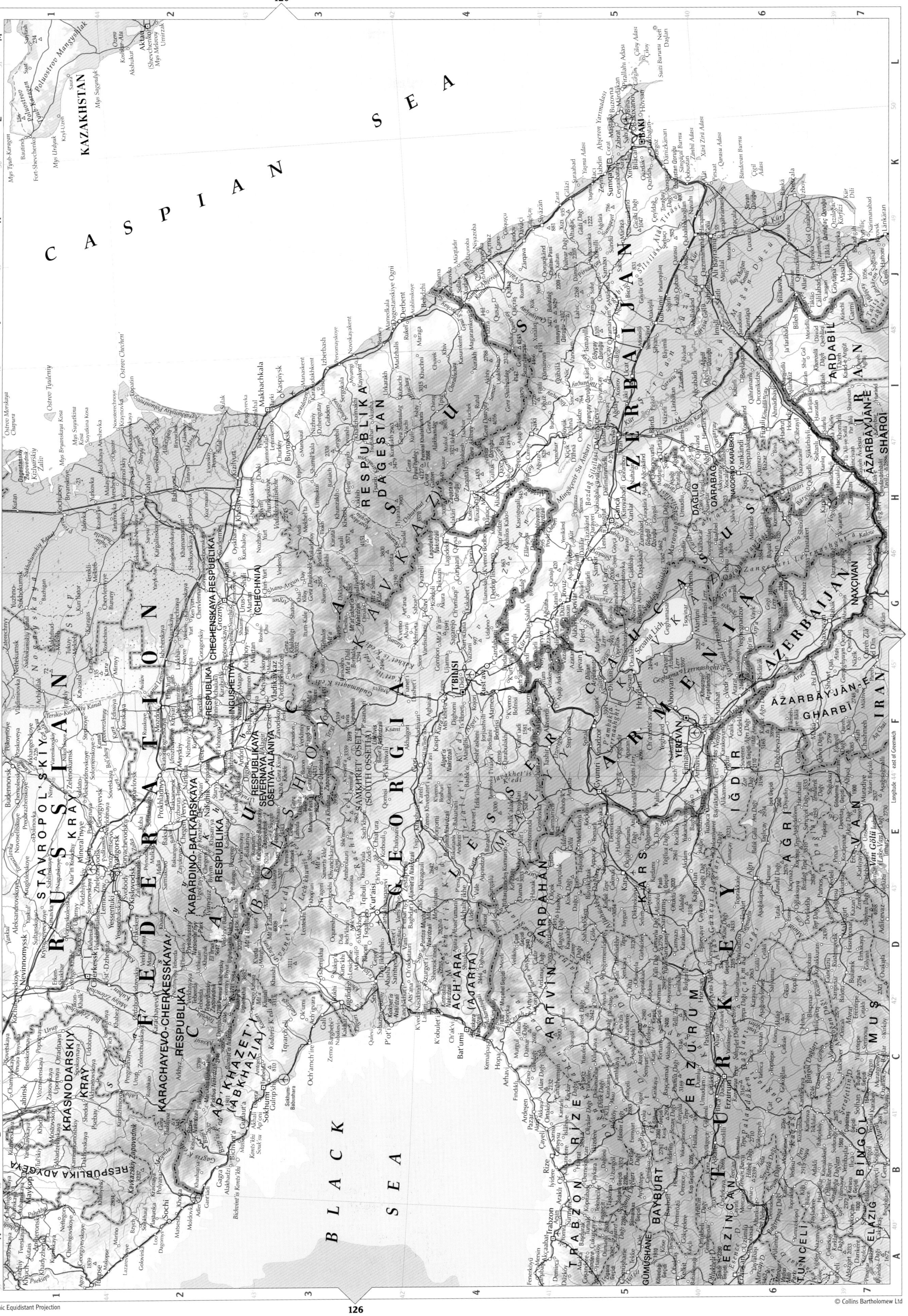

1:3 000 000

Conic Equidistant Projection

© Collins Bartholomew Ltd

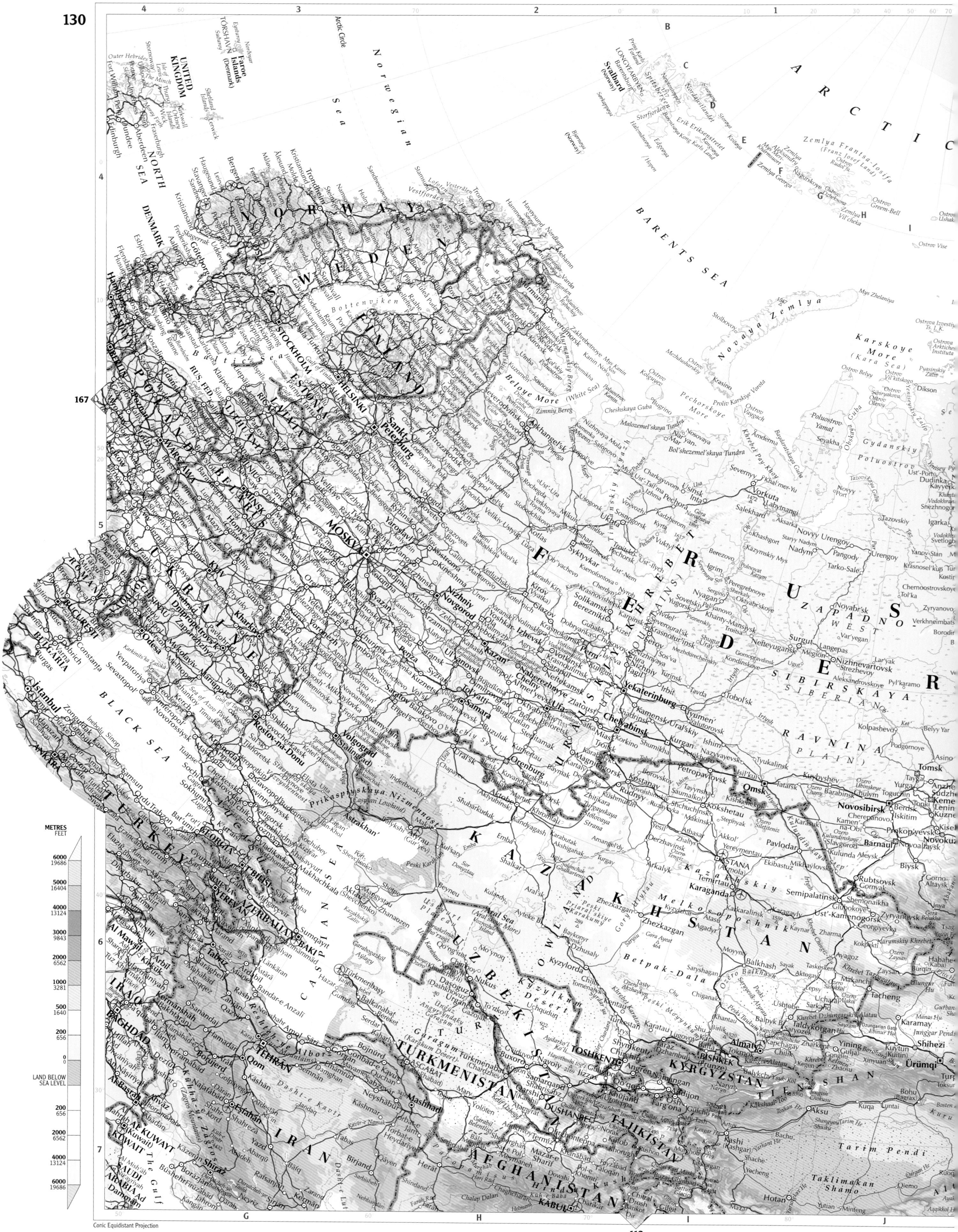
ARCTIC
BARENTS SEA
Norwegian Sea
NORTH SEA
NORWAY
SWEDEN
FINLAND
DENMARK
UNITED KINGDOM
Faroe Islands (Denmark)
Svalbard (Norway)
Zemlya Frantsa-Iosifa (Franz Josef Land)
Novaya Zemlya
Karskoye More (Kara Sea)
Beloye More (White Sea)
Pechorskoye More
ESTONIA
LATVIA
LITHUANIA
BELARUS
POLAND
UKRAINE
ROMANIA
BULGARIA
MOLDOVA
BLACK SEA
Sea of Azov
TURKEY
GEORGIA
ARMENIA
AZERBAIJAN
CASPIAN SEA
RUSSIAN FEDERATION
ZAPADNO-SIBIRSKAYA RAVNINA (WEST SIBERIAN PLAIN)
URAL MOUNTAINS
KAZAKHSTAN
UZBEKISTAN
TURKMENISTAN
KYRGYZSTAN
TAJIKISTAN
AFGHANISTAN
IRAN
IRAQ
KUWAIT
SAUDI ARABIA
The Gulf
Aral Sea
TIEN SHAN
Taklimakan Shamo
Tarim Pendi
Kazakhskiy Melkosopochnik
Betpak-Dala
Kyzylkum Desert
Garagum (Karakum Desert)
Prikaspiyskaya Nizmennost' (Caspian Lowland)
MOSKVA
Sankt-Peterburg
STOCKHOLM
HELSINKI
TALLINN
RIGA
VILNIUS
MINSK
WARSZAWA
KYIV
CHIȘINĂU
BUCUREȘTI
İstanbul
ANKARA
T'BILISI
YEREVAN
BAKI
TEHRĀN
BAGHDĀD
AL KUWAYT
ASTANA (Akmola)
TOSHKENT
BISHKEK
DUSHANBE
KĀBUL
ASGABAT
Almaty
Novosibirsk
Omsk
Yekaterinburg
Chelyabinsk
Volgograd
Samara
Kazan'
Nizhniy Novgorod
Perm'
Ufa
Rostov-na-Donu
Kharkiv
Odesa
Astrakhan'
Mashhad
Karaganda
Ürümqi
METRES
FEET
6000 19686
5000 16404
4000 13124
3000 9843
2000 6562
1000 3281
500 1640
200 656
0 0
LAND BELOW SEA LEVEL
200 656
2000 6562
4000 13124
6000 19686
Conic Equidistant Projection

167
112

RUSSIAN FEDERATION

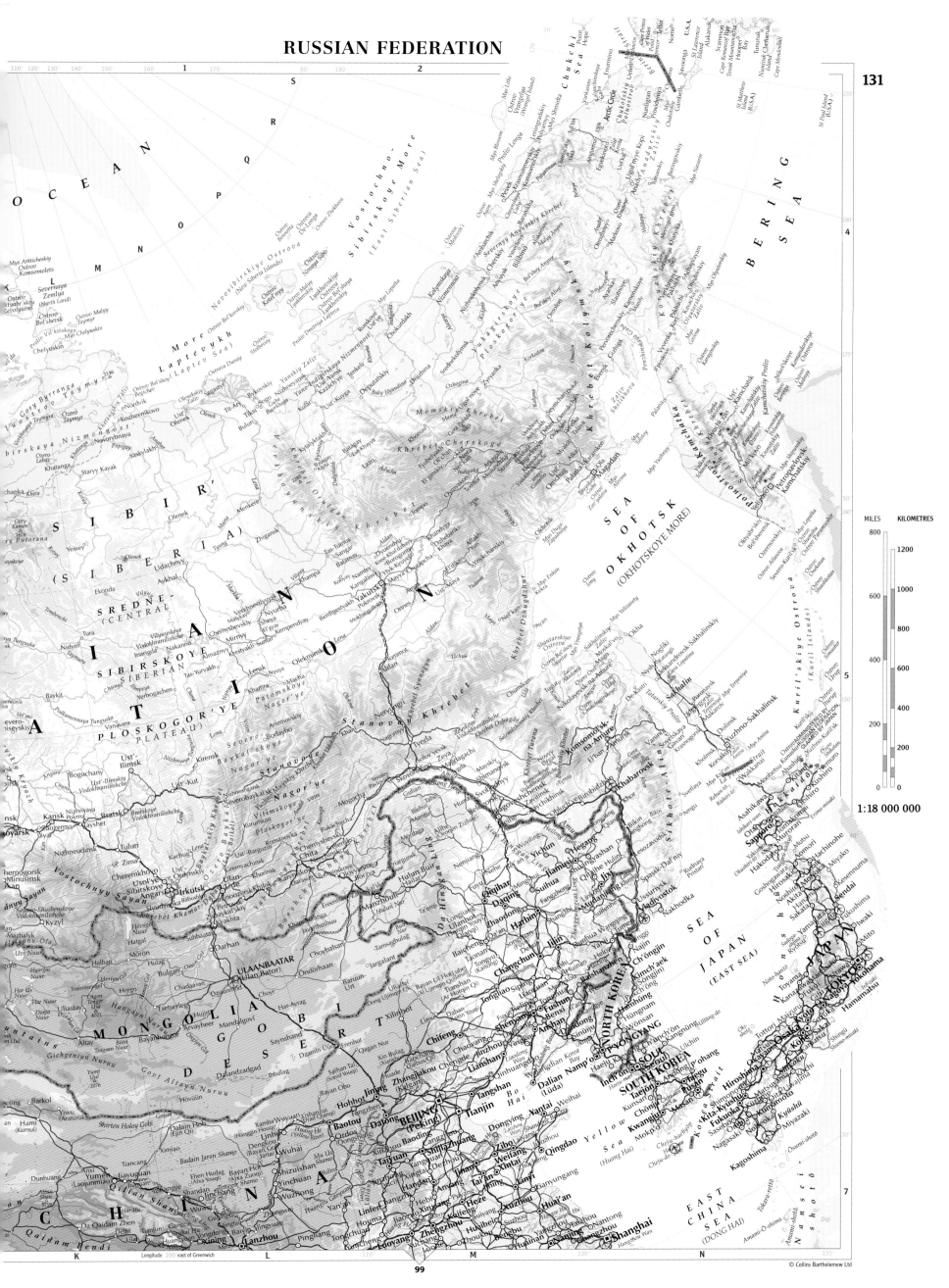

ARCTIC OCEAN
SIBIR' (SIBERIA)
SREDNE-SIBIRSKOYE PLOSKOGOR'YE
(CENTRAL SIBERIAN PLATEAU)
Vostochno-Sibirskoye More
(East Siberian Sea)
More Laptevykh
(Laptev Sea)
Novosibirskiye Ostrova
(New Siberian Islands)
Severnaya Zemlya
(North Land)
BERING SEA
SEA OF OKHOTSK
(OKHOTSKOYE MORE)
SEA OF JAPAN
(EAST SEA)
EAST CHINA SEA
(DONG HAI)
Yellow Sea
(Huang Hai)
Bo Hai
Chukchi Sea
Kamchatka
Sakhalin
Kuril'skiye Ostrova
(Kuril Islands)
Hokkaidō
Honshū
JAPAN
TŌKYŌ
NORTH KOREA
P'YŎNGYANG
SOUTH KOREA
SEOUL
MONGOLIA
ULAANBAATAR
(Ulan Bator)
GOBI DESERT
CHINA
BEIJING
(Peking)
Shanghai
Tianjin
Harbin
Vladivostok
Khabarovsk
Irkutsk
Yakutsk
Magadan
Petropavlovsk-Kamchatskiy
Yuzhno-Sakhalinsk
Chita
Sapporo
Lanzhou
Xining
Ozero Baykal
(Lake Baikal)
Khrebet Cherskogo
Verkhoyanskiy Khrebet
Stanovoy Khrebet
Arctic Circle
MILES
KILOMETRES
1:18 000 000
Longitude 100° east of Greenwich

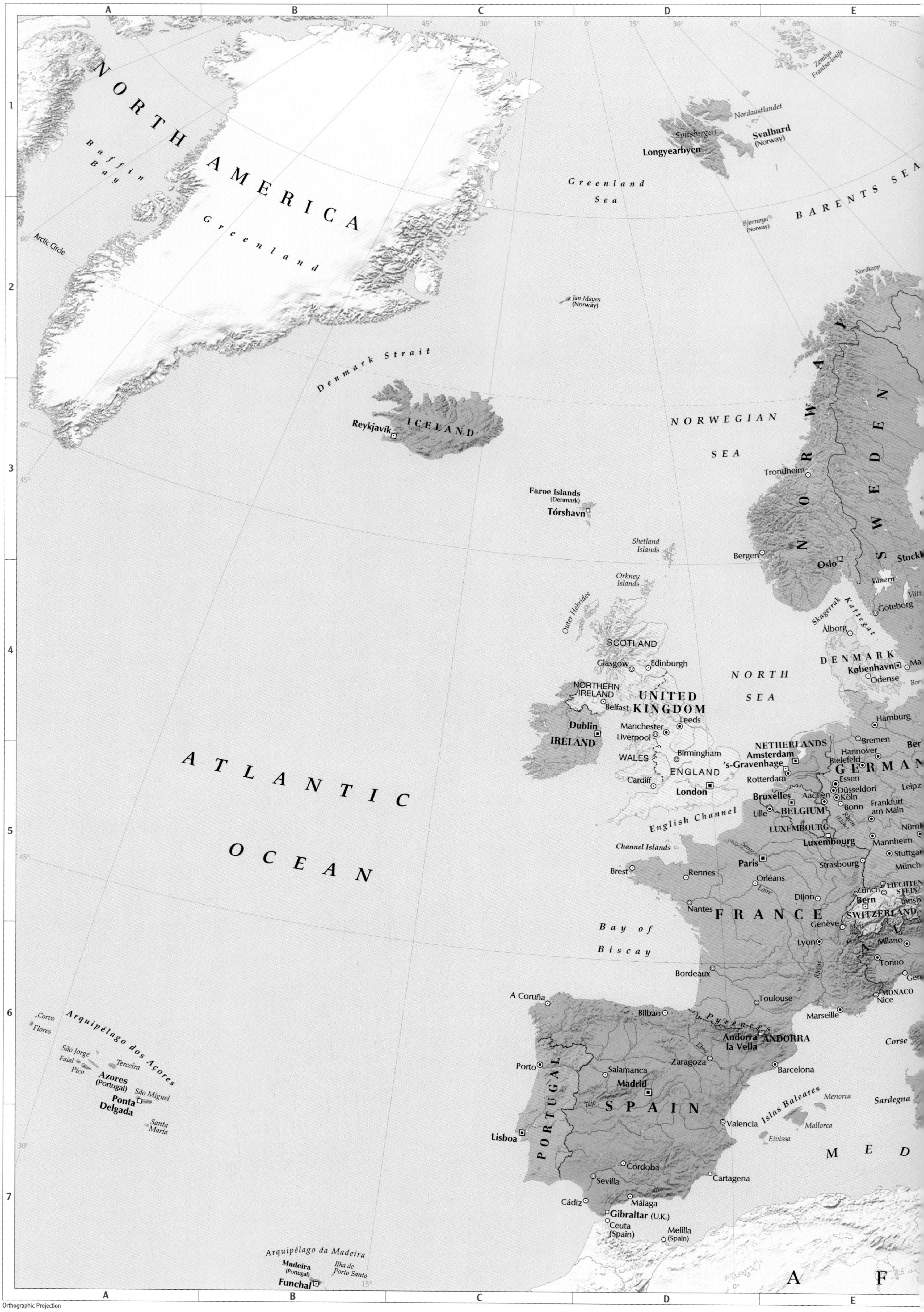

NORTH AMERICA

Baffin Bay

Greenland

Greenland Sea

Longyearbyen

Spitsbergen

Svalbard
(Norway)

Nordaustlandet

Zemlya Frantsa-Josifa

BARENTS SEA

Bjørnøya
(Norway)

Jan Mayen
(Norway)

Denmark Strait

ICELAND

Reykjavík

NORWEGIAN SEA

Nordkapp

Trondheim

N O R W A Y

Faroe Islands
(Denmark)

Tórshavn

Bergen

S W E D E N

Oslo □ Stockh

Shetland Islands

Vänern

Vätt

Göteborg

Orkney Islands

Skagerrak *Kattegat*

Ålborg

Outer Hebrides

DENMARK

København Ma

SCOTLAND

NORTH SEA

Odense Bor

Glasgow Edinburgh

Hamburg

NORTHERN
IRELAND

**UNITED
KINGDOM**

Belfast

Leeds

Bremen

Ber

Manchester

Hannover

Dublin

Liverpool

Bielefeld

GERMAN

IRELAND

Birmingham

Amsterdam

Essen

Leipz

WALES

ENGLAND

'**s-Gravenhage**

Düsseldorf

Cardiff

Rotterdam

Bruxelles Aachen □ **Köln**

London

Bonn

BELGIUM

Frankfurt
am Main

Nürn

English Channel

Lille

LUXEMBOURG

Mannheim

Channel Islands

Luxembourg

Stuttgart

Paris □

Strasbourg

Münch

Brest

Rennes

Orléans

Zürich LIECHTEN
STEIN

Dijon

Bern Inšb

ATLANTIC

Nantes F R A N C E

SWITZERLAND

OCEAN

Genève

Loire

Milano

Lyon

Torino

*Bay of
Biscay*

Bordeaux

MONACO
Nice

Rhône

Gen

Toulouse

Marseille

A Coruña

Bilbao

Pyrenees

Corse

Corvo

Flores

Arquipélago dos Açores

Porto

Zaragoza

Andorra ANDORRA
la Vella

Ebro

Barcelona

São Jorge

Faial *Terceira*

Pico

Azores
(Portugal)

São Miguel

Salamanca

P O R T U G A L

Madrid □

S P A I N

Islas Baleares

Menorca

Sardegna

**Ponta
Delgada**

*Santa
Maria*

Tejo

Valencia

Eivissa

Mallorca

Córdoba

Cartagena

M E D

Sevilla

Lisboa

Cádiz

Málaga

Gibraltar (U.K.)

Ceuta
(Spain)

Melilla
(Spain)

Arquipélago da Madeira

Madeira
(Portugal)

*Ilha de
Porto Santo*

Funchal □

A

F

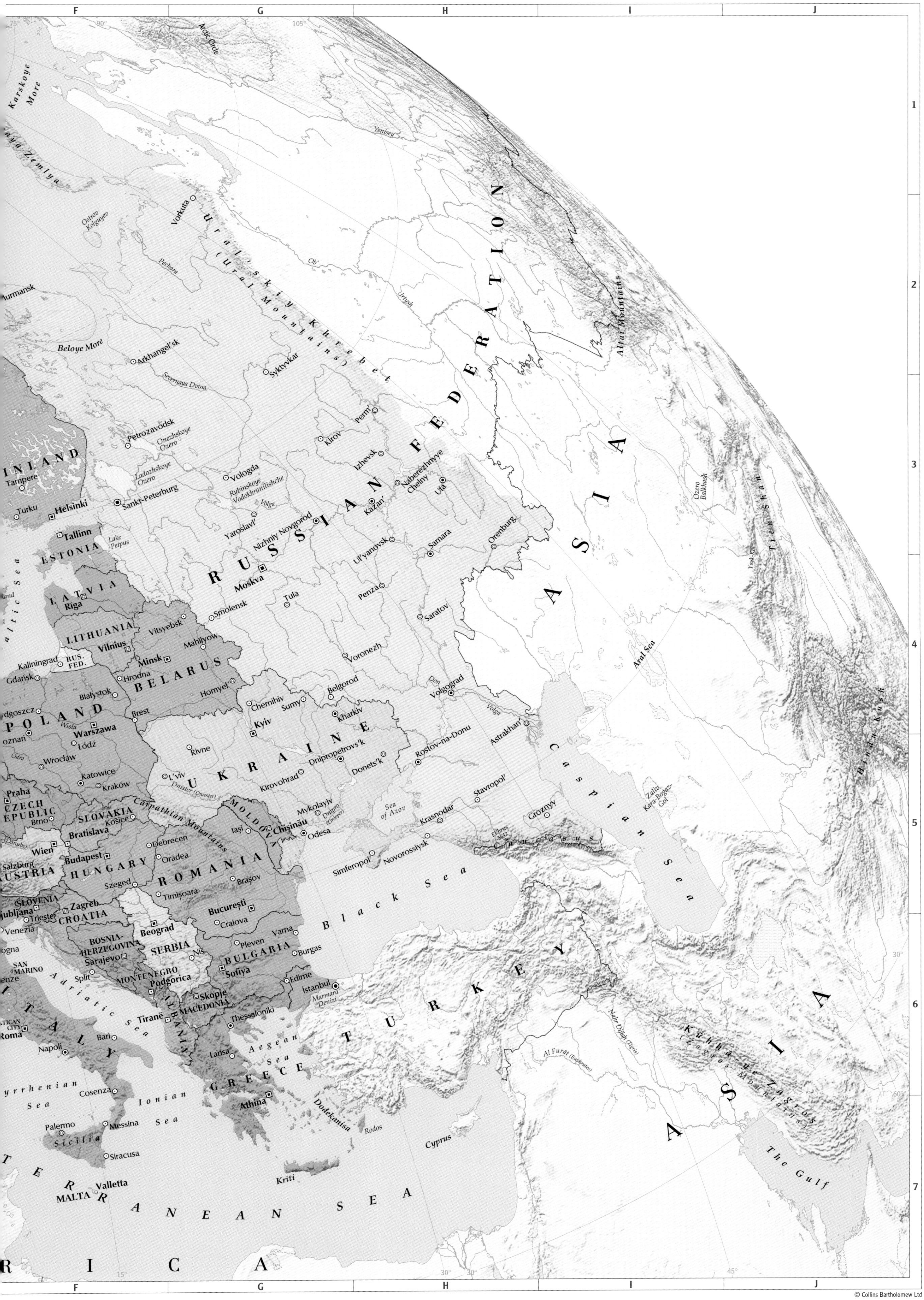

Karskoye More

Novaya Zemlya

Ostrov Kolguyev

Murmansk

Vorkuta

Arctic Circle

Ural'skiy Khrebet (Ural Mountains)

Ob'

Yenisey

Irtysh

Altai Mountains

Pechora

R U S S I A N   F E D E R A T I O N

A S I A

Beloye More

Arkhangel'sk

Severnaya Dvina

Syktyvkar

INLAND

Tampere

Turku

Helsinki

Petrozavodsk

Onezhskoye Ozero

Vologda

Perm'

Kirov

Izhevsk

Naberezhnyye Chelny

Ufa

Ladozhskoye Ozero

Rybinskoye Vodokhranilishche

Volga

Orenburg

Ozero Balkhash

Ysyk-Köl

Tien Shan

Tallinn

Sankt-Peterburg

Yaroslavl'

Nizhniy Novgorod

Kazan'

ESTONIA

Lake Peipus

Baltic Sea

LATVIA

Riga

Moskva

Ul'yanovsk

Samara

R U S S I A

LITHUANIA

Vilnius

Vitsyebsk

Smolensk

Tula

Penza

Saratov

Aral Sea

Caspian Sea

Kaliningrad RUS. FED.

Minsk

Hrodna

Mahilyow

Voronezh

Belgorod

Don

Volgograd

Astrakhan'

Hindu Kush

Gdańsk

BELARUS

Homyel'

Chernihiv

Sumy

Kharkiv

Volga

Białystok

Brest

Kyiv

Rostov-na-Donu

Stavropol'

Grozny

Zaliv Kara-Bogaz-Gol

Bydgoszcz

P O L A N D

Warszawa

Łódź

Rivne

U K R A I N E

Dnipropetrovs'k

Donets'k

Krasnodar

Caucasus

Caspian Sea

Poznań

Wrocław

Katowice

Kraków

L'viv

Dnister (Dniester)

Kirovohrad

Sea of Azov

Dnipro (Dnieper)

Novorossiysk

Elbrus

PRAHA

CZECH REPUBLIC

Brno

SLOVAKIA

Košice

Carpathian Mountains

MOLDOVA

Iaşi

Chişinău

Mykolayiv

Simferopol

Bratislava

Debrecen

Odesa

Black Sea

Wien

Budapest

Oradea

ROMANIA

Salzburg

AUSTRIA

HUNGARY

Szeged

Timişoara

Braşov

Danube

SLOVENIA

Zagreb

CROATIA

Bucureşti

Craiova

Ljubljana

Trieste

Venezia

Beograd

Pleven

Varna

ognia

SAN MARINO

BOSNIA-HERZEGOVINA

Sarajevo

SERBIA

Niš

BULGARIA

Burgas

Split

MONTENEGRO

Podgorica

Sofiya

Edirne

Firenze

Adriatic Sea

Skopje

MACEDONIA

Istanbul

Marmara Denizi

VATICAN CITY

Roma

I T A L Y

Tiranë

ALBANIA

Thessaloniki

T U R K E Y

Kühha-ye Zagros

Bari

Napoli

Larisa

Aegean Sea

A S I A

Cosenza

Tyrrhenian Sea

Ionian Sea

G R E E C E

Athina

Dodekanisa

Al Furāt (Euphrates)

Kühha-ye Zagros Mountains

Palermo

Messina

Sicilia

Siracusa

Rodos

Cyprus

The Gulf

Kriti

Nahr Dijlah (Tigris)

Valletta

MALTA

M E D I T E R R A N E A N   S E A

FRICA

RICA

© Collins Bartholomew Ltd

MILES

KILOMETRES

1:15 000 000

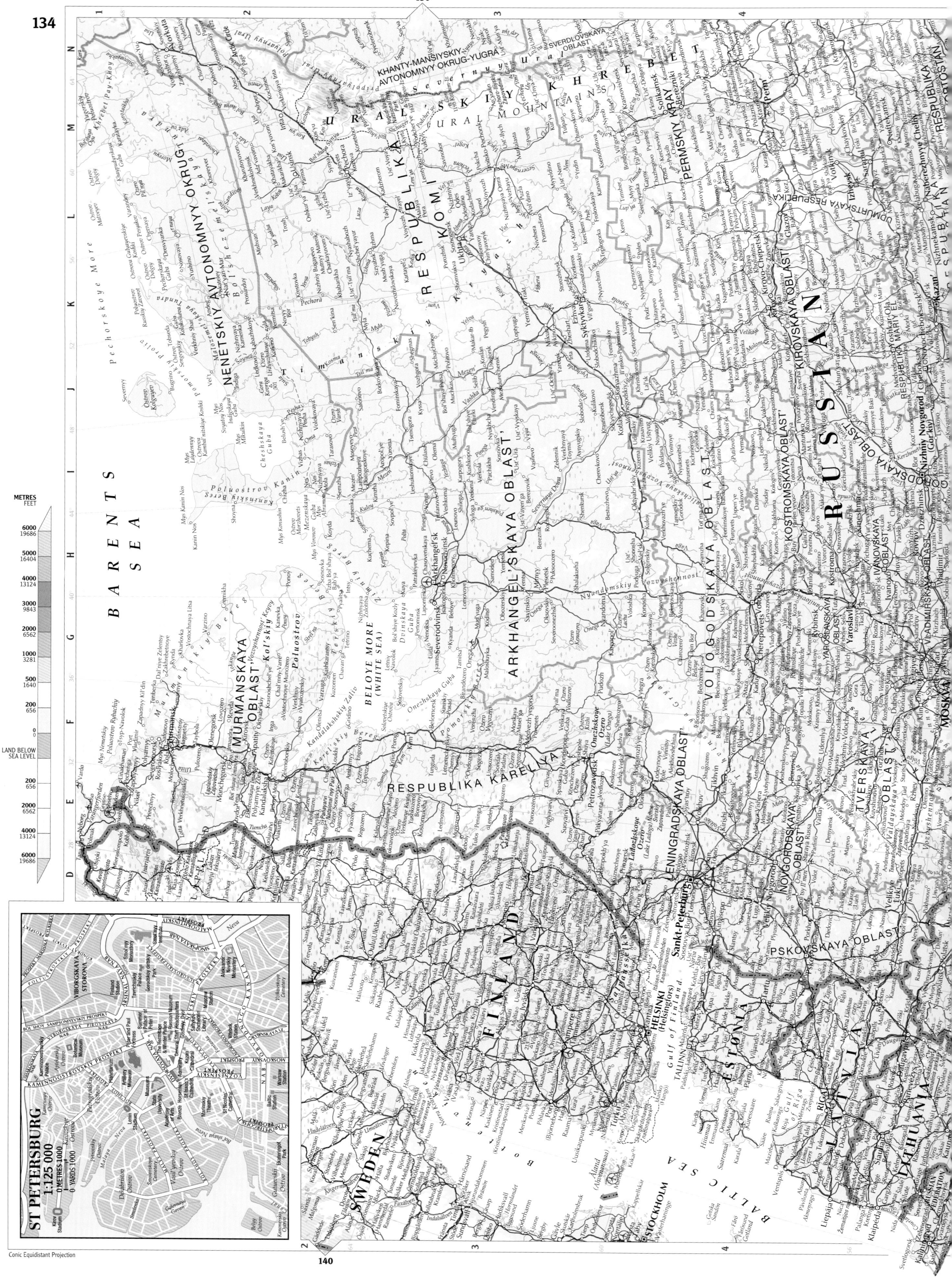

ST PETERSBURG
1:125 000

Conic Equidistant Projection

130
140
METRES
FEET
6000
19686
16404
4000
13124
3000
9843
2000
6562
1000
3281
1640
200
656
LAND BELOW
SEA LEVEL
200
656
2000
6562
4000
13124
6000
19686
BARENTS SEA
BELOYE MORE
(WHITE SEA)
NENETSKIY AVTONOMNYY OKRUG
RESPUBLIKA KOMI
ARKHANGEL'SKAYA OBLAST'
MURMANSKAYA OBLAST'
RESPUBLIKA KARELIYA
VOLOGODSKAYA OBLAST'
LENINGRADSKAYA OBLAST'
KOSTROMSKAYA OBLAST'
KIROVSKAYA OBLAST'
PERMSKIY KRAY
UDMURTSKAYA RESPUBLIKA
NOVGORODSKAYA OBLAST'
PSKOVSKAYA OBLAST'
TVERSKAYA OBLAST'
YAROSLAVSKAYA OBLAST'
IVANOVSKAYA OBLAST'
VLADIMIRSKAYA OBLAST'
KHANTY-MANSIYSKIY AVTONOMNYY OKRUG-YUGRA
SVERDLOVSKAYA OBLAST'
URAL MOUNTAINS
RUSSIA
FINLAND
SWEDEN
ESTONIA
LATVIA
LITHUANIA
Gulf of Finland
BALTIC SEA
Sankt-Peterburg
HELSINKI
TALLINN
STOCKHOLM
Arkhangel'sk
Murmansk
Petrozavodsk
Vologda
Yaroslavl'
Kostroma
Nizhniy Novgorod
Perm'
Kazan'
Riga
Tartu
MOSKVA
0 METRES 1000
0 YARDS 1000

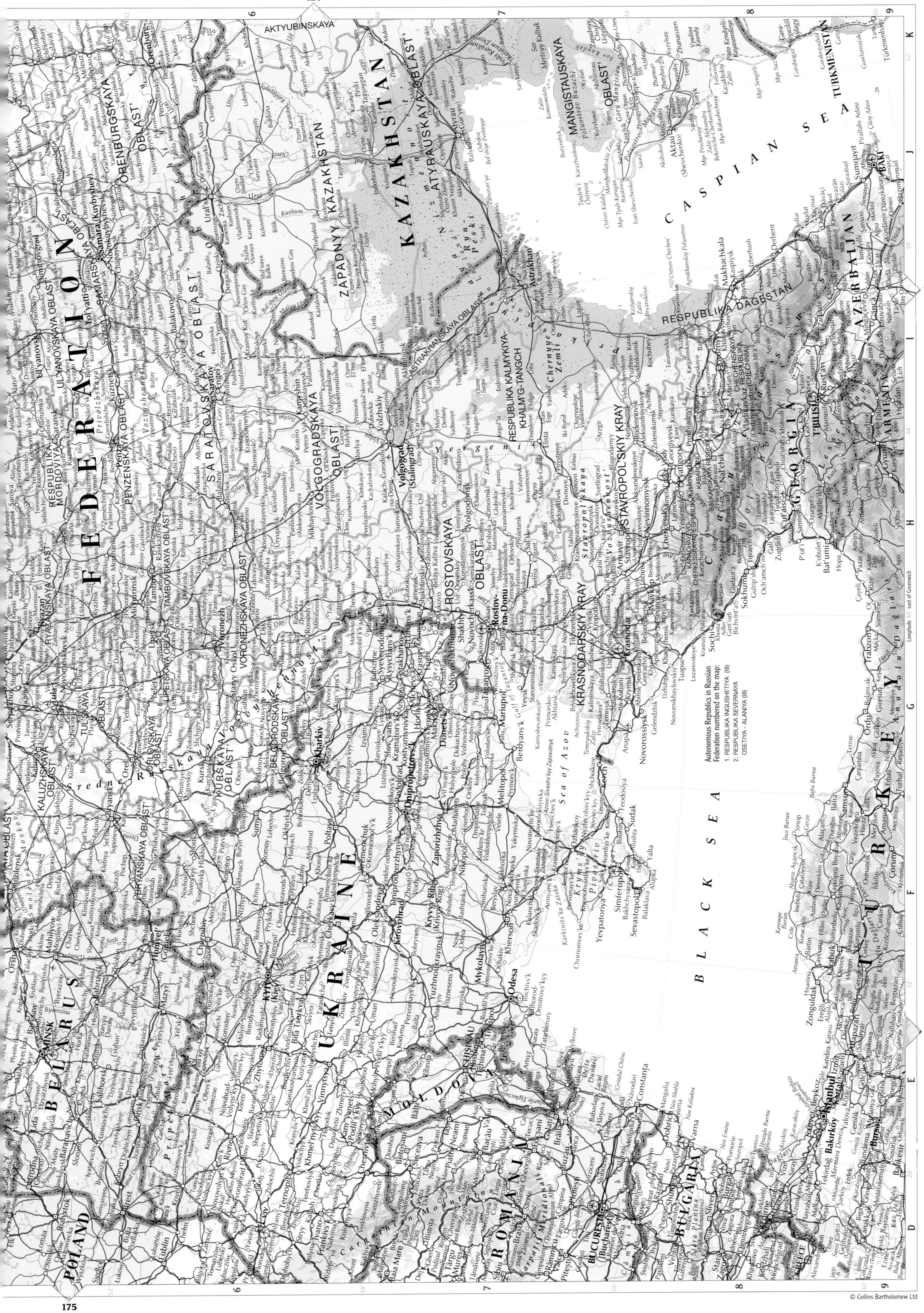

Autonomous Republics in Russian
Federation numbered on the map:
1. RESPUBLIKA INGUSHETIYA (8)
2. RESPUBLIKA SEVERNAYA
   OSETIYA - ALANIYA (8)

MILES   KILOMETRES

1:7 200 000

© Collins Bartholomew Ltd

138

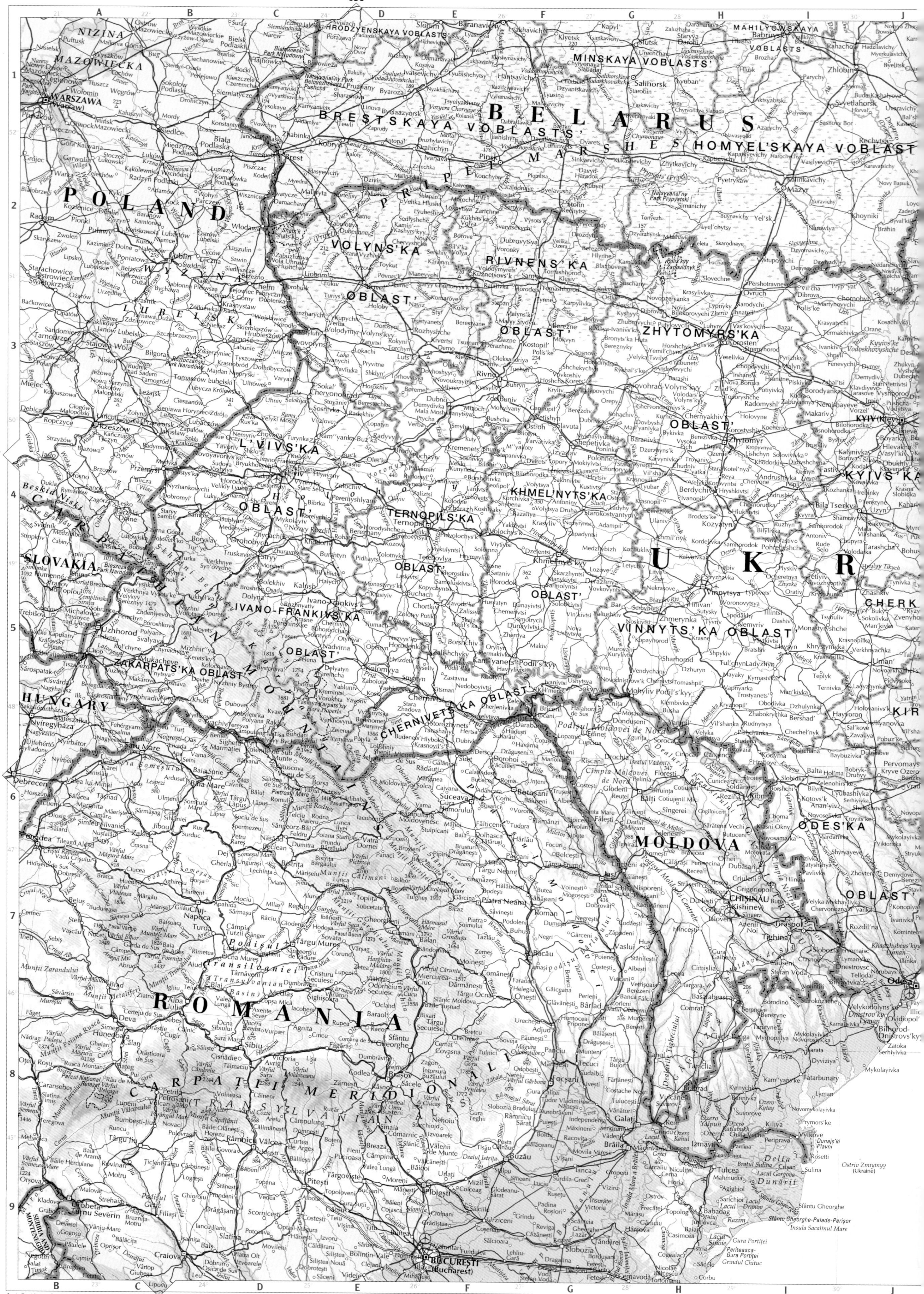
POLAND
BELARUS
UKR
SLOVAKIA
HUNGARY
ROMANIA
MOLDOVA
SERBIA AND MONTENEGRO
MAZOWIECKA
LUBELSKA
BRESTSKAYA VOBLASTS'
HRODZYENSKAYA VOBLASTS'
MINSKAYA VOBLASTS'
MAHILYOWSKAYA VOBLASTS'
HOMYEL'SKAYA VOBLAST
VOLYNS'KA OBLAST'
RIVNENS'KA OBLAST'
ZHYTOMYRS'KA OBLAST'
L'VIVS'KA OBLAST'
TERNOPILS'KA OBLAST'
KHMEL'NYTS'KA OBLAST'
IVANO-FRANKIVS'KA OBLAST'
ZAKARPATS'KA OBLAST
CHERNIVETS'KA OBLAST'
VINNYTS'KA OBLAST'
KYIVS'KA
CHERK
KIR
ODES'KA OBLAST'
PRIPET MARSHES
CARPATHIAN MOUNTAINS
CARPAȚII MERIDIONALI
TRANSYLVANIAN ALPS
Podișul Transilvaniei (Transylvanian Basin)
Warszawa (Warsaw)
Brest
Lublin
Rzeszów
L'viv
Rivne
Zhytomyr
Kyiv (Kiev)
Vinnytsya
Chernivtsi
Chișinău (Kishinev)
Iași
Cluj-Napoca
Brașov
Sibiu
Bucuresti (Bucharest)
Galați
Brăila
Ploiești
Craiova
Odesa
Ostriv Zmiyinyy (Ukraine)
Delta Dunării
Conic Equidistant Projection

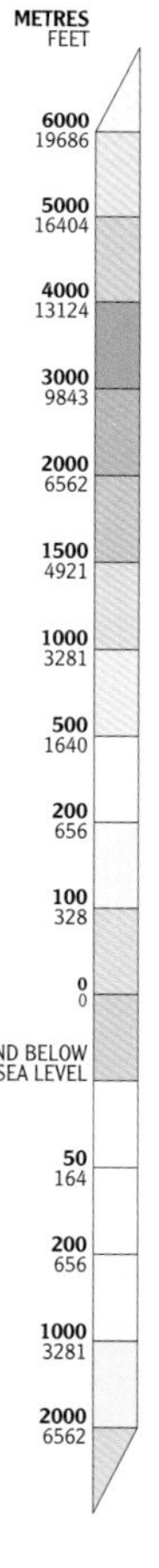
METRES
FEET
6000
19686
5000
16404
4000
13124
3000
9843
2000
6562
1500
4921
1000
3281
500
1640
200
656
100
328
0
0
LAND BELOW SEA LEVEL
50
164
200
656
1000
3281
2000
6562

197

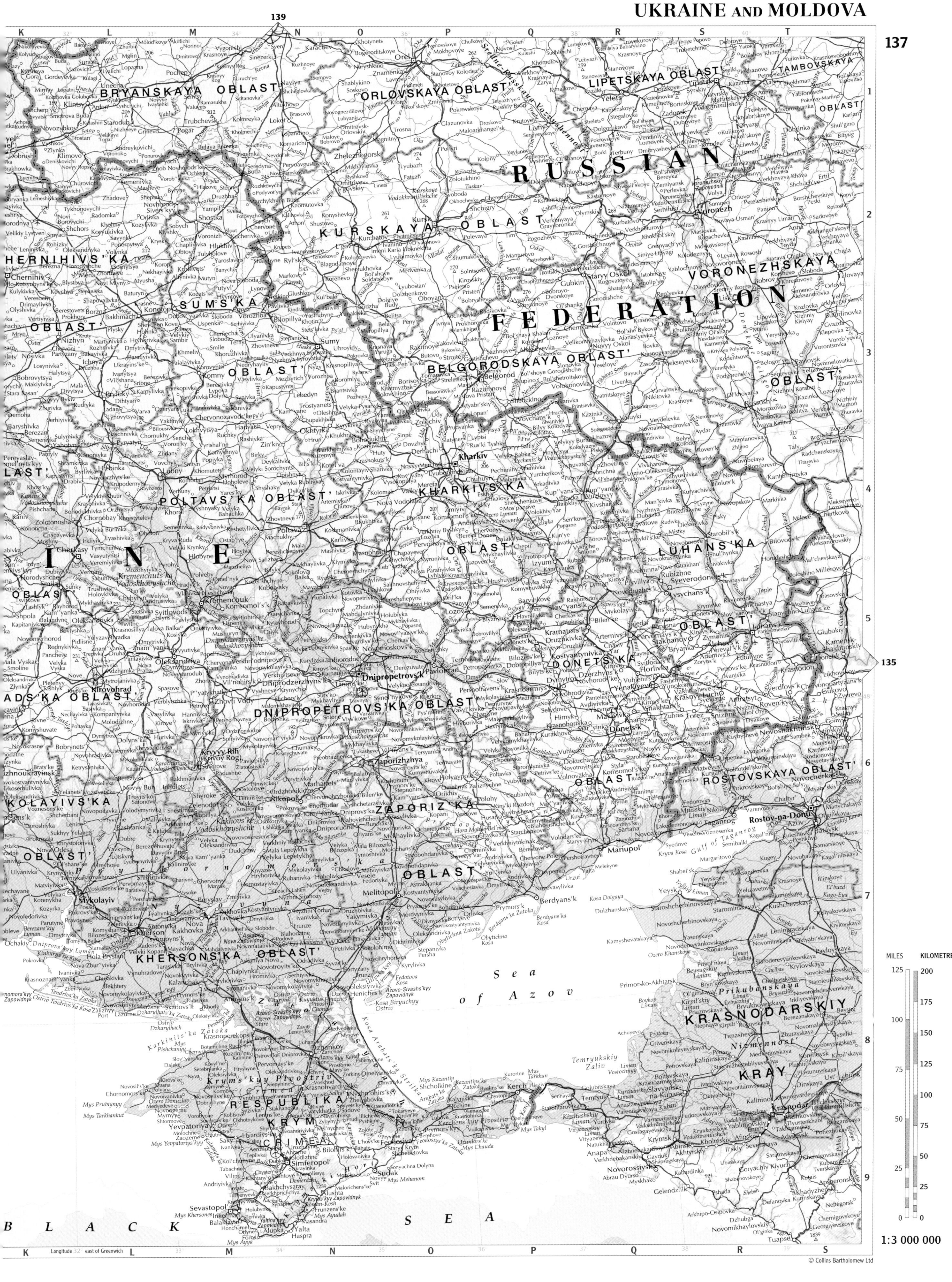

RUSSIAN

FEDERATION

BRYANSKAYA OBLAST
ORLOVSKAYA OBLAST'
LIPETSKAYA OBLAST
TAMBOVSKAYA OBLAST
KURSKAYA OBLAST
BELGORODSKAYA OBLAST'
VORONEZHSKAYA OBLAST'
ROSTOVSKAYA OBLAST'
KRASNODARSKIY KRAY

HERNIHIVS'KA OBLAST'
SUMS'KA OBLAST'
POLTAVS'KA OBLAST'
KHARKIVS'KA OBLAST'
LUHANS'KA OBLAST'
DONETS'KA OBLAST'
DNIPROPETROVS'KA OBLAST'
ZAPORIZ'KA OBLAST'
KHERSONS'KA OBLAST'
KOLAYIVS'KA OBLAST'
ADS'KA OBLAST'
KIROVOHRAD

RESPUBLIKA KRYM (CRIMEA)

U K R A I N E

Kharkiv
Sumy
Poltava
Dnipropetrovs'k
Dniprodzerzhyns'k
Zaporizhzhya
Kryvyy Rih
Krivoy Rog
Mykolayiv
Kherson
Kakhovka
Nova Kakhovka
Melitopol'
Berdyans'k
Mariupol'
Donets'k
Horlivka
Kremenchuk
Kirovohrad
Cherkasy
Chernihiv
Nizhyn
Konotop
Simferopol'
Sevastopol'
Yevpatoriya
Yalta
Alushta
Sudak
Bakhchysaray
Voronezh
Staryy Oskol
Belgorod
Kursk
Orel
Yelets
Rostov-na-Donu
Novocherkassk
Taganrog
Krasnodar
Novorossiysk
Anapa
Yeysk
Primorsko-Akhtarsk

Sea of Azov

Gulf of Taganrog

B L A C K   S E A

Temryukskiy Zaliv

Kerch

MILES   KILOMETRES
125 — 200
100 — 150
75 — 125
        100
50 — 75
25 — 50
        25
0 — 0

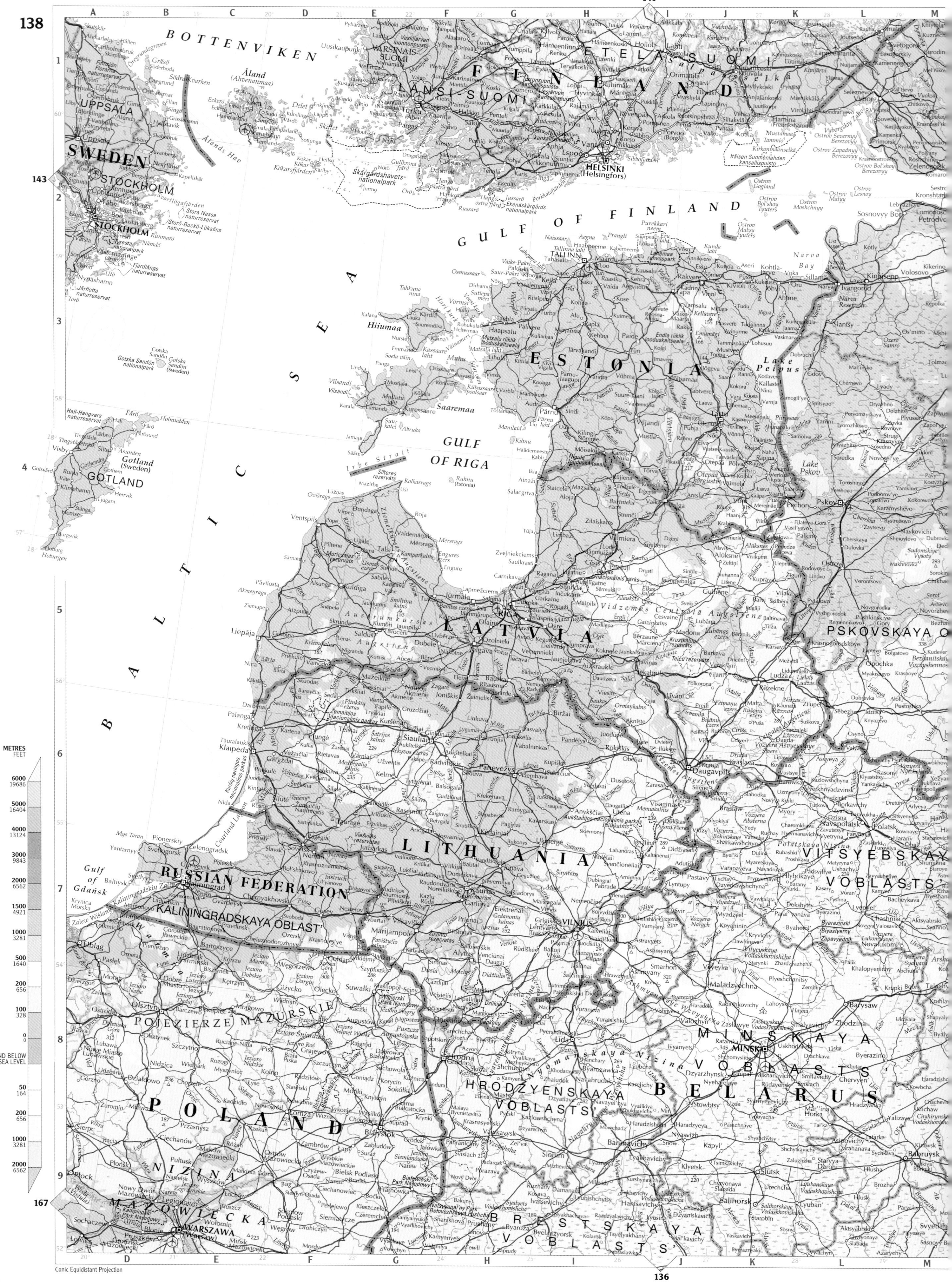

BOTTENVIKEN

SWEDEN

UPPSALA

STOCKHOLM

FINLAND

LÄNSI-SUOMI

VARSINAIS-SUOMI

ETELÄ-SUOMI

HELSINKI (Helsingfors)

GULF OF FINLAND

TALLINN

ESTONIA

Hiiumaa

Saaremaa

Lake Peipus

Lake Pskov

GULF OF RIGA

GOTLAND

Gotland (Sweden)

BALTIC SEA

RIGA

LATVIA

PSKOVSKAYA O

Vidzemes Centrālā Augstiene

LITHUANIA

VILNIUS

RUSSIAN FEDERATION

KALININGRADSKAYA OBLAST'

Gulf of Gdańsk

VITSYEBSKAYA VOBLASTS'

MINSKAYA VOBLASTS'

MINSK

BELARUS

HRODZYENSKAYA VOBLASTS'

POJEZIERZE MAZURSKIE

POLAND

NIZINA MAZOWIECKA

WARSZAWA (Warsaw)

BRESTSKAYA VOBLASTS'

METRES	FEET
6000	19686
5000	16404
4000	13124
3000	9843
2000	6562
1500	4921
1000	3281
500	1640
200	656
100	328
0	0

LAND BELOW SEA LEVEL

50	164
200	656
1000	3281
2000	6562

Conic Equidistant Projection

LADOZHSKOYE OZERO (LAKE LADOGA)

LENINGRADSKAYA OBLAST'

VOLOGODSKAYA OBLAST'

Ozero Beloye

NOVGORODSKAYA OBLAST'

Ozero Il'men'

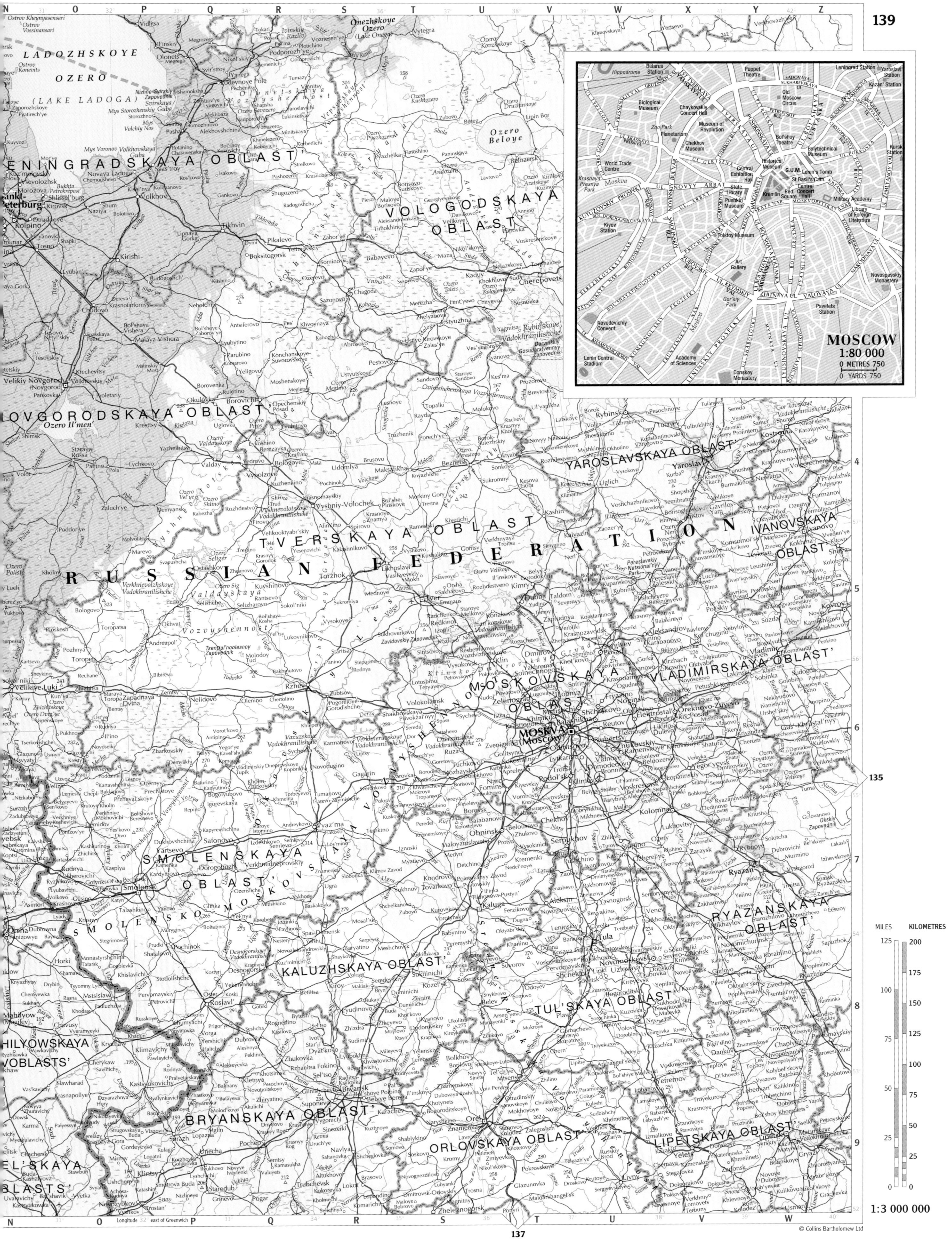

RUSSIAN FEDERATION

TVERSKAYA OBLAST'

Valdayskaya Vozvyshennost'

YAROSLAVSKAYA OBLAST'

Yaroslavl'

IVANOVSKAYA OBLAST'

MOSKOVSKAYA OBLAST'

MOSKVA Moscow

VLADIMIRSKAYA OBLAST'

SMOLENSKAYA OBLAST'

Smolensk

Smolensko-Moskovskaya Vozvyshennost'

KALUZHSKAYA OBLAST'

Kaluga

TUL'SKAYA OBLAST'

Tula

RYAZANSKAYA OBLAST'

Ryazan'

BRYANSKAYA OBLAST'

Bryansk

ORLOVSKAYA OBLAST'

Orel

LIPETSKAYA OBLAST'

Moscow inset

MOSCOW
1:80 000

0 METRES 750
0 YARDS 750

Hippodrome · Belorus Station · Puppet Theatre · Leningrad Station · Yaroslavl' Station · Kazan' Station

Biological Museum · Chaykovskiy Concert Hall · Museum of Revolution · Chekhov Museum · Old Moscow Circus · Kursk Station

World Trade Centre · Zoo Park · Planetarium · Bol'shoy Theatre · Historical Museum · Pushkin Museum · G.U.M. Lenin's Tomb · Polytechnical Museum

Krasnaya Presnya Park · Central Library · Red Square · Central Concert Hall · Military Academy · Library of Foreign Literature

Kiyev Station · Kremlin · St Basil's Cath. · Tolstoy Museum · Art Gallery · Gor'ky Park · Pavelets Station · Novospasskiy Monastery

Novodevichiy Convent · Academy of Sciences · Donskoy Monastery

Lenin Central Stadium

Scale

MILES / KILOMETRES

125 / 200
100 / 175
75 / 150
50 / 125
25 / 100

1:3 000 000

Longitude 32 east of Greenwich

© Collins Bartholomew Ltd

138

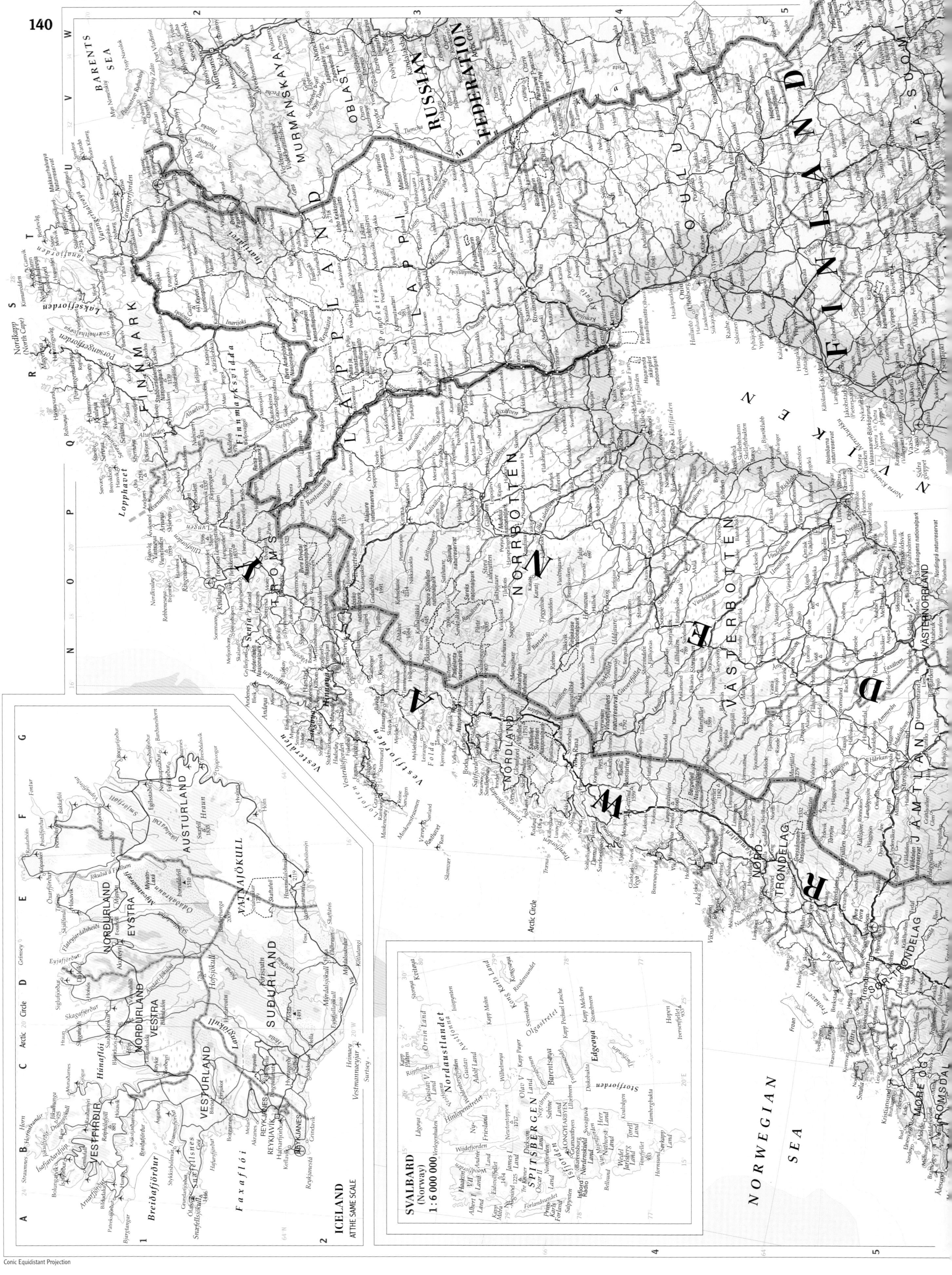
BARENTS SEA
RUSSIAN FEDERATION
MURMANSKAYA OBLAST
FINLAND
SUOMI
OULU
LAPPI
LAPLAND
FINNMARK
TROMS
NORRBOTTEN
VÄSTERBOTTEN
VÄSTERNORRLAND
JÄMTLAND
NORDLAND
NORD-TRØNDELAG
SØR-TRØNDELAG
MØRE OG ROMSDAL
NORWEGIAN SEA
Arctic Circle
ICELAND
AT THE SAME SCALE
VESTFIRÐIR
VESTURLAND
NORÐURLAND VESTRA
NORÐURLAND EYSTRA
AUSTURLAND
SUÐURLAND
REYKJANES
REYKJAVÍK
VATNAJÖKULL
Faxaflói
Breiðafjörður
SVALBARD
(Norway)
1:6 000 000
Nordaustlandet
SPITSBERGEN
Barentsøya
Edgeøya
LONGYEARBYEN

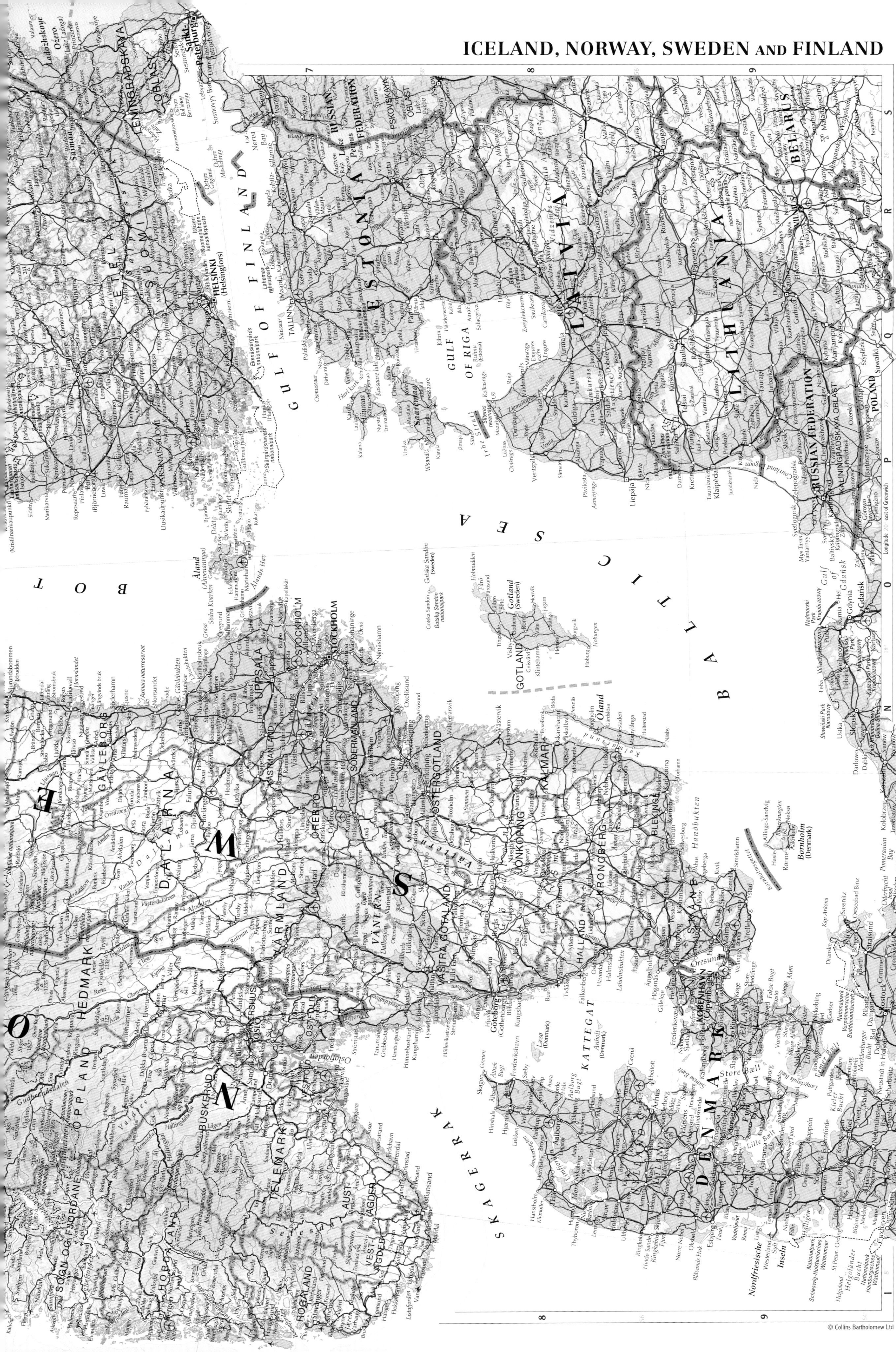

METRES
FEET
LAND BELOW SEA LEVEL
MILES
KILOMETRES
1:4 000 000
167
BALTIC SEA
GULF OF FINLAND
GULF OF RIGA
SKAGERRAK
KATTEGAT
ESTONIA
LATVIA
LITHUANIA
BELARUS
RUSSIAN FEDERATION
POLAND
GERMANY
DENMARK

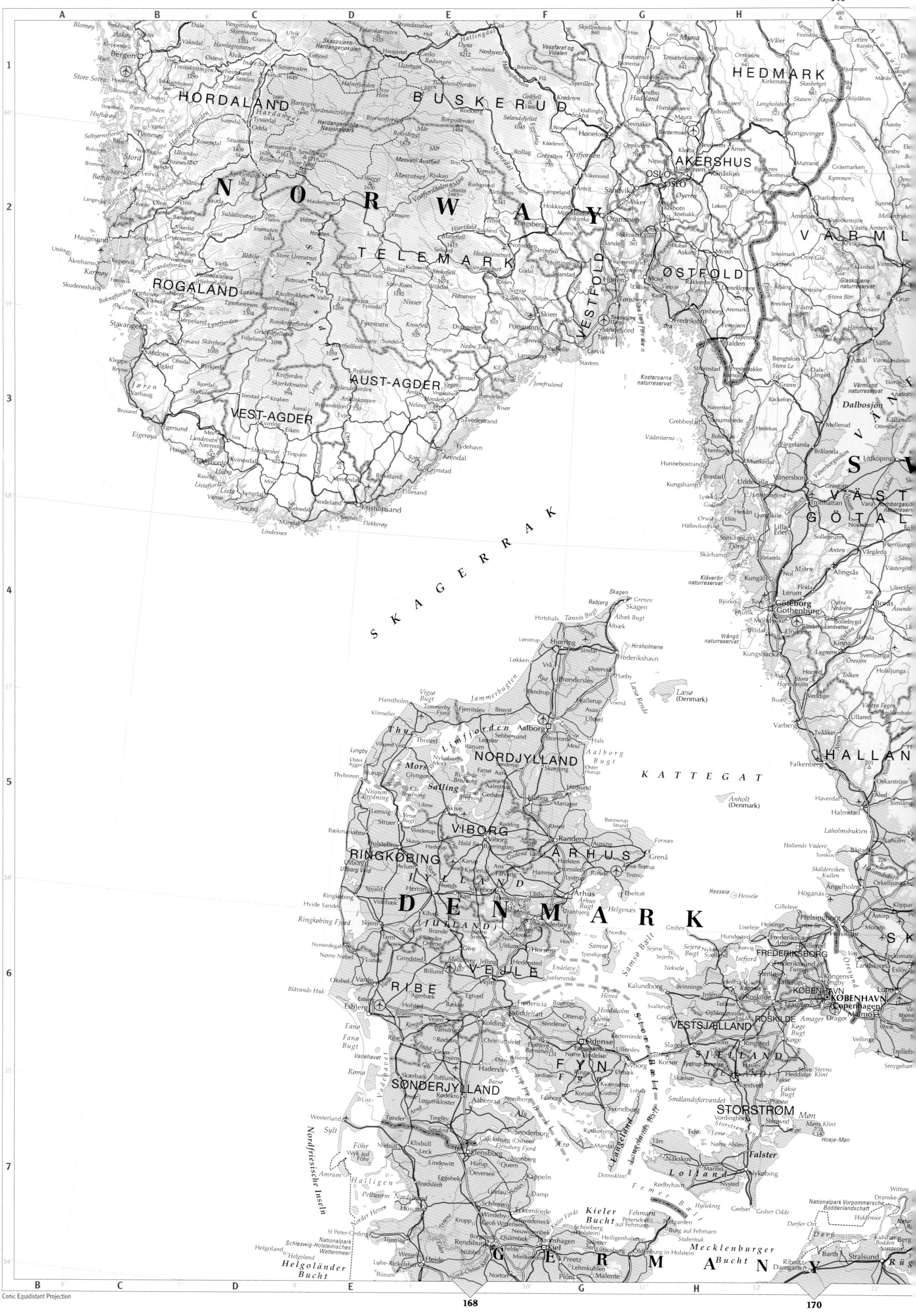

HORDALAND

BUSKERUD

HEDMARK

Bergen

AKERSHUS
OSLO
Oslo

N O R W A Y

TELEMARK

VESTFOLD

ØSTFOLD

VARML

ROGALAND

Stavanger

AUST-AGDER

VEST-AGDER

Kristiansand

S K A G E R R A K

Skagen

HALLAN

Frederikshavn

K A T T E G A T

Läsö
(Denmark)

Thy

Aalborg

NORDJYLLAND

Aalborg
Bugt

Mors

Anholt
(Denmark)

Salling

VIBORG

ÅRHUS

Randers

Hessela

RINGKØBING

Århus

Halmstad

Viborg

Ringkøbing Fjord

D E N M A R K

(JYLLAND)

VEJLE

RIBE

FYN

Esbjerg

Kolding

Odense

VESTSJÆLLAND

KØBENHAVN
Copenhagen

ROSKILDE

SJÆLLAND

SØNDERJYLLAND

STORSTRØM

Møn

Falster

Lolland

G E R M A N Y

Conic Equidistant Projection

METRES / FEET

6000 / 19686
5000 / 16404
4000 / 13124
3000 / 9843
2000 / 6562
1500 / 4921
1000 / 3281
500 / 1640
200 / 656
100 / 328
0 / 0

LAND BELOW SEA LEVEL

50 / 164
200 / 656
1000 / 3281
2000 / 6562

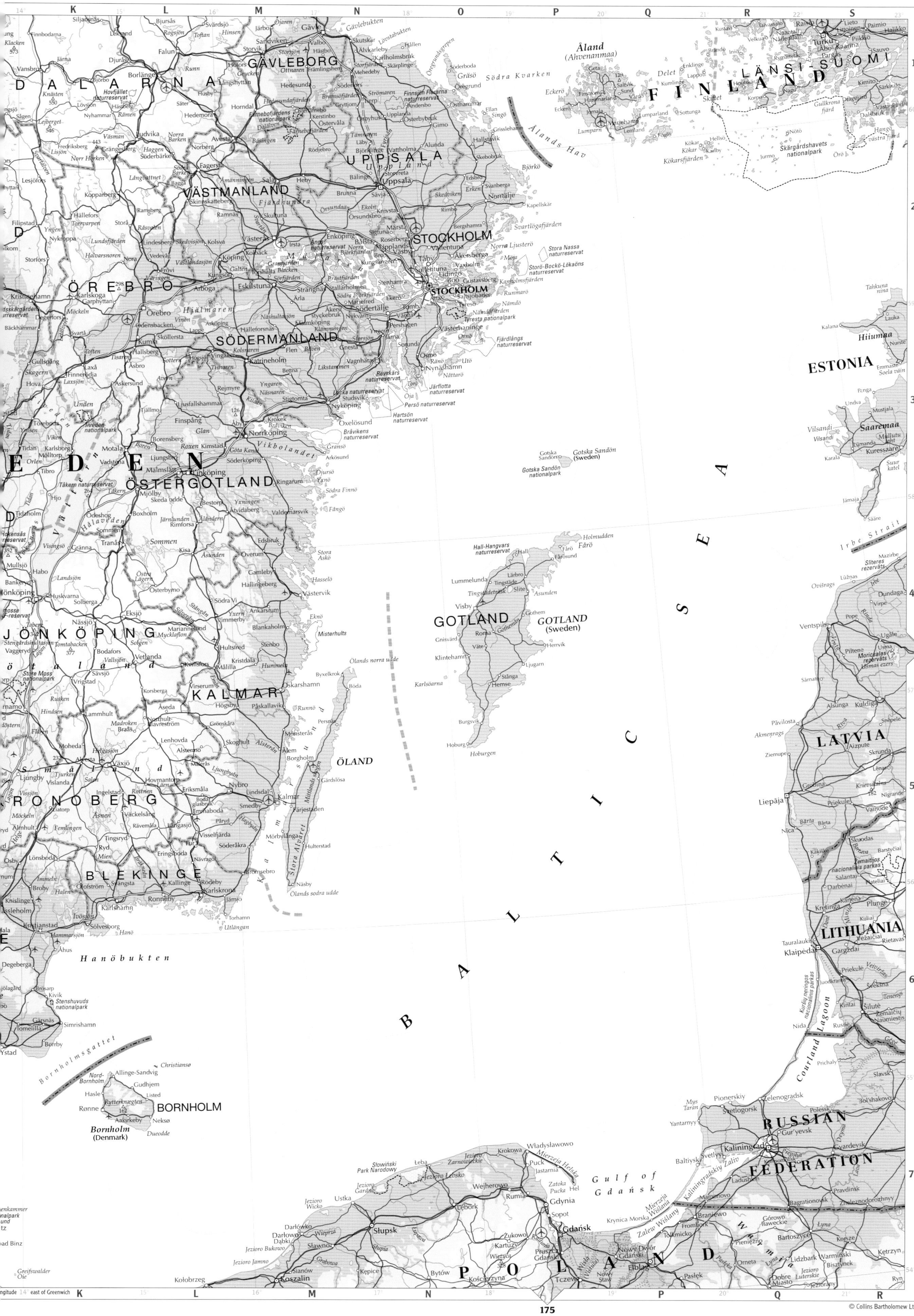

138

1:2 250 000

© Collins Bartholomew Ltd

K L M N O P Q R S
1 2 3 4 5 6 7
DALARNA
GÄVLEBORG
UPPSALA
VÄSTMANLAND
STOCKHOLM
ÖREBRO
SÖDERMANLAND
ÖSTERGOTLAND
JÖNKÖPING
KALMAR
KRONOBERG
BLEKINGE
SWEDEN
FINLAND
LÄNSI-SUOMI
Åland (Ahvenanmaa)
Ålands Hav
Södra Kvarken
ESTONIA
Hiiumaa
Saaremaa
Irbe Strait
LATVIA
LITHUANIA
RUSSIAN FEDERATION
POLAND
BALTIC SEA
GOTLAND
GOTLAND (Sweden)
Gotska Sandön (Sweden)
ÖLAND
BORNHOLM
Bornholm (Denmark)
Hanöbukten
Bornholmsgattet
Gulf of Gdańsk
Courland Lagoon
Stockholm
Uppsala
Gävle
Västerås
Örebro
Norrköping
Linköping
Jönköping
Kalmar
Karlskrona
Visby
Turku
Ventspils
Liepāja
Klaipėda
Kaliningrad
Gdańsk
Gdynia
Słupsk
Koszalin
Elbląg
MILES KILOMETRES

144

NORWAY

SOGN OG FJORDANE

HORDALAND

ROGALAND

Bergen

N O R T H   S E A

SHETLAND ISLANDS

Herma Ness
Unst
Haroldswick
Baltasound
Fetlar
Yell
Hillswick
Out Skerries
Whalsay
Isle of Noss
St Magnus Bay
Walls
Scalloway
Burra
Papa Stour
Bressay
Mousa
Sumburgh Head
Yell Sound

Fair Isle

Foula

ORKNEY ISLANDS

Papa
Westray
North Ronaldsay
Sanday
Eday
Rousay
The North Sound
Stronsay
Westray Firth
Shapinsay
Stromness
Kirkwall
Birsay
Hoy
St Margaret's Hope
South Ronaldsay
Longhope
Burray
Brough Ness
Ward Hill
Dunnet Head
Pentland Firth
Duncansby Head
John o'Groats

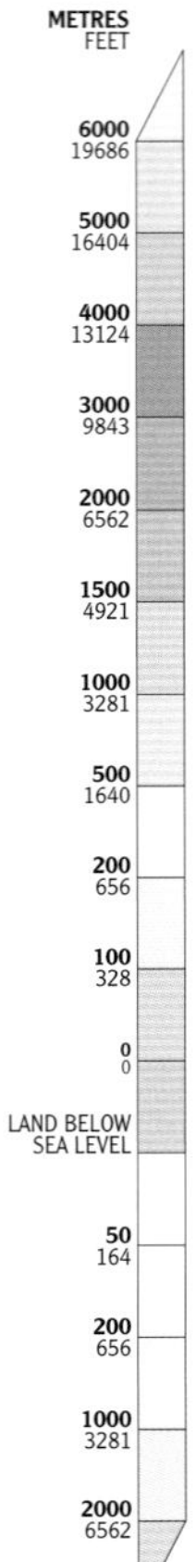

METRES / FEET

6000	19686
5000	16404
4000	13124
3000	9843
2000	6562
1500	4921
1000	3281
500	1640
200	656
100	328
0	0

LAND BELOW SEA LEVEL

50	164
200	656
1000	3281
2000	6562

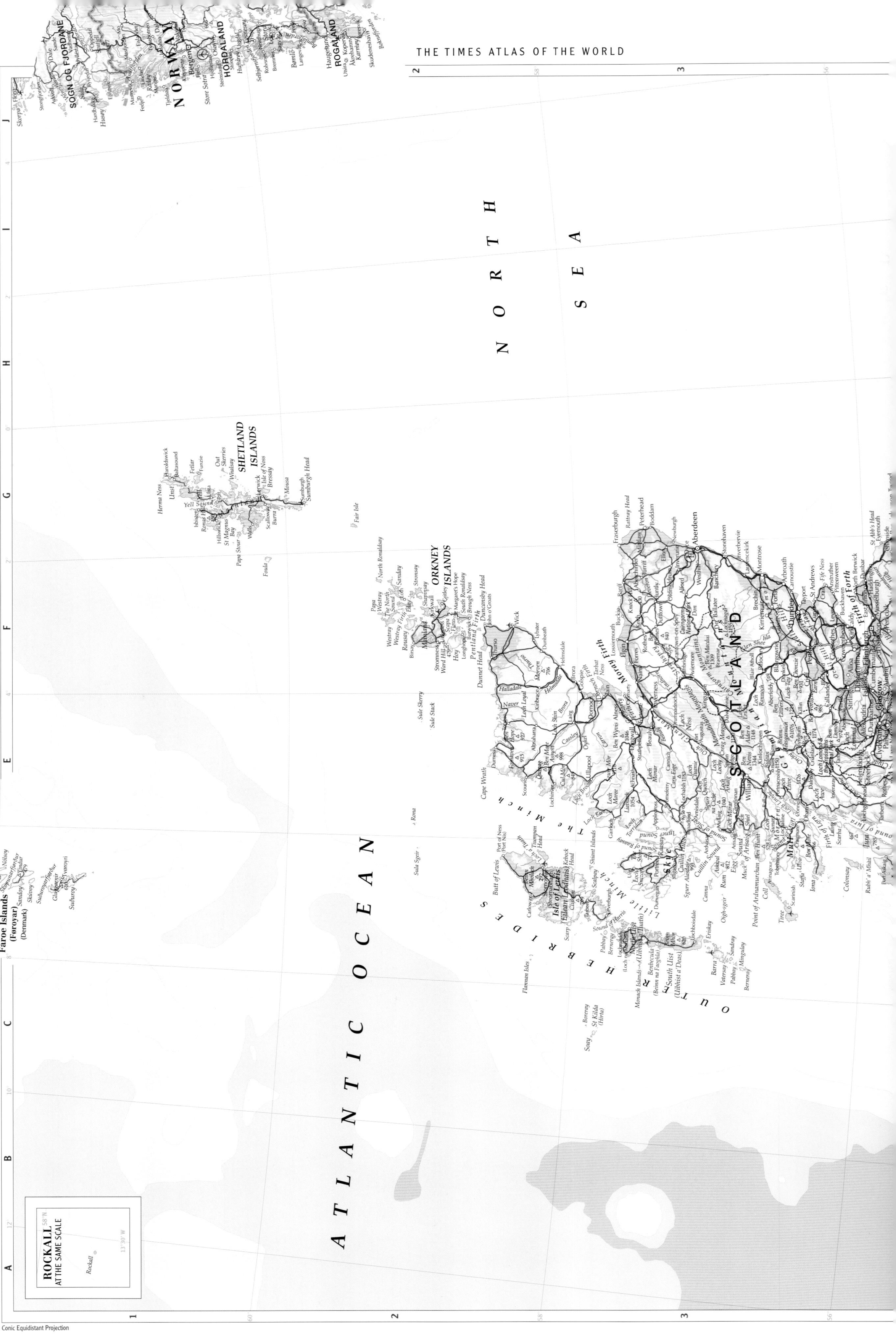

Faroe Islands
(Føroyar)
(Denmark)

TÓRSHAVN

A T L A N T I C   O C E A N

SCOTLAND

Fraserburgh
Rattray Head
Peterhead
Aberdeen
Stonehaven
Elgin
Inverness
Moray Firth
Montrose
Arbroath
St Andrews
Firth of Forth

Cape Wrath

The Minch

Butt of Lewis
Port of Ness

Isle of Lewis
Stornoway

O U T E R   H E B R I D E S

Skye

Little Minch

North Uist
Benbecula
South Uist
Barra

St Kilda
(Hirta)

Rockall

Conic Equidistant Projection

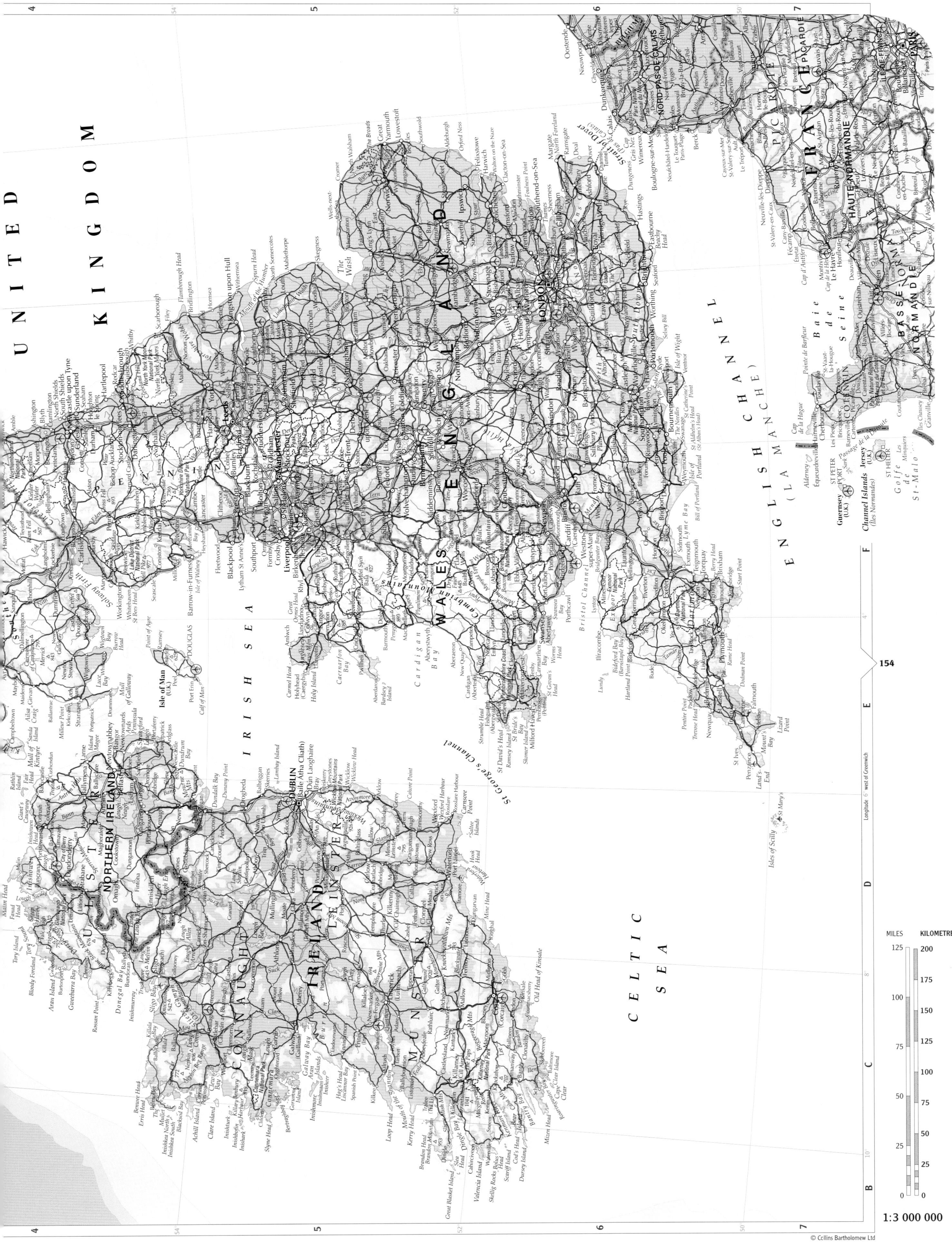

154

MILES   KILOMETRES

1:3 000 000

© Collins Bartholomew Ltd

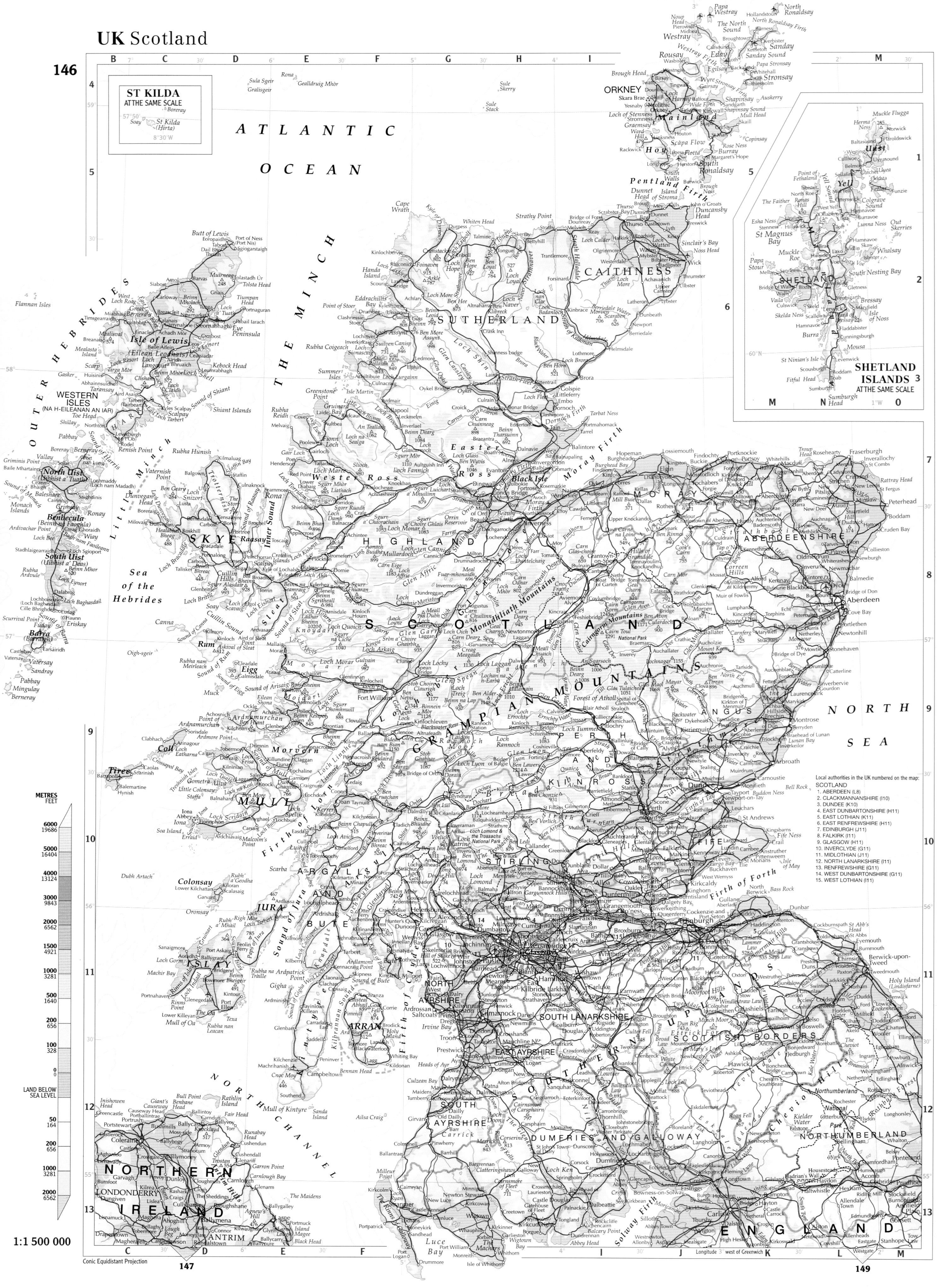
ST KILDA
AT THE SAME SCALE
ATLANTIC OCEAN
OUTER HEBRIDES
THE MINCH
WESTERN ISLES
(NA H-EILEANAN AN IAR)
Isle of Lewis
(Eilean Leodhais)
Sea of the Hebrides
SKYE
ORKNEY
Mainland
Hoy
Pentland Firth
CAITHNESS
SUTHERLAND
HIGHLAND
Wester Ross
Easter Ross
Moray Firth
Black Isle
MORAY
ABERDEENSHIRE
Aberdeen
SCOTLAND
GRAMPIAN MOUNTAINS
Cairngorm Mountains
Monadhliath Mountains
PERTH AND KINROSS
ANGUS
Dundee
NORTH SEA
Firth of Forth
FIFE
STIRLING
Edinburgh
Glasgow
ARGYLL AND BUTE
MULL
JURA
ISLAY
ARRAN
NORTH AYRSHIRE
EAST AYRSHIRE
SOUTH AYRSHIRE
SOUTH LANARKSHIRE
SCOTTISH BORDERS
SOUTHERN UPLANDS
DUMFRIES AND GALLOWAY
NORTHUMBERLAND
ENGLAND
Solway Firth
NORTH CHANNEL
NORTHERN IRELAND
SHETLAND ISLANDS
AT THE SAME SCALE
SHETLAND
Local authorities in the UK numbered on the map:
SCOTLAND
1. ABERDEEN (L8)
2. CLACKMANNANSHIRE (I10)
3. DUNDEE (K10)
4. EAST DUNBARTONSHIRE (H11)
5. EAST LOTHIAN (K11)
6. EAST RENFREWSHIRE (H11)
7. EDINBURGH (J11)
8. FALKIRK (I11)
9. GLASGOW (H11)
10. INVERCLYDE (G11)
11. MIDLOTHIAN (J11)
12. NORTH LANARKSHIRE (I11)
13. RENFREWSHIRE (G11)
14. WEST DUNBARTONSHIRE (G11)
15. WEST LOTHIAN (I11)
METRES
FEET
LAND BELOW SEA LEVEL
Conic Equidistant Projection
Longitude 3° west of Greenwich
147
149

1:1 500 000

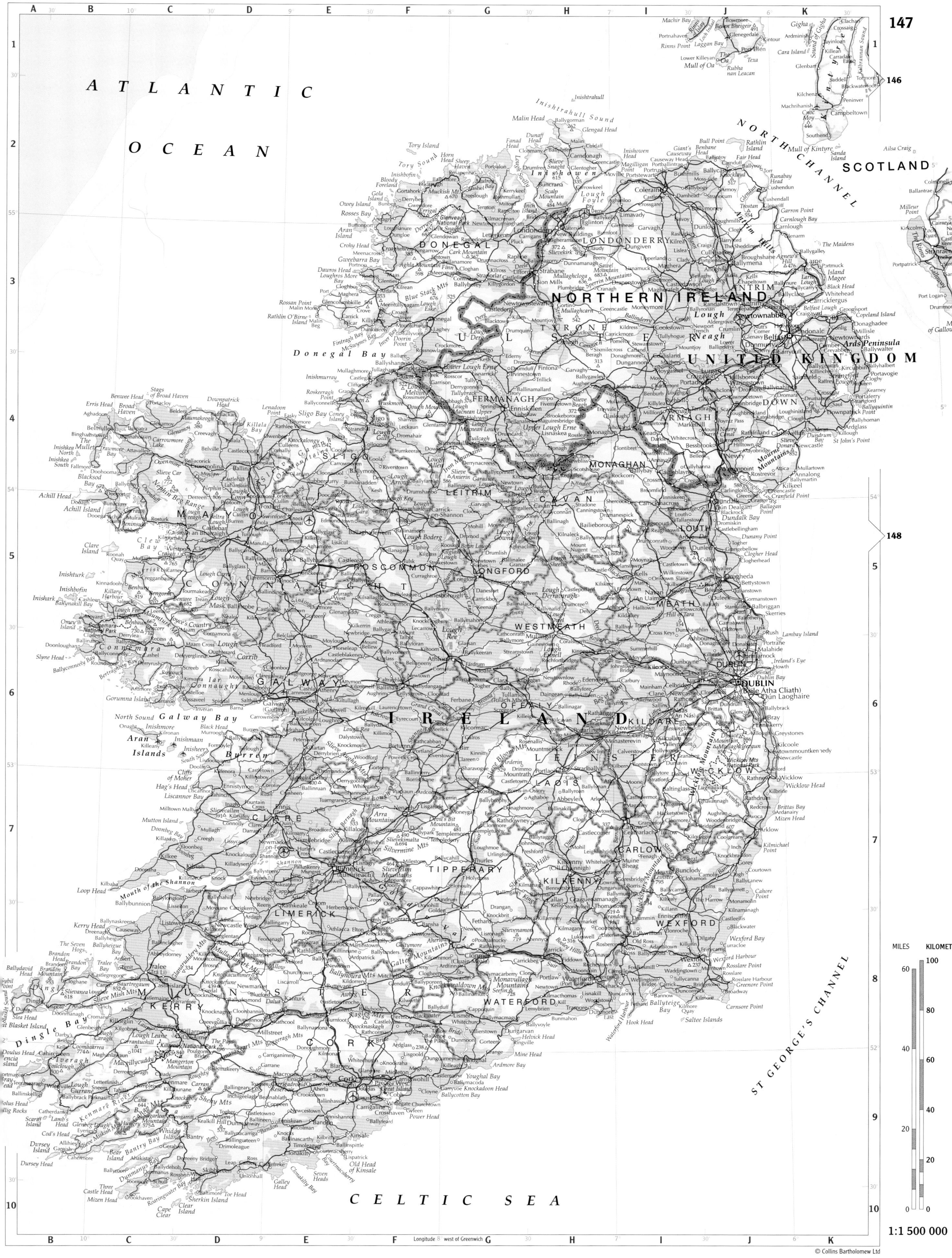

A T L A N T I C

O C E A N

SCOTLAND

NORTH CHANNEL

DONEGAL

ULSTER

NORTHERN IRELAND

LONDONDERRY

TYRONE

FERMANAGH

ANTRIM

ARMAGH

DOWN

UNITED KINGDOM

MONAGHAN

CAVAN

LEITRIM

SLIGO

MAYO

ROSCOMMON

LONGFORD

LOUTH

MEATH

WESTMEATH

CONNAUGHT

GALWAY

I R E L A N D

DUBLIN
(Baile Átha Cliath)
Dún Laoghaire

KILDARE

OFFALY

LAOIS

WICKLOW

LEINSTER

Galway Bay

Aran
Islands

CLARE

TIPPERARY

CARLOW

KILKENNY

Mouth of the Shannon

LIMERICK

WEXFORD

KERRY

MUNSTER

WATERFORD

CORK

Dingle Bay

C E L T I C   S E A

ST GEORGE'S CHANNEL

Longitude   west of Greenwich

MILES	KILOMETRES
60	100
	80
40	60
20	40
	20
0	0

1:1 500 000

© Collins Bartholomew Ltd

148

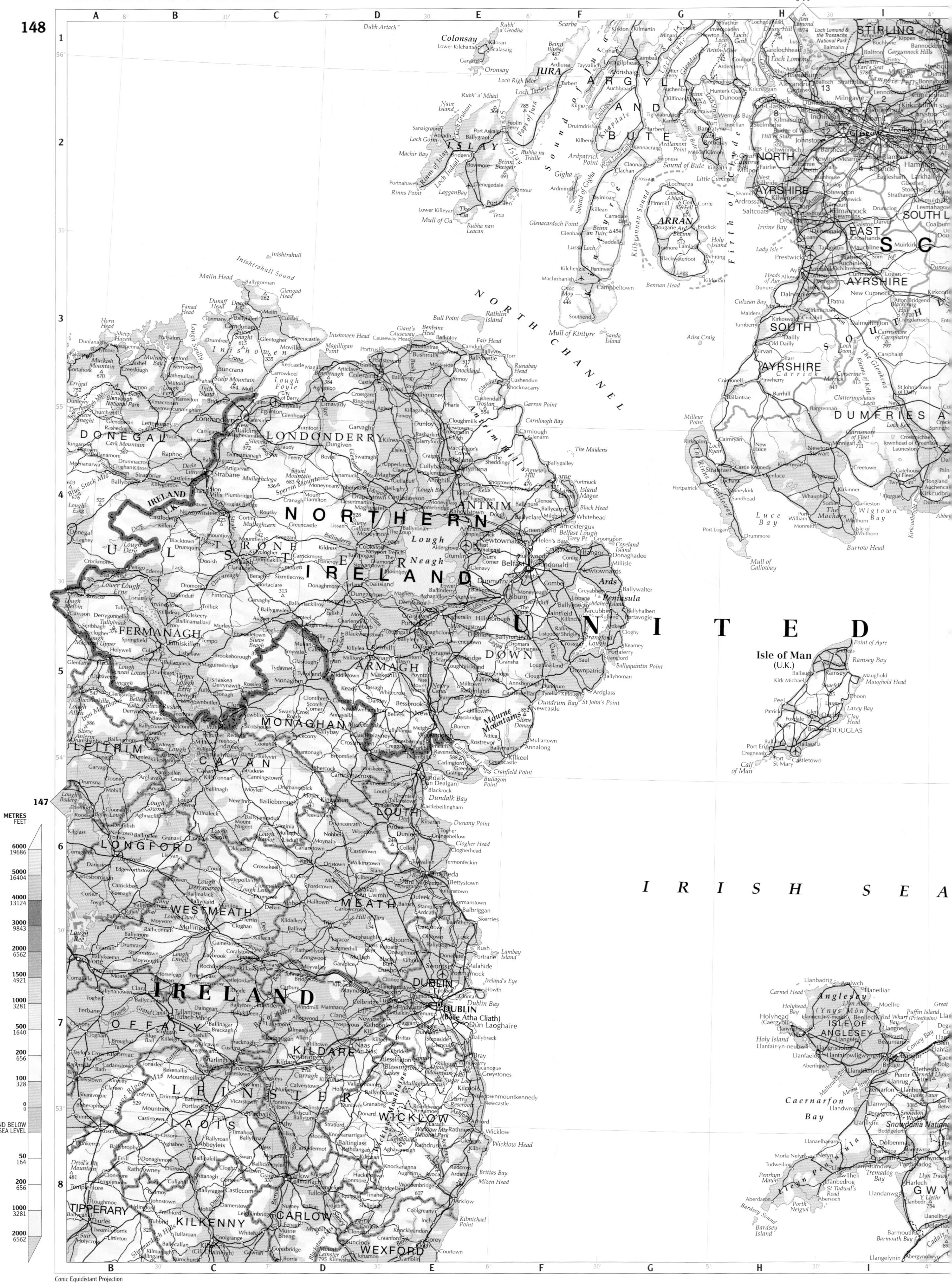

NORTHERN IRELAND

IRELAND

ULSTER

LEINSTER

DONEGAL

TYRONE

LONDONDERRY

ANTRIM

FERMANAGH

ARMAGH

DOWN

MONAGHAN

CAVAN

LEITRIM

LONGFORD

WESTMEATH

MEATH

LOUTH

OFFALY

KILDARE

DUBLIN

LAOIS

WICKLOW

TIPPERARY

KILKENNY

CARLOW

WEXFORD

ARGYLL AND BUTE

NORTH AYRSHIRE

EAST AYRSHIRE

SOUTH AYRSHIRE

SOUTH LANARKSHIRE

DUMFRIES AND GALLOWAY

STIRLING

JURA

ISLAY

ARRAN

COLONSAY

Isle of Man (U.K.)

DOUGLAS

Anglesey (Ynys Môn)

ISLE OF ANGLESEY

GWYNEDD

NORTH CHANNEL

IRISH SEA

Dublin Bay

Dundalk Bay

Belfast Lough

Lough Neagh

Firth of Clyde

Caernarfon Bay

Snowdonia National Park

DUBLIN (Baile Átha Cliath)

BELFAST

Londonderry

Conic Equidistant Projection

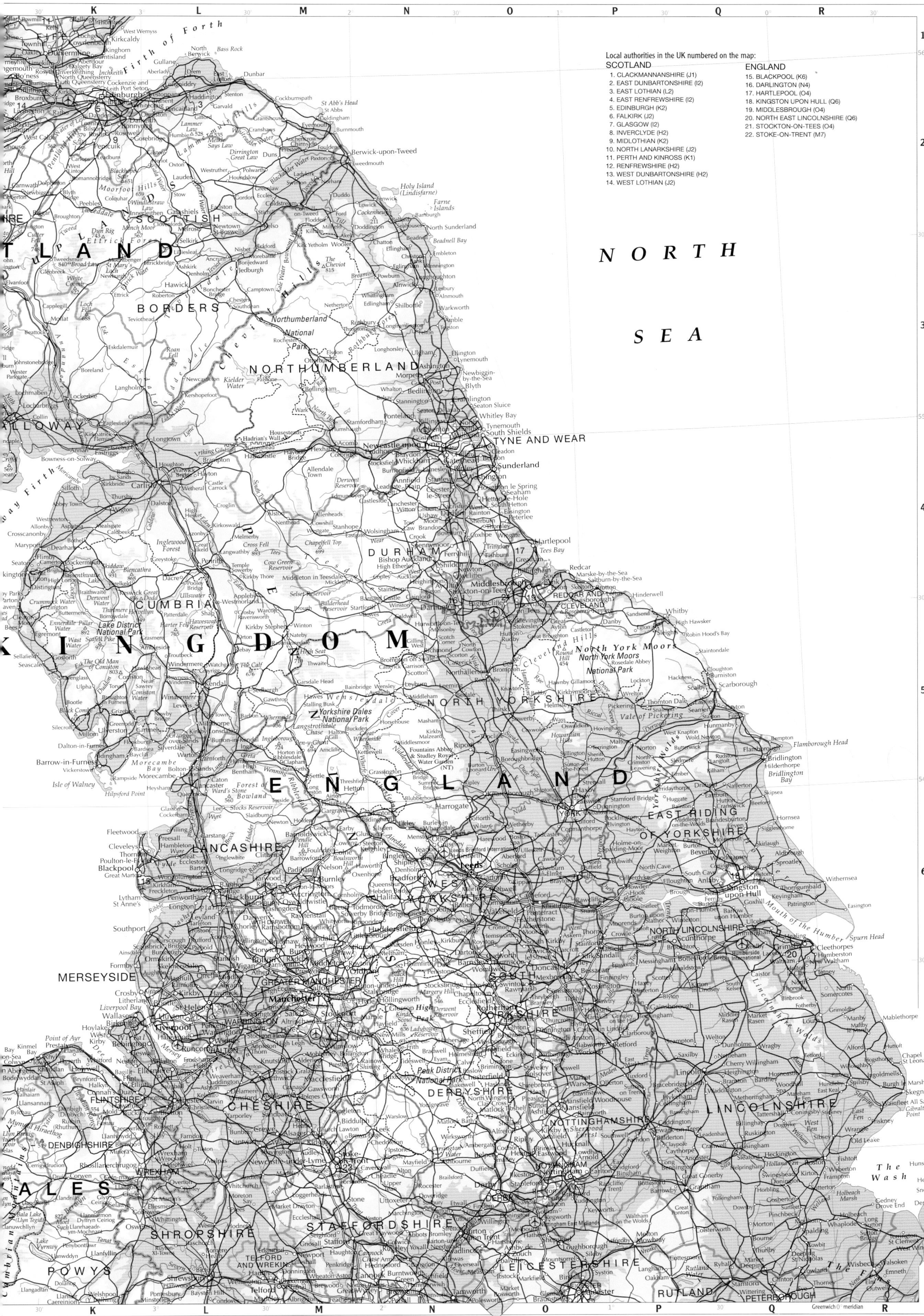

N O R T H

S E A

MILES   KILOMETRES

1:1 200 000

© Collins Bartholomew Ltd

Local authorities in the UK numbered on the map:
SCOTLAND
1. CLACKMANNANSHIRE (J1)
2. EAST DUNBARTONSHIRE (I2)
3. EAST LOTHIAN (L2)
4. EAST RENFREWSHIRE (I2)
5. EDINBURGH (K2)
6. FALKIRK (J2)
7. GLASGOW (I2)
8. INVERCLYDE (H2)
9. MIDLOTHIAN (K2)
10. NORTH LANARKSHIRE (J2)
11. PERTH AND KINROSS (K1)
12. RENFREWSHIRE (H2)
13. WEST DUNBARTONSHIRE (H2)
14. WEST LOTHIAN (J2)
ENGLAND
15. BLACKPOOL (K6)
16. DARLINGTON (N4)
17. HARTLEPOOL (O4)
18. KINGSTON UPON HULL (Q6)
19. MIDDLESBROUGH (O4)
20. NORTH EAST LINCOLNSHIRE (Q6)
21. STOCKTON-ON-TEES (O4)
22. STOKE-ON-TRENT (M7)
SCOTTISH BORDERS
NORTHUMBERLAND
TYNE AND WEAR
DURHAM
CUMBRIA
NORTH YORKSHIRE
KINGDOM
ENGLAND
EAST RIDING OF YORKSHIRE
LANCASHIRE
WEST YORKSHIRE
NORTH LINCOLNSHIRE
MERSEYSIDE
GREATER MANCHESTER
SOUTH YORKSHIRE
DERBYSHIRE
CHESHIRE
LINCOLNSHIRE
NOTTINGHAMSHIRE
FLINTSHIRE
DENBIGHSHIRE
WREXHAM
SHROPSHIRE
STAFFORDSHIRE
TELFORD AND WREKIN
LEICESTERSHIRE
RUTLAND
PETERBOROUGH
POWYS
WALES
Firth of Forth
The Wash
Mouth of the Humber
North York Moors National Park
Yorkshire Dales National Park
Lake District National Park
Peak District National Park
Northumberland National Park
Newcastle upon Tyne
Sunderland
Middlesbrough
Leeds
Manchester
Liverpool
Sheffield
Nottingham
Derby
Lincoln
Blackpool
Kingston upon Hull
Berwick-upon-Tweed
Carlisle
Edinburgh
Greenwich 0° meridian

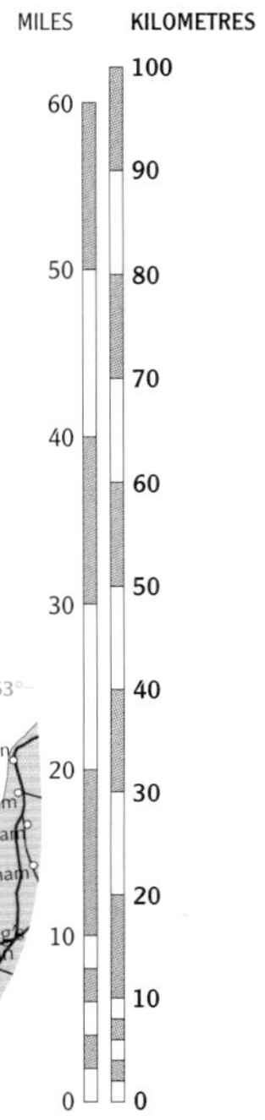

147

IRELAND

IRISH SEA

St George's Channel

CARDIGAN BAY

WALES

GWYNEDD
ISLE OF ANGLESEY
CONWY
DENBIGHSHIRE
FLINTSHIRE
WREXHAM
CEREDIGION
POWYS
PEMBROKESHIRE
CARMARTHENSHIRE
NEATH PORT TALBOT
SWANSEA
VALE OF GLAMORGAN

UNITED

CHESHIRE
SHROPSHIRE
HEREFORDSHIRE
MONMOUTHSHIRE
GLOUCESTER
SOMERSET

Bristol Channel

Lundy

DEVON
CORNWALL
DORSET

Exmoor National Park
Dartmoor National Park
Bodmin Moor

Land's End
Lizard Point
Mount's Bay

Local authorities in the UK numbered on the map:

ENGLAND	WALES
1. BATH AND N.E. SOMERSET (H5)	24. BLAENAU GWENT (F4)
2. BRACKNELL FOREST (K5)	25. BRIDGEND (E4)
3. BRIGHTON AND HOVE (L6)	26. CAERPHILLY (F4)
4. BRISTOL (G5)	27. CARDIFF (F5)
5. BOURNEMOUTH (I6)	28. MERTHYR TYDFIL (F4)
6. GREATER MANCHESTER (H1)	29. NEWPORT (G4)
7. LUTON (L4)	30. RHONDDA CYNON TAFF (F4)
8. MILTON KEYNES (K3)	31. TORFAEN (F4)
9. NOTTINGHAM (J2)	
10. PLYMOUTH (D7)	
11. POOLE (I6)	
12. PORTSMOUTH (J6)	
13. READING (J5)	
14. SLOUGH (K4)	
15. SOUTHAMPTON (J6)	
16. SOUTHEND (N4)	
17. STOKE-ON-TRENT (H1)	
18. SWINDON (I4)	
19. THURROCK (M5)	
20. TORBAY (E7)	
21. WEST MIDLANDS (I3)	
22. WINDSOR AND MAIDENHEAD (K5)	
23. WOKINGHAM (K5)	

METRES / FEET

6000	19686
5000	16404
4000	13124
3000	9843
2000	6562
1500	4921
1000	3281
500	1640
200	656
100	328
0	0

LAND BELOW SEA LEVEL

50	164
200	656
1000	3281
2000	6562

ISLES OF SCILLY
CONTINUATION AT THE SAME SCALE

Isles of Scilly
Bryher St Martin's
Tresco St Mary's
Annet Gugh
St Agnes
Western Rocks

Conic Equidistant Projection

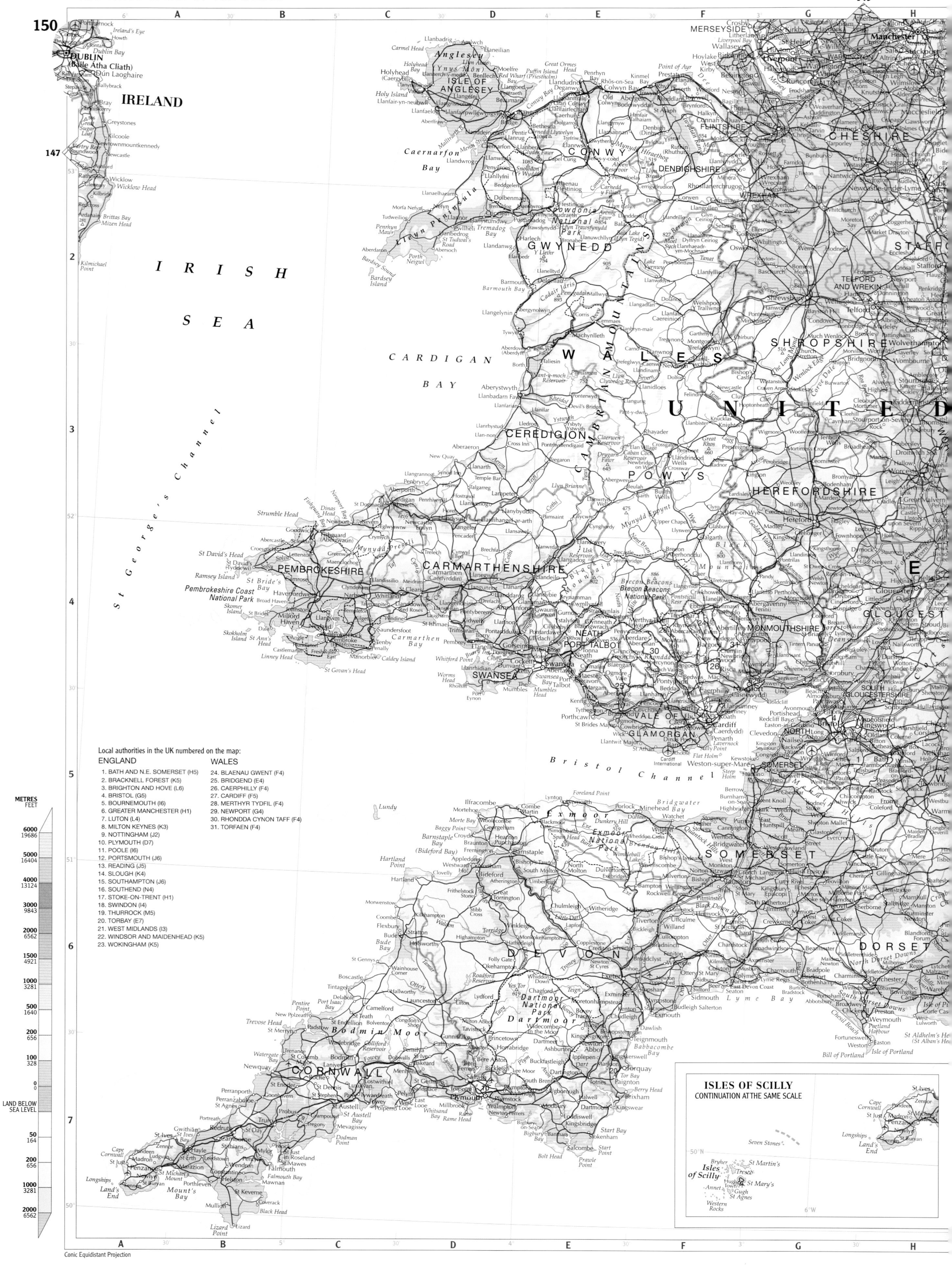

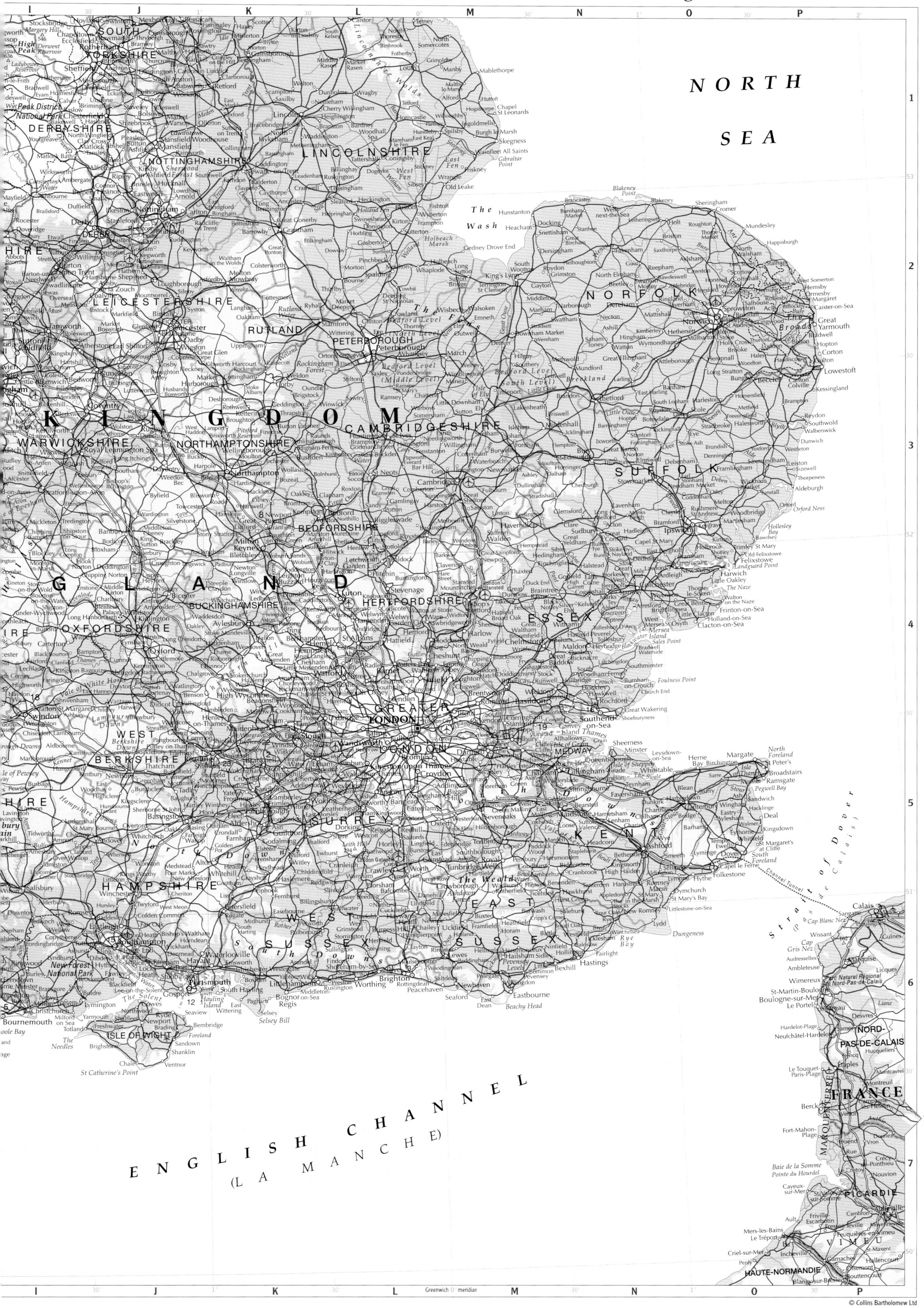

NORTH SEA

The Wash

ENGLISH CHANNEL (LA MANCHE)

Strait of Dover (Pas de Calais)

UNITED KINGDOM

ENGLAND

SOUTH YORKSHIRE
DERBYSHIRE
NOTTINGHAMSHIRE
LINCOLNSHIRE
LEICESTERSHIRE
RUTLAND
NORFOLK
CAMBRIDGESHIRE
SUFFOLK
NORTHAMPTONSHIRE
WARWICKSHIRE
BEDFORDSHIRE
HERTFORDSHIRE
BUCKINGHAMSHIRE
OXFORDSHIRE
ESSEX
GREATER LONDON
LONDON
MEDWAY
KENT
SURREY
WEST BERKSHIRE
HAMPSHIRE
WEST SUSSEX
EAST SUSSEX
ISLE OF WIGHT

The Fens
Sherwood
Peak District National Park
Lincolnshire Wolds
Breckland
The Broads
The Weald
North Downs
South Downs
New Forest National Park

Sheffield
Nottingham
Derby
Leicester
Peterborough
Northampton
Cambridge
Norwich
Great Yarmouth
Lowestoft
Ipswich
Colchester
Harwich
Chelmsford
Southend-on-Sea
London
Croydon
Margate
Ramsgate
Dover
Folkestone
Canterbury
Maidstone
Ashford
Guildford
Brighton
Worthing
Eastbourne
Hastings
Portsmouth
Southampton
Bournemouth
Newport
Salisbury
Oxford
Swindon
Milton Keynes
Luton
St Albans
Stevenage
Watford

FRANCE

NORD-PAS-DE-CALAIS
PICARDIE
HAUTE-NORMANDIE
VIMEU

Calais
Boulogne-sur-Mer
Le Touquet-Paris-Plage
Montreuil
Abbeville
Cap Gris Nez
Cap Blanc Nez
Baie de la Somme

Greenwich 0 meridian

MILES	KILOMETRES
60	100
50	90
	80
40	70
	60
30	50
	40
20	30
10	20
	10
0	0

1:1 200 000

© Collins Bartholomew Ltd

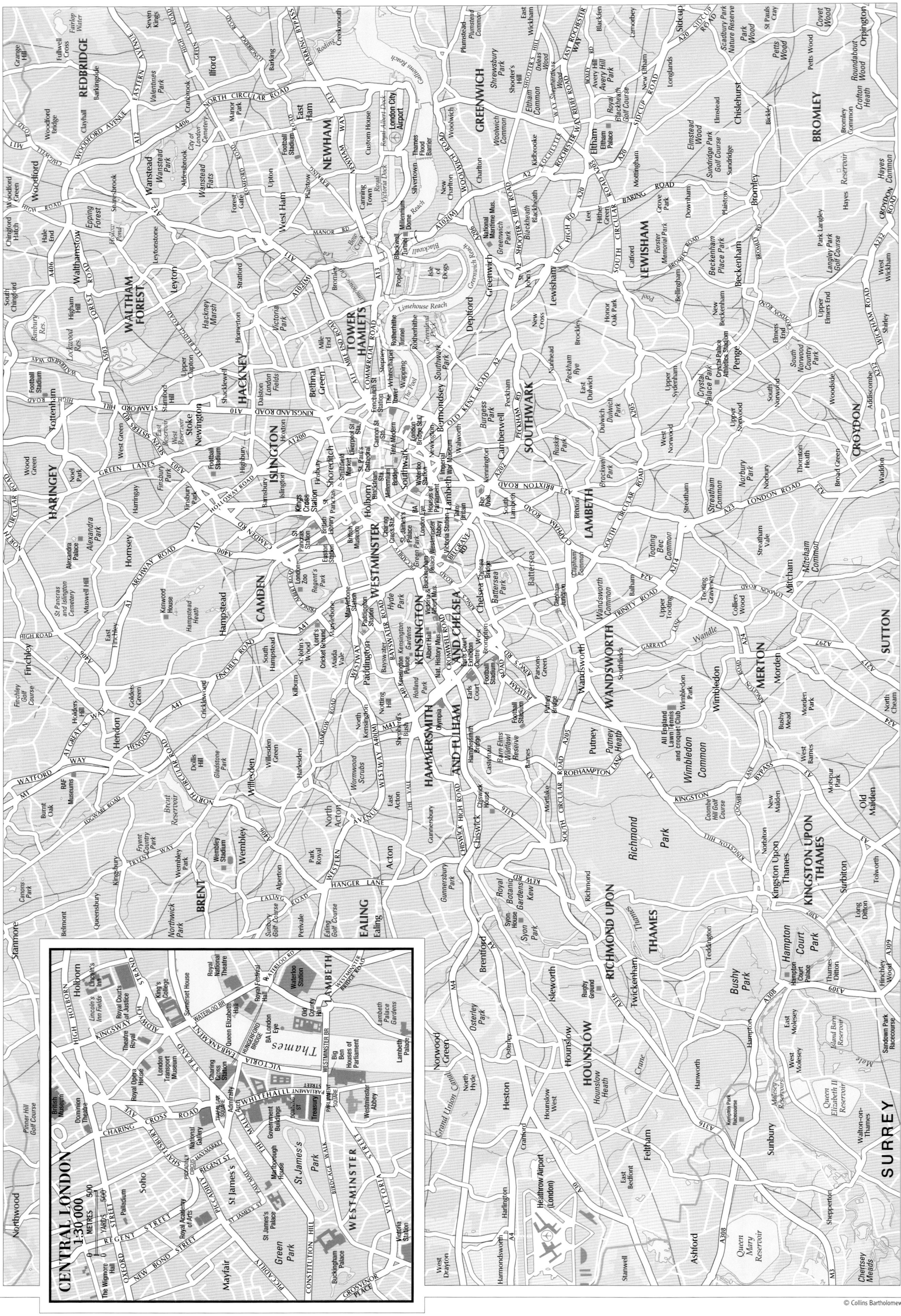

1:125 000

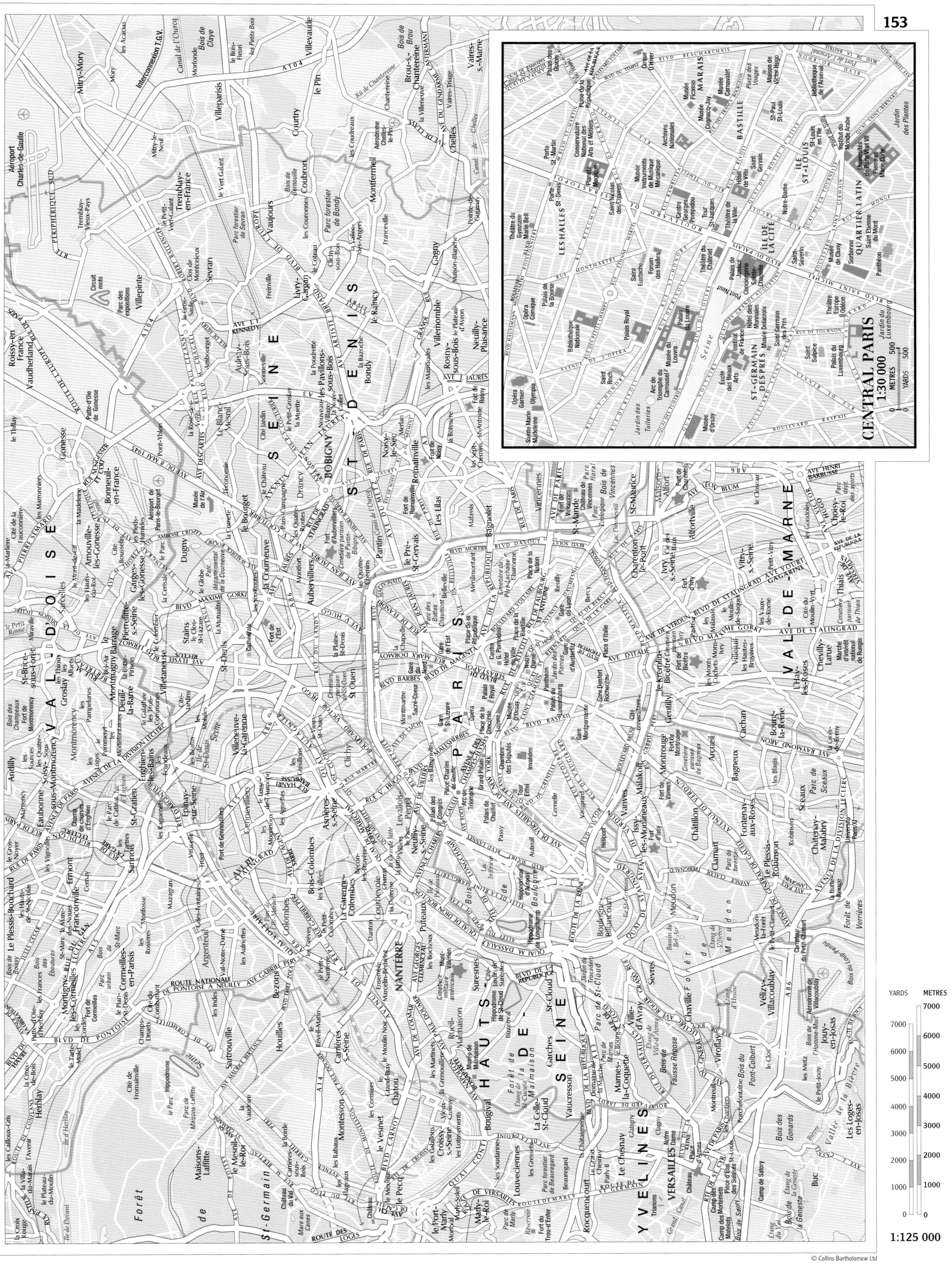

CENTRAL PARIS
1:30 000

1:125 000

© Collins Bartholomew Ltd

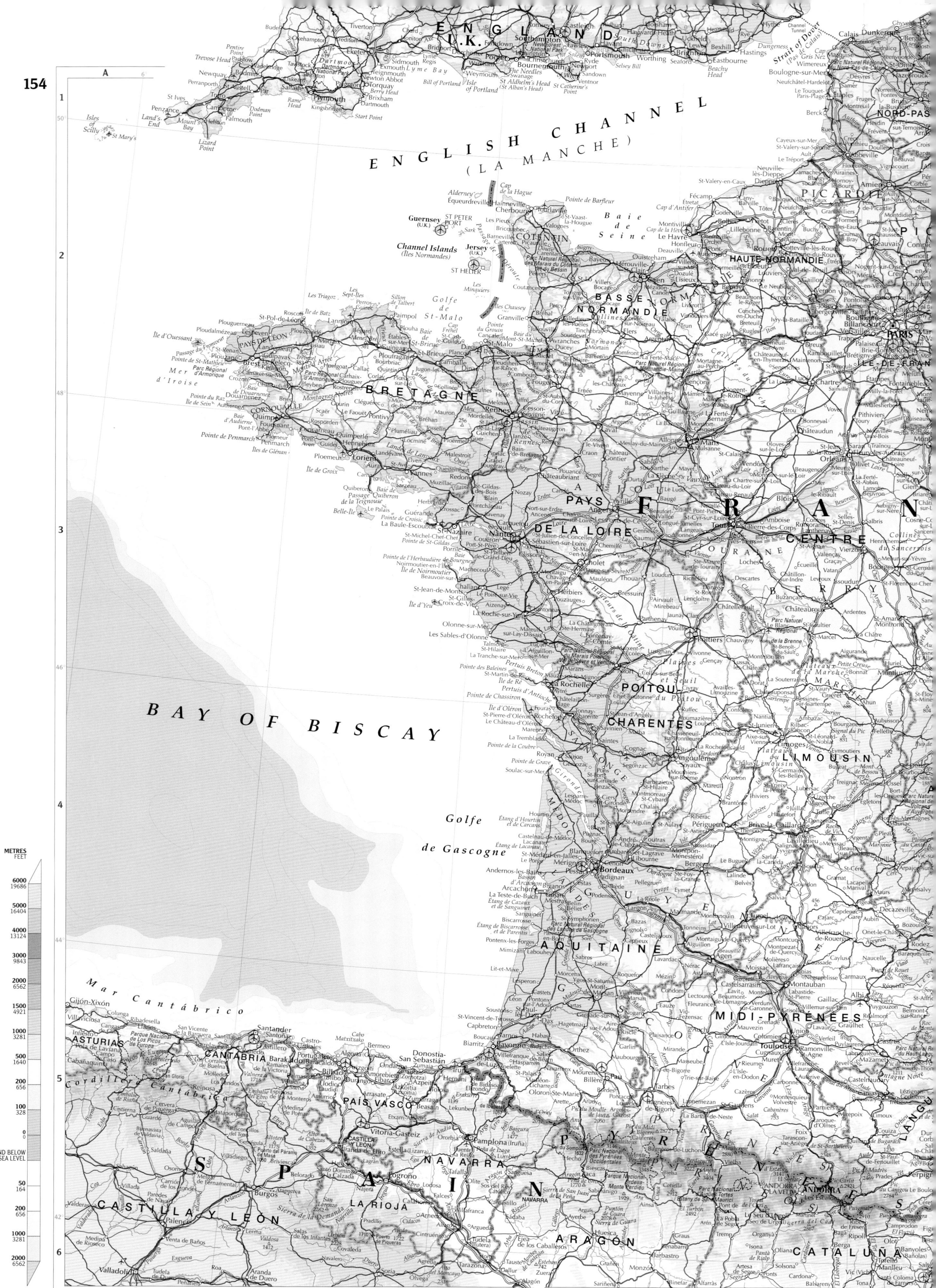

ENGLAND

U.K.

ENGLISH CHANNEL
(LA MANCHE)

NORD-PAS

PICARDIE

PARIS

ÎLE-DE-FRANCE

HAUTE-NORMANDIE

Baie de Seine

COTENTIN

BASSE-NORMANDIE

Channel Islands
(Îles Normandes)

Guernsey (U.K.)
ST PETER PORT

Jersey (U.K.)
ST HELIER

Golfe de St-Malo

Mer d'Iroise

PAYS DE LÉON

BRETAGNE

CORNOUAILLE

Rennes

Nantes

ANJOU

PAYS DE LA LOIRE

F R A N C E

CENTRE

TOURAINE

BERRY

Poitiers

POITOU

CHARENTES

La Rochelle

BAY OF BISCAY

LIMOUSIN

MARCHE

Golfe de Gascogne

Bordeaux

GUYENNE

PÉRIGORD

AQUITAINE

MIDI-PYRÉNÉES

Toulouse

LANGUE

Mar Cantábrico

ASTURIAS

CANTABRIA

Cordillera Cantábrica

PAÍS VASCO

Bilbao

San Sebastián

NAVARRA

Pamplona (Iruña)

Bayonne

Pau

P Y R É N É E S

ANDORRA
LA VELLA

ANDORRA

S P A I N

CASTILLA Y LEÓN

LA RIOJA

Burgos

Logroño

ARAGÓN

CATALUÑA

METRES / FEET
6000 / 19686
5000 / 16404
4000 / 13124
3000 / 9843
2000 / 6562
1500 / 4921
1000 / 3281
500 / 1640
200 / 656
100 / 328
0 / 0
LAND BELOW SEA LEVEL
50 / 164
200 / 656
1000 / 3281
2000 / 6562

Conic Equidistant Projection

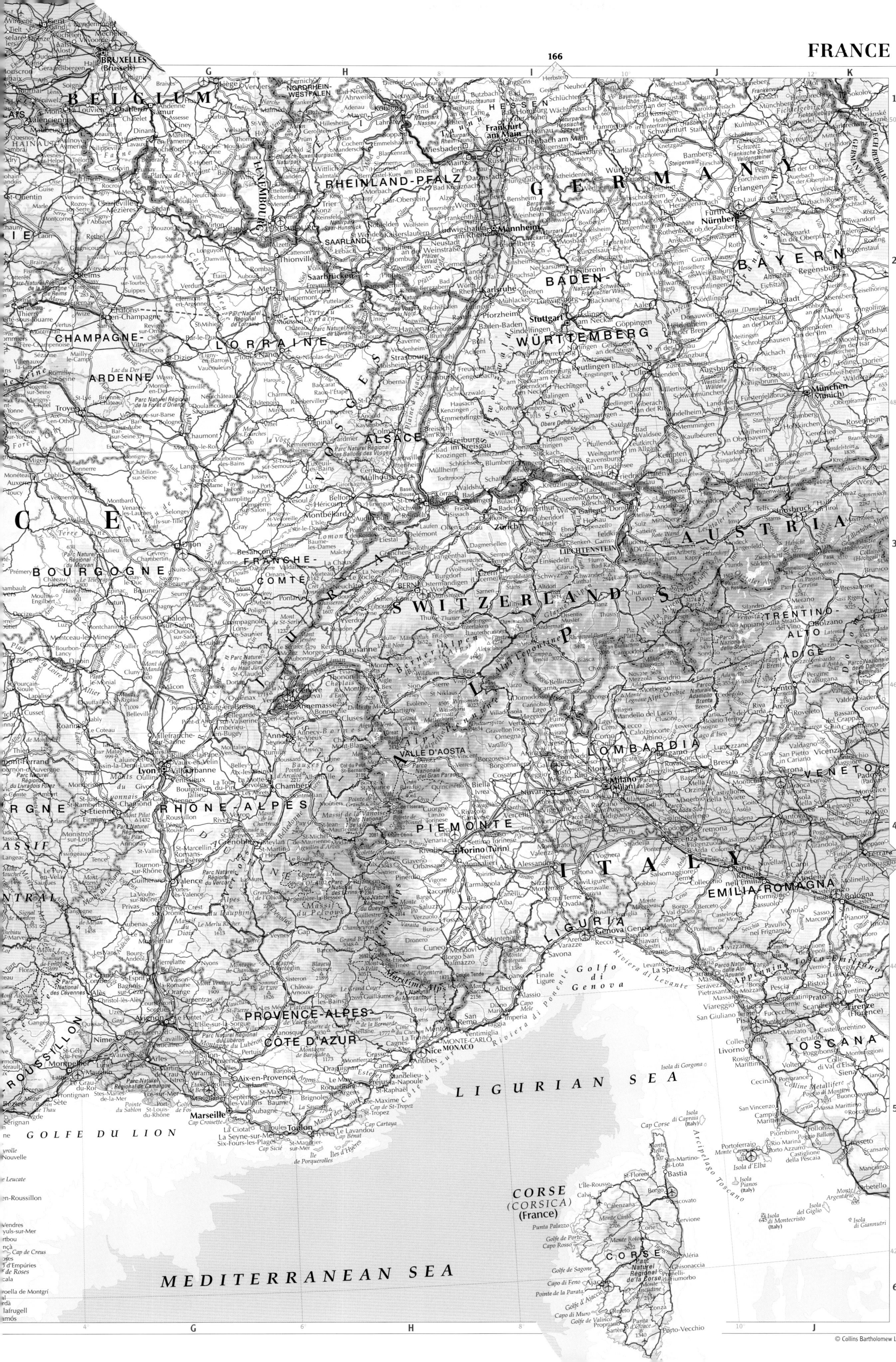

BELGIUM

GERMANY

NORDRHEIN-WESTFALEN

HESSE

RHEINLAND-PFALZ

LUXEMBOURG

SAARLAND

BAYERN

BADEN-WÜRTTEMBERG

CHAMPAGNE-ARDENNE

LORRAINE

ARDENNE

ALSACE

AUSTRIA

BOURGOGNE

FRANCHE-COMTÉ

SWITZERLAND

LIECHTENSTEIN

TRENTINO-ALTO ADIGE

VALLE D'AOSTA

LOMBARDIA

VENETO

RHÔNE-ALPES

PIEMONTE

ITALY

EMILIA-ROMAGNA

PROVENCE-ALPES-CÔTE D'AZUR

LIGURIA

TOSCANA

ROUSSILLON

Marseille

GOLFE DU LION

LIGURIAN SEA

MONACO

CORSE (CORSICA) (France)

CORSE

MEDITERRANEAN SEA

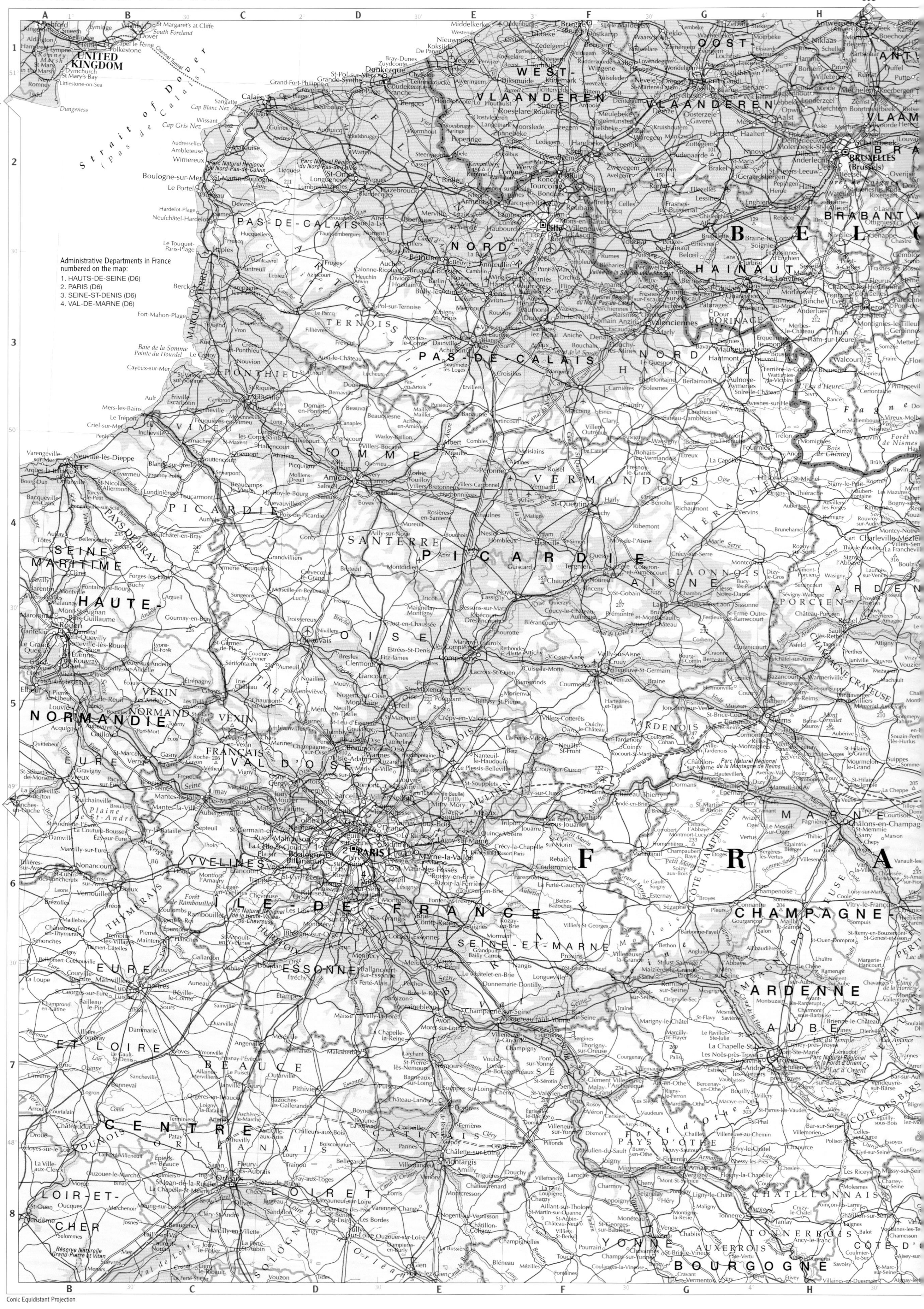

Administrative Departments in France
numbered on the map:
1. HAUTS-DE-SEINE (D6)
2. PARIS (D6)
3. SEINE-ST-DENIS (D6)
4. VAL-DE-MARNE (D6)

METRES	FEET
6000	19686
5000	16404
4000	13124
3000	9843
2000	6562
1500	4921
1000	3281
500	1640
200	656
100	328
0	0

LAND BELOW
SEA LEVEL

METRES	FEET
50	164
200	656
1000	3281
2000	6562

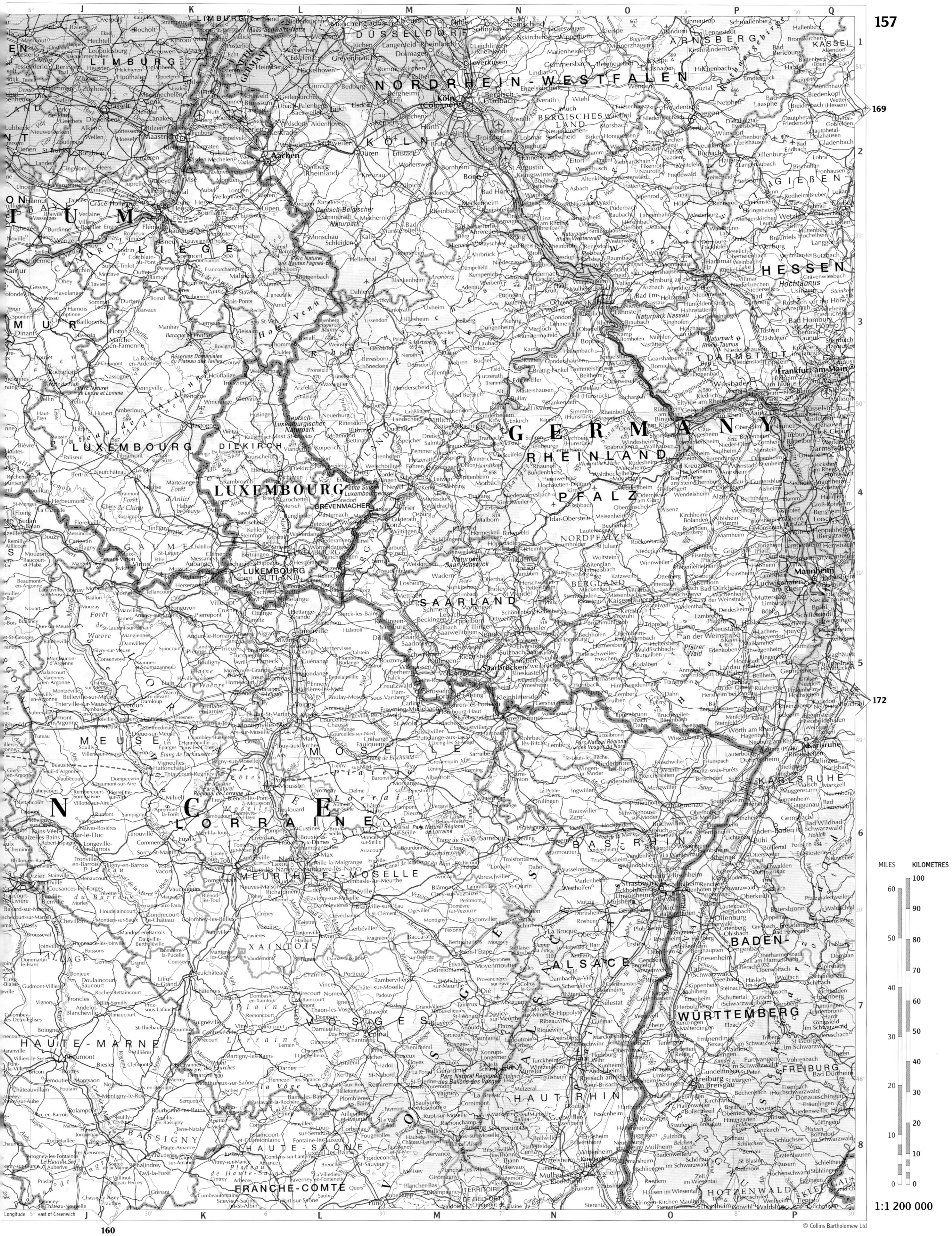

MILES   KILOMETRES

1:1 200 000

© Collins Bartholomew Ltd

E N G L I S H   C H A N N E L

CHANNEL ISLANDS
(ÎLES NORMANDES)

Alderney
Burhou
St Anne
Cap de la Hague
Auderville
Urville
Nacqueville
Querqueville
Tourlaville
Cap Lévy

Équeurdreville-Hanneville
Octeville
Cherbourg
La Glacerie
Quettehou

Flamanville
Brix
Valognes

Vale
Herm
St Sampson
ST PETER PORT
St Pierre in the Wood
St Peter
Vazon
Torteval
St Martin
Sark

Guernsey
(U.K.)

Bricquebec
Parc Naturel Régional des

St John
Les Écréhou
St Ouen
St Martin
ST HELIER
St Brelade
St Saviour
St Clement

Jersey
(U.K.)

COTENTIN

Carteret
Barneville-Carteret
Cap de Carteret
Portbail

La Haye-du-Puits
du Cotentin et du

Lessay
Périers

Blainville-sur-Mer
Coutainville
Créances

MA

Les Minquiers

Passage de la Déroute

Réserve Naturelle des Sept-Îles
Les Triagoz
Pointe du Château
Sillon de Talbert
Île de Bréhat
Pointe de l'Arcouest

Les Sept-Îles
Plougrescant
Penvénan
Pleubian
Paimpol

Île Grande
Trébeurden
Tréguier
Lézardrieux
Lanmodez

Golfe de St-Malo

Île de Batz
Roscoff
Santec
Baie de Morlaix
Pointe de Primel
Baie de Lannion
Lannion
Ploumanac'h

TRÉGORROIS

Lanvollon
Étables-sur-Mer
Binic

Baie de St-Brieuc
Sables-d'Or-les-Pins
Cap Fréhel
Rothéneuf
St-Cast-le-Guildo
St-Malo
Dinard
Cancale

Pointe du Grouin
Baie du Mont-St-Michel
Le Val-St-Père
Genêts
St-Pair-sur-Mer
Granville
Donville-les-Bains
Villedieu-les-Poêles

Îles Chausey

Île d'Ouessant
Parc Régional d'Armorique

PAYS DE LÉON

St-Pol-de-Léon
Carantec
St-Thégonnec
Morlaix

Guingamp
Ploumagoar

CÔTES D'ARMOR

Dinan
Fougères

Île de Molène
Passage du Fromveur
Île de Beniguet
Pointe de St-Mathieu
Parc Régional d'Armorique

Brest
Rade de Brest
Plougastel-Daoulas
Daoulas

FINISTÈRE

Monts d'Arrée

Callac

Quintin
Corlay

BRETAGNE

Mûr-de-Bretagne
Lac de Guerlédan

Loudéac

ILLE-ET-VILAINE

Rennes

Mer d'Iroise
Cap de la Chèvre
Île de Sein
Pointe du Raz
Le Cap
Audierne

CORNOUAILLE

Douarnenez
Baie de Douarnenez

Châteaulin
Montagne St-Michel

Carhaix-Plouguer

Le Faouet
Gourin

Pontivy
Rohan

Josselin
Ploërmel

Montfort-sur-Meu

Quimper
Pont-l'Abbé
Plomelin

Concarneau
Quimperlé

Scaër

Guiscriff

Guémené-sur-Scorff

MORBIHAN

Landes de Lanvaux

Malestroit

Redon

Pointe de Penmarch
Penmarch
Guilvinec
Lesconil

Pont-Aven
Moëlan-sur-Mer
Clohars-Carnoët

Lorient
Hennebont
Lanester
Port-Louis

Baud

Locminé

La Gacilly

Île de Groix

Ploemeur
Larmor-Plage

Étel
Quiberon
Auray
Vannes

Questembert
Allaire
St-Nicolas-de-Redon

Châteaubriant
Derval

Passage de la Teignouse

Presqu'île de Quiberon
St-Pierre-Quiberon
Quiberon

Carnac
La Trinité-sur-Mer
Baie de Quiberon
St-Gildas-de-Rhuys
Presqu'île de Rhuys

Damgan
La Roche-Bernard
Pénestin

Vilaine

Nozay

Île d'Houat
Île Hœdic

Piriac-sur-Mer
La Turballe

GRANDE BRIÈRE
Parc Naturel Régional de Brière
Guérande
La Baule

LOIRE-ATLANTIQUE

Belle-Île
Le Palais
Sauzon
Locmaria

Pointe de Croisic
Le Croisic
Le Pouliguen
Batz-sur-Mer
St-Nazaire
St-Brevin-les-Pins
St-Père-en-Retz

Pornic
St-Michel-Chef-Chef

Nantes

PAYS DE RETZ

BAY OF BISCAY

Pointe de St-Gildas
Préfailles

Baie de Bourgneuf
Bourgneuf-en-Retz

Machecoul

Pointe de l'Herbaudière
Île de Noirmoutier
Noirmoutier-en-l'Île
La Guérinière
Barbâtre
Beauvoir-sur-Mer
Fromentine
La Barre-de-Monts
St-Gervais
St-Jean-de-Monts
Notre-Dame-de-Monts

VENDÉE

Port-Joinville
St-Hilaire-de-Riez
Croix-de-Vie
St-Gilles-Croix-de-Vie

Île d'Yeu
Pointe de Grosse Terre

Brétignolles-sur-Mer

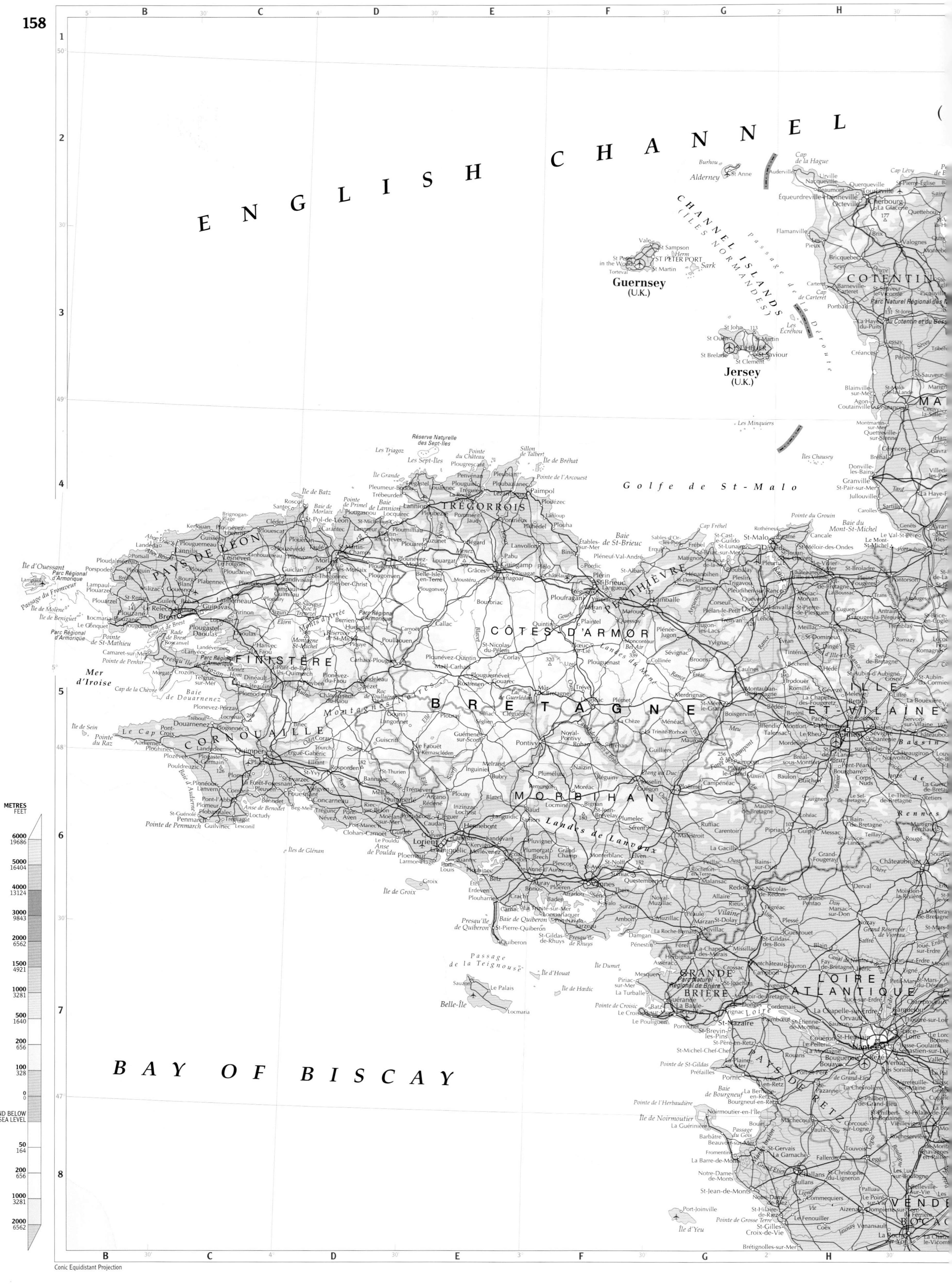

METRES
FEET
6000 / 19686
5000 / 16404
4000 / 13124
3000 / 9843
2000 / 6562
1500 / 4921
1000 / 3281
500 / 1640
200 / 656
100 / 328
0 / 0
LAND BELOW SEA LEVEL
50 / 164
200 / 656
1000 / 3281
2000 / 6562

Conic Equidistant Projection

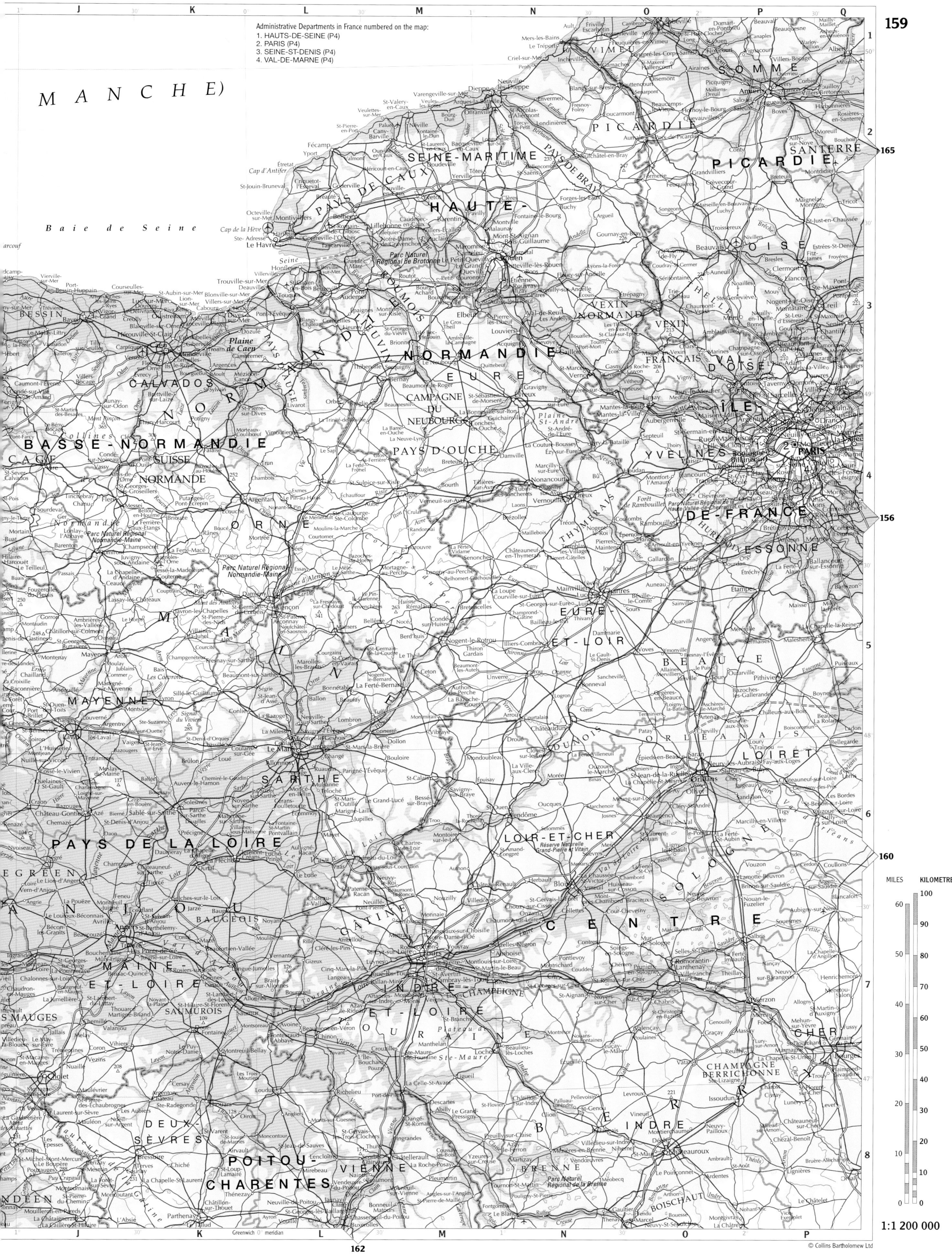

Administrative Departments in France numbered on the map:
1. HAUTS-DE-SEINE (P4)
2. PARIS (P4)
3. SEINE-ST-DENIS (P4)
4. VAL-DE-MARNE (P4)

MILES   KILOMETRES

1:1 200 000

© Collins Bartholomew Ltd

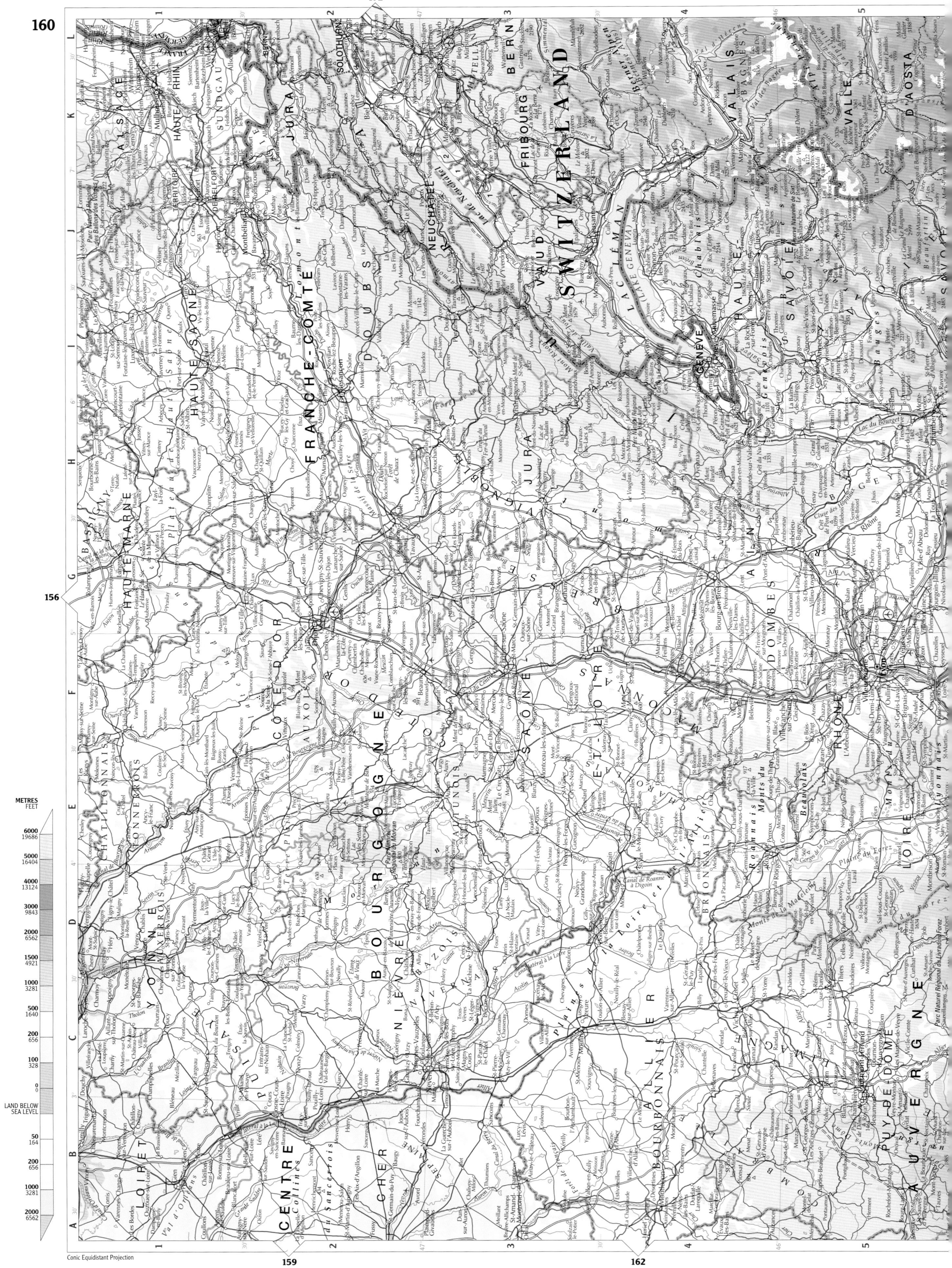

156

METRES
FEET

6000
19686

5000
16404

4000
13124

3000
9843

2000
6562

1500
4921

1000
3281

500
1640

200
656

100
328

0
0

LAND BELOW
SEA LEVEL

50
164

200
656

1000
3281

2000
6562

Conic Equidistant Projection

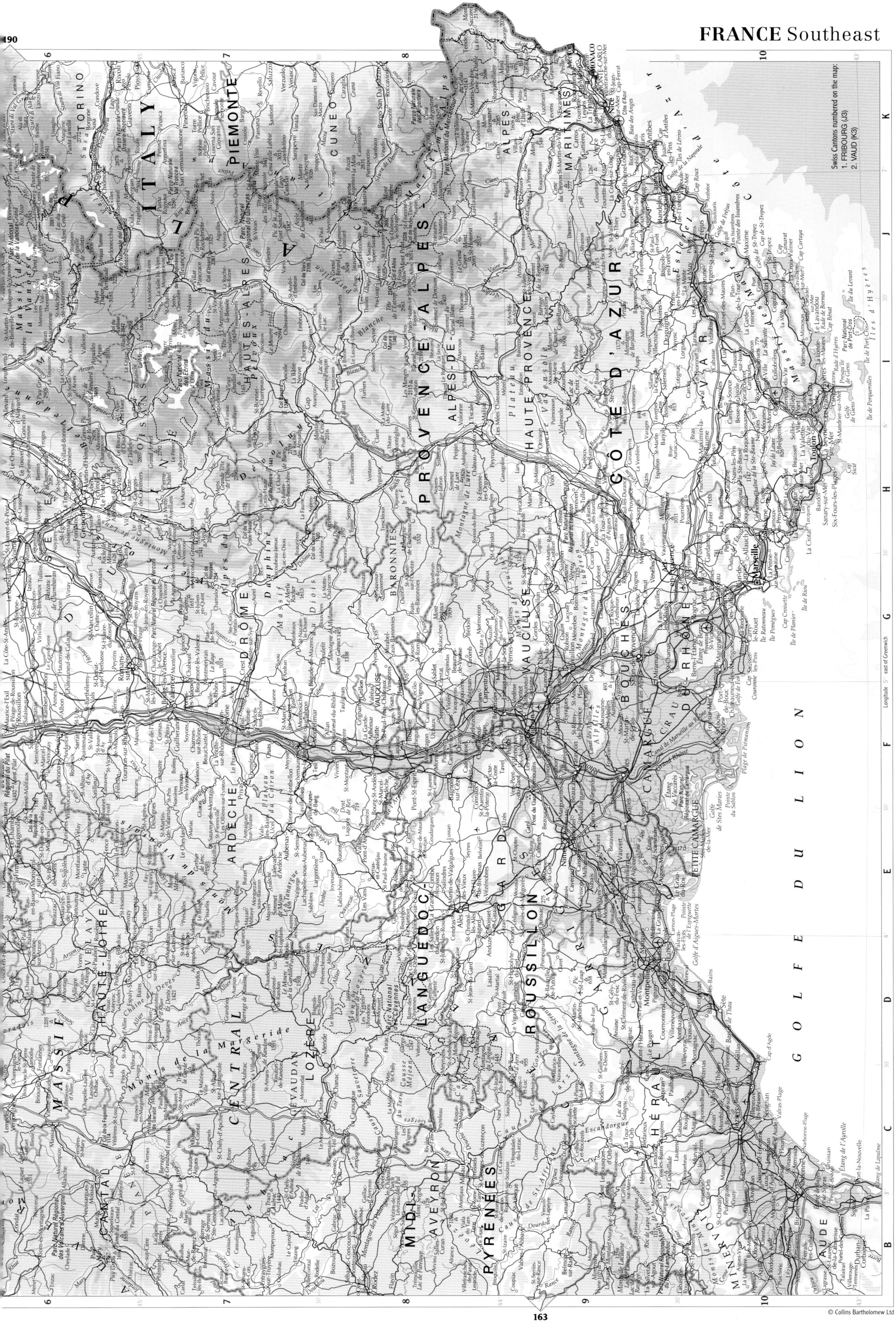

Swiss Cantons numbered on the map:
1. FRIBOURG (J3)
2. VAUD (K3)

MILES   KILOMETRES

1:1 200 000

© Collins Bartholomew Ltd

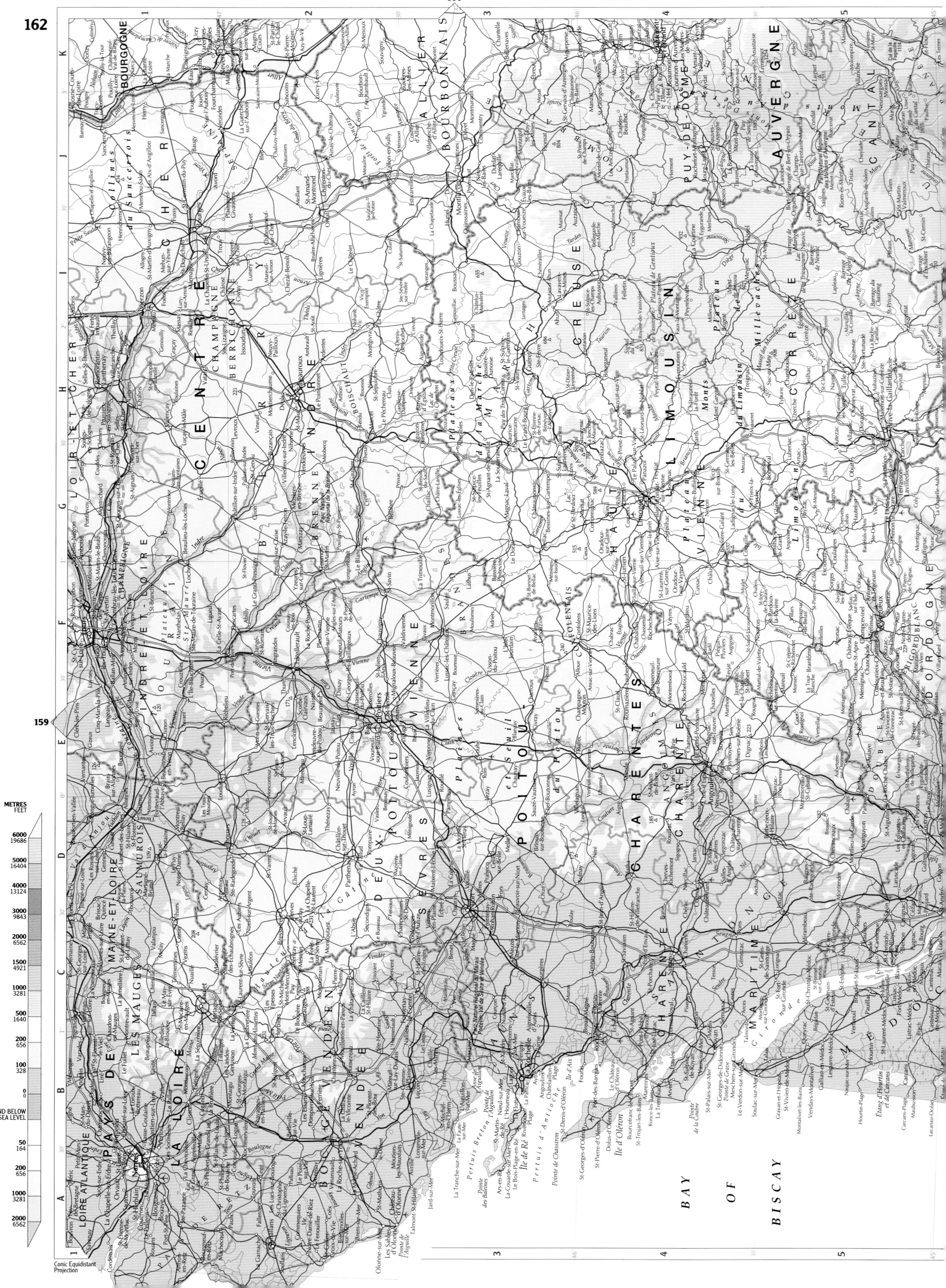

METRES / FEET

METRES	FEET
6000	19686
5000	16404
4000	13124
3000	9843
2000	6562
1500	4921
1000	3281
500	1640
200	656
100	328
0	0

LAND BELOW SEA LEVEL

50	164
200	656
1000	3281
2000	6562

Conic Equidistant Projection

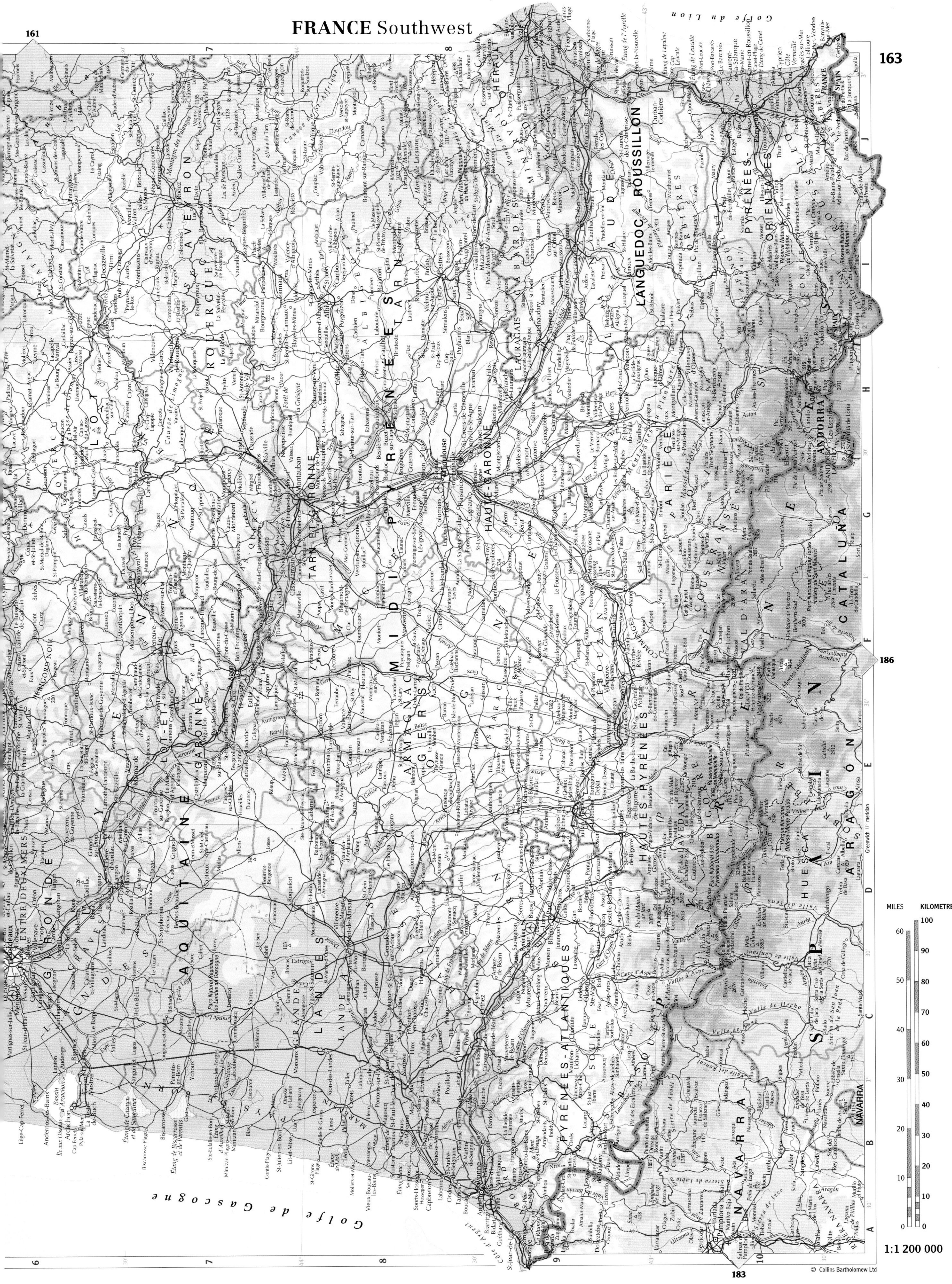
161
163
186
183
AQUITAINE
LANDES
GIRONDE
AVEYRON
HAUTE-GARONNE
TARN-ET-GARONNE
PYRÉNÉES-ATLANTIQUES
HAUTES-PYRÉNÉES
PYRÉNÉES-ORIENTALES
LANGUEDOC-ROUSSILLON
MIDI-PYRÉNÉES
ARIÈGE
AUDE
HÉRAULT
TARN
LOT
GERS
LOT-ET-GARONNE
ANDORRA
CATALUÑA
ARAGÓN
NAVARRA
HUESCA
SPAIN
FRANCE
Golfe de Gascogne
Golfe du Lion
Toulouse
Bordeaux
Montauban
Pamplona
Perpignan
Carcassonne
Narbonne
Albi
Castres
Rodez
Auch
Tarbes
Pau
Bayonne
Mont-de-Marsan
Agen
Foix
Andorra la Vella
Arcachon
MILES
KILOMETRES
1:1 200 000
© Collins Bartholomew Ltd

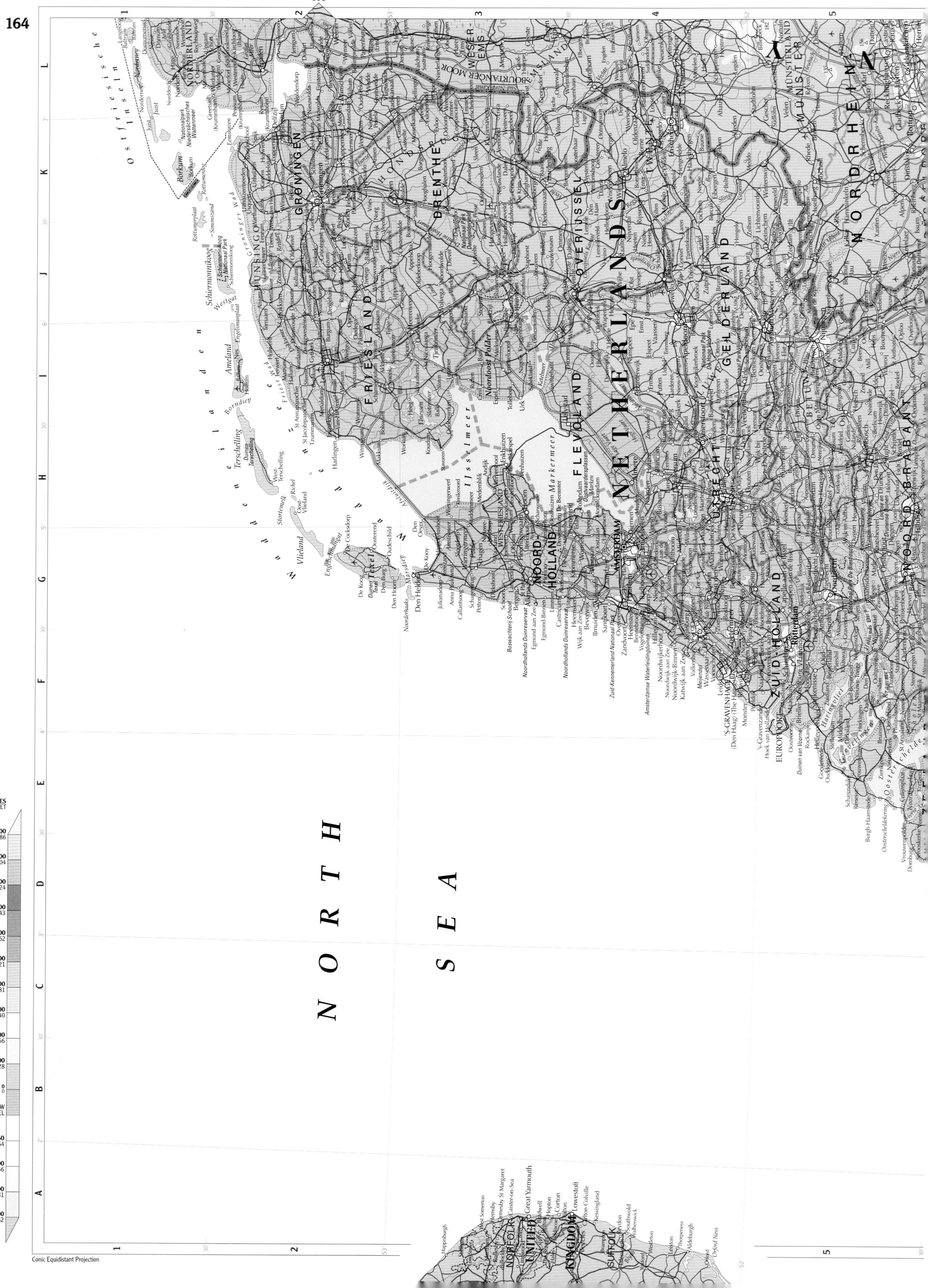

168

NORTH

SEA

NETHERLANDS

GRONINGEN

FRIESLAND

DRENTHE

OVERIJSSEL

FLEVOLAND

GELDERLAND

NOORD-HOLLAND

ZUID-HOLLAND

UTRECHT

NOORD-BRABANT

NORDRHEIN

MÜNSTER

WESER-EMS

IJsselmeer

Markermeer

Noordoost Polder

Waddenzee

Ostfriesische Inseln

Ameland

Terschelling

Vlieland

Texel

UNITED KINGDOM

NORFOLK

SUFFOLK

Great Yarmouth

Lowestoft

'S-GRAVENHAGE
(Den Haag) The Hague

AMSTERDAM

Rotterdam

EUROPOORT

METRES	FEET
6000	19686
5000	16404
4000	13124
3000	9843
2000	6562
1500	4921
1000	3281
500	1640
200	656
100	328
0	0

LAND BELOW
SEA LEVEL

50	164
200	656
1000	3281
2000	6562

Conic Equidistant Projection

NETHERLANDS, BELGIUM AND LUXEMBOURG

WESTFALEN

LIMBURG

ANTWERPEN

VLAAMS-BRABANT

BRABANT WALLON

LIÈGE

OOST-VLAANDEREN

WEST-VLAANDEREN

B E L G I U M

HAINAUT

NAMUR

LUXEMBOURG

DIEKIRCH

LUXEMBOURG

RHEINLAND-PFALZ

SAARLAND

PAS-DE-CALAIS

NORD

SOMME

PICARDIE

F R A N C E

AISNE

ARDENNE

CHAMPAGNE-ARDENNE

MEURTHE-ET-MOSELLE

MEUSE

LORRAINE

Bruxelles
(Brussel)

Luxembourg

157

MILES   KILOMETRES

60   100
      90
50   80
      70
40   60
      50
30
      40
20   30

10   20
      10
0   0

1:1 200 000

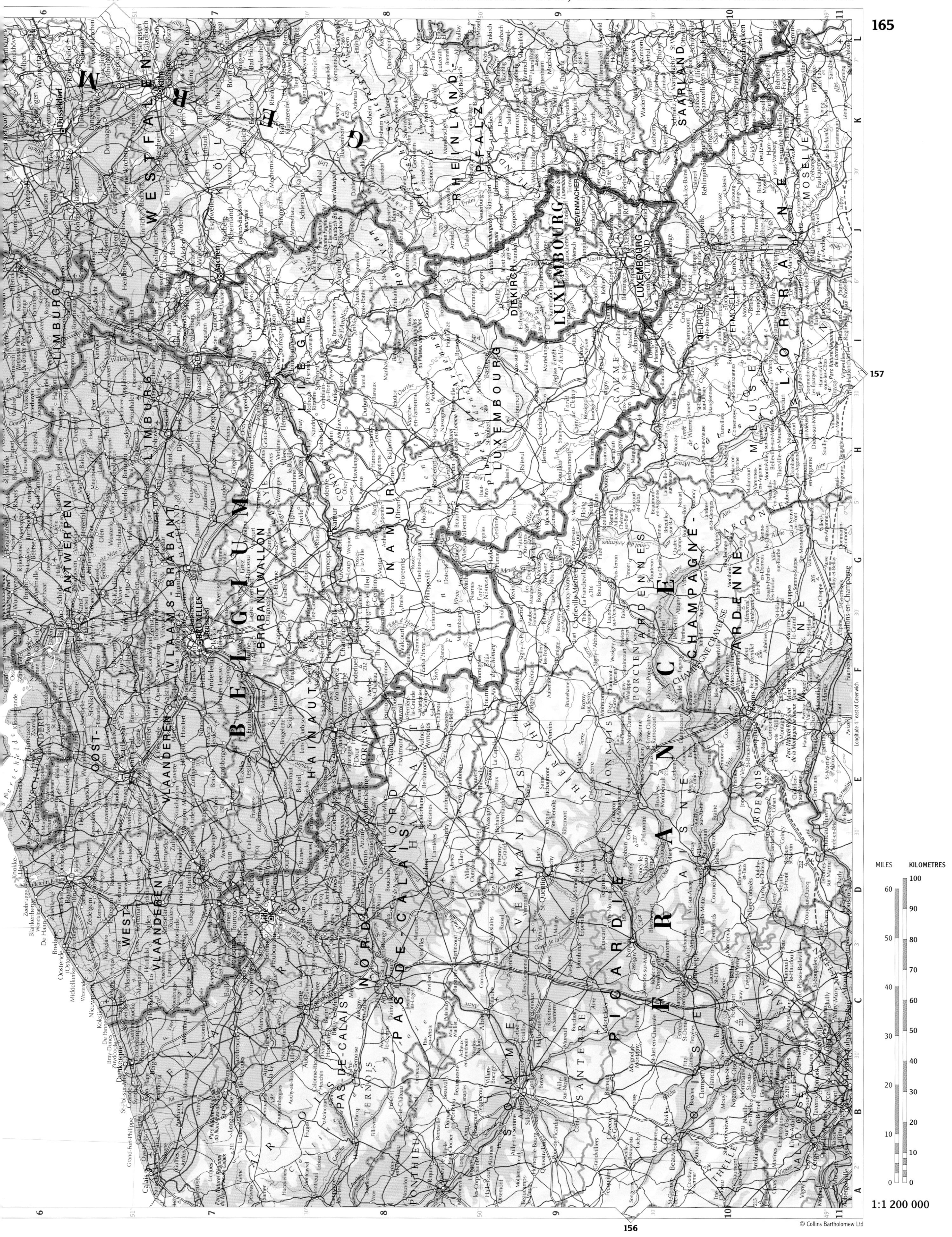

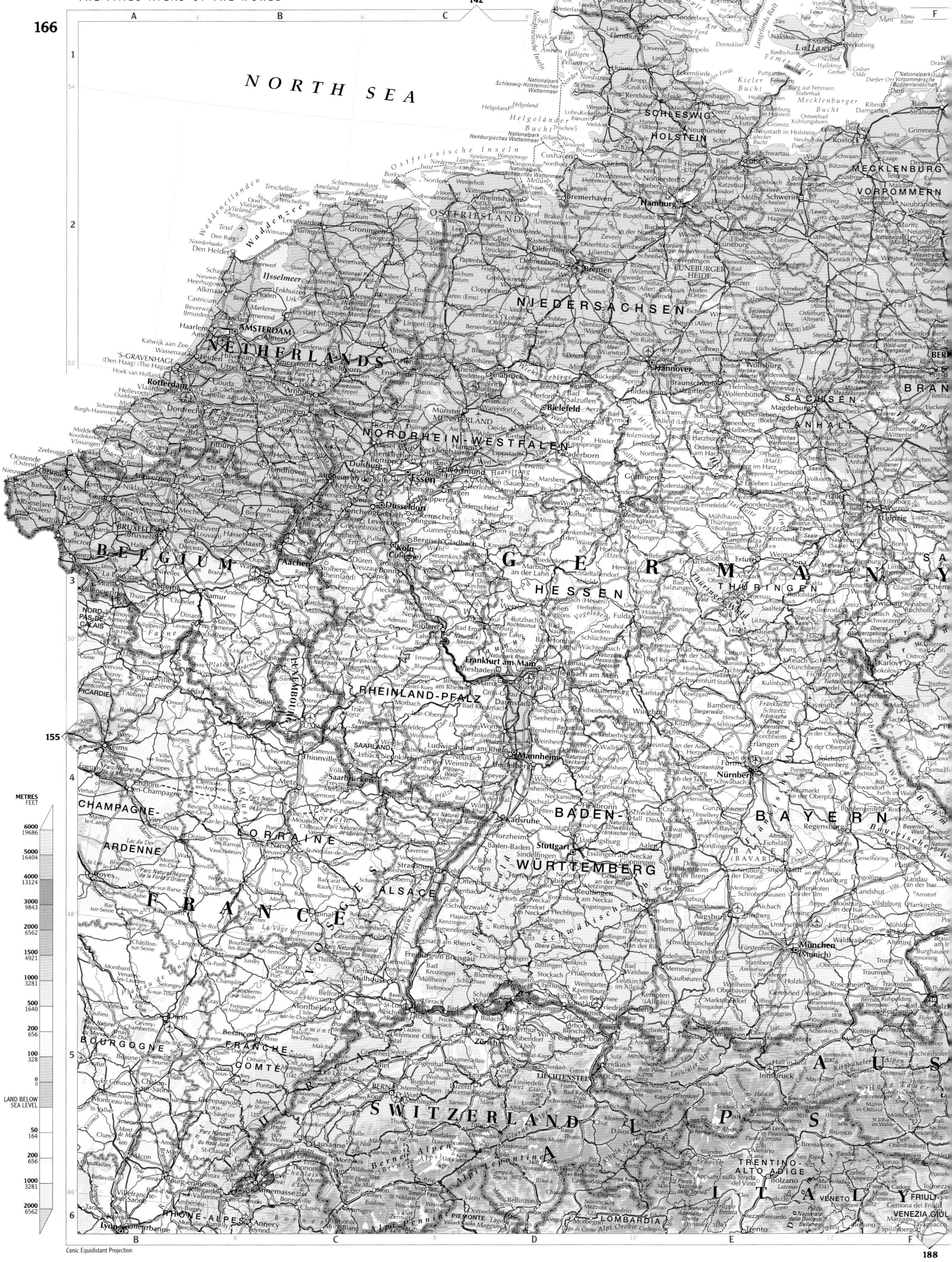

NORTH SEA

DENMARK

SCHLESWIG-HOLSTEIN

MECKLENBURG-VORPOMMERN

NIEDERSACHSEN

NETHERLANDS

Hamburg

Bremen

AMSTERDAM

'S-GRAVENHAGE
(Den Haag) (The Hague)

Rotterdam

Ijsselmeer

Den Helder

Groningen

NORDRHEIN-WESTFALEN

MÜNSTERLAND

Essen

Düsseldorf

Köln
(Cologne)

BELGIUM

BRUXELLES
(Brussels)

Aachen

Bonn

GERMANY

HESSEN

Hannover

SACHSEN-ANHALT

Magdeburg

THÜRINGEN

Erfurt

Frankfurt am Main
Wiesbaden

Offenbach am Main

RHEINLAND-PFALZ

Mannheim

Nürnberg

BAYERN
(BAVARIA)

SAARLAND

Saarbrücken

LUXEMBOURG

NORD-PAS-DE-CALAIS

PICARDIE

CHAMPAGNE-ARDENNE

LORRAINE

ALSACE

FRANCE

VOSGES

BADEN-WÜRTTEMBERG

Stuttgart

Karlsruhe

Baden-Baden

Strasbourg

München
(Munich)

Augsburg

BOURGOGNE

FRANCHE-COMTÉ

Dijon

RHÔNE-ALPES

Lyon

SWITZERLAND

BERN

LIECHTENSTEIN

ALPS

AUSTRIA

Innsbruck

ITALY

LOMBARDIA

TRENTINO-ALTO ADIGE

Bolzano

PIEMONTE

VENETO

FRIULI-VENEZIA GIULIA

Trento

METRES / FEET

6000 / 19686
5000 / 16404
4000 / 13124
3000 / 9843
2000 / 6562
1500 / 4921
1000 / 3281
500 / 1640
200 / 656
100 / 328
0

LAND BELOW SEA LEVEL

50 / 164
200 / 656
1000 / 3281
2000 / 6562

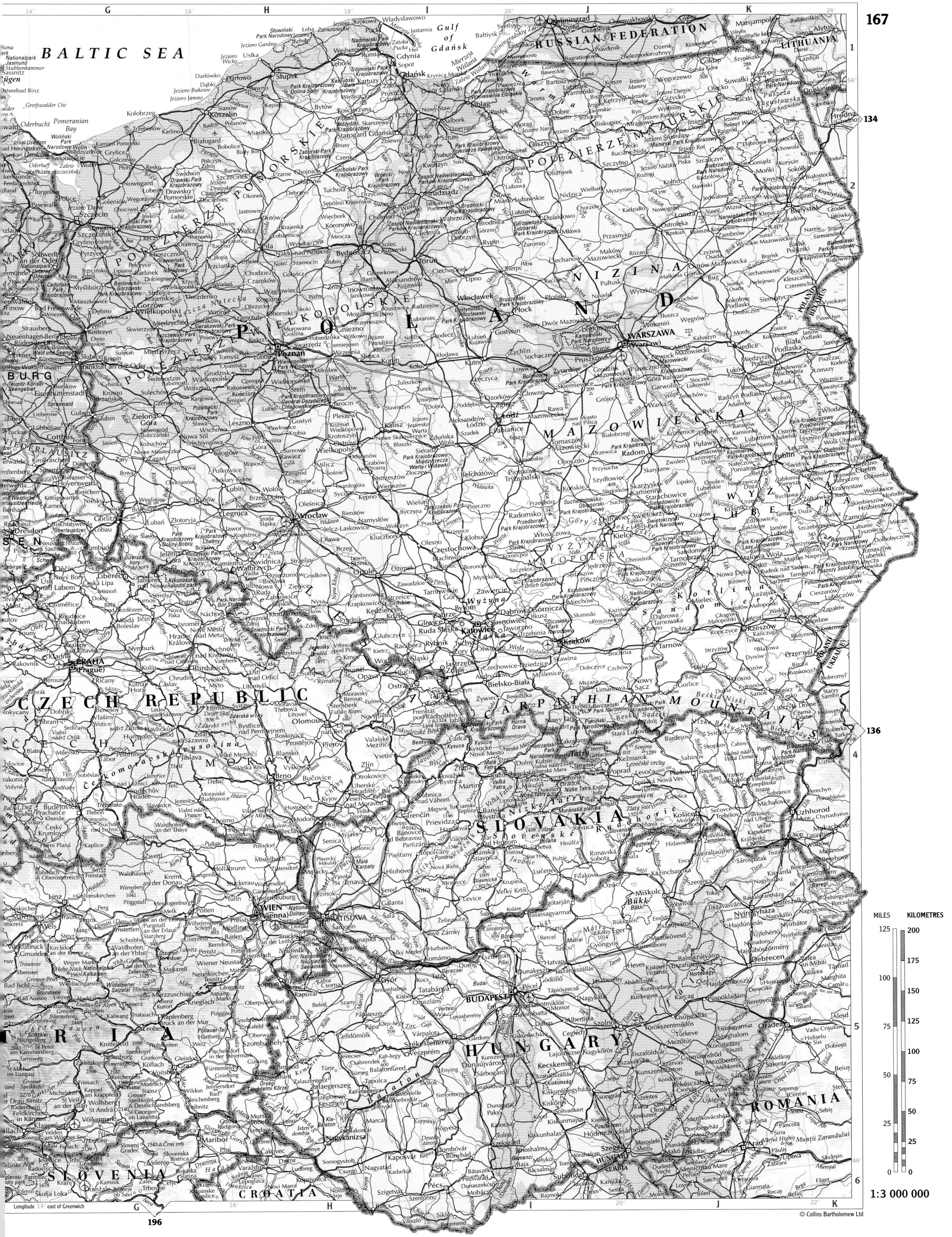
BALTIC SEA
Gulf of Gdańsk
RUSSIAN FEDERATION
LITHUANIA
POLAND
WARSZAWA (Warsaw)
Gdańsk
Poznań
Wrocław
Łódź
Kraków
Katowice
Lublin
Szczecin
Bydgoszcz
Toruń
Białystok
Olsztyn
Rzeszów
Kielce
Radom
Częstochowa
Opole
Zielona Góra
Gorzów Wielkopolski
Koszalin
Słupsk
Elbląg
Suwałki
Hrodna (Grodno)
Berlin
Dresden
Cottbus
Frankfurt an der Oder
CZECH REPUBLIC
PRAHA (Prague)
Brno
Ostrava
Olomouc
Plzeň
MORAVA
SLOVAKIA
BRATISLAVA
Košice
Žilina
Banská Bystrica
CARPATHIAN MOUNTAINS
Tatry
HUNGARY
BUDAPEST
Debrecen
Miskolc
Szeged
Pécs
Győr
Balaton
WIEN (Vienna)
Linz
Graz
Klagenfurt
Maribor
SLOVENIA
CROATIA
SERBIA
ROMANIA
Oradea
Arad
UKRAINE
BELARUS
Uzhhorod
POMORSKIE
WIELKOPOLSKIE
POJEZIERZE MAZURSKIE
NIZINA MAZOWIECKA
WYŻYNA LUBELSKA
WYŻYNA MAŁOPOLSKA
Longitude 14° east of Greenwich
134
136
196
MILES
KILOMETRES
1:3 000 000
© Collins Bartholomew Ltd

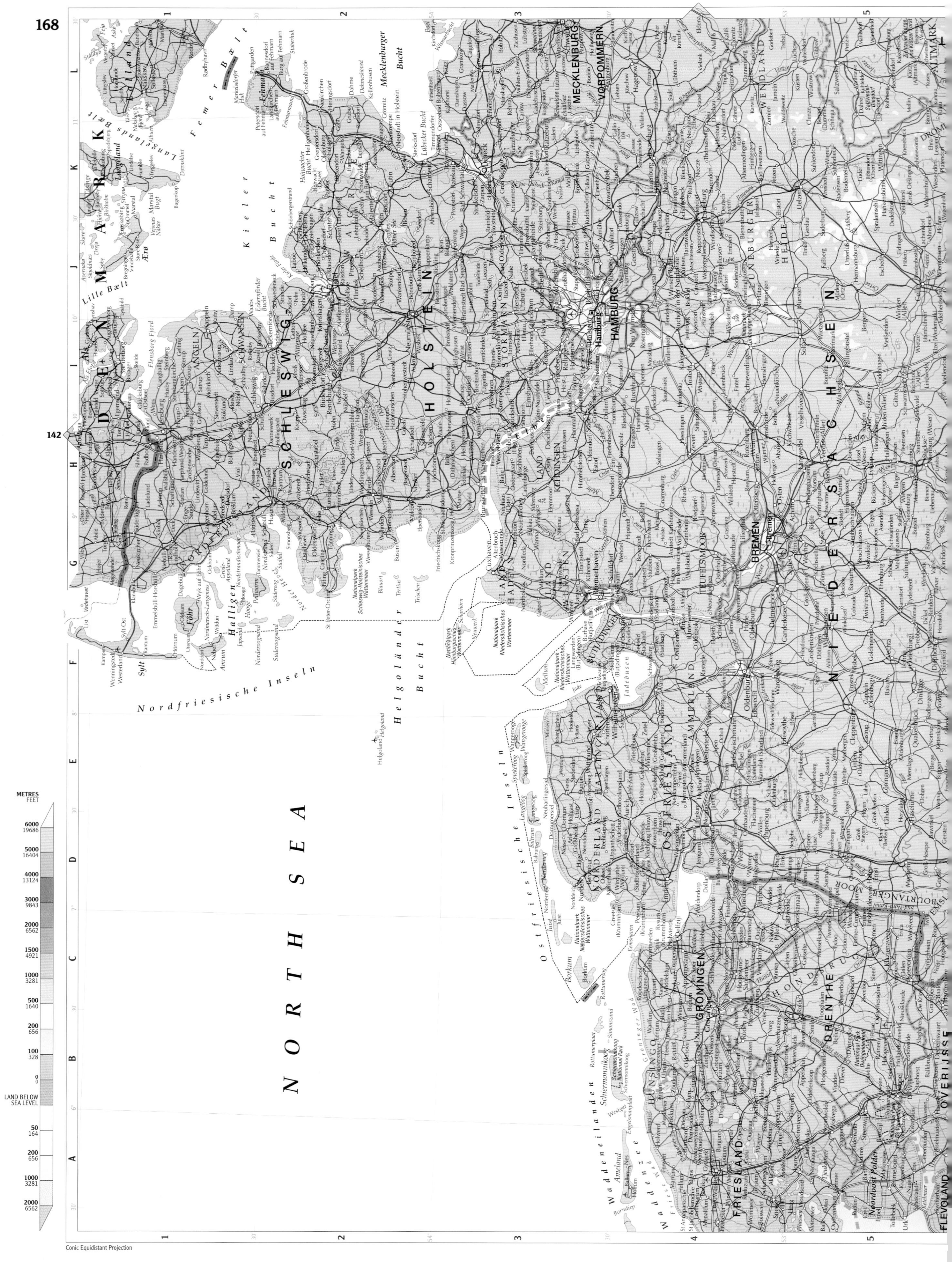
168
142
NORTH SEA
Nordfriesische Inseln
Ostfriesische Inseln
Helgoländer Bucht
Kieler Bucht
Mecklenburger Bucht
Femer Bælt
Lille Bælt
DENMARK
SCHLESWIG
HOLSTEIN
NIEDERSACHSEN
HAMBURG
BREMEN
MECKLENBURG-VORPOMMERN
GRONINGEN
FRIESLAND
DRENTHE
OVERIJSSEL
FLEVOLAND
ALTMARK
LÜNEBURGER HEIDE
Sylt
Föhr
Amrum
Helgoland
Borkum
Ameland
Schiermonnikoog
Fehmarn
Langeland
Ærø
Cuxhaven
Wilhelmshaven
Bremerhaven
Oldenburg
Emden
Lübeck
Kiel
Flensburg
Neumünster
METRES
FEET
6000
19686
5000
16404
4000
13124
3000
9843
2000
6562
1500
4921
1000
3281
500
1640
200
656
100
328
0
0
LAND BELOW SEA LEVEL
50
164
200
656
1000
3281
2000
6562

Conic Equidistant Projection

171

173

172

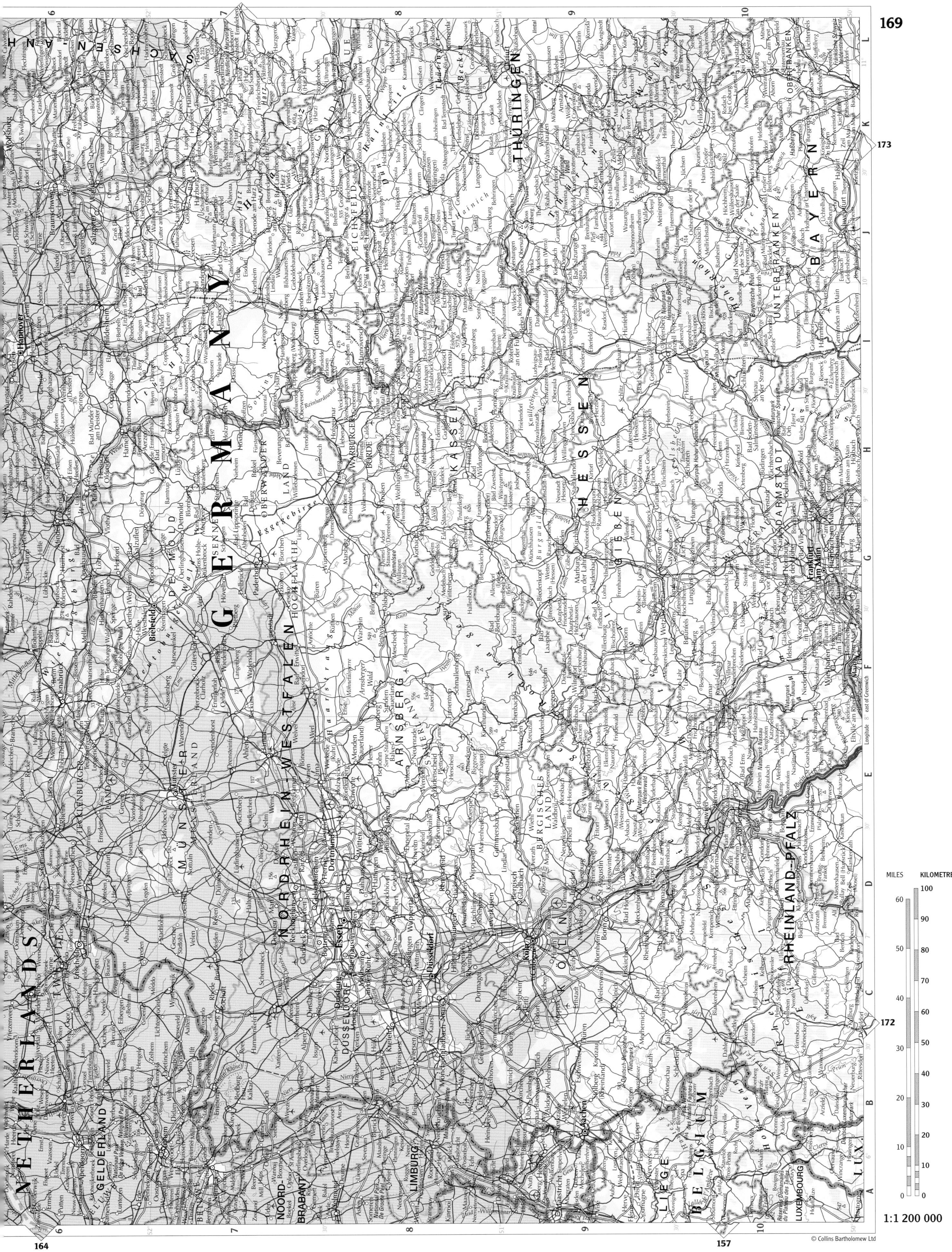

GERMANY

NETHERLANDS

BELGIUM

LUXEMBOURG

SACHSEN-ANHALT

NIEDERSACHSEN

NORDRHEIN-WESTFALEN

HESSEN

THÜRINGEN

BAYERN

RHEINLAND-PFALZ

UNTERFRANKEN

OBERFRANKEN

DARMSTADT

GIEßEN

KASSEL

ARNSBERG

MÜNSTERLAND

DETMOLD

GELDERLAND

NOORD-BRABANT

LIMBURG

LIÈGE

Hannover

Bielefeld

Göttingen

Köln

Düsseldorf

Essen

Dortmund

Wuppertal

Bonn

Aachen

Maastrichт

Frankfurt am Main

MILES   KILOMETRES

60   100
      90
50   80
      70
40   60
      50
30   40
20   30
      20
10
      10
0   0

1:1 200 000

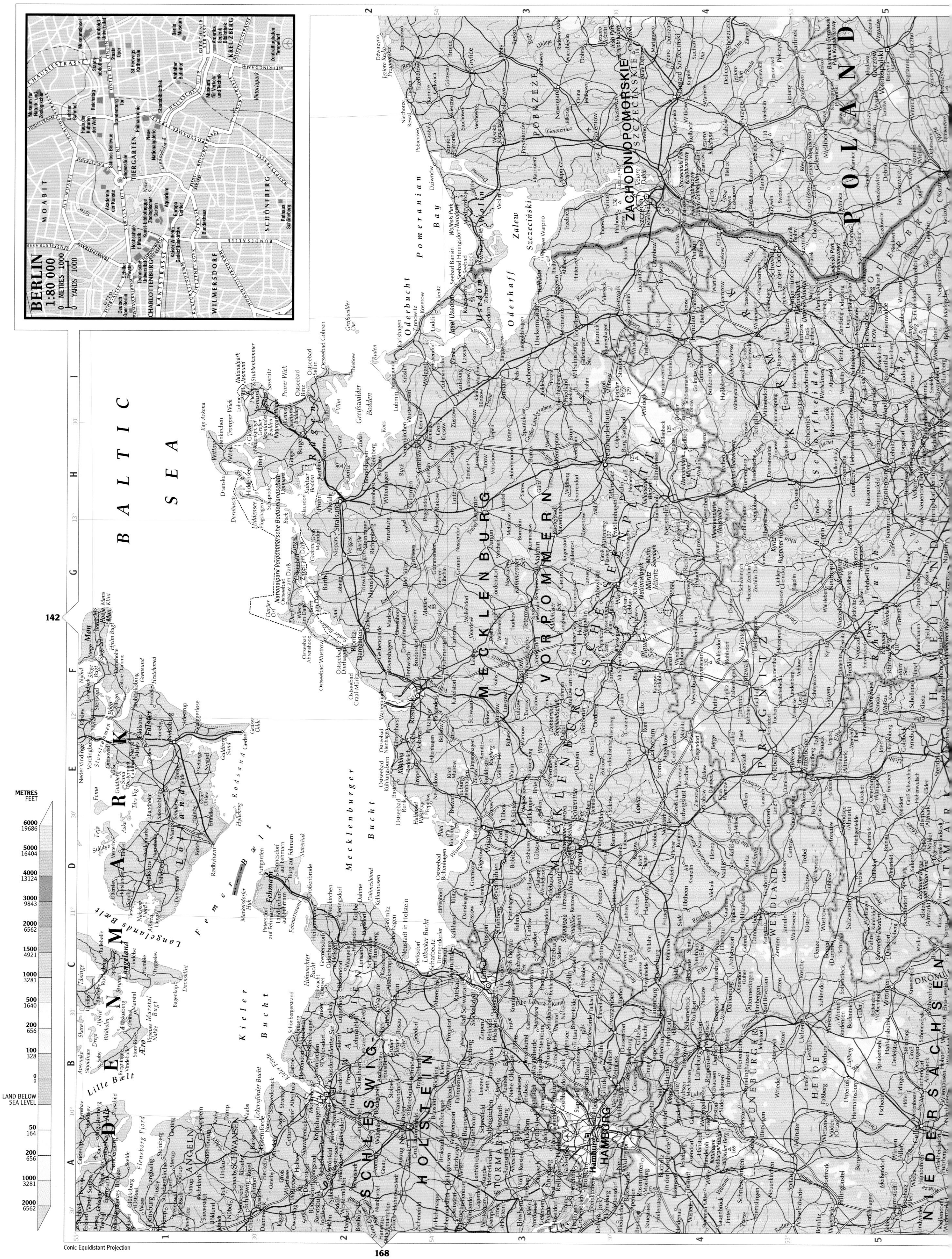

BERLIN
1:80 000

MECKLENBURG

VORPOMMERN

POLAND

BALTIC SEA

DENMARK

SCHLESWIG-HOLSTEIN

NIEDERSACHSEN

HAMBURG

ZACHODNIOPOMORSKIE

Pomeranian Bay

142

Conic Equidistant Projection

174

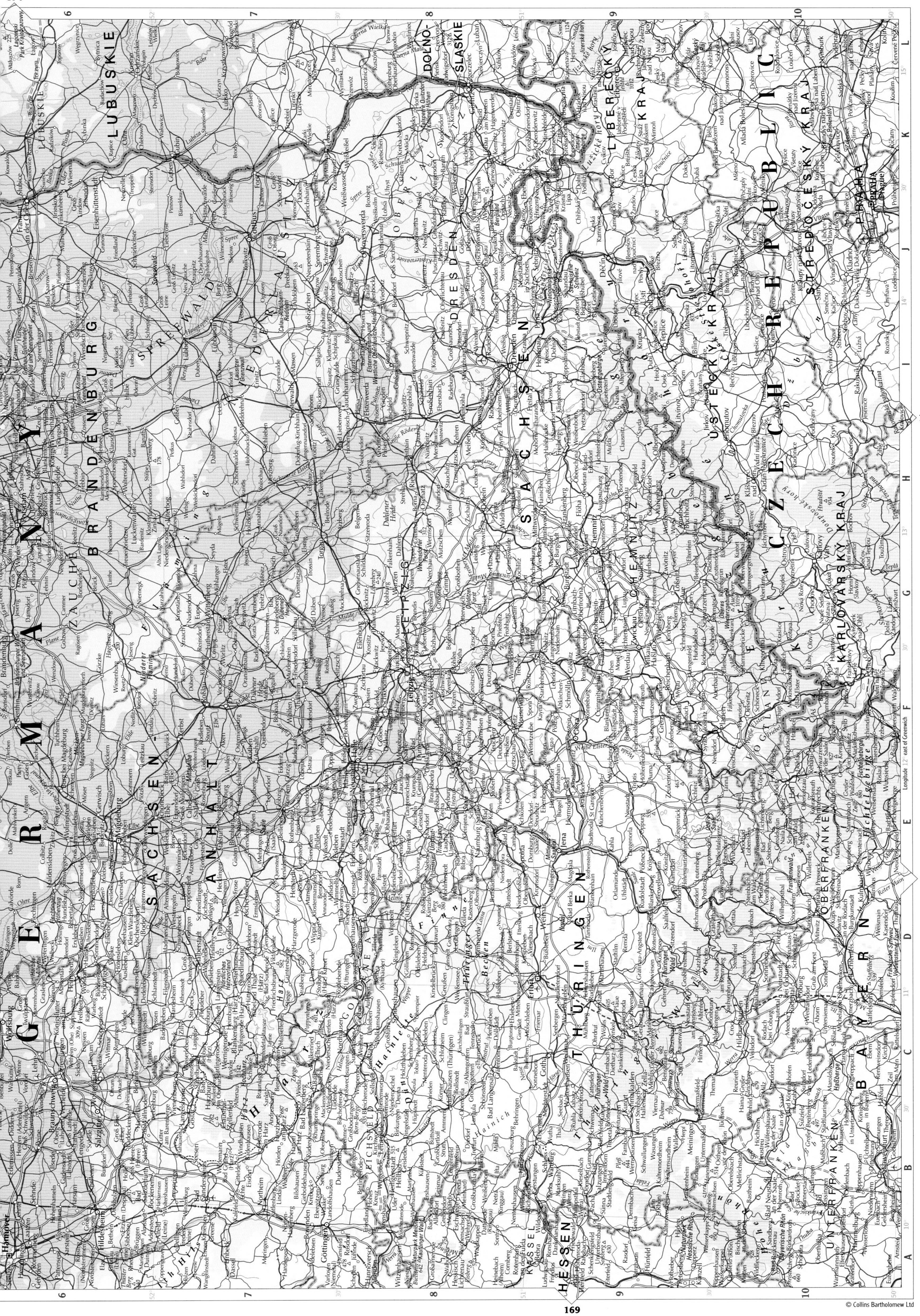

176

173

GERMANY

LUBUSKIE

DOLNO- ŚLĄSKIE

LIBERECKÝ KRAJ

BRANDENBURG

SPREEWALD

OBERLAUSITZ

NIEDERLAUSITZ

ZAUCHE

DRESDEN

ÚSTECKÝ KRAJ

KARLOVARSKÝ KRAJ

STŘEDOČESKÝ KRAJ

ČZECH REPUBLIC

PRAHA

SACHSEN

CHEMNITZ

SACHSEN-ANHALT

LEIPZIG

VOGTLAND

THÜRINGEN

HARZ

EICHSFELD

GOLDENE AUE

KASSEL

HESSEN

OBERFRANKEN

BAYERN

UNTERFRANKEN

Longitude 12° east of Greenwich

MILES	KILOMETRES
60	100
	90
50	80
	70
40	60
30	50
	40
20	30
10	20
	10
0	0

1:1 200 000

BELGIUM
LIÈGE

RHEINLAND

PFALZ

HESSEN

DARMSTADT

Frankfurt am Main

LUXEMBOURG
LUXEMBOURG

NORDPFÄLZER
BERGLAND

SAARLAND

Mannheim
Ludwigshafen am Rhein
Heidelberg

Saarbrücken

MOSELLE

KARLSRUHE

STUTTGART

LORRAINE

Karlsruhe

Baden-Baden

BAS-RHIN

MEURTHE-ET-MOSELLE

Strasbourg

BADEN-WÜRTTEMBERG

Stuttgart

ALSACE

TÜBINGEN

F R A N C E

VOSGES

HAUT-RHIN

FREIBURG

Colmar

Freiburg im Breisgau

Mulhouse

HAUTE-SAÔNE

SCHAFFHAUSEN

HOTZENWALD

LINZGAU

TERRITOIRE
DE BELFORT

Belfort

SUNDGAU

THURGAU

FRANCHE-COMTÉ

ZÜRICH

AARGAU

Zürich

APPENZELL
AUSSERRHODEN
APPENZELL
INNERRHODEN

DOUBS

JURA

SOLOTHURN

BASELLANDSCHAFT

BERN

S W I T Z E R L A N D

SANKT
GALLEN

VORARLBERG

LUZERN

ZUG

SCHWYZ

GLARUS

LIECHTENSTEIN

NEUCHÂTEL

VAUD

Conic Equidistant Projection

METRES	FEET
6000	19686
5000	16404
4000	13124
3000	9843
2000	6562
1500	4921
1000	3281
500	1640
200	656
100	328
0	0

LAND BELOW
SEA LEVEL

50	164
200	656
1000	3281
2000	6562

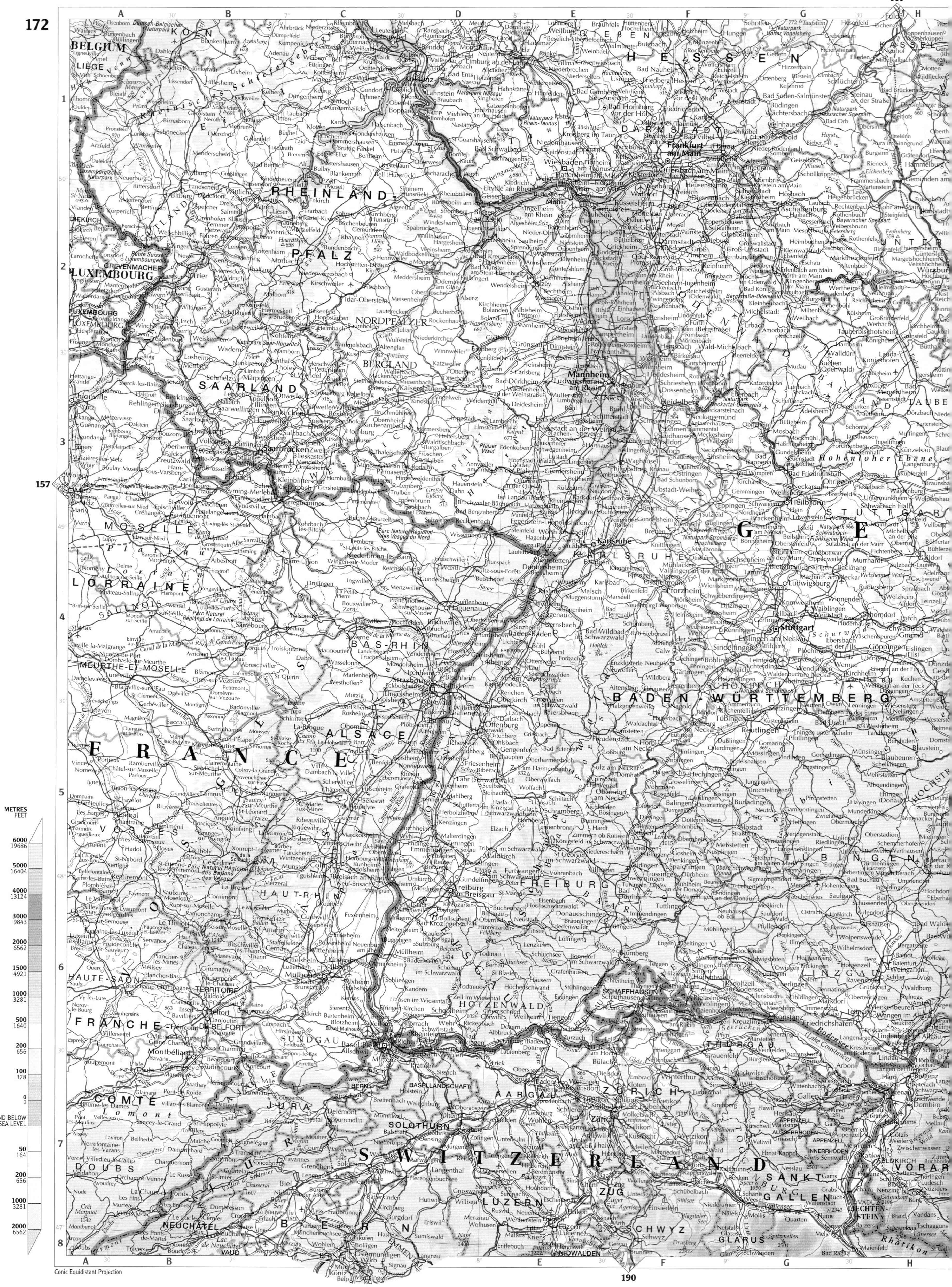

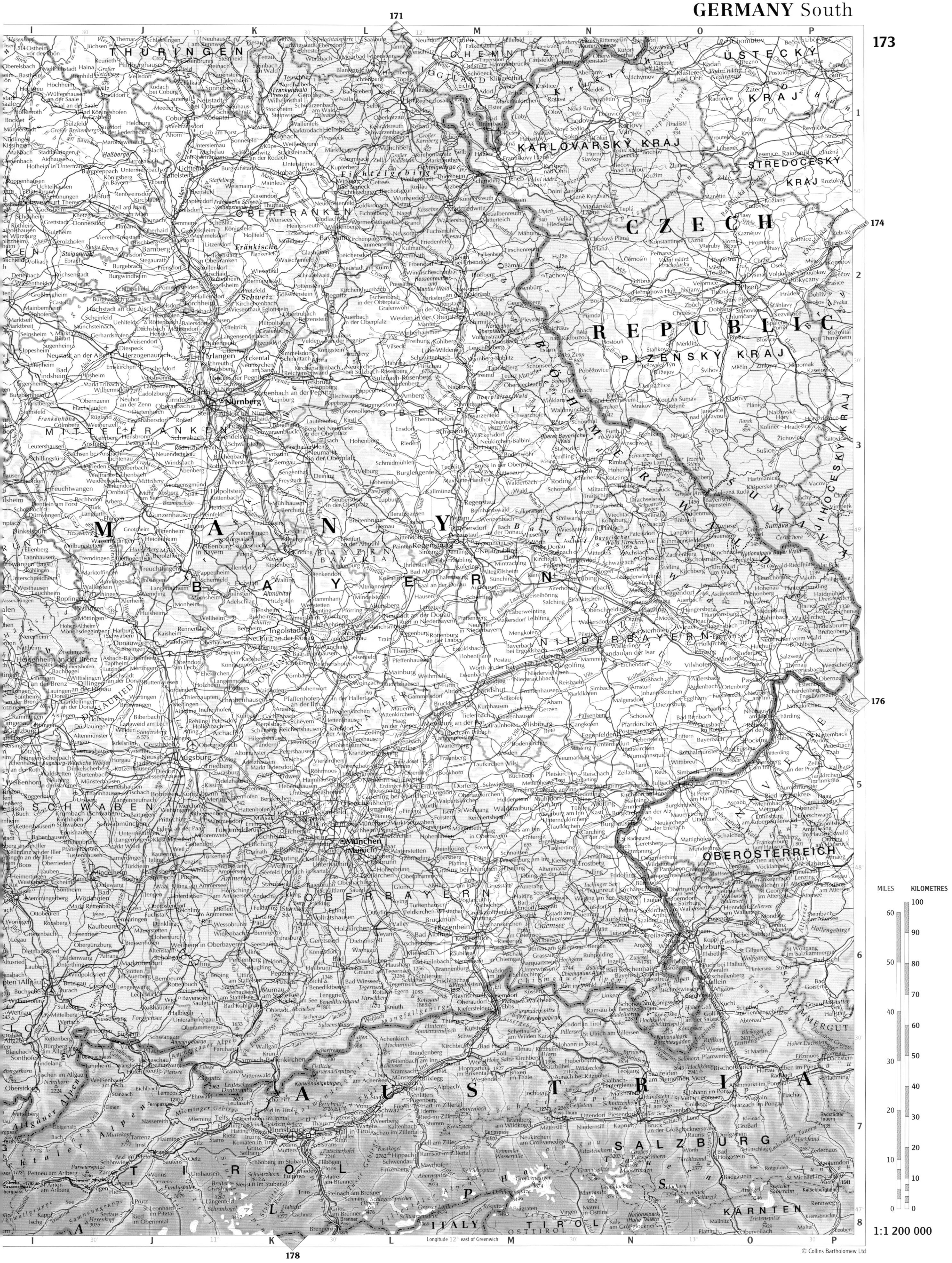
171
174
176
178
THÜRINGEN
OBERFRANKEN
MITTELFRANKEN
OBERPFALZ
NIEDERBAYERN
OBERBAYERN
SCHWABEN
GERMANY
BAYERN
(BAVARIA)
CZECH
REPUBLIC
KARLOVARSKÝ KRAJ
PLZEŇSKÝ KRAJ
ÚSTECKÝ KRAJ
STŘEDOČESKÝ KRAJ
JIHOČESKÝ KRAJ
AUSTRIA
OBERÖSTERREICH
SALZBURG
TIROL
KÄRNTEN
ITALY
Nürnberg
München (Munich)
Augsburg
Regensburg
Ingolstadt
Landshut
Passau
Plzeň
Salzburg
Innsbruck
Bamberg
Bayreuth
Erlangen
Rosenheim
Chiemsee
Longitude 12° east of Greenwich
MILES
KILOMETRES

1:1 200 000

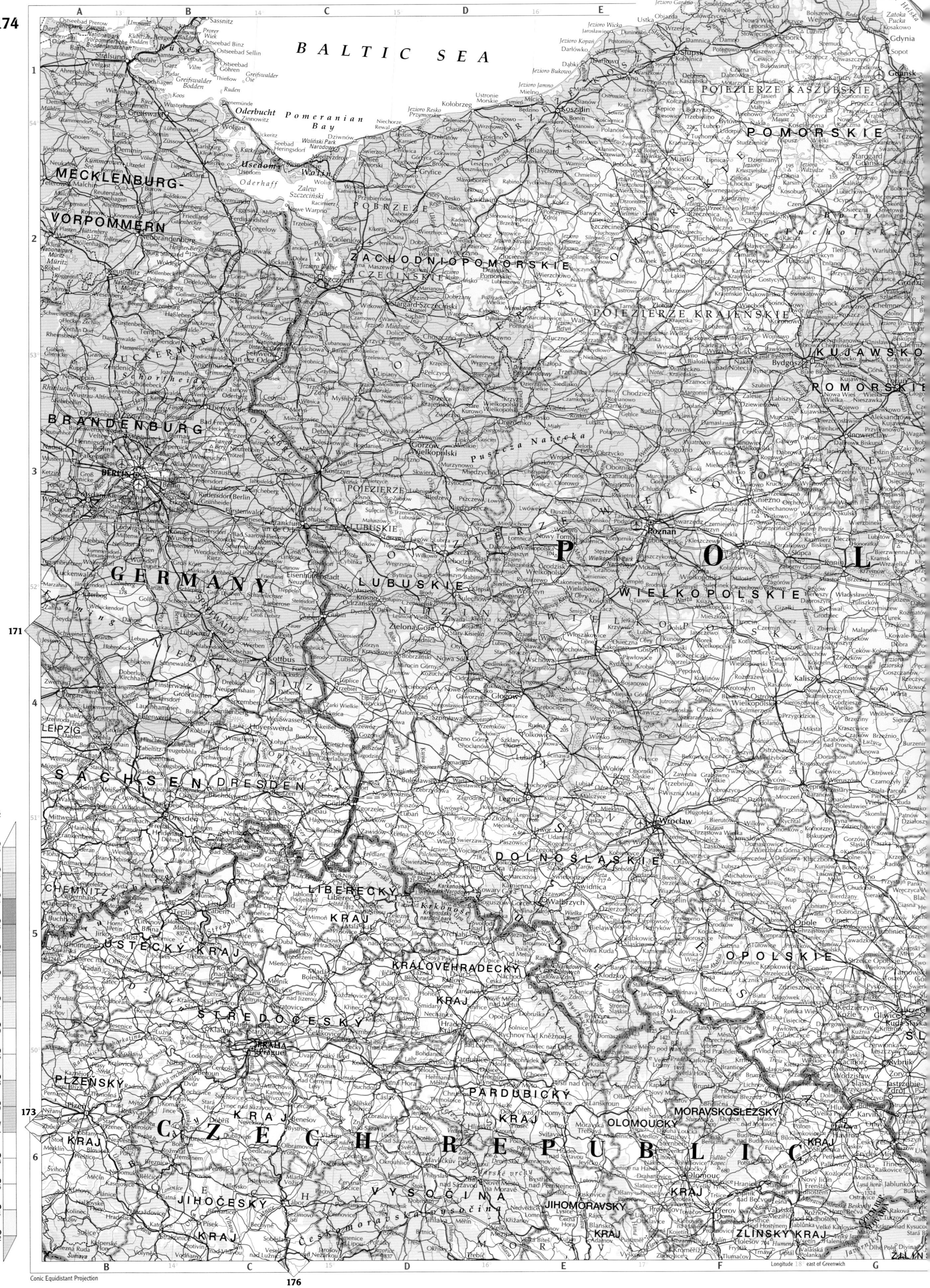

BALTIC SEA

Pomeranian
Bay

MECKLENBURG

VORPOMMERN

BRANDENBURG

GERMANY

LEIPZIG

SACHSEN

DRESDEN

CHEMNITZ

ÚSTECKÝ KRAJ

PLZEŇSKÝ

KRAJ

STŘEDOČESKÝ

PRAHA

JIHOČESKÝ

KRAJ

CZECH REPUBLIC

VYSOČINA

ZACHODNIOPOMORSKIE

SZCZECIŃSKIE

POJEZIERZE KRAJEŃSKIE

POJEZIERZE KASZUBSKIE

POMORSKIE

KUJAWSKO-

POMORSKIE

POJEZIERZE

LUBUSKIE

LUBUSKIE

WIELKOPOLSKIE

Poznań

P O L

Wrocław

DOLNOŚLĄSKIE

OPOLSKIE

LIBERECKÝ

KRAJ

KRÁLOVÉHRADECKÝ

KRAJ

PARDUBICKÝ

KRAJ

OLOMOUCKÝ

KRAJ

MORAVSKOSLEZSKÝ

KRAJ

JIHOMORAVSKÝ

KRAJ

ZLÍNSKÝ KRAJ

Berlin

Dresden

METRES
FEET

6000
19686

5000
16404

4000
13124

3000
9843

2000
6562

1500
4921

1000
3281

500
1640

200
656

100
328

0
0
LAND BELOW
SEA LEVEL

50
164

200
656

1000
3281

2000
6562

Longitude 18 east of Greenwich

Conic Equidistant Projection

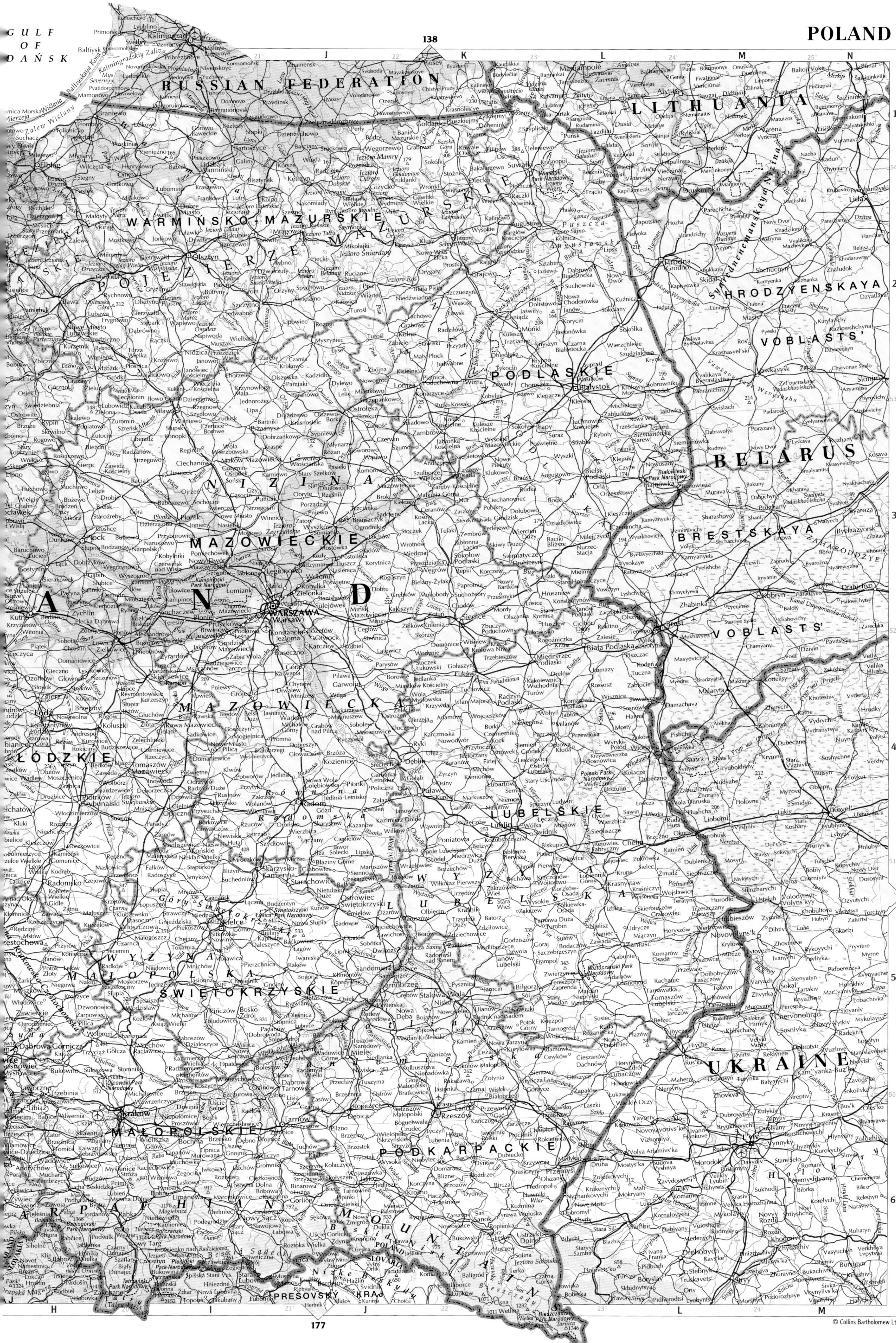
GULF OF GDAŃSK
RUSSIAN FEDERATION
LITHUANIA
BELARUS
UKRAINE
SLOVAKIA
Kaliningrad
WARMIŃSKO-MAZURSKIE
POJEZIERZE MAZURSKIE
PODLASKIE
MAZOWIECKIE
NIZINA MAZOWIECKA
WARSZAWA (Warsaw)
ŁÓDZKIE
LUBELSKIE
WYŻYNA LUBELSKA
WYŻYNA MAŁOPOLSKA
ŚWIĘTOKRZYSKIE
MAŁOPOLSKIE
PODKARPACKIE
CARPATHIAN MOUNTAINS
HRODZYENSKAYA VOBLASTS'
BRESTSKAYA VOBLASTS'
PREŠOVSKÝ KRAJ
Białystok
Lublin
Kraków
Rzeszów
Brest
Hrodna
L'viv
138
136
177

MILES
KILOMETRES
60
40
20
0
100
80
60
40
20
0

1:1 800 000

171
173
178
191
METRES
FEET
6000
19686
5000
16404
4000
13124
3000
9843
2000
6562
1500
4921
1000
3281
500
1640
200
656
100
328
0
0
LAND BELOW
SEA LEVEL
50
164
200
656
1000
3281
2000
6562
CZECH REPUBLIC
GERMANY
AUSTRIA
ITALY
SLOVENIA
CROATIA
SACHSEN
CHEMNITZ
ÚSTECKÝ KRAJ
LIBERECKÝ KRAJ
KRÁLOVÉHRADECKÝ KRAJ
DOLNOŚLĄSKIE
KARLOVARSKÝ KRAJ
STŘEDOČESKÝ KRAJ
PARDUBICKÝ KRAJ
OLOMOUCKÝ KRAJ
PLZEŇSKÝ KRAJ
VYSOČINA
JIHOČESKÝ KRAJ
JIHOMORAVSKÝ KRAJ
OBERFRANKEN
OBERPFALZ
BAYERN
NIEDERBAYERN
OBERBAYERN
NIEDERÖSTERREICH
OBERÖSTERREICH
BRATISLAVSKÝ KRAJ
BURGENLAND
GYŐR-MOSON
SOPRON
VAS
ZALA
TIROL
SALZBURG
STEIERMARK
KÄRNTEN
VENETO
FRIULI-VENEZIA GIULIA
BELLUNO
PORDENONE
UDINE
TREVISO
PRAHA (Prague)
WIEN (Vienna)
LJUBLJANA
ZAGREB
BRATISLAVA
Salzburg
Graz
Linz
Plzeň
Passau
Klagenfurt
Maribor
Villach
Gulf of Trieste

Conic Equidistant Projection

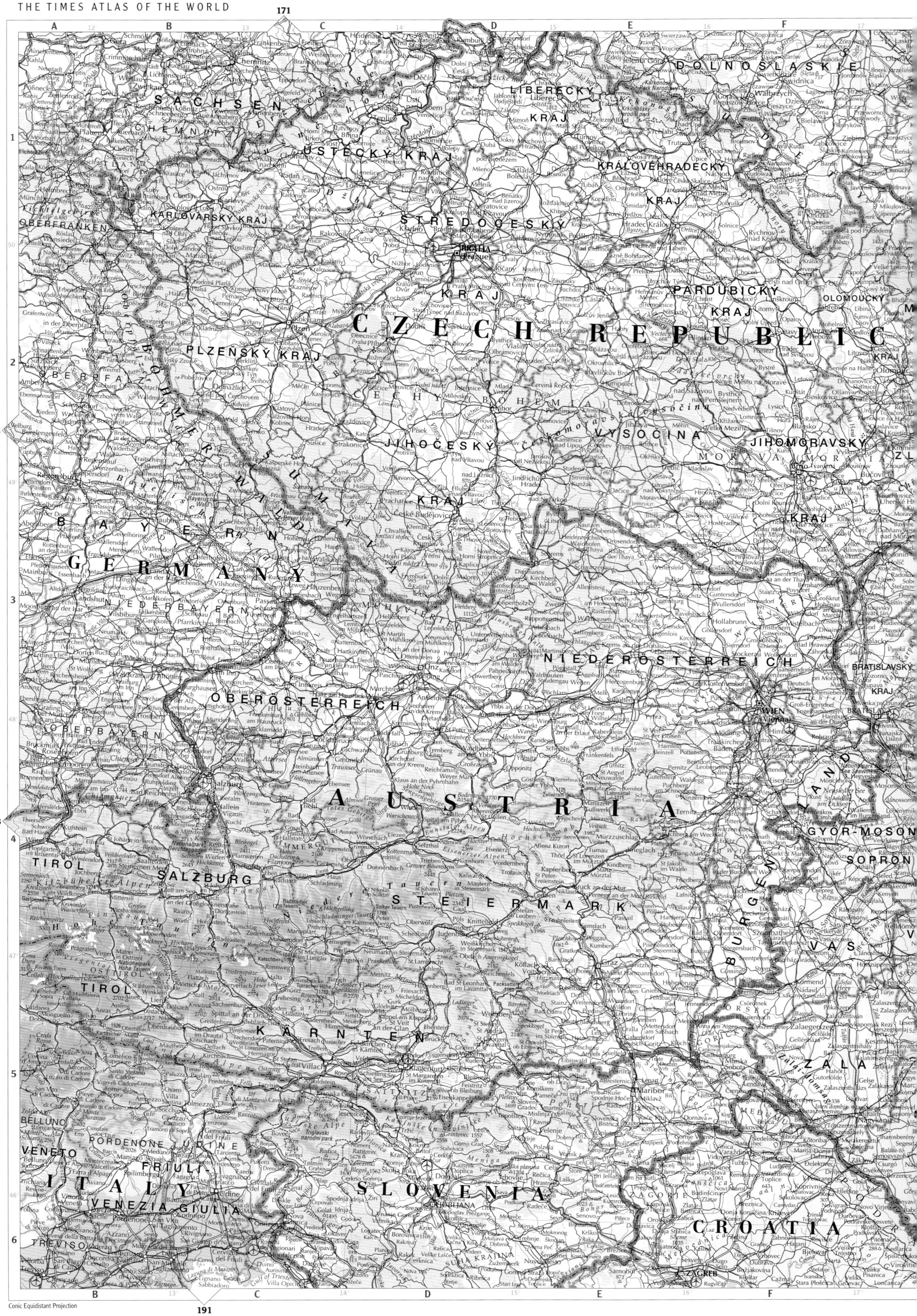

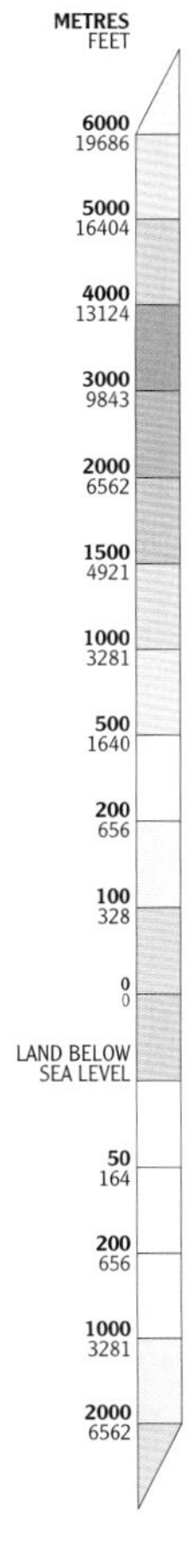

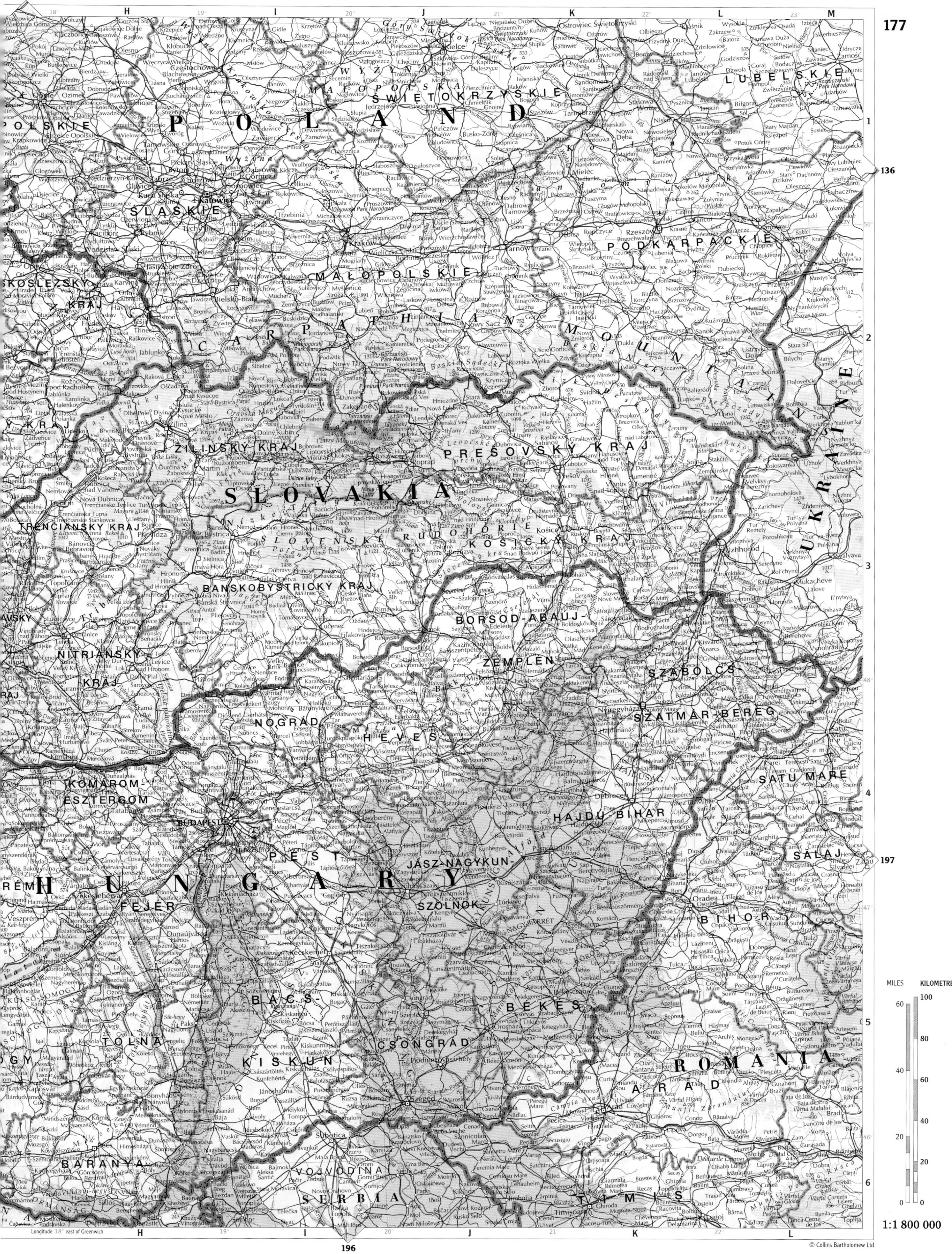

POLAND

ŚWIETOKRZYSKIE

LUBELSKIE

ŚLĄSKIE

MAŁOPOLSKIE

PODKARPACKIE

KOSLEZSKY KRAJ

CARPATHIAN MOUNTAINS

UKRAINE

ŽILINSKÝ KRAJ

PREŠOVSKÝ KRAJ

SLOVAKIA

TRENČIANSKY KRAJ

SLOVENSKÉ RUDOHORIE

KOŠICKÝ KRAJ

BANSKOBYSTRICKÝ KRAJ

NITRIANSKY KRAJ

BORSOD-ABAUJ-

ZEMPLÉN

SZABOLCS-

SZATMÁR-BEREG

NÓGRÁD

HEVES

SATU MARE

KOMÁROM-ESZTERGOM

HAJDÚ-BIHAR

SÁLAJ

BUDAPEST

PEST

JÁSZ-NAGYKUN-

HUNGARY

197

FEJÉR

SZOLNOK

Oradea

BIHOR

BÁCS-

BÉKÉS

TOLNA

KISKUN

CSONGRÁD

ROMANIA

ARAD

BARANYA

VOJVODINA

SERBIA

TIMIŞ

© Collins Bartholomew Ltd

MILES   KILOMETRES

60   100

80

40   60

40

20   20

0   0

1:1 800 000

178

172

GERMANY

BADEN

WÜRTTEMBERG

TÜBINGEN

STUTTGART

MITTELFRANKEN

SCHWABEN

BAYERN

OBERPFALZ

NIEDERBAYERN

OBERBAYERN

München
Munich

VORARLBERG

ALLGÄU

TIROL

ALPS

A U S T R I A

SALZBURG

OSTTIROL

TIROL

GRAUBÜNDEN

SWITZERLAND

UNTERENGADIN

OBERENGADIN

BOLZANO

TRENTINO-ALTO ADIGE

FRIULI

VENEZIA GIULIA

BELLUNO

PORDENONE

VENETO

TREVISO

TRENTO

I T A L Y

LOMBARDIA

BRESCIA

BERGAMO

SONDRIO

VICENZA

Scale (left margin):

METRES / FEET
6000 / 19686
5000 / 16404
4000 / 13124
3000 / 9843
2000 / 6562
1500 / 4921
1000 / 3281
500 / 1640
200 / 656
100 / 328
0 / 0
LAND BELOW SEA LEVEL
50 / 164
200 / 656
1000 / 3281
2000 / 6562

Longitude 12 east of Greenwich

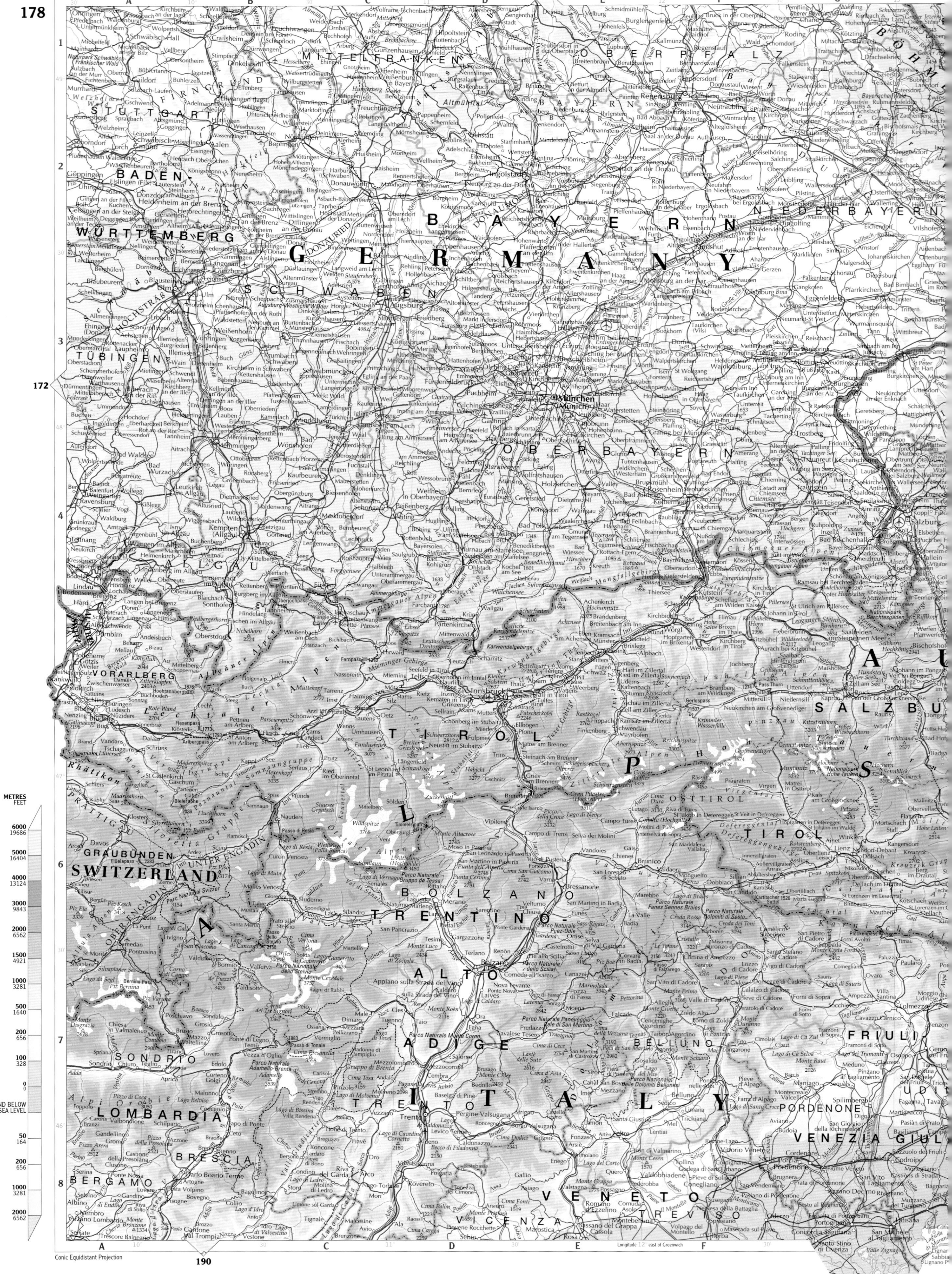

177

1:1 200 000

© Collins Bartholomew Ltd

CZECH REPUBLIC
JIHOČESKÝ KRAJ
VYSOČINA
JIHOMORAVSKÝ KRAJ
NIEDERÖSTERREICH
WIEN
STEIERMARK
KÄRNTEN
BURGENLAND
HUNGARY
GYŐR-MOSON-SOPRON
VAS
ZALA
SLOVENIA
CROATIA
SLOVAKIA
174
191
MILES
KILOMETRES

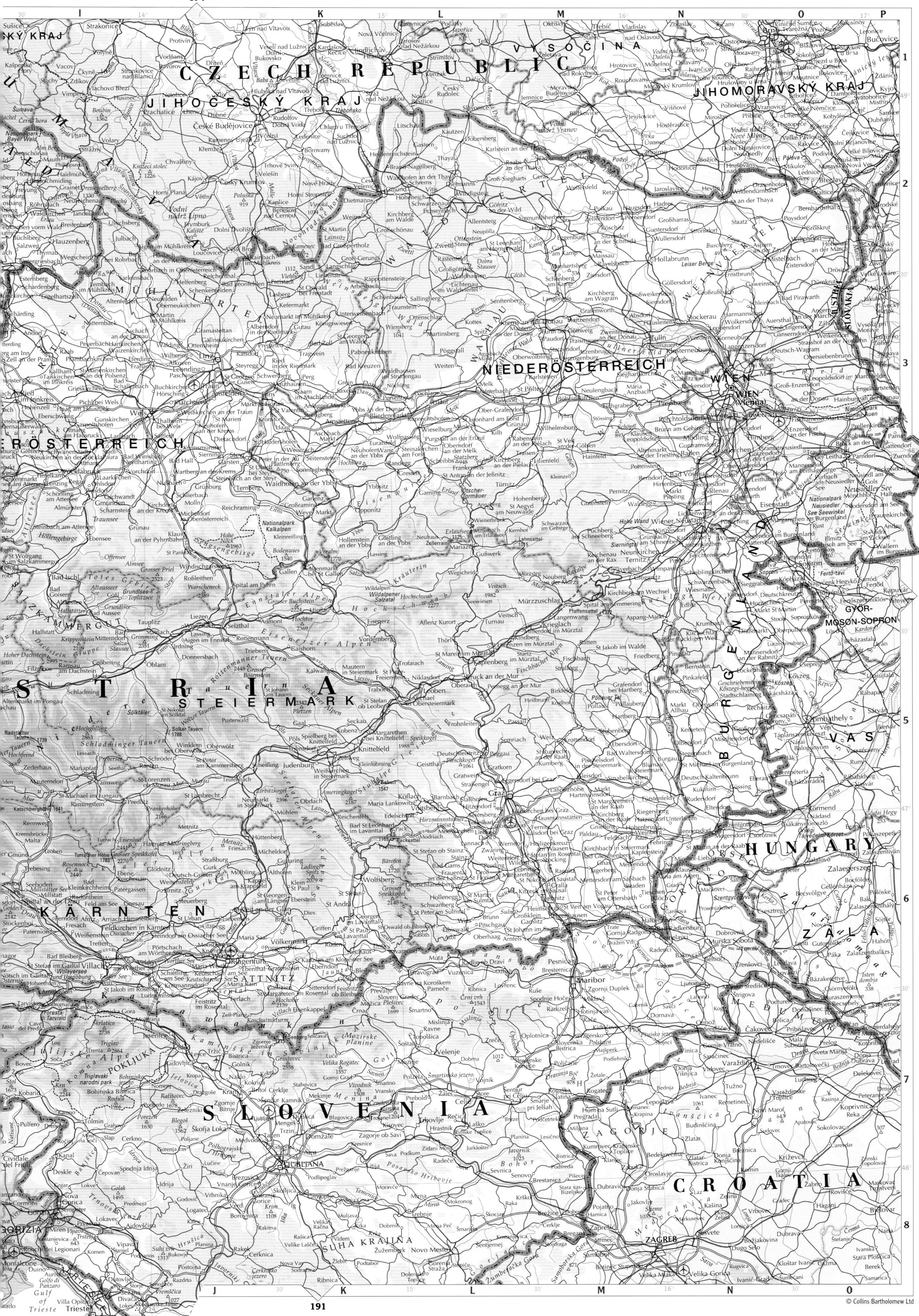

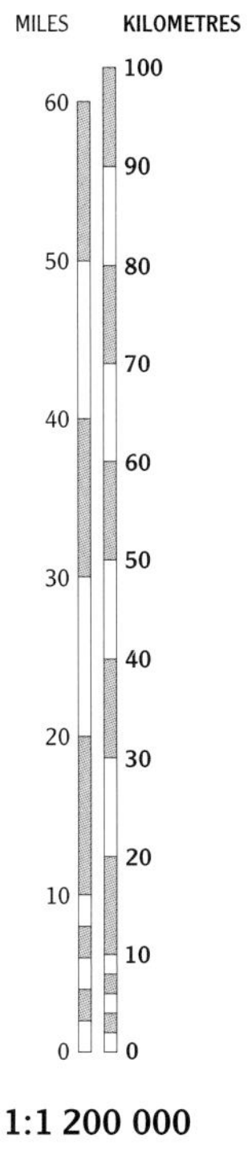

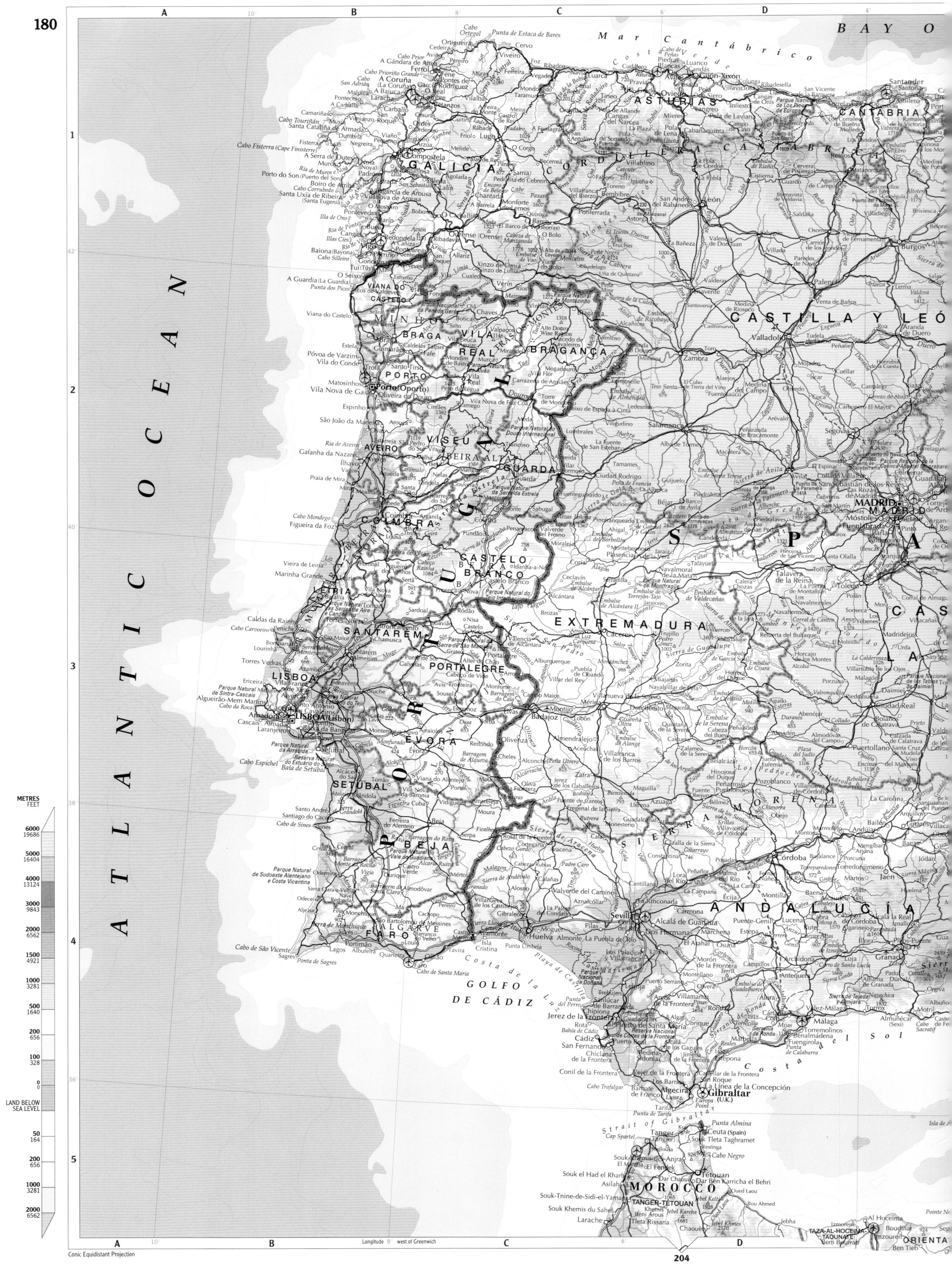
A
B
C
D
BAY O
Mar Cantábrico
Costa Verde
ATLANTIC OCEAN
GALICIA
ASTURIAS
CANTABRIA
CORDILLERA CANTÁBRICA
CASTILLA Y LEÓ
PORTUGAL
ESPA
EXTREMADURA
ANDALUCÍA
CAS
LA
VIANA DO CASTELO
BRAGA
VILA REAL
BRAGANÇA
PORTO
VISEU
AVEIRO
GUARDA
COIMBRA
CASTELO BRANCO
LEIRIA
SANTARÉM
PORTALEGRE
LISBOA
SETÚBAL
ÉVORA
BEJA
FARO
ALGARVE
SIERRA MORENA
GOLFO DE CÁDIZ
Costa de la Luz
Costa del Sol
Strait of Gibraltar
MOROCCO
TANGER-TETOUAN
TAZA-AL-HOCEIMA-TAOUNATE
ORIENTA
A Coruña
Santiago de Compostela
Lugo
Ourense
Vigo
Pontevedra
Oviedo
Gijón-Xixón
Santander
León
Burgos
Palencia
Valladolid
Zamora
Salamanca
Segovia
Ávila
MADRID
Toledo
Cáceres
Badajoz
Mérida
Porto (Oporto)
Coimbra
LISBOA (Lisbon)
Sevilla
Córdoba
Huelva
Cádiz
Jerez de la Frontera
Málaga
Granada
Jaén
Ciudad Real
Gibraltar (U.K.)
Ceuta (Spain)
Tanger
Tetouan
Cabo Fisterra (Cape Finisterre)
Cabo de São Vicente
Cabo Trafalgar
METRES
FEET
6000 19686
5000 16404
4000 13124
3000 9843
2000 6562
1500 4921
1000 3281
500 1640
200 656
100 328
0 0
LAND BELOW SEA LEVEL
50 164
200 656
1000 3281
2000 6562
Longitude 8° west of Greenwich

Conic Equidistant Projection

204

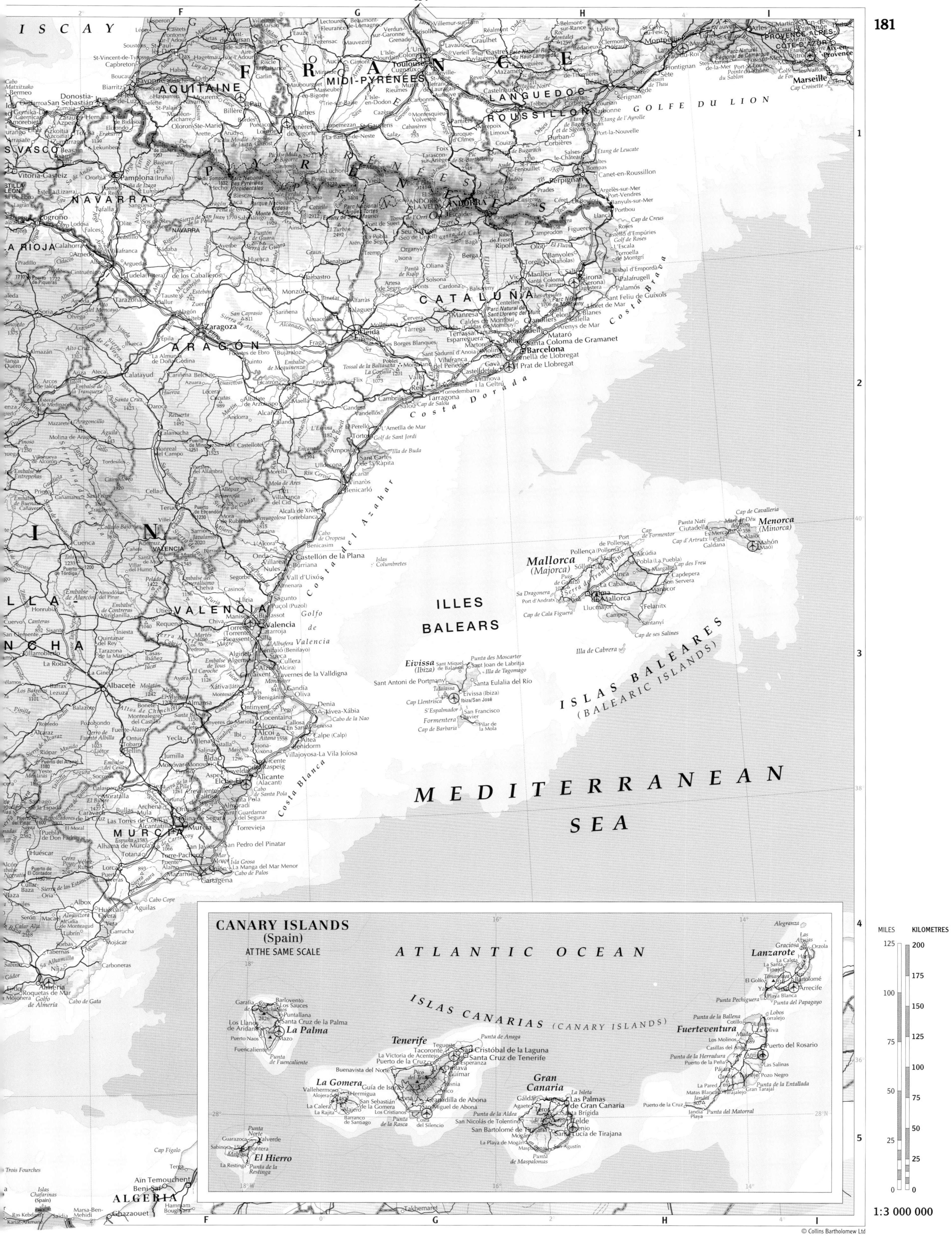

MEDITERRANEAN SEA

ILLES BALEARS

ISLAS BALEARES (BALEARIC ISLANDS)

CANARY ISLANDS
(Spain)
AT THE SAME SCALE

ATLANTIC OCEAN

ISLAS CANARIAS (CANARY ISLANDS)

1:3 000 000

MILES KILOMETRES

© Collins Bartholomew Ltd

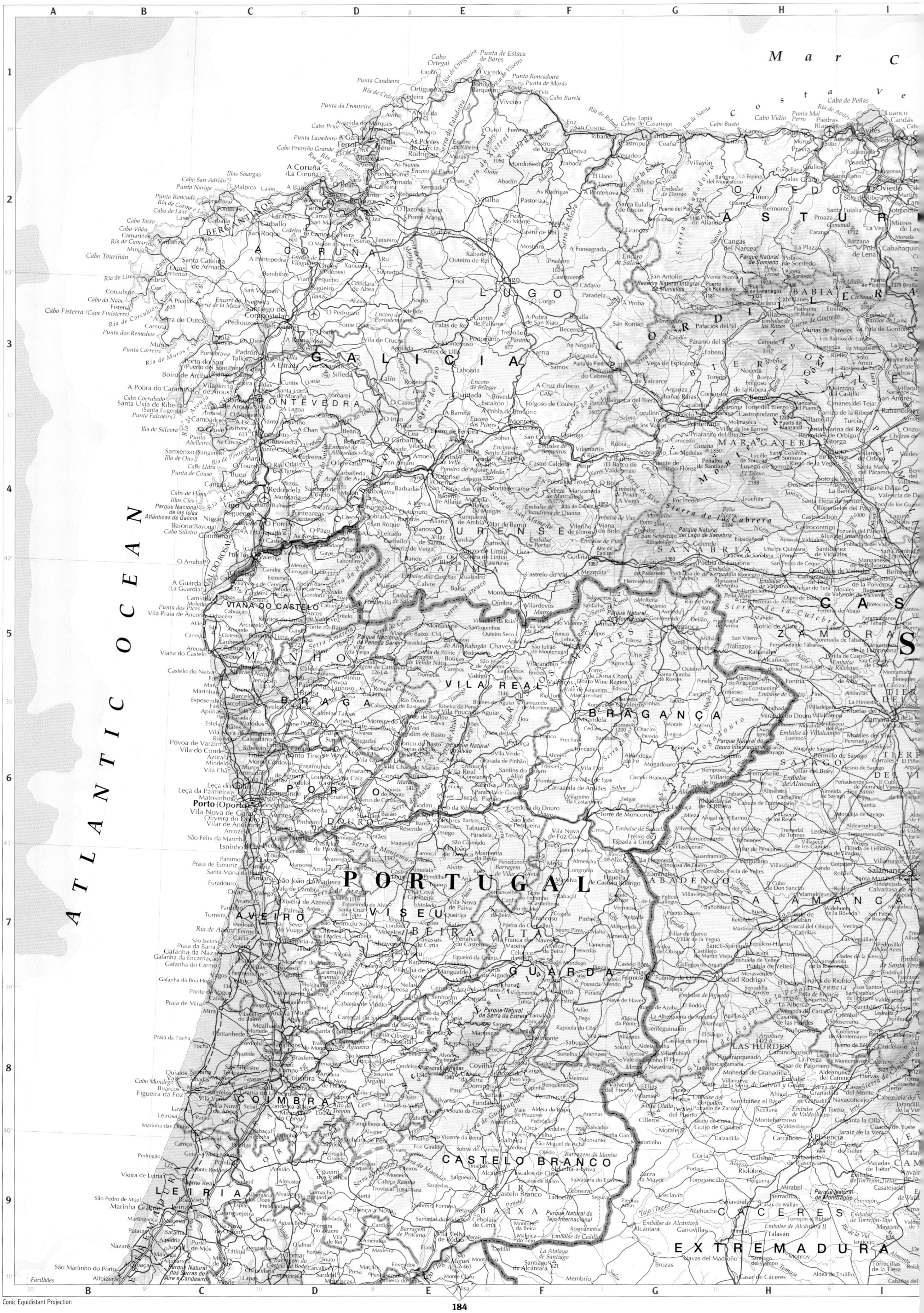

ATLANTIC OCEAN

PORTUGAL

GALICIA

A CORUÑA
LUGO
PONTEVEDRA
OURENSE
VIANA DO CASTELO
MINHO
BRAGA
VILA REAL
BRAGANÇA
PORTO
DOURO
AVEIRO
VISEU
BEIRA ALTA
GUARDA
COIMBRA
BEIRA LITORAL
LEIRIA
CASTELO BRANCO
BEIRA BAIXA
CÁCERES
EXTREMADURA
SALAMANCA
ZAMORA

Porto (Oporto)
Santiago de Compostela
A Coruña (La Coruña)
Viana do Castelo
Vila Nova de Gaia

Cabo Fisterra (Cape Finisterre)
Cabo Ortegal

Conic Equidistant Projection

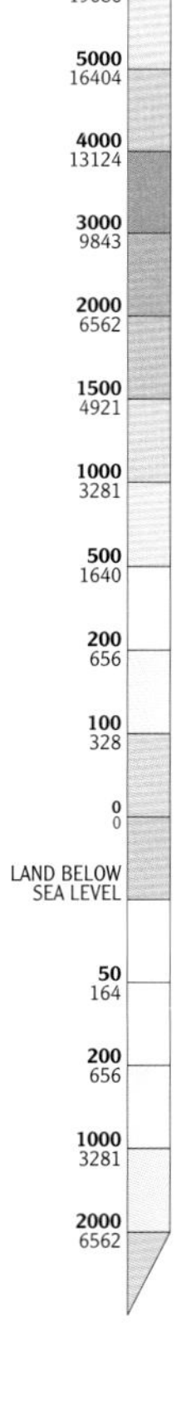

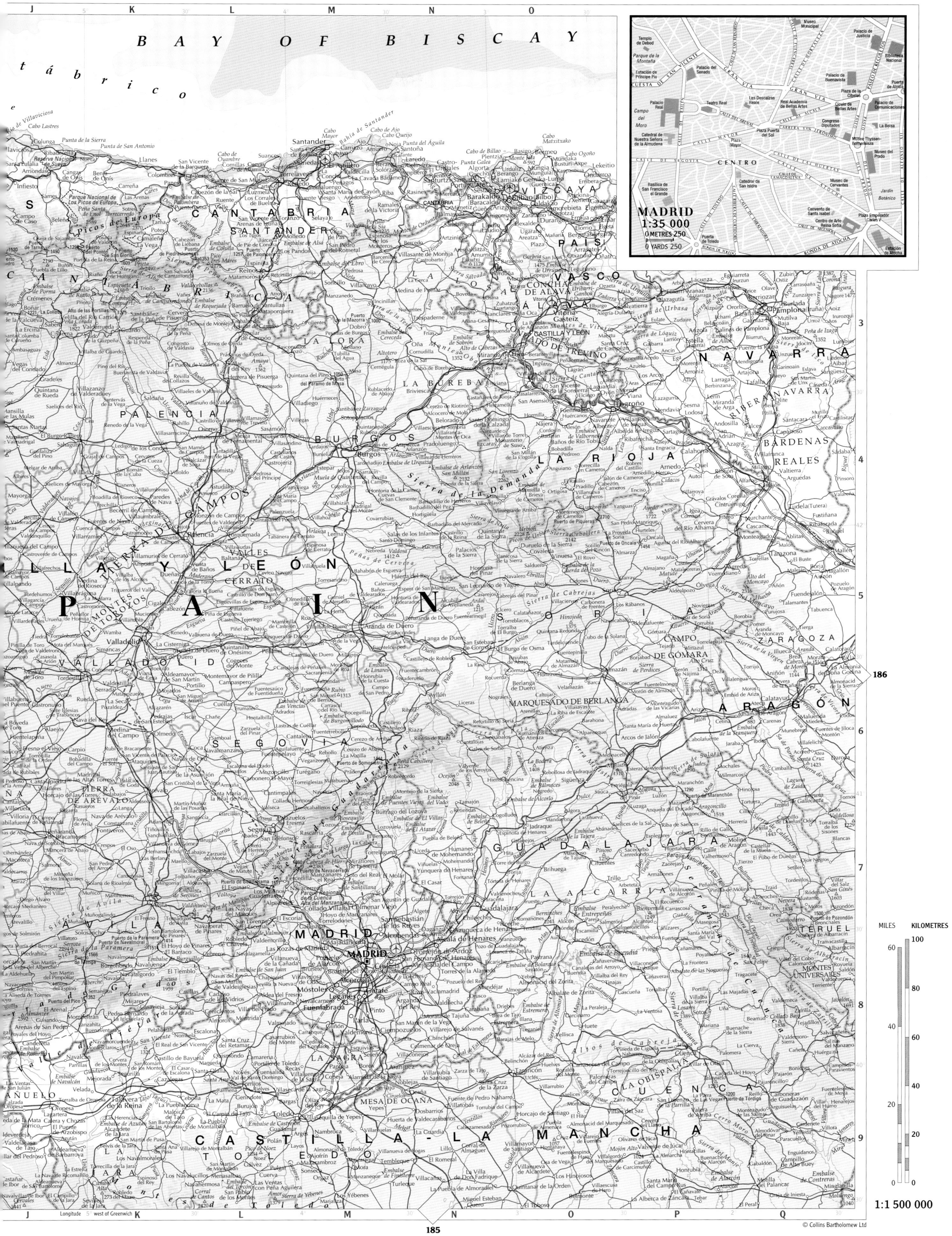

© Collins Bartholomew Ltd

1:1 500 000

BAY OF BISCAY
CANTABRIA
SANTANDER
PAÍS VASCO
VIZCAYA
ÁLAVA
NAVARRA
LA RIOJA
BURGOS
PALENCIA
CASTILLA Y LEÓN
SPAIN
VALLADOLID
SORIA
ZARAGOZA
ARAGÓN
SEGOVIA
GUADALAJARA
MADRID
ÁVILA
TOLEDO
CUENCA
CASTILLA - LA MANCHA
TERUEL
Bilbao
Santander
Vitoria-Gasteiz
Pamplona
Logroño
Burgos
Palencia
Valladolid
Segovia
Ávila
Guadalajara
Toledo
Cuenca
MADRID
1:35 000
CENTRO
MILES
KILOMETRES
186
Longitude west of Greenwich

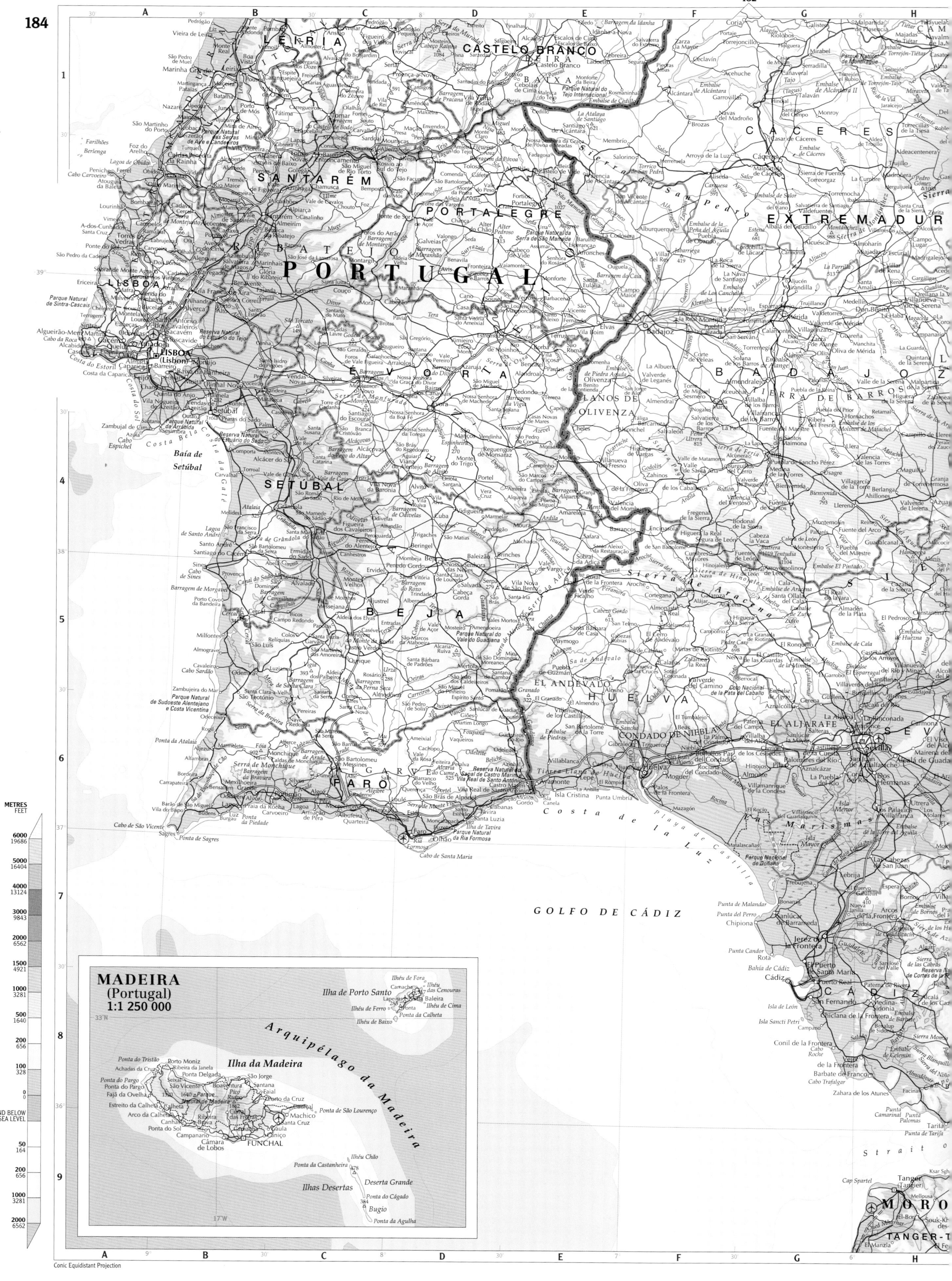
182
A B C D E F G H
1 4 5 6 7 8 9
LEIRIA
CASTELO BRANCO
BEIRA BAIXA
SANTARÉM
PORTALEGRE
RIBATEJO
PORTUGAL
LISBOA
LISBOA (Lisbon)
ÉVORA
ALENTEJO
SETÚBAL
BEJA
ALGARVE
FARO
CÁCERES
EXTREMADURA
BADAJOZ
HUELVA
SEVILLA
CÁDIZ
CONDADO DE NIBLA
EL ANDEVALO
EL ALJARAFE
LLANOS DE OLIVENZA
TIERRA DE BARROS
Sierra de San Pedro
Sierra de Aracena
Baía de Setúbal
Costa Bela
Costa da Galé
Costa do Estoril
Costa de la Luz
Playa de Castilla
Las Marismas
GOLFO DE CÁDIZ
Parque Nacional de Doñana
Parque Natural de Sintra-Cascais
Parque Natural do Vale do Guadiana
Parque Natural de Sudoeste Alentejano e Costa Vicentina
Parque Natural da Ria Formosa
Cabo de São Vicente
Cabo de Santa Maria
Cabo da Roca
Cabo Espichel
Cabo Carvoeiro
Cabo Trafalgar
Strait
Tanger (Tangier)
MOROCCO
TANGER-TETOUAN
MADEIRA
(Portugal)
1:1 250 000
Arquipélago da Madeira
Ilha da Madeira
Ilha de Porto Santo
Ilhas Desertas
Deserta Grande
Bugio
FUNCHAL
METRES
FEET
6000 19686
5000 16404
4000 13124
3000 9843
2000 6562
1500 4921
1000 3281
500 1640
200 656
100 328
0 0
LAND BELOW SEA LEVEL
50 164
200 656
1000 3281
2000 6562

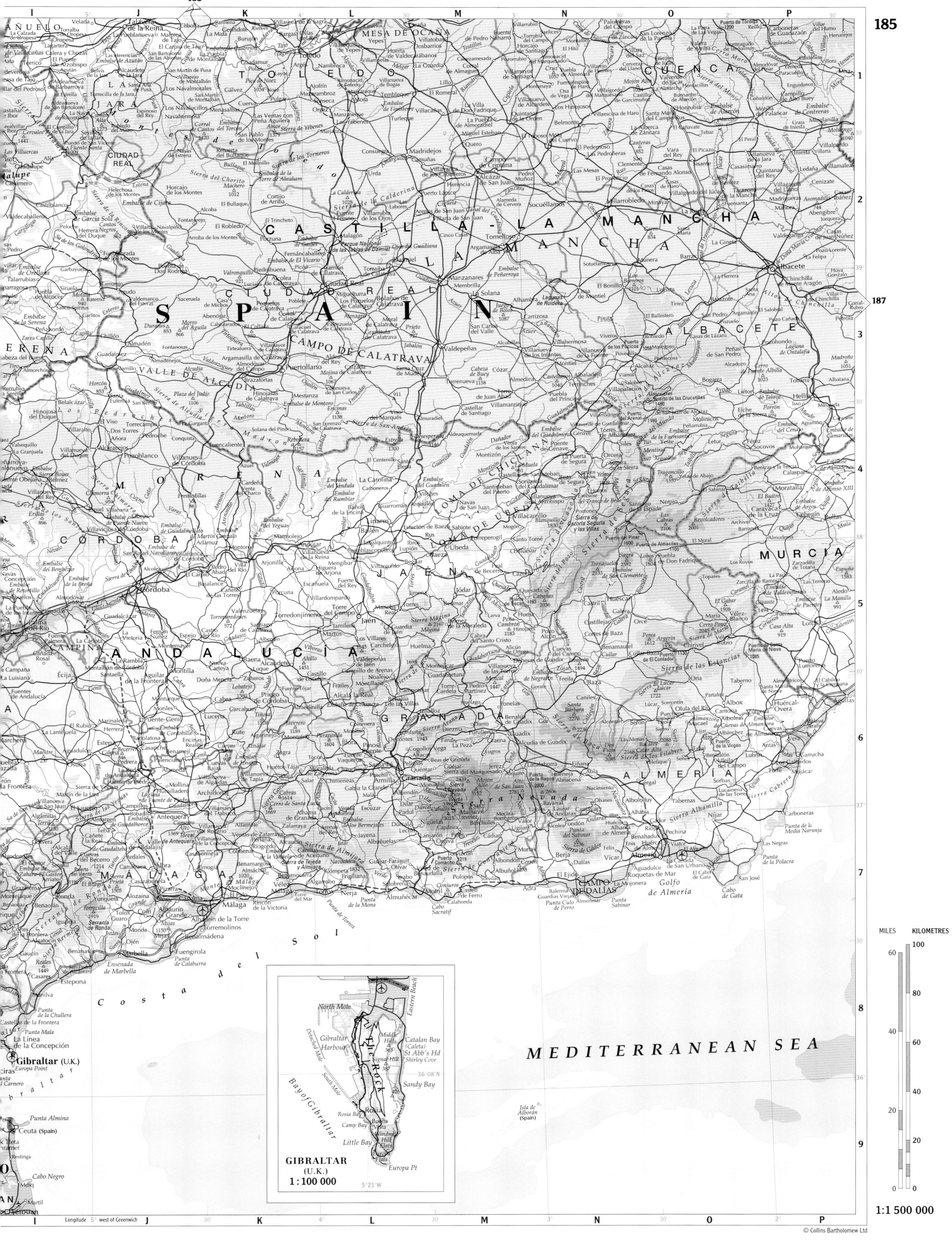

SPAIN

CASTILLA-LA MANCHA

LA MANCHA

ANDALUCÍA

TOLEDO
CUENCA
CIUDAD REAL
ALBACETE
CÓRDOBA
JAÉN
MURCIA
GRANADA
ALMERÍA
MÁLAGA

MEDITERRANEAN SEA

Costa del Sol

Gibraltar (U.K.)
Europa Point

Ceuta (Spain)

North Mole
Gibraltar Harbour
Detached Mole
The Rock
Middle Hill
Catalan Bay (Caleta)
St Abb's Hd
Shirley Cove
Eastern Beach
Sandy Bay
Signal Hill
Windmill Hill
Flats
Europa Pt
Rosia Bay
Camp Bay
Little Bay
Bay of Gibraltar
36°08′N

Isla de Alborán (Spain)

MILES   KILOMETRES

1:1 500 000

163

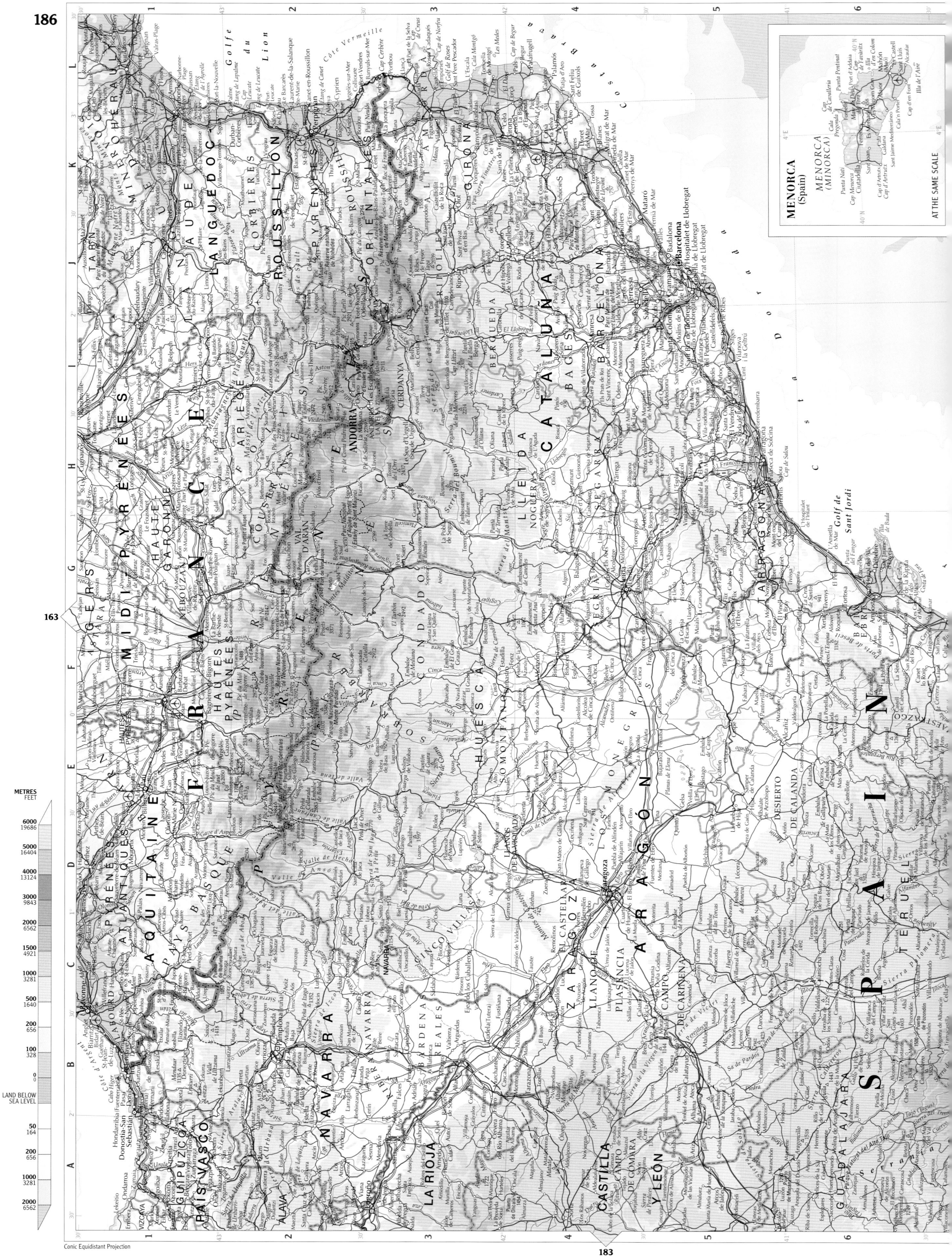
METRES
FEET
6000 19686
5000 16404
4000 13124
3000 9843
2000 6562
1500 4921
1000 3281
500 1640
200 656
100 328
0 0
LAND BELOW SEA LEVEL
50 164
200 656
1000 3281
2000 6562
MENORCA (Spain)
AT THE SAME SCALE
FRANCE
SPAIN
ANDORRA
ARAGÓN
CATALUÑA
NAVARRA
PAÍS VASCO
LA RIOJA
CASTILLA Y LEÓN
LANGUEDOC-ROUSSILLON
MIDI-PYRÉNÉES
AQUITAINE
PYRÉNÉES
Golfe du Lion
Barcelona
Zaragoza
Perpignan
Pamplona/Iruña

Conic Equidistant Projection

183

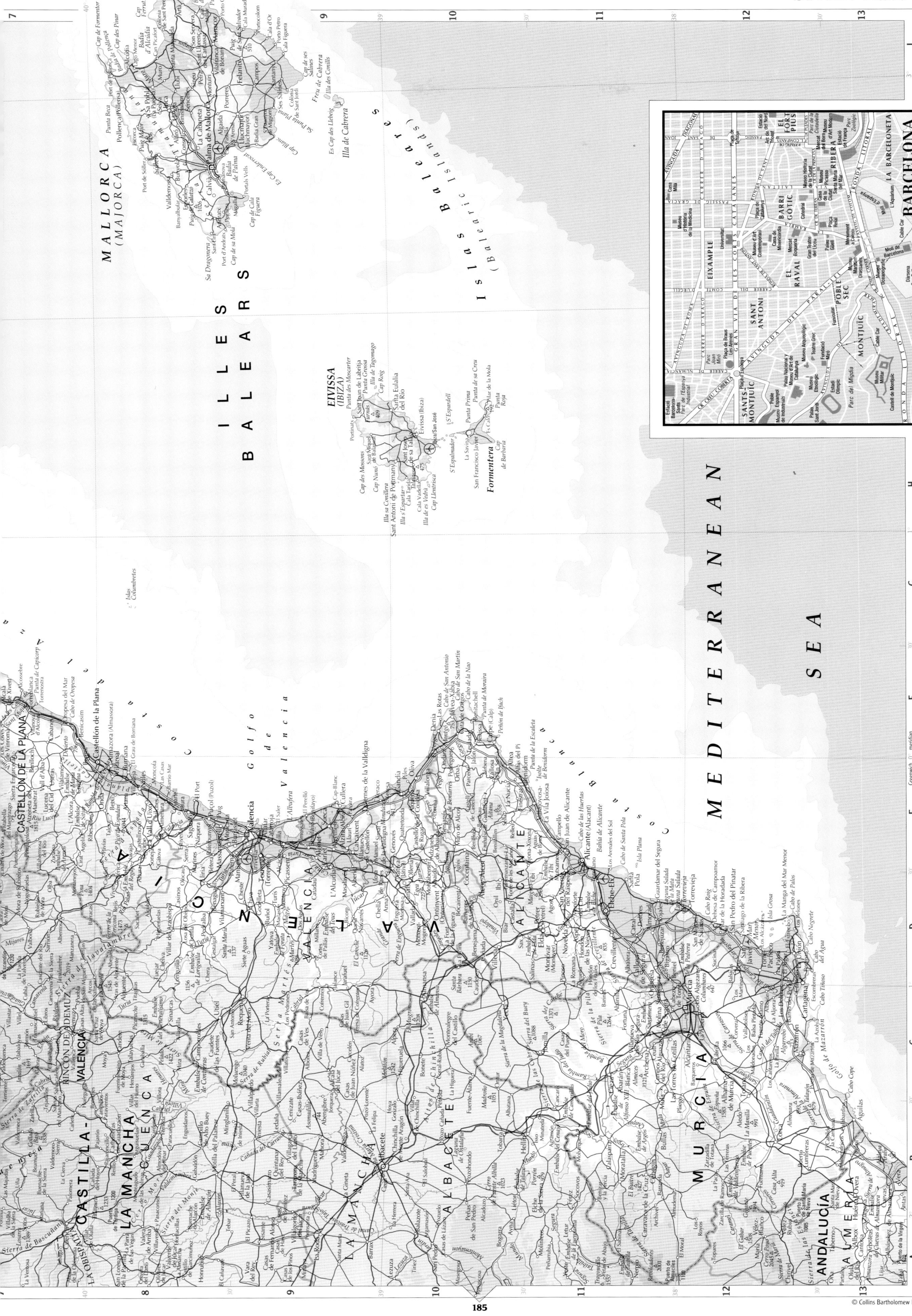
MEDITERRANEAN
SEA
ILLES BALEARS
Islas Baleares
(Balearic Islands)
MALLORCA
(MAJORCA)
Palma de Mallorca
EIVISSA
(IBIZA)
Formentera
BARCELONA
1:60 000
CASTILLA-LA MANCHA
VALENCIA
MURCIA
ALICANTE
ALBACETE
CUENCA
ANDALUCÍA
ALMERÍA
Golfo de Valencia
Valencia
Alicante
Murcia
Cartagena
Albacete
Castellón de la Plana
Greenwich meridian

MILES KILOMETRES

1:1 500 000

185

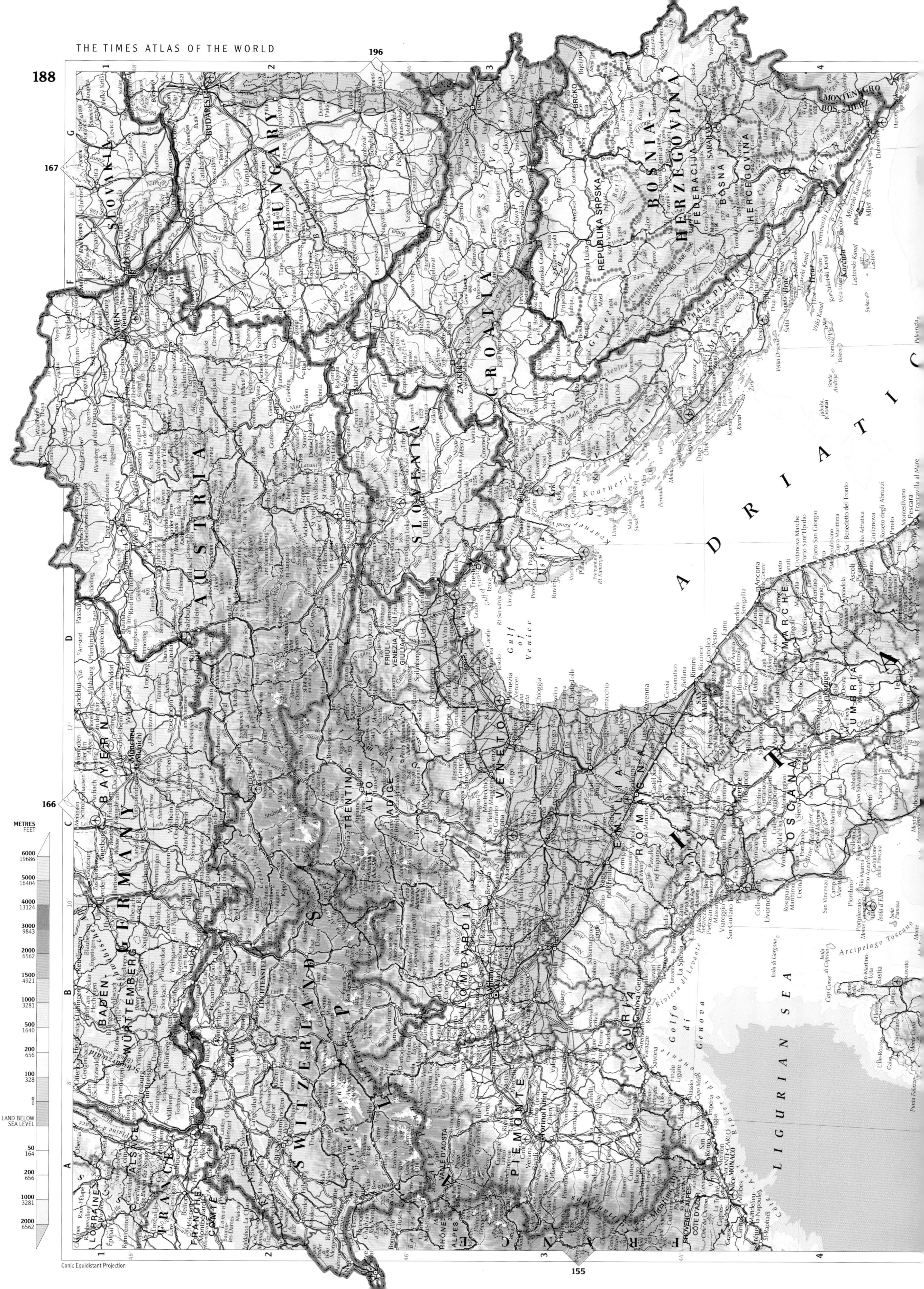
196
167
166
155
SLOVAKIA
HUNGARY
AUSTRIA
GERMANY
BAYERN
BADEN-WÜRTTEMBERG
SWITZERLAND
LIECHTENSTEIN
FRANCE
ALSACE
LORRAINE
FRANCHE-COMTÉ
RHÔNE-ALPES
PROVENCE-ALPES-CÔTE D'AZUR
SLOVENIA
CROATIA
BOSNIA-HERZEGOVINA
REPUBLIKA SRPSKA
FEDERACIJA BOSNA I HERCEGOVINA
DAYTON ACCORD LINE 1995
MONTENEGRO
ITALY
TRENTINO-ALTO ADIGE
FRIULI-VENEZIA GIULIA
VENETO
LOMBARDIA
PIEMONTE
VALLE D'AOSTA
LIGURIA
EMILIA-ROMAGNA
TOSCANA
MARCHE
UMBRIA
SAN MARINO
MONACO
A D R I A T I C
Gulf of Venice
LIGURIAN SEA
Golfo di Genova
Arcipelago Toscano
METRES
FEET
6000
19686
5000
16404
4000
13124
3000
9843
2000
6562
1500
4921
1000
3281
500
1640
200
656
100
328
0
0
LAND BELOW SEA LEVEL
50
164
200
656
1000
3281
2000
6562

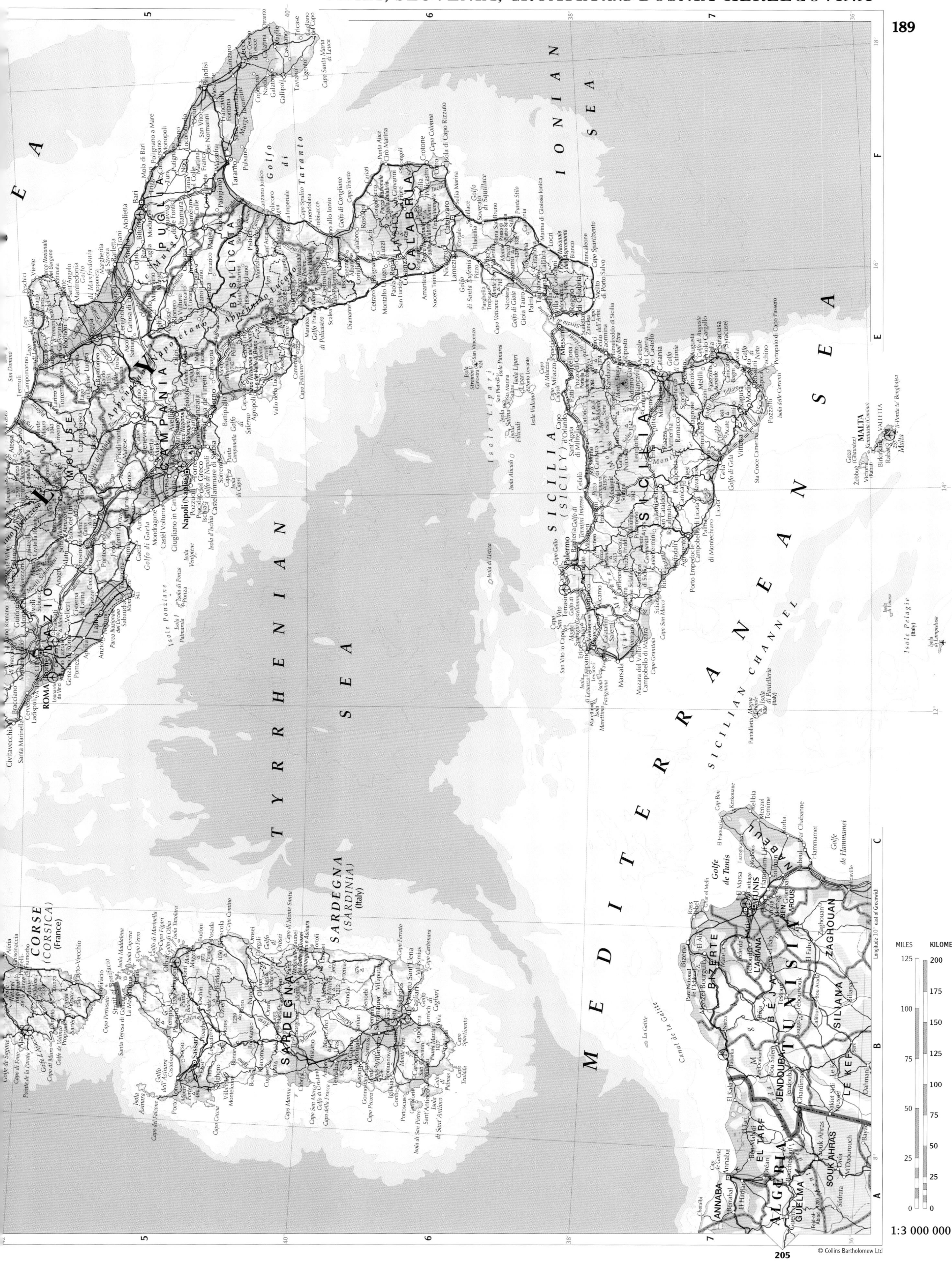

1:3 000 000

© Collins Bartholomew Ltd

TYRRHENIAN SEA
IONIAN SEA
MEDITERRANEAN SEA
SICILIAN CHANNEL
SARDEGNA (SARDINIA) (Italy)
CORSE (CORSICA) (France)
SICILIA (SICILY)
MALTA
VALLETTA
TUNISIA
ALGERIA
LAZIO
MOLISE
CAMPANIA
PUGLIA
BASILICATA
CALABRIA
SICILIA
SARDEGNA
ROMA
Napoli
Palermo
Bari
Taranto
Brindisi
Lecce
Catania
Messina
Siracusa
Cagliari
Sassari
TUNIS
BIZERTE
ANNABA
Golfo di Taranto
Golfo di Squillace
Golfo di Policastro
Golfo di Gaeta
Golfe de Tunis
Golfe de Hammamet
Isole Eolie o Lipari
Isole Ponziane
Isole Pelagie
Canal de la Galite
MILES | KILOMETRES
205

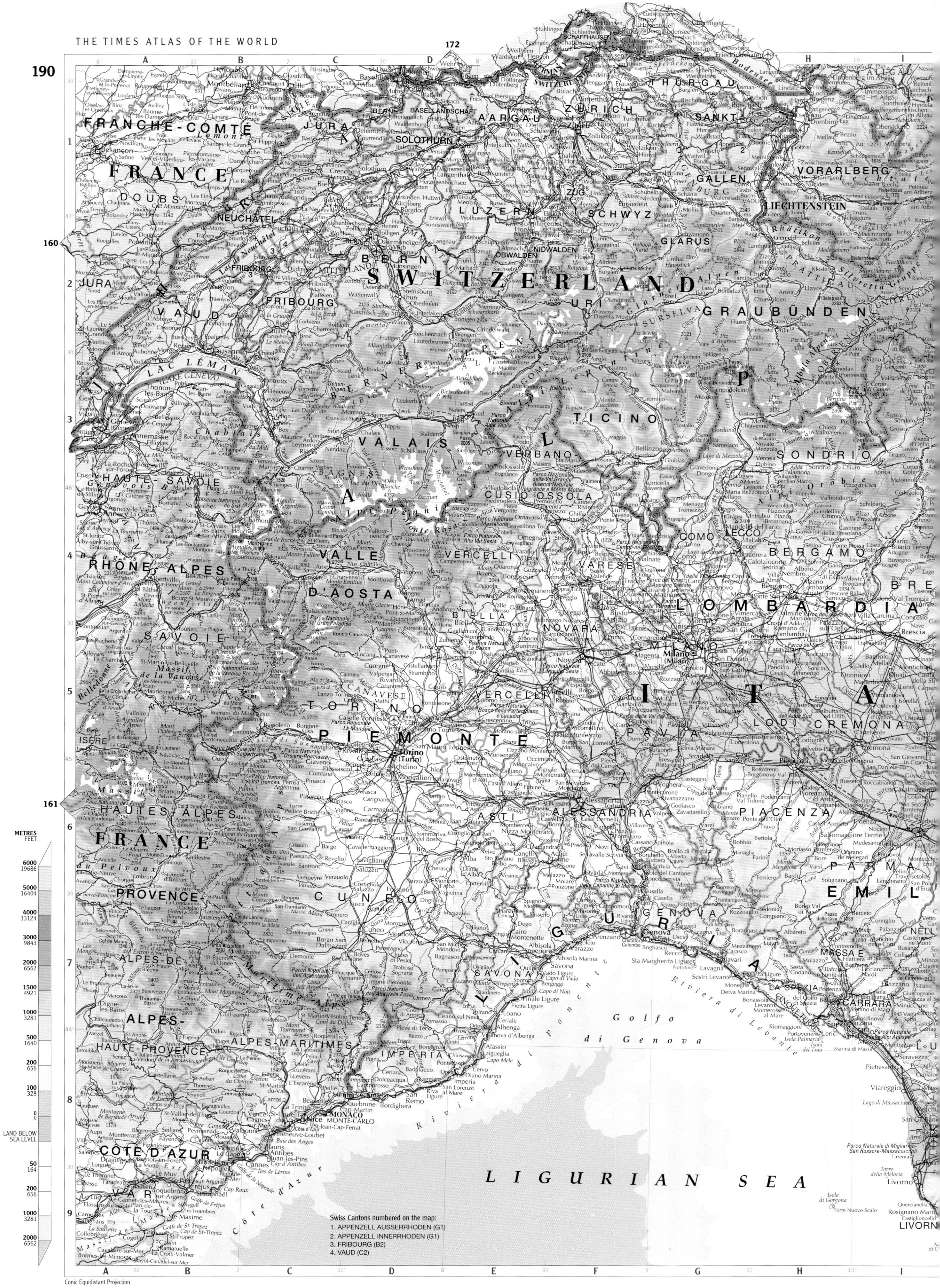

Swiss Cantons numbered on the map:
1. APPENZELL AUSSERRHODEN (G1)
2. APPENZELL INNERRHODEN (G1)
3. FRIBOURG (B2)
4. VAUD (C2)

METRES
FEET

6000
19686

5000
16404

4000
13124

3000
9843

2000
6562

1500
4921

1000
3281

500
1640

200
656

100
328

0

LAND BELOW
SEA LEVEL

50
164

200
656

1000
3281

2000
6562

Conic Equidistant Projection

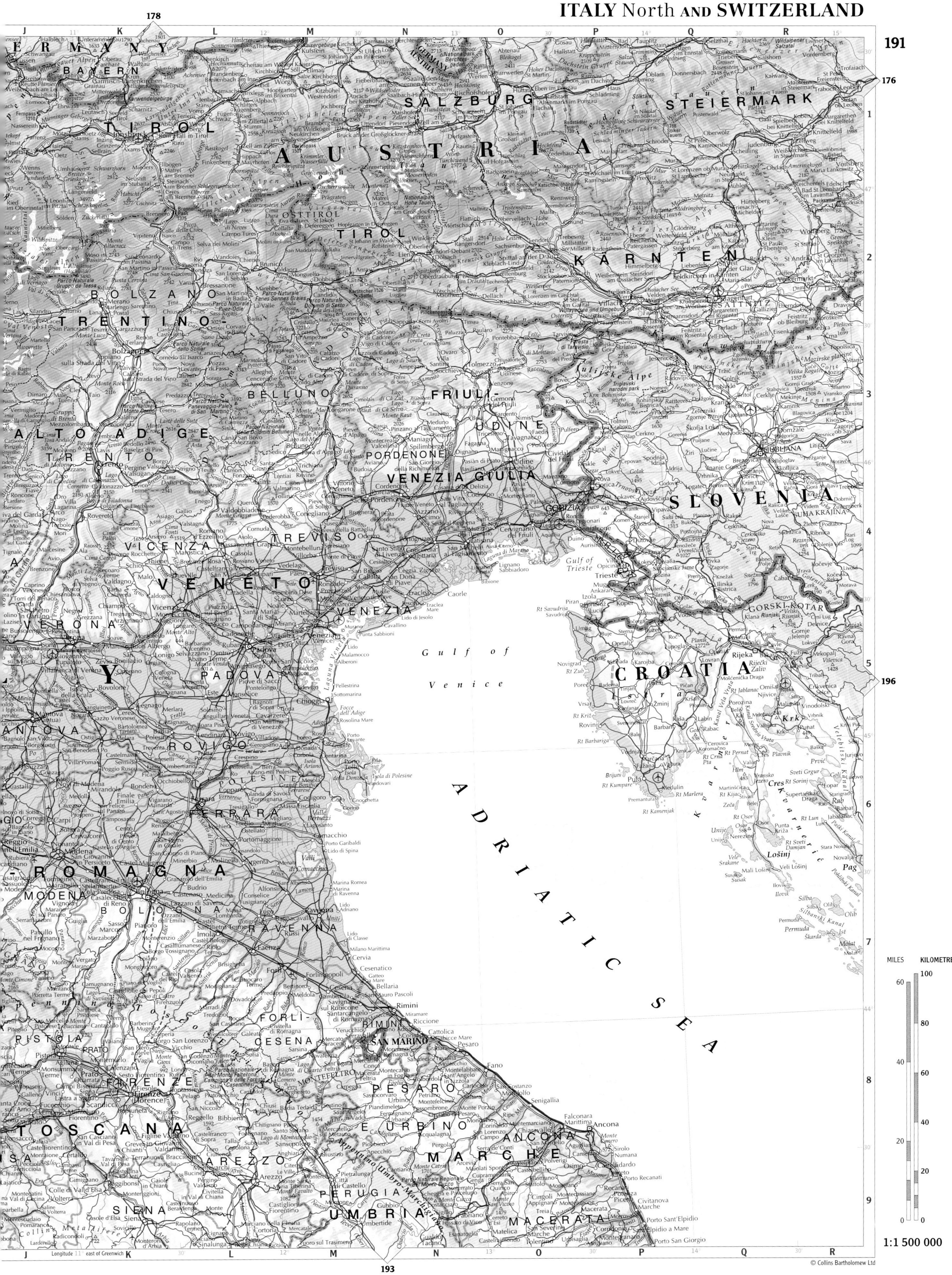

178

GERMANY
BAYERN

TIROL

SALZBURG

STEIERMARK

AUSTRIA

OSTTIROL

TIROL

KÄRNTEN

BOLZANO

TRENTINO

ALTO ADIGE

TRENTO

BELLUNO

FRIULI-
UDINE

PORDENONE

VENEZIA GIULIA

SLOVENIA

SUMA KRAJINA

VICENZA

TREVISO

GOBIZIA

VENETO

VERONA

VENEZIA

Gulf of
Trieste

Trieste

PADOVA

Venezia
Venice

CROATIA

GORSKI KOTAR

Rijeka

ROVIGO

Gulf of

Venice

Krk

MANTOVA

POLESINE

FERRARA

ROMAGNA

MODENA

BOLOGNA

RAVENNA

A D R I A T I C   S E A

Cres

Lošinj

Pag

TOSCANA

FIRENZE
Florence

FORLI-

CESENA

RIMINI

San Marino

SAN MARINO

PESARO

PISTOIA

PRATO

URBINO

ANCONA

AREZZO

MARCHE

SIENA

PERUGIA

UMBRIA

MACERATA

MILES   KILOMETRES
60   100
      80
40   60
      40
20   20
0   0

1:1 500 000

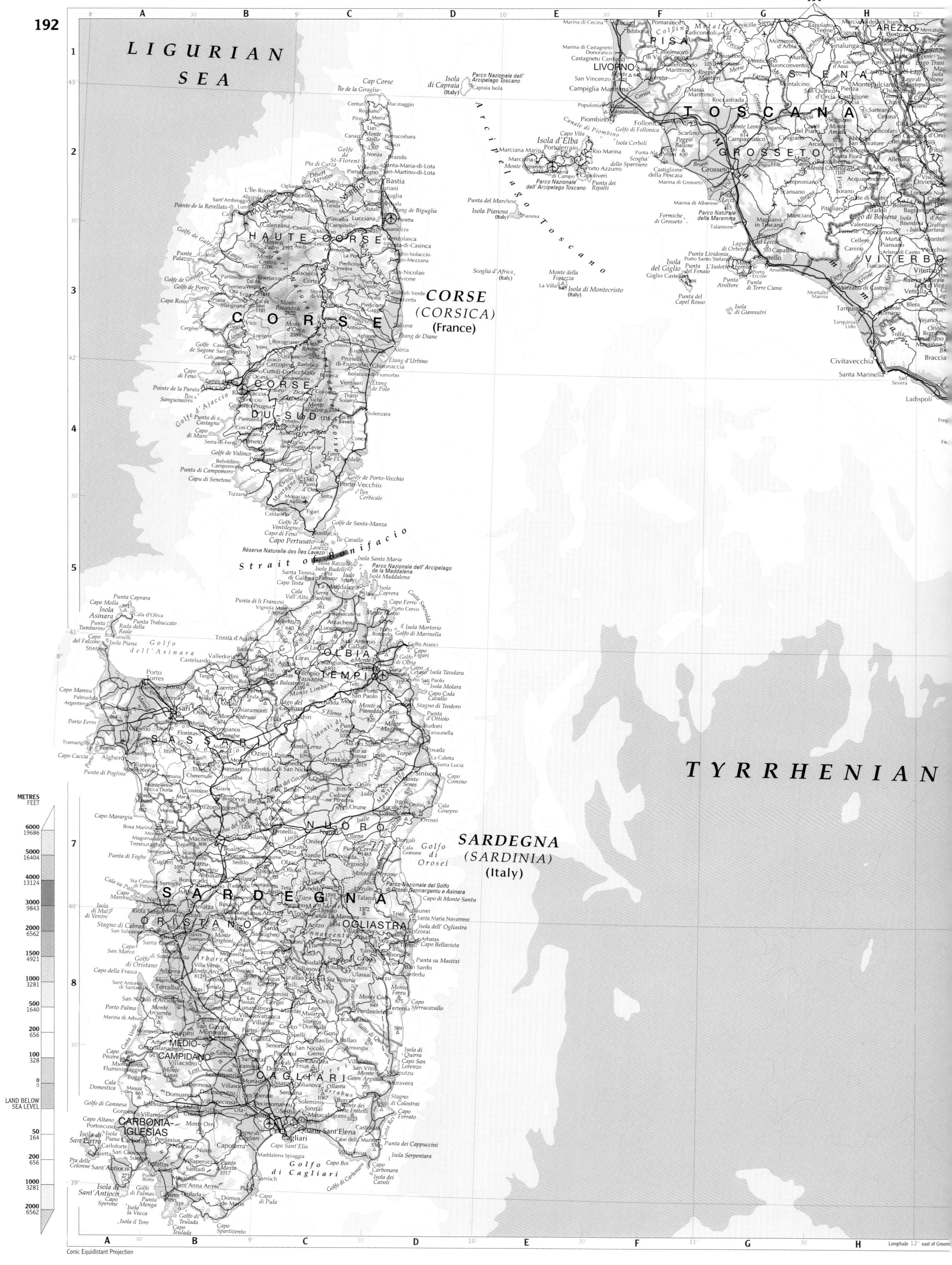

LIGURIAN

SEA

PISA
LIVORNO

TOSCANA

GROSSETO

Cap Corse
Île de la Giraglia

Parco Nazionale dell'
Arcipelago Toscano
Isola
di Capraia
(Italy)

CORSE
(CORSICA)
(France)

HAUTE-CORSE

CORSE

Isola d'Elba

Golfo di Follonica

Arcipelago Toscano

Parco Nazionale dell'
Arcipelago Toscano

Isola Pianosa
(Italy)

Scoglio d'Africa

Isola di Montecristo
(Italy)

Isola
del Giglio

CORSE
DU SUD

Isola
di Giannutri

VITERBO

Civitavecchia

Santa Marinella

Golfe d'Ajaccio

Ladispoli

Bonifacio
Capo Pertusato
Réserve Naturelle des Îles Lavezzi

Strait of Bonifacio

Isola Santa Maria

Parco Nazionale dell' Arcipelago
de la Maddalena

La Maddalena

Isola
Asinara

Golfo
dell'Asinara

OLBIA-
TEMPIO

TYRRHENIAN

Porto Torres

SASSARI

Alghero

NUORO

Golfo
di
Orosei

SARDEGNA
(SARDINIA)
(Italy)

ORISTANO

OGLIASTRA

Golfo di
Oristano

MEDIO-
CAMPIDANO

CAGLIARI

CARBONIA-
IGLESIAS

Cagliari

Golfo
di Cagliari

Golfo di Palmas

Capo
Teulada

Capo
Spartivento

METRES
FEET

6000
19686

5000
16404

4000
13124

3000
9843

2000
6562

1500
4921

1000
3281

500
1640

200
656

100
328

0
0

LAND BELOW
SEA LEVEL

50
164

200
656

1000
3281

2000
6562

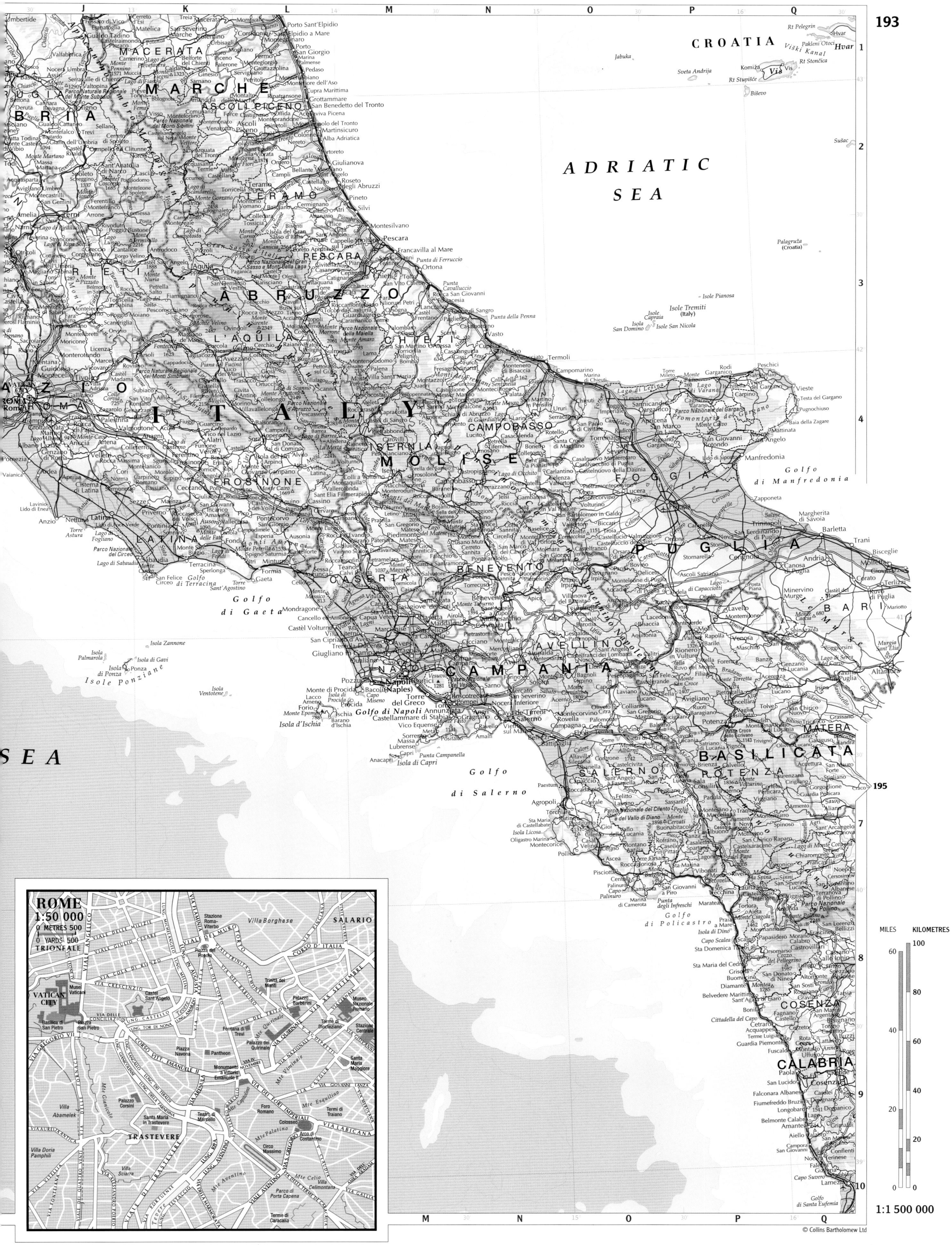

CROATIA

ADRIATIC
SEA

MARCHE

MACERATA

ASCOLI PICENO

TERAMO

ABRUZZO

L'AQUILA

RIETI

ITALY

FROSINONE

LATINA

CASERTA

ISERNIA

MOLISE

CAMPOBASSO

CHIETI

PESCARA

FOGGIA

PUGLIA

BENEVENTO

AVELLINO

CAMPANIA

NAPOLI
(Naples)

BARI

MATERA

BASILICATA

POTENZA

SALERNO

Golfo
di Napoli

Golfo
di Salerno

Golfo
di Policastro

COSENZA

CALABRIA

Isole Tremiti
(Italy)

Golfo
di Manfredonia

SEA

Isole Ponziane

Golfo
di Gaeta

ROME 1:50 000
0 METRES 500
0 YARDS 500

TRIONFALE

SALARIO

VATICAN CITY

TRASTEVERE

MILES KILOMETRES

1:1 500 000

© Collins Bartholomew Ltd

195

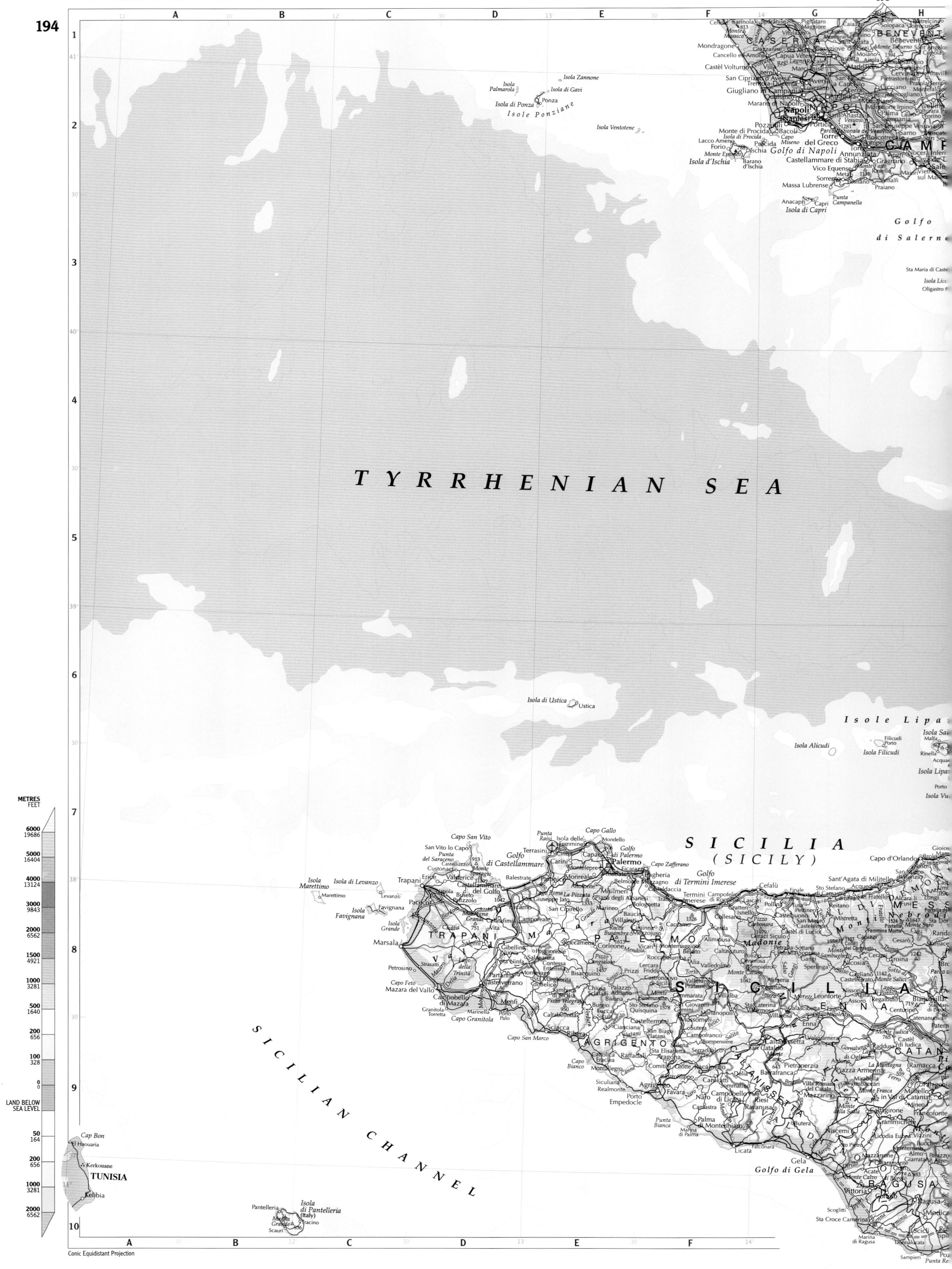

TYRRHENIAN SEA

SICILIA (SICILY)

SICILIAN CHANNEL

Golfo di Napoli

Golfo di Salerno

Isole Ponziane

Isola di Ponza
Isola Palmarola
Isola di Gavi
Isola Zannone
Isola Ventotene

Napoli
Pozzuoli
Ischia
Isola d'Ischia
Procida
Isola di Procida
Monte Epomeo
Lacco Ameno
Forio
Barano d'Ischia
Sorrento
Massa Lubrense
Anacapri
Capri
Isola di Capri
Punta Campanella

CASERTA
BENEVENTO
CAMP...

Castellammare di Stabia
Torre del Greco
Torre Annunziata
Vico Equense

Isola di Ustica
Ustica

Isole Lipa...
Isola Alicudi
Isola Filicudi
Filicudi Porto
Rinella

Capo San Vito
San Vito lo Capo
Punta del Saraceno
Custonaci
Isola di Levanzo
Isola Marettimo
Marettimo
Levanzo
Isola Favignana
Favignana
Isola Grande
Trapani
Erice
Marsala
Petrosino
Mazara del Vallo
Campobello di Mazara
Capo Feto
Granitola Torretta
Capo Granitola
Marinella
Porto Palo

TRAPANI

Capo Gallo
Mondello
Punta Raisi
Isola delle Femmine
Golfo di Castellammare
Terrasini
Carini
Castellammare del Golfo
Partinico
Monreale
PALERMO
Bagheria
Capo Zafferano
Golfo di Termini Imerese
Termini Imerese
Cefalù

Capo d'Orlando
Sant'Agata di Militello
Sto Stefano

PALERMO

MAZARA

Salemi
Gibellina
Castelvetrano
Santa Ninfa
Partanna
Calatafimi

Corleone
Contessa Entellina

Sciacca
Menfi
Ribera

AGRIGENTO
Agrigento
Porto Empedocle
Favara
Naro
Canicattì
Palma di Montechiaro
Licata

CALTANISSETTA
ENNA
Enna
CATAN...

Gela
Golfo di Gela

RAGUSA
Vittoria

Capo San Marco
Capo Bianco
Punta Bianca

Cap Bon
El Haouaria
Kerkouane

TUNISIA

Kelibia

Pantelleria
Isola di Pantelleria (Italy)
Grande A
Scauri
Tracino

Conic Equidistant Projection

METRES / FEET

6000	19686
5000	16404
4000	13124
3000	9843
2000	6562
1500	4921
1000	3281
500	1640
200	656
100	328
0	0

LAND BELOW SEA LEVEL

50	164
200	656
1000	3281
2000	6562

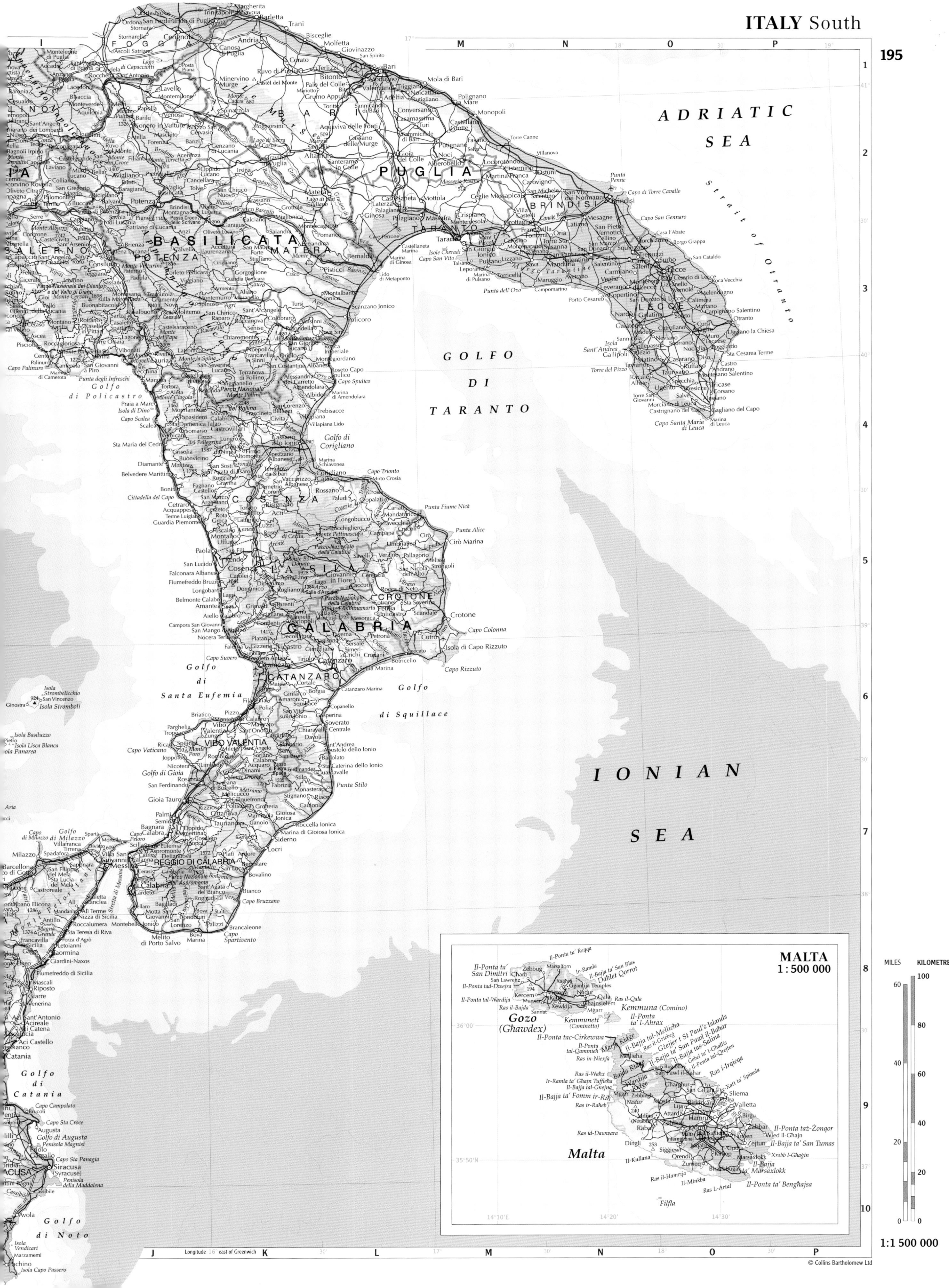

ADRIATIC
SEA

Strait of Otranto

PUGLIA

BARI

BRINDISI

LECCE

GOLFO
DI
TARANTO

BASILICATA
POTENZA   MATERA

SALERNO

COSENZA

SILA

CROTONE

CALABRIA

Golfo
di
Santa Eufemia

VIBO VALENTIA

Golfo di Gioia

CATANZARO

Golfo
di Squillace

IONIAN

SEA

REGGIO DI CALABRIA

Golfo
di Milazzo di Milazzo

Golfo
di
Catania

Catania

Golfo
di Augusta

Siracusa
(Syracuse)

Golfo
di Noto

MALTA
1 : 500 000

Gozo
(Ghawdex)

Kemmuna (Comino)

Malta

14°10'E   14°20'   14°30'

35°50'

36°00'

MILES   KILOMETRES

1 : 1 500 000

Longitude 16 east of Greenwich

© Collins Bartholomew Ltd

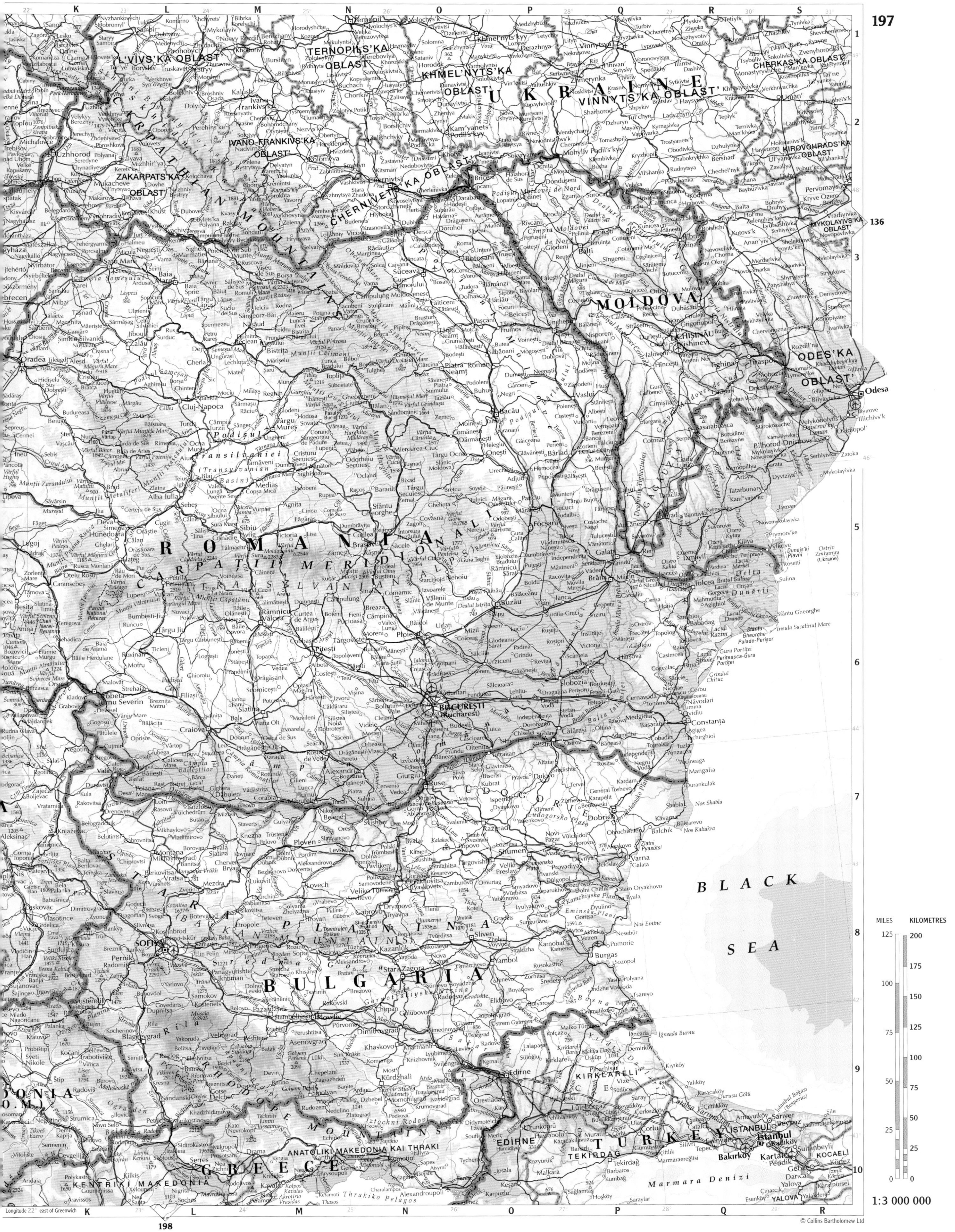

Longitude 22 east of Greenwich

1:3 000 000

© Collins Bartholomew Ltd

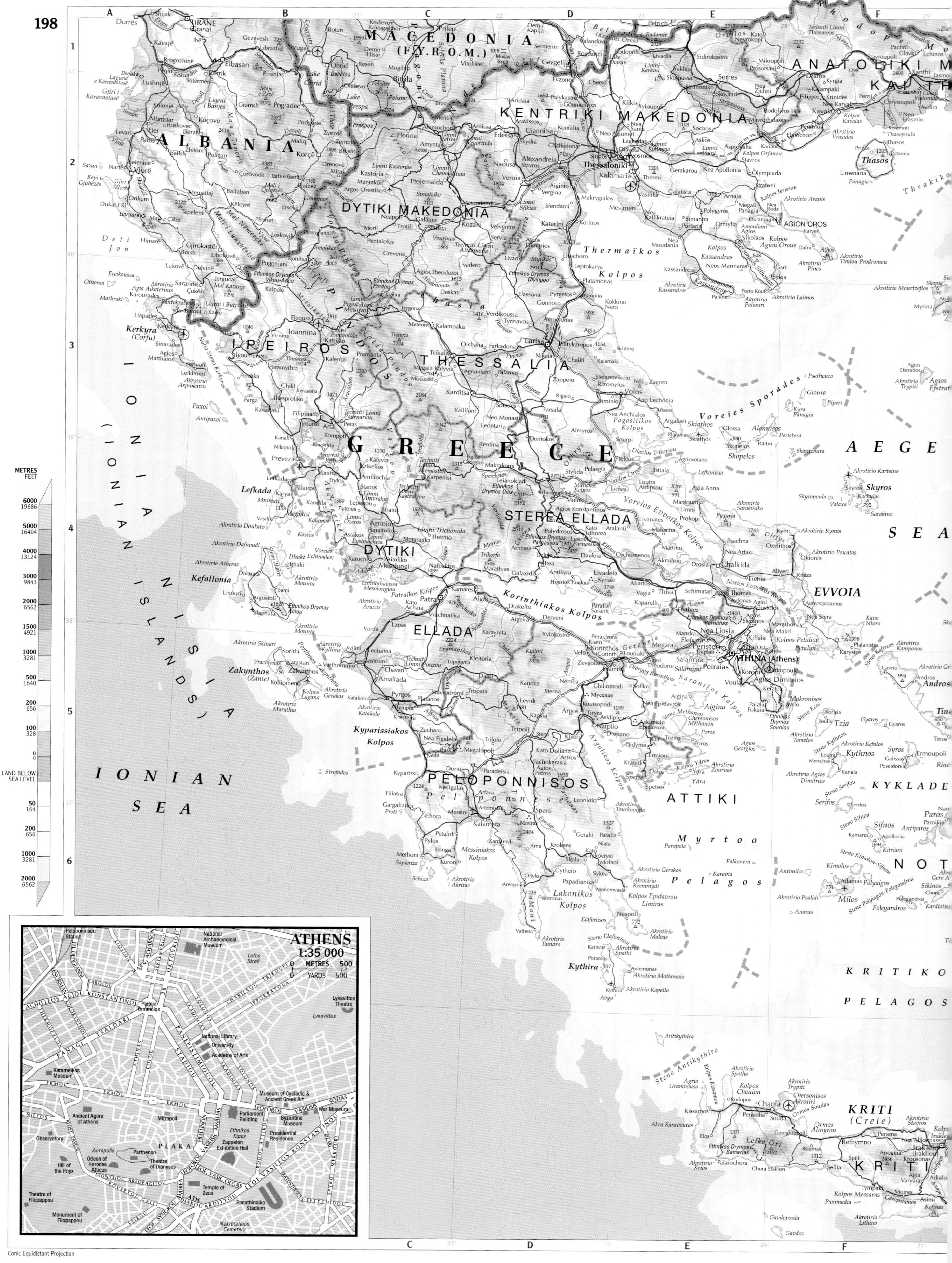

ALBANIA

MACEDONIA (F.Y.R.O.M.)

KENTRIKI MAKEDONIA

DYTIKI MAKEDONIA

ANATOLIKI MAKAI...

IPEIROS

THESSALIA

GREECE

STEREA ELLADA

DYTIKI

ELLADA

PELOPONNISOS

ATTIKI

EVVOIA

AEGE... SEA

IONIAN ISLANDS (IONIA NISIA)

IONIAN SEA

Thermaïkos Kolpos

Pagasitikos Kolpos

Voreies Sporades

Skyros

Voreios Evvoïkos Kolpos

Korinthiakos Kolpos

Patraikos Kolpos

Saronikos Kolpos

Argolikos Kolpos

Lakonikos Kolpos

Messiniakos Kolpos

Kyparissiakos Kolpos

Myrtoo Pelagos

KYKLADE...

NOT...

KRITIKO PELAGOS

KRITI (Crete)

Kerkyra (Corfu)

Kefallonia

Zakynthos (Zante)

Ithaki

Lefkada

Paxoi

Antipaxoi

Thasos

Skiathos

Skopelos

Alonnisos

Skyros

Andros

Kythnos

Serifos

Sifnos

Milos

Folegandros

Kythira

Antikythira

Thessaloniki

Kalamaria

Veroia

Katerini

Larisa

Volos

Ioannina

Arta

Agrinio

Patra

Pyrgos

Kalamata

Sparti

Tripoli

Argos

Nafplio

Korinthos

ATHINA (Athens)

Peiraias

Chalkida

AGION OROS

Chersonisos Kassandras

Chersonisos Sithonias

ATHENS
1:35 000
METRES 500
YARDS 500

National Archaeological Museum

Lykavittos

Lykavittos Theatre

National Library

University

Academy of Arts

Museum of Cycladic & Ancient Greek Art

War Museum

Byzantine Museum

Presidential Residence

Zappeion Exhibition Hall

Keramikos Museum

Ancient Agora of Athens

Observatory

Acropolis

Parthenon

Odeon of Herodes Atticus

Theatre of Dionysos

Hill of the Pnyx

Theatre of Filopappou

Monument of Filopappou

Temple of Zeus

Panathinaiko Stadium

Mitropoli

PLAKA

Peloponnisou Station

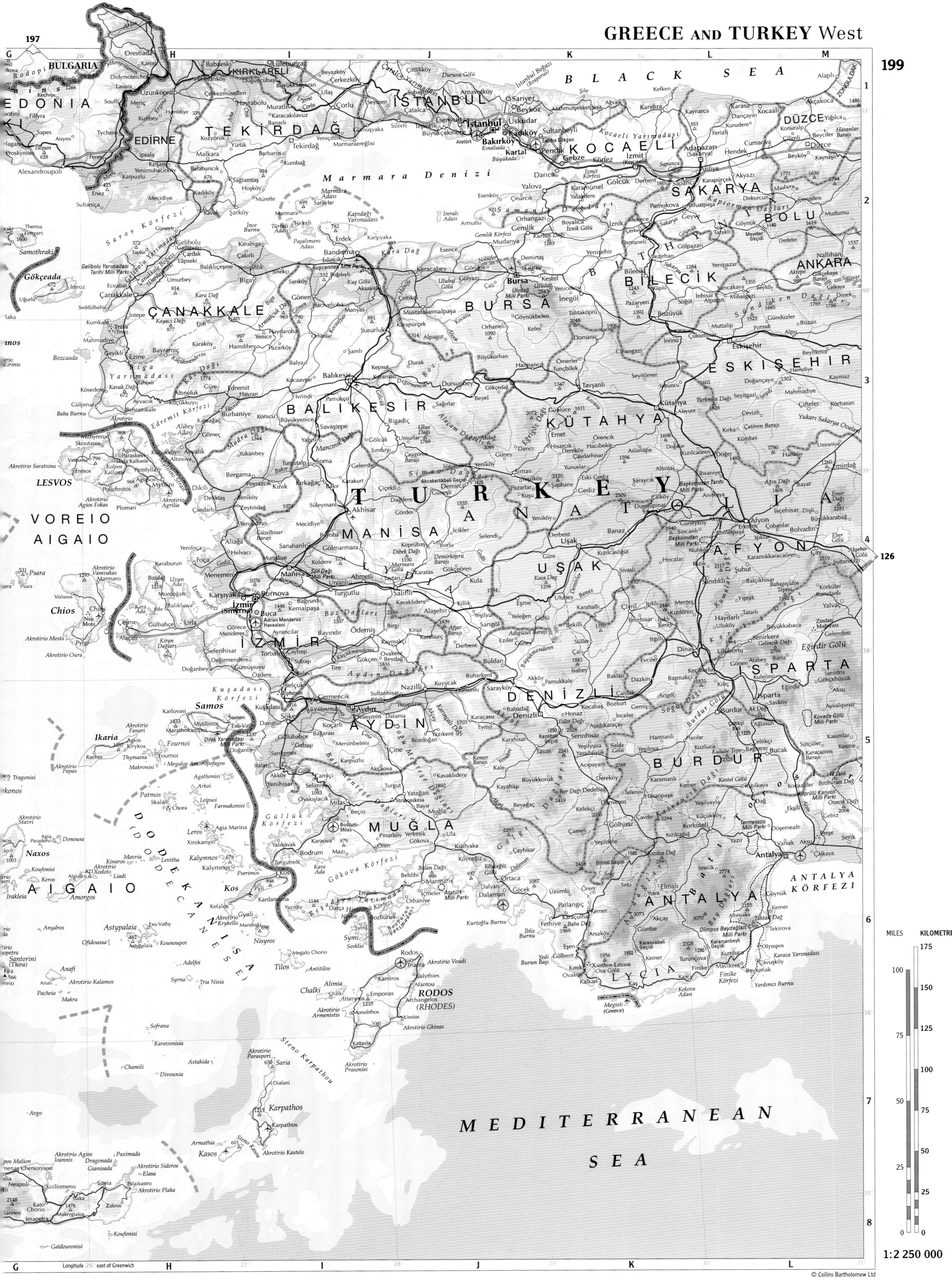
BLACK SEA
Marmara Denizi
MEDITERRANEAN SEA
TURKEY
ANATOLIA
BULGARIA
EDIRNE
KIRKLARELİ
TEKİRDAĞ
İSTANBUL
KOCAELİ
SAKARYA
DÜZCE
BOLU
ANKARA
BİLECİK
BURSA
ÇANAKKALE
BALIKESİR
KÜTAHYA
ESKİŞEHİR
MANİSA
UŞAK
AFYON
İZMİR
AYDIN
DENİZLİ
ISPARTA
BURDUR
MUĞLA
ANTALYA
VOREIO AIGAIO
AIGAIO
DODEKANISA (DODECANESE)
LESVOS
Chios
Samos
Ikaria
Naxos
Kos
RODOS (RHODES)
Karpathos
Samothraki
Gökçeada
Bozcaada
ANTALYA KÖRFEZİ
LYCIA
LYDIA
Istanbul
Bursa
İzmir
Antalya
Denizli
Eskişehir
Afyon
Kütahya
Uşak
Isparta
Burdur
Aydın
Manisa
Balıkesir
Muğla
Bodrum
Fethiye
Çanakkale
Edirne
Tekirdağ
Kırklareli
Izmit
Adapazarı
Bilecik
Bolu
126
197
MILES
KILOMETRES
1:2 250 000
Longitude 26° east of Greenwich
© Collins Bartholomew Ltd

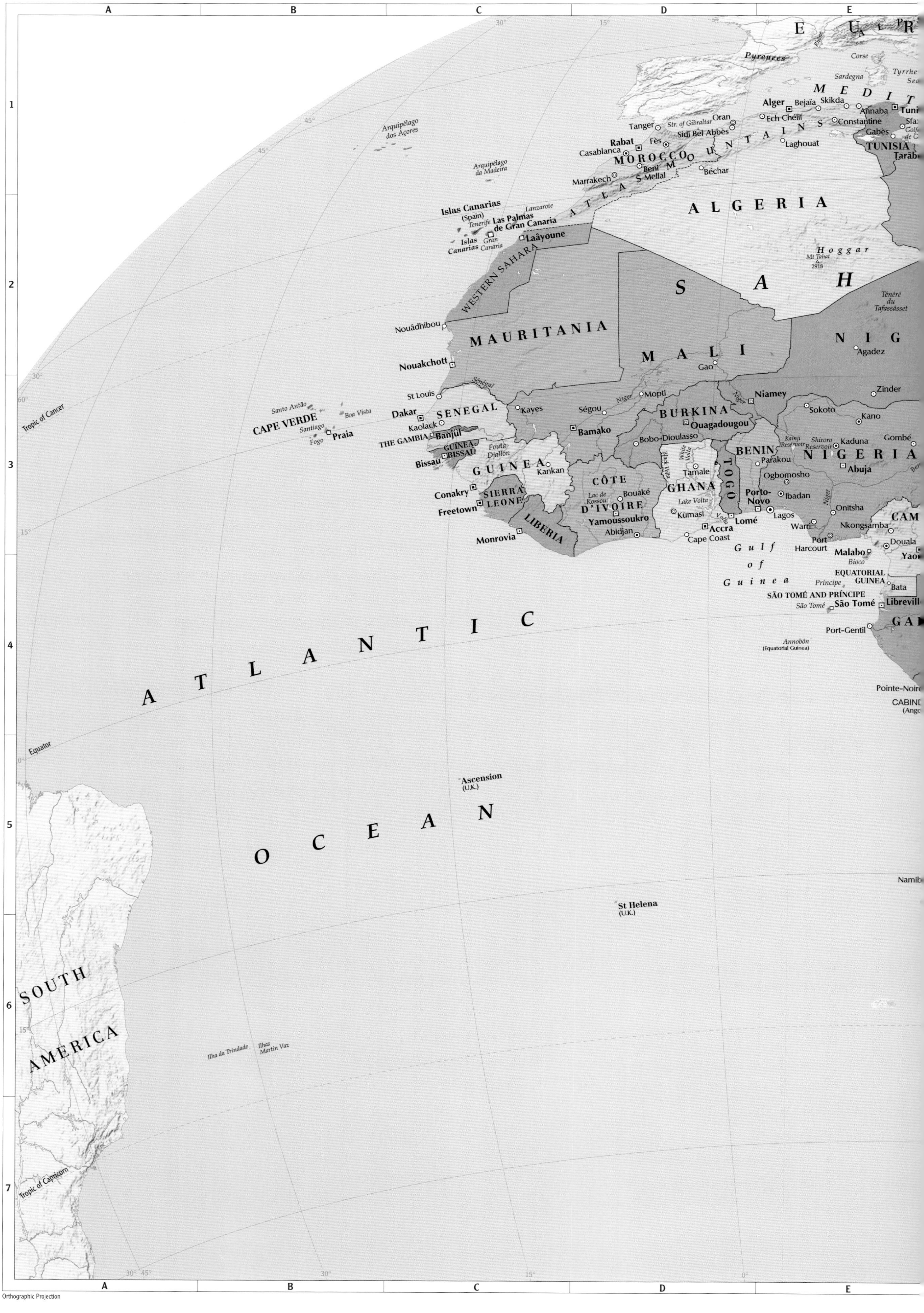
ATLANTIC
OCEAN
SOUTH
AMERICA
Tropic of Cancer
Equator
Tropic of Capricorn
Arquipélago dos Açores
Arquipélago da Madeira
Islas Canarias (Spain)
Lanzarote
Tenerife
Las Palmas de Gran Canaria
Islas Canarias
Gran Canaria
Laâyoune
WESTERN SAHARA
MOROCCO
Rabat
Casablanca
Fès
Marrakech
Beni Mellal
Tanger
Str. of Gibraltar
Oran
Sidi Bel Abbès
ATLAS MOUNTAINS
Béchar
ALGERIA
Alger
Bejaïa
Skikda
Annaba
Ech Chélif
Constantine
Laghouat
TUNISIA
Tunis
Sfax
Gabès
Golfe de Gabès
Tarabulus
Pyrenees
Rhône
Corse
Sardegna
Tyrrhenian Sea
MEDITERRANEAN
EUROPE
Hoggar
Mt Tahat 2918
SAHARA
Ténéré du Tafassâsset
NIGER
Agadez
Zinder
Niamey
MAURITANIA
Nouâdhibou
Nouakchott
St Louis
Sénégal
MALI
Gao
Mopti
Ségou
Niger
Kayes
Bamako
SENEGAL
Dakar
Kaolack
THE GAMBIA
Banjul
GUINEA-BISSAU
Bissau
Fouta Djallon
GUINEA
Kankan
Conakry
SIERRA LEONE
Freetown
LIBERIA
Monrovia
CAPE VERDE
Santo Antão
Boa Vista
Santiago
Fogo
Praia
BURKINA
Ouagadougou
Bobo-Dioulasso
CÔTE D'IVOIRE
Lac de Kossou
Bouaké
Yamoussoukro
Abidjan
GHANA
Black Volta
White Volta
Tamale
Lake Volta
Kumasi
Volta
Accra
Cape Coast
TOGO
Lomé
BENIN
Parakou
Porto-Novo
Kainji Reservoir
Shiroro Reservoir
NIGERIA
Sokoto
Kano
Kaduna
Gombe
Abuja
Ogbomosho
Ibadan
Lagos
Niger
Onitsha
Warri
Port Harcourt
Nkongsamba
Douala
Yaoundé
CAMEROON
Malabo
Bioco
EQUATORIAL GUINEA
Bata
Príncipe
SÃO TOMÉ AND PRÍNCIPE
São Tomé
Libreville
GABON
Port-Gentil
Annobón (Equatorial Guinea)
Gulf of Guinea
Pointe-Noire
CABINDA (Angola)
Namibe
Ascension (U.K.)
St Helena (U.K.)
Ilha da Trindade
Ilhas Martin Vaz

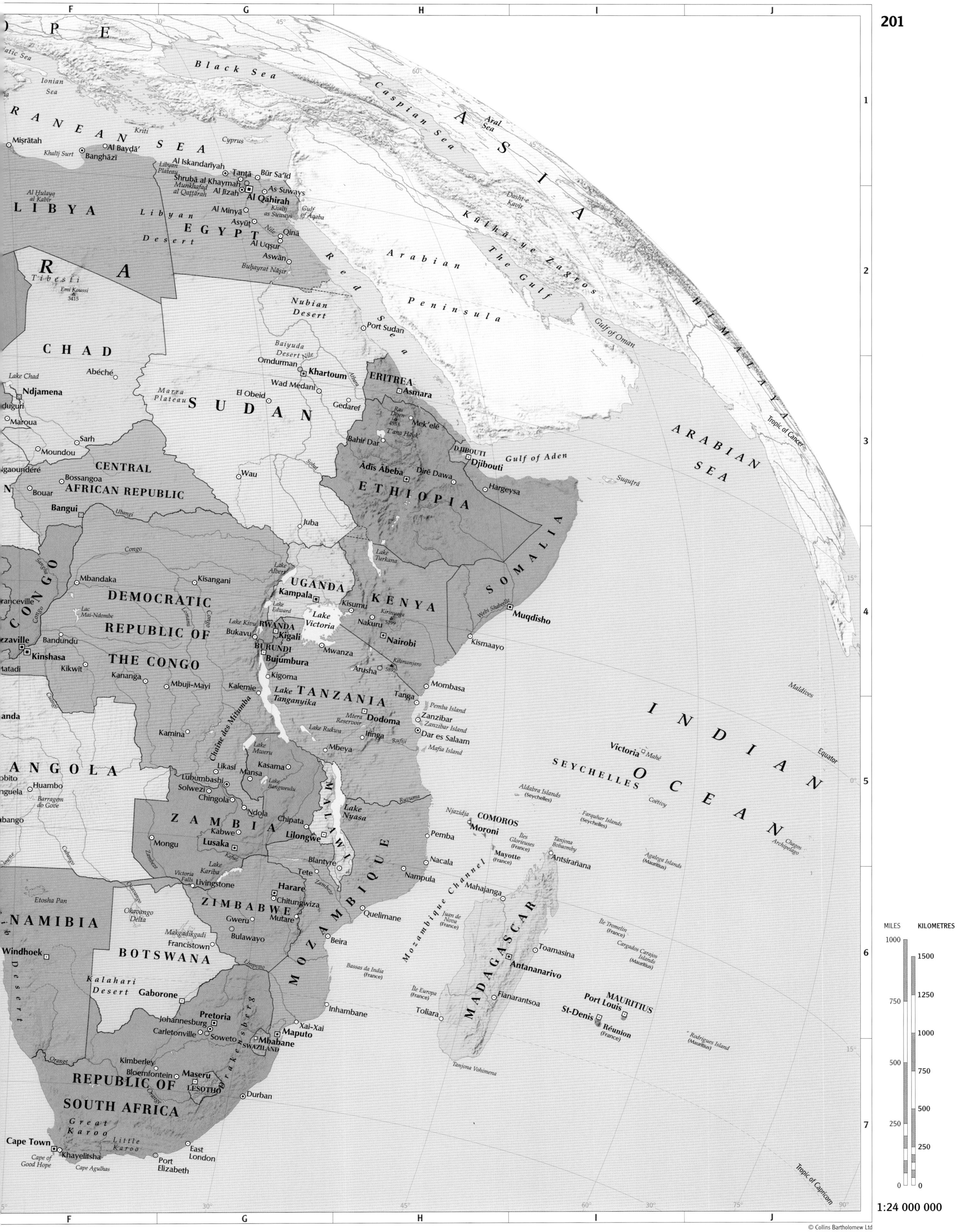

EUROPE

Mişrātah
Al Baydā'
Khalīj Surt
Banghāzī

LIBYA

Al Hulayq al Kabīr

Tibesti
Emi Koussi 3415

RA

SAHARA

CHAD

Lake Chad
Ndjamena
Maiduguri
Maroua
Sarh
Ngaoundéré
Bouar

CENTRAL
AFRICAN REPUBLIC

Bossangoa
Bangui

Ubangi

Mbandaka

DEMOCRATIC

REPUBLIC OF

THE CONGO

Franceville
Brazzaville
Kinshasa
Matadi
Kikwit
Kananga
Mbuji-Mayi

Luanda

ANGOLA

Lobito
Benguela
Huambo

Kamina

Lubumbashi
Likasi
Solwezi
Chingola
Ndola

ZAMBIA

Mongu
Kabwe
Lusaka

Livingstone
Victoria Falls

NAMIBIA

Etosha Pan
Okavango Delta

Windhoek

BOTSWANA

Kalahari Desert
Gaborone

Pretoria
Johannesburg
Carletonville
Soweto
Mbabane
SWAZILAND

Kimberley
Bloemfontein
Maseru
LESOTHO

REPUBLIC OF
SOUTH AFRICA

Great Karoo
Little Karoo

Cape Town
Khayelitsha
Cape of Good Hope
Cape Agulhas

East London
Port Elizabeth

Black Sea
Ionian Sea
Kriti
Cyprus

MEDITERRANEAN SEA

Libyan Plateau
Al Iskandarīyah
Tanta
Būr Sa'īd
Shubrā al Khaymah
Munūfīyah
al Qattārah
Al Jīzah
Al Qāhirah
As Suways
Gulf of Aqaba
Al Minyā
Khalīj as Suways
Asyūt
Libyan Desert
Al Uqsur
Qina
Aswān
Buhayrat Nāşir

EGYPT

Nile

Nubian Desert

Baiyuda Desert
Nile
Omdurman
Khartoum
El Obeid
Wad Medani
Gedaref

SUDAN

Marra Plateau

Wau

Juba

UGANDA
Kampala

Lake Albert
Lake Edward
Lake Kivu
RWANDA
Kigali
Bukavu
BURUNDI
Bujumbura
Kigoma
Kalemie

Kisangani

Lac Mai-Ndombe

Kisumu

Lake Victoria
Mwanza

Nakuru

KENYA

Nairobi

Arusha
Kilimanjaro 5892

Mombasa

TANZANIA

Lake Tanganyika

Dodoma
Mtera Reservoir
Iringa
Lake Rukwa
Mbeya

Dar es Salaam
Zanzibar
Zanzibar Island
Pemba Island

Mafia Island

Kasama
Mansa
Lake Bangweulu
Chipata
Lake Nyasa

MALAWI

Lilongwe
Lake Kariba
Blantyre
Tete

Harare
Chitungwiza
Mutare

ZIMBABWE

Gweru
Bulawayo

Beira

MOZAMBIQUE

Quelimane
Nacala
Nampula

Mozambique Channel

Inhambane

Xai-Xai
Maputo

Durban

Red Sea

ERITREA
Asmara
Ras Dejen
Mek'elē
T'ana Hāyk'
Bahir Dar
Ādīs Ābeba
Dirē Dawa

DJIBOUTI
Djibouti

ETHIOPIA

Hargeysa

SOMALIA

Wabē Shabēlē

Muqdisho

Kismaayo

Lake Turkana

Gulf of Aden

ASIA

Caspian Sea
Aral Sea

Dasht-e Kavīr

Kūhhā-ye Zāgros

The Gulf

Gulf of Oman

Arabian Peninsula

ARABIAN SEA

Suqutrā

Tropic of Cancer

HIMALAYA

INDIAN OCEAN

Maldives

Equator

SEYCHELLES

Victoria
Mahé

Aldabra Islands (Seychelles)
Coëtivy

Farquhar Islands (Seychelles)

Îles Glorieuses (France)

COMOROS
Njazidja
Moroni
Pemba

Mayotte (France)

Juan de Nova (France)

Mahajanga

MADAGASCAR

Antananarivo

Fianarantsoa

Toliara

Antsirañana

Toamasina

Tanjona Bobaomby

Agalega Islands (Mauritius)

Tromelin (France)

Cargados Carajos Islands (Mauritius)

MAURITIUS
Port Louis
St-Denis
Réunion (France)

Chagos Archipelago

Rodrigues Island (Mauritius)

Bassas da India (France)

Île Europa (France)

Tanjona Vohimena

Tropic of Capricorn

© Collins Bartholomew Ltd

MILES   KILOMETRES

1000   1500

750   1250
          1000

500   750

250   500
          250

0   0

1:24 000 000

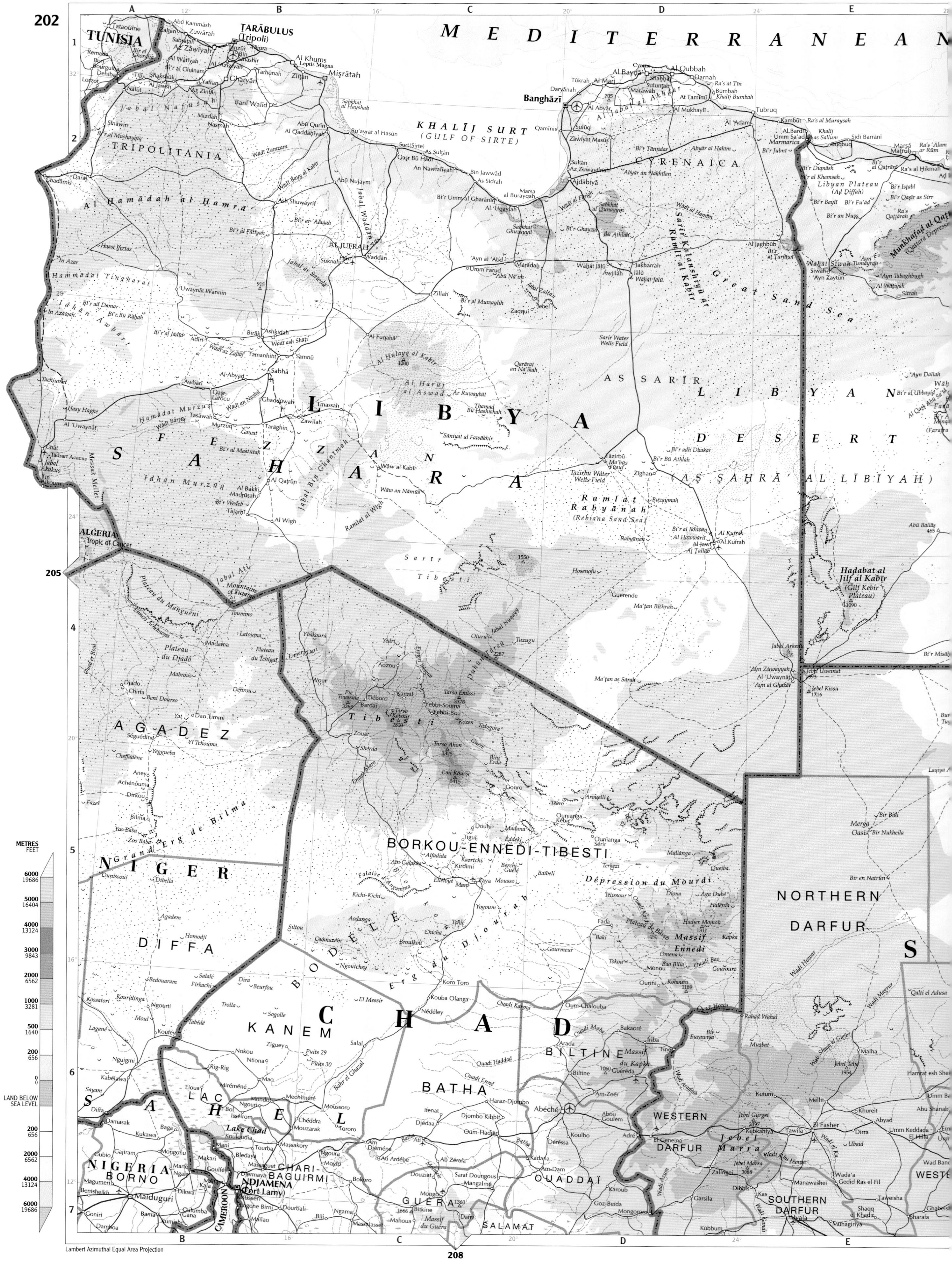

MEDITERRANEAN

TUNISIA

Abū Kammāsh
Zaltan
Zuwārah
TARĀBULUS
(Tripoli)
Az Zāwiyah
Sabrātah
Al Khums
Leptis Magna
Bi'r al Ghanam
Tarhūnah
Zlītan
Misrātah

Banghāzī

Al Bayḍā' Al Qubbah
Cyrene Shahhāt Darnah
Al Marj Sulunṭah Ra's at Tīn
Daryānah Marāwah Būmbah
Al Akhḍar At Tamīmī Khalīj Bumbah
Al Abyār

KHALĪJ SURT
(GULF OF SIRTE)

Qamīnis
Zāwiyat Masūs
Sulṭān Abyār al Ḥakīm
Az Zuwayṭīnah
Ajdābiyā

CYRENAICA

Tubruq
Kambūt Ra's al Murayṣah
Umm Sa'ad as Sallūm Sīdī Barrānī
Bi'r Jubni Marmarica Buqbuq

Libyan Plateau
(Aḍ Ḍiffah)

L I B Y A

S A H A R A

F E Z Z A N

ALGERIA
Tropic of Cancer

Great Sand Sea

LIBYAN

DESERT

(AS SAHRĀ' AL LĪBĪYAH)

Ramlat
Rabyānah
(Rebiana Sand Sea)

Hadabat al
Jilf al Kabīr
(Gilf Kebir
Plateau)

AGADEZ

Tibesti

NIGER

BORKOU-ENNEDI-TIBESTI

Dépression du Mourdi

NORTHERN

DARFUR

DIFFA

Massif
Ennedi

C H A D

KANEM

BILTINE

Lake Chad

BATHA

WESTERN

DARFUR

NIGERIA
BORNO

NDJAMENA
(Fort Lamy)

CHARI-
BAGUIRMI

GUERA

SALAMAT

OUADDAÏ

SOUTHERN
DARFUR

CAMEROUN

METRES
FEET

6000
19686

5000
16404

4000
13124

3000
9843

2000
6562

1000
3281

500
1640

200
656

0

LAND BELOW
SEA LEVEL

200
656

2000
6562

4000
13124

6000
19686

Lambert Azimuthal Equal Area Projection

208

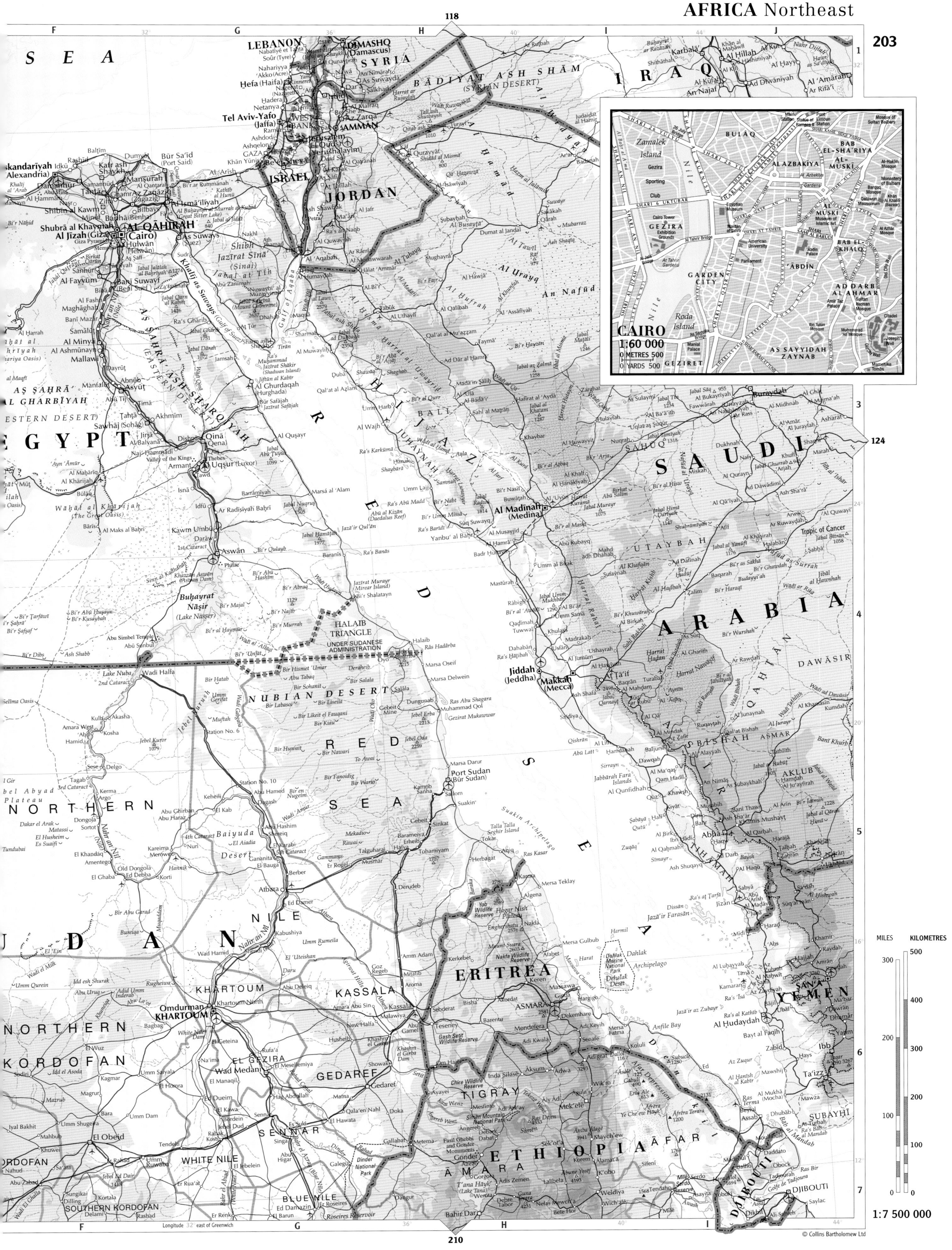

F G 118 H I J

SEA

LEBANON
DIMASHQ (Damascus)
SYRIA
Soûr (Tyre)
Nahariyya
Hefa (Haifa)
'Akko (Acre)
Nazareth
Dar'a
Al Mafraq
Az Zarqa
Netanya
Tel Aviv-Yafo (Jaffa)
Ashdod
Ashqelon
'AMMAN
GAZA
ISRAEL
Jerusalem (Yerushalayim)
JORDAN
Al Karak
Ma'an
Petra
Shawbak

BADIYAT ASH SHAM
(SYRIAN DESERT)

IRAQ
Karbala'
Al Hillah
An Najaf
Ad Diwaniyah

Skandarîyah
Alexandria
Damanhûr
Rashîd
Dumyat
Bûr Sa'îd (Port Said)
Mansûrah
Katr ash Shaykh
Samannûd
Az Zaqaziq
Al Isma'îlîyah
Al 'Arîsh
Khan Yûnis

Shubrâ al Khaymah
AL QAHIRAH
Al Jizah (Giza)
Cairo
Hulwan
Helwan
As Suways (Suez)

EGYPT

Al Minyâ
Banî Suwayf (Beni Suef)
Al Fashn
Al Fayyûm

AS SAHRA' ASH SHARQIYAH
(EASTERN DESERT)

AS SAHRA' AL GHARBIYAH
(WESTERN DESERT)

Asyût
Abnûb
Mallawî
Dayrût

HIJAZ

Qinâ (Qena)
Uqsur (Luxor)
Thebes
Valley of the Kings

Aswân
Buhayrat Nasir (Lake Nasser)
Abu Simbel Temple

RED SEA

HALAIB TRIANGLE
UNDER SUDANESE ADMINISTRATION

Halaib
Ras Hadarba

NUBIAN DESERT

Lake Nuba
Wadi Halfa
2nd Cataract

NORTHERN

SAUDI

ARABIA

Al Madinah (Medina)

Tropic of Cancer

Jiddah (Jeddah)
Makkah (Mecca)
At Ta'if

Port Sudan (Bûr Sudan)
Suakin

ASIR

NILE

Atbara
Berber
Ed Damer

SUDAN

KHARTOUM
Omdurman
KHARTOUM North

NORTHERN
KORDOFAN

El Obeid

WHITE NILE

SENNAR

BLUE NILE

SOUTHERN KORDOFAN

EL GEZIRA

Wad Medani

GEDAREF
Gedaref

KASSALA
Kassala

ERITREA

ASMARA
Massawa

Dahlak Archipelago

TIGRAY

AMARA

ETHIOPIA

AFAR

Gonder
Bahir Dar
Tana Hayk' (Lake Tana)

YEMEN
SAN'A'
Al Hudaydah
Ibb
Ta'izz

SUBAYHI

DJIBOUTI
DJIBOUTI

Longitude 32 east of Greenwich

210

1:7 500 000

© Collins Bartholomew Ltd

CAIRO 1:60 000
0 METRES 500
0 YARDS 500

Zamalek Island
Gezira
Sporting Club
BULAQ
AL AZBAKIYA
AL MUSKI
BAB EL-SHA'RIYA
GEZIRA
Cairo Tower
Egyptian Museum
GARDEN CITY
'ABDIN
AS SAYYIDAH ZAYNAB
Roda Island
AD DARB AL AHMAR
BAB EL KHALQ

MILES KILOMETRES
300 500
400
200 300
200
100 100
0 0

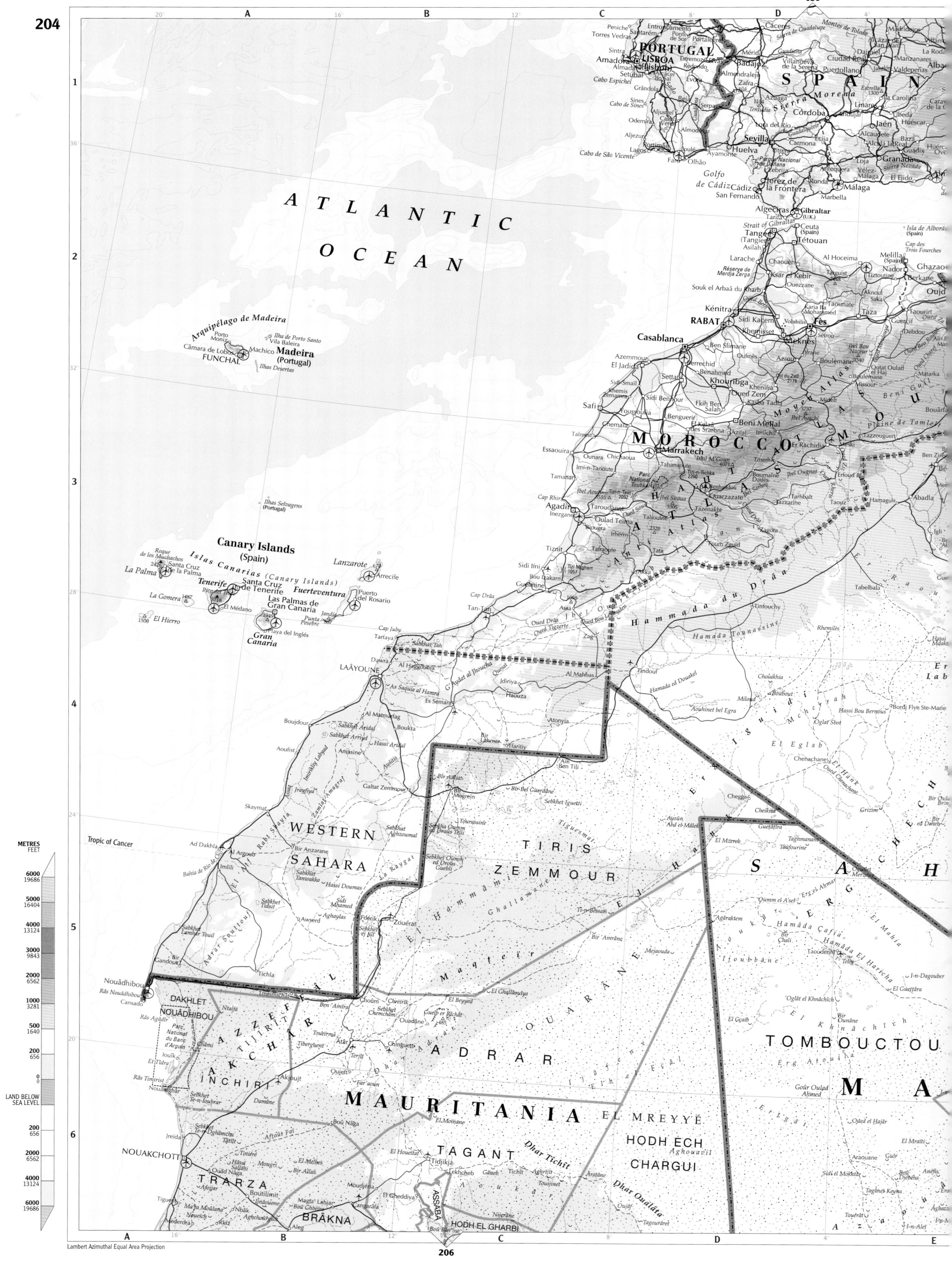

ATLANTIC
OCEAN

PORTUGAL
LISBOA
Lisbon
SPAIN

Peniche
Entroncamento
Torres Vedras
Cáceres
Montes de Toledo

Amadora
Estremoz
Portalegre
Badajoz
Mérida
Ciudad Real
Puertollano
Valdepeñas

Setúbal
Redondo
Almendralejo
Villanueva de la Serena

Grândola
Beja
Serpa
Azuaga
Córdoba
Linares
La Carolina

Sines
Odemira
Aljustrel
Peñarroya-Pueblonuevo
Andújar
Jaén
Huéscar

Cabo de São Vicente
Lagos
Ayamonte
Huelva
Écija
Sevilla
Carmona
Alcalá la Real
Guadix
Baza

Golfo
de Cádiz
Cádiz
Jerez de la Frontera
Ronda
Málaga
Vélez-Málaga
El Ejido
Granada
Sierra Nevada

San Fernando
Algeciras
Gibraltar (U.K.)
Marbella
Strait of Gibraltar
Ceuta (Spain)
Tarifa
Isla de Alborán (Spain)

Tánger (Tangier)
Asilah
Tétouan
Melilla (Spain)
Cap des Trois Fourches
Nador
Ghazaouet

Larache
Chaouen
Al Hoceima
Targuist
Aknoul
Berkane
Oujda

Réserve de Merdja Zerga
Ksar el Kébir
Ouezzane
Taounate
Taza
Taourirt

Souk el Arbâa du Rharb
Taza

Kénitra
Sidi Kacem
Volubilis
Fès
Sefrou
Guercif
Debdou

RABAT
Khemisset
Meknès
MOROCCO

Casablanca
Ben Slimane
Oulmès
Azrou
Ifrane
Boulemane
Bouârfa

Azemmour
Berrechid
Benahmed
Boujad
Khenifra
Midelt
Jbel Bou Naceur

El Jadida
Settat
Oued Zem
Khouribga
Kasba Tadla
Er Rachidia
Moyen Atlas

Safi
Sidi Smaïl
Khemis Zemamra
Sidi Bennour
Fkih Ben Salah
Beni Mellal
Jbel Ayachi

Chemaia
El Kelaâ des Srarhna
Azilal
HAUT ATLAS
Jbel M'Goun 4071
Tinerhir

Essaouira
Ounara
Chichaoua
Marrakech
Imlil Toubkal
Toubkal 4167
Toundoute
Boumalne
Dades
Tarhbalt

Cap Rhir
Tamanar
Imi-n-Tanoute
Taliouine
Ouarzazate
Jbel Siroua
Tazenakht
Agdz

Agadir
Taroudannt
Aoulouz
Foum Zguid

Inezgane
Oulad Teima
Biougra
Irherm
Tata
Anti Atlas
Tafraoute
Foum Zguid

Tiznit
Tata
Abadla

Sidi Ifni
Bou Izakarn
Tin Mghert
Hamaguir

Guelmine
Assa
Hamada du Drâa

Tan-Tan
Oued Drâa
Oued Bou Kerch
Zag
Hamada Tounassine

Tarfaya
Sabkhat Tah
Oued Tigzerte

Dawra
Al Hagounia
G. Oudat al Jhoucha
Quésat
Al Mahbas
Tindouf

LAÂYOUNE
As Saquia al Hamra
Es Semara
Idiriya
Haouza
Hamada ed Douakel

Al Matmarfag
Boukta
Atonyia

Boujdour
Sabkhat Aridal
Hassi Aridal
Bir Lharmar
Tfariti
Aïn Ben Tili

Aoulist
Amasine
Haïlis
Bir Bel Guerdâne
Sebkhet Iguetti

Jraufiya
Zemul Amagrar
Galtat Zemmour
Bir Mogrein

Skaymat

WESTERN
SAHARA
TIRIS
ZEMMOUR
Tiguesmat
Ayoûn Abd el-Mâlek

Ad Dakhla
Bir Anzarane
Sabkhat Aghzoumal
Zouérat
Fdérik

Bahía de Río de Oro
Imlili
Sebkhet Oumm ed Drous Telli

SAHARA

OUARÂNE

TOMBOUCTOU

Nouâdhibou
Ras Nouâdhibou
Cansado
Tichla
Tmeïmichât

DAKHLET
NOUÂDHIBOU
Ntalfa
Ben Amîra
Choûm
Atâr
ADRAR

Ras Agadir
Parc National du Banc d'Arguin
Toûteï
Inchiri

INCHIRI
Akjoujt
Ouadâne
Chinguetti

MAURITANIA
EL MREYYÉ
HODH ECH
CHARGUI

NOUAKCHOTT
TAGANT
Tidjikja
Tichit
Oualâta
Dhar Tichît

TRARZA
ASSABA
Dhar Oualâta

BRÂKNA
HODH EL GHARBI

Arquipélago de Madeira
Ilha de Porto Santo
Vila Baleira
Porto Moniz
Câmara de Lobos
Machico
Madeira (Portugal)
FUNCHAL
Ilhas Desertas

Ilhas Selvagens (Portugal)

Canary Islands
(Spain)
Islas Canarias (Canary Islands)
Roque de los Muchachos 2426
La Palma
Santa Cruz de la Palma
Lanzarote
Arrecife
Tenerife
Santa Cruz de Tenerife
Fuerteventura
La Gomera
Pico del Teide
El Médano
Las Palmas de Gran Canaria
Puerto del Rosario
El Hierro
Gran Canaria
Playa del Inglés
Punta de Maspalomas

Tropic of Cancer

METRES FEET	
6000	19686
5000	16404
4000	13124
3000	9843
2000	6562
1000	3281
500	1640
200	656
0	
LAND BELOW SEA LEVEL	
200	656
2000	6562
4000	13124
6000	19686

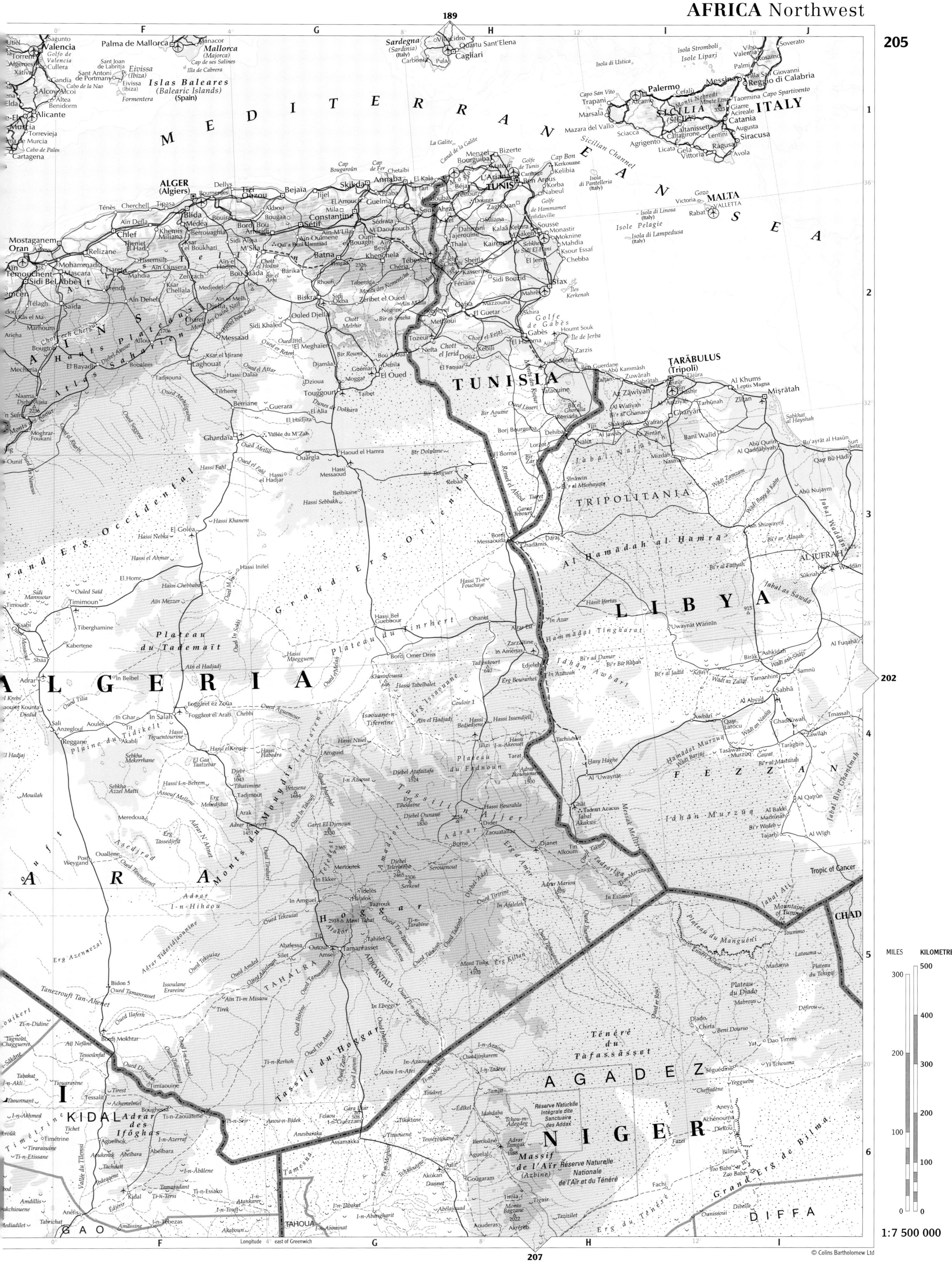
189
MEDITERRANEAN SEA
Palma de Mallorca
Mallorca
(Majorca)
Islas Baleares
(Balearic Islands)
(Spain)
Eivissa
(Ibiza)
Formentera
Valencia
Alicante
Murcia
Cartagena
Sardegna
(Sardinia)
(Italy)
Cagliari
Isola di Ustica
Isola Stromboli
Isole Lipari
Palermo
Trapani
Marsala
Mazara del Vallo
Agrigento
SICILIA
(SICILY)
ITALY
Messina
Reggio di Calabria
Catania
Siracusa
Ragusa
Sicilian Channel
Isola di Pantelleria
(Italy)
Isola di Linosa
(Italy)
Isole Pelagie
Isola di Lampedusa
(Italy)
Gozo
MALTA
VALLETTA
Victoria
Rabat
La Galite
Canal de la Galite
Bizerte
Menzel Bourguiba
Golfe de Tunis
Cap Bon
Kelibia
L'Ariana
TUNIS
Golfe de Hammamet
Sousse
Monastir
Mahdia
Kairouan
Sfax
Îles Kerkenah
Golfe de Gabès
Gabès
Houmt Souk
Île de Jerba
Zarzis
Medenine
Tataouine
TUNISIA
Tozeur
Nefta
Chott el Jerid
Kebili
Douz
Gafsa
Kasserine
ALGER
(Algiers)
Tizi Ouzou
Bejaïa
Jijel
Skikda
Annaba
El Kala
Constantine
Sétif
Guelma
Souk Ahras
Batna
Biskra
Tébessa
Khenchela
Blida
Médéa
Chlef
Mostaganem
Oran
Relizane
Mascara
Sidi Bel Abbès
Tiaret
Saïda
M'Sila
Bou Saâda
Djelfa
Aïn Témouchent
Chott el Hodna
Chott Melrhir
Hauts Plateaux
Atlas Saharien
Tell
Messaad
Laghouat
El Bayadh
Mecheria
Naama
Aïn Sefra
Touggourt
El Oued
Ouargla
Ghardaïa
Hassi Messaoud
El Goléa
Timimoun
Adrar
In Salah
Reggane
Aoulef
Grand Erg Occidental
Grand Erg Oriental
Plateau du Tademaït
Plateau du Tinrhert
Plateau du Tidikelt
ALGERIA
SAHARA
Tanezrouft
Tamanrasset
Hoggar
Tassili n' Ajjer
Djanet
Illizi
In Amenas
In Guezzam
Bordj Mokhtar
Tassili du Hoggar
Adrar des Iforas
KIDAL
Kidal
GAO
Tessalit
TAHOUA
AGADEZ
NIGER
Massif de l'Aïr
Réserve Naturelle Intégrale dite Sanctuaire des Addax
Réserve Naturelle Nationale de l'Aïr et du Ténéré
Ténéré du Tafassâsset
Grand Erg de Bilma
Bilma
Plateau du Djado
Djado
DIFFA
Arlit
Agadez
Assamakka
TARĀBULUS
(Tripoli)
Az Zawiyah
Misratah
Al Khums
Ghadāmis
Jabal Nafusah
TRIPOLITANIA
Al Hamadah al Hamra
LIBYA
Sabhā
Ubari
Murzuq
FEZZAN
Idhan Awbari
Idhan Murzuq
Ghat
AL JUFRAH
Waddan
Tropic of Cancer
CHAD
Plateau du Manguéni
Longitude east of Greenwich
202
207
MILES
KILOMETRES
1:7 500 000
© Collins Bartholomew Ltd

SAHARA

MAURITANIA

INCHIRI

ADRAR

AKCHÂR

DAKHLET
NOUADHIBOU

EL MREYYÉ

HODH
ECH CHARGUI

TAGANT

TRARZA

BRÂKNA

ASSABA

HODH
EL GHARBI

GORGOL

GUIDIMAKA

TOMBOUCTOU

NOUAKCHOTT

St-Louis

DAKAR

SENEGAL

THE GAMBIA

BANJUL

KAYES

KOULIKORO

SÉGOU

MALI

MOPTI

BAMAKO

SIKASSO

GUINEA-BISSAU

BISSAU

MOYENNE-GUINÉE

GUINEA

HAUTE
GUINÉE

BURKINA

OUAGADOUGOU

GUINÉE-
MARITIME

CONAKRY

FOUTA
DJALLON

GUINÉE-FORESTIERE

UPPER
WEST

UPPER E

NORTHE

GHAN

BRONG-AHAFC

SIERRA
LEONE

FREETOWN
WESTERN AREA

NORTHERN

EASTERN

SOUTHERN

CÔTE
D'IVOIRE

YAMOUSSOUKRO

ASHANTI

KUMASI

WESTERN

CENTRA

LIBERIA

MONROVIA

Abidjan

ATLANTIC OCEAN

Cape
Three Points

Cape
Palmas

METRES / FEET

METRES	FEET
6000	19686
5000	16404
4000	13124
3000	9843
2000	6562
1000	3281
500	1640
200	656
0	0

LAND BELOW
SEA LEVEL

200	656
2000	6562
4000	13124
6000	19686

CAPE VERDE
AT THE SAME SCALE

Santo
Antão

São Vicente

Mindelo

Santa
Luzia

São
Nicolau

Sal

Boa
Vista

Ilhas do Cabo Verde

Santiago

Maio

PRAIA

Fogo

Brava

Equator

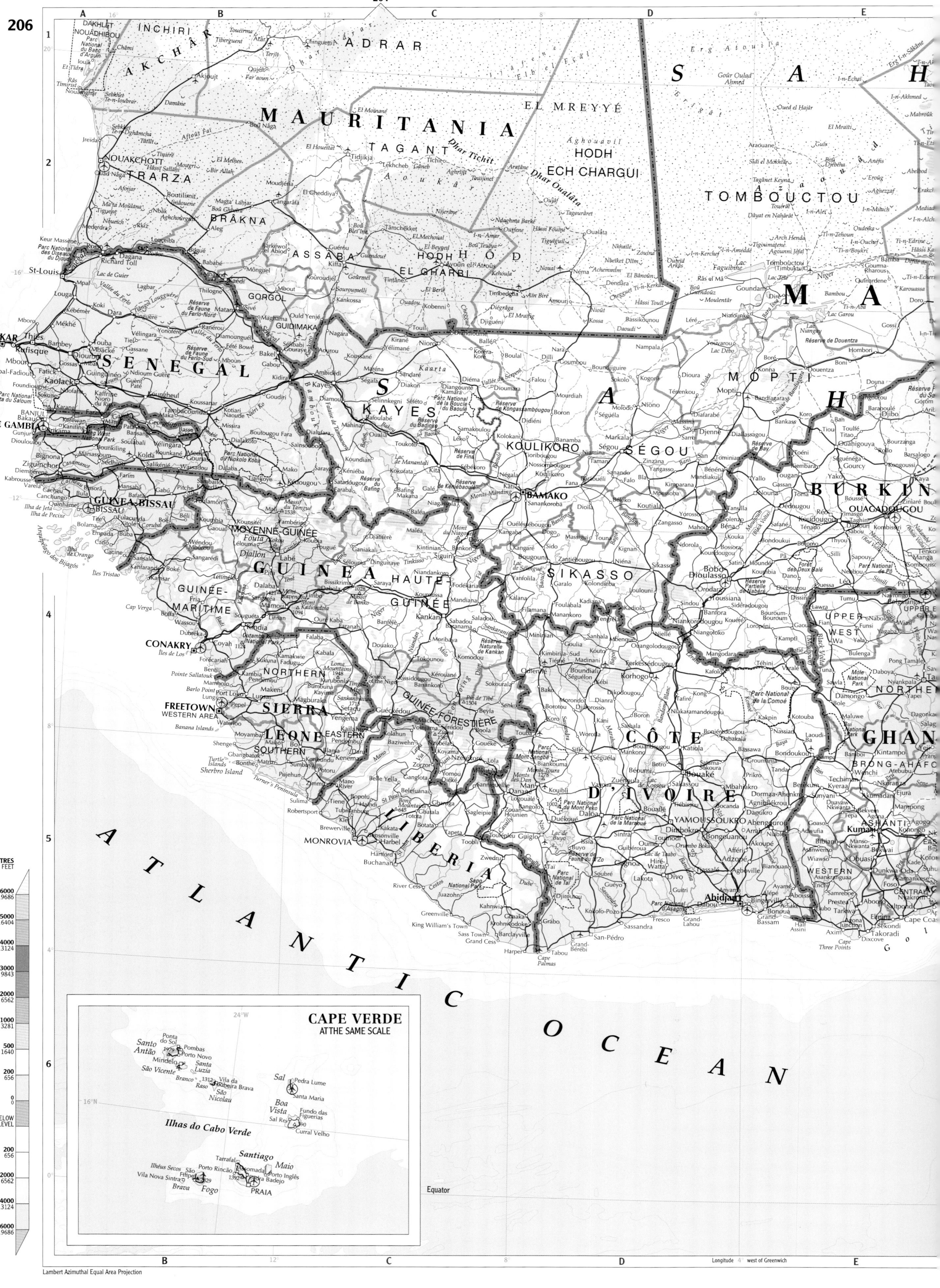

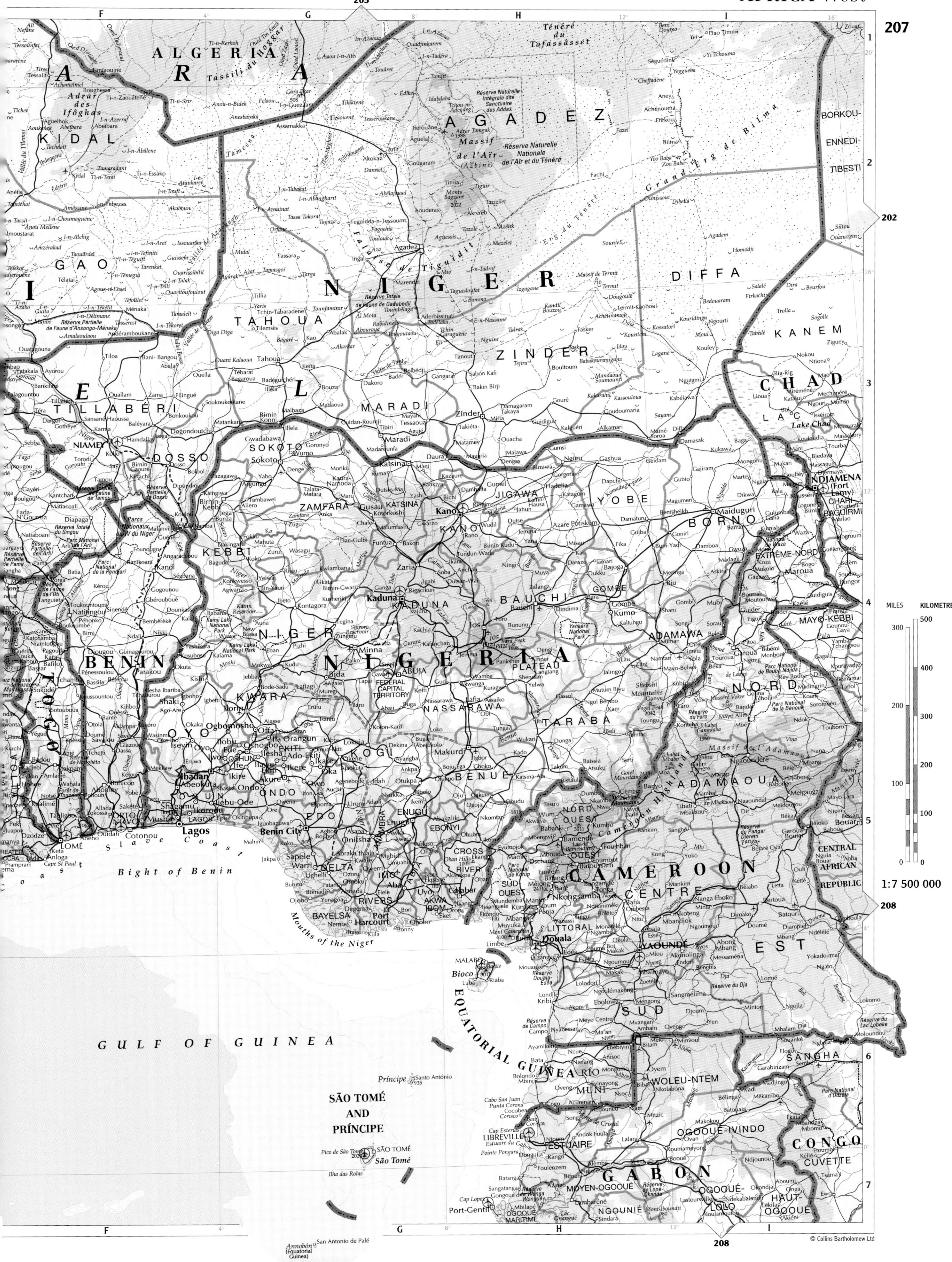
205
202
208
208
ALGERIA
NIGER
AGADEZ
TAHOUA
ZINDER
MARADI
DIFFA
TILLABÉRI
DOSSO
KANEM
CHAD
LAC
BORKOU-ENNEDI-TIBESTI
GAO
KIDAL
NIAMEY
NIGERIA
SOKOTO
KATSINA
KANO
JIGAWA
YOBE
BORNO
ZAMFARA
KEBBI
KADUNA
BAUCHI
GOMBE
ADAMAWA
NIGER
PLATEAU
KWARA
OYO
OSUN
EKITI
ONDO
OGUN
LAGOS
KOGI
NASSARAWA
FEDERAL CAPITAL TERRITORY
ABUJA
TARABA
BENUE
EDO
ANAMBRA
ENUGU
EBONYI
DELTA
IMO
ABIA
CROSS RIVER
AKWA IBOM
RIVERS
BAYELSA
BENIN
TOGO
CAMEROON
EXTRÊME-NORD
NORD
ADAMAOUA
NORD OUEST
OUEST
SUD OUEST
LITTORAL
CENTRE
EST
SUD
CENTRAL AFRICAN REPUBLIC
MAYO-KEBBI
EQUATORIAL GUINEA
RÍO MUNI
GABON
WOLEU-NTEM
ESTUAIRE
MOYEN-OGOOUÉ
OGOOUÉ-IVINDO
OGOOUÉ-LOLO
HAUT-OGOOUÉ
NGOUNIÉ
OGOOUÉ MARITIME
CONGO
CUVETTE
SANGHA
SÃO TOMÉ AND PRÍNCIPE
São Tomé
Príncipe
Annobón (Equatorial Guinea)
GULF OF GUINEA
Bight of Benin
Slave Coast
Mouths of the Niger
Lake Chad
Grand Erg de Bilma
Ténéré du Tafassâsset
Massif de l'Aïr
Tassili du Hoggar
Adrar des Ifôghas
Cameroon Highlands
Massif de l'Adamaoua
Lagos
Kano
Kaduna
Maiduguri
Zinder
Maradi
Agadez
Tahoua
Sokoto
Douala
YAOUNDÉ
LIBREVILLE
MALABO
Bioco
Port Harcourt
Benin City
Ibadan
Ogbomosho
Jos
Cotonou
PORTO NOVO
LOMÉ
NDJAMENA (Fort Lamy)
Maroua
Garoua
Ngaoundéré
Port-Gentil
Calabar
Enugu
MILES
KILOMETRES
1:7 500 000

202

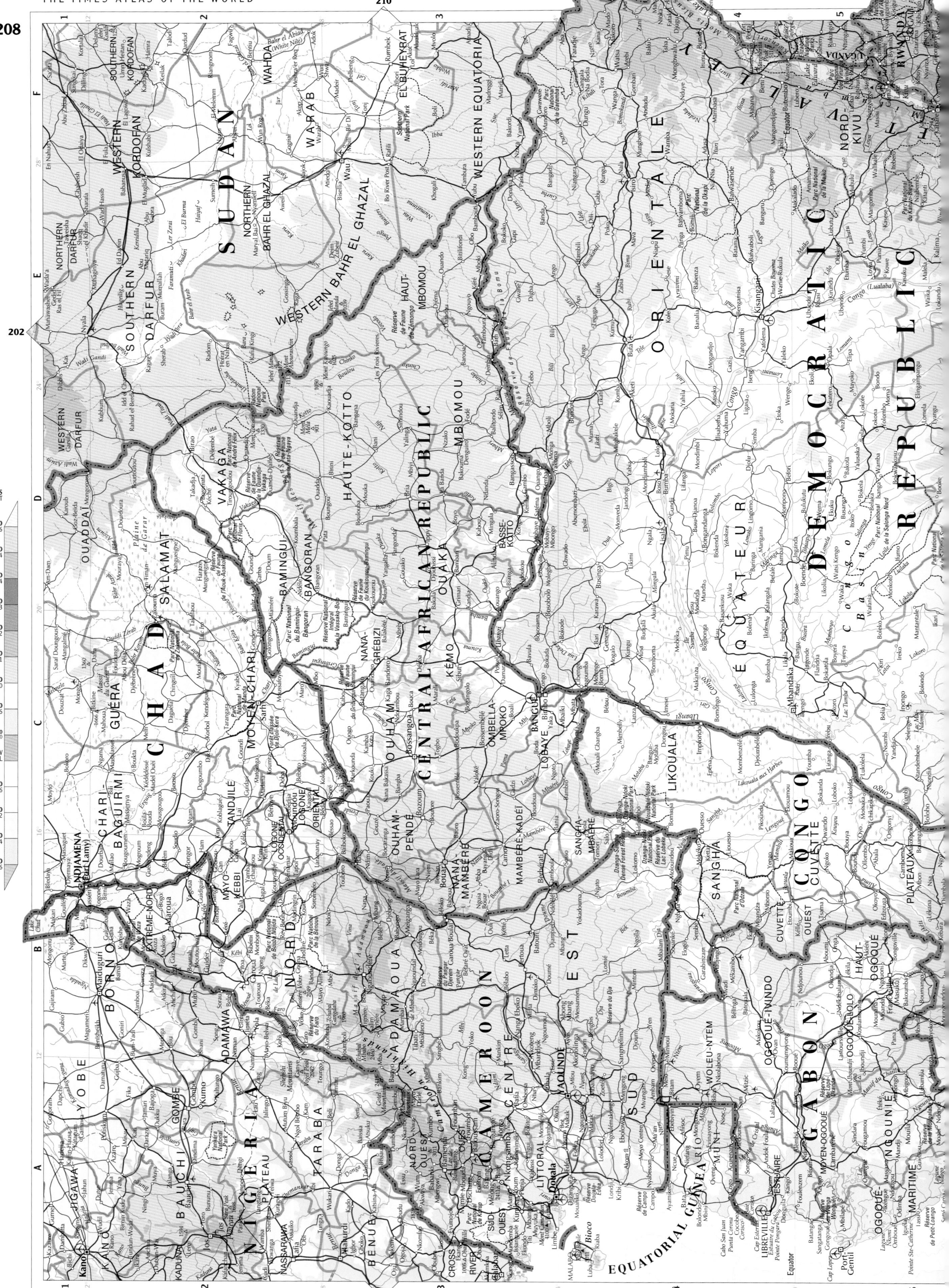

METRES
FEET

6000	19686
5000	16404
4000	13124
3000	9843
2000	6562
1000	3281
500	1640
200	656
0	0

LAND BELOW
SEA LEVEL

200	656
2000	6562
4000	13124
6000	19686

SUDAN

CHAD

CENTRAL AFRICAN REPUBLIC

CAMEROON

NIGERIA

DEMOCRATIC REPUBLIC

CONGO

GABON

EQUATORIAL GUINEA

WESTERN KORDOFAN

NORTHERN KORDOFAN

SOUTHERN KORDOFAN

NORTHERN DARFUR

SOUTHERN DARFUR

WESTERN DARFUR

WARAB

BAHR EL GHAZAL

WESTERN BAHR EL GHAZAL

WESTERN EQUATORIA

ORIENTALE

NORD KIVU

MANIEMA

SUD KIVU

ÉQUATEUR

OUADDAÏ

SALAMAT

GUÉRA

CHARI-BAGUIRMI

VAKAGA

BAMINGUI-BANGORAN

HAUTE-KOTTO

MBOMOU

HAUT-MBOMOU

BASSE-KOTTO

OUAKA

KÉMO

NANA-GRÉBIZI

OMBELLA-MPOKO

LOBAYE

SANGHA-MBAÉRÉ

NANA-MAMBÉRÉ

MAMBÉRÉ-KADÉI

OUHAM

OUHAM-PENDÉ

MOYEN-CHARI

TANDJILÉ

MAYO-KEBBI

LOGONE ORIENTAL

LOGONE OCCIDENTAL

NORD

ADAMAOUA

ADAMAWA

EXTRÊME-NORD

BORNO

YOBE

BAUCHI

GOMBE

JIGAWA

KANO

KADUNA

PLATEAU

NASSARAWA

TARABA

BENUE

CROSS RIVER

CENTRE

EST

SUD

OUEST

LITTORAL

NORD-OUEST

SUD-OUEST

NDJAMENA (Ndjamena)

KINSHASA

Kano

Kisangani

LIBREVILLE

Douala

YAOUNDÉ

BANGUI

Bioco

WOLEU-NTEM

OGOOUÉ-IVINDO

OGOOUÉ-MARITIME

NGOUNIÉ

MOYEN-OGOOUÉ

ESTUAIRE

HAUT-OGOOUÉ

OGOOUÉ-LOLO

PLATEAUX

CUVETTE

CUVETTE OUEST

SANGHA

LIKOUALA

NTEM

Lambert Azimuthal Equal Area Projection

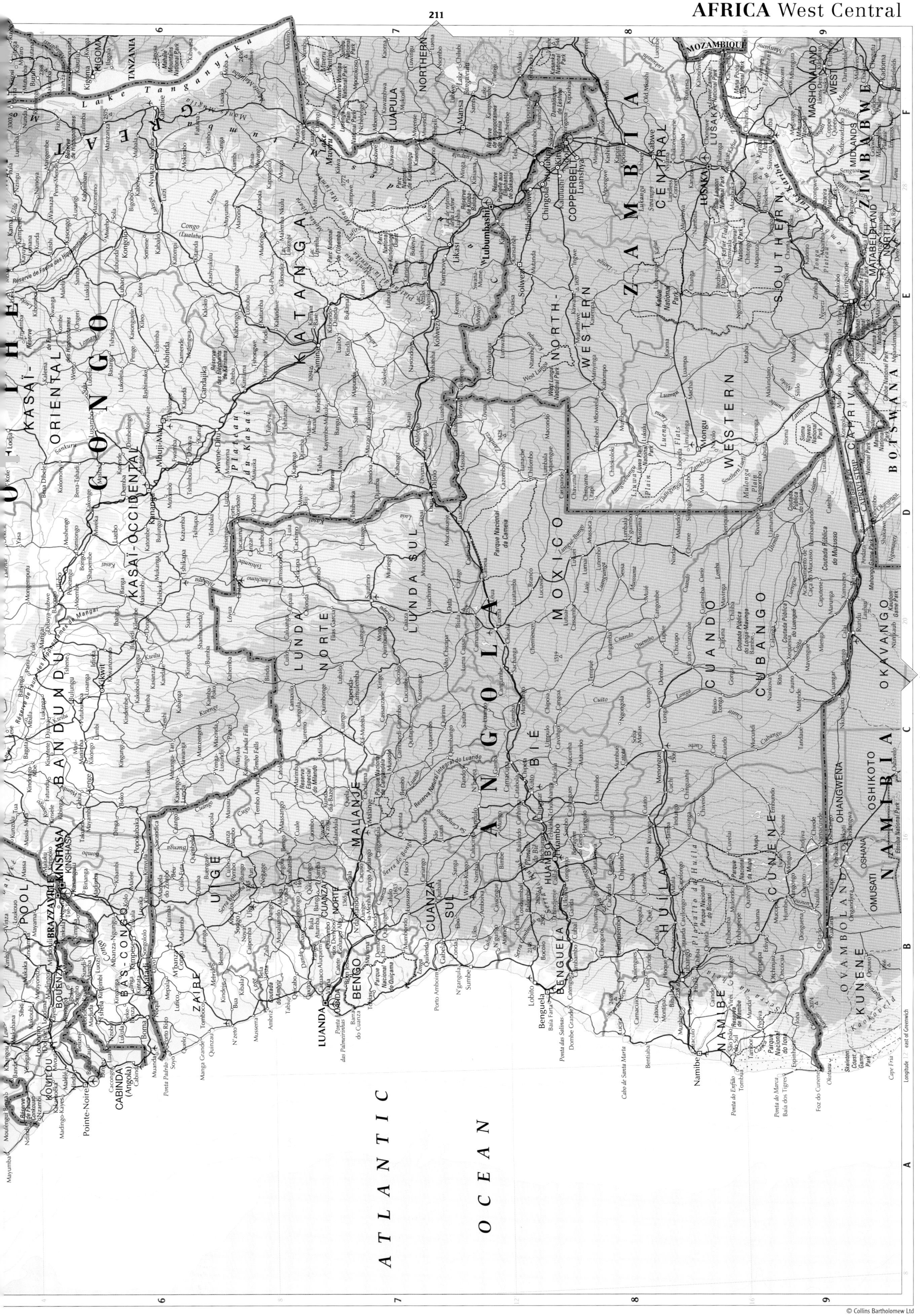

211

212

MILES   KILOMETRES

300   500

400

200   300

100   200

100

0   0

© Collins Bartholomew Ltd

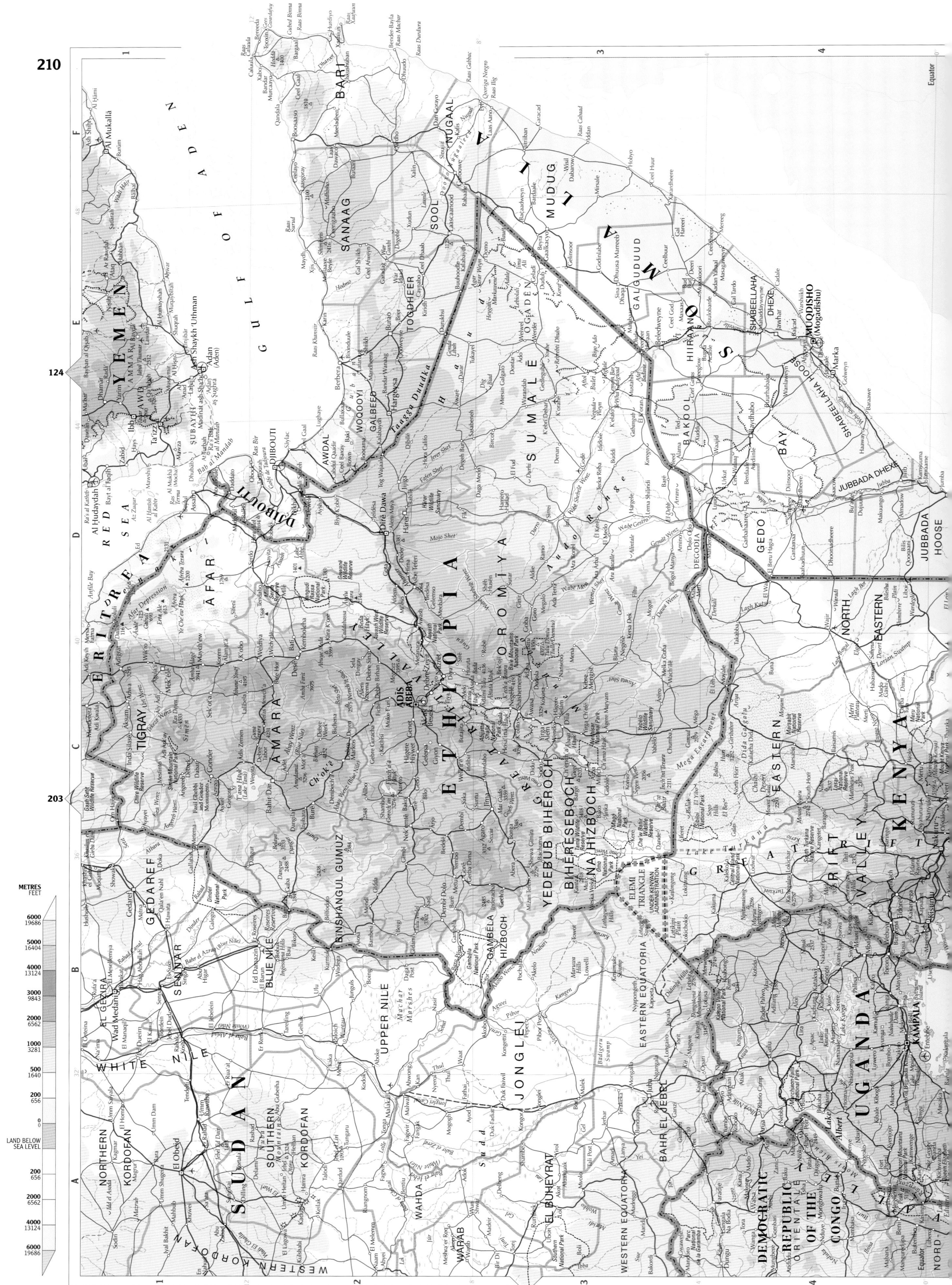

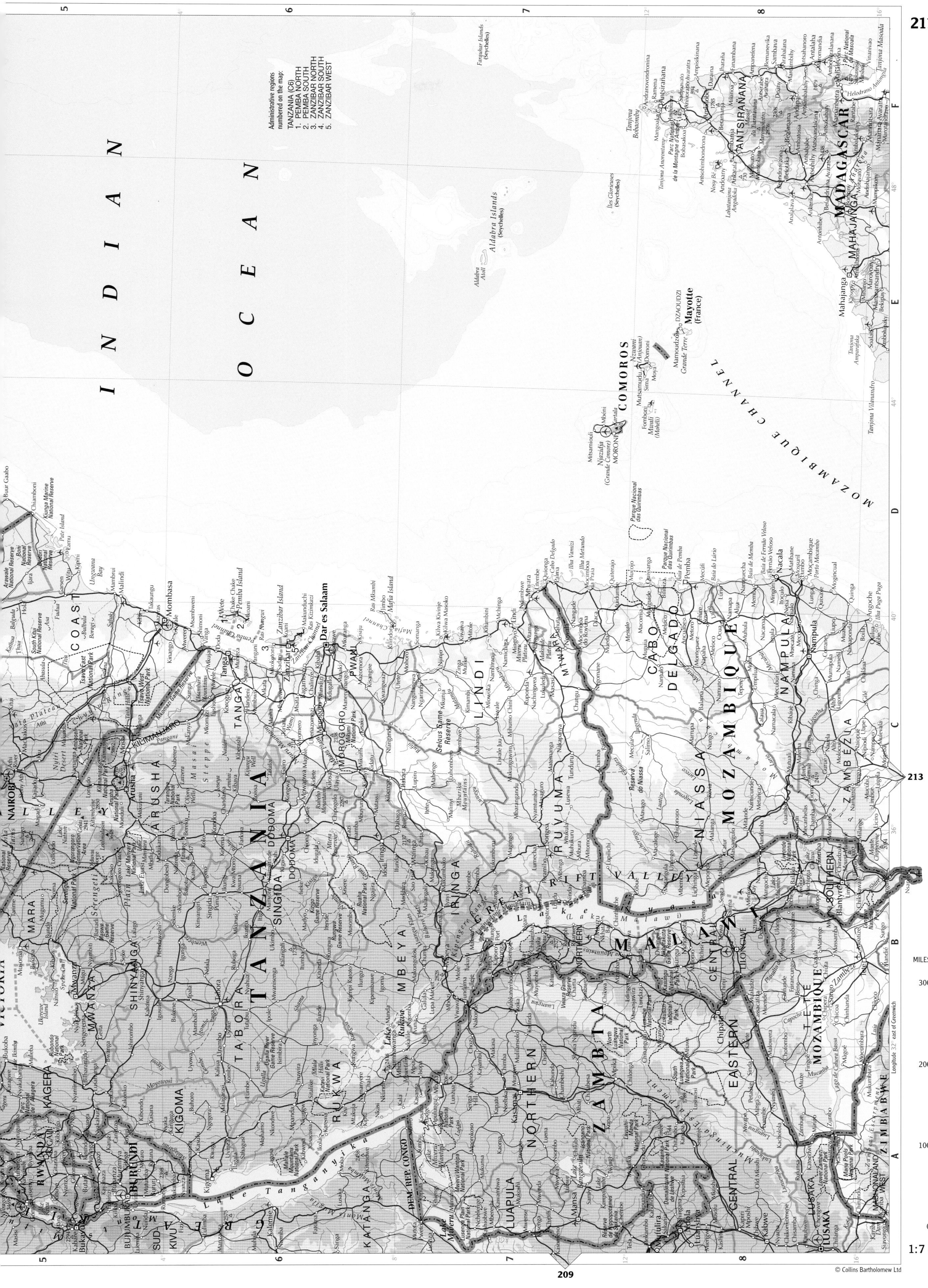

213

209

Administrative regions
numbered on the map:
TANZANIA (C6)
1. PEMBA NORTH
2. PEMBA SOUTH
3. ZANZIBAR NORTH
4. ZANZIBAR SOUTH
5. ZANZIBAR WEST

MILES   KILOMETRES

300   500

400

200   300

200

100   100

0   0

1:7 500 000

© Collins Bartholomew Ltd

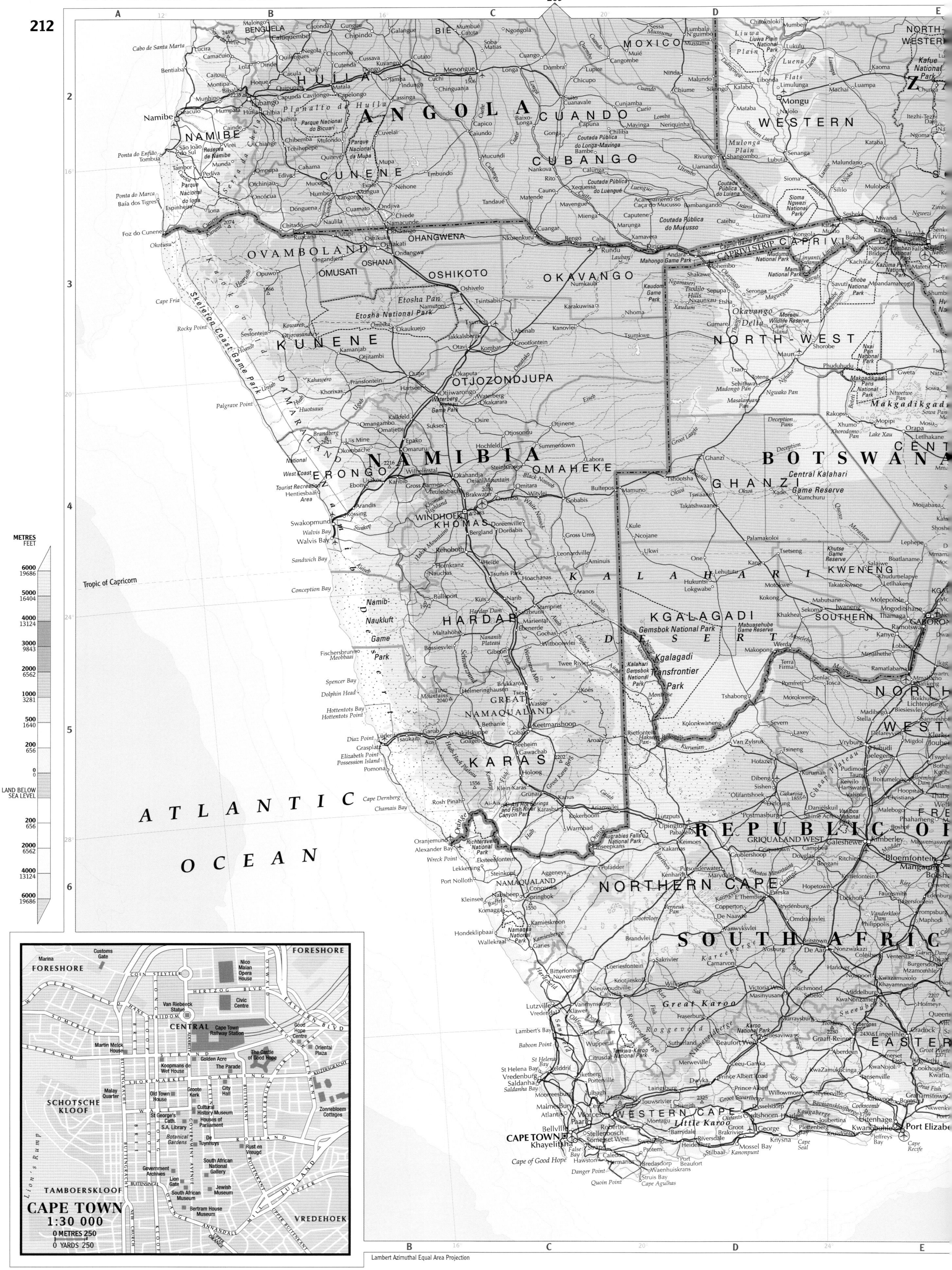

ANGOLA

HUÍLA
BENGUELA
BIÉ
MOXICO
CUANDO
CUBANGO
CUNENE
NAMIBE
WESTERN

NAMIBIA
OVAMBOLAND
OHANGWENA
OMUSATI
OSHANA
OSHIKOTO
OKAVANGO
CAPRIVI STRIP CAPRIVI
KUNENE
OTJOZONDJUPA
ERONGO
OMAHEKE
KHOMAS
HARDAP
KARAS
GREAT NAMAQUALAND

Etosha Pan
Etosha National Park
WINDHOEK
Walvis Bay
Swakopmund

BOTSWANA
NORTH-WEST
GHANZI
Central Kalahari
Game Reserve
KWENENG
SOUTHERN
KGALAGADI
KALAHARI DESERT
Okavango Delta
Makgadikgadi

Tropic of Capricorn

ATLANTIC

OCEAN

Skeleton Coast Game Park

Namib-Naukluft Game Park

Gemsbok National Park
Kgalagadi Transfrontier Park

REPUBLIC OF
SOUTH AFRICA
NORTHERN CAPE
GRIQUALAND WEST
WESTERN CAPE
EASTERN
NAMAQUALAND

Kimberley
Bloemfontein
Port Elizabeth

Great Karoo
Little Karoo

CAPE TOWN
Cape of Good Hope
Cape Agulhas

METRES FEET
6000 19686
5000 16404
4000 13124
3000 9843
2000 6562
1000 3281
500 1640
200 656
0
LAND BELOW SEA LEVEL
200 656
2000 6562
4000 13124
6000 19686

CAPE TOWN
1:30 000
0 METRES 250
0 YARDS 250

FORESHORE
CENTRAL
TAMBOERSKLOOF
VREDEHOEK
SCHOTSCHE KLOOF
Marina
Customs Gate
Nico Malan Opera House
Civic Centre
Van Riebeeck Statue
Cape Town Railway Station
Golden Acre
The Parade
The Castle of Good Hope
Good Hope Centre
Oriental Plaza
Malay Quarter
City Hall
Groote Kerk
St George's Cath.
S.A. Library
Cultural History Museum
Houses of Parliament
Botanical Gardens
South African National Gallery
South African Museum
Jewish Museum
Bertram House Museum
Koopmans de Wet House
Martin Melck House
Old Town House
Government Archives
Lion Gate
Lion's Rump

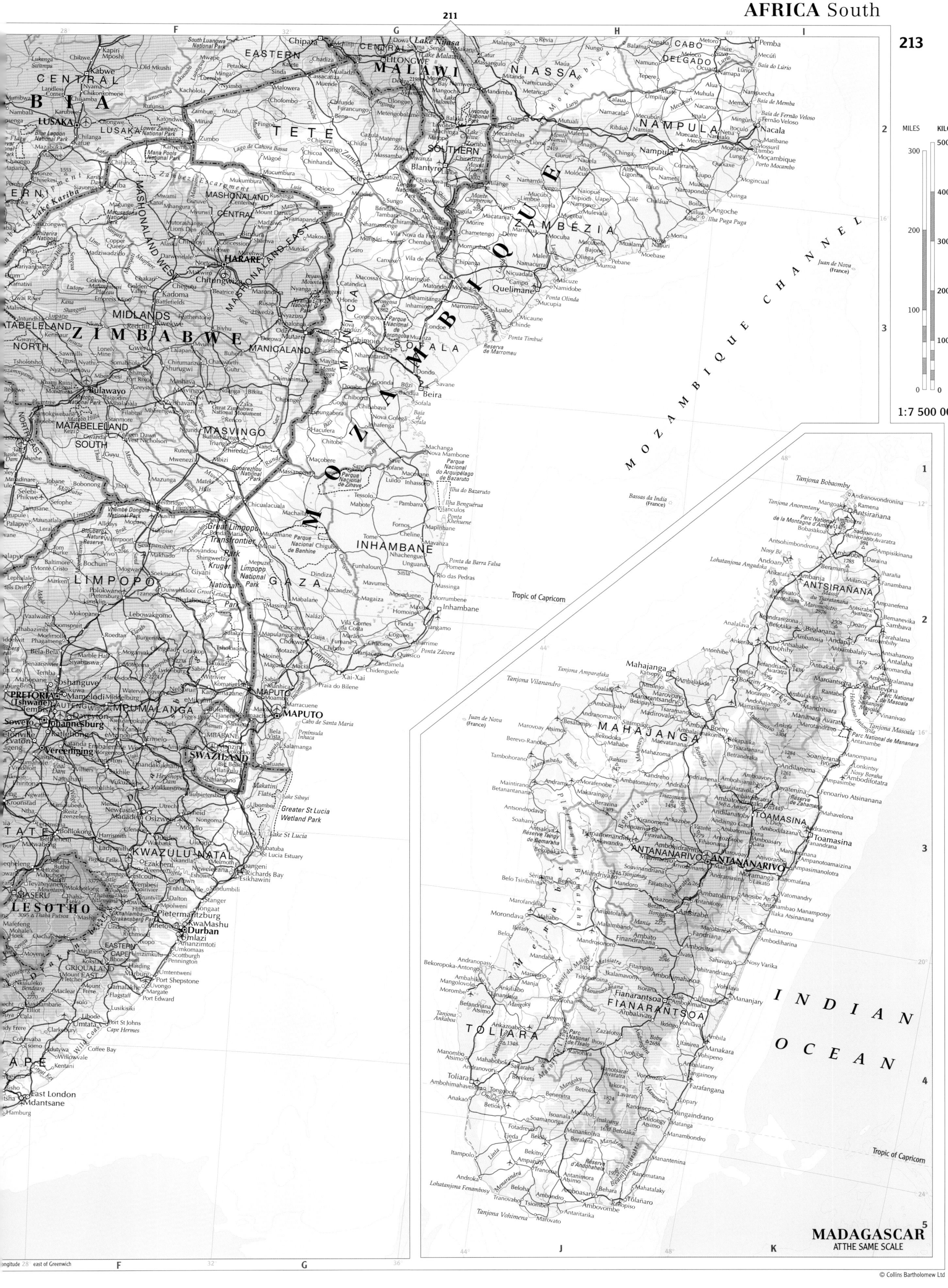

ZAMBIA

ZIMBABWE

MOZAMBIQUE

MALAWI

NIASSA

NAMPULA

CABO DELGADO

ZAMBÉZIA

SOFALA

MANICA

TETE

SOUTHERN

CENTRAL

EASTERN

LUSAKA

HARARE

Bulawayo

MATABELELAND NORTH

MATABELELAND SOUTH

MIDLANDS

MASHONALAND WEST

MASHONALAND CENTRAL

MASHONALAND EAST

MANICALAND

MASVINGO

LIMPOPO

GAZA

INHAMBANE

MPUMALANGA

GAUTENG

PRETORIA (Tshwane)

Johannesburg

Soweto

Vereeniging

MAPUTO

MBABANE

SWAZILAND

KWAZULU NATAL

Durban

Pietermaritzburg

LESOTHO

MASERU

EASTERN CAPE

FREE STATE

NORTH WEST

Quelimane

Beira

Blantyre

Nacala

Nampula

Pemba

MOZAMBIQUE CHANNEL

Tropic of Capricorn

Inhambane

Xai-Xai

East London

Wild Coast

Greater St Lucia Wetland Park

Kruger National Park

MADAGASCAR

ANTSIRAÑANA

MAHAJANGA

TOAMASINA

ANTANANARIVO

FIANARANTSOA

TOLIARA

Mahajanga

Toamasina

Antananarivo

Antsirabe

Fianarantsoa

Toliara

Antsirañana

Morondava

Tanjona Bobaomby

Tanjona Vohimena

INDIAN OCEAN

Tropic of Capricorn

1:7 500 000

MILES   KILOMETRES

300   500

400

200   300

200

100

100

0   0

MADAGASCAR
AT THE SAME SCALE

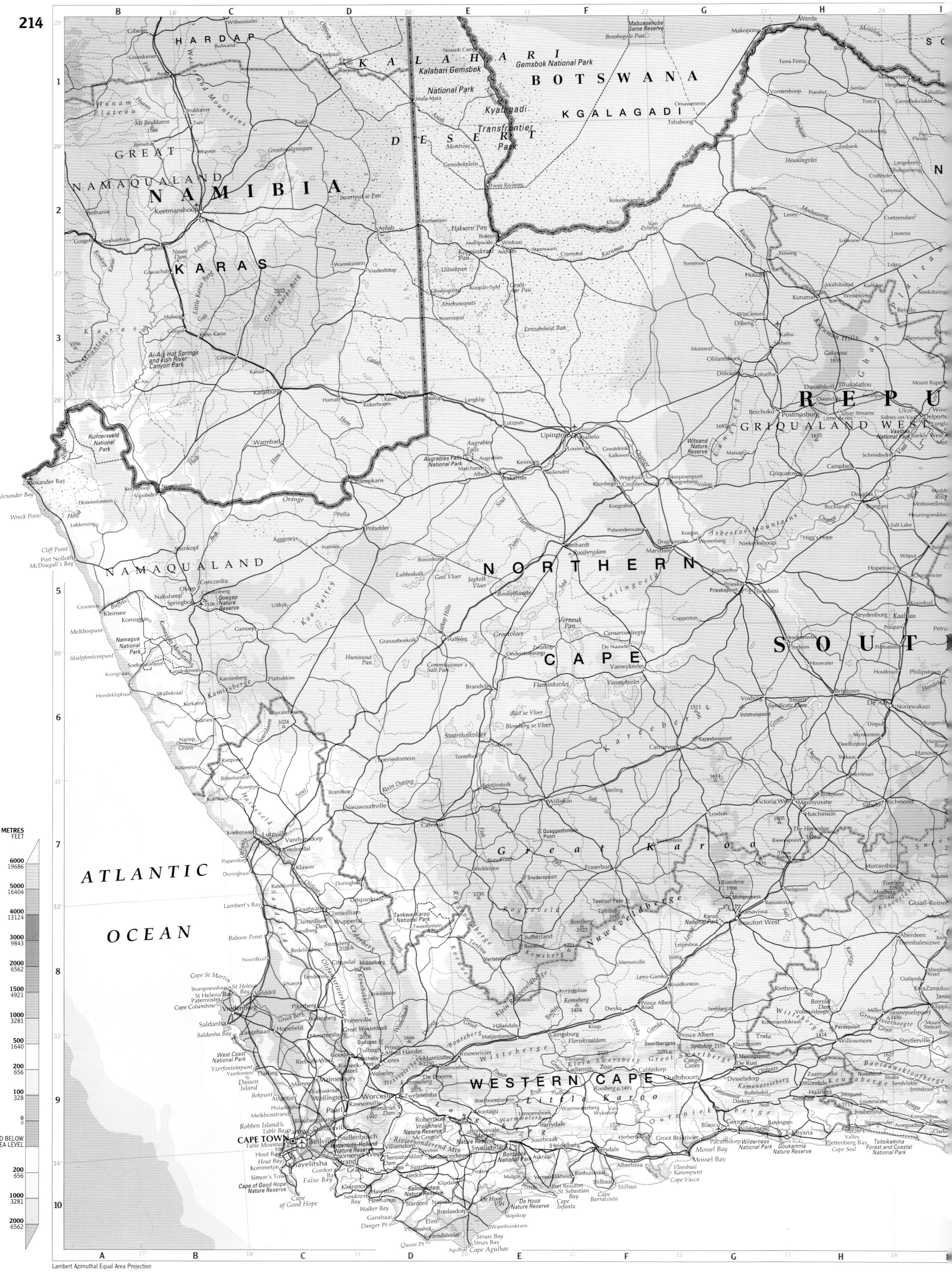

HARDAP

NAMAQUALAND

N A M I B I A

KARAS

K A L A H A R I

D E S E R T

Kalahari Gemsbok
National Park

Gemsbok National Park

B O T S W A N A

KGALAGADI

Kgalagadi
Transfrontier
Park

GREAT

REPU

GRIQUALAND WEST

N O R T H E R N

C A P E

S O U T

ATLANTIC

OCEAN

G r e a t   K a r o o

WESTERN CAPE

Little Karoo

CAPE TOWN

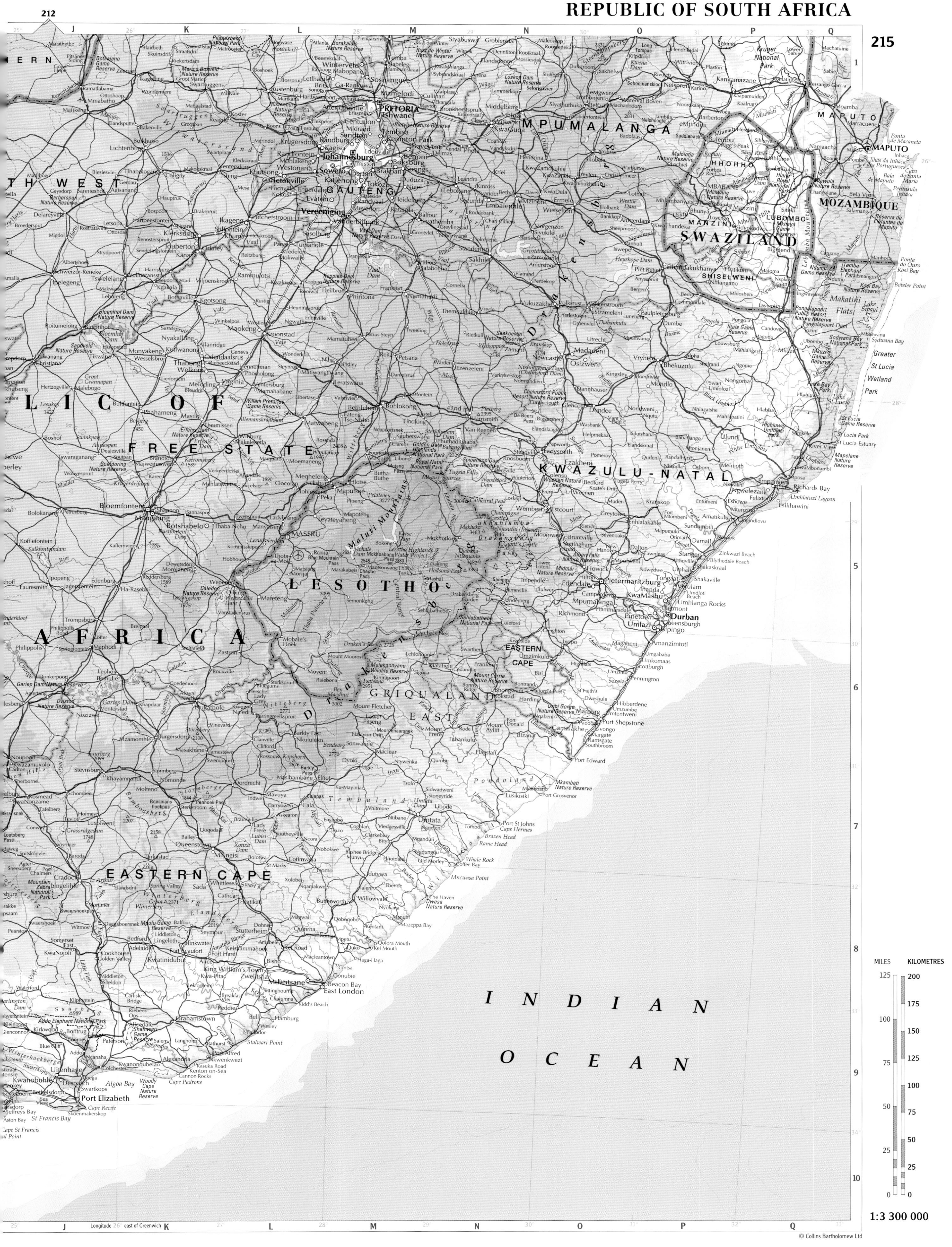
212
215
MPUMALANGA
GAUTENG
PRETORIA
Tshwane
Johannesburg
Soweto
Vereeniging
MAPUTO
MOZAMBIQUE
SWAZILAND
MBABANE
HHOHHO
MANZINI
LUBOMBO
SHISELWENI
FREE STATE
Bloemfontein
Mangaung
LESOTHO
MASERU
KWAZULU-NATAL
Pietermaritzburg
Durban
EASTERN CAPE
GRIQUALAND EAST
East London
Port Elizabeth
Algoa Bay
INDIAN OCEAN
MILES
KILOMETRES
1:3 300 000
Longitude east of Greenwich

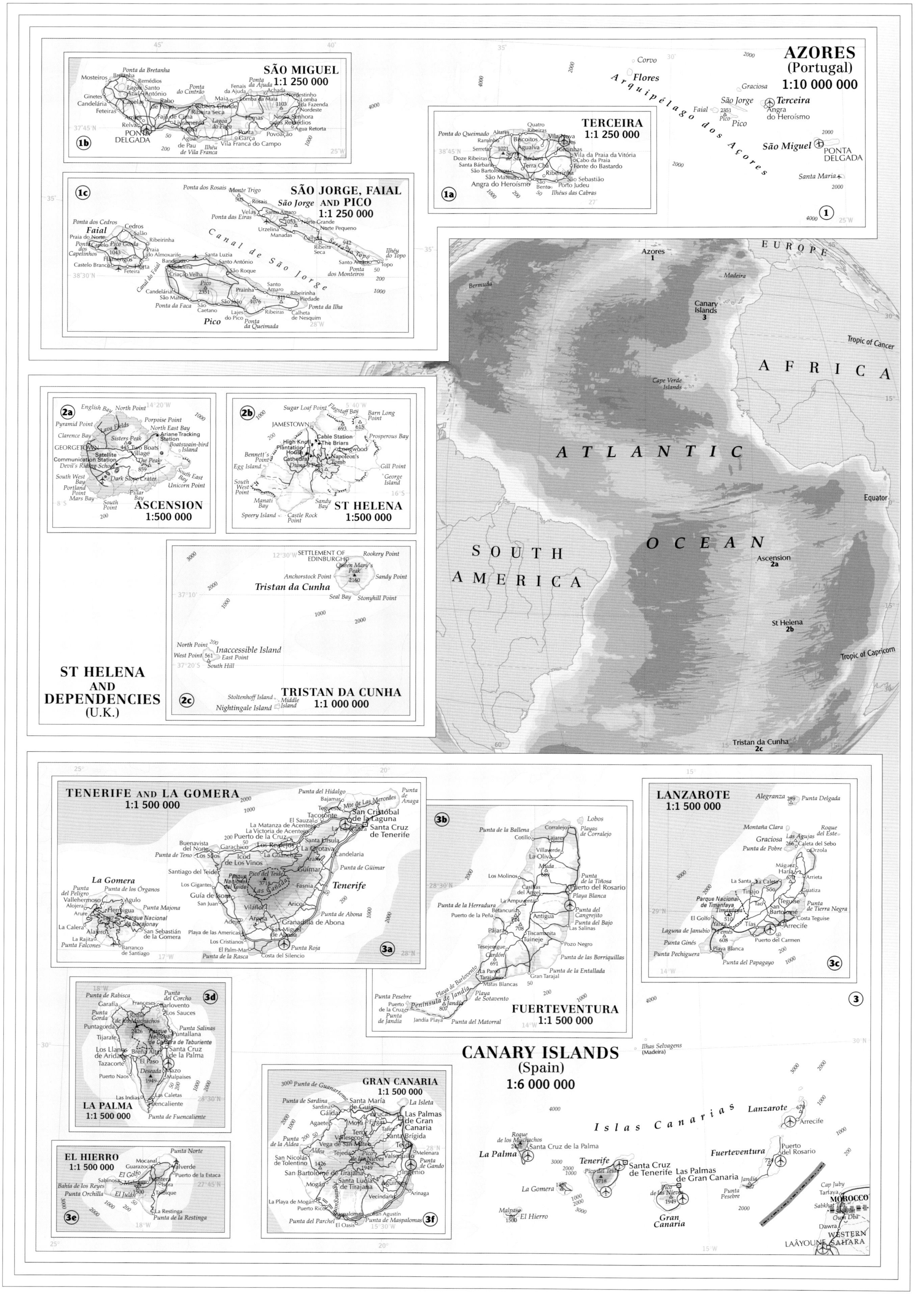

AZORES
(Portugal)
1:10 000 000

Arquipélago dos Açores

SÃO MIGUEL
1:1 250 000

PONTA
DELGADA

TERCEIRA
1:1 250 000

Angra
do Heroísmo

Angra do Heroísmo

SÃO JORGE, FAIAL
AND PICO
1:1 250 000

Canal de São Jorge

Faial

Pico

ASCENSION
1:500 000

JAMESTOWN

ST HELENA
1:500 000

Tristan da Cunha

ST HELENA
AND
DEPENDENCIES
(U.K.)

Inaccessible Island

TRISTAN DA CUNHA
1:1 000 000

EUROPE

Azores
1

Bermuda

Madeira

Canary
Islands
3

Cape Verde
Islands

A F R I C A

Tropic of Cancer

A T L A N T I C

SOUTH
AMERICA

O C E A N

Ascension
2a

Equator

St Helena
2b

Tropic of Capricorn

Tristan da Cunha
2c

TENERIFE AND LA GOMERA
1:1 500 000

Santa Cruz
de Tenerife

La Gomera

Tenerife

Parque Nacional
del Teide

San Sebastián
de la Gomera

LANZAROTE
1:1 500 000

Arrecife

FUERTEVENTURA
1:1 500 000

LA PALMA
1:1 500 000

Santa Cruz
de la Palma

EL HIERRO
1:1 500 000

Valverde

GRAN CANARIA
1:1 500 000

Las Palmas
de Gran
Canaria

CANARY ISLANDS
(Spain)
1:6 000 000

Ilhas Selvagens
(Madeira)

I s l a s   C a n a r i a s

Lanzarote

Arrecife

La Palma

Santa Cruz de la Palma

Fuerteventura

Puerto
del Rosario

Tenerife

Santa Cruz
de Tenerife

Las Palmas
de Gran Canaria

La Gomera

El Hierro

*Gran
Canaria*

MOROCCO

WESTERN
SAHARA

LAÂYOUNE

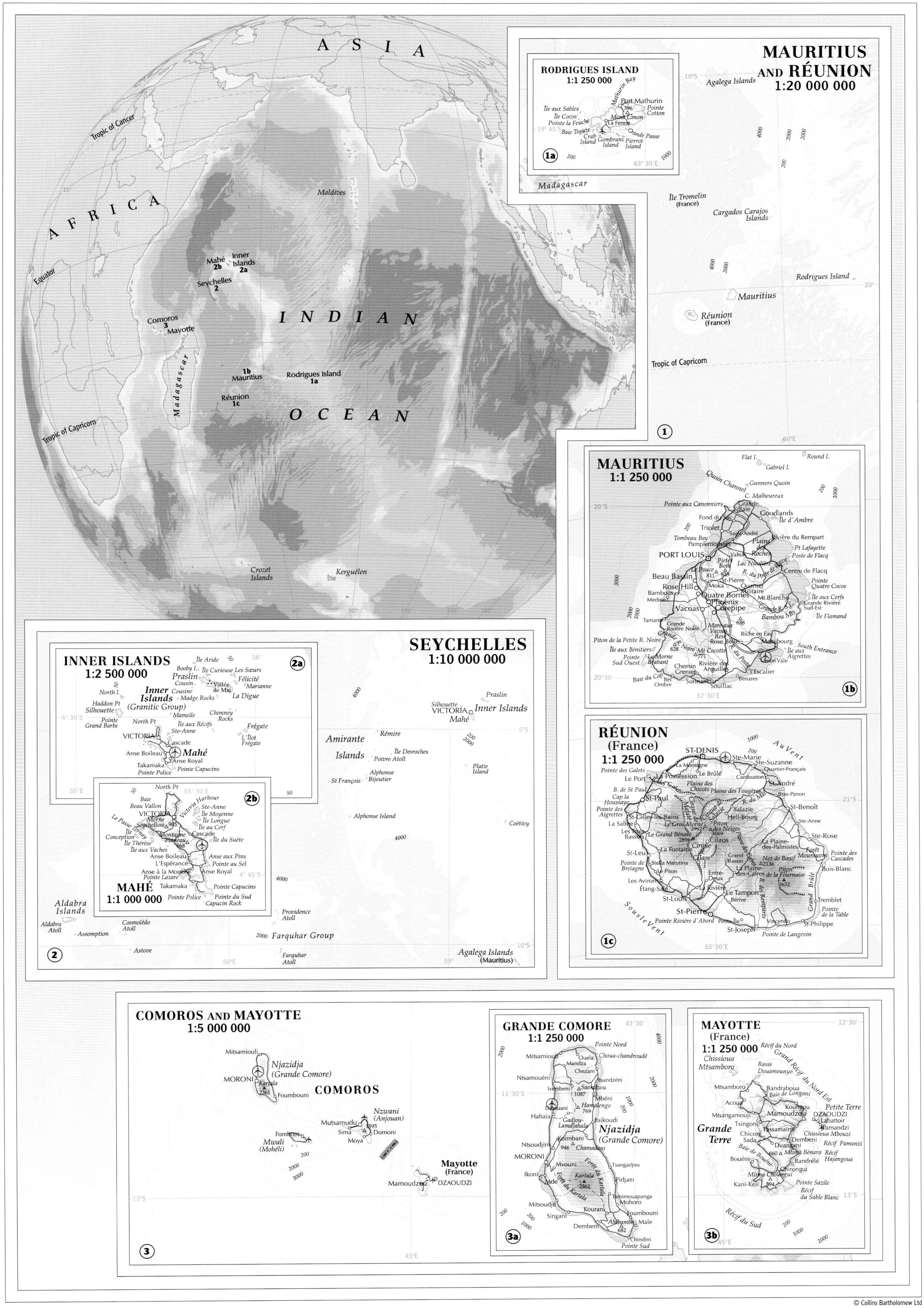

ASIA

AFRICA

Tropic of Cancer

15°

Equator

Maldives

Mahé
2b
Inner
Islands
2a

Seychelles
2

INDIAN

Comoros
3
Mayotte

Madagascar

1b
Mauritius

Rodrigues Island
1a

Réunion
1c

OCEAN

Tropic of Capricorn

Crozet
Islands
Kerguélen

(1)

RODRIGUES ISLAND
1:1 250 000

Île aux Sables
Île Cocos
Pointe la Fouche
19° 45′
Crab
Island
Gombrani
Island
Mount Limon
La Ferme
Grande Passe
Pierrot
Island
Port Mathurin
396
Pointe
Cotton
Baie Topaze
200
1000

63° 30′E

(1a)

Madagascar

MAURITIUS
AND RÉUNION
1:20 000 000

Agalega Islands

10°S

4000
2000

2000

Île Tromelin
(France)

Cargados Carajos
Islands

4000
2000

Rodrigues Island

20°

Mauritius

Réunion
(France)

Tropic of Capricorn

60°E

MAURITIUS
1:1 250 000

Flat I.
Gabriel I.
Round I.

Quoin Channel
Gunners Quoin
C. Malheureux
1000
200
Pointe aux Canonniers
Grande
Baie
Goodlands
Île d'Ambre
20°S
Fond du Sac
Triolet
Saint André
Rivière du Rempart
Tombeau Bay
Pamplemousses
Plaine
des
Roches
Pt Lafayette
Poste de Flacq
PORT LOUIS
Pieter
Both
811
Vallée
R. du Poste de Flacq
Centre de Flacq
Beau Bassin
826
St-Pierre
Pointe
Quatre Cocos
Rose Hill
Moka
Quartier
Militaire
Île aux Cerfs
Bambous
Quatre Bornes
Mt Blanche
Grande Rivière
Sud-Est
Medine
Curepipe
Phoenix
Bambou Mtn
Île Flamand
Vacoas
Tamarin
Grande
Rivière Noire
Mare aux
Vacoas
Riche en Eau
3000
828
Mt Cocotte
Mahebourg
South Entrance
Piton de la Petite R. Noire
Noire
771
Île aux
Aigrettes
Île aux Bénitiers
Rose Belle
Pointe
Sud Ouest
Le Morne
Brabant
Rivière des
Anguilles
L'Escalier
Chemin
Grenier
Bon Vale
Baie du Cap
Surinam
Benares
Ombre
Souillac

20°30′
57° 30′E
(1b)

RÉUNION
(France)
1:1 250 000

Au Vent
1000
St-DENIS
Ste-Marie
La Montagne
Ste-Suzanne
Pointe des Galets
Le Brûlé
Quartier-Français
Le Port
La Possession
St-André
B. de St Paul
Plaine des
Cilaos
Plaine des Fougères
Cambuston
Cap la
Houssaye
Bras-Panon
St-Paul
Plaine des
Chicots
St-Benoît
21°S
St-Gilles-les-Bains
Le Gros Morne
Salazie
Pointe des
Aigrettes
3069
La Saline
Hell-Bourg
Piton
des Neiges
Les
Avirons
Le Grand Bénard
2896
Cirque
Gilaos
Ste-Rose
St-Leu
La Fontaine
Cilaos
Plaine-
des-Palmistes
Forêt
Mourouvin
Stella Matutina
Entre-
Deux
Grand
Bassin
Nez de Boeuf
2136
Pointe des
Cascades
Les Aviron
Piton
Plaine
des-Cafres de la Fournaise
Bois-Blanc
St-Louis
2632
Le Tampon
Étang-Salé
Rivière
Bérive
St-Pierre
Pointe
de la Table
Sous
le
Vent
Pointe Rivière d'Abord
Petite Île
St-Philippe
St-Joseph
Pointe de Langevin
55° 30′E
(1c)

SEYCHELLES
1:10 000 000

INNER ISLANDS
1:2 500 000

Île Aride
56°
(2a)
Booby I.
Praslin
Les Soeurs
North I.
Cousin
Cousine
Vallée
de Mai
Marianne
Inner
Islands
(Granitic Group)
Félicité
Chimney
Rocks
Madge Rocks
La Digue
Haddon Pt
Silhouette
4° 30′S
Mamelle
Pointe
Grand Barbe
North Pt
Île aux Récifs
Frégate
VICTORIA
Ste-Anne
L'Îlot
Frégate
Cascade
Anse Boileau
Mahé
Takamaka
Anse Royal
Pointe Police
Pointe Capucins

55°E
4000
2000
2000

Amirante
Islands

Rémire
5°S
Île Desroches
Poivre Atoll

St François
Alphonse
Bijoutier
Platte
Island

Alphonse Island

Coëtivy

4000

(2b)
North Pt
50′
Baie
Beau Vallon
Victoria Harbour
Ste-Anne
Le Passe
Morne
Seychellois
905
VICTORIA
Île Moyenne
Île Longue
Île
Conception
Montagne
Posée
Île au Cerf
Île Thérèse
Plateau
Île aux Vaches
Île au Suette
Anse Boileau
Anse aux Pins
L'Espérance
Pointe au Sel
Anse à la Mouche
Anse Royal
Pointe Lazare
Pointe Capucins
Takamaka
MAHÉ
Pointe du Sud
1:1 000 000
Pointe Police
Capucin Rock

Aldabra
Islands

Aldabra
Atoll
Cosmoledo
Atoll
Assomption
Astove

Providence
Atoll

4000

Farquhar Group

Farquhar
Atoll

Agalega Islands
(Mauritius)
10°S

(2)
50°E
55°

COMOROS AND MAYOTTE
1:5 000 000

Mitsamiouli
Njazidja
(Grande Comore)
MORONI
Karthala
2361
Foumbouni
COMOROS

Mutsamudu
Nzwani
(Anjouan)
Fomboni
Sima
595
Domoni
Mwali
(Mohéli)
Moya
200
3000

Mayotte
(France)
Mamoudzou
DZAOUDZI

13°S

(3)
45°E

GRANDE COMORE
1:1 250 000

43° 30′
Pointe Nord
4000
Mitsamiouli
Choua-chandroudé
Ouela
Mandza
Ntsamouéni
Chezani
Bandzéni
2000
Ivembéni
Saolitzou
1087
11° 30′
M'Béni
Hamalengo
769
Hahaïa
Itsikoudi
Gadjou-
Lamdjahale
Koimbani
2000
946
Chamadani
Ntsoudjini
MORONI
Mvouni
Forêt de Karthala
Tsangadjou
Ikoni
946
Pidjani
Fadé
Karthala
Mitsoudjé
2361
Kourani
Singani
Voumbouni
Tsimimouapanga
Mohoro
Male
Dembeni
682
Chindini
Pointe Sud

200
1000
(3a)
45°

MAYOTTE
(France)
1:1 250 000

12° 30′
Récif du Nord
Chissioua
Mtsamboro
Rassi
Douamounyo
Grand Récif du Nord Est
Bandraboua
Baie de Longani
Mtsamboro
Koungou
Mamoudzou
Petite Terre
DZAOUDZI
Tsingoni
Passamainty
Labattoir
Chiconi
Sada
Pamandzi
Dembeni
Grande
Combani
Récif Pamanzi
Terre
Baie de Bouéni
660
Ongojou
Bandrélé
Bouéni
Chirongui
Récif
Hajangoua
Mlima Choungui
594
Kani-Kéli
Pointe Sazile
Récif
du Sable Blanc
Récif du Sud
13°S

(3b)
2000

© Collins Bartholomew Ltd

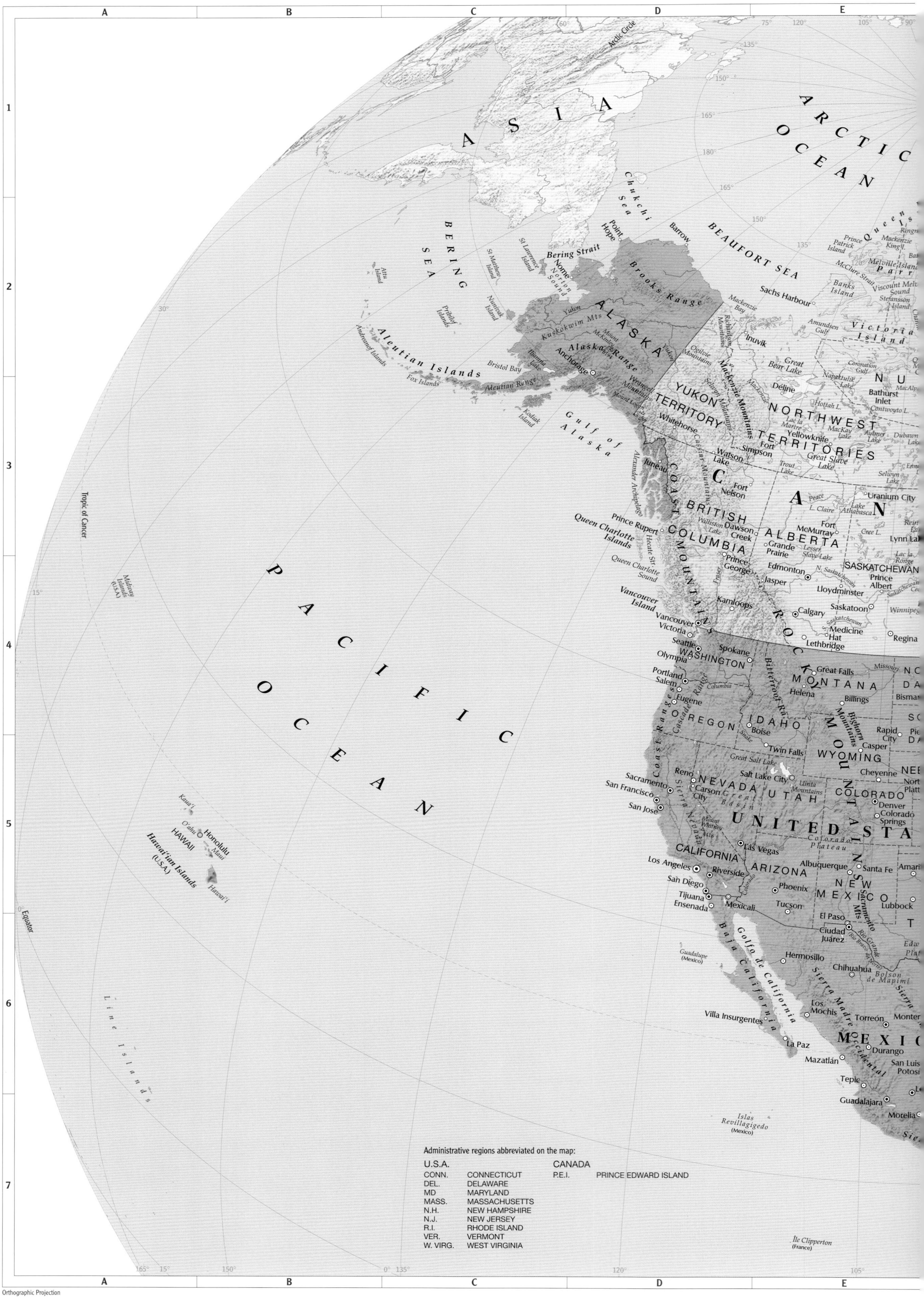

ASIA

ARCTIC OCEAN

Arctic Circle

Chukchi Sea

BEAUFORT SEA

BERING SEA

Bering Strait

Nome

Barrow

Brooks Range

Sachs Harbour

ALASKA

Alaska Range

Anchorage

YUKON TERRITORY

Mackenzie Mountains

Inuvik

Déline

Great Bear Lake

NORTHWEST TERRITORIES

NU

Whitehorse

Fort Simpson

Yellowknife

Great Slave Lake

Uranium City

CAN

Aleutian Islands

Gulf of Alaska

Juneau

Fort Nelson

BRITISH COLUMBIA

ALBERTA

McMurray

SASKATCHEWAN

Prince Rupert

Queen Charlotte Islands

Prince George

Grande Prairie

Edmonton

Jasper

Lloydminster

Prince Albert

Vancouver Island

Kamloops

Calgary

Saskatoon

Winnipeg

Vancouver

Victoria

Seattle

WASHINGTON

Spokane

Medicine Hat

Lethbridge

Regina

Olympia

Great Falls

MONTANA

Portland

Salem

OREGON

Helena

Billings

Bismarck

IDAHO

Boise

WYOMING

Casper

Cheyenne

NEBRASKA

Reno

NEVADA

Salt Lake City

UTAH

Denver

COLORADO

Colorado Springs

San Francisco

Sacramento

Carson City

San Jose

UNITED STATES

PACIFIC OCEAN

Kaua'i

O'ahu

Honolulu

HAWAII

Hawaiian Islands (U.S.A.)

Maui

Hawai'i

Las Vegas

CALIFORNIA

ARIZONA

Los Angeles

Riverside

Albuquerque

Santa Fe

NEW MEXICO

San Diego

Tijuana

Phoenix

Ensenada

Mexicali

Tucson

El Paso

Lubbock

Ciudad Juárez

Guadalupe (Mexico)

Hermosillo

Chihuahua

Baja California

Villa Insurgentes

Los Mochis

Torreón

La Paz

MEXICO

Durango

Mazatlán

San Luis Potosí

Tepic

Guadalajara

Islas Revillagigedo (Mexico)

Morelia

Île Clipperton (France)

Tropic of Cancer

Midway Islands (U.S.A.)

Line Islands

Equator

Administrative regions abbreviated on the map:

U.S.A.		CANADA	
CONN.	CONNECTICUT	P.E.I.	PRINCE EDWARD ISLAND
DEL.	DELAWARE		
MD	MARYLAND		
MASS.	MASSACHUSETTS		
N.H.	NEW HAMPSHIRE		
N.J.	NEW JERSEY		
R.I.	RHODE ISLAND		
VER.	VERMONT		
W. VIRG.	WEST VIRGINIA		

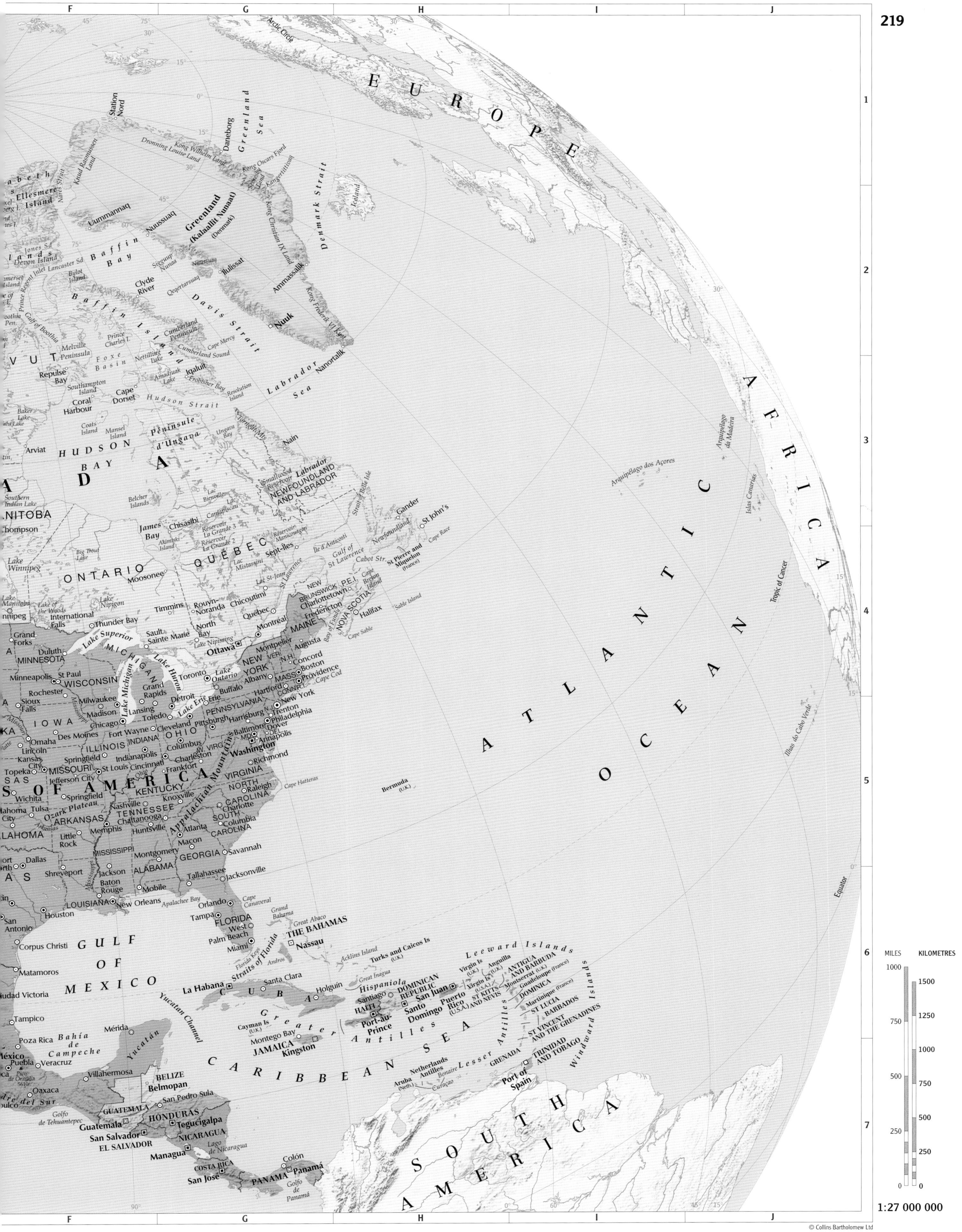
F
G
H
I
J
1
2
3
4
5
6
7
E U R O P E
A F R I C A
ATLANTIC OCEAN
S O U T H A M E R I C A
Arctic Circle
Station Nord
Greenland Sea
Daneborg
Kong Wilhelm Land
Dronning Louise Land
Knud Rasmussen Land
Kong Oscars Fjord
Kangertittivaq
Kong Christian IX Land
Denmark Strait
Iceland
Greenland (Kalaallit Nunaat) (Denmark)
Uummannaq
Nuussuaq
Ellesmere Island
Nares Strait
Jones Sd
Devon Island
Lancaster Sd
Baffin Bay
Bylot Island
Prince Regent Inlet
Somerset Island
Clyde River
Sisimiut
Ilulissat
Qeqertarsuaq
Ammassalik
Kong Frederik VI Kyst
Nuuk
Davis Strait
Baffin Island
Gulf of Boothia
Prince Charles I.
Melville Peninsula
Cumberland Peninsula
Cape Mercy
Cumberland Sound
Foxe Basin
Nettilling Lake
Amadjuak Lake
Iqaluit
Frobisher Bay
Resolution Island
Labrador Sea
Nanortalik
Repulse Bay
Southampton Island
Coral Harbour
Cape Dorset
Hudson Strait
Baker Lake
Coats Island
Mansel Island
Péninsule d'Ungava
Ungava Bay
Torngat Mts
Nain
Arviat
HUDSON BAY
CANADA
Smallwood Reservoir
Labrador
NEWFOUNDLAND AND LABRADOR
Strait of Belle Isle
Belcher Islands
Lac Bienville
Southern Indian Lake
MANITOBA
Thompson
James Bay
Chisasibi
Akimiski Island
Réservoir La Grande 3
Réservoir La Grande 2
Réservoir Manicouagan
Île d'Anticosti
Gander
Newfoundland
St John's
Cape Race
Big Trout Lake
QUÉBEC
Lac Mistassini
Sept-Îles
Gulf of St Lawrence
Cabot Str.
St Pierre and Miquelon (France)
Lake Winnipeg
ONTARIO
Moosonee
Lac St-Jean
St Lawrence
NEW BRUNSWICK
P.E.I.
Cape Breton Island
Charlottetown
NOVA SCOTIA
Sable Island
Lake Manitoba
Lake of the Woods
Lake Nipigon
Timmins
Rouyn-Noranda
Chicoutimi
Québec
Fredericton
Halifax
Bay of Fundy
Cape Sable
Winnipeg
International Falls
Thunder Bay
Sault Sainte Marie
North Bay
Montréal
Lake Superior
Lake Nipissing
Ottawa
MAINE
Montpelier
Augusta
Grand Forks
Duluth
MINNESOTA
MICHIGAN
Lake Huron
NEW YORK
VERMONT
N.H.
Concord
Boston
Providence
Cape Cod
St Paul
Minneapolis
WISCONSIN
Toronto
Lake Ontario
Albany
MASS.
Rochester
Sioux Falls
Milwaukee
Grand Rapids
Detroit
Buffalo
Hartford
CONN.
R.I.
New York
Lake Michigan
Madison
Lansing
Lake Erie
Erie
Toledo
PENNSYLVANIA
Harrisburg
Trenton
Philadelphia
IOWA
Chicago
Cleveland
Pittsburgh
Baltimore
Dover
DEL.
Des Moines
Fort Wayne
OHIO
MD.
Annapolis
Omaha
ILLINOIS
INDIANA
Columbus
W. VIRGINIA
Washington
Lincoln
Springfield
Indianapolis
Charleston
Kansas City
Cincinnati
Frankfort
Richmond
Topeka
MISSOURI
St Louis
Jefferson City
VIRGINIA
UNITED STATES OF AMERICA
KANSAS
Appalachian Mountains
NORTH CAROLINA
Raleigh
Wichita
Springfield
KENTUCKY
Knoxville
Cape Hatteras
Bermuda (U.K.)
Oklahoma City
Tulsa
Ozark Plateau
Nashville
TENNESSEE
Charlotte
SOUTH CAROLINA
Columbia
ARKANSAS
Chattanooga
OKLAHOMA
Memphis
Huntsville
Atlanta
Little Rock
MISSISSIPPI
Montgomery
Macon
GEORGIA
Savannah
Dallas
ALABAMA
Shreveport
Jackson
Tallahassee
Jacksonville
TEXAS
Baton Rouge
Mobile
LOUISIANA
New Orleans
Apalachee Bay
Orlando
Cape Canaveral
Houston
Tampa
FLORIDA
West Palm Beach
Grand Bahama
Great Abaco
THE BAHAMAS
San Antonio
Miami
Nassau
Corpus Christi
GULF OF MEXICO
Florida Keys
Straits of Florida
Andros
Acklins Island
Turks and Caicos Is (U.K.)
Leeward Islands
Matamoros
La Habana
Santa Clara
Great Inagua
CUBA
Holguín
Hispaniola
DOMINICAN REPUBLIC
San Juan
Virgin Is (U.K.)
Virgin Is (U.S.A.)
Anguilla (U.K.)
ANTIGUA AND BARBUDA
ST KITTS AND NEVIS
Montserrat (U.K.)
Guadeloupe (France)
DOMINICA
Martinique (France)
ST LUCIA
BARBADOS
Ciudad Victoria
Yucatan Channel
Santiago
HAITI
Port-au-Prince
Santo Domingo
Puerto Rico (U.S.A.)
Tampico
Mérida
Cayman Is (U.K.)
Greater Antilles
Lesser Antilles
Windward Islands
Bahía de Campeche
Yucatán
Montego Bay
JAMAICA
Kingston
CARIBBEAN SEA
ST VINCENT AND THE GRENADINES
GRENADA
TRINIDAD AND TOBAGO
Poza Rica
México
Puebla
Veracruz
Pico de Orizaba
5610
Villahermosa
BELIZE
Belmopan
Aruba (Neth.)
Netherlands Antilles
Bonaire
Curaçao
Port of Spain
Oaxaca
Sierra Madre del Sur
San Pedro Sula
Golfo de Tehuantepec
GUATEMALA
HONDURAS
Guatemala
Tegucigalpa
San Salvador
EL SALVADOR
NICARAGUA
Lago de Nicaragua
Managua
COSTA RICA
San José
Colón
PANAMA
Panamá
Golfo de Panamá
Arquipélago dos Açores
Arquipélago da Madeira
Islas Canarias
Tropic of Cancer
Ilhas do Cabo Verde
Equator
MILES
KILOMETRES
1000
750
500
250
0
1500
1250
1000
750
500
250
0
1:27 000 000

131

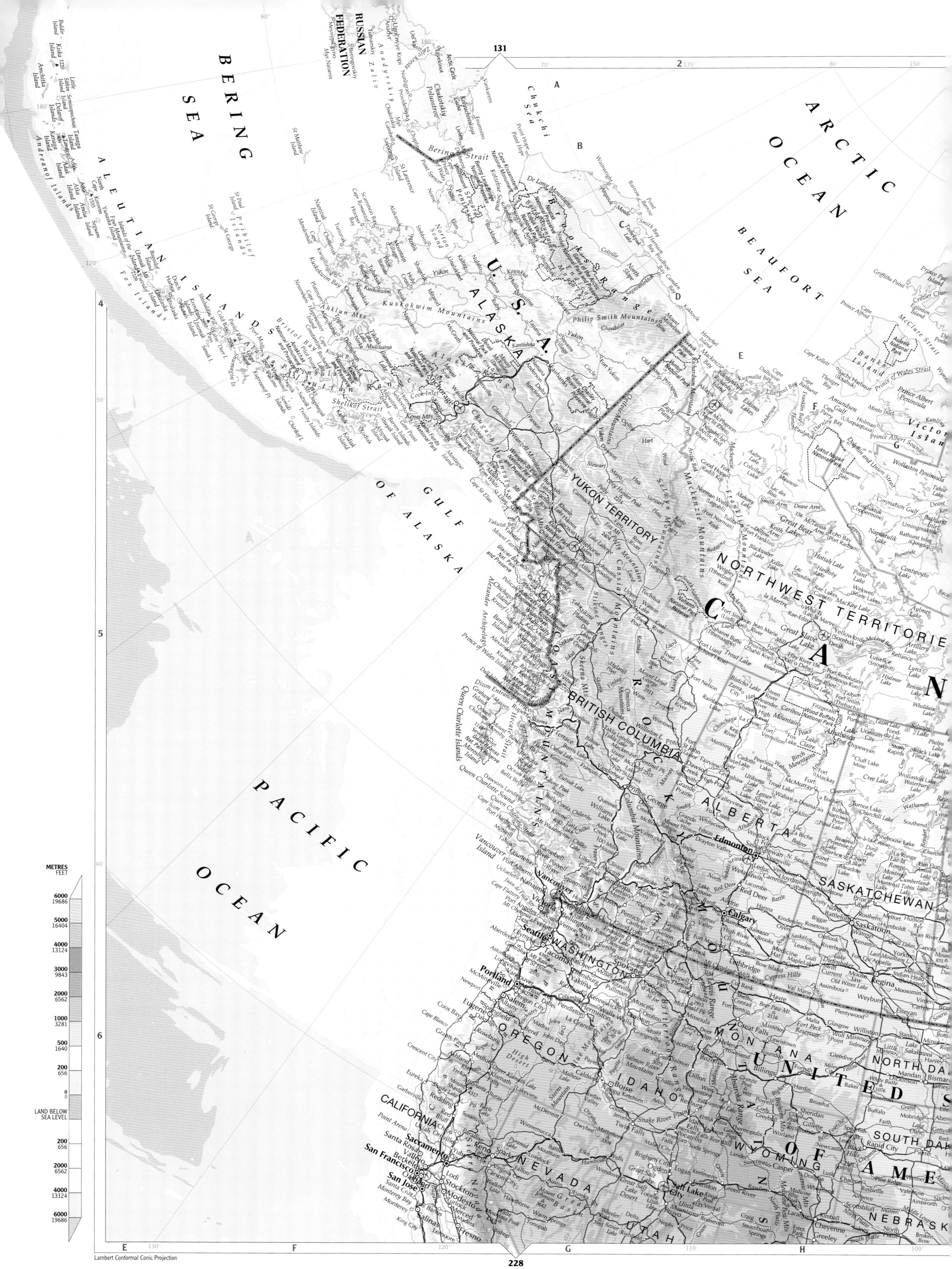
BERING SEA
ARCTIC OCEAN
BEAUFORT SEA
Chukchi Sea
RUSSIAN FEDERATION
Bering Strait
ALEUTIAN ISLANDS
Andreanof Islands
Fox Islands
Pribilof Islands
U.S.A.
ALASKA
Brooks Range
Philip Smith Mountains
Kuskokwim Mountains
Alaska Range
Anchorage
GULF OF ALASKA
Bristol Bay
Shelikof Strait
Cook Inlet
YUKON TERRITORY
NORTHWEST TERRITORIES
Mackenzie Mountains
Selwyn Mountains
Great Bear Lake
Great Slave Lake
Yellowknife
CANADA
Banks Island
Amundsen Gulf
Prince of Wales Strait
BRITISH COLUMBIA
ALBERTA
SASKATCHEWAN
COAST MOUNTAINS
ROCKY MOUNTAINS
Queen Charlotte Islands
Vancouver Island
Edmonton
Calgary
Vancouver
Saskatoon
Regina
PACIFIC OCEAN
WASHINGTON
Seattle
Tacoma
Spokane
Portland
OREGON
Eugene
IDAHO
Boise
MONTANA
Billings
Great Falls
WYOMING
Casper
NORTH DAKOTA
SOUTH DAKOTA
NEBRASKA
CALIFORNIA
Sacramento
San Francisco
Oakland
San Jose
Stockton
Modesto
Fresno
NEVADA
Reno
UTAH
Salt Lake City
Great Salt Lake
UNITED STATES OF AMERICA
METRES
FEET
6000 19686
5000 16404
4000 13124
3000 9843
2000 6562
1000 3281
500 1640
200 656
0 0
LAND BELOW SEA LEVEL
200 656
2000 6562
4000 13124
6000 19686

Lambert Conformal Conic Projection

228

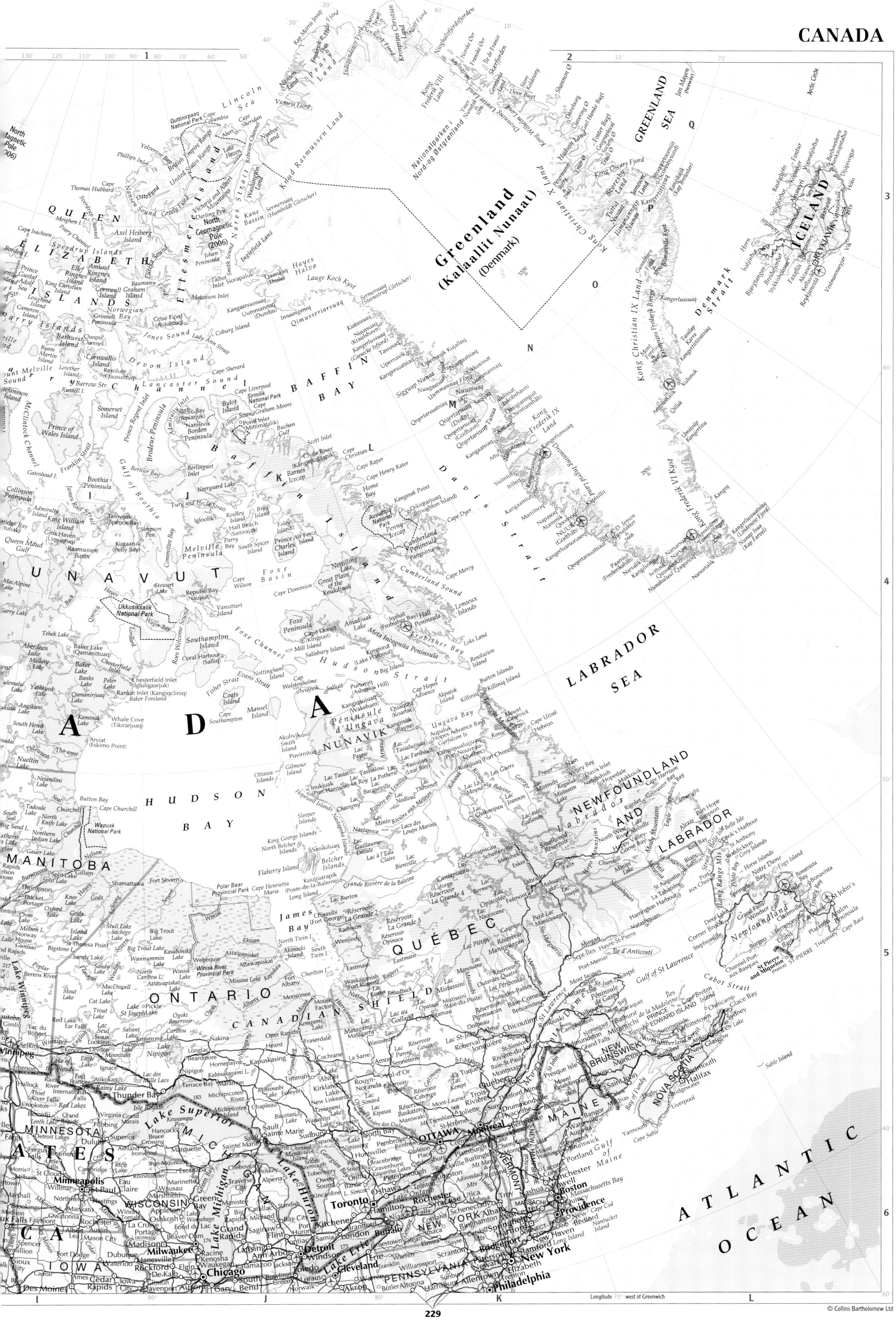

1:15 000 000

© Collins Bartholomew Ltd

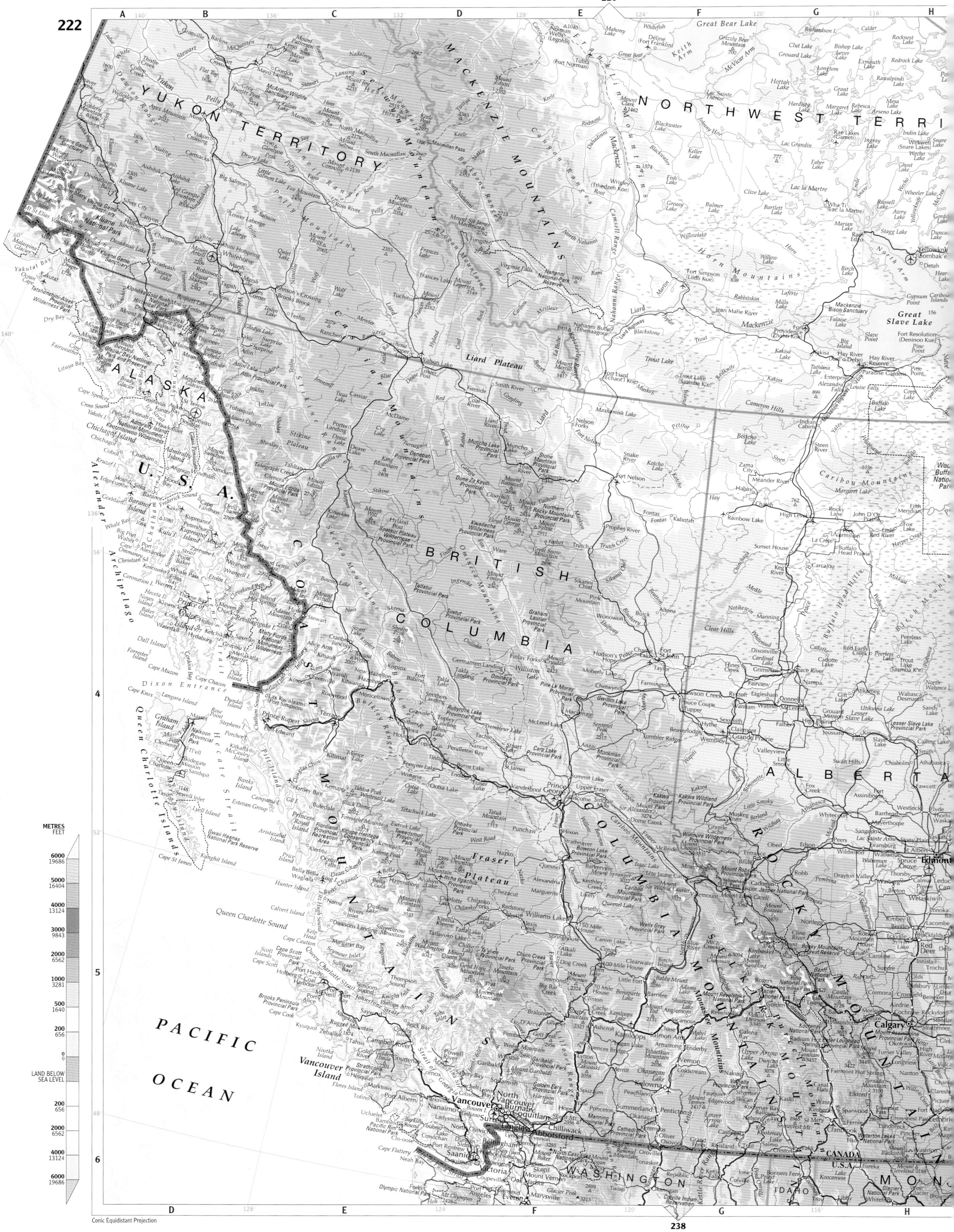

PACIFIC

OCEAN

YUKON TERRITORY

ALASKA

U.S.A.

BRITISH

COLUMBIA

NORTHWEST TERRI

ALBERTA

MACKENZIE MOUNTAINS

ROCKY MOUNTAINS

COAST MOUNTAINS

Great Bear Lake

Great Slave Lake

Queen Charlotte Islands

Vancouver Island

Queen Charlotte Sound

Alexander Archipelago

Dixon Entrance

Hecate Strait

Fraser Plateau

WASHINGTON

IDAHO

MON

CANADA
U.S.A.

Vancouver

Calgary

Edmon

Whitehorse

METRES	FEET
6000	19686
5000	16404
4000	13124
3000	9843
2000	6562
1000	3281
500	1640
200	656
0	0

LAND BELOW
SEA LEVEL

200	656
2000	6562
4000	13124
6000	19686

Conic Equidistant Projection

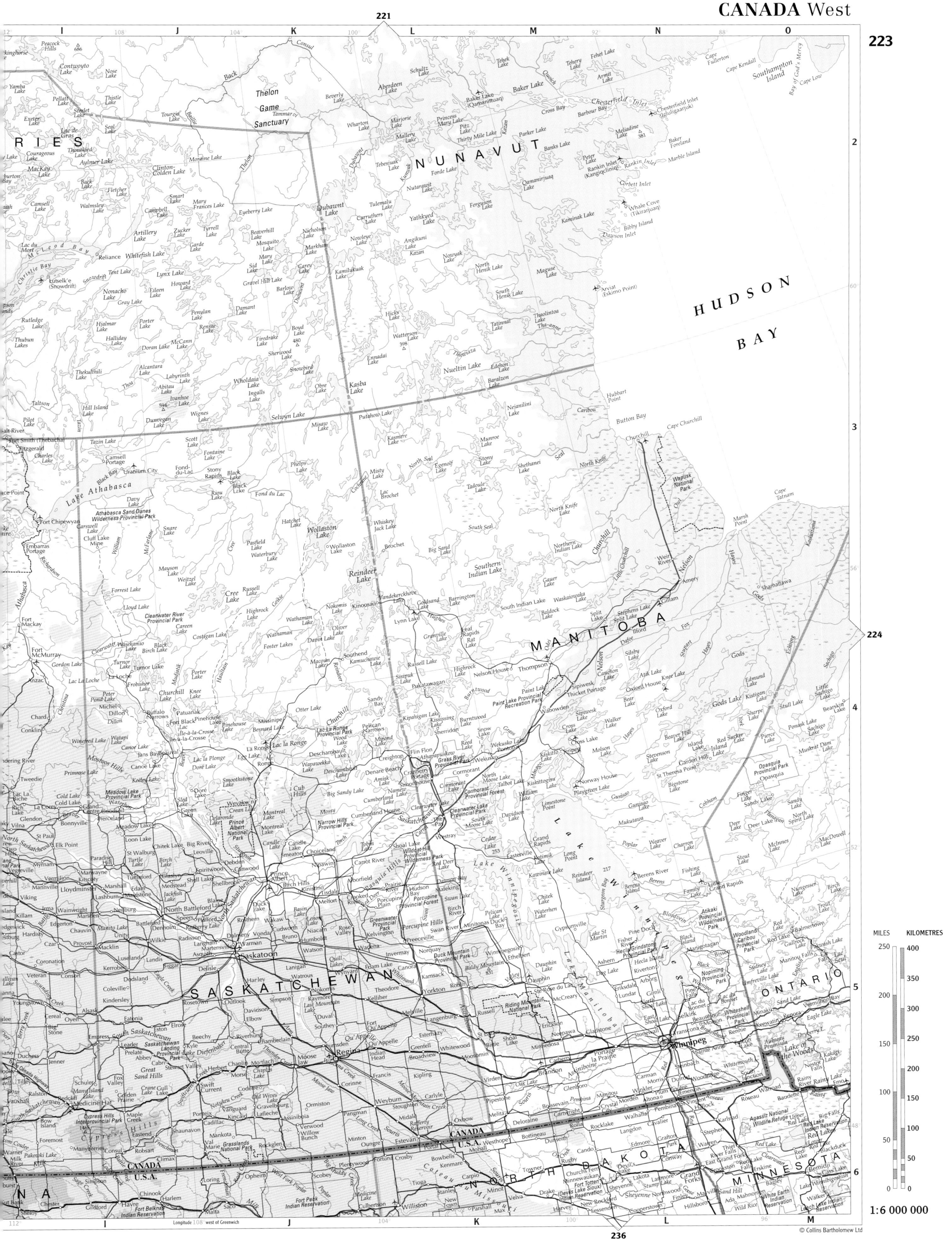

HUDSON

BAY

N U N A V U T

RIES

MANITOBA

SASKATCHEWAN

ONTARIO

Saskatoon

Regina

Winnipeg

NORTH DAKOTA

MINNESOTA

CANADA
U.S.A.

MILES   KILOMETRES

250   400

350

200   300

250

150   250

200

100   150

100

50   50

0   0

1:6 000 000

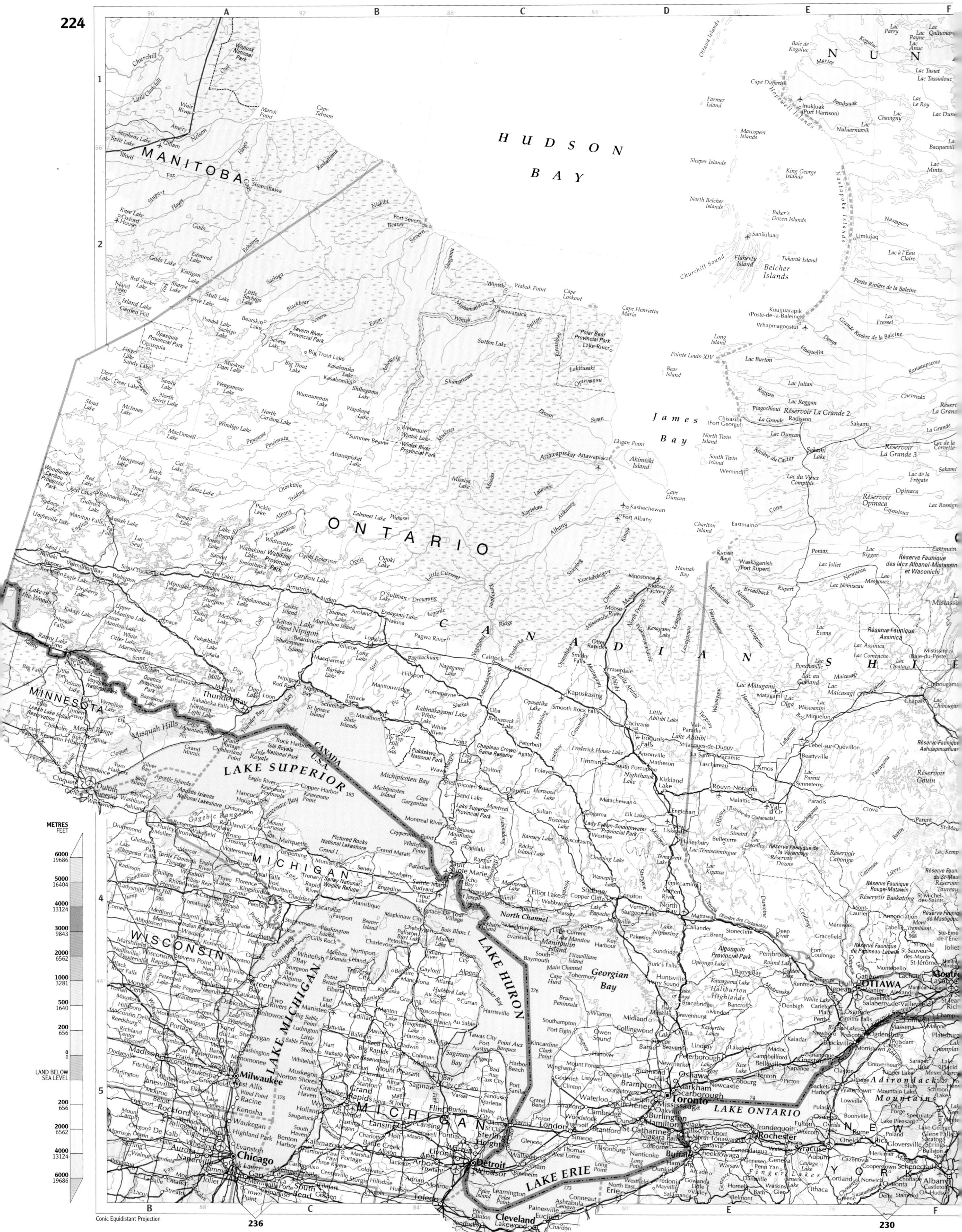

MANITOBA

HUDSON BAY

NUN

ONTARIO

CANADIAN SHIELD

James Bay

Belcher Islands

Polar Bear Provincial Park

MINNESOTA

WISCONSIN

MICHIGAN

LAKE SUPERIOR

LAKE MICHIGAN

LAKE HURON

Georgian Bay

LAKE ONTARIO

LAKE ERIE

Chicago

Milwaukee

Detroit

Toronto

Ottawa

Buffalo

Rochester

Cleveland

NEW YORK

Adirondack Mountains

CANADA
U.S.A.

Duluth

Thunder Bay

Sault Sainte Marie

Sudbury

Algonquin Provincial Park

Réservoir La Grande 2

Réservoir La Grande 3

Conic Equidistant Projection

METRES FEET
6000 19686
5000 16404
4000 13124
3000 9843
2000 6562
1000 3281
500 1640
200 656
0
LAND BELOW SEA LEVEL
200 656
2000 6562
4000 13124
6000 19686

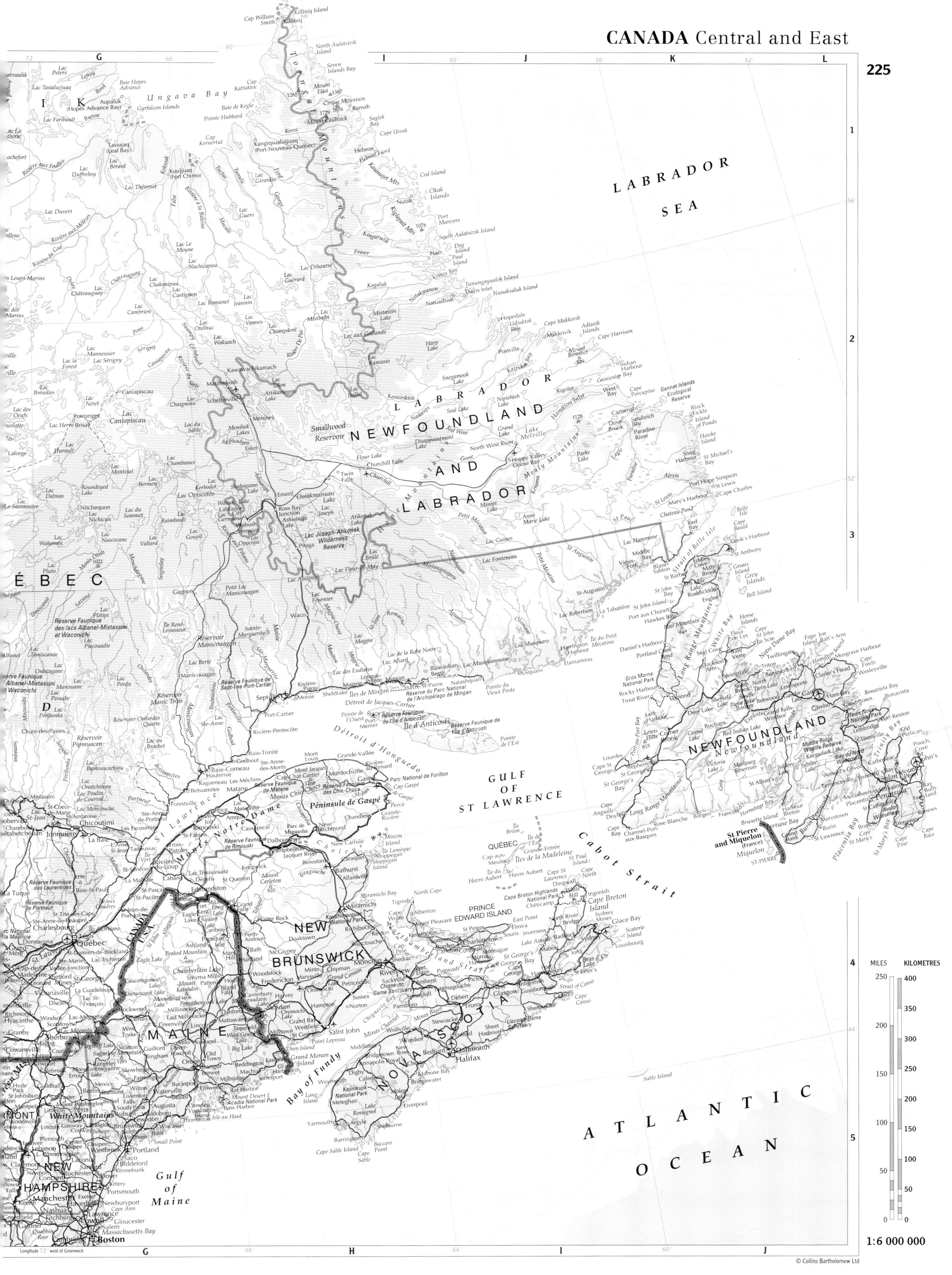

LABRADOR

SEA

Ungava Bay

LABRADOR

NEWFOUNDLAND

AND

LABRADOR

NEWFOUNDLAND

Newfoundland

GULF

OF

ST LAWRENCE

QUÉBEC

Cabot Strait

Gros Morne
National Park

St Pierre
and Miquelon
(France)

ST-PIERRE

NEW

BRUNSWICK

PRINCE
EDWARD ISLAND

Cape Breton
Island

NOVA SCOTIA

MAINE

White Mountains

NEW
HAMPSHIRE

Bay of Fundy

Halifax

Gulf
of
Maine

Sable Island

ATLANTIC

OCEAN

Boston

MILES   KILOMETRES
250   400
         350
200   300
         250
150   200
100   150
         100
50   50
0   0

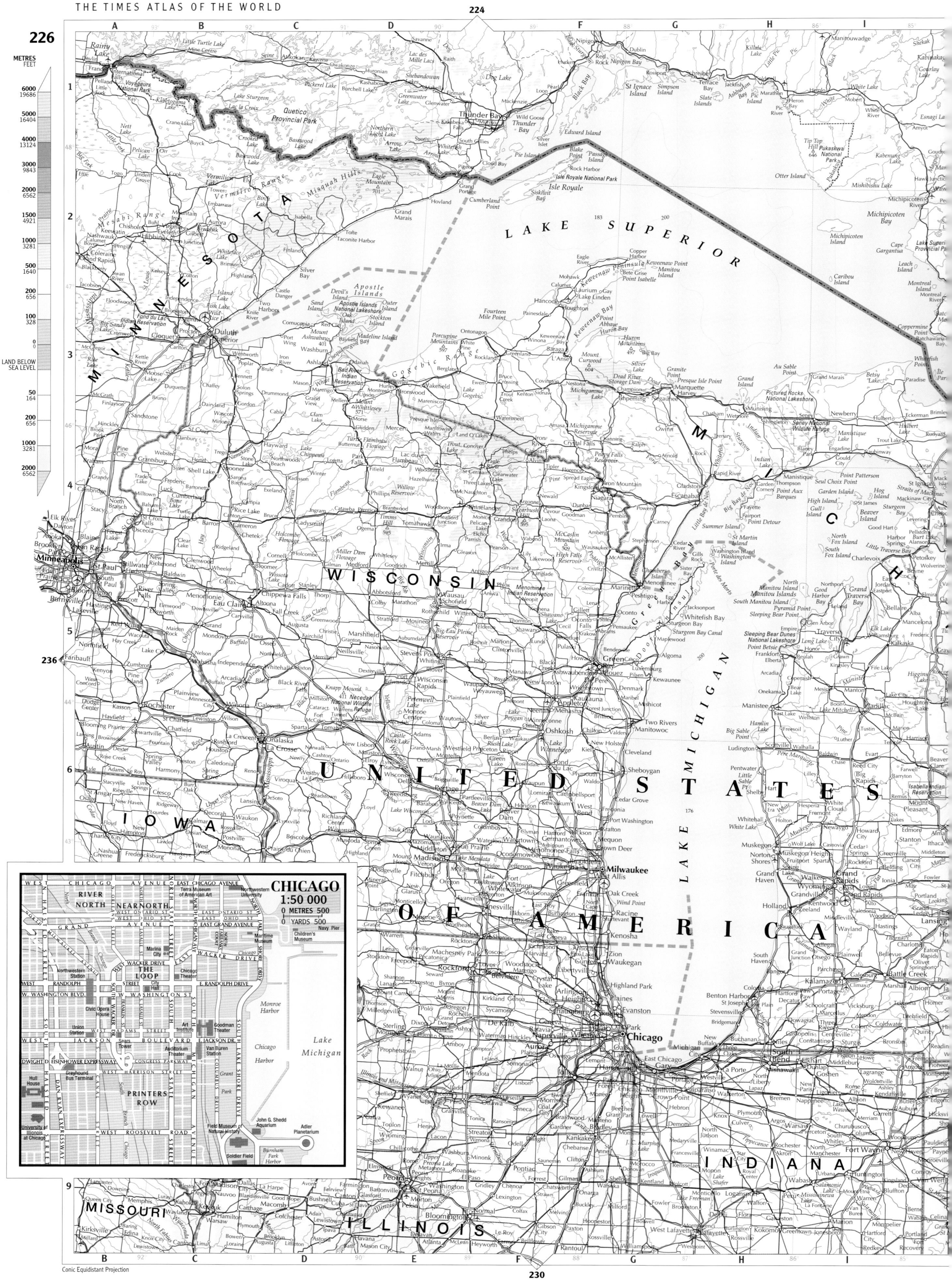

226

METRES
FEET

6000	19686
5000	16404
4000	13124
3000	9843
2000	6562
1500	4921
1000	3281
500	1640
200	656
0	0

LAND BELOW
SEA LEVEL

50	164
200	656
1000	3281
2000	6562

LAKE SUPERIOR

MINNESOTA

MICHIGAN

WISCONSIN

UNITED STATES

OF AMERICA

IOWA

Lake Michigan

Milwaukee

Chicago

MISSOURI

ILLINOIS

INDIANA

236

CHICAGO 1:50 000

0 METRES 500
0 YARDS 500

RIVER NORTH

NEAR NORTH

THE LOOP

PRINTERS ROW

Lake Michigan

Chicago Harbor

Monroe Harbor

Burnham Park Harbor

Conic Equidistant Projection

THE GREAT LAKES

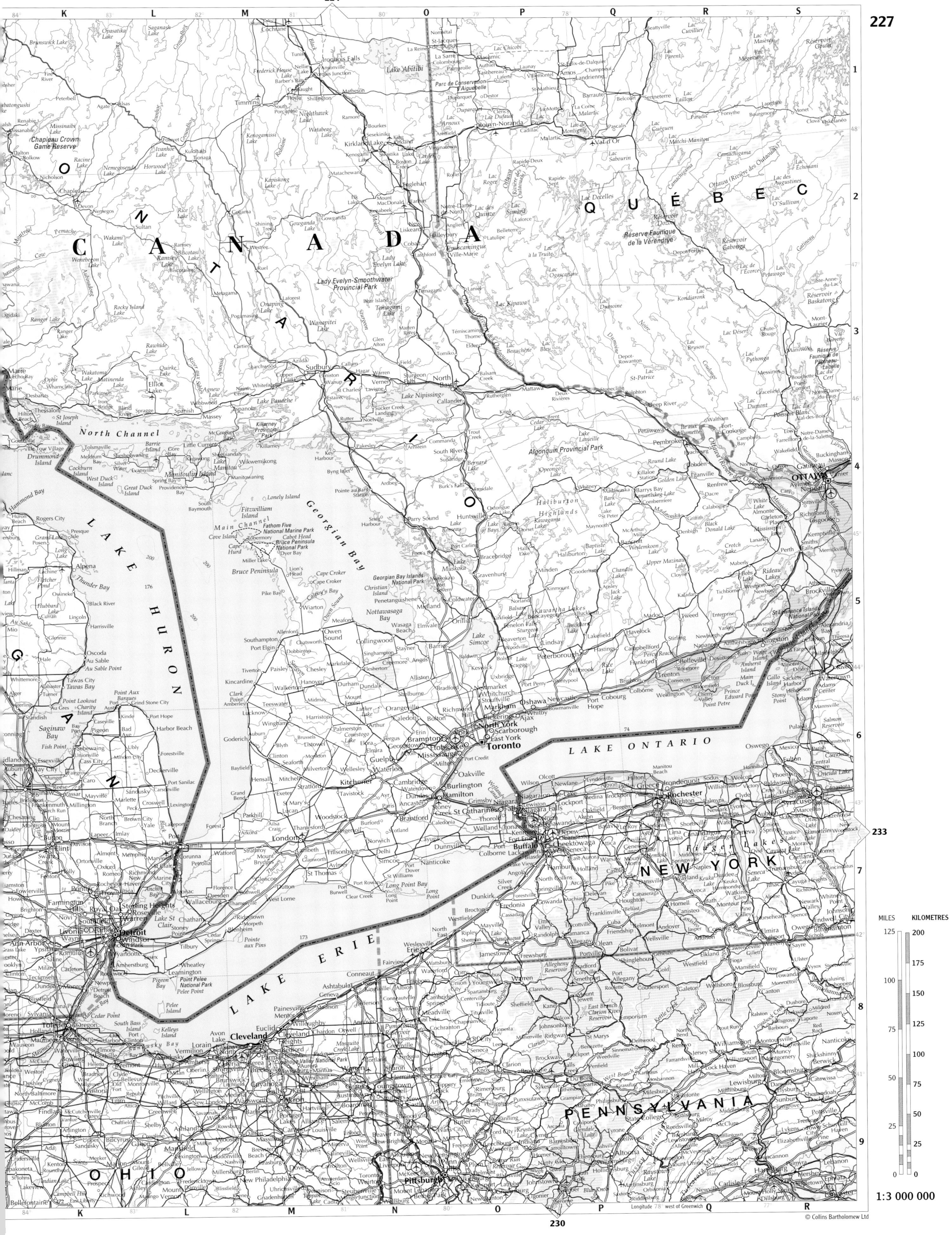

CANADA

ONTARIO

QUÉBEC

LAKE HURON

Georgian Bay

North Channel

LAKE ONTARIO

LAKE ERIE

MICHIGAN

NEW YORK

PENNSYLVANIA

OHIO

Toronto

Ottawa

Buffalo

Detroit

Cleveland

Pittsburgh

Sudbury

Lake Nipissing

Algonquin Provincial Park

Bruce Peninsula National Park

Georgian Bay Islands National Park

Point Pelee National Park

Lake Simcoe

Lake Abitibi

Finger Lakes

1:3 000 000

MILES   KILOMETRES
125   200
         175
100   150
         125
75   100
50   75
         50
25
         25
0   0

© Collins Bartholomew Ltd

224

230

233

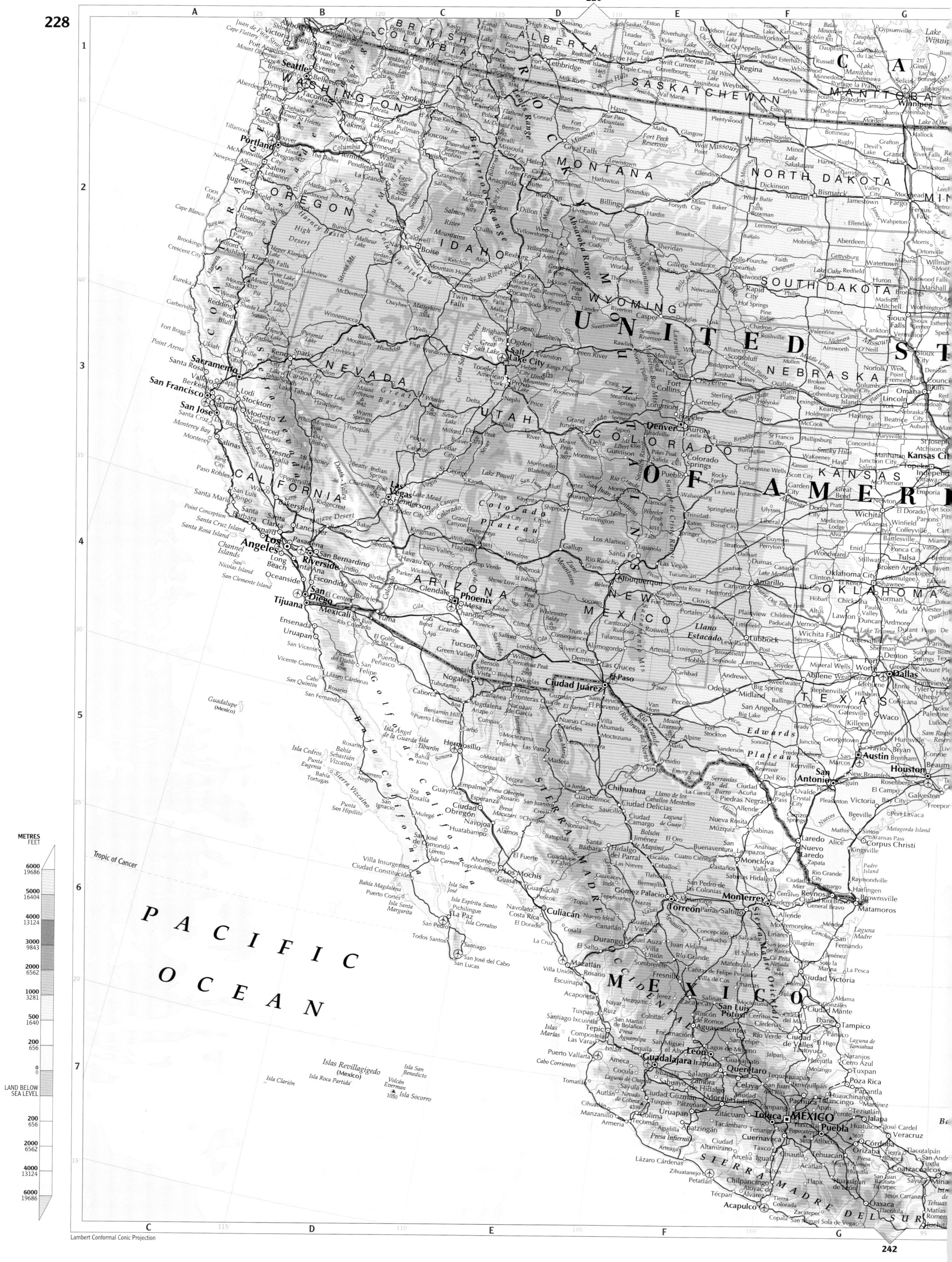
220
242
PACIFIC
OCEAN
UNITED STATES OF AMERICA
MEXICO
CANADA
BRITISH COLUMBIA
ALBERTA
SASKATCHEWAN
MANITOBA
WASHINGTON
OREGON
IDAHO
MONTANA
NORTH DAKOTA
SOUTH DAKOTA
WYOMING
NEBRASKA
NEVADA
UTAH
COLORADO
KANSAS
CALIFORNIA
ARIZONA
NEW MEXICO
OKLAHOMA
TEXAS
ROCKY MOUNTAINS
SIERRA MADRE OCCIDENTAL
SIERRA MADRE ORIENTAL
SIERRA MADRE DEL SUR
Golfo de California
Baja California
Colorado Plateau
Great Basin
Llano Estacado
Edwards Plateau
Tropic of Cancer
Islas Revillagigedo (Mexico)
Guadalupe (Mexico)
Seattle
Portland
Sacramento
San Francisco
San Jose
Los Angeles
San Diego
Tijuana
Las Vegas
Phoenix
Salt Lake City
Denver
Boise
Helena
Cheyenne
Santa Fe
Albuquerque
El Paso
Ciudad Juárez
Chihuahua
Hermosillo
Monterrey
Torreón
Culiacán
Guadalajara
León
San Luis Potosí
MÉXICO
Puebla
Acapulco
Veracruz
Dallas
Austin
San Antonio
Houston
Oklahoma City
Kansas City
Winnipeg
Omaha
Lincoln
Topeka
Bismarck
Pierre
Vancouver
Victoria
METRES
FEET
6000
19686
5000
16404
4000
13124
3000
9843
2000
6562
1000
3281
500
1640
200
656
0
0
LAND BELOW SEA LEVEL
200
656
2000
6562
4000
13124
6000
19686

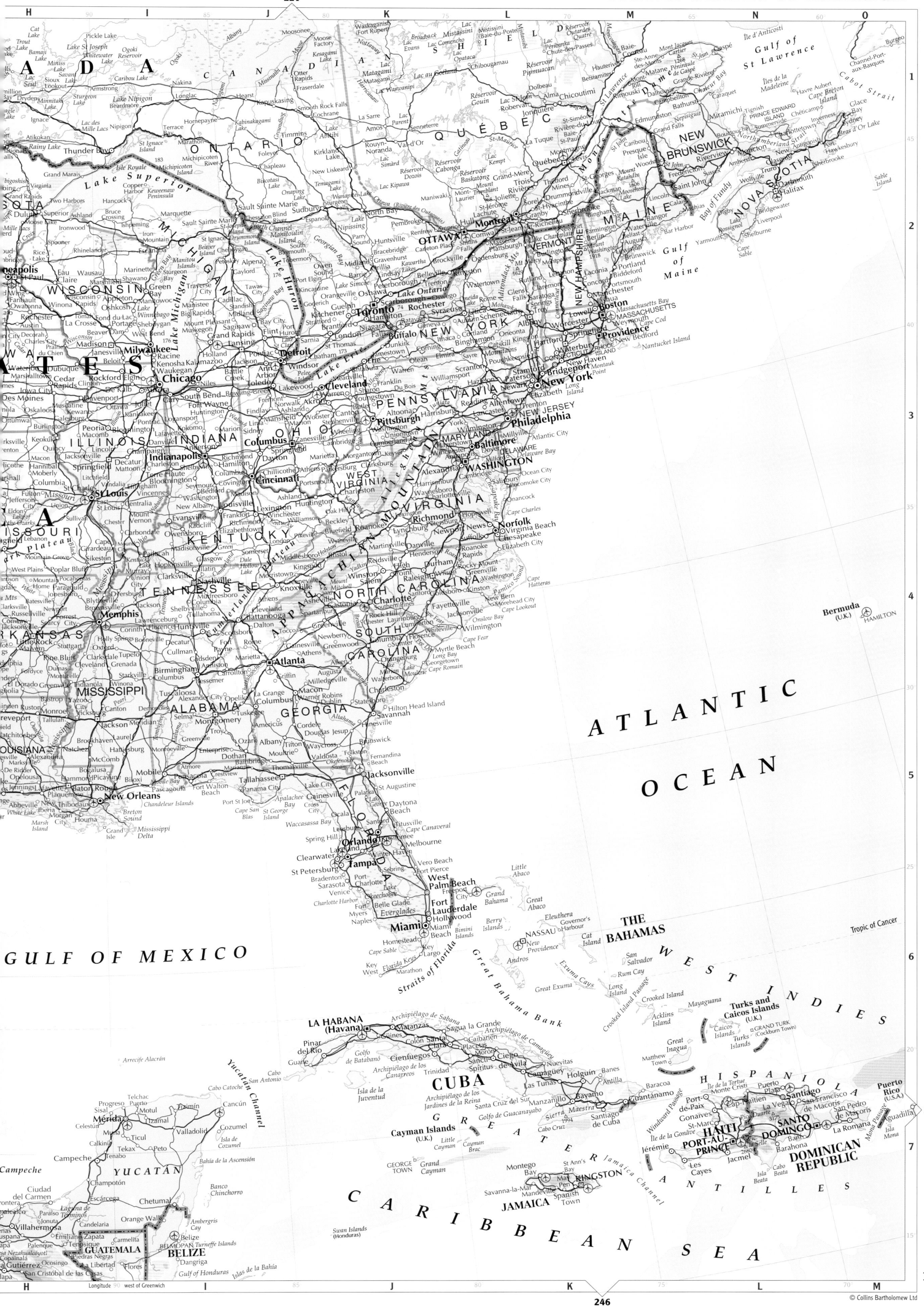

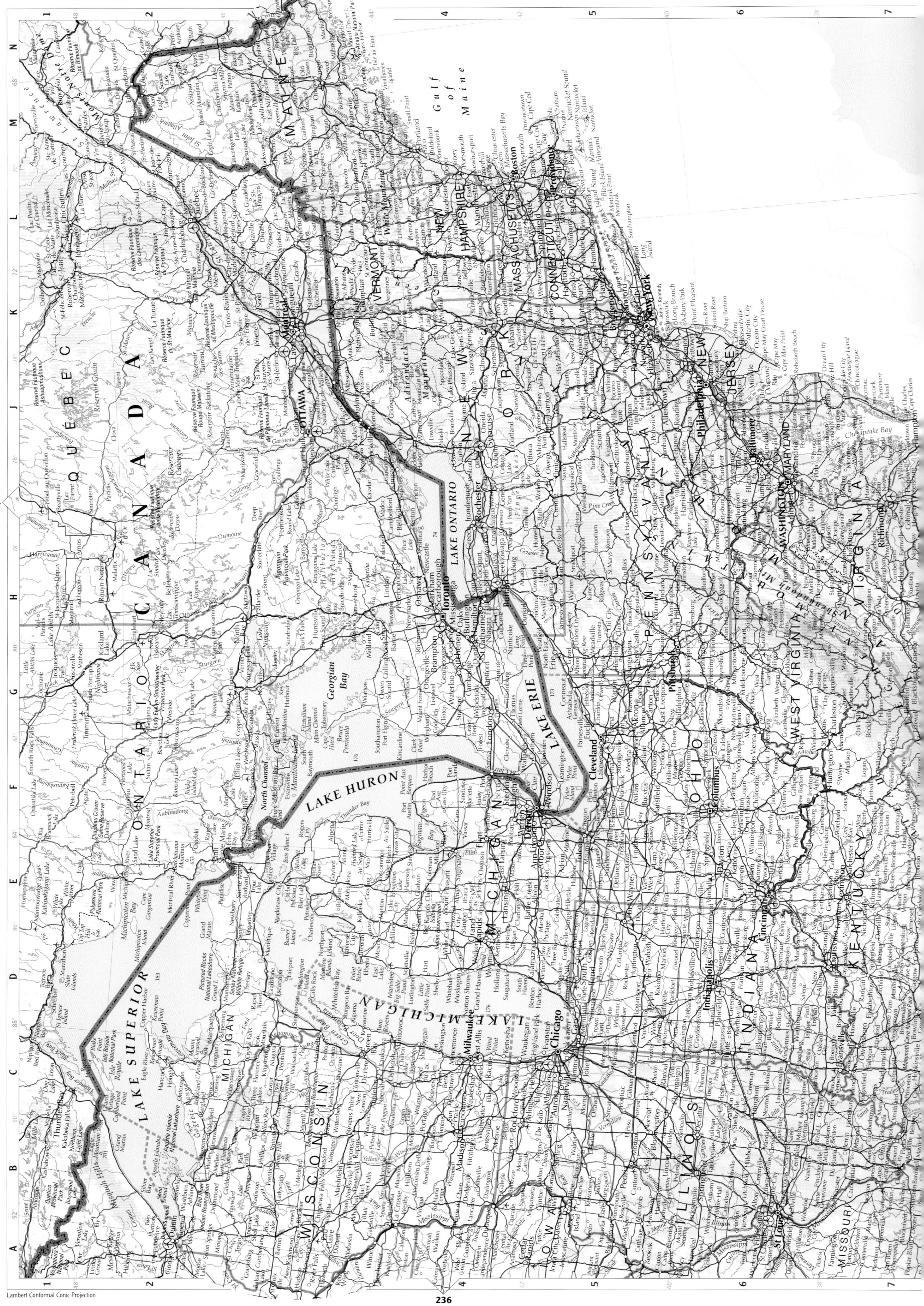

BERMUDA
(U.K.)
1:500 000

NEW PROVIDENCE
(The Bahamas)
1:500 000

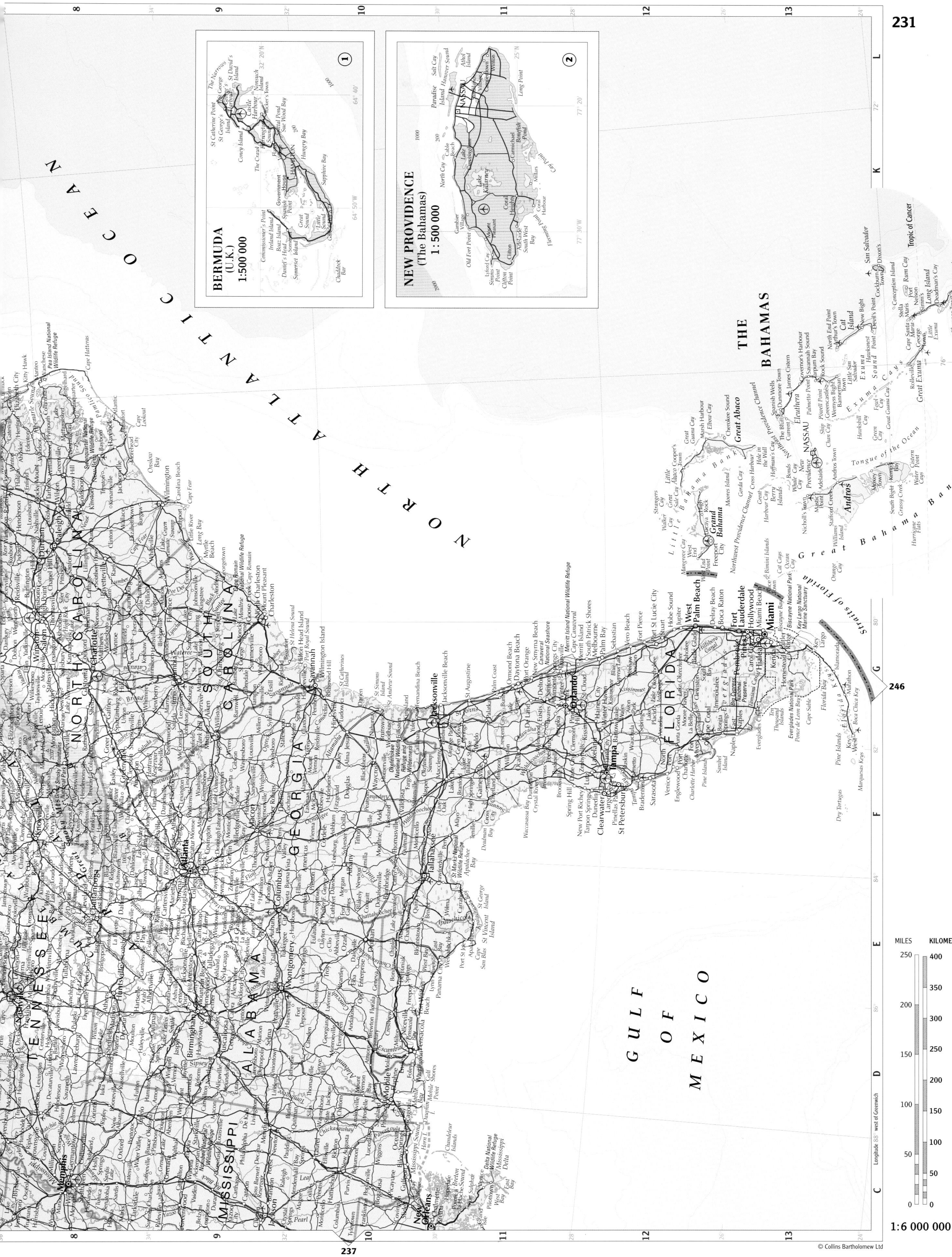

NORTH ATLANTIC OCEAN

THE BAHAMAS

NASSAU

Grand Bahama
Freeport

Great Abaco

Andros

Eleuthera

Great Exuma

Long Island

Cat Island

Rum Cay

San Salvador

Tropic of Cancer

NORTH CAROLINA

SOUTH CAROLINA

TENNESSEE

GEORGIA

ALABAMA

MISSISSIPPI

FLORIDA

Atlanta

Charlotte

Raleigh

Columbia

Charleston

Savannah

Jacksonville

Orlando

Tampa

St Petersburg

Miami

Fort Lauderdale

West Palm Beach

Birmingham

Montgomery

Mobile

New Orleans

Tallahassee

Memphis

Nashville

Knoxville

Cape Hatteras

Cape Fear

GULF OF MEXICO

Straits of Florida

Key West

Everglades National Park

Longitude 88° west of Greenwich

MILES   KILOMETRES
250   400
200   350
         300
150   250
         200
100   150
50   100
         50
0   0

1:6 000 000

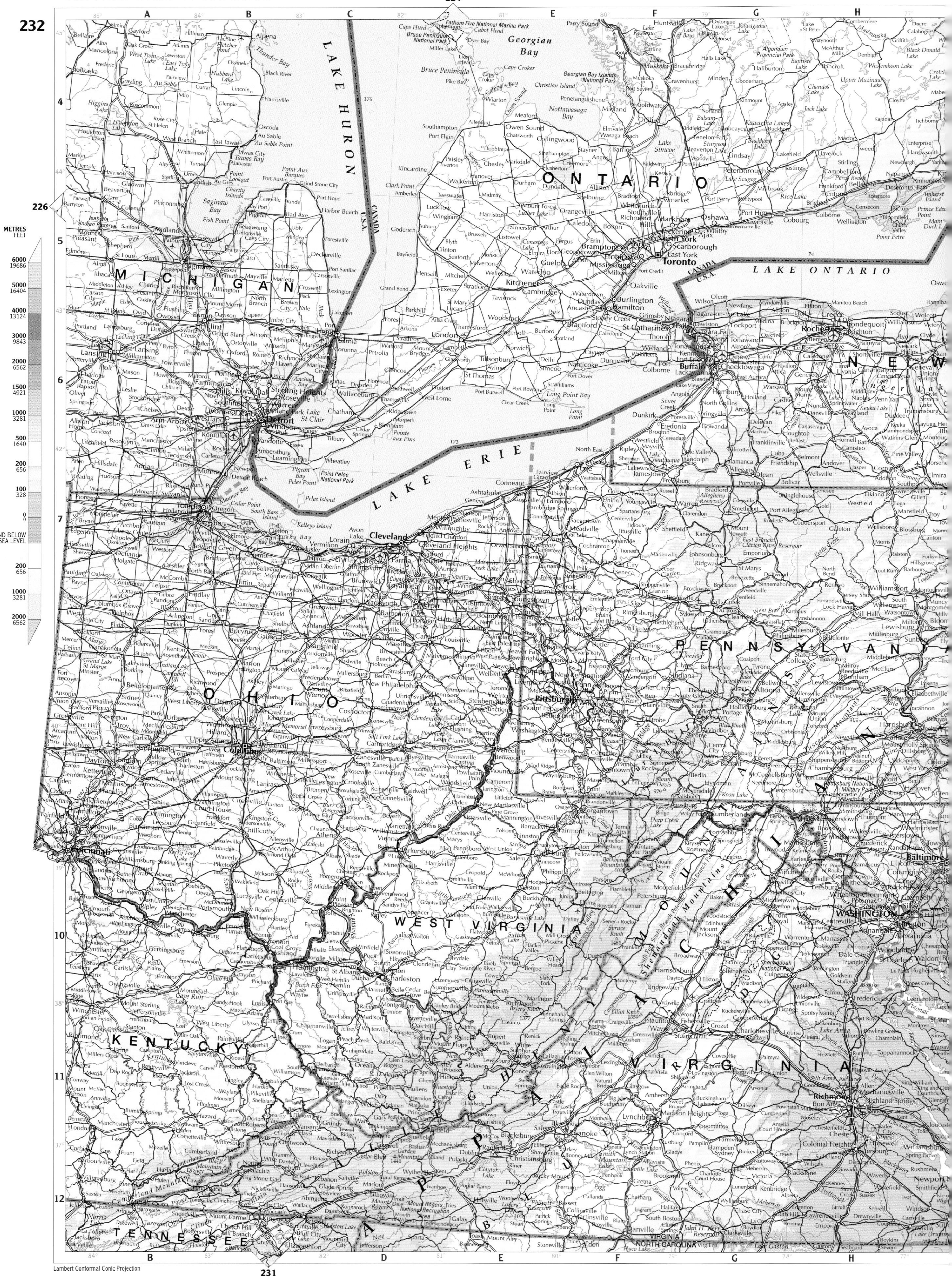

METRES
FEET

6000
19686

5000
16404

4000
13124

3000
9843

2000
6562

1500
4921

1000
3281

500
1640

200
656

100
328

0

LAND BELOW
SEA LEVEL

200
656

1000
3281

2000
6562

Lambert Conformal Conic Projection

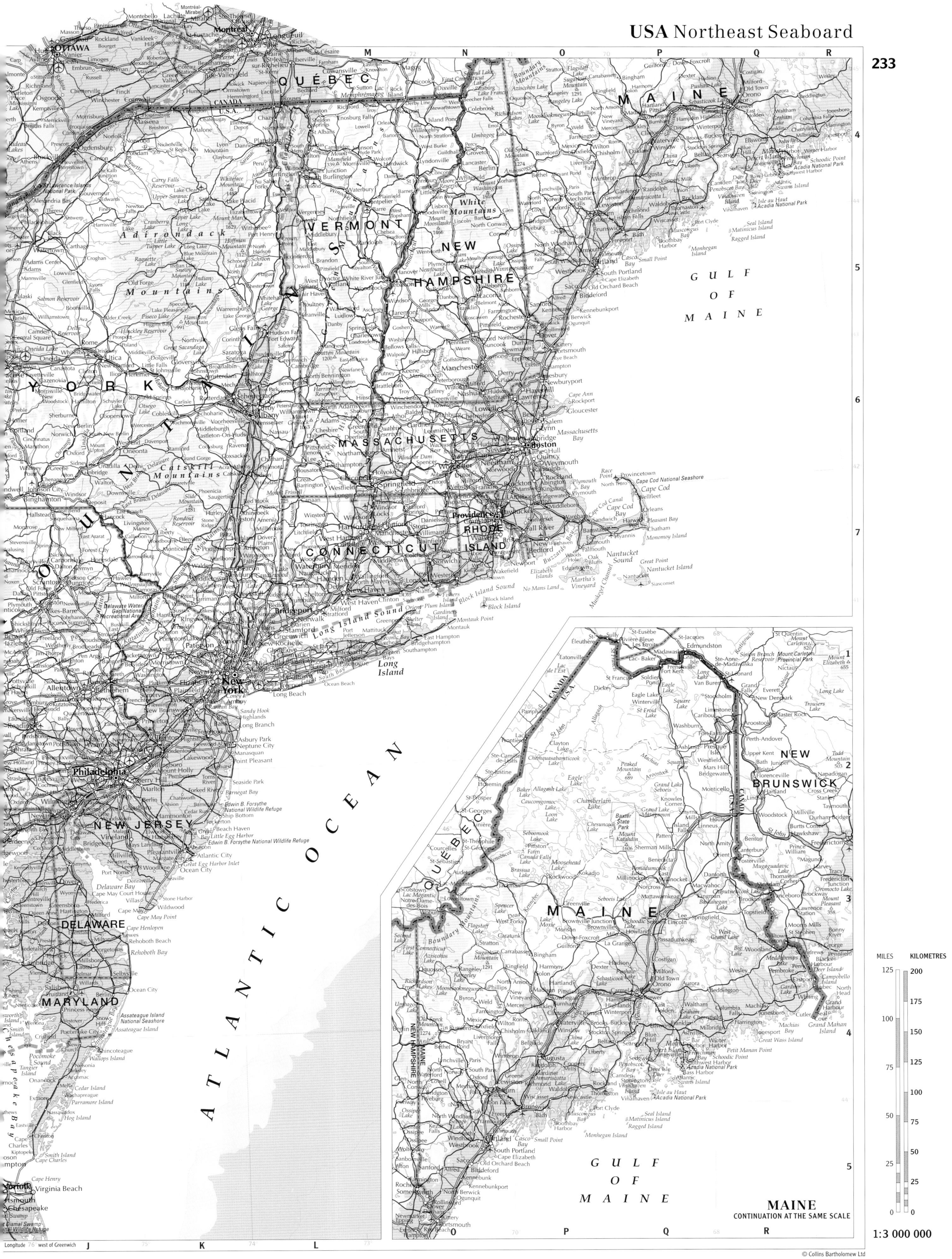

MAINE
CONTINUATION AT THE SAME SCALE

1:3 000 000

MILES   KILOMETRES

© Collins Bartholomew Ltd

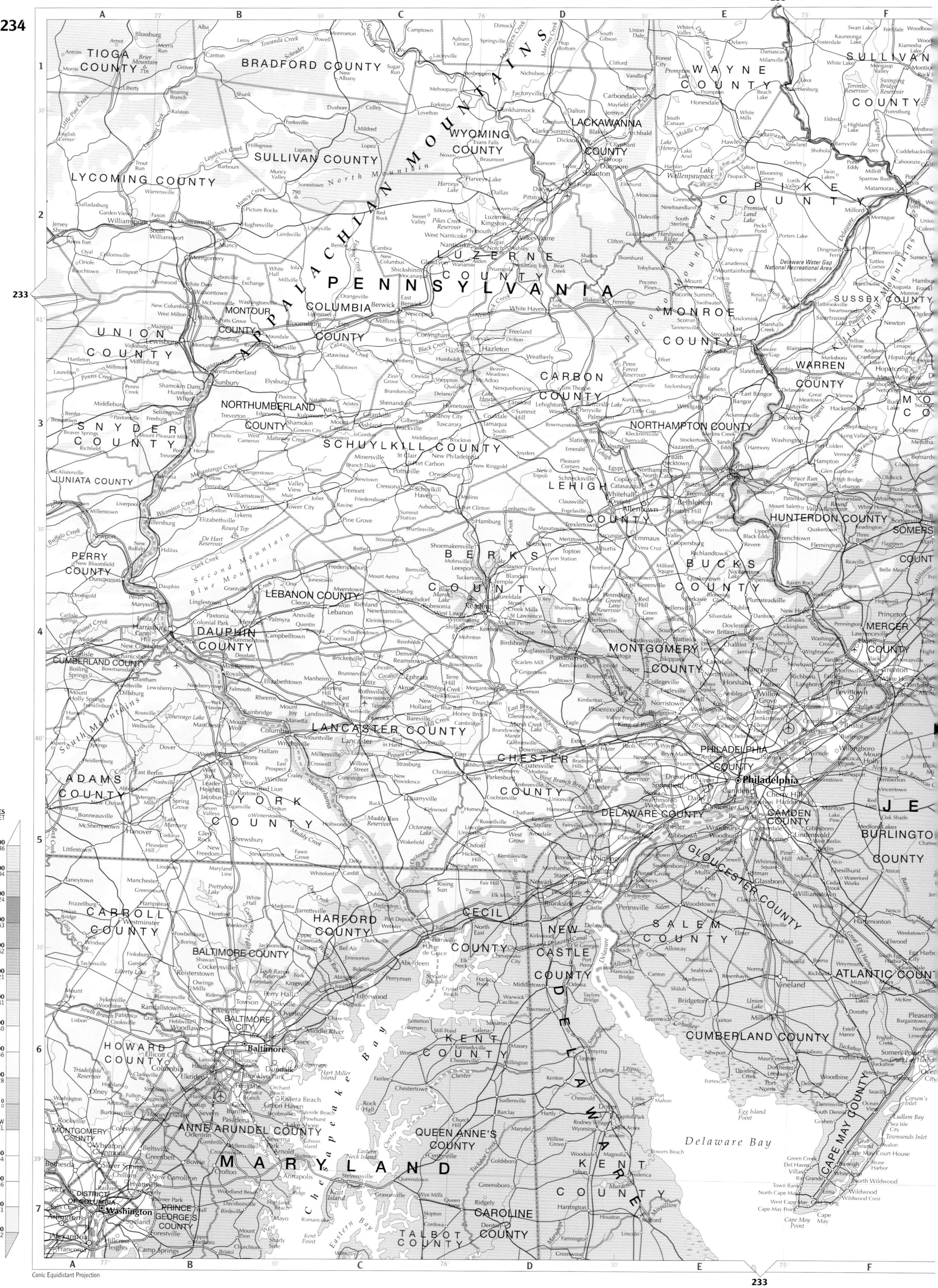

PENNSYLVANIA

MARYLAND

APPALACHIAN MOUNTAINS

Counties (Pennsylvania): TIOGA COUNTY, BRADFORD COUNTY, SULLIVAN COUNTY, LYCOMING COUNTY, WYOMING COUNTY, LACKAWANNA COUNTY, WAYNE COUNTY, SULLIVAN COUNTY, PIKE COUNTY, LUZERNE COUNTY, UNION COUNTY, COLUMBIA COUNTY, MONROE COUNTY, WARREN COUNTY, SNYDER COUNTY, NORTHUMBERLAND COUNTY, SCHUYLKILL COUNTY, CARBON COUNTY, NORTHAMPTON COUNTY, JUNIATA COUNTY, LEHIGH COUNTY, HUNTERDON COUNTY, SOMERSET COUNTY, PERRY COUNTY, BERKS COUNTY, BUCKS COUNTY, LEBANON COUNTY, DAUPHIN COUNTY, MONTGOMERY COUNTY, MERCER COUNTY, CUMBERLAND COUNTY, LANCASTER COUNTY, CHESTER COUNTY, PHILADELPHIA COUNTY, DELAWARE COUNTY, CAMDEN COUNTY, ADAMS COUNTY, YORK COUNTY, GLOUCESTER COUNTY, BURLINGTON COUNTY

Counties (Maryland / Delaware / NJ): CARROLL COUNTY, BALTIMORE COUNTY, CECIL COUNTY, NEW CASTLE COUNTY, SALEM COUNTY, ATLANTIC COUNTY, HOWARD COUNTY, BALTIMORE CITY, KENT COUNTY, CUMBERLAND COUNTY, HARFORD COUNTY, ANNE ARUNDEL COUNTY, QUEEN ANNE'S COUNTY, MONTGOMERY COUNTY, PRINCE GEORGE'S COUNTY, KENT COUNTY, CAPE MAY COUNTY, TALBOT COUNTY, CAROLINE COUNTY

DISTRICT OF COLUMBIA

Washington, Baltimore, Philadelphia, Wilmington, Allentown, Bethlehem, Reading, Harrisburg, Lancaster, York, Wilkes-Barre, Scranton, Alexandria

Chesapeake Bay, Delaware Bay, Eastern Bay

Scale legend:

METRES / FEET

METRES	FEET
6000	19686
5000	16404
4000	13124
3000	9843
2000	6562
1500	4921
1000	3281
500	1640
200	656
100	328
0	0

LAND BELOW SEA LEVEL

50	164
200	656
1000	3281
2000	6562

Conic Equidistant Projection

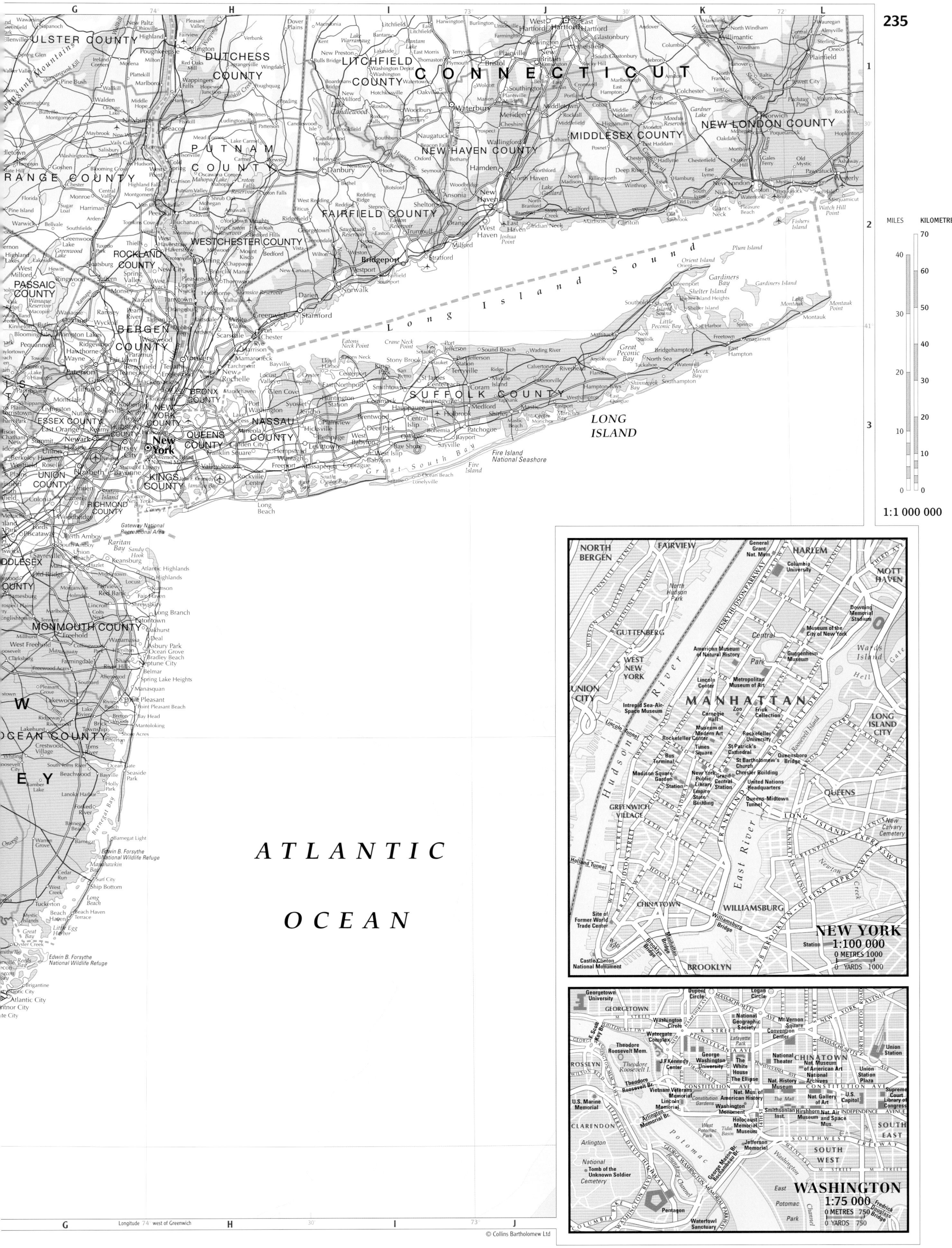

MILES KILOMETRES

1:1 000 000

NEW YORK 1:100 000
Station ▪ 0 METRES 1000
0 YARDS 1000

WASHINGTON 1:75 000
0 METRES 750
0 YARDS 750

ATLANTIC

OCEAN

© Collins Bartholomew Ltd

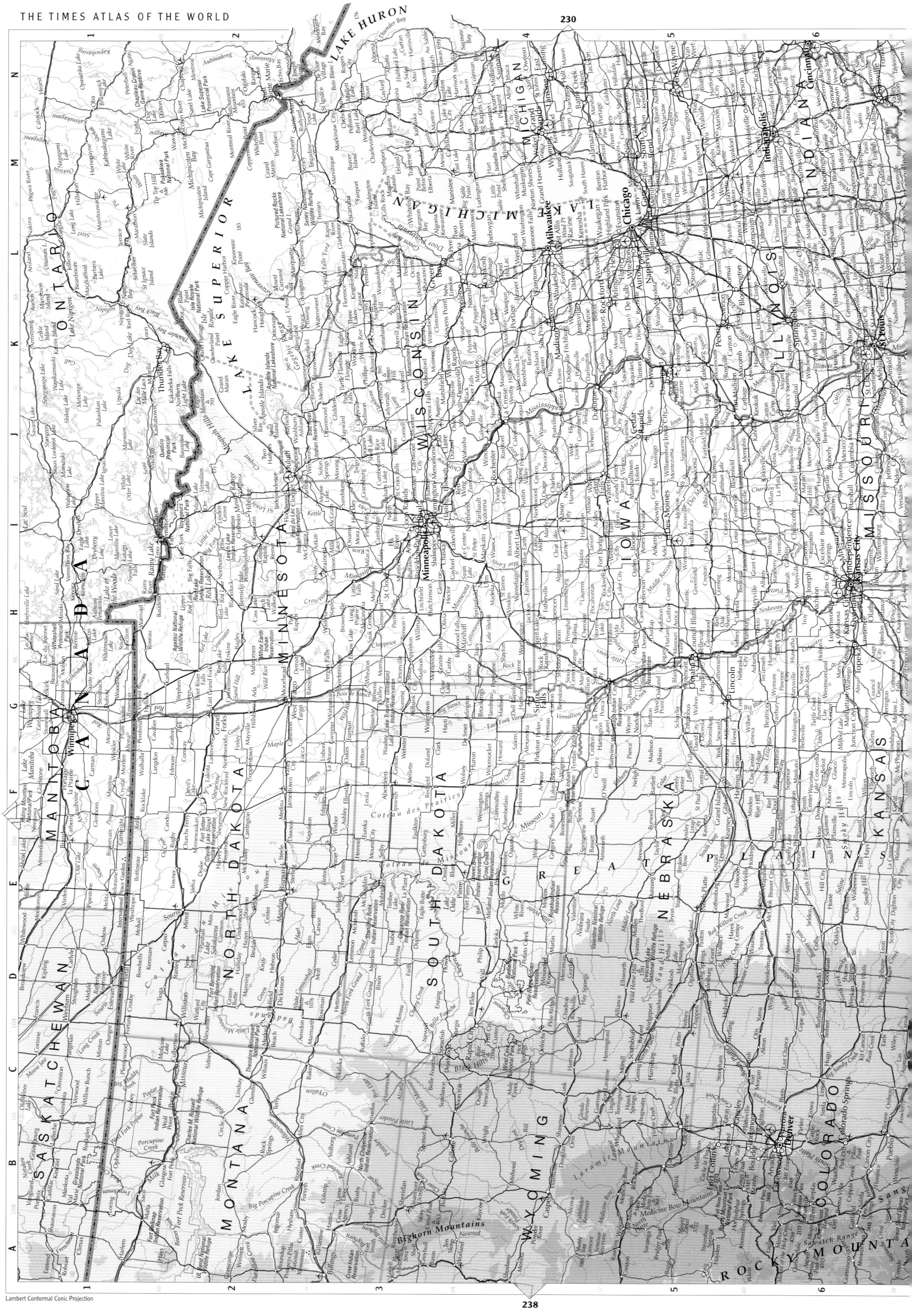

Lambert Conformal Conic Projection

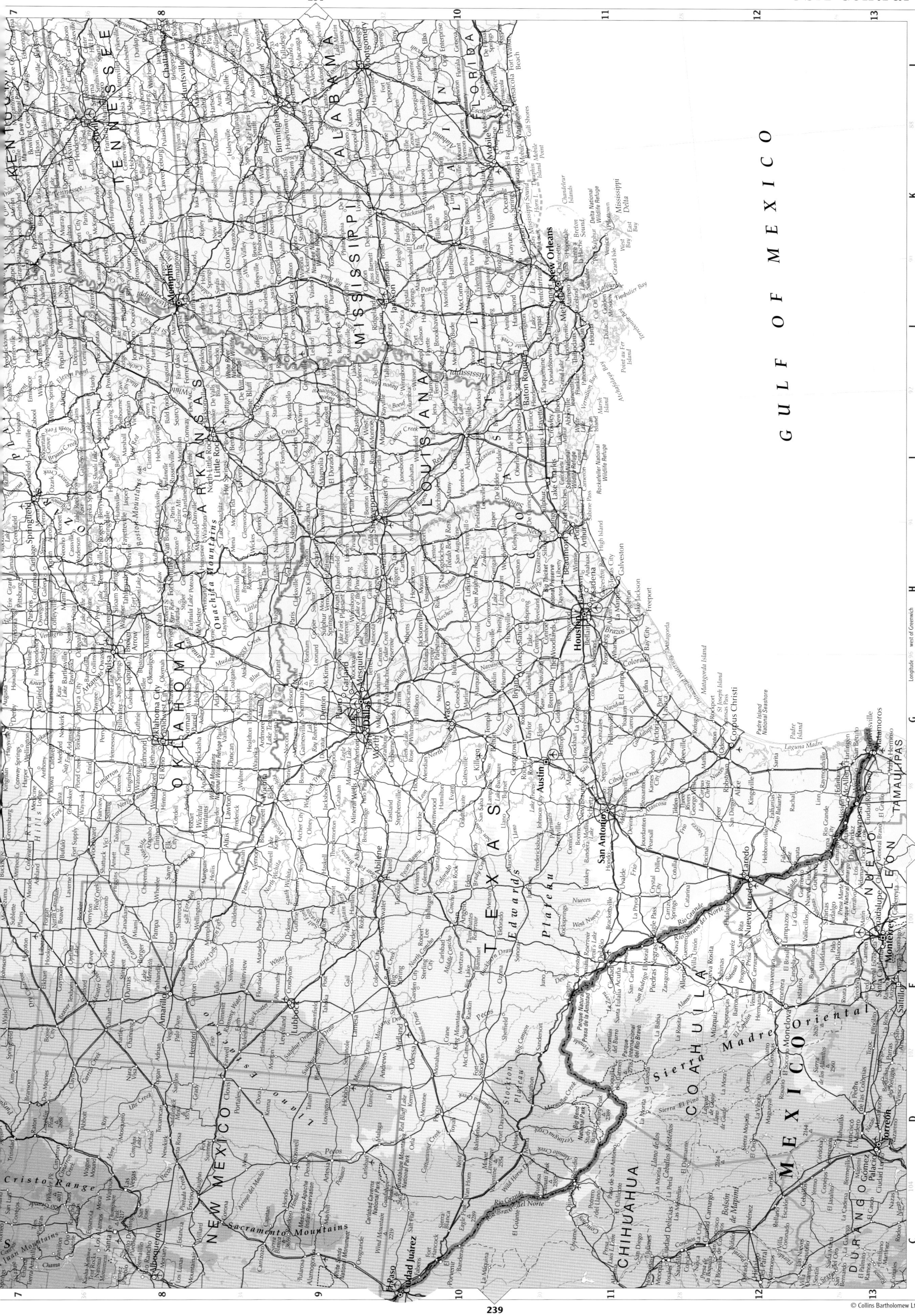

© Collins Bartholomew Ltd

1:6 000 000

MILES   KILOMETRES

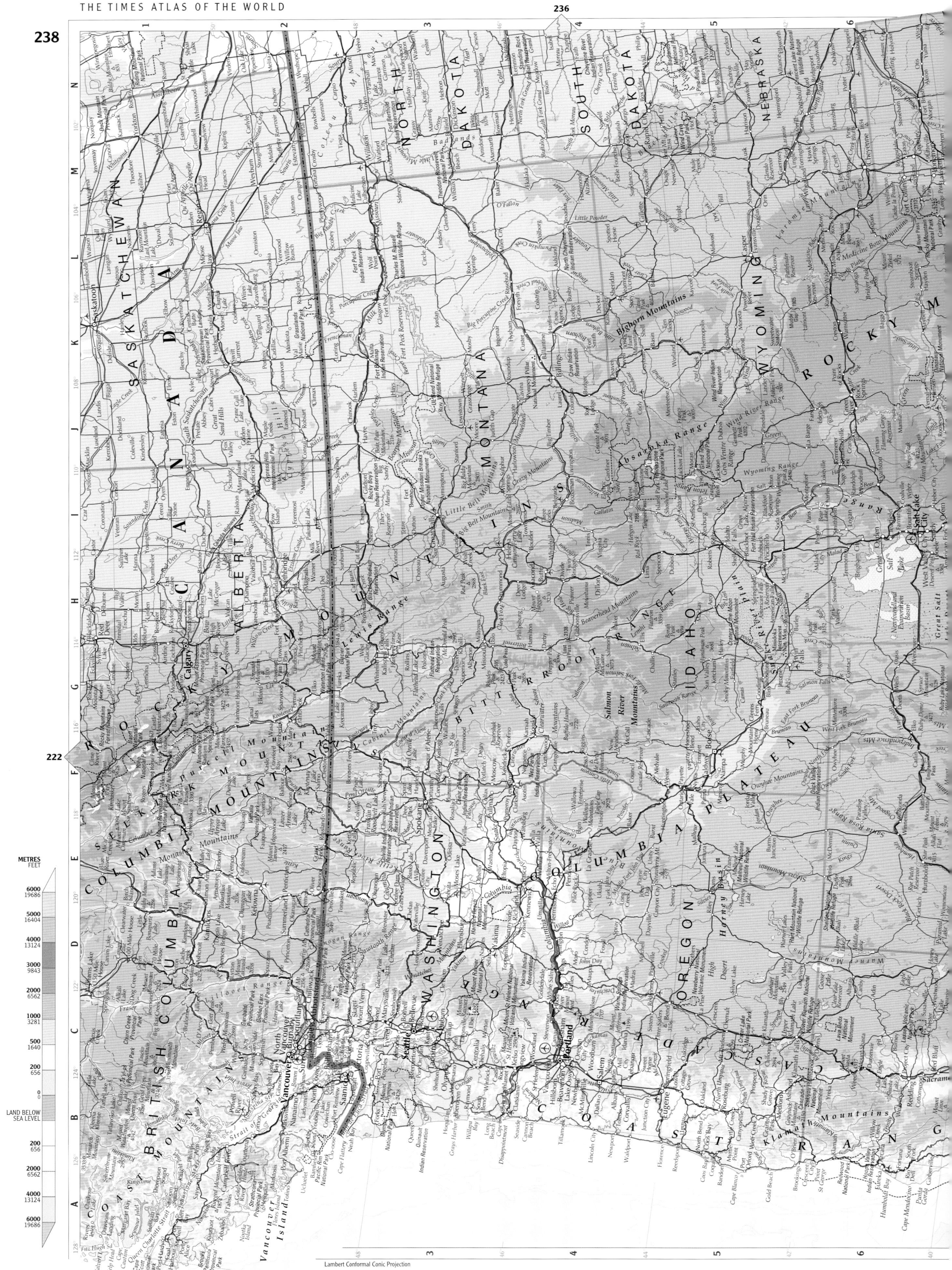

METRES
FEET

6000
19686

5000
16404

4000
13124

3000
9843

2000
6562

1000
3281

500
1640

200
656

0
0

LAND BELOW
SEA LEVEL

200
656

2000
6562

4000
13124

6000
19686

Lambert Conformal Conic Projection

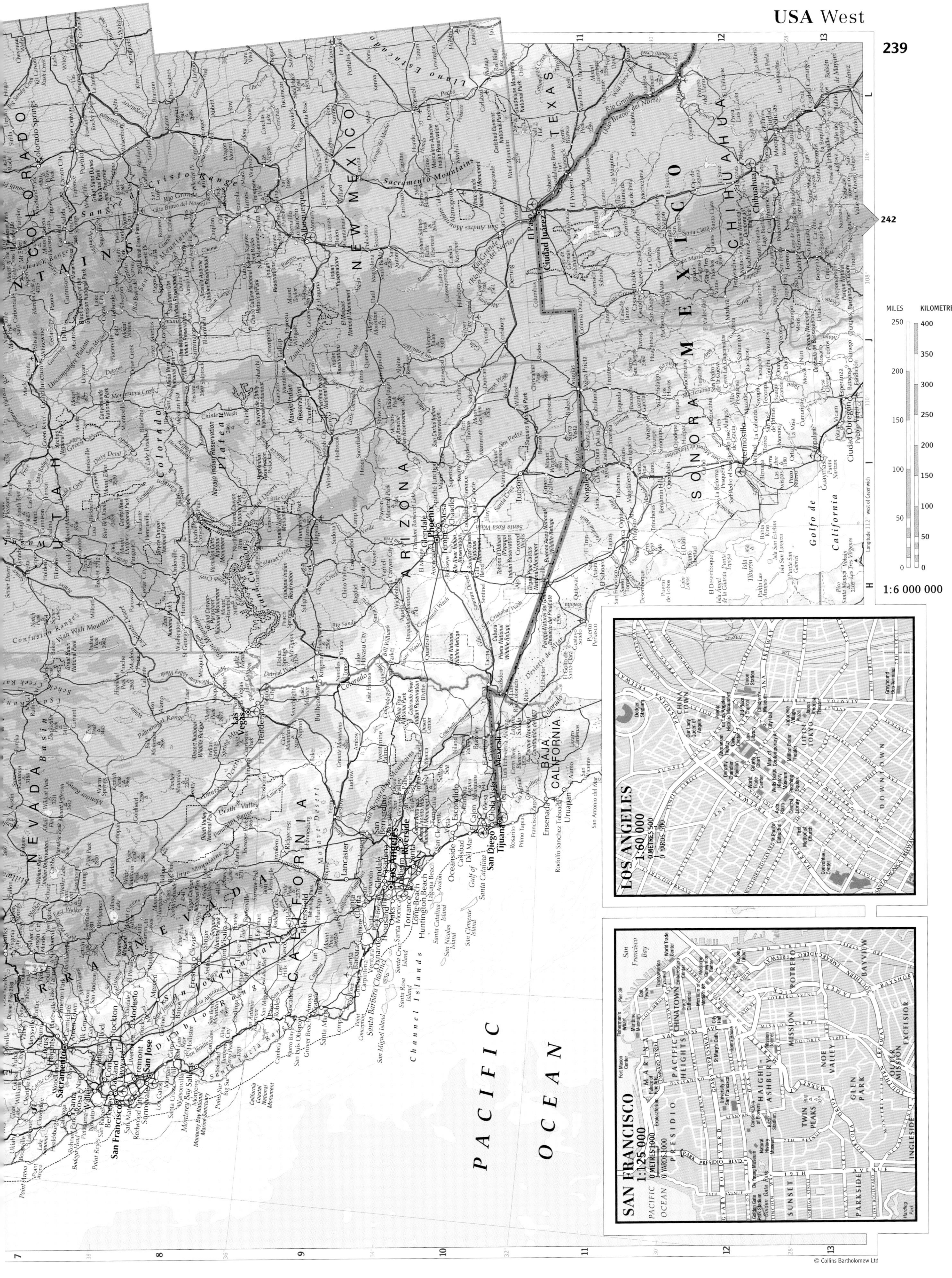
COLORADO
UTAH
NEVADA
CALIFORNIA
ARIZONA
NEW MEXICO
TEXAS
SONORA
CHIHUAHUA
BAJA CALIFORNIA
MEXICO
PACIFIC OCEAN
Golfo de California
Channel Islands
Sierra Nevada
San Joaquin Valley
Mojave Desert
Colorado Plateau
Great Basin
Sangre de Cristo Range
Sacramento Mountains
Llano Estacado
Los Angeles
San Francisco
San Diego
Las Vegas
Phoenix
Tucson
Albuquerque
El Paso
Ciudad Juárez
Chihuahua
Hermosillo
Tijuana
Mexicali
Sacramento
San Jose
Fresno
242
MILES
KILOMETRES
1:6 000 000
LOS ANGELES
1:60 000
SAN FRANCISCO
1:125 000
7
8
9
10
11
12
13

Map legend

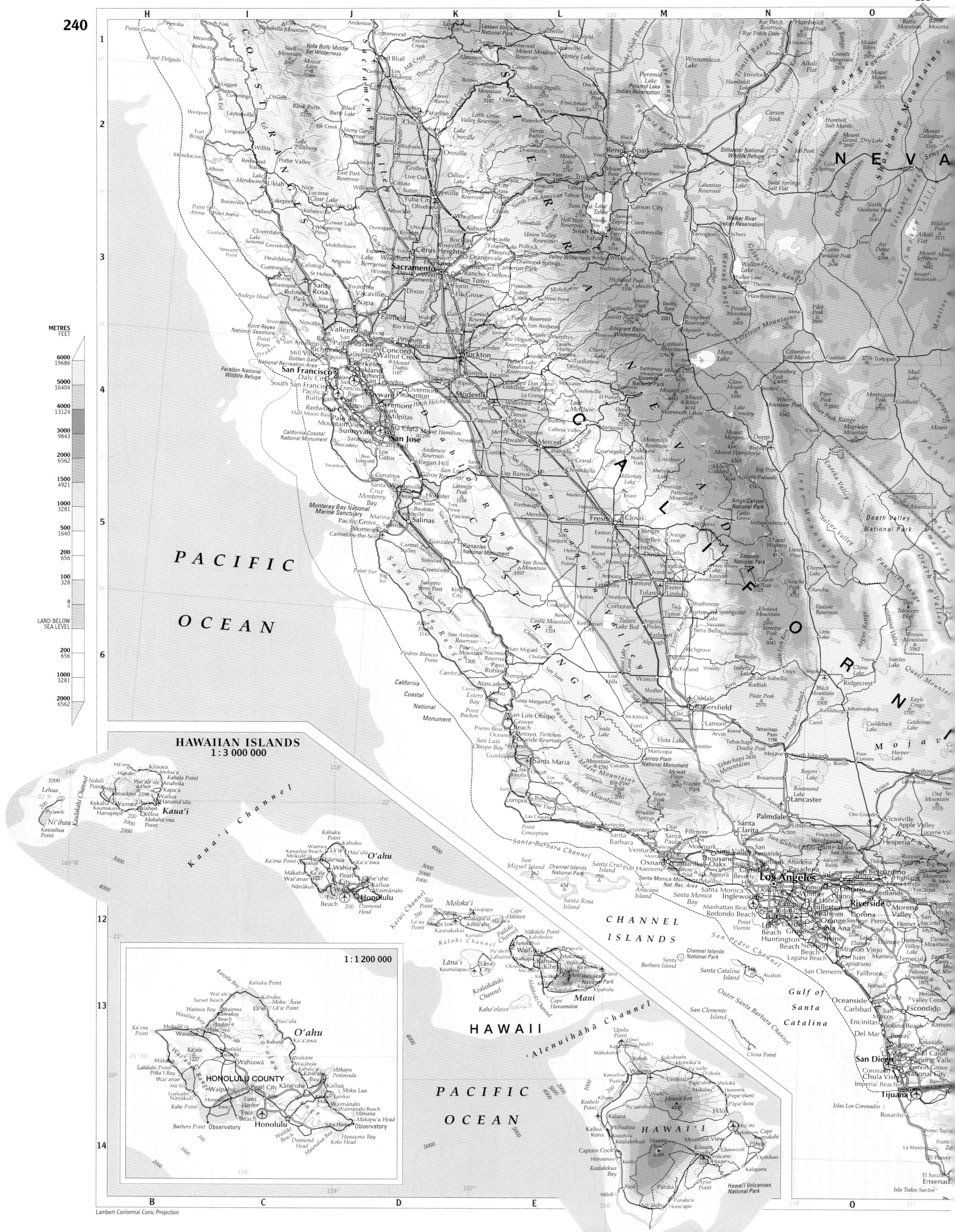

METRES / FEET

6000 / 19686
5000 / 16404
4000 / 13124
3000 / 9843
2000 / 6562
1500 / 4921
1000 / 3281
500 / 1640
200 / 656
100 / 328
0 / 0
LAND BELOW SEA LEVEL
200 / 656
1000 / 3281
2000 / 6562

PACIFIC OCEAN

NEVADA

CALIFORNIA

HAWAIIAN ISLANDS
1:3 000 000

Kaua'i

O'ahu

Honolulu

Moloka'i

Lāna'i

Maui

HAWAII

HAWAI'I

Mauna Kea

Hilo

Kailua Kona

Hawai'i Volcanoes National Park

CHANNEL ISLANDS

Los Angeles

San Diego

Tijuana

Gulf of Santa Catalina

HONOLULU COUNTY
1:1 200 000

O'ahu

Pearl Harbor

Honolulu

PACIFIC OCEAN

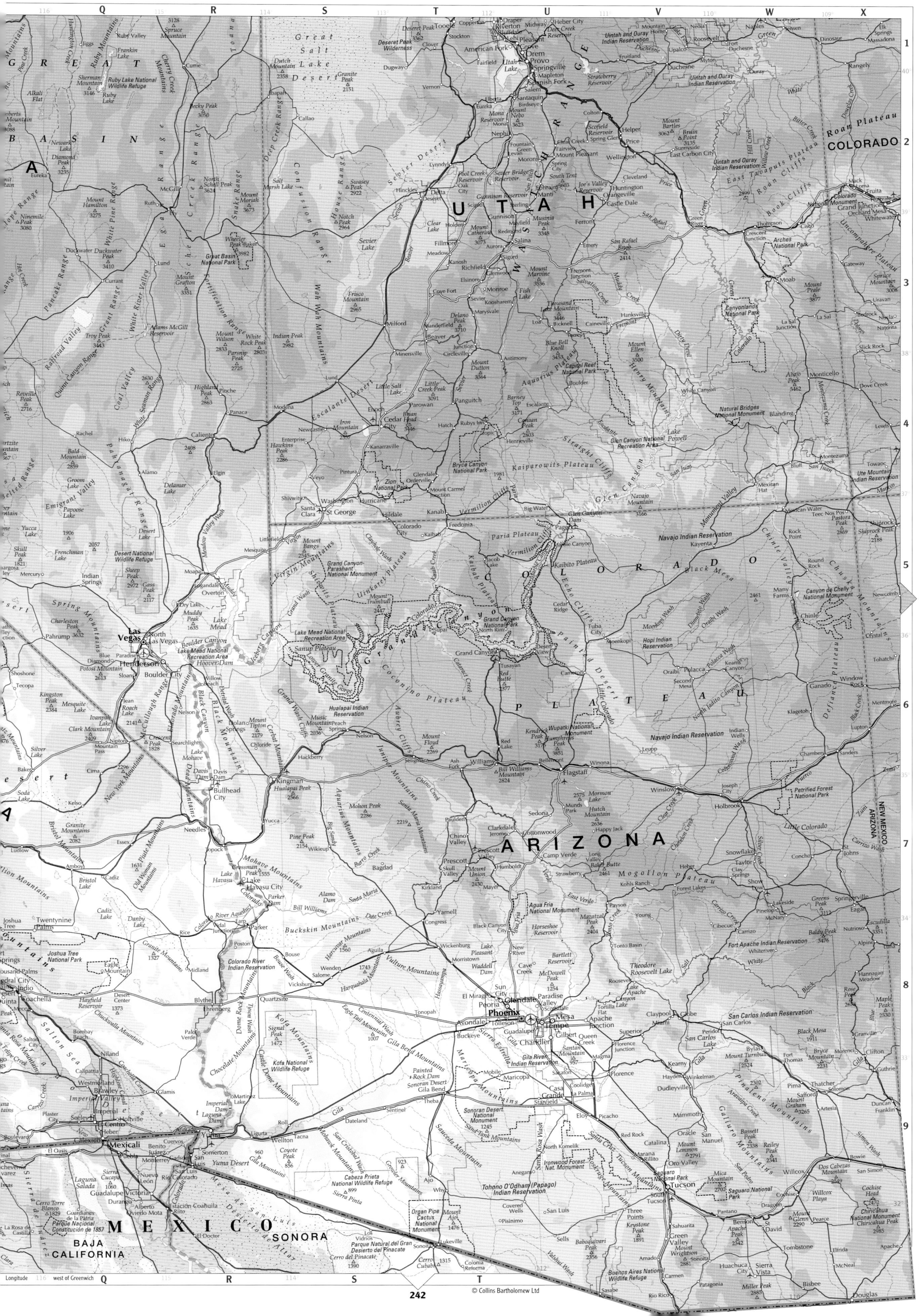

COLORADO

UTAH

ARIZONA

NEW MEXICO

MEXICO

BAJA CALIFORNIA

SONORA

GREAT BASIN

Great Salt Lake

Great Salt Lake Desert

WASATCH RANGE

Las Vegas

North Las Vegas

Henderson

Boulder City

Phoenix

Mesa

Tempe

Chandler

Gilbert

Glendale

Peoria

Scottsdale

Sun City

Avondale

Tucson

Yuma

Mexicali

San Luis Río Colorado

239

Longitude 116 west of Greenwich

MILES   KILOMETRES

125   200

100   150

75   125

          100

50   75

25   50
          25

0   0

1:3 000 000

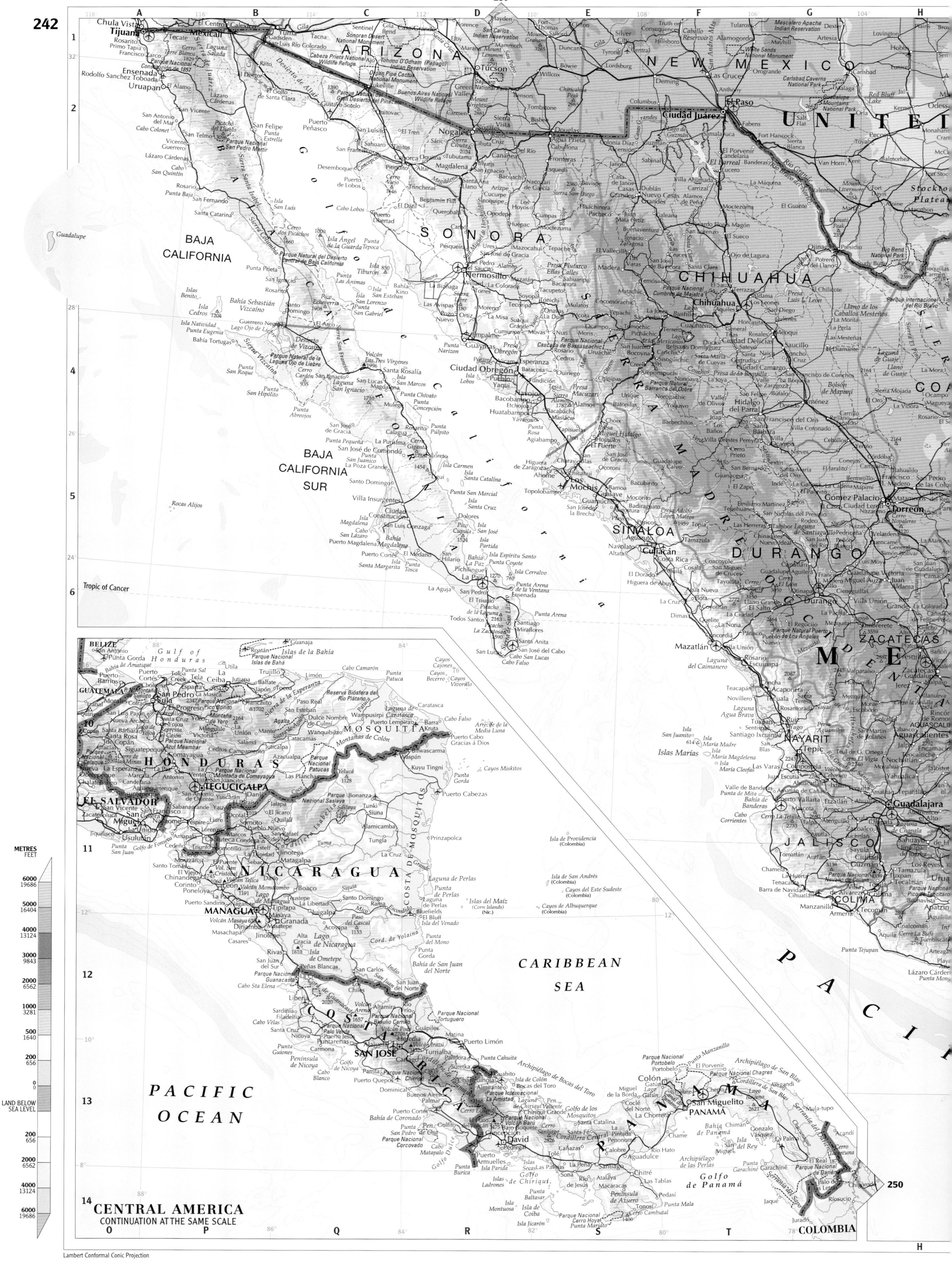

ARIZONA

NEW MEXICO

UNITED

BAJA CALIFORNIA

BAJA CALIFORNIA SUR

SONORA

CHIHUAHUA

SINALOA

DURANGO

ZACATECAS

ME

NAYARIT

JALISCO

COLIMA

Tropic of Cancer

Tijuana

Mexicali

Ensenada

Hermosillo

Ciudad Obregón

Ciudad Juárez

El Paso

Tucson

Nogales

Chihuahua

Ciudad Delicias

Mochis

Culiacán

Gómez Palacio

Torreón

Durango

Mazatlán

Tepic

Guadalajara

El Centro

Gulf of California

Golfo de California

PACIFIC OCEAN

PACI

METRES / FEET

METRES	FEET
6000	19686
5000	16404
4000	13124
3000	9843
2000	6562
1000	3281
500	1640
200	656
0	0

LAND BELOW SEA LEVEL

200	656
2000	6562
4000	13124
6000	19686

BELIZE

GUATEMALA

HONDURAS

EL SALVADOR

NICARAGUA

COSTA RICA

PANAMÁ

COLOMBIA

Gulf of Honduras

Islas de la Bahía

MOSQUITIA

COSTA DE MOSQUITOS

TEGUCIGALPA

MANAGUA

SAN JOSÉ

SAN JOSÉ

Lago de Managua

Lago de Nicaragua

CARIBBEAN SEA

PACIFIC OCEAN

Golfo de Panamá

Isla de Providencia (Colombia)

Isla de San Andrés (Colombia)

Cayos del Este Sudeste (Colombia)

Cayos de Albuquerque (Colombia)

Islas del Maíz (Corn Islands) (Nic.)

250

CENTRAL AMERICA
CONTINUATION AT THE SAME SCALE

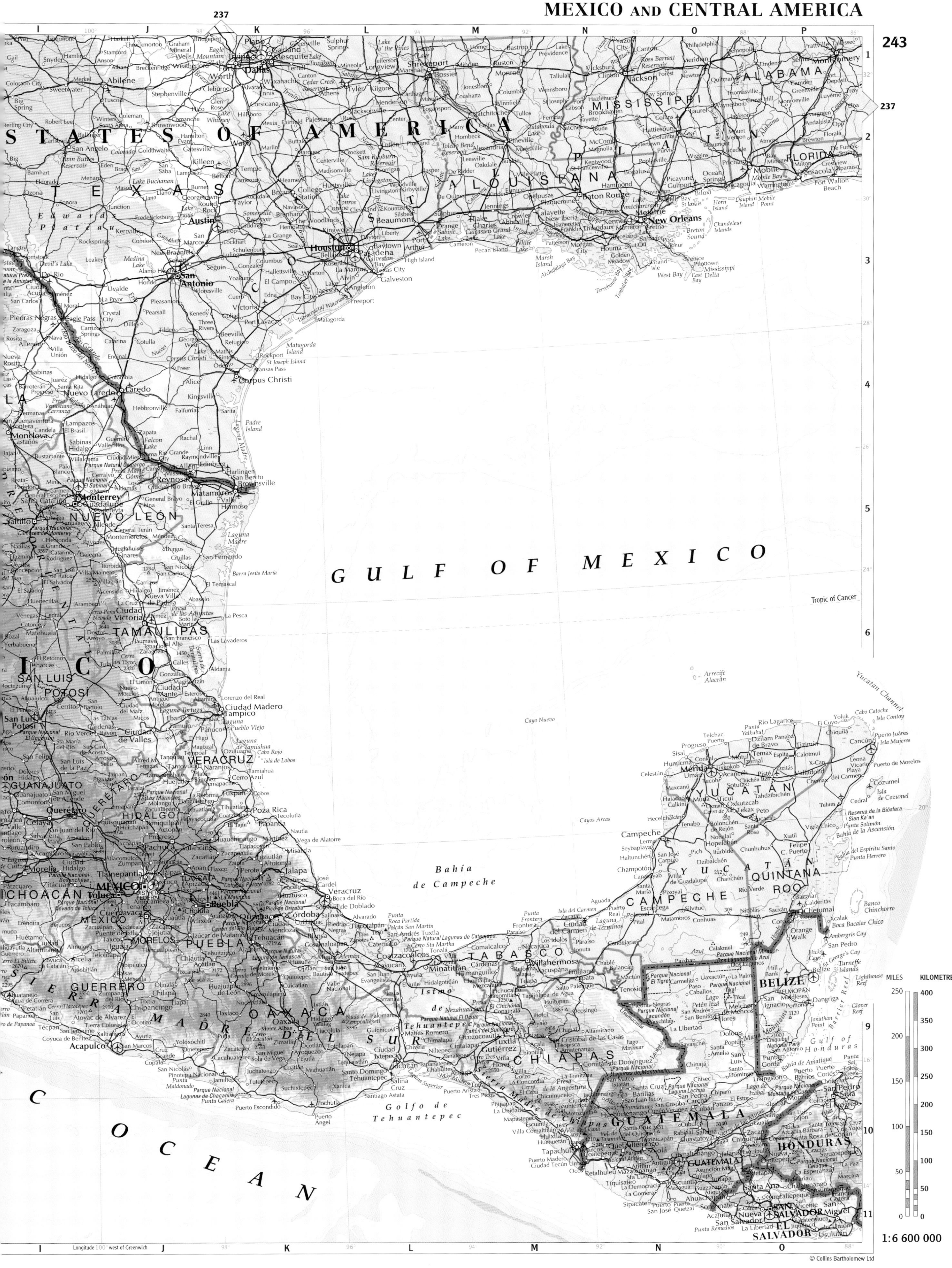

237

STATES OF AMERICA

TEXAS

MISSISSIPPI

ALABAMA

LOUISIANA

FLORIDA

Dallas
Fort Worth
Shreveport
Jackson
Mobile
Pensacola
New Orleans
Baton Rouge
Houston
Pasadena
Galveston
Austin
San Antonio
Corpus Christi
Brownsville

Edwards Plateau

Piedras Negras
Eagle Pass
Nuevo Laredo
Laredo

Matamoros
Reynosa
Monterrey
Guadalupe
NUEVO LEÓN
Saltillo

TAMAULIPAS

GULF OF MEXICO

Tropic of Cancer

SAN LUIS POTOSÍ
San Luis Potosí
Ciudad Victoria
Ciudad Madero
Tampico
Ciudad de Valles

GUANAJUATO
Querétaro
HIDALGO
Poza Rica
VERACRUZ

MÉXICO
Toluca
MICHOACÁN
Morelia
MORELOS
Cuernavaca
PUEBLA
Puebla
TLAXCALA
Orizaba
Córdoba
Veracruz
Boca del Río

Bahía de Campeche

Yucatan Channel

Cancún
Isla Mujeres
Río Lagartos
Mérida
YUCATÁN
Cozumel
Valladolid
Tulum

Reserva de la Biósfera
Sian Ka'an

QUINTANA ROO
Campeche
CAMPECHE
Chetumal

GUERRERO
OAXACA
Oaxaca
SIERRA MADRE DEL SUR
Acapulco

Coatzacoalcos
Minatitlán
TABASCO
Villahermosa

Istmo de Tehuantepec
Golfo de Tehuantepec

CHIAPAS
Tuxtla Gutiérrez

BELIZE
BELMOPAN

Gulf of Honduras

GUATEMALA
GUATEMALA

HONDURAS

SAN SALVADOR
EL SALVADOR

PACIFIC OCEAN

MILES   KILOMETRES

250   400
350
200   300
250
150   200
100   150
50   100
50
0   0

1:6 600 000

PACIFIC

OCEAN

DURANGO

SINALOA

ZACATECAS

NAYARIT

JALISCO

COLIMA

MICHOACÁN

AGUASCALIENTES

SAN LUIS POTOSÍ

GUANAJUATO

COAHUILA

SIERRA MADRE OCCIDENTAL

Mazatlán

Durango

Guadalajara

Tepic

León

San Luis Potosí

Morelia

Manzanillo

Colima

Puerto Vallarta

Islas Marías

Isla María Madre
Isla María Magdalena
Isla María Cleofas
Isla San Juanito
Isla Isabela

Bahía de Banderas

Cabo Corrientes

Laguna de Chapala

Tropic of Cancer

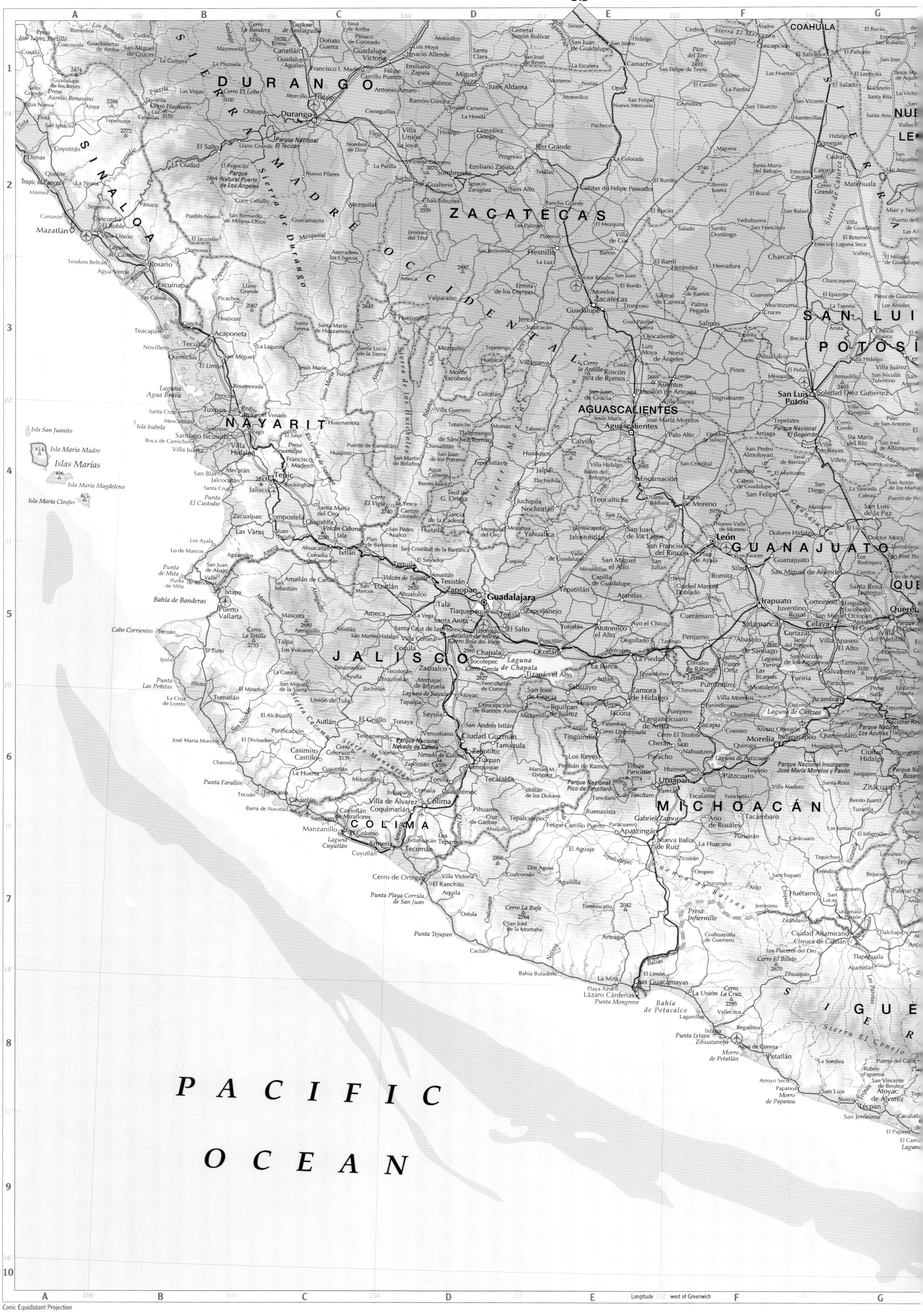

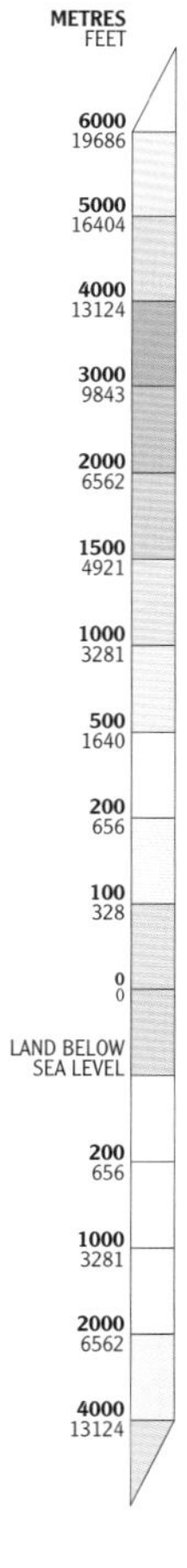

METRES / FEET
6000 / 19686
5000 / 16404
4000 / 13124
3000 / 9843
2000 / 6562
1500 / 4921
1000 / 3281
500 / 1640
200 / 656
100 / 328
0 / 0
LAND BELOW SEA LEVEL
200 / 656
1000 / 3281
2000 / 6562
4000 / 13124

Conic Equidistant Projection

Longitude 102 west of Greenwich

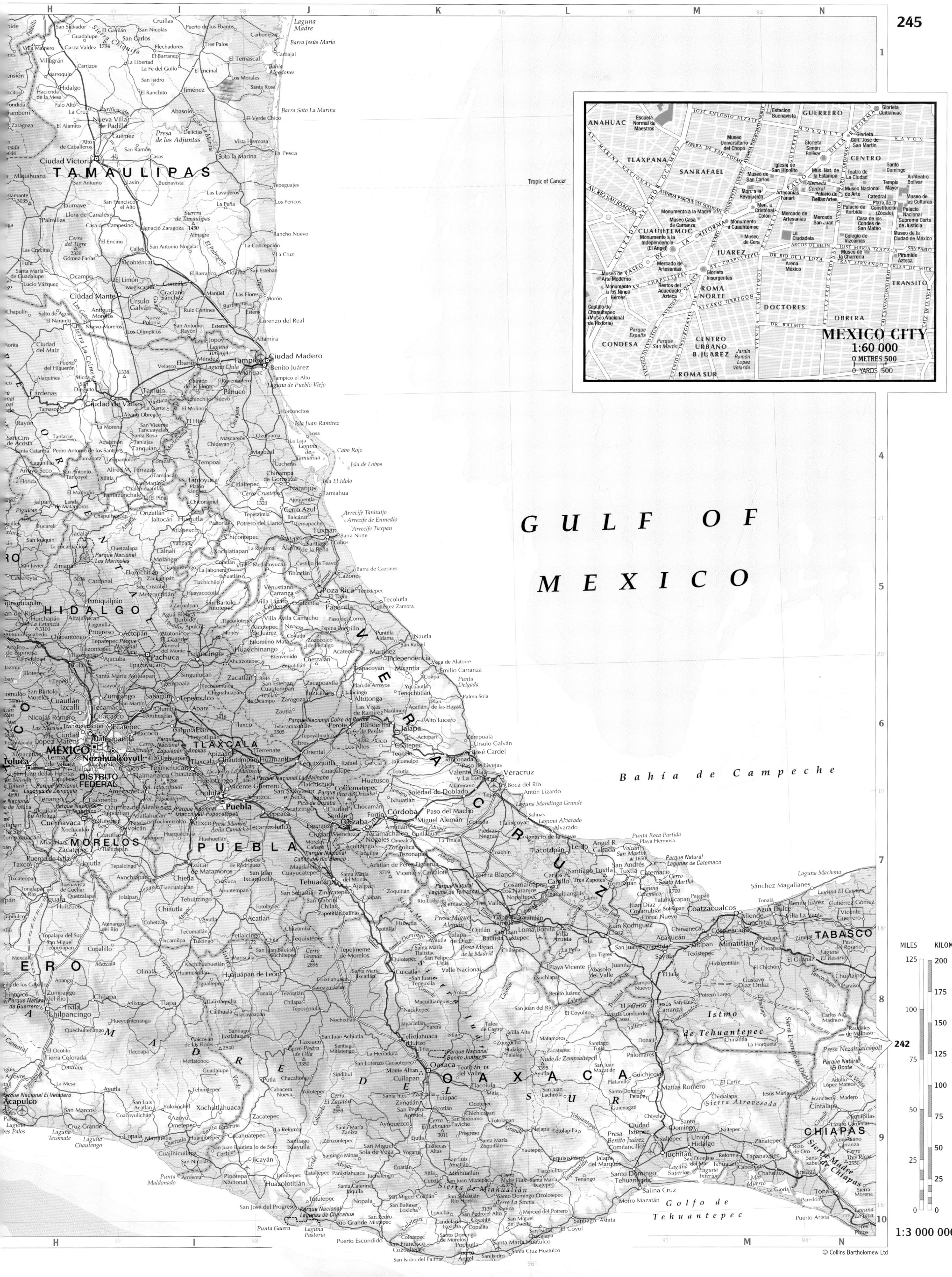

TAMAULIPAS

HIDALGO

GULF OF MEXICO

VERACRUZ

Tropic of Cancer

Tampico
Ciudad Madero
Ciudad Victoria

Ciudad de Valles

Tuxpan

Poza Rica
Papantla

Pachuca
Tulancingo

MEXICO
DISTRITO FEDERAL
Nezahualcóyotl
Toluca

TLAXCALA

Puebla
Cholula

MORELOS
Cuernavaca

PUEBLA

Bahía de Campeche

Veracruz
Córdoba
Orizaba

Coatzacoalcos
Minatitlán

TABASCO

Istmo de Tehuantepec

Acapulco
Chilpancingo

OAXACA

Oaxaca

SIERRA MADRE DEL SUR

CHIAPAS

SIERRA MADRE DE CHIAPAS

Golfo de Tehuantepec

MEXICO CITY
1:60 000
0 METRES 500
0 YARDS 500

ANAHUAC
TLAXPANA
SAN RAFAEL
GUERRERO
CENTRO
TRANSITO
CUAUHTEMOC
JUAREZ
ROMA NORTE
DOCTORES
OBRERA
CONDESA
CENTRO URBANO B. JUAREZ
ROMA SUR

MILES   KILOMETRES
125   200
          175
100   150
          125
75   100
          75
50
          50
25
          25
0   0

1:3 000 000

© Collins Bartholomew Ltd

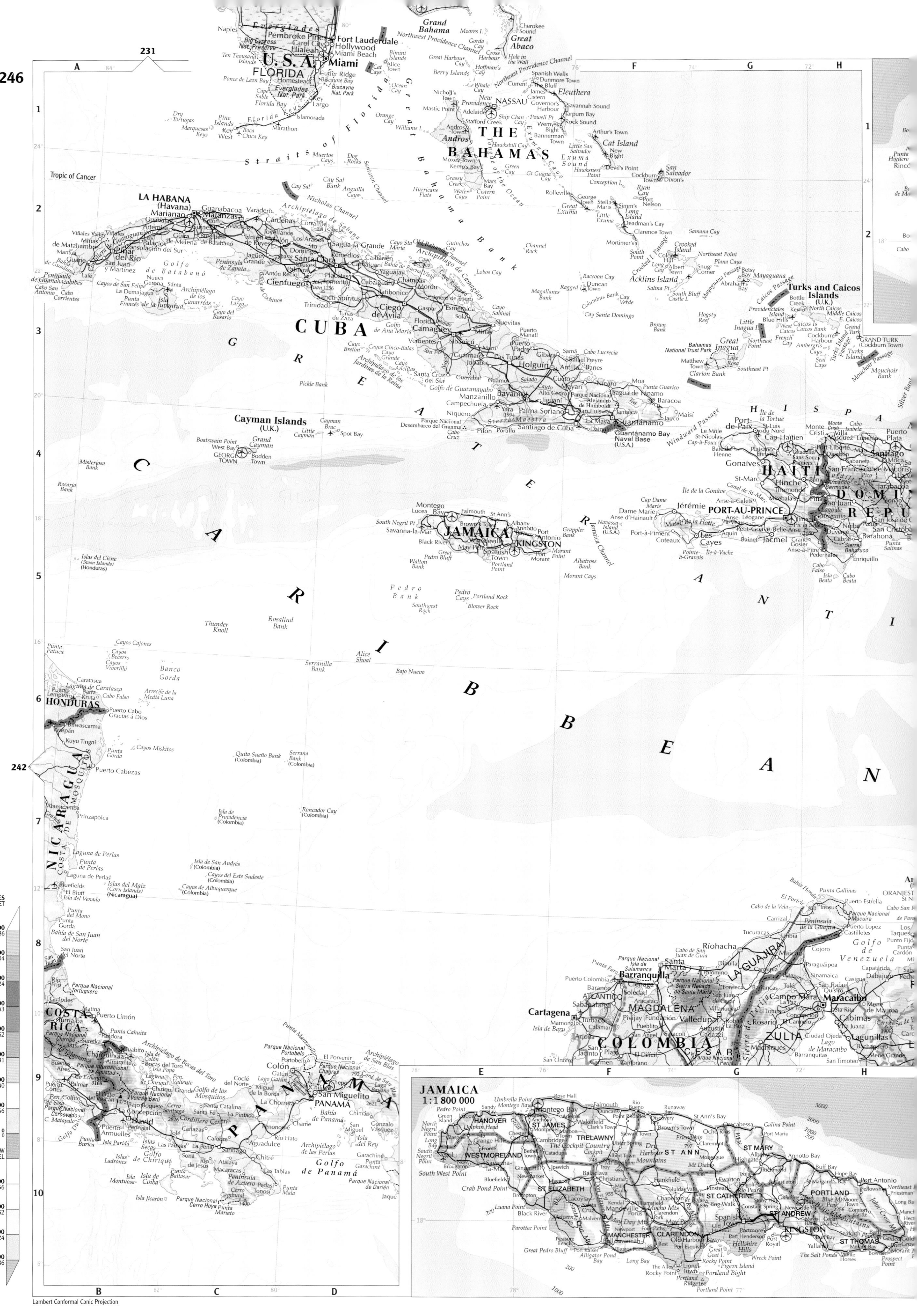

231

A 84 B 82 C 80 D

U.S.A.
FLORIDA

Naples
Everglades
Big Cypress
Nat. Preserve
Pembroke Pines
Hollywood
Hialeah
Miami Beach
Miami
Fort Lauderdale
Ten Thousand
Islands
Homestead
Carol City
Everglades
Nat. Park
Cutler Ridge
Biscayne
Nat. Park
Ponce de Leon Bay
Sable
Cape
Florida Bay
Key
Largo
Islamorada
Marathon
Boca
Chica Key
Key West
Marquesas
Keys
Dry
Tortugas
Pine
Islands

Grand Bahama
Moores I.
West End
Northwest Providence Channel
Great
Abaco
Cherokee
Sound
Hole in
the Wall
Grand
Bahama

Freeport
Grand Harbour
Cross
Harbour
Great Harbour

Bimini
Islands
Cat
Cays
Alice
Town
Gun
Cay
Berry
Islands
Whale
Cay
Nichol's
Town
Andros
Town
Mastic Point
Nicholl's Town
Fresh Creek
NASSAU
New Providence
Spanish Wells
Dunmore Town
Harbour I.
Eleuthera
Rock Sound
Cat Island
Arthur's Town
New Bight
San Salvador
Cockburn Town
Dixon's
Rum Cay
Conception I.

THE BAHAMAS

Governor's Harbour
Gt Exuma
George Town
Rolleville
Long Island
Clarence Town
Samana Cay
Mortimer's
Acklins Island
Crooked Island
Plana Cays
Mayaguana
Betsy Bay
Abraham's Bay

Turks and Caicos Islands (U.K.)
Providenciales
North Caicos
Middle Caicos
East Caicos
South Caicos
GRAND TURK (Cockburn Town)
Salt Cay

Straits of Florida

Tropic of Cancer

LA HABANA (Havana)
Marianao
Guanabacoa
Matanzas
Cárdenas
Varadero
Jovellanos
Colón
Los Arabos
Sagua la Grande
Remedios
Caibarién
Santa Clara
Sancti Spíritus
CUBA
Ciego de Ávila
Cienfuegos
Trinidad
Morón
Nuevitas
Camagüey
Las Tunas
Holguín
Bayamo
Manzanillo
Santiago de Cuba
Guantánamo
Guantánamo Bay Naval Base (U.S.A.)
Sierra Maestra
Pinar del Río
San Juan y Martínez
Nueva Gerona
Isla de la Juventud

Golfo de Batabanó

Península de Zapata

Cayman Islands (U.K.)
Grand Cayman
GEORGE TOWN
Little Cayman
Cayman Brac

Golfo de Guacanayabo

Windward Passage

HAITI
PORT-AU-PRINCE
Cap-Haïtien
Gonaïves
St-Marc
Hinche
Jérémie
Les Cayes
Jacmel
Île de la Gonâve

DOMINICAN REPUBLIC
Santiago
Puerto Plata

HISPANIOLA

Montego Bay
Falmouth
St Ann's
JAMAICA
KINGSTON
Spanish Town
Savanna-la-Mar
Black River
May Pen
Port Antonio
Morant Point
South Negril Pt
Portland Point

Pedro Bank

Rosalind Bank
Thunder Knoll

Serranilla Bank
Alice Shoal

Quita Sueño Bank
(Colombia)
Serrana Bank
(Colombia)
Bajo Nuevo

HONDURAS
Puerto Cabezas
Cabo Gracias á Dios
Cayos Miskitos

NICARAGUA
Prinzapolca
Bluefields
El Bluff
Islas del Maíz
(Corn Islands)
(Nicaragua)
Laguna de Perlas

Isla de Providencia
(Colombia)
Roncador Cay
(Colombia)
Isla de San Andrés
(Colombia)
Cayos del Este Sudeste
(Colombia)
Cayos de Albuquerque
(Colombia)

COSTA RICA
Puerto Limón
David
PANAMA
PANAMÁ
Colón
Parque Nacional Portobelo
Archipiélago de San Blas
Golfo de Panamá
Golfo de los Mosquitos

COLOMBIA
Cartagena
Barranquilla
Santa Marta
Ríohacha
Valledupar
Maicao
Punta Gallinas
Península de la Guajira
LA GUAJIRA
MAGDALENA
ATLÁNTICO
CESAR
Golfo de Venezuela
Maracaibo
Cabimas
ZULIA
Lago de Maracaibo
Lagunillas

C A R I B B E A N **S E A**

METRES / FEET
6000 19686
5000 16404
4000 13124
3000 9843
2000 6562
1000 3281
500 1640
200 656
0
LAND BELOW SEA LEVEL
200 656
2000 6562
4000 13124
6000 19686

242

JAMAICA
1:1 800 000

E 78 F 76 G 74 H

Montego Bay
HANOVER
ST JAMES
TRELAWNY
ST ANN
ST MARY
PORTLAND
WESTMORELAND
Savanna-la-Mar
ST ELIZABETH
MANCHESTER
CLARENDON
ST CATHERINE
ST ANDREW
KINGSTON
ST THOMAS
Spanish Town
The Cockpit Country
Blue Mountains
Port Antonio
Morant Bay
Black River
Mandeville
May Pen
Portland Point
Portland Bight

Lambert Conformal Conic Projection

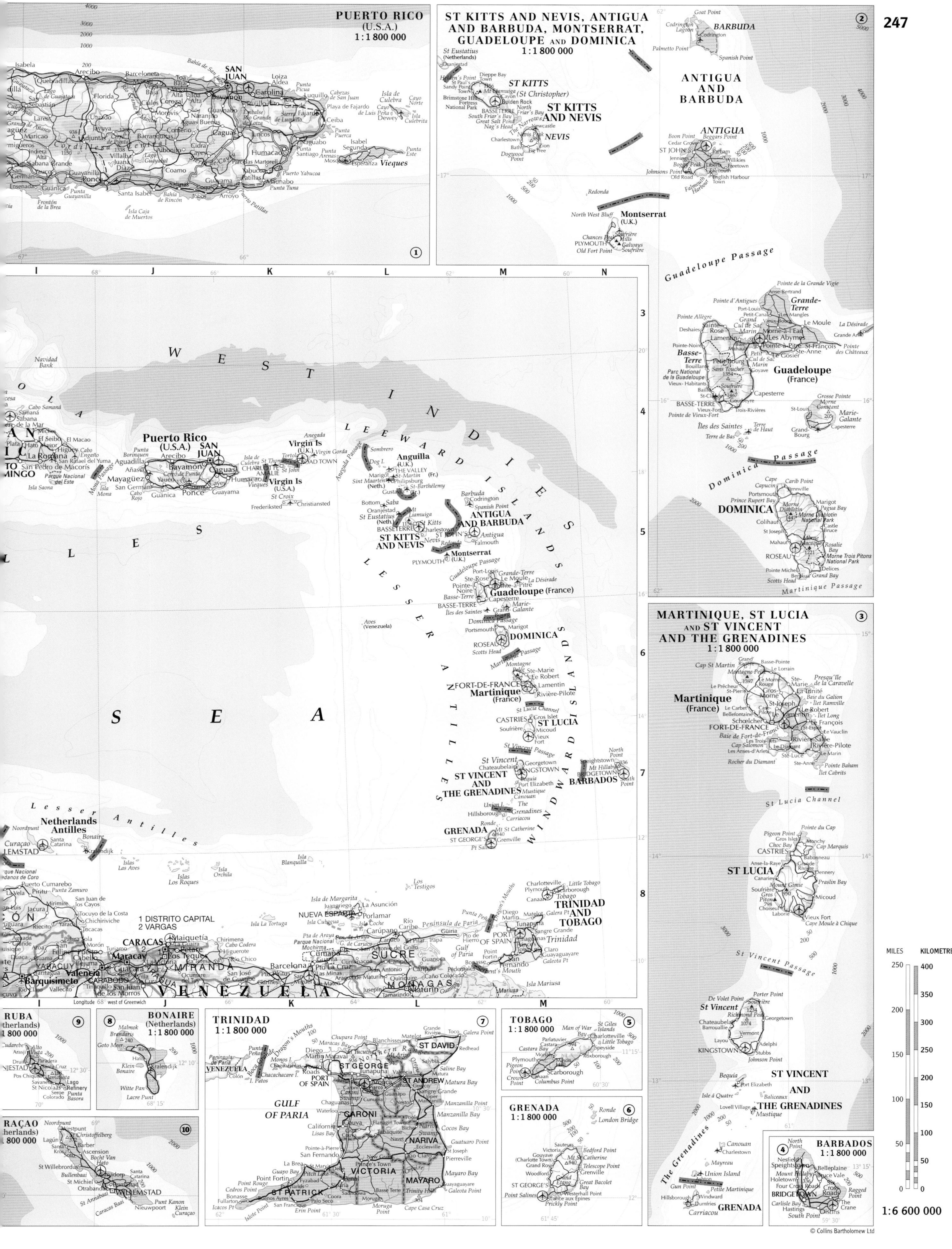
PUERTO RICO
(U.S.A.)
1 : 1 800 000
ST KITTS AND NEVIS, ANTIGUA AND BARBUDA, MONTSERRAT, GUADELOUPE AND DOMINICA
1 : 1 800 000
ST KITTS AND NEVIS
ANTIGUA AND BARBUDA
Montserrat
(U.K.)
Guadeloupe Passage
Guadeloupe
(France)
Dominica Passage
DOMINICA
Martinique Passage
MARTINIQUE, ST LUCIA AND ST VINCENT AND THE GRENADINES
1 : 1 800 000
Martinique
(France)
St Lucia Channel
ST LUCIA
St Vincent Passage
ST VINCENT AND THE GRENADINES
GRENADA
WEST INDIES
LEEWARD ISLANDS
LESSER ANTILLES
WINDWARD ISLANDS
SEA
Puerto Rico
(U.S.A.)
Virgin Is
(U.K.)
Virgin Is
(U.S.A.)
Anguilla
(U.K.)
TRINIDAD AND TOBAGO
BARBADOS
Netherlands Antilles
VENEZUELA
1 DISTRITO CAPITAL
2 VARGAS
ARUBA
(Netherlands)
1 : 1 800 000
BONAIRE
(Netherlands)
1 : 1 800 000
CURAÇAO
(Netherlands)
1 : 1 800 000
TRINIDAD
1 : 1 800 000
GULF OF PARIA
TOBAGO
1 : 1 800 000
GRENADA
1 : 1 800 000
BARBADOS
1 : 1 800 000
MILES
KILOMETRES
1:6 600 000

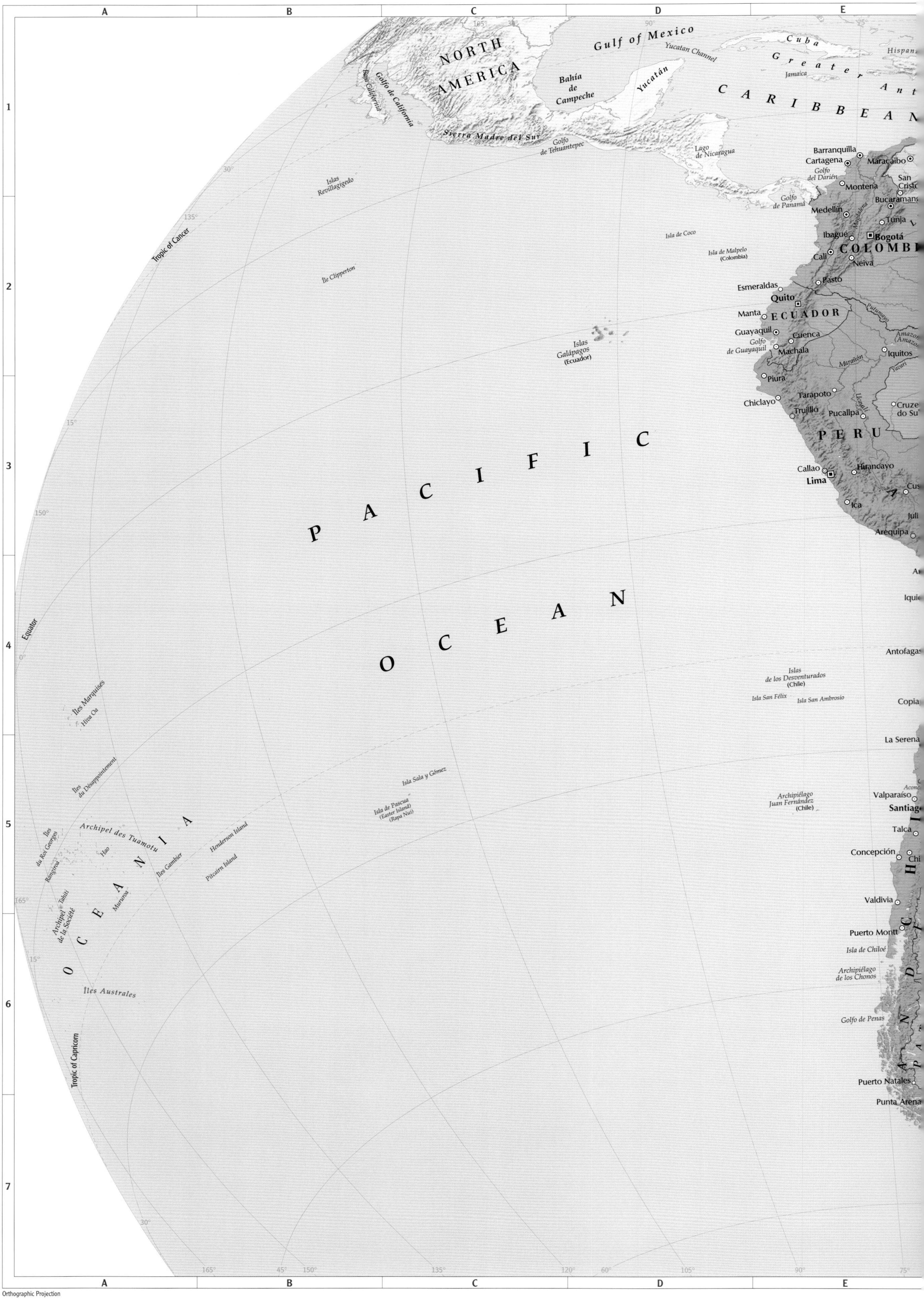

	A	B	C	D	E

NORTH AMERICA

Gulf of Mexico

Cuba

Hispan

Yucatan Channel

G r e a t e r

Bahía
de
Campeche

Yucatán

Ant

Jamaica

C A R I B B E A N

Golfo de California

Sierra Madre del Sur

Golfo
de Tehuantepec

Lago
de Nicaragua

Barranquilla

Cartagena

Maracaibo

*Golfo
del Darién*

San
Crist

Montería

Bucaraman

Islas
Revillagigedo

Medellín

*Golfo
de Panamá*

Tunja

Bogotá

Tropic of Cancer

135°

Ile Clipperton

Isla de Coco

Ibagué

Cali

COLOMBIA

Neiva

Isla de Malpelo
(Colombia)

Esmeraldas

Pasto

Quito

30°

Manta

ECUADOR

Islas
Galápagos
(Ecuador)

Guayaquil

Cuenca

Amazon

*Golfo
de Guayaquil*

Machala

Iquitos

Piura

Marañón

Tarapoto

Cruze
do Su

Chiclayo

15°

Trujillo

Pucallpa

P A C I F I C

P E R U

150°

Callao

Huancayo

Lima

Cus

Ica

Juli

O C E A N

Arequipa

A

Iquiqu

Equator

0°

Antofagas

*Islas
de los Desventurados
(Chile)*

Isla San Félix

Isla San Ambrosio

Copiap

Iles Marquises

Hiva Oa

La Serena

Iles du Désappointement

Isla Sala y Gómez

*Archipiélago
Juan Fernández
(Chile)*

Valparaíso

Acon

Santiag

Isla de Pascua
(Easter Island)
(Rapa Nui)

Archipel des Tuamotu

Talca

Iles

du Roi George

Hao

Concepción

Ch

Henderson Island

165°

Rangiroa

Tahiti

Archipel

de la Société

Moorea

Iles Gambier

Pitcairn Island

Valdivia

Puerto Montt

Isla de Chiloé

15°

O C E A N I A

*Archipiélago
de los Chonos*

Iles Australes

Golfo de Penas

Tropic of Capricorn

Puerto Natales

Punta Arena

30°

	A	B	C	D	E

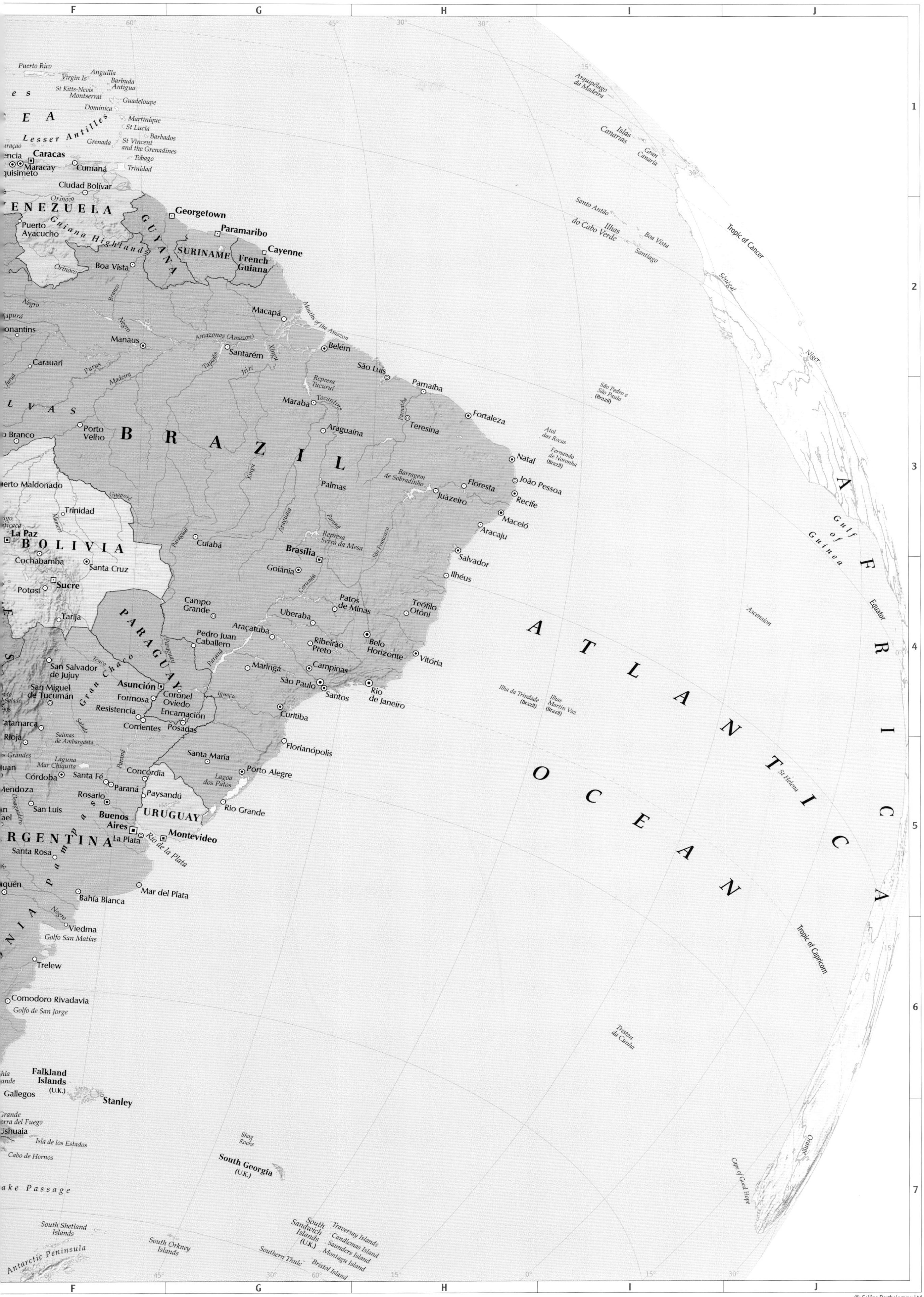

Puerto Rico
Virgin Is · Anguilla
Barbuda
St Kitts-Nevis · Antigua
Montserrat
Dominica
Guadeloupe

Lesser Antilles
Martinique
St Lucia
Grenada · Barbados
St Vincent
and the Grenadines
Tobago
Trinidad

Caracas
Maracay · Cumaná
quisimeto

Ciudad Bolívar

ENEZUELA
Orinoco
Puerto
Ayacucho
Guiana Highlands
GUYANA
Georgetown
Paramaribo
SURINAME
French
Guiana · **Cayenne**
Boa Vista
Orinoco

Georgetown

Macapá

Negro
Branco

Manaus
Amazonas (Amazon)
Santarém
Tapajós
Iriri

*Represa
Tucuruí*

Belém

Meuths of the Amazon

Carauari
Purus
Madeira

São Luís
Parnaíba

Maraba
Tocantins

Teresina
Fortaleza

Porto
Velho
Xingu

Araguaína
Parnaíba

Natal
João Pessoa
Recife

B R A Z I L

Palmas
*Barragem
de Sobradinho*

Floresta
Juàzeiro

Maceió
Aracaju

Cuiabá

Brasília
Goiânia
Salvador

Ilhéus

Campo
Grande

Patos
de Minas
Uberaba
Teófilo
Otôni

Araçatuba
Ribeirão
Preto
Belo
Horizonte

Maringá
Campinas
Vitória

São Paulo
Santos
Rio
de Janeiro

Curitiba

Florianópolis

Santa Maria

Concórdia
Porto Alegre
*Lagoa
dos Patos*

A T L A N T I C

O C E A N

Tropic of Capricorn

*Arquipélago
da Madeira*

*Islas
Canárias*
*Gran
Canária*

Tropic of Cancer

Santo Antão
*Ilhas
do Cabo Verde*
Boa Vista
Santiago

*São Pedro e
São Paulo
(Brazil)*

*Atol
das Rocas*
*Fernando
de Noronha
(Brazil)*

A F R I C A

*Gulf
of
Guinea*

Equator

Ascension

*Ilha da Trindade
(Brazil)*
*Ilhas
Martin Vaz
(Brazil)*

St Helena

Tristan
da Cunha

Niger

Senegal

MILES   KILOMETRES
1000   1500
        1250
750   1000
500   750
        500
250   250
0   0

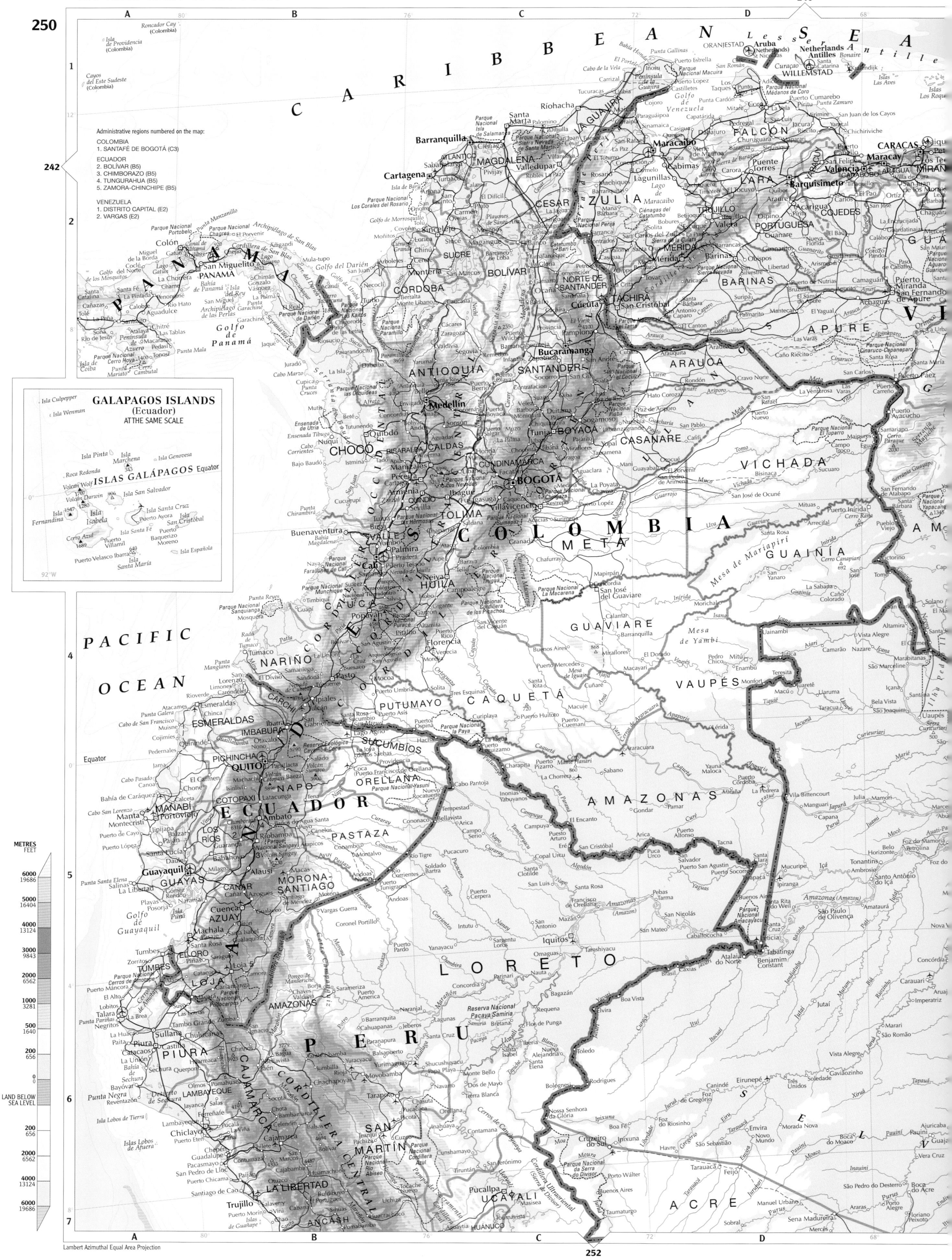

Administrative regions numbered on the map:

COLOMBIA
1. SANTAFÉ DE BOGOTÁ (C3)

ECUADOR
2. BOLÍVAR (B5)
3. CHIMBORAZO (B5)
4. TUNGURAHUA (B5)
5. ZAMORA-CHINCHIPE (B5)

VENEZUELA
1. DISTRITO CAPITAL (E2)
2. VARGAS (E2)

GALAPAGOS ISLANDS
(Ecuador)
AT THE SAME SCALE

Isla Culpepper
Isla Wenman
Isla Pinta   Isla Marchena   Isla Genovesa
Roca Redonda
Volcán Wolf 1707 Isla San Salvador
Darwin 906
1547 Isla Santa Cruz
Isla Fernandina   Cerro Azul Isla Isabela 1689 Puerto Ayora
Puerto Villamil 640
Isla Santa Fé
San Cristóbal
Baquerizo Moreno
Puerto Velasco Ibarra
Isla Santa María   Isla Española

ISLAS GALÁPAGOS   Equator

92°W

CARIBBEAN SEA

Lesser Antilles

PACIFIC

OCEAN

PANAMA

COLOMBIA

ECUADOR

VENEZUELA

PERU

ANDES

CORDILLERA CENTRAL

AMAZONAS

Equator

METRES / FEET
6000 / 19686
5000 / 16404
4000 / 13124
3000 / 9843
2000 / 6562
1000 / 3281
500 / 1640
200 / 656
0 / 0
LAND BELOW SEA LEVEL
200 / 656
2000 / 6562
4000 / 13124
6000 / 19686

247

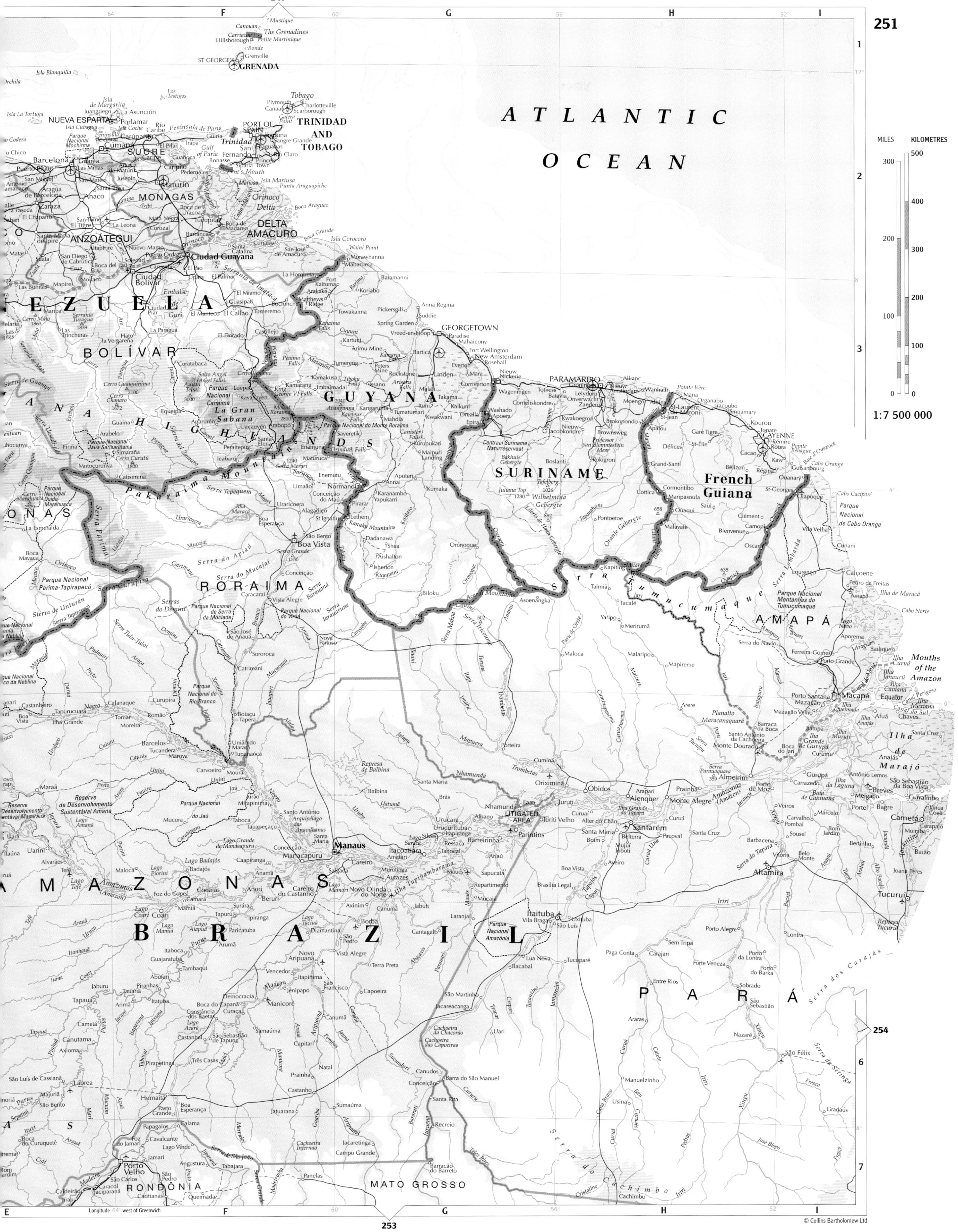

F · G · H · I

ATLANTIC
OCEAN

MILES · KILOMETRES

1:7 500 000

GRENADA

The Grenadines
Carriacou
Hillsborough · Petite Martinique
ST GEORGE'S
Ronde
Grenville
Mustique
Canouan

Tobago
Plymouth · Scarborough
Charlotteville
Canaan
Galera Point
TRINIDAD AND TOBAGO
PORT OF SPAIN
San Fernando
Trinidad
Gulf of Paria
Península de Paria

NUEVA ESPARTA
Isla de Margarita
La Asunción
Porlamar
Isla Coche
Isla Cubagua

Barcelona
Puerto La Cruz
SUCRE
Cumaná
MONAGAS
Maturín
ANZOÁTEGUI
El Tigre
Anaco

Orinoco
Delta
Boca de Uracoa
DELTA AMACURO
Boca Grande

Ciudad Guayana
Ciudad Bolívar
Embalse de Guri

VENEZUELA
BOLÍVAR

GEORGETOWN
New Amsterdam
GUYANA

La Gran Sabana
Santa Elena
GUIANA HIGHLANDS

Pakaraima Mountains

PARAMARIBO
Nieuw Nickerie
SURINAME

CAYENNE
French Guiana
St-Laurent
Kourou

Boa Vista
RORAIMA

Serra Parima

Parque Nacional Pico da Neblina

AMAPÁ
Macapá
Equator

Mouths of the Amazon

Ilha de Marajó

Parque Nacional Montanhas do Tumucumaque

A M A Z O N A S

B R A Z I L

Manaus
Manacapuru

RONDÔNIA
Porto Velho

MATO GROSSO

P A R Á

Santarém
Altamira
Tucuruí

Serra dos Carajás

253

254

METRES / FEET

METRES	FEET
6000	19686
5000	16404
4000	13124
3000	9843
2000	6562
1000	3281
500	1640
200	656
0	0

LAND BELOW SEA LEVEL

200	656
2000	6562
4000	13124
6000	19686

PACIFIC

OCEAN

Tropic of Capricorn

JUAN FERNÁNDEZ ISLANDS
(Chile)
AT THE SAME SCALE

San Juan   Isla
Bautista   Robinson
1650   Crusoe
Isla
Alejandro Selkirk
Isla Santa Clara

Archipiélago Juan Fernández

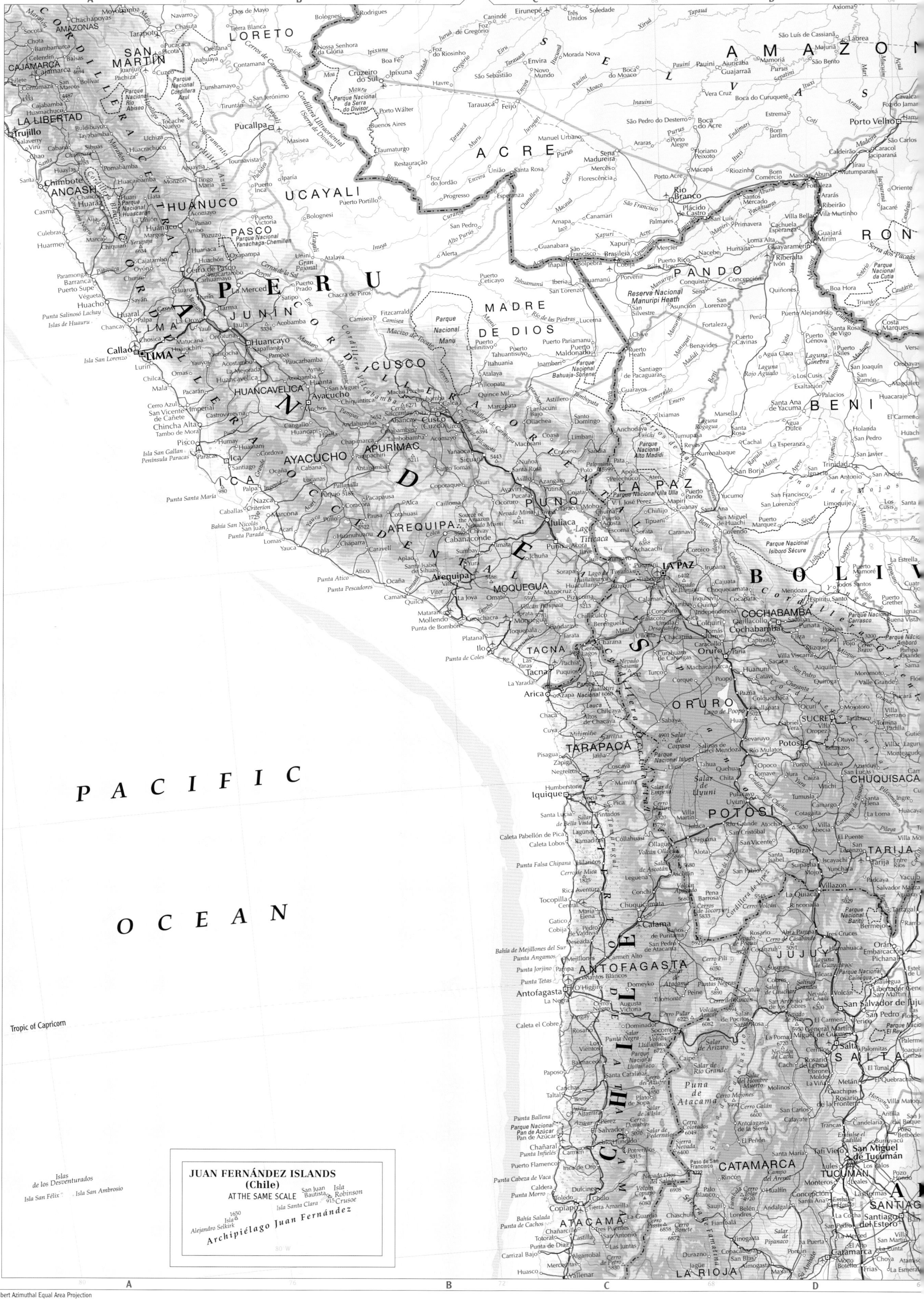

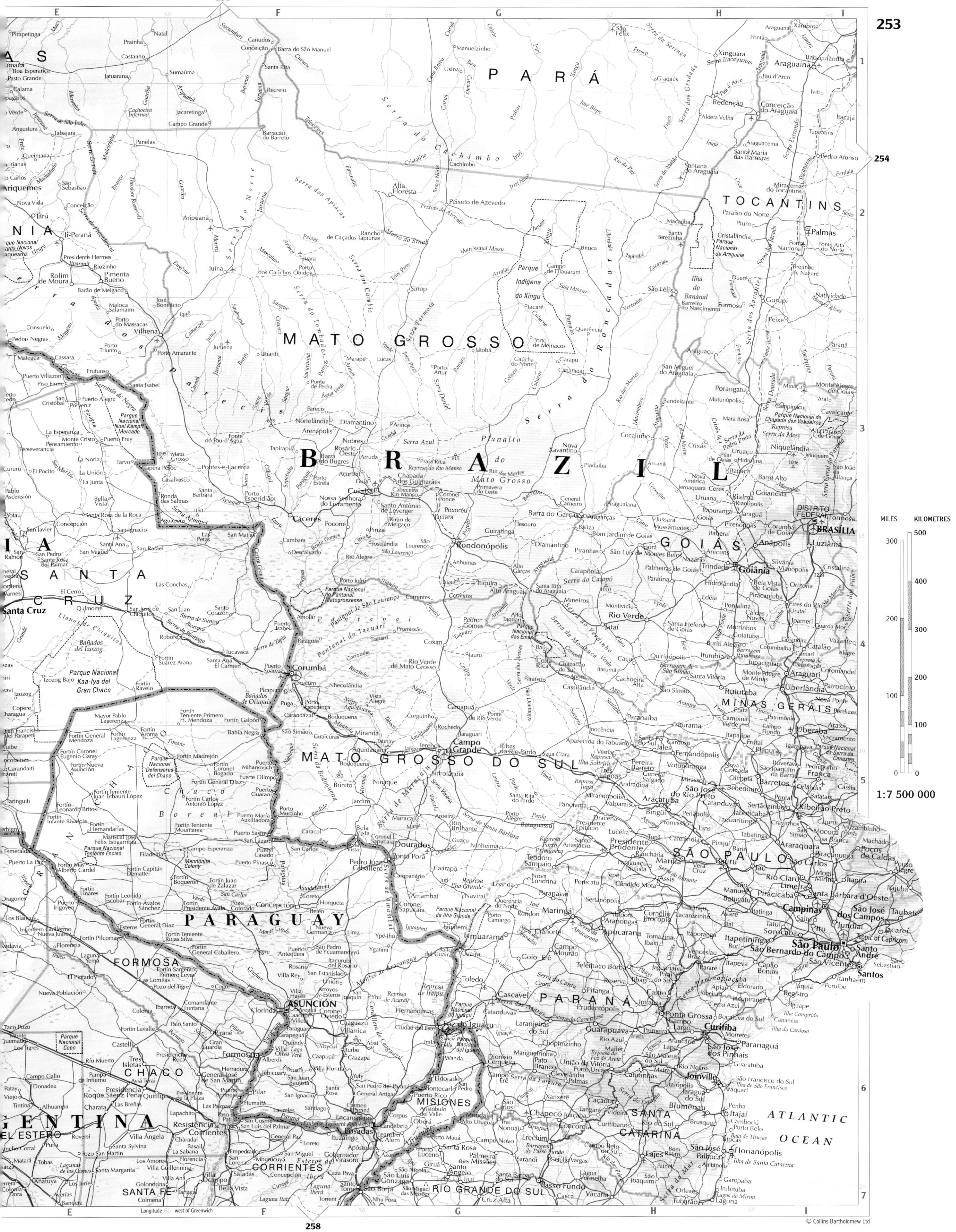

251

PARÁ

TOCANTINS

MATO GROSSO

B R A Z I L

GOIÁS

DISTRITO FEDERAL

BRASÍLIA

Goiânia

Anápolis

Luziânia

MINAS GERAIS

Uberlândia

Uberaba

Araguari

MATO GROSSO DO SUL

Campo Grande

SÃO PAULO

São Paulo

Campinas

São José dos Campos

Santos

São Bernardo do Campo

Santo André

São Vicente

Tropic of Capricorn

PARANÁ

Curitiba

Ponta Grossa

Joinville

SANTA CATARINA

Blumenau

Florianópolis

Itajaí

ATLANTIC OCEAN

RIO GRANDE DO SUL

Passo Fundo

Lajes

PARAGUAY

ASUNCIÓN

CHACO

FORMOSA

CORRIENTES

MISIONES

Posadas

Resistencia

Corrientes

SANTA FÉ

ARGENTINA

SANTA CRUZ

Santa Cruz

BOLIVIA

RONDÔNIA

Ji-Paraná

Vilhena

Parque Nacional Noel Kempff Mercado

Parque Nacional Kaa-Iya del Gran Chaco

Pantanal

Corumbá

Cuiabá

Rondonópolis

Planalto do Mato Grosso

Serra dos Parecis

Serra do Roncador

Serra do Norte

Ilha do Bananal

Palmas

Parque Indígena do Xingu

Parque Nacional de Araguaia

MILES   KILOMETRES

300   500

400

200   300

200

100   100

0   0

1:7 500 000

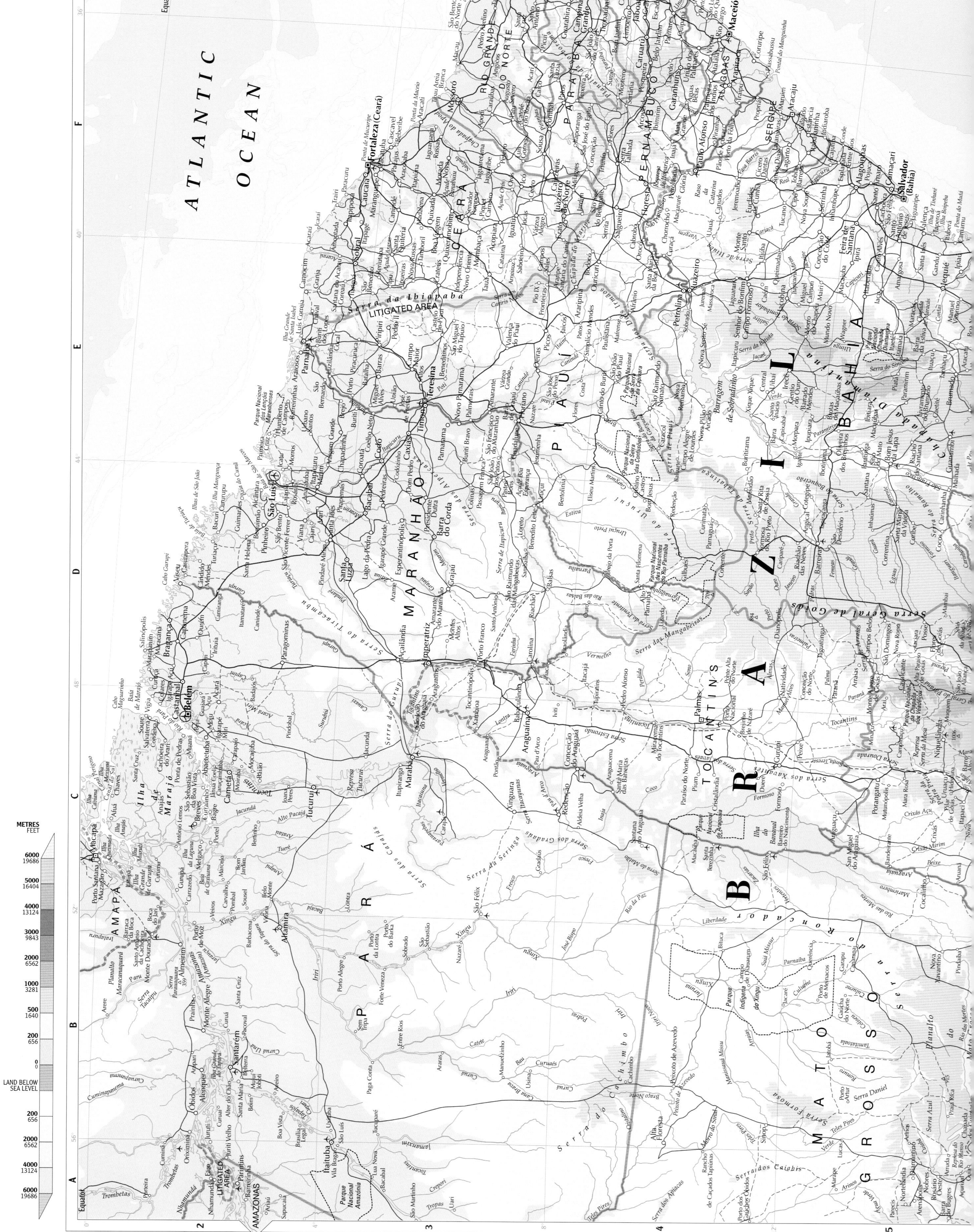

ATLANTIC

OCEAN

Equator

B R A Z I L

MARANHÃO

PIAUÍ

CEARÁ

RIO GRANDE DO NORTE

PARAÍBA

PERNAMBUCO

ALAGOAS

SERGIPE

BAHIA

TOCANTINS

PARÁ

AMAPÁ

AMAZONAS

MATO GROSSO

Serra Geral de Goiás

Serra dos Caiapós

Serra do Roncador

Natal
João Pessoa
Recife
Olinda
Maceió
Aracaju
Salvador (Bahia)
Camaçari
Fortaleza (Ceará)
Teresina
São Luís
Belém
Macapá
Santarém
Imperatriz
Marabá
Palmas
Araguaína
Parnaíba

LITIGATED AREA

Serra da Ibiapaba

Serra do Tiracambu

Ilha de Marajó

Chapada Diamantina

Parque Nacional Amazônia

Parque Indígena do Xingu

METRES	FEET
6000	19686
5000	16404
4000	13124
3000	9843
2000	6562
1000	3281
500	1640
200	656
0	0

LAND BELOW SEA LEVEL

200	656
2000	6562
4000	13124
6000	19686

Lambert Azimuthal Equal Area Projection

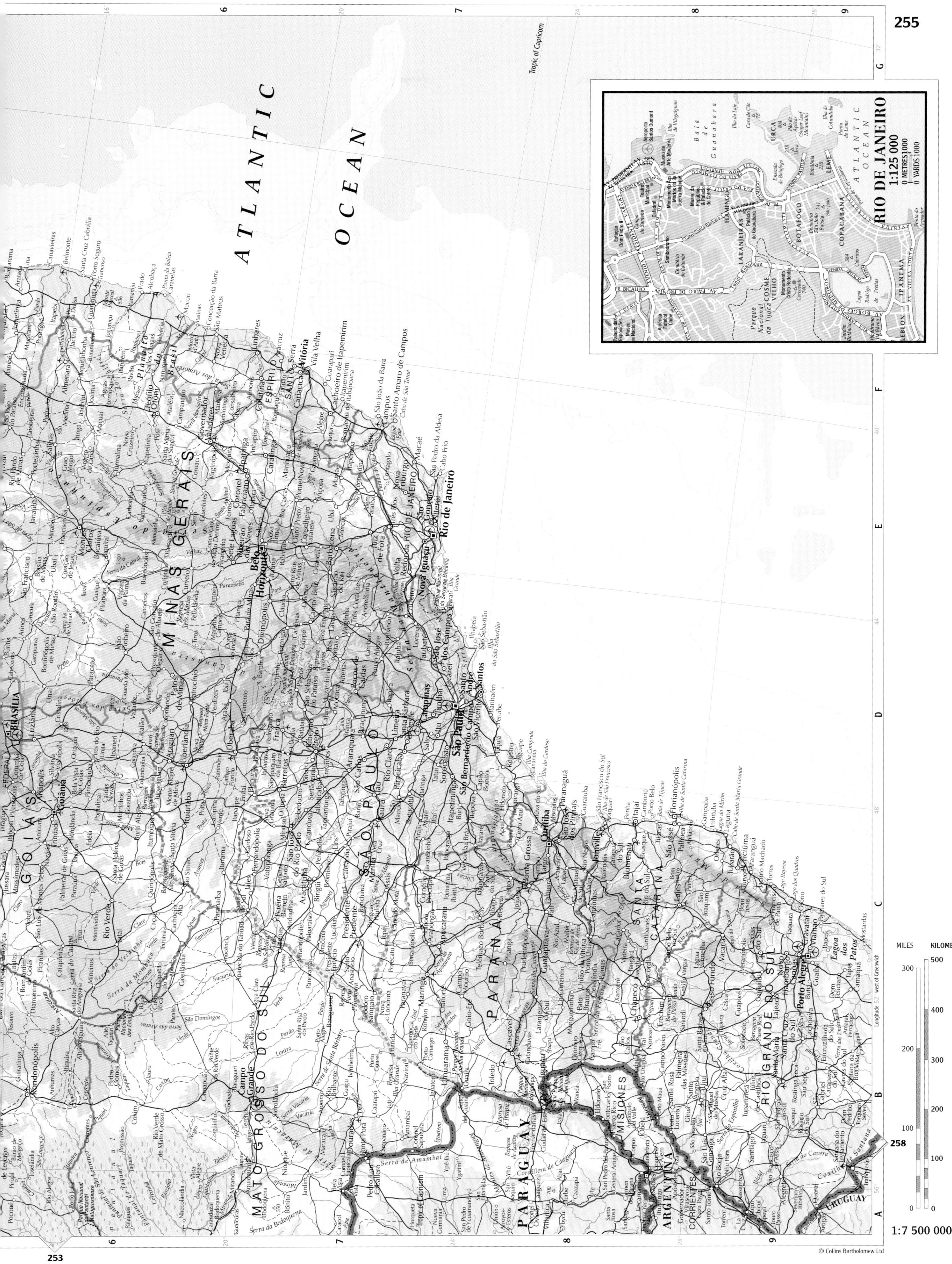

ATLANTIC

OCEAN

RIO DE JANEIRO
1:125 000

MINAS GERAIS

ESPÍRITO SANTO

Vitória
Vila Velha

RIO DE JANEIRO

Rio de Janeiro

Belo Horizonte

BRASÍLIA

DISTRITO FEDERAL

GOIÁS

Goiânia

MATO GROSSO DO SUL

Campo Grande

SÃO PAULO

São Paulo
São Bernardo do Campo
Santos

Campinas

PARANÁ

Curitiba

SANTA CATARINA

Florianópolis

RIO GRANDE DO SUL

Porto Alegre

PARAGUAY

ARGENTINA

CORRIENTES

MISIONES

URUGUAY

Tropic of Capricorn

Longitude 52° west of Greenwich

MILES   KILOMETRES
300   500
          400
200   300
          200
100   100
0   0

MATO GROSSO

GOIÁS

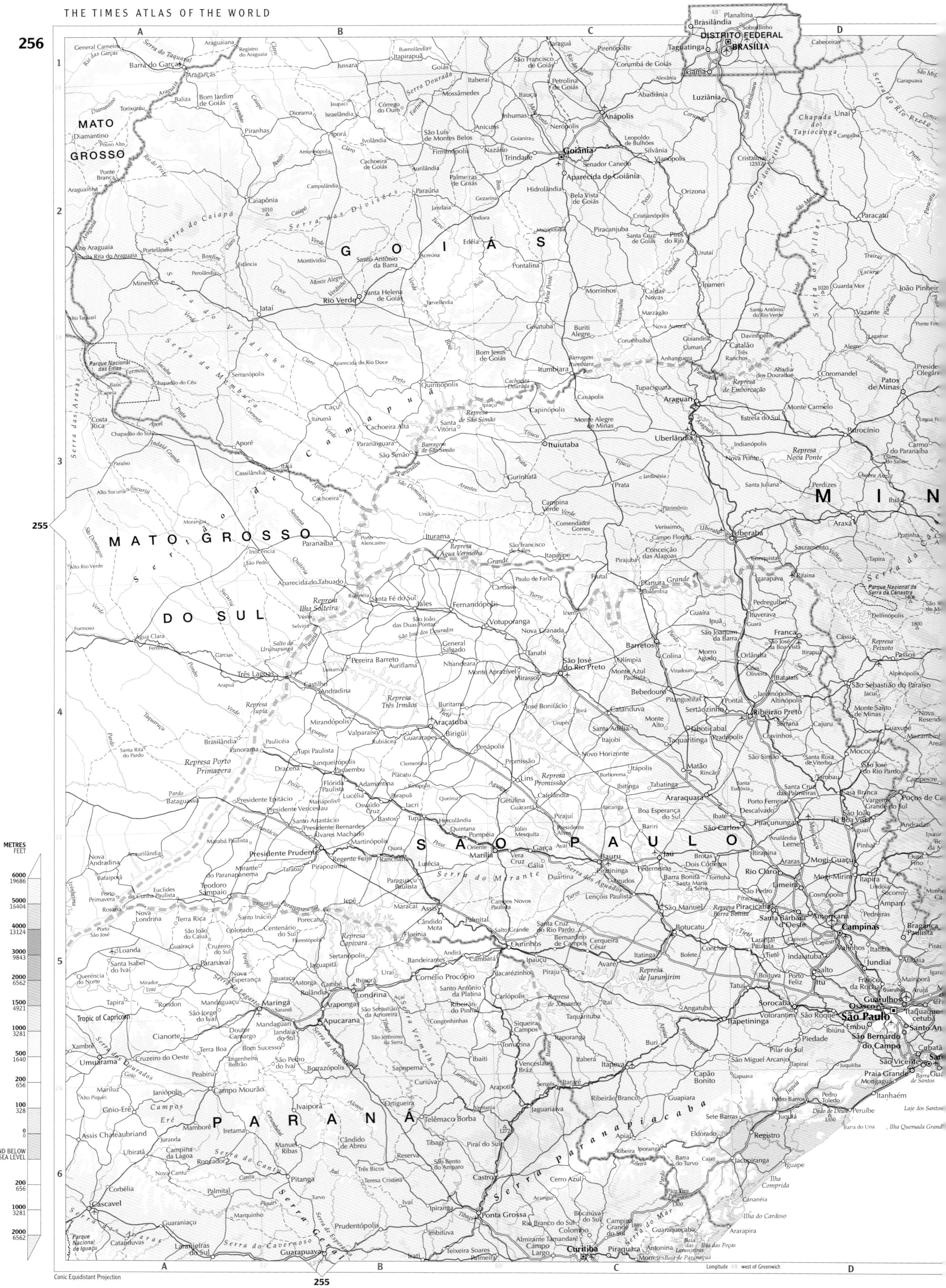

DISTRITO FEDERAL

BRASÍLIA

Goiânia

Anápolis

Luziânia

M I N

Uberlândia

Uberaba

Ituiutaba

Araguari

MATO GROSSO DO SUL

Paranaíba

Três Lagoas

SÃO PAULO

São José do Rio Preto

Ribeirão Preto

Araraquara

Bauru

Franca

Campinas

Presidente Prudente

São Paulo

Osasco

São Bernardo do Campo

Sorocaba

Jundiaí

Guarulhos

PARANÁ

Maringá

Londrina

Apucarana

Cascavel

Campo Mourão

Ponta Grossa

Curitiba

METRES / FEET

6000 / 19686
5000 / 16404
4000 / 13124
3000 / 9843
2000 / 6562
1500 / 4921
1000 / 3281
500 / 1640
200 / 656
100 / 328
0 / 0
LAND BELOW SEA LEVEL
200 / 656
1000 / 3281
2000 / 6562

Tropic of Capricorn

Conic Equidistant Projection

Longitude 48 west of Greenwich

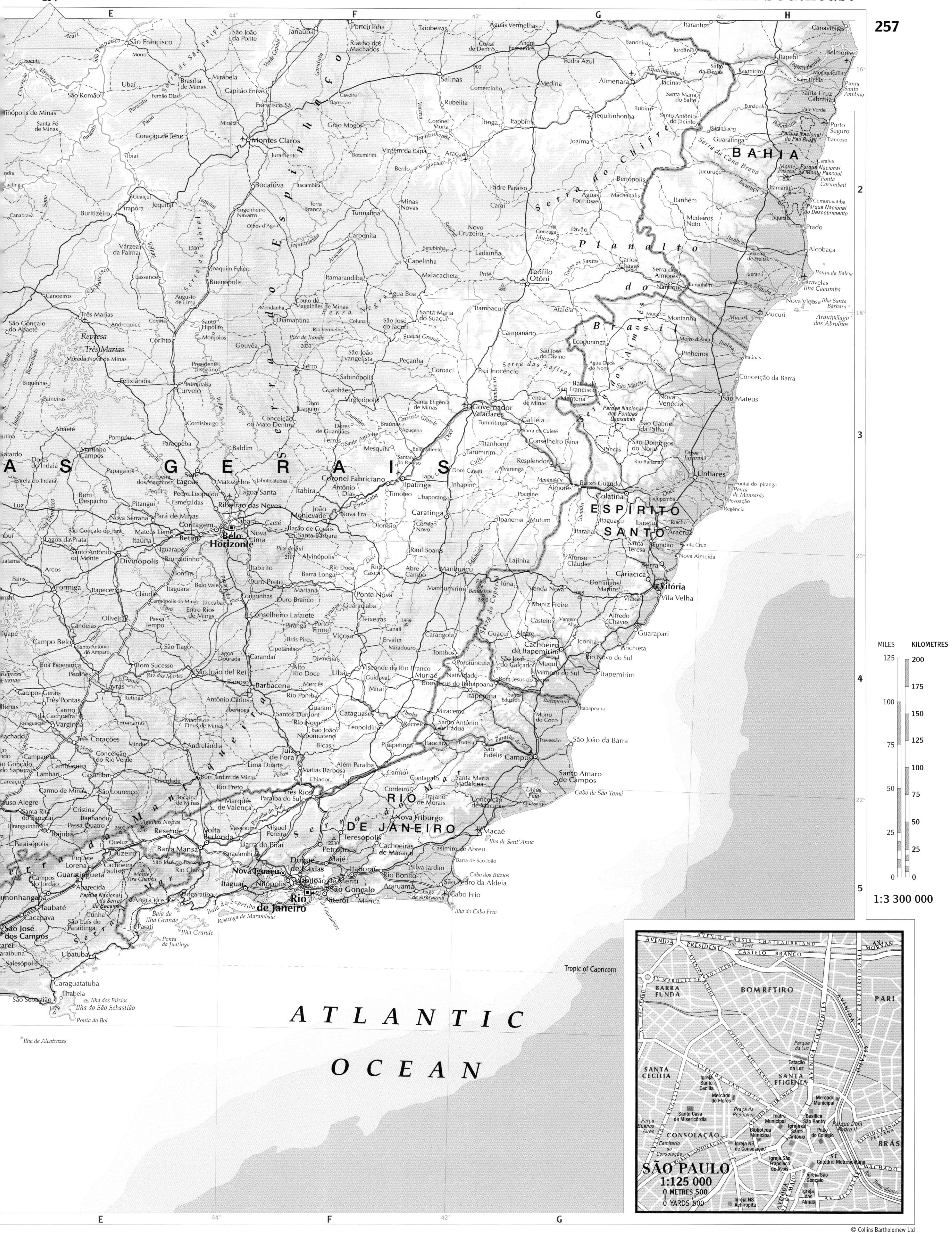

MINAS GERAIS

BAHIA

ESPIRITO SANTO

RIO DE JANEIRO

Belo Horizonte

Rio de Janeiro

Vitória

São Paulo

Tropic of Capricorn

ATLANTIC

OCEAN

MILES KILOMETRES

125 — 200
100 — 150
75 — 100
50 — 75
25 — 50
0 — 0

1:3 300 000

SÃO PAULO
1:125 000
0 METRES 500
0 YARDS 500

© Collins Bartholomew Ltd

255

METRES
FEET

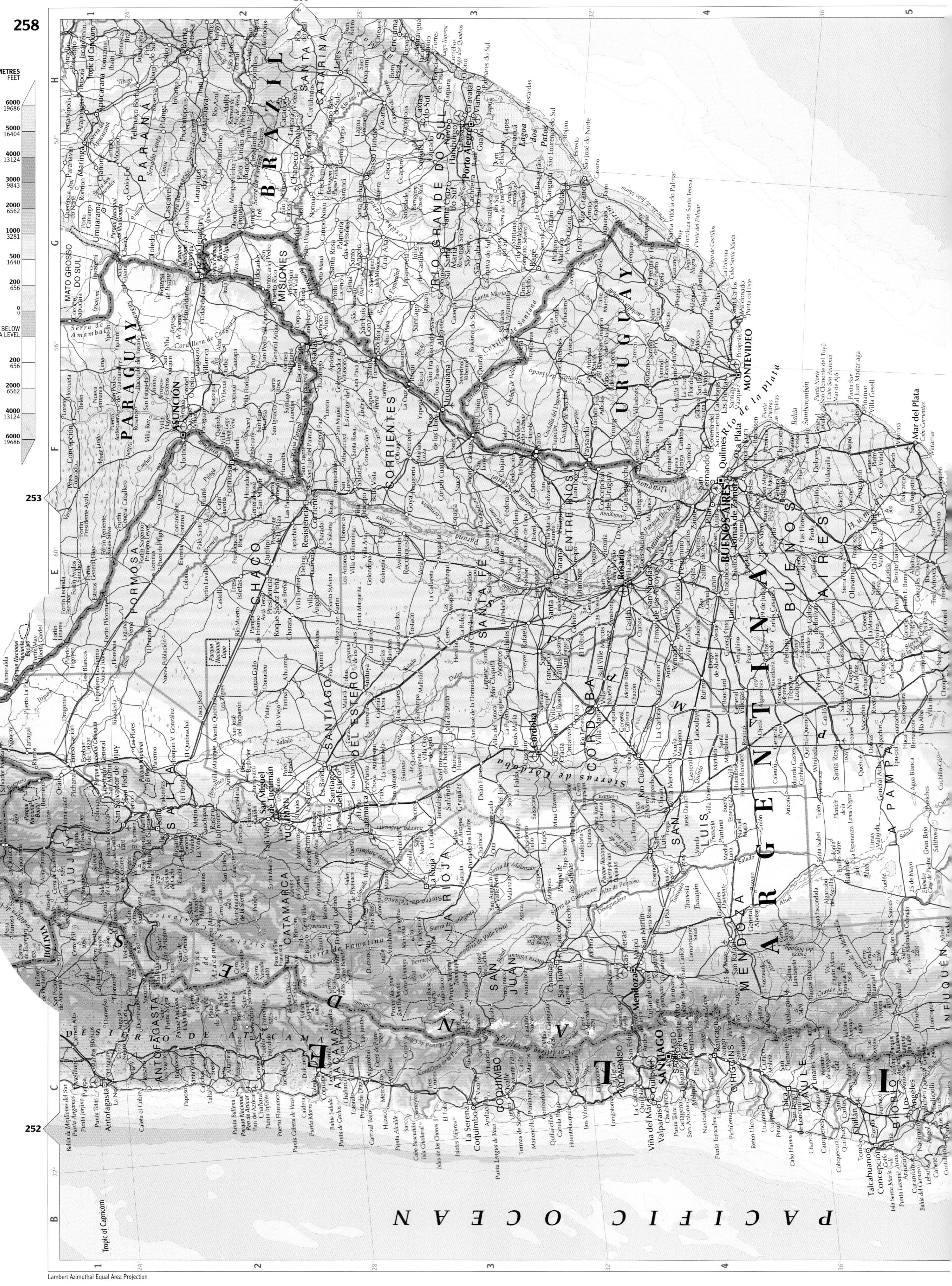

METRES	FEET
6000	19686
5000	16404
4000	13124
3000	9843
2000	6562
1000	3281
500	1640
200	656
0	0

LAND BELOW
SEA LEVEL

200	656
2000	6562
4000	13124
6000	19686

253

252

BRAZIL

PARANÁ

SANTA CATARINA

RIO GRANDE DO SUL

MATO GROSSO DO SUL

PARAGUAY

ASUNCIÓN

MISIONES

URUGUAY

MONTEVIDEO

CORRIENTES

ENTRE RÍOS

BUENOS AIRES

Buenos Aires

Mar del Plata

Río de la Plata

FORMOSA

CHACO

SANTIAGO DEL ESTERO

SANTA FE

Rosario

CÓRDOBA

Córdoba

BOLIVIA

SALTA

JUJUY

TUCUMÁN

CATAMARCA

LA RIOJA

SAN LUIS

SAN JUAN

MENDOZA

Mendoza

LA PAMPA

A R G E N T I N A

DESIERTO DE ATACAMA

ANTOFAGASTA

ATACAMA

COQUIMBO

SANTIAGO

Valparaíso

NEUQUÉN

C H I L E

Tropic of Capricorn

PACIFIC OCEAN

Lambert Azimuthal Equal Area Projection

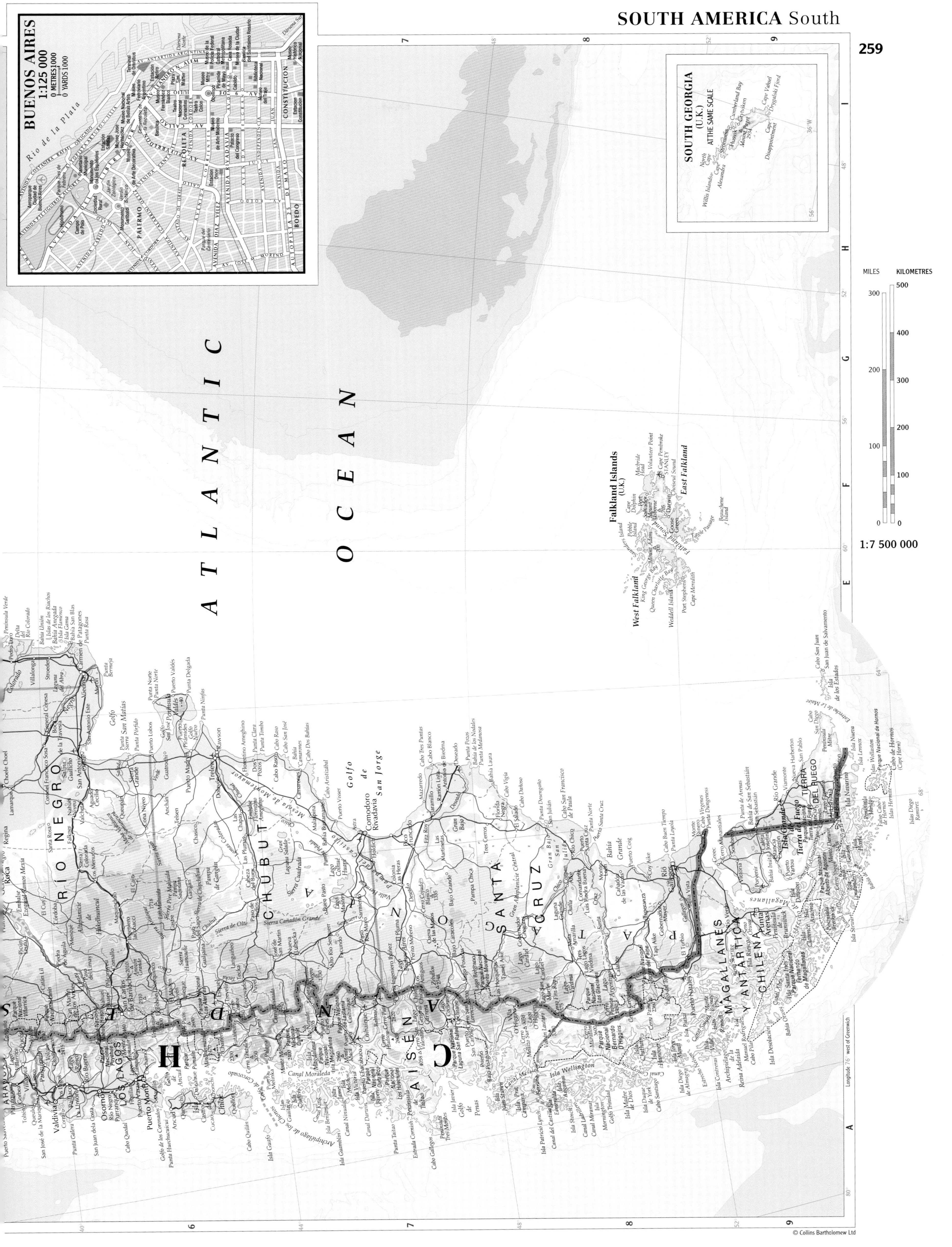
BUENOS AIRES
1:125 000
SOUTH GEORGIA
(U.K.)
AT THE SAME SCALE
ATLANTIC
OCEAN
Falkland Islands
(U.K.)
West Falkland
East Falkland
STANLEY
RÍO NEGRO
CHUBUT
SANTA CRUZ
AISÉN
MAGALLANES Y ANTÁRTICA CHILENA
TIERRA DEL FUEGO
LOS LAGOS
Golfo San Jorge
Comodoro Rivadavia
Puerto Montt
Punta Arenas
Río Gallegos
Isla Grande de Tierra del Fuego
Cabo de Hornos (Cape Horn)
MILES
KILOMETRES
1:7 500 000
Longitude 76° west of Greenwich

PACIFIC OCEAN

COQUIMBO

VALPARAISO

SANTIAGO

O'HIGGINS

MAULE

BÍOBÍO

ARAUCANÍA

SAN JUAN

LA RIOJA

SAN LUIS

MENDOZA

ARGEN **TINA**

PAMPA SECA

LA PAMPA

NEUQUÉN

RIO NEGRO

C O R D I L L E R A   D E   L O S   A N D E S

Cordillera de la Costa

La Serena
Coquimbo
Ovalle
Illapel
Valparaíso
Viña del Mar
Santiago
San Bernardo
Rancagua
San Fernando
Curicó
Talca
Linares
Chillán
Los Ángeles
Temuco
Mendoza
Godoy Cruz
San Rafael
General Alvear
San Luis
Mercedes
Neuquén
General Roca
Cipolletti

Cerro Aconcagua 6959
Cerro Mercedario 6770

METRES FEET
6000 19686
5000 16404
4000 13124
3000 9843
2000 6562
1500 4921
1000 3281
500 1640
200 656
100 328
0 0
LAND BELOW SEA LEVEL
200 656
1000 3281
2000 6562

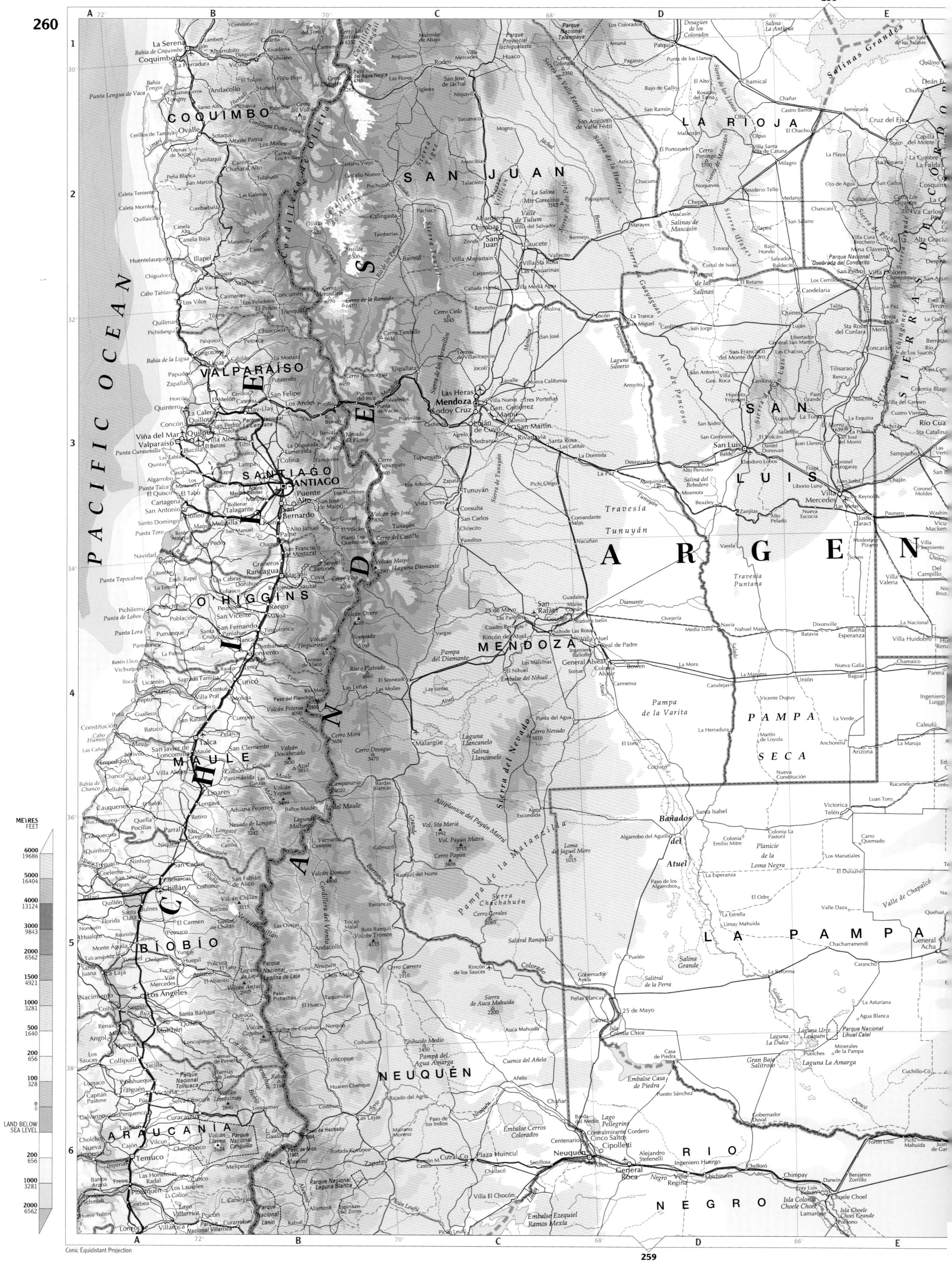

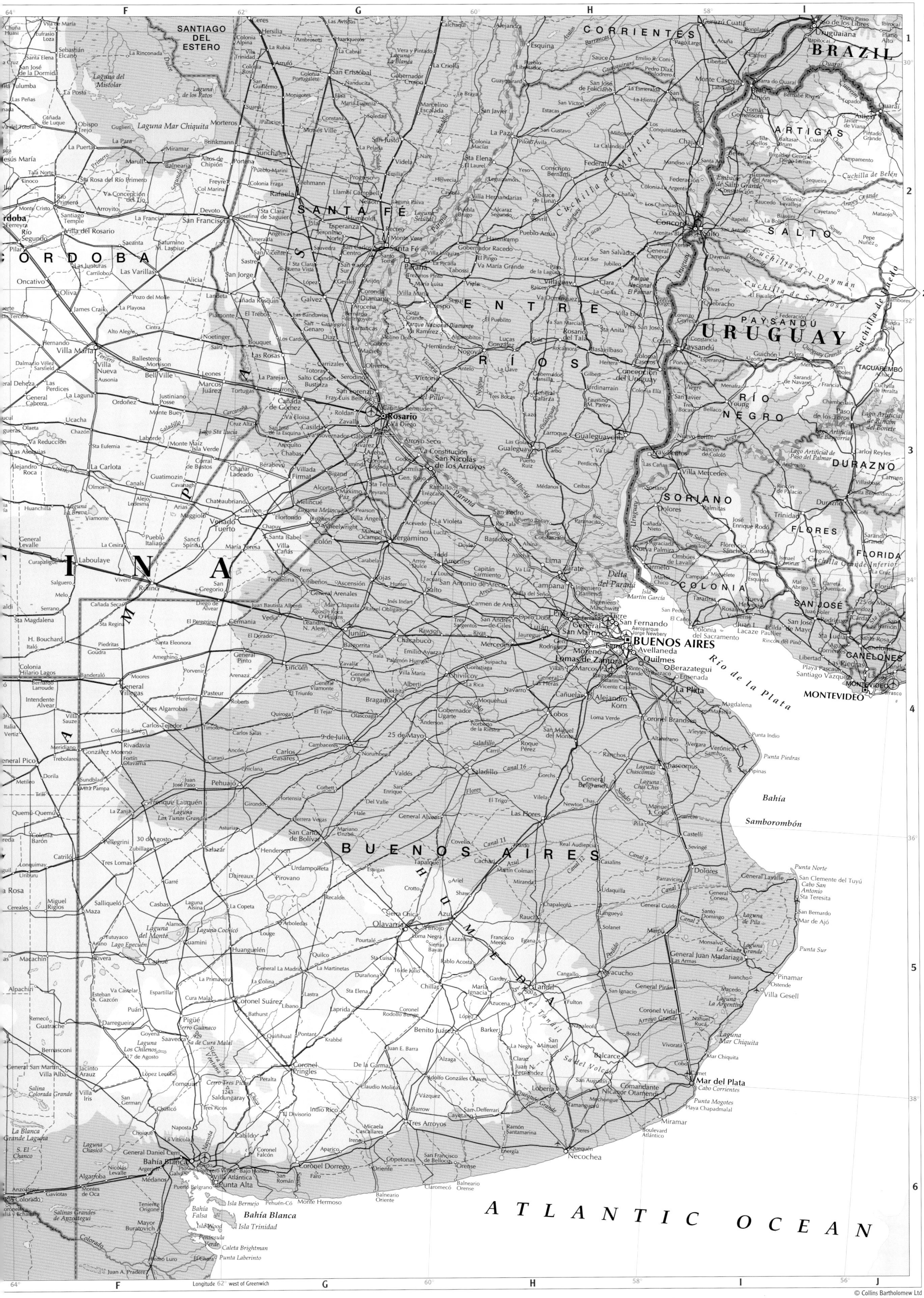

MILES   KILOMETRES

1:3 300 000

© Collins Bartholomew Ltd

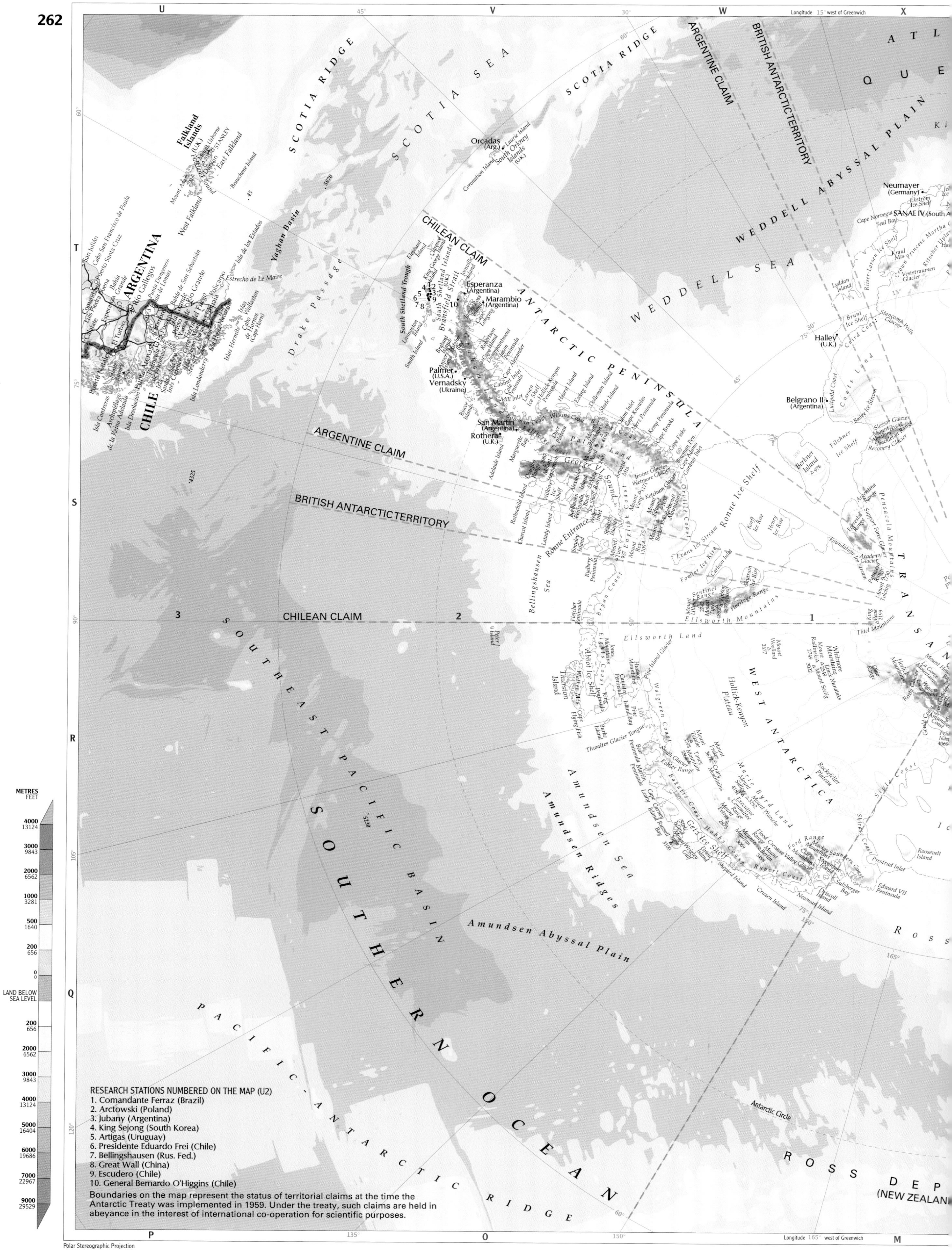

RESEARCH STATIONS NUMBERED ON THE MAP (U2)
1. Comandante Ferraz (Brazil)
2. Arctowski (Poland)
3. Jubany (Argentina)
4. King Sejong (South Korea)
5. Artigas (Uruguay)
6. Presidente Eduardo Frei (Chile)
7. Bellingshausen (Rus. Fed.)
8. Great Wall (China)
9. Escudero (Chile)
10. General Bernardo O'Higgins (Chile)

Boundaries on the map represent the status of territorial claims at the time the
Antarctic Treaty was implemented in 1959. Under the treaty, such claims are held in
abeyance in the interest of international co-operation for scientific purposes.

Polar Stereographic Projection

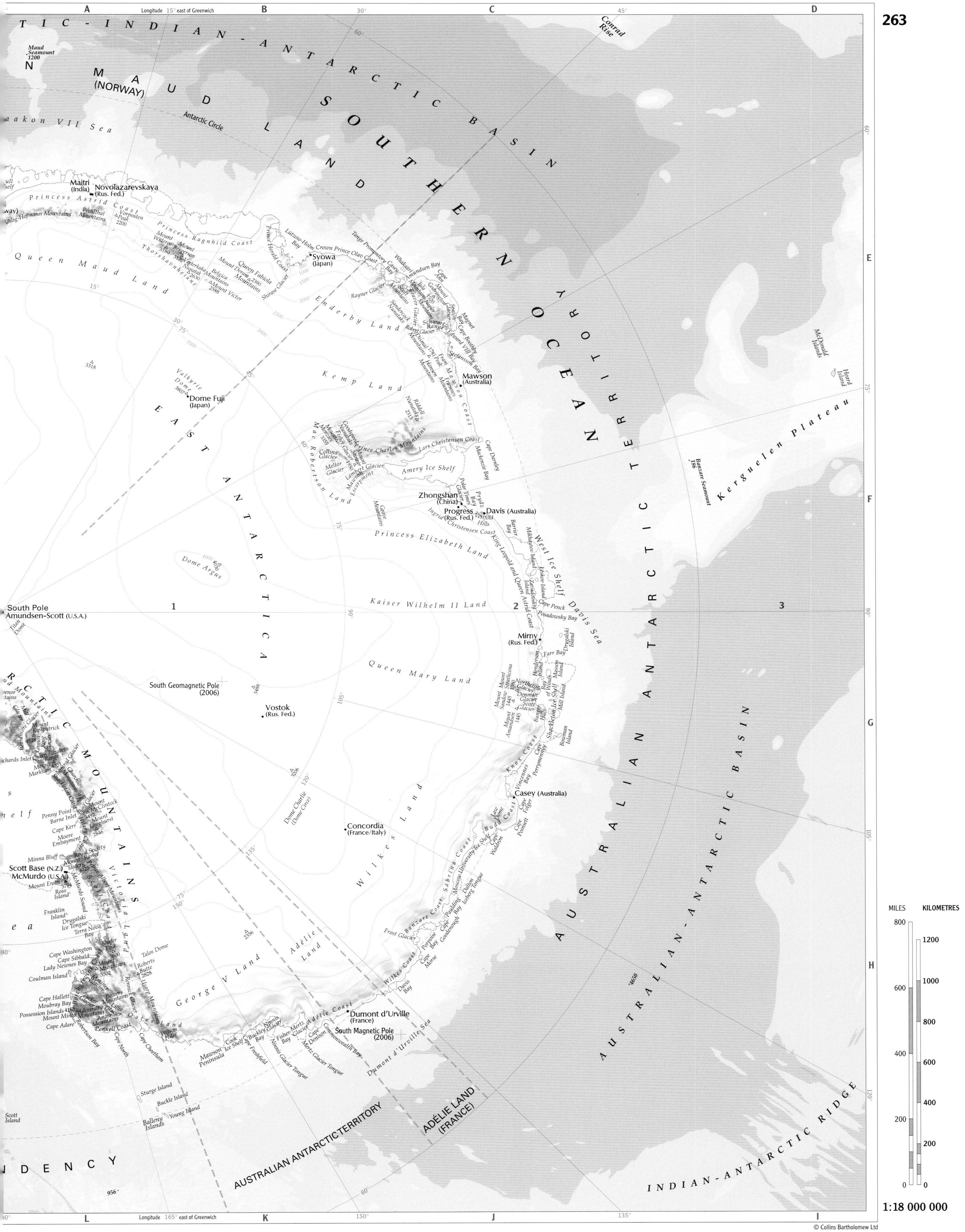
Longitude 15° east of Greenwich
A
B
C
D
E
F
G
H
1
2
3
SOUTHERN OCEAN
INDIAN-ANTARCTIC BASIN
Conrad Rise
Maud Seamount 1200
Haakon VII Sea
Antarctic Circle
MAUD (NORWAY)
DRONNING MAUD LAND
Maitri (India)
Novolazarevskaya (Rus. Fed.)
Princess Astrid Coast
Wohlthat Mountains
Princess Ragnhild Coast
Prince Harald Coast
Lützow-Holm Bay
Crown Prince Olav Coast
Syowa (Japan)
Queen Maud Land
Queen Fabiola Mountains
Belgica Mountains
Sør Rondane Mountains
Shirase Glacier
Enderby Land
Amundsen Bay
Rayner Glacier
Kemp Land
Mawson (Australia)
Mawson Coast
Valkyrie Dome 3807
Dome Fuji (Japan)
EAST ANTARCTICA
Prince Charles Mountains
Lars Christensen Coast
Mac Robertson Land
Lambert Glacier
Amery Ice Shelf
Mackenzie Bay
Cape Darnley
Zhongshan (China)
Progress (Rus. Fed.)
Davis (Australia)
Prydz Bay
Vestfold Hills
Ingrid Christensen Coast
Princess Elizabeth Land
Gamburtsev Mountains
Dome Argus 4093
AUSTRALIAN ANTARCTIC TERRITORY
West Ice Shelf
Davis Sea
Kerguelen plateau
Banzare Seamount 186
McDonald Islands
Heard Island
South Pole
Amundsen-Scott (U.S.A.)
Kaiser Wilhelm II Land
King Leopold and Queen Astrid Coast
Posadowsky Bay
Mirny (Rus. Fed.)
Drygalski Island
Queen Mary Land
Shackleton Ice Shelf
South Geomagnetic Pole (2006)
Vostok (Rus. Fed.)
Knox Coast
Vincennes Bay
Casey (Australia)
Budd Coast
Dome Charlie (Dome Circe)
Concordia (France/Italy)
Wilkes Land
Sabrina Coast
Moscow University Ice Shelf
AUSTRALIAN-ANTARCTIC BASIN
Banzare Coast
Frost Glacier
Porpoise Bay
Wilkes Coast
Adélie Land
George V Land
Dumont d'Urville (France)
Adélie Coast
South Magnetic Pole (2006)
Dumont d'Urville Sea
Commonwealth Bay
Mertz Glacier Tongue
Ninnis Glacier Tongue
Cook Ice Shelf
Mawson Peninsula
Oates Land
Pennell Coast
Cape Adare
Robertson Bay
Cape North
Cape Cheetham
TRANSANTARCTIC MOUNTAINS
Victoria Land
Scott Base (N.Z.)
McMurdo (U.S.A.)
Mount Erebus 3794
Ross Island
Minna Bluff
Moore Embayment
Cape Kerr
Barne Inlet
Penny Point
Mount Markham
Richards Inlet
Mount Kirkpatrick 4528
Franklin Island
Drygalski Ice Tongue
Terra Nova Bay
Talos Dome
Cape Washington
Cape Sibbald
Lady Newnes Bay
Coulman Island
Cape Hallett
Moubray Bay
Possession Islands
Mount Minto
Sturge Island
Buckle Island
Young Island
Balleny Islands
Scott Island
AUSTRALIAN ANTARCTIC TERRITORY
ADÉLIE LAND (FRANCE)
DEPENDENCY
INDIAN-ANTARCTIC RIDGE
Longitude 165° east of Greenwich
L
K
J
I
956
4650
MILES
KILOMETRES
800
600
400
200
0
1200
1000
800
600
400
200
0
1:18 000 000

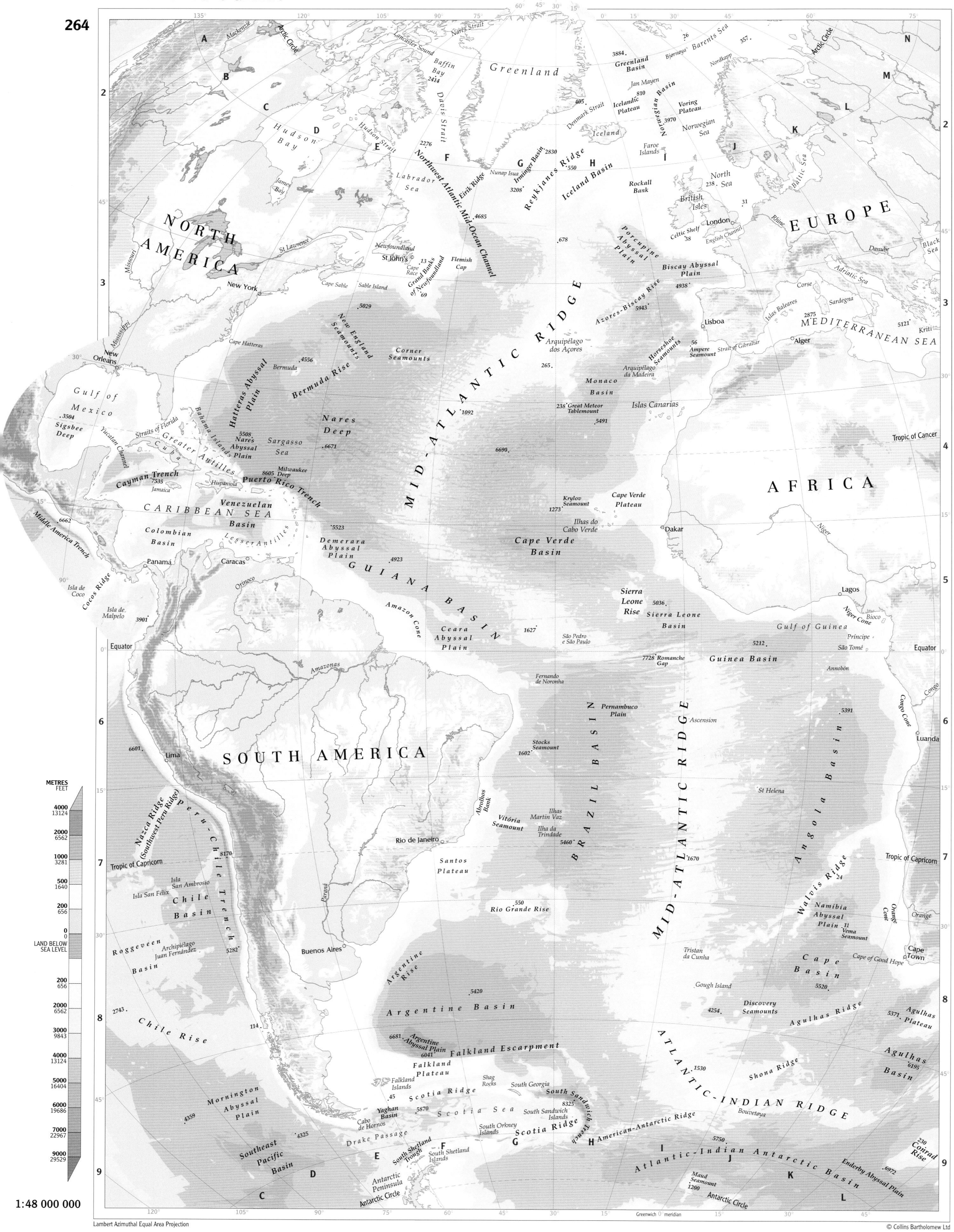

NORTH AMERICA
SOUTH AMERICA
EUROPE
AFRICA

Greenland

Seas, Bays, Straits & Channels
Arctic Circle
Mackenzie
Baffin Bay
Lancaster Sound
Nares Strait
Barents Sea
Greenland Basin
Bjørnøya
Nordkapp
Davis Strait
Hudson Strait
Hudson Bay
James Bay
Denmark Strait
Iceland
Icelandic Plateau
Jan Mayen
Norwegian Basin
Voring Plateau
Norwegian Sea
Faroe Islands
Baltic Sea
North Sea
Nunap Isua
Imminger Basin
Reykjanes Ridge
Iceland Basin
Rockall Bank
British Isles
Rhine
Black Sea

Labrador Sea
Eirik Ridge
Northwest Atlantic Mid-Ocean Channel
Newfoundland
St John's
Cape Race
Grand Banks of Newfoundland
Flemish Cap
Porcupine Abyssal Plain
Celtic Shelf
London
English Channel
Danube
Adriatic Sea
Corse

St Lawrence
St Lawrence
Cape Sable
Sable Island
Biscay Abyssal Plain
Azores-Biscay Rise
Lisboa
Islas Baleares
Sardegna
MEDITERRANEAN SEA
Kriti

New Orleans
Cape Hatteras
New England Seamounts
Corner Seamounts
Bermuda
Bermuda Rise
Hatteras Abyssal Plain
Arquipélago dos Açores
Horseshoe Seamounts
Arquipélago da Madeira
Ampere Seamount
Strait of Gibraltar
Alger

Gulf of Mexico
Sigsbee Deep
Straits of Florida
Yucatán Channel
Greater Antilles
Cuba
Bahama Islands
Sargasso Sea
Nares Deep
Nares Abyssal Plain
Monaco Basin
Great Meteor Tablemount
Islas Canarias
Tropic of Cancer

Cayman Trench
Jamaica
Hispaniola
Milwaukee Deep
Puerto Rico Trench
Krylov Seamount
Cape Verde Plateau
AFRICA

Middle America Trench
CARIBBEAN SEA
Venezuelan Basin
Lesser Antilles
Colombian Basin
Panamá
Caracas
Orinoco
Demerara Abyssal Plain
Ilhas do Cabo Verde
Cape Verde Basin
Dakar

Isla de Coco
Cocos Ridge
Isla de Malpelo
GUIANA BASIN
Amazon Cone
Ceara Abyssal Plain
São Pedro e São Paulo
Sierra Leone Rise
Sierra Leone Basin
Gulf of Guinea
Lagos
Príncipe
Bioco
Niger Cone

Equator
Amazonas
Fernando de Noronha
Romanche Gap
Guinea Basin
São Tomé
Annobón
Congo
Congo Cone
Luanda

SOUTH AMERICA
Lima
Nazca Ridge
Peru-Chile Trench
(Southwest Peru Ridge)
Pernambuco Plain
Ascension
BRAZIL BASIN
Stocks Seamount
MID-ATLANTIC RIDGE
St Helena
Angola Basin

Tropic of Capricorn
Isla San Ambrosio
Isla San Félix
Chile Basin
Abrolhos Bank
Vitória Seamount
Ilhas Martin Vaz
Ilha da Trindade
Walvis Ridge
Namibia Abyssal Plain
Vema Seamount
Orange Cone
Orange
Tropic of Capricorn

Rio de Janeiro
Santos Plateau
Rio Grande Rise
Tristan da Cunha
Cape Basin
Cape Town
Cape of Good Hope

Roggeveen Basin
Archipiélago Juan Fernández
Gough Island
Discovery Seamounts
Agulhas Ridge
Agulhas Plateau
Agulhas Basin

Argentine Rise
Buenos Aires
Paraná
Argentine Basin
Chile Rise

Mornington Abyssal Plain
Cabo de Hornos
Yaghan Basin
Argentine Abyssal Plain
Falkland Escarpment
Falkland Plateau
Falkland Islands
Shag Rocks
South Georgia
South Sandwich Islands
Shona Ridge
Conrad Rise

Southeast Pacific Basin
Drake Passage
South Shetland Trough
South Shetland Islands
Scotia Ridge
Scotia Sea
South Orkney Islands
Scotia Ridge
South Sandwich Trench
American-Antarctic Ridge
ATLANTIC-INDIAN RIDGE
Bouvetøya
Maud Seamount
Enderby Abyssal Plain

Antarctic Peninsula
Antarctic Circle
Atlantic-Indian Antarctic Basin
Antarctic Circle

MID-ATLANTIC RIDGE

Scale 1:48 000 000

METRES / FEET
4000 / 13124
2000 / 6562
1000 / 3281
500 / 1640
200 / 656
0 / 0
LAND BELOW SEA LEVEL
200 / 656
2000 / 6562
3000 / 9843
4000 / 13124
5000 / 16404
6000 / 19686
7000 / 22967
9000 / 29529

Lambert Azimuthal Equal Area Projection

© Collins Bartholomew Ltd

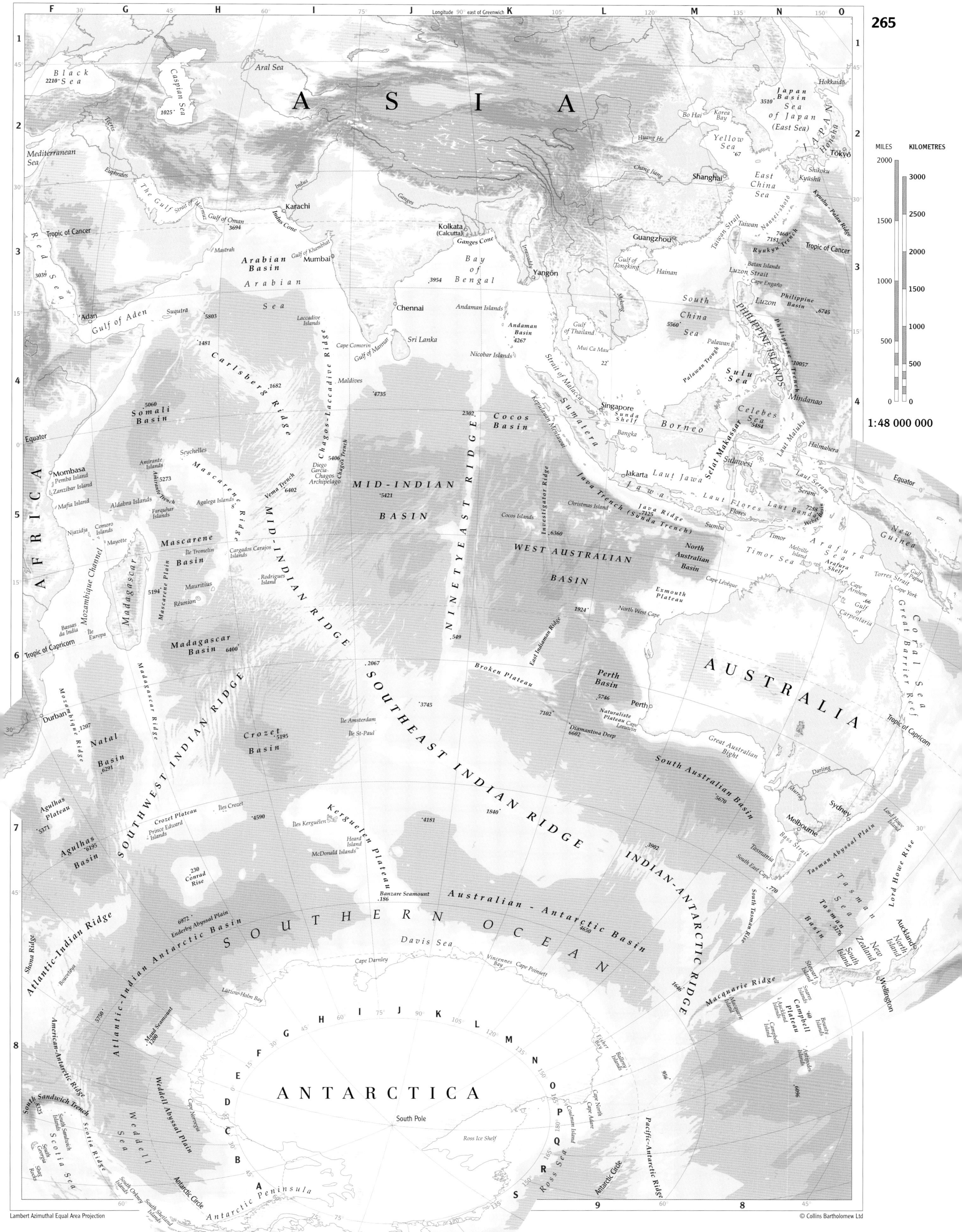

A S I A

AUSTRALIA

ANTARCTICA

AFRICA

New Guinea

Seas and Oceans

Black Sea 2210
Caspian Sea 1025
Aral Sea
Mediterranean Sea
Red Sea 3039
Gulf of Aden
The Gulf
Gulf of Oman 3694
Strait of Hormuz
Arabian Sea
Gulf of Khambhat 3954
Bay of Bengal
Gulf of Mannar
Gulf of Thailand
Andaman Basin 4267
South China Sea 5560
Gulf of Tongking
Sea of Japan (East Sea) 3510
Japan Basin
Bo Hai
Korea Bay
Yellow Sea 67
East China Sea
Philippine Basin 6745
Philippine Trench 10057
Sulu Sea 5484
Celebes Sea
Laut Jawa
Laut Flores
Laut Banda 7288
Arafura Sea
Timor Sea
Gulf of Carpentaria
Coral Sea
Great Australian Bight
Tasman Sea

Land / Islands

Hokkaidō
Honshū
Tōkyō
Shikoku
Kyūshū
Nansei-shotō
Ryūkyū Trench 7460 / 7181
Taiwan
Taiwan Strait
Batan Islands
Luzon Strait
Cape Engaño
Luzon
PHILIPPINE ISLANDS
Mindanao
Palawan
Palawan Trough
Borneo
Sulawesi
Halmahera
Laut Maluku
Laut Seram
Seram
Sumatera
Java (Jawa)
Java Ridge 2125
Sumba
Christmas Island 6360
Cocos Islands
Timor
Melville Island
Bangka
Singapore
Sunda Shelf
Jakarta
North Australian Basin
Exmouth Plateau
North West Cape 1924
Cape Lévêque
Cape Arnhem
Cape York
Torres Strait
Gulf of Papua
Great Barrier Reef
Tropic of Capricorn
Perth Basin 5746
Perth
Naturaliste Plateau
Cape Leeuwin
Diamantina Deep 6602
South Australian Basin 5670
Darling
Murray
Sydney
Melbourne
Tasmania
Bass Strait
South East Cape 770
Tasman Basin 5376
Tasman Abyssal Plain
Lord Howe Rise
South Tasman Rise
Lord Howe Island
Auckland
North Island
Wellington
South Island
New Zealand
Stewart Island
Snares Islands
Auckland Islands
Campbell Plateau
Campbell Island 60
Bounty Islands 6096
Macquarie Ridge
Macquarie Island
Balleny Islands
Fisher Basin
Cape North
Cape Adare
Cape Colbeck
Ross Sea
Ross Ice Shelf
Pacific-Antarctic Ridge 956

India region

Karachi
Indus
Indus Cone 3694
Ganges
Ganges Cone
Kolkata (Calcutta)
Mastrah
Arabian Basin
Mumbai 5803
Chennai
Sri Lanka
Cape Comorin
Maldives 4735
Laccadive Islands
Chagos-Laccadive Ridge
Carlsberg Ridge 1481 / 1682
Somali Basin 5060
Mombasa
Pemba Island
Zanzibar Island
Mafia Island
Njazidja
Comoro Islands
Mayotte
Aldabra Islands
Farquhar Islands
Amirante Islands 5273
Amirante Trench
Seychelles
Mascarene Plain
Île Tromelin
Agalega Islands
Cargados Carajos Islands
Mascarene Basin 5194
Rodrigues Island
Mauritius
Réunion
Mascarene Ridge
MID-INDIAN RIDGE
Vema Trench 5406 / 6402
Diego Garcia
Chagos Archipelago
Chagos Trench
MID-INDIAN BASIN 5421
NINETYEAST RIDGE 2302
COCOS BASIN
WEST AUSTRALIAN BASIN
Investigator Ridge
Strait of Malacca
Sunda Shelf
Yangôn
Irrawaddy
Mekong
Guangzhou
Shanghai
Chang Jiang
Huang He
Hainan
Andaman Islands
Nicobar Islands
Kepulauan Mentawai
Java Trench (Sunda Trench)
Mui Ca Mau 22
East Indaman Ridge
Broken Plateau 2067 / 3745 / 549
Madagascar Basin 6400
Madagascar
Madagascar Ridge
SOUTHWEST INDIAN RIDGE
SOUTHEAST INDIAN RIDGE
INDIAN-ANTARCTIC RIDGE 1666
Australian-Antarctic Basin 4650
Crozet Basin 5195
Île Amsterdam
Île St-Paul
Îles Crozet 4590
Îles Kerguélen
Kerguelen Plateau 4181 / 1840
Heard Island
McDonald Islands
Crozet Plateau
Prince Edward Islands
Conrad Rise 230
Banzare Seamount 186
Enderby Abyssal Plain 6972
Atlantic-Indian Antarctic Basin
Davis Sea
Cape Darnley
Vincennes Bay
Cape Poinsett
Lützow-Holm Bay
Cape Norvegia
Ross Ice Shelf
South Pole
Antarctic Circle
Antarctic Peninsula
Weddell Sea
Weddell Abyssal Plain
Maud Seamount 1380
Atlantic-Indian Ridge
Shona Ridge
Bouvetøya
South Sandwich Trench 8325
South Sandwich Islands
Scotia Sea
Scotia Ridge
South Georgia
South Orkney Islands
South Shetland Islands
American-Antarctic Ridge
Agulhas Plateau 5371
Agulhas Basin 6195
Durban
Mozambique Ridge 1207
Natal Basin 6291
Mozambique Channel
Basses da India
Île Europa
Tropic of Cancer
Tropic of Capricorn
Equator
Longitude 90° east of Greenwich
SOUTHERN OCEAN

Scale

MILES
2000
1500
1000
500
0

KILOMETRES
3000
2500
2000
1500
1000
500
0

1:48 000 000

Lambert Azimuthal Equal Area Projection

© Collins Bartholomew Ltd

A
B
C
D
E
F
G
H
90°
105°
120°
135°
150°
165°E
180°
Arctic Circle
Ostrov Vrangelya
Chukchi Sea
Bering Strait
Anadyrskiy Zaliv
St Lawrence Island
Heilong Jiang
Sea of Okhotsk
Kamchatka Basin
Ostrov Beringa
Ostrov Mednyy
Bering Sea
Aleutian Basin
Bowers Ridge
Nunivak Island
Pribilof Islands
Attu Island
Aleutian Islands
Andreanof Islands
Aleutian Trench
7822
7679
Sakhalin
3916
Kuril Basin
Kuril'skiye Ostrova
Kuril Trench
9550
Hokkaidō
ASIA
Tropic of Cancer
Ganges
Kolkata (Calcutta)
Huang He
Bo Hai
Korea Bay
Yellow Sea
67
3510
Sea of Japan (East Sea)
Japan Basin
JAPAN
Honshū
Tōkyō
Japan Trench
8412
Chang Jiang
Shanghai
East China Sea
Kyushu
Shikoku
Nansei-shotō
Ganges Cone
Bay of Bengal
Irrawaddy
Guangzhou
Taiwan Strait
Taiwan
7460
7181
Ryukyu Trench
Gulf of Tongking
Hainan
Luzon Strait
Batan Islands
Cape Engaño
Luzon
Philippine Basin
6745
Yangon
3954
Chennai
Andaman Islands
Mekong
South China Sea
5560
PHILIPPINE ISLANDS
Philippine Trench
10057
Andaman Basin
4267
Gulf of Thailand
Sri Lanka
Nicobar Islands
Mui Ca Mau
Palawan
Palawan Trough
Sulu Sea
Mindanao
22
Kyushu - Palau Ridge
West Mariana Basin
South Honshu Ridge
Izu-Ogasawara Trench
Ramapo Deep
9780
Ogasawara-shotō
Kazan-rettō
9156
Mariana Ridge
Mariana Trench
Saipan
Rota
Guam
Challenger Deep
10920
NORTHWEST PACIFIC BASIN
Emperor Seamount Chain
6671
1240
Emperor Trough
Chinook Trough
7900
6345
18
Kure Atoll
104
Midway Islands
Laysan Island
Gardner Pinnacles
Necker Island
Hawaiian Ridge
Mapmakers Seamounts
MID-PACIFIC MOUNTAINS
Wake Island
1823
Magellan Seamounts
East Mariana Basin
1564
Johnston Atoll
Nonouti
MICRONESIA
Enewetak
Bikini
Rongelap
Gaferut
Pikelot
Hall Islands
Chuuk
Pohnpei
Kwajalein
Wotje
Ailinglaplap
Marshall Islands
Taongi
6530
Palau Islands
8054
Palau Trench
8967
Yap Trench
Eauripik Rise
Caroline Islands
Mortlock Islands
Kosrae
West Caroline Basin
East Caroline Basin
New Guinea Rise
Celebes Sea
5484
Laut Maluku
Halmahera
Strait of Malacca
Kepulauan Mentawai
Sumatera
Singapore
Sunda Shelf
Borneo
Selat Makasar
Sulawesi
Kapingamarangi
Kapingamarangi Rise
Central Pacific Basin
Palmyra Atoll
6957
Equator
0°
Cocos Basin
2302
Bangka
Laut Seram
Seram
7208
Admiralty Islands
New Ireland
Bismarck Sea
Melanesian Basin
Nauru
Banaba
Abaiang
Butaritari
Gilbert Ridge
Nonouti
Tabiteuea
Onotoa
Howland Island
Baker Island
McKean
Phoenix Islands
Kanton
Rawaki
Nikumaroro
Orona
Manra
POLYNESIA
Laut Banda
7288
Weber Basin
New Guinea
New Britain
New Britain Trench
8940
Bougainville Island
Solomon Islands
Solomon Sea
MELANESIA
Nanumea
Vaitupu
Nukufetau
Funafuti
Nukulaelae
Atafu
Tokelau
Fakaofo
Laut Jawa
Jakarta
Jawa
Laut Flores
Flores
Timor
Sumba
Arafura Sea
Arafura Shelf
Melville Island
Gulf of Papua
Torres Strait
Cape York
D'Entrecasteaux Islands
Guadalcanal
San Cristobal
8322
South Solomon Trench
Santa Cruz Islands
Rennell
Louisiade Archipelago
Coral Sea Basin
Rotuma
Swains Island
13
Pukapuka
Nassau
Îles Wallis
Savai'i
Upolu
Suwarrow
Îles de Hoorn
Tutuila
Samoa Basin
Mid-Indian Basin
6
Java Ridge
Java Trench (Sunda Trench)
7125
Investigator Ridge
Christmas Island
Timor Sea
Cape Arnhem
66
Gulf of Carpentaria
Great Barrier Reef
Banks Islands
Espiritu Santo
Malakula
Ambrym
Éfaté
Erromango
Tanna
Anatom
Vanua Levu
Fiji Islands
Viti Levu
Vava'u Group
Tofua
Tonga Trench
Niue
Palmerston
Coral Sea
Cocos Islands
North Australian Basin
6360
Cape Lévêque
7073
Îles Loyauté
Hunter Island
7633
Nouvelle Calédonie
Île des Pins
New Hebrides Trench
Tongatapu Group
Horizon Deep
10800
NINETYEAST RIDGE
WEST AUSTRALIAN BASIN
Exmouth Plateau
New Caledonia Trough
Norfolk Island Ridge
Lord Howe Rise
South Fiji Basin
AUSTRALIA
North West Cape
1924
15°
Norfolk Island
Kermadec Islands
Kermadec Trench
10047
Louisville Ridge
SOUTH PACIFIC
Lord Howe Island
Darling
Sydney
Tasman Abyssal Plain
Tasman Sea
Auckland
North Island
New Zealand
Wellington
East Indiaman Ridge
Great Australian Bight
Murray
Melbourne
Perth Basin
Perth
Naturaliste Plateau
Cape Leeuwin
5746
Bass Strait
Tasman Basin
5176
Chatham Rise
Chatham Islands
South Island
Tropic of Capricorn
7
549
Broken Plateau
7102
Diamantina Deep
6602
5670
South Australian Basin
Tasmania
South East Cape
770
Bounty Trough
Bounty Islands
Antipodes Islands
Stewart Island
Snares Islands
60
Campbell Plateau
Auckland Islands
Campbell Island
6096
South Tasman Rise
Macquarie Ridge
Macquarie Island
2067
30°
3902
INDIAN - ANTARCTIC RIDGE
1646
SOUTHEAST INDIAN RIDGE
SOUTHERN
956
Île Amsterdam
Île St-Paul
8
1840
Australian - Antarctic Basin
4650
Fisher Bay
Balleny Islands
Cape North
Cape Adare
Ross Sea
Antarctic Circle
Vincennes Bay
Cape Poinsett
4181
9
10
45°
60°
120°
150°
165°E
180°
Ross Ice Shelf
ANTARCTICA

METRES
FEET
4000
13124
2000
6562
1000
3281
500
1640
200
656
0
0
LAND BELOW SEA LEVEL
200
656
2000
6562
3000
9843
4000
13124
5000
16404
6000
19686
7000
22967
9000
29529

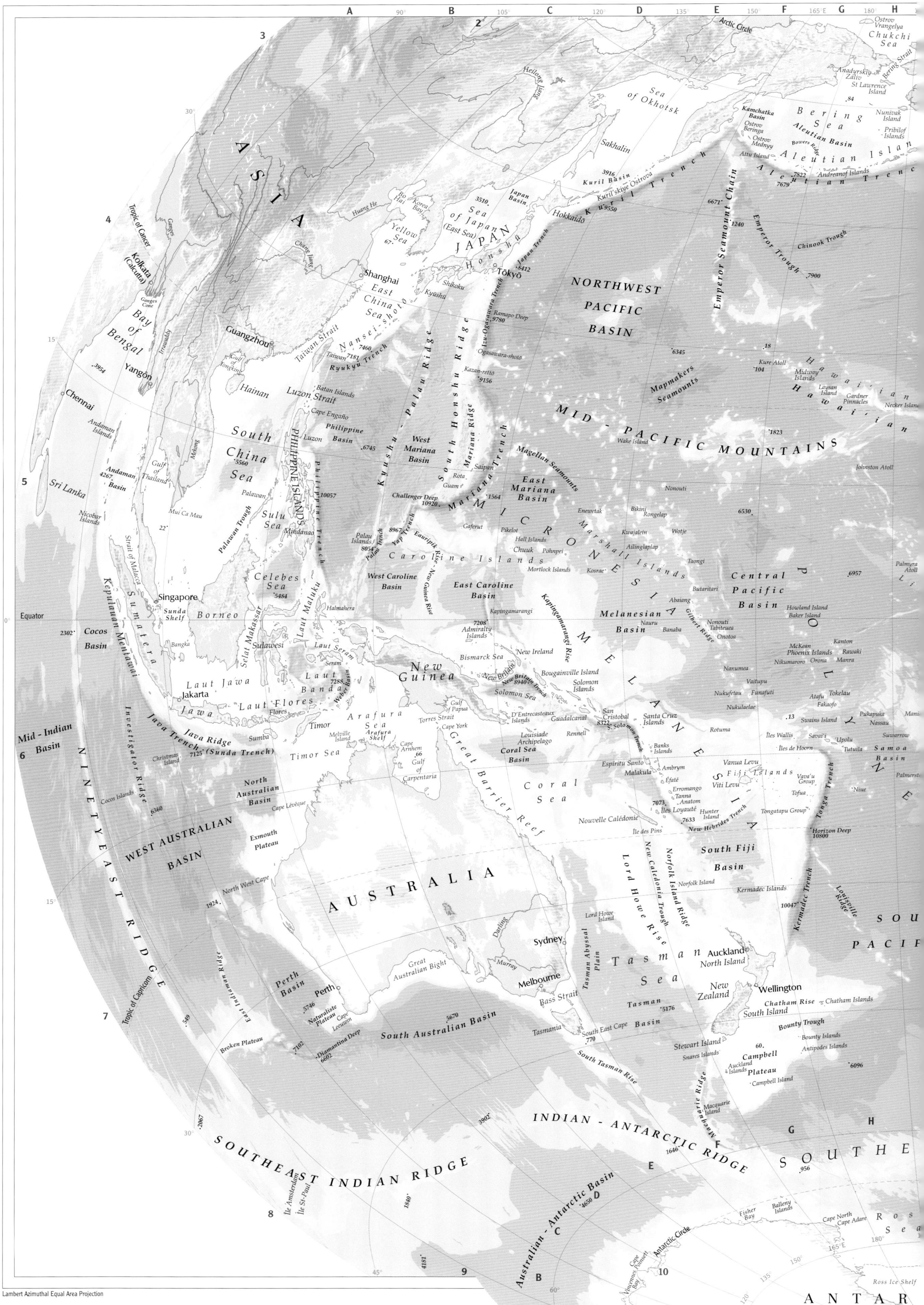

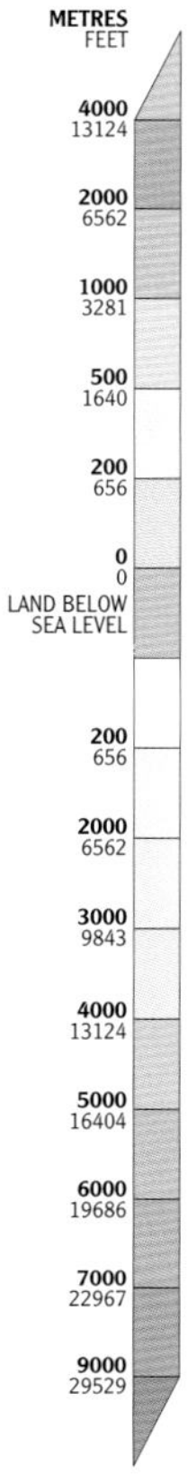

Lambert Azimuthal Equal Area Projection

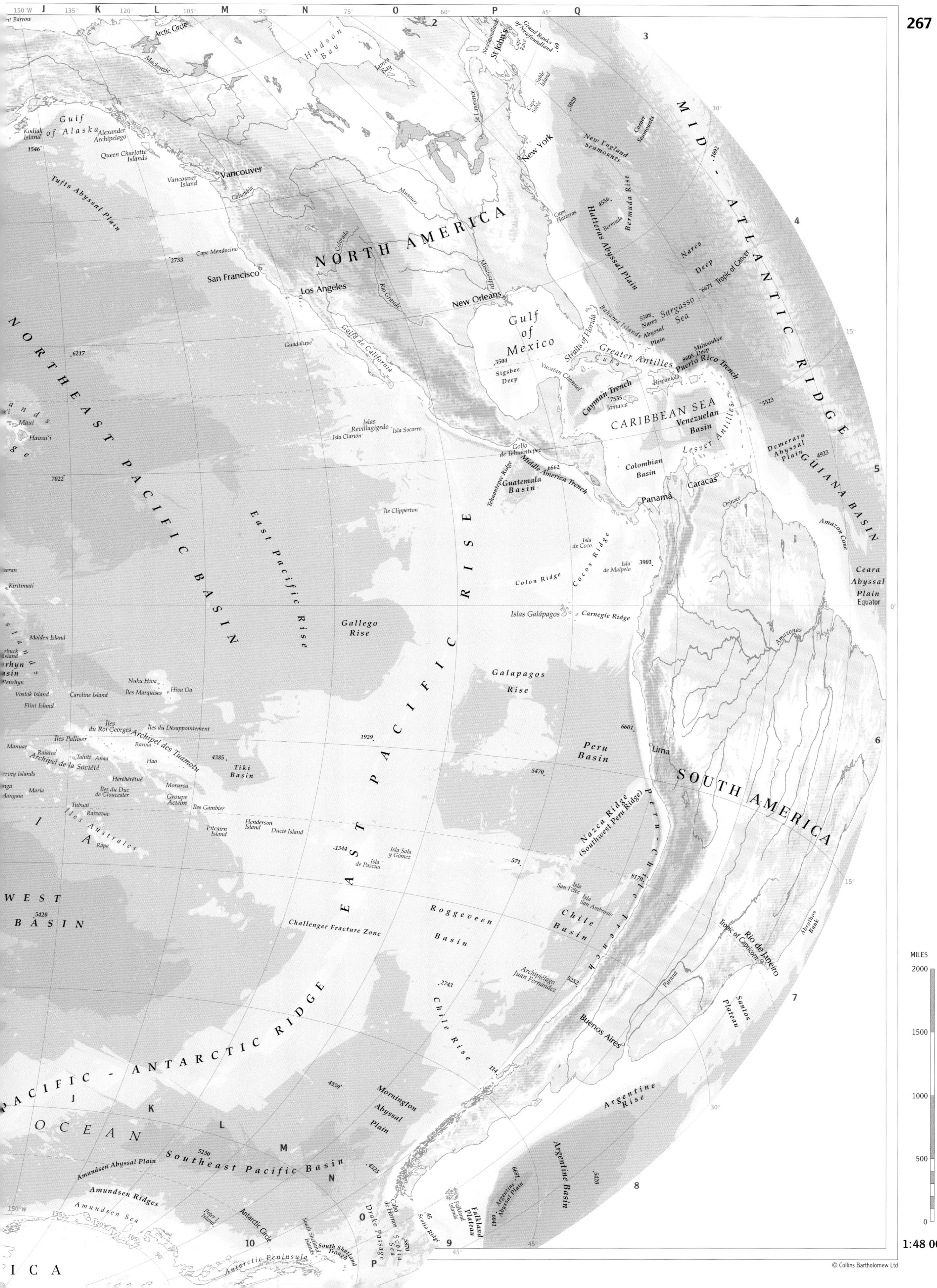

Point Barrow

Arctic Circle

Mackenzie

Hudson Bay

James Bay

Newfoundland

Grand Banks of Newfoundland

St John's

Cape Sable

Corner Seamounts

MID - ATLANTIC RIDGE

Gulf of Alaska

Kodiak Island

Alexander Archipelago

Queen Charlotte Islands

1546

Vancouver Island

Vancouver

Columbia

Missouri

New York

New England Seamounts

Bermuda Rise

4556

Bermuda

NORTH AMERICA

Cape Hatteras

Hatteras Abyssal Plain

Nares Deep

1002

Tufts Abyssal Plain

2733

Cape Mendocino

San Francisco

Los Angeles

Rio Grande

Colorado

New Orleans

Mississippi

Gulf of Mexico

Straits of Florida

Bahama Islands

Cuba

5508

Nares Abyssal Plain

Sargasso Sea

6671

Tropic of Cancer

4

Milwaukee Deep

Nares Deep

5523

Puerto Rico Trench

NORTHEAST PACIFIC BASIN

6217

Guadalupe

Golfo de California

Sigsbee Deep

3504

Yucatan Channel

Greater Antilles

8605

5

Maui

Hawai'i

Islas Revillagigedo

Isla Socorro

Isla Clarión

7022

Cayman Trench

7535

Jamaica

Hispaniola

CARIBBEAN SEA

Venezuelan Basin

Lesser Antilles

Demerara Abyssal Plain

4923

GUIANA BASIN

Kiritimati

East Pacific Rise

Île Clipperton

Golfo de Tehuántepec

Tehuantepec Ridge

Middle America Trench

6662

Guatemala Basin

Colombian Basin

Caracas

Panamá

Colon Ridge

Cocos Ridge

Isla de Coco

Isla de Malpelo

3901

Orinoco

Amazon Cone

Ceara Abyssal Plain

Equator

0

EAST PACIFIC RISE

Gallego Rise

Islas Galápagos

Carnegie Ridge

Amazonas

Malden Island

Vostok Island

Flint Island

Penrhyn

Caroline Island

Nuku Hiva

Iles Marquises

Hiva Oa

Galapagos Rise

Manuae

Raiatea

Tahiti

Anaa

Hao

Îles du Roi Georges

Îles du Désappointement

Raroia

Archipel des Tuamotu

4385

Tiki Basin

1929

6601

Peru Basin

Lima

SOUTH AMERICA

Archipel de la Société

Hérehérétué

Hervey Islands

Maria

Mangaia

Îles du Duc de Gloucester

Moruroa

Groupe Actéon

Îles Gambier

5470

Îles Australes

Tubuai

Raivavae

Rapa

Pitcairn Island

Henderson Island

Ducie Island

1344

Isla Sala y Gómez

Isla de Pascua

571

Nazca Ridge (Southwest Peru Ridge)

Peru-Chile Trench

15

WEST BASIN

5420

Challenger Fracture Zone

Roggeveen Basin

San Félix

Isla San Ambrosio

8170

Chile Basin

EAST PACIFIC RISE

2743

Archipiélago Juan Fernández

5252

Chile Rise

Río de Janeiro

Tropic of Capricorn

Abrolhos Bank

Santos Plateau

PACIFIC - ANTARCTIC RIDGE

Buenos Aires

Paraná

OCEAN

4359

Mornington Abyssal Plain

Argentine Rise

30

Amundsen Abyssal Plain

Southeast Pacific Basin

5230

4325

Argentine Basin

Amundsen Ridges

Amundsen Sea

Peter I Island

Antarctic Circle

Drake Passage

Falkland Plateau

Falkland Islands

5420

8

150°W

135°

120°

Antarctic Peninsula

South Shetland Islands

South Sandwich Trench

Scotia Sea

Scotia Ridge

45°

9

ICA

MILES

2000

1500

1000

500

KILOMETRES

3000

2500

2000

1500

1000

500

0

0

1:48 000 000

© Collins Bartholomew Ltd

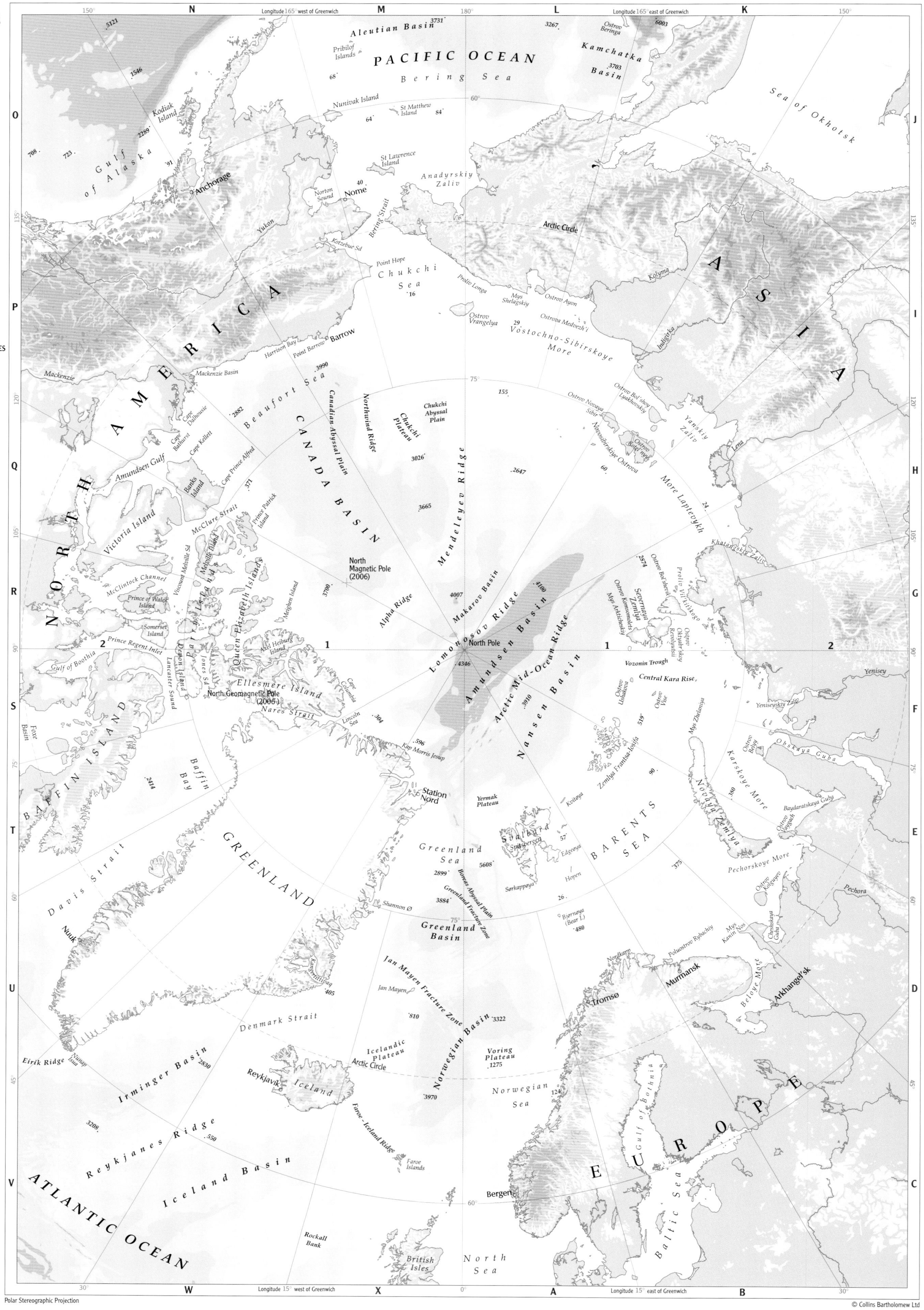

ARCTIC OCEAN

MILES KILOMETRES

1000
750
500
250
0

1500
1250
1000
750
500
250
0

1:24 000 000

METRES FEET

4000 / 13124
2000 / 6562
1000 / 3281
500 / 1640
200 / 656
0 / 0
LAND BELOW SEA LEVEL
200 / 656
2000 / 6562
3000 / 9843
4000 / 13124
5000 / 16404
6000 / 19686
7000 / 22967
9000 / 29529

PACIFIC OCEAN

Bering Sea

Aleutian Basin

Kamchatka Basin

Sea of Okhotsk

ASIA

Arctic Circle

Chukchi Sea

Vostochno-Sibirskoye More

More Laptevykh

Beaufort Sea

CANADA BASIN

Mendeleyev Ridge

North Magnetic Pole (2006)

Makarov Basin

Lomonosov Ridge

North Pole

Amundsen Basin

Nansen Basin

Arctic Mid-Ocean Ridge

NORTH AMERICA

Ellesmere Island

North Geomagnetic Pole (2006)

BAFFIN ISLAND

Baffin Bay

GREENLAND

Greenland Sea

Svalbard

BARENTS SEA

Novaya Zemlya

Karskoye More

Davis Strait

Denmark Strait

Iceland

Reykjavik

Greenland Basin

Norwegian Basin

Norwegian Sea

EUROPE

Reykjanes Ridge

Iceland Basin

ATLANTIC OCEAN

British Isles

North Sea

Baltic Sea

Gulf of Bothnia

Murmansk

Arkhangel'sk

Tromso

Bergen

GLOSSARY

Geographical term	Language	Meaning
A		
-á	Icelandic	river
-å	Danish	river
Āb	Farsi	river
Abajo	Spanish	lower
Abbaye	French	abbey
Abhainn	Gaelic	river
Abyār	Arabic	wells
Açude	Portuguese	reservoir
Adası	Azeri, Turkish	island
Adrar	Berber	hills, mountains
Agia, Agios	Greek	saint
Agioi	Greek	saints
Aiguille	French	peak
Ain, 'Ain, 'Aïn, Aïn, 'Aïn	Arabic	spring, well
Akra	Greek	cape, point
Ala-	Finnish	lower
Allt	Gaelic	river
Alpi	Italian	mountain range
Alpe	Slovene	mountain range
Alpen	German	mountain range
Alpes	French	mountain range
Alt-	German	old
Alta	Italian, Portuguese, Spanish	upper
Altiplanicie	Spanish	high plain
Alto	Italian, Portuguese, Spanish	upper
Alto	Spanish	summit
-älv, -älven	Swedish	river
Ano	Greek	upper
Anou, Ânou	Berber	well
Anse	French	bay
Ao	Thai	bay
Archipel	French	archipelago
Archipiélago	Spanish	archipelago
Arenas	Spanish	sands
Argelanots'	Armenian	reserve
Arkhipelag	Russian	archipelago
Arquipélago	Portuguese	archipelago
Arrecife	Spanish	reef
Arriba	Spanish	upper
Arroio	Portuguese	watercourse
Arroyo	Spanish	watercourse
Augstiene	Latvian	hill region
Aust-	Norwegian	east, eastern
Austur-	Icelandic	east, eastern
Avtonomnaya, Avtonomnyy	Russian	autonomous
Āw	Kurdish	river
'Ayn	Arabic	spring, waterhole, well
B		
Baai, -baai	Afrikaans, Dutch	bay
Bāb	Arabic	strait
Bad	German	spa
Badia	Catalan	bay
Bādiyah	Arabic	desert
Bælt	Danish	strait
Bagh	Gaelic	bay
Bahia	Portuguese	bay
Bahía	Spanish	bay
Bahr, Baḩr, Baḩr	Arabic	bay, lake, canal, river, watercourse
Bahra, Baḩra	Arabic	lagoon, lake
Baía	Portuguese	bay
Baie	French	bay
Baixa, Baixo	Portuguese	lower
Baja	Spanish	lower
Bajja	Maltese	bay
Bajo	Spanish	depression, lower
Bālā	Farsi	upper
Ban	Laotian, Thai	village
Banc	Welsh	hill
Banco	Spanish	shoal
Bandao	Chinese	peninsula
Bandar	Arabic, Farsi, Somali	anchorage, inlet, port, harbour
Bandar	Malay	port, town
Banī	Arabic	desert
Banjaran	Malay	mountain range
Baraj, Barajı	Turkish	dam
Barat	Indonesian, Malay	west, western
Barra	Portuguese, Spanish	sandbank, sandbar, spit
Barrage	French	dam
Barragem	Portuguese	dam, reservoir
Barranco	Spanish	gorge, ravine
Baruun	Mongolian	west, western
Bas, Basse	French	lower
Bassin	French	basin
Bāṭin, Baṭn	Arabic	depression
-beek	Afrikaans, Dutch	river
Beg, Beag	Gaelic, Irish	small
Bei	Chinese	north, northern

Geographical term	Language	Meaning
bei	German	at, near
Beinn	Gaelic	mountain
Belogor'ye	Russian	mountain range
Ben	Gaelic	mountain
Bereg	Russian	coastal area
-berg, -berge	German, Norwegian, Swedish, Afrikaans	mountain, mountains
Besar	Indonesian, Malay	big
Bi'ār	Arabic	wells
Bir, Bi'r, Bîr	Arabic	waterhole, well
Birkat	Arabic	waterhole, well
-bjerg	Danish	hill
Boca	Portuguese, Spanish	mouth
Bodden	German	bay
Boğazı	Turkish	strait, pass
Bois	French	forest, wood
Boloto	Russian	marsh
Bol'shaya, Bol'shiye, Bol'shoy, Bol'shoye	Russian	big
-bong	Korean	mountain
Boquerón	Spanish	pass
Bory	Polish	woods
-botn	Norwegian	valley floor
-botten	Swedish	valley floor
Böyük	Azeri	big
Braţul	Romanian	arm, branch
-bre, -breen	Norwegian	glacier
Bredning	Danish	bay
Breg	Croatian, Serbian	hill
-bron	Afrikaans	spring, well
Brücke	German	bridge
Bucht	German	bay
Bugt	Danish	bay
-bugten	Danish	bay
Bukhta	Russian	bay
Bukit	Indonesian, Malay	hill, mountain
-bukt, -bukta	Norwegian	bay
-bukten	Swedish	bay
Bulag	Mongolian	spring
Bulak	Russian, Uighur	spring
Bum	Burmese	mountain
Burnu, Burun	Turkish	cape, point
Büyük	Turkish	big
Bwlch	Welsh	pass
C		
Cabo	Portuguese, Spanish	cape, point
Cachoeira	Portuguese	waterfall
Caka	Tibetan	salt lake
Cala	Catalan, Italian	bay
Caleta	Spanish	inlet
Câmpia	Romanian	plain
Campo	Italian, Spanish	plain
Cañada, Cañadón	Spanish	ravine, gorge
Canal	French, Portuguese, Spanish	canal, channel
Caño	Spanish	river
Cañon	Spanish	canyon
Caol	Gaelic	hill
Cap	Catalan, French	cape, point
Capo	Italian	cape, point
Carn	Welsh	hill
Castell	Catalan	castle
Causse	French	limestone plateau
Çay, -çay, Çayı, -çayı	Azeri, Turkish	river
Cayo	Spanish	island
Cefn	Welsh	hill, ridge
Cerro	Spanish	hill, mountain, peak
Česká, České, Český	Czech	Czech
Chaco	Spanish	plain
Chāh	Farsi	river
Chaîne	French	mountain range
Cham	Kurdish	river
Chapada	Portuguese	hills, uplands
Château	French	castle, palace
Chau	Chinese	island
Chaung	Burmese	river
Chāy	Kurdish	river
Chhu	Dzongkha (Bhutan)	river
Chiang	Thai	town
Chink	Russian	hill range
Chiyā	Kurdish	mountain, hill range
Chott	Arabic	salt lake
Chuan	Chinese	river
Chuŏr Phnum	Cambodian	mountain range
Ci	Indonesian	river
Ciénaga	Spanish	marshy lake
Cima	Italian	peak
Cime	French	peak
Città	Italian	city
Ciudad	Spanish	town, city
Cnoc	Gaelic	hill
Co	Tibetan	lake
Col	French	pass
Collado	Spanish	mountain
Colle	Italian	pass
Colline	French	hill
Cona	Tibetan	lake
Cordillera	Spanish	mountain range

Geographical term	Language	Meaning
Corno	Italian	peak
Coronel	Spanish	colonel
Costa	Catalan, Italian, Portuguese, Spanish	coastal area
Côte	French	coast, hill region, slope
Coutada	Portuguese	reserve
Coxilha	Portuguese	mountain pasture
Cratère	French	crater
Creag	Gaelic	mountain
Cruz	Spanish	cross
Cu Lao	Vietnamese	island
Cuchilla	Spanish	mountain range
Cuenca	Spanish	deep valley, river basin
Cueva	Spanish	cave
Cumbre	Spanish	mountain
-cun	Chinese	village
D		
Da	Chinese	big
Da	Vietnamese	river
Dağ, Dağı	Azeri, Turkish	hill(s), mountain(s)
Dāgh	Farsi	mountain(s)
Dağları	Turkish	mountains
-dake	Japanese	hill, mountain
-dal	Afrikaans, Danish, Swedish	valley
-dal, -dalen	Norwegian	valley
-dalur	Icelandic	valley
-dan	Korean	cape, point
Danau	Indonesian, Malay	lake
Dao	Chinese	island
Đao	Vietnamese	island
Daqq	Farsi	salt flat, salt lake
-dara	Tajik	river
Darreh	Farsi	valley
Dar'ya	Russian	river
Daryācheh	Farsi	lake
Dashan	Chinese	mountain
Dasht	Farsi	desert
Dataran Tinggi	Malay	plateau
Davan	Kazakh	pass
Dawḩat	Arabic	bay
Dayr	Arabic	monastery
Dealul	Romanian	hill, mountain
Dealurile	Romanian	hills
Deh	Farsi	village
Deir	Arabic	monastery
Denizi	Turkish	sea
Deresi	Turkish	river
Desierto	Spanish	desert
Détroit	French	channel
-diep	Dutch	channel
Dingzi	Chinese	hill, small mountain
Djebel	Arabic	mountain
-do	Korean	island
Dolna, Dolni	Bulgarian	lower
Dolna, Dolne, Dolny	Polish	lower
Dolní	Czech	lower
Dong	Chinese	east, eastern
-dong	Korean	village
Donja, Donji	Croatian, Serbian	lower
Dorf	German	village
-dorp	Afrikaans, Dutch	village
Druim	Gaelic	hill, mountain
Dund	Mongolian	middle, central
Düzü	Azeri	plain
-dyngja	Icelandic	hill, mountain
Dzüün	Mongolian	east, eastern
E		
Eilean	Gaelic	island
-elv, -elva	Norwegian	river
Embalse	Spanish	reservoir
'Emeq	Hebrew	plain
Ensenada	Spanish	bay
Erg, 'Erg, 'Erg	Arabic	sand dunes
Eski	Turkish	old
Estany	Catalan	pond
Estero	Spanish	estuary, inlet, lagoon
Estrada	Spanish	bay
Estrecho	Spanish	strait
Étang	French	lagoon, lake
-ey, -eyjar	Icelandic	island, islands
-eyri	Icelandic	sandbar
ežeras	Lithuanian	lake
ezers	Latvian	lake
F		
Falaise	French	cliff, escarpment
Farihy	Malagasy	lake
Fayḑat	Arabic	waterhole
-fell	Icelandic	hill, mountain
Fels	German	rock
Feng	Chinese	mountain
Fiume	Italian	river

Geographical term	Language	Meaning
-fjäll, -fjällen, -fjället	Swedish	hill(s), mountain(s)
-fjallgarður	Icelandic	mountains
-fjara	Icelandic	beach
-fjell, -fjellet	Norwegian	mountain
-fjöll	Icelandic	hill(s), mountain(s)
Fjord, -fjord, -fjorden	Danish, Norwegian, Swedish	fjord
-fjörður	Icelandic	fjord
Fliegu	Maltese	channel
-fljót	Icelandic	river
-flói	Icelandic	bay
-fócsatorna	Hungarian	canal
Foel	Welsh	hill
Förde	German	inlet
Forêt	French	forest
Forst	German	forest
-foss	Icelandic	waterfall
-foss, -fossen	Norwegian	rapids, waterfall
Fuente	Spanish	source, well
Fulayj	Arabic	watercourse

G

-gan	Japanese	rock
Gang	Dzongkha (Bhutan)	mountain
Gang	Chinese	bay, river
-gang	Korean	river
Gaoyuan	Chinese	plateau
Gardaneh	Farsi	pass
-gat	Dutch	channel
-gata	Japanese	inlet, lagoon, lake
Gau	German	district
Gave	French	torrent
-gawa	Japanese	river
Gebel	Arabic	mountain
Gebergte	Dutch	mountain range
Gebiet	German	district, region
Gebirge	German	mountains
Geodha	Gaelic	inlet
Gezâ'ir	Arabic	islands
Gezirat	Arabic	island
Ghard	Arabic	sand dunes
Ghubba	Arabic	bay
Gjiri	Albanian	bay
Gletscher	German	glacier
Gobernador	Spanish	governor
Gobi	Mongolian	desert
Gol	Mongolian	river
Göl	Azeri	lake
Golets	Russian	mountain
Golf	Catalan	gulf
Golfe	French	bay, gulf
Golfo	Italian, Spanish	bay, gulf
Gölü	Azeri, Turkish	lake
Gora	Bulgarian, Croatian, Russian, Serbian	mountain(s)
Gorges	French	gorge
Górka	Polish	hill
Gornja, Gornje, Gornji	Croatian, Serbian	upper
Gorno-	Russian	mountainous
Gory	Russian	mountains
Góry	Polish	mountains
Gou	Chinese	river
Graben	German	trench
-grad	Bulgarian, Croatian, Russian, Serbian	town
Grand, Grande	French	big
-gród	Polish	town
Groot	Afrikaans, Dutch	big
Gross, Grosse, Grossen, Grosser (also Groß-)	German	big
Grotta	Italian	cave
Grotte	French	cave
Grotte	Italian	caves
Groupe	French	group
Grund	German	ground, valley
Gruppo	Italian	group
Gryada	Russian	mountains
Guan	Chinese	pass
Guba	Russian	bay, gulf
Gubed	Somali	bay
-guntō	Japanese	islands
Gunung	Indonesian, Malay	mountain
Guri	Albanian	peak

H

Ḥafar	Arabic	wells
Hafen	German	port, harbour
Haff	German	bay
Hai	Chinese	lake, sea
Haixia	Chinese	channel, strait
-háls	Icelandic	ridge
-halvøya	Norwegian	peninsula
Hamada, Hammada	Arabic	plateau
-hamn	Norwegian, Swedish	port, harbour
-hamrar	Icelandic	cliffs
Hāmūn	Farsi	marsh, salt pan
-hantō	Japanese	peninsula
Har	Hebrew	mountain
Hara	Belorussian	hill
Hardt	German	wooded hills
Ḥarrat, Ḥarrāt	Arabic	lava field
Hassi	Arabic	well
-haug, -haugen	Norwegian	hill
-havn	Danish, Faroese, Norwegian	bay, harbour, port
Hawr	Arabic	lake, impermanent lake, marsh
Hāyk'	Amharic	lake
He	Chinese	river
-hegység	Hungarian	hills, mountains
-hei	Norwegian	heath, moor
-heide	Dutch	heath, marsh
Heide	German	heath, moor
-heiði	Icelandic	heath

Geographical term	Language	Meaning
Helodrano	Malagasy	bay
Higashi-	Japanese	east, eastern
-hisar	Turkish	castle
Ḥiṣn	Arabic	fort
Hka	Burmese	river
-hnjúkur	Icelandic	hill
-ho	Korean	lake
-hø	Norwegian	peak
Hoch	German	high
Hoek	Dutch	cape, point
-höfði	Icelandic	hill, mountain
-höfn	Icelandic	cove
Hög	Swedish	height, high
-högda	Norwegian	height
Höhe	German	height
Hohen-	German	high
Hoi, Hoi Hap	Chinese	bay, channel, harbour, inlet
-høj, -høje	Danish	hill, hills
Hon	Vietnamese	island
Hoog	Dutch	high
Hora, Hory	Czech, Ukrainian	mountain(s)
-horn	Icelandic	cape, point, peak
Horn, -horn	German	mountain, peak
Horná, Horné, Horní, Horný	Czech	upper
Ḥorvot	Hebrew	ruins
-hot	Mongolian	town
-hrad	Czech	town
-hraun	Icelandic	lava field
Hu	Chinese	lake

I

Idd	Arabic	well
Île	French	island
Ilha, Ilhéu	Portuguese	island
Illa	Catalan	island
im	German	in
imeni	Russian	in the name of
Inish	Irish	island
Insel, Inseln	German	island, islands
Insula	Romanian	island
Irq, 'Irq	Arabic	hill, sand dune, sand dunes
Isla	Spanish	island
Iso-	Finnish	big
Isola, Isole	Italian	island, islands
Isolte	Catalan	island
Isthme	French	isthmus
Istmo	Spanish	isthmus
-iwa	Japanese	island

J

Jabal	Arabic	mountain
järv	Estonian	lake
-järvi	Finnish	lake
Jasiired	Somali	island
Jaun-	Latvian	new
-jaure	Lappish	lake
Jazīrah, Jazīreh, Jazīrat	Arabic	island
Jbel, Jebel	Arabic	mountain
Jezero, jezero	Croatian, Serbian, Slovene	lake
Jezioro	Polish	lake
Jiang	Chinese	river
Jiao	Chinese	cape, point
Jibāl	Arabic	mountains
-jima	Japanese	island
Jing	Chinese	well
-jõgi	Estonian	river
-joki	Finnish	river
-jokka	Lappish	river
-jökull, jökullen	Icelandic, Norwegian	glacier, ice cap

K

Kaap	Afrikaans	cape, point
-kai	Japanese	bay, channel
-kaigan	Japanese	coastal area
-kaikyō	Japanese	channel, strait
Kali	Indonesian, Malay	river
kalnas, kalnis	Lithuanian	hill
Kalns	Latvian	hill
Kamen'	Russian	rock
Kamm	German	ridge, crest
Kâmpóng	Cambodian	town, village
-kanaal	Dutch	canal
Kanal	German, Russian	canal
Kanał	Polish	canal
Kanalı	Azeri	canal
Kaôh	Cambodian	island
Kap	Danish	cape, point
Kapp	Norwegian	cape, point
Karang	Indonesian, Malay	reef
Kato	Greek	lower
Kavīr	Farsi	salt desert
-kawa	Japanese	river
Kecil	Indonesian, Malay	small
K'edi	Georgian	hills
Kefar	Hebrew	village
Kepi	Albanian	cape, point
Kepulauan	Indonesian	islands
Keski-	Finnish	middle, central
Khabrah, Khabrat	Arabic	impermanent lake
Khalīg, Khalīj	Arabic	bay, gulf
Khao	Thai	peak
Khashm	Arabic	hill
Khawr	Arabic	bay, channel
Khor, Khōr	Arabic	bay
Khowr	Farsi	bay, inlet
Khrebet	Russian	mountain range
Kis-	Hungarian	small
Kita-	Japanese	north, northern
Klein	Afrikaans	small
Klein, Kleine, Kleiner	German	small

Geographical term	Language	Meaning
Klint	Danish	cliff
-kloof	Afrikaans	pass
Knock	Irish	hill
-ko	Japanese	lake
Ko	Thai	island
-kōchi, -kōgen	Japanese	plateau
Koh	Farsi	mountain
Kok	Chinese	cape, point
Köl	Kazakh, Kyrgyz	lake
Kolpos	Greek	gulf
Koog	German	polder (reclaimed land)
-kop	Afrikaans	hill, mountain
Kopf	German	hill
Körfezi	Turkish	bay, gulf
körgustik	Estonian	upland
Kosa	Russian, Ukrainian	spit
Kou	Chinese	river mouth
-köy	Turkish	village
Kraj	Croatian, Czech, Polish, Serbian	region
Krajobrazowy	Polish	regional
Kray	Russian	territory
Kryazh	Russian	hills, ridge
Kuala	Malay	river mouth
Küçük	Turkish	small
Kuduk	Uighur	well
Kūh	Farsi	mountain
Kūhhā	Farsi	mountain range
Kul'	Russian	lake
-kül	Tajik	lake
-küla	Estonian	village
Kum	Russian	sandy desert
-kundo	Korean	islands
Kuppe	German	hill top
kurk	Estonian	channel, strait
K'vemo	Georgian	upper
-kvísl, kvíslar	Icelandic	river, rivers
-kylä	Finnish	village
Kyun	Burmese	island

L

La	Tibetan	pass
Lac	French	lake
Lacul	Romanian	lake
Laem	Thai	cape, point
Lago	Italian, Portuguese, Spanish	lake
Lagoa	Portuguese	lagoon
Laguna	Spanish	lagoon, lake
Lagune	French	lagoon
laht	Estonian	bay
-laid	Estonian	island
Lam	Thai	river
Län	Swedish	county
Land	German	province
Lande	French	heath, sandy moor
Las	Polish	wood, forest
Laut	Indonesian, Malay	sea
Lerr	Armenian	mountain
Lerrnashght'a	Armenian	mountains
Lich	Armenian	lake
Liedao	Chinese	islands
Liel-	Latvian	big
Lille	Danish, Norwegian	small
Liman	Russian	bay, lagoon, lake
Limni	Greek	lagoon, lake
Limnothalassa	Greek	inlet, lagoon
Ling	Chinese	mountain range
Liqeni	Albanian	lake
Llano	Spanish	plain, prairie
Llyn	Welsh	lake
Loch, Lochan	Gaelic	lake, small lake
Lohatanjona	Malagasy	cape, point
Loi	Burmese	mountain
looduskaitseala	Estonian	reserve
Luonnonpuisto	Finnish	nature reserve
-luoto	Finnish	rocky island
Lyman	Ukrainian	bay, lake

M

Macizo	Spanish	mountain range
Madh	Albanian	big
Madīnat	Arabic	town
Mae, Mae Nam	Thai	river
mägi	Estonian	hill
Măgura	Romanian	hill, mountain
Maḥaṭṭat	Arabic	station
Maja	Albanian	mountain
Mal	Albanian	mountain(s)
Mala	Croatian, Serbian	small
Malá	Czech, Slovak	small
Mali	Albanian	mountain
Mali	Croatian, Serbian, Ukrainian	small
Malo	Croatian, Serbian	small
Maloye	Russian	small
Maly, Malyya	Belorussian	small
-man	Korean	bay
Mar	Spanish	lagoon, lake
Marais	French	marsh, swamp
Mare	Italian	sea
Mare	Romanian	big
marios	Lithuanian	lake
Marsa	Arabic	anchorage, bay, inlet
Marsch	German	fen, marsh
Masabb	Arabic	estuary
Massif	French	mountains, upland
Maʻṭan	Arabic	well
Mayor	Spanish	higher, larger
Maz-	Latvian	small
Meall	Gaelic	hill, mountain
Meer	Dutch, German	lake
Mega, Megalo-	Greek	big
Men	Chinese	gate

Geographical term	Language	Meaning
Menor	Portuguese, Spanish	smaller, lesser
Mersa	Arabic	anchorage, inlet
Mesa, Meseta	Spanish	tableland
Mesto	Croatian, Serbian	town
Město	Czech	town
Mets	Armenian	big
Mezzo	Italian	middle, central
Miao	Chinese	temple
Miasto	Polish	town
Mic, Mica	Romanian	small
Mikra, Mikri	Greek	small
Mina'	Arabic	port, harbour
Minami-	Japanese	south, southern
-mine	Japanese	mountain
-misaki	Japanese	cape, point
Mishāsh	Arabic	well
Mittel-, Mitten-	German	middle, central
Moel	Welsh	hill
Monasterio	Spanish	monastery
Moni	Greek	monastery
Mont	French	hill, mountain
Montagna	Italian	mountain
Montagne	French	mountain
Monte	Italian, Portuguese, Spanish	hill, mountain
Monti	Italian	mountains
Moor	German	marsh, moor, swamp
Moos	German	marsh, moss
More	Russian	sea
Mörön	Mongolian	river
Morro	Portuguese	hill
Morro	Spanish	cape, point
-mose	Danish	marsh, moor
Moyen	French	middle, central
Mt'a	Georgian	mountain
Muang	Laotian, Thai	town
Muara	Indonesian, Malay	estuary
Mui	Vietnamese	cape, point
Mun	Chinese	channel
Munții	Romanian	mountains
Mynydd	Welsh	mountain
-mýri	Icelandic	marsh
Mys	Russian	cape, point

N

na	Croatian, Czech, Russian, Serbian, Slovak, Slovene	on
Nacional	Portuguese, Spanish	national
nacionalinis	Lithuanian	national
nad	Czech, Polish, Slovak	above, over
-nada	Japanese	bay, gulf
Nafūd	Arabic	desert, sand dunes
Nagor'ye	Russian	mountains, plateau
Nagy-	Hungarian	big
Nahr	Arabic	river
Nakhon	Thai	town
Nakrdzali	Georgian	reserve
Nam	Burmese, Laotian	river
Nam	Korean, Vietnamese	south, southern
Nan	Chinese	south, southern
Nanshan	Chinese	mountain range
Narodowy	Polish	national
Nationaal	Dutch	national
Naturreservat	Norwegian, Swedish	nature reserve
Natuurreservaat	Dutch	nature reserve
Naviglio	Italian	canal
Nawa-	Urdu	new
Nazionale	Italian	national
Neder-	Dutch	lower
Nehri	Turkish	river
Nei	Chinese	inner
Nek	Afrikaans	pass
-nes	Icelandic	cape, point
Neu-	German	new
Neuf, Neuve	French	new
Nevado, Nevada	Spanish	snow-covered mountain(s)
Nieder-	German	lower
Nieuw, Nieuwe, Nieuwer	Dutch	new
nina	Estonian	cape, point
Nishi-	Japanese	west, western
Nizhneye, Nizhniy, Nizhniye, Nizhnyaya	Russian	lower
Nizina	Belorussian	lowland
Nízke	Slovak	low
Nizmennost'	Russian	lowland
Nižní	Czech	lower
Nižný	Slovak	lower
Noguera	Catalan	river
Noord	Dutch	north, northern
Nord	French, German	north, northern
Nord-, Nordre	Danish	north, northern
Norður	Icelandic	north, northern
Norra	Swedish	north, northern
Nørre	Danish	north, northern
Norte	Portuguese, Spanish	north, northern
Nos	Bulgarian, Russian	cape, point, spit
Nosy	Malagasy	island
Nou	Romanian	new
Nouveau, Nouvelle	French	new
Nova	Bulgarian, Croatian, Portuguese, Serbian, Slovene, Ukrainian	new
Nová	Czech	new
Novaya	Russian	new
Nové	Czech, Slovak	new
Novi	Bulgarian, Croatian, Serbian, Ukrainian	new
Novo	Portuguese, Slovene	new
Novo-, Novoye	Russian	new
Novy	Belorussian	new
Nový	Czech	new
Novyy, Novyye	Russian, Ukrainian	new
Novyya	Belorussian	new
Nowa, Nowe, Nowy	Polish	new
Nueva, Nuevo	Spanish	new
-numa	Japanese	lake

Geographical term	Language	Meaning
-núpur	Icelandic	hill
Nur	Chinese, Mongolian	lake
Nuruu	Mongolian	mountain range
Nuur	Mongolian	lake
Ny-	Danish, Norwegian, Swedish	new

O

-ø	Danish	island
-ö	Swedish	island
oaivi, oaivve	Lappish	hill, mountain
Obanbari	Tajik	reservoir
Ober-	German	upper
Oblast'	Russian, Ukrainian	administrative division
-odde	Danish, Norwegian	cape, point
Oeste	Spanish	west, western
Okrug	Russian	administrative district
-ön	Swedish	island
Öndör-	Mongolian	upper
-oog	German	island
Oost, Ooster	Dutch	east, eastern
-öræfi	Icelandic	lava field
Oriental	Spanish	east, eastern
Ormos	Greek	bay
Oros	Greek	mountain
-ós	Icelandic	river mouth
Ost-	German	east, eastern
Øster-	Danish, Norwegian	east, eastern
Östra-	Swedish	east, eastern
Ostriv	Ukrainian	island
Ostrov, Ostrova	Russian	island, islands
Oud, Oude, Ouden, Ouder	Dutch	old
Oued	Arabic	watercourse
Ovası	Turkish	plain
Over-	Danish, Dutch	upper
Över-, Övre-	Norwegian, Swedish	upper
-oy	Faroese	island
Ozero	Russian, Ukrainian	lake

P

-pää	Finnish	hill
Pampa	Spanish	plain
Pantà	Catalan	reservoir
Pantanal	Portuguese	marsh
Pao	Chinese	small lake
Parbat	Urdu	mountain
Parc	French	park
Parc Naturel	French	nature reserve
Parco	Italian	park
parkas	Lithuanian	park
Parque	Portuguese, Spanish	park
-pas	Afrikaans	pass
Paso	Spanish	pass
Paß	German	pass
Passage	French	channel
Passe	French	channel
Passo	Italian	pass
Pasul	Romanian	pass
Pegunungan	Indonesian, Malay	mountain range
Pelabuhan	Malay	port, harbour
Pen	Welsh	hill
Peña	Spanish	cliff, rock
Pendi	Chinese	basin
Península	Spanish	peninsula
Péninsule	French	peninsula
Penisola	Italian	peninsula
Pereval	Russian	pass
Pervo-, Pervyy	Russian	first
Peski	Russian	desert
Petit, Petite	French	small
Phou	Laotian	mountain
Phu	Thai, Vietnamese	mountain
Phumĭ	Cambodian	town, village
Pic	Catalan, French	peak
Picacho	Spanish	peak
Pico	Spanish	peak
Pik	Russian	peak
Pingyuan	Chinese	plain
Pivostriv	Ukrainian	peninsula
Pizzo	Italian	peak
-plaat	Dutch	flat, sandbank, shoal
Plage	French	beach
Plaine	French	plain
Planalto	Portuguese	plateau
Planina	Bulgarian, Croatian, Serbian	mountain(s)
Platforma	Romanian	plateau
Plato	Bulgarian, Russian	plateau
Playa	Spanish	beach
Plaza	Spanish	market-place, square
Ploskogor'ye	Russian	plateau
Po	Chinese	lake
pod	Czech, Russian, Slovak	under, sub-, near
Podişul	Romanian	plateau
Pointe	French	cape, point
Pojezierze	Polish	area of lakes
Polje	Croatian, Serbian	plain
Poluostrov	Russian	peninsula
Pont	French	bridge
Ponta	Maltese, Portuguese	cape, point
Ponte	Portuguese	bridge
poolsaar	Estonian	peninsula
Porogi	Russian	rapids
Port	Catalan, French, Maltese, Russian	port, harbour
Portella	Italian	pass
Portillo	Spanish	gap, pass
Porto	Italian, Portuguese, Spanish	bay, port, harbour, pass
Pradesh	Hindi	state

Geographical term	Language	Meaning
Praia	Portuguese	beach, shore
Prêk	Cambodian	lake, river
près	French	near, beside
Presa	Spanish	reservoir
Presqu'île	French	peninsula
Pri-	Russian	near, by
Proliv	Russian	channel, strait
Protoka	Russian	channel, watercourse
Pueblo	Spanish	village
Puente	Spanish	bridge
Puerta	Spanish	narrow pass
Puerto	Spanish	pass, port, harbour
Puig	Catalan	hill, mountain
Puk-	Korean	north, northern
Pulau	Indonesian, Malay	island
Pulau-pulau	Indonesian, Malay	islands
Puncak	Indonesian, Malay	hill, mountain, summit
Punta	Italian, Spanish	cape, point
Punta	Italian	hill, mountain
Puntan	Marshallese	cape, point
Puy	French	peak

Q

Qã'	Arabic	depression, salt flat, impermanent lake
Qabr	Arabic	tomb
Qafa	Albanian	pass
Qala	Maltese	bay
Qalamat	Arabic	well
Qalti	Arabic	well
Qāret	Arabic	hill
Qatorkühi	Tajik	mountain range
Qi	Chinese	banner (administrative division)
Qiao	Chinese	bridge
Qiryat	Hebrew	town
Qolleh	Farsi	mountain
Qoor, Qooriga	Somali	bay
qoruğu	Azeri	reserve
Qu	Tibetan	river
Quan	Chinese	spring, well
Quebrada	Spanish	ravine, river
Qullai	Tajik	mountain
Qundao	Chinese	islands

R

Raas	Somali	cape, point
Rade	French	harbour
rags	Latvian	cape, point
Rambla	Catalan	river
Ramla	Maltese	bay, harbour
Ramlat	Arabic	sandy desert
-rani	Icelandic	spur
Ras	Arabic, Maltese	cape, point
Ra's	Arabic, Farsi	cape, point
Rãs, Räs	Arabic	cape, point
Ravnina	Russian	plain
Récif	French	reef
Represa	Portuguese, Spanish	reservoir
Reserva	Portuguese, Spanish	reserve
Réserve de Faune, Réserve Faunique	French	wildlife reserve
Réserve Naturelle	French	nature reserve
Reshteh	Farsi	mountain range
Respublika	Russian	republic
-rettö	Japanese	island chain, island group
rezervatas	Lithuanian	reserve
-ri	Korean	village
Ri	Tibetan	mountain
Ría	Spanish	estuary, inlet, river mouth
Ribeirão, Ribeiro	Portuguese	river
Rio	Portuguese	river
Río	Spanish	river
Riserva	Italian	reserve
-rivier	Afrikaans	river
Riviera	Italian	coastal area
Rivière	French	river
Roca	Spanish	rock
Rocher	French	rock
Rt	Croatian, Serbian	cape, point
Rū, Rūbār	Kurdish	river
Rubh', Rubha	Gaelic	cape, point
Rūd, Rūdkhāneh	Farsi	river
Rujm	Arabic	hill

S

-saar	Estonian	island
-saari	Finnish	island
Sabkhat, Sabkhet	Arabic	impermanent lake, salt flat, salt marsh
Sadd, Saddat	Arabic	dam
Sagar, Sagara	Hindi	lake
Şaghîr, Şaghïr	Arabic	small
Şahrã'	Arabic	desert
-saki	Japanese	cape, point
Salar, Salina	Spanish	salt pan
Salto	Portuguese, Spanish	waterfall
San	Italian, Maltese, Portuguese, Spanish	saint
San	Laotian	mountain
-san	Japanese, Korean	mountain
-sanchi	Japanese	mountain range
-sandur	Icelandic	sandy area
Sankt	German, Russian	saint
-sanmaek	Korean	mountain range
-sanmyaku	Japanese	mountain range
Sant	Catalan	saint
Sant'	Italian	saint

Geographical term	Language	Meaning
Santa	Italian, Portuguese, Spanish	saint
Santo	Italian, Portuguese, Spanish	saint
São	Portuguese	saint
Sar	Kurdish	mountain
Sarīr	Arabic	desert
Satu	Romanian	village
Say	Kyrgyz	river
Schloß	German	castle, mansion
Scoglio	Italian	reef, rock
Sebkha, Sebkhet	Arabic	salt flat, salt marsh
See, -see	German	lake
-şehir	Turkish	town
Selat	Indonesian, Malay	channel, strait
Selatan	Indonesian, Malay	south, southern
-selkä	Finnish	lake, open water, ridge
Selo	Croatian, Russian, Serbian	village
Selva	Portuguese, Spanish	forest
Semenanjung	Indonesian, Malay	peninsula
Seno	Spanish	bay, sound
Serra	Catalan, Portuguese	hills, mountains
Serranía	Spanish	mountain range
-seter	Norwegian	mountain pasture
-seto	Japanese	channel, strait
Severnaya, Severnoye, Severnyy, Severo-	Russian	north, northern
Sfântu	Romanian	saint
Sgeir	Gaelic	island
Sgor, Sgorach, Sgorr, Sgurr	Gaelic	hill
Shahr	Farsi	town
Sha'ib, Sha'īān	Arabic	watercourse
Shamo	Chinese	desert
Shan	Chinese	hill(s), mountain(s)
Shang	Chinese	next to, upper
Shankou	Chinese	pass
Sharm	Arabic	bay
Shaṭṭ	Arabic	estuary, river mouth, watercourse
Shën-	Albanian	saint
Shet'	Amharic	watercourse
Shi	Chinese	city
-shima	Japanese	island
-sho	Japanese	island
-shotō	Japanese	islands
Shui	Chinese	river
Shui Tong	Chinese	reservoir
Shuiku	Chinese	reservoir
Sierra	Spanish	mountain range
Silsiläsi	Azeri	hills
-sjø	Norwegian	lake
-sjö, -sjön	Swedish	lake
-sjór	Icelandic	lake
-sker	Icelandic	island
-skog	Norwegian	wood
Slieau	Manx	hill, mountain
Slieve	Irish	hill, mountain
Sloboda	Russian	large village
Sø	Danish, Norwegian	lake
Söder, Södra	Swedish	south, southern
Solonchak	Russian	salt lake
Sommet	French	peak, summit
Sønder-, Søndre	Danish	south, southern
Sông	Vietnamese	river
Sopka	Russian	hill, mountain, volcano
Sør-	Norwegian	south, southern
Sor	Russian	salt pan
sous	French	under
Sovkhoz	Russian	state farm
Spitze	German	peak
Sredna, Sredno	Bulgarian	middle, central
Sredne-, Sredneye, Sredniy, Srednyaya	Russian	middle, central
Sron	Gaelic	hill
Stac	Gaelic	hill, stack
-stad	Afrikaans, Norwegian, Swedish	town
-stadt	German	town
-staður	Icelandic	town
Stagno	Italian	lagoon, lake
Stara, Stari	Croatian, Serbian, Ukrainian	old
Stará, Staré, Starý	Czech	old
Staraya, Stary, Staryya	Belorussian	old
Staraya, Staroye, Staryy, Staryye	Russian	old
Stare, Staro-, Staryy	Ukrainian	old
Stausee	German	reservoir
Steno	Greek	strait
Step'	Russian	plain, steppe
Stob	Gaelic	hill, mountain
Stœng	Cambodian	river
Stór-, Stóra, Stóri	Icelandic	big
Stor, Stora	Swedish	big
Store	Danish	big
Strand	Danish, German	beach
-strand	Norwegian, Swedish	beach
Straße	German	street
Stretta	Italian	strait
-strönd	Icelandic	beach
Sud	French	south, southern
Süd-, Süder-	German	south, southern
Suður-	Icelandic	south, southern
Suid	Afrikaans	south, southern
-suidō	Japanese	channel, strait
Sul	Portuguese	south, southern
sul, sull'	Italian	on
Sund	Swedish	strait, sound
Sungai	Indonesian, Malay	river
-suo	Finnish	marsh, swamp
Superior	Spanish	upper
Süq	Arabic	market
Sur	Spanish	south, southern
sur	French	on
Suur	Estonian	big
Sveti	Croatian, Serbian	saint
Syðra, Syðri	Icelandic	south, southern
sýsla	Icelandic	county

Geographical term	Language	Meaning
Szent-	Hungarian	saint
-sziget	Hungarian	island

T

Geographical term	Language	Meaning
-tag	Uighur	mountain
-take	Japanese	hill, mountain
Tal	German	valley
Tall	Arabic	hill
Tanjona	Malagasy	cape, point
Tanjong, Tanjung	Indonesian, Malay	cape, point
Tao	Chinese	island
Tassili	Berber	plateau
Tau	Russian	mountain(s)
Taung	Burmese	mountain
Tba	Georgian	lake
Techniti Limni	Greek	reservoir
tekojärvi	Finnish	reservoir
Tell	Arabic	hill, mountain
Teluk, Telukan	Indonesian, Malay	bay, gulf
Tengah	Indonesian, Malay	middle, central
Teniente	Spanish	lieutenant
Tepe, Tepesi	Turkish	hill, mountain
Terara	Amharic	mountain
Terre	French	land
Thale	Thai	lake
Thamad	Arabic	well
Tierra	Spanish	land
Timur	Indonesian, Malay	east, eastern
-tind, -tinden	Norwegian	peak
-tindar	Icelandic	peak
-tindur	Faroese, Icelandic	peak
Tir'at	Arabic	canal, river, watercourse
Tizi	Berber	pass
-tjåkkå	Lappish	mountain
-tjårro	Lappish	mountain
-tó	Hungarian	lake
-tō	Japanese	island
-to	Korean	island
-töge	Japanese	pass
-tong	Korean	village
Tônlé	Cambodian	lake, river
Too	Kyrgyz	mountain range
-topp, -toppen	Norwegian	peak
T'ou	Chinese	cape, point
Tsentral'nyy	Russian	central
Tso	Tibetan	lake
Tsqalsats'avi	Georgian	reservoir
Tsui	Chinese	cape, point
Túnel	Spanish	tunnel
-tunturi	Finnish	treeless mountain

U

Geographical term	Language	Meaning
Über-	German	upper
-udden	Swedish	cape, point
Ugheltekhili	Georgian	pass
Új-	Hungarian	new
Ujung	Indonesian	cape, point
Unter-, unter	German	below, lower
'Uqlat	Arabic	well
-ura	Japanese	inlet
'Urayq, 'Urūq	Arabic	sand dunes
Ust'-, Ust'ye	Russian	river mouth
Utara	Indonesian, Malay	north, northern
Uttar	Hindi	north, northern
Uul	Mongolian	mountain range
Uval	Russian	hills
'Uyūn	Arabic	springs

V

Geographical term	Language	Meaning
v	Czech	in
-vaara, -vaarat	Finnish	hill(s), mountain(s)
Vaart, -vaart	Dutch	canal
-vaðall	Icelandic	inlet
-våg	Norwegian	bay
-vágur	Faroese	bay
Väike-	Estonian	small
väin	Estonian	bay, channel, strait
Val	French, Portuguese, Spanish	valley
Vale	Portuguese, Romanian	valley
Vall	Catalan, Spanish	valley
Valle	Italian, Spanish	valley
Vallée	French	valley
Valli	Italian	valleys
Vallon	French	small valley
Vârful	Romanian	hill, mountain
-város	Hungarian	town
-varre	Norwegian	mountain
Väster, Västra	Swedish	west, western
-vatn	Icelandic	lake
-vatn, -vatnet	Norwegian	lake
-vatten, -vattnet	Swedish	lake
Vaux	French	valleys
Vechi	Romanian	old
veehoidla	Estonian	lake
-veld	Afrikaans	field
Velha, Velho	Portuguese	old
Velika	Croatian, Slovene, Serbian	big
Velikaya, Velikiy, Velikiye	Russian	big
Velike	Slovene	big
Veliki	Croatian, Serbian	big
Velká, Velké, Velký	Czech	big
Veľká, Veľké, Veľký	Slovak	big
-vellir	Icelandic	plain
Velyka	Ukrainian	big
Verkhne-, Verkhneye, Verkhniy, Verkhnyaya	Russian	upper
-vesi	Finnish	lake, water
Viaduc	French	viaduct
-vidda	Norwegian	plateau

Geographical term	Language	Meaning
Vieja, Viejo	Spanish	old
Vieux	French	old
Vig	Danish	bay
-vik	Icelandic	bay
-vik	Norwegian	bay, inlet
Vila	Portuguese	small town
Ville	French	town
Vinh	Vietnamese	bay
-víz	Hungarian	river
-víztároló	Hungarian	reservoir
-vlei	Afrikaans	lake, salt pan
-vloer	Afrikaans	salt pan
Voblasts'	Belorussian	province
Vodaskhovishcha	Belorussian	reservoir
Vodná nádrž	Slovak	reservoir
Vodní nádrž	Czech	reservoir
Vodokhranilishche	Russian	reservoir
Vodoskhovyshche	Ukrainian	reservoir
-vogur	Icelandic	bay
Volcán	Spanish	volcano
Vostochno-, Vostochnyy	Russian	east, eastern
-võtn	Icelandic	lakes
Vozvyshennost'	Russian	hills, upland
Vozyera	Belorussian	lake
Vpadina	Russian	depression
Vrchovina	Czech	hills, mountain region
Vrŭkh	Bulgarian	hill, mountain
Vulkan	Russian	volcano
Vyalikaya, Vyalikaye, Vyaliki, Vyalikiya	Belorussian	big
Vyerkhnya	Belorussian	upper
Vysokaya, Vysokoye	Russian	upper

W

Geographical term	Language	Meaning
-waard	Dutch	polder (reclaimed land)
Wad	Dutch	sandflat
Wadi, Wādi, Wādī	Arabic	watercourse
Wai	Chinese	outer
Wald	German	forest
Wan	Chinese	bay
-wan	Japanese	bay
Wand	German	cliff
Wasser	German	water
Wāw	Arabic	well
Webi	Somali	river
Wenz	Amharic	river, watercourse
Wielka, Wielki, Wielkie, Wielko-	Polish	big
-woud	Dutch	wood, forest
Wysoka, Wysoki, Wysokie	Polish	upper
Wyżna	Polish	lowland
Wzvyshsha	Belorussian	upland

X

Geographical term	Language	Meaning
Xé	Vietnamese	river
Xi	Chinese	river, west, western
Xia	Chinese	gorge, lower
Xian	Chinese	county
Xiao	Chinese	small

Y

Geographical term	Language	Meaning
Yam	Hebrew	lake, sea
-yama	Japanese	mountain
Yang	Chinese	channel
Yangi	Russian	new
Yarımadası	Azeri, Turkish	peninsula
Yazovir	Bulgarian	reservoir
Ye	Burmese	island
Yeni	Turkish	new
Yli-	Finnish	upper
Ynys	Welsh	island
Yoma	Burmese	mountain range
You	Chinese	right
Ytra-, Ytri-	Icelandic	outer
Ytre-	Norwegian	outer
Ytter-	Norwegian, Swedish	outer
Yuan	Chinese	spring
Yumco	Tibetan	lake
Yunhe	Chinese	canal
Yuzhno-, Yuzhnyy	Russian	south, southern

Z

Geographical term	Language	Meaning
Za-	Russian	behind, beyond
-zaki	Japanese	cape, point
Zalew	Polish	bay
Zaliv	Russian	bay, gulf, inlet
-zan	Japanese	mountain
Zand	Dutch	sandbank, sandhill
Zangbo	Tibetan	river
Zapadnaya, Zapadno-, Zapadnyy	Russian	west, western
Zapavyednik	Belorussian	reserve
Zapovednik	Russian	reserve
Zapovidnyk	Ukrainian	reserve
Zatoka	Polish, Ukrainian	bay, gulf, lagoon
-zee	Dutch	lake, sea
Zemlya	Russian	land
Zemo	Georgian	upper
Zhen	Chinese	town
Zhong	Chinese	middle, central
Zhou	Chinese	island
Zizhiqu	Chinese	autonomous region
Zuid, Zuider	Dutch	south, southern
Zuo	Chinese	left

INTRODUCTION TO THE INDEX

The index includes names shown on the maps in the Atlas of the World. Each entry includes the country or geographical area in which the feature is located, a page number and an alphanumeric reference. Additional details within the entries are explained below. Abbreviations used in the index are explained in the table below.

REFERENCING

Names are referenced by page number, the first element of each entry, and by a grid reference. The grid reference correlates to the alphanumeric values which appear within each map frame. These reflect the graticule on the map – the letter relates to longitude divisions, the number to latitude divisions.

Names are generally referenced to the largest scale map page on which they appear. For large geographical features, including countries, the reference is to the largest scale map on which the feature appears in its entirety, or on which the majority of it appears.

Rivers are referenced to their lowest downstream point – either their mouth or their confluence with another river. The river name will generally be positioned as close to this point as possible, but may not necessarily be in the same grid square.

ALTERNATIVE NAMES

Alternative names or name forms appear as cross-references and refer the user to the entry for the map form of the name.

For rivers with multiple names – for example those which flow through several countries – all alternative name forms are included within the main index entries, with details of the countries in which each form applies. Different types of name used are: alternative forms or spellings currently in use (alt.); English conventional name forms normally used in English-language contexts (conv.); and long names – full forms of names which are most commonly used in the abbreviated form.

ADMINISTRATIVE QUALIFIERS

Entries within the following countries include the main administrative division in which they occur: Australia, Canada, China, India, Serbia, UK and USA. Administrative divisions are also included to differentiate duplicate names – entries of exactly the same name and feature type within the one country – where these division names are shown on the maps. In such cases, duplicate names are alphabetized in the order of the administrative division names.

Additional qualifiers are included for names within selected geographical areas, to indicate more clearly their location. In particular, this has been applied to island nations to indicate the island group, or individual island, on which a feature occurs.

DESCRIPTORS

Entries, other than those for towns and cities, include a descriptor indicating the type of geographical feature. Descriptors are not included where the type of feature is implicit in the name itself, unless there is a town or city of exactly the same name.

INSETS

Entries relating to names appearing on insets are indicated by a small box symbol: ▫, followed by an inset number if there is more than one inset on the page, or by a grid reference if the inset has its own alphanumeric values.

NAME FORMS AND ALPHABETICAL ORDER

Name forms are as they appear on the maps, with additional alternative forms included as cross-references. Names appear in full in the index, although they may appear in abbreviated form on the maps.

The Icelandic characters Þ and þ are transliterated and alphabetized as 'Th' and 'th'. The German character ß is alphabetized as 'ss'. Names beginning with Mac or Mc are alphabetized exactly as they appear. The terms Saint, Sainte, etc, are abbreviated to St, Ste, etc, but alphabetized as if in the full form.

Name form policies are explained in the Introduction to the Atlas (pp 66-67).

NUMERICAL ENTRIES

Entries beginning with numerals appear at the beginning of the index, in numerical order. Elsewhere, numerals appear before 'a'.

PERMUTED TERMS

Names beginning with generic, geographical terms are permuted – the descriptive term is placed after, and the index alphabetized by, the main part of the name. For example, Lake Superior is indexed as Superior, Lake; Mount Everest as Everest, Mount. This policy is applied to all languages. Permuting has not been applied to names of towns, cities or administrative divisions beginning with such geographical terms. These remain in their full form, for example, Lake Isabella, California, USA. The definite article, for example La, Le, Les (French); El, Las, Los (Spanish); Al, Ar, As (Arabic), is not permuted in any language.

INDEX ABBREVIATIONS

A.C.T.	Australian Capital Territory	est.	estuary	Moz.	Mozambique	rf	reef
admin. dist.	administrative district	Eth.	Ethiopia	MS	Mississippi	RI	Rhode Island
admin. div.	administrative division	Fin.	Finland	MT	Montana	Rus. Fed.	Russian Federation
admin. reg.	administrative region	FL	Florida	mt.	mountain	S.	South
Afgh.	Afghanistan	for.	forest	mts	mountains	S.A.	South Australia
AK	Alaska	Fr. Guiana	French Guiana	mun.	municipality	Sask.	Saskatchewan
AL	Alabama	Fr. Polynesia	French Polynesia	N.	North	SC	South Carolina
Alg.	Algeria	g.	gulf	N.B.	New Brunswick	SD	South Dakota
alt.	alternative name form	GA	Georgia	NC	North Carolina	sea chan.	sea channel
Alta	Alberta	Gd Bahama	Grand Bahama	ND	North Dakota	Sing.	Singapore
Andhra Prad.	Andhra Pradesh	Ger.	Germany	NE	Nebraska	str.	strait
AR	Arkansas	Guat.	Guatemala	Neth.	Netherlands	Switz.	Switzerland
Arg.	Argentina	hd	headland	Nfld.	Newfoundland	Tajik.	Tajikistan
Arun. Prad.	Arunachal Pradesh	Heilong.	Heilongjiang	NH	New Hampshire	Tanz.	Tanzania
Austr.	Australia	HI	Hawaii	Nic.	Nicaragua	Tas.	Tasmania
aut. comm.	autonomous community	Hima. Prad.	Himachal Pradesh	NJ	New Jersey	terr.	territory
aut. div.	autonomous division	H.K.	Hong Kong	NM	New Mexico	Thai.	Thailand
aut. prov.	autonomous province	Hond.	Honduras	N.S.	Nova Scotia	TN	Tennessee
aut. reg.	autonomous region	i.	island	N.S.W.	New South Wales	Trin. and Tob.	Trinidad and Tobago
aut. rep.	autonomous republic	is	islands	N.T.	Northern Territory	tun.	tunnel
AZ	Arizona	IA	Iowa	NV	Nevada	Turkm.	Turkmenistan
Azer.	Azerbaijan	ID	Idaho	N.W.T.	Northwest Territories	TX	Texas
b.	bay	IL	Illinois	NY	New York	U.A.E.	United Arab Emirates
Bangl.	Bangladesh	imp. l.	impermanent lake	N.Z.	New Zealand	U.K.	United Kingdom
B.C.	British Columbia	IN	Indiana	OH	Ohio	Ukr.	Ukraine
B.I.O.T.	British Indian Ocean Territory	Indon.	Indonesia	OK	Oklahoma	Uru.	Uruguay
Bol.	Bolivia	isth.	isthmus	Ont.	Ontario	U.S.A.	United States of America
Bos.-Herz.	Bosnia-Herzegovina	Kazakh.	Kazakhstan	OR	Oregon	UT	Utah
Bulg.	Bulgaria	KS	Kansas	PA	Pennsylvania	Uttar Prad.	Uttar Pradesh
c.	cape	KY	Kentucky	Pak.	Pakistan	Uzbek.	Uzbekistan
CA	California	Kyrg.	Kyrgyzstan	Para.	Paraguay	VA	Virginia
Can.	Canada	l.	lake	P.E.I.	Prince Edward Island	val.	valley
C.A.R.	Central African Republic	LA	Louisiana	pen.	peninsula	Venez.	Venezuela
CO	Colorado	lag.	lagoon	Phil.	Philippines	Vic.	Victoria
Col.	Colombia	Lith.	Lithuania	plat.	plateau	vol.	volcano
conv.	conventional name form	Lux.	Luxembourg	P.N.G.	Papua New Guinea	vol. crater	volcanic crater
CT	Connecticut	MA	Massachusetts	Pol.	Poland	VT	Vermont
Czech Rep.	Czech Republic	Madag.	Madagascar	Port.	Portugal	W.	West, Western
DC	District of Columbia	Madh. Prad.	Madhya Pradesh	pref.	prefecture	W.A.	Western Australia
DE	Delaware	Mahar.	Maharashtra	prov.	province	WA	Washington
Dem. Rep. Congo	Democratic Republic of the Congo	Man.	Manitoba	Qld	Queensland	WI	Wisconsin
depr.	depression	Maur.	Mauritania	Que.	Québec	WV	West Virginia
dept	department	MD	Maryland	r.	river	WY	Wyoming
des.	desert	ME	Maine	r. mouth	river mouth	Y.T.	Yukon Territory
Dom. Rep.	Dominican Republic	Mex.	Mexico	reg.	region		
E.	East, Eastern	MI	Michigan	Rep.	Republic		
Equat. Guinea	Equatorial Guinea	MN	Minnesota	research stn	research station		
esc.	escarpment	MO	Missouri	resr	reservoir		

1st Cataract to Afonso Cláudio

274

1

203 G3 **1st Cataract** *rapids* Egypt
85 J2 **1st Three Mile Opening** *sea chan. Qld* Austr.
203 F4 **2nd Cataract** *rapids* Sudan
85 I2 **2nd Three Mile Opening** *sea chan. Qld* Austr.
203 F5 **3rd Cataract** *rapids* Sudan
203 G5 **4th Cataract** *rapids* Sudan
203 G5 **5th Cataract** *rapids* Sudan
261 G4 **9 de Julio** Arg.
261 G5 **16 de Julio** Arg.
261 F5 **17 de Agosto** Arg.
261 G4 **25 de Mayo** *Buenos Aires* Arg.
260 D5 **25 de Mayo** *La Pampa* Arg.
260 C4 **25 de Mayo** *Mendoza* Arg.
261 I4 **25 de Mayo** Uru.
129 K6 **26 Bakı Komissari** Azer.
261 F5 **30 de Agosto** Arg.
215 N4 **42nd Hill** S. Africa
222 F5 **70 Mile House** *B.C.* Can.
222 F5 **100 Mile House** *B.C.* Can.
222 F4 **150 Mile House** *B.C.* Can.

A

156 D1 **Aa** *r.* France
169 B7 **Aa** *r.* Ger.
169 E7 **Aa** *r.* Ger.
142 F6 **Aabenraa** Denmark
172 F6 **Aach** Ger.
172 G6 **Aach** *r.* Ger.
169 B9 **Aachen** Ger.
210 E4 **Aadan Yabaal** Somalia
190 F1 **Aadorf** Switz.
143 K6 **Aakirkeby** *Bornholm* Denmark
142 F4 **Aalborg** Denmark
142 G5 **Aalborg Bugt** *b.* Denmark
173 I4 **Aalen** Ger.
142 F5 **Aalestrup** Denmark
Aalesund Norway *see* **Ålesund**
Aaley Lebanon *see* **Aley**
164 G4 **Aalsmeer** Neth.
165 F7 **Aalst** Belgium
165 H6 **Aalst** Neth.
164 K5 **Aalten** Neth.
165 D6 **Aalter** Belgium
Aanaar Fin. *see* **Inari**
140 R5 **Äänekoski** Fin.
214 G2 **Aansluit** S. Africa
Aar *r.* Switz. *see* **Aare**
113 □1 **Aarah** *i. N. Male* Maldives
190 E1 **Aarau** Switz.
190 C1 **Aarberg** Switz.
190 D1 **Aarburg** Switz.
165 D6 **Aardenburg** Neth.
190 E1 **Aare** *r.* Switz.
140 Q3 **Aareavaara** Sweden
190 E1 **Aargau** *canton* Switz.
Aarhus Denmark *see* **Århus**
164 I6 **Aarle** Neth.
Aarlen Belgium *see* **Arlon**
182 D2 **A Armada** Spain
142 F5 **Aars** Denmark
165 G7 **Aarschot** Belgium
165 F6 **Aartselaar** Belgium
142 G6 **Aarup** Denmark
172 D7 **Aarwangen** Switz.
221 M3 **Aasiaat** Greenland
Aath Belgium *see* **Ath**
140 Q3 **Aavasaksa** Fin.
108 C2 **Aba** *Sichuan* China
208 F4 **Aba** Dem. Rep. Congo
177 H4 **Aba** Hungary
207 G5 **Aba** Nigeria
124 G2 **Abā ad Dūd** Saudi Arabia
125 J6 **Abā al Afan** *oasis* Saudi Arabia
128 D9 **Abā al Hinshan** Saudi Arabia
251 G6 **Abacaxis** *r.* Brazil
122 C6 **Ābādān** Iran
122 H2 **Abadan** Turkm.
122 C6 **Ābādān, Jazīrah** *i.* Iran/Iraq
122 F3 **Abadan Tappeh** Iran
122 E6 **Ābādeh** Iran
122 E7 **Ābādeh Ţashk** Iran
182 G7 **Abadengo** *reg.* Spain
183 L7 **Abades** Spain
256 D3 **Abadia dos Dourados** Brazil
256 C2 **Abadiânia** Brazil
182 F2 **Abadín** Spain
204 E3 **Abadla** Alg.
177 J4 **Abádszalók** Hungary
129 B1 **Abadzekhskaya** Rus. Fed.
257 E3 **Abaeté** Brazil
257 E3 **Abaeté** *r.* Brazil
254 C2 **Abaetetuba** Brazil
107 O2 **Abagaytuy** Rus. Fed.
Abagnar Qi *Nei Mongol* China *see* **Xilinhot**
Abag Qi *Nei Mongol* China *see* **Xin Hot**
253 G6 **Abaí** Para.
77 H1 **Abaiang** *atoll* Kiribati
182 D2 **A Baiuca** Spain
207 G4 **Abaji** Nigeria
241 W4 **Abajo Peak** *UT* U.S.A.
207 H5 **Abakaliki** Nigeria
98 F1 **Abakan** Rus. Fed.
98 E1 **Abakanskiy Khrebet** *mts* Rus. Fed.
208 B5 **Abala** Congo
207 F3 **Abala** Niger
207 G3 **Abalak** Niger
205 G5 **Abalessa** Alg.
138 N7 **Abalyanka** *r.* Belarus
126 G3 **Abana** Turkey
183 P7 **Abánades** Spain
252 B3 **Abancay** Peru
208 A5 **Abanga** *r.* Gabon
187 C11 **Abanilla** Spain
191 L5 **Abano Terme** Italy
252 E4 **Abapó** Bol.
187 C11 **Abarán** Spain
Abariringa *atoll Phoenix Is* Kiribati *see* **Kanton**
122 E6 **Abarkūh, Kavīr-e** *des.* Iran
122 E6 **Abarqū** Iran
182 E3 **A Barrela** Spain
Abarshahr Iran *see* **Neyshābūr**
177 J4 **Abasár** Hungary
129 D3 **Abasha** Georgia
102 V2 **Abashiri** Japan
102 V3 **Abashiri-ko** *l.* Japan
102 V2 **Abashiri-wan** *b.* Japan
244 F5 **Abasolo** *Guanajuato* Mex.
245 I1 **Abasolo** *Tamaulipas* Mex.
245 L8 **Abasolo del Valle** Mex.
129 D4 **Abast'umani** Georgia
211 C5 **Abasula** *waterhole* Kenya
91 K9 **Abau** P.N.G.
177 K3 **Abaújszántó** Hungary
138 E4 **Abava** *r.* Latvia
121 O3 **Abay** *Karagandinskaya Oblast'* Kazakh.
Abay *Vostochnyy Kazakhstan* Kazakh. *see* **Karaul**
Abaya, Lake Eth. *see* **Ābaya Hāyk'**
210 C3 **Ābaya Hāyk'** *l.* Eth.
Abay Bazar Kazakh. *see* **Abay**
210 B2 **Ābay Wenz** *r.* Eth. *alt.* **Azraq, Bahr el (Sudan),** *conv.* **Blue Nile**
98 F1 **Abaza** Rus. Fed.
208 B3 **Abba** C.A.R.
192 H2 **Abbadia San Salvatore** Italy
127 P8 **Abbāsābād** *Fārs* Iran
122 H5 **Abbāsābād** *Khorāsān* Iran
122 G3 **'Abbāsābad** Iran
122 F5 **Abbāsābād Mehr Jān** Iran
192 B7 **Abbasanta** *Sardegna* Italy
Abbatis Villa France *see* **Abbeville**
226 F3 **Abbaye, Point** *MI* U.S.A.
210 D2 **Abbe, Lake** Djibouti/Eth.
151 N4 **Abberton Reservoir** *England* U.K.
156 C3 **Abbeville** France
231 E10 **Abbeville** *AL* U.S.A.
231 F10 **Abbeville** *GA* U.S.A.
237 I11 **Abbeville** *LA* U.S.A.
231 F8 **Abbeville** *SC* U.S.A.
223 I5 **Abbey** *Sask.* Can.
147 C8 **Abbeydorney** Ireland
147 D8 **Abbeyfeale** Ireland
146 I13 **Abbey Head** *Scotland* U.K.
147 H7 **Abbeyleix** Ireland
149 K4 **Abbey Town** *Cumbria, England* U.K.
190 F5 **Abbiategrasso** Italy
140 O4 **Abborrträsk** Sweden
85 K6 **Abbot, Mount** *Qld* Austr.
85 K5 **Abbot Bay** *Qld* Austr.
262 R2 **Abbot Ice Shelf** Antarctica
151 I2 **Abbots Bromley** *Staffordshire, England* U.K.
150 G6 **Abbotsbury** *Dorset, England* U.K.
222 F5 **Abbotsford** *B.C.* Can.
226 D5 **Abbotsford** *WI* U.S.A.
151 L4 **Abbots Langley** *Hertfordshire, England* U.K.
234 B5 **Abbotstown** *PA* U.S.A.
239 L8 **Abbott** *NM* U.S.A.
232 E11 **Abbott** *VA* U.S.A.
232 E10 **Abbott** *WV* U.S.A.
123 O4 **Abbottabad** Pak.
138 M7 **Abchuha** Belarus
164 G4 **Abcoude** Neth.
177 G4 **Abda** Hungary
127 J5 **'Abd al 'Azīz, Jabal** *hill* Syria
125 K9 **'Abd al Kūrī** *i.* Yemen
127 N9 **'Abd Allah, Khawr** *sea chan.* Iraq/Kuwait
128 G8 **Abd al Ma'asīr** *well* Saudi Arabia
122 B5 **Ābdānān** Iran
134 J5 **Abdi** Rus. Fed.
122 G4 **Abdolabād** Iran
122 G3 **Abdollāhābād** *Khorāsān* Iran
122 E4 **Abdollāhābād** *Semnān* Iran
120 E1 **Abdulino** Rus. Fed.
202 D6 **Abéché** Chad
122 G5 **Ab-e Garm, Chashmeh-ye** *spring* Iran
105 H6 **Abe-gawa** *r.* Japan
207 F2 **Abeïbara** Mali
207 F2 **Abeïbara** *well* Mali
183 O5 **Abejar** Spain
187 D8 **Abejuela** Spain
207 G5 **Abejukolo** Nigeria
184 B4 **Abela** Port.
207 G2 **Abélajouad** *well* Niger
206 E2 **Abelbod** *well* Mali
165 C7 **Abele** Belgium
182 C4 **Abelleiro, Punta** *pt* Spain
Abellinum Italy *see* **Avellino**
81 H7 **Abel Tasman National Park** *South I.* N.Z.
140 K4 **Abelvær** Norway
77 H1 **Abemama** *atoll Gilbert Is* Kiribati
212 C3 **Abenab** Namibia
173 J3 **Abenberg** Ger.
185 P2 **Abengibre** Spain
206 E5 **Abengourou** Côte d'Ivoire
185 K3 **Abenójar** Spain
Åbenrå Denmark *see* **Aabenraa**
173 L4 **Abens** *r.* Ger.
173 L4 **Abensberg** Ger.
207 F5 **Abeokuta** Nigeria
210 B3 **Abera** Eth.
150 D3 **Aberaeron** *Ceredigion, Wales* U.K.
150 F4 **Aberaman** *Rhondda Cynon Taff, Wales* U.K.
150 E4 **Aberavon** *Neath Port Talbot, Wales* U.K.
158 B4 **Aber Benoît** *inlet* France
150 F4 **Abercanaid** *Merthyr Tydfil, Wales* U.K.
150 B4 **Abercastle** *Pembrokeshire, Wales* U.K.
146 K7 **Aberchirder** *Aberdeenshire, Scotland* U.K.
Abercorn Zambia *see* **Mbala**
83 L5 **Abercrombie** *r. N.S.W.* Austr.
83 L6 **Abercrombie River National Park** *N.S.W.* Austr.
150 F4 **Abercynon** *Rhondda Cynon Taff, Wales* U.K.
150 F4 **Aberdare** *Rhondda Cynon Taff, Wales* U.K.
210 C5 **Aberdare National Park** Kenya
150 C2 **Aberdaron** *Gwynedd, Wales* U.K.
Aberdaugleddau *Pembrokeshire, Wales* U.K. *see* **Milford Haven**
83 M5 **Aberdeen** *N.S.W.* Austr.
109 □J7 **Aberdeen** *H.K.* China
214 I8 **Aberdeen** S. Africa
146 L8 **Aberdeen** *Aberdeen, Scotland* U.K.
146 L8 **Aberdeen** *admin. div. Scotland* U.K.
234 C6 **Aberdeen** *MD* U.S.A.
237 K9 **Aberdeen** *MS* U.S.A.
232 B10 **Aberdeen** *OH* U.S.A.
236 F3 **Aberdeen** *SD* U.S.A.
238 C3 **Aberdeen** *WA* U.S.A.
Aberdeen Island *H.K.* China *see* **Ap Lei Chau**
223 L1 **Aberdeen Lake** *Nunavut* Can.
214 I8 **Aberdeen Road** S. Africa
146 K8 **Aberdeenshire** *admin. div. Scotland* U.K.
146 J10 **Aberdour** *Fife, Scotland* U.K.
150 D2 **Aberdovey** *Gwynedd, Wales* U.K.
Aberdyfi *Gwynedd, Wales* U.K. *see* **Aberdovey**
146 I9 **Aberfeldy** *Perth and Kinross, Scotland* U.K.
150 D1 **Aberffraw** *Isle of Anglesey, Wales* U.K.
149 O6 **Aberford** *West Yorkshire, England* U.K.
146 H10 **Aberfoyle** *Stirling, Scotland* U.K.
150 F4 **Abergavenny** *Monmouthshire, Wales* U.K.
210 C1 **Ābergelē** Eth.
150 E1 **Abergele** *Conwy, Wales* U.K.
Abergwaun *Pembrokeshire, Wales* U.K. *see* **Fishguard**
150 E3 **Abergwesyn** *Powys, Wales* U.K.
150 E2 **Abergynolwyn** *Gwynedd, Wales* U.K.
Aberhonddu *Powys, Wales* U.K. *see* **Brecon**
150 E4 **Aberkenfig** *Bridgend, Wales* U.K.
146 K10 **Aberlady** *East Lothian, Scotland* U.K.
146 K9 **Aberlemno** *Angus, Scotland* U.K.
146 J8 **Aberlour** *Moray, Scotland* U.K.
Abermaw *Gwynedd, Wales* U.K. *see* **Barmouth**
Abermaw *Wales* U.K. *see* **Barmouth**
237 E9 **Abernathy** *TX* U.S.A.
146 J10 **Abernethy** *Perth and Kinross, Scotland* U.K.
Aberpennar *Wales* U.K. *see* **Mountain Ash**
150 C3 **Aberporth** *Ceredigion, Wales* U.K.
150 C2 **Abersoch** *Gwynedd, Wales* U.K.
150 F4 **Abersychan** *Torfaen, Wales* U.K.
176 B1 **Abertamy** Czech Rep.
Abertawe *Swansea, Wales* U.K. *see* **Swansea**
Aberteifi *Ceredigion, Wales* U.K. *see* **Cardigan**
150 F4 **Abertillery** *Blaenau Gwent, Wales* U.K.
184 H2 **Abertura** Spain
146 I10 **Aberuthven** *Perth and Kinross, Scotland* U.K.
158 B4 **Aber Vrac'h** *inlet* France
150 D3 **Aberystwyth** *Ceredigion, Wales* U.K.
Abeshr Chad *see* **Abéché**
134 M2 **Abez'** Rus. Fed.
178 G6 **Abfaltersbach** Austria
122 H8 **Āb Gāh** Iran
135 I6 **Abganerovo** Rus. Fed.
124 F6 **Abhā** Saudi Arabia
124 E3 **Abhā, Jabal** *hill* Saudi Arabia
146 B7 **Abhainnsuidhe** *Western Isles, Scotland* U.K.
116 H9 **Abhanpur** *Chhattisgarh* India
122 C3 **Abhar** Iran
122 C4 **Abhar Rūd** *r.* Iran
207 G5 **Abia** *state* Nigeria
203 G6 **Abiad, Bahr el** *r.* Sudan/Uganda *alt.* **Jebel, Bahr el** *conv.* **White Nile**
183 P8 **Abia de la Obispalía** Spain
210 C3 **Ābīata Hāyk'** *l.* Eth.
250 B2 **Abibe, Serranía de** *mts* Col.
206 D5 **Abidjan** Côte d'Ivoire
186 E3 **Abiego** Spain
214 E3 **Abiekwasputs** *salt pan* S. Africa
210 C3 **Abijatta-Shalla National Park** Eth.
105 L4 **Abiko** Japan
168 G1 **Abild** Denmark
236 G6 **Abilene** *KS* U.S.A.
237 F9 **Abilene** *TX* U.S.A.
159 M8 **Abilly** France
151 J4 **Abingdon** *Oxfordshire, England* U.K.
234 C6 **Abingdon** *MD* U.S.A.
232 C12 **Abingdon** *VA* U.S.A.
Abingdon Island *Islas Galápagos* Ecuador *see* **Pinta, Isla**
146 I12 **Abington** *South Lanarkshire, Scotland* U.K.
233 O6 **Abington** *MA* U.S.A.
234 E4 **Abington** *PA* U.S.A.
85 L5 **Abington Reef** *Coral Sea Is Terr.* Austr.
135 G7 **Abinsk** Rus. Fed.
183 N5 **Abión** *r.* Spain
Ab-i-Panja *r.* Afgh./Tajik. *see* **Panj**
140 O2 **Abisko nationalpark** *nat. park* Sweden
223 J2 **Abitau Lake** *N.W.T.* Can.
224 D3 **Abitibi** *r. Ont.* Can.
224 D3 **Abitibi, Lake** *Ont./Que.* Can.
Abkhazia *aut. rep.* Georgia *see* **Ap'khazet'i**
122 G4 **Ab Khūr** Iran
185 N6 **Abla** Spain
156 C6 **Ablis** France
183 Q5 **Ablitas** Spain
203 F3 **Abnūb** Egypt
Åbo Fin. *see* **Turku**
186 C2 **Abodi, Sierra de** *mts* Spain
116 E4 **Abohar** *Punjab* India
182 D5 **Aboim das Choças** Port.
206 E5 **Aboisso** Côte d'Ivoire
210 B2 **Aboke** Sudan
207 F5 **Abomey** Benin
216 □3a **Abona, Punta de** *pt Tenerife* Canary Is
160 J4 **Abondance** France
94 B2 **Abongabong, Gunung** *mt.* Indon.
207 I6 **Abong Mbang** Cameroon
177 J4 **Abony** Hungary
206 E5 **Abooso** Ghana
125 K7 **Aboot** Oman
92 B7 **Aborlan** *Palawan* Phil.
104 G3 **Abō-tōge** *pass* Japan
208 C2 **Abou Déia** Chad
202 D6 **Abou Goulem** Chad
208 B5 **Aboumi** Gabon
208 E2 **Abourasséin, Mont** *mt.* C.A.R.
207 G3 **Abouraya** *well* Niger
129 F5 **Abovyan** Armenia
146 K8 **Aboyne** *Aberdeenshire, Scotland* U.K.
125 I3 **Abqaiq** Saudi Arabia
259 B9 **Abra, Canal** *sea chan.* Chile
259 E6 **Abra, Laguna del** *l.* Arg.
124 H8 **Abrād, Wādī** *watercourse* Yemen
182 D6 **Abragão** Port.
246 G2 **Abraham's Bay** *Mayaguana* Bahamas
207 G5 **Abraka** Nigeria
177 L4 **Abram** Romania
149 L6 **Abram** *Greater Manchester, England* U.K.
134 H2 **Abramov, Mys** *pt* Rus. Fed.
137 U2 **Abramovka** Rus. Fed.
226 F5 **Abrams** *WI* U.S.A.
177 L4 **Abrămuț** Romania
184 C2 **Abrantes** Port.
258 D1 **Abra Pampa** Arg.
129 G6 **Äbraqunis** Azer.
137 Q9 **Abrau Dyurso** Rus. Fed.
182 E7 **Abraveses** Port.
257 F4 **Abre Campo** Brazil
182 F6 **Abreiro** Port.
242 C4 **Abreojos, Punta** *pt* Mex.
186 I4 **Abrera** Spain
157 N6 **Abreschviller** France
160 C4 **Abrest** France
203 F4 **'Abri** Sudan
161 J7 **Abriès** France
257 H3 **Abrolhos, Arquipélago dos** *is* Brazil
264 G7 **Abrolhos Bank** *sea feature* S. Atlantic Ocean
139 S3 **Abrosovo** Rus. Fed.
185 N6 **Abrucena** Spain
197 L4 **Abrud** Romania
138 F3 **Abruka** *i.* Estonia
Abruzzi *admin. reg.* Italy *see* **Abruzzo**
193 L3 **Abruzzo** *admin. reg.* Italy
193 L4 **Abruzzo, Parco Nazionale d'** *nat. park* Italy
124 F7 **'Abs** Yemen
262 W1 **Absalom, Mount** Antarctica
178 E5 **Absam** Austria
238 I4 **Absaroka Range** *mts WY* U.S.A.
173 J3 **Absberg** Ger.
179 M3 **Absdorf** Austria
235 G6 **Absecon** *NJ* U.S.A.
235 G6 **Absecon Bay** *NJ* U.S.A.
129 K5 **Abşeron Yarımadası** *pen.* Azer.
138 K6 **Absterna, Vozyera** *l.* Belarus
128 F4 **Abtar, Jabal al** *hills* Syria
179 H4 **Abtenau** Austria
172 H4 **Abtsgmünd** Ger.
103 I12 **Abu** Japan
128 F3 **Abū aḍ Ḍuhūr** Syria
125 K3 **Abū al Abyaḍ** *i.* U.A.E.
128 G6 **Abū al Ḥusayn, Qā'** *imp. l.* Jordan
125 I2 **Abū 'Alī** *i.* Saudi Arabia
124 C3 **Abū al Kizān** *rf* Saudi Arabia
128 E8 **Abū 'Āmūd, Wādī** *watercourse* Jordan
124 F7 **Abū 'Arīsh** Saudi Arabia
202 E3 **Abū Ballāṣ** *hill* Egypt
124 G7 **Abū Dā'ir** *des.* Yemen
203 G6 **Abu Deleiq** Sudan
Abu Dhabi U.A.E. *see* **Abū Ẓabī**
124 D4 **Abū Ḍībā'** *waterhole* Saudi Arabia
128 G2 **Abū Du'ān** Syria
128 B10 **Abū Durbah** Egypt
251 F6 **Abufari** Brazil
208 E2 **Abu Gabra** Sudan
203 H6 **Abu Gamel** Sudan
203 G5 **Abu Ghirban** Sudan
210 A2 **Abu Gubeiha** Sudan
128 B10 **Abū Ḥād, Wādī** *watercourse* Egypt
128 G6 **Abū Ḥafnah, Wādī** *watercourse* Jordan
128 E7 **Abū Ḥallūfah, Jabal** *hill* Jordan
203 G5 **Abu Hamed** Sudan
202 E6 **Abu Hamra, Wadi** *watercourse* Sudan
203 G5 **Abu Haraz** Sudan
203 G5 **Abu Hashim** Sudan
128 B10 **Abū Ḥaṣwah, Jabal** *hill* Egypt
113 □2 **Abuhera** *i. Addu Atoll* Maldives
203 G6 **Abu Higar** Sudan
207 G4 **Abuja** Nigeria
128 C10 **Abū Jalūm, Ra's** *pt* Egypt
125 H3 **Abū Jifān** *well* Saudi Arabia
128 D8 **Ābū Jurdhān** Jordan
127 J6 **Abū Kamāl** Syria
202 A1 **Abū Kammāsh** Libya
175 M2 **Abukhava** Belarus
105 L1 **Abukuma-gawa** *r.* Japan
105 M2 **Abukuma-kōchi** *plat.* Japan
203 F6 **Abu La'ot** *watercourse* Sudan
124 E6 **Abū Latt** *i.* Saudi Arabia
124 C3 **Abū Madd, Ra's** *hd* Saudi Arabia
208 E2 **Abu Matariq** Sudan
126 D8 **Abu Mena** *tourist site* Egypt
208 D4 **Abumombazi** Dem. Rep. Congo
125 L3 **Abu Musa** *i.* The Gulf
Abū Mūsá, Jazīreh-ye *i.* The Gulf *see* **Abu Musa**
252 D2 **Abunã** *r.* Bol.
252 D2 **Abunā** Brazil
250 E5 **Abunai** Brazil
202 C2 **Abū Nā'im** *well* Libya
210 C1 **Ābune Yosēf** *mt.* Eth.
202 B2 **Abū Nujaym** Libya
128 F4 **Abū Qa'ṭūr** Syria
126 E8 **Abū Qīr, Khalīj** *b.* Egypt
202 B2 **Abū Qurīn** Libya
124 C2 **Abū Rāqah** *well* Saudi Arabia
128 C9 **Abū Rawthah, Jabal** *mt.* Egypt
104 E4 **Aburazaka-tōge** *pass* Japan
208 F4 **Aburo** *mt.* Dem. Rep. Congo
116 D7 **Abu Road** *Rajasthan* India
124 D4 **Abū Rubayq** Saudi Arabia
128 B10 **Abū Rudays** Egypt
128 G4 **Abū Rujmayn, Jabal** *mts* Syria
124 E3 **Abū Salīm, Birkat** *waterhole* Saudi Arabia
128 F10 **Abū Sallah, Wādī** *watercourse* Saudi Arabia
125 I3 **Abū Sawādah** *well* Saudi Arabia
203 H4 **Abu Shagara, Ras** *pt* Sudan
202 E6 **Abu Shanab** Sudan
203 F4 **Abu Simbel Temple** *tourist site* Egypt
127 L8 **Abū Şukhayr** Iraq
203 F4 **Abū Sunbul** Egypt
102 R4 **Abuta** Japan
203 G4 **Abu Tabaq** *well* Sudan
124 C2 **Abū Ţāqah** Saudi Arabia
128 B9 **Abū Ţarfā', Wādī** *watercourse* Egypt
81 E10 **Abut Head** *South I.* N.Z.
203 F3 **Abū Tīj** Egypt
203 G3 **Abū Ţuyūr, Jabal** *mt.* Egypt
203 F6 **Abu Uruq** *well* Sudan
128 C8 **Abū 'Uwayqilah** *well* Egypt
210 C2 **Abuye Meda** *mt.* Eth.
92 E6 **Abuyog** *Leyte* Phil.
203 F6 **Abu Zabad** Sudan
125 L3 **Abū Ẓabī** U.A.E.
122 C6 **Abūzam** Iran
203 G2 **Abū Zanīmah** Egypt
122 D5 **Abū Zeydābād** Iran
210 B2 **Abwong** Sudan
143 M3 **Åby** Sweden
202 E6 **Abyad** Sudan
128 F4 **Abyaḍ, Jabal al** *mts* Syria
124 G9 **Abyān** *governorate* Yemen
202 D2 **Abyār al Hakīm** *well* Libya
202 D2 **Abyār an Nakhīlan** *well* Libya
86 E6 **Abydos** *W.A.* Austr.
208 F2 **Abyei** Sudan
127 O5 **Ābyek** Iran
140 P4 **Åbyn** Sweden
Abyssinia *country* Africa *see* **Ethiopia**
120 H1 **Abzakovo** Rus. Fed.
120 G2 **Abzanovo** Rus. Fed.
202 C6 **Ab Zérafa** Chad
250 C4 **Acacias** Col.
Acacus, Jabal *mts* Libya *see* **Akakus, Jabal**
Academician Vernadskiy *research stn* Antarctica *see* **Vernadsky**
Academy Bay Rus. Fed. *see* **Akademii, Zaliv**
262 T1 **Academy Glacier** Antarctica
Acadia *prov.* Can. *see* **Nova Scotia**
233 □Q4 **Acadia National Park** *ME* U.S.A.
256 B5 **Açaí** Brazil
254 D3 **Açailândia** Brazil
254 F4 **Acajutiba** Brazil
243 O11 **Acajutla** El Salvador
243 M9 **Acala** Mex.
Acamarachi *mt.* Chile *see* **Pili, Cerro**
244 G5 **Acambaro** Mex.
245 H6 **Acambay** Mex.
209 D9 **Acampamento de Caça do Mucusso** Angola
243 O7 **Acancéh** Mex.
250 B2 **Acandí** Col.
182 D4 **A Cañiza** Spain
244 B3 **Acaponeta** Mex.
244 B3 **Acaponeta** *r.* Mex.
245 H9 **Acapulco** Mex.
Acapulco de Juárez Mex. *see* **Acapulco**
254 C2 **Acará** Brazil
254 C2 **Acará** *r.* Brazil
251 F6 **Acará, Lago** *l.* Brazil
251 G4 **Acarai Mountains** *hills* Brazil/Guyana
254 C2 **Acará Miri** *r.* Brazil
254 E2 **Acaraú** Brazil
254 E2 **Acaraú** *r.* Brazil
253 G6 **Acaray, Represa de** *resr* Para.
182 C2 **A Carballa** Spain
254 F3 **Acarí** Brazil
257 E1 **Acari** *r.* Brazil
252 B3 **Acarí** Peru
252 B3 **Acarí** *r.* Peru
250 D2 **Acarigua** Venez.
182 D2 **A Carreira** Spain
197 K3 **Acâș** Romania
194 G9 **Acate** *Sicilia* Italy
245 J5 **Acateno** Mex.
245 I7 **Acatlan** Mex.
245 K6 **Acatlán** Mex.
244 D5 **Acatlán de Juárez** Mex.
245 K7 **Acatlán de Pérez Figueroa** Mex.
245 J7 **Acatzingo** Mex.
258 D2 **Acay, Nevado de** *mt.* Arg.
245 M8 **Acayucán** Mex.
193 O5 **Accadia** Italy
190 B7 **Acceglio** Italy
193 Q7 **Accettura** Italy
Accho Israel *see* **'Akko**
193 L3 **Acciano** Italy
233 J11 **Accomac** *VA* U.S.A.
Accomack *VA* U.S.A. *see* **Accomac**
163 C10 **Accous** France
206 E5 **Accra** Ghana
149 M6 **Accrington** *Lancashire, England* U.K.
193 K2 **Accumoli** Italy
261 G3 **Aceba** Arg.
182 G8 **Acebo** Spain
184 H2 **Acedera** Spain
183 P3 **Acedo** Spain
258 G3 **Aceguá** Brazil
94 B2 **Aceh** *admin. dist.* Indon.
182 G9 **Acehuche** Spain
182 H8 **Aceituna** Spain
183 Q6 **Acered** Spain
193 P6 **Acerenza** Italy
193 O6 **Acerno** Italy
193 M6 **Acerra** Italy
184 G3 **Aceuchal** Spain
261 G3 **Acevedo** Arg.
178 G3 **Ach** Austria
173 K4 **Ach** *r.* Ger.
173 K6 **Ach** *r.* Ger.
252 C4 **Achacachi** Bol.
216 □1b **Achada** *São Miguel* Azores
184 □ **Achadas da Cruz** Madeira
146 C6 **Achadh Mòr** *Western Isles, Scotland* U.K.
250 D3 **Achaguas** Venez.
116 F9 **Achalpur** *Mahar.* India
114 F4 **Achampet** *Andhra Prad.* India
100 J4 **Achan** Rus. Fed.
182 D4 **A Chan** Spain
114 G4 **Achanta** *Andhra Prad.* India
261 I3 **Achar** Uru.
129 D4 **Ach'ara** *aut. rep.* Georgia
146 E9 **Acharacle** *Highland, Scotland* U.K.
129 C4 **Acharistsqali** *r.* Georgia
146 J6 **Achavanich** *Highland, Scotland* U.K.
131 S3 **Achayvayam** Rus. Fed.
202 A5 **Achegour** *well* Niger
Acheh *admin. dist.* Indon. *see* **Aceh**
165 H6 **Achel** Belgium
198 C4 **Acheloos** *r.* Greece
205 F5 **Achemelmel** *well* Mali
206 D2 **Achemmîm** *well* Maur.
100 E6 **Acheng** *Heilong.* China
178 E4 **Achenkirch** Austria
207 I2 **Achénouma** Niger
178 E5 **Achensee** *l.* Austria
172 E4 **Achern** Ger.
207 H3 **Achétinamou** *well* Niger
156 E3 **Acheux-en-Amiénois** France
146 G6 **Achfary** *Highland, Scotland* U.K.
116 H9 **Achhota** *Chhattisgarh* India
104 G5 **Achi** Japan
156 E3 **Achicourt** France
129 C3 **Ach'igvara** Georgia
129 F1 **Achikulak** Rus. Fed.
147 B5 **Achill Head** Ireland
147 B5 **Achill Island** Ireland
147 C5 **Achill Sound** Ireland
146 F6 **Achiltibuie** *Highland, Scotland* U.K.
168 H4 **Achim** Ger.
Achin *admin. dist.* Indon. *see* **Aceh**
131 K4 **Achinsk** Rus. Fed.
146 F8 **Achintee** *Highland, Scotland* U.K.
260 E3 **Achiras** Arg.
121 M6 **Achisay** Kazakh.
129 I3 **Achisu** Rus. Fed.
134 L4 **Achit** Rus. Fed.
106 B2 **Achit Nuur** *l.* Mongolia
129 G2 **Achkhoy-Martan** Rus. Fed.
199 G6 **Achlada, Akrotirio** *pt* Greece
128 B3 **Achna** Cyprus
146 F7 **Achnasheen** *Highland, Scotland* U.K.
139 O9 **Achosa-Rudnya** Belarus
146 D9 **Achosnich** *Highland, Scotland* U.K.
173 N4 **Achslach** Ger.
172 H5 **Achstetten** Ger.
168 H1 **Achtrup** Ger.
135 G7 **Achuyevo** Rus. Fed.
195 I8 **Aci Castello** *Sicilia* Italy
195 I8 **Aci Catena** *Sicilia* Italy
199 K5 **Acıgöl** *l.* Turkey
129 H4 **Acınohur** *depr.* Azer.
199 K5 **Acıpayam** Turkey
195 I8 **Acireale** *Sicilia* Italy
195 I8 **Aci Sant'Antonio** *Sicilia* Italy
237 K9 **Ackerman** *MS* U.S.A.
234 E3 **Ackermanville** *PA* U.S.A.
236 I4 **Ackley** *IA* U.S.A.
246 F2 **Acklins Island** Bahamas
149 O6 **Ackworth Moor Top** *West Yorkshire, England* U.K.
151 P2 **Acle** *Norfolk, England* U.K.
252 B3 **Acobamba** *Huancavelica* Peru
252 B2 **Acobamba** *Junín* Peru
160 C3 **Acolin** *r.* France
252 C3 **Acomayo** *Cusco* Peru
252 A2 **Acomayo** *Huánuco* Peru
149 M4 **Acomb** *Northumberland, England* U.K.
260 B3 **Aconcagua** *r.* Chile
260 B3 **Aconcagua, Cerro** *mt.* Arg.
254 F3 **Acopiara** Brazil
252 C3 **Acora** Peru
216 □1 **Açores, Arquipélago dos** *is* N. Atlantic Ocean
182 D2 **A Coruña** Spain
182 D2 **A Coruña** *prov.* Spain
252 B3 **Acostambo** Peru
217 □3b **Acoua** Mayotte
242 □Q12 **Acoyapa** Nic.
194 H6 **Acquacalda** *Isole Lipari* Italy
191 N8 **Acqualagna** Italy
195 L4 **Acquaniti** *r.* Italy
192 H2 **Acquapendente** Italy
193 P9 **Acquappesa** Italy
195 K6 **Acquaro** Italy
190 F3 **Acquarossa** Switz.
193 K2 **Acquasanta Terme** Italy
193 J2 **Acquasparta** Italy
193 L2 **Acquaviva Picena** Italy
194 H7 **Acquedolci** *Sicilia* Italy
156 B5 **Acquigny** France
190 E6 **Acqui Terme** Italy
233 K6 **Acra** *NY* U.S.A.
Acragas *Sicilia* Italy *see* **Agrigento**
82 E5 **Acraman, Lake** *salt flat S.A.* Austr.
252 D2 **Acre** *r.* Brazil
252 C2 **Acre** *state* Brazil
Acre Israel *see* **'Akko**
256 B2 **Acreúna** Brazil
195 K5 **Acri** Italy
182 F3 **A Cruz do Incio** Spain
177 H4 **Ács** Hungary
177 I4 **Acsa** Hungary
Actaeon Group *is Arch. des Tuamotu* Fr. Polynesia *see* **Actéon, Groupe**
79 □9 **Actéon, Groupe** *is Arch. des Tuamotu* Fr. Polynesia
245 I7 **Acteopan** Mex.
227 N6 **Acton** *Ont.* Can.
151 N3 **Acton** *Suffolk, England* U.K.
240 N7 **Acton** *CA* U.S.A.
245 I5 **Actopán** Mex.
245 K6 **Actopan** Mex.
252 D1 **Açuã** *r.* Brazil
257 F3 **Açuçena** Brazil
245 H5 **Aculco de Espinosa** Mex.
245 J7 **Acultzingo** Mex.
261 I1 **Acuña** Arg.
256 C6 **Acungui** Brazil
Acunum Acusio France *see* **Montélimar**
207 H6 **Acurenam** Equat. Guinea
253 F3 **Açurizal** Brazil
193 K4 **Acuto** Italy
207 F5 **Ada** Ghana
196 I5 **Ada** *Vojvodina* Serbia
236 G2 **Ada** *MN* U.S.A.
232 B8 **Ada** *OH* U.S.A.
237 G8 **Ada** *OK* U.S.A.
210 C3 **Ādaba** Eth.
Adabazar Turkey *see* **Adapazarı**
78 □1 **Adacao** Guam
205 H5 **Adaf, Djebel** *mts* Alg.
137 Q8 **Adagum** *r.* Rus. Fed.
186 E3 **Adahuesca** Spain
226 D9 **Adair** *IL* U.S.A.
183 K5 **Adaja** *r.* Spain
140 O4 **Adak** Sweden
220 A4 **Adak** *AK* U.S.A.
220 A4 **Adak Island** *AK* U.S.A.
129 B6 **Adaklı** *Bingöl* Turkey
128 F1 **Adaklı** *Gaziantep* Turkey
210 E3 **Adale** *well* Eth.
Adalia Turkey *see* **Antalya**
125 M4 **Adam** Oman
259 F8 **Adam, Mount** *hill* Falkland Is
256 B4 **Adamantina** Brazil
207 I5 **Adamaoua** *prov.* Cameroon
207 I5 **Adamaoua, Massif de l'** *mts* Cameroon
198 F6 **Adamas** *Milos* Greece
207 H4 **Adamawa** *state* Nigeria
197 P6 **Adamclisi** Romania
190 J3 **Adamello** *mt.* Italy
190 I3 **Adamello-Brenta, Parco Naturale** *nature res.* Italy
83 L7 **Adaminaby** *N.S.W.* Austr.
210 C3 **Ādamī Tulu** Eth.
174 E6 **Adamov** Czech Rep.
120 H2 **Adamovka** Rus. Fed.
175 K4 **Adamów** *Lubelskie* Pol.
175 L5 **Adamów** *Lubelskie* Pol.
175 K5 **Adamówka** Pol.
136 G4 **Adampil'** Ukr.
232 C10 **Adams** *KY* U.S.A.
233 L6 **Adams** *MA* U.S.A.
226 B6 **Adams** *MN* U.S.A.
233 I5 **Adams** *NY* U.S.A.
226 E6 **Adams** *WI* U.S.A.
262 T2 **Adams, Cape** Antarctica
81 E10 **Adams, Mount** *South I.* N.Z.
114 F8 **Adam's Bridge** *sea feature* India/Sri Lanka
233 I5 **Adams Center** *NY* U.S.A.
234 A5 **Adams County** *county PA* U.S.A.
222 G5 **Adams Lake** *B.C.* Can.
241 Q3 **Adams McGill Reservoir** *NV* U.S.A.
222 D4 **Adams Mountain** *AK* U.S.A.
Adam's Peak Sri Lanka *see* **Sri Pada**
240 L2 **Adams Peak** *CA* U.S.A.
147 I8 **Adamstown** Ireland
234 C4 **Adamstown** *PA* U.S.A.
185 J4 **Adamuz** Spain
124 G9 **'Adan** Yemen
124 G9 **'Adan** *governorate* Yemen
126 G5 **Adana** Turkey
128 D1 **Adana** *prov.* Turkey
Adana Yemen *see* **'Adan**
124 G9 **'Adan aş Şughrá** Yemen
197 O3 **Adâncata** Romania
177 H5 **Ádánd** Hungary
183 K7 **Adanero** Spain
95 L5 **Adang, Teluk** *b.* Indon.
207 G5 **Adani** Nigeria
182 F8 **Adão** Port.
199 L2 **Adapazarı** Turkey
124 G9 **Adaran, Jabal** *mt.* Yemen
147 E7 **Adare** Ireland
263 L2 **Adare, Cape** Antarctica
124 B5 **Adarmo, Khawr** *watercourse* Sudan
102 R9 **Adatara-san** *vol.* Japan
210 D3 **Ada Terra** Eth.
85 J8 **Adavale** *Qld* Austr.
138 H4 **Ādaži** Latvia
123 M3 **Adban** Afgh.
117 I9 **Adbhar** *Chhattisgarh* India
190 H5 **Adda** *r.* Italy
202 F2 **Aḍ Ḍab'ah** Egypt
Ad Dabbah Sudan *see* **Ed Debba**
124 E4 **Ad Dafīnah** Saudi Arabia
127 L7 **Ad Daghghārah** Iraq
124 H5 **Ad Dahnā'** *des.* Saudi Arabia
125 M5 **Ad Dākhilīyah** *admin. reg.* Oman
204 B5 **Ad Dakhla** Western Sahara
124 G9 **Aḍ Ḍāli'** Yemen
124 G9 **Aḍ Ḍāli'** *governorate* Yemen
Ad Damir Sudan *see* **Ed Damer**
125 J2 **Ad Dammām** Saudi Arabia
114 F5 **Addanki** *Andhra Prad.* India
190 H4 **Adda Nord, Parco dell'** *park* Italy
126 E8 **Ad Daqahlīyah** *governorate* Egypt
124 C2 **Ad Dār al Ḥamrā'** Saudi Arabia
124 F7 **Ad Darb** Saudi Arabia
190 H5 **Adda Sud, Parco dell'** *park* Italy
114 H4 **Addatigala** *Andhra Prad.* India
124 G3 **Ad Dawādimī** Saudi Arabia
125 J3 **Ad Dawḥah** Qatar
127 K6 **Ad Dawr** Iraq
128 F4 **Ad Daww** *plain* Syria
207 H2 **Addax, Réserve Naturelle Intégrale dite Sanctuaire des** *nature res.* Niger
127 M8 **Ad Dayr** Iraq
151 J3 **Adderbury** *Oxfordshire, England* U.K.
124 H2 **Ad Dibdibah** *plain* Saudi Arabia
125 J7 **Ad Dibīn** Yemen
Aḍ Ḍiffah *plat.* Egypt/Libya *see* **Libyan Plateau**
125 J6 **Ad Dikākah** *des.* Saudi Arabia
125 H4 **Ad Dilam** Saudi Arabia
149 N6 **Addingham** *West Yorkshire, England* U.K.
124 H3 **Ad Dir'īyah** Saudi Arabia
Addis Ababa Eth. *see* **Ādīs Ābeba**
232 H6 **Addison** *NY* U.S.A.
127 L8 **Ad Dīwānīyah** Iraq
Ad Dīwānīyah *governorate* Iraq *see* **Al Qādisīyah**
151 L5 **Addlestone** *Surrey, England* U.K.
215 J9 **Addo** S. Africa
215 J9 **Addo Elephant National Park** S. Africa
113 □2 **Addu Atoll** Maldives
127 K8 **Ad Duwayd** *well* Saudi Arabia
124 G2 **Ad Duwayḥirah** Saudi Arabia
Ad Duwaym Sudan *see* **Ed Dueim**
125 J4 **Ad Duwayris** *well* Saudi Arabia
216 □3a **Adeje** *Tenerife* Canary Is
231 F10 **Adel** *GA* U.S.A.
236 H5 **Adel** *IA* U.S.A.
82 G6 **Adelaide** *S.A.* Austr.
84 C2 **Adelaide** *r. N.T.* Austr.
246 E1 **Adelaide** *New Prov.* Bahamas
215 K8 **Adelaide** S. Africa
262 T2 **Adelaide Island** Antarctica
84 C2 **Adelaide River** *N.T.* Austr.
190 D3 **Adelboden** Switz.
169 I7 **Adelebsen** Ger.
86 G3 **Adele Island** *W.A.* Austr.
195 L1 **Adelfia** Italy
199 H6 **Adelfoi** *i.* Greece
168 J5 **Adelheidsdorf** Ger.
261 E3 **Adelia María** Arg.
Adélie Coast *reg.* Antarctica *see* **Adélie Land**
263 J2 **Adélie Land** *reg.* Antarctica
172 H4 **Adelmannsfelden** Ger.
83 L6 **Adelong** *N.S.W.* Austr.
87 F10 **Adelong Aboriginal Reserve** *W.A.* Austr.
246 □ **Adelphi** Jamaica
247 □3 **Adelphi** St Vincent
173 K4 **Adelschlag** Ger.
173 J2 **Adelsdorf** Ger.
172 G3 **Adelsheim** Ger.
173 J5 **Adelsried** Ger.
173 K5 **Adelzhausen** Ger.
187 C7 **Ademuz** Spain
Aden Yemen *see* **'Adan**
118 F7 **Aden, Gulf of** Somalia/Yemen
232 E8 **Adena** *OH* U.S.A.
169 C10 **Adenau** Ger.
168 J4 **Adendorf** Ger.
214 I8 **Adendorp** S. Africa
169 I7 **Adenstedt** Ger.
207 G3 **Aderbissinat** Niger
Aderno *Sicilia* Italy *see* **Adrano**
116 C8 **Adesar** *Gujarat* India
210 C2 **Ādēt** Eth.
Adhámas *Milos* Greece *see* **Adamas**
125 M3 **Adhan, Jabal** *mt.* U.A.E.
124 G8 **Adhanah, Wādī** *watercourse* Yemen
125 L3 **Adh Dhayd** U.A.E.
124 G2 **Adh Dhāyūf** *well* Saudi Arabia
127 J9 **'Adhfā'** *well* Saudi Arabia
123 N5 **Adhi Kot** Pak.
128 E8 **'Ādhirīyāt, Jibāl al** *mts* Jordan
116 C8 **Adhoi** *Gujarat* India
91 H7 **Adi** *i. Papua* Indon.
206 E5 **Adiaké** Côte d'Ivoire
210 C1 **Ādī Ārk'ay** Eth.
184 E4 **Adiça, Serra da** *hills* Port.
250 D2 **Adícora** Venez.
124 D8 **Ādī Da'iro** Eth.
203 F6 **'Adid Umm Inderab** *well* Sudan
191 M5 **Adige** *r.* Italy
Adigey Autonomous Oblast *aut. rep.* Rus. Fed. *see* **Adygeya, Respublika**
210 C1 **Ādīgrat** Eth.
199 K4 **Adıgüzel Barajı** *resr* Turkey
203 H6 **Adi Keyih** Eritrea
203 H6 **Adi Kwala** Eritrea
114 F3 **Adilabad** *Andhra Prad.* India
210 B4 **Adilang** Uganda
127 K4 **Adilcevaz** Turkey
238 D6 **Adin** *CA* U.S.A.
Adîncata Romania *see* **Adâncata**
165 C6 **Adinkerke** Belgium
202 B3 **Adīrī** Libya
233 K4 **Adirondack Mountains** *NY* U.S.A.
210 C2 **Ādīs Ābeba** Eth.
210 C1 **Ādīs Zemen** Eth.
Adi Ugri Eritrea *see* **Mendefera**
126 I5 **Adıyaman** Turkey
Adjaria *aut. rep.* Georgia *see* **Ach'ara**
205 F5 **Adjelman, Oued** *watercourse* Alg.
197 P4 **Adjud** Romania
210 A4 **Adjumani** Uganda
247 □1 **Adjuntas** Puerto Rico
245 I2 **Adjuntas, Presa de las** *resr* Mex.
225 J2 **Adlavik Islands** *Nfld and Lab.* Can.
129 A2 **Adler** Rus. Fed.
149 L6 **Adlington** *Lancashire, England* U.K.
190 F1 **Adliswil** Switz.
173 M4 **Adlkofen** Ger.
86 H3 **Admiralty Gulf** *W.A.* Austr.
86 H3 **Admiralty Gulf Aboriginal Reserve** *W.A.* Austr.
221 J2 **Admiralty Inlet** *Nunavut* Can.
221 H3 **Admiralty Island** *Nunavut* Can.
220 E4 **Admiralty Island** *AK* U.S.A.
220 E4 **Admiralty Island National Monument-Kootznoowoo Wilderness** *nat. park AK* U.S.A.
82 □2 **Admiralty Islands** *Lord Howe I.* Austr.
91 K7 **Admiralty Islands** P.N.G.
263 L2 **Admiralty Mountains** Antarctica
179 J4 **Admont** Austria
199 I4 **Adnan Menderes Havaalani** *airport* Turkey
210 E3 **Ādo** Eth.
207 G5 **Ado-Ekiti** Nigeria
104 D5 **Adogawa** Japan
104 D5 **Ado-gawa** *r.* Japan
208 F2 **Adok** Sudan
261 G6 **Adolfo Gonzáles Chaves** Arg.
245 N9 **Adolfo López Mateos** Mex.
140 N3 **Adolfsström** Sweden
86 J3 **Adolphus Island** *W.A.* Austr.
93 C8 **Adonara** *i.* Indon.
114 E5 **Adoni** *Andhra Prad.* India
177 H4 **Adony** Hungary
171 F10 **Adorf** *Sachsen* Ger.
171 G9 **Adorf** *Sachsen* Ger.
169 G8 **Adorf (Diemelsee)** Ger.
184 A2 **A-dos-Cunhados** Port.
100 M3 **Ado-Tymovo** *Sakhalin* Rus. Fed.
182 E6 **Adoufe** Port.
163 A8 **Adour** *r.* France
117 K8 **Adra** *W. Bengal* India
185 M7 **Adra** Spain
185 N7 **Adra** *r.* Spain
128 E5 **'Adrā'** Syria
183 P6 **Adradas** Spain
183 L6 **Adrados** Spain
Adramyttium Turkey *see* **Edremit**
Adramyttium, Gulf of Turkey *see* **Edremit Körfezi**
194 H8 **Adrano** *Sicilia* Italy
205 E4 **Adrar** Alg.
205 G4 **Adrar** *mts* Alg.
Adrar *hills* Mali *see* **Ifôghas, Adrar des**
204 C5 **Adrar** *admin. reg.* Maur.
Adrar des Iforas *hills* Mali *see* **Ifôghas, Adrar des**
205 G5 **Adrar Tedjorart** *well* Alg.
128 B2 **Adras Dağı** *mt.* Turkey
123 J5 **Adraskand** *r.* Afgh.
123 M1 **Adrasmon** Tajik.
202 D6 **Adré** Chad
191 M5 **Adria** Italy
227 J8 **Adrian** *MI* U.S.A.
237 D8 **Adrian** *TX* U.S.A.
Adrianople Turkey *see* **Edirne**
Adrianopolis Turkey *see* **Edirne**
188 D3 **Adriatic Sea** Europe
162 F3 **Adriers** France
147 C9 **Adrigole** Ireland
Adua Eth. *see* **Ādwa**
260 B5 **Aduana Pejerrey** Chile
164 J2 **Aduard** Neth.
190 G3 **Adula Gruppe** *mts* Switz.
Adunara *i.* Indon. *see* **Adonara**
114 E8 **Adur** *Kerala* India
208 F4 **Adusa** Dem. Rep. Congo
202 E5 **Adusa, Qalti el** *well* Sudan
138 J6 **Adutiškis** Lith.
Aduwa Eth. *see* **Ādwa**
86 G6 **Adverse Well** *W.A.* Austr.
210 C1 **Ādwa** Eth.
149 O6 **Adwick le Street** *South Yorkshire, England* U.K.
206 E5 **Adwufia** Ghana
131 O3 **Adycha** *r.* Rus. Fed.
129 C1 **Adyge-Khabl'** Rus. Fed.
Adygeya *aut. rep.* Rus. Fed. *see* **Adygeya, Respublika**
129 B1 **Adygeya, Respublika** *aut. rep.* Rus. Fed.
135 G7 **Adygeysk** Rus. Fed.
Adygeyskaya Avtonomnaya Oblast' *aut. rep.* Rus. Fed. *see* **Adygeya, Respublika**
135 I7 **Adyk** Rus. Fed.
187 E10 **Adzaneta de Albaida** Spain
137 L5 **Adzhamka** Ukr.
Adzharia *aut. rep.* Georgia *see* **Ach'ara**
206 E5 **Adzopé** Côte d'Ivoire
134 M2 **Adz'va** *r.* Rus. Fed.
134 L2 **Adz'vavom** Rus. Fed.
199 F4 **Aegean Sea** Greece/Turkey
Aegeri, Lake of Switz. *see* **Ägerisee**
Aegina *i.* Greece *see* **Aigina**
138 H2 **Aegna** *i.* Estonia
138 I2 **Aegviidu** Estonia
Aegyptus *country* Africa *see* **Egypt**
Aela Jordan *see* **Al 'Aqabah**
Aelana Jordan *see* **Al 'Aqabah**
Aelia Capitolina Israel/West Bank *see* **Jerusalem**
Aelönlaplap *atoll* Marshall Is *see* **Ailinglaplap**
Aenus Turkey *see* **Enez**
142 G7 **Ærø** *i.* Denmark
137 N8 **Aeroflots'kyy** Ukr.
150 D3 **Aeron** *r. Wales* U.K.
168 J1 **Ærøskøbing** Denmark
169 H6 **Aerzen** Ger.
182 C3 **A Escusa** Spain
Aesernia Italy *see* **Isernia**
182 C4 **A Esfarrapada** Spain
182 D3 **A Estrada** Spain
198 C2 **Aetos** Greece
141 Q6 **Äetsä** Fin.
79 □9a **Afaahiti** *Tahiti* Fr. Polynesia
203 H5 **Afabet** Eritrea
210 E3 **Afaf Badane** *well* Eth.
Afal *watercourse* Saudi Arabia *see* **'Ifāl, Wādī**
127 L5 **Afan** Iran
137 R3 **Afanas'yevka** Rus. Fed.
134 K4 **Afanas'yevo** Rus. Fed.
Afándou *Rodos* Greece *see* **Afantou**
199 J6 **Afantou** *Rodos* Greece
210 D1 **Āfar** *admin. reg.* Eth.
125 M4 **Afar** Oman
203 I6 **Afar Depression** Eritrea/Eth.
79 □9a **Afareaitu** *Moorea* Fr. Polynesia
210 D2 **Āfdem** Eth.
182 E2 **A Feira do Monte** Spain
158 G6 **Aff** *r.* France
206 E5 **Afféri** Côte d'Ivoire
193 K4 **Affile** Italy
173 J5 **Affing** Ger.
190 E1 **Affoltern am Albis** Switz.
Affreville Alg. *see* **Khemis Miliana**
146 F8 **Affric, Loch** *l. Scotland* U.K.
Afghānestān *country* Asia *see* **Afghanistan**
123 K5 **Afghanistan** *country* Asia
210 E4 **Afgooye** Somalia
78 □2 **Afi, Mount** Samoa
78 □2 **Afiamalu** Samoa
124 F4 **'Afīf** Saudi Arabia
182 C5 **Afife** Port.
207 G5 **Afikpo** Nigeria
139 R4 **Afim'ino** Rus. Fed.
137 R9 **Afipskiy** Rus. Fed.
128 D6 **Afiq** Syria
198 E3 **Afissos** Greece
Afiun Karahissar Turkey *see* **Afyon**
122 D4 **Afjeh** Iran
140 K5 **Åfjord** Norway
165 D6 **Afleidingskanaal van de Leie** *canal* Belgium
179 L4 **Aflenz Kurort** Austria
205 F2 **Aflou** Alg.
210 D4 **Afmadow** Somalia
220 C4 **Afognak Island** *AK* U.S.A.
206 B2 **Afojjar** *well* Maur.
182 F2 **A Fonsagrada** Spain
257 G4 **Afonso Cláudio** Brazil

Akzhal to Alice

276

121 S3 **Akzhal** *Vostochnyy Kazakhstan* Kazakh.
120 G2 **Akzhar** Kazakh.
120 K5 **Akzhar** *Kyzylordinskaya Oblast'* Kazakh.
121 T4 **Akzhar** *Vostochnyy Kazakhstan* Kazakh.
121 N6 **Akzhar** *Zhambylskaya Oblast'* Kazakh.
121 O4 **Akzhartas** Kazakh.
121 L5 **Akzhaykyn, Ozero** *salt l.* Kazakh.
126 I5 **Akziyaret** Turkey
142 E1 **Ål** Norway
138 M9 **Ala** *r.* Belarus
191 K4 **Ala** Italy
128 E3 **'Alā, Jabal al** *hills* Syria
192 C6 **Alà, Monti di** *mts Sardegna* Italy
125 I2 **Al 'Abā** Saudi Arabia
231 D10 **Alabama** *r. AL* U.S.A.
231 D9 **Alabama** *state* U.S.A.
231 D9 **Alabaster** *AL* U.S.A.
227 K5 **Alabaster** *MI* U.S.A.
81 C11 **Alabaster, Lake** *South I.* N.Z.
127 L9 **Al 'Abţīyah** *well* Iraq
121 N7 **Ala-Buka** Kyrg.
202 B3 **Al Abyaḑ** Libya
202 D1 **Al Abyār** Libya
195 L6 **Alaca** *r.* Italy
126 G3 **Alaca** Turkey
129 C4 **Alaca Dağı** *mt.* Turkey
126 H4 **Alacahan** Turkey
126 G3 **Alaçam** Turkey
199 J3 **Alaçam Dağları** *mts* Turkey
128 A2 **Alacami** Turkey
Alacant Spain *see* **Alicante**
199 H4 **Alaçatı** Turkey
243 O6 **Alacrán, Arrecife** *rf* Mex.
197 N9 **Aladag** *mt.* Bulg.
126 F5 **Aladağ** Turkey
129 D5 **Aladağ** *mt.* Turkey
127 K4 **Ala Dag** *mt.* Turkey
127 K4 **Ala Dağlar** *mts* Turkey
126 G5 **Ala Dağları** *mts* Turkey
202 D2 **Al 'Adam** Libya
192 C6 **Alà dei Sardi** *Sardegna* Italy
190 C5 **Ala di Stura** Italy
183 J6 **Alaejos** Spain
110 E6 **Ala'er** *Xinjiang* China
124 H5 **Al Aflāj** *reg.* Saudi Arabia
251 F4 **Alagadiço** Brazil
114 F7 **Alagapuram** *Tamil Nadu* India
Alagez *mt.* Armenia *see* **Aragats Lerr**
106 D4 **Alag Hayrhan Uul** *mt.* Mongolia
106 E9 **Alag Hu** *l. Qinghai* China
129 F2 **Alagir** Rus. Fed.
190 D4 **Alagna Valsesia** Italy
161 C6 **Alagnon** *r.* France
182 C3 **A Lagoa** Spain
254 F4 **Alagoas** *state* Brazil
254 F5 **Alagoinhas** Brazil
186 C4 **Alagón** Spain
182 G9 **Alagón** *r.* Spain
110 I5 **Ala Gou** *r.* China
129 D4 **Alagöz Dağı** *mt.* Turkey
92 E8 **Alah** *r. Mindanao* Phil.
94 D5 **Alahanpanjang** *Sumatera* Indon.
140 Q5 **Alahärmä** Fin.
127 N9 **Al Aḩmadī** Kuwait
Alaid, Ostrov *i. Kuril'skiye O-va* Rus. Fed. *see* **Atlasova, Ostrov**
163 I9 **Alaigne** France
186 □ **Alaior** Spain
123 N2 **Alai Range** *mts* Asia
122 E4 **Ālaivān** Iran
128 D3 **Ālājah** Syria
125 M6 **Al 'Ajā'iz** *well* Oman
125 I2 **Al Ajām** Saudi Arabia
184 F5 **Alájar** Spain
140 Q5 **Alajärvi** Fin.
140 P2 **Alajaure naturreservat** *nature res.* Sweden
216 □3a **Alajero** *La Gomera* Canary Is
124 F2 **Al Ajfar** Saudi Arabia
138 K2 **Alajõgi** *r.* Estonia
128 C8 **Al 'Ajrūd** *well* Egypt
242 □Q12 **Alajuela** Costa Rica
122 B2 **Alajujeh** Iran
213 □J4 **Alak Ambohimaha** Madag.
220 B3 **Alakanuk** *AK* U.S.A.
129 B2 **Alakhadzi** Georgia
124 C1 **Al Akhḑar** Saudi Arabia
129 I4 **Alakhundag, Gora** *mt.* Rus. Fed.
116 G4 **Alaknanda** *r.* India
121 S4 **Alakol', Ozero** *salt l.* Kazakh.
Ala Kul *salt l.* Kazakh. *see* **Alakol', Ozero**
140 U3 **Alakurtti** Rus. Fed.
140 R3 **Alakylä** Fin.
240 □E13 **'Alalākeiki Channel** *HI* U.S.A.
203 F2 **Al 'Alamayn** Egypt
251 F5 **Alalaú** *r.* Brazil
124 E6 **Al 'Alayyah** Saudi Arabia
Alalia *Corse* France *see* **Aléria**
210 D3 **Alama** Somalia
127 K5 **Al 'Amādīyah** Iraq
91 K3 **Alamagan** *i.* N. Mariana Is
Alamaguan *i.* N. Mariana Is *see* **Alamagan**
124 G3 **Al'Amār** Saudi Arabia
127 M8 **Al 'Amārah** Iraq
202 E2 **'Alam ar Rūm, Ra's** *pt* Egypt
122 E8 **'Alāmarvdasht** Iran
122 E7 **'Alāmarvdasht** *watercourse* Iran
210 C1 **Ālamat'ā** Eth.
122 A2 **Alamdar** Iran
185 J6 **Alameda** Spain
240 J4 **Alameda** *CA* U.S.A.
185 M2 **Alameda de Cervera** Spain
183 M8 **Alameda de la Sagra** Spain
127 L9 **Al Amghar** *waterhole* Iraq
242 □Q11 **Alamicamba** Nic.
185 J3 **Alamillo** Spain
92 B3 **Alaminos** *Luzon* Phil.
126 D8 **Al 'Āmirīyah** Egypt
239 L12 **Alamito Creek** *r. TX* U.S.A.
242 H4 **Alamítos, Sierra de los** *mt.* Mex.
124 F5 **Al Amlah** Saudi Arabia
245 J5 **Álamo** Mex.
184 E4 **Álamo** *r.* Port.
184 H8 **Alamo** *r.* Spain
231 F9 **Alamo** *GA* U.S.A.
241 Q4 **Alamo** *NV* U.S.A.
237 K8 **Alamo** *TN* U.S.A.
241 S7 **Alamo Dam** *AZ* U.S.A.
239 L10 **Alamogordo** *NM* U.S.A.
237 F11 **Alamo Heights** *TX* U.S.A.
250 A6 **Alamor** Ecuador
261 F5 **Alamos** Arg.
242 D3 **Alamos** *Sonora* Mex.
242 E4 **Álamos** *Sonora* Mex.
243 I4 **Alamos** *r.* Mex.
242 E4 **Álamos, Sierra** *mts* Mex.
239 L8 **Alamosa** *CO* U.S.A.
239 K10 **Alamosa** *watercourse NM* U.S.A.
239 L9 **Alamosa Creek** *r. NM* U.S.A.
242 F2 **Alamos de Peña** Mex.
114 F5 **Alampur** *Andhra Prad.* India
191 R5 **Alan** Croatia
124 G9 **Al 'Anad** Yemen
140 S3 **Ala-Nampa** Fin.
140 M4 **Alanäs** Sweden
127 J6 **Al Anbār** *governorate* Iraq
141 O6 **Åland** *is Åland* Fin.
170 E4 **Aland** *r.* Ger.
114 E4 **Aland** *Karnataka* India
122 A2 **Aland** *r.* Iran
129 C4 **Alan Dağı** *mt.* Turkey
128 F3 **Al Andarīn** Syria
143 L3 **Åländern** *l.* Sweden
Åland Islands *Åland* Fin. *see* **Åland**
111 L11 **Alando** *Xizang* China
184 E3 **Alandroal** Port.
141 O7 **Ålands Hav** *sea chan.* Fin./Sweden
114 G6 **Alandur** *Tamil Nadu* India
95 L2 **Alang** *Kalimantan* Indon.
95 L6 **Alangalang, Tanjung** *pt* Indon.
94 D3 **Alang Besar** *i.* Indon.
184 G3 **Alange** Spain
184 G3 **Alange, Embalse de** *resr* Spain
94 F5 **Alanggantang** *i.* Indon.
Alania *aut. reg.* Georgia *see* **Samkhret' Oset'i**
184 H4 **Alanís** Spain
226 J4 **Alanson** *MI* U.S.A.
207 I4 **Alantika Mountains** Cameroon/Nigeria
126 F5 **Alanya** Turkey
122 F6 **'Alā' od Dīn** Iran
177 H5 **Alap** Hungary
231 F10 **Alapaha** *r. GA* U.S.A.
114 F7 **Alapakam** *Tamil Nadu* India
199 M1 **Alaplı** Turkey
Alappuzha *Kerala* India *see* **Alleppey**
116 G6 **Alapur** *Uttar Prad.* India
128 D9 **Al 'Aqabah** Jordan
128 D9 **'Alāqān** Saudi Arabia
124 E5 **Al 'Aqīq** Saudi Arabia
245 H3 **Alaquines** Mex.
125 I4 **Al 'Āqūlah** *well* Saudi Arabia
125 J2 **Al 'Arabiyah** *i. Ash Sharqīyah* Saudi Arabia
122 D8 **Al 'Arabiyah** *i.* Saudi Arabia
125 J2 **Al 'Arabiyah** *i.* Saudi Arabia
Al 'Arabīyah as Sa'ūdīyah *country* Asia *see* **Saudi Arabia**
183 J7 **Alaraz** Spain
183 P9 **Alarcón** Spain
183 P9 **Alarcón, Embalse de** *resr* Spain
183 L3 **Alar del Rey** Spain
204 B5 **Al Argoub** Western Sahara
124 F7 **Al 'Āriḑah** Saudi Arabia
124 F6 **Al Arīn** Saudi Arabia
203 G2 **Al 'Arīsh** Egypt
187 K8 **Alaró** Spain
124 G3 **Al Arţāwī** Saudi Arabia
124 G2 **Al Arţāwīyah** Saudi Arabia
95 L9 **Alas** *Sumbawa* Indon.
95 L9 **Alas, Selat** *sea chan.* Indon.
199 J4 **Alaşehir** Turkey
129 G5 **Äläsgärli** Azer.
Alashiya *country* Asia *see* **Cyprus**
203 F3 **Al Ashmūnayn** Egypt
127 K8 **Al 'Āshūrīyah** *well* Iraq
220 D3 **Alaska** *state* U.S.A.
213 F3 **Alaska** Zimbabwe
220 D4 **Alaska, Gulf of** *AK* U.S.A.
222 A2 **Alaska Highway** Can./U.S.A.
220 B4 **Alaska Peninsula** *AK* U.S.A.
220 D3 **Alaska Range** *mts AK* U.S.A.
95 K9 **Alas Purwo, Taman Nasional** *nat. park* Indon.
124 D1 **Al 'Assāfīyah** Saudi Arabia
190 E7 **Alassio** Italy
141 Q6 **Alastaro** Fin.
129 K6 **Älät** Azer.
Alat Uzbek. *see* **Olot**
192 B4 **Alata** *Corse* France
Alataw Shankou *pass* China/Kazakh. *see* **Dzungarian Gate**
187 C9 **Alatoz** Spain
193 K4 **Alatri** Italy
129 J5 **Älät Tirāsi** *plat.* Azer.
177 J4 **Alattyán** Hungary
124 F1 **Al Atwā'** *well* Saudi Arabia
135 I5 **Alatyr'** Rus. Fed.
135 I5 **Alatyr'** *r.* Rus. Fed.
138 I4 **Alauksts** *l.* Latvia
250 B5 **Alausí** Ecuador
183 O3 **Álava** *prov.* Spain
129 F4 **Alaverdi** Armenia
122 D5 **'Alavī** Iran
140 R4 **Alavieska** Fin.
140 T4 **Ala-Vuokki** Fin.
140 Q5 **Alavus** Fin.
150 D1 **Alaw, Llyn** *resr Wales* U.K.
84 E3 **Alawa Aboriginal Land** *res. N.T.* Austr.
125 M4 **Al Awābī** Oman
96 C2 **Alawbum** Myanmar
124 G3 **Al 'Awdah** Saudi Arabia
82 H6 **Alawoona** *S.A.* Austr.
124 E2 **Al Awshazīyah** Saudi Arabia
Alaykel' Kyrg. *see* **Kök-Art**
Alaykuu *Osh* Kyrg. *see* **Kök-Art**
Alay Kyrka Toosu *mts* Asia *see* **Alai Range**
125 M4 **Al 'Ayn** Oman
124 D3 **Al 'Ayn** Saudi Arabia
125 L3 **Al 'Ayn** U.A.E.
128 D8 **Al 'Aynā** Jordan
Alayskiy Khrebet *mts* Asia *see* **Alai Range**
199 L3 **Alayunt** Turkey
129 H4 **Alazani** *r.* Azer./Georgia
131 Q2 **Alazeya** *r.* Rus. Fed.
127 L7 **Al 'Azīzīyah** Iraq
202 B1 **Al 'Azīzīyah** Libya
128 E7 **Al Azraq al Janūbī** Jordan
172 E6 **Alb** *r.* Ger.
190 E6 **Alba** Italy
186 C6 **Alba** Spain
226 J5 **Alba** *MI* U.S.A.
234 B1 **Alba** *PA* U.S.A.
81 C11 **Alba, Mount** *South I.* N.Z.
183 K3 **Alba, Sierra de** *mts* Spain
193 L2 **Alba Adriatica** Italy
124 E2 **Al Ba'ā'ith** Saudi Arabia
128 F2 **Al Bāb** Syria
185 P2 **Albacete** Spain
185 P3 **Albacete** *prov.* Spain
128 D10 **Al Bad'** Saudi Arabia
124 D2 **Al Badā'i'** Saudi Arabia
183 I7 **Alba de Tormes** Spain
124 H5 **Al Badī'** Saudi Arabia
127 L8 **Al Bādiyah al Janūbīyah** *des.* Iraq
142 G4 **Ålbæk** Denmark
142 G4 **Ålbæk Bugt** *b.* Denmark
192 B8 **Albagiara** *Sardegna* Italy
124 E5 **Al Bāḩah** Egypt
124 E5 **Al Bāḩah** Saudi Arabia
124 E5 **Al Bāḩah** *prov.* Saudi Arabia
128 D3 **Al Bahlūlīyah** Syria
128 A10 **Al Baḩr al Aḩmar** *governorate* Egypt
Al Bahrayn *country* Asia *see* **Bahrain**
187 E10 **Albaida** Spain
197 L4 **Alba Iulia** Romania
125 J3 **Al Bajā'** *well* U.A.E.
124 F3 **Al Ba'jah** Saudi Arabia
114 G3 **Albaka** *Andhra Prad.* India
124 H3 **Al Bakhrā** *well* Saudi Arabia
202 B3 **Al Bakkī** Libya
185 N3 **Albaladejo** Spain
184 G2 **Albalá del Caudillo** Spain
128 B10 **Al Balā'im** Egypt
128 B10 **Al Balā'im** *b.* Egypt
161 F7 **Alba-la-Romaine** France
186 E5 **Albalate de Arzobispo** Spain
186 F4 **Albalate de Cinca** Spain
183 P8 **Albalate de las Nogueras** Spain
183 O8 **Albalate de Zorita** Spain
186 E4 **Albalatillo** Spain
203 F3 **Al Balyanā** Egypt
163 I8 **Alban** France
185 O6 **Albánchez** Spain
225 F3 **Albanel, Lac** *l. Que.* Can.
193 O7 **Albanella** Italy
225 F3 **Albanel-Mistassini et Waconichi, Réserve Faunique des lacs** *nature res. Que.* Can.
196 H9 **Albania** *country* Europe
251 G5 **Albano** Brazil
193 J4 **Albano, Lago** *l.* Italy
193 Q6 **Albano di Lucania** Italy
193 J4 **Albano Laziale** Italy
87 D13 **Albany** *W.A.* Austr.
224 D2 **Albany** *r. Ont.* Can.
246 □ **Albany** Jamaica
231 E10 **Albany** *GA* U.S.A.
236 H5 **Albany** *MO* U.S.A.
233 L6 **Albany** *NY* U.S.A.
232 C9 **Albany** *OH* U.S.A.
238 C4 **Albany** *OR* U.S.A.
237 F9 **Albany** *TX* U.S.A.
186 K3 **Albanyà** Spain
85 L9 **Albany Downs** *Qld* Austr.
258 G4 **Albardão do João Maria** *coastal area* Brazil
202 E2 **Al Bardī** Libya
260 C2 **Albardón** Arg.
190 H3 **Albaredo per San Marco** Italy
182 D4 **Albarellos, Embalse de** *resr* Spain
161 C7 **Albaret-le-Comtal** France
190 H7 **Albareto** Italy
161 C7 **Albaret-Ste-Marie** France
128 H9 **Al Bāridah** *hills* Saudi Arabia
160 G5 **Albarine** *r.* France
205 H4 **Al Barkāt** *well* Libya
161 E9 **Albaron** France
183 R8 **Albarracín** Spain
183 Q8 **Albarracín, Sierra de** *mts* Spain
184 F2 **Albarragena** *r.* Spain
124 G3 **Al Barrah** Saudi Arabia
124 G3 **Al Barūd** Saudi Arabia
137 R7 **Albasi** *r.* Rus. Fed.
127 M8 **Al Başrah** Iraq
127 M8 **Al Başrah** *governorate* Iraq
150 D6 **Albaston** *Cornwall, England* U.K.
185 P3 **Albatana** Spain
186 G4 **Albatàrrec** Spain
187 D11 **Albatera** Spain
127 L8 **Al Baţḩa'** *marsh* Iraq
125 M4 **Al Bāţinah** *admin. reg.* Oman
125 M3 **Al Bāţinah** *reg.* Oman
125 I2 **Al Bāţinah** *i.* Saudi Arabia
246 F5 **Albatross Bank** *sea feature* Jamaica
85 H2 **Albatross Bay** *Qld* Austr.
83 J9 **Albatross Island** *Tas.* Austr.
80 I5 **Albatross Point** *North I.* N.Z.
203 F2 **Al Bawītī** Egypt
202 D1 **Al Bayḑā'** Libya
124 G9 **Al Bayḑā'** Yemen
124 G8 **Al Bayḑā'** *governorate* Yemen
92 D5 **Albay Gulf** *Luzon* Phil.
172 E6 **Albbruck** Ger.
157 N6 **Albe** *r.* France
192 G2 **Albegna** *r.* Italy
186 F4 **Albelda** Spain
183 P4 **Albelda de Iregua** Spain
186 E3 **Albella** Spain
231 G8 **Albemarle** *NC* U.S.A.
Albemarle Island *Islas Galápagos* Ecuador *see* **Isabela, Isla**
231 I8 **Albemarle Sound** *sea chan. NC* U.S.A.
183 P7 **Albendea** Spain
185 K5 **Albendín** Spain
190 E7 **Albenga** Italy
160 H5 **Albens** France
187 D7 **Albentosa** Spain
183 K9 **Alberche** *r.* Spain
253 F6 **Alberdi** Para.
82 E2 **Alberga** *watercourse S.A.* Austr.
182 D7 **Albergaria-a-Velha** Port.
182 C9 **Albergaria dos Doze** Port.
190 B5 **Albergian, Monte** *mt.* Italy
187 E9 **Alberic** Spain
183 P4 **Alberite** Spain
179 J3 **Alberndorf in der Riedmark** Austria
184 D5 **Albernoa** Port.
186 E3 **Albero Alto** Spain
195 M2 **Alberobello** Italy
191 M5 **Alberoni** Italy
178 A5 **Alberschwende** Austria
168 H2 **Albersdorf** Ger.
83 K5 **Albert** *N.S.W.* Austr.
84 G4 **Albert** *r. Qld* Austr.
156 E4 **Albert** France
82 G6 **Albert, Lake** *S.A.* Austr.
210 A4 **Albert, Lake** Dem. Rep. Congo/Uganda
Albert, Parc National *nat. park* Dem. Rep. Congo *see* **Virunga, Parc National des**
222 H4 **Alberta** *prov.* Can.
232 H12 **Alberta** *VA* U.S.A.
192 B3 **Albertacce** *Corse* France
190 G6 **Alberta Ligure** Italy
215 O5 **Albert Falls Nature Reserve** S. Africa
261 G4 **Alberti** Arg.
140 □ **Albert I Land** *reg.* Svalbard
214 F10 **Albertinia** S. Africa
177 I4 **Albertirsa** Hungary
165 H7 **Albert Kanaal** *canal* Belgium
236 I4 **Albert Lea** *MN* U.S.A.
210 B4 **Albert Nile** *r.* Sudan/Uganda
259 C9 **Alberto de Agostini, Parque Nacional** *nat. park* Chile
225 H4 **Alberton** *P.E.I.* Can.
215 M2 **Alberton** S. Africa
238 G3 **Alberton** *MT* U.S.A.
241 Q9 **Alberto Oviedo Mota** Mex.
215 J3 **Albertshoek** S. Africa
173 I2 **Albertshofen** Ger.
246 F2 **Albert Town** Bahamas
246 □ **Albert Town** Jamaica
81 D11 **Albert Town** *South I.* N.Z.
Albertville Dem. Rep. Congo *see* **Kalemie**
160 I5 **Albertville** France
231 D8 **Albertville** *AL* U.S.A.
186 E4 **Alberuela de Tubo** Spain
186 G4 **Albesa** Spain
197 P3 **Albeşti** *Botoşani* Romania
197 P4 **Albeşti** *Vaslui* Romania
157 M6 **Albestroff** France
163 I8 **Albi** France
236 I5 **Albia** *IA* U.S.A.
124 D4 **Al Bi'ār** Saudi Arabia
163 G7 **Albias** France
125 I3 **Al Bīḑah** *des.* Saudi Arabia
195 K4 **Albidona** Italy
163 H8 **Albigeois** *reg.* France
191 L5 **Albignasego** Italy
251 H3 **Albina** Suriname
124 C2 **Al Binī** Saudi Arabia
190 H4 **Albino** Italy
240 I2 **Albion** *CA* U.S.A.
230 E5 **Albion** *IN* U.S.A.
226 J7 **Albion** *MI* U.S.A.
236 F5 **Albion** *NE* U.S.A.
234 F5 **Albion** *NJ* U.S.A.
232 G5 **Albion** *NY* U.S.A.
232 E7 **Albion** *PA* U.S.A.
124 G3 **Al Bīr** Saudi Arabia
124 C1 **Al Bi'r** Saudi Arabia
183 J4 **Albires** Spain
124 E6 **Al Birk** Saudi Arabia
124 E4 **Al Birkah** Saudi Arabia
172 E2 **Albisheim (Pfrimm)** Ger.
190 F7 **Albisola Marina** Italy
190 F7 **Albisola Superiore** Italy
124 H5 **Al Biyāḑh** *reg.* Saudi Arabia
164 G5 **Alblasserdam** Neth.
192 C7 **Albo, Monte** *mts Sardegna* Italy
187 F7 **Albocàsser** Spain
185 N6 **Alboloduy** Spain
161 F6 **Albon** France
185 M7 **Albondón** Spain
185 M9 **Alborán, Isla de** *i.* Spain
187 C9 **Alborea** Spain
Ålborg Denmark *see* **Aalborg**
122 C3 **Alborz, Reshteh-ye** *mts* Iran
197 M6 **Albota** Romania
185 O6 **Albox** Spain
177 H2 **Albrechtice** Czech Rep.
150 H2 **Albrighton** *Shropshire, England* U.K.
85 K7 **Albro** *Qld* Austr.
172 G5 **Albstadt** Ger.
173 H4 **Albuch** *hills* Ger.
125 J2 **Al Budayyi'** Bahrain
168 K1 **Albuen** *pen.* Denmark
184 C6 **Albufeira** Port.
126 E8 **Al Buḩayrah** *governorate* Egypt
187 C12 **Albujón** Spain
124 F2 **Al Bukayrīyah** Saudi Arabia
190 G2 **Albula** *r.* Switz.
190 H3 **Albula Alpen** *mts* Switz.
185 M7 **Albuñol** Spain
185 L7 **Albuñuelas** Spain
239 K9 **Albuquerque** *NM* U.S.A.
246 C7 **Albuquerque, Cayos de** *is* Caribbean Sea
128 E4 **Al Burayj** Syria
125 L3 **Al Buraymī** Oman
233 L4 **Alburg** *VT* U.S.A.
128 C9 **Al Burj** Jordan
193 O6 **Alburno, Monte** *mt.* Italy
184 F2 **Alburquerque** Spain
234 D3 **Alburtis** *PA* U.S.A.
83 K7 **Albury** *N.S.W.* Austr.
81 E11 **Albury** *South I.* N.Z.
127 J6 **Al Buşayrah** Syria
126 I9 **Al Busayţā'** *plain* Saudi Arabia
127 M8 **Al Buşayyah** Iraq
124 G1 **Al Bushūk** *well* Saudi Arabia
124 G2 **Al Buţayn** *plain* Saudi Arabia
124 D3 **Al Buwayr** Saudi Arabia
125 M6 **Al Buwī** *well* Oman
160 I5 **Alby-sur-Chéran** France
252 B3 **Alca** Peru
184 A3 **Alcabideche** Port.
187 E9 **Alcácer** Spain
184 B4 **Alcácer do Sal** Port.
184 C4 **Alcáçovas** Port.
184 C4 **Alcáçovas** *r.* Port.
185 P3 **Alcadozo** Spain
186 D6 **Alcaine** Spain
182 F9 **Alcains** Port.
184 H6 **Alcalá de Guadaira** Spain
186 D3 **Alcalá de Gurrea** Spain
183 N8 **Alcalá de Henares** Spain
187 D7 **Alcalá de la Selva** Spain
187 C9 **Alcalá del Júcar** Spain
184 H8 **Alcalá de los Gazules** Spain
184 H5 **Alcalá del Río** Spain
185 I7 **Alcalá del Valle** Spain
187 F7 **Alcalà de Xivert** Spain
185 L6 **Alcalá la Real** Spain
258 C3 **Alcalde, Punta** *pt* Chile
194 D8 **Alcamo** *Sicilia* Italy
186 F4 **Alcampell** Spain
186 F4 **Alcanadre** *r.* Spain
186 F6 **Alcanar** Spain
184 B2 **Alcanede** Port.
184 B2 **Alcanena** Port.
184 B2 **Alcanhões** Port.
182 H5 **Alcañices** Spain
186 E5 **Alcañiz** Spain
254 D2 **Alcântara** Brazil
182 G9 **Alcántara** Spain
182 G9 **Alcántara, Embalse de** *resr* Spain
182 H9 **Alcántara II, Embalse de** *resr* Spain
223 I2 **Alcantara Lake** *N.W.T.* Can.
187 C12 **Alcantarilla** Spain
183 P7 **Alcantud** Spain
185 J4 **Alcaracejos** Spain
194 H7 **Alcara li Fusi** *Sicilia* Italy
185 O3 **Alcaraz** Spain
185 N3 **Alcaraz, Sierra de** *mts* Spain
261 H2 **Alcaraz Segundo** Arg.
184 D6 **Alcaria do Cume** *hill* Port.
184 D5 **Alcaria Ruiva** Port.
180 C4 **Alcaria Ruiva** *hill* Port.
184 E4 **Alcarrache** *r.* Port./Spain
186 G4 **Alcarràs** Spain
257 E6 **Alcatrazes, Ilha de** *i.* Brazil
185 K7 **Alcaucín** Spain
185 K5 **Alcaudete** Spain
183 K9 **Alcaudete de la Jara** Spain
186 □ **Alcaufar** Spain
163 C9 **Alçay-Alçabéhéty-Sunharette** France
184 F3 **Alcazaba** *r.* Spain
183 O8 **Alcázar del Rey** Spain
185 M2 **Alcázar de San Juan** Spain
183 K6 **Alcazarén** Spain
Alcazarquivir Morocco *see* **Ksar el Kebir**
151 I3 **Alcester** *Warwickshire, England* U.K.
137 R5 **Alchevs'k** Ukr.
260 E3 **Alcira** Arg.
Alcira *Valencia* Spain *see* **Alzira**
185 K2 **Alcoba** Spain
257 H2 **Alcobaça** Brazil
182 C9 **Alcobaça** Port.
183 M7 **Alcobendas** Spain
184 B2 **Alcobertas** Port.
Alcocebre Spain *see* **Alcossebre**
183 O8 **Alcocer** Spain
183 N4 **Alcocero de Mola** Spain
184 B3 **Alcochete** Port.
184 B2 **Alcoentre** Port.
182 D7 **Alcofra** Port.
185 J5 **Alcolea** *Andalucía* Spain
185 N7 **Alcolea** *Andalucía* Spain
185 K3 **Alcolea de Calatrava** Spain
186 F4 **Alcolea de Cinca** Spain
183 P6 **Alcolea del Pinar** Spain
184 H5 **Alcolea del Río** Spain
186 G4 **Alcoletge** Spain
184 H2 **Alcollarín** Spain
184 E3 **Alconchel** Spain
184 G4 **Alconera** Spain
185 N6 **Alcóntar** Spain
84 E7 **Alcoota** *N.T.* Austr.
183 M8 **Alcorcón** Spain
186 E6 **Alcorisa** Spain
183 O6 **Alcorlo, Embalse de** *resr* Spain
184 F2 **Alcorneo** *r.* Port./Spain
183 Q7 **Alcoroches** Spain
261 G3 **Alcorta** Arg.
187 F7 **Alcossebre** Spain
184 E6 **Alcoutim** Port.
238 K5 **Alcova** *WY* U.S.A.
186 H5 **Alcover** Spain
187 E10 **Alcoy-Alcoi** Spain
177 H4 **Alcsútdoboz** Hungary
186 E4 **Alcubierre** Spain
186 D4 **Alcubierre, Sierra de** *mts* Spain
183 N5 **Alcubilla de Avellaneda** Spain
185 M3 **Alcubillas** Spain
187 D8 **Alcublas** Spain
187 L8 **Alcúdia** Spain
185 J3 **Alcudia** *r.* Spain
187 L8 **Alcúdia, Badia d'** *b.* Spain
185 J3 **Alcudia, Sierra de** *mts* Spain
185 J3 **Alcudia, Valle de** *reg.* Spain
Alcudia de Carlet Spain *see* **L'Alcudia**
185 M6 **Alcudia de Guadix** Spain
181 E4 **Alcudia de Monteagud** Spain
184 G2 **Alcuéscar** Spain
217 □2 **Aldabra Atoll** *Aldabra Is* Seychelles
217 □2 **Aldabra Islands** Seychelles
242 G3 **Aldama** *Chihuahua* Mex.
245 I3 **Aldama** *Tamaulipas* Mex.
131 N4 **Aldan** Rus. Fed.
131 N3 **Aldan** *r.* Rus. Fed.
151 I5 **Aldbourne** *Wiltshire, England* U.K.
149 Q6 **Aldbrough** *East Riding of Yorkshire, England* U.K.
151 O3 **Alde** *r. England* U.K.
216 □3f **Aldea** *r. Gran Canaria* Canary Is
216 □3f **Aldea, Punta de la** *pt Gran Canaria* Canary Is
184 H1 **Aldeacentenera** Spain
182 G6 **Aldeadávila, Embalse de** *resr* Port./Spain
182 G6 **Aldeadávila de la Ribera** Spain
184 G2 **Aldea del Cano** Spain
183 L8 **Aldea del Fresno** Spain
182 G7 **Aldea del Obispo** Spain
185 L3 **Aldea del Rey** Spain
182 I9 **Aldea de Trujillo** Spain
183 P5 **Aldealafuente** Spain
183 P5 **Aldealpozo** Spain
183 K5 **Aldeamayor de San Martín** Spain
183 J9 **Aldeanueva de Barbarroya** Spain
182 I6 **Aldeanueva de Figueroa** Spain
182 I8 **Aldeanueva del Camino** Spain
183 J9 **Aldeanueva de San Bartolomé** Spain
185 M4 **Aldeaquemada** Spain
182 I6 **Aldearrodrigo** Spain
183 K6 **Aldeaseca** Spain
182 I7 **Aldeatejada** Spain
183 L7 **Aldeavieja** Spain
164 I2 **Aldeboarn** Neth.
151 P3 **Aldeburgh** *Suffolk, England* U.K.
182 H7 **Aldehuela de la Bóveda** Spain
182 H7 **Aldehuela de Yeltes** Spain
184 D2 **Aldeia da Mata** Port.
182 G8 **Aldeia da Ponte** Port.
182 F8 **Aldeia do Bispo** Port.
184 C5 **Aldeia dos Elvas** Port.
184 C5 **Aldeia dos Palheiros** Port.
254 C4 **Aldeia Velha** Brazil
182 G8 **Aldeia Velha** *Guarda* Port.
184 C2 **Aldeia Velha** *Portalegre* Port.
209 B7 **Aldeia Viçosa** Angola
234 C2 **Alden** *PA* U.S.A.
151 L4 **Aldenham** *Hertfordshire, England* U.K.
169 B9 **Aldenhoven** Ger.
191 K4 **Aldeno** Italy
151 I5 **Alderbury** *Wiltshire, England* U.K.
233 J5 **Alder Creek** *NY* U.S.A.
147 J3 **Aldergrove** *Northern Ireland* U.K.
151 I6 **Alderholt** *Dorset, England* U.K.
149 M7 **Alderley Edge** *Cheshire, England* U.K.
158 G2 **Alderney** *i.* Channel Is
240 K6 **Alder Peak** *CA* U.S.A.
173 O4 **Aldersbach** Ger.
151 K5 **Aldershot** *Hampshire, England* U.K.
232 E11 **Alderson** *WV* U.S.A.
125 K4 **Al Dhafrah** *reg.* U.A.E.
210 D3 **Aldie** Eth.
196 J9 **Aldinci** Macedonia
172 F5 **Aldingen** Ger.
149 K5 **Aldingham** *Cumbria, England* U.K.
151 N5 **Aldington** *Kent, England* U.K.
215 P5 **Aldinville** S. Africa
186 G6 **Aldover** Spain
151 I2 **Aldridge** *West Midlands, England* U.K.
163 B9 **Aldudes** France
142 I5 **Åled** Sweden
185 P5 **Aledo** Spain
236 J5 **Aledo** *IL* U.S.A.
206 B2 **Aleg** Maur.
216 □3c **Alegranza** *i.* Canary Is
257 G4 **Alegre** *Espírito Santo* Brazil
256 D3 **Alegre** *Minas Gerais* Brazil
255 B9 **Alegrete** Brazil
184 E2 **Alegrete** Port.
183 P3 **Alegría-Dulantzi** Spain
239 J9 **Alegros Mountain** *NM* U.S.A.
261 H1 **Alejandra** Arg.
261 H4 **Alejandro Korn** Arg.
261 F3 **Alejandro Roca** Arg.
252 □ **Alejandro Selkirk, Isla** *i.* S. Pacific Ocean
260 D6 **Alejandro Stefenelli** Arg.
261 F3 **Alejo Ledesma** Arg.
139 Q1 **Alekhovshchina** Rus. Fed.
100 K1 **Aleksandra, Mys** *hd* Rus. Fed.
120 D6 **Aleksandra Bekovicha-Cherkasskoga, Zaliv** *b.* Kazakh.
Aleksandriya Ukr. *see* **Oleksandriya**
129 I2 **Aleksandriyskaya** Rus. Fed.
129 H2 **Aleksandro-Nevskaya** Rus. Fed.
139 X8 **Aleksandro-Nevskiy** Rus. Fed.
Aleksandropol Armenia *see* **Gyumri**
139 V5 **Aleksandrov** Rus. Fed.
196 J7 **Aleksandrovac** Serbia
Aleksandrov Dar Ukr. *see* **Rakhmanivka**
120 C2 **Aleksandrov Gay** Rus. Fed.
135 K5 **Aleksandrovka** *Orenburgskaya Oblast'* Rus. Fed.
120 G1 **Aleksandrovka** *Respublika Bashkortostan* Rus. Fed.
137 S7 **Aleksandrovka** *Rostovskaya Oblast'* Rus. Fed.
197 M7 **Aleksandrovo** *Lovech* Bulg.
197 N8 **Aleksandrovo** *Stara Zagora* Bulg.
134 L4 **Aleksandrovsk** Rus. Fed.
Aleksandrovsk Ukr. *see* **Zaporizhzhya**
139 T2 **Aleksandrovskaya** Rus. Fed.
Aleksandrovskiy Rus. Fed. *see* **Aleksandrovsk**
129 D1 **Aleksandrovskoye** *Stavropol'skiy Kray* Rus. Fed.
127 L1 **Aleksandrovskoye** *Stavropol'skiy Kray* Rus. Fed.
130 I3 **Aleksandrovskoye** *Tomskaya Oblast'* Rus. Fed.
100 M3 **Aleksandrovsk-Sakhalinskiy** *Sakhalin* Rus. Fed.
175 I3 **Aleksandrów** Pol.
174 G3 **Aleksandrów Kujawski** Pol.
175 H4 **Aleksandrów Łódzki** Pol.
130 F1 **Aleksandry, Zemlya** *i. Zemlya Frantsa-Iosifa* Rus. Fed.
177 I6 **Aleksa Šantić** *Vojvodina* Serbia
129 J4 **Alekseyevka** Azer.
Alekseyevka *Akmolinskaya Oblast'* Kazakh. *see* **Akkol'**
121 P2 **Alekseyevka** *Pavlodarskaya Oblast'* Kazakh.
Alekseyevka *Vostochnyy Kazakhstan* Kazakh. *see* **Terekty**
100 E2 **Alekseyevka** *Amurskaya Oblast'* Rus. Fed.
135 G6 **Alekseyevka** *Belgorodskaya Oblast'* Rus. Fed.
135 G6 **Alekseyevka** *Belgorodskaya Oblast'* Rus. Fed.
139 P8 **Alekseyevka** *Bryanskaya Oblast'* Rus. Fed.
137 T4 **Alekseyevo-Lozovskoye** Rus. Fed.
135 H6 **Alekseyevskaya** Rus. Fed.
139 U7 **Aleksin** Rus. Fed.
197 J7 **Aleksinac** Serbia
139 W6 **Aleksino-Shatur** Rus. Fed.
143 M5 **Ålem** Sweden
207 I7 **Alembé** Congo
208 A5 **Alèmbé** Gabon
210 C2 **'Alem Ketema** Eth.
210 D2 **'Alem Maya** Eth.
257 F4 **Além Paraíba** Brazil
140 K5 **Ålen** Norway
159 L5 **Alençon** France
159 L5 **Alençon, Campagne d'** *plain* France
160 D3 **Alène** *r.* France
251 H5 **Alenquer** Brazil
184 B2 **Alenquer** Port.
184 B2 **Alenquer** *r.* Port.
184 C4 **Alentejo** *reg.* Port.
240 □E14 **'Alenuihāhā Channel** *HI* U.S.A.
163 J10 **Alénya** France
Alep Syria *see* **Ḩalab**
206 E5 **Alépé** Côte d'Ivoire
Aleppo Syria *see* **Ḩalab**
114 F4 **Aler** *r.* India
173 J4 **Alerheim** Ger.
192 D3 **Aléria** *Corse* France
186 E3 **Alerre** Spain
221 L1 **Alert** *Nunavut* Can.
252 C2 **Alerta** Peru
222 E5 **Alert Bay** *B.C.* Can.
161 E8 **Alès** France
192 B8 **Ales** *Sardegna* Italy
197 K3 **Aleşd** Romania
Aleshki Ukr. *see* **Tsyurupyns'k**
139 Q8 **Aleshnya** Rus. Fed.
Alesia France *see* **Alise-Ste-Reine**
Aleşkirt Turkey *see* **Eleşkirt**
183 O4 **Alesón** Spain
190 F6 **Alessandria** Italy
190 F6 **Alessandria** *prov.* Italy
195 K4 **Alessandria del Carretto** Italy
195 O4 **Alessano** Italy
Alessio Albania *see* **Lezhë**
140 I5 **Ålesund** Norway
163 I9 **Alet-les-Bains** France
Aletrium Italy *see* **Alatri**
190 D3 **Aletschhorn** *mt.* Switz.
266 G2 **Aleutian Basin** *sea feature* Bering Sea
220 A4 **Aleutian Islands** *AK* U.S.A.
220 C4 **Aleutian Range** *mts AK* U.S.A.
266 H2 **Aleutian Trench** *sea feature* N. Pacific Ocean
131 Q4 **Alevina, Mys** *c.* Rus. Fed.
Alevişik Turkey *see* **Samandağı**
236 D2 **Alexander** *ND* U.S.A.
262 T2 **Alexander, Cape** Antarctica
84 F2 **Alexander, Mount** *hill N.T.* Austr.
87 C7 **Alexander, Mount** *hill W.A.* Austr.
220 E4 **Alexander Archipelago** *is AK* U.S.A.
214 A4 **Alexander Bay** *b.* Namibia/S. Africa
214 A4 **Alexander Bay** S. Africa
231 E9 **Alexander City** *AL* U.S.A.
262 T2 **Alexander Island** Antarctica
122 E3 **Alexander's Wall** *tourist site* Iran
122 F3 **Alexander's Wall** *tourist site* Iran
83 J7 **Alexandra** *Vic.* Austr.
84 G5 **Alexandra** *r. Qld* Austr.
81 D12 **Alexandra** *South I.* N.Z.
259 □ **Alexandra, Cape** S. Georgia
115 M5 **Alexandra Channel** *Andaman & Nicobar Is* India
222 G2 **Alexandra Falls** *N.W.T.* Can.
Alexandra Land *i. Zemlya Frantsa-Iosifa* Rus. Fed. *see* **Aleksandry, Zemlya**
198 D2 **Alexandreia** Greece
Alexandretta Turkey *see* **İskenderun**
Alexandria Afgh. *see* **Ghaznī**
84 F5 **Alexandria** *N.T.* Austr.
222 F4 **Alexandria** *B.C.* Can.
224 F4 **Alexandria** *Ont.* Can.
197 N7 **Alexandria** Romania
215 K9 **Alexandria** S. Africa
Alexandria Turkm. *see* **Mary**
146 G11 **Alexandria** *West Dunbartonshire, Scotland* U.K.
232 A10 **Alexandria** *KY* U.S.A.
237 I10 **Alexandria** *LA* U.S.A.
236 H3 **Alexandria** *MN* U.S.A.
236 G4 **Alexandria** *SD* U.S.A.
234 A7 **Alexandria** *VA* U.S.A.
Alexandria Arachoton Afgh. *see* **Kandahār**
Alexandria Areion Afgh. *see* **Herāt**
233 J4 **Alexandria Bay** *NY* U.S.A.
Alexandria Prophthasia Afgh. *see* **Farāh**
82 G6 **Alexandrina, Lake** *S.A.* Austr.
199 G2 **Alexandroupoli** Greece
256 C2 **Alexânia** Brazil
225 J2 **Alexis** *r. Nfld and Lab.* Can.
222 F4 **Alexis Creek** *B.C.* Can.
128 D5 **Aley** Lebanon
121 T1 **Aley** *r.* Rus. Fed.
122 G3 **Aleyak** Iran
121 T1 **Aleysk** Rus. Fed.
195 O3 **Alezio** Italy
169 D10 **Alf** Ger.
185 L6 **Alfacar** Spain
186 G6 **Alfacs, Port dels** *b.* Spain
202 C5 **Alfadida** *well* Chad
187 E9 **Alfafar** Spain
182 G8 **Alfaiates** Port.
186 D4 **Alfajarín** Spain
245 H5 **Alfajayucan** Mex.
186 C6 **Alfambra** Spain
186 C7 **Alfambra** *r.* Spain
184 B6 **Alfambras** Port.
186 C5 **Alfamén** Spain
182 G6 **Alfândega da Fé** Port.
186 F4 **Alfántega** Spain
125 I8 **Al Fardah** Yemen
182 C8 **Alfarelos** Port.
185 K6 **Alfarnate** Spain
183 Q4 **Alfaro** Spain
186 G4 **Alfarràs** Spain
125 I3 **Al Farūq** *reg.* Saudi Arabia
122 B7 **Al Farwānīyah** Kuwait
127 M9 **Al Farwānīyah** Kuwait
Al Fas Morocco *see* **Fès**
203 F2 **Al Fashn** Egypt
197 P7 **Alfatar** Bulg.
127 K6 **Al Fatḩah** Iraq
125 K7 **Al Fatk** Yemen
127 N9 **Al Fāw** Iraq
203 F2 **Al Fayyūm** Egypt
126 E9 **Al Fayyūm** *governorate* Egypt
124 F8 **Al Fāzih** Yemen
172 H4 **Alfdorf** Ger.
193 M4 **Alfedena** Italy
198 C5 **Alfeios** *r.* Greece
182 B9 **Alfeizerão** Port.
169 I7 **Alfeld (Leine)** Ger.
182 C6 **Alfena** Port.
257 E4 **Alfenas** Brazil
184 C6 **Alferce** Port.
121 Q1 **Alferovka** Rus. Fed.
184 C2 **Alferrarede** Port.
169 E5 **Alfhausen** Ger.
127 N9 **Al Finţās** Kuwait
Alfíos *r.* Greece *see* **Alfeios**
128 A8 **Al Firdān** Egypt
177 J5 **Alföld** *plain* Hungary
191 M7 **Alfonsine** Italy
185 P4 **Alfonso XIII, Embalse de** *resr* Spain
146 K8 **Alford** *Aberdeenshire, Scotland* U.K.
149 R7 **Alford** *Lincolnshire, England* U.K.
186 G5 **Alforja** Spain
233 K3 **Alfred** *Ont.* Can.
233 □O5 **Alfred** *ME* U.S.A.
87 H8 **Alfred and Marie Range** *hills W.A.* Austr.
245 I4 **Alfred M. Terrazas** Mex.
257 G4 **Alfredo Chaves** Brazil
80 J7 **Alfredton** *North I.* N.Z.
149 O7 **Alfreton** *Derbyshire, England* U.K.
141 N6 **Alfta** Sweden
125 M3 **Al Fujayrah** U.A.E.
184 C4 **Alfundão** Port.
202 C3 **Al Fuqahā'** Libya
118 F3 **Al Furāt** *r.* Iraq/Syria *alt.* **Fırat (Turkey),** *conv.* **Euphrates**
124 G3 **Al Furūthi** Saudi Arabia
120 G3 **Alga** Kazakh.
120 E2 **Algabas** Kazakh.
187 K8 **Algaida** Spain
192 B2 **Algajola** *Corse* France
185 I6 **Algámitas** Spain
184 H7 **Algar** Spain
142 B3 **Ålgård** Norway
185 K6 **Algarinejo** Spain
261 F6 **Algarroba** Arg.
258 C3 **Algarrobal** Chile
260 B1 **Algarrobito** Chile
261 G3 **Algarrobitos** Arg.
260 B3 **Algarrobo** Chile
185 K7 **Algarrobo** Spain
187 C12 **Algarrobo** *hill* Spain
260 D5 **Algarrobo del Aguilla** Arg.
184 C6 **Algarve** *reg.* Port.
135 H5 **Algasovo** Rus. Fed.
185 I7 **Algatocín** Spain
100 I1 **Algazeya** Rus. Fed.
185 I8 **Algeciras** Spain
Algeciras, Bahía de *b.* Gibraltar/Spain *see* **Gibraltar, Bay of**
187 E9 **Algemesí** Spain
203 H5 **Algena** Eritrea
205 F1 **Alger** Alg.
227 J5 **Alger** *MI* U.S.A.
205 F3 **Algeria** *country* Africa
169 I6 **Algermissen** Ger.
186 G4 **Algerri** Spain
183 N7 **Algete** Spain
129 G4 **Alget'i** *r.* Georgia
129 F4 **Alget'is Nakrdzali** *nature res.* Georgia
Algha Kazakh. *see* **Alga**
125 M4 **Al Ghāfāt** Oman
127 L8 **Al Ghammās** Iraq
126 E8 **Al Gharbīyah** *governorate* Egypt
Al Ghardaqah Egypt *see* **Al Ghurdaqah**
124 E5 **Al Gharīth** Saudi Arabia
124 G2 **Al Ghāţ** Saudi Arabia
128 D7 **Al Ghawr** *plain* Jordan/West Bank
128 D8 **Al Ghawr** *plain* Jordan/West Bank
125 K7 **Al Ghayḑah** Yemen
124 H4 **Al Ghayl** Saudi Arabia
192 A6 **Alghero** *Sardegna* Italy
125 M6 **Al Ghubr** *reg.* Oman
203 G3 **Al Ghurdaqah** *Al Baḩr al Aḩmar* Egypt
125 J3 **Al Ghuwayr** *well* Qatar
125 I3 **Al Ghwaybiyah** Saudi Arabia
184 C6 **Algibre** *r.* Port.
Algiers Alg. *see* **Alger**
187 E9 **Alginet** Spain
215 J9 **Algoa Bay** S. Africa
250 D5 **Algodón** *r.* Peru
185 I7 **Algodonales** Spain
245 J1 **Algodones, Bahía** *b.* Mex.
183 M9 **Algodor** *r.* Spain
226 G5 **Algoma** *WI* U.S.A.
236 H4 **Algona** *IA* U.S.A.
227 L7 **Algonac** *MI* U.S.A.
224 E4 **Algonquin Park** *Ont.* Can.
227 P4 **Algonquin Provincial Park** *Ont.* Can.
183 O7 **Algora** Spain
183 O2 **Algorta** Spain
261 I3 **Algorta** Uru.
182 G6 **Algoso** Port.
184 C6 **Algoz** Port.
157 L5 **Algrange** France
140 N4 **Älgsjö** Sweden
186 G4 **Alguaire** Spain
187 C11 **Alguazas** Spain
Algueirao Moz. *see* **Hacufera**
184 A3 **Algueirão-Mem Martins** Port.
187 D11 **Algueña** Spain
127 K9 **Al Habakah** *well* Saudi Arabia
127 K7 **Al Ḩabbānīyah** Iraq
185 N7 **Alhabia** Spain
124 G1 **Al Ḩadaqah** *well* Saudi Arabia
182 C8 **Alhadas** Port.
124 F4 **Al Ḩadbah** *reg.* Saudi Arabia
125 J2 **Al Ḩadd** Bahrain
124 G5 **Al Ḩaddār** Saudi Arabia
127 K9 **Al Ḩadhālīl** *plat.* Saudi Arabia
128 E3 **Al Ḩadīdīyah** Syria
127 K6 **Al Ḩadīthah** Iraq
128 F7 **Al Ḩadīthah** Saudi Arabia
127 K6 **Al Ḩaḑr** Iraq
124 E1 **Al Ḩafár** *well* Saudi Arabia
128 E3 **Al Ḩaffah** Syria
204 B4 **Al Haggounia** Western Sahara
124 H3 **Al Ḩā'ir** Saudi Arabia
125 N4 **Al Ḩajar** Oman
125 M3 **Al Ḩajar al Gharbī** *mts* Oman
125 N4 **Al Ḩajar ash Sharqī** *mts* Oman
125 H7 **Al Ḩajr** Yemen
125 M7 **Al Ḩallānīyah** *i.* Oman
185 L6 **Alhama** *r.* Spain
183 Q4 **Alhama** *r.* Spain
128 G7 **Al Ḩamād** *plain* Asia
185 N7 **Alhama de Almería** Spain
183 Q6 **Alhama de Aragón** Spain
185 L6 **Alhama de Granada** Spain
187 C12 **Alhama de Murcia** Spain
124 H4 **Al Ḩamar** Saudi Arabia
185 M3 **Alhambra** Spain
125 I8 **Al Ḩāmi** Yemen
128 D4 **Al Ḩamīdīyah** Syria
185 O7 **Alhamilla, Sierra** *hills* Spain
203 F2 **Al Ḩammām** Egypt
127 K8 **Al Ḩammām** *well* Iraq
124 D4 **Al Ḩamrā'** Saudi Arabia
128 E4 **Al Ḩamrāt** Syria
124 E3 **Al Ḩanākīyah** Saudi Arabia
184 A3 **Alhandra** Port.
124 F9 **Al Ḩanīsh al Kabīr** *i.* Yemen
127 L9 **Al Haniyah** *esc.* Iraq
128 F3 **Al Ḩānūtah** Syria
124 F7 **Al Ḩaqū** Saudi Arabia
124 H4 **Al Ḩariq** Saudi Arabia
203 F2 **Al Ḩarrah** Egypt
128 G8 **Al Ḩarrah** *reg.* Saudi Arabia
202 C3 **Al Ḩarūj al Aswad** *hills* Libya
128 D8 **Al Ḩasā** Jordan
125 I3 **Al Ḩasa** *reg.* Saudi Arabia
127 J5 **Al Ḩasakah** Syria
124 C3 **Al Ḩasāni** *i.* Saudi Arabia
127 L7 **Al Ḩāshimīyah** Iraq
124 G5 **Al Ḩasī** *well* Saudi Arabia
125 L7 **Al Ḩāsikīyah** *i.* Oman
124 G2 **Al Ḩatīfah** *plain* Saudi Arabia
185 J7 **Alhaurín de la Torre** Spain
185 J7 **Alhaurín el Grande** Spain
125 I5 **Al Ḩawāyā** *des.* Saudi Arabia
128 G9 **Al Hawi** *salt pan* Saudi Arabia
124 E5 **Al Ḩawīyah** Saudi Arabia
124 D1 **Al Ḩawjā'** Saudi Arabia
125 H9 **Al Ḩawrā** Yemen
125 H4 **Al Ḩawţah** *reg.* Saudi Arabia
202 D3 **Al Ḩawwārīī** *oasis* Libya
124 F3 **Al Ḩayd** Saudi Arabia
127 M7 **Al Ḩayy** Iraq
126 D9 **Al Ḩayz** Egypt
126 H8 **Al Hazīm** Jordan
124 C1 **Al Ḩazm** Saudi Arabia
124 G7 **Al Ḩazm al Jawf** Yemen
214 E4 **Alheit** S. Africa
185 L6 **Alhendín** Spain
125 K6 **Al Ḩibāk** *des.* Saudi Arabia
128 E5 **Al Ḩījānah** Syria
127 L7 **Al Ḩillah** Iraq
Al Ḩillah *governorate* Iraq *see* **Bābil**
124 H4 **Al Ḩillah** Saudi Arabia
124 H4 **Al Ḩilwah** Saudi Arabia
125 I2 **Al Ḩimārah** *well* Saudi Arabia
127 L7 **Al Hindīyah** Iraq
125 I2 **Al Ḩinnāh** Saudi Arabia
126 I8 **Al Ḩinw** *mt.* Saudi Arabia
125 J4 **Al Hirrah** *well* Saudi Arabia
128 H2 **Al Hīshah** Syria
124 G7 **Al Ḩishwah** *hills* Yemen
124 B1 **Al Ḩismā** *plain* Saudi Arabia
128 D6 **Al Ḩiṣn** Jordan
124 G9 **Al Ḩiṣn** Yemen
204 E2 **Al Hoceima** Morocco
180 D5 **Al Hoceima** *prov.* Morocco
182 E7 **Alhões** Port.
183 O7 **Alhóndiga** Spain
258 E2 **Alhuampa** Arg.
124 F8 **Al Ḩudaydah** Yemen
124 F8 **Al Ḩudaydah** *governorate* Yemen
124 F1 **Al Ḩudūd ash Shamālīyah** *prov.* Saudi Arabia
125 I2 **Al Ḩufayrah** *well* Saudi Arabia
124 G3 **Al Ḩufayyirah** Saudi Arabia
124 D1 **Al Ḩufrah** *reg.* Saudi Arabia
125 I3 **Al Hufūf** Saudi Arabia
124 D1 **Al Ḩūj** *hills* Saudi Arabia
202 C3 **Al Ḩulayq al Kabīr** *hills* Libya
126 G9 **Al Ḩumayḑah** Saudi Arabia
124 G9 **Al Ḩumayshah** Yemen
125 L4 **Al Ḩumrah** *reg.* U.A.E.
125 I3 **Al Ḩunayy** Saudi Arabia
124 G3 **Al Ḩurayyiq** Saudi Arabia
125 M3 **Al Husayfīn** Oman
125 M5 **Al Huwatsah** Oman
125 J3 **Al Huwaylah** Qatar
125 H8 **Al Ḩuwaymi** Yemen
124 E3 **Al Ḩuwayyiţ** Saudi Arabia
128 E3 **Al Ḩuwayz** *Ḩamāh* Syria
128 E3 **Al Ḩuwayz** *Ḩamāh* Syria
124 G4 **Al Huwwah** Saudi Arabia
111 D10 **Ali** *Xizang* China
195 I7 **Alì** *Sicilia* Italy
194 F8 **Alia** *Sicilia* Italy
185 I2 **Alía** Spain
123 M3 **'Alīābād** Afgh.
129 H4 **Äliabad** Azer.
122 F3 **'Alīābād** *Golestān* Iran
122 F7 **'Alīābād** *Hormozgan* Iran
122 H5 **'Alīābād** *Khorāsān* Iran
122 I6 **'Alīābād** *Khorāsān* Iran
122 B3 **'Alīābād** *Kordestān* Iran
122 B4 **'Alīābād** *Kordestān* Iran
122 D4 **'Alīābād** *Qom* Iran
122 D4 **Alīābād, Kūh-e** *mt.* Iran
186 D6 **Aliaga** Spain
199 H4 **Aliağa** Turkey
187 C8 **Aliaguilla** Spain
198 C2 **Aliakmona, Techniti Limni** *l.* Greece
198 D2 **Aliakmonas** *r.* Greece
122 B5 **'Alī al Gharbī** Iraq
93 E8 **Aliambata** East Timor
193 Q7 **Aliano** Italy
198 E4 **Aliartos** Greece
114 C3 **Alibag** *Mahar.* India
123 M9 **Ali Bandar** Pak.
129 G5 **Älibäyli** Azer.
129 J6 **Äli Bayramlı** Azer.
199 H3 **Alibey Adası** *i.* Turkey
210 C2 **Ālībo** Eth.
196 I5 **Alibunar** *Vojvodina* Serbia
129 I5 **Älicançay** *r.* Azer.
187 E11 **Alicante** Spain
187 D10 **Alicante** *prov.* Spain
187 E11 **Alicante, Bahía de** *b.* Spain
85 J7 **Alice** *Qld* Austr.
85 H3 **Alice** *r. Qld* Austr.
85 J8 **Alice** *watercourse Qld* Austr.
215 K8 **Alice** S. Africa
237 F12 **Alice** *TX* U.S.A.

Amakazari-yama to Anivorano

278

105 G2 Amakazari-yama mt. Japan
103 H14 Amakusa-Kami-shima i. Japan
103 G14 Amakusa-nada b. Japan
103 H14 Amakusa-Shimo-shima i. Japan
125 L6 Amal Oman
142 I2 Åmål Sweden
207 F3 Amalaoulaou well Mali
114 H4 Amalapuram Andhra Prad. India
99 K1 Amalat r. Rus. Fed.
193 N6 Amalfi Italy
215 J3 Amalia S. Africa
198 C5 Amaliada Greece
116 E9 Amalner Mahar. India
175 L1 Amalvas l. Lith.
91 I7 Amamapare Papua Indon.
253 G5 Amambaí Brazil
253 G5 Amambaí, Serra de hills Brazil/Para.
102 □G18 Amami-Ō-shima i. Nansei-shotō Japan
102 □F20 Amami-shotō is Japan
208 E5 Amamula Dem. Rep. Congo
141 M6 Amån r. Sweden
260 D2 Amaná Arg.
251 E5 Amanã, Lago l. Brazil
250 E5 Amana, Reserva de Desenvolvimento Sustentável nature res. Brazil
84 B4 Amanbidji Aboriginal Land res. N.T. Austr.
157 L8 Amance France
157 K8 Amance r. France
156 H7 Amance, Lac l. France
160 I2 Amancey France
232 C9 Amanda OH U.S.A.
193 K2 Amandola Italy
120 H3 Amangel'dy Aktyubinskaya Oblast' Kazakh.
120 K2 Amangel'dy Kostanayskaya Oblast' Kazakh.
120 K1 Amankaragay Kazakh.
Amankeldi Aktyubinskaya Oblast' Kazakh. see Amangel'dy
Amankeldi Kostanayskaya Oblast' Kazakh. see Amangel'dy
143 M2 Åmänningen l. Sweden
120 I4 Amanotkel' Kazakh.
Amanqaraghay Kazakh. see Amankaragay
193 Q9 Amantea Italy
213 E3 Amanzamnyama watercourse Zimbabwe
215 O6 Amanzimtoti S. Africa
252 C2 Amapa Brazil
251 I4 Amapá Brazil
251 I4 Amapá state Brazil
245 K7 Amapa r. Mex.
242 □P11 Amapala Hond.
251 I4 Amapari r. Brazil
210 C2 Āmara admin. reg. Eth.
203 G6 Amara Abu Sin Sudan
197 L6 Amaradia r. Romania
'Amārah Iraq see Al 'Amārah
255 B9 Amaral Ferrador Brazil
254 E3 Amarante Brazil
182 D6 Amarante Port.
254 D3 Amarante do Maranhão Brazil
96 C4 Amarapura Myanmar
114 F7 Amaravati r. India
203 F4 Amara West Sudan
106 J3 Amardalay Mongolia
182 D5 Amarela, Serra mts Port.
184 E4 Amareleja Port.
182 D5 Amares Port.
254 F5 Amargosa Brazil
239 F8 Amargosa watercourse CA U.S.A.
241 P5 Amargosa Desert NV U.S.A.
240 P5 Amargosa Range mts CA U.S.A.
241 P5 Amargosa Valley NV U.S.A.
185 M2 Amarguillo r. Spain
Amargura Island Tonga see Fonualei
237 E8 Amarillo TX U.S.A.
258 C4 Amarillo, Cerro mt. Arg.
116 H8 Amarkantak Chhattisgarh India
193 M3 Amaro, Monte mt. Italy
195 K6 Amaroni Italy
84 G7 Amaroo, Lake salt flat Qld Austr.
116 H8 Amarpur Madh. Prad. India
117 M8 Amarpur Tripura India
116 G8 Amarwara Madh. Prad. India
226 F3 Amasa MI U.S.A.
104 E1 Ama-saki pt Japan
193 K5 Amaseno Italy
193 K5 Amaseno r. Italy
129 E5 Amasia Armenia
Amasia Turkey see Amasya
204 B4 Amasine Western Sahara
126 F3 Amasra Turkey
207 F2 Amâssine well Mali
126 G3 Amasya Turkey
82 C2 Amata S.A. Austr.
251 G5 Amatari Brazil
250 D5 Amataurá Brazil
243 M9 Amatenango Mex.
244 G7 Amatepec Mex.
215 P5 Amatikulu S. Africa
242 □O10 Amatique, Bahía de b. Guat.
244 D5 Amatitán Mex.
245 K7 Amatlán Mex.
244 C5 Amatlán de Cañas Mex.
195 K6 Amato r. Italy
215 K8 Amatola Range mts S. Africa
193 K2 Amatrice Italy
105 L5 Amatsu-Kominato Japan
235 H2 Amawalk NY U.S.A.
165 H7 Amay Belgium
183 L3 Amaya mt. Spain
100 B2 Amazar Rus. Fed.
100 B2 Amazar r. Rus. Fed.
251 I4 Amazon r. S. America
251 I4 Amazon r. S. America alt. Amazonas
251 I4 Amazon, Mouths of the Brazil
252 C3 Amazon, Source of the Peru
251 E6 Amazonas state Brazil
250 D5 Amazonas dept Col.
250 B6 Amazonas dept Peru
251 I4 Amazonas r. S. America
251 I4 Amazonas r. S. America conv. Amazon
251 E4 Amazonas state Venez.
264 F5 Amazon Cone sea feature S. Atlantic Ocean
251 G6 Amazónia, Parque Nacional nat. park Brazil
123 O4 Amb Pak.
210 C1 Āmba Ālagē mt. Eth.
114 D3 Ambad Mahar. India
210 C2 Amba Farit mt. Eth.
213 □I4 Ambahikily Madag.
114 E3 Ambajogai Mahar. India
116 F4 Ambala Haryana India
213 □J3 Ambalajanakomby Madag.
213 □J2 Ambalakida Madag.
213 □K2 Ambalakirajy Madag.
114 G9 Ambalangoda Sri Lanka
213 □J4 Ambalatany Madag.
213 □J4 Ambalavao Madag.
84 E7 Ambalindum N.T. Austr.
207 H6 Ambam Cameroon
213 □K2 Ambanja Madag.
122 H6 Ambar Iran
131 R3 Ambarchik Rus. Fed.
162 D6 Ambarès-et-Lagrave France
258 D3 Ambargasta, Salinas de salt pan Arg.
134 F2 Ambarnyy Rus. Fed.
183 J3 Ambasaguas Spain
114 E8 Ambasamudram Tamil Nadu India
117 M8 Ambassa Tripura India
85 J8 Ambathala Qld Austr.
250 B5 Ambato Ecuador
258 D3 Ambato, Sierra mts Arg.
213 □J3 Ambato Boeny Madag.
213 □J4 Ambato Finandrahana Madag.
213 □J4 Ambatolahy Madag.
213 □J3 Ambatolampy Madag.
213 □J3 Ambatomainty Madag.
213 □J3 Ambatomanoina Madag.
213 □K3 Ambatondrazaka Madag.
213 □K2 Ambatosia Madag.
213 □K3 Ambatosoratra Madag.
162 G4 Ambazac France
162 G4 Ambazac, Monts d' hills France
Ambejogai Mahar. India see Ambajogai
123 O4 Ambela Pak.
93 E5 Ambelau i. Maluku Indon.
Ambelón Greece see Ampelonas
Amber Rajasthan India see Amer
173 L3 Amberg Ger.
226 G4 Amberg WI U.S.A.
149 O7 Ambergate Derbyshire, England U.K.
243 P8 Ambergris Cay i. Belize
246 H3 Ambergris Cays is Turks and Caicos Is
160 G5 Ambérieu-en-Bugey France
227 M5 Amberley Ont. Can.
81 G10 Amberley South I. N.Z.
165 I8 Amberloup Belgium
160 D5 Ambert France
162 C5 Ambès France
116 H9 Ambgaon Mahar. India
163 I8 Ambialet France
Ambianum France see Amiens
206 C3 Ambidédi Mali
160 D4 Ambierle France
116 D9 Ambika r. India
117 I8 Ambikapur Chhattisgarh India
92 C5 Ambil i. Phil.
213 □J4 Ambila Madag.
159 L7 Ambillou France
213 □K2 Ambilobe Madag.
222 D3 Ambition, Mount B.C. Can.
156 D5 Amblainville France
149 N3 Amble Northumberland, England U.K.
150 H3 Amblecote West Midlands, England U.K.
220 C3 Ambler AK U.S.A.
234 E4 Ambler PA U.S.A.
149 L5 Ambleside Cumbria, England U.K.
156 C2 Ambleteuse France
165 I8 Amblève r. Belgium
165 I8 Amblève, Vallée de l' val. Belgium
117 K9 Ambo Orissa India
252 A2 Ambo Peru
213 □J5 Amboasary Madag.
213 □K3 Amboasary Gara Madag.
213 □K3 Amboavory Madag.
78 □3a Ambo Channel Kwajalein Marshall Is
213 □K3 Ambodifotatra Madag.
213 □K4 Ambodiharina Madag.
213 □K3 Ambodilazana Madag.
213 □J3 Ambohidratrimo Madag.
213 □K3 Ambohijanahary Madag.
213 □J4 Ambohimahasoa Madag.
213 □I4 Ambohimahavelona Madag.
213 □J3 Ambohipaky Madag.
213 □K2 Ambohitra mt. Madag.
213 □K2 Ambohitralanana Madag.
Amboina Maluku Indon. see Ambon
162 F1 Amboise France
209 B7 Amboiva Angola
158 F6 Ambon France
93 F5 Ambon Maluku Indon.
93 E5 Ambon i. Maluku Indon.
213 □J5 Ambondro Madag.
156 H5 Ambonnay France
252 D4 Amboró, Parque Nacional nat. park Bol.
211 C5 Amboseli National Park Kenya
213 □J4 Ambositra Madag.
213 □J5 Ambovombe Madag.
Ambow i. Fiji see Bau
241 Q7 Amboy CA U.S.A.
226 E8 Amboy IL U.S.A.
159 O8 Ambrault France
Ambre, Cap d' c. Madag. see Bobaomby, Tanjona
217 □1b Ambre, Île d' i. Mauritius
159 J5 Ambrières-les-Vallées France
Ambrim i. Vanuatu see Ambrym
209 B6 Ambriz Angola
209 B6 Ambriz, Coutada do nature res. Angola
Ambrizete Angola see N'zeto
129 E3 Ambrolauri Georgia
160 G4 Ambronay France
151 J4 Ambrosden Oxfordshire, England U.K.
261 G2 Ambrosetti Arg.
250 D5 Ambrosio Brazil
78 □5 Ambrym i. Vanuatu
95 J9 Ambulu Jawa Indon.
95 J8 Ambunten Jawa Indon.
114 F6 Ambur Tamil Nadu India
85 L9 Amby Qld Austr.
220 A4 Amchitka Island AK U.S.A.
142 E2 Åmdals Verk Norway
202 D6 Am-Dam Chad
205 F5 Amded, Oued watercourse Alg.
130 H3 Amderma Rus. Fed.
207 E2 Amdillis well Mali
202 C6 Am Djéména Chad
111 J10 Amdo Xizang China
244 G5 Amealco Mex.
244 C5 Ameca Jalisco Mex.
244 D3 Ameca Zacatecas Mex.
244 B5 Ameca r. Mex.
245 I6 Amecameca Mex.
210 C2 Amedamit mt. Eth.
261 F4 Ameghino Arg.
190 H7 Ameglia Italy
179 I2 Ameisberg hill Austria
184 D6 Ameixial Port.
165 J8 Amel Belgium
164 I2 Ameland i. Neth.
193 I2 Amelia Italy
232 H11 Amelia Court House VA U.S.A.
163 J11 Amélie-les-Bains-Palalda France
168 J4 Amelinghausen Ger.
116 H6 Amellu Uttar Prad. India
182 D9 Amêndoa Port.
184 D5 Amendoeira Port.
195 L4 Amendolara Italy
195 J8 Amendolea r. Italy
233 L7 Amenia NY U.S.A.
203 F5 Amentego Sudan
111 B13 Amer Rajasthan India
186 K3 Amer Spain
205 H4 Amer, Erg d' des. Alg.
187 L8 Amer, Punta pt Spain
173 M6 Amerang Ger.
182 E4 A Merca Spain
240 K3 American, North Fork r. CA U.S.A.
256 D5 Americana Brazil
264 H9 American-Antarctic Ridge sea feature S. Atlantic Ocean
238 H5 American Falls ID U.S.A.
238 H5 American Falls Reservoir ID U.S.A.
241 U1 American Fork UT U.S.A.
78 □2 American Samoa terr. S. Pacific Ocean
231 E9 Americus GA U.S.A.
179 K5 Ameringkogel mt. Austria
164 H5 Amerongen Neth.
164 H4 Amersfoort Neth.
215 N3 Amersfoort S. Africa
151 K4 Amersham Buckinghamshire, England U.K.
223 M3 Amery Man. Can.
263 E2 Amery Ice Shelf Antarctica
236 I4 Ames IA U.S.A.
151 I5 Amesbury Wiltshire, England U.K.
233 O6 Amesbury MA U.S.A.
116 D7 Amet Rajasthan India
116 H6 Amethi Uttar Prad. India
186 A1 Amezketa Spain
182 F4 A Mezquita Spain
198 C4 Amfilochia Greece
198 D4 Amfissa Greece
159 M3 Amfreville-la-Campagne France
131 O3 Amga Rus. Fed.
107 P2 Amgalang Nei Mongol China
100 J6 Amgu Rus. Fed.
131 T3 Amguema Rus. Fed.
205 G4 Amguid Alg.
99 O1 Amgun' r. Rus. Fed.
225 H4 Amherst N.S. Can.
233 M6 Amherst MA U.S.A.
232 C7 Amherst OH U.S.A.
232 F11 Amherst VA U.S.A.
86 I5 Amherst, Mount hill W.A. Austr.
227 K7 Amherstburg Ont. Can.
232 D11 Amherstdale WV U.S.A.
227 R5 Amherst Island Ont. Can.
227 R5 Amherstview Ont. Can.
105 L3 Ami Japan
184 B2 Amiais de Baixo Port.
192 H2 Amiata, Monte mt. Italy
Amida Turkey see Diyarbakır
236 D2 Amidon ND U.S.A.
184 D4 Amieira Port.
182 E9 Amieira do Tejo Port.
156 D4 Amiens France
127 J7 'Amīj, Wādī watercourse Iraq
126 H5 Amik Ovası marsh Turkey
125 K6 Amilḩayt, Ramlat des. Oman
125 K6 Amilḩayt, Wādī al r. Oman
156 E8 Amilly France
122 E6 'Amīnābād Iran
Amíndhaion Greece see Amyntaio
Amindivi atoll India see Amini
114 C7 Amindivi Islands Lakshadweep India
114 C7 Amini atoll India
210 D3 Amino Eth.
104 B4 Amino Japan
212 C4 Aminuis Namibia
128 D4 Amioun Lebanon
116 G5 Amipshahr Uttar Prad. India
123 L4 Amīr, Band-e lakes Afgh.
122 D5 Amīrābād Eşfahān Iran
122 B5 Amīrābād Īlām Iran
Amirabad Iran see Fūlād Maïalleh
217 □2 Amirante Islands Seychelles
265 H5 Amirante Trench sea feature Indian Ocean
123 J7 Amir Chah Pak.
223 K4 Amisk Lake Sask. Can.
Amistad, Represa de resr Mex./U.S.A. see Amistad Reservoir
243 I3 Amistad Reservoir Mex./U.S.A.
Amisus Turkey see Samsun
237 J10 Amite LA U.S.A.
237 J10 Amite Creek r. MS U.S.A.
85 N9 Amity Point Qld Austr.
116 E8 Amjhera Madh. Prad. India
116 G9 Amla Madh. Prad. India
124 F6 Amlaḩ, Jabal al hill Saudi Arabia
207 F5 Amlamé Togo
122 D3 Amlash Iran
117 J6 Amlekhganj Nepal
142 E3 Åmli Norway
220 A4 Amlia Island AK U.S.A.
150 D1 Amlwch Isle of Anglesey, Wales U.K.
203 H5 'Amm Adam Sudan
128 D7 'Ammān Jordan
122 F2 Ammanazar Turkm.
150 E4 Ammanford Carmarthenshire, Wales U.K.
134 E2 Ämmänsaari Fin.
124 G8 'Ammār reg. Yemen
128 E6 'Ammār, Tall hill Syria
140 N4 Ammarnäs Sweden
84 E6 Ammaroo N.T. Austr.
82 D2 Ammaroodinna watercourse S.A. Austr.
221 O3 Ammassalik Greenland
173 K6 Ammer r. Ger.
140 N5 Ammerån r. Sweden
172 F4 Ammerbuch Ger.
178 C5 Ammergauer Alpen mts Austria/Ger.
173 J6 Ammergebirge nature res. Ger.
168 E4 Ammerland reg. Ger.
169 J8 Ammern Ger.
168 J3 Ammersbek Ger.
157 N7 Ammerschwihr France
173 K6 Ammersee l. Ger.
198 C2 Ammochori Greece
128 B3 Ammochostos Cyprus
128 C3 Ammochostos Bay Cyprus
124 F9 Am Nābiyah Yemen
Amne Machin Range mts China see A'nyêmaqên Shan
157 L5 Amnéville France
Amnok-kang r. China/N. Korea see Yalu Jiang
116 D9 Amod Gujarat India
182 E4 Amoeiro Spain
108 D7 Amo Jiang r. Yunnan China
122 E3 Amol Iran
253 F4 Amolar Brazil
137 N2 Amon' Rus. Fed.
182 C5 Amonde Port.
169 G9 Amöneburg Ger.
254 F2 Amontada Brazil
183 L9 Amor mt. Spain
172 G2 Amorbach Ger.
183 O2 Amorebieta País Vasco Spain
258 F3 Amores r. Arg.
199 G6 Amorgos i. Greece
256 B2 Amorinópolis Brazil
237 K8 Amory MS U.S.A.
224 E3 Amos Que. Can.
142 H6 Åmose r. Denmark
142 F2 Åmot Buskerud Norway
142 D2 Åmot Telemark Norway
141 N6 Åmot Sweden
Amota i. Vanuatu see Mota
250 A6 Amotape, Cerros de mts Peru
142 I2 Åmotfors Sweden
163 C8 Amou France
198 E2 Amouliani i. Greece
205 F2 Amour, Djebel mts Alg.
206 D2 Amourj Maur.
Amoy Fujian China see Xiamen
245 I6 Amozoc Mex.
95 K5 Ampah Kalimantan Indon.
93 B4 Ampana Sulawesi Indon.
213 □K2 Ampanefena Madag.
115 H3 Ampani Orissa India
213 □J5 Ampanihy Madag.
213 □K3 Ampanotoamaizina Madag.
213 □J2 Amparafaka, Tanjona pt Madag.
213 □K3 Amparafaravola Madag.
114 G9 Amparai Sri Lanka
256 D5 Amparo Brazil
213 □K3 Ampasimanolotra Madag.
213 □K3 Ampasimbe Madag.
178 D5 Ampass Austria
198 D3 Ampelonas Greece
95 L9 Ampenan Lombok Indon.
173 L5 Amper r. Ger.
207 H4 Amper Nigeria
264 I3 Ampere Seamount sea feature N. Atlantic Ocean
191 N3 Ampezzo Italy
173 M5 Ampfing Ger.
173 P5 Ampflwang im Hausruckwald Austria
90 D3 Amphitrite Group is Paracel Is
93 B4 Ampibaku Sulawesi Indon.
213 □K2 Ampisikinana Madag.
Ampitsikinana Madag. see Ampisikinana
160 E5 Amplepuis France
93 B4 Ampoa Sulawesi Indon.
151 I5 Amport Hampshire, England U.K.
186 G6 Amposta Spain
151 L3 Ampthill Bedfordshire, England U.K.
183 K5 Ampudia Spain
183 N2 Ampuero Spain
161 I9 Ampus France
106 H9 Amqog Gansu China
225 H3 Amqui Que. Can.
114 F4 Amrabad Andhra Prad. India
124 F3 'Amrah, Jabal hill Saudi Arabia
124 F8 'Amrān Yemen
124 F7 'Amrān governorate Yemen
Amraoti Mahar. India see Amravati
116 F9 Amravati Mahar. India
116 C9 Amreli Gujarat India
123 M8 Amri Pak.
117 N7 Amring Assam India
190 G1 Amriswil Switz.
116 E4 Amritsar Punjab India
116 G5 Amroha Uttar Prad. India
168 F1 Amrum i. Ger.
205 G5 Amsel Alg.
140 O4 Åmsele Sweden
164 G3 Amstelmeer l. Neth.
164 G4 Amstelveen Neth.
164 G4 Amsterdam Neth.
215 O2 Amsterdam S. Africa
233 K6 Amsterdam NY U.S.A.
232 E8 Amsterdam OH U.S.A.
265 J7 Amsterdam, Île i. Indian Ocean
164 H5 Amsterdam-Rijnkanaal canal Neth.
164 F4 Amsterdamse Waterleidingduinen nature res. Neth.
179 K3 Amstetten Austria
172 H4 Amstetten Ger.
235 K1 Amston CT U.S.A.
208 D2 Am Timan Chad
129 C2 Amtqeli Georgia
172 H6 Amtzell Ger.
250 C4 Amú r. Col.
111 I10 Amu Co l. Xizang China
120 H5 Amudar'ya r. Asia
Amudaryo r. Asia see Amudar'ya
221 I2 Amund Ringnes Island Nunavut Can.
263 G2 Amundsen, Mount Antarctica
267 K10 Amundsen Abyssal Plain sea feature Southern Ocean
268 B1 Amundsen Basin sea feature Arctic Ocean
263 D2 Amundsen Bay Antarctica
262 O1 Amundsen Coast Antarctica
262 N1 Amundsen Glacier Antarctica
220 F2 Amundsen Gulf N.W.T. Can.
267 K10 Amundsen Ridges sea feature Southern Ocean
263 A1 Amundsen-Scott research stn Antarctica
262 Q2 Amundsen Sea Antarctica
95 K6 Amuntai Kalimantan Indon.
100 C2 Amur Heilong. China
100 I4 Amur r. Rus. Fed. alt. Heilong Jiang (China)
203 G5 'Amur, Wadi watercourse Sudan
93 D3 Amurang Sulawesi Indon.
Amur Oblast admin. div. Rus. Fed. see Amurskaya Oblast'
183 O2 Amurrio Spain
100 J3 Amursk Rus. Fed.
100 F2 Amurskaya Oblast' admin. div. Rus. Fed.
137 N8 Amurs'ke Ukr.
120 H1 Amurskiy Rus. Fed.
100 L2 Amurskiy Liman str. Rus. Fed.
100 G5 Amurzet Rus. Fed.
195 K7 Amusa r. Italy
183 L4 Amusco Spain
100 C1 Amutkachi Rus. Fed.
198 C4 Amvrakia, Limni l. Greece
198 B4 Amvrakikos Kolpos b. Greece
137 R6 Amvrosiyivka Ukr.
Amyderya r. Asia see Amudar'ya
198 C2 Amyntaio Greece
226 J1 Amyot Ont. Can.
197 Q7 Amzacea Romania
207 F2 Amzérakad well Mali
202 D6 Am-Zoer Chad
96 B5 An Myanmar
199 I1 Ana r. Turkey
79 □9 Anaa atoll Arch. des Tuamotu Fr. Polynesia
93 B5 Anabanua Sulawesi Indon.
131 M2 Anabar r. Rus. Fed.
83 H6 Ana Branch r. N.S.W. Austr.
128 D6 Anabtā West Bank
240 M7 Anacapa Island CA U.S.A.
193 M6 Anacapri Italy
251 E2 Anaco Venez.
238 H3 Anaconda MT U.S.A.
238 C2 Anacortes WA U.S.A.
92 C3 Anacuao, Mount Phil.
237 F8 Anadarko OK U.S.A.
182 D8 Anadia Port.
126 H3 Anadolu Dağları mts Turkey
131 S3 Anadyr' Rus. Fed.
131 S3 Anadyr' r. Rus. Fed.
Anadyr, Gulf of Rus. Fed. see Anadyrskiy Zaliv
131 T3 Anadyrskiy Zaliv b. Rus. Fed.
199 G6 Anafi Greece
199 G6 Anafi i. Greece
216 □3a Anaga, Punta de pt Tenerife Canary Is
254 E5 Anagé Brazil
193 K4 Anagni Italy
Anagnia Italy see Anagni
127 J6 'Ānah Iraq
240 O8 Anaheim CA U.S.A.
222 E4 Anahim Lake B.C. Can.
240 □B11 Anahola HI U.S.A.
243 I4 Anáhuac Nuevo León Mex.
245 J3 Anáhuac Veracruz Mex.
237 H11 Anahuac TX U.S.A.
240 □C12 'Anahulu r. HI U.S.A.
114 E7 Anaimalai Hills India
114 E7 Anai Mudi Peak Kerala India
Anaiteum i. Vanuatu see Anatom
251 I5 Anajás Brazil
251 I5 Anajás, Ilha i. Brazil
254 D2 Anajatuba Brazil
213 □I4 Anakao Madag.
115 H4 Anakapalle Andhra Prad. India
85 K7 Anakie Qld Austr.
213 □J2 Analalava Madag.
213 □K3 Analamaitso mts Madag.
256 D5 Analândia Brazil
213 □I4 Analavelona mts Madag.
234 E2 Analomink PA U.S.A.
251 F5 Anamã Brazil
246 D3 Ana María, Golfo de b. Cuba
94 F3 Anambas, Kepulauan is Indon.
207 G5 Anambra state Nigeria
104 E1 Anamizu Japan
Anamooka i. Tonga see Nomuka
236 J4 Anamosa IA U.S.A.
251 G4 Anamu r. Brazil
126 F5 Anamur Turkey
105 G5 Anan Nagano Japan
104 A8 Anan Tokushima Japan
183 O3 Añana-Gesaltza Spain
116 D8 Anand Gujarat India
117 K9 Anandapur Orissa India
116 F4 Anandpur Punjab India
117 K8 Anandpur r. W. Bengal India
198 F6 Ananes i. Greece
121 Q6 Anan'ev Kyrg.
82 C2 Anangu Pitjantjatjara Aboriginal Lands res. S.A. Austr.
93 D6 Anano i. Indon.
114 E5 Anantapur Andhra Prad. India
116 E3 Anantnag Jammu and Kashmir
116 G6 Anant Peth Madh. Prad. India
Ananyev Ukr. see Anan'yiv
Anan'yevo Kyrg. see Anan'ev
136 I6 Anan'yiv Ukr.
135 G7 Anapa Rus. Fed.
195 I9 Anapo r. Sicilia Italy
198 G8 Anapodiaris r. Kriti Greece
256 C2 Anápolis Brazil
251 I5 Anapú r. Brazil
Anár Fin. see Inari
122 F6 Anār Iran
122 E5 Anārak Iran
122 D4 Anarbar r. Iran
122 G4 Anarbat Iran
177 L3 Anarcs Hungary
123 I5 Anardara Afgh.
263 L2 Anare Mountains Antarctica
82 □3 Anare Station S. Pacific Ocean
147 B8 Anascaul Ireland
247 □1 Añasco Puerto Rico
247 □1 Añasco, Río Grande de r. Puerto Rico
140 P4 Ånäset Sweden
137 R6 Anastasiyevka Rus. Fed.
137 Q8 Anastasiyevskaya Rus. Fed.
91 K3 Anatahan i. N. Mariana Is
Anatajan i. N. Mariana Is see Anatahan
199 J4 Anatolia reg. Turkey
198 G1 Anatoliki Makedonia kai Thraki admin. reg. Greece
78 □5 Anatom i. Vanuatu
258 E3 Añatuya Arg.
84 F7 Anatye Aboriginal Land res. N.T. Austr.
251 F4 Anauá r. Brazil
256 A5 Anaurilândia Brazil
251 F5 Anavilhanas, Arquipélago das is Brazil
183 J7 Anaya de Alba Spain
Anaypazari Turkey see Gülnar
128 E10 Anaz mts Saudi Arabia
122 C2 'Anbarān Iran
106 E6 Anbei Gansu China
Anbu Guangdong China see Chao'an
122 C3 Anbūh Iran
122 F8 Anbūr-e Kālārī Iran
101 E9 Anbyon N. Korea
182 C8 Ançã Port.
182 F3 Ancares, Serra dos mts Spain
252 A2 Ancash dept Peru
227 O6 Ancaster Ont. Can.
151 K2 Ancaster Lincolnshire, England U.K.
258 D3 Ancasti, Sierra mts Arg.
161 D7 Ance r. France
161 I7 Ancelle France
158 I7 Ancenis France
157 J6 Ancerville France
259 D6 Anchán Arg.
108 E3 Anchang Sichuan China
207 H4 Anchau Nigeria
257 G4 Anchieta Brazil
252 C3 Anchodaya Bol.
220 D3 Anchorage AK U.S.A.
Anchorage Island atoll Cook Is see Suwarrow
85 M1 Anchorage Reefs P.N.G.
227 L7 Anchor Bay MI U.S.A.
260 E4 Anchorena Arg.
216 □2c Anchorstock Point Tristan da Cunha S. Atlantic Ocean
246 □ Anchovy Jamaica
Anchuthengu Kerala India see Anjengo
Anci Hebei China see Langfang
175 L1 Ančia l. Lith.
138 F6 Ančia r. Lith.
183 P3 Ancín Spain
246 D3 Anclitas, Cayo i. Cuba
An Cóbh Ireland see Cobh
261 G4 Ancón Arg.
252 A2 Ancón Peru
191 P8 Ancona Italy
191 N9 Ancona prov. Italy
156 D4 Ancre r. France
146 K11 Ancrum Scottish Borders, Scotland U.K.
211 C8 Ancuabe Moz.
213 G3 Ancuaze Moz.
259 B6 Ancud Chile
259 B6 Ancud, Golfo de g. Chile
156 H8 Ancy-le-Franc France
Ancyra Turkey see Ankara
100 D5 Anda Heilong. China
Anda Heilong. China see Daqing
93 D1 Anda i. Indon.
141 I6 Anda Norway
260 B5 Andacollo Arg.
260 B2 Andacollo Chile
84 E8 Andado N.T. Austr.
252 B3 Andahuaylas Peru
213 □K3 Andaingo Gara Madag.
117 K8 Andal W. Bengal India
Andalaly Rus. Fed. see Nozhay-Yurt
258 D2 Andalgalá Arg.
191 K3 Andalo Italy
140 I5 Åndalsnes Norway
185 K5 Andalucía aut. comm. Spain
Andalusia S. Africa see Jan Kempdorp
Andalusia aut. comm. Spain see Andalucía
231 D10 Andalusia AL U.S.A.
125 N5 Andām, Wādī r. Oman
97 A9 Andaman and Nicobar Islands union terr. India
113 H9 Andaman and Nicobar Islands union terr. India
265 K4 Andaman Basin sea feature Indian Ocean
115 M6 Andaman Islands Andaman & Nicobar Is India
97 B9 Andaman Sea Indian Ocean
115 M6 Andaman Strait Andaman & Nicobar Is India
82 F4 Andamooka S.A. Austr.
161 F6 Andance France
213 □K2 Andapa Madag.
212 D3 Andara Namibia
123 M4 Andarāb Afgh.
185 N7 Andarax r. Spain
123 N3 Andarob Tajik.
179 P4 Andau Austria
182 I5 Andavías Spain
108 F7 Ande Guangxi China
124 E8 Andeba Ye Midir Zerf Chaf pt Eritrea
173 K6 Andechs Ger.
190 G2 Andeer Switz.
134 K2 Andeg Rus. Fed.
Andegavum France see Angers
190 F1 Andelfingen Switz.
156 B5 Andelle r. France
157 J7 Andelot-Blancheville France
160 H3 Andelot-en-Montagne France
178 A5 Andelsbuch Austria
164 I5 Andelst Neth.
140 N2 Andenes Norway
165 H8 Andenne Belgium
207 F3 Andéramboukane Mali
140 N2 Ånderdalen Nasjonalpark nat. park Norway
165 F7 Anderlecht Belgium
165 F8 Anderlues Belgium
190 F2 Andermatt Switz.
169 D10 Andernach Ger.
163 B6 Andernos-les-Bains France
Anderob Tajik. see Andarob
143 N1 Andersbo Sweden
78 □1 Andersen Airforce Base Guam
261 G4 Anderson Arg.
220 F3 Anderson r. N.W.T. Can.
220 D3 Anderson AK U.S.A.
240 J1 Anderson CA U.S.A.
230 E5 Anderson IN U.S.A.
237 H7 Anderson MO U.S.A.
231 F8 Anderson SC U.S.A.
83 K9 Anderson Bay Tas. Austr.
240 K4 Anderson Reservoir CA U.S.A.
232 B9 Andersonville OH U.S.A.
169 E5 Andervenne Ger.
250 C3 Andes Col.
252 B3 Andes mts S. America
184 E5 Andévalo, Sierra de hills Spain
140 N2 Andfjorden sea chan. Norway
Andhíparos i. Greece see Antiparos
114 C3 Andhra Lake India
114 F4 Andhra Pradesh state India
129 H3 Andi Rus. Fed.
183 Q3 Andía, Sierra de mts Spain
164 H3 Andijk Neth.
121 O7 Andijon Andijon Uzbek.
121 O7 Andijon admin. div. Uzbek.
Andijon Wiloyati admin. div. Uzbek. see Andijon
Andikíra Greece see Antikyra
Andikithira i. Greece see Antikythira
213 □K3 Andilamena Madag.
213 □K3 Andilanatoby Madag.
157 K8 Andilly-en-Bassigny France
122 C5 Andīmeshk Iran
Andímilos i. Greece see Antimilos
109 I4 Anding Hunan China
Andípaxoi i. Greece see Antipaxoi
Andípsara i. Greece see Antipsara
256 B5 Andirá Brazil
111 F8 Andir He r. China
126 H5 Andırın Turkey
111 F8 Andirlangar Xinjiang China
129 H3 Andiyskoye Koysu r. Rus. Fed.
114 E7 Andiyur Tamil Nadu India
Andizhan Andijon Uzbek. see Andijon
Andizhan Oblast admin. div. Uzbek. see Andijon
123 K3 Andkhui r. Afgh.
123 K3 Andkhvoy Afgh.
157 N7 Andlau France
157 O6 Andlau r. France
186 A1 Andoain Spain
213 □K2 Andoany Madag.
250 B5 Andoas Peru
250 B5 Andoas Nuevo Ecuador
177 G5 Andocs Hungary
139 U2 Andoga r. Rus. Fed.
139 U2 Andogskaya Gryada hills Rus. Fed.
213 □J5 Andohahela, Réserve d' nature res. Madag.
213 □K2 Andohajango Madag.
208 A4 Andok Foula Gabon
114 F4 Andol Andhra Prad. India
114 E4 Andola Karnataka India
157 N7 Andolsheim France
Andong Liaoning China see Dandong
101 F10 Andong S. Korea
107 P9 Andongwei Shandong China
85 H2 Andoom Qld Austr.
179 I3 Andorf Austria
177 J4 Andornaktálya Hungary
190 E4 Andorno Micca Italy
186 I2 Andorra country Europe
186 E6 Andorra Spain
186 I2 Andorra, Valls d' val. Andorra
186 I2 Andorra la Vella Andorra
Andorra la Vieja Andorra see Andorra la Vella
183 Q4 Andosilla Spain
159 J5 Andouillé France
177 H4 Andovce Slovakia
151 J5 Andover Hampshire, England U.K.
235 K1 Andover CT U.S.A.
233 N6 Andover MA U.S.A.
233 N5 Andover NH U.S.A.
234 F3 Andover NJ U.S.A.
232 H6 Andover NY U.S.A.
232 E7 Andover OH U.S.A.
140 M2 Andøya i. Norway
139 U2 Andozero, Ozero l. Rus. Fed.
161 E6 Andrable r. France
256 D5 Andradas Brazil
241 R9 Andrade CA U.S.A.
256 B4 Andradina Brazil
Andraitx Spain see Andratx
213 □J3 Andramasina Madag.
213 □J3 Andramy Madag.
195 O4 Andrano Italy
213 □J3 Andranomavo Madag.
213 □K3 Andranomena Madag.
213 □I4 Andranopasy Madag.
213 □K2 Andranovondronina Madag.
213 □J4 Andranovory Madag.
187 J8 Andratx Spain
220 A4 Andreanof Islands AK U.S.A.
139 P5 Andreapol' Rus. Fed.
148 I5 Andreas Isle of Man
140 □ Andrée Land reg. Svalbard
208 D2 André Félix, Parc National de nat. park C.A.R.
257 G1 André Fernandes Brazil
257 E4 Andrelândia Brazil
257 E3 Andrequicé Brazil
261 I3 Andresito Uru.
175 H4 Andrespol Pol.
163 E9 Andrest France
223 H4 Andrew Alta Can.
96 B5 Andrew Bay Myanmar
231 H9 Andrews SC U.S.A.
237 D9 Andrews TX U.S.A.
121 S5 Andreyevka Almatinskaya Oblast' Kazakh.
120 D1 Andreyevka Rus. Fed.
Andreyevskoye Rus. Fed. see Dneprovskoye
137 M1 Andreykovichi Rus. Fed.
139 R6 Andreykovo Rus. Fed.
160 E5 Andrézieux-Bouthéon France
193 Q5 Andria Italy
213 □J3 Andriamena Madag.
213 □J3 Andriba Madag.
177 L4 Andrid Romania
214 I9 Andrieskraal S. Africa
214 E2 Andriesvale S. Africa
213 □J4 Andringitra mts Madag.
137 P7 Andrivka Ukr.
136 G3 Andriyevychi Ukr.
137 P6 Andriyivka Dnipropetrovs'ka Oblast' Ukr.
137 Q6 Andriyivka Donets'ka Oblast' Ukr.
137 P4 Andriyivka Kharkivs'ka Oblast' Ukr.
137 M9 Andriyivka Respublika Krym Ukr.
137 M3 Andriyivka Sums'ka Oblast' Ukr.
137 P6 Andriyivka Zaporiz'ka Oblast' Ukr.
213 □J5 Androka Madag.
213 □K2 Androna reg. Madag.
139 W4 Androniki Rus. Fed.
Andropov Rus. Fed. see Rybinsk
246 D1 Andros i. Bahamas
198 F5 Andros Andros Greece
198 F5 Andros i. Greece
233 P5 Androscoggin r. ME/NH U.S.A.
120 C1 Androsovka Rus. Fed.
246 E1 Andros Town Andros Bahamas
114 C7 Andrott i. India
Andrushevka Ukr. see Andrushivka
136 I3 Andrushivka Ukr.
136 I4 Andrushky Ukr.
175 H6 Andrychów Pol.
175 K3 Andrzejewo Pol.
140 O2 Andselv Norway
140 P1 Andsnes Norway
208 F4 Andudu Dem. Rep. Congo
122 G6 Andūhjerd Iran
185 K4 Andújar Spain
209 C7 Andulo Angola
161 D8 Anduze France
129 E1 Andzhiyevskiy Rus. Fed.
87 J7 Anec, Lake salt flat W.A. Austr.
259 C6 Anecón Grande mt. Arg.
Āneen-Kio N. Pacific Ocean see Wake Island
207 F2 Anéfis Mali
206 E2 Anéfis well Mali
247 K4 Anegada i. Virgin Is (U.K.)
259 E6 Anegada, Bahía b. Arg.
247 L4 Anegada Passage Virgin Is (U.K.)
241 T9 Anegam AZ U.S.A.
207 F5 Aného Togo
Aneityum i. Vanuatu see Anatom
'Aneiza, Jabal hill Iraq see 'Unayzah, Jabal
78 □3b Aneju i. Majuro Marshall Is
114 E6 Anekal Karnataka India
78 □5 Anelghowhat Vanuatu
260 C6 Añelo Arg.
128 A2 Anemourıon tourist site Turkey
78 □3b Anemwanot i. Majuro Marshall Is
136 I7 Anenii Noi Moldova
205 G6 Anesbaraka well Alg.
156 B6 Anet France
Anetchom, Île i. Vanuatu see Anatom
186 G2 Aneto mt. Spain
Ānewetak atoll Marshall Is see Enewetak
207 I2 Aney Niger
Aneytioum, Île i. Vanuatu see Anatom
203 I6 Anfile Bay Eritrea
178 B8 Anfo Italy
109 J5 Anfu Jiangxi China
114 E7 Angadippuram Kerala India
213 □J2 Angadoka, Lohatanjona hd Madag.
83 I8 Angahook Lorne State Park nature res. Vic. Austr.
84 C3 Angalarri r. N.T. Austr.
202 C5 Angamma, Falaise d' esc. Chad
259 B8 Angamos, Isla i. Chile
252 C5 Angamos, Punta pt Chile
244 G6 Angangueo Mex.
107 R3 Ang'angxi Heilong. China
98 H1 Angara r. Rus. Fed.
207 F4 Angaradébou Benin
84 E7 Angarapa Aboriginal Land res. N.T. Austr.
98 H1 Angarsk Rus. Fed.
84 D8 Angas Downs N.T. Austr.
86 J7 Angas Range hills W.A. Austr.
82 G6 Angaston S.A. Austr.
92 C4 Angat Luzon Phil.
Angatau atoll Arch. des Tuamotu Fr. Polynesia see Fangatau
256 C5 Angatuba Brazil
92 □ Angaur i. Palau
141 M5 Ånge Sweden
182 C7 Angeja Port.
251 F3 Angel, Salto waterfall Venez.
242 C3 Ángel de la Guarda, Isla i. Mex.
92 C4 Angeles Luzon Phil.
Angel Falls Venez. see Angel, Salto
142 I5 Ängelholm Sweden
140 R2 Angeli Fin.
261 G2 Angelica Arg.
237 H10 Angelina r. TX U.S.A.
85 K9 Angellala Creek r. Qld Austr.
168 I1 Angeln reg. Ger.
87 D7 Angelo r. W.A. Austr.
245 L7 Angel R. Cabada Mex.
240 L3 Angels Camp CA U.S.A.
143 J5 Angelstad Sweden
160 E1 Angely France
173 N6 Anger Ger.
210 C1 Āngereb Eth.
210 C1 Āngereb Wenz r. Eth.
140 N5 Ångermanälven r. Sweden
170 J4 Angermünde Ger.
171 E6 Angern Ger.
179 O3 Angern an der March Austria
159 J7 Angers France
156 D7 Angerville France
161 K9 Anges, Baie des b. France
95 L5 Anggana Kalimantan Indon.
191 M8 Anghiari Italy
254 D4 Angical Brazil
254 F3 Angicos Brazil
223 L2 Angikuni Lake Nunavut Can.
240 M6 Angiola CA U.S.A.
198 E2 Angistis r. Greece
97 F8 Angkor tourist site Cambodia
162 C5 Anglade France
162 I5 Anglards-de-Salers France
150 B4 Angle Pembrokeshire, Wales U.K.
81 B13 Anglem, Mount hill Stewart I. N.Z.
222 G5 Anglemont B.C. Can.
163 J8 Anglès France
186 K4 Anglès Spain
150 D1 Anglesey i. Wales U.K.
186 H4 Anglesona Spain
159 M8 Angles-sur-l'Anglin France
163 A9 Anglet France
237 H11 Angleton TX U.S.A.
227 O2 Angliers Que. Can.
159 L8 Angliers France
162 F2 Anglin r. France
Anglo-Egyptian Sudan country Africa see Sudan
192 B6 Anglona reg. Sardegna Italy
156 G6 Anglure France
Angmagssalik Greenland see Ammassalik
94 □ Ang Mo Kio Sing.
208 E3 Ango Dem. Rep. Congo
213 H3 Angoche Moz.
122 G8 Angohrān Iran
162 G5 Angoisse France
260 A5 Angol Chile
209 C7 Angola country Africa
230 E5 Angola IN U.S.A.
232 F6 Angola NY U.S.A.
264 I7 Angola Basin sea feature S. Atlantic Ocean
213 G2 Angonia, Planalto de plat. Moz.
220 E4 Angoon AK U.S.A.
Angora Turkey see Ankara
244 G3 Angostura San Luis Potosí Mex.
242 E5 Angostura Sinaloa Mex.
162 E4 Angoulême France
162 B3 Angoulins France
162 D4 Angoumois reg. France
216 □1a Angra do Heroísmo Terceira Azores
257 E5 Angra dos Reis Brazil
121 N7 Angren Uzbek.
193 N6 Angri Italy
114 C4 Angria's Bank sea feature India
159 J6 Angrie France
143 M2 Ängsö naturreservat nature res. Sweden
97 E7 Ang Thong Thai.
97 D10 Ang Thong Marine National Park Thai.
208 E4 Angu Dem. Rep. Congo
260 C2 Angualasto Arg.
107 R4 Anguang Jilin China
186 E3 Angüés Spain
183 O4 Anguiano Spain
261 F5 Anguil Arg.
247 L4 Anguilla terr. West Indies
246 D2 Anguilla Cays is Bahamas
193 I3 Anguillara Sabazia Italy
191 L5 Anguillara Veneta Italy
225 J4 Anguille, Cape Nfld and Lab. Can.
183 P6 Anguita Spain
117 J9 Angul Orissa India
107 N6 Anguli Nur l. China
107 N7 Anguo Hebei China
84 F2 Angurugu N.T. Austr.
227 O5 Angus Ont. Can.
146 K9 Angus admin. div. Scotland U.K.
253 E2 Angustura Brazil
240 J3 Angwin CA U.S.A.
256 C3 Anhanguera Brazil
165 G8 Anhée Belgium
142 H5 Anholt i. Denmark
109 H4 Anhua Hunan China
109 K2 Anhui prov. China
255 B6 Anhumas Brazil
Anhwei prov. China see Anhui
102 R7 Ani Japan
129 E5 Ani tourist site Turkey
191 I7 Ania r. Italy
220 C3 Aniak AK U.S.A.
220 C4 Aniakchak National Monument and Preserve nat. park AK U.S.A.
161 D9 Aniane France
156 F3 Aniche France
256 C2 Anicuns Brazil
Ánidhros i. Greece see Anydros
207 F5 Anié Togo
163 C10 Anie, Pic d' mt. France
193 J4 Aniene r. Italy
178 H4 Anif Austria
103 □2 Ani-jima i. Ogasawara-shotō Japan
120 I2 Anikhovka Rus. Fed.
134 H4 Anikovo Rus. Fed.
105 L3 Animaki-san hill Japan
239 J8 Animas r. CO U.S.A.
96 C7 Anin Myanmar
197 J5 Anina Romania
117 O5 Anini Arun. Prad. India
183 Q6 Aniñón Spain
139 U7 Anishino Rus. Fed.
207 H6 Añisoc Equat. Guinea
92 E6 Anitaguipan Point Samar Phil.
255 C8 Anitápolis Brazil
199 L4 Anıtkaya Turkey
128 A2 Anıtlı Turkey
100 M5 Aniva Sakhalin Rus. Fed.
100 M5 Aniva, Mys c. Sakhalin Rus. Fed.
100 M5 Aniva, Zaliv b. Sakhalin Rus. Fed.
213 □K3 Anivorano Madag.

213 □K2 Anivorano Avaratra Madag.
226 E4 Aniwa WI U.S.A.
78 □5 Aniwa i. Vanuatu
156 F4 Anizy-le-Château France
116 E8 Anjad Madh. Prad. India
114 D5 Anjadip i. India
213 □J3 Anjafy mt. Madag.
141 S6 Anjalankoski Fin.
116 F9 Anjangaon Mahar. India
116 C8 Anjar Gujarat India
114 E8 Anjengo Kerala India
109 L3 Anji Zhejiang China
116 G9 Anji Mahar. India
Anjiang Hunan China see Qianyang
110 G4 Anjihai Xinjiang China
122 F5 Anjir Avand Iran
104 F6 Anjō Japan
122 G4 Anjoman Iran
159 K6 Anjou reg. France
162 D1 Anjou, Val d' val. France
Anjouan i. Comoros see Nzwani
213 □J3 Anjozorobe Madag.
99 M4 Anjŭ N. Korea
164 J2 Anjum Neth.
123 N4 Anjuman reg. Afgh.
207 G3 Anka Nigeria
213 □I4 Ankaboa, Tanjona pt Madag.
108 G2 Ankang Shaanxi China
126 F4 Ankara Turkey
199 M2 Ankara prov. Turkey
191 P4 Ankaran Slovenia
213 □J3 Ankaratra mts Madag.
143 M4 Ankarsrum Sweden
140 N4 Ankarsund Sweden
213 □K2 Ankatafa Madag.
213 □J3 Ankavandra Madag.
213 □J4 Ankazoabo Madag.
213 □J3 Ankazobe Madag.
213 □J3 Ankazomiriotra Madag.
236 I5 Ankeny IA U.S.A.
213 □J2 Ankerika Madag.
170 G4 Ankershagen Ger.
97 I8 An Khê Vietnam
213 □I4 Ankiliabo Madag.
170 I3 Anklam Ger.
116 D9 Ankleshwar Gujarat India
Anklesvar Gujarat India see Ankleshwar
213 □K3 Ankofa mt. Madag.
178 H5 Ankogel mt. Austria
114 D5 Ankola Karnataka India
106 J9 Ankouzhen Gansu China
139 W5 An'kovo Rus. Fed.
207 G5 Ankpa Nigeria
168 E5 Ankum Ger.
149 Q6 Anlaby East Riding of Yorkshire, England U.K.
173 K4 Anlauter r. Ger.
160 D3 Anlezy France
165 I9 Anlier, Forêt d' for. Belgium
Anling Henan China see Yanling
97 H9 An Lôc Vietnam
207 F5 Anloga Ghana
108 E6 Anlong Guizhou China
97 G7 Ânlong Vêng Cambodia
109 I3 Anlu Hubei China
232 E9 Anmoore WV U.S.A.
An Muileann gCearr Ireland see Mullingar
101 E10 Anmyŏn-do i. S. Korea
263 D2 Ann, Cape Antarctica
233 O6 Ann, Cape MA U.S.A.
135 H6 Anna Rus. Fed.
187 D9 Anna Spain
232 A8 Anna OH U.S.A.
232 H10 Anna, Lake VA U.S.A.
91 H6 Anna, Pulo i. Palau
205 G1 Annaba Alg.
189 A7 Annaba prov. Alg.
179 L4 Annaberg Austria
171 H9 Annaberg-Buchholtz Ger.
124 F3 An Nabhānīyah Saudi Arabia
128 F7 An Nabk Saudi Arabia
128 E4 An Nabk Syria
171 H7 Annaburg Ger.
147 E7 Annacotty Ireland
124 E1 An Nafūd des. Saudi Arabia
147 F2 Annagry Ireland
171 I7 Annahütte Ger.
251 G4 Annai Guyana
127 L8 An Najaf Iraq
127 K8 An Najaf governorate Iraq
105 I3 Annaka Japan
147 H4 Annalee r. Ireland
147 K4 Annalong Northern Ireland U.K.
96 G5 Annam reg. Vietnam
96 G5 Annam Highlands mts Laos/Vietnam
148 E7 Annamoe Ireland
146 J13 Annan Dumfries and Galloway, Scotland U.K.
146 J13 Annan r. Scotland U.K.
128 G4 'Annān, Wādī al watercourse Syria
106 C7 Annanba Gansu China
146 J12 Annandale val. Scotland U.K.
234 F3 Annandale NJ U.S.A.
232 H10 Annandale VA U.S.A.
164 G3 Anna Paulowna Neth.
86 F5 Anna Plains W.A. Austr.
234 C7 Annapolis MD U.S.A.
225 H4 Annapolis Royal N.S. Can.
117 J5 Annapurna Conservation Area nature res. Nepal
117 I5 Annapurna I mt. Nepal
125 I2 An Naqīrah well Saudi Arabia
227 K7 Ann Arbor MI U.S.A.
251 G3 Anna Regina Guyana
171 D7 Annarode Ger.
An Nás Ireland see Naas
202 B3 An Nashū, Wādī watercourse Libya
127 M8 An Nāşirīyah Iraq
215 J4 Annaspan imp. l. S. Africa
128 F5 An Naşrānī, Jabal mts Syria
202 C2 An Nawfalīyah Libya
147 I4 Annayalla Ireland
146 G12 Annbank South Ayrshire, Scotland U.K.
193 Q9 Annea r. Italy
87 E9 Annean, Lake salt flat W.A. Austr.
234 B7 Anne Arundel County county MD U.S.A.
Anne Arundel Town MD U.S.A. see Annapolis
160 I5 Annecy France
160 I5 Annecy, Lac d' l. France
160 I5 Annecy-le-Vieux France
Annel Fin. see Angeli
225 I2 Anne Marie Lake Nfld and Lab. Can.
160 I4 Annemasse France
164 K2 Annen Neth.
162 F5 Annesse-et-Beaulieu France
150 □ Annet i. England U.K.
222 D4 Annette Island AK U.S.A.
161 F6 Anneyron France
149 N4 Annfield Plain Durham, England U.K.
148 H2 Annick r. Scotland U.K.
85 I3 Annie r. Qld Austr.
138 J2 Annikvere Estonia
128 F6 An Nimārah Syria
124 F6 An Nimāş Saudi Arabia
108 D6 Anning Yunnan China
108 C5 Anning He r. Sichuan China
139 X9 Annino Lipetskaya Oblast' Rus. Fed.
139 U2 Annino Vologodskaya Oblast' Rus. Fed.
124 F3 An Nīr, Jabal hills Saudi Arabia
231 E9 Anniston AL U.S.A.
207 G7 Annobón i. Equat. Guinea
156 E2 Annœullin France
161 F6 Annonay France
190 G4 Annone, Lago di l. Italy
161 J9 Annot France
246 □ Annotto Bay Jamaica
148 F5 Annsborough Northern Ireland U.K.
125 I2 An Nu'ayrīyah Saudi Arabia
127 L7 An Nu'mānīyah Iraq
125 J3 An Nuqay'ah Qatar
126 H6 An Nuşayrīyah, Jabal mts Syria
232 B11 Annville KY U.S.A.
234 B4 Annville PA U.S.A.
172 D3 Annweiler am Trifels Ger.
104 D6 Anō Japan
78 □6 Anoano Malaita Solomon Is
186 A1 Anoeta Spain
198 F7 Anogeia Kriti Greece
226 A4 Anoka MN U.S.A.
198 E3 Ano Lechonia Greece
183 Q5 Añón Spain
Anonima atoll Micronesia see Namonuito
139 X6 Anopino Rus. Fed.
156 H4 Anor France
185 J4 Añora Spain
251 F5 Anori Brazil
211 F8 Anorontany, Tanjona hd Madag.
213 □K3 Anosibe An'Ala Madag.
205 G5 Anou I-n-Atei well Alg.
157 M7 Anould France
207 F2 Ânou Mellene well Mali
205 G6 Anou-n-Bidek well Alg.
183 M9 Añover de Tajo Spain
Anóyia Kriti Greece see Anogeia
109 I5 Anping Hunan China
108 H8 Anpu Guangdong China
108 G8 Anpu Gang b. China
109 K3 Anqing Anhui China
107 P8 Anqiu Shandong China
183 P7 Anquela del Ducado Spain
178 G6 Anras Austria
109 I5 Anren Hunan China
169 F7 Anröchte Ger.
An Rubha pen. Scotland U.K. see Eye Peninsula
165 I7 Ans Belgium
142 F5 Ans Denmark
162 F4 Ansac-sur-Vienne France
107 K8 Ansai Shaanxi China
173 J3 Ansbach Ger.
160 F5 Anse France
246 G4 Anse-à-Galets Haiti
217 □2b Anse à la Mouche Mahé Seychelles
246 H4 Anse-à-Pitre Haiti
246 G4 Anse-à-Veau Haiti
124 C7 Anseba Shet watercourse Eritrea
247 □2 Anse-Bertrand Guadeloupe
217 □2b Anse Boileau Mahé Seychelles
246 F4 Anse d'Hainault Haiti
192 G3 Ansedonia Italy
247 □3 Anse-la-Raye St Lucia
165 G8 Anseremme Belgium
83 K8 Anser Group is Tas. Austr.
250 C3 Anserma Col.
217 □2b Anse Royal Mahé Seychelles
179 J3 Ansfelden Austria
146 I9 An Sgarsoch mt. Scotland U.K.
107 R6 Anshan Liaoning China
108 E5 Anshun Guizhou China
108 D4 Anshunchang Sichuan China
182 D9 Ansião Port.
191 M3 Ansiei r. Italy
260 C2 Ansilta mt. Arg.
260 C2 Ansilta, Cordillera de mts Arg.
258 G3 Ansina Uru.
126 H8 An Sirhān, Wādī watercourse Saudi Arabia
140 N5 Ansjö Sweden
236 F5 Ansley NE U.S.A.
186 D2 Ansó Spain
186 D2 Ansó, Valle de val. Spain
237 F9 Anson TX U.S.A.
84 C2 Anson Bay N.T. Austr.
82 □1 Anson Bay Norfolk I.
207 F3 Ansongo Mali
207 F3 Ansongo-Ménaka, Réserve Partielle de Faune d' nature res. Mali
235 I2 Ansonia CT U.S.A.
232 A8 Ansonia OH U.S.A.
224 D3 Ansonville Ont. Can.
171 H9 Ansprung Ger.
232 D10 Ansted WV U.S.A.
146 K10 Anstruther Fife, Scotland U.K.
Ansu Hebei China see Xushui
151 P2 Ant r. England U.K.
116 F7 Anta Rajasthan India
252 B3 Anta Peru
252 B3 Antabamba Peru
126 H5 Antakya Turkey
213 □K2 Antalaha Madag.
199 L6 Antalya Turkey
199 L5 Antalya prov. Turkey
199 L6 Antalya Körfezi g. Turkey
213 □K3 Antanambao Manampotsy Madag.
213 □K3 Antanambe Madag.
213 □J3 Antananarivo Madag.
213 □J3 Antananarivo prov. Madag.
213 □J3 Antanifotsy Madag.
213 □J5 Antanimora Atsimo Madag.
An tAonach Ireland see Nenagh
262 Antarctica continent
262 T2 Antarctic Peninsula Antarctica
213 □J5 Antaritarika Madag.
182 F7 Antas Port.
185 P6 Antas Spain
185 P6 Antas r. Spain
182 E3 Antas de Ulla Spain
146 F7 An Teallach mt. Scotland U.K.
261 G3 Antelo Arg.
241 P2 Antelope Range mts NV U.S.A.
142 I3 Anten l. Sweden
162 D4 Antenne r. France
185 J6 Antequera Spain
178 F6 Anterselva di Sopra Italy
234 A2 Antes Fort PA U.S.A.
161 J10 Anthéor France
178 H4 Anthering Austria
160 D2 Anthien France
237 F7 Anthony KS U.S.A.
239 K10 Anthony NM U.S.A.
82 D3 Anthony, Lake salt flat S.A. Austr.
84 E4 Anthony Lagoon N.T. Austr.
204 C3 Anti Atlas mts Morocco
161 K9 Antibes France
161 K9 Antibes, Cap d' c. France
225 I3 Anticosti, Île d' i. Que. Can.
Anticosti Island Que. Can. see Anticosti, Île d'
159 L2 Antifer, Cap d' c. France
226 E4 Antigo WI U.S.A.
225 I4 Antigonish N.S. Can.
247 □2 Antigua i. Antigua and Barbuda
216 □3b Antigua Fuerteventura Canary Is
Antigua Guat. see Antigua Guatemala
Antigua country West Indies see Antigua and Barbuda
247 □2 Antigua and Barbuda country West Indies
243 N10 Antigua Guatemala Guat.
247 □2 Antigues, Pointe d' pt Guadeloupe
245 H3 Antiguo-Morelos Mex.
198 D4 Antikyra Greece
198 E7 Antikythira i. Greece
198 E7 Antikythiro, Steno sea chan. Greece
Anti Lebanon mts Lebanon/Syria see Sharqī, Jabal ash
258 D2 Antilla Arg.
246 F3 Antilla Cuba
195 I8 Antillo Sicilia Italy
198 F6 Antimilos i. Greece
241 U3 Antimony UT U.S.A.
An tInbhear Mór Ireland see Arklow
240 K3 Antioch CA U.S.A.
226 F7 Antioch IL U.S.A.
128 A2 Antiocheia ad Cragum tourist site Turkey
Antiochia Turkey see Antakya
250 C3 Antioquia Col.
250 C3 Antioquia dept Col.
198 G5 Antiparos i. Greece
198 B3 Antipaxoi i. Greece
139 Q6 Antipino Rus. Fed.
77 H6 Antipodes Islands N.Z.
199 G4 Antipsara i. Greece
192 C3 Antisanti Corse France
199 I6 Antitilos i. Greece
Antium Italy see Anzio
237 H8 Antlers OK U.S.A.
An t-Òb Western Isles, Scotland U.K. see Leverburgh
252 C5 Antofagasta Chile
252 C5 Antofagasta admin. reg. Chile
258 D2 Antofagasta de la Sierra Arg.
165 D7 Antoing Belgium
177 H3 Antol Slovakia
190 G6 Antola, Monte mt. Italy
213 □J2 Antonhibe Madag.
256 C6 Antonina Brazil
136 F4 Antoniny Ukr.
195 L5 Antonio r. Italy
244 C1 Antonio Amaro Mex.
257 F4 Antônio Carlos Brazil
259 D7 Antonio de Biedma Arg.
257 F3 Antônio Dias Brazil
António Enes Moz. see Angoche
251 I5 Antônio Lemos Brazil
136 I4 Antoniv Ukr.
137 L3 Antonivka Chernihivs'ka Oblast' Ukr.
137 L7 Antonivka Khersons'ka Oblast' Ukr.
177 L3 Antonivka Zakarpats'ka Oblast' Ukr.
137 O6 Antonivka Zaporiz'ka Oblast' Ukr.
245 L6 Antón Lizardo Mex.
162 F5 Antonne-et-Trigonant France
246 C2 Antón Recio Cuba
156 D6 Antony France
136 D1 Antopal' Belarus
161 E7 Antraigues-sur-Volane France
158 I5 Antrain France
137 S5 Antratsyt Ukr.
147 J3 Antrim Northern Ireland U.K.
147 J3 Antrim county Northern Ireland U.K.
234 A1 Antrim PA U.S.A.
147 J2 Antrim Hills Northern Ireland U.K.
86 J5 Antrim Plateau W.A. Austr.
193 K3 Antrodoco Italy
134 H4 Antropovo Rus. Fed.
213 □K2 Antsahabe Madag.
213 □K2 Antsahanoro Madag.
213 □K2 Antsakabary Madag.
213 □J3 Antsalova Madag.
213 □K2 Antsambalahy Madag.
Antseranana Madag. see Antsirañana
139 Q3 Antsiferovo Rus. Fed.
213 □J3 Antsirabe Madag.
213 □K2 Antsirabe Avaratra Madag.
213 □K2 Antsirañana Madag.
213 □K2 Antsirañana prov. Madag.
138 J4 Antsla Estonia
213 □J2 Antsohihy Madag.
213 □K2 Antsohimbondrona Madag.
213 □J3 Antsondrodava Madag.
140 Q3 Anttis Sweden
141 S6 Anttola Fin.
Antu Jilin China see Songjiang
An Tuc Vietnam see An Khê
260 B5 Antuco Chile
260 B5 Antuco, Volcán vol. Chile
124 F8 Antufash, Jazīrat i. Yemen
Antufush Island Yemen see Antufash, Jazīrat
160 E3 Antully France
Antunnacum Ger. see Andernach
Antwerp Belgium see Antwerpen
233 J4 Antwerp NY U.S.A.
165 F6 Antwerpen Belgium
165 G6 Antwerpen prov. Belgium
186 A1 Antzuola Spain
An Uaimh Ireland see Navan
224 F1 Anuc, Lac l. Que. Can.
100 H7 Anuchino Rus. Fed.
259 C6 Anueque, Sierra mts Arg.
101 E11 Anŭi S. Korea
116 D5 Anupgarh Rajasthan India
114 G8 Anuradhapura Sri Lanka
84 E6 Anurrete Aboriginal Land res. N.T. Austr.
122 F8 Anveh Iran
Anvers Belgium see Antwerpen
262 T2 Anvers Island Antarctica
222 C2 Anvil Range mts Y.T. Can.
156 D3 Anvin France
109 L6 Anxi Fujian China
106 D6 Anxi Gansu China
Anxian Sichuan China see Anchang
108 E3 Anxian Sichuan China
109 I4 Anxiang Hunan China
107 N7 Anxin Hebei China
82 E5 Anxious Bay S.A. Austr.
Anxur Italy see Terracina
206 D5 Anyama Côte d'Ivoire
Anyang Guangxi China see Du'an
107 N8 Anyang Henan China
101 E10 Anyang S. Korea
94 F8 Anyar Jawa Indon.
199 G6 Anydros i. Greece
106 F9 A'nyêmaqên Shan mts China
109 J4 Anyi Jiangxi China
138 I6 Anykščiai Lith.
215 O3 Anysspruit S. Africa
109 I5 Anyuan Jiangxi China
109 J6 Anyuan Jiangxi China
134 L3 An'yudin Rus. Fed.
108 E3 Anyue Sichuan China
100 J4 Anyuy r. Rus. Fed.
131 R3 Anyuysk Rus. Fed.
190 E3 Anza r. Italy
223 I3 Anzac Alta Can.
222 F4 Anzac B.C. Can.
186 D3 Anzánigo Spain
193 O5 Anzano di Puglia Italy
161 C6 Anzat-le-Luguet France
107 M8 Anze Shanxi China
165 D7 Anzegem Belgium
205 F4 Anzeglouf Alg.
173 L2 Anzelberg hill Ger.
160 K4 Anzère Switz.
130 J4 Anzhero-Sudzhensk Rus. Fed.
208 D5 Anzi Dem. Rep. Congo
193 P6 Anzi Italy
156 F3 Anzin France
176 A3 Anzing Ger.
193 J5 Anzio Italy
261 F6 Anzoátegui Arg.
251 E2 Anzoátegui state Venez.
261 F6 Anzoátegui, Salinas Grandes de salt pan Arg.
185 J6 Anzur r. Spain
105 K4 Aoba Japan
78 □5 Aoba i. Vanuatu
104 B4 Aoba-yama hill Japan
202 C5 Aodanga well Chad
104 B5 Aogaki Japan
103 Q14 Aoga-shima i. Japan
Aohan Qi Nei Mongol China see Xinhui
183 R3 Aoiz Spain
97 D10 Ao Kham, Laem pt Thai.
105 H3 Aoki Japan
78 □6 Aola Guadalcanal Solomon Is
Aomen Macau China see Macao
102 R6 Aomori Japan
102 S6 Aomori pref. Japan
146 F8 Aonach Buidhe hill Scotland U.K.
111 E10 A'ong Co l. Xizang China
198 B2 Aoos r. Greece
97 D10 Ao Phang Nga National Park Thai.
146 D11 Aoradh Argyll and Bute, Scotland U.K.
79 □9a Aorai mt. Tahiti Fr. Polynesia
81 E10 Aoraki South I. N.Z.
81 E10 Aoraki mt. South I. N.Z.
81 E10 Aoraki/Mount Cook National Park South I. N.Z.
97 G8 Aôral, Phnum mt. Cambodia
Aorangi mt. South I. N.Z. see Aoraki
81 J8 Aorangi Mountains North I. N.Z.
81 G7 Aorere r. South I. N.Z.
183 R3 Aós Spain
104 A8 Ao-shima i. Japan
190 C4 Aosta Italy
160 H5 Aoste France
80 I5 Aotea Harbour North I. N.Z.
Aotearoa country Oceania see New Zealand
207 H2 Aouderas Niger
204 B4 Aoufist Western Sahara
204 D4 Aouhinet bel Egra well Alg.
208 C2 Aouk, Bahr r. C.A.R./Chad
208 D2 Aoukalé r. C.A.R./Chad
208 D2 Aouk-Aoakole, Réserve de Faune de l' nature res. C.A.R.
204 D5 Aoukâr reg. Mali/Maur.
207 F2 Aoukenek well Mali
205 F4 Aoulef Alg.
204 C3 Aoulime, Jbel mt. Morocco
206 C3 Aourou Mali
161 G7 Aouste-sur-Sye France
Aoxi Jiangxi China see Le'an
103 L11 Aoya Japan
104 D6 Aoyama Japan
Aoyang Jiangxi China see Shanggao
202 C4 Aozou Chad
253 F5 Apa r. Brazil
197 L3 Apa Romania
210 B4 Apac Uganda
179 M6 Apače Slovenia
241 W10 Apache AZ U.S.A.
237 F8 Apache OK U.S.A.
241 U8 Apache, Lake AZ U.S.A.
241 U8 Apache Junction AZ U.S.A.
241 V10 Apache Peak AZ U.S.A.
252 D5 Apagado, Volcán vol. Bol.
177 K4 Apagy Hungary
197 L4 Apahida Romania
256 C5 Apaiaí r. Brazil
Apaiang atoll Kiribati see Abaiang
177 I4 Apaj Hungary
231 E11 Apalachee Bay FL U.S.A.
231 E11 Apalachicola FL U.S.A.
231 E11 Apalachicola r. FL U.S.A.
231 E11 Apalachicola Bay FL U.S.A.
206 E5 Apam Ghana
Apamama atoll Gilbert Is Kiribati see Abemama
Apamea Turkey see Dinar
245 I6 Apan Mex.
157 L8 Apance r. France
245 H8 Apango Mex.
250 D5 Apaporis r. Col.
95 L6 Apar, Teluk b. Indon.
129 F5 Aparan Armenia
257 E5 Aparecida Brazil
256 C2 Aparecida de Goiânia Brazil
256 B3 Aparecida do Rio Doce Brazil
256 B4 Aparecida do Tabuado Brazil
177 H5 Aparhant Hungary
261 G6 Aparico Arg.
Aparima South I. N.Z. see Riverton
81 C13 Aparima r. South I. N.Z.
92 C2 Aparri Luzon Phil.
251 F3 Aparurén Venez.
259 D6 Apas, Sierra hills Arg.
138 H5 Apaščia r. Lith.
244 G5 Apaseo El Grande Mex.
79 □9 Apataki atoll Arch. des Tuamotu Fr. Polynesia
177 K5 Apateu Romania
177 J5 Apátfalva Hungary
196 G5 Apatin Vojvodina Serbia
134 F2 Apatity Rus. Fed.
251 H3 Apatou Fr. Guiana
179 O7 Apatovac Croatia
244 E6 Apatzingán Mex.
245 H7 Apaxtla Mex.
138 J4 Ape Latvia
191 M8 Apecchio Italy
253 E2 Apediá r. Brazil
182 D4 A Pedreira Spain
164 I4 Apeldoorn Neth.
169 H6 Apelern Ger.
168 E4 Apen Ger.
170 D5 Apenburg Ger.
168 I4 Apensen Ger.
252 D3 Apere r. Bol.
182 E4 A Peroxa Spain
222 B2 Apex Mountain Y.T. Can.
208 E4 Api Dem. Rep. Congo
116 H4 Api mt. Nepal
Api i. Vanuatu see Epi
93 B4 Api, Tanjung pt Indon.
250 C3 Apia Col.
Apia atoll Kiribati see Abaiang
78 □2 Apia Samoa
253 F2 Apiacas, Serra dos hills Brazil
256 C6 Apiaí Brazil
251 F4 Apiaú, Serra do mts Brazil
193 N5 Apice Italy
182 C3 A Picota Spain
78 □6 Apio Malaita Solomon Is
245 H7 Apipilulco Mex.
191 O9 Apiro Italy
237 D6 Apishapa r. CO U.S.A.
80 J6 Apiti North I. N.Z.
245 I6 Apizaco Mex.
242 H5 Apizolaya Mex.
129 C2 Ap'khazet'i aut. rep. Georgia
252 B4 Aplao Peru
109 □J7 Ap Lei Chau i. H.K. China
92 E8 Apo, Mount vol. Mindanao Phil.
182 F3 A Pobla de Brollón Spain
182 F3 A Pobra de San Xiao Spain
182 F4 A Pobra de Trives Spain
182 C3 A Pobra do Caramiñal Spain
137 Q2 Apochka r. Rus. Fed.
254 F3 Apodi Brazil
254 F3 Apodi, Chapada do hills Brazil
92 C5 Apo East Passage Phil.
251 G3 Apoera Suriname
171 E8 Apolda Ger.
Apollinopolis Magna Egypt see Idfū
83 I8 Apollo Bay Vic. Austr.
Apollonia Bulg. see Sozopol
198 F6 Apollonia Sifnos Greece
252 C3 Apolo Bol.
182 F2 A Pontenova Spain
182 C2 A Pontepedra Spain
231 G11 Apopka FL U.S.A.
255 B6 Aporé Goiás Brazil
256 B3 Aporé Mato Grosso do Sul Brazil
256 B3 Aporé r. Brazil
251 I4 Aporema Brazil
177 H5 Apostag Hungary
226 D3 Apostle Islands WI U.S.A.
226 D2 Apostle Islands National Lakeshore nature res. WI U.S.A.
221 N3 Apostolens Tommelfinger mt. Greenland
258 G2 Apóstoles Arg.
128 C3 Apostolos Andreas, Cape Cyprus
137 M6 Apostolove Ukr.
251 G3 Apoteri Guyana
Apoucaroua atoll Arch. des Tuamotu Fr. Polynesia see Pukarua
92 C5 Apo West Passage Phil.
232 C12 Appalachia VA U.S.A.
232 B12 Appalachian Mountains U.S.A.
Appalla i. Fiji see Kabara
164 J3 Appelscha Neth.
Appenines mts Italy
Appennino mts Italy see Appenines
193 K3 Appennino Abruzzese mts Italy
193 M4 Appennino Campano mts Italy
193 P6 Appennino Lucano mts Italy
193 O5 Appennino Napoletano mts Italy
191 I8 Appennino Tosco-Emiliano mts Italy
191 M9 Appennino Umbro-Marchigiano mts Italy
172 D4 Appenweier Ger.
190 G1 Appenzell Switz.
190 G1 Appenzell Ausserrhoden canton Switz.
190 G1 Appenzell Innerrhoden canton Switz.
191 K3 Appiano sulla Strada del Vino Italy
192 B3 Appietto Corse France
191 O9 Appignano Italy
164 K2 Appingedam Neth.
149 M4 Appleby-in-Westmorland Cumbria, England U.K.
146 E8 Applecross Highland, Scotland U.K.
150 D5 Appledore Devon, England U.K.
151 N5 Appledore Kent, England U.K.
236 G3 Appleton MN U.S.A.
226 F5 Appleton WI U.S.A.
149 L7 Appleton Thorn Warrington, England U.K.
240 O7 Apple Valley CA U.S.A.
156 G8 Appoigny France
232 G11 Appomattox VA U.S.A.
161 G6 Apprieu France
78 □1 Apra Harbor inlet Guam
78 □1 Apra Heights Guam
139 U6 Aprelevka Rus. Fed.
160 H2 Apremont France
157 K6 Apremont-la-Forêt France
190 I3 Aprica Italy
193 O4 Apricena Italy
195 K5 Aprigliano Italy
193 J4 Aprilia Italy
182 G3 A Proba Spain
117 O5 Aprunyi Arun. Prad. India
129 A1 Apsheronsk Rus. Fed.
Apsheronskaya Rus. Fed. see Apsheronsk
Apsheronskiy Poluostrov pen. Azer. see Abşeron Yarımadası
82 H7 Apsley Vic. Austr.
227 P5 Apsley Ont. Can.
84 C1 Apsley Strait N.T. Austr.
161 G9 Apt France
190 I7 Apuane, Alpi mts Italy
240 □F14 'Āpua Point HI U.S.A.
256 B5 Apucarana Brazil
256 B5 Apucarana, Serra da hills Brazil
245 I5 Apulco Mex.
182 C6 Apúlia Port.
Apulum Romania see Alba Iulia
92 B7 Apurahuan Palawan Phil.
92 □ Apurashokoru i. Palau
250 E3 Apure r. Venez.
250 D3 Apure state Venez.
252 B3 Apurímac dept Peru
252 B3 Apurimac r. Peru
250 D3 Apurito Venez.
Aq"a Georgia see Sokhumi
'Aqaba Jordan see Al 'Aqabah
124 B1 Aqaba, Gulf of Asia
127 K8 'Aqabah, Birkat al well Iraq
128 B8 'Aqabah, Wādī al watercourse Egypt
Aqadyr Kazakh. see Agadyr'
110 D6 Aqal Xinjiang China
Aqbalyq Kazakh. see Akbalyk
Aqbaūyr Kazakh. see Akbauyr
Aqbeyit Kazakh. see Akbeit
123 L3 Āqchah Afgh.
127 L4 Aq Chai r. Iran
122 E5 'Aqdā Iran
122 B3 Aqdoghmish r. Iran
127 N5 Āq Gadūk, Gardaneh-ye pass Iran
203 H5 Aqiq Sudan
124 D6 Aqiq, Khalîg b. Sudan
124 E3 Aqiq, Wādī al watercourse Saudi Arabia
106 B6 Aqitag mt. Xinjiang China
Aqköl Akmolinskaya Oblast' Kazakh. see Akkol'
Aqköl Atyrauskaya Oblast' Kazakh. see Akkol'
124 C3 Aqla well Saudi Arabia
Aqmola Kazakh. see Astana
Aqmola Oblysy admin. div. Kazakh. see Akmolinskaya Oblast'
122 F3 Āq Qal'eh Iran
111 E8 Aqqan Xinjiang China
111 G8 Aqqan Xinjiang China
111 I8 Aqqikkol Hu salt l. China
Aqqystaū Kazakh. see Akkistau
128 D6 'Aqraba West Bank
127 K5 'Aqrah Iraq
128 G7 'Aqran hill Saudi Arabia
Aqsay Kazakh. see Aksay
Aqsayqin Hit terr. Asia see Aksai Chin
Aqshataū Kazakh. see Akchatau
Aqshī Kazakh. see Akshiy
120 H6 Aqsho'laq Uzbek.
Aqshuqyr Kazakh. see Akshukur
Aqsū Akmolinskaya Oblast' Kazakh. see Aksu
Aqsū Almatinskaya Oblast' Kazakh. see Aksu
Aqsū Pavlodarskaya Oblast' Kazakh. see Aksu
Aqsūat Kazakh. see Aksuat
Aqsū-Ayuly Kazakh. see Aksu-Ayuly
Aqtas Kazakh. see Aktas
Aqtaū Kazakh. see Aktau
Aqtöbe Kazakh. see Aktobe
Aqtöbe Oblysy admin. div. Kazakh. see Aktyubinskaya Oblast'
Aqtoghay Karagandinskaya Oblast' Kazakh. see Aktogay
Aqtoghay Pavlodarskaya Oblast' Kazakh. see Aktogay
Aquae Grani Ger. see Aachen
Aquae Gratianae France see Aix-les-Bains
Aquae Mortuae France see Aigues-Mortes
Aquae Sextiae France see Aix-en-Provence
Aquae Statiellae Italy see Acqui Terme
241 S7 Aquarius Mountains AZ U.S.A.
241 U4 Aquarius Plateau UT U.S.A.
195 L2 Aquaviva delle Fonti Italy
235 J3 Aquebogue NY U.S.A.
253 F5 Aquidabánmi r. Para.
253 G5 Aquidauana Brazil
253 F4 Aquidauana r. Brazil
244 D7 Aquila Mex.
179 H8 Aquilêia Italy
242 F3 Aquiles Mex.
193 O6 Aquilonia Italy
186 E3 Aquilué Spain
246 G4 Aquin Haiti
Aquincum Hungary see Budapest
193 L5 Aquino Italy
Aquinum Italy see Aquino
Aquiry r. Brazil see Acre
Aquisgranum Ger. see Aachen
245 H4 Aquismón Mex.
163 D7 Aquitaine admin. reg. France
Aqzhal Kazakh. see Akzhal
Aqzhar Kazakh. see Akzhar
Aqzhayqyn Köli salt l. Kazakh. see Akzhaykyn, Ozero
117 J7 Ara Bihar India
186 F3 Ara r. Spain
210 D3 Āra Ārba Eth.
123 K6 Arab Afgh.
231 D8 Arab AL U.S.A.
208 F2 Arab, Bahr el watercourse Sudan
203 F2 'Arab, Khalīj al b. Egypt
122 G5 'Arabābād Iran
210 D3 Ara Bacalle well Eth.
128 A9 'Arabah, Wādī watercourse Egypt
125 J7 'Arabah, Wādī r. Yemen
128 D9 'Arabah, Wādī al watercourse Israel/Jordan
128 D3 'Arab al Mulk Syria
137 N8 Arabats'ka Strilka, Kosa spit Ukr.
Arabatskaya Strelka spit Ukr. see Arabats'ka Strilka, Kosa
137 O8 Arabats'ka Zatoka b. Ukr.
251 E3 Arabelo Venez.
187 C10 Arabí mt. Spain
265 I4 Arabian Basin sea feature Indian Ocean
Arabian Gulf Asia see The Gulf
125 M6 Arabian Oryx Sanctuary tourist site Saudi Arabia
125 J5 Arabian Peninsula Asia
119 J6 Arabian Sea Indian Ocean
129 J4 Arablinskoye Rus. Fed.
210 D3 Ara Bonel Eth.
251 F3 Arabopó Venez.
129 J5 Äräb Qubalı Azer.
163 G10 Arac r. France
126 F3 Araç Turkey
251 F5 Araça r. Brazil
254 F4 Aracaju Brazil
253 G6 Aracanguy, Montes de hills Para.
258 D2 Aracar, Volcán vol. Arg.
246 F8 Aracataca Col.
254 F3 Aracati Brazil
254 E5 Aracatu Brazil
256 B4 Araçatuba Brazil
184 F5 Aracena Spain
184 G5 Aracena, Embalse de resr Spain
259 C9 Aracena, Isla i. Chile
184 E5 Aracena, Sierra de hills Spain
198 C3 Arachthos r. Greece
78 □6 Aracides, Cape Malaita Solomon Is
197 J8 Aračinovo Macedonia
254 F3 Aracoiaba Brazil
257 G3 Aracruz Brazil
257 F2 Araçuaí Brazil
257 F2 Araçuaí r. Brazil
128 D7 'Arad Israel
196 J4 Arad Romania
177 K5 Arad county Romania
202 D6 Arada Chad
182 D7 Arada, Serra de mts Port.
125 K4 'Arādah U.A.E.
122 E4 Arādān Iran
184 B6 Arade r. Port.
184 C6 Arade, Barragem de resr Port.
202 D6 Aradeib, Wadi watercourse Sudan
195 O3 Aradeo Italy
177 J5 Aradului, Câmpia plain Romania
216 □3a Arafo Tenerife Canary Is
105 I3 Arafune-yama mt. Japan
76 D2 Arafura Sea Austr./Indon.
266 D6 Arafura Shelf sea feature Austr./Indon.
256 A1 Aragarças Brazil
129 F5 Aragats Lerr mt. Armenia
105 H1 Ara-gawa r. Japan
105 K4 Ara-gawa r. Japan
163 E10 Aragnouet France
183 Q6 Aragón aut. comm. Spain
183 Q4 Aragón r. Spain
186 C4 Aragón, Canal Imperial de Spain
194 F9 Aragona Sicilia Italy
183 P7 Aragoncillo Spain
183 P7 Aragoncillo mt. Spain
250 E2 Aragua state Venez.
254 C4 Araguacema Brazil
254 C5 Araguaçu Brazil
251 E2 Aragua de Barcelona Venez.
251 F2 Aragua de Maturín Venez.
256 C Araguaia r. Brazil
254 C4 Araguaia, Parque Nacional de nat. park Brazil
256 B1 Araguaiana Brazil
254 C3 Araguaína Brazil
256 A2 Araguainha Brazil
253 H1 Araguana Brazil
251 F2 Araguao, Boca r. mouth Venez.
251 F2 Araguapiche, Punta pt Venez.
256 C3 Araguari Brazil
256 C3 Araguari r. Brazil
251 I4 Araguari r. Brazil
254 C3 Araguatins Brazil
129 F4 Aragvi r. Georgia
124 F9 'Ārah, Ra's pt Yemen
125 L7 'Ārah, Wādī r. Oman
254 D5 Arai Brazil
105 H2 Arai Niigata Japan
104 G6 Arai Shizuoka Japan
183 P3 Araia Spain
254 E2 Araiosos Brazil
205 F4 Arak Alg.
122 C4 Arāk Iran
128 G4 Arak Syria
105 K1 Arakai-yama mt. Japan
251 F3 Arakaka Guyana
96 A4 Arakan state Myanmar
96 B4 Arakan Yoma mts Myanmar
102 □1 Arakawa Okinawa Japan
Arakhthos r. Greece see Arachthos
104 F3 Araki-gawa r. Japan
80 M5 Arakihi hill North I. N.Z.
114 F6 Arakkonam Tamil Nadu India
129 B5 Araklı Turkey
129 F6 Arak's r. Armenia
alt. Aras Nehri (Turkey),
alt. Araz (Azerbaijan/Iran),
conv. Aras, hist. Araxes
129 I4 Arakul Rus. Fed.
111 J7 Aral Qinghai China
Aral Kazakh. see Aral'sk
Aral Tajik. see Vose
186 A1 Aralar, Sierra de mts Spain
129 F6 Aralık Turkey
120 I5 Aral Sea salt l. Kazakh./Uzbek.
120 I4 Aral'sk Kazakh.
Aral'skoye More salt l. Kazakh./Uzbek. see Aral Sea
120 C3 Aralsor, Ozero l. Kazakh.
120 E3 Aralsor, Ozero salt l. Kazakh.
Aral Tengizi salt l. Kazakh./Uzbek. see Aral Sea
106 B3 Araltobe Xinjiang China
85 J7 Aramac Qld Austr.
85 J7 Aramac Creek watercourse Qld Austr.
124 H3 Aramah plat. Saudi Arabia
182 C3 A Ramallosa Spain
245 H1 Aramberri Mex.
254 D3 Arame Brazil
91 J8 Aramia r. P.N.G.
163 C9 Aramits France
161 F9 Aramon France
129 H5 Aran Azer.
114 F3 Aran r. India
186 G2 Aran, Val d' reg. Spain
185 M6 Arana, Sierra mts Spain
129 J6 Ārānchī Iran
260 C2 Arancibia Arg.
183 R5 Aranda r. Spain
183 M5 Aranda de Duero Spain
183 Q5 Aranda de Moncayo Spain
127 M6 Arandān Iran
244 E5 Arandas Mex.
196 I6 Aranđelovac Serbia
212 B4 Arandis Namibia
116 I9 Arang Chhattisgarh India
182 F8 Aranhas Port.
114 F6 Arani Tamil Nadu India
147 E3 Aran Island Ireland
147 C6 Aran Islands Ireland
183 M8 Aranjuez Spain
261 F5 Arano Arg.
212 C5 Aranos Namibia
237 G12 Aransas Pass TX U.S.A.
114 F7 Arantangi Tamil Nadu India
256 B3 Arantes r. Brazil
182 I9 Arañuelo, Campo reg. Spain
77 H1 Aranuka atoll Gilbert Is Kiribati
97 F8 Aranyaprathet Thai.
177 L3 Aranyosapáti Hungary
183 N8 Aranzueque Spain
103 H14 Arao Japan
206 E2 Araouane Mali
237 F8 Arapaho OK U.S.A.
236 F5 Arapahoe NE U.S.A.
251 H5 Arapari Brazil
81 I8 Arapawa Island South I. N.Z.
261 I2 Arapey Grande r. Uru.
126 I4 Arapgir Turkey
250 B5 Arapicos Ecuador
182 I7 Arapiles Spain
254 F4 Arapiraca Brazil
198 F2 Arapis, Akrotirio pt Greece
256 B5 Arapongas Brazil
256 C6 Arapoti Brazil
Arapsun Turkey see Gülşehir
256 A4 Arapuá Brazil
80 J5 Arapuni North I. N.Z.
255 C8 Araquari Brazil
127 J8 'Ar'ar Saudi Arabia
127 K8 'Ar'ar, Wādī watercourse Iraq/Saudi Arabia
251 F5 Arara r. Brazil
250 C5 Araracuara Col.
250 C5 Araracuara, Cerros de hills Col.
117 J6 Araraj Bihar India
255 C9 Araranguá Brazil
256 C6 Ararapira Brazil
256 C4 Araraquara Brazil
252 C2 Araras Amazonas Brazil
251 H6 Araras Pará Brazil
252 D2 Ararás Brazil
256 D5 Araras São Paulo Brazil
254 E3 Araras, Açude resr Brazil
256 A3 Araras, Serra das hills Brazil
256 A6 Araras, Serra das mts Brazil
129 F6 Ararat Armenia
83 I7 Ararat Vic. Austr.
Ararat, Mount Turkey see Ağrı Dağı
254 D2 Arari Brazil
117 K6 Araria Bihar India
254 E3 Araripe Brazil
254 E3 Araripe, Chapada do hills Brazil
254 E3 Araripina Brazil
257 F5 Araruama Brazil
257 F5 Araruama, Lago de lag. Brazil
127 L4 Aras r. Asia
alt. Arak's (Armenia),
alt. Aras Nehri (Turkey),
alt. Araz (Azerbaijan/Iran),
hist. Araxes
183 P3 Aras Spain
127 K4 Aras Turkey
102 □1 Ara-saki c. Okinawa Japan
122 F4 Arāsavān Iran
187 C8 Aras de Alpuente Spain
106 I2 Ar-Asgat Mongolia
129 G6 Aras Govşaghyuyn resr Azer./Iran
129 D6 Aras Güneyi Dağları mts Turkey
104 E4 Arashima-dake mt. Japan
247 □9 Arasji Aruba
129 C6 Aras Nehri r. Turkey
alt. Arak's (Armenia),
alt. Araz (Azerbaijan/Iran),
conv. Aras, hist. Araxes
260 E4 Arata Arg.
255 F5 Arataca Brazil
206 C2 Araţâne well Maur.
251 I5 Arataú r. Brazil
Aratürük Xinjiang China see Yiwu
94 D1 Arau Malaysia
252 D2 Arauã r. Brazil
251 F6 Arauá r. Brazil
251 F6 Arauá r. Brazil
250 D3 Arauca Col.
250 D3 Arauca dept Col.
250 E3 Arauca r. Venez.
260 A6 Araucanía admin. reg. Chile
255 C8 Araucária Brazil
258 B5 Arauco Chile
258 B5 Arauco, Golfo de b. Chile
161 E6 Araules France
250 D3 Arauquita Col.
250 D2 Araure Venez.
241 V9 Aravaipa Creek watercourse AZ U.S.A.
116 D7 Aravalli Range mts India
138 I2 Aravete Estonia
183 P5 Araviana r. Spain
160 I5 Aravis mts France
160 I5 Aravis, Col des pass France
198 D2 Aravissos Greece
78 □6 Arawa P.N.G.
211 D5 Arawale National Reserve nature res. Kenya
Arawata r. South I. N.Z. see Arawhata
80 L5 Arawhana mt. North I. N.Z.
81 C11 Arawhata r. South I. N.Z.
256 D3 Araxá Brazil
198 C4 Araxos, Akrotirio pt Greece
Araya Spain see Araia
251 E2 Araya, Península de pen. Venez.
247 K8 Araya, Punta de pt Venez.
126 E4 Arayıt Dağı mt. Turkey
129 J6 Araz r. Azer.
alt. Arak's (Armenia),
alt. Aras Nehri (Turkey),
conv. Aras, hist. Araxes
182 C8 Arazede Port.
186 C4 Arba r. Spain
186 C3 Arba de Biel r. Spain
186 C3 Arba de Luesia r. Spain
Arbailu Iraq see Arbīl
210 C3 Ārba Minch Eth.
163 F10 Arbas France
127 L6 Arbat Iraq
192 D8 Arbatax Sardegna Italy
134 J4 Arbazh Rus. Fed.
186 G4 Arbeca Spain
157 K8 Arbecey France
190 G3 Arbedo Switz.
Arbela Iraq see Arbīl
160 H4 Arbent France
163 D10 Arbéost France
173 J3 Arberg Ger.
Arberth Pembrokeshire, Wales U.K. see Narberth
179 K2 Arbesbach Austria
183 P7 Arbeteta Spain
191 K9 Arbia r. Italy
127 L5 Arbīl Iraq
127 K6 Arbīl governorate Iraq
183 P3 Arbizu Spain
143 L2 Arboga Sweden
160 H3 Arbois France
185 O6 Arboleas Spain
261 G5 Arboledas Arg.
250 B2 Arboletes Col.
261 I3 Arbolito Uru.
190 G1 Arbon Switz.
192 B8 Arborea Sardegna Italy
192 B8 Arborea reg. Sardegna Italy
223 K4 Arborfield Sask. Can.
223 L5 Arborg Man. Can.
190 E5 Arborio Italy
141 N6 Arbrå Sweden
146 K9 Arbroath Angus, Scotland U.K.
186 K4 Arbúcies Spain
240 J2 Arbuckle CA U.S.A.
123 J7 Arbu Lut, Dasht-e des. Afgh.
163 C9 Arbus France
192 B8 Arbus Sardegna Italy
137 K6 Arbuzynka Ukr.
161 G9 Arc r. France
161 I5 Arc r. France
163 B6 Arcachon France
163 B6 Arcachon, Bassin d' inlet France
232 G6 Arcade NY U.S.A.
231 G12 Arcadia FL U.S.A.
237 I9 Arcadia LA U.S.A.
226 H5 Arcadia MI U.S.A.
232 G8 Arcadia PA U.S.A.
226 C5 Arcadia WI U.S.A.
160 I5 Arcalod, Pointe d' mt. France
232 A9 Arcanum OH U.S.A.
243 N7 Arcas, Cayos is Mex.
238 B6 Arcata CA U.S.A.
240 O3 Arc Dome mt. NV U.S.A.
193 L4 Arce Italy
244 G7 Arcelia Mex.
164 J6 Arcen Neth.
157 J8 Arc-en-Barrois France
162 C4 Arces France
156 G7 Arces-Dilo France
160 H2 Arc-et-Senans France
191 N8 Arcevia Italy
Archangel Rus. Fed. see Arkhangel'sk
Archangel Oblast admin. div. Rus. Fed. see Arkhangel'skaya Oblast'
199 J6 Archangelos Rodos Greece
197 K7 Archar r. Bulg.
234 D2 Archbald PA U.S.A.
232 A7 Archbold OH U.S.A.
187 C11 Archena Spain
85 H2 Archer r. Qld Austr.
85 I2 Archer Bend National Park Qld Austr.
237 F9 Archer City TX U.S.A.
157 M7 Arches France
241 W3 Arches National Park UT U.S.A.

Arch Henda to Aschbach Markt

280

206 E2 Arch Henda well Mali
162 D4 Archiac France
185 K6 Archidona Spain
84 G5 Archie Creek r. Qld Austr.
225 I3 Archipélago de Mingan, Réserve du Parc National de l' nat. park Que. Can.
177 L5 Archiş Romania
185 P4 Archivel Spain
192 B8 Arci, Monte hill Italy
192 H2 Arcidosso Italy
192 C5 Arcipelago de la Maddalena, Parco Nazionale dell' nat. park Sardegna Italy
192 E2 Arcipelago Toscano, Parco Nazionale dell' nat. park Italy
156 H6 Arcis-sur-Aube France
122 C2 Ärçivan Azer.
82 E3 Arckaringa watercourse S.A. Austr.
160 H2 Arc-lès-Gray France
122 G2 Arçman Turkm.
191 J4 Arco Italy
238 H5 Arco ID U.S.A.
260 B6 Arco, Paso de pass Chile
184 □ Arco da Calheta Madeira
182 E6 Arco de Baúlhe Port.
190 H7 Arcola Italy
232 H10 Arcola VA U.S.A.
160 I3 Arçon France
160 D4 Arconce r. France
159 L5 Arçonnay France
257 E4 Arcos Brazil
184 D3 Arcos Port.
183 M4 Arcos Spain
183 P6 Arcos de Jalón Spain
184 H7 Arcos de la Frontera Spain
187 C8 Arcos de las Salinas Spain
182 D5 Arcos de Valdevez Port.
114 F6 Arcot Tamil Nadu India
158 E4 Arcouest, Pointe de l' pt France
254 F4 Arcoverde Brazil
182 C5 Arcozelo Braga Port.
182 E7 Arcozelo Guarda Port.
182 C6 Arcozelo Porto Port.
182 C5 Arcozelo Viana do Castelo Port.
160 G2 Arc-sur-Tille France
221 J2 Arctic Bay Nunavut Can.
Arctic Institute Islands Rus. Fed. see Arkticheskogo Instituta, Ostrova
268 B1 Arctic Mid-Ocean Ridge sea feature Arctic Ocean
268 Arctic Ocean
220 E3 Arctic Red r. N.W.T. Can.
Arctic Red River N.W.T. Can. see Tsiigehtchic
262 N8 Arctowski research stn Antarctica
192 B8 Arcuentu, Monte hill Italy
186 F3 Arcusa Spain
160 D1 Arcy-sur-Cure France
197 O9 Arda r. Bulg. alt. Ardas (Greece)
190 I5 Arda r. Italy
122 C2 Ardabīl Iran
122 B2 Ardabīl prov. Iran
179 K3 Ardagger Markt Austria
147 D8 Ardagh Ireland
127 K3 Ardahan Turkey
129 D4 Ardahan prov. Turkey
122 H3 Ardāk Iran
122 E6 Ardakān Fārs Iran
122 E5 Ardakān Yazd Iran
122 D6 Ardal Iran
141 I6 Årdal Norway
183 N5 Ardal mt. Spain
185 J7 Ardales Spain
142 D3 Ardalsknapen hill Norway
141 I6 Årdalstangen Norway
147 J7 Ardanairy Ireland
163 B10 Ardanaz Spain
129 D4 Ardanuç Turkey
192 B6 Ardara Sardegna Italy
147 F3 Ardara Ireland
197 O9 Ardas r. Greece alt. Arda (Bulgaria)
128 F8 Ard aş Şawwān plain Jordan
135 H5 Ardatov Nizhegorodskaya Oblast' Rus. Fed.
135 I5 Ardatov Respublika Mordoviya Rus. Fed.
148 D8 Ardattin Ireland
227 N4 Ardbeg Ont. Can.
146 F11 Ard Bheinn hill Scotland U.K.
148 E6 Ardcath Ireland
146 D10 Ardchiavaig Argyll and Bute, Scotland U.K.
147 F7 Ardconry Ireland
193 J4 Ardea Italy
161 E7 Ardèche dept France
161 F8 Ardèche r. France
161 E8 Ardèche, Gorges de l' France
147 I5 Ardee Ireland
146 G10 Arden Argyll and Bute, Scotland U.K.
235 G2 Arden NY U.S.A.
82 F5 Arden, Mount hill S.A. Austr.
165 G9 Ardenne, Plateau de l' Belgium
Ardennes plat. Belgium see Ardenne, Plateau de l'
156 I4 Ardennes dept France
156 H5 Ardennes r. France
157 I4 Ardennes, Canal des France
162 H2 Ardentes France
146 G10 Ardentinny Argyll and Bute, Scotland U.K.
240 K3 Arden Town CA U.S.A.
147 G6 Arderin hill Ireland
146 H7 Ardersier Highland, Scotland U.K.
161 C6 Ardes France
129 C4 Ardeşen Turkey
122 E5 Ardestān Iran
190 I2 Ardez Switz.
147 C8 Ardfert Ireland
147 G8 Ardfinnan Ireland
146 H7 Ardgay Highland, Scotland U.K.
147 F8 Ardglass Ireland
147 K4 Ardglass Northern Ireland U.K.
129 B6 Ardıcın Dağı mt. Turkey
184 E4 Ardila r. Port.
197 N9 Ardino Bulg.
146 B8 Ardivachar Point Scotland U.K.
80 L5 Ardkeen North I. N.Z.
147 K4 Ardkeen Northern Ireland U.K.
146 F11 Ardlamont Point Scotland U.K.
151 N4 Ardleigh Essex, England U.K.
83 K6 Ardlethan N.S.W. Austr.
146 G10 Ardlui Argyll and Bute, Scotland U.K.
146 E10 Ardlussa Argyll and Bute, Scotland U.K.
146 F7 Ardmair Highland, Scotland U.K.
146 E11 Ardminish Argyll and Bute, Scotland U.K.
146 E9 Ardmolich Highland, Scotland U.K.
147 C6 Ardmore Ireland
237 G8 Ardmore OK U.S.A.
234 E4 Ardmore PA U.S.A.
147 G9 Ardmore Bay Ireland
146 D9 Ardmore Point Scotland U.K.
147 E7 Ardnacrusha Ireland
146 D9 Ardnamurchan pen. Scotland U.K.
146 D9 Ardnamurchan, Point of Scotland U.K.
147 E6 Ardnasodan Ireland
137 L1 Ardon' Rus. Fed.
129 F2 Ardon Rus. Fed.
129 F2 Ardon r. Rus. Fed.
190 C3 Ardon Switz.
165 D7 Ardooie Belgium
195 K7 Ardore Italy
147 E8 Ardpatrick Ireland
146 E11 Ardpatrick Point Scotland U.K.
147 E6 Ardrahan Ireland
156 C2 Ardres France
146 F10 Ardrishaig Argyll and Bute, Scotland U.K.
82 F6 Ardrossan S.A. Austr.
146 G11 Ardrossan North Ayrshire, Scotland U.K.
148 D7 Ardscull Ireland
235 H2 Ardsley NY U.S.A.
147 L4 Ards Peninsula Northern Ireland U.K.
147 H3 Ardstraw Northern Ireland U.K.
197 L3 Ardusat Romania
146 E8 Ardvasar Highland, Scotland U.K.
146 A8 Ardvule, Rubha pt Scotland U.K.
140 L5 Åre Sweden
256 D4 Areado Brazil
183 O2 Areatza Spain
208 F4 Arebi Dem. Rep. Congo
160 J5 Arèches France
247 □1 Arecibo Puerto Rico
261 H3 Areco r. Arg.
197 M5 Arefu Romania
258 F2 Areguá Para.
254 F3 Areia Branca Brazil
182 D9 Areias Port.
92 □ Arekalong Peninsula Palau
136 C2 Arekhava Belarus
139 N7 Arekhawsk Belarus
Arel Belgium see Arlon
Arelas France see Arles
Arelate France see Arles
142 H2 Aremark Norway
169 C10 Aremberg hill Ger.
186 G3 Arén Spain
92 C7 Arena rf Phil.
240 I3 Arena, Point CA U.S.A.
242 E6 Arena, Punta pt Mex.
242 E5 Arena de la Ventana, Punta pt Mex.
258 D2 Arenal, Campo del plain Arg.
185 O4 Arenal, Puerto del pass Spain
242 □Q12 Arenal, Volcán vol. Costa Rica
92 D5 Arena Point Luzon Phil.
253 F3 Arenápolis Brazil
247 □1 Arenas, Punta pt Puerto Rico
259 C9 Arenas, Punta de pt Arg.
183 L2 Arenas de Iguña Spain
185 L7 Arenas del Rey Spain
185 M2 Arenas de San Juan Spain
183 J8 Arenas de San Pedro Spain
261 G4 Arenaza Arg.
142 E3 Arendal Norway
165 H6 Arendonk Belgium
170 D5 Arendsee l. Ger.
170 D5 Arendsee (Altmark) Ger.
163 C7 Arengosse France
150 E2 Arenig Fawr hill Wales U.K.
183 O6 Arenillas Spain
261 I2 Arenitas Blancas Uru.
187 D7 Arenos, Embalse de resr Spain
185 K4 Arenosillo r. Spain
185 K4 Arenoso r. Spain
169 I8 Arenshausen Ger.
195 K5 Arente r. Italy
186 K4 Arenys de Mar Spain
190 F7 Arenzano Italy
198 D6 Areopoli Greece
182 C5 Areosa Port.
242 F4 Areponapuchi Mex.
252 C4 Arequipa Peru
252 B3 Arequipa dept Peru
261 G3 Arequito Arg.
190 H4 Arera, Pizzo mt. Italy
251 H5 Arere Brazil
210 C3 Ārēro Eth.
163 B6 Arès France
182 D2 Ares Spain
138 L9 Aresa r. Belarus
173 K4 Aresing Ger.
183 N2 Arespalditza Spain
122 F5 Arestān Iran
163 C9 Arette France
163 C10 Arette-Pierre-St-Martin France
183 J7 Arevalillo Spain
183 K6 Arevalillo r. Spain
183 K6 Arévalo Spain
183 K6 Arévalo, Tierra de reg. Spain
184 D2 Arez Port.
124 D8 Areza Eritrea
Arezzaf well Mali see Aghezzaf
191 L9 Arezzo Italy
191 L8 Arezzo prov. Italy
126 I8 'Arfajah well Saudi Arabia
198 D5 Arfara Greece
163 I9 Arfons France
183 Q4 Arga r. Spain
84 F6 Argadargada N.T. Austr.
107 L4 Argalant Mongolia
198 E3 Argalasti Greece
184 H3 Argallanes, Sierra de los hills Spain
185 I4 Argallón Spain
185 M2 Argamasilla de Alba Spain
185 K3 Argamasilla de Calatrava Spain
185 O3 Argamasón Spain
110 I6 Argan Xinjiang China
183 N8 Arganda del Rey Spain
182 D8 Arganil Port.
182 G3 Arganza Spain
92 D7 Argao Cebu Phil.
116 F9 Argaon Mahar. India
107 J4 Argatay Mongolia
193 L4 Argatone, Monte mt. Italy
190 G4 Argegno Italy
Argel Alg. see Alger
163 D9 Argelès-Gazost France
163 K10 Argelès-sur-Mer France
161 B10 Argeliers France
187 E7 Argelita Spain
172 H6 Argen r. Ger.
172 H6 Argenbühl Ger.
159 K3 Argences France
161 J10 Argens r. France
191 L6 Argenta Italy
159 K4 Argentan France
192 G3 Argentario, Monte hill Italy
162 H5 Argentat France
186 C6 Argente Spain
190 B7 Argentera Italy
190 C7 Argentera, Cima dell' mt. Italy
190 C7 Argentera, Parco Naturale dell' nature res. Italy
156 D6 Argenteuil France
172 D2 Argenthal Ger.
192 A6 Argentiera Sardegna Italy
160 J5 Argentière France
190 D8 Argentina r. Italy
258 D4 Argentina country S. America
262 V1 Argentina Range mts Antarctica
160 I6 Argentine France
264 F9 Argentine Abyssal Plain sea feature S. Atlantic Ocean
264 G8 Argentine Basin sea feature S. Atlantic Ocean
Argentine Republic country S. America see Argentina
264 F8 Argentine Rise sea feature S. Atlantic Ocean
259 B8 Argentino, Lago l. Arg.
162 D1 Argenton r. France
159 K8 Argenton-Château France
Argentoratum France see Strasbourg
159 J5 Argentre France
159 I5 Argentré-du-Plessis France
159 P6 Argent-sur-Sauldre France
261 F6 Argerich Arg.
185 O5 Argerín mt. Spain
197 O6 Argeş r. Romania
183 L9 Argés Spain
197 M6 Argeşel r. Romania
123 K6 Arghandab r. Afgh.
123 K6 Arghastan r. Afgh.
148 B6 Arghavas Ireland
203 F5 Argo Sudan
198 D5 Argolikos Kolpos b. Greece
160 I5 Argonay France
157 I5 Argonne reg. France
226 F4 Argonne WI U.S.A.
198 D5 Argos Greece
185 P4 Argos r. Spain
226 H8 Argos IN U.S.A.
185 P4 Argos, Embalse de resr Spain
198 C2 Argos Orestiko Greece
198 B4 Argostoli Kefallonia Greece
158 I5 Argouges France
Argovie canton Switz. see Aargau
129 E2 Argudan Rus. Fed.
183 Q4 Arguedas Spain
156 C4 Argueil France
185 O4 Arguellite Spain
158 G4 Arguenon r. France
186 E3 Arguís Spain
183 Q9 Arguisuelas Spain
182 I6 Argujillo Spain
100 B2 Argun' r. China/Rus. Fed.
129 H2 Argun r. Georgia/Rus. Fed.
129 G2 Argun Rus. Fed.
207 G3 Argungu Nigeria
100 A3 Argunsk Rus. Fed.
107 O2 Argunskiy Khrebet mts Rus. Fed.
240 O6 Argus Range mts CA U.S.A.
106 H4 Arguut Mongolia
225 H5 Argyle N.S. Can.
226 C9 Argyle IA U.S.A.
226 E7 Argyle WI U.S.A.
86 J4 Argyle, Lake W.A. Austr.
146 F10 Argyll reg. Scotland U.K.
146 F11 Argyll and Bute admin. div. Scotland U.K.
Argyrokastron Albania see Gjirokastër
124 G8 Arḩab reg. Yemen
106 G3 Arhangay prov. Mongolia
129 C4 Arhavi Turkey
Ar Horqin Qi Nei Mongol China see Tianshan
142 G5 Århus Denmark
142 G5 Århus county Denmark
142 G5 Århus Bugt b. Denmark
142 G5 Århus-Tirstrup airport Denmark
80 I5 Aria North I. N.Z.
195 H7 Aria, Monte hill Isole Lipari Italy
100 I6 Ariadnoye Rus. Fed.
93 D1 Ariaga i. Indon.
83 K6 Ariah Park N.S.W. Austr.
103 H13 Ariake-kai b. Japan
212 C6 Ariamsvlei Namibia
216 □2a Ariane Tracking Station research stn Ascension S. Atlantic Ocean
191 M6 Ariano, Isola d' i. Italy
193 O5 Ariano Irpino Italy
191 M6 Ariano nel Polesine Italy
261 F3 Arias Arg.
113 D11 Ari Atoll Maldives
251 G5 Ariaú Brazil
186 C2 Aribe Spain
251 F2 Aribí r. Venez.
206 E3 Aribinda Burkina
252 C4 Arica Chile
250 D5 Arica Col.
250 C5 Arica Peru
250 D2 Aricagua Venez.
193 J4 Ariccia Italy
216 □3a Arico Tenerife Canary Is
87 G12 Arid, Cape W.A. Austr.
104 B7 Arida Japan
104 B7 Arida-gawa r. Japan
129 E6 Arı Dağı mt. Turkey
198 D2 Aridaia Greece
204 B4 Aridal, Sabkhat salt pan Western Sahara
217 □2a Aride, Île i. Inner Islands Seychelles
Arid Island North I. N.Z. see Rakitu Island
163 G10 Ariège dept France
163 G8 Ariège r. France
261 H5 Ariel Arg.
197 L4 Arieş r. Romania
177 L5 Arieşeni Romania
197 L4 Arieşul Mic r. Romania
199 L2 Arifiye Turkey
106 G1 Arigiyn Gol r. Mongolia
128 E3 Arīḩā Syria
Arīḩā West Bank see Jericho
183 M3 Arija Spain
261 G2 Arijón Arg.
236 E5 Arikaree r. CO U.S.A.
196 I7 Arilje Serbia
251 F6 Arimã Brazil
247 □7 Arima Trin. and Tob.
104 F3 Arimine-ko resr Japan
Ariminum Italy see Rimini
251 G3 Arimu Mine Guyana
124 F6 'Arīn, Wādī al watercourse Saudi Arabia
216 □3f Arinaga Gran Canaria Canary Is
146 C9 Arinagour Argyll and Bute, Scotland U.K.
186 D5 Ariño Spain
253 G3 Arinos Mato Grosso Brazil
257 D1 Arinos Minas Gerais Brazil
253 F2 Arinos r. Brazil
160 H4 Arinthod France
244 F6 Ario de Rosáles Mex.
138 G6 Ariogala Lith.
247 □7 Aripo, Mount hill Trin. and Tob.
250 D3 Ariporo r. Col.
253 F2 Aripuanã Brazil
251 F6 Aripuanã r. Brazil
253 E2 Ariquemes Brazil
255 B6 Ariranhá r. Brazil
146 E9 Arisaig Highland, Scotland U.K.
146 E9 Arisaig, Sound of sea chan. Scotland U.K.
251 G3 Arisaru Falls Guyana
128 B7 'Arīsh, Wādī al watercourse Egypt
250 D2 Arismendi Venez.
244 G3 Arista Mex.
222 D4 Aristazabal Island B.C. Can.
234 C3 Aristes PA U.S.A.
259 D7 Aristizábal, Cabo c. Arg.
258 G2 Aristóbulo del Valle Arg.
123 O6 Aritwala Pak.
192 C8 Aritzo Sardegna Italy
213 □J3 Arivonimamo Madag.
Arixang Xinjiang China see Wenquan
210 C4 Ariya waterhole Kenya
114 F7 Ariyalur Tamil Nadu India
182 E7 Ariz Port.
183 P6 Ariza Spain
258 D2 Arizaro, Salar de salt flat Arg.
163 G9 Arize r. France
163 G10 Arize, Massif de l' mts France
183 O2 Arizgoiti Spain
183 Q3 Arizola Spain
260 E4 Arizona Arg.
241 U7 Arizona state U.S.A.
242 D2 Arizpe Mex.
124 G3 'Arjah Saudi Arabia
142 I2 Årjäng Sweden
95 K8 Arjasa Jawa Indon.
140 N3 Arjeplog Sweden
210 C2 Ārjo Eth.
250 C2 Arjona Col.
185 K5 Arjona Spain
185 K5 Arjonilla Spain
117 I9 Arjuni Chhattisgarh India
116 H9 Arjuni Mahar. India
135 H6 Arkadak Rus. Fed.
237 I8 Arkadelphia AR U.S.A.
137 Q4 Arkadivka Ukr.
131 P3 Arkagala Rus. Fed.
146 F9 Arkaig, Loch l. Scotland U.K.
114 E6 Arkalgud Karnataka India
198 G7 Arkalochori Kriti Greece
121 L2 Arkalyk Kazakh.
237 J9 Arkansas r. AR U.S.A.
237 I8 Arkansas state U.S.A.
237 J9 Arkansas City AR U.S.A.
237 G7 Arkansas City KS U.S.A.
197 K8 Arkata r. Bulg.
111 I8 Arkatag Shan mts China
222 C2 Arkell, Mount Y.T. Can.
202 E4 Arkenu, Jabal mt. Libya
134 H2 Arkhangel'sk Rus. Fed.
134 H3 Arkhangel'skaya Oblast' admin. div. Rus. Fed.
135 L5 Arkhangel'skoye Respublika Bashkortostan Rus. Fed.
129 F1 Arkhangel'skoye Stavropol'skiy Kray Rus. Fed.
139 U8 Arkhangel'skoye Tul'skaya Oblast' Rus. Fed.
137 T2 Arkhangel'skoye Voronezhskaya Oblast' Rus. Fed.
137 M7 Arkhanhel's'ka Sloboda Ukr.
137 M6 Arkhanhel's'ke Ukr.
100 F4 Arkhara Rus. Fed.
100 F4 Arkhara r. Rus. Fed.
129 H4 Arkhilos Kalo Georgia
137 R9 Arkhipo-Osipovka Rus. Fed.
139 Y5 Arkhipovka Ivanovskaya Oblast' Rus. Fed.
100 H7 Arkhipovka Primorskiy Kray Rus. Fed.
139 O7 Arkhipovka Smolenskaya Oblast' Rus. Fed.
129 F2 Arkhonskaya Rus. Fed.
129 C2 Arkhyz Rus. Fed.
Árki i. Greece see Arkoi
129 J6 Ärkivan Azer.
146 G6 Arkle hill Scotland U.K.
147 J7 Arklow Ireland
199 H5 Arkoi i. Greece
227 M6 Arkona Ont. Can.
170 H1 Arkona, Kap c. Ger.
Arkonam Tamil Nadu India see Arakkonam
143 M3 Arkösund Sweden
131 K1 Arkticheskiy, Mys c. Rus. Fed.
130 J2 Arkticheskogo Instituta, Ostrova is Rus. Fed.
134 J4 Arkul' Rus. Fed.
143 M2 Ärla Sweden
161 D6 Arlanc France
122 F2 Arlandag mt. Turkm.
183 L4 Arlanza r. Spain
183 N4 Arlanzón Spain
183 L4 Arlanzón r. Spain
183 N4 Arlanzón, Embalse de resr Spain
183 O8 Arlas r. Spain
178 B5 Arlbergpass pass Austria
168 D3 Arle (Großheide) Ger.
161 D7 Arlempdes France
192 H3 Arlena di Castro Italy
161 F9 Arles France
151 L3 Arlesey Bedfordshire, England U.K.
147 H7 Arless Ireland
163 J11 Arles-sur-Tech France
160 E2 Arleuf France
156 F3 Arleux France
207 F4 Arli Burkina
207 F4 Arli, Parc National de l' nat. park Burkina
207 F4 Arli, Réserve Partielle de l' nature res. Burkina
226 E8 Arlington IL U.S.A.
235 H1 Arlington NY U.S.A.
232 B8 Arlington OH U.S.A.
238 D4 Arlington OR U.S.A.
236 G3 Arlington SD U.S.A.
234 A7 Arlington VA U.S.A.
226 E6 Arlington WI U.S.A.
226 F7 Arlington Heights IL U.S.A.
207 G2 Arlit Niger
165 I9 Arlon Belgium
84 E7 Arltunga N.T. Austr.
190 F4 Arluno Italy
160 I5 Arly r. France
138 M6 Arlyeya Belarus
223 J5 Arm r. Sask. Can.
184 C6 Armação de Pêra Port.
232 C6 Armada MI U.S.A.
87 C12 Armadale W.A. Austr.
146 I11 Armadale West Lothian, Scotland U.K.
244 G3 Armadillo Mex.
93 D1 Armadores i. Indon.
Armageddon tourist site Israel see Tel Megiddo
147 I4 Armagh Northern Ireland U.K.
147 I4 Armagh county Northern Ireland U.K.
163 E8 Armagnac reg. France
125 J7 Armah, Wādī r. Yemen
183 P7 Armallones Spain
182 E6 Armamar Port.
156 G8 Armance r. France
156 G8 Armançon r. France
246 H4 Armando Bermudez nat. park Dom. Rep.
203 G3 Armant Egypt
140 Q3 Armasjärvi Sweden
199 H7 Armathia i. Greece
129 F5 Armavir Armenia
135 H7 Armavir Rus. Fed.
121 M2 Armavirskiy Kazakh.
163 B9 Armendarits France
129 F5 Armenia country Asia
250 C3 Armenia Col.
199 I6 Armenistis, Akrotirio pt Rodos Greece
139 X4 Armenki Rus. Fed.
190 E4 Armeno Italy
Armenopolis Romania see Gherla
245 I9 Armenta Mex.
183 J7 Armenteros Spain
156 E2 Armentières France
193 Q7 Armento Italy
244 D7 Armeria Mex.
244 D7 Armería r. Mex.
189 E7 Armi, Capo dell' c. Italy
83 M4 Armidale N.S.W. Austr.
185 L6 Armilla Spain
261 G3 Arminda Arg.
238 I3 Armington MT U.S.A.
161 C10 Armissan France
149 N8 Armitage Staffordshire, England U.K.
223 N1 Armit Lake Nunavut Can.
240 M5 Armona CA U.S.A.
116 H9 Armori Mahar. India
158 D5 Armorique, Parc Régional d' park France
236 F4 Armour SD U.S.A.
147 J2 Armoy Northern Ireland U.K.
172 E2 Armsheim Ger.
261 G3 Armstrong Arg.
84 C4 Armstrong r. N.T. Austr.
222 G5 Armstrong B.C. Can.
224 B3 Armstrong Ont. Can.
222 C2 Armstrong, Mount Y.T. Can.
Armstrong Island Cook Is see Rarotonga
232 E9 Armstrong Mills OH U.S.A.
100 J5 Armu r. Rus. Fed.
183 L6 Armuña Spain
192 C8 Armungia Sardegna Italy
182 I3 Armunia Spain
114 F3 Armur Andhra Prad. India
199 I3 Armutçuk Dağı mts Turkey
199 J2 Armutlu Turkey
Armutova Turkey see Gömeç
137 M7 Armyans'k Ukr.
Armyanskaya S.S.R. country Asia see Armenia
142 E7 Arnå r. Denmark
198 D6 Arna Greece
162 G5 Arnac-Pompadour France
190 D4 Arnad Italy
144 D1 Árnafjall hill Faroe Is
159 L6 Arnage France
198 E2 Arnaia Greece
128 A3 Arnaoutis, Cape Cyprus
140 □A1 Arnarfjörður inlet Iceland
225 G1 Arnaud r. Que. Can.
Arnauti, Cape Cyprus see Arnaoutis, Cape
199 J1 Arnavutköy Turkey
123 N4 Arnawai Pak.
160 E2 Arnay-le-Duc France
173 N3 Arnbruck Ger.
149 M5 Arncliffe North Yorkshire, England U.K.
150 H6 Arne Dorset, England U.K.
170 F5 Arneburg Ger.
183 P4 Arnedillo Spain
183 P4 Arnedo Spain
182 D3 Arnego r. Spain
163 B9 Arnéguy France
254 E3 Arneiroz Brazil
140 P4 Arnemark Sweden
164 E6 Arnemuiden Neth.
142 H1 Årnes Norway
186 F6 Arnes Spain
237 F7 Arnett OK U.S.A.
179 L6 Arnfels Austria
164 I5 Arnhem Neth.
84 F2 Arnhem, Cape N.T. Austr.
84 F2 Arnhem Bay N.T. Austr.
84 D2 Arnhem Land reg. N.T. Austr.
84 E2 Arnhem Land Aboriginal Land res. N.T. Austr.
78 □3b Arniel i. Majuro Marshall Is
138 I6 Arnionys 1 Lith.
146 E8 Arnisdale Highland, Scotland U.K.
198 C2 Arnissa Greece
191 I8 Arno r. Italy
82 F5 Arno Bay S.A. Austr.
182 D4 Arnoia r. Spain
146 C6 Arnol Western Isles, Scotland U.K.
149 O7 Arnold Nottinghamshire, England U.K.
234 B6 Arnold MD U.S.A.
226 G3 Arnold MI U.S.A.
236 J6 Arnold MO U.S.A.
225 K4 Arnold's Cove Nfld and Lab. Can.
179 I6 Arnoldstein Austria
162 I1 Arnon r. France
Arnon r. Jordan see Mawjib, Wādī al
177 J3 Arnót Hungary
234 A1 Arnot PA U.S.A.
227 O1 Arnoux, Lac l. Que. Can.
140 P1 Arnøya i. Norway
Arnoya r. Spain see Arnoia
224 E4 Arnprior Ont. Can.
148 I1 Arnprior Stirling, Scotland U.K.
169 F8 Arnsberg Ger.
169 F8 Arnsberg admin. reg. Ger.
169 F8 Arnsberger Wald hills Ger.
173 N3 Arnschwang Ger.
171 I8 Arnsdorf bei Dresden Ger.
169 K9 Arnstadt Ger.
227 O4 Arnstein Ont. Can.
171 A11 Arnstein Ger.
173 N4 Arnstorf Ger.
227 O1 Arntfield Que. Can.
183 M2 Arnuero Spain
251 E3 Aro r. Venez.
247 I8 Aroa Venez.
79 □9a Aroa, Pointe pt Moorea Fr. Polynesia
212 C5 Aroab Namibia
261 G3 Arocena Arg.
184 F5 Aroche Spain
184 E4 Aroche, Sierra de hills Spain
255 B7 Aroeira Brazil
182 D7 Arões Aveiro Port.
182 D6 Arões Braga Port.
177 J4 Ároktő Hungary
224 C3 Aroland Ont. Can.
190 C3 Arolla Switz.
169 H8 Arolsen Ger.
203 H6 Aroma Sudan
240 K5 Aromas CA U.S.A.
159 J5 Aron France
160 C3 Aron r. France
159 J5 Aron r. France
116 F7 Aron Madh. Prad. India
216 □3a Arona Tenerife Canary Is
190 F4 Arona Italy
233 □R2 Aroostook N.B. Can.
233 □R2 Aroostook r. ME U.S.A.
78 □6 Aropa P.N.G.
77 H2 Arorae i. Gilbert Is Kiribati
81 □3 Arorangi Rarotonga Cook Is
Arore i. Gilbert Is Kiribati see Arorae
92 D5 Aroroy Masbate Phil.
242 E3 Aros r. Mex.
182 D5 Arosa Port.
190 H2 Arosa Switz.
Arosa, Ría de est. Spain see Arousa, Ría de
Arossi i. Solomon Is see San Cristobal
182 D7 Arouca Port.
247 □7 Arouca Trin. and Tob.
202 D5 Arouelli well Chad
182 C3 Arousa, Illa de i. Spain
182 B4 Arousa, Ría de est. Spain
129 F6 Arp'a r. Armenia
129 E5 Arpa r. Armenia/Turkey
121 P7 Arpa Kyrg.
127 K3 Arpaçay Turkey
128 C2 Arpaçsakarlar Turkey
156 D6 Arpajon France
163 I6 Arpajon-sur-Cère France
193 L4 Arpino Italy
Arpinum Italy see Arpino
Arqalyq Kazakh. see Arkalyk
193 K2 Arquata del Tronto Italy
190 F6 Arquata Scrivia Italy
163 I10 Arques Languedoc-Roussillon France
156 D2 Arques Nord-Pas-de-Calais France
186 K4 Arques, Puig d' hill Spain
156 B4 Arques-la-Bataille France
185 M4 Arquillos Spain
213 G4 Arquipélago de Bazaruto, Parque Nacional de nat. park Moz.
216 □1 Arquipélago dos Açores aut. reg. N. Atlantic Ocean
123 K9 Arra r. Pak.
128 D7 Ar Rabbah Jordan
184 B3 Arrábida, Parque Natural da nature res. Port.
85 H9 Arrabury Qld Austr.
173 N3 Arrach Ger.
157 M6 Arracourt France
203 G3 Ar Radīsīyah Baḩrī Egypt
158 F6 Arradon France
124 G3 Ar Raghbah Saudi Arabia
206 E5 Arrah Côte d'Ivoire
Arrah Bihar India see Ara
127 K7 Ar Raḩḩālīyah Iraq
124 G9 Ar Rāhidah Yemen
254 D5 Arraias Brazil
254 B4 Arraias r. Brazil
254 D5 Arraias, Serra de hills Brazil
184 D3 Arraiolos Port.
127 K7 Ar Ramādī Iraq
128 D9 Ar Ramlah Jordan
147 F7 Arra Mountains hills Ireland
128 E6 Ar Ramthā Jordan
146 F11 Arran i. Scotland U.K.
157 K5 Arrancy-sur-Crusne France
184 A3 Arranhó Port.
128 H3 Ar Raqqah Syria
128 G2 Ar Raqqah governorate Syria
210 D3 Arraro well Eth.
156 E3 Arras France
124 D4 Ar Ra's al Abyaḑ pt Saudi Arabia
183 P2 Arrasate Spain
Arrasate Spain see Arrasate
163 D10 Arras-en-Lavedan France
128 D8 Ar Rashādīyah Jordan
124 F3 Ar Rass Saudi Arabia
128 E4 Ar Rastān Syria
163 F7 Arrats r. France
163 B9 Arraute-Charritte France
127 K9 Ar Rawḑ well Saudi Arabia
124 E2 Ar Rawḑah Ḩā'il Saudi Arabia
124 F5 Ar Rawḑah Makkah Saudi Arabia
125 H8 Ar Rawḑah Yemen
124 F5 Ar Rawshan Saudi Arabia
125 I8 Ar Rāwuk Yemen
125 L4 Ar Rayḩānī Oman
124 G4 Ar Rayn Saudi Arabia
125 J3 Ar Rayyān Qatar
124 D4 Ar Rayyān Al Madīnah Saudi Arabia
124 D5 Ar Rayyān Makkah Saudi Arabia
163 E10 Arreau France
250 D4 Arrecifal Col.
216 □3c Arrecife Lanzarote Canary Is
261 G4 Arrecifes Arg.
183 M2 Arredondo Spain
158 C5 Arrée, Monts d' hills France
156 I7 Arrentières France
142 I6 Arresø l. Denmark
Arretium Italy see Arezzo
179 I6 Arriach Austria
245 N9 Arriagá Mex.
244 F4 Arriaga Mex.
185 I7 Arriate Spain
261 G4 Arribeños Arg.
216 □3c Arrieta Lanzarote Canary Is
127 M8 Ar Rifā'ī Iraq
182 D7 Arrifana Aveiro Port.
182 D8 Arrifana Coimbra Port.
182 F7 Arrifana Guarda Port.
216 □1b Arrifes São Miguel Azores
156 I6 Arrigny France
183 O2 Arrigorriaga Spain
127 L8 Ar Rihāb salt flat Iraq
125 K5 Ar Rimāl des. Saudi Arabia
232 G11 Arrington VA U.S.A.
87 C10 Arrino W.A. Austr.
183 J2 Arriondas Spain
124 H3 Ar Riyāḑ Saudi Arabia
124 G3 Ar Riyāḑ prov. Saudi Arabia
204 B4 Arriyd, Sabkhat salt pan Western Sahara
185 J2 Arroba de los Montes Spain
182 H8 Arrobuey mt. Spain
146 G10 Arrochar Argyll and Bute, Scotland U.K.
258 G4 Arroio Grande Brazil
159 J3 Arromanches-les-Bains France
184 E2 Arronches Port.
193 J2 Arrone Italy
192 H3 Arrone r. Italy
193 I4 Arrone r. Italy
183 P3 Arroniz Spain
163 D8 Arros r. France
190 E7 Arroscia r. Italy
156 B7 Arrou France
160 D4 Arroux r. France
226 E1 Arrow r. Ont. Can.
150 G3 Arrow r. England U.K.
147 F4 Arrow, Lough l. Ireland
238 J3 Arrow Creek r. MT U.S.A.
226 D1 Arrow Lake Ont. Can.
81 E10 Arrowsmith, Mount South I. N.Z.
84 F2 Arrowsmith, Point N.T. Austr.
81 C11 Arrowtown South I. N.Z.
183 L3 Arroyal Spain
261 G4 Arroy Dulce Arg.
261 F2 Arroyito Córdoba Arg.
260 D3 Arroyito Mendoza Arg.
247 □1 Arroyo Puerto Rico
184 F1 Arroyo de la Luz Spain
184 G3 Arroyo de San Serván Spain
240 L6 Arroyo Grande CA U.S.A.
184 G4 Arroyomolinos de León Spain
261 G3 Arroyo Seco Arg.
244 F8 Arroyo Seco Guerrero Mex.
245 H4 Arroyo Seco Querétaro Mex.
253 F6 Arroyos-y-Esteros Para.
124 D4 Ar Rubaḑ Saudi Arabia
124 G2 Ar Rubay'iyah Saudi Arabia
253 F3 Arruda Brazil
184 A3 Arruda dos Vinhos Port.
261 G2 Arrufó Arg.
124 F3 Ar Rumādīyat Saudi Arabia
125 J3 Ar Rumaythah Bahrain
127 L8 Ar Rumaythah Iraq
128 D6 Ar Rummān Jordan
124 H1 Ar Ruq'ī well Saudi Arabia
128 G3 Ar Ruşāfah Syria
128 E6 Ar Ruşayfah Jordan
125 M4 Ar Rustāq Oman
127 J7 Ar Ruţbah Iraq
202 C3 Ar Ruwaybāt well Libya
124 G2 Ar Ruwayḑah Ar Riyāḑ Saudi Arabia
124 G4 Ar Ruwayḑah Ar Riyāḑ Saudi Arabia
128 F3 Ar Ruwayḑah Syria
84 F6 Arruwurra Aboriginal Land res. N.T. Austr.
157 L5 Arry France
122 B3 Ars Iran
199 K6 Arsaköy Turkey
122 F1 Ärsarybaba Erezi hills Turkm.
186 I3 Arsèguel Spain
122 E7 Arsenajān Iran
222 H1 Arseno Lake N.W.T. Can.
162 A3 Ars-en-Ré France
100 M5 Arsent'evka Rus. Fed.
100 H6 Arsen'yev Rus. Fed.
139 T8 Arsen'yevo Rus. Fed.
121 O2 Arshaly Kazakh.
121 S3 Arshaly Kazakh.
138 M7 Arshanskaye Wzvyshsha hills Belarus
191 L4 Arsiè Italy
191 K4 Arsiero Italy
114 E6 Arsikere Karnataka India
129 A5 Arsin Turkey
134 J4 Arsk Rus. Fed.
Arslanbob Kyrg. see Arstanban
193 K3 Arsoli Italy
160 F5 Ars-sur-Formans France
157 L5 Ars-sur-Moselle France
123 O1 Arstanban Kyrg.
78 □5 Art, Île i. New Caledonia
198 B3 Arta Greece
187 L8 Artà Spain
183 Q3 Artajona Spain
129 G3 Art'ana Georgia
187 E8 Artana Spain
190 C4 Artanavaz r. Italy
159 M7 Artannes-sur-Indre France
129 F6 Artashat Armenia
243 I5 Arteaga Coahuila Mex.
244 E7 Arteaga Michoacán Mex.
100 H7 Artem Rus. Fed.
160 H5 Artemare France
246 B2 Artemisa Cuba
198 D5 Artemisia Greece
137 R6 Artemivka Donets'ka Oblast' Ukr.
137 Q4 Artemivka Kharkivs'ka Oblast' Ukr.
137 O4 Artemivka Poltavs'ka Oblast' Ukr.
137 R5 Artemivs'k Donets'ka Oblast' Ukr.
137 R5 Artemivs'k Luhans'ka Oblast' Ukr.
Artemovsk Ukr. see Artemivs'k
131 M4 Artemovskiy Irkutskaya Oblast' Rus. Fed.
100 H7 Artemovskiy Primorskiy Kray Rus. Fed.
191 L3 Artèn Italy
193 J4 Artena Italy
156 C7 Artenay France
171 D8 Artern (Unstrut) Ger.
186 I4 Artés Spain
186 H4 Artesa de Segre Spain
241 W9 Artesia AZ U.S.A.
239 L10 Artesia NM U.S.A.
190 F1 Arth Switz.
163 I8 Arthès France
163 D9 Arthez-d'Asson France
163 C9 Arthez-de-Béarn France
159 O8 Arthon France
158 H7 Arthon-en-Retz France
87 C8 Arthur r. W.A. Austr.
227 N6 Arthur Ont. Can.
236 E5 Arthur NE U.S.A.
232 B12 Arthur TN U.S.A.
82 F4 Arthur, Lake salt flat S.A. Austr.
215 J8 Arthur, Lake S. Africa
232 E8 Arthur, Lake PA U.S.A.
83 K9 Arthur Lake Tas. Austr.
83 J9 Arthur Pieman Protected Area nature res. Tas. Austr.
85 M7 Arthur Point Qld Austr.
81 F9 Arthur's Pass South I. N.Z.
81 F9 Arthur's Pass National Park South I. N.Z.
246 F1 Arthur's Town Cat I. Bahamas
148 D3 Articlave Northern Ireland U.K.
186 D2 Artieda Spain
186 G2 Arties Spain
148 C4 Artigarvan Northern Ireland U.K.
262 U2 Artigas research stn Antarctica
261 I2 Artigas Uru.
261 I2 Artigas dept Uru.
163 G9 Artigat France
129 E5 Art'ik Armenia
223 I2 Artillery Lake N.W.T. Can.
212 E5 Artisia Botswana
163 C9 Artix France
138 J1 Artjärvi Fin.
168 J4 Artlenburg Ger.
190 I4 Artogne Italy
156 C2 Artois reg. France
156 C2 Artois, Collines d' hills France
127 K4 Artos Dağı mt. Turkey
126 H3 Artova Turkey
186 □ Artrutx, Cap d' c. Spain
Artsakh aut. reg. Azer. see Dağlıq Qarabağ
106 G4 Arts Bogd Uul mts Mongolia
Artsiz Ukr. see Artsyz
136 I8 Artsyz Ukr.
161 I9 Artuby r. France
Artur de Paiva Angola see Kuvango
110 C7 Artux Xinjiang China
127 J3 Artvin Turkey
129 C4 Artvin prov. Turkey
122 H3 Artyk Turkm.
183 N2 Artziniega Spain
208 F4 Aru Dem. Rep. Congo
91 H8 Aru, Kepulauan is Indon.
182 F4 A Rúa Spain
210 A4 Arua Uganda
250 E6 Aruajá Brazil
254 C5 Aruanã Brazil
247 □9 Aruba terr. West Indies
216 □3f Arucas Gran Canaria Canary Is
129 F5 Aruch Armenia
163 D9 Arudy France
79 □9a Arue Tahiti Fr. Polynesia
256 D5 Arujá Brazil
78 □6 Aruliho Guadalcanal Solomon Is
251 F6 Arumã Brazil
102 □1 Arume Okinawa Japan
102 □1 Arume-wan b. Okinawa Japan
117 K6 Arun r. Nepal
117 N6 Arunachal Pradesh state India
81 F10 Arundel South I. N.Z.
151 K6 Arundel West Sussex, England U.K.
107 S3 Arun Gol r. China
Arun Qi Nei Mongol China see Naji
114 F8 Aruppukkottai Tamil Nadu India
216 □3a Arure La Gomera Canary Is
93 B3 Arus, Tanjung pt Indon.
211 C5 Arusha Tanz.
211 C5 Arusha admin. reg. Tanz.
211 C5 Arusha National Park Tanz.
95 I6 Arut r. Indon.
251 E5 Aruti Brazil
208 D4 Aruwimi r. Dem. Rep. Congo
236 C6 Arvada CO U.S.A.
147 G5 Arvagh Ireland
161 I6 Arvan r. France
106 H3 Arvayheer Mongolia
160 I4 Arve r. France
162 B4 Arvert France
163 D6 Arveyres France
116 G9 Arvi Mahar. India
223 M2 Arviat Nunavut Can.
230 L1 Arvida Que. Can.
140 O4 Arvidsjaur Sweden
161 B8 Arvieu France
161 J7 Arvieux France
142 I2 Arvika Sweden
140 P1 Årviksand Norway
240 N6 Arvin CA U.S.A.
195 K5 Arvo, Lago l. Italy
232 G11 Arvonia VA U.S.A.
124 G4 Arwā' Saudi Arabia
128 D4 Arwād i. Syria
93 E7 Arwala Maluku Indon.
107 P3 Arxan Nei Mongol China
110 G5 Arxan Xinjiang China
Aryanah Tunisia see L'Ariana
134 K4 Aryazh Rus. Fed.
121 M1 Arykbalyk Kazakh.
Aryqbayq Kazakh. see Arykbalyk
121 M6 Arys' Kazakh.
121 M6 Arys' r. Kazakh.
121 L5 Arys, Ozero salt l. Kazakh.
192 C5 Arzachena Sardegna Italy
163 D8 Arzacq-Arraziguet France
135 H5 Arzamas Rus. Fed.
192 D8 Arzana Sardegna Italy
125 K3 Arzanah i. U.A.E.
158 E6 Arzano France
169 E10 Arzbach Ger.
171 F10 Arzberg Bayern Ger.
171 H7 Arzberg Sachsen Ger.
163 I9 Arzens France
205 E2 Arzew Alg.
169 B10 Arzfeld Ger.
135 I7 Arzgir Rus. Fed.
191 K4 Arzignano Italy
Arzila Morocco see Asilah
178 C5 Arzl im Pitztal Austria
161 D6 Arzon r. France
182 D3 Arzúa Spain
165 I6 As Belgium
176 B1 Aš Czech Rep.
211 C5 Asa waterhole Kenya
142 I4 Åsa Sweden
142 G4 Asaa Denmark
214 B1 Asab Namibia
105 G6 Asaba Japan
207 G5 Asaba Nigeria
128 G2 Asad, Buḩayrat al resr Syria
123 N4 Asadābād Afgh.
122 C4 Asadābād Hamadān Iran
122 H4 Asadābād Khorāsān Iran
122 E6 Asadābād Yazd Iran
129 H5 Aşağı Ağcakänd Azer.
129 G4 Aşağı Äskipara Azer.
129 G5 Aşağı Ayıblı Azer.
129 E5 Aşağı Dağ mt. Turkey
129 E6 Aşağıdalören Turkey
199 K5 Aşağıkaraçay Turkey
129 C5 Aşağıkatıklı Turkey
129 I4 Aşağı Köynük Azer.
129 E6 Aşağıküpkıran Turkey
129 H5 Aşağı Oratağ Azer.
129 F7 Aşağısağmallı Turkey
129 C6 Aşağısöylemez Turkey
206 D5 Asagny, Parc National d' nat. park Côte d'Ivoire
104 A5 Asago Japan
94 C3 Asahan r. Indon.
104 F5 Asahi Aichi Japan
105 M4 Asahi Chiba Japan
104 D4 Asahi Fukui Japan
104 F3 Asahi Gifu Japan
105 M3 Asahi Ibaraki Japan
105 K5 Asahi Kanagawa Japan
104 E5 Asahi Mie Japan
105 G3 Asahi Nagano Japan
104 G2 Asahi Toyama Japan
102 Q8 Asahi-dake mt. Japan
102 T3 Asahi-dake vol. Japan
103 K12 Asahi-gawa r. Japan
102 T3 Asahikawa Japan
105 J1 Asahi-take mt. Japan
105 K4 Asaka Japan
121 O7 Asaka Uzbek.
105 L1 Asakawa Japan
104 E5 Asake-gawa r. Japan
128 A9 'Asal Egypt
210 D1 Āsalē l. Eth.
122 C3 Asālem Iran
122 E6 'Asalū, Chāh-e well Iran
104 E7 Asamaga-take hill Japan
206 E5 Asamankese Ghana
105 I3 Asama-yama vol. Japan
78 □1 Asan Guam
206 E5 Asankranguaa Ghana
101 E10 Asan-man b. S. Korea
117 K8 Asansol W. Bengal India
206 E5 Asanwenso Ghana
105 K4 Asao Japan
107 O3 Asar Nei Mongol China
105 H3 Asashina Japan
163 C9 Asasp-Arros France
78 □2 Asau Samoa
Asava i. Fiji see Yasawa
210 D2 Āsayita Eth.
169 D9 Asbach Ger.
173 J4 Asbach-Bäumenheim Ger.
230 L3 Asbestos Que. Can.
Asbestos Hill Que. Can. see Purtuniq
214 G5 Asbestos Mountains S. Africa
210 D2 Āsbe Teferi Eth.
143 L3 Åsbro Sweden
233 K8 Asbury Park NJ U.S.A.
163 A9 Ascain France
Ascalon Israel see Ashqelon
193 O7 Ascea Italy
261 G4 Ascensión Arg.
253 E3 Ascensión Bol.
242 F2 Ascensión Chihuahua Mex.
245 H1 Ascensión Nuevo León Mex.
Ascension atoll Micronesia see Pohnpei
247 □10 Ascension Curaçao Neth. Antilles
216 □2a Ascension i. S. Atlantic Ocean
243 P8 Ascensión, Bahía de la b. Mex.
173 N3 Ascha Ger.
173 M3 Ascha r. Ger.
179 J3 Aschach an der Donau Austria
172 G2 Aschaffenburg Ger.
178 E5 Aschau im Zillertal Austria
173 M6 Aschau in Chiemgau Ger.
179 K3 Aschbach Markt Austria

Ascheberg to Aumont-Aubrac
281

169 E7 Ascheberg Ger.
168 J2 Ascheberg (Holstein) Ger.
173 O4 Aschenstein hill Ger.
156 D7 Aschères-le-Marché France
171 D7 Aschersleben Ger.
173 L5 Aschheim Ger.
191 L9 Asciano Italy
195 K5 Ascione, Colle d' pass Italy
192 C3 Asco Corse France
261 E2 Ascochinga Arg.
193 L2 Ascoli Piceno Italy
193 L2 Ascoli Piceno prov. Italy
193 P5 Ascoli Satriano Italy
190 F3 Ascona Switz.
151 K5 Ascot Windsor and Maidenhead, England U.K.
252 C5 Ascotán Chile
252 C5 Ascotán, Salar de salt flat Chile
163 H10 Ascou France
182 C4 As Covas Spain
Asculum Italy see Ascoli Piceno
Asculum Picenum Italy see Ascoli Piceno
233 M5 Ascutney VT U.S.A.
113 □1 Asdhu i. N. Male Maldives
Asdu i. N. Male Maldives see Asdhu
140 M2 Åse Norway
Āseb Eritrea see Assab
143 L4 Åseda Sweden
205 F4 Asedjrad plat. Alg.
120 E1 Asekeyevo Rus. Fed.
210 C3 Āsela Eth.
140 N4 Åsele Sweden
141 L6 Åsen Sweden
210 C3 Āsendabo Eth.
168 H5 Asendorf Niedersachsen Ger.
168 I4 Asendorf Niedersachsen Ger.
197 M8 Asenovgrad Bulg.
142 D3 Åseral Norway
138 J2 Aseri Estonia
182 C3 A Serra de Outes Spain
244 C2 Aserradero los Charcos Mex.
122 G4 Aşfāk Iran
128 E6 Aşfar, Jabal al mt. Jordan
128 E5 Aşfar, Tall al hill Syria
156 H5 Asfeld France
151 K2 Asfordby Leicestershire, England U.K.
122 H3 Aşgabat Turkm.
140 □C1 Ásgarður Iceland
151 O5 Ash Kent, England U.K.
151 K5 Ash Surrey, England U.K.
134 L5 Asha Rus. Fed.
104 G2 Ashahi-dake mt. Japan
206 E5 Ashanti admin. reg. Ghana
134 L4 Ashap Rus. Fed.
124 G3 Asharat Saudi Arabia
124 F3 Ash 'arīyah Saudi Arabia
235 L2 Ashaway RI U.S.A.
147 J5 Ashbourne Ireland
149 N7 Ashbourne Derbyshire, England U.K.
231 F10 Ashburn GA U.S.A.
87 C6 Ashburton watercourse W.A. Austr.
81 F10 Ashburton South I. N.Z.
81 F11 Ashburton r. South I. N.Z.
150 E6 Ashburton Devon, England U.K.
226 H1 Ashburton Bay Ont. Can.
84 D5 Ashburton Range hills N.T. Austr.
151 I4 Ashbury Oxfordshire, England U.K.
151 J2 Ashby de la Zouch Leicestershire, England U.K.
121 L5 Ashchikol', Ozero salt l. Kazakh.
121 N6 Ashchikol', Ozero salt l. Kazakh.
150 H4 Ashchurch Gloucestershire, England U.K.
Ashchysay Kazakh. see Achisay
150 G5 Ashcott Somerset, England U.K.
222 F5 Ashcroft B.C. Can.
128 C7 Ashdod Israel
237 H9 Ashdown AR U.S.A.
151 M5 Ashdown Forest reg. England U.K.
231 H8 Asheboro NC U.S.A.
237 G8 Asher OK U.S.A.
223 L5 Ashern Man. Can.
231 F8 Asheville NC U.S.A.
138 M4 Ashevo Rus. Fed.
224 C2 Asheweig r. Ont. Can.
83 M3 Ashford N.S.W. Austr.
147 J6 Ashford Ireland
148 E8 Ashford r. Ireland
151 I6 Ashford Hampshire, England U.K.
151 N5 Ashford Kent, England U.K.
151 L5 Ashford Surrey, England U.K.
241 T6 Ash Fork AZ U.S.A.
80 J7 Ashhurst North I. N.Z.
102 T3 Ashibetsu Japan
105 I4 Ashigawa Japan
105 J3 Ashikaga Japan
103 H14 Ashikita Japan
151 N2 Ashill Norfolk, England U.K.
149 N3 Ashington Northumberland, England U.K.
105 J5 Ashino-ko l. Japan
105 J2 Ashio Japan
105 J3 Ashio-sanchi mts Japan
226 F6 Ashippun WI U.S.A.
102 S6 Ashiro Japan
105 I4 Ashiwada Japan
104 B6 Ashiya Japan
103 K14 Ashizuri-misaki pt Japan
103 J14 Ashizuri-Uwakai Kokuritsu-kōen nat. park Japan
122 F6 Ashkazar Iran
Ashkelon Israel see Ashqelon
Ashkhabad Turkm. see Aşgabat
Ashkhabadskaya Oblast' admin. div. Turkm. see Ahal
202 B3 Ashkīdah Libya
146 K12 Ashkirk Scottish Borders, Scotland U.K.
226 G9 Ashkum IL U.S.A.
123 N4 Ashkun reg. Afgh.
231 E9 Ashland AL U.S.A.
237 F7 Ashland KS U.S.A.
232 C10 Ashland KY U.S.A.
233 □Q2 Ashland ME U.S.A.
237 K8 Ashland MS U.S.A.
238 K4 Ashland MT U.S.A.
236 G5 Ashland NE U.S.A.
233 N5 Ashland NH U.S.A.
232 C8 Ashland OH U.S.A.
238 C5 Ashland OR U.S.A.
234 C3 Ashland PA U.S.A.
232 H11 Ashland VA U.S.A.
226 D3 Ashland WI U.S.A.
231 D7 Ashland City TN U.S.A.
83 L3 Ashley N.S.W. Austr.
81 G10 Ashley r. South I. N.Z.
151 M3 Ashley Cambridgeshire, England U.K.
226 I8 Ashley IN U.S.A.
226 J6 Ashley MI U.S.A.
236 F2 Ashley ND U.S.A.
232 C8 Ashley OH U.S.A.
234 D2 Ashley PA U.S.A.
86 G2 Ashmore and Cartier Islands terr. Austr.
86 G2 Ashmore Reef Ashmore & Cartier Is Austr.
138 I7 Ashmyanskaye Wzvyshsha hills Belarus
138 I7 Ashmyany Hrodzyenskaya Voblasts' Belarus
138 J7 Ashmyany Hrodzyenskaya Voblasts' Belarus
116 F7 Ashoknagar Madh. Prad. India
102 U3 Ashoro Japan
129 E4 Ashots'k' Armenia
124 G7 Ashqar, Barqā al reg. Yemen
128 C7 Ashqelon Israel
124 F6 Ash Sha'ār Saudi Arabia
127 K8 Ash Shabakah Iraq
203 F4 Ash Shabb well Egypt
127 J5 Ash Shaddādah Syria
124 E5 Ash Shafa Saudi Arabia
128 A8 Ash Shallūfah Egypt
Ash Sham Syria see Dimashq
125 M2 Ash Sha'm U.A.E.
127 L8 Ash Shanāfīyah Iraq
127 J9 Ash Shaqīq well Saudi Arabia
124 G3 Ash Sha'rā' Saudi Arabia
128 D8 Ash Sharāh mts Jordan
125 H7 Ash Sharawrah Saudi Arabia
125 L3 Ash Shāriqah U.A.E.
127 K6 Ash Sharqāţ Iraq
126 E8 Ash Sharqīyah governorate Egypt
125 N5 Ash Sharqīyah admin. reg. Oman
125 N4 Ash Sharqīyah reg. Oman
125 J5 Ash Sharqīyah prov. Saudi Arabia
127 M8 Ash Shaţrah Iraq
128 A9 Ash Shaţţ Egypt
128 D8 Ash Shawbak Jordan
124 E1 Ash Shaybānī well Saudi Arabia
124 B1 ash Shaykh Humayd Saudi Arabia
128 G3 Ash Shaykh Ibrāhīm Syria
124 G9 Ash Shaykh 'Uthman Yemen
128 F9 Ash Shiblīyāt hill Saudi Arabia
125 I8 Ash Shiḩr Yemen
125 M3 Ash Shināş Oman
125 K6 Ash Shişar well Oman
124 F2 Ash Shu'āybah Saudi Arabia
124 G1 Ash Shu'bah Saudi Arabia
124 F3 Ash Shubaykīyah Saudi Arabia
125 H2 Ash Shumlūl Saudi Arabia
124 F7 Ash Shuqayq Saudi Arabia
Ash Shurayf Saudi Arabia see Khaybar
202 B2 Ash Shuwayrif Libya
116 F8 Ashta Madh. Prad. India
114 D4 Ashta Mahar. India
232 E7 Ashtabula OH U.S.A.
129 F5 Ashtarak Armenia
114 D3 Ashti Mahar. India
114 F3 Ashti Mahar. India
116 G9 Ashti Mahar. India
214 E9 Ashton S. Africa
247 □3 Ashton St Vincent
149 L7 Ashton Cheshire, England U.K.
238 I4 Ashton ID U.S.A.
226 E8 Ashton IL U.S.A.
234 A6 Ashton MD U.S.A.
149 M7 Ashton-under-Lyne Greater Manchester, England U.K.
129 I4 Ashty Rus. Fed.
225 H2 Ashuanipi r. Nfld and Lab. Can.
225 H2 Ashuanipi Lake Nfld and Lab. Can.
230 K1 Ashuapmushuan r. Que. Can.
224 F3 Ashuapmushuan, Réserve Faunique nature res. Que. Can.
Ashur Iraq see Ash Sharqāţ
151 I6 Ashurst Hampshire, England U.K.
151 M5 Ashurst Kent, England U.K.
231 D9 Ashville AL U.S.A.
233 □Q4 Ashville ME U.S.A.
232 G8 Ashville PA U.S.A.
226 D3 Ashwabay, Mount hill WI U.S.A.
226 F5 Ashwaubenon WI U.S.A.
150 G5 Ashwick Somerset, England U.K.
128 E4 'Āşī r. Lebanon alt. 'Āşī, Nahr al (Syria), alt. Asi (Turkey), hist. Orontes
128 E3 Asi r. Turkey alt. 'Āşī (Lebanon), alt. 'Āşī, Nahr al (Syria), hist. Orontes
128 E2 'Āşī, Nahr al r. Syria alt. 'Āşī (Lebanon), alt. Asi (Turkey), hist. Orontes
88 Asia continent
191 L4 Asiago Italy
92 D5 Asid Gulf Masbate Phil.
244 E3 Asientos Mex.
114 F3 Asifabad Andhra Prad. India
115 I3 Asika Orissa India
141 R6 Asikkala Fin.
204 D2 Asilah Morocco
252 C3 Asillo Peru
198 G7 Asimi Kriti Greece
186 C3 Asín Spain
192 B6 Asinara, Golfo dell' b. Sardegna Italy
192 A5 Asinara, Isola i. Sardegna Italy
116 E7 Asind Rajasthan India
130 J4 Asino Rus. Fed.
139 N7 Asintorf Belarus
138 L8 Asipovichy Belarus
122 E8 Asīr Iran
124 E5 'Asīr prov. Saudi Arabia
124 E5 'Asīr reg. Saudi Arabia
Asisium Italy see Assisi
138 E1 Askainen Fin.
116 E2 Askale Jammu and Kashmir
127 J4 Aşkale Turkey
137 M7 Askaniya Nova Ukr.
137 M7 Askaniya Nova Zapovidnyk nature res. Ukr.
120 H1 Askarovo Rus. Fed.
147 E7 Askeaton Ireland
215 L7 Askeaton S. Africa
142 G2 Asker Norway
129 A7 Asker Dağı mt. Turkey
149 O6 Askern South Yorkshire, England U.K.
143 K3 Askersund Sweden
214 E2 Askham S. Africa
147 F4 Askill Ireland
142 H2 Askim Norway
127 K5 Askī Mawşil Iraq
134 L4 Askino Rus. Fed.
207 I4 Askira Nigeria
146 D9 Askival hill Scotland U.K.
98 F1 Askiz Rus. Fed.
198 E5 Asklipieio Greece
198 E5 Asklipieio Epidavrou tourist site Greece
168 L1 Askø i. Denmark
141 R6 Askola Fin.
143 M2 Äsköping Sweden
198 E2 Askos Greece
116 H5 Askot Uttaranchal India
142 B1 Askøy i. Norway
214 E10 Askraal S. Africa
141 H6 Askvoll Norway
129 H6 Askyaran Azer.
124 G5 Aslam, Wādī watercourse Saudi Arabia
199 K3 Aslanapa Turkey
122 B2 Aşlāndūz Iran
138 M8 Aslik r. Belarus
Aslóközpont Hungary see Mórahalom
123 N4 Asmar Afgh.
123 N4 Asmar reg. Afgh.
124 F6 Asmar reg. Saudi Arabia
203 H6 Asmara Eritrea
124 E2 Asmarah, Jabal mts Saudi Arabia
182 D2 As Mariñas reg. Spain
Āsmera Eritrea see Asmara
143 K5 Åsnen l. Sweden
182 D2 As Neves Galicia Spain
182 D4 As Neves Galicia Spain
182 F3 As Nogais Spain
193 L1 Aso r. Italy
105 L4 Asō Japan
251 G4 Asoenangka Brazil
103 I14 Aso-Kuju Kokuritsu-kōen nat. park Japan
190 I5 Asola Italy
191 L4 Asolo Italy
185 P2 Asomadilla hill Spain
117 O5 Asonli Arun. Prad. India
198 D5 Asopos r. Greece
198 E4 Asopos r. Greece
210 B2 Āsosa Eth.
103 I14 Aso-san vol. Japan
203 H4 Asoteriba, Jebel mt. Sudan
238 F3 Asotin WA U.S.A.
177 I5 Ásotthalom Hungary
103 G12 Asō-wan b. Japan
134 L4 Aspa Rus. Fed.
179 H3 Aspach Austria
179 N4 Aspang-Markt Austria
122 C3 Aspar Iran
121 O6 Aspara Kazakh.
179 N2 Asparn an der Zaya Austria
197 P8 Asparukhovo Bulg.
140 M5 Aspås Sweden
149 K4 Aspatria Cumbria, England U.K.
187 D11 Aspe Spain
163 C10 Aspe, Vallée d' val. France
140 N5 Aspeå Sweden
239 K7 Aspen CO U.S.A.
164 H5 Asperen Neth.
142 H2 Asperen l. Norway
172 G4 Asperg Ger.
237 E9 Aspermont TX U.S.A.
234 A5 Aspers PA U.S.A.
163 F9 Aspet France
163 E10 Aspin, Col d' pass France
129 E4 Aspindza Georgia
161 C9 Aspiran France
81 C11 Aspiring, Mount South I. N.Z.
182 E2 As Pontes de García Rodríguez Spain
161 H7 Aspremont France
161 H7 Aspres-sur-Buëch France
163 I6 Asprières France
Aspro, Cape Cyprus see Aspron, Cape
198 B3 Asprokavos, Akrotirio pt Kerkyra Greece
195 J7 Aspromonte, Parco Nazionale dell' nat. park Italy
128 A4 Aspron, Cape Cyprus
Aspropotamos r. Greece see Acheloos
198 E2 Asprovalta Greece
116 E8 Aspur Rajasthan India
223 J4 Asquith Sask. Can.
182 F2 As Rodrigas Spain
191 K4 Assa r. Italy
204 C3 Assa Morocco
129 G2 Assa r. Rus. Fed.
128 F3 As Sa'an Syria
203 I6 Assab Eritrea
206 C2 Assaba admin. reg. Maur.
124 E2 Aş Sab'ān Saudi Arabia
128 H3 As Sabkhah Syria
125 I2 As Sabsab well Saudi Arabia
102 R5 Assabu Japan
128 E5 Aş Şafā lava field Syria
Aş Şafāqis Tunisia see Sfax
203 F2 Aş Şaff Egypt
128 D7 Aş Şāfī Jordan
128 F2 As Safīrah Syria
124 D3 Aş Şafrā Saudi Arabia
124 F2 Aş Şafrā Saudi Arabia
125 I2 Aş Şaḩāf Saudi Arabia
124 F8 Aş Şaḩīf Yemen
Aş Şaḩrā' des. Egypt/Libya see Libyan Desert
203 F3 Aş Şaḩrā' al Gharbīyah des. Egypt
203 G3 Aş Şaḩrā' ash Sharqīyah des. Egypt
207 H4 Assaiko Nigeria
Assake Uzbek. see Asaka
120 G6 Assake-Audan, Vpadina depr. Uzbek.
203 I7 'Assal, Lac l. Djibouti
125 H3 As Salamiyah Saudi Arabia
126 F8 Aş Şāliḩīyah Egypt
127 J6 Aş Şāliḩīyah Syria
126 B8 As Sallūm Egypt
127 L8 As Salmān Iraq
128 D6 As Salţ Jordan
117 M6 Assam state India
207 G2 Assamakka Niger
127 L8 As Samāwah Iraq
128 E6 As Samrā' Jordan
172 H3 Assamstadt Ger.
125 J5 Aş Şanām reg. Saudi Arabia
128 E5 Aş Şanamayn Syria
204 B4 Assaq watercourse Western Sahara
204 B4 As Saquia al Hamra watercourse Western Sahara
124 G2 As Sarīf well Saudi Arabia
202 D3 As Sarīr reg. Libya
163 D9 Assat France
233 J10 Assateague Island MD U.S.A.
233 J11 Assateague Island National Seashore nature res. VA U.S.A.
124 G4 As Sawādah reg. Saudi Arabia
125 L7 As Sawdā i. Oman
124 D2 Aş Şawrah Al Madīnah Saudi Arabia
124 B2 Aş Şawrah Tabūk Saudi Arabia
124 H4 As Sayḩ Saudi Arabia
124 E5 As Sayl al Kabīr Saudi Arabia
165 F7 Asse Belgium
161 H9 Asse r. France
214 I9 Assegaaibos S. Africa
192 C9 Assemini Sardegna Italy
164 K2 Assen Neth.
164 G4 Assendelft Neth.
165 E6 Assenede Belgium
142 F6 Assens Denmark
158 G7 Assérac France
193 L3 Assergi Italy
165 H8 Assesse Belgium
202 C2 As Sidrah Libya
163 H6 Assier France
125 N4 As Sīfah Oman
225 H2 Assigny, Lac l. Nfld and Lab. Can.
125 J3 As Sikak Saudi Arabia
125 J4 As Sila' U.A.E.
223 J5 Assiniboia Sask. Can.
223 L5 Assiniboine r. Man./Sask. Can.
222 H5 Assiniboine, Mount Alta/B.C. Can.
224 F3 Assinica, Réserve Faunique nature res. Que. Can.
256 B5 Assis Brazil
256 A6 Assis Chateaubriand Brazil
193 J1 Assisi Italy
169 F9 Aßlar Ger.
178 G6 Assling Austria
173 M6 Aßling Ger.
190 G4 Asso Italy
206 □ Assomada Santiago Cape Verde
217 □2 Assomption i. Aldabra Is Seychelles
163 D9 Asson France
194 G8 Assoro Sicilia Italy
205 F4 Assouf Mellene watercourse Alg.
127 M9 Aş Şubayḩīyah Kuwait
124 F6 As Subaykhah Saudi Arabia
125 I8 As Sufāl Yemen
124 G1 Aş Şufayrī well Saudi Arabia
128 G4 As Sukhnah Syria
127 L6 As Sulaymānīyah Iraq
127 L6 As Sulaymānīyah governorate Iraq
124 E2 As Sulaymī Saudi Arabia
124 G5 As Sulayyil Saudi Arabia
125 I3 Aş Şulb reg. Saudi Arabia
202 C2 As Sulţān Libya
184 E2 Assumar Port.
124 H2 Aş Şummān plat. Saudi Arabia
125 I5 Aş Şummān plat. Saudi Arabia
124 E5 As Sūq Saudi Arabia
As Sūrīyah country Asia see Syria
127 J6 Aş Şuwar Syria
128 E6 As Suwaydā' Syria
128 E6 As Suwaydā' governorate Syria
125 N4 As Suwayḩ Oman
125 M4 As Suwayq Oman
127 L7 Aş Şuwayrah Iraq
124 E4 As Suwayriqīyah Saudi Arabia
203 G2 As Suways Egypt
128 A9 As Suways governorate Egypt
124 G8 As Suwwādīyah Yemen
146 F6 Assynt, Loch l. Scotland U.K.
141 K6 Asta r. Norway
191 L3 Asta, Cima d' mt. Italy
Astacus Turkey see İzmit
163 F7 Astaffort France
199 H7 Astakida i. Greece
198 C4 Astakos Greece
Astalu Island Pak. see Astola Island
121 N2 Astana Kazakh.
122 C3 Astaneh Iran
122 C2 Āstārā Iran
163 E8 Astarac reg. France
163 F9 Astarac, Barrage de l' dam France
142 J1 Åsteby Sweden
179 J3 Asten Austria
165 I6 Asten Neth.
Asterabad Iran see Gorgān
190 E6 Asti Italy
190 E6 Asti prov. Italy
260 D2 Astica Arg.
191 L4 Astico r. Italy
177 L4 Aştileu Romania
252 C3 Astillero Peru
Astin Tag mts China see Altun Shan
Astipálaia i. Greece see Astypalaia
123 J9 Astola Island Pak.
163 H10 Aston r. France
215 I10 Aston Bay S. Africa
151 K4 Aston Clinton Buckinghamshire, England U.K.
116 E2 Astor Jammu and Kashmir
123 P4 Astor r. Pak.
256 B5 Astorga Brazil
182 H4 Astorga Spain
226 D9 Astoria IL U.S.A.
238 C3 Astoria OR U.S.A.
142 I5 Åstorp Sweden
217 □2 Astove i. Aldabra Is Seychelles
259 D7 Astra Arg.
Astrabad Iran see Gorgān
Astrakhan' Kazakh. see Astrakhanka
120 C4 Astrakhan' Rus. Fed.
Astrakhan' Bazar Azer. see Cälilabad
121 M2 Astrakhanka Kazakh.
137 O7 Astrakhanka Ukr.
Astrakhan Oblast admin. div. Rus. Fed. see Astrakhanskaya Oblast'
120 B4 Astrakhanskaya Oblast' admin. div. Rus. Fed.
138 I7 Astravyets Belarus
129 J5 Astraxanka Azer.
Astrida Rwanda see Butare
78 □6 Astrolabe, Cape Malaita Solomon Is
78 □5 Astrolabe, Récifs de l' rf New Caledonia
198 D5 Astros Greece
138 M6 Astrowna Belarus
138 H8 Astryna Belarus
139 O8 Astsyer r. Belarus
183 L4 Astudillo Spain
193 J5 Astura r. Italy
261 F5 Asturias Arg.
182 H1 Asturias airport Spain
182 H2 Asturias aut. comm. Spain
Asturica Augusta Spain see Astorga
151 I3 Astwood Bank Worcestershire, England U.K.
199 H6 Astypalaia Greece
199 H6 Astypalaia i. Greece
121 T3 Asubulak Kazakh.
Asūbulaq Kazakh. see Asubulak
78 □2 Asuisui, Cape Samoa
104 C7 Asuka Japan
104 F5 Asuke Japan
252 D2 Asunción Bol.
239 H11 Asunción r. Mex.
91 K3 Asuncion i. N. Mariana Is
253 F6 Asunción Para.
243 O10 Asunción Mita Guat.
143 O4 Åsunden i. Sweden
142 J4 Åsunden l. Sweden
143 L4 Åsunden l. Sweden
192 B8 Asuni Sardegna Italy
104 D3 Asuwa-gawa r. Japan
138 L5 Asvyeya Belarus
138 L5 Asvyeyskaye, Vozyera l. Belarus
210 A4 Aswa r. Uganda
125 M3 Aswad Oman
124 D5 Aswad, Ar Ra's al pt Saudi Arabia
125 L5 Aswad, Wādī watercourse Oman
203 G3 Aswān Egypt
124 A3 Aswān governorate Egypt
203 G3 Aswān, Khazzān dam Egypt
Aswan Dam Egypt see Aswān, Khazzān
203 F3 Asyūţ Egypt
126 E10 Asyūţ governorate Egypt
177 J3 Aszaló Hungary
79 □8a Ata i. Tonga
250 E3 Atabapo r. Col./Venez.
121 M6 Atabay Kazakh.
199 L5 Atabey Turkey
258 C2 Atacama admin. reg. Chile
258 C2 Atacama, Desierto de des. Chile
258 D2 Atacama, Puna de plat. Arg.
252 C5 Atacama, Salar de salt flat Chile
250 B4 Atacames Ecuador
250 C4 Ataco Col.
205 G4 Atafaitafa, Djebel mt. Alg.
81 □1 Atafu atoll Tokelau
81 □1 Atafu i. Tokelau
104 C5 Atago-san hill Japan
105 K5 Atago-yama hill Japan
79 □9a Ataiti Tahiti Fr. Polynesia
121 M7 Atakent Kazakh.
128 C2 Atakent Turkey
129 J5 Atakişili Azer.
205 G5 Atakor mts Alg.
207 F4 Atakora, Chaîne de l' mts Benin
207 F5 Atakpamé Togo
254 G4 Atalaia Brazil
184 B4 Atalaia hill Port.
184 B6 Atalaia, Ponta da pt Port.
250 D6 Atalaia do Norte Brazil
Atalándi Greece see Atalanti
198 E4 Atalanti Greece
242 □S13 Atalaya Panama
252 C3 Atalaya Madre de Dios Peru
252 B2 Atalaya Ucayali Peru
185 P6 Atalaya Arabe hill Spain
257 G3 Ataléia Brazil
76 C2 Atambua Timor Indon.
105 J5 Atami Japan
258 E3 Atamisqui Arg.
221 M3 Atammik Greenland
123 K3 Atamyrat Turkm.
Ataniya Turkey see Adana
177 J4 Átány Hungary
183 M4 Atapuerca tourist site Spain
93 D8 Atapupu Timor Indon.
124 H8 'Ataq Yemen
128 A9 'Atāqah, Jabal hill Egypt
183 K6 Ataquines Spain
204 B5 Atâr Maur.
96 C6 Ataran r. Myanmar
245 H4 Atarjea Mex.
Atas i. Cocos Is see South Island
240 L6 Atascadero CA U.S.A.
237 F11 Atascosa watercourse TX U.S.A.
121 N3 Atasu Kazakh.
79 □8a Atata i. Tonga
111 I7 Atatan He r. China
126 D3 Atatürk airport Turkey
199 J6 Atatürk Milli Parkı nat. park Turkey
93 D8 Ataúro, Ilha de i. East Timor
Atáviros mt. Rodos Greece see Attavyros
122 H1 Atayap Turkm.
128 B2 Atayurt Turkey
203 G5 Atbara Sudan
203 G5 Atbara r. Sudan
121 M2 Atbasar Kazakh.
121 P7 At-Bashy Kyrg.
237 J11 Atchafalaya Bay LA U.S.A.
236 H6 Atchison KS U.S.A.
234 F5 Atco NJ U.S.A.
183 Q6 Atea Spain
206 E5 Atebubu Ghana
183 Q6 Ateca Spain
182 E6 Atei Port.
182 F4 A Teixeira Spain
193 M4 Ateleta Italy
193 P6 Atella Italy
193 P6 Atella r. Italy
244 D5 Atemajac de Brizuela Mex.
105 I1 Atema-yama mt. Japan
252 C3 Aten Bol.
193 P7 Atena Lucana Italy
245 H7 Atenango del Río Mex.
244 C4 Atengo r. Mex.
244 C5 Atenguillo Mex.
244 C5 Atenguillo r. Mex.
244 D6 Atenquique Mex.
Ateransk Kazakh. see Atyrau
193 L3 Aterno r. Italy
122 E4 Āteshān Iran
123 I5 Āteshkhāneh, Kūh-e hill Afgh.
193 M3 Atessa Italy
124 G7 'Aţfayn, Wādī watercourse Yemen
234 D5 Atglen PA U.S.A.
165 E7 Ath Belgium
222 H4 Athabasca Alta Can.
222 I3 Athabasca r. Alta Can.
223 I3 Athabasca, Lake Alta/Sask. Can.
223 I3 Athabasca Sand Dunes Wilderness Provincial Park nature res. Sask. Can.
117 J9 Athagarh Orissa India
232 C10 Athalia OH U.S.A.
223 K4 Athapapuskow Lake Man. Can.
123 O6 Atharan Hazari Pak.
147 I5 Athboy Ireland
147 D8 Athea Ireland
Athenae Greece see Athina
147 E6 Athenry Ireland
227 S5 Athens Ont. Can.
Athens Greece see Athina
231 D8 Athens AL U.S.A.
231 F9 Athens GA U.S.A.
233 L6 Athens NY U.S.A.
232 C9 Athens OH U.S.A.
232 I7 Athens PA U.S.A.
231 E8 Athens TN U.S.A.
237 H9 Athens TX U.S.A.
169 K7 Athenstedt Ger.
198 B4 Atheras, Akrotirio pt Kefallonia Greece
150 D6 Atherington Devon, England U.K.
151 I2 Atherstone Warwickshire, England U.K.
85 J4 Atherton Qld Austr.
149 M6 Atherton Greater Manchester, England U.K.
211 C5 Athi r. Kenya
156 E4 Athies France
156 G4 Athies-sous-Laon France
198 E5 Athina Greece
Athínai Greece see Athina
211 C5 Athi River Kenya
159 K4 Athis-de-l'Orne France
156 D6 Athis-Mons France
147 E8 Athlacca Ireland
147 F5 Athleague Ireland
147 G6 Athlone Ireland
128 G6 Athnā', Wādī al watercourse Jordan
114 D4 Athni Karnataka India
81 C12 Athol South I. N.Z.
233 M6 Athol MA U.S.A.
231 □2 Athol Island New Prov. Bahamas
146 H9 Atholl, Forest of reg. Scotland U.K.
198 F2 Athos mt. Greece
Athos, Mount admin. div. Greece see Agion Oros
203 G2 Ath Thamad Egypt
127 K6 Ath Tharthār, Wādī r. Iraq
128 E9 Ath Thāyat mt. Saudi Arabia
124 G2 Ath Thumāmī well Saudi Arabia
147 I7 Athy Ireland
202 C6 Ati Chad
202 B4 Ati, Jabal mts Libya
122 H4 Aţīābād Iran
210 B4 Atiak Uganda
80 K5 Atiamuri North I. N.Z.
202 C6 Ati Ardébé Chad
256 D5 Atibaia Brazil
252 B4 Atico Peru
252 B4 Atico, Punta pt Peru
208 E3 Atiedo Sudan
183 O6 Atienza Spain
244 F7 Atijo Mex.
223 L5 Atikaki Provincial Wilderness Park Man. Can.
222 H4 Atikameg Alta Can.
224 D2 Atikameg r. Ont. Can.
223 M4 Atik Lake Man. Can.
224 B3 Atikokan Ont. Can.
225 H2 Atikonak Lake Nfld and Lab. Can.
79 □9a Atimaono Tahiti Fr. Polynesia
92 C4 Atimonan Luzon Phil.
193 L4 Atina Italy
243 O10 Atiquizaya El Salvador
114 F7 Atirampattinam Tamil Nadu India
243 N10 Atitlán Guat.
243 N10 Atitlán, Parque Nacional nat. park Guat.
81 □2 Atiu i. Cook Is
Atjeh admin. dist. Indon. see Aceh
124 H2 'Atk, Wādī al watercourse Saudi Arabia
131 Q3 Atka Rus. Fed.
220 A4 Atka AK U.S.A.
220 A4 Atka Island AK U.S.A.
177 I4 Atkár Hungary
135 I6 Atkarsk Rus. Fed.
237 I8 Atkins AR U.S.A.
93 G4 Atkri Papua Indon.
245 H6 Atlacomulco Mex.
215 L1 Atlanta S. Africa
231 E9 Atlanta GA U.S.A.
226 E9 Atlanta IL U.S.A.
227 J4 Atlanta MI U.S.A.
237 H9 Atlanta TX U.S.A.
126 F4 Atlantı Turkey
236 H5 Atlantic IA U.S.A.
233 □Q4 Atlantic ME U.S.A.
231 I8 Atlantic NC U.S.A.
233 K9 Atlantic City NJ U.S.A.
234 F6 Atlantic County county NJ U.S.A.
235 G4 Atlantic Highlands NJ U.S.A.
262 X2 Atlantic-Indian-Antarctic Basin sea feature S. Atlantic Ocean
263 H3 Atlantic-Indian-Antarctic Basin sea feature S. Atlantic Ocean
265 D8 Atlantic-Indian Ridge sea feature Southern Ocean
250 C2 Atlántico dept Col.
264 Atlantic Ocean
238 J5 Atlantic Peak WY U.S.A.
214 C9 Atlantis S. Africa
245 I4 Atlapexco Mex.
234 C3 Atlas PA U.S.A.
106 E5 Atlas Bogd mt. Mongolia
Atlas Méditerranéen mts Alg. see Atlas Tellien
204 D3 Atlas Mountains Africa
131 Q4 Atlasova, Ostrov i. Kuril'skiye O-va Rus. Fed.
205 F2 Atlas Saharien mts Alg.
205 F2 Atlas Tellien mts Alg.
245 I7 Atlatlahucan Mex.
222 C3 Atlin B.C. Can.
222 C3 Atlin Lake B.C./Y.T. Can.
222 C3 Atlin Provincial Park B.C. Can.
128 C6 'Atlit Israel
245 I7 Atlixco Mex.
245 I8 Atlixtac Mex.
114 F5 Atmakur Andhra Prad. India
114 F5 Atmakur Andhra Prad. India
231 D10 Atmore AL U.S.A.
141 K6 Atna Norway
116 F9 Atner Madh. Prad. India
84 F7 Atnetye Aboriginal Land res. N.T. Austr.
114 E4 Atnur Karnataka India
103 I12 Atō Japan
252 D5 Atocha Bol.
237 G8 Atoka OK U.S.A.
209 B7 Atome Angola
204 C4 Atonyia Western Sahara
78 □6 Atori Malaita Solomon Is
245 I5 Atotonico El Grande Mex.
244 D1 Atotonilco Durango Mex.
244 E1 Atotonilco Zacatecas Mex.
244 E5 Atotonilco el Alto Mex.
96 H6 Atouat mt. Laos
184 A2 Atouguia da Baleia Port.
204 D5 Atouila, Erg des. Mali
244 D5 Atoyac Mex.
245 I7 Atoyac r. Mex.
245 J9 Atoyac r. Mex.
245 K6 Atoyac r. Mex.
244 G8 Atoyac de Álvarez Mex.
114 D4 Atpadi Mahar. India
Atqan Xinjiang China see Aqqan
220 C2 Atqasuk AK U.S.A.
117 L7 Atrai r. India
122 G3 Atrak, Rūd-e r. Turkm. see Atrek
142 I5 Ätran r. Sweden
116 G6 Atranh Uttar Prad. India
250 B2 Atrato r. Col.
245 M9 Atravesada, Sierra mts Mex.
122 G3 Atrek r. Iran
193 L2 Atri Italy
Atria Italy see Adria
193 N6 Atripalda Italy
Atropatene country Asia see Azerbaijan
129 D3 Ats'ana Georgia
198 G3 Atsiki Limnos Greece
234 F5 Atsion NJ U.S.A.
105 J5 Atsugi Japan
207 H5 Atsuku Nigeria
104 F6 Atsumi Aichi Japan
102 Q8 Atsumi Yamagata Japan
104 F6 Atsumi-hantō pen. Japan
102 S3 Atsuta Japan
125 L3 Aţ Ţaff reg. U.A.E.
128 D8 Aţ Ţafīlah Jordan
124 E5 Aţ Ţā'if Saudi Arabia
177 H5 Attala Hungary
Attalea Turkey see Antalya
Attalia Turkey see Antalya
231 D8 Attalla AL U.S.A.
202 D3 At Tallāb oasis Libya
127 K6 At Ta'mīm governorate Iraq
202 D1 At Tamīmī Libya
148 C8 Attanagh Ireland
97 H7 Attapu Laos
205 G2 Attar, Oued el watercourse Alg.
195 □ Attard Malta
147 C4 Attavalley Ireland
199 I6 Attavyros mt. Rodos Greece
224 D2 Attawapiskat Ont. Can.
224 D2 Attawapiskat r. Ont. Can.
224 C2 Attawapiskat Lake Ont. Can.
203 H2 Aţ Ţawīl mts Saudi Arabia
124 E5 Aţ Ţāwlah Saudi Arabia
124 F1 At Taysīyah plat. Saudi Arabia
128 D8 Aţ Ţayyibah Jordan
80 H7 Attempt Hill South I. N.Z.
169 E8 Attendorn Ger.
173 L4 Attenkirchen Ger.
215 M1 Atteridgeville S. Africa
179 I4 Attersee Austria
179 I4 Attersee l. Austria
165 I9 Attert Belgium
165 J9 Attert r. Lux.
147 J4 Attica Northern Ireland U.K.
230 D5 Attica IN U.S.A.
232 G6 Attica NY U.S.A.
232 C7 Attica OH U.S.A.
156 F5 Attichy France
193 I2 Attigliano Italy
160 G4 Attignat France
156 I5 Attigny France
225 H2 Attikamagen Lake Nfld and Lab. Can.
198 E5 Attiki admin. reg. Greece
128 A7 Aţ Ţīnah Egypt
114 E8 Attingal Kerala India
233 N7 Attleboro MA U.S.A.
151 O2 Attleborough Norfolk, England U.K.
151 O2 Attlebridge Norfolk, England U.K.
179 I3 Attnang Austria
123 O5 Attock City Pak.
Attopeu Laos see Attapu
221 M3 Attu Greenland
126 H9 Aţ Ţubayq reg. Saudi Arabia
266 G2 Attu Island AK U.S.A.
124 G2 Aţ Ţulayḩī well Saudi Arabia
83 M4 Attunga N.S.W. Austr.
At Tūnisīyah country Africa see Tunisia
203 G2 Aţ Ţūr Egypt
114 E7 Attur Tamil Nadu India
114 F7 Attur Tamil Nadu India
124 F9 At Turbah Ta'izz Yemen
124 G9 At Turbah Ta'izz Yemen
124 E2 Aţ Ţuwayyah well Saudi Arabia
147 E6 Attymon Ireland
261 H3 Atucha Arg.
125 I8 Atūd Yemen
260 D5 Atuel r. Arg.
162 F5 Atur France
143 L3 Åtvidaberg Sweden
117 L6 Atwari Bangl.
240 L4 Atwater CA U.S.A.
236 E6 Atwood KS U.S.A.
135 I5 Atyashevo Rus. Fed.
120 D4 Atyrau Kazakh.
Atyrau Oblast admin. div. Kazakh. see Atyrauskaya Oblast'
Atyraū Oblysy admin. div. Kazakh. see Atyrauskaya Oblast'
120 D4 Atyrauskaya Oblast' admin. div. Kazakh.
135 H5 Atyur'yevo Rus. Fed.
137 L2 Atyusha Ukr.
192 C8 Atzara Sardegna Italy
179 M3 Atzenbrugg Austria
171 E7 Atzendorf Ger.
187 E7 Atzeneta del Maestrat Spain
178 A5 Au Austria
190 H1 Au Switz.
250 E5 Auati-Paraná r. Brazil
173 I2 Aub Ger.
169 H10 Aubach r. Ger.
161 H10 Aubagne France
161 E9 Aubais France
165 I9 Aubange Belgium
92 D3 Aubarede Point Luzon Phil.
162 H5 Aubazines France
159 M4 Aube France
156 H7 Aube dept France
156 G6 Aube r. France
213 H3 Aúbe Moz.
165 I7 Aubel Belgium
161 E7 Aubenas France
156 H4 Aubenton France
156 C6 Aubergenville France
156 H5 Aubérive France
157 J8 Auberive France
162 E5 Aubeterre-sur-Dronne France
156 F6 Aubetin r. France
156 B5 Aubevoye France
163 F8 Aubiet France
161 G8 Aubignan France
159 L6 Aubigné-Racan France
161 H8 Aubignosc France
156 E3 Aubigny-en-Artois France
159 P7 Aubigny-sur-Nère France
163 I6 Aubin France
224 D4 Aubinadong r. Ont. Can.
163 D10 Aubisque, Col d' pass France
190 A2 Aubonne Switz.
161 E9 Aubord France
157 K5 Auboué France
161 B7 Aubrac mts France
157 J5 Aubreville France
241 T6 Aubrey Cliffs mts AZ U.S.A.
220 F3 Aubry Lake N.W.T. Can.
85 M8 Auburn r. Qld Austr.
227 M6 Auburn Ont. Can.
231 E9 Auburn AL U.S.A.
240 K3 Auburn CA U.S.A.
236 K6 Auburn IL U.S.A.
230 E5 Auburn IN U.S.A.
233 N6 Auburn MA U.S.A.
233 □O4 Auburn ME U.S.A.
227 J6 Auburn MI U.S.A.
236 H5 Auburn NE U.S.A.
232 I6 Auburn NY U.S.A.
234 C3 Auburn PA U.S.A.
238 C3 Auburn WA U.S.A.
234 C1 Auburn Center PA U.S.A.
226 D5 Auburndale WI U.S.A.
85 M8 Auburn Range hills Qld Austr.
162 I4 Aubusson France
156 F3 Auby France
260 C5 Auca Mahuida Arg.
260 C5 Auca Mahuida, Sierra de mt. Arg.
163 G8 Aucamville France
138 F5 Auce Latvia
163 F8 Auch France
146 J9 Auchallater Aberdeenshire, Scotland U.K.
148 G2 Auchbraad Argyll and Bute, Scotland U.K.
96 C2 Auche Myanmar
156 D2 Auchel France
146 L9 Auchenblae Aberdeenshire, Scotland U.K.
146 F11 Auchenbreck Argyll and Bute, Scotland U.K.
146 I13 Auchencairn Dumfries and Galloway, Scotland U.K.
146 L11 Auchencrow Scottish Borders, Scotland U.K.
207 G5 Auchi Nigeria
146 H12 Auchinleck East Ayrshire, Scotland U.K.
146 K9 Auchmull Angus, Scotland U.K.
146 L8 Auchnagatt Aberdeenshire, Scotland U.K.
146 J8 Aucholzie Aberdeenshire, Scotland U.K.
146 K9 Auchronie Angus, Scotland U.K.
146 I10 Auchterarder Perth and Kinross, Scotland U.K.
146 J10 Auchtermuchty Fife, Scotland U.K.
156 D2 Auchy-au-Bois France
80 I3 Auckland North I. N.Z.
80 I3 Auckland admin. reg. North I. N.Z.
77 G6 Auckland Islands N.Z.
163 D10 Aucun France
161 A10 Aude dept France
161 C10 Aude r. France
224 C3 Auden Ont. Can.
Audenarde Belgium see Oudenaarde
163 B6 Audenge France
158 H2 Auderville France
233 □O3 Audet Que. Can.
160 H2 Audeux France
158 B5 Audierne France
158 C6 Audierne, Baie d' b. France
160 J2 Audincourt France
150 G2 Audlem Cheshire, England U.K.
149 M7 Audley Staffordshire, England U.K.
210 D3 Audo mts Eth.
163 C8 Audon France
156 C2 Audresselles France
138 H3 Audru Estonia
156 D2 Audruicq France
236 H5 Audubon IA U.S.A.
234 E5 Audubon NJ U.S.A.
157 K5 Audun-le-Roman France
171 G9 Aue Ger.
168 E4 Aue r. Ger.
169 J5 Aue r. Ger.
173 O4 Auerbach Bayern Ger.
171 F9 Auerbach Sachsen Ger.
171 G9 Auerbach Sachsen Ger.
173 L2 Auerbach in der Oberpfalz Ger.
171 G10 Auersberg mt. Ger.
179 O3 Auersthal Austria
171 G9 Auerswalde Ger.
121 S3 Auezov Kazakh.
156 B4 Auffay France
173 M4 Aufhausen Ger.
85 K8 Augathella Qld Austr.
147 H4 Augher Northern Ireland U.K.
147 I4 Aughnacloy Northern Ireland U.K.
147 F6 Aughrim Galway Ireland
147 J7 Aughrim Wicklow Ireland
149 L6 Aughton Lancashire, England U.K.
149 O7 Aughton South Yorkshire, England U.K.
162 F4 Augignac France
Augila Libya see Awjilah
214 E4 Augrabies S. Africa
214 E4 Augrabies Falls S. Africa
214 E4 Augrabies Falls National Park S. Africa
227 K5 Au Gres MI U.S.A.
173 J5 Augsburg Ger.
178 C3 Augsburg airport Ger.
173 J5 Augsburg-Westliche Wälder park Ger.
138 I4 Augšlīgatne Latvia
138 J5 Augšzemes augstiene hills Latvia
87 C13 Augusta W.A. Austr.
195 I9 Augusta Sicilia Italy
237 J8 Augusta AR U.S.A.
231 F9 Augusta GA U.S.A.
226 D9 Augusta IL U.S.A.
237 G7 Augusta KS U.S.A.
232 A10 Augusta KY U.S.A.
233 □P4 Augusta ME U.S.A.
238 H3 Augusta MT U.S.A.
234 F2 Augusta NJ U.S.A.
226 C5 Augusta WI U.S.A.
232 G9 Augusta WV U.S.A.
195 I9 Augusta, Golfo di b. Sicilia Italy
Augusta Auscorum France see Auch
Augusta Taurinorum Italy see Torino
Augusta Treverorum Ger. see Trier
252 C6 Augusta Victoria Chile
Augusta Vindelicorum Ger. see Augsburg
168 I1 Augustenborg Denmark
246 G8 Augustin Cadazzi Col.
220 C4 Augustine Island AK U.S.A.
227 S2 Augustines, Lac des l. Que. Can.
Augusto Cardosa Moz. see Metangula
257 E3 Augusto de Lima Brazil
Augustodunum France see Autun
254 F3 Augusto Severo Brazil
175 K2 Augustów Pol.
175 L3 Augustowo Pol.
175 L2 Augustowska, Puszcza for. Pol.
175 L2 Augustowski, Kanał canal Pol.
87 D8 Augustus, Mount W.A. Austr.
171 H9 Augustusburg Ger.
86 H3 Augustus Island W.A. Austr.
169 H6 Auhagen Ger.
173 L4 Au in der Hallertau Ger.
157 I7 Aujon r. France
Aujuittuq Nunavut Can. see Grise Fiord
124 E8 Aukan Island Eritrea
222 C3 Auke Bay AK U.S.A.
78 □6 Auki Malaita Solomon Is
168 I2 Aukrug Ger.
138 J6 Aukštaitijos nacionalinis parkas nat. park Lith.
138 G6 Aukštelkai Lith.
138 G6 Aukštelkė Lith.
140 O4 Auktsjaur Sweden
220 G2 Aulavik National Park N.W.T. Can.
86 G7 Auld, Lake salt flat W.A. Austr.
146 I7 Auldearn Highland, Scotland U.K.
169 K8 Auleben Ger.
190 H7 Aulella r. Italy
172 H6 Aulendorf Ger.
193 O6 Auletta Italy
Auliye Ata Kazakh. see Taraz
120 K1 Auliyekol' Kazakh.
190 H7 Aulla Italy
192 C4 Aullène Corse France
160 C5 Aulnat France
160 C5 Aulnat airport France
162 D3 Aulnay France
156 E6 Aulnay-sous-Bois France
158 C5 Aulne r. France
223 M5 Aulneau Peninsula Ont. Can.
157 L6 Aulnois sur-Seille France
156 G3 Aulnoye-Aymeries France
Aulon Albania see Vlorë
163 F9 Aulon France
92 □ Aulong i. Palau
170 E5 Aulosen Ger.
156 B3 Ault France
146 E7 Aultbea Highland, Scotland U.K.
146 G7 Aultguish Inn Highland, Scotland U.K.
92 □ Auluptagel i. Palau
163 G10 Aulus-les-Bains France
171 E9 Auma Ger.
156 C4 Aumale France
160 B3 Aumance r. France
157 K5 Aumetz France
160 H3 Aumont France
161 C7 Aumont-Aubrac France

Bad Münstereifel to Balotra

283

169 C9 Bad Münstereifel Ger.
171 K7 Bad Muskau Ger.
169 G10 Bad Nauheim Ger.
116 E8 Badnawar Madh. Prad. India
169 H6 Bad Nenndorf Ger.
116 F9 Badnera Mahar. India
169 D9 Bad Neuenahr-Ahrweiler Ger.
169 J10 Bad Neustadt an der Saale Ger.
169 G6 Bad Oeynhausen Ger.
195 L6 Badolato Italy
185 J6 Badolatosa Spain
168 J3 Bad Oldesloe Ger.
108 H3 Badong Hubei China
97 H10 Ba Đông Vietnam
157 M6 Badonviller France
169 H10 Bad Orb Ger.
107 O8 Badou Shandong China
207 F5 Badou Togo
196 H6 Badovinci Serbia
172 E5 Bad Peterstal Ger.
179 O3 Bad Pirawarth Austria
215 O1 Badplaas S. Africa
169 H7 Bad Pyrmont Ger.
124 F7 Badr Saudi Arabia
179 M6 Bad Radkersburg Austria
190 H1 Bad Ragaz Switz.
127 L7 Badrah Iraq
172 G3 Bad Rappenau Ger.
173 N6 Bad Reichenhall Ger.
124 D4 Badr Ḥunayn Saudi Arabia
Badrinath Peaks Uttaranchal India see Chaukhamba
226 D3 Bad River Indian Reservation res. WI U.S.A.
169 F6 Bad Rothenfelde Ger.
171 J6 Bad Saarow-Pieskow Ger.
169 K7 Bad Sachsa Ger.
172 D6 Bad Säckingen Ger.
169 J6 Bad Salzdetfurth Ger.
169 I9 Bad Salzschlirf Ger.
169 G6 Bad Salzuflen Ger.
169 J9 Bad Salzungen Ger.
179 K6 Bad Sankt Leonhard im Lavanttal Austria
169 F7 Bad Sassendorf Ger.
179 I3 Bad Schallerbach Austria
171 J9 Bad Schandau Ger.
171 G7 Bad Schmiedeberg Ger.
172 F3 Bad Schönborn Ger.
172 H5 Bad Schussenried Ger.
169 F10 Bad Schwalbach Ger.
168 K3 Bad Schwartau Ger.
168 J3 Bad Segeberg Ger.
151 I3 Badsey Worcestershire, England U.K.
172 D2 Bad Sobernheim Ger.
169 H10 Bad Soden-Salmünster Ger.
169 I8 Bad Sooden-Allendorf Ger.
171 E10 Bad Steben Ger.
171 D7 Bad Suderode Ger.
171 E8 Bad Sulza Ger.
170 G2 Bad Sülze Ger.
169 K8 Bad Tennstedt Ger.
173 L6 Bad Tölz Ger.
109 L5 Badu Fujian China
172 H4 Bad Überkingen Ger.
91 J9 Badu Island Qld Austr.
186 C5 Badules Spain
114 G9 Badulla Sri Lanka
172 G5 Bad Urach Ger.
114 F5 Badvel Andhra Prad. India
169 G10 Bad Vilbel Ger.
179 N4 Bad Vöslau Austria
172 H6 Bad Waldsee Ger.
179 N5 Bad Waltersdorf Austria
173 L6 Bad Wiessee Ger.
172 F4 Bad Wildbad im Schwarzwald Ger.
169 H8 Bad Wildungen Ger.
170 E5 Bad Wilsnack Ger.
172 G3 Bad Wimpfen Ger.
179 I3 Bad Wimsbach-Neydharting Austria
173 I2 Bad Windsheim Ger.
173 J6 Bad Wörishofen Ger.
172 H6 Bad Wurzach Ger.
179 K3 Bad Zell Austria
100 I3 Badzhal Rus. Fed.
100 H4 Badzhal'skiy Khrebet mts Rus. Fed.
169 H8 Bad Zwesten Ger.
168 F4 Bad Zwischenahn Ger.
Bae Cinmel Conwy, Wales U.K. see Kinmel Bay
Bae Colwyn Conwy, Wales U.K. see Colwyn Bay
140 □B1 Bæir Iceland
170 E4 Baek Ger.
142 F6 Bække Denmark
142 E5 Bækmarksbro Denmark
165 I7 Baelen Belgium
186 I3 Baells, Pantà de la resr Spain
185 K5 Baena Spain
Bae Penrhyn Conwy, Wales U.K. see Penrhyn Bay
169 B9 Baesweiler Ger.
250 B5 Baeza Ecuador
185 M5 Baeza Spain
207 H5 Bafang Cameroon
206 B3 Bafatá Guinea-Bissau
123 O4 Baffa Pak.
221 L2 Baffin Bay sea Can./Greenland
221 L3 Baffin Island Nunavut Can.
207 H5 Bafia Cameroon
207 F4 Bafilo Togo
206 C3 Bafing r. Guinea/Mali
206 C3 Bafing, Réserve du nature res. Mali
206 C3 Bafing Makana Mali
164 K2 Baflo Neth.
206 C3 Bafoulabé Mali
207 H5 Bafoussam Cameroon
122 F6 Bāfq Iran
126 G3 Bafra Turkey
126 G3 Bafra Burnu pt Turkey
122 G7 Bāft Iran
208 E4 Bafwaboli Dem. Rep. Congo
208 E4 Bafwamboma Dem. Rep. Congo
208 E4 Bafwasende Dem. Rep. Congo
177 I4 Bag Hungary
207 I3 Baga Nigeria
186 I3 Bagà Spain
106 G4 Baga Bogd Uul mts Mongolia
92 C4 Bagac Bay Luzon Phil.
117 J6 Bagaha Bihar India
95 M2 Bagahak, Gunung hill Malaysia
195 J7 Bagaladi Italy
114 D4 Bagalkot Karnataka India
177 K4 Bagamér Hungary
211 C6 Bagamoyo Tanz.
121 Q1 Bagan Rus. Fed.
Bagan Datoh Malaysia see Bagan Datuk
94 D3 Bagan Datuk Malaysia
92 F8 Baganga Mindanao Phil.
212 D3 Bagani Namibia
92 D8 Baganian Peninsula Mindanao Phil.
94 D2 Bagan Serai Malaysia
94 D3 Bagansiapiapi Sumatera Indon.
107 K3 Baganuur Mongolia
190 I6 Baganza r. Italy
111 K11 Bagar Xizang China
121 T3 Bagar watercourse Kazakh.
199 I5 Bağarası Turkey
161 E8 Bagard France
207 G3 Bagaré well Niger
207 G3 Bagaroua Niger
209 C5 Bagata Dem. Rep. Congo
250 C6 Bagazán Peru
203 F6 Bagbag Sudan
241 S7 Bagdad AZ U.S.A.
Bagdadi Georgia see Baghdat'i
258 G3 Bagé Brazil
160 F4 Bâgé-le-Châtel France
168 K1 Bagenkop Denmark
114 E6 Bagepalli Karnataka India
117 L8 Bagerhat Bangl.
163 J10 Bages France
186 I4 Bages reg. Spain
161 B10 Bages et de Sigean, Étang de lag. France
116 G5 Bageshwar Uttaranchal India
114 E4 Bagevadi Karnataka India
143 L2 Baggå Sweden
238 K6 Baggs WY U.S.A.
150 D5 Baggy Point England U.K.
116 E8 Bagh Madh. Prad. India
123 O5 Bagh Pak.
122 F6 Bāgh, Chāh-e well Iran
Bàgh a'Chaisteil Scotland U.K. see Castlebay
123 K7 Baghak Pak.
146 B8 Baghasdail, Loch inlet Scotland U.K.
122 I3 Baghbaghū Iran
127 L7 Baghdād Iraq
127 L7 Baghdād governorate Iraq
129 D3 Baghdat'i Georgia
122 G7 Bāgh-e Bābū'īyeh Iran
122 C6 Bāgh-e Malek Iran
Bagherhat Bangl. see Bagerhat
194 F7 Bagheria Sicilia Italy
122 G6 Bāghīn Iran
123 M3 Baghlān Afgh.
123 M4 Baghlān prov. Afgh.
122 B2 Bāghlī Da hill Iran
146 B8 Bagh nam Faoileann b. Scotland U.K.
129 E5 Baghramyan Armenia
123 K5 Baghrān Afgh.
123 L8 Baghwana Pak.
150 F1 Bagillt Flintshire, Wales U.K.
94 G6 Baginda, Tanjung pt Indon.
129 A6 Bağırpaşa Dağı mts Turkey
Bağırsak Deresi r. Syria/Turkey see Sājūr, Nahr
129 C7 Bağlar Turkey
236 H2 Bagley MN U.S.A.
117 I5 Baglung Nepal
141 J6 Bagn Norway
191 L7 Bagnacavallo Italy
163 I6 Bagnac-sur-Célé France
195 J7 Bagnara Calabra Italy
190 G6 Bagnaria Italy
191 O4 Bagnaria Arsa Italy
190 E7 Bagnasco Italy
156 E7 Bagneaux-sur-Loing France
163 E9 Bagnères-de-Bigorre France
163 F10 Bagnères-de-Luchon France
190 C3 Bagnes reg. Switz.
190 C3 Bagnes, Val des val. Switz.
190 H3 Bagni di Masino Italy
191 J3 Bagni di Rabbi Italy
191 L8 Bagno di Romagna Italy
159 K4 Bagnoles-de-l'Orne France
193 M4 Bagnoli del Trigno Italy
191 L5 Bagnoli di Sopra Italy
193 O6 Bagnoli Irpino Italy
191 J6 Bagnolo in Piano Italy
190 I5 Bagnolo Mella Italy
161 K7 Bagnolo Piemonte Italy
191 J5 Bagnolo San Vito Italy
161 J9 Bagnols-en-Forêt France
161 D7 Bagnols-les-Bains France
161 F8 Bagnols-sur-Cèze France
190 I7 Bagnone Italy
192 I2 Bagnoregio Italy
117 K7 Bagnuiti r. Nepal
Bago Myanmar see Pegu
Bago admin. div. Myanmar see Pegu
92 D6 Bago Negros Phil.
176 F5 Bagod Hungary
206 D3 Bagoé r. Côte d'Ivoire/Mali
190 I4 Bagolino Italy
Bagong Guizhou China see Sansui
138 D7 Bagrationovsk Rus. Fed.
Bagrax Xinjiang China see Bohu
Bagrax Hu l. China see Bosten Hu
251 I5 Bagre Brazil
199 L5 Bağsaray Turkey
151 K5 Bagshot Surrey, England U.K.
250 B6 Bagua Peru
260 E4 Bagual Arg.
207 G4 Bagudo Nigeria
186 C5 Báguena Spain
92 C3 Baguio Luzon Phil.
92 E8 Baguio Mindanao Phil.
92 D3 Baguio Point Luzon Phil.
Bagur Spain see Begur
Bagur, Cabo c. Spain see Begur, Cap de
176 G4 Bágyogszovát Hungary
199 I4 Bağyurdu Turkey
207 H2 Bagzane, Monts mts Niger
183 M5 Bahabón de Esgueva Spain
137 R4 Bahachka Ukr.
111 F13 Bahadurganj Nepal
116 F5 Bahadurgarh Haryana India
123 N5 Bahadur Khel Pak.
247 □3 Baham, Pointe pt Martinique
Bahāmabād Iran see Rafsanjān
Bahamas country West Indies see The Bahamas
123 L8 Bahara Pak.
117 L7 Baharampur W. Bengal India
123 M9 Bahardipur Pak.
Bahariya Oasis Egypt see Bahrīyah, Wāḥāt al
122 G2 Baharly Turkm.
137 N8 Bahate Ukr.
137 P6 Bahatyr Ukr.
95 L3 Bahau r. Indon.
94 E3 Bahau Malaysia
95 K6 Bahaur Kalimantan Indon.
123 O7 Bahawalnagar Pak.
123 N7 Bahawalpur Pak.
128 D2 Bahçe Adana Turkey
126 H5 Bahçe Osmaniye Turkey
129 B6 Bahçeköy Turkey
199 H3 Bahçeli Çanakkale Turkey
129 C5 Bahçeli Erzurum Turkey
108 F3 Ba He r. China
Bäherden Turkm. see Baharly
116 G5 Baheri Uttar Prad. India
211 B6 Bahi Tanz.
Bahia Brazil see Salvador
257 G1 Bahia state Brazil
242 □P9 Bahía, Islas de la is Hond.
261 F6 Bahía Blanca Arg.
244 E7 Bahía Bufadero Mex.
259 D7 Bahía Bustamante Arg.
250 A5 Bahía de Caráquez Ecuador
92 B7 Bahia Honda Point Palawan Phil.
242 D3 Bahía Kino Mex.
259 D8 Bahía Laura Arg.
253 F5 Bahía Negra Para.
259 E6 Bahía San Blas Arg.
242 B4 Bahía Tortugas Mex.
183 K4 Bahíllo Spain
210 C2 Bahir Dar Eth.
116 E5 Bahl Haryana India
125 M4 Bahlā Oman
197 P3 Bahlui r. Romania
122 C7 Bahmanshīr, Khowr-e r. Iran
122 D7 Bahman Yārī-ye Gharbī Iran
93 B5 Bahomonte Sulawesi Indon.
176 G3 Báhoň Slovakia
124 E6 Bahr Saudi Arabia
116 H6 Bahraich Uttar Prad. India
125 J2 Bahrain country Asia
125 J3 Bahrain, Gulf of Asia
122 C3 Bahrāmābād Iran
122 C3 Bahrām Beyg Iran
116 H6 Bahramghat Uttar Prad. India
122 G7 Bahrāmjerd Iran
129 I6 Bährämtäpä Azer.
171 D6 Bahrdorf Ger.
210 A3 Bahr el Jebel state Sudan
168 G5 Bahrenborstel Ger.
203 F3 Bahrīyah, Wāḥāt al oasis Egypt
116 F6 Bahror Rajasthan India
252 C3 Bahuaja-Sonene, Parque Nacional nat. park Peru
93 C5 Bahubulu i. Indon.
123 I9 Bāhū Kālāt Iran
139 N7 Bahushewsk Belarus
197 O3 Baia Suceava Romania
197 Q6 Baia Tulcea Romania
197 K6 Baia de Aramă Romania
197 L4 Baia de Arieș Romania
177 L5 Baia de Criș Romania
193 Q4 Baia della Zagare Italy
209 A9 Baía dos Tigres Angola
209 B8 Baía Farta Angola
197 L3 Baia Mare Romania
251 I5 Baião Brazil
182 D6 Baião Port.
183 O3 Baias r. Spain
197 L3 Baia Sprie Romania
194 D8 Baiata r. Sicilia Italy
122 F5 Baiazeh Iran
117 K5 Baiba Xizang China
202 D5 Baïbeli well Chad
208 B3 Baïbokoum Chad
Baicheng Henan China see Xiping
107 R4 Baicheng Jilin China
110 E6 Baicheng Xinjiang China
197 N5 Băicoi Romania
Baidoa Somalia see Baydhabo
111 H10 Baidoi Co l. Xizang China
109 K6 Baidu Guangdong China
110 L6 Baidunzi Gansu China
106 I8 Baidunzi Gansu China
Baie-aux-Feuilles Que. Can. see Tasiujaq
225 G3 Baie-Comeau Que. Can.
246 G4 Baie de Henne Haiti
Baie-du-Poste Que. Can. see Mistissini
225 I3 Baie-Johan-Beetz Que. Can.
247 □2 Baie-Mahault b. Guadeloupe
172 H6 Baienfurt Ger.
173 K5 Baierbrunn Ger.
172 E4 Baiersbronn Ger.
173 K2 Baiersdorf Ger.
225 G4 Baie-St-Paul Que. Can.
225 H3 Baie-Trinité Que. Can.
225 J3 Baie Verte Nfld and Lab. Can.
162 D5 Baignes-Ste-Radegonde France
160 F1 Baigneux-les-Juifs France
261 G4 Baigorrita Arg.
107 O7 Baigou He r. China
Baiguan Zhejiang China see Shangyu
109 J3 Baiguo Hubei China
109 I5 Baiguo Hunan China
183 R3 Baigura mt. Spain
108 B5 Baihanchang Yunnan China
116 H8 Baihar Madh. Prad. India
100 F7 Baihe Jilin China
108 H2 Baihe Shaanxi China
109 I2 Bai He r. China
107 O6 Bai He r. China
Baiji Iraq see Bayjī
110 G4 Baijiantan Xinjiang China
116 F3 Baijnath Hima. Prad. India
116 G5 Baijnath Uttaranchal India
Baikal, Lake Rus. Fed. see Baykal, Ozero
116 H7 Baikanthpur Madh. Prad. India
110 G4 Baikouquan Xinjiang China
117 I8 Baikunthpur Chhattisgarh India
107 Q3 Bailang Nei Mongol China
149 N6 Baildon West Yorkshire, England U.K.
Baile Ailein Scotland U.K. see Balallan
Baile Átha Cliath Ireland see Dublin
Baile Átha Luain Ireland see Athlone
197 M5 Băile Govora Romania
197 K6 Băile Herculane Romania
146 B7 Baile Mhartainn Western Isles, Scotland U.K.
185 L4 Bailén Spain
197 M5 Băile Olănești Romania
197 L6 Băilești Romania
197 L6 Băileștilor, Câmpia plain Romania
215 K7 Bailey S. Africa
87 G10 Bailey Range hills W.A. Austr.
232 C12 Baileyton TN U.S.A.
109 J3 Bailianhe Shuiku resr China
108 H6 Bailicun Guangxi China
147 I5 Bailieborough Ireland
107 L6 Bailingmiao Nei Mongol China
251 I4 Bailique Brazil
156 B7 Bailleau-le-Pin France
156 E2 Bailleul France
223 J1 Baillie r. Nunavut Can.
247 □2 Baillif Guadeloupe
165 H8 Baillonville Belgium
186 D2 Bailo Spain
Bailong Gansu China see Hadapu
108 E2 Bailong Jiang r. Gansu/Qinghai China
209 B8 Bailundo Angola
108 C2 Baima Qinghai China
Baima Xizang China see Baxoi
109 K3 Baima Jian mt. Anhui China
108 G9 Baimajing Hainan China
149 Q7 Bain r. England U.K.
Bainang Xizang China see Norkyung
149 M5 Bainbridge North Yorkshire, England U.K.
231 E10 Bainbridge GA U.S.A.
233 J6 Bainbridge NY U.S.A.
232 B9 Bainbridge OH U.S.A.
234 B4 Bainbridge PA U.S.A.
158 H6 Bain-de-Bretagne France
172 H6 Baindt Ger.
114 D6 Bainduru Karnataka India
246 G4 Bainet Haiti
111 J11 Baingoin Xizang China
Baini Guizhou China see Yuqing
161 D6 Bains France
157 L7 Bains-les-Bains France
158 G6 Bains-sur-Oust France
149 P6 Bainton East Riding of Yorkshire, England U.K.
182 C2 Baio Spain
182 C4 Baiona Spain
108 C2 Baiqên Qinghai China
100 E5 Baiquan Heilong. China
128 E8 Bā'ir Jordan
128 F7 Bā'ir, Wādī watercourse Jordan/Saudi Arabia
111 F9 Bairab Co l. China
117 J6 Bairagnia Bihar India
237 F9 Baird TX U.S.A.
220 C3 Baird Mountains AK U.S.A.
77 H1 Bairiki Kiribati
107 P5 Bairin Qiao Nei Mongol China
Bairin Youqi Nei Mongol China see Daban
Bairin Zuoqi Nei Mongol China see Lindong
121 M6 Bairkum Kazakh.
83 K7 Bairnsdale Vic. Austr.
184 D3 Bairro dos Canaviais Port.
158 I5 Bais Bretagne France
159 K5 Bais Pays de la Loire France
92 D7 Bais Negros Phil.
163 E7 Baïse r. France
108 F4 Baisha Chongqing China
108 G9 Baisha Hainan China
109 J5 Baisha Jiangxi China
108 G3 Baisha Sichuan China
Baishan Guangxi China see Mashan
101 E8 Baishan Jilin China
110 K6 Bai Shan mt. Gansu China
100 E7 Baishanzhen Jilin China
107 Q6 Baishi Shuiku resr Liaoning China
107 K9 Baishui Shaanxi China
108 E2 Baishui Jiang r. Sichuan China
191 J7 Baiso Italy
197 L4 Băișoara Romania
138 G6 Baisogala Lith.
207 H5 Baissia Nigeria
177 L5 Băița Romania
116 H5 Baitadi Nepal
108 A2 Baitang Qinghai China
96 G5 Bai Thương Vietnam
197 M3 Băiuț Romania
161 F7 Baix France
184 A3 Baixa da Banheira Port.
163 J10 Baixas France
186 F6 Baix Ebre reg. Spain
Baixi Sichuan China see Yibin
107 N8 Baixiang Hebei China
107 Q5 Baixingt Nei Mongol China
216 □1c Baixo, Ilhéu de i. Azores
184 □ Baixo, Ilhéu de i. Madeira
257 G3 Baixo Guandu Brazil
209 C8 Baixo-Longa Angola
107 O7 Baiyang Dian resr China
110 I5 Baiyanghe Xinjiang China
Baiyashi Hunan China see Dong'an
106 I8 Baiyin Gansu China
108 B3 Baiyü Sichuan China
203 G5 Baiyuda Desert Sudan
108 C2 Baiyügoinba Qinghai China
107 J8 Baiyu Shan mts China
177 H5 Baja Hungary
242 B3 Baja, Punta pt Mex.
242 B2 Baja California pen. Mex.
242 B3 Baja California state Mex.
242 C5 Baja California Sur state Mex.
260 B6 Bajado del Agrio Arg.
122 C3 Bājalān Iran
216 □3a Bajamar Tenerife Canary Is
243 I4 Bajan Mex.
116 H5 Bajang Nepal
94 G3 Bajau i. Indon.
123 N4 Bajaur reg. Pak.
93 B8 Bajawa Flores Indon.
117 L8 Baj Baj W. Bengal India
177 H4 Bajč Slovakia
195 □ Bajda Ridge Malta
122 H3 Bājgīrān Iran
124 F8 Bājil Yemen
196 H7 Bajina Bašta Serbia
117 M7 Bajitpur Bangl.
196 H5 Bajmok Vojvodina Serbia
177 H4 Bajna Hungary
116 E8 Bajna Madh. Prad. India
216 □3b Bajo, Punta del pt Fuerteventura Canary Is
250 B3 Bajo Baudó Col.
242 □R13 Bajo Boquete Panama
259 C7 Bajo Caracoles Arg.
260 D2 Bajo de Gallo Arg.
207 H4 Bajoga Nigeria
259 C7 Bajo Grande Arg.
184 H6 Bajo Guadalquivir, Canal del Spain
261 G6 Bajo Hondo Buenos Aires Arg.
260 E2 Bajo Hondo La Rioja Arg.
213 H3 Bajone Moz.
246 D6 Bajo Nuevo sea feature Col.
85 M7 Bajool Qld Austr.
177 H4 Bajót Hungary
183 J6 Bajoz r. Spain
117 J9 Bajrakot Orissa India
196 I8 Bajram Curri Albania
177 I6 Bajša Vojvodina Serbia
176 F5 Bak Hungary
177 G4 Baka Slovakia
95 J5 Baka, Bukit mt. Indon.
208 C3 Bakaba Chad
208 D3 Bakala C.A.R.
175 K1 Bakałarzewo Pol.
134 K5 Bakaly Rus. Fed.
121 Q5 Bakanas Kazakh.
121 R4 Bakanas watercourse Kazakh.
202 D6 Bakaoré Chad
191 R5 Bakar Croatia
206 A3 Bakau Gambia
95 L6 Bakaucengal Kalimantan Indon.
95 L3 Bakayan, Gunung mt. Indon.
137 L3 Bakayivka Ukr.
164 I6 Bakel Neth.
206 B3 Bakel Senegal
241 P6 Baker CA U.S.A.
238 H4 Baker ID U.S.A.
237 J10 Baker LA U.S.A.
238 L3 Baker MT U.S.A.
241 R2 Baker NV U.S.A.
238 F4 Baker OR U.S.A.
232 G9 Baker WV U.S.A.
238 D2 Baker, Mount vol. WA U.S.A.
241 U7 Baker Butte mt. AZ U.S.A.
223 N2 Baker Foreland hd Nunavut Can.
77 I1 Baker Island N. Pacific Ocean
222 C4 Baker Island AK U.S.A.
87 I9 Baker Lake salt flat W.A. Austr.
223 M1 Baker Lake Nunavut Can.
223 M1 Baker Lake l. Nunavut Can.
233 □P2 Baker Lake l. ME U.S.A.
85 L6 Bakers Creek Qld Austr.
224 E1 Baker's Dozen Islands Nunavut Can.
240 N6 Bakersfield CA U.S.A.
231 F7 Bakersville NC U.S.A.
215 K1 Bakerville S. Africa
97 H8 Bâ Kêv Cambodia
149 N7 Bakewell Derbyshire, England U.K.
125 M2 Bakhā Oman
139 Q8 Bakhany Rus. Fed.
Bakharden Turkm. see Baharly
122 I4 Bākharz mts Iran
116 C7 Bakhasar Rajasthan India
Bakhchisaray Ukr. see Bakhchysaray
137 M9 Bakhchysaray Ukr.
100 F3 Bakhirevo Rus. Fed.
137 L2 Bakhmach Ukr.
Bakhmut Ukr. see Artemivs'k
137 R5 Bakhmut r. Ukr.
139 R5 Bakhmutovo Rus. Fed.
130 J3 Bakhta Rus. Fed.
Bākhtarān Iran see Kermānshāh
Bākhtarān prov. Iran see Kermānshāh
122 E7 Bakhtegan, Daryācheh-ye l. Iran
122 C5 Bakhtiari Country reg. Iran
117 J7 Bakhtiyarpur Bihar India
121 T4 Bakhty Kazakh.
251 G3 Bakhuis Gebergte mts Suriname
129 K5 Bakı Azer.
202 D5 Baki well Chad
210 D2 Baki Somalia
207 H3 Bakin Birji Niger
199 I3 Bakır Turkey
199 I4 Bakır r. Turkey
199 J2 Bakırköy Turkey
129 K5 Bakıxanov Azer.
140 □F1 Bakkaflói b. Iceland
164 J2 Bakkeveen Neth.
199 K5 Baklan Turkey
139 O6 Baklanovo Rus. Fed.
116 E3 Bakloh Hima. Prad. India
206 D4 Bako Côte d'Ivoire
210 C2 Bako Oromīya Eth.
210 C3 Bako YeDebub Bihēroch Bihēreseboch na Hizboch Eth.
95 I4 Bako National Park Malaysia
94 B3 Bakongan Sumatera Indon.
177 K4 Bakonszeg Hungary
177 G4 Bakony hills Hungary
177 G4 Bakonybél Hungary
177 G4 Bakonynána Hungary
177 H4 Bakonysárkány Hungary
177 G4 Bakonyszentkirály Hungary
177 G4 Bakonyszombathely Hungary
210 D4 Bakool admin. reg. Somalia
208 F3 Bakordi Sudan
207 G4 Bakori Nigeria
208 D5 Bakota Dem. Rep. Congo
208 D3 Bakouma C.A.R.
208 B5 Bakoumba Gabon
179 N6 Bakovci Slovenia
171 K10 Bakov nad Jizerou Czech Rep.
206 C3 Bakoy r. Mali
123 M8 Bakrani Pak.
177 H6 Baksa Hungary
129 E2 Baksan Rus. Fed.
129 F2 Baksan r. Rus. Fed.
129 E2 Baksanenok Rus. Fed.
129 E2 Baksanges Rus. Fed.
177 L4 Baktalórántháza Hungary
Baku Azer. see Bakı
208 F4 Baku Dem. Rep. Congo
168 F5 Bakum Ger.
94 F4 Bakung i. Indon.
138 H9 Bakuny Belarus
129 E4 Bakuriani Georgia
129 E4 Bakurianis Andeziti Georgia
262 P2 Bakutis Coast Antarctica
Baky Azer. see Bakı
131 P3 Baky Uyandino r. Rus. Fed.
126 F4 Balâ Turkey
150 E2 Bala Gwynedd, Wales U.K.
252 C3 Bala, Cerros de mts Bol.
92 A7 Balabac Phil.
92 A8 Balabac i. Phil.
95 L1 Balabac Strait Malaysia/Phil.
122 E5 Balābād, Gardaneh-ye pass Iran
95 L6 Balabalangan, Kepulauan atolls Indon.
199 H2 Balabancık Turkey
139 T6 Balabanovo Rus. Fed.
78 □5 Balabio i. New Caledonia
123 J5 Bālā Bolūk Afgh.
137 O6 Balabyne Ukr.
197 P5 Bălăceanu Romania
197 L6 Bălăcița Romania
246 □ Balaclava Jamaica
127 L6 Balad Iraq
122 D7 Bālā Deh Iran
122 D3 Baladeh Māzandarān Iran
122 D3 Baladeh Māzandarān Iran
100 H2 Baladek Rus. Fed.
116 H9 Balaghat Madh. Prad. India
114 D3 Balaghat Range hills India
192 B2 Balagne reg. Corse France
186 G4 Balaguer Spain
116 F6 Balahera Rajasthan India
122 H6 Bālā Ḥowẓ Iran
95 I5 Balaiberkuak Kalimantan Indon.
95 I4 Balaikarangan Kalimantan Indon.
94 D4 Balaipungut Sumatera Indon.
95 I6 Balairiam Kalimantan Indon.
163 D10 Balaïtous mt. France
211 B8 Balaka Malawi
129 H4 Balakän Azer.
208 C3 Balakété C.A.R.
134 H4 Balakhna Rus. Fed.
139 V5 Balakirevo Rus. Fed.
82 G6 Balaklava S.A. Austr.
137 M9 Balaklava Ukr.
Balakleya Ukr. see Balakliya
137 P4 Balakliya Ukr.
120 B1 Balakovo Rus. Fed.
150 E2 Bala Lake Wales U.K.
146 C6 Balallan Western Isles, Scotland U.K.
213 H2 Balama Moz.
95 L1 Balambangan i. Malaysia
123 J4 Bālā Morghāb Afgh.
157 I4 Balan Champagne-Ardenne France
160 G5 Balan Rhône-Alpes France
116 C6 Balan Rajasthan India
197 N4 Bălan Romania
243 N9 Balancán Mex.
Balanda Rus. Fed. see Kalininsk
199 J6 Balan Dağı hill Turkey
137 K5 Balandyne Ukr.
136 H6 Bălănești Moldova
92 C4 Balanga Luzon Phil.
208 C4 Balangala Dem. Rep. Congo
114 G9 Balangoda Sri Lanka
93 C4 Balantak Sulawesi Indon.
116 F9 Balapur Mahar. India
117 K8 Balarampur W. Bengal India
161 D10 Balaruc-les-Bains France
93 B5 Balase r. Indon.
197 P4 Bălășești Romania
120 C2 Balashi Rus. Fed.
139 U6 Balashikha Rus. Fed.
135 H6 Balashov Rus. Fed.
116 D8 Balasinor Gujarat India
177 I3 Balassagyarmat Hungary
177 J5 Balástya Hungary
199 I5 Balat Turkey
176 G5 Baláta-tó l. Hungary
177 G5 Balaton l. Hungary
Balaton, Lake Hungary see Balaton
177 H4 Balatonalmádi Hungary
177 G5 Balatonboglár Hungary
177 G5 Balaton-felvidék hills Hungary
177 G5 Balatonföldvár Hungary
177 G5 Balatonfüred Hungary
177 H4 Balatonfűzfő Hungary
177 H4 Balatonkenese Hungary
176 G5 Balatonkeresztúr Hungary
177 G5 Balatonlelle Hungary
177 H5 Balatonszabadi Hungary
177 G5 Balatonszemes Hungary
176 G5 Balatonszentgyörgy Hungary
177 H5 Balatonvilágos Hungary
93 C8 Balauring Indon.
185 O3 Balazote Spain
138 G7 Balbieriškis Lith.
160 E5 Balbigny France
251 G5 Balbina Brazil
251 G5 Balbina, Represa de resr Brazil
146 H7 Balblair Highland, Scotland U.K.
147 J5 Balbriggan Ireland
177 L4 Balc Romania
210 E4 Balcad Somalia
82 G4 Balcanoona S.A. Austr.
261 H5 Balcarce Arg.
146 I13 Balcary Point Scotland U.K.
245 J4 Balcázar Mex.
197 Q7 Balchik Bulg.
199 L4 Balçıkhisar Turkey
128 A2 Balcılar Turkey
81 D13 Balclutha South I. N.Z.
151 L5 Balcombe West Sussex, England U.K.
260 D3 Balde Arg.
260 E2 Baldecito Arg.
190 E1 Baldegger See l. Switz.
149 M4 Balderhead Reservoir England U.K.
149 P7 Balderton Nottinghamshire, England U.K.
87 D13 Bald Head W.A. Austr.
257 F3 Baldim Brazil
237 J8 Bald Knob AR U.S.A.
232 D11 Bald Knob WV U.S.A.
241 Q4 Bald Mountain NV U.S.A.
151 L4 Baldock Hertfordshire, England U.K.
223 L3 Baldock Lake Man. Can.
179 H6 Baldramsdorf Austria
151 N6 Baldslow East Sussex, England U.K.
192 C5 Baldu r. Italy
227 O5 Baldwin Ont. Can.
231 F10 Baldwin FL U.S.A.
226 I6 Baldwin MI U.S.A.
226 B5 Baldwin WI U.S.A.
233 I5 Baldwinsville NY U.S.A.
233 M6 Baldwinville MA U.S.A.
222 G5 Baldy Mount B.C. Can.
223 K5 Baldy Mountain hill Man. Can.
241 W8 Baldy Peak AZ U.S.A.
107 L2 Bal'dzhikan Rus. Fed.
191 P5 Bale Croatia
94 D6 Bale Indon.
Bâle Switz. see Basel
206 C3 Baléa Mali
187 H9 Baleares, Islas is Spain
Baleares Insulae is Spain see Baleares, Islas
Balearic Islands is Spain see Baleares, Islas
95 J3 Baleh r. Malaysia
257 H2 Baleia, Ponta da pt Brazil
224 E2 Baleine, Grande Rivière de la r. Que. Can.
224 E2 Baleine, Petite Rivière de la r. Que. Can.
225 H1 Baleine, Rivière à la r. Que. Can.
162 A3 Baleines, Pointe des pt France
184 D4 Baleizão Port.
146 C10 Balemartine Argyll and Bute, Scotland U.K.
210 C3 Bale Mountains National Park Eth.
165 H6 Balen Belgium
197 N6 Băleni Romania
92 D5 Baleno Masbate Phil.
92 C4 Baler Luzon Phil.
92 C4 Baler Bay Luzon Phil.
185 N7 Balerma Spain
210 C4 Balesa well Kenya
146 B7 Baleshare i. Scotland U.K.
117 K9 Baleshwar Orissa India
141 I6 Balestrand Norway
194 E7 Balestrate Sicilia Italy
192 C6 Balestrieri, Punta mt. Italy
207 F3 Baléyara Niger
134 K4 Balezino Rus. Fed.
242 □P10 Balfate Hond.
85 J6 Balfe's Creek Qld Austr.
222 G5 Balfour B.C. Can.
81 C12 Balfour South I. N.Z.
215 K8 Balfour Eastern Cape S. Africa
215 M2 Balfour Mpumalanga S. Africa
146 K4 Balfour Orkney, Scotland U.K.
86 F7 Balfour Downs W.A. Austr.
146 H10 Balfron Stirling, Scotland U.K.
106 E3 Balgatay Mongolia
168 H5 Balge Ger.
86 I6 Balgo W.A. Austr.
86 J6 Balgo Aboriginal Reserve W.A. Austr.
146 D7 Balgown Highland, Scotland U.K.
211 C5 Balguda well Kenya
110 H5 Balguntay Xinjiang China
125 I8 Bālḥaf Yemen
210 D1 Balho Djibouti
116 D7 Bali Rajasthan India
116 D7 Bali Rajasthan India
95 K9 Bali i. Indon.
95 K9 Bali prov. Indon.
124 C2 Bali reg. Saudi Arabia
95 K8 Bali, Laut sea Indon.
95 K9 Bali, Selat sea chan. Indon.
92 D7 Baliangao Mindanao Phil.
117 K9 Baliapal Orissa India
95 K9 Bali Barat, Taman Nasional nat. park Bali Indon.
247 □3 Baliceaux i. St Vincent
117 K8 Balichak W. Bengal India
94 C3 Balige Sumatera Indon.
175 K6 Baligród Pol.
117 I9 Baliguda Orissa India
107 P6 Balihan Nei Mongol China
199 I3 Balıkesir Turkey
199 J3 Balıkesir prov. Turkey
127 K4 Balık Gölü l. Turkey
128 H3 Balīkh r. Syria/Turkey
199 I2 Balıklıçeşme Turkey
199 H4 Balıklıova Turkey
95 L5 Balikpapan Kalimantan Indon.
95 L5 Balikpapan, Teluk b. Indon.
197 M5 Bălilești Romania
92 B9 Balimbing Phil.
114 H3 Balimila Reservoir India
91 J8 Balimo P.N.G.
107 R2 Balin Nei Mongol China
94 D2 Baling Malaysia
143 N2 Bälinge Sweden
172 F5 Balingen Ger.
95 J3 Balingian Sarawak Malaysia
95 J3 Balingian r. Malaysia
177 H4 Balinka Hungary
Balinqiao Nei Mongol China see Bairin Qiao
177 K6 Balinț Romania
92 C2 Balintang Channel Phil.
146 I7 Balintore Highland, Scotland U.K.
Balira r. Andorra/Spain see Valira
Bali Sea Indon. see Bali, Laut
208 D3 Balitondo C.A.R.
92 C9 Baliungan i. Phil.
256 A2 Baliza Brazil
168 H3 Balje Ger.
124 E6 Baljurshī Saudi Arabia
164 I3 Balk Neth.
122 F1 Balkan admin. div. Turkm.
122 F2 Balkanabat Turkm.
Balkan Mountains Bulg./Serbia see Stara Planina
Balkan Oblast admin. div. Turkm. see Balkan
177 K4 Balkány Hungary
121 M1 Balkashino Kazakh.
164 J3 Balkbrug Neth.
123 L3 Balkh Afgh.
123 L3 Balkh prov. Afgh.
123 L3 Balkhab r. Afgh.
121 P4 Balkhash Kazakh.
Balkhash, Lake Kazakh. see Balkhash, Ozero
121 O5 Balkhash, Ozero l. Kazakh.
114 F3 Balkonda Andhra Prad. India
120 B4 Balkuduk Kazakh.
117 M7 Balla Bangl.
Balla Balla Zimbabwe see Mbalabala
198 B2 Ballaban Albania
148 H5 Ballabeg Isle of Man
190 G4 Ballabio Italy
146 F9 Ballachulish Highland, Scotland U.K.
87 G12 Balladonia W.A. Austr.
83 L4 Balladoran N.S.W. Austr.
147 J5 Ballagan Point Ireland
147 E5 Ballaghaderreen Ireland
156 D6 Ballancourt-sur-Essonne France
140 N2 Ballangen Norway
159 M7 Ballan-Miré France
238 J4 Ballantine MT U.S.A.
146 G12 Ballantrae South Ayrshire, Scotland U.K.
192 C8 Ballao Sardegna Italy
83 I7 Ballarat Vic. Austr.
87 F10 Ballard, Lake salt flat W.A. Austr.
114 F3 Ballarpur Mahar. India
148 H5 Ballasalla Isle of Man
146 J8 Ballater Aberdeenshire, Scotland U.K.
148 H5 Ballaugh Isle of Man
82 □1 Ball Bay Norfolk I.
206 C3 Ballé Mali
159 K6 Ballée France
258 C2 Ballena, Punta pt Chile
216 □3b Ballena, Punta de la pt Fuerteventura Canary Is
146 I12 Ballencleuch Law hill Scotland U.K.
259 C9 Ballenero, Canal sea chan. Chile
263 K2 Balleny Islands Antarctica
159 J3 Balleroy France
142 I6 Ballerup Denmark
261 F3 Ballesteros Arg.
117 J7 Ballia Uttar Prad. India
148 C8 Ballickmoyler Ireland
83 N3 Ballina N.S.W. Austr.
147 D4 Ballina Ireland
147 B6 Ballinaboy Ireland
147 H6 Ballinagar Ireland
147 H5 Ballinagh Ireland
147 H7 Ballinakill Ireland
147 H5 Ballinalack Ireland
147 G5 Ballinalee Ireland
147 G4 Ballinamallard Northern Ireland U.K.
147 F5 Ballinameen Ireland
147 G4 Ballinamore Ireland
147 G8 Ballinamult Ireland
147 E9 Ballinascarthy Ireland
147 F6 Ballinasloe Ireland
147 C8 Ballinclogher Ireland
147 E6 Ballinderreen Ireland
147 F6 Ballinderry Ireland
147 J3 Ballinderry Northern Ireland U.K.
147 I3 Ballinderry r. Northern Ireland U.K.
147 E5 Ballindine Ireland
147 D6 Ballindooly Ireland
147 E9 Ballineen Ireland
147 E8 Ballingarry Limerick Ireland
147 G7 Ballingarry Tipperary Ireland
147 D9 Ballingeary Ireland
237 F10 Ballinger TX U.S.A.
146 J10 Ballingry Fife, Scotland U.K.
147 D9 Ballingurteen Ireland
147 E9 Ballinhassig Ireland
147 E5 Ballinlough Ireland
146 I9 Ballinluig Perth and Kinross, Scotland U.K.
147 D5 Ballinrobe Ireland
147 E7 Ballinruan Ireland
147 B9 Ballinskelligs Ireland
147 E9 Ballinspittle Ireland
147 J2 Ballintoy Northern Ireland U.K.
146 J9 Ballintuim Perth and Kinross, Scotland U.K.
147 G7 Ballinure Ireland
147 I5 Ballivor Ireland
173 I4 Ballmertshofen Ger.
186 F4 Ballobar Spain
146 G11 Balloch West Dunbartonshire, Scotland U.K.
159 L5 Ballon France
148 D8 Ballon Ireland
157 M8 Ballon d'Alsace mt. France
157 M8 Ballons des Vosges, Parc Naturel Régional des nature res. France
177 I5 Ballószög Hungary
159 I6 Ballots France
198 A2 Ballsh Albania
82 □2 Ball's Pyramid i. Lord Howe I. Austr.
169 K8 Ballstädt Ger.
233 L5 Ballston Spa NY U.S.A.
164 I2 Ballum Neth.
147 F3 Ballure Ireland
234 D4 Bally PA U.S.A.
147 E8 Ballyagran Ireland
147 I4 Ballybay Ireland
147 G3 Ballybofey Ireland
147 J5 Ballyboghil Ireland
147 I2 Ballybogy Northern Ireland U.K.
147 J6 Ballybrack Dublin Ireland
147 B9 Ballybrack Kerry Ireland
147 G7 Ballybrophy Ireland
147 C7 Ballybunnion Ireland
147 G7 Ballycahill Ireland
147 H7 Ballycallan Ireland
147 J7 Ballycanew Ireland
147 I7 Ballycarney Ireland
147 D5 Ballycarra Ireland
147 K3 Ballycarry Northern Ireland U.K.
147 D4 Ballycastle Ireland
147 J2 Ballycastle Northern Ireland U.K.
147 K3 Ballyclare Northern Ireland U.K.
147 B6 Ballyconneely Ireland
147 B6 Ballyconneely Bay Ireland
147 G4 Ballyconnell Cavan Ireland
147 E4 Ballyconnell Sligo Ireland
147 G9 Ballycotton Bay Ireland
147 C4 Ballycroy Ireland
147 G6 Ballycumber Ireland
147 F6 Ballydangan Ireland
147 F6 Ballydavid Ireland
147 B8 Ballydavid Head Ireland
147 D9 Ballydehob Ireland
147 D8 Ballydesmond Ireland
147 F8 Ballyduff Ireland
147 D5 Ballyfarnagh Ireland
147 F4 Ballyfarnan Ireland
147 F9 Ballyfeard Ireland
148 C7 Ballyfin Ireland
147 F6 Ballyforan Ireland
147 H6 Ballyfore Ireland
147 K3 Ballygalley Northern Ireland U.K.
147 F5 Ballygar Ireland
147 J7 Ballygarrett Ireland
147 H4 Ballygawley Northern Ireland U.K.
147 D5 Ballyglass Mayo Ireland
147 E5 Ballyglass Mayo Ireland
147 H2 Ballygorman Ireland
147 K3 Ballygowan Northern Ireland U.K.
146 D11 Ballygrant Argyll and Bute, Scotland U.K.
147 I8 Ballyhack Ireland
147 E8 Ballyhaght Ireland
147 D7 Ballyhahill Ireland
148 C5 Ballyhaise Ireland
147 L4 Ballyhalbert Northern Ireland U.K.
147 E5 Ballyhaunis Ireland
147 C8 Ballyheigue Ireland
147 C8 Ballyheigue Bay Ireland
147 F8 Ballyhooly Ireland
147 K4 Ballyhornan Northern Ireland U.K.
147 E8 Ballyhoura Mountains hills Ireland
147 H5 Ballyjamesduff Ireland
147 G6 Ballykeeran Ireland
147 H2 Ballykelly Northern Ireland U.K.
147 H6 Ballykilleen Ireland
147 F8 Ballylanders Ireland
147 F5 Ballyleague Ireland
148 D5 Ballyleny Northern Ireland U.K.
147 H2 Ballyliffen Ireland
147 D7 Ballylongford Ireland
147 H7 Ballylynan Ireland
147 G8 Ballymacarberry Ireland
147 C8 Ballymacelligott Ireland
147 H7 Ballymack Ireland
148 C5 Ballymackilroy Northern Ireland U.K.
147 G8 Ballymacmague Ireland
147 G9 Ballymacoda Ireland
147 H3 Ballymagorry Northern Ireland U.K.
147 G5 Ballymahon Ireland
147 D9 Ballymakeery Ireland
147 K4 Ballymartin Northern Ireland U.K.
147 J3 Ballymena Northern Ireland U.K.
147 F5 Ballymoe Ireland
147 I2 Ballymoney Northern Ireland U.K.
147 G2 Ballymore Donegal Ireland
147 G6 Ballymore Westmeath Ireland
147 E4 Ballymote Ireland
147 I7 Ballymurphy Ireland
147 F5 Ballymurry Ireland
147 I8 Ballynabola Ireland
147 D9 Ballynacarriga Ireland
148 B6 Ballynacarrigy Ireland
147 H5 Ballynafid Ireland
147 C6 Ballynahinch Ireland
147 K4 Ballynahinch Northern Ireland U.K.
147 G6 Ballynahowen Ireland
147 B5 Ballynakill Bay Ireland
147 E8 Ballynamona Ireland
147 C8 Ballynaskreena Ireland
147 E7 Ballyneety Ireland
148 E7 Ballynockan Ireland
147 F8 Ballynoe Ireland
147 K3 Ballynure Northern Ireland U.K.
147 F8 Ballyporeen Ireland
147 L4 Ballyquintin Point Northern Ireland U.K.
147 H7 Ballyragget Ireland
147 H7 Ballyroan Ireland
147 I3 Ballyronan Northern Ireland U.K.
147 C9 Ballyroon Ireland
147 F3 Ballyshannon Ireland
147 E7 Ballysteen Ireland
147 I8 Ballyteige Bay Ireland
147 I6 Ballytore Ireland
147 D6 Ballyvaughan Ireland
147 F6 Ballyvoneen Ireland
147 J2 Ballyvoy Northern Ireland U.K.
147 G8 Ballyvoyle Ireland
147 L3 Ballywalter Northern Ireland U.K.
148 E5 Ballyward Northern Ireland U.K.
147 I8 Ballywilliam Ireland
146 E8 Balmacara Highland, Scotland U.K.
259 C7 Balmaceda Aisén Chile
252 C6 Balmaceda Antofagasta Chile
146 G10 Balmaha Stirling, Scotland U.K.
Balmartin Western Isles, Scotland U.K. see Baile Mhartainn
183 N2 Balmaseda Spain
177 K4 Balmazújváros Hungary
190 C5 Balme Italy
146 L8 Balmedie Aberdeenshire, Scotland U.K.
Balmer Rajasthan India see Barmer
223 M5 Balmertown Ont. Can.
190 D3 Balmhorn mt. Switz.
82 H7 Balmoral Vic. Austr.
81 G9 Balmoral South I. N.Z.
237 D10 Balmorhea TX U.S.A.
190 E4 Balmuccia Italy
146 F8 Balnacra Highland, Scotland U.K.
146 D10 Balnahard Argyll and Bute, Scotland U.K.
146 H7 Balnapaling Highland, Scotland U.K.
261 F2 Balnearia Arg.
186 E2 Balneario de Panticosa Huesca Spain
261 H6 Balneario Orense Arg.
261 G6 Balneario Oriente Arg.
93 C4 Baloa Sulawesi Indon.
190 E5 Balocco Italy
123 L7 Balochistan prov. Pak.
119 I4 Balochistan reg. Pak.
116 H9 Balod Chhattisgarh India
117 I8 Baloda Chhattisgarh India
116 I9 Baloda Bazar Chhattisgarh India
176 F4 Balogunyom Hungary
95 G6 Balok, Teluk b. Indon.
209 B8 Balombo Angola
83 L3 Balonne r. Qld Austr.
93 D2 Balontohe i. Indon.
156 H8 Balot France
177 I5 Balotaszállás Hungary
116 D7 Balotra Rajasthan India

Barnwell to Beaucouzé
285

231 G9 Barnwell SC U.S.A.
207 G4 Baro Nigeria
Baroda Gujarat India see Vadodara
116 F7 Baroda Madh. Prad. India
215 J7 Baroda S. Africa
214 I9 Baroe S. Africa
179 K6 Bärofen mt. Austria
116 H7 Baronda Madh. Prad. India
190 E4 Barone, Monte mt. Italy
108 B3 Barong Sichuan China
192 D7 Baronia reg. Sardegna Italy
139 P8 Baron'ki Belarus
161 G8 Baronnies reg. France
87 I8 Barons Range hills W.A. Austr.
157 M6 Baronville France
78 □6 Barora Fa i. Solomon Is
78 □6 Barora Ite i. Solomon Is
208 E3 Baroua C.A.R.
210 B2 Baro Wenz r. Eth.
123 O3 Barowghīl, Kowtal-e pass Afgh.
138 K6 Barowka Belarus
117 N6 Barpathar Assam India
117 M6 Barpeta Assam India
Bar Pla Soi Thai. see Chon Buri
125 I3 Barqā ad Dumrān esc. Saudi Arabia
128 E10 Barqā Damaj well Saudi Arabia
128 C10 Barqah, Jabal mt. Egypt
187 C12 Barqueros Spain
226 H4 Barques, Point Aux MI U.S.A.
227 L5 Barques, Point Aux MI U.S.A.
184 C2 Barquinha Port.
250 D2 Barquisimeto Venez.
157 N7 Barr France
146 G12 Barr South Ayrshire, Scotland U.K.
254 E4 Barra Brazil
146 A9 Barra i. Scotland U.K.
146 B8 Barra, Sound of sea chan. Scotland U.K.
83 M4 Barraba N.S.W. Austr.
256 C5 Barra Bonita Brazil
256 C5 Barra Bonita, Represa resr Brazil
251 H5 Barraca da Boca Brazil
253 F2 Barracão do Barreto Brazil
187 D7 Barracas Spain
186 C6 Barrachina Spain
232 E9 Barrackville WV U.S.A.
214 F10 Barracouta, Cape S. Africa
254 E5 Barra da Estiva Brazil
245 J5 Barra de Cazones Mex.
244 C6 Barra de Navidad Mex.
256 D6 Barra de Santos inlet Brazil
257 G3 Barra de São Francisco Brazil
257 G5 Barra de São João Brazil
253 F3 Barra do Bugres Brazil
254 D3 Barra do Corda Brazil
209 B7 Barra do Cuanza Angola
257 G3 Barra do Cuieté Brazil
256 A1 Barra do Garças Brazil
254 E4 Barrado Mendes Brazil
257 F5 Barra do Piraí Brazil
261 I2 Barra do Quaraí Brazil
253 F1 Barra do São Manuel Brazil
256 C6 Barra do Turvo Brazil
256 D6 Barra do Una Brazil
213 G4 Barra Falsa, Ponta da pt Moz.
194 G9 Barrafranca Sicilia Italy
Barraigh i. Scotland U.K. see Barra
242 □R10 Barra Kruta Hond.
182 D4 Barral Spain
192 C9 Barrali Sardegna Italy
257 F4 Barra Longa Brazil
257 E5 Barra Mansa Brazil
203 G3 Barrāmīyah Egypt
163 E8 Barran France
123 O6 Barrana Pak.
252 A2 Barranca Peru
250 C2 Barranca Venez.
250 C3 Barrancabermeja Col.
242 F4 Barranca del Cobre, Parque Natural nature res. Mex.
260 C5 Barrancas Neuquén Arg.
261 G3 Barrancas Santa Fé Arg.
260 C5 Barrancas r. Arg.
261 H2 Barrancas r. Arg.
246 G8 Barrancas Col.
250 D2 Barrancas Barinas Venez.
251 F2 Barrancas Monagas Venez.
250 C2 Barranco de Loba Col.
216 □3a Barranco de Santiago La Gomera Canary Is
184 D6 Barranco do Velho Port.
184 F4 Barrancos Port.
185 P4 Barranda Spain
245 J5 Barra Norte Mex.
250 C2 Barranquilla Atlántico Col.
250 C4 Barranquilla Guaviare Col.
250 B6 Barranquita Peru
247 □1 Barranquitas Puerto Rico
250 C2 Barranquitas Venez.
146 C10 Barrapoll Argyll and Bute, Scotland U.K.
254 E3 Barras Brazil
227 Q1 Barraute Que. Can.
185 O2 Barrax Spain
233 M6 Barre MA U.S.A.
233 M4 Barre VT U.S.A.
193 L4 Barrea, Lago di l. Italy
260 C2 Barreal Arg.
161 D8 Barre-des-Cévennes France
161 I7 Barre des Ecrins mt. France
254 D5 Barreiras Brazil
251 G5 Barreirinha Brazil
254 E2 Barreirinhas Brazil
255 B5 Barreiro r. Brazil
184 A3 Barreiro Port.
254 C4 Barreiro do Nascimento Brazil
254 G4 Barreiros Brazil
161 I9 Barrême France
115 M6 Barren Island Andaman & Nicobar Is India
Barren Island Kiribati see Starbuck Island
220 C4 Barren Islands AK U.S.A.
256 C4 Barretos Brazil
240 P9 Barrett CA U.S.A.
86 I5 Barrett, Mount hill W.A. Austr.
222 H4 Barrhead Alta Can.
146 H11 Barrhead East Renfrewshire, Scotland U.K.
81 F10 Barrhill South I. N.Z.
146 G12 Barrhill South Ayrshire, Scotland U.K.
124 F7 Barrī i. Saudi Arabia
186 J4 Barriada Nueva Spain
224 E4 Barrie Ont. Can.
182 C3 Barrié de la Maza, Encoro de resr Spain
227 L4 Barrie Island Ont. Can.
80 J3 Barrier, Cape North I. N.Z.
263 F2 Barrier Bay Antarctica
222 F5 Barrière B.C. Can.
82 H4 Barrier Range hills N.S.W. Austr.
243 O9 Barrier Reef Belize
78 □1 Barrigada Guam
225 H5 Barrington N.S. Can.
214 G9 Barrington S. Africa
83 M5 Barrington, Mount N.S.W. Austr.
Barrington Island Islas Galápagos Ecuador see Santa Fé, Isla
223 K3 Barrington Lake Man. Can.
83 M5 Barrington Tops National Park N.S.W. Austr.
83 J3 Barringun N.S.W. Austr.
187 D12 Barrio del Peral Spain
187 E8 Barrio Mar Spain
182 I3 Barrios de Luna, Embalse de resr Spain
182 E6 Barrô Port.
254 C5 Barro Alto Brazil
182 E8 Barroca Port.
257 F2 Barrocão Brazil
182 D4 Barroças e Taias Port.
157 J6 Barrois, Plateau du France
257 H2 Barrolândia Brazil
226 C4 Barron WI U.S.A.
226 C4 Barronett WI U.S.A.
184 G3 Barros, Tierra de reg. Spain
260 A6 Barros Arana Chile
182 C5 Barroselas Port.
257 F4 Barroso Brazil
243 I4 Barroterán Mex.
247 □3 Barrouallie St Vincent
261 G6 Barrow Arg.
147 I8 Barrow r. Ireland
220 C2 Barrow AK U.S.A.
220 C2 Barrow, Point AK U.S.A.
151 K2 Barrowby Lincolnshire, England U.K.
84 D6 Barrow Creek N.T. Austr.
149 M6 Barrowford Lancashire, England U.K.
149 K5 Barrow-in-Furness Cumbria, England U.K.
86 C6 Barrow Island W.A. Austr.
86 C6 Barrow Island Nature Reserve W.A. Austr.
85 J3 Barrow Point Qld Austr.
87 I9 Barrow Range hills W.A. Austr.
221 I2 Barrow Strait Nunavut Can.
149 Q6 Barrow upon Humber North Lincolnshire, England U.K.
87 F9 Barr Smith Range hills W.A. Austr.
182 G6 Barruecopardo Spain
183 L3 Barruelo de Santullan Spain
150 F5 Barry Vale of Glamorgan, Wales U.K.
214 E9 Barrydale S. Africa
83 K7 Barry Mountains Vic. Austr.
224 E4 Barrys Bay Ont. Can.
232 A5 Barryton MI U.S.A.
80 J5 Barryville North I. N.Z.
234 F2 Barryville NY U.S.A.
177 L5 Bârsa Romania
163 D6 Barsac France
120 H5 Barsakel'mes, Poluostrov pen. Kazakh.
120 I5 Barsakel'messkiy Zapovednik nature res. Kazakh.
206 E3 Barsalogo Burkina
116 D5 Barsalpur Rajasthan India
197 M3 Bârsana Romania
168 J3 Barsbüttel Ger.
121 R3 Barshatas Kazakh.
Barshi Mahar. India see Barsi
114 D3 Barsi Mahar. India
169 H6 Barsinghausen Ger.
142 F6 Barsø i. Denmark
117 K7 Barsoi Bihar India
168 E4 Barßel Ger.
240 O7 Barstow CA U.S.A.
138 E5 Barstyčiai Lith.
139 U7 Barsuki Rus. Fed.
114 G3 Barsur Chhattisgarh India
156 I7 Bar-sur-Aube France
156 H7 Bar-sur-Seine France
138 E5 Bārta Latvia
138 E5 Bārta r. Latvia
123 N2 Bartang Tajik.
123 N3 Bartang r. Tajik.
160 K1 Bartenheim France
172 H3 Bartenstein Ger.
170 G2 Barth Ger.
170 G2 Barthe r. Ger.
172 H4 Bartholomä Ger.
237 I9 Bartholomew, Bayou r. LA U.S.A.
Bartholomew Island Vanuatu see Malo
251 G3 Bartica Guyana
126 F3 Bartın Turkey
85 J4 Bartle Frere, Mount Qld Austr.
232 C10 Bartles OH U.S.A.
241 V2 Bartles, Mount UT U.S.A.
237 G7 Bartlesville OK U.S.A.
236 F5 Bartlett NE U.S.A.
233 N4 Bartlett NH U.S.A.
222 G2 Bartlett Lake N.W.T. Can.
241 U8 Bartlett Reservoir AZ U.S.A.
80 L5 Bartletts North I. N.Z.
175 I2 Bartniki Pol.
175 L1 Bartninkai Lith.
149 L6 Barton Lancashire, England U.K.
233 M4 Barton VT U.S.A.
151 L4 Barton-le-Clay Bedfordshire, England U.K.
151 I2 Barton-under-Needwood Staffordshire, England U.K.
149 Q6 Barton-upon-Humber North Lincolnshire, England U.K.
226 E9 Bartonville IL U.S.A.
143 Q7 Bartoszyce Pol.
231 G12 Bartow FL U.S.A.
140 N3 Barturte mt. Sweden
138 E5 Bartuva r. Lith.
250 C2 Baru, Isla de i. Col.
175 H3 Baruchowo Pol.
117 L8 Baruipur W. Bengal India
184 E2 Barulho Port.
192 C8 Barumini Sardegna Italy
94 D3 Barumun r. Indon.
106 E8 Barun Qinghai China
95 J9 Barung i. Indon.
Barunga N.T. Austr. see Bamyili
107 N1 Barun-Torey, Ozero l. Rus. Fed.
94 C3 Barus Sumatera Indon.
171 I6 Baruth Brandenburg Ger.
171 K8 Baruth Sachsen Ger.
106 J2 Baruunharaa Mongolia
106 I5 Baruunsuu Mongolia
106 D2 Baruunturuun Mongolia
107 M3 Baruun-Urt Mongolia
115 I3 Baruva Andhra Prad. India
146 C6 Barvas Western Isles, Scotland U.K.
165 H8 Barvaux Belgium
168 G5 Barver Ger.
137 Q5 Barvinkove Ukr.
117 J8 Barwa Jharkhand India
116 F8 Barwah Madh. Prad. India
116 C8 Barwala Gujarat India
116 E5 Barwala Haryana India
116 E8 Barwani Madh. Prad. India
116 G7 Barwa Sagar Uttar Prad. India
168 K5 Barwedel Ger.
Barwéli Mali see Baraouéli
174 E2 Barwice Pol.
83 K4 Barwon r. N.S.W. Austr.
139 R7 Baryatino Rus. Fed.
139 U6 Barybino Rus. Fed.
174 E4 Barycz r. Pol.
Barygaza Gujarat India see Bharuch
138 L7 Barysaw Belarus
135 I5 Barysh Rus. Fed.
137 K3 Baryshivka Ukr.
125 N4 Barzamān Oman
182 I2 Bárzana Spain
177 L5 Bârzava Romania
123 K3 Basaga Turkm.
122 F8 Bāsa'īdū Iran
258 F2 Basail Arg.
97 G9 Basăk, Tônlé r. Cambodia
85 J5 Basalt r. Qld Austr.
Basalt Island H.K. China see Fo Shek Chau
209 E6 Basanga Dem. Rep. Congo
208 C4 Basankusu Dem. Rep. Congo
117 K6 Basantpur Bihar India
114 E3 Basar Mahar. India
136 H7 Basarabeasca Moldova
197 Q6 Basarabi Romania
Basargechar Armenia see Vardenis
261 H3 Basavilbaso Arg.
92 D7 Basay Negros Phil.
129 C5 Başçakmak Turkey
197 O5 Bâsca Mică r. Romania
186 K3 Bàscara Spain
157 K4 Bascharage Lux.
150 G2 Baschurch Shropshire, England U.K.
193 L2 Basciano Italy
92 C1 Basco Phil.
82 E5 Bascombe Well Conservation Park nature res. S.A. Austr.
183 M3 Basconcillos del Tozo Spain
209 B6 Bas-Congo prov. Dem. Rep. Congo
163 D8 Bascons France
163 E8 Bascous France
258 C3 Bascuñán, Cabo c. Chile
183 P8 Bascuñana, Sierra de mts Spain
168 H4 Basdahl Ger.
170 H5 Basdorf Ger.
129 A5 Başdurak Turkey
165 E7 Basècles Belgium
84 D8 Basedow Range hills N.T. Austr.
190 D1 Basel Switz.
191 K3 Baselga di Pinè Italy
193 N5 Baselice Italy
190 D1 Basellandschaft canton Switz.
160 L1 Basel-Mulhouse airport France
161 E6 Bas-en-Basset France
193 Q6 Basentello r. Italy
193 R7 Basento r. Italy
163 F10 Baserca, Embalse de resr Spain
197 P3 Başeu r. Romania
92 E6 Basey Samar Phil.
122 H8 Bashākerd, Kūhhā-ye mts Iran
Bashan Jiangxi China see Chongren
Bashanta Rus. Fed. see Gorodovikovsk
222 H4 Bashaw Alta Can.
121 U2 Bashchelakskiy Khrebet mts Rus. Fed.
215 M8 Bashee r. S. Africa
215 M7 Bashee Bridge S. Africa
123 N4 Bashgul r. Afgh.
122 D7 Bāshī Iran
90 F2 Bashi Channel Taiwan
209 E6 Bashimuke Dem. Rep. Congo
110 H1 Bashkaus r. Rus. Fed.
Bashkiria aut. rep. Rus. Fed. see Bashkortostan, Respublika
Bashkirskaya A.S.S.R. aut. rep. Rus. Fed. see Bashkortostan, Respublika
120 G1 Bashkirskiy Zapovednik nature res. Rus. Fed.
129 F4 Bashk'oi Georgia
120 G1 Bashkortostan, Respublika aut. rep. Rus. Fed.
135 H5 Bashmakovo Rus. Fed.
Bāsh Qal'eh Iran see Pīsh Qal'eh
122 D6 Bāsht Iran
137 L6 Bashtanka Ukr.
125 K9 Bashūri, Ra's pt Suquṭrā Yemen
116 F6 Basi Rajasthan India
117 J8 Basia Jharkhand India
183 O2 Basigo Spain
85 M1 Basilaki Island P.N.G.
92 C8 Basilan i. Phil.
92 D8 Basilan Strait Phil.
151 M4 Basildon Essex, England U.K.
237 I10 Basile LA U.S.A.
207 H6 Basile, Pico vol. Equat. Guinea
191 O3 Basiliano Italy
193 P6 Basilicata admin. reg. Italy
195 I6 Basiluzzo, Isola i. Isole Lipari Italy
238 J4 Basin WY U.S.A.
143 M1 Bäsingen l. Sweden
151 J5 Basingstoke Hampshire, England U.K.
223 J4 Basin Lake Sask. Can.
127 L6 Bāsīra r. Iraq
122 H6 Başīrān Iran
117 L8 Basirhat W. Bengal India
128 D3 Basīṭ, Ra's al pt Syria
137 O2 Basivka Ukr.
188 E3 Baška Croatia
177 H2 Baška Czech Rep.
233 □R3 Baskahegan Lake ME U.S.A.
139 R7 Baskakovka Rus. Fed.
127 L4 Başkale Turkey
224 F4 Baskatong, Réservoir resr Que. Can.
86 G4 Baskerville, Cape W.A. Austr.
199 L4 Başkomutan Milli Parkı nat. park Turkey
199 L4 Başkomutan Tarıhı Milli Parkı nat. park Turkey
129 B5 Başköy Erzurum Turkey
128 A2 Başköy Karaman Turkey
135 I6 Baskunchak, Ozero l. Rus. Fed.
129 I4 Baş Layski Azer.
Basle Switz. see Basel
129 H6 Başlıbel Azer.
149 N7 Baslow Derbyshire, England U.K.
199 L5 Başmakçı Turkey
114 E3 Basmat Mahar. India
129 J6 Baş Muğan Kanalı canal Azer.
94 E5 Baso i. Indon.
116 F8 Basoda Madh. Prad. India
190 E3 Basodino mt. Italy/Switz.
208 D4 Basoko Dem. Rep. Congo
209 D6 Basongo Dem. Rep. Congo
Basora, Punt pt Aruba see Basora, Punta
247 □9 Basora, Punta pt Aruba
211 B6 Basotu Tanz.
129 I5 Baş Qärvänd Azer.
Basque Country aut. comm. Spain see País Vasco
163 F7 Bas-Quercy reg. France
Basra Iraq see Al Başrah
157 O6 Bas-Rhin dept France
Bass, Îlots de is Îs Australes Fr. Polynesia see Marotiri
192 C5 Bassacutena Sardegna Italy
192 C5 Bassacutena r. Italy
198 C5 Bassae tourist site Greece
223 H5 Bassano Alta Can.
191 L4 Bassano del Grappa Italy
192 I3 Bassano Romano Italy
207 F4 Bassar Togo
265 G6 Bassas da India rf Indian Ocean
114 C6 Bassas de Pedro Padua Bank sea feature India
206 D4 Bassawa Côte d'Ivoire
190 C1 Bassecourt Switz.
158 I7 Basse-Goulaine France
96 B6 Bassein Myanmar
96 B6 Bassein r. Myanmar
208 D3 Basse-Kotto pref. C.A.R.
159 K4 Basse-Normandie admin. reg. France
149 K4 Bassenthwaite Lake England U.K.
247 □3 Basse-Pointe Martinique
Basses-Alpes dept France see Alpes-de-Haute-Provence
206 B3 Basse Santa Su Gambia
161 H9 Basses Gorges du Verdon France
Basses-Pyrénées dept France see Pyrénées-Atlantiques
247 □2 Basse-Terre Guadeloupe
247 □2 Basse-Terre i. Guadeloupe
247 □2 Basseterre St Kitts and Nevis
247 □7 Basse Terre Trin. and Tob.
236 F4 Bassett NE U.S.A.
232 F12 Bassett VA U.S.A.
241 V9 Bassett Peak AZ U.S.A.
233 □Q4 Bass Harbor ME U.S.A.
193 K4 Bassiano Italy
163 G10 Bassiès, Pic Rouge de mt. France
157 J8 Bassigny reg. France
206 D3 Bassikounou Maur.
207 F4 Bassila Benin
151 L3 Bassingbourn Cambridgeshire, England U.K.
149 P7 Bassingham Lincolnshire, England U.K.
202 D5 Basso, Plateau de Chad
163 E8 Bassoues France
146 K10 Bass Rock i. Scotland U.K.
83 K8 Bass Strait Tas./Vic. Austr.
168 G5 Bassum Ger.
224 B3 Basswood Lake Ont. Can.
226 C1 Basswood Lake MN U.S.A.
160 H5 Bassy France
142 I5 Båstad Sweden
122 F8 Bastak Iran
127 Q5 Bastam Iran
122 B3 Bastānābād Iran
193 J2 Bastardo Italy
192 C3 Bastelica Corse France
192 B4 Bastelicaccia Corse France
163 C8 Bastennes France
169 J10 Bastheim Ger.
117 I6 Basti Uttar Prad. India
192 C2 Bastia Corse France
Bastia airport Corse France see Poretta
193 J1 Bastia Italy
232 D11 Bastian VA U.S.A.
165 I8 Bastogne Belgium
170 E2 Bastorf Ger.
256 B4 Bastos Brazil
237 J9 Bastrop LA U.S.A.
237 G10 Bastrop TX U.S.A.
140 P4 Bastuträsk Sweden
136 F1 Bastyn' Belarus
94 E5 Basu, Tanjung pt Indon.
123 K9 Basul r. Pak.
Basuo Hainan China see Dongfang
Basutoland country Africa see Lesotho
139 O8 Basya r. Belarus
128 A2 Başyayla Turkey
Bas-Zaïre prov. Dem. Rep. Congo see Bas-Congo
188 F4 Bat mt. Croatia
125 M4 Bat, Al Khutm and Al Ayn tourist site Oman
207 H6 Bata Equat. Guinea
177 H5 Báta Hungary
177 L5 Bata Romania
92 C4 Bataan Peninsula Luzon Phil.
246 B2 Batabanó, Golfo de b. Cuba
92 C2 Batac Luzon Phil.
242 E4 Batacosa Mex.
131 O3 Batagay Rus. Fed.
131 O3 Batagay-Alyta Rus. Fed.
256 A4 Bataguassu Brazil
256 A5 Bataiporã Brazil
197 M9 Batak Bulg.
95 K7 Batakan Kalimantan Indon.
116 E4 Batala Punjab India
254 E3 Batalha Brazil
182 C9 Batalha Port.
94 F4 Batam i. Indon.
208 E4 Batama Dem. Rep. Congo
131 N3 Batamay Rus. Fed.
120 H2 Batamshinskiy Kazakh.
Batamshy Kazakh. see Batamshinskiy
109 M1 Batan Jiangsu China
92 D1 Batan i. Phil.
92 E5 Batan i. Phil.
108 B3 Batang Sichuan China
95 H8 Batang Jawa Indon.
208 A5 Batanga Gabon
208 C3 Batangafo C.A.R.
95 J4 Batang Ai National Park Malaysia
92 C5 Batangas Luzon Phil.
94 F5 Batanghari r. Indon.
93 G4 Batangpele i. Papua Indon.
95 I4 Batangtarang Kalimantan Indon.
94 C4 Batangtoru Sumatera Indon.
92 D1 Batan Islands Phil.
93 G4 Batanta i. Papua Indon.
177 K5 Batăr Romania
177 H5 Bátaszék Hungary
256 D4 Batatais Brazil
260 E4 Batavia Arg.
Batavia Jawa Indon. see Jakarta
251 H3 Batavia Suriname
226 F8 Batavia IL U.S.A.
232 G6 Batavia NY U.S.A.
232 A9 Batavia OH U.S.A.
139 P8 Batayeva Rus. Fed.
135 G7 Bataysk Rus. Fed.
92 C6 Batbatan i. Phil.
227 J2 Batchawana Ont. Can.
227 J3 Batchawana r. Ont. Can.
226 J3 Batchawana Bay Ont. Can.
224 C4 Batchawana Mountain hill Ont. Can.
84 C2 Batchelor N.T. Austr.
97 F8 Bătdâmbâng Cambodia
186 F5 Batea Spain
94 A2 Bateemeucica, Gunung mt. Indon.
209 B5 Batéké, Plateaux Congo
83 M6 Batemans Bay N.S.W. Austr.
140 S1 Båteng Norway
185 J3 Baterno Spain
82 □1 Bates, Mount hill Norfolk I.
231 G9 Batesburg SC U.S.A.
87 F9 Bates Range hills W.A. Austr.
237 J8 Batesville AR U.S.A.
237 K8 Batesville MS U.S.A.
139 N3 Batetskiy Rus. Fed.
225 H4 Bath N.B. Can.
227 R5 Bath Ont. Can.
246 □ Bath Jamaica
247 □2 Bath St Kitts and Nevis
150 H5 Bath Bath and North East Somerset, England U.K.
226 D9 Bath IL U.S.A.
233 □P5 Bath ME U.S.A.
232 H6 Bath NY U.S.A.
234 E3 Bath PA U.S.A.
202 C6 Batha pref. Chad
202 C6 Batha watercourse Chad
150 H5 Bath and North East Somerset admin. div. England U.K.
150 H5 Batheaston Bath and North East Somerset, England U.K.
150 H5 Bathford Bath and North East Somerset, England U.K.
146 I11 Bathgate West Lothian, Scotland U.K.
116 E4 Bathinda Punjab India
164 J4 Bathmen Neth.
261 G5 Bathurst Arg.
83 L5 Bathurst N.S.W. Austr.
225 H4 Bathurst N.B. Can.
Bathurst Gambia see Banjul
215 K9 Bathurst S. Africa
220 F2 Bathurst, Cape N.W.T. Can.
85 J3 Bathurst Bay Qld Austr.
220 H3 Bathurst Inlet Nunavut Can.
220 H3 Bathurst Inlet inlet Nunavut Can.
84 C1 Bathurst Island N.T. Austr.
221 I2 Bathurst Island Nunavut Can.
123 I4 Bathyz Döwlet Gorugy nature res. Turkm.
210 D2 Batī Eth.
207 F4 Batia Benin
206 E4 Batié Burkina
93 B5 Batikala, Tanjung pt Indon.
79 □7 Batiki i. Fiji
157 K5 Batilly France
199 I5 Batı Menteşe Dağları mts Turkey
124 H1 Bāṭin, Wādī al watercourse Asia
177 H6 Batina Croatia
254 E4 Batista, Serra da hills Brazil
199 L6 Batı Toroslar mts Turkey
177 J2 Batizovce Slovakia
121 N7 Batken Kyrg.
121 N8 Batken admin. div. Kyrg.
129 H3 Batlaich Rus. Fed.
122 E5 Bāṭlāq-e Gavkhūnī marsh Iran
149 N6 Batley West Yorkshire, England U.K.
83 L6 Batlow N.S.W. Austr.
127 J5 Batman Turkey
205 G2 Batna Alg.
105 L2 Batō Japan
196 J6 Batočina Serbia
94 □ Batok, Bukit Sing.
94 □ Batok, Bukit hill Sing.
209 E9 Batoka Zambia
97 D11 Batong, Ko i. Thai.
237 J10 Baton Rouge LA U.S.A.
177 I4 Bátonyterenye Hungary
242 F4 Batopilas Mex.
177 H4 Bátorove Kosihy Slovakia
175 K5 Batorz Pol.
116 E3 Batote Jammu and Kashmir
208 B4 Batouala Gabon
207 I5 Batouri Cameroon
177 H3 Bátovce Slovakia
Batrā' tourist site Jordan see Petra
124 C3 Batrā, Jabal mt. Saudi Arabia
128 D9 Batrā', Jabal al mt. Jordan
177 L5 Bătrâna, Vârful mt. Romania
97 H9 Ba Tri Vietnam
128 D4 Batroûn Lebanon
140 T1 Båtsfjord Norway
234 F5 Batsto r. NJ U.S.A.
Battambang Cambodia see Bătdâmbâng
169 G8 Battenberg (Eder) Ger.
190 D1 Bätterkinden Switz.
116 E4 Batti Punjab India
114 G9 Batticaloa Sri Lanka
115 M8 Batti Malv i. Andaman & Nicobar Is India
193 N6 Battipaglia Italy
223 I4 Battle r. Alta/Sask. Can.
151 M6 Battle East Sussex, England U.K.
84 C3 Battle Creek r. N.T. Austr.
223 I5 Battle Creek r. Can./U.S.A.
226 I7 Battle Creek MI U.S.A.
213 F3 Battlefields Zimbabwe
223 I4 Battleford Sask. Can.
240 P1 Battle Mountain NV U.S.A.
240 O1 Battle Mountain mt. NV U.S.A.
177 K5 Battonya Hungary
116 E1 Battura Glacier Jammu and Kashmir
210 C3 Batu mt. Eth.
95 J3 Batu, Bukit mt. Malaysia
94 C5 Batu, Pulau-pulau is Indon.
95 M3 Batu, Tanjung pt Indon.
93 C7 Batuata i. Indon.
95 K4 Batuayau, Bukit mt. Indon.
94 G6 Batubetumbang Indon.
95 K3 Batu Bora, Bukit mt. Malaysia
260 B4 Batuco Chile
93 B4 Batudaka i. Indon.
94 D2 Batu Gajah Malaysia
93 C4 Batuhitam, Tanjung pt Indon.
93 C4 Batui Sulawesi Indon.
92 E9 Batulaki Mindanao Phil.
95 L6 Batulicin Kalimantan Indon.
95 K4 Batulilangmebang, Gunung mt. Indon.
Batum Georgia see Bat'umi
129 C4 Bat'umi Georgia
94 D6 Batumonga Indon.
94 E4 Batu Pahat Malaysia
94 D2 Batu Putih, Gunung mt. Malaysia
94 F7 Baturaja Sumatera Indon.
95 I9 Baturetno Jawa Indon.
139 P6 Baturino Rus. Fed.
137 L2 Baturyn Ukr.
94 D5 Batusangkar Sumatera Indon.
177 H5 Bátya Hungary
175 M5 Batyatychi Ukr.
135 I5 Batyrevo Rus. Fed.
Batys Qazaqstan Oblysy admin. div. Kazakh. see Zapadnyy Kazakhstan
158 C4 Batz, Île de i. France
158 G7 Batz-sur-Mer France
251 H6 Bau r. Brazil
79 □7a Bau i. Fiji
95 I4 Bau Sarawak Malaysia
210 B2 Bau Sudan
93 C6 Baubau Sulawesi Indon.
93 E8 Baucau East Timor
207 H4 Bauchi Nigeria
207 H4 Bauchi state Nigeria
194 F8 Baucina Sicilia Italy
158 E6 Baud France
236 H1 Baudette MN U.S.A.
250 B3 Baudo, Serranía de mts Col.
Baudouinville Dem. Rep. Congo see Moba
161 I9 Bauduen France
190 F2 Bauen Switz.
82 □3 Bauer Bay S. Pacific Ocean
210 E3 Bauet well Eth.
159 K6 Baugé France
159 K6 Baugeois reg. France
160 I5 Bauges mts France
151 J5 Baughurst Hampshire, England U.K.
160 B2 Baugy France
85 L8 Bauhinia Qld Austr.
Baukau East Timor see Baucau
93 B6 Baula Sulawesi Indon.
172 G3 Bauland reg. Ger.
225 K3 Bauld, Cape Nfld and Lab. Can.
158 H6 Baulon France
221 J2 Baumann Fiord inlet Nunavut Can.
160 I2 Baume-les-Dames France
172 C2 Baumholder Ger.
169 K11 Baunach Ger.
169 K11 Baunach r. Ger.
78 □6 Baunani Malaita Solomon Is
116 E3 Baundal Hima. Prad. India
192 D7 Baunei Sardegna Italy
147 C8 Baurtregaum hill Ireland
256 C5 Bauru Brazil
256 A3 Baús Brazil
169 C10 Bausendorf Ger.
125 N4 Baushar Oman
138 H5 Bauska Latvia
120 D5 Bautino Kazakh.
171 J8 Bautzen Ger.
121 N6 Bauyrzhan Momyshuly Kazakh.
122 E6 Bavānāt Iran
160 J2 Bavans France
Bavaria reg. Ger. see Bayern
156 G3 Bavay France
114 C4 Bavda Mahar. India
164 G5 Bavel Neth.
192 C4 Bavella, Col de pass France
143 M2 Båven l. Sweden
190 F4 Baveno Italy
214 H9 Baviaanskloofberge mts S. Africa
160 J1 Bavilliers France
242 E2 Bavispe Mex.
242 E3 Bavispe r. Mex.
116 D8 Bavla Gujarat India
139 W5 Bavleny Rus. Fed.
135 K5 Bavly Rus. Fed.
176 D2 Bavorov Czech Rep.
208 C3 Bavula Dem. Rep. Congo
96 B3 Baw Myanmar
116 F5 Bawal Haryana India
95 I6 Bawal i. Indon.
95 J5 Bawan Kalimantan Indon.
95 H5 Bawang, Tanjung pt Indon.
83 K7 Baw Baw National Park Vic. Austr.
151 O2 Bawdeswell Norfolk, England U.K.
151 O3 Bawdsey Suffolk, England U.K.
96 C3 Bawdwin Myanmar
95 J7 Bawean i. Indon.
168 D5 Bawinkel Ger.
206 E4 Bawku Ghana
96 C5 Bawlake Myanmar
148 B5 Bawnboy Ireland
108 C4 Bawolung Sichuan China
149 O7 Bawtry South Yorkshire, England U.K.
108 D2 Baxi Sichuan China
Baxian Chongqing China see Banan
Baxian Hebei China see Bazhou
110 J7 Baxkorgan Xinjiang China
231 F10 Baxley GA U.S.A.
108 A3 Baxoi Xizang China
233 □Q2 Baxter State Park ME U.S.A.
Bay Xinjiang China see Baicheng
210 D4 Bay admin. reg. Somalia
92 C4 Bay, Laguna de lag. Luzon Phil.
206 E3 Bay, Réserve de nature res. Mali
206 E5 Baya r. Côte d'Ivoire
189 B8 Bayad Alg.
246 E3 Bayamo Cuba
247 □1 Bayamón Puerto Rico
129 H5 Bayan Azer.
100 E5 Bayan Heilong. China
106 E9 Bayan Qinghai China
Bayan Qinghai China see Hualong
95 L9 Bayan Lombok Indon.
106 H3 Bayan Arhangay Mongolia
106 D3 Bayan Govĭ-Altay Mongolia
107 L2 Bayan Hentiy Mongolia
123 K4 Bāyan, Band-e mts Afgh.
116 F6 Bayana Rajasthan India
121 P2 Bayanaul Kazakh.
106 F3 Bayanbulag Bayanhongor Mongolia
106 F4 Bayanbulag Bayanhongor Mongolia
107 K3 Bayanbulag Hentiy Mongolia
110 G3 Bayanbulak Xinjiang China
110 G5 Bayanbulak Xinjiang China
107 K3 Bayandelger Mongolia
95 H4 Bayang, Pegunungan mts Indon.
208 C4 Bayanga C.A.R.
208 B3 Bayanga-Didi C.A.R.
Bayan Gol Nei Mongol China see Dengkou
106 D4 Bayangol Mongolia
106 H1 Bayangol Rus. Fed.
108 A1 Bayan Har Shan mt. Qinghai China
106 D9 Bayan Har Shan mts China
106 E9 Bayan Har Shankou pass Qinghai China
106 G3 Bayanhongor Mongolia
106 F4 Bayanhongor prov. Mongolia
106 I7 Bayan Hot Nei Mongol China
106 G3 Bayanhushuu Mongolia
106 E2 Bayan-Kol Rus. Fed.
106 I6 Bayan Mod Nei Mongol China
106 I6 Bayan Nuru Nei Mongol China
242 □T13 Bayano, Lago l. Panama
107 K6 Bayan Obo Nei Mongol China
106 A2 Bayan-Ölgiy prov. Mongolia
106 D4 Bayan-Ovoo Govĭ-Altay Mongolia
107 L2 Bayan-Ovoo Hentiy Mongolia
107 M3 Bayan-Ovoo Hentiy Mongolia
107 M6 Bayan Qagan Nei Mongol China
107 Q4 Bayan Qagan Nei Mongol China
106 F4 Bayansayr Mongolia
106 E8 Bayan Shan mt. China
110 G5 Bayansumküre Xinjiang China
107 O2 Bayan Tal Nei Mongol China
106 G4 Bayanteeg Mongolia
107 P2 Bayan Tohoi Nei Mongol China
106 I3 Bayantöhöm Mongolia
107 O4 Bayan Ul Hot Nei Mongol China
107 K6 Bayan Us Nei Mongol China
106 A2 Bayan Uul mts Mongolia
185 N6 Bayárcal Spain
236 D5 Bayard NE U.S.A.
232 F9 Bayard WV U.S.A.
161 I7 Bayard, Col pass France
157 J6 Bayard-sur-Marne France
107 M3 Bayasgalant Mongolia
199 L4 Bayat Afyon Turkey
Bayat Antalya Turkey see Akçay
92 D7 Bayawan Negros Phil.
122 F6 Bayāz Iran
92 E6 Baybay Leyte Phil.
231 I8 Bayboro NC U.S.A.
232 C7 Bay Bridge OH U.S.A.
225 K4 Bay Bulls Nfld and Lab. Can.
127 J3 Bayburt Turkey
129 B5 Bayburt prov. Turkey
136 I5 Baybuzivka Ukr.
97 H10 Bay Canh, Hon i. Vietnam
120 E4 Baychunas Kazakh.
227 K6 Bay City MI U.S.A.
237 G11 Bay City TX U.S.A.
149 K5 Baycliff Cumbria, England U.K.
124 D3 Baydā, Jabal al hill Saudi Arabia
130 H3 Baydaratskaya Guba Rus. Fed.
210 D4 Baydhabo Somalia
106 F3 Baydrag Mongolia
106 F4 Baydrag Gol r. Mongolia
225 K3 Bay du Nord Wilderness nature res. Nfld and Lab. Can.
Baydzhansay Kazakh. see Bayzhansay
208 D3 Baye Dem. Rep. Congo
156 G6 Baye France
122 D3 Bāyeh Iran
157 I7 Bayel France
207 G5 Bayelsa state Nigeria
173 O5 Bayerbach Ger.
173 M4 Bayerbach bei Ergoldsbach Ger.
173 O3 Bayerisch Eisenstein Ger.
169 I10 Bayerische Rhön park Ger.
172 G2 Bayerischer Spessart park Ger.
173 M3 Bayerischer Wald mts Ger.
173 N3 Bayerischer Wald nat. park Ger.
173 N6 Bayerisch Gmain Ger.
171 C10 Bayern reg. Ger.
178 D2 Bayern reg. Ger.
173 K6 Bayersoien Ger.
173 O4 Bayer Wald, Nationalpark nat. park Ger.
159 J3 Bayeux France
139 O7 Bayeva Belarus
121 S1 Bayevo Rus. Fed.
227 M6 Bayfield Ont. Can.
226 D3 Bayfield WI U.S.A.
120 F3 Bayganin Kazakh.
121 L5 Baygekum Kazakh.
120 J1 Baygora Kazakh.
137 S1 Baygora r. Rus. Fed.
261 I3 Baygorria, Lago Artificial de resr Uru.
124 G8 Bayḥan al Qiṣab Yemen
235 G4 Bay Head NJ U.S.A.
107 O9 Bayiji Jiangsu China
129 I5 Bäyimli Azer.
199 I4 Bayındır Turkey
199 J5 Bayır Turkey
Bay Islands is Hond. see Bahía, Islas de la
111 L12 Bayizhen Xizang China
127 K6 Bayjī Iraq
Baykadam Kazakh. see Saudakent
106 I1 Baykal, Ozero l. Rus. Fed.
100 F2 Baykal-Amur Magistral Rus. Fed.
Baykal Range mts Rus. Fed. see Baykal'skiy Khrebet
106 I1 Baykal'sk Rus. Fed.
98 I1 Baykal'skiy Khrebet mts Rus. Fed.
106 I1 Baykal'skiy Zapovednik nature res. Rus. Fed.
127 J4 Baykan Turkey
120 J5 Bay-Khozha Kazakh.
134 L5 Baykibashevo Rus. Fed.
131 K3 Baykit Rus. Fed.
Baykonur Kazakh. see Baykonyr
120 L4 Baykonur Karagandinskaya Oblast' Kazakh.
120 J5 Baykonyr Gorod Baykonyr Kazakh.
84 G4 Bayley Point Aboriginal Reserve Qld Austr.
120 H1 Baymak Rus. Fed.
231 D10 Bay Minette AL U.S.A.
125 K4 Baynūna'h reg. U.A.E.
Bayo Spain see Baio
80 I2 Bay of Islands Maritime and Historic Park nature res. North I. N.Z.
80 K4 Bay of Plenty admin. reg. North I. N.Z.
92 C3 Bayombong Luzon Phil.
157 L7 Bayon France
Bayona Galicia Spain see Baiona
163 B9 Bayonne France
235 G3 Bayonne NJ U.S.A.
92 C6 Bayo Point Panay Phil.
250 A6 Bayóvar Peru
92 B6 Bay Point Phil.
227 K6 Bay Port MI U.S.A.
235 I3 Bayport NY U.S.A.
Bayqadam Kazakh. see Saudakent
Bayqongyr Kazakh. see Baykonyr
137 N4 Bayrak Ukr.
129 E5 Bayraktutan Turkey
123 J3 Baýramaly Turkm.
199 H3 Bayramiç Turkey
173 L2 Bayreuth Ger.
234 C7 Bay Ridge MD U.S.A.
173 M6 Bayrischzell Ger.
Bayrūt Lebanon see Beirut
224 E4 Bays, Lake of Ont. Can.
237 K10 Bay St Louis MS U.S.A.
124 F7 Baysh watercourse Saudi Arabia
Bayshonas Kazakh. see Baychunas
235 I3 Bay Shore NY U.S.A.
234 C6 Bayside Beach MD U.S.A.
237 K10 Bay Springs MS U.S.A.
150 G2 Bayston Hill Shropshire, England U.K.
Baysun Uzbek. see Boysun
121 L8 Baysuntau, Gory mts Uzbek.
124 F8 Bayt al Faqīh Yemen
106 B4 Baytik Shan mts China
Bayt Lahm West Bank see Bethlehem
237 H11 Baytown TX U.S.A.
93 C5 Bayu Sulawesi Indon.
183 O5 Bayubas de Abajo Spain
94 E5 Bayunglincir Sumatera Indon.
80 K6 Bay View North I. N.Z.
235 G5 Bayville NJ U.S.A.
235 H3 Bayville NY U.S.A.
202 B2 Bayy al Kabīr, Wādī watercourse Libya
Bayyrqum Kazakh. see Bairkum
121 M6 Bayzhansay Kazakh.
185 N5 Baza Spain
185 N5 Baza r. Spain
185 N6 Baza, Sierra de mts Spain
176 F5 Bázakerettye Hungary
136 F4 Bazaliya Ukr.
156 H5 Bazancourt France
136 I2 Bazar Ukr.
123 M4 Bāzārak Afgh.
120 D3 Bazarchulan Kazakh.
129 I4 Bazardyuzyu, Gora mt. Azer./Rus. Fed.
122 C3 Bāzār-e Māsāl Iran
127 L4 Bāzargān Iran
121 M8 Bazarkhanym, Gora mt. Uzbek.
121 O7 Bazar-Korgon Kyrg.
Bazar Kurgan Kyrg. see Bazar-Korgon
120 B1 Bazarnyy Karabulak Rus. Fed.
135 I5 Bazarnyy Syzgan Rus. Fed.
Bazarshulan Kazakh. see Bazarchulan
120 D3 Bazartobe Kazakh.
213 G4 Bazaruto, Ilha do i. Moz.
163 D7 Bazas France
137 N6 Bazavluk r. Ukr.
123 K8 Bazdar Pak.
157 I4 Bazeilles France
163 E9 Bazet France
129 G1 Bazhigan Rus. Fed.
108 F3 Bazhong Sichuan China
107 O7 Bazhou Hebei China
Bazhou Sichuan China see Bazhong
163 H9 Baziège France
163 E9 Bazillac France
224 F4 Bazin r. Que. Can.
206 C4 Baziwehn Liberia
122 I8 Bazmān Iran
122 I7 Bazmān, Kūh-e mt. Iran
160 D2 Bazoches France
159 K4 Bazoches-au-Houlme France
156 D7 Bazoches-les-Gallerandes France
159 L4 Bazoches-sur-Hoëne France
122 D6 Bāzoft, Āb-e r. Iran
160 D2 Bazois reg. France
159 J5 Bazougers France
159 J6 Bazouges France
158 H5 Bazouges-la-Pérouse France
186 C1 Baztán, Valle del val. France/Spain
128 E4 Bcharré Lebanon
Bé, Nossi i. Madag. see Bé, Nosy
213 □K2 Bé, Nosy i. Madag.
97 H9 Be, Sông r. Vietnam
236 D2 Beach ND U.S.A.
227 R4 Beachburg Ont. Can.
232 D8 Beach City OH U.S.A.
235 G3 Beach Glen NJ U.S.A.
235 G5 Beach Haven NJ U.S.A.
235 G5 Beach Haven Terrace NJ U.S.A.
234 E1 Beach Lake PA U.S.A.
82 H7 Beachport S.A. Austr.
235 G5 Beachwood NJ U.S.A.
151 M6 Beachy Head England U.K.
87 D11 Beacon W.A. Austr.
233 L7 Beacon NY U.S.A.
215 L8 Beacon Bay S. Africa
235 I2 Beacon Falls CT U.S.A.
83 K9 Beaconsfield Tas. Austr.
151 K4 Beaconsfield Buckinghamshire, England U.K.
149 N2 Beadnell Northumberland, England U.K.
149 N2 Beadnell Bay England U.K.
148 B3 Beagh, Lough l. Ireland
259 C9 Beagle, Canal sea chan. Arg.
86 G3 Beagle Bank rf W.A. Austr.
86 G4 Beagle Bay W.A. Austr.
86 G4 Beagle Bay Aboriginal Reserve W.A. Austr.
84 B2 Beagle Gulf N.T. Austr.
87 C10 Beagle Island W.A. Austr.
213 □K2 Bealanana Madag.
Béal an Átha Ireland see Ballina
Béal Átha na Sluaighe Ireland see Ballinasloe
147 E9 Bealnablath Ireland
237 E9 Beals Creek r. TX U.S.A.
150 G6 Beaminster Dorset, England U.K.
213 □J5 Beampingaratra mts Madag.
183 Q8 Beamud Spain
213 □K2 Beandrarezona Madag.
238 H6 Bear r. ID U.S.A.
147 C9 Beara reg. Ireland
Bearalváhki Norway see Berlevåg
234 D2 Bear Creek PA U.S.A.
237 E7 Bear Creek r. KS U.S.A.
224 C3 Beardmore Ont. Can.
263 L1 Beardmore Glacier Antarctica
236 J5 Beardstown IL U.S.A.
Bear Island i. Arctic Ocean see Bjørnøya
227 N3 Bear Island Ont. Can.
224 D2 Bear Island i. Nunavut Can.
147 C9 Bear Island i. Ireland
182 D4 Beariz Spain
223 L4 Bear Lake l. Man. Can.
226 H5 Bear Lake MI U.S.A.
238 I5 Bear Lake l. ID U.S.A.
116 G7 Bearma r. Madh. Prad. India
236 D4 Bear Mountain SD U.S.A.
163 C9 Béarn reg. France
Bearnaraigh i. Scotland U.K. see Berneray
Bearnaraigh i. Western Isles, Scotland U.K. see Berneray
238 J2 Bear Paw Mountain MT U.S.A.
238 J2 Bearpaw Mountains MT U.S.A.
262 Q2 Bear Peninsula Antarctica
146 H11 Bearsden East Dunbartonshire, Scotland U.K.
223 N4 Bearskin Lake Ont. Can.
151 N5 Bearsted Kent, England U.K.
116 E4 Beas r. India
184 F6 Beas Spain
186 A1 Beasain Spain
185 M6 Beas de Granada Spain
185 N4 Beas de Segura Spain
246 H5 Beata, Cabo c. Dom. Rep.
246 H5 Beata, Isla i. Dom. Rep.
236 G5 Beatrice NE U.S.A.
213 F3 Beatrice Zimbabwe
84 F3 Beatrice, Cape N.T. Austr.
146 J12 Beattock Dumfries and Galloway, Scotland U.K.
222 F3 Beatton r. B.C. Can.
240 P5 Beatty NV U.S.A.
224 E3 Beattyville Que. Can.
232 B11 Beattyville KY U.S.A.
217 □1b Beau Bassin Mauritius
161 F9 Beaucaire France
156 C4 Beaucamps-le-Vieux France
156 C7 Beauce reg. France
161 F7 Beauchastel France
227 P3 Beauchêne, Lac l. Que. Can.
259 F9 Beauchene Island Falkland Is
160 J2 Beaucourt France
159 J7 Beaucouzé France

Beaudéan to Benito Juarez

286

163 E9 **Beaudéan** France
85 N9 **Beaudesert** *Qld* Austr.
Beauduc, Golfe de *b.* France *see* **Stes Maries, Golfe des**
159 L5 **Beaufay** France
83 I7 **Beaufort** *Vic.* Austr.
160 G3 **Beaufort** *Franche-Comté* France
160 J5 **Beaufort** *Rhône-Alpes* France
95 K2 **Beaufort** *Sabah* Malaysia
147 C8 **Beaufort** Ireland
231 I8 **Beaufort** *NC* U.S.A.
231 G9 **Beaufort** *SC* U.S.A.
162 D1 **Beaufort-en-Vallée** France
160 J5 **Beaufortin** *mts* France
Beaufort Island *H.K.* China *see* **Lo Chau**
220 F2 **Beaufort Sea** Can./U.S.A.
214 G8 **Beaufort West** S. Africa
156 C8 **Beaugency** France
233 L3 **Beauharnois** *Que.* Can.
161 I8 **Beaujeu** *Provence-Alpes-Côte d'Azur* France
160 F4 **Beaujeu** *Rhône-Alpes* France
160 E4 **Beaujolais, Monts du** *hills* France
161 E9 **Beaulieu** France
159 N7 **Beaulieu-lès-Loches** France
162 H6 **Beaulieu-sur-Dordogne** France
160 B1 **Beaulieu-sur-Loire** France
160 D3 **Beaulon** France
146 H8 **Beauly** *Highland, Scotland* U.K.
146 H8 **Beauly** *r. Scotland* U.K.
146 H8 **Beauly Firth** *est. Scotland* U.K.
163 E8 **Beaumarchés** France
150 D1 **Beaumaris** *Isle of Anglesey, Wales* U.K.
145 E5 **Beaumaris Castle** *tourist site Wales* U.K.
161 G8 **Beaumes-de-Venise** France
159 M3 **Beaumesnil** France
156 E3 **Beaumetz-lès-Loges** France
165 F8 **Beaumont** Belgium
163 F6 **Beaumont** *Aquitaine* France
160 C5 **Beaumont** *Auvergne* France
158 H2 **Beaumont** *Basse-Normandie* France
159 L8 **Beaumont** *Poitou-Charentes* France
81 D12 **Beaumont** *South I.* N.Z.
240 P8 **Beaumont** *CA* U.S.A.
237 K10 **Beaumont** *MS* U.S.A.
234 D2 **Beaumont** *PA* U.S.A.
237 H10 **Beaumont** *TX* U.S.A.
163 F8 **Beaumont-de-Lomagne** France
161 H9 **Beaumont-de-Pertuis** France
157 J4 **Beaumont-en-Argonne** France
159 L7 **Beaumont-en-Véron** France
159 M6 **Beaumont-la-Ronce** France
159 M3 **Beaumont-le-Roger** France
159 M5 **Beaumont-les-Autels** France
161 F7 **Beaumont-lès-Valence** France
156 D5 **Beaumont-sur-Oise** France
159 L5 **Beaumont-sur-Sarthe** France
160 F2 **Beaune** France
156 D7 **Beaune-La Rolande** France
159 J7 **Beaupréau** France
156 D3 **Beauquesne** France
165 G8 **Beauraing** Belgium
160 K5 **Beauregard, Lago di** *l.* Italy
161 G6 **Beaurepaire** France
160 G3 **Beaurepaire-en-Bresse** France
161 H7 **Beaurières** France
223 L5 **Beauséjour** *Man.* Can.
157 J6 **Beausite** France
161 K9 **Beausoleil** France
78 □5 **Beautemps Beaupré** *atoll Îles Loyauté* New Caledonia
156 F4 **Beautor** France
156 D5 **Beauvais** France
223 J4 **Beauval** *Sask.* Can.
156 D3 **Beauval** France
217 □2b **Beau Vallon, Baie** *b. Mahé* Seychelles
161 J8 **Beauvezer** France
163 F7 **Beauville** France
158 G8 **Beauvoir-sur-Mer** France
162 D3 **Beauvoir-sur-Niort** France
161 E9 **Beauvoisin** France
161 E6 **Beauzac** France
163 G8 **Beauzelle** France
223 J4 **Beaver** *r. Alta/Sask.* Can.
224 C2 **Beaver** *r. Ont.* Can.
222 C2 **Beaver** *r. Y.T.* Can.
222 E3 **Beaver** *r. Y.T.* Can.
237 E7 **Beaver** *OK* U.S.A.
241 T3 **Beaver** *UT* U.S.A.
237 E7 **Beaver** *r. OK* U.S.A.
241 T2 **Beaver** *r. UT* U.S.A.
236 F5 **Beaver City** *NE* U.S.A.
222 A2 **Beaver Creek** *Y.T.* Can.
237 I7 **Beaver Creek** *r. MO* U.S.A.
238 K2 **Beaver Creek** *r. MT* U.S.A.
236 E2 **Beaver Creek** *r. ND* U.S.A.
236 F5 **Beaver Creek** *r. NE* U.S.A.
230 D7 **Beaver Dam** *KY* U.S.A.
226 F6 **Beaver Dam** *WI* U.S.A.
226 F6 **Beaver Dam Lake** *WI* U.S.A.
232 E8 **Beaver Falls** *PA* U.S.A.
263 D2 **Beaver Glacier** Antarctica
238 H4 **Beaverhead** *r. MT* U.S.A.
238 H4 **Beaverhead Mountains** *MT* U.S.A.
223 H4 **Beaverhill Lake** *Alta* Can.
223 M4 **Beaver Hill Lake** *Man.* Can.
223 J2 **Beaverhill Lake** *N.W.T.* Can.
226 I4 **Beaver Island** *MI* U.S.A.
237 I7 **Beaver Lake** *resr AR* U.S.A.
222 G4 **Beaverlodge** *Alta* Can.
234 D3 **Beaver Meadows** *PA* U.S.A.
232 F8 **Beaver Run Reservoir** *PA* U.S.A.
234 A3 **Beaver Springs** *PA* U.S.A.
224 E4 **Beaverton** *Ont.* Can.
226 J6 **Beaverton** *MI* U.S.A.
238 C4 **Beaverton** *OR* U.S.A.
234 A3 **Beavertown** *PA* U.S.A.
116 E6 **Beawar** *Rajasthan* India
260 D3 **Beazley** Arg.
177 J5 **Beba Veche** Romania
260 D3 **Bebedero, Salina del** *salt pan* Arg.
208 C2 **Bébédjia** Chad
256 C4 **Bebedouro** Brazil
254 F3 **Beberibe** Brazil
171 D6 **Bebertal** Ger.
149 K7 **Bebington** *Merseyside, England* U.K.
208 C2 **Béboto** Chad
169 I9 **Bebra** Ger.
108 A3 **Bêca** *Qinghai* China
187 K8 **Beca, Punta** *pt* Spain
160 J5 **Becca du Lac** *mt.* France
151 P3 **Beccles** *Suffolk, England* U.K.
191 K4 **Becco di Filadonna** *mt.* Italy
182 I8 **Becedas** Spain
186 F6 **Beceite** Spain
196 I5 **Bečej** *Vojvodina* Serbia
182 F3 **Becerreá** Spain
185 J6 **Becerrero** *hill* Spain
183 K4 **Becerril de Campos** Spain
242 □R10 **Becerro, Cayos** *is* Hond.
204 E3 **Béchar** Alg.
220 C4 **Becharof Lake** *AK* U.S.A.
172 D2 **Becherbach** Ger.
158 H5 **Bécherel** France
134 G4 **Bechevinka** Rus. Fed.
173 J3 **Bechhofen** *Bayern* Ger.
172 C3 **Bechhofen** *Rheinland-Pfalz* Ger.
171 J10 **Bechlín** Czech Rep.
234 D4 **Bechtelsville** *PA* U.S.A.
172 E2 **Bechtheim** Ger.
Bechuanaland *country* Africa *see* **Botswana**
176 D2 **Bechyně** Czech Rep.
177 K6 **Becicherecu Mic** Romania
183 J4 **Becilla de Valderaduey** Spain
199 I5 **Beçin** Turkey
168 I4 **Beckdorf** Ger.
169 H6 **Beckedorf** Ger.
168 G5 **Beckeln** Ger.
262 T1 **Becker, Mount** Antarctica
172 B3 **Beckingen** Ger.
149 P7 **Beckingham** *Nottinghamshire, England* U.K.
232 D11 **Beckley** *WV* U.S.A.
177 G3 **Beckov** Slovakia
81 D11 **Becks** *South I.* N.Z.
169 F7 **Beckum** Ger.
241 R2 **Becky Peak** *NV* U.S.A.
197 M3 **Beclean** Romania
93 D8 **Beco** East Timor
159 J7 **Bécon-les-Granits** France
171 I10 **Bečov** Czech Rep.
176 B1 **Bečov nad Teplou** Czech Rep.
176 F5 **Becsehely** Hungary
176 F5 **Becsvölgye** Hungary
177 G2 **Bečva** *r.* Czech Rep.
210 D2 **Beda Hāyk'** *l.* Eth.
149 N5 **Bedale** *North Yorkshire, England* U.K.
208 C2 **Bédan** Chad
161 C9 **Bédarieux** France
161 F8 **Bédarrides** France
169 C9 **Bedburg** Ger.
169 B7 **Bedburg-Hau** Ger.
150 F4 **Beddau** *Rhondda Cynon Taff, Wales* U.K.
150 D1 **Beddgelert** *Gwynedd, Wales* U.K.
151 M6 **Beddingham** *East Sussex, England* U.K.
233 □Q4 **Beddington** *ME* U.S.A.
Bedeau Alg. *see* **Râs el Ma**
158 H5 **Bédée** France
179 M7 **Bedekovčina** Croatia
Bedel', Pereval *pass* China/Kyrg. *see* **Bedel Pass**
210 C2 **Bedelē** Eth.
110 D6 **Bedel Pass** China/Kyrg.
210 D2 **Bedēsa** Eth.
134 L5 **Bedeyeva Polyana** Rus. Fed.
225 I4 **Bedford** *N.S.* Can.
233 M3 **Bedford** *Que.* Can.
215 K8 **Bedford** *Eastern Cape* S. Africa
215 O4 **Bedford** *KwaZulu-Natal* S. Africa
151 L3 **Bedford** *Bedfordshire, England* U.K.
236 H5 **Bedford** *IA* U.S.A.
230 D6 **Bedford** *IN* U.S.A.
230 E6 **Bedford** *KY* U.S.A.
235 H2 **Bedford** *NY* U.S.A.
232 G8 **Bedford** *PA* U.S.A.
232 F11 **Bedford** *VA* U.S.A.
85 J3 **Bedford, Cape** *Qld* Austr.
86 I4 **Bedford Downs** *W.A.* Austr.
232 D7 **Bedford Heights** *OH* U.S.A.
235 H2 **Bedford Hills** *NY* U.S.A.
151 L3 **Bedford Level (Middle Level)** *lowland England* U.K.
151 L2 **Bedford Level (North Level)** *lowland England* U.K.
151 M3 **Bedford Level (South Level)** *lowland England* U.K.
247 □6 **Bedford Point** Grenada
151 L3 **Bedfordshire** *admin. div. England* U.K.
83 K5 **Bedgerebong** *N.S.W.* Austr.
116 C8 **Bedi** *Gujarat* India
129 F4 **Bediani** Georgia
94 G6 **Bedinggong** Indon.
175 H4 **Będków** Pol.
116 D7 **Bedla** *Rajasthan* India
149 N3 **Bedlington** *Northumberland, England* U.K.
175 H3 **Bedlno** Pol.
185 M5 **Bedmar** Spain
179 M7 **Bednja** Croatia
188 F2 **Bednja** *r.* Croatia
161 G8 **Bédoin** France
94 □ **Bedok** Sing.
94 □ **Bedok, Sungai** *r.* Sing.
94 □ **Bedok Jetty** Sing.
94 □ **Bedok Reservoir** Sing.
191 K3 **Bedollo** Italy
190 H6 **Bedonia** Italy
207 I3 **Bedouaram** *well* Niger
84 G8 **Bedourie** *Qld* Austr.
163 C9 **Bedous** France
241 X3 **Bedrock** *CO* U.S.A.
163 H6 **Béduer** France
164 K2 **Bedum** Neth.
150 F4 **Bedwas** *Caerphilly, Wales* U.K.
151 J3 **Bedworth** *Warwickshire, England* U.K.
175 H5 **Będzin** Pol.
174 D1 **Będzino** Pol.
146 B8 **Bee, Loch** *l. Scotland* U.K.
85 J9 **Beechal Creek** *watercourse Qld* Austr.
226 G8 **Beecher** *IL* U.S.A.
233 N3 **Beecher Falls** *VT* U.S.A.
232 C10 **Beech Fork Lake** *WV* U.S.A.
83 K7 **Beechworth** *Vic.* Austr.
223 J5 **Beechy** *Sask.* Can.
168 J5 **Beedenbostel** Ger.
149 Q6 **Beeford** *East Riding of Yorkshire, England* U.K.
164 I5 **Beek** *Gelderland* Neth.
164 I5 **Beek** *Noord-Brabant* Neth.
164 I4 **Beekbergen** Neth.
87 C10 **Beekeepers Nature Reserve** *W.A.* Austr.
171 G6 **Beelitz** Ger.
234 F2 **Beemerville** *NJ* U.S.A.
171 D6 **Beendorf** Ger.
85 N9 **Beenleigh** *Qld* Austr.
170 H4 **Beenz** Ger.
210 E2 **Beer** Somalia
150 F6 **Beer** *Devon, England* U.K.
172 F2 **Beerfelden** Ger.
87 D10 **Beeringgnurding, Mount** *hill W.A.* Austr.
128 D8 **Be'ér Menuḥa** Israel
165 D6 **Beernem** Belgium
128 C9 **Be'ér Ora** Israel
164 I5 **Beers** Neth.
165 G6 **Beerse** Belgium
165 F7 **Beersel** Belgium
Beersheba Israel *see* **Be'ér Sheva'**
128 C7 **Be'ér Sheva'** Israel
128 C7 **Be'ér Sheva'** *watercourse* Israel
165 C6 **Beerst** Belgium
164 L2 **Beerta** Neth.
214 H9 **Beervlei Dam** S. Africa
171 E7 **Beesenstedt** Ger.
171 J6 **Beeskow** Ger.
215 L1 **Beestekraal** S. Africa
169 E6 **Beesten** Ger.
151 J2 **Beeston** *Nottinghamshire, England* U.K.
84 D4 **Beetaloo** *N.T.* Austr.
262 T2 **Beethoven Peninsula** Antarctica
151 N2 **Beetley** *Norfolk, England* U.K.
164 J2 **Beetsterzwaag** Neth.
170 D5 **Beetzendorf** Ger.
171 G6 **Beetzsee** *l.* Ger.
237 G11 **Beeville** *TX* U.S.A.
208 D4 **Befale** Dem. Rep. Congo
213 □I4 **Befandriana Atsimo** Madag.
213 □K2 **Befandriana Avaratra** Madag.
213 □J4 **Befasy** Madag.
208 D4 **Befori** Dem. Rep. Congo
213 □J4 **Befotaka** *Fianarantsoa* Madag.
213 □K2 **Befotaka** *Mahajanga* Madag.
147 J3 **Beg, Lough** *l. Northern Ireland* U.K.
83 L7 **Bega** *N.S.W.* Austr.
93 D5 **Bega** *Maluku* Indon.
197 J5 **Bega** *r.* Romania
163 C8 **Bégaar** France
162 C5 **Bégadan** France
117 M8 **Begamganj** Bangl.
158 E4 **Bégard** France
123 M7 **Begari** *r.* Pak.
177 K5 **Begécsivíztároló** *resr* Hungary
247 □2 **Beggars Point** Antigua and Barbuda
Begicheva, Ostrov *i.* Rus. Fed. *see* **Bol'shoy Begichev, Ostrov**
185 L5 **Begíjar** Spain
165 G6 **Begijnendijk** Belgium
163 C6 **Bègles** France
158 D6 **Beg-Meil** France
142 G1 **Begna** *r.* Norway
182 E2 **Begonte** Spain
206 E5 **Begoro** Ghana
Begovat Uzbek. *see* **Bekobod**
116 E7 **Begun** *Rajasthan* India
186 L4 **Begur** Spain
186 L4 **Begur, Cap de** *c.* Spain
117 K7 **Begusarai** *Bihar* India
122 H5 **Behābād** Iran
251 I3 **Béhague, Pointe** *pt* Fr. Guiana
213 □J5 **Behara** Madag.
122 D6 **Behbehān** Iran
111 J8 **Behleg** *Qinghai* China
168 K3 **Behlendorf** Ger.
222 D4 **Behm Canal** *sea chan. AK* U.S.A.
199 H3 **Behramkale** Turkey
262 T2 **Behrendt Mountains** Antarctica
157 M5 **Behren-lès-Forbach** France
170 G2 **Behren-Lübchin** Ger.
169 K8 **Behringen** Ger.
122 E7 **Behrūsī** Iran
122 E3 **Behshahr** Iran
123 L4 **Behsūd** Afgh.
215 I8 **Behulpsaam** S. Africa
100 E4 **Bei'an** *Heilong.* China
Bei'ao *Zhejiang* China *see* **Dongtou**
108 F2 **Beiba** *Shaanxi* China
108 F4 **Beibei** *Chongqing* China
108 E3 **Beichuan** *Sichuan* China
Beida Libya *see* **Al Bayḍā'**
106 F7 **Beida He** *r. Gansu* China
106 G7 **Beida Shan** *mts Nei Mongol* China
171 G9 **Beierfeld** Ger.
Beigang Taiwan *see* **Peikang**
149 O7 **Beighton** *South Yorkshire, England* U.K.
210 B2 **Beigi** Eth.
190 F7 **Beigua, Monte** *mt.* Italy
108 G8 **Beihai** *Guangxi* China
111 L8 **Bei Hulsan Hu** *salt l. Qinghai* China
109 I7 **Bei Jiang** *r.* China
107 O7 **Beijing** *Beijing* China
107 O6 **Beijing** *mun.* China
164 K3 **Beilen** Neth.
108 H7 **Beiliu** *Guangxi* China
173 K3 **Beilngries** Ger.
171 H7 **Beilrode** Ger.
172 G3 **Beilstein** Ger.
111 K9 **Beilu He** *r. Qinghai* China
106 C9 **Beiluheyan** *Qinghai* China
172 H5 **Beimerstetten** Ger.
208 B2 **Béinamar** Chad
190 D5 **Beinasco** Italy
156 H5 **Beine-Nauroy** France
190 D7 **Beinette** Italy
107 Q6 **Beining** *Liaoning* China
148 F2 **Beinn an Tuirc** *hill Scotland* U.K.
146 E8 **Beinn Bhan** *hill Scotland* U.K.
146 D11 **Beinn Bheigeir** *hill Scotland* U.K.
148 F1 **Beinn Bhreac** *hill Argyll and Bute, Scotland* U.K.
146 F10 **Beinn Bhreac** *hill Argyll and Bute, Scotland* U.K.
146 F11 **Beinn Bhreac** *hill Argyll and Bute, Scotland* U.K.
146 D8 **Beinn Bhreac** *hill Highland, Scotland* U.K.
146 G10 **Beinn Bhuidhe** *hill Scotland* U.K.
146 F10 **Beinn Chapull** *hill Scotland* U.K.
146 G7 **Beinn Dearg** *mt. Highland, Scotland* U.K.
146 I9 **Beinn Dearg** *mt. Perth and Kinross, Scotland* U.K.
146 G9 **Beinn Dorain** *mt. Scotland* U.K.
144 E3 **Beinn Heasgarnich** *mt. Scotland* U.K.
146 G10 **Beinn Ime** *mt. Scotland* U.K.
146 G6 **Beinn Leoid** *hill Scotland* U.K.
146 C6 **Beinn Mholach** *hill Scotland* U.K.
146 F10 **Beinn Mhòr** *hill Scotland* U.K.
146 B8 **Beinn Mhòr** *hill Western Isles, Scotland* U.K.
146 C7 **Beinn Mhòr** *hill Western Isles, Scotland* U.K.
Beinn na Faoghla *i. Scotland* U.K. *see* **Benbecula**
146 G9 **Beinn na Lap** *hill Scotland* U.K.
146 E8 **Beinn na Seamraig** *hill Scotland* U.K.
146 E9 **Beinn Resipol** *hill Scotland* U.K.
146 E8 **Beinn Sgritheall** *hill Scotland* U.K.
146 F9 **Beinn Sgulaird** *hill Scotland* U.K.
146 H7 **Beinn Tharsuinn** *hill Scotland* U.K.
146 H9 **Beinn Udlamain** *mt. Scotland* U.K.
190 E1 **Beinwil** Switz.
108 F6 **Beipan Jiang** *r. Guizhou* China
107 Q6 **Beipiao** *Liaoning* China
213 G3 **Beira** Moz.
Beira *prov.* Moz. *see* **Sofala**
184 E2 **Beirã** Port.
182 E7 **Beira Alta** *reg.* Port.
182 F9 **Beira Baixa** *reg.* Port.
182 D8 **Beira Litoral** *reg.* Port.
183 Q4 **Beire** Spain
109 J2 **Beiru He** *r.* China
128 D5 **Beirut** Lebanon
222 H5 **Beiseker** *Alta* Can.
106 F6 **Beishan** *Nei Mongol* China
106 D6 **Bei Shan** *mts* China
107 M7 **Beitai Ding** *mts* China
213 F4 **Beitbridge** Zimbabwe
146 G11 **Beith** *North Ayrshire, Scotland* U.K.
128 D7 **Beit Jālā** West Bank
140 K5 **Beitstadfjorden** *sea chan.* Norway
110 H3 **Beitun** *Xinjiang* China
197 K4 **Beiuş** Romania
100 D4 **Beixing** *Heilong.* China
Beizhen *Liaoning* China *see* **Beining**
254 C2 **Beja** Brazil
184 D4 **Beja** Port.
184 C5 **Beja** *admin. dist.* Port.
205 H1 **Béja** Tunisia
189 B7 **Béja** *admin. div.* Tunisia
205 G1 **Bejaïa** Alg.
182 I8 **Béjar** Spain
122 H4 **Bejestān** Iran
123 M7 **Beji** *r.* Pak.
187 D8 **Bejís** Spain
244 G7 **Bejucos** Mex.
247 I8 **Bejuma** Venez.
207 I6 **Bek** *r.* Cameroon
207 I5 **Béka** *Adamaoua* Cameroon
207 I5 **Béka** *Est* Cameroon
207 I4 **Béka** *Nord* Cameroon
Bekabad Uzbek. *see* **Bekobod**
114 D6 **Bekal** *Kerala* India
213 □J3 **Bekapaika** Madag.
94 G8 **Bekasi** *Jawa* Indon.
120 E4 **Bekbike** Kazakh.
209 E7 **Beke** Dem. Rep. Congo
177 K5 **Békés** Hungary
177 K5 **Békés** *county* Hungary
177 K5 **Békéscsaba** Hungary
177 J5 **Békéssámson** Hungary
177 J5 **Békésszentandrás** Hungary
134 G3 **Beketovskaya** Rus. Fed.
137 L7 **Bekhtery** Ukr.
199 K4 **Bekilli** Turkey
213 □J5 **Bekily** Madag.
213 □J3 **Bekipay** Madag.
213 □J5 **Bekitro** Madag.
102 W3 **Bekkai** Japan
119 J1 **Bekobod** Uzbek.
213 □J3 **Bekodoka** Madag.
210 C3 **BeK'ojī** Eth.
213 □J3 **Bekopaka** Madag.
213 □I4 **Bekoropoka-Antongo** Madag.
135 H5 **Bekovo** Rus. Fed.
206 E5 **Bekwai** Ghana
206 E5 **Bekyem** Ghana
117 J7 **Bela** *Bihar* India
116 H7 **Bela** *Uttar Prad.* India
123 L8 **Bela** Pak.
177 H2 **Belá** Slovakia
123 M7 **Belab** *r.* Pak.
213 F5 **Bela-Bela** S. Africa
207 I5 **Bélabo** Cameroon
162 G2 **Bélâbre** France
196 J6 **Bela Crkva** *Vojvodina* Serbia
177 H3 **Beladice** Slovakia
177 H2 **Belá-Dulice** Slovakia
95 J3 **Belaga** *Sarawak* Malaysia
121 S2 **Bel'agash** Kazakh.
158 F5 **Bel Air** *hill* France
234 C5 **Bel Air** *MD* U.S.A.
208 D5 **Belaka** Dem. Rep. Congo
185 I3 **Belalcázar** Spain
176 B2 **Bělá nad Radbuzou** Czech Rep.
93 D3 **Belang** *Sulawesi* Indon.
93 E4 **Belangbelang** *i. Maluku* Indon.
197 K7 **Bela Palanka** Serbia
177 J3 **Bélapátfalva** Hungary
176 D1 **Bělá pod Bezdězem** Czech Rep.
176 G1 **Bělá pod Pradědem** Czech Rep.
114 D3 **Belapur** *Mahar.* India
135 E5 **Belarus** *country* Europe
183 Q3 **Belascoáin** Spain
Belasica *mts* Bulg./Macedonia *see* **Belasitsa**
197 K9 **Belasitsa** *mts* Bulg./Macedonia
Belau *country* N. Pacific Ocean *see* **Palau**
209 B6 **Bela Vista** *Bengo* Angola
Bela Vista *Huambo* Angola *see* **Katchiungo**
250 E4 **Bela Vista** *Amazonas* Brazil
253 F5 **Bela Vista** *Mato Grosso do Sul* Brazil
213 G5 **Bela Vista** Moz.
256 C2 **Bela Vista de Goiás** Brazil
94 C3 **Belawan** *Sumatera* Indon.
210 C2 **Belaya** *mt.* Eth.
137 O2 **Belaya** Rus. Fed.
131 S3 **Belaya** *r.* Rus. Fed.
137 S8 **Belaya** *r.* Rus. Fed.
137 M1 **Belaya Berezka** Rus. Fed.
135 H7 **Belaya Glina** Rus. Fed.
135 H6 **Belaya Kalitva** Rus. Fed.
134 J4 **Belaya Kholunitsa** Rus. Fed.
95 L5 **Belayan** *r.* Indon.
95 K4 **Belayan, Gunung** *mt.* Indon.
139 W5 **Belaya Rechka** Rus. Fed.
Belaya Tserkva Ukr. *see* **Bila Tserkva**
182 D7 **Belazaima do Chão** Port.
207 G3 **Belbédji** Niger
190 F6 **Belbo** *r.* Italy
163 H10 **Belcaire** France
234 C6 **Belcamp** *MD* U.S.A.
163 I7 **Belcastel** France
197 P3 **Belceşti** Romania
175 H4 **Bełchatów** Pol.
172 D6 **Belchen** *mt.* Ger.
232 C11 **Belcher** *KY* U.S.A.
224 E1 **Belcher Islands** *Nunavut* Can.
123 K4 **Belchiragh** Afgh.
186 D5 **Belchite** Spain
176 C2 **Bělčice** Czech Rep.
126 H4 **Belcik** Turkey
147 E6 **Belclare** Ireland
227 Q1 **Belcourt** *Que.* Can.
117 L8 **Beldanga** *W. Bengal* India
175 J2 **Bełdany, Jezioro** *l.* Pol.
240 K1 **Belden** *CA* U.S.A.
147 C4 **Belderg** Ireland
199 J6 **Beldibi** Turkey
226 I6 **Belding** *MI* U.S.A.
Beleapani *rf* India *see* **Cherbaniani Reef**
120 F1 **Belebey** Rus. Fed.
176 G4 **Beled** Hungary
210 E3 **Beledweyne** Somalia
206 C5 **Belefuanai** Liberia
191 Q6 **Belej** Croatia
122 E2 **Belek** Turkm.
206 D3 **Béléko** Mali
207 I5 **Bélèl** Cameroon
207 I4 **Belel** Nigeria
254 C2 **Belém** Brazil
208 B2 **Bélèm** Chad
258 D2 **Belén** Arg.
253 F5 **Belén** Para.
128 A2 **Belen** *Antalya* Turkey
126 H5 **Belen** *Hatay* Turkey
261 I2 **Belén** Uru.
239 K9 **Belen** *NM* U.S.A.
261 I2 **Belén, Cuchilla de** *hills* Uru.
183 N7 **Beleña, Embalse de** *resr* Spain
244 E4 **Belén del Refugio** Mex.
197 N7 **Belene** Bulg.
137 P3 **Belenikhino** Rus. Fed.
183 J2 **Beleño** Spain
78 □5 **Belep, Îles** *is* New Caledonia
182 E3 **Belesar, Encoro de** *resr* Spain
163 H10 **Bélesta** France
139 T8 **Belev** Rus. Fed.
199 I4 **Belevi** Turkey
176 F5 **Belezna** Hungary
81 G10 **Belfast** *South I.* N.Z.
215 O1 **Belfast** S. Africa
147 K3 **Belfast** *Northern Ireland* U.K.
233 □P4 **Belfast** *ME* U.S.A.
232 G6 **Belfast** *NY* U.S.A.
148 E4 **Belfast International** *airport Northern Ireland* U.K.
147 K3 **Belfast Lough** *inlet Northern Ireland* U.K.
165 J6 **Belfeld** Neth.
236 D2 **Belfield** *ND* U.S.A.
210 B2 **Bēlfodiyo** Eth.
149 N2 **Belford** *Northumberland, England* U.K.
160 J1 **Belfort** France
163 H7 **Belfort-du-Quercy** France
193 K1 **Belforte del Chienti** Italy
114 D5 **Belgaum** *Karnataka* India
161 I10 **Belgentier** France
171 H8 **Belgern** Ger.
171 G8 **Belgershain** Ger.
Belgian Congo *country* Africa *see* **Congo, Democratic Republic of the**
Belgicafjella *mts* Antarctica *see* **Belgica Mountains**
263 C2 **Belgica Mountains** Antarctica
België *country* Europe *see* **Belgium**
190 G5 **Belgioioso** Italy
Belgique *country* Europe *see* **Belgium**
165 F7 **Belgium** *country* Europe
192 C2 **Belgodère** *Corse* France
135 G6 **Belgorod** Rus. Fed.
Belgorod-Dnestrovskyy Ukr. *see* **Bilhorod-Dnistrovs'kyy**
Belgorod Oblast *admin. div.* Rus. Fed. *see* **Belgorodskaya Oblast'**
135 G6 **Belgorodskaya Oblast'** *admin. div.* Rus. Fed.
Belgrade Serbia *see* **Beograd**
233 □P4 **Belgrade** *ME* U.S.A.
238 I4 **Belgrade** *MT* U.S.A.
262 V1 **Belgrano II** *research stn* Antarctica
81 G8 **Belgrove** *South I.* N.Z.
163 C7 **Belhade** France
205 G3 **Belhirane** Alg.
156 B6 **Belhomert-Guéhouville** France
191 Q5 **Beli** Croatia
206 B4 **Béli** Guinea-Bissau
207 H5 **Beli** Nigeria
186 H4 **Belianes** Spain
179 O7 **Belica** Croatia
194 D8 **Belice** *r. Sicilia* Italy
184 E6 **Beliche** *r.* Port.
194 F8 **Belici** *r. Sicilia* Italy
196 I8 **Beli Drim** *r.* Albania/Serbia
129 J4 **Belidzhi** Rus. Fed.
Beliliou *i.* Palau *see* **Peleliu**
197 O7 **Beli Lom** *r.* Bulg.
188 G3 **Beli Manastir** Croatia
94 F7 **Belimbing** *Sumatera* Indon.
97 I14 **Belimbing, Tanjung** *pt* Indon.
163 C7 **Belin-Béliet** France
183 N8 **Belinchón** Spain
208 B4 **Bélinga** Gabon
232 F9 **Belington** *WV* U.S.A.
Belingwe Zimbabwe *see* **Mberengwa**
135 H5 **Belinskiy** Rus. Fed.
197 J5 **Belinţ** Romania
94 F5 **Belinyu** Indon.
197 K6 **Beli Timok** *r.* Serbia
175 N2 **Belitsa** Belarus
197 L9 **Belitsa** Bulg.
137 O2 **Belitsa** Rus. Fed.
95 H6 **Belitung** *i.* Indon.
177 L5 **Beliu** Romania
209 B6 **Belize** Angola
243 O9 **Belize** Belize
243 O9 **Belize** *country* Central America
251 H3 **Bélizon** Fr. Guiana
Beljak Austria *see* **Villach**
197 J6 **Beljanica** *mt.* Serbia
131 O2 **Bel'kovskiy, Ostrov** *i. Novosibirskiye O-va* Rus. Fed.
85 M9 **Bell** *Qld* Austr.
83 L5 **Bell** *r. N.S.W.* Austr.
224 E3 **Bell** *r. Que.* Can.
169 D10 **Bell** Ger.
215 L9 **Bell** S. Africa
169 D10 **Bell (Hunsrück)** Ger.
82 D5 **Bell, Point** *S.A.* Austr.
193 P6 **Bella** Italy
222 D4 **Bella Bella** *B.C.* Can.
162 G3 **Bellac** France
160 I5 **Bellacha, Mont** *mt.* France
261 I3 **Bellaco** Uru.
222 E4 **Bella Coola** *B.C.* Can.
222 E4 **Bella Coola** *r. B.C.* Can.
147 C4 **Bellacorick** Ireland
252 D2 **Bella Flor** Bol.
147 I3 **Bellaghy** *Northern Ireland* U.K.
190 G4 **Bellagio** Italy
147 E5 **Bellahy** Ireland
226 I5 **Bellaire** *MI* U.S.A.
237 H11 **Bellaire** *TX* U.S.A.
147 F5 **Bellanagare** Ireland
147 G4 **Bellanaleck** *Northern Ireland* U.K.
147 F3 **Bellanamore** Ireland
147 F6 **Bellaneeny** Ireland
190 G3 **Bellano** Italy
193 L2 **Bellante** Italy
191 M7 **Bellaria** Italy
114 E5 **Bellary** *Karnataka* India
83 L3 **Bellata** *N.S.W.* Austr.
261 I2 **Bella Unión** Uru.
148 B5 **Bellavally Gap** *pass* Ireland
147 D5 **Bellavary** Ireland
258 F3 **Bella Vista** *Corrientes* Arg.
259 C8 **Bella Vista** *Santa Cruz* Arg.
253 E3 **Bella Vista** Bol.
253 F5 **Bella Vista** Para.
250 B6 **Bellavista** *Cajamarca* Peru
250 C5 **Bellavista** *Loreto* Peru
192 D8 **Bellavista, Capo** *c. Sardegna* Italy
252 C5 **Bella Vista, Salar de** *salt flat* Chile
80 I6 **Bell Block** *North I.* N.Z.
85 M6 **Bell Cay** *rf Qld* Austr.
186 G4 **Bellclaire d'Urgell** Spain
232 D10 **Belle** *WV* U.S.A.
246 G4 **Belle-Anse** Haiti
171 E7 **Belleben** Ger.
161 H6 **Belledonne** *mts* France
147 F4 **Belleek** *Northern Ireland* U.K.
147 J4 **Belleek** *Northern Ireland* U.K.
157 L7 **Bellefontaine** France
247 □3 **Bellefontaine** Martinique
232 B8 **Bellefontaine** *OH* U.S.A.
232 H8 **Bellefonte** *PA* U.S.A.
236 D3 **Belle Fourche** *SD* U.S.A.
236 D3 **Belle Fourche** *r. SD* U.S.A.
156 D8 **Bellegarde** *Centre* France
161 F9 **Bellegarde** *Languedoc-Roussillon* France
162 I4 **Bellegarde-en-Marche** France
160 H4 **Bellegarde-sur-Valserine** France
231 G12 **Belle Glade** *FL* U.S.A.
158 E7 **Belle-Île** *i.* France
225 K3 **Belle Isle** *i. Nfld and Lab.* Can.
225 J3 **Belle Isle, Strait of** *Nfld and Lab.* Can.
158 E4 **Belle-Isle-en-Terre** France
159 M5 **Bellême** France
234 F4 **Belle Mead** *NJ* U.S.A.
241 U6 **Bellemont** *AZ* U.S.A.
160 C4 **Bellenaves** France
173 I5 **Bellenberg** Ger.
156 B4 **Bellencombre** France
247 □4 **Belleplaine** Barbados
160 C4 **Bellerive-sur-Allier** France
157 M6 **Belles-Forêts** France
224 E4 **Belleterre** *Que.* Can.
156 F5 **Belleu** France
160 J4 **Bellevaux** France
160 G3 **Bellevesvre** France
224 E4 **Belleville** *Ont.* Can.
160 F4 **Belleville** France
236 G6 **Belleville** *KS* U.S.A.
235 G3 **Belleville** *NJ* U.S.A.
160 B1 **Belleville-sur-Loire** France
157 J5 **Belleville-sur-Meuse** France
158 I8 **Belleville-sur-Vie** France
230 B4 **Bellevue** *IA* U.S.A.
226 I7 **Bellevue** *MI* U.S.A.
236 H5 **Bellevue** *NE* U.S.A.
232 C7 **Bellevue** *OH* U.S.A.
238 C3 **Bellevue** *WA* U.S.A.
161 D6 **Bellevue-la-Montagne** France
160 H5 **Belley** France
206 C5 **Belle Yella** Liberia
226 F9 **Bellflower** *IL* U.S.A.
172 E3 **Bellheim** Ger.
160 J2 **Bellherbe** France
160 H4 **Bellignat** France
Bellin *Que.* Can. *see* **Kangirsuk**
83 N4 **Bellingen** *N.S.W.* Austr.
149 M3 **Bellingham** *Northumberland, England* U.K.
238 C2 **Bellingham** *WA* U.S.A.
262 U2 **Bellingshausen** *research stn* Antarctica
Bellingshausen Island *atoll Arch. de la Société* Fr. Polynesia *see* **Motu One**
262 S2 **Bellingshausen Sea** Antarctica
164 L2 **Bellingwolde** Neth.
190 F4 **Bellinzago Novarese** Italy
190 G3 **Bellinzona** Switz.
225 K3 **Bell Island** *Nfld and Lab.* Can.
222 D4 **Bell Island Hot Springs** *AK* U.S.A.
193 N6 **Bellizzi** Italy
234 E5 **Bellmawr** *NJ* U.S.A.
250 C3 **Bello** Col.
183 R7 **Bello** Spain
163 C8 **Bellocq** France
78 □6 **Bellona** *i.* Solomon Is
159 K4 **Bellou-en-Houlme** France
233 M5 **Bellows Falls** *VT* U.S.A.
123 M7 **Bellpat** Pak.
186 H4 **Bellpuig** Spain
146 L10 **Bell Rock** *i. Scotland* U.K.
146 H11 **Bellshill** *North Lanarkshire, Scotland* U.K.
140 □ **Bellsund** *inlet* Svalbard
191 M3 **Belluno** Italy
191 M3 **Belluno** *prov.* Italy
114 E6 **Belluru** *Karnataka* India
235 G2 **Bellvale** *NY* U.S.A.
186 I3 **Bellver de Cerdanya** Spain
261 F3 **Bell Ville** Arg.
214 C9 **Bellville** S. Africa
232 C8 **Bellville** *OH* U.S.A.
237 G11 **Bellville** *TX* U.S.A.
232 G8 **Bellwood** *PA* U.S.A.
222 H5 **Belly** *r. Alta* Can.
169 F6 **Belm** Ger.
235 G4 **Belmar** *NJ* U.S.A.
177 K5 **Bélmegyer** Hungary
185 I4 **Bélmez** Spain
185 M5 **Bélmez de la Moraleda** Spain
83 M5 **Belmont** *N.S.W.* Austr.
163 E8 **Belmont** France
214 I5 **Belmont** S. Africa
146 □O1 **Belmont** *Shetland, Scotland* U.K.
233 N5 **Belmont** *NH* U.S.A.
232 G6 **Belmont** *NY* U.S.A.
160 E4 **Belmont-de-la-Loire** France
257 H1 **Belmonte** Brazil
182 F8 **Belmonte** Port.
182 H2 **Belmonte** *Asturias* Spain
183 O9 **Belmonte** *Castilla-La Mancha* Spain
193 Q9 **Belmonte Calabro** Italy
193 M4 **Belmonte del Sannio** Italy
193 J3 **Belmonte in Sabina** Italy
194 E7 **Belmonte Mezzagno** *Sicilia* Italy
161 B9 **Belmont-sur-Rance** France
243 O9 **Belmopan** Belize
85 H5 **Belmore Creek** *r. Qld* Austr.
147 C4 **Belmullet** Ireland
213 □J4 **Belo** Madag.
255 E5 **Belo Campo** Brazil
165 E7 **Belœil** Belgium
121 T1 **Beloglazovo** Rus. Fed.
100 F3 **Belogorsk** Rus. Fed.
Belogorsk Ukr. *see* **Bilohirs'k**
137 T3 **Belogor'ye** Rus. Fed.
197 K7 **Belogradchik** Bulg.
213 □J5 **Beloha** Madag.
250 E5 **Belo Horizonte** *Amazonas* Brazil
257 F3 **Belo Horizonte** *Minas Gerais* Brazil
236 F6 **Beloit** *KS* U.S.A.
226 E7 **Beloit** *WI* U.S.A.
254 F4 **Belo Jardim** Brazil
Belokamensk Ukr. *see* **Inkerman**
208 B3 **Béloko** C.A.R.
121 U2 **Belokurikha** Rus. Fed.
217 □1b **Bel Ombre** Mauritius
251 I5 **Belo Monte** *Pará* Brazil
Belo Monte *Piauí* Brazil *see* **Batalha**
134 F2 **Belomorsk** Rus. Fed.
117 M8 **Belonia** *Tripura* India
139 W7 **Beloomut** Rus. Fed.
257 F3 **Belo Oriente** Brazil
Beloozersk Belarus *see* **Byelaazyorsk**
139 V6 **Beloozerskiy** Rus. Fed.
93 B5 **Belopa** *Sulawesi* Indon.
Belopol'ye Ukr. *see* **Bilopillya**
183 N4 **Belorado** Spain
135 G7 **Belorechensk** Rus. Fed.
Belorechenskaya Rus. Fed. *see* **Belorechensk**
126 H5 **Belören** *Adıyaman* Turkey
126 F5 **Belören** *Konya* Turkey
120 H1 **Beloretsk** Rus. Fed.
Belorussia *country* Europe *see* **Belarus**
Belorusskaya S.S.R. *country* Europe *see* **Belarus**
197 P7 **Beloslav** Bulg.
Belostok Pol. *see* **Białystok**
129 F3 **Belot'i** Georgia
177 G2 **Bělotín** Czech Rep.
197 K7 **Belotintsi** Bulg.
213 □J3 **Belo Tsiribihina** Madag.
121 T2 **Belousovka** Kazakh.
139 T6 **Belousovo** Rus. Fed.
257 E4 **Belo Vale** Brazil
197 M8 **Belovo** Bulg.
100 F3 **Beloyarovo** Rus. Fed.
134 G2 **Beloye** Rus. Fed.
139 U1 **Beloye, Ozero** *l.* Rus. Fed.
140 V3 **Beloye More** Rus. Fed.
134 G2 **Beloye More** *sea* Rus. Fed.
134 K4 **Beloyevo** Rus. Fed.
120 F1 **Belozerka** Rus. Fed.
139 U1 **Belozersk** Rus. Fed.
Belozerskoye Ukr. *see* **Bilozers'ke**
190 C2 **Belp** Switz.
172 D8 **Belp** *airport* Switz.
194 H8 **Belpasso** *Sicilia* Italy
163 H9 **Belpech** France
149 O7 **Belper** *Derbyshire, England* U.K.
232 D9 **Belpre** *OH* U.S.A.
149 N3 **Belsay** *Northumberland, England* U.K.
175 I4 **Belsk Duży** Pol.
139 X7 **Bel'skoye** Rus. Fed.
82 G4 **Beltana** *S.A.* Austr.
82 F3 **Belt Bay** *salt flat S.A.* Austr.
241 P4 **Belted Range** *mts NV* U.S.A.
251 H5 **Belterra** Brazil
106 F1 **Beltes Gol** *r.* Mongolia
169 D10 **Beltheim** Ger.
179 N6 **Beltinci** Slovenia
177 L4 **Beltiug** Romania
151 P2 **Belton** *Norfolk, England* U.K.
236 H6 **Belton** *MO* U.S.A.
237 G10 **Belton** *TX* U.S.A.
120 I6 **Beltov** Uzbek.
147 D5 **Beltra** *Mayo* Ireland
147 E4 **Beltra** *Sligo* Ireland
147 D5 **Beltra Lough** *l.* Ireland
164 K4 **Beltrum** Neth.
Bel'ts' Moldova *see* **Bălţi**
234 B6 **Beltsville** *MD* U.S.A.
Bel'tsy Moldova *see* **Bălţi**
147 H4 **Belturbet** Ireland
234 D3 **Beltzville Lake** *PA* U.S.A.
192 B8 **Belu** *r. Sardegna* Italy
112 G2 **Belukha, Gora** *mt.* Kazakh./Rus. Fed.
114 D6 **Belur** *Karnataka* India
95 L2 **Beluran** *Sabah* Malaysia
177 H2 **Beluša** Slovakia
134 I2 **Belush'ye** Rus. Fed.
232 D10 **Belva** *WV* U.S.A.
192 B4 **Belvédère-Campomoro** *Corse* France
193 P8 **Belvedere Marittimo** Italy
184 D1 **Belver** Port.
186 F4 **Belver de Cinca** Spain
163 G6 **Belvès** France
163 I9 **Belvèze-du-Razès** France
161 E8 **Belvézet** France
226 F7 **Belvidere** *IL* U.S.A.
234 E3 **Belvidere** *NJ* U.S.A.
147 D4 **Belville** Ireland
183 K9 **Belvís de la Jara** Spain
178 B7 **Belviso, Lago** *l.* Italy
85 K6 **Belyando** *r. Qld* Austr.
85 K6 **Belyando Crossing** *Qld* Austr.
120 G2 **Belyayevka** Rus. Fed.
Belyayevka Ukr. *see* **Bilyayivka**
139 O6 **Belyayevo** Rus. Fed.
84 C2 **Belyuen** *N.T.* Austr.
139 P6 **Belyy** Rus. Fed.
130 I2 **Belyy, Ostrov** *i.* Rus. Fed.
110 H1 **Belyy Bom** Rus. Fed.
139 R8 **Belyye Berega** Rus. Fed.
139 U6 **Belyye Stolby** Rus. Fed.
139 U5 **Belyy Gorodok** Rus. Fed.
137 R3 **Belyy Kolodez'** Rus. Fed.
130 J4 **Belyy Yar** Rus. Fed.
158 E6 **Belz** France
136 D3 **Belz** Ukr.
175 L5 **Bełżec** Pol.
171 G6 **Belzig** Ger.
237 J9 **Belzoni** *MS* U.S.A.
175 K4 **Bełżyce** Pol.
213 □K2 **Bemanevika** Madag.
213 □J3 **Bemaraha, Plateau du** Madag.
209 B6 **Bembe** Angola
207 F4 **Bembèrèkè** Benin
185 I5 **Bembézar** *r.* Spain
185 I5 **Bembézar, Embalse del** *resr* Spain
182 H3 **Bembibre** *Castilla y León* Spain
182 C2 **Bembibre** *Galicia* Spain
209 C7 **Bembo** Angola
151 J6 **Bembridge** *Isle of Wight, England* U.K.
236 H2 **Bemidji** *MN* U.S.A.
237 K8 **Bemis** *TN* U.S.A.
164 I5 **Bemmel** Neth.
182 H6 **Bemposta** *Bragança* Port.
184 C2 **Bemposta** *Santarém* Port.
149 Q5 **Bempton** *East Riding of Yorkshire, England* U.K.
206 D3 **Béna** Burkina
186 F3 **Benabarre** Spain
209 D6 **Bena Dibele** Dem. Rep. Congo
95 K5 **Benagin** *Kalimantan* Indon.
187 D8 **Benaguasil** Spain
185 O7 **Benahadux** Spain
185 I7 **Benahavís** Spain
204 D2 **Benahmed** Morocco
146 J7 **Ben Aigan** *hill Scotland* U.K.
185 I4 **Benajarafe** *r.* Spain
146 H9 **Ben Alder** *mt. Scotland* U.K.
83 J7 **Benalla** *Vic.* Austr.
185 J7 **Benalmádena** Spain
185 M6 **Benalúa de Guadix** Spain
185 L6 **Benalúa de las Villas** Spain
184 H8 **Benalup de Sidonia** Spain
185 K7 **Benamargosa** Spain
185 N5 **Benamaurel** Spain
185 J6 **Benamejí** Spain
204 B5 **Ben 'Amîra** *well* Maur.
185 K7 **Benamocarra** Spain
185 I7 **Benaocaz** Spain
185 I7 **Benaoján** Spain
Benares *Uttar Prad.* India *see* **Varanasi**
217 □1b **Benares** Mauritius
205 H1 **Ben Arous** Tunisia
189 B7 **Ben Arous** *admin. div.* Tunisia
187 E7 **Benasal** Spain
187 E10 **Benasau** Spain
186 G2 **Benasque** Spain
162 E2 **Benassay** France
161 I10 **Bénat, Cap** *c.* France
176 D1 **Benátky nad Jizerou** Czech Rep.
209 D6 **Bena-Tshadi** Dem. Rep. Congo
184 B3 **Benavente** Port.
182 I4 **Benavente** Spain
252 D3 **Benavides** Bol.
182 I4 **Benavides de Orbigo** Spain
184 D2 **Benavila** Port.
146 J8 **Ben Avon** *mt. Scotland* U.K.
147 J2 **Benbane Head** *Northern Ireland* U.K.
147 C5 **Benbaun** *hill* Ireland
146 B8 **Benbecula** *i. Scotland* U.K.
83 M7 **Ben Boyd National Park** *N.S.W.* Austr.
147 F4 **Benbulben** *hill* Ireland
147 I4 **Benburb** *Northern Ireland* U.K.
147 C5 **Benbury** *hill* Ireland
184 E3 **Bencatel** Port.
109 M2 **Bencha** *Jiangsu* China
Bencheng *Hebei* China *see* **Luannan**
146 I10 **Ben Chonzie** *hill Scotland* U.K.
147 C5 **Bencorr** *hill* Ireland
146 F10 **Ben Cruachan** *mt. Scotland* U.K.
87 D11 **Bencubbin** *W.A.* Austr.
238 D4 **Bend** *OR* U.S.A.
215 L7 **Bendearg** *mt.* S. Africa
209 C5 **Bendela** Dem. Rep. Congo
83 M4 **Bendemeer** *N.S.W.* Austr.
Bender Moldova *see* **Tighina**
210 F2 **Bender-Bayla** Somalia
226 G5 **Benderville** *WI* U.S.A.
Bendery Moldova *see* **Tighina**
168 I4 **Bendestorf** Ger.
82 G4 **Bendieuta** *watercourse S.A.* Austr.
83 J7 **Bendigo** *Vic.* Austr.
83 L7 **Bendoc** *Vic.* Austr.
169 E10 **Bendorf** Ger.
Bendzin Pol. *see* **Będzin**
138 G5 **Bēne** Latvia
213 G2 **Bene** Moz.
164 H5 **Beneden-Leeuwen** Neth.
225 J2 **Benedict, Mount** *hill Nfld and Lab.* Can.
233 □Q3 **Benedicta** *ME* U.S.A.
173 K6 **Benediktbeuren** Ger.
173 K6 **Benediktenwand** *mt.* Ger.
184 B2 **Benedita** Port.
254 E3 **Beneditinos** Brazil
254 D3 **Benedito Leite** Brazil
182 I5 **Benegiles** Spain
163 D9 **Bénéjacq** France
187 D10 **Benejama** Spain
187 D11 **Benejúzar** Spain
206 D3 **Bénéna** Mali
151 N5 **Benenden** *Kent, England* U.K.
213 □J4 **Benenitra** Madag.
176 D2 **Benešov** Czech Rep.
179 K2 **Benešov nad Černou** Czech Rep.
176 D1 **Benešov nad Ploučnicí** Czech Rep.
163 B8 **Bénesse-Maremne** France
195 K7 **Benestare** Italy
157 M6 **Bénestroff** France
162 C3 **Benet** France
192 C7 **Benetutti** *Sardegna* Italy
190 D6 **Bene Vagienna** Italy
162 H3 **Bénévent-l'Abbaye** France
193 N5 **Benevento** Italy
193 N5 **Benevento** *prov.* Italy
Beneventum Italy *see* **Benevento**
232 G7 **Benezette** *PA* U.S.A.
157 O7 **Benfeld** France
234 A3 **Benfer** *PA* U.S.A.
184 B2 **Benfica do Ribatejo** Port.
96 E5 **Beng, Nam** *r.* Laos
Benga *i.* Fiji *see* **Beqa**
211 B8 **Benga** Malawi
113 G8 **Bengal, Bay of** *sea* Indian Ocean
208 E4 **Bengamisa** Dem. Rep. Congo
207 I6 **Bengbis** Cameroon
109 K2 **Bengbu** *Anhui* China
146 C7 **Ben Geary** *hill Scotland* U.K.
195 □ **Benghajsa, Il-Ponta ta'** *pt* Malta
Benghazi Libya *see* **Banghāzī**
107 P9 **Beng He** *r.* China
Benghisa Point Malta *see* **Benghajsa, Il-Ponta ta'**
94 E4 **Bengkalis** *Sumatera* Indon.
94 E4 **Bengkalis** *i.* Indon.
95 H4 **Bengkayang** *Kalimantan* Indon.
94 E6 **Bengkulu** *Sumatera* Indon.
94 D6 **Bengkulu** *prov.* Indon.
95 L6 **Bengkung** *Kalimantan* Indon.
209 C9 **Bengo** *Cuando Cubango* Angola
209 B7 **Bengo** *Uíge* Angola
209 B7 **Bengo** *prov.* Angola
93 G5 **Bengoi** *Seram* Indon.
147 C5 **Bengorm** *hill* Ireland
142 I2 **Bengtsfors** Sweden
209 B8 **Benguela** Angola
209 B8 **Benguela** *prov.* Angola
205 H2 **Ben Guerdane** Tunisia
204 D2 **Benguerir** Morocco
213 G4 **Benguérua, Ilha** *i.* Moz.
Benha *Qalyūbīyah* Egypt *see* **Banhā**
146 G6 **Ben Hee** *hill Scotland* U.K.
146 D9 **Ben Hiant** *hill Scotland* U.K.
146 G6 **Ben Hope** *hill Scotland* U.K.
146 H6 **Ben Horn** *hill Scotland* U.K.
252 D3 **Beni** *dept* Bol.
252 D2 **Beni** *r.* Bol.
208 F4 **Beni** Dem. Rep. Congo
117 I5 **Beni** Nepal
204 E3 **Beni-Abbès** Alg.
183 K2 **Benia de Onís** Spain
223 H2 **Beniah Lake** *N.W.T.* Can.
187 E10 **Beniarrés** Spain
187 E10 **Beniarrés, Embalse de** *resr* Spain
180 D5 **Beni Boufrah** Morocco
186 F7 **Benicarló** Spain
187 F7 **Benicasim** Spain
240 J3 **Benicia** *CA* U.S.A.
187 E10 **Benidorm** Spain
187 E10 **Benidorm, Isolte de** *i.* Spain
207 I1 **Beni Dourso** *well* Niger
187 D11 **Beniel** Spain
187 E9 **Benifaió** Spain
186 G6 **Benifallet** Spain
187 E10 **Benifallim** Spain
Benifayo *Valencia* Spain *see* **Benifaió**
181 F3 **Benigánim** Spain
158 B5 **Beniguet, Île de** *i.* France
204 E2 **Beni Guil** *reg.* Morocco
187 E10 **Benilloba** Spain
204 D2 **Beni Mellal** Morocco
207 F4 **Benin** *country* Africa
207 G5 **Benin** *r.* Nigeria
207 F5 **Benin, Bight of** *g.* Africa
207 G5 **Benin City** Nigeria
205 E3 **Beni-Ounif** Alg.
205 E2 **Beni-Saf** Alg.
207 I4 **Benisheikh** Nigeria
187 F10 **Benissa** Spain
186 G5 **Benissanet** Spain
Beni Suef *Banī Suwayf* Egypt *see* **Banī Suwayf**
187 F10 **Benitachell** Spain
114 E4 **Benithora** *r.* India
217 □1b **Bénitiers, Île aux** *i.* Mauritius
Benito *r.* Equat. Guinea *see* **Mbini**
242 B3 **Benito, Islas** *is* Mex.
261 H5 **Benito Juárez** Arg.
241 R9 **Benito Juárez** *Baja California* Mex.
244 G6 **Benito Juarez** *Michoacán* Mex.

Benito Juarez to Bidbid
287

244 F2 **Benito Juarez** *San Luis Potosí* Mex.
245 N7 **Benito Juárez** *Tabasco* Mex.
245 J3 **Benito Juárez** *Veracruz* Mex.
245 L8 **Benito Juárez** *Veracruz* Mex.
244 D4 **Benito Juárez** *Zacatecas* Mex.
245 K8 **Benito Juárez, Parque Nacional** *nat. park* Mex.
245 L9 **Benito Juárez, Presa** *resr* Mex.
92 C3 **Benito Soliven** *Luzon* Phil.
185 O6 **Benizalón** Spain
185 P4 **Benizar y la Tercia** Spain
250 D6 **Benjamim Constant** Brazil
237 F9 **Benjamin** *TX* U.S.A.
259 B7 **Benjamín, Isla** *i.* Chile
242 D2 **Benjamín Hill** Mex.
260 E6 **Benjamín Zorrillo** Arg.
91 H8 **Benjina** *Maluku* Indon.
102 R4 **Benkei-misaki** *pt* Japan
236 E5 **Benkelman** *NE* U.S.A.
190 G1 **Benken** Switz.
146 H6 **Ben Klibreck** *hill Scotland* U.K.
188 E3 **Benkovac** Croatia
197 P7 **Benkovski** Bulg.
146 H9 **Ben Lawers** *mt. Scotland* U.K.
146 H10 **Ben Ledi** *hill Scotland* U.K.
150 D1 **Benllech** *Isle of Anglesey, Wales* U.K.
187 F7 **Benlloch** Spain
83 M4 **Ben Lomond** *mt. N.S.W.* Austr.
146 G10 **Ben Lomond** *hill Scotland* U.K.
240 J4 **Ben Lomond** *CA* U.S.A.
83 K9 **Ben Lomond National Park** *Tas.* Austr.
146 H6 **Ben Loyal** *hill Scotland* U.K.
146 G10 **Ben Lui** *mt. Scotland* U.K.
215 L6 **Ben Macdhui** *mt.* Lesotho
144 F3 **Ben Macdui** *mt. Scotland* U.K.
189 A7 **Ben Mahidi** Alg.
84 F4 **Benmara** *N.T.* Austr.
81 F10 **Ben More** *mt. South I.* N.Z.
146 D10 **Ben More** *hill Scotland* U.K.
146 G10 **Ben More** *mt. Scotland* U.K.
81 E11 **Benmore, Lake** *South I.* N.Z.
146 G6 **Ben More Assynt** *hill Scotland* U.K.
81 E11 **Benmore Peak** *South I.* N.Z.
146 F12 **Bennan Head** *Scotland* U.K.
171 D7 **Benndorf** Ger.
164 G4 **Bennebroek** Neth.
169 K7 **Benneckenstein (Harz)** Ger.
164 I4 **Bennekom** Neth.
222 C3 **Bennett** *B.C.* Can.
226 C3 **Bennett** *WI* U.S.A.
84 C7 **Bennett, Lake** *salt flat N.T.* Austr.
131 P2 **Bennetta, Ostrov** *i. Novosibirskiye O-va* Rus. Fed.
Bennett Island *Novosibirskiye O-va* Rus. Fed. *see* Bennetta, Ostrov
222 C3 **Bennett Lake** *B.C.* Can.
147 H7 **Bennettsbridge** Ireland
216 □2b **Bennett's Point** St Helena
231 H8 **Bennettsville** *SC* U.S.A.
146 F9 **Ben Nevis** *mt. Scotland* U.K.
80 J5 **Benneydale** *North I.* N.Z.
233 N5 **Bennington** *NH* U.S.A.
233 L6 **Bennington** *VT* U.S.A.
171 E8 **Bennstedt** Ger.
171 D8 **Bennungen** Ger.
158 C6 **Bénodet** France
158 C6 **Benodet, Anse de** *b.* France
81 D11 **Ben Ohau Range** *mts South I.* N.Z.
94 □ **Benoi Basin** *dock* Sing.
215 M2 **Benoni** S. Africa
207 I4 **Bénoué** *r.* Cameroon
207 I4 **Bénoué, Parc National de la** *nat. park* Cameroon
208 C2 **Bénoye** Chad
182 F8 **Benquerença** Port.
163 C8 **Benquet** France
146 J8 **Ben Rinnes** *hill Scotland* U.K.
184 B6 **Bensafrim** Port.
171 F6 **Bensdorf** Ger.
169 K9 **Benshausen** Ger.
172 F2 **Bensheim** Ger.
204 D2 **Ben Slimane** Morocco
151 J4 **Benson** *Oxfordshire, England* U.K.
241 V10 **Benson** *AZ* U.S.A.
236 H3 **Benson** *MN* U.S.A.
206 C5 **Bensonville** Liberia
232 D9 **Bens Run** *WV* U.S.A.
146 F9 **Ben Starav** *mt. Scotland* U.K.
122 H8 **Bent** Iran
94 D2 **Benta Seberang** Malaysia
164 K4 **Bentelo** Neth.
93 B7 **Benteng** *Sulawesi* Indon.
96 G5 **Ben Thuy** Vietnam
206 B4 **Benti** Guinea
209 B8 **Bentiaba** Angola
180 E5 **Ben Tieb** Morocco
84 G4 **Bentinck Island** *Qld* Austr.
97 D9 **Bentinck Island** Myanmar
146 J9 **Ben Tirran** *hill Scotland* U.K.
208 F2 **Bentiu** Sudan
128 D5 **Bent Jbaïl** Lebanon
222 H4 **Bentley** *Alta* Can.
149 O6 **Bentley** *South Yorkshire, England* U.K.
232 E8 **Bentleyville** *PA* U.S.A.
253 F4 **Bento Gomes** *r.* Brazil
233 □R3 **Benton** *N.B.* Can.
237 I8 **Benton** *AR* U.S.A.
240 N4 **Benton** *CA* U.S.A.
236 K6 **Benton** *IL* U.S.A.
237 K7 **Benton** *KY* U.S.A.
237 I9 **Benton** *LA* U.S.A.
237 K7 **Benton** *MO* U.S.A.
234 C2 **Benton** *PA* U.S.A.
231 E8 **Benton** *TN* U.S.A.
Bentong Malaysia *see* Bentung
226 H7 **Benton Harbor** *MI* U.S.A.
237 H7 **Bentonville** *AR* U.S.A.
232 B10 **Bentonville** *OH* U.S.A.
97 H9 **Bên Tre** Vietnam
139 O5 **Bentsy** Rus. Fed.
94 D3 **Bentung** Malaysia
170 F2 **Bentwisch** Ger.
170 H3 **Bentzin** Ger.
93 C6 **Benua** *Sulawesi* Indon.
94 G4 **Benua** *i.* Indon.
95 J4 **Benuamartinus** *Kalimantan* Indon.
207 G5 **Benue** *r.* Nigeria
207 H5 **Benue** *state* Nigeria
94 E3 **Benum, Gunung** *mt.* Malaysia
177 I3 **Beňuš** Slovakia
146 G10 **Ben Vorlich** *hill Argyll and Bute, Scotland* U.K.
146 H10 **Ben Vorlich** *hill Perth and Kinross/Stirling, Scotland* U.K.
209 E7 **Benwa** Zambia
147 C5 **Benwee** *hill* Ireland
147 C4 **Benwee Head** Ireland
232 E8 **Benwood** *WV* U.S.A.
146 G7 **Ben Wyvis** *mt. Scotland* U.K.
107 R6 **Benxi** *Liaoning* China
204 E3 **Ben Zireg** Alg.
185 I9 **Benzu** Morocco
93 E1 **Beo** *Sulawesi* Indon.
196 I6 **Beograd** Serbia
116 H7 **Beohari** *Madh. Prad.* India
206 D5 **Béoumi** Côte d'Ivoire
94 E7 **Bepagut, Gunung** *mt.* Indon.
103 I13 **Beppu** Japan
103 I13 **Beppu-wan** *b.* Japan
79 □7a **Beqa** *i.* Fiji
247 □3 **Bequia** *i.* St Vincent
254 D2 **Bequimão** Brazil
117 L7 **Bera** Bangl.
94 E3 **Bera, Tasik** *l.* Malaysia
261 G3 **Berabevú** Arg.
116 E7 **Berach** *r.* India
186 B1 **Bera de Bidasoa** Spain
147 H3 **Beragh** *Northern Ireland* U.K.
213 □J5 **Beraketa** Madag.
213 □K2 **Beramanja** Madag.
196 H8 **Berane** Montenegro
183 M2 **Beranga** Spain
95 L6 **Berangas** *Kalimantan* Indon.
183 O2 **Berango** Spain
183 O3 **Berantevilla** Spain
225 G1 **Bérard, Lac** *l. Que.* Can.
116 F8 **Berasia** *Madh. Prad.* India
94 C3 **Berastagi** *Sumatera* Indon.
198 A2 **Berat** Albania
163 G9 **Bérat** France
95 L5 **Beratus, Gunung** *mt.* Indon.
173 L3 **Beratzhausen** Ger.
95 L3 **Berau** *r.* Indon.
91 H7 **Berau, Teluk** *b. Papua* Indon.
213 □J3 **Beravina** Madag.
261 H4 **Berazategui** Arg.
94 F5 **Berbak, Taman Nasional** *nat. park* Indon.
186 E4 **Berbegal** Spain
203 G5 **Berber** Sudan
210 E2 **Berbera** Somalia
208 B3 **Berbérati** C.A.R.
215 P3 **Berbice** S. Africa
183 Q3 **Berbinzana** Spain
183 N2 **Bercedo** Spain
177 I4 **Bercel** Hungary
156 G7 **Bercenay-en-Othe** France
183 J5 **Bercero** Spain
190 H6 **Berceto** Italy
165 E7 **Berchem** Belgium
190 B2 **Bercher** Switz.
192 C6 **Berchidda** *Sardegna* Italy
202 C5 **Berchi-Guélé** *well* Chad
173 K3 **Berching** Ger.
120 H3 **Berchogur** Kazakh.
173 O6 **Berchtesgaden** Ger.
173 N6 **Berchtesgaden, Nationalpark** *nat. park* Ger.
173 N6 **Berchtesgadener Alpen** *mts* Ger.
185 M7 **Bérchules** Spain
182 I4 **Bercianos del Páramo** Spain
156 C3 **Berck** France
177 L4 **Bercu** Romania
129 G5 **Berd** Armenia
137 P7 **Berda** *r.* Ukr.
210 D4 **Berdaale** Somalia
159 M5 **Berd'huis** France
Berdichev Ukr. *see* **Berdychiv**
131 N3 **Berdigestyakh** Rus. Fed.
130 J4 **Berdsk** Rus. Fed.
182 G2 **Berducedo** Spain
186 D2 **Berdún** Spain
137 P7 **Berdyans'k** Ukr.
137 P7 **Berdyans'ka Kosa** *spit* Ukr.
Berdyanskaya Kosa *spit* Ukr. *see* **Berdyans'ka Kosa**
137 P7 **Berdyans'ka Zatoka** *b.* Ukr.
136 H4 **Berdychiv** Ukr.
208 C2 **Béré** Chad
232 A11 **Berea** *KY* U.S.A.
232 D7 **Berea** *OH* U.S.A.
150 D7 **Bere Alston** *Devon, England* U.K.
93 F2 **Berebere** *Maluku* Indon.
Béréby Côte d'Ivoire *see* **Grand-Bérébi**
210 F2 **Bereeda** Somalia
150 D7 **Bere Ferrers** *Devon, England* U.K.
139 U1 **Bereg** Rus. Fed.
177 L3 **Beregdaróc** Hungary
Beregovo Ukr. *see* **Berehove**
100 E1 **Beregovoy** Rus. Fed.
190 G5 **Bereguardo** Italy
136 E5 **Berehomet** Ukr.
137 O8 **Berehove** *Respublika Krym* Ukr.
136 B5 **Berehove** *Zakarpats'ka Oblast'* Ukr.
91 K8 **Bereina** P.N.G.
179 O8 **Berek** Croatia
137 P4 **Bereka** Ukr.
137 P4 **Bereka** *r.* Ukr.
177 K4 **Berekböszörmény** Hungary
122 F2 **Bereket** Turkm.
213 □J4 **Bereketa** Madag.
177 J4 **Berekfürdő** Hungary
211 B6 **Bereku** Tanz.
247 □2 **Berekua** Dominica
206 E5 **Berekum** Ghana
121 V3 **Berel'** Kazakh.
177 H6 **Beremend** Hungary
139 W5 **Berendeyevo** Rus. Fed.
252 C4 **Berenguela** Bol.
Berenice Libya *see* **Banghāzī**
223 L4 **Berens** *r. Man.* Can.
223 L4 **Berens Island** *Man.* Can.
223 L4 **Berens River** *Man.* Can.
213 □J4 **Berenty** Madag.
150 H6 **Bere Regis** *Dorset, England* U.K.
225 H4 **Beresford** *N.B.* Can.
236 G4 **Beresford** *SD* U.S.A.
136 E3 **Berestechko** Ukr.
197 P4 **Bereşti** Romania
137 M3 **Berestivka** Ukr.
137 O4 **Berestova** *r.* Ukr.
137 P5 **Berestove** *Kharkivs'ka Oblast'* Ukr.
137 P6 **Berestove** *Zaporiz'ka Oblast'* Ukr.
137 O4 **Berestoven'ka** Ukr.
137 L2 **Berestovets'** Ukr.
136 E3 **Berestyane** Ukr.
177 K4 **Berettyó** *r.* Hungary
177 K4 **Berettyóújfalu** Hungary
213 □J3 **Berevo** Madag.
213 □J3 **Berevo-Ranobe** Madag.
Bereza Belarus *see* **Byaroza**
137 K3 **Berezan'** Ukr.
137 K7 **Berezanka** Ukr.
137 S8 **Berezanskaya** Rus. Fed.
137 K7 **Berezans'kiy Lyman** *l.* Ukr.
139 Q4 **Berezayka** Rus. Fed.
136 G3 **Berezdiv** Ukr.
197 Q4 **Berezeni** Romania
136 D4 **Berezhany** Ukr.
Berezino *Minskaya Voblasts'* Belarus *see* **Byerazino**
Berezino *Vitsyebskaya Voblasts'* Belarus *see* **Byerazino**
120 C2 **Berezino** Kazakh.
137 L3 **Berezivka** *Chernihivs'ka Oblast'* Ukr.
137 L6 **Berezivka** *Kirovohrads'ka Oblast'* Ukr.
136 J6 **Berezivka** *Odes'ka Oblast'* Ukr.
136 G4 **Berezivka** *Zhytomyrs'ka Oblast'* Ukr.
136 H3 **Berezivka** *Zhytomyrs'ka Oblast'* Ukr.
137 K2 **Berezna** Ukr.
136 F2 **Berezne** Ukr.
137 L6 **Bereznehuvate** Ukr.
134 H3 **Bereznik** Rus. Fed.
134 L4 **Berezniki** Rus. Fed.
136 G3 **Bereznyky** Ukr.
Berezov Rus. Fed. *see* **Berezovo**
134 L3 **Berezovaya** *r.* Rus. Fed.
136 G2 **Berezove** Ukr.
134 I3 **Berezovik** Rus. Fed.
Berezovka Belarus *see* **Byarozawka**
100 E3 **Berezovka** *Amurskaya Oblast'* Rus. Fed.
139 V8 **Berezovka** *Lipetskaya Oblast'* Rus. Fed.
120 H1 **Berezovka** *Orenburgskaya Oblast'* Rus. Fed.
134 L4 **Berezovka** *Permskaya Oblast'* Rus. Fed.
Berezovka Ukr. *see* **Berezivka**
130 H3 **Berezovo** Rus. Fed.
100 I3 **Berezovyy** Rus. Fed.
136 I7 **Berezyne** Ukr.
172 H6 **Berg** *Baden-Württemberg* Ger.
171 E10 **Berg** *Bayern* Ger.
173 K6 **Berg** *Bayern* Ger.
169 C9 **Berg** *Rheinland-Pfalz* Ger.
165 J9 **Berg** Lux.
172 E4 **Berg (Pfalz)** Ger.
171 D8 **Berga** *Sachsen-Anhalt* Ger.
171 F9 **Berga** *Thüringen* Ger.
186 I3 **Berga** Spain
199 I3 **Bergama** Turkey
190 H4 **Bergamo** Italy
190 H4 **Bergamo** *prov.* Italy
186 E6 **Bergantes, Riu** *r.* Spain
182 C2 **Bergantiños** *reg.* Spain
183 P2 **Bergara** Spain
172 H6 **Bergatreute** Ger.
173 K3 **Berg bei Neumarkt in der Oberpfalz** Ger.
179 I2 **Berg bei Rohrbach** Austria
141 N6 **Bergby** Sweden
170 E4 **Berge** *Brandenburg* Ger.
168 E5 **Berge** *Niedersachsen* Ger.
186 E6 **Berge** Spain
190 E7 **Bergeggi** Italy
173 N6 **Bergen** *Bayern* Ger.
170 H2 **Bergen** *Mecklenburg-Vorpommern* Ger.
168 I5 **Bergen** *Niedersachsen* Ger.
164 G3 **Bergen** Neth.
142 B1 **Bergen** Norway
215 O3 **Bergen** S. Africa
232 H5 **Bergen** *NY* U.S.A.
168 K5 **Bergen (Dumme)** Ger.
235 G3 **Bergen County** *county NJ* U.S.A.
235 H3 **Bergenfield** *NJ* U.S.A.
164 F6 **Bergen op Zoom** Neth.
164 K3 **Bergentheim** Neth.
163 E6 **Bergerac** France
156 H6 **Bergères-lès-Vertus** France
263 B2 **Bergerson, Mount** Antarctica
160 F4 **Bergesserin** France
165 H6 **Bergeyk** Neth.
170 H5 **Bergfelde** Ger.
80 H1 **Berghan Point** *North I.* N.Z.
164 I5 **Bergharen** Neth.
172 D5 **Berghaupten** Ger.
178 H4 **Bergheim** Austria
173 K4 **Bergheim** Ger.
169 H8 **Bergheim (Edertal)** Ger.
169 C9 **Bergheim (Erft)** Ger.
164 I5 **Berghem** Neth.
171 H6 **Bergholz-Rehbrücke** Ger.
172 H5 **Berghülen** Ger.
178 H6 **Berg im Drautal** Austria
169 D9 **Bergisches Land** *reg.* Ger.
169 D9 **Bergisch Gladbach** Ger.
169 E7 **Bergkamen** Ger.
173 K5 **Bergkirchen** Ger.
212 C4 **Bergland** Namibia
226 E3 **Bergland** *MI* U.S.A.
140 N4 **Bergnäs** Sweden
140 O3 **Bergnäsviken** Sweden
169 E8 **Bergneustadt** Ger.
Bergomum Italy *see* **Bergamo**
232 E10 **Bergoo** *WV* U.S.A.
169 J10 **Bergrheinfeld** Ger.
143 O2 **Bergshamra** Sweden
141 N6 **Bergsjö** Sweden
172 G2 **Bergstraße-Odenwald** *park* Ger.
140 P4 **Bergsviken** Sweden
173 I2 **Bergtheim** Ger.
186 I3 **Bergueda** *reg.* Spain
183 N3 **Berguenda** Spain
156 D2 **Bergues** France
190 H2 **Bergün** Switz.
215 N4 **Bergville** S. Africa
171 G7 **Bergwitz** Ger.
107 L3 **Berh** Mongolia
94 E5 **Berhala, Selat** *sea chan.* Indon.
Berhampur *W. Bengal* India *see* **Baharampur**
197 P4 **Berheci** *r.* Romania
177 H4 **Berhida** Hungary
94 G6 **Berikat, Tanjung** *pt* Indon.
129 J3 **Berikey** Rus. Fed.
257 F2 **Berilo** Brazil
131 R4 **Beringa, Ostrov** *i.* Rus. Fed.
87 D8 **Beringarra** *W.A.* Austr.
165 I6 **Beringe** Neth.
184 D4 **Beringel** Port.
165 H6 **Beringen** Belgium
220 B3 **Bering Land Bridge National Preserve** *nature res. AK* U.S.A.
131 S3 **Beringovskiy** Rus. Fed.
220 A4 **Bering Sea** N. Pacific Ocean
220 B3 **Bering Strait** Rus. Fed./U.S.A.
151 J4 **Berinsfield** *Oxfordshire, England* U.K.
123 I9 **Berīs, Ra's** *pt* Iran
Berislav Ukr. *see* **Beryslav**
217 □1c **Bérive** Réunion
136 J6 **Berizky** Ukr.
185 N7 **Berja** Spain
169 J9 **Berka** Ger.
140 K5 **Berkåk** Norway
204 E2 **Berkane** Morocco
164 F5 **Berkel** Neth.
164 J4 **Berkel** *r.* Neth.
86 I3 **Berkeley** *r. W.A.* Austr.
150 H4 **Berkeley** *Gloucestershire, England* U.K.
240 J4 **Berkeley** *CA* U.S.A.
235 G3 **Berkeley Heights** *NJ* U.S.A.
232 G9 **Berkeley Springs** *WV* U.S.A.
168 K3 **Berkenthin** Ger.
151 K4 **Berkhamsted** *Hertfordshire, England* U.K.
173 I5 **Berkheim** Ger.
164 H3 **Berkhout** Neth.
262 U1 **Berkner Island** Antarctica
197 L7 **Berkovitsa** Bulg.
234 D4 **Berks County** *county PA* U.S.A.
151 J5 **Berkshire Downs** *hills England* U.K.
233 L6 **Berkshire Hills** *MA* U.S.A.
151 I3 **Berkswell** *West Midlands, England* U.K.
164 J3 **Berkum** Neth.
165 G6 **Berlaar** Belgium
156 G3 **Berlaimont** France
222 G4 **Berland** *r. Alta* Can.
184 H4 **Berlanga** Spain
183 O6 **Berlanga de Duero** Spain
165 F6 **Berlare** Belgium
184 A2 **Berlenga** *i.* Port.
140 T1 **Berlevåg** Norway
164 H5 **Berlicum** Neth.
164 I2 **Berlikum** Neth.
170 H5 **Berlin** Ger.
171 H5 **Berlin** *land* Ger.
235 J1 **Berlin** *CT* U.S.A.
233 J10 **Berlin** *MD* U.S.A.
233 □N4 **Berlin** *NH* U.S.A.
234 F5 **Berlin** *NJ* U.S.A.
232 D8 **Berlin** *OH* U.S.A.
232 G9 **Berlin** *PA* U.S.A.
226 F6 **Berlin** *WI* U.S.A.
262 O1 **Berlin, Mount** Antarctica
169 J8 **Berlingerode** Ger.
221 J2 **Berlinguet Inlet** *Nunavut* Can.
81 F8 **Berlins** *South I.* N.Z.
234 D3 **Berlinsville** *PA* U.S.A.
196 J6 **Berlişte** Romania
171 D8 **Berlstedt** Ger.
83 M7 **Bermagui** *N.S.W.* Austr.
172 G6 **Bermatingen** Ger.
122 G2 **Berme** Turkm.
259 E6 **Bermeja, Punta** *pt* Arg.
185 I8 **Bermeja, Sierra** *mts* Spain
185 L7 **Bermejales, Embalse de los** *resr* Spain
242 H5 **Bermejíllo** Mex.
260 D2 **Bermejo** Arg.
260 D3 **Bermejo** *r.* Arg.
258 F2 **Bermejo** *r.* Arg./Bol.
252 D5 **Bermejo** Bol.
261 G6 **Bermejo, Isla** *i.* Arg.
225 G2 **Bermen, Lac** *l. Que.* Can.
183 O2 **Bermeo** Spain
182 H6 **Bermillo de Sayago** Spain
231 □1 **Bermuda** *terr.* N. Atlantic Ocean
264 E4 **Bermuda Rise** *sea feature* N. Atlantic Ocean
190 C2 **Bern** Switz.
190 D2 **Bern** *canton* Switz.
261 I2 **Bernabé Rivera** Uru.
163 E9 **Bernac-Dessus** France
195 L3 **Bernalda** Italy
239 K9 **Bernalillo** *NM* U.S.A.
161 J9 **Bernarde, Sommet de la** *mt.* France
256 C5 **Bernardino de Campos** Brazil
227 O4 **Bernard Lake** *Ont.* Can.
261 G3 **Bernardo de Irigoyen** Arg.
261 F4 **Bernardo Larroude** Arg.
259 B8 **Bernardo O'Higgins, Parque Nacional** *nat. park* Chile
183 L6 **Bernardos** Spain
234 F3 **Bernardsville** *NJ* U.S.A.
176 D2 **Bernartice** Czech Rep.
261 F5 **Bernasconi** Arg.
172 E6 **Bernau** *Baden-Württemberg* Ger.
170 I5 **Bernau** *Brandenburg* Ger.
173 M6 **Bernau am Chiemsee** Ger.
161 J6 **Bernaude, Roche** *mt.* France/Italy
156 D3 **Bernaville** France
159 M3 **Bernay** France
173 J6 **Bernbeuren** Ger.
171 E7 **Bernburg (Saale)** Ger.
179 N4 **Berndorf** Austria
168 F4 **Berne** Ger.
Berne Switz. *see* **Bern**
226 J9 **Berne** *IN* U.S.A.
177 H3 **Bernecebaráti** Hungary
183 P3 **Bernedo** Spain
190 C3 **Berner Alpen** *mts* Switz.
146 B7 **Berneray** *i. Western Isles, Scotland* U.K.
146 A9 **Berneray** *i. Western Isles, Scotland* U.K.
Bernese Alps *mts* Switz. *see* **Berner Alpen**
182 I4 **Bernesga** *r.* Spain
160 J4 **Bernex** France
173 K3 **Berngau** Ger.
179 O2 **Bernhardsthal** Austria
173 M3 **Bernhardswald** Ger.
221 J2 **Bernier Bay** *Nunavut* Can.
87 B8 **Bernier Island** *W.A.* Austr.
161 H6 **Bernin** France
190 I3 **Bernina Pass** Switz.
183 O7 **Berninches** *mt.* Spain
146 D8 **Bernisdale** *Highland, Scotland* U.K.
165 E8 **Bernissart** Belgium
170 E3 **Bernitt** Ger.
172 C2 **Bernkastel-Kues** Ger.
163 D7 **Bernos-Beaulac** France
173 K6 **Bernried** *Bayern* Ger.
173 N4 **Bernried** *Bayern* Ger.
171 J8 **Bernsdorf** Ger.
173 I4 **Bernstadt** *Baden-Württemberg* Ger.
171 K8 **Bernstadt** *Sachsen* Ger.
232 A11 **Bernstadt** *KY* U.S.A.
179 N5 **Bernstein** Austria
234 C4 **Bernville** *PA* U.S.A.
Beroea Greece *see* **Veroia**
Beroea Syria *see* **Ḥalab**
190 E1 **Beromünster** Switz.
213 □J4 **Beroroha** Madag.
176 D2 **Beroun** Czech Rep.
176 D2 **Berounka** *r.* Czech Rep.
Berovina Madag. *see* **Beravina**
197 K9 **Berovo** Macedonia
191 L6 **Berra** Italy
189 A7 **Berrahal** Alg.
161 B10 **Berre** *r.* France
161 G10 **Berre, Étang de** *lag.* France
204 D2 **Berrechid** Morocco
161 G10 **Berre-l'Étang** France
82 H6 **Berri** *S.A.* Austr.
205 F2 **Berriane** Alg.
161 E8 **Berrias-et-Casteljau** France
83 L7 **Berridale** *N.S.W.* Austr.
146 I6 **Berriedale** *Highland, Scotland* U.K.
146 I6 **Berriedale Water** *r. Scotland* U.K.
158 D5 **Berrien** France
83 J6 **Berrigan** *N.S.W.* Austr.
183 Q3 **Berriozar** Spain
184 F5 **Berrocal** Spain
260 E3 **Berrotarán** Arg.
205 F1 **Berrouaghia** Alg.
150 F5 **Berrow** *Somerset, England* U.K.
156 H5 **Berru** France
83 M6 **Berry** *N.S.W.* Austr.
162 H2 **Berry** *reg.* France
160 B3 **Berry, Canal du** France
156 G5 **Berry-au-Bac** France
223 I5 **Berry Creek** *r. Alta* Can.
240 J3 **Berryessa, Lake** *CA* U.S.A.
150 F7 **Berry Head** *England* U.K.
246 E1 **Berry Islands** Bahamas
234 B3 **Berrysburg** *PA* U.S.A.
237 I7 **Berryville** *AR* U.S.A.
232 H9 **Berryville** *VA* U.S.A.
214 B2 **Berseba** Namibia
168 E5 **Bersenbrück** Ger.
136 I5 **Bershad'** Ukr.
162 C5 **Berson** France
191 J4 **Bersone** Italy
171 I7 **Berste** *r.* Ger.
120 I1 **Bersuat** Rus. Fed.
129 C4 **Berta** *r.* Turkey
94 E2 **Bertam** Malaysia
182 C3 **Bertamirans** Spain
225 G3 **Berté, Lac** *l. Que.* Can.
171 J8 **Berthelsdorf** Ger.
161 B8 **Bertholène** France
156 E3 **Bertincourt** France
251 I5 **Bertinho** Brazil
191 M7 **Bertinoro** Italy
165 I8 **Bertogne** Belgium
254 E3 **Bertolínia** Brazil
257 G2 **Bertópolis** Brazil
207 I5 **Bertoua** Cameroon
147 C6 **Bertraghboy Bay** Ireland
165 J9 **Bertrange** Lux.
157 M7 **Bertrichamps** France
165 H9 **Bertrix** Belgium
191 M6 **Bertuzzi, Valle** *lag.* Italy
77 H2 **Beru** *atoll Gilbert Is* Kiribati
168 D3 **Berumbur** Ger.
120 I7 **Beruniy** Uzbek.
251 F5 **Beruri** Brazil
114 F9 **Beruwala** Sri Lanka
197 K3 **Berveni** Romania
146 L9 **Bervie Water** *r. Scotland* U.K.
159 L3 **Berville-sur-Mer** France
83 J8 **Berwick** *Vic.* Austr.
233 O5 **Berwick** *ME* U.S.A.
227 R8 **Berwick** *PA* U.S.A.
149 M2 **Berwick-upon-Tweed** *Northumberland, England* U.K.
150 F2 **Berwyn** *hills Wales* U.K.
234 E4 **Berwyn** *PA* U.S.A.
137 M7 **Beryslav** Ukr.
Berytus Lebanon *see* **Beirut**
197 J6 **Berzasca** Romania
138 J5 **Bērzaune** Latvia
138 G6 **Beržė** *r.* Lith.
176 G5 **Berzence** Hungary
175 L1 **Berźniki** Pol.
185 I2 **Berzocana** Spain
138 K5 **Bērzpils** Latvia
161 C7 **Bès** *r.* France
95 L3 **Besah** *Kalimantan* Indon.
213 □J3 **Besalampy** Madag.
186 K3 **Besalú** Spain
160 I2 **Besançon** France
183 K3 **Besande** Spain
93 C8 **Besar** *i.* Indon.
95 K6 **Besar, Gunung** *mt.* Indon.
94 D2 **Besar, Gunung** *mt.* Malaysia
183 L2 **Besaya** *r.* Spain
120 F4 **Besbay** Kazakh.
160 D3 **Besbre** *r.* France
186 K4 **Bescanó** Spain
139 O9 **Besed'** *r.* Rus. Fed.
137 P2 **Besedino** Rus. Fed.
169 F10 **Beselich-Obertiefenbach** Ger.
177 H3 **Bešeňov** Slovakia
177 J4 **Besenyőtelek** Hungary
177 J4 **Besenyszög** Hungary
94 E3 **Beserah** Malaysia
121 N7 **Beshariq** Uzbek.
Besharyk Uzbek. *see* **Beshariq**
120 K8 **Beshkent** Uzbek.
116 F8 **Beshnagar** *Madh. Prad.* India
122 F7 **Beshneh** Iran
129 F4 **Besht'asheni** Georgia
Besh-Ter, Gora *mt.* Kyrg./Uzbek. *see* Besh-Ter Toosu
121 N6 **Besh-Ter Toosu** *mt.* Kyrg./Uzbek.
Beshtor Toghi *mt.* Kyrg./Uzbek. *see* Besh-Ter Toosu
186 G2 **Besiberri Sud** *mt.* Spain
93 D8 **Besikama** *Timor* Indon.
120 K8 **Beşir** Turkm.
127 J5 **Beşiri** Turkey
94 C2 **Besitang** *Sumatera* Indon.
175 J6 **Beskid Niski** *hills* Pol.
175 I6 **Beskid Sądecki** *mts* Pol.
Beskra Alg. *see* **Biskra**
177 H2 **Beskydy** *park* Czech Rep.
129 F2 **Beslan** Rus. Fed.
197 L9 **Beslet** *mt.* Bulg.
197 K8 **Besna Kobila** *mt.* Serbia
223 J4 **Besnard Lake** *Sask.* Can.
126 H5 **Besni** Turkey
121 P3 **Besoba** Kazakh.
128 C7 **Besor** *watercourse* Israel
190 F4 **Besozzo** Italy
Beşparmak Dağları *mts* Cyprus *see* **Pentadaktylos Range**
139 U7 **Besputa** *r.* Rus. Fed.
149 O6 **Bessacarr** *South Yorkshire, England* U.K.
Bessa Monteiro Angola *see* **Kindeje**
208 B3 **Bessan** C.A.R.
161 C10 **Bessan** France
208 B3 **Béssao** Chad
Bessarabka Moldova *see* **Basarabeasca**
160 C4 **Bessay-sur-Allier** France
121 M6 **Bessaz, Gora** *mt.* Kazakh.
147 J4 **Bessbrook** *Northern Ireland* U.K.
161 I6 **Besse** France
160 B5 **Besse-et-St-Anastaise** France
161 E8 **Bessèges** France
231 D9 **Bessemer** *AL* U.S.A.
226 D3 **Bessemer** *MI* U.S.A.
232 E8 **Bessemer** *PA* U.S.A.
160 F5 **Bessenay** France
172 G2 **Bessenbach** Ger.
159 M6 **Bessé-sur-Braye** France
161 I10 **Besse-sur-Issole** France
120 E5 **Besshoky, Gora** *hill* Kazakh.
163 H8 **Bessières** France
159 J3 **Bessin** *reg.* France
162 G3 **Bessines-sur-Gartempe** France
129 C1 **Besskorbnaya** Rus. Fed.
137 P3 **Bessonovka** *Belgorodskaya Oblast'* Rus. Fed.
135 I5 **Bessonovka** *Penzenskaya Oblast'* Rus. Fed.
162 I4 **Bessou, Mont de** *hill* France
164 H5 **Best** Neth.
120 F3 **Bestamak** *Aktyubinskaya Oblast'* Kazakh.
121 R3 **Bestamak** *Vostochnyy Kazakhstan* Kazakh.
171 I6 **Bestensee** Ger.
215 N4 **Besters** S. Africa
121 O1 **Bestobe** Kazakh.
143 L3 **Bestorp** Sweden
134 H3 **Bestuzhevo** Rus. Fed.
169 F8 **Bestwig** Ger.
84 D3 **Beswick** *N.T.* Austr.
84 D3 **Beswick Aboriginal Land** *res. N.T.* Austr.
213 □J3 **Betafo** Madag.
213 □J3 **Betanantanana** Madag.
216 □3b **Betancuria** *Fuerteventura* Canary Is
252 D4 **Betanzos** Bol.
182 D2 **Betanzos** Spain
182 D2 **Betanzos, Ría de** *est.* Spain
207 I5 **Bétaré Oya** Cameroon
250 B3 **Beté** Col.
226 G2 **Bete Grise** *MI* U.S.A.
210 C2 **Bete Hor** Eth.
186 B1 **Betelu** Spain
187 E8 **Bétera** Spain
207 F4 **Bétérou** Benin
94 F5 **Betet** *i.* Indon.
183 P7 **Beteta** Spain
128 C7 **Bet Guvrin** Israel
204 D2 **Beth, Oued** *r.* Morocco
215 N2 **Bethal** S. Africa
212 C5 **Bethanie** Namibia
235 J2 **Bethany** *CT* U.S.A.
236 H5 **Bethany** *MO* U.S.A.
237 G8 **Bethany** *OK* U.S.A.
117 I6 **Bethari** Nepal
177 K6 **Bethausen** Romania
220 B3 **Bethel** *AK* U.S.A.
235 I2 **Bethel** *CT* U.S.A.
233 □O4 **Bethel** *ME* U.S.A.
232 A10 **Bethel** *OH* U.S.A.
234 C4 **Bethel** *PA* U.S.A.
169 I6 **Betheln** Ger.
232 E8 **Bethel Park** *PA* U.S.A.
215 J9 **Bethelsdorp** S. Africa
246 □ **Bethel Town** Jamaica
156 H5 **Bétheny** France
151 N5 **Bethersden** *Kent, England* U.K.
150 D1 **Bethesda** *Gwynedd, Wales* U.K.
234 A7 **Bethesda** *MD* U.S.A.
232 D8 **Bethesda** *OH* U.S.A.
215 I7 **Bethesdaweg** S. Africa
156 E5 **Béthisy-St-Pierre** France
80 K4 **Bethlehem** *North I.* N.Z.
215 M4 **Bethlehem** S. Africa
234 E3 **Bethlehem** *PA* U.S.A.
128 D7 **Bethlehem** West Bank
163 G10 **Bethmale** France
156 G6 **Bethon** France
235 I3 **Bethpage** *NY* U.S.A.
215 J6 **Bethulie** S. Africa
156 E2 **Béthune** France
156 B4 **Béthune** *r.* France
123 M7 **Beti** Pak.
250 D2 **Betijoque** Venez.
257 E3 **Betim** Brazil
213 □J4 **Betioky** Madag.
95 J9 **Betiri, Gunung** *mt.* Indon.
Bet Lehem West Bank *see* **Bethlehem**
139 Q7 **Betlitsa** Rus. Fed.
116 E8 **Betma** *Madh. Prad.* India
156 F6 **Beton-Bazoches** France
95 I4 **Betong** *Sarawak* Malaysia
97 E12 **Betong** Thai.
84 H8 **Betoota** *Qld* Austr.
210 C2 **Beto Shet'** *r.* Eth.
208 C4 **Bétou** Congo
121 N4 **Betpak-Dala** Kazakh.
121 N5 **Betpak-Dala** *plain* Kazakh.
213 □J3 **Betrandraka** Madag.
213 □J4 **Betroka** Madag.
157 O6 **Betschdorf** France
128 D6 **Bet She'an** Israel
225 G3 **Betsiamites** *Que.* Can.
225 G3 **Betsiamites** *r. Que.* Can.
213 □J2 **Betsiboka** *r.* Madag.
226 H5 **Betsie, Point** *MI* U.S.A.
104 E3 **Betsu-zan** *mt.* Japan
246 G2 **Betsy Bay** *Mayaguana* Bahamas
226 I3 **Betsy Lake** *MI* U.S.A.
157 L5 **Bettelainville** France
178 E5 **Bettelwurf** *mt.* Austria
165 J9 **Bettembourg** Lux.
165 J9 **Bettendorf** Lux.
234 C6 **Betterton** *MD* U.S.A.
117 J6 **Bettiah** *Bihar* India
215 N2 **Bettiesdam** S. Africa
172 A2 **Bettingen** Ger.
143 M3 **Bettna** Sweden
190 H6 **Bettola** Italy
158 H5 **Betton** France
193 J1 **Bettona** Italy
146 H5 **Bettyhill** *Highland, Scotland* U.K.
147 J5 **Bettystown** Ireland
116 F9 **Betul** *Madh. Prad.* India
93 D8 **Betun** *Timor* Indon.
95 J4 **Betung Kerihun National Park** Indon.
164 I5 **Betuwe** *reg.* Neth.
116 G7 **Betwa** *r.* India
150 E1 **Betws-y-coed** *Conwy, Wales* U.K.
187 E8 **Betxi** Spain
138 G6 **Betygala** Lith.
174 E2 **Betyń, Jezioro** *l.* Pol.
156 E5 **Betz** France
169 E9 **Betzdorf** Ger.
165 J9 **Betzdorf** Lux.
173 K2 **Betzenstein** Ger.
173 I6 **Betzigau** Ger.
209 B6 **Béu** Angola
161 J8 **Beuil** France
83 I6 **Beulah** *Vic.* Austr.
150 E3 **Beulah** *Powys, Wales* U.K.
226 H5 **Beulah** *MI* U.S.A.
236 E2 **Beulah** *ND* U.S.A.
151 M5 **Beult** *r. England* U.K.
164 I5 **Beuningen** Neth.
169 J8 **Beuren** Ger.
202 B6 **Beurfou** *well* Chad
172 F5 **Beuron** Ger.
157 I7 **Beurville** France
Beuthen Pol. *see* **Bytom**
160 E3 **Beuvray, Mont** *hill* France
160 D2 **Beuvron** *r.* France
159 N7 **Beuvron** *r.* France
156 E2 **Beuvry** France
159 L3 **Beuzeville** France
193 J2 **Bevagna** Italy
190 B2 **Bevaix** Switz.
169 E6 **Bever** *r.* Ger.
161 L9 **Bévéra** *r.* France
87 D12 **Beverley** *W.A.* Austr.
149 Q6 **Beverley** *East Riding of Yorkshire, England* U.K.
233 O6 **Beverly** *MA* U.S.A.
234 F4 **Beverly** *NJ* U.S.A.
232 D9 **Beverly** *OH* U.S.A.
240 N7 **Beverly Hills** *CA* U.S.A.
223 K1 **Beverly Lake** *Nunavut* Can.
169 H7 **Bevern** Ger.
168 G4 **Beverstedt** Ger.
169 H7 **Beverungen** Ger.
164 G4 **Beverwijk** Neth.
156 C7 **Béville-le-Comte** France
150 H3 **Bewdley** *Worcestershire, England* U.K.
151 M5 **Bewl Water** *resr England* U.K.
190 C3 **Bex** Switz.
172 C3 **Bexbach** Ger.
151 M6 **Bexhill** *East Sussex, England* U.K.
199 J5 **Beyağaç** Turkey
127 M6 **Beyānlū** Iran
199 I1 **Beyazköy** Turkey
Beyce Turkey *see* **Orhaneli**
163 D6 **Beychac-et-Caillau** France
199 M2 **Beyciler** Turkey
199 J4 **Beydağ** Turkey
199 L6 **Bey Dağları** *mts* Turkey
129 B7 **Beydoğan** Turkey
199 J3 **Beyel** Turkey
171 E6 **Beyendorf** Ger.
199 L6 **Beykonak** Turkey
199 M2 **Beyköy** *Bolu* Turkey
199 L2 **Beyköy** *Eskişehir* Turkey
199 K1 **Beykoz** Turkey
206 C4 **Beyla** Guinea
Beylagan Azer. *see* **Beyläqan**
129 I6 **Beyläqan** Azer.
199 M3 **Beylikova** Turkey
203 I6 **Beylul** Eritrea
163 G6 **Beynac-et-Cazenac** France
162 H5 **Beynat** France
165 I7 **Beyne-Heusay** Belgium
120 F5 **Beyneu** Kazakh.
160 G5 **Beynost** France
199 I4 **Beyoba** Turkey
103 Q15 **Beyoneisu-retsugan** *i.* Japan
103 Q15 **Beyoneisu Retugan** *i.* Japan
126 E3 **Beypazarı** Turkey
126 H4 **Beypınarı** Turkey
114 D7 **Beypore** *Kerala* India
210 E3 **Beyra** Somalia
122 E8 **Beyram** Iran
Beyrouth Lebanon *see* **Beirut**
126 E5 **Beyşehir** Turkey
126 E5 **Beyşehir Gölü** *l.* Turkey
137 S8 **Beysug** Rus. Fed.
137 R7 **Beysug** *r.* Rus. Fed.
137 R7 **Beysugskiy Liman** *lag.* Rus. Fed.
137 R8 **Beysuzhek** *r.* Rus. Fed.
100 D2 **Beytonovo** Rus. Fed.
127 K5 **Beytüşşebap** Turkey
161 G7 **Bez** *r.* France
122 G4 **Bezameh** Iran
187 C7 **Bezas** Spain
178 A5 **Bezau** Austria
134 J4 **Bezbozhnik** Rus. Fed.
196 G5 **Bezdan** *Vojvodina* Serbia
160 G2 **Bèze** France
129 E2 **Bezengi** Rus. Fed.
122 G7 **Bezenjān** Iran
176 G4 **Bezenye** Hungary
138 M5 **Bezhanitskaya Vozvyshennost'** *hills* Rus. Fed.
138 M5 **Bezhanitsy** Rus. Fed.
197 M7 **Bezhanovo** Bulg.
139 T4 **Bezhetsk** Rus. Fed.
139 T4 **Bezhetskiy Verkh** *reg.* Rus. Fed.
129 H3 **Bezhta** Rus. Fed.
161 C10 **Béziers** France
175 I1 **Bezledy** Pol.
Bezmein Turkm. *see* **Abadan**
161 F9 **Bezouce** France
177 L3 **Bežovce** Slovakia
Bezwada *Andhra Prad.* India *see* **Vijayawada**
116 C7 **Bhabhar** *Gujarat* India
117 I7 **Bhabhua** *Bihar* India
116 E8 **Bhabra** *Madh. Prad.* India
116 C8 **Bhachau** *Gujarat* India
116 C7 **Bhachbhar** *Rajasthan* India
116 B9 **Bhadar** *r.* India
116 E3 **Bhadarwah** Jammu and Kashmir
123 P6 **Bhadaur** *Punjab* India
116 F7 **Bhadaura** *Madh. Prad.* India
117 J6 **Bhadgaon** Nepal
117 I7 **Bhadohi** *Uttar Prad.* India
116 E5 **Bhadra** *Rajasthan* India
114 G4 **Bhadrachalam** *Andhra Prad.* India
Bhadrachalam Road Station *Andhra Prad.* India *see* **Kottagudem**
116 D7 **Bhadrajan** *Rajasthan* India
117 K9 **Bhadrak** *Orissa* India
114 D6 **Bhadra Reservoir** India
114 D6 **Bhadravati** *Karnataka* India
123 L7 **Bhag** Pak.
111 C10 **Bhaga** *r.* India
117 K7 **Bhagalpur** *Bihar* India
117 L8 **Bhagirathi** *r.* India
114 E3 **Bhainsa** *Andhra Prad.* India
116 F9 **Bhainsdehi** *Madh. Prad.* India
117 M7 **Bhairab Bazar** Bangl.
117 I6 **Bhairawa** Nepal
Bhairawaha Nepal *see* **Bhairawa**
119 I4 **Bhairi Hol** *mt.* Pak.
123 N6 **Bhakkar** Pak.
Bhaktapur Nepal *see* **Bhadgaon**
Bhaleshear *i. Scotland* U.K. *see* **Baleshare**
114 E3 **Bhalki** *Karnataka* India
123 O5 **Bhalwal** Pak.
116 F9 **Bhamgarh** *Madh. Prad.* India
96 C2 **Bhamo** Myanmar
114 G3 **Bhamragarh** *Mahar.* India
116 G9 **Bhandara** *Mahar.* India
116 G7 **Bhander** *Madh. Prad.* India
116 H6 **Bhangaha** *Uttar Prad.* India
116 B8 **Bhangor** *Gujarat* India
115 I3 **Bhanjanagar** *Orissa* India
116 E7 **Bhanpura** *Madh. Prad.* India
116 G8 **Bhanrer Range** *hills Madh. Prad.* India
116 H9 **Bhanupratappur** *Chhattisgarh* India
Bharat *country* Asia *see* **India**
116 F6 **Bharatpur** *Rajasthan* India
117 J6 **Bharatpur** Nepal
117 N6 **Bhareli** *r.* India
123 J9 **Bhari** *r.* Pak.
116 G6 **Bharthana** *Uttar Prad.* India
116 D9 **Bharuch** *Gujarat* India
116 H9 **Bhatapara** *Chhattisgarh* India
Bhatarsaigh *i. Scotland* U.K. *see* **Vatersay**
114 C3 **Bhatghar Lake** India
117 L8 **Bhatiapara Ghat** Bangl.
Bhatinda *Punjab* India *see* **Bathinda**
114 D6 **Bhatkal** *Karnataka* India
Bhatnair *Rajasthan* India *see* **Hanumangarh**
117 L8 **Bhatpara** *W. Bengal* India
123 O5 **Bhaun Gharibwal** Pak.
114 E7 **Bhavani** *Tamil Nadu* India
114 E7 **Bhavani** *r.* India
114 E7 **Bhavani Sagar** *l.* India
116 D9 **Bhavnagar** *Gujarat* India
123 O6 **Bhawana** Pak.
115 H3 **Bhawanipatna** *Orissa* India
Bhearnaraigh, Eilean *i. Western Isles, Scotland* U.K. *see* **Berneray**
Bheemavaram *Andhra Prad.* India *see* **Bhimavaram**
215 O3 **Bhekuzulu** S. Africa
116 H7 **Bhelki** *Madh. Prad.* India
123 O5 **Bhera** Pak.
116 H5 **Bheri** *r.* Nepal
114 D3 **Bhigvan** *Mahar.* India
116 H9 **Bhilai** *Chhattisgarh* India
116 D7 **Bhildi** *Gujarat* India
116 E7 **Bhilwara** *Rajasthan* India
114 E4 **Bhima** *r.* India
116 C6 **Bhimar** *Rajasthan* India
114 G4 **Bhimavaram** *Andhra Prad.* India
123 P5 **Bhimbar** Pak.
116 H8 **Bhimlath** *Madh. Prad.* India
117 K6 **Bhimnagar** *Bihar* India
117 J6 **Bhimphedi** Nepal
116 G6 **Bhind** *Madh. Prad.* India
116 E7 **Bhindar** *Rajasthan* India
116 H6 **Bhinga** *Uttar Prad.* India
114 D3 **Bhingar** *Mahar.* India
116 D7 **Bhinmal** *Rajasthan* India
114 C3 **Bhiwandi** *Mahar.* India
116 F5 **Bhiwani** *Haryana* India
116 G6 **Bhogaipur** *Uttar Prad.* India
116 B9 **Bhogat** *Gujarat* India
116 F8 **Bhojpur** *Madh. Prad.* India
117 K6 **Bhojpur** Nepal
116 E9 **Bhokardan** *Mahar.* India
117 M8 **Bhola** Bangl.
116 G6 **Bhongaon** *Uttar Prad.* India
114 F4 **Bhongir** *Andhra Prad.* India
215 N6 **Bhongweni** S. Africa
116 F8 **Bhopal** *Madh. Prad.* India
114 G3 **Bhopalpatnam** *Chhattisgarh* India
114 C3 **Bhor** *Mahar.* India
Bhrigukaccha *Gujarat* India *see* **Bharuch**
117 J9 **Bhuban** *Orissa* India
117 J9 **Bhubaneshwar** *Orissa* India
Bhubaneswar *Orissa* India *see* **Bhubaneshwar**
117 N7 **Bhuban Hills** India
116 B8 **Bhuj** *Gujarat* India
96 D6 **Bhumiphol Dam** Thai.
215 P2 **Bhunya** Swaziland
116 E9 **Bhusawal** *Mahar.* India
117 M6 **Bhutan** *country* Asia
116 C6 **Bhuttewala** *Rajasthan* India
114 F7 **Bhuvanagiri** *Tamil Nadu* India
250 E5 **Biá** *r.* Brazil
209 E7 **Bia, Monts** *mts* Dem. Rep. Congo
96 F5 **Bia, Phou** *mt.* Laos
122 G8 **Bīabān** *mts* Iran
210 E3 **Biad** *well* Eth.
174 F4 **Biadki** Pol.
111 B9 **Biafo Glacier** Jammu and Kashmir
Biafra, Bight of *g.* Africa *see* **Benin, Bight of**
91 I7 **Biak** *Papua* Indon.
93 C4 **Biak** *Sulawesi* Indon.
91 I7 **Biak** *i. Papua* Indon.
174 F5 **Biała** Pol.
175 I5 **Biała** *r.* Pol.
174 F5 **Biała** *r.* Pol.
174 G4 **Biała-Parcela Pierwsza** Pol.
175 K2 **Biała Piska** Pol.
175 L3 **Biała Podlaska** Pol.
175 I4 **Biała Rawska** Pol.
174 F2 **Białe Błota** Pol.
175 K4 **Białka** *r.* Pol.
175 I4 **Białobrzegi** *Mazowieckie* Pol.
175 K5 **Białobrzegi** *Podkarpackie* Pol.
174 D2 **Białogard** Pol.
174 F2 **Białośliwie** Pol.
175 L3 **Białowieski Park Narodowy** *nat. park* Pol.
175 L3 **Białowieża** Pol.
174 E2 **Biały Bór** Pol.
175 I6 **Biały Dunajec** Pol.
175 L2 **Białystok** Pol.
194 F9 **Bianca, Punta** *pt Sicilia* Italy
194 H8 **Biancavilla** *Sicilia* Italy
195 K7 **Bianco** Italy
191 L5 **Bianco, Canale** *canal* Italy
194 E9 **Bianco, Capo** *c. Sicilia* Italy
190 D4 **Bianco, Corno** *mt.* Italy
Bianco, Monte *mt.* France/Italy *see* **Blanc, Mont**
107 Q9 **Biandangang Kou** *r. mouth* China
190 E5 **Biandrate** Italy
208 D3 **Bianga** C.A.R.
206 D5 **Biankouma** Côte d'Ivoire
206 E5 **Bianouan** Côte d'Ivoire
160 I3 **Bians-les-Usiers** France
190 E5 **Bianzè** Italy
107 R4 **Bianzhao** *Jilin* China
Bianzhuang *Shandong* China *see* **Cangshan**
92 E8 **Biao** *Mindanao* Phil.
116 F8 **Biaora** *Madh. Prad.* India
187 D10 **Biar** Spain
122 F3 **Bīārjmand** Iran
93 D2 **Biaro** *i.* Indon.
163 A9 **Biarritz** France
Biarritz *airport* France *see* **Parme**
163 B8 **Biarrotte** France
162 H6 **Biars-sur-Cère** France
124 G3 **Bi'ār Tabrāk** *well* Saudi Arabia
163 B7 **Bias** *Aquitaine* France
163 F7 **Bias** *Aquitaine* France
190 F3 **Biasca** Switz.
261 I2 **Biassini** Uru.
177 H4 **Biatorbágy** Hungary
203 F2 **Bibā** Egypt
102 S3 **Bibai** Japan
209 B8 **Bibala** Angola
208 A4 **Bibas** Gabon
83 L7 **Bibbenluke** *N.S.W.* Austr.
191 L8 **Bibbiena** Italy
191 J9 **Bibbona** Italy
223 M2 **Bibby Island** *Nunavut* Can.
207 I4 **Bibémi** Cameroon
172 E5 **Biberach** Ger.
172 H5 **Biberach an der Riß** Ger.
173 J4 **Biberbach** Ger.
173 J3 **Bibert** *r.* Ger.
206 E5 **Bibiani** Ghana
114 G9 **Bibile** Sri Lanka
191 O4 **Bibione** Italy
139 P5 **Bibirevo** Rus. Fed.
117 M7 **Bibiyana** *r.* Bangl.
172 E2 **Biblis** Ger.
Biblos Lebanon *see* **Jbail**
136 D4 **Bibrka** Ukr.
151 I4 **Bibury** *Gloucestershire, England* U.K.
138 J5 **Bicānu ezers** *l.* Latvia
257 F4 **Bicas** Brazil
177 M4 **Bicaz** *Maramureş* Romania
197 O4 **Bicaz** *Neamţ* Romania
193 O5 **Biccari** Italy
126 E4 **Biçer** Turkey
151 J4 **Bicester** *Oxfordshire, England* U.K.
116 D7 **Bichabhera** *Rajasthan* India
247 □7 **Biche** Trin. and Tob.
210 C2 **Bichena** Eth.
Bicheng *Chongqing* China *see* **Bishan**
83 L9 **Bicheno** *Tas.* Austr.
100 I5 **Bichevaya** Rus. Fed.
207 H3 **Bichi** Nigeria
100 K2 **Bichi** *r.* Rus. Fed.
173 K6 **Bichl** Ger.
178 C5 **Bichlbach** Austria
114 C5 **Bicholim** *Goa* India
117 J6 **Bichraltar** Nepal
107 J1 **Bichura** Rus. Fed.
129 B2 **Bichvint'a** Georgia
129 B2 **Bichvint'is Konts'khi** *pt* Georgia
172 F2 **Bickenbach** Ger.
151 I3 **Bickenhill** *West Midlands, England* U.K.
84 F2 **Bickerton Island** *N.T.* Austr.
150 D7 **Bickleigh** *Devon, England* U.K.
150 E6 **Bickleigh** *Devon, England* U.K.
151 N4 **Bicknacre** *Essex, England* U.K.
241 U3 **Bicknell** *UT* U.S.A.
129 J5 **Bico** Azer.
93 F3 **Bicoli** *Halmahera* Indon.
187 D9 **Bicorp** Spain
184 C5 **Bicos** Port.
177 H4 **Bicske** Hungary
150 G2 **Bicton** *Shropshire, England* U.K.
209 B8 **Bicuari, Parque Nacional do** *nat. park* Angola
114 D3 **Bid** *Mahar.* India
207 G4 **Bida** Nigeria
163 B9 **Bidache** France
95 M2 **Bidadari, Tanjung** *pt* Malaysia
114 E4 **Bidar** *Karnataka* India
163 A9 **Bidart** France
116 E6 **Bidasar** *Rajasthan* India
125 N4 **Bidbid** Oman

Biddeford to Black River

288

233 □O5 **Biddeford** ME U.S.A.
151 N5 **Biddenden** Kent, England U.K.
164 I4 **Biddinghuizen** Neth.
149 M7 **Biddulph** Staffordshire, England U.K.
146 F9 **Bidean nam Bian** mt. Scotland U.K.
150 D5 **Bideford** Devon, England U.K.
Bideford Bay England U.K. see **Barnstaple Bay**
191 M7 **Bidente** r. Italy
151 I3 **Bidford-on-Avon** Warwickshire, England U.K.
140 Q2 **Bidjovagge** Norway
122 G7 **Bīdkhan, Kūh-e** mt. Iran
122 H4 **Bidokht** Iran
205 F5 **Bidon 5** tourist site Alg.
163 C9 **Bidos** France
163 B8 **Bidouze** r. France
177 K3 **Bidovce** Slovakia
100 G5 **Bidzhan** Rus. Fed.
100 H5 **Bidzhar** r. Rus. Fed.
Bié Angola see **Kuito**
209 C8 **Bié** prov. Angola
209 B8 **Bié, Planalto do** plat. Angola
169 H10 **Bieber** Ger.
172 E2 **Biebesheim am Rhein** Ger.
175 K2 **Biebrza** r. Pol.
175 K2 **Biebrzański Park Narodowy** nat. park Pol.
175 J6 **Biecz** Pol.
169 G9 **Biedenkopf** Ger.
171 E6 **Biederitz** Ger.
186 D3 **Biel** Spain
190 C1 **Biel** Switz.
177 I1 **Bielańsko-Tyniecki Park Krajobrazowy** Pol.
175 K3 **Bielany-Żyłaki** Pol.
174 E5 **Bielawa** Pol.
169 G6 **Bielefeld** Ger.
177 H2 **Biele Karpaty** park Slovakia
178 B6 **Bielerhöhe** pass Austria
190 C1 **Bieler See** l. Switz.
174 C2 **Bielice** Pol.
175 I5 **Bieliny Kapitulne** Pol.
Bielitz Pol. see **Bielsko-Biała**
190 E4 **Biella** Italy
190 E4 **Biella** prov. Italy
163 D9 **Bielle** France
186 F2 **Bielsa** Spain
175 H3 **Bielsk** Pol.
175 H6 **Bielsko-Biała** Pol.
175 L3 **Bielsk Podlaski** Pol.
169 I8 **Bielstein** hill Ger.
168 J4 **Bienenbüttel** Ger.
97 H9 **Biên Hoa** Vietnam
174 D4 **Bieniów** Pol.
160 H4 **Bienne** r. France
Bienne Switz. see **Biel**
190 I4 **Bienno** Italy
185 N3 **Bienservida** Spain
184 G4 **Bienvenida** Spain
184 G4 **Bienvenida** hill Spain
183 P7 **Bienvenida** mt. Spain
245 J5 **Bienvenido** Mex.
251 H4 **Bienvenue** Fr. Guiana
225 F2 **Bienville, Lac** l. Que. Can.
177 H1 **Bierawa** Pol.
174 G5 **Bierawka** r. Pol.
85 J9 **Bierbank** Qld Austr.
174 G5 **Bierdzany** Pol.
171 E7 **Biere** Ger.
190 A2 **Bière** Switz.
186 E3 **Bierge** Spain
159 J6 **Bierné** France
163 G10 **Biert** France
175 H5 **Bieruń** Pol.
174 F4 **Bierutów** Pol.
174 G3 **Bierzwienna-Długa** Pol.
174 D2 **Bierzwnik** Pol.
186 E2 **Biescas** Spain
170 E5 **Biese** r. Ger.
170 I5 **Biesenthal** Ger.
174 E1 **Biesiekierz** Pol.
215 J2 **Biesiesvlei** S. Africa
157 J7 **Biesles** France
174 E1 **Biesowice** Pol.
214 H7 **Biesrespoort** S. Africa
173 J6 **Biessenhofen** Ger.
175 K6 **Bieszczady** mts Pol.
175 K6 **Bieszczadzki Park Narodowy** nat. park Pol.
172 E4 **Bietigheim** Ger.
172 G4 **Bietigheim-Bissingen** Ger.
170 I4 **Bietikow** Ger.
190 D3 **Bietschhorn** mt. Switz.
165 H9 **Bièvre** Belgium
175 H3 **Bieżuń** Pol.
193 O4 **Biferno** r. Italy
208 A5 **Bifoun** Gabon
140 □C1 **Bifröst** Iceland
102 T2 **Bifuka** Japan
240 I2 **Big** r. CA U.S.A.
199 I2 **Biga** Turkey
199 I2 **Biga** r. Turkey
199 J3 **Bigadiç** Turkey
261 G3 **Bigand** Arg.
163 C6 **Biganos** France
187 D11 **Bigastro** Spain
199 H3 **Biga Yarımadası** pen. Turkey
238 I3 **Big Baldy Mountain** MT U.S.A.
222 F5 **Big Bar Creek** B.C. Can.
81 C11 **Big Bay** b. South I. N.Z.
226 G3 **Big Bay** MI U.S.A.
78 □5 **Big Bay** b. Vanuatu
226 G4 **Big Bay de Noc** MI U.S.A.
240 P7 **Big Bear Lake** CA U.S.A.
238 I3 **Big Belt Mountains** MT U.S.A.
215 P2 **Big Bend** Swaziland
237 D11 **Big Bend National Park** TX U.S.A.
237 J9 **Big Black** r. MS U.S.A.
236 G6 **Big Blue** r. NE U.S.A.
150 E7 **Bigbury Bay** England U.K.
150 E7 **Bigbury-on-Sea** Devon, England U.K.
80 □ **Big Bush** Chatham Is S. Pacific Ocean
237 E11 **Big Canyon** watercourse TX U.S.A.
246 C1 **Big Cypress National Preserve** nature res. FL U.S.A.
231 G13 **Big Cypress National Preserve** nature res. FL U.S.A.
82 H6 **Big Desert Wilderness Park** nature res. Vic. Austr.
226 E5 **Big Eau Pleine Reservoir** WI U.S.A.
78 □3a **Bigej** i. Kwajalein Marshall Is
78 □3a **Bigej Channel** Kwajalein Marshall Is
234 D5 **Big Elk Creek** r. MD U.S.A.
106 E4 **Biger Nuur** salt l. Mongolia
236 I1 **Big Falls** MN U.S.A.
226 A1 **Big Fork** r. MN U.S.A.
223 J4 **Biggar** Sask. Can.
146 I11 **Biggar** South Lanarkshire, Scotland U.K.
224 F3 **Biggar, Lac** l. Que. Can.
78 □3a **Biggarenn** i. Kwajalein Marshall Is
215 N4 **Biggarsberg** S. Africa
86 H3 **Bigge Island** W.A. Austr.
85 N8 **Biggenden** Qld Austr.
222 B3 **Bigger, Mount** B.C. Can.
78 □3a **Biggerann** i. Kwajalein Marshall Is
169 E8 **Biggesee** l. Ger.
151 M5 **Biggin Hill** Greater London, England U.K.
151 L3 **Biggleswade** Bedfordshire, England U.K.
240 K2 **Biggs** CA U.S.A.
238 D4 **Biggs** OR U.S.A.
238 H4 **Big Hole** r. MT U.S.A.
238 K3 **Bighorn** r. MT/WY U.S.A.
238 K4 **Bighorn Mountains** WY U.S.A.
208 D4 **Bigi** Dem. Rep. Congo
78 □3a **Bigi** i. Kwajalein Marshall Is
139 W8 **Bigil'dino** Rus. Fed.
129 I5 **Bığır** Azer.
221 K3 **Big Island** i. Nunavut Can.
222 G2 **Big Island** i. N.W.T. Can.
232 F11 **Big Island** VA U.S.A.
222 C2 **Big Kalzas Lake** Y.T. Can.
237 E10 **Big Lake** TX U.S.A.
233 □R3 **Big Lake** l. ME U.S.A.
238 H5 **Big Lost** r. ID U.S.A.
Big Moggy Island Stewart I. N.Z. see **Mokinui Island**
238 L2 **Big Muddy Creek** r. MT U.S.A.
158 F6 **Bignan** France
190 F3 **Bignasco** Switz.
206 A3 **Bignona** Senegal
209 E6 **Bigobo** Dem. Rep. Congo
163 D10 **Bigorre** reg. France
232 F11 **Big Otter** r. VA U.S.A.
240 N4 **Big Pine** CA U.S.A.
240 M7 **Big Pine Peak** CA U.S.A.
238 K3 **Big Porcupine Creek** r. MT U.S.A.
222 C3 **Big Port Walter** AK U.S.A.
226 I6 **Big Rapids** MI U.S.A.
226 E5 **Big Rib** r. WI U.S.A.
223 J4 **Big River** Sask. Can.
226 H5 **Big Sable Point** MI U.S.A.
222 C2 **Big Salmon** Y.T. Can.
222 C2 **Big Salmon** r. Y.T. Can.
223 L3 **Big Sand Lake** Man. Can.
238 I2 **Big Sandy** MT U.S.A.
238 J6 **Big Sandy** r. WY U.S.A.
241 S7 **Big Sandy** watercourse AZ U.S.A.
236 D6 **Big Sandy Creek** r. CO U.S.A.
223 J4 **Big Sandy Lake** Sask. Can.
226 A3 **Big Sandy Lake** MN U.S.A.
236 G4 **Big Sioux** r. SD U.S.A.
240 O3 **Big Smokey Valley** NV U.S.A.
81 B14 **Big South Cape Island** Stewart I. N.Z.
237 E9 **Big Spring** TX U.S.A.
236 D5 **Big Springs** NE U.S.A.
223 I5 **Big Stone** Alta Can.
236 G3 **Big Stone City** SD U.S.A.
232 C12 **Big Stone Gap** VA U.S.A.
223 M4 **Bigstone Lake** Man. Can.
237 J9 **Big Sunflower** r. MS U.S.A.
240 K5 **Big Sur** CA U.S.A.
237 H10 **Big Thicket National Preserve** nature res. TX U.S.A.
238 J4 **Big Timber** MT U.S.A.
224 B2 **Big Trout Lake** Ont. Can.
224 B2 **Big Trout Lake** l. Ont. Can.
186 C2 **Bigüézal** Spain
192 C2 **Biguglia** Corse France
192 C2 **Biguglia, Étang de** lag. Corse France
222 H4 **Big Valley** Alta Can.
241 U4 **Big Water** UT U.S.A.
227 O4 **Bigwin** Ont. Can.
188 E3 **Bihać** Bos.-Herz.
117 J7 **Bihar** state India
177 K4 **Biharia** Romania
117 K7 **Bihariganj** Bihar India
177 K4 **Biharkeresztes** Hungary
177 K4 **Biharnagybajom** Hungary
117 J7 **Bihar Sharif** Bihar India
177 K5 **Biharugra** Hungary
177 K5 **Biharugraihalastavak** lakes Hungary
177 L5 **Bihor** county Romania
197 K4 **Bihor, Vârful** mt. Romania
102 V3 **Bihoro** Japan
177 L5 **Bihorului, Munții** mts Romania
117 N6 **Bihpuriagaon** Assam India
120 F4 **Biikzhal** Kazakh.
116 E9 **Bijagarh** Madh. Prad. India
206 A4 **Bijagós, Arquipélago dos** is Guinea-Bissau
116 E7 **Bijainagar** Rajasthan India
116 F6 **Bijaipur** Madh. Prad. India
114 D4 **Bijapur** Karnataka India
122 B4 **Bījār** Iran
114 G3 **Bijarpur** Chhattisgarh India
116 G7 **Bijawar** Madh. Prad. India
116 E3 **Bijbehara** Jammu and Kashmir
188 G3 **Bijeljina** Bos.-Herz.
188 E3 **Bijelolasica** mt. Croatia
196 H7 **Bijelo Polje** Montenegro
116 H8 **Bijeraghogarh** Madh. Prad. India
Bijiang Yunnan China see **Zhiziluo**
108 E5 **Bijie** Guizhou China
114 G3 **Bijji** Chhattisgarh India
117 M6 **Bijni** Assam India
116 G5 **Bijnor** Uttar Prad. India
123 N7 **Bijnot** Pak.
116 E7 **Bijolia** Rajasthan India
217 □2 **Bijoutier** i. Seychelles
125 J3 **Bijrān** well Saudi Arabia
125 J3 **Bijrān, Khashm** hill Saudi Arabia
116 D6 **Bikampur** Rajasthan India
116 D5 **Bikaner** Rajasthan India
120 J5 **Bikbauli** Kazakh.
128 D5 **Bikfaiya** Lebanon
100 I5 **Bikin** Rus. Fed.
100 I5 **Bikin** r. Rus. Fed.
213 F4 **Bikita** Zimbabwe
210 B2 **Bikori** Sudan
208 C5 **Bikoro** Dem. Rep. Congo
108 E2 **Bikou** Gansu China
108 E2 **Bikou Shuiku** resr Gansu China
177 I6 **Bikovo** Vojvodina Serbia
117 J7 **Bikramganj** Bihar India
137 R4 **Bila** r. Ukr.
137 S4 **Bila** r. Ukr.
92 E7 **Bilaa Point** Mindanao Phil.
129 K5 **Biläcarı** Azer.
125 N5 **Bilād Banī Bū 'Alī** Oman
125 N4 **Bilād Banī Bū Ḥasan** Oman
124 E5 **Bilād Ghāmid** reg. Saudi Arabia
124 E5 **Bilād Zahrān** reg. Saudi Arabia
137 M6 **Bila Krynytsya** Ukr.
129 B7 **Bilaloğlu** Turkey
207 E3 **Bilanga** Burkina
95 M4 **Bilangbilangan** i. Indon.
116 D6 **Bilara** Rajasthan India
116 G5 **Bilari** Uttar Prad. India
116 I8 **Bilaspur** Chhattisgarh India
116 F4 **Bilaspur** Hima. Prad. India
129 J6 **Biläsuvar** Azer.
129 J6 **Biläsuvar** Azer.
92 C9 **Bilatan** i. Phil.
136 J4 **Bila Tserkva** Ukr.
97 D7 **Bilauktaung Range** mts Myanmar/Thai.
183 O2 **Bilbao** Spain
203 F2 **Bilbays** Egypt
Bilbo Spain see **Bilbao**
197 N3 **Bilbor** Romania
146 J6 **Bilbster** Highland, Scotland U.K.
107 L1 **Bil'chir** Rus. Fed.
140 □B1 **Bíldudalur** Iceland
175 M6 **Bile** Ukr.
188 G4 **Bileća** Bos.-Herz.
199 K2 **Bilecik** Turkey
199 L2 **Bilecik** prov. Turkey
188 G4 **Bilečko Jezero** resr Bos.-Herz./Montenegro
196 I5 **Biled** Romania
129 J6 **Bīleh Savār** Iran
177 G2 **Bílé Karpaty** park Czech Rep.
137 Q5 **Bilen'ke** Donets'ka Oblast' Ukr.
137 O6 **Bilen'ke** Zaporiz'ka Oblast' Ukr.
210 D4 **Bilesha Plain** Kenya
175 K5 **Biłgoraj** Pol.
211 A5 **Bilharamulo** Tanz.
116 H6 **Bilhaur** Uttar Prad. India
136 J7 **Bilhorod-Dnistrovs'kyy** Ukr.
208 C2 **Bili** Chad
208 E3 **Bili** Dem. Rep. Congo
208 D3 **Bili** r. Dem. Rep. Congo
131 R3 **Bilibino** Rus. Fed.
211 D8 **Bilibiza** Moz.
129 B6 **Bilice** Turkey
Bīlikōl l. Kazakh. see **Biylikol', Ozero**
96 C6 **Bilin** Myanmar
176 C1 **Bílina** Czech Rep.
193 Q6 **Bilioso** r. Italy
92 E6 **Biliran** i. Phil.
198 B2 **Bilisht** Albania
210 D4 **Bilis Qooqaani** Somalia
95 M2 **Bilit** Sabah Malaysia
107 R7 **Biliu He** r. China
177 M3 **Bilky** Ukr.
238 L5 **Bill** WY U.S.A.
87 C9 **Billabalong** W.A. Austr.
Billabong Creek r. N.S.W. Austr. see **Moulamein Creek**
87 C9 **Billabong Roadhouse** W.A. Austr.
183 O2 **Billao, Cabo de** c. Spain
142 H4 **Billdal** Sweden
168 J3 **Bille** r. Ger.
169 D7 **Billerbeck** Ger.
163 D9 **Billère** France
151 M4 **Billericay** Essex, England U.K.
160 H4 **Billiat** France
82 H6 **Billiat Conservation Park** nature res. S.A. Austr.
172 G3 **Billigheim** Ger.
86 I5 **Billiluna** W.A. Austr.
86 I5 **Billiluna Aboriginal Reserve** W.A. Austr.
264 J2 **Billingford** Norfolk, England U.K.
149 O4 **Billingham** Stockton-on-Tees, England U.K.
149 Q7 **Billinghay** Lincolnshire, England U.K.
238 J4 **Billings** MT U.S.A.
151 L5 **Billingshurst** West Sussex, England U.K.
Billiton i. Indon. see **Belitung**
151 P2 **Billockby** Norfolk, England U.K.
150 G6 **Bill of Portland** hd England U.K.
160 C5 **Billom** France
142 F6 **Billund** Denmark
141 J9 **Billund** airport Denmark
241 R7 **Bill Williams** r. AZ U.S.A.
241 T6 **Bill Williams Mountain** AZ U.S.A.
160 C4 **Billy** France
207 I2 **Bilma** Niger
210 C2 **Bīlo** Eth.
85 M8 **Biloela** Qld Austr.
176 F5 **Bilo Gora** hills Croatia
137 N8 **Bilohirs'k** Ukr.
136 F3 **Bilohir"ya** Ukr.
136 F4 **Bilohorodka** Khmel'nyts'ka Oblast' Ukr.
136 J3 **Bilohorodka** Kyivs'ka Oblast' Ukr.
251 G4 **Biloku** Guyana
137 R4 **Bilokurakyne** Ukr.
114 E3 **Biloli** Mahar. India
137 S4 **Biloluts'k** Ukr.
137 N2 **Bilopillya** Ukr.
136 F3 **Bilotyn** Ukr.
137 L3 **Bilousivka** Ukr.
177 H2 **Bílovec** Czech Rep.
177 G2 **Bílovice** Czech Rep.
137 S4 **Bilovods'k** Ukr.
237 K10 **Biloxi** MS U.S.A.
137 L7 **Bilozerka** Ukr.
137 Q5 **Bilozers'ke** Ukr.
84 G8 **Bilpa Morea Claypan** salt flat Qld Austr.
169 J7 **Bilshausen** Ger.
136 D4 **Bil'shivtsi** Ukr.
116 G5 **Bilsi** Uttar Prad. India
137 N3 **Bil's'k** Ukr.
136 E2 **Bil's'ka Volya** Ukr.
146 J11 **Bilston** Midlothian, Scotland U.K.
164 H4 **Bilthoven** Neth.
202 D6 **Biltine** Chad
202 D6 **Biltine** pref. Chad
140 P2 **Bilto** Norway
149 Q6 **Bilton** East Riding of Yorkshire, England U.K.
96 C6 **Bilugyun Island** Myanmar
137 O4 **Bilukhivka** Ukr.
93 C3 **Bilungala** Sulawesi Indon.
242 □R10 **Bilwascarma** Nic.
136 J7 **Bilyayivka** Ukr.
175 K6 **Bilychi** Ukr.
137 N4 **Bilyky** Ukr.
136 I4 **Bilylivka** Ukr.
136 I6 **Bilyne** Ukr.
137 Q5 **Bilyts'ke** Ukr.
136 D5 **Bilyy Cheremosh** r. Ukr.
137 Q3 **Bilyy Kolodyaz'** Ukr.
165 I7 **Bilzen** Belgium
208 E4 **Bima** r. Dem. Rep. Congo
95 M9 **Bima** Sumbawa Indon.
95 M9 **Bima, Teluk** b. Sumbawa Indon.
209 B7 **Bimbe** Angola
207 F4 **Bimbila** Ghana
208 C3 **Bimbo** C.A.R.
246 D1 **Bimini Islands** Bahamas
115 H4 **Bimlipatam** Andhra Prad. India
129 H6 **Binä** Dağlıq Qarabağ Azer.
129 L5 **Binä** Azer.
173 N5 **Bina** r. Ger.
177 H4 **Bíňa** Slovakia
127 N5 **Bināb** Iran
186 F4 **Binaced** Spain
116 G7 **Bina-Etawa** Madh. Prad. India
93 F5 **Binaija, Gunung** mt. Seram Indon.
92 D6 **Binalbagan** Negros Phil.
122 H3 **Bīnālūd, Kūh-e** mts Iran
209 B6 **Binanga** Dem. Rep. Congo
122 H4 **Binar** pass Iran
175 J6 **Binarowa** Pol.
156 B8 **Binas** France
190 G5 **Binasco** Italy
95 I3 **Binatang** Sarawak Malaysia
85 K6 **Binbee** Qld Austr.
126 H4 **Binboğa Daği** mt. Turkey
149 Q7 **Binbrook** Lincolnshire, England U.K.
165 F8 **Binche** Belgium
107 P8 **Bincheng** Shandong China
Bincheng Shandong China see **Binzhou**
108 C6 **Binchuan** Yunnan China
208 B2 **Binder** Chad
116 H6 **Bindki** Uttar Prad. India
173 L2 **Bindlach** Ger.
85 L9 **Bindle** Qld Austr.
Bindloe Island Islas Galápagos Ecuador see **Marchena, Isla**
209 C6 **Bindu** Dem. Rep. Congo
213 F3 **Bindura** Zimbabwe
186 F4 **Binefar** Spain
148 D3 **Binevenagh** hill Northern Ireland U.K.
213 E3 **Binga** Zimbabwe
213 G3 **Binga, Monte** mt. Moz.
83 M3 **Bingara** N.S.W. Austr.
114 C7 **Bingaram** i. India
84 F3 **Bing Bong** N.T. Austr.
106 H8 **Bingcaowan** Gansu China
172 G5 **Bingen** Ger.
172 D2 **Bingen am Rhein** Ger.
164 J5 **Bingerden** Neth.
206 E5 **Bingerville** Côte d'Ivoire
151 K2 **Bingham** Nottinghamshire, England U.K.
233 □P3 **Bingham** ME U.S.A.
147 B4 **Binghamstown** Ireland
233 J6 **Binghamton** NY U.S.A.
202 B3 **Bin Ghanīmah, Jabal** hills Libya
202 B1 **Bin Ghashir** Libya
149 N6 **Bingley** West Yorkshire, England U.K.
Bingmei Guizhou China see **Congjiang**
127 J4 **Bingöl** Turkey
129 B6 **Bingöl** prov. Turkey
127 J4 **Bingol Dağı** mt. Turkey
129 C6 **Bingöl Dağları** mts Turkey
Bingxi Jiangxi China see **Yushan**
108 B4 **Bingzhongluo** Yunnan China
97 I8 **Binh Đinh** Vietnam
96 H4 **Binh Gia** Vietnam
158 F4 **Binic** France
92 D7 **Binicuil** Negros Phil.
202 C4 **Bini Erda** well Chad
186 D2 **Biniés** Spain
117 I9 **Binika** Orissa India
187 K8 **Binissalem** Spain
94 C3 **Binjai** Sumatera Indon.
202 C2 **Bin Jawwād** Libya
210 F2 **Binna, Raas** pt Somalia
83 L4 **Binnaway** N.S.W. Austr.
146 G9 **Binnein Mòr** mt. Scotland U.K.
168 H5 **Binnen** Ger.
93 D7 **Binongko** i. Indon.
129 D6 **Binpınar** Turkey
117 K8 **Binpur** W. Bengal India
81 F10 **Binser, Mount** South I. N.Z.
210 B2 **Bīnshangul Gumuz** admin. reg. Eth.
173 J4 **Binswangen** Ger.
94 F4 **Bintan** i. Indon.
94 D2 **Bintang, Bukit** mts Malaysia
92 C5 **Bintuan** Phil.
94 E7 **Bintuhan** Sumatera Indon.
95 J3 **Bintulu** Sarawak Malaysia
92 C5 **Binubusan** Luzon Phil.
100 E6 **Binxian** Heilong. China
107 K9 **Binxian** Shaanxi China
Binxian Shandong China see **Bincheng**
108 G7 **Binyang** Guangxi China
207 G4 **Bin-Yauri** Nigeria
170 I2 **Binz, Ostseebad** Ger.
172 D6 **Binzen** Ger.
Binzhou Guangxi China see **Binyang**
Binzhou Heilong. China see **Binxian**
107 P8 **Binzhou** Shandong China
260 A5 **Biobío** admin. reg. Chile
260 A5 **Biobío** r. Chile
207 H6 **Bioco** i. Equat. Guinea
188 E4 **Biograd na Moru** Croatia
196 H8 **Biogradska Gora** nat. park Montenegro
Bioko i. Equat. Guinea see **Bioco**
188 F4 **Biokovo** park Croatia
160 G6 **Biol** France
190 C4 **Bionaz** Italy
186 H4 **Biosca** Spain
161 K9 **Biot** France
186 C3 **Biota** Spain
204 C3 **Biougra** Morocco
168 E5 **Bippen** Ger.
111 K10 **Bi Qu** r. Qinghai China
257 E3 **Biquinhas** Brazil
Bir Mahar. India see **Bid**
210 D2 **Bir, Ras** pt Djibouti
100 H4 **Bira** Rus. Fed.
100 H4 **Bira** r. Rus. Fed.
124 C2 **Bi'r Abā al 'Ajjāj** well Saudi Arabia
203 G4 **Bi'r Abraq** well Egypt
126 C8 **Bi'r Abū Baṭṭah** well Egypt
128 A9 **Bi'r Abū Daraj** well Egypt
203 F5 **Bir Abu Garad** well Sudan
203 G4 **Bi'r Abū Hashīm** well Egypt
203 F4 **Bi'r Abū Ḥuṣayn** well Egypt
128 G2 **Bi'r Abū Jady** oasis Syria
202 E3 **Bi'r Abū Minqār** well Egypt
202 A3 **Bi'r ad Damar** well Libya
128 A8 **Bi'r ad Duwaydār** well Egypt
202 D3 **Bi'r adh Dhakar** well Libya
123 I8 **Bīrag, Kūh-e** mts Iran
204 C4 **Bîr Aïdiat** well Maur.
202 B3 **Birāk** Libya
100 G4 **Birakan** Rus. Fed.
128 B7 **Bi'r al 'Abd** Egypt
124 D3 **Bi'r al Amīr** well Saudi Arabia
124 D3 **Bi'r al Aṭbaq** well Saudi Arabia
124 D4 **Bi'r al 'Awādī** well Saudi Arabia
202 B2 **Bi'r al Fātīyah** well Libya
202 B1 **Bi'r al Ghanam** Libya
128 G4 **Bi'r al Ḥalbā** well Syria
203 G4 **Bi'r al Ḥaymūr** well Egypt
124 E3 **Bi'r al Ḥisw** well Saudi Arabia
202 D3 **Bi'r al Ikhwān** well Libya
202 B3 **Bi'r al Jadīd** well Libya
124 F5 **Bi'r al Jāhilīyah** well Saudi Arabia
128 B8 **Bi'r al Jifjāfah** well Egypt
202 E2 **Bi'r al Khamsah** well Egypt
206 B2 **Bir Allah** well Maur.
128 B9 **Bi'r al Māliḥah** well Egypt
203 H3 **Bi'r al Mashī** well Saudi Arabia
202 B3 **Bi'r al Mastūtah** well Libya
127 J7 **Bi'r al Mulūsi** Iraq
128 G4 **Bi'r al Munbaṭiḥ** well Syria
202 A2 **Bi'r al Mushayqīq** well Libya
202 C2 **Bi'r al Muwaylih** well Libya
202 E2 **Bi'r al Qaṭrānī** well Egypt
124 C2 **Bi'r al Qurr** well Saudi Arabia
202 E3 **Bi'r al Ubbayiḍ** well Egypt
128 C10 **Bi'r al 'Udayd** well Egypt
204 C5 **Bir 'Amrâne** well Maur.
134 G3 **Birandozero** Rus. Fed.
202 E2 **Bi'r an Nuṣṣ** well Egypt
204 B5 **Bir Anzarane** Western Sahara
208 D2 **Birao** C.A.R.
205 H2 **Bir Aouine** well Tunisia
202 B2 **Bi'r ar 'Alaqah** well Libya
124 E3 **Bi'r 'Arja** well Saudi Arabia
126 B8 **Bi'r ar Rābiyah** well Egypt
203 G2 **Bi'r ar Rummānah** Egypt
124 F4 **Bi'r as Sakhā** well Saudi Arabia
128 C9 **Bi'r as Sawrah** well Egypt
110 J6 **Biratar Bulak** spring China
117 K6 **Biratnagar** Nepal
102 T4 **Biratori** Japan
202 E2 **Bi'r aṭ Ṭarfāwī** well Libya
125 J4 **Bi'r 'Azīz** well Saudi Arabia
124 F6 **Bi'raz Zurq** well Saudi Arabia
128 F4 **Bi'r Başīrī** well Syria
128 C8 **Bi'r Bayḍā'** well Egypt
124 C2 **Bi'r Baydā** well Saudi Arabia
202 E2 **Bi'r Baylī** well Egypt
204 C4 **Bîr Bel Guerdâne** well Maur.
204 E4 **Bir Ben Takoul** well Alg.
202 E5 **Bir Bidi** well Sudan
202 D3 **Bi'r Bū Athlah** well Libya
124 D3 **Bi'r Budayy** well Saudi Arabia
202 A3 **Bi'r Bū Rāḥah** well Libya
124 E5 **Bi'r Buraym** well Saudi Arabia
126 I5 **Bi'r Buṭaymān** Syria
222 H3 **Birch** r. Alta Can.
204 D5 **Bir Chali** well Mali
223 J4 **Birch Hills** Sask. Can.
151 O5 **Birchington** Kent, England U.K.
83 I6 **Birchip** Vic. Austr.
177 L6 **Birchiș** Romania
222 G5 **Birch Island** B.C. Can.
222 G2 **Birch Lake** N.W.T. Can.
223 M5 **Birch Lake** Ont. Can.
223 I4 **Birch Lake** Sask. Can.
226 C2 **Birch Lake** MN U.S.A.
222 H3 **Birch Mountains** Y.T. Can.
223 K4 **Birch River** Man. Can.
232 E10 **Birch River** WV U.S.A.
227 K6 **Birch Run** MI U.S.A.
226 C4 **Birchwood** WI U.S.A.
210 D3 **Bircot** Eth.
175 K6 **Bircza** Pol.
147 F7 **Birdhill** Ireland
208 F3 **Bir Di** Sudan
203 F4 **Bi'r Dibs** well Egypt
234 C4 **Bird in Hand** PA U.S.A.
202 E2 **Bi'r Diqnāsh** well Egypt
Bird Island N. Mariana Is see **Farallon de Medinilla**
205 H3 **Bir Dolmane** well Alg.
234 D4 **Birdsboro** PA U.S.A.
241 U2 **Birdseye** UT U.S.A.
84 G8 **Birdsville** Qld Austr.
234 B7 **Birdsville** MD U.S.A.
84 D3 **Birdum** r. N.T. Austr.
126 H5 **Birecik** Turkey
204 E4 **Bir ed Deheb** well Alg.
205 G2 **Bir el Arbi** well Alg.
205 H2 **Bir el Ghoralia** well Tunisia
205 E4 **Bir El Hadjaj** well Alg.
Birendranagar Nepal see **Surkhet**
211 A5 **Birenga** Rwanda
202 E5 **Bir en Natrûn** well Sudan
203 G5 **Bir en Nugeim** well Sudan
205 G2 **Bir es Smeha** well Alg.
94 B2 **Bireun** Sumatera Indon.
125 I4 **Bi'r Fāḍil** well Saudi Arabia
124 C1 **Bi'r Fajr** well Saudi Arabia
203 G5 **Bir Fanoidig** well Sudan
125 I4 **Bi'r Fardān** well Saudi Arabia
202 E2 **Bi'r Fu'ād** well Egypt
202 D6 **Bir Furawiya** well Sudan
204 A5 **Bir Gandouz** Western Sahara
124 G4 **Bi'r Ghawdah** well Saudi Arabia
202 D2 **Bi'r Ghayzal** well Libya
199 J4 **Birgi** Turkey
195 □ **Birgu** Malta
125 J6 **Bir Hādī** oasis Saudi Arabia
128 H4 **Bi'r Ḥajal** well Syria
210 C2 **Birhan** mt. Eth.
124 F4 **Bi'r Haraqī** well Saudi Arabia
128 B8 **Bi'r Ḥasanah** well Egypt
203 G4 **Bir Hatab** well Sudan
124 D3 **Bi'r Ḥaymir** well Saudi Arabia
124 D2 **Bi'r Ḥayzān** well Saudi Arabia
203 G4 **Bir Hismet 'Umar** well Sudan
124 F4 **Bi'r Ḥudūf** well Saudi Arabia
203 G4 **Bir Huwait** well Sudan
124 E3 **Bi'r Ḥuwaymidah** well Saudi Arabia
92 E5 **Biri** i. Phil.
124 C3 **Bi'r Ibn Ghunayn** well Saudi Arabia
Bi'r Ibn Hirmās Saudi Arabia see **Al Bi'r**
125 I4 **Bir Ibn Juhayyim** Saudi Arabia
124 F6 **Bi'r Ibn Sarrār** well Saudi Arabia
124 G6 **Bi'r Īdīmah** well Saudi Arabia
256 B4 **Birigüi** Brazil
128 E3 **Bīrīn** Syria
129 G4 **Birinci Şıxlı** Azer.
208 D3 **Birini** C.A.R.
202 E2 **Bi'r Isṭabl** well Egypt
122 H5 **Bīrjand** Iran
124 C2 **Bi'r Jaydah** well Saudi Arabia
124 G8 **Bi'r Jifah** well Yemen
202 E2 **Bi'r Jubnī** well Libya
124 F5 **Bi'r Jugjug** well Saudi Arabia
125 M4 **Birkat al Mawz** Oman
142 E3 **Birkeland** Norway
172 F2 **Birkenau** Ger.
172 F4 **Birkenfeld** Baden-Württemberg Ger.
172 H2 **Birkenfeld** Bayern Ger.
172 C2 **Birkenfeld** Rheinland-Pfalz Ger.
149 K7 **Birkenhead** Merseyside, England U.K.
169 E9 **Birken-Honigsessen** Ger.
170 H5 **Birkenwerder Berlin** Ger.
168 L1 **Birket** Denmark
179 M5 **Birkfeld** Austria
168 J1 **Birkholm** i. Denmark
124 C2 **Bi'r Khurbah** well Saudi Arabia
124 E4 **Bi'r Khuwārah** well Saudi Arabia
203 G4 **Bir Kiau** well Sudan
127 L5 **Bīrkim** Iraq
195 □ **Birkirkara** Malta
82 C2 **Birksgate Range** hills S.A. Austr.
169 J8 **Birkungen** Ger.
203 F4 **Bi'r Kusaybah** well Egypt
137 N3 **Birky** Ukr.
203 G4 **Bir Labasoi** well Sudan
Bîrlad Romania see **Bârlad**
128 B7 **Bi'r Lahfān** well Egypt
204 C4 **Bir Lahmar** Western Sahara
121 O5 **Birlik** Zhambylskaya Oblast' Kazakh.
121 O6 **Birlik** Zhambylskaya Oblast' Kazakh.
203 G4 **Bir Likeit el Fauqani** well Sudan
203 G4 **Bir Liseila** well Sudan
203 G4 **Bi'r Majal** well Egypt
123 M5 **Birmal** reg. Afgh.
124 F4 **Bi'r Malīyah** well Saudi Arabia
151 I3 **Birmingham** West Midlands, England U.K.
231 D9 **Birmingham** AL U.S.A.
202 E4 **Bi'r Misāḥa** well Egypt
117 J8 **Birmitrapur** Orissa India
204 C4 **Bîr Mogreïn** Maur.
128 G4 **Bi'r Muḥaymid al Wazwaz** well Syria
128 D9 **Bi'r Mujayfil** well Saudi Arabia
203 G4 **Bi'r Murrah** well Egypt
124 C3 **Bi'r Nabt** well Saudi Arabia
203 F2 **Bi'r Nāḥid** oasis Egypt
203 G4 **Bi'r Najīb** well Egypt
124 D3 **Bi'r Nasīf** Saudi Arabia
203 G4 **Bir Nawari** well Sudan
178 G6 **Birnbaum** Austria
178 G5 **Birnhorn** mt. Austria
207 F4 **Birni** Benin
78 □5 **Birnie** i. Kiribati
207 F3 **Birnin-Gaouré** Niger
207 G4 **Birnin-Gwari** Nigeria
207 G3 **Birnin-Kebbi** Nigeria
207 G3 **Birnin Konni** Niger
207 H4 **Birnin Kudu** Nigeria
207 H3 **Birniwa** Nigeria
202 E5 **Bir Nukheila** well Sudan
100 H4 **Birobidzhan** Rus. Fed.
100 H4 **Birofel'd** Rus. Fed.
163 F6 **Biron** France
92 B7 **Birong** Palawan Phil.
204 E4 **Bir Ould Brini** well Alg.
204 E5 **Bir Ounâne** well Mali
117 K6 **Birpur** Bihar India
202 E2 **Bi'r Qaşīr as Sirr** well Egypt
203 G3 **Bi'r Qulayb** well Egypt
147 G6 **Birr** Ireland
128 B8 **Bi'r Rawḍ Sālim** well Egypt
169 C10 **Birresborn** Ger.
83 K3 **Birrie** r. N.S.W. Austr.
84 B5 **Birrindudu** N.T. Austr.
205 G2 **Bir Roumi** well Alg.
127 K7 **Bi'r Sābil** Iraq
203 F4 **Bi'r Şafşaf** well Egypt
203 F4 **Bi'r Şaḥrā'** well Egypt
203 G4 **Bir Salala** well Sudan
Bîrsana Romania see **Bârsana**
146 J4 **Birsay** Orkney, Scotland U.K.
190 D1 **Birse** r. Switz.
203 G4 **Bi'r Shalatayn** Egypt
128 H2 **Bi'r Shamandūr** well Syria
Birshoghyr Kazakh. see **Berchogur**
134 K5 **Birsk** Rus. Fed.
203 G4 **Bir Sohanit** well Sudan
151 J2 **Birstall** Leicestershire, England U.K.
169 H10 **Birstein** Ger.
138 H7 **Birštonas** Lith.
128 C9 **Bi'r Tābah** Egypt
124 H4 **Bir Ṭalḥah** well Saudi Arabia
205 H3 **Bir Tanguer** well Alg.
202 D2 **Bi'r Tānjidar** well Libya
203 F4 **Bi'r Ṭarfāwī** well Egypt
140 P2 **Birtavarre** Norway
128 B9 **Bi'r Thāl** well Egypt
85 I2 **Birthday Mountain** hill Qld Austr.
223 K5 **Birtle** Man. Can.
149 N4 **Birtley** Tyne and Wear, England U.K.
111 K11 **Biru** Xizang China
128 A9 **Bi'r Udayb** well Egypt
136 H6 **Biruința** Moldova
Biruintsa Moldova see **Ștefan Vodă**
202 C2 **Bi'r Umm al Gharāniq** Libya
124 A3 **Bi'r Umm Fawākhīr** well Egypt
124 C3 **Bi'r Umm Missā** well Saudi Arabia
Biruni Uzbek. see **Beruniy**
203 G4 **Bi'r 'Unjāt** well Egypt
114 D6 **Birur** Karnataka India
124 H4 **Bi'r Usaylīlah** well Saudi Arabia
203 G5 **Bir Wario** well Sudan
202 B3 **Bi'r Wedeb** well Libya
124 F5 **Bi'r Wurshah** well Saudi Arabia
137 R3 **Biryuch** Rus. Fed.
129 I2 **Biryuchek** Rus. Fed.
138 H5 **Biržai** Lith.
205 H3 **Bir Zar** well Tunisia
195 □ **Birżebbuġa** Malta
179 M6 **Biš** Slovenia
93 E4 **Bisa** i. Maluku Indon.
193 O5 **Bisaccia** Italy
194 E8 **Bisacquino** Sicilia Italy
104 E5 **Bisai** Japan
116 G5 **Bisalpur** Uttar Prad. India
116 E5 **Bisau** Rajasthan India
186 D2 **Bisaurín** mt. Spain
241 W10 **Bisbee** AZ U.S.A.
Biscari Sicilia Italy see **Acate**
163 B7 **Biscarrosse** France
163 B7 **Biscarrosse et de Parentis, Étang de** l. France
163 B7 **Biscarrosse-Plage** France
154 B4 **Biscay, Bay of** sea France/Spain
264 I3 **Biscay Abyssal Plain** sea feature N. Atlantic Ocean
231 G13 **Biscayne Bay** FL U.S.A.
231 G13 **Biscayne National Park** FL U.S.A.
193 R5 **Bisceglie** Italy
173 J2 **Bischberg** Ger.
172 G2 **Bischbrunn** Ger.
157 O6 **Bischheim** France
169 F9 **Bischoffen** Ger.
169 J8 **Bischofferode** Ger.
173 L1 **Bischofsgrün** Ger.
172 E2 **Bischofsheim** Ger.
169 J10 **Bischofsheim an der Rhön** Ger.
178 H5 **Bischofshofen** Austria
173 O4 **Bischofsmais** Ger.
171 J8 **Bischofswerda** Ger.
173 N6 **Bischofswiesen** Ger.
190 G1 **Bischofszell** Switz.
157 M6 **Bischwald, Étang de** l. France
157 O6 **Bischwiller** France
262 T2 **Biscoe Islands** Antarctica
216 □1a **Biscoitos** Terceira Azores
224 D4 **Biscotasi Lake** Ont. Can.
224 D4 **Biscotasing** Ont. Can.
102 □1 **Bise** Okinawa Japan
208 E3 **Bisellia** Sudan
193 L2 **Bisenti** Italy
192 H2 **Bisentina, Isola** i. Italy
134 L4 **Biser** Rus. Fed.
134 K4 **Biserovo** Rus. Fed.
134 L4 **Bisert'** r. Rus. Fed.
197 O7 **Bisertsi** Bulg.
188 E4 **Biševo** i. Croatia
102 □1 **Bise-zaki** pt Okinawa Japan
108 D7 **Bisezhai** Yunnan China
203 H6 **Bisha** Eritrea
124 F6 **Bīshah** reg. Saudi Arabia
124 G5 **Bīshah, Wādī** watercourse Saudi Arabia
108 F4 **Bishan** Chongqing China
Bishbek Kyrg. see **Bishkek**
127 N7 **Bīsheh** Iran
117 P5 **Bishemnagar** Arun. Prad. India
121 P6 **Bishkek** Kyrg.
117 K8 **Bishnupur** W. Bengal India
215 L8 **Bisho** S. Africa
240 N4 **Bishop** CA U.S.A.
81 B13 **Bishop and Clerks Islands** Stewart I. N.Z.
149 N4 **Bishop Auckland** Durham, England U.K.
146 H11 **Bishopbriggs** East Dunbartonshire, Scotland U.K.
222 G1 **Bishop Lake** N.W.T. Can.
150 G3 **Bishop's Castle** Shropshire, England U.K.
150 H4 **Bishop's Cleeve** Gloucestershire, England U.K.
150 F5 **Bishop's Hull** Somerset, England U.K.
151 J3 **Bishop's Itchington** Warwickshire, England U.K.
150 F5 **Bishop's Lydeard** Somerset, England U.K.
151 M4 **Bishop's Stortford** Hertfordshire, England U.K.
150 D5 **Bishop's Tawton** Devon, England U.K.
150 E6 **Bishopsteignton** Devon, England U.K.
151 J6 **Bishop's Waltham** Hampshire, England U.K.
146 H11 **Bishopton** Renfrewshire, Scotland U.K.
231 G8 **Bishopville** SC U.S.A.
126 I6 **Bishrī, Jabal** hills Syria
100 C2 **Bishui** Heilong. China
Bishui Henan China see **Biyang**
215 N6 **Bisi** S. Africa
193 Q8 **Bisignano** Italy
250 D3 **Bisinaca** Col.
172 F5 **Bisingen** Ger.
205 G2 **Biskra** Alg.
175 K4 **Biskupice** Lubelskie Pol.
174 G4 **Biskupice** Opolskie Pol.
177 I3 **Biskupice** Slovakia
175 H2 **Biskupiec** Warmińsko-Mazurskie Pol.
175 I2 **Biskupiec** Warmińsko-Mazurskie Pol.
150 H4 **Bisley** Gloucestershire, England U.K.
92 F7 **Bislig** Mindanao Phil.
92 F7 **Bislig Bay** Mindanao Phil.
236 E2 **Bismarck** ND U.S.A.
91 K7 **Bismarck Archipelago** is P.N.G.
76 E2 **Bismarck Range** mts P.N.G.
91 K7 **Bismarck Sea** P.N.G.
170 E5 **Bismark (Altmark)** Ger.
127 J5 **Bismil** Turkey
141 J6 **Bismo** Norway
236 D3 **Bison** SD U.S.A.
122 B4 **Bīsotūn** Iran
140 N5 **Bispgården** Sweden
168 J4 **Bispingen** Ger.
115 H3 **Bissamcuttak** Orissa India
206 B4 **Bissau** Guinea-Bissau
207 H5 **Bissaula** Nigeria
165 J9 **Bissen** Lux.
169 F6 **Bissendorf** Ger.
168 I5 **Bissendorf (Wedemark)** Ger.
223 M5 **Bissett** Man. Can.
206 C4 **Bissikrima** Guinea
178 C7 **Bissina, Lago di** l. Italy
173 J4 **Bissingen** Ger.
206 B3 **Bissorã** Guinea-Bissau
190 E6 **Bistagno** Italy
222 G3 **Bistcho Lake** Alta Can.
196 I9 **Bistra** mt. Macedonia
196 I8 **Bistra** mt. Macedonia/Serbia
197 K5 **Bistra** r. Romania
197 L7 **Bistreț** Romania
197 L7 **Bistreț, Lacul** l. Romania
179 M7 **Bistrica** Šmarje pri Jelšah Slovenia
179 J7 **Bistrica** Tržič Slovenia
197 M3 **Bistrița** Romania
197 M3 **Bistrița** r. Romania
197 O4 **Bistrița** r. Romania
197 M3 **Bistrița Bârgăului** Romania
197 N3 **Bistriței, Munții** mts Romania
197 L9 **Bistritsa** r. Bulg.
92 C6 **Bisucay** i. Phil.
116 H6 **Biswan** Uttar Prad. India
125 M4 **Bīsyah** Oman
143 Q7 **Bisztynek** Pol.
113 □1 **Bitadhoo** i. S. Male Maldives
Bitadoo i. S. Male Maldives see **Bitadhoo**
208 A4 **Bitam** Gabon
210 C3 **Bitata** Eth.
172 B2 **Bitburg** Ger.
157 N5 **Bitche** France
195 L1 **Bitetto** Italy
116 H6 **Bithur** Uttar Prad. India
199 K2 **Bithynia** reg. Turkey
120 D2 **Bitik** Kazakh.
208 E3 **Bitilifondi** C.A.R.
208 C2 **Bitkine** Chad
127 K4 **Bitlis** Turkey
196 J9 **Bitola** Macedonia
Bitolj Macedonia see **Bitola**
195 L1 **Bitonto** Italy
124 G4 **Bitrān, Jabal** hill Saudi Arabia
114 C7 **Bitra Par** rf India
157 N8 **Bitschwiller-lès-Thann** France
241 W2 **Bitter Creek** r. UT U.S.A.
238 J6 **Bitter Creek** r. WY U.S.A.
171 F7 **Bitterfeld** Ger.
214 C7 **Bitterfontein** S. Africa
238 G3 **Bitterroot** r. MT U.S.A.
238 G3 **Bitterroot Range** mts ID U.S.A.
240 L5 **Bitterwater** CA U.S.A.
192 C7 **Bitti** Sardegna Italy
171 E6 **Bittkau** Ger.
150 H5 **Bitton** South Gloucestershire, England U.K.
207 E4 **Bittou** Burkina
254 B4 **Bituca** Brazil
93 D3 **Bitung** Sulawesi Indon.
215 M7 **Bityi** S. Africa
135 G6 **Bityug** r. Rus. Fed.
172 G5 **Bitz** Ger.
207 I4 **Biu** Nigeria
209 D7 **Biula** Angola
183 Q3 **Biurrun** Spain
215 P3 **Bivane** r. S. Africa
190 H3 **Bivio** Switz.
197 P3 **Bivolari** Romania
194 E8 **Bivona** Sicilia Italy
226 B2 **Biwabik** MN U.S.A.
104 C5 **Biwa-ko** l. Japan
104 D5 **Biwa-ko Kokutei-kōen** park Japan
Biwmares Wales U.K. see **Beaumaris**
197 N4 **Bixad** Romania
210 E2 **Bixinduule** Somalia
146 □N2 **Bixter** Shetland, Scotland U.K.
121 U1 **Biya** r. Rus. Fed.
Biyang Anhui China see **Yixian**
109 I2 **Biyang** Henan China
210 D2 **Bīye K'obē** Eth.
121 N6 **Biylikol', Ozero** l. Kazakh.
210 E3 **Biyo Ado** well Eth.
121 U1 **Biysk** Rus. Fed.
215 N6 **Bizana** S. Africa
161 B10 **Bizanet** France
163 D9 **Bizanos** France
178 A5 **Bizau** Austria
161 B10 **Bize-Minervois** France
103 L12 **Bizen** Japan
Bizerta Tunisia see **Bizerte**
205 H1 **Bizerte** Tunisia
189 B7 **Bizerte** admin. div. Tunisia
122 H8 **Bīzhanābād** Iran
140 □A1 **Bjargtangar** hd Iceland
140 N2 **Bjarkøy** Norway
143 J5 **Bjärnum** Sweden
143 J6 **Bjärsjölagård** Sweden
140 O5 **Bjästa** Sweden
196 H8 **Bjelasica** mts Montenegro
188 G4 **Bjelašnica** mts Bos.-Herz.
188 F3 **Bjelovar** Croatia
140 N2 **Bjerkvik** Norway
168 K1 **Bjerreby** Denmark
142 F5 **Bjerringbro** Denmark
140 M3 **Bjøllånes** Norway
142 G1 **Bjoneroa** Norway
143 K1 **Björbo** Sweden
142 C3 **Bjordal** Norway
140 K5 **Bjørgan** Norway
142 H2 **Bjørkelangen** Norway
140 N3 **Björkfjället** mts Sweden
140 O2 **Björkliden** Sweden
143 N1 **Björklinge** Sweden
142 H1 **Bjørknes** Akershus Norway
140 T2 **Bjørknes** Finnmark Norway
142 H4 **Björkö** Sweden
143 P2 **Björkö** i. Sweden
140 O4 **Björksele** Sweden
141 J5 **Bjorli** Norway
140 O5 **Björna** Sweden
142 B1 **Bjørnafjorden** b. Norway
142 C2 **Bjørnanuten** mt. Norway
Björneborg Fin. see **Pori**
142 D1 **Bjornesfjorden** l. Norway
140 T2 **Bjørnevatn** Norway
140 O2 **Bjørnfjell** Norway
268 B2 **Bjørnøya** i. Arctic Ocean
140 U2 **Bjørnstad** Norway
142 I1 **Bjurberget** Sweden
140 O5 **Bjurholm** Sweden
140 P4 **Bjuröklubb** pt Sweden
143 L1 **Bjursås** Sweden
206 D3 **Bla** Mali
146 D8 **Bla Bheinn** hill Scotland U.K.
160 F4 **Blacé** France
196 I8 **Blace** Kosovo Serbia
196 J7 **Blace** Serbia
174 G5 **Blachownia** Pol.
223 L5 **Black** r. Man. Can.
224 D3 **Black** r. Ont. Can.
226 H1 **Black** r. Ont. Can.
246 □ **Black** r. Jamaica
Black Mauritius see **Grande Rivière Noire**
229 H3 **Black** r. AR U.S.A.
237 J8 **Black** r. AR U.S.A.
241 V8 **Black** r. AZ U.S.A.
227 L7 **Black** r. MI U.S.A.
231 H9 **Black** r. SC U.S.A.
226 C5 **Black** r. WI U.S.A.
146 L11 **Blackadder Water** r. Scotland U.K.
85 J8 **Blackall** Qld Austr.
224 B3 **Black Bay** Ont. Can.
223 I3 **Black Bay** Sask. Can.
224 B2 **Blackbear** r. Ont. Can.
226 A2 **Blackberry** MN U.S.A.
223 J3 **Black Birch Lake** Sask. Can.
82 □1 **Blackbourne, Point** Norfolk I.
151 I4 **Black Bourton** Oxfordshire, England U.K.
85 H4 **Blackbull** Qld Austr.
148 E7 **Black Bull** Ireland
146 L8 **Blackburn** Aberdeenshire, Scotland U.K.
149 M6 **Blackburn** Blackburn with Darwen, England U.K.
146 I11 **Blackburn** West Lothian, Scotland U.K.
149 M6 **Blackburn with Darwen** admin. div. England U.K.
85 N9 **Blackbutt** Qld Austr.
240 J2 **Black Butte** mt. CA U.S.A.
240 J2 **Black Butte Lake** CA U.S.A.
241 R6 **Black Canyon** gorge AZ U.S.A.
241 T7 **Black Canyon City** AZ U.S.A.
239 K7 **Black Canyon of the Gunnison National Park** CO U.S.A.
262 T2 **Black Coast** Antarctica
149 K5 **Black Combe** hill England U.K.
148 I3 **Blackcraig Hill** Scotland U.K.
226 F5 **Black Creek** WI U.S.A.
234 C2 **Black Creek** r. PA U.S.A.
241 W6 **Black Creek** watercourse AZ U.S.A.
222 E4 **Black Dome** mt. B.C. Can.
227 R4 **Black Donald Lake** Ont. Can.
150 F6 **Black Down Hills** England U.K.
85 L7 **Blackdown Tableland National Park** Qld Austr.
236 H2 **Blackduck** MN U.S.A.
143 M2 **Blacken** b. Sweden
222 H4 **Blackfalds** Alta Can.
238 H2 **Blackfeet Indian Reservation** res. MT U.S.A.
151 J6 **Blackfield** Hampshire, England U.K.
238 H5 **Blackfoot** ID U.S.A.
238 H3 **Black Foot** r. MT U.S.A.
238 I5 **Blackfoot Reservoir** ID U.S.A.
146 I10 **Blackford** Perth and Kinross, Scotland U.K.
Black Forest mts Ger. see **Schwarzwald**
147 D6 **Black Head** Ireland
150 B7 **Black Head** England U.K.
147 K3 **Black Head** Northern Ireland U.K.
149 N6 **Black Hill** England U.K.
84 D8 **Black Hill Range** hills N.T. Austr.
220 H5 **Black Hills** SD U.S.A.
238 L4 **Black Hills** SD U.S.A.
146 J11 **Blackhope Scar** hill Scotland U.K.
223 L5 **Black Island** Man. Can.
146 H7 **Black Isle** pen. Scotland U.K.
223 J3 **Black Lake** Sask. Can.
223 J3 **Black Lake** l. Sask. Can.
227 J4 **Black Lake** l. MI U.S.A.
148 B5 **Blacklion** Ireland
146 J9 **Blacklunans** Perth and Kinross, Scotland U.K.
247 □4 **Blackman's** Barbados
241 W8 **Black Mesa** mt. AZ U.S.A.
241 V5 **Black Mesa** ridge AZ U.S.A.
150 E5 **Blackmoor Gate** Devon, England U.K.
151 M4 **Blackmore** Essex, England U.K.
150 E4 **Black Mountain** hills Wales U.K.
240 O6 **Black Mountain** CA U.S.A.
232 C12 **Black Mountain** KY U.S.A.
150 F4 **Black Mountains** hills Wales U.K.
241 R6 **Black Mountains** AZ U.S.A.
212 C4 **Black Nossob** watercourse Namibia
151 N4 **Black Notley** Essex, England U.K.
Black Pagoda Orissa India see **Konarka**
Black Point H.K. China see **Lan Kok Tsui**
149 K6 **Blackpool** Blackpool, England U.K.
83 I7 **Black Range State Park** nature res. Vic. Austr.
246 □ **Black River** Jamaica

Black River to Bol'shoye Mikhaylovskoye
289

227 K5 Black River MI U.S.A.
233 J4 Black River NY U.S.A.
Black River r. Vietnam see Đa, Sông
226 D5 Black River Falls WI U.S.A.
Black Rock hill Jordan see 'Unāb, Jabal al
147 J5 Blackrock Ireland
238 E6 Black Rock Desert NV U.S.A.
232 E11 Blacksburg VA U.S.A.
135 G8 Black Sea Asia/Europe
238 J6 Blacks Fork r. WY U.S.A.
233 □S3 Blacks Harbour N.B. Can.
231 F10 Blackshear GA U.S.A.
147 B4 Blacksod Bay Ireland
240 M2 Black Springs NV U.S.A.
147 I7 Blackstairs Mountains hills Ireland
222 F2 Blackstone r. N.W.T. Can.
232 G11 Blackstone VA U.S.A.
226 F1 Black Sturgeon r. Ont. Can.
83 M4 Black Sugarloaf mt. N.S.W. Austr.
225 K2 Black Tickle Nfld and Lab. Can.
147 G3 Blacktown Northern Ireland U.K.
215 P4 Black Umfolozi r. S. Africa
83 M4 Blackville N.S.W. Austr.
206 E4 Black Volta r. Africa alt. Mouhoun, alt. Volta Noire
85 L7 Blackwater Qld Austr.
85 J8 Blackwater watercourse Qld Austr.
222 E2 Blackwater r. N.W.T. Can.
147 I3 Blackwater r. N. Ireland/Ireland
147 J8 Blackwater Ireland
147 I5 Blackwater r. Ireland
147 G8 Blackwater r. Ireland
151 N4 Blackwater r. England U.K.
146 H6 Black Water r. Highland, Scotland U.K.
146 H7 Black Water r. Highland, Scotland U.K.
232 I12 Blackwater r. VA U.S.A.
237 E9 Blackwater watercourse NM/TX U.S.A.
146 F12 Blackwaterfoot North Ayrshire, Scotland U.K.
222 F2 Blackwater Lake N.W.T. Can.
146 G9 Blackwater Reservoir Scotland U.K.
148 D5 Blackwatertown Northern Ireland U.K.
87 C13 Blackwood r. W.A. Austr.
150 F4 Blackwood Caerphilly, Wales U.K.
85 K6 Blackwood National Park Qld Austr.
165 H6 Bladel Neth.
85 I7 Bladensburg National Park Qld Austr.
150 E2 Blaenau Ffestiniog Gwynedd, Wales U.K.
150 F4 Blaenau Gwent admin. div. Wales U.K.
150 F4 Blaenavon Torfaen, Wales U.K.
150 E4 Blaengarw Bridgend, Wales U.K.
150 E4 Blaengwrach Neath Port Talbot, Wales U.K.
140 L4 Blåfjellshatten mt. Norway
150 G5 Blagdon North Somerset, England U.K.
163 G8 Blagnac France
163 J4 Blagny France
121 T4 Blagodarnoye Kazakh.
135 H7 Blagodarnyy Rus. Fed.
121 O2 Blagodatnoye Kazakh.
137 N2 Blagodatnoye Rus. Fed.
197 L8 Blagoevgrad Bulg.
121 L1 Blagoveshchenka Kazakh.
121 R1 Blagoveshchenka Rus. Fed.
100 E3 Blagoveshchensk Amurskaya Oblast' Rus. Fed.
134 L5 Blagoveshchensk Respublika Bashkortostan Rus. Fed.
Blagoveshchenskoye Severnyy Kazakhstan Kazakh. see Blagoveshchenka
179 K7 Blagovica Slovenia
137 N7 Blahodatne Khersons'ka Oblast' Ukr.
137 K6 Blahodatne Mykolayivs'ka Oblast' Ukr.
137 N6 Blahovishchenka Zaporiz'ka Oblast' Ukr.
137 P6 Blahovishchenka Zaporiz'ka Oblast' Ukr.
173 N3 Blaibach Ger.
146 F9 Blaich Highland, Scotland U.K.
173 I6 Blaichach Ger.
222 H5 Blaikiston, Mount B.C. Can.
162 H7 Blain France
232 H8 Blain PA U.S.A.
226 A4 Blaine MN U.S.A.
238 C2 Blaine WA U.S.A.
223 J4 Blaine Lake Sask. Can.
162 F3 Blainville-sur-l'Eau France
158 H3 Blainville-sur-Mer France
159 K3 Blainville-sur-Orne France
236 G5 Blair NE U.S.A.
226 C5 Blair WI U.S.A.
85 K7 Blair Athol Qld Austr.
146 I9 Blair Atholl Perth and Kinross, Scotland U.K.
215 K1 Blairbeth S. Africa
146 J9 Blairgowrie Perth and Kinross, Scotland U.K.
232 F12 Blairs VA U.S.A.
240 L2 Blairsden CA U.S.A.
234 F3 Blairstown NJ U.S.A.
231 F8 Blairsville GA U.S.A.
232 F8 Blairsville PA U.S.A.
157 I6 Blaise r. France
157 I7 Blaiserives France
160 F2 Blaisy-Bas France
197 L4 Blaj Romania
163 F9 Blajan France
177 L5 Blăjeni Romania
120 I2 Blak Rus. Fed.
Blakang Mati, Pulau i. Sing. see Sentosa
231 E10 Blakely GA U.S.A.
234 D2 Blakely PA U.S.A.
150 H4 Blakeney Gloucestershire, England U.K.
151 O2 Blakeney Norfolk, England U.K.
151 N2 Blakeney Point England U.K.
226 F1 Blake Point MI U.S.A.
234 D2 Blakeslee PA U.S.A.
206 C5 Blama Sierra Leone
95 K9 Blambangan, Semenanjung pen. Indon.
157 M6 Blâmont France
163 I8 Blan France
187 K9 Blanc, Cap c. Spain
163 B8 Blanc, Étang l. France
160 J5 Blanc, Mont mt. France/Italy
187 C11 Blanca Spain
261 G6 Blanca, Bahía b. Arg.
252 A2 Blanca, Cordillera mts Peru
185 J7 Blanca, Sierra mts Spain
239 L10 Blanca, Sierra mt. NM U.S.A.
159 Q6 Blancafort France
239 L8 Blanca Peak CO U.S.A.
183 R7 Blancas Spain
148 E7 Blanchardstown Ireland
161 I8 Blanche r. France
161 I8 Blanche ridge France
82 E5 Blanche, Cape S.A. Austr.
82 G3 Blanche, Lake salt flat S.A. Austr.
86 G7 Blanche, Lake salt flat W.A. Austr.
78 □6 Blanche Channel New Georgia Is Solomon Is
232 B9 Blanchester OH U.S.A.
82 G6 Blanchetown S.A. Austr.
247 □7 Blanchisseuse Trin. and Tob.
156 C2 Blanc Nez, Cap c. France
258 C3 Blanco r. Arg.
252 D3 Blanco r. Bol.
250 C6 Blanco r. Peru
214 G9 Blanco S. Africa
185 I5 Blanco r. Spain
242 □Q13 Blanco, Cabo c. Costa Rica
Blanco, Cabo c. Spain see Blanc, Cap
238 B5 Blanco, Cape OR U.S.A.
225 J3 Blanc-Sablon Que. Can.
83 K5 Bland r. N.S.W. Austr.
232 D11 Bland VA U.S.A.
140 □C1 Blanda r. Iceland
150 H6 Blandford Camp Dorset, England U.K.
150 H6 Blandford Forum Dorset, England U.K.
241 W4 Blanding UT U.S.A.
226 D9 Blandinsville IL U.S.A.
234 D4 Blandon PA U.S.A.
186 K4 Blanes Spain
226 I3 Blaney Park MI U.S.A.
94 □ Blangah, Telok b. Sing.
94 B3 Blangkejeren Sumatera Indon.
94 B3 Blangpidie Sumatera Indon.
159 L3 Blangy-le-Château France
156 C4 Blangy-sur-Bresle France
176 D2 Blanice r. Czech Rep.
176 D2 Blanice r. Czech Rep.
176 D2 Blaník park Czech Rep.
143 M4 Blankaholm Sweden
170 E3 Blankenberg Ger.
165 C6 Blankenberge Belgium
169 K7 Blankenburg (Harz) Ger.
171 H6 Blankenfelde Ger.
172 E8 Blankenhain Sachsen Ger.
171 D9 Blankenhain Thüringen Ger.
169 C10 Blankenheim Nordrhein-Westfalen Ger.
171 D7 Blankenheim Sachsen-Anhalt Ger.
169 D10 Blankenrath Ger.
170 H4 Blankensee Ger.
171 E10 Blankenstein Ger.
163 C6 Blanquefort France
251 E2 Blanquilla, Isla i. Venez.
184 H8 Blanquilla, Sierra mts Spain
185 N4 Blanquillo mt. Spain
176 C2 Blansko Czech Rep.
211 B8 Blantyre Malawi
162 E5 Blanzac-Porcheresse France
160 C5 Blanzat France
160 E3 Blanzay France
160 E3 Blanzy France
164 H4 Blaricum Neth.
147 E9 Blarney Ireland
232 G6 Blasdell NY U.S.A.
142 C2 Blåsjø l. Norway
141 I6 Blaskavlen mt. Norway
147 A8 Blasket Sound sea chan. Ireland
140 L5 Blåstöten mt. Sweden
174 G4 Blaszki Pol.
176 C2 Blatná Czech Rep.
176 G3 Blatné Slovakia
165 E7 Blaton Belgium
140 N4 Blattniksele Sweden
93 C3 Blau Sulawesi Indon.
172 H5 Blaubeuren Ger.
172 H3 Blaufelden Ger.
168 G2 Blauort i. Ger.
172 H5 Blaustein Ger.
142 E6 Blåvands Huk pt Denmark
Blaven hill Scotland U.K. see Bla Bheinn
158 E6 Blavet r. France
134 B2 Blåviksjön Sweden
161 D6 Blavozy France
149 N4 Blaydon Tyne and Wear, England U.K.
162 C5 Blaye France
163 D5 Blaye-les-Mines France
161 I8 Blayeul Sommet mt. France
83 L5 Blayney N.S.W. Austr.
84 C2 Blaze, Point N.T. Austr.
175 L6 Blazhiv Ukr.
136 G2 Blazhove Ukr.
175 J4 Błażiny Górne Pol.
179 O1 Blažovice Czech Rep.
175 K6 Błażowa Pol.
188 K4 Blázquez Spain
151 O5 Blean Kent, England U.K.
168 K4 Bleckede Ger.
186 E3 Blecua Spain
179 J7 Bled Slovenia
202 B6 Bledaya Chad
175 I4 Bledów Pol.
175 J4 Błędów Pol.
174 D3 Bledzew Pol.
95 J8 Blega Jawa Indon.
179 J7 Blegoš mt. Slovenia
165 D7 Bléharies Belgium
169 B10 Bleialf Ger.
179 B6 Bleiburg Austria
169 K8 Bleicherode Ger.
169 F10 Bleidenstadt Ger.
140 M2 Bleik Norway
179 K2 Bleikogel mt. Austria
171 E9 Bleilochtalsperre resr Ger.
165 G4 Bleiswijk Neth.
168 K2 Blekendorf Ger.
143 K5 Blekinge county Sweden
150 G1 Blencathra hill England U.K.
156 D2 Blendecques France
168 H5 Blender Ger.
156 E8 Bléneau France
224 D5 Blenheim Ont. Can.
81 H8 Blenheim South I. N.Z.
151 J4 Blenheim Palace tourist site England U.K.
157 L6 Blénod-lès-Pont-à-Mousson France
157 K6 Blénod-lès-Toul France
161 H8 Bléone r. France
192 I3 Blera Italy
156 F4 Blérancourt France
162 F1 Bléré France
165 J6 Blerick Neth.
165 J6 Blesa Spain
164 G5 Bleskensgraaf Neth.
161 C6 Blesle France
214 I3 Blesmanspos S. Africa
147 I6 Blessington Ireland
147 I6 Blessington Lakes Ireland
160 D3 Blet France
151 K3 Bletchley Milton Keynes, England U.K.
142 F2 Bletoppen mt. Norway
160 G3 Bleterans France
227 P3 Bleu, Lac l. Que. Can.
208 F4 Bleus, Monts mts Dem. Rep. Congo
151 J4 Blewbury Oxfordshire, England U.K.
168 G3 Blexen (Nordenham) Ger.
177 J3 Blh r. Slovakia
205 F1 Blida Alg.
168 I4 Bliedersdorf Ger.
172 C3 Blies r. Ger.
172 C3 Blieskastel Ger.
81 B11 Bligh Sound inlet South I. N.Z.
79 □7a Bligh Water b. Fiji
156 I7 Bligny France
160 F2 Bligny-sur-Ouche France
164 L2 Blijham Neth.
182 I2 Blimea Spain
179 K3 Blindenmarkt Austria
170 I4 Blindow Ger.
224 D4 Blind River Ont. Can.
215 K8 Blinkwater S. Africa
82 G4 Blinman S.A. Austr.
190 E3 Blinnenhorn mt. Italy/Switz.
235 I2 Bliss ID U.S.A.
227 K8 Blissfield MI U.S.A.
232 D8 Blissfield OH U.S.A.
151 K3 Blisworth Northamptonshire, England U.K.
95 J9 Blitar Jawa Indon.
174 G4 Bliżanów Pol.
173 N3 Bliżejov Czech Rep.
172 G3 Blížkovice Czech Rep.
175 J6 Blizne Pol.
Bliznetsy Ukr. see Blyznyuky
Bliznyuki Ukr. see Blyznyuky
175 I4 Bliżyn Pol.
233 N7 Block Island RI U.S.A.
233 N7 Block Island i. RI U.S.A.
233 N7 Block Island Sound sea chan. RI U.S.A.
151 I3 Blockley Gloucestershire, England U.K.
215 O3 Bloedrivier S. Africa
215 K5 Bloemfontein S. Africa
215 J3 Bloemhof S. Africa
215 J3 Bloemhof Dam S. Africa
215 J3 Bloemhof Dam Nature Reserve S. Africa
159 N6 Blois France
164 I3 Blokzijl Neth.
169 H7 Blomberg Ger.
214 E6 Blomberg se Vloer salt pan S. Africa
142 A1 Blomøy i. Norway
140 □C1 Blöndulón l. Iceland
140 □C1 Blönduós Iceland
95 L9 Blongas Lombok Indon.
175 H3 Błonie Łódzkie Pol.
175 I3 Błonie Mazowieckie Pol.
171 G7 Blönsdorf Ger.
159 L3 Blonville-sur-Mer France
84 B8 Bloods Range mts N.T. Austr.
223 I10 Bloodsworth Island MD U.S.A.
223 L5 Bloodvein r. Man. Can.
147 F2 Bloody Foreland pt Ireland
226 C4 Bloomer WI U.S.A.
227 Q6 Bloomfield Ont. Can.
236 I5 Bloomfield IA U.S.A.
230 D6 Bloomfield IN U.S.A.
237 K7 Bloomfield MO U.S.A.
239 K8 Bloomfield NM U.S.A.
85 J3 Bloomfield River Qld Austr.
235 G1 Bloomingburg NY U.S.A.
235 G2 Bloomingdale NJ U.S.A.
234 E4 Blooming Glen PA U.S.A.
235 G2 Blooming Grove NY U.S.A.
234 E2 Blooming Grove PA U.S.A.
226 A6 Blooming Prairie MN U.S.A.
226 F9 Bloomington IL U.S.A.
230 D6 Bloomington IN U.S.A.
226 A5 Bloomington MN U.S.A.
227 R8 Bloomsburg PA U.S.A.
85 L6 Bloomsbury Qld Austr.
234 E3 Bloomsbury NJ U.S.A.
95 I8 Blora Jawa Indon.
227 Q8 Blossburg PA U.S.A.
221 P3 Blosseville Kyst coastal area Greenland
131 S2 Blossom, Mys pt Rus. Fed.
160 K1 Blotzheim France
213 F4 Blouberg Nature Reserve S. Africa
214 C9 Bloubergstrand S. Africa
215 K4 Bloudrif S. Africa
231 E10 Blountstown FL U.S.A.
232 C12 Blountville TN U.S.A.
163 E9 Blousson-Sérian France
176 C2 Blovice Czech Rep.
170 E3 Blowatz Ger.
246 E5 Blower Rock i. Jamaica
151 J3 Bloxham Oxfordshire, England U.K.
149 N6 Blubberhouses North Yorkshire, England U.K.
178 A5 Bludenz Austria
178 A5 Bludesch Austria
222 D3 Blue r. B.C. Can.
237 H9 Blue r. OK U.S.A.
241 W8 Blue watercourse AZ U.S.A.
148 B7 Blue Ball Ireland
234 C4 Blue Ball PA U.S.A.
234 E4 Blue Bell PA U.S.A.
241 U3 Blue Bell Knoll mt. UT U.S.A.
222 F3 Blueberry r. B.C. Can.
215 J9 Blue Cliff S. Africa
Blue Creek r. Mex. see Azul
231 G12 Blue Cypress Lake FL U.S.A.
241 Q5 Blue Diamond NV U.S.A.
236 H4 Blue Earth MN U.S.A.
236 H3 Blue Earth r. MN U.S.A.
232 D11 Bluefield VA U.S.A.
232 D11 Bluefield WV U.S.A.
246 □ Bluefields Jamaica
242 □R11 Bluefields Nic.
147 D8 Blueford Ireland
215 L6 Bluegums S. Africa
233 O4 Blue Hill ME U.S.A.
236 F5 Blue Hill NE U.S.A.
246 G3 Blue Hills Turks and Caicos Is
232 G8 Blue Knob hill PA U.S.A.
209 E8 Blue Lagoon National Park Zambia
234 C4 Blue Marsh Lake PA U.S.A.
225 J3 Blue Mountain hill Nfld and Lab. Can.
117 N8 Blue Mountain Mizoram India
234 B4 Blue Mountain ridge PA U.S.A.
233 J4 Blue Mountain Lake NY U.S.A.
215 L5 Blue Mountain Pass Lesotho
232 F9 Blue Mountain Peak Jamaica
83 L5 Blue Mountains N.S.W. Austr.
246 □ Blue Mountains Jamaica
81 D13 Blue Mountains South I. N.Z.
238 E3 Blue Mountains OR U.S.A.
83 M5 Blue Mountains National Park N.S.W. Austr.
84 F2 Blue Mud Bay N.T. Austr.
203 G6 Blue Nile r. Eth./Sudan alt. Abay Wenz (Ethiopia), alt. Azraq, Bahr el (Sudan)
210 B2 Blue Nile state Sudan
223 G2 Bluenose Lake Nunavut Can.
236 G6 Blue Rapids KS U.S.A.
231 E8 Blue Ridge GA U.S.A.
232 F11 Blue Ridge VA U.S.A.
232 E12 Blue Ridge mts VA U.S.A.
222 G4 Blue River B.C. Can.
147 F3 Blue Stack Mountains hills Ireland
232 E11 Bluestone Lake WV U.S.A.
85 L7 Bluff Qld Austr.
81 C13 Bluff South I. N.Z.
241 W4 Bluff UT U.S.A.
232 C12 Bluff City TN U.S.A.
241 U1 Bluffdale UT U.S.A.
86 I4 Bluff Face Range hills W.A. Austr.
81 C13 Bluff Harbour South I. N.Z.
Bluff Island H.K. China see Sha Tong Hau Shan
87 E13 Bluff Knoll mt. W.A. Austr.
87 C9 Bluff Point W.A. Austr.
230 E5 Bluffton IN U.S.A.
232 B8 Bluffton OH U.S.A.
179 N5 Blumau in Steiermark Austria
172 F6 Blumberg Baden-Württemberg Ger.
170 I5 Blumberg Brandenburg Ger.
255 C8 Blumenau Brazil
170 I3 Blumenhagen Ger.
170 F4 Blumenholz Ger.
170 F4 Blumenthal Ger.
190 D3 Blümlisalp mt. Switz.
236 E3 Blunt SD U.S.A.
222 F5 Blustry Mountain B.C. Can.
238 D5 Bly OR U.S.A.
137 K6 Blyestova Ukr.
84 E2 Blyth r. N.T. Austr.
227 M6 Blyth Ont. Can.
149 N3 Blyth Northumberland, England U.K.
149 O7 Blyth Nottinghamshire, England U.K.
151 O3 Blyth r. England U.K.
146 J11 Blyth Bridge Scottish Borders, Scotland U.K.
241 R8 Blythe CA U.S.A.
215 P5 Blythedale Beach S. Africa
237 K8 Blytheville AR U.S.A.
87 J9 Blyth Range hills W.A. Austr.
149 P7 Blyton Lincolnshire, England U.K.
137 P5 Blyznyuky Ukr.
142 F2 Bø Norway
190 C5 Bo Sierra Leone
92 C5 Boac Phil.
242 □Q11 Boaco Nic.
182 H7 Boada Spain
186 K3 Boadella, Pantà de resr Spain
183 M8 Boadilla del Monte Spain
182 H4 Boadilla de Rioseco Spain
253 E1 Boa Esperança Amazonas Brazil
257 E4 Boa Esperança Minas Gerais Brazil
251 F4 Boa Esperança Roraima Brazil
254 E3 Boa Esperança, Açude resr Brazil
256 C4 Boa Esperança do Sul Brazil
252 B1 Boa Fé Brazil
252 D2 Boa Hora Brazil
107 M9 Bo'ai Henan China
108 F7 Bo'ai Yunnan China
148 B4 Boa Island Northern Ireland U.K.
182 G2 Boal Spain
182 D5 Boalhosa Port.
208 C3 Boali C.A.R.
232 B8 Boalsburg PA U.S.A.
215 Q2 Boane Moz.
93 E5 Boano i. Maluku Indon.
93 E5 Boano, Selat sea chan. Maluku Indon.
254 E5 Boa Nova Brazil
191 L5 Boara Pisani Italy
232 E7 Boardman OH U.S.A.
235 I1 Boardmans Bridge CT U.S.A.
146 H7 Boath Highland, Scotland U.K.
212 E4 Boatlaname Botswana
85 K9 Boatman Qld Austr.
146 I8 Boat of Garten Highland, Scotland U.K.
216 □2a Boatswain-bird Island Ascension S. Atlantic Ocean
246 C4 Boatswain Point Cayman Is
184 □ Boaventura Madeira
254 F3 Boa Viagem Brazil
251 F5 Boa Vista Amazonas Brazil
251 E5 Boa Vista Amazonas Brazil
251 F4 Boa Vista Pará Brazil
251 F4 Boa Vista Roraima Brazil
206 □ Boa Vista i. Cape Verde
182 C9 Boa Vista Port.
231 □1 Boaz Island Bermuda
83 K5 Bobadah N.S.W. Austr.
185 J6 Bobadilla Andalucía Spain
183 O4 Bobadilla La Rioja Spain
183 J6 Bobadilla del Campo Spain
108 H7 Bobai Guangxi China
213 □K1 Bobaomby, Tanjona c. Madag.
213 □K2 Bobasakoa Madag.
171 F7 Bobbau Ger.
115 H3 Bobbili Andhra Prad. India
190 G6 Bobbio Italy
190 C6 Bobbio Pellice Italy
227 P5 Bobcaygeon Ont. Can.
170 E3 Bobenheim-Roxheim Ger.
136 F2 Bober r. Ukr.
136 B4 Boberka Ukr.
183 P4 Bobia mt. Spain
182 G2 Bobia, Sierra de la mts Spain
174 E2 Bobięcińskie Wielkie, Jezioro l. Pol.
156 D6 Bobigny France
173 K6 Böbing Ger.
173 J5 Bobingen Ger.
170 D3 Bobitz Ger.
139 W6 Bobkovo Rus. Fed.
173 J2 Böblingen Ger.
175 M4 Bobly Ukr.
206 D4 Bobo-Dioulasso Burkina
174 E2 Bobolice Pol.
92 E5 Bobon Samar Phil.
213 F4 Bobonong Botswana
182 D4 Boborás Spain
177 L4 Bobota Romania
Bobotov Kuk mt. Montenegro see Durmitor
197 L8 Bobovdol Bulg.
177 L3 Bobove Ukr.
175 I6 Bobowa Pol.
175 I2 Bobowo Pol.
121 N7 Boboyob, Gora mt. Uzbek.
138 M7 Bobr Belarus
138 L7 Bobr r. Belarus
174 D3 Bóbr r. Pol.
173 O3 Böbrach Ger.
Bobriki Rus. Fed. see Novomoskovsk
Bobrinets Ukr. see Bobrynets'
135 H6 Bobrov Rus. Fed.
177 I2 Bobrov Slovakia
177 I2 Bobrovec Slovakia
Bobrovitsa Ukr. see Bobrovytsya
137 Q2 Bobrovo-Dvorskoye Rus. Fed.
137 K3 Bobrovytsya Ukr.
174 D3 Bobrowice Pol.
174 E2 Bobrówko Pol.
174 G3 Bobrowniki Kujawsko-Pomorskie Pol.
175 L2 Bobrowniki Podlaskie Pol.
175 H2 Bobrowo Pol.
Bobruysk Belarus see Babruysk
138 J9 Bobryk r. Belarus
136 J6 Bobryk-Druhyy Ukr.
137 L5 Bobrynets' Ukr.
137 P2 Bobryshevo Rus. Fed.
137 O6 Bobs Lake Ont. Can.
108 D2 Bobso Sichuan China
222 F8 Bobtown PA U.S.A.
210 B2 Bobuk Sudan
250 D2 Bobures Venez.
213 □J4 Boby mt. Madag.
179 M4 Boč hill Slovenia
181 H7 Bocacara Spain
231 G13 Boca Chica Key i. FL U.S.A.
244 B4 Boca de Camichín Mex.
183 K3 Boca de Huérgano Spain
253 D6 Boca de la Travesía Arg.
251 E2 Boca del Pao Venez.
245 K6 Boca del Río Mex.
251 F2 Boca de Macareo Venez.
251 E2 Boca de Uracoa Venez.
252 D2 Boca do Acre Brazil
252 E2 Boca do Capanã Brazil
252 F6 Boca do Curuquetê Brazil
251 I5 Boca do Jari Brazil
252 C1 Boca do Moaco Brazil
159 I4 Bocage reg. France
162 F2 Bocage Vendéen reg. France
247 □7 Boca Grande r. mouth Trin. and Tob./Venez.
257 E5 Bocaina de Minas Brazil
187 D10 Bocairent Spain
252 E2 Bocaiúva Brazil
256 C6 Bocaiúva do Sul Brazil
251 E4 Boca Mavaca Venez.
206 D5 Bocanda Côte d'Ivoire
177 J6 Bočar Vojvodina Serbia
208 B3 Bocaranga C.A.R.
231 G12 Boca Raton FL U.S.A.
245 J1 Bocas Mex.
242 □R13 Bocas del Toro Panama
242 □R13 Bocas del Toro, Archipiélago de is Panama
195 L5 Bocchigliero Italy
183 M6 Bocequillas Spain
176 F5 Bocfölde Hungary
176 F5 Bochinche Venez.
175 I6 Bochnia Pol.
165 J6 Bocholt Belgium
168 E6 Bocholt Ger.
176 C1 Bochov Czech Rep.
169 D8 Bochum Ger.
213 F4 Bochum S. Africa
170 G3 Bock i. Ger.
169 J6 Bockenem Ger.
173 K6 Bockhorn Bayern Ger.
168 F4 Bockhorn Niedersachsen Ger.
168 E4 Bockhorst Ger.
175 L5 Boćki Pol.
192 B3 Bocognano Corse France
209 B6 Bocoio Angola
177 J4 Boconád Hungary
242 F4 Bocoyna Mex.
165 G8 Bocq r. Belgium
177 J3 Bőcs Hungary
177 L6 Bocșa Caraș-Severin Romania
177 L4 Bocșa Sălaj Romania
177 K5 Bocsig Romania
174 F4 Boczów Pol.
208 C4 Boda C.A.R.
143 M3 Böda Sweden
141 K6 Boda Sweden
175 L5 Bodaczów Pol.
143 K5 Bodafors Sweden
143 L5 Boda glasbruk Sweden
177 H4 Bodajk Hungary
87 B1 Bodalla N.S.W. Austr.
87 E11 Bodallin W.A. Austr.
131 M4 Bodaybo Rus. Fed.
146 M8 Boddam Aberdeenshire, Scotland U.K.
146 □N3 Boddam Shetland, Scotland U.K.
246 C4 Bodden Town Cayman Is
170 I3 Boddin Ger.
87 D10 Boddington W.A. Austr.
171 E7 Bode r. Ger.
240 I3 Bodega Head CA U.S.A.
172 E4 Bodegraven Neth.
172 F5 Bodelshausen Ger.
150 F1 Bodelwyddan Denbighshire, Wales U.K.
140 P4 Boden Sweden
171 H6 Bodenfelde Ger.
150 G3 Bodenham Herefordshire, England U.K.
172 E2 Bodenheim Ger.
173 M5 Bodenkirchen Ger.
173 O3 Bodenmais Ger.
172 G6 Bodensee l. Ger./Switz.
168 K5 Bodenteich Ger.
169 I7 Bodenwerder Ger.
179 K4 Bodenwies mt. Austria
173 M3 Bodenwöhr Ger.
147 G5 Boderg, Lough l. Ireland
207 G4 Bode-Sadu Nigeria
197 O3 Bodești Romania
240 N6 Bodfish CA U.S.A.
114 E3 Bodhan Andhra Prad. India
117 J7 Bodh Gaya Bihar India
151 J3 Bodicote Oxfordshire, England U.K.
240 M3 Bodie CA U.S.A.
114 F7 Bodinayakkanur Tamil Nadu India
184 F4 Bodión r. Spain
172 G6 Bodman Ger.
150 C7 Bodmin Cornwall, England U.K.
150 C6 Bodmin Moor moorland England U.K.
172 H6 Bodnegg Ger.
140 M3 Bodø Norway
254 F3 Bodocó Brazil
172 H6 Bodolz Ger.
258 F4 Bodonal de la Sierra Spain
106 C4 Bodonchiyn Gol watercourse Mongolia
253 F4 Bodoquena Mato Grosso do Sul Brazil
253 F5 Bodoquena Mato Grosso do Sul Brazil
253 F5 Bodoquena, Serra da hills Brazil
208 C3 Bodoukpa C.A.R.
177 K3 Bodrog r. Hungary
177 K3 Bodroghalom Hungary
199 I5 Bodrum Turkey
126 C5 Bodrum-Milas airport Turkey
140 M5 Bodsjö Sweden
140 P3 Bodträskfors Sweden
113 □1 Boduhali i. N. Male Maldives
177 J3 Bodva r. Hungary
177 J3 Bodva r. Slovakia
177 J3 Bódvaszilas Hungary
175 I3 Bodzanów Pol.
175 I5 Bodzentyn Pol.
163 F7 Boé France
206 B4 Boé Guinea-Bissau
165 F6 Boechout Belgium
183 K5 Boecillo Spain
183 L4 Boedo r. Spain
163 L4 Boëge France
214 G4 Boegoeberg S. Africa
164 I5 Boekel Neth.
165 E6 Boëkhoute Belgium
160 E5 Boën France
208 D5 Boende Dem. Rep. Congo
93 B6 Bo Epinang Sulawesi Indon.
214 E9 Boerboonfontein S. Africa
237 F11 Boerne TX U.S.A.
215 K9 Boesmans r. S. Africa
215 K7 Boesmans hoekpas pass S. Africa
237 J10 Boeuf r. LA U.S.A.
182 H3 Boeza Spain
182 G3 Boeza r. Spain
256 C5 Bofete Brazil
206 B4 Boffa Guinea
161 F7 Boffres France
169 H7 Boffzen Ger.
147 G5 Bofin Lough l. Ireland
142 F2 Bøfjell hill Norway
140 T1 Boftsa Norway
117 O5 Boga Arun. Prad. India
177 J5 Bogács Hungary
182 G7 Bogajo Spain
210 D4 Bogal, Lagh watercourse Kenya/Somalia
96 B6 Bogale Myanmar
96 B7 Bogale r. Myanmar
237 K10 Bogalusa LA U.S.A.
83 K3 Bogan r. N.S.W. Austr.
207 E3 Bogandé Burkina
83 K5 Bogan Gate N.S.W. Austr.
208 C3 Bogangolo C.A.R.
93 C3 Bogani Nani Wartabone, Taman Nasional nat. park Indon.
85 K7 Bogantungan Qld Austr.
185 O3 Bogarra Spain
196 H6 Bogatić Serbia
130 H3 Bogatye Saby Rus. Fed.
174 C5 Bogatynia Pol.
129 I2 Bogatyrevka Rus. Fed.
126 G4 Boğazlıyan Turkey
208 C4 Bogbonga Dem. Rep. Congo
111 H11 Bogcang Zangbo r. Xizang China
177 K6 Bogda Romania
110 I5 Bogda Feng mt. Xinjiang China
197 M8 Bogdan mt. Bulg.
197 N7 Bogdana Romania
197 K9 Bogdanci Macedonia
177 K5 Bogdand Romania
174 D3 Bogdaniec Pol.
Bogdanovka Georgia see Ninotsminda
120 E1 Bogdanovka Rus. Fed.
106 A5 Bogda Shan mts China
100 A3 Bogdat' Rus. Fed.
121 O1 Bogembay Kazakh.
173 N4 Bogen Ger.
140 N2 Bogen Norway
142 G6 Bogense Denmark
83 M3 Boggabilla Qld Austr.
83 M4 Boggabri N.S.W. Austr.
78 □3a Boggenatjen i. Kwajalein Marshall Is
147 D8 Boggeragh Mountains hills Ireland
78 □3a Boggerik i. Kwajalein Marshall Is
87 D7 Boggola hill W.A. Austr.
247 □2 Boggy Peak hill Antigua and Barbuda
Boghari Alg. see Ksar el Boukhari
123 K6 Boghra Dam Afgh.
91 J7 Bogia P.N.G.
85 K6 Bogie r. Qld Austr.
146 K8 Bogie r. Scotland U.K.
190 G7 Bogliasco Italy
142 H6 Bognæs nature res. Denmark
190 E3 Bognanco Italy
146 K7 Bogniebrae Aberdeenshire, Scotland U.K.
151 K6 Bognor Regis West Sussex, England U.K.
156 I4 Bogny-sur-Meuse France
207 I4 Bogo Cameroon
142 J6 Bogø i. Denmark
170 F1 Bogø i. Denmark
92 E6 Bogo Cebu Phil.
Bogodukhov Ukr. see Bohodukhiv
121 M1 Bogodukhovka Kazakh.
147 H6 Bog of Allen reg. Ireland
100 I5 Bogoladza, Khrebet mts Rus. Fed.
210 D3 Bogol Manya Eth.
121 M1 Bogolyubovo Kazakh.
139 P6 Bogolyubovo Smolenskaya Oblast' Rus. Fed.
139 X5 Bogolyubovo Vladimirskaya Oblast' Rus. Fed.
83 K7 Bogong, Mount Vic. Austr.
94 G8 Bogor Jawa Indon.
197 N8 Bogorovo Bulg.
139 R3 Bogoroditsk Rus. Fed.
139 S8 Bogoroditskoye Rus. Fed.
134 H4 Bogorodsk Rus. Fed.
100 L2 Bogorodskoye Khabarovskiy Kray Rus. Fed.
134 J4 Bogorodskoye Kirovskaya Oblast' Rus. Fed.
220 B4 Bogoslof Island AK U.S.A.
250 C3 Bogotá Col.
177 K3 Bogota hill Slovakia
130 J4 Bogotol Rus. Fed.
134 I4 Bogovarovo Rus. Fed.
Bogoyavlenskoye Rus. Fed. see Pervomayskiy
117 L7 Bogra Bangl.
131 K4 Boguchany Rus. Fed.
135 H6 Boguchar Rus. Fed.
137 T4 Boguchar r. Rus. Fed.
175 J6 Boguchwała Pol.
206 B2 Bogué Maur.
237 K10 Bogue Chitto r. MS U.S.A.
Boguslav Ukr. see Bohuslav
175 H4 Boguslaw Pol.
246 □ Bog Walk Jamaica
177 H5 Bogyiszló Hungary
95 K4 Boh r. Indon.
107 P7 Bo Hai g. China
107 O7 Bohai Haixia sea chan. China
156 F4 Bohain-en-Vermandois France
107 O7 Bohai Wan b. China
158 C5 Bohars France
136 D5 Bohdan Ukr.
137 O7 Bohdanivka Ukr.
179 M3 Böheimkirchen Austria
Bohemia reg. Czech Rep. see Čechy
235 I3 Bohemia NY U.S.A.
86 I5 Bohemia Downs W.A. Austr.
86 I5 Bohemia Downs Aboriginal Reserve W.A. Austr.
Bohemian Forest mts Ger. see Böhmer Wald
147 F7 Boher Ireland
148 B7 Boheraphuca Ireland
207 F5 Bohicon Benin
179 I7 Bohinjska Bistrica Slovenia
179 I7 Bohinjsko jezero l. Slovenia
138 J6 Bohinskaye, Vozyera l. Belarus
171 E8 Böhl Ger.
171 F8 Böhlen Ger.
171 F8 Böhlitz-Ehrenberg Ger.
215 M4 Bohlokong S. Africa
168 H5 Böhme Ger.
168 H5 Böhme r. Ger.
Böhmen reg. Czech Rep. see Čechy
173 M2 Böhmer Wald mts Ger.
169 F6 Bohmte Ger.
170 F5 Böhne Ger.
137 O3 Bohodukhiv Ukr.
137 L4 Bohodukhivka Ukr.
92 E7 Bohol i. Phil.
147 D5 Bohola Ireland
92 E7 Bohol Sea Phil.
92 D7 Bohol Strait Phil.
176 G5 Böhönye Hungary
179 L7 Bohor mt. Slovenia
136 D5 Bohorodchany Ukr.
107 K4 Böhöt Mongolia
183 J8 Bohoyo Spain
116 E1 Bohrt Jammu and Kashmir
110 H6 Bohu Xinjiang China
177 H2 Bohumín Czech Rep.
176 G2 Bohuňovice Czech Rep.
142 H3 Bohuslän reg. Sweden
136 J4 Bohuslav Ukr.
176 C2 Bohutín Czech Rep.
163 C10 Boí France
192 C9 Boi, Capo c. Sardegna Italy
257 E5 Boi, Ponta do pt Brazil
251 F5 Boiaçu Brazil
177 L4 Boianu Mare Romania
214 H4 Boichoko S. Africa
91 J8 Boigu Island Qld Austr.
215 K2 Boikhutso S. Africa
213 H3 Boila Moz.
86 G4 Boileau, Cape W.A. Austr.
234 A4 Boiling Springs PA U.S.A.
251 H5 Boim Brazil
210 B2 Boing Sudan
96 A3 Boinu r. Myanmar
254 F5 Boipeba, Ilha i. Brazil
182 C3 Boiro de Arriba Spain
256 B3 Bois r. Brazil
220 F3 Bois, Lac des l. N.W.T. Can.
217 □1c Bois-Blanc Réunion
226 J3 Bois Blanc Island MI U.S.A.
258 C3 Boischaut reg. France
156 D7 Boiscommun France
160 I3 Bois-d'Amont France
236 C3 Bois de Sioux r. MN U.S.A.
238 F5 Boise ID U.S.A.
238 F5 Boise r. ID U.S.A.
237 D7 Boise City OK U.S.A.
158 G5 Boisgervilly France
156 B5 Bois-Guillaume France
156 E7 Bois-le-Roi France
161 E9 Boisseron France
163 I6 Boisset France
161 E8 Boisset-et-Gaujac France
223 K5 Boissevain Man. Can.
163 I8 Boisson France
191 M3 Boite r. Italy
215 J3 Boitumelong S. Africa
256 D5 Boituva Brazil
170 I4 Boitzenburg Ger.
162 E2 Boivre r. France
168 I4 Boize r. Ger.
168 K4 Boizenburg Ger.
174 D4 Bojadła Pol.
193 M5 Bojano Italy
175 J5 Bojanów Pol.
174 E4 Bojanowo Pol.
92 C2 Bojeador, Cape Luzon Phil.
177 H3 Bojná Slovakia
177 H3 Bojnice Slovakia
197 J7 Bojnik Serbia
122 G3 Bojnurd Iran
95 I8 Bojonegoro Jawa Indon.
94 G8 Bojong Jawa Indon.
207 H5 Boju-Ega Nigeria
258 H3 Bojuru Brazil
208 C3 Bokada Dem. Rep. Congo
117 N6 Bokajan Assam India
120 D5 Bokanda Congo
Bo'kantov tog'lari hills Uzbek.
116 J8 Bokaro Jharkhand India
93 B3 Bokat Sulawesi Indon.
208 C5 Bokatola Dem. Rep. Congo
206 B4 Boké Guinea
121 S3 Boke Kazakh.
168 G4 Bokel Ger.
208 D5 Bokela Dem. Rep. Congo
208 D4 Bokenda Dem. Rep. Congo
215 L5 Bokfontein S. Africa
83 K3 Bokhara r. N.S.W. Austr.
Bo Kheo Cambodia see Bå Kêv
207 I5 Bokito Cameroon
168 I1 Boklund Ger.
142 B2 Boknafjorden sea chan. Norway
209 B6 Boko Congo
209 C6 Boko Dem. Rep. Congo
177 H4 Bokod Hungary
208 C4 Bokode Dem. Rep. Congo
208 E3 Bokoko Dem. Rep. Congo
208 A5 Bokolo Gabon
Bokombayevskoye Kyrg. see Bökönbaev
121 Q6 Bökönbaev Kyrg.
Bokonbayevo Kyrg. see Bökönbaev
215 M5 Bokong Lesotho
177 K4 Bököny Hungary
202 C6 Bokoro Chad
208 C5 Bokoro Dem. Rep. Congo
209 B6 Boko-Songho Congo
208 D5 Bokote Dem. Rep. Congo
Bokovo-Antratsit Ukr. see Antratsyt
135 H6 Bokovskaya Rus. Fed.
214 C9 Bokpunt pt S. Africa
97 D9 Bokpyin Myanmar
215 M2 Boksburg S. Africa
139 Q2 Boksitogorsk Rus. Fed.
214 E2 Bokspits S. Africa
100 J3 Boktor Rus. Fed.
208 D5 Bokungu Dem. Rep. Congo
122 H2 Bokurdak Turkm.
208 D5 Bokwankusu Dem. Rep. Congo
202 B6 Bol Chad
208 C2 Bola, Bahr watercourse Chad
93 C4 Bolaang Sulawesi Indon.
244 D5 Bolaños r. Mex.
209 E5 Bolaiti Dem. Rep. Congo
206 B4 Bolama Guinea-Bissau
123 L7 Bolan r. Pak.
208 E3 Bolanda, Jebel mt. Sudan
172 E2 Bolanden Ger.
160 I2 Bolandoz France
117 I9 Bolangir Orissa India
190 H7 Bolano Italy
244 C4 Bolaños r. Mex.
78 □1 Bolanos, Mount Guam
185 L3 Bolaños de Calatrava Spain
123 L7 Bolan Pass Pak.
183 O8 Bolarque, Embalse de resr Spain
162 F3 Bolbec France
207 F3 Bolbol Niger
177 H5 Bölcske Hungary
122 D6 Boldajī Iran
170 I3 Boldekow Ger.
168 H1 Bolderslev Denmark
177 I5 Boldogkőváralja Hungary
149 O4 Boldon Tyne and Wear, England U.K.
151 I6 Boldre Hampshire, England U.K.
197 P5 Boldu Romania
122 H1 Boldumsaz Turkm.
177 K6 Boldur Romania
177 J5 Boldva Hungary
110 F4 Bole Xinjiang China
206 E4 Bole Ghana
186 D3 Bolea Spain
136 C4 Bolekhiv Ukr.
208 C5 Boleko Dem. Rep. Congo
100 I3 Bolen Rus. Fed.
208 C4 Bolena Dem. Rep. Congo
177 G3 Boleráz Slovakia
175 I5 Bolesław Pol.
174 D4 Bolesławiec Dolnośląskie Pol.
174 G4 Bolesławiec Łódzkie Pol.
174 C3 Boleszkowice Pol.
135 J5 Bolgar Rus. Fed.
206 E4 Bolgatanga Ghana
138 L5 Bolgatovo Rus. Fed.
Bolgrad Ukr. see Bolhrad
136 H8 Bolhrad Ukr.
100 G6 Boli Heilong. China
208 F3 Boli Sudan
208 C5 Bolia Dem. Rep. Congo
140 P4 Boliden Sweden
Bolifuri i. S. Male Maldives see Bolifushi
113 □1 Bolifushi i. S. Male Maldives
175 J5 Bolimów Pol.
167 J2 Bolimowski Park Krajobrazowy Pol.
92 B3 Bolinao Luzon Phil.
197 N6 Bolintin-Vale Romania
250 B3 Bolívar Antioquia Col.
250 B4 Bolívar Cauca Col.
250 C2 Bolívar dept Col.
252 A1 Bolívar Peru
237 I7 Bolivar MO U.S.A.
232 G6 Bolivar NY U.S.A.
237 K8 Bolivar TN U.S.A.
251 F3 Bolívar state Venez.
252 D4 Bolivia country S. America
197 J7 Boljevac Serbia
128 B1 Bolkar Dağları mts Turkey
139 T8 Bolkhov Rus. Fed.
227 K1 Bolkow Ont. Can.
170 E2 Bölkow Ger.
174 E5 Bolków Pol.
172 H4 Boll Ger.
142 I4 Bollebygd Sweden
260 B3 Bollenar Chile
161 F8 Bollène France
190 D5 Bollengo Italy
190 C2 Bolligen Switz.
168 H1 Bollingstedt Ger.
149 M7 Bollington Cheshire, England U.K.
141 N6 Bollnäs Sweden
83 K3 Bollon Qld Austr.
142 I2 Bollsbyn Sweden
172 D6 Bollschweil Ger.
140 N5 Bollstabruk Sweden
166 E3 Bollstedt Ger.
184 F6 Bollullos Par del Condado Spain
157 N8 Bollwiller France
143 J5 Bolmen l. Sweden
151 I3 Bolnhurst Bedfordshire, England U.K.
129 F4 Bolnisi Georgia
92 D6 Bolo Panay Phil.
208 C5 Bolobo Dem. Rep. Congo
92 C8 Bolod Islands Phil.
100 I3 Bolodzhak Rus. Fed.
191 K7 Bologna Italy
191 K7 Bologna prov. Italy
157 J7 Bologne France
250 C6 Bolognesi Loreto Peru
252 B2 Bolognesi Ucayali Peru
194 E8 Bolognetta Sicilia Italy
193 K2 Bolognola Italy
139 O5 Bologovo Rus. Fed.
139 R4 Bologoye Rus. Fed.
215 J5 Bolokanang S. Africa
139 U7 Bolokhovo Rus. Fed.
208 C4 Bolomba Dem. Rep. Congo
208 D4 Bolomba r. Dem. Rep. Congo
Bolon' Rus. Fed. see Achan
243 O7 Bolonchén de Rejón Mex.
208 C5 Bolondo Dem. Rep. Congo
207 H6 Bolondo Equat. Guinea
92 D8 Bolong Mindanao Phil.
209 B7 Bolongongo Angola
192 B7 Bolotana Sardegna Italy
139 P2 Bolotovo Rus. Fed.
215 L7 Bolotwa S. Africa
96 H7 Bolovens, Phouphieng plat. Laos
208 B4 Bolozo Congo
252 C2 Bolpebra Bol.
117 K8 Bolpur W. Bengal India
129 J6 Bolqarçay r. Azer.
258 C3 Bolsa, Cerro mt. Arg.
192 H2 Bolsena Italy
192 H2 Bolsena, Lago di l. Italy
138 E7 Bol'shakovo Rus. Fed.
129 H1 Bol'shaya Areshevka Rus. Fed.
134 J4 Bol'shaya Atnya Rus. Fed.
137 R1 Bol'shaya Bereyka Rus. Fed.
137 R1 Bol'shaya Boyevka Rus. Fed.
120 D1 Bol'shaya Chernigovka Rus. Fed.
120 K1 Bol'shaya Churakovka Kazakh.
120 D1 Bol'shaya Glushitsa Rus. Fed.
134 F2 Bol'shaya Imandra, Ozero l. Rus. Fed.
137 Q3 Bol'shaya Khalan' Rus. Fed.
134 I4 Bol'shaya Kokshaga r. Rus. Fed.
139 Q5 Bol'shaya Kosha Rus. Fed.
137 U1 Bol'shaya Lipovitsa Rus. Fed.
135 H7 Bol'shaya Martinovka Rus. Fed.
Bol'shaya Novoselka Ukr. see Velyka Novosilka
134 M1 Bol'shaya Oyu r. Rus. Fed.
134 J2 Bol'shaya Pyssa Rus. Fed.
134 M2 Bol'shaya Rogovaya r. Rus. Fed.
134 L2 Bol'shaya Synya r. Rus. Fed.
Bol'shaya Tsarevshchina Rus. Fed. see Volzhskiy
134 K4 Bol'shaya Usa Rus. Fed.
139 P3 Bol'shaya Vishera Rus. Fed.
121 R2 Bol'shaya Vladimirovka Kazakh.
137 R3 Bol'she Bykovo Rus. Fed.
137 S6 Bol'shekrepinskaya Rus. Fed.
121 U3 Bol'shenarymskoye Kazakh.
139 S4 Bol'she-Ploskoye Rus. Fed.
131 Q4 Bol'sheretsk Rus. Fed.
137 Q3 Bol'shetroitskoye Rus. Fed.
131 L2 Bol'shevik, Ostrov i. Severnaya Zemlya Rus. Fed.
134 K2 Bol'shezemel'skaya Tundra lowland Rus. Fed.
120 H4 Bol'shiye Barsuki, Peski des. Kazakh.
134 I3 Bol'shiye Chirki Rus. Fed.
134 G2 Bol'shiye Kozly Rus. Fed.
139 U8 Bol'shiye Medvedki Rus. Fed.
120 D4 Bol'shiye Peshnyye, Ostrova is Kazakh.
137 S6 Bol'shiye Saly Rus. Fed.
121 R6 Bol'shoy Aksu Kazakh.
120 K2 Bol'shoy Aksuat, Ozero salt l. Kazakh.
131 Q3 Bol'shoy Aluy r. Rus. Fed.
131 R3 Bol'shoy Anyuy r. Rus. Fed.
131 M2 Bol'shoy Begichev, Ostrov i. Rus. Fed.
138 L1 Bol'shoy Berezovyy, Ostrov i. Rus. Fed.
121 T3 Bol'shoy Bukon' Kazakh.
139 V6 Bol'shoye Alekseyevskoye Rus. Fed.
139 P6 Bol'shoye Beresnevo Rus. Fed.
137 Q3 Bol'shoye Gorodishche Rus. Fed.
135 I5 Bol'shoye Ignatovo Rus. Fed.
139 W7 Bol'shoye Korovino Rus. Fed.
139 V5 Bol'shoye Mikhaylovskoye Rus. Fed.

Bol'shoye Murashkino to Bovey

290

134 I5 **Bol'shoye Murashkino** Rus. Fed.
140 V2 **Bol'shoye Ozerko** Rus. Fed.
139 R8 **Bol'shoye Polpino** Rus. Fed.
139 W9 **Bol'shoye Popovo** Rus. Fed.
134 G4 **Bol'shoye Selo** Rus. Fed.
137 O2 **Bol'shoye Soldatskoye** Rus. Fed.
121 R1 **Bol'shoye Topol'noye, Ozero** *salt l.* Rus. Fed.
139 Q3 **Bol'shoye Zaborov'ye** Rus. Fed.
139 V7 **Bol'shoye Zhokovo** Rus. Fed.
120 F2 **Bol'shoy Ik** *r.* Rus. Fed.
120 B2 **Bol'shoy Irgiz** *r.* Rus. Fed.
100 H7 **Bol'shoy Kamen'** Rus. Fed.
Bol'shoy Kavkaz *mts* Asia/Europe *see* **Caucasus**
139 W9 **Bol'shoy Khomutets** Rus. Fed.
139 Q1 **Bol'shoy Kokovichi** Rus. Fed.
129 F1 **Bol'shoy Levoberezhnyy, Kanal** *canal* Rus. Fed.
131 P2 **Bol'shoy Lyakhovskiy, Ostrov** *i. Novosibirskiye O-va* Rus. Fed.
134 L2 **Bol'shoy Patok** *r.* Rus. Fed.
131 K3 **Bol'shoy Porog** Rus. Fed.
131 O4 **Bol'shoy Shantar, Ostrov** *i.* Rus. Fed.
Bol'shoy Tokmak Kyrg. *see* **Tokmok**
Bol'shoy Tokmak Ukr. *see* **Tokmak**
139 O4 **Bol'shoy Tuder** *r.* Rus. Fed.
138 K2 **Bol'shoy Tyuters, Ostrov** *i.* Estonia
120 C3 **Bol'shoy Uzen'** *r.* Kazakh./Rus. Fed.
129 C1 **Bol'shoy Zelenchuk** *r.* Rus. Fed.
242 G4 **Bolsón de Mapimí** *des.* Mex.
149 O7 **Bolsover** *Derbyshire, England* U.K.
164 I2 **Bolsward** Neth.
174 G1 **Bolszewo** Pol.
186 F3 **Boltaña** Spain
149 O5 **Boltby** *North Yorkshire, England* U.K.
170 D3 **Boltenhagen, Ostseebad** Ger.
150 E7 **Bolt Head** *England* U.K.
190 C2 **Boltigen** Switz.
227 O6 **Bolton** *Ont.* Can.
92 E8 **Bolton** *Mindanao* Phil.
149 M6 **Bolton** *Greater Manchester, England* U.K.
149 L5 **Bolton-le-Sands** *Lancashire, England* U.K.
139 P7 **Boltutino** Rus. Fed.
137 N5 **Boltyshka** Ukr.
126 E3 **Bolu** Turkey
199 M2 **Bolu** *prov.* Turkey
140 □B1 **Bolungarvík** Iceland
111 K8 **Boluntay** *Qinghai* China
109 J7 **Boluo** *Guangdong* China
147 B9 **Bolus Head** Ireland
139 R8 **Bolva** *r.* Rus. Fed.
199 M4 **Bolvadin** Turkey
150 C6 **Bolventor** *Cornwall, England* U.K.
177 H6 **Bóly** Hungary
197 O8 **Bolyarovo** Bulg.
191 K3 **Bolzano** Italy
191 K2 **Bolzano** *prov.* Italy
209 B6 **Boma** Dem. Rep. Congo
83 M6 **Bomaderry** *N.S.W.* Austr.
207 G5 **Bomadi** Nigeria
108 B4 **Bomai** *Sichuan* China
165 I8 **Bomal** Belgium
208 C4 **Bomassa** Congo
193 M3 **Bomba** Italy
83 L7 **Bombala** *N.S.W.* Austr.
184 A2 **Bombarral** Port.
Bombay *Mahar.* India *see* **Mumbai**
80 I4 **Bombay** *North I.* N.Z.
241 Q8 **Bombay Beach** *CA* U.S.A.
91 H7 **Bomberai, Semenanjung** *pen. Papua* Indon.
209 B5 **Bombo** *r.* Dem. Rep. Congo
210 B4 **Bombo** Uganda
207 G6 **Bom Bom, Ilha** *i.* São Tomé and Príncipe
208 C4 **Bomboma** Dem. Rep. Congo
252 D2 **Bom Comércio** Brazil
257 E3 **Bom Despacho** Brazil
117 N6 **Bomdila** *Arun. Prad.* India
150 G2 **Bomere Heath** *Shropshire, England* U.K.
111 L12 **Bomi** *Xizang* China
208 E4 **Bomili** Dem. Rep. Congo
252 D2 **Bom Jardim** *Amazonas* Brazil
251 I5 **Bom Jardim** *Pará* Brazil
254 G3 **Bom Jardim** *Pernambuco* Brazil
256 A2 **Bom Jardim de Goiás** Brazil
257 E4 **Bom Jardim de Minas** Brazil
209 B7 **Bom Jesus** Angola
254 D4 **Bom Jesus** *Piauí* Brazil
255 C9 **Bom Jesus** *Rio Grande do Sul* Brazil
254 E4 **Bom Jesus da Gurgueia, Serra do** *hills* Brazil
254 E5 **Bom Jesus da Lapa** Brazil
256 C3 **Bom Jesus de Goiás** Brazil
257 G4 **Bom Jesus do Itabapoana** Brazil
257 G4 **Bom Jesus do Norte** Brazil
142 B2 **Bomlafjorden** *sea chan.* Norway
168 I5 **Bomlitz** Ger.
142 B2 **Bømlo** *i.* Norway
208 E4 **Bomokandi** *r.* Dem. Rep. Congo
208 C4 **Bomongo** Dem. Rep. Congo
163 J10 **Bompas** France
194 F9 **Bompensiere** *Sicilia* Italy
194 G8 **Bompietro** *Sicilia* Italy
255 C8 **Bom Retiro** Brazil
257 E4 **Bom Sucesso** *Minas Gerais* Brazil
256 B5 **Bom Sucesso** *Paraná* Brazil
208 D3 **Bomu, Réserve de Faune de la** *nature res.* Dem. Rep. Congo
205 H1 **Bon, Cap** *c.* Tunisia
97 C10 **Bon, Ko** *i.* Thai.
Bona Alg. *see* **Annaba**
160 C2 **Bona** France
122 B3 **Bonāb** Iran
163 F10 **Bonac-Irazein** France
190 G2 **Bonaduz** Switz.
232 H11 **Bon Air** *VA* U.S.A.
247 □8 **Bonaire** *i.* Neth. Antilles
83 N3 **Bonalbo** *N.S.W.* Austr.
195 K7 **Bonamico** *r.* Italy
94 C4 **Bonandolok** *Sumatera* Indon.
242 □Q11 **Bonanza** Nic.
184 G7 **Bonanza** Spain
246 H4 **Bonao** Dom. Rep.
86 H3 **Bonaparte Archipelago** *is W.A.* Austr.
222 F5 **Bonaparte Lake** *B.C.* Can.
183 J3 **Boñar** Spain
146 H7 **Bonar Bridge** *Highland, Scotland* U.K.
192 B7 **Bonarcado** *Sardegna* Italy
247 □7 **Bonasse** Trin. and Tob.
190 H7 **Bonassola** Italy
225 K3 **Bonavista** *Nfld and Lab.* Can.
225 K3 **Bonavista Bay** *Nfld and Lab.* Can.
160 H2 **Bonboillon** France
82 E4 **Bon Bon** *S.A.* Austr.
159 J5 **Bonchamp-lès-Laval** France
146 K12 **Bonchester Bridge** *Scottish Borders, Scotland* U.K.
190 C1 **Boncourt** Switz.
137 S4 **Bondarevo** Rus. Fed.
135 H5 **Bondari** Rus. Fed.
191 K6 **Bondeno** Italy
208 D5 **Bondo** *Équateur* Dem. Rep. Congo
208 D4 **Bondo** *Orientale* Dem. Rep. Congo
92 D5 **Bondoc Peninsula** *Luzon* Phil.
93 A8 **Bondokodi** *Sumba* Indon.
172 F4 **Bondorf** Ger.
206 E4 **Bondoukou** Côte d'Ivoire
206 E4 **Bondoukui** Burkina
95 J8 **Bondowoso** *Jawa* Indon.
231 I13 **Bonds Cay** *i.* Bahamas
226 F5 **Bonduel** *WI* U.S.A.
156 F2 **Bondues** France
134 K3 **Bondyug** Rus. Fed.
Bondyuzhskiy Rus. Fed. *see* **Mendeleyevsk**
Bône Alg. *see* **Annaba**
93 C6 **Bone** *Sulawesi* Indon.
93 B6 **Bone, Teluk** *b.* Indon.
168 J2 **Bönebüttel** Ger.
207 G6 **Bone de Jókei, Ilha** *i.* São Tomé and Príncipe
231 □2 **Bonefish Pond** *New Prov.* Bahamas
193 N4 **Bonefro** Italy
214 E7 **Bonekraal** S. Africa
226 B4 **Bone Lake** *WI* U.S.A.
93 C6 **Bonelipu** *Sulawesi* Indon.
169 E7 **Bönen** Ger.
163 F7 **Bon-Encontre** France
93 B7 **Bonerate** *Sulawesi* Indon.
93 B7 **Bonerate** *i.* Indon.
93 B7 **Bonerate, Kepulauan** *is* Indon.
146 I10 **Bo'ness** *Falkirk, Scotland* U.K.
236 F4 **Bonesteel** *SD* U.S.A.
187 C10 **Bonete** Spain
258 C2 **Bonete, Cerro** *mt.* Arg.
257 E4 **Bonfim** Brazil
256 A2 **Bonfim** *r.* Brazil
257 E2 **Bonfinópolis de Minas** Brazil
210 C3 **Bonga** Eth.
92 C5 **Bongabong** *Mindoro* Phil.
117 M6 **Bongaigaon** *Assam* India
208 D4 **Bongandanga** Dem. Rep. Congo
214 H5 **Bongani** S. Africa
92 B9 **Bongao** Phil.
85 N9 **Bongaree** *Qld* Austr.
111 E10 **Bongba** *Xizang* China
111 J11 **Bong Co** *l.* China
93 B4 **Bongka** *r.* Indon.
206 C5 **Bong Mountains** *hills* Liberia
209 D6 **Bongo** Dem. Rep. Congo
92 E8 **Bongo** *i.* Phil.
208 D2 **Bongo, Massif des** *mts* C.A.R.
209 B7 **Bongo, Serra do** *mts* Angola
213 □J3 **Bongolava** *mts* Madag.
208 B2 **Bongor** Chad
206 D5 **Bongouanou** Côte d'Ivoire
208 B5 **Bongoville** Gabon
97 I7 **Bông Sơn** Vietnam
237 G9 **Bonham** *TX* U.S.A.
140 O5 **Bönhamn** Sweden
206 E3 **Boni** Mali
183 Q9 **Boniches** Spain
206 D4 **Boniérédougou** Côte d'Ivoire
174 G3 **Boniewo** Pol.
192 C5 **Bonifacio** *Corse* France
Bonifacio, Bocche di *str.* France/Italy *see* Bonifacio, Strait of
Bonifacio, Bouches de *str.* France/Italy *see* Bonifacio, Strait of
192 B5 **Bonifacio, Strait of** France/Italy
193 P8 **Bonifati** Italy
231 E10 **Bonifay** *FL* U.S.A.
190 D2 **Bönigen** Switz.
174 E1 **Bonin** Pol.
211 D5 **Boni National Reserve** *nature res.* Kenya
Bonin Islands N. Pacific Ocean *see* **Ogasawara-shotō**
231 G12 **Bonita Springs** *FL* U.S.A.
253 F5 **Bonito** Brazil
256 B2 **Bonito** *r.* Brazil
146 K12 **Bonjedward** *Scottish Borders, Scotland* U.K.
94 D4 **Bonjol** *Sumatera* Indon.
207 F3 **Bonkoukou** Niger
169 D9 **Bonn** Ger.
Bonna Ger. *see* **Bonn**
163 H9 **Bonnac** France
192 B6 **Bonnanaro** *Sardegna* Italy
162 H3 **Bonnat** France
160 F3 **Bonnay** France
172 E6 **Bonndorf im Schwarzwald** Ger.
161 H7 **Bonne** *r.* France
234 A5 **Bonneauville** *PA* U.S.A.
163 E9 **Bonnefont** France
238 F2 **Bonners Ferry** *ID* U.S.A.
142 G5 **Bønnerup Strand** Denmark
223 M5 **Bonnet, Lac du** *resr Man.* Can.
159 L5 **Bonnétable** France
159 M8 **Bonneuil-Matours** France
156 B7 **Bonneval** *Centre* France
160 J5 **Bonneval** *Rhône-Alpes* France
161 K6 **Bonneval-sur-Arc** France
160 I3 **Bonnevaux** France
160 I4 **Bonneville** France
82 H7 **Bonney, Lake** *S.A.* Austr.
156 C5 **Bonnières-sur-Seine** France
87 E11 **Bonnie Rock** *W.A.* Austr.
161 G9 **Bonnieux** France
214 E9 **Bonnievale** S. Africa
172 G3 **Bönnigheim** Ger.
168 I3 **Bönningstedt** Ger.
163 C8 **Bonnut** France
207 G5 **Bonny** Nigeria
146 I10 **Bonnybridge** *Falkirk, Scotland* U.K.
85 J4 **Bonny Glen Aboriginal Holding** *res. Qld* Austr.
215 N6 **Bonny Ridge** S. Africa
146 J11 **Bonnyrigg** *Midlothian, Scotland* U.K.
233 □S3 **Bonny River** *N.B.* Can.
160 B1 **Bonny-sur-Loire** France
223 I4 **Bonnyville** *Alta* Can.
158 F6 **Bono** France
192 C7 **Bono** *Sardegna* Italy
92 A7 **Bonobono** *Palawan* Phil.
103 H15 **Bōno-misaki** *pt* Japan
Bononia Italy *see* **Bologna**
192 B7 **Bonorva** *Sardegna* Italy
206 E5 **Bonoua** Côte d'Ivoire
261 I1 **Bonpland** Arg.
81 C11 **Bonpland, Mount** *South I.* N.Z.
240 O8 **Bonsall** *CA* U.S.A.
160 I4 **Bons-en-Chablais** France
83 M3 **Bonshaw** *N.S.W.* Austr.
160 E5 **Bonson** France
95 L4 **Bontang** *Kalimantan* Indon.
214 F8 **Bontberg** *mt.* S. Africa
214 D9 **Bonteberg** *mts* S. Africa
214 E10 **Bontebok National Park** S. Africa
206 B5 **Bonthe** Sierra Leone
92 C3 **Bontoc** *Luzon* Phil.
93 B7 **Bontomatane** *Sulawesi* Indon.
93 A6 **Bontosunggu** *Sulawesi* Indon.
215 N6 **Bontrand** S. Africa
215 J9 **Bontrug** S. Africa
177 G4 **Bőny** Hungary
177 H5 **Bonyhád** Hungary
84 B7 **Bonython Range** *hills N.T.* Austr.
143 O2 **Boo** Sweden
93 F4 **Boo, Kepulauan** *is Papua* Indon.
217 □2a **Booby Island** *Inner Islands* Seychelles
170 J4 **Boock** Ger.
87 G8 **Boodie Boodie Range** *hills W.A.* Austr.
82 D4 **Bookabie** *S.A.* Austr.
241 W2 **Book Cliffs** *ridge UT* U.S.A.
208 D5 **Booke** Dem. Rep. Congo
237 E7 **Booker** *TX* U.S.A.
206 C4 **Boola** Guinea
83 L3 **Boolba** *Qld* Austr.
82 G5 **Booleroo Centre** *S.A.* Austr.
147 H8 **Booley Hills** Ireland
83 J5 **Booligal** *N.S.W.* Austr.
87 C8 **Boologooro** *W.A.* Austr.
83 L3 **Boomi** *N.S.W.* Austr.
226 I5 **Boon** *MI* U.S.A.
85 N9 **Boonah** *Qld* Austr.
239 L7 **Boone** *CO* U.S.A.
236 I4 **Boone** *IA* U.S.A.
231 G7 **Boone** *NC* U.S.A.
232 C12 **Boone Lake** *TN* U.S.A.
232 F11 **Boones Mill** *VA* U.S.A.
237 I8 **Booneville** *AR* U.S.A.
232 B11 **Booneville** *KY* U.S.A.
237 K8 **Booneville** *MS* U.S.A.
247 □2 **Boon Point** Antigua and Barbuda
215 L1 **Boons** S. Africa
232 H9 **Boonsboro** *MD* U.S.A.
235 G3 **Boonton** *NJ* U.S.A.
106 F4 **Böön Tsagaan Nuur** *salt l.* Mongolia
240 I3 **Boonville** *CA* U.S.A.
230 D6 **Boonville** *IN* U.S.A.
236 I6 **Boonville** *MO* U.S.A.
233 J5 **Boonville** *NY* U.S.A.
252 D3 **Boopi** *r.* Bol.
87 F11 **Boorabin National Park** *W.A.* Austr.
210 D2 **Boorama** Somalia
83 J6 **Booroorban** *N.S.W.* Austr.
83 L6 **Boorowa** *N.S.W.* Austr.
83 I7 **Boort** *Vic.* Austr.
165 G7 **Boortmeerbeek** Belgium
156 B5 **Boos** France
173 I5 **Boos** Ger.
210 F2 **Boosaaso** Somalia
168 J2 **Boostedt** Ger.
233 □P5 **Boothbay Harbor** *ME* U.S.A.
263 D2 **Boothby, Cape** Antarctica
221 J3 **Boothia, Gulf of** *Nunavut* Can.
221 I2 **Boothia Peninsula** *Nunavut* Can.
149 K5 **Bootle** *Cumbria, England* U.K.
149 L7 **Bootle** *Merseyside, England* U.K.
208 A5 **Booué** Gabon
173 I4 **Bopfingen** Ger.
206 C5 **Bopolu** Liberia
169 E10 **Boppard** Ger.
111 J11 **Boqê** *Xizang* China
258 G3 **Boqueirão** Brazil
254 D5 **Boqueirão, Serra do** *hills* Brazil
247 □1 **Boquerón** Puerto Rico
242 G4 **Boquilla, Presa de la** *resr* Mex.
242 H3 **Boquillas del Carmen** Mex.
242 H5 **Boquillas del Refugio** Mex.
176 B2 **Bor** Czech Rep.
134 I4 **Bor** Rus. Fed.
197 K6 **Bor** Serbia
210 A3 **Bor** Sudan
126 G5 **Bor** Turkey
210 D4 **Bor, Lagh** *watercourse* Kenya/Somalia
79 □9 **Bora-Bora** *is Arch. de la Société* Fr. Polynesia
129 J7 **Boradigah** Azer.
211 C5 **Boragi** *waterhole* Kenya
213 □K3 **Boraha, Nosy** *i.* Madag.
238 H4 **Borah Peak** *ID* U.S.A.
116 H9 **Borai** *Chhattisgarh* India
215 L1 **Borakalalo Nature Reserve** S. Africa
Boran Kazakh. *see* **Buran**
156 D5 **Boran-sur-Oise** France
96 E7 **Boraphet, Bung** *l.* Thai.
Boraraigh *i. Western Isles, Scotland* U.K. *see* **Boreray**
142 I4 **Borås** Sweden
117 I9 **Borasambar** *Orissa* India
122 D7 **Borāzjān** Iran
251 G6 **Borba** Brazil
184 E3 **Borba** Port.
190 F6 **Borbera** *r.* Italy
182 G8 **Borbollón, Embalse del** *resr* Spain
92 E6 **Borbon** *Cebu* Phil.
190 E6 **Borbore** *r.* Italy
256 C4 **Borborema** Brazil
254 F3 **Borborema, Planalto da** *plat.* Brazil
197 N3 **Borca** Romania
197 P6 **Borcea, Braţul** *watercourse* Romania
Borchalo Georgia *see* **Marneuli**
169 G7 **Borchen** Ger.
263 K2 **Borchgrevink Coast** Antarctica
127 J3 **Borçka** Turkey
164 K4 **Borculo** Neth.
86 G4 **Borda, Cape** *W.A.* Austr.
256 D5 **Borda da Mata** Brazil
199 K5 **Bor Dağı** *mt.* Turkey
183 P6 **Bordalba** Spain
177 I5 **Bordány** Hungary
163 C6 **Bordeaux** France
116 G8 **Bordehi** *Madh. Prad.* India
203 G6 **Bordein** Sudan
184 B6 **Bordeira** Port.
168 G1 **Bordelum** Ger.
87 E13 **Borden** *W.A.* Austr.
225 I4 **Borden-Carleton** *P.E.I.* Can.
221 G2 **Borden Island** *N.W.T.* Can.
221 J2 **Borden Peninsula** *Nunavut* Can.
234 F4 **Bordentown** *NJ* U.S.A.
163 E10 **Bordères-Louron** France
163 E9 **Bordères-sur-l'Échez** France
83 N3 **Border Ranges National Park** *N.S.W.* Austr.
Borders *admin. div. Scotland* U.K. *see* **Scottish Borders**
82 H7 **Bordertown** *S.A.* Austr.
163 D9 **Bordes** *Aquitaine* France
163 E9 **Bordes** *Midi-Pyrénées* France
168 J2 **Bordesholm** Ger.
140 □C1 **Borðeyri** Iceland
190 D8 **Bordighera** Italy
186 K3 **Bordils** Spain
194 D8 **Bordino** *r. Sicilia* Italy
205 G1 **Bordj Bou Arréridj** Alg.
204 E4 **Bordj Flye Ste-Marie** Alg.
205 H3 **Bordj Messaouda** Alg.
205 F5 **Bordj Mokhtar** Alg.
Bordj Omar Driss Alg. *see* **Bordj Omer Driss**
205 G3 **Bordj Omer Driss** Alg.
186 E6 **Bordón** Spain
144 D1 **Borðoy** *i.* Faroe Is
121 P6 **Bordu** Kyrg.
Bordunskiy Kyrg. *see* **Bordu**
197 P6 **Borduşani** Romania
190 H6 **Bore** Italy
206 E3 **Boré** Mali
262 X2 **Boreas Nunatak** Antarctica
151 N4 **Boreham** *Essex, England* U.K.
151 L4 **Borehamwood** *Hertfordshire, England* U.K.
173 O3 **Borek** *hill* Czech Rep.
175 I5 **Borek** Pol.
174 F5 **Borek Strzeliński** Pol.
174 F4 **Borek Wielkopolski** Pol.
225 G1 **Borel** *r. Que.* Can.
146 J12 **Boreland** *Dumfries and Galloway, Scotland* U.K.
136 E3 **Boremel'** Ukr.
143 L3 **Boren** *l.* Sweden
143 L3 **Borensberg** Sweden
146 C8 **Boreraig** *Highland, Scotland* U.K.
146 B7 **Boreray** *i. Western Isles, Scotland* U.K.
146 □1 **Boreray** *i. Western Isles, Scotland* U.K.
179 O2 **Bořetice** Czech Rep.
172 A2 **Borg** Ger.
Borgå Fin. *see* **Porvoo**
140 M4 **Borgafjäll** Sweden
140 □G1 **Borgarfjörður** Iceland
140 □C1 **Borgarnes** Iceland
140 L4 **Børgefjell Nasjonalpark** *nat. park* Norway
169 H7 **Borgentreich** Ger.
168 E5 **Börger** Ger.
164 K3 **Borger** Neth.
237 E8 **Borger** *TX* U.S.A.
187 L8 **Borges** *r.* Spain
190 F6 **Borghetto di Borbera** Italy
143 M5 **Borgholm** *Öland* Sweden
169 F6 **Borgholzhausen** Ger.
195 L6 **Borgia** Italy
146 H5 **Borgie** *r. Scotland* U.K.
165 H7 **Borgloon** Belgium
192 C2 **Borgo** *Corse* France
191 J8 **Borgo a Mozzano** Italy
190 E5 **Borgo d'Ale** Italy
191 J5 **Borgoforte** Italy
190 D4 **Borgofranco d'Ivrea** Italy
195 O3 **Borgo Grappa** Italy
190 F5 **Borgo-lavezzaro** Italy
190 E4 **Borgomanero** Italy
190 D8 **Borgomaro** Italy
190 C5 **Borgone Susa** Italy
190 G5 **Borgonovo Val Tidone** Italy
191 K6 **Borgo Panigale** *airport* Italy
193 K3 **Borgorose** Italy
190 C7 **Borgo San Dalmazzo** Italy
191 K8 **Borgo San Lorenzo** Italy
190 F5 **Borgo San Martino** Italy
190 E4 **Borgosesia** Italy
191 L7 **Borgo Tossignano** Italy
190 H7 **Borgo Val di Taro** Italy
191 K3 **Borgo Valsugana** Italy
193 K3 **Borgo Velino** Italy
190 E5 **Borgo Vercelli** Italy
170 H5 **Borgsdorf** Ger.
142 E1 **Borgsjåbrotet** *mt.* Norway
168 I2 **Borgstedt** Ger.
146 H13 **Borgue** *Dumfries and Galloway, Scotland* U.K.
116 E8 **Bori** *Madh. Prad.* India
116 G9 **Bori** *Mahar.* India
116 E9 **Bori** *r.* India
207 G5 **Bori** Nigeria
96 F5 **Borikhan** Laos
Börili Kazakh. *see* **Burli**
139 S8 **Borilovo** Rus. Fed.
165 E8 **Borinage** *reg.* Belgium
234 B5 **Boring** *MD* U.S.A.
197 M9 **Borino** Bulg.
247 □1 **Borinquen, Punta** *pt* Puerto Rico
139 W9 **Borinskoye** Rus. Fed.
Borislav Ukr. *see* **Boryslav**
135 H6 **Borisoglebsk** Rus. Fed.
139 W4 **Borisoglebskiy** Rus. Fed.
Borisov Belarus *see* **Barysaw**
135 G6 **Borisovka** Rus. Fed.
139 T6 **Borisovo** Rus. Fed.
139 T2 **Borisovo-Sudskoye** Rus. Fed.
Borispol' Ukr. *see* **Boryspil'**
208 E3 **Bo River Post** Sudan
213 □J2 **Boriziny** Madag.
188 F3 **Borja** *mts* Bos.-Herz.
250 B6 **Borja** Peru
183 Q5 **Borja** Spain
183 P5 **Borjabad** Spain
122 G4 **Borjak** Iran
179 H7 **Borjana** Slovenia
Borjas Blancas Spain *see* **Les Borges Blanques**
205 H2 **Borj Bourguiba** Tunisia
129 E4 **Borjomi** Georgia
129 E4 **Borjomis Nakrdzali** *nature res.* Georgia
138 L6 **Borkavichy** Belarus
123 M3 **Borkeh** Afgh.
169 C7 **Borken** Ger.
169 H8 **Borken (Hessen)** Ger.
140 N2 **Borkenes** Norway
171 G6 **Borkheide** Ger.
175 M3 **Borki** Belarus
175 K4 **Borki** Pol.
137 R1 **Borki** Rus. Fed.
202 C5 **Borkou** *reg.* Chad
202 C5 **Borkou-Ennedi-Tibesti** *pref.* Chad
134 J2 **Borkovskaya** Rus. Fed.
175 I4 **Borkowice** Pol.
168 C3 **Borkum** Ger.
168 C3 **Borkum** *i.* Ger.
143 L1 **Borlänge** Sweden
141 I6 **Borlaug** Norway
199 J4 **Borlu** Turkey
161 I10 **Bormes, Rade de** *inlet* France
161 I10 **Bormes-les-Mimosas** France
190 F6 **Bormida** *r.* Italy
190 I3 **Bormio** Italy
171 D6 **Born** Ger.
171 G8 **Borna** *Sachsen* Ger.
171 H8 **Borna** *Sachsen* Ger.
170 G2 **Born am Darß** Ger.
169 J8 **Born-Berge** *hill* Ger.
164 I2 **Borndiep** *sea chan.* Neth.
205 G4 **Borne** Alg.
160 I4 **Borne** *r.* France
164 K4 **Borne** Neth.
156 D5 **Bornel** France
165 F6 **Bornem** Belgium
90 D6 **Borneo** *i.* Asia
164 K4 **Bornerbroek** Neth.
160 J5 **Bornes** *mts* France
182 G6 **Bornes** Port.
182 F6 **Bornes, Serra de** *mts* Port.
182 E5 **Bornes de Aguiar** Port.
174 E2 **Borne Sulinowo** Pol.
169 C9 **Bornheim** Ger.
169 E10 **Bornhofen** Ger.
143 K6 **Bornholm** *county* Denmark
143 L7 **Bornholm** *i. Bornholm* Denmark
143 K6 **Bornholmsgattet** *str.* Denmark/Sweden
168 J2 **Bornhöved** Ger.
169 E10 **Bornich** Ger.
207 I4 **Borno** *state* Nigeria
184 H7 **Bornos** Spain
184 H7 **Bornos, Embalse de** *resr* Spain
183 O7 **Bornova** *r.* Spain
199 I4 **Bornova** Turkey
168 J4 **Börnsen** Ger.
171 D8 **Bornstedt** Ger.
183 Q5 **Borobia** Spain
95 H8 **Borobudur** *tourist site* Indon.
177 L5 **Borod** Romania
137 N5 **Borodayivka** Ukr.
130 J3 **Borodino** *Krasnoyarskiy Kray* Rus. Fed.
139 S6 **Borodino** *Moskovskaya Oblast'* Rus. Fed.
139 S6 **Borodino** *Moskovskaya Oblast'* Rus. Fed.
136 I7 **Borodino** Ukr.
138 M1 **Borodinskoye** Rus. Fed.
136 I3 **Borodyanka** Ukr.
131 O3 **Borogontsy** Rus. Fed.
110 F4 **Borohoro Shan** *mts* China
176 F1 **Borohrádek** Czech Rep.
139 V3 **Borok** Rus. Fed.
93 C3 **Boroko** *Sulawesi* Indon.
139 T4 **Borok-Sulezhskiy** Rus. Fed.
208 D2 **Boromata** C.A.R.
137 N3 **Boromlya** Ukr.
137 O3 **Boromlya** *r.* Ukr.
206 E4 **Boromo** Burkina
206 D4 **Boron** Côte d'Ivoire
206 D3 **Boron** Mali
240 O7 **Boron** *CA* U.S.A.
114 H3 **Borondi** *Orissa* India
92 E6 **Borongan** *Samar* Phil.
174 G5 **Boronów** Pol.
192 B7 **Borore** *Sardegna* Italy
85 M8 **Bororen** *Qld* Austr.
174 G5 **Boroszów** Pol.
177 I5 **Borota** Hungary
206 D4 **Borotou** Côte d'Ivoire
149 O5 **Boroughbridge** *North Yorkshire, England* U.K.
151 M5 **Borough Green** *Kent, England* U.K.
137 Q4 **Borova** *Kharkivs'ka Oblast'* Ukr.
136 J3 **Borova** *Kyivs'ka Oblast'* Ukr.
137 R5 **Borova** *r.* Ukr.
197 L7 **Borovan** Bulg.
176 D3 **Borovany** Czech Rep.
136 E2 **Borove** *Rivnens'ka Oblast'* Ukr.
136 G2 **Borove** *Rivnens'ka Oblast'* Ukr.
139 Q3 **Borovenka** Rus. Fed.
139 Q3 **Borovichi** Rus. Fed.
121 U1 **Borovlyanka** Rus. Fed.
179 J8 **Borovnica** Slovenia
188 G3 **Borovo Selo** Croatia
134 J4 **Borovoy** *Kirovskaya Oblast'* Rus. Fed.
134 F2 **Borovoy** *Respublika Kareliya* Rus. Fed.
134 K3 **Borovoy** *Respublika Komi* Rus. Fed.
121 N1 **Borovoye** Kazakh.
139 T6 **Borovsk** Rus. Fed.
120 K1 **Borovskoy** Kazakh.
175 J5 **Borów** Pol.
175 J5 **Borowa** Pol.
175 J4 **Borowie** Pol.
183 M8 **Borox** Spain
257 E3 **Borrachudo** *r.* Brazil
256 B5 **Borrazópolis** Brazil
143 K6 **Borrby** Sweden
170 F1 **Borre** Denmark
241 P8 **Borrego Springs** *CA* U.S.A.
170 G3 **Borrentin** Ger.
162 G6 **Borrèze** France
187 E7 **Borriol** Spain
216 □3b **Borriquillas, Punta de las** *pt Fuerteventura* Canary Is
147 I7 **Borris** Ireland
147 G7 **Borris-in-Ossory** Ireland
147 F7 **Borrisokane** Ireland
84 F4 **Borroloola** *N.T.* Austr.
149 K4 **Borrowdale** *Cumbria, England* U.K.
177 K4 **Borş** Romania
140 K5 **Børsa** Norway
197 L4 **Borşa** *Cluj* Romania
197 M3 **Borşa** *Maramureş* Romania
177 K3 **Borša** Slovakia
116 D8 **Borsad** *Gujarat* India
120 G6 **Borsakelmas sho'rxogi** *salt marsh* Uzbek.
165 G6 **Borsbeek** Belgium
171 G8 **Borsdorf** Ger.
197 N4 **Borsec** Romania
140 R1 **Børselv** Norway
198 A2 **Borsh** Albania
137 T2 **Borshchevskiye Peski** Rus. Fed.
136 I6 **Borshchi** Ukr.
136 F5 **Borshchiv** Ukr.
136 E4 **Borshchivka** Ukr.
107 K2 **Borshchovochnyy Khrebet** *mts* Rus. Fed.
175 M6 **Borshchovychi** Ukr.
127 L7 **Borsippa** *tourist site* Iraq
120 D1 **Borskoye** Rus. Fed.
Borský Jur Slovakia *see* **Borský Svätý Jur**
179 P2 **Borský Svätý Jur** Slovakia
177 K3 **Borsod-Abaúj-Zemplén** *county* Hungary
177 J3 **Borsodbóta** Hungary
177 J3 **Borsodnádasd** Hungary
177 J3 **Borsodszentgyörgy** Hungary
165 E6 **Borssele** Neth.
169 K6 **Börßum** Ger.
168 G5 **Borstel** Ger.
171 H9 **Borstendorf** Ger.
Bortala *Xinjiang* China *see* **Bole**
110 F4 **Bortala He** *r.* China
150 D3 **Borth** *Ceredigion, Wales* U.K.
192 B7 **Bortigali** *Sardegna* Italy
192 C6 **Bortigiadas** *Sardegna* Italy
162 I5 **Bort-les-Orgues** France
162 J5 **Bort-les-Orgues, Barrage de** *dam* France
106 C4 **Bor-Üdzüür** Mongolia
122 D6 **Borūjen** Iran
122 C5 **Borūjerd** Iran
106 F6 **Bor Ul Shan** *mts* China
122 H4 **Borun** Iran
197 N8 **Borushtitsa** Bulg.
192 B6 **Borutta** *Sardegna* Italy
146 D8 **Borve** *Highland, Scotland* U.K.
136 B4 **Borynya** Ukr.
136 C4 **Boryslav** Ukr.
136 J3 **Boryspil'** Ukr.
175 K4 **Borzechów** Pol.
174 F4 **Borzęciczki** Pol.
137 L2 **Borzenka** *r.* Ukr.
136 B5 **Borzhava** *r.* Ukr.
Borzhomi Georgia *see* **Borjomi**
137 L2 **Borzna** Ukr.
190 G7 **Borzonasca** Italy
177 H4 **Börzsöny** *hills* Hungary
177 H4 **Börzsönyi** *park* Hungary
107 O1 **Borzya** Rus. Fed.
107 N1 **Borzya** *r.* Rus. Fed.
174 F1 **Borzytuchom** Pol.
192 B7 **Bosa** *Sardegna* Italy
177 G3 **Bošáca** Slovakia
121 O4 **Bosaga** Kazakh.
Bosagha Kazakh. *see* **Bosaga**
Bosaginskiy Kazakh. *see* **Bosaga**
192 A7 **Bosa Marina** *Sardegna* Italy
197 O3 **Bosanci** Romania
188 F3 **Bosanska Dubica** Bos.-Herz.
188 F3 **Bosanska Gradiška** Bos.-Herz.
188 F3 **Bosanska Kostajnica** Bos.-Herz.
188 F3 **Bosanska Krupa** Bos.-Herz.
188 G3 **Bosanski Brod** Bos.-Herz.
188 F3 **Bosanski Novi** Bos.-Herz.
188 F3 **Bosanski Petrovac** Bos.-Herz.
188 G3 **Bosanski Šamac** Bos.-Herz.
188 F3 **Bosansko Grahovo** Bos.-Herz.
177 H3 **Bošany** Slovakia
176 G4 **Bősárkány** Hungary
168 J2 **Bosau** Ger.
215 K4 **Bosberg** *mt.* S. Africa
150 H3 **Bosbury** *Herefordshire, England* U.K.
150 C6 **Boscastle** *Cornwall, England* U.K.
233 N5 **Boscawen** *NH* U.S.A.
Boscawen Island Tonga *see* **Niuatoputopu**
261 H5 **Bosch** Arg.
193 I1 **Bosco** Italy
226 D6 **Boscobel** *WI* U.S.A.
191 K4 **Bosco Chiesanuova** Italy
190 E5 **Bosco della Partecipiano e Lucedio, Parco Naturale** *nature res.* Italy
190 F6 **Bosco Marengo** Italy
193 M6 **Boscotrecase** Italy
168 J2 **Bösdorf** Ger.
214 E5 **Bosduiflaagte** *salt pan* S. Africa
108 F7 **Bose** *Guangxi* China
168 E4 **Bösel** Ger.
244 G6 **Bosencheve, Parque Nacional** *nat. park* Mex.
151 K6 **Bosham** *West Sussex, England* U.K.
Boshchakul' Kazakh. *see* **Bozshakol'**
100 M4 **Boshnyakovo** *Sakhalin* Rus. Fed.
215 L1 **Boshoek** S. Africa
215 J4 **Boshof** S. Africa
122 G5 **Boshruyeh** Iran
197 K8 **Bosilegrad** Serbia
Bosiljgrad Serbia *see* **Bosilegrad**
172 F5 **Bösingen** Ger.
120 I1 **Boskol'** Kazakh.
164 G4 **Boskoop** Neth.
176 F2 **Boskovice** Czech Rep.
251 H3 **Boslanti** Suriname
188 G3 **Bosna** *r.* Bos.-Herz.
197 P8 **Bosna** *hills* Bulg.
Bosna i Hercegovina *country* Europe *see* **Bosnia-Herzegovina**
Bosna Saray Bos.-Herz. *see* **Sarajevo**
Bosnia and Herzegovina, Federation of *aut. div.* Bos.-Herz. *see* **Federacija Bosna i Hercegovina**
188 F3 **Bosnia-Herzegovina** *country* Europe
208 D4 **Boso** Dem. Rep. Congo
214 G1 **Bosobogolo Pan** *salt pan* Botswana
208 C3 **Bosobolo** Dem. Rep. Congo
105 L5 **Bōsō-hantō** *pen.* Japan
208 D3 **Bososama** Dem. Rep. Congo
Bosost Spain *see* **Bòssost**
179 O1 **Bošovice** Czech Rep.
215 K2 **Bospoort** S. Africa
Bosporus *str.* Turkey *see* **İstanbul Boğazı**
Bossaga Turkm. *see* **Basaga**
208 C3 **Bossangoa** C.A.R.
141 M6 **Bössbod** Sweden
208 C3 **Bossembélé** C.A.R.
Bossemptélé C.A.R. *see* **Bossentélé**
208 C3 **Bossentélé** C.A.R.
162 E6 **Bosset** France
214 E5 **Bossiekom** S. Africa
237 I9 **Bossier City** *LA* U.S.A.
212 C5 **Bossiesvlei** Namibia
206 D4 **Bossora** Burkina
186 G2 **Bòssost** Spain
215 L1 **Bosspruit** S. Africa
86 F5 **Bossut, Cape** *W.A.* Austr.
111 G8 **Bostan** *Xinjiang* China
122 B6 **Bostān** Iran
123 L6 **Bostan** Pak.
120 C3 **Bostandyk** Kazakh.
122 F8 **Bostāneh, Ra's-e** *pt* Iran
110 H6 **Bosten Hu** *l.* China
147 E6 **Boston** Ireland
151 L2 **Boston** *Lincolnshire, England* U.K.
233 N6 **Boston** *MA* U.S.A.
82 E6 **Boston Bay** *S.A.* Austr.
227 O1 **Boston Creek** *Ont.* Can.
237 H8 **Boston Mountains** *AR* U.S.A.
149 O6 **Boston Spa** *West Yorkshire, England* U.K.
188 G3 **Bosut** *r.* Croatia
164 G3 **Boswachterij Schoorl** *nature res.* Neth.
226 G9 **Boswell** *IN* U.S.A.
232 F8 **Boswell** *PA* U.S.A.
116 C8 **Botad** *Gujarat* India
137 M8 **Botanichne** Ukr.
206 C5 **Botata** Liberia
140 N5 **Boteå** Sweden
215 Q2 **Boteler Point** S. Africa
197 N5 **Boteni** Romania
151 O3 **Botesdale** *Suffolk, England* U.K.
212 E4 **Boteti** *r.* Botswana
135 D8 **Botev** *mt.* Bulg.
197 L8 **Botevgrad** Bulg.
215 K3 **Bothaville** S. Africa
168 I4 **Bothel** Ger.
149 K4 **Bothel** *Cumbria, England* U.K.
238 C3 **Bothell** *WA* U.S.A.
150 G6 **Bothenhampton** *Dorset, England* U.K.
141 O6 **Bothnia, Gulf of** Fin./Sweden
83 K10 **Bothwell** *Tas.* Austr.
227 M7 **Bothwell** *Ont.* Can.
182 E5 **Boticas** Port.
188 G4 **Botin** *mt.* Bos.-Herz.
179 M8 **Botinec Stupnički** Croatia
137 O7 **Botiyeve** Ukr.
177 L4 **Botiz** Romania
232 A8 **Botkins** *OH* U.S.A.
135 I6 **Botkul', Ozero** *l.* Kazakh./Rus. Fed.
129 H3 **Botlikh** Rus. Fed.
207 H6 **Bot Makak** Cameroon
136 I7 **Botna** *r.* Moldova
186 C4 **Botorrita** Spain
197 O3 **Botoşani** Romania
107 O7 **Botou** *Hebei* China
195 L6 **Botricello** Italy
206 D5 **Botro** Côte d'Ivoire
215 J1 **Botsalano Game Reserve** *nature res.* S. Africa
235 I2 **Botsford** *CT* U.S.A.
215 K5 **Botshabelo** S. Africa
140 P4 **Botsmark** Sweden
142 D2 **Botsvatn** *l.* Norway
212 D5 **Botswana** *country* Africa
195 K5 **Botte Donato, Monte** *mt.* Italy
169 G8 **Bottendorf (Burgwald)** Ger.
168 K5 **Bottendorf (Obernholz)** Ger.
140 Q4 **Bottenviken** *g.* Fin./Sweden
151 K2 **Bottesford** *Leicestershire, England* U.K.
149 P6 **Bottesford** *North Lincolnshire, England* U.K.
192 C7 **Bottidda** *Sardegna* Italy
236 E1 **Bottineau** *ND* U.S.A.
246 G3 **Bottle Creek** Turks and Caicos Is
247 L5 **Bottom** *Saba* Neth. Antilles
169 C7 **Bottrop** Ger.
256 C5 **Botucatu** Brazil
257 F2 **Botumirim** Brazil
196 I9 **Botun** Macedonia
Botushany Moldova *see* **Butuceni**
225 K3 **Botwood** *Nfld and Lab.* Can.
172 D5 **Bötzingen** Ger.
206 D5 **Bouaflé** Côte d'Ivoire
156 B5 **Bouafles** France
180 D5 **Bou Ahmed** Morocco
206 D5 **Bouaké** Côte d'Ivoire
205 F2 **Boualem** Alg.
206 D4 **Bouandougou** Côte d'Ivoire
208 C5 **Bouanga** Congo
208 B3 **Bouar** C.A.R.
189 B7 **Bou Arada** Tunisia
204 E2 **Bouârfa** Morocco
205 G2 **Bou Aroua** Alg.
158 H7 **Bouaye** France
207 I4 **Bouba Ndjida, Parc National de** *nat. park* Cameroon
176 C2 **Boubín** *mt.* Czech Rep.
206 C2 **Boû Bleï'îne** *well* Maur.
204 D4 **Boubout** *well* Alg.
208 C3 **Bouca** C.A.R.
163 B8 **Boucau** France
84 E2 **Boucaut Bay** *N.T.* Austr.
161 G10 **Bouc-Bel-Air** France
159 K4 **Boucé** France
156 F3 **Bouchain** France
189 A7 **Bouchegouf** Alg.
159 J7 **Bouchemaine** France
Boucher, Île *i. Îles Loyauté* New Caledonia *see* **Tiga**
233 L3 **Boucherville** *Que.* Can.
161 G9 **Bouches-du-Rhône** *dept* France
227 S3 **Bouchette** *Que.* Can.
156 E4 **Bouchoir** France
206 C3 **Boucle du Baoulé, Parc National de la** *nat. park* Mali
225 H4 **Bouctouche** *N.B.* Can.
208 A5 **Bouda** Gabon
165 D6 **Boudewijn Kanaal** *canal* Belgium
117 J9 **Boudh** *Orissa* India
180 E5 **Boudinar** Morocco
206 E2 **Boû Djébéha** *well* Mali
208 C3 **Boudoua** C.A.R.
190 B2 **Boudry** Switz.
156 G3 **Boué** France
217 □3b **Bouéni** Mayotte
217 □3b **Bouéni, Baie de** *b.* Mayotte
209 B6 **Bouenza** *admin. reg.* Congo
209 B6 **Bouenza** *r.* Congo
159 K6 **Bouessay** France
159 O8 **Bouesse** France
208 C3 **Boufore** C.A.R.
205 G1 **Bougaa** Alg.
86 I2 **Bougainville, Cape** *W.A.* Austr.
93 G4 **Bougainville, Selat** *sea chan. Papua* Indon.
91 L8 **Bougainville Island** P.N.G.
85 K3 **Bougainville Reef** *Coral Sea Is Terr.* Austr.
78 □6 **Bougainville Strait** Solomon Is
205 G1 **Bougaroûn, Cap** *c.* Alg.
206 B2 **Boû Ghbeïra** *spring* Maur.
207 F2 **Boughessa** Mali
Bougie Alg. *see* **Bejaïa**
163 E7 **Bouglon** France
208 B2 **Bougoumen** Chad
206 D4 **Bougouni** Mali
205 F2 **Bougtob** Alg.
158 H7 **Bouguenais** France
206 D2 **Boû Guendoûz** *well* Mali
163 G8 **Bouillac** France
247 □2 **Bouillante** Guadeloupe
161 E9 **Bouillargues** France
165 H9 **Bouillon** Belgium
156 G7 **Bouilly** France
158 G8 **Bouin** France
205 F1 **Bouira** Alg.
204 C3 **Bou Izakarn** Morocco
160 I3 **Boujailles** France
161 C10 **Boujan-sur-Libron** France
204 B4 **Boujdour** Western Sahara
205 F2 **Bou Kahil, Djebel** *mts* Alg.
207 F4 **Boukoumbé** Benin
204 B4 **Boukra** Western Sahara
208 C2 **Boukta** Chad
208 C2 **Boula Bouda** Chad
206 C3 **Boulal** Mali
157 L5 **Boulay-Moselle** France
162 F5 **Boulazac** France
161 F9 **Boulbon** France
87 F11 **Boulder** *W.A.* Austr.
238 L6 **Boulder** *CO* U.S.A.
238 H3 **Boulder** *MT* U.S.A.
241 U4 **Boulder** *UT* U.S.A.
241 R5 **Boulder Canyon** *gorge NV* U.S.A.
241 R6 **Boulder City** *NV* U.S.A.
204 C3 **Bou Legmaden, Oued** *watercourse* Alg./Morocco
204 D2 **Boulemane** *Fez-Boulmane* Morocco
204 D2 **Boulemane** *Fez-Boulmane* Morocco
241 P9 **Boulevard** *CA* U.S.A.
261 H6 **Boulevard Atlántico** Arg.
207 F3 **Boulgou** Burkina
Boulhaut Morocco *see* **Ben Slimane**
84 G7 **Boulia** *Qld* Austr.
157 K5 **Bouligny** France
163 G8 **Bouloc** France
Boulogne France *see* **Boulogne-sur-Mer**
158 H7 **Boulogne** *r.* France
156 D6 **Boulogne-Billancourt** France
163 F9 **Boulogne-sur-Gesse** France
156 C2 **Boulogne-sur-Mer** France
159 M6 **Bouloire** France
208 E3 **Boulou** *r.* C.A.R.
208 D3 **Boulouba** C.A.R.
77 G4 **Bouloupari** New Caledonia
161 J10 **Boulouris** France
206 E3 **Boulsa** Burkina
149 M6 **Boulsworth Hill** *England* U.K.
157 I5 **Boult-aux-Bois** France
207 H3 **Boultoum** Niger
156 I4 **Boulzicourt** France
204 D3 **Boumalne Dadès** Morocco
208 B5 **Boumango** Gabon
207 I6 **Boumba** *r.* Cameroon
208 B3 **Boumbé I** *r.* C.A.R.
205 F1 **Boumerdes** Alg.
186 H3 **Boumort** *mt.* Spain
186 H3 **Boumort, Serra del** *mts* Spain
206 E4 **Bouna** Côte d'Ivoire
204 E2 **Bou Naceur, Jbel** *mt.* Morocco
206 B2 **Boû Nâga** Maur.
233 □O3 **Boundary Mountains** *ME* U.S.A.
240 N4 **Boundary Peak** *NV* U.S.A.
234 F3 **Bound Brook** *NJ* U.S.A.
206 D4 **Boundiali** Côte d'Ivoire
208 B5 **Boundji** Congo
206 D3 **Boundjiguire** Mali
208 D3 **Boungou** C.A.R.
208 D3 **Boungou** *r.* C.A.R.
163 F6 **Bouniagues** France
206 B3 **Bounkiling** Senegal
96 E4 **Boun Nua** Laos
238 I6 **Bountiful** *UT* U.S.A.
84 G4 **Bountiful Island** *Qld* Austr.
77 H6 **Bounty Islands** N.Z.
266 G9 **Bounty Trough** *sea feature* S. Pacific Ocean
261 G3 **Bouquet** Arg.
78 □5 **Bourail** New Caledonia
205 H4 **Bourarhet, Erg** *des.* Alg.
160 E4 **Bourbince** *r.* France
Bourbon *reg.* France *see* **Bourbonnais**
Bourbon *terr.* Indian Ocean *see* **Réunion**
160 D3 **Bourbon-Lancy** France
160 C3 **Bourbon-l'Archambault** France
160 B4 **Bourbonnais** *reg.* France
157 K8 **Bourbonne-les-Bains** France
156 D2 **Bourbourg** France
160 G5 **Bourbre** *r.* France
158 E5 **Bourbriac** France
162 B4 **Bourcefranc-le-Chapus** France
161 G7 **Bourdeaux** France
162 F5 **Bourdeilles** France
160 C1 **Bourdon, Réservoir du** *resr* France
157 M6 **Bourdonnay** France
206 E2 **Bourem** Mali
Bouressa Mali *see* **Boughessa**
162 F3 **Bouresse** France
162 C5 **Bourg** France
159 M3 **Bourg-Achard** France
162 H4 **Bourganeuf** France
161 F6 **Bourg-Argental** France
158 H6 **Bourgbarré** France
158 B5 **Bourg-Blanc** France
161 G6 **Bourg-de-Péage** France
160 E4 **Bourg-de-Thizy** France
163 F7 **Bourg-de-Visa** France
156 A4 **Bourg-Dun** France
160 G4 **Bourg-en-Bresse** France
162 I1 **Bourges** France
233 J3 **Bourget** *Ont.* Can.
160 H5 **Bourget, Lac du** *l.* France
156 G5 **Bourg-et-Comin** France
160 B5 **Bourg-Lastic** France
161 F7 **Bourg-lès-Valence** France
163 H11 **Bourg-Madame** France
227 S1 **Bourgmont** *Que.* Can.
158 G7 **Bourgneuf, Baie de** *b.* France
159 J7 **Bourgneuf-en-Mauges** France
158 H7 **Bourgneuf-en-Retz** France
156 H5 **Bourgogne** France
156 G8 **Bourgogne** *admin. reg.* France
156 H8 **Bourgogne, Canal de** France
160 G5 **Bourgoin-Jallieu** France
161 F8 **Bourg-St-Andéol** France
163 H8 **Bourg-St-Bernard** France
160 J5 **Bourg-St-Maurice** France
159 M3 **Bourgtheroulde-Infreville** France
159 K3 **Bourguébus** France
159 L7 **Bourgueil** France
83 J4 **Bourke** *N.S.W.* Austr.
227 N1 **Bourkes** *Ont.* Can.
157 K7 **Bourmont** France
161 G6 **Bourne** *r.* France
151 L2 **Bourne** *Lincolnshire, England* U.K.
151 I6 **Bournemouth** *Bournemouth, England* U.K.
151 I6 **Bournemouth** *admin. div. England* U.K.
159 I8 **Bournezeau** France
161 C6 **Bournoncle-St-Pierre** France
182 D5 **Bouro** Port.
160 J1 **Bourogne** France
204 E2 **Bou Rouhat, Oued** *watercourse* Morocco
206 E4 **Bouroum-Bouroum** Burkina
207 I4 **Bourrah** Cameroon
163 E7 **Bourran** France
163 D7 **Bourriot-Bergonce** France
165 J9 **Bourscheid** Lux.
164 L2 **Bourtange** Neth.
168 D5 **Bourtanger Moor** *reg.* Ger.
159 M4 **Bourth** France
150 H5 **Bourton** *Dorset, England* U.K.
151 I4 **Bourton-on-the-Water** *Gloucestershire, England* U.K.
208 D2 **Bourtoutou** Chad
206 E3 **Bourzanga** Burkina
205 G2 **Bou Saâda** Alg.
189 B7 **Bou Salem** Tunisia
241 R8 **Bouse** *AZ* U.S.A.
241 R7 **Bouse Wash** *watercourse AZ* U.S.A.
162 I3 **Boussac** France
206 E3 **Boussé** Burkina
163 F9 **Boussens** France
160 H2 **Boussières** France
208 C2 **Bousso** Chad
156 H3 **Boussois** France
165 E8 **Boussu** Belgium
165 G7 **Boutersem** Belgium
206 C2 **Boû Tezâya** *well* Maur.
206 B2 **Boutilimit** Maur.
162 C4 **Boutonne** *r.* France
206 B3 **Boutougou Fara** Senegal
156 C4 **Bouttencourt** France
190 B3 **Bouveret** Switz.
Bouvet Island *terr.* S. Atlantic Ocean *see* **Bouvetøya**
264 J9 **Bouvetøya** *terr.* S. Atlantic Ocean
161 G7 **Bouvières** France
158 H7 **Bouvron** France
157 L6 **Bouxières-aux-Dames** France
157 N6 **Bouxwiller** France
156 H5 **Bouy** France
204 E3 **Bou Yala** Alg.
207 G3 **Bouza** Niger
159 N8 **Bouzanne** *r.* France
157 M5 **Bouzonville** France
156 H5 **Bouzy** France
195 J7 **Bova** Italy
195 K7 **Bovalino** Italy
195 J8 **Bova Marina** Italy
179 I7 **Bovec** Slovenia
182 F3 **Bóveda** *Galicia* Spain
183 N3 **Boveda** *País Vasco* Spain
190 I4 **Bovegno** Italy
169 I7 **Bovenden** Ger.
Boven Kapuas Mountains Indon./Malaysia *see* **Kapuas Hulu, Pegunungan**
164 H3 **Bovenkarspel** Neth.
164 J3 **Bovensmilde** Neth.
156 D4 **Boves** France
190 D7 **Boves** Italy
150 E6 **Bovey** *r. England* U.K.
226 A2 **Bovey** *MN* U.S.A.

Bovey Tracey to Brompton
291

150 E6 Bovey Tracey Devon, England U.K.
148 D4 Boviel Northern Ireland U.K.
165 I8 Bovigny Belgium
193 K4 Boville Ernica Italy
150 H6 Bovington Camp Dorset, England U.K.
193 O5 Bovino Italy
191 K5 Bovolone Italy
261 H2 Bovril Arg.
168 I1 Bovrup Denmark
137 L5 Bovtyshka Ukr.
86 J4 Bow r. W.A. Austr.
238 I2 Bow r. Alta Can.
223 I5 Bow r. Alta Can.
Bowa Sichuan China see Muli
236 D1 Bowbells ND U.S.A.
149 N4 Bowburn Durham, England U.K.
246 □ Bowden Jamaica
232 F10 Bowden WV U.S.A.
Bowditch atoll Tokelau see Fakaofo
260 D4 Bowen Arg.
85 L6 Bowen Qld Austr.
85 K6 Bowen r. Qld Austr.
226 C9 Bowen IL U.S.A.
83 L7 Bowen, Mount Vic. Austr.
85 J7 Bowen Downs Qld Austr.
222 F5 Bowen Island B.C. Can.
83 K7 Bowen Mountains Vic. Austr.
84 D1 Bowen Strait N.T. Austr.
85 M9 Bowenville Qld Austr.
234 E6 Bowers Beach DE U.S.A.
263 K2 Bowers Mountains Antarctica
266 G2 Bowers Ridge sea feature Bering Sea
149 M4 Bowes Durham, England U.K.
85 J6 Bowie Qld Austr.
241 W9 Bowie AZ U.S.A.
234 B7 Bowie MD U.S.A.
237 G9 Bowie TX U.S.A.
223 I5 Bow Island Alta Can.
149 L6 Bowland, Forest of reg. England U.K.
230 D7 Bowling Green KY U.S.A.
236 J6 Bowling Green MO U.S.A.
232 B7 Bowling Green OH U.S.A.
232 H10 Bowling Green VA U.S.A.
85 K5 Bowling Green, Cape Qld Austr.
85 K5 Bowling Green Bay Qld Austr.
85 K5 Bowling Green Bay National Park Qld Austr.
236 D2 Bowman ND U.S.A.
222 F5 Bowman, Mount B.C. Can.
262 T2 Bowman Coast Antarctica
263 G2 Bowman Island Antarctica
262 T2 Bowman Peninsula Antarctica
234 B4 Bowmansdale PA U.S.A.
234 D3 Bowmanstown PA U.S.A.
234 C4 Bowmansville PA U.S.A.
227 P6 Bowmanville Ont. Can.
149 M2 Bowmont Water r. England/Scotland U.K.
146 D11 Bowmore Argyll and Bute, Scotland U.K.
210 D2 Bown Somalia
149 K4 Bowness-on-Solway Cumbria, England U.K.
149 L5 Bowness-on-Windermere Cumbria, England U.K.
Bowo Sichuan China see Bomai
Bowo Xizang China see Bomi
83 N4 Bowraville N.S.W. Austr.
86 I4 Bow River Aboriginal Reserve W.A. Austr.
222 F4 Bowron r. B.C. Can.
222 F4 Bowron Lake Provincial Park B.C. Can.
222 D3 Bowser Lake B.C. Can.
150 H5 Box Wiltshire, England U.K.
172 H3 Boxberg Baden-Württemberg Ger.
171 K8 Boxberg Sachsen Ger.
171 I8 Boxdorf Ger.
236 D3 Box Elder SD U.S.A.
236 D3 Box Elder r. SD U.S.A.
143 L3 Boxholm Sweden
107 P8 Boxing Shandong China
164 I5 Boxmeer Neth.
164 H5 Boxtel Neth.
126 G3 Boyabat Turkey
250 C3 Boyacá dept Col.
197 O8 Boyadzhik Bulg.
199 K2 Boyalıca Turkey
Boyalık Turkey see Çiçekdağı
197 L8 Boyana tourist site Bulg.
109 K4 Boyang Jiangxi China
139 R8 Boyanovichi Rus. Fed.
197 O8 Boyanovo Bulg.
87 C12 Boyanup W.A. Austr.
136 J3 Boyarka Ukr.
83 N3 Boyd r. N.S.W. Austr.
87 H8 Boyd Lagoon salt flat W.A. Austr.
223 K2 Boyd Lake N.W.T. Can.
232 G12 Boydton VA U.S.A.
236 H5 Boyer r. IA U.S.A.
208 C5 Boyera Dem. Rep. Congo
234 D4 Boyertown PA U.S.A.
232 H12 Boykins VA U.S.A.
137 Q8 Boykov Liman l. Rus. Fed.
222 H4 Boyle Alta Can.
147 F5 Boyle Ireland
85 M7 Boyne r. Qld Austr.
85 M8 Boyne r. Qld Austr.
147 J5 Boyne r. Ireland
226 I4 Boyne City MI U.S.A.
156 D7 Boynes France
123 L3 Boyni Qara Afgh.
208 D3 Boyo C.A.R.
208 E4 Boyoma, Chutes waterfall Dem. Rep. Congo
121 L8 Boysun Uzbek.
253 E5 Boyuibe Bol.
129 I5 Böyük Dähnä Azer.
122 A1 Böyük Hinaldağ mt. Azer.
129 H6 Böyük İşıqlı Dağ mt. Armenia
87 D12 Boyup Brook W.A. Austr.
199 L3 Bozan Turkey
121 T3 Bozanbay Kazakh.
129 B5 Bozan Dağı mt. Turkey
Bozashy Tübegi pen. Kazakh. see Buzachi, Poluostrov
199 J6 Bozburun Turkey
199 M5 Bozburun Dağ mt. Turkey
199 J6 Bozburun Yarımadası pen. Turkey
199 H3 Bozcaada i. Turkey
128 E2 Bozdağ mt. Turkey
199 H4 Bozdağ mt. Turkey
199 J3 Boz Dağ mts Turkey
Bozdag, Khrebet hills Azer. see Bozdağ Silsiläsi
199 I4 Boz Dağları mts Turkey
129 H5 Bozdağ Silsiläsi hills Azer.
129 E6 Bozdağ Tepe mt. Turkey
199 J5 Bozdoğan Turkey
151 K3 Bozeat Northamptonshire, England U.K.
161 J6 Bozel France
238 I4 Bozeman MT U.S.A.
Bozen Italy see Bolzano
175 H3 Bożewo Pol.
109 J2 Bozhou Anhui China
176 F3 Božice Czech Rep.
179 N8 Božjakovina Croatia
126 F5 Bozkır Turkey
Bozköl Kazakh. see Boskol'
199 K5 Bozkurt Turkey
122 H5 Boznābād Iran
Bozoglan mts Turkey see Bolkar Dağları
161 B8 Bozouls France
208 C3 Bozoum C.A.R.
126 I5 Bozova Turkey
197 K6 Bozovici Romania
122 B3 Bozqūsh, Kūh-e mts Iran
121 P2 Bozshakol' Kazakh.
121 L3 Boztumsyk Kazakh.
199 L3 Bozüyük Turkey
128 A2 Bozyazı Turkey
190 I5 Bozzolo Italy
190 D6 Bra Italy
148 H5 Braaid Isle of Man
146 I9 Braan r. Scotland U.K.
143 L4 Braås Sweden
262 T2 Brabant Island Antarctica
165 G7 Brabant Wallon prov. Belgium
188 F4 Brač i. Croatia
146 D8 Bracadale Highland, Scotland U.K.
146 C8 Bracadale, Loch b. Scotland U.K.
Bracara Port. see Braga
192 I3 Bracciano Italy
192 I3 Bracciano, Lago di l. Italy
224 E4 Bracebridge Ont. Can.
149 P7 Bracebridge Heath Lincolnshire, England U.K.
162 C5 Brach France
169 E9 Brachbach Ger.
225 G3 Brachet, Lac au l. Que. Can.
159 O6 Bracieux France
148 C7 Brackagh Ireland
140 M5 Bräcke Sweden
168 J4 Brackel Ger.
172 G3 Brackenheim Ger.
237 E11 Brackettville TX U.S.A.
188 F4 Bracki Kanal sea chan. Croatia
151 J3 Brackley Northamptonshire, England U.K.
147 H6 Bracknagh Ireland
151 K5 Bracknell Bracknell Forest, England U.K.
151 K5 Bracknell Forest admin. div. England U.K.
253 G2 Braço Norte r. Brazil
197 K4 Brad Romania
193 R7 Bradano r. Italy
231 F12 Bradenton FL U.S.A.
227 O5 Bradford Ont. Can.
149 N6 Bradford West Yorkshire, England U.K.
232 A8 Bradford OH U.S.A.
232 G7 Bradford PA U.S.A.
233 M5 Bradford VT U.S.A.
234 C1 Bradford County county PA U.S.A.
234 D4 Bradford Hills PA U.S.A.
150 H5 Bradford-on-Avon Wiltshire, England U.K.
151 J6 Brading Isle of Wight, England U.K.
226 G8 Bradley IL U.S.A.
235 G4 Bradley Beach NJ U.S.A.
232 B7 Bradner OH U.S.A.
150 F6 Bradninch Devon, England U.K.
150 G6 Bradpole Dorset, England U.K.
149 M6 Bradshaw Greater Manchester, England U.K.
232 D11 Bradshaw WV U.S.A.
86 H3 Bradshaw, Mount hill W.A. Austr.
149 N7 Bradwell Derbyshire, England U.K.
151 P2 Bradwell Norfolk, England U.K.
151 N4 Bradwell Waterside Essex, England U.K.
237 F10 Brady TX U.S.A.
237 F10 Brady Creek r. TX U.S.A.
222 B3 Brady Glacier AK U.S.A.
175 L4 Bradzyatsin Belarus
146 □N2 Brae Shetland, Scotland U.K.
146 H7 Braeantra Highland, Scotland U.K.
146 K9 Braehead of Lunan Angus, Scotland U.K.
82 G5 Braemar S.A. Austr.
146 J8 Braemar Aberdeenshire, Scotland U.K.
194 G9 Braemi r. Sicilia Italy
182 D5 Braga Port.
182 D5 Braga admin. dist. Port.
261 G4 Bragado Arg.
254 D2 Bragança Brazil
182 G5 Bragança Port.
182 G5 Bragança admin. dist. Port.
256 D5 Bragança Paulista Brazil
226 A4 Braham MN U.S.A.
136 J2 Brahin Belarus
136 J2 Brahinka r. Belarus
168 K4 Brahlstorf Ger.
117 P6 Brahmakund Arun. Prad. India
117 M8 Brahmanbaria Bangl.
117 K9 Brahmani r. India
115 I3 Brahmapur Orissa India
117 M8 Brahmaputra r. Asia
alt. Dihang (India),
alt. Jamuna (Bangladesh),
alt. Yarlung Zangbo (China)
116 F3 Brahmaur Hima. Prad. India
83 L6 Braidwood N.S.W. Austr.
226 F8 Braidwood IL U.S.A.
178 F6 Braies, Lago di l. Italy
197 P5 Brăila Romania
197 P6 Brăilei, Insula Mare a i. Romania
151 I2 Brailsford Derbyshire, England U.K.
156 G5 Braine France
165 F7 Braine-l'Alleud Belgium
165 F7 Braine-le-Comte Belgium
236 H2 Brainerd MN U.S.A.
159 L7 Brain-sur-Allonnes France
151 N4 Braintree Essex, England U.K.
149 K4 Braithwaite Cumbria, England U.K.
84 D1 Braithwaite Point N.T. Austr.
165 H7 Braives Belgium
213 F4 Brak r. Limpopo S. Africa
214 E9 Brak r. Western Cape S. Africa
214 C4 Brak watercourse S. Africa
168 F4 Brake (Unterweser) Ger.
165 E7 Brakel Belgium
169 H7 Brakel Ger.
164 H5 Brakel Neth.
206 B2 Brâkna admin. reg. Maur.
143 L5 Bräkneån r. Sweden
215 M2 Brakpan S. Africa
214 H7 Brakpoort S. Africa
215 K2 Brakspruit S. Africa
212 C4 Brakwater Namibia
142 I3 Brålanda Sweden
174 F4 Bralin Pol.
190 G6 Brallo di Pregola Italy
222 F5 Bralorne B.C. Can.
163 I9 Bram France
161 J6 Bramans France
178 F5 Bramberg am Wildkogel Austria
82 E5 Bramfield S.A. Austr.
151 O3 Bramford Suffolk, England U.K.
116 G9 Bramhapuri Mahar. India
149 O7 Bramley South Yorkshire, England U.K.
142 E6 Bramming Denmark
134 B3 Brämön i. Sweden
224 E5 Brampton Ont. Can.
151 L3 Brampton Cambridgeshire, England U.K.
149 L4 Brampton Cumbria, England U.K.
151 P3 Brampton Suffolk, England U.K.
169 D6 Bramsche Niedersachsen Ger.
169 F6 Bramsche Niedersachsen Ger.
143 N1 Bramsöfjärden l. Sweden
168 G4 Bramstedt Ger.
85 I2 Bramwell Qld Austr.
182 I2 Braña Caballo mt. Spain
171 I9 Braňany Czech Rep.
177 H3 Branč Slovakia
195 K8 Brancaleone Italy
151 N2 Brancaster Norfolk, England U.K.
225 K4 Branch Nfld and Lab. Can.
234 C3 Branch Dale PA U.S.A.
234 F2 Branchville NJ U.S.A.
209 D8 Branco Angola
251 F5 Branco r. Roraima Brazil
253 E2 Branco r. Brazil
206 □ Branco i. Cape Verde
178 A5 Brand Austria
173 L2 Brand Ger.
247 □8 Brandaris hill Bonaire Neth. Antilles
212 B4 Brandberg mt. Namibia
141 N5 Brändbo Sweden
142 G1 Brandbu Norway
142 F6 Brande Denmark
168 I3 Brande-Hörnerkirchen Ger.
178 E5 Brandenberg Austria
171 G6 Brandenburg Ger.
171 H5 Brandenburg land Ger.
230 D7 Brandenburg KY U.S.A.
171 F6 Brandenburger Wald- und Seengebiet park Ger.
171 H9 Brand-Erbisdorf Ger.
162 F3 Brandes reg. France
149 Q6 Brandesburton East Riding of Yorkshire, England U.K.
215 K4 Brandfort S. Africa
171 H7 Brandis Brandenburg Ger.
171 G8 Brandis Sachsen Ger.
214 D7 Brandkop S. Africa
179 L2 Brand-Nagelberg Austria
141 P6 Brändö Åland Fin.
192 C2 Brando Corse France
85 K5 Brandon Qld Austr.
223 L5 Brandon Man. Can.
147 B8 Brandon Ireland
149 N4 Brandon Durham, England U.K.
151 N3 Brandon Suffolk, England U.K.
237 K9 Brandon MS U.S.A.
236 G4 Brandon SD U.S.A.
233 L5 Brandon VT U.S.A.
147 B8 Brandon Bay Ireland
147 B8 Brandon Head Ireland
147 I7 Brandon Hill Ireland
147 B8 Brandon Mountain hill Ireland
234 C3 Brandonville PA U.S.A.
232 F9 Brandonville WV U.S.A.
170 H2 Brandshagen Ger.
234 A4 Brandtsville PA U.S.A.
214 E6 Brandvlei S. Africa
214 D9 Brandvlei Dam resr S. Africa
140 O2 Brandvoll Norway
176 D1 Brandýs nad Labem-Stará Boleslav Czech Rep.
234 D5 Brandywine Creek, East Branch r. PA U.S.A.
234 D5 Brandywine Creek, West Branch r. DE U.S.A.
234 D4 Brandywine Manor PA U.S.A.
235 J2 Branford CT U.S.A.
231 F11 Branford FL U.S.A.
160 G3 Branges France
94 □ Brani, Pulau i. Sing.
179 I8 Branica r. Slovenia
143 P7 Braniewo Pol.
179 I8 Branik Slovenia
177 L6 Brănișca Romania
156 F8 Branlin r. France
140 P4 Brännberg Sweden
163 D6 Branne France
173 M6 Brannenburg Ger.
183 L3 Brañosera Spain
262 T2 Bransfield Strait Antarctica
151 I6 Bransgore Hampshire, England U.K.
175 K3 Brańsk Pol.
237 D7 Branson CO U.S.A.
149 Q7 Branston Lincolnshire, England U.K.
175 J3 Brańszczyk Pol.
95 J8 Brantas r. Indon.
224 D5 Brantford Ont. Can.
151 O4 Brantham Suffolk, England U.K.
177 G1 Brantice Czech Rep.
231 D10 Brantley AL U.S.A.
162 F5 Brantôme France
137 O3 Brantsivka Ukr.
226 D4 Brantwood WI U.S.A.
137 K3 Branytsya Ukr.
190 H3 Branzi Italy
183 M6 Braojos Spain
190 I4 Braone Italy
251 G5 Brás Brazil
161 H10 Bras France
196 J8 Brasaljce Kosovo Serbia
225 I4 Bras d'Or Lake N.S. Can.
182 D8 Brasfemes Port.
250 D6 Brasil Brazil
Brasil country S. America see Brazil
257 G2 Brasil, Planalto do plat. Brazil
256 A4 Brasilândia Mato Grosso do Sul Brazil
256 C1 Brasilândia Minas Gerais Brazil
257 D2 Brasilândia Minas Gerais Brazil
252 C2 Brasileia Brazil
256 D1 Brasília Brazil
257 E2 Brasília de Minas Brazil
251 H5 Brasília Legal Brazil
138 H4 Brasla r. Latvia
Braslav Belarus see Braslaw
138 K6 Braslaw Belarus
197 N5 Brașov Romania
139 R9 Brasovo Rus. Fed.
217 □1c Bras-Panon Réunion
257 F4 Brás Pires Brazil
207 G5 Brass Nigeria
163 I8 Brassac France
161 C6 Brassac-les-Mines France
165 F6 Brasschaat Belgium
95 L2 Brassey, Banjaran mts Malaysia
84 E7 Brassey, Mount N.T. Austr.
87 G8 Brassey Range hills W.A. Austr.
233 □P3 Brassua Lake ME U.S.A.
160 D2 Brassy France
142 H3 Brastad Sweden
173 P2 Břasy Czech Rep.
197 N8 Bratan mt. Bulg.
197 K4 Bratca Romania
176 G3 Bratislava Slovakia
176 G3 Bratislavský kraj admin. reg. Slovakia
175 J5 Bratkowice Pol.
131 L4 Bratsk Rus. Fed.
137 K6 Brats'ke Mykolayivs'ka Oblast' Ukr.
137 M8 Brats'ke Respublika Krym Ukr.
Bratskoye Rus. Fed. see Nogamirzin-Yurt
131 L4 Bratskoye Vodokhranilishche resr Rus. Fed.
136 H5 Bratslav Ukr.
233 M6 Brattleboro VT U.S.A.
142 I1 Brattmon Sweden
150 H5 Bratton Wiltshire, England U.K.
140 I5 Brattvåg Norway
188 G3 Bratunac Bos.-Herz.
169 E10 Braubach Ger.
162 C5 Braud-et-St-Louis France
242 □R12 Braulio Carrillo, Parque Nacional nat. park Costa Rica
257 F3 Braúnas Brazil
178 H3 Braunau am Inn Austria
172 B2 Brauneberg Ger.
169 F9 Braunfels Ger.
169 K7 Braunlage Ger.
172 E6 Bräunlingen Ger.
172 H3 Braunsbach Ger.
171 E8 Braunsbedra Ger.
169 K6 Braunschweig Ger.
151 J3 Braunston Northamptonshire, England U.K.
151 J2 Braunstone Leicestershire, England U.K.
150 D5 Braunton Devon, England U.K.
215 L7 Braunville S. Africa
206 □ Brava i. Cape Verde
185 O5 Bravatas r. Spain
232 E9 Brave PA U.S.A.
136 H6 Bravicea Moldova
143 M3 Bråviken inlet Sweden
143 N3 Bråvikens naturreservat nature res. Sweden
252 D4 Bravo, Cerro mt. Bol.
243 K5 Bravo del Norte, Río r. Mex./U.S.A.
alt. Rio Grande
184 B6 Bravura, Barragem da resr Port.
241 Q9 Brawley CA U.S.A.
147 J6 Bray Ireland
214 H1 Bray S. Africa
151 K4 Bray Windsor and Maidenhead, England U.K.
150 E6 Bray r. England U.K.
156 E1 Bray-Dunes France
159 M6 Braye r. France
147 B9 Bray Head Ireland
136 H4 Brayiliv Ukr.
221 K3 Bray Island Nunavut Can.
156 F7 Bray-sur-Seine France
149 O6 Brayton North Yorkshire, England U.K.
185 K3 Brazatortas Spain
222 H4 Brazeau r. Alta Can.
222 G4 Brazeau, Mount Alta Can.
215 N7 Brazen Head S. Africa
160 G2 Brazey-en-Plaine France
177 L5 Brazii Romania
254 C4 Brazil country S. America
230 D6 Brazil IN U.S.A.
264 H7 Brazil Basin sea feature S. Atlantic Ocean
237 H11 Brazos r. TX U.S.A.
209 B6 Brazzaville Congo
188 G3 Brčko Bos.-Herz.
174 G2 Brda r. Pol.
174 G3 Brdów Pol.
176 C2 Brdy hills Czech Rep.
Bré Ireland see Bray
183 Q5 Brea Spain
84 G7 Breadalbane Qld Austr.
146 H10 Breadalbane reg. Scotland U.K.
87 H8 Breaden, Lake salt flat W.A. Austr.
183 N8 Brea de Tajo Spain
215 K9 Breakfast Vlei S. Africa
81 A12 Breaksea Island South I. N.Z.
81 A12 Breaksea Sound inlet South I. N.Z.
85 N8 Breaksea Spit Qld Austr.
158 H5 Bréal-sous-Montfort France
150 G4 Bream Gloucestershire, England U.K.
80 I2 Bream Bay North I. N.Z.
80 I2 Bream Head North I. N.Z.
149 M2 Breamish r. England U.K.
80 I3 Bream Tail c. North I. N.Z.
146 B6 Breanais Western Isles, Scotland U.K.
258 C2 Breas Chile
146 C6 Breascleit Western Isles, Scotland U.K.
151 J2 Breaston Derbyshire, England U.K.
159 L2 Bréauté France
197 N5 Breaza Romania
95 H8 Brebes Jawa Indon.
95 H8 Brebes, Tanjung pt Indon.
161 K9 Brec d'Utelle mt. France
158 I4 Brécey France
158 F6 Brech France
156 D5 Brêche r. France
150 D4 Brechfa Carmarthenshire, Wales U.K.
146 K9 Brechin Angus, Scotland U.K.
165 G6 Brecht Belgium
239 K7 Breckenridge CO U.S.A.
236 G2 Breckenridge MN U.S.A.
237 F9 Breckenridge TX U.S.A.
169 D8 Breckerfeld Ger.
151 N3 Breckland lowland England U.K.
259 B9 Brecknock, Península pen. Chile
232 D7 Brecksville OH U.S.A.
176 F3 Břeclav Czech Rep.
150 F4 Brecon Powys, Wales U.K.
150 F4 Brecon Beacons reg. Wales U.K.
150 F4 Brecon Beacons National Park Wales U.K.
164 G5 Breda Neth.
186 K4 Breda Spain
143 J4 Bredaryd Sweden
214 E10 Bredasdorp S. Africa
83 L6 Bredbo N.S.W. Austr.
168 E5 Breddenberg Ger.
170 F5 Breddin Ger.
168 H4 Breddorf Ger.
142 E6 Brede r. Denmark
151 N6 Brede r. England U.K.
165 C6 Bredene Belgium
170 H4 Bredereiche Ger.
150 H3 Bredon Worcestershire, England U.K.
168 G1 Bredstedt Ger.
140 O5 Bredträsk Sweden
140 M3 Bredviken Sweden
120 I1 Bredy Rus. Fed.
165 I6 Bree Belgium
214 E10 Breede r. S. Africa
170 E4 Breese Ger.
164 G3 Breezand Neth.
232 G9 Breezewood PA U.S.A.
172 F6 Breg r. Ger.
197 J9 Bregalnica r. Macedonia
179 M8 Bregana Croatia
191 L4 Breganze Italy
178 A4 Bregenz Austria
178 A5 Bregenzer Wald mts Austria
168 J1 Bregninge Denmark
197 K6 Bregovo Bulg.
191 J4 Breguzzo Italy
158 H4 Bréhal France
158 F5 Bréhan France
158 F4 Bréhat, Île de i. France
169 J8 Brehme Ger.
171 F7 Brehna Ger.
140 □A1 Breiðafjörður b. Iceland
140 B1 Breiðafjörður nature res. Iceland
140 □F1 Breiðdalsvík Iceland
157 N5 Breidenbach France
169 F9 Breidenbach Ger.
236 E2 Breien ND U.S.A.
168 I2 Breiholz Ger.
190 G2 Breil Switz.
161 L9 Breil-sur-Roya France
215 K6 Breipaal S. Africa
172 D5 Breisach am Rhein Ger.
172 D6 Breisgau reg. Ger.
190 D1 Breitenbach Switz.
169 I9 Breitenbach am Herzberg Ger.
178 E5 Breitenbach am Inn Austria
173 P4 Breitenberg Ger.
173 I5 Breitenbrunn Bayern Ger.
173 L3 Breitenbrunn Bayern Ger.
168 I3 Breitenburg Ger.
168 K3 Breitenfelde Ger.
171 E7 Breitenhagen Ger.
178 C5 Breitenwang Austria
169 J8 Breitenworbis Ger.
178 D5 Breiter Grieskogel mt. Austria
170 H4 Breiter Luzinsee l. Ger.
172 E6 Breitnau Ger.
169 F9 Breitscheid Hessen Ger.
169 D9 Breitscheid Rheinland-Pfalz Ger.
169 J9 Breitungen Ger.
140 Q1 Breivikbotn Norway
140 O2 Breivikeidet Norway
184 B6 Brejeira, Serra da mts Port.
254 C4 Brejinho de Nazaré Brazil
254 E2 Brejo Brazil
254 E4 Brejo r. Brazil
254 D4 Brejo da Porta Brazil
168 G1 Breklum Ger.
140 J5 Brekstad Norway
158 B5 Brélès France
190 H4 Brembo r. Italy
168 G4 Bremen Ger.
168 G4 Bremen land Ger.
231 E9 Bremen GA U.S.A.
226 H8 Bremen IN U.S.A.
232 C9 Bremen OH U.S.A.
87 E13 Bremer Bay W.A. Austr.
87 E13 Bremer Bay b. W.A. Austr.
168 G3 Bremerhaven Ger.
87 F12 Bremer Range hills W.A. Austr.
Bremersdorp Swaziland see Manzini
238 C3 Bremerton WA U.S.A.
168 H4 Bremervörde Ger.
190 E1 Bremgarten Switz.
169 D10 Bremm Ger.
142 B2 Bremnes Norway
162 A2 Brem-sur-Mer France
175 J5 Breń r. Pol.
185 J5 Breña, Embalse de la resr Spain
216 □3d Breña Alta La Palma Canary Is
150 F5 Brendon Hills England U.K.
184 H5 Brenes Spain
237 G10 Brenham TX U.S.A.
184 E4 Brenhas r. Port.
150 E1 Brenig, Llyn resr Wales U.K.
140 L4 Brenna Norway
174 G6 Brenna Pol.
160 G3 Brenne r. France
159 M7 Brenne r. France
159 N8 Brenne reg. France
162 G2 Brenne, Parc Naturel Régional de la nature res. France
191 L2 Brennero Italy
Brennero, Passo di pass Austria/Italy see Brenner Pass
Brennerpaß pass Austria/Italy see Brenner Pass
178 E6 Brenner Pass pass Austria/Italy
140 P2 Brennes Norway
140 P2 Brennfjell Norway
190 I4 Breno Italy
160 H4 Brénod France
163 H8 Brens France
172 F2 Brensbach Ger.
224 E4 Brent Ont. Can.
191 M5 Brenta r. Italy
191 J3 Brenta, Gruppo di mts Italy
150 G5 Brent Knoll Somerset, England U.K.
151 M4 Brentwood Essex, England U.K.
235 I3 Brentwood NY U.S.A.
173 I4 Brenz r. Ger.
191 J4 Brenzone Italy
190 I4 Brescia Italy
190 I4 Brescia prov. Italy
165 E6 Breskens Neth.
Breslau Pol. see Wrocław
156 B3 Bresle r. France
156 D5 Bresles France
225 G2 Brésolles, Lac l. Que. Can.
190 G5 Bressana Bottarone Italy
191 L2 Bressanone Italy
146 □N2 Bressay i. Scotland U.K.
160 G4 Bresse reg. France
163 G8 Bressols France
162 D2 Bressuire France
136 C1 Brest Belarus
158 C5 Brest France
158 C5 Brest, Rade de inlet France
179 L8 Brestanica Slovenia
179 M6 Bresternica Slovenia
Brest-Litovsk Belarus see Brest
Brest Oblast admin. div. Belarus see Brestskaya Voblasts'
197 J7 Brestovac Serbia
177 K6 Brestovăț Romania
Brestskaya Oblast' admin. div. Belarus see Brestskaya Voblasts'
138 I9 Brestskaya Voblasts' admin. div. Belarus
158 F5 Bretagne admin. reg. France
217 □1c Bretagne, Pointe de pt Réunion
163 E8 Bretagne-d'Armagnac France
250 C6 Bretana Peru
142 G2 Bretangen b. Norway
216 □1b Bretanha São Miguel Azores
216 □1b Bretanha, Ponta da pt São Miguel Azores
197 O4 Brețcu Romania
158 H5 Breteil France
163 H6 Bretenoux France
159 M4 Breteuil Haute-Normandie France
156 D4 Breteuil Picardie France
158 H8 Brétignolles-sur-Mer France
156 D6 Brétigny-sur-Orge France
171 J8 Bretnig Ger.
182 I5 Bretocino Spain
222 H4 Breton Alta Can.
246 D3 Breton, Cayo i. Cuba
159 M5 Bretoncelles France
237 K11 Breton Sound b. LA U.S.A.
235 G4 Breton Woods NJ U.S.A.
172 F3 Bretten Ger.
150 G1 Bretton Flintshire, Wales U.K.
159 K3 Brettville-sur-Laize France
172 D2 Bretzenheim Ger.
172 G3 Bretzfeld Ger.
252 B2 Breu r. Brazil/Peru
172 G2 Breuberg-Neustadt Ger.
157 L8 Breuches France
157 L8 Breuchin r. France
94 A2 Breueh, Pulau i. Indon.
164 I5 Breugel Neth.
190 D4 Breuil-Cervinia Italy
162 C4 Breuil-Magné France
156 B6 Breuilpont France
164 H4 Breukelen Neth.
169 H8 Breuna Ger.
157 K7 Breuvannes-en-Bassigny France
231 F8 Brevard NC U.S.A.
251 I5 Breves Brazil
142 F2 Brevik Norway
142 I2 Breviken Sweden
160 J4 Brévon r. France
169 H7 Brevörde Ger.
83 K3 Brewarrina N.S.W. Austr.
233 □Q4 Brewer ME U.S.A.
206 C5 Brewerville Liberia
150 H2 Brewood Staffordshire, England U.K.
236 F5 Brewster NE U.S.A.
235 H2 Brewster NY U.S.A.
232 D8 Brewster OH U.S.A.
238 E2 Brewster WA U.S.A.
Brewster, Kap c. Greenland see Kangikajik
83 J5 Brewster, Lake imp. l. N.S.W. Austr.
231 D10 Brewton AL U.S.A.
215 N2 Breyten S. Africa
139 U3 Breytovo Rus. Fed.
177 I2 Breza Slovakia
179 L7 Breze Slovenia
Brezhnev Rus. Fed. see Naberezhnyye Chelny
176 F3 Březí Czech Rep.
188 E3 Brežice Slovenia
179 N7 Breznica Croatia
177 K2 Breznica Slovakia
176 C2 Březnice Czech Rep.
197 K8 Breznik Bulg.
197 L6 Breznița-Motru Romania
197 L9 Breznitsa Bulg.
171 H10 Březno Czech Rep.
177 I3 Brezno Slovakia
156 B6 Brézolles France
177 G2 Březová Czech Rep.
177 G3 Brezová pod Bradlom Slovakia
177 L3 Brezovec Slovakia
179 J7 Brezovica Slovenia
197 N8 Brezovo Bulg.
188 F3 Brezovo Polje plain Croatia
208 D3 Bria C.A.R.
100 I2 Briakan Rus. Fed.
162 G4 Briance r. France
161 J7 Briançon France
241 T4 Brian Head mt. UT U.S.A.
150 E3 Brianne, Llyn resr Wales U.K.
235 H2 Briarcliff Manor NY U.S.A.
160 B1 Briare France
156 E8 Briare, Canal de France
163 H8 Briatexte France
195 K6 Briatico Italy
85 N9 Bribie Island Qld Austr.
161 K7 Bric Bouchet mt. France/Italy
136 G5 Briceni Moldova
161 J7 Bric Froid mt. France/Italy
Brichany Moldova see Briceni
190 C6 Bricherasio Italy
147 E5 Brickeens Ireland
234 C4 Brickerville PA U.S.A.
234 F6 Bricksboro NJ U.S.A.
235 G4 Brick Township NJ U.S.A.
157 I7 Bricon France
158 H3 Bricquebec France
147 G8 Bride r. Ireland
161 J6 Brides-les-Bains France
151 O5 Bridge Kent, England U.K.
235 K3 Bridgehampton NY U.S.A.
147 I7 Bridgeland Ireland
226 H8 Bridgeman MI U.S.A.
147 H2 Bridgend Ireland
146 K9 Bridgend Angus, Scotland U.K.
146 D11 Bridgend Argyll and Bute, Scotland U.K.
150 E4 Bridgend Bridgend, Wales U.K.
146 J8 Bridgend Moray, Scotland U.K.
150 E4 Bridgend admin. div. Wales U.K.
146 I10 Bridge of Allan Stirling, Scotland U.K.
146 H9 Bridge of Balgie Perth and Kinross, Scotland U.K.
146 J9 Bridge of Cally Perth and Kinross, Scotland U.K.
146 J9 Bridge of Craigisla Angus, Scotland U.K.
146 L8 Bridge of Don Aberdeen, Scotland U.K.
146 K9 Bridge of Dun Angus, Scotland U.K.
146 K9 Bridge of Dye Aberdeenshire, Scotland U.K.
146 J10 Bridge of Earn Perth and Kinross, Scotland U.K.
146 I5 Bridge of Forss Highland, Scotland U.K.
146 G9 Bridge of Orchy Argyll and Bute, Scotland U.K.
146 □M2 Bridge of Walls Shetland, Scotland U.K.
146 G11 Bridge of Weir Renfrewshire, Scotland U.K.
231 E8 Bridgeport AL U.S.A.
240 M3 Bridgeport CA U.S.A.
233 L7 Bridgeport CT U.S.A.
227 K6 Bridgeport MI U.S.A.
236 D5 Bridgeport NE U.S.A.
234 E4 Bridgeport PA U.S.A.
237 G9 Bridgeport TX U.S.A.
240 M3 Bridgeport Reservoir CA U.S.A.
238 J4 Bridger MT U.S.A.
238 K6 Bridger Peak WY U.S.A.
234 E6 Bridgeton NJ U.S.A.
87 D12 Bridgetown W.A. Austr.
247 □4 Bridgetown Barbados
225 H4 Bridgetown N.S. Can.
147 I8 Bridgetown Ireland
233 J10 Bridgeville DE U.S.A.
83 K10 Bridgewater Tas. Austr.
225 H4 Bridgewater N.S. Can.
233 O7 Bridgewater MA U.S.A.
233 □R2 Bridgewater ME U.S.A.
233 J6 Bridgewater NY U.S.A.
232 G10 Bridgewater VA U.S.A.
82 H8 Bridgewater, Cape Vic. Austr.
150 H2 Bridgnorth Shropshire, England U.K.
233 □O4 Bridgton ME U.S.A.
150 F5 Bridgwater Somerset, England U.K.
150 F5 Bridgwater Bay England U.K.
176 G2 Břidličná Czech Rep.
149 Q5 Bridlington East Riding of Yorkshire, England U.K.
149 Q5 Bridlington Bay England U.K.
83 K9 Bridport Tas. Austr.
150 G6 Bridport Dorset, England U.K.
162 E4 Brie France
156 E7 Brie reg. France
158 D5 Briec France
156 E6 Brie-Comte-Robert France
169 D10 Briedel Ger.
Brieg Pol. see Brzeg
164 F5 Brielle Neth.
156 I7 Brienne-le-Château France
160 E4 Briennon France
156 G7 Brienon-sur-Armançon France
190 E2 Brienz Switz.
193 P7 Brienza Italy
190 E2 Brienzer Rothorn mt. Switz.
190 D2 Brienzer See l. Switz.
158 G7 Brière, Parc Naturel Régional de nature res. France
234 A1 Brier Mountain hill PA U.S.A.
232 E10 Briery Knob mt. WV U.S.A.
171 J6 Briescht Ger.
170 G5 Brieselang Ger.
171 J6 Briesen Ger.
171 I8 Brieske Ger.
171 K6 Brieskow-Finkenheerd Ger.
171 K7 Briesnig Ger.
168 J4 Brietlingen Ger.
157 I5 Brieuilles-sur-Bar France
183 O4 Brieva de Cameros Spain
157 K5 Briey France
190 D3 Brig Switz.
172 F6 Brigach r. Ger.
261 I2 Brigadier General Diego Lamas Uru.
235 G6 Brigantine NJ U.S.A.
149 Q6 Brigg North Lincolnshire, England U.K.
238 L6 Briggsdale CO U.S.A.
226 E6 Briggsville WI U.S.A.
149 K4 Brigham Cumbria, England U.K.
238 H6 Brigham City UT U.S.A.
149 N6 Brighouse West Yorkshire, England U.K.
151 J6 Brighstone Isle of Wight, England U.K.
83 K7 Bright Vic. Austr.
151 O4 Brightlingsea Essex, England U.K.
261 F6 Brightman, Caleta inlet Arg.
227 Q5 Brighton Ont. Can.
81 E12 Brighton South I. N.Z.
151 L6 Brighton Brighton and Hove, England U.K.
238 L7 Brighton CO U.S.A.
227 K7 Brighton MI U.S.A.
232 H5 Brighton NY U.S.A.
232 C10 Brighton WV U.S.A.
151 L6 Brighton and Hove admin. div. England U.K.
85 H7 Brighton Downs Qld Austr.
81 H8 Brightwater South I. N.Z.
160 F5 Brignais France
163 F8 Brignemont France
158 C4 Brignogan-Plage France
161 I10 Brignoles France
146 H10 Brig o'Turk Stirling, Scotland U.K.
151 K3 Brigstock Northamptonshire, England U.K.
183 O7 Brihuega Spain
191 P6 Brijuni nat. park Croatia
206 A3 Brikama Gambia
226 F5 Brillion WI U.S.A.
157 J6 Brillon-en-Barrois France
169 G8 Brilon Ger.
149 O7 Brimington Derbyshire, England U.K.
226 J3 Brimley MI U.S.A.
140 □G1 Brimnes Iceland
226 C2 Brimson MN U.S.A.
247 □2 Brimstone Hill Fortress National Park St Kitts and Nevis
184 D4 Brinches Port.
182 H6 Brincones Spain
195 N2 Brindisi Italy
195 N2 Brindisi prov. Italy
193 P6 Brindisi Montagna Italy
82 D4 Bring, Lake salt flat S.A. Austr.
188 E3 Brinje Croatia
237 J8 Brinkley AR U.S.A.
261 F2 Brinkmann Arg.
168 E4 Brinkum Niedersachsen Ger.
168 G4 Brinkum Niedersachsen Ger.
82 G5 Brinkworth S.A. Austr.
160 C2 Brinon-sur-Beuvron France
159 P6 Brinon-sur-Sauldre France
149 O7 Brinsley Nottinghamshire, England U.K.
157 L6 Brin-sur-Seille France
149 O7 Brinsworth South Yorkshire, England U.K.
161 C7 Brion France
225 I4 Brion, Île i. Que. Can.
183 O3 Briones Spain
160 E4 Brionnais reg. France
159 M3 Brionne France
161 C6 Brioude France
162 D3 Brioux-sur-Boutonne France
159 K4 Briouze France
225 G2 Brisay Que. Can.
85 N9 Brisbane Qld Austr.
191 L7 Brisighella Italy
159 K7 Brissac-Quincé France
233 □R2 Bristol N.B. Can.
150 G5 Bristol Bristol, England U.K.
150 G5 Bristol admin. div. England U.K.
233 M7 Bristol CT U.S.A.
231 E10 Bristol FL U.S.A.
234 B7 Bristol MD U.S.A.
233 N5 Bristol NH U.S.A.
234 F4 Bristol PA U.S.A.
233 N7 Bristol RI U.S.A.
232 C12 Bristol TN U.S.A.
233 L4 Bristol VT U.S.A.
220 B4 Bristol Bay AK U.S.A.
150 D5 Bristol Channel est. England U.K.
249 G7 Bristol Island S. Sandwich Is
241 Q7 Bristol Lake CA U.S.A.
241 P7 Bristol Mountains CA U.S.A.
151 O2 Briston Norfolk, England U.K.
237 G8 Bristow OK U.S.A.
150 G6 Brit r. England U.K.
Britannia Island Îles Loyauté New Caledonia see Maré
182 D5 Britelo Port.
262 S2 British Antarctic Territory Antarctica
222 F5 British Columbia prov. Can.
221 J1 British Empire Range mts Nunavut Can.
British Guiana country S. America see Guyana
88 C7 British Indian Ocean Territory terr. Indian Ocean
264 J6 British Isles N. Atlantic Ocean
British Solomon Islands country S. Pacific Ocean see Solomon Islands
179 J7 Britof Slovenia
Brito Godins Angola see Kiwaba N'zogi
215 L1 Brits S. Africa
214 H6 Britstown S. Africa
147 J6 Brittas Ireland
147 J7 Brittas Bay Ireland
146 D8 Brittle, Loch b. Scotland U.K.
236 G3 Britton SD U.S.A.
170 I5 Britz Ger.
162 H5 Brive-la-Gaillarde France
161 D6 Brives-Charensac France
183 N3 Briviesca Spain
158 H2 Brix France
178 F5 Brixen im Thale Austria
150 E7 Brixham Torbay, England U.K.
Brixia Italy see Brescia
178 E5 Brixlegg Austria
151 K3 Brixworth Northamptonshire, England U.K.
191 P4 Brkini reg. Slovenia
Brlik Zhambylskaya Oblast' Kazakh. see Birlik
171 K9 Brniště Czech Rep.
176 F2 Brno Czech Rep.
143 N2 Bro Sweden
Broach Gujarat India see Bharuch
231 G8 Broad r. SC U.S.A.
233 K5 Broadalbin NY U.S.A.
87 F11 Broad Arrow W.A. Austr.
224 E3 Broadback r. Que. Can.
150 F6 Broadclyst Devon, England U.K.
83 J7 Broadford Vic. Austr.
147 E7 Broadford Clare Ireland
147 E8 Broadford Limerick Ireland
146 E8 Broadford Highland, Scotland U.K.
147 C4 Broad Haven b. Ireland
150 B4 Broad Haven Pembrokeshire, Wales U.K.
150 H3 Broadheath Worcestershire, England U.K.
146 J12 Broad Law hill Scotland U.K.
150 H6 Broadmayne Dorset, England U.K.
84 E4 Broadmere N.T. Austr.
151 N6 Broad Oak East Sussex, England U.K.
123 Q4 Broad Peak China/Jammu and Kashmir
85 L7 Broad Sound sea chan. Qld Austr.
85 M7 Broad Sound Channel Qld Austr.
85 L7 Broadsound Range hills Qld Austr.
151 O5 Broadstairs Kent, England U.K.
238 L4 Broadus MT U.S.A.
223 K5 Broadview Sask. Can.
83 N3 Broadwater N.S.W. Austr.
236 D5 Broadwater NE U.S.A.
147 J8 Broadway Ireland
151 I3 Broadway Worcestershire, England U.K.
232 G10 Broadway VA U.S.A.
150 H6 Broadwey Dorset, England U.K.
150 G6 Broadwindsor Dorset, England U.K.
80 H2 Broadwood North I. N.Z.
168 I1 Broager Denmark
143 K5 Broby Sweden
190 C2 Broc Switz.
163 C7 Brocas France
138 F5 Brocēni Latvia
146 D8 Brochel Highland, Scotland U.K.
223 K3 Brochet Man. Can.
223 K3 Brochet, Lac l. Man. Can.
149 L6 Brock r. England U.K.
168 I4 Brockel Ger.
168 J5 Bröckel Ger.
169 K7 Brocken mt. Ger.
151 I6 Brockenhurst Hampshire, England U.K.
221 G2 Brock Island N.W.T. Can.
86 D7 Brockman, Mount W.A. Austr.
232 H5 Brockport NY U.S.A.
232 G7 Brockport PA U.S.A.
233 N6 Brockton MA U.S.A.
234 C3 Brockton PA U.S.A.
169 F6 Brockum Ger.
224 F4 Brockville Ont. Can.
233 □R3 Brockway N.B. Can.
232 G7 Brockway PA U.S.A.
150 H4 Brockworth Gloucestershire, England U.K.
232 F6 Brocton NY U.S.A.
174 E2 Broczyno Pol.
198 C2 Brod Macedonia
196 J9 Brod Macedonia
176 G2 Brodek u Přerova Czech Rep.
Broderick Falls Kenya see Webuye
170 F2 Broderstorf Ger.
136 H4 Brodets'ke Ukr.
221 J2 Brodeur Peninsula Nunavut Can.
226 E7 Brodhead WI U.S.A.
234 E3 Brodhead r. PA U.S.A.
234 E3 Brodheadsville PA U.S.A.
146 F11 Brodick North Ayrshire, Scotland U.K.
232 G12 Brodnax VA U.S.A.
175 H2 Brodnica Kujawsko-Pomorskie Pol.
174 E3 Brodnica Wielkopolskie Pol.
167 I2 Brodnicki Park Krajobrazowy Pol.
176 G3 Brodské Slovakia
174 C4 Brody Lubuskie Pol.
174 D3 Brody Lubuskie Pol.
136 E3 Brody Ukr.
215 J2 Broedersput S. Africa
164 J6 Broekhuizenvorst Neth.
215 J6 Broekpoort r. S. Africa
159 M3 Broglie France
169 D10 Brohl Ger.
170 I3 Brohm Ger.
160 G2 Broin France
174 D3 Brójce Pol.
174 D2 Brojce Pol.
175 J3 Brok Pol.
175 J3 Brok r. Pol.
168 H3 Brokdorf Ger.
142 E2 Brokefjell mt. Norway
87 D13 Broke Inlet W.A. Austr.
237 H7 Broken Arrow OK U.S.A.
83 M5 Broken Bay N.S.W. Austr.
236 F5 Broken Bow NE U.S.A.
237 H8 Broken Bow OK U.S.A.
237 H8 Broken Bow Reservoir OK U.S.A.
232 H10 Brokenburg VA U.S.A.
223 L5 Brokenhead r. Man. Can.
82 H4 Broken Hill N.S.W. Austr.
Broken Hill Zambia see Kabwe
265 K7 Broken Plateau sea feature Indian Ocean
251 H3 Brokopondo Suriname
Brokopondo Stuwmeer resr Suriname see Professor van Blommestein Meer
168 I3 Brokstedt Ger.
194 H7 Brolo Sicilia Italy
173 J3 Brombachsee l. Ger.
Bromberg Pol. see Bydgoszcz
168 K5 Brome Ger.
150 G3 Bromfield Shropshire, England U.K.
151 K3 Bromham Bedfordshire, England U.K.
150 H5 Bromham Wiltshire, England U.K.
151 L5 Bromley Greater London, England U.K.
142 F1 Bromma Norway
161 B7 Brommat France
143 J3 Brommö i. Sweden
140 O1 Bromnes Norway
95 J8 Bromo Tengger Semeru, Taman Nasional nat. park Indon.
246 □ Brompton Jamaica

Brompton to Burgpreppach

292

149 O5 **Brompton** *North Yorkshire, England* U.K.
149 N5 **Brompton on Swale** *North Yorkshire, England* U.K.
143 M5 **Brömsebro** Sweden
150 H3 **Bromsgrove** *Worcestershire, England* U.K.
169 G8 **Bromskirchen** Ger.
150 G3 **Bromyard** *Herefordshire, England* U.K.
160 F5 **Bron** France
150 E2 **Bronaber** *Gwynedd, Wales* U.K.
183 Q7 **Bronchales** Spain
142 F4 **Brønderslev** Denmark
206 E5 **Brong-Ahafo** *admin. reg.* Ghana
190 G5 **Broni** Italy
171 K7 **Bronice** Pol.
215 M1 **Bronkhorstspruit** S. Africa
139 V6 **Bronnitsy** Rus. Fed.
140 L4 **Brønnøysund** Norway
231 F11 **Bronson** *FL* U.S.A.
226 I8 **Bronson** *MI* U.S.A.
194 H8 **Bronte** *Sicilia* Italy
235 H3 **Bronx County** *county NY* U.S.A.
136 G3 **Bronyts'ka Huta** Ukr.
190 H4 **Bronzone, Monte** *mt.* Italy
151 O2 **Brooke** *Norfolk, England* U.K.
232 H10 **Brooke** *VA* U.S.A.
147 H4 **Brookeborough** *Northern Ireland* U.K.
92 A7 **Brooke's Point** *Palawan* Phil.
235 I1 **Brookfield** *CT* U.S.A.
236 I6 **Brookfield** *MO* U.S.A.
226 F6 **Brookfield** *WI* U.S.A.
237 J10 **Brookhaven** *MS* U.S.A.
238 B5 **Brookings** *OR* U.S.A.
236 G3 **Brookings** *SD* U.S.A.
234 D5 **Brookland Terrace** *DE* U.S.A.
233 N6 **Brookline** *MA* U.S.A.
226 D9 **Brooklyn** *IL* U.S.A.
227 J7 **Brooklyn** *MI* U.S.A.
234 B6 **Brooklyn Park** *MD* U.S.A.
226 A4 **Brooklyn Park** *MN* U.S.A.
232 G11 **Brookneal** *VA* U.S.A.
226 A4 **Brook Park** *MN* U.S.A.
223 I5 **Brooks** *Alta* Can.
233 □P4 **Brooks** *ME* U.S.A.
232 E11 **Brooks** *WV* U.S.A.
262 T2 **Brooks, Cape** Antarctica
222 C2 **Brooks Brook** *Y.T.* Can.
234 D5 **Brookside** *DE* U.S.A.
222 E5 **Brooks Peninsula Provincial Park** *B.C.* Can.
220 D3 **Brooks Range** *mts AK* U.S.A.
226 H9 **Brookston** *IN* U.S.A.
226 B3 **Brookston** *MN* U.S.A.
231 F11 **Brooksville** *FL* U.S.A.
232 A10 **Brooksville** *KY* U.S.A.
87 D12 **Brookton** *W.A.* Austr.
233 □R3 **Brookton** *ME* U.S.A.
230 E6 **Brookville** *IN* U.S.A.
232 F7 **Brookville** *PA* U.S.A.
146 F7 **Broom, Loch** *inlet Scotland* U.K.
86 G4 **Broome** *W.A.* Austr.
87 D12 **Broomehill** *W.A.* Austr.
147 I4 **Broomfield** Ireland
151 M4 **Broomfield** *Essex, England* U.K.
158 G5 **Broons** France
161 B8 **Broquiès** France
146 I6 **Brora** *Highland, Scotland* U.K.
146 I6 **Brora** *r. Scotland* U.K.
146 I6 **Brora, Loch** *l. Scotland* U.K.
143 K6 **Brösarp** Sweden
150 H2 **Broseley** *Shropshire, England* U.K.
136 D5 **Broshniv Osada** Ukr.
147 D8 **Brosna** Ireland
147 G6 **Brosna** *r.* Ireland
162 D5 **Brossac** France
140 N2 **Brøstadbotn** Norway
197 N3 **Broşteni** Romania
232 F12 **Brosville** *VA* U.S.A.
256 C5 **Brotas** Brazil
184 C3 **Brotas** Port.
254 E5 **Brotas de Macaúbas** Brazil
115 M7 **Brothers** *is Andaman & Nicobar Is* India
238 D5 **Brothers** *OR* U.S.A.
82 □3 **Brothers Point** S. Pacific Ocean
186 E2 **Broto** Spain
159 M3 **Brotonne, Parc Naturel Régional de** *nature res.* France
157 J7 **Brottes** France
149 P4 **Brotton** *Redcar and Cleveland, England* U.K.
156 B7 **Brou** France
149 M4 **Brough** *Cumbria, England* U.K.
149 P6 **Brough** *East Riding of Yorkshire, England* U.K.
146 J5 **Brough** *Highland, Scotland* U.K.
148 B7 **Broughal** Ireland
146 J4 **Brough Head** *Scotland* U.K.
146 K5 **Brough Ness** *pt Scotland* U.K.
147 J3 **Broughshane** *Northern Ireland* U.K.
150 G1 **Broughton** *Flintshire, Wales* U.K.
151 K3 **Broughton** *Northamptonshire, England* U.K.
149 P6 **Broughton** *North Lincolnshire, England* U.K.
146 J11 **Broughton** *Scottish Borders, Scotland* U.K.
151 J2 **Broughton Astley** *Leicestershire, England* U.K.
149 K5 **Broughton in Furness** *Cumbria, England* U.K.
Broughton Island *Nunavut* Can. *see* **Qikiqtarjuaq**
146 K4 **Broughtown** *Orkney, Scotland* U.K.
202 C5 **Broulkou** *well* Chad
176 F1 **Broumov** Czech Rep.
157 I7 **Brousseval** France
157 M7 **Brouvelieures** France
164 E5 **Brouwershaven** Neth.
136 J3 **Brovary** Ukr.
85 M9 **Brovinia** *Qld* Austr.
142 F4 **Brovst** Denmark
236 H2 **Browerville** *MN* U.S.A.
87 E11 **Brown, Lake** *salt flat W.A.* Austr.
82 G5 **Brown, Mount** *hill S.A.* Austr.
82 D5 **Brown, Point** *S.A.* Austr.
246 F3 **Brown Bank** *sea feature* Bahamas
227 L6 **Brown City** *MI* U.S.A.
85 I4 **Brown Creek** *r. Qld* Austr.
226 G6 **Brown Deer** *WI* U.S.A.
149 M7 **Brown Edge** *Staffordshire, England* U.K.
87 H8 **Browne Range** *hills W.A.* Austr.
237 D9 **Brownfield** *TX* U.S.A.
151 I2 **Brownhills** *West Midlands, England* U.K.
238 H2 **Browning** *MT* U.S.A.
240 O6 **Brown Mountain** *CA* U.S.A.
226 B6 **Brownsdale** *MN* U.S.A.
234 F5 **Browns Mills** *NJ* U.S.A.
246 □ **Brown's Town** Jamaica
230 D6 **Brownstown** *IN* U.S.A.
234 C4 **Brownstown** *PA* U.S.A.
236 G3 **Browns Valley** *MN* U.S.A.
230 D7 **Brownsville** *KY* U.S.A.
232 F8 **Brownsville** *PA* U.S.A.
237 K8 **Brownsville** *TN* U.S.A.
237 G13 **Brownsville** *TX* U.S.A.
251 H3 **Brownsweg** Suriname
233 □P3 **Brownville** *ME* U.S.A.
233 □P3 **Brownville Junction** *ME* U.S.A.
237 F10 **Brownwood** *TX* U.S.A.
243 J2 **Brownwood, Lake** *TX* U.S.A.
86 G3 **Browse Island** *W.A.* Austr.
146 J11 **Broxburn** *West Lothian, Scotland* U.K.
190 C2 **Broye** *r.* Switz.
156 G6 **Broyes** France
171 J10 **Brozany** Czech Rep.
182 G9 **Brozas** Spain
138 M9 **Brozha** Belarus
190 I4 **Brozzo** Italy
176 E2 **Brtnice** Czech Rep.
146 I9 **Bruar Water** *r. Scotland* U.K.
156 E3 **Bruay-la-Bussière** France
Bruce Barbados *see* **Bruce Vale**
237 K9 **Bruce** *MS* U.S.A.
226 C4 **Bruce** *WI* U.S.A.
86 E7 **Bruce, Mount** *W.A.* Austr.
226 E3 **Bruce Crossing** *MI* U.S.A.
227 M5 **Bruce Peninsula** *Ont.* Can.
227 M4 **Bruce Peninsula National Park** *Ont.* Can.
87 E11 **Bruce Rock** *W.A.* Austr.
247 □4 **Bruce Vale** Barbados
157 O6 **Bruche** *r.* France
168 H5 **Bruchhausen-Vilsen** Ger.
169 G10 **Bruchköbel** Ger.
172 C3 **Bruchmühlbach** Ger.
172 F3 **Bruchsal** Ger.
172 D3 **Bruchweiler-Bärenbach** Ger.
171 G6 **Brück** Ger.
178 G5 **Bruck an der Großglocknerstraße** Austria
179 O3 **Bruck an der Leitha** Austria
179 L5 **Bruck an der Mur** Austria
173 L4 **Bruckberg** Ger.
172 C2 **Brücken** Ger.
172 C3 **Brücken (Pfalz)** Ger.
173 M3 **Bruck in der Oberpfalz** Ger.
179 K6 **Brückl** Austria
173 L6 **Bruckmühl** Ger.
195 I9 **Brucoli** *Sicilia* Italy
175 H3 **Brudzeń Duży** Pol.
167 I2 **Brudzeński Park Krajobrazowy** Pol.
174 G3 **Brudzew** Pol.
150 G5 **Brue** *r. England* U.K.
161 H9 **Brue-Auriac** France
170 E3 **Brüel** Ger.
159 P8 **Bruère-Allichamps** France
165 E7 **Brugelette** Belgium
Bruges Belgium *see* **Brugge**
190 E1 **Brugg** Switz.
165 D6 **Brugge** Belgium
169 I6 **Brüggen** *Niedersachsen* Ger.
169 B8 **Brüggen** *Nordrhein-Westfalen* Ger.
190 H7 **Brugnato** Italy
191 N4 **Brugnera** Italy
163 G8 **Bruguières** France
140 I5 **Bruhagen** Norway
172 F3 **Brühl** *Baden-Württemberg* Ger.
169 C9 **Brühl** *Nordrhein-Westfalen* Ger.
232 B10 **Bruin** *KY* U.S.A.
232 F7 **Bruin** *PA* U.S.A.
164 F5 **Bruinisse** Neth.
241 V2 **Bruin Point** *mt. UT* U.S.A.
117 P5 **Bruint** *Arun. Prad.* India
212 C5 **Brukkaros** Namibia
214 B1 **Brukkaros, Mount** Namibia
222 G4 **Brûlé** *Alta* Can.
226 C3 **Brule** *WI* U.S.A.
225 I2 **Brûlé, Lac** *l. Que.* Can.
159 K6 **Brûlon** France
165 G9 **Brûly** Belgium
257 E4 **Brumadinho** Brazil
254 E5 **Brumado** Brazil
157 O6 **Brumath** France
85 M1 **Brumer Islands** P.N.G.
164 J4 **Brummen** Neth.
177 H2 **Brumov-Bylnice** Czech Rep.
177 G1 **Brumovice** Czech Rep.
141 K6 **Brumunddal** Norway
192 F2 **Bruna** *r.* Italy
147 J5 **Brú Na Bóinne** *tourist site* Ireland
170 D5 **Brunau** Ger.
151 O2 **Brundall** *Norfolk, England* U.K.
151 O3 **Brundish** *Suffolk, England* U.K.
Brundisium Italy *see* **Brindisi**
238 G5 **Bruneau** *ID* U.S.A.
238 G5 **Bruneau** *r. ID* U.S.A.
238 G5 **Bruneau, East Fork** *r. ID/NV* U.S.A.
238 G5 **Bruneau, West Fork** *r. ID/NV* U.S.A.
156 H4 **Brunehamel** France
95 K2 **Brunei** *country* Asia
Brunei Brunei *see* **Bandar Seri Begawan**
95 K2 **Brunei Bay** Malaysia
183 M8 **Brunete** Spain
84 E5 **Brunette Downs** *N.T.* Austr.
225 K4 **Brunette Island** *Nfld and Lab.* Can.
140 M5 **Brunflo** Sweden
191 L2 **Brunico** Italy
163 H7 **Bruniquel** France
179 L6 **Brunn** Austria
Brünn Czech Rep. *see* **Brno**
170 H3 **Brunn** Ger.
143 N2 **Brunna** Sweden
179 N3 **Brunn am Gebirge** Austria
190 F1 **Brunnen** Switz.
81 F9 **Brunner, Lake** *South I.* N.Z.
234 C4 **Brunnerville** *PA* U.S.A.
223 J4 **Bruno** *Sask.* Can.
226 B3 **Bruno** *MN* U.S.A.
168 H3 **Brunsbüttel** Ger.
165 I7 **Brunssum** Neth.
157 N8 **Brunstatt** France
Brunswick Ger. *see* **Braunschweig**
231 G10 **Brunswick** *GA* U.S.A.
232 H9 **Brunswick** *MD* U.S.A.
233 □P5 **Brunswick** *ME* U.S.A.
236 I6 **Brunswick** *MO* U.S.A.
232 D7 **Brunswick** *OH* U.S.A.
259 C9 **Brunswick, Península de** *pen.* Chile
86 H3 **Brunswick Bay** *W.A.* Austr.
83 N3 **Brunswick Heads** *N.S.W.* Austr.
87 C12 **Brunswick Junction** *W.A.* Austr.
224 D3 **Brunswick Lake** *Ont.* Can.
176 G2 **Bruntál** Czech Rep.
262 W2 **Brunt Ice Shelf** Antarctica
215 O5 **Bruntville** S. Africa
83 K10 **Bruny Island** *Tas.* Austr.
196 J7 **Brus** Serbia
Brusa Turkey *see* **Bursa**
178 D7 **Brusago** Italy
142 B3 **Brusand** Norway
134 H3 **Brusenets** Rus. Fed.
170 D3 **Brüsewitz** Ger.
236 D5 **Brush** *CO* U.S.A.
233 K4 **Brushton** *NY* U.S.A.
190 I3 **Brusio** Switz.
177 I3 **Brusno** Slovakia
139 S4 **Brusovo** Rus. Fed.
255 C8 **Brusque** Brazil
161 B9 **Brusque** France
Brussel Belgium *see* **Bruxelles**
Brussels Belgium *see* **Bruxelles**
227 M6 **Brussels** *Ont.* Can.
170 J4 **Brüssow** Ger.
177 L4 **Brusturi** Romania
197 O3 **Brusturi-Drăgăneşti** Romania
174 F2 **Brusy** Pol.
136 I3 **Brusyliv** Ukr.
83 K7 **Bruthen** *Vic.* Austr.
150 H5 **Bruton** *Somerset, England* U.K.
169 D10 **Bruttig-Fankel** Ger.
165 F7 **Bruxelles** Belgium
157 M7 **Bruyères** France
156 G4 **Bruyères-et-Montbérault** France
158 H5 **Bruz** France
250 D2 **Bruzual** Venez.
195 K7 **Bruzzano, Capo** *c.* Italy
177 H2 **Brvnište** Slovakia
175 I3 **Brwinów** Pol.
236 M5 **Bryan** *OH* U.S.A.
237 G10 **Bryan** *TX* U.S.A.
82 G5 **Bryan, Mount** *hill S.A.* Austr.
262 S2 **Bryan Coast** Antarctica
137 R5 **Bryanka** Ukr.
139 R8 **Bryansk** Rus. Fed.
129 I1 **Bryanskaya Kosa, Mys** *pt* Rus. Fed.
139 Q8 **Bryanskaya Oblast'** *admin. div.* Rus. Fed.
Bryansk Oblast *admin. div.* Rus. Fed. *see* **Bryanskaya Oblast'**
129 H1 **Bryanskoye** Rus. Fed.
237 I8 **Bryant** *AR* U.S.A.
226 E4 **Bryant** *WI* U.S.A.
237 I7 **Bryant Creek** *r. MO* U.S.A.
233 □O4 **Bryant Pond** *ME* U.S.A.
241 T4 **Bryce Canyon National Park** *UT* U.S.A.
241 W8 **Bryce Mountain** *AZ* U.S.A.
150 □ **Bryher** *i. England* U.K.
137 M7 **Brylivka** Ukr.
150 F1 **Brymbo** *Wrexham, Wales* U.K.
139 S8 **Bryn'** Rus. Fed.
150 E4 **Brynamman** *Carmarthenshire, Wales* U.K.
Brynbuga *Wales* U.K. *see* **Usk**
142 B3 **Bryne** Norway
150 F1 **Brynford** *Flintshire, Wales* U.K.
175 H5 **Brynica** *r.* Pol.
135 G7 **Bryn'kovskaya** Rus. Fed.
150 F4 **Brynmawr** *Blaenau Gwent, Wales* U.K.
234 E4 **Bryn Mawr** *PA* U.S.A.
227 Q3 **Bryson, Lac** *l. Que.* Can.
231 F8 **Bryson City** *NC* U.S.A.
135 G7 **Bryukhovetskaya** Rus. Fed.
136 C4 **Bryukhovychi** Ukr.
196 I5 **Brzava** *r.* Serbia
174 F5 **Brzeg** Pol.
174 E4 **Brzeg Dolny** Pol.
174 G3 **Brześć Kujawski** Pol.
Brześć nad Bugiem Belarus *see* **Brest**
175 I6 **Brzesko** Pol.
175 H6 **Brzeszcze** Pol.
174 G3 **Brzezie** *Kujawsko-Pomorskie* Pol.
174 E2 **Brzezie** *Pomorskie* Pol.
175 H4 **Brzeziny** *Łódzkie* Pol.
175 J6 **Brzeziny** *Podkarpackie* Pol.
174 G4 **Brzeziny** *Wielkopolskie* Pol.
175 H6 **Brzeźnica** *Małopolskie* Pol.
175 J5 **Brzeźnica** *Podkarpackie* Pol.
174 G4 **Brzeźnio** Pol.
175 L4 **Brzeźno** *Lubelskie* Pol.
174 G3 **Brzeźno** *Wielkopolskie* Pol.
174 D2 **Brzeźno** *Zachodniopomorskie* Pol.
175 J6 **Brzostek** Pol.
177 J3 **Brzotín** Slovakia
175 J4 **Brzóza** Pol.
175 K6 **Brzozów** Pol.
175 K2 **Brzozówka** *r.* Pol.
175 H2 **Brzuze** Pol.
175 K5 **Brzyska Wola** Pol.
156 C6 **Bû** France
124 G7 **Bū** *well* Yemen
209 B6 **Bua** Angola
79 □7 **Bua** *Vanua Levu* Fiji
142 I4 **Bua** Sweden
210 D4 **Bu'aale** Somalia
92 E6 **Buad** *i.* Phil.
159 J4 **Buais** France
78 □6 **Buala** *Sta Isabel* Solomon Is
Buandougou Côte d'Ivoire *see* **Bouandougou**
93 D2 **Buang** *i.* Indon.
182 C8 **Buarcos** Port.
94 D4 **Buatan** *Sumatera* Indon.
202 D2 **Bū Athlah** *well* Libya
125 J3 **Bu'ayj** *well* Saudi Arabia
202 B2 **Bu'ayrāt al Hasūn** Libya
206 B4 **Buba** Guinea-Bissau
186 E2 **Búbal, Embalse de** *resr* Spain
211 A5 **Bubanza** Burundi
173 K2 **Bubenreuth** Ger.
213 F4 **Bubi** *r.* Zimbabwe
127 N9 **Būbiyān, Jazīrat** *i.* Kuwait
158 E6 **Bubry** France
92 C8 **Bubuan** *i.* Phil.
92 C9 **Bubuan** *i.* Phil.
149 P6 **Bubwith** *East Riding of Yorkshire, England* U.K.
79 □7 **Buca** *Vanua Levu* Fiji
199 I4 **Buca** Turkey
199 L5 **Bucak** Turkey
177 G3 **Bučany** Slovakia
129 I4 **Bucaq** Azer.
250 C3 **Bucaramanga** Col.
245 H4 **Bucareli** Mex.
92 E7 **Bucas Grande** *i.* Phil.
86 G4 **Buccaneer Archipelago** *is W.A.* Austr.
194 H9 **Buccheri** *Sicilia* Italy
193 M3 **Bucchianico** Italy
191 K7 **Bucciana, Monte** *mt.* Italy
190 G5 **Buccinasco** Italy
193 O6 **Buccino** Italy
197 O3 **Bucecea** Romania
197 N5 **Bucegi, Munţii** *mts* Romania
184 A3 **Bucelas** Port.
160 H2 **Bucey-lès-Gy** France
173 I5 **Buch** Ger.
136 E4 **Buchach** Ukr.
173 M5 **Buch am Erlbach** Ger.
83 L7 **Buchan** *Vic.* Austr.
84 F5 **Buchanan** *watercourse N.T.* Austr.
206 C5 **Buchanan** Liberia
231 E9 **Buchanan** *GA* U.S.A.
226 H8 **Buchanan** *MI* U.S.A.
235 H2 **Buchanan** *NY* U.S.A.
232 F11 **Buchanan** *VA* U.S.A.
85 J6 **Buchanan, Lake** *salt flat Qld* Austr.
87 G8 **Buchanan, Lake** *salt flat W.A.* Austr.
237 F10 **Buchanan, Lake** *TX* U.S.A.
221 K2 **Buchan Gulf** *Nunavut* Can.
225 J3 **Buchans** *Nfld and Lab.* Can.
Bucharest Romania *see* **Bucureşti**
173 M5 **Buchbach** Ger.
178 A5 **Buchboden** Austria
169 D10 **Büchel** Ger.
168 K4 **Büchen** Ger.
172 G2 **Buchen (Odenwald)** Ger.
172 E6 **Buchenbach** Ger.
173 K3 **Büchenbach** Ger.
173 I6 **Buchenberg** Ger.
172 C2 **Büchenbeuren** Ger.
170 F4 **Buchholz** Ger.
168 I5 **Buchholz (Aller)** Ger.
169 D9 **Buchholz (Westerwald)** Ger.
179 J3 **Buchkirchen** Austria
173 P4 **Büchlberg** Ger.
173 J5 **Buchloe** Ger.
176 G2 **Buchlovice** Czech Rep.
146 H10 **Buchlyvie** *Stirling, Scotland* U.K.
168 I4 **Bucholz in der Nordheide** Ger.
240 L6 **Buchon, Point** *CA* U.S.A.
190 G1 **Buchs** Switz.
260 A5 **Buchupureo** Chile
156 B4 **Buchy** France
197 N4 **Bucin, Pasul** *pass* Romania
191 L9 **Bucine** Italy
234 C5 **Buck** *PA* U.S.A.
237 E10 **Buckburn Draw** *watercourse TX* U.S.A.
151 L3 **Buckden** *Cambridgeshire, England* U.K.
149 M5 **Buckden** *North Yorkshire, England* U.K.
169 H6 **Bückeburg** Ger.
168 H5 **Bücken** Ger.
241 T8 **Buckeye** *AZ* U.S.A.
150 E7 **Buckfastleigh** *Devon, England* U.K.
232 E10 **Buckhannon** *WV* U.S.A.
232 F9 **Buckhannon** *r. WV* U.S.A.
146 J10 **Buckhaven** *Fife, Scotland* U.K.
227 P5 **Buckhorn** *Ont.* Can.
227 P5 **Buckhorn Lake** *Ont.* Can.
146 K7 **Buckie** *Moray, Scotland* U.K.
227 S4 **Buckingham** *Que.* Can.
244 C4 **Buckingham** Mex.
151 K3 **Buckingham** *Buckinghamshire, England* U.K.
234 E4 **Buckingham** *PA* U.S.A.
232 G11 **Buckingham** *VA* U.S.A.
84 E2 **Buckingham Bay** *N.T.* Austr.
151 K4 **Buckinghamshire** *admin. div. England* U.K.
220 B3 **Buckland** *AK* U.S.A.
214 H5 **Bucklands** S. Africa
85 L8 **Buckland Tableland** *reg. Qld* Austr.
82 F5 **Buckleboo** *S.A.* Austr.
151 J5 **Bucklebury** *West Berkshire, England* U.K.
263 K2 **Buckle Island** Antarctica
82 □3 **Buckles Bay** S. Pacific Ocean
84 F6 **Buckley** *watercourse Qld* Austr.
150 F1 **Buckley** *Flintshire, Wales* U.K.
226 F9 **Buckley** *IL* U.S.A.
263 J2 **Buckley Bay** Antarctica
179 M4 **Bucklige Welt** *reg.* Austria
237 F7 **Bucklin** *KS* U.S.A.
Buckner Bay *Okinawa* Japan *see* **Nakagusuku-wan**
170 J5 **Buckow Märkische Schweiz** Ger.
146 L8 **Bucksburn** *Aberdeen, Scotland* U.K.
234 E4 **Bucks County** *county PA* U.S.A.
241 S7 **Buckskin Mountains** *AZ* U.S.A.
240 K2 **Bucks Mountain** *CA* U.S.A.
233 □Q4 **Bucksport** *ME* U.S.A.
170 F5 **Bückwitz** Ger.
176 G2 **Bučovice** Czech Rep.
209 B6 **Buco-Zau** Angola
177 K4 **Bucsa** Hungary
197 N6 **Bucşani** Romania
197 O6 **Bucureşti** Romania
156 G4 **Bucy-lès-Pierrepont** France
232 C8 **Bucyrus** *OH* U.S.A.
175 H4 **Buczek** Pol.
140 I5 **Bud** Norway
139 R8 **Buda** Rus. Fed.
186 G6 **Buda, Illa de** *i.* Spain
171 L6 **Budachów** Pol.
177 H4 **Budai** *park* Hungary
139 N9 **Buda-Kashalyova** Belarus
177 H4 **Budakeszi** Hungary
96 B3 **Budalin** Myanmar
177 H4 **Budaörs** Hungary
177 I4 **Budapest** Hungary
116 G5 **Budaun** *Uttar Prad.* India
83 M6 **Budawang National Park** *N.S.W.* Austr.
124 F4 **Budayyi'ah** *well* Saudi Arabia
210 E3 **Bud Bud** Somalia
87 C10 **Budd, Mount** *hill W.A.* Austr.
83 J4 **Budda** *N.S.W.* Austr.
263 H2 **Budd Coast** Antarctica
171 D6 **Büddenstedt** Ger.
210 D3 **Buddi** Eth.
234 F3 **Budd Lake** *NJ* U.S.A.
146 K10 **Buddon Ness** *pt Scotland* U.K.
192 C6 **Buddusò** *Sardegna* Italy
150 C6 **Bude** *Cornwall, England* U.K.
237 J10 **Bude** *MS* U.S.A.
150 C6 **Bude Bay** *England* U.K.
165 I6 **Budel** Neth.
192 C5 **Budelli, Isola** *i. Sardegna* Italy
168 I2 **Büdelsdorf** Ger.
136 E5 **Budenets'** Ukr.
169 F10 **Budenheim** Ger.
129 F1 **Budennovsk** Rus. Fed.
Budennoye Rus. Fed. *see* **Krasnogvardeyskoye**
184 B6 **Budens** Port.
85 N9 **Buderim** *Qld* Austr.
197 O6 **Budeşti** Romania
123 M9 **Budhapur** Pak.
123 P7 **Budhlada** *Punjab* India
183 O7 **Budia** Spain
177 I3 **Budiná** Slovakia
122 G8 **Būdīng** Iran
169 H10 **Büdingen** Ger.
179 N7 **Budinšćina** Croatia
177 G2 **Budišov nad Budišovkou** Czech Rep.
128 B9 **Budīyah, Jabal** *hills* Egypt
128 B9 **Budīyah, Jabal** *mt.* Egypt
208 C4 **Budjala** Dem. Rep. Congo
174 F5 **Budkowiczanka** *r.* Pol.
150 F6 **Budleigh Salterton** *Devon, England* U.K.
139 P2 **Budogoshch'** Rus. Fed.
191 N3 **Budoia** Italy
106 C9 **Budongquan** *Qinghai* China
192 D6 **Budoni** *Sardegna* Italy
191 L6 **Budrio** Italy
175 J1 **Budry** Pol.
Búdszentmihály Hungary *see* **Tiszavasvári**
125 I4 **Budū, Ḩadabat al** *plain* Saudi Arabia
125 I4 **Budū', Sabkhat al** *salt pan* Saudi Arabia
197 K4 **Budureasa** Romania
177 L4 **Buduslău** Romania
196 G8 **Budva** Montenegro
175 K1 **Būdviečiai** Lith.
Budweis Czech Rep. *see* **České Budějovice**
171 J10 **Budyně nad Ohří** Czech Rep.
138 M6 **Budzilava** Belarus
175 H4 **Budziszewice** Pol.
175 H6 **Budzów** Pol.
174 E3 **Budzyń** Pol.
207 H5 **Buea** Cameroon
161 H8 **Buëch** *r.* France
240 L7 **Buellton** *CA* U.S.A.
186 C6 **Bueña** Spain
234 F5 **Buena** *NJ* U.S.A.
183 P9 **Buenache de Alarcón** Spain
183 P8 **Buenache de la Sierra** Spain
260 E4 **Buena Esperanza** Arg.
250 B4 **Buenaventura** Col.
242 F3 **Buenaventura** Mex.
183 K8 **Buenaventura** Spain
252 E4 **Buena Vista** Bol.
185 □ **Buena Vista** Gibraltar
244 E6 **Buenavista** *Michoacán* Mex.
245 I2 **Buenavista** *Tamaulipas* Mex.
Buena Vista *i.* N. Mariana Is *see* **Tinian**
92 E7 **Buenavista** *Mindanao* Phil.
92 C5 **Buenavista** Phil.
239 K7 **Buena Vista** *CO* U.S.A.
231 E9 **Buena Vista** *GA* U.S.A.
232 F11 **Buena Vista** *VA* U.S.A.
246 D2 **Buena Vista, Bahía de** *b.* Cuba
245 H7 **Buenavista de Cuéllar** Mex.
216 □3a **Buenavista del Norte** *Tenerife* Canary Is
183 K3 **Buenavista de Valdavia** Spain
183 O8 **Buendía** Spain
183 O8 **Buendia, Embalse de** *resr* Spain
209 B6 **Buenga** *r.* Angola
209 B6 **Buengas** Angola
256 B1 **Buenolândia** Brazil
257 E2 **Buenópolis** Brazil
261 H4 **Buenos Aires** Arg.
261 G5 **Buenos Aires** *prov.* Arg.
252 B2 **Buenos Aires** Brazil
250 D5 **Buenos Aires** *Amazonas* Col.
250 C4 **Buenos Aires** *Guaviare* Col.
242 □R13 **Buenos Aires** Costa Rica
259 B7 **Buenos Aires, Lago** *l.* Arg./Chile
241 U10 **Buenos Aires National Wildlife Refuge** *nature res. AZ* U.S.A.
247 □7 **Buenos Ayres** Trin. and Tob.
259 C7 **Buen Pasto** Arg.
259 C8 **Buen Tiempo, Cabo** *c.* Arg.
255 F5 **Buerarema** Brazil
250 B4 **Buesaco** Col.
160 J4 **Buet, Le Mont** *mt.* France
182 C4 **Bueu** Spain
185 M3 **Buey, Cabeza de** *mt.* Spain
187 C11 **Buey, Sierra del** *mts* Spain
242 G4 **Búfalo** Mex.
222 H2 **Buffalo** *r. Alta/N.W.T.* Can.
236 I3 **Buffalo** *MN* U.S.A.
237 I7 **Buffalo** *MO* U.S.A.
232 G6 **Buffalo** *NY* U.S.A.
232 D9 **Buffalo** *OH* U.S.A.
237 F7 **Buffalo** *OK* U.S.A.
236 D3 **Buffalo** *SD* U.S.A.
237 G10 **Buffalo** *TX* U.S.A.
226 C5 **Buffalo** *WI* U.S.A.
238 K4 **Buffalo** *WY* U.S.A.
237 I7 **Buffalo** *r. AR* U.S.A.
231 D8 **Buffalo** *r. TN* U.S.A.
226 C5 **Buffalo** *r. WI* U.S.A.
234 A4 **Buffalo Creek** *r. PA* U.S.A.
222 G3 **Buffalo Head Hills** *Y.T.* Can.
222 G3 **Buffalo Head Prairie** *Alta* Can.
238 G4 **Buffalo Hump** *mt. ID* U.S.A.
222 H2 **Buffalo Lake** *N.W.T.* Can.
223 I4 **Buffalo Narrows** *Sask.* Can.
213 F4 **Buffalo Range** Zimbabwe
240 O1 **Buffalo Valley** *NV* U.S.A.
246 □ **Buff Bay** Jamaica
215 O4 **Buffels** *r. KwaZulu-Natal* S. Africa
214 E9 **Buffels** *r. Western Cape* S. Africa
214 B5 **Buffels** *watercourse* S. Africa
214 G9 **Buffelsdrif** S. Africa
213 E4 **Buffels Drift** S. Africa
160 F4 **Buffières** France
169 K8 **Bufleben** Ger.
231 E8 **Buford** *GA* U.S.A.
197 N6 **Buftea** Romania
170 H1 **Bug** *pen.* Ger.
175 L4 **Bug** *r.* Pol.
250 B4 **Buga** Col.
106 D3 **Buga** Mongolia
207 G4 **Buga** Nigeria
Buga Buga *i.* Vanuatu *see* **Toga**
177 I5 **Bugac** Hungary
210 B5 **Bugala Island** Uganda
83 L4 **Bugaldie** *N.S.W.* Austr.
207 G5 **Bugana** Nigeria
107 J2 **Bugant** Mongolia
163 I10 **Bugarach, Pic de** *mt.* France
Bugaz Ukr. *see* **Zatoka**
151 J3 **Bugbrooke** *Northamptonshire, England* U.K.
210 E3 **Bugda Acable** Somalia
199 I2 **Buğdaylı** Turkey
122 F2 **Bugdaýly** Turkm.
162 H4 **Bugeat** France
95 I8 **Bugel, Tanjung** *pt* Indon.
160 H5 **Bugey** *reg.* France
165 F6 **Buggenhout** Belgium
192 A9 **Buggerru** *Sardegna* Italy
172 D6 **Buggingen** Ger.
195 □ **Buġibba** Malta
184 □ **Bugio** *i.* Madeira
129 C7 **Buğlan Geçidi** *pass* Turkey
193 L3 **Bugnara** Italy
163 C9 **Bugnein** France
188 F3 **Bugojno** Bos.-Herz.
140 T2 **Bugøyfjord** Norway
134 J1 **Bugrino** Rus. Fed.
92 A7 **Bugsuk** *i.* Phil.
107 Q2 **Bugt** *Nei Mongol* China
92 C2 **Buguey** *Luzon* Phil.
92 D5 **Bugui Point** *Masbate* Phil.
135 K5 **Bugul'ma** Rus. Fed.
120 I4 **Bugun'** Kazakh.
Bügür *Xinjiang* China *see* **Luntai**
120 E1 **Buguruslan** Rus. Fed.
177 I4 **Bugyi** Hungary
117 N6 **Buha** *Arun. Prad.* India
122 F6 **Būhābād** Iran
199 J5 **Buharkent** Turkey
213 F3 **Buhera** Zimbabwe
106 F8 **Buh He** *r.* China
92 D5 **Buhi** *Luzon* Phil.
172 E4 **Bühl** Ger.
238 G5 **Buhl** *ID* U.S.A.
226 B2 **Buhl** *MN* U.S.A.
172 E4 **Bühlertal** Ger.
172 H3 **Bühlertann** Ger.
172 H3 **Bühlerzell** Ger.
169 K7 **Bühne** Ger.
211 A6 **Buhoro** Tanz.
211 B7 **Buhoro Flats** *plain* Tanz.
136 F3 **Buhryn** Ukr.
127 K5 **Bühtan** *r.* Turkey
211 B6 **Buhu** *r.* Tanz.
197 O4 **Buhuşi** Romania
191 O3 **Buia** Italy
222 F3 **Buick** *B.C.* Can.
146 E10 **Buie, Loch** *b. Scotland* U.K.
150 F3 **Builth Wells** *Powys, Wales* U.K.
260 B3 **Buin** Chile
122 D4 **Bū'īn** Iran
78 □6 **Buin** P.N.G.
206 E4 **Bui National Park** Ghana
135 J5 **Buinsk** Rus. Fed.
122 B4 **Bu'in Soflā** Iran
122 D4 **Bu'in Zahrā** Iran
107 O3 **Buir Nur** *l.* Mongolia
161 G8 **Buis-les-Baronnies** France
164 J2 **Buitenpost** Neth.
212 C4 **Buitepos** Namibia
183 M7 **Buitrago del Lozoya** Spain
138 I7 **Būivydžiai** Lith.
185 K5 **Bujalance** Spain
197 J8 **Bujanovac** Serbia
186 E5 **Bujaraloz** Spain
191 P5 **Buje** Croatia
197 N7 **Bujoru** Romania
211 A5 **Bujumbura** Burundi
179 O5 **Bük** Hungary
174 E3 **Buk** Pol.
99 K1 **Bukachacha** Rus. Fed.
175 M6 **Bukachivtsi** Ukr.
111 J8 **Buka Daban** *mt. Qinghai/Xinjiang* China
91 L8 **Buka Island** P.N.G.
212 E3 **Bukalo** Namibia
209 E7 **Bukama** Dem. Rep. Congo
122 B3 **Būkān** Iran
139 R8 **Bukan'** Rus. Fed.
122 E6 **Būkand** Iran
121 S1 **Bukanskoye** Rus. Fed.
208 F5 **Bukavu** Dem. Rep. Congo
209 C6 **Bukedi** Dem. Rep. Congo
211 B6 **Bukene** Tanz.
209 E7 **Bukeya** Dem. Rep. Congo
Bukhara *Buxoro* Uzbek. *see* **Buxoro**
Bukhara Oblast *admin. div.* Uzbek. *see* **Buxoro**
138 M6 **Bukhava** Belarus
Bukhoro Uzbek. *see* **Buxoro**
Bukhoro Wiloyati *admin. div.* Uzbek. *see* **Buxoro**
100 B1 **Bukhta** Rus. Fed.
121 U3 **Bukhtarminskoye Vodokhranilishche** *resr* Kazakh.
93 D2 **Bukide** *i.* Indon.
211 B5 **Bukima** Tanz.
95 J5 **Bukit Baka-Bukit Raya, Taman Nasional** *nat. park* Indon.
95 J6 **Bukitlidi** *Kalimantan* Indon.
94 □ **Bukit Timah** Sing.
94 D5 **Bukittinggi** *Sumatera* Indon.
177 J3 **Bükk** *mts* Hungary
177 J4 **Bükkábrány** Hungary
177 J4 **Bükkalja** *hills* Hungary
114 E5 **Bukkapatnam** *Andhra Prad.* India
177 J3 **Bükki** *nat. park* Hungary
177 G5 **Bükkösd** Hungary
177 J4 **Bükkzsérc** Hungary
171 F7 **Buko** Ger.
211 A5 **Bukoba** Tanz.
138 H6 **Bukonys** Lith.
177 H2 **Bukovec** Czech Rep.
179 J8 **Bukovje** Slovenia
177 L2 **Bukovské vrchy** *hills* Slovakia
175 K5 **Bukowa** *r.* Pol.
174 F3 **Bukowe** Pol.
174 F4 **Bukowice** Pol.
174 G2 **Bukowiec** *Kujawsko-Pomorskie* Pol.
174 D3 **Bukowiec** *Lubuskie* Pol.
171 L6 **Bukowiec** *hill* Pol.
174 F1 **Bukowina** Pol.
175 I6 **Bukowina Tatrzańska** Pol.
174 G4 **Bukownica** Pol.
175 H5 **Bukowno** Pol.
174 F2 **Bukowo** Pol.
143 M7 **Bukowo, Jezioro** *lag.* Pol.
175 K6 **Bukowsko** Pol.
Bükreş Romania *see* **Bucureşti**
94 F5 **Buku, Tanjung** *pt* Indon.
107 L2 **Bukukun** Rus. Fed.
94 □ **Bukum, Pulau** *i.* Sing.
136 J4 **Buky** Ukr.
122 E6 **Būl, Kūh-e** *mt.* Iran
206 B3 **Bula** Guinea-Bissau
93 G5 **Bula** *Seram* Indon.
209 B7 **Bula Atumba** Angola
190 F1 **Bülach** Switz.
107 K2 **Bulag** Mongolia
107 J2 **Bulagtay** Mongolia
83 N5 **Bulahdelah** *N.S.W.* Austr.
92 C6 **Bulalacao** *i.* Phil.
94 E4 **Bulan** *i.* Indon.
92 D5 **Bulan** *Luzon* Phil.
92 C8 **Bulan** *i.* Phil.
126 I3 **Bulancak** Turkey
116 F5 **Bulandshahr** *Uttar Prad.* India
127 K4 **Bulanık** Turkey
120 F1 **Bulanovo** Rus. Fed.
203 F3 **Būlāq** Egypt
100 L3 **Bulava** Rus. Fed.
93 C3 **Bulawa, Gunung** *mt.* Indon.
213 F4 **Bulawayo** Zimbabwe
121 N1 **Bulayevo** Kazakh.
126 H5 **Bulbul** Syria
208 E2 **Bulbul, Wadi** *watercourse* Sudan
211 C5 **Bulbula** *waterhole* Kenya
199 J4 **Buldan** Turkey
116 F9 **Buldhana** *Mahar.* India
252 A2 **Buldibuyo** Peru
220 A4 **Buldir Island** *AK* U.S.A.
116 F4 **Buldur** *Hima. Prad.* India
120 E2 **Buldurta** Kazakh.
Buldyrty Kazakh. *see* **Buldurta**
123 J8 **Buleda** *reg.* Pak.
210 E3 **Bulei** *well* Eth.
215 P1 **Bulembu** Swaziland
206 E4 **Bulenga** Ghana
151 I5 **Bulford** *Wiltshire, England* U.K.
106 H2 **Bulgan** *Bulgan* Mongolia
Bulgan *Hovd* Mongolia *see* **Bürenhayrhan**
106 C3 **Bulgan** *Hovd* Mongolia
106 G1 **Bulgan** *Hövsgöl* Mongolia
106 H4 **Bulgan** *Ömnögovĭ* Mongolia
106 H2 **Bulgan** *prov.* Mongolia
106 B3 **Bulgan Gol** *r.* Mongolia
Bulgar Rus. Fed. *see* **Bolgar**
197 Q7 **Bŭlgarevo** Bulg.
197 N8 **Bulgaria** *country* Europe
Bŭlgariya *country* Europe *see* **Bulgaria**
124 E3 **Bulghah** Saudi Arabia
193 O7 **Bulgheria, Monte** *mt.* Italy
157 K7 **Bulgnéville** France
129 D5 **Bulgurlu** Turkey
137 M9 **Bulhanak** *r.* Ukr.
93 F3 **Buli** *Halmahera* Indon.
93 F3 **Buli, Teluk** *b. Halmahera* Indon.
92 A7 **Buliluyan, Cape** *Palawan* Phil.
210 A4 **Bulisa** Uganda
168 G3 **Bülkau** Ger.
151 J3 **Bulkington** *Warwickshire, England* U.K.
222 D4 **Bulkley Ranges** *mts B.C.* Can.
175 I3 **Bulkowo** Pol.
Bulla, Ostrov *is* Azer. *see* **Xärä Zirä Adası**
185 K3 **Bullaque** *r.* Spain
185 P4 **Bullas** Spain
85 I9 **Bullawarra, Lake** *salt flat Qld* Austr.
210 E2 **Bullaxaar** Somalia
169 D10 **Bullay** Ger.
246 □ **Bull Bay** Jamaica
190 C2 **Bulle** Switz.
83 H4 **Bullea, Lake** *salt flat N.S.W.* Austr.
247 □10 **Bullenbaai** *b. Curaçao* Neth. Antilles
81 F8 **Buller** *r. South I.* N.Z.
85 I4 **Bulleringa National Park** *Qld* Austr.
87 E11 **Bullfinch** *W.A.* Austr.
241 R6 **Bullhead City** *AZ* U.S.A.
83 M6 **Bulli** *N.S.W.* Austr.
165 J8 **Büllingen** Belgium
241 P7 **Bullion Mountains** *CA* U.S.A.
140 P4 **Bullmark** Sweden
84 B3 **Bullo** *r. N.T.* Austr.
183 P7 **Bullones** *r.* Spain
83 I3 **Bulloo** *watercourse Qld* Austr.
83 I3 **Bulloo Downs** *Qld* Austr.
83 I3 **Bulloo Lake** *salt flat Qld* Austr.
147 J2 **Bull Point** *Northern Ireland* U.K.
80 J7 **Bulls** *North I.* N.Z.
246 □ **Bull Savannah** Jamaica
235 I1 **Bulls Bridge** *CT* U.S.A.
237 I7 **Bull Shoals Lake** *AR* U.S.A.
212 C5 **Büllsport** Namibia
235 G1 **Bullville** *NY* U.S.A.
156 E3 **Bully-les-Mines** France
84 E2 **Bulman** *N.T.* Austr.
84 E2 **Bulman Gorge** *N.T.* Austr.
222 F2 **Bulmer Lake** *N.W.T.* Can.
151 N3 **Bulmer Tye** *Essex, England* U.K.
260 A5 **Bulnes** Chile
94 □ **Buloh, Pulau** *i.* Sing.
83 I7 **Buloke, Lake** *dry lake Vic.* Austr.
91 K8 **Bulolo** P.N.G.
196 I9 **Bulqizë** Albania
192 C7 **Bultei** *Sardegna* Italy
215 K4 **Bultfontein** S. Africa
95 L3 **Bulu, Gunung** *mt.* Indon.
92 E8 **Buluan** *Mindanao* Phil.
93 B6 **Bulubulu** *Sulawesi* Indon.
210 C3 **Buluk** *well* Kenya
93 B6 **Bulukumba** *Sulawesi* Indon.
208 D5 **Bulukutu** Dem. Rep. Congo
131 N2 **Bulun** Rus. Fed.
123 P2 **Bulungkol** *Xinjiang* China
209 C6 **Bulungu** *Bandundu* Dem. Rep. Congo
209 D6 **Bulungu** *Kasaï-Occidental* Dem. Rep. Congo
129 E2 **Bulungu** Rus. Fed.
121 L8 **Bulung'ur** Uzbek.
92 E5 **Bulusan** *Luzon* Phil.
214 C1 **Bulwana** Namibia
215 N5 **Bulwer** S. Africa
177 L5 **Bulz** Romania
192 B6 **Bulzi** *Sardegna* Italy
78 □6 **Buma** *Malaita* Solomon Is
209 C6 **Bumba** *Bandundu* Dem. Rep. Congo
208 D4 **Bumba** *Équateur* Dem. Rep. Congo
202 D1 **Būmbah** Libya
202 D1 **Bumbah, Khalīj** *b.* Libya
106 I6 **Bumbat** *Nei Mongol* China
106 I3 **Bumbat** Mongolia
197 L5 **Bumbeşti-Jiu** Romania
206 C4 **Bumbuna** Sierra Leone
96 C1 **Bumhkang** Myanmar
96 C1 **Bumpha Bum** *mt.* Myanmar
209 C5 **Buna** Dem. Rep. Congo
210 C4 **Buna** Kenya
147 C5 **Bunacurry** Ireland
125 J4 **Bunayyān** *well* Saudi Arabia
211 A5 **Bunazi** Tanz.
147 F2 **Bunbeg** Ireland
87 C12 **Bunbury** *W.A.* Austr.
149 L7 **Bunbury** *Cheshire, England* U.K.
147 I7 **Bunclody** Ireland
147 H2 **Buncrana** Ireland
211 B5 **Bunda** Tanz.
85 N8 **Bundaberg** *Qld* Austr.
83 K3 **Bundaleer** *Qld* Austr.
83 M4 **Bundarra** *N.S.W.* Austr.
168 D4 **Bunde** Ger.
169 G6 **Bünde** Ger.
172 C2 **Bundenbach** Ger.
168 D4 **Bunderhee** Ger.
84 E6 **Bundey** *watercourse N.T.* Austr.
116 E7 **Bundi** *Rajasthan* India
210 A4 **Bundibugyo** Uganda
83 N3 **Bundjalung National Park** *N.S.W.* Austr.
147 F4 **Bundoran** Ireland
117 J8 **Bundu** *Jharkhand* India
210 A3 **Bunduqiya** Sudan
196 H9 **Bunë** *r.* Albania/Montenegro
122 C6 **Būneh** *i.* Iran
125 I1 **Būneh Dara** *b.* Iran
123 O4 **Buner** *reg.* Pak.
207 H3 **Bunga** *r.* Nigeria
104 C5 **Bunga-dake** *mt.* Japan
94 C6 **Bungalaut, Selat** *sea chan.* Indon.
151 O3 **Bungay** *Suffolk, England* U.K.
83 L6 **Bungendore** *N.S.W.* Austr.
263 G2 **Bunger Hills** Antarctica
93 C6 **Bungi** *Sulawesi* Indon.
85 L9 **Bungil Creek** *r. Qld* Austr.
93 B5 **Bungku** *Sulawesi* Indon.
Bungle Bungle National Park *W.A.* Austr. *see* **Purnululu National Park**
209 B6 **Bungo** Angola
210 B4 **Bungoma** Kenya
111 J10 **Bungona'og** *Xizang* China
103 J13 **Bungo-suidō** *sea chan.* Japan
103 I13 **Bungo-Takada** Japan
Bunguran, Kepulauan *is* Indon. *see* **Natuna, Kepulauan**
Bunguran, Pulau *i.* Indon. *see* **Natuna Besar**
94 G8 **Buni, Ci** *r.* Indon.
208 F4 **Bunia** Dem. Rep. Congo
183 M4 **Buniel** Spain
177 L6 **Bunila** Romania
87 G11 **Buningonia** *well W.A.* Austr.
207 I4 **Buni-Yadi** Nigeria
116 E2 **Bunji** Jammu and Kashmir
237 J7 **Bunker** *MO* U.S.A.
85 N7 **Bunker Group** *atolls Qld* Austr.
209 E7 **Bunkeya** Dem. Rep. Congo
237 I10 **Bunkie** *LA* U.S.A.
141 L6 **Bunkris** Sweden
147 H8 **Bunmahon** Ireland
147 C4 **Bunnahowen** Ireland
147 E4 **Bunnanadden** Ireland
231 G11 **Bunnell** *FL* U.S.A.
164 H4 **Bunnik** Neth.
147 D4 **Bunnyconnellan** Ireland
80 J7 **Bunnythorpe** *North I.* N.Z.
187 D9 **Buñol** Spain
164 H4 **Bunschoten-Spakenburg** Neth.
111 F11 **Bünsum** *Xizang* China
207 G3 **Bunsuru** *watercourse* Nigeria
177 L5 **Bunteşti** Romania
87 D10 **Buntine** *W.A.* Austr.
151 L4 **Buntingford** *Hertfordshire, England* U.K.
95 K5 **Buntok** *Kalimantan* Indon.
95 K5 **Buntokecil** *Kalimantan* Indon.
183 R5 **Buñuel** Spain
207 H4 **Bununu** Nigeria
85 M9 **Bunya Mountains National Park** *Qld* Austr.
126 G4 **Bünyan** Turkey
187 K8 **Bunyola** Spain
95 L3 **Bunyu** *i.* Indon.
207 G3 **Bunza** Nigeria
188 F3 **Buoač** Bos.-Herz.
Buoddobohki Fin. *see* **Patoniva**
193 P7 **Buonabitacolo** Italy
193 N5 **Buonalbergo** Italy
192 G1 **Buonconvento** Italy
97 I8 **Buôn Hô** Vietnam
97 I8 **Buôn Ma Thuôt** Vietnam
193 P8 **Buonvicino** Italy
131 O2 **Buorkhaya, Guba** *b.* Rus. Fed.
111 H12 **Bup** *r.* China
124 F2 **Buqay'ā** Saudi Arabia
Buqayq Saudi Arabia *see* **Abqaiq**
202 E2 **Buqbuq** Egypt
Buqtyrma Bögeni *resr* Kazakh. *see* **Bukhtarminskoye Vodokhranilishche**
211 C5 **Bura** Kenya
210 F2 **Buraan** Somalia
122 H9 **Burak** Iran
87 D11 **Burakin** *W.A.* Austr.
208 E2 **Buram** Sudan
121 U3 **Buran** Kazakh.
94 □ **Buran Darat** *rf* Sing.
116 H4 **Burang** *Xizang* China
257 G2 **Buranhaém** Brazil
257 H2 **Buranhaém** *r.* Brazil
120 F2 **Burannoye** Rus. Fed.
191 N8 **Burano** *r.* Italy
128 E5 **Burāq** Syria
92 E6 **Burauen** *Leyte* Phil.
123 O4 **Burawai** Pak.
116 E9 **Buray** *r.* India
124 F2 **Buraydah** Saudi Arabia
134 K5 **Burayevo** Rus. Fed.
169 F9 **Burbach** Ger.
151 I5 **Burbage** *Wiltshire, England* U.K.
186 C5 **Burbáguena** Spain
240 N7 **Burbank** *CA* U.S.A.
192 C9 **Burcei** *Sardegna* Italy
137 O6 **Burchak** Ukr.
226 D1 **Burchell Lake** *Ont.* Can.
83 K5 **Burcher** *N.S.W.* Austr.
210 E2 **Burco** Somalia
164 I2 **Burdaard** Neth.
123 K2 **Burdalyk** Turkm.
85 K5 **Burdekin** *r. Qld* Austr.
85 K6 **Burdekin Falls** *Qld* Austr.
160 H4 **Burdet, Mont** *mt.* France
Burdigala France *see* **Bordeaux**
165 H7 **Burdinne** Belgium
199 L5 **Burdur** Turkey
199 L5 **Burdur** *prov.* Turkey
199 L5 **Burdur Gölü** *l.* Turkey
Burdwan *W. Bengal* India *see* **Barddhaman**
210 C2 **Burē** *Āmara* Eth.
210 B2 **Burē** *Oromīya* Eth.
151 P2 **Bure** *r. England* U.K.
161 H7 **Bure, Pic de** *mt.* France
140 P4 **Bureå** Sweden
100 H3 **Bureinskiy Khrebet** *mts* Rus. Fed.
203 F5 **Bureiqa** *well* Sudan
183 L3 **Burejo** *r.* Spain
182 F1 **Burela, Cabo** *c.* Spain
169 G7 **Büren** Ger.
164 H5 **Buren** Neth.
190 C1 **Büren an der Aare** Switz.
106 B3 **Bürenhayrhan** Mongolia
107 L3 **Bürentsogt** Mongolia
260 A5 **Bureo** *r.* Chile
151 N4 **Bures** *Suffolk, England* U.K.
100 F4 **Bureya** *r.* Rus. Fed.
Bureya-Pristan' Rus. Fed. *see* **Novobureyskiy**
Bureya Range *mts* Rus. Fed. *see* **Bureinskiy Khrebet**
100 I3 **Bureyinski Zapovednik** *nature res.* Rus. Fed.
227 N6 **Burford** *Ont.* Can.
151 I4 **Burford** *Oxfordshire, England* U.K.
128 A7 **Būr Fu'ād** Egypt
163 E9 **Burg** France
171 J7 **Burg** Ger.
168 H3 **Burg (Dithmarschen)** Ger.
106 I2 **Burgaltay** Mongolia
182 I5 **Burganes de Valverde** Spain
197 P8 **Burgas** Bulg.
179 N5 **Burgau** Austria
173 I5 **Burgau** Ger.
184 B6 **Burgau** Port.
170 D2 **Burg auf Fehmarn** Ger.
231 I8 **Burgaw** *NC* U.S.A.
171 E6 **Burg bei Magdeburg** Ger.
173 I6 **Burgberg im Allgäu** Ger.
173 I3 **Burgbernheim** Ger.
169 D10 **Burgbrohl** Ger.
169 J6 **Burgdorf** *Niedersachsen* Ger.
169 J6 **Burgdorf** *Niedersachsen* Ger.
190 D1 **Burgdorf** Switz.
173 J2 **Burgebrach** Ger.
171 E9 **Bürgel** Ger.
179 N5 **Burgenland** *land* Austria
225 J4 **Burgeo** *Nfld and Lab.* Can.
215 K6 **Burgersdorp** S. Africa
213 F5 **Burgersfort** S. Africa
214 I6 **Burgerville** S. Africa
87 F11 **Burges, Mount** *hill W.A.* Austr.
233 I11 **Burgess** *VA* U.S.A.
151 L6 **Burgess Hill** *West Sussex, England* U.K.
202 E4 **Burget Tuyur** *waterhole* Sudan
173 J2 **Burghaslach** Ger.
169 I9 **Burghaun** Ger.
173 N5 **Burghausen** Ger.
149 K4 **Burgh by Sands** *Cumbria, England* U.K.
151 J5 **Burghclere** *Hampshire, England* U.K.
146 J7 **Burghead** *Moray, Scotland* U.K.
146 I7 **Burghead Bay** *Scotland* U.K.
173 K4 **Burgheim** Ger.
151 J5 **Burghfield Common** *West Berkshire, England* U.K.
164 E5 **Burgh-Haamstede** Neth.
150 G3 **Burghill** *Herefordshire, England* U.K.
149 R7 **Burgh le Marsh** *Lincolnshire, England* U.K.
194 E8 **Burgio** *Sicilia* Italy
194 H9 **Burgio, Serra di** *hill Sicilia* Italy
178 H3 **Burgkirchen** Austria
173 N5 **Burgkirchen an der Alz** Ger.
171 D10 **Burgkunstadt** Ger.
190 G1 **Bürglen** *Thurgau* Switz.
190 F2 **Bürglen** *Uri* Switz.
173 M3 **Burglengenfeld** Ger.
173 J3 **Burgoberbach** Ger.
183 K8 **Burgohondo** Spain
183 M6 **Burgomillodo, Embalse de** *resr* Spain
192 B7 **Burgos** *Sardegna* Italy
243 J5 **Burgos** Mex.
183 M4 **Burgos** Spain
183 M4 **Burgos** *prov.* Spain
169 K10 **Burgpreppach** Ger.

Cantil to Cascina
295

240 O6 Cantil CA U.S.A.
92 E7 Cantilan Mindanao Phil.
184 H5 Cantillana Spain
183 L6 Cantimpalos Spain
254 E4 Canto do Buriti Brazil
190 C5 Cantoira Italy
Canton Guangdong China see Guangzhou
150 F5 Canton Cardiff, Wales U.K.
231 E8 Canton GA U.S.A.
226 D9 Canton IL U.S.A.
236 J5 Canton MO U.S.A.
237 K9 Canton MS U.S.A.
234 E6 Canton NJ U.S.A.
233 J4 Canton NY U.S.A.
232 D8 Canton OH U.S.A.
227 R8 Canton PA U.S.A.
236 G4 Canton SD U.S.A.
237 H9 Canton TX U.S.A.
226 C4 Canton WI U.S.A.
Canton Island atoll Phoenix Is Kiribati see Kanton
185 O6 Cantoria Spain
185 J2 Cantos Negros hill Spain
256 A6 Cantu r. Brazil
190 G4 Cantù Italy
256 B6 Cantu, Serra do hills Brazil
Cantuaria Kent, England U.K. see Canterbury
253 F1 Canudos Amazonas Brazil
254 F4 Canudos Bahia Brazil
261 H4 Cañuelas Arg.
251 F6 Canumã Amazonas Brazil
251 G6 Canumã Amazonas Brazil
82 H7 Canunda National Park S.A. Austr.
Canusium Italy see Canosa di Puglia
251 E6 Canutama Brazil
237 C12 Canutillo Mex.
81 H8 Canvastown South I. N.Z.
151 N4 Canvey Island Essex, England U.K.
223 J4 Canwood Sask. Can.
213 G3 Canxixe Moz.
159 M2 Cany-Barville France
187 D9 Cànyoles r. Spain
222 B2 Canyon Y.T. Can.
237 E8 Canyon TX U.S.A.
238 E4 Canyon City OR U.S.A.
240 K2 Canyon Creek r. CA U.S.A.
240 K1 Canyondam CA U.S.A.
241 W5 Canyon de Chelly National Monument nat. park AZ U.S.A.
238 I3 Canyon Ferry Lake MT U.S.A.
241 U8 Canyon Lake AZ U.S.A.
241 W3 Canyonlands National Park UT U.S.A.
222 E2 Canyon Ranges mts N.W.T. Can.
238 C5 Canyonville OR U.S.A.
209 D6 Canzar Angola
96 H3 Cao Băng Vietnam
Caocheng Shandong China see Caoxian
106 G8 Cao Daban Qinghai China
Caohai Guizhou China see Weining
Caohe Hubei China see Qichun
101 D8 Cao He r. China
110 G6 Caohu Xinjiang China
110 G6 Caohu Xinjiang China
Caojiahe Hubei China see Qichun
108 B6 Caojian Yunnan China
146 C9 Caolas Argyll and Bute, Scotland U.K.
Caolas Scalpaigh Western Isles, Scotland U.K. see Kyles Scalpay
146 E11 Caolisport, Loch inlet Scotland U.K.
209 C7 Caombo Angola
191 L3 Caorame r. Italy
191 N4 Caorle Italy
107 N9 Caoxian Shandong China
Caozhou Shandong China see Heze
92 C9 Cap i. Phil.
217 □1b Cap, Baie du b. Mauritius
247 □3 Cap, Pointe du pt St Lucia
227 L6 Capac MI U.S.A.
193 O7 Capaccio Italy
193 P5 Capacciotti, Lago di l. Italy
194 E7 Capaci Sicilia Italy
246 G4 Cap-à-Foux c. Haiti
209 D7 Capaia Angola
Çapakçur Turkey see Bingöl
192 G3 Capalbio Italy
177 L5 Căpâlna Romania
93 D4 Capalulu, Selat sea chan. Indon.
250 D5 Capana Brazil
250 E3 Capanaparo r. Venez.
254 D2 Capanema Brazil
192 E2 Capanne, Monte mt. Italy
190 F6 Capanne di Marcarolo, Parco Naturale delle nature res. Italy
191 J8 Capannoli Italy
191 J8 Capannori Italy
256 C6 Capão Bonito Brazil
257 G4 Caparaó, Serra do mts Brazil
184 A3 Caparica Port.
250 D3 Caparo r. Venez.
182 D7 Caparrosa Port.
183 Q4 Caparroso Spain
92 C4 Capas Luzon Phil.
197 L5 Căpățânii, Munții mts Romania
250 D2 Capatárida Venez.
225 I4 Cap-aux-Meules Que. Can.
187 E9 Cap-Blanc Spain
163 B8 Capbreton France
225 H3 Cap-Chat Que. Can.
163 I10 Capcir reg. France
161 D10 Cap d'Agde France
186 □ Cap d'Artrutx Spain
225 F4 Cap-de-la-Madeleine Que. Can.
163 I6 Capdenac France
163 I6 Capdenac-Gare France
186 □ Cap d'en Font Spain
187 L8 Capdepera Spain
85 K6 Cape r. Qld Austr.
87 G12 Cape Arid National Park W.A. Austr.
Cape Bald N.B. Can. see Cap-Pelé
83 L9 Cape Barren Island Tas. Austr.
264 J8 Cape Basin sea feature S. Atlantic Ocean
82 F6 Cape Borda S.A. Austr.
86 I3 Cape Bougainville Aboriginal Reserve W.A. Austr.
225 I4 Cape Breton Highlands National Park N.S. Can.
225 I4 Cape Breton Island N.S. Can.
225 K2 Cape Charles Nfld and Lab. Can.
233 I11 Cape Charles VA U.S.A.
206 E5 Cape Coast Ghana
Cape Coast Castle Ghana see Cape Coast
233 O7 Cape Cod Bay MA U.S.A.
233 O7 Cape Cod Canal MA U.S.A.
233 P7 Cape Cod National Seashore nature res. MA U.S.A.
231 F12 Cape Coral FL U.S.A.
84 E4 Cape Crawford N.T. Austr.
227 M5 Cape Croker Ont. Can.
221 K3 Cape Dorset Nunavut Can.
233 □O5 Cape Elizabeth ME U.S.A.
222 C3 Cape Fanshaw AK U.S.A.
231 I8 Cape Fear r. NC U.S.A.
82 F6 Cape Gantheaume Conservation Park nature res. S.A. Austr.
225 I4 Cape George N.S. Can.
237 K7 Cape Girardeau MO U.S.A.
Cape Juby Morocco see Tarfaya
220 B3 Cape Krusenstern National Monument nat. park AK U.S.A.
87 C12 Capel W.A. Austr.
151 M5 Capel Kent, England U.K.
151 L5 Capel Surrey, England U.K.
256 A3 Capela Brazil
216 □1b Capelas São Miguel Azores
150 E1 Capel Curig Conwy, Wales U.K.
87 G12 Cape Le Grand National Park W.A. Austr.
257 F2 Capelinha Brazil
216 □1c Capelinhos, Ponta dos pt Faial Azores
184 E3 Capelins Port.
85 L7 Capella Qld Austr.
164 G5 Capelle aan de IJssel Neth.
151 O5 Capel le Ferne Kent, England U.K.
165 J9 Capellen Lux.
216 □1c Capelo Faial Azores
86 □2 Capelok, Pulu i. Cocos Is
209 B8 Capelongo Huíla Angola
Capelongo Huíla Angola see Kuvango
192 F3 Capel Rosso, Punta del Italy
151 O3 Capel St Mary Suffolk, England U.K.
234 F7 Cape May NJ U.S.A.
234 F6 Cape May County county NJ U.S.A.
234 F6 Cape May Court House NJ U.S.A.
234 F7 Cape May Point NJ U.S.A.
234 F7 Cape May Point pt NJ U.S.A.
85 J3 Cape Melville National Park Qld Austr.
209 C7 Capenda-Camulemba Angola
163 J9 Capendu France
214 C10 Cape of Good Hope Nature Reserve S. Africa
85 L6 Cape Palmerston National Park Qld Austr.
86 B7 Cape Range hills W.A. Austr.
86 B7 Cape Range National Park W.A. Austr.
231 H9 Cape Romain National Wildlife Refuge nature res. SC U.S.A.
225 H5 Cape Sable Island N.S. Can.
225 J3 Cape St George Nfld and Lab. Can.
222 D5 Cape Scott Provincial Park B.C. Can.
161 C10 Capestang France
247 □2 Capesterre Guadeloupe
193 L3 Capestrano Italy
214 C9 Cape Town S. Africa
85 J3 Cape Tribulation National Park Qld Austr.
85 K5 Cape Upstart National Park Qld Austr.
206 □ Cape Verde country N. Atlantic Ocean
264 G5 Cape Verde Basin sea feature N. Atlantic Ocean
264 G4 Cape Verde Plateau sea feature N. Atlantic Ocean
233 I4 Cape Vincent NY U.S.A.
225 H4 Cape Wolfe P.E.I. Can.
85 I2 Cape York Peninsula Qld Austr.
163 B6 Cap Ferret France
246 G4 Cap-Haïtien Haiti
250 E4 Capibara Venez.
209 C8 Capico Angola
187 F7 Capicorp, Punta de pt Spain
185 M7 Capileira Spain
185 I3 Capilla Spain
244 E5 Capilla de Guadalupe Mex.
260 E2 Capilla del Monte Arg.
261 H4 Capilla del Señor Arg.
254 D2 Capim Brazil
254 C2 Capim r. Brazil
182 F8 Capinha Port.
256 C3 Capinópolis Brazil
252 D4 Capinota Bol.
193 K4 Capistrello Italy
239 L10 Capitan NM U.S.A.
261 G3 Capitán Bermudez Arg.
260 A6 Capitán Pastene Chile
261 H4 Capitán Sarmiento Arg.
257 F2 Capitão Enéas Brazil
251 F6 Capitari Brazil
234 D6 Capitol Park DE U.S.A.
241 U3 Capitol Reef National Park UT U.S.A.
256 B5 Capivara, Represa resr Brazil
256 D5 Capivari Brazil
256 D5 Capivari r. Brazil
254 F5 Capivari r. Brazil
254 E4 Capixaba Brazil
194 G8 Capizzi Sicilia Italy
177 L4 Căpleni Romania
188 F4 Čapljina Bos.-Herz.
186 I3 Cap Llitzet mt. Spain
92 C6 Capnoyan i. Phil.
213 G2 Capoche r. Moz./Zambia
192 H2 Capodimonte Italy
190 I3 Capo di Ponte Italy
193 M6 Capodochino airport Italy
194 H7 Capo d'Orlando Sicilia Italy
251 G6 Capoeira Brazil
251 G6 Capoeiras, Cachoeira das waterfall Brazil
192 E2 Capoliveri Italy
191 L8 Capolona Italy
195 I10 Capo Passero, Isola i. Sicilia Italy
193 O6 Caposele Italy
192 B9 Capoterra Sardegna Italy
163 H10 Capoulet France
193 K3 Cappadocia Italy
147 E7 Cappagh Ireland
147 F7 Cappamore Ireland
147 F7 Cappawhite Ireland
168 G3 Cappel Ger.
225 H4 Cap-Pelé N.B. Can.
193 M3 Cappelle sul Tavo Italy
168 F5 Cappeln (Oldenburg) Ger.
146 J12 Capplegill Dumfries and Galloway, Scotland U.K.
147 G8 Cappoquin Ireland
192 D9 Cappuccini, Punta dei pt Sardegna Italy
193 M4 Capracotta Italy
192 D1 Capraia, Isola di i. Italy
193 P3 Capraia, Isole is Italy
192 D1 Capraia Isola Italy
192 I3 Capranica Italy
192 A5 Caprara, Punta pt Sardegna Italy
192 I3 Caprarola Italy
192 C5 Caprera, Isola i. Sardegna Italy
193 M6 Capri Italy
193 M6 Capri, Isola di i. Italy
193 M5 Capriati a Volturno Italy
85 M7 Capricorn, Cape Qld Austr.
85 M7 Capricorn Channel Qld Austr.
85 N7 Capricorn Group atolls Qld Austr.
190 G4 Caprino Bergamasco Italy
191 J4 Caprino Veronese Italy
212 D3 Caprivi admin. reg. Namibia
212 D3 Caprivi Game Park nature res. Namibia
Capsa Tunisia see Gafsa
240 □F14 Captain Cook HI U.S.A.
163 D7 Captieux France
232 E9 Captina r. OH U.S.A.
193 M5 Capua Italy
256 D6 Capuava Brazil
247 □2 Capucin, Cape Dominica
217 □2b Capucin Rock i. Mahé Seychelles
217 □2b Capucins, Pointe pt Mahé Seychelles
245 H6 Capulhuac Mex.
244 G4 Capulín Mex.
209 C8 Capuna Angola
209 B8 Capunda Cavilongo Angola
209 D9 Caputene Angola
171 G6 Caputh Ger.
146 J9 Caputh Perth and Kinross, Scotland U.K.
163 E9 Capvern-les-Bains France
250 C4 Caquetá dept Col.
250 D5 Caquetá r. Col. alt. Japurá (Brazil)
250 C3 Cáqueza Col.
183 N8 Carabaña Spain
92 C5 Carabao i. Phil.
252 C3 Carabaya, Cordillera de mts Peru
261 G4 Carabelas Arg.
251 F5 Carabinani r. Brazil
250 E2 Carabobo state Venez.
197 M6 Caracal Romania
251 F4 Caracarai Brazil
250 E2 Caracas Venez.
247 □10 Caracas Baai b. Curaçao Neth. Antilles
253 F5 Caracol Mato Grosso do Sul Brazil
254 E4 Caracol Piauí Brazil
252 D2 Caracol Rondônia Brazil
246 G8 Caracolí Col.
252 D4 Caracollo Bol.
244 F6 Carácuaro Mex.
185 K3 Caracuel de Calatrava Spain
92 F8 Caraga Mindanao Phil.
83 K5 Caragabal N.S.W. Austr.
147 C8 Caragh, Lough l. Ireland
190 C7 Caraglio Italy
257 E5 Caraguatatuba Brazil
259 B5 Carahue Chile
257 G2 Caraí Brazil
147 K1 Cara Island Scotland U.K.
257 H2 Caraiva Brazil
251 H6 Carajari Brazil
251 I6 Carajás, Serra dos hills Brazil
Carales Sardegna Italy see Cagliari
Caralis Sardegna Italy see Cagliari
Caralps Spain see Queralbs
163 H8 Caraman France
193 M3 Caramanico Terme Italy
185 P5 Caramel r. Spain
92 D5 Caramoan Peninsula Luzon Phil.
182 D7 Caramulo Port.
182 D7 Caramulo mt. Port.
182 D8 Caramulo, Serra do mts Port.
253 F3 Caraná r. Brazil
252 D3 Caranavi Bol.
260 E5 Carancho Arg.
177 L5 Cărand Romania
257 F4 Carandaí Brazil
253 E5 Carandaiti Bol.
253 F4 Carandazal Brazil
182 H2 Caranga Spain
257 F4 Carangola Brazil
182 C9 Caranguejeira Port.
197 K5 Caransebeș Romania
158 D4 Carantec France
163 F10 Carants, Tuc de les mt. Spain
251 I5 Carapajó Brazil
250 C5 Cara Paraná r. Col.
253 F6 Carapeguá Para.
193 P5 Carapelle Italy
193 P5 Carapelle r. Italy
193 P5 Carapellotto r. Italy
82 F5 Carappee Hill S.A. Austr.
225 H4 Caraquet N.B. Can.
250 C3 Carare r. Col.
190 G7 Carasco Italy
197 J5 Carașova Romania
177 L4 Carastelec Romania
94 F6 Carat, Tanjung pt Indon.
242 □R10 Caratasca Hond.
242 □R10 Caratasca, Laguna de lag. Hond.
257 F3 Caratinga Brazil
250 D5 Caratué r. Col.
233 □P3 Caratunk ME U.S.A.
250 E6 Carauari Brazil
254 F3 Caraúbas Brazil
Carauná mt. Brazil see Grande, Serra
185 P4 Caravaca de la Cruz Spain
190 H5 Caravaggio Italy
257 H2 Caravelas Brazil
252 B3 Caravelí Peru
247 □3 Caravelle, Presqu'île de la pen. Martinique
245 J1 Carbajal Mex.
182 I5 Carbajales de Alba Spain
182 D4 Carballeda de Avia Spain
182 C2 Carballo Galicia Spain
182 E4 Carballo Galicia Spain
182 H6 Carbellino Spain
223 L5 Carberry Man. Can.
261 H3 Carbo Arg.
242 D3 Carbó Mex.
194 D8 Carboi r. Sicilia Italy
192 D9 Carbonara, Capo c. Sardegna Italy
192 C9 Carbonara, Golfo di b. Sardegna Italy
194 G8 Carbonara, Pizzo mt. Italy
163 D6 Carbon-Blanc France
234 D3 Carbon County county PA U.S.A.
239 K7 Carbondale CO U.S.A.
237 K7 Carbondale IL U.S.A.
234 D1 Carbondale PA U.S.A.
225 K4 Carbonear Nfld and Lab. Can.
183 O5 Carbonera de Frentes Spain
245 J1 Carboneras Mex.
185 P7 Carboneras Spain
183 Q9 Carboneras de Guadazaón Spain
183 L6 Carbonero El Mayor Spain
185 L4 Carboneros Spain
192 B9 Carbonia Sardegna Italy
192 B9 Carbonia-Iglesias prov. Sardegna Italy
191 M2 Carbonìn Italy
257 F2 Carbonita Brazil
163 G9 Carbonne France
146 D8 Carbost Highland, Scotland U.K.
146 D8 Carbost Highland, Scotland U.K.
147 I6 Carbury Ireland
182 H8 Carcaboso Spain
185 K6 Carcabuey Spain
187 E9 Carcaixent Spain
222 G3 Carcajou Alta Can.
222 D1 Carcajou r. N.W.T. Can.
197 Q5 Carcaliu Romania
162 B5 Carcans France
162 B5 Carcans-Plage France
182 G5 Carção Port.
92 D6 Carcar Cebu Phil.
261 G3 Carcarañá r. Arg.
190 E7 Carcare Italy
163 I9 Carcassonne France
183 R4 Carcastillo Spain
187 C9 Carcelén Spain
161 I10 Carcès France
187 C11 Carche, Sierra del mts Spain
185 L5 Carchelejo Spain
250 B4 Carchi prov. Ecuador
190 E4 Carcoforo Italy
149 O6 Carcroft South Yorkshire, England U.K.
222 C2 Carcross Y.T. Can.
163 H6 Cardaillac France
199 H2 Çardak Çanakkale Turkey
199 K5 Çardak Denizli Turkey
261 I4 Cardal Uru.
Cardamomes, Chaîne des mts Cambodia see Cardamom Range
114 E7 Cardamom Hills India
96 F8 Cardamom Range mts Cambodia
186 J4 Cardedeu Spain
192 D8 Cardedu Sardegna Italy
185 K4 Cardeña Spain
183 M4 Cardeñadijo Spain
246 C2 Cárdenas Cuba
245 H3 Cárdenas San Luis Potosí Mex.
243 M8 Cárdenas Tabasco Mex.
183 Q9 Cardenete Spain
183 K7 Cardeñosa Spain
83 I3 Cardenyabba watercourse N.S.W. Austr.
195 J7 Cardeto Italy
Çardi Turkey see Harmancık
259 C8 Cardiel, Lago l. Arg.
150 F5 Cardiff Cardiff, Wales U.K.
150 F4 Cardiff admin. div. Wales U.K.
234 C5 Cardiff MD U.S.A.
150 F5 Cardiff International airport Wales U.K.
150 C3 Cardigan Ceredigion, Wales U.K.
150 C2 Cardigan Bay Wales U.K.
182 D9 Cardigos Port.
233 J4 Cardinal Ont. Can.
195 K6 Cardinale Italy
222 G3 Cardinal Lake Alta Can.
232 C8 Cardington OH U.S.A.
193 L4 Cardito Italy
216 □3b Cardón hill Fuerteventura Canary Is
242 C4 Cardón, Cerro hill Mex.
186 I4 Cardona Spain
261 I3 Cardona Uru.
245 H5 Cardonal Mex.
186 I4 Cardoner r. Spain
244 B1 Cardos Mex.
256 C4 Cardoso Brazil
256 D6 Cardoso, Ilha do i. Brazil
81 D11 Cardrona South I. N.Z.
81 C11 Cardrona, Mount South I. N.Z.
146 G11 Cardross Argyll and Bute, Scotland U.K.
222 H5 Cardston Alta Can.
85 K5 Cardwell Qld Austr.
257 E5 Careaçu Brazil
223 I3 Careen Lake Sask. Can.
191 K4 Carega, Cima mt. Italy
197 K3 Carei Romania
177 L4 Careilor, Câmpia plain Romania
251 G5 Careiro Brazil
251 F5 Careiro do Castanho Brazil
260 B2 Carén Coquimbo Chile
260 B2 Carén Coquimbo Chile
183 Q6 Carenas Spain
158 I3 Carentan France
158 G6 Carentoir France
183 K2 Cares r. Spain
179 O7 Carevdar Croatia
232 B8 Carey OH U.S.A.
87 G10 Carey, Lake salt flat W.A. Austr.
87 C8 Carey Downs W.A. Austr.
223 K2 Carey Lake N.W.T. Can.
217 □1 Cargados Carajos Islands Mauritius
146 I12 Cargenbridge Dumfries and Galloway, Scotland U.K.
192 B3 Cargèse Corse France
158 D5 Carhaix-Plouguer France
252 A2 Carhuamayo Peru
261 F5 Carhué Arg.
182 F8 Caria Port.
254 F4 Cariacá r. Brazil
257 G4 Cariacica Brazil
247 L8 Cariaco Venez.
247 K8 Cariaco, Golfo de b. Venez.
250 B6 Cariamanga Ecuador
209 B7 Cariango Angola
195 L5 Cariati Italy
246 B4 Caribbean Sea N. Atlantic Ocean
222 F4 Cariboo Mountains B.C. Can.
222 F4 Cariboo Mountains Provincial Park B.C. Can.
223 M3 Caribou r. Man. Can.
222 E2 Caribou r. N.W.T. Can.
233 □Q2 Caribou ME U.S.A.
226 I2 Caribou Island Ont. Can.
222 H2 Caribou Islands N.W.T. Can.
224 B3 Caribou Lake Ont. Can.
222 H3 Caribou Mountains Alta Can.
247 □2 Carib Point Dominica
242 F4 Carichic Mex.
92 E6 Carigara Leyte Phil.
92 E6 Carigara Bay Leyte Phil.
157 J4 Carignan France
190 D6 Carignano Italy
83 K4 Carinda N.S.W. Austr.
186 C5 Cariñena Spain
186 C5 Cariñena, Campo de reg. Spain
254 E5 Carinhanha Brazil
254 E5 Carinhanha r. Brazil
194 E7 Carini Sicilia Italy
146 B7 Carinish Western Isles, Scotland U.K.
182 E1 Cariño Spain
193 L5 Carinola Italy
Carinthia land Austria see Kärnten
209 D8 Caripande Angola
254 D4 Cariparé Brazil
251 F2 Caripe Venez.
251 F2 Caripito Venez.
254 E3 Cariris Novos, Serra dos hills Brazil
251 F2 Caris r. Venez.
190 E5 Carisio Italy
191 J3 Carisolo Italy
253 E2 Caritianas Brazil
177 L6 Cârjiți Romania
147 G3 Cark Mountain hill Ireland
163 G9 Carla-Bayle France
Carlabhagh Scotland U.K. see Carloway
Carlabhagh Western Isles, Scotland U.K. see Carloway
147 I3 Carland Northern Ireland U.K.
147 I5 Carlanstown Ireland
193 N4 Carlantino Italy
161 B7 Carlat France
195 I9 Carlentini Sicilia Italy
187 D9 Carlet Spain
227 K7 Carleton MI U.S.A.
225 H4 Carleton, Mount hill N.B. Can.
224 E4 Carleton Place Ont. Can.
215 L2 Carletonville S. Africa
197 N3 Cârlibaba Romania
238 F6 Carlin NV U.S.A.
86 E6 Carlindie Aboriginal Reserve W.A. Austr.
157 M5 Carling France
147 J4 Carlingford Ireland
147 J4 Carlingford Lough inlet Ireland/U.K.
236 K6 Carlinville IL U.S.A.
149 L4 Carlisle Cumbria, England U.K.
232 A10 Carlisle KY U.S.A.
233 K6 Carlisle NY U.S.A.
227 Q9 Carlisle PA U.S.A.
247 □4 Carlisle Bay Barbados
215 K9 Carlisle Bridge S. Africa
87 I10 Carlisle Lakes salt flat W.A. Austr.
234 A4 Carlisle Springs PA U.S.A.
163 H10 Carlit, Pic mt. France
192 A9 Carloforte Sardegna Italy
195 K5 Carlopoli Italy
256 C5 Carlópolis Brazil
146 J11 Carlops Scottish Borders, Scotland U.K.
245 L7 Carlos A. Carrillo Mex.
245 N8 Carlos A. Madrazo Mex.
261 G4 Carlos Casares Arg.
257 G2 Carlos Chagas Brazil
261 I3 Carlos Reyles Uru.
261 G4 Carlos Salas Arg.
261 F4 Carlos Tejedor Arg.
168 K3 Carlow Ger.
147 I7 Carlow Ireland
147 I7 Carlow county Ireland
146 C6 Carloway Western Isles, Scotland U.K.
Carlsbad Czech Rep. see Karlovy Vary
240 O8 Carlsbad CA U.S.A.
239 L10 Carlsbad NM U.S.A.
237 E10 Carlsbad TX U.S.A.
239 L10 Carlsbad Caverns National Park NM U.S.A.
172 E3 Carlsberg Ger.
265 H4 Carlsberg Ridge sea feature Indian Ocean
171 G10 Carlsfeld Ger.
262 S1 Carlson Inlet Antarctica
215 I7 Carlton S. Africa
151 J2 Carlton Nottinghamshire, England U.K.
226 B3 Carlton MN U.S.A.
151 P3 Carlton Colville Suffolk, England U.K.
86 J3 Carlton Hill W.A. Austr.
215 I7 Carlton Hills S. Africa
149 O7 Carlton in Lindrick Nottinghamshire, England U.K.
146 I11 Carluke South Lanarkshire, Scotland U.K.
163 G6 Carlux France
223 K5 Carlyle Sask. Can.
236 K6 Carlyle IL U.S.A.
236 K6 Carlyle Lake IL U.S.A.
222 B2 Carmacks Y.T. Can.
190 D6 Carmagnola Italy
223 L5 Carman Man. Can.
Carmana Iran see Kermān
150 D4 Carmarthen Carmarthenshire, Wales U.K.
150 C4 Carmarthen Bay Wales U.K.
150 D4 Carmarthenshire admin. div. Wales U.K.
163 I7 Carmaux France
230 D6 Carmel IN U.S.A.
233 □P4 Carmel ME U.S.A.
233 L7 Carmel NY U.S.A.
Carmel, Mount hill Israel see Karmel, Har
240 K5 Carmel-by-the-Sea CA U.S.A.
150 C1 Carmel Head Wales U.K.
243 N9 Carmelita Guat.
261 H3 Carmelo Uru.
240 K5 Carmel Valley CA U.S.A.
261 G3 Carmen Arg.
258 C2 Carmen Chile
250 C2 Carmen Col.
243 I5 Carmen Mex.
242 F2 Carmen r. Mex.
92 E7 Carmen Bohol Phil.
261 I3 Carmen Uru.
241 U10 Carmen AZ U.S.A.
242 D5 Carmen, Isla i. Mex.
243 N8 Carmen, Isla del i. Mex.
183 L9 Carmena Spain
252 C5 Carmen Alto Chile
261 H4 Carmen de Areco Arg.
253 F6 Carmen del Paraná Para.
259 E6 Carmen de Patagones Arg.
182 I3 Cármenes Spain
260 D4 Carmensa Arg.
236 K6 Carmi IL U.S.A.
195 O3 Carmiano Italy
231 □2 Carmichael New Prov. Bahamas
240 K3 Carmichael CA U.S.A.
85 L6 Carmila Qld Austr.
257 F4 Carmo Brazil
257 E4 Carmo da Cachoeira Brazil
257 E5 Carmo de Minas Brazil
256 D3 Carmo do Paranaíba Brazil
87 E12 Carmody, Lake salt flat W.A. Austr.
Carmona Angola see Uíge
242 □Q13 Carmona Hond.
184 H6 Carmona Spain
184 G2 Carmonita Spain
257 E4 Carmópolis do Minas Brazil
146 K9 Carmyllie Angus, Scotland U.K.
158 E6 Carnac France
146 G8 Carn a' Chuilinn hill Scotland U.K.
147 I4 Carnagh Northern Ireland U.K.
87 C10 Carnamah W.A. Austr.
87 B8 Carnarvon W.A. Austr.
214 G6 Carnarvon S. Africa
214 F6 Carnarvonleegte salt pan S. Africa
85 K8 Carnarvon National Park Qld Austr.
87 F8 Carnarvon Range hills W.A. Austr.
85 L8 Carnarvon Range mts Qld Austr.
146 K10 Carnbee Fife, Scotland U.K.
146 G7 Carn Chuinneag hill Scotland U.K.
146 G8 Carn Dearg hill Highland, Scotland U.K.
146 H8 Carn Dearg hill Highland, Scotland U.K.
147 H2 Carndonagh Ireland
147 J2 Carnduff Northern Ireland U.K.
146 J8 Carn Ealasaid hill Scotland U.K.
150 E1 Carnedd Llywelyn mt. Wales U.K.
150 E2 Carnedd y Filiast hill Wales U.K.
87 G8 Carnegie W.A. Austr.
87 G9 Carnegie, Lake salt flat W.A. Austr.
267 N6 Carnegie Ridge sea feature S. Pacific Ocean
146 F8 Carn Eige mt. Scotland U.K.
146 I8 Carne na Loine hill Scotland U.K.
258 B5 Carnero, Bahía del b. Chile
185 I8 Carnero, Punta del pt Spain
82 E4 Carnes S.A. Austr.
231 F8 Carnesville GA U.S.A.
147 J7 Carnew Ireland
226 G4 Carney MI U.S.A.
262 P2 Carney Island Antarctica
234 E5 Carneys Point NJ U.S.A.
146 K8 Carnferg hill Scotland U.K.
149 L5 Carnforth Lancashire, England U.K.
146 I8 Carn Glas-choire hill Scotland U.K.
115 M8 Car Nicobar i. Andaman & Nicobar Is India
156 F3 Carnières France
138 H4 Carnikava Latvia
147 K3 Carnlough Northern Ireland U.K.
147 K2 Carnlough Bay Northern Ireland U.K.
146 J8 Carn Mòr hill Scotland U.K.
147 E6 Carnmore Ireland
150 E2 Carno Powys, Wales U.K.
146 H8 Carn Odhar hill Scotland U.K.
158 D5 Carnoët France
161 D9 Carnon-Plage France
208 B3 Carnot C.A.R.
76 D5 Carnot, Cape S.A. Austr.
182 B3 Carnota Spain
86 G4 Carnot Bay W.A. Austr.
161 I10 Carnoules France
146 K9 Carnoustie Angus, Scotland U.K.
161 H10 Carnoux-en-Provence France
147 J8 Carnsore Point Ireland
148 D5 Carnteel Northern Ireland U.K.
146 I11 Carnwath South Lanarkshire, Scotland U.K.
227 K6 Caro MI U.S.A.
251 F4 Caroaebe r. Brazil
Caroch mt. Spain see El Caroche
85 N5 Carola Cay rf Coral Sea Is Terr. Austr.
231 G13 Carol City FL U.S.A.
193 Q9 Carolei Italy
260 D3 Carolina Arg.
254 D3 Carolina Brazil
247 □1 Carolina Puerto Rico
215 O2 Carolina S. Africa
231 I8 Carolina Beach NC U.S.A.
222 H4 Caroline Alta Can.
234 D7 Caroline County county MD U.S.A.
82 □3 Caroline Cove b. S. Pacific Ocean
267 I6 Caroline Island atoll Kiribati
266 E5 Caroline Islands N. Pacific Ocean
81 B12 Caroline Peak South I. N.Z.
158 H4 Carolles France
214 B5 Carolusberg S. Africa
161 G8 Caromb France
190 H3 Carona Italy
250 B4 Carondelet Ecuador
247 □7 Caroni Trinidad Trin. and Tob.
247 □7 Caroni Trinidad Trin. and Tob.
247 □7 Caroni county Trin. and Tob.
251 F2 Caroní r. Venez.
194 G7 Caronia Sicilia Italy
247 □7 Caroni Swamp Trin. and Tob.
250 D2 Carora Venez.
197 R5 C. A. Rosetti Romania
195 M3 Carosino Italy
195 N2 Carovigno Italy
193 M4 Carovilli Italy
227 R4 Carp Ont. Can.
190 H6 Carpaneto Piacentino Italy
177 I2 Carpathian Mountains Europe
Carpații mts Europe see Carpathian Mountains
197 K5 Carpații Meridionali mts Romania
191 M8 Carpegna Italy
190 I5 Carpenedolo Italy
84 G3 Carpentaria, Gulf of N.T./Qld Austr.
85 J5 Carpentaria Downs Qld Austr.
260 C2 Carpentiría Arg.
161 G8 Carpentras France
191 J6 Carpi Italy
195 O3 Carpignano Salentino Italy
190 E4 Carpignano Sesia Italy
254 G3 Carpina Brazil
191 M9 Carpina r. Italy
177 L5 Cărpinet Romania
190 I7 Carpineti Italy
193 K4 Carpineto Romano Italy
196 I5 Cărpiniș Romania
193 P4 Carpino Italy
193 M4 Carpinone Italy
240 M7 Carpinteria CA U.S.A.
183 J6 Carpio Spain
236 E1 Carpio ND U.S.A.
159 K3 Carpiquet France
222 F4 Carp Lake Provincial Park B.C. Can.
158 I7 Carquefou France
161 I10 Carqueiranne France
184 F2 Carquesa hill Spain
147 D5 Carra, Lough l. Ireland
233 □O3 Carrabassett ME U.S.A.
231 E11 Carrabelle FL U.S.A.
147 E5 Carracastle Ireland
182 G3 Carracedelo Spain
146 F11 Carradale East Argyll and Bute, Scotland U.K.
Carraig na Siuire Ireland see Carrick-on-Suir
250 C2 Carraipía Col.
182 D2 Carral Spain
147 D9 Carran hill Ireland
183 M8 Carranque Spain
147 C9 Carrantuohill mt. Ireland
184 B6 Carrapateira Port.
182 F7 Carrapichana Port.
190 I7 Carrara Italy
147 C6 Carraroe Ireland
186 E6 Carrascal mt. Spain
182 I7 Carrascal del Obispo Spain
183 M6 Carrascal del Río Spain
252 D4 Carrasco, Parque Nacional nat. park Bol.
183 P7 Carrascosa Spain
183 O8 Carrascosa del Campo Spain
187 C12 Carrascoy, Sierra de mts Spain
83 J6 Carrathool N.S.W. Austr.
185 J7 Carratraca Spain
182 F6 Carrazeda de Ansiães Port.
251 I5 Carrazedo Brazil
182 F5 Carrazedo de Montenegro Port.
86 J4 Carr Boyd Range hills W.A. Austr.
146 I8 Carrbridge Highland, Scotland U.K.
182 C5 Carreço Port.
184 B2 Carregado Port.
182 E8 Carregal do Sal Port.
182 D9 Carregueiros Port.
182 B3 Carreiro, Punta pt Spain
184 D5 Carreiros r. Port.
183 K2 Carreña Spain
260 C5 Carrero, Cerro mt. Arg.
163 C9 Carresse-Cassaber France
261 I4 Carreta Quemada Uru.
Carrhae Turkey see Harran
247 □3 Carriacou i. Grenada
183 M2 Carriazo Spain
147 E3 Carrick Donegal Ireland
147 I8 Carrick Wexford Ireland
146 G12 Carrick reg. Scotland U.K.
147 H8 Carrickbeg Ireland
147 G5 Carrickboy Ireland
147 K3 Carrickfergus Northern Ireland U.K.
147 I5 Carrickmacross Ireland
147 H3 Carrickmore Northern Ireland U.K.
147 F5 Carrick-on-Shannon Ireland
147 H8 Carrick-on-Suir Ireland
182 C9 Carriço Port.
82 G5 Carrieton S.A. Austr.
147 E9 Carrigadrohid Reservoir Ireland
147 F9 Carrigaline Ireland
147 G5 Carrigallen Ireland
147 D9 Carriganimmy Ireland
147 H3 Carrigans Ireland
147 D8 Carrigkerry Ireland
147 F9 Carrigtwohill Ireland
261 H4 Carril Arg.
242 H4 Carrillo Mex.
261 F2 Carrilobo Arg.
236 F2 Carrington ND U.S.A.
182 D2 Carrio Spain
183 K4 Carrion r. Spain
185 L2 Carrión de Calatrava Spain
184 G6 Carrión de los Céspedes Spain
183 K4 Carrión de los Condes Spain
250 C2 Carrizal Col.
242 F2 Carrizal Mex.
258 C3 Carrizal Bajo Chile
261 G3 Carrizales Arg.
241 V7 Carrizo AZ U.S.A.
244 D4 Carrizo Colorado Mex.
237 D7 Carrizo Creek r. TX U.S.A.
241 V8 Carrizo Creek watercourse AZ U.S.A.
241 Q8 Carrizo Creek watercourse CA U.S.A.
182 I3 Carrizo de la Ribera Spain
240 M7 Carrizo Plain National Monument nat. park CA U.S.A.
245 H1 Carrizos Mex.
185 N3 Carrizosa Spain
237 F11 Carrizo Springs TX U.S.A.
241 W7 Carrizo Wash watercourse AZ/NM U.S.A.
239 L10 Carrizozo NM U.S.A.
185 O2 Carro hill Spain
186 F3 Carrodilla, Sierra de mts Spain
236 H4 Carroll IA U.S.A.
234 A5 Carroll County county MD U.S.A.
237 K9 Carrollton AL U.S.A.
231 E9 Carrollton GA U.S.A.
236 J6 Carrollton IL U.S.A.
230 E6 Carrollton KY U.S.A.
236 I6 Carrollton MO U.S.A.
237 K9 Carrollton MS U.S.A.
232 D8 Carrollton OH U.S.A.
232 G8 Carrolltown PA U.S.A.
85 H4 Carron r. Qld Austr.
146 H7 Carron r. Highland, Scotland U.K.
146 E8 Carron, Loch inlet Scotland U.K.
146 I12 Carronbridge Dumfries and Galloway, Scotland U.K.
260 E5 Carro Quemado Arg.
161 K9 Carros France
223 K4 Carrot r. Sask. Can.
223 K4 Carrot River Sask. Can.
159 K4 Carrouges France
147 H2 Carrowkeel Ireland
147 E6 Carrowmore Ireland
147 C4 Carrowmore Lake Ireland
147 E4 Carrowneden Ireland
232 I12 Carrsville VA U.S.A.
190 D7 Carrù Italy
223 K2 Carruthers Lake Nunavut Can.
237 K7 Carruthersville MO U.S.A.
147 K3 Carryduff Northern Ireland U.K.
233 K4 Carry Falls Reservoir NY U.S.A.
161 G10 Carry-le-Rouet France
162 C5 Cars France
163 G6 Carsac-Aillac France
146 E10 Carsaig Argyll and Bute, Scotland U.K.
126 H3 Çarşamba Turkey
129 A4 Çarşıbaşı Turkey
149 N7 Carsington Water resr England U.K.
193 K3 Carsoli Italy
86 I3 Carson r. W.A. Austr.
236 E2 Carson ND U.S.A.
240 M2 Carson r. NV U.S.A.
226 J6 Carson City MI U.S.A.
240 M2 Carson City NV U.S.A.
86 I3 Carson Escarpment W.A. Austr.
240 N2 Carson Lake NV U.S.A.
86 I3 Carson River Aboriginal Reserve W.A. Austr.
240 N2 Carson Sink l. NV U.S.A.
227 L6 Carsonville MI U.S.A.
160 K1 Carspach France
146 H12 Carsphairn Dumfries and Galloway, Scotland U.K.
146 I11 Carstairs South Lanarkshire, Scotland U.K.
Carstensz-top mt. Papua Indon. see Jaya, Puncak
223 I3 Carswell Lake Sask. Can.
260 B3 Cartagena Chile
250 C2 Cartagena Col.
187 D12 Cartagena Spain
250 C3 Cartago Col.
242 □R13 Cartago Costa Rica
185 J7 Cártama Spain
184 B2 Cartaxo Port.
184 E6 Cartaya Spain
161 J10 Cartaya, Cap c. France
162 C5 Cartelègue France
85 I2 Carter, Mount hill Qld Austr.
158 H3 Carteret France
235 G3 Carteret NJ U.S.A.
158 H3 Carteret, Cap de c. France
Carteret Group is P.N.G. see Kilinailau Islands
Carteret Island Solomon Is see Malaita
85 H7 Carters Range hills Qld Austr.
231 E8 Cartersville GA U.S.A.
81 J8 Carterton North I. N.Z.
151 I4 Carterton Oxfordshire, England U.K.
183 L2 Cartes Spain
205 H1 Carthage tourist site Tunisia
226 C9 Carthage IL U.S.A.
237 H7 Carthage MO U.S.A.
231 C9 Carthage MS U.S.A.
231 H8 Carthage NC U.S.A.
233 J5 Carthage NY U.S.A.
231 E7 Carthage TN U.S.A.
237 H9 Carthage TX U.S.A.
Carthago tourist site Tunisia see Carthage
Carthago Nova Spain see Cartagena
227 M3 Cartier Ont. Can.
86 G2 Cartier Island Ashmore & Cartier Is Austr.
149 L5 Cartmel Cumbria, England U.K.
191 N8 Cartoceto Italy
223 L5 Cartwright Man. Can.
225 J2 Cartwright Nfld and Lab. Can.
251 F2 Caruachi Venez.
254 G4 Caruarú Brazil
254 C2 Caruçambaba Brazil
182 G4 Carucedo Spain
193 N4 Carunchio Italy
197 O4 Cărunta, Vârful mt. Romania
251 F2 Carúpano Venez.
254 D2 Carutapera Brazil
182 D9 Carvalhal Santarém Port.
184 B4 Carvalhal Setúbal Port.
251 I5 Carvalho Brazil
182 F6 Carvalho de Egas Port.
232 B11 Carver KY U.S.A.
182 G6 Carviçais Port.
156 E3 Carvin France
184 A2 Carvoeira Port.
251 F5 Carvoeiro Brazil
184 C6 Carvoeiro Port.
184 A2 Carvoeiro, Cabo c. Port.
85 K8 Carwell Qld Austr.
129 J4 Çarxı Azer.
231 H8 Cary NC U.S.A.
83 I3 Caryapundy Swamp Qld Austr.
232 A12 Caryville TN U.S.A.
226 C5 Caryville WI U.S.A.
185 P5 Casa Alta hill Spain
185 K7 Casabermeja Spain
258 D1 Casabindo, Cerro de mt. Arg.
260 B3 Casablanca Chile
204 D2 Casablanca Morocco
256 D4 Casa Branca Brazil
184 C3 Casa Branca Évora Port.
184 D3 Casa Branca Portalegre Port.
193 N4 Casacalenda Italy
247 □7 Casa Cruz, Cape Trin. and Tob.
242 E2 Casa de Janos Mex.
245 I2 Casa del Campesino Mex.
185 K3 Casa de Michos Spain
260 D6 Casa de Piedra Arg.
260 D6 Casa de Piedra, Embalse resr Arg.
193 M5 Casagiove Italy
192 B3 Casaglione Corse France
241 U9 Casa Grande AZ U.S.A.
195 O3 Casa l'Abate Italy
193 M3 Casalanguida Italy
183 O3 Casalarreina Spain
193 N3 Casalbordino Italy
193 O5 Casalbore Italy
193 P7 Casalbuono Italy
190 H5 Casalbuttano ed Uniti Italy
190 F6 Casàl Cermelli Italy
191 K7 Casalecchio di Reno Italy
261 G3 Casalegno Arg.
190 E5 Casale Monferrato Italy
193 P7 Casaletto Spartano Italy
191 L7 Casalfiumanese Italy
191 J6 Casalgrande Italy
190 D6 Casalgrasso Italy
184 B2 Casalinho Port.
261 H5 Casalins Arg.
190 I6 Casalmaggiore Italy
193 O4 Casalnuovo Monterotaro Italy
190 H5 Casalpusterlengo Italy
253 E3 Casalvasco Brazil
193 O4 Casalvecchio di Puglia Italy
193 O7 Casàl Velino Italy
206 A3 Casamance r. Senegal
195 L2 Casamassima Italy
192 C2 Casamozza Corse France
250 D3 Casanare dept Col.
250 D3 Casanare r. Col.
185 J7 Casarabonela Spain
195 O3 Casarano Italy
182 H9 Casar de Cáceres Spain
182 H8 Casar de Palomero Spain
183 N5 Casarejos Spain
242 □P12 Casares Nic.
185 I8 Casares Spain
182 H2 Casares Spain
182 H8 Casares de las Hurdes Spain
185 J6 Casariche Spain
183 L8 Casarrubios del Monte Spain
191 N4 Casarsa della Delizia Italy
190 G7 Casarza Ligure Italy
245 I2 Casas Mex.
187 C7 Casas Altas Spain
185 O2 Casas de Benitez Spain
185 I2 Casas de Don Pedro Spain
185 O2 Casas de Fernando Alonso Spain
185 O2 Casas de Haro Spain
187 C9 Casas de Juan Gil Spain
185 P2 Casas de Juan Núñez Spain
185 O3 Casas de Lázaro Spain
182 I8 Casas del Monte Spain
185 O2 Casas de los Pinos Spain
187 C11 Casas del Puerto Spain
182 H9 Casas de Millán Spain
187 C9 Casas de Ves Spain
242 F2 Casas Grandes Mex.
242 F2 Casas Grandes r. Mex.
185 Q2 Casas-Ibáñez Spain
185 O2 Casasimarro Spain
184 E3 Casas Novas de Mares Port.
183 J5 Casasola de Arión Spain
182 I9 Casatejada Spain
190 G4 Casatenovo Italy
183 K8 Casavieja Spain
261 F5 Casbas Arg.
255 B9 Casca Brazil
242 E3 Cascada de Bassaseachic, Parque Nacional nat. park Mex.
87 F12 Cascade W.A. Austr.
81 C11 Cascade r. South I. N.Z.
217 □2b Cascade Mahé Seychelles
236 J4 Cascade IA U.S.A.
238 F4 Cascade ID U.S.A.
238 I3 Cascade MT U.S.A.
82 □1 Cascade Bay Norfolk I.
81 C11 Cascade Point South I. N.Z.
228 B2 Cascade Range mts Can./U.S.A.
238 F4 Cascade Reservoir ID U.S.A.
217 □1c Cascades, Pointe des pt Réunion
238 D5 Cascade-Siskiyou National Monument nat. park OR U.S.A.
184 A3 Cascais Port.
242 □Q12 Cascal, Paso del pass Nic.
183 Q4 Cascante Spain
187 C7 Cascante del Río Spain
225 H3 Cascapédia r. Que. Can.
254 F3 Cascavel Ceará Brazil
256 A6 Cascavel Paraná Brazil
193 K2 Cascia Italy
191 J8 Casciana Terme Italy
190 J8 Cascina Italy

215 M5 **Central Range** mts Lesotho
91 J7 **Central Range** mts P.N.G.
Central Russian Upland hills Rus. Fed. see **Sredne-Russkaya Vozvyshennost'**
Central Siberian Plateau Rus. Fed. see **Sredne-Sibirskoye Ploskogor'ye**
233 I5 **Central Square** NY U.S.A.
235 G2 **Central Valley** NY U.S.A.
235 L1 **Central Village** CT U.S.A.
207 H5 **Centre** prov. Cameroon
231 H1 **Centre** admin. reg. France
231 E8 **Centre** AL U.S.A.
160 E3 **Centre, Canal du** France
217 □1b **Cente de Flacq** Mauritius
81 B13 **Centre Island** South I. N.Z.
231 D9 **Centreville** AL U.S.A.
234 C6 **Centreville** MD U.S.A.
226 I8 **Centreville** MI U.S.A.
132 C2 **Centreville** VA U.S.A.
141 **Centuri Corse** France
215 M1 **Centurion** S. Africa
194 H8 **Centuripe** Sicilia Italy
231 D10 **Century** FL U.S.A.
109 H7 **Cenxi** Guangxi China
Ceos i. Greece see **Tzia**
163 G6 **Ceos** Greece U.K. see **Keose**
193 M3 **Céou** r. France
193 Q7 **Cepagatti** Italy
Cephaloedium Sicilia Italy see **Cefalù**
Cephalonia i. Greece see **Kefalonia**
138 H8 **Čepkeliu** nature res. Lith.
182 E7 **Cepões** Port.
181 I7 **Čepovan** Slovenia
156 E7 **Cepoy** France
194 H1 **Ceppaloni** Italy
193 L4 **Ceprano** Italy
95 I8 **Cepu** Jawa Indon.
196 H6 **Cer** hills Serbia
194 H8 **Cerami** Sicilia Italy
194 G8 **Cerami** r. Sicilia Italy
Ceram Sea Indon. see **Seram, Laut**
190 F5 **Cerano** Italy
175 K5 **Ceranów** Pol.
159 L6 **Cérans-Foulletourte** France
195 J7 **Cerasi** Italy
193 L3 **Ceraso** Italy
192 D6 **Ceraso, Capo** c. Sardegna Italy
177 L6 **Cerbăl** Romania
241 R6 **Cerbat Mountains** AZ U.S.A.
163 K11 **Cerbère** France
163 J5 **Cerbère, Cap** c. France/Spain
192 C4 **Cerbicale, Îles** is Corse France
Cerbol r. Spain see **Cervol, Riu**
192 F2 **Cerboli, Isola i.** Italy
184 B2 **Cercal** Lisboa Port.
184 B5 **Cercal** Setúbal Port.
184 B5 **Cercal** hill Port.
184 B5 **Cercal, Serra de** mts Port.
176 D2 **Čerčany** Czech Rep.
182 L7 **Cercedilla** Spain
193 N5 **Cercemaggiore** Italy
193 L3 **Cerchio** Italy
176 B2 **Cerchov** mt. Czech Rep.
160 D3 **Cercy-la-Tour** France
194 F8 **Cerda** Sicilia Italy
163 I11 **Cerdagne** reg. France
Cerdagne reg. France see **Cerdanya**
186 I3 **Cerdanya** reg. Spain
186 J5 **Cerdanyola del Vallès** Spain
182 D3 **Cerdedo** Spain
182 E8 **Cerdeira** Port.
163 H6 **Cère** r. France
191 K5 **Cerea** Italy
223 I3 **Cereal** Alta Can.
261 F5 **Cereales** Arg.
177 I3 **Cered** Hungary
Ceredigion admin. div. Wales U.K.
191 L5 **Ceregnano** Italy
174 F3 **Cerekwica** Pol.
158 I4 **Cérences** France
195 L5 **Cerenzia** Italy
261 G1 **Ceres** Arg.
254 C4 **Ceres** Brazil
190 C5 **Ceres** Italy
214 D9 **Ceres** S. Africa
234 C4 **Ceres** CA U.S.A.
161 K6 **Ceresole, Lago di** l. Italy
190 C5 **Ceresole Reale** Italy
191 L5 **Ceresone** r. Italy
156 H9 **Cérêt** France
250 C2 **Cereté** Col.
183 M6 **Cerezo de Abajo** Spain
183 M6 **Cerezo de Arriba** Spain
183 O2 **Cerezo de Ríotirón** Spain
217 □2b **Cerf, Île au** i. Inner Islands Seychelles
227 S3 **Cerf, Lac du** l. Que. Can.
165 F8 **Cerfontaine** Belgium
217 □1b **Cerfs, Îles aux** is Mauritius
177 K2 **Čergov** mts Slovakia
156 D5 **Cergy** France
171 L10 **Cerhenice** Czech Rep.
111 G11 **Cêri** Xizang China
190 D8 **Ceriale** Italy
190 E7 **Cerignola** Italy
Cerigo i. Greece see **Kythira**
126 F4 **Çerikli** Turkey
129 B5 **Cerillos** Chile
260 B2 **Cerillos de Tamaya** Chile
160 B3 **Céringgolêb** Xizang China see **Dongco**
156 F7 **Cerisiers** France
159 J3 **Cerisy-la-Forêt** France
158 I3 **Cerisy-la-Salle** France
159 J8 **Cerizay** France
191 K4 **Cerkno mt.** Slovenia
126 F3 **Çerkeş** Turkey
199 K2 **Çerkeşli** Turkey
199 J1 **Çerkezmüsellim** Turkey
179 M8 **Cerklje** Brežice Slovenia
179 J7 **Cerklje** Kranj Slovenia
188 E3 **Cerknica** Slovenia
179 I8 **Cerkniško jezero** l. Slovenia
179 I7 **Cerkno** Slovenia
174 D1 **Cerkwica** Pol.
128 D5 **Çerme** Turkey
197 J4 **Cermei** Romania
193 L2 **Cerminara** Italy
162 I4 **Çermik** Turkey
197 O5 **Cerna** r. Romania
197 K5 **Cerna** r. Romania
197 K6 **Cerna** r. Romania
197 M6 **Cerna** r. Romania
184 D4 **Cernache do Bonjardim** Port.
182 H5 **Cernadilla, Embalse de** resr Spain
176 F2 **Černá Hora** Czech Rep.
176 □3 **Černá Hora** mt. Czech Rep.
197 O5 **Cernat** Romania
197 Q6 **Cernavodă** Romania
157 N1 **Cernay** France
156 I5 **Cernay-en-Dormois** France
176 C1 **Černčice** Czech Rep.
183 M3 **Cérnegula** Spain
179 N6 **Černelavci** Slovenia
190 D1 **Cernier** Switz.
177 H3 **Černík** Slovakia
177 H3 **Černíny** hill Slovakia
190 G4 **Cernobbio** Italy
176 D2 **Černošice** Czech Rep.
176 B1 **Černošín** Czech Rep.
191 J5 **Cerovac** Croatia
177 I3 **Cerovica** Slovakia
256 C5 **Cerqueira César** Brazil
176 F2 **Černá r.** France
176 □3 **Černá Hora** mt. Czech Rep.
197 O5 **Cernat** Romania
127 J5 **Ceylanpınar** Turkey
129 K5 **Ceyranbatan** Azer.
197 Q6 **Cernăuți** Ukr. see **Chernivtsi**
197 O5 **Cernavodă** Romania
Ceylon country Asia see **Sri Lanka**
155 I5 **Cernay-en-Dormois** Azer.
176 L1 **Cernčice** Azer.
183 M3 **Ceyranbatan** Azer.
160 G4 **Ceyzériat** France
181 F8 **Cézac** France
190 J3 **Cernier** Switz.
177 H3 **Čermná** Slovakia
177 H3 **Černíny** hill Czech Rep.
122 E6 **Chābahār** Iran
176 D2 **Černošice** Czech Rep.
122 F4 **Chabanais** France
160 H3 **Chabeuil** France
122 H5 **Chalain, Lac de** l. France
256 C5 **Chabet el Ameur** Alg.
160 K5 **Chalap Dalan** mts Afgh.
156 E7 **Chalaronne** r. France
183 L8 **Chaláte** Mex.
160 I3 **Chalamont** France
160 D5 **Chalais** Switz.
159 O7 **Chabris** France

190 I7 **Cerreto, Passo del** pass Italy
191 N9 **Cerreto d'Esi** Italy
193 J2 **Cerreto di Spoleto** Italy
193 N5 **Cerreto Sannita** Italy
150 E1 **Cerrigydrudion** Conwy, Wales U.K.
258 D2 **Cerrillos** Arg.
244 G5 **Cerritos** Guanajuato Mex.
244 G3 **Cerritos** San Luis Potosí Mex.
193 M4 **Cerro al Volturno** Italy
256 C6 **Cerro Azul** Brazil
245 J4 **Cerro Azul** Peru
252 A3 **Cerro Azul** Peru
184 H5 **Cerro del Hiero** Spain
245 D7 **Cerro de Ortega** Mex.
252 A2 **Cerro de Pasco** Peru
244 D7 **Cerro Gordo** Mex.
242 □S4 **Cerro Hoya, Parque Nacional** nat. park Panama
259 C9 **Cerro Manantiales** Chile
185 M7 **Cerrón** mt. Spain
250 D2 **Cerrón, Cerro** mt. Venez.
252 C5 **Cerro Negro** Chile
242 F4 **Cerro Prieto** Mex.
260 C6 **Cerros Colorados, Embalse** resr Arg.
250 A5 **Cerros de Amotape, Parque Nacional** nat. park Peru
251 G6 **Cerro, Cachoeira da** waterfall Brazil
252 B2 **Chacra de Piros** Peru
202 C6 **Chad** country Africa
202 B6 **Chad, Lake** Africa
106 H3 **Chadaasan** Mongolia
98 F1 **Chadan** Rus. Fed.
231 □1 **Chaddock Bar** rf Bermuda
234 D5 **Chadds Ford** PA U.S.A.
213 C2 **Chadiza** Zambia
161 D6 **Chadrac** France
236 D4 **Chadron** NE U.S.A.
234 C7 **Chadwick Bar** MD U.S.A.
123 M7 **Chae Hom** Thai.
121 P7 **Chaek** Kyrg.
101 D9 **Chaeryŏng** N. Korea
96 D5 **Chae Son National Park** Thai.
160 H5 **Chafarinas, Islas** is N. Africa
207 G4 **Chafe** Nigeria
237 K7 **Chaffee** MO U.S.A.
259 B7 **Chaffers, Isla i.** Chile
160 E3 **Chaffey** WI U.S.A.
123 J7 **Chafurray** Col.
122 I6 **Chagai Hills** Afgh./Pak.
114 F5 **Chagalamarri** Andhra Prad. India
120 K5 **Chagan** Kyzylordinskaya Oblast' Kazakh.
120 I1 **Chagan** Vostochnyy Kazakhstan Kazakh.
129 J5 **Chaganuzun** Rus. Fed.
150 E6 **Chagford** Devon, England U.K.
111 L9 **Chaggur** Qinghai China
123 K4 **Chagha Khûr** mt. Iran
121 M1 **Chaghcharān** Afgh.
139 S2 **Chagoda** Rus. Fed.
139 S2 **Chagoda** r. Rus. Fed.
265 I5 **Chagos Archipelago** is B.I.O.T.
265 I5 **Chagos-Laccadive Ridge** sea feature Indian Ocean
265 I5 **Chagos Trench** sea feature Indian Ocean
100 C7 **Chagra** r. Rus. Fed.
120 C1 **Chagra** r. Rus. Fed.
242 □T13 **Chagres, Parque Nacional** nat. park Panama
251 G4 **Chaguanas** Trin. and Tob.
250 E2 **Chaguaramas** Venez.
99 D1 **Chagyllyshor, Vpadina** depr. Turkm.
136 I8 **Chah** r. Ukr.
123 N6 **Chahah Burjal** Afgh.
122 H5 **Chāhak** Iran
129 F2 **Chah 'Ali** Iran
123 N3 **Chāh 'Ali Akbar** Iran
123 K4 **Chaharbagh** Afgh.
122 D5 **Chahār Mahāll va Bakhtīārī** prov. Iran
122 D7 **Chahār Rūstā'ī** Iran
122 F4 **Chāhār Ţāq** Iran
122 F4 **Chāh Baba** well Iran
122 E5 **Chāh Badam** Iran
122 D8 **Chāh Bahār, Khalīj-e** b. Iran
121 M1 **Chahchaheh** Turkm.
122 D5 **Chāh-e Ab** Afgh.
122 D7 **Chāh-e Dow Chāh** Iran
122 G4 **Chāh-e Khoshāb** Iran
122 G4 **Chāh-e Nūklok** Iran
211 A7 **Chāh-e Rāh** Iran
122 F5 **Chāh-e Rig** Afgh.
122 I7 **Chāh-e Shīrin** Iran
122 D7 **Chāh Sorkh** Iran
245 M9 **Chahuites** Mex.
117 J8 **Chaibasa** Jharkhand India
225 H2 **Chaidamu** China
100 D5 **Chaigoubu** Hebei China
91 J7 **Chaihe** Nei Mongol China
100 D7 **Chai He** r. China
117 L5 **Chailley** France
117 M5 **Chailley** East Sussex, England U.K.
161 H6 **Chaillac** France
159 J5 **Chailland** France
161 H6 **Chaillé-les-Marais** France
161 H7 **Chailley** France
96 E7 **Chainat** Thai.
111 H9 **Chainjoin Co** l. Xizang China
156 H6 **Châlons-en-Champagne** France
95 F3 **Chainat** Thai.
126 G7 **Chai Si** r. Thai.
116 F7 **Chaitén** Chile
259 B7 **Chaitén** Chile
110 D7 **Chaiwopu** Xinjiang China
96 D10 **Chaiya** Thai.
96 E7 **Chaiyaphum** Thai.
259 C6 **Chaiyan** Arg.
123 L8 **Chaj Doab** lowland Pak.
261 I2 **Chajari** Arg.
117 K7 **Chakai** Bihar India
117 J6 **Chakai** Pak.
122 I7 **Chak Amru** Pak.
213 A3 **Chakari** Zimbabwe
260 B3 **Chakaria** Bangl.
123 O4 **Chakdarra** Pak.
211 O4 **Chake Chake** Tanz.
116 I5 **Chakhānsūr** Afgh.
177 J7 **Chakia** Uttar Prad. India
117 I7 **Chak Jhumra** Pak.
221 I5 **Chakku** Pak.
227 I2 **Chakonipau, Lac** l. Que. Can.
159 O7 **Chakradharpur** Jharkhand India
117 K8 **Chakulia** Jharkhand India
129 C4 **Ch'ak'vi** Georgia
215 N5 **Chala** Peru
252 B3 **Chala** Tanz.
211 A6 **Chalabesa** Zambia
163 J10 **Chalabre** France
160 H3 **Chaladinki** Georgia see **Sabazho**
160 H3 **Chalain, Lac de** l. France
156 G7 **Chalais** Switz.
160 K5 **Chalap Dalan** mts Afgh.
156 E7 **Chalaronne** r. France
245 L8 **Chalateng** mt. El Salvador
157 M8 **Chalampé** France
210 C4 **Chalbi Desert** Kenya
259 O7 **Chabris** France

244 D2 **Chalchihuites** Mex.
245 I6 **Chalco** Mex.
100 A2 **Chaldonka** Rus. Fed.
151 K6 **Chale** Isle of Wight, England U.K.
162 F4 **Chalencon** France
161 F7 **Chalenon** France
111 K7 **Chalengkou** Qinghai China
156 E7 **Châlette-sur-Loing** France
225 H3 **Chaleur Bay** inlet N.B./Que. Can.
Chaleurs, Baie de inlet N.B./Que. Can. see **Chaleur Bay**
234 E4 **Chalfont** PA U.S.A.
151 K4 **Chalfont St Peter** Buckinghamshire, England U.K.
150 H4 **Chalford** Gloucestershire, England U.K.
151 J4 **Chalgrove** Oxfordshire, England U.K.
259 C8 **Chalía** r. Arg.
175 H3 **Chalin** Pol.
157 J8 **Chalindrey** France
109 I5 **Chaling** Hunan China
211 C6 **Chalinze** Tanz.
114 E7 **Chalisgaon** Mahar. India
114 E7 **Chalisseri** Kerala India
160 B3 **Chalivoy-Milon** France
Chalk, Ozero salt l. Kazakh. see **Shalkar, Ozero**
199 I6 **Chalki** Notio Aigaio Greece
198 D3 **Chalki** Thessalia Greece
198 E4 **Chalkida** Greece
198 D2 **Chalkidona** Greece
121 R6 **Chalkudysu** Kazakh.
234 C6 **Challacó** Arg.
114 E5 **Challakere** Karnataka India
158 I8 **Challans** France
252 C4 **Challapata** Bol.
266 E5 **Challenger Deep** sea feature N. Pacific Ocean
267 L8 **Challenger Fracture Zone** sea feature S. Pacific Ocean
160 H5 **Challes-les-Eaux** France
161 H6 **Challis** ID U.S.A.
237 K11 **Chalmette** LA U.S.A.
134 G2 **Chal'mny-Varre** Rus. Fed.
160 D3 **Chalmoux** France
160 E3 **Chaloire** r. France
162 C1 **Chalonnes-sur-Loire** France
156 H6 **Châlons-en-Champagne** France
Chālons-sur-Marne France see **Châlons-en-Champagne**
160 F3 **Chalon-sur-Saône** France
163 C8 **Chalosse** reg. France
161 C8 **Chaloveni** Georgia
116 E1 **Chalt** Jammu and Kashmir
129 J5 **Chaltan Pass** Azer.
261 H2 **Chañar** Entre Ríos Arg.
260 C2 **Chañar** La Rioja Arg.
260 C6 **Chañar** San Juan Arg.
226 F5 **Channing** S. Africa
258 D8 **Channing** TX U.S.A.
182 E3 **Chanoia** Spain
260 B2 **Chañaral, Isla i.** Chile
260 B2 **Chañaral Alto** Chile
122 H3 **Chanarān** Iran
258 C2 **Chañarcillo** Chile
261 F3 **Chañar Ladeado** Arg.
260 B1 **Chañaras, Cerro** mt. Venez.
59 F4 **Chañi** Arg.
122 D3 **Chanaumaa** Port.
162 B2 **Chança** r. Port./Spain see **Chanza**
260 E2 **Chanza** Port.
244 A2 **Chiamaico** Arg.
212 E4 **Chamais Bay** Namibia
161 G7 **Chamalières** France
161 G7 **Chamaloc** France
122 G3 **Chaman** Bid Iran
243 O8 **Chanchén** Mex.
260 A4 **Chanco** Chile
250 A4 **Chanco, Bahia de** b. Chile
252 A2 **Chancos** Peru
242 □R13 **Chanda** Mahar. India see **Chandrapur**
97 E8 **Chandalar** r. AK U.S.A.
211 C6 **Chandama** Tanz.
116 D2 **Chandan Chauki** Uttar Prad. India
117 I9 **Chandarpur** Chhattisgarh India
115 H5 **Chandausi** Uttar Prad. India
117 K9 **Chandbali** Orissa India
116 F4 **Chandeleur Islands** LA U.S.A.
237 K11 **Chandeleur Sound** LA U.S.A.
116 F4 **Chandeleur Islands** LA U.S.A.
241 W6 **Chandler** AZ U.S.A.
84 C2 **Chandler** Que. Can.
232 H9 **Chandler** OK U.S.A.
231 □3 **Chandler** Nei Mongol China
226 O4 **Chandler** Que. Can.
241 U8 **Chandler** AZ U.S.A.
237 G8 **Chandler** OK U.S.A.
121 O1 **Chandler** CA U.S.A.
109 K7 **Chandler** Guangdong China
254 C5 **Chapada Diamantina, Parque Nacional** nat. park Brazil
255 B6 **Chapada do Céu** Brazil
253 G3 **Chapada dos Guimarães** Brazil
254 D5 **Chapada dos Veadeiros, Parque Nacional da** nat. park Brazil
226 I4 **Chapais** Que. Can.
244 D5 **Chapala** Mex.
244 D4 **Chapala, Laguna de** l. Mex.
250 C2 **Chapaleca, Valle de** val. Col.
259 C6 **Chapaleofú** Arg.
252 D3 **Chapana** Bol.
252 C3 **Chapare** r. Bol.
250 C3 **Chaparral** Col.
122 E7 **Chāpāri, Kowtal-e** pass Afgh.
250 C2 **Chaparral** Col.
160 G4 **Chapareillan** France
252 B3 **Chaparra** Peru

149 J2 **Champany** Falkirk, Scotland U.K.
260 E2 **Champaqui, Cerro** mt. Arg.
252 D4 **Champara** mt. Peru
96 C5 **Champasak** Laos
156 G6 **Champaubert** France
116 H5 **Champawat** Uttaranchal India
162 F5 **Champcevinel** France
162 D3 **Champdeniers-St-Denis** France
160 E1 **Champ-d'Oiseau** France
162 B2 **Champdôr, Lac** l. Que. Can.
157 N7 **Champ du Feu** mt. France
159 M7 **Champeigne** reg. France
190 B3 **Champéix** France
160 D1 **Champéry** Switz.
160 F3 **Champforgeuil** France
159 K5 **Champgenéteux** France
117 N8 **Champhai** Mizoram India
161 G6 **Champier** France
156 F8 **Champigné** France
157 L6 **Champignelles** France
156 I7 **Champignol-lez-Mondeville** France
156 G2 **Champigny** France
222 H5 **Champion** Alta Can.
233 L4 **Champion** NY U.S.A.
232 I10 **Champlain** VA U.S.A.
224 E7 **Champlain, Canal** NY U.S.A.
160 C2 **Champlemy** France
107 Q7 **Champlitte** France
160 E4 **Champoléon** France
160 D5 **Champoly** France
243 N8 **Champotón** Mex.
156 B7 **Champrond-en-Gâtine** France
107 N9 **Champsecret** France
161 B6 **Champs-Sur-Tarentaine-Marchal** France
107 M9 **Champs-sur-Yonne** France
160 L3 **Champtoceaux** France
114 C7 **Chamrajnagar** Karnataka India
161 H6 **Chamrousse** France
156 H5 **Chamusca** Port.
111 J9 **Chamyn Co** l. Qinghai China
184 C2 **Chamusca** Port.
135 I5 **Chamzinka** Rus. Fed.
97 E11 **Chana** Thai.
161 C8 **Chanac** France
116 E1 **Chanak** Turkey see **Çanakkale**
225 J4 **Chanal** Mex.
246 E2 **Channel-Port-aux-Basques** Nfld and Lab. Can.
108 A7 **Channel Tunnel** France/U.K.
151 J4 **Channing** TX U.S.A.
182 E3 **Chanos** Spain
131 S3 **Chantada** Spain
158 H5 **Chantepie** France
162 B2 **Chanthaburi** Thai.
156 D5 **Chantilly** France
162 B2 **Chantonnay** France
157 L7 **Chantraine** France
162 B2 **Chantrans** France
159 J4 **Chanu** France
115 M8 **Chanumla** Andaman & Nicobar Is India
237 H7 **Chanute** KS U.S.A.
130 I4 **Chanuwala** Rus. Fed.
120 C4 **Chany, Ozero** salt l. Rus. Fed.
184 C5 **Chanza** r. Port./Spain
252 A2 **Chao** Peru
184 □ **Chão** Ilhéu i. Madeira
105 G3 **Chao'an** Guangdong China
107 O7 **Chaobai Xinhe** r. China
109 K3 **Chaohu** Anhui China
105 N3 **Chao Hu** l. China
109 L3 **Chao Phraya** r. Thai.
97 E8 **Chaor** Nei Mongol China
160 A2 **Chaouen** Morocco
156 H7 **Chaource** France
109 K7 **Chaoyang** Guangdong China
247 □3 **Chaoyang** Heilong. China see **Jiayin**
109 L3 **Chaoyang** Jilin China see **Huinan**
107 Q6 **Chaoyang** Liaoning China
101 K4 **Chaoyangcun** Nei Mongol China
111 H9 **Chaozhou** Hu r. Xizang China
109 K7 **Chaozhou** Guangdong China
254 C5 **Chapada Diamantina, Parque Nacional** nat. park Brazil
258 D7 **Charata** Arg.
242 E4 **Charay** Mex.

252 C4 **Charana** Bol.
250 C5 **Charapita** Col.
258 E2 **Charata** Arg.
242 E4 **Charay** Mex.
204 D2 **Charbonneau** France
161 K6 **Charbonnel, Pointe de** mt. France
244 F2 **Charcas** Mex.
160 H2 **Charcenne** France
160 H4 **Charco** Mex.
244 G3 **Charco Blanco** Arg.
262 S2 **Charcot Island** Antarctica
223 I4 **Chard** Alta Can.
150 G6 **Chard** Somerset, England U.K.
223 I4 **Chardara** Kazakh.
121 L7 **Chardara, Step'** plain Kazakh.
121 M7 **Chardarinskoye Vodokhranilishche** resr Kazakh./Uzbek.
122 B5 **Chardâval** Iran
122 F3 **Chardeh** Iran
232 D7 **Chardon** OH U.S.A.
150 G6 **Chardstock** Devon, England U.K.
Chardzhev Lebapskaya Oblast' Turkm. see **Türkmenabat**
Chardzhou Turkm. see **Türkmenabat**
Chardzhouskaya Oblast' admin. div. Turkm. see **Lebap**
205 F2 **Charef, Oued** watercourse Morocco
162 E4 **Charente** dept France
162 C4 **Charente** r. France
162 C4 **Charente-Maritime** dept France
160 B3 **Charenton-du-Cher** France
159 M3 **Charentonne** r. France
129 F5 **Ch'arents'avan** Armenia
150 H4 **Charfield** South Gloucestershire, England U.K.
122 E7 **Chari** Iran
160 H2 **Chargey-lès-Gray** France
208 B1 **Chari** r. Cameroon/Chad
122 G6 **Chari** Iran
202 C3 **Chari-Baguirmi** pref. Chad
123 M4 **Chārīkār** Afgh.
117 K6 **Charikot** Nepal
151 N5 **Charing** Kent, England U.K.
236 I5 **Chariton** r. IA U.S.A.
236 I6 **Chariton** r. IA U.S.A.
237 K5 **Charity** Guyana
137 M6 **Charlvne** Ukr.
Chärjew Turkm. see **Türkmenabat**
127 O8 **Charkas** Iran
123 L3 **Charkhab** Afgh.
116 G3 **Chār Kent** India
116 F5 **Charkhari** Uttar Prad. India
151 J4 **Charkhari** Haryana India
Charkhlik Xinjiang China see **Ruoqiang**
Charlbury Oxfordshire, England U.K. see
215 N2 **Charl Cilliers** S. Africa
147 I4 **Charlemont** Northern Ireland U.K.
165 F8 **Charleroi** Belgium
233 J11 **Charles, Cape** VA U.S.A.
225 G4 **Charlesbourg** Que. Can.
226 B6 **Charles City** IA U.S.A.
232 H11 **Charles City** VA U.S.A.
254 □ **Charles Island** Islas Galápagos Ecuador see **Santa María, Isla**
238 K3 **Charles Lake** Alta Can.
238 K3 **Charles M. Russell National Wildlife Refuge** nat. res. MT U.S.A.
84 C2 **Charles Point** N.T. Austr.
81 F10 **Charleston** South I. N.Z.
237 H8 **Charleston** AR U.S.A.
231 □3 **Charleston** IA U.S.A.
237 K7 **Charleston** MO U.S.A.
231 I8 **Charleston** SC U.S.A.
232 D10 **Charleston** WV U.S.A.
241 Q10 **Charleston Peak** NV U.S.A.
147 E5 **Charlestown** Ireland
215 N3 **Charlestown** S. Africa
247 □2 **Charlestown** St Kitts and Nevis
247 □3 **Charlestown St Vincent**
235 M3 **Charlestown** MD U.S.A.
233 M5 **Charlestown** NH U.S.A.
235 I2 **Charlestown** NY U.S.A.
232 H9 **Charlestown of Aberlour** Moray, Scotland U.K. see **Aberlour**
Charleville Qld Austr.
Charleville Ireland see **Rathluire**
114 E7 **Charleville-Mézières** France
226 I4 **Charlevoix** MI U.S.A.
227 H6 **Charlie Lake** B.C. Can.
160 G4 **Charlieu** France
226 J7 **Charlotte** MI U.S.A.
226 I8 **Charlotte** NC U.S.A.
247 K4 **Charlotte Amalie** Virgin Is (U.S.A.)
95 G1 **Charlotte Bank** sea feature S. China Sea
232 I10 **Charlotte Court House** VA U.S.A.
231 F12 **Charlotte Harbor** b. FL U.S.A.
222 E4 **Charlotte Lake** B.C. Can.
142 I2 **Charlottenberg** Sweden
232 G10 **Charlottesville** VA U.S.A.
83 J7 **Charlton** Vic. Austr.
150 H4 **Charlton** Hampshire, England U.K.
224 E2 **Charlton Island** Nunavut Can.
150 H4 **Charlton Kings** Gloucestershire, England U.K.
151 L5 **Charlwood** Surrey, England U.K.
138 L6 **Charmé** France
161 F7 **Charmes** France
157 L7 **Charmes** France
161 G6 **Charmes-sur-Rhône** France
150 H6 **Charmey** Switz.
Charminster Dorset, England U.K.
157 L7 **Charmois-l'Orgueilleux** France
156 H7 **Charmont-sous-Barbuise** France
150 G6 **Charmouth** Dorset, England U.K.
156 H5 **Charmoy** France
156 I7 **Charnay-lès-Mâcon** France
184 A3 **Charneca** Port.
184 A2 **Charneca** Port.
175 H5 **Charnia** r. W.A. Austr.
156 I5 **Charny** France
138 I7 **Charny-Orgerus** France
175 K6 **Charny-sur-Meuse** France
157 J5 **Charolais** reg. France
138 L6 **Charolles** France
134 P4 **Charoláis, Monts du** mts France
190 C4 **Charquemont** France
137 P3 **Charret** Switz.
190 J2 **Charroux** France
137 M7 **Charsk** Kazakh. see **Shar**
175 H5 **Charstnitsa** Pol.
233 B10 **Charters** KY U.S.A.
83 L4 **Charters Towers** Qld Austr.
156 D6 **Chartham** Kent, England U.K.
161 H5 **Chartres** France
190 C4 **Chartreuse, Massif de la** mts France
190 C4 **Charvensod** Italy
160 I4 **Charvonnex** France

Chilluévar to Cirocha
299

185 M4 Chilluévar Spain
234 B7 Chillum MD U.S.A.
117 L7 Chilmari Bangl.
116 D6 Chilo Rajasthan India
259 B6 Chiloé, Isla de i. Chile
Chiloé, Isla Grande de i. Chile see Chiloé, Isla de
183 N7 Chiloeches Spain
209 D8 Chilombo Angola
211 A8 Chilonga Zambia
238 D5 Chiloquin OR U.S.A.
245 H8 Chilpancingo Mex.
116 H8 Chilpi Chhattisgarh India
232 B6 Chilson MI U.S.A.
245 K8 Chiltepec Mex.
83 K7 Chiltern Vic. Austr.
151 K4 Chiltern Hills England U.K.
226 F5 Chilton WI U.S.A.
209 D7 Chiluage Angola
209 F7 Chilubi Zambia
211 B7 Chilumba Malawi
109 M6 Chilung Taiwan
211 B8 Chilwa, Lake Malawi
211 B7 Chimala Tanz.
245 M9 Chimalapa Mex.
243 N10 Chimaltenango Guat.
244 D4 Chimaltitán Mex.
242 □T13 Chimán Panama
213 G3 Chimanimani Zimbabwe
109 □J7 Chi Ma Wan H.K. China
165 F8 Chimay Belgium
165 F8 Chimay, Bois de for. Belgium
211 A7 Chimba Zambia
260 B4 Chimbarongo Chile
260 C2 Chimbas Arg.
Chimbay Uzbek. see Chimboy
250 B5 Chimborazo mt. Ecuador
252 A2 Chimbote Peru
120 H6 Chimboy Uzbek.
185 L6 Chimeneas Spain
123 P6 Chimian Pak.
250 C2 Chimichaguá Col.
Chimishliya Moldova see Cimişlia
Chimkent Kazakh. see Shymkent
Chimkentskaya Oblast' admin. div. Kazakh. see Yuzhnyy Kazakhstan
217 □2a Chimney Rocks is Inner Islands Seychelles
213 G3 Chimoio Moz.
185 J4 Chimorra hill Spain
185 J4 Chimorra, Sierra mts Spain
260 D6 Chimpay Arg.
123 M2 Chimtargha, Qullai mt. Tajik.
Chimtorga, Gora mt. Tajik. see Chimtargha, Qullai
121 N7 Chimyon Uzbek.
96 A4 Chin state Myanmar
98 E4 China country Asia
243 J5 China Mex.
China, Republic of country Asia see Taiwan
China Bakir r. Myanmar see To
242 G5 Chinacates Mex.
243 N9 Chinajá Guat.
240 O6 China Lake CA U.S.A.
233 □P4 China Lake ME U.S.A.
245 M7 Chinameca Mex.
245 J4 Chinampa de Gorostiza Mex.
190 C6 Chinanale Italy
242 □P11 Chinandega Nic.
245 M8 Chinantla Mex.
240 N9 China Point CA U.S.A.
239 L12 Chinati Peak TX U.S.A.
Chinaz Uzbek. see Chinoz
250 B4 Chinca Ecuador
252 A3 Chincha Alta Peru
222 G3 Chinchaga r. Alta Can.
85 M9 Chinchilla Qld Austr.
185 P3 Chinchilla de Monte Aragón Spain
114 E4 Chincholi Karnataka India
183 N8 Chinchón Spain
243 P8 Chinchorro, Banco sea feature Mex.
260 B3 Chincolco Chile
233 J11 Chincoteague VA U.S.A.
233 J11 Chincoteague Bay MD/VA U.S.A.
213 H3 Chinde Moz.
217 □3a Chindini Njazidja Comoros
101 E11 Chindo S. Korea
101 E11 Chin-do i. S. Korea
160 H5 Chindrieux France
108 A2 Chindu Qinghai China
96 B4 Chindwin r. Myanmar
102 □1 Chinen Okinawa Japan
116 E3 Chineni Jammu and Kashmir
Chinese Turkestan aut. reg. China see Xinjiang Uygur Zizhiqu
213 H2 Chinga Moz.
250 C3 Chingaza, Parque Nacional nat. park Col.
151 L4 Chingford Greater London, England U.K.
Chinghai prov. China see Qinghai
101 D9 Chinghwa N. Korea
120 F2 Chingirlau Kazakh.
121 R3 Chingiz-Tau, Khrebet mts Kazakh.
Chingleput Tamil Nadu India see Chengalpattu
209 E8 Chingola Zambia
209 C8 Chinguanja Angola
209 C8 Chinguar Angola
204 B5 Chinguețți Maur.
208 C2 Chinguil Chad
101 F11 Chinhae S. Korea
213 G2 Chinhanda Moz.
213 F3 Chinhoyi Zimbabwe
Chini Hima. Prad. India see Kalpa
252 C3 Chiñijo Bol.
Chining Shandong China see Jining
123 O6 Chiniot Pak.
242 E4 Chinipas Mex.
97 G8 Chinit, Stœng r. Cambodia
101 F11 Chinju S. Korea
208 D3 Chinko r. C.A.R.
241 W5 Chinle AZ U.S.A.
241 W5 Chinle Valley AZ U.S.A.
241 W5 Chinle Wash watercourse AZ U.S.A.
109 L6 Chinmen Taiwan
109 L6 Chinmen Tao i. Taiwan
114 G5 Chinna Ganjam Andhra Prad. India
114 E8 Chinnamanur Tamil Nadu India
Chinnamp'o N. Korea see Namp'o
114 F7 Chinna Salem Tamil Nadu India
151 K4 Chinnor Oxfordshire, England U.K.
114 F3 Chinnur Andhra Prad. India
105 H4 Chino Japan
240 O7 Chino CA U.S.A.
241 T7 Chino Creek watercourse AZ U.S.A.
87 E12 Chinocup, Lake salt flat W.A. Austr.
87 E12 Chinocup Nature Reserve W.A. Austr.
162 E1 Chinon France
238 J2 Chinook MT U.S.A.
266 H3 Chinook Trough sea feature N. Pacific Ocean
241 T7 Chino Valley AZ U.S.A.
121 M7 Chinoz Uzbek.
211 B7 Chinsali Zambia
114 G3 Chintalnar Chhattisgarh India
114 F6 Chintamani Karnataka India
197 L4 Chinteni Romania
211 B7 Chintheche Malawi
245 I3 Chintón de las Flores Mex.
250 C2 Chinú Col.
165 H9 Chiny Belgium
165 H9 Chiny, Forêt de for. Belgium
209 D8 Chinyama Litapi Zambia
134 K3 Chin'yavoryk Rus. Fed.
213 G3 Chioco Moz.
191 M5 Chioggia Italy
190 B5 Chiomonte Italy
211 B6 Chiona Tanz.
199 H4 Chios Chios Greece
199 G4 Chios i. Greece
199 H4 Chios Strait Greece
243 N10 Chipam Guat.
213 G3 Chipanga Moz.
211 B8 Chipata Zambia
111 C9 Chip Chap r. China/India
259 C6 Chipchihua, Sierra de mts Arg.
213 G2 Chipera Moz.
209 C8 Chipeta Angola
97 H9 Chiphu Cambodia
209 F7 Chipili Zambia
209 B8 Chipindo Angola
107 O8 Chiping Shandong China
Chipinga Zimbabwe see Chipinge
213 G4 Chipinge Zimbabwe
184 G7 Chipiona Spain
231 E10 Chipley FL U.S.A.
114 C4 Chiplun Mahar. India
225 H4 Chipman N.B. Can.
211 C6 Chipogolo Tanz.
209 C8 Chipoia Angola
150 H5 Chippenham Wiltshire, England U.K.
213 G3 Chipperone, Monte mt. Moz.
236 H3 Chippewa r. MN U.S.A.
226 B5 Chippewa r. WI U.S.A.
226 C4 Chippewa, Lake WI U.S.A.
226 C5 Chippewa Falls WI U.S.A.
151 I3 Chipping Campden Gloucestershire, England U.K.
151 I4 Chipping Norton Oxfordshire, England U.K.
151 M4 Chipping Ongar Essex, England U.K.
150 H4 Chipping Sodbury South Gloucestershire, England U.K.
190 D3 Chippis Switz.
186 E5 Chiprana Spain
197 K7 Chiprovtsi Bulg.
209 F8 Chipundu Central Zambia
209 F8 Chipundu Luapula Zambia
Chipuriro Zimbabwe see Guruve
115 H3 Chipurupalle Andhra Prad. India
115 H4 Chipurupalle Andhra Prad. India
233 □R3 Chiputneticook Lakes Can./U.S.A.
252 A2 Chiquian Peru
243 O9 Chiquibul National Park Belize
243 P7 Chiquilá Mex.
244 D5 Chiquilistlán Mex.
243 O10 Chiquimula Guat.
250 C3 Chiquinquira Col.
252 B3 Chiquintirca Peru
261 G4 Chiquita, Mar l. Arg.
245 H1 Chiquita, Sierra mts Mex.
244 F7 Chiquito r. Mex.
253 E4 Chiquitos, Llanos de plain Bol.
135 H6 Chir r. Rus. Fed.
161 C7 Chirac France
114 G5 Chirada Andhra Prad. India
211 B8 Chiradzulu Malawi
129 I4 Chirag Rus. Fed.
129 J4 Chirakhchay r. Rus. Fed.
114 D7 Chirakkal Kerala India
114 G5 Chirala Andhra Prad. India
213 G3 Chiramba Moz.
250 B3 Chirambirá, Punta pt Col.
123 K4 Chiras Afgh.
111 B12 Chirawa Rajasthan India
150 F2 Chirbury Shropshire, England U.K.
121 M7 Chirchiq Uzbek.
121 M7 Chirchiq r. Uzbek.
213 F4 Chiredzi Zimbabwe
210 C1 Chire Wildlife Reserve nature res. Eth.
202 B4 Chirfa Niger
250 E2 Chirgua r. Venez.
241 W9 Chiricahua National Monument nat. park AZ U.S.A.
241 W10 Chiricahua Peak AZ U.S.A.
250 C2 Chiriguaná Col.
220 C4 Chirikof Island AK U.S.A.
247 J8 Chirimena Venez.
250 B6 Chirinos Peru
242 □R13 Chiriquí, Golfo de b. Panama
242 □R13 Chiriquí, Laguna de b. Panama
246 C9 Chiriquí, Punta pt Panama
242 □R13 Chiriquí Grande Panama
101 E11 Chiri-san mt. S. Korea
101 E11 Chiri-san National Park S. Korea
185 O5 Chirivel Spain
129 G2 Chiri-Yurt Rus. Fed.
150 F2 Chirk Wrexham, Wales U.K.
146 L11 Chirnside Scottish Borders, Scotland U.K.
217 □3b Chirongui Mayotte
123 L2 Chiroqchi Uzbek.
160 F4 Chiroubles France
78 □6 Chirovanga Choiseul Solomon Is
197 N8 Chirpan Bulg.
242 □R13 Chirripó, Parque Nacional nat. park Costa Rica
213 F3 Chirumanzu Zimbabwe
213 F3 Chirundu Zimbabwe
244 F5 Chiruntzio Mex.
122 E8 Chīrūyeh Iran
104 F5 Chiryū Japan
209 F8 Chisamba Zambia
209 E8 Chisasa Zambia
224 E2 Chisasibi Que. Can.
261 I4 Chis Chis, Laguna l. Arg.
243 N10 Chisec Guat.
209 E9 Chisekesi Zambia
151 I4 Chiseldon Swindon, England U.K.
197 O6 Chiselet Romania
211 B7 Chisenga Malawi
Chishima-retto is Rus. Fed. see Kuril'skiye Ostrova
135 K5 Chishmy Rus. Fed.
222 H4 Chisholm Alta Can.
233 □O4 Chisholm ME U.S.A.
226 B2 Chisholm MN U.S.A.
123 O7 Chishtian Mandi Pak.
108 E4 Chishui Guizhou China
108 E5 Chishuihe Sichuan China
108 E4 Chishui He r. China
Chisimaio Somalia see Kismaayo
136 H6 Chişinău Moldova
177 L5 Chişindia Romania
197 J4 Chişineu-Criş Romania
177 L4 Chişlaz Romania
190 D6 Chisola r. Italy
190 C6 Chisone r. Italy
217 □3b Chissioua Mbouzi i. Mayotte
217 □3b Chissioua Mtsamboro i. Mayotte
134 J5 Chistopol' Rus. Fed.
121 L1 Chistopol'ye Kazakh.
Chistyakovo Ukr. see Torez
121 N1 Chistyakovskoye Kazakh.
175 K1 Chistye-Prudy Rus. Fed.
252 D5 Chita Bol.
250 C3 Chita Col.
104 E6 Chita Japan
99 J1 Chita Rus. Fed.
211 B7 Chita Tanz.
122 D6 Chitab Iran
209 B9 Chitado Angola
104 E6 Chita-hantō pen. Japan
Chitaldrug Karnataka India see Chitradurga
116 C7 Chitalwana Rajasthan India
211 A8 Chitambo Zambia
107 L1 Chitanga Rus. Fed.
Chita Oblast admin. div. Rus. Fed. see Chitinskaya Oblast'
209 D6 Chitato Angola
104 E6 Chita-wan b. Japan
134 J3 Chitayevo Rus. Fed.
223 J4 Chitek Lake Sask. Can.
223 L4 Chitek Lake l. Man. Can.
209 C8 Chitembo Angola
191 L8 Chitignano Italy
100 A3 Chitinskaya Oblast' admin. div. Rus. Fed.
211 B7 Chitipa Malawi
Chitkul Hima. Prad. India see Chhitkul
213 G4 Chitobe Moz.
209 D8 Chitokoloki Zambia
209 E9 Chitongo Zambia
Chitor Rajasthan India see Chittaurgarh
102 S4 Chitose Japan
114 E5 Chitradurga Karnataka India
116 H7 Chitrakoot Uttar Prad. India
123 N4 Chitral Pak.
123 N4 Chitral r. Pak.
114 F5 Chitravati r. India
242 □S14 Chitré Panama
116 C8 Chitrod Gujarat India
117 M8 Chittagong Bangl.
117 M8 Chittagong admin. div. Bangl.
117 K8 Chittaranjan W. Bengal India
116 E7 Chittaurgarh Rajasthan India
114 F6 Chittoor Andhra Prad. India
Chittorgarh Rajasthan India see Chittaurgarh
114 E7 Chittur Kerala India
211 B8 Chitungulu Zambia
213 F3 Chitungwiza Zimbabwe
211 C7 Chiulezi r. Moz.
Chiu Lung H.K. China see Kowloon
209 D8 Chiume Angola
213 H2 Chiúre Novo Moz.
190 H3 Chiuro Italy
191 L2 Chiusa Italy
190 D7 Chiusa di Pesio Italy
191 O3 Chiusaforte Italy
194 E8 Chiusa Sclafani Sicilia Italy
190 D8 Chiusavecchia Italy
192 G1 Chiusdino Italy
190 D5 Chiusella r. Italy
192 H1 Chiusi Italy
192 H1 Chiusi, Lago di l. Italy
191 L8 Chiusi della Verna Italy
213 G2 Chiúta Moz.
187 D9 Chiva Spain
190 D5 Chivasso Italy
242 D4 Chívato, Punta pt Mex.
252 C3 Chivay Peru
252 C3 Chive Bol.
209 C8 Chiveio Angola
245 M9 Chivela Mex.
213 F3 Chivhu Zimbabwe
213 F4 Chivi Zimbabwe
261 G4 Chivilcoy Arg.
109 I8 Chixi Guangdong China
Chiyirchik, Pereval pass Kyrg. see Chyyyrchyk Ashuusu
105 J3 Chiyoda Gunma Japan
105 L3 Chiyoda Ibaraki Japan
105 K3 Chiyogawa Japan
213 E3 Chizarira Hills Zimbabwe
213 E3 Chizarira National Park Zimbabwe
162 D3 Chizé France
134 I2 Chizha Rus. Fed.
120 C2 Chizha Vtoraya Kazakh.
109 K3 Chizhou Anhui China
103 L11 Chizu Japan
Chkalov Rus. Fed. see Orenburg
137 N6 Chkalove Ukr.
121 N1 Chkalovo Kazakh.
Chkalovo Rus. Fed. see Kurchaloy
134 H4 Chkalovsk Rus. Fed.
Chkalovskaya Oblast' admin. div. Rus. Fed. see Orenburgskaya Oblast'
137 P4 Chkalovs'ke Ukr.
100 H6 Chkalovskoye Rus. Fed.
129 D3 Ch'khari Georgia
177 G2 Chlebičov Czech Rep.
177 I2 Chlebnice Slovakia
174 C3 Chlebowo Pol.
205 F1 Chlef Alg.
175 I4 Chlewiska Pol.
177 K3 Chlmec r. Slovakia
175 K6 Chłopice Pol.
241 R6 Chloride AZ U.S.A.
174 E3 Chludowo Pol.
173 O2 Chlumčany Czech Rep.
176 C1 Chlumec Czech Rep.
176 E1 Chlumec nad Cidlinou Czech Rep.
176 D3 Chlum u Třeboně Czech Rep.
100 L2 Chlya, Ozero l. Rus. Fed.
177 H2 Chmeľová hill Slovakia
175 I5 Chmielnik Pol.
174 E2 Chmielno Pol.
175 K4 Chmiel Pierwszy Pol.
94 □ Choa Chu Kang Sing.
94 □ Choa Chu Kang hill Sing.
97 G7 Chŏâm Khsant Cambodia
260 B2 Choapa Chile
260 B2 Choapa r. Chile
212 E3 Chobe admin. dist. Botswana
212 E3 Chobe National Park Botswana
174 E4 Chobienia Pol.
174 D3 Chobienice Pol.
96 G4 Chô Bo Vietnam
245 J6 Chocamán Mex.
247 □3 Choc Bay St Lucia
176 F1 Choceň Czech Rep.
175 H3 Choceń Pol.
101 E10 Choch'iwŏn S. Korea
177 G3 Chocholná-Velčice Slovakia
96 G4 Chơ Chu Vietnam
174 D4 Chocianów Pol.
174 D2 Chociwel Pol.
250 B3 Chocó dept Col.
241 Q8 Chocolate Mountains AZ/CA U.S.A.
250 C3 Chocontá Col.
231 D10 Choctawhatchee r. FL U.S.A.
174 F4 Chocz Pol.
174 F1 Choczewo Pol.
114 G4 Chodavaram Andhra Prad. India
175 H3 Chodecz Pol.
175 K4 Chodel Pol.
175 J4 Chodelka r. Pol.
101 D9 Cho-do i. N. Korea
176 B1 Chodov Czech Rep.
176 B2 Chodová Planá Czech Rep.
175 K3 Chodów Mazowieckie Pol.
175 H3 Chodów Wielkopolskie Pol.
110 I1 Chodro Rus. Fed.
174 E3 Chodzież Pol.
260 E6 Choele Choel Arg.
260 E6 Choele Choel Grande, Isla i. Arg.
213 F2 Chofombo Moz.
105 K4 Chōfu Japan
122 D7 Choghādak Iran
122 E7 Choghān Iran
116 E2 Chogo Lungma Glacier Jammu and Kashmir
Chogori Feng mt. China/Jammu and Kashmir see K2
135 I7 Chograyskoye Vodokhranilishche resr Rus. Fed.
223 J4 Choiceland Sask. Can.
261 F6 Choique Arg.
78 □6 Choiseul i. Solomon Is
247 □3 Choiseul St Lucia
259 F8 Choiseul Sound sea chan. Falkland Is
160 I5 Choisy France
242 E4 Choix Mex.
174 C3 Chojna Pol.
174 F2 Chojnice Pol.
174 D4 Chojnów Pol.
136 A1 Chojnowski Park Krajobrazowy Pol.
102 R7 Chōkai-san vol. Japan
210 C2 Ch'ok'ē mts Eth.
129 D3 Ch'okhatauri Georgia
121 P6 Chokpar Kazakh.
121 Q6 Chok-Tal Kyrg.
Chokue Moz. see Chókwé
131 P2 Chokurdakh Rus. Fed.
213 G5 Chókwé Moz.
108 B3 Cho La pass Sichuan China
240 L6 Cholame CA U.S.A.
240 L6 Cholame Creek r. CA U.S.A.
108 B2 Chola Shan mts Sichuan China
260 A6 Cholchol Chile
162 C1 Cholet France
260 A5 Cholguán Chile
242 □P10 Choloma Hond.
121 P6 Cholpon Kyrg.
121 Q6 Cholpon-Ata Kyrg.
151 J4 Cholsey Oxfordshire, England U.K.
245 I6 Cholula Mex.
242 □P11 Choluteca Hond.
209 E9 Choma Zambia
101 F10 Chŏmch'ŏn S. Korea
161 D6 Chomelix France
161 F7 Chomérac France
111 I12 Chomo Ganggar mt. Xizang China
96 G4 Chơ Moi Vietnam
117 L6 Chomo Lhari mt. Bhutan
96 D5 Chom Thong Thai.
116 E6 Chomun Rajasthan India
176 C1 Chomutov Czech Rep.
176 C1 Chomutovka r. Czech Rep.
131 L3 Chona r. Rus. Fed.
105 L5 Chōnan Japan
101 E10 Ch'ŏnan S. Korea
97 E8 Chon Buri Thai.
259 B6 Chonchi Chile
250 A5 Chone Ecuador
Chong'an Fujian China see Wuyishan
101 D9 Ch'ŏngch'ŏn-gang r. N. Korea
101 F11 Ch'ongdo S. Korea
Chonggye Xizang China see Qonggyai
103 G11 Chŏngja S. Korea
101 F8 Ch'ŏngjin N. Korea
101 D9 Chŏngju N. Korea
101 E10 Ch'ŏngju S. Korea
97 F8 Chông Kal Cambodia
107 N6 Chongli Hebei China
Chonglong Sichuan China see Zizhong
109 M3 Chongming Shanghai China
109 M3 Chongming Dao i. China
209 B8 Chongoroi Angola
101 E9 Chŏngp'yŏng N. Korea
108 F4 Chongqing Chongqing China
Chongqing Sichuan China see Chongzhou
108 F3 Chongqing mun. China
109 J5 Chongren Jiangxi China
101 E11 Chŏngŭp S. Korea
209 F8 Chongwe Zambia
109 J4 Chongyang Hubei China
109 L5 Chongyang Xi r. China
109 J6 Chongyi Jiangxi China
108 D3 Chongzhou Sichuan China
108 F7 Chongzuo Guangxi China
137 N7 Chonhar, Pivostriv pen. Ukr.
101 E11 Chŏnju S. Korea
107 N4 Chonogol Mongolia
259 B7 Chonos, Archipiélago de los is Chile
245 N8 Chontalpa Mex.
97 H9 Chơn Thanh Vietnam
117 K5 Cho Oyu mt. China/Nepal
157 I3 Chooz France
136 B5 Chop Ukr.
117 I7 Chopan Uttar Prad. India
116 E9 Chopda Mahar. India
255 B8 Chopimzinho Brazil
136 H3 Chopovychi Ukr.
233 I10 Choptank r. MD U.S.A.
122 C6 Choqāy Zanbil tourist site Iran
252 D4 Choquecamata Bol.
123 M9 Chor Pak.
198 G6 Chora Greece
198 G6 Chora Greece
198 C5 Chora Greece
126 C5 Chora tourist site Greece
199 H5 Chorá tourist site Greece
198 F7 Chora Sfakion Kriti Greece
161 I7 Chorges France
185 K2 Chorito, Sierra del mts Spain
149 L6 Chorley Lancashire, England U.K.
151 K4 Chorleywood Hertfordshire, England U.K.
136 I6 Chorna Ukr.
137 M9 Chorna r. Ukr.
136 D5 Chorna Tysa Ukr.
136 E1 Chornaye, Vozyera l. Belarus
175 M5 Chorniyiv Ukr.
137 L4 Chornobay Ukr.
136 J2 Chornobyl' Ukr.
177 L3 Chornoholova Ukr.
137 J7 Chornomors'ke Odes'ka Oblast' Ukr.
135 F7 Chornomors'ke Respublika Krym Ukr.
137 K7 Chornomors'kyy Zapovidnyk nature res. Ukr.
136 I4 Chornorudka Ukr.
137 L3 Chornukhy Ukr.
137 J5 Chornyy Tashlyk r. Ukr.
129 C4 Chorokhi r. Georgia/Turkey
258 C3 Choros, Islas de los is Chile
175 K2 Choroszcz Pol.
85 I7 Chorregon Qld Austr.
254 F4 Chorrochó Brazil
136 E4 Chortkiv Ukr.
123 L3 Chorvoq Uzbek.
121 M7 Chorvoq suv ombori resr Kazakh./Uzbek.
116 C9 Chorwad Gujarat India
101 E9 Ch'ŏrwŏn S. Korea
175 I2 Chorzele Pol.
174 G5 Chorzów Pol.
101 D8 Ch'osan N. Korea
Chōsen-kaikyō sea chan. Japan/S. Korea see Nishi-suidō
105 M4 Chōshi Japan
259 B5 Choshuenco, Volcán vol. Chile
252 A2 Chosica Peru
260 B5 Chos Malal Arg.
260 D3 Chosmes Arg.
174 D2 Choszczno Pol.
250 B6 Chota Peru
117 I8 Chota Nagpur reg. Chhattisgarh India
177 K2 Chotča Slovakia
238 H3 Choteau MT U.S.A.
176 E2 Chotěboř Czech Rep.
173 O2 Chotěšov Czech Rep.
123 N7 Choti Pak.
116 C8 Chotila Gujarat India
177 H4 Chotín Slovakia
217 □3a Choua-chandroudé i. Comoros
204 D4 Chouikhia well Alg.
156 H5 Chouilly France
204 B5 Choûm Maur.
184 C2 Chouto Port.
159 N6 Chouzy-sur-Cisse France
240 L4 Chowchilla CA U.S.A.
114 D7 Chowghat Kerala India
82 H5 Chowilla Regional Reserve nature res. S.A. Austr.
222 G4 Chown, Mount Alta Can.
258 D3 Choya Arg.
121 V2 Choya Rus. Fed.
107 N3 Choybalsan Mongolia
160 H2 Choye France
107 K3 Choyr Mongolia
182 I3 Chozas de Abajo Spain
Chozas de la Sierra Spain see Soto del Real
211 B7 Chozi Zambia
176 E2 Chrast Czech Rep.
176 C2 Chrást Czech Rep.
176 D1 Chrastava Czech Rep.
204 B5 Chreïrîk well Maur.
171 J9 Chřibská Czech Rep.
176 G2 Chřiby hills Czech Rep.
236 L6 Chrisman IL U.S.A.
215 O2 Chrissiesmeer S. Africa
81 G10 Christchurch South I. N.Z.
151 I6 Christchurch Dorset, England U.K.
221 L2 Christian, Cape Nunavut Can.
246 □ Christiana Jamaica
215 J3 Christiana S. Africa
234 D5 Christiana PA U.S.A.
Christiania Norway see Oslo
227 N5 Christian Island Ont. Can.
232 E11 Christiansburg VA U.S.A.
142 F6 Christiansfeld Denmark
Christianshåb Greenland see Qasigiannguit
143 L6 Christiansø i. Denmark
222 C4 Christian Sound sea chan. AK U.S.A.
247 K5 Christiansted Virgin Is (U.S.A.)
226 D5 Christie WI U.S.A.
223 I2 Christie Bay N.W.T. Can.
223 I3 Christina r. Alta Can.
81 C11 Christina, Mount South I. N.Z.
149 L7 Christleton Cheshire, England U.K.
86 H5 Christmas Creek W.A. Austr.
86 H5 Christmas Creek r. W.A. Austr.
86 □1 Christmas Island terr. Indian Ocean
Christmas Island atoll Kiribati see Kiritimati
149 N2 Christon Bank Northumberland, England U.K.
87 I8 Christopher, Lake salt flat W.A. Austr.
176 E2 Chrudim Czech Rep.
175 H3 Chruślin Pol.
128 A3 Chrysochou Bay Cyprus
Chrysochous, Kolpos b. Cyprus see Chrysochou Bay
198 F2 Chrysoupoli Greece
148 I2 Chryston North Lanarkshire, Scotland U.K.
175 H5 Chrzanów Pol.
174 F4 Chrząstowa Wielka Pol.
174 G5 Chrząstowice Pol.
174 E3 Chrzypsko Wielkie Pol.
Chu Kazakh. see Shu
121 L5 Chu r. Kazakh.
117 L8 Chuadanga Bangl.
Chuanhui Henan China see Zhoukou
109 M3 Chuansha Shanghai China
108 B4 Chubalung Sichuan China
137 P6 Chubarivka Ukr.
Chubarovka Ukr. see Polohy
139 T6 Chubarovo Rus. Fed.
Chubartau Kazakh. see Barshatas
238 H5 Chubbuck ID U.S.A.
137 R7 Chuburka r. Rus. Fed.
104 G3 Chūbu-Sangaku Kokuritsu-kōen nat. park Japan
259 C6 Chubut prov. Arg.
259 D6 Chubut r. Arg.
106 F9 Chubxi Qinghai China
244 F6 Chucándiro Mex.
177 H2 Chuchelná Czech Rep.
135 H5 Chuchkovo Rus. Fed.
241 Q8 Chuckwalla Mountains CA U.S.A.
261 E3 Chucul Arg.
260 D2 Chucuma Arg.
242 □U13 Chucunaque r. Panama
150 E6 Chudleigh Devon, England U.K.
136 H3 Chudniv Ukr.
174 G5 Chudoba Pol.
139 O2 Chudovo Rus. Fed.
Chudskoye, Ozero l. Estonia/Rus. Fed. see Peipus, Lake
138 J9 Chudzin Belarus
220 D3 Chugach Mountains AK U.S.A.
103 J12 Chūgoku-sanchi mts Japan
Chugqênsumdo Qinghai China see Jigzhi
Chuguchak Xinjiang China see Tacheng
Chuguyev Ukr. see Chuhuyiv
100 H6 Chuguyevka Rus. Fed.
238 L6 Chugwater WY U.S.A.
Chuhai Guangdong China see Zhuhai
137 P4 Chuhuyiv Ukr.
121 P5 Chu-Iliyskiye Gory mts Kazakh.
Chuimatan Gansu China see Jishishan
Chujiang Hunan China see Shimen
108 B4 Chuka Xizang China
Chukai Malaysia see Cukai
100 J2 Chukchagirskoye, Ozero l. Rus. Fed.
Chukchi Peninsula Rus. Fed. see Chukotskiy Poluostrov
268 M1 Chukchi Plateau sea feature Arctic Ocean
220 A3 Chukchi Sea Rus. Fed./U.S.A.
134 H4 Chukhloma Rus. Fed.
131 T3 Chukotskiy, Mys c. Rus. Fed.
131 T3 Chukotskiy Poluostrov pen. Rus. Fed.
137 L7 Chulakivka Ukr.
Chulakkurgan Kazakh. see Sholakkorgan
Chulaktau Kazakh. see Karatau
96 E6 Chulaphon Reservoir Thai.
134 I2 Chulasa Rus. Fed.
240 O9 Chula Vista CA U.S.A.
187 D8 Chulilla Spain
139 T8 Chulkovo Rus. Fed.
185 I8 Chullera, Punta de la pt Spain
150 E6 Chulmleigh Devon, England U.K.
252 C6 Chulo Chile
250 A6 Chulucanas Peru
123 Q4 Chulung Pass Pak.
106 G2 Chuluut Gol r. Mongolia
130 J4 Chulym Rus. Fed.
110 H1 Chulyshman r. Rus. Fed.
134 M2 Chum Rus. Fed.
252 C3 Chuma Bol.
137 N6 Chumaky Ukr.
116 G3 Chumar Jammu and Kashmir
210 C3 Chumba Eth.
258 D3 Chumbicha Arg.
108 A2 Chumda Qinghai China
121 U3 Chumek Kazakh.
197 N8 Chumerna mt. Bulg.
100 I1 Chumikan Rus. Fed.
129 G4 Ch'umlaqi Georgia
96 F6 Chum Phae Thai.
97 D9 Chumphon Thai.
96 E7 Chum Saeng Thai.
260 E2 Chuña Arg.
131 K4 Chuna r. Rus. Fed.
261 E1 Chuña Huasi Arg.
109 L4 Chun'an Zhejiang China
140 V3 Chuna-Tundra plain Rus. Fed.
101 E10 Ch'unch'ŏn S. Korea
117 L8 Chunchura W. Bengal India
121 R6 Chundzha Kazakh.
209 E8 Chunga Zambia
Chung-hua Jen-min Kung-ho-kuo country Asia see China
Chung-hua Min-kuo country Asia see Taiwan
101 E10 Ch'ungju S. Korea
Chungking Chongqing China see Chongqing
Ch'ungmu S. Korea see T'ongyŏng
101 D9 Chŭngsan N. Korea
211 C7 Chungu Tanz.
109 M7 Chungyang Shanmo mts Taiwan
100 G7 Chunhua Jilin China
108 G1 Chunhua Shaanxi China
243 O8 Chunhuhux Mex.
Chunxi Jiangsu China see Gaochun
131 K3 Chunya r. Rus. Fed.
211 B7 Chunya Tanz.
97 G10 Chuôi, Hon i. Vietnam
Chuosijia Sichuan China see Guanyinqiao
134 F2 Chupa Rus. Fed.
137 N3 Chupakhivka Ukr.
247 □7 Chupara Point Trin. and Tob.
122 B3 Chūplū Iran
136 J4 Chupyra Ukr.
252 C5 Chuquicamata Chile
252 D5 Chuquisaca dept Bol.
Chuqung Qinghai China see Chindu
190 H2 Chur Switz.
117 N7 Churachandpur Manipur India
134 K4 Churaki Rus. Fed.
122 F7 Chūrān Iran
131 O3 Churapcha Rus. Fed.
134 K5 Churayevo Rus. Fed.
151 M3 Church End Essex, England U.K.
148 B4 Church Hill Ireland
234 D6 Church Hill MD U.S.A.
232 C12 Church Hill TN U.S.A.
223 M3 Churchill Man. Can.
223 M3 Churchill r. Man. Can.
225 I2 Churchill r. Nfld and Lab. Can.
223 M3 Churchill, Cape Man. Can.
225 I2 Churchill Falls Nfld and Lab. Can.
223 I4 Churchill Lake Sask. Can.
263 K1 Churchill Mountains Antarctica
222 E3 Churchill Peak B.C. Can.
224 E1 Churchill Sound sea chan. Nunavut Can.
149 M7 Church Lawton Cheshire, England U.K.
236 F1 Churchs Ferry ND U.S.A.
150 G2 Church Stretton Shropshire, England U.K.
234 B7 Churchton MD U.S.A.
147 E8 Churchtown Cork Ireland
147 F9 Churchtown Cork Ireland
234 D4 Churchtown PA U.S.A.
234 C5 Churchville MD U.S.A.
232 F10 Churchville VA U.S.A.
106 B1 Chureg-Tag, Gora mt. Rus. Fed.
117 J6 Churia Ghati Hills Nepal
139 N6 Churilovo Rus. Fed.
252 A2 Churin Peru
129 H3 Churkey Rus. Fed.
129 H3 Churkeyskoye Vodokhranilishche resr Rus. Fed.
222 F5 Churn Creek Provincial Park B.C. Can.
134 I4 Churov Rus. Fed.
137 L1 Churovichi Rus. Fed.
116 E5 Churu Rajasthan India
Churubay Nura Kazakh. see Abay
226 I8 Churubusco IN U.S.A.
250 D2 Churuguara Venez.
102 U4 Chūrui Japan
123 K1 Churuk Uzbek.
244 F7 Churumuco Mex.
190 H2 Churwalden Switz.
137 N7 Churyuk, Ostriv i. Ukr.
97 I8 Chu Sê Vietnam
116 G3 Chushul Jammu and Kashmir
241 W5 Chuska Mountains NM U.S.A.
134 L4 Chusovaya r. Rus. Fed.
134 L4 Chusovoy Rus. Fed.
134 L3 Chusovskoye Rus. Fed.
Chust Ukr. see Khust
121 N7 Chust Uzbek.
225 G3 Chute-des-Passes Que. Can.
227 R3 Chute-Rouge Que. Can.
117 N6 Chutia Assam India
137 O4 Chutove Ukr.
109 M6 Chutung Taiwan
78 □4a Chuuk is Micronesia
134 L3 Chuval Rus. Fed.
Chuvashia aut. rep. Rus. Fed. see Chuvashskaya Respublika
Chuvashskaya A.S.S.R. aut. rep. Rus. Fed. see Chuvashskaya Respublika
135 I5 Chuvashskaya Respublika aut. rep. Rus. Fed.
129 I4 Chuvek Rus. Fed.
101 F10 Chuwang-san National Park S. Korea
108 C6 Chuxiong Yunnan China
121 P6 Chüy admin. div. Kyrg.
258 G4 Chuy Uru.
Chuyskaya Oblast' admin. div. Kyrg. see Chüy
160 F5 Chuzelles France
105 J2 Chūzenji-ko l. Japan
109 L2 Chuzhou Anhui China
109 L2 Chuzhou Jiangsu China
104 D5 Chūzu Japan
176 D3 Chvalšiny Czech Rep.
127 L6 Chwārtā Iraq
174 G1 Chwaszczyno Pol.
Chwitffordd Flintshire, Wales U.K. see Whitford
Chwitffordd Wales U.K. see Whitford
174 G6 Chybie Pol.
136 K6 Chychykliya r. Ukr.
138 M8 Chyhirynskaye Vodaskhovishcha resr Belarus
137 L4 Chyhyryn Ukr.
Chymyshliya Moldova see Cimişlia
136 B5 Chynadiyeve Ukr.
171 J10 Chyňava Czech Rep.
175 J4 Chynów Pol.
175 M2 Chyrvonae Syalo Belarus
138 L9 Chyrvonaya Slabada Belarus
138 K9 Chyrvonaya Slabada Belarus
136 G1 Chyrvonaye, Vozyera l. Belarus
137 N9 Chysten'ke Ukr.
137 P8 Chystopillya Ukr.
Chystyakove Ukr. see Torez
211 C5 Chyulu Range mts Kenya
121 O7 Chyyyrchyk Ashuusu pass Kyrg.
175 M6 Chyzhykiv Ukr.
196 J5 Ciacova Romania
Ciadâr-Lunga Moldova see Ciadîr-Lunga
136 H7 Ciadîr-Lunga Moldova
163 F9 Ciadoux France
193 P8 Ciagola, Monte mt. Italy
247 □1 Ciales Puerto Rico
192 C4 Ciamannacce Corse France
95 H8 Ciamis Jawa Indon.
193 J4 Ciampino Italy
193 J4 Ciampino airport Italy
194 E8 Cianciana Sicilia Italy
94 G8 Cianjur Jawa Indon.
256 A5 Cianorte Brazil
161 K9 Cians r. France
174 G5 Ciasna Pol.
174 F3 Ciążeń Pol.
94 G8 Cibadak Jawa Indon.
177 J5 Cibakháza Hungary
95 H8 Cibatu Jawa Indon.
241 V7 Cibecue AZ U.S.A.
94 G8 Cibinong Jawa Indon.
211 A5 Cibitoke Burundi
237 G11 Cibolo Creek r. TX U.S.A.
184 C3 Ciborro Port.
242 D2 Cibuta Mex.
242 D2 Cibuta, Sierra mt. Mex.
190 G7 Cicagna Italy
188 D3 Čićarija mts Croatia
193 N6 Cicciano Italy
126 G4 Çiçekdağı Turkey
128 D2 Çiçekli İçel Turkey
199 J3 Çiçekli Manisa Turkey
193 O7 Cicerale Italy
226 G8 Cicero IL U.S.A.
254 F4 Cícero Dantas Brazil
196 J7 Ćićevac Serbia
174 E4 Cicha Woda r. Pol.
175 L3 Cicibór Duży Pol.
177 G4 Čičov Slovakia
183 Q4 Cidacos r. Spain
94 G8 Cidaun Jawa Indon.
126 F3 Cide Turkey
176 E1 Cidlina r. Czech Rep.
183 O5 Cidones Spain
247 □1 Cidra Puerto Rico
175 I3 Ciechanów Pol.
175 K3 Ciechanowiec Pol.
174 G3 Ciechocinek Pol.
246 D3 Ciego de Ávila Cuba
175 I4 Cielądz Pol.
260 C3 Cielo, Cerro mt. Arg.
94 G8 Ciemas Jawa Indon.
183 M8 Ciempozuelos Spain
250 C2 Ciénaga Col.
250 D2 Ciénagas del Catatumbo nat. park Venez.
243 I5 Ciénega Mex.
244 C1 Cieneguillas Mex.
246 C2 Cienfuegos Cuba
174 F3 Cienin Zaborny Pol.
175 J4 Ciepielów Pol.
174 E5 Ciepłowody Pol.
163 F10 Cier-de-Luchon France
177 G3 Čierna Voda Slovakia
177 K3 Čierna voda r. Slovakia
177 H3 Čierne Kľačany Slovakia
177 I3 Čierny Balog Slovakia
163 F10 Cierp-Gaud France
174 F2 Cierznie Pol.
182 C4 Cíes, Illas is Spain
175 L5 Cieszanów Pol.
174 F4 Cieszków Pol.
174 G6 Cieszyn Śląskie Pol.
174 F4 Cieszyn Wielkopolskie Pol.
163 E9 Cieutat France
162 G4 Cieux France
187 C11 Cieza Spain
175 I6 Ciężkowice Pol.
128 F2 Çiflikköy Turkey
199 M3 Çifteler Turkey
Çiftlik Turkey see Kelkit
129 C6 Çiftlikköy Erzurum Turkey
199 J1 Çiftlikköy İstanbul Turkey
183 O7 Cifuentes Spain
183 K5 Cigales Spain
177 K3 Cigánd Hungary
129 C6 Çiğdemli Turkey
94 F8 Cigeulis Jawa Indon.
129 K6 Çigil Adası i. Azer.
190 E5 Cigliano Italy
183 M10 Cigüela r. Spain
126 F4 Cihanbeyli Turkey
199 K3 Cihangazi Turkey
244 C6 Cihuatlán Mex.
185 J2 Cijara, Embalse de resr Spain
177 J6 Čik r. Serbia
Cikai Yunnan China see Gongshan
95 H8 Cikalong Jawa Indon.
198 A2 Çikes, Maja e mt. Albania
79 □7 Cikobia i. Fiji
188 F4 Čikola r. Croatia
95 H8 Cilacap Jawa Indon.
94 G8 Cilangkahan Jawa Indon.
217 □1c Cilaos Réunion
217 □1c Cilaos, Cirque de vol. crater Réunion
127 K3 Çıldır Turkey
127 K3 Çıldır Gölü l. Turkey
128 F2 Çıldıroba Turkey
95 H8 Ciledug Jawa Indon.
193 O7 Cilento e del Vallo di Diano, Parco Nazionale del nat. park Italy
129 A5 Çilhorozdağı Geçidi pass Turkey
109 H4 Cili Hunan China
128 B2 Cilicia reg. Turkey
Cilician Gates pass Turkey see Gülek Boğazı
197 M7 Cilieni Romania
199 M2 Çilimli Turkey
Cill Airne Ireland see Killarney
183 Q7 Cillas Spain
Cill Chainnigh Ireland see Kilkenny
146 B8 Cille Bhrighde Western Isles, Scotland U.K.
182 G8 Cilleros Spain
129 F6 Çilli Geçidi pass Turkey
Cill Mhantáin Ireland see Wicklow
122 F1 Çilmämmetgum des. Turkm.
127 L5 Cilo Dağı mt. Turkey
129 L5 Çiloy Azer.
129 L5 Çiloy Adası i. Azer.
150 E4 Cilybebyll Neath Port Talbot, Wales U.K.
150 E3 Cilycwm Carmarthenshire, Wales U.K.
241 Q6 Cima CA U.S.A.
184 □ Cima, Ilhéu de i. Madeira
94 G8 Cimahi Jawa Indon.
182 I3 Cimanes del Tejar Spain
237 E7 Cimarron KS U.S.A.
239 L8 Cimarron NM U.S.A.
237 G7 Cimarron r. OK U.S.A.
239 L8 Cimarron Creek r. CO U.S.A.
183 Q6 Cimballa Spain
194 F8 Ciminna Sicilia Italy
192 I3 Cimino, Monte mt. Italy
136 H7 Cimişlia Moldova
191 M3 Cimolais Italy
191 J7 Cimone, Monte mt. Italy
Cîmpeni Romania see Câmpeni
Cîmpia Turzii Romania see Câmpia Turzii
Cîmpina Romania see Câmpina
Cîmpulung Romania see Câmpulung
Cîmpulung la Tisa Romania see Câmpulung la Tisa
Cîmpulung Moldovenesc Romania see Câmpulung Moldovenesc
94 F7 Cina, Tanjung c. Indon.
127 J5 Çınar Turkey
199 K2 Çınarcık Turkey
250 E3 Cinaruco r. Venez.
250 E3 Cinaruco-Capanaparo, Parque Nacional nat. park Venez.
186 F3 Cinca r. Spain
186 F5 Cinca r. Spain
188 F4 Cincar mt. Bos.-Herz.
236 M6 Cincinnati OH U.S.A.
233 J6 Cincinnatus NY U.S.A.
246 D3 Cinco-Balas, Cayos is Cuba
185 M2 Cinco Casas Spain
Cinco de Outubro Angola see Xá-Muteba
260 C6 Cinco Saltos Arg.
186 C3 Cinco Villas reg. Spain
186 E6 Cinctorres Spain
197 M5 Cincu Romania
150 H4 Cinderford Gloucestershire, England U.K.
199 J5 Çine Turkey
199 I5 Çine r. Turkey
182 I3 Ciñera Spain
165 H8 Ciney Belgium
182 D6 Cinfães Port.
191 O9 Cingoli Italy
192 G2 Cinigiano Italy
190 G4 Cinisello Balsamo Italy
194 E7 Cinisi Sicilia Italy
177 I3 Cinobaňa Slovakia
159 L7 Cinq-Mars-la-Pile France
195 K7 Cinquefrondi Italy
115 M7 Cinque Island Andaman & Nicobar Is India
190 H7 Cinque Terre reg. Italy
245 N9 Cintalapa Mex.
163 H9 Cintegabelle France
192 B3 Cinto, Monte mt. France
261 F3 Cintra Arg.
216 □1b Cintrão, Ponta do pt São Miguel Azores
157 K8 Cintrey France
183 Q4 Cintruénigo Spain
215 M8 Cintsa S. Africa
256 B5 Cinzas r. Brazil
197 O6 Ciolpani Romania
177 L6 Ciordan, Dealul hill Romania
188 F4 Čiovo i. Croatia
95 H8 Cipatuja Jawa Indon.
Ciping Jiangxi China see Jinggangshan
254 F4 Cipó Brazil
257 E3 Cipo r. Brazil
260 D6 Cipolletti Arg.
257 F4 Cipotânea Brazil
129 H5 Çıraqdärä Azer.
187 E7 Cirat Spain
94 G8 Cirata, Waduk resr Jawa Indon.
182 I3 Cirbanal mt. Spain
193 N5 Circello Italy
193 K5 Circeo, Monte hill Italy
193 J5 Circeo, Parco Nazionale del nat. park Italy
220 D3 Circle AK U.S.A.
238 L3 Circle MT U.S.A.
232 C9 Circleville OH U.S.A.
241 T3 Circleville UT U.S.A.
95 H8 Cirebon Jawa Indon.
151 I4 Cirencester Gloucestershire, England U.K.
Cirene tourist site Libya see Cyrene
94 D5 Cirenti Sumatera Indon.
157 I7 Cirey-sur-Blaise France
157 M6 Cirey-sur-Vezouze France
183 Q5 Ciria Spain
190 D5 Ciriè Italy
193 Q7 Cirigliano Italy
136 H5 Ciripcău Moldova
138 J5 Cirišs l. Latvia
195 □ Cirkewwa, Il-Ponta tac- pt Malta
195 M5 Cirò Italy
177 K3 Cirocha r. Slovakia

Column 1

116 H6 Colonelganj Uttar Prad. India
246 F2 Colonel Hill Bahamas
242 A4 Colonet, Cabo c. Mex.
258 E2 Colonia Arg.
91 I5 Colonia Yap Micronesia
261 I4 Colonia dept Uru.
235 G3 Colonia NJ U.S.A.
　Colonia Agrippina Ger. see Köln
261 G2 Colonia Alpina Arg.
260 D4 Colonia Alvear Arg.
261 F5 Colonia Barón Arg.
261 E3 Colonia Biagorria Arg.
260 D3 Colonia Caseros Arg.
260 D5 Colonia Chica, Isla i. Arg.
260 E6 Colonia Choele Choel, Isla i. Arg.
261 I4 Colonia del Sacramento Uru.
187 L8 Colònia de Sant Jordi Spain
187 L9 Colònia de Sant Pere Spain
258 E3 Colonia Díaz Mex.
258 E3 Colonia Dora Arg.
261 H3 Colonia Elía Arg.
261 G2 Colonia Emilio Mitre Arg.
261 F4 Colonia Fraga Arg.
261 G2 Colonia Hilario Lagos Arg.
　Colonia Julia Fenestris Italy see Fano
261 H2 Colonia La Argentina Arg.
260 D6 Colonia La Pastoril Arg.
259 C7 Colonia Las Heras Arg.
261 I2 Colonia Lavalleja Uru.
232 H11 Colonial Heights VA U.S.A.
234 B4 Colonial Park NJ U.S.A.
260 C6 Colonia Macías Arg.
261 E6 Colonia Portugalete Arg.
241 T10 Colonia Reforma Mex.
261 G2 Colonia Rosa Arg.
261 F4 Colonia Seré Arg.
261 I2 Colonia Suiza Uru.
195 M5 Colonna, Capo c. Italy
192 A9 Colonne, Punta delle pt Sardegna Italy
193 L2 Colonnella Italy
　Colon Ridge sea feature Pacific Ocean
146 D10 Colonsay i. Scotland U.K.
261 F6 Colorada Grande, Salina salt l. Arg.
260 C2 Colorado r. Arg.
260 F6 Colorado r. Arg.
258 D3 Colorado r. Arg.
256 B5 Colorado Brazil
260 B4 Colorado r. Chile
245 J9 Colorado r. Mex.
242 B2 Colorado r. Mex./U.S.A.
237 G11 Colorado r. TX U.S.A.
241 X2 Colorado state U.S.A.
260 D2 Colorado, Cerro mt. Arg.
259 C5 Colorado, Delta del Río Arg.
241 S5 Colorado City AZ U.S.A.
237 E9 Colorado City TX U.S.A.
241 P8 Colorado Desert CA U.S.A.
241 X2 Colorado National Monument nat. park CO U.S.A.
241 W4 Colorado Plateau CO U.S.A.
241 R7 Colorado River Aqueduct CA U.S.A.
241 R8 Colorado River Indian Reservation res. AZ/CA U.S.A.
258 C5 Colorados, Cerro mt. Arg.
239 L7 Colorado Springs CO U.S.A.
190 I6 Colorno Italy
184 C5 Colos Port.
　Colosae Turkey see Honaz
192 D9 Colostrai, Stagno di lag. Sardegna Italy
161 H9 Colostre r. France
260 C3 Colotepec Mex.
245 J10 Colotepec r. Mex.
244 D3 Colotlán Mex.
170 H3 Cölpin Ger.
252 D4 Colquechaca Bol.
146 J11 Colquhar Scottish Borders, Scotland U.K.
252 D4 Colquiri Bol.
231 E10 Colquitt GA U.S.A.
129 K4 Colquıçsu Azer.
157 N7 Colroy-la-Grande France
232 C11 Colson KY U.S.A.
151 K2 Colsterworth Lincolnshire, England U.K.
238 K4 Colstrip MT U.S.A.
151 O2 Coltishall Norfolk, England U.K.
240 O7 Colton CA U.S.A.
233 K4 Colton NY U.S.A.
235 U2 Colton UT U.S.A.
187 C12 Columbares hill Spain
233 K1 Columbia CT U.S.A.
235 E7 Columbia KY U.S.A.
237 I9 Columbia LA U.S.A.
234 B6 Columbia MD U.S.A.
236 I6 Columbia MO U.S.A.
237 K10 Columbia MS U.S.A.
233 I8 Columbia NC U.S.A.
234 B3 Columbia NJ U.S.A.
234 B4 Columbia PA U.S.A.
231 G9 Columbia SC U.S.A.
231 D8 Columbia TN U.S.A.
234 C5 Columbia r. WA U.S.A.
221 K1 Columbia, Cape Nunavut Can.
234 A7 Columbia, District of admin. dist. U.S.A.
222 G4 Columbia, Mount Alta/B.C. Can.
242 A3 Columbia, Sierra mts Mex.
230 E5 Columbia City IN U.S.A.
234 C2 Columbia county county PA U.S.A.
233 □R4 Columbia Falls ME U.S.A.
238 D3 Columbia Falls MT U.S.A.
222 E4 Columbia Mountains B.C. Can.
231 D9 Columbiana AL U.S.A.
232 E3 Columbiana OH U.S.A.
238 E3 Columbia Plateau U.S.A.
240 B1 Columbine, Cape S. Africa
187 G8 Columbretes, Islas is Spain
230 E5 Columbus GA U.S.A.
230 E6 Columbus IN U.S.A.
236 E3 Columbus KS U.S.A.
237 H7 Columbus MS U.S.A.
237 K8 Columbus MS U.S.A.
237 G7 Columbus NC U.S.A.
238 J4 Columbus NE U.S.A.
241 S6 Columbus NM U.S.A.
235 G5 Columbus OH U.S.A.
234 C2 Columbus PA U.S.A.
231 K11 Columbus NM U.S.A.
232 B9 Columbus PA U.S.A.
232 G11 Columbus PA U.S.A.
246 F3 Columbus Bank sea feature Bahamas
231 C10 Columbus Grove OH U.S.A.
247 □5 Columbus Point Trin. and Tob.
240 N3 Columbus Salt Marsh NV U.S.A.
257 F2 Coluna Brazil
240 J2 Colusa CA U.S.A.
183 J2 Colungo Spain
80 J3 Colville North I. N.Z.
222 D2 Colville r. AK U.S.A.
80 J3 Colville, Cape North I. N.Z.
87 I10 Colville, Lake salt flat W.A. Austr.
80 J3 Colville Channel North I. N.Z.
220 F3 Colville Indian Reservation res. U.S.A.
220 F3 Colville Lake N.W.T. Can.
151 I2 Colwich Staffordshire, England U.K.
150 D3 Colwyn Bay Conwy, Wales U.K.
161 G5 Colze France
150 F6 Colyton Devon, England U.K.
191 M6 Comacchio Italy
191 M6 Comacchio, Valli di lag. Italy
84 G5 Comacho, Puerto pass Spain
111 J12 Comai Xizang China
244 D6 Comalcalco Mex.
245 I4 Comales r. Mex.
245 I4 Comallo Arg.
197 O6 Comana Romania
246 F3 Comana de Sus Romania
237 C6 Comanche TX U.S.A.
258 E2 Comandante Ferraz research stn Antarctica
258 F2 Comandante Fontana Arg.
256 C8 Comandante Luis Piedra Buena Arg.

Column 2

261 I6 Comandante Nicanor Otamendi Arg.
260 C3 Comandante Salas Arg.
181 H1 Comanegra, Puig de mt. Spain
197 O4 Comăneşti Romania
186 H2 Coma Pedrosa, Pic de mt. Andorra
197 N5 Comarnic Romania
242 □P10 Comayagua Hond.
231 G9 Combahee r. SC U.S.A.
157 K8 Combeaufontaine France
160 I5 Combe de Savoie val. France
150 D5 Combe Martin Devon, England U.K.
226 J7 Comber Northern Ireland U.K.
96 A5 Combermere Bay Myanmar
151 M3 Comberton Cambridgeshire, England U.K.
150 G6 Combe St Nicholas Somerset, England U.K.
165 I8 Comblain-au-Pont Belgium
156 E3 Comblanchien France
160 I5 Combles France
160 D5 Combloux France
94 E4 Comboré i. Indon.
190 I3 Combourg, Monte mt. Italy/Switz.
158 H5 Combourg France
160 A4 Combrailles reg. France
158 C6 Combrit France
160 C5 Combronde France
260 E3 Comechingones, Sierra de mts Arg.
191 N2 Comeglians Italy
191 N2 Comelico Superiore Italy
224 F3 Comencho, Lac l. Que. Can.
184 D2 Comenda Port.
256 C3 Comendador Gomes Brazil
257 G2 Comercinho Brazil
247 □1 Comerio Puerto Rico
191 M8 Comero, Monte mt. Italy
85 L7 Comet r. Qld Austr.
85 L7 Comet Qld Austr.
237 F10 Comfort TX U.S.A.
232 D10 Comfort WV U.S.A.
246 □ Comfort Castle Jamaica
117 M8 Comilla Bangl.
183 L2 Comines Spain
165 C7 Comines Belgium
192 D6 Comino, Capo c. Sardegna Italy
　Comino i. Malta see Kemmuna
　Cominotti i. Malta see Kemmunett
194 H10 Comiso Sicilia Italy
243 M9 Comitán de Domínguez Mex.
194 F9 Comitini Sicilia Italy
137 J6 Comloşu Mare Romania
235 I3 Commack NY U.S.A.
227 O4 Commanda Ont. Can.
147 G3 Commeen Ireland
160 G3 Commenailles France
163 C7 Commensacq France
158 H8 Commentry France
159 J5 Commer France
157 K6 Commercy France
163 F10 Comminges reg. France
231 □1 Commissioner's Point Bermuda
214 D6 Commissioner's Salt Pan S. Africa
221 J3 Committee Bay Nunavut Can.
215 O3 Commondale S. Africa
263 J2 Commonwealth Bay Antarctica
　Commonwealth Territory admin. div. Austr. see Jervis Bay Territory
234 C5 Como Italy
234 C4 Como, Lago di l. Italy
227 N6 Como, Lago di l. Italy
234 B4 Comoapan Mex.
157 L8 Como r. France
260 A4 Coney r. France
231 □1 Coney Island Bermuda
147 E4 Coney Island Sing. see Serangoon, Pulau
235 H3 Coney Island NY U.S.A.
157 K5 Conflans-en-Jarnisy France
163 I10 Conflans-sur-Lanterne France
244 G5 Comonfort Mex.
190 G4 Como Italy
190 G4 Como, Lago di l. Italy
190 G4 Como, Lago di
245 L7 Comoapan Mex.
111 I12 Como Chamling l. China
260 B3 Comodoro Arturo Merino Benítez airport Chile
259 D7 Comodoro Rivadavia Arg.
206 E4 Comoé, Parc National de la nat. park Côte d'Ivoire
206 E4 Comoé r. Côte d'Ivoire
244 G5 Comonfort Mex.
　Comores country Africa see Comoros
114 E8 Comorin, Cape India
217 □3 Comoro country Africa
222 E5 Comox B.C. Can.
185 L7 Cómpeta Spain
190 H6 Compiano Italy
156 E5 Compiègne France
162 F4 Compolibat France
184 D4 Comporta Port.
244 C4 Compostela Mex.
92 F8 Compostela Mindanao Phil.
162 G4 Compreignac France
181 H4 Comprida, Ilha i. Brazil
157 K5 Comps-sur-Artuby France
240 N8 Compton CA U.S.A.
226 E8 Compton IL U.S.A.
183 K3 Compuerto, Embalse de resr Spain
198 B2 Comrat Moldova
149 M7 Comrie Perth and Kinross, Scotland U.K.
208 B5 Comstock TX U.S.A.
191 L1 Comunanza Italy
96 C6 Comuna r. Sicilia Italy
96 C6 Cona, Sông r. Vietnam
97 I8 Cona, Sông r. Vietnam
111 J13 Cona Xizang China
128 E1 Çona Turkey
206 B4 Conakry Guinea
250 B5 Conambo Ecuador
250 B5 Conambo r. Ecuador
259 D6 Conara Junction Tas. Austr.
83 K9 Conay Chile
192 C4 Conca Corse France
260 D4 Concarán Arg.
257 F4 Concarneau France
256 D6 Concas Sardegna Italy
192 D6 Conceição Amazonas Brazil
182 H3 Conceição Port.
183 K3 Conceição r. Brazil
253 F1 Conceição Mato Grosso Brazil
253 E2 Conceição Rondônia Brazil
253 E2 Conceição r. Brazil
256 F4 Conceição r. Brazil
257 F4 Conceição da Barra Brazil
256 C3 Conceição das Alagoas Brazil
254 C4 Conceição do Araguaia Brazil
259 E12 Conceição do Macabu Brazil
254 D5 Conceição do Mato Dentro Brazil
253 E5 Conceição do Maú Brazil
254 D5 Conceição do Norte Brazil
149 O7 Conceição do Rio Verde Brazil
258 F3 Concepción Corrientes Arg.
252 D2 Concepción Tucumán Arg.
252 D2 Concepción Beni Bol.
224 D4 Concepción Santa Cruz Bol.
149 K5 Concepción Chile
244 C2 Concepción Mex.
242 C2 Concepción r. Mex.
253 F5 Concepción Para.
185 M7 Concepción Venez.
259 B8 Concepción, Canal sea chan. Chile
223 I4 Concepción, Punta pt Mex.
260 E3 Concepción de Buenos Aires Mex.
261 H3 Concepción del Uruguay Arg.
159 K5 Conception, Île i. Seychelles
147 K3 Conception, Point Can.
246 F2 Conception Bay Namibia
261 I2 Concepción Italy
213 F4 Concesio Zimbabwe
183 N2 Concha Spain

Column 3

183 O3 Concha de Álava reg. Spain
256 C5 Conchas Brazil
239 L9 Conchas U.S.A.
182 E5 Conchas, Embalse das resr Spain
242 G4 Conchas Lake NM U.S.A.
156 A6 Conches-en-Ouche France
252 C5 Conchi Chile
242 G4 Concho Mex.
241 W7 Concho r. TX U.S.A.
237 F10 Concho r. TX U.S.A.
243 K5 Conchos r. Nuevo León/Tamaulipas Mex.
232 F8 Conchos r. Mex.
260 B3 Concón Chile
240 J4 Concord CA U.S.A.
147 C5 Concord Ireland
84 C8 Concord MA U.S.A.
233 N5 Concord NC U.S.A.
230 E6 Concord NH U.S.A.
147 C7 Concord VA U.S.A.
232 G11 Concord VT U.S.A.
262 I2 Concord VT U.S.A.
　Concordia research stn Antarctica
261 I2 Concórdia Arg.
250 E6 Concórdia Amazonas Brazil
255 B8 Concórdia Santa Catarina Brazil
250 C3 Concordia Antioquia Col.
250 C4 Concordia Meta Col.
244 A2 Concordia Mex.
250 C6 Concordia Peru
214 B5 Concordia S. Africa
236 E6 Concordia KS U.S.A.
191 N4 Concordia Sagittaria Italy
123 O3 Concord Peak Afgh.
163 G6 Concorès France
163 H7 Concots France
163 I6 Concumén Chile
163 I9 Con Cuông Vietnam
256 D3 Conda Angola
256 D3 Condado lag. Spain
185 J4 Condado de Niebla reg. Spain
238 I2 Condado de Treviño reg. Spain
264 U9 Condamine r. Qld Austr.
237 H10 Condamine r. Qld Austr.
237 H10 Condamine, Qld Austr.
191 L6 Consandolo Italy
261 H2 Consejo Bernardí Arg.
165 J9 Consdorf Lux.
242 Q5 Consecon Ont. Can.
243 O8 Consejo Belize
257 F4 Conselheiro Lafaiete Brazil
257 G3 Conselheiro Pena Brazil
191 L6 Conselice Italy
147 K8 Consell Spain
257 J5 Consenvoye France
149 N4 Consett Durham, England U.K.
234 C4 Conshohocken PA U.S.A.
246 B2 Consolación del Sur Cuba
97 H10 Côn Sơn, Đảo i. Vietnam
223 I4 Consort Alta Can.
184 C2 Constância Port.
261 I4 Constancia Uru.
251 F6 Constância dos Baetas Brazil
197 Q6 Constanţa Romania
　Constanţa airport Romania see Kogălniceanu
186 H1 Constanti Spain
　Constantia Ger. see Konstanz
　Constantia tourist site Cyprus see Salamis
182 H5 Constantim Bragança Port.
182 E5 Constantim Vila Real Port.
184 H5 Constantina Spain
205 G1 Constantine Alg.
222 F3 Constantine, Cape AK U.S.A.
226 I8 Constantine MI U.S.A.
220 C4 Constantinople Turkey see Istanbul
246 □ Constant Spring Jamaica
261 G2 Constanza Arg.
114 G6 Constitución Chile
258 D3 Constitución Uru.
177 L5 Constitución de 1857, Parque Nacional nat. park Mex.
185 L2 Consuegra Spain
253 E3 Consuelo Brazil
245 K10 Consuelo Mex.
245 K10 Consul r. Mex.
250 C5 Consul Sask. Can.
242 Q10 Copán tourist site Hond.
195 L6 Copanello Italy
187 C13 Cope, Cabo c. Spain
147 L3 Copeland Island Northern Ireland U.K.
226 I5 Copenhagen Denmark see København
253 E4 Copere Bol.
150 H6 Copertino Italy
261 G6 Copetonas Arg.
83 M3 Copeton Reservoir N.S.W. Austr.
85 I6 Côpi Pî, Phou mt. Laos/Vietnam
193 L3 Copiague NY U.S.A.
258 C2 Copiapó Chile
258 C2 Copiapó, Volcán vol. Chile
146 K5 Copinsay i. Scotland U.K.
82 G4 Copley S.A. Austr.
149 O6 Copley Durham, England U.K.
253 E6 Copo, Parque Nacional nat. park Arg.
184 G6 Copons Spain
252 C2 Coporaque Peru
190 G5 Coppa r. Italy
147 E9 Copparo Italy
85 M4 Coppename r. Suriname
197 M4 Coppename r. Suriname
151 L4 Coppenhall Cheshire, England U.K.
147 F9 Coppet Switz.
85 L6 Copplestone Devon, England U.K.
197 M4 Copp Lake salt flat S.A. Austr.
151 L5 Copthorne Surrey, England U.K.
147 F9 Copthorne Hampshire, England U.K.
85 L6 Conway National Park Qld Austr.

Column 4

227 N1 Connaught Ont. Can.
147 D5 Connaught reg. Ireland
147 F8 Connaught reg. Ireland
232 E7 Conneaut OH U.S.A.
232 E7 Conneaut Lake PA U.S.A.
232 K2 Conneautville PA U.S.A.
233 N7 Connecticut r. U.S.A.
146 F10 Connecticut state U.S.A.
84 F7 Connel Argyll and Bute, Scotland U.K.
　Connellis Lagoon Conservation Reserve nature res. N.T. Austr.
232 F8 Connellsville PA U.S.A.
147 C6 Connemara Qld Austr.
147 C5 Connemara reg. Ireland
147 C5 Connemara National Park Ireland
84 C8 Conner, Mount hill N.T. Austr.
159 L5 Connerré France
230 E6 Connersville IN U.S.A.
147 D7 Connolly Ireland
83 M4 Connolly Basin N.S.W. Austr.
147 C7 Connolly, Mount Y.T. Can.
85 L6 Connors Range hill Qld Austr.
83 J5 Conoble N.S.W. Austr.
234 B4 Conodoguinet Creek r. PA U.S.A.
250 C5 Conocarno Ecuador
250 C5 Cononaco r. Ecuador
146 H7 Conon Bridge Highland, Scotland U.K.
84 C3 Coolibah N.T. Austr.
241 U9 Coolidge AZ U.S.A.
177 K5 Conop Romania
177 I6 Çonoplja Vojvodina Serbia
226 E3 Conover WI U.S.A.
170 H4 Conow Ger.
234 C5 Conowingo MD U.S.A.
234 B3 Conques France
163 I9 Conques-sur-Orbiel France
256 D3 Conquista Brazil
185 J4 Conquista Spain
238 I2 Conrad MT U.S.A.
264 U9 Conrad Rise sea feature Southern Ocean
237 H10 Conroe, Lake TX U.S.A.
191 L6 Consandolo Italy
261 H2 Consejo Bernardí Arg.
165 J9 Consdorf Lux.
242 Q5 Consecon Ont. Can.
243 O8 Consejo Belize
257 F4 Conselheiro Lafaiete Brazil
257 G3 Conselheiro Pena Brazil
191 L6 Conselice Italy
147 K8 Consell Spain
257 J5 Consenvoye France
149 N4 Consett Durham, England U.K.
234 C4 Conshohocken PA U.S.A.
246 B2 Consolación del Sur Cuba
97 H10 Côn Sơn, Đảo i. Vietnam
223 I4 Consort Alta Can.
184 C2 Constância Port.
261 I4 Constancia Uru.
251 F6 Constância dos Baetas Brazil
197 Q6 Constanţa Romania
　Constanţa airport Romania see Kogălniceanu
186 H1 Constanti Spain
　Constantia Ger. see Konstanz
　Constantia tourist site Cyprus see Salamis
182 H5 Constantim Bragança Port.
182 E5 Constantim Vila Real Port.
184 H5 Constantina Spain
205 G1 Constantine Alg.
222 F3 Constantine, Cape AK U.S.A.
226 I8 Constantine MI U.S.A.
220 C4 Constantinople Turkey see Istanbul
246 □ Constant Spring Jamaica
261 G2 Constanza Arg.

Column 5

81 □2 Cook Islands S. Pacific Ocean
150 H3 Cookley Worcestershire, England U.K.
79 □8a Cook Point Tongatapu Tonga
79 □8a Cook's Bay Moorea Fr. Polynesia
85 J3 Cook's Cairn hill Scotland U.K.
85 J3 Cook's Harbour Nfld and Lab. Can.
147 I3 Cooks Passage Qld Austr.
147 I3 Cookstown Northern Ireland U.K.
81 I7 Cook Strait South I. N.Z.
234 A6 Cooksville MD U.S.A.
156 D6 Cooktown Qld Austr.
147 F4 Coola Ireland
83 K4 Coolabah N.S.W. Austr.
159 L5 Cooladdi Qld Austr.
83 L4 Coolah N.S.W. Austr.
83 M4 Coolah Tops National Park N.S.W. Austr.
83 K6 Coolamon N.S.W. Austr.
156 H6 Coole France
148 C6 Coole Ireland
87 F11 Coolgardie W.A. Austr.
147 H7 Coolgreany Ireland
147 J7 Coolgreany Ireland
84 C3 Coolibah N.T. Austr.
241 U9 Coolidge AZ U.S.A.
186 G4 Coolis Spain
187 K5 Coolola Italy
232 A12 Corbin KY U.S.A.
234 F6 Corbin City NJ U.S.A.
186 G4 Corbins Spain
177 I6 Çorbola Italy
232 C9 Coolroebeg Ireland
85 N9 Coolum Beach Qld Austr.
83 L7 Cooma N.S.W. Austr.
147 B9 Coomacarrabaran N.S.W. Austr.
82 G6 Coomalbidgup W.A. Austr.
83 L4 Coonamble N.S.W. Austr.
87 G11 Coonana S.A. Austr.
87 G11 Coonana Aboriginal Reserve W.A. Austr.
82 E4 Coonawarra S.A. Austr.
259 D6 Coondambo S.A. Austr.
259 B6 Coondapoor Karnataka India see Kundapura
86 E6 Coongan r. W.A. Austr.
86 E6 Coongan Aboriginal Reserve W.A. Austr.
85 J9 Coongoola Qld Austr.
82 E2 Coongra watercourse Qld Austr.
235 I3 Coon Rapids MN U.S.A.
84 D2 Cooper r. S.A. Austr.
82 F3 Cooper TX U.S.A.
　Cooper Creek watercourse Qld/S.A. Austr.
232 G6 Cooperdale OH U.S.A.
83 N4 Coopernook N.S.W. Austr.
191 H5 Coopersburg PA U.S.A.
233 □P4 Coopers Mills ME U.S.A.
231 I12 Cooper's Town Bahamas
236 F2 Cooperstown ND U.S.A.
233 K6 Cooperstown NY U.S.A.
83 L7 Coorabambra National Park Vic. Austr.
247 □7 Coora Trin. and Tob.
82 D4 Coorabie S.A. Austr.
82 D8 Coor-de-Wandy hill W.A. Austr.
82 G7 Coorong National Park S.A. Austr.
87 D10 Coorow W.A. Austr.
85 N9 Cooroy Qld Austr.
85 N9 Coosa r. AL U.S.A.
238 B5 Coos Bay OR U.S.A.
238 B5 Coos Bay b. OR U.S.A.
83 L6 Cootamundra N.S.W. Austr.
147 H4 Coothill Ireland
114 C6 Cooum r. India
85 M9 Cooyar Qld Austr.
147 J6 Cooyar Ireland
245 K10 Copala Mex.
244 D5 Copalillo Mex.
245 I7 Copalis Mex.
250 C5 Copan Mex.

Column 6

78 □5 Coral Sea S. Pacific Ocean
266 F6 Coral Sea Basin S. Pacific Ocean
77 T3 Coral Sea Islands Territory terr. Austr.
147 N6 Coralstown Ireland
235 I3 Coram NY U.S.A.
232 E5 Coramba Italy
186 J5 Corandi PA U.S.A.
129 K5 Corat Azer.
185 J3 Coraopolis PA U.S.A.
186 K3 Corat Azer.
186 J5 Cornellà de Llobregat Spain
186 J5 Cornellà de Terri Spain
182 H2 Corateca Spain
33 K8 Corner Brook Nfld and Lab. Can.
81 I7 Corner Inlet b. Vic. Austr.
185 P5 Corneros r. Spain
264 F3 Corner Seamounts sea feature N. Atlantic Ocean
136 H6 Corneşti Moldova
186 H4 Corbalá France
184 G2 Corbán Spain
186 D7 Corbally Ireland
147 D4 Corbell France
192 I2 Corbara, Lago di l. Italy
232 B11 Cornettsville KY U.S.A.
177 L6 Corneu, Vârful hill Romania
146 K7 Cornhill Aberdeenshire, Scotland U.K.
149 M2 Cornhill-on-Tweed Northumberland, England U.K.
190 M6 Cornholme West Yorkshire, England U.K.
197 O3 Corni Romania
192 F2 Cornia r. Italy
190 I7 Corniglio Italy
156 H5 Cornillet, Mont hill France
157 M8 Corrimont France
231 I7 Corning AR U.S.A.
240 J2 Corning CA U.S.A.
236 I4 Corning IA U.S.A.
232 H6 Corning NY U.S.A.
232 C9 Corning OH U.S.A.
85 □7 Cornish watercourse Austr.
259 B7 Cornish, Estrada b. Chile
　Corn Islands is Nic. see Maíz, Islas del
193 J2 Corno r. Italy
193 L3 Corno, Monte mt. Italy
190 I3 Corno di Campo mt. Italy/Switz.
158 C5 Cornouaille reg. France
226 C3 Cornucopia WI U.S.A.
191 M4 Cornuda Italy
159 L9 Cornus France
161 C9 Cornus France
224 F3 Cornwall Ont. Can.
225 I4 Cornwall P.E.I. Can.
246 □ Cornwall parish Jamaica
　Cornwall admin. div. England U.K.
235 G2 Cornwall NY U.S.A.
234 C4 Cornwall PA U.S.A.
150 □ Cornwall, Cape England U.K.
221 I2 Cornwallis Island Nunavut Can.
221 I2 Cornwallis Island Nunavut Can.
235 G2 Cornwall on Hudson NY U.S.A.
82 F3 Corny Point S.A. Austr.
250 D2 Coro Venez.
182 F5 Coroa, Serra da mts Port.
257 F3 Coroatá Brazil
254 D3 Coroatá Brazil
252 C4 Corocoro Bol.
251 F2 Corocoro, Isla i. Venez.
147 D7 Corofin Ireland
81 I7 Coroglen North I. N.Z.
256 D3 Coroico Bol.
255 B8 Coromandel Brazil
81 I7 Coromandel North I. N.Z.
114 G7 Coromandel Coast India
81 I7 Coromandel Forest Park nature res. North I. N.Z.
81 I7 Coromandel Peninsula North I. N.Z.
81 I7 Coromandel Range hills North I. N.Z.
92 C5 Coron France
92 C5 Coron Phil.
185 K3 Corona r. Port.
183 R3 Corona r. Spain
241 V8 Corona CA U.S.A.
239 L9 Corona NM U.S.A.
207 H6 Corona Port.

Column 7

169 I8 Cornberg Ger.
159 K7 Corné France
191 K3 Corneliano Italy
163 J10 Corneilla-del-Vercol France
215 M3 Cornélia S. Africa
256 F5 Cornélio Procópio Brazil
225 J5 Cornélio Brazil
184 J5 Cornélio Brazil
186 J5 Cornellà de Llobregat Spain
186 J5 Cornellà de Terri Spain
182 H2 Coranzuli Arg.
226 C4 Cornell WI U.S.A.
33 K8 Corner Brook Nfld and Lab. Can.
81 I7 Corner Inlet b. Vic. Austr.
185 P5 Corneros r. Spain
264 F3 Corner Seamounts sea feature N. Atlantic Ocean
136 H6 Corneşti Moldova
191 K4 Corneto Italy see Tarquinia
232 B11 Cornettsville KY U.S.A.
177 L6 Cornu, Vârful hill Romania
146 K7 Cornhill Aberdeenshire, Scotland U.K.
149 M2 Cornhill-on-Tweed Northumberland, England U.K.
190 M6 Cornholme West Yorkshire, England U.K.
197 O3 Corni Romania
192 F2 Cornia r. Italy
190 I7 Corniglio Italy
156 H5 Cornillet, Mont hill France
157 M8 Corrimont France
231 I7 Corning AR U.S.A.
240 J2 Corning CA U.S.A.
236 I4 Corning IA U.S.A.
232 H6 Corning NY U.S.A.
232 C9 Corning OH U.S.A.
197 Q6 Corbu Romania
186 G4 Corbins Spain
226 C3 Corbola Italy
161 G6 Corbigny France
232 A12 Corbin KY U.S.A.
234 F6 Corbin City NJ U.S.A.
186 G4 Corbins Spain
177 I6 Çorbola Italy
186 L4 Corça Spain
259 B7 Corcaigh Ireland see Cork
160 C2 Corcelles-lès-Cîteaux France
193 I3 Corchuela Spain
216 □3d Corcho, Punta del pt La Palma Canary Is
147 D8 Corcomroe Ireland
183 L3 Corcorán CA U.S.A.
240 M5 Corcoran CA U.S.A.
158 C5 Corcoué-sur-Logne France
259 C6 Corcovado Arg.
259 B6 Corcovado, Golfo de sea chan. Chile
242 □R13 Corcovado, Parque Nacional nat. park Costa Rica
183 B3 Corcubión, Ría de b. Spain
182 B3 Corcubión, Ría de b. Spain
　Corcyra i. Greece see Kerkyra
147 D8 Cordal Ireland
85 N8 Cordalba Qld Austr.
231 F10 Cordele GA U.S.A.
240 J3 Cordelia CA U.S.A.
237 F8 Cordell OK U.S.A.
158 C4 Cordemais France
191 M4 Cordenòns Italy
158 H6 Cordes France
191 M4 Cordigmano Italy
252 E1 Cordillera Azul, Parque Nacional nat. park Peru
250 C4 Cordillera de los Picachos, Parque Nacional nat. park Col.
92 D6 Cordilleras Range mts Panay Phil.
261 E2 Cordillo Downs S.A. Austr.
261 E2 Córdoba Arg.
259 C6 Córdoba Río Negro Arg.
261 E3 Córdoba prov. Arg.
245 J4 Córdoba Durango Mex.
245 J4 Córdoba Mex.
185 J5 Córdoba prov. Spain
260 E3 Córdoba, Sierras de hills Spain
260 E3 Córdoba, Sierras de mts Arg.
184 G2 Cordobilla de Lácara Spain
252 B3 Córdoba Peru
220 D3 Cordova AK U.S.A.
234 C6 Cordova MD U.S.A.
222 C4 Cordova Bay AK U.S.A.
183 Q7 Corduente Spain
261 G5 Corduba Spain see Córdoba
223 I4 Coronation Alta Can.
220 G3 Coronation Gulf Nunavut Can.
262 U2 Coronation Island S. Orkney Is Atlantic Ocean
222 C4 Coronation Island W.A. Austr.
86 H3 Coronation Islands W.A. Austr.
92 C6 Coron Bay Phil.
261 G2 Coronda Arg.
261 E4 Coronel Altagaray Arg.
261 E6 Coronel Bogado Arg.
251 G3 Coronel Bogado Para.
261 H4 Coronel Brandsen Arg.
261 F6 Coronel Dorrego Arg.
256 C6 Coronel Fabriciano Brazil
261 E6 Coronel Falcón Arg.
261 F6 Coronel Francisco Sosa Arg.
261 E6 Coronel Juliá y Echarrán Arg.
260 E3 Coronel Moldes Córdoba Arg.
261 E5 Coronel Moldes Salta Arg.
261 F6 Coronel Murta Brazil
261 F6 Coronel Oviedo Para.
253 K3 Coronel Ponce Brazil
252 B3 Coronel Portillo Peru
261 G5 Coronel Pringles Arg.
256 C5 Coronel Rodolfo Bunge Arg.
253 G5 Coronel Sapucaia Mato Grosso do Sul Brazil
261 E5 Coronel Suárez Arg.
261 I5 Coronel Vidal Arg.
147 D8 Coroneo Mex.
81 □1 Coronet Peak South I. N.Z.
192 B2 Corovodë Albania
81 K3 Corowa N.S.W. Austr.
243 O8 Corozal Belize
254 I4 Corozal Col.
247 □1 Corozal Puerto Rico
257 C8 Corozal Panama Venez.
255 C8 Corpen Aike Arg.
161 H7 Corps France
158 H6 Corps-Nuds France
237 G11 Corpus Christi TX U.S.A.
237 G11 Corpus Christi, Lake TX U.S.A.
252 D4 Corque Bol.
259 B5 Corral Chile
187 E7 Corral mt. Spain
183 N9 Corral de Almaguer Spain
185 K5 Corral de Bustos Arg.
183 R8 Corral de Calatrava Spain
186 L9 Corral de Cantos mt. Spain
183 L9 Corral de Isaac r. Arg.
216 □3f Corralejo Fuerteventura Canary Is
237 C13 Corrales Mex.
244 F5 Corrales de Rábago Mex.
261 E5 Corrales de Ujo Spain
259 C8 Corrales Mex.
161 H7 Corps France
158 K3 Corral Nuevo Mex.
185 Q3 Corral-Rubio Spain
162 □ Corrandibby Range hills W.A. Austr.
213 H2 Corrane Moz.
192 D7 Corràsi, Punta mt. Sardegna Italy

Column 8

169 I8 Cornberg Ger.
159 K7 Corné France
191 K3 Corneliano Italy
163 J10 Corneilla-del-Vercol France
215 M3 Cornélia S. Africa
256 F5 Cornélio Procópio Brazil
250 E4 Coromoto Venez.
250 E4 Coromoto Venez.
197 O7 Corund Romania
192 I7 Coruña, A Spain see A Coruña
185 K5 Coruche Port.
147 D8 Corumá r. Brazil
253 J2 Corumbá Brazil
256 C2 Corumbá r. Brazil
256 C2 Corumbá de Goiás Brazil
253 J2 Corumbá, Parque Nacional nat. park Brazil
256 C4 Corumbataí r. Brazil
253 I9 Corumbiara Brazil
253 F2 Corumbiara r. Brazil
256 C4 Corupá Brazil
238 B4 Corvallis OR U.S.A.
151 L1 Corve r. England U.K.
216 □1a Corvo i. Azores
185 P5 Corvera Spain
151 O3 Corton Suffolk, England U.K.
191 L8 Cortona Italy
184 C5 Coruche Port.
185 Q4 Corvera de Asturias Spain
193 O7 Coruno Italy
161 B9 Corvol-l'Orgueilleux France
225 H4 Cornwall P.E.I. Can.
151 M3 Coton Cambridgeshire, England U.K.
256 C6 Cotia Brazil
256 C6 Cotia r. Brazil
237 G11 Corpus Christi, Lake TX U.S.A.
252 D4 Corque Bol.
191 K3 Cossato Italy
159 K6 Cossé-le-Vivien France
161 H9 Corps France
252 D5 Correntina Brazil
254 D5 Correntina Brazil
254 D5 Correntina Brazil

162 H5	Correntina r. Brazil see Éguas
162 H5	Corrèze France
162 G5	Corrèze dept France
162 G5	Corrèze r. France
147 D6	Corrib, Lough l. Ireland
191 P9	Corridonia Italy
146 F11	Corrie North Ayrshire, Scotland U.K.
258 F2	Corrientes Arg.
261 H1	Corrientes prov. Arg.
258 F2	Corrientes r. Arg.
250 C5	Corrientes r. Peru
261 I6	Corrientes, Cabo c. Arg.
250 B3	Corrientes, Cabo c. Col.
246 A3	Corrientes, Cabo c. Cuba
244 B5	Corrientes, Cabo c. Mex.
237 H10	Corrigan TX U.S.A.
87 D12	Corrigin W.A. Austr.
151 M4	Corringham Thurrock, England U.K.
150 E2	Corris Gwynedd, Wales U.K.
251 G3	Corriverton Guyana
156 G6	Corrobert France
182 B3	Corrubedo, Cabo c. Spain
232 F7	Corry PA U.S.A.
83 K7	Corryong Vic. Austr.
190 D7	Corsaglia r. Italy
190 O4	Corsano Italy
192 C3	Corse admin. reg. France
192 A3	Corse i. France
192 C1	Corse, Cap c. Corse France
192 B2	Corse, Parc Naturel Régional de la nature res. Corse France
192 B4	Corse-du-Sud dept Corse France
146 H12	Corserine hill Scotland U.K.
158 G5	Corseul France
150 H5	Corsham Wiltshire, England U.K.
	Corsica i. France see Corse
237 G9	Corsicana TX U.S.A.
190 G5	Corsico Italy
208 A4	Corsico, Baie de b. Gabon
146 I12	Corsock Dumfries and Galloway, Scotland U.K.
234 F6	Corson's Inlet N.J. U.S.A.
	Cort Adelaer, Kap c. Greenland see Kangeq
195 K6	Cortale Italy
244 B3	Cortazar Mex.
192 C3	Corte Corse France
184 F3	Corte de Peleas Spain
182 D4	Cortegada Spain
184 F5	Cortegana Spain
190 E6	Cortemilia Italy
190 I3	Corteno Golgi Italy
190 G5	Cortenova Italy
183 R5	Cortes Spain
	Cortes, Sea of g. Mex. see California, Golfo de
186 D6	Cortes de Aragón Spain
185 N5	Cortes de Baza Spain
185 I7	Cortes de la Frontera Spain
184 H7	Cortes de la Frontera, Reserva Nacional de nature res. Spain
187 D9	Cortes de Pallás Spain
239 J8	Cortez CO U.S.A.
241 P1	Cortez Mountains NV U.S.A.
184 C3	Cortiçadas do Lavre Port.
186 G5	Cortina i. Italy
185 K2	Cortijo de Arriba Spain
245 I9	Cortijos r. Mex.
185 N4	Cortijos Nuevos Spain
191 M2	Cortina d'Ampezzo Italy
233 I6	Cortland NY U.S.A.
232 E7	Cortland OH U.S.A.
178 E8	Cortona Italy
151 P2	Corton Suffolk, England U.K.
191 L9	Cortona Italy
206 B4	Corubal r. Guinea-Bissau
184 B3	Coruche Port.
129 C4	Çoruh Turkey see Artvin
127 J3	Çoruh r. Turkey
182 G3	Corullón Spain
126 G3	Çorum Turkey
253 F4	Corumbá Brazil
256 C1	Corumbá r. Brazil
256 C1	Corumbá de Goiás Brazil
256 C3	Corumbaíba Brazil
256 B5	Corumbataí r. Brazil
257 H2	Corumbaú, Ponta pt Brazil
192 N4	Corund Romania
177 L4	Corund r. Romania
232 C6	Corunna Ont. Can.
227 J7	Corunna MI U.S.A.
	Corunna Spain see A Coruña
254 F4	Coruripe Brazil
238 C4	Corvallis OR U.S.A.
191 L2	Corvara in Badia Italy
150 G3	Corve Dale val. England U.K.
187 C12	Corvera Spain
224 F2	Corvette, Lac de la l. Que. Can.
193 J4	Corvia, Cofa hill Italy
216 □11	Corvo i. Azores
150 F2	Corwen Denbighshire, Wales U.K.
236 I5	Corydon IA U.S.A.
230 E6	Corydon IN U.S.A.
151 N4	Coryton Thurrock, England U.K.
232 G7	Coryville PA U.S.A.
	Cos i. Greece see Kos
186 C6	Cosa Spain
245 L7	Cosalá Mex.
245 I7	Cosamaloapan Mex.
129 A5	Cosandere Turkey
151 J2	Cosby Leicestershire, England U.K.
252 C4	Coscaya Chile
193 J2	Coscerno, Monte mt. Italy
195 L4	Coscile r. Italy
245 J6	Coscomatepec Mex.
183 P6	Coscurita Spain
	Cosentia Italy see Cosenza
193 Q9	Cosenza Italy
193 Q9	Cosenza prov. Italy
197 O6	Cogeni Romania
195 L4	Coșerie r. Italy
146 I9	Coshieville Perth and Kinross, Scotland U.K.
232 D8	Coshocton OH U.S.A.
244 E3	Cosío Mex.
190 D7	Cosio di Arroscia Italy
183 M8	Coslada Spain
217 □2	Cosmolédo Atoll Aldabra Is Seychelles
87 G10	Cosmo Newbery Aboriginal Reserve W.A. Austr.
256 D5	Cosmópolis Brazil
160 B2	Cosne-Cours-sur-Loire France
160 B4	Cosne-d'Allier France
245 M8	Cosoleacaque Mex.
195 J7	Cosoleto Italy
260 E2	Cosquín Arg.
190 E4	Cossato Italy
177 I8	Cossebaude Ger.
191 J9	Cosse-le-Vivien France
192 B7	Cossoine Sardegna Italy
156 B8	Cosson r. France
190 B2	Cossonay Switz.
254 E3	Costa Brazil
184 A4	Costa Bela coastal area Port.
187 E11	Costa Blanca coastal area Spain
186 L5	Costa Brava coastal area Spain
191 N9	Costache Negri Romania
197 P5	Costache Negri Romania
193 K4	Costa de Caparica Port.
184 B4	Costa da Galé coastal area Port.
186 G6	Costa de Fora coastal area Spain
184 E6	Costa de la Luz coastal area Spain
187 E8	Costa del Azahar coastal area Spain
216 □3a	Costa del Silencio Tenerife Canary Is
185 I8	Costa del Sol coastal area Spain
242 □R11	Costa de Mosquitos coastal area Nic.
184 A3	Costa de Estoril coastal area Port.
186 J5	Costa Dorada coastal area Spain
184 A3	Costa do Sol coastal area Port.
261 G3	Costa Grande Arg.

252 B3	Costa Marques Brazil
192 D9	Costa Rei coastal area Sardegna Italy
256 C5	Costa Rica Brazil
246 A8	Costa Rica country Central America
242 F5	Costa Rica Mex.
192 D5	Costa Smeralda coastal area Sardegna Italy
216 □3c	Costa Teguise Lanzarote Canary Is
192 A9	Costa Verde coastal area Sardegna Italy
182 G2	Costa Verde coastal area Spain
190 I4	Costa Volpino Italy
177 K6	Coştei Romania
147 C6	Costelloe Ireland
	Costermansville Dem. Rep. Congo see Bukavu
151 I2	Costessey Norfolk, England U.K.
136 G6	Costeşti Moldova
197 M6	Costeşti Argeş Romania
197 P4	Costeşti Vaslui Romania
190 C1	Costigan Switz.
233 □Q3	Costigan ME U.S.A.
223 J3	Costigan Lake Sask. Can.
190 C6	Costigliole d'Asti Italy
186 C5	Costigliole Saluzzo Italy
197 L6	Coşuştea r. Romania
252 B3	Cotabambas Peru
92 E8	Cotabato Mindanao Phil.
161 G10	Cotacajes r. Bol.
250 D5	Cotagaita Bol.
190 C1	Cotahuasi Peru
190 C1	Cotahuasi r. Peru
257 C4	Cotaxé r. Brazil
245 K7	Cotaxtla Mex.
160 B2	Côte, Mount AK U.S.A.
236 F3	Coteau des Prairies slope SD U.S.A.
236 D1	Coteau du Missouri slope ND U.S.A.
236 E3	Coteau du Missouri slope SD U.S.A.
233 K4	Coteau Station Que. Can.
246 F4	Côtes, Baie des i. Haiti
156 G6	Côte Champenoise reg. France
163 A9	Côte d'Argent coastal area France
161 K9	Côte d'Azur airport France
161 K9	Côte d'Azur coastal area France
156 H7	Côte d'Ivoire country Africa
206 D5	Côte-d'Or dept France
156 I8	Côte-d'Or reg. France
160 F3	Côte Française de Somalis country Africa see Djibouti
254 D4	Coteṭipe Brazil
158 F3	Cotentin pen. France
158 F5	Côtes de Meuse ridge France
157 K6	Côtes de Moselle hills France
	Côtes-du-Nord dept France see Côtes-d'Armor
163 K10	Côte Vermeille coastal area France
150 D4	Cothi r. Wales U.K.
150 D4	Cothi r. Wales U.K.
192 D3	Cotiaeum Turkey see Kütahya
192 D3	Coti-Chiavari Corse France
186 F2	Cotiella mt. Spain
161 I9	Cotignac France
244 E6	Cotija Mex.
216 □3b	Cotillo Fuerteventura Canary Is
251 F4	Cotingo r. Brazil
136 H6	Cotiujeni Moldova
136 H6	Cotiujenii Mici Moldova
197 M6	Cotmeana r. Romania
96 H4	Cô Tô, Quân Đao is Vietnam
257 F3	Coto, Pointe pt Rodrigues I. Mauritius see Cotton, Pointe
162 D5	Coutras France
227 L6	Côte d'Or dept France

Cuacos de Yuste to Damasak
303

182 I8 Cuacos de Yuste Spain
259 C7 Cuadrada, Sierra hills Arg.
260 C4 Cuadro Berregas Arg.
182 I3 Cuadros Spain
245 I9 Cuajinicuilapa Mex.
209 C7 Cuale Angola
182 E5 Cualedro Spain
209 B9 Cuamato Angola
213 H2 Cuamba Moz.
209 D9 Cuando r. Angola/Zambia
209 C8 Cuando Cubango prov. Angola
209 C9 Cuangar Angola
209 C8 Cuango Cuando Cubango Angola
209 C7 Cuango Lunda Norte Angola
209 C6 Cuango Uíge Angola
209 C6 Cuango r. Angola alt. Kwango (Dem. Rep. Congo)
209 B7 Cuanza r. Angola
209 B7 Cuanza Norte prov. Angola
209 B7 Cuanza Sul prov. Angola
261 I2 Cuareim r. Uru.
261 I2 Cuaró Uru.
261 I2 Cuaro r. Uru.
186 D4 Cuarte de Huerva Spain
261 F3 Cuarto r. Arg.
209 C9 Cuatir r. Angola
Cuatretonda Spain see Quatretonda
242 H4 Cuatro Ciénegas Mex.
252 E4 Cuatro Ojos Bol.
260 E3 Cuatro Vientos Arg.
242 F3 Cuauhtémoc Chihuahua Mex.
244 D6 Cuauhtémoc Colima Mex.
244 D1 Cuauhtémoc Durango Mex.
244 C6 Cuautitlán Mex.
245 I7 Cuautla Mex.
245 H6 Cuautlán Izcalli Mex.
245 I7 Cuayuca Mex.
184 D4 Cuba Port.
226 D9 Cuba IL U.S.A.
239 K8 Cuba NM U.S.A.
232 G6 Cuba NY U.S.A.
232 B9 Cuba OH U.S.A.
246 C3 Cuba country West Indies
241 T10 Cubabi, Cerro mt. Mex.
251 E2 Cubagua, Isla i. Venez.
209 B8 Cubal Angola
209 B7 Cubal r. Angola
182 D4 Cubalhão Port.
209 D9 Cubango r. Angola/Namibia
250 C3 Cubara Col.
256 D5 Cubatão Brazil
186 G4 Cubells Spain
223 J4 Cub Hills Sask. Can.
182 H2 Cubia r. Spain
185 L6 Cubillas r. Spain
183 M4 Cubillo r. Spain
162 F5 Cubjac France
187 C7 Cubla Spain
183 N3 Cubo de Bureba Spain
183 P5 Cubo de la Solana Spain
136 H6 Cubolta r. Moldova
126 F3 Çubuk Turkey
243 N10 Cubulco Guat.
162 D6 Cubzac-les-Ponts France
186 C5 Cucalón Spain
259 B6 Cucao Chile
241 Q9 Cucapa, Sierra mts Mex.
191 N9 Cucco, Monte mt. Italy
192 C7 Cuccuru su Pirastru hill Sardegna Italy
245 J4 Cucharas Mex.
209 C8 Cuchi Angola
261 I3 Cuchilla de Peralta Uru.
258 G4 Cuchilla Grande hills Uru.
261 I3 Cuchilla Grande Inferior hills Uru.
260 E6 Cuchillo-Có Arg.
151 L5 Cuckfield West Sussex, England U.K.
151 M6 Cuckmere r. England U.K.
197 N4 Cucu, Vârful mt. Romania
250 E4 Cucuí Brazil
209 C7 Cucumbi Angola
161 G9 Cucuron France
242 D2 Cucurpe Mex.
250 B3 Cucurrupí Col.
250 C3 Cúcuta Col.
186 D5 Cucutas hill Spain
197 P5 Cudalbi Romania
247 □9 Cudarebe pt Aruba
114 F7 Cuddalore Tamil Nadu India
114 F5 Cuddapah Andhra Prad. India
85 H8 Cuddapan, Lake salt flat Qld Austr.
240 O6 Cuddeback Lake CA U.S.A.
234 F2 Cuddebackville NY U.S.A.
194 D8 Cuddia r. Sicilia Italy
149 L7 Cuddington Cheshire, England U.K.
128 H2 Cudi watercourse Turkey
128 G2 Cudi Dağı hill Turkey
182 H1 Cudillero Spain
163 D7 Cudos France
223 J4 Cudworth Sask. Can.
149 O6 Cudworth South Yorkshire, England U.K.
87 D9 Cue W.A. Austr.
209 C8 Cuebe r. Angola
209 D8 Cueio r. Angola
247 □1 Cuelebrita, Isla i. Puerto Rico
183 L6 Cuéllar Spain
209 C8 Cuemba Angola
250 B5 Cuenca Ecuador
92 C5 Cuenca Luzon Phil.
183 P8 Cuenca Spain
183 P9 Cuenca prov. Spain
183 P7 Cuenca, Serranía de mts Spain
183 M7 Cuenca Alta del Manzanares, Parque Regional de la park Spain
244 E7 Cuenca de Balsas basin Mex.
183 J4 Cuenca de Campos Spain
260 C6 Cuenca del Añelo reg. Arg.
242 H5 Cuencamé Mex.
244 F5 Cuerámaro Mex.
183 O5 Cuerda del Pozo, Embalse de la resr Spain
183 M7 Cuerda Larga ridge Spain
245 H7 Cuernavaca Mex.
237 G11 Cuero TX U.S.A.
161 I10 Cuers France
183 L9 Cuerva Spain
183 P7 Cuervo r. Spain
241 R9 Cuervos Mex.
246 F3 Cueto Cuba
245 J5 Cuetzalán Mex.
185 K6 Cuevas Altas hill Spain
185 K6 Cuevas Bajas Spain
185 P6 Cuevas de Almanzora Spain
185 P6 Cuevas de Almanzora, Embalse resr Spain
185 I7 Cuevas del Becerro Spain
185 N5 Cuevas del Campo Spain
183 M4 Cuevas de San Clemente Spain
186 C7 Cuevas Labradas Spain
252 E5 Cuevo Bol.
183 K4 Cueza r. Spain
151 L4 Cuffley Hertfordshire, England U.K.
158 I7 Cugand France
161 H10 Cuges-les-Pins France
197 L5 Cugir Romania
197 L5 Cugir r. Romania
192 B7 Cuglieri Sardegna Italy
163 G8 Cugnaux France
209 C6 Cugo r. Angola
158 H5 Cuguen France
253 F3 Cuiabá Brazil
253 F4 Cuiabá r. Brazil
245 K8 Cuicatlan Mex.
245 M8 Cuichapa Mex.
Cuihua Yunnan China see Daguan
Cuijiang Fujian China see Ninghua
164 I5 Cuijk Neth.
243 N10 Cuilapa Guat.
245 K9 Cuilapan Mex.
147 G4 Cuilcagh hill Ireland/U.K.
146 D8 Cuillin Hills Scotland U.K.
146 D8 Cuillin Sound sea chan. Scotland U.K.
209 C7 Cuilo Angola
209 B6 Cuilo-Futa Angola
209 B6 Cuilo Pombo Angola
100 F5 Cuiluan Heilong. China
209 B6 Cuimba Angola
160 G4 Cuiseaux France
156 F5 Cuise-la-Motte France
160 F3 Cuisery France
257 G3 Cuité r. Brazil
245 K7 Cuitláhuac Mex.
209 D9 Cuito r. Angola
209 C8 Cuito Cuanavale Angola
244 F6 Cuitzeo Mex.
244 F6 Cuitzeo, Laguna de l. Mex.
251 F5 Cuiuni r. Brazil
236 J6 Cuivre r. MO U.S.A.
245 K9 Cuixtla Mex.
92 C8 Cujangan i. Phil.
197 K6 Cujmir Romania
94 E2 Cukai Malaysia
198 B3 Çukë Albania
129 E6 Çukurbağ Turkey
127 K5 Çukurca Turkey
129 A5 Çukurçayır Turkey
199 L3 Çukurhisar Turkey
129 A6 Çukurköy Turkey
128 D2 Çukurova plat. Turkey
136 H6 Cula r. Moldova
107 O8 Culai Shan mt. Shandong China
162 I2 Culan France
146 J8 Culardoch hill Scotland U.K.
92 D6 Culasi Panay Phil.
238 L2 Culbertson MT U.S.A.
236 E5 Culbertson NE U.S.A.
146 H7 Culbokie Highland, Scotland U.K.
83 K6 Culcairn N.S.W. Austr.
177 M4 Culciu Romania
147 H2 Culdaff Ireland
146 K8 Culdrain Aberdeenshire, Scotland U.K.
247 □1 Culebra, Isla de i. Puerto Rico
182 H5 Culebra, Sierra de la mts Spain
252 A2 Culebras Peru
247 □1 Culebrinas r. Puerto Rico
164 H5 Culemborg Neth.
129 G7 Culfa Azer.
242 F5 Culiacán Mex.
92 B6 Culion Phil.
92 B6 Culion i. Phil.
148 B5 Culkey Northern Ireland U.K.
187 E7 Culla Spain
148 C8 Cullahill Ireland
185 N5 Cullar r. Spain
185 N5 Cúllar-Baza Spain
147 I4 Cullaville Northern Ireland U.K.
147 D4 Culleens Ireland
146 K7 Cullen Moray, Scotland U.K.
237 I9 Cullen LA U.S.A.
85 H1 Cullen Point Qld Austr.
187 E9 Cullera Spain
146 H7 Cullicudden Highland, Scotland U.K.
147 D5 Cullin Ireland
147 D5 Cullin, Lough l. Ireland
215 M1 Cullinan S. Africa
146 E10 Cullipool Argyll and Bute, Scotland U.K.
146 □N1 Cullivoe Shetland, Scotland U.K.
231 D8 Cullman AL U.S.A.
85 J7 Culloden Creek watercourse Qld Austr.
150 F6 Cullompton Devon, England U.K.
190 B3 Cully Switz.
147 J3 Cullybackey Northern Ireland U.K.
147 I4 Cullyhanna Northern Ireland U.K.
146 F6 Cul Mòr hill Scotland U.K.
147 H2 Culmore Northern Ireland U.K.
150 F6 Culmstock Devon, England U.K.
146 F7 Culnacraig Highland, Scotland U.K.
146 D7 Culnaknock Highland, Scotland U.K.
185 N7 Culo de Perro, Punta pt Spain
160 H5 Culoz France
232 H10 Culpeper VA U.S.A.
250 □ Culpepper, Isla i. Islas Galápagos Ecuador
146 H7 Culrain Highland, Scotland U.K.
146 □M2 Culswick Shetland, Scotland U.K.
146 I11 Culter Fell hill Scotland U.K.
146 L8 Cults Aberdeen, Scotland U.K.
254 B4 Culuene r. Brazil
226 H8 Culver IN U.S.A.
87 H12 Culver, Point W.A. Austr.
81 G9 Culverden South I. N.Z.
146 G12 Culzean Bay Scotland U.K.
254 D2 Cumã, Baía do inlet Brazil
129 E6 Cumaçay Turkey
251 E2 Cumaná Venez.
247 L8 Cumanacoa Venez.
199 L2 Cumaova Turkey
256 C3 Cumari Brazil
129 H4 Cumay Azer.
250 B4 Cumbal, Nevado de vol. Col.
232 C12 Cumberland KY U.S.A.
232 G9 Cumberland MD U.S.A.
232 D9 Cumberland OH U.S.A.
232 G11 Cumberland VA U.S.A.
226 B4 Cumberland WI U.S.A.
232 B12 Cumberland r. KY U.S.A.
Cumberland, Cape Vanuatu see Nahoï, Cap
230 E7 Cumberland, Lake KY U.S.A.
259 □ Cumberland Bay S. Georgia
234 E6 Cumberland County county NJ U.S.A.
234 A4 Cumberland County county PA U.S.A.
223 K4 Cumberland House Sask. Can.
85 L6 Cumberland Islands Qld Austr.
223 K4 Cumberland Lake Sask. Can.
232 B12 Cumberland Mountains KY/TN U.S.A.
221 L3 Cumberland Peninsula Nunavut Can.
231 E8 Cumberland Plateau KY/TN U.S.A.
226 E2 Cumberland Point MI U.S.A.
221 L3 Cumberland Sound sea chan. Nunavut Can.
146 I11 Cumbernauld North Lanarkshire, Scotland U.K.
183 K9 Cumbre Alta mt. Spain
259 C7 Cumbre Negro mt. Arg.
242 F3 Cumbres de Majalca, Parque Nacional nat. park Mex.
243 I5 Cumbres de Monterey, Parque Nacional nat. park Mex.
184 F4 Cumbres de San Bartolomé Spain
184 F4 Cumbres Mayores Spain
149 K4 Cumbria admin. div. England U.K.
114 F5 Cumbum Andhra Prad. India
184 C6 Cumeada Port.
190 C6 Cumiana Italy
182 E6 Cumieira Port.
251 G5 Cuminá Brazil
251 H5 Cuminapanema r. Brazil
146 L7 Cuminestown Aberdeenshire, Scotland U.K.
170 E4 Cumlosen Ger.
231 E8 Cumming GA U.S.A.
240 I2 Cummings CA U.S.A.
82 E6 Cummins S.A. Austr.
86 I5 Cummins Range hills W.A. Austr.
83 L5 Cumnock N.S.W. Austr.
146 H12 Cumnock East Ayrshire, Scotland U.K.
151 J4 Cumnor Oxfordshire, England U.K.
242 E2 Cumpas Mex.
260 B4 Cumpeo Chile
126 F5 Çumra Turkey
242 E3 Cumuripa Mex.
257 H2 Cumuruxatiba Brazil
247 □7 Cumuto Trin. and Tob.
251 I4 Cunani Brazil
250 C4 Cuñaré Col.
159 K7 Cunault France
260 A6 Cunco Chile
87 G11 Cundeelee Aboriginal Reserve W.A. Austr.
87 D11 Cunderdin W.A. Austr.
250 C3 Cundinamarca dept Col.
215 N4 Cundycleugh S. Africa
163 E6 Cunegès France
243 N10 Cunén Guat.
209 B9 Cunene prov. Angola
209 A9 Cunene r. Angola/Namibia alt. Kunene
190 D7 Cuneo Italy
190 D7 Cuneo prov. Italy
171 K8 Cunewalde Ger.
156 I7 Cunfin France
82 E5 Cungena S.A. Austr.
97 I8 Cung Sơn Vietnam
126 I4 Çüngüş Turkey
257 E5 Cunha Brazil
182 F7 Cunha Port.
209 C8 Cunhinga Angola
136 H6 Cunicea Moldova
186 I5 Cunit Spain
209 D8 Cunjamba Angola
160 D5 Cunlhat France
83 J3 Cunnamulla Qld Austr.
231 □2 Cunningham, Lake New Prov. Bahamas
146 □N2 Cunningsburgh Shetland, Scotland U.K.
252 B1 Cunshamayo Peru
182 C3 Cuntis Spain
197 J6 Cununa mt. Romania
247 □7 Cunupia Trin. and Tob.
190 D5 Cuorgnè Italy
146 J10 Cupar Fife, Scotland U.K.
251 H5 Cupari r. Brazil
177 L4 Cupari, Dealul hill Romania
136 G5 Cupcina Moldova
193 N3 Cupello Italy
250 B3 Cupica Col.
193 L1 Cupra Marittima Italy
191 O9 Cupramontana Italy
196 J7 Ćuprija Serbia
242 D5 Cupula, Pico mt. Mex.
163 H8 Cuq-Toulza France
244 D5 Cuquio Mex.
251 F6 Curaça Brazil
254 F4 Curaçá Brazil
250 D6 Curaçá r. Brazil
247 □10 Curaçao i. Neth. Antilles
260 B6 Curacautín Chile
260 B3 Curacaví Chile
260 E6 Curacó r. Arg.
209 B8 Curaculo Angola
252 C4 Curahuara de Carangas Bol.
261 F5 Cura Malal Arg.
261 F5 Cura Malal, Sierra de hills Arg.
258 B5 Curanilahue Chile
252 C2 Curanja r. Peru
261 F4 Curapaligüe Arg.
250 C5 Curaray r. Ecuador
260 B6 Curarrehue Chile
261 F4 Curarú Arg.
251 F3 Curatabaca Venez.
177 L5 Curățele Romania
260 B3 Curaumilla, Punta pt Chile
258 F3 Curaya r. Arg.
82 F4 Curdlawidny Lagoon salt flat S.A. Austr.
250 D5 Curé r. Col.
160 D1 Cure r. France
190 E4 Cureggio Italy
217 □1b Curepipe Mauritius
260 A4 Curepto Chile
160 E3 Curgy France
Curia Switz. see Chur
251 F2 Curiapo Venez.
260 B4 Curicó Chile
250 E5 Curicuriari, Serra hill Brazil
250 E5 Curieuriari r. Brazil
217 □2a Curieuse, Île i. Inner Islands Seychelles
254 D4 Curimata Brazil
195 K6 Curinga Italy
250 C4 Curiplaya Col.
256 C6 Curitiba Brazil
255 C8 Curitibanos Brazil
256 B6 Curiúva Brazil
83 M4 Curlewis N.S.W. Austr.
82 G4 Curnamona S.A. Austr.
209 A8 Curoca r. Angola
190 F5 Curone r. Italy
191 J2 Curon Venosta Italy
182 F5 Curopos Port.
83 M4 Currabubula N.S.W. Austr.
147 J8 Curracloe Ireland
147 I6 Curragh Ireland
147 F5 Curraghroe Ireland
147 E5 Curragh West Ireland
147 F8 Curraglass Ireland
184 □ Curral das Freiras Madeira
257 G1 Curral de Dentro Brazil
251 I5 Curralinho Brazil
82 E2 Curralulla watercourse S.A. Austr.
206 □ Curral Velho Cape Verde
227 K5 Curran MI U.S.A.
147 B9 Currane, Lough l. Ireland
241 Q3 Currant NV U.S.A.
83 J4 Curranyalpa N.S.W. Austr.
182 C3 Currás Spain
85 H8 Currawilla Qld Austr.
83 J3 Currawinya National Park Qld Austr.
246 E1 Current Eleuthera Bahamas
237 J7 Current r. MO U.S.A.
83 I8 Currie Tas. Austr.
241 R1 Currie NV U.S.A.
231 I7 Currituck NC U.S.A.
147 E5 Curry Ireland
150 G5 Curry Rivel Somerset, England U.K.
195 O3 Cursi Italy
177 L6 Curtea Romania
197 M5 Curtea de Argeș Romania
196 J4 Curtici Romania
87 G11 Curtin W.A. Austr.
85 N8 Curtis Channel Qld Austr.
83 K8 Curtis Group is Tas. Austr.
85 M7 Curtis Island Qld Austr.
77 I5 Curtis Island N.Z.
177 L4 Curtuișeni Romania
251 H5 Curuá Brazil
251 H6 Curuá r. Brazil
251 I4 Curuá, Ilha i. Brazil
254 B3 Curuaés r. Brazil
251 H5 Curuaí Brazil
251 H5 Curuapanema r. Brazil
251 H5 Curuá Una r. Brazil
254 D2 Curuçá Brazil
251 I5 Curumu Brazil
94 E6 Curup Sumatera Indon.
251 F5 Curupira Brazil
251 E4 Curupira, Serra mts Brazil/Venez.
253 E3 Cururú Bol.
253 F1 Cururu r. Brazil
254 D2 Cururupu Brazil
251 F3 Curutú, Cerro mt. Venez.
261 H1 Curuzú Cuatiá Arg.
257 E3 Curvelo Brazil
226 F3 Curwood, Mount hill MI U.S.A.
192 C2 Curza, Punta di pt Corse France
193 N5 Cusano Mutri Italy
252 C3 Cusco Peru
252 B3 Cusco dept Peru
147 J2 Cushendall Northern Ireland U.K.
147 J2 Cushendun Northern Ireland U.K.
148 C7 Cushina Ireland
237 G7 Cushing OK U.S.A.
190 I7 Cusna, Monte mt. Italy
162 F4 Cussac France
162 C5 Cussac-Fort-Médoc France
161 D7 Cussac-sur-Loire France
212 B2 Cussava Angola
160 C4 Cusset France
231 E9 Cusseta GA U.S.A.
160 E2 Cussy-les-Forges France
238 K3 Custer MT U.S.A.
236 D4 Custer SD U.S.A.
157 L6 Custines France
194 D7 Custonaci Sicilia Italy
209 C8 Cutato Angola
238 H2 Cut Bank MT U.S.A.
238 H2 Cut Bank Creek r. MT U.S.A.
212 B2 Cutenda Angola
231 E10 Cuthbert GA U.S.A.
84 D2 Cuthbertson Falls N.T. Austr.
191 J7 Cutigliano Italy
240 M5 Cutler CA U.S.A.
233 □R4 Cutler ME U.S.A.
231 G13 Cutler Ridge FL U.S.A.
194 H8 Cutò r. Sicilia Italy
237 J11 Cut Off LA U.S.A.
147 E6 Cutra, Lough l. Ireland
260 C6 Cutral-Co Arg.
195 L5 Cutro Italy
195 O3 Cutrofiano Italy
83 J3 Cuttaburra Creek r. Qld Austr.
117 J9 Cuttack Orissa India
192 B4 Cuttoli-Corticchiato Corse France
244 G7 Cutzamala r. Mex.
244 G7 Cutzamala de Pinzón Mex.
209 B8 Cuvelai Angola
208 B5 Cuvette admin. reg. Congo
208 B5 Cuvette Ouest admin. reg. Congo
87 B8 Cuvier, Cape W.A. Austr.
80 J3 Cuvier Island North I. N.Z.
227 R1 Cuvillier, Lac l. Que. Can.
163 I9 Cuxac-Cabardès France
161 B10 Cuxac-d'Aude France
129 J6 Çuxanlı Azer.
168 G3 Cuxhaven Ger.
129 J5 Çuxuryurd Azer.
252 C4 Cuya Chile
232 D7 Cuyahoga Falls OH U.S.A.
232 D7 Cuyahoga Valley National Park OH U.S.A.
240 M7 Cuyama CA U.S.A.
240 L7 Cuyama r. CA U.S.A.
92 C4 Cuyapo Luzon Phil.
92 C6 Cuyo Phil.
92 C6 Cuyo i. Phil.
92 C6 Cuyo East Passage Phil.
92 C6 Cuyo Islands Phil.
92 C6 Cuyo West Passage Phil.
251 G3 Cuyuni r. Guyana
Cuyutingni Nic. see Kuyu Tingni
244 C7 Cuyutlán Mex.
244 C7 Cuyutlán, Laguna lag. Mex.
162 H6 Cuzance France
Cuzco Cusco Peru see Cusco
252 A1 Cuzco San Martín Peru
185 J4 Cuzna r. Spain
163 F6 Cuzorn France
171 K9 Cvikov Czech Rep.
150 F4 Cwm Blaenau Gwent, Wales U.K.
150 E4 Cwmafan Neath Port Talbot, Wales U.K.
150 F3 Cwmbach Powys, Wales U.K.
150 F4 Cwmbrân Torfaen, Wales U.K.
150 E4 Cwmllynfell Neath Port Talbot, Wales U.K.
211 A5 Cyangugu Rwanda
174 C3 Cybinka Pol.
174 D2 Cybowo Pol.
170 K5 Cychry Pol.
Cyclades is Greece see Kyklades
175 L4 Cyców Pol.
Cydonia Kriti Greece see Chania
Cydweli Carmarthenshire, Wales U.K. see Kidwelly
Cydweli Wales U.K. see Kidwelly
83 K10 Cygnet Tas. Austr.
232 B7 Cygnet OH U.S.A.
Cymru admin. div. U.K. see Wales
150 E3 Cynghordy Carmarthenshire, Wales U.K.
150 D4 Cynin r. Wales U.K.
232 A10 Cynthiana KY U.S.A.
150 D4 Cynwyl Elfed Carmarthenshire, Wales U.K.
223 I5 Cypress Hills Sask. Can.
223 I5 Cypress Hills Interprovincial Park B.C. Can.
128 B3 Cyprus country Asia
202 D3 Cyrenaica reg. Libya
202 D1 Cyrene tourist site Libya
156 F2 Cysoing France
Cythera i. Greece see Kythira
150 D4 Cywyn r. Wales U.K.
174 E3 Czacz Pol.
174 G4 Czajków Pol.
174 E2 Czaplinek Pol.
223 I4 Czar Alta Can.
175 J5 Czarna Podkarpackie Pol.
175 K5 Czarna Podkarpackie Pol.
175 H4 Czarna r. Pol.
175 H5 Czarna r. Pol.
175 J5 Czarna r. Pol.
175 L2 Czarna Białostocka Pol.
174 F1 Czarna Dąbrówka Pol.
175 K6 Czarna Górna Pol.
175 L2 Czarna Hańcza r. Pol.
175 I5 Czarna Nida r. Pol.
174 G3 Czarna Struga r. Pol.
174 G2 Czarna Woda Pol.
175 H5 Czarnca Pol.
174 E2 Czarne Pol.
175 J2 Czarnia Pol.
174 E3 Czarnków Pol.
170 K5 Czarnów Pol.
174 G4 Czarnożyły Pol.
175 H6 Czarny Dunajec Pol.
177 I2 Czarny Dunajec r. Pol.
174 G4 Czastary Pol.
175 I6 Czchów Pol.
175 H6 Czechowice-Dziedzice Pol.
176 E2 Czech Republic country Europe
174 E2 Czechy Pol.
175 J4 Czekarzewice Pol.
175 K4 Czemierniki Pol.
174 E3 Czempiń Pol.
175 L3 Czeremcha Pol.
174 F4 Czermin Pol.
174 D4 Czerna Mała r. Pol.
174 D4 Czerna Wielka r. Pol.
174 F4 Czernica Pol.
174 E2 Czernica r. Pol.
175 I2 Czernice Borowe Pol.
174 F3 Czerniejewo Pol.
175 I4 Czerniewice Pol.
174 G3 Czernikowo Pol.
174 E4 Czernina Pol.
Czernowitz Ukr. see Chernivtsi
174 F2 Czersk Pol.
174 D3 Czerwieńsk Pol.
175 J3 Czerwin Pol.
175 I3 Czerwińsk nad Wisłą Pol.
174 G5 Czerwionka-Leszczyny Pol.
174 E3 Czerwonak Pol.
171 L8 Czerwona Woda Pol.
175 J3 Czerwonka Włościańska Pol.
175 H4 Czestków Pol.
175 H5 Częstochowa Pol.
174 F4 Czeszów Pol.
174 E2 Człopa Pol.
174 F2 Człuchów Pol.
174 F3 Czmoń Pol.
171 K8 Czorneboh hill Ger.
175 I6 Czorsztyn, Jezioro resr Pol.
175 I3 Czosnów Pol.
175 J6 Czudec Pol.
175 L3 Czyże Pol.
175 K3 Czyżew-Osada Pol.

D

96 G4 Đa, Sông r. Vietnam
169 E9 Daaden Ger.
107 S4 Da'an Jilin China
92 D6 Daanbantayan Phil.
164 K4 Daarle Neth.
111 D11 Daba Xizang China
128 D7 Ḍabāb, Jabal aḍ mt. Jordan
211 B7 Dabaga Tanz.
250 D2 Dabajuro Venez.
206 D4 Dabakala Côte d'Ivoire
107 P5 Daban Nei Mongol China
106 G8 Daban Shan mts China
108 D4 Dabao Sichuan China
177 I4 Dabas Hungary
108 G2 Daba Shan mts China
210 C1 Dabat Eth.
Dabba Sichuan China see Daocheng
250 B3 Dabeiba Col.
96 C6 Dabein Myanmar
170 E3 Dabel Ger.
116 D8 Dabhoi Gujarat India
114 C4 Dabhol Mahar. India
128 E7 Ḍab'ī, Wādī aḍ watercourse Jordan
174 D3 Dąbie Lubuskie Pol.
174 G3 Dąbie Wielkopolskie Pol.
174 C2 Dąbie, Jezioro l. Pol.
106 D7 Dabiegai Gansu China
109 J3 Dabie Shan mts China
143 M7 Dąbki Pol.
128 E9 Dabl, Wādī watercourse Saudi Arabia
157 N6 Dabo France
116 G7 Daboh Madh. Prad. India
206 C4 Dabola Guinea
206 D5 Dabou Côte d'Ivoire
206 E4 Daboya Ghana
107 K7 Dabqig Nei Mongol China
116 G7 Dabra Madh. Prad. India
138 J9 Dabraslawka Belarus
175 M3 Dabravolya Belarus
174 C3 Dąbroszyn Lubuskie Pol.
174 G3 Dąbroszyn Wielkopolskie Pol.
174 F3 Dąbrowa Kujawsko-Pomorskie Pol.
174 F5 Dąbrowa Opolskie Pol.
174 F5 Dąbrowa Opolskie Pol.
175 L2 Dąbrowa Białostocka Pol.
174 G3 Dąbrowa Biskupia Pol.
174 G2 Dąbrowa Chełmińska Pol.
175 H5 Dąbrowa Górnicza Pol.
175 I5 Dąbrowa Tarnowska Pol.
175 H3 Dąbrowice Pol.
174 D3 Dąbrówka Wielkopolska Pol.
175 I2 Dąbrówno Pol.
106 D8 Dabsan Qinghai China
111 L8 Dabsan Hu salt l. Qinghai China
109 K6 Dabu Guangdong China
Dabu Guangxi China see Liucheng
175 M3 Dabuchyn Belarus
197 M7 Dăbuleni Romania
Dacca Bangl. see Dhaka
173 K5 Dachau Ger.
173 K5 Dachauer Moos marsh Ger.
106 G7 Dachechang Nei Mongol China
107 P6 Dachengzi Liaoning China
114 F4 Dachepalle Andhra Prad. India
175 L5 Dachnów Pol.
169 J8 Dachrieden Ger.
173 J2 Dachsbach Ger.
179 I4 Dachstein Gruppe mts Austria
Dachuan Sichuan China see Dazhou
176 E2 Dačice Czech Rep.
227 R4 Dacre Ont. Can.
149 L4 Dacre Cumbria, England U.K.
177 H4 Dad Hungary
175 I2 Dadaj, Jezioro l. Pol.
78 □6 Dadale Sta Isabel Solomon Is
251 G4 Dadanawa Guyana
129 C6 Dadaş Turkey
128 F2 Dādāt Syria
126 F3 Daday Turkey
210 D1 Daddato Djibouti
231 F11 Dade City FL U.S.A.
231 E9 Dadeville AL U.S.A.
123 L7 Dadhar Pak.
122 I8 Dādkān Iran
Dadong Liaoning China see Donggang
163 H8 Dadou r. France
116 D9 Dadra Dadra India
Dadra Mahar. India see Achalpur
116 D9 Dadra and Nagar Haveli union terr. India
123 L8 Dadu Pak.
108 D4 Dadu He r. Sichuan China
Daedalus Reef Saudi Arabia see Abū al Kizān
Daegu S. Korea see Taegu
Daejŏn S. Korea see Taejŏn
92 D4 Daet Luzon Phil.
108 E5 Dafang Guizhou China
109 M2 Dafeng Jiangsu China
100 E7 Dafengman Jilin China
125 K4 Dafīr U.A.E.
117 N6 Dafla Hills India
114 D4 Daflapur Mahar. India
198 D5 Dafni Dytiki Ellas Greece
198 F2 Dafni Kentriki Makedonia Greece
198 B4 Dafnoudi, Akrotirio pt Kefallonia Greece
223 M4 Dafoe r. Man. Can.
208 C2 Dafra Chad
226 J3 Dafter MI U.S.A.
177 H4 Dág Hungary
116 E8 Dag Rajasthan India
199 L5 Dağ Turkey
210 D3 Daga Medo Eth.
206 B2 Dagana Senegal
183 N7 Daganzo de Arriba Spain
210 B2 Daga Post Sudan
203 G5 Dagash Sudan
93 E2 Dagasuli i. Maluku Indon.
106 H9 Dagcanglhamo Gansu China
129 G5 Dağ Cäyir Azer.
129 D5 Dağcı Turkey
138 K5 Dagda Latvia
199 J4 Dağdere Turkey
Dage Hebei China see Fengning
168 G1 Dagebüll Ger.
Dagenraad atoll Arch. des Tuamotu Fr. Polynesia see Manihi
129 I3 Dagestan, Respublika aut. rep. Rus. Fed.
Dagestanskaya A.S.S.R. aut. rep. Rus. Fed. see Dagestan, Respublika
129 J3 Dagestanskiye Ogni Rus. Fed.
129 I1 Dagestanskiy Zapovednik nature res. Rus. Fed.
Dagezhen Hebei China see Fengning
215 J8 Daggaboersnek S. Africa
81 A12 Dagg Sound inlet South I. N.Z.
Daghestan aut. rep. Rus. Fed. see Dagestan, Respublika
125 N4 Daghmar Oman
163 G6 Daglan France
129 H6 Dağlıq Qarabağ aut. reg. Azer.
111 J12 Daglung Xizang China
111 K11 Dagma Xizang China
108 A3 Dagmala Shan mts Xizang China
166 C5 Dagmersellen Luzern Switz.
190 D1 Dagmersellen Luzern Switz.
Dagö i. Estonia see Hiiumaa
129 A2 Dagomys Rus. Fed.
Dagon Myanmar see Yangôn
81 C11 Dagon mt. South I. N.Z.
206 E4 Dagonkadi Ghana
129 B5 Dağönü Turkey
128 B2 Dağpazarı Turkey
129 E5 Dağpınar Turkey
111 H11 Dagrag Zangbo r. Xizang China
108 B2 Dagtog Qinghai China
107 O7 Dagu Tianjin China
108 D5 Daguan Yunnan China
208 C2 Daguéla Chad
107 Q8 Dagu He r. China
100 F6 Daguokui Shan hill Heilong. China
92 C3 Dagupan Luzon Phil.
106 D8 Dagur Qinghai China
84 C4 Daguragu N.T. Austr.
84 C4 Daguragu Aboriginal Land res. N.T. Austr.
96 C5 Dagwin Myanmar
Dagxoi Sichuan China see Yidun
Dagxoi Sichuan China see Sowa
111 J12 Dagzê Xizang China
111 H11 Dagzê Co salt l. China
111 I12 Dagzhuka Xizang China
124 D5 Dahabān Saudi Arabia
222 E2 Dahadinni r. N.W.T. Can.
Dahalach, Isole is Eritrea see Dahlak Archipelago
Dahana des. Saudi Arabia see Ad Dahnā'
114 C3 Dahanu Mahar. India
Dahe Guangxi China see Ziyuan
106 F9 Daheba Qinghai China
100 F5 Daheiding Shan mt. China
107 L6 Dahei He r. China
106 C5 Dahei Shan mt. Xinjiang China
100 D7 Dahei Shan mts China
109 L6 Daheng Fujian China
Daheyan Xinjiang China see Turpan Zhan
100 H5 Dahezhen Heilong. China
124 E7 Dahīn, Ḩarrat ad lava field Saudi Arabia
107 O5 Da Hinggan Ling mts China
114 D4 Dahivadi Mahar. India
124 G5 Daḩl, Nafūd ad des. Saudi Arabia
203 I6 Dahlak Archipelago is Eritrea
203 I5 Dahlak Marine National Park Eritrea
125 H2 Daḩl al Furayy well Saudi Arabia
124 F5 Daḩlat Shabāb Saudi Arabia
169 C10 Dahlem Ger.
171 H8 Dahlen Ger.
168 K4 Dahlenburg Ger.
171 H8 Dahlener Heide reg. Ger.
171 E6 Dahlenwarsleben Ger.
195 □ Daħlet Qorrot b. Gozo Malta
125 H2 Daḩl Iftākh well Saudi Arabia
231 F8 Dahlonega GA U.S.A.
171 I5 Dahlwitz-Hoppegarten Ger.
124 G7 Dahm, Ramlat des. Saudi Arabia/Yemen
205 H2 Dahmani Tunisia
171 H7 Dahme Brandenburg Ger.
170 D2 Dahme Schleswig-Holstein Ger.
171 I6 Dahme r. Ger.
170 D2 Dahmeshöved hd Ger.
172 D3 Dahn Ger.
116 E8 Dahod Gujarat India
Dahomey country Africa see Benin
111 D9 Dahongliutan Aksai Chin
Dahra Senegal see Dara
168 K5 Dähre Ger.
108 G7 Dahua Guangxi China
127 K5 Dahūk Iraq
127 K5 Dahūk governorate Iraq
127 K5 Dahūk, Buḩayrat l. Iraq
125 J7 Ḑaḩyah, Wādī r. Yemen
93 F7 Dai i. Maluku Indon.
105 I4 Daibosatsu-rei mt. Japan
107 O7 Daicheng Hebei China
Daido r. N. Korea see Taedong-gang
105 L2 Daigo Japan
107 M6 Dai Hai l. China
78 □6 Dai Island Solomon Is
94 F5 Daik Indon.
140 N4 Daikanvik Sweden
96 C6 Daik-U Myanmar
97 I8 Đai Lanh, Mui pt Vietnam
Dail Bho Thuath Scotland U.K. see North Dell
116 H5 Dailekh Nepal
232 F10 Dailey WV U.S.A.
146 G12 Dailly South Ayrshire, Scotland U.K.
122 H5 Daim Iran
103 K10 Daimanji-san hill Japan
185 L2 Daimiel Spain
104 F2 Daimon Japan
105 H3 Daimon-tōge pass Japan
105 H5 Daimugen-zan mt. Japan
175 M1 Dainava Lith.
147 H6 Daingean Ireland
237 H9 Daingerfield TX U.S.A.
104 E3 Dainichiga-take vol. Japan
104 E3 Dainichi-gawa r. Japan
104 D3 Dainichi-zan mt. Japan
108 A2 Dainkog Sichuan China
85 J4 Daintree Qld Austr.
85 J4 Daintree National Park Qld Austr.
156 E3 Dainville France
157 K7 Dainville-Bertheléville France
104 E7 Daiō Japan
104 E7 Daiō-zaki pt Japan
246 F4 Daiquiri Cuba
261 G5 Daireaux Arg.
Dairen Liaoning China see Dalian
146 K10 Dairsie Fife, Scotland U.K.
235 F1 Dairyland NY U.S.A.
226 B3 Dairyland WI U.S.A.
103 K11 Dai-sen vol. Japan
103 K11 Daisen-Oki Kokuritsu-kōen nat. park Japan
102 T3 Daisetsu-zan Kokuritsu-kōen nat. park Japan
109 N3 Daishan Zhejiang China
104 C6 Daitō Ōsaka Japan
105 H6 Daitō Shizuoka Japan
105 K2 Daiya-gawa r. Japan
Daiyue Shanxi China see Shanyin
109 L6 Daiyun Shan mts China
246 H4 Dajabón Dom. Rep.
123 N7 Dajal Pak.
104 E5 Dajan Japan
84 G6 Dajarra Qld Austr.
Dajie Yunnan China see Jiangchuan
108 C3 Dajin Chuan r. Sichuan China
106 H8 Dajing Gansu China
106 D8 Da Juh Qinghai China
206 A3 Dakar Senegal
203 F5 Dakar el Arak well Sudan
128 A10 Dakhal, Wādī ad watercourse Egypt
203 F3 Dākhilah, Wāḩāt ad oasis Egypt
117 M8 Dakhin Shahbazpur Island Bangl.
Dakhla Western Sahara see Ad Dakhla
Dakhla Oasis Egypt see Dākhilah, Wāḩāt ad
204 A5 Dakhlet Nouâdhibou admin. reg. Maur.
129 B1 Dakhovskaya Rus. Fed.
207 G4 Dakingari Nigeria
107 K2 Dakituy Rus. Fed.
97 I8 Đâk Lăk, Cao Nguyên plat. Vietnam
115 M9 Dakoank Andaman & Nicobar Is India
138 L9 Dakol'ka r. Belarus
116 D8 Dakor Gujarat India
207 G3 Dakoro Niger
236 H4 Dakota City IA U.S.A.
236 G4 Dakota City NE U.S.A.
196 I8 Đakovica Kosovo Serbia
188 G3 Đakovo Croatia
100 E2 Daktuy Rus. Fed.
209 D7 Dala Angola
177 J5 Đala Vojvodina Serbia
78 □6 Dala Malaita Solomon Is
178 B5 Dalaas Austria
206 B4 Dalaba Guinea
206 B3 Dalaba Senegal
146 B8 Dalabrog Western Isles, Scotland U.K.
Dalad Qi Nei Mongol China see Shulinzhao
Dalai Jilin China see Da'an
106 G6 Dalain Hob Nei Mongol China
107 O5 Dalai Nur l. China
122 B4 Dālā Khānī, Kūh-e mt. Iran
122 D7 Dālakī Iran
122 D7 Dalaki, Rūd-e r. Iran
128 B10 Ḑalal, Jabal mt. Egypt
143 N1 Dalälven r. Sweden
199 J5 Dalama Turkey
107 M6 Dalamamiao Nei Mongol China
199 J6 Dalaman Turkey
199 J6 Dalaman r. Turkey
106 I5 Dalandzadgad Mongolia
92 C6 Dalanganem Islands Phil.
110 F6 Dalaoba Xinjiang China
Dalap-Uliga-Darrit Majuro Marshall Is see Delap-Uliga-Djarrit
143 K1 Dalarna county Sweden
141 L6 Dalarna reg. Sweden
95 I3 Dalat Sarawak Malaysia
97 I9 Đa Lat Vietnam
Dalatando Angola see N'dalatando
116 E8 Dalauda Madh. Prad. India
106 H5 Dalay Mongolia
123 K7 Dalbandin Pak.
146 I13 Dalbeattie Dumfries and Galloway, Scotland U.K.
85 K6 Dalbeg Qld Austr.
170 D3 Dalberg-Wendelstorf Ger.
226 A4 Dalbo MN U.S.A.
142 I3 Dalbosjön l. Sweden
85 M9 Dalby Qld Austr.
148 H5 Dalby Isle of Man
142 J6 Dalby Sweden
259 B6 Dalcahue Chile
142 B1 Dale Hordaland Norway
141 H6 Dale Sogn og Fjordane Norway
150 B4 Dale Pembrokeshire, Wales U.K.
232 H10 Dale City VA U.S.A.
229 I3 Dale Hollow Lake TN U.S.A.
169 B10 Daleiden Ger.
137 M8 Daleke Ukr.
164 K3 Dalen Neth.
179 N1 Dalešice, Vodní nádrž resr Czech Rep.
215 M2 Daleside S. Africa
175 I5 Daleszyce Pol.
96 A5 Dalet Myanmar
96 A4 Daletme Myanmar
231 E10 Daleville AL U.S.A.
234 D2 Daleville PA U.S.A.
141 M6 Dalfors Sweden
164 J3 Dalfsen Neth.
122 H8 Dalgān Iran
87 D9 Dalgaranger, Mount hill W.A. Austr.
83 L7 Dalgety N.S.W. Austr.
87 C8 Dalgety r. W.A. Austr.
146 J10 Dalgety Bay Fife, Scotland U.K.
151 N3 Dalham Suffolk, England U.K.
237 D7 Dalhart TX U.S.A.
225 H3 Dalhousie N.B. Can.
116 F3 Dalhousie Hima. Prad. India
220 F2 Dalhousie, Cape N.W.T. Can.
107 L9 Dali Shaanxi China
108 C6 Dali Yunnan China
128 B3 Dali Cyprus
107 Q7 Dalian Liaoning China
Daliang Guangdong China see Shunde
106 G8 Daliang Qinghai China
108 D4 Daliang Shan mts Sichuan China
107 Q7 Dalian Wan b. China
185 N7 Dalías Spain
185 N7 Dalías, Campo de reg. Spain
Daliburgh Western Isles, Scotland U.K. see Dalabrog
129 H6 Dälidağ mt. Azer.
107 L8 Dali He r. China
175 H4 Dalików Pol.
129 H5 Dälilär Azer.
129 H5 Dälimämmädli Azer.
107 R5 Dalin Nei Mongol China
Dalinghe Liaoning China see Linghai
107 Q6 Daling He r. China
101 E8 Dalizi Jilin China
188 G3 Dalj Croatia
146 J11 Dalkeith Midlothian, Scotland U.K.
117 K7 Dalkola W. Bengal India
85 N8 Dallarnil Qld Austr.
146 J7 Dallas Moray, Scotland U.K.
238 C4 Dallas OR U.S.A.
234 D2 Dallas PA U.S.A.
237 G9 Dallas TX U.S.A.
226 C9 Dallas City IL U.S.A.
234 B5 Dallastown PA U.S.A.
Dalles City OR U.S.A. see The Dalles
170 H5 Dallgow Ger.
116 H9 Dalli Chhattisgarh India
220 E4 Dall Island AK U.S.A.
210 D1 Dallol vol. Eth.
207 F3 Dallol Bosso watercourse Mali/Niger
125 K3 Dalmā i. U.A.E.
188 E3 Dalmacija reg. Croatia
261 F3 Dalmacio Vélez Sarsfield Arg.
146 G10 Dalmally Argyll and Bute, Scotland U.K.
177 H5 Dalmand Hungary
225 G2 Dalmas, Lac l. Que. Can.
Dalmatia reg. Croatia see Dalmacija
234 B3 Dalmatia PA U.S.A.
116 H6 Dalmau Uttar Prad. India
146 H12 Dalmellington East Ayrshire, Scotland U.K.
223 J4 Dalmeny Sask. Can.
117 K8 Dalmi Jharkhand India
190 H4 Dalmine Italy
146 H7 Dalnavie Highland, Scotland U.K.
100 I6 Dal'negorsk Rus. Fed.
100 H6 Dal'nerechensk Rus. Fed.
134 I5 Dal'neye Konstantinovo Rus. Fed.
134 G1 Dal'niye Zelentsy Rus. Fed.
Dalny Liaoning China see Dalian
206 D5 Daloa Côte d'Ivoire
85 M1 Daloloia Group is P.N.G.
108 F5 Dalou Shan mts China
171 G10 Dalovice Czech Rep.
124 G3 Dalqān well Saudi Arabia
146 G11 Dalry North Ayrshire, Scotland U.K.
146 G12 Dalrymple East Ayrshire, Scotland U.K.
85 K6 Dalrymple, Lake Qld Austr.
85 L6 Dalrymple, Mount Qld Austr.
138 F1 Dalsbruk Fin.
142 I3 Dals Långed Sweden
157 L5 Dalstein France
149 L4 Dalston Cumbria, England U.K.
117 J7 Daltenganj Jharkhand India
224 C3 Dalton Ont. Can.
215 O5 Dalton S. Africa
231 E8 Dalton GA U.S.A.
233 L6 Dalton MA U.S.A.
232 D8 Dalton OH U.S.A.
234 D1 Dalton PA U.S.A.
Daltonganj Jharkhand India see Daltenganj
263 I2 Dalton Iceberg Tongue Antarctica
149 K5 Dalton-in-Furness Cumbria, England U.K.
227 J1 Dalton Mills Ont. Can.
147 E8 Dalua r. Ireland
94 D4 Daludalu Sumatera Indon.
101 C9 Dalu Dao i. China
161 J8 Daluis France
108 C8 Daluo Yunnan China
109 I7 Daluo Shan mt. Guangdong China
92 C2 Dalupiri i. Phil.
140 □D1 Dalvík Iceland
87 D11 Dalwallinu W.A. Austr.
146 H9 Dalwhinnie Highland, Scotland U.K.
84 C2 Daly r. N.T. Austr.
199 J6 Dalyan Turkey
240 J4 Daly City CA U.S.A.
138 J6 Dalyokiya Belarus
84 C2 Daly River N.T. Austr.
84 C3 Daly River/Port Keats Aboriginal Land res. N.T. Austr.
147 F6 Dalystown Ireland
84 D4 Daly Waters N.T. Austr.
136 C2 Damachava Belarus
207 H3 Damagaram Takaya Niger
129 D4 Damal Turkey
209 F8 Damalisques de Leshwe nature res. Dem. Rep. Congo
116 D9 Daman Daman India
116 C9 Daman and Diu union terr. India
138 I9 Damanava Belarus
206 B2 Damâne well Maur.
122 D5 Dāmaneh Iran
203 F2 Damanhūr Egypt
223 J2 Damant Lake N.W.T. Can.
Damão Daman India see Daman
122 C4 Damaq Iran
107 N6 Damaqun Shan mts China
93 E2 Damar Sulawesi Indon.
93 F4 Damar i. Maluku Indon.
93 F7 Damar i. Maluku Indon.
129 C4 Damar Turkey
208 C3 Damara C.A.R.
212 C4 Damaraland reg. Namibia
233 □P4 Damariscotta Lake ME U.S.A.
94 □ Damar Laut, Pulau i. Sing.
Damas Syria see Dimashq
207 I3 Damasak Nigeria

Delbrück to Dillingham

305

169 G7 **Delbrück** Ger.
222 H4 **Delburne** *Alta* Can.
260 E4 **Del Campillo** Arg.
197 K9 **Delčevo** Macedonia
164 K4 **Delden** Neth.
111 H12 **Dêlêg** *Xizang* China
83 L7 **Delegate** *N.S.W.* Austr.
182 I9 **Deleitosa** Spain
179 O7 **Đelekovec** Croatia
208 D2 **Délembé** C.A.R.
190 C1 **Delémont** Switz.
141 P6 **Delet** *b.* Fin.
240 J2 **Delevan** *CA* U.S.A.
232 G6 **Delevan** *NY* U.S.A.
256 D4 **Delfinópolis** Brazil
164 F4 **Delft** Neth.
114 F8 **Delft Island** Sri Lanka
164 K2 **Delfzijl** Neth.
240 H1 **Delgada, Point** *CA* U.S.A.
245 K6 **Delgada, Punta** *pt* Mex.
211 D7 **Delgado, Cabo** *c.* Moz.
106 F3 **Delgermörön** Mongolia
106 G2 **Delger Mörön** *r.* Mongolia
203 F4 **Delgo** Sudan
234 F6 **Del Haven** *NJ* U.S.A.
227 N7 **Delhi** *Ont.* Can.
106 E8 **Delhi** *Qinghai* China
116 F5 **Delhi** *Delhi* India
111 C12 **Delhi** *admin. div.* India
240 L4 **Delhi** *CA* U.S.A.
239 L8 **Delhi** *CO* U.S.A.
237 J9 **Delhi** *LA* U.S.A.
233 K6 **Delhi** *NY* U.S.A.
106 E8 **Delhi Nongchang** *Qinghai* China
94 F8 **Deli** *i.* Indon.
127 K4 **Deli** *r.* Turkey
194 F9 **Delia** *Sicilia* Italy
194 D8 **Delia** *r. Sicilia* Italy
195 J7 **Delianuova** Italy
126 G4 **Delice** Turkey
126 G3 **Delice** *r.* Turkey
247 □2 **Delices** Dominica
251 H3 **Délices** Fr. Guiana
193 O5 **Deliceto** Italy
245 I2 **Delicias** Mex.
122 D4 **Delījān** Iran
199 H4 **Deliktaş** Turkey
222 F1 **Déljne** *N.W.T.* Can.
Delingha *Qinghai* China *see* **Delhi**
Delingha Nongchang *Qinghai* China *see* **Delhi Nongchang**
168 J3 **Delingsdorf** Ger.
223 J5 **Delisle** *Sask.* Can.
94 C3 **Delitua** *Sumatera* Indon.
171 F7 **Delitzsch** Ger.
178 H6 **Dellach** Austria
178 H6 **Dellach im Drautal** Austria
160 K1 **Delle** France
169 I7 **Delligsen** Ger.
190 I5 **Dello** Italy
236 G4 **Dell Rapids** *SD* U.S.A.
205 F1 **Dellys** Alg.
240 O9 **Del Mar** *CA* U.S.A.
233 J10 **Delmar** *DE* U.S.A.
215 M2 **Delmas** S. Africa
157 L6 **Delme** France
168 G4 **Delmenhorst** Ger.
234 F6 **Delmont** *NJ* U.S.A.
232 F8 **Delmont** *PA* U.S.A.
84 E7 **Delmore Downs** *N.T.* Austr.
188 E3 **Delnice** Croatia
239 K8 **Del Norte** *CO* U.S.A.
131 Q2 **De-Longa, Ostrova** *is* *Novosibirskiye O-va* Rus. Fed.
De Long Islands *Novosibirskiye O-va* Rus. Fed. *see* **De-Longa, Ostrova**
220 B3 **De Long Mountains** *AK* U.S.A.
De Long Strait Rus. Fed. *see* **Longa, Proliv**
83 K9 **Deloraine** *Tas.* Austr.
223 K5 **Deloraine** *Man.* Can.
149 M6 **Delph** *Greater Manchester, England* U.K.
198 D4 **Delphi** *tourist site* Greece
230 D5 **Delphi** *IN* U.S.A.
232 A8 **Delphos** *OH* U.S.A.
214 I4 **Delportshoop** S. Africa
231 G12 **Delray Beach** *FL* U.S.A.
242 D2 **Del Río** Mex.
237 E11 **Del Rio** *TX* U.S.A.
141 N6 **Delsbo** Sweden
207 G5 **Delta** *state* Nigeria
239 J7 **Delta** *CO* U.S.A.
232 A7 **Delta** *OH* U.S.A.
234 C5 **Delta** *PA* U.S.A.
241 T2 **Delta** *UT* U.S.A.
251 F2 **Delta Amacuro** *state* Venez.
85 H4 **Delta Downs** *Qld* Austr.
206 A3 **Delta du Saloum, Parc National du** *nat. park* Senegal
220 D3 **Delta Junction** *AK* U.S.A.
237 K11 **Delta National Wildlife Refuge** *nature res. LA* U.S.A.
233 J5 **Delta Reservoir** *NY* U.S.A.
186 G6 **Deltebre** Spain
231 G11 **Deltona** *FL* U.S.A.
83 M3 **Delungra** *N.S.W.* Austr.
164 L4 **De Lutte** Neth.
116 C9 **Delvada** *Gujarat* India
261 G4 **Del Valle** Arg.
168 H2 **Delve** Ger.
147 H5 **Delvin** Ireland
198 B3 **Delvinë** Albania
136 D5 **Delyatyn** Ukr.
120 F1 **Dema** *r.* Rus. Fed.
95 I8 **Demak** *Jawa* Indon.
183 N4 **Demanda, Sierra de la** *mts* Spain
157 J6 **Demange-aux-Eaux** France
Demavend *mt.* Iran *see* **Damāvand, Qolleh-ye**
209 D6 **Demba** Dem. Rep. Congo
209 B7 **Demba Chio** Angola
138 H6 **Dembava** Lith.
210 C2 **Dembech'a** Eth.
217 □3a **Dembeni** *Njazidja* Comoros
217 □3b **Dembeni** Mayotte
210 C2 **Dembī** Eth.
208 E3 **Dembia** C.A.R.
210 B2 **Dembī Dolo** Eth.
177 K3 **Demecser** Hungary
164 H4 **De Meern** Neth.
170 E3 **Demen** Ger.
165 F6 **Demer** *r.* Belgium
Demerara Guyana *see* **Georgetown**
264 F5 **Demerara Abyssal Plain** *sea feature* S. Atlantic Ocean
137 N9 **Demerdzhi** *mt.* Ukr.
139 O6 **Demidov** Rus. Fed.
139 X6 **Demidovo** Rus. Fed.
160 F3 **Demigny** France
239 K10 **Deming** *NM* U.S.A.
251 F5 **Demini** *r.* Brazil
251 F4 **Demini, Serras do** *mts* Brazil
199 J3 **Demirci** *Manisa* Turkey
129 A5 **Demirci** *Trabzon* Turkey
196 J9 **Demir Hisar** Macedonia
197 K9 **Demir Kapija** Macedonia
129 E5 **Demirkent** Turkey
199 J4 **Demirköprü Barajı** *resr* Turkey
197 P9 **Demirköy** Turkey
199 K4 **Demirler** *r.* Turkey
129 A5 **Demirözü** Turkey
126 F5 **Demirtaş** *Antalya* Turkey
199 K2 **Demirtaş** *Bursa* Turkey
215 I9 **Demistkraal** S. Africa
170 H3 **Demmin** Ger.
251 F6 **Democracia** Brazil
190 C7 **Demonte** Italy
231 D9 **Demopolis** *AL* U.S.A.
230 D5 **Demotte** *IN* U.S.A.
94 E7 **Dempo, Gunung** *vol.* Indon.
87 G12 **Dempster, Point** *W.A.* Austr.
116 G3 **Dêmqog** Jammu and Kashmir
163 E8 **Dému** France
137 P5 **Demuryne** Ukr.
139 P6 **Demyakhi** Rus. Fed.
Dem'yanovka Kazakh. *see* **Uzynkol'**
134 I3 **Dem'yanovo** Rus. Fed.
139 P4 **Demyansk** Rus. Fed.
136 J3 **Demydiv** Ukr.
136 E3 **Demydivka** Ukr.
136 J6 **Demydove** Ukr.
137 R3 **Demyno-Oleksandrivka** Ukr.
214 F6 **De Naawte** S. Africa
156 F3 **Denain** France
240 L4 **Denair** *CA* U.S.A.
203 I6 **Denakil** *reg.* Eritrea/Eth.
Denali *mt. AK* U.S.A. *see* **McKinley, Mount**
220 C3 **Denali National Park and Preserve** *AK* U.S.A.
210 D3 **Denan** Eth.
223 K4 **Denare Beach** *Sask.* Can.
163 I8 **Dénat** France
224 E4 **Denbigh** *Ont.* Can.
150 F1 **Denbigh** *Denbighshire, Wales* U.K.
150 F1 **Denbighshire** *admin. div. Wales* U.K.
164 F5 **Den Bommel** Neth.
Den Bosch Neth. *see* **'s-Hertogenbosch**
164 G2 **Den Burg** Neth.
149 N6 **Denby Dale** *West Yorkshire, England* U.K.
96 E6 **Den Chai** Thai.
95 G6 **Dendang** Indon.
206 D2 **Dendâra** Maur.
165 F7 **Denderleeuw** Belgium
165 F6 **Dendermonde** Belgium
164 H4 **Den Dolder** Neth.
165 F6 **Dendre** *r.* Belgium
164 H5 **Den Dungen** Neth.
164 L4 **Denekamp** Neth.
196 J8 **Đeneral Janković** *Kosovo* Serbia
222 E3 **Denetiah Provincial Park** *nat. park B.C.* Can.
134 L3 **Denezhkin Kamen', Gora** *mt.* Rus. Fed.
207 H3 **Dengas** Niger
207 G3 **Denge** Nigeria
92 □ **Denges Passage** Palau
107 M9 **Dengfeng** *Henan* China
111 G12 **Dênggar** *Xizang* China
207 H4 **Dengi** Nigeria
Dengjiabu *Jiangxi* China *see* **Yujiang**
Dêngka *Gansu* China *see* **Têwo**
Dêngkagoin *Gansu* China *see* **Têwo**
107 J6 **Dengkou** *Nei Mongol* China
111 L11 **Dêngqên** *Xizang* China
109 J7 **Dengta** *Guangdong* China
163 D9 **Denguin** France
208 D3 **Denguiro** C.A.R.
Dengxian *Henan* China *see* **Dengzhou**
111 E10 **Dêngzê** *Xizang* China
109 I2 **Dengzhou** *Henan* China
Dengzhou *Shandong* China *see* **Penglai**
Den Haag Neth. *see* **'s-Gravenhage**
87 B8 **Denham** *W.A.* Austr.
86 J3 **Denham** *r. W.A.* Austr.
164 K4 **Den Ham** Neth.
151 L4 **Denham** *Buckinghamshire, England* U.K.
246 □ **Denham, Mount** *hill* Jamaica
84 G4 **Denham Island** *Qld* Austr.
85 L7 **Denham Range** *mts Qld* Austr.
87 B8 **Denham Sound** *sea chan. W.A.* Austr.
164 G3 **Den Helder** Neth.
223 I4 **Denholm** *Sask.* Can.
146 K12 **Denholm** *Scottish Borders, Scotland* U.K.
149 N6 **Denholme** *West Yorkshire, England* U.K.
164 G2 **Den Hoorn** Neth.
187 F10 **Denia** Spain
82 D5 **Denial Bay** *S.A.* Austr.
82 D5 **Denial Bay** *b. S.A.* Austr.
83 J6 **Deniliquin** *N.S.W.* Austr.
117 P6 **Dening** *Arun. Prad.* India
Deninoo Kue *N.W.T.* Can. *see* **Fort Resolution**
238 E6 **Denio** *NV* U.S.A.
137 K1 **Deniskovichi** Rus. Fed.
236 H4 **Denison** *IA* U.S.A.
237 G9 **Denison** *TX* U.S.A.
263 J2 **Denison, Cape** Antarctica
86 J5 **Denison Plains** *W.A.* Austr.
120 I1 **Denisovka** Kazakh.
114 G9 **Deniyaya** Sri Lanka
199 K5 **Denizli** Turkey
199 K5 **Denizli** *prov.* Turkey
161 J8 **Denjuan, Sommet de** *mt.* France
172 G4 **Denkendorf** *Baden-Württemberg* Ger.
173 K4 **Denkendorf** *Bayern* Ger.
172 F5 **Denkingen** *Baden-Württemberg* Ger.
172 G6 **Denkingen** *Baden-Württemberg* Ger.
173 J6 **Denklingen** Ger.
169 K6 **Denkte** Ger.
83 M5 **Denman** *N.S.W.* Austr.
263 G2 **Denman Glacier** Antarctica
87 D13 **Denmark** *W.A.* Austr.
142 G5 **Denmark** *country* Europe
226 G5 **Denmark** *WI* U.S.A.
Denmark Fjord *inlet* Greenland *see* **Danmark Fjord**
221 P3 **Denmark Strait** Greenland/Iceland
151 J6 **Denmead** *Hampshire, England* U.K.
247 □3 **Dennery** St Lucia
171 H7 **Dennewitz** Ger.
215 N1 **Dennilton** S. Africa
151 O3 **Dennington** *Suffolk, England* U.K.
86 J6 **Dennis, Lake** *salt flat W.A.* Austr.
232 D8 **Dennison** *OH* U.S.A.
234 F6 **Dennisville** *NJ* U.S.A.
146 I10 **Denny** *Falkirk, Scotland* U.K.
164 H3 **Den Oever** Neth.
121 L8 **Denov** Uzbek.
Denow Uzbek. *see* **Denov**
95 K9 **Denpasar** *Bali* Indon.
93 B5 **Densongi** *Sulawesi* Indon.
170 H4 **Densow** Ger.
190 D3 **Dent Blanche** *mt.* Switz.
161 E8 **Dent de Rez** *hill* France
165 D7 **Dentergem** Belgium
173 I3 **Dentlein am Forst** Ger.
149 M7 **Denton** *Greater Manchester, England* U.K.
234 D7 **Denton** *MD* U.S.A.
237 G9 **Denton** *TX* U.S.A.
161 J6 **Dent Parrachée** *mt.* France
87 C13 **D'Entrecasteaux, Point** *W.A.* Austr.
77 G3 **D'Entrecasteaux, Récifs** *rf* New Caledonia
91 L8 **D'Entrecasteaux Islands** P.N.G.
87 C13 **D'Entrecasteaux National Park** *W.A.* Austr.
190 B3 **Dents du Midi** *mt.* Switz.
151 M2 **Denver** *Norfolk, England* U.K.
238 L7 **Denver** *CO* U.S.A.
234 C4 **Denver** *PA* U.S.A.
224 E2 **Denys** *r. Que.* Can.
136 I2 **Denysovychi** Ukr.
172 D5 **Denzlingen** Ger.
117 J7 **Deo** *Bihar* India
116 F5 **Deoband** *Uttar Prad.* India
115 H3 **Deobhog** *Chhattisgarh* India
234 B4 **Deodate** *PA* U.S.A.
117 I7 **Deogaon** *Uttar Prad.* India
116 G9 **Deogarh** *Madh. Prad.* India
117 J9 **Deogarh** *Orissa* India
116 D7 **Deogarh** *Rajasthan* India
116 G7 **Deogarh** *Uttar Prad.* India
116 I8 **Deogarh** *mt. Madh. Prad.* India
117 K7 **Deoghar** *Jharkhand* India
116 G9 **Deoli** *Mahar.* India
117 K8 **Deoli** *Orissa* India
116 E7 **Deolia** *Rajasthan* India
162 H2 **Déols** France
116 G8 **Deori** *Madh. Prad.* India
117 I6 **Deoria** *Uttar Prad.* India
116 E2 **Deosai, Plains of** Jammu and Kashmir
116 I8 **Deosil** *Chhattisgarh* India
117 M6 **Deothang** Bhutan
100 E2 **Dep** *r.* Rus. Fed.
116 E8 **Depalpur** *Madh. Prad.* India
165 C6 **De Panne** Belgium
225 H2 **De Pas, Rivière** *r. Que.* Can.
226 F5 **De Pere** *WI* U.S.A.
232 G6 **Depew** *NY* U.S.A.
233 J6 **Deposit** *NY* U.S.A.
227 R2 **Depot-Forbes** *Que.* Can.
227 Q3 **Depot-Rowanton** *Que.* Can.
111 D9 **Depsang Point** *hill* Aksai Chin
226 E8 **Depue** *IL* U.S.A.
131 O3 **Deputatskiy** Rus. Fed.
111 J11 **Dêqên** *Xizang* China
111 J12 **Dêqên** *Xizang* China
Dêqên *Xizang* China *see* **Dagzê**
108 B4 **Dêqên** *Yunnan* China
109 H7 **Deqing** *Guangdong* China
109 M3 **Deqing** *Zhejiang* China
237 H8 **De Queen** *AR* U.S.A.
237 I10 **De Quincy** *LA* U.S.A.
156 I6 **Der, Lac du** *l.* France
210 C2 **Dera** Eth.
116 F4 **Dera** *Hima. Prad.* India
123 M7 **Dera Bugti** Pak.
123 N6 **Dera Ghazi Khan** Pak.
203 G4 **Deraheib** *reg.* Sudan
123 N6 **Dera Ismail Khan** Pak.
123 N6 **Derajat** *reg.* Pak.
263 C2 **Deram, Mount** Antarctica
123 N7 **Derawar Fort** Pak.
136 F3 **Derazhne** Ukr.
136 G4 **Derazhnya** Ukr.
171 E6 **Derben** Ger.
129 J3 **Derbent** Rus. Fed.
199 L2 **Derbent** *Kocaeli* Turkey
199 J4 **Derbent** *Manisa* Turkey
199 K4 **Derbent** *Uşak* Turkey
Derbent Uzbek. *see* **Darband**
Derbesiye Turkey *see* **Şenyurt**
100 B3 **Derbur** *Nei Mongol* China
83 K9 **Derby** *Tas.* Austr.
86 G4 **Derby** *W.A.* Austr.
215 L1 **Derby** S. Africa
151 J2 **Derby** *Derby, England* U.K.
151 J2 **Derby** *admin. div. England* U.K.
235 I2 **Derby** *CT* U.S.A.
237 G7 **Derby** *KS* U.S.A.
233 M3 **Derby Line** *VT* U.S.A.
149 N7 **Derbyshire** *admin. div. England* U.K.
129 C5 **Derebaşı** Turkey
177 K4 **Derecske** Hungary
151 N2 **Dereham** *Norfolk, England* U.K.
128 A1 **Dereiçi** Turkey
177 J5 **Derekegyház** Hungary
128 A2 **Dereköy** *Antalya* Turkey
199 K5 **Dereköy** *Denizli* Turkey
199 K3 **Dereköy** *Kütahya* Turkey
169 K7 **Derenburg** Ger.
169 H7 **Derental** Ger.
202 D6 **Déréssa** Chad
139 P2 **Dereva** Rus. Fed.
137 O5 **Derezuvate** Ukr.
147 H3 **Derg** *r.* Ireland/U.K.
147 G3 **Derg, Lough** *l.* Ireland
147 F7 **Derg, Lough** *l.* Ireland
120 C2 **Dergachi** Rus. Fed.
Dergachi Ukr. *see* **Derhachi**
82 H7 **Dergholm State Park** *nature res. Vic.* Austr.
137 P3 **Derhachi** Ukr.
116 G7 **Deri** *Uttar Prad.* India
237 I10 **De Ridder** *LA* U.S.A.
164 G3 **De Rijp** Neth.
127 J5 **Derik** Turkey
129 B6 **Derinçay** Turkey
129 B6 **Derindere** Turkey
126 G4 **Derinkuyu** Turkey
137 M5 **Deriyivka** Ukr.
210 D4 **Derkali** *well* Kenya
137 S5 **Derkul** *r.* Rus. Fed./Ukr.
169 J9 **Dermbach** Ger.
120 J5 **Dermentobe** Kazakh.
Derna Libya *see* **Darnah**
177 L4 **Derna** Romania
212 B5 **Dernberg, Cape** Namibia
129 B5 **Dernekpazarı** Turkey
136 E3 **Derno** Ukr.
108 B4 **Dêrong** *Sichuan* China
158 G3 **Déroute, Passage de la** *str.* Channel Is/France
120 C9 **Derow** Iran
147 H5 **Derravaragh, Lough** *l.* Ireland
213 H3 **Derre** Moz.
147 D4 **Derreen** Ireland
147 C9 **Derreendaragh** Ireland
147 D9 **Derreeny Bridge** Ireland
147 F4 **Derry** Ireland
147 I7 **Derry** *r.* Ireland
Derry *Northern Ireland* U.K. *see* **Londonderry**
233 N6 **Derry** *NH* U.S.A.
147 F2 **Derrybeg** Ireland
147 E6 **Derrybrien** Ireland
147 D6 **Derryerglinna** Ireland
147 G4 **Derrygonnelly** *Northern Ireland* U.K.
147 F7 **Derrygoolin** Ireland
147 C6 **Derrylea** Ireland
148 B5 **Derrylin** *Northern Ireland* U.K.
147 G4 **Derrynacreeve** Ireland
147 D9 **Derrynasaggart Mountains** *hills* Ireland
148 C5 **Derrynawilt** *Northern Ireland* U.K.
147 C6 **Derryrush** Ireland
148 E5 **Derrytrasna** *Northern Ireland* U.K.
147 F3 **Derryveagh Mountains** *hills* Ireland
197 O3 **Dersca** Romania
151 N2 **Dersingham** *Norfolk, England* U.K.
107 M5 **Derst** *Nei Mongol* China
106 G6 **Derstei** *Nei Mongol* China
168 D5 **Dersum** Ger.
111 D10 **Dêrub** *Xizang* China
203 H5 **Derudeb** Sudan
214 G9 **De Rust** S. Africa
193 I2 **Deruta** Italy
146 D9 **Dervaig** *Argyll and Bute, Scotland* U.K.
158 H6 **Derval** France
198 D4 **Derveni** Greece
188 F3 **Derventa** Bos.-Herz.
190 G3 **Dervio** Italy
83 K10 **Derwent** *r. Tas.* Austr.
151 J2 **Derwent** *r. Derbyshire, England* U.K.
149 P6 **Derwent** *r. England* U.K.
149 N7 **Derwent Reservoir** *Derbyshire, England* U.K.
149 N4 **Derwent Reservoir** *Durham/Northumberland, England* U.K.
149 K4 **Derwent Water** *l. England* U.K.
137 O1 **Deryugino** Rus. Fed.
139 R5 **Derza** *r.* Rus. Fed.
120 E1 **Derzhavino** Rus. Fed.
121 L2 **Derzhavinsk** Kazakh.
Derzhavinskiy Kazakh. *see* **Derzhavinsk**
197 L7 **Desa** Romania
260 D3 **Desaguadero** Arg.
260 D4 **Desaguadero** *r.* Arg.
252 C4 **Desaguadero** *r.* Bol.
260 C4 **Desague, Cerro** *mt.* Arg.
260 D1 **Desagües de los Colorados** *marsh* Arg.
161 F7 **Désaignes** France
190 E5 **Desana** Italy
79 □9 **Désappointement, Îles du** *is* *Arch. des Tuamotu* Fr. Polynesia
237 J8 **Des Arc** *AR* U.S.A.
240 O2 **Desatoya Mountains** *NV* U.S.A.
227 K3 **Desbarats** *Ont.* Can.
151 K3 **Desborough** *Northamptonshire, England* U.K.
260 B4 **Descabezado, Volcán** *vol.* Chile
253 F4 **Descalvado** *Mato Grosso* Brazil
256 D4 **Descalvado** *São Paulo* Brazil
182 H8 **Descargamaría** Spain
162 F2 **Descartes** France
223 K4 **Deschambault Lake** *Sask.* Can.
223 K4 **Deschambault Lake** *l. Sask.* Can.
238 D4 **Deschutes** *r. OR* U.S.A.
257 H2 **Descombrimento, Parque Nacional do** *nat. park* Brazil
210 C2 **Desē** Eth.
216 □3d **Deseada** *vol. La Palma* Canary Is
252 C5 **Deseada** Chile
259 D7 **Deseado** Arg.
259 D7 **Deseado** *r.* Arg.
177 G5 **Deseda-tározó** *l.* Hungary
246 B2 **Desembarco del Granma National Park** *tourist site* Cuba
242 C2 **Desemboque** Mex.
259 D8 **Desengaño, Punta** *pt* Arg.
191 J5 **Desenzano del Garda** Italy
241 T2 **Deseret** *UT* U.S.A.
241 T1 **Deseret Peak** *UT* U.S.A.
241 T1 **Deseret Peak Wilderness** *nature res. UT* U.S.A.
227 Q5 **Deseronto** *Ont.* Can.
227 R3 **Désert, Lac** *l. Que.* Can.
184 □ **Deserta Grande** *i.* Madeira
184 □ **Desertas, Ilhas** *is* Madeira
123 M7 **Desert Canal** Pak.
241 Q8 **Desert Center** *CA* U.S.A.
241 P8 **Desert Hot Springs** *CA* U.S.A.
160 B4 **Désertines** France
239 G8 **Desert Lake** *NV* U.S.A.
148 D4 **Desertmartin** *Northern Ireland* U.K.
241 Q5 **Desert National Wildlife Refuge** *nature res. NV* U.S.A.
241 U5 **Desert View** *AZ* U.S.A.
185 M4 **Desesperada** *mt.* Spain
161 C6 **Desges** France
247 □2 **Deshaies** *i.* Guadeloupe
232 B7 **Deshler** *OH* U.S.A.
116 D6 **Deshnok** *Rajasthan* India
260 D2 **Desiderio Tello** Arg.
187 F7 **Desierto** *hill* Spain
242 B3 **Desierto Central de Baja California, Parque Natural del** *nature res.* Mex.
190 G4 **Desio** Italy
198 C3 **Deskati** Greece
179 I7 **Deskle** Slovenia
236 G3 **De Smet** *SD* U.S.A.
236 I5 **Des Moines** *IA* U.S.A.
237 D7 **Des Moines** *NM* U.S.A.
228 H2 **Des Moines** *r. IA* U.S.A.
136 H4 **Desna** *r.* Rus. Fed./Ukr.
137 J3 **Desna** *r.* Rus. Fed./Ukr.
136 J3 **Desna** Ukr.
197 L7 **Desnățui** *r.* Romania
139 Q7 **Desnogorsk** Rus. Fed.
139 Q7 **Desnogorskoye Vodokhranilishche** *resr* Rus. Fed.
259 C7 **Desnudo, Cerro** *mt.* Arg.
259 B9 **Desolación, Isla** *i.* Chile
92 E6 **Desolation Point** Phil.
240 L3 **Desolation Valley Wilderness** *nature res. CA* U.S.A.
226 C6 **DeSoto** *WI* U.S.A.
215 J9 **Despatch** S. Africa
106 C1 **Despen** Rus. Fed.
260 E2 **Despeñaderos** Arg.
226 G7 **Des Plaines** *IL* U.S.A.
196 J6 **Despotovac** Serbia
217 □2 **Desroches, Île** *i.* Seychelles
171 F7 **Dessau** Ger.
165 H6 **Dessel** Belgium
160 J2 **Dessoubre** *r.* France
Dessye Eth. *see* **Desē**
164 J4 **De Steeg** Neth.
165 E6 **Destelbergen** Belgium
227 P1 **Destor** *Que.* Can.
82 F6 **D'Estrees Bay** *S.A.* Austr.
182 H4 **Destriana** Spain
222 B2 **Destruction Bay** *Y.T.* Can.
192 C7 **Desulo** *Sardegna* Italy
252 A6 **Desventurados, Islas de los** *is* S. Pacific Ocean
156 C2 **Desvres** France
174 D3 **Deszczno** Pol.
177 J5 **Deszk** Hungary
196 J5 **Deta** Romania
222 H2 **Detah** *N.W.T.* Can.
139 T7 **Detchino** Rus. Fed.
213 E3 **Dete** Zimbabwe
168 E4 **Detern** Ger.
198 A2 **Deti Jon** *b.* Albania/Greece
196 I7 **Đetinja** *r.* Serbia
177 J4 **Detk** Hungary
177 G6 **Detkovac** Croatia
169 G7 **Detmold** Ger.
169 G7 **Detmold** *admin. reg.* Ger.
226 H4 **Detour, Point** *MI* U.S.A.
227 K4 **De Tour Village** *MI* U.S.A.
241 R5 **Detrital Wash** *watercourse AZ* U.S.A.
227 K7 **Detroit** *MI* U.S.A.
227 K8 **Detroit Beach** *MI* U.S.A.
236 H2 **Detroit Lakes** *MN* U.S.A.
Dett Zimbabwe *see* **Dete**
173 I2 **Dettelbach** Ger.
172 G4 **Dettingen an der Erms** Ger.
173 I5 **Dettingen an der Iller** Ger.
170 G2 **Dettmannsdorf** Ger.
169 K6 **Dettum** Ger.
157 N6 **Dettwiller** France
97 G7 **Det Udom** Thai.
177 I3 **Detva** Slovakia
83 L6 **Deua National Park** *N.S.W.* Austr.
171 F8 **Deuben** Ger.
156 E2 **Deûle, Canal de la** *r.* France
169 J8 **Deuna** Ger.
165 I6 **Deurne** Neth.
165 J8 **Deutsch-Belgischer Naturpark** *nature res.* Belgium
168 J4 **Deutsch Evern** Ger.
179 L5 **Deutschfeistritz** Austria
179 M6 **Deutsch Goritz** Austria
179 J6 **Deutsch-Griffen** Austria
170 G5 **Deutschhof** Ger.
179 N5 **Deutsch Kaltenbrunn** Austria
179 O4 **Deutschkreutz** Austria
Deutschland *country* Europe *see* **Germany**
179 L6 **Deutschlandsberg** Austria
169 B11 **Deutsch-Luxemburgischer Naturpark** *nature res.* Ger.
171 H9 **Deutschneudorf** Ger.
179 O3 **Deutsch-Wagram** Austria
171 F8 **Deutzen** Ger.
227 P3 **Deux-Rivières** *Ont.* Can.
159 K8 **Deux-Sèvres** *dept* France
197 K5 **Deva** Romania
183 K2 **Deva** *r.* Spain
Deva *Cheshire, England* U.K. *see* **Chester**
114 E4 **Devadurga** *Karnataka* India
114 F8 **Devakottai** *Tamil Nadu* India
237 J8 **De Valls Bluff** *AR* U.S.A.
Devana *Aberdeen, Scotland* U.K. *see* **Aberdeen**
114 E6 **Devanhalli** *Karnataka* India
114 F4 **Devarkonda** *Andhra Prad.* India
177 J4 **Dévaványa** Hungary
177 J4 **Dévaványai** *park* Hungary
Deve Bair *pass* Macedonia *see* **Velbŭzhdki Prokhod**
176 G4 **Devecser** Hungary
126 G4 **Develi** Turkey
164 J4 **Deventer** Neth.
190 E3 **Devero** *r.* Italy
146 K7 **Deveron** *r. Scotland* U.K.
197 K6 **Devesel** Romania
129 E6 **Devetaş** Turkey
176 E2 **Devét Skal** *hill* Czech Rep.
116 D8 **Devgadh Bariya** *Gujarat* India
114 C4 **Devgarh** *Mahar.* India
Devghar *Jharkhand* India *see* **Deoghar**
116 C6 **Devikot** *Rajasthan* India
156 I4 **Deville** France
81 G7 **Devil River Peak** *South I.* N.Z.
237 E11 **Devils** *r. TX* U.S.A.
81 H8 **Devil's Backbone** *mt. South I.* N.Z.
147 G7 **Devil's Bit Mountain** *hill* Ireland
150 E3 **Devil's Bridge** *Ceredigion, Wales* U.K.
240 M3 **Devil's Gate** *pass CA* U.S.A.
226 D2 **Devil's Island** *WI* U.S.A.
236 F1 **Devil's Lake** *ND* U.S.A.
237 E11 **Devil's Lake** *l. TX* U.S.A.
220 E4 **Devil's Paw** *mt. AK* U.S.A.
240 M4 **Devil's Peak** *CA* U.S.A.
246 F1 **Devil's Point** *Cat I.* Bahamas
216 □2a **Devil's Riding School** *vol. crater Ascension* S. Atlantic Ocean
222 C3 **Devil's Thumb** *mt.* Can./U.S.A.
197 M9 **Devin** Bulg.
237 F11 **Devine** *TX* U.S.A.
137 R2 **Devitsa** *r.* Rus. Fed.
151 I5 **Devizes** *Wiltshire, England* U.K.
116 E7 **Devli** *Rajasthan* India
226 A1 **Devlin** *Ont.* Can.
197 P7 **Devnya** Bulg.
247 □3 **De Volet Point** St Vincent
196 H10 **Devoll** *r.* Albania
161 H7 **Dévoluy** *mts* France
227 K2 **Devon** *Ont.* Can.
215 M2 **Devon** S. Africa
150 E6 **Devon** *admin. div. England* U.K.
149 P7 **Devon** *r. England* U.K.
146 I10 **Devon** *r. Scotland* U.K.
221 I2 **Devon Island** *Nunavut* Can.
83 K9 **Devonport** *Tas.* Austr.
240 O7 **Devore** *CA* U.S.A.
261 F2 **Devoto** Arg.
126 E3 **Devrek** Turkey
135 F8 **Devrekâni** Turkey
126 G3 **Devrez** *r.* Turkey
114 C4 **Devrukh** *Mahar.* India
94 A3 **Dewa, Tanjung** *pt* Indon.
95 M7 **Dewakang Besar** *i.* Indon.
117 L7 **Dewanganj** Bangl.
116 F8 **Dewas** *Madh. Prad.* India
164 J3 **De Weerribben, Nationaal Park** *nat. park* Neth.
210 D2 **Dewelē** Eth.
215 K5 **Dewetsdorp** S. Africa
247 □1 **Dewey** Puerto Rico
164 J3 **De Wijk** Neth.
237 J8 **De Witt** *AR* U.S.A.
236 J5 **De Witt** *IA* U.S.A.
233 I5 **DeWitt** *NY* U.S.A.
149 N6 **Dewsbury** *West Yorkshire, England* U.K.
109 K4 **Dexing** *Jiangxi* China
111 L12 **Dêxing** *Xizang* China
233 □P3 **Dexter** *ME* U.S.A.
227 K7 **Dexter** *MI* U.S.A.
226 B6 **Dexter** *MN* U.S.A.
237 K7 **Dexter** *MO* U.S.A.
239 L10 **Dexter** *NM* U.S.A.
233 I4 **Dexter** *NY* U.S.A.
226 D5 **Dexterville** *WI* U.S.A.
108 E3 **Deyang** *Sichuan* China
82 C3 **Dey-Dey Lake** *salt flat S.A.* Austr.
122 G5 **Deyhuk** Iran
137 N3 **Deykalivka** Ukr.
122 C3 **Deylaman** Iran
143 R7 **Deyma** *r.* Rus. Fed.
Deynau Turkm. *see* **Galkynyş**
91 I8 **Deyong, Tanjung** *pt Papua* Indon.
122 C6 **Dez** *r.* Iran
122 C5 **Dez, Sadd-e** *resr* Iran
183 P6 **Deza** Spain
182 D3 **Deza** *r.* Spain
222 B2 **Dezadeash** *Y.T.* Can.
222 B2 **Dezadeash Lake** *Y.T.* Can.
122 C5 **Dezfūl** Iran
131 U3 **Dezhneva, Mys** *c.* Rus. Fed.
107 O8 **Dezhou** *Shandong* China
Dezhou *Sichuan* China *see* **Dechang**
Dezh Shāhpūr Iran *see* **Marīvān**
177 L5 **Dezna** Romania
190 I4 **Dezzo** *r.* Italy
129 D3 **Dghnorisa** Georgia
129 D4 **Dghvani** Georgia
117 I6 **Dhabarau** *Uttar Prad.* India
117 J6 **Dhading** Nepal
203 G2 **Dhahab** Egypt
128 C10 **Dhahab, Marsá** *b.* Egypt
124 F5 **Dhahab, Wādī** *watercourse* Saudi Arabia
128 D6 **Dhahab, Wādī adh** *r.* Syria
125 J7 **Dhaḥawn, Wādī** *r.* Yemen
128 C7 **Dhāhiriya** West Bank
124 G3 **Dhahlān, Jabal** *hill* Saudi Arabia
Dhahran Saudi Arabia *see* **Aẓ Ẓahrān**
117 M8 **Dhaka** Bangl.
117 M8 **Dhaka** *admin. div.* Bangl.
117 K8 **Dhalbhum** *reg. Jharkhand* India
117 M8 **Dhaleswari** *r.* Bangl.
117 N7 **Dhaleswari** *r.* India
114 D4 **Dhalgaon** *Mahar.* India
Dhali Cyprus *see* **Dali**
124 G8 **Dhamār** Yemen
124 G8 **Dhamār** *governorate* Yemen
117 K9 **Dhamara** *Orissa* India
116 E8 **Dhamnod** *Madh. Prad.* India
116 G7 **Dhamoni** *Madh. Prad.* India
116 G5 **Dhampur** *Uttar Prad.* India
116 H9 **Dhamtari** *Chhattisgarh* India
123 M9 **Dhana** Pak.
123 N6 **Dhana Sar** Pak.
117 K8 **Dhanbad** *Jharkhand* India
116 D8 **Dhandhuka** *Gujarat* India
116 D7 **Dhanera** *Gujarat* India
116 H5 **Dhangarhi** Nepal
116 H5 **Dhang Range** *mts* Nepal
117 K6 **Dhankuta** Nepal
116 E5 **Dhansia** *Rajasthan* India
114 F8 **Dhanushkodi** *Tamil Nadu* India
116 F3 **Dhaola Dhar** *mts* India
116 E9 **Dhaoli** *Madh. Prad.* India
116 E8 **Dhar** *Madh. Prad.* India
206 B2 **Ḍhar Adrar** *hills* Maur.
115 I3 **Dharakota** *Orissa* India
116 D9 **Dharampur** *Gujarat* India
117 K6 **Dharan Bazar** Nepal
114 E7 **Dharapuram** *Tamil Nadu* India
123 M8 **Dhareja** Pak.
116 C9 **Dhari** *Gujarat* India
117 N7 **Dharmanagar** *Tripura* India
114 F6 **Dharmapuri** *Tamil Nadu* India
114 E5 **Dharmavaram** *Andhra Prad.* India
117 I8 **Dharmjaygarh** *Chhattisgarh* India
116 E4 **Dharmkot** *Punjab* India
117 K9 **Dharmsala** *Orissa* India
210 F2 **Dharoor** *watercourse* Somalia
206 D2 **Ḍhar Oualâta** *hills* Maur.
206 C2 **Ḍhar Tîchît** *hills* Maur.
83 M5 **Dharug National Park** *N.S.W.* Austr.
114 E3 **Dharur** *Mahar.* India
114 D5 **Dharwad** *Karnataka* India
Dharwar *Karnataka* India *see* **Dharwad**
116 F3 **Dharwas** *Hima. Prad.* India
116 C9 **Dhasa** *Gujarat* India
116 G7 **Dhasan** *r. Madh. Prad.* India
126 H9 **Dhāt al Ḥājj** Saudi Arabia
117 I5 **Dhaulagiri** *mt.* Nepal
116 G7 **Dhaura** *Uttar Prad.* India
116 H6 **Dhaurahra** *Uttar Prad.* India
Dhávlia Greece *see* **Davleia**
Dhawlagiri *mt.* Nepal *see* **Dhaulagiri**
Dhebar Lake India *see* **Jaisamand Lake**
128 B3 **Dhekelia Sovereign Base Area** *military base* Cyprus
117 N6 **Dhekiajuli** *Assam* India
117 O6 **Dhemaji** *Assam* India
117 J9 **Dhenkanal** *Orissa* India
Dheskáti Greece *see* **Deskati**
Dhiafánion *Karpathos* Greece *see* **Diafani**
Dhiakoptón Greece *see* **Diakofto**
128 D7 **Dhībān** Jordan
Dhídhima Greece *see* **Didyma**
Dhidhimótikhon Greece *see* **Didymoteicho**
113 □1 **Dhiffushi** *i. N. Male* Maldives
113 □1 **Dhigufinolhu** *i. S. Male* Maldives
117 N6 **Dhing** *Assam* India
Dhíorix Korínthou *b.* Greece *see* **Korinthou, Dioryga**
127 M8 **Dhī Qār** *governorate* Iraq
128 E7 **Dhirwah, Wādī adh** *watercourse* Jordan
Dhodhekánisos *is* Greece *see* **Dodekanisa**
Dhofar *admin. reg.* Oman *see* **Ẓufār**
Dhokós *i.* Greece *see* **Dokos**
116 C9 **Dhola** *Gujarat* India
116 D8 **Dholera** *Gujarat* India
116 D8 **Dholka** *Gujarat* India
116 F6 **Dholpur** *Rajasthan* India
Dhomokós Greece *see* **Domokos**
114 E5 **Dhone** *Andhra Prad.* India
210 D4 **Dhoomadheere** Somalia
148 I5 **Dhoon** Isle of Man
116 C9 **Dhoraji** *Gujarat* India
116 B8 **Dhori** *Gujarat* India
Dhragonádha *i.* Greece *see* **Dragonada**
Dhragónisos *i.* Greece *see* **Tragonisi**
116 C8 **Dhrangadhra** *Gujarat* India
116 C8 **Dhrol** *Gujarat* India
172 B2 **Dhron** Ger.
Dhrosiá Greece *see* **Drosia**
124 F9 **Dhubāb** Yemen
117 L7 **Dhubri** *Assam* India
Dhuburi *Assam* India *see* **Dhubri**
123 O5 **Dhudial** Pak.
116 E9 **Dhule** *Mahar.* India
Dhulia *Mahar.* India *see* **Dhule**
117 K7 **Dhulian** *W. Bengal* India
123 O5 **Dhulian** Pak.
116 G8 **Dhuma** *Madh. Prad.* India
117 J6 **Dhunche** Nepal
210 F2 **Dhuudo** Somalia
210 E3 **Dhuusa Marreeb** Somalia
124 D2 **Dhuwaybān** *basin* Saudi Arabia
Dhytikí Ellás *admin. reg.* Greece *see* **Dytiki Ellada**
Dhytikí Makedhonía *admin. reg.* Greece *see* **Dytiki Makedonia**
198 G7 **Dia** *i.* Greece
161 K8 **Diable, Cime du** *mt.* France
246 □ **Diablo, Mount** *hill* Jamaica
240 K4 **Diablo, Mount** *CA* U.S.A.
242 B2 **Diablo, Picacho del** *mt.* Mex.
240 K4 **Diablo Range** *mts CA* U.S.A.
211 C7 **Diaca** Moz.
199 I7 **Diafani** *Karpathos* Greece
206 D3 **Diafarabé** Mali
260 B2 **Diaguitas** Chile
206 D3 **Diaka** *r.* Mali
198 D4 **Diakofto** Greece
206 C3 **Diakon** Mali
177 G3 **Diakovce** Slovakia
206 C3 **Dialafara** Mali
206 B3 **Dialakoto** Senegal
206 E3 **Diallassagou** Mali
247 □3 **Diamant, Rocher du** *i.* Martinique
261 G3 **Diamante** Arg.
260 D4 **Diamante** *r.* Arg.
193 P8 **Diamante** Italy
260 C4 **Diamante, Laguna** *l.* Arg.
260 C4 **Diamante, Pampa del** *plain* Arg.
261 G3 **Diamante, Parque Nacional** *nat. park* Arg.
85 G9 **Diamantina** *watercourse Qld* Austr.
251 F6 **Diamantina** *Amazonas* Brazil
257 F3 **Diamantina** *Minas Gerais* Brazil
254 E5 **Diamantina, Chapada** *plat.* Brazil
265 K7 **Diamantina Deep** *sea feature* Indian Ocean
85 H7 **Diamantina Gates National Park** *Qld* Austr.
85 H7 **Diamantina Lakes** *Qld* Austr.
256 A2 **Diamantino** *Mato Grosso* Brazil
253 F3 **Diamantino** *Mato Grosso* Brazil
256 A2 **Diamantino** *r.* Brazil
117 L8 **Diamond Harbour** *W. Bengal* India
240 □D12 **Diamond Head** *HI* U.S.A.
240 □D12 **Diamond Head** *HI* U.S.A.
85 M4 **Diamond Islets** *Coral Sea Is Terr.* Austr.
241 Q2 **Diamond Peak** *NV* U.S.A.
240 L3 **Diamond Springs** *CA* U.S.A.
240 O8 **Diamond Valley Lake** *resr CA* U.S.A.
238 I6 **Diamondville** *WY* U.S.A.
206 C3 **Diamou** Mali
206 B3 **Diamounguél** Senegal
216 □2b **Diana's Peak** *hill* St Helena
109 H8 **Dianbai** *Guangdong* China
Dianbu *Anhui* China *see* **Feidong**
108 C6 **Diancang Shan** *mt. Yunnan* China
108 D6 **Dian Chi** *l.* China
206 C3 **Diandioumé** Mali
192 D3 **Diane, Étang de** *lag. Corse* France
85 L3 **Diane Bank** *sea feature Coral Sea Is Terr.* Austr.
206 C3 **Diangounté Kamara** Mali
206 C5 **Diani** *r.* Guinea
108 F3 **Dianjiang** *Chongqing* China
190 E6 **Diano d'Alba** Italy
190 E8 **Diano Marina** Italy
254 D4 **Dianópolis** Brazil
206 D4 **Dianra** Côte d'Ivoire
Dianyang *Yunnan* China *see* **Shidian**
107 R5 **Diaobingshan** *Liaoning* China
107 P8 **Diaokou** *Shandong* China
100 G6 **Diaoling** *Heilong.* China
207 F3 **Diapaga** Burkina
128 A4 **Diarizos** *r.* Cyprus
206 C4 **Diatifèrè** Guinea
198 D2 **Diavata** Greece
115 M6 **Diavolo, Mount** *hill Andaman & Nicobar Is* India
261 G3 **Diaz** Arg.
212 B5 **Diaz Point** Namibia
125 M3 **Dibā al Ḥiṣn** U.A.E.
125 N4 **Ḍibab** Oman
Dibang *r.* India *see* **Dingba Qu**
209 D6 **Dibaya** Dem. Rep. Congo
209 C6 **Dibaya-Lubwe** Dem. Rep. Congo
202 E6 **Dibbis** Sudan
151 J6 **Dibden** *Hampshire, England* U.K.
199 J4 **Dibek Dağı** *mt.* Turkey
207 I2 **Dibella** *well* Niger
214 G3 **Dibeng** S. Africa
210 D2 **Dībīlē** Eth.
124 E2 **Ḍibīy, Jabal** *hills* Saudi Arabia
217 □3a **Dibouani** *Njazidja* Comoros
136 I2 **Dibrova** *Kyivs'ka Oblast'* Ukr.
136 G2 **Dibrova** *Zhytomyrs'ka Oblast'* Ukr.
117 O6 **Dibrugarh** *Assam* India
Dibse Syria *see* **Dibsī**
128 G3 **Dibsī** Syria
250 C2 **Dibulla** Col.
168 F5 **Dickel** Ger.
237 E9 **Dickens** *TX* U.S.A.
233 □P1 **Dickey** *ME* U.S.A.
236 D2 **Dickinson** *ND* U.S.A.
231 D7 **Dickson** *TN* U.S.A.
234 D2 **Dickson City** *PA* U.S.A.
140 □ **Dickson Land** *reg.* Svalbard
127 K5 **Dicle** *r.* Turkey *alt.* **Dijlah, Nahr (Iraq/Syria),** *conv.* **Tigris**
191 L8 **Dicomano** Italy
210 C4 **Dida Galgalu** *reg.* Kenya
124 G2 **Dīdah** *well* Saudi Arabia
164 J5 **Didam** Neth.
151 J4 **Didcot** *Oxfordshire, England* U.K.
169 J6 **Didderse** Ger.
205 H4 **Dider** Alg.
129 G3 **Didi Borbalo, Mt'a** Georgia
92 D2 **Didicas** *i.* Phil.
206 C3 **Didiéni** Mali
129 D3 **Didi Inch'khuri** Georgia
129 D3 **Didi Jikhaishi** Georgia
129 F4 **Didi Lilo** Georgia
210 B3 **Didinga Hills** Sudan
136 I3 **Didivshchyna** Ukr.
211 D5 **Dido** *waterhole* Kenya
222 H5 **Didsbury** *Alta* Can.
210 C3 **Didu** Eth.
116 E6 **Didwana** *Rajasthan* India
213 □K3 **Didy** Madag.
198 E5 **Didyma** Greece
199 H1 **Didymoteicho** Greece
138 J6 **Didžiasalis** Lith.
138 H7 **Didžiulis** *l.* Lith.
161 G7 **Die** France
169 D10 **Dieblich** Ger.
206 E4 **Diébougou** Burkina
172 F2 **Dieburg** Ger.
177 L5 **Dieci** Romania
Dieciséis de Julio Arg. *see* **16 de Julio**
Diecisiete de Agosto Arg. *see* **17 de Agosto**
Diedenhofen France *see* **Thionville**
173 J5 **Diedorf** *Bayern* Ger.
169 J8 **Diedorf** *Thüringen* Ger.
223 I5 **Diefenbaker, Lake** *Sask.* Can.
162 I5 **Diège** *r.* France
183 J7 **Diego Álvaro** Spain
259 B8 **Diego de Almagro, Isla** *i.* Chile
261 F4 **Diego de Alvear** Arg.
265 I5 **Diego Garcia** *atoll* B.I.O.T.
247 □7 **Diego Martin** Trin. and Tob.
259 C9 **Diego Ramirez, Islas** *is* Chile
Diégo Suarez Madag. *see* **Antsirañana**
206 C3 **Diégrâga** *well* Maur.
206 C5 **Diéké** Guinea
170 F3 **Diekhof** Ger.
169 I6 **Diekholzen** Ger.
165 J9 **Diekirch** Lux.
165 I9 **Diekirch** *admin. dist.* Lux.
190 E1 **Dielsdorf** Switz.
206 C3 **Diéma** Mali
206 A3 **Diembéreng** Senegal
169 H7 **Diemel** *r.* Ger.
169 G8 **Diemelsee** *park* Ger.
169 G8 **Diemel-Stausee** *resr* Ger.
164 G4 **Diemen** Neth.
160 G5 **Diémoz** France
Điên Biên Vietnam *see* **Điên Biên Phu**
96 F4 **Điên Biên Phu** Vietnam
96 G5 **Diên Châu** Vietnam
172 E2 **Dienheim** Ger.
97 I8 **Diên Khanh** Vietnam
161 B6 **Dienne** France
138 H5 **Dienvidsusēja** *r.* Latvia
156 I7 **Dienville** France
169 G6 **Diepenau** Ger.
165 H7 **Diepenbeek** Belgium
164 K4 **Diepenheim** Neth.
164 J4 **Diepenveen** Neth.
168 F5 **Diepholz** Ger.
156 B4 **Dieppe** France
247 □2 **Dieppe Bay Town** St Kitts and Nevis
214 H6 **Dieput** S. Africa
169 E9 **Dierdorf** Ger.
164 J4 **Dieren** Neth.
170 F2 **Dierhagen, Ostseebad** Ger.
237 H8 **Dierks** *AR* U.S.A.
106 J7 **Di'er Nonchang Qu** *r.* China
100 D6 **Di'er Songhua Jiang** *r.* China
168 K5 **Diesdorf** Ger.
171 F8 **Dieskau** Ger.
173 J2 **Diespeck** Ger.
164 H6 **Diessen** Neth.
173 K6 **Dießen am Ammersee** Ger.
190 F1 **Diessenhofen** Switz.
165 H7 **Diest** Belgium
179 J3 **Dietachdorf** Austria
173 I5 **Dietenheim** Ger.
173 J3 **Dietenhofen** Ger.
173 N4 **Dietersburg** Ger.
173 L3 **Dietfurt an der Altmühl** Ger.
190 E1 **Dietikon** Switz.
172 F5 **Dietingen** Ger.
179 K2 **Dietmanns** *Niederösterreich* Austria
179 L2 **Dietmanns** *Niederösterreich* Austria
173 I6 **Dietmannsried** Ger.
173 L6 **Dietramszell** Ger.
169 G10 **Dietzenbach** Ger.
169 F9 **Dietzhölztal-Ewersbach** Ger.
157 J5 **Dieue-sur-Meuse** France
161 G7 **Dieulefit** France
157 L6 **Dieulouard** France
157 M6 **Dieuze** France
138 I7 **Dieveniškės** Lith.
164 J3 **Diever** Neth.
179 K6 **Diex** Austria
169 F10 **Diez** Ger.
185 M6 **Diezma** Spain
207 I3 **Diffa** Niger
207 I2 **Diffa** *dept* Niger
165 I9 **Differdange** Lux.
124 D7 **Difnein** *i.* Eritrea
210 E3 **Dig** *well* Eth.
207 F3 **Diga Diga** *well* Niger
115 I3 **Digapahandi** *Orissa* India
208 E3 **Digba** Dem. Rep. Congo
117 O6 **Digboi** *Assam* India
225 H4 **Digby** *N.S.* Can.
141 M6 **Digerbergen** *hill* Sweden
142 J1 **Digerberget** *hill* Sweden
116 E6 **Diggi** *Rajasthan* India
117 K9 **Digha** *W. Bengal* India
129 F4 **Dighomi** Georgia
236 E6 **Dighton** *KS* U.S.A.
114 E3 **Diglur** *Mahar.* India
162 E4 **Dignac** France
191 N3 **Dignano** Italy
161 I8 **Digne-les-Bains** France
156 B6 **Digny** France
160 D4 **Digoin** France
92 D3 **Digollorin Point** *Luzon* Phil.
191 N2 **Digòn** *r.* Italy
129 E5 **Digor** Turkey
129 F2 **Digora** Rus. Fed.
92 E8 **Digos** *Mindanao* Phil.
116 F9 **Digras** *Mahar.* India
123 M9 **Digri** Pak.
91 I8 **Digul** *r. Papua* Indon.
106 F7 **Diguojiadan** *Qinghai* China
206 E5 **Digya National Park** Ghana
111 L13 **Dihang** *r.* India *alt.* **Jamuna (Bangladesh),** *alt.* **Yarlung Zangbo (China),** *conv.* **Brahmaputra**
225 H1 **Dihourse, Lac** *l. Que.* Can.
175 M5 **Dihtiv** Ukr.
137 L3 **Dihtyari** Ukr.
124 C4 **Diib, Wadi** *watercourse* Sudan
207 I4 **Diibao** Cameroon
210 D4 **Diinsoor** Somalia
127 M8 **Dijlah, Nahr** *r.* Iraq/Syria *alt.* **Dicle (Turkey),** *conv.* **Tigris**
165 G7 **Dijle** *r.* Belgium
160 G2 **Dijon** France
Dijon *airport* France *see* **Longvic**
208 C2 **Dik** Chad
140 N4 **Dikanäs** Sweden
129 I6 **Dīkdāsh** Iran
116 E7 **Diken** *Madh. Prad.* India
210 D2 **Dikhil** Djibouti
117 O6 **Dikho** *r.* India
199 H3 **Dikili** Turkey
165 C7 **Dikkebus** Belgium
129 G3 **Diklosmta** *mt.* Rus. Fed.
129 D5 **Dikmeköyü** Turkey
206 D4 **Dikodougou** Côte d'Ivoire
165 C6 **Diksmuide** Belgium
130 J2 **Dikson** Rus. Fed.
207 I3 **Dikwa** Nigeria
210 C3 **Dīla** Eth.
185 L6 **Dilar** Spain
185 L6 **Dilar** *r.* Spain
122 H6 **Dilaram** Iran
165 F7 **Dilbeek** Belgium
129 B5 **Dilek Dağı** *mt.* Turkey
199 I5 **Dilek Yarımadası Milli Parkı** *nat. park* Turkey
208 E4 **Dili** Dem. Rep. Congo
93 D8 **Dili** East Timor
207 I3 **Dilia** *watercourse* Niger
129 F5 **Dilijan** Armenia
129 F5 **Dilijan Argelanots'** *nature res.* Armenia
97 I9 **Di Linh** Vietnam
81 H9 **Dilion Cone** *mt. South I.* N.Z.
129 E4 **Dilit'i** Georgia
Dilizhan Armenia *see* **Dilijan**
169 F9 **Dillenburg** Ger.
237 F11 **Dilley** *TX* U.S.A.
206 D3 **Dilli** Mali
142 G2 **Dilling** Norway
203 F6 **Dilling** Sudan
172 B3 **Dillingen (Saar)** Ger.
173 I4 **Dillingen an der Donau** Ger.
220 C4 **Dillingham** *AK* U.S.A.

Đông Văn to Dumbrăveni
307

108 E7 Đông Văn Vietnam
Dongxiang Sichuan China see Xuanhan
106 H9 Dongxiangzu Gansu China
108 F8 Dongxing Guangxi China
100 E5 Dongxing Heilong. China
109 M4 Dongyang Zhejiang China
107 P8 Dongying Shandong China
109 J7 Dongyuan Guangdong China
106 H7 Dongzhen Gansu China
109 K3 Dongzhi Anhui China
260 B4 Doñihue Chile
151 L2 Donington Lincolnshire, England U.K.
237 J7 Doniphan MO U.S.A.
196 J8 Donja Dubnica Kosovo Serbia
179 O7 Donja Dubrava Croatia
179 N7 Donja Konjšćina Croatia
179 M8 Donja Stubica Croatia
179 N7 Donja Višnjica Croatia
179 N8 Donja Zelina Croatia
222 A2 Donjek r. Y.T. Can.
157 J7 Donjeux France
188 G3 Donji Miholjac Croatia
197 K6 Donji Milanovac Serbia
188 F3 Donji Vakuf Bos.-Herz.
188 E3 Donji Zemunik Croatia
164 J2 Donkerbroek Neth.
215 J6 Donkerpoort S. Africa
117 M9 Donmanick Islands Bangl.
140 L3 Dønna i. Norway
225 G4 Donnacona Que. Can.
194 H10 Donnalucata Sicilia Italy
190 D4 Donnas Italy
222 G4 Donnelly Alta Can.
80 H2 Donnellys Crossing North I. N.Z.
156 F7 Donnemarie-Dontilly France
240 L2 Donner Pass CA U.S.A.
179 J5 Donnersbach Austria
172 D2 Donnersberg hill Ger.
173 I2 Donnersdorf Ger.
150 H2 Donnington Telford and Wrekin, England U.K.
87 C12 Donnybrook W.A. Austr.
147 F7 Donohill Ireland
157 N6 Donon mt. France
192 C9 Donori Sardegna Italy
186 B1 Donostia-San Sebastián Spain
147 E9 Donoughmore Ireland
199 G5 Donousa i. Greece
226 G9 Donovan IL U.S.A.
137 Q6 Dons'ke Ukr.
137 T6 Donskoy Rostovskaya Oblast' Rus. Fed.
139 V8 Donskoy Tul'skaya Oblast' Rus. Fed.
139 V9 Donskoye Lipetskaya Oblast' Rus. Fed.
135 H7 Donskoye Stavropol'skiy Kray Rus. Fed.
137 S3 Donskoye Belogor'ye hills Rus. Fed.
92 D5 Donsol Luzon Phil.
96 C6 Donthami r. Myanmar
137 L8 Donuzlav, Ozero l. Ukr.
158 H4 Donville-les-Bains France
120 G4 Donyztau, Sor dry lake Kazakh.
163 F7 Donzac France
122 D4 Donzdorf Ger.
191 M6 Donzella, Isola della i. Italy
162 H5 Donzenac France
161 F8 Donzère France
160 C2 Donzy France
147 B5 Dooagh Ireland
147 E4 Doocastle Ireland
147 B5 Dooega Ireland
147 C5 Dooghbeg Ireland
147 B4 Doogort Ireland
147 C4 Doohooma Ireland
148 C4 Dooish Northern Ireland U.K.
86 E6 Dooleena hill W.A. Austr.
147 D6 Doolin Ireland
84 G4 Doomadgee Qld Austr.
84 G4 Doomadgee Aboriginal Reserve Qld Austr.
147 F7 Doon Ireland
146 G12 Doon r. Scotland U.K.
146 H12 Doon, Loch l. Scotland U.K.
147 C7 Doonaha Ireland
147 C7 Doonbeg Ireland
147 C7 Doonbeg r. Ireland
147 C7 Doonbeg Bay Ireland
86 J4 Doon Doon Aboriginal Reserve W.A. Austr.
147 B6 Doonloughan Ireland
147 B8 Doonmanagh Ireland
147 F3 Doorin Point Ireland
164 H4 Doorn Neth.
164 I4 Doornspijk Neth.
226 G5 Door Peninsula WI U.S.A.
210 F2 Dooxo Nugaaleed val. Somalia
174 E3 Dopiewo Pol.
117 K11 Doqêmo Xizang China
111 J12 Doqoi Xizang China
108 A1 Do Qu r. Qinghai China
123 I6 Dor watercourse Afgh.
128 C6 Dor Israel
139 S6 Dor Rus. Fed.
237 D9 Dora NM U.S.A.
86 G7 Dora, Lake salt flat W.A. Austr.
190 E5 Dora Baltea r. Italy
160 J5 Dora di Ferret r. Italy
160 K5 Dora di Veny r. Italy
242 G4 Dorado Mex.
122 D8 Do Rāhak Iran
123 N3 Dorah Pass Pak.
117 J8 Doranda Jharkhand India
223 I2 Doran Lake N.W.T. Can.
190 D5 Dora Riparia r. Italy
253 E5 D'Orbigny Bol.
Dorbiljin Xinjiang China see Emin
Dorbod Heilong. China see Taikang
Dorbod Qi Nei Mongol China see Ulan Hua
196 J8 Đorče Petrov Macedonia
150 H6 Dorchester Dorset, England U.K.
234 F6 Dorchester NJ U.S.A.
212 C4 Dordabis Namibia
156 E7 Dordives France
162 F5 Dordogne dept France
160 B5 Dordogne r. France
151 I2 Dordon Warwickshire, England U.K.
164 G5 Dordrecht Neth.
215 L7 Dordrecht S. Africa
160 C4 Dore r. France
160 B6 Dore, Monts mts France
212 C4 Doreenville Namibia
223 J4 Doré Lake Sask. Can.
223 J4 Doré Lake l. Sask. Can.
161 D6 Dore-l'Église France
178 A5 Doren Austria
169 H6 Dörentrup Ger.
146 H8 Dores Highland, Scotland U.K.
257 F3 Dores de Guanhães Brazil
257 E3 Dores do Indaiá Brazil
206 E3 Dorey Mali
173 M5 Dorfen Ger.
178 H5 Dorfgastein Austria
168 I5 Dorfmark Ger.
170 D3 Dorf Mecklenburg Ger.
192 D7 Dorgali Sardegna Italy
106 C9 Dorgê Co l. Qinghai China
106 C2 Dörgön Mongolia
177 K5 Dorgoș Romania
123 K6 Dori r. Afgh.
207 E3 Dori Burkina
261 F4 Dorila Arg.
214 C7 Doring r. S. Africa
214 D8 Doring r. S. Africa
214 C7 Doringbaai S. Africa
214 D7 Doringbos S. Africa
198 C5 Dorio Greece
84 C3 Dorisvale N.T. Austr.
151 L5 Dorking Surrey, England U.K.
157 N6 Dorlisheim France
206 E5 Dormaa-Ahenkro Ghana
169 C8 Dormagen Ger.
177 J4 Dormánd Hungary
156 G5 Dormans France
190 F4 Dormelletto Italy
172 F5 Dormettingen Ger.
100 I5 Dormidontovka Rus. Fed.
114 G4 Dornakal Andhra Prad. India
179 M7 Dornava Slovenia
169 H8 Dörnberg (Habichtswald) Ger.
178 A5 Dornbirn Austria
171 E8 Dornburg (Saale) Ger.
169 F9 Dornburg-Frickhofen Ger.
168 H3 Dornbusch Ger.
170 H1 Dornbusch pen. Ger.
169 J9 Dorndorf Ger.
171 E8 Dorndorf-Steudnitz Ger.
186 E5 Dornelas Port.
160 C3 Dornes France
169 I8 Dörnhagen (Fuldabrück) Ger.
172 H5 Dornhan Ger.
146 E8 Dornie Highland, Scotland U.K.
171 F6 Dörnitz Ger.
190 F5 Dorno Italy
146 H7 Dornoch Highland, Scotland U.K.
146 H7 Dornoch Firth est. Scotland U.K.
107 N2 Dornod prov. Mongolia
107 K4 Dornogovĭ prov. Mongolia
234 B3 Dornsife PA U.S.A.
172 H5 Dornstadt Ger.
172 E5 Dornstetten Ger.
168 D3 Dornum Ger.
168 D3 Dornumersiel Ger.
206 E2 Doro Mali
197 O6 Dorobanțu Romania
138 N4 Dorobino Rus. Fed.
177 H4 Dorog Hungary
177 I4 Dorogháza Hungary
139 Q7 Dorogobuzh Rus. Fed.
134 I2 Dorogorskoye Rus. Fed.
197 O3 Dorohoi Romania
175 L4 Dorohusk Pol.
139 T6 Dorokhovo Rus. Fed.
122 H5 Dorokhsh Iran
177 L4 Dorolț Romania
116 G1 Dörö Nuur salt l. Mongolia
137 K6 Doroshivka Ukr.
Dorostol Bulg. see Silistra
136 E3 Dorosyni Ukr.
140 N4 Dorotea Sweden
234 F6 Dorothy NJ U.S.A.
213 F3 Dorowa Zimbabwe
Dorpat Estonia see Tartu
168 D5 Dörpen Ger.
87 B8 Dorre Island W.A. Austr.
83 N4 Dorrigo N.S.W. Austr.
238 D6 Dorris CA U.S.A.
227 P4 Dorset Ont. Can.
150 H6 Dorset admin. div. England U.K.
232 E7 Dorset OH U.S.A.
150 F6 Dorset and East Devon Coast tourist site U.K.
111 I10 Dorsoidong Co l. Xizang China
169 K6 Dorstadt Ger.
169 C7 Dorsten Ger.
160 H4 Dortan France
169 D7 Dortmund Ger.
169 E7 Dortmund-Ems-Kanal canal Ger.
232 C11 Dorton KY U.S.A.
126 H5 Dörtyol Turkey
174 G4 Doruchów Pol.
129 D6 Dorukdibi Turkey
139 G8 Dorum Ger.
208 E3 Doruma Dem. Rep. Congo
122 G4 Dorūneh Iran
122 G4 Dorūneh, Kūh-e mts Iran
168 H5 Dörverden Ger.
Dorylaeum Turkey see Eskişehir
172 H3 Dörzbach Ger.
244 E7 Dos Aguas Mex.
187 D9 Dos Aguas Spain
122 G7 Do Sārī Iran
259 D7 Dos Bahías, Cabo c. Arg.
183 N9 Dosbarrios Spain
241 W9 Dos Cabezas Mountain AZ U.S.A.
250 C6 Dos de Mayo Peru
199 L5 Döşemealtı Turkey
123 J5 Do Shākh, Kūh-e mt. Afgh.
184 H6 Dos Hermanas Spain
105 J4 Dōshi Japan
117 O6 Dosing Arun. Prad. India
243 O9 Dos Lagunos Guat.
96 H4 Do Son Vietnam
240 L5 Dos Palos CA U.S.A.
197 M9 Dospat Bulg.
197 M9 Dospat r. Bulg.
185 N6 Dos Picos mt. Spain
259 D6 Dos Pozos Arg.
172 F5 Dosse r. Ger.
172 F3 Dossenheim Ger.
208 C2 Dosséo, Bahr r. Chad
207 F3 Dosso Niger
207 F3 Dosso dept Niger
207 F3 Dosso, Réserve Partielle de nature res. Niger
190 E3 Dossola, Val val. Italy
120 E4 Dossor Kazakh.
121 M7 Do'stlik Uzbek.
185 J4 Dos Torres Spain
121 T5 Dostyk Kazakh.
Dostyq Kazakh. see Dostyk
231 E10 Dothan AL U.S.A.
172 F5 Dötlingen Ger.
156 F5 Dottignies Belgium
172 F5 Dotternhausen Ger.
172 E5 Dottingen Switz.
156 F5 Douai France
204 D4 Douakel, Hamada ed plat. Alg.
206 C4 Douako Guinea
207 H5 Douala Cameroon
207 H6 Douala-Edéa, Réserve nature res. Cameroon
158 C5 Douarnenez France
158 C5 Douarnenez, Baie de b. France
162 E5 Double reg. France
Double Island H.K. China see Wong Wan Chau
85 N8 Double Island Point Qld Austr.
237 E9 Double Mountain Fork r. TX U.S.A.
240 N6 Double Peak CA U.S.A.
85 K4 Double Point Qld Austr.
231 D8 Double Springs AL U.S.A.
176 E2 Doubrava r. Czech Rep.
160 I3 Doubs France
160 I2 Doubs dept France
160 G3 Doubs r. France/Switz.
86 H3 Doubtful Bay W.A. Austr.
87 E13 Doubtful Island Bay W.A. Austr.
81 B12 Doubtful Sound South I. N.Z.
81 A12 Doubtful Sound inlet South I. N.Z.
80 H1 Doubtless Bay North I. N.Z.
Doucan Shaanxi China see Fuping
156 F8 Douchy France
156 F3 Douchy-les-Mines France
160 I3 Doucier France
159 M2 Doudeville France
162 D1 Doué-la-Fontaine France
206 E3 Douentza Mali
206 E3 Douentza, Réserve de nature res. Mali
148 G2 Dougarie North Ayrshire, Scotland U.K.
205 H1 Dougga tourist site Tunisia
81 B14 Doughboy Bay Stewart I. N.Z.
84 F6 Dough Mountain hill Ireland
145 E4 Douglas Isle of Man
80 I6 Douglas North I. N.Z.
147 F9 Douglas Ireland
214 H5 Douglas S. Africa
146 I11 Douglas South Lanarkshire, Scotland U.K.
222 C3 Douglas AK U.S.A.
241 W10 Douglas AZ U.S.A.
231 F10 Douglas GA U.S.A.
238 L5 Douglas WY U.S.A.
83 L9 Douglas Apsley National Park Tas. Austr.
148 G2 Douglas Bridge Northern Ireland U.K.
222 D4 Douglas Channel B.C. Can.
82 F3 Douglas Creek watercourse S.A. Austr.
241 X1 Douglas Creek r. CO U.S.A.
262 T2 Douglas Range mts Antarctica
Douglas Reef i. Japan see Okino-Tori-shima
234 D4 Douglassville PA U.S.A.
146 K9 Douglastown Angus, Scotland U.K.
231 E9 Douglasville GA U.S.A.
207 H3 Dougoulé well Niger
202 C5 Douhi Chad
Douhudi Hubei China see Gong'an
198 B4 Doukato, Akrotirio pt Lefkada Greece
157 J7 Doulaincourt-Saucourt France
Douliu Taiwan see Touliu
156 D3 Doullens France
158 H3 Doulus Head Ireland
208 D2 Doum C.A.R.
208 D4 Douma Benin
207 F4 Doumé Cameroon
207 I5 Doumé r. Cameroon
109 I7 Doumen Guangdong China
206 E3 Dounan Mali
146 J4 Dounby Orkney, Scotland U.K.
146 H10 Doune Stirling, Scotland U.K.
146 G10 Doune Hill Scotland U.K.
207 F4 Dounkassa Benin
146 I5 Dounreay Highland, Scotland U.K.
176 C1 Doupovské hory mts Czech Rep.
165 E8 Dour Belgium
256 C3 Dourada, Cachoeira waterfall Brazil
256 B2 Dourada, Serra hills Brazil
254 C5 Dourada, Serra mts Brazil
255 B7 Dourados Brazil
255 B7 Dourados r. Brazil
255 A5 Dourados, Serra dos hills Brazil
208 B2 Dourbali Chad
161 C8 Dourbie r. France
161 C8 Dourbies France
156 D6 Dourdan France
161 A7 Dourdou r. France
161 B9 Dourdou r. France
208 D2 Dourdoura Chad
163 I9 Dourgne France
156 C3 Douriez France
182 C6 Douro r. Port. alt. Duero (Spain)
182 D6 Douro Internacional, Parque Natural do nature res. Port.
Doushi Hubei China see Gong'an
109 J6 Doushui Shuiku resr China
155 I5 Doussard France
256 A5 Doutor Camargo Brazil
160 I4 Douvaine France
158 I3 Douvres-la-Délivrande France
159 K3 Douvres r. France
161 F6 Doux r. France
205 H2 Douz Tunisia
163 D8 Douze r. France
202 C6 Douzilac Chad
162 E5 Douzillac France
156 E5 Douzy France
191 L7 Dovadola Italy
136 H3 Dovbysh Ukr.
151 I2 Dove r. Derbyshire/Staffordshire, England U.K.
149 P5 Dove r. North Yorkshire, England U.K.
151 O3 Dove r. Suffolk, England U.K.
225 J2 Dove Brook Nfld and Lab. Can.
221 P2 Dove Bugt b. Greenland
241 X4 Dove Creek CO U.S.A.
83 K10 Dover Tas. Austr.
151 O5 Dover Kent, England U.K.
234 D6 Dover DE U.S.A.
233 □O5 Dover NH U.S.A.
234 F4 Dover NJ U.S.A.
232 D8 Dover OH U.S.A.
234 B5 Dover PA U.S.A.
231 D7 Dover TN U.S.A.
87 H12 Dover, Point W.A. Austr.
145 H6 Dover, Strait of France/U.K.
233 □P3 Dover-Foxcroft ME U.S.A.
151 I2 Doveridge Derbyshire, England U.K.
235 H1 Dover Plains NY U.S.A.
150 E2 Dovey r. Wales U.K.
122 C6 Doveyrich, Rūd-e r. Iran/Iraq
136 E5 Dovhe Ukr.
136 E3 Dovhoshyyi Ukr.
175 L1 Dovine r. Lith.
142 G7 Dovnsklint cliff Denmark
141 J5 Dovrefjell mts Norway
141 J5 Dovrefjell Sunndalsfjella nat. park Norway
137 O3 Dovzhyk Ukr.
Dow, Lake Botswana see Xau, Lake
211 B8 Dowa Malawi
226 H8 Dowagiac MI U.S.A.
146 I9 Dowally Perth and Kinross, Scotland U.K.
122 F6 Dow Chāhī Iran
122 H3 Dowgha'ī Iran
92 C4 Dowi, Tanjung pt Indon.
122 F3 Dow Kūh mt. Iran
123 J5 Dowlatābād Afgh.
123 K3 Dowlatābād Afgh.
122 E7 Dowlatābād Būshehr Iran
122 E6 Dowlatābād Fārs Iran
122 F7 Dowlatābād Fārs Iran
122 G3 Dowlatābād Khorāsān Iran
122 H4 Dowlatābād Khorāsān Iran
123 J3 Dowlatābād Khorāsān Iran
123 H3 Dowl at Yār Afgh.
147 K4 Down county Northern Ireland U.K.
240 N8 Downey CA U.S.A.
151 M2 Downham Market Norfolk, England U.K.
240 L2 Downieville CA U.S.A.
226 B9 Downing MO U.S.A.
234 D4 Downingtown PA U.S.A.
147 K4 Downpatrick Northern Ireland U.K.
147 L4 Downpatrick Head Ireland
236 F6 Downs KS U.S.A.
233 K6 Downsville NY U.S.A.
226 C5 Downsville WI U.S.A.
151 I6 Downton Wiltshire, England U.K.
222 E4 Downton, Mount B.C. Can.
147 E4 Dowra Ireland
122 C5 Dow Rūd Iran
122 B4 Dow Sar Iran
151 L2 Dowsby Lincolnshire, England U.K.
123 M4 Dowshī Afgh.
184 B5 Dowsk Belarus
139 N5 Dowsk Belarus
111 L12 Doxong Xizang China
160 B4 Doyet France
261 H3 Doyle Arg.
240 L1 Doyle CA U.S.A.
225 J4 Doyles Nfld and Lab. Can.
234 E4 Doylestown PA U.S.A.
197 M7 Doyrentsi Bulg.
122 G8 Dozdān r. Iran
103 J10 Dōzen is Japan
216 □1a Doze Ribeiras Terceira Azores
224 E4 Dozois, Réservoir resr Que. Can.
159 K3 Dozulé France
129 G5 Dprabak Armenia
204 C3 Drâa, Cap c. Morocco
204 C3 Drâa, Hammada du plat. Alg.
204 C3 Drâa, Oued watercourse Morocco
137 L4 Drabiv Ukr.
137 K4 Drabivka Ukr.
161 F6 Drac r. France
256 B4 Dracena Brazil
197 J9 Dračevo Macedonia
171 J7 Drachhausen Ger.
138 L8 Drachkava Belarus
173 O3 Drachselsried Ger.
164 J2 Drachten Neth.
197 P6 Dragalina Romania
177 L5 Drăgan r. Romania
140 M4 Drägan l. Sweden
177 L5 Drăgănești Romania
197 M6 Drăgănești-Olt Romania
197 N6 Drăgănești-Vlașca Romania
197 M6 Drăgășani Romania
168 J4 Drage Ger.
177 L5 Drăgești Romania
214 G5 Draghoender S. Africa
197 K8 Dragoman Bulg.
199 H7 Dragonada i. Greece
Dragonera, Isla i. Spain see Sa Dragonera
258 E1 Dragones Arg.
193 M5 Dragoni Italy
87 E12 Dragon Rocks Nature Reserve W.A. Austr.
247 □7 Dragon's Mouths str. Trin. and Tob./Venez.
241 V9 Dragoon AZ U.S.A.
142 I6 Dragør Denmark
197 P6 Dragoș Vodă Romania
141 Q6 Dragsfjärd Fin.
161 I9 Draguignan France
197 O2 Drăgușeni Botoșani Romania
197 P5 Drăgușeni Galați Romania
176 G2 Drahanovice Czech Rep.
136 E1 Drahichyn Belarus
171 I7 Drahnsdorf Ger.
83 N3 Drake N.S.W. Austr.
236 E2 Drake ND U.S.A.
168 H5 Drakenburg Ger.
215 M5 Drakensberg mts Lesotho/S. Africa
213 F5 Drakensberg mts S. Africa
215 N5 Drakensberg Garden S. Africa
215 M6 Draken's Rock mt. S. Africa
264 E9 Drake Passage S. Atlantic Ocean
240 I4 Drakes Bay CA U.S.A.
129 G5 Drakhtik Armenia
136 I8 Drakulya r. Ukr.
198 F1 Drama Greece
142 G2 Drammen Norway
156 D6 Drancy France
97 H8 Drang, Prêk r. Cambodia
140 □B1 Drangajökull ice cap Iceland
147 G7 Drangan Ireland
142 F2 Drangedal Norway
116 H6 Drangme Chhu r. Bhutan
168 G3 Drangstedt Ger.
197 R6 Dranov, Lacul l. Romania
160 J4 Dranse r. France
170 G4 Dranse Ger.
168 G5 Dransfeld Ger.
241 U1 Draper UT U.S.A.
164 B8 Draper, Mount AK U.S.A.
147 I3 Draperstown Northern Ireland U.K.
Drapsaca Afgh. see Kunduz
116 E2 Dras Jammu and Kashmir
123 O3 Drasan Pak.
179 O2 Drasenhofen Austria
179 N4 Draßmarkt Austria
179 K6 Drau r. Austria alt. Drava (Croatia), alt. Dráva (Hungary)
188 G3 Drava r. Croatia alt. Drau (Austria), alt. Dráva (Hungary)
188 G3 Dráva r. Hungary alt. Drau (Austria), alt. Drava (Croatia)
177 G6 Drávafok Hungary
188 E2 Dravinja r. Slovenia
188 E2 Dravograd Slovenia
174 D2 Drawa r. Pol.
174 D2 Drawieński Park Narodowy nat. park Pol.
174 D2 Drawno Pol.
167 H2 Drawski Park Krajobrazowy Pol.
174 E3 Drawsko Pol.
174 E2 Drawsko, Jezioro l. Pol.
174 E2 Drawsko Pomorskie Pol.
151 O2 Drayton Norfolk, England U.K.
151 J4 Drayton Oxfordshire, England U.K.
222 H4 Drayton Valley Alta Can.
179 O2 Drążdżewo Pol.
179 M6 Dražen Vrh Slovenia
179 J7 Dražgoše Slovenia
123 N6 Drazinda Pak.
189 A7 Dréan Alg.
168 F5 Drebber Ger.
171 J7 Drebkau Ger.
160 E3 Drée r. France
147 G3 Dreenagh Ireland
170 F5 Dreetz Ger.
150 D4 Drefach Carmarthenshire, Wales U.K.
177 I3 Drégelypalánk Hungary
146 G11 Dreghorn North Ayrshire, Scotland U.K.
169 G10 Dreieich Ger.
178 F5 Dreiherrnspitze mt. Austria
176 D1 Dreileben Ger.
172 B2 Dreis Ger.
172 D5 Dreisam r. Ger.
173 P4 Dreisesselberg mt. Ger.
169 I10 Dreistelzberge hill Ger.
168 J1 Drejø i. Denmark
175 K4 Drelów Pol.
169 H7 Drelsdorf Ger.
149 L1 Drem East Lothian, Scotland U.K.
191 P3 Drenchia Italy
188 G3 Drenovci Croatia
189 B2 Drenovë Albania
197 K7 Drenovets Bulg.
170 I4 Drense Ger.
169 E7 Drensteinfurt Ger.
164 K3 Drenthe prov. Neth.
164 J3 Drentse Hoofdvaart canal Neth.
168 G5 Drentwede Ger.
198 D3 Drepano Greece
227 L7 Dresden Ont. Can.
171 I8 Dresden Ger.
171 J8 Dresden admin. reg. Ger.
232 K7 Dresden OH U.S.A.
134 K1 Dresvyanka Rus. Fed.
138 M6 Dretun' Belarus
174 E1 Dretyń Pol.
164 F5 Dreumel Neth.
156 C6 Dreux France
176 C2 Dřevnice r. Czech Rep.
141 L6 Drevsjø Norway
168 F5 Drewitz Ger.
176 F6 Drewitzer See l. Ger.
174 G1 Drewnica Pol.
171 I8 Drewnyville VA U.S.A.
234 E5 Drexel Hill PA U.S.A.
174 D3 Drezdenko Pol.
138 K5 Dricēni Latvia
138 K6 Dridža l. Latvia
164 H4 Driebergen Neth.
184 D3 Driebes Spain
169 F9 Driedorf Ger.
179 K6 Driencov Slovakia
188 H2 Driesum Neth.
149 Q5 Driffield East Riding of Yorkshire, England U.K.
151 I4 Driffield Gloucestershire, England U.K.
234 D3 Drifton PA U.S.A.
232 G7 Driftwood PA U.S.A.
238 I5 Driggs ID U.S.A.
85 M9 Drillham Qld Austr.
137 K2 Drimaylivka Ukr.
147 G6 Drimmo Ireland
146 E9 Drimnin Highland, Scotland U.K.
147 D9 Drimoleague Ireland
196 H8 Drin r. Albania
188 G3 Drina r. Bos.-Herz./Serbia
196 E3 Drincea r. Romania
196 I8 Drini i Zi r. Albania
196 H9 Drinit, Gjiri i b. Albania
198 B2 Drino r. Albania
232 B11 Drip Rock KY U.S.A.
147 E9 Driscoll Ireland
262 O1 Driscoll Island Antarctica
Drissa Belarus see Vyerkhnyadzvinsk
179 J1 Dříteň Czech Rep.
140 J5 Driva Norway
176 F3 Drnholec Czech Rep.
188 F4 Drniš Croatia
179 O7 Drnje Croatia
176 J3 Dro Italy
191 J4 Drøbak Norway
142 G2 Drobeta-Turnu Severin Romania
197 K6 Drobie r. France
161 E8 Drobin Pol.
176 H3 Drobysheve Ukr.
137 Q4 Drocea, Vârful hill Romania
177 L5 Drochia Moldova
136 G5 Drochia Moldova
168 H3 Drochtersen Ger.
164 J2 Drogeham Neth.
147 J5 Drogheda Ireland
Drogichin Belarus see Drahichyn
Drogobych Ukr. see Drohobych
175 K3 Drohiczyn Pol.
136 C4 Drohobych Ukr.
Droichead Átha Ireland see Drogheda
Droichead Nua Ireland see Newbridge
150 H3 Droitwich Spa Worcestershire, England U.K.
Drokiya Moldova see Drochia
117 M6 Drokung Arun. Prad. India
169 E8 Drolshagen Ger.
147 F4 Dromahair Ireland
83 J8 Dromana Vic. Austr.
147 J4 Dromara Northern Ireland U.K.
161 G7 Drôme dept France
161 F7 Drôme r. France
159 J3 Drôme r. France
83 M7 Dromedary, Cape N.S.W. Austr.
234 A4 Dromgold PA U.S.A.
147 J5 Dromiskin Ireland
168 K5 Drömling reg. Ger.
147 G5 Dromod Ireland
147 H3 Dromore Northern Ireland U.K.
147 J4 Dromore Northern Ireland U.K.
147 E4 Dromore West Ireland
190 C7 Dronero Italy
149 O7 Dronfield Derbyshire, England U.K.
146 H12 Drongan East Ayrshire, Scotland U.K.
165 E6 Drongen Belgium
162 D5 Dronne r. France
163 H6 Dronning Ingrid Land reg. Greenland
221 P2 Dronning Louise Land reg. Greenland
Dronning Maud Land reg. Antarctica see Queen Maud Land
164 I3 Dronten Neth.
164 G3 Droogmakerij De Beemster tourist site Neth.
163 D6 Dropt r. France
179 M2 Drosendorf Austria
123 N4 Drosh Pak.
198 E4 Drosia Greece
179 O2 Drösing Austria
126 T5 Droskovo Rus. Fed.
156 B7 Droué France
107 M1 Drovyanaya Rus. Fed.
224 C3 Drowning r. Ont. Can.
171 F8 Droyßig Ger.
136 G2 Drozdyn' Ukr.
123 N6 Drug Pak.
150 F2 Druid Denbighshire, Wales U.K.
247 □9 Druif Aruba
148 F2 Druimdrishaig Argyll and Bute, Scotland U.K.
138 J6 Drūkšiu ežeras l. Belarus/Lith.
Druk-Yul country Asia see Bhutan
157 N6 Drulingen France
147 E7 Drumandoora Ireland
147 H5 Drumanespick Ireland
147 K4 Drumaness Northern Ireland U.K.
146 F6 Drumbeg Highland, Scotland U.K.
147 J4 Drumbilla Ireland
147 G4 Drumcard Northern Ireland U.K.
148 I2 Drumclog South Lanarkshire, Scotland U.K.
147 J6 Drumcondra Ireland
147 I5 Drumconrath Ireland
147 H5 Drumcree Ireland
147 G4 Drumduff Northern Ireland U.K.
160 H5 Drumettaz-Clarafond France
147 H2 Drumfree Ireland
147 F5 Drumharlow, Lough l. Ireland
223 H5 Drumheller Alta Can.
147 F4 Drumkeeran Ireland
148 B5 Drumlea Ireland
147 H2 Drumlish Ireland
146 L9 Drumlithie Aberdeenshire, Scotland U.K.
147 I8 Drummin Ireland
Drummond atoll Gilbert Is Kiribati see Tabiteuea
238 H3 Drummond MT U.S.A.
226 C3 Drummond WI U.S.A.
232 I12 Drummond, Lake VA U.S.A.
Drummond Island Phoenix Is Kiribati see McKean
227 K4 Drummond Island MI U.S.A.
85 K8 Drummond Range hills Qld Austr.
225 F4 Drummondville Que. Can.
146 G13 Drummore Dumfries and Galloway, Scotland U.K.
147 G3 Drumnacross Ireland
146 H8 Drumnadrochit Highland, Scotland U.K.
148 C4 Drumnakilly Northern Ireland U.K.
147 H3 Drumquin Northern Ireland U.K.
148 B7 Drumraney Ireland
147 F4 Drumshanbo Ireland
148 B6 Drumsna Ireland
164 H5 Drunen Neth.
148 C5 Drung Ireland
222 C2 Drury Lake Y.T. Can.
190 F1 Drusberg mt. Switz.
157 O6 Drusenheim France
Druskieniki Lith. see Druskininkai
138 H8 Druskininkai Lith.
138 I4 Drusti Latvia
164 I5 Druten Neth.
138 N8 Druts' r. Belarus
138 K6 Druya Belarus
160 C1 Druyes-les-Belles-Fontaines France
175 H4 Drużbice Pol.
Druzhba Kazakh. see Dostyk
175 J1 Druzhba Rus. Fed.
137 L3 Druzhba Chernihivs'ka Oblast' Ukr.
137 M1 Druzhba Sums'ka Oblast' Ukr.
137 N7 Druzhbivka Ukr.
131 P3 Druzhina Rus. Fed.
139 U1 Druzhinnoye, Ozero l. Rus. Fed.
137 Q5 Druzhkivka Donets'ka Oblast' Ukr. see Druzhkivka
Druzhkovka Kharkivs'ka Oblast' Ukr. see Lozova
139 N2 Druzhnaya Gorka Rus. Fed.
136 E1 Druzhylavichy Belarus
175 H1 Druzno, Jezioro l. Pol.
177 K3 Družstevná pri Hornáde Slovakia
175 J4 Drwalew Pol.
174 F4 Drwęca r. Pol.
175 H2 Drwęckie, Jezioro l. Pol.
175 I5 Drwinia Pol.
84 D3 Dry r. N.T. Austr.
197 N8 Dryanovo Bulg.
137 S1 Dryazgi Rus. Fed.
138 L3 Dryazhno Rus. Fed.
222 B3 Dry Bay AK U.S.A.
223 M5 Dryberry Lake Ont. Can.
139 O7 Drybin Belarus
150 G4 Drybrook Gloucestershire, England U.K.
237 E7 Dry Cimarron r. KS U.S.A.
224 A3 Dryden Ont. Can.
233 I6 Dryden NY U.S.A.
232 C12 Dryden VA U.S.A.
238 L5 Dry Fork r. WY U.S.A.
259 □ Drygalski Fjord inlet S. Georgia
263 L1 Drygalski Ice Tongue Antarctica
263 G2 Drygalski Island Antarctica
175 K2 Drygały Pol.
150 E3 Drygarn Fawr hill Wales U.K.
246 □ Dry Harbour Mountains hills Jamaica
215 I3 Dry Harts r. S. Africa
241 R5 Dry Lake NV U.S.A.
240 O2 Dry Lake l. NV U.S.A.
146 H10 Drymen Stirling, Scotland U.K.
138 K6 Drysa r. Belarus
86 I3 Drysdale r. W.A. Austr.
84 E1 Drysdale Island N.T. Austr.
86 I3 Drysdale River National Park W.A. Austr.
Drysyvaty Vozyera l. Belarus/Lith. see Drūkšiu ežeras
231 F13 Dry Tortugas is FL U.S.A.
174 G3 Drzewce Pol.
174 E2 Drzewiany Pol.
175 I4 Drzewica Pol.
174 E2 Drzonowo Zachodniopomorskie Pol.
170 L2 Drzonowo Zachodniopomorskie Pol.
174 G2 Drzycim Pol.
207 H5 Dschang Cameroon
208 D4 Dua r. Dem. Rep. Congo
122 C4 Dūāb r. Iran
227 I6 Duaca Venez.
192 B7 Dualchi Sardegna Italy
108 G7 Du'an Guangxi China
Duancun Shanxi China see Wuxiang
217 □3b Duangani Mayotte
85 L7 Duaringa Qld Austr.
117 M6 Duars reg. Assam India
246 H4 Duarte, Pico mt. Dom. Rep.
256 C5 Duartina Brazil
182 H6 Duas Igrejas Port.
206 E5 Duayaw-Nkwanta Ghana
176 D1 Dubá Czech Rep.
124 B2 Dubā Saudi Arabia
Dubai U.A.E. see Dubayy
240 I1 Dubakella Mountain CA U.S.A.
136 I6 Dubăsari Moldova
136 I6 Dubău Moldova
223 L2 Dubawnt r. Nunavut Can.
223 K2 Dubawnt Lake N.W.T./Nunavut Can.
Dubayshī Oman
125 M4 Dubayy U.A.E.
125 L3 Dubbagh, Jabal ad mt. Saudi Arabia
124 B2 Dubbo N.S.W. Austr.
83 L5 Dube r. Liberia
206 D5 Dubechne Ukr.
136 D2 Dubeczno Pol.
175 L4 Duben Ger.
171 I7 Düben Ger.
171 F7 Dübendorf Switz.
190 F1 Dübener Heide park Ger.
171 G7 Dübener Heide reg. Ger.
171 F7 Dubeninki Pol.
175 K1 Dubenskiy Rus. Fed.
135 I5 Dubesar' Moldova see Dubăsari
120 G2 Dubh Artach i. Scotland U.K.
146 C10 Dubí Czech Rep.
171 I9 Dubičiai Lith.
138 H7 Dubiecko Pol.
175 K6 Dubienka Pol.
175 L4 Dubinės, Maja e mt. Albania
196 H8 Dubingiai Lith.
138 I6 Dubino Ukr.
190 G3 Dubivka Ukr.
136 F5 Dubiyivka Ukr.
137 K4 Dubki Rus. Fed.
129 H2 Dubky Ukr.
137 N9 Dublán Mex.
242 F2 Dublin Ont. Can.
226 G1 Dublin Ireland
147 J6 Dublin county Ireland
147 J6 Dublin GA U.S.A.
231 F9 Dublin MD U.S.A.
234 C5 Dublin PA U.S.A.
234 E4 Dublin VA U.S.A.
232 E11 Dublin Bay Ireland
147 J6 Dublovice Czech Rep.
176 D2 Dublyany L'vivs'ka Oblast' Ukr.
136 C4 Dublyany L'vivs'ka Oblast' Ukr.
136 D4 Dubna Moskovskaya Oblast' Rus. Fed.
137 M2 Dubna Belarus
138 J5 Dubna r. Latvia
139 U5 Dubna Moskovskaya Oblast' Rus. Fed.
139 T7 Dubna Tul'skaya Oblast' Rus. Fed.
176 G3 Dubňany Czech Rep.
176 D2 Dubné Czech Rep.
177 H4 Dubnica nad Váhom Slovakia
136 E3 Dubno Ukr.
238 I4 Dubois ID U.S.A.
232 G7 Du Bois PA U.S.A.
238 J5 Dubois WY U.S.A.
Dubossary Moldova see Dubăsari
139 T8 Dubovaya Roshcha Rus. Fed.
136 C5 Dubove Ukr.
177 J2 Dubovica Slovakia
137 O5 Dubovi Hryady Ukr.
139 V8 Dubovka Tul'skaya Oblast' Rus. Fed.
135 I6 Dubovka Volgogradskaya Oblast' Rus. Fed.
Dubovoye Moldova see Dubău
139 X6 Dubovoye, Ozero l. Rus. Fed.
135 H7 Dubovskoye Rus. Fed.
137 M2 Dubov"yazivka Ukr.
129 J5 Dübrar Dağı mt. Azer.
179 O8 Dubrava Croatia
177 I2 Dúbrava Slovakia
179 M8 Dúbrava Croatia
177 I3 Dúbravy Slovakia
206 B4 Dubréka Guinea
Dubris Kent, England U.K. see Dover
136 G3 Dubrivka Ukr.
139 W7 Dubrovichi Rus. Fed.
139 Q8 Dubrovka Bryanskaya Oblast' Rus. Fed.
138 L5 Dubrovka Pskovskaya Oblast' Rus. Fed.
138 M4 Dubrovka Pskovskaya Oblast' Rus. Fed.
188 G4 Dubrovnik Croatia
121 M1 Dubrovnoye Kazakh.
175 L6 Dubrovytsya L'vivs'ka Oblast' Ukr.
136 F2 Dubrovytsya Rivnens'ka Oblast' Ukr.
139 N7 Dubrowna Belarus
121 S6 Dubun Kazakh.
230 B4 Dubuque IA U.S.A.
136 J5 Dubynove Ukr.
138 G6 Dubysa r. Lith.
158 G6 Duc, Étang au l. France
97 H9 Đuc Bôn Vietnam
97 H9 Duc de Gloucester, Îles du is Arch. des Tuamotu Fr. Polynesia
79 □9 Duc de Gloucester, Îles du is Arch. des Tuamotu Fr. Polynesia
158 I4 Ducey France
109 K4 Duchang Jiangxi China
85 N1 Duchateau Entrance sea chan. P.N.G.
Duchong Guangdong China see Yunan
170 I3 Ducherow Ger.
241 V1 Duchesne UT U.S.A.
241 W1 Duchesne r. UT U.S.A.
84 E6 Duchess Qld Austr.
223 I5 Duchess Alta Can.
171 I9 Duchov Czech Rep.
85 I2 Ducie r. Qld Austr.
267 K7 Ducie Island atoll Pitcairn Is
231 D7 Duck r. TN U.S.A.
223 K4 Duck Bay Man. Can.
86 D7 Duck Creek r. W.A. Austr.
151 M4 Duck End Essex, England U.K.
223 J4 Duck Lake Sask. Can.
222 K5 Duck Mountain Provincial Park Man. Can.
238 F6 Duck Valley Indian Reservation res. ID/NV U.S.A.
241 Q3 Duckwater NV U.S.A.
241 Q3 Duckwater Peak NV U.S.A.
159 M3 Duclair France
97 H9 Đuc Linh Vietnam
247 □3 Ducos Martinique
97 I7 Đuc Phổ Vietnam
96 G5 Đuc Tho Vietnam
250 C4 Duda r. Col.
177 G4 Dudar Hungary
137 M6 Dudchany Ukr.
149 M2 Duddo Northumberland, England U.K.
149 K5 Duddon r. England U.K.
165 J10 Dudelange Lux.
169 C11 Dudeldorf Ger.
169 J7 Duderstadt Ger.
196 I4 Dudeștii Vechi Romania
117 I7 Dudhi Uttar Prad. India
117 M7 Dudhnai Assam India
116 H5 Dudhwa Uttar Prad. India
177 H3 Dudince Slovakia
190 C2 Düdingen Switz.
130 J3 Dudinka Rus. Fed.
150 H2 Dudley West Midlands, England U.K.
241 V9 Dudleyville AZ U.S.A.
114 E3 Dudna r. India
139 S8 Dudorovskiy Rus. Fed.
116 E6 Dudu Rajasthan India
210 E3 Dudub Eth.
215 M2 Duduza S. Africa
188 F2 Duďvah r. Slovakia
146 L8 Dudwick, Hill of Scotland U.K.
100 M3 Due Sakhalin Rus. Fed.
206 D5 Duékoué Côte d'Ivoire
94 E6 Duen, Bukit vol. Indon.
183 K5 Dueñas Spain
143 L7 Dueodde pt Bornholm Denmark
254 C4 Duerê Brazil
182 I4 Duerna r. Spain
160 F5 Duerne France
182 G6 Duero r. Spain alt. Douro (Portugal)
191 L4 Dueville Italy
227 P1 Dufault, Lac l. Que. Can.
165 G6 Duffel Belgium
224 E1 Dufferin, Cape Que. Can.
238 E6 Duffer Peak NV U.S.A.
151 J2 Duffield Derbyshire, England U.K.
232 C12 Duffield VA U.S.A.
78 □6 Duff Islands Santa Cruz Is Solomon Is
225 G1 Duffreboy, Lac l. Que. Can.
146 J8 Dufftown Moray, Scotland U.K.
190 D4 Dufourspitze mt. Italy/Switz.
223 L5 Dufrost Man. Can.
84 H5 Dugald r. Qld Austr.
188 E3 Duga Resa Croatia
131 P4 Duga-Zapadnaya, Mys c. Rus. Fed.
100 F2 Dugda Rus. Fed.
128 E9 Dughdash mts Saudi Arabia
Dughoba Uzbek. see Dugob
188 E3 Dugi Otok i. Croatia
188 F4 Dugi Rat Croatia
139 T7 Dugna Rus. Fed.
157 J5 Dugny-sur-Meuse France
121 L8 Dugob Uzbek.
188 F4 Dugopolje Croatia
188 F3 Dugo Selo Croatia
107 K7 Dugui Qarag Nei Mongol China
199 I1 Düğüncübaşı Turkey
241 T1 Dugway UT U.S.A.
108 H2 Du He r. China
163 D8 Duhort-Bachen France
202 C4 Duhūn Tārsū mts Chad/Libya
251 E4 Duida-Marahuaca, Parque Nacional nat. park Venez.
85 H2 Duifken Point Qld Austr.
164 H2 Duinen Terschelling nature res. Neth.
164 G2 Duinen Texel nature res. Neth.
164 F5 Duinen van Voorne nature res. Neth.
169 I6 Duingen Ger.
191 P4 Duino Italy
122 D5 Duir Iran
169 C8 Duisburg Ger.
250 C3 Duitama Col.
164 J5 Duiven Neth.
213 F4 Duiwelskloof S. Africa
108 D3 Dujiangyan Sichuan China
210 D4 Dujuuma Somalia
131 Q3 Dukat Rus. Fed.
197 K8 Dukat mt. Serbia
215 K6 Dukathole S. Africa
198 A2 Dukat i Ri Albania
222 D4 Duke Island AK U.S.A.
Duke of Clarence atoll Tokelau see Nukunonu
Duke of Gloucester Islands Arch. des Tuamotu Fr. Polynesia see Duc de Gloucester, Îles du
Duke of York atoll Tokelau see Atafu
210 A3 Duk Fadiat Sudan
210 A3 Duk Faiwil Sudan
125 J3 Dukhān Qatar
124 F3 Dukhnah Saudi Arabia
120 C1 Dukhovnitskoye Rus. Fed.
139 P6 Dukhovshchina Rus. Fed.
139 O6 Dukhovshehinskaya Vozvyshennost' hills Rus. Fed.
123 M6 Duki Pak.
100 I3 Duki Rus. Fed.
100 I3 Duki r. Rus. Fed.
207 H4 Dukku Nigeria
175 J6 Dukla Pol.
Dukou Sichuan China see Panzhihua
138 J6 Dūkštas Lith.
212 E4 Dukwe Botswana
106 J2 Dulaanhaan Mongolia
122 H7 Dūlab Iran
237 J11 Dulac LA U.S.A.
106 F8 Dulan Qinghai China
Dulawan Mindanao Phil. see Datu Piang
261 F2 Dulce r. Arg.
183 O7 Dulce r. Spain
239 K8 Dulce NM U.S.A.
242 □R13 Dulce, Golfo b. Costa Rica
242 □Q10 Dulce Nombre de Culmí Hond.
258 C2 Dulcinea Chile
107 M1 Dul'durga Rus. Fed.
147 J5 Duleek Ireland
131 O3 Dulgalakh r. Rus. Fed.
197 P7 Dŭlgopol Bulg.
85 I1 Dulhunty r. Qld Austr.
138 K6 Dulina Belarus
111 E9 Dulishi Hu salt l. China
95 J3 Dulit, Pegunungan mts Malaysia
108 G6 Duliu Jiang r. China
92 E6 Duljugan Point Leyte Phil.
117 N7 Dullabchara Assam India
151 M3 Dullingham Cambridgeshire, England U.K.
215 O1 Dullstroom S. Africa
169 D7 Dülmen Ger.
116 D5 Dulmera Rajasthan India
146 I8 Dulnain r. Scotland U.K.
146 I8 Dulnain Bridge Highland, Scotland U.K.
138 L4 Dulovka Rus. Fed.
197 P7 Dulovo Bulg.
128 G2 Dulq Maghār Syria
226 B3 Duluth MN U.S.A.
236 I2 Duluth/Superior airport MN U.S.A.
150 E5 Dulverton Somerset, England U.K.
139 X4 Dulyapino Rus. Fed.
128 E5 Dūmā Syria
92 D7 Dumaguete Negros Phil.
94 D4 Dumai Sumatera Indon.
129 A5 Dumanlı Turkey
129 E5 Dumanlı Dağı mt. Turkey
129 B6 Dumanlı Tepe mt. Turkey
92 D8 Dumanquilas Bay Mindanao Phil.
92 C6 Dumaran i. Phil.
93 D1 Dumarchen i. Indon.
83 M3 Dumaresq r. N.S.W. Austr.
237 J9 Dumas AR U.S.A.
237 E8 Dumas TX U.S.A.
126 I9 Dumat al Jandal Al Jawf Saudi Arabia
128 E5 Dumayr Syria
128 E5 Dumayr, Jabal mts Syria
Dumbakh Iran see Dom Bākh
146 G11 Dumbarton West Dunbartonshire, Scotland U.K.
215 O3 Dumbe S. Africa
78 □5 Dumbéa New Caledonia
177 I3 Dumbier mt. Slovakia
87 D12 Dumbleyung W.A. Austr.
87 D12 Dumbleyung, Lake salt flat W.A. Austr.
207 H5 Dumbo Cameroon
177 L6 Dumbrava Romania
197 M4 Dumbrava Roşie Romania
197 P5 Dumbrăveni Vrancea Romania

Column 1

197 N5 **Dumbrăviţa** Braşov Romania
177 K6 **Dumbrăviţa** Timiş Romania
182 B2 **Dumbria** Spain
116 G3 **Dumchele** Jammu and Kashmir
94 G4 **Dumdum** i. Indon.
171 Q6 **Dum Duma** Assam India
197 P4 **Dumeşti** Romania
158 F7 **Dumet, Île** i. France
247 □³ **Dumfries** Grenada
146 I12 **Dumfries** Dumfries and Galloway, Scotland U.K.
146 I12 **Dumfries and Galloway** admin. div. Scotland U.K.
139 S8 **Duminichi** Kaluzhskaya Oblast' Rus. Fed.
139 S8 **Duminichi** Kaluzhskaya Oblast' Rus. Fed.
197 M3 **Dumitra** Romania
117 K7 **Dumka** Jharkhand India
129 C5 **Dumlu** Turkey
129 C5 **Dumlu Dağı** mt. Turkey
129 D4 **Dumluçay** Turkey
199 K4 **Dumlupınar** Turkey
114 G4 **Dummagudem** Andhra Prad. India
168 F5 **Dümmer** i. Ger.
169 F5 **Dümmer, Naturpark** nature res. Ger.
170 F3 **Dummerstorf** Ger.
93 D3 **Dumoga** Sulawesi Indon.
224 E4 **Dumoine** r. Que. Can.
227 Q3 **Dumoine, Lac** l. Que. Can.
227 R3 **Dumont, Lac** l. Que. Can.
263 J2 **Dumont d'Urville** research stn Antarctica
263 I2 **Dumont d'Urville Sea** Antarctica
169 C10 **Dumpelfeld** Ger.
117 J7 **Dumraon** Bihar India
124 F7 **Dumsuk** i. Saudi Arabia
203 F2 **Dumyāt** Egypt
126 E8 **Dumyāţ** governorate Egypt
163 H9 **Dun** France
169 J8 **Dun** ridge Ger.
188 G3 **Duna** r. Hungary
  alt. Donau (Austria/Germany),
  alt. Dunaj (Slovakia),
  alt. Dunărea (Romania),
  alt. Dunav (Serbia),
  conv. Danube
175 I5 **Dunajec** r. Pol.
175 G3 **Dunajská Lužná** Slovakia
177 G4 **Dunajská Streda** Slovakia
136 I3 **Dunajs'ki Plavni** nature res. Ukr.
177 I4 **Dunakeszi** Hungary
176 G4 **Dunakiliti** Hungary
83 K10 **Dunalley** Tas. Austr.
147 J5 **Dunany Point** Ireland
177 I5 **Dunapataj** Hungary
197 R5 **Dunărea** r. Romania
  alt. Donau (Austria/Germany),
  alt. Dunaj (Hungary),
  alt. Dunaj (Slovakia),
  alt. Dunav (Serbia),
  conv. Danube
197 R5 **Dunării, Delta** Romania
177 G4 **Dunaszeg** Hungary
177 H5 **Dunaszekcső** Hungary
177 H5 **Dunaszentgyörgy** Hungary
176 G4 **Dunasziget** Hungary
177 I5 **Dunatetétlen** Hungary
177 I5 **Duna-Tisza Köze** reg. Hungary
177 H5 **Dunaújváros** Hungary
197 P6 **Dunav** r. Serbia
  alt. Donau (Austria/Germany),
  alt. Duna (Hungary),
  alt. Dunaj (Slovakia),
  alt. Dunărea (Romania),
  conv. Danube
177 I4 **Dunavarsány** Hungary
177 H5 **Dunavecse** Hungary
197 K7 **Dunavtsi** Bulg.
131 N2 **Dunay, Ostrova** is Rus. Fed.
136 F4 **Dunayivtsi** Khmel'nyts'ka Oblast' Ukr.
136 F5 **Dunayivtsi** Khmel'nyts'ka Oblast' Ukr.
81 C12 **Dunback** South I. N.Z.
85 I4 **Dunbar** Qld Austr.
146 K10 **Dunbar** East Lothian, Scotland U.K.
232 F9 **Dunbar** PA U.S.A.
226 F4 **Dunbar** WI U.S.A.
232 D10 **Dunbar** WV U.S.A.
146 J6 **Dunbeath** Highland, Scotland U.K.
146 I10 **Dunblane** Stirling, Scotland U.K.
147 J6 **Dunboyne** Ireland
222 F5 **Duncan** B.C. Can.
241 W9 **Duncan** AZ U.S.A.
237 G8 **Duncan** OK U.S.A.
224 D2 **Duncan, Cape** Nunavut Can.
224 E2 **Duncan, Lac** l. Que. Can.
222 G5 **Duncan Lake** B.C. Can.
222 H2 **Duncan Lake** N.W.T. Can.
147 I8 **Duncannon** Ireland
227 Q9 **Duncannon** PA U.S.A.
147 D8 **Duncan Bridge** Ireland
115 M7 **Duncan Passage** Andaman & Nicobar Is India
246 □ **Duncans** Jamaica
146 J5 **Duncansby Head** Scotland U.K.
246 F2 **Duncan Town** Bahamas
151 J3 **Dunchurch** Warwickshire, England U.K.
147 I8 **Duncormick** Ireland
138 F4 **Dundaga** Latvia
146 E10 **Dun da Ghaoithe** hill Scotland U.K.
227 N5 **Dundalk** Ont. Can.
147 J4 **Dundalk** Ireland
234 B6 **Dundalk** MD U.S.A.
147 J5 **Dundalk Bay** Ireland
224 E5 **Dundas** Ont. Can.
Dundas Greenland see Uummannaq
87 F12 **Dundas, Lake** salt flat W.A. Austr.
222 D4 **Dundas Island** B.C. Can.
87 G12 **Dundas Nature Reserve** W.A. Austr.
220 G2 **Dundas Peninsula** N.W.T. Can.
84 C1 **Dundas Strait** N.T. Austr.
107 L3 **Dundbürd** Mongolia
Dún Dealgan Ireland see Dundalk
215 O4 **Dundee** S. Africa
146 K10 **Dundee** Dundee, Scotland U.K.
146 K10 **Dundee** admin. div. Scotland U.K.
227 K8 **Dundee** MI U.S.A.
232 I6 **Dundee** NY U.S.A.
106 I4 **Dundgovi** prov. Mongolia
107 O5 **Dund Hot** Nei Mongol China
147 K3 **Dundonald** Northern Ireland U.K.
146 G11 **Dundonald** South Ayrshire, Scotland U.K.
85 J9 **Dundoo** Qld Austr.
146 G8 **Dundreggan** Highland, Scotland U.K.
146 I13 **Dundrennan** Dumfries and Galloway, Scotland U.K.
147 J6 **Dundrum** Dublin Ireland
147 F7 **Dundrum** Tipperary Ireland
147 K4 **Dundrum** Northern Ireland U.K.
147 K4 **Dundrum Bay** Northern Ireland U.K.
116 I6 **Dundwa Range** mts India/Nepal
224 F1 **Dune, Lac** l. Que. Can.

Column 2

146 I11 **Duneaton Water** r. Scotland U.K.
146 L8 **Dunecht** Aberdeenshire, Scotland U.K.
81 E12 **Dunedin** South I. N.Z.
231 F11 **Dunedin** FL U.S.A.
83 L5 **Dunedoo** N.S.W. Austr.
121 S3 **Dunenbay** Kazakh.
163 F7 **Dunes** France
222 E3 **Dune za Keyih Provincial Park** nat. park B.C. Can.
148 B3 **Dunfanaghy** Ireland
146 J10 **Dunfermline** Fife, Scotland U.K.
147 I3 **Dungannon** Northern Ireland U.K.
Dún Garbhán Ireland see Dungarvan
116 E5 **Dungargarh** Rajasthan India
116 D7 **Dungarpur** Rajasthan India
147 H7 **Dungarvan** Kilkenny Ireland
147 G8 **Dungarvan** Waterford Ireland
173 N4 **Dungau** reg. Ger.
111 J11 **Dung Co** l. Xizang China
151 N6 **Dungeness** hd England U.K.
259 C9 **Dungeness, Punta** pt Arg.
231 G10 **Düngenheim** Ger.
147 I3 **Dungiven** Northern Ireland U.K.
147 F3 **Dungloe** Ireland
83 M5 **Dungog** N.S.W. Austr.
96 I7 **Dung Quất, Vung** b. Vietnam
208 F4 **Dungu** Dem. Rep. Congo
94 E2 **Dungun** Malaysia
203 H4 **Dungunab** Sudan
Dunhou Jiangxi China see Ji'an
100 F7 **Dunhua** Jilin China
110 L6 **Dunhuang** Gansu China
158 E5 **Dunières** France
174 E1 **Duninowo** Pol.
85 L8 **Dunkeld** Qld Austr.
83 I7 **Dunkeld** Vic. Austr.
146 I9 **Dunkeld** Perth and Kinross, Scotland U.K.
147 E6 **Dunkellin** r. Ireland
179 L3 **Dunkelsteiner Wald** for. Austria
156 D1 **Dunkerque** France
147 G7 **Dunkerrin** Ireland
150 E5 **Dunkery Hill** England U.K.
147 F3 **Dunkineely** Ireland
Dunkirk France see Dunkerque
151 N5 **Dunkirk** NY U.S.A.
232 B8 **Dunkirk** IN U.S.A.
85 K4 **Dunk Island** Qld Austr.
206 C5 **Dunkwa** Ghana
147 J6 **Dún Laoghaire** Ireland
236 H5 **Dunlap** IA U.S.A.
231 E8 **Dunlap** TN U.S.A.
147 I6 **Dunlavin** Ireland
147 J5 **Dunleer** Ireland
162 H3 **Dun-le-Palestel** France
160 E2 **Dun-les-Places** France
148 A3 **Dunlewy** Ireland
146 G11 **Dunlop** East Ayrshire, Scotland U.K.
147 J2 **Dunloy** Northern Ireland U.K.
145 D4 **Dunluce** tourist site Northern Ireland U.K.
147 C9 **Dunmanus** Ireland
147 D9 **Dunmanway** Ireland
84 D4 **Dunmarra** N.T. Austr.
147 G8 **Dunmoon** Ireland
147 E5 **Dunmore** Ireland
234 D2 **Dunmore** PA U.S.A.
232 F10 **Dunmore** WV U.S.A.
147 I8 **Dunmore** Ireland
246 E1 **Dunmore Town** Eleuthera Bahamas
Dunmore East Ireland see Dunmore
147 K3 **Dunmurry** Northern Ireland U.K.
147 I5 **Dunmurry** Ireland
146 I5 **Dunnamanagh** Northern Ireland U.K.
231 F11 **Dunnellon** FL U.S.A.
146 J5 **Dunnet** Scotland, Scotland U.K.
146 J5 **Dunnet Bay** Scotland U.K.
146 J5 **Dunnet Head** Scotland U.K.
240 K3 **Dunnigan** CA U.S.A.
146 I10 **Dunning** Perth and Kinross, Scotland U.K.
236 E3 **Dunning** NE U.S.A.
172 F5 **Dunningen** Ger.
149 P6 **Dunnington** York, England U.K.
87 E12 **Dunn Rock Nature Reserve** W.A. Austr.
87 E8 **Dunns Range** hills W.A. Austr.
227 O7 **Dunnville** Ont. Can.
156 B8 **Dunois** France
83 I7 **Dunolly** Vic. Austr.
146 G11 **Dunoon** Argyll and Bute, Scotland U.K.
147 B8 **Dunquin** Ireland
146 J11 **Dun Rig** hill Scotland U.K.
146 L11 **Duns** Scottish Borders, Scotland U.K.
123 K4 **Dunsa** Afgh.
123 J3 **Duşak** Turkm.
115 I6 **Dusetos** Lith.
113 K7 **Dushan** Pak.
102 F6 **Dushan** Guizhou China
123 M2 **Dushanbe** Tajik.
110 I4 **Dushanzi** Xinjiang China
137 L1 **Dushatine** Rus. Fed.
177 I Georgia
107 N6 **Dushkou** Hebei China
227 R8 **Dushore** PA U.S.A.
138 G7 **Dusia** l. Lith.
81 A12 **Dusky Sound** inlet South I. N.Z.
175 M1 **Dusmenys** Lith.
175 H5 **Dusocin** Pol.
174 G2 **Dusocin** Pol.
100 I3 **Dusse-Alin', Khrebet** mts Rus. Fed.
86 J3 **Dussejour, Cape** W.A. Austr.
169 C9 **Düsseldorf** Ger.
169 B7 **Düsseldorf** admin. reg. Ger.
106 I1 **Dzelter** Mongolia
138 J4 **Dzeni** Latvia
172 G5 **Dußlingen** Ger.
169 E11 **Düßnitz** Ger.
123 M3 **Düsti** Tajik.
238 F3 **Dusty** WY U.S.A.
174 E5 **Duszniki-Zdrój** Pol.

Column 3

244 C1 **Durango** state Mex.
183 O2 **Durango** Spain
239 K8 **Durango** CO U.S.A.
244 B2 **Durango, Sierra de** mts Mex.
123 L6 **Durani** reg. Afgh.
197 Q7 **Durankulak** Bulg.
191 M3 **Durazno, Monte** mt. Italy
261 G5 **Durazno** Uru.
237 K9 **Durant** MS U.S.A.
237 G8 **Durant** OK U.S.A.
163 E6 **Duras** France
161 I7 **Durant** r. Spain
157 I8 **Duravel** France
128 E4 **Duraykish** Syria
261 G5 **Durazno** Arg.
261 G5 **Durazno** Uru.
261 I3 **Durazno** dept. Uru.
172 E4 **Durazzo** Albania see Durrës
163 G9 **Durban** France
215 P5 **Durban** S. Africa
161 B11 **Durban-Corbières** France
214 C9 **Durban S.** Africa
172 E5 **Durbheim** Ger.
232 F10 **Durbin** WV U.S.A.
157 L7 **Durbion** r. France
123 K7 **Durbin** Pak.
165 H8 **Durbuy** Belgium
185 M7 **Durcal** r. Spain
177 H2 **Durčiná** Slovakia
160 B4 **Durdat-Larequille** France
159 M2 **Durdent** r. France
127 I4 **Durdura, Raas** pt Somalia
110 I3 **Düre** Xinjiang China
169 B9 **Düren** Ger.
122 G5 **Düren** Iran
122 G5 **Düren, Küh-e** mt. Iran
161 D9 **Duret** France
116 H9 **Durg** Chhattisgarh India
117 M7 **Durgapur** Bangl.
117 K8 **Durgapur** W. Bengal India
227 N5 **Durham** Ont. Can.
149 N4 **Durham** Durham, England U.K.
149 M4 **Durham** admin. div. England U.K.
240 K2 **Durham** CA U.S.A.
235 J2 **Durham** CT U.S.A.
231 H8 **Durham** NC U.S.A.
233 □O5 **Durham** NH U.S.A.
80 □ **Durham** Chatham Is S. Pacific Ocean
233 □S2 **Durham Bridge** N.B. Can.
85 H9 **Durham Downs** Qld Austr.
149 O4 **Durham Tees Valley** airport England U.K.
210 D3 **Durhi** well Eth.
94 D4 **Duri** Sumatra Indon.
95 H5 **Duri** Sumatra Indon.
146 I12 **Durisdeer** Dumfries and Galloway, Scotland U.K.
Durlas Ireland see Thurles
136 H6 **Durleşti** Moldova
179 M7 **Durmanec** Croatia
171 E1 **Durme** r. Belgium
172 H5 **Durmersheim** Ger.
196 H7 **Durmitor** mt. Montenegro
196 G7 **Durmitor** nat. park Montenegro
146 G5 **Durness** Highland, Scotland U.K.
146 G5 **Durness, Kyle of** inlet Scotland U.K.
179 O3 **Dürnkrut** Austria
Durocortorum France see Reims
85 L8 **Durong South** Qld Austr.
210 D2 **Durostorum** Bulg. see Silistra
178 G7 **Durovernum** Kent, England U.K. see Canterbury
196 H9 **Durrës** Albania
172 I5 **Dürrlauingen** Ger.
171 H7 **Dürrnhaar** Ger.
173 I6 **Durran** Ireland
173 I3 **Dürrwangen** Ger.
147 F11 **Dursey Head** Ireland
147 B9 **Dursey Island** Ireland
150 H4 **Dursley** Gloucestershire, England U.K.
199 J3 **Dursunbey** Turkey
159 K6 **Durtal** France
173 Q3 **Duru** Guizhou China see
208 F4 **Duru** r. Dem. Rep. Congo
138 F2 **Duruca** Turkey
183 O3 **Duruelo de la Sierra** Spain
122 I5 **Durukhsi** Somalia
210 E2 **Duruksu** Turkey
199 J1 **Durusu Gölü** l. Turkey
128 E6 **Duruz, Jabal ad** mt. Syria
91 I7 **D'Urville, Tanjung** pt Papua Indon.
80 H7 **D'Urville Island** South I. N.Z.
234 D2 **Duryea** PA U.S.A.
146 □N2 **Dury Voe** inlet Scotland U.K.
123 K4 **Dusa** Afgh.

Column 4

199 M2 **Düzce** Turkey
199 M1 **Düzce** prov. Turkey
129 G4 **Düz Cırdaxan** Azer.
123 J6 **Duzdab** Iran see Zāhedān
129 A5 **Düzköy** Turkey
136 F1 **Dvarets** Belarus
197 N7 **Dve Mogili** Bulg.
138 J5 **Dviete** Latvia
134 G2 **Dvinskaya Guba** g. Rus. Fed.
139 O5 **Dvin'ye, Ozero** l. Rus. Fed.
188 F3 **Dvor** Croatia
177 Q2 **Dvorce** Czech Rep.
137 Q4 **Dvorichna** Ukr.
137 V5 **Dvoriki** Rus. Fed.
177 H4 **Dvory nad Žitavou** Slovakia
139 W6 **Dvoyni** Rus. Fed.
176 F1 **Dvůr Králové nad Labem** Czech Rep.
209 D6 **Dwangwa** Malawi
116 B8 **Dwarka** Gujarat India
215 J2 **Dwarsberg** S. Africa
123 N5 **Dwehi** Pak.
195 □ **Dwejra, Il-Ponta ta** pt Gozo Malta
87 D12 **Dwellingup** W.A. Austr.
215 M8 **Dwesa Nature Reserve** S. Africa
215 O6 **Dweshula** S. Africa
226 F2 **Dwight** IL U.S.A.
175 J5 **Dwikozy** Pol.
164 J3 **Dwingelderveld, Nationaal Park** Neth.
164 J3 **Dwingeloo** Neth.
238 G3 **Dworshak Reservoir** ID U.S.A.
214 F9 **Dwyka** S. Africa
214 F9 **Dwyka** r. S. Africa
137 T4 **D'yachenkovo** Rus. Fed.
134 H4 **D'yakonovo** Kostromskaya Oblast' Rus. Fed.
137 O2 **D'yakonovo** Kurskaya Oblast' Rus. Fed.
137 S6 **Dyakove** Ukr.
193 J9 **Dyakovo** Rus. Fed.
189 B9 **D'yakovo** Rus. Fed.
137 O2 **D'yat'kovo** Rus. Fed.
121 T5 **Dyaul Island** P.N.G.
123 I2 **Dyce** Aberdeen, Scotland U.K.
174 L8 **Dyce** Aberdeen, Scotland U.K.
175 K6 **Dydia** Pol.
100 G4 **Dydy** Rus. Fed.
221 L3 **Dyer, Cape** Nunavut Can.
227 M4 **Dyer Bay** Ont. Can.
262 T2 **Dyer Plateau** Antarctica
237 K7 **Dyersburg** TN U.S.A.
83 J7 **Dyeville** North I. N.Z.
176 B2 **Dyje** r. Austria/Czech Rep.
137 J2 **Dykanka** r. Ukr.
129 F2 **Dykhtau, Gora** mt. Rus. Fed.
176 B2 **Dyleň** hill Czech Rep.
174 F3 **Dylewska Góra** hill Pol.
129 P2 **Dylym** Rus. Fed.
151 I5 **Dymchurch** Kent, England U.K.
136 J3 **Dymer** Ukr.
139 Q2 **Dymi** Rus. Fed.
150 H4 **Dymock** Gloucestershire, England U.K.
137 L5 **Dymytrove** Kirovohrads'ka Oblast' Ukr.
137 L5 **Dymytrove** Kirovohrads'ka Oblast' Ukr.
142 E1 **Dyna** inl. Norway
83 J3 **Dynevor Downs** Qld Austr.
175 K6 **Dynów** Pol.
160 E4 **Dyoki** S. Africa
140 N2 **Dyrøyhamn** Norway
Dyrrhachium Albania see Durrës
85 L7 **Dysart** Qld Austr.
150 F1 **Dyserth** Denbighshire, Wales U.K.
173 P3 **Dyška** Czech Rep.
138 F4 **Dysna** r. Lith.
214 G9 **Dysselsdorp** S. Africa
198 B4 **Dytiki Ellada** admin. reg. Greece
198 C2 **Dytiki Makedonia** admin. reg. Greece
131 O3 **Dyurtyuli** Rus. Fed.
175 J5 **Dyulino** Bulg.
106 K7 **Dzaanhushuu** Mongolia
106 J2 **Dzag** Mongolia
106 I2 **Dzag Gol** r. Mongolia
106 F4 **Dzalaa** Mongolia
208 C4 **Dzanga-Ndoki, Parc National** Congo
208 C4 **Dzanga-Sangha, Réserve Spéciale de Forêt Dense de** nature res. C.A.R.
125 J2 **Dzaoudzi** Mayotte
175 M1 **Dzaukčiai** Lith.
106 D2 **Dzavhan** prov. Mongolia
106 D2 **Dzavhan Gol** r. Mongolia
176 C1 **Džbán** mts Czech Rep.
240 O6 **Dzeg** Mongolia
223 M6 **Dzelter** Mongolia
233 □Q1 **Dzeni** Latvia
233 □P2 **Dzerzhinsk** Homyel'skaya Voblasts' Belarus see Dzyarzhynsk
233 □Q1 **Dzerzhinsk** Minskaya Voblasts' Belarus see Dzyarzhynsk
226 D2 **Dzerzhinsk** Rus. Fed.
237 E10 **Dzerzhyns'k** Donets'ka Oblast' Ukr.
217 □3b **Dzerzhyns'k** Zhytomyrs'ka Oblast' Ukr.
100 I2 **Dzhagdy, Khrebet** mts Rus. Fed.
100 I4 **Dzhaki-Unakhta Yakbyyana, Khrebet** mts Rus. Fed.
120 K5 **Dzhalagash** Kazakh.
129 J12 **Dzhalalabad** Azer. see Cälilabad
222 G5 **Dzhalal-Abad** Kyrg. see Jalal-Abad
241 S8 **Dzhalal-Abadskaya Oblast'** admin. div. Kyrg. see Jalal-Abad
100 C2 **Dzhalinda** Rus. Fed.
151 K4 **Dzhambeyty** Kazakh. see Zhympity
87 F8 **Dzhambul** Kazakh. see Taraz
134 K5 **Dzhambul** r. Rus. Fed.
138 I3 **Dzhambul** Kazakh. see
123 J5 **Dzhanga** Turkm. see Jaña
120 D3 **Dzhangala** Kazakh.
134 K5 **Dzhanibek** Kazakh.
129 J12 **Dzhebel** Azer.
86 I6 **Dzhebel** Bulg.
207 M7 **Dzheti-Oguz** Kyrg. see Jeti-Ögüz
82 F4 **Dzhetygara** Kazakh. see Zhitikara
238 I1 **Dzhezkazgan** Kazakh. see Zhezkazgan
82 F4 **Dzhidinskiy, Khrebet** mts Mongolia/Rus. Fed.
241 J3 **Dzhirgatal'** Tajik. see Jirgatol
175 J3 **Dzhizak** Uzbek. see Jizzax
223 J5 **Dzhokhar Ghala** Rus. Fed. see Groznyy
146 J10 **Dzhordzhiashvili** Georgia see Jorjiashvili
134 C6 **Dzhubga** Rus. Fed.
131 N3 **Dzhugdzhur, Khrebet** mts Rus. Fed.
123 J7 **Dzhul'fa** Azer. see Culfa
121 U3 **Dzhulynka** Ukr. see Juma
121 T5 **Dzhungarskiy Alatau, Khrebet** mts China/Kazakh.
151 K2 **Dzhungarskiye Vorota** val. Kazakh.
146 H7 **Dzhuma** Uzbek. see Juma
80 M4 **Dzhurin** Ukr. see Zhuryn
235 K2 **Dzhurinskaya, Mys** Rus. Fed.
233 J7 **Dzialoszyce** Pol.
174 G4 **Działdowo** Pol.
174 E3 **Działoszyce** Pol.
174 G4 **Działoszyn** Pol.
243 O8 **Dzibalchén** Mex.
175 I2 **Dziemiany** Pol.
175 I2 **Dzierzązna** r. Pol.
174 E3 **Dzierżążno Wielkie** Pol.
174 F5 **Dzierżoniów** Pol.
174 E2 **Dzierzgoń** Pol.
174 F3 **Dziewierzewo** Pol.
243 O7 **Dzilam de Bravo** Mex.
209 D2 **Dziua** Alg.
243 O7 **Dzilam** Mex.
18 I8 **Dzitbalché** Mex.
174 C2 **Dziwna** r. Belarus
174 D2 **Dziwnów** Pol.
137 L5 **Dzmitravichy** Belarus
207 F5 **Dzodze** Ghana
130 J3 **Dzoogol** Mongolia
129 F5 **Dzoraget** r. Armenia
138 M7 **Dzoraget** Homyel'skaya Voblasts' Belarus
135 I5 **Dzoyga** r. Armenia
106 J2 **Dzuunbayan** Mongolia
106 J2 **Dzuunbayan** Mongolia
106 J3 **Dzuunmod** Mongolia
207 J3 **Dzuyl** Mongolia
175 I2 **Dziwierzuty** Pol.
175 I5 **Dzwola** Pol.
136 I1 **Dzwonowice** Pol.
139 I8 **Dzyanisavichy** Belarus
139 O8 **Dzyarzhynsk** Belarus
138 H8 **Dzyarzhynskaya Hara** h. Belarus
138 J7 **Dzyarzhynsk** Minskaya Voblasts' Belarus
136 F1 **Dzyatavichy** Belarus
146 H7 **Dzyatlavichy** Belarus
138 I8 **Dzyerkawshchyna** Belarus
136 I2 **Dzyornavichy** Belarus

Column 5

100 K3 **Dzhaur** r. Rus. Fed.
131 O3 **Dzhebariki-Khaya** Rus. Fed.
197 N9 **Dzhebel** Bulg.
130 K1 **Dzhelon** r. Rus. Fed.
129 A5 **Dzhidzhu** Turkey
136 F1 **Dzhelondi** Tajik. see Jelondi
129 K8 **Dzhergalan** Kyrg. see Jyrgalang
134 G2 **Dzheti-Oguz** Kyrg. see Jeti-Ögüz
139 O5 **Dzhetygara** Kazakh. see Zhitikara
177 Q2 **Dzhezkazgan** Kazakh. see Zhezkazgan
137 Q4 **Dzhidinskiy** Rus. Fed.
137 V5 **Dzhugdzhur** Rus. Fed.
177 H4 **Dzhul'fa** Azer. see Culfa
139 W6 **Dzhulynka** Ukr.
120 K6 **Dzhetysay** Kazakh.
137 V5 **Dzhugdzhur** Rus. Fed.
129 F2 **Dzhukhta** r. Rus. Fed.
131 N2 **Dzhulukul, Ozero** l. Rus. Fed.
136 F4 **Dzhurmut** r. Rus. Fed.
80 M4 **Dzhuryn** Rus. Fed.
235 K2 **Dzhusaly** Kazakh.
146 J10 **Dzialoszyce** Pol.

Column 6

81 D12 **Earnscleugh** South I. N.Z.
81 C11 **Earnslaw, Mount** South I. N.Z.
146 B9 **Earsairidh** Western Isles, Scotland U.K.
237 D8 **Earth** TX U.S.A.
146 E10 **Easdale** Argyll and Bute, Scotland U.K.
151 K6 **Easebourne** West Sussex, England U.K.
149 O4 **Easington** Durham, England U.K.
149 R6 **Easington** East Riding of Yorkshire, England U.K.
149 O5 **Easingwold** North Yorkshire, England U.K.
147 E4 **Easky** Ireland
231 F8 **Easley** SC U.S.A.
87 G10 **East, Mount** hill W.A. Austr.
263 H1 **East Antarctica** reg. Antarctica
233 J7 **East Ararat** PA U.S.A.
232 G6 **East Aurora** NY U.S.A.
146 H12 **East Ayrshire** admin. div. Scotland U.K.
84 B3 **East Baines** r. N.T. Austr.
234 E3 **East Bangor** PA U.S.A.
237 K11 **East Bay** l. LA U.S.A.
231 E10 **East Bay** inlet FL U.S.A.
151 O4 **East Bergholt** Suffolk, England U.K.
235 I3 **East Berlin** CT U.S.A.
234 B5 **East Berlin** PA U.S.A.
234 C2 **East Berwick** PA U.S.A.
81 I8 **Eastbourne** North I. N.Z.
151 M6 **Eastbourne** East Sussex, England U.K.
232 F8 **East Branch** NY U.S.A.
233 J7 **East Branch Clarion River Reservoir** PA U.S.A.
151 K2 **East Bridgford** Nottinghamshire, England U.K.
149 O5 **Eastburn** East Riding of Yorkshire, England U.K.
246 H3 **East Caicos** i. Turks and Caicos Is
80 M4 **East Cape** North I. N.Z.
80 M4 **East Cape** Rus. Fed. see Dezhneva, Mys
241 V2 **East Carbon City** UT U.S.A.
266 E5 **East Caroline Basin** sea feature N. Pacific Ocean
226 G3 **East Chicago** IL U.S.A.
99 M5 **East China Sea** N. Pacific Ocean
80 I3 **East Coast Bays** North I. N.Z.
150 G6 **East Coker** Somerset, England U.K.
223 H5 **East Coulee** Alta Can.
151 M6 **East Dean** East Sussex, England U.K.
151 L6 **East Dereham** England U.K. see Dereham
146 H11 **East Dunbartonshire** admin. div. Scotland U.K.
241 W2 **East Tavaputs Plateau** UT U.S.A.
232 B4 **East Tawas** MI U.S.A.
93 D8 **East Timor** country Asia
117 J7 **Tons** r. India
83 J4 **East Toorale** N.S.W. Austr.
227 F7 **East Troy** WI U.S.A.
227 J5 **East Twin Lake** MI U.S.A.
241 U7 **East Verde** r. AZ U.S.A.
236 C5 **East Vanier**
233 J11 **Eastville** VA U.S.A.
240 M3 **East Walker** r. NV U.S.A.
151 K6 **East Wittering** West Sussex, England U.K.
150 H6 **Eastwood** Nottinghamshire, England U.K.
151 J5 **East Woodhay** Hampshire, England U.K.
227 O6 **East York** Ont. Can.
96 I6 **Ea Sup** Vietnam
97 H8 **Etat** Vietnam
146 C5 **Eatharna, Loch** inlet Scotland U.K.
87 C12 **Eaton** W.A. Austr.
238 L6 **Eaton** CO U.S.A.
234 E1 **Eaton** NY U.S.A.
238 L6 **Eaton** CO U.S.A.
151 L3 **Eaton Bray** Bedfordshire, England U.K.
223 I5 **Eatonia** Sask. Can.
235 I1 **Eaton Neck** NY U.S.A.
235 I1 **Eaton Neck Point** NY U.S.A.
150 I3 **Eaton Socon** Cambridgeshire, England U.K.
232 F9 **Eatonton** GA U.S.A.
235 G4 **Eatontown** NJ U.S.A.
233 □P1 **Eatonville** Que. Can.
226 C5 **Eau Claire** WI U.S.A.
224 F1 **Eau Claire, Lac à l'** l. Que. Can.
163 J7 **Eauze** France
91 J5 **Eauripik** atoll Micronesia
266 E5 **Eauripik-Rise-New Guinea Rise** sea feature N. Pacific Ocean
163 D10 **Eaux-Bonnes** France
163 C9 **Eaux** France
78 □3a **Ebadon** i. Kwajalein Marshall Is
240 O2 **Eagate** NV U.S.A.
78 □3a **Ebadon** i. Kwajalein Marshall Is
226 F1 **Eagle** AK U.S.A.
220 E3 **Eagle** AK U.S.A.
239 K7 **Eagle** CO U.S.A.
234 B4 **Eagle** PA U.S.A.
240 O6 **Eagle Butte** SD U.S.A.
236 C2 **Eagle Crags** mt. OR U.S.A.
240 O6 **Eagle Crags** mt. CA U.S.A.
223 M4 **Eagle Lake** l. Ont. Can.
233 O1 **Eagle Lake** l. ME U.S.A.
233 O1 **Eagle Lake** l. CA U.S.A.
233 □Q1 **Eagle Lake** ME U.S.A.
233 □Q1 **Eagle Lake** l. ME U.S.A.
240 O2 **Eagle Mountain** hill MN U.S.A.
237 E11 **Eagle Mountain Lake** TX U.S.A.
237 E11 **Eagle Pass** TX U.S.A.
259 F9 **Eagle Passage** Falkland Is
236 C5 **Eagle Peak** CA U.S.A.
102 I7 **Eagle Plain** Y.T. Can.
236 C5 **Eagle Point** S. Pacific Ocean
236 I2 **Eagle River** MI U.S.A.
226 E4 **Eagle River** WI U.S.A.
240 O4 **Eaglescliffe** Stockton-on-Tees, England U.K.
80 M4 **Eagle Tail Mountains** AZ U.S.A.
241 J12 **Eaglesfield** Dumfries and Galloway, Scotland U.K.
222 G4 **Eaglesham** Alta Can.
146 H11 **Eaglesham** East Renfrewshire, Scotland U.K.
241 R7 **Eagle Tail Mountains** AZ U.S.A.
151 L4 **Ealing** Greater London, England U.K.
151 J6 **Eamont** r. England U.K.
87 B8 **Earaheedy** W.A. Austr.
87 F8 **Eardisley** Herefordshire, England U.K.
151 I3 **Ear Falls** Ont. Can.
235 I1 **Earith** Cambridgeshire, England U.K.
151 I3 **Earl Barton** Northamptonshire, England U.K.
151 I3 **Earl Colne** Essex, England U.K.
215 I5 **Earl Shilton** Leicestershire, England U.K.
150 I3 **Earls Barton** Northamptonshire, England U.K.
151 K3 **Earl Soham** Suffolk, England U.K.
146 H10 **Earl's Seat** hill Scotland U.K.
146 K11 **Earlston** Scottish Borders, Scotland U.K.
235 K2 **Earl Stonham** Suffolk, England U.K.
224 E5 **Earlton** Ont. Can.
146 J10 **Earn** r. Scotland U.K.

Column 7

231 F9 **Eastman** GA U.S.A.
266 F5 **East Mariana Basin** sea feature Pacific Ocean
149 P7 **East Markham** Nottinghamshire, England U.K.
85 J7 **Eastmere** Qld Austr.
233 L5 **East Middlebury** VT U.S.A.
233 □Q3 **East Millinocket** ME U.S.A.
235 I1 **East Morris** CT U.S.A.
231 G12 **East Naples** FL U.S.A.
235 I3 **East Northport** NY U.S.A.
149 P6 **Eastoft** North Lincolnshire, England U.K.
150 H6 **Easton** Dorset, England U.K.
240 M5 **Easton** CA U.S.A.
235 I2 **Easton** CT U.S.A.
234 I3 **Easton** DE U.S.A.
235 G3 **Easton** PA U.S.A.
150 G5 **Easton-in-Gordano** North Somerset, England U.K.
235 I4 **Easton** MD U.S.A.
235 G3 **East Reservoir** CT U.S.A.
267 L8 **East Pacific Ridge** S. Pacific Ocean
267 L4 **East Pacific Rise** sea feature S. Pacific Ocean
East Pakistan country Asia see Bangladesh
232 E8 **East Palatine** OH U.S.A.
240 J2 **East Park Reservoir** CA U.S.A.
226 E9 **East Peoria** IL U.S.A.
234 C4 **East Petersburg** PA U.S.A.
82 □7 **East Point** Lord Howe I. Austr.
225 I4 **East Point** P.E.I. Can.
216 □3c **East Point** i. Tristan da Cunha S. Atlantic Ocean
233 □S4 **Eastport** ME U.S.A.
226 I4 **Eastport** MI U.S.A.
234 I3 **Eastport** CT U.S.A.
234 B5 **East Prospect** PA U.S.A.
151 L6 **East Preston** West Sussex, England U.K.
235 I2 **East Quogue** NY U.S.A.
240 O1 **East Range** mts NV U.S.A.
146 H11 **East Renfrewshire** admin. div. Scotland U.K.
East Retford England U.K. see Retford
149 P7 **East Retford** Nottinghamshire, England U.K. see Retford
231 E8 **East Ridge** TN U.S.A.
149 Q6 **East Riding of Yorkshire** admin. div. England U.K.
146 J13 **Eastriggs** Dumfries and Galloway, Scotland U.K.
151 O5 **East Ruston** England U.K.
230 B6 **East St. Louis** IL U.S.A.
266 N4 **East Sea** N. Pacific Ocean see Japan, Sea of
235 I3 **East Setauket** NY U.S.A.
223 L5 **East Siberian Sea** Rus. Fed. see Vostochno-Sibirskoye More
234 D2 **East Side** PA U.S.A.
240 M6 **East Side Canal** r. CA U.S.A.
233 I10 **East Stroudsburg** PA U.S.A.
151 M6 **East Sussex** admin. div. England U.K.
241 W2 **East Tavaputs Plateau** UT U.S.A.
232 B4 **East Tawas** MI U.S.A.
93 D8 **East Timor** country Asia
117 J7 **East Tons** r. India
83 J4 **East Toorale** N.S.W. Austr.
227 F7 **East Troy** WI U.S.A.
227 J5 **East Twin Lake** MI U.S.A.
241 U7 **East Verde** r. AZ U.S.A.
236 C5 **Eastville** VA U.S.A.
233 J11 **Eastville** VA U.S.A.
240 M3 **East Walker** r. NV U.S.A.
151 K6 **East Wittering** West Sussex, England U.K.
150 H6 **Eastwood** Nottinghamshire, England U.K.
151 J5 **East Woodhay** Hampshire, England U.K.
227 O6 **East York** Ont. Can.
96 I6 **Ea Sup** Vietnam
97 H8 **Ea Sup** Vietnam
146 C5 **Eatharna, Loch** inlet Scotland U.K.
87 C12 **Eaton** W.A. Austr.
234 E1 **Eaton** NY U.S.A.
238 L6 **Eaton** CO U.S.A.
151 L3 **Eaton Bray** Bedfordshire, England U.K.
223 I5 **Eatonia** Sask. Can.
235 I1 **Eaton Neck** NY U.S.A.
235 I1 **Eaton Neck Point** NY U.S.A.
150 I3 **Eaton Socon** Cambridgeshire, England U.K.
232 F9 **Eatonton** GA U.S.A.
235 G4 **Eatontown** NJ U.S.A.
233 □P1 **Eatonville** Que. Can.
226 C5 **Eau Claire** WI U.S.A.
224 F1 **Eau Claire, Lac à l'** l. Que. Can.
163 J7 **Eauze** France
91 J5 **Eauripik** atoll Micronesia
266 E5 **Eauripik-Rise-New Guinea Rise** sea feature N. Pacific Ocean
163 D10 **Eaux-Bonnes** France
163 C9 **Eaux** France
78 □3a **Ebadon** i. Kwajalein Marshall Is
240 O2 **Eagate** NV U.S.A.
182 B3 **Ebano** Mex.
245 I4 **Ebano** Mex.
78 □3a **Ebadon** Marshall Is
151 I4 **Ebbesbourne Wake** Wiltshire, England U.K.
150 F4 **Ebbw Vale** Blaenau Gwent, Wales U.K.
207 I4 **Ebebiyin** Equat. Guinea
169 K6 **Ebeleben** Ger.
142 I2 **Ebeltoft** Denmark
178 E5 **Ebene am Achensee** Austria
215 M8 **Ebende** S. Africa
178 I6 **Ebenerde** Namibia
179 H6 **Ebene Reichenau** Austria
178 I5 **Ebenfurth** Austria
178 D5 **Ebenfurth** Austria
169 K10 **Ebensfeld** Ger.
178 H5 **Ebensee** Austria
172 H5 **Ebenweiler** Ger.
172 N5 **Eberbach** Ger.
198 □ **Eber Gölü** l. Turkey
199 J3 **Eber Gölü** l. Turkey
193 J7 **Ebergötzen** Ger.
172 E3 **Eberhardzell** Ger.
173 K2 **Ebermannstadt** Ger.
173 K2 **Ebermannstadt** Ger.
169 K10 **Ebern** Ger.
173 I5 **Ebersbach** Ger.
172 H3 **Ebersbach** Sachsen Ger.
179 I2 **Ebersbach** Sachsen Ger.
172 F3 **Ebersbach an der Fils** Ger.
179 K4 **Eberschwang** Austria
179 K2 **Ebersdorf** Austria
170 F3 **Ebersdorf** Ger.
179 K2 **Ebersmunster** France
171 E10 **Ebersdorf** Thüringen Ger.
173 K5 **Eberstein** Austria
175 I3 **Eberswalde-Finow** Ger.
277 K3 **Ebetsu** Japan
102 J3 **Ebetsu** Japan
78 □2 **Ebeye** Kwajalein Marshall Is
102 S3 **Ebino** Japan
105 D5 **Ebino** Japan
103 H14 **Ebino** Japan
110 H14 **Ebino** Japan
127 N6 **Ebi Nor** salt l. China
181 G1 **Ebnat** Switz.
179 J7 **Ebnat** tourist site Switz.
178 E5 **Ebnat-Kappel** Switz.
209 B6 **Ebo** Angola
193 I6 **Eboli** Italy
207 H5 **Ebolowa** Cameroon
208 F3 **Ebola** r. Dem. Rep. Congo
207 H5 **Ebonyi** state Nigeria

Ebrach to Ellezelles
309

173 I2 Ebrach Ger.
122 A3 Ebrāhīm Ḩeşār Iran
Ebre r. Spain see Ebro
179 N4 Ebreichsdorf Austria
160 C4 Ébreuil France
183 O5 Ebrillos r. Spain
172 D6 Ebringen Ger.
183 N3 Ebro r. Spain
183 M2 Ebro, Embalse del resr Spain
187 C7 Ebrón r. Spain
169 G9 Ebsdorfergrund-Dreihausen Ger.
169 G9 Ebsdorfergrund-Rauischholzhausen Ger.
168 J4 Ebstorf Ger.
Eburacum York, England U.K. see York
Eburodunum France see Embrun
Ebusus i. Spain see Eivissa
245 H6 Ecatepec Mex.
165 F7 Écaussinnes-d'Enghien Belgium
Ecbatana Iran see Hamadān
146 J12 Ecclefechan Dumfries and Galloway, Scotland U.K.
149 M7 Eccles Greater Manchester, England U.K.
146 L11 Eccles Scottish Borders, Scotland U.K.
232 D11 Eccles WV U.S.A.
149 O7 Ecclesfield South Yorkshire, England U.K.
150 H2 Eccleshall Staffordshire, England U.K.
149 L6 Eccleston Lancashire, England U.K.
247 □7 Ecclesville Trin. and Tob.
199 H2 Eceabat Turkey
92 C3 Echague Luzon Phil.
190 B2 Echallens Switz.
246 B9 Echandi, Cerro mt. Costa Rica
Echaot'l Koe N.W.T. Can. see Fort Liard
183 Q3 Echarri Spain
Echarri-Aranaz Spain see Etxarri-Aranatz
159 L4 Échauffour France
129 G3 Echeda Rus. Fed.
Echeng Hubei China see Ezhou
160 I1 Échenoz-la-Méline France
242 C3 Echeverria, Pico mt. Mex.
104 D5 Echigawa Japan
105 J1 Echigo-Sanzan-Tadami Kokutei-kōen park Japan
162 C4 Échillais France
173 L5 Eching Bayern Ger.
173 M4 Eching Bayern Ger.
198 F1 Echinos Greece
162 D3 Échiré France
161 H6 Échirolles France
104 D4 Echizen Japan
105 I5 Echizen-dake mt. Japan
104 D3 Echizen-Kaga-kaigan Kokutei-kōen park Japan
104 C4 Echizen-misaki pt Japan
Echmiadzin Armenia see Ejmiatsin
238 E4 Echo OR U.S.A.
83 K10 Echo, Lake Tas. Austr.
220 G3 Echo Bay N.W.T. Can.
224 C4 Echo Bay Ont. Can.
241 U5 Echo Cliffs esc. AZ U.S.A.
223 M4 Echoing r. Man./Ont. Can.
227 S2 Échouani, Lac l. Que. Can.
162 E5 Échourgnac France
179 L2 Echsenbach Austria
165 I6 Echt Neth.
146 L8 Echt Aberdeenshire, Scotland U.K.
169 J7 Echte Ger.
165 J9 Echternach Lux.
83 J7 Echuca Vic. Austr.
169 G10 Echzell Ger.
185 I5 Écija Spain
261 I4 Ecilda Paullier Uru.
148 H1 Eck, Loch l. Scotland U.K.
196 I5 Ečka Vojvodina Serbia
171 E8 Eckartsberga Ger.
157 O6 Eckbolsheim France
173 K2 Eckental Ger.
226 I3 Eckerman MI U.S.A.
168 I2 Eckernförde Ger.
168 J1 Eckernförder Bucht b. Ger.
141 O6 Eckerö Åland Fin.
138 C1 Eckerö i. Fin.
173 L2 Eckersdorf Ger.
146 L11 Eckford Scottish Borders, Scotland U.K.
149 O7 Eckington Derbyshire, England U.K.
150 H3 Eckington Worcestershire, England U.K.
232 D11 Eckman WV U.S.A.
222 H4 Eckville Alta Can.
168 F3 Eckwarden (Butjadingen) Ger.
157 I6 Éclaron-Braucourt-Ste-Livière France
221 J2 Eclipse Sound sea chan. Nunavut Can.
159 L6 Écommoy France
257 G3 Ecoporanga Brazil
227 R2 Écorce, Lac de l' l. Que. Can.
156 C5 Écos France
159 K4 Écouché France
159 J6 Écouflant France
156 B5 Écouis France
161 I7 Écrins, Parc National des nat. park France
157 K6 Écrouves France
177 G4 Écs Hungary
177 I4 Ecséd Hungary
177 I4 Ecseg Hungary
177 J4 Ecsegfalva Hungary
177 I4 Ecser Hungary
250 B5 Ecuador country S. America
244 E5 Ecuandureo Mex.
162 G1 Écueillé France
160 F3 Écuisses France
156 H6 Écury-sur-Coole France
203 I6 Ed Eritrea
142 H3 Ed Sweden
223 I4 Edam Sask. Can.
164 H3 Edam Neth.
146 K4 Eday i. Scotland U.K.
208 E2 Ed Da'ein Sudan
203 F6 Ed Dair, Jebel mt. Sudan
210 B2 Ed Damazin Sudan
203 G5 Ed Damer Sudan
203 F5 Ed Debba Sudan
202 C5 Eddeki well Chad
168 H3 Eddelak Ger.
171 E7 Edderitz Ger.
146 H7 Edderton Highland, Scotland U.K.
225 J3 Eddies Cove Nfld and Lab. Can.
146 F6 Eddrachillis Bay Scotland U.K.
203 G6 Ed Dueim Sudan
83 L9 Eddystone Point Tas. Austr.
237 K7 Eddyville KY U.S.A.
164 I4 Ede Neth.
207 G5 Ede Nigeria
207 H6 Edéa Cameroon
165 F6 Edegem Belgium
223 L2 Edehon Lake Nunavut Can.
256 C2 Edéia Brazil
177 J3 Edelény Hungary
179 L5 Edelschrott Austria
169 J6 Edemissen Ger.
83 L7 Eden N.S.W. Austr.
148 F4 Eden Northern Ireland U.K.
149 K4 Eden r. England U.K.
232 F12 Eden NC U.S.A.
237 F10 Eden TX U.S.A.
238 J5 Eden WY U.S.A.
93 E7 Eden, Tanjung pt Maluku Indon.
151 M5 Edenbridge Kent, England U.K.
215 J5 Edenburg S. Africa
81 C13 Edendale South I. N.Z.
215 O5 Edendale S. Africa
147 H6 Edenderry Ireland
149 M6 Edenfield Lancashire, England U.K.
82 H7 Edenhope Vic. Austr.
172 E3 Edenkoben Ger.
226 A5 Eden Prairie MN U.S.A.
231 I7 Edenton NC U.S.A.
215 M2 Edenvale S. Africa
215 L3 Edenville S. Africa
169 H8 Eder r. Ger.
169 H8 Edermünde Ger.
147 G3 Ederny Northern Ireland U.K.
169 G8 Eder-Stausee resr Ger.
198 D2 Edessa Greece
Edessa Turkey see Şanlıurfa
140 L5 Edevik Sweden
168 E4 Edewecht Ger.
168 E4 Edewechterdamm Ger.
Edfu Egypt see Idfū
236 G5 Edgar NE U.S.A.
86 F6 Edgar, Mount hill W.A. Austr.
86 G5 Edgar Ranges hills W.A. Austr.
233 O7 Edgartown MA U.S.A.
80 K4 Edgecumbe North I. N.Z.
80 K5 Edgecumbe, Mount hill North I. N.Z.
Edgecumbe Island Santa Cruz Is Solomon Is see Utupua
231 G9 Edgefield SC U.S.A.
Edge Island Svalbard see Edgeøya
236 F2 Edgeley ND U.S.A.
234 C6 Edgemere MD U.S.A.
236 D4 Edgemont SD U.S.A.
140 □ Edgeøya i. Svalbard
223 I4 Edgerton Alta Can.
232 A7 Edgerton OH U.S.A.
232 H12 Edgerton VA U.S.A.
226 E7 Edgerton WI U.S.A.
222 G5 Edgewood B.C. Can.
234 C6 Edgewood MD U.S.A.
234 B3 Edgewood PA U.S.A.
147 G5 Edgeworthstown Ireland
78 □3a Edgigen i. Kwajalein Marshall Is
150 H2 Edgmond Telford and Wrekin, England U.K.
Édhessa Greece see Edessa
81 D12 Edievale South I. N.Z.
169 D10 Ediger-Eller Ger.
207 G2 Édîkel well Niger
129 E4 Edik'ilisa Georgia
236 I5 Edina MO U.S.A.
232 E7 Edinboro PA U.S.A.
237 F12 Edinburg TX U.S.A.
232 G10 Edinburg VA U.S.A.
146 J11 Edinburgh Edinburgh, Scotland U.K.
146 J11 Edinburgh admin. div. Scotland U.K.
199 I2 Edincik Turkey
136 G5 Edineţ Moldova
211 B8 Edingeni Malawi
172 F3 Edingen-Neckarhausen Ger.
126 C3 Edirne Turkey
199 H1 Edirne prov. Turkey
129 F3 Edisa Georgia
234 E4 Edison PA U.S.A.
129 F1 Edissiya Rus. Fed.
231 G9 Edisto r. SC U.S.A.
238 I3 Edith, Mount MT U.S.A.
82 F6 Edithburgh S.A. Austr.
222 G4 Edith Cavell, Mount Alta Can.
Edith Ronne Land ice feature Antarctica see Ronne Ice Shelf
87 F8 Edith Withnell, Lake salt flat W.A. Austr.
209 B9 Ediva Angola
205 H4 Edjeleh Libya
207 F2 Édjérir watercourse Mali
87 G10 Edjudina W.A. Austr.
173 M5 Edling Ger.
149 N3 Edlingham Northumberland, England U.K.
179 N4 Edlitz Austria
237 G8 Edmond OK U.S.A.
238 C3 Edmonds WA U.S.A.
147 E5 Edmondstown Ireland
85 J4 Edmonton Qld Austr.
222 H4 Edmonton Alta Can.
230 E7 Edmonton KY U.S.A.
226 I6 Edmore MI U.S.A.
236 F1 Edmore ND U.S.A.
149 N4 Edmundbyers Durham, England U.K.
223 M4 Edmund Lake Man. Can.
225 G4 Edmundston N.B. Can.
237 G11 Edna TX U.S.A.
222 C4 Edna Bay AK U.S.A.
Edo Japan see Tōkyō
207 G5 Edo state Nigeria
105 K4 Edo-gawa r. Japan
190 I3 Edolo Italy
128 D8 Edom reg. Israel/Jordan
105 L4 Edosaki Japan
199 I3 Edremit Turkey
199 H3 Edremit Körfezi b. Turkey
106 E4 Edrengiyn Nuruu mts Mongolia
182 G5 Edrosa Port.
182 G5 Edroso Port.
143 O2 Edsbro Sweden
143 M3 Edsbruk Sweden
141 M6 Edsbyn Sweden
140 N5 Edsele Sweden
222 G4 Edson Alta Can.
260 E4 Eduardo Castex Arg.
222 D1 Eduni, Mount N.W.T. Can.
83 J6 Edward r. N.S.W. Austr.
85 H3 Edward r. Qld Austr.
208 F5 Edward, Lake Dem. Rep. Congo/Uganda
262 T1 Edward, Mount Antarctica
86 K7 Edward, Mount N.T. Austr.
Edwardesabad Pak. see Bannu
84 E3 Edward Island N.T. Austr.
226 F1 Edward Island Ont. Can.
85 H3 Edward River Aboriginal Reserve Qld Austr.
233 J4 Edwards NY U.S.A.
81 A12 Edwardson Sound inlet South I. N.Z.
237 E10 Edwards Plateau TX U.S.A.
236 K6 Edwardsville IL U.S.A.
263 D2 Edward VIII Bay Antarctica
262 N1 Edward VII Peninsula Antarctica
235 G5 Edwin B. Forsythe National Wildlife Refuge nature res. NJ U.S.A.
149 O7 Edwinstowe Nottinghamshire, England U.K.
222 D3 Edziza, Mount B.C. Can.
Edzo N.W.T. Can. see Rae-Edzo
208 B5 Edzouga Congo
164 J4 Eefde Neth.
165 E6 Eeklo Belgium
240 H1 Eel r. CA U.S.A.
240 I1 Eel, South Fork r. CA U.S.A.
164 K2 Eelde-Paterswolde Neth.
164 H4 Eem r. Neth.
164 H4 Eemnes Neth.
164 K2 Eemshaven pt Neth.
164 K2 Eemskanaal canal Neth.
214 C8 Eendekuil S. Africa
164 J2 Eenrum Neth.
214 E3 Eenzamheid Pan salt pan S. Africa
164 J4 Eerbeek Neth.
165 D6 Eernegem Belgium
165 H6 Eersel Neth.
Eesti country Europe see Estonia
78 □5 Éfaté i. Vanuatu
179 J3 Eferding Austria
173 K2 Effeltrich Ger.
226 A2 Effie MN U.S.A.
151 L5 Effingham Surrey, England U.K.
236 K6 Effingham IL U.S.A.
234 E3 Effort PA U.S.A.
190 F1 Effretikon Switz.
126 F3 Eflâni Turkey
172 D6 Efringen-Kirchen Ger.
Efsus Turkey see Afşin
197 K6 Eftimie Murgu Romania
93 F4 Eftorobi i. Papua Indon.
107 L2 Eg Mongolia
183 Q4 Ega r. Spain
261 H5 Egana Arg.
241 R3 Egan Range mts NV U.S.A.
227 Q4 Eganville Ont. Can.
207 G4 Egbe Nigeria
187 D10 Egea hill Spain
Egedesminde Greenland see Aasiaat
171 D7 Egeln Ger.
173 K5 Egenhofen Ger.
223 K3 Egenolf Lake Man. Can.
Egentliga Finland reg. Fin. see Varsinais-Suomi
171 F10 Eger r. Ger.
173 J4 Eger r. Ger.
177 J4 Eger Hungary
177 J4 Egerbakta Hungary
177 J3 Egercsehi Hungary
86 □1 Egeria Point Christmas I.
168 I1 Egernsund Denmark
142 C3 Egersund Norway
87 D8 Egerton, Mount hill W.A. Austr.
176 F5 Egervár Hungary
168 J4 Egestorf Ger.
178 A5 Egg Austria
168 H1 Eggebek Ger.
142 F2 Eggedøla r. Norway
169 G7 Eggegebirge hills Ger.
179 M2 Eggenburg Austria
173 N5 Eggenfelden Ger.
172 E3 Eggenstein-Leopoldshafen Ger.
168 E5 Eggermühlen Ger.
171 E7 Eggersdorf Ger.
179 M5 Eggersdorf bei Graz Austria
170 I5 Eggersdorf bei Strausberg Ger.
170 J3 Eggesin Ger.
226 G4 Egg Harbor WI U.S.A.
234 F5 Egg Harbor City NJ U.S.A.
172 E6 Eggingen Ger.
216 □2b Egg Island St Helena
234 E6 Egg Island Point NJ U.S.A.
190 D2 Eggiwil Switz.
223 J4 Egg Lake Sask. Can.
173 O4 Egglham Ger.
173 K2 Eggolsheim Ger.
173 M6 Eggstätt Ger.
140 L2 Eggum Norway
151 K5 Egham Surrey, England U.K.
165 G7 Eghezée Belgium
183 Q3 Egiarreta Spain
146 K4 Egilsay i. Scotland U.K.
140 □F1 Egilsstaðir Iceland
Eğin Turkey see Kemaliye
86 E6 Eginbah W.A. Austr.
Egindibulaq Kazakh. see Yegindybulak
121 P2 Egindy Kazakh.
173 O4 Eging am See Ger.
199 L5 Eğirdir Turkey
199 L5 Eğirdir Gölü l. Turkey
106 H2 Egiyn Gol r. Mongolia
162 I5 Égletons France
173 L6 Egling Ger.
173 J5 Egling an der Paar Ger.
149 N3 Eglingham Northumberland, England U.K.
147 H2 Eglinton Northern Ireland U.K.
220 G2 Eglinton Island N.W.T. Can.
172 F6 Eglisau Switz.
148 D5 Eglish Northern Ireland U.K.
173 K2 Egloffstein Ger.
150 E2 Eglwys Fach Ceredigion, Wales U.K.
150 C3 Eglwyswrw Pembrokeshire, Wales U.K.
164 G3 Egmond aan Zee Neth.
164 G3 Egmond-Binnen Neth.
80 H6 Egmont, Cape North I. N.Z.
Egmont, Mount vol. North I. N.Z. see Taranaki, Mount
80 I6 Egmont National Park North I. N.Z.
80 I6 Egmont Village North I. N.Z.
191 K3 Egna Italy
149 J5 Egremont Cumbria, England U.K.
199 K3 Eğrigöz Dağı mts Turkey
156 F7 Égriselles-le-Bocage France
149 P5 Egton North Yorkshire, England U.K.
142 F6 Egtved Denmark
250 E3 Egua Col.
254 D5 Éguas r. Brazil
92 C8 Eguet Point Phil.
Eguiarreta Spain see Egiarreta
161 G9 Éguilles France
156 I7 Éguilly-sous-Bois France
157 N7 Eguisheim France
162 H3 Éguzon, Barrage d' dam France
162 H3 Éguzon-Chantôme France
131 T3 Egvekinot Rus. Fed.
177 J4 Egyek Hungary
179 O5 Egyházasfalu Hungary
177 H5 Egyházaskozár Hungary
176 F4 Egyházasrádóc Hungary
203 F2 Egypt country Africa
234 D3 Egypt PA U.S.A.
Ehcel well Mali see Agous-n-Ehsel
128 D4 Ehden Lebanon
173 J2 Ehebach r. Ger.
173 K4 Ehekirchen Ger.
106 G7 Ehen Hudag Nei Mongol China
103 J13 Ehime pref. Japan
173 J3 Ehingen Ger.
172 H5 Ehingen (Donau) Ger.
171 E6 Ehle r. Ger.
169 H8 Ehlen (Habichtswald) Ger.
172 F4 Ehningen Ger.
168 K5 Ehra-Lessien Ger.
241 R8 Ehrenberg AZ U.S.A.
84 C7 Ehrenberg Range hills N.T. Austr.
169 J10 Ehrenberg-Wüstensachsen Ger.
168 G5 Ehrenburg Ger.
179 M6 Ehrenhausen Austria
169 F9 Ehringshausen Ger.
178 C5 Ehrwald Austria
103 H15 Ei Japan
79 □9 Eiao i. Fr. Polynesia
183 P2 Eibar Spain
173 I2 Eibelstadt Ger.
171 G10 Eibenstock Ger.
164 K4 Eibergen Neth.
179 L6 Eibiswald Austria
173 K7 Eibsee l. Ger.
172 E2 Eich Ger.
173 K5 Eichenau Ger.
171 D6 Eichenbarleben Ger.
169 I10 Eichenberg hill Ger.
172 G2 Eichenbühl Ger.
173 N4 Eichendorf Ger.
169 I10 Eichenzell Ger.
179 M3 Eichgraben Austria
171 F10 Eichigt Ger.
169 J8 Eichsfeld reg. Ger.
173 K4 Eichstätt Ger.
172 D5 Eichstetten Ger.
171 I6 Eichwalde Ger.
171 E7 Eickendorf Ger.
168 J5 Eicklingen Ger.
140 I5 Eide Norway
168 G2 Eider r. Ger.
142 D1 Eidfjord Norway
144 D1 Eiði Faroe Is
140 J5 Eidsvåg Norway
85 M8 Eidsvold Qld Austr.
142 H1 Eidsvoll Norway
140 □ Eidsvollfjellet mt. Svalbard
169 C10 Eifel hills Ger.
172 F6 Eigeltingen Ger.
104 D5 Eigenji Japan
190 E2 Eiger mt. Switz.
142 B3 Eigerøya i. Norway
146 D9 Eigg i. Scotland U.K.
146 D9 Eigg, Sound of sea chan. Scotland U.K.
114 C9 Eight Degree Channel India/Maldives
262 R2 Eights Coast Antarctica
86 F5 Eighty Mile Beach W.A. Austr.
104 D3 Eiheiji Japan
165 I7 Eijsden Neth.
142 B1 Eikelandsosen Norway
142 D3 Eiken Norway
142 F2 Eikeren l. Norway
146 F9 Eil, Loch inlet Scotland U.K.
Eilat Israel see Elat
83 J7 Eildon Vic. Austr.
83 K7 Eildon, Lake Vic. Austr.
223 J2 Eileen Lake N.W.T. Can.
171 G8 Eilenburg Ger.
171 D7 Eilenstedt Ger.
251 G4 Eilerts de Haan, Natuurreservaat nature res. Suriname
251 G4 Eilerts de Haan Gebergte mts Suriname
92 □ Eil Malk i. Palau
171 D6 Eilsleben Ger.
169 I6 Eime Ger.
169 I7 Eimen Ger.
Eimeo i. Fr. Polynesia see Moorea
168 J5 Eimke Ger.
142 G1 Eina Norway
146 C6 Einacleit Western Isles, Scotland U.K.
85 J5 Einasleigh Qld Austr.
85 I4 Einasleigh r. Qld Austr.
142 G1 Einavatnet l. Norway
169 I7 Einbeck Ger.
165 H6 Eindhoven Neth.
214 D1 Eindpaal Namibia
171 E7 Eine r. Ger.
172 F2 Einhausen Ger.
146 G7 Einig r. Scotland U.K.
96 B6 Einme Myanmar
171 G9 Einsiedel Ger.
190 F1 Einsiedeln Switz.
157 L6 Einville-au-Jard France
128 D8 Ein Yahav Israel
216 □1c Eiras, Ponta das pt São Jorge Azores
264 G2 Eirik Ridge sea feature N. Atlantic Ocean
Eiriosgaigh i. Scotland U.K. see Eriskay
250 D6 Eiru r. Brazil
250 D6 Eirunepé Brazil
169 I8 Eisberg hill Ger.
165 J9 Eisch r. Lux.
165 I7 Eisden Belgium
169 J7 Eisdorf Ger.
212 D3 Eiseb watercourse Namibia
173 M5 Eiselfing Ger.
169 J9 Eisenach Ger.
172 E6 Eisenbach (Hochschwarzwald) Ger.
171 E9 Eisenberg Ger.
172 E2 Eisenberg (Pfalz) Ger.
179 K4 Eisenerz Austria
179 J4 Eisenerzer Alpen mts Austria
Eisenhower, Mount Alta Can. see Castle Mountain
179 I6 Eisenhut mt. Austria
171 K6 Eisenhüttenstadt Ger.
179 K7 Eisenkappel Austria
179 O4 Eisenstadt Austria
179 K4 Eisenwurzen reg. Austria
169 K10 Eisfeld Ger.
146 E8 Eishort, Loch inlet Scotland U.K.
138 H7 Eišiškės Lith.
144 J1 Eislandet Norway
171 E7 Eisleben Lutherstadt Ger.
172 H4 Eislingen (Fils) Ger.
80 J4 Eistow North I. N.Z.
Eitape P.N.G. see Aitape
173 K4 Eitensheim Ger.
169 I9 Eiterfeld Ger.
169 D9 Eitorf Ger.
169 I6 Eitzum (Despetal) Ger.
141 H6 Eivinvik Norway
187 H10 Eivissa Spain
187 I9 Eivissa i. Spain
182 F4 Eixe, Serra do mts Spain
182 C7 Eixo Port.
182 D6 Eja Port.
186 C3 Ejea de los Caballeros Spain
213 □J5 Ejeda Madag.
Ejin Horo Qi Nei Mongol China see Altan Shiret
Ejin Qi Nei Mongol China see Dalain Hob
204 B5 Ej Jill, Sebkhet salt flat Maur.
Ejmiadzin Armenia see Ejmiatsin
129 F5 Ejmiatsin Armenia
186 D6 Ejulve Spain
206 E5 Ejura Ghana
245 K9 Ejutla Mex.
238 L4 Ekalaka MT U.S.A.
207 H5 Ekang Nigeria
215 M1 Ekangala S. Africa
208 B4 Ékata Gabon
103 J13 Ekawasaki Japan
141 Q7 Ekenäs Fin.
142 J3 Ekenäs Sweden
141 Q7 Ekenäskärgårds nationalpark nat. park Fin.
122 F2 Ekerem Turkm.
165 F6 Ekeren Belgium
143 N2 Ekerö Sweden
207 G5 Eket Nigeria
80 J7 Eketahuna North I. N.Z.
Ekhínos Greece see Echinos
Ekhmîm Egypt see Akhmīm
121 P2 Ekibastuz Kazakh.
100 H2 Ekimchan Rus. Fed.
128 H2 Ekinyazı Turkey
207 G5 Ekiti state Nigeria
143 M4 Eknö i. Sweden
208 E5 Ekoli Dem. Rep. Congo
143 N2 Ekoln l. Sweden
131 L3 Ekonda Rus. Fed.
207 H5 Ekondo Titi Cameroon
140 V3 Ekostrovskaya Imandra, Ozero l. Rus. Fed.
208 C4 Ekouamou Congo
207 G5 Ekpoma Nigeria
165 E6 Eksaarde Belgium
165 H6 Eksel Belgium
Eksere Turkey see Gündoğmuş
142 J1 Ekshärad Sweden
199 L5 Ekşili Turkey
143 K4 Eksjö Sweden
100 C1 Ekskavatornyy Rus. Fed.
214 B4 Eksteenfontein S. Africa
262 X2 Ekström Ice Shelf Antarctica
140 O4 Ekträsk Sweden
208 D5 Ekuku Dem. Rep. Congo
224 D2 Ekwan r. Ont. Can.
224 D2 Ekwan Point Ont. Can.
96 C5 Ela Myanmar
El Aaiún Western Sahara see Laâyoune
260 B5 El Abanico Chile
203 F6 El Abbasiya Sudan
198 D6 Elafonisos i. Greece
198 D6 Elafonisou, Steno sea chan. Greece
206 D2 El Aghlâf well Maur.
244 E7 El Aguaje Mex.
128 C3 Elaia, Cape Cyprus
203 G5 El Aiadia well Sudan
198 F2 Elaiochori Greece
204 A5 El 'Aïouej well Maur.
El 'Alamein Egypt see Al 'Alamayn
245 H2 El Alamito Mex.
242 A2 El Alamo Mex.
244 C6 El Alcihuatl Mex.
187 D12 El Algar Spain
205 G2 El Alia Alg.
189 B7 El Alia Tunisia
184 G6 El Aljarafe reg. Spain
184 E5 El Almendro Spain
185 O7 El Alquián Spain
258 D3 El Alto Catamarca Arg.
260 D2 El Alto La Rioja Arg.
250 A6 El Alto Peru
156 C6 Élancourt France
184 E5 El Andévalo reg. Spain
215 O1 Elands r. S. Africa
213 F5 Elands r. S. Africa
215 K8 Elandsberg mt. S. Africa
215 N1 Elandsdoorn S. Africa
215 J8 Elandsdrif S. Africa
215 O4 Elandskraal S. Africa
215 N4 Elandslaagte S. Africa
215 K1 Elandsputte S. Africa
150 E3 Elan Village Powys, Wales U.K.
Elar Armenia see Abovyan
184 H6 El Arahal Spain
El Araïche Morocco see Larache
242 C3 El Arco Mex.
183 J8 El Arenal Castilla y León Spain
El Arenal Illes Balears Spain see S'Arenal
205 E2 El Aricha Alg.
85 K4 El Arish Qld Austr.
205 G1 El Arrouch Alg.
199 H7 Elasa i. Greece
El Asnam Alg. see Chlef
198 D3 Elassona Greece
183 M2 El Astillero Spain
128 C9 Elat Israel
183 N7 El Atazar, Embalse de resr Spain
204 B5 El 'Aṭf reg. Western Sahara
91 K5 Elato atoll Micronesia
126 I4 Elazığ Turkey
129 A7 Elazığ prov. Turkey
231 D10 Elba AL U.S.A.
192 E2 Elba, Isola d' i. Italy
185 O3 El Ballestero Spain
100 J3 El'ban Rus. Fed.
250 C2 El Banco Col.
206 D2 El Bânoûn well Maur.
182 I8 El Barco de Ávila Spain
El Barco de Valdeorras Spain see O Barco
183 K8 El Barraco Spain
245 I1 El Barranco Tamaulipas Mex.
245 I3 El Barranco Tamaulipas Mex.
242 F2 El Barreal salt l. Mex.
244 E2 El Barril Mex.
210 B2 El Barun Sudan
196 I9 Elbasan Albania
126 G4 Elbaşı Turkey
203 G5 El Bauga Sudan
250 D2 El Baúl Venez.
205 F2 El Bayadh Alg.
168 H3 Elbe r. Ger.
alt. Labe (Czech Rep.)
238 C3 Elbe WA U.S.A.
171 E6 Elbe-Havel-Kanal canal Ger.
206 C2 'Elb el Fçâl des. Maur.
260 B3 El Belloto airport Chile
168 K3 Elbe-Lübeck-Kanal canal Ger.
128 E4 El Béqaa val. Lebanon
169 D6 Elbergen Ger.
206 C2 El Berié well Maur.
183 M7 El Berrueco Spain
239 K7 Elbert, Mount CO U.S.A.
226 H5 Elberta MI U.S.A.
241 U2 Elberta UT U.S.A.
231 F8 Elberton GA U.S.A.
210 D4 El Beru Hagia Somalia
210 C4 El Bes well Kenya
156 B5 Elbeuf France
128 F2 Elbeyli Turkey
206 C2 El Beyyeḍ well Maur.
204 C5 El Beyyeḍ well Maur.
182 F4 El Bierzo reg. Spain
178 B5 Elbigenalp Austria
244 F7 El Billete, Cerro mt. Mex.
Elbing Pol. see Elbląg
169 K7 Elbingerode (Harz) Ger.
126 H4 Elbistan Turkey
184 I9 El-Biutz Morocco
143 P7 Elbląg Pol.
175 H1 Elbląski, Kanał canal Pol.
242 □R11 El Bluff Nic.
182 G8 El Bodón Spain
260 A4 El Boldo Chile
El Bollo Spain see O Bolo
259 C6 El Bolsón Arg.
185 N3 El Bonillo Spain
244 E3 El Bordo Mex.
184 H9 El-Borj Morocco
205 H3 El Borma Tunisia
185 I7 El Bosque Spain
El Boulaïda Alg. see Blida
223 J5 Elbow Sask. Can.
231 I12 Elbow Cay i. Bahamas
236 G2 Elbow Lake MN U.S.A.
244 F2 El Bozal Mex.
243 I4 El Brasil Mex.
129 D2 El'brus Rus. Fed.
129 D2 El'brus mt. Rus. Fed.
129 D2 El'brusskiy Rus. Fed.
171 J9 Elbsandstein Gebirge hills Ger.
208 F3 El Buheyrat state Sudan
185 P4 El Buitre mt. Spain
185 K2 El Bullaque Spain
164 I4 Elburg Neth.
185 J7 El Burgo Spain
183 O3 Elburgo Spain
186 D4 El Burgo de Ebro Spain
183 N5 El Burgo de Osma Spain
183 J4 El Burgo Ranero Spain
208 E2 El Burma well Sudan
244 E2 El Burrito Mex.
Elburz Mountains Iran see Alborz, Reshteh-ye
183 Q5 El Buste Spain
137 S7 El'buzd r. Rus. Fed.
182 H7 El Cabaco Spain
185 P6 El Cabildo y la Campana Spain
185 O7 El Cabo de Gata Spain
258 D2 El Cadillal, Embalse resr Arg.
259 C6 El Cain Arg.
240 P9 El Cajon CA U.S.A.
242 □P10 El Cajón, Represa dam Hond.
251 F3 El Callao Venez.
El Caló Spain see Es Caló
245 G8 El Camotal, Sierra mts Mex.
183 J9 El Campillo de la Jara Spain
El Campo Spain see Campo Lugar
237 G11 El Campo TX U.S.A.
183 J7 El Campo de Peñaranda Spain
183 P9 El Cañavate Spain
244 G1 El Canelo Mex.
261 I4 El Caño Uru.
250 D3 El Canton Venez.
237 E12 El Capulin r. Mex.
244 F1 El Cardito Mex.
250 D2 El Carmelo Venez.
258 D2 El Carmen Jujuy Arg.
260 C1 El Carmen San Juan Arg.
252 E3 El Carmen Beni Bol.
253 F4 El Carmen Santa Cruz Bol.
260 B5 El Carmen Chile
250 B5 El Carmen Ecuador
250 E4 El Carmen Venez.
245 N7 El Carmen, Laguna l. Mex.
187 D9 El Caroche mt. Spain
185 K5 El Carpio Spain
183 L9 El Carpio de Tajo Spain
244 G9 El Carrizal Mex.
183 N7 El Casar Spain
183 K8 El Casar de Escalona Spain
242 G5 El Casco Mex.
187 D7 El Castellar Spain
186 C4 El Castellar reg. Spain
184 G5 El Castillo de las Guardas Spain
243 M10 El Cebú, Cerro mt. Mex.
185 L4 El Centenillo Spain
241 Q9 El Centro CA U.S.A.
253 E4 El Cerro Bol.
184 F5 El Cerro de Andévalo Spain
260 E2 El Chacho Arg.
261 F6 El Chanco, Salina salt pan Arg.
251 E2 El Chaparro Venez.
245 H3 El Chapulín Mex.
261 F6 El Chara Arg.
187 D11 Elche, Embalse de resr Spain
185 O4 Elche de la Sierra Spain
187 D11 Elche-Elx Spain
245 M8 El Chichón Mex.
243 M9 El Chichónal vol. Mex.
245 I5 El Chico, Parque Nacional nat. park Mex.
242 G3 El Chilicote Mex.
173 I5 Elchingen Ger.
226 E4 Elcho WI U.S.A.
84 E1 Elcho Island N.T. Austr.
183 O3 Elciego Spain
244 G5 El Cimatario, Parque Nacional nat. park Mex.
El Coca Ecuador see Coca
250 C3 El Cocuy, Parque Nacional nat. park Col.
185 K3 El Collado hill Spain
244 C6 El Colomo Mex.
244 G8 El Conejo, Sierra mts Mex.
186 J5 El Congost r. Spain
185 O5 El Contador, Puerto de pass Spain
184 H6 El Coronil Spain
245 M8 El Corte r. Mex.
245 L10 El Coyol Mex.
245 L8 El Coyolito Mex.
182 H7 El Cubo de Don Sancho Spain
182 I6 El Cubo de Tierra del Vino Spain
184 G7 El Cuervo Spain
244 B4 El Custodio, Punta pt Mex.
259 C5 El Cuy Arg.
243 P7 El Cuyo Mex.
187 D11 Elda Spain
187 D10 Elda, Embalse de resr Spain
210 B4 Eldama Ravine Kenya
186 L3 El Daró r. Spain
242 C3 El Dátil Mex.
210 D3 El Debb well Eth.
227 O3 Eldee Ont. Can.
170 D4 Eldena Ger.
226 E8 Eldena IL U.S.A.
82 □3 Elder, Mount hill S. Pacific Ocean
226 E5 Elderon WI U.S.A.
239 H12 El Desemboque Mex.
140 □D2 Eldhraun lava field Iceland
242 H3 El Diamante Mex.
250 C2 El Difícil Col.
131 O3 El'dikan Rus. Fed.
168 J5 Eldingen Ger.
244 C6 El Divisadero Mex.
250 B4 El Diviso Col.
261 G6 El Divisorio Arg.
El Djezair Alg. see Alger
242 B2 El Doctor Mex.
236 I6 Eldon MO U.S.A.
236 I4 Eldora IA U.S.A.
234 F6 Eldora NJ U.S.A.
261 G4 El Dorado Arg.
258 G2 Eldorado Arg.
256 C6 Eldorado Brazil
250 D4 El Dorado Col.
242 F5 El Dorado Mex.
237 I9 El Dorado AR U.S.A.
237 G7 El Dorado KS U.S.A.
237 E10 Eldorado TX U.S.A.
251 F3 El Dorado Venez.
241 R6 Eldorado Mountains NV U.S.A.
210 B4 Eldoret Kenya
234 F1 Eldred NY U.S.A.
260 E5 El Durazno Arg.
Elea, Cape Cyprus see Elaia, Cape
232 D10 Eleanor WV U.S.A.
238 I4 Electric Peak MT U.S.A.
198 E4 Elefsina Greece
204 D4 El Eglab plat. Alg.
203 F5 El 'Ein well Sudan
138 G5 Eleja Latvia
185 N7 El Ejido Spain
177 K5 Elek Hungary
Elek r. Rus. Fed. see Ilek
121 V2 Elekmonar Rus. Fed.
138 H7 Elektrėnai Lith.
139 V6 Elektrogorsk Rus. Fed.
139 V6 Elektrostal' Rus. Fed.
139 V6 Elektrougli Rus. Fed.
207 G5 Elele Nigeria
210 B3 Elemi Triangle terr. Africa
197 N8 Elena Bulg.
186 E5 Elena, Planas de plain Spain
250 C5 El Encanto Col.
241 P9 El Encinal Baja California Mex.
245 I1 El Encinal Tamaulipas Mex.
245 H2 El Encino Mex.
169 K7 Elend Ger.
260 D3 Eleodoro Lobos Arg.
198 B3 Eleousa Greece
244 G3 El Epazote Mex.
114 C3 Elephanta Caves tourist site Mahar. India
239 K10 Elephant Butte Reservoir NM U.S.A.
262 U2 Elephant Island Antarctica
114 G8 Elephant Pass Sri Lanka
117 N9 Elephant Point Bangl.
183 L7 El Escorial Spain
197 L9 Eleshnitsa Bulg.
127 K4 Eleşkirt Turkey
184 G5 El Esparragal, Embalse resr Spain
183 L7 El Espinar Spain
243 O10 El Estor Guat.
187 D12 El Estrecho Spain
261 I2 El Eucaliptus Uru.
246 E1 Eleuthera i. Bahamas
226 C5 Eleva WI U.S.A.
237 J7 Eleven Point r. MO U.S.A.
183 O2 Elexalde Spain
189 B7 El Fahs Tunisia
El Faiyûm Egypt see Al Fayyūm
205 H2 El Faouar Tunisia
202 E6 El Fasher Sudan
180 D5 El Fendek Morocco
El Ferrol Spain see Ferrol
El Ferrol del Caudillo Spain see Ferrol
169 I10 Elfershausen Ger.
186 L3 El Fluvià r. Spain
186 H5 El Francolí r. Spain
206 B2 El Freïoua well Maur.
183 K7 El Fresno Spain
241 W10 Elfrida AZ U.S.A.
210 D3 El Fud Eth.
242 E4 El Fuerte Mex.
208 F2 El Fula Sudan
141 K5 Elgå Norway
205 F4 El Gaa Taatzebar basin Alg.
185 O5 El Gabar mt. Spain
186 H5 El Gaià r. Spain
210 C4 Elgal waterhole Kenya
244 G5 El Gallo Mex.
184 G5 El Garrobo Spain
185 I7 El Gastor Spain
245 I1 El Gavilán Mex.
204 D5 El Gçaib well Mali
118 C6 El Geili Sudan
202 D6 El Geneina Sudan
169 H8 Elgershausen (Schauenburg) Ger.
183 P2 Elgeta Spain
203 G6 El Geteina Sudan
203 G6 El Gezira state Sudan
203 F5 El Ghaba Sudan
204 C5 El Ghallâouîya well Maur.
206 C2 El Gheddiya Maur.
142 H2 Elgheia hill Norway
El Ghor plain Jordan/West Bank see Al Ghawr
146 J7 Elgin Moray, Scotland U.K.
226 F7 Elgin IL U.S.A.
236 E2 Elgin ND U.S.A.
241 R4 Elgin NV U.S.A.
238 F4 Elgin OR U.S.A.
237 G10 Elgin TX U.S.A.
85 K7 Elgin Down Qld Austr.
131 P3 El'ginskiy Rus. Fed.
203 F5 El Gir well Sudan
El Gîza Egypt see Al Jīzah
244 G4 El Gogorrón, Parque Nacional nat. park Mex.
183 P2 Elgoibar Spain
146 D8 Elgol Highland, Scotland U.K.
205 F3 El Goléa Alg.
216 □3c El Golfo Lanzarote Canary Is
216 □3e El Golfo b. El Hierro Canary Is
242 B2 El Golfo de Santa Clara Mex.
210 B4 Elgon, Mount Uganda
140 U2 Elgoras, Gora hill Rus. Fed.
141 K5 Elgpiggen mt. Norway
186 F3 El Grado Spain
186 F3 El Grado, Embalse de resr Spain
184 E5 El Granado Spain
187 E8 El Grau de Borriana Spain
244 C6 El Grullo Jalisco Mex.
243 J5 El Grullo Tamaulipas Mex.
245 N8 El Guanal Mex.
242 G2 El Guante Mex.
205 H2 El Guetar Tunisia
204 E5 El Gueṭṭâra well Mali
131 M3 El'gyay Rus. Fed.
189 A7 El Hadjar Alg.
205 G2 El Hadjira Alg.
205 H2 El Hamma Tunisia
204 C5 El Ḥammâmi reg. Maur.
204 D4 El Hank reg. Alg.
204 C5 El Ḥank esc. Mali/Maur.
189 C7 El Haouaria Tunisia
124 B9 El Hasira Sudan
242 □R13 El Hato del Volcán Panama
203 G6 El Hawata Sudan
El Hazim Jordan see Al Hazīm
216 □3e El Hierro i. Canary Is
245 I4 El Higo Mex.
202 E6 El Hilla Sudan
183 O9 El Hito Spain
205 F3 El Homr Alg.
203 F6 El Homra Sudan
206 C2 El Houeïtat well Maur.
183 L7 El Hoyo de Pinares Spain
260 B5 El Huecu Arg.
203 F5 El Husheim well Sudan
207 H3 Eli well Niger
93 G8 Eliase Maluku Indon.
209 D7 Elias Garcia Angola
246 H4 Elías Piña Dom. Rep.
193 L2 Elice Italy
Elichpur Mahar. India see Achalpur
232 A8 Elida OH U.S.A.
245 J4 El Idolo, Isla i. Mex.
146 K10 Elie Fife, Scotland U.K.
114 C7 Elikalpeni Bank sea feature India
198 D4 Elikonas mts Greece
208 E5 Elila Dem. Rep. Congo
209 E5 Elila r. Dem. Rep. Congo
214 D10 Elim S. Africa
220 B3 Elim AK U.S.A.
138 J1 Elimäki Fin.
Elimberrum France see Auch
234 A2 Elimsport PA U.S.A.
244 G6 El Infiernillo Mex.
Eling Guizhou China see Yinjiang
151 J6 Eling Hampshire, England U.K.
208 E5 Elingampangu Dem. Rep. Congo
197 L8 Elin Pelin Bulg.
129 F2 Elin-Yurt Rus. Fed.
193 P4 Elio, Monte d' hill Italy
225 I1 Eliot, Mount Nfld and Lab. Can.
208 E5 Elipa Dem. Rep. Congo
208 D4 Elisabetha Dem. Rep. Congo
Élisabethville Dem. Rep. Congo see Lubumbashi
254 E4 Eliseu Martins Brazil
El Iskandarîya Egypt see Al Iskandarīyah
135 I7 Elista Rus. Fed.
178 H4 Elixhausen Austria
110 C7 Elixku Xinjiang China
233 K8 Elizabeth NJ U.S.A.
232 D9 Elizabeth WV U.S.A.
86 I4 Elizabeth, Mount hill W.A. Austr.
233 □S1 Elizabeth, Mount hill N.B. Can.
231 I7 Elizabeth City NC U.S.A.
84 G5 Elizabeth Creek r. Qld Austr.
Elizabeth Island Pitcairn Is see Henderson Island
233 O7 Elizabeth Islands MA U.S.A.
212 B5 Elizabeth Point Namibia
77 F4 Elizabeth Reef Austr.
232 C12 Elizabethton TN U.S.A.
237 K7 Elizabethtown IL U.S.A.
230 E7 Elizabethtown KY U.S.A.
231 H8 Elizabethtown NC U.S.A.
233 L4 Elizabethtown NY U.S.A.
234 B4 Elizabethtown PA U.S.A.
227 R9 Elizabethville PA U.S.A.
186 B1 Elizondo Spain
244 B2 El Jacuixtle Mex.
204 C2 El Jadida Morocco
242 G4 El Jaralito Mex.
182 G8 Eljas Spain
245 H5 El Jazmin Mex.
203 G6 El Jebelein Sudan
205 H2 El Jem Tunisia
242 □P11 El Jicaro Nic.
244 G8 El Jilguero Mex.
245 M8 El Juile Mex.
216 □3e El Julán slope El Hierro Canary Is
222 H5 Elk r. B.C. Can.
175 K2 Ełk Pol.
175 K2 Ełk r. Pol.
234 D6 Elk r. MD U.S.A.
231 D8 Elk r. TN U.S.A.
El Kaa Lebanon see Qaa
203 G5 El Kab Sudan
236 J4 Elkader IA U.S.A.
205 H1 El Kala Alg.
118 C6 El Kamlin Sudan
203 G5 El Karabi Sudan
138 I4 Elkas kalns hill Latvia
232 B11 Elkatawa KY U.S.A.
203 G6 El Kawa Sudan
237 F8 Elk City OK U.S.A.
240 J2 Elk Creek CA U.S.A.
84 E6 Elkedra N.T. Austr.
84 F6 Elkedra watercourse N.T. Austr.
204 D2 El Kelaâ des Srarhna Morocco
169 E9 Elkenroth Ger.
210 D3 Ēl Kerē Eth.
222 H5 Elkford B.C. Can.
240 K3 Elk Grove CA U.S.A.
El Khalil West Bank see Hebron
203 F5 El Khandaq Sudan
El Khârga Egypt see Al Khārijah
230 E5 Elkhart IN U.S.A.
237 E7 Elkhart KS U.S.A.
El Khartûm Sudan see Khartoum
El Khenachich esc. Mali see El Khnâchîch
204 D5 El Khnâchîch esc. Mali
226 F7 Elkhorn WI U.S.A.
236 G5 Elkhorn r. NE U.S.A.
232 C11 Elkhorn City KY U.S.A.
129 F2 El'khotovo Rus. Fed.
197 O8 Elkhovo Bulg.
Elki Turkey see Beytüşşebap
231 G7 Elkin NC U.S.A.
232 F10 Elkins WV U.S.A.
234 E4 Elkins Park PA U.S.A.
223 H4 Elk Island National Park Y.T. Can.
224 D4 Elk Lake Ont. Can.
226 I5 Elk Lake l. MI U.S.A.
232 H7 Elkland PA U.S.A.
234 D5 Elk Mills MD U.S.A.
238 K6 Elk Mountain WY U.S.A.
234 D5 Elk Neck MD U.S.A.
222 H5 Elko B.C. Can.
238 G6 Elko NV U.S.A.
210 E3 Ēl K'oran Eth.
223 I4 Elk Point Alta Can.
236 G4 Elk Point SD U.S.A.
234 B6 Elkridge MD U.S.A.
226 A4 Elk River MN U.S.A.
El Ksaib Ounane well Mali see El Gçaib
241 X1 Elk Springs CO U.S.A.
230 D7 Elkton KY U.S.A.
234 D5 Elkton MD U.S.A.
232 G10 Elkton VA U.S.A.
232 D10 Elkview WV U.S.A.
245 K9 El Labrador, Cerro mt. Mex.
208 F2 El Lagowa Sudan
143 O1 Ellan Sweden
129 H4 Elläryoğu Dağı hill Azer.
Ellas country Europe see Greece
261 G2 El Laurel Arg.
87 C8 Ellavalla W.A. Austr.
231 E9 Ellaville GA U.S.A.
178 D5 Ellbögen Austria
158 D6 Ellé r. France
171 F10 Ellefeld Ger.
221 H2 Ellef Ringnes Island Nunavut Can.
210 C4 Ēl Lēh Eth.
210 D5 El Lein well Kenya
128 E1 Ellek Turkey
87 D13 Elleker W.A. Austr.
202 C5 Elléloyé well Chad
241 V3 Ellen, Mount UT U.S.A.
116 E5 Ellenabad Haryana India
173 I3 Ellenberg Ger.
232 D9 Ellenboro WV U.S.A.
233 L4 Ellenburg Depot NY U.S.A.
233 J10 Ellendale DE U.S.A.
236 F2 Ellendale ND U.S.A.
238 D3 Ellensburg WA U.S.A.
235 G1 Ellenville NY U.S.A.
244 B1 El León, Cerro mt. Mex.
244 G1 El Leoncito Mex.
78 □3a Eller i. Kwajalein Marshall Is
168 I3 Ellerau Ger.
168 I3 Ellerbek Ger.
168 I3 Ellerhoop Ger.
81 C11 Ellery, Lake South I. N.Z.
81 G10 Ellesmere South I. N.Z.
150 G2 Ellesmere Shropshire, England U.K.
81 G10 Ellesmere, Lake South I. N.Z.
221 J2 Ellesmere Island Nunavut Can.
149 L7 Ellesmere Port Cheshire, England U.K.
165 E7 Ellezelles Belgium

Elliant to Ermelo

310

158 D6 **Elliant** France
221 H3 **Ellice** *r. Nunavut* Can.
Ellice Island *atoll* Tuvalu *see* **Funafuti**
Ellice Islands *country* S. Pacific Ocean *see* **Tuvalu**
234 B6 **Ellicott City** *MD* U.S.A.
232 G6 **Ellicottville** *NY* U.S.A.
231 E8 **Ellijay** *GA* U.S.A.
244 F7 **El Limón** *Guerrero* Mex.
244 B3 **El Limón** *Nayarit* Mex.
245 I3 **El Limón** *Tamaulipas* Mex.
173 J3 **Ellingen** Ger.
149 N2 **Ellingham** *Northumberland, England* U.K.
Ellington *Viti Levu* Fiji *see* **Nakorokula**
149 N3 **Ellington** *Northumberland, England* U.K.
215 L7 **Elliot** S. Africa
85 K5 **Elliot, Mount** *Qld* Austr.
215 M7 **Elliotdale** S. Africa
232 F10 **Elliot Knob** *mt. VA* U.S.A.
224 D4 **Elliot Lake** *Ont.* Can.
82 F3 **Elliot Price Conservation Park** *nature res. S.A.* Austr.
82 □3 **Elliot Reef** S. Pacific Ocean
84 D4 **Elliott** *N.T.* Austr.
238 G4 **Ellis** *ID* U.S.A.
236 F6 **Ellis** *KS* U.S.A.
82 E5 **Elliston** *S.A.* Austr.
232 E11 **Elliston** *VA* U.S.A.
237 K10 **Ellisville** *MS* U.S.A.
244 G4 **El Llano** Mex.
182 F2 **El Llano** Spain
186 I4 **El Llobregat** *r.* Spain
178 F4 **Ellmau** Austria
146 L8 **Ellon** *Aberdeenshire, Scotland* U.K.
116 E9 **Ellora Caves** *tourist site Mahar.* India
260 D4 **El Loro** Arg.
142 H3 **Ellös** Sweden
182 I8 **El Losar del Barco** Spain
149 P6 **Elloughton** *East Riding of Yorkshire, England* U.K.
169 K7 **Ellrich** Ger.
261 G2 **Ellsa** Arg.
236 F6 **Ellsworth** *KS* U.S.A.
233 □Q4 **Ellsworth** *ME* U.S.A.
236 D4 **Ellsworth** *NE* U.S.A.
226 B5 **Ellsworth** *WI* U.S.A.
262 R1 **Ellsworth Land** *reg.* Antarctica
262 S1 **Ellsworth Mountains** Antarctica
173 I4 **Ellwangen (Jagst)** Ger.
232 E8 **Ellwood City** *PA* U.S.A.
168 F4 **Ellwürden** Ger.
168 H3 **Elm** Ger.
190 G2 **Elm** Switz.
151 M2 **Elm** *Cambridgeshire, England* U.K.
175 I1 **Elma** *r.* Pol.
247 I4 **El Macao** Dom. Rep.
245 H4 **El Madroño** Mex.
El Maestral *reg.* Spain *see* **El Maestrazgo**
186 F7 **El Maestrazgo** *reg.* Spain
204 E5 **El Mahia** *reg.* Mali
259 C6 **El Maitén** Arg.
129 D6 **Elmakaya** Turkey
128 B2 **Elmakuz Dağı** *mt.* Turkey
199 K6 **Elmali** Turkey
239 K9 **El Malpais National Monument** *nat. park NM* U.S.A.
203 G6 **El Manaqil** Sudan
250 E4 **El Mango** Venez.
El Manşūra Egypt *see* **Al Manşūrah**
251 F3 **El Manteco** Venez.
180 D5 **El Manzla** Morocco
189 C7 **El Marsa** Tunisia
244 F1 **El Mascaron, Sierra** *mts* Mex.
186 G5 **El Masroig** Spain
244 F4 **El Mastranto** Mex.
206 C2 **El Mechouat** *well* Maur.
216 □3a **El Médano** *Tenerife* Canary Is
245 I5 **El Médano** Mex.
210 D3 **El Medo** Eth.
205 G2 **El Meghaïer** Alg.
208 F2 **El Melemm** Sudan
208 B2 **El Melhes** *well* Maur.
260 B3 **El Melón** Chile
178 C5 **Elmen** Austria
170 D3 **Elmenhorst** *Mecklenburg-Vorpommern* Ger.
170 F2 **Elmenhorst** *Mecklenburg-Vorpommern* Ger.
170 H2 **Elmenhorst** *Mecklenburg-Vorpommern* Ger.
168 J3 **Elmenhorst** *Schleswig-Holstein* Ger.
168 K3 **Elmenhorst** *Schleswig-Holstein* Ger.
234 E5 **Elmer** *NJ* U.S.A.
203 G6 **El Mesellemiya** Sudan
202 C6 **El Messir** *well* Chad
244 E2 **El Mezquite** Mex.
234 D2 **Elmhurst** *PA* U.S.A.
251 F3 **El Miamo** Venez.
244 G7 **El Milagro de Guadalupe** Mex.
206 E5 **Elmina** Ghana
128 D4 **El Mina** Lebanon
227 N6 **Elmira** *Ont.* Can.
225 I4 **Elmira** *P.E.I.* Can.
226 J4 **Elmira** *MI* U.S.A.
227 H7 **Elmira** *NY* U.S.A.
244 C5 **El Mirador** Mex.
245 I6 **El Mirador, Cerro** *mt.* Mex.
241 T8 **El Mirage** *AZ* U.S.A.
206 C2 **El Moïnane** *well* Maur.
183 M7 **El Molar** Spain
185 K2 **El Molinillo** Spain
245 I4 **El Molino** Mex.
243 I3 **El Moral** Mex.
185 O5 **El Moral** Spain
83 J7 **Elmore** *Vic.* Austr.
227 B7 **Elmore** *OH* U.S.A.
186 H5 **El Morell** Spain
260 E3 **El Morro** *mt.* Arg.
206 C3 **El Mraïfig** *well* Maur.
206 E2 **El Mraïti** *well* Mali
206 D2 **El Mreyyé** *reg.* Maur.
235 H2 **Elmsford** *NY* U.S.A.
168 I3 **Elmshorn** Ger.
172 D3 **Elmstein** Ger.
151 N3 **Elmswell** *Suffolk, England* U.K.
208 E2 **El Muglad** Sudan
187 C10 **El Mugrón** *mt.* Spain
227 O5 **Elmvale** *Ont.* Can.
226 E9 **Elmwood** *IL* U.S.A.
226 B5 **Elmwood** *WI* U.S.A.
204 D4 **El Mzereb** *well* Mali
245 H3 **El Naranjo** Mex.
244 D7 **El Naranjo** *r.* Mex.
163 J10 **Elne** France
140 I5 **Elnesvågen** Norway
92 B6 **El Nido** *Palawan* Phil.
260 C4 **El Nihuel** Arg.
216 □3f **El Oasis** *Gran Canaria* Canary Is
241 O9 **El Oasis** Mex.
203 F6 **El Obeid** Sudan
245 N9 **El Ocote, Parque Natural** *nature res.* Mex.
245 H8 **El Ocotito** Mex.
203 F6 **El Odaiya** Sudan
250 D5 **El Odre** Arg.
208 B4 **Elogo** Congo
227 N6 **Elora** *Ont.* Can.
158 C5 **Elorn** *r.* France
250 B5 **El Oro** *prov.* Ecuador
242 H4 **El Oro** *Coahuila* Mex.
244 G6 **El Oro** *México* Mex.
183 O2 **Elorrio** Spain
261 G3 **Elortondo** Arg.
183 Q3 **Elorz** Spain
198 E7 **Elos** *Kriti* Greece
183 K7 **El Oso** Spain
177 H5 **Előszállás** Hungary
244 A2 **Elota** Mex.
244 A2 **Elota** *r.* Mex.
205 G2 **El Oued** Alg.
245 I5 **Eloxochitlán** Mex.
241 U9 **Eloy** *AZ* U.S.A.
157 M7 **Éloyes** France
251 F3 **El Palmar** Venez.
261 H2 **El Palmar, Parque Nacional** *nat. park* Arg.
242 G5 **El Palmito** Mex.
216 □3a **El Palm-Mar** *Tenerife* Canary Is
185 K7 **El Palo** Spain
244 G1 **El Pañuelo** Mex.
251 F2 **El Pao** *Bolívar* Venez.
250 D2 **El Pao** *Cojedes* Venez.
244 G8 **El Papayo** Mex.
93 F5 **Elpaputih, Teluk** *b. Seram* Indon.
242 □P11 **El Paraíso** Hond.
245 L8 **El Paraíso** Mex.
216 □3d **El Paso** *La Palma* Canary Is
226 F9 **El Paso** *IL* U.S.A.
El Paso *KS* U.S.A. *see* **Derby**
239 K11 **El Paso** *TX* U.S.A.
182 G8 **El Payo** Spain
185 N2 **El Pedernoso** Spain
245 I3 **El Pedregoso** *r.* Mex.
184 F5 **El Pedroso** Spain
183 J6 **El Pedroso de la Armuña** Spain
244 G3 **El Peñasco** Mex.
258 D2 **El Peñón** Arg.
260 B3 **El Peñón** *mt.* Chile
183 Q9 **El Peral** Spain
182 I6 **El Perdigón** Spain
261 F4 **El Peregrino** Arg.
186 G6 **El Perelló** *Cataluña* Spain
187 E9 **El Perelló** *Valencia* Spain
168 H2 **Elpersbüttel** Ger.
147 F5 **Elphin** Ireland
146 F6 **Elphin** *Highland, Scotland* U.K.
Elphinstone *i.* Myanmar *see* **Thayawthadangyi Kyun**
185 O2 **El Picazo** Spain
251 F2 **El Pilar** Venez.
Elpin Armenia *see* **Yelp'in**
245 I4 **El Piñal** Mex.
186 G5 **El Pinell de Bray** Spain
182 I6 **El Piñero** Spain
261 H2 **El Pingo** Arg.
242 H3 **El Pino, Sierra** *mts* Mex.
258 E2 **El Pintado** Arg.
184 H4 **El Pintado, Embalse** *resr* Spain
186 H5 **El Pla de Santa María** Spain
260 B3 **El Plomo, Nevado** *mt.* Chile
259 C7 **El Pluma** Arg.
186 D6 **El Pobo** Spain
183 Q7 **El Pobo de Dueñas** Spain
253 E3 **El Pocito** Bol.
187 E8 **El Port** Spain
240 M4 **El Portal** *CA* U.S.A.
186 L3 **El Port de la Selva** Spain
250 C1 **El Portete** *b.* Col.
260 D2 **El Portezuelo** Arg.
250 B7 **El Portugues** Peru
250 D3 **El Porvenir** Col.
240 P9 **El Porvenir** Mex.
242 G2 **El Porvenir** Mex.
242 □T13 **El Porvenir** Panama
245 H4 **El Potosí, Parque Nacional** *nat. park* Mex.
186 J5 **El Prat de Llobregat** Spain
El Progreso Guat. *see* **Guastatoya**
242 □P10 **El Progreso** Hond.
185 N2 **El Provencio** Spain
261 H3 **El Pueblito** Arg.
252 D5 **El Puente** Bol.
242 □P11 **El Puente** Nic.
183 N2 **El Puente** Spain
183 J9 **El Puente de Arzobispo** Spain
El Puerto de Andraitx Spain *see* **Port d'Andratx**
184 G7 **El Puerto de Santa María** Spain
El Qâhira Egypt *see* **Al Qāhirah**
128 D5 **El Qasimiye** *r.* Lebanon
El Quds Israel/West Bank *see* **Jerusalem**
258 D2 **El Quebrachal** Arg.
244 G3 **El Quelital** Mex.
260 B1 **Elqui** *r.* Chile
250 D3 **El Quisco** Chile
244 D7 **El Ranchito** *Michoacán* Mex.
245 H4 **El Ranchito** *Tamaulipas* Mex.
183 O4 **El Rasillo** Spain
242 □U13 **El Real** Panama
184 G5 **El Real de la Jara** Spain
183 K8 **El Real de San Vicente** Spain
183 P7 **El Recuenco** Spain
244 G4 **El Refugio** Mex.
244 B2 **El Regocijo** Mex.
237 G8 **El Reno** *OK* U.S.A.
260 D3 **El Retamo** Arg.
244 G2 **El Retorno** Mex.
258 D2 **El Rey, Parque Nacional** *nat. park* Arg.
240 M7 **El Rio** *CA* U.S.A.
244 A2 **El Roble** Mex.
185 K2 **El Robledo** Spain
184 G6 **El Rocío** Spain
183 N9 **El Romeral** Spain
184 E6 **El Rompido** Spain
184 G5 **El Ronquillo** Spain
245 N8 **El Rosario, Laguna** *l.* Mex.
223 I5 **Elrose** *Sask.* Can.
226 C5 **Elroy** *WI* U.S.A.
183 O5 **El Royo** Spain
185 J6 **El Rubio** Spain
244 G1 **El Rucio** *Nuevo León* Mex.
244 E2 **El Rucio** *Zacatecas* Mex.
222 C2 **Elsa** *Y.T.* Can.
196 E5 **Elsa** *r. Sicilia* Italy
191 J8 **Elsa** *r.* Italy
243 J4 **El Sabinal, Parque Nacional** *nat. park* Mex.
186 C3 **El Sabinar** *Aragón* Spain
185 O4 **El Sabinar** *Murcia* Spain
242 G2 **El Sahuaro** Mex.
259 D8 **El Salado** Arg.
244 G1 **El Salado** Mex.
187 E9 **El Saler** Spain
185 P3 **El Salobral** Spain
244 B2 **El Salto** *Durango* Mex.
244 D5 **El Salto** *Jalisco* Mex.
243 O11 **El Salvador** *country* Central America
258 C2 **El Salvador** Chile
244 D5 **El Salvador** *Jalisco* Mex.
244 G2 **El Salvador** *Zacatecas* Mex.
92 E7 **El Salvador** *Mindanao* Phil.
250 D3 **El Samán de Apure** Venez.
186 G4 **Els Arcs** Spain
227 L1 **Elsas** *Ont.* Can.
Elsass *reg.* France *see* **Alsace**
185 I6 **El Saucejo** Spain
182 G8 **El Saugo** Spain
242 F4 **El Sauz** *Chihuahua* Mex.
244 C4 **El Sauz** *Nayarit* Mex.
216 □3a **El Sauzal** *Tenerife* Canary Is
240 P10 **El Sauzal** Mex.
172 G2 **Elsava** *r.* Ger.
178 H4 **Elsbethen** Austria
149 M3 **Elsdon** *Northumberland, England* U.K.
168 H4 **Elsdorf** *Niedersachsen* Ger.
169 C9 **Elsdorf** *Nordrhein-Westfalen* Ger.
168 I2 **Elsdorf-Westermühlen** Ger.
169 G6 **Else** *r.* Ger.
247 I4 **El Seibo** Dom. Rep.
165 J8 **Elsenborn** Belgium
173 L4 **Elsendorf** Ger.
172 G2 **Elsenfeld** Ger.
172 F3 **Elsenz** *r.* Ger.
186 I2 **El Serrat** Andorra
83 J2 **Elsey** *N.T.* Austr.
168 F4 **Elsfleth** Ger.
84 D2 **El Sharana** *N.T.* Austr.
226 J6 **Elsie** *MI* U.S.A.
Elsinore Denmark *see* **Helsingør**
240 O8 **Elsinore** *CA* U.S.A.
241 T3 **Elsinore** *UT* U.S.A.
240 O8 **Elsinore Lake** *CA* U.S.A.
165 I7 **Elsloo** Neth.
234 D5 **Elsmere** *DE* U.S.A.
140 P2 **Elsnes** Norway
171 G7 **Elsnig** Ger.
171 G7 **Elsnigk** Ger.
242 H4 **El Socorro** Mex.
186 G5 **El Soleràs** Spain
260 C4 **El Sosneado** Arg.
164 I4 **Elspeet** Neth.
186 I4 **Els Prats de Rei** Spain
164 I5 **Elst** *Gelderland* Neth.
164 H5 **Elst** *Utrecht* Neth.
151 K5 **Elstead** *Surrey, England* U.K.
171 G7 **Elster** Ger.
171 F9 **Elsterberg** Ger.
171 I8 **Elsterniederung und Westliche Oberlausitzer Heide** *park* Ger.
171 I8 **Elsterwerda** Ger.
151 L4 **Elstree** *Hertfordshire, England* U.K.
242 F3 **El Sueco** Mex.
260 B3 **El Tabo** Chile
245 J5 **El Tajín** *tourist site* Mex.
250 C3 **El Tama, Parque Nacional** *nat. park* Venez.
205 H1 **El Tarf** Alg.
189 B7 **El Tarf** *prov.* Alg.
244 F6 **El Tecolote, Cerro** *mt.* Mex.
244 C2 **El Tecuán, Parque Nacional** *nat. park* Mex.
261 G4 **El Tejar** Arg.
182 H4 **El Teleno** *mt.* Spain
245 I1 **El Temascal** Mex.
179 N5 **Eltendorf** Austria
245 H6 **El Tepozteco, Parque Nacional** *nat. park* Mex.
186 L3 **El Ter** *r.* Spain
171 G9 **Elterlein** Ger.
80 I6 **Eltham** *North I.* N.Z.
183 L8 **El Tiemblo** Spain
251 E2 **El Tigre** Venez.
243 N9 **El Tigre, Parque Nacional** *nat. park* Guat.
173 J2 **Eltmann** Ger.
183 O9 **El Toboso** Spain
250 D2 **El Tocuyo** Venez.
258 C3 **El Tofo** *Coquimbo* Chile
260 B2 **El Tololo** Chile
147 F8 **Elton** Ireland
120 B3 **El'ton** Rus. Fed.
151 L2 **Elton** *Cambridgeshire, England* U.K.
149 L7 **Elton** *Cheshire, England* U.K.
120 B3 **El'ton, Ozero** *l.* Rus. Fed.
238 E3 **Eltopia** *WA* U.S.A.
182 I8 **El Torno** Spain
260 B5 **El Toro** *Biobío* Chile
250 C2 **El Totumo** Venez.
261 G3 **El Trébol** Arg.
245 H9 **El Treinta** Mex.
242 C2 **El Tren** Mex.
261 H4 **El Trigo** Arg.
185 K2 **El Trincheto** Spain
261 G4 **El Triunfo** Arg.
244 D7 **El Triunfo** Mex.
247 □7 **El Tucuche** *hill* Trin. and Tob.
244 B5 **El Tuito** Mex.
184 F6 **El Tumbalejo** Spain
258 D2 **El Tunal** Arg.
250 D3 **El Tuparro, Parque Nacional** *nat. park* Col.
259 B8 **El Turbio** Chile
186 G3 **El Turbón** *mt.* Spain
169 F10 **Eltville am Rhein** Ger.
206 E5 **Elubo** Ghana
114 G4 **Eluru** *Andhra Prad.* India
203 G5 **El 'Uteishan** *well* Sudan
138 J3 **Elva** Estonia
246 I3 **El Vallecillo** Mex.
146 I12 **Elvanfoot** *South Lanarkshire, Scotland* U.K.
Elvanlı Turkey *see* **Tömük**
184 E3 **Elvas** Port.
140 O2 **Elvebakken** Norway
140 N2 **Elvegard** Norway
245 H9 **El Veladero, Parque Nacional** *nat. park* Mex.
158 F6 **Elven** France
244 C4 **El Venado** Mex.
186 I5 **El Vendrell** Spain
245 J1 **El Verde Chico** Mex.
187 F10 **El Verger** Spain
234 D4 **Elverson** *PA* U.S.A.
141 K6 **Elverum** Norway
185 L2 **El Vicario, Embalse de** *resr* Spain
250 C3 **El Viejo** *mt.* Col.
242 □P11 **El Viejo** Nic.
244 C4 **El Vigía, Cerro** *mt.* Mex.
183 M7 **El Villar, Embalse de** *resr* Spain
149 P6 **Elvington** *York, England* U.K.
250 C6 **Elvira** Brazil
86 J4 **Elvire** *r. W.A.* Austr.
86 I5 **Elvire Aboriginal Reserve** *W.A.* Austr.
185 J4 **El Viso** Spain
184 H6 **El Viso del Alcor** Spain
140 U2 **Elvnes** Norway
190 E5 **Elvo** *r.* Italy
260 D3 **El Volcán** Arg.
260 B3 **El Volcán** Chile
210 D4 **El Wak** Kenya
226 F8 **Elwood** *IL* U.S.A.
230 E5 **Elwood** *IN* U.S.A.
236 F5 **Elwood** *NE* U.S.A.
235 I3 **Elwood** *NJ* U.S.A.
210 A2 **El Wurl** *watercourse* Sudan
203 F6 **El Wuz** Sudan
169 K8 **Elxleben** Ger.
151 M3 **Ely** *Cambridgeshire, England* U.K.
150 F5 **Ely** *Cardiff, Wales* U.K.
226 C2 **Ely** *MN* U.S.A.
241 R2 **Ely** *NV* U.S.A.
151 M3 **Ely, Isle of** *reg. England* U.K.
250 D3 **El Yagual** Venez.
191 I4 **El Yibo** *well* Kenya
210 C3 **Elyria** *OH* U.S.A.
232 C7 **Elyria** *OH* U.S.A.
227 R9 **Elysburg** *PA* U.S.A.
169 F10 **Elz** Ger.
172 D5 **Elz** *r.* Ger.
245 J9 **El Zacatón, Cerro** *mt.* Mex.
172 E5 **Elzach** Ger.
242 G5 **El Zape** Mex.
169 I6 **Elze** Ger.
168 I5 **Elze (Wedemark)** Ger.
78 □5 **Émaé** *i.* Vanuatu
160 H2 **Émagny** France
138 K3 **Emajõgi** *r.* Estonia
122 H3 **Emāmrūd** Iran
122 F3 **Emām Qolī** Iran
123 M3 **Emām Şaḩeb** Afgh.
122 F3 **Emām Taqī** Iran
143 M4 **Emån** *r.* Sweden
215 Q2 **Emangusi** S. Africa
78 □5 **Émao** *i.* Vanuatu
E. Martínez Mex. *see* **Emiliano Martínez**
256 A3 **Emas, Parque Nacional das** *nat. park* Brazil
121 T4 **Emazar** Kazakh.
120 H3 **Emba** Kazakh.
120 E4 **Emba** *r.* Kazakh.
215 N5 **Embalenhle** S. Africa
258 D1 **Embarcación** Arg.
223 I3 **Embarras Portage** *Alta* Can.
226 B2 **Embarrass** *MN* U.S.A.
Embetsu Japan *see* **Enbetsu**
Embi Kazakh. *see* **Emba**
94 □ **Embiah, Mount** *hill* Sing.
183 Q7 **Embid** Spain
183 Q6 **Embid de Ariza** Spain
Embira *r.* Brazil *see* **Envira**
149 N2 **Embleton** *Northumberland, England* U.K.
146 I7 **Embo** *Highland, Scotland* U.K.
Émbonas *Rodos* Greece *see* **Emponas**
208 C4 **Embondo** Dem. Rep. Congo
256 D3 **Emborcação, Represa de** *resr* Brazil
Emborion Greece *see* **Emporeio**
172 F7 **Embrach** Switz.
234 D5 **Embreeville** *PA* U.S.A.
233 J3 **Embrun** *Ont.* Can.
161 I7 **Embrun** France
168 J4 **Embsen** Ger.
256 B3 **Embu** Brazil
210 C5 **Embu** Kenya
113 □1 **Embudhu** *i. S. Male* Maldives
113 □1 **Embudhu Finolhu** *i. S. Male* Maldives
209 C9 **Embundo** Angola
168 D4 **Emden** Ger.
199 I6 **Emecik** Turkey
Emei *Sichuan* China *see* **Emeishan**
108 D4 **Emeishan** *Sichuan* China
108 D4 **Emei Shan** *mt. Sichuan* China
121 S4 **Emel'** *r.* Kazakh.
85 L7 **Emerald** *Qld* Austr.
83 J7 **Emerald** *Vic.* Austr.
234 D3 **Emerald** *PA* U.S.A.
221 G2 **Emerald Isle** *i. N.W.T.* Can.
225 H2 **Emeril** *Nfld and Lab.* Can.
Emerita Augusta Spain *see* **Mérida**
252 D3 **Emero** *r.* Bol.
223 L5 **Emerson** *Man.* Can.
232 B10 **Emerson** *KY* U.S.A.
241 U3 **Emery** *UT* U.S.A.
Emesa Syria *see* **Ḩimş**
199 K3 **Emet** Turkey
215 O1 **eMgwenya** S. Africa
240 M3 **Emigrant Basin Wilderness** *nature res. CA* U.S.A.
240 L2 **Emigrant Gap** *CA* U.S.A.
238 F6 **Emigrant Pass** *NV* U.S.A.
241 Q4 **Emigrant Valley** *NV* U.S.A.
202 C5 **Emi Koussi** *mt.* Chad
222 G3 **Emile** *r. N.W.T.* Can.
261 G2 **Emilia** Arg.
242 G5 **Emiliano Martínez** Mex.
243 N9 **Emiliano Zapata** *Chiapas* Mex.
244 D1 **Emiliano Zapata** *Durango* Mex.
244 D2 **Emiliano Zapata** *Zacatecas* Mex.
190 K7 **Emilia-Romagna** *admin. reg.* Italy
261 G4 **Emilio Ayarza** Arg.
245 K6 **Emilio Carranza** *Veracruz* Mex.
244 D1 **Emilio Carranza** *Zacatecas* Mex.
261 H2 **Emilio R. Coni** Arg.
190 C4 **Emilius, Monte** *mt.* Italy
110 F3 **Emin** *Xinjiang* China
197 P8 **Emine, Nos** *pt* Bulg.
237 J7 **Eminence** *MO* U.S.A.
110 F3 **Emin He** *r.* China
197 P8 **Eminska Planina** *hills* Bulg.
128 B1 **Emirdağ** Turkey
199 M4 **Emir Dağı** *mt.* Turkey
199 K4 **Emirhisar** Turkey
83 K9 **Emita** *Tas.* Austr.
215 P1 **eMjindini** S. Africa
168 I2 **Emkendorf** Ger.
232 F7 **Emlenton** *PA* U.S.A.
168 C5 **Emlichheim** Ger.
147 F8 **Emly** Ireland
143 L5 **Emmaboda** Sweden
Emmahaven *Sumatera* Indon. *see* **Telukbayur**
247 □10 **Emmastad** *Curaçao* Neth. Antilles
138 F3 **Emmaste** Estonia
139 T5 **Emmaus** Rus. Fed.
234 E3 **Emmaus** *PA* U.S.A.
83 M3 **Emmaville** *N.S.W.* Austr.
190 D1 **Emme** *r.* Switz.
164 I3 **Emmeloord** Neth.
168 G1 **Emmelsbüll-Horsbüll** Ger.
169 E10 **Emmelshausen** Ger.
164 K3 **Emmen** Neth.
172 E7 **Emmen** Switz.
172 D5 **Emmendingen** Ger.
190 D1 **Emmental** *reg.* Switz.
169 H6 **Emmer** *r.* Ger.
164 L3 **Emmer-Compascuum** Neth.
164 K3 **Emmer-Erfscheidenveen** Neth.
169 B7 **Emmerich** Ger.
173 K5 **Emmering** Ger.
173 N5 **Emmerting** Ger.
85 J8 **Emmet** *Qld* Austr.
236 H4 **Emmetsburg** *IA* U.S.A.
238 F5 **Emmett** *ID* U.S.A.
232 C5 **Emmett** *MI* U.S.A.
114 E5 **Emmiganuru** *Andhra Prad.* India
232 H9 **Emmitsburg** *MD* U.S.A.
234 C6 **Emmorton** *MD* U.S.A.
151 M2 **Emneth** *Norfolk, England* U.K.
223 M5 **Emo** *Ont.* Can.
177 J4 **Emőd** Hungary
Emona Slovenia *see* **Ljubljana**
237 H9 **Emory** *TX* U.S.A.
237 D11 **Emory Peak** *TX* U.S.A.
206 B4 **Empada** Guinea-Bissau
242 D4 **Empalme** Mex.
244 G5 **Empalme Escobedo** Mex.
181 E4 **Empandadas** *mt.* Spain
215 P4 **Empangeni** S. Africa
258 F2 **Empedrado** Arg.
260 A4 **Empedrado** Chile
164 H5 **Empel** Neth.
266 G2 **Emperor Seamount Chain** *sea feature* N. Pacific Ocean
266 G2 **Emperor Trough** *sea feature* N. Pacific Ocean
252 C5 **Empexa, Salar de** *salt flat* Bol.
172 F5 **Empfingen** Ger.
Empingham Reservoir *England* U.K. *see* **Rutland Water**
226 H5 **Empire** *MI* U.S.A.
93 F8 **Emplawas** *Maluku* Indon.
191 J8 **Empoli** Italy
198 I5 **Emponas** *Rodos* Greece
199 G6 **Emporeio** Greece
236 G3 **Emporia** *KS* U.S.A.
232 H12 **Emporia** *VA* U.S.A.
232 G7 **Emporium** *PA* U.S.A.
223 I5 **Empress** *Alta* Can.
213 F3 **Empress Mine** Zimbabwe
165 H8 **Emptinne** Belgium
Empty Quarter *des.* Saudi Arabia *see* **Rub' al Khālī**
161 F6 **Empurany** France
168 D4 **Ems** *r.* Ger.
172 H4 **Ems** *r.* Ger.
169 D6 **Emsbüren** Ger.
227 O4 **Emsdale** *Ont.* Can.
169 E6 **Emsdetten** Ger.
168 D4 **Ems-Jade-Kanal** *canal* Ger.
173 J2 **Emskirchen** Ger.
168 E4 **Emsland** *reg.* Ger.
164 I4 **Emst** Neth.
168 F5 **Emstek** Ger.
151 K6 **Emsworth** *Hampshire, England* U.K.
215 O1 **Emthonjeni** S. Africa
168 G5 **Emtinghausen** Ger.
85 H4 **Emu Creek** *r. Qld* Austr.
138 J3 **Emumägi** *hill* Estonia
84 F3 **Emu Park** *Qld* Austr.
100 D2 **Emur He** *r.* China
100 B2 **Emur Shan** *mts* China
147 I4 **Emyvale** Ireland
215 N2 **eMzinoni** S. Africa
104 F5 **Ena** Japan
140 L5 **Enafors** Sweden
250 D4 **Enambú** Col.
251 F3 **Enamuna** Brazil
141 N6 **Enånger** Sweden
91 I7 **Enarotali** *Papua* Indon.
97 F1 **Ena-san** *mt.* Japan
121 Q3 **Enbek** Kazakh.
102 Q3 **Enbetsu** Japan
186 F6 **Encanadé** *mt.* Spain
255 B9 **Encantadas, Serra das** *hills* Brazil
92 C4 **Encanto, Cape** *Luzon* Phil.
244 E4 **Encarnación** Mex.
253 G6 **Encarnación** Para.
162 I5 **Enchanet, Barrage d'** *dam* France
206 E5 **Enchi** Ghana
185 P2 **Encina** *r.* Spain
186 C5 **Encinacorba** Spain
237 F11 **Encinal** *TX* U.S.A.
183 L6 **Encinas** *mt.* Spain
183 J8 **Encinas de Abajo** Spain
185 L3 **Encinasola** Spain
185 K6 **Encinas Reales** Spain
182 G4 **Encinedo** Spain
240 O8 **Encinitas** *CA* U.S.A.
239 L9 **Encino** *NM* U.S.A.
183 P3 **Enciso** Spain
260 D3 **Encón** Arg.
250 D2 **Encontrados** Venez.
82 G6 **Encounter Bay** *S.A.* Austr.
255 E5 **Encruzilhada** Brazil
255 B9 **Encruzilhada do Sul** Brazil
177 K3 **Encs** Hungary
177 L4 **Encsencs** Hungary
222 E4 **Endako** *B.C.* Can.
94 E3 **Endau** *r.* Malaysia
90 B6 **Endau-Rompin National Park** Malaysia
93 B8 **Ende** *Flores* Indon.
93 B8 **Ende** *i.* Indon.
85 H1 **Endeavour Strait** *Qld* Austr.
162 G6 **Endelave** *i.* Denmark
77 I2 **Enderbury** *i.* Kiribati
222 G5 **Enderby** *B.C.* Can.
Enderby *atoll* Micronesia *see* **Puluwat**
151 J2 **Enderby** *Leicestershire, England* U.K.
264 L9 **Enderby Abyssal Plain** *sea feature* Southern Ocean
86 D6 **Enderby Island** *W.A.* Austr.
263 D2 **Enderby Land** *reg.* Antarctica
187 K9 **Enderrocat, Es Cap** *c.* Spain
220 C3 **Endicott Mountains** *AK* U.S.A.
252 D2 **Endimari** *r.* Brazil
190 H4 **Endine, Lago di** *l.* Italy
172 D5 **Endingen** Ger.
138 J3 **Endla riiklik looduskaitseala** *nature res.* Estonia
207 I6 **Endom** Cameroon
177 I3 **Endrefalva** Hungary
182 I7 **Endrinal** Spain
163 H10 **Endron, Pique d'** *mt.* France
227 R7 **Endwell** *NY* U.S.A.
138 I4 **Endzele** Latvia
252 B2 **Ene** *r.* Peru
87 C10 **Eneabba** *W.A.* Austr.
142 H2 **Enebakk** Norway
191 L4 **Enego** Italy
137 F9 **Enem** Rus. Fed.
251 G3 **Enemutu** Brazil
EnenKio N. Pacific Ocean *see* **Wake Island**
120 H2 **Energetik** Rus. Fed.
261 H6 **Energía** Arg.
Energodar Ukr. *see* **Enerhodar**
137 N6 **Enerhodar** Ukr.
176 G4 **Enese** Hungary
266 G6 **Enewetak** *atoll* Marshall Is
199 H2 **Enez** Turkey
128 D4 **Enfe** Lebanon
182 C3 **Enfesta** Spain
209 A8 **Enfião, Ponta do** *pt* Angola
205 H1 **Enfidaville** Tunisia
225 I4 **Enfield** *N.S.* Can.
151 L4 **Enfield** *Greater London, England* U.K.
231 I7 **Enfield** *NC* U.S.A.
226 I3 **Engadine** *MI* U.S.A.
140 J5 **Engan** Norway
247 I4 **Engaño, Cabo** *c.* Dom. Rep.
265 M3 **Engaño, Cape** *Luzon* Phil.
Engaños, Río de los *r.* Col. *see* **Yari**
102 U2 **Engaru** Japan
215 L5 **Engcobo** S. Africa
169 D6 **Engden** Ger.
128 D7 **En Gedi** Israel
190 E2 **Engelberg** Switz.
231 J8 **Engelhard** *NC* U.S.A.
179 O3 **Engelhartstetten** Austria
179 I2 **Engelhartszell** Austria
120 B2 **Engel's** Rus. Fed.
173 N5 **Engelsberg** Ger.
164 G2 **Engelschmangat** *sea chan.* Neth.
171 F8 **Engelsdorf** Ger.
169 D9 **Engelskirchen** Ger.
164 J2 **Engelsmanplaat** *i.* Neth.
172 F6 **Engen** Ger.
256 A5 **Engenheiro Beltrão** Brazil
257 F2 **Engenheiro Navarro** Brazil
82 E3 **Engenina** *watercourse S.A.* Austr.
169 G6 **Enger** Ger.
141 K6 **Engerdal** Norway
170 D5 **Engersen** Ger.
169 G8 **Enge-Sande** Ger.
161 G8 **Enggano** *i.* Indon.
203 H5 **Enghershatu** *mt.* Eritrea
165 F7 **Enghien** Belgium
222 C3 **Engineer** *B.C.* Can.
165 H7 **Engis** Belgium
94 E6 **Engkilili** *Sarawak* Malaysia
95 I4 **England** *admin. div.* U.K.
149 O8 **Englebright Reservoir** *CA* U.S.A.
240 K2 **Englee** *Nfld and Lab.* Can.
225 K3 **Englefontaine** France
156 G3 **Englehart** *Ont.* Can.
224 E4 **Englewood** *FL* U.S.A.
231 F12 **Englewood** *NJ* U.S.A.
235 H3 **Englewood** *OH* U.S.A.
232 A9 **English** *r. Ont.* Can.
223 M5 **English** *IN* U.S.A.
230 D6 **English Bay** *Ascension* S. Atlantic Ocean
216 □2a **English Bazar** *W. Bengal* India *see* **Ingraj Bazar**
234 A2 **English Center** *PA* U.S.A.
145 G7 **English Channel** France/U.K.
262 S2 **English Coast** Antarctica
234 F6 **English Creek** *NJ* U.S.A.
247 □2 **English Harbour Town** Antigua and Barbuda
235 G4 **Englishtown** *NJ* U.S.A.
163 G10 **Engomer** France
134 F2 **Engozero** Rus. Fed.
172 G5 **Engstingen** Ger.
187 D10 **Enguera, Serra de** *mts* Spain
183 O9 **Enguídanos** Spain
138 G4 **Engure** Latvia
138 G4 **Engures ezers** *l.* Latvia
129 C3 **Enguri** *r.* Georgia
128 D8 **'En Hazeva** Israel
215 O4 **Enhlalakahle** S. Africa
237 G7 **Enid** *OK* U.S.A.
78 □3b **Enigu** *i. Majuro* Marshall Is
172 G5 **Eningen unter Achalm** Ger.
198 D3 **Enipeas** *r.* Greece
102 S4 **Eniwa** Japan
Eniwetok *atoll* Marshall Is *see* **Enewetak**
185 N7 **Enix** Spain
Enjiang *Jiangxi* China *see* **Yongfeng**
131 P4 **Enkan, Mys** *pt* Rus. Fed.
Enkeldoorn Zimbabwe *see* **Chivhu**
157 O5 **Enkenbach** Ger.
164 H3 **Enkhuizen** Neth.
172 G5 **Enkirch** Ger.
138 D1 **Enklinge** *Åland* Fin.
143 L4 **Enköping** Sweden
Enle *Yunnan* China *see* **Zhenyuan**
245 J4 **Enmedio, Arrecife de** *rf* Mex.
194 G8 **Enna** Italy
194 H8 **Enna** *prov. Sicilia* Italy
190 H4 **Enna** *r.* Italy
223 K2 **Ennadai Lake** *Nunavut* Can.
203 F6 **En Nahud** Sudan
205 E3 **En Namous, Oued** *watercourse* Alg.
207 H3 **E-n-Nassamé** *well* Niger
202 C6 **Enné, Ouadi** *watercourse* Chad
202 D5 **Ennedi, Massif** *mts* Chad
147 H6 **Ennell, Lough** *l.* Ireland
169 D8 **Ennepetal** Ger.
215 L2 **Ennerdale** S. Africa
149 K4 **Ennerdale Water** *l. England* U.K.
202 B4 **Enneri Achelouma** *watercourse* Niger
202 C5 **Enneri Maro** *watercourse* Chad
202 B4 **Enneri Ouri** *watercourse* Chad
202 C4 **Enneri Yebigué** *watercourse* Chad
157 L5 **Ennery** France
246 G4 **Ennery** Haiti
160 C5 **Ennezat** France
83 J3 **Enngonia** *N.S.W.* Austr.
169 F7 **Enniger** Ger.
150 F5 **Enniggerloh** Ger.
236 C3 **Ening** *SD* U.S.A.
147 E8 **Ennis** Ireland
238 I4 **Ennis** *MT* U.S.A.
237 G9 **Ennis** *TX* U.S.A.
147 I7 **Enniscorthy** Ireland
147 E9 **Enniskean** Ireland
147 J6 **Enniskerry** Ireland
147 G4 **Enniskillen** *Northern Ireland* U.K.
147 D7 **Ennistymon** Ireland
78 □3a **Enniwetak** *i. Kwajalein* Marshall Is
128 D5 **Enn Nâqoûra** Lebanon
179 J3 **Enns** Austria
179 K3 **Enns** *r.* Austria
179 J4 **Ennstaler Alpen** *mts* Austria
78 □3a **Ennubuj** *i. Kwajalein* Marshall Is
78 □3a **Ennumennet** *i. Kwajalein* Marshall Is
114 G6 **Ennur** *Tamil Nadu* India
78 □3a **Ennylabagan** *i. Kwajalein* Marshall Is
140 U5 **Eno** Fin.
241 S4 **Enoch** *UT* U.S.A.
94 E5 **Enok** *Sumatera* Indon.
234 B4 **Enola** *PA* U.S.A.
140 T5 **Enonkoski** Fin.
140 Q2 **Enontekiö** Fin.
231 G8 **Enoree** *r. SC* U.S.A.
233 M4 **Enosburg Falls** *VT* U.S.A.
109 I7 **Enping** *Guangdong* China
93 A5 **Enrekang** *Sulawesi* Indon.
92 C3 **Enrile** *Luzon* Phil.
246 H5 **Enriquillo** Dom. Rep.
246 H4 **Enriquillo, Lago de** *l.* Dom. Rep.
164 I3 **Ens** Neth.
83 K7 **Ensay** *Vic.* Austr.
164 K4 **Enschede** Neth.
173 L3 **Ensdorf** Ger.
169 F8 **Ense** Ger.
261 I4 **Ensenada** Arg.
242 A2 **Ensenada** *Baja California* Mex.
242 E6 **Ensenada** *Baja California Sur* Mex.
247 □1 **Ensenada** Puerto Rico
250 B3 **Ensenada de Utria** *nat. park* Col.
172 C3 **Ensheim** Ger.
108 G3 **Enshi** *Hubei* China
104 G7 **Enshū-nada** *g.* Japan
157 N8 **Ensisheim** France
231 D10 **Ensley** *FL* U.S.A.
151 J4 **Enstone** *Oxfordshire, England* U.K.
161 G10 **Ensuès-la-Redonne** France
216 □3b **Entallada, Punta de la** *pt Fuerteventura* Canary Is
210 B4 **Entebbe** Uganda
164 K4 **Enter** Neth.
146 I12 **Enterkinfoot** *Dumfries and Galloway, Scotland* U.K.
222 G2 **Enterprise** *N.W.T.* Can.
227 R5 **Enterprise** *Ont.* Can.
231 E10 **Enterprise** *AL* U.S.A.
238 F4 **Enterprise** *OR* U.S.A.
241 S4 **Enterprise** *UT* U.S.A.
92 B6 **Enterprise Point** *Palawan* Phil.
222 E4 **Entiako Provincial Park** *B.C.* Can.
95 J4 **Entimau, Bukit** *hill* Malaysia
190 E2 **Entlebuch** Switz.
190 C7 **Entracque** Italy
184 C5 **Entradas** Port.
161 F8 **Entraigues-sur-la-Sorgue** France
160 C2 **Entrains-sur-Nohain** France
159 J6 **Entrammes** France
222 G4 **Entrance** *Alta* Can.
84 B3 **Entrance Island** *N.T.* Austr.
161 J8 **Entraunes** France
161 B7 **Entraygues-sur-Truyère** France
78 □5 **Entrecasteaux, Récifs d'** *rf* New Caledonia
217 □1c **Entre-Deux** Réunion
163 D6 **Entre-deux-Mers** *reg.* France
183 O7 **Entrepeñas, Embalse de** *resr* Spain
261 H3 **Entre Ríos** *prov.* Arg.
252 D5 **Entre Ríos** Bol.
254 F4 **Entre Rios** *Bahia* Brazil
251 H6 **Entre Rios** *Pará* Brazil
Entre Rios Moz. *see* **Malema**
257 E4 **Entre Rios de Minas** Brazil
161 J9 **Entrevaux** France
184 C2 **Entroncamento** Port.
244 G1 **Entronque San Roberto** Mex.
212 E3 **Entuba** Zimbabwe
215 P4 **Entumeni** S. Africa
207 G5 **Enugu** Nigeria
207 G5 **Enugu** *state* Nigeria
131 T3 **Enurmino** Rus. Fed.
186 I2 **Envalira, Port d'** *pass* Andorra
162 H5 **Envendos** Port.
156 B4 **Envermeu** France
250 C3 **Envigado** Col.
252 C1 **Envira** Brazil
252 C1 **Envira** *r.* Brazil
209 E5 **Enyamba** Dem. Rep. Congo
177 H5 **Enying** Hungary
81 F10 **Enys, Mount** *South I.* N.Z.
172 G3 **Enz** *r.* Ger.
190 J6 **Enza** *r.* Italy
105 I4 **Enzan** Japan
179 O3 **Enzersdorf an der Fischa** Austria
172 E4 **Enzklösterle** Ger.
78 □5 **Eo** *atoll Îles Loyauté* New Caledonia
182 F2 **Eo** *r.* Spain
Eochaill Ireland *see* **Youghal**
232 C11 **Eolia** *KY* U.S.A.
Eooa *i.* Tonga *see* **'Eua**
146 D5 **Eoropaidh** *Western Isles, Scotland* U.K.
159 L3 **Épagnes** France
212 C4 **Epako** Namibia
190 B2 **Épalinges** Switz.
245 I5 **Epazoyucan** Mex.
164 I5 **Epe** Neth.
207 F5 **Epe** Nigeria
261 F5 **Epecuén, Lago** *l.* Arg.
208 C4 **Epéna** Congo
177 J5 **Eperjes** Hungary
156 G5 **Épernay** France
156 D6 **Épernon** France
172 F5 **Epfendorf** Ger.
199 I5 **Ephesus** *tourist site* Turkey
241 U2 **Ephraim** *UT* U.S.A.
234 C4 **Ephrata** *PA* U.S.A.
238 E3 **Ephrata** *WA* U.S.A.
78 □5 **Epi** *i.* Vanuatu
Epidamnus Albania *see* **Durrës**
198 E6 **Epidavrou Limiras, Kolpos** *b.* Greece
156 C8 **Épieds-en-Beauce** France
161 I6 **Épierre** France
181 F2 **Épila** Spain
160 F3 **Épinac** France
157 L7 **Épinal** France
251 G3 **Epira** Guyana
Epirus *admin. reg.* Greece *see* **Ipeiros**
160 D2 **Épiry** France
128 A4 **Episkopi** Cyprus
128 A4 **Episkopi Bay** Cyprus
Episkopis, Kolpos *b.* Cyprus *see* **Episkopi Bay**
244 G5 **Epitacio Huerta** Mex.
160 E1 **Époisses** France
193 L6 **Epomeo, Monte** *vol.* Italy
172 B3 **Eppelborn** Ger.
172 F3 **Eppelheim** Ger.
172 D3 **Eppenbrunn** Ger.
171 H9 **Eppendorf** Ger.
172 F2 **Eppertshausen** Ger.
156 F4 **Eppeville** France
151 M4 **Epping** *Essex, England* U.K.
233 □N5 **Epping** *NH* U.S.A.
172 F3 **Eppingen** Ger.
85 K7 **Epping Forest National Park** *Qld* Austr.
173 J5 **Eppishausen** Ger.
169 F10 **Eppstein** Ger.
150 F3 **Eppynt, Mynydd** *hills Wales* U.K.
151 L5 **Epsom** *Surrey, England* U.K.
156 C5 **Epte** *r.* France
159 M6 **Épuisay** France
260 E5 **Epu-pel** Arg.
259 C6 **Epuyén** Arg.
149 P6 **Epworth** *North Lincolnshire, England* U.K.
122 E6 **Eqlīd** Iran
208 D4 **Équateur** *prov.* Dem. Rep. Congo
207 H6 **Equatorial Guinea** *country* Africa
251 F3 **Equeipa** Venez.
158 H2 **Équeurdreville-Hainneville** France
191 J8 **Era** *r.* Italy
85 J9 **Erac Creek** *watercourse Qld* Austr.
191 N4 **Eraclea** Italy
191 N4 **Eraclea Mare** Italy
206 E2 **Erakchiouene** *well* Mali
186 B1 **Erakurri** *mt.* Spain
116 G8 **Eran** *Madh. Prad.* India
92 A7 **Eran** *Palawan* Phil.
92 A7 **Eran Bay** *Palawan* Phil.
116 E9 **Erandol** *Mahar.* India
215 M1 **Erasmia** S. Africa
Erawadi *r.* Myanmar *see* **Irrawaddy**
97 D7 **Erawan National Park** Thai.
190 G4 **Erba** Italy
203 H4 **Erba, Jebel** *mt.* Sudan
126 H3 **Erbaa** Turkey
172 H5 **Erbach** *Baden-Württemberg* Ger.
172 G2 **Erbach** *Hessen* Ger.
173 M2 **Erbendorf** Ger.
172 C2 **Erbeskopf** *hill* Ger.
190 F5 **Erbognone** *r.* Italy
158 I6 **Erbray** France
128 B3 **Ercan** *airport* Cyprus
163 G10 **Ercé** France
127 K4 **Erçek** Turkey
260 A6 **Ercilla** Chile
127 K4 **Erciş** Turkey
126 G4 **Erciyes Dağı** *mt.* Turkey
177 H4 **Ercsi** Hungary
177 H4 **Érd** Hungary
Erdaobaihe *Jilin* China *see* **Baihe**
106 C9 **Erdaogou** *Qinghai* China
100 E7 **Erdao Jiang** *r.* China
171 E8 **Erdeborn** Ger.
199 I2 **Erdek** Turkey
126 G5 **Erdemli** Turkey
106 F2 **Erdenet** *Hövsgöl* Mongolia
106 I2 **Erdenet** *Orhon* Mongolia
106 G3 **Erdenetsogt** *Bayanhongor* Mongolia
106 J5 **Erdenetsogt** *Ömnögovĭ* Mongolia
158 E6 **Erdeven** France
173 L4 **Erding** Ger.
173 L5 **Erdinger Moos** *marsh* Ger.
171 H9 **Erdmannsdorf** Ger.
135 I7 **Erdniyevskiy** Rus. Fed.
158 H7 **Erdre** *r.* France
173 K5 **Erdweg** Ger.
250 C5 **Eré** Peru
256 A6 **Eré, Campos** *hills* Brazil
156 C5 **Éréac** France
251 E3 **Erebato** *r.* Venez.
263 L1 **Erebus, Mount** *vol.* Antarctica
127 L8 **Erech** *tourist site* Iraq
255 B8 **Erechim** Brazil
107 N2 **Ereentsav** Mongolia
126 G5 **Ereğli** *Konya* Turkey
126 E3 **Ereğli** *Zonguldak* Turkey
Erego Moz. *see* **Errego**
194 G8 **Erei, Monti** *mts Sicilia* Italy
198 A3 **Ereikoussa** *i.* Greece
93 C6 **Ereke** *Sulawesi* Indon.
Erementaū Kazakh. *see* **Yereymentau**
244 G7 **Eréndira** Mex.
110 G5 **Erenhaberga Shan** *mts* China
107 M5 **Erenhot** *Nei Mongol* China
196 E8 **Erenik** *r.* Serbia
129 D7 **Erentepe** Turkey
182 G5 **Eresk** Iran
183 K6 **Eresma** *r.* Spain
199 G5 **Eresos** *Lesvos* Greece
198 E4 **Eretria** Greece
Erevan Armenia *see* **Yerevan**
261 G3 **Erézcano** Arg.
168 H2 **Erfde** Ger.
215 K4 **Erfenis Dam** *resr* S. Africa
215 K4 **Erfenis Dam Nature Reserve** S. Africa
204 D3 **Erfoud** Morocco
169 C9 **Erftstadt** Ger.
171 D9 **Erfurt** Ger.
129 I4 **Ergani** Turkey
204 D5 **'Erg Chech** *des.* Alg./Mali
107 K5 **Ergel** Mongolia
204 D5 **'Erg el Aḩmar** *des.* Mali
138 I4 **Ērgeme** Latvia
199 H2 **Ergene** *r.* Turkey
199 H2 **Ergenehir** Ger.
205 E5 **'Erg I-n-Sâkâne** *des.* Mali
138 I5 **Ērgļi** Latvia
173 M4 **Ergolding** Ger.
173 M4 **Ergoldsbach** Ger.
109 I6 **Ergu** *Heilong.* China
150 F5 **Ergué-Gabéric** France
208 B2 **Erguig** *r.* Chad
107 Q1 **Ergun** *Nei Mongol* China
Ergun He *r.* China/Rus. Fed. *see* **Argun'**
Ergun Youqi *Nei Mongol* China *see* **Ergun**
108 C6 **Er Hai** *l.* China
173 N5 **Erharting** Ger.
203 H5 **Erheib** Sudan
101 D1 **Erhulai** *Liaoning* China
182 I4 **Eria** *r.* Spain
146 G6 **Eriboll** *Highland, Scotland* U.K.
146 G6 **Eriboll, Loch** *inlet Scotland* U.K.
164 K3 **Erica** Neth.
194 D7 **Erice** *Sicilia* Italy
183 Q3 **Erice** Spain
184 A3 **Ericeira** Port.
146 J9 **Ericht** *r. Scotland* U.K.
146 H9 **Ericht, Loch** *l. Scotland* U.K.
223 L5 **Erickson** *Man.* Can.
232 E6 **Erie** *PA* U.S.A.
227 N7 **Erie, Lake** Can./U.S.A.
Erieddu *i. N. Male* Maldives *see* **Eriyadhu**
206 D2 **'Erîgât** *des.* Mali
130 D2 **Erik Eriksenstretet** *sea chan.* Svalbard
Erikoússa *i.* Greece *see* **Ereikoussa**
223 L5 **Eriksdale** *Man.* Can.
143 L5 **Eriksmåla** Sweden
185 I4 **Erillas** *hill* Spain
Erímanthos Óros *mts* Greece *see* **Erymanthos**
102 U4 **Erimo** Japan
102 U5 **Erimo-misaki** *c.* Japan
227 N6 **Erin** *Ont.* Can.
231 D7 **Erin** *TN* U.S.A.
173 O5 **Ering** Ger.
143 L5 **Eringsboda** Sweden
247 □7 **Erin Point** Trin. and Tob.
146 B8 **Eriskay** *i. Scotland* U.K.
172 H6 **Eriskirch** Ger.
146 C6 **Erisort, Loch** *inlet Scotland* U.K.
151 N3 **Eriswell** *Suffolk, England* U.K.
190 D1 **Eriswil** Switz.
Erithraí Greece *see* **Erythres**
Erithropótamos *r.* Greece *see* **Erythropotamos**
203 H6 **Eritrea** *country* Africa
113 □1 **Eriyadhu** *i. N. Male* Maldives
Eriyadu *i. N. Male* Maldives *see* **Eriyadhu**
121 O8 **Erkech-Tam** Kyrg.
169 B8 **Erkelenz** Ger.
156 D2 **Erkelsbrugge** France
143 O2 **Erken** *l.* Sweden
129 C1 **Erken-Shakhar** Rus. Fed.
173 I5 **Erkheim** Ger.
199 L4 **Erkmen** Turkey
171 I6 **Erkner** Ger.
124 C6 **Erkowit** Sudan
178 F4 **Erl** Austria
183 D3 **Erla** Spain
190 C1 **Erlach** Switz.
173 K2 **Erlangen** Ger.
109 H2 **Erlangping** *Henan* China
173 P4 **Erlau** *r.* Ger.
179 L3 **Erlauf** Austria
179 L3 **Erlauf** *r.* Austria
179 L4 **Erlaufsee** *l.* Austria
171 F10 **Erlbach** Ger.
84 D8 **Erldunda** *N.T.* Austr.
172 G2 **Erlenbach am Main** Ger.
169 G10 **Erlensee** Ger.
190 E7 **Erli** Italy
87 F9 **Erlistoun** *watercourse W.A.* Austr.
100 F7 **Erlong Shan** *mt.* China
234 F7 **Erma** *NJ* U.S.A.
Ermak Kazakh. *see* **Aksu**
107 M2 **Ermana, Khrebet** *mts* Rus. Fed.
164 I4 **Ermelo** Neth.
182 E6 **Ermelo** Port.

Ermelo to Fajão
311

215 N2 Ermelo S. Africa
126 F5 Ermenek Turkey
128 B2 Ermenek r. Turkey
182 C6 Ermesinde Port.
184 C4 Ermidas do Sado Port.
202 E6 Ermil Sudan
198 E5 Ermioni Greece
244 D3 Ermita de los Correas Mex.
156 D6 Ermont France
198 F5 Ermoupoli Syros Greece
172 G4 Erms r. Ger.
171 D7 Ermsleben Ger.
183 O2 Ermua Spain
82 D2 Ernabella S.A. Austr.
114 E8 Ernakulam Kerala India
169 F9 Erndtebrück Ger.
147 F4 Erne r. Ireland/U.K.
159 J5 Ernée France
159 J5 Ernée r. France
87 G9 Ernest Giles Range hills W.A. Austr.
222 C4 Ernest Sound sea chan. AK U.S.A.
179 N2 Ernstbrunn Austria
172 A2 Ernz Noire r. Lux.
114 E7 Erode Tamil Nadu India
78 □3b Eroj i. Majuro Marshall Is
173 I5 Erolzheim Ger.
85 I9 Eromanga Qld Austr.
212 B4 Erongo admin. reg. Namibia
206 E2 'Eroûg well Mali
164 I5 Erp Neth.
177 K4 Érpatak Hungary
169 D9 Erpel Ger.
129 H3 Erpeli Rus. Fed.
106 C5 Erpu Xinjiang China
Erqu Shaanxi China see Zhouzhi
165 F8 Erquelinnes Belgium
158 G4 Erquy France
87 C9 Errabiddy Hills W.A. Austr.
204 D3 Er Rachidia Morocco
203 F6 Er Rahad Sudan
146 D10 Erraid i. Scotland U.K.
114 E5 Erramala Hills India
204 E3 Er Raoui des. Alg.
186 C1 Erratzu Spain
213 H3 Errego Moz.
210 B2 Er Renk Sudan
186 B1 Errenteria Spain
186 A1 Errezil Spain
183 P2 Erribera Spain
147 F2 Errigal hill Ireland
147 G7 Errill Ireland
170 E1 Errindlev Denmark
83 L7 Errinundra National Park Vic. Austr.
147 B4 Erris Head Ireland
190 E6 Erro r. Italy
186 C2 Erro r. Spain
146 H9 Errochty, Loch l. Scotland U.K.
146 I9 Errochty Water r. Scotland U.K.
203 G5 Er Rogel Sudan
146 H8 Errogie Highland, Scotland U.K.
233 □N4 Errol NH U.S.A.
78 □5 Erromango i. Vanuatu
Erronan i. Vanuatu see Futuna
210 B2 Er Roseires Sudan
203 G6 Er Rua'at Sudan
177 H5 Érsekcsanád Hungary
198 B2 Ersekë Albania
177 I3 Érsekvadkert Hungary
169 J8 Ershausen Ger.
100 D2 Ershiyizhan Heilong. China
Ersis Turkey see Kılıçkaya
236 G2 Erskine MN U.S.A.
143 S1 Erstan b. Fin.
157 O7 Erstein France
190 F2 Erstfeld Switz.
210 D1 Erta Ale vol. Eth.
106 B3 Ertai Xinjiang China
135 H6 Ertil' Rus. Fed.
172 G5 Ertingen Ger.
Ertis Kazakh. see Irtyshsk
Ertis r. Kazakh./Rus. Fed. see Irtysh
110 G2 Ertix He r. China/Kazakh.
191 M3 Erto Italy
78 □3a Eru i. Kwajalein Marshall Is
82 G4 Erudina S.A. Austr.
207 G4 Erufu Nigeria
127 K5 Eruh Turkey
192 B6 Erula Sardegna Italy
138 I2 Eru laht b. Estonia
207 F5 Eruwa Nigeria
258 G4 Erval Brazil
257 F4 Ervália Brazil
159 K6 Erve r. France
182 F6 Ervedosa do Douro Port.
184 C5 Ervidel Port.
156 E3 Ervillers France
182 F5 Ervões Port.
156 G7 Ervy-le-Châtel France
231 F7 Erwin TN U.S.A.
169 F7 Erwitte Ger.
170 E5 Erxleben Sachsen-Anhalt Ger.
171 D6 Erxleben Sachsen-Anhalt Ger.
198 C5 Erymanthos mts Greece
198 C5 Erymanthos r. Greece
198 E4 Erythres Greece
199 H1 Erythropotamos r. Greece
108 B5 Eryuan Yunnan China
196 H9 Erzen r. Albania
Erzerum Turkey see Erzurum
171 H9 Erzgebirge mts Czech Rep./Ger.
100 E4 Erzhan Heilong. China
172 F2 Erzhausen Ger.
106 D1 Erzin Rus. Fed.
126 H5 Erzin Turkey
126 I4 Erzincan Turkey
129 A6 Erzincan prov. Turkey
127 J4 Erzurum Turkey
129 C5 Erzurum prov. Turkey
138 F6 Eržvilkas Lith.
91 L8 Esa-ala P.N.G.
191 N9 Esanatoglia Italy
102 S5 Esan-misaki pt Japan
195 M5 Esaro r. Italy
193 Q8 Esaro r. Italy
102 R5 Esashi Hokkaidō Japan
102 T2 Esashi Hokkaidō Japan
102 S7 Esashi Iwate Japan
142 E6 Esbjerg Denmark
142 E6 Esbjerg airport Denmark
156 E6 Esbly France
Esbo Fin. see Espoo
254 G4 Escada Brazil
182 E3 Escairón Spain
92 D6 Escalante Negros Phil.
183 N2 Escalante Spain
241 U4 Escalante UT U.S.A.
241 V4 Escalante r. UT U.S.A.
241 S4 Escalante Desert UT U.S.A.
192 C8 Escalaplano Sardegna Italy
186 G3 Escales, Embassament d' resr Spain
187 E10 Escaleta, Punta de la pt Spain
182 G7 Escalhão Port.
163 B9 Escaliers, Pic des mt. France
186 H2 Escaló Spain
187 I10 Es Caló Spain
242 G4 Escalón Mex.
240 L4 Escalon CA U.S.A.
183 L8 Escalona Spain
183 L6 Escalona del Prado Spain
182 F9 Escalos de Baixo Port.
182 F9 Escalos de Cima Port.
183 O6 Escalote r. Spain
231 D10 Escambia r. FL U.S.A.
183 O7 Escamilla Spain
226 G4 Escanaba MI U.S.A.
187 D7 Escandón, Puerto de pass Spain
161 C9 Escandorgue ridge France
185 K5 Escañuela Spain
81 B13 Escape Reefs South I. N.Z.
243 N8 Escárcega Mex.
183 N8 Escariche Spain
182 F8 Escarigo Port.
186 C2 Escároz Spain
92 D2 Escarpada Point Luzon Phil.
186 □ Es Castell Spain
163 G8 Escatalens France
186 E5 Escatrón Spain
156 F3 Escaudain France
165 D7 Escaut r. Belgium
164 H5 Esch Neth.
173 I6 Eschach r. Ger.
157 O7 Eschau France
172 G2 Eschau Ger.
169 G10 Eschborn Ger.
168 C5 Esche Ger.
168 J4 Escheburg Ger.
168 J5 Eschede Ger.
190 E1 Eschenbach Switz.
173 L2 Eschenbach in der Oberpfalz Ger.
169 F9 Eschenburg-Eibelshausen Ger.
169 I8 Eschenstruth (Helsa) Ger.
169 I7 Eschershausen Ger.
178 D6 Eschio r. Italy
173 N3 Eschlkam Ger.
190 D2 Escholzmatt Switz.
165 I10 Esch-sur-Alzette Lux.
165 I9 Esch-sur-Sûre Lux.
169 J8 Eschwege Ger.
169 B9 Eschweiler Ger.
247 I4 Escocesa, Bahía b. Dom. Rep.
252 C3 Escoma Bol.
187 D12 Escombreras Spain
237 E11 Escondido r. Mex.
242 □R11 Escondido r. Nic.
240 O8 Escondido CA U.S.A.
187 K8 Escorca Spain
186 D6 Escorihuela Spain
163 B9 Escos France
163 I10 Escouloubre France
163 B7 Escource France
163 B7 Escource r. France
161 J9 Escragnolles France
186 D6 Escucha Spain
241 W8 Escudilla mt. AZ U.S.A.
244 B3 Escuinapa Mex.
243 N10 Escuintla Guat.
243 M10 Escuintla Mex.
250 D2 Escuque Venez.
184 H2 Escurial Spain
186 D5 Escuriza r. Spain
160 C4 Escurolles France
256 D2 Escurso r. Brazil
183 K8 Escusa mt. Spain
185 L6 Escúzar Spain
207 H6 Eséka Cameroon
131 O3 Ese-Khayya Rus. Fed.
199 K6 Eşen Turkey
199 K6 Eşen r. Turkey
199 J2 Esence Turkey
129 A6 Esence Dağları mts Turkey
129 F6 Eşengöl Dağı mt. Iran/Turkey
122 E3 Esenguly Turkm.
122 E3 Esenguly Döwlet Gorugy nature res. Turkm.
199 J2 Esenköy Turkey
128 C2 Esenpınar Turkey
168 E3 Esens Ger.
129 B5 Esenyurt Erzurum Turkey
199 J1 Esenyurt İstanbul Turkey
186 F3 Ésera r. Spain
122 D5 Eşfahān Iran
122 E5 Eşfahān prov. Iran
123 J8 Esfandak Iran
122 E6 Esfandārān Iran
122 G3 Esfarayen, Reshteh-ye mts Iran
122 H5 Esfīdeh Iran
182 E4 Esgos Spain
183 K5 Esgueva r. Spain
183 L5 Esguevillas de Esgueva Spain
122 H8 Es'hak Iran
108 D6 Eshan Yunnan China
146 □M2 Esha Ness hd Scotland U.K.
151 L5 Esher Surrey, England U.K.
129 B2 Eshera Georgia
209 E6 Eshimba Dem. Rep. Congo
123 M3 Eshkamesh Afgh.
122 E8 Eshkanān Iran
215 P4 Eshowe S. Africa
122 D4 Eshtehārd Iran
213 F4 Esigodini Zimbabwe
215 Q4 Esikhawini S. Africa
Esil Kazakh. see Yesil'
Esil r. Kazakh./Rus. Fed. see Ishim
191 O8 Esino r. Italy
129 B5 Esirçölü Tepe mt. Turkey
215 O3 eSizameleni S. Africa
85 N9 Esk Qld Austr.
83 K9 Esk r. Tas. Austr.
149 K5 Esk r. Cumbria, England U.K.
149 K4 Esk r. England/Scotland U.K.
146 J11 Esk r. Midlothian/Scottish Borders, Scotland U.K.
80 K6 Eskdale North I. N.Z.
146 J12 Eskdale val. Scotland U.K.
146 J12 Eskdalemuir Dumfries and Galloway, Scotland U.K.
147 F3 Eske, Lough l. Ireland
Eskene Kazakh. see Iskininskiy
225 H2 Esker Nfld and Lab. Can.
137 P4 Eskhar Ukr.
140 □F1 Eskifjörður Iceland
199 K3 Eski Gediz Turkey
170 E1 Eskilstrup Denmark
143 M2 Eskilstuna Sweden
220 E3 Eskimo Lakes N.W.T. Can.
Eskimo Point Nunavut Can. see Arviat
121 O7 Eski-Nookat Kyrg.
126 F3 Eskipazar Turkey
199 L3 Eskişehir Turkey
199 M3 Eskişehir prov. Turkey
183 N2 Eskutxi mt. Spain
183 H6 Esla r. Spain
Esla, Embalse de resr Spain see Ricobayo, Embalse de
122 B4 Eslāmābād-e Gharb Iran
122 H4 Eslām Qal'eh Iran
173 N2 Eslarn Ger.
183 R3 Eslava Spain
199 K5 Esler Dağı mt. Turkey
169 F8 Eslohe (Sauerland) Ger.
142 J6 Eslöv Sweden
122 G7 Esmā'īlī-ye Soflá Iran
199 J4 Eşme Turkey
129 D5 Eşmeçayır Turkey
129 D6 Esmer Turkey
261 G2 Esmeralda Arg.
260 B3 Esmeralda Chile
246 D3 Esmeralda Cuba
259 B8 Esmeralda, Isla i. Chile
257 E3 Esmeraldas Brazil
250 B4 Esmeraldas Ecuador
250 B4 Esmeraldas prov. Ecuador
252 D3 Esmeraldo r. Bol.
186 □ Es Mercadal Spain
186 □ Es Migjorn Gran Spain
232 G11 Esmont VA U.S.A.
182 C7 Esmoriz Port.
224 C3 Esnagami Lake Ont. Can.
226 J1 Esnagi Lake Ont. Can.
156 F3 Esnes France
165 I7 Esneux Belgium
187 D8 Espada, Serra d' mts Spain
187 E8 Espadán, Pico de mt. Spain
182 H4 Espadañedo Spain
122 I8 Espakeh Iran
Espalha r. Brazil see São Francisco
161 B7 Espalion France
Espalmador, Isla i. Spain see S'Espalmador
161 D6 Espaly-St-Marcel France
España country Europe see Spain
227 M3 Espanola Ont. Can.
239 K8 Espanola NM U.S.A.
250 □ Española, Isla i. Islas Galápagos Ecuador
184 G3 Esparragalejo Spain
185 I3 Esparragosa Spain
186 I4 Esparreguera Spain
161 H9 Esparron France
242 □P10 Esparta Hond.
187 H10 Espartar, Illa s' i. Spain
261 F5 Espartillar Arg.
240 J3 Esparto CA U.S.A.
186 C2 Esparza de Salazar Spain
121 P6 Espe Kazakh.
182 G7 Espeja Spain
183 N5 Espeja de San Marcelino Spain
185 J5 Espejo Spain
183 N5 Espejón Spain
164 I3 Espel Neth.
163 B9 Espelette France
169 G6 Espelkamp Ger.
169 H8 Espenau Ger.
184 H7 Espera Spain
184 E2 Esperança Port.
256 B6 Esperança, Serra de mts Brazil
87 F12 Esperance W.A. Austr.
87 F13 Esperance Bay W.A. Austr.
254 D3 Esperantinópolis Brazil
262 U2 Esperanza research stn Antarctica
259 C8 Esperanza Santa Cruz Arg.
261 G2 Esperanza Santa Fé Arg.
245 J7 Esperanza Puebla Mex.
242 E4 Esperanza Sonora Mex.
252 C2 Esperanza Peru
92 E6 Esperanza Masbate Phil.
247 □1 Esperanza Puerto Rico
261 I3 Esperanza Uru.
242 □P10 Esperanza, Sierra de la mts Hond.
163 I10 Espéraza France
193 L5 Esperia Italy
163 I10 Espezel France
184 A4 Espichel, Cabo c. Port.
185 J4 Espiel Spain
255 C8 Espigão, Serra do mts Brazil
261 G5 Espigas Arg.
183 K3 Espigüete mt. Spain
161 E9 Espiguette, Pointe de l' pt France
245 J5 Espina Mex.
183 K2 Espinama Spain
161 I8 Espinasses France
243 I4 Espinazo Mex.
245 M8 Espinazo del Diablo, Sierra mts Mex.
260 B6 Espinazo del Zorro Arg.
257 F2 Espinhaço, Serra do mts Brazil
184 B6 Espinhaço de Cão, Serra do mts Port.
182 D8 Espinhal Port.
209 B9 Espinheira Angola
184 D4 Espinheira hill Port.
182 C6 Espinho Port.
255 B9 Espinilho, Serra do hills Brazil
183 L2 Espinilla Spain
251 E2 Espino Venez.
255 E5 Espinosa Brazil
183 M5 Espinosa de Cerrato Spain
183 N7 Espinosa de Henares Spain
183 M2 Espinosa de los Monteros Spain
183 K9 Espinoso del Rey Spain
161 B9 Espinouse, Monts de l' mts France
163 J10 Espira-de-l'Agly France
Espirito Santo Brazil see Vila Velha
257 G3 Espírito Santo state Brazil
184 D5 Espírito Santo Port.
92 C3 Espiritu Luzon Phil.
252 D4 Espiritu Santo Bol.
244 F3 Espíritu Santo Mex.
78 □5 Espíritu Santo i. Vanuatu
243 P8 Espíritu Santo, Bahía del b. Mex.
242 D5 Espíritu Santo, Isla i. Mex.
243 O7 Espita Mex.
182 C9 Espite Port.
254 F4 Esplanada Brazil
183 P7 Esplegares Spain
186 J5 Esplugues de Llobregat Spain
186 F4 Esplús Spain
186 L3 Espolla Spain
161 C10 Espondeilham France
186 K3 Esponellà Spain
141 R6 Espoo Fin.
187 K8 Esporles Spain
182 C5 Esposende Port.
186 H2 Espot Spain
160 I1 Esprels France
185 P5 Espuña mt. Spain
187 B12 Espuña, Sierra de mts Spain
213 G4 Espungabera Moz.
234 C2 Espy PA U.S.A.
242 E2 Esqueda Mex.
259 C6 Esquel Arg.
222 F5 Esquimalt B.C. Can.
261 H2 Esquina Arg.
243 O10 Esquipulas Guat.
183 M8 Esquivias Spain
140 P3 Esrange Sweden
142 I5 Esrum Sø l. Denmark
210 A1 Es Samalat Sudan
93 E1 Essang Sulawesi Indon.
204 C3 Essaouira Morocco
159 L4 Essay France
207 H5 Essé Cameroon
168 I5 Essel Ger.
204 C4 Es Semara Western Sahara
165 F6 Essen Belgium
169 D8 Essen Ger.
168 E5 Essen (Oldenburg) Ger.
173 M4 Essenbach Ger.
87 F8 Essendon, Mount hill W.A. Austr.
160 J1 Essert France
227 L7 Essex Ont. Can.
151 N4 Essex admin. div. England U.K.
241 Q7 Essex CA U.S.A.
235 K2 Essex CT U.S.A.
233 O6 Essex MA U.S.A.
234 C6 Essex MD U.S.A.
233 L4 Essex NY U.S.A.
235 G3 Essex County county NJ U.S.A.
233 L4 Essex Junction VT U.S.A.
Essexvale Zimbabwe see Esigodini
227 K6 Essexville MI U.S.A.
173 I4 Essingen Ger.
150 H2 Essington Staffordshire, England U.K.
172 G4 Esslingen am Neckar Ger.
131 Q4 Esso Rus. Fed.
156 F5 Essômes-sur-Marne France
156 D6 Essonne dept France
156 D6 Essonne r. France
156 I7 Essoyes France
207 H5 Essu Cameroon
138 J2 Essu Estonia
203 F5 Es Suaifi well Sudan
203 G6 Es Suki Sudan
207 I5 Est prov. Cameroon
157 L7 Est, Canal de l' France
225 I4 Est, Île de l' i. Que. Can.
233 □P1 Est, Lac de l' l. Que. Can.
225 I3 Est, Pointe de l' pt Que. Can.
182 E1 Estaca de Bares, Punta de pt Spain
261 H2 Estacas Arg.
244 G2 Estación Catorce Mex.
241 R9 Estación Coahuila Mex.
185 L4 Estación de Baeza Spain
244 G2 Estación Laguna Seca Mex.
186 F3 Estadilla Spain
259 D9 Estados, Isla de los i. Arg.
163 J10 Estagel France
92 D3 Estagno Point Luzon Phil.
122 F7 Eşţahbān Iran
161 B7 Estaing France
227 N3 Estaire Ont. Can.
156 E2 Estaires France
256 B2 Estância Goiás Brazil
254 F4 Estância Sergipe Brazil
239 K9 Estancia NM U.S.A.
259 C9 Estancia Camerón Chile
259 C9 Estancia Carmen Arg.
185 O5 Estancias, Sierra de las mts Spain
122 I6 Estand, Kūh-e mt. Iran
163 D8 Estang France
122 H7 Estārm Iran
182 C7 Estarreja Port.
186 D2 Estarrón r. Spain
186 H2 Estats, Pic d' mt. France/Spain
190 B2 Estavayer-le-Lac Switz.
215 N5 Estcourt S. Africa
168 I3 Este r. Ger.
191 L5 Este Italy
247 I4 Este, Parque Nacional del nat. park Dom. Rep.
247 □1 Este, Punta pt Puerto Rico
186 D4 Esteban hill Spain
261 F5 Esteban A. Gazcón Arg.
258 D1 Esteban de Urizar Arg.
Esteban Echeverria Arg. see Monte Grande
170 D5 Estedt Ger.
182 C6 Estela Port.
242 □P11 Estelí Nic.
183 P3 Estella Spain
234 F6 Estell Manor NJ U.S.A.
184 G2 Estena hill Spain
185 J2 Estena r. Spain
173 I2 Estenfeld Ger.
185 J6 Estepa Spain
183 M4 Estepar Spain
185 I8 Estepona Spain
185 J3 Esteras r. Spain
183 P6 Esteras de Medinaceli Spain
186 D6 Estercuel Spain
161 J9 Esterel reg. France
163 B9 Estérençuby France
173 K6 Estergebirge mts Ger.
223 K5 Esterhazy Sask. Can.
208 A4 Esterias, Cap c. Gabon
156 G6 Esternay France
179 I2 Esternberg Austria
245 J3 Estero Mex.
240 K6 Estero Bay CA U.S.A.
190 C8 Esteron r. Italy
245 I3 Esteros Mex.
253 E5 Esteros Para.
186 H2 Esterri d'Aneu Spain
168 E5 Esterwegen Ger.
238 L6 Estes Park CO U.S.A.
250 A1 Este Sudeste, Cayos del is Col.
223 K5 Estevan Sask. Can.
222 D4 Estevan Group is B.C. Can.
236 H4 Estherville IA U.S.A.
161 E6 Estiavreilles France
231 G9 Estill SC U.S.A.
163 F7 Estillac France
165 F8 Estinnes-au-Mont Belgium
156 G7 Estissac France
257 D5 Estiva Brazil
254 D3 Estiva r. Brazil
160 B4 Estivareilles France
187 E8 Estivella Spain
184 D6 Estói Port.
184 C6 Estômbar Port.
223 I5 Eston Sask. Can.
149 O4 Eston Redcar and Cleveland, England U.K.
138 I3 Estonia country Europe
Estonskaya S.S.R. country Europe see Estonia
168 H3 Estorf Niedersachsen Ger.
168 H5 Estorf Niedersachsen Ger.
184 A3 Estoril Port.
161 I9 Estoublon France
160 F5 Estrablin France
156 E5 Estrées-St-Denis France
258 H3 Estreito Brazil
182 E9 Estreito Port.
184 □ Estreito da Calheta Madeira
184 E4 Estrela Port.
182 E8 Estrela, Serra da mts Port.
257 E3 Estrela do Indaiá Brazil
256 D3 Estrela do Sul Brazil
185 L4 Estrella mt. Spain
242 B2 Estrella, Punta pt Mex.
241 T8 Estrella, Sierra mts AZ U.S.A.
78 □6 Estrella Bay Sta Isabel Solomon Is
252 D2 Estrema Brazil
182 B10 Estremadura reg. Port.
183 N8 Estremera Spain
183 N8 Estremera, Canal de Spain
183 O8 Estremera, Embalse de resr Spain
184 D3 Estremoz Port.
183 O6 Estriégala Spain
163 C8 Estrigon r. France
254 C4 Estrondo, Serra hills Brazil
208 A4 Estuaire prov. Gabon
184 B4 Estuário do Sado, Reserva Natural do nature res. Port.
184 B3 Estuário do Tejo, Reserva Natural do nature res. Port.
122 C4 Estūh Iran
Esu Cameroon see Essu
208 D4 Esumba, Île i. Dem. Rep. Congo
159 M7 Esvres France
177 K4 Esztár Hungary
177 H4 Esztergom Hungary
158 F4 Étables-sur-Mer France
82 G3 Etadunna S.A. Austr.
162 F4 Étagnac France
116 G6 Etah Uttar Prad. India
157 K5 Étain France
160 C1 Étais-la-Sauvin France
160 F1 Étalante France
165 I9 Étalle Belgium
225 J3 Étamamiou Que. Can.
156 D7 Étampes France
82 G2 Etamunbanie, Lake salt flat S.A. Austr.
217 □1c Étang-Salé Réunion
160 E3 Étang-sur-Arroux France
156 C2 Étaples France
162 B4 Étaules France
162 C5 Étauliers France
116 F7 Etawah Rajasthan India
116 G6 Etawah Uttar Prad. India
78 □3a Etcharai i. Kwajalein Marshall Is
242 E4 Etchojoa Mex.
208 A5 Étéké Gabon
158 E6 Étel France
141 S6 Etelä-Suomi prov. Fin.
161 I6 Étendard, Pic de l' mt. France
160 I2 Éternoz France
215 O2 Ethandakukhanya S. Africa
165 I9 Ethe Belgium
87 E8 Ethel watercourse W.A. Austr.
223 K5 Ethelbert Man. Can.
86 F7 Ethel Creek W.A. Austr.
85 I3 Ethel Creek r. Qld Austr.
214 G5 E'Thembini S. Africa
85 I4 Etheridge r. Qld Austr.
210 C3 Ethiopia country Africa
199 H3 Etili Turkey
126 F4 Etimesğut Turkey
160 H3 Étival France
157 M7 Étival-Clairefontaine France
146 F10 Etive, Loch inlet Scotland U.K.
156 H8 Étivey France
245 K8 Etla Mex.
141 K6 Etna r. Norway
195 I8 Etna, Monte vol. Sicilia Italy
Etna, Mount vol. Sicilia Italy see Etna, Monte
194 H8 Etna, Parco dell' park Italy
142 B2 Etne Norway
227 O6 Etobicoke Ont. Can.
156 G6 Étoges France
161 G10 Étoile, Chaîne de l' hills France
161 F7 Étoile-sur-Rhône France
208 D4 Etoka Dem. Rep. Congo
220 E4 Etolin Island AK U.S.A.
85 L6 Eton Qld Austr.
151 K5 Eton Windsor and Maidenhead, England U.K.
Etorofu-tō i. Kuril'skiye O-va Rus. Fed. see Iturup, Ostrov
212 B3 Etosha National Park Namibia
212 C3 Etosha Pan salt pan Namibia
208 B4 Etoumbi Congo
235 F4 Etra NJ U.S.A.
156 D7 Étréchy France
122 F3 Etrek Turkm.
156 C5 Étrépagny France
159 L2 Étretat France
156 G4 Étreux France
197 M8 Etropole Bulg.
190 C4 Etroubles Italy
163 C10 Etsaut France
212 D3 Etsha Botswana
165 J9 Ettelbruck Lux.
78 □4a Etten i. Chuuk Micronesia
172 D5 Ettenheim Ger.
164 G5 Etten-Leur Neth.
146 H8 Etteridge Highland, Scotland U.K.
171 D8 Ettersburg Ger.
206 A2 Et Tīdra i. Maur.
151 I3 Ettington Warwickshire, England U.K.
172 E4 Ettlingen Ger.
146 J12 Ettrick Scottish Borders, Scotland U.K.
149 L2 Ettrickbridge Scottish Borders, Scotland U.K.
146 J11 Ettrick Forest reg. Scotland U.K.
146 K11 Ettrick Water r. Scotland U.K.
169 D10 Ettringen Ger.
114 E8 Ettumanur Kerala India
208 E5 Etumba Dem. Rep. Congo
160 H2 Étuz France
151 I2 Etwall Derbyshire, England U.K.
186 B1 Etxalar Spain
Etxarri Spain see Echarri
183 P3 Etxarri-Aranatz Spain
244 C5 Etzatlán Mex.
223 I5 Etzicom Coulee r. Alta Can.
156 B3 Eu France
79 □8a 'Eua i. Tonga
83 K5 Euabalong N.S.W. Austr.
79 □8a 'Euaiki i. Tonga
Eubarca, Cabo c. Spain see Mossons, Cap des
172 H2 Eubigheim Ger.
Euboea i. Greece see Evvoia
87 J11 Eucla W.A. Austr.
232 D7 Euclid OH U.S.A.
254 F4 Euclides da Cunha Brazil
256 A5 Euclides da Cunha Paulista Brazil
83 L7 Eucumbene, Lake N.S.W. Austr.
225 H3 Eudistes, Lac des l. Que. Can.
237 J9 Eudora AR U.S.A.
82 G6 Eudunda S.A. Austr.
'Eueiki i. Tonga see 'Euaiki
169 J10 Euerbach Ger.
169 J10 Euerdorf Ger.
231 E10 Eufaula AL U.S.A.
237 H8 Eufaula OK U.S.A.
237 H8 Eufaula Lake resr OK U.S.A.
261 F1 Eufrasio Loza Arg.
178 H4 Eugendorf Austria
238 C4 Eugene OR U.S.A.
253 F2 Eugênia r. Brazil
242 B4 Eugenia, Punta pt Mex.
163 D8 Eugénie-les-Bains France
163 A10 Eugi, Embalse de resr Spain
83 L5 Eugowra N.S.W. Austr.
183 P3 Eulate Spain
83 J3 Eulo Qld Austr.
182 E2 Eume r. Spain
182 E2 Eume, Encoro do resr Spain
257 H2 Eunápolis Brazil
85 L6 Eungella Qld Austr.
85 L6 Eungella National Park Qld Austr.
237 I10 Eunice LA U.S.A.
237 D9 Eunice NM U.S.A.
165 J7 Eupen Belgium
171 G7 Euper Ger.
118 F3 Euphrates r. Asia alt. Al Furāt (Iraq/Syria), alt. Fırat (Turkey)
237 K9 Eupora MS U.S.A.
141 Q6 Eura Fin.
141 P6 Eurajoki Fin.
173 K5 Eurasburg Bayern Ger.
173 K6 Eurasburg Bayern Ger.
179 K3 Euratsfeld Austria
156 B5 Eure dept France
156 B5 Eure r. France
156 B7 Eure-et-Loir dept France
238 B6 Eureka CA U.S.A.
237 G7 Eureka KS U.S.A.
238 G2 Eureka MT U.S.A.
241 Q2 Eureka NV U.S.A.
232 C10 Eureka OH U.S.A.
236 F3 Eureka SD U.S.A.
241 T2 Eureka UT U.S.A.
221 J2 Eureka Sound sea chan. Nunavut Can.
237 I7 Eureka Springs AR U.S.A.
240 O4 Eureka Valley CA U.S.A.
82 H4 Eurinilla watercourse S.A. Austr.
83 H4 Euriowie N.S.W. Austr.
83 J7 Euroa Vic. Austr.
85 L8 Eurombah Qld Austr.
85 L8 Eurombah Creek r. Qld Austr.
201 H6 Europa, Île i. Indian Ocean
183 J2 Europa, Picos de mts Spain
Europa, Punta de pt Gibraltar see Europa Point
185 □ Europa Flats Gibraltar
185 □ Europa Point Gibraltar
132 Europe continent
164 F5 Europoort reg. Neth.
157 J6 Eurville-Bienville France
169 C9 Euskirchen Ger.
169 I10 Eußenheim Ger.
231 G11 Eustis FL U.S.A.
83 I6 Euston N.S.W. Austr.
231 D9 Eutaw AL U.S.A.
168 K2 Eutin Ger.
172 F5 Eutingen im Gäu Ger.
222 E4 Eutsuk Lake B.C. Can.
171 G7 Eutzsch Ger.
157 K6 Euville France
84 E4 Eva Downs N.T. Austr.
209 B9 Evale Angola
190 D4 Evançon r. Italy
215 N2 Evander S. Africa
224 E3 Evans, Lac l. Que. Can.
236 C6 Evans, Mount CO U.S.A.
222 H4 Evansburg Alta Can.
232 E8 Evans City PA U.S.A.
234 C2 Evans Falls PA U.S.A.
83 N3 Evans Head N.S.W. Austr.
262 S1 Evans Ice Stream Antarctica
221 J3 Evans Strait Nunavut Can.
226 G7 Evanston IL U.S.A.
238 I6 Evanston WY U.S.A.
224 D4 Evansville Ont. Can.
230 D7 Evansville IN U.S.A.
226 E7 Evansville WI U.S.A.
238 K5 Evansville WY U.S.A.
237 F10 Evant TX U.S.A.
146 H7 Evanton Highland, Scotland U.K.
Eva Perón Arg. see La Plata
Eva Perón prov. Arg. see La Pampa
226 I6 Evart MI U.S.A.
215 L2 Evaton S. Africa
160 A4 Évaux-les-Bains France
122 F8 Evaz Iran
129 F6 Evci Turkey
199 K4 Evciler Turkey
128 C1 Evcili Turkey
226 B2 Eveleth MN U.S.A.
237 J7 Evening Shade AR U.S.A.
151 J4 Evenlode r. England U.K.
131 Q3 Evensk Rus. Fed.
140 N2 Evenskjær Norway
82 E4 Everard, Lake salt flat S.A. Austr.
84 D7 Everard, Mount N.T. Austr.
82 D2 Everard, Mount S.A. Austr.
82 D2 Everard Range hills S.A. Austr.
150 G5 Evercreech Somerset, England U.K.
164 H5 Everdingen Neth.
Everek Turkey see Develi
117 K6 Everest, Mount China/Nepal
233 □R1 Everett N.B. Can.
232 G8 Everett PA U.S.A.
238 C3 Everett WA U.S.A.
165 E6 Evergem Belgium
231 G12 Everglades swamp FL U.S.A.
231 G13 Everglades City FL U.S.A.
231 G13 Everglades National Park FL U.S.A.
231 D10 Evergreen AL U.S.A.
228 D7 Everman, Volcán vol. Mex.
238 C2 Everson WA U.S.A.
251 G3 Everton Guyana
141 L6 Evertsberg Sweden
85 I7 Evesham Qld Austr.
151 I3 Evesham Worcestershire, England U.K.
151 I3 Evesham, Vale of val. England U.K.
169 K6 Evessen Ger.
160 J4 Évian-les-Bains France
140 Q5 Evijärvi Fin.
207 H6 Evinayong Equat. Guinea
232 F11 Evington VA U.S.A.
198 C4 Evinos r. Greece
192 B3 Evisa Corse France
142 D3 Evje Norway
190 D3 Evolène Switz.
184 D3 Évora Port.
184 D3 Évora admin. dist. Port.
184 D3 Évora-Monte Port.
100 J3 Evoron, Ozero l. Rus. Fed.
198 D2 Evosmos Greece
122 A2 Evowghlī Iran
158 H5 Évran France
159 I7 Èvre r. France
159 J3 Évrecy France
156 B5 Évreux France
159 K5 Évron France
126 C3 Evros r. Greece/Turkey
199 H2 Evros r. Greece alt. Meriç (Turkey), alt. Maritsa (Bulgaria)
198 D6 Evrotas r. Greece
156 D6 Évry France
128 A3 Evrychou Cyprus
Evrykhou Cyprus see Evrychou
100 J3 Evur r. Rus. Fed.
198 F4 Evvoia i. Greece
198 D1 Evzonoi Greece
240 □C12 'Ewa HI U.S.A.
240 □D12 'Ewa Beach HI U.S.A.
85 J5 Ewan Qld Austr.
246 □ Ewarton Jamaica
210 D4 Ewaso Ngiro r. Kenya
214 H2 Ewbank S. Africa
146 E7 Ewe, Loch b. Scotland U.K.
151 L5 Ewell Surrey, England U.K.
226 E3 Ewen MI U.S.A.
Ewenkizu Zizhiqi Nei Mongol China see Bayan Tohoi
151 L5 Ewhurst Surrey, England U.K.
234 F4 Ewing NJ U.S.A.
262 T2 Ewing Island Antarctica
110 H5 Ewirgol Xinjiang China
208 B5 Ewo Congo
252 D3 Exaltación Bol.
198 D5 Examilia Greece
215 L4 Excelsior S. Africa
240 M3 Excelsior Mountain CA U.S.A.
240 N3 Excelsior Mountains NV U.S.A.
236 H6 Excelsior Springs MO U.S.A.
234 B2 Exchange PA U.S.A.
162 G5 Excideuil France
150 F6 Exe r. England U.K.
150 E5 Exebridge Somerset, England U.K.
262 P1 Executive Committee Range mts Antarctica
226 C4 Exeland WI U.S.A.
83 M6 Exeter N.S.W. Austr.
227 M6 Exeter Ont. Can.
150 E6 Exeter Devon, England U.K.
240 M5 Exeter CA U.S.A.
233 □O6 Exeter NH U.S.A.
223 I1 Exeter Lake N.W.T. Can.
161 J6 Exilles Italy
164 K3 Exloo Neth.
159 L4 Exmes France
150 F6 Exminster Devon, England U.K.
150 E5 Exmoor hills England U.K.
150 E5 Exmoor National Park England U.K.
233 J11 Exmore VA U.S.A.
86 C6 Exmouth W.A. Austr.
150 F6 Exmouth Devon, England U.K.
83 L4 Exmouth, Mount N.S.W. Austr.
86 C7 Exmouth Gulf W.A. Austr.
222 H1 Exmouth Lake N.W.T. Can.
265 L6 Exmouth Plateau sea feature Indian Ocean
199 H6 Exo Vathy Notio Aigaio Greece
85 L8 Expedition National Park Qld Austr.
85 L8 Expedition Range mts Qld Austr.
225 K3 Exploits r. Nfld and Lab. Can.
222 H5 Exshaw Alta Can.
234 D4 Exton PA U.S.A.
245 H4 Extoraz r. Mex.
182 N10 Extremadura aut. comm. Spain
207 I4 Extrême-Nord prov. Cameroon
182 D5 Extremo Port.
246 E1 Exuma Cays is Bahamas
246 F1 Exuma Sound sea chan. Bahamas
135 G7 Eya r. Rus. Fed.
149 N7 Eyam Derbyshire, England U.K.
208 D5 Eyangu Dem. Rep. Congo
211 B5 Eyasi, Lake salt l. Tanz.
Eyawadi r. Myanmar see Irrawaddy
161 H6 Eybens France
162 H5 Eyburie France
163 G10 Eycheil France
142 E3 Eydehavn Norway
168 G5 Eydelstedt Ger.
151 L2 Eye Peterborough, England U.K.
151 O3 Eye Suffolk, England U.K.
223 J2 Eyeberry Lake N.W.T. Can.
134 M2 Eyelenoborsk Rus. Fed.
146 L11 Eyemouth Scottish Borders, Scotland U.K.
146 D6 Eye Peninsula Scotland U.K.
147 C9 Eyeries Ireland
161 G8 Eygues r. France
161 H8 Eyguians France
161 G9 Eyguières France
162 I4 Eygurande France
162 E5 Eygurande-et-Gardedeuil France
140 □D2 Eyjafjallajökull ice cap Iceland
140 □D1 Eyjafjörður inlet Iceland
210 F3 Eyl Somalia
Eylau Rus. Fed. see Bagrationovsk
163 E6 Eymet France
199 J5 Eymir Turkey
162 H4 Eymoutiers France
122 B5 'Eyn Gazān Iran
Eynihal Turkey see Kale
146 B8 Eynort, Loch inlet Scotland U.K.
151 M5 Eynsford Kent, England U.K.
151 J4 Eynsham Oxfordshire, England U.K.
161 F9 Eyragues France
162 C5 Eyrans France
163 B6 Eyre r. France
82 F3 Eyre (North), Lake salt flat S.A. Austr.
147 F6 Eyrecourt Ireland
84 G9 Eyre Creek watercourse Qld Austr.
162 H5 Eyrein France
81 C12 Eyre Mountains South I. N.Z.
81 C12 Eyre Peak South I. N.Z.
82 E5 Eyre Peninsula S.A. Austr.
161 F7 Eyrieux r. France
163 C6 Eysines France
168 H5 Eystrup Ger.
130 A3 Eysturoy i. Faroe Is
144 D1 Eysturoy i. Faroe Is
151 O5 Eythorne Kent, England U.K.
211 C5 Eyuku waterhole Kenya
207 H5 Eyumojok Cameroon
122 E4 Eyvānakī Iran
160 F6 Eyzin-Pinet France
215 O4 Ezakheni S. Africa
215 N2 eZamokuhle S. Africa
183 O4 Ezcaray Spain
161 K9 Èze France
232 B11 Ezel KY U.S.A.
215 M3 Ezenzeleni S. Africa
260 C6 Ezequiel Ramos Mexía, Embalse resr Arg.
138 K5 Ezernieki Latvia
138 K5 Ežezers l. Latvia
109 J3 Ezhou Hubei China
134 J3 Ezhva Rus. Fed.
199 J4 Eziler Turkey
199 H3 Ezine Turkey
126 H3 Ezinepazar Turkey
186 B1 Ezkurra Spain
Ezo i. Japan see Hokkaidō
128 A4 Ezousa r. Cyprus
127 M8 Ezra's Tomb tourist site Iraq
156 B6 Ézy-sur-Eure France

F

79 □9a Faaa Tahiti Fr. Polynesia
142 G6 Faaborg Denmark
114 C10 Faadhippolhu Atoll Maldives
113 D10 Faadhippolhu Atoll Maldives
210 D4 Faafxadhuun Somalia
179 I6 Faaker See l. Austria
79 □9a Faaone Tahiti Fr. Polynesia
Faarava atoll Arch. des Tuamotu Fr. Polynesia see Fakarava
79 □9a Faaupo, Pointe pt Moorea Fr. Polynesia
186 F5 Fabara Spain
163 G9 Fabas France
239 K11 Fabens TX U.S.A.
94 □ Faber, Mount hill Sing.
222 G2 Faber Lake N.W.T. Can.
182 G3 Fabero Spain
177 L4 Fábiánháza Hungary
175 H3 Fabianki Pol.
177 J5 Fábiánsebestyén Hungary
177 I3 Fabova hoľa mt. Slovakia
161 D9 Fabrègues France
191 N9 Fabriano Italy
193 I3 Fabrica di Roma Italy
185 O3 Fábricas de San Juan de Alcaraz Spain
195 K7 Fabrizia Italy
192 I2 Fabro Italy
216 □1c Faca, Ponta da pt Pico Azores
250 C3 Facatativá Col.
209 D6 Facauma Angola
182 C5 Facha Port.
207 H2 Fachi Niger
184 H8 Facinas Spain
85 M7 Facing Island Qld Austr.
78 □1 Facpi Point Guam
234 D1 Factoryville PA U.S.A.
259 C7 Facundo Arg.
202 D5 Fada Chad
184 E2 Fadagosa Port.
122 F7 Fadāmī Iran
207 F3 Fada-N'Gourma Burkina
177 H5 Fadd Hungary
127 J6 Fadghāmī Syria
125 J4 Faḑīlah well Saudi Arabia
124 G9 Faḑli reg. Yemen
205 H4 Fadnoun, Plateau du Alg.
206 C4 Fadugu Sierra Leone
191 O3 Faedis Italy
191 L7 Faenza Italy
Færingehavn Greenland see Kangerluarsoruseq
Færoerne terr. N. Atlantic Ocean see Faroe Islands
Faeroes terr. N. Atlantic Ocean see Faroe Islands
Faesulae Italy see Fiesole
192 G2 Faete, Monte hill Italy
208 C3 Fafa r. C.A.R.
79 □8a Fafa i. Tonga
93 G5 Fafanlap Papua Indon.
182 D6 Fafe Port.
210 E3 Fafen Shet' watercourse Eth.
210 D5 Fafi waterhole Kenya
207 F3 Faga watercourse Burkina
191 O3 Fagagna Italy
78 □2 Fagaloa Bay Samoa
78 □2 Fagamalo Samoa
197 M5 Făgăraş Romania
Fagatau atoll Arch. des Tuamotu Fr. Polynesia see Fangatau
78 □2 Fagatogo American Samoa
140 J5 Fagerhaug Norway
141 J6 Fagernes Norway
143 L2 Fagersta Sweden
197 K5 Făget Romania
93 G4 Fagita Papua Indon.
259 C9 Fagnano, Lago l. Arg./Chile
193 Q8 Fagnano Castello Italy
165 F8 Fagne reg. Belgium
156 H6 Fagnières France
207 G2 Fagochia well Niger
206 D2 Faguibine, Lac l. Mali
140 □E2 Fagurhólsmýri Iceland
210 A2 Fagwir Jonglei Sudan
208 F2 Fagwir Wahda Sudan
148 C3 Fahan Ireland
205 G3 Fahl, Oued el watercourse Alg.
122 D6 Fahlīān, Rūdkhāneh-ye watercourse Iran
122 F6 Fahraj Iran
168 I1 Fahrdorf Ger.
168 J3 Fahrenkrug Ger.
173 L5 Fahrenzhausen Ger.
171 H6 Fahrland Ger.
125 M4 Fahūd, Jabal hill Oman
216 □1c Faial i. Azores
184 □ Faial Madeira
216 □1c Faial, Canal do sea chan. Azores
193 M5 Faicchio Italy
78 □4a Faichuk is Chuuk Micronesia
203 G2 Fā'id Egypt
169 D10 Faid Ger.
190 F3 Faido Switz.
182 G5 Failde Port.
227 R1 Faillon, Lac l. Que. Can.
165 H7 Faimes Belgium
160 E1 Fain-lès-Montbard France
157 J6 Fains-Véel France
220 D3 Fairbanks AK U.S.A.
232 A9 Fairborn OH U.S.A.
236 G5 Fairbury NE U.S.A.
226 D5 Fairchild WI U.S.A.
81 C13 Fairfax South I. N.Z.
232 H10 Fairfax VA U.S.A.
233 L4 Fairfax VT U.S.A.
81 E12 Fairfield South I. N.Z.
240 J3 Fairfield CA U.S.A.
235 I2 Fairfield CT U.S.A.
236 J5 Fairfield IA U.S.A.
238 G5 Fairfield ID U.S.A.
236 K6 Fairfield IL U.S.A.
232 A9 Fairfield OH U.S.A.
237 G10 Fairfield TX U.S.A.
241 T1 Fairfield UT U.S.A.
232 F11 Fairfield VA U.S.A.
235 I2 Fairfield County county CT U.S.A.
151 I4 Fairford Gloucestershire, England U.K.
227 K6 Fairgrove MI U.S.A.
233 O7 Fairhaven MA U.S.A.
235 G4 Fair Haven NJ U.S.A.
233 L5 Fair Haven VT U.S.A.
147 J2 Fair Head Northern Ireland U.K.
234 D5 Fair Hill MD U.S.A.
92 A6 Fairie Queen sea feature Phil.
146 □M3 Fair Isle i. Scotland U.K.
235 G3 Fair Lawn NJ U.S.A.
234 C6 Fairlee MD U.S.A.
233 M5 Fairlee VT U.S.A.
234 F4 Fairless Hills PA U.S.A.
81 E11 Fairlie South I. N.Z.
146 G11 Fairlie North Ayrshire, Scotland U.K.
85 J3 Fairlight Qld Austr.
151 N6 Fairlight East Sussex, England U.K.
236 H4 Fairmont MN U.S.A.
232 E9 Fairmont WV U.S.A.
222 H5 Fairmont Hot Springs B.C. Can.
151 J6 Fair Oak Hampshire, England U.K.
237 J8 Fair Oaks AR U.S.A.
226 H7 Fair Plain MI U.S.A.
239 L7 Fairplay CO U.S.A.
226 H4 Fairport MI U.S.A.
234 E6 Fairton NJ U.S.A.
85 J3 Fairview Qld Austr.
222 G3 Fairview Alta Can.
226 D9 Fairview IL U.S.A.
232 B10 Fairview KY U.S.A.
227 J5 Fairview MI U.S.A.
235 G4 Fairview NJ U.S.A.
235 H1 Fairview NY U.S.A.
237 F7 Fairview OK U.S.A.
232 E6 Fairview PA U.S.A.
241 U2 Fairview UT U.S.A.
226 D6 Fairview WI U.S.A.
109 □J7 Fairview Park H.K. China
234 D5 Fairville PA U.S.A.
222 B3 Fairweather, Cape AK U.S.A.
222 B3 Fairweather, Mount Can./U.S.A.
148 C4 Fairy Water r. Northern Ireland U.K.
91 J5 Fais i. Micronesia
123 O6 Faisalabad Pak.
156 I4 Faissault France
236 D3 Faith SD U.S.A.
193 M6 Faito, Monte mt. Italy
Faizabad Badakhshān Afgh. see Feyzābād
123 K3 Faizabad Fāryāb Afgh.
116 I6 Faizabad Uttar Prad. India
184 □ Fajã da Ovelha Madeira
216 □1b Fajã de Cima São Miguel Azores
182 E8 Fajão Port.

Fajarda to Fimber

312

184 B3 Fajarda Port.
247 □1 Fajardo Puerto Rico
126 I9 Fajr, Wādī watercourse Saudi Arabia
175 K4 Fajsławice Pol.
177 H5 Fajsz Hungary
81 □1 Fakaofo atoll Tokelau
Fakaofu atoll Tokelau see Fakaofo
79 □9 Fakarava atoll Arch. des Tuamotu Fr. Polynesia
134 K4 Fakel Rus. Fed.
151 N2 Fakenham Norfolk, England U.K.
140 M5 Fåker Sweden
120 C3 Fakeyevo Kazakh.
91 H7 Fakfak Papua Indon.
122 E6 Fakhrabad Iran
117 M6 Fakiragram Assam India
197 P8 Fakiyska Reka r. Bulg.
142 I6 Fakse Denmark
142 I6 Fakse Bugt b. Denmark
107 R5 Faku Liaoning China
150 C7 Fal r. England U.K.
206 C4 Falaba Sierra Leone
182 E2 Faladoira, Serra da mts Spain
207 F3 Falagountou Burkina
159 K4 Falaise France
222 G2 Falaise Lake N.W.T. Can.
117 L6 Falakata W. Bengal India
96 A3 Falam Myanmar
122 D5 Falavarjan Iran
191 L3 Falcade Italy
147 F2 Falcarragh Ireland
183 Q4 Falces Spain
197 Q4 Fălciu Romania
157 M5 Falck France
191 L8 Falco, Monte mt. Italy
182 B3 Falcoeira, Punta c. Spain
250 D2 Falcón state Venez.
194 G9 Falconara Sicilia Italy
193 Q9 Falconara Albanese Italy
191 O8 Falconara Marittima Italy
195 I7 Falcone Sicilia Italy
192 A6 Falcone, Capo del c. Sardegna Italy
192 C5 Falcone, Punta pt Sardegna Italy
216 □3a Falcones, Punta pt La Gomera Canary Is
223 M5 Falcon Lake Man. Can.
243 J4 Falcon Lake l. Mex./U.S.A.
260 E2 Falda del Carmen Arg.
81 □1 Fale Tokelau
78 □2 Falealupo Samoa
78 □2 Falefa Samoa
78 □2 Falelatai Samoa
78 □2 Falelima Samoa
206 B3 Falémé r. Mali/Senegal
134 J4 Falenki Rus. Fed.
193 I3 Faleria Italy
Falerii Italy see Civita Castellana
193 Q9 Falerna Italy
193 K1 Falerone Italy
Faleshty Moldova see Fălești
136 G6 Fălești Moldova
78 □2 Fale'ula Samoa
237 F12 Falfurrias TX U.S.A.
222 G4 Falher Alta Can.
124 D7 Falkat watercourse Eritrea
169 J8 Falken Ger.
173 M2 Falkenberg Bayern Ger.
173 N5 Falkenberg Bayern Ger.
170 I5 Falkenberg Brandenburg Ger.
171 H7 Falkenberg Brandenburg Ger.
142 I5 Falkenberg Sweden
170 F4 Falkenhagen Ger.
171 G8 Falkenhain Ger.
170 H5 Falkensee Ger.
173 M3 Falkenstein Bayern Ger.
171 F10 Falkenstein Sachsen Ger.
170 H5 Falkenthal Ger.
146 I11 Falkirk Falkirk, Scotland U.K.
146 I11 Falkirk admin. div. Scotland U.K.
146 J10 Falkland Fife, Scotland U.K.
264 F9 Falkland Escarpment sea feature S. Atlantic Ocean
259 F8 Falkland Islands terr. S. Atlantic Ocean
264 F9 Falkland Plateau sea feature S. Atlantic Ocean
259 E9 Falkland Sound sea chan. Falkland Is
259 D6 Falkner Arg.
198 E6 Falkonera i. Greece
142 J3 Falköping Sweden
175 I4 Fałków Pol.
237 H7 Fall r. KS U.S.A.
232 C12 Fall Branch TN U.S.A.
240 O8 Fallbrook CA U.S.A.
226 C5 Fall Creek WI U.S.A.
190 C4 Fallère, Monte mt. Italy
158 H8 Falleron France
140 P4 Fällfors Sweden
262 T2 Fallieres Coast Antarctica
146 I10 Fallin Stirling, Scotland U.K.
168 I5 Fallingbostel Ger.
147 B4 Fallmore Ireland
215 L9 Fallodon S. Africa
240 N2 Fallon NV U.S.A.
233 N7 Fall River MA U.S.A.
238 L6 Fall River Pass CO U.S.A.
234 D2 Falls PA U.S.A.
234 A7 Falls Church VA U.S.A.
236 H5 Falls City NE U.S.A.
232 G7 Falls Creek PA U.S.A.
234 F4 Fallsington PA U.S.A.
234 C5 Fallston MD U.S.A.
190 F3 Falmenta Italy
247 □2 Falmouth Antigua and Barbuda
246 □ Falmouth Jamaica
150 B7 Falmouth Cornwall, England U.K.
232 A10 Falmouth KY U.S.A.
233 O7 Falmouth MA U.S.A.
233 □O5 Falmouth ME U.S.A.
234 B4 Falmouth PA U.S.A.
232 H10 Falmouth VA U.S.A.
150 B7 Falmouth Bay England U.K.
247 □2 Falmouth Harbour Antigua and Barbuda
206 D3 Falo Mali
206 D3 Falou Mali
261 F6 Falsa, Bahía b. Arg.
252 C5 Falsa Chipana, Punta pt Chile
225 G1 False r. Que. Can.
214 C10 False Bay S. Africa
215 Q3 False Bay Park S. Africa
220 B4 False Pass AK U.S.A.
117 K9 False Point India
186 G5 Falset Spain
246 H5 Falso, Cabo c. Dom. Rep.
242 □R10 Falso, Cabo c. Hond.
259 C9 Falso Cabo de Hornos c. Chile
142 H7 Falster i. Denmark
149 M3 Falstone Northumberland, England U.K.
197 O3 Fălticeni Romania
143 L1 Falun Sweden
191 M2 Falzarego, Passo di pass Italy
93 G4 Fam, Kepulauan is Papua Indon.
Famagusta Cyprus see Ammochostos
Famagusta Bay Cyprus see Ammochostos Bay
182 F8 Famalicão Port.
258 D3 Famatina Arg.
258 C3 Famatina, Sierra de mts Arg.
169 J9 Fambach Ger.
157 L5 Fameck France
122 C4 Famenin Iran
165 G8 Famenne val. Belgium
87 G8 Fame Range hills W.A. Austr.
223 M5 Family Lake Man. Can.
86 I7 Family Well W.A. Austr.
122 D7 Fāmūr, Daryācheh-ye l. Iran
206 D3 Fana Mali
147 G2 Fanad Head Ireland
78 □4a Fanaik i. Chuuk Micronesia
80 J2 Fanal Island North I. N.Z.
213 □K2 Fanambana Madag.
78 □4a Fanan i. Chuuk Micronesia
78 □4a Fanananei, Mochun sea chan. Chuuk Micronesia
213 □K3 Fanandrana Madag.
191 J7 Fanano Italy
78 □4a Fanapanges i. Chuuk Micronesia
199 H5 Fanari, Akrotirio pt Ikaria Greece
109 L3 Fanchang Anhui China
213 □J4 Fandriana Madag.
147 J5 Fane r. Ireland
191 M2 Fanes Sennes Braies, Parco Naturale nature res. Italy
78 □4a Fanew, Mochun sea chan. Chuuk Micronesia
96 D5 Fang Thai.
210 A2 Fangak Sudan
186 G6 Fangar, Punta del pt Spain
79 □9 Fangatau atoll Arch. des Tuamotu Fr. Polynesia
79 □9 Fangataufa atoll Arch. des Tuamotu Fr. Polynesia
79 □8a Fanga Uta inlet Tongatapu Tonga
Fangcheng Guangxi China see Fangchenggang
109 I2 Fangcheng Henan China
108 G8 Fangchenggang Guangxi China
108 G3 Fangdou Shan mts China
109 M7 Fangliao Taiwan
192 B3 Fango r. Corse France
143 M3 Fångö i. Sweden
109 M7 Fangshan Taiwan
108 H2 Fangxian Hubei China
100 F6 Fangzheng Heilong. China
196 H9 Fani i Vogël r. Albania
138 K8 Fanipal' Belarus
163 I9 Fanjeaux France
108 G3 Fankuai Sichuan China
Fankuaidian Sichuan China see Fankuai
109 □J7 Fanling H.K. China
186 E2 Fanlo Spain
146 F7 Fannich, Loch l. Scotland U.K.
Fanning Island atoll Kiribati see Tabuaeran
140 J5 Fannrem Norway
122 H8 Fannūj Iran
142 E6 Fanø i. Denmark
191 O8 Fano Italy
142 E6 Fanø Bugt b. Denmark
78 □4a Fanos i. Chuuk Micronesia
Fanoualie i. Tonga see Fonualei
109 K3 Fanshan Anhui China
109 M5 Fanshan Zhejiang China
107 M7 Fanshi Shanxi China
177 K5 Fântâna Rece hill Romania
177 K5 Fântânele Romania
Fanum Fortunae Italy see Fano
182 C5 Fão Port.
122 D7 Faqīh Aḥmadān Iran
Farab Turkm. see Farap
206 C3 Faraba Mali
Farab-Pristan' Turkm. see Jeýhun
208 F4 Faradje Dem. Rep. Congo
Faradofay Madag. see Tôlañaro
213 □J4 Farafangana Madag.
206 B3 Farafenni Gambia
193 M3 Fara Filiorum Petri Italy
202 F3 Farāfirah, Wāḥāt al oasis Egypt
Farafra Oasis Egypt see Farāfirah, Wāḥāt al
122 E6 Farāgheh Iran
123 J5 Farāh Afgh.
123 I5 Farāh prov. Afgh.
Farahābād Iran see Khezerābād
213 □K2 Farahalana Madag.
123 I6 Farah Rūd watercourse Afgh.
193 J3 Fara in Sabina Italy
123 M4 Farakhulm Afgh.
244 B6 Farallón, Punta pt Mex.
91 K3 Farallon de Medinilla i. N. Mariana Is
91 J2 Farallon de Pajaros vol. N. Mariana Is
250 B4 Farallones de Cali, Parque Nacional nat. park Col.
240 I4 Farallon National Wildlife Refuge nature res. CA U.S.A.
182 I5 Faramontanos de Tábara Spain
208 E2 Faramuti I. Sudan
206 C4 Faranah Guinea
123 P4 Faranshat Jammu and Kashmir
197 O4 Faraoani Romania
206 B2 Far'aoun well Maur.
123 J2 Farap Turkm.
125 L7 Fararah Oman
124 E7 Farasān Saudi Arabia
124 E7 Farasān, Jazā'ir is Saudi Arabia
193 M3 Fara San Martino Italy
186 C3 Farasdues Spain
213 □J3 Faratsiho Madag.
91 J5 Faraulep atoll Micronesia
197 M3 Farcău, Vârful mt. Romania
173 K6 Farchant Ger.
165 G8 Farciennes Belgium
177 L6 Fârdea Romania
185 N5 Fardes r. Spain
147 G6 Fardrum Ireland
157 M5 Farébersviller France
151 J6 Fareham Hampshire, England U.K.
156 F6 Faremoutiers France
Farewell, Cape Greenland see Nunap Isua
80 G7 Farewell, Cape South I. N.Z.
80 G7 Farewell Spit South I. N.Z.
193 J3 Farfa r. Italy
142 I3 Färgelanda Sweden
Farghona Uzbek. see Farg'ona
Farghona Wiloyati admin. div. Uzbek. see Farg'ona
231 F10 Fargo GA U.S.A.
236 G2 Fargo ND U.S.A.
121 N7 Farg'ona Uzbek.
121 N7 Farg'ona admin. div. Uzbek.
163 D6 Fargues-St-Hilaire France
163 E7 Fargues-sur-Ourbise France
168 H1 Fårhus Denmark
236 I3 Faribault MN U.S.A.
225 G1 Faribault, Lac l. Que. Can.
116 F5 Faridabad Haryana India
116 E4 Faridkot Punjab India
117 L8 Faridpur Bangl.
116 G5 Faridpur Uttar Prad. India
202 C2 Fārigh, Wādī al watercourse Libya
141 M6 Färila Sweden
182 A10 Farilhões i. Port.
206 B3 Farim Guinea-Bissau
122 H4 Farīmān Iran
151 I4 Faringdon Oxfordshire, England U.K.
149 L6 Farington Lancashire, England U.K.
254 D3 Farinha r. Brazil
190 H6 Farini Italy
125 J6 Fāris, Qalamat oasis Saudi Arabia
182 H6 Fariza de Sayago Spain
143 M5 Färjestaden Öland Sweden
198 D3 Farkadona Greece
Farkhar Afgh. see Farkhato
123 M3 Farkhato Afgh.
123 M3 Farkhor Tajik.
211 B6 Farkwa Tanz.
85 L6 Farleigh Qld Austr.
151 J5 Farleigh Wallop Hampshire, England U.K.
186 D4 Farlete Spain
192 G1 Farma r. Italy
122 C4 Farmahin Iran
199 I5 Farmakonisi i. Greece
150 H5 Farmborough Bath and North East Somerset, England U.K.
226 F9 Farmer City IL U.S.A.
224 D1 Farmer Island Nunavut Can.
237 I9 Farmerville LA U.S.A.
235 G4 Farmingdale NJ U.S.A.
222 F4 Farmington B.C. Can.
235 J1 Farmington CT U.S.A.
234 D7 Farmington DE U.S.A.
226 D9 Farmington IL U.S.A.
233 □O4 Farmington ME U.S.A.
237 J7 Farmington MO U.S.A.
233 □N5 Farmington NH U.S.A.
239 J8 Farmington NM U.S.A.
238 I6 Farmington UT U.S.A.
232 B6 Farmington Hills MI U.S.A.
235 I3 Farmingville NY U.S.A.
177 I4 Farmos Hungary
222 E4 Far Mountain B.C. Can.
232 G11 Farmville VA U.S.A.
177 H3 Farná Slovakia
151 K5 Farnborough Hampshire, England U.K.
149 L7 Farndon Cheshire, England U.K.
149 P7 Farndon Nottinghamshire, England U.K.
143 M1 Färnebofjärden l. Sweden
143 M1 Färnebofjärdens nationalpark nat. park Sweden
149 N2 Farne Islands England U.K.
192 H2 Farnese Italy
233 M3 Farnham Que. Can.
151 K5 Farnham Surrey, England U.K.
232 I11 Farnham VA U.S.A.
87 I8 Farnham, Lake salt flat W.A. Austr.
222 G5 Farnham, Mount B.C. Can.
151 K4 Farnham Royal Buckinghamshire, England U.K.
171 E8 Farnstädt Ger.
149 M6 Farnworth Greater Manchester, England U.K.
261 G6 Faro Arg.
251 G5 Faro Brazil
207 I4 Faro r. Cameroon
222 C2 Faro Y.T. Can.
184 D6 Faro Port.
184 C6 Faro admin. dist. Port.
182 E3 Faro mt. Spain
143 P4 Fårö Gotland Sweden
143 P4 Fårö i. Sweden
246 F8 Faro, Punta pt Col.
207 I4 Faro, Réserve du nature res. Cameroon
182 E4 Faro, Serra do mts Spain
144 D1 Faroe Islands terr. N. Atlantic Ocean
190 C4 Faroma, Monte mt. Italy
143 P4 Fårösund Gotland Sweden
217 □2 Farquhar Atoll Seychelles
217 □2 Farquhar Group is Seychelles
87 G9 Farquharson Tableland hills W.A. Austr.
146 H8 Farr Highland, Scotland U.K.
191 M3 Farra d'Alpago Italy
232 H7 Farrandsville PA U.S.A.
147 C8 Farranfore Ireland
146 G8 Farrar r. Scotland U.K.
85 H8 Farrars Creek watercourse Qld Austr.
124 F6 Farrāsh, Jabal al hill Saudi Arabia
122 E7 Farrāshband Iran
263 G2 Farr Bay Antarctica
227 S4 Farrellton Que. Can.
260 B3 Farrelones Chile
122 H5 Farrokhī Iran
Farruch, Cabo c. Spain see Ferrutx, Cap
Farrukhabad Uttar Prad. India see Fatehgarh
122 E7 Fārs prov. Iran
129 B1 Fars r. Rus. Fed.
122 F5 Farsakh Iran
198 D3 Farsala Greece
198 D3 Farsaliotis r. Greece
123 J5 Fārsī Afgh.
122 D8 Fārsī, Jazīreh-ye i. Būshehr Iran
127 O9 Fārsī, Jazīreh-ye i. Būshehr Iran
142 F5 Farsø Denmark
238 J5 Farson WY U.S.A.
142 C3 Farsund Norway
125 J8 Fartak, Jabal mts Yemen
125 K8 Fartak, Ra's c. Yemen
197 P5 Fărtănești Romania
256 B2 Fartura r. Brazil
255 B8 Fartura, Serra da mts Brazil
122 H3 Fārūj Iran
122 G3 Farūmād Iran
142 F5 Fårvang Denmark
Farvel, Kap c. Greenland see Nunap Isua
226 J6 Farwell MI U.S.A.
237 D8 Farwell TX U.S.A.
123 K3 Fāryāb prov. Afgh.
122 G8 Fāryāb Hormozgan Iran
122 G7 Fāryāb Kermān Iran
138 L6 Farynava Belarus
122 E7 Fasā Iran
195 M2 Fasano Italy
141 K5 Fåset Norway
137 R5 Fashchivka Ukr.
128 A2 Faşikan Geçidi pass Turkey
210 C1 Fasil Ghebbi and Gonder Monuments tourist site Eth.
216 □3a Fasnia Tenerife Canary Is
168 J5 Faßberg Ger.
123 I9 Fāsteh, Ra's-e pt Iran
136 I3 Fastiv Ukr.
Fastov Ukr. see Fastiv
208 F4 Fataki Dem. Rep. Congo
193 K5 Fate, Monte delle mt. Italy
116 E5 Fatehabad Haryana India
116 F7 Fatehgarh Madh. Prad. India
116 G6 Fatehgarh Uttar Prad. India
116 F4 Fatehgarh Sahib Punjab India
116 E7 Fatehnagar Rajasthan India
116 E6 Fatehpur Rajasthan India
116 H7 Fatehpur Uttar Prad. India
123 N6 Fatehpur Pak.
116 F6 Fatehpur Sikri Uttar Prad. India
182 F8 Fatela Port.
215 L4 Fateng-Tse-Ntsho S. Africa
137 N1 Fateyevka Rus. Fed.
137 O1 Fatezh Rus. Fed.
122 F7 Fatḥābād Iran
210 A2 Fathai Sudan
227 M4 Fathom Five National Marine Park Ont. Can.
206 A3 Fatick Senegal
182 C9 Fátima Port.
Fattoilep atoll Micronesia see Faraulep
Fatuhiva i. Fr. Polynesia see Fatu Hiva
79 □9 Fatu Hiva i. Fr. Polynesia
209 F6 Fatuma Dem. Rep. Congo
209 C6 Fatundu Dem. Rep. Congo
78 □6 Fauabu Malaita Solomon Is
160 I4 Faucille, Col de la pass France
157 M8 Faucogney-et-la-Mer France
161 C9 Faugères France
147 H2 Faughan r. Northern Ireland U.K.
190 J8 Fauglia Italy
163 E7 Fauguerolles France
172 G2 Faulbach Ger.
146 I11 Fauldhouse West Lothian, Scotland U.K.
170 G3 Faulenrost Ger.
236 F3 Faulkton SD U.S.A.
157 M5 Faulquemont France
156 D2 Fauquembergues France
222 G5 Fauquier B.C. Can.
187 E8 Faura Spain
87 B8 Faure Island W.A. Austr.
215 J5 Fauresmith S. Africa
78 □6 Fauro i. Solomon Is
140 M3 Fauske Norway
222 H4 Faust Alta Can.
261 H3 Faustino M. Parera Arg.
159 M2 Fauville-en-Caux France
163 F6 Faux France
162 H4 Faux-la-Montagne France
182 F6 Favaios Port.
190 G7 Favale di Malvaro Italy
191 M9 Favalto, Monte mt. Italy
194 F9 Favara Sicilia Italy
187 E9 Favara Spain
186 □ Favàritx, Cap de c. Spain
160 I5 Faverges France
157 L8 Faverney France
161 C7 Faverolles France
151 N5 Faversham Kent, England U.K.
157 K7 Favières France
194 C8 Favignana Sicilia Italy
194 C8 Favignana, Isola i. Sicilia Italy
222 H4 Fawcett Alta Can.
151 J6 Fawley Hampshire, England U.K.
224 B2 Fawn r. Ont. Can.
234 C5 Fawn Grove PA U.S.A.
215 O5 Fawnleas S. Africa
124 F2 Fawwārah Saudi Arabia
140 □B1 Faxaflói b. Iceland
140 N5 Faxälven r. Sweden
234 B2 Faxon PA U.S.A.
202 C5 Faya Chad
78 □5 Fayaoué Îles Loyauté New Caledonia
156 D8 Fay-aux-Loges France
163 H6 Faycelles France
124 F2 Fayd Saudi Arabia
158 H7 Fay-de-Bretagne France
161 J9 Fayence France
231 D9 Fayette AL U.S.A.
226 H4 Fayette MI U.S.A.
236 I6 Fayette MO U.S.A.
237 J10 Fayette MS U.S.A.
232 A7 Fayette OH U.S.A.
237 H7 Fayetteville AR U.S.A.
231 E9 Fayetteville GA U.S.A.
231 H8 Fayetteville NC U.S.A.
233 I5 Fayetteville NY U.S.A.
232 H9 Fayetteville PA U.S.A.
231 D8 Fayetteville TN U.S.A.
232 D10 Fayetteville WV U.S.A.
124 F7 Fayfā Saudi Arabia
127 N9 Faylakah i. Kuwait
157 K8 Fayl-la-Forêt France
157 M8 Faymont France
186 F5 Fayón Spain
128 B10 Fayrān well Egypt
128 B10 Fayrān, Wādī watercourse Egypt
128 C10 Fayranī, Jabal mt. Egypt
161 E7 Fay-sur-Lignon France
91 L5 Fayu i. Micronesia
128 E9 Fazair al Ghrazi watercourse Saudi Arabia
191 P6 Fažana Croatia
207 F4 Fazao Malfakassa, Parc National de nat. park Togo
207 H2 Fazeï well Niger
151 I2 Fazeley Staffordshire, England U.K.
116 E4 Fazilka Punjab India
123 N7 Fazilpur Pak.
125 I2 Fazrān, Jabal hill Saudi Arabia
204 B5 Fdérik Maur.
Fead Group is P.N.G. see Nuguria Islands
147 C8 Feale r. Ireland
231 I9 Fear, Cape NC U.S.A.
146 E7 Fearnmore Highland, Scotland U.K.
163 C9 Féas France
234 E4 Feasterville PA U.S.A.
240 K3 Feather r. CA U.S.A.
240 K2 Feather, North Fork r. CA U.S.A.
81 J8 Featherston North I. N.Z.
150 H2 Featherstone Staffordshire, England U.K.
149 O6 Featherstone West Yorkshire, England U.K.
213 F3 Featherstone Zimbabwe
159 L2 Fécamp France
192 G1 Feccia r. Italy
157 N7 Fecht r. France
188 G3 Federacija Bosna i Hercegovina aut. div. Bos.-Herz.
261 I2 Federación Arg.
261 I3 Federación Uru.
261 H2 Federal Arg.
207 G4 Federal Capital Territory admin. div. Nigeria
Federal District admin. dist. Brazil see Distrito Federal
Federal District admin. dist. Mex. see Distrito Federal
Federal District admin. dist. Venez. see Distrito Capital
233 J10 Federalsburg MD U.S.A.
172 H5 Federsee l. Ger.
144 J1 Fedje Norway
137 O7 Fedorivka Ukr.
Fedorov Kazakh. see Fedorovka
120 J1 Fedorovka Kostanayskaya Oblast' Kazakh.
121 Q1 Fedorovka Pavlodarskaya Oblast' Kazakh.
120 D2 Fedorovka Zapadnyy Kazakhstan Kazakh.
120 F1 Fedorovka Respublika Bashkortostan Rus. Fed.
137 R6 Fedorovka Rostovskaya Oblast' Rus. Fed.
120 C1 Fedorovka Samarskaya Oblast' Rus. Fed.
135 I6 Fedorovka Saratovskaya Oblast' Rus. Fed.
137 R8 Fedorovskaya Rus. Fed.
139 W5 Fedorovskoye Rus. Fed.
137 O7 Fedotova Kosa spit Ukr.
139 X6 Fedotovo Rus. Fed.
116 D6 Fedusar Rajasthan India
147 C5 Fee, Lough l. Ireland
147 C5 Feeagh, Lough l. Ireland
146 H8 Feehlin r. Scotland U.K.
147 H3 Feeny Northern Ireland U.K.
210 E3 Feerfeer Somalia
78 □4a Fefan i. Chuuk Micronesia
158 G6 Fégréac France
177 J4 Fegyvernek Hungary
177 L4 Fehérgyarmat Hungary
177 K5 Fehér-Körös r. Hungary
177 J5 Fehér-tó l. Hungary
177 J5 Fehér-tó l. Hungary
177 H4 Fehérvárcsurgó Hungary
223 M1 Fehet Lake Nunavut Can.
170 D2 Fehmarn i. Ger.
Fehmarn Belt str. Denmark/Ger. see Femer Bælt
168 K2 Fehmarnsund sea chan. Ger.
170 G5 Fehrbellin Ger.
179 N6 Fehring Austria
257 G4 Feia, Lagoa lag. Brazil
Feicheng Shandong China see Feixian
109 K3 Feidong Anhui China
156 G3 Feignies France
252 C2 Feijó Brazil
184 A3 Feijó Port.
172 D2 Feilbingert Ger.
80 J7 Feilding North I. N.Z.
171 E10 Feilitzsch Ger.
160 F4 Feillens France
138 J5 Feimaņu ezers l. Latvia
109 □J7 Fei Ngo Shan hill H.K. China
Feio r. Brazil see Aguapeí
Feira Zambia see Luangwa
254 F5 Feira de Santana Brazil
160 I5 Feissons-sur-Isère France
179 J6 Feistritz im Rosental Austria
179 K6 Feistritz ob Bleiburg Austria
184 D6 Feiteira Port.
109 K3 Feixi Anhui China
107 O9 Feixian Shandong China
107 N8 Feixiang Hebei China
205 H2 Fejaj, Chott el salt l. Tunisia
189 A7 Fejd-el-Abiod pass Alg.
177 H4 Fejér county Hungary
142 H7 Fejø i. Denmark
126 G5 Feke Turkey
177 K5 Fekete-Körös r. Hungary
187 L9 Felanitx Spain
205 G6 Felaou well Alg.
170 J4 Felchow Ger.
169 J9 Felda r. Ger.
173 K6 Feldafing Ger.
179 I6 Feld am See Austria
179 M6 Feldbach Austria
160 K1 Feldbach France
170 H4 Feldberg Ger.
172 E6 Feldberg mt. Ger.
168 I2 Felde Ger.
177 J4 Feldebrő Hungary
178 A5 Feldkirch Austria
172 H7 Feldkirch admin. reg. Austria
173 L5 Feldkirchen Ger.
179 L5 Feldkirchen bei Graz Austria
179 J6 Feldkirchen in Kärnten Austria
173 L6 Feldkirchen-Westerham Ger.
197 M3 Feldru Romania
182 G6 Felgar Port.
182 D6 Felgueiras Port.
177 J5 Felgyő Hungary
261 H2 Feliciano r. Arg.
217 □2a Félicité i. Inner Islands Seychelles
232 A10 Felicity OH U.S.A.
113 D11 Felidhu Atoll Maldives
113 □1 Felidhu Channel Maldives
150 F3 Felindre Powys, Wales U.K.
161 D6 Félines France
190 I6 Felino Italy
244 C1 Felipe Carrillo Puerto Durango Mex.
244 E6 Felipe Carrillo Puerto Michoacán Mex.
243 O8 Felipe C. Puerto Mex.
193 O7 Felitto Italy
185 N7 Félix Spain
179 N4 Felixdorf Austria
257 E3 Felixlândia Brazil
151 O4 Felixstowe Suffolk, England U.K.
215 P4 Felixton S. Africa
190 E6 Felizzano Italy
172 B2 Fell Ger.
146 J12 Fell, Loch hill Scotland U.K.
191 O3 Fella r. Italy
172 G4 Fellbach Ger.
162 I4 Felletin France
149 N4 Felling Tyne and Wear, England U.K.
246 □ Fellowship Jamaica
232 F9 Fellowsville WV U.S.A.
168 J2 Felm Ger.
177 K5 Felnac Romania
Fels Lux. see Larochette
169 H8 Felsberg Ger.
Felsina Italy see Bologna
177 K3 Felsődobsza Hungary
177 I4 Felsőlajos Hungary
177 H5 Felsőnyék Hungary
177 G6 Felsőszentmárton Hungary
177 J4 Felsőtárkány Hungary
179 O6 Felső-Válicka r. Hungary
177 J3 Felsőzsolca Hungary
168 H1 Felsted Denmark
151 M4 Felsted Essex, England U.K.
149 N3 Felton Northumberland, England U.K.
234 D6 Felton DE U.S.A.
234 B5 Felton PA U.S.A.
191 L3 Feltre Italy
151 N3 Feltwell Norfolk, England U.K.
193 K2 Fema, Monte mt. Italy
254 D5 Femeas r. Brazil
168 K1 Femer Bælt str. Denmark/Ger.
216 □3c Femés hill Lanzarote Canary Is
143 K5 Femlingen l. Sweden
195 L5 Femminamorta, Monte mt. Italy
194 H8 Femmina Morta, Portella pass Italy
142 H7 Femø i. Denmark
142 H2 Femsjøen l. Norway
141 K5 Femunden l. Norway
141 L5 Femundsmarka Nasjonalpark nat. park Norway
147 I7 Fenagh Carlow Ireland
148 B5 Fenagh Leitrim Ireland
192 F3 Fenaio, Punta del pt Italy
216 □1b Fenais da Ajuda São Miguel Azores
213 □J5 Fenambosy, Lohatanjona pt Madag.
78 □1 Fena Valley Reservoir Guam
160 G2 Fénay France
163 H9 Fendeille France
182 D2 Fene Spain
227 P5 Fenelon Falls Ont. Can.
78 □4a Feneppi i. Chuuk Micronesia
128 D2 Fener Burnu hd Turkey
Fénérive Madag. see Fenoarivo Atsinanana
129 A4 Fenerköyü Turkey
190 C5 Fenestrelle Italy
157 N6 Fénétrange France
159 J6 Feneu France
136 J3 Fenevychi Ukr.
199 G2 Fengari mt. Samothraki Greece
Fengcheng Fujian China see Yongding
Fengcheng Fujian China see Lianjiang
Fengcheng Fujian China see Anxi
Fengcheng Guangdong China see Xinfeng
Fengcheng Guangxi China see Fengshan
Fengcheng Guizhou China see Tianzhu
109 J4 Fengcheng Jiangxi China
101 D8 Fengcheng Liaoning China
Fengchuan Jiangxi China see Fengxin
108 F4 Fengdu Chongqing China
Fenggang Fujian China see Shaxian
108 F5 Fenggang Guizhou China
Fenggang Jiangxi China see Yihuang
106 J9 Fenggeling Gansu China
109 M4 Fenghua Zhejiang China
108 G5 Fenghuang Hunan China
Fengjiaba Sichuan China see Wangcang
108 G3 Fengjie Chongqing China
109 H7 Fengkai Guangdong China
109 M7 Fenglin Taiwan
Fengming Shaanxi China see Qishan
107 P7 Fengnan Hebei China
107 O6 Fengning Hebei China
Fengqi Shaanxi China see Luochuan
108 B6 Fengqing Yunnan China
107 N9 Fengqiu Henan China
107 P7 Fengrun Hebei China
Fengshan Fujian China see Luoyuan
108 F6 Fengshan Guangxi China
Fengshan Hubei China see Luotian
Fengshan Yunnan China see Fengqing
109 J6 Fengshuba Shuiku resr China
100 C2 Fengshui Shan mt. Heilong. China
109 K2 Fengtai Anhui China
108 D3 Fengtongzai Giant Panda Reserve nature res. China
108 B7 Fengwei Yunnan China
Fengweiba Yunnan China see Fengwei
107 O9 Fengxian Jiangsu China
108 F2 Fengxian Shaanxi China
109 M3 Fengxian Shanghai China
Fengxiang Heilong. China see Luobei
Fengxiang Yunnan China see Lincang
109 J4 Fengxin Jiangxi China
109 K2 Fengyang Anhui China
Fengyi Guizhou China see Zheng'an
Fengyi Sichuan China see Maoxian
107 K9 Fengyuan Shaanxi China
109 M6 Fengyüan Taiwan
107 M6 Fengzhen Nei Mongol China
107 L9 Fen He r. China
107 L7 Fenhe Shuiku resr China
117 M8 Feni Bangl.
91 L7 Feni Islands P.N.G.
162 D2 Fenioux France
190 C4 Fenis Italy
147 C8 Fenit Ireland
150 F6 Feniton Devon, England U.K.
117 M8 Fenny r. Bangl./India
192 B4 Feno, Capo di c. Corse France
192 C5 Feno, Capo di c. Corse France
213 □K3 Fenoarivo Atsinanana Madag.
213 □J3 Fenoarivo Be Madag.
163 G8 Fenouillet France
163 I10 Fenouillet reg. France
109 L4 Fenshui Zhejiang China
151 L3 Fenstanton Cambridgeshire, England U.K.
173 M3 Fensterbach r. Ger.
227 K7 Fenton MI U.S.A.
81 □1 Fenua Fale Tokelau
81 □1 Fenua Loa i. Tokelau
81 □1 Fenua Loa i. Tokelau
Fenua Ura atoll Arch. de la Société Fr. Polynesia see Manuae
146 H11 Fenwick East Ayrshire, Scotland U.K.
149 N2 Fenwick Northumberland, England U.K.
232 E10 Fenwick WV U.S.A.
108 F1 Fenxiang Shaanxi China
107 L8 Fenyang Shanxi China
177 L3 Fényeslitke Hungary
109 J5 Fenyi Jiangxi China
150 B7 Feock Cornwall, England U.K.
137 O8 Feodosiya Ukr.
137 O8 Feodosiys'ka Zatoka b. Ukr.
138 M3 Feofilova Pustyn' Rus. Fed.
146 D11 Feolin Ferry Argyll and Bute, Scotland U.K.
147 E8 Feonanagh Ireland
205 G1 Fer, Cap de c. Alg.
78 □6 Fera i. Solomon Is
160 H3 Fer-à-Cheval, Cirque du corrie France
Férai Greece see Feres
147 G6 Ferbane Ireland
171 F6 Ferchland Ger.
195 K6 Ferdinandea Italy
170 I3 Ferdinandshof Ger.
122 H5 Ferdows Iran
156 G6 Fère-Champenoise France
197 N3 Feredeului, Obcina ridge Romania
156 G5 Fère-en-Tardenois France
158 G7 Férel France
193 J2 Ferentillo Italy
193 K4 Ferentino Italy
199 H2 Feres Greece
185 P4 Férez Spain
Fergana Oblast admin. div. Uzbek. see Farg'ona
Fergana Range mts Kyrg. see Fergana Too Tizmegi
121 O7 Fergana Too Tizmegi mts Kyrg.
Ferganskiy Khrebet mts Kyrg. see Fergana Too Tizmegi
227 N6 Fergus Ont. Can.
147 E7 Fergus r. Ireland
236 G2 Fergus Falls MN U.S.A.
223 L2 Ferguson Lake Nunavut Can.
84 C3 Fergusson r. N.T. Austr.
91 L8 Fergusson Island P.N.G.
184 F3 Feria, Sierra de hills Spain
205 H2 Fériana Tunisia
199 L2 Ferizli Turkey
140 □C1 Ferjukot Iceland
206 D4 Ferkessédougou Côte d'Ivoire
194 H9 Ferla Sicilia Italy
179 J6 Ferlach Austria
206 B3 Ferlo, Vallée du watercourse Senegal
206 B3 Ferlo-Nord, Réserve de Faune du nature res. Senegal
206 B3 Ferlo-Sud, Réserve de Faune du nature res. Senegal
147 G4 Fermanagh county Northern Ireland U.K.
182 C7 Fermelã Port.
182 C7 Fermentelos Port.
191 N8 Fermignano Italy
193 L1 Fermo Italy
225 H2 Fermont Que. Can.
182 H6 Fermoselle Spain
147 F8 Fermoy Ireland
148 B3 Fern, Lough l. Ireland
185 L2 Fernáncaballero Spain
250 □ Fernandina, Isla i. Islas Galápagos Ecuador
231 G10 Fernandina Beach FL U.S.A.
259 B9 Fernando de Magallanes, Parque Nacional nat. park Chile
264 G6 Fernando de Noronha i. Brazil
256 B4 Fernandópolis Brazil
Fernando Poó i. Equat. Guinea see Bioco
185 J5 Fernán Núñez Spain
257 E2 Fernão Dias Brazil
213 I2 Fernão Veloso Moz.
213 I2 Fernão Veloso, Baía de b. Moz.
234 B6 Ferndale MD U.S.A.
234 F1 Ferndale NY U.S.A.
238 C2 Ferndale WA U.S.A.
179 I6 Ferndorf Austria
151 I6 Ferndown Dorset, England U.K.
146 I8 Ferness Highland, Scotland U.K.
160 I4 Ferney-Voltaire France
80 K6 Fernhill North I. N.Z.
150 H3 Fernhill Heath Worcestershire, England U.K.
151 K5 Fernhurst West Sussex, England U.K.
222 H5 Fernie B.C. Can.
179 M6 Fernitz Austria
83 K3 Fernlee Qld Austr.
240 M2 Fernley NV U.S.A.
178 C5 Fernpass pass Austria
234 D2 Fernridge PA U.S.A.
147 I7 Ferns Ireland
238 F3 Fernwood ID U.S.A.
195 K6 Feroleto Antico Italy
Ferozepore Punjab India see Firozpur
161 B10 Ferrals-les-Corbières France
195 K3 Ferrandina Italy
191 L6 Ferrara Italy
191 L6 Ferrara prov. Italy
191 M6 Ferrarese r. Italy
192 D9 Ferrato, Capo c. Sardegna Italy
193 N4 Ferrazzano Italy
261 G4 Ferré Arg.
182 F1 Ferreira Spain
184 C4 Ferreira do Alentejo Port.
182 D9 Ferreira do Zêzere Port.
251 I4 Ferreira-Gomes Brazil
256 A4 Ferreiros Brazil
184 A2 Ferrel Port.
232 C10 Ferrellsburg WV U.S.A.
250 B6 Ferreñafe Peru
182 H5 Ferreras de Abajo Spain
182 H5 Ferreras de Arriba Spain
190 D6 Ferrere Italy
186 □ Ferreries Spain
186 C5 Ferreruela de Huerva Spain
182 H5 Ferreruela de Tábara Spain
160 K1 Ferrette France
261 E2 Ferreyra Arg.
237 J10 Ferriday LA U.S.A.
190 H6 Ferriere Italy
156 H3 Ferrière-la-Grande France
165 I8 Ferrières Belgium
156 E7 Ferrières France
161 C6 Ferrières-St-Mary France
163 H10 Ferrières-sur-Ariège France
194 H9 Ferro r. Sicilia Italy
195 L4 Ferro r. Italy
192 D5 Ferro, Capo c. Sardegna Italy
184 □ Ferro, Ilhéu de i. Madeira
192 A6 Ferro, Porto b. Sardegna Italy
182 D2 Ferrol Spain
182 D2 Ferrol, Ría de inlet Spain
241 U2 Ferron UT U.S.A.
257 F3 Ferros Brazil
192 D8 Ferru, Monte hill Sardegna Italy
193 M3 Ferruccio, Punta di pt Italy
232 E12 Ferrum VA U.S.A.
187 L8 Ferrutx, Cap c. Spain
147 I8 Ferrycarrig Ireland
146 L9 Ferryden Angus, Scotland U.K.
149 N4 Ferryhill Durham, England U.K.
225 K4 Ferryland Nfld and Lab. Can.
Ferryville Tunisia see Menzel Bourguiba
172 A2 Ferschweiler Ger.
120 H1 Fershampenuaz Rus. Fed.
192 A6 Fertilia Sardegna Italy
179 O4 Fertő l. Austria/Hungary
179 O4 Fertőd Hungary
176 F4 Fertőrákos Hungary
176 F4 Fertőszentmiklós Hungary
179 O4 Fertőszéplak Hungary
176 F4 Fertő-tavi nat. park Hungary
182 D6 Fervença Port.
182 C3 Fervenza, Encoro da resr Spain
164 I2 Ferwert Neth.
139 T7 Ferzikovo Rus. Fed.
204 D2 Fès Morocco
209 C6 Feshi Dem. Rep. Congo
146 I8 Feshiebridge Highland, Scotland U.K.
236 F2 Fessenden ND U.S.A.
157 O8 Fessenheim France
156 G4 Festieux France
161 H7 Festre, Col du pass France
93 F4 Fet Dom, Tanjung pt Papua Indon.
206 B3 Fété Bowé Senegal
216 □1c Feteira Faial Azores
216 □1b Feteiras São Miguel Azores
197 P6 Fetești Romania
197 P6 Fetești-Gară Romania
146 □N1 Fethaland, Point of Scotland U.K.
147 G8 Fethard Tipperary Ireland
147 I8 Fethard Wexford Ireland
Fethiye Malatya Turkey see Yazıhan
199 K6 Fethiye Muğla Turkey
120 E6 Fetisovo Kazakh.
146 □O1 Fetlar i. Scotland U.K.
194 D8 Feto, Capo c. Sicilia Italy
146 K9 Fettercairn Aberdeenshire, Scotland U.K.
173 K3 Feucht Ger.
173 I3 Feuchtwangen Ger.
163 E7 Feugarolles France
225 G1 Feuilles, Rivière aux r. Que. Can.
156 C4 Feuquières France
156 C3 Feuquières-en-Vimeu France
160 E5 Feurs France
100 G2 Fevral'sk Rus. Fed.
126 H5 Fevzipaşa Turkey
162 G4 Feytiat France
123 N3 Feyzābād Afgh.
122 F6 Feyẕābād Kermān Iran
122 H4 Feyẕābād Khorāsān Iran
Fez Morocco see Fès
202 B3 Fezzan reg. Libya
150 E2 Ffestiniog Gwynedd, Wales U.K.
150 D3 Ffostrasol Ceredigion, Wales U.K.
Ffynnon Taf Wales U.K. see Taff's Well
163 H8 Fiac France
258 D2 Fiambalá Arg.
258 D2 Fiambala r. Arg.
193 K3 Fiamignano Italy
206 E4 Fian Ghana
213 □J4 Fianarantsoa Madag.
213 □J4 Fianarantsoa prov. Madag.
208 B2 Fianga Chad
190 D5 Fiano Italy
193 J3 Fiano Romano Italy
191 O9 Fiastra r. Italy
193 K1 Fiastra, Lago di l. Italy
191 J4 Fiavè Italy
184 E5 Ficalho hill Port.
194 E7 Ficarazzi Sicilia Italy
191 K6 Ficarolo Italy
210 C2 Fichē Eth.
173 L2 Fichtelberg Ger.
171 F10 Fichtelgebirge hills Ger.
171 F10 Fichtelgebirge park Ger.
173 M2 Fichtelnaab r. Ger.
172 H4 Fichtenberg Ger.
215 L4 Ficksburg S. Africa
192 I2 Ficulle Italy
194 G9 Ficuzza r. Sicilia Italy
125 M4 Fidā Oman
125 K6 Fidā oasis Saudi Arabia
146 J8 Fiddich r. Scotland U.K.
147 H8 Fiddown Ireland
190 I6 Fidenza Italy
142 C3 Fidjeland Norway
176 G2 Fidlův Kopec hill Czech Rep.
206 C4 Fié r. Guinea
178 E6 Fiè allo Sciliar Italy
178 G5 Fieberbrunn Austria
193 K1 Fiegni, Monte mt. Italy
222 G5 Field B.C. Can.
227 N3 Field Ont. Can.
232 B12 Field KY U.S.A.
84 D2 Field Island N.T. Austr.
138 J5 Fiemanka r. Latvia
197 N5 Fieni Romania
198 A2 Fier Albania
160 H5 Fier r. France
178 E7 Fiera di Primiero Italy
84 G5 Fiery Creek r. Qld Austr.
196 I8 Fierzes, Liqeni i resr Albania
190 E3 Fiesch Switz.
191 K8 Fiesole Italy
191 L6 Fiesso Umbertiano Italy
146 K10 Fife admin. div. Scotland U.K.
226 I5 Fife Lake MI U.S.A.
146 K10 Fife Ness pt Scotland U.K.
83 K5 Fifield N.S.W. Austr.
226 D4 Fifield WI U.S.A.
Fifth Cataract rapids Sudan see 5th Cataract
222 H3 Fifth Meridian Alta Can.
181 F5 Figalo, Cap c. Alg.
161 I9 Figaniéres France
192 B2 Figarella r. Corse France
192 C5 Figari Corse France
192 D6 Figari, Capo c. Sardegna Italy
163 I6 Figeac France
191 K8 Figline Valdarno Italy
247 □2 Fig Tree St Kitts and Nevis
184 C4 Figueira r. Port.
182 C8 Figueira da Foz Port.
182 G7 Figueira de Castelo Rodrigo Port.
184 C4 Figueira dos Cavaleiros Port.
184 D2 Figueira e Barros Port.
182 E7 Figueiredo de Alva Port.
184 D1 Figueiró r. Port.
182 F7 Figueiró da Granja Port.
182 D9 Figueiró dos Vinhos Port.
Figueras Spain see Figueres
186 K3 Figueres Spain
182 H5 Figueruela de Arriba Spain
205 E2 Figuig Morocco
207 I4 Figuil Cameroon
128 E9 Fiha al 'Ināb reg. Saudi Arabia
213 □J3 Fihaonana Madag.
79 □7 Fiji country S. Pacific Ocean
266 G7 Fiji Islands S. Pacific Ocean
164 F5 Fijnaart Neth.
210 D2 Fīk' Eth.
207 H4 Fika Nigeria
185 N6 Filabres, Sierra de los mts Spain
213 F4 Filabusi Zimbabwe
242 □Q12 Filadelfia Costa Rica
195 K6 Filadelfia Italy
253 E5 Filadelfia Para.
177 I3 Fiľakovo Slovakia
206 D4 Filamana Mali
138 L4 Filatova-Gora Rus. Fed.
190 H7 Filattiera Italy
262 V1 Filchner Ice Shelf Antarctica
193 K4 Filettino Italy
149 Q5 Filey North Yorkshire, England U.K.
129 I4 Filfili Azer.
195 □ Filfla i. Malta
193 P6 Filiano Italy
197 L6 Filiași Romania
198 B3 Filiates Greece
198 C5 Filiatra Greece
Filibe Bulg. see Plovdiv
194 H6 Filicudi, Isola i. Isole Lipari Italy
194 H6 Filicudi Porto Isole Lipari Italy
207 F3 Filingué Niger
Filipinas country Asia see Philippines
175 K1 Filipów Pol.
100 J1 Filippa, Mys hd Rus. Fed.
198 B3 Filippiada Greece
198 F1 Filippoi tourist site Greece
143 K2 Filipstad Sweden
190 H2 Filisur Switz.
140 J5 Fillan Norway
156 D3 Fillièvres France
160 I4 Fillinges France
Fillíra Greece see Fillyra
240 N7 Fillmore CA U.S.A.
241 T3 Fillmore UT U.S.A.
151 I3 Fillongley Warwickshire, England U.K.
199 G1 Fillyra Greece
245 H8 Filo de los Caballos Mex.
245 J5 Filomeno Mata Mex.
199 G5 Filotio Naxos Greece
191 O9 Filottrano Italy
172 G4 Fils r. Ger.
168 E4 Filsum Ger.
150 G4 Filton South Gloucestershire, England U.K.
210 D3 Filtu Eth.
179 I5 Filzmoos Austria
149 P5 Fimber East Riding of Yorkshire, England U.K.

Fimbull Ice Shelf to Fos
313

263 A2 Fimbull Ice Shelf Antarctica
122 D5 Fin Iran
206 C3 Fina, Réserve de nature res. Mali
194 G7 Finale Sicilia Italy
191 K6 Finale Emilia Italy
190 E7 Finale Ligure Italy
185 N6 Fiñana Spain
146 K9 Finavon Angus, Scotland U.K.
232 F11 Fincastle VA U.S.A.
233 J3 Finch Ont. Can.
210 C2 Finch'a'ā Hāyk' l. Eth.
151 K5 Finchampstead Wokingham, England U.K.
85 L6 Finch Hatton Qld Austr.
151 M4 Finchingfield Essex, England U.K.
151 I2 Findern Derbyshire, England U.K.
146 I7 Findhorn Moray, Scotland U.K.
146 I7 Findhorn r. Scotland U.K.
127 J5 Findık Turkey
129 C4 Findıklı Turkey
232 B7 Findlay OH U.S.A.
146 K7 Findochty Moray, Scotland U.K.
151 L6 Findon West Sussex, England U.K.
233 J4 Fine NY U.S.A.
151 K3 Finedon Northamptonshire, England U.K.
195 L3 Finese, Monte hill Italy
187 E10 Finestrat Spain
186 J3 Finestres, Serra mts Spain
83 L9 Fingal Tas. Austr.
223 M4 Finger Lake Ont. Can.
232 I6 Finger Lakes NY U.S.A.
116 I9 Fingeshwar Chhattisgarh India
213 F2 Fingoè Moz.
163 G8 Finhan France
161 D8 Finiels, Sommet de mt. France
199 L6 Finike Turkey
199 L6 Finike Körfezi b. Turkey
177 L5 Finiş Romania
158 D5 Finistère dept France
Finisterre Spain see Fisterra
Finisterre, Cabo c. Spain see Fisterra, Cabo
Finisterre, Cape Spain see Fisterra, Cabo
183 M9 Finisterre, Embalse de resr Spain
84 E8 Finke N.T. Austr.
84 E9 Finke watercourse N.T. Austr.
82 E4 Finke, Mount hill S.A. Austr.
84 F8 Finke Aboriginal Land res. N.T. Austr.
84 C2 Finke Bay N.T. Austr.
82 E2 Finke Flood Flats lowland S.A. Austr.
84 D8 Finke Gorge National Park N.T. Austr.
178 E5 Finkenberg Austria
179 I6 Finkenstein Austria
234 B6 Finksburg MD U.S.A.
140 S5 Finland country Europe
226 C2 Finland MN U.S.A.
138 F2 Finland, Gulf of Europe
222 E3 Finlay r. B.C. Can.
222 E3 Finlay, Mount B.C. Can.
222 F4 Finlay Forks B.C. Can.
226 B3 Finlayson MN U.S.A.
83 J6 Finley N.S.W. Austr.
236 G2 Finley ND U.S.A.
226 E1 Finmark Ont. Can.
147 H3 Finn r. Ireland
143 K1 Finnbodarna Sweden
171 D8 Finne ridge Ger.
147 H5 Finnea Ireland
169 E8 Finnentrop Ger.
143 K3 Finnerödja Sweden
85 J3 Finnigan, Mount Qld Austr.
151 O3 Finningham Suffolk, England U.K.
149 P7 Finningley South Yorkshire, England U.K.
84 C2 Finniss r. N.T. Austr.
82 E5 Finniss, Cape S.A. Austr.
82 F3 Finniss Springs Aboriginal Land res. S.A. Austr.
140 R1 Finnmark county Norway
140 Q2 Finnmarksvidda reg. Norway
143 N1 Finnsjön Florama naturreservat nature res. Sweden
142 I1 Finnskog Norway
140 N2 Finnsnes Norway
170 I5 Finowfurt Ger.
170 I5 Finowkanal canal Ger.
125 N4 Fins Oman
91 K8 Finschhafen P.N.G.
173 L5 Finsing Ger.
143 L3 Finspång Sweden
190 E2 Finsteraarhorn mt. Switz.
171 I7 Finsterwalde Ger.
164 L2 Finsterwolde Neth.
146 J4 Finstown Orkney, Scotland U.K.
141 O6 Finström Åland Fin.
168 I4 Fintel Ger.
177 K2 Fintice Slovakia
Fîntînele Romania see Fântânele
147 H4 Fintona Northern Ireland U.K.
147 F3 Fintown Ireland
147 E3 Fintragh Bay Ireland
146 H10 Fintry Stirling, Scotland U.K.
85 H7 Finucane Range hills Qld Austr.
147 C8 Finuge Ireland
147 J2 Finvoy Northern Ireland U.K.
193 J2 Fionchi, Monte mt. Italy
146 F7 Fionn Loch l. Scotland U.K.
146 D10 Fionnphort Argyll and Bute, Scotland U.K.
192 H3 Fiora r. Italy
191 J6 Fiorano Modenese Italy
81 B12 Fiordland National Park South I. N.Z.
222 D4 Fiordland Provincial Recreation Area park B.C. Can.
190 H6 Fiorenzuola d'Arda Italy
193 L2 Fiori, Montagna dei mt. Italy
124 G1 Fir reg. Saudi Arabia
199 G6 Fira Greece
118 D2 Firat r. Turkey
alt. Al Furāt (Iraq/Syria),
conv. Euphrates
129 A6 Firat Nehri r. Turkey
213 □J3 Firavahana Madag.
128 C9 Fir'awn, Jazīrat i. Egypt
240 L5 Firebaugh CA U.S.A.
223 J2 Firedrake Lake N.W.T. Can.
235 I3 Fire Island NY U.S.A.
235 I3 Fire Island National Seashore nature res. NY U.S.A.
191 K8 Firenze Italy
191 K8 Firenze prov. Italy
191 K7 Firenzuola Italy
227 K1 Fire River Ont. Can.
222 E3 Fireside B.C. Can.
236 G4 Firesteel Creek r. SD U.S.A.
216 □3f Firgas Gran Canaria Canary Is
251 E3 Firiña Venez.
127 L8 Firk, Sha'īb watercourse Iraq
207 I3 Firkachi well Niger
175 K4 Firlej Pol.
261 G3 Firmat Arg.
163 I6 Firmi France
256 B2 Firminópolis Brazil
161 E6 Firminy France
193 Q8 Firmo Italy
Firmum Italy see Fermo
Firmum Picenum Italy see Fermo
173 I4 Firngrund reg. Ger.
139 Q4 Firovo Rus. Fed.
123 N7 Firoza Pak.
116 G6 Firozabad Uttar Prad. India
123 K4 Firozkoh reg. Afgh.
116 F6 Firozpur Haryana India
116 E4 Firozpur Punjab India
168 E4 Firrel Ger.
100 M5 Firsovo Rus. Fed.
First Cataract rapids Egypt see 1st Cataract
233 □N3 First Connecticut Lake NH U.S.A.
146 □N2 Firth Shetland, Scotland U.K.
122 E7 Fīrūzābād Iran
Firuzabad Iran see Rāsk
122 G3 Fīrūzeh Iran
122 E4 Fīrūzkūh Iran
186 E2 Fiscal Spain
173 J5 Fischach Ger.
179 O3 Fischamend Markt Austria
179 M5 Fischbach Austria
172 C2 Fischbach Ger.
173 L6 Fischbachau Ger.
172 D3 Fischbach bei Dahn Ger.
179 L5 Fischbacher Alpen mts Austria
170 F5 Fischbeck Ger.
173 I7 Fischen im Allgäu Ger.
212 B5 Fischersbrunn Namibia
212 C6 Fish watercourse Namibia
214 E6 Fish r. S. Africa
149 O4 Fishburn Durham, England U.K.
82 C4 Fisher S.A. Austr.
263 J2 Fisher Bay Antarctica
263 E2 Fisher Glacier Antarctica
223 L5 Fisher River Man. Can.
235 L2 Fishers Island NY U.S.A.
221 J3 Fisher Strait Nunavut Can.
232 G10 Fishersville VA U.S.A.
150 C4 Fishguard Pembrokeshire, Wales U.K.
150 C3 Fishguard Bay Wales U.K.
233 I10 Fishing Creek MD U.S.A.
234 C3 Fishing Creek r. PA U.S.A.
223 M4 Fishing Lake Man. Can.
235 H1 Fishkill NY U.S.A.
235 H2 Fishkill Creek r. NY U.S.A.
222 F2 Fish Lake N.W.T. Can.
226 B3 Fish Lake MN U.S.A.
241 U3 Fish Lake UT U.S.A.
227 K6 Fish Point MI U.S.A.
151 M2 Fishtoft Lincolnshire, England U.K.
141 H5 Fiskå Norway
262 T2 Fiske, Cape Antarctica
140 M2 Fiskebøl Norway
Fiskenæsset Greenland see Qeqertarsuatsiaat
156 G5 Fismes France
182 B3 Fisterra Spain
182 B3 Fisterra, Cabo c. Spain
213 □J4 Fitampito Madag.
233 N6 Fitchburg MA U.S.A.
226 E7 Fitchburg WI U.S.A.
235 K1 Fitchville CT U.S.A.
232 C7 Fitchville OH U.S.A.
183 Q4 Fitero Spain
146 □N3 Fitful Head Scotland U.K.
Fitíai Greece see Fyteies
142 B2 Fitjar Norway
78 □2 Fito, Mount vol. Samoa
163 J10 Fitou France
252 B2 Fitzcarrald Peru
223 I3 Fitzgerald Alta Can.
231 F10 Fitzgerald GA U.S.A.
87 E12 Fitzgerald River National Park W.A. Austr.
222 D5 Fitz Hugh Sound sea chan. B.C. Can.
156 D5 Fitz-James France
84 C3 Fitzmaurice r. N.T. Austr.
259 D7 Fitz Roy Arg.
85 M7 Fitzroy r. Qld Austr.
86 G4 Fitzroy r. W.A. Austr.
259 B8 Fitz Roy, Cerro mt. Arg.
84 C3 Fitzroy Aboriginal Land res. N.T. Austr.
86 H5 Fitzroy Crossing W.A. Austr.
224 D4 Fitzwilliam Island Ont. Can.
193 K4 Fiuggi Italy
191 J7 Fiumalbo Italy
193 O5 Fiumarella r. Italy
Fiume Croatia see Rijeka
193 Q9 Fiumefreddo Bruzio Italy
195 I8 Fiumefreddo di Sicilia Sicilia Italy
195 M5 Fiume Nicà, Punta pt Italy
191 N4 Fiume Veneto Italy
192 I4 Fiumicino Italy
192 C4 Fium'Orbo r. Corse France
146 E9 Fiunary Highland, Scotland U.K.
81 A12 Five Fingers Peninsula South I. N.Z.
81 E12 Five Forks South I. N.Z.
147 H4 Fivemiletown Northern Ireland U.K.
240 L5 Five Points CA U.S.A.
81 C12 Five Rivers South I. N.Z.
190 I7 Fivizzano Italy
161 D6 Fix-St-Geneys France
209 F6 Fizi Dem. Rep. Congo
Fizuli Azer. see Füzuli
140 N4 Fjällsjönäs Sweden
143 M2 Fjärdhundra reg. Sweden
143 O2 Fjärdlångs naturreservat nature res. Sweden
170 E1 Fjelde Denmark
142 B1 Fjell Norway
140 N2 Fjellbu Norway
142 F4 Fjerritslev Denmark
204 D2 Fkih Ben Salah Morocco
142 F1 Flå Norway
179 H5 Flachau Austria
173 J3 Flachslanden Ger.
168 D4 Flachsmeer Ger.
146 □N2 Fladdabister Shetland, Scotland U.K.
142 E6 Fladså r. Denmark
169 J9 Fladungen Ger.
140 □D2 Flaga Iceland
163 I6 Flagnac France
215 N7 Flagstaff S. Africa
241 U6 Flagstaff AZ U.S.A.
216 □2b Flagstaff Bay St Helena
233 □O3 Flagstaff Lake ME U.S.A.
234 F3 Flagtown NJ U.S.A.
224 E1 Flaherty Island Nunavut Can.
160 J4 Flaine France
140 P3 Flakaberg Sweden
141 I6 Flåm Norway
217 □1b Flamand, Île i. Mauritius
158 H2 Flamanville France
197 O3 Flămânzi Romania
226 C4 Flambeau r. WI U.S.A.
149 Q5 Flamborough East Riding of Yorkshire, England U.K.
149 Q5 Flamborough Head England U.K.
259 E6 Flamenco, Isla i. Arg.
216 □1c Flamengos Faial Azores
186 G3 Flamicell r. Spain
171 F6 Fläming hills Ger.
238 J6 Flaming Gorge Reservoir WY U.S.A.
214 F6 Flaminksvlei salt pan S. Africa
223 M4 Flanagan r. Ont. Can.
247 □7 Flanagin Town Trin. and Tob.
165 C7 Flanders reg. Europe
235 J3 Flanders NY U.S.A.
156 D2 Flandre reg. France
236 G3 Flandreau SD U.S.A.
208 C5 Flandria Dem. Rep. Congo
232 C11 Flannagan Lake VA U.S.A.
146 A6 Flannan Isles Scotland U.K.
143 K4 Flåren l. Sweden
140 M4 Flåsjön l. Sweden
161 I10 Flassans-sur-Issole France
222 E2 Flat r. N.W.T. Can.
226 I7 Flat r. MI U.S.A.
234 F2 Flatbrookville NJ U.S.A.
140 □E1 Flateyjardalsheiði reg. Iceland
220 G5 Flathead r. MT U.S.A.
238 G3 Flathead Indian Reservation res. MT U.S.A.
238 G3 Flathead Lake MT U.S.A.
150 F5 Flat Holm i. Wales U.K.
238 H4 Flatiron mt. ID U.S.A.
217 □1b Flat Island Mauritius
90 E4 Flat Island S. China Sea
232 B12 Flat Lick KY U.S.A.
81 B12 Flat Mountain South I. N.Z.
81 J8 Flat Point North I. N.Z.
178 H6 Flattach Austria
85 J3 Flattery, Cape Qld Austr.
238 B2 Flattery, Cape WA U.S.A.
179 J6 Flattnitz Austria
222 B2 Flat Top mt. Y.T. Can.
231 □1 Flatts Village Bermuda
238 K3 Flatwillow Creek r. MT U.S.A.
232 C10 Flatwoods KY U.S.A.
232 E10 Flatwoods WV U.S.A.
178 D5 Flaurling Austria
142 E2 Flåvatnet l. Norway
157 L6 Flavigny-sur-Moselle France
160 F1 Flavigny-sur-Ozerain France
161 B8 Flavin France
190 G1 Flawil Switz.
178 B5 Flaxenpass pass Austria
161 I9 Flayosc France
245 I1 Flechadores Mex.
171 D6 Flechtingen Ger.
171 D6 Flechtinger Höhenzug park Ger.
168 I2 Fleckeby Ger.
170 G4 Flecken Zechlin Ger.
151 J2 Fleckney Leicestershire, England U.K.
231 □2 Fleeming Point New Prov. Bahamas
170 F3 Fleesensee l. Ger.
151 K5 Fleet Hampshire, England U.K.
146 H7 Fleet r. Scotland U.K.
146 H7 Fleet, Loch b. Scotland U.K.
170 D5 Fleetmark Ger.
85 J7 Fleetwood Qld Austr.
149 K6 Fleetwood Lancashire, England U.K.
234 D4 Fleetwood PA U.S.A.
172 G3 Flein Ger.
142 C3 Flekkefjord Norway
142 E3 Flekkerøy i. Norway
165 H7 Flémalle Belgium
232 B10 Flemingsburg KY U.S.A.
234 F3 Flemington NJ U.S.A.
264 G2 Flemish Cap sea feature N. Atlantic Ocean
151 N3 Flempton Suffolk, England U.K.
143 M2 Flen Sweden
168 I1 Flensborg Fjord inlet Denmark/Ger.
168 H1 Flensburg Ger.
Flensburger Förde inlet Denmark/Ger. see Flensborg Fjord
165 I7 Fléron Belgium
159 J4 Flers France
227 N5 Flesherton Ont. Can.
93 D3 Flesko, Tanjung pt Indon.
170 E5 Flessau Ger.
223 I2 Fletcher Lake N.W.T. Can.
262 S2 Fletcher Peninsula Antarctica
227 K5 Fletcher Pond l. MI U.S.A.
163 F8 Fleurance France
225 J3 Fleur de Lys Nfld and Lab. Can.
225 H3 Fleur-de-May, Lac l. Nfld and Lab. Can.
162 F3 Fleuré France
160 F4 Fleurie France
190 B2 Fleurier Switz.
165 G8 Fleurus Belgium
161 C10 Fleury France
156 C8 Fleury-les-Aubrais France
156 B5 Fleury-sur-Andelle France
159 K3 Fleury-sur-Orne France
157 K5 Fléville-Lixières France
164 H4 Flevoland prov. Neth.
150 C6 Flexbury Cornwall, England U.K.
169 I10 Flieden Ger.
178 C5 Fließ Austria
149 J4 Flimby Cumbria, England U.K.
190 G2 Flims Switz.
151 M5 Flimwell East Sussex, England U.K.
85 H4 Flinders r. Qld Austr.
87 C4 Flinders r. W.A. Austr.
87 C13 Flinders Bay W.A. Austr.
82 F6 Flinders Chase National Park S.A. Austr.
85 J3 Flinders Group is Qld Austr.
85 J3 Flinders Group National Park Qld Austr.
82 E5 Flinders Island S.A. Austr.
83 L8 Flinders Island Tas. Austr.
85 L5 Flinders Passage Qld Austr.
82 F5 Flinders Ranges mts S.A. Austr.
82 G4 Flinders Ranges National Park S.A. Austr.
85 L4 Flinders Reefs Coral Sea Is Terr. Austr.
156 F3 Flines-lez-Raches France
223 K4 Flin Flon Man. Can.
150 F1 Flint Flintshire, Wales U.K.
227 K6 Flint MI U.S.A.
231 E10 Flint r. GA U.S.A.
227 K6 Flint r. MI U.S.A.
168 J2 Flintbek Ger.
267 I6 Flint Island Kiribati
85 L9 Flinton Qld Austr.
150 F1 Flintshire admin. div. Wales U.K.
232 G9 Flintstone MD U.S.A.
157 K6 Flirey France
178 B5 Flirsch Austria
142 I1 Flisa Norway
141 L6 Flisa r. Norway
142 D2 Fliseggi mt. Norway
151 L3 Flitwick Bedfordshire, England U.K.
186 G5 Flix Spain
186 G5 Flix, Pantà de resr Spain
156 D3 Flixecourt France
156 I4 Flize France
142 I4 Floda Sweden
149 M2 Flodden Northumberland, England U.K.
156 G8 Flogny-la-Chapelle France
171 H9 Flöha Ger.
171 H9 Flöha r. Ger.
157 I4 Floing France
163 C6 Floirac France
262 P1 Flood Range mts Antarctica
226 D3 Floodwood MN U.S.A.
149 L5 Flookburgh Cumbria, England U.K.
84 C2 Flora r. N.T. Austr.
226 H9 Flora IN U.S.A.
161 D8 Florac France
157 L5 Florange France
85 K4 Flora Reef Coral Sea Is Terr. Austr.
84 G5 Floraville Qld Austr.
250 C6 Flor de Punga Peru
165 G8 Floreffe Belgium
227 L7 Florence Ont. Can.
Florence Italy see Firenze
231 D8 Florence AL U.S.A.
241 U8 Florence AZ U.S.A.
239 L7 Florence CO U.S.A.
236 G6 Florence KS U.S.A.
234 F4 Florence NJ U.S.A.
238 B5 Florence OR U.S.A.
231 H8 Florence SC U.S.A.
226 F4 Florence WI U.S.A.
241 U8 Florence Junction AZ U.S.A.
233 □R2 Florenceville N.B. Can.
258 E2 Florencia Formosa Arg.
258 F3 Florencia Santa Fé Arg.
250 C4 Florencia Col.
261 I3 Florencio Sánchez Uru.
165 G8 Florennes Belgium
161 C10 Florensac France
Florentia Italy see Firenze
259 D6 Florentino Ameghino Arg.
259 D6 Florentino Ameghino, Embalse resr Arg.
165 H9 Florenville Belgium
261 H4 Flores r. Arg.
216 □1 Flores i. Azores
254 F3 Flores Pernambuco Brazil
254 E3 Flores Piauí Brazil
243 G3 Flores Guat.
93 B8 Flores i. Indon.
261 I3 Flores dept Uru.
93 A7 Flores, Laut sea Indon.
252 F2 Florescência Brazil
183 J7 Flores de Ávila Spain
254 D5 Flores de Goiás Brazil
Floreshty Moldova see Florești
222 E5 Flores Island B.C. Can.
Flores Sea Indon. see Flores, Laut
254 F4 Floresta Brazil
194 H8 Floresta Sicilia Italy
136 H6 Florești Moldova
256 B5 Florestópolis Brazil
237 F11 Floresville TX U.S.A.
235 G3 Florham Park NJ U.S.A.
254 E3 Floriano Brazil
252 D2 Floriano Peixoto Brazil
255 C8 Florianópolis Brazil
252 E4 Florida Bol.
260 A5 Florida Chile
246 D3 Florida Cuba
247 □1 Florida Puerto Rico
261 I4 Florida Uru.
261 I4 Florida dept Uru.
235 G2 Florida NY U.S.A.
231 F10 Florida state U.S.A.
231 G14 Florida, Straits of Bahamas/U.S.A.
231 G13 Florida Bay FL U.S.A.
182 I6 Florida de Liébana Spain
78 □6 Florida Islands Solomon Is
231 G13 Florida Keys is FL U.S.A.
259 D8 Florida Negra Arg.
256 B4 Flórida Paulista Brazil
195 I9 Floridia Sicilia Italy
237 C12 Florido r. Mex.
197 L3 Florii, Vârful hill Romania
240 K3 Florin CA U.S.A.
198 C2 Florina Greece
192 B6 Florinas Sardegna Italy
256 B5 Florínia Brazil
214 F9 Floriskraaldam l. S. Africa
236 J6 Florissant MO U.S.A.
141 H6 Florø Norway
169 H10 Flörsbach Ger.
169 F10 Flörsheim am Main Ger.
172 E2 Flörsheim-Dalsheim Ger.
169 G10 Florstadt Ger.
173 M2 Floß Ger.
173 M2 Flossenbürg Ger.
146 J5 Flotta i. Scotland U.K.
163 I9 Floure France
225 H2 Flour Lake Nfld and Lab. Can.
226 B6 Floyd IA U.S.A.
232 E12 Floyd VA U.S.A.
241 T6 Floyd, Mount AZ U.S.A.
237 E9 Floydada TX U.S.A.
178 B6 Fluchthorn mt. Austria/Switz.
190 H2 Flüelapass pass Switz.
190 F2 Flüelen Switz.
164 I3 Fluessen l. Neth.
190 E2 Flühli Switz.
93 E4 Fluk Maluku Indon.
186 E4 Flúmen r. Spain
192 D9 Flumendosa r. Sardegna Italy
193 O5 Flumeri Italy
160 J5 Flumet France
192 D7 Flumineddu r. Sardegna Italy
192 C8 Flumineddu r. Italy
192 B9 Fluminimaggiore Sardegna Italy
190 G1 Flums Switz.
Flushing Neth. see Vlissingen
232 B5 Flushing MI U.S.A.
232 D8 Flushing OH U.S.A.
192 B7 Flussio Sardegna Italy
91 J8 Fly r. P.N.G.
262 R2 Flying Fish, Cape Antarctica
86 □1 Flying Fish Cove Christmas I.
84 E3 Flying Fox Creek r. N.T. Austr.
79 □8 Foa i. Tonga
223 K5 Foam Lake Sask. Can.
190 E4 Fobello Italy
188 G4 Foča Bos.-Herz.
199 H4 Foça Turkey
165 H8 Focant Belgium
191 M5 Focce dell'Adige r. mouth Italy
146 J7 Fochabers Moray, Scotland U.K.
215 L2 Fochville S. Africa
168 I2 Fockbek Ger.
197 P5 Focșani Romania
197 P3 Focuri Romania
208 D3 Fodé C.A.R.
206 C4 Fodékaria Guinea
159 P7 Foëcy France
84 F3 Foelsche r. N.T. Austr.
109 I7 Fogang Guangdong China
84 C2 Fog Bay N.T. Austr.
234 D3 Fogelsville PA U.S.A.
205 F4 Foggâret el Arab Alg.
205 F4 Foggâret ez Zoûa Alg.
193 P5 Foggia Italy
193 P5 Foggia prov. Italy
192 A7 Foghe, Punta di pt Sardegna Italy
93 E5 Fogi Buru Indon.
191 N8 Foglia r. Italy
193 J5 Fogliano, Lago di lag. Italy
141 P6 Föglö Åland Fin.
206 □ Fogo i. Cape Verde
225 K3 Fogo Island Nfld and Lab. Can.
121 M6 Fogolevo Kazakh.
179 K5 Fohnsdorf Austria
168 G1 Föhr i. Ger.
171 F6 Fohrde Ger.
172 B2 Föhren Ger.
184 B6 Fóia hill Port.
191 L9 Foiano della Chiana Italy
177 L4 Foieni Romania
147 B9 Foilclough hill Ireland
146 G6 Foinaven hill Scotland U.K.
163 H10 Foix France
163 G10 Foix reg. France
186 I5 Foix r. Spain
134 K4 Foki Rus. Fed.
139 R8 Fokino Rus. Fed.
207 G4 Fokku Nigeria
177 H5 Foktő Hungary
142 D1 Folarskarnuten mt. Norway
140 M3 Folda sea chan. Norway
177 J5 Földeák Hungary
140 L4 Foldereid Norway
177 K4 Földes Hungary
140 K4 Foldfjorden sea chan. Norway
198 F6 Folegandros Greece
198 F6 Folegandros i. Greece
213 E4 Foley Botswana
231 D10 Foley AL U.S.A.
236 I3 Foley MN U.S.A.
224 D3 Foleyet Ont. Can.
221 K3 Foley Island Nunavut Can.
85 L7 Foleyvale Qld Austr.
Folgares Angola see Capelongo
191 K4 Folgaria Italy
263 H2 Folger, Cape Antarctica
182 F3 Folgoso de Courel Spain
182 H3 Folgoso de la Ribera Spain
193 L2 Folignano Italy
193 J2 Foligno Italy
151 O5 Folkestone Kent, England U.K.
151 L2 Folkingham Lincolnshire, England U.K.
231 F10 Folkston GA U.S.A.
141 K5 Folldal Norway
191 M4 Follina Italy
140 M5 Föllinge Sweden
192 F2 Follonica Italy
192 F2 Follonica, Golfo di b. Italy
142 F2 Follsjå l. Norway
150 D6 Folly Gate Devon, England U.K.
157 M5 Folschviller France
232 E9 Folsom WV U.S.A.
240 K3 Folsom Lake CA U.S.A.
217 □3 Fomboni Mwali Comoros
246 D2 Fomento Cuba
135 H7 Fomin Rus. Fed.
134 H5 Fominki Rus. Fed.
134 J2 Fominskaya Rus. Fed.
134 J3 Fominskiy Rus. Fed.
134 H4 Fominskoye Rus. Fed.
195 □ Fomm ir-Riħ, Il-Bajja ta' b. Malta
183 N3 Foncea hill Spain
233 K6 Fonda NY U.S.A.
223 J3 Fond-du-Lac Sask. Can.
223 J3 Fond du Lac r. Sask. Can.
226 F6 Fond du Lac WI U.S.A.
226 B3 Fond du Lac Indian Reservation res. MN U.S.A.
217 □1b Fond du Sac Mauritius
232 B12 Fonde KY U.S.A.
182 D5 Fondevila Spain
193 K5 Fondi Italy
193 K5 Fondi, Lago di l. Italy
185 N7 Fondón Spain
185 M6 Fonelas Spain
186 C5 Fonfría Aragón Spain
182 H5 Fonfría Castilla y León Spain
206 C4 Fon Going ridge Guinea
192 C7 Fonni Sardegna Italy
163 E6 Fonroque France
Fonsagrada Spain see A Fonsagrada
250 C2 Fonseca Col.
242 □O11 Fonseca, Golfo do b. Central America
163 G8 Fonsorbes France
157 M8 Fontaine Franche-Comté France
161 H6 Fontaine Rhône-Alpes France
156 E7 Fontainebleau France
160 G1 Fontaine-Française France
223 J3 Fontaine Lake Sask. Can.
156 B4 Fontaine-le-Bourg France
159 M2 Fontaine-le-Dun France
160 G2 Fontaine-lès-Dijon France
157 L8 Fontaine-lès-Luxeuil France
165 F8 Fontaine-l'Évêque Belgium
160 F3 Fontaines Bourgogne France
156 F8 Fontaines Bourgogne France
161 L8 Fontan France
234 C4 Fontana PA U.S.A.
183 N7 Fontanar Spain
185 J2 Fontanarejo Spain
190 I6 Fontanellato Italy
193 L5 Fontanelle r. Italy
161 E9 Fontanès France
225 G2 Fontanges Que. Can.
190 G6 Fontanigorda Italy
161 C6 Fontannes France
185 J3 Fontanosas Spain
222 F3 Fontas B.C. Can.
222 F3 Fontas r. B.C. Can.
Font Blanca, Pic de mt. France/Spain see Port, Pic du
251 E5 Fonte Boa Brazil
193 L3 Fontecchio Italy
193 K3 Fontecellese, Monte mt. Italy
182 D3 Fonte Díaz Spain
216 □1a Fonte do Bastardo Terceira Azores
253 F3 Fonte do Pau-d'Agua Brazil
207 H5 Fontem Cameroon
162 C3 Fontenay-le-Comte France
156 E6 Fontenay-Trésigny France
225 I3 Fonteneau, Lac l. Que. Can.
160 C1 Fontenoy France
157 L8 Fontenoy-le-Château France
157 K6 Fontenoy-sur-Moselle France
182 D9 Fontes Port.
159 L7 Fontevraud-l'Abbaye France
159 M8 Fontgombault France
191 K4 Fonti, Cima mt. Italy
216 □1a Fontinhas Terceira Azores
183 K7 Fontiveros Spain
157 K5 Fontoy France
163 I10 Font-Romeu-Odeillo-Via France
161 J7 Font Sancte, Pic de la mt. France
147 I6 Fontstown Ireland
140 □F1 Fontur pt Iceland
161 F9 Fontvieille France
Fonuafo'ou i. Tonga see Fonuafu'u
79 □8 Fonuafu'u i. Tonga
81 □4 Fonuakula Niue
77 I3 Fonualei i. Tonga
78 □4a Fonuchu i. Chuuk Micronesia
177 G5 Fonyód Hungary
186 F3 Fonz Spain
191 L3 Fonzaso Italy
Foochow Fujian China see Fuzhou
241 T2 Fool Creek Reservoir UT U.S.A.
227 O4 Foot's Bay Ont. Can.
108 G2 Foping Shaanxi China
190 H3 Foppolo Italy
184 □ Fora, Ilhéu de i. Madeira
193 J3 Forano Italy
122 F4 Forat Iran
187 D9 Forata, Embalse de resr Spain
Foraulep atoll Micronesia see Faraulep
157 M5 Forbach France
172 E4 Forbach Ger.
83 L5 Forbes N.S.W. Austr.
222 G4 Forbes, Mount Alta Can.
81 A12 Forbes, Mount South I. N.Z.
117 K6 Forbesganj Bihar India
215 P2 Forbes Reef Swaziland
161 I10 Forcalcueiret France
186 E6 Forcall Spain
161 H9 Forcalquier France
182 D3 Forcarei Spain
Forcary Spain see Forcarei
193 K2 Force Italy
172 D5 Forchheim Baden-Württemberg Ger.
173 K2 Forchheim Bayern Ger.
172 H3 Forchtenberg Ger.
179 N4 Forchtenstein Austria
190 C3 Forclaz, Col de la pass Switz.
225 H1 Ford r. Que. Can.
146 F10 Ford Argyll and Bute, Scotland U.K.
149 M2 Ford Northumberland, England U.K.
226 G4 Ford r. MI U.S.A.
84 B2 Ford, Cape N.T. Austr.
240 M6 Ford City CA U.S.A.
232 F8 Ford City PA U.S.A.
142 B2 Førde Hordaland Norway
141 H6 Førde Sogn og Fjordane Norway
223 L2 Forde Lake Nunavut Can.
80 J6 Fordell North I. N.Z.
171 E7 Förderstedt Ger.
151 M3 Fordham Cambridgeshire, England U.K.
151 I6 Fordingbridge Hampshire, England U.K.
192 B8 Fordongianus Sardegna Italy
146 L9 Fordoun Aberdeenshire, Scotland U.K.
262 O1 Ford Range mts Antarctica
235 G3 Fords NJ U.S.A.
83 J3 Fords Bridge N.S.W. Austr.
147 I5 Fordstown Ireland
146 K7 Fordyce Aberdeenshire, Scotland U.K.
237 I9 Fordyce AR U.S.A.
206 B4 Forécariah Guinea
221 O3 Forel, Mont mt. Greenland
151 J6 Foreland hd England U.K.
150 E5 Foreland Point England U.K.
237 H9 Foreman AR U.S.A.
223 I5 Foremost Alta Can.
193 P6 Forenza Italy
222 E4 Foresight Mountain B.C. Can.
224 D5 Forest Ont. Can.
237 K9 Forest MS U.S.A.
232 B8 Forest OH U.S.A.
232 F11 Forest VA U.S.A.
223 H4 Forestburg Alta Can.
234 F1 Forestburg NY U.S.A.
234 E1 Forest City PA U.S.A.
85 H5 Forest Creek r. Qld Austr.
83 K6 Forest Hill N.S.W. Austr.
85 J8 Forest Hill Qld Austr.
240 L2 Foresthill CA U.S.A.
83 L10 Forestier Peninsula Tas. Austr.
226 F5 Forest Junction WI U.S.A.
226 B4 Forest Lake MN U.S.A.
241 V7 Forest Lakes AZ U.S.A.
231 E9 Forest Park GA U.S.A.
240 K2 Forest Ranch CA U.S.A.
151 M5 Forest Row East Sussex, England U.K.
225 G3 Forestville Que. Can.
240 J3 Forestville CA U.S.A.
234 B7 Forestville MD U.S.A.
227 L6 Forestville MI U.S.A.
232 F6 Forestville NY U.S.A.
142 B2 Føresvik Norway
206 E4 Forêt des Deux Balé nat. park Burkina
207 F5 Forêt de Togodo nature res. Togo
156 H7 Forêt d'Orient, Parc Naturel Régional de la nature res. France
160 D5 Forez, Monts du mts France
160 D5 Forez, Plaine du plain France
146 K9 Forfar Angus, Scotland U.K.
237 E7 Forgan OK U.S.A.
156 C4 Forges-les-Eaux France
173 J6 Forggensee l. Ger.
146 J7 Forgie Moray, Scotland U.K.
225 H3 Forillon, Parc National de nat. park Que. Can.
193 N6 Forino Italy
193 L6 Forio Italy
171 D10 Föritz Ger.
182 C5 Forjães Port.
234 C6 Fork MD U.S.A.
237 K8 Forked Deer r. TN U.S.A.
233 K9 Forked River NJ U.S.A.
147 J4 Forkhill Northern Ireland U.K.
238 B3 Forks WA U.S.A.
234 C1 Forkston PA U.S.A.
234 B1 Forksville PA U.S.A.
232 G11 Fork Union VA U.S.A.
140 □ Forlandsundet str. Svalbard
191 M7 Forlì Italy
191 M8 Forlì-Cesena prov. Italy
191 M7 Forlimpopoli Italy
236 G2 Forman ND U.S.A.
190 E3 Formazza Italy
149 K6 Formby Merseyside, England U.K.
187 H10 Formentera i. Spain
187 L8 Formentor, Cap de c. Spain
156 C4 Formerie France
Former Yugoslav Republic of Macedonia country Europe see Macedonia
193 L5 Formia Italy
187 D7 Formiche Alto Spain
192 F2 Formiche di Grosseto is Italy
193 M5 Formicola Italy
257 E4 Formiga Brazil
191 J6 Formigine Italy
191 L6 Formignana Italy
163 I10 Formiguères France
258 F2 Formosa Arg.
258 F2 Formosa prov. Arg.
Formosa country Asia see Taiwan
255 D5 Formosa Brazil
184 D7 Formosa, Ria lag. Port.
253 G3 Formosa, Serra hills Brazil
254 D4 Formosa do Rio Preto Brazil
Formosa Strait China/Taiwan see Taiwan Strait
182 C8 Formoselha Port.
256 A4 Formoso Mato Grosso do Sul Brazil
254 D5 Formoso Minas Gerais Brazil
254 C4 Formoso Tocantins Brazil
256 A3 Formoso r. Brazil
254 C4 Formoso r. Brazil
254 D5 Formoso r. Brazil
147 D6 Formoyle Ireland
142 G5 Fornæs c. Denmark
192 A5 Fornelli Sardegna Italy
186 □ Fornells Spain
186 K4 Fornells de la Selva Spain
191 N2 Forni Avoltri Italy
191 N3 Forni di Sopra Italy
191 N3 Forni di Sotto Italy
190 C5 Forno Alpi Graie Italy
178 F7 Forno di Zoldo Italy
213 G4 Fornos Moz.
182 G6 Fornos Port.
182 E7 Fornos de Algodres Port.
190 I6 Fornovo di Taro Italy
193 M3 Foro r. Italy
140 K5 Forolshogna mt. Norway
137 M9 Foros Ukr.
184 C3 Foros de Vale Figueira Port.
184 C2 Foros do Arrão Port.
Føroyar terr. N. Atlantic Ocean see Faroe Islands
177 I5 Forráskút Hungary
146 I7 Forres Moray, Scotland U.K.
87 J11 Forrest W.A. Austr.
86 J3 Forrest r. W.A. Austr.
226 F9 Forrest IL U.S.A.
262 U1 Forrestal Range mts Antarctica
237 J8 Forrest City AR U.S.A.
222 C4 Forrester Island AK U.S.A.
223 I3 Forrest Lake Sask. Can.
87 J10 Forrest Lakes salt flat W.A. Austr.
226 E7 Forreston IL U.S.A.
Forrest River Mission W.A. Austr. see Oombulgurri
177 K3 Forró Hungary
162 D3 Fors France
142 C3 Forsand Norway
85 I5 Forsayth Qld Austr.
140 N2 Forsbakken Norway
150 H2 Forsbrook Staffordshire, England U.K.
142 J2 Forshaga Sweden
146 I6 Forsinard Highland, Scotland U.K.
140 O3 Forsnäs Sweden
141 Q6 Forssa Fin.
172 F3 Forst Baden-Württemberg Ger.
171 K7 Forst Brandenburg Ger.
83 N5 Forster N.S.W. Austr.
173 L5 Forstern Ger.
173 L5 Forstinning Ger.
231 F9 Forsyth GA U.S.A.
237 I7 Forsyth MO U.S.A.
238 K3 Forsyth MT U.S.A.
227 R1 Forsythe Que. Can.
81 I7 Forsyth Island South I. N.Z.
84 G4 Forsyth Islands Qld Austr.
85 I7 Forsyth Range hills Qld Austr.
123 O7 Fort Abbas Pak.
224 D2 Fort Albany Ont. Can.
252 D2 Fortaleza Pando Bol.
252 D3 Fortaleza Pando Bol.
254 F2 Fortaleza Brazil
258 G4 Fortaleza de Santa Teresa Uru.
186 D6 Fortanete Spain
241 V8 Fort Apache Indian Reservation res. AZ U.S.A.
Fort Archambault Chad see Sarh
232 G9 Fort Ashby WV U.S.A.
222 H4 Fort Assiniboine Alta Can.
226 F7 Fort Atkinson WI U.S.A.
146 G8 Fort Augustus Highland, Scotland U.K.
222 E4 Fort Babine B.C. Can.
215 K8 Fort Beaufort S. Africa
238 J2 Fort Belknap Indian Reservation res. MT U.S.A.
238 I3 Fort Benton MT U.S.A.
236 D2 Fort Berthold Indian Reservation res. ND U.S.A.
223 J4 Fort Black Sask. Can.
Fort Brabant N.W.T. Can. see Tuktoyaktuk
240 I2 Fort Bragg CA U.S.A.
Fort Carillon NY U.S.A. see Ticonderoga
Fort Carnot Madag. see Ikongo
Fort Charlet Alg. see Djanet
Fort Chimo Que. Can. see Kuujjuaq
223 I3 Fort Chipewyan Alta Can.
238 L6 Fort Collins CO U.S.A.
85 H6 Fort Constantine Qld Austr.
224 E4 Fort-Coulonge Que. Can.
233 K4 Fort Covington NY U.S.A.
Fort Crampel C.A.R. see Kaga Bandoro
Fort-Dauphin Madag. see Tôlañaro
237 D10 Fort Davis TX U.S.A.
247 □3 Fort-de-France Martinique
247 □3 Fort-de-France, Baie de b. Martinique
Fort de Kock Sumatera Indon. see Bukittinggi
Fort de Polignac Alg. see Illizi
231 D9 Fort Deposit AL U.S.A.
236 H4 Fort Dodge IA U.S.A.
215 N6 Fort Donald S. Africa
241 W1 Fort Duchesne UT U.S.A.
192 A6 Forte, Monte hill Italy
233 L5 Fort Edward NY U.S.A.
209 D6 Forte Nordeste Angola
227 P7 Fort Erie Ont. Can.
86 D6 Fortescue r. W.A. Austr.
234 E6 Fortescue NJ U.S.A.
251 H6 Forte Veneza Brazil
191 L2 Fortezza Italy
192 E3 Fortezza, Monte della hill Italy
233 □R2 Fort Fairfield ME U.S.A.
Fort Flatters Alg. see Bordj Omer Driss
Fort Foureau Cameroon see Kousséri
226 A1 Fort Frances Ont. Can.
Fort Franklin N.W.T. Can. see Déline
231 E10 Fort Gaines GA U.S.A.
Fort Gardel Alg. see Zaouatallaz
239 L8 Fort Garland CO U.S.A.
232 C10 Fort Gay WV U.S.A.
Fort George Que. Can. see Chisasibi
237 H8 Fort Gibson Lake OK U.S.A.
220 F3 Fort Good Hope N.W.T. Can.
Fort Gouraud Maur. see Fdérik
146 I11 Forth South Lanarkshire, Scotland U.K.
144 F3 Forth r. Scotland U.K.
146 J10 Forth, Firth of est. Scotland U.K.
Fort Hall Kenya see Murang'a
238 H5 Fort Hall Indian Reservation res. ID U.S.A.
239 L11 Fort Hancock TX U.S.A.
215 K8 Fort Hare S. Africa
Fort Hertz Myanmar see Putao
241 R3 Fortification Range mts NV U.S.A.
245 K7 Fortín Mex.
253 E5 Fortín Aroma Para.
253 E5 Fortín Ávalos Sánchez Para.
253 F5 Fortín Boquerón Para.
253 E5 Fortín Capitán Demattei Para.
253 F5 Fortín Carlos Antonio López Para.
253 F5 Fortín Coronel Bogado Para.
253 E5 Fortín Coronel Eugenio Garay Para.
146 H9 Fortingall Perth and Kinross, Scotland U.K.
253 F4 Fortín Galpón Para.
253 F6 Fortín General Caballero Para.
253 F5 Fortín General Díaz Para.
253 E5 Fortín General Diaz Para.
253 E5 Fortín General Mendoza Para.
253 E5 Fortín Hernandarías Para.
253 E5 Fortín Infante Rivarola Para.
253 F5 Fortín Juan de Zalazar Para.
253 E5 Fortín Lagerenza Para.
258 E2 Fortín Lavalle Arg.
253 E5 Fortín Leonardo Britos Para.
253 E5 Fortín Leonida Escobar Para.
253 E5 Fortín Linares Para.
253 F5 Fortín Madrejón Para.
253 E5 Fortín May Alberto Gardel Para.
253 E5 Fortín Nueva Asunción Para.
261 F4 Fortín Olavarría Arg.
258 E1 Fortín Pilcomayo Arg.
253 F5 Fortín Presidente Ayala Para.
253 E4 Fortín Ravelo Bol.
258 F2 Fortín Sargento Primero Leyes Arg.
253 E4 Fortín Suárez Arana Bol.
253 E5 Fortín Teniente Juan Echauri López Para.
253 F5 Fortín Teniente Mountania Para.
253 F4 Fortín Teniente Primero H. Mendoza Para.
253 E6 Fortín Teniente Rojas Silva Para.
260 E6 Fortín Uno Arg.
184 E2 Fortios Port.
Fort Jameson Zambia see Chipata
Fort Johnston Malawi see Mangochi
233 □Q1 Fort Kent ME U.S.A.
238 D5 Fort Klamath OR U.S.A.
Fort Lamy Chari-Baguirmi Chad see Ndjamena
Fort Laperrine Alg. see Tamanrasset
238 L5 Fort Laramie WY U.S.A.
231 G12 Fort Lauderdale FL U.S.A.
235 H3 Fort Lee NJ U.S.A.
222 F2 Fort Liard N.W.T. Can.
246 H4 Fort-Liberté Haiti
232 H9 Fort Loudon PA U.S.A.
223 I3 Fort Mackay Alta Can.
222 H5 Fort Macleod Alta Can.
226 C9 Fort Madison IA U.S.A.
156 C3 Fort-Mahon-Plage France
Fort Manning Malawi see Mchinji
226 D5 Fort McCoy WI U.S.A.
223 I3 Fort McMurray Alta Can.
220 E3 Fort McPherson N.W.T. Can.
235 H2 Fort Montgomery NY U.S.A.
236 D5 Fort Morgan CO U.S.A.
215 O5 Fort Mtombeni S. Africa
123 N7 Fort Munro Pak.
231 G12 Fort Myers FL U.S.A.
222 F3 Fort Nelson B.C. Can.
222 F3 Fort Nelson r. B.C. Can.
Fort Norman N.W.T. Can. see Tulita
Fort Orange NY U.S.A. see Albany
193 O4 Fortore r. Italy
231 E8 Fort Payne AL U.S.A.
238 K2 Fort Peck MT U.S.A.
238 L2 Fort Peck Indian Reservation res. MT U.S.A.
238 K3 Fort Peck Reservoir MT U.S.A.
231 G12 Fort Pierce FL U.S.A.
236 E3 Fort Pierre SD U.S.A.
210 A4 Fort Portal Uganda
222 G2 Fort Providence N.W.T. Can.
223 K5 Fort Qu'Appelle Sask. Can.
Fort Randall AK U.S.A. see Cold Bay
232 A8 Fort Recovery OH U.S.A.
222 H2 Fort Resolution N.W.T. Can.
213 F3 Fort Rixon Zimbabwe
81 C13 Fortrose South I. N.Z.
146 H7 Fortrose Highland, Scotland U.K.
Fort Rosebery Zambia see Mansa
Fort Rousset Congo see Owando
Fort Rupert Que. Can. see Waskaganish
222 E4 Fort St James B.C. Can.
222 F3 Fort St John B.C. Can.
Fort Sandeman Pak. see Zhob
222 H4 Fort Saskatchewan Alta Can.
237 H7 Fort Scott KS U.S.A.
224 C1 Fort Severn Ont. Can.
120 D5 Fort-Shevchenko Kazakh.
222 F2 Fort Simpson N.W.T. Can.
223 H2 Fort Smith N.W.T. Can.
237 H8 Fort Smith AR U.S.A.
238 K4 Fort Smith MT U.S.A.
237 D10 Fort Stockton TX U.S.A.
239 L9 Fort Sumner NM U.S.A.
237 F7 Fort Supply OK U.S.A.
241 W8 Fort Thomas AZ U.S.A.
236 F2 Fort Totten (Devils Lake Sioux) Indian Reservation res. ND U.S.A.
Fort Trinquet Maur. see Bîr Mogreïn
187 C11 Fortuna Spain
238 B6 Fortuna CA U.S.A.
236 D1 Fortuna ND U.S.A.
225 K4 Fortune Bay Nfld and Lab. Can.
150 H6 Fortuneswell Dorset, England U.K.
231 F9 Fort Valley GA U.S.A.
222 G3 Fort Vermilion Alta Can.
Fort Victoria Zimbabwe see Masvingo
Fort Walton FL U.S.A. see Fort Walton Beach
231 D10 Fort Walton Beach FL U.S.A.
Fort Ware B.C. Can. see Ware
234 E4 Fort Washington PA U.S.A.
230 E5 Fort Wayne IN U.S.A.
251 G3 Fort Wellington Guyana
96 A3 Fort White Myanmar
146 F9 Fort William Highland, Scotland U.K.
239 J9 Fort Wingate NM U.S.A.
237 G9 Fort Worth TX U.S.A.
236 E2 Fort Yates ND U.S.A.
234 D2 Forty Fort PA U.S.A.
85 J5 Forty Mile Scrub National Park Qld Austr.
Forty-Second Hill S. Africa see 42nd Hill
220 D3 Fort Yukon AK U.S.A.
Forum Iulii France see Fréjus
122 F8 Forūr, Jazīreh-ye i. Iran
140 L4 Forvik Norway
195 I8 Forza d'Agrò Sicilia Italy
163 F10 Fos France

F.Y.R.O.M. to Gaweinstal 315

F.Y.R.O.M. country Europe see Macedonia
198 C4 Fyteies Greece
146 L8 Fyvie Aberdeenshire, Scotland U.K.
247 □7 Fyzabad Trin. and Tob.

G

113 □1 Gaafaru i. N. Male Maldives
113 □1 Gaafaru Atoll N. Male Maldives
113 □1 Gaafaru Channel Maldives
189 B7 Gaâfour Tunisia
179 K5 Gaal Austria
210 E3 Gaalkacyo Somalia
95 J4 Gaat r. Malaysia
214 B3 Gab watercourse Namibia
123 J2 Gabakly Turkm.
183 Q9 Gabaldón Spain
210 E3 Gabangab well Eth.
163 E8 Gabarret France
163 C8 Gabas r. France
Gabasumdo Qinghai China see Tongde
210 F2 Gabbac, Raas pt Somalia
240 O3 Gabbs NV U.S.A.
240 N3 Gabbs Valley Range mts NV U.S.A.
177 G4 Gabčíkovo Slovakia
123 I9 Gabd Pak.
209 B7 Gabela Angola
179 K5 Gaberl pass Austria
Gaberones Botswana see Gaborone
176 E5 Gabersdorf Austria
205 H2 Gabès Tunisia
205 H2 Gabès, Golfe de g. Tunisia
203 G4 Gabgaba, Wadi watercourse Sudan
209 C6 Gabia Dem. Rep. Congo
185 L6 Gabia la Grande Spain
161 C9 Gabian France
191 N8 Gabicce Mare Italy
175 H3 Gąbin Pol.
245 K7 Gabino Barreda Mex.
80 M5 Gable End Foreland hd North I. N.Z.
173 J5 Gablingen Ger.
179 N3 Gablitz Austria
208 A5 Gabon country Africa
208 A4 Gabon, Estuaire du est. Gabon
212 E5 Gaborone Botswana
261 G3 Gaboto Arg.
206 B3 Gabou Senegal
161 B8 Gabriac France
217 □1b Gabriel Island Mauritius
252 D4 Gabriel Vera Bol.
182 H8 Gabriel y Galán, Embalse de resr Spain
244 E6 Gabriel Zamora Mex.
122 H9 Gābrīk Iran
122 H9 Gābrīk watercourse Iran
179 M7 Gabrnik Slovenia
197 L7 Gabrovnitsa Bulg.
197 N8 Gabrovo Bulg.
208 E4 Gabu Dem. Rep. Congo
206 B3 Gabú Guinea-Bissau
210 D1 Gabuli vol. Eth.
190 D4 Gaby Italy
175 K5 Gać Pol.
159 L4 Gacé France
173 K5 Gachenbach Ger.
127 O5 Gach Sār Iran
122 D6 Gachsārān Iran
188 G4 Gacko Bos.-Herz.
129 G5 Gädäbäy Azer.
207 G3 Gadabedji, Réserve Totale de Faune de nature res. Niger
114 D5 Gadag Karnataka India
116 H9 Gadchiroli Mahar. India
140 M4 Gäddede Sweden
108 B2 Gadê Qinghai China
170 D3 Gadebusch Ger.
169 J6 Gadenstedt (Lahstedt) Ger.
191 L2 Gadera r. Italy
Gades Spain see Cádiz
116 C8 Gadhada Gujarat India
116 C9 Gadhada Gujarat India
123 L9 Gadhap Pak.
116 B8 Gadhka Gujarat India
116 C9 Gadhra Gujarat India
129 K5 Gädi Dağı mt. Azer.
217 □3a Gadjou-Lamdjahala depr. Njazidja Comoros
190 E2 Gadmen Switz.
192 C8 Gadoni Sardegna Italy
185 O7 Gádor Spain
185 N7 Gádor, Sierra de mts Spain
177 J5 Gádoros Hungary
123 L8 Gadra Balochistan Pak.
123 N9 Gadra Sindh Pak.
231 D8 Gadsden AL U.S.A.
241 R9 Gadsden AZ U.S.A.
114 E4 Gadwal Andhra Prad. India
Gadyach Ukr. see Hadyach
123 J2 Gadyn Turkm.
208 C3 Gadzi C.A.R.
197 K7 Gadžin Han Serbia
184 A2 Gaeiras Port.
221 P2 Gael Hamke Bugt b. Greenland
150 F4 Gaer Powys, Wales U.K.
197 N6 Găeşti Romania
193 L5 Gaeta Italy
193 L5 Gaeta, Golfo di g. Italy
182 C7 Gafanha da Boa Hora Port.
182 C7 Gafanha da Encarnação Port.
182 C7 Gafanha da Nazaré Port.
182 C7 Gafanha do Carmo Port.
184 C3 Gafanhoeira Port.
Gafaru i. N. Male Maldives see Gaafaru
Gafaru Atoll N. Male Maldives see Gaafaru Atoll
Gafaru Channel Maldives see Gaafaru Channel
91 K5 Gaferut i. Micronesia
184 D2 Gáfete Port.
231 G8 Gaffney SC U.S.A.
205 H2 Gafsa Tunisia
93 F4 Gag i. Papua Indon.
208 B2 Gagal Chad
116 E9 Gagaon Madh. Prad. India
139 S6 Gagarin Rus. Fed.
121 M7 Gagarin Uzbek.
197 Q5 Găgăuzia reg. Moldova
170 D3 Gägelow Ger.
207 G3 Gagere watercourse Nigeria
172 E4 Gaggenau Ger.
195 I8 Gaggi Sicilia Italy
191 J7 Gaggio Montano Italy
190 E4 Gaglianico Italy
194 H8 Gagliano Castelferrato Sicilia Italy
195 O4 Gagliano del Capo Italy
161 E8 Gagnières France
206 D5 Gagnoa Côte d'Ivoire
225 G3 Gagnon Que. Can.
Gago Coutinho Angola see Lumbala N'guimbo
129 B2 Gagra Georgia
129 B2 Gagris K'edi hills Georgia
106 E8 Gahai Qinghai China
212 C6 Gaiab watercourse Namibia
117 L7 Gaibandha Bangl.
197 P4 Găiceana Romania
199 G8 Gaïdouronisi i. Greece
172 F6 Gaienhofen Ger.
178 I6 Gail r. Austria
237 E9 Gail TX U.S.A.
172 H4 Gaildorf Ger.
172 F6 Gailingen Ger.
163 H8 Gaillac France
161 B8 Gaillac-d'Aveyron France
235 J2 Gaillard, Lake CT U.S.A.
Gaillimh Ireland see Galway
156 B5 Gaillon France
178 G6 Gailtaler Alpen mts Austria
173 K4 Gaimersheim Ger.
177 L5 Găina mt. Romania
111 J11 Gaindainqoinkor Xizang China
231 E7 Gainesboro TN U.S.A.
147 H6 Gainestown Ireland
231 F11 Gainesville FL U.S.A.
231 F8 Gainesville GA U.S.A.
237 I7 Gainesville MO U.S.A.
237 G9 Gainesville TX U.S.A.
149 N4 Gainford Durham, England U.K.
149 P7 Gainsborough Lincolnshire, England U.K.
191 K9 Gaiole in Chianti Italy
87 E13 Gairdner r. W.A. Austr.
82 E4 Gairdner, Lake salt flat S.A. Austr.
146 E7 Gairloch Highland, Scotland U.K.
146 E7 Gair Loch b. Scotland U.K.
192 D8 Gairo Sardegna Italy
211 C6 Gairo Tanz.
146 K4 Gairsay i. Scotland U.K.
191 L2 Gais Italy
190 G1 Gais Switz.
179 K4 Gaishorn Austria
173 L6 Gaißach Ger.
172 H7 Gaißau Austria
232 H9 Gaithersburg MD U.S.A.
Gaixian Liaoning China see Gaizhou
107 R6 Gaizhou Liaoning China
138 I5 Gaiziņkalns hill Latvia
177 H4 Gaja r. Hungary
94 D1 Gajah Hutan, Bukit hill Malaysia
102 □G17 Gaja-jima i. Nansei-shotō Japan
183 O7 Gajanejos Spain
115 H3 Gajapatinagaram Andhra Prad. India
123 K8 Gajar Pak.
176 F3 Gajary Slovakia
207 H4 Gaji r. Nigeria
207 I3 Gajiram Nigeria
117 L7 Gajol W. Bengal India
214 H3 Gakarosa mt. S. Africa
207 H5 Gakem Nigeria
177 I6 Gakovo Vojvodina Serbia
116 D1 Gakuch Jammu and Kashmir
111 I12 Gala Xizang China
Galaasiya Uzbek. see Galaosiyo
111 I12 Gala Co l. China
175 L1 Gaładuś, Jezioro l. Pol.
176 G5 Galambok Hungary
163 E9 Galan France
258 D2 Galán, Cerro mt. Arg.
211 D5 Galana r. Kenya
122 F3 Galand Iran
197 N3 Gălăneşti Romania
94 F4 Galang Besar i. Indon.
209 C8 Galangue Angola
140 Q2 Gálaniitu Norway
177 G3 Galanta Slovakia
120 K8 Galaosiyo Uzbek.
183 M7 Galapagar Spain
250 □ Galápagos, Islas is Pacific Ocean
Galapagos Islands is Pacific Ocean see Galápagos, Islas
267 M6 Galapagos Rise sea feature Pacific Ocean
184 F5 Galaroza Spain
210 C4 Galas well Kenya
146 K11 Galashiels Scottish Borders, Scotland U.K.
197 P7 Galata Bulg.
80 K5 Galatea North I. N.Z.
197 Q5 Galaţi Romania
195 O3 Galatina Italy
198 C2 Galatini Greece
198 E2 Galatista Greece
195 O3 Galatone Italy
187 K8 Galatzó, Puig de mt. Spain
149 L2 Gala Water r. Scotland U.K.
232 E12 Galax VA U.S.A.
198 D4 Galaxidi Greece
Galaymor Turkm. see Galaýmor
123 J4 Galaýmor Turkm.
147 F8 Galbally Ireland
183 P3 Galbarra Spain
85 H4 Galbraith Qld Austr.
216 □3f Gáldar Gran Canaria Canary Is
141 J6 Galdhøpiggen mt. Norway
206 C3 Galé Mali
183 N2 Galea, Punta pt Spain
242 F2 Galeana Chihuahua Mex.
243 I5 Galeana Nuevo León Mex.
191 L8 Galeata Italy
203 G6 Galegu Sudan
122 E8 Galeh Dār Iran
93 E3 Galela Halmahera Indon.
220 C3 Galena AK U.S.A.
236 J4 Galena IL U.S.A.
237 H7 Galena KS U.S.A.
234 D6 Galena MD U.S.A.
237 I7 Galena MO U.S.A.
222 G5 Galena Bay B.C. Can.
170 I3 Galenbecker See l. Ger.
182 G4 Galende Spain
247 □7 Galeota Point Trin. and Tob.
185 N5 Galera Spain
185 N5 Galera r. Spain
259 B6 Galera, Punta pt Chile
250 A4 Galera, Punta pt Ecuador
245 J10 Galera, Punta pt Mex.
247 □7 Galera Point Trin. and Tob.
192 B3 Galéria Corse France
192 A3 Galéria, Golfe de b. Corse France
236 J5 Galesburg IL U.S.A.
226 I7 Galesburg MI U.S.A.
235 K2 Gales Ferry CT U.S.A.
215 I4 Galeshewe S. Africa
226 C5 Galesville WI U.S.A.
232 H7 Galeton PA U.S.A.
217 □1c Galets, Pointe des pt Réunion
217 □1c Galets, Rivière des r. Réunion
174 G4 Galewice Pol.
147 C8 Galey r. Ireland
177 I4 Galga r. Hungary
177 I4 Galgagyörk Hungary
177 I4 Galgamácsa Hungary
162 D6 Galgon France
210 E3 Galguduud admin. reg. Somalia
210 E3 Gal Hareeri Somalia
129 C3 Gali Georgia
256 C5 Gália Brazil
222 F5 Galiano Island B.C. Can.
161 I6 Galibier, Col du pass France
197 L6 Galicea Mare Romania
134 H4 Galich Rus. Fed.
134 H4 Galichskaya Vozvyshennost' hills Rus. Fed.
182 E3 Galicia aut. comm. Spain
196 I9 Galičica nat. park Macedonia
129 C3 Galidzga r. Georgia
85 J7 Galilee, Lake salt flat Qld Austr.
Galilee, Sea of l. Israel see Kinneret, Yam
257 G3 Galiléia Brazil
190 I8 Galileo airport Italy
207 I5 Galim Tignère Cameroon
178 A5 Galinakopf mt. Austria/Liechtenstein
246 □ Galina Point Jamaica
244 G5 Galindo Mex.
182 C4 Galiñeiro hill Spain
175 I1 Galiny Pol.
232 C8 Galion OH U.S.A.
247 □3 Galion, Baie du b. Martinique
198 F5 Galissas Syros Greece
182 H9 Galisteo Spain
205 H1 Galite, Canal de la sea chan. Tunisia
139 U8 Galitsa Rus. Fed.
241 V9 Galiuro Mountains AZ U.S.A.
84 E2 Galiwinku N.T. Austr.
123 J2 Galkynyş Turkm.
203 H6 Gallabat Sudan
121 L7 G'allaorol Uzbek.
190 F4 Gallarate Italy
156 C6 Gallardon France
161 E9 Gallargues-le-Montueux France
236 I6 Gallatin MO U.S.A.
231 D7 Gallatin TN U.S.A.
238 I4 Gallatin r. MT U.S.A.
114 G9 Galle Sri Lanka
186 D4 Gállego r. Spain
185 N6 Gallegón r. Spain
267 L6 Gallego Rise sea feature Pacific Ocean
259 C8 Gallegos r. Arg.
259 B7 Gallegos, Cabo c. Chile
182 G7 Gallegos de Argañan Spain
183 J7 Gallegos de Solmirón Spain
191 J8 Galleno Italy
193 I3 Gallese Italy
147 E9 Galley Head Ireland
Gallia country Europe see France
162 C5 Gallian-en-Médoc France
190 F5 Galliate Italy
193 J4 Gallicano nel Lazio Italy
170 F3 Gallin Mecklenburg-Vorpommern Ger.
168 K3 Gallin Mecklenburg-Vorpommern Ger.
250 D1 Gallinas, Punta pt Col.
191 L4 Gallio Italy
195 O3 Gallipoli Italy
Gallipoli Turkey see Gelibolu
232 C10 Gallipolis OH U.S.A.
186 E6 Gallipuén, Embalse de resr Spain
140 P3 Gällivare Sweden
179 K6 Gallizien Austria
179 J3 Gallneukirchen Austria
183 P7 Gallo r. Spain
140 M5 Gällö Sweden
194 E7 Gallo, Capo c. Sicilia Italy
190 I2 Gallo, Lago di l. Italy
183 Q7 Gallocanta, Laguna de l. Spain
232 I5 Gallo Island NY U.S.A.
193 L5 Galluccio Italy
232 C10 Gallup KY U.S.A.
239 J9 Gallup NM U.S.A.
183 R5 Gallur Spain
192 B6 Gallura reg. Sardegna Italy
207 G4 Galma watercourse Nigeria
146 D9 Galmisdale Highland, Scotland U.K.
148 B8 Galmoy Ireland
Galne Chechenskaya Respublika Rus. Fed. see Ken'yurt
Galne Chechenskaya Respublika Rus. Fed. see Kalinovskaya
83 L6 Galong N.S.W. Austr.
114 G8 Galoya Sri Lanka
114 G9 Gal Oya National Park Sri Lanka
147 G6 Galros Ireland
210 E2 Gal Shiikh Somalia
175 L1 Galstas l. Lith.
146 H11 Galston East Ayrshire, Scotland U.K.
240 K3 Galt CA U.S.A.
210 E4 Gal Tardo Somalia
204 B4 Galtat Zemmour Western Sahara
147 F8 Galtee Mountains hills Ireland
192 D7 Galtelli Sardegna Italy
143 M2 Galten l. Sweden
178 B6 Galtür Austria
147 F8 Galtymore hill Ireland
122 F7 Galūgāh, Kūh-e mts Iran
122 H4 Galūgāh-e Āsīyeh Iran
211 B7 Galula Tanz.
226 D8 Galva IL U.S.A.
260 A6 Galvarino Chile
186 D6 Galve Spain
183 N6 Galve de Sorbe Spain
184 D2 Galveias Port.
226 H9 Galveston IN U.S.A.
237 H11 Galveston TX U.S.A.
237 H11 Galveston Bay TX U.S.A.
261 G3 Galvez Arg.
183 L9 Gálvez Spain
116 H5 Galwa Nepal
147 D6 Galway Ireland
147 D6 Galway county Ireland
147 D6 Galway Bay Ireland
247 □2 Galways Soufrière vol. Montserrat
93 F4 Gam i. Papua Indon.
93 G4 Gam i. Papua Indon.
96 G4 Gâm, Sông r. Vietnam
256 C2 Gamá Brazil
259 E6 Gama, Isla i. Arg.
156 C4 Gamaches France
104 F6 Gamagōri Japan
215 O6 Gamalakhe S. Africa
93 E3 Gamalama vol. Maluku Indon.
163 C8 Gamarde-les-Bains France
250 C2 Gamarra Col.
Gámas Fin. see Kaamanen
177 G5 Gamás Hungary
207 H3 Gamawa Nigeria
260 E5 Gamay Arg.
92 E5 Gamay Bay Samar Phil.
209 C7 Gamba Angola
Gamba Xizang China see Gongbalou
208 A5 Gamba Gabon
206 E4 Gambaga Ghana
190 I5 Gambara Italy
195 J7 Gambarie Italy
191 J8 Gambassi Terme Italy
193 N4 Gambatesa Italy
210 B2 Gambēla Eth.
210 B3 Gambēla Hizboch admin. reg. Eth.
210 B3 Gambēla National Park Eth.
220 A3 Gambell AK U.S.A.
234 B6 Gamber MD U.S.A.
191 M7 Gambettola Italy
Gambia country Africa see The Gambia
206 A3 Gambia r. Gambia
206 B3 Gambie r. Senegal
84 C1 Gambier, Cape N.T. Austr.
Gambier, Île i. Arch. des Tuamotu Fr. Polynesia see Mangareva
79 □9 Gambier, Îles is Arch. des Tuamotu Fr. Polynesia
82 F6 Gambier Islands S.A. Austr.
Gambier Islands Arch. des Tuamotu Fr. Polynesia see Gambier, Îles
231 □2 Gambier Village New Prov. Bahamas
225 K3 Gambo Nfld and Lab. Can.
208 D3 Gambo C.A.R.
190 F5 Gambolò Italy
208 B5 Gamboma Congo
85 I4 Gamboola Qld Austr.
208 B3 Gamboula C.A.R.
234 B6 Gambrills MD U.S.A.
157 O6 Gambsheim France
Gamda Sichuan China see Zamtang
Gameti N.W.T. Can. see Rae Lakes
179 L4 Gaming Austria
129 H5 Gamış Dağı mt. Azer.
214 F9 Gamka r. S. Africa
93 E3 Gamkunoro, Gunung vol. Halmahera Indon.
Gamlakarleby Fin. see Kokkola
143 M4 Gamleby Sweden
151 L3 Gamlingay Cambridgeshire, England U.K.
179 M6 Gamlitz Austria
203 G5 Gammams well Sudan
173 L4 Gammelsdorf Ger.
140 Q4 Gammelstaden Sweden
172 G5 Gammertingen Ger.
82 G4 Gammon Ranges National Park S.A. Austr.
104 D5 Gamō Japan
214 C5 Gamoep S. Africa
182 I2 Gamonal mt. Spain
100 G7 Gamova, Mys pt Rus. Fed.
114 G9 Gampaha Sri Lanka
114 G9 Gampola Sri Lanka
190 G1 Gams Switz.
123 I7 Gamshadzai Kūh mts Iran
108 B3 Gamtog Xizang China
215 J9 Gamtoos r. S. Africa
210 C3 Gamud mt. Eth.
140 T1 Gamvik Norway
163 D9 Gan France
113 □2 Gan Addu Atoll Maldives
113 □2 Gan i. Addu Atoll Maldives
108 C2 Gana Sichuan China
241 W6 Ganado AZ U.S.A.
161 H8 Ganagobie France
203 G5 Gananita Sudan
224 E4 Gananoque Ont. Can.
129 H5 Gäncä Azer.
129 H5 Gäncäçay r. Azer.
110 I6 Gancaohu Xinjiang China
108 G9 Gancheng Hainan China
Gand Belgium see Gent
209 B8 Ganda Angola
111 L11 Ganda Xizang China
93 A5 Gandadiwata, Bukit mt. Indon.
116 H9 Gandai Chhattisgarh India
209 D6 Gandajika Dem. Rep. Congo
117 I6 Gandak Barrage dam Nepal
123 I5 Gandalak Afgh.
116 E2 Gandarbal Jammu and Kashmir
182 D6 Gandarela Port.
123 M7 Gandari Mountain Pak.
123 I5 Gandarra Afgh.
123 L7 Gandava Pak.
190 H4 Gandellino Italy
225 K3 Gander Nfld and Lab. Can.
221 M5 Gander r. Nfld and Lab. Can.
168 G4 Ganderkesee Ger.
225 K3 Gander Lake Nfld and Lab. Can.
186 F5 Gandesa Spain
116 D9 Gandevi Gujarat India
116 C8 Gandhidham Gujarat India
116 D8 Gandhinagar Gujarat India
116 E7 Gandhi Sagar resr India
208 E2 Gandi, Wadi watercourse Sudan
187 E10 Gandía Spain
190 H4 Gandino Italy
216 □3f Gando, Punta de pt Gran Canaria Canary Is
122 D6 Gandomān Iran
129 J4 Gändov Azer.
182 C4 Gandra Viana do Castelo Port.
182 D5 Gandra Viana do Castelo Port.
254 F5 Gandu Brazil
106 H9 Gandu Qinghai China
140 T1 Gandvik Norway
Gandzha Azer. see Gäncä
206 C2 Gâneb well Maur.
182 C4 Ganfei Port.
117 L7 Ganga r. India alt. Padma (Bangladesh), conv. Ganges
207 G4 Ganga Nigeria
114 G9 Ganga r. Sri Lanka
Ganga Cone sea feature Indian Ocean see Ganges Cone
114 E3 Gangakher Mahar. India
208 F4 Gangala Na Bodia Dem. Rep. Congo
259 C6 Gangán Arg.
259 C6 Gangán, Pampa de plain Arg.
116 D5 Ganganagar Rajasthan India
114 D3 Gangapur Mahar. India
116 E7 Gangapur Rajasthan India
116 F6 Gangapur Rajasthan India
207 H3 Gangara Niger
117 L9 Ganga Sagar W. Bengal India
116 C7 Ganga Sera Rajasthan India
114 D5 Gangavali r. India
96 B3 Gangaw Myanmar
114 E5 Gangawati Karnataka India
96 C3 Gangaw Range mts Myanmar
106 G8 Gangca Qinghai China
116 E8 Gangdhar Rajasthan India
111 F11 Gangdisê Shan mts Xizang China
117 L8 Ganges r. Bangl./India alt. Ganga (India), alt. Padma (Bangladesh)
161 D9 Ganges France
117 L9 Ganges, Mouths of the Bangl./India
265 J3 Ganges Cone sea feature Indian Ocean
194 G8 Gangi Sicilia Italy
194 G8 Gangi r. Sicilia Italy
173 N5 Gangkofen Ger.
206 C5 Ganglota Liberia
106 E7 Gangou Qinghai China
106 I9 Gangouyi Gansu China
Gangra Turkey see Çankırı
116 E7 Gangrar Rajasthan India
117 L6 Gangtok Sikkim India
106 I9 Gangu Gansu China
107 N8 Gangziyao Hebei China
107 S2 Gan He r. China
110 I4 Ganhezi Xinjiang China
93 F4 Gani Halmahera Indon.
206 C4 Ganiakali Guinea
115 I3 Ganjam Orissa India
122 D6 Ganjgūn Iran
109 K4 Gan Jiang r. China
107 R5 Ganjig Nei Mongol China
107 L9 Ganjing Shaanxi China
107 N4 Ganjur Sum Nei Mongol China
139 Q2 Gankovo Rus. Fed.
108 D4 Ganluo Sichuan China
107 R3 Gannan Heilong. China
160 C4 Gannat France
225 J2 Gannet Islands Ecological Reserve nature res. Nfld and Lab. Can.
238 J5 Gannett Peak WY U.S.A.
136 F3 Gannopil' Ukr.
236 F3 Gannvalley SD U.S.A.
111 K8 Ganq Qinghai China
107 K8 Ganquan Shaanxi China
214 D10 Gansbaai S. Africa
169 D10 Gänsehals hill Ger.
179 O3 Gänserndorf Austria
165 F7 Ganshoren Belgium
108 F4 Ganshui Chongqing China
106 E6 Gansu prov. China
210 D4 Gantamaa Somalia
106 I8 Gantang Nei Mongol China
117 I9 Gantapara Orissa India
86 G4 Gantheaume Point W.A. Austr.
129 B2 Gant'iadi Ap'khazet'i Georgia
129 F4 Gant'iadi Georgia
Ganting Shaanxi China see Huxian
190 C2 Gantrisch mt. Switz.
Gantsevichi Belarus see Hantsavichy
95 H6 Gantung Indon.
109 J6 Ganxian Jiangxi China
116 F8 Ganyal r. Madh. Prad. India
207 I4 Ganye Nigeria
214 I2 Ganyesa S. Africa
107 P9 Ganyu Jiangsu China
120 C4 Ganyushkino Kazakh.
Ganzhe Fujian China see Minhou
109 J6 Ganzhou Jiangxi China
210 A3 Ganzi Sudan
170 F4 Ganzlin Ger.
207 E2 Gao Mali
207 F2 Gao admin. reg. Mali
109 J4 Gao'an Jiangxi China
106 H8 Gaoba Gansu China
107 N7 Gaocheng Hebei China
Gaocheng Sichuan China see Litang
109 L3 Gaochun Jiangsu China
Gaocun Hunan China see Mayang
109 M4 Gaojian Zhejiang China
106 H8 Gaolan Gansu China
Gaoleshan Hubei China see Xianfeng
Gaoliangjian Jiangsu China see Hongze
108 B6 Gaoligong Shan mts China
107 K9 Gaoling Shaanxi China
107 P8 Gaomi Shandong China
109 H5 Gaomutang Hunan China
107 M9 Gaoping Shanxi China
107 O8 Gaoqing Shandong China
106 F7 Gaotai Gansu China
107 O8 Gaotang Shandong China
Gaotangling Hunan China see Wangcheng
Gaoting Zhejiang China see Daishan
107 K7 Gaotouyao Nei Mongol China
206 E4 Gaoua Burkina
206 B4 Gaoual Guinea
Gaoxian Sichuan China see Wenjiang
Gaoxiong Taiwan see Kaohsiung
107 N7 Gaoyang Hebei China
109 I7 Gaoyao Guangdong China
107 N8 Gaoyi Hebei China
109 L2 Gaoyou Jiangsu China
109 L2 Gaoyou Hu l. China
108 H8 Gaozhou Guangdong China
161 I7 Gap France
234 C5 Gap PA U.S.A.
80 □ Gap, Point Chatham Is S. Pacific Ocean
92 C4 Gapan Luzon Phil.
161 I10 Gapeau r. France
208 E3 Gapi Dem. Rep. Congo
84 E2 Gapuwiyak N.T. Austr.
111 F12 Gaqoi Xizang China
117 K5 Gaqung Xizang China
98 D5 Gar Xizang China
123 J8 Gar Pak.
100 F2 Gar' r. Rus. Fed.
177 I5 Gara Hungary
147 F5 Gara, Lough l. Ireland
205 H3 Garaa Tebourt well Tunisia
187 C8 Garaballa Spain
123 K2 Garabekewül Turkm.
123 J3 Garabil Belentligi hills Turkm.
208 B4 Garabinzam Congo
161 C7 Garabit, Viaduc de France
122 E1 Garabogaz Turkm.
122 E1 Garabogazköl Turkm.
122 E1 Garabogazköl Aýlagy b. Turkm.
Garabogazköl Aylagy b. Turkm. see Garabogazköl Aýlagy
122 E1 Garabogazköl Bogazy sea chan. Turkm.
210 F3 Garacad Somalia
216 □3a Garachico Tenerife Canary Is
242 □T13 Garachiné Panama
242 □T13 Garachiné, Punta pt Panama
210 E2 Garadag Somalia
148 D7 Garadice Ireland
147 G4 Garadice Lough l. Ireland
205 G6 Gara Ekar hill Alg.
216 □3d Garafía La Palma Canary Is
183 P2 Garagarza Spain
122 I6 Garāgheh Iran
250 C3 Garagoa Col.
122 E2 Garagöl Turkm.
Garagum des. Kazakh. see Karakum, Peski
122 I2 Garagum des. Turkm.
123 I3 Garagum Kanaly canal Turkm.
193 Q6 Garaguso Italy
83 L3 Garah N.S.W. Austr.
123 O4 Garai Pak.
216 □3a Garajonay, Parque Nacional de nat. park La Gomera Canary Is
206 D4 Garalo Mali
Garamätnyyaz Turkm. see Garamätnyýaz
123 K3 Garamätnyýaz Turkm.
208 F4 Garamba r. Dem. Rep. Congo
208 F3 Garamba, Parc National de la nat. park Dem. Rep. Congo
106 G8 Garang Qinghai China
254 F4 Garanhuns Brazil
215 L1 Ga-Rankuwa S. Africa
254 B5 Garapu Brazil
256 D2 Garapuava Brazil
208 D2 Garar, Plaine de plain Chad
116 G7 Garautha Uttar Prad. India
161 G8 Garaux, Rocher mt. France
84 F4 Garawa Aboriginal Land res. N.T. Austr.
208 D2 Garba C.A.R.
210 D4 Garbahaarrey Somalia
175 J4 Garbatka-Letnisko Pol.
210 C4 Garba Tula Kenya
185 J2 Garbayuela Spain
240 I1 Garberville CA U.S.A.
122 D5 Garbosh, Kūh-e mt. Iran
197 O5 Gârbova, Vârful hill Romania
175 K4 Garbów Pol.
169 I6 Garbsen Ger.
116 H4 Garbyang Uttaranchal India
256 C5 Garça Brazil
256 A1 Garças, Rio das r. Brazil
197 P4 Gârceni Romania
173 N5 Garching an der Alz Ger.
173 L5 Garching bei München Ger.
160 C2 Garchizy France
186 G5 Garcia Spain
244 D5 García, Cerro mt. Mex.
244 D4 Garcia de la Cadena Mex.
256 A4 Garcias Brazil
185 I2 Garcia Sola, Embalse de resr Spain
184 H2 Garciaz Spain
183 J7 Garcihernández Spain
183 L7 Garcillán Spain
197 O4 Gârcina Romania
183 O8 Garcinarro Spain
161 E8 Gard dept France
161 F9 Gard r. France
191 J4 Garda Italy
191 J5 Garda, Lago di l. Italy
129 G4 Gardabani Georgia
197 K4 Gârda de Sus Romania
161 G10 Gardanne France
189 A7 Garde, Cap de c. Alg.
174 G2 Gardeja Pol.
223 J2 Garde Lake N.W.T. Can.
170 D5 Gardelegen Ger.
191 L2 Gardena r. Italy
236 E7 Garden City KS U.S.A.
235 H3 Garden City NY U.S.A.
237 E10 Garden City TX U.S.A.
226 H4 Garden Corners MI U.S.A.
240 O8 Garden Grove CA U.S.A.
223 M4 Garden Hill Man. Can.
87 C12 Garden Island W.A. Austr.
226 I4 Garden Island MI U.S.A.
232 D11 Garden Mountain VA U.S.A.
234 A2 Garden View PA U.S.A.
164 I4 Garderen Neth.
142 G1 Gardermoen airport Norway
261 H5 Gardey Arg.
123 M5 Gardēz Afgh.
Gardinas Belarus see Hrodna
233 □P4 Gardiner ME U.S.A.
238 I4 Gardiner MT U.S.A.
84 D7 Gardiner, Mount N.T. Austr.
84 B5 Gardiner Range hills N.T. Austr.
235 K2 Gardiners Bay NY U.S.A.
235 K2 Gardiners Island NY U.S.A.
84 D7 Gardiner's Range mts N.T. Austr.
168 G2 Garding Ger.
Gardner atoll Micronesia see Faraulep
226 F8 Gardner IL U.S.A.
233 N6 Gardner MA U.S.A.
262 T1 Gardner Inlet Antarctica
Gardner Island atoll Phoenix Is Kiribati see Nikumaroro
235 K1 Gardner Lake CT U.S.A.
233 □R4 Gardner Lake ME U.S.A.
75 H2 Gardner Pinnacles is HI U.S.A.
240 M3 Gardnerville NV U.S.A.
143 N7 Gardno, Jezioro lag. Pol.
161 E8 Gardon d'Alès r. France
161 D8 Gardon de St-Jean r. France
191 J4 Gardone Riviera Italy
190 I4 Gardone Val Trompia Italy
163 E6 Gardonne France
177 H4 Gárdony Hungary
163 H9 Gardouch France
140 N4 Gardsjönås Sweden
143 M5 Gärdslösa Öland Sweden
Gáregasnjárga Fin. see Karigasniemi
163 C7 Garein France
148 H1 Gare Loch inlet Scotland U.K.
146 G10 Garelochhead Argyll and Bute, Scotland U.K.
Gares Spain see Puente la Reina
188 F3 Garešnica Croatia
190 E7 Garessio Italy
78 □5 Garet, Mount vol. Vanuatu
205 G4 Garet El Djenoun mt. Alg.
251 H3 Gare Tigre Fr. Guiana
239 K7 Garfield CO U.S.A.
235 G3 Garfield NJ U.S.A.
149 O6 Garforth West Yorkshire, England U.K.
193 Q8 Garga r. Italy
198 C5 Gargalianoi Greece
184 H2 Gargáligas Spain
185 H2 Gargáligas r. Spain
186 D6 Gargallo Spain
162 H4 Gargan, Mont hill France
193 P4 Gargano, Parco Nazionale del nat. park Italy
182 I8 Garganta la Olla Spain
224 C4 Gargantua, Cape Ont. Can.
127 N8 Gargar Iran
161 G9 Gargas France
191 K2 Gargazzone Italy
178 A6 Gargellen Austria
156 D6 Garges-lès-Gonesse France
162 H2 Gargilesse-Dampierre France
191 J4 Gargnano Italy
161 D8 Gargo mt. France
149 M6 Gargrave North Yorkshire, England U.K.
146 H10 Gargunnock Hills Scotland U.K.
Gargunsa Xizang China see Gar
138 E6 Gargždai Lith.
116 G8 Garhakota Madh. Prad. India
117 K8 Garhbeta W. Bengal India
116 G8 Garhi Madh. Prad. India
116 E8 Garhi Rajasthan India
123 L7 Garhi Khairo Pak.
116 G7 Garhi Malehra Madh. Prad. India
116 G5 Garhmuktesar Uttar Prad. India
116 F4 Garhshankar Punjab India
117 I7 Garhwa Jharkhand India
193 L5 Gari r. Italy
255 C9 Garibaldi Brazil
222 F5 Garibaldi B.C. Can.
222 F5 Garibaldi, Mount B.C. Can.
222 F5 Garibaldi Provincial Park B.C. Can.
215 J6 Gariep Dam resr S. Africa
215 J6 Gariep Dam Nature Reserve S. Africa
214 B6 Garies S. Africa
193 L5 Garigliano r. Italy
183 Q3 Garínoain Spain
210 C5 Garissa Kenya
138 H4 Garkalne Latvia
111 H10 Garkung Caka l. Xizang China
Gârla Mare r. Moldova see Gîrla Mare
237 G9 Garland TX U.S.A.
190 F5 Garlasco Italy
179 K4 Garlenz Austria
138 G7 Garliava Lith.
197 Q6 Gârliciu Romania
146 H13 Garlieston Dumfries and Galloway, Scotland U.K.
163 D8 Garlin France
185 I3 Garlitos Spain
147 I5 Garlowcross Ireland
168 J4 Garlstorf Ger.
Garm Tajik. see Gharm
123 K5 Garmab Afgh.
122 G4 Garmab Iran
122 H5 Garm Ab, Chashmeh-ye spring Iran
122 C6 Garmdasht Iran
122 F5 Garmeh Eşfahān Iran
122 G3 Garmeh Khorāsān Iran
122 C2 Garmī Iran
173 K7 Garmisch-Partenkirchen Ger.
146 E10 Garmony Argyll and Bute, Scotland U.K.
122 E7 Garmosht Iran
122 E4 Garmsar Iran
123 J6 Garmsel reg. Afgh.
123 J6 Garmushki Afgh.
236 I4 Garner IA U.S.A.
232 C11 Garner KY U.S.A.
236 H6 Garnett KS U.S.A.
147 B9 Garnish Ireland
122 H7 Gārnow Iran
83 I5 Garnpung Lake imp. l. N.S.W. Austr.
117 M7 Garo Hills Meghalaya India
186 G2 Garona r. Spain
163 C6 Garonne r. France
163 E7 Garonne, Canal latéral à la France
161 E9 Garons France
210 F2 Garoowe Somalia
255 C9 Garopaba Brazil
116 E7 Garoth Madh. Prad. India
206 E2 Garou, Lac l. Mali
207 I4 Garoua Cameroon
207 I5 Garoua Boulai Cameroon
143 K2 Garphyttan Sweden
143 K2 Garphyttans nationalpark nat. park Sweden
111 K10 Gar Qu r. Qinghai China
111 K10 Garqu Yan Qinghai China
182 I3 Garrafe de Torio Spain
163 B10 Garralda Spain
147 D9 Garrane Ireland
183 P5 Garray Spain
261 F5 Garré Arg.
168 F5 Garrel Ger.
92 □ Garreru i. Palau
226 I8 Garrett IN U.S.A.
161 D9 Garrigues reg. France
147 F4 Garrison Northern Ireland U.K.
232 B10 Garrison KY U.S.A.
236 I2 Garrison MN U.S.A.
236 E2 Garrison ND U.S.A.
235 H2 Garrison NY U.S.A.
147 J5 Garristown Ireland
129 E4 Garnarrich Armenia
245 L7 Garro Mex.
147 K2 Garron Point Northern Ireland U.K.
182 G9 Garrovillas Spain
185 P6 Garrucha Spain
186 D6 Garrucha, Sierra de la mts Spain
123 K7 Garruk Pak.
146 G8 Garry r. Scotland U.K.
146 G8 Garry, Loch l. Highland, Scotland U.K.
122 I3 Garryçyrla Turkm.
221 H3 Garry Lake Nunavut Can.
146 C6 Garrynahine Western Isles, Scotland U.K.
215 L7 Garryowen S. Africa
147 F9 Garryvoe Ireland
173 M5 Gars am Inn Ger.
179 M2 Gars am Kamp Austria
149 M5 Garsdale Head Cumbria, England U.K.
211 D5 Garsen Kenya
Garshy Turkm. see Garşy
202 D6 Garsila Sudan
143 K6 Gärsnäs Sweden
149 L6 Garstang Lancashire, England U.K.
168 J4 Garstedt Ger.
179 J3 Garsten Austria
81 C12 Garston South I. N.Z.
122 E1 Garşy Turkm.
Gartar Sichuan China see Qianning
162 F2 Gartempe r. France
150 E3 Garth Powys, Wales U.K.
150 F2 Garthmyl Powys, Wales U.K.
146 G10 Gartocharn West Dunbartonshire, Scotland U.K.
Gartog Xizang China see Markam
Gartok Xizang China see Garyarsa
170 D4 Gartow Ger.
172 F4 Gärtringen Ger.
170 J4 Gartz Ger.
212 C5 Garub Namibia
92 □ Garusuun Palau
95 G8 Garut Jawa Indon.
147 G5 Garvagh Ireland
147 I3 Garvagh Northern Ireland U.K.
147 H4 Garvaghy Northern Ireland U.K.
146 K11 Garvald East Lothian, Scotland U.K.
146 H8 Garvamore Highland, Scotland U.K.
184 C5 Garvão Port.
146 D10 Garvard Argyll and Bute, Scotland U.K.
146 G7 Garve Highland, Scotland U.K.
81 C12 Garvie Mountains South I. N.Z.
175 J4 Garwolin Pol.
111 E10 Gar Xincun Xizang China
230 D5 Gary IN U.S.A.
232 D11 Gary WV U.S.A.
111 E11 Garyarsa Xizang China
108 B3 Garyi Sichuan China
103 J12 Garyū-zan mt. Japan
170 H2 Garz Ger.
258 E3 Garza Arg.
111 D10 Gar Zangbo r. China
245 H1 Garza Valdez Mex.
108 B3 Garzê Sichuan China
250 C4 Garzón Col.
Gasan-Kuli Turkm. see Esenguly
174 F3 Gąsawa Pol.
178 B6 Gaschurn Austria
171 F8 Gaschwitz Ger.
163 C8 Gascogne reg. France
154 C5 Gascogne, Golfe de g. France/Spain
236 J6 Gasconade r. MO U.S.A.
Gascony reg. France see Gascogne
Gascony, Gulf of France/Spain see Gascogne, Golfe de
87 C8 Gascoyne r. W.A. Austr.
87 D8 Gascoyne, Mount hill W.A. Austr.
87 C8 Gascoyne Junction W.A. Austr.
183 O8 Gascueña Spain
Gascuña, Golfo de g. France/Spain see Gascogne, Golfe de
111 H11 Gase Xizang China
113 □1 Gasfinolhu i. N. Male Maldives
124 C8 Gash and Setit prov. Eritrea
116 F2 Gasherbrum I mt. Jammu and Kashmir
123 Q4 Gasherbrum II mt. China/Jammu and Kashmir
203 H6 Gash Setit Wildlife Reserve nature res. Eritrea
123 I8 Gasht Iran
111 J7 Gas Hu salt l. China
207 H3 Gashua Nigeria
146 B7 Gasker i. Scotland U.K.
175 K2 Gąski Pol.
156 C5 Gasny France
175 I3 Gąsocin Pol.
246 D3 Gaspar Cuba
94 G6 Gaspar, Selat sea chan. Indon.
225 H3 Gaspé Que. Can.
225 H3 Gaspé, Baie de b. Que. Can.
225 H3 Gaspé, Cap c. Que. Can.
225 H3 Gaspé, Péninsule de pen. Que. Can.
195 L6 Gasperina Italy
179 I3 Gaspoltshofen Austria
206 E3 Gassan Burkina
102 R8 Gassan vol. Japan
206 B3 Gassane Senegal
232 E10 Gassaway WV U.S.A.
164 K3 Gasselte Neth.
164 K3 Gasselternijveen Neth.
185 L2 Gasset, Embalse de resr Spain
161 J10 Gassin France
207 H4 Gassol Nigeria
241 Q5 Gass Peak NV U.S.A.
178 H5 Gasteiner Tal val. Austria
Gasteiz Spain see Vitoria-Gasteiz
100 M4 Gastello Sakhalin Rus. Fed.
179 L2 Gastern Austria
163 B7 Gastes France
232 H12 Gaston NC U.S.A.
232 H12 Gaston, Lake NC U.S.A.
231 G8 Gastonia NC U.S.A.
198 C5 Gastouni Greece
259 C6 Gastre Arg.
182 G8 Gata Spain
185 O7 Gata, Cabo de c. Spain
128 B4 Gata, Cape Cyprus
182 G8 Gata, Sierra de mts Spain
187 F10 Gata de Gorgos Spain
222 E3 Gataga r. B.C. Can.
196 J5 Gătaia Romania
Gatas, Akra c. Cyprus see Gata, Cape
139 N2 Gatchina Rus. Fed.
232 C12 Gate City VA U.S.A.
146 H13 Gatehouse of Fleet Dumfries and Galloway, Scotland U.K.
177 I5 Gátér Hungary
171 D7 Gatersleben Ger.
149 N4 Gateshead Tyne and Wear, England U.K.
221 H2 Gateshead Island Nunavut Can.
220 C3 Gates of the Arctic National Park and Preserve AK U.S.A.
231 I7 Gatesville NC U.S.A.
237 G10 Gatesville TX U.S.A.
241 X3 Gateway CO U.S.A.
235 G4 Gateway National Recreational Area park NJ U.S.A.
252 C5 Gatico Chile
156 E7 Gâtinais reg. France
159 L7 Gâtine reg. France
224 F4 Gatineau Que. Can.
224 F4 Gatineau r. Que. Can.
185 J4 Gato r. Spain
Gatong Xizang China see Jomda
Gatooma Zimbabwe see Kadoma
187 D8 Gátova Spain
179 O3 Gattendorf Austria
191 M7 Gatteo a Mare Italy
161 K9 Gattières France
190 E4 Gattinara Italy
85 N9 Gatton Qld Austr.
250 B2 Gatún Panama
242 □S13 Gatún, Lago l. Panama
122 C5 Gatvand Iran
79 □7 Gau i. Fiji
172 E2 Gau-Algesheim Ger.
254 B5 Gaúcha do Norte Brazil
156 F4 Gauchy France
185 I7 Gaucín Spain
185 J7 Gaudalteba, Embalse de resr Spain
223 L3 Gauer Lake Man. Can.
Gauhati Assam India see Guwahati
138 H4 Gauja r. Latvia
138 I7 Gauja r. Lith.
138 I4 Gaujas nacionālais parks nat. park Latvia
172 H2 Gaukönigshofen Ger.
Gaul country Europe see France
184 □ Gaula Madeira
140 K5 Gaula r. Norway
232 D10 Gauley Bridge WV U.S.A.
165 I9 Gaume reg. Belgium
172 E2 Gau-Odernheim Ger.
141 I6 Gaupne Norway
Gaurdak Turkm. see Gowurdak
114 E6 Gauribidanur Karnataka India
117 M8 Gaurnadi Bangl.
142 E2 Gausta mt. Norway
215 M2 Gauteng prov. S. Africa
173 K5 Gauting Ger.
186 E4 Gautizalema r. Spain
123 K4 Gauzan Afgh.
186 J5 Gavà Spain
127 P9 Gāvakān Iran
190 I4 Gavardo Italy
122 H3 Gavāreshg Iran
163 D10 Gavarnie France
163 D10 Gavarnie, Cirque de corrie France/Spain
129 G5 Gavarr Armenia
123 I9 Gavāter Iran
177 K3 Gávavencsellő Hungary
122 E8 Gāvbandī Iran
122 E8 Gāvbūs, Kūh-e mts Iran
198 F8 Gavdopoula i. Greece
198 F8 Gavdos i. Greece
163 B8 Gave r. France
182 D4 Gave Port.
163 D9 Gave d'Arrens r. France
163 C9 Gave d'Aspe r. France
163 B8 Gave d'Oloron r. France
163 C9 Gave d'Ossau r. France
122 B4 Gāveh Rūd r. Iran
165 E7 Gavere Belgium
190 F6 Gavi Italy
193 K6 Gavi, Isola di i. Italy
255 E5 Gavião r. Brazil
184 D2 Gavião Port.
250 D6 Gaviãozinho Brazil
122 B4 Gavīleh Iran
261 F6 Gaviotas Arg.
190 F4 Gavirate Italy
122 E5 Gav Khūnī Iran
143 N1 Gävle Sweden
143 M1 Gävleborg county Sweden
143 N1 Gävlebukten b. Sweden
192 C7 Gavoi Sardegna Italy
192 F2 Gavorrano Italy
158 I4 Gavray France
135 H5 Gavrilovka Vtoraya Rus. Fed.
139 X5 Gavrilov Posad Rus. Fed.
139 W4 Gavrilov-Yam Rus. Fed.
198 F5 Gavrio Andros Greece
212 C5 Gawachab Namibia
96 C1 Gawai Myanmar
117 J7 Gawan Jharkhand India
202 B3 Gawat well Libya
179 O3 Gaweinstal Austria

Gäwers to Girna

316

122 H3 **Gäwers** Turkm.
116 F9 **Gawilgarh Hills** India
82 G6 **Gawler** *S.A.* Austr.
82 E5 **Gawler Ranges** *hills S.A.* Austr.
175 K1 **Gawliki Wielkie** Pol.
174 D4 **Gaworzyce** Pol.
149 M7 **Gawsworth** *Cheshire, England* U.K.
149 M5 **Gawthrop** *Cumbria, England* U.K.
207 G4 **Gawu** Nigeria
122 F2 **Gäwür** *watercourse* Turkm.
106 G5 **Gaxun Nur** *salt l. Nei Mongol* China
120 H2 **Gay** Rus. Fed.
226 F2 **Gay** *MI* U.S.A.
117 J7 **Gaya** *Bihar* India
95 L1 **Gaya** *i.* Malaysia
95 M2 **Gaya** *i.* Malaysia
207 F4 **Gaya** Niger
Gayá *r.* Spain *see* **El Gaià**
100 F7 **Gaya He** *r.* China
116 D2 **Gayal Gah** Jammu and Kashmir
95 K8 **Gayam** *Jawa* Indon.
210 A5 **Gayaza** Uganda
148 C7 **Gaybrook** Ireland
204 C4 **G'Aydat al Jhoucha** *ridge* Western Sahara
137 Q9 **Gayduk** Rus. Fed.
207 F3 **Gayéri** Burkina
226 J4 **Gaylord** *MI* U.S.A.
236 H3 **Gaylord** *MN* U.S.A.
85 M8 **Gayndah** *Qld* Austr.
139 T4 **Gaynovo** Rus. Fed.
134 K3 **Gayny** Rus. Fed.
Gaysin Ukr. *see* **Haysyn**
151 N2 **Gayton** *Norfolk, England* U.K.
134 G4 **Gayutino** Rus. Fed.
Gayvoron Ukr. *see* **Hayvoron**
122 D5 **Gaz** *Eşfahān* Iran
122 G8 **Gaz** *Hormozgan* Iran
128 C7 **Gaza** *terr.* Asia
128 C7 **Gaza** Gaza
213 G4 **Gaza** *prov.* Moz.
122 G6 **Gazak** Iran
121 M7 **Gazalkent** Uzbek.
123 L7 **Gazan** Pak.
207 I4 **Gazawa** Cameroon
78 □5 **Gazelle, Récif de la** *rf* New Caledonia
122 F5 **Gazestān** Iran
208 E4 **Gazi** Dem. Rep. Congo
126 H5 **Gaziantep** Turkey
128 F2 **Gaziantep** *prov.* Turkey
Gazibenli Turkey *see* **Yahyalı**
122 I5 **Gazik** Iran
129 E5 **Gaziler** Turkey
Gazimağusa Cyprus *see* **Ammochostos**
100 B2 **Gazimur** *r.* Rus. Fed.
107 L2 **Gazimuro-Ononskiy Khrebet** *mts* Rus. Fed.
100 A3 **Gazimurskiy Khrebet** *mts* Rus. Fed.
126 F5 **Gazipaşa** Turkey
196 I8 **Gazivode Jezero** *l.* Serbia
120 J7 **Gazli** Uzbek.
122 H8 **Gaz Māhū** Iran
122 E3 **Gazmāsarā** Iran
123 I1 **Gazojak** Turkm.
Gazojak Turkm. *see* **Gazojak**
183 Q3 **Gazolaz** Spain
191 J5 **Gazoldo degli Ippoliti** Italy
191 K5 **Gazzo Veronese** Italy
191 J5 **Gazzuolo** Italy
206 D5 **Gbaaka** Liberia
208 D3 **Gbadolite** Dem. Rep. Congo
206 B5 **Gbangbatok** Sierra Leone
206 C5 **Gbarnga** Liberia
206 C5 **Gbatala** Liberia
177 H4 **Gbelce** Slovakia
176 G3 **Gbely** Slovakia
207 F4 **Gbéroubouè** Benin
207 H5 **Gboko** Nigeria
208 D4 **Gbwado** Dem. Rep. Congo
143 O7 **Gdańsk** Pol.
175 H1 **Gdańsk, Gulf of** Pol./Rus. Fed.
Gdańska, Zatoka *g.* Pol./Rus. Fed. *see* **Gdańsk, Gulf of**
Gdingen Pol. *see* **Gdynia**
138 K3 **Gdov** Rus. Fed.
175 I6 **Gdów** Pol.
143 O7 **Gdynia** Pol.
186 C7 **Gea de Albarracín** Spain
140 Q2 **Geaidnouvuohppi** Norway
146 H8 **Geal Charn** *hill Highland, Scotland* U.K.
146 J8 **Geal Charn** *hill Highland, Scotland* U.K.
146 E4 **Gealldruig Mhòr** *i. Scotland* U.K.
163 I11 **Géant, Pic du** *mt.* France
78 □3a **Gea Passage** *Kwajalein* Marshall Is
238 D5 **Gearhart Mountain** *OR* U.S.A.
Gearraidh na h-Aibhne *Scotland* U.K. *see* **Garrynahine**
Gearraidh na h-Aibhne *Western Isles, Scotland* U.K. *see* **Garrynahine**
148 C7 **Geashill** Ireland
234 F6 **Geat Sound** *b. NJ* U.S.A.
163 D8 **Geaune** France
Geavvú Fin. *see* **Kevo**
93 F3 **Gebe** *i. Maluku* Indon.
203 H5 **Gebeit** Sudan
203 H4 **Gebeit Mine** Sudan
169 K8 **Gebesee** Ger.
169 E9 **Gebhardshain** Ger.
174 E3 **Gębice** Pol.
199 L5 **Gebiz** Turkey
210 C2 **Gebre Guracha** Eth.
129 E5 **Gebze** Turkey
210 B3 **Gech'a** Eth.
Gecheng *Chongqing* China *see* **Chengkou**
172 F4 **Gechingen** Ger.
129 C6 **Geçitkale** Cyprus *see* **Lefkonikon**
94 D6 **Gedang, Gunung** *mt.* Indon.
138 H7 **Gedanoniu kalnas** *hill* Lith.
203 G6 **Gedaref** Sudan
203 G6 **Gedaref** *state* Sudan
203 G6 **Gedi** *Rajasthan* India
151 K3 **Geddington** *Northamptonshire, England* U.K.
177 H5 **Gēderlak** Hungary
169 H10 **Gedern** Ger.
202 E6 **Gedid Ras el Fil** Sudan
165 G9 **Gedinne** Belgium
199 K4 **Gediz** Turkey
199 H4 **Gediz** *r.* Turkey
210 E3 **Gedlegubē** Eth.
151 M2 **Gedney Drove End** *Lincolnshire, England* U.K.
210 C2 **Gēdo** Eth.
210 D4 **Gedo** *admin. reg.* Somalia
95 I4 **Gedong** *Sarawak* Malaysia
94 □ **Gedong, Tanjong** *pt* Sing.
163 E10 **Gèdre** France
142 H7 **Gedser** Denmark
142 H7 **Gedser Odde** *c.* Denmark
142 F5 **Gedsted** Denmark
94 F7 **Gedungpakuan** *Sumatera* Indon.
Gedzheti Georgia *see* **Gejet'i**
165 H6 **Geel** Belgium
83 J8 **Geelong** *Vic.* Austr.
87 B10 **Geelvink Channel** *W.A.* Austr.
214 E5 **Geel Vloer** *salt pan* S. Africa
165 I7 **Geer** *r.* Belgium
168 J4 **Geertruidenberg** Neth.
168 D5 **Geeste** Ger.
168 G3 **Geeste** *r.* Ger.
164 K4 **Geesteren** Neth.
170 E5 **Geestgottberg** Ger.
168 J4 **Geesthacht** Ger.
165 H7 **Geetbets** Belgium
171 E10 **Geffell** Ger.
210 C2 **Gefersa** Eth.
164 H5 **Geffen** Neth.
171 E10 **Gefrees** Ger.
138 E6 **Gégé** *r.* Lith.
Gegechkori Georgia *see* **Martvili**
177 K3 **Gégény** Hungary
129 F5 **Geghadir** Armenia
129 F5 **Geghama Lerrnashght'a** *mts* Armenia
129 G5 **Geghamasar** Armenia
138 H7 **Gegužinė** Lith.
111 E10 **Gê'gyai** *Xizang* China
78 □3a **Gehh** *i. Kwajalein* Marshall Is
168 F5 **Gehrde** Ger.
169 I6 **Gehrden** Ger.
171 D9 **Gehren** Ger.
109 L3 **Ge Hu** *l.* China
207 H3 **Geidam** Nigeria
172 G2 **Geiersberg** *hill* Ger.
173 N3 **Geiersthal** Ger.
234 D4 **Geigertown** *PA* U.S.A.
223 K3 **Geikie** *r. Sask.* Can.
224 B3 **Geikie Island** *Ont.* Can.
85 I2 **Geikie Range** *hills Qld* Austr.
169 B9 **Geilenkirchen** Ger.
142 E1 **Geilo** Norway
104 D6 **Geinō** Japan
141 I5 **Geiranger** Norway
169 I9 **Geisa** Ger.
169 H10 **Geiselbach** Ger.
173 M4 **Geiselhöring** Ger.
173 I2 **Geiselwind** Ger.
173 L4 **Geisenfeld** Ger.
173 M5 **Geisenhausen** Ger.
172 D2 **Geisenheim** Ger.
171 I9 **Geising** Ger.
172 F6 **Geisingen** Ger.
169 J8 **Geisleden** Ger.
172 F5 **Geislingen** Ger.
172 H4 **Geislingen an der Steige** Ger.
169 J8 **Geismar** Ger.
157 O6 **Geispolsheim** France
178 F5 **Geißstein** *mt.* Austria
179 L5 **Geisthal** Austria
Geisum, Gezâ'ir *is* Egypt *see* **Qaysūm, Juzur**
211 B5 **Geita** Tanz.
171 G8 **Geithain** Ger.
140 L4 **Geittind** *mt.* Norway
129 D3 **Gejet'i** Georgia
108 D7 **Gejiu** *Yunnan* China
122 G2 **Gekdepe** Turkm.
210 A3 **Gel** *r.* Sudan
208 F2 **Gel** *watercourse* Sudan
194 G9 **Gela** *Sicilia* Italy
194 G9 **Gela** *r. Sicilia* Italy
194 G9 **Gela, Golfo di** *g. Sicilia* Italy
111 J10 **Gêladaindong** *mt. Qinghai* China
210 E3 **Geladī** Eth.
211 C5 **Gelai** *vol.* Tanz.
95 I6 **Gelam** *i.* Indon.
161 K8 **Gelas, Cime du** *mt.* France/Italy
170 F2 **Gelbensande** Ger.
173 I2 **Gelchsheim** Ger.
164 J4 **Gelderland** *prov.* Neth.
164 H5 **Geldermalsen** Neth.
169 B7 **Geldern** Ger.
169 J10 **Geldersheim** Ger.
165 I6 **Geldrop** Neth.
165 I7 **Geleen** Neth.
199 I3 **Gelembe** Turkey
210 D2 **Gelemso** Eth.
171 G9 **Gelenau** Ger.
199 M4 **Gelendost** Turkey
135 G7 **Gelendzhik** Rus. Fed.
210 B2 **Gelhak** Sudan
199 H2 **Gelibolu** Turkey
199 H2 **Gelibolu Yarımadası** *pen.* Turkey
199 H2 **Gelibolu Yarımadası Tarihi Milli Parkı** *nat. park* Turkey
Gelidonya Burnu *pt* Turkey *see* **Yardımcı Burnu**
199 L4 **Gelincik Dağı** *mt.* Turkey
204 E4 **Gelib** Somalia
163 E7 **Gelise** *r.* France
176 F5 **Gellénháza** Hungary
150 F4 **Gelligaer** *Caerphilly, Wales* U.K.
78 □3a **Gellinam** *i. Kwajalein* Marshall Is
122 G5 **Gelmord** Iran
169 H10 **Gelnhausen** Ger.
177 J3 **Gelnica** Slovakia
163 D9 **Gelos** France
163 C8 **Geloux** *r.* France
142 E6 **Gels** *r.* Denmark
186 E5 **Gelsa** Spain
176 F5 **Gelse** Hungary
169 D7 **Gelsenkirchen** Ger.
172 K5 **Geltendorf** Ger.
190 C3 **Gelten-Iffigen** *nature res.* Switz.
168 I1 **Gelting** Ger.
171 G6 **Geltow** Ger.
94 E6 **Gelumbang** *Sumatera* Indon.
94 E3 **Gemas** Malaysia
165 G7 **Gembloux** Belgium
207 H5 **Gembu** Nigeria
160 G2 **Gemeaux** France
208 C4 **Gemena** Dem. Rep. Congo
177 H5 **Gemenci** *park* Hungary
161 H10 **Gémenos** France
126 H4 **Gemerek** Turkey
177 J3 **Gemerská Hôrka** Slovakia
177 J3 **Gemerská Poloma** Slovakia
164 I5 **Gemert** Neth.
Geminokağı Cyprus *see* **Karavostasi**
199 K5 **Gemiş** Turkey
199 K2 **Gemlik** Turkey
199 J2 **Gemlik Körfezi** *b.* Turkey
140 □B1 **Gemlufall** Iceland
172 F3 **Gemmingen** Ger.
191 O3 **Gemona del Friuli** Italy
162 C4 **Gémozac** France
212 D5 **Gemsbok National Park** Botswana
214 E2 **Gemsbokplein** *well* S. Africa
214 I1 **Gemsbokvlakte** S. Africa
172 C2 **Gemünden** Ger.
169 G9 **Gemünden (Wohra)** Ger.
169 I10 **Gemünden am Main** Ger.
185 I8 **Genal** *r.* Spain
210 E3 **Genalē Wenz** *r.* Eth.
165 F7 **Genappe** Belgium
185 N4 **Génave** Spain
122 D7 **Genāveh** Iran
193 J4 **Genazzano** Italy
129 B7 **Genç** Turkey
162 E3 **Gençay** France
176 F4 **Gencsapáti** Hungary
210 C2 **Gendea** *r.* Eth.
111 C14 **Gendoli** *Rajasthan* India
160 H2 **Gendrey** France
164 J5 **Gendringen** Neth.
164 I5 **Gendt** Neth.
160 E3 **Généland** France
164 J3 **Genemuiden** Neth.
260 E5 **General Acha** Arg.
261 G5 **General Alvear** *Buenos Aires* Arg.
260 D4 **General Alvear** *Mendoza* Arg.
261 G4 **General Arenales** Arg.
253 F6 **General Artigas** Para.
261 H4 **General Belgrano** Arg.
262 **General Belgrano II** *research stn* Antarctica *see* **Belgrano II**
262 U2 **General Bernardo O'Higgins** *research stn* Antarctica
243 J5 **General Bravo** Mex.
261 F3 **General Cabrera** Arg.
261 H2 **General Campos** Arg.
256 A1 **General Carneiro** Brazil
259 B7 **General Carrera, Lago** *l.* Arg./Chile
261 I5 **General Conesa** *Buenos Aires* Arg.
259 D6 **General Conesa** *Rio Negro* Arg.
261 G4 **General Daniel Cerri** Arg.
261 F3 **General Deheza** Arg.
167 H2 **General Dezydery Chłapowskiego, Park Krajobrazowy imieniu** Pol.
243 I5 **General Escobeda** Mex.
General Freire Angola *see* **Muxaluando**
261 H3 **General Galarza** Arg.
261 I5 **General Guido** Arg.
260 C3 **General Gutiérrez** Arg.
187 C8 **Generalísimo, Embalse del** *resr* Spain
258 F2 **General José de San Martín** Arg.
261 I5 **General Juan Madariaga** Arg.
252 C4 **General Lagos** Chile
261 G5 **General La Madrid** Arg.
261 H4 **General Las Heras** Arg.
261 I5 **General Lavalle** Arg.
261 F4 **General Levalle** Arg.
92 F7 **General Luna** Phil.
92 E6 **General MacArthur** *Samar* Phil.
General Machado Angola *see* **Camacupa**
261 I4 **General Mansilla** Arg.
258 D2 **General Martín Miguel de Güemes** Arg.
261 G4 **General O'Brien** Arg.
258 F2 **General Paz** Arg.
261 F4 **General Pico** Arg.
261 G4 **General Pinto** Arg.
261 I5 **General Pirán** Arg.
260 D6 **General Roca** Arg.
261 H4 **General Rodríguez** Arg.
261 G3 **General Rojo** Arg.
253 E4 **General Saavedra** Bol.
256 B4 **General Salgado** Brazil
General San Martín *research stn* Antarctica *see* **San Martín**
261 H4 **General San Martín** *Buenos Aires* Arg.
261 F5 **General San Martín** *La Pampa* Arg.
92 E8 **General Santos** *Mindanao* Phil.
244 D1 **General Simón Bolívar** Mex.
243 J5 **General Terán** Mex.
197 Q7 **General Toshevo** Bulg.
242 F3 **General Trias** Mex.
261 G4 **General Viamonte** Arg.
261 F4 **General Villegas** Arg.
232 H7 **Genesee** *PA* U.S.A.
232 H5 **Genesee** *r. NY* U.S.A.
232 H6 **Geneseo** *NY* U.S.A.
182 H2 **Genestoso** Spain
210 C2 **Genet** Eth.
158 I4 **Genêts** France
215 L3 **Geneva** S. Africa
Geneva Switz. *see* **Genève**
231 E10 **Geneva** *AL* U.S.A.
226 F8 **Geneva** *IL* U.S.A.
236 G5 **Geneva** *NE* U.S.A.
232 H6 **Geneva** *NY* U.S.A.
232 E7 **Geneva** *OH* U.S.A.
Geneva, Lake France/Switz. *see* **Léman, Lac**
226 F7 **Geneva, Lake** *WI* U.S.A.
190 A3 **Genève** Switz.
160 I4 **Genève** *canton* Switz.
183 P3 **Genevilla** Spain
160 I5 **Genevois** *mts* France
Genf Switz. *see* **Genève**
191 N9 **Genga** Italy
Gengda *Sichuan* China *see* **Gana**
172 E5 **Gengenbach** Ger.
109 I7 **Genglou** *Guangdong* China
108 B7 **Gengma** *Yunnan* China
Gengqing *Sichuan* China *see* **Dêgê**
209 D5 **Gengwa** Dem. Rep. Congo
Gengxuan *Yunnan* China *see* **Gengma**
107 P1 **Gen He** *r.* China
210 B3 **Geni** *r.* Sudan
175 L1 **Geniai** Lith.
Genichesk Ukr. *see* **Heniches'k**
185 I5 **Genil** *r.* Spain
198 F1 **Genisea** Greece
163 D6 **Génissac** France
160 H4 **Génissiat, Barrage de** *dam* France
116 D8 **Genji** *Rajasthan* India
165 I7 **Genk** Belgium
103 H13 **Genkai-nada** *b.* Japan
160 G2 **Genlis** France
192 C8 **Gennargentu, Monti del** *mts Sardegna* Italy
192 C9 **Genn'Argiolas, Monte** *hill* Italy
164 I5 **Gennep** Neth.
162 D1 **Gennes** France
83 L7 **Genoa** *Vic.* Austr.
Genoa Italy *see* **Genova**
226 F7 **Genoa** *IL* U.S.A.
161 D8 **Genolhac** France
192 C8 **Genoni** *Sardegna* Italy
162 H3 **Genouillac** France
162 E3 **Genouillé** France
159 O7 **Genouilly** France
190 F7 **Genova** Italy
190 G7 **Genova** *prov.* Italy
190 F7 **Genova, Golfo di** *g.* Italy
187 E10 **Genovés** Spain
250 □ **Genovesa, Isla** *i. Islas Galápagos* Ecuador
163 E6 **Gensac** France
165 E6 **Gent** Belgium
94 G8 **Genteng** *Jawa* Indon.
95 J8 **Genteng** *i.* Indon.
171 F6 **Genthin** Ger.
94 D3 **Genting Highlands** Malaysia
254 E4 **Gentio do Ouro** Brazil
162 I4 **Gentioux, Plateau de** France
162 H4 **Gentioux-Pigerolles** France
Genua Italy *see* **Genova**
193 Q6 **Genzano di Lucania** Italy
193 J4 **Genzano di Roma** Italy
197 L4 **Geoagiu** *r.* Romania
210 D4 **Geodha, Rubh' a'** *pt Scotland* U.K.
87 C12 **Geographe Bay** *W.A.* Austr.
87 B8 **Geographe Channel** *W.A.* Austr.
221 P2 **Geographical Society Ø** *i.* Greenland
Geok-Tepe Turkm. *see* **Gëkdepe**
130 F1 **Georga, Zemlya** *i. Zemlya Frantsa-Iosifa* Rus. Fed.
86 D6 **George** *r. W.A.* Austr.
225 H1 **George** *r. Que.* Can.
214 G9 **George** S. Africa
225 I4 **George, Cape** *N.S.* Can.
83 L6 **George, Lake** *N.S.W.* Austr.
82 G7 **George, Lake** *S.A.* Austr.
86 G7 **George, Lake** *salt flat W.A.* Austr.
210 A4 **George, Lake** Uganda
231 G11 **George, Lake** *FL* U.S.A.
233 L5 **George, Lake** *NY* U.S.A.
84 C7 **George Gills Range** *mts N.T.* Austr.
150 D5 **Georgeham** *Devon, England* U.K.
216 □2b **George Island** St Helena
George Land *i. Zemlya Frantsa-Iosifa* Rus. Fed. *see* **Georga, Zemlya**
173 M2 **Georgenberg** Ger.
173 K3 **Georgensgmünd** Ger.
233 M5 **Georges Mills** *NH* U.S.A.
81 B11 **George Sound** *inlet South I.* N.Z.
85 I5 **Georgetown** *Qld* Austr.
83 K9 **George Town** *Tas.* Austr.
246 F2 **George Town** *Gt Exuma* Bahamas
224 E5 **Georgetown** *Ont.* Can.
246 C4 **George Town** Cayman Is
206 B3 **Georgetown** Gambia
251 G3 **Georgetown** Guyana
94 D2 **George Town** Malaysia
216 □2a **Georgetown** *Ascension* S. Atlantic Ocean
247 □3 **Georgetown** St Vincent
235 I2 **Georgetown** *CT* U.S.A.
233 J10 **Georgetown** *DE* U.S.A.
231 E10 **Georgetown** *GA* U.S.A.
230 E4 **Georgetown** *KY* U.S.A.
232 B10 **Georgetown** *OH* U.S.A.
231 H9 **Georgetown** *SC* U.S.A.
237 G10 **Georgetown** *TX* U.S.A.
262 T2 **George VI Sound** *sea chan.* Antarctica
263 K2 **George V Land** *reg.* Antarctica
237 F11 **George West** *TX* U.S.A.
129 E4 **Georgia** *country* Asia
231 F9 **Georgia** *state* U.S.A.
222 E5 **Georgia, Strait of** *B.C.* Can.
231 D10 **Georgiana** *AL* U.S.A.
224 D4 **Georgian Bay** *Ont.* Can.
227 O5 **Georgian Bay Islands National Park** *Ont.* Can.
Georgi Dimitrov, Yazovir *resr* Bulg. *see* **Koprinka, Yazovir**
84 G8 **Georgina** *watercourse Qld* Austr.
198 F7 **Georgioupoli** *Kriti* Greece
Georgi Traykov Bulg. *see* **Dolni Chiflik**
Georgiu-Dezh Rus. Fed. *see* **Liski**
120 G2 **Georgiyevka** *Aktyubinskaya Oblast'* Kazakh.
121 S3 **Georgiyevka** *Vostochnyy Kazakhstan* Kazakh.
Georgiyevka *Zhambylskaya Oblast'* Kazakh. *see* **Korday**
129 E1 **Georgiyevsk** Rus. Fed.
134 I4 **Georgiyevskoye** *Kostromskaya Oblast'* Rus. Fed.
129 A1 **Georgiyevskoye** *Krasnodarskiy Kray* Rus. Fed.
139 T2 **Georgiyevskoye** *Vologodskaya Oblast'* Rus. Fed.
168 D5 **Georgsdorf** Ger.
168 D4 **Georgsheil** Ger.
169 F6 **Georgsmarienhütte** Ger.
Georg von Neumayer *research stn* Antarctica *see* **Neumayer**
178 C6 **Gepatsch, Stausee** *resr* Austria
163 D9 **Ger** *Aquitaine* France
159 J4 **Ger** *Basse-Normandie* France
186 I3 **Ger** Spain
171 F9 **Gera** Ger.
165 E7 **Geraardsbergen** Belgium
169 K9 **Geraberg** Ger.
172 H3 **Gerabronn** Ger.
195 K7 **Gerace** Italy
195 K7 **Gerace** *r.* Italy
194 G8 **Geraci Siculo** *Sicilia* Italy
147 C9 **Gerahies** Ireland
198 E2 **Gerakarou** Greece
198 B5 **Gerakas, Akrotirio** *pt Zakynthos* Greece
198 E6 **Gerakas, Akrotirio** *pt* Greece
198 D6 **Geraki** Greece
256 B6 **Geral, Serra** *mts* Brazil
254 D4 **Geral de Goiás, Serra** *hills* Brazil
81 F11 **Geraldine** *South I.* N.Z.
254 D5 **Geral do Paraná, Serra** *hills* Brazil
87 C10 **Geraldton** *W.A.* Austr.
93 E1 **Gerama** *i.* Indon.
198 E5 **Gerania** *mts* Greece
128 C7 **Gerar** *watercourse* Israel
157 M7 **Gérardmer** France
179 M2 **Geras** Austria
179 N3 **Gerasdorf bei Wien** Austria
122 F8 **Gerāsh** Iran
156 H7 **Géraudot** France
210 B2 **Gerba Dima** Eth.
240 J1 **Gerber** *CA* U.S.A.
157 M7 **Gerbéviller** France
161 E7 **Gerbier de Jonc** *mt.* France
171 E7 **Gerbstedt** Ger.
176 G4 **Gércé** Hungary
172 H2 **Gerchsheim** Ger.
127 J5 **Gercüş** Turkey
168 J5 **Gerdau** Ger.
215 K2 **Gerdau** S. Africa
Gerdauen Rus. Fed. *see* **Zheleznodorozhnyy**
177 H4 **Gerecsei** *park* Hungary
126 F3 **Gerede** Turkey
126 F3 **Gerede** *r.* Turkey
184 G5 **Gerena** Spain
177 J5 **Gerendás** Hungary
182 D5 **Gerês, Serra do** *mts* Port.
177 H5 **Geresdlak** Hungary
123 K6 **Gereshk** Afgh.
179 G3 **Geretsberg** Austria
173 K6 **Geretsried** Ger.
185 N6 **Gérgal** Spain
129 I3 **Gergebil'** Rus. Fed.
192 C8 **Gergei** *Sardegna* Italy
177 K3 **Gergely-hegy** *hill* Hungary
162 F3 **Gergy** France
173 J2 **Gerhardshofen** Ger.
94 D2 **Gerik** Malaysia
122 H5 **Gerimenj** Iran
183 L9 **Gerindote** Spain
236 D5 **Gering** *NE* U.S.A.
171 G8 **Geringswalde** Ger.
177 J4 **Gerje** *r.* Hungary
177 H5 **Gerjen** Hungary
238 E6 **Gerlach** *NV* U.S.A.
177 J2 **Gerlachovský štít** *mt.* Slovakia
172 G4 **Gerlingen** Ger.
178 G5 **Gerlos** Austria
178 F5 **Gerlospass** *pass* Austria
225 H2 **Germaine, Lac** *l. Que.* Can.
261 F4 **Germania** Arg.
Germania *country* Europe *see* **Germany**
221 Q2 **Germania Land** *reg.* Greenland
Germanicea Turkey *see* **Kahramanmaraş**
222 E4 **Germansen Landing** *B.C.* Can.
German South-West Africa *country* Africa *see* **Namibia**
232 H9 **Germantown** *MD* U.S.A.
232 A9 **Germantown** *OH* U.S.A.
237 K8 **Germantown** *TN* U.S.A.
226 F6 **Germantown** *WI* U.S.A.
166 E3 **Germany** *country* Europe
172 E3 **Germaringen** Ger.
157 J7 **Germay** France
199 I5 **Germencik** Turkey
173 K5 **Germering** Ger.
172 E3 **Germersheim** Ger.
158 D8 **Germigny-des-Prés** France
215 M2 **Germiston** S. Africa
183 O2 **Gernika-Lumo** Spain
172 D1 **Gernrode** *Sachsen-Anhalt* Ger.
169 J8 **Gernrode** *Thüringen* Ger.
172 E4 **Gernsbach** Ger.
172 E2 **Gernsheim** Ger.
104 F4 **Gero** Japan
198 G6 **Gero Angeli, Akrotirio** *pt* Greece
190 H3 **Gerola Alta** Italy
171 E10 **Geroldsgrün** Ger.
173 K5 **Gerolsbach** Ger.
169 C10 **Gerolstein** Ger.
173 I2 **Gerolzhofen** Ger.
Gerona Spain *see* **Girona**
198 F7 **Geropotamos** *r. Kriti* Greece
191 R4 **Gerovo** Croatia
165 G8 **Gerpinnes** Belgium
192 C9 **Gerrei** *reg. Sardegna* Italy
Gerri Spain *see* **Guerri de la Sal**
Gerrit Denys *is* P.N.G. *see* **Lihir Group**
163 E8 **Gers** *dept* France
163 F7 **Gers** *r.* France
190 F2 **Gersau** Switz.
169 E9 **Gersfeld (Rhön)** Ger.
172 C3 **Gersheim** Ger.
114 D5 **Gersoppa** *Karnataka* India
128 E3 **Gersten** Ger.
178 F3 **Gerstetten** Ger.
157 O7 **Gerstheim** France
173 J5 **Gersthofen** Ger.
169 J9 **Gerstungen** Ger.
170 I4 **Gerswalde** Ger.
163 H9 **Geruanne** *r.* France
171 G6 **Gerwisch** Ger.
Géryville Alg. *see* **El Bayadh**
160 C5 **Gerzat** France
111 G10 **Gêrzê** *Xizang* China
126 G3 **Gerze** Turkey
172 H2 **Gescher** Ger.
179 N5 **Geschriebenstein** *hill* Austria
169 K9 **Geschwenda** Ger.
169 G7 **Geseke** Ger.
192 G8 **Gesico** *Sardegna* Italy
Gesoriacum France *see* **Boulogne-sur-Mer**
157 I4 **Gespunsart** France
173 J5 **Gessertshausen** Ger.
261 G2 **Gessler** Arg.
160 I3 **Gesso** *r.* Italy
223 H6 **Gestalgar** Spain
159 I7 **Gesté** France
192 C8 **Gesturi** *Sardegna* Italy
193 O5 **Gesualdo** Italy
165 H8 **Gesves** Belgium
177 K4 **Geszt** Hungary
177 J4 **Gesztéréd** Hungary
141 O6 **Geta** *Åland* Fin.
186 H6 **Getafe** Spain
107 L9 **Getai** *Shaanxi* China
122 E4 **Getcheh, Kūh-e** *hills* Iran
165 H7 **Gete** *r.* Belgium
197 L6 **Getic, Podișul** *plat.* Romania
158 I7 **Gétigné** France
129 G5 **Getik** *r.* Armenia
168 I2 **Gettorf** Ger.
234 A5 **Gettysburg** *PA* U.S.A.
236 F3 **Gettysburg** *SD* U.S.A.
232 H9 **Gettysburg National Military Park** *nat. park PA* U.S.A.
108 F6 **Getu He** *r.* China
256 C4 **Getulina** Brazil
255 B8 **Getúlio Vargas** Brazil
262 P2 **Getz Ice Shelf** Antarctica
165 I7 **Geul** *r.* Neth.
94 B3 **Geumapang** *r.* Indon.
94 B2 **Geumpang** *Sumatera* Indon.
94 B2 **Geureudong, Gunung** *vol.* Indon.
83 L5 **Geurie** *N.S.W.* Austr.
122 H8 **Gevān-e Tāleb Khānī** Iran
127 K4 **Gevaş** Turkey
161 C7 **Gévaudan** *reg.* France
169 D8 **Gevelsberg** Ger.
158 H5 **Gévezé** France
197 K9 **Gevgelija** Macedonia
186 E2 **Gévora** *r.* Spain
114 D3 **Gevrai** *Mahar.* India
160 F2 **Gevrey-Chambertin** France
210 D2 **Gewanē Wildlife Reserve** *nature res.* Eth.
160 I4 **Gex** France
Gexianzhuang *Hebei* China *see* **Qinghe**
Gey Iran *see* **Nīkshahr**
128 A2 **Geydik Dağları** *mts* Turkey
171 G9 **Geyer** Ger.
129 B3 **Geyikli** Turkey
94 □ **Geylang** Sing.
94 □ **Geylang** *r.* Sing.
117 M6 **Geylegphug** Bhutan
215 J2 **Geysdorp** S. Africa
240 J3 **Geyserville** *CA* U.S.A.
199 L2 **Geyve** Turkey
189 C2 **Gezira** *state* Sudan
198 B1 **Gezavesh** Albania
106 G7 **Gezidong** *Qinghai* China
122 F8 **Gezir** Iran
179 L2 **Gföhl** Austria
195 □ **Ġgantija Temples** *Gozo* Malta
214 H3 **Ghaap Plateau** S. Africa
128 F5 **Ghabāghib** Syria
202 E6 **Ghabeish** Sudan
127 K6 **Ghadaf, Wādī al** *watercourse* Iraq
128 E7 **Ghadaf, Wādī al** *watercourse* Jordan
123 N4 **Ghadai** Pak.
Ghadamès Libya *see* **Ghadāmis**
202 A2 **Ghadāmis** Libya
202 B3 **Ghaddūwah** Libya
122 E3 **Ghaem Shahr** Iran
125 L5 **Ghāfah, Ramlat al** *des.* Saudi Arabia
123 O7 **Ghaggar, Dry Bed of** *watercourse* Pak.
117 J7 **Ghaghara** *r.* India
78 □6 **Ghaghe** *i.* Solomon Is
117 J8 **Ghaghra** *Jharkhand* India
195 □ **Ghajn, Xrobb l-** *pt* Malta
123 L8 **Ghaibi Dero** Pak.
195 □ **Ghajnsielem** *Gozo* Malta
195 □ **Ghajn Tuffieha, Ir-Ramla ta'** *b.* Malta
123 I6 **Ghaland** Iran
120 J3 **Ghalkarteniz, Solonchak** *salt marsh* Kazakh.
208 E2 **Ghallah, Wadi El** *watercourse* Sudan
Ghalloarol Uzbek. *see* **G'allaorol**
195 □ **Ghallis, Ġebel ta' l-** *is* Malta
206 E4 **Ghana** *country* Africa
125 L3 **Ghanādah, Rās** *pt* U.A.E.
125 M6 **Ghānah** *well* Oman
125 K6 **Ghanim** *well* Saudi Arabia
116 D6 **Ghanliala** *Rajasthan* India
116 C8 **Ghantila** *Gujarat* India
116 C9 **Ghantwar** *Gujarat* India
125 I2 **Ghanwā** Saudi Arabia
212 D4 **Ghanzi** Botswana
212 D4 **Ghanzi** *admin. dist.* Botswana
Ghap'an Armenia *see* **Kapan**
125 I2 **Ghār, Ras al** *pt* Saudi Arabia
Gharakach' Armenia *see* **Lusashogh**
124 F5 **Gharāmil, Jabal al** *hill* Saudi Arabia
128 D8 **Gharandal** Jordan
128 A9 **Gharandal, Wādī** *watercourse* Egypt
195 □ **Għarb** *Gozo* Malta
205 F2 **Ghardaïa** Alg.
189 B7 **Ghardimaou** Tunisia
129 C7 **Ghar el Melh** Tunisia
123 K4 **Gharghārib** Afgh.
116 C6 **Gharghoda** *Chhattisgarh* India
117 I8 **Gharghur Malta**
195 □ **Għargħur** Malta
203 G2 **Ghārib, Jabal** *mt.* Egypt
128 B10 **Ghārib, Ra's** *pt* Egypt
123 N2 **Gharm** Tajik.
125 M6 **Gharm, Wādī** *r.* Oman
125 I3 **Ghār Mihnān** Saudi Arabia
123 L4 **Gharo** Pak.
122 C4 **Gharq Ābād** Iran
202 B1 **Gharyān** Libya
126 H7 **Gharz, Wādī al** *watercourse* Syria
125 M7 **Gharzaut** *i.* Oman
183 O2 **Ghāt** Libya
202 A3 **Ghatampur** *Uttar Prad.* India
116 H6 **Ghatere** *Sta Isabel* Solomon Is
78 □6 **Ghatgan** *Orissa* India
117 J9 **Ghatol** *Rajasthan* India
116 E8 **Ghatsila** *Jharkhand* India
117 K8 **Ghauspur** Pak.
123 M7 **Ghawdex** *i.* Malta *see* **Gozo**
124 G8 **Ghayman** Yemen
202 C6 **Ghazal, Bahr el** *watercourse* Chad
208 F2 **Ghazal, Bahr el** *r.* Sudan
Ghazalkent Uzbek. *see* **G'azalkent**
204 E2 **Ghazaouet** Alg.
116 F5 **Ghaziabad** *Uttar Prad.* India
117 I7 **Ghazipur** *Uttar Prad.* India
125 M2 **Ghazira, Ghubbat al** *inlet* Oman
123 L6 **Ghazluna** Pak.
Ghazna Afgh. *see* **Ghaznī**
123 M5 **Ghaznī** Afgh.
123 L5 **Ghaznī** *prov.* Afgh.
123 L5 **Ghazni** *r.* Afgh.
123 J5 **Ghazoor** Afgh.
124 E2 **Ghazzālah** Saudi Arabia
122 G5 **Ghebar Gumbad** Iran
190 I5 **Ghedi** Italy
197 K5 **Ghelari** Romania
197 O5 **Ghelinta** Romania
125 J3 **Ghemeis, Ras** *pt* U.A.E.
Ghent Belgium *see* **Gent**
232 D11 **Ghent** *WV* U.S.A.
Gheorghe Gheorghiu-Dej Romania *see* **Onești**
197 P6 **Gheorghe Lazăr** Romania
197 N4 **Gheorgheni** Romania
114 D4 **Gherdi** *Mahar.* India
197 L3 **Gherla** Romania
190 F4 **Ghiffa** Italy
Ghijduwon Uzbek. *see* **G'ijduvon**
192 B7 **Ghilarza** *Sardegna* Italy
123 L6 **Ghilzai** *reg.* Afgh.
126 I8 **Ghinah, Wādī al** *watercourse* Saudi Arabia
177 K5 **Ghioroc** Romania
197 L6 **Ghioroiu** Romania
177 K6 **Ghiroda** Romania
165 F7 **Ghislenghien** Belgium
190 G3 **Ghisonaccia** *Corse* France
192 C3 **Ghisoni** *Corse* France
123 L5 **Ghizao** Afgh.
116 D1 **Ghizar** Jammu and Kashmir
177 K6 **Ghizela** Romania
116 C3 **Ghizri Creek** *inlet* Pak.
78 □6 **Ghizunabeana Islands** Solomon Is
114 C3 **Ghod** *Mahar.* India
114 D3 **Ghod** *r.* India
116 D9 **Gholvad** *Mahar.* India
123 L9 **Ghorabari** Pak.
117 L7 **Ghoraghat** Bangl.
123 K5 **Ghorak** Afgh.
123 M4 **Ghorband** *r.* Afgh.
222 H2 **Ghost Lake** *N.W.T.* Can.
116 C6 **Ghotaru** *Rajasthan* India
123 M8 **Ghotki** Pak.
123 K4 **Ghowr** *prov.* Afgh.
125 K9 **Ghubbah** *Suquṭrā* Yemen
Ghudamis Libya *see* **Ghadāmis**
123 O2 **Ghūdara** Tajik.
117 H7 **Ghugri** *r.* India
114 F3 **Ghugus** *Mahar.* India
Ghukasyan Armenia *see* **Ashots'k'**
123 M9 **Ghulam Mohammed Barrage** Pak.
128 F4 **Ghunthur** Syria
128 F7 **Ghurayfah** *hill* Saudi Arabia
122 F7 **Ghūrī** Iran
123 I4 **Ghurian** Afgh.
124 G3 **Ghurrab, Jabal** *hill* Saudi Arabia
124 F4 **Ghurūb, Jabal** *hill* Saudi Arabia
116 H8 **Ghutipari** *Madh. Prad.* India
128 G9 **Ghuwayṭah, Nafūd al** *des.* Saudi Arabia
125 M4 **Ghuzayn** Oman
202 C2 **Ghuzayyil, Sabkhat** *salt marsh* Libya
Ghuzor Uzbek. *see* **G'uzor**
156 E1 **Ghyvelde** France
135 H7 **Giaginskaya** Rus. Fed.
128 B3 **Gialias** *r.* Cyprus
97 H8 **Gia Nghia** Vietnam
96 H6 **Gianh, Sông** *r.* Vietnam
198 I5 **Gianisada** *i.* Greece
198 D2 **Giannitsa** Greece
192 G3 **Giannutri, Isola di** *i.* Italy
193 J2 **Giano dell'Umbria** Italy
215 N5 **Giant's Castle** *mt.* S. Africa
147 I2 **Giant's Causeway** *lava field Northern Ireland* U.K.
235 K2 **Giant's Neck** *CT* U.S.A.
95 K9 **Gianyar** *Bali* Indon.
97 G10 **Gia Rai** Vietnam
195 I8 **Giardini-Naxos** *Sicilia* Italy
196 J5 **Giarmata** Romania
194 H9 **Giarratana** *Sicilia* Italy
195 I8 **Giarre** *Sicilia* Italy
162 I4 **Giat** France
192 B7 **Giave** *Sardegna* Italy
190 C5 **Giaveno** Italy
190 D4 **Giavino, Monte** *mt.* Italy
192 B9 **Giba** *Sardegna* Italy
184 H7 **Gibalbín** *hill* Spain
246 E3 **Gibara** Cuba
184 H5 **Gibarrayo** *hill* Spain
86 I3 **Gibb** *r. W.A.* Austr.
236 F5 **Gibbon** *NE* U.S.A.
238 H4 **Gibbonsville** *ID* U.S.A.
86 I4 **Gibb River** *W.A.* Austr.
86 I4 **Gibb River Aboriginal Reserve** *W.A.* Austr.
234 F5 **Gibbsboro** *NJ* U.S.A.
231 □1 **Gibb's Hill** Bermuda
234 E5 **Gibbstown** *NJ* U.S.A.
194 D8 **Gibellina Nuova** *Sicilia* Italy
212 C5 **Gibeon** Namibia
159 K3 **Giberville** France
140 O2 **Gibostad** Norway
162 A2 **Giboule** *r.* France
184 F6 **Gibraleón** Spain
185 I8 **Gibraltar** Europe
185 □ **Gibraltar, Bay of** Gibraltar/Spain
184 H8 **Gibraltar, Campo de** *reg.* Spain
204 D2 **Gibraltar, Strait of** Morocco/Spain
185 □ **Gibraltar Harbour** Gibraltar
149 R7 **Gibraltar Point** *England* U.K.
83 N3 **Gibraltar Range National Park** *N.S.W.* Austr.
87 F12 **Gibson** *W.A.* Austr.
231 F9 **Gibson** *GA* U.S.A.
226 F9 **Gibson City** *IL* U.S.A.
87 G8 **Gibson Desert** *W.A.* Austr.
87 H8 **Gibson Desert Nature Reserve** *W.A.* Austr.
234 C6 **Gibson Island** *MD* U.S.A.
222 F5 **Gibsons** *B.C.* Can.
175 L1 **Giby** Pol.
129 K5 **Gicăki Dağı** *mt.* Azer.
106 D4 **Gichgeniyn Nuruu** *mts* Mongolia
210 B2 **Gīdamī** Eth.
123 L7 **Gidar** Pak.
134 K4 **Gidayevo** Rus. Fed.
210 B2 **Gidda** Eth.
114 F5 **Giddalur** *Andhra Prad.* India
237 G10 **Giddings** *TX* U.S.A.
Giddi Pass *hill* Egypt *see* **Jiddī, Jabal al**
140 O5 **Gideälven** *r.* Sweden
175 H5 **Gidle** Pol.
210 C3 **Gīdolē** Eth.
172 H2 **Giebelstadt** Ger.
169 J7 **Gieboldehausen** Ger.
175 H4 **Gieczno** Pol.
168 K2 **Giekau** Ger.
167 K3 **Giełczew** *r.* Pol.
175 I4 **Gielniów** Pol.
170 G3 **Gielow** Ger.
156 E8 **Gien** France
173 I4 **Giengen an der Brenz** Ger.
161 I10 **Giens, Golfe de** *b.* France
161 I10 **Giens, Presqu'île de** *pen.* France
161 H6 **Gières** France
165 G6 **Gierle** Belgium
171 E7 **Gierslében** Ger.
169 K8 **Gierstädt** Ger.
175 I2 **Gierzwałd** Pol.
Giesecke Isfjord *inlet* Greenland *see* **Kangerlussuaq**
169 I7 **Gieselwerder (Oberweser)** Ger.
169 G9 **Gießen** Ger.
169 G9 **Gießen** *admin. reg.* Ger.
164 K2 **Gieten** Neth.
175 I1 **Gietrzwałd** Pol.
159 O7 **Gièvres** France
122 G3 **Gifan** Iran
Gifatin Island Egypt *see* **Jiftūn al Kabīr**
149 L2 **Gifford** *East Lothian, Scotland* U.K.
163 I7 **Giffou** *r.* France
160 I4 **Giffre** *r.* France
169 K6 **Gifhorn** Ger.
222 G4 **Gift Lake** *Alta* Can.
104 E5 **Gifu** Japan
104 E4 **Gifu** *pref.* Japan
135 H7 **Gigant** Rus. Fed.
242 D4 **Giganta, Cerro** *mt.* Mex.
250 C4 **Gigante** Col.
185 P5 **Gigante** *mt.* Spain
161 D9 **Gigean** France
146 E11 **Gigha** *i. Scotland* U.K.
146 E11 **Gigha, Sound of** *sea chan. Scotland* U.K.
197 L7 **Gighera** Romania
192 F3 **Giglio, Isola del** *i.* Italy
192 F3 **Giglio Castello** Italy
161 D9 **Gignac** *Languedoc-Roussillon* France
161 H9 **Gignac** *Provence-Alpes-Côte d'Azur* France
190 C4 **Gignod** Italy
161 G8 **Gigondas** France
120 K7 **G'ijduvon** Uzbek.
182 I1 **Gijón-Xixón** Spain
163 I8 **Gijou** *r.* France
211 A5 **Gikongoro** Rwanda
239 K9 **Gila** *r. AZ* U.S.A.
93 F2 **Gila, Tanjung** *pt Maluku* Indon.
239 K9 **Gila Bend** *AZ* U.S.A.
241 S8 **Gila Bend Mountains** *AZ* U.S.A.
241 R9 **Gila Mountains** *AZ* U.S.A.
122 C3 **Gīlān** *prov.* Iran
122 A4 **Gīlān-e Gharb** Iran
241 U8 **Gila River Indian Reservation** *res. AZ* U.S.A.
197 L4 **Gilău** Romania
129 K5 **Giläzi** Azer.
149 P6 **Gilberdyke** *East Riding of Yorkshire, England* U.K.
261 H3 **Gilbert** Arg.
85 H4 **Gilbert** *r. Qld* Austr.
241 U8 **Gilbert** *AZ* U.S.A.
226 B2 **Gilbert** *MN* U.S.A.
232 D11 **Gilbert** *WV* U.S.A.
Gilbert Islands *country* Pacific Ocean *see* **Kiribati**
234 C3 **Gilberton** *PA* U.S.A.
85 I5 **Gilbert Range** *mts Qld* Austr.
266 G6 **Gilbert Ridge** *sea feature* Pacific Ocean
85 I5 **Gilbert River** *Qld* Austr.
234 D4 **Gilbertsville** *PA* U.S.A.
232 B7 **Gilboa** *OH* U.S.A.
255 A7 **Gilbués** Brazil
122 G4 **Gil Chashmeh** Iran
173 K5 **Gilching** Ger.
238 I2 **Gildford** *MT* U.S.A.
213 H3 **Gilé** Moz.
Gilead *reg.* Jordan *see* **Jil'ād**
185 J6 **Gilena** Spain
87 E10 **Giles, Lake** *salt flat W.A.* Austr.
84 C4 **Giles Creek** *r. N.T.* Austr.
87 J8 **Giles Meteorological Station** *W.A.* Austr.
84 D6 **Giles Range** *mts N.T.* Austr.
161 K9 **Gilette** France
Gilf Kebir Plateau Egypt *see* **Jilf al Kabīr, Haḍabat al**
147 J4 **Gilford** *Northern Ireland* U.K.
83 M3 **Gilgai** *N.S.W.* Austr.
83 L4 **Gilgandra** *N.S.W.* Austr.
129 K4 **Gilgilçay** Azer.
83 L3 **Gil Gil Creek** *r. N.S.W.* Austr.
116 E2 **Gilgit** Jammu and Kashmir
116 E2 **Gilgit** *r.* Jammu and Kashmir
83 K5 **Gilgunnia** *N.S.W.* Austr.
93 G8 **Gili Iyang** *i.* Indon.
95 K9 **Gilimanuk** *Bali* Indon.
Gilindire Turkey *see* **Aydıncık**
222 D4 **Gil Island** *B.C.* Can.
147 F4 **Gill, Lough** *l.* Ireland
223 M3 **Gillam** *Man.* Can.
149 P5 **Gillamoor** *North Yorkshire, England* U.K.
142 I5 **Gilleleje** Denmark
84 E7 **Gillen** *watercourse N.T.* Austr.
87 H9 **Gillen, Lake** *salt flat W.A.* Austr.
169 C10 **Gillenfeld** Ger.
82 F5 **Gilles, Lake** *salt flat S.A.* Austr.
81 D10 **Gillespies Point** *South I.* N.Z.
232 I7 **Gillett** *PA* U.S.A.
226 F5 **Gillett** *WI* U.S.A.
238 L4 **Gillette** *WY* U.S.A.
140 M5 **Gillhov** Sweden
85 H6 **Gilliat** *Qld* Austr.
85 H6 **Gilliat** *r. Qld* Austr.
150 H5 **Gillingham** *Dorset, England* U.K.
151 N5 **Gillingham** *Medway, England* U.K.
149 N5 **Gilling West** *North Yorkshire, England* U.K.
216 □2b **Gill Point** St Helena
146 J5 **Gills** *Highland, Scotland* U.K.
226 G4 **Gills Rock** *WI* U.S.A.
160 I5 **Gilly-sur-Isère** France
160 D3 **Gilly-sur-Loire** France
235 K1 **Gilman** *CT* U.S.A.
226 G9 **Gilman** *IL* U.S.A.
226 D4 **Gilman** *WI* U.S.A.
237 I9 **Gilmer** *TX* U.S.A.
146 I10 **Gilmerton** *Perth and Kinross, Scotland* U.K.
221 K4 **Gilmour Island** *Nunavut* Can.
197 L6 **Gilort** *r.* Romania
240 K4 **Gilroy** *CA* U.S.A.
169 H9 **Gilserberg** Ger.
149 L4 **Gilsland** *Northumberland, England* U.K.
146 K11 **Gilston** *Scottish Borders, Scotland* U.K.
168 I5 **Gilten** Ger.
91 J8 **Giluwe, Mount** P.N.G.
150 F4 **Gilwern** *Monmouthshire, Wales* U.K.
164 G5 **Gilze** Neth.
210 B2 **Gīmbī** Eth.
247 □3 **Gimie, Mount** *vol.* St Lucia
195 L6 **Gimigliano** Italy
223 L5 **Gimli** *Man.* Can.
143 O1 **Gimo** Sweden
163 F9 **Gimone, Barrage de la** *dam* France
163 G8 **Gimone** *r.* France
163 F8 **Gimont** France
160 C3 **Gimouille** France
165 H9 **Gimsnevis** France
203 H6 **Ginda** Eritrea
85 L7 **Gindie** *Qld* Austr.
252 D3 **Ginebra, Laguna** *l.* Bol.
192 D7 **Ginepro, Cala** *b. Sardegna* Italy
216 □3c **Ginés, Punta** *pt Lanzarote* Canary Is
161 B10 **Ginestas** France
216 □1b **Ginetes** *São Miguel* Azores
140 □ **Ginevrabotnen** *str.* Svalbard
114 G9 **Gin Ganga** *r.* Sri Lanka
114 F6 **Gingee** *Tamil Nadu* India
165 H7 **Gingelom** Belgium
172 H4 **Gingen an der Fils** Ger.
246 □ **Ginger Hill** Jamaica
85 M8 **Gin Gin** *Qld* Austr.
87 C11 **Gingin** *W.A.* Austr.
215 P5 **Gingindlovu** S. Africa
92 E7 **Gingoog** *Mindanao* Phil.
170 H2 **Gingst** Ger.
210 D3 **Ginir** Eth.
138 G6 **Ginkūnai** Lith.
163 I10 **Ginoles** France
195 L2 **Ginosa** Italy
195 I6 **Ginostra** *Isole Lipari* Italy
102 □1 **Ginowan** *Okinawa* Japan
193 I3 **Gintota** *Sri Lanka*
Ginzo de Limia *Galicia* Spain *see* **Xinzo de Limia**
184 D6 **Giões** Port.
198 G7 **Giofyros** *r. Kriti* Greece
193 O7 **Gioi** Italy
195 J6 **Gioia, Golfo di** *b.* Italy
193 L4 **Gioia dei Marsi** Italy
195 L2 **Gioia del Colle** Italy
193 M5 **Gioia Sannitica** Italy
195 J7 **Gioia Tauro** Italy
195 K7 **Gioiosa Ionica** Italy
194 H7 **Gioiosa Marea** *Sicilia* Italy
Gióna Óros *mts* Greece *see* **Gkiona**
190 F5 **Giornico** Switz.
198 F3 **Gioura** *i.* Greece
193 I3 **Giovenco** *r.* Italy
191 J3 **Giovetto** *mt.* Italy
178 C7 **Giovetto, Lago di** *l.* Italy
191 K8 **Giovi, Monte** *hill* Italy
191 N3 **Giovinazzo** Italy
224 F2 **Gipouloux** *r. Que.* Can.
83 J8 **Gippsland** *reg. Vic.* Austr.
113 □1 **Giraavaru** *i. N. Male* Maldives
116 C6 **Girab** *Rajasthan* India
192 C1 **Giraglia, Île de la** *i. Corse* France
177 K2 **Giraltovce** Slovakia
122 H8 **Girān** Iran
157 L7 **Girancourt** France
122 H7 **Girān Rīg** *mt.* Iran
116 G9 **Girar** *Mahar.* India
237 H7 **Girard** *KS* U.S.A.
232 E7 **Girard** *OH* U.S.A.
232 E6 **Girard** *PA* U.S.A.
225 H1 **Girardin, Lac** *l. Que.* Can.
234 C3 **Girardville** *PA* U.S.A.
192 D8 **Girasole** *Sardegna* Italy
Giravaru *i. N. Male* Maldives *see* **Giraavaru**
122 G4 **Girdab** Iran
123 M6 **Girdao** Pak.
123 K8 **Girdar Dhor** *r.* Pak.
123 I6 **Girdi** Iran
207 I4 **Girei** Nigeria
126 I3 **Giresun** Turkey
Girgenti *Sicilia* Italy *see* **Agrigento**
208 C4 **Giri** *r.* Dem. Rep. Congo
210 C4 **Giribabor** *well* Kenya
117 K7 **Giridih** *Jharkhand* India
195 K6 **Girifalco** Italy
83 K4 **Girilambone** *N.S.W.* Austr.
177 K4 **Girișu de Criș** Romania
136 G6 **Girla Mare** *r.* Moldova
116 E9 **Girna** *r.* India

Gir National Park to Gormaz
317

116 C9 Gir National Park India
Girne Cyprus see Keryneia
177 K6 Giroc Romania
169 E10 Girod Ger.
192 A3 Girolata, Golfe de b. Corse France
157 M8 Giromagny France
250 B5 Girón Ecuador
Giron Sweden see Kiruna
186 K4 Girona Spain
186 K3 Girona prov. Spain
163 D6 Gironde dept France
162 C4 Gironde est. France
163 D6 Gironde-sur-Dropt France
261 G4 Girondo Arg.
186 I3 Gironella Spain
123 O5 Girot Pak.
163 G8 Girou r. France
163 H8 Giroussens France
151 M3 Girton Cambridgeshire, England U.K.
255 B9 Giruá Brazil
146 G12 Girvan South Ayrshire, Scotland U.K.
134 F3 Girvas Rus. Fed.
116 H7 Girwan Uttar Prad. India
80 M5 Gisborne North I. N.Z.
80 M5 Gisborne admin. reg. North I. N.Z.
149 M6 Gisburn Lancashire, England U.K.
222 F4 Giscome B.C. Can.
211 A5 Gisenyi Rwanda
142 J4 Gislaved Sweden
156 C5 Gisors France
Gisozi Burundi see Kisosi
Gissar Tajik. see Hisor
123 L2 Gissar Range mts Tajik./Uzbek.
Gissarskiy Khrebet mts Tajik./Uzbek. see Gissar Range
193 N3 Gissi Italy
165 C6 Gistel Belgium
182 H3 Gistredo, Sierra de mts Spain
190 E2 Giswil Switz.
211 A5 Gitarama Rwanda
211 A5 Gitega Burundi
169 J7 Gittelde Ger.
Giuba r. Somalia see Jubba
197 L6 Giubega Romania
190 G3 Giubiasco Switz.
191 J4 Giudicarie, Valli val. Italy
193 M6 Giugliano in Campania Italy
193 K4 Giuliano di Roma Italy
193 L2 Giulianova Italy
190 I7 Giuncugnano Italy
197 N4 Giurgeului, Munții mts Romania
197 N7 Giurgiu Romania
122 G3 Givar Iran
142 F6 Give Denmark
156 C5 Giverny France
157 I3 Givet France
160 F5 Givors France
165 F8 Givry Belgium
160 F3 Givry France
157 I6 Givry-en-Argonne France
213 F4 Giyani S. Africa
210 C2 Giyon Eth.
Giza Al Jīzah Egypt see Al Jīzah
174 F3 Gizałki Pol.
122 B4 Gīzeh Rūd r. Iran
129 F2 Gizel' Rus. Fed.
159 L7 Gizeux France
131 R3 Gizhiga Rus. Fed.
193 L3 Gizio r. Italy
78 □6 Gizo New Georgia Is Solomon Is
78 □6 Gizo i. New Georgia Is Solomon Is
175 J1 Giżycko Pol.
193 Q10 Gizzeria Italy
196 I8 Gjalicë e Lumës, Mal mt. Albania
141 I6 Gjerde Norway
142 F3 Gjerstad Norway
198 B2 Gjirokastër Albania
221 I3 Gjoa Haven Nunavut Can.
140 □C1 Gjögur Iceland
140 J5 Gjøra Norway
141 K6 Gjøvik Norway
198 A2 Gjuhëzës, Kepi i pt Albania
199 J6 Gkinas, Akrotirio pt Rodos Greece
198 D4 Gkiona mts Greece
225 J4 Glace Bay N.S. Can.
190 D4 Glacier, Monte mt. Italy
222 C3 Glacier Bay AK U.S.A.
220 E4 Glacier Bay National Park and Preserve AK U.S.A.
222 G5 Glacier National Park B.C. Can.
238 H2 Glacier National Park MT U.S.A.
238 D2 Glacier Peak vol. WA U.S.A.
169 C7 Gladbeck Ger.
169 G9 Gladenbach Ger.
232 D12 Glade Spring VA U.S.A.
140 K4 Gladstad Norway
85 M7 Gladstone Qld Austr.
82 G5 Gladstone S.A. Austr.
83 L9 Gladstone Tas. Austr.
223 L5 Gladstone Man. Can.
81 J8 Gladstone North I. N.Z.
226 G4 Gladstone MI U.S.A.
234 F3 Gladstone NJ U.S.A.
232 G11 Gladstone VA U.S.A.
226 J6 Gladwin MI U.S.A.
232 F11 Gladys VA U.S.A.
222 C3 Gladys Lake B.C. Can.
160 J2 Glainans France
146 J9 Glamis Angus, Scotland U.K.
241 Q9 Glamis CA U.S.A.
188 F3 Glamoč Bos.-Herz.
179 J6 Glan r. Austria
172 D2 Glan r. Ger.
92 E9 Glan Mindanao Phil.
143 L3 Glan l. Sweden
150 E4 Glanaman Carmarthenshire, Wales U.K.
147 C8 Glanaruddery Mountains hills Ireland
161 H7 Glandage France
162 G5 Glandon France
161 I6 Glandon r. France
169 F6 Glandorf Ger.
162 F4 Glane r. France
169 E6 Glane r. Ger.
179 J6 Glanegg Austria
164 K4 Glanerbrug Neth.
147 F9 Glanmire Ireland
227 M7 Glanworth Ont. Can.
190 E2 Glarner Alpen mts Switz.
172 F8 Glärnisch mts Switz.
147 J3 Glarryford Northern Ireland U.K.
190 G1 Glarus Switz.
190 G2 Glarus canton Switz.
146 G6 Glas Bheinn hill Scotland U.K.
150 F3 Glasbury Powys, Wales U.K.
146 G7 Glascarnoch, Loch l. Scotland U.K.
236 G6 Glasco KS U.S.A.
142 I2 Glasfjorden l. Sweden
226 E9 Glasford IL U.S.A.
246 □ Glasgow Jamaica
146 H11 Glasgow Glasgow, Scotland U.K.
146 H11 Glasgow admin. div. Scotland U.K.
234 D5 Glasgow DE U.S.A.
230 E7 Glasgow KY U.S.A.
238 K2 Glasgow MT U.S.A.
232 F11 Glasgow VA U.S.A.
171 I9 Glashütte Ger.
173 K2 Glashütten Ger.
169 F10 Gläshütten Ger.
142 I2 Glaskogens naturreservat nature res. Norway
147 I4 Glaslough Ireland
223 I4 Glaslyn Sask. Can.
146 J9 Glas Maol mt. Scotland U.K.
146 G7 Glass, Loch l. Scotland U.K.
147 G6 Glassan Ireland
234 E5 Glassboro NJ U.S.A.
148 I2 Glassford South Lanarkshire, Scotland U.K.
240 N4 Glass Mountain CA U.S.A.
149 K4 Glasson Cumbria, England U.K.
222 C3 Glass Peninsula AK U.S.A.
150 G5 Glastonbury Somerset, England U.K.
235 J1 Glastonbury CT U.S.A.
146 I9 Glas Tulaichean mt. Scotland U.K.
190 E1 Glatt r. Switz.
171 H8 Glaubitz Ger.
171 G9 Glauchau Ger.
197 N6 Glavacioc r. Romania
197 O8 Glavan Bulg.
197 P4 Glăvănești Romania
197 O7 Glavinitsa Bulg.
198 F1 Glavki Greece
196 J8 Glavnik Kosovo Serbia
129 I2 Glavnyy Kut Rus. Fed.
139 O6 Glazomichi Rus. Fed.
207 F5 Glazoué Benin
134 K4 Glazov Rus. Fed.
139 T9 Glazunovka Rus. Fed.
139 N6 Glazunovo Rus. Fed.
226 E4 Gleason WI U.S.A.
222 H5 Gleichen Alta Can.
171 E8 Gleina Ger.
179 K5 Gleinalpe mt. Austria
179 M5 Gleisdorf Austria
Gleiwitz Pol. see Gliwice
160 F5 Gleizé France
151 N3 Glemsford Suffolk, England U.K.
140 L5 Glen Sweden
233 □N4 Glen NH U.S.A.
148 F2 Glenacardoch Point Scotland U.K.
146 F8 Glen Affric val. Scotland U.K.
227 N3 Glen Afton Ont. Can.
80 J4 Glen Afton North I. N.Z.
232 H11 Glen Allen VA U.S.A.
147 E5 Glenamaddy Ireland
147 C4 Glenamoy Ireland
147 C4 Glenamoy r. Ireland
158 D6 Glénan, Îles de is France
226 I5 Glen Arbor MI U.S.A.
147 J2 Glenariff Northern Ireland U.K.
147 K3 Glenarm Northern Ireland U.K.
146 H10 Glen Artney val. Scotland U.K.
146 I8 Glen Avon val. Scotland U.K.
81 F11 Glenavy South I. N.Z.
147 J3 Glenavy Northern Ireland U.K.
146 E11 Glenbarr Argyll and Bute, Scotland U.K.
146 E9 Glenbeg Highland, Scotland U.K.
147 C9 Glenbeg Lough l. Ireland
147 C8 Glenbeigh Ireland
223 L5 Glenboro Man. Can.
146 J12 Glenbreck Scottish Borders, Scotland U.K.
146 D8 Glenbrittle Highland, Scotland U.K.
234 D1 Glenburn PA U.S.A.
234 B6 Glen Burnie MD U.S.A.
146 F8 Glen Cannich val. Scotland U.K.
241 U4 Glen Canyon gorge UT U.S.A.
241 U5 Glen Canyon Dam AZ U.S.A.
241 V4 Glen Canyon National Recreation Area park UT U.S.A.
146 I12 Glencaple Dumfries and Galloway, Scotland U.K.
146 J10 Glencarse Perth and Kinross, Scotland U.K.
146 G6 Glen Cassley val. Scotland U.K.
146 J9 Glen Clova val. Scotland U.K.
224 D5 Glencoe Ont. Can.
215 O4 Glencoe S. Africa
146 F9 Glencoe Highland, Scotland U.K.
146 F9 Glen Coe val. Scotland U.K.
236 H3 Glencoe MN U.S.A.
147 E3 Glencolumbkille Ireland
215 J9 Glenconnor S. Africa
235 H3 Glen Cove NY U.S.A.
147 J6 Glencullen Ireland
227 J3 Glendale Ont. Can.
241 T8 Glendale AZ U.S.A.
240 N7 Glendale CA U.S.A.
241 T4 Glendale UT U.S.A.
232 G8 Glendale Lake PA U.S.A.
82 E4 Glendambo S.A. Austr.
146 F10 Glendaruel val. Scotland U.K.
146 I8 Glen Dee val. Scotland U.K.
85 L6 Glenden Qld Austr.
238 L3 Glendive MT U.S.A.
223 I4 Glendon Alta Can.
234 E3 Glendon PA U.S.A.
238 L5 Glendo Reservoir WY U.S.A.
147 G3 Glendowan Ireland
147 F8 Glenduff Ireland
147 J2 Glendun r. Northern Ireland U.K.
146 I10 Gleneagles Perth and Kinross, Scotland U.K.
148 E8 Glenealy Ireland
146 D11 Glenegedale Argyll and Bute, Scotland U.K.
82 H8 Glenelg r. Vic. Austr.
146 E8 Glenelg Highland, Scotland U.K.
146 J10 Glenfarg Perth and Kinross, Scotland U.K.
147 G4 Glenfarne Ireland
146 I8 Glen Feshie val. Scotland U.K.
151 J2 Glenfield Leicester, England U.K.
233 J5 Glenfield NY U.S.A.
146 F9 Glenfinnan Highland, Scotland U.K.
147 H2 Glengad Head Ireland
234 F3 Glen Gardner NJ U.S.A.
147 C9 Glengarriff Ireland
146 F8 Glen Garry val. Highland, Scotland U.K.
146 H9 Glen Garry val. Perth and Kinross, Scotland U.K.
87 E9 Glengarry Range hills W.A. Austr.
148 B5 Glengavlen Ireland
246 □ Glengoffe Jamaica
84 G8 Glengyle Qld Austr.
81 C13 Glenham South I. N.Z.
147 H2 Glenhead Northern Ireland U.K.
84 D7 Glen Helen N.T. Austr.
86 J4 Glen Hill Aboriginal Reserve W.A. Austr.
83 M3 Glen Innes N.S.W. Austr.
146 K8 Glenkindie Aberdeenshire, Scotland U.K.
146 G13 Glenluce Dumfries and Galloway, Scotland U.K.
146 H9 Glen Lyon val. Scotland U.K.
234 C2 Glen Lyon PA U.S.A.
222 C2 Glenlyon Peak Y.T. Can.
80 I4 Glen Massey North I. N.Z.
234 D4 Glenmoore PA U.S.A.
146 G8 Glen More val. Scotland U.K.
85 L9 Glenmorgan Qld Austr.
146 J9 Glen Muick val. Scotland U.K.
80 I4 Glen Murray North I. N.Z.
240 J2 Glenn CA U.S.A.
241 V10 Glenn, Mount AZ U.S.A.
147 C5 Glennagevlagh Ireland
220 D3 Glennallen AK U.S.A.
146 F9 Glen Nevis val. Scotland U.K.
227 K5 Glennie MI U.S.A.
232 I11 Glenns VA U.S.A.
238 G5 Glenns Ferry ID U.S.A.
148 F4 Glenoe Northern Ireland U.K.
222 D3 Glenora B.C. Can.
85 H4 Glenore Qld Austr.
84 G7 Glenormiston Qld Austr.
87 F10 Glenorn Aboriginal Reserve W.A. Austr.
146 G6 Glen Oykel val. Scotland U.K.
83 N4 Glenreagh N.S.W. Austr.
233 K3 Glen Robertson Ont. Can.
234 B5 Glen Rock PA U.S.A.
232 D11 Glen Rogers WV U.S.A.
237 G9 Glen Rose TX U.S.A.
146 J10 Glenrothes Fife, Scotland U.K.
86 I4 Glenroy W.A. Austr.
233 L5 Glens Falls NY U.S.A.
148 D4 Glenshane Pass Northern Ireland U.K.
146 J9 Glen Shee val. Scotland U.K.
146 F8 Glen Shiel val. Scotland U.K.
234 E4 Glenside PA U.S.A.
146 G9 Glen Spean val. Scotland U.K.
234 F2 Glen Spey NY U.S.A.
147 F3 Glenties Ireland
147 H2 Glentogher Ireland
146 H8 Glen Tromie val. Scotland U.K.
81 F10 Glentunnel South I. N.Z.
147 G2 Glenveagh National Park Ireland
232 E10 Glenville WV U.S.A.
148 H5 Glen Vine Isle of Man
226 E1 Glenwater Ont. Can.
232 F11 Glen Wilton VA U.S.A.
237 I8 Glenwood AR U.S.A.
240 □F14 Glenwood HI U.S.A.
236 H5 Glenwood IA U.S.A.
236 H3 Glenwood MN U.S.A.
235 G2 Glenwood NJ U.S.A.
239 J10 Glenwood NM U.S.A.
241 U3 Glenwood UT U.S.A.
232 C10 Glenwood WV U.S.A.
226 B4 Glenwood City WI U.S.A.
239 K7 Glenwood Springs CO U.S.A.
160 J2 Glère France
171 F8 Glesien Ger.
146 □N2 Gletness Shetland, Scotland U.K.
190 E2 Gletsch Switz.
Glevum Gloucestershire, England U.K. see Gloucester
170 G2 Glewitz Ger.
226 D3 Glidden WI U.S.A.
171 J6 Glienicke Ger.
Glikí Greece see Glyki
147 D7 Glin Ireland
188 F3 Glina r. Bos.-Herz./Croatia
188 F3 Glina Croatia
168 J3 Glinde Ger.
171 G6 Glindow Ger.
139 R8 Glinishchevo Rus. Fed.
136 G6 Glinjeni Moldova
139 P7 Glinka Rus. Fed.
175 I3 Glinojeck Pol.
151 L2 Glinton Peterborough, England U.K.
141 J6 Glittertinden mt. Norway
174 G5 Gliwice Pol.
174 G5 Gliwicki, Kanał canal Pol.
179 K6 Globasnitz Austria
241 V8 Globe AZ U.S.A.
177 L6 Glodea, Vârful hill Romania
197 O6 Glodeanu-Sărat Romania
136 G6 Glodeni Moldova
197 M4 Glodeni Romania
179 J6 Glödnitz Austria
174 E2 Głodowa Pol.
Glodyany Moldova see Glodeni
Glogau Pol. see Głogów
179 M4 Gloggnitz Austria
190 G2 Glogn r. Switz.
196 I8 Glogovac Kosovo Serbia
174 E4 Głogów Pol.
174 F5 Głogówek Pol.
175 J5 Głogów Małopolski Pol.
174 G2 Głogowo Pol.
140 L3 Glomfjord Norway
140 O4 Glommersträsk Sweden
173 L6 Glonn Ger.
173 L5 Glonn r. Ger.
178 C6 Glorenza Italy
254 F4 Glória Brazil
184 B2 Glória do Ribatejo Port.
217 □2 Glorieuses, Îles is Indian Ocean
Glorioso Islands Indian Ocean see Glorieuses, Îles
159 M4 Glos-la-Ferrière France
198 E3 Glossa Greece
149 N7 Glossop Derbyshire, England U.K.
171 E7 Glöthe Ger.
135 I5 Glotovka Rus. Fed.
83 M4 Gloucester N.S.W. Austr.
91 K8 Gloucester New Britain P.N.G.
150 H4 Gloucester Gloucestershire, England U.K.
233 O6 Gloucester MA U.S.A.
232 I11 Gloucester VA U.S.A.
150 H4 Gloucester, Vale of val. England U.K.
234 E5 Gloucester City NJ U.S.A.
234 E5 Gloucester County county NJ U.S.A.
85 L6 Gloucester Island Qld Austr.
232 I11 Gloucester Point VA U.S.A.
150 H4 Gloucestershire admin. div. England U.K.
147 F9 Glounthaune Ireland
243 P9 Glover Reef Belize
233 K5 Gloversville NY U.S.A.
225 K3 Glovertown Nfld and Lab. Can.
175 J4 Głowaczów Pol.
174 F1 Główczyce Pol.
170 H1 Glowe Ger.
170 F5 Glöwen Ger.
175 H4 Głowno Pol.
174 F5 Głubczyce Pol.
100 I5 Glubinnoye Rus. Fed.
137 T5 Glubokaya r. Rus. Fed.
135 H6 Glubokiy Rostovskaya Oblast' Rus. Fed.
135 H7 Glubokiy Rostovskaya Oblast' Rus. Fed.
Glubokoye Belarus see Hlybokaye
121 T2 Glubokoye Kazakh.
138 M1 Glubokoye, Ozero l. Rus. Fed.
174 F5 Głuchołazy Pol.
175 I4 Głuchów Pol.
168 I1 Glücksburg (Ostsee) Ger.
168 H3 Glückstadt Ger.
144 D1 Gluggarnir hill Faroe Is
161 F7 Gluiras France
Glukhov Ukr. see Hlukhiv
94 A2 Glumpangminyeuk Sumatera Indon.
149 N6 Glusburn North Yorkshire, England U.K.
137 N2 Glushkovo Rus. Fed.
174 E5 Głuszyca Pol.
174 G3 Głuszyńskie, Jezioro l. Pol.
150 D1 Glyder Fawr hill Wales U.K.
198 B3 Glyki Greece
150 F2 Glyn Ceiriog Wrexham, Wales U.K.
150 E4 Glyncorrwg Neath Port Talbot, Wales U.K.
Glynebwy Wales U.K. see Ebbw Vale
142 E5 Glyngøre Denmark
147 K3 Glynn Northern Ireland U.K.
150 E4 Glynneath Neath Port Talbot, Wales U.K.
Glyn-Nedd Wales U.K. see Glynneath
120 B2 Gmelinka Rus. Fed.
179 I6 Gmünd Kärnten Austria
179 K2 Gmünd Niederösterreich Austria
173 L6 Gmund am Tegernsee Ger.
179 I4 Gmunden Austria
232 D8 Gnadenhutten OH U.S.A.
141 N5 Gnarp Sweden
168 H4 Gnarrenburg Ger.
179 M6 Gnas Austria
147 D8 Gneevgullia Ireland
171 G8 Gneisenaustadt Schildau Ger.
195 □ Ġnejna, Il-Bajja tal- b. Malta
179 I6 Gnesau Austria
Gnesen Pol. see Gniezno
143 N2 Gnesta Sweden
142 H5 Gniben pt Denmark
179 M6 Gniebing Austria
174 G2 Gniew Pol.
174 G1 Gniewino Pol.
174 G3 Gniewkowo Pol.
175 I5 Gnieździska Pol.
174 F3 Gniezno Pol.
143 O4 Gnisvärd Gotland Sweden
196 J8 Gnjilane Kosovo Serbia
191 M6 Gnocchetta Italy
170 G3 Gnoien Ger.
174 F5 Gnojna Pol.
175 I6 Gnojnik Pol.
175 I5 Gnojno Pol.
150 H2 Gnosall Staffordshire, England U.K.
173 J3 Gnotzheim Ger.
87 D12 Gnowangerup W.A. Austr.
87 D10 Gnows Nest Range hills W.A. Austr.
168 I2 Gnutz Ger.
114 C5 Goa Goa India
114 D5 Goa state India
212 C5 Goageb Namibia
83 M7 Goalen Head N.S.W. Austr.
117 M6 Goalpara Assam India
93 A8 Goang Flores Indon.
206 E5 Goaso Ghana
146 F11 Goat Fell hill Scotland U.K.
247 □2 Goat Point Antigua and Barbuda
210 D3 Goba Eth.
212 C4 Gobabis Namibia
Gobannium Monmouthshire, Wales U.K. see Abergavenny
212 C5 Gobas Namibia
260 C5 Gobernador Ayala Arg.
261 G2 Gobernador Crespo Arg.
260 D6 Gobernador Duval Arg.
259 C8 Gobernador Gregores Arg.
261 H3 Gobernador Mansilla Arg.
259 C8 Gobernador Mayer Arg.
261 G2 Gobernador Racedo Arg.
261 G4 Gobernador Ugarte Arg.
258 F3 Gobernador Virasoro Arg.
106 J4 Gobi Desert China/Mongolia
139 Q8 Gobiki Rus. Fed.
179 I3 Göblberg hill Austria
104 B8 Gobō Japan
150 F2 Gobowen Shropshire, England U.K.
Gobustan Azer. see Qobustan
199 J6 Göcek Turkey
169 B7 Goch Ger.
212 C5 Gochas Namibia
169 J10 Gochsheim Ger.
97 H9 Go Công Vietnam
179 O6 Göcsej hills Hungary
177 I4 Göd Hungary
171 J8 Göda Ger.
117 L7 Godagari Bangl.
142 F2 Godal Norway
151 K5 Godalming Surrey, England U.K.
114 G4 Godavari r. India
114 H4 Godavari, Cape India
114 H4 Godavari, Mouths of the India
225 H3 Godbout Que. Can.
225 H3 Godbout r. Que. Can.
117 K7 Godda Jharkhand India
222 C3 Goddard AK U.S.A.
240 N4 Goddard, Mount CA U.S.A.
172 F2 Goddelau Ger.
169 G8 Goddelsheim (Lichtenfels) Ger.
210 D3 Godē Eth.
184 C3 Godeal hill Port.
197 L7 Godech Bulg.
234 F2 Godeffroy NY U.S.A.
178 F8 Godega di Sant'Urbano Italy
129 F6 Gödekli Turkey
187 D9 Godelleta Spain
224 D5 Goderich Ont. Can.
159 L2 Goderville France
Godhavn Greenland see Qeqertarsuaq
116 D8 Godhra Gujarat India
116 B8 Godia Creek b. Gujarat India
190 G6 Godiasco Italy
182 E6 Godim Port.
210 E3 Godinlabe Somalia
175 H1 Godkowo Pol.
81 E10 Godley r. South I. N.Z.
151 L3 Godmanchester Cambridgeshire, England U.K.
104 E5 Gōdo Japan
93 D4 Godo, Gunung mt. Indon.
184 E4 Godolín r. Port./Spain
177 I4 Gödöllő Hungary
179 J8 Godovič Slovenia
261 G3 Godoy Arg.
260 C3 Godoy Cruz Arg.
177 G5 Gödre Hungary
223 M3 Gods r. Man. Can.
223 M4 Gods Lake Man. Can.
223 O2 God's Mercy, Bay of Nunavut Can.
151 L5 Godstone Surrey, England U.K.
Godthåb Greenland see Nuuk
140 O2 Godučohkka mt. Sweden
Godwin-Austen, Mount China/Jammu and Kashmir see K2
174 G4 Godziesze Wielkie Pol.
175 K5 Godziszów Pol.
215 K6 Goedemoed S. Africa
164 E5 Goedereede Neth.
Goedgegun Swaziland see Nhlangano
214 C5 Goegap Nature Reserve S. Africa
224 E3 Goéland, Lac au l. Que. Can.
225 I2 Goélands, Lac aux l. Que. Can.
164 E5 Goes Neth.
227 J3 Goetzville MI U.S.A.
233 N5 Goffstown NH U.S.A.
179 L2 Göfritz an der Wild Austria
224 D4 Gogama Ont. Can.
103 J12 Gō-gawa r. Japan
226 E3 Gogebic, Lake MI U.S.A.
226 E3 Gogebic Range hills MI U.S.A.
128 H2 Gögeç Turkey
172 H4 Göggingen Ger.
129 G6 Gogi Lerr mt. Armenia/Azer.
138 J1 Gogland, Ostrov i. Rus. Fed.
213 G4 Gogoi Moz.
139 O7 Gogolevka Rus. Fed.
174 G5 Gogolin Pol.
197 K6 Gogoșu Romania
207 F4 Gogounou Benin
Gogra Jharkhand India see Ghaghra
Gogra r. India see Ghaghara
208 F2 Gogrial Sudan
116 D7 Gogunda Rajasthan India
116 G6 Gohad Madh. Prad. India
116 F5 Gohana Haryana India
116 F8 Goharganj Madh. Prad. India
168 K2 Göhl Ger.
171 F7 Gohrau Ger.
168 K4 Göhrde Ger.
170 I2 Göhren, Ostseebad Ger.
170 G4 Göhren-Lebbin Ger.
254 G3 Goiana Brazil
256 C3 Goiandira Brazil
255 C5 Goianésia Brazil
256 C2 Goiânia Brazil
254 G3 Goianinha Brazil
256 C2 Goianira Brazil
256 B1 Goiás Brazil
256 B2 Goiás state Brazil
256 C3 Goiatuba Brazil
111 E10 Goicangmai Xizang China
92 □ Goikul Palau
146 G10 Goil, Loch inlet Scotland U.K.
108 C2 Goincang Qinghai China
142 J5 Göinge reg. Sweden
256 A6 Goio r. Brazil
256 A6 Goio-Erê Brazil
209 E6 Goi-Pula Dem. Rep. Congo
164 H5 Goirle Neth.
182 D8 Góis Port.
158 G8 Gois, Passage du France
191 J5 Goito Italy
186 B1 Goizueta Spain
210 C3 Gojeb Wenz r. Eth.
104 C7 Gojō Japan
102 R7 Gojōme Japan
123 O6 Gojra Pak.
175 H4 Gojść Pol.
105 K3 Goka Japan
114 D4 Gokak Karnataka India
114 D5 Gokarn Karnataka India
128 A1 Gök Çay r. Turkey
199 G2 Gökçeada i. Turkey
199 J3 Gökçedağ Turkey
129 A5 Gökçedere Turkey
199 L5 Gökçehüyük Turkey
199 M2 Gökçekaya Barajı resr Turkey
199 I4 Gökçen Turkey
199 J4 Gökçeören Turkey
129 B6 Gökçeşeyh Turkey
Gökdepe Turkm. see Gëkdepe
128 A2 Gökdere r. Turkey
168 H2 Gokels Ger.
126 G3 Gökirmak r. Turkey
122 G1 Goklenkuy, Solonchak salt l. Turkm.
129 C6 Gököğlan Turkey
199 J5 Gökova Muğla Turkey
Gökova Muğla Turkey see Ula
199 I6 Gökova Körfezi b. Turkey
123 J9 Gokprosh Hills Pak.
129 D6 Göksu r. Turkey
126 H4 Göksun Turkey
126 G5 Göksu Nehri r. Turkey
128 B2 Göksu Parkı Turkey
96 C3 Gokteik Myanmar
128 A2 Göktepe Turkey
213 F3 Gokwe Zimbabwe
142 E1 Gol Norway
176 G5 Gola Croatia
117 J8 Gola Jharkhand India
116 H5 Gola Uttar Prad. India
175 J4 Gołąb Pol.
191 Q4 Golac Slovenia
Golada Spain see Agolada
117 N6 Golaghat Assam India
147 F2 Gola Island Ireland
179 I8 Golak mt. Slovenia
117 L6 Golakganj Assam India
128 D5 Golan hills Syria
174 F3 Gołańcz Pol.
175 K4 Gołaszyn Pol.
122 G7 Golbāf Iran
123 M4 Golbahār Afgh.
126 H5 Gölbaşı Turkey
199 K6 Gölbent Turkey
157 L7 Golbey France
114 F4 Golconda Andhra Prad. India
237 K7 Golconda IL U.S.A.
238 F6 Golconda NV U.S.A.
199 I3 Gölcük Balıkesir Turkey
Gölçük Turkey see Etili
199 K2 Gölcük Kocaeli Turkey
199 J3 Gölcük r. Turkey
176 E2 Golčův Jeníkov Czech Rep.
175 H5 Gołcza Pol.
174 C2 Golczewo Pol.
232 H7 Gold PA U.S.A.
172 G7 Goldach Switz.
175 K1 Gołdap Pol.
175 J1 Gołdapa r. Pol.
169 H10 Goldbach Ger.
238 B5 Gold Beach OR U.S.A.
170 E5 Goldbeck Ger.
170 F3 Goldberg Ger.
150 G4 Goldcliff Newport, Wales U.K.
Gold Coast country Africa see Ghana
83 N3 Gold Coast Qld Austr.
206 E5 Gold Coast coastal area Ghana
179 H6 Goldeck mt. Austria
178 H5 Goldegg Austria
168 H1 Goldelund Ger.
222 G5 Golden B.C. Can.
147 G8 Golden Ireland
80 G7 Golden Bay South I. N.Z.
238 D4 Goldendale WA U.S.A.
81 G8 Golden Downs South I. N.Z.
222 F5 Golden Ears Provincial Park B.C. Can.
169 K7 Goldene Aue reg. Ger.
215 M4 Golden Gate Highlands National Park S. Africa
240 J4 Golden Gate National Recreation Area park CA U.S.A.
246 □ Golden Grove Jamaica
222 E5 Golden Hinde mt. B.C. Can.
224 E4 Golden Lake Ont. Can.
237 J11 Golden Meadow LA U.S.A.
151 K5 Golden Pot Hampshire, England U.K.
223 I5 Golden Prairie Sask. Can.
247 □2 Golden Rock airport St Kitts and Nevis
168 F5 Goldenstedt Ger.
116 F2 Golden Throne mt. Jammu and Kashmir
147 F7 Golden Vale lowland Ireland
215 J8 Golden Valley S. Africa
150 G3 Golden Valley val. England U.K.
213 F3 Golden Valley Zimbabwe
240 O4 Goldfield NV U.S.A.
173 L1 Goldkronach Ger.
175 J1 Gołdopiwo, Jezioro l. Pol.
222 E5 Gold River B.C. Can.
223 K3 Goldsand Lake Man. Can.
234 D6 Goldsboro MD U.S.A.
231 I8 Goldsboro NC U.S.A.
240 P6 Goldstone Lake CA U.S.A.
86 E6 Goldsworthy W.A. Austr.
237 F10 Goldthwaite TX U.S.A.
129 E7 Göldüzü Turkey
232 H10 Goldvein VA U.S.A.
127 K3 Göle Turkey
184 C2 Golegã Port.
170 K5 Golenice Pol.
174 C2 Goleniów Pol.
123 J5 Golestān Afgh.
122 F3 Golestān prov. Iran
174 G6 Goleszów Pol.
240 M7 Goleta CA U.S.A.
242 □R13 Golfito Costa Rica
192 D6 Golfo Aranci Sardegna Italy
192 C7 Golfo di Orosei Gennargentu e Asinara, Parco Nazionale del nat. park Sardegna Italy
199 J6 Gölgeli Dağları mts Turkey
199 K5 Gölhisar Turkey
191 Q5 Goli hill Croatia
191 R6 Goli i. Croatia
237 G11 Goliad TX U.S.A.
196 I7 Golija nat. park Serbia
196 I7 Golija Planina mts Serbia
174 G3 Golina Pol.
107 Q4 Golin Baixing Nei Mongol China
161 B7 Golinhac France
139 U6 Golitsyno Rus. Fed.
126 H3 Gölköy Turkey
173 I2 Gollach r. Ger.
Gollel Swaziland see Lavumisa
179 N3 Göllersdorf Austria
172 E2 Göllheim Ger.
170 I4 Gollin Ger.
170 E3 Göllin Ger.
178 H4 Golling an der Salzach Austria
171 D8 Göllingen Ger.
170 I4 Gollmitz Ger.
171 G6 Golm Ger.
199 I4 Gölmarmara Turkey
169 I7 Golmbach Ger.
171 H6 Golmberg hill Ger.
186 G4 Golmes Spain
106 D8 Golmud Qinghai China
106 D8 Golmud He r. China
179 J7 Golnik Slovenia
192 D2 Golo r. Corse France
92 C5 Golo i. Phil.
139 X6 Golobino Rus. Fed.
121 L7 Golodnaya Step' plain Uzbek.
Gologory hills Ukr. see Holohory
258 E3 Golondrina Arg.
185 I2 Golondrinos, Sierra de los mts Spain
208 C2 Golongosso C.A.R.
139 X7 Golovanovo Rus. Fed.
128 D2 Gölovası Turkey
137 O3 Golovchino Rus. Fed.
129 A2 Golovinka Rus. Fed.
100 N7 Golovnino Kuril'skiye O-va Rus. Fed.
122 D5 Golpāyegān Iran
199 L2 Gölpazarı Turkey
182 I6 Golpejas Spain
179 O4 Gols Austria
179 M3 Gölsen r. Austria
146 I7 Golspie Highland, Scotland U.K.
171 I7 Golßen Ger.
179 K7 Golte mts Slovenia
171 F9 Göltzsch r. Ger.
175 H2 Golub-Dobrzyń Pol.
137 Q8 Golubitskaya Rus. Fed.
121 P1 Golubovka Kazakh.
174 F4 Gołuchów Pol.
139 U8 Golun' Rus. Fed.
209 B7 Golungo Alto Angola
122 I5 Gol Vardeh Iran
210 E4 Golweyn Somalia
197 M9 Golyama Syutkya mt. Bulg.
197 M8 Golyama Zhelyazna Bulg.
197 M9 Golyam Perelik mt. Bulg.
197 M9 Golyam Persenk mt. Bulg.
129 D7 Gölyanı Turkey
Golyashi Belarus see Sasnovy Bor
199 J2 Gölyazı Turkey
175 I3 Gołymin-Ośrodek Pol.
139 O7 Golynki Rus. Fed.
Golyshi Rus. Fed. see Vetluzhskiy
129 B5 Gölyurt Geçidi pass Turkey
170 J5 Golzow Brandenburg Ger.
171 G6 Golzow Brandenburg Ger.
208 F5 Goma Dem. Rep. Congo
211 A5 Goma Uganda
172 G5 Gomadingen Ger.
116 F2 Goma Hanu Jammu and Kashmir
111 I11 Gomang Co salt l. China
106 G9 Gomangxung Qinghai China
104 C7 Gomanodan-zan mt. Japan
183 P5 Gómara Spain
183 P5 Gómara, Campo de reg. Spain
172 G5 Gomaringen Ger.
116 I7 Gomati r. India
94 □ Gombak, Bukit hill Sing.
208 F4 Gombari Dem. Rep. Congo
207 H4 Gombe Nigeria
207 H4 Gombe state Nigeria
211 A6 Gombe r. Tanz.
199 K6 Gömbe Turkey
211 A6 Gombe Stream National Park Tanz.
207 I4 Gombi Nigeria
129 G4 Gombori Georgia
206 E4 Gomboussougou Burkina
217 □1a Gombrani Island Rodrigues I. Mauritius
Gombroon Iran see Bandar-e 'Abbās
199 H3 Gömeç Turkey
182 I6 Gomecello Spain
Gomel' Belarus see Homyel'
Gomel Oblast admin. div. Belarus see Homyel'skaya Voblasts'
Gomel'skaya Oblast' admin. div. Belarus see Homyel'skaya Voblasts'
184 C5 Gomes Aires Port.
146 D10 Gometra i. Scotland U.K.
245 H2 Gómez Farías Mex.
242 H5 Gómez Palacio Mex.
250 A5 Gómez Rendón Ecuador
122 E3 Gomīshān Iran
171 E6 Gommern Ger.
111 G10 Gomo Xizang China
111 G10 Gomo Co salt l. China
139 R1 Gomorovichi Rus. Fed.
190 E3 Goms reg. Switz.
93 E4 Gomumu i. Maluku Indon.
175 H4 Gomunice Pol.
Gonabad Iran see Jūymand
246 G4 Gonaïves Haiti
213 F4 Gonarezhou National Park Zimbabwe
246 G4 Gonâve, Île de la i. Haiti
122 E5 Gonbad, Chāh-e well Iran
122 F3 Gonbad-e Kavus Iran
177 K3 Gönc Hungary
182 F8 Gonçalo Port.
161 H6 Goncelin France
116 I6 Gonda Uttar Prad. India
116 C9 Gondal Gujarat India
210 E2 Gonda Libah well Eth.
250 C5 Gondar Col.
Gondar Eth. see Gonder
182 D6 Gondar Braga Port.
182 D6 Gondar Porto Port.
172 F3 Gondelsheim Ger.
210 C1 Gonder Eth.
129 E6 Gönderme Geçidi pass Turkey
169 D10 Gondershausen Ger.
182 G5 Gondesende Port.
208 C2 Gondey Chad
116 H9 Gondia Mahar. India
182 C6 Gondomar Port.
182 C4 Gondomar Spain
169 D10 Gondorf Ger.
182 D5 Gondoriz Port.
157 K6 Gondrecourt-le-Château France
157 K6 Gondreville France
157 M6 Gondrexange, Étang de l. France
163 E8 Gondrin France
199 I2 Gönen Balıkesir Turkey
199 L5 Gönen Isparta Turkey
199 I2 Gönen r. Turkey
161 I10 Gonfaron France
159 L2 Gonfreville-l'Orcher France
209 C8 Gonga Angola
109 I3 Gong'an Hubei China
111 I12 Gongbalou Xizang China
111 K12 Gongbo'gyamda Xizang China
106 E7 Gongchakou Gansu China
Gongchang Gansu China see Longxi
108 H6 Gongcheng Guangxi China
111 J12 Gonggar Xizang China
108 C4 Gongga Shan mt. Sichuan China
106 G8 Gonghe Qinghai China
Gonghe Yunnan China see Mouding
107 N6 Gonghui Hebei China
Gongjiang Jiangxi China see Yudu
110 F5 Gongliu Xinjiang China
207 I4 Gongola r. Nigeria
83 K4 Gongolgon N.S.W. Austr.
208 A5 Gongoué Gabon
106 E6 Gongpoquan Gansu China
108 E4 Gongquan Sichuan China
108 B5 Gongshan Yunnan China
108 D6 Gongwang Shan mts Yunnan China
Gongxian Henan China see Gongyi
Gongxian Sichuan China see Gongquan
107 M9 Gongyi Henan China
100 D7 Gongzhuling Jilin China
192 C8 Goni Sardegna Italy
261 I3 Goñi Uru.
175 K2 Goniądz Pol.
207 I4 Goniri Nigeria
Gonjo Xizang China see Kasha
108 B3 Gonjo Xizang China
192 A9 Gonnesa Sardegna Italy
192 A9 Gonnesa, Golfo di b. Sardegna Italy
198 D3 Gonnoi Greece
192 B9 Gonnosfanadiga Sardegna Italy
192 B8 Gonnosnò Sardegna Italy
102 S6 Gonohe Japan
103 G13 Gōnoura Japan
160 I2 Gonsans France
215 M8 Gonubie S. Africa
177 G4 Gönyű Hungary
191 J6 Gonzaga Italy
245 I3 Gonzáles Mex.
240 K5 Gonzales CA U.S.A.
237 G11 Gonzales TX U.S.A.
261 F4 González Moreno Arg.
244 D2 González Ortega Mex.
242 □T13 Gonzalo Vásquez Panama
100 D2 Gonzha Rus. Fed.
232 H11 Goochland VA U.S.A.
232 F11 Goode VA U.S.A.
263 I2 Goodenough, Cape Antarctica
91 L8 Goodenough Island P.N.G.
227 P5 Gooderham Ont. Can.
226 I4 Good Harbor Bay MI U.S.A.
226 I4 Good Hart MI U.S.A.
215 J1 Good Hope Botswana
226 D9 Good Hope IL U.S.A.
214 C10 Good Hope, Cape of S. Africa
222 E5 Good Hope Mountain B.C. Can.
238 G5 Gooding ID U.S.A.
236 E6 Goodland KS U.S.A.
217 □1b Goodlands Mauritius
226 F4 Goodman WI U.S.A.
83 K3 Goodooga N.S.W. Austr.
84 D2 Goodparla N.T. Austr.
226 D4 Goodrich WI U.S.A.
223 I4 Goodsoil Sask. Can.
263 E2 Goodspeed Nunataks nunataks Antarctica
150 C3 Goodwick Pembrokeshire, Wales U.K.
225 G2 Goodwood r. Que. Can.
81 E12 Goodwood South I. N.Z.
149 P6 Goole East Riding of Yorkshire, England U.K.
83 J6 Goolgowi N.S.W. Austr.
82 G6 Goolwa S.A. Austr.
84 D1 Goomadeer r. N.T. Austr.
87 D11 Goomalling W.A. Austr.
83 J3 Goombalie N.S.W. Austr.
85 N9 Goomeri Qld Austr.
213 G3 Goonda Moz.
83 M3 Goondiwindi Qld Austr.
87 F10 Goongarrie, Lake salt flat W.A. Austr.
87 F10 Goongarrie National Park W.A. Austr.
150 B7 Goonhavern Cornwall, England U.K.
85 K6 Goonyella Qld Austr.
164 K4 Goor Neth.
87 D11 Goorly, Lake salt flat W.A. Austr.
225 I2 Goose r. Nfld and Lab. Can.
236 G2 Goose r. ND U.S.A.
Goose Bay Nfld and Lab. Can. see Happy Valley-Goose Bay
81 H9 Goose Bay South I. N.Z.
231 G9 Goose Creek SC U.S.A.
238 H5 Goose Creek r. ID/NV U.S.A.
259 F8 Goose Green Falkland Is
238 D6 Goose Lake CA U.S.A.
240 M6 Goose Lake Canal r. CA U.S.A.
114 E5 Gooty Andhra Prad. India
115 J3 Gop Orissa India
117 L8 Gopalganj Bangl.
117 J6 Gopalganj Bihar India
115 I3 Gopalpur Orissa India
183 O3 Gopegi Spain
116 G4 Gopeshwar Uttaranchal India
114 E7 Gopichettipalayam Tamil Nadu India
116 I7 Gopiganj Uttar Prad. India
174 G3 Gopło, Jezioro l. Pol.
172 H4 Göppingen Ger.
108 A4 Goqên Xizang China
185 N6 Gor Spain
185 M5 Gor r. Spain
174 E4 Góra Dolnośląskie Pol.
175 I3 Góra Mazowieckie Pol.
Goradiz Azer. see Horadiz
185 M6 Gorafe Spain
129 G2 Goragorskiy Rus. Fed.
175 K5 Goraj Pol.
175 J4 Góra Kalwaria Pol.
117 I6 Gorakhpur Uttar Prad. India
129 H5 Goranboy Azer.
175 J4 Góra Puławska Pol.
177 H1 Góra Świętej Anny, Park Krajobrazowy Pol.
174 D2 Gorawino Pol.
188 G4 Goražde Bos.-Herz.
139 U8 Gorbachevo Rus. Fed.
260 A6 Gorbea Chile
177 K4 Görbeháza Hungary
183 O2 Gorbeia mt. Spain
100 A2 Gorbitsa Rus. Fed.
261 H4 Gorchs Arg.
134 H4 Gorchukha Rus. Fed.
177 H6 Görcsöny Hungary
175 I6 Gorczański Park Narodowy nat. park Pol.
246 B6 Gorda, Banco sea feature Hond.
216 □3d Gorda, Punta pt La Palma Canary Is
242 □R10 Gorda, Punta pt Nic.
240 H1 Gorda, Punta pt CA U.S.A.
185 K6 Gorda, Sierra mts Spain
246 E1 Gorda Cay i. Bahamas
141 L6 Gördalen Sweden
183 J4 Gordaliza del Pino Spain
190 H7 Gordana r. Italy
161 G9 Gordes France
199 J4 Gördes Turkey
139 O9 Gordeyevka Rus. Fed.
190 F3 Gordola Switz.
87 D13 Gordon r. W.A. Austr.
146 K11 Gordon Scottish Borders, Scotland U.K.
236 D4 Gordon NE U.S.A.
234 C3 Gordon PA U.S.A.
226 C3 Gordon WI U.S.A.
259 C9 Gordon, Isla i. Chile
83 K10 Gordon, Lake Tas. Austr.
190 G3 Gordona Italy
84 C1 Gordon Bay N.T. Austr.
84 C4 Gordon Creek r. N.T. Austr.
86 J5 Gordon Downs W.A. Austr.
223 I3 Gordon Lake Alta Can.
222 H2 Gordon Lake N.W.T. Can.
222 C2 Gordon Landing Y.T. Can.
214 C10 Gordon's Bay S. Africa
232 G10 Gordonsville VA U.S.A.
85 J4 Gordonvale Qld Austr.
234 C4 Gordonville PA U.S.A.
208 C3 Goré Chad
210 B2 Gorē Eth.
81 C13 Gore South I. N.Z.
232 G9 Gore VA U.S.A.
227 L4 Gore Bay Ont. Can.
146 J11 Gorebridge Midlothian, Scotland U.K.
199 I4 Görece Turkey
139 U7 Gorelki Rus. Fed.
129 E4 Gorelovka Georgia
135 H5 Goreloye Rus. Fed.
126 G4 Göreme Milli Parkı nat. park Turkey
179 L8 Gorenja Straža Slovenia
179 J7 Gorenja vas Slovenia
220 C4 Gore Point AK U.S.A.
147 I7 Goresbridge Ireland
139 S6 Goretovo Rus. Fed.
147 J7 Gorey Ireland
122 H7 Gorg Iran
122 F3 Gorgān Iran
122 E3 Gorgān, Khalīj-e b. Iran
122 E3 Gorgān, Rūd-e r. Iran
Gorgany mts Ukr. see Horhany
86 E6 Gorge Range hills W.A. Austr.
85 J5 Gorge Range mts Qld Austr.
81 C13 Gorge Road South I. N.Z.
214 B3 Gorges Namibia
176 G5 Gőrgeteg Hungary
193 Q7 Gorgoglione Italy
206 B2 Gorgol admin. reg. Maur.
190 H9 Gorgona, Isola di i. Italy
190 G4 Gorgonzola Italy
210 C1 Gorgora Eth.
207 H3 Gorgoram Nigeria
187 F10 Gorgos r. Spain
197 R5 Gorgova, Lacul l. Romania
129 C6 Görgü Turkey
233 N4 Gorham NH U.S.A.
129 F4 Gori Georgia
196 H8 Gorica Montenegro
179 O7 Goričan Croatia
179 N6 Goričko reg. Slovenia
164 G5 Gorinchem Neth.
151 J4 Goring Oxfordshire, England U.K.
191 M6 Gorino Italy
129 H6 Goris Armenia
173 J6 Görisried Ger.
197 P8 Goritsa Bulg.
139 T4 Goritsy Rus. Fed.
170 I4 Göritz Ger.
191 P4 Gorizia Italy
191 P4 Gorizia prov. Italy
179 L8 Gorjanci mts Slovenia
139 V5 Gorka Rus. Fed.
129 F1 Gor'kaya Balka r. Rus. Fed.
117 J6 Gorkha Nepal
Gorki Belarus see Horki
134 I4 Gorki Rus. Fed.
Gor'kiy Rus. Fed. see Nizhniy Novgorod
Gor'kovskaya Oblast' admin. div. Rus. Fed. see Nizhegorodskaya Oblast'
139 N4 Gor'kovskoye Vodokhranilishche resr Rus. Fed.
121 S1 Gor'koye, Ozero salt l. Rus. Fed.
121 S1 Gor'koye, Ozero salt l. Rus. Fed.
170 D4 Gorleben Ger.
142 H6 Gørlev Denmark
175 J6 Gorlice Pol.
171 K8 Görlitz Ger.
170 D4 Gorlosen Ger.
Gorlovka Ukr. see Horlivka
139 W8 Gorlovo Rus. Fed.
171 I7 Görlsdorf Ger.
146 D11 Gorm, Loch l. Scotland U.K.
147 J5 Gormanstown Ireland
183 O5 Gormaz Spain

Gormi to Great Rann of Kachchh
318

116 G6 Gormi Madh. Prad. India
170 H3 Görmin Ger.
Gorna Dzhumaya Bulg. see Blagoevgrad
194 I9 Gornalunga r. Sicilia Italy
197 N7 Gorna Oryakhovitsa Bulg.
171 H9 Gornau Ger.
197 M7 Gorni Dŭbnik Bulg.
188 E2 Gornja Radgona Slovenia
197 J7 Gornja Toponica Serbia
191 R5 Gornje Jelenje Croatia
179 N7 Gornje Vratno Croatia
177 J6 Gornji Breg Vojvodina Serbia
179 K7 Gornji Grad Slovenia
197 J7 Gornji Matejevac Serbia
196 I6 Gornji Milanovac Serbia
179 N8 Gornji Tkalec Croatia
188 F4 Gornji Vakuf Bos.-Herz.
175 I5 Górno Pol.
197 N7 Gorno Ablanovo Bulg.
121 U2 Gorno-Altaysk Rus. Fed.
Gorno-Altayskaya Avtonomnaya Oblast' aut. rep. Rus. Fed. see Altay, Respublika
Gorno-Badakhshan aut. rep. Tajik. see Kŭhistoni Badakhshon
130 H3 Gornopravdinsk Rus. Fed.
197 N8 Gornotrakiyska Nizina lowland Bulg.
134 L4 Gornozavodsk Permskaya Oblast' Rus. Fed.
100 L5 Gornozavodsk Sakhalin Rus. Fed.
110 E1 Gornyak Altayskiy Kray Rus. Fed.
139 W8 Gornyak Ryazanskaya Oblast' Rus. Fed.
Gornyak Ukr. see Hirnyk
100 H6 Gornye Klyuchi Rus. Fed.
100 J3 Gornyy Khabarovskiy Kray Rus. Fed.
137 T6 Gornyy Rostovskaya Oblast' Rus. Fed.
120 C2 Gornyy Saratovskaya Oblast' Rus. Fed.
Gornyy Altay aut. rep. Rus. Fed. see Altay, Respublika
Gornyy Badakhshan aut. rep. Tajik. see Kŭhistoni Badakhshon
135 I6 Gornyy Balykley Rus. Fed.
210 D3 Goro Eth.
Goro i. Fiji see Koro
191 M6 Goro Italy
210 C2 Goroch'an mt. Eth.
Gorodenka Ukr. see Horodenka
134 H4 Gorodets Rus. Fed.
137 R2 Gorodishche Belgorodskaya Oblast' Rus. Fed.
135 I5 Gorodishche Penzenskaya Oblast' Rus. Fed.
135 I6 Gorodishche Volgogradskaya Oblast' Rus. Fed.
Gorodishche Ukr. see Horodyshche
Gorodok Minskaya Voblasts' Belarus see Haradok
Gorodok Vitsyebskaya Voblasts' Belarus see Haradok
Gorodok Rus. Fed. see Zakamensk
Gorodok Khmel'nyts'ka Oblast' Ukr. see Horodok
Gorodok L'vivs'ka Oblast' Ukr. see Horodok
135 H7 Gorodovikovsk Rus. Fed.
91 K8 Goroka P.N.G.
82 H7 Goroke Vic. Austr.
134 H4 Gorokhovets Rus. Fed.
206 E3 Gorom Gorom Burkina
91 H7 Gorong, Kepulauan is Indon.
213 G3 Gorongosa Moz.
213 G3 Gorongosa mt. Moz.
213 G3 Gorongosa, Parque Nacional de nat. park Moz.
93 C3 Gorontalo Sulawesi Indon.
93 C3 Gorontalo prov. Indon.
207 G3 Goronyo Nigeria
177 G1 Gór Opawskich, Park Krajobrazowy Pol.
261 H4 Gorostiaga Arg.
207 F3 Goroubi watercourse Niger
207 F3 Gorouol r. Burkina/Niger
143 Q7 Górowo Iławeckie Pol.
164 J2 Gorredijk Neth.
190 G6 Gorreto Italy
159 J5 Gorron France
169 K8 Görsbach Ger.
150 D4 Gorseinon Swansea, Wales U.K.
135 G6 Gorshechnoye Rus. Fed.
174 G2 Górsk Pol.
191 Q5 Gorski Kotar reg. Croatia
Gorskoye Ukr. see Hirs'ke
176 F1 Gór Sowich, Park Krajobrazowy Pol.
164 J4 Gorssel Neth.
174 E5 Gór Stołowych, Park Narodowy nat. park Pol.
147 E6 Gort Ireland
148 C4 Gortaclare Northern Ireland U.K.
147 F2 Gortahork Ireland
147 E5 Gorteen Galway Ireland
148 C8 Gorteen Kilkenny Ireland
147 F5 Gorteen Sligo Ireland
147 G8 Gorteen Waterford Ireland
147 F6 Gorteeny Ireland
147 H3 Gortin Northern Ireland U.K.
197 O5 Goru, Vârful mt. Romania
199 J2 Görükle Turkey
147 C6 Gorumna Island Ireland
257 F1 Gorutuba r. Brazil
122 G7 Gorveh Iran
172 E6 Görwihl Ger.
172 F2 Gorxheimertal Ger.
129 G2 Goryacheistochnenskaya Chechenskaya Respublika Rus. Fed.
Goryacheistochnenskaya Stavropol'skiy Kray Rus. Fed. see Goryachevodskiy
129 E1 Goryachevodskiy Rus. Fed.
129 A1 Goryachiy Klyuch Rus. Fed.
Goryn' r. Ukr. see Horyn'
100 J3 Goryun r. Rus. Fed.
123 J5 Gorzanak Afgh.
193 K2 Gorzano, Monte mt. Italy
157 L5 Gorze France
171 E7 Görzig Ger.
171 F6 Görzke Ger.
175 H4 Gorzkowice Pol.
175 L5 Gorzków-Osada Pol.
174 E2 Górzna Pol.
167 I2 Górznieńsko-Lidzbarski Park Krajobrazowy Pol.
175 H2 Górzno Pol.
174 G4 Gorzów Śląski Pol.
174 D3 Gorzów Wielkopolski Pol.
174 C3 Górzyca Lubuskie Pol.
174 D2 Górzyca Zachodniopomorskie Pol.
175 J5 Gorzyce Podkarpackie Pol.
175 K5 Gorzyce Podkarpackie Pol.
174 G6 Gorzyce Śląskie Pol.
174 C4 Górzyn Pol.
174 D3 Gorzyń Pol.
Gosainthan mt. Xizang China see Xixabangma Feng
191 L3 Gosaldo Italy
179 I4 Gosau Austria
151 L2 Gosberton Lincolnshire, England U.K.
174 D3 Gościm Pol.
174 D1 Gościno Pol.
174 D4 Gósciszów Pol.
179 M6 Gosdorf Austria
104 C7 Gose Japan
171 E8 Goseck Ger.
176 F5 Gősfai Hegy hill Hungary
151 N4 Gosfield Essex, England U.K.
83 M5 Gosford N.S.W. Austr.
149 K5 Gosforth Cumbria, England U.K.
149 N3 Gosforth Tyne and Wear, England U.K.
123 K8 Goshanak Pak.
172 F5 Gosheim Ger.
240 M5 Goshen CA U.S.A.
230 E5 Goshen IN U.S.A.
233 M5 Goshen NH U.S.A.
234 F6 Goshen NJ U.S.A.
233 K7 Goshen NY U.S.A.
232 F11 Goshen VA U.S.A.
104 A7 Goshiki Japan
Goshoba Turkm. see Goşoba
102 R6 Goshogawara Japan
169 J7 Goslar Ger.
175 H3 Goślice Pol.
158 I5 Gosné France
122 F1 Goşoba Turkm.
188 E3 Gospić Croatia
151 J6 Gosport Hampshire, England U.K.
206 A3 Gossas Senegal
190 G1 Gossau St Gallen Switz.
172 F7 Gossau Zürich Switz.
84 E5 Gosse watercourse N.T. Austr.
179 M6 Gössendorf Austria
206 E3 Gossi Mali
208 E2 Gossinga Sudan
179 I4 Gößl Austria
171 F9 Gößnitz Ger.
173 K2 Gößweinstein Ger.
137 Q8 Gostagayevskaya Rus. Fed.
137 P3 Gostishchevo Rus. Fed.
196 I9 Gostivar Macedonia
179 K4 Göstling an der Ybbs Austria
174 F2 Gostycyn Pol.
174 F4 Gostyń Wielkopolskie Pol.
174 C1 Gostyń Zachodniopomorskie Pol.
175 H3 Gostynin Pol.
167 I2 Gostynińsko-Włocławski Park Krajobrazowy Pol.
108 B2 Gosu Sichuan China
174 F4 Goszcz Pol.
174 G4 Goszczanów Pol.
175 I4 Goszczyn Pol.
210 D2 Gota Eth.
142 H4 Götaälven r. Sweden
143 M3 Göta Kanal canal Sweden
143 K5 Götaland reg. Sweden
142 H4 Göteborg Sweden
142 I4 Göteborg-Landvetter airport Sweden
207 H5 Gotel Mountains Cameroon/Nigeria
Gotemba Shizuoka Japan see Gotenba
105 I5 Gotenba Shizuoka Japan
142 J3 Götene Sweden
Gotenhafen Pol. see Gdynia
191 R4 Goteniška gora mts Slovenia
169 K9 Gotha Ger.
151 J2 Gotham Nottinghamshire, England U.K.
143 O4 Gothem Gotland Sweden
143 O4 Gothemån r. Gotland Sweden
Gothenburg Sweden see Göteborg
236 E5 Gothenburg NE U.S.A.
207 F3 Gothèye Niger
143 O4 Gotland county Sweden
143 O4 Gotland i. Gotland Sweden
247 □8 Goto Meer Bonaire Neth. Antilles
103 F14 Gotō-rettō is Japan
197 L9 Gotse Delchev Bulg.
143 P3 Gotska Sandön Gotland Sweden
143 P3 Gotska Sandön i. Gotland Sweden
143 P3 Gotska Sandön nationalpark nat. park Gotland Sweden
103 J12 Gōtsu Japan
190 H7 Gottero, Monte mt. Italy
173 N4 Gotteszell Ger.
173 N4 Gottfrieding Ger.
169 I7 Göttingen Ger.
172 F6 Gottmadingen Ger.
140 O5 Gottne Sweden
222 F5 Gott Peak B.C. Can.
Gottwaldow Czech Rep. see Zlín
122 E2 Goturdepe Turkm.
Gotval'd Ukr. see Zmiyiv
179 O3 Götzendorf an der Leitha Austria
178 A5 Götzis Austria
208 D3 Gouako C.A.R.
158 E5 Gouarec France
164 G4 Gouda Neth.
214 D9 Gouda S. Africa
161 E8 Goudargues France
260 C4 Goudge Arg.
151 M5 Goudhurst Kent, England U.K.
206 B3 Goudiri Senegal
207 H3 Goudoumaria Niger
261 F4 Goudra Arg.
226 J1 Goudreau Ont. Can.
206 C4 Gouéké Guinea
158 C5 Gouesnou France
158 F4 Gouet r. France
207 G2 Goûgaram Niger
264 I8 Gough Island S. Atlantic Ocean
160 I1 Gouhenans France
224 F3 Gouin, Réservoir resr Que. Can.
214 G10 Goukamma Nature Reserve S. Africa
161 B7 Goul r. France
226 J3 Goulais River Ont. Can.
83 L6 Goulburn N.S.W. Austr.
83 J7 Goulburn r. Vic. Austr.
84 D1 Goulburn Islands N.T. Austr.
83 M5 Goulburn River National Park N.S.W. Austr.
87 D8 Gould, Mount hill W.A. Austr.
226 I3 Gould City MI U.S.A.
262 O1 Gould Coast Antarctica
234 E2 Gouldsboro PA U.S.A.
158 B5 Goulet de Brest sea chan. France
207 I3 Goulféy Cameroon
206 D4 Goulia Côte d'Ivoire
Goulou atoll Micronesia see Ngulu
161 G9 Goult France
206 D3 Goumbou Mali
198 D2 Goumenissa Greece
160 J2 Goumois France
207 I4 Gouna Cameroon
208 D2 Gounda C.A.R.
206 E2 Goundam Mali
208 C2 Goundi Chad
208 B2 Gounou-Gan Chad
208 B2 Gounou-Gaya Chad
225 G2 Goupil, Lac l. Que. Can.
206 B3 Gouraye Maur.
163 B8 Gourbera France
247 □2 Gourbeyre Guadeloupe
206 E3 Gourcy Burkina
161 J9 Gourdan, Montagne de mt. France
163 F9 Gourdan-Polignan France
163 G6 Gourdon Midi-Pyrénées France
161 J9 Gourdon Provence-Alpes-Côte d'Azur France
146 L9 Gourdon Aberdeenshire, Scotland U.K.
207 H3 Gouré Niger
163 D10 Gourette France
156 H6 Gourgançon France
158 D5 Gourin France
117 M7 Gouripur Bangl.
214 F10 Gourits r. S. Africa
226 J1 Gourlay Lake Ont. Can.
206 E2 Gourma-Rharous Mali
206 C2 Goûrmél well Maur.
202 D5 Gourmeur well Chad
156 C5 Gournay-en-Bray France
202 C5 Gouro Chad
204 D5 Goûr Oulad Ahmed reg. Mali
202 D5 Gourouro well Chad
156 D5 Goussainville France
162 E5 Gout-Rossignol France
164 I2 Goutum Neth.
257 F3 Gouvêa Brazil
182 E8 Gouveia Port.
233 J4 Gouverneur NY U.S.A.
156 D5 Gouvieux France
165 I8 Gouvy Belgium
247 □6 Gouyave Grenada
208 C3 Gouzé C.A.R.
162 I3 Gouzon France
182 D6 Gove Port.
236 E6 Gove KS U.S.A.
209 B8 Gove, Barragem do resr Angola
197 L8 Govedartsi Bulg.
131 R4 Govena, Mys hd Rus. Fed.
84 F2 Gove Peninsula N.T. Austr.
Goverla, Gora mt. Ukr. see Hoverla, Hora
257 G3 Governador Valadares Brazil
92 F8 Governor Generoso Mindanao Phil.
246 E1 Governor's Harbour Eleuthera Bahamas
235 G3 Governor's Island National Monument nat. park NY U.S.A.
106 D4 Govĭ-Altay prov. Mongolia
106 F4 Govĭ Altayn Nuruu mts Mongolia
117 I7 Govind Ballash Pant Sagar resr India
116 H7 Govindgarh Madh. Prad. India
116 F4 Govind Sagar resr India
232 G6 Gowanda NY U.S.A.
85 J8 Gowan Range hills Qld Austr.
111 H11 Gowaqungo Xizang China
123 K7 Gowārān Afgh.
175 I4 Gowarczów Pol.
122 F6 Gowd-e Ahmar Iran
122 F8 Gowdeh, Rūd-e watercourse Iran
81 G8 Gowenbridge South I. N.Z.
234 B3 Gowen City PA U.S.A.
150 D4 Gower pen. Wales U.K.
82 □2 Gower, Mount hill Lord Howe I. Austr.
227 N2 Gowganda Ont. Can.
227 N2 Gowganda Lake Ont. Can.
174 F1 Gowidlino Pol.
174 C2 Gowienica r. Pol.
123 M5 Gowmal Kalay Afgh.
147 G5 Gowna, Lough l. Ireland
175 J3 Goworowo Pol.
147 H7 Gowran Ireland
123 L3 Gowurdak Turkm.
149 L7 Gowy r. England U.K.
149 Q6 Goxhill North Lincolnshire, England U.K.
258 F3 Goya Arg.
247 □2 Goyave Guadeloupe
129 I5 Göyçay Azer.
129 I5 Göyçay r. Azer.
129 I5 Göyçay Qoruğu nature res. Azer.
84 E2 Goyder r. N.T. Austr.
84 E8 Goyder watercourse N.T. Austr.
82 G2 Goyder Lagoon salt flat S.A. Austr.
261 F5 Goyena Arg.
129 H5 Göygöl Azer.
129 H5 Göygöl Qoruğu nature res. Azer.
129 J5 Göylär Çöl Azer.
122 F1 Goýmatdag hills Turkm.
199 L6 Göynük Antalya Turkey
127 J4 Göynük Bingöl Turkey
199 L2 Göynük Bolu Turkey
199 L2 Göynük r. Turkey
199 K3 Göynükbelen Turkey
102 S7 Goyō-zan mt. Japan
129 J6 Göytäpä Azer.
123 J4 Gozareh Afgh.
202 D6 Goz-Beïda Chad
128 D2 Gözcüler Turkey
175 J4 Gózd Pol.
174 D4 Gozdnica Pol.
174 C3 Gozdowice Pol.
126 I4 Gözene Turkey
105 L2 Gozen-yama Japan
111 E9 Gozha Co salt l. China
128 E2 Gözkaya Turkey
195 □ Gozo i. Malta
203 G5 Goz Regeb Sudan
190 E4 Gozzano Italy
214 I8 Graaff-Reinet S. Africa
214 C8 Graafwater S. Africa
170 F2 Graal-Müritz, Ostseebad Ger.
172 E3 Graben-Neudorf Ger.
178 H3 Grabensee l. Austria
173 N6 Grabenstätt Ger.
169 J10 Grabfeld plain Ger.
175 G4 Grabia r. Pol.
175 H4 Grabica Pol.
206 D5 Grabo Côte d'Ivoire
214 D10 Grabouw S. Africa
197 K6 Grabovica Serbia
170 E4 Grabow Mecklenburg-Vorpommern Ger.
171 E6 Grabow Sachsen-Anhalt Ger.
170 G2 Grabow inlet Ger.
175 H3 Grabów Pol.
143 M7 Grabowa r. Pol.
170 G3 Grabowhöfe Ger.
175 L5 Grabowiec Lubelskie Pol.
175 J4 Grabowiec Mazowieckie Pol.
175 J4 Grabów nad Pilicą Pol.
174 G4 Grabów nad Prosną Pol.
174 F2 Grabówno Pol.
174 F4 Grabowno Wielkie Pol.
175 K2 Grabowo Podlaskie Pol.
175 K1 Grabowo Warmińsko-Mazurskie Pol.
190 G1 Grabs Switz.
188 E3 Gračac Croatia
188 G3 Gračanica Bos.-Herz.
196 H8 Gračanica Jezero l. Montenegro
162 H1 Graçay France
87 E12 Grace, Lake salt flat W.A. Austr.
224 E4 Gracefield Que. Can.
165 H7 Grâce-Hollogne Belgium
85 M7 Gracemere Qld Austr.
158 E4 Grâces France
139 X9 Grachevka Lipetskaya Oblast' Rus. Fed.
120 E1 Grachevka Orenburgskaya Oblast' Rus. Fed.
121 R2 Grachi Kazakh.
245 I3 Graciano Sánchez Mex.
242 □O10 Gracias Hond.
216 □1c Graciosa i. Azores
216 □3c Graciosa i. Canary Is
179 N6 Grad Slovenia
188 G3 Gradačac Bos.-Herz.
191 N8 Gradara Italy
254 C3 Gradaús Brazil
254 C4 Gradaús, Serra dos hills Brazil
179 N8 Gradec Croatia
183 J3 Gradefes Spain
197 O8 Gradets Bulg.
163 C6 Gradignan France
197 O8 Gradishte hill Bulg.
Gradiška Bos.-Herz. see Bosanska Gradiška
188 G3 Gradište Croatia
197 O6 Grădiştea Romania
191 O4 Grado Italy
182 H2 Grado Spain
178 H8 Grado, Laguna di lag. Italy
192 H2 Gradoli Italy
237 D8 Grady NM U.S.A.
146 J5 Graemsay i. Scotland U.K.
185 M6 Graena Spain
173 K5 Gräfelfing Ger.
173 K2 Gräfenberg Ger.
169 I10 Gräfendorf Ger.
179 M5 Grafendorf bei Hartberg Austria
171 F7 Gräfenhainichen Ger.
172 E6 Grafenhausen Ger.
169 K9 Gräfenroda Ger.
179 J6 Grafenstein Austria
171 D9 Gräfenthal Ger.
169 K8 Gräfentonna Ger.
173 L2 Grafenwöhr Ger.
179 M3 Grafenworth Austria
192 I2 Graffignano Italy
151 L3 Grafham Water resr England U.K.
169 K6 Grafhorst Ger.
171 D9 Gräfinau-Angstedt Ger.
173 L5 Grafing bei München Ger.
142 F1 Gråfjell mt. Norway
173 N4 Grafling Ger.
173 K5 Grafrath Ger.
140 L5 Gräftåvallen Sweden
83 N3 Grafton N.S.W. Austr.
236 G1 Grafton ND U.S.A.
232 C7 Grafton OH U.S.A.
226 G6 Grafton WI U.S.A.
232 E9 Grafton WV U.S.A.
85 J4 Grafton, Cape Qld Austr.
241 R3 Grafton, Mount NV U.S.A.
85 K4 Grafton Passage Qld Austr.
142 F1 Grågalten hill Norway
193 N6 Gragnano Italy
231 H7 Graham NC U.S.A.
237 F9 Graham TX U.S.A.
241 W9 Graham, Mount AZ U.S.A.
Graham Bell Island Zemlya Frantsa-Iosifa Rus. Fed. see Greem-Bell, Ostrov
222 C4 Graham Island B.C. Can.
221 I2 Graham Island Nunavut Can.
233 □Q4 Graham Lake ME U.S.A.
262 T2 Graham Land reg. Antarctica
222 F3 Graham Laurier Provincial Park B.C. Can.
221 K2 Graham Moore, Cape Nunavut Can.
215 K9 Grahamstown S. Africa
Grahovo Bos.-Herz. see Bosansko Grahovo
179 I7 Grahovo Slovenia
148 D8 Graigue Ireland
147 I7 Graiguenamanagh Ireland
151 N5 Grain Medway, England U.K.
151 N5 Grain, Isle of pen. England U.K.
173 K7 Grainau Ger.
173 P4 Grainet Ger.
161 B7 Graissac France
161 C9 Graissessac France
183 Q9 Graja de Iniesta Spain
95 K9 Grajagan Jawa Indon.
183 J4 Grajal de Campos Spain
254 D3 Grajaú Brazil
254 D2 Grajaú r. Brazil
175 K2 Grajewo Pol.
134 J4 Grakhovo Rus. Fed.
146 D4 Gralisgeir i. Scotland U.K.
179 M6 Gralla Austria
142 F6 Gram Denmark
197 K8 Gramada mt. Serbia
179 J3 Gramastettan Austria
163 H6 Gramat France
163 H6 Gramat, Causse de hills France
197 P8 Gramatikovo Bulg.
179 N3 Gramatneusiedl Austria
161 H9 Grambois France
170 J4 Grambow Ger.
170 D3 Gramkow Ger.
170 G2 Grammendorf Ger.
194 H9 Grammichele Sicilia Italy
Grammont Belgium see Geraardsbergen
190 D8 Grammont, Mont mt. Italy
198 B2 Grammos mt. Greece
232 G8 Grampian PA U.S.A.
146 G9 Grampian Mountains Scotland U.K.
83 I7 Grampians National Park Vic. Austr.
150 C7 Grampound Cornwall, England U.K.
164 K3 Gramsbergen Neth.
196 I10 Gramsh Albania
170 J4 Gramzow Ger.
Gran Hungary see Esztergom
190 D6 Grana r. Italy
190 F5 Grana r. Italy
214 D6 Granaatboskolk S. Africa
147 J6 Granabeg Ireland
250 C4 Granada Col.
242 □Q12 Granada Nic.
185 L6 Granada Spain
185 M6 Granada prov. Spain
236 D6 Granada CO U.S.A.
216 □3a Granadilla de Abona Tenerife Canary Is
184 E5 Granado hill Spain
259 C8 Gran Altiplanicie Central plain Arg.
147 H5 Granard Ireland
191 K6 Granarolo dell'Emilia Italy
178 G5 Granatspitze mt. Austria
185 L3 Granátula de Calatrava Spain
259 D7 Gran Bajo depr. Arg.
260 D6 Gran Bajo Salitroso salt flat Arg.
259 C8 Gran Bajo San Julián val. Arg.
190 B5 Gran Bosco di Salbertrand, Parco Naturale del nature res. Italy
237 G9 Granbury TX U.S.A.
225 F4 Granby Que. Can.
238 K6 Granby CO U.S.A.
216 □3f Gran Canaria i. Canary Is
157 J8 Grancey-le-Château-Nouvelle France
253 E6 Gran Chaco reg. Arg./Para.
247 □7 Gran Couva Trin. and Tob.
157 J7 Grand France
230 D4 Grand r. MO U.S.A.
236 E3 Grand r. SD U.S.A.
236 D3 Grand, North Fork r. SD U.S.A.
236 D3 Grand, South Fork r. SD U.S.A.
161 H7 Grand Armet mt. France
182 G2 Grandas Spain
Grand Atlas mts Morocco see Haut Atlas
246 D1 Grand Bahama i. Bahamas
157 N8 Grand Ballon mt. France
225 K4 Grand Bank Nfld and Lab. Can.
264 F3 Grand Banks of Newfoundland sea feature N. Atlantic Ocean
206 E5 Grand-Bassam Côte d'Ivoire
217 □1c Grand Bassin Réunion
247 □2 Grand Bay b. Dominica
237 K10 Grand Bay AL U.S.A.
225 H4 Grand Bay-Westfield N.B. Can.
224 D5 Grand Bend Ont. Can.
161 J8 Grand Bérard mt. France
206 D5 Grand-Bérébi Côte d'Ivoire
232 B6 Grand Blanc MI U.S.A.
247 □2 Grand-Bourg Guadeloupe
217 □1c Grand Brûlé coastal area Réunion
159 I3 Grandcamp-Maisy France
Grand Canal China see Da Yunhe
147 H6 Grand Canal Ireland
Grand Canary i. Canary Is see Gran Canaria
241 T5 Grand Canyon AZ U.S.A.
241 T5 Grand Canyon gorge AZ U.S.A.
241 T5 Grand Canyon National Park AZ U.S.A.
241 S5 Grand Canyon-Parashant National Monument nat. park AZ U.S.A.
246 C4 Grand Cayman i. Cayman Is
223 I4 Grand Centre Alta Can.
206 C5 Grand Cess Liberia
158 F6 Grand-Champ France
160 J1 Grand-Charmont France
160 H5 Grand Colombier mt. France
190 C4 Grand Combin mt. Switz.
238 E3 Grand Coulee WA U.S.A.
156 B5 Grand-Couronne France
247 □2 Grand Cul de Sac Marin b. Guadeloupe
226 E8 Grand Detour IL U.S.A.
260 C5 Grande r. Arg.
253 E4 Grande r. Bol.
252 E4 Grande r. Bol.
256 B3 Grande r. Brazil
254 E4 Grande r. Brazil
194 E8 Grande r. Sicilia Italy
244 E6 Grande r. Jalisco/Michoacán Mex.
245 K8 Grande r. Mex.
245 L9 Grande r. Mex.
245 N9 Grande r. Mex.
242 □R11 Grande r. Nic.
252 B3 Grande r. Peru
187 D9 Grande r. Spain
185 J7 Grande r. Spain
185 L4 Grande r. Spain
261 I5 Grande, Arroyo r. Arg.
259 C8 Grande, Bahía b. Arg.
246 D3 Grande, Cayo i. Cuba
244 G2 Grande, Cerro mt. Mex.
245 J8 Grande, Cerro mt. Mex.
250 C2 Grande, Ciénaga lag. Col.
158 D4 Grande, Île i. France
257 E5 Grande, Ilha i. Brazil
194 C8 Grande, Isola i. Sicilia Italy
161 K6 Grande, Lago l. Italy
194 D8 Grande, Montagna hill Italy
260 D5 Grande, Salina salt flat Arg.
253 E2 Grande, Serra hills Brazil
251 F4 Grande, Serra mt. Brazil
260 E2 Grande, Sierra mts Arg.
247 □2 Grande Anse Guadeloupe
217 □1b Grande Baie Mauritius
217 □2a Grande Barbe, Pointe pt Inner Islands Seychelles
191 M6 Grande Bonifica Ferrarese i. Italy
158 G7 Grande Brière reg. France
222 G4 Grande Cache Alta Can.
161 J6 Grande Casse, Pointe de la mt. France
Grande Comore i. Comoros see Njazidja
251 F5 Grande de Manacapuru, Lago l. Brazil
225 I4 Grande-Entrée Que. Can.
163 C7 Grande Lande reg. France
163 C7 Grande Leyre r. France
159 M3 Grande Mare l. France
217 □1a Grande Passe Rodrigues I. Mauritius
222 G4 Grande Prairie Alta Can.
207 I2 Grand Erg de Bilma des. Niger
205 E3 Grand Erg Occidental des. Alg.
205 G3 Grand Erg Oriental des. Alg.
225 H3 Grande-Rivière Que. Can.
247 □3 Grande Rivière St Lucia
247 □7 Grande Rivière Trin. and Tob.
217 □1b Grande Rivière Noire Mauritius
217 □1b Grande Rivière Noire r. Mauritius
217 □1b Grande Rivière South East r. Mauritius
217 □1b Grande Rivière Sud-Est Mauritius
217 □1b Grande Rivière Sud-Est r. Mauritius
190 C4 Grande Rochère mt. Italy
238 F3 Grande Ronde r. OR U.S.A.
260 E2 Grandes, Salinas salt marsh Arg.
258 D1 Grandes, Salinas salt marsh Arg.
160 A2 Grande Sauldre r. France
242 C2 Gran Desierto del Pinacate, Parque Natural del nature res. Mex.
160 K5 Grandes Jorasses mts France/Italy
161 I6 Grandes Rousses mts France
156 D1 Grande-Synthe France
247 □6 Grand Étang l. Grenada
247 □2 Grande-Terre i. Guadeloupe
217 □3b Grande Terre i. Mayotte
161 H7 Grande Tête de l'Obiou mt. France
158 G8 Grand Etier r. France
190 D4 Grande Tournalin mt. Italy
163 I6 Grande-Vabre France
225 H3 Grande-Vallée Que. Can.
247 □2 Grande Vigie, Pointe de la pt Guadeloupe
190 C4 Grand Eyvia r. Italy
225 H4 Grand Falls N.B. Can.
225 K3 Grand Falls-Windsor Nfld and Lab. Can.
222 G5 Grand Forks B.C. Can.
236 G2 Grand Forks ND U.S.A.
156 D1 Grand-Fort-Philippe France
158 H6 Grand-Fougeray France
163 D10 Grand Gabizos mt. France
233 K6 Grand Gorge NY U.S.A.
246 H4 Grand Gosier Haiti
225 H4 Grand Harbour N.B. Can.
226 H6 Grand Haven MI U.S.A.
222 G1 Grandin, Lac l. N.W.T. Can.
236 F5 Grand Island NE U.S.A.
226 H3 Grand Island i. MI U.S.A.
237 J11 Grand Isle LA U.S.A.
233 □Q1 Grand Isle ME U.S.A.
241 X2 Grand Junction CO U.S.A.
226 H7 Grand Junction MI U.S.A.
206 D5 Grand-Lahou Côte d'Ivoire
225 H4 Grand Lake N.B. Can.
225 I2 Grand Lake Nfld and Lab. Can.
225 J3 Grand Lake Nfld and Lab. Can.
237 I11 Grand Lake LA U.S.A.
237 J11 Grand Lake LA U.S.A.
227 K4 Grand Lake MI U.S.A.
233 □Q2 Grand Lake Matagamon ME U.S.A.
232 A8 Grand Lake St Marys OH U.S.A.
233 □Q2 Grand Lake Seboeis ME U.S.A.
159 I8 Grand Lay r. France
226 J7 Grand Ledge MI U.S.A.
158 H7 Grand-Lieu, Lac de l. France
159 I8 Grand Maine r. France
225 H4 Grand Manan Island N.B. Can.
226 I3 Grand Marais MI U.S.A.
226 D2 Grand Marais MN U.S.A.
226 E6 Grand Marsh WI U.S.A.
225 F4 Grand-Mère Que. Can.
156 E6 Grand Morin r. France
184 B4 Grândola Port.
184 C4 Grândola r. Port.
184 B4 Grândola, Serra de mts Port.
222 B3 Grand Pacific Glacier B.C. Can.
78 □5 Grand Passage New Caledonia
161 H6 Grand Pic de Belledonne mt. France
156 B8 Grand-Pierre et Vitan, Réserve Naturelle nature res. France
226 E2 Grand Portage MN U.S.A.
157 I5 Grandpré France
156 E6 Grandpuits-Bailly-Carrois France
223 L4 Grand Rapids Man. Can.
226 I7 Grand Rapids MI U.S.A.
226 A2 Grand Rapids MN U.S.A.
217 □3b Grand Récif du Nord Est rf Mayotte
158 I6 Grand Réservoir de Vioreau resr France
161 F10 Grand Rhône r. France
161 D7 Grandrieu France
160 E4 Grandris France
247 □3 Grand' Rivière Martinique
161 J6 Grand Roc Noir mt. France
247 □6 Grand Roy Grenada
Grand St Bernard, Col du pass Italy/Switz. see Great St Bernard Pass
251 H3 Grand-Santi Fr. Guiana
190 B2 Grandson Switz.
238 I5 Grand Teton mt. WY U.S.A.
238 I5 Grand Teton National Park WY U.S.A.
226 I5 Grand Traverse Bay MI U.S.A.
246 H3 Grand Turk Turks and Caicos Is
246 H3 Grand Turk i. Turks and Caicos Is
161 C7 Grandval, Barrage de dam France
215 P2 Grand Valley Swaziland
160 I1 Grandvelle-et-le-Perrenot France
226 C3 Grand View WI U.S.A.
160 J1 Grandvillars France
226 I7 Grandville MI U.S.A.
157 M7 Grandvillers France
156 C4 Grandvilliers France
241 R5 Grand Wash watercourse AZ U.S.A.
241 R6 Grand Wash Cliffs mts AZ U.S.A.
226 A4 Grandy MN U.S.A.
161 F7 Grane France
186 E4 Grañén Spain
260 B4 Graneros Chile
147 E7 Graney, Lough l. Ireland
143 M2 Granfjärden b. Sweden
147 J5 Grange Louth Ireland
147 E4 Grange Sligo Ireland
147 G9 Grange Waterford Ireland
160 J4 Grange, Mont de mt. France
147 J5 Grangebellow Ireland
147 I7 Grangeford Ireland
246 □ Grange Hill Jamaica
146 I10 Grangemouth Falkirk, Scotland U.K.
161 E6 Grangent, Barrage de dam France
149 L5 Grange-over-Sands Cumbria, England U.K.
238 J6 Granger WY U.S.A.
143 L1 Grängesberg Sweden
157 M7 Granges-sur-Vologne France
150 F5 Grangetown Cardiff, Wales U.K.
238 F4 Grangeville ID U.S.A.
258 F2 Gran Guardia Arg.
140 P3 Granhult Sweden
160 H6 Granier, Col du pass France
161 H6 Granier, Mont mt. France
222 E4 Granisle B.C. Can.
234 B6 Granite MD U.S.A.
236 J6 Granite City IL U.S.A.
236 H3 Granite Falls MN U.S.A.
240 O1 Granite Mountain NV U.S.A.
241 Q7 Granite Mountains CA U.S.A.
241 Q8 Granite Mountains CA U.S.A.
238 J4 Granite Peak MT U.S.A.
241 S1 Granite Peak UT U.S.A.
226 G3 Granite Point MI U.S.A.
Granitic Group is Seychelles see Inner Islands
121 O6 Granitogorsk Kazakh.
194 D8 Granitola, Capo c. Sicilia Italy
194 D8 Granitola-Torretta Sicilia Italy
81 F8 Granity South I. N.Z.
254 E2 Granja Brazil
184 E4 Granja Port.
182 I5 Granja de Moreruela Spain
184 H4 Granja de Torrehermosa Spain
182 C8 Granja do Ulmeiro Port.
259 D7 Gran Laguna Salada l. Arg.
239 K12 Gran Morelos Mex.
142 I3 Grann l. Sweden
143 K3 Gränna Sweden
186 J4 Granollers Spain
174 E3 Granowo Pol.
252 B2 Gran Pajonal plain Peru
244 E3 Gran Pánfilo Natera Mex.
190 C4 Gran Paradiso mt. Italy
190 C4 Gran Paradiso, Parco Nazionale del nat. park Italy
178 E6 Gran Pilastro mt. Austria/Italy
Gran San Bernardo, Colle del pass Italy/Switz. see Great St Bernard Pass
193 K2 Gran Sasso d'Italia mts Italy
193 L3 Gran Sasso e Monti della Laga, Parco Nazionale del nat. park Italy
171 F8 Granschütz Ger.
170 H4 Gransee Ger.
148 E5 Gransha Northern Ireland U.K.
143 M3 Gransö i. Sweden
236 E5 Grant NE U.S.A.
240 N3 Grant, Mount NV U.S.A.
240 O2 Grant, Mount NV U.S.A.
216 □3b Gran Tarajal Fuerteventura Canary Is
236 H5 Grant City MO U.S.A.
151 K2 Grantham Lincolnshire, England U.K.
234 B4 Grantham PA U.S.A.
262 P2 Grant Island Antarctica
84 D1 Grant Island N.T. Austr.
222 G1 Grant Lake N.W.T. Can.
226 D5 Granton WI U.S.A.
146 I8 Grantown-on-Spey Highland, Scotland U.K.
226 G8 Grant Park IL U.S.A.
241 Q3 Grant Range mts NV U.S.A.
239 K9 Grants NM U.S.A.
226 B4 Grantsburg WI U.S.A.
146 L11 Grantshouse Scottish Borders, Scotland U.K.
238 C5 Grants Pass OR U.S.A.
232 D10 Grantsville WV U.S.A.
234 B4 Grantville PA U.S.A.
222 B2 Granville Y.T. Can.
158 H4 Granville France
241 W8 Granville AZ U.S.A.
226 E8 Granville IL U.S.A.
233 L5 Granville NY U.S.A.
232 C8 Granville OH U.S.A.
223 K3 Granville Lake Man. Can.
142 C1 Granvin Norway
170 E3 Granzin Ger.
257 F2 Grão Mogol Brazil
240 O5 Grapevine Mountains NV U.S.A.
191 L4 Grappa, Monte mt. Italy
246 F4 Grappler Bank sea feature Caribbean Sea
223 I1 Gras, Lac de l. N.W.T. Can.
140 T1 Grasbakken Norway
168 G4 Grasberg Ger.
213 F5 Graskop S. Africa
171 D6 Grasleben Ger.
142 I1 Gräsmarken Sweden
149 K5 Grasmere Cumbria, England U.K.
143 O1 Gräsö i. Sweden
234 C7 Grasonville MD U.S.A.
212 B5 Grasplatz Namibia
223 L3 Grass r. Man. Can.
233 K4 Grass r. NY U.S.A.
193 Q6 Grassano Italy
173 M6 Grassau Ger.
161 J9 Grasse France
232 G7 Grassflat PA U.S.A.
149 N5 Grassington North Yorkshire, England U.K.
227 J7 Grass Lake MI U.S.A.
223 J5 Grasslands National Park Sask. Can.
81 I8 Grassmere, Lake South I. N.Z.
87 F12 Grass Patch W.A. Austr.
238 J3 Grassrange MT U.S.A.
215 J7 Grassridgedam l. S. Africa
223 K4 Grass River Provincial Park Man. Can.
240 K2 Grass Valley CA U.S.A.
83 J9 Grassy Tas. Austr.
236 D2 Grassy Butte ND U.S.A.
246 E2 Grassy Creek r. Andros Bahamas
168 I1 Gråsten Denmark
142 I3 Grästorp Sweden
186 G5 Gratallops Spain
140 N2 Gratangsbotn Norway
163 G9 Gratens France
163 G8 Gratentour France
226 D7 Gratiot WI U.S.A.
179 L5 Gratkorn Austria
140 O4 Gråträsk Sweden
194 F8 Gratteri Sicilia Italy
179 L5 Gratwein Austria
190 H2 Graubünden canton Switz.
Graudenz Pol. see Grudziądz
169 E10 Grauer Kopf hill Ger.
163 H8 Graulhet France
171 I8 Graupa Ger.
186 F3 Graus Spain
183 Q4 Grávalos Spain
254 G4 Gravata Brazil
255 C9 Gravataí Brazil
140 L2 Gravdal Norway
164 I5 Grave Neth.
162 B4 Grave, Pointe de pt France
190 G3 Gravedona Italy
223 J5 Gravelbourg Sask. Can.
223 K2 Gravel Hill Lake N.W.T. Can.
156 D2 Gravelines France
190 E4 Gravellona Toce Italy
157 L5 Gravelotte France
224 E4 Gravenhurst Ont. Can.
169 F10 Grävenwiesbach Ger.
238 G3 Grave Peak ID U.S.A.
138 K5 Gräveri Latvia
163 C6 Graves reg. France
83 M3 Gravesend N.S.W. Austr.
151 M5 Gravesend Kent, England U.K.
237 H7 Gravette AR U.S.A.
156 B5 Gravigny France
193 R6 Gravina r. Italy
195 L3 Gravina di Matera r. Italy
193 Q6 Gravina in Puglia Italy
222 D4 Gravina Island AK U.S.A.
246 G4 Gravois, Pointe-à- pt Haiti
192 B4 Gravona r. Corse France
226 I5 Grawn MI U.S.A.
160 H2 Gray France
231 F9 Gray GA U.S.A.
232 A12 Gray KY U.S.A.
233 □O5 Gray ME U.S.A.
232 C12 Gray TN U.S.A.
162 B5 Grayan-et-l'Hôpital France
238 C5 Grayback Mountain OR U.S.A.
223 I2 Gray Lake N.W.T. Can.
222 E3 Grayling r. B.C. Can.
226 J5 Grayling MI U.S.A.
149 L5 Grayrigg Cumbria, England U.K.
151 M5 Grays Thurrock, England U.K.
238 B3 Grays Harbor inlet WA U.S.A.
151 K5 Grayshott Hampshire, England U.K.
238 I5 Grays Lake ID U.S.A.
232 C10 Grayson KY U.S.A.
230 D6 Grayville IL U.S.A.
137 O3 Grayvoron Rus. Fed.
179 L5 Graz Austria
161 E6 Grazac France
185 I7 Grazalema Spain
175 H2 Grążawy Pol.
194 G1 Grazzanise Italy
197 K8 Grdelica Serbia
163 H6 Gréalou France
222 F2 Greasy Lake N.W.T. Can.
246 □ Great r. Jamaica
246 E1 Great Abaco i. Bahamas
Great Ararat mt. Turkey see Büyük Ağrı Dağı
76 C5 Great Australian Bight g. Austr.
149 O5 Great Ayton North Yorkshire, England U.K.
247 □6 Great Bacolet Bay Grenada
151 N4 Great Baddow Essex, England U.K.
246 D1 Great Bahama Bank sea feature Bahamas
80 J3 Great Barrier Island North I. N.Z.
85 J1 Great Barrier Reef Qld Austr.
85 K4 Great Barrier Reef Marine Park (Cairns Section) Qld Austr.
85 M6 Great Barrier Reef Marine Park (Capricorn Section) Qld Austr.
85 L5 Great Barrier Reef Marine Park (Central Section) Qld Austr.
85 J2 Great Barrier Reef Marine Park (Far North Section) Qld Austr.
233 L6 Great Barrington MA U.S.A.
151 N3 Great Barton Suffolk, England U.K.
85 J5 Great Basalt Wall National Park Qld Austr.
241 P2 Great Basin NV U.S.A.
241 R3 Great Basin National Park NV U.S.A.
235 G6 Great Bay NJ U.S.A.
222 E1 Great Bear r. N.W.T. Can.
222 G1 Great Bear Lake N.W.T. Can.
Great Belt sea chan. Denmark see Store Bælt
236 F6 Great Bend KS U.S.A.
233 J7 Great Bend PA U.S.A.
151 O4 Great Bentley Essex, England U.K.
146 C6 Great Bernera i. Scotland U.K.
151 N2 Great Bircham Norfolk, England U.K.
Great Bitter Lake Egypt see Murrah al Kubrá, Al Buhayrah al
147 A8 Great Blasket Island Ireland
149 O5 Great Broughton North Yorkshire, England U.K.
149 K4 Great Clifton Cumbria, England U.K.
97 A7 Great Coco Island Cocos Is
151 N3 Great Cornard Suffolk, England U.K.
148 H2 Great Cumbrae i. Scotland U.K.
233 I12 Great Dismal Swamp National Wildlife Refuge nature res. VA U.S.A.
76 E5 Great Dividing Range mts Austr.
149 K4 Great Dodd hill England U.K.
227 L4 Great Duck Island Ont. Can.
151 M4 Great Dunmow Essex, England U.K.
Great Eastern Erg des. Alg. see Grand Erg Oriental
149 L6 Great Eccleston Lancashire, England U.K.
234 F6 Great Egg Harbor r. NJ U.S.A.
234 F6 Great Egg Harbor Inlet NJ U.S.A.
151 N2 Great Ellingham Norfolk, England U.K.
246 C3 Greater Antilles is Caribbean Sea
Greater Khingan Mountains China see Da Hinggan Ling
151 L4 Greater London admin. div. England U.K.
149 M6 Greater Manchester admin. div. England U.K.
215 Q3 Greater St Lucia Wetland Park nature res. S. Africa
90 B8 Greater Sunda Islands Indon.
125 L2 Greater Tunb i. The Gulf
80 H1 Great Exhibition Bay North I. N.Z.
246 F2 Great Exuma i. Bahamas
238 I3 Great Falls MT U.S.A.
215 L9 Great Fish r. S. Africa
213 E7 Great Fish Point S. Africa
80 J7 Greatford North I. N.Z.
117 J7 Great Gandak r. India
Great Ganges atoll Cook Is see Manihiki
151 J2 Great Glen Leicestershire, England U.K.
246 □ Great Goat Island Jamaica
151 K2 Great Gonerby Lincolnshire, England U.K.
151 L3 Great Gransden Cambridgeshire, England U.K.
246 E1 Great Guana Cay i. Bahamas
231 I12 Great Guana Cay i. Bahamas
151 K5 Greatham Hampshire, England U.K.
149 O4 Greatham Hartlepool, England U.K.
246 E1 Great Harbour Cay i. Bahamas
149 M6 Great Harwood Lancashire, England U.K.
151 I2 Great Haywood Staffordshire, England U.K.
151 N4 Great Horkesley Essex, England U.K.
246 G3 Great Inagua i. Bahamas
147 F9 Great Island Ireland
214 H8 Great Karoo plat. S. Africa
215 M8 Great Kei r. S. Africa
85 M7 Great Keppel Island Qld Austr.
83 K9 Great Lake Tas. Austr.
213 F4 Great Limpopo Transfrontier Park nat. park Africa
151 K3 Great Linford Milton Keynes, England U.K.
150 H3 Great Malvern Worcestershire, England U.K.
149 K6 Great Marton Blackpool, England U.K.
234 F3 Great Meadows NJ U.S.A.
80 J3 Great Mercury Island North I. N.Z.
264 H4 Great Meteor Tablemount sea feature N. Atlantic Ocean
232 A9 Great Miami r. OH U.S.A.
151 K4 Great Missenden Buckinghamshire, England U.K.
212 C5 Great Namaqualand reg. Namibia
115 N9 Great Nicobar i. Andaman & Nicobar Is India
91 J8 Great North East Channel Austr./P.N.G.
150 E1 Great Ormes Head Wales U.K.
151 M2 Great Ouse r. England U.K.
83 L10 Great Oyster Bay Tas. Austr.
85 K5 Great Palm Islands Qld Austr.
235 K3 Great Peconic Bay NY U.S.A.
246 □ Great Pedro Bluff pt Jamaica
236 E4 Great Plains NE U.S.A.
233 O7 Great Point MA U.S.A.
151 K2 Great Ponton Lincolnshire, England U.K.
Great Rann of Kachchh marsh India see Kachchh, Rann of

150 F3 Great Rhos hill Wales U.K.
210 B5 Great Rift Valley Africa
211 C6 Great Ruaha r. Tanz.
233 K5 Great Sacandaga Lake NY U.S.A.
160 K5 Great St Bernard Pass Italy/Switz.
231 H12 Great Sale Cay i. Bahamas
149 L4 Great Salkeld Cumbria, England U.K.
238 H6 Great Salt Lake UT U.S.A.
241 S1 Great Salt Lake Desert UT U.S.A.
247 □2 Great Salt Pond l. St Kitts and Nevis
151 M4 Great Sampford Essex, England U.K.
236 B6 Great Sand Dunes National Park and Preserve CO U.S.A.
223 I5 Great Sand Hills Sask. Can.
202 E2 Great Sand Sea des. Egypt/Libya
86 G6 Great Sandy Desert W.A. Austr.
Great Sandy Island Qld Austr. see Fraser Island
86 C6 Great Sandy Island Nature Reserve W.A. Austr.
79 □7 Great Sea Reef Fiji
151 M3 Great Shelford Cambridgeshire, England U.K.
222 H2 Great Slave Lake N.W.T. Can.
231 E8 Great Smoky Mountains NC/TN U.S.A.
231 F8 Great Smoky Mountains National Park NC/TN U.S.A.
222 E3 Great Snow Mountain B.C. Can.
231 □1 Great Sound b. Bermuda
235 I3 Great South Bay NY U.S.A.
151 O5 Great Stour r. England U.K.
148 E7 Great Sugar Loaf hill Ireland
150 D6 Great Torrington Devon, England U.K.
Great Usutu r. Africa see Usutu
87 J10 Great Victoria Desert W.A. Austr.
82 B3 Great Victoria Desert Conservation Park nature res. S.A. Austr.
87 J10 Great Victoria Desert Nature Reserve W.A. Austr.
151 N4 Great Wakering Essex, England U.K.
262 U2 Great Wall research stn Antarctica
107 P6 Great Wall tourist site China
151 M4 Great Waltham Essex, England U.K.
233 □R4 Great Wass Island ME U.S.A.
Great Western Erg des. Alg. see Grand Erg Occidental
83 K9 Great Western Tiers mts Tas. Austr.
97 C9 Great West Torres Islands Myanmar
149 N5 Great Whernside hill England U.K.
214 D9 Great Winterhoek mt. S. Africa
150 H2 Great Wyrley Staffordshire, England U.K.
151 P2 Great Yarmouth Norfolk, England U.K.
151 N3 Great Yeldham Essex, England U.K.
213 F4 Great Zimbabwe National Monument tourist site Zimbabwe
142 H3 Grebbestad Sweden
169 H9 Grebenau Ger.
169 J8 Grebendorf (Meinhard) Ger.
169 H10 Grebenhain Ger.
Grebenkovskiy Ukr. see Hrebinka
129 H2 Grebenskaya Rus. Fed.
Grebenski Rus. Fed. see Grebenskaya
169 H8 Grebenstein Ger.
168 J2 Grebin Ger.
175 J3 Grębków Pol.
139 W7 Grebnevo Rus. Fed.
174 E4 Grębocice Pol.
174 G2 Grębocin Pol.
175 J5 Grębów Pol.
Grebyonka Ukr. see Hrebinka
193 J3 Greccio Italy
193 O5 Greci Italy
197 Q5 Greci, Vârful hill Romania
Greco, Cape Cyprus see Greko, Cape
189 D5 Greco, Monte mt. Italy
173 K3 Greding Ger.
182 I8 Gredos, Sierra de mts Spain
259 C9 Greec Chile
198 C3 Greece country Europe
232 H5 Greece NY U.S.A.
238 L6 Greeley CO U.S.A.
234 F2 Greeley PA U.S.A.
236 F5 Greely Center NE U.S.A.
221 J1 Greely Fiord inlet Nunavut Can.
130 H1 Greem-Bell, Ostrov i. Zemlya Frantsa-Iosifa Rus. Fed.
229 M1 Green r. N.B. Can.
230 D7 Green r. KY U.S.A.
236 D2 Green r. ND U.S.A.
241 W3 Green r. WY U.S.A.
226 F5 Green Bay WI U.S.A.
226 G4 Green Bay b. WI U.S.A.
234 B6 Greenbelt MD U.S.A.
232 E11 Greenbrier r. WV U.S.A.
87 D12 Greenbushes W.A. Austr.
83 M7 Green Cape N.S.W. Austr.
231 I13 Greencastle Bahamas
147 I2 Greencastle Ireland
147 H3 Greencastle Northern Ireland U.K.
147 J4 Greencastle Northern Ireland U.K.
230 D6 Greencastle IN U.S.A.
232 H9 Greencastle PA U.S.A.
246 E1 Green Cay i. Bahamas
231 G11 Green Cove Springs FL U.S.A.
234 F6 Green Creek NJ U.S.A.
169 I7 Greene Ger.
226 B7 Greene IA U.S.A.
233 □O4 Greene ME U.S.A.
233 J6 Greene NY U.S.A.
231 F7 Greeneville TN U.S.A.
240 K5 Greenfield CA U.S.A.
236 H5 Greenfield IA U.S.A.
230 E6 Greenfield IN U.S.A.
233 M6 Greenfield MA U.S.A.
237 I7 Greenfield MO U.S.A.
232 B9 Greenfield OH U.S.A.
226 F7 Greenfield WI U.S.A.
235 G1 Greenfield Park NY U.S.A.
148 J2 Greengairs North Lanarkshire, Scotland U.K.
151 J5 Greenham West Berkshire, England U.K.
234 B6 Green Haven MD U.S.A.
87 C11 Green Head W.A. Austr.
87 C11 Green Head hd W.A. Austr.
149 L4 Greenhead Northumberland, England U.K.
84 D1 Greenhill Island N.T. Austr.
81 C13 Greenhills South I. N.Z.
246 □ Green Island Jamaica
147 K3 Greenisland Northern Ireland U.K.
92 B6 Green Island Bay Palawan Phil.
91 L7 Green Islands P.N.G.
223 J4 Green Lake Sask. Can.
222 F5 Green Lake l. B.C. Can.
81 B12 Green Lake l. South I. N.Z.
226 F6 Green Lake WI U.S.A.
221 N2 Greenland terr. N. America
226 E3 Greenland MI U.S.A.
268 X2 Greenland Basin sea feature Arctic Ocean
81 D12 Greenland Reservoir South I. N.Z.
218 G1 Greenland Sea Greenland/Svalbard
234 E4 Green Lane PA U.S.A.
234 D4 Green Lane Reservoir PA U.S.A.
146 L11 Greenlaw Scottish Borders, Scotland U.K.
146 I10 Greenloaning Perth and Kinross, Scotland U.K.
146 I12 Green Lowther hill Scotland U.K.
82 E6 Greenly Island S.A. Austr.
234 B5 Greenmount MD U.S.A.
233 M4 Green Mountains VT U.S.A.
146 G11 Greenock Inverclyde, Scotland U.K.
149 K5 Greenodd Cumbria, England U.K.
147 J4 Greenore Ireland
147 J8 Greenore Point Ireland
87 C10 Greenough W.A. Austr.
87 C10 Greenough r. W.A. Austr.
82 □3 Green Point S. Pacific Ocean
235 G2 Green Pond NJ U.S.A.
233 M7 Greenport NY U.S.A.
241 V3 Green River UT U.S.A.
238 J6 Green River WY U.S.A.
231 D9 Greensboro AL U.S.A.
231 F9 Greensboro GA U.S.A.
234 D7 Greensboro MD U.S.A.
231 H7 Greensboro NC U.S.A.
230 E6 Greensburg IN U.S.A.
237 F7 Greensburg KS U.S.A.
230 E7 Greensburg KY U.S.A.
237 J10 Greensburg LA U.S.A.
232 F8 Greensburg PA U.S.A.
241 W7 Greens Peak NM U.S.A.
146 E7 Greenstone Point Scotland U.K.
231 H8 Green Swamp NC U.S.A.
226 I9 Greentown IN U.S.A.
234 E2 Greentown PA U.S.A.
236 K6 Greenup IL U.S.A.
232 C10 Greenup KY U.S.A.
85 J5 Greenvale Qld Austr.
233 K3 Green Valley Ont. Can.
241 V10 Green Valley AZ U.S.A.
222 D4 Greenville B.C. Can.
206 C5 Greenville Liberia
231 D10 Greenville AL U.S.A.
240 L1 Greenville CA U.S.A.
231 F10 Greenville FL U.S.A.
231 E9 Greenville GA U.S.A.
236 K6 Greenville IL U.S.A.
230 D7 Greenville KY U.S.A.
233 □P3 Greenville ME U.S.A.
226 I6 Greenville MI U.S.A.
237 J7 Greenville MO U.S.A.
237 J9 Greenville MS U.S.A.
231 I8 Greenville NC U.S.A.
233 N6 Greenville NH U.S.A.
236 M5 Greenville OH U.S.A.
232 E7 Greenville PA U.S.A.
231 F8 Greenville SC U.S.A.
237 G9 Greenville TX U.S.A.
232 F10 Greenville VA U.S.A.
226 D1 Greenwater Lake Ont. Can.
223 K4 Greenwater Provincial Park Sask. Can.
150 C4 Greenway Pembrokeshire, Wales U.K.
Greenwich atoll Micronesia see Kapingamarangi
151 L5 Greenwich Greater London, England U.K.
235 H2 Greenwich CT U.S.A.
234 E6 Greenwich NJ U.S.A.
233 L5 Greenwich NY U.S.A.
232 C7 Greenwich OH U.S.A.
237 H8 Greenwood AR U.S.A.
234 D7 Greenwood DE U.S.A.
230 D6 Greenwood IN U.S.A.
237 J9 Greenwood MS U.S.A.
231 F8 Greenwood SC U.S.A.
226 D5 Greenwood WI U.S.A.
235 G2 Greenwood Lake NY U.S.A.
235 G2 Greenwood Lake l. NJ U.S.A.
231 F8 Greer SC U.S.A.
237 I8 Greers Ferry Lake AR U.S.A.
148 D8 Greese r. Ireland
168 D3 Greetsiel (Krummhörn) Ger.
250 D6 Gregório r. Brazil
84 G5 Gregory r. Qld Austr.
227 J7 Gregory MI U.S.A.
236 F4 Gregory SD U.S.A.
82 G3 Gregory, Lake salt flat S.A. Austr.
86 I6 Gregory, Lake salt flat W.A. Austr.
87 E8 Gregory, Lake salt flat W.A. Austr.
84 G5 Gregory Downs Qld Austr.
84 C4 Gregory National Park N.T. Austr.
85 I5 Gregory Range hills Qld Austr.
86 F6 Gregory Range hills W.A. Austr.
178 H6 Greifenburg Austria
171 H8 Greifendorf Ger.
190 F1 Greifensee l. Switz.
169 F9 Greifenstein Ger.
170 I4 Greiffenberg Ger.
170 H2 Greifswald Ger.
170 I2 Greifswalder Bodden b. Ger.
170 I2 Greifswalder Oie i. Ger.
179 K3 Grein Austria
171 F9 Greiz Ger.
128 C4 Greko, Cape Cyprus
168 K2 Gremersdorf Ger.
134 G1 Gremikha Rus. Fed.
139 V7 Gremyachev Rus. Fed.
134 L4 Gremyachinsk Permskaya Oblast' Rus. Fed.
98 I1 Gremyachinsk Respublika Buryatiya Rus. Fed.
137 S2 Gremyach'ye Rus. Fed.
142 G5 Grenå Denmark
237 K9 Grenada MS U.S.A.
247 □6 Grenada country West Indies
237 K9 Grenada Lake resr MS U.S.A.
163 G8 Grenade France
163 D8 Grenade-sur-l'Adour France
157 K8 Grenant France
190 C1 Grenchen Switz.
142 G4 Grenen spit Denmark
83 L5 Grenfell N.S.W. Austr.
223 K5 Grenfell Sask. Can.
161 H6 Grenoble France
140 U2 Grense-Jakobselv Norway
247 □6 Grenville Grenada
85 I1 Grenville, Cape Qld Austr.
Grenville Island Fiji see Rotuma
172 D6 Grenzach-Wyhlen Ger.
161 H9 Gréoux-les-Bains France
170 F2 Gresenhorst Ger.
123 K8 Greshag Pak.
123 L8 Greshak Pak.
238 C4 Gresham OR U.S.A.
163 H7 Grésigne, Forêt de la reg. France
95 J8 Gresik Jawa Indon.
146 D6 Gress Western Isles, Scotland U.K.
140 L4 Gressåmoen Nasjonalpark nat. park Norway
190 C4 Gressan Italy
161 H6 Gresse r. France
168 K4 Gresse Ger.
161 H7 Gresse-en-Vercors France
190 D4 Gressoney-la-Trinite Italy
179 L4 Gresten Austria
160 H5 Grésy-sur-Aix France
160 I5 Grésy-sur-Isère France
149 L5 Greta r. England U.K.
192 G2 Gretano r. Italy
146 J13 Gretna Dumfries and Galloway, Scotland U.K.
237 J11 Gretna LA U.S.A.
232 F12 Gretna VA U.S.A.
173 I2 Grettstadt Ger.
169 K8 Greußen Ger.
157 K7 Greux France
191 K8 Greve r. Italy
191 K8 Greve in Chianti Italy
164 E5 Grevelingen sea chan. Neth.
168 K4 Greven Mecklenburg-Vorpommern Ger.
169 E6 Greven Nordrhein-Westfalen Ger.
198 C2 Grevena Greece
165 I6 Grevenbicht Neth.
169 C8 Grevenbroich Ger.
165 J9 Grevenmacher Lux.
165 J9 Grevenmacher admin. dist. Lux.
170 D3 Grevesmühlen Ger.
225 J4 Grey r. Nfld and Lab. Can.
81 F9 Grey r. South I. N.Z.
84 F2 Grey, Cape N.T. Austr.
147 K3 Greyabbey Northern Ireland U.K.
238 J4 Greybull WY U.S.A.
238 J4 Greybull r. WY U.S.A.
222 C2 Grey Hunter Peak Y.T. Can.
225 K3 Grey Islands Nfld and Lab. Can.
215 M2 Greylingstad S. Africa
233 L6 Greylock, Mount MA U.S.A.
81 F9 Greymouth South I. N.Z.
148 F4 Grey Point Northern Ireland U.K.
83 I3 Grey Range hills Qld Austr.
87 C8 Grey's Plains W.A. Austr.
149 L4 Greystoke Cumbria, England U.K.
213 F4 Greystone Zimbabwe
147 J6 Greystones Ireland
214 D10 Greyton S. Africa
81 J8 Greytown North I. N.Z.
215 O5 Greytown S. Africa
165 G7 Grez-Doiceau Belgium
159 J6 Grez-en-Bouère France
191 K4 Grezzana Italy
179 I7 Grgar Slovenia
198 F5 Gria, Akrotirio pt Andros Greece
Griais Scotland U.K. see Gress
135 H6 Gribanovskiy Rus. Fed.
208 C2 Gribingui r. C.A.R.
208 C3 Gribingui-Bamingui, Réserve de Faune du nature res. C.A.R.
134 F2 Gridino Rus. Fed.
240 K2 Gridley CA U.S.A.
226 F9 Gridley IL U.S.A.
171 E6 Grieben Ger.
183 Q8 Griegos Spain
157 O6 Gries France
178 D5 Gries am Brenner Austria
172 E5 Griesbach Ger.
173 O5 Griesbach im Rottal Ger.
172 F2 Griesheim Ger.
179 I3 Grieskirchen Austria
171 K7 Grießen Ger.
173 M6 Griesstätt Ger.
179 K6 Griffen Austria
231 E9 Griffin GA U.S.A.
83 K6 Griffith N.S.W. Austr.
227 Q4 Griffith Ont. Can.
220 F2 Griffiths Point N.W.T. Can.
232 D10 Griffithsville WV U.S.A.
Grigan i. N. Mariana Is see Agrihan
192 B8 Grighini, Monte hill Italy
Grigioni canton Switz. see Graubünden
138 I7 Grigiškės Lith.
190 G4 Grigna mt. Italy
190 I4 Grigna r. Italy
161 F8 Grignan France
191 L3 Grigno Italy
191 L3 Grigno r. Italy
163 D7 Grignols France
160 F5 Grigny France
136 I6 Grigoriopol Moldova
183 K4 Grijota Spain
164 J2 Grijpskerk Neth.
Grik Malaysia see Gerik
161 F8 Grillon France
83 J9 Grim, Cape Tas. Austr.
193 Q9 Grimaldi Italy
208 D3 Grimari C.A.R.
161 J10 Grimaud France
146 A7 Griminis Point Scotland U.K.
171 G8 Grimma Ger.
170 H2 Grimmen Ger.
179 I4 Grimming mt. Austria
170 I5 Grimnitzsee l. Ger.
149 R7 Grimoldby Lincolnshire, England U.K.
146 B8 Grimsay i. Scotland U.K.
227 O6 Grimsby Ont. Can.
149 Q6 Grimsby North East Lincolnshire, England U.K.
190 E2 Grimsel nature res. Switz.
140 □E1 Grímsey i. Iceland
222 G3 Grimshaw Alta Can.
140 □E1 Grímsstaðir Iceland
142 E3 Grimstad Norway
151 N2 Grimston Norfolk, England U.K.
142 B2 Grindafjord Norway
141 J6 Grindaheim Norway
140 □B2 Grindavík Iceland
190 E2 Grindelwald Switz.
142 E6 Grindsted Denmark
227 L5 Grind Stone City MI U.S.A.
197 O6 Grindu Ialomița Romania
197 Q5 Grindu Tulcea Romania
197 Q6 Grindul Chituc spit Romania
197 O4 Grindușu, Vârful mt. Romania
139 Q9 Grinevo Rus. Fed.
149 P7 Gringley on the Hill Nottinghamshire, England U.K.
236 I5 Grinnell IA U.S.A.
221 I2 Grinnell Peninsula Nunavut Can.
183 M8 Griñón Spain
178 C5 Grins Austria
197 N3 Grințieș Romania
188 E2 Grintovec mt. Slovenia
178 D5 Grinzens Austria
183 R5 Grío r. Spain
Griomasaigh i. Scotland U.K. see Grimsay
215 N6 Griqualand East reg. S. Africa
214 H4 Griqualand West reg. S. Africa
214 H4 Griquatown S. Africa
Grischun canton Switz. see Graubünden
221 J2 Grise Fiord Nunavut Can.
186 C4 Grisén Spain
Grishino Ukr. see Krasnoarmiys'k
191 L5 Grisignano di Zocco Italy
94 E6 Grisik Sumatera Indon.
156 C2 Gris Nez, Cap c. France
193 P8 Grisolia Italy
163 G8 Grisolles France
Grisons canton Switz. see Graubünden
143 O1 Grisslehamn Sweden
146 K5 Gritley Orkney, Scotland U.K.
137 R8 Grivenskaya Rus. Fed.
149 K5 Grizebeck Cumbria, England U.K.
204 E4 Grizim well Alg.
222 F1 Grizzly Bear Mountain hill N.W.T. Can.
188 F3 Grmeč mts Bos.-Herz.
225 K3 Groais Island Nfld and Lab. Can.
165 G6 Grobbendonk Belgium
173 K5 Gröbenzell Ger.
171 F8 Gröbers Ger.
138 E5 Grobiņa Latvia
215 N1 Groblersdal S. Africa
214 G4 Groblershoop S. Africa
179 I5 Gröbming Austria
171 E7 Gröbzig Ger.
196 I6 Grocka Serbia
168 G1 Gröde-Appelland i. Ger.
175 K4 Gródek Lubelskie Pol.
175 L2 Gródek Podlaskie Pol.
171 I8 Gröden Ger.
178 H4 Grödig Austria
171 H8 Gröditz Ger.
175 I2 Gródki Pol.
174 F5 Grodków Pol.
Grodnenskaya Oblast' admin. div. Belarus see Hrodzyenskaya Voblasts'
Grodnenskaya Vozvyshennost' hills Belarus see Hrodnyendskaye Wzvyshsha
Grodno Belarus see Hrodna
Grodno Oblast admin. div. Belarus see Hrodzyenskaya Voblasts'
175 H2 Grodziczno Pol.
174 G3 Grodziec Pol.
175 K3 Grodzisk Pol.
175 I3 Grodzisk Mazowiecki Pol.
174 E3 Grodzisk Wielkopolski Pol.
214 H6 Groen watercourse Northern Cape S. Africa
214 B6 Groen watercourse S. Africa
164 K4 Groenlo Neth.
215 O3 Groenvlei S. Africa
237 G10 Groesbeck TX U.S.A.
164 I5 Groesbeek Neth.
140 □B1 Gröf Iceland
85 J4 Groganville Qld Austr.
169 H6 Grohnde (Emmerthal) Ger.
177 L6 Grohot, Vârful hill Romania
171 F8 Groitzsch Ger.
158 E6 Groix France
158 E6 Groix, Île de i. France
175 I4 Grójec Pol.
175 I2 Grom Pol.
174 D4 Gromadka Pol.
189 C7 Grombalia Tunisia
168 K2 Grömitz Ger.
175 I6 Gromnik Pol.
190 H4 Gromo Italy
168 G1 Grønå r. Denmark
169 I6 Gronau (Leine) Ger.
169 D6 Gronau (Westfalen) Ger.
193 Q8 Grondo r. Italy
173 I6 Grönenbach Ger.
140 L4 Grong Norway
171 D7 Gröningen Ger.
164 K2 Groningen Neth.
164 K2 Groningen prov. Neth.
251 H3 Groningen Suriname
164 J2 Groninger Wad tidal flat Neth.
Grønland terr. N. America see Greenland
Grønnedal Greenland see Kangilinnguit
175 H1 Gronowo Pol.
143 L4 Grönskåra Sweden
170 F1 Grønsund sea chan. Denmark
237 E8 Groom TX U.S.A.
241 Q4 Groom Lake NV U.S.A.
147 K3 Groomsport Northern Ireland U.K.
214 I9 Groot r. Eastern Cape S. Africa
214 D8 Groot r. Western Cape S. Africa
214 F9 Groot r. Western Cape S. Africa
214 E3 Groot-Aar Pan salt pan S. Africa
214 C8 Groot Berg r. S. Africa
215 J7 Groot Brak r. S. Africa
214 G10 Groot Brakrivier S. Africa
215 N2 Grootdraaidam dam S. Africa
214 F4 Grootdrink S. Africa
164 H3 Grootebroek Neth.
84 F2 Groote Eylandt i. N.T. Austr.
84 F3 Groote Eylandt Aboriginal Land res. N.T. Austr.
164 J2 Grootegast Neth.
212 C3 Grootfontein Namibia
215 J4 Groot-Grannapan salt pan S. Africa
212 C5 Groot Karas Berg plat. Namibia
212 D4 Groot Laagte watercourse Botswana/Namibia
213 F4 Groot Letaba r. S. Africa
215 K1 Groot Marico S. Africa
214 B5 Grootmis S. Africa
215 K1 Grootpan S. Africa
214 H9 Grootrivierhoogte mts S. Africa
214 F9 Groot Swartberge mts S. Africa
214 C2 Grootvaalgraspan salt pan Namibia
215 M2 Grootvlei S. Africa
214 E5 Grootvloer salt pan S. Africa
215 K8 Groot Winterberg mt. S. Africa
215 I9 Groot-Winterhoekberge mts S. Africa
190 F5 Gropello Cairoli Italy
197 P5 Gropeni Romania
187 D12 Grosa, Isla i. Spain
161 I9 Gros Bessillon hill France
160 F2 Grosbois-en-Montagne France
161 K6 Groscavallo Italy
190 I3 Grosio Italy
247 □3 Gros Islet St Lucia
247 □3 Gros-Morne Martinique
225 J3 Gros Morne National Park Nfld and Lab. Can.
160 F3 Grosne r. France
178 B7 Grosotto Italy
247 □3 Gros Piton mt. St Lucia
187 I9 Grossa, Punta pt Spain
173 J5 Großaitingen Ger.
169 I8 Großalmerode Ger.
171 E6 Groß Ammensleben Ger.
178 H5 Großarl Austria
212 C4 Gross Barmen Namibia
169 J8 Großbartloff Ger.
171 H6 Großbeeren Ger.
168 D5 Groß Berßen Ger.
172 F2 Groß-Bieberau Ger.
169 J8 Großbodungen Ger.
171 G8 Großbothen Ger.
172 G4 Großbottwar Ger.
171 D9 Großbreitenbach Ger.
169 I6 Großburgwedel (Burgwedel) Ger.
169 J8 Großburschla Ger.
170 I5 Groß Dölln Ger.
171 J8 Großdubrau Ger.
169 H5 Große Aue r. Ger.
172 F4 Große Enz r. Ger.
173 N4 Große Laaber r. Ger.
172 H5 Große Lauter r. Ger.
169 J6 Groß Elbe (Elbe) Ger.
172 F5 Grosselfingen Ger.
168 I3 Großenaspe Ger.
170 D2 Großenbrode Ger.
169 G9 Großen-Buseck Ger.
169 K8 Großenehrich Ger.
179 O3 Groß Engersdorf Austria
169 K8 Großengottern Ger.
171 I8 Großenhain Ger.
168 F5 Großenkneten Ger.
169 I9 Großenlüder Ger.
168 J3 Großensee Ger.
171 F9 Großenstein Ger.
168 H1 Großenwiehe Ger.
179 O3 Groß-Enzersdorf Austria
247 □2 Grosse Pointe Guadeloupe
173 O3 Großer Arber mt. Ger.
169 K9 Großer Beerberg hill Ger.
179 J5 Grosser Bösenstein mt. Austria
169 J10 Großer Breitenberg hill Ger.
179 K4 Grosser Buchstein mt. Austria
172 D3 Großer Eyberg hill Ger.
169 K10 Großer Gleichberg hill Ger.
170 H1 Großer Jasmunder Bodden b. Ger.
171 F10 Großer Kornberg hill Ger.
170 H3 Großer Landgraben r. Ger.
178 E5 Grosser Löffler mt. Austria
171 I6 Großer Müggelsee l. Ger.
171 H8 Große Röder r. Ger.
176 C2 Großer Osser mt. Czech Rep./Ger.
168 J2 Großer Plöner See l. Ger.
179 J4 Grosser Priel mt. Austria
173 O4 Großer Rachel mt. Ger.
171 I6 Großer Selchower See l. Ger.
179 I6 Grosser Speikkofel mt. Austria
179 K6 Grosser Speikkogel mt. Austria
171 E10 Großer Waldstein hill Ger.
168 D4 Großes Meer l. Ger.
178 G5 Großes Wiesbachhorn mt. Austria
158 H8 Grosse Terre, Pointe de pt France
192 G2 Grosseto Italy
192 G2 Grosseto prov. Italy
192 B4 Grosseto-Prugna Corse France
100 K5 Grossevichi Rus. Fed.
173 M4 Große Vils r. Ger.
170 I4 Groß Fredenwalde Ger.
169 K8 Großfurra Ger.
170 E5 Groß Garz Ger.
172 E2 Groß-Gerau Ger.
179 K2 Groß-Gerungs Austria
169 I6 Groß Giesen Ger.
171 H6 Groß Glienicke Ger.
178 G5 Großglockner mt. Austria
173 N6 Großgmain Ger.
170 E4 Groß Godems Ger.
179 L2 Großgöttfritz Austria
168 K3 Groß Grönau Ger.
173 J3 Großhabersdorf Ger.
168 J3 Großhansdorf Ger.
179 N2 Großharras Austria
169 J6 Groß Heere (Heere) Ger.
171 K9 Großhennersdorf Ger.
171 E8 Großheringen Ger.
168 D5 Groß-Hesepe Ger.
172 G2 Großheubach Ger.
168 G5 Groß Ippener Ger.
173 M6 Großkarolinenfeld Ger.
171 E8 Großkayna Ger.
170 H2 Groß Kiesow Ger.
179 L6 Großklein Austria
171 F8 Großkorbetha Ger.
171 I6 Groß Köris Ger.
171 J8 Großkoschen Ger.
171 G6 Groß Kreutz Ger.
179 O2 Großkrut Austria
168 J2 Groß Kummerfeld Ger.
170 E4 Groß Laasch Ger.
169 J6 Groß Lafferde (Lahstedt) Ger.
173 I2 Großlangheim Ger.
171 F8 Großlehna Ger.
171 J6 Groß Leine Ger.
171 J6 Groß Leuthen Ger.
171 K6 Groß Lindow Ger.
169 C10 Großlittgen Ger.
169 K8 Großlohra Ger.
171 I8 Großmehlen Ger.
173 L4 Großmehring Ger.
170 I3 Groß Miltzow Ger.
170 G2 Groß Mohrdorf Ger.
171 D8 Großmonra Ger.
171 E7 Groß Mühlingen Ger.
171 I8 Großnaundorf Ger.
171 G7 Groß Naundorf Ger.
170 H4 Groß Nemerow Ger.
168 J5 Groß Oesingen Ger.
171 H9 Großolbersdorf Ger.
171 D7 Großörner Ger.
171 J7 Groß Oßnig Ger.
172 G2 Großostheim Ger.
179 N5 Großpetersdorf Austria
170 G3 Groß Plasten Ger.
171 D7 Groß Quenstedt Ger.
179 K4 Großraming Austria
171 J7 Großräschen Ger.
172 H2 Großrinderfeld Ger.
172 E2 Groß-Rohrheim Ger.
171 J8 Großröhrsdorf Ger.
171 E7 Groß Rosenburg Ger.
172 B3 Großrosseln Ger.
171 D8 Großrudestedt Ger.
179 N3 Großrußbach Austria
179 L6 Groß Sankt Florian Austria
171 J8 Groß Särchen Ger.
171 K7 Groß Schacksdorf Ger.
171 H9 Großschirma Ger.
179 K2 Großschönau Austria
171 K9 Großschönau Ger.
170 I5 Groß Schönebeck Ger.
170 E5 Groß Schwechten Ger.
171 K8 Großschweidnitz Ger.
169 J6 Groß Schwülper (Schwülper) Ger.
179 L2 Groß-Siegharts Austria
168 I1 Großsolt Ger.
168 D5 Groß Stavern Ger.
171 G8 Großsteinberg Ger.
170 D3 Groß Stieten Ger.
171 G7 Großtreben Ger.
169 K6 Groß Twülpstedt Ger.
212 C4 Gross Ums Namibia
172 F2 Groß-Umstadt Ger.
178 F5 Großvenediger mt. Austria
172 G2 Großwallstadt Ger.
190 E1 Grosswangen Switz.
170 E4 Groß Warnow Ger.
169 K8 Großwechsungen Ger.
179 M3 Großweikersdorf Austria
170 F4 Groß Welle Ger.
168 I2 Groß Wittensee Ger.
170 F3 Groß Wokern Ger.
170 F5 Großwudicke Ger.
170 G3 Groß Wüstenfelde Ger.
170 I5 Groß Ziethen Ger.
172 F2 Groß-Zimmern Ger.
157 M6 Grostenquin France
188 E3 Grosuplje Slovenia
263 L1 Grosvenor Mountains Antarctica
238 I5 Gros Ventre Range mts WY U.S.A.
225 J2 Groswater Bay Nfld and Lab. Can.
165 F6 Grote Nete r. Belgium
235 K2 Groton CT U.S.A.
233 I6 Groton NY U.S.A.
236 F3 Groton SD U.S.A.
193 J4 Grottaferrata Italy
195 M2 Grottaglie Italy
193 L2 Grottammare Italy
193 L1 Grottazzolina Italy
194 F9 Grotte Sicilia Italy
192 H2 Grotte di Castro Italy
195 K7 Grotteria Italy
232 G10 Grottoes VA U.S.A.
195 K2 Grottole Italy
164 I2 Grou Neth.
222 G1 Grouard Lake N.W.T. Can.
222 G4 Grouard Mission Alta Can.
158 H4 Grouin, Pointe du pt France
206 E5 Groumania Côte d'Ivoire
224 D3 Groundhog r. Ont. Can.
237 H7 Grove OK U.S.A.
232 B9 Grove City OH U.S.A.
232 E7 Grove City PA U.S.A.
231 D10 Grove Hill AL U.S.A.
141 L5 Grövelsjön Sweden
263 F2 Grove Mountains Antarctica
234 B1 Grover PA U.S.A.
240 L6 Grover Beach CA U.S.A.
233 N4 Groveton NH U.S.A.
237 H10 Groveton TX U.S.A.
234 F4 Groveville NJ U.S.A.
140 N2 Grovfjord Norway
241 S9 Growler Mountains AZ U.S.A.
197 P7 Grozd'ovo Bulg.
129 G2 Groznyy Rus. Fed.
171 D10 Grub am Forst Ger.
142 C3 Grubbåfjellet mt. Norway
165 J6 Grubbenvorst Neth.
170 D2 Grube Ger.
188 F3 Grubišno Polje Croatia
174 G2 Gruczno Pol.
Grudovo Bulg. see Sredets
175 I2 Grudusk Pol.
174 G2 Grudziądz Pol.
190 F6 Grue r. Italy
157 L7 Gruey-lès-Surance France
190 D5 Grugliasco Italy
146 E7 Gruinard Bay Scotland U.K.
146 D11 Gruinart, Loch inlet Scotland U.K.
161 C10 Gruissan France
182 H2 Grullos Spain
140 □ Grumantbyen Svalbard
197 O3 Grumăzești Romania
171 I8 Grumbach Ger.
193 P7 Grumento Nova Italy
195 L1 Grumo Appula Italy
142 J2 Grums Sweden
171 G9 Grüna Ger.
179 M3 Grünau Niederösterreich Austria
179 I4 Grünau Oberösterreich Austria
212 C5 Grünau Namibia
171 I6 Grünau-Grünheider Wald und Seengebiet park Ger.
179 M4 Grünbach am Schneeberg Austria
169 G9 Grünberg Ger.
Grünberg Pol. see Zielona Góra
179 J4 Grünburg Austria
141 L5 Grundagssätern Sweden
140 □B1 Grundarfjörður Iceland
141 L6 Grundforsen Sweden
179 I4 Grundlsee l. Austria
179 I4 Grundlsee nature res. Austria
214 B1 Grundorner Namibia
140 O5 Grundsuna Sweden
232 C11 Grundy VA U.S.A.
236 I4 Grundy Center IA U.S.A.
170 H5 Grüneberg Ger.
168 I3 Grünendeich Ger.
171 I8 Grünewald Ger.
171 I7 Grünewalde Ger.
171 I6 Grünheide Ger.
244 F1 Gruñidora Mex.
172 H6 Grünkraut Ger.
171 J6 Grunow Ger.
172 H2 Grünsfeld Ger.
172 E2 Grünstadt Ger.
191 K2 Gruppo de Tessa, Parco Naturale nature res. Italy
160 D3 Grury France
174 G2 Gruta Pol.
146 □N3 Grutness Shetland, Scotland U.K.
237 E7 Gruver TX U.S.A.
190 C2 Gruyère, Lac de la l. Switz.
190 C2 Gruyères Switz.
138 G5 Gruzdžiai Lith.
Gruzinskaya S.S.R. country Asia see Georgia
139 W9 Gryazi Rus. Fed.
139 W7 Gryaznoye Rus. Fed.
134 H4 Gryazovets Rus. Fed.
175 I6 Grybów Pol.
143 M1 Grycken l. Sweden
174 D2 Gryfice Pol.
174 C2 Gryfino Pol.
174 D4 Gryfów Śląski Pol.
174 F3 Grylewo Pol.
140 N2 Gryllefjord Norway
142 B2 Grytenuten hill Norway
143 N1 Gryttjom Sweden
259 □ Grytviken S. Georgia
175 I2 Gryźliny Pol.
174 E3 Grzebienisko Pol.
174 G3 Grzegorzew Pol.
174 E2 Grzmiąca Pol.
174 C2 Grzybno Pol.
174 G3 Grzymiszew Pol.
174 G2 Grzywna Pol.
178 D5 Gschnitz Austria
179 I4 Gschwandt Austria
172 H4 Gschwend Ger.
190 C3 Gstaad Switz.
173 M6 Gstadt am Chiemsee Ger.
190 C3 Gsteig Switz.
117 J8 Gua Jharkhand India
191 L5 Guà r. Italy
242 □R13 Guabito Panama
244 C2 Guacamayita Mex.
246 E3 Guacanayabo, Golfo de b. Cuba
247 J8 Guacara Venez.
250 D3 Guacharía r. Col.
244 A1 Guachimetas de Arriba Mex.
258 D2 Guachipas Arg.
255 B7 Guaçu Brazil
257 G4 Guaçuí Brazil
185 M5 Guadahortuna Spain
185 N5 Guadahortuna r. Spain
184 G6 Guadaira r. Spain
184 H6 Guadairilla r. Spain
184 F3 Guadajira r. Spain
184 H5 Guadajoz Spain
185 J5 Guadajoz r. Spain
244 D5 Guadalajara Mex.
183 N7 Guadalajara Spain
183 P7 Guadalajara prov. Spain
187 C7 Guadalaviar r. Spain
184 I5 Guadalbacar r. Spain
185 L5 Guadalbullón r. Spain
184 H7 Guadalcacín, Embalse de resr Spain
78 □6 Guadalcanal i. Solomon Is
184 H4 Guadalcanal Spain
185 J5 Guadalcázar Spain
184 H3 Guadalefra r. Spain
185 L4 Guadalén r. Spain
185 M4 Guadalén, Embalse del resr Spain
185 N5 Guadalentín r. Spain
185 Q5 Guadalentín r. Spain
260 D4 Guadales Arg.
187 E10 Guadalest, Embalse de resr Spain
184 G7 Guadalete r. Spain
185 K7 Guadalhorce r. Spain
185 J7 Guadalhorce, Embalse de resr Spain
185 L5 Guadalimar r. Spain
185 I5 Guadalmazán r. Spain
185 J4 Guadalmellato, Embalse de resr Spain
185 N4 Guadalmena r. Spain
185 N4 Guadalmena, Embalse del resr Spain
185 J3 Guadalmez Spain
185 J3 Guadalmez r. Spain
186 E5 Guadalope r. Spain
185 G7 Guadalquivir r. Spain
254 E3 Guadalupe Brazil
243 I5 Guadalupe Nuevo León Mex.
245 J6 Guadalupe Puebla Mex.
245 H1 Guadalupe Tamaulipas Mex.
244 E3 Guadalupe Zacatecas Mex.
245 I9 Guadalupe Mex.
242 A3 Guadalupe i. Mex.
241 P9 Guadalupe watercourse Mex.
250 B6 Guadalupe Peru
185 I2 Guadalupe Spain
241 U8 Guadalupe AZ U.S.A.
240 L7 Guadalupe CA U.S.A.
237 G11 Guadalupe r. TX U.S.A.
237 G11 Guadalupe r. TX U.S.A.
184 H2 Guadalupe, Sierra de mts Spain
244 C1 Guadalupe Aguilera Mex.
239 K11 Guadalupe Bravos Mex.
244 A1 Guadalupe de los Reyes Mex.
239 L11 Guadalupe Mountains National Park TX U.S.A.
237 C10 Guadalupe Peak TX U.S.A.
241 Q9 Guadalupe Victoria Baja California Mex.
244 C1 Guadalupe Victoria Durango Mex.
242 F4 Guadalupe y Calvo Mex.
185 I5 Guadalvacarejo r. Spain
183 O8 Guadamajud r. Spain
185 I3 Guadamatilla r. Spain
184 H3 Guadamez r. Spain
183 L9 Guadamur Spain
183 L7 Guadarrama Spain
183 L9 Guadarrama r. Spain
250 D2 Guadarrama Venez.
183 L7 Guadarrama, Puerto de pass Spain
183 L7 Guadarrama, Sierra de mts Spain
183 Q9 Guadazaón r. Spain
247 □2 Guadeloupe terr. West Indies
247 □ Guadeloupe, Parc National de la nat. park Guadeloupe
247 □2 Guadeloupe Passage Caribbean Sea
184 G7 Guadiamar r. Spain
185 E6 Guadiana r. Port./Spain
246 A2 Guadiana, Bahía de b. Cuba
185 M2 Guadiana, Canal del Spain
185 M5 Guadiana Menor r. Spain
185 I8 Guadiaro r. Spain
185 I5 Guadiato r. Spain
183 P8 Guadiela r. Spain
183 J8 Guadiervas r. Spain
185 M6 Guadix Spain
259 B6 Guafo, Isla i. Chile
92 C4 Guagua Luzon Phil.
255 C9 Guaíba Brazil
247 □7 Guaico Trin. and Tob.
257 E2 Guaiçuí Brazil
253 F5 Guaicuras Brazil
250 B4 Guaillabamba r. Ecuador
246 E3 Guáimaro Cuba
251 F3 Guaina Venez.
250 D4 Guainía dept Col.
250 E4 Guainía r. Col./Venez.
251 F3 Guaiquinima, Cerro mt. Venez.
255 B8 Guaíra Brazil
256 C4 Guaíra Brazil
256 A5 Guairaçá Brazil
259 B6 Guaitecas, Islas is Chile
106 H6 Guaizihu Nei Mongol China
254 C2 Guajará Açu Brazil
252 D2 Guajará Mirim Brazil
251 F6 Guajaratuba Brazil
183 L9 Guajaraz r. Spain
185 L7 Guájar-Faraguit Spain
252 D1 Guajarraã Brazil
247 □1 Guajataca r. Puerto Rico
247 □1 Guajataca, Lago de l. Puerto Rico
242 H3 Guaje, Laguna de l. Mex.
242 H4 Guaje, Llano de plain Mex.
250 D2 Guajira, Península de la pen. Col.
250 B5 Gualaceo Ecuador
240 I3 Gualala CA U.S.A.
243 O10 Gualán Guat.
250 B5 Gualaquiza Ecuador
193 J2 Gualdo Cattaneo Italy
191 N9 Gualdo Tadino Italy
261 H3 Gualeguay Arg.
261 H3 Gualeguay r. Arg.
261 H3 Gualeguaychu Arg.
259 D6 Gualicho, Salina salt flat Arg.
259 C6 Gualjaina Arg.
252 C4 Guallatiri vol. Chile
260 B4 Gualleco Chile
260 B6 Gualletue, Lago de l. Chile
244 D2 Gualterio Mex.
191 J6 Gualtieri Italy
91 J4 Guam terr. N. Pacific Ocean
247 I8 Guama Venez.
259 B7 Guamblin, Isla i. Chile
261 F5 Guamini Arg.
246 E3 Guamo Cuba
251 E3 Guampí, Sierra de mts Venez.
242 E5 Guamúchil Mex.
94 D2 Gua Musang Malaysia
107 O7 Gu'an Hebei China
246 B2 Guanabacoa Cuba
252 C2 Guanabara Brazil
257 F5 Guanabara, Baía de b. Brazil
242 □Q12 Guanacaste, Cordillera de mts Costa Rica
242 □Q12 Guanacaste, Parque Nacional nat. park Costa Rica
242 G5 Guanacevi Mex.
261 F5 Guanaco, Cerro hill Arg.
246 A2 Guanahacabibes, Península de pen. Cuba
242 □Q9 Guanaja Hond.
246 B2 Guanajay Cuba
244 F4 Guanajuato Mex.
244 G4 Guanajuato state Mex.
244 F4 Guanajuato, Sierra de mts Mex.
254 E5 Guanambi Brazil
244 F3 Guaname Mex.
250 B7 Guañape, Islas de is Peru
247 □7 Guanapo Trin. and Tob.
260 B2 Guanaqueros Chile
250 D2 Guanare Venez.
250 E2 Guanare Viejo r. Venez.
250 D2 Guanarito Venez.
250 D2 Guanarito r. Venez.
216 □3f Guanarteme, Punta de pt Gran Canaria Canary Is
252 D3 Guanay Bol.
258 C3 Guandacol Arg.
107 L9 Guandaokou Henan China
107 L8 Guandi Shan mt. Shanxi China
257 G3 Guandu r. Brazil
109 I6 Guandu Guangdong China
246 A2 Guane Cuba
108 F3 Guang'an Sichuan China
109 K5 Guangchang Jiangxi China
109 L3 Guangde Anhui China
109 J7 Guangdong prov. China
109 L4 Guangfeng Jiangxi China
109 I8 Guanghai Guangdong China
108 E3 Guanghan Sichuan China
Guanghua Hubei China see Laohekou
107 N7 Guangling Shanxi China
108 C5 Guangmao Shan mt. Yunnan China
Guangming Sichuan China see Xide
109 L3 Guangming Ding mt. Anhui China
108 E6 Guangnan Yunnan China
109 I7 Guangning Guangdong China
Guangning Liaoning China see Beining
107 P8 Guangrao Shandong China
109 J3 Guangshan Henan China
109 I3 Guangshui Hubei China
Guangxi aut. reg. China see Guangxi Zhuangzu Zizhiqu
108 G7 Guangxi Zhuangzu Zizhiqu aut. reg. China
108 E2 Guangyuan Sichuan China
109 K5 Guangze Fujian China
109 I7 Guangzhou Guangdong China
107 N8 Guangzong Hebei China
257 F3 Guanhães Brazil
257 F3 Guanhães r. Brazil
107 P9 Guan He r. China
107 P9 Guanhe Kou r. mouth China
247 □1 Guánica Puerto Rico
246 A2 Guaniguanico, Cordillera de mts Cuba
251 F2 Guanipa r. Venez.
108 E6 Guanling Guizhou China
108 G3 Guanmian Shan mts China
251 F2 Guanoca Venez.
108 H2 Guanpo Henan China
101 D8 Guanshui Liaoning China
Guansuo Guizhou China see Guanling
260 B1 Guanta Chile
251 E2 Guanta Venez.
246 F3 Guantánamo Cuba
246 F4 Guantánamo Bay Naval Base military base Cuba
107 N8 Guantao Hebei China
108 E2 Guanting Gansu China
106 H9 Guanting Qinghai China
107 N6 Guanting Shuiku resr China
Guanxian Sichuan China see Dujiangyan
109 H6 Guanyang Guangxi China
108 C3 Guanyinqiao Sichuan China
107 P9 Guanyun Jiangsu China
Guapay r. Bol. see Grande
257 E4 Guapé Brazil
250 B4 Guapí Col.
256 C6 Guapiara Brazil
242 □R12 Guápiles Costa Rica
247 □7 Guapo Bay Trin. and Tob.
252 D3 Guaporé r. Bol./Brazil
255 C9 Guaporé Brazil
Guaporé state Brazil see Rondônia
252 C4 Guaqui Bol.
256 D4 Guará Brazil
254 D5 Guará r. Brazil
186 E3 Guara, Sierra de mts Spain
254 G3 Guarabira Brazil
257 F4 Guaraciaba Brazil
250 B5 Guaranda Ecuador
257 F4 Guarani Brazil
256 A6 Guaraniaçu Brazil
256 C4 Guarantã Brazil
257 G4 Guarapari Brazil
256 B6 Guarapuava Brazil
256 C6 Guaraqueçaba Brazil
256 B4 Guararapes Brazil
257 H2 Guaratinga Brazil
257 E5 Guaratinguetá Brazil
255 C8 Guaratuba Brazil
252 C3 Guarayos Bol.
216 □3e Guarazoca El Hierro Canary Is
193 K4 Guarcino Italy
182 F7 Guarda Port.
182 F7 Guarda admin. dist. Port.
Guardafui, Cape Somalia see Gwardafuy, Gees
185 N5 Guardal r. Spain
187 D11 Guardamar del Segura Spain
256 D2 Guarda Mor Brazil
250 E2 Guardatinajas Venez.
195 K6 Guardavalle Italy
258 E3 Guardia Escolta Arg.
193 M3 Guardiagrele Italy
193 N4 Guardialfiera, Lago di l. Italy
241 Q9 Guardianes de la Patria Mex.
193 Q7 Guardia Perticara Italy
193 Q9 Guardia Piemontese Italy
193 N5 Guardia Sanframondi Italy
185 N7 Guardias Viejas Spain
186 I3 Guardiola de Berguedà Spain
183 K3 Guardo Spain
182 H6 Guardramiro Spain
182 E9 Guardunha, Serra de mts Port.
184 G3 Guareña Spain
183 J6 Guareña r. Spain
186 E3 Guarga r. Spain
253 E1 Guariba r. Brazil
250 E2 Guárico state Venez.
246 F3 Guarico, Punta pt Cuba
185 J7 Guaro Spain
185 L4 Guarrizas r. Spain
250 D3 Guarrojo r. Col.
185 L4 Guarromán Spain
256 D5 Guarujá Brazil
256 D5 Guarulhos Brazil
256 D5 Guarulhos airport Brazil
246 H8 Guasare r. Venez.
242 E5 Guasave Mex.
250 D3 Guasdualito Venez.
192 C8 Guasila Sardegna Italy
251 F3 Guasipati Venez.
191 J6 Guastalla Italy
243 O10 Guastatoya Guat.
117 L9 Guasuba r. India

Guatemala to Hailar He

320

243 N10 Guatemala country Central America
243 N10 Guatemala Guat.
267 M5 Guatemala Basin sea feature Pacific Ocean
Guatemala City Guat. see Guatemala
261 F3 Guatimozin Arg.
216 □3c Guatiza Lanzarote Canary Is
261 F5 Guatrache Arg.
259 D6 Guatrochi Arg.
247 □7 Guatuaro Point Trin. and Tob.
250 D4 Guaviare dept Col.
250 E3 Guaviare r. Col.
256 D4 Guaxupé Brazil
250 D3 Guayabal Col.
246 E3 Guayabal Cuba
247 □1 Guayabal, Lago l. Puerto Rico
260 D2 Guayaguas, Sierra da mts Arg.
247 □7 Guayaguayare Trin. and Tob.
245 J3 Guayalejo r. Mex.
247 □1 Guayama Puerto Rico
247 □1 Guayanilla Puerto Rico
247 □1 Guayanilla, Punta pt Puerto Rico
250 E3 Guayapo, Serranía mts Venez.
250 B5 Guayaquil Ecuador
250 A5 Guayaquil, Golfo de g. Ecuador
252 D2 Guayaramerín Bol.
250 A5 Guayas prov. Ecuador
258 D1 Guayatayoc, Laguna de imp. l. Arg.
242 D4 Guaymas Mex.
247 □1 Guaynabo Puerto Rico
261 H2 Guayquirard Arg.
261 H2 Guayquiraró r. Arg.
243 N10 Guazacapán Guat.
106 D6 Guazhou Gansu China
210 B2 Guba Eth.
120 H6 Gubadag Turkm.
134 L4 Gubakha Rus. Fed.
Gûbâl Island Egypt see Jūbāl, Jazīrat
210 E2 Guban plain Somalia
92 E5 Gubat Luzon Phil.
148 B5 Gubaveeny Ireland
114 E6 Gubbi Karnataka India
191 N9 Gubbio Italy
129 I3 Gubden Rus. Fed.
134 L3 Gubdor Rus. Fed.
210 F2 Gubed Binna b. Somalia
107 O6 Gubeikou Beijing China
171 K7 Guben Ger.
197 N8 Gŭbene Bulg.
175 J1 Guber r. Pol.
174 C4 Gubin Pol.
139 S6 Gubino Rus. Fed.
207 I3 Gubio Nigeria
135 G6 Gubkin Rus. Fed.
106 H8 Gucheng Gansu China
106 F6 Gucheng Gansu China
107 N8 Gucheng Hebei China
109 H2 Gucheng Hubei China
107 L9 Gucheng Shanxi China
114 E7 Gudalur Tamil Nadu India
129 F3 Gudamaqris K'edi hills Georgia
186 D7 Gudar Spain
187 D7 Gudar, Sierra de mts Spain
Gudara Tajik. see Ghŭdara
115 H3 Gudari Orissa India
129 B2 Gudaut'a Georgia
141 J6 Gudbrandsdalen val. Norway
123 M7 Guddu Barrage Pak.
142 G5 Gudenå r. Denmark
169 H8 Gudensberg Ger.
129 H2 Gudermes Rus. Fed.
168 I1 Guderup Denmark
143 K6 Gudhjem Bornholm Denmark
207 H4 Gudi Nigeria
114 G4 Gudivada Andhra Prad. India
114 F6 Gudiyattam Tamil Nadu India
195 □ Gudja Malta
142 G6 Gudme Denmark
157 J7 Gudmont-Villiers France
100 F7 Gudong He r. China
168 K3 Gudow Ger.
123 J8 Gudri r. Pak.
126 F3 Güdül Turkey
114 F5 Gudur Andhra Prad. India
114 F5 Gudur Andhra Prad. India
141 I6 Gudvangen Norway
100 H4 Gudzhal r. Rus. Fed.
138 G6 Gudžiūnai Lith.
225 G1 Gué, Rivière du r. Que. Can.
157 N8 Guebwiller France
Guecho Spain see Algorta
206 C4 Guéckédou Guinea
158 F6 Guégon France
227 Q1 Guéguen, Lac l. Que. Can.
185 M6 Güéjar-Sierra Spain
204 C5 Guelb er Rîchât hill Maur.
208 B2 Guélengdeng Chad
205 G1 Guelma Alg.
189 A7 Guelma prov. Alg.
204 C3 Guelmine Morocco
224 D5 Guelph Ont. Can.
205 E5 Guem waterhole Mali
205 G2 Guémar Alg.
157 N7 Guémar France
158 H6 Guémené-Penfao France
158 E5 Guémené-sur-Scorff France
245 H2 Guémez Mex.
157 L5 Guénange France
206 C2 Guendour well Maur.
207 F4 Guéné Benin
183 N2 Güeñes Spain
158 H6 Guenrouet France
206 B3 Guènt Paté Senegal
158 G6 Guer France
208 C2 Guéra pref. Chad
208 C2 Guéra, Massif du mts Chad
158 G7 Guérande France
205 G2 Guerara Alg.
225 H1 Guérard, Lac l. Que. Can.
204 E2 Guercif Morocco
202 C5 Guéré watercourse Chad
202 D6 Guéréda Chad
202 D4 Guerende Libya
162 H3 Guéret France
160 C2 Guérigny France
207 F4 Guérin-Kouka Togo
158 E5 Guerlédan, Lac de l. France
240 J3 Guerneville CA U.S.A.
Guernica Spain see Gernika-Lumo
158 F3 Guernsey terr. Channel Is
238 L5 Guernsey WY U.S.A.
206 C2 Guérou Maur.
184 E6 Guerreiros do Rio Port.
261 I4 Guerrero Arg.
237 E11 Guerrero Coahuila Mex.
243 J4 Guerrero Tamaulipas Mex.
244 G8 Guerrero state Mex.
184 F3 Guerrero r. Spain
245 H8 Guerrero, Parque Natural de nature res. Mex.
242 B4 Guerrero Negro Mex.
163 E10 Guerreys, Pic de mt. France
186 H3 Guerri de la Sal Spain
225 H1 Guers, Lac l. Que. Can.
204 E3 Guerzim Alg.
186 C2 Güesa Spain
204 D4 Guețâțîra well Mali
163 A9 Guéthary France
160 E3 Gueugnon France
206 D5 Guéyo Côte d'Ivoire
Gufeng Fujian China see Pingnan
Gufu Hubei China see Xingshan
129 F5 Gugark' Armenia
210 C3 Gugē mt. Eth.
78 □3a Gugegwe i. Kwajalein Marshall Is
123 O6 Gugera Pak.
122 E4 Gügerd, Kūh-e mts Iran
150 □ Gugh i. England U.K.
261 F2 Guglieri Arg.
172 F3 Güglingen Ger.
193 N4 Guglionesi Italy
210 C2 Gugu mts Eth.
91 K3 Guguan i. N. Mariana Is
94 F8 Guhakolak, Tanjung pt Indon.
109 K3 Guhe Anhui China
122 H8 Gūh Kūh mt. Iran
170 G4 Gühlen-Glienicke Ger.
Guhuai Henan China see Pingyu
253 F3 Guia Brazil
182 C9 Guia Port.
216 □3a Guía de Isora Tenerife Canary Is
182 G4 Guiana mt. Spain
264 F5 Guiana Basin sea feature N. Atlantic Ocean
249 F2 Guiana Highlands reg. Guyana/Venez.
250 E3 Guiana Highlands mts S. America
206 D5 Guibéroua Côte d'Ivoire
156 B6 Guichainville France
158 H6 Guichen France
82 G7 Guichen Bay S.A. Austr.
Guichi Anhui China see Chizhou
245 L8 Guichicovi Mex.
261 I3 Guichón Uru.
158 D4 Guiclan France
207 G3 Guidan-Roumji Niger
208 C2 Guidari Chad
106 G9 Guide Qinghai China
158 E6 Guidel France
149 N3 Guide Post Northumberland, England U.K.
207 I4 Guider Cameroon
207 H3 Guidiguir Niger
207 I4 Guidiguis Cameroon
206 B3 Guidimaka admin. reg. Maur.
108 F5 Guiding Guizhou China
191 J5 Guidizzolo Italy
109 I6 Guidong Hunan China
193 J4 Guidonia-Montecelio Italy
257 F4 Guidoval Brazil
245 L9 Guienagati Mex.
206 B2 Guier, Lac de l. Senegal
160 H5 Guiers r. France
208 A5 Guietsou Gabon
108 G7 Guigang Guangxi China
191 J7 Guiglia Italy
206 D5 Guiglo Côte d'Ivoire
158 H6 Guignen France
156 E6 Guignes France
156 G5 Guignicourt France
247 J8 Güigüe Venez.
213 G5 Guija Moz.
108 H7 Gui Jiang r. China
109 M4 Guiji Shan mts China
182 H8 Guijo de Coria Spain
182 H8 Guijo de Galisteo Spain
182 H8 Guijo de Granadilla Spain
182 I7 Guijuelo Spain
161 J7 Guil r. France
151 K5 Guildford Surrey, England U.K.
233 N4 Guildhall VT U.S.A.
146 J10 Guildtown Perth and Kinross, Scotland U.K.
158 B5 Guilers France
235 J2 Guilford CT U.S.A.
233 □P3 Guilford ME U.S.A.
161 F7 Guilherand France
Guilherme Capelo Angola see Cacongo
182 D5 Guilhofrei Port.
108 H6 Guilin Guangxi China
221 K4 Guillaume-Delisle, Lac l. Que. Can.
161 J8 Guillaumes France
184 G5 Guillena Spain
161 J7 Guillestre France
158 G5 Guilliers France
160 E1 Guillon France
163 C6 Guillos France
158 C6 Guilvinec France
216 □3a Güímar Tenerife Canary Is
216 □3a Güímar, Punta de pt Tenerife Canary Is
254 D2 Guimarães Brazil
182 D6 Guimarães Port.
92 D6 Guimaras i. Phil.
92 D6 Guimaras Strait Phil.
107 O9 Guimeng Ding mt. Shandong China
207 F4 Guinagourou Benin
106 G9 Guinan Qinghai China
246 D2 Guinchos Cay i. Cuba
92 E7 Guindulman Bohol Phil.
206 C4 Guinea country Africa
207 G6 Guinea, Gulf of Africa
264 I5 Guinea Basin sea feature N. Atlantic Ocean
206 B4 Guinea-Bissau country Africa
Guinea-Conakry country Africa see Guinea
Guinea Ecuatorial country Africa see Equatorial Guinea
Guiné-Bissau country Africa see Guinea-Bissau
Guinée country Africa see Guinea
206 C4 Guinée-Forestière admin. reg. Guinea
206 B4 Guinée-Maritime admin. reg. Guinea
246 B2 Güines Cuba
156 C2 Guînes France
225 I2 Guines, Lac l. Nfld and Lab. Can.
158 E4 Guingamp France
206 B3 Guinguinéo Senegal
242 □Q13 Guiones, Punta pt Costa Rica
158 C5 Guipavas France
108 H7 Guiping Guangxi China
158 H6 Guipry France
186 A1 Guipúzcoa prov. Spain
206 E2 Guîr well Mali
246 B2 Güira de Melena Cuba
255 B6 Guiratinga Brazil
251 F2 Güiria Venez.
251 I3 Guisanbourg Fr. Guiana
183 J8 Guisando Spain
161 J7 Guisane r. France
149 O4 Guisborough Redcar and Cleveland, England U.K.
156 F4 Guiscard France
158 D5 Guiscriff France
156 G4 Guise France
149 N6 Guiseley West Yorkshire, England U.K.
Guishan Yunnan China see Xinping
207 F2 Guissefa well Mali
158 C4 Guissény France
186 H4 Guissona Spain
151 N2 Guist Norfolk, England U.K.
182 E2 Guitiriz Spain
162 D5 Guîtres France
206 D5 Guitri Côte d'Ivoire
92 E6 Guiuan Samar Phil.
140 S2 Guivi hill Fin.
Guixi Chongqing China see Dianjiang
108 F5 Guiyang Guizhou China
109 I5 Guiyang Hunan China
109 I6 Guiyang Hunan China
108 F5 Guizhou prov. China
109 H7 Guizi Guangdong China
163 B6 Gujan-Mestras France
116 D8 Gujarat state India
129 E4 Gujaret'i Georgia
123 O5 Gujar Khan Pak.
207 H4 Gujba Nigeria
Gujerat state India see Gujarat
107 M8 Gujiao Shanxi China
123 P5 Gujranwala Pak.
123 P5 Gujrat Pak.
Gukasyan Armenia see Ashots'k'
135 G6 Gukovo Rus. Fed.
122 A3 Gük Tappeh Iran
116 F3 Gulabgarh Jammu and Kashmir
129 H6 Gülablı Azer.
106 H8 Gulang Gansu China
Gulân Islands Egypt see Qul'ân, Jazâ'ir
83 L4 Gulargambone N.S.W. Austr.
199 H4 Gülbahçe Turkey
121 M7 Gulbahor Uzbek.
114 E4 Gulbarga Karnataka India
94 □ Gul Basin dock Sing.
138 J4 Gulbene Latvia
Gul'cha Kyrg. see Gülchö
121 O7 Gülchö Kyrg.
128 D2 Gülcihan Turkey
129 C4 Gül dağı mt. Turkey
170 E1 Guldborg Denmark
170 E1 Guldborg Sund str. Denmark
128 B1 Güldere Turkey
129 A6 Güleç Turkey
126 G5 Gülek Turkey
118 C2 Gülek Boğazı pass Turkey
Gulf of Chihli China see Bo Hai
237 K10 Gulfport MS U.S.A.
231 D10 Gulf Shores AL U.S.A.
83 L5 Gulgong N.S.W. Austr.
113 □1 Gulhi i. S. Male Maldives
100 C2 Gulian Heilong. China
108 E5 Gulin Sichuan China
123 L6 Gulistan Pak.
Gulistan Uzbek. see Guliston
121 M7 Guliston Uzbek.
92 □ Gulitel hill Palau
170 E4 Gülitz Ger.
107 R2 Guliya Shan mt. Nei Mongol China
Gulja Xinjiang China see Yining
123 M6 Gul Kach Pak.
135 H7 Gul'kevichi Rus. Fed.
224 B3 Gull r. Ont. Can.
148 D4 Gulladuff Northern Ireland U.K.
146 K10 Gullane East Lothian, Scotland U.K.
141 I6 Gullbrå Norway
226 I4 Gull Island MI U.S.A.
141 Q7 Gullkrona fjärd b. Fin.
223 I5 Gull Lake Sask. Can.
142 H3 Gullmarn inlet Sweden
223 M5 Gullrock Lake Ont. Can.
143 K3 Gullspång Sweden
129 D6 Güllü Erzurum Turkey
199 K4 Güllü Uşak Turkey
199 I5 Güllübahçe Turkey
129 H4 Güllük Azer.
199 I5 Güllük Turkey
199 I5 Güllük Körfezi b. Turkey
126 F5 Gülnar Turkey
165 I7 Gulpen Neth.
170 F5 Gülper See l. Ger.
199 H3 Gülpınar Turkey
123 I4 Gulran Afgh.
129 C3 Gulrip'shi Georgia
126 G4 Gülşehir Turkey
121 P4 Gul'shat Kazakh.
170 H3 Gültz Ger.
Gulü Henan China see Xincai
210 B4 Gulu Uganda
197 N8 Gŭlŭbovo Bulg.
85 M9 Guluguba Qld Austr.
207 I4 Gulumba Gana Nigeria
84 F1 Guluwuru Island N.T. Austr.
146 F9 Gulvain hill Scotland U.K.
211 C6 Gulwe Tanz.
197 M7 Gulyantsi Bulg.
134 K1 Gulyayevskiye Koshki, Ostrova is Rus. Fed.
170 F3 Gülzow Mecklenburg-Vorpommern Ger.
168 J4 Gülzow Schleswig-Holstein Ger.
Guma Xinjiang China see Pishan
123 N6 Gumal r. Pak.
212 D3 Gumare Botswana
123 M6 Gumbaz Pak.
Gumbinnen Rus. Fed. see Gusev
210 A3 Gumbiri mt. Sudan
122 F2 Gumdag Turkm.
207 H3 Gumel Nigeria
Gümgüm Turkey see Varto
183 M5 Gumiel de Hizán Spain
183 M5 Gumiel de Mercado Spain
129 C2 Gumist'is Nakrdzali nature res. Georgia
117 J8 Gumla Jharkhand India
Gumma Japan see Gunma
Gumma pref. Japan see Gunma
169 E8 Gummersbach Ger.
94 B2 Gumpang r. Indon.
169 J9 Gumpelstadt Ger.
207 H3 Gumsi Nigeria
170 F5 Gumtow Ger.
126 I3 Gümüşhane Turkey
129 A5 Gümüşhane prov. Turkey
199 I4 Gümüşsuyu Turkey
199 J1 Gümüşyaka Turkey
116 F7 Guna Madh. Prad. India
Gunan Chongqing China see Qijiang
177 I6 Gunaroš Vojvodina Serbia
210 C2 Guna Terara mt. Eth.
83 J6 Gunbar N.S.W. Austr.
Gund r. Tajik. see Gunt
83 J4 Gundabooka National Park N.S.W. Austr.
83 L6 Gundagai N.S.W. Austr.
116 H9 Gundardehi Chhattisgarh India
172 D5 Gundelfingen Ger.
173 I4 Gundelfingen an der Donau Ger.
172 G3 Gundelsheim Baden-Württemberg Ger.
173 J2 Gundelsheim Bayern Ger.
114 E6 Gunderi Karnataka India
157 O6 Gundershoffen France
208 D4 Gundji Dem. Rep. Congo
114 G5 Gundlakamma r. India
114 E7 Gundlupet Karnataka India
126 F5 Gündoğmuş Turkey
Gundorovka Rus. Fed. see Donetsk
199 L3 Gündüzler Turkey
129 D6 Gündüzü Turkey
199 J3 Güneşli Turkey
199 K4 Güney Denizli Turkey
199 J3 Güney Kütahya Turkey
126 J4 Güneydoğu Toroslar plat. Turkey
199 L4 Güneyköy Turkey
199 H2 Güneyli Turkey
129 B5 Güneysu Turkey
128 A2 Güneyyurt Turkey
96 D1 Gunglilap Myanmar
209 C6 Gungu Dem. Rep. Congo
209 B8 Gungue Angola
129 H3 Gunib Rus. Fed.
223 L4 Gunisao r. Man. Can.
223 L4 Gunisao Lake Man. Can.
188 G3 Gunja Croatia
206 A3 Gunjur Gambia
199 K3 Günlüce Turkey
105 J3 Gunma Japan
105 I2 Gunma pref. Japan
140 N4 Gunnarn Sweden
140 P3 Gunnarsbyn Sweden
85 J4 Gunnawarra Qld Austr.
221 P3 Gunnbjørn Fjeld nunatak Greenland
83 M4 Gunnedah N.S.W. Austr.
217 □1b Gunners Quoin Mauritius
149 P6 Gunness North Lincolnshire, England U.K.
83 L6 Gunning N.S.W. Austr.
150 D6 Gunnislake Cornwall, England U.K.
239 K7 Gunnison CO U.S.A.
241 U2 Gunnison UT U.S.A.
239 J7 Gunnison r. CO U.S.A.
241 U2 Gunnison Reservoir UT U.S.A.
84 C2 Gunn Point N.T. Austr.
Gunong Ayer Sarawak Malaysia see Gunung Ayer
247 □3 Gun Point Grenada
84 G5 Gunpowder Creek r. Qld Austr.
234 C6 Gunpowder Falls r. MD U.S.A.
Güns Hungary see Kőszeg
114 E3 Gun Sangari Mahar. India
179 I3 Gunskirchen Austria
171 D8 Günstedt Ger.
123 N3 Gunt r. Tajik.
114 E5 Guntakal Andhra Prad. India
169 K7 Güntersberge Ger.
172 E2 Guntersblum Ger.
179 N2 Guntersdorf Austria
172 H2 Güntersleben Ger.
231 D8 Guntersville AL U.S.A.
182 E3 Guntin de Pallares Spain
179 N3 Guntramsdorf Austria
114 G4 Guntur Andhra Prad. India
84 G4 Gununa Qld Austr.
93 E7 Gunungapi i. Maluku Indon.
95 I3 Gunung Ayer Sarawak Malaysia
95 L6 Gunungbatubesar Kalimantan Indon.
95 H4 Gunung Gading National Park Malaysia
94 G8 Gunung Gede Pangrango, Taman Nasional nat. park Indon.
94 G8 Gunung Halimun, Taman Nasional nat. park Indon.
94 B3 Gunung Leuser, Taman Nasional nat. park Indon.
95 K2 Gunung Mulu National Park Malaysia
95 H4 Gunung Niyut, Suaka Margasatwa nature res. Indon.
95 I5 Gunung Palung, Taman Nasional nat. park Indon.
95 L9 Gunung Rinjani, Taman Nasional nat. park Lombok Indon.
94 B4 Gunungsitoli Indon.
94 F7 Gunungsugih Sumatera Indon.
94 C4 Gunungtua Sumatera Indon.
115 H3 Gunupur Orissa India
126 E4 Günyüzü Turkey
173 I5 Günz r. Ger.
Gunza Angola see Porto Amboim
173 I5 Günzburg Ger.
173 J3 Gunzenhausen Ger.
106 I8 Guochengyi Gansu China
109 J2 Guo He r. China
109 K2 Guo He r. China
106 I9 Guojia Gansu China
108 H3 Guojiaba Hubei China
107 O6 Guojiatun Hebei China
Guoluezhen Henan China see Lingbao
Guovdageaidnu Norway see Kautokeino
109 K2 Guoyang Anhui China
Guozhen Shaanxi China see Baoji
116 D1 Gupis Jammu and Kashmir
100 J3 Gur r. Rus. Fed.
197 O5 Gura Caliței Romania
Guradu i. S. Male Maldives see Guraidhu
136 H7 Gura Galbenei Moldova
177 L5 Gurahonț Romania
197 N3 Gura Humorului Romania
113 □1 Guraidhu i. S. Male Maldives
116 E2 Gurais Jammu and Kashmir
197 Q6 Gura Portiței sea chan. Romania
207 G4 Gurara r. Nigeria
177 L6 Gurasada Romania
197 N6 Gura Șuții Romania
197 O5 Gura Teghii Romania
208 E4 Gurba r. Dem. Rep. Congo
107 M5 Gurban Obo Nei Mongol China
122 H1 Gurbansoltan Eje Turkm.
110 H4 Gurbantünggüt Shamo des. China
129 F6 Gürbulak Turkey
129 D5 Gürbüzler Turkey
116 E3 Gurdaspur Punjab India
122 I9 Gurdim Iran
237 I9 Gurdon AR U.S.A.
Gurdzhaani Georgia see Gurjaani
199 H3 Güre Balıkesir Turkey
199 K4 Güre Uşak Turkey
129 L5 Gürgān Azer.
Gurgan Iran see Gorgān
116 F5 Gurgaon Haryana India
202 E6 Gurgei, Jebel mt. Sudan
197 M4 Gurghiu r. Romania
197 M4 Gurghiului, Munții mts Romania
254 E3 Gurgueia r. Brazil
116 C7 Gurha Rajasthan India
251 F3 Guri, Embalse de resr Venez.
84 D1 Gurig National Park N.T. Austr.
256 C3 Gurinhatã Brazil
129 G4 Gurjaani Georgia
179 J6 Gurk Austria
179 K6 Gurk r. Austria
122 H7 Gur Khar Iran
179 J6 Gurktal val. Austria
179 I6 Gurktaler Alpen mts Austria
120 I7 Gurlan Uzbek.
Gurlen Uzbek. see Gurlan
114 E4 Gurmatkal Karnataka India
226 G7 Gurnee IL U.S.A.
150 E4 Gurnos Powys, Wales U.K.
213 G3 Guro Moz.
127 K4 Gürpınar Turkey
114 F6 Gurramkonda Andhra Prad. India
186 D3 Gurrea de Gállego Spain
199 K2 Gürsu Bursa Turkey
129 C4 Gürsu Rize Turkey
123 L3 Gurşunmagdan Kärhanasy Turkm.
Gu-ru i. S. Male Maldives see Gulhi
Guru i. S. Male Maldives see Gulhi
213 H2 Gurué Moz.
126 H4 Gürün Turkey
251 I5 Gurupá Brazil
251 I5 Gurupa, Ilha Grande de i. Brazil
254 C4 Gurupi Brazil
254 D2 Gurupi, Cabo c. Brazil
254 C3 Gurupi, Serra do hills Brazil
116 D7 Guru Sikhar mt. Rajasthan India
213 F3 Guruve Zimbabwe
Guruwe Zimbabwe see Guruve
114 F4 Guruzala Andhra Prad. India
106 H5 Gurvan Sayan Uul mts Mongolia
Gur'yev Kazakh. see Atyrau
138 D7 Gur'yevsk Rus. Fed.
Gur'yevskaya Oblast' admin. div. Kazakh. see Atyrauskaya Oblast'
123 K5 Gurz Afgh.
139 Y7 Gus' r. Rus. Fed.
207 G3 Gusau Nigeria
170 D4 Gusborn Ger.
171 E6 Güsen Ger.
138 F7 Gusev Rus. Fed.
139 X6 Gusevskiy Rus. Fed.
123 J3 Guşgy r. Turkm.
101 C9 Gushan Liaoning China
137 Q2 Gushchino Rus. Fed.
109 J2 Gushi Henan China
207 E4 Gushiegu Ghana
102 □1 Gushikami Okinawa Japan
102 □D20 Gushikawa Nansei-shotō Japan
102 □1 Gushikawa Okinawa Japan
196 H8 Gusinje Montenegro
139 O7 Gusino Rus. Fed.
106 J1 Gusinoozersk Rus. Fed.
106 J1 Gusinoye, Ozero l. Rus. Fed.
117 K8 Guskara W. Bengal India
139 X6 Gus'-Khrustal'nyy Rus. Fed.
170 J5 Gusow Ger.
192 B8 Guspini Sardegna Italy
190 I4 Gussago Italy
179 N5 Güssing Austria
190 I5 Gussola Italy
179 L4 Gußwerk Austria
140 □ Gustav Adolf Land reg. Svalbard
Gustav Holm, Kap c. Greenland see Tasiilap Karra
247 L5 Gustavia St Barthélémy West Indies
237 F12 Gustavo Díaz Ordaz Mex.
245 M8 Gustavo Diaz Ordaz Mex.
242 C2 Gustavo Sotelo Mex.
143 O2 Gustavsberg Sweden
220 E4 Gustavus AK U.S.A.
140 □ Gustav V Land reg. Svalbard
171 E7 Güsten Ger.
172 B2 Gusterath Ger.
240 L4 Gustine CA U.S.A.
170 F3 Güstrow Ger.
102 □C22 Gusukube Nansei-shotō Japan
172 E5 Gutach (Schwarzwaldbahn) Ger.
197 L3 Gutâiului, Munții mts Romania
111 L12 Gutang Xizang China
179 K3 Gutau Austria
146 □N1 Gutcher Shetland, Scotland U.K.
179 M4 Gutenstein Austria
171 H6 Güterfelde Ger.
171 E7 Güterglück Ger.
169 F7 Gütersloh Ger.
241 W9 Guthrie AZ U.S.A.
230 D7 Guthrie KY U.S.A.
237 G8 Guthrie OK U.S.A.
237 E9 Guthrie TX U.S.A.
236 H5 Guthrie Center IA U.S.A.
234 D4 Guthriesville PA U.S.A.
109 K6 Gutian Fujian China
109 L5 Gutian Fujian China
109 L5 Gutian Shuiku resr China
252 E4 Gutiérrez Bol.
245 N7 Gutiérrez Gómez Mex.
245 J5 Gutiérrez Zamora Mex.
Guting Shandong China see Yutai
172 A2 Gutland reg. Ger./Lux.
165 J9 Gutland reg. Lux.
129 H4 Guton, Gora mt. Azer./Rus. Fed.
176 F5 Gutorfölde Hungary
170 F3 Gutow Ger.
190 E2 Guttannen Switz.
179 K6 Guttaring Austria
236 J4 Guttenberg IA U.S.A.
213 F3 Gutu Zimbabwe
170 H3 Gützkow Ger.
129 B7 Güveçli Turkey
140 N4 Guvertfjället mts Sweden
117 M6 Guwahati Assam India
127 K5 Guwēr Iraq
Guwlumayak Turkm. see Guwlumaýak
122 E1 Guwlumaýak Turkm.
169 H8 Guxhagen Ger.
109 J5 Guxian Jiangxi China
251 G3 Guyana country S. America
Guyane Française terr. S. America see French Guiana
Guyang Hunan China see Guzhang
107 L6 Guyang Nei Mongol China
160 F3 Guye r. France
163 C6 Guyenne reg. France
83 N4 Guy Fawkes River National Park N.S.W. Austr.
Guyi Guangxi China see Sanjiang
237 E7 Guymon OK U.S.A.
122 E7 Gūyom Iran
Guyong Fujian China see Jiangle
83 M4 Guyra N.S.W. Austr.
225 I4 Guysborough N.S. Can.
213 F4 Guyu Zimbabwe
107 N6 Guyuan Hebei China
106 J9 Guyuan Ningxia China
129 K5 Güzdäk Azer.
129 C6 Güzelhisar Turkey
199 I4 Güzelhisar Barajı resr Turkey
129 C6 Güzelkent Turkey
128 C2 Güzeloluk Turkey
Güzelyurt Cyprus see Morfou
108 G4 Guzhang Hunan China
109 K2 Guzhen Anhui China
Guzhou Guizhou China see Rongjiang
242 F2 Guzmán Mex.
242 F2 Guzmán, Lago de l. Mex.
121 L8 G'uzor Uzbek.
138 E7 Gvardeysk Rus. Fed.
Gvardeyskoye Rus. Fed. see Elin-Yurt
142 F2 Gvarv Norway
100 J5 Gvasyugi Rus. Fed.
137 T3 Gvazda Rus. Fed.
96 B6 Gwa Myanmar
83 L4 Gwabegar N.S.W. Austr.
207 G4 Gwada Nigeria
207 G3 Gwadabawa Nigeria
123 J9 Gwadar Pak.
123 J9 Gwadar West Bay Pak.
Gwador Pak. see Gwadar
222 D4 Gwaii Haanas National Park Reserve B.C. Can.
213 E3 Gwai River Zimbabwe
116 G4 Gwaldam Uttaranchal India
123 M6 Gwal Haidarzai Pak.
116 E7 Gwalior Madh. Prad. India
116 G6 Gwalior Madh. Prad. India
213 F4 Gwanda Zimbabwe
208 E3 Gwane Dem. Rep. Congo
210 F2 Gwardafuy, Gees c. Somalia
207 G4 Gwarzo Nigeria
123 K7 Gwash Pak.
123 I9 Gwatar Bay Pak.
150 E4 Gwaun-Cae-Gurwen Neath Port Talbot, Wales U.K.
208 F3 Gwawele Dem. Rep. Congo
213 E3 Gwayi Zimbabwe
213 E3 Gwayi r. Zimbabwe
174 E2 Gwda r. Pol.
174 E2 Gwda Wielka Pol.
96 B2 Gwedaukkon Myanmar
147 F3 Gweebarra Bay Ireland
147 F2 Gweedore Ireland
Gwelo Zimbabwe see Gweru
213 F3 Gweru Zimbabwe
212 E4 Gweta Botswana
222 F4 Gwillim Lake Provincial Park B.C. Can.
226 G3 Gwinn MI U.S.A.
236 G2 Gwinner ND U.S.A.
150 B7 Gwithian Cornwall, England U.K.
207 I4 Gwoza Nigeria
83 L3 Gwydir r. N.S.W. Austr.
150 D1 Gwynedd admin. div. Wales U.K.
150 E1 Gwytherin Conwy, Wales U.K.
160 H2 Gy France
111 K11 Gyablung Xizang China
111 K12 Gyaca Xizang China
111 F10 Gyaco Xizang China
Gyaijêpozhanggê Qinghai China see Zhidoi
111 L11 Gyai Qu r. Xizang China
108 A2 Gyairong Qinghai China
Gyaisi Sichuan China see Jiulong
177 I4 Gyál Hungary
199 I6 Gyali i. Greece
111 E10 Gyamug Xizang China
Gyandzha Azer. see Gäncä
111 H9 Gyangnyi Caka salt l. China
111 G11 Gyangrang Xizang China
Gyangtse Xizang China see Gyangzê
111 I12 Gyangzê Xizang China
111 E11 Gya'nyima Xizang China
116 G8 Gyaraspur Madh. Prad. India
106 E9 Gyaring Qinghai China
111 I11 Gyaring Co l. China
106 E9 Gyaring Hu l. Qinghai China
117 O5 Gyarishing Arun. Prad. India
176 G4 Gyarmat Hungary
198 F5 Gyaros Greece
198 F5 Gyaros i. Greece
Gyaurs Turkm. see Gäwers
Gydan, Khrebet mts Rus. Fed. see Kolymskiy, Khrebet
130 I2 Gydanskiy Poluostrov pen. Rus. Fed.
214 D9 Gydopas pass S. Africa
Gyêgu Qinghai China see Yushu
176 G5 Gyékényes Hungary
111 K12 Gyêmdong Xizang China
177 H4 Gyermely Hungary
111 G11 Gyêsar Co l. Xizang China
156 H7 Gyé-sur-Seine France
Gyêwa Xizang China see Zabqung
168 H4 Gyhum Ger.
108 A4 Gyigang Xizang China
111 K11 Gyimda Xizang China
111 E9 Gyipug Xizang China
111 G12 Gyirong Xizang China
111 G12 Gyirong Xizang China
108 A3 Gyitang Xizang China
Gyixong Xizang China see Gonggar
111 L10 Gyiza Qinghai China
Gyldenløve Fjord inlet Greenland see Umiiviip Kangertiva
142 H6 Gyldenløveshøj hill Denmark
147 F9 Gyleen Ireland
140 Q3 Gyljen Sweden
85 N9 Gympie Qld Austr.
96 B5 Gyobingauk Myanmar
105 J3 Gyōda Japan
177 J5 Gyomaendrőd Hungary
177 G4 Gyömöre Hungary
177 I4 Gyömrő Hungary
177 I4 Gyöngyös Hungary
176 F4 Gyöngyös r. Hungary
177 G6 Gyöngyös r. Romania
177 I4 Gyöngyöshalász Hungary
177 I4 Gyöngyöspata Hungary
177 H5 Gyönk Hungary
177 G4 Győr Hungary
176 G4 Győr-Moson-Sopron county Hungary
177 G4 Győrság Hungary
Győrszentmárton Hungary see Pannonhalma
177 L4 Győrtelek Hungary
177 G4 Győrújbarát Hungary
177 G4 Győrújfalu Hungary
222 H2 Gypsum Point N.W.T. Can.
223 L5 Gypsumville Man. Can.
225 G1 Gyrfalcon Islands Que. Can.
198 D6 Gytheio Greece
164 I2 Gytsjerk Neth.
177 K5 Gyula Hungary
Gyulafehérvár Romania see Alba Iulia
177 L3 Gyulaháza Hungary
177 H5 Gyulaj Hungary
129 J4 Gyul'gerychay r. Rus. Fed.
Gyümai Qinghai China see Darlag
129 E5 Gyumri Armenia
111 D10 Gyungcang Xizang China
197 O9 Gyurgen Bair hill Turkey
123 K3 Gyzylaýak Turkm.
120 J9 Gyzylbaýdak Turkm.
Gyzylbaydak Turkm. see Gyzylbaýdak
122 E2 Gyzylsuw Turkm.
139 R6 Gzhat' r. Rus. Fed.
Gzhatsk Rus. Fed. see Gagarin
195 □ Għira Malta
175 I3 Gzy Pol.

H

117 L6 Ha Bhutan
138 H2 Haabneeme Estonia
165 G7 Haacht Belgium
138 H3 Häädemeeste Estonia
179 K3 Haag Austria
179 I3 Haag am Hausruck Austria
173 L5 Haag an der Amper Ger.
173 M5 Haag in Oberbayern Ger.
140 □ Haakon VII Land reg. Svalbard
164 K4 Haaksbergen Neth.
165 F7 Haaltert Belgium
106 C2 Haanhöhiy Uul mts Mongolia
138 K4 Haanja Estonia
79 □8 Ha'ano i. Tonga
79 □8 Ha'apai Group is Tonga
134 D3 Haapajärvi Fin.
140 R4 Haapavesi Fin.
79 □9a Haapiti Moorea Fr. Polynesia
138 G3 Haapsalu Estonia
173 L5 Haar Ger.
173 O4 Haarbach Ger.
172 D3 Haardt hills Ger.
172 C2 Haardtkopf hill Ger.
164 G4 Haarlem Neth.
214 H9 Haarlem S. Africa
169 E7 Haarstrang ridge Ger.
81 D10 Haast South I. N.Z.
81 D10 Haast r. South I. N.Z.
84 C7 Haast Bluff N.T. Austr.
81 C11 Haast Range mts South I. N.Z.
164 G5 Haastrecht Neth.
84 C7 Haasts Bluff Aboriginal Land res. N.T. Austr.
210 D4 Haaway Somalia
123 L9 Hab r. Pak.
173 K6 Habach Ger.
110 H2 Habahe Xinjiang China
Habai Group is Tonga see Ha'apai Group
Habana Cuba see La Habana
114 G8 Habarane Sri Lanka
125 J4 Habarōn well Saudi Arabia
173 N1 Habartov Czech Rep.
125 K7 Ḩabarūt Oman
163 C8 Habas France
210 C4 Habaswein Kenya
124 G7 Ḩabawnāh, Wādī watercourse Saudi Arabia
222 G3 Habay Alta Can.
165 I9 Habay-la-Neuve Belgium
124 H8 Ḩabbān Yemen
127 K7 Ḩabbānīyah, Hawr al l. Iraq
123 L9 Hab Chauki Pak.
124 E6 Habhab ash Shaykh, Ḩarrat lava field Saudi Arabia
178 D5 Habicht mt. Austria
169 H8 Habichtswald park Ger.
117 M7 Habiganj Bangl.
104 C6 Habikino Japan
107 N5 Habirag Nei Mongol China
143 K4 Habo Sweden
102 S2 Haboro Japan
177 I2 Habovka Slovakia
117 L8 Habra W. Bengal India
176 E2 Habry Czech Rep.
157 N8 Habsheim France
125 J7 Ḩabshīyah, Jabal mts Yemen
250 C5 Hacha Col.
260 B6 Hachado, Paso de pass Arg./Chile
169 E9 Hachenburg Ger.
105 H3 Hachibuse-yama mt. Japan
103 Q13 Hachijō-jima i. Japan
104 E5 Hachikai Japan
104 E4 Hachiman Japan
105 L5 Hachiman-misaki c. Japan
102 Q6 Hachimori Japan
104 G3 Hachimori-yama mt. Japan
102 S6 Hachinohe Japan
105 J4 Hachiōji Japan
102 Q6 Hachiryū Japan
129 H6 Hacıalılı Azer.
199 K3 Hacıbekir Turkey
126 G4 Hacıbektaş Turkey
245 H1 Hacienda de la Mesa Mex.
129 E6 Hacıhalit Turkey
Hacıköy Turkey see Çekerek
199 L5 Hacılar Turkey
183 N5 Hacinas Spain
127 J4 Hacıömer Turkey
128 E2 Hacıpaşa Turkey
129 J6 Hacıqabul Gölü l. Azer.
129 J6 Hacıqährämanlı Azer.
199 I2 Hacıvelioba Turkey
129 K5 Hacı Zeynalabdin Azer.
82 G4 Hack, Mount S.A. Austr.
241 S6 Hackberry AZ U.S.A.
172 D2 Hackenheim Ger.
235 G3 Hackensack NJ U.S.A.
232 E10 Hacker Valley WV U.S.A.
147 I7 Hacketstown Ireland
234 F3 Hackettstown NJ U.S.A.
151 K3 Hackleton Northamptonshire, England U.K.
151 O5 Hacklinge Kent, England U.K.
149 P5 Hackness North Yorkshire, England U.K.
234 D6 Hack Point MD U.S.A.
209 B7 Haco Angola
213 G4 Hacufera Moz.
175 J6 Haczów Pol.
110 F6 Hadadong Xinjiang China
114 D5 Hadagalli Karnataka India
169 F10 Hadamar Ger.
123 L6 Hada Mountains Afgh.
124 E5 Ḩaḑan, Ḩarrat lava field Saudi Arabia
105 J5 Hadano Japan
106 I9 Hadapu Gansu China
124 E6 Ḩadārah i. Saudi Arabia
203 H4 Hadârba, Râs pt Sudan
107 P2 Hadat Nei Mongol China
107 S2 Hadayang Nei Mongol China
125 N4 Ḩadd, Ra's al pt Oman
202 C6 Haddad, Ouadi watercourse Chad
151 K4 Haddenham Buckinghamshire, England U.K.
146 K11 Haddington East Lothian, Scotland U.K.
151 P2 Haddiscoe Norfolk, England U.K.
234 E5 Haddonfield NJ U.S.A.
217 □2a Haddon Point Inner Islands Seychelles
207 H3 Hadejia Nigeria
207 I3 Hadejia watercourse Nigeria
142 G1 Hadeland reg. Norway
128 C6 Ḩadera Israel
128 C6 Ḩadera r. Israel
142 F6 Haderslev Denmark
142 E5 Haderup Denmark
114 E3 Hadgaon Mahar. India
124 E4 Ḩādhah Saudi Arabia
125 I5 Ḩādh Banī Zaynān des. Saudi Arabia
113 D11 Hadhdhunmathi Atoll Maldives
Hadhramaut reg. Yemen see Ḩaḑramawt
128 E8 Hādī, Jabal al mts Jordan
125 K9 Hadībоh Suquṭrā Yemen
111 H8 Hadilik Xinjiang China
126 F5 Hadım Turkey
202 D5 Hadjer Momou mt. Chad
151 N3 Hadleigh Suffolk, England U.K.
150 H2 Hadley Telford and Wrekin, England U.K.
221 H2 Hadley Bay Nunavut Can.
235 K2 Hadlyme CT U.S.A.
171 D7 Hadmersleben Ger.
157 L7 Hadol France
108 E8 Ha Đông Vietnam
126 H8 Ḩadraj, Wādī watercourse Saudi Arabia
125 I7 Ḩaḑramawt governorate Yemen
125 H8 Ḩaḑramawt reg. Yemen
125 I7 Ḩaḑramawt, Wādī watercourse Yemen
Hadranum Sicilia Italy see Adrano
179 N2 Hadres Austria
Hadria Italy see Adria
149 M3 Hadrian's Wall tourist site England U.K.
Hadrumetum Tunisia see Sousse
129 I6 Hadrut Azer.
140 M2 Hadseløy i. Norway
142 G5 Hadsten Denmark
142 G5 Hadsund Denmark
137 M3 Hadyach Ukr.
139 N8 Hadzilavichy Belarus
102 □1 Haebaru Okinawa Japan
261 I3 Haedo, Cuchilla de hills Uru.
101 D9 Haeju N. Korea
101 D10 Haeju-man b. N. Korea
165 I6 Haelen Neth.
240 □B11 Hā'ena HI U.S.A.
101 E11 Haenam S. Korea
124 H3 Ḩafar al 'Atk well Saudi Arabia
124 G1 Ḩafar al Bāţin Saudi Arabia
125 M3 Ḩaffah, Ra's pt Oman
170 J3 Haffküste park Ger.
223 J4 Hafford Sask. Can.
126 H4 Hafik Turkey
128 E7 Ḩafīrah, Qā' al salt pan Jordan
128 D7 Ḩafīrah, Wādī al watercourse Jordan
124 D2 Ḩafirat al 'Aydā Saudi Arabia
124 H3 Hafirat Nasah Saudi Arabia
125 L4 Ḩafīt Oman
125 L3 Ḩafīt, Jabal mt. U.A.E.
123 O5 Hafizabad Pak.
117 N7 Haflong Assam India
140 □C1 Hafnarfjörður Iceland
179 L3 Hafnerbach Austria
122 C6 Haft Gel Iran
129 J7 Haftoni Azer.
122 E8 Haftvān Iran
140 □B1 Hafursfjörður b. Iceland
Haga Myanmar see Haka
203 G6 Hag Abdullah Sudan
105 I6 Hagachi-zaki pt Japan
215 M8 Haga-Haga S. Africa
179 O8 Haganj Croatia
227 N3 Hagar Ont. Can.
114 E5 Hagari r. India
203 H5 Hagar Nish Plateau Eritrea
78 □1 Hagåtña Guam
143 M5 Hagbyån r. Sweden
168 D3 Hage Ger.
165 G7 Hageland reg. Belgium
171 G6 Hagelberg hill Ger.
220 B4 Hagemeister Island AK U.S.A.
169 D8 Hagen Ger.
169 E6 Hagen am Teutoburger Wald Ger.
172 E3 Hagenbach Ger.
169 H6 Hagenburg Ger.
178 H5 Hagengebirge mts Austria
168 G4 Hagen im Bremischen Ger.
170 D4 Hagenow Ger.
222 E4 Hagensborg B.C. Can.
171 K8 Hagenwerder Ger.
210 C2 Hägere Hiywet Eth.
210 C3 Hägere Selam Eth.
232 C11 Hagerhill KY U.S.A.
232 H9 Hagerstown MD U.S.A.
163 C8 Hagetaubin France
163 C8 Hagetmau France
143 J1 Hagfors Sweden
143 L1 Haggen l. Sweden
140 M5 Häggenås Sweden
238 H3 Haggin, Mount MT U.S.A.
140 L5 Häggsjön Sweden
140 M5 Häggsjövik Sweden
103 I12 Hagi Japan
96 G3 Ha Giang Vietnam
104 F4 Hagiwara Japan
150 G3 Hagley Herefordshire, England U.K.
150 H3 Hagley Worcestershire, England U.K.
HaGolan hills Syria see Golan
157 L5 Hagondange France
147 D7 Hag's Head Ireland
233 L5 Hague NY U.S.A.
158 H2 Hague, Cap de la c. France
157 O6 Haguenau France
217 □3a Hahaïa Njazidja Comoros
103 □2 Hahajima-rettō is Ogasawara-shotō Japan
169 J7 Hahausen Ger.
173 L2 Hahnbach Ger.
172 F2 Hähnlein Ger.
169 F10 Hahnstätten Ger.
176 F5 Hahót Hungary
211 C5 Hai Tanz.
94 C1 Hai, Ko i. Thai.
108 H8 Hai'an Guangdong China
109 M2 Hai'an Jiangsu China
Haian Shanmo mts Taiwan see T'aitung Shan
212 C6 Haib watercourse Namibia
172 G2 Haibach Bayern Ger.
173 N3 Haibach Bayern Ger.
104 C6 Haibara Nara Japan
105 H6 Haibara Shizuoka Japan
Haibowan Nei Mongol China see Wuhai
Haicheng Guangdong China see Haifeng
107 R6 Haicheng Liaoning China
Haicheng Ningxia China see Haiyuan
116 H6 Haidargarh Uttar Prad. India
173 M2 Haidenaab r. Ger.
179 J3 Haidershofen Austria
106 C9 Haiding Hu salt l. Qinghai China
173 P4 Haidmühle Ger.
96 H4 Hai Dương Vietnam
Haifa Israel see Ḩefa
109 J7 Haifeng Guangdong China
87 I11 Haig W.A. Austr.
169 F9 Haiger Ger.
172 F5 Haigerloch Ger.
107 O7 Hai He r. China
106 G8 Haihu Qinghai China
Haikakan country Asia see Armenia
Haikang Guangdong China see Leizhou
103 G13 Haiki Japan
108 H8 Haikou Hainan China
124 E2 Ḩā'il Saudi Arabia
124 E2 Ḩā'il prov. Saudi Arabia
124 F2 Ḩā'il, Wādī watercourse Saudi Arabia
117 N7 Hailakandi Assam India
Hailar Nei Mongol China see Hulun Buir
107 O2 Hailar He r. China

Hailey to Ḩarūrī, 'Irq al 321

238 G5 Hailey ID U.S.A.
224 E4 Haileybury Ont. Can.
100 F6 Hailin Heilong. China
109 H8 Hailing Dao i. Guangdong China
Hailong Jilin China see Meihekou
107 P5 Hails Nei Mongol China
151 M6 Hailsham East Sussex, England U.K.
100 E5 Hailun Heilong. China
140 R4 Hailuoto Fin.
140 R4 Hailuoto i. Fin.
109 M3 Haimen Jiangsu China
173 L5 Haimhausen Ger.
102 □A22 Haimi Nansei-shotō Japan
178 C5 Haiming Austria
173 N5 Haiming Ger.
169 K10 Haina Ger.
169 G8 Haina (Kloster) Ger.
108 H9 Hainan i. China
99 I8 Hainan prov. China
96 C4 Hai-nang Myanmar
Hainan Strait China see Qiongzhou Haixia
165 F8 Hainaut prov. Belgium
156 F3 Hainaut reg. France
179 O3 Hainburg an der Donau Austria
206 C5 Haindi Liberia
220 E4 Haines AK U.S.A.
231 G11 Haines City FL U.S.A.
222 B2 Haines Junction Y.T. Can.
234 F5 Hainesport NJ U.S.A.
222 B2 Haines Road Can./U.S.A.
179 M3 Hainfeld Austria
169 J8 Hainich ridge Ger.
171 H9 Hainichen Ger.
169 K8 Hainleite ridge Ger.
96 H4 Hai Phong Vietnam
Haiphong Vietnam see Hai Phong
100 I5 Haiqing Heilong. China
106 G8 Hairag Qinghai China
157 J6 Haironville France
109 L6 Haitan Dao i. China
172 F4 Haiterbach Ger.
246 G4 Haiti country West Indies
108 G9 Haitou Hainan China
97 I8 Hai Triêu Vietnam
179 M3 Haitzendorf Austria
240 O5 Haiwee Reservoir CA U.S.A.
203 H5 Haiya Sudan
208 E2 Haiyaf I. Sudan
109 I8 Haiyan Guangdong China
106 G8 Haiyan Qinghai China
109 M3 Haiyan Zhejiang China
Haiyang Anhui China see Xiuning
107 Q8 Haiyang Shandong China
Haiyou Zhejiang China see Sanmen
106 I8 Haiyuan Ningxia China
107 P9 Haizhou Wan b. China
122 F4 Hāj Ali Qoli, Kavīr-e salt l. Iran
217 □3b Hajangoua, Récif rf Mayotte
124 D4 Ḩajar Saudi Arabia
124 D2 Ḩajar, Jibāl mts Saudi Arabia
206 E2 Ḩajâr, Oued el well Mali
177 K4 Hajdú-Bihar county Hungary
177 K4 Hajdúböszörmény Hungary
177 K4 Hajdúdorog Hungary
177 K4 Hajdúhadház Hungary
177 K4 Hajdúnánás Hungary
177 K4 Hajdúság reg. Hungary
177 K4 Hajdúsámson Hungary
177 K4 Hajdúszoboszló Hungary
177 K4 Hajdúszovát Hungary
125 L9 Ḩajhir mt. Suquṭrā Yemen
122 F4 Haji Abdulla, Chāh well Iran
102 P8 Hajiki-zaki pt Japan
123 L7 Haji Mahesar Pak.
117 J7 Hajipur Bihar India
125 I3 Hajir reg. Saudi Arabia
124 F8 Ḩājir Yemen
122 D4 Ḩājjābād-e Māsileh Iran
124 F8 Ḩajjah Yemen
124 F7 Ḩajjah governorate Yemen
122 F7 Ḩājjīābād Fārs Iran
122 F3 Ḩājjīābād Iran
122 F7 Ḩājjīābād Hormozgan Iran
122 F5 Ḩājjīābād-e Zarrīn Iran
177 H4 Hajmáskér Hungary
175 L3 Hajnówka Pol.
117 M6 Hajo Assam India
177 I5 Hajós Hungary
125 I8 Ḩājr, Wādī watercourse Yemen
124 E5 Ḩajrah Saudi Arabia
177 G3 Hájske Slovakia
106 F5 Haju Nei Mongol China
107 J3 Hajuu-Us Mongolia
96 A3 Haka Myanmar
240 □F14 Hakalau HI U.S.A.
129 H6 Häkäri r. Azer.
103 Q9 Hakase-yama mt. Japan
81 E11 Hakataramea South I. N.Z.
81 F10 Hakatere South I. N.Z.
Hakatere r. South I. N.Z. see Ashburton
142 H4 Hakefjord sea chan. Sweden
259 C6 Hakelhuincul, Altiplanicie de plat. Arg.
80 □ Hakepa, Mount hill Chatham Is S. Pacific Ocean
Hakha Myanmar see Haka
128 D8 Hakippa, Har hill Israel
127 K5 Hakkârі Turkey
140 P3 Hakkas Sweden
104 C7 Hakken-zan mt. Japan
102 R6 Hakkōda-san mt. Japan
105 H6 Hakkō-san hill Japan
102 T2 Hako-dake mt. Japan
102 R5 Hakodate Japan
102 R5 Hakodate-wan b. Japan
105 J5 Hakone Japan
105 J5 Hakone-tōge pass Japan
212 C4 Hakos Mountains Namibia
214 E2 Hakseen Pan salt pan S. Africa
129 C6 Haksever Turkey
105 G2 Hakuba Japan
104 E2 Hakui Japan
81 □4 Hakupu Niue
104 D6 Hakusan Japan
104 D2 Haku-san vol. Japan
104 E3 Haku-san Kokuritsu-kōen nat. park Japan
105 H4 Hakushū Japan
Hal Belgium see Halle
123 M9 Hala Pak.
128 D8 Ḩalā', Jabal al mt. Jordan
128 F2 Ḩalab Syria
128 F2 Ḩalab governorate Syria
124 G4 Halabān Saudi Arabia
127 L6 Ḩalabja Iraq
123 K2 Halaç Turkm.
Halach Turkm. see Halaç
243 N7 Halachó Mex.
81 □4 Halagigie Point Niue
100 D6 Halahai Jilin China
136 G5 Halahora de Sus Moldova
203 H4 Halaib Sudan
203 G4 Halaib Triangle terr. Egypt/Sudan
96 I7 Ha Lam Vietnam
125 M7 Ḩalāniyāt, Juzur al is Oman
125 L7 Ḩalāniyāt, Khalīj al b. Oman
176 G4 Halászi Hungary
126 H9 Ḩālat 'Ammār Saudi Arabia
197 O3 Hălăuceşti Romania
143 K3 Hålaveden hills Sweden
240 □E12 Hālawa HI U.S.A.
240 □E12 Hālawa, Cape HI U.S.A.
128 E4 Halba Lebanon
106 E2 Halban Mongolia
171 I6 Halbe Ger.
179 M6 Halbenrain Austria
171 D7 Halberstadt Ger.
150 F6 Halberton Devon, England U.K.
173 J6 Halblech Ger.
179 O4 Halbturn Austria
92 C5 Halcon, Mount Mindoro Phil.
215 M6 Halcyon Drift S. Africa
142 H2 Halden Norway
171 D6 Haldensleben Ger.
173 I6 Haldenwang Ger.
117 L8 Haldi r. W. Bengal India
117 L8 Haldia W. Bengal India
117 L6 Haldibari W. Bengal India
142 F5 Hald Sø I. Denmark
116 G5 Haldwani Uttaranchal India
261 G5 Hale Arg.
84 E8 Hale watercourse N.T. Austr.
107 L6 Hale Nei Mongol China
149 M7 Hale Greater Manchester, England U.K.
227 K5 Hale MI U.S.A.
87 D9 Hale, Mount hill W.A. Austr.
240 □E13 Haleakalā National Park HI U.S.A.
129 E5 Halefoğlu Turkey
122 E8 Ḩāleh Iran
240 □C12 Hale'iwa HI U.S.A.
165 H7 Halen Belgium
143 K5 Halen I. Sweden
202 D5 Halénia well Chad
177 H2 Halenkov Czech Rep.
Haleparki Deresi r. Syria/Turkey see Quwayq, Nahr
151 P2 Hales Norfolk, England U.K.
150 H3 Halesowen West Midlands, England U.K.
151 O3 Halesworth Suffolk, England U.K.
234 B6 Halethorpe MD U.S.A.
149 L7 Halewood Merseyside, England U.K.
122 D7 Haleyleh Iran
231 D8 Haleyville AL U.S.A.
206 E5 Half Assini Ghana
126 H5 Halfeti Turkey
173 M6 Halfing Ger.
81 C13 Halfmoon Bay Stewart I. N.Z.
82 □3 Half Moon Bay b. S. Pacific Ocean
240 J4 Half Moon Bay CA U.S.A.
82 D4 Half Moon Lake salt flat S.A. Austr.
222 F3 Halfway r. B.C. Can.
232 H9 Halfway MD U.S.A.
164 G4 Halfweg Neth.
214 E6 Halfweg S. Africa
142 J1 Halgån r. Sweden
107 P3 Halhgol Mongolia
124 E6 Ḩalī Saudi Arabia
124 E6 Ḩalī, Wādī watercourse Saudi Arabia
127 I6 Ḩalībīyah Syria
227 P4 Haliburton Ont. Can.
224 E4 Haliburton Highlands hills Ont. Can.
177 I3 Halič Slovakia
Halicarnassus Turkey see Bodrum
139 P8 Halichy Rus. Fed.
225 I4 Halifax N.S. Can.
149 N6 Halifax West Yorkshire, England U.K.
231 I7 Halifax NC U.S.A.
234 B4 Halifax PA U.S.A.
232 G12 Halifax VA U.S.A.
85 K5 Halifax, Mount Qld Austr.
85 K5 Halifax Bay Qld Austr.
138 G1 Halikko Fin.
110 E5 Halik Shan mts Xinjiang China
129 C6 Halilçavuş Turkey
122 D7 Halīleh, Ra's-e pt Iran
129 B5 Halilkaya Turkey
93 D8 Halilulik Timor Indon.
128 E4 Ḩalīmah mt. Lebanon/Syria
82 C3 Halinor Lake salt flat S.A. Austr.
128 F2 Ḩalīsah Syria
107 K6 Haliut Nei Mongol China
125 I7 Ḩalīyā well Yemen
114 D5 Haliyal Karnataka India
146 J5 Halkirk Highland, Scotland U.K.
150 F1 Halkyn Flintshire, Wales U.K.
Hall atoll Gilbert Is Kiribati see Maiana
143 O4 Hall Gotland Sweden
148 H2 Hall East Renfrewshire, Scotland U.K.
234 B7 Hall MD U.S.A.
140 N5 Hälla Sweden
144 F2 Halladale r. Scotland U.K.
234 B4 Hallam PA U.S.A.
142 I4 Halland county Sweden
151 M6 Halland East Sussex, England U.K.
142 I5 Hallandsåsen hills Sweden
142 I5 Hallands Väderö i. Sweden
101 E12 Halla-san mt. S. Korea
101 E12 Halla-san National Park S. Korea
221 J3 Hall Beach Nunavut Can.
173 L5 Hallbergmoos Ger.
165 G6 Halle Antwerpen Belgium
165 F7 Halle Vlaams-Brabant Belgium
169 I7 Halle Ger.
171 E8 Halle (Saale) Ger.
169 F6 Halle (Westfalen) Ger.
143 K2 Hällefors Sweden
143 M2 Hälleforsnäs Sweden
178 H4 Hallein Austria
140 M5 Hallen Sweden
143 N1 Hållen Sweden
169 G8 Hallenberg Ger.
156 C4 Hallencourt France
171 E8 Halle-Neustadt Ger.
173 J2 Hallerndorf Ger.
173 L5 Hallertau reg. Ger.
263 L2 Hallett, Cape Antarctica
237 G11 Hallettsville TX U.S.A.
142 H3 Hälleviksstrand Sweden
262 W1 Halley research stn Antarctica
262 X2 Hallgreen, Mount Antarctica
143 O4 Hall-Hangvars naturreservat nature res. Gotland Sweden
236 D2 Halliday ND U.S.A.
223 I2 Halliday Lake N.W.T. Can.
168 G1 Halligen is Ger.
142 G1 Hallingby Norway
142 E1 Hallingdal val. Norway
142 F2 Hallingdalselva r. Norway
143 M4 Hallingeberg Sweden
178 E5 Hall in Tirol Austria
266 F5 Hall Islands Micronesia
138 I3 Halliste r. Estonia
140 O4 Hällnäs Sweden
236 G1 Hallock MN U.S.A.
150 H3 Hallow Worcestershire, England U.K.
221 L3 Hall Peninsula Nunavut Can.
86 H3 Hall Point W.A. Austr.
234 B2 Halls PA U.S.A.
143 L2 Hallsberg Sweden
86 I5 Halls Creek W.A. Austr.
227 P4 Halls Lake Ont. Can.
173 J2 Hallstadt Ger.
179 I4 Hallstatt Austria
179 I4 Hallstätter See I. Austria
143 O1 Hallstavik Sweden
233 J7 Hallstead PA U.S.A.
147 I5 Halltown Ireland
165 D7 Halluin Belgium
164 I2 Hallum Neth.
140 N3 Hällvik Sweden
140 M5 Hallviken Sweden
190 E1 Hallwiler See I. Switz.
150 C6 Hallworthy Cornwall, England U.K.
101 F11 Hallyŏ Haesang National Park S. Korea
177 L5 Hălmăgel Romania
177 L5 Hălmagiu Romania
93 F3 Halmahera i. Maluku Indon.
93 F4 Halmahera, Laut sea Maluku Indon.
Halmahera Sea Maluku Indon. see Halmahera, Laut
177 L4 Halmăşd Romania
197 L3 Halmeu Romania
142 I5 Halmstad Sweden
142 D1 Halnefjorden I. Norway
116 D8 Halol Gujarat India
96 H4 Ha Long Vietnam
108 F8 Ha Long, Vinh b. Vietnam
175 M3 Halowchytsy Belarus
188 E2 Haloze reg. Slovenia
142 G5 Hals Denmark
195 □ Hal Saflieni Hypogeum tourist site Malta
171 H9 Halsbrücke Ger.
169 E10 Halsenbach Ger.
Hälsingborg Sweden see Helsingborg
151 N4 Halstead Essex, England U.K.
168 I3 Halstenbek Ger.
164 F5 Halsteren Neth.
157 L5 Halstroff France
140 R5 Halsua Fin.
106 D7 Haltang He r. China
169 D7 Haltern Ger.
151 K4 Halton Buckinghamshire, England U.K.
149 L5 Halton Lancashire, England U.K.
149 L7 Halton admin. div. England U.K.
149 M5 Halton Gill North Yorkshire, England U.K.
243 N8 Haltunchén Mex.
149 M4 Haltwhistle Northumberland, England U.K.
125 K3 Ḩālūl i. Qatar
93 B9 Halura i. Indon.
116 C8 Halvad Gujarat India
122 G5 Ḩalvān Iran
143 K2 Halvarsnoren I. Sweden
169 D8 Halver Ger.
130 D2 Halvmåneøya i. Svalbard
150 E7 Halwell Devon, England U.K.
175 L2 Halyanka Belarus
136 D4 Halych Ukr.
137 L3 Halytsya Ukr.
176 B2 Halže Czech Rep.
208 B2 Ham Chad
156 F4 Ham France
214 D4 Ham watercourse Namibia
146 □L2 Ham Shetland, Scotland U.K.
214 D4 Hamab Namibia
103 J12 Hamada Japan
122 C4 Hamadān Iran
122 C4 Hamadān prov. Iran
204 E3 Hamaguir Alg.
128 E3 Ḩamāh Syria
128 F3 Ḩamāh governorate Syria
102 □1 Hamahiga-jima i. Okinawa Japan
104 E7 Hamajima Japan
105 G6 Hamakita Japan
217 □3a Hamalengo hill Njazidja Comoros
128 E2 Hamam Turkey
102 S3 Hamamasu Japan
104 G6 Hamamatsu Japan
104 G6 Hamana-ko I. Japan
105 H6 Hamaoka Japan
184 H4 Hamapega hill Spain
140 □B1 Hamar Iceland
141 K6 Hamar Norway
124 H4 Ḩamar, Wādī al watercourse Saudi Arabia
125 M6 Ḩamar Nafūr i. Oman
140 M2 Hamarøy Norway
140 M2 Hamarøy i. Norway
103 L11 Hamasaka Japan
124 D8 Hamasien prov. Eritrea
203 G3 Ḩamāṭah, Jabal mt. Egypt
102 T1 Hamatonbetsu Japan
157 N5 Hambach France
114 G9 Hambantota Sri Lanka
140 □ Hambergbukta b. Svalbard
168 K3 Hamberge Ger.
168 G4 Hambergen Ger.
82 E5 Hambidge Conservation Park nature res. S.A. Austr.
151 K4 Hambleden Buckinghamshire, England U.K.
151 J6 Hamble-le-Rice Hampshire, England U.K.
149 L6 Hambleton Lancashire, England U.K.
232 F9 Hambleton WV U.S.A.
149 O5 Hambleton Hills England U.K.
172 F3 Hambrücken Ger.
168 I5 Hambühren Ger.
168 I3 Hamburg Ger.
168 I3 Hamburg land Ger.
215 L9 Hamburg S. Africa
237 J9 Hamburg AR U.S.A.
235 K2 Hamburg CT U.S.A.
236 H5 Hamburg IA U.S.A.
234 F2 Hamburg NJ U.S.A.
232 G6 Hamburg NY U.S.A.
234 D3 Hamburg PA U.S.A.
168 F3 Hamburgisches Wattenmeer, Nationalpark nat. park Ger.
142 H3 Hamburgsund Sweden
158 I4 Hambye France
124 C3 Ḩamḑ, Wādī al watercourse Saudi Arabia
124 F6 Ḩamdah Saudi Arabia
207 F3 Hamdallay Niger
124 E6 Ḩamdānah Saudi Arabia
233 M7 Hamden CT U.S.A.
199 I3 Hamdibey Turkey
128 D1 Hamdili Turkey
168 I2 Hamdorf Ger.
141 Q6 Hämeenkangas moorland Fin.
138 I1 Hämeenkoski Etelä-Suomi Fin.
Hämeenkoski Fin. see Koski
141 Q6 Hämeenkyrö Fin.
141 R6 Hämeenlinna Fin.
HaMelaḩ, Yam salt l. Asia see Dead Sea
168 H5 Hämelhausen Ger.
87 C9 Hamelin W.A. Austr.
87 C13 Hamelin, Cape W.A. Austr.
87 C9 Hamelin Pool b. W.A. Austr.
169 H6 Hameln Ger.
210 D3 Hamero Hadad Eth.
171 D6 Hamersleben Ger.
86 D7 Hamersley W.A. Austr.
87 E11 Hamersley Lakes salt flat W.A. Austr.
86 D7 Hamersley Range mts W.A. Austr.
170 E5 Hämerten Ger.
101 F8 Hamgyŏng-sanmaek mts N. Korea
101 E9 Hamhŭng N. Korea
106 C5 Hami Xinjiang China
179 M8 Hamica Croatia
122 C6 Ḩamīd Iran
203 F4 Hamid Sudan
199 H1 Hamidiye Turkey
199 L3 Hamıdiye Turkey
84 H7 Hamilton Qld Austr.
84 E9 Hamilton S.A. Austr.
84 G7 Hamilton watercourse Qld Austr.
82 E2 Hamilton watercourse S.A. Austr.
231 □1 Hamilton Bermuda
224 E5 Hamilton Ont. Can.
Hamilton r. Nfld and Lab. Can. see Churchill
80 J4 Hamilton North I. N.Z.
146 H11 Hamilton South Lanarkshire, Scotland U.K.
231 D8 Hamilton AL U.S.A.
231 E9 Hamilton GA U.S.A.
226 C9 Hamilton IL U.S.A.
238 G3 Hamilton MT U.S.A.
235 G4 Hamilton NJ U.S.A.
233 J6 Hamilton NY U.S.A.
232 A9 Hamilton OH U.S.A.
237 F10 Hamilton TX U.S.A.
82 □3 Hamilton, Mount hill S. Pacific Ocean
240 K4 Hamilton, Mount CA U.S.A.
241 Q2 Hamilton, Mount NV U.S.A.
81 C12 Hamilton Burn South I. N.Z.
240 J2 Hamilton City CA U.S.A.
84 D7 Hamilton Downs N.T. Austr.
225 J2 Hamilton Inlet Nfld and Lab. Can.
233 K5 Hamilton Mountain NY U.S.A.
148 D5 Hamilton's Bawn Northern Ireland U.K.
225 K3 Hamilton Sound sea chan. Nfld and Lab. Can.
202 D2 Hamīm, Wādī al watercourse Libya
141 S6 Hamina Fin.
127 J8 Ḩāmir, Wādī al watercourse Saudi Arabia
116 F4 Hamirpur Hima. Prad. India
116 H7 Hamirpur Uttar Prad. India
Hamitabat Turkey see Isparta
142 C1 Hamlagrovatnet I. Norway
231 H8 Hamlet NC U.S.A.
82 G6 Hamley Bridge S.A. Austr.
234 E2 Hamlin PA U.S.A.
237 E9 Hamlin TX U.S.A.
232 C10 Hamlin WV U.S.A.
226 H5 Hamlin Lake MI U.S.A.
97 H10 Ham Luông, Sông r. mouth Vietnam
169 E7 Hamm Nordrhein-Westfalen Ger.
172 E2 Hamm Rheinland-Pfalz Ger.
169 E9 Hamm (Sieg) Ger.
168 H3 Hammah Ger.
127 K5 Ḩammām al 'Alīl Iraq
181 F5 Hammam Boughrara Alg.
189 C7 Hammamet Tunisia
205 H1 Hammamet, Golfe de g. Tunisia
189 C7 Hammam-Lif Tunisia
215 M1 Hammanskraal S. Africa
127 M8 Ḩammār, Hawr al imp. l. Iraq
141 O6 Hammarland Åland Fin.
215 O5 Hammarsdale S. Africa
143 K6 Hammarsjön I. Sweden
140 N5 Hammarstrand Sweden
165 F6 Hamme Belgium
142 F5 Hammel Denmark
169 I10 Hammelburg Ger.
170 H4 Hammelspring Ger.
165 G7 Hamme-Mille Belgium
171 F10 Hammerbrücke Ger.
140 M5 Hammerdal Sweden
140 Q1 Hammerfest Norway
151 I2 Hammerwich Staffordshire, England U.K.
169 C7 Hamminkeln Ger.
82 G5 Hammond S.A. Austr.
230 D5 Hammond IN U.S.A.
237 J10 Hammond LA U.S.A.
238 L4 Hammond MT U.S.A.
227 J4 Hammond Bay MI U.S.A.
232 H6 Hammondsport NY U.S.A.
225 J3 Hammone, Lac I. Que. Can.
234 F5 Hammonton NJ U.S.A.
146 □N1 Hamnavoe Shetland, Scotland U.K.
146 □N2 Hamnavoe Shetland, Scotland U.K.
146 □N2 Hamnavoe Shetland, Scotland U.K.
97 G9 Ham Ninh Vietnam
165 I8 Hamoir Belgium
165 H8 Hamois Belgium
165 I6 Hamont Belgium
234 D5 Hamorton PA U.S.A.
81 E12 Hampden South I. N.Z.
233 □Q4 Hampden Highlands ME U.S.A.
232 G11 Hampden Sydney VA U.S.A.
114 E5 Hampi Karnataka India
140 P3 Håmpjåkk Sweden
157 M6 Hampont France
151 I6 Hampreston Dorset, England U.K.
151 J5 Hampshire admin. div. England U.K.
151 I5 Hampshire Downs hills England U.K.
234 B5 Hampstead MD U.S.A.
225 H4 Hampton N.B. Can.
237 I9 Hampton AR U.S.A.
236 I4 Hampton IA U.S.A.
233 □O6 Hampton NH U.S.A.
234 F3 Hampton NJ U.S.A.
231 G9 Hampton SC U.S.A.
233 I11 Hampton VA U.S.A.
235 J3 Hampton Bays NY U.S.A.
87 I12 Hampton Tableland reg. W.A. Austr.
125 M4 Hamrā Oman
208 F2 Hamra Sudan
202 A2 Ḩamrā', Al Ḩamādah al plat. Libya
124 F1 Ḩamrā, Birkat al well Saudi Arabia
Hamra, Vâdii watercourse Syria/Turkey see Ḩimār, Wādī al
125 I3 Ḩamrā Jūdah plat. Saudi Arabia
202 E6 Hamrat esh Sheikh Sudan
127 L6 Ḩamrīn, Jabal hills Iraq
195 □ Ḩamrun Malta
238 J6 Hams Fork r. WY U.S.A.
129 A5 Hamsiköy Turkey
157 M5 Ham-sous-Varsberg France
151 N5 Hamstreet Kent, England U.K.
165 F8 Ham-sur-Heure Belgium
97 H9 Ham Tân Vietnam
116 F3 Hamta Pass Hima. Prad. India
127 K4 Hamur Turkey
105 J4 Hamura Japan
Hamwic Southampton, England U.K. see Southampton
121 N7 Hamza Uzbek.
128 A1 Hamzalar Turkey
165 H8 Han, Grotte de cave Belgium
176 G2 Haná r. Czech Rep.
240 □E13 Hāna HI U.S.A.
246 C2 Hanábana r. Cuba
212 D4 Hanahai watercourse Botswana/Namibia
124 C3 Ḩanak Saudi Arabia
129 D4 Hanak Turkey
Hanakpınar Turkey see Çınar
240 □B11 Hanalei HI U.S.A.
240 □E13 Hanamaioa, Cape HI U.S.A.
102 S7 Hanamaki Japan
240 □B12 Hanamā'ulu HI U.S.A.
105 L4 Hanamigawa Japan
214 B1 Hanam Plateau Namibia
211 B6 Hanang mt. Tanz.
Hananui hill Stewart I. N.Z. see Anglem, Mount
240 □B12 Hanapēpē HI U.S.A.
103 □3 Hanare-iwa i. Japan
169 G10 Hanau Ger.
240 □D12 Hanauma Bay HI U.S.A.
105 L2 Hanawa Japan
Hânceşti Moldova see Hînceşti
Hanchang Hunan China see Pingjiang
138 I8 Hanchary Belarus
107 L9 Hancheng Shaanxi China
156 C6 Hanches France
109 I3 Hanchuan Hubei China
232 G9 Hancock MD U.S.A.
226 F2 Hancock MI U.S.A.
233 J7 Hancock NY U.S.A.
234 E5 Hancocks Bridge NJ U.S.A.
104 E6 Handa Japan
146 F6 Handa Island Scotland U.K.
107 N8 Handan Hebei China
168 I4 Handeloh Ger.
211 C6 Handeni Tanz.
168 H1 Handewitt Ger.
Handian Shanxi China see Changzhi
177 H3 Handlová Slovakia
168 J4 Handorf Ger.
168 E5 Handrup Ger.
82 □3 Handspike Point S. Pacific Ocean
105 K4 Haneda airport Japan
HaNegev des. Israel see Negev
128 D8 Haneqarot watercourse Israel
168 H2 Hanerau-Hademarschen Ger.
Hanfeng Chongqing China see Kaixian
240 M5 Hanford CA U.S.A.
238 E3 Hanford Reach National Monument nat. park WA U.S.A.
114 D5 Hangal Karnataka India
96 C7 Hangan Myanmar
101 E10 Han-gang r. S. Korea
106 E2 Hangayn Nuruu mts Mongolia
Hangchow Zhejiang China see Hangzhou
Hangchuan Fujian China see Guangze
171 I6 Hangelsberg Ger.
Hanggin Houqi Nei Mongol China see Xamba
Hanggin Qi Nei Mongol China see Xin
Hangö Fin. see Hanko
138 G2 Hangö östra fjärd b. Fin.
138 F2 Hangö västra fjärd b. Fin.
107 O7 Hangu Tianjin China
123 N5 Hangu Pak.
106 E8 Hangya Qinghai China
109 M3 Hangzhou Zhejiang China
109 M3 Hangzhou Wan b. China
150 G5 Hanham South Gloucestershire, England U.K.
127 J4 Hani Turkey
125 I2 Ḩanīdh Saudi Arabia
199 J2 Hanife r. Turkey
177 K3 Haniska Slovakia
Hanji Gansu China see Linxia
Hanjia Chongqing China see Pengshui
109 K7 Han Jiang r. China
106 I8 Hanjiaoshui Ningxia China
100 D2 Hanjiayuanzi Heilong. China
123 I8 Hanjīrak Iran
140 S5 Hankasalmi Fin.
168 K5 Hankensbüttel Ger.
215 I9 Hankey S. Africa
141 Q7 Hanko Fin.
199 L3 Hanköy Turkey
241 V3 Hanksville UT U.S.A.
116 G3 Hanle Jammu and Kashmir
223 J5 Hanley Sask. Can.
150 H3 Hanley Castle Worcestershire, England U.K.
81 G9 Hanmer Forest Park nature res. South I. N.Z.
81 G9 Hanmer Springs South I. N.Z.
85 J3 Hann r. Qld Austr.
86 I4 Hann r. W.A. Austr.
86 H3 Hann, Mount hill W.A. Austr.
223 I5 Hanna Alta Can.
175 L4 Hanna Pol.
241 W8 Hannagan Meadow AZ U.S.A.
224 D3 Hannah Bay Ont. Can.
236 J6 Hannibal MO U.S.A.
232 I5 Hannibal NY U.S.A.
232 E9 Hannibal OH U.S.A.
203 G5 Hannik well Sudan
137 M5 Hannivka Ukr.
105 J4 Hannō Japan
157 K5 Hannonville-sous-les-Côtes France
169 I6 Hannover Ger.
169 I8 Hannoversch Münden Ger.
84 D7 Hann Range mts N.T. Austr.
165 H7 Hannut Belgium
143 K5 Hanö i. Sweden
143 K6 Hanöbukten b. Sweden
Hanoi Vietnam see Ha Nôi
96 G4 Ha Nôi Vietnam
104 A8 Hanoura Japan
224 D4 Hanover Ont. Can.
Hanover Ger. see Hannover
246 □ Hanover parish Jamaica
214 I7 Hanover S. Africa
235 K1 Hanover CT U.S.A.
233 M5 Hanover NH U.S.A.
232 C8 Hanover OH U.S.A.
234 B5 Hanover PA U.S.A.
232 H11 Hanover VA U.S.A.
259 B8 Hanover, Isla i. Chile
234 B4 Hanoverdale PA U.S.A.
214 I6 Hanover Road S. Africa
231 □2 Hanover Sound sea chan. New Prov. Bahamas
176 G4 Hanság hill Hungary
176 G4 Hansagi park Hungary
165 E6 Hansbeke Belgium
263 D2 Hansen Mountains Antarctica
170 D3 Hanshagen Ger.
109 H4 Hanshou Hunan China
109 J3 Han Shui r. China
116 F5 Hansi Haryana India
151 K3 Hanslope Milton Keynes, England U.K.
140 O2 Hansnes Norway
84 D6 Hanson watercourse N.T. Austr.
82 F4 Hanson, Lake salt flat S.A. Austr.
80 □ Hanson Bay Chatham Is S. Pacific Ocean
232 C12 Hansonville VA U.S.A.
168 J4 Hanstedt Niedersachsen Ger.
168 J4 Hanstedt Niedersachsen Ger.
142 E4 Hanstholm Denmark
107 P4 Han Sum Nei Mongol China
157 L6 Han-sur-Nied France
Hantengri Feng mt. Kazakh./Kyrg. see Khan-Tengri, Pik
177 H5 Hantos Hungary
138 J9 Hantsavichy Belarus
116 I7 Hanumana Madh. Prad. India
116 E5 Hanumangarh Rajasthan India
125 L7 Hanūn well Oman
177 K2 Hanušovce nad Topľou Slovakia
176 F1 Hanušovice Czech Rep.
106 H2 Hanuy Gol r. Mongolia
158 C5 Hanvec France
83 K6 Hanwood N.S.W. Austr.
150 G2 Hanwood Shropshire, England U.K.
106 E7 Hanxia Gansu China
Hanyang Hubei China see Caidian
108 G2 Hanyin Shaanxi China
105 K3 Hanyū Japan
Hanyuan Gansu China see Xihe
108 D4 Hanyuan Sichuan China
122 I9 Hanzaram Iran
108 F2 Hanzhong Shaanxi China
79 □9 Hao atoll Arch. des Tuamotu Fr. Polynesia
Haomen Qinghai China see Menyuan
117 L8 Haora W. Bengal India
205 G2 Haoud el Hamra Alg.
185 I9 Haouz, Jebel el hill Morocco
204 C4 Haouza Western Sahara
140 R4 Haparanda Sweden
140 Q4 Haparanda skärgård nationalpark nat. park Sweden
165 H6 Hapert Neth.
117 N6 Hapoli Arun. Prad. India
173 K3 Happburg Ger.
151 P2 Happisburgh Norfolk, England U.K.
84 F6 Happy Creek watercourse N.T. Austr.
241 U7 Happy Jack AZ U.S.A.
225 I2 Happy Valley-Goose Bay Nfld and Lab. Can.
164 I5 Haps Neth.
101 F8 Hapsu N. Korea
116 F5 Hapur Uttar Prad. India
126 G9 Ḩaql Saudi Arabia
125 J4 Ḩaqshah well Saudi Arabia
203 I5 Ḩaqw Saudi Arabia
105 H4 Hara Japan
210 D2 Hara Alol mt. Djibouti
125 I3 Ḩaraḑ well Saudi Arabia
124 F7 Ḩaraḑ Yemen
128 D9 Ḩarad, Jabal al mt. Jordan
125 I3 Ḩaradh Saudi Arabia
138 J7 Haradok Minskaya Voblasts' Belarus
138 M6 Haradok Vitsyebskaya Voblasts' Belarus
138 M6 Haradotskaye Wzvyshsha hills Belarus
140 P3 Harads Sweden
138 J8 Haradzishcha Brestskaya Voblasts' Belarus
138 M8 Haradzishcha Mahilyowskaya Voblasts' Belarus
175 M3 Haradzyets Belarus
138 J8 Haradzyeya Belarus
117 I6 Haraiya Uttar Prad. India
124 F7 Ḩarajā Saudi Arabia
102 R9 Haramachi Japan
110 H3 Haramgai Xinjiang China
116 E2 Haramukh mt. Jammu and Kashmir
Haran Turkey see Harran
138 M6 Harany Belarus
123 O6 Harappa Road Pak.
213 F3 Harare Zimbabwe
215 J5 Ha-Rasebei S. Africa
125 L6 Ḩarāsīs, Jiddat al des. Oman
175 K5 Harasiuki Pol.
203 H5 Harat i. Eritrea
122 F6 Harāt Iran
125 K6 Ḩaraym well Saudi Arabia
107 K4 Har-Ayrag Mongolia
202 C6 Haraz-Djombo Chad
208 D2 Haraze-Mangueigne Chad
138 M6 Harbacheva Belarus
169 I7 Harbarnsen Ger.
206 C5 Harbel Liberia
100 E6 Harbin Heilong. China
171 D6 Harbke Ger.
171 D6 Harbke-Allertal park Ger.
151 O5 Harbledown Kent, England U.K.
123 L7 Harboi Hills Pak.
156 E4 Harbonnières France
227 L6 Harbor Beach MI U.S.A.
226 J4 Harbor Springs MI U.S.A.
146 D6 Harbost Western Isles, Scotland U.K.
225 K4 Harbour Breton Nfld and Lab. Can.
173 J4 Harburg (Schwaben) Ger.
151 J3 Harbury Warwickshire, England U.K.
86 G7 Harbutt Range hills W.A. Austr.
116 H8 Harchoka Chhattisgarh India
241 S8 Harcuvar Mountains AZ U.S.A.
178 A5 Hard Austria
116 F8 Harda Madh. Prad. India
125 I7 Ḩarḑah, Wādī r. Yemen
142 C1 Hardanger reg. Norway
142 B2 Hardangerfjorden sea chan. Norway
142 D1 Hardangervidda Nasjonalpark nat. park Norway
122 D5 Hardank Iran
212 C5 Hardap admin. reg. Namibia
212 C5 Hardap Dam Namibia
141 H6 Hardbakke Norway
231 G9 Hardeeville SC U.S.A.
179 M2 Hardegg Austria
169 I7 Hardegsen Ger.
156 C2 Hardelot-Plage France
95 K2 Harden, Bukit mt. Indon.
164 K3 Hardenberg Neth.
164 I4 Harderwijk Neth.
214 C7 Hardeveld mts S. Africa
87 D7 Hardey r. W.A. Austr.
172 G2 Hardheim Ger.
236 J6 Hardin IL U.S.A.
238 K4 Hardin MT U.S.A.
86 D6 Harding r. W.A. Austr.
215 N6 Harding S. Africa
234 F6 Harding Lakes NJ U.S.A.
86 H4 Harding Range hills W.A. Austr.
87 D9 Harding Range hills W.A. Austr.
151 K3 Hardingstone Northamptonshire, England U.K.
164 G5 Hardinxveld-Giessendam Neth.
223 I4 Hardisty Alta Can.
222 G1 Hardisty Lake N.W.T. Can.
116 H6 Hardoi Uttar Prad. India
172 E5 Hardt Ger.
Hardwar Uttaranchal India see Haridwar
231 F9 Hardwick GA U.S.A.
233 M4 Hardwick VT U.S.A.
82 F6 Hardwicke Bay S.A. Austr.
234 E2 Hardwood Ridge PA U.S.A.
237 J7 Hardy AR U.S.A.
Hardy, Mount North I. N.Z. see Rangipoua
259 C9 Hardy, Península pen. Chile
225 K3 Hare Bay Nfld and Lab. Can.
151 L4 Harefield Greater London, England U.K.
142 I2 Harefjorden I. Sweden
149 J2 Hare Hill Scotland U.K.
140 I5 Hareid Norway
165 D7 Harelbeke Belgium
164 K2 Haren Neth.
168 D5 Haren (Ems) Ger.
Hareøen i. Greenland see Qeqertarsuatsiaq
210 D2 Hārer Eth.
210 D2 Hārer Wildlife Sanctuary nature res. Eth.
151 M4 Hare Street Hertfordshire, England U.K.
210 C2 Hareto Eth.
149 N6 Harewood West Yorkshire, England U.K.
128 D5 Harf el Mreffi mt. Lebanon
159 L2 Harfleur France
234 C5 Harford County county MD U.S.A.
107 P2 Hargant Nei Mongol China
Hargeisa Somalia see Hargeysa
210 D3 Hargele Eth.
172 D2 Hargesheim Ger.
210 E2 Hargeysa Somalia
197 N4 Harghita, Munţii mts Romania
197 N4 Harghita-Mădăraş, Vârful mt. Romania
203 H6 Hargigo Eritrea
165 H8 Hargimont Belgium
157 I3 Hargnies France
127 J4 Harhal Dağları mts Turkey
107 J7 Harhatan Nei Mongol China
106 H3 Harhorin Mongolia
106 E7 Har Hu I. Qinghai China
216 □3c Haría Lanzarote Canary Is
124 G8 Ḩarīb Yemen
204 D5 Ḩaricha, Ḩamâda El des. Mali
116 G5 Haridwar Uttaranchal India
128 C8 Ḩarif, Har mt. Israel
114 D5 Harihar Karnataka India
81 E10 Harihari South I. N.Z.
114 D6 Hariharpur Karnataka India
116 C8 Harij Gujarat India
138 F2 Hari kurk sea chan. Estonia
128 E2 Ḩārim Syria
104 A6 Harima Japan
104 A6 Harima-nada b. Japan
117 L9 Haringhat r. Bangl.
164 F5 Haringvliet est. Neth.
140 S5 Harinkaa Fin.
104 G2 Harinoki-dake mt. Japan
114 E8 Haripad Kerala India
123 O5 Haripur Pak.
128 E6 Ḩarīr, Wādī adh r. Syria
123 I3 Hari Rūd r. Afgh./Iran
124 F6 Ḩarjab, Wādī watercourse Saudi Arabia
141 M6 Härjåsjön Sweden
141 Q6 Harjavalta Fin.
141 L5 Härjedalen reg. Sweden
140 Q4 Harjufjärden b. Sweden
176 F4 Harka Hungary
177 I5 Harkakötöny Hungary
140 M5 Hårkan r. Sweden
177 H6 Harkány Hungary
236 H5 Harlan IA U.S.A.
232 B12 Harlan KY U.S.A.
236 F5 Harlan County Lake NE U.S.A.
197 O3 Hârlău Romania
150 D2 Harlech Gwynedd, Wales U.K.
238 J2 Harlem MT U.S.A.
151 O3 Harleston Norfolk, England U.K.
234 E4 Harleysville PA U.S.A.
164 H2 Harlingen Neth.
237 G12 Harlingen TX U.S.A.
168 E3 Harlinger Land reg. Ger.
151 L4 Harlington Bedfordshire, England U.K.
151 M4 Harlow Essex, England U.K.
238 J3 Harlowton MT U.S.A.
156 F4 Harly France
232 F10 Harman WV U.S.A.
199 K3 Harmancık Turkey
199 K5 Harmanlı Turkey
179 N3 Harmannsdorf Austria
234 B6 Harmans MD U.S.A.
164 G4 Harmelen Neth.
203 I5 Harmil i. Eritrea
233 □P4 Harmony ME U.S.A.
226 B6 Harmony MN U.S.A.
234 E3 Harmony NJ U.S.A.
168 K2 Harmsdorf Schleswig-Holstein Ger.
168 K3 Harmsdorf Schleswig-Holstein Ger.
114 E6 Harnahalli Karnataka India
114 C4 Harnai Mahar. India
123 L6 Harnai Pak.
156 E3 Harnes France
238 E5 Harney Basin OR U.S.A.
238 E5 Harney Lake OR U.S.A.
140 N5 Härnösand Sweden
107 O2 Har Nuden Nei Mongol China
106 C2 Har Nuur I. Mongolia
106 E2 Har Nuur I. Mongolia
183 O3 Haro Spain
136 I1 Harochychy Belarus
232 C11 Harold KY U.S.A.
146 □O1 Haroldswick Shetland, Scotland U.K.
157 L7 Haroué France
114 D5 Harpanahalli Karnataka India
151 L4 Harpenden Hertfordshire, England U.K.
206 D5 Harper Liberia
237 F7 Harper KS U.S.A.
222 H3 Harper Creek r. Alta Can.
240 O6 Harper Lake CA U.S.A.
232 H9 Harpers Ferry WV U.S.A.
225 I2 Harp Lake Nfld and Lab. Can.
151 K3 Harpole Northamptonshire, England U.K.
168 G5 Harpstedt Ger.
Harqin Qi Nei Mongol China see Jinshan
Harqin Zuoqi Mongolzu Zizhixian Liaoning China see Dachengzi
241 S8 Harquahala Mountains AZ U.S.A.
116 G8 Harrai Madh. Prad. India
128 H2 Harran Turkey
123 N7 Harrand Pak.
124 E4 Ḩarrāt Kishb lava field Saudi Arabia
146 J4 Harray, Loch of I. Scotland U.K.
224 E3 Harricanaw r. Ont./Que. Can.
146 I10 Harrietfield Perth and Kinross, Scotland U.K.
151 N5 Harrietsham Kent, England U.K.
235 G2 Harriman NY U.S.A.
233 M6 Harriman Reservoir VT U.S.A.
83 N4 Harrington N.S.W. Austr.
234 D7 Harrington DE U.S.A.
233 □R4 Harrington ME U.S.A.
225 J3 Harrington Harbour Que. Can.
231 □1 Harrington Sound inlet Bermuda
146 C7 Harris reg. Scotland U.K.
82 E4 Harris, Lake salt flat S.A. Austr.
84 B8 Harris, Mount N.T. Austr.
146 B7 Harris, Sound of sea chan. Scotland U.K.
215 K3 Harrisburg S. Africa
237 J8 Harrisburg AR U.S.A.
237 K7 Harrisburg IL U.S.A.
236 D5 Harrisburg NE U.S.A.
232 B9 Harrisburg OH U.S.A.
227 R9 Harrisburg PA U.S.A.
168 H1 Harrislee Ger.
87 D12 Harrismith W.A. Austr.
215 N4 Harrismith S. Africa
81 C11 Harris Mountains South I. N.Z.
237 I7 Harrison AR U.S.A.
226 J5 Harrison MI U.S.A.
236 D4 Harrison NE U.S.A.
235 H3 Harrison NY U.S.A.
225 J2 Harrison, Cape Nfld and Lab. Can.
220 C2 Harrison Bay AK U.S.A.
237 J10 Harrisonburg LA U.S.A.
232 G10 Harrisonburg VA U.S.A.
222 F5 Harrison Lake B.C. Can.
234 B6 Harrisonville MD U.S.A.
236 H6 Harrisonville MO U.S.A.
227 N6 Harriston Ont. Can.
227 K5 Harrisville MI U.S.A.
233 J4 Harrisville NY U.S.A.
232 D9 Harrisville WV U.S.A.
Harrodsville North I. N.Z. see Otorohanga
149 N6 Harrogate North Yorkshire, England U.K.
232 B12 Harrogate TN U.S.A.
227 R5 Harrowsmith Ont. Can.
236 I6 Harry S. Truman Reservoir MO U.S.A.
141 M6 Harsa Sweden
106 E9 Har Sai Shan mt. Qinghai China
177 J4 Harsány Hungary
168 I4 Harsefeld Ger.
197 M6 Hârseşti Romania
169 F7 Harsewinkel Ger.
122 B4 Harsīn Iran
126 I3 Harşit r. Turkey
171 D7 Harsleben Ger.
197 P6 Hârşova Romania
140 O3 Harsprånget Sweden
140 N2 Harstad Norway
151 M3 Harston Cambridgeshire, England U.K.
116 F8 Harsud Madh. Prad. India
169 I6 Harsum Ger.
140 K4 Harsvik Norway
220 E3 Hart r. Y.T. Can.
226 H6 Hart MI U.S.A.
82 F4 Hart, Lake salt flat S.A. Austr.
86 H4 Hart, Mount hill W.A. Austr.
177 I5 Harta Hungary
107 R5 Hartao Liaoning China
214 E4 Hartbees watercourse S. Africa
215 K2 Hartbeesfontein S. Africa
215 L1 Hartbeespoort S. Africa
179 M5 Hartberg Austria
142 D1 Harteigan mt. Norway
168 J3 Hartenholm Ger.
156 F5 Hartennes-et-Taux France
171 G9 Hartenstein Ger.
149 L5 Harter Fell hill England U.K.
151 M5 Hartfield East Sussex, England U.K.
206 C5 Hartford Liberia
233 M7 Hartford CT U.S.A.
230 D7 Hartford KY U.S.A.
226 H7 Hartford MI U.S.A.
236 G4 Hartford SD U.S.A.
226 F6 Hartford WI U.S.A.
230 E5 Hartford City IN U.S.A.
171 G8 Hartha Ger.
172 E3 Harthausen Ger.
172 D6 Hartheim Ger.
149 J2 Harthill North Lanarkshire, Scotland U.K.
197 M5 Hârtibaciu r. Romania
178 E5 Hart im Zillertal Austria
236 G4 Hartington NE U.S.A.
179 I3 Hartkirchen Austria
225 H4 Hartland N.B. Can.
150 D6 Hartland Devon, England U.K.
233 □P4 Hartland ME U.S.A.
150 C5 Hartland Point England U.K.
150 H3 Hartlebury Worcestershire, England U.K.
149 O4 Hartlepool Hartlepool, England U.K.
149 O4 Hartlepool admin. div. England U.K.
234 A3 Hartleton PA U.S.A.
151 M5 Hartley Kent, England U.K.
237 D8 Hartley TX U.S.A.
Hartley Zimbabwe see Chegutu
222 D4 Hartley Bay B.C. Can.
151 K5 Hartley Wintney Hampshire, England U.K.
234 D6 Hartly DE U.S.A.
173 O3 Hartmanice Czech Rep.
171 E9 Hartmannsdorf Ger.
234 C6 Hart Miller Island MD U.S.A.
238 E5 Hart Mountain National Wildlife Refuge nature res. OR U.S.A.
141 S6 Hartola Fin.
214 I4 Harts r. S. Africa
235 H2 Hartsdale NY U.S.A.
212 C4 Hartseer Namibia
231 D8 Hartselle AL U.S.A.
173 I4 Härtsfeld hills Ger.
151 I2 Hartshill Warwickshire, England U.K.
151 I2 Hartshorne Derbyshire, England U.K.
237 H8 Hartshorne OK U.S.A.
143 N3 Hartsö naturreservat nature res. Sweden
84 E7 Harts Range N.T. Austr.
84 E7 Harts Range mts N.T. Austr.
231 G8 Hartsville SC U.S.A.
231 D7 Hartsville TN U.S.A.
215 I3 Hartswater S. Africa
237 I7 Hartville MO U.S.A.
232 D8 Hartville OH U.S.A.
151 K3 Hartwell Northamptonshire, England U.K.
231 F8 Hartwell GA U.S.A.
231 F8 Hartwell Reservoir GA/SC U.S.A.
83 K10 Hartz Mountains National Park Tas. Austr.
104 D3 Harue Japan
93 F5 Haruku i. Maluku Indon.
105 I3 Haruna Japan
105 G5 Haruno Japan
114 F6 Harur Tamil Nadu India
125 H2 Ḩarūrī, 'Irq al des. Saudi Arabia

Hohenthann to Huaco

324

173 M4 Hohenthann Ger.
171 F7 Hohenthurm Ger.
179 I6 Hohenthurn Austria
231 D8 Hohenwald TN U.S.A.
170 F3 Hohen Wangelin Ger.
173 K4 Hohenwart Ger.
171 E9 Hohenwartetalsperre resr Ger.
173 N3 Hohenwarth Ger.
168 I2 Hohenwestedt Ger.
170 E5 Hohenwulsch Ger.
179 I3 Hohenzell Austria
179 I5 Hoher Dachstein mt. Austria
Hoh Ereg Nei Mongol China see Wuchuan
178 H4 Hoher Göll mt. Austria/Ger.
169 I10 Hohe Rhön mts Ger.
178 B5 Hoher Ifen mt. Austria/Ger.
169 H10 Hoher Vogelsberg, Naturpark nature res. Ger.
178 F5 Hohe Salve mt. Austria
169 H8 Hohes Gras hill Ger.
169 J8 Hohes Kreuz Ger.
178 F5 Hohe Tauern mts Austria
178 G5 Hohe Tauern, Nationalpark nat. park Austria
165 J8 Hohe Venn moorland Belgium
179 M4 Hohe Wand nature res. Austria
190 D2 Hohgant mt. Switz.
107 L6 Hohhot Nei Mongol China
172 E4 Hohloh hill Ger.
169 E9 Höhn Ger.
168 I2 Hohn Ger.
168 J5 Hohne Ger.
157 N7 Hohneck mt. France
168 K4 Hohnstorf (Elbe) Ger.
207 F5 Hohoe Ghana
109 □J7 Ho Hok Shan H.K. China
103 H12 Hōhoku Japan
137 M4 Hoholeve Ukr.
137 K3 Hoholiv Ukr.
137 N7 Hoholivka Ukr.
106 C9 Hoh Sai Hu l. Qinghai China
168 K2 Hohwacht (Ostsee) Ger.
168 K2 Hohwachter Bucht b. Ger.
111 J9 Hoh Xil Hu salt l. China
111 I9 Hoh Xil Shan mts China
106 F8 Hoh Yanhu salt l. Qinghai China
96 I7 Hôi An Vietnam
106 F9 Hoika Qinghai China
210 A4 Hoima Uganda
168 J3 Hoisdorf Ger.
236 F6 Hoisington KS U.S.A.
106 E8 Hoit Taria Qinghai China
122 G2 Hojagala Turkm.
117 N7 Hojai Assam India
123 K2 Hojambaz Turkm.
168 G1 Højer Denmark
103 J13 Hōjo Japan
96 E4 Hok r. Myanmar
143 J4 Hökensås hills Sweden
143 K3 Hökensås naturreservat nature res. Sweden
80 H2 Hokianga Harbour North I. N.Z.
105 L2 Hōki-gawa r. Japan
80 J7 Hokio Beach North I. N.Z.
81 E9 Hokitika South I. N.Z.
100 M7 Hokkaidō i. Japan
102 T3 Hokkaidō pref. Japan
142 F2 Hokksund Norway
122 G3 Hokmābād Iran
81 C13 Hokonui South I. N.Z.
81 C12 Hokonui Hills South I. N.Z.
105 M3 Hokota Japan
104 A6 Hokudan Japan
104 E4 Hokunō Japan
105 H1 Hokura-gawa r. Japan
104 E5 Hokusei Japan
142 E1 Hol Buskerud Norway
140 N2 Hol Nordland Norway
211 C5 Hola Kenya
177 J3 Hoľa mt. Slovakia
114 E5 Holalkere Karnataka India
252 D3 Holanda Bol.
137 L7 Hola Prystan' Ukr.
174 F6 Holasovice Czech Rep.
142 H6 Holbæk Denmark
215 O2 Holbank S. Africa
151 M2 Holbeach Lincolnshire, England U.K.
151 M2 Holbeach Marsh England U.K.
222 D5 Holberg B.C. Can.
168 H1 Holbøl Denmark
85 L5 Holborne Island Qld Austr.
83 K6 Holbrook N.S.W. Austr.
151 O4 Holbrook Suffolk, England U.K.
241 V7 Holbrook AZ U.S.A.
235 I3 Holbrook NY U.S.A.
226 C4 Holcombe WI U.S.A.
226 C4 Holcombe Flowage resr WI U.S.A.
223 H4 Holden Alta Can.
149 M6 Holden Lancashire, England U.K.
241 T2 Holden UT U.S.A.
237 G8 Holdenville OK U.S.A.
149 Q6 Holderness pen. England U.K.
259 C7 Holdich Arg.
168 F5 Holdorf Ger.
236 F5 Holdrege NE U.S.A.
168 L1 Holeby Denmark
246 E1 Hole in the Wall pt Gt Abaco Bahamas
114 E6 Hole Narsipur Karnataka India
177 G2 Holešov Czech Rep.
247 □4 Holetown Barbados
214 A4 Holgat watercourse S. Africa
232 A7 Holgate OH U.S.A.
182 H9 Holguera Spain
246 E3 Holguín Cuba
176 G3 Holíč Slovakia
176 E1 Holice Czech Rep.
137 M2 Holinka Ukr.
141 L6 Höljes Sweden
179 N2 Hollabrunn Austria
169 E6 Hollage (Wallenhorst) Ger.
Holland country Europe see Netherlands
226 H7 Holland MI U.S.A.
232 G6 Holland NY U.S.A.
232 B7 Holland OH U.S.A.
237 J9 Hollandale MS U.S.A.
246 □ Holland Bay Jamaica
151 L2 Holland Fen reg. England U.K.
Hollandia Papua Indon. see Jayapura
151 O4 Holland-on-Sea Essex, England U.K.
164 K3 Hollandscheveld Neth.
164 F5 Hollands Diep est. Neth.
146 L4 Hollandstoun Scotland U.K.
165 I9 Hollange Belgium
169 J6 Holle Ger.
171 E8 Holleben Ger.
173 K5 Hollenbach Ger.
168 K3 Hollenbek Ger.
179 L6 Hollenegg Austria
179 I4 Höllengebirge hills Austria
168 I4 Hollenstedt Ger.
179 K4 Hollenstein an der Ybbs Austria
151 O3 Hollesley Bay England U.K.
232 G5 Holley NY U.S.A.
173 K2 Hollfeld Ger.
262 T2 Hollick-Kenyon Peninsula Antarctica
262 Q1 Hollick-Kenyon Plateau Antarctica
232 G8 Hollidaysburg PA U.S.A.
168 H2 Hollingstedt Ger.
151 N6 Hollington East Sussex, England U.K.
149 N7 Hollingworth Greater Manchester, England U.K.
222 C4 Hollis AK U.S.A.
237 F8 Hollis OK U.S.A.
240 K5 Hollister CA U.S.A.
190 F2 Holloch Karst nature res. Switz.
177 K3 Hollóháza Hungary
177 I3 Hollókő Hungary
141 R6 Hollola Fin.
164 I2 Hollum Neth.
227 K7 Holly MI U.S.A.
148 H3 Hollybush East Ayrshire, Scotland U.K.
150 H3 Hollybush Worcestershire, England U.K.
81 B11 Hollyford r. South I. N.Z.
235 G5 Holly Park NJ U.S.A.
237 K8 Holly Springs MS U.S.A.
147 I6 Hollywood Ireland
240 N7 Hollywood CA U.S.A.
231 G13 Hollywood FL U.S.A.
168 I3 Holm Ger.
140 L4 Holm Norway
136 I6 Hol'ma Ukr.
220 G2 Holman N.W.T. Can.
235 G4 Holmdel NJ U.S.A.
215 N2 Holmdene S. Africa
149 P6 Holme-on-Spalding-Moor East Riding of Yorkshire, England U.K.
235 H1 Holmes NY U.S.A.
149 M7 Holmes Chapel Cheshire, England U.K.
149 N7 Holmesfield Derbyshire, England U.K.
85 K4 Holmes Reef Coral Sea Is Terr. Austr.
142 G2 Holmestrand Norway
232 D8 Holmesville OH U.S.A.
149 N6 Holmfirth West Yorkshire, England U.K.
Holmgard Rus. Fed. see Velikiy Novgorod
Holm Ø i. Greenland see Kiatassuaq
140 P5 Holmöarna naturreservat nature res. Sweden
134 C3 Holmön i. Sweden
140 P5 Holmsund Sweden
141 N6 Holmsveden Sweden
143 P3 Holmudden pt Gotland Sweden
136 E2 Holoby Ukr.
177 L5 Holod Romania
197 K4 Holod r. Romania
175 L5 Hołodowska Pol.
136 D4 Holohory hills Ukr.
128 C6 Holon Israel
212 C5 Holoog Namibia
86 H2 Holothuria Banks rf W.A. Austr.
173 P2 Holoubkov Czech Rep.
137 N9 Holovanivka Ukr.
136 J5 Holovanivs'k Ukr.
136 B4 Holovets'ko Ukr.
137 L4 Holovkivka Ukr.
175 M4 Holovne Ukr.
136 H3 Holovyne Ukr.
85 H3 Holroyd r. Qld Austr.
87 G9 Holroyd Bluff hills W.A. Austr.
142 I4 Holsljunga Sweden
215 M3 Holspruit r. S. Africa
168 G4 Holste Ger.
142 E5 Holstebro Denmark
142 E6 Holsted Denmark
190 D1 Hölstein Switz.
236 H4 Holstein IA U.S.A.
Holsteinsborg Greenland see Sisimiut
232 B12 Holston r. TN U.S.A.
232 D12 Holston Lake TN U.S.A.
150 D6 Holsworthy Devon, England U.K.
151 O2 Holt Norfolk, England U.K.
150 H5 Holt Wiltshire, England U.K.
150 G1 Holt Wrexham, Wales U.K.
226 J7 Holt MI U.S.A.
164 J4 Holten Neth.
168 E3 Holtgast Ger.
170 D3 Holthusen Ger.
168 E4 Holtland Ger.
236 H6 Holton KS U.S.A.
226 H6 Holton MI U.S.A.
149 Q6 Holton le Clay Lincolnshire, England U.K.
168 E4 Holtrop (Großefehn) Ger.
168 I2 Holtsee Ger.
241 Q9 Holtville CA U.S.A.
234 C5 Holtwood PA U.S.A.
240 □F14 Hōlualoa HI U.S.A.
137 O5 Holubivka Ukr.
137 M9 Holubynka Ukr.
164 I2 Holwerd Neth.
164 K2 Holwierde Neth.
147 G7 Holycross Ireland
220 C3 Holy Cross AK U.S.A.
239 K7 Holy Cross, Mount of the CO U.S.A.
150 C1 Holyhead Isle of Anglesey, Wales U.K.
150 C1 Holyhead Bay Wales U.K.
149 N2 Holy Island England U.K.
146 F11 Holy Island Scotland U.K.
150 C1 Holy Island Wales U.K.
236 D5 Holyoke CO U.S.A.
233 M6 Holyoke MA U.S.A.
Holy See Europe see Vatican City
150 F1 Holywell Flintshire, Wales U.K.
147 G4 Holywell Northern Ireland U.K.
146 I12 Holywood Dumfries and Galloway, Scotland U.K.
147 K3 Holywood Northern Ireland U.K.
169 E10 Holzappel Ger.
171 H7 Holzdorf Ger.
169 I7 Holzen Ger.
172 G4 Holzgerlingen Ger.
171 F8 Holzhausen Ger.
169 E10 Holzhausen an der Haide Ger.
173 I5 Holzheim Bayern Ger.
173 J4 Holzheim Bayern Ger.
173 J4 Holzheim Bayern Ger.
169 G10 Holzheim Hessen Ger.
173 L6 Holzkirchen Ger.
169 H7 Holzminden Ger.
169 K8 Holzthaleben Ger.
171 F7 Holzweißig Ger.
169 E7 Holzwickede Ger.
214 C4 Hom watercourse Namibia
122 C5 Homā Iran
210 B5 Homa Bay Kenya
96 B2 Homalin Myanmar
222 E5 Homathko r. B.C. Can.
Homāyūnshahr Iran see Khomeynīshahr
169 H8 Homberg (Efze) Ger.
169 G9 Homberg (Ohm) Ger.
Hombetsu Japan see Honbetsu
156 E4 Hombleux France
206 E3 Hombori Mali
157 L5 Hombourg-Budange France
157 M5 Hombourg-Haut France
258 D2 Hombre Muerto, Salar del salt flat Arg.
172 C3 Homburg Ger.
182 C4 Home, Cabo de pt Spain
221 L3 Home Bay Nunavut Can.
157 K5 Homécourt France
85 K5 Home Hill Qld Austr.
86 □2 Home Island Cocos Is
182 D5 Homem r. Port.
80 I2 Home Point North I. N.Z.
220 C4 Homer AK U.S.A.
231 F8 Homer GA U.S.A.
237 I9 Homer LA U.S.A.
226 J7 Homer MI U.S.A.
233 I6 Homer NY U.S.A.
232 F8 Homer City PA U.S.A.
151 O3 Homersfield Suffolk, England U.K.
231 F10 Homerville GA U.S.A.
85 J6 Homestead Qld Austr.
231 G13 Homestead FL U.S.A.
234 D3 Hometown PA U.S.A.
234 D5 Homeville PA U.S.A.
81 J8 Homewood North I. N.Z.
231 D9 Homewood AL U.S.A.
140 L4 Hommelstø Norway
140 K5 Hommelvik Norway
114 E4 Homnabad Karnataka India
197 P4 Homocea Romania
207 I2 Homodji well Niger
213 G4 Homoine Moz.
177 I5 Homokmégy Hungary
177 G5 Homokszentgyörgy Hungary
177 M4 Homoroade Romania
177 L3 Homorod r. Romania
Homs Libya see Al Khums
Homs Syria see Ḥimş
137 K1 Homyel' Belarus
Homyel Oblast admin. div. Belarus see Homyel'skaya Voblasts'
139 M9 Homyel'skaya Voblasts' admin. div. Belarus
232 D11 Honaker VA U.S.A.
Honan prov. China see Henan
240 □F14 Hōnaunau HI U.S.A.
114 E6 Honavalli Karnataka India
114 D5 Honavar Karnataka India
199 K5 Honaz Turkey
102 U3 Honbetsu Japan
136 J2 Honcharivs'ke Ukr.
137 M9 Honcharne Ukr.
97 G9 Hon Chông Vietnam
250 C3 Honda Col.
117 J9 Honda Orissa India
250 C1 Honda, Bahía b. Col.
92 B7 Honda Bay Palawan Phil.
117 J9 Hondapa Orissa India
186 B1 Hondarribia Spain
213 G3 Honde Moz.
214 I6 Hondeblaf r. S. Africa
214 B6 Hondeklipbaai S. Africa
243 O8 Hondo r. Belize/Mex.
103 H14 Hondo Japan
239 L10 Hondo NM U.S.A.
237 F11 Hondo TX U.S.A.
239 L10 Hondo r. NM U.S.A.
187 D11 Hondón de las Nieves Spain
187 D11 Hondón de los Frailes Spain
156 E2 Hondschoote France
164 K2 Hondsrug reg. Neth.
246 A6 Honduras country Central America
242 □P9 Honduras, Gulf of Belize/Hond.
190 D4 Hône Italy
142 G1 Hønefoss Norway
232 H6 Honeoye Falls NY U.S.A.
234 E1 Honesdale PA U.S.A.
245 I5 Honey Mex.
234 D4 Honey Brook PA U.S.A.
240 L1 Honey Lake salt l. CA U.S.A.
159 L3 Honfleur France
96 H4 Hong, Mouths of the Vietnam
96 H4 Hông, Sông r. Vietnam
109 J3 Hong'an Hubei China
106 H8 Hongchengzi Gansu China
101 E10 Hongch'ŏn S. Korea
107 J8 Hongde Gansu China
110 J7 Honggouzi Qinghai China
106 H8 Honggu Gansu China
109 J7 Honghai Wan b. China
108 D7 Honghe Yunnan China
109 J2 Hong He r. China
109 I4 Honghu Hubei China
109 I4 Hong Hu l. China
Hongjialou Shandong China see Licheng
108 G5 Hongjiang Hunan China
108 G5 Hongjiang Hunan China
Hongjiang Sichuan China see Wangcang
109 □J7 Hong Kong H.K. China
109 J7 Hong Kong special admin. reg. China
109 □J7 Hong Kong Harbour sea chan. H.K. China
109 □J7 Hong Kong Island H.K. China
106 F6 Hongliu Daquan well Nei Mongol China
106 D6 Hongliuhe Gansu China
107 K7 Hongliu He r. China
110 J7 Hongliuquan Qinghai China
Hongliuwan Gansu China see Aksay
106 H7 Hongliuyuan Gansu China
110 L6 Hongliuyuan Gansu China
97 G9 Hông Ngư Vietnam
107 M4 Hongor Nei Mongol China
107 M4 Hongor Mongolia
Hongqiao Hunan China see Qidong
Hongqiao Hunan China see Qidong
109 M3 Hongqiao airport China
106 C5 Hongqicun Xinjiang China
Hongqizhen Hainan China see Wuzhishan
108 B4 Hongshan Yunnan China
106 I7 Hongshansi Nei Mongol China
100 E7 Hongshi Jilin China
108 H7 Hongshui He r. China
107 L8 Hongtong Shanxi China
104 C8 Hongū Japan
225 H3 Honguedo, Détroit d' sea chan. Que. Can.
Hongwansi Gansu China see Sunan
101 E8 Hongwŏn N. Korea
107 R4 Hongxing Jilin China
106 H7 Hongyashan Shuiku resr Gansu China
108 D2 Hongyuan Sichuan China
109 L2 Hongze Jiangsu China
109 L2 Hongze Hu l. China
78 □6 Honiara Guadalcanal Solomon Is
150 F6 Honiton Devon, England U.K.
102 R7 Honjō Akita Japan
105 G3 Honjo Japan
105 J3 Honjō Saitama Japan
141 Q6 Honkajoki Fin.
105 H5 Honkawane Japan
149 N6 Honley West Yorkshire, England U.K.
114 D5 Honnali Karnataka India
140 R1 Honningsvåg Norway
240 □F13 Honoka'a HI U.S.A.
240 □E13 Honokahua HI U.S.A.
80 L4 Honokawa mt. North I. N.Z.
240 □D12 Honolulu HI U.S.A.
240 □ Honolulu County county HI U.S.A.
240 □F14 Honomū HI U.S.A.
226 H5 Honor MI U.S.A.
174 G3 Honoratka Pol.
240 □C12 Honouliuli HI U.S.A.
174 B3 Hönow Ger.
183 P9 Honrubia Spain
183 M6 Honrubia de la Cuesta Spain
103 K11 Honshū i. Japan
183 P9 Hontacillas Spain
183 L6 Hontalbilla Spain
183 O9 Hontanaya Spain
163 D8 Hontanx France
177 H3 Hontianske Nemce Slovakia
183 M4 Hontoria de la Cantera Spain
183 N5 Hontoria del Pinar Spain
183 M5 Hontoria de Valdearados Spain
240 □F14 Honu'apo HI U.S.A.
114 D4 Honwad Karnataka India
151 N5 Hoo Medway, England U.K.
238 D4 Hood, Mount vol. OR U.S.A.
222 C3 Hood Bay AK U.S.A.
Hood Island Islas Galápagos Ecuador see Española, Isla
87 E13 Hood Point W.A. Austr.
238 D4 Hood River OR U.S.A.
164 G4 Hoofddorp Neth.
168 G1 Hooge Ger.
168 G1 Hooge i. Ger.
165 F6 Hoogerheide Neth.
164 J3 Hoogersmilde Neth.
164 J3 Hoogeveen Neth.
164 K2 Hoogezand-Sappemeer Neth.
164 G5 Hooge Zwaluwe Neth.
164 K3 Hooghalen Neth.
Hooghly r. mouth India see Hugli
164 H3 Hoogkarspel Neth.
164 J5 Hoog-Keppel Neth.
164 J2 Hoogkerk Neth.
164 H4 Hoogland Neth.
168 C5 Hoogstede Ger.
165 G6 Hoogstraten Belgium
164 F5 Hoogvliet Neth.
149 P6 Hook East Riding of Yorkshire, England U.K.
151 K5 Hook Hampshire, England U.K.
237 E7 Hooker OK U.S.A.
84 C5 Hooker Creek watercourse N.T. Austr.
84 C4 Hooker Creek Aboriginal Land res. N.T. Austr.
147 I8 Hook Head Ireland
151 J4 Hook Norton Oxfordshire, England U.K.
Hook of Holland Neth. see Hoek van Holland
85 N8 Hook Point Qld Austr.
85 L5 Hook Reef Qld Austr.
168 F3 Hooksiel Ger.
240 □D12 Ho'olehua HI U.S.A.
106 H4 Hoolt Mongolia
220 E4 Hoonah AK U.S.A.
238 C6 Hoopa Valley Indian Reservation res. CA U.S.A.
220 B3 Hooper Bay AK U.S.A.
233 I10 Hooper Island MD U.S.A.
226 G9 Hoopeston IL U.S.A.
215 J3 Hoopstad S. Africa
142 J6 Höör Sweden
164 H3 Hoorn Neth.
77 I3 Hoorn, Îles de is Wallis and Futuna Is
164 G5 Hoornaar Neth.
105 H4 Hōō-san mt. Japan
233 L6 Hoosick NY U.S.A.
241 R5 Hoover Dam AZ/NV U.S.A.
232 C8 Hoover Memorial Reservoir OH U.S.A.
106 G4 Höövör Mongolia
140 □C1 Hóp lag. Iceland
127 J3 Hopa Turkey
234 F3 Hopatcong NJ U.S.A.
234 F3 Hopatcong, Lake NJ U.S.A.
234 D1 Hop Bottom PA U.S.A.
222 F5 Hope B.C. Can.
81 H8 Hope South I. N.Z.
81 G9 Hope r. South I. N.Z.
150 F1 Hope Flintshire, Wales U.K.
237 I9 Hope AR U.S.A.
234 F3 Hope NJ U.S.A.
82 G3 Hope, Lake salt flat S.A. Austr.
87 F12 Hope, Lake salt flat W.A. Austr.
146 G6 Hope, Loch l. Scotland U.K.
220 B3 Hope, Point AK U.S.A.
246 □ Hope Bay Jamaica
225 I2 Hopedale Nfld and Lab. Can.
237 K11 Hopedale LA U.S.A.
214 C9 Hopefield S. Africa
Hopei prov. China see Hebei
243 O8 Hopelchén Mex.
146 J7 Hopeman Moray, Scotland U.K.
225 I2 Hope Mountains Nfld and Lab. Can.
140 □ Hopen i. Svalbard
225 G1 Hopes Advance, Baie b. Que. Can.
221 L3 Hopes Advance, Cap c. Que. Can.
Hopes Advance Bay Que. Can. see Aupaluk
83 I6 Hopetoun Vic. Austr.
87 F12 Hopetoun W.A. Austr.
214 I5 Hopetown S. Africa
85 J3 Hope Vale Qld Austr.
85 J3 Hope Vale Aboriginal Reserve Qld Austr.
233 N7 Hope Valley RI U.S.A.
234 F4 Hopewell NJ U.S.A.
232 H11 Hopewell VA U.S.A.
224 E1 Hopewell Islands Nunavut Can.
235 H1 Hopewell Junction NY U.S.A.
178 F5 Hopfgarten im Brixental Austria
178 G6 Hopfgarten in Defereggen Austria
241 V6 Hopi Indian Reservation res. AZ U.S.A.
96 C2 Hopin Myanmar
83 I8 Hopkins r. Vic. Austr.
87 J8 Hopkins, Lake salt flat W.A. Austr.
230 D7 Hopkinsville KY U.S.A.
235 L2 Hopkinton RI U.S.A.
240 I3 Hopland CA U.S.A.
79 □8a Hopohoponga, Mui pt Tongatapu Tonga
96 C4 Hopong Myanmar
172 C2 Hoppstädten Ger.
140 S1 Hopseidet Norway
169 E6 Hopsten Ger.
151 P2 Hopton Norfolk, England U.K.
151 N3 Hopton Suffolk, England U.K.
150 G3 Hoptonheath Shropshire, England U.K.
209 B8 Hoque Angola
238 C3 Hoquiam WA U.S.A.
106 G9 Hor Qinghai China
111 E11 Hor Xizang China
136 J3 Hora Ukr.
210 D2 Hora Califo Eth.
129 I6 Horadiz Azer.
104 E4 Horado Japan
104 G6 Hōrai Japan
104 G6 Hōraiji-san hill Japan
151 M6 Horam East Sussex, England U.K.
127 K3 Horasan Turkey
176 C2 Horažďovice Czech Rep.
172 F5 Horb am Neckar Ger.
170 F1 Horbelev Denmark
151 L2 Horbling Lincolnshire, England U.K.
157 N7 Horbourg-Wihr France
178 A4 Hörbranz Austria
143 J6 Hörby Sweden
183 J6 Horcajo de las Torres Spain
185 J2 Horcajo de los Montes Spain
183 O9 Horcajo de Santiago Spain
183 J7 Horcajo Medianero Spain
242 G3 Horcasitas Mex.
183 N7 Horche Spain
260 B3 Horcón Chile
185 J3 Horcón hill Spain
245 J4 Horconcitos Mex.
258 D2 Horcones r. Arg.
142 C2 Horda Norway
142 C1 Hordaland county Norway
169 J7 Hörden Ger.
151 I6 Hordle Hampshire, England U.K.
150 D3 Horeb Ceredigion, Wales U.K.
80 H2 Horeke North I. N.Z.
197 L5 Horezu Romania
173 J5 Horgau Ger.
190 F1 Horgen Switz.
172 H6 Horgenzell Ger.
106 F2 Horgo Mongolia
196 H4 Horgoš Vojvodina Serbia
136 C5 Horhany mts Ukr.
106 I5 Hörh Uul mts Mongolia
197 Q5 Horia Romania
176 E1 Hořice Czech Rep.
226 F6 Horicon WI U.S.A.
105 G3 Horigane Japan
107 L6 Horinger Nei Mongol China
105 I1 Horinouchi Japan
179 O4 Horitschon Austria
106 G4 Horiult Mongolia
266 H7 Horizon Deep sea feature S. Pacific Ocean
179 J7 Horjul Slovenia
171 K8 Horka Ger.
139 N7 Horki Belarus
151 L5 Horley Surrey, England U.K.
262 Q1 Horlick Mountains Antarctica
171 I7 Hörlitz Ger.
137 R5 Horlivka Ukr.
122 I7 Hormak Iran
247 □1 Hormigueros Puerto Rico
183 O4 Hormilla Spain
122 G8 Hormoz i. Iran
122 F8 Hormoz, Kūh-e mt. Iran
122 G8 Hormozgān prov. Iran
122 F8 Hormūd-e Bāgh Iran
122 F8 Hormūd-e Mīr Khūnd Iran
122 G8 Hormuz, Strait of Iran/Oman
179 M2 Horn Austria
222 G2 Horn r. N.W.T. Can.
140 □B1 Horn c. Iceland
Horn, Cape Chile see Hornos, Cabo de
184 G3 Hornachos Spain
185 I5 Hornachuelos Spain
167 J4 Hornád r. Slovakia
177 I2 Horna Orava park Slovakia
176 G3 Horná Potôň Slovakia
177 H3 Horná Štubňa Slovakia
140 N3 Hornavan l. Sweden
172 C3 Hornbach Ger.
169 G7 Horn-Bad Meinberg Ger.
237 I10 Hornbeck LA U.S.A.
172 E5 Hornberg Ger.
142 J3 Hornborgasjöns naturreservat nature res. Sweden
238 C6 Hornbrook CA U.S.A.
169 K6 Hornburg Ger.
149 L5 Hornby Lancashire, England U.K.
149 Q7 Horncastle Lincolnshire, England U.K.
143 M1 Horndal Sweden
151 J6 Horndean Hampshire, England U.K.
Horne, Îles de is Wallis and Futuna Is see Hoorn, Îles de
168 I3 Horneburg Ger.
140 O5 Hörnefors Sweden
232 H6 Hornell NY U.S.A.
224 C3 Hornepayne Ont. Can.
235 F4 Hornerstown NJ U.S.A.
177 G3 Horné Saliby Slovakia
177 H2 Horné Srnie Slovakia
147 F2 Horn Head Ireland
177 H2 Horní Bečva Czech Rep.
177 G2 Horní Benešov Czech Rep.
171 J10 Horní Beřkovice Czech Rep.
176 C2 Horní Bříza Czech Rep.
176 E2 Horní Cerekev Czech Rep.
176 C1 Horní Jiřetín Czech Rep.
242 E4 Hornillos Mex.
176 G2 Horní Moštěnice Czech Rep.
141 I6 Hornindal Norway
151 O2 Horning Norfolk, England U.K.
176 D3 Horní Planá Czech Rep.
171 J10 Horní Počaply Czech Rep.
172 E4 Hornisgrinde mt. Ger.
85 I1 Horn Island Qld Austr.
237 K10 Horn Island MS U.S.A.
176 B1 Horní Slavkov Czech Rep.
176 D3 Horní Stropnice Czech Rep.
212 C4 Hornkranz Namibia
222 F2 Horn Mountains N.W.T. Can.
185 N4 Hornos Spain
259 D9 Hornos, Cabo de c. Chile
259 D9 Hornos, Parque Nacional de nat. park Chile
137 K1 Hornostayivka Chernihivs'ka Oblast' Ukr.
137 M6 Hornostayivka Khersons'ka Oblast' Ukr.
137 P8 Hornostayivka Respublika Krym Ukr.
171 K7 Hornow Ger.
156 C4 Hornoy-le-Bourg France
222 D2 Horn Peak Y.T. Can.
83 M5 Hornsby N.S.W. Austr.
149 Q6 Hornsea East Riding of Yorkshire, England U.K.
141 N6 Hornslandet pen. Sweden
142 G5 Hornslet Denmark
170 E3 Hornstorf Ger.
140 □B1 Hornstrandir reg. Iceland
140 □ Hornsund inlet Svalbard
168 F1 Hörnum Ger.
177 I3 Horný Tisovník Slovakia
177 L4 Horoatu Crasnei Romania
136 E5 Horodenka Ukr.
136 F2 Horodets' Ukr.
175 M5 Horodło Pol.
137 K2 Horodnya Ukr.
136 G3 Horodnytsya Ukr.
136 F4 Horodok Khmel'nyts'ka Oblast' Ukr.
136 C4 Horodok L'vivs'ka Oblast' Ukr.
137 K4 Horodyshche Cherkas'ka Oblast' Ukr.
137 K2 Horodyshche Chernihivs'ka Oblast' Ukr.
137 S4 Horodyshche Luhans'ka Oblast' Ukr.
136 E4 Horodyshche Ternopils'ka Oblast' Ukr.
102 T2 Horokanai Japan
136 D3 Horokhiv Ukr.
137 Q4 Horokhuvatka Ukr.
171 J10 Horoměřice Czech Rep.
177 L3 Horonda Ukr.
102 S1 Horonobe Japan
110 F5 Horo Shan mts China
102 T4 Horoshiri-dake mt. Japan
102 T1 Horoshiri-yama hill Japan
176 C2 Hořovice Czech Rep.
107 Q5 Horqin Shadi reg. China
Horqin Youyi Qianqi Nei Mongol China see Ulanhot
Horqin Zuoyi Houqi Nei Mongol China see Ganjig
Horqin Zuoyi Zhongqi Nei Mongol China see Baokang
253 F5 Horqueta Para.
150 D6 Horrabridge Devon, England U.K.
156 I7 Horre, Étang de la l. France
170 E1 Horreby Denmark
142 I4 Horred Sweden
151 N3 Horringer Suffolk, England U.K.
87 C10 Horrocks W.A. Austr.
111 J11 Horru Xizang China
86 □2 Horsburgh Island Cocos Is
179 J3 Hörsching Austria
238 L6 Horse Creek r. WY U.S.A.
222 F4 Horsefly B.C. Can.
227 R7 Horseheads NY U.S.A.
149 N5 Horsehouse North Yorkshire, England U.K.
225 K3 Horse Islands Nfld and Lab. Can.
169 J8 Hörsel r. Ger.
147 E6 Horseleap Galway Ireland
147 G6 Horseleap Westmeath Ireland
142 F6 Horsens Denmark
84 E8 Horseshoe Bend N.T. Austr.
238 F5 Horseshoe Bend ID U.S.A.
241 U7 Horseshoe Reservoir AZ U.S.A.
264 H3 Horseshoe Seamounts sea feature N. Atlantic Ocean
151 O2 Horsford Norfolk, England U.K.
149 N6 Horsforth West Yorkshire, England U.K.
83 I7 Horsham Vic. Austr.
151 L5 Horsham West Sussex, England U.K.
234 E4 Horsham PA U.S.A.
136 H3 Horshchyk Ukr.
171 D6 Hörsingen Ger.
168 L1 Horslunde Denmark
151 M5 Horsmonden Kent, England U.K.
176 B2 Horšovský Týn Czech Rep.
169 H10 Horst hill Ger.
165 J6 Horst Neth.
168 I3 Horst (Holstein) Ger.
151 O2 Horstead Norfolk, England U.K.
168 H4 Horstedt Ger.
169 E6 Hörstel Ger.
169 D6 Horstmar Ger.
199 J5 Horsunlu Turkey
177 I4 Hort Hungary
216 □1c Horta Faial Azores
142 G2 Horten Norway
261 G4 Hortensia Arg.
183 O6 Hortezuela Spain
183 N4 Hortigüela Spain
177 K4 Hortobágy Hungary
177 J4 Hortobágy-Berettyó canal Hungary
177 K4 Hortobágyi nat. park Hungary
220 F3 Horton r. N.W.T. Can.
151 J6 Horton Heath Hampshire, England U.K.
149 M5 Horton in Ribblesdale North Yorkshire, England U.K.
168 I1 Høruphav Denmark
139 N9 Horval' Belarus
190 E1 Horw Switz.
149 L6 Horwich Greater Manchester, England U.K.
224 D3 Horwood Lake Ont. Can.
139 O8 Hory Belarus
136 F2 Horyn' r. Ukr.
175 L5 Horyniec-Zdrój Pol.
175 L5 Horyszów Pol.
104 C6 Hōryūji tourist site Japan
210 C3 Hosa'ina Eth.
169 H10 Hösbach Ger.
114 E6 Hosdurga Karnataka India
95 J3 Hose, Pegunungan mts Malaysia
171 J8 Hosena Ger.
169 H9 Hosenfeld Ger.
202 D4 Hosenofu well Libya
122 B4 Ḥoseynābād Iran
122 F4 Ḥoseynīān, Band-e mts Iran
122 C6 Ḥoseynīyeh Iran
123 J8 Hoshab Pak.
116 F8 Hoshangabad Madh. Prad. India
136 F3 Hoshcha Ukr.
116 E4 Hoshiarpur Punjab India
106 H2 Höshööt Arhangay Mongolia
106 A2 Höshööt Bayan-Ölgiy Mongolia
165 J8 Hosingen Lux.
91 L8 Hoskins New Britain P.N.G.
199 I2 Hoşköy Turkey
104 G6 Hosoe Japan
114 E5 Hospet Karnataka India
163 F10 Hospice de France France
Hospitalet Cataluña Spain see L'Hospitalet de l'Infant
Hospitalet Cataluña Spain see L'Hospitalet de Llobregat
140 T4 Hossa Fin.
163 B8 Hosseger France
207 I4 Hosséré Vokre mt. Cameroon
198 D4 Hossios Luckas tourist site Greece
172 G6 Hoßkirch Ger.
177 K4 Hosszúpályi Hungary
176 G4 Hosszúpereszteg Hungary
186 K4 Hostalríc Spain
Hostalrich Spain see Hostalríc
259 C9 Hoste, Isla i. Chile
163 C7 Hostens France
176 F3 Hostěradice Czech Rep.
177 H3 Hostie Slovakia
176 E1 Hostinné Czech Rep.
176 D1 Hostivice Czech Rep.
171 J10 Hoštka Czech Rep.
176 C1 Hostomice Czech Rep.
173 N2 Hostouň Czech Rep.
168 H1 Hostrupskov Denmark
114 E6 Hosur Tamil Nadu India
140 M5 Hotagen r. Sweden
Hotahudo East Timor see Hatudo
105 G3 Hotaka Japan
104 G3 Hotaka-dake mt. Japan
105 J2 Hotaka-yama mt. Japan
111 E8 Hotan Xinjiang China
110 E6 Hotan He watercourse China
214 G3 Hotazel S. Africa
235 I1 Hotchkissville CT U.S.A.
241 P3 Hot Creek r. NV U.S.A.
241 P3 Hot Creek Range mts NV U.S.A.
171 D6 Hötensleben Ger.
87 D12 Hotham r. W.A. Austr.
84 C2 Hotham, Cape N.T. Austr.
93 G5 Hoti Seram Indon.
140 N4 Hoting Sweden
179 M7 Hotinja vas Slovenia
79 □9a Hotopuu Tahiti Fr. Polynesia
237 I8 Hot Springs AR U.S.A.
Hot Springs NM U.S.A. see Truth or Consequences
236 D4 Hot Springs SD U.S.A.
238 K6 Hot Sulphur Springs CO U.S.A.
222 G1 Hottah Lake N.W.T. Can.
246 F4 Hotte, Massif de la mts Haiti
212 B5 Hottentots Bay Namibia
214 C9 Hottentots-Holland Nature Reserve S. Africa
212 B5 Hottentots Point Namibia
165 H8 Hotton Belgium
172 E6 Hotzenwald reg. Ger.
78 □5 Houaïlu New Caledonia
158 F7 Houat, Île d' i. France
156 E3 Houdain France
156 C6 Houdan France
157 J6 Houdelaincourt France
157 K7 Houécourt France
163 E7 Houeillès France
163 E9 Houeydets France
165 I8 Houffalize Belgium
94 □ Hougang Sing.
85 K5 Houghton r. Qld Austr.
149 L4 Houghton Cumbria, England U.K.
226 F2 Houghton MI U.S.A.
232 G6 Houghton NY U.S.A.
226 J5 Houghton Lake MI U.S.A.
226 J5 Houghton Lake l. MI U.S.A.
149 O4 Houghton le Spring Tyne and Wear, England U.K.
151 K4 Houghton Regis Bedfordshire, England U.K.
96 F4 Houie Moc, Phou mt. Laos
157 M6 Houillères de la Sarve, Canal des France
159 K3 Houlgate France
233 □R2 Houlton ME U.S.A.
107 L9 Houma Shanxi China
79 □8a Houma Tongatapu Tonga
79 □8a Houma Tonga
237 J11 Houma LA U.S.A.
109 J7 Houmen Guangdong China
205 H2 Houmt Souk Tunisia
206 E4 Houndé Burkina
146 K11 Houndslow Scottish Borders, Scotland U.K.
156 E2 Houplines France
156 C3 Hourdel, Pointe du pt France
106 F8 Houri Qinghai China
146 E8 Hourn, Loch inlet Scotland U.K.
162 B5 Hourtin France
162 B5 Hourtin et de Carcans, Étang d' l. France
162 B5 Hourtin-Plage France
233 L6 Housatonic MA U.S.A.
235 I2 Housatonic r. CT U.S.A.
241 S2 House Range mts UT U.S.A.
149 M3 Housesteads tourist site England U.K.
222 E4 Houston B.C. Can.
234 E7 Houston DE U.S.A.
226 C6 Houston MN U.S.A.
237 J7 Houston MO U.S.A.
237 K9 Houston MS U.S.A.
237 H11 Houston TX U.S.A.
214 C10 Hout Bay S. Africa
214 C10 Hout Bay b. S. Africa
164 H4 Houten Neth.
165 H6 Houthalen Belgium
165 C7 Houthulst Belgium
214 I6 Houtkraal S. Africa
87 B10 Houtman Abrolhos is W.A. Austr.
146 J5 Houton Orkney, Scotland U.K.
141 P6 Houtskär Fin.
214 H6 Houwater S. Africa
110 H5 Houxia Xinjiang China
165 H8 Houyet Belgium
106 G8 Houzihe Qinghai China
142 G6 Hov Denmark
142 G1 Hov Norway
143 K3 Hova Sweden
106 B3 Hovd Hovd Mongolia
106 H4 Hovd Övörhangay Mongolia
106 C3 Hovd prov. Mongolia
142 E3 Hovdefjell hill Norway
142 D2 Hovden park Norway
106 C2 Hovd Gol r. Mongolia
151 L6 Hove Brighton and Hove, England U.K.
169 G7 Hövelhof Ger.
136 D5 Hoverla, Hora mt. Ukr.
151 O2 Hoveton Norfolk, England U.K.
122 C6 Hoveyzeh Iran
143 L1 Hovfjället naturreservat nature res. Sweden
149 P5 Hovingham North Yorkshire, England U.K.
226 E2 Hovland MN U.S.A.
143 L5 Hovmantorp Sweden
129 L5 Hövsan Azer.
107 K5 Hövsgöl Mongolia
106 G1 Hövsgöl prov. Mongolia
106 G1 Hövsgöl Nuur l. Mongolia
137 M4 Hovtva Ukr.
137 M4 Hovtva r. Ukr.
106 H5 Hövüün Mongolia
202 D6 Howa, Ouadi watercourse Chad/Sudan
202 E5 Howar, Wadi watercourse Sudan
85 N8 Howard Qld Austr.
237 G7 Howard KS U.S.A.
236 G3 Howard SD U.S.A.
226 F5 Howard WI U.S.A.
226 I6 Howard City MI U.S.A.
234 B6 Howard County county MD U.S.A.
149 O5 Howardian Hills England U.K.
84 E2 Howard Island N.T. Austr.
223 J2 Howard Lake N.W.T. Can.
84 C2 Howard Springs N.T. Austr.
149 P6 Howden East Riding of Yorkshire, England U.K.
226 I8 Howe IN U.S.A.
83 L7 Howe, Cape Vic. Austr.
262 O1 Howe, Mount Antarctica
227 K7 Howell MI U.S.A.
146 K9 Howe of the Mearns reg. Scotland U.K.
236 D3 Howes SD U.S.A.
233 L3 Howick Que. Can.
215 O5 Howick S. Africa
82 G2 Howitt, Lake salt flat S.A. Austr.
233 □Q3 Howland ME U.S.A.
77 I1 Howland Island N. Pacific Ocean
83 K6 Howlong N.S.W. Austr.
Howrah W. Bengal India see Haora
147 J6 Howth Ireland
122 H5 Ḥowẕ well Iran
122 F5 Ḥowẕ-e Gīvar Iran
122 G5 Ḥowẕ-e Khān well Iran
122 G6 Ḥowẕ-e Panj Iran
122 F5 Ḥowẕ-e Panj waterhole Iran
122 F5 Ḥowz i-Mian i-Tak Iran
96 H6 Hô Xa Vietnam
236 E6 Hoxie KS U.S.A.
169 H7 Höxter Ger.
110 H3 Hoxtolgay Xinjiang China
110 H5 Hoxud Xinjiang China
146 J5 Hoy i. Scotland U.K.
168 H5 Hoya Ger.
105 K4 Hōya Japan
185 P3 Hoya Gonzalo Spain
141 I6 Høyanger Norway
171 J8 Hoyerswerda Ger.
149 K7 Hoylake Merseyside, England U.K.
149 O7 Hoyland South Yorkshire, England U.K.
140 L4 Høylandet Norway
227 M1 Hoyle Ont. Can.
171 D7 Hoym Ger.
183 M7 Hoyo de Manzanares Spain
106 I6 Hoyor Amt Nei Mongol China
182 G8 Hoyos Spain
183 J8 Hoyos del Espino Spain
140 T5 Höytiäinen l. Fin.
126 I4 Hozat Turkey
185 I8 Hozgarganta r. Spain
138 G8 Hozha Belarus
104 C5 Hozu-gawa r. Japan
104 E5 Hozumi Japan
96 C6 Hpa-an Myanmar
96 C5 Hpapun Myanmar
136 I5 Hrabove Ukr.
137 Q3 Hrachivka Ukr.
173 O2 Hracholusky, Vodní nádrž resr Czech Rep.
176 E1 Hradec Králové Czech Rep.
177 G2 Hradec nad Moravicí Czech Rep.
176 F2 Hradec nad Svitavou Czech Rep.
173 P2 Hrádek Czech Rep.
176 D1 Hrádek nad Nisou Czech Rep.
176 C2 Hradešice Czech Rep.
176 C1 Hradiště hill Czech Rep.
177 H3 Hradište Slovakia
137 M4 Hradyz'k Ukr.
138 L8 Hradzyanka Belarus
175 L2 Hrandzichy Belarus
176 B1 Hranice Karlovarský kraj Czech Rep.
177 G2 Hranice Olomoucký kraj Czech Rep.
137 Q6 Hranitne Donets'ka Oblast' Ukr.
136 I3 Hranitne Zhytomyrs'ka Oblast' Ukr.
177 J3 Hranovnica Slovakia
188 G4 Hrasnica Bos.-Herz.
179 L7 Hrastnik Slovenia
140 □C1 Hraun Iceland
140 □F1 Hraun slope Iceland
138 I7 Hrawzhyshki Belarus
129 F5 Hrazdan Armenia
171 J9 Hrazený hill Czech Rep.
137 L3 Hrebinka Ukr.
136 J4 Hrebinky Ukr.
191 R5 Hreljin Croatia
137 M1 Hrem"yach Ukr.
137 L6 Hreyhove Ukr.
177 J3 Hrhov Slovakia
175 L6 Hrimne Ukr.
177 I3 Hriňová Slovakia
Hristós Ikaria Greece see Raches
136 H5 Hristovaia Moldova
171 I9 Hrob Czech Rep.
177 I3 Hrochoť Slovakia
176 E2 Hrochův Týnec Czech Rep.
138 G8 Hrodna Belarus
Hrodna Oblast admin. div. Belarus see Hrodzyenskaya Voblasts'
175 L2 Hrodnyendskaye Wzvyshsha hills Belarus
138 I8 Hrodzyenskaya Voblasts' admin. div. Belarus
137 N7 Hromivka Ukr.
173 O2 Hromnice Czech Rep.
177 H4 Hron r. Slovakia
177 I3 Hronec Slovakia
176 F1 Hronov Czech Rep.
177 H3 Hronský Beňadik Slovakia
176 F2 Hrotovice Czech Rep.
171 G10 Hroznětín Czech Rep.
175 L5 Hrubieszów Pol.
175 M4 Hrudky Ukr.
137 N3 Hrun' Ukr.
137 N3 Hrun' r. Ukr.
137 P4 Hrushuvakha Ukr.
179 J8 Hrušica mts Slovenia
176 F3 Hrušky Czech Rep.
177 I3 Hrusov Slovakia
176 F3 Hrušovany nad Jevišovkou Czech Rep.
179 O1 Hrušovany u Brna Czech Rep.
177 I2 Hruštín Slovakia
175 K3 Hruszniew Pol.
Hrvatska country Europe see Croatia
188 F3 Hrvatska Kostajnica Croatia
Hrvatsko Grahovo Bos.-Herz. see Bosansko Grahovo
137 L2 Hryhorivka Chernihivs'ka Oblast' Ukr.
137 P5 Hryhorivka Dnipropetrovs'ka Oblast' Ukr.
137 M7 Hryhorivka Khersons'ka Oblast' Ukr.
136 F4 Hrymayliv Ukr.
136 D6 Hrynyava Ukr.
136 H4 Hryshkivtsi Ukr.
137 M8 Hryshyne Ukr.
136 G4 Hrytsiv Ukr.
96 C3 Hsenwi Myanmar
Hsiang Chang i. H.K. China see Hong Kong Island
Hsiang Kang H.K. China see Hong Kong
96 C4 Hsi-hseng Myanmar
96 D4 Hsin, Nam r. Myanmar
Hsin-chia-p'o country Asia see Singapore
Hsin-chia-p'o Sing. see Singapore
109 M6 Hsinchu Taiwan
Hsinking Jilin China see Changchun
109 M7 Hsinying Taiwan
96 C3 Hsipaw Myanmar
Hsi-sha Ch'un-tao is S. China Sea see Paracel Islands
109 L7 Hsiyüp'ing Yü i. Taiwan
109 M6 Hsüeh Shan mt. Taiwan
109 K6 Hua'an Fujian China
212 B4 Huab watercourse Namibia
107 N8 Huabei Pingyuan plain China
252 A2 Huacaibamba Peru
252 E3 Huacaraje Bol.
252 E5 Huacaya Bol.
109 J6 Huacheng Guangdong China
252 E3 Huachi Bol.
107 K8 Huachi Gansu China
242 E2 Huachinera Mex.
252 A2 Huacho Peru
252 B2 Huachón Peru
100 G5 Huachuan Heilong. China
241 V10 Huachuca City AZ U.S.A.
260 C2 Huaco Arg.

Huacrachuco to Ignacio Zaragoza 325

252 A2 **Huacrachuco** Peru
252 C4 **Huacullani** Peru
107 M6 **Huade** Nei Mongol China
100 E7 **Huadian** Jilin China
109 I7 **Huadu** Guangdong China
Huafeng Fujian China see Hua'an
106 E6 **Huahai** Gansu China
110 L7 **Huahaizi** Qinghai China
97 D8 **Hua Hin** Thai.
79 □9 **Huahine** i. Arch. de la Société Fr. Polynesia
107 N6 **Huai'an** Hebei China
109 L2 **Huai'an** Jiangsu China
109 K2 **Huaibei** Anhui China
109 J2 **Huaibin** Henan China
Huaicheng Guangdong China see **Huaiji**
Huaicheng Jiangsu China see **Chuzhou**
Huaide Jilin China see **Gongzhuling**
100 D7 **Huaidezhen** Jilin China
Huaidian Henan China see **Shenqiu**
96 G6 **Huai Had National Park** Thai.
109 L2 **Huai He** r. China
108 G5 **Huaihua** Hunan China
109 I7 **Huaiji** Guangdong China
96 D7 **Huai Kha Khaeng Wildlife Reserve** nature res. Thai.
107 N6 **Huailai** Hebei China
96 D5 **Huai Nam Dung National Park** Thai.
109 K2 **Huainan** Anhui China
109 K3 **Huaining** Anhui China
Huaining Hubei China see **Wuhan**
107 M7 **Huairen** Shanxi China
107 O6 **Huairou** Beijing China
109 J2 **Huaiyang** Henan China
109 L2 **Huaiyin** Jiangsu China
Huaiyin Jiangsu China see **Huai'an**
109 K2 **Huaiyuan** Anhui China
108 G6 **Huaiyuan** Guangxi China
106 I9 **Huajialing** Gansu China
244 B3 **Huajicori** Mex.
244 C4 **Huajimic** Mex.
245 J8 **Huajuápan de León** Mex.
244 G6 **Huajúmbaro** Mex.
93 E7 **Huaki** Maluku Indon.
243 J5 **Hualahuises** Mex.
241 S6 **Hualapai Indian Reservation** res. AZ U.S.A.
241 S6 **Hualapai Peak** AZ U.S.A.
258 D2 **Hualfín** Arg.
109 M6 **Hualien** Taiwan
252 B3 **Hualla** Peru
250 C6 **Huallaga** r. Peru
106 H8 **Hualong** Qinghai China
260 A5 **Hualqui** Chile
252 A1 **Huamachuco** Peru
252 B3 **Huamani** Peru
245 J6 **Huamantla** Mex.
209 B8 **Huambo** Angola
209 B8 **Huambo** prov. Angola
214 B1 **Huams** watercourse Namibia
245 I8 **Huamuxtitlán** Mex.
100 G5 **Huanan** Heilong. China
250 B6 **Huancabamba** r. Peru
259 C6 **Huancache, Sierra** mts Arg.
252 B3 **Huancapi** Peru
252 B3 **Huancavelica** Peru
252 B3 **Huancavelica** dept Peru
252 B3 **Huancayo** Peru
Huancheng Gansu China see **Huanxian**
261 F3 **Huanchilla** Arg.
109 J5 **Huangbei** Jiangxi China
Huangcaoba Guizhou China see **Xingyi**
106 G8 **Huangcheng** Gansu China
109 J2 **Huangchuan** Henan China
109 J3 **Huanggang** Hubei China
Huang Hai sea N. Pacific Ocean see **Yellow Sea**
107 P8 **Huang He** r. China
107 P8 **Huanghe Kou** r. mouth China
107 O7 **Huanghua** Hebei China
109 M2 **Huangjiajian** Jiangsu China
108 D5 **Huanglianguan** Sichuan China
107 K9 **Huangling** Shaanxi China
108 G9 **Huangliu** Hainan China
107 K9 **Huanglong** Shaanxi China
109 L5 **Huanglonggang** Fujian China
Huanglongsi Henan China see **Kaifeng**
109 L5 **Huangmao Jian** mt. Zhejiang China
109 J3 **Huangmei** Hubei China
100 E7 **Huangnihe** Jilin China
109 J3 **Huangpi** Hubei China
108 F5 **Huangping** Guizhou China
108 H8 **Huangpo** Guangdong China
109 L5 **Huangqi** Fujian China
107 M6 **Huangqi Hai** l. China
109 L4 **Huangshan** Anhui China
109 K3 **Huang Shan** mts Anhui China
108 D2 **Huangshengguan** Sichuan China
109 J3 **Huangshi** Hubei China
106 H8 **Huang Shui** r. China
107 J8 **Huangtu Gaoyuan** plat. China
261 G5 **Huanguelén** Arg.
107 Q8 **Huangxian** Shandong China
109 M4 **Huangyan** Zhejiang China
106 H8 **Huangyang** Gansu China
106 G8 **Huangyuan** Qinghai China
106 G8 **Huangzhong** Qinghai China
Huangzhou Hubei China see **Huanggang**
108 D6 **Huaning** Yunnan China
106 D6 **Huaniushan** Gansu China
108 G6 **Huanjiang** Guangxi China
107 J8 **Huan Jiang** r. China
245 I9 **Huanjintepec** Mex.
261 G2 **Huanqueros** Arg.
101 D8 **Huanren** Liaoning China
Huanshan Zhejiang China see **Yuhuan**
252 B3 **Huanta** Peru
107 P8 **Huantai** Shandong China
252 A2 **Huánuco** Peru
252 A2 **Huánuco** dept Peru
252 B3 **Huanuhuanu** Peru
252 D4 **Huanuni** Bol.
244 E4 **Huanusco** Mex.
107 J8 **Huanxian** Gansu China
108 C5 **Huaping** Yunnan China
109 N6 **Huap'ing Yü** i. Taiwan
245 I7 **Huaquechula** Mex.
252 D4 **Huar** Bol.
252 A2 **Huaral** Peru
252 A2 **Huaráz** Peru
260 B6 **Huaren Chenque** Arg.
252 A2 **Huari** Peru
252 A2 **Huariaca** Peru
250 B6 **Huarmaca** Peru
252 A2 **Huarmey** Peru
252 A3 **Huarochiri** Peru
252 A2 **Huaron** Peru
109 I4 **Huarong** Hunan China
Huarte-Araquil Spain see **Uharte-Arakil**
250 B5 **Huasaga** r. Peru
252 A2 **Huascarán, Parque Nacional** nat. park Peru
258 C3 **Huasco** Chile
107 L9 **Hua Shan** mt. Shaanxi China
107 N6 **Huashaoying** Hebei China
106 F9 **Huashixia** Qinghai China
Huashugou Gansu China see **Jingtieshan**
242 E4 **Huatabampo** Mex.
107 Q6 **Huatong** Liaoning China
245 K6 **Huatusco** Mex.
245 I5 **Huauchinango** Mex.
252 A2 **Huauru, Islas de** is Peru
245 K7 **Huautla** Mex.
Huaxian Guangdong China see **Huadu**
107 N9 **Huaxian** Henan China
107 K9 **Huaxian** Shaanxi China
245 I5 **Huayacocotla** Mex.
Huayang Anhui China see **Jixi**
252 A2 **Huaylas** Peru
244 C4 **Huaynamota** Mex.
Huayuan Hubei China see **Xiaochang**
108 G4 **Huayuan** Hunan China
96 E4 **Huayxay** Laos
Huazangsi Gansu China see **Tianzhu**
106 G7 **Huazhaizi** Gansu China
108 H8 **Huazhou** Guangdong China
245 J9 **Huazolotitlán** Mex.
222 B2 **Hubbard, Mount** Can./U.S.A.
225 H1 **Hubbard, Pointe** pt Que. Can.
227 K5 **Hubbard Lake** MI U.S.A.
223 M3 **Hubbart Point** Man. Can.
109 I3 **Hubei** prov. China
114 D5 **Hubli** Karnataka India
177 I2 **Hubová** Slovakia
175 M5 **Hubyn** Ukr.
137 O5 **Hubynykha** Ukr.
261 E5 **Hucal** Arg.
101 E8 **Huch'ang** N. Korea
169 B8 **Hückelhoven** Ger.
169 D8 **Hückeswagen** Ger.
149 O7 **Hucknall** Nottinghamshire, England U.K.
156 C2 **Hucqueliers** France
175 L5 **Huczwa** r. Pol.
203 G4 **Ḩuḑayn, Wādī** watercourse Egypt
124 D2 **Huḑb Ḩumar** mts Saudi Arabia
149 N6 **Huddersfield** West Yorkshire, England U.K.
169 F5 **Hüde** Ger.
168 F4 **Hude (Oldenburg)** Ger.
107 Q2 **Huder** Nei Mongol China
197 O2 **Hudeşti** Romania
113 □1 **Hudhuveli** i. N. Male Maldives
141 N6 **Hudiksvall** Sweden
233 N6 **Hudson** MA U.S.A.
233 I10 **Hudson** MD U.S.A.
233 □Q3 **Hudson** ME U.S.A.
227 J8 **Hudson** MI U.S.A.
233 N6 **Hudson** NH U.S.A.
233 L6 **Hudson** NY U.S.A.
226 B5 **Hudson** WI U.S.A.
233 L8 **Hudson** r. NY U.S.A.
Hudson, Baie d' sea Can. see **Hudson Bay**
259 B7 **Hudson, Cerro** vol. Chile
Hudson, Détroit d' str. Nunavut/Que. Can. see **Hudson Strait**
237 H7 **Hudson, Lake** OK U.S.A.
223 K4 **Hudson Bay** Sask. Can.
221 J4 **Hudson Bay** sea Can.
235 G3 **Hudson County** county NJ U.S.A.
233 L5 **Hudson Falls** NY U.S.A.
Hudson Island Tuvalu see **Nanumanga**
221 P2 **Hudson Land** reg. Greenland
262 R2 **Hudson Mountains** Antarctica
222 F3 **Hudson's Hope** B.C. Can.
221 K3 **Hudson Strait** Nunavut/Que. Can.
96 H6 **Huê** Vietnam
182 H7 **Huebra** r. Spain
183 R5 **Huecha** r. Spain
259 B6 **Huechucuicui, Punta** pt Chile
185 N7 **Huécija** Spain
197 L4 **Huedin** Romania
243 M10 **Huehuetán** Mex.
243 N10 **Huehuetenango** Guat.
245 I7 **Huehuetlán** Mex.
244 B1 **Huehueto, Cerro** mt. Mex.
245 I6 **Huejotzingo** Mex.
244 D3 **Huejúcar** Mex.
244 D3 **Huejuqilla** Mex.
245 I4 **Huejutla** Mex.
185 M6 **Huélago** Spain
158 D5 **Huelgoat** France
185 M5 **Huelma** Spain
184 F6 **Huelva** Spain
184 F5 **Huelva** prov. Spain
184 G6 **Huelva** r. Spain
184 E6 **Huelva, Tierra Llana de** plain Spain
183 O8 **Huelves** Spain
185 N6 **Huéneja** Spain
260 B2 **Huentelauquén** Chile
242 D3 **Huépac** Mex.
260 B5 **Huepil** Chile
260 A5 **Huequén** Chile
185 O7 **Huércal de Almería** Spain
185 P6 **Huércal-Overa** Spain
183 O4 **Huércanos** Spain
239 L7 **Huerfano** r. CO U.S.A.
183 Q8 **Huérguina** Spain
183 M3 **Huérmeces** Spain
260 D2 **Huerta, Sierra de la** mts Arg.
183 N5 **Huerta del Rey** Spain
183 M9 **Huerta de Valdecarábanos** Spain
183 P7 **Huertahernando** Spain
187 E11 **Huertas, Cabo de las** c. Spain
244 F1 **Huertecillas** Mex.
186 E4 **Huerto** Spain
186 D4 **Huerva** r. Spain
185 M5 **Huesa** Spain
186 D5 **Huesa del Común** Spain
186 E3 **Huesca** Spain
186 E3 **Huesca** prov. Spain
185 N5 **Huéscar** Spain
244 G7 **Huétamo** Mex.
183 O8 **Huete** Spain
185 K6 **Huétor-Tájar** Spain
260 A6 **Hueva Toltén** Chile
245 H8 **Hueycantenango** Mex.
245 I6 **Hueyotlipan** Mex.
231 D9 **Hueytown** AL U.S.A.
184 H5 **Huezna** r. Spain
184 H5 **Huezna, Embalse de** resr Spain
172 E6 **Hüfingen** Ger.
142 B1 **Huftarøy** i. Norway
Hufūf Saudi Arabia see **Al Hufūf**
208 E2 **Hugeilig** l. Sudan
149 P6 **Huggate** East Riding of Yorkshire, England U.K.
84 E8 **Hugh** watercourse N.T. Austr.
85 J6 **Hughenden** Qld Austr.
261 G3 **Hughes** Arg.
82 B4 **Hughes** S.A. Austr.
223 K3 **Hughes** r. Man. Can.
262 T2 **Hughes Bay** Antarctica
232 I10 **Hughesville** MD U.S.A.
227 R8 **Hughesville** PA U.S.A.
240 L4 **Hughson** CA U.S.A.
150 □ **Hugh Town** Isles of Scilly, England U.K.
173 K6 **Huglfing** Ger.
117 K9 **Hugli** r. mouth India
236 D6 **Hugo** CO U.S.A.
237 H8 **Hugo** OK U.S.A.
237 E7 **Hugoton** KS U.S.A.
177 I3 **Hugyag** Hungary
Huhehot Nei Mongol China see **Hohhot**
Huhhot Nei Mongol China see **Hohhot**
251 E3 **Huhucunya** Venez.
215 I2 **Huhudi** S. Africa
140 U5 **Huhus** Fin.
109 L6 **Hui'an** Fujian China
106 J8 **Hui'anpu** Ningxia China
80 K5 **Huiarau Range** mts North I. N.Z.
212 C5 **Huib-Hoch Plateau** Namibia
109 J6 **Huichang** Jiangxi China
245 H5 **Huichapán** Mex.
Huicheng Anhui China see **Shexian**
Huicheng Guangdong China see **Huilai**
244 C3 **Huicholes, Sierra de los** mts Mex.
101 E8 **Huich'ŏn** N. Korea
109 J7 **Huidong** Guangdong China
108 D5 **Huidong** Sichuan China
100 E7 **Huifa He** r. China
107 P2 **Huihe** Nei Mongol China
165 F6 **Huijbergen** Neth.
109 J2 **Huiji He** r. China
209 B8 **Huíla** Angola
209 B8 **Huíla** prov. Angola
250 C4 **Huila** dept Col.
250 C4 **Huila, Nevado de** vol. Col.
209 B8 **Huíla, Planalto da** plat. Angola
109 K7 **Huilai** Guangdong China
108 D5 **Huili** Sichuan China
Huilongzhen Jiangsu China see **Qidong**
244 F6 **Huimangaro** Mex.
243 M9 **Huimanguillo** Mex.
244 G5 **Huimilpan** Mex.
107 O8 **Huimin** Shandong China
252 C4 **Huiñaimarca, Lago de** l. Bol./Peru
100 E7 **Huinan** Jilin China
Huinan Shanghai China see **Nanhui**
260 E4 **Huinca Renancó** Arg.
106 I9 **Huining** Gansu China
106 J7 **Huinong** Ningxia China
173 J4 **Huisheim** Ger.
150 G5 **Huish Episcopi** Somerset, England U.K.
Huishi Gansu China see **Huining**
108 F5 **Huishui** Guizhou China
146 B7 **Huisinis** Western Isles, Scotland U.K.
159 L5 **Huisne** r. France
159 N6 **Huisseau-sur-Cosson** France
164 I5 **Huissen** Neth.
106 B9 **Huiten Nur** l. China
108 G5 **Huitong** Hunan China
141 Q6 **Huittinen** Fin.
243 M9 **Huitupan** Mex.
244 D4 **Huitzila** Mex.
245 K8 **Huitzo** Mex.
245 H7 **Huitzuco** Mex.
108 F2 **Huixian** Gansu China
107 M9 **Huixian** Henan China
243 M10 **Huixtla** Mex.
108 D5 **Huize** Yunnan China
164 H4 **Huizen** Neth.
109 J7 **Huizhou** Guangdong China
106 G2 **Hujirt** Arhangay Mongolia
106 H3 **Hujirt** Övörhangay Mongolia
106 I3 **Hujirt** Töv Mongolia
124 E3 **Hujr** Saudi Arabia
80 J7 **Hukanui** North I. N.Z.
81 F9 **Hukarere** South I. N.Z.
96 C1 **Hukawng Valley** Myanmar
109 K4 **Hukou** Jiangxi China
212 D4 **Hukuntsi** Botswana
100 E6 **Hulan** Heilong. China
107 R3 **Hulan Ergi** Heilong. China
100 E6 **Hulan He** r. China
124 E2 **Hulayfah** Saudi Arabia
128 G4 **Ḩulayḩilah** well Syria
226 I3 **Hulbert** MI U.S.A.
226 I3 **Hulbert Lake** MI U.S.A.
232 B12 **Hulen** KY U.S.A.
Huliao Guangdong China see **Dabu**
122 B5 **Hulilan** Iran
100 H6 **Hulin** Heilong. China
176 G2 **Hulín** Czech Rep.
107 Q4 **Hulingol** Nei Mongol China
107 S4 **Hulin Gol** r. China
Hulin Rocks is Northern Ireland U.K. see **The Maidens**
224 F4 **Hull** Que. Can.
Hull Kingston upon Hull, England U.K. see **Kingston upon Hull**
233 O6 **Hull** MA U.S.A.
150 H4 **Hullavington** Wiltshire, England U.K.
151 N4 **Hullbridge** Essex, England U.K.
169 G6 **Hüllhorst** Ger.
Hull Island atoll Phoenix Is Kiribati see **Orona**
138 G3 **Hullo** Estonia
165 I7 **Hulsberg** Neth.
169 H6 **Hülsede** Ger.
165 G6 **Hulshout** Belgium
165 F6 **Hulst** Neth.
143 M5 **Hulterstad** Öland Sweden
143 L4 **Hultsfred** Sweden
107 Q6 **Huludao** Liaoning China
107 K9 **Hulu He** r. China
111 J9 **Hulu Hu** salt l. Qinghai China
113 □1 **Huluk** i. N. Male Maldives
Hulumeedhoo i. Addu Atoll Maldives see **Midu**
107 P2 **Hulun Buir** Nei Mongol China
107 O2 **Hulun Nur** l. China
203 F2 **Ḩulwān** Egypt
Ḩulwān Egypt see **Ḩulwān**
137 P6 **Hulyaypole** Ukr.
100 E3 **Huma** Heilong. China
247 □1 **Humacao** Puerto Rico
100 E3 **Huma He** r. China
258 D1 **Humahuaca** Arg.
252 D2 **Humaita** Bol.
253 E1 **Humaitá** Brazil
253 F6 **Humaitá** Para.
183 N7 **Humanes de Mohernando** Spain
215 I10 **Humansdorp** S. Africa
Humåtak Guam see **Umatac**
252 B3 **Humay** Peru
125 L4 **Humaym** well U.A.E.
124 G3 **Humayyān, Jabal** hill Saudi Arabia
209 B9 **Humbe** Angola
209 B8 **Humbe, Serra do** mts Angola
149 R6 **Humber, Mouth of the** England U.K.
149 Q6 **Humberside International** airport England U.K.
149 Q6 **Humberston** North East Lincolnshire, England U.K.
252 C5 **Humberstone** Chile
254 E2 **Humberto de Campos** Brazil
149 L2 **Humbie** East Lothian, Scotland U.K.
168 K1 **Humble** Denmark
261 G2 **Humboldt** Arg.
223 J4 **Humboldt** Sask. Can.
241 T7 **Humboldt** AZ U.S.A.
236 H5 **Humboldt** NE U.S.A.
240 N1 **Humboldt** NV U.S.A.
234 C3 **Humboldt** PA U.S.A.
237 K8 **Humboldt** TN U.S.A.
240 N1 **Humboldt** r. NV U.S.A.
78 □5 **Humboldt, Mont** mt. New Caledonia
238 B6 **Humboldt Bay** CA U.S.A.
Humboldt Gletscher glacier Greenland see **Sermersuaq**
240 N1 **Humboldt Lake** NV U.S.A.
81 C11 **Humboldt Mountains** South I. N.Z.
240 N1 **Humboldt Range** mts NV U.S.A.
240 O2 **Humbolt Salt Marsh** NV U.S.A.
85 J9 **Humeburn** Qld Austr.
261 G5 **Humeda** plain Arg.
109 I7 **Hu Men** sea chan. China
177 G2 **Humenec** hill Czech Rep.
177 K3 **Humenné** Slovakia
83 K6 **Hume Reservoir** N.S.W. Austr.
157 J8 **Humes-Jorquenay** France
185 J6 **Humilladero** Spain
188 F4 **Humina** reg. Bos.-Herz.
188 F3 **Humka, Gora** hill Croatia
143 M4 **Hummeln** l. Sweden
164 J4 **Hummelo** Neth.
234 B4 **Hummelstown** PA U.S.A.
234 B3 **Hummels Wharf** PA U.S.A.
81 E12 **Hummock** hill South I. N.Z.
179 M7 **Hum na Sutli** Croatia
260 A4 **Humos, Cabo** c. Chile
209 B8 **Humpata** Angola
Humphrey Island atoll Cook Is see **Manihiki**
240 N4 **Humphreys, Mount** CA U.S.A.
241 U6 **Humphreys Peak** AZ U.S.A.
176 E2 **Humpolec** Czech Rep.
141 Q6 **Humppila** Fin.
84 C2 **Humpty Doo** N.T. Austr.
149 M3 **Humshaugh** Northumberland, England U.K.
202 B2 **Hūn** Libya
140 □C1 **Húnaflói** b. Iceland
109 H5 **Hunan** prov. China
100 G7 **Hunchun** Jilin China
100 G7 **Hunchun He** r. China
177 J2 **Huncovce** Slovakia
171 F7 **Hundeluft** Ger.
173 N4 **Hunderdorf** Ger.
142 H6 **Hundested** Denmark
123 O6 **Hundewali** Pak.
171 D6 **Hundisburg** Ger.
149 R7 **Hundleby** Lincolnshire, England U.K.
150 C4 **Hundleton** Pembrokeshire, Wales U.K.
141 J6 **Hundorp** Norway
232 E9 **Hundred** WV U.S.A.
171 G9 **Hundshübel** Ger.
168 I1 **Hundslev** Denmark
178 G5 **Hundstein** mt. Austria
197 K5 **Hunedoara** Romania
169 I9 **Hünfeld** Ger.
169 F10 **Hünfelden-Kirberg** Ger.
79 □8 **Hunga** i. Vava'u Gp Tonga
79 □8 **Hunga Ha'apai** i. Tonga
177 H4 **Hungary** country Europe
79 □8 **Hunga Tonga** i. Tonga
169 G10 **Hungen** Ger.
173 J4 **Hungerberg** hill Ger.
83 J3 **Hungerford** Qld Austr.
151 I5 **Hungerford** West Berkshire, England U.K.
109 □J7 **Hung Fa Leng** hill H.K. China
106 C2 **Hüngiy Gol** r. Mongolia
101 E9 **Hŭngnam** N. Korea
231 □1 **Hungry Bay** Bermuda
147 C9 **Hungry Hill** Ireland
238 H2 **Hungry Horse Reservoir** MT U.S.A.
109 □I7 **Hung Shui Kiu** H.K. China
209 C8 **Hungulo** Angola
114 E4 **Hungund** Karnataka India
96 H4 **Hưng Yên** Vietnam
107 R6 **Hun He** r. China
146 D7 **Hunish, Rubha** pt Scotland U.K.
214 D6 **Hunissout Pan** salt pan S. Africa
Hunjiang Jilin China see **Baishan**
101 D8 **Hun Jiang** r. China
149 Q5 **Hunmanby** North Yorkshire, England U.K.
142 H3 **Hunnebostrand** Sweden
165 I6 **Hunsel** Neth.
164 J2 **Hunsingo** reg. Neth.
214 B3 **Huns Mountains** Namibia
157 O6 **Hunspach** France
151 M2 **Hunstanton** Norfolk, England U.K.
114 E6 **Hunsur** Karnataka India
227 M1 **Hunta** Ont. Can.
169 F4 **Hunte** r. Ger.
261 G4 **Hunter** Arg.
83 M5 **Hunter** r. N.S.W. Austr.
81 F11 **Hunter** South I. N.Z.
81 D11 **Hunter** r. South I. N.Z.
82 □1 **Hunter, Point** c. Norfolk I.
234 F3 **Hunterdon County** county NJ U.S.A.
117 J7 **Hunterganj** Jharkhand India
83 J9 **Hunter Island** Tas. Austr.
222 D5 **Hunter Island** B.C. Can.
77 H4 **Hunter Island** S. Pacific Ocean
83 J9 **Hunter Islands** Tas. Austr.
81 B12 **Hunter Mountains** South I. N.Z.
96 A5 **Hunter's Bay** Myanmar
146 G11 **Hunter's Quay** Argyll and Bute, Scotland U.K.
234 A4 **Hunters Run** PA U.S.A.
233 K3 **Huntingdon** Que. Can.
151 L3 **Huntingdon** Cambridgeshire, England U.K.
232 H8 **Huntingdon** PA U.S.A.
237 K7 **Huntingdon** TN U.S.A.
230 E5 **Huntington** IN U.S.A.
238 F4 **Huntington** OR U.S.A.
241 V2 **Huntington** UT U.S.A.
232 C10 **Huntington** WV U.S.A.
240 N8 **Huntington Beach** CA U.S.A.
241 Q1 **Huntington Creek** r. NV U.S.A.
235 I3 **Huntington Station** NY U.S.A.
168 F5 **Huntlosen** Ger.
80 J4 **Huntly** North I. N.Z.
146 K8 **Huntly** Aberdeenshire, Scotland U.K.
238 K4 **Hunt Mountain** WY U.S.A.
82 F3 **Hunt Peninsula** S.A. Austr.
224 E4 **Huntsville** Ont. Can.
231 D8 **Huntsville** AL U.S.A.
237 I7 **Huntsville** AR U.S.A.
236 I6 **Huntsville** MO U.S.A.
237 H10 **Huntsville** TX U.S.A.
203 G2 **Hunū, Kathīb al** des. Egypt
128 A8 **Hunū, Kathīb al** hill Egypt
243 O7 **Hunucmá** Mex.
177 J5 **Hunya** Hungary
Hunyani r. Moz./Zimbabwe see **Manyame**
107 M7 **Hunyuan** Shanxi China
116 E1 **Hunza** Jammu and Kashmir
116 E1 **Hunza** reg. Jammu and Kashmir
123 P4 **Hunza** r. Pak.
164 K2 **Hunze** r. Neth.
110 E4 **Huocheng** Xinjiang China
Huoer Xizang China see **Hor**
107 M9 **Huojia** Henan China
100 D4 **Huolongmen** Heilong. China
Huolu Hebei China see **Luquan**
78 □5 **Huon** i. New Caledonia
96 G5 **Hương Khê** Vietnam
91 K8 **Huon Peninsula** P.N.G.
83 K10 **Huonville** Tas. Austr.
109 K2 **Huoqiu** Anhui China
109 K3 **Huoshan** Anhui China
Huoshao Tao i. Taiwan see **Lü Tao**
212 B4 **Huotsaus** waterhole Namibia
Huoxian Shanxi China see **Huozhou**
107 L8 **Huozhou** Shanxi China
137 N4 **Hupalivka** Ukr.
Hupeh prov. China see **Hubei**
169 J8 **Hüpstedt** Ger.
122 G6 **Hūr** Iran
122 B2 **Hurānd** Iran
Huras i. S. Male Maldives see **Embudhu Finolhu**
225 G2 **Hurault, Lac** l. Que. Can.
128 B8 **Ḩuraydīn, Wādī** watercourse Egypt
124 H3 **Ḩuraymilā'** Saudi Arabia
125 H4 **Ḩuraysān** reg. Saudi Arabia
177 H4 **Hurbanovo** Slovakia
224 D4 **Hurd, Cape** Ont. Can.
142 H1 **Hurdalssjøen** l. Norway
Hurd Island Gilbert Is Kiribati see **Arorae**
210 F2 **Hurdiyo** Somalia
82 □3 **Hurd Point** S. Pacific Ocean
107 Q5 **Hure** Nei Mongol China
106 H2 **Hüremt** Mongolia
106 H3 **Hürent** Mongolia
156 C6 **Hurepoix** reg. France
Hure Qi Nei Mongol China see **Hure**
Hurghada Al Baḩr al Aḩmar Egypt see **Al Ghurdaqah**
210 C4 **Huri** mt. Kenya
160 A4 **Huriel** France
137 M5 **Hurivka** Ukr.
226 F1 **Hurkett** Ont. Can.
106 E8 **Hurleg** Qinghai China
106 E8 **Hurleg Hu** l. Qinghai China
147 E7 **Hurler's Cross** Ireland
233 K7 **Hurley** NY U.S.A.
226 D3 **Hurley** WI U.S.A.
233 J10 **Hurlock** MD U.S.A.
87 E12 **Hurlstone, Lake** salt flat W.A. Austr.
123 K7 **Hurmagai** Pak.
240 L5 **Huron** CA U.S.A.
232 C7 **Huron** OH U.S.A.
236 F3 **Huron** SD U.S.A.
227 L5 **Huron, Lake** Can./U.S.A.
226 F3 **Huron Bay** MI U.S.A.
227 J4 **Huron Beach** MI U.S.A.
184 H7 **Hurones, Embalse de los** resr Spain
226 D1 **Huronian** Ont. Can.
226 G3 **Huron Mountains** hills MI U.S.A.
241 S4 **Hurricane** UT U.S.A.
246 D2 **Hurricane Flats** sea feature Bahamas
151 J5 **Hursley** Hampshire, England U.K.
151 J5 **Hurstbourne Tarrant** Hampshire, England U.K.
151 M5 **Hurst Green** East Sussex, England U.K.
151 L6 **Hurstpierpoint** West Sussex, England U.K.
260 B2 **Hurtado** Chile
260 B2 **Hurtado** r. Chile
183 P4 **Hurteles** Spain
169 C9 **Hürth** Ger.
231 E9 **Hurtsboro** AL U.S.A.
95 J4 **Hurung, Gunung** mt. Indon.
81 H9 **Hurunui** r. South I. N.Z.
142 E5 **Hurup** Denmark
168 I1 **Hürup** Ger.
210 C2 **Huruta** Eth.
149 N5 **Hurworth-on-Tees** Darlington, England U.K.
137 O3 **Hur"yiv Kozachok** Ukr.
123 M6 **Husain Nika** Pak.
137 P6 **Husarka** Ukr.
177 K5 **Husasău de Tinca** Romania
140 □E1 **Húsavík** Norðurland eystra Iceland
140 □C1 **Húsavík** Vestfirðir Iceland
124 G7 **Husayn** reg. Yemen
151 J3 **Husbands Bosworth** Leicestershire, England U.K.
168 I1 **Husby** Ger.
143 M1 **Husby** Sweden
Huseyinabat Turkey see **Alaca**
Huseyinli Turkey see **Kızılırmak**
Hushan Zhejiang China see **Cixi**
136 C2 **Hushcha** Ukr.
203 G6 **Husheib** Sudan
197 Q4 **Huşi** Romania
176 C2 **Husinec** Czech Rep.
137 N3 **Huska** r. Ukr.
143 K4 **Huskvarna** Sweden
220 C3 **Huslia** AK U.S.A.
Husn Jordan see **Al Ḩişn**
125 H7 **Ḩuşn Āl 'Abr** Yemen
142 B2 **Husnes** Norway
144 J1 **Husøy** i. Norway
117 J7 **Hussainabad** Jharkhand India
176 F3 **Hustopeče** Czech Rep.
168 H5 **Husum** Niedersachsen Ger.
168 H2 **Husum** Schleswig-Holstein Ger.
140 O5 **Husum** Sweden
259 □ **Husvik** S. Georgia
136 F4 **Husyatyn** Ukr.
137 Q4 **Husynka** Ukr.
175 K3 **Huszlew** Pol.
175 I4 **Huta** Pol.
106 H2 **Hutag** Mongolia
122 G6 **Hūtak** Iran
94 C4 **Hutanopan** Sumatera Indon.
117 J8 **Hutar** Jharkhand India
124 E2 **Hutaym, Ḩarrat** lava field Saudi Arabia
214 H7 **Hutchinson** S. Africa
236 G6 **Hutchinson** KS U.S.A.
236 H3 **Hutchinson** MN U.S.A.
241 U7 **Hutch Mountain** AZ U.S.A.
124 F7 **Ḩūth** Yemen
96 D6 **Huthi** Myanmar
100 H6 **Hutou** Heilong. China
87 C10 **Hutt** r. W.A. Austr.
83 I6 **Huttah Kulkyne National Park** N.S.W. Austr.
178 H5 **Hüttau** Austria
179 K6 **Hüttenberg** Austria
170 G3 **Hüttenberg** hill Ger.
169 G9 **Hüttenberg-Hochelheim** Ger.
169 K7 **Hüttenrode** Ger.
173 O4 **Hutthurm** Ger.
173 I4 **Hüttlingen** Ger.
149 R7 **Huttoft** Lincolnshire, England U.K.
150 G5 **Hutton** North Somerset, England U.K.
85 L8 **Hutton, Mount** hill Qld Austr.
149 Q6 **Hutton Cranswick** East Riding of Yorkshire, England U.K.
87 G8 **Hutton Range** hills W.A. Austr.
149 O5 **Hutton Rudby** North Yorkshire, England U.K.
178 H5 **Hüttschlag** Austria
190 D1 **Huttwil** Switz.
110 H4 **Hutubi** Xinjiang China
110 H4 **Hutubi He** r. China
107 O7 **Hutuo He** r. China
137 O3 **Huty** Ukr.
168 J4 **Hützel** Ger.
113 D11 **Huvadhu Atoll** Maldives
123 I8 **Hūvār** Iran
Hüvek Turkey see **Bozova**
168 E5 **Hüven** Ger.
122 H8 **Hūvīān, Kūh-e** mts Iran
125 J3 **Ḩuwār** i. The Gulf
124 G7 **Huwaymil** des. Saudi Arabia
126 H9 **Huwaytat** reg. Saudi Arabia
175 K6 **Huwniki** Pol.
109 J5 **Huxi** Jiangxi China
107 K9 **Huxian** Shaanxi China
86 I5 **Huxley, Mount** hill W.A. Austr.
81 D11 **Huxley, Mount** South I. N.Z.
165 H7 **Huy** Belgium
136 H3 **Huyba** r. Ukr.
149 L7 **Huyton** Merseyside, England U.K.
100 C3 **Huyuan** Heilong. China
136 H3 **Huyva** Ukr.
109 M4 **Huzhen** Zhejiang China
100 C3 **Huzhong** Heilong. China
109 M3 **Huzhou** Zhejiang China
106 G8 **Huzhu** Qinghai China
114 F4 **Huzurnagar** Andhra Prad. India
140 □F1 **Hvalnes** Iceland
140 □B1 **Hvammsfjörður** inlet Iceland
140 □E1 **Hvannadalshnúkur** vol. Iceland
188 F4 **Hvar** Croatia
188 F4 **Hvar** i. Croatia
137 O5 **Hvardiys'ke** Dnipropetrovs'ka Oblast' Ukr.
137 N8 **Hvardiys'ke** Respublika Krym Ukr.
188 F4 **Hvarski Kanal** sea chan. Croatia
140 □C1 **Hveragerði** Iceland
142 E5 **Hvide Sande** Denmark
140 □C2 **Hvíta** r. Iceland
140 □D1 **Hvítárvatn** l. Iceland
142 F2 **Hvittingfoss** Norway
136 E5 **Hvizdets'** Ukr.
137 M2 **Hvyntove** Ukr.
101 F8 **Hwadae** N. Korea
212 E3 **Hwange** Zimbabwe
212 E3 **Hwange National Park** Zimbabwe
Hwang Ho r. China see **Huang He**
101 D9 **Hwangju** N. Korea
213 F3 **Hwedza** Zimbabwe
Hwlffordd Pembrokeshire, Wales U.K. see **Haverfordwest**
104 C5 **Hyakuriga-take** hill Japan
233 O7 **Hyannis** MA U.S.A.
236 E4 **Hyannis** NE U.S.A.
106 C2 **Hyargas Nuur** salt l. Mongolia
234 B7 **Hyattsville** MD U.S.A.
232 F12 **Hyco Lake** NC U.S.A.
222 C4 **Hydaburg** AK U.S.A.
81 E12 **Hyde** South I. N.Z.
149 M7 **Hyde** Greater Manchester, England U.K.
87 E12 **Hyden** W.A. Austr.
232 B11 **Hyden** KY U.S.A.
233 M4 **Hyde Park** VT U.S.A.
222 D4 **Hyder** AK U.S.A.
114 F4 **Hyderabad** Andhra Prad. India
123 M9 **Hyderabad** Pak.
Hydra i. Greece see **Ydra**
161 I10 **Hyères** France
161 I11 **Hyères, Îles d'** is France
161 I10 **Hyères, Rade d'** g. France
138 K6 **Hyermanavichy** Belarus
101 F8 **Hyesan** N. Korea
222 D3 **Hyland** r. Y.T. Can.
83 N4 **Hyland, Mount** N.S.W. Austr.
84 B2 **Hyland Bay** N.T. Austr.
222 D3 **Hyland Post** B.C. Can.
142 H7 **Hyllekrog** i. Denmark
141 H6 **Hyllestad** Norway
142 J4 **Hyltebruk** Sweden
157 L7 **Hymont** France
232 G9 **Hyndman** PA U.S.A.
238 G5 **Hyndman Peak** ID U.S.A.
146 C10 **Hynish** Argyll and Bute, Scotland U.K.
104 A5 **Hyōgo** pref. Japan
103 L11 **Hyōno-sen** mt. Japan
Hyrcania Iran see **Gorgān**
Hyrra Banda C.A.R. see **Ira Banda**
140 T4 **Hyrynsalmi** Fin.
238 K3 **Hysham** MT U.S.A.
222 G4 **Hythe** Alta Can.
151 J6 **Hythe** Hampshire, England U.K.
151 O5 **Hythe** Kent, England U.K.
103 I14 **Hyūga** Japan
141 R6 **Hyvinkää** Fin.
175 K6 **Hyżne** Pol.

I

204 E4 **Iabès, Erg** des. Alg.
256 C4 **Iacanga** Brazil
254 D5 **Iaciara** Brazil
252 C2 **Iaco** r. Brazil
197 M4 **Iacobeni** Sibiu Romania
197 N3 **Iacobeni** Suceava Romania
256 B4 **Iacri** Brazil
254 E5 **Iaçu** Brazil
Iadera Croatia see **Zadar**
232 D11 **Iaeger** WV U.S.A.
213 □J4 **Iakora** Madag.
Ialbuzi Rus. Fed. see **El'brus**
136 E9 **Ialomița** r. Romania
197 P6 **Ialomița** r. Romania
197 P6 **Ialomiței, Balta** marsh Romania
136 H7 **Ialoveni** Moldova
136 H7 **Ialpug** r. Moldova
197 P5 **Ianca** Romania
197 M6 **Iancu Jianu** Romania
129 D3 **Ianet'i** Georgia
257 F3 **Iapu** Brazil
197 L4 **Iara** r. Romania
251 F4 **Iarauarune, Serra** mts Brazil
147 D6 **Iar Connaught** reg. Ireland
136 H7 **Iargara** Moldova
197 P3 **Iași** Romania
198 G1 **Iasmos** Greece
92 B4 **Iba** Luzon Phil.
207 F5 **Ibadan** Nigeria
250 C3 **Ibagué** Col.
184 H2 **Ibahernando** Spain
256 B5 **Ibaiti** Brazil
210 A5 **Ibanda** Uganda
197 M4 **Ibănești** Romania
186 C1 **Ibañeta, Puerto de** pass Spain
209 D6 **Ibanga** Kasaï-Occidental Dem. Rep. Congo
208 E5 **Ibanga** Sud-Kivu Dem. Rep. Congo
241 S1 **Ibapah** UT U.S.A.
196 I7 **Ibar** r. Serbia
103 K12 **Ibara** Japan
105 L3 **Ibaraki** Ibaraki Japan
104 C6 **Ibaraki** Ōsaka Japan
105 L3 **Ibaraki** pref. Japan
250 B4 **Ibarra** Ecuador
186 A1 **Ibarra** Spain
258 F2 **Ibarreta** Arg.
256 D4 **Ibaté** Brazil
124 G8 **Ibb** Yemen
124 G8 **Ibb** governorate Yemen
208 F3 **Ibba** watercourse Sudan
169 E6 **Ibbenbüren** Ger.
207 F2 **Ibdeqqene** watercourse Mali
183 Q6 **Ibdes** Spain
198 A1 **Ibë** Albania
183 M4 **Ibeas de Juarros** Spain
258 F3 **Iberá, Esteros del** marsh Arg.
258 F3 **Iberá, Laguna** l. Arg.
250 C6 **Iberia** Loreto Peru
252 C2 **Iberia** Madre de Dios Peru
257 F4 **Ibertioga** Brazil
233 L3 **Iberville** Que. Can.
225 F2 **Iberville, Lac d'** l. Que. Can.
140 N2 **Ibestad** Norway
207 G4 **Ibeto** Nigeria
94 B2 **Ibi** Sumatera Indon.
207 H4 **Ibi** Nigeria
187 D10 **Ibi** Spain
256 D3 **Ibiá** Brazil
257 E2 **Ibiaí** Brazil
254 E2 **Ibiapaba, Serra da** hills Brazil
182 G2 **Ibias** r. Spain
255 F5 **Ibicaraí** Brazil
255 A9 **Ibicuí** Brazil
255 A9 **Ibicuí** r. Brazil
161 E8 **Ibie** r. France
104 E5 **Ibigawa** Japan
104 E5 **Ibi-gawa** r. Japan
254 F4 **Ibimirim** Brazil
208 F4 **Ibina** r. Dem. Rep. Congo
256 B5 **Ibiporã** Brazil
256 C4 **Ibirá** Brazil
257 G3 **Ibiraçu** Brazil
257 G2 **Ibiranhém** Brazil
261 I1 **Ibirocaí** Brazil
104 D5 **Ibi-Sekigahara-Yōrō Kokutei-kōen** park Japan
254 E5 **Ibitiara** Brazil
256 C4 **Ibitinga** Brazil
256 D5 **Ibiúna** Brazil
Ibiza Illes Balears Spain see **Eivissa**
Ibiza i. Spain see **Eivissa**
187 H10 **Ibiza/San José** airport Spain
194 H9 **Iblei, Monti** mts Sicilia Italy
199 J6 **İblis Burnu** pt Turkey
124 G2 **Ibn Buşayyiş** well Saudi Arabia
124 E6 **Ibn Ḩādī** Saudi Arabia
163 D9 **Ibos** France
254 E5 **Ibotirama** Brazil
208 A5 **Iboundji** Gabon
208 A5 **Iboundji, Mont** hill Gabon
125 N4 **Ibrā'** Oman
208 E2 **Ibra, Wadi** watercourse Sudan
Ibrala Turkey see **Yeşildere**
135 I5 **Ibresi** Rus. Fed.
125 M4 **Ibrī** Oman
185 M4 **Ibros** Spain
151 J2 **Ibstock** Leicestershire, England U.K.
93 E3 **Ibu** Halmahera Indon.
102 □1 **Ibu** Okinawa Japan
92 C1 **Ibuhos** i. Phil.
104 D5 **Ibuki** Japan
104 D4 **Ibuki-sanchi** mts Japan
104 D5 **Ibuki-yama** mt. Japan
103 H15 **Ibusuki** Japan
250 E5 **Içá** r. Brazil
252 B3 **Ica** Peru
252 B3 **Ica** dept Peru
251 F3 **Icabarú** Venez.
247 □7 **Icacos Point** Trin. and Tob.
243 O8 **Icaiché** Mex.
250 E4 **Içana** Brazil
250 E4 **Içana** r. Brazil
254 F2 **Icaraí** Brazil
Icaria i. Greece see **Ikaria**
254 D2 **Icatu** Brazil
241 R5 **Iceberg Canyon** gorge NV U.S.A.
İçel İçel Turkey see **Mersin**
221 Q3 **Iceland** country Europe
264 H2 **Iceland Basin** sea feature N. Atlantic Ocean
264 I1 **Icelandic Plateau** sea feature N. Atlantic Ocean
256 C4 **Icem** Brazil
117 J7 **Ichak** Jharkhand India
114 D4 **Ichalkaranji** Mahar. India
115 I3 **Ichchapuram** Andhra Prad. India
173 I5 **Ichenhausen** Ger.
172 D5 **Ichenheim** Ger.
103 I14 **Ichifusa-yama** mt. Japan
105 L5 **Ichihara** Japan
105 L2 **Ichikai** Japan
105 K4 **Ichikawa** Chiba Japan
104 A5 **Ichikawa** Hyōgo Japan
104 A6 **Ichi-kawa** r. Japan
105 I4 **Ichikawadaimon** Japan
252 D4 **Ichilo** r. Bol.
104 E5 **Ichinomiya** Aichi Japan
104 F6 **Ichinomiya** Aichi Japan
105 L5 **Ichinomiya** Chiba Japan
104 A7 **Ichinomiya** Hyōgo Japan
105 I4 **Ichinomiya** Yamanashi Japan
102 S8 **Ichinoseki** Japan
131 Q4 **Ichinskiy, Vulkan** vol. Rus. Fed.
104 D6 **Ichishi** Japan
Ichkeria aut. rep. Rus. Fed. see **Chechenskaya Respublika**
189 B7 **Ichkeul, Parc National de l'** nat. park Tunisia
137 L3 **Ichnya** Ukr.
101 E9 **Ich'ŏn** N. Korea
101 E10 **Ich'ŏn** S. Korea
165 D6 **Ichtegem** Belgium
169 K9 **Ichtershausen** Ger.
252 C4 **Ichuña** Peru
199 J4 **İcikler** Turkey
173 K6 **Icking** Ger.
151 N6 **Icklesham** East Sussex, England U.K.
151 N3 **Icklingham** Suffolk, England U.K.
199 J6 **İçmeler** Turkey
254 F3 **Icó** Brazil
216 □3a **Icod de Los Vinos** Tenerife Canary Is
122 H1 **Içoguz** Turkm.
257 G4 **Iconha** Brazil
Iconium Turkey see **Konya**
Icosium Alg. see **Alger**
Iculisma France see **Angoulême**
222 C3 **Icy Strait** AK U.S.A.
ıd Turkey see **Narman**
81 E11 **Ida, Mount** South I. N.Z.
207 H2 **Idabdaba** well Niger
237 H9 **Idabel** OK U.S.A.
124 D8 **Idaga Hamus** Eth.
236 H4 **Ida Grove** IA U.S.A.
207 G5 **Idah** Nigeria
238 G4 **Idaho** state U.S.A.
238 G5 **Idaho City** ID U.S.A.
238 H5 **Idaho Falls** ID U.S.A.
85 J8 **Idalia National Park** Qld Austr.
Idalion Cyprus see **Dali**
238 C4 **Idanha** OR U.S.A.
182 F9 **Idanha, Barragem da** resr Port.
182 F9 **Idanha-a-Nova** Port.
116 D8 **Idar** Gujarat India
172 C2 **Idar-Oberstein** Ger.
172 C2 **Idarwald** for. Ger.
81 D12 **Ida Valley** South I. N.Z.
207 H3 **Iday** well Niger
210 F3 **Iddan** Somalia
195 □ **Id-Dawwara, Ras** pt Malta
203 F6 **Idd el Asoda** well Sudan
208 E2 **Idd el Chanam** Sudan
203 F5 **Idd esh Shurak** well Sudan
104 C6 **Ide** Japan
142 H2 **Idefjorden** inlet Norway/Sweden
205 G5 **Idelès** Alg.
170 E5 **Iden** Ger.
106 F2 **Ider** Mongolia
106 G2 **Ideriyn Gol** r. Mongolia
170 E1 **Idestrup** Denmark
203 G3 **Idfū** Egypt
Idhra i. Greece see **Ydra**
Ídhras, Kólpos sea chan. Greece see **Ydras, Kolpos**
Idi Amin Dada, Lake Dem. Rep. Congo/Uganda see **Edward, Lake**
186 A1 **Idiazabal** Spain
191 L6 **Idice** r. Italy
210 D3 **Ididole** Eth.
209 C6 **Idiofa** Dem. Rep. Congo
220 C3 **Iditarod** AK U.S.A.
140 Q2 **Idivuoma** Sweden
203 F2 **Idkū** Egypt
149 P7 **Idle** r. England U.K.
128 E3 **Idlib** Syria
128 E3 **Idlib** governorate Syria
151 I5 **Idmiston** Wiltshire, England U.K.
183 R3 **Idocin** Spain
211 B6 **Idodi** Tanz.
177 J6 **Iđoš** Vojvodina Serbia
Idra i. Greece see **Ydra**
84 D8 **Idracowra** N.T. Austr.
141 L6 **Idre** Sweden
188 E2 **Idrija** Slovenia
188 D2 **Idrijca** r. Slovenia
138 L5 **Idritsa** Rus. Fed.
190 I4 **Idro** Italy
190 J4 **Idro, Lago d'** l. Italy
163 D9 **Idron-Ousse-Sendets** France
168 I1 **Idstedt** Ger.
169 F10 **Idstein** Ger.
211 B6 **Idugala** Tanz.
114 E8 **Idukki** Kerala India
215 M8 **Idutywa** S. Africa
240 P8 **Idyllwild** CA U.S.A.
Idzhevan Armenia see **Ijevan**
102 □1 **Ie** Okinawa Japan
138 H5 **Iecava** Latvia
138 G5 **Iecava** r. Latvia
102 □1 **Ie-jima** i. Okinawa Japan
256 B5 **Iepê** Brazil
165 C7 **Ieper** Belgium
197 K3 **Ier** r. Romania
199 G7 **Ierapetra** Kriti Greece
198 E2 **Ierissou, Kolpos** b. Greece
140 R2 **Iešjávri** l. Norway
102 □1 **Ie-suidō** str. Okinawa Japan
211 C7 **Ifakara** Tanz.
124 B1 **'Ifāl, Wādī** watercourse Saudi Arabia
91 J5 **Ifalik** atoll Micronesia
Ifaluk atoll Micronesia see **Ifalik**
213 □J4 **Ifanadiana** Madag.
213 □J4 **Ifanirea** Madag.
207 G5 **Ife** Nigeria
202 C6 **Ifenat** Chad
207 H2 **Iferouâne** Niger
205 G4 **Ifetesene** mt. Alg.
173 K6 **Iffeldorf** Ger.
158 G5 **Iffendic** France
172 E4 **Iffezheim** Ger.
85 H5 **Iffley** Qld Austr.
140 S1 **Ifjord** Norway
207 F2 **Ifôghas, Adrar des** hills Mali
207 G5 **Ifon** Nigeria
82 D4 **Ifould Lake** salt flat S.A. Austr.
204 D2 **Ifrane** Morocco
159 K3 **Ifs** France
169 J8 **Ifta** Ger.
208 D5 **Ifumo** Dem. Rep. Congo
211 B7 **Ifunda** Tanz.
179 K8 **Ig** Slovenia
104 D6 **Iga** Japan
207 G4 **Igabi** Nigeria
177 G5 **Igal** Hungary
196 G8 **Igalo** Montenegro
95 I3 **Igan** Sarawak Malaysia
95 I3 **Igan** r. Malaysia
210 B4 **Iganga** Uganda
177 H5 **Igar** Hungary
256 D4 **Igarapava** Brazil
254 D2 **Igarape Açú** Brazil
254 D3 **Igarapé Grande** Brazil
254 C2 **Igarapé Miri** Brazil
256 D5 **Igaratá** Brazil
254 E4 **Igarité** Brazil
130 J3 **Igarka** Rus. Fed.
114 C3 **Igatpuri** Mahar. India
207 G4 **Igbetti** Nigeria
207 F4 **Igboho** Nigeria
207 H5 **Igbor** Nigeria
127 M4 **Igdir** Iran
127 L4 **Iğdır** Turkey
129 F6 **Iğdır** prov. Turkey
159 M5 **Igé** France
183 P4 **Igea** Spain
172 B2 **Igel** Ger.
173 K2 **Igensdorf** Ger.
172 H3 **Igersheim** Ger.
172 E3 **Iggelheim** Ger.
173 O4 **Iggensbach** Ger.
141 N6 **Iggesund** Sweden
197 L4 **Ighiu** Romania
190 H2 **Igis** Switz.
260 C2 **Iglesia** Arg.
192 B9 **Iglesias** Sardegna Italy
192 A8 **Iglesiente** reg. Sardegna Italy
204 E3 **Igli** Alg.
173 J5 **Igling** Ger.
134 L5 **Iglino** Rus. Fed.
221 J3 **Igloolik** Nunavut Can.
Igluligaarjuk Nunavut Can. see **Chesterfield Inlet**
224 B3 **Ignace** Ont. Can.
244 C1 **Ignacio Allende** Mex.
245 L7 **Ignacio de la Llave** Mex.
242 F3 **Ignacio Zaragosa** Mex.
245 I2 **Ignacio Zaragoza** Tamaulipas Mex.

Ignacio Zaragoza to Ipswich

326

244 D2 Ignacio Zaragoza Zacatecas Mex.
138 J6 Ignalina Lith.
100 C2 Ignashino Rus. Fed.
126 C3 İğneada Turkey
126 D3 İğneada Burnu pt Turkey
177 L5 Ignești Romania
157 L7 Igney France
115 M7 Ignoitijala Andaman & Nicobar Is India
160 G1 Ignon r. France
134 H4 Igodovo Rus. Fed.
93 G4 Igom Papua Indon.
211 B6 Igoma Tanz.
211 A6 Igombe r. Tanz.
139 Q6 Igorevskaya Rus. Fed.
160 E2 Igornay France
198 B3 Igoumenitsa Greece
134 K4 Igra Rus. Fed.
186 E3 Igriés Spain
130 H3 Igrim Rus. Fed.
255 B8 Iguaçu r. Brazil
256 A6 Iguaçu, Parque Nacional do nat. park Brazil
Iguaçu, Saltos do waterfall Arg./Brazil see Iguaçu Falls
258 G2 Iguaçu Falls Arg./Brazil
255 E5 Iguaí Brazil
250 C4 Iguaje, Mesa de hills Col.
245 H7 Iguala Mex.
186 I4 Igualada Spain
185 I7 Igualeja Spain
245 I8 Igualtepec Mex.
256 D6 Iguape Brazil
256 B5 Iguaraçu Brazil
257 E4 Iguarapé Brazil
257 E4 Iguatama Brazil
255 B7 Iguatemi Brazil
255 B7 Iguatemi r. Brazil
254 F3 Iguatu Brazil
Iguazú, Cataratas do waterfall Arg./Brazil see Iguaçu Falls
258 G2 Iguazú, Parque Nacional del nat. park Arg.
208 A5 Iguéla Gabon
182 H3 Igueña Spain
160 E4 Iguerande France
204 C4 Iguetti, Sebkhet salt flat Maur.
204 D4 Iguidi, Erg des. Alg./Maur.
211 B6 Igunga Tanz.
207 G5 Iguobazuwa Nigeria
213 F3 Iguri Zimbabwe
211 B5 Igusule Tanz.
Iguvium Italy see Gubbio
213 □K2 Iharaña Madag.
176 G5 Iharosberény Hungary
114 C9 Ihavandhippolhu Atoll Maldives
107 J5 Ihbulag Mongolia
102 □E19 Iheya-jima i. Nansei-shotō Japan
106 I3 Ihhayrhan Mongolia
205 F5 Ihiala Nigeria
205 G5 Ihirène, Oued watercourse Alg.
177 J2 Ihľany Slovakia
168 E4 Ihlowerhörn (Ihlow) Ger.
136 H2 Ihnatpil' Ukr.
163 B9 Iholdy France
213 □J4 Ihosy Madag.
168 D4 Ihrhove Ger.
172 D5 Ihringen Ger.
173 L4 Ihrlerstein Ger.
199 L3 İhsaniye Turkey
106 J2 Ihsuuj Mongolia
105 H3 Ih Tal Nei Mongol China
105 G4 Iida Japan
102 G9 Iide-san mt. Japan
105 G4 Iijima Japan
140 R4 Iijoki r. Fin.
104 D7 Iinan Japan
105 M4 Iioka Japan
140 S5 Iisalmi Fin.
104 D7 Iitaka Japan
138 J1 Iitti Fin.
105 H2 Iiyama Japan
103 H13 Iizuka Japan
204 C5 Ijâfene des. Maur.
211 D5 Ijara Kenya
207 F5 Ijebu-Ode Nigeria
95 K9 Ijen-Merapi-Maelang, Cagar Alam nature res. Jawa Indon.
129 G5 Ijevan Armenia
164 I2 IJlst Neth.
164 G4 IJmuiden Neth.
206 B2 Ijinouene well Maur.
206 D5 Ijoubbâne des. Mali
164 I3 IJssel r. Neth.
164 H3 IJsselmeer l. Neth.
164 I3 IJsselmuiden Neth.
164 H4 IJsselstein Neth.
255 B9 Ijuí Brazil
258 G6 Ijuí r. Brazil
165 E6 IJzendijke Neth.
165 C7 IJzer r. Belgium alt. Yser (France)
Ikaahuk N.W.T. Can. see Sachs Harbour
141 Q6 Ikaalinen Fin.
215 K1 Ikageleng S. Africa
215 L2 Ikageng S. Africa
213 □J3 Ikahavo hill Madag.
105 I3 Ikaho Japan
213 □J4 Ikalamavony Madag.
Ikaluktutiak Nunavut Can. see Cambridge Bay
81 F9 Ikamatua South I. N.Z.
209 D5 Ikanda-Nord Dem. Rep. Congo
207 H5 Ikang Nigeria
207 H4 Ikara Nigeria
207 G5 Ikare Nigeria
208 C5 Ikari Dem. Rep. Congo
199 H5 Ikaria i. Greece
104 C6 Ikaruga Japan
142 F5 Ikast Denmark
208 C4 Ikau Dem. Rep. Congo
105 H5 Ikawa Japan
81 E11 Ikawai South I. N.Z.
80 K5 Ikawhenua Range mts North I. N.Z.
104 D4 Ikeda Fukui Japan
104 E5 Ikeda Gifu Japan
102 U4 Ikeda Hokkaidō Japan
105 G3 Ikeda Nagano Japan
104 C5 Ikeda Ōsaka Japan
103 K12 Ikeda Tokushima Japan
103 K13 Ikegawa Japan
102 D4 Ikegoya-yama mt. Japan
103 □C2 Ikei-jima i. Okinawa Japan
207 F5 Ikeja Nigeria
208 D5 Ikela Dem. Rep. Congo
208 C4 Ikelemba r. Dem. Rep. Congo
209 E7 Ikelenge Zambia
207 G5 Ikem Nigeria
208 C5 Ikengo Dem. Rep. Congo
208 A5 Ikengue Gabon
207 G5 Ikere Nigeria
Ikerre Nigeria see Ikere
176 F4 Ikervár Hungary
129 I4 Ikhrek Rus. Fed.
197 L8 Ikhtiman Bulg.
215 I4 Ikhutseng S. Africa
126 F3 İkiağiz Turkey
128 H1 İkiağiz Turkey
135 I7 Iki-Burul Rus. Fed.
211 A5 Ikimba, Lake Tanz.
207 G5 Ikire Nigeria
103 G13 Iki-shima i. Japan
103 G13 Iki-suidō sea chan. Japan
129 B5 İkizdere Turkey
138 H4 Ikla Estonia
211 A6 Ikola Tanz.
207 F5 Ikom Nigeria
104 C6 Ikoma Japan
211 B5 Ikoma Tanz.
213 □J4 Ikongo Madag.
217 □3a Ikoni Njazidja Comoros
129 C1 Ikon-Khalk Rus. Fed.
213 □J3 Ikopa r. Madag.
137 S3 Ikorets r. Rus. Fed.
207 F5 Ikorodu Nigeria
208 E5 Ikosi Dem. Rep. Congo
207 G5 Ikot Ekpene Nigeria
205 H4 Ikouhaouene, Adrar mt. Alg.
Ikpiarjuk Nunavut Can. see Arctic Bay
177 G4 Ikrény Hungary
101 E11 Iksan S. Korea
104 F2 Ikuji-hana pt Japan
211 B6 Ikungi Tanz.
211 B6 Ikungu Tanz.
104 A5 Ikuno Japan
105 G3 Ikusaka Japan
136 E3 Ikva r. Ukr.
205 F5 Ilaferh, Oued watercourse Alg.
211 A6 Ilagala Tanz.
92 C3 Ilagan Luzon Phil.
210 C4 Ilaisamis Kenya
114 F8 Ilaiyankudi Tamil Nadu India
213 □K3 Ilaka Atsinanana Madag.
122 B5 Īlām Iran
122 B5 Īlām prov. Iran
117 K6 Ilam Nepal
109 M6 Ilan Taiwan
174 C3 Ilanka r. Pol.
190 G2 Ilanz Switz.
207 G4 Ila Orangun Nigeria
137 O5 Ilarionove Ukr.
207 F5 Ilaro Nigeria
252 C4 Ilave Peru
175 H2 Iława Pol.
207 G5 Ilawe-Ekiti Nigeria
175 H2 Iławskie, Pojezierze reg. Pol.
122 G7 Īlazārān, Kūh-e mt. Iran
195 □ Il-Bajda, Ras pt Gozo Malta
106 F4 Il Bogd Uul mts Mongolia
192 D8 Ilbono Sardegna Italy
150 G6 Ilchester Somerset, England U.K.
199 H4 Ildır Turkey
121 Q5 Ile r. China/Kazakh.
223 J4 Île-à-la-Crosse Sask. Can.
223 J4 Île-à-la-Crosse, Lac l. Sask. Can.
246 G4 Île-à-Vache i. Haiti
209 D6 Ilebo Dem. Rep. Congo
225 I3 Île d'Anticosti, Réserve Faunique de l' nature res. Que. Can.
156 E6 Île-de-France admin. reg. France
211 B7 Ileje Tanz.
120 E2 Ilek Kazakh.
120 E2 Ilek r. Rus. Fed.
137 O3 Ilek-Pen'kovka Rus. Fed.
147 D9 Ilen r. Ireland
Ilerda prov. Spain see Lleida
210 C3 Ileret Kenya
Île Royale i. N.S. Can. see Cape Breton Island
Ilesa Nigeria see Ilesha
207 G5 Ilesha Nigeria
207 F4 Ilesha Ibariba Nigeria
134 J5 Ilet' r. Rus. Fed.
143 H3 Ileza Rus. Fed.
169 K7 Ilfeld Ger.
223 M3 Ilford Man. Can.
151 M4 Ilford Greater London, England U.K.
85 J7 Ilfracombe Qld Austr.
150 D5 Ilfracombe Devon, England U.K.
126 F3 Ilgaz Turkey
126 F3 Ilgaz Dağları mts Turkey
126 E4 Ilgın Turkey
175 M1 Ilgis l. Lith.
195 □ Il-Griebeġ, Ras pt Malta
216 □1c Ilha, Ponta da pt Pico Azores
257 E5 Ilhabela Brazil
251 E6 Ilha Grande Brazil
257 E5 Ilha Grande, Baía da b. Brazil
255 B7 Ilha Grande, Parque Nacional da nat. park Brazil
255 B7 Ilha Grande, Represa resr Brazil
195 □ Il-Ħamrija, Ras pt Malta
256 B4 Ilha Solteira, Represa resr Brazil
182 C7 Ílhavo Port.
255 F5 Ilhéus Brazil
Ili r. China/Kazakh. see Ile
Ili Kazakh. see Kapchagay
197 K5 Ilia Romania
220 C4 Iliamna Lake AK U.S.A.
126 I4 İliç Turkey
129 B6 Ilica Bingöl Turkey
126 D3 Ilıca Erzurum Turkey
129 C1 Il'ich Rus. Fed.
Il'ichevsk Azer. see Şärur
Il'ichevsk Ukr. see Illichivs'k
Ilici Spain see Elche-Elx
210 F3 Ilig, Raas pt Somalia
92 E7 Iligan Mindanao Phil.
92 E7 Iligan Bay Mindanao Phil.
92 D2 Iligan Point Luzon Phil.
Ili He r. China/Kazakh. see Ile
188 G4 Ilijaš Bos.-Herz.
221 P2 Ilimanangip Nunaa i. Greenland
131 L3 Ilimpeya r. Rus. Fed.
120 G3 Il'inka Kazakh.
139 T7 Il'inka Kaluzhskaya Oblast' Rus. Fed.
121 U2 Il'inka Respublika Altay Rus. Fed.
106 D1 Il'inka Respublika Tyva Rus. Fed.
139 O6 Il'ino Rus. Fed.
134 K4 Il'inskiy Permskaya Oblast' Rus. Fed.
139 P1 Il'inskiy Respublika Kareliya Rus. Fed.
100 M5 Il'inskiy Sakhalin Rus. Fed.
134 I3 Il'insko-Podomskoye Rus. Fed.
137 S7 Il'inskoye Krasnodarskiy Kray Rus. Fed.
139 S8 Il'inskoye Orlovskaya Oblast' Rus. Fed.
139 U5 Il'inskoye Tverskaya Oblast' Rus. Fed.
139 V4 Il'inskoye Yaroslavskaya Oblast' Rus. Fed.
139 W5 Il'inskoye-Khovanskoye Rus. Fed.
92 C5 Ilin Strait Phil.
Il'intsy Ukr. see Illintsi
93 E8 Ilomar East Timor
233 J5 Ilion NY U.S.A.
250 □D12 'Īlio Point HI U.S.A.
188 E3 Ilirska Bistrica Slovenia
129 H4 İlisu Qoruğu nature res. Azer.
Ilium tourist site Turkey see Truva
138 K7 Iliya r. Belarus
Iliysk Kazakh. see Kapchagay
177 L3 Ilk Hungary
114 E5 Ilkal Karnataka India
151 J2 Ilkeston Derbyshire, England U.K.
149 N6 Ilkley West Yorkshire, England U.K.
195 □ Il-Kullana pt Malta
157 O6 Ill r. France
183 O8 Illana Spain
92 D8 Illana Bay Mindanao Phil.
190 D2 Illapel Chile
260 B2 Illapel r. Chile
185 N7 Illar Spain
191 K5 Illasi r. Italy
163 D6 Illats France
82 D2 Illbillee, Mount hill S.A. Austr.
160 F5 Ille r. France
158 D2 Ille-et-Rance, Canal d' France
158 F5 Ille-et-Vilaine dept France
207 G3 Iléla Niger
207 G3 Illela Nigeria
173 H5 Iller r. Ger.
173 I5 Illerrieden Ger.
173 I5 Illertissen Ger.
183 G3 Illes Balears aut. comm. Spain
183 M8 Illescas Spain
245 G4 Illescas Uru.
163 J10 Ille-sur-Têt France
137 O8 Illicheve Ukr.
136 J7 Illichivs'k Ukr.
156 B7 Illiers-Combray France
252 D4 Illimani, Nevado de mt. Bol.
172 F4 Illingen Baden-Württemberg Ger.
172 C3 Illingen Saarland Ger.
137 J6 Illinka Odes'ka Oblast' Ukr.
137 M8 Illinka Respublika Krym Ukr.
226 D9 Illinois r. IL U.S.A.
233 C3 Illinois state U.S.A.
226 E8 Illinois and Mississippi Canal IL U.S.A.
136 I4 Illintsi Ukr.
205 H4 Illizi Alg.
157 O6 Illkirch-Graffenstaden France
192 C3 Illmensee Ger.
179 O4 Illmitz Austria
84 E8 Illogwa watercourse N.T. Austr.
185 L6 Íllora Spain
192 B7 Illorai Sardegna Italy
173 L3 Illschwang Ger.
183 Q5 Illueca Spain
157 N8 Illzach France
171 E8 Ilm r. Ger.
173 L4 Ilm r. Ger.
87 I10 Ilma, Lake salt flat W.A. Austr.
124 G6 'Ilmān, Jabal al hill Saudi Arabia
139 O3 Il'men', Ozero l. Rus. Fed.
171 J6 Ilmenau Ger.
168 J4 Ilmenau r. Ger.
195 □ Il-Minkba pt Malta
92 B6 Il-Minkba pt Malta
150 G6 Ilminster Somerset, England U.K.
178 F8 Il Montello mt. Italy
171 D9 Ilmtal park Ger.
136 G5 Il'nytsya Ukr.
252 C4 Ilo Peru
207 G5 Ilobu Nigeria
92 B6 Iloc i. Phil.
260 A4 Iloca Chile
92 D6 Iloilo Panay Phil.
92 D6 Iloilo Strait Phil.
140 U5 Ilomantsi Fin.
211 B6 Ilongero Tanz.
207 G4 Ilorin Nigeria
188 F3 Ilovačka r. Croatia
134 H6 Ilovka Rus. Fed.
137 R6 Ilovays'k Ukr.
197 K9 Ilovica Macedonia
191 R7 Ilovik Croatia
188 E3 Ilovik i. Croatia
137 R3 Ilovka Rus. Fed.
135 H6 Ilovlya Rus. Fed.
135 H6 Ilovlya r. Rus. Fed.
175 I3 Iłów Pol.
174 D4 Iłowa Pol.
175 I2 Iłowo Osada Pol.
134 G4 Ilpendam Neth.
131 R3 Il'pyrskoye Rus. Fed.
195 □ Il-Qala, Ras pt Gozo Malta
141 N6 Ilsbo Sweden
169 K6 Ilse r. Ger.
169 J6 Ilsede Ger.
169 K7 Ilsenburg (Harz) Ger.
172 G3 Ilsfeld Ger.
172 H3 Ilshofen Ger.
150 E6 Ilsington Devon, England U.K.
137 R9 Il'skiy Rus. Fed.
192 A8 Il Toro, Isola i. Sardegna Italy
138 J6 Ilūkste Latvia
221 M3 Ilulissat Greenland
211 B6 Ilunde Tanz.
211 B6 Ilungu Tanz.
Ilva i. Italy see Elba, Isola d'
195 □ Il-Wahx, Ras pt Malta
138 K7 Il'ya Belarus
Il'yaly Turkm. see Gurbansoltan Eje
134 L3 Ilych r. Rus. Fed.
177 K3 Ilyushino Rus. Fed.
179 M5 Ilz Austria
173 O4 Ilz r. Ger.
175 J4 Iłża Pol.
175 J4 Iłżanka r. Pol.
103 J12 Imabari Japan
103 G12 Imabetsu Japan
251 G5 Imabú r. Brazil
104 D4 Imadate Japan
102 R4 Imagane Japan
105 K2 Imaichi Japan
104 D4 Imajō Japan
213 H2 Imala Moz.
127 L8 Imām al Ḩamzah Iraq
123 J3 İmam-baba Turkm.
126 G5 İmamoğlu Turkey
Iman Rus. Fed. see Dal'nerechensk
100 H6 Iman r. Rus. Fed.
134 F2 Imandra Rus. Fed.
121 M1 Imantau, Ozero l. Kazakh.
103 G13 Imari Japan
206 E3 Imasgo Burkina
Imassogo Burkina see Imasgo
252 C3 Imata Peru
251 F3 Imataca, Serranía de mts Venez.
141 T6 Imatra Fin.
138 I5 Imavere Estonia
105 J5 Imazu Japan
250 B4 Imbabura prov. Ecuador
251 F3 Imbaimadai Guyana
Imba-numa l. Japan see Inba-numa
255 C9 Imbituba Brazil
256 B6 Imbituva Brazil
196 L6 İmecik Turkey
177 H4 Imef Slovakia
imeni 26 Bakinskikh Komissarov Azer. see Uzboy
134 H4 imeni Babushkina Rus. Fed.
imeni Chapayevka Turkm. see S. A. Nyýazow Adyndaky
131 P3 imeni Gastello Rus. Fed.
imeni G. I. Petrovskogo Ukr. see Horodyshche
imeni Gor'kogo Rus. Fed.
139 X5 imeni G. Ya. Sedova Ukr. see Syedove
imeni Kalinina Tajik. see Cheshtebe
137 O2 imeni Karla Libknekhta Rus. Fed.
imeni Khamzy Khakikmzade Uzbek. see Hamza
imeni Kirova Kazakh. see Kopbirlik
imeni Kirova Donets'ka Oblast' Ukr. see Kirovs'k
imeni Kirova Donets'ka Oblast' Ukr. see Kirove
imeni L. M. Kaganovicha Ukr. see Popasna
134 I4 imeni M. I. Kalinina Rus. Fed.
imeni Petra Stuchki Latvia see Aizkraukle
100 J2 imeni Poliny Osipenko Rus. Fed.
imeni Voroshilova Kyrg. see Tash-Bashat
139 T3 imeni Zhelyabova Rus. Fed.
137 O5 imeny Lenina, Ozero l. Ukr.
191 L3 Imèr Italy
194 G8 Imera r. Sicilia Italy
251 E4 Imeri, Serra mts Brazil
208 C4 Imese Dem. Rep. Congo
210 D3 Īmī Eth.
207 D2 Imilchil Morocco
204 C3 Imi-n-Tanoute Morocco
204 B4 Imirikliy Labyad reg. Western Sahara
129 J6 İmişli Azer. see İmişli
116 D1 Imit Jammu and Kashmir
101 E11 Imja-do i. S. Korea
101 E10 Imjin-gang r. N. Korea/S. Korea
227 K6 Imlay City MI U.S.A.
204 B5 Imlili Western Sahara
169 J9 Immelborn Ger.
143 K5 Immeln l. Sweden
172 F6 Immendingen Ger.
169 H8 Immenhausen Ger.
173 L2 Immenreuth Ger.
172 G6 Immenstaad am Bodensee Ger.
173 I6 Immenstadt im Allgäu Ger.
149 Q6 Immingham North East Lincolnshire, England U.K.
231 G12 Immokalee FL U.S.A.
207 G5 Imo state Nigeria
191 J8 Imola Italy
188 F4 Imotski Croatia
175 I5 Impendle S. Africa
250 E6 Imperatriz Amazonas Brazil
254 D3 Imperatriz Maranhão Brazil
190 E8 Imperia Italy
190 D7 Imperia prov. Italy
260 A6 Imperial r. Chile
252 A3 Imperial Peru
241 O9 Imperial CA U.S.A.
240 G2 Imperial NE U.S.A.
240 G3 Imperial Beach CA U.S.A.
241 R9 Imperial Dam AZ/CA U.S.A.
241 Q9 Imperial Valley plain CA U.S.A.
86 E4 Imperieuse Reef W.A. Austr.
208 C4 Impfondo Congo
117 N7 Imphal Manipur India
160 C3 Imphy France
151 M3 Impington Cambridgeshire, England U.K.
191 K8 Impruneta Italy
199 J2 İmralı Adası i. Turkey
124 G9 Imrān Yemen
177 I5 Imrehegy Hungary
199 G2 İmroz Gökeada Turkey
İmroz i. Turkey see Gökçeada
ımrun Turkey see Pütürge
101 E11 Imsil S. Korea
178 C5 Imst Austria
128 E6 Imtān Syria
242 D2 Imuris Mex.
92 B6 Imuruan Bay Palawan Phil.
175 M3 Imyanin Belarus
180 E5 Imzouren Morocco
100 H4 In r. Rus. Fed.
105 L4 Ina Fukushima Japan
105 I4 Ina Ibaraki Japan
105 G4 Ina Nagano Japan
174 C2 Ina r. Pol.
207 F2 I-n-Âbâlene well Mali
207 G2 I-n-Abangharit well Niger
105 H4 Inabe Japan
104 E5 Inabu Japan
216 □2c Inaccessible Island Tristan da Cunha S. Atlantic Ocean
104 D5 Inae Japan
205 H5 In Afaleleh well Alg.
92 B7 Inagauan Palawan Phil.
104 B6 Inagawa Japan
104 B6 Ina-gawa r. Japan
105 L4 Inage Japan
147 D7 Inagh Ireland
105 K4 Inagi Japan
213 H2 Inago Moz.
252 B1 Inahuaya Peru
254 F4 Inajá Brazil
253 H2 Inajá r. Brazil
253 H2 Inaja, Serra do hills Brazil
207 E2 I-n-Akhmed well Mali
205 E5 I-n-Akli well Mali
78 □6 Inakona Guadalcanal Solomon Is
Inalahan Guam see Inarajan
207 F2 I-n-Alakam well Mali
206 E2 I-n-Alchi well Mali
207 F2 I-n-Alchig well Mali
206 E2 I-n-Aleï well Mali
206 C2 I-n-'Amar well Maur.
Inamba-jima i. Japan see Inanba-jima
252 C3 Inambari Peru
252 C3 Inambari r. Peru
205 F4 I-n-Amedde well Mali
205 H3 In Aménas Alg.
205 G5 In Amguel Alg.
104 A6 Inami Hyōgo Japan
104 E4 Inami Toyama Japan
104 E8 Inami Wakayama Japan
95 L1 Inanam Sabah Malaysia
103 Q13 Inanba-jima i. Japan
177 K3 Inánes Hungary
215 O5 Inanda S. Africa
81 F8 Inangahua Junction South I. N.Z.
91 H7 Inanwatan Papua Indon.
252 C2 Iñapari Peru
78 □1 Inarajan Guam
207 F2 I-n-Areï well Mali
140 U5 Inari Itä-Suomi Fin.
140 S2 Inari Lappi Fin.
131 L3 Inarigda Rus. Fed.
140 R2 Inarijärvi l. Fin.
140 S2 Inarijoki r. Fin./Norway
207 G2 I-n-Arouinat well Niger
104 G6 Inasa Japan
207 F2 I-n-Atankarer well Mali
252 D2 Inauini r. Brazil
102 S5 Inawashiro-ko l. Japan
205 G4 In Azaoua well Alg.
205 G5 In-Azaoua well Alg.
207 G1 I-n-Azaoua watercourse Niger
202 A2 In Azar well Libya
205 G4 Inazawa Japan
202 A3 In Azāwah well Libya
207 E2 I-n-Azerraf well Mali
105 L4 Inba Japan
105 L4 Inba-numa l. Japan
205 F4 In Belbel Alg.
187 K8 Inca Spain
252 C3 Inca de Oro Chile
129 I2 İnce Burnu pt Turkey
126 G2 İnce Burun pt Turkey
199 K5 İnceler Turkey
147 C8 Inch Kerry Ireland
147 J7 Inch Wexford Ireland
146 H7 Inchbare Angus, Scotland U.K.
81 F9 Inchbonnie South I. N.Z.
122 G3 Incheh Iran
173 K4 Inchenhofen Ger.
147 F6 Incheville France
147 D9 Inchigeelagh Ireland
210 C3 Inch'īnī Terara mt. Eth.
146 H11 Inchinnan Renfrewshire, Scotland U.K.
204 B5 Inchiri admin. reg. Maur.
147 H2 Inch Island Ireland
149 K1 Inchkeith i. Scotland U.K.
101 E10 Inch'ŏn S. Korea
213 G3 Inchope Moz.
207 F2 I-n-Choumaguene well Mali
146 J10 Inchture Perth and Kinross, Scotland U.K.
183 M3 Incinillas Spain
Incio Spain see A Cruz do Incio
128 D2 Incirli Adana Turkey
Incirli Sakarya Turkey see Karasu
213 G3 Incomati r. Moz.
165 G7 Incourt Belgium
192 C4 Incudine, Monte mt. France
138 G5 Inčukalns Latvia
146 H4 Indaal, Loch b. Scotland U.K.
205 E4 I-n-Dagouber well Mali
257 E3 Indaiá r. Brazil
256 A3 Indaiá Grande r. Brazil
256 D5 Indaiatuba Brazil
141 N5 Indalsälven r. Sweden
141 H6 Indalstø Norway
244 G6 Indaparapeo Mex.
116 G7 Indargarh Madh. Prad. India
116 F7 Indargarh Rajasthan India
96 B3 Indaw Sagaing Myanmar
96 C4 Indaw Shan Myanmar
96 C2 Indawgyi, Lake Myanmar
242 G5 Indé Mex.
Indefatigable Island Islas Galápagos Ecuador see Santa Cruz, Isla
207 F3 I-n-Délimane well Mali
240 N5 Independence CA U.S.A.
236 J4 Independence IA U.S.A.
237 H7 Independence KS U.S.A.
232 E6 Independence KY U.S.A.
226 E3 Independence MN U.S.A.
236 H6 Independence MO U.S.A.
232 D12 Independence VA U.S.A.
226 C5 Independence WI U.S.A.
221 P1 Independence Fjord inlet Greenland
238 F6 Independence Mountains NV U.S.A.
252 D4 Independencia Bol.
254 E3 Independência Brazil
244 E5 Independencia Mex.
197 P6 Independența Călărași Romania
197 Q7 Independența Constanța Romania
197 P5 Independența Galați Romania
107 R3 Inder Nei Mongol China
120 D3 Inder, Ozero salt l. Kazakh.
210 B3 Inderacha Eth.
120 D3 Inderborskiy Kazakh.
114 E4 Indi Karnataka India
113 H6 India country Asia
226 H3 Indian r. MI U.S.A.
232 F8 Indiana PA U.S.A.
230 D5 Indiana state U.S.A.
265 L8 Indian-Antarctic Ridge sea feature Southern Ocean
230 D6 Indianapolis IN U.S.A.
222 G3 Indian Cabins Alta Can.
Indian Desert India/Pak. see Thar Desert
232 B11 Indian Fields KY U.S.A.
225 J2 Indian Harbour Nfld and Lab. Can.
223 K5 Indian Head Sask. Can.
233 K5 Indian Lake NY U.S.A.
226 H4 Indian Lake l. MI U.S.A.
233 K5 Indian Lake l. NY U.S.A.
232 B8 Indian Lake l. OH U.S.A.
232 G8 Indian Lake l. PA U.S.A.
235 J2 Indian Neck CT U.S.A.
213 □G5 Indian Ocean OCEAN
236 I5 Indianola IA U.S.A.
237 J9 Indianola MS U.S.A.
256 D3 Indianópolis Brazil
241 S3 Indian Peak UT U.S.A.
226 J4 Indian River MI U.S.A.
241 Q5 Indian Springs NV U.S.A.
241 V6 Indian Wells AZ U.S.A.
256 B2 Indiara Brazil
254 F4 Indiaroba Brazil
210 C2 Indibir Eth.
247 □1 Indiera Alta Puerto Rico
134 J2 Indiga Rus. Fed.
131 P2 Indigirka r. Rus. Fed.
134 J2 Indigskaya Guba b. Rus. Fed.
196 I5 Inđija Vojvodina Serbia
96 B3 Indin Myanmar
222 H1 Indin Lake N.W.T. Can.
242 □R12 Indio r. Nic.
241 P8 Indio CA U.S.A.
261 G6 Indio Rico Arg.
116 G9 Indira Priyadarshini Pench National Park India
77 G3 Indispensable Reefs Solomon Is
78 □6 Indispensable Strait Solomon Is
90 C3 Indo-China reg. Asia
137 O8 Indol r. Ukr.
139 U1 Indomanka r. Rus. Fed.
90 D7 Indonesia country Asia
116 E8 Indore Madh. Prad. India
94 E5 Indragiri r. Indon.
95 H8 Indramayu Jawa Indon.
95 H8 Indramayu, Tanjung pt Indon.
94 D6 Indrapura Sumatera Indon.
Indrapura, Gunung vol. Indon. see Kerinci, Gunung
94 D6 Indrapura, Tanjung pt Indon.
115 G3 Indravati r. India
159 O8 Indre dept France
162 E1 Indre r. France
159 M7 Indre-et-Loire dept France
140 U1 Indre Kiberg Norway
142 C1 Indre Samlen b. Norway
82 D2 Indulkana S.A. Austr.
209 C8 Indungo Angola
Indur Andhra Prad. India see Nizamabad
138 G8 Indura Belarus
114 F4 Indurti Andhra Prad. India
123 L10 Indus r. China/Pak. alt. Shiquan He (China)
123 L9 Indus, Mouths of the Pak.
265 I3 Indus Cone sea feature Indian Ocean
215 L7 Indwe S. Africa
215 L8 Indwe r. S. Africa
197 P8 Indzhe Voyvoda Bulg.
104 B4 Ine Japan
215 G5 In Ebeggi well Alg.
126 F3 İnebolu Turkey
207 E5 I-n-Échaï well Mali
199 K2 İnegöl Turkey
205 G4 In Ekker Alg.
150 B8 Ineris vol. Flores Indon.
261 G4 Ines Indart Arg.
197 J4 Ineu Arad Romania
177 L4 Ineu Bihor Romania
Inevi Turkey see Cihanbeyli
232 C11 Inez KY U.S.A.
204 C3 Inezgane Morocco
205 H5 In Ezzane well Alg.
214 E10 Infanta, Cape S. Africa
250 C3 Infantas Col.
Infantes Spain see Villanueva de los Infantes
245 M9 Inferior, Laguna lag. Mex.
253 E2 Infernão, Cachoeira waterfall Brazil
258 C2 Infielés, Punta pt Chile
244 F7 Infiernillo, Presa resr Mex.
183 J2 Infiesto Spain
193 O8 Infreschi, Punta degli pt Italy
96 E4 Ing, Nam Mae r. Thai.
209 D6 Inga Dem. Rep. Congo
141 R6 Ingå Fin.
134 F2 Inga Rus. Fed.
96 B6 Ingabu Myanmar
207 G2 Ingal Niger
84 D6 Ingallanna watercourse N.T. Austr.
240 L2 Ingalls CA U.S.A.
223 J2 Ingalls Lake N.W.T. Can.
208 D5 Inganda Dem. Rep. Congo
151 M4 Ingatestone Essex, England U.K.
172 H3 Ingelfingen Ger.
172 E2 Ingelheim am Rhein Ger.
165 D7 Ingelmunster Belgium
142 H3 Ingelstad Sweden
208 C5 Ingende Dem. Rep. Congo
260 D4 Ingeniero Balloffet Arg.
258 E1 Ingeniero Guillermo Nueva Juárez Arg.
260 D6 Ingeniero Huergo Arg.
259 C6 Ingeniero Jacobacci Arg.
260 E4 Ingeniero Luiggi Arg.
261 H4 Ingeniero Maschwitz Arg.
261 H4 Ingeniero Otamendi Arg.
222 E3 Ingenika r. B.C. Can.
216 □3f Ingenio Gran Canaria Canary Is
252 B3 Ingenio r. Peru
224 D5 Ingersoll Ont. Can.
210 B2 Ingessana Hills Sudan
106 H2 Ingettolgoy Mongolia
Ingezi Zimbabwe see Ngezi
93 F3 Inggelang i. Maluku Indon.
85 K5 Ingham Qld Austr.
205 F4 In Ghar Alg.
120 L8 Ingichka Uzbek.
183 O3 Inglares r. Spain
149 M5 Ingleborough hill England U.K.
221 K2 Inglefield Land reg. Greenland
149 N4 Ingleton Durham, England U.K.
149 M5 Ingleton North Yorkshire, England U.K.
149 L6 Inglewhite Lancashire, England U.K.
83 M3 Inglewood Qld Austr.
83 I7 Inglewood Vic. Austr.
80 H6 Inglewood North I. N.Z.
240 N8 Inglewood CA U.S.A.
149 L4 Inglewood Forest England U.K.
84 F2 Inglis Island N.T. Austr.
107 N1 Ingoda r. Rus. Fed.
96 C2 Ingoka Pum mt. Myanmar
172 G2 Ingoldingen Ger.
149 R7 Ingoldmells Lincolnshire, England U.K.
221 Q1 Ingolf Fjord inlet Greenland
173 K4 Ingolstadt Ger.
82 B3 Ingomar S.A. Austr.
238 K3 Ingomar MT U.S.A.
225 I4 Ingonish N.S. Can.
117 L7 Ingraj Bazar W. Bengal India
146 M12 Ingram Northumberland, England U.K.
232 F12 Ingram VA U.S.A.
226 D4 Ingram WI U.S.A.
159 J7 Ingrandes Pays de la Loire France
159 M8 Ingrandes Poitou-Charentes France
222 G1 Ingray Lake N.W.T. Can.
252 E5 Ingre Bol.
156 C8 Ingré France
263 F2 Ingrid Christensen Coast Antarctica
205 G6 I-n-Guezzam Alg.
158 E6 Inguiniel France
207 F3 I-n-Guita well Mali
Ingul r. Ukr. see Inhul
Ingulets Ukr. see Inhulets'
140 L4 Ingulsvatn Norway
Ingushetia aut. rep. Rus. Fed. see Ingushetiya, Respublika
129 G3 Ingushetiya, Respublika aut. rep. Rus. Fed.
215 Q3 Ingwavuma S. Africa
Ingwavuma r. Swaziland see Ngwavuma
209 E8 Ingwe Zambia
157 N6 Ingwiller France
215 Q1 Inhaca Moz.
213 G5 Inhaca, Peninsula pen. Moz.
215 Q1 Inhaca e dos Portugueses, Ilhas da nature res. Moz.
213 G4 Inhafenga Moz.
213 G4 Inhambane Moz.
213 G4 Inhambane prov. Moz.
254 F4 Inhambupe Brazil
213 G3 Inhaminga Moz.
213 G3 Inhamitanga Moz.
257 F3 Inhapim Brazil
213 G4 Inharrime Moz.
213 G4 Inhassoro Moz.
254 D5 Inhaúmas Brazil
205 F5 I-n-Hihaou, Adrar hills Alg.
199 L2 İnhisar Turkey
137 K6 Inhul r. Ukr.
137 M6 Inhulets' Ukr.
137 L7 Inhulets' r. Ukr.
256 C2 Inhumas Brazil
93 B8 Inielika vol. Flores Indon.
185 P2 Iniesta Spain
257 E3 Inimutaba Brazil
138 E1 Iniö Fin.
250 E4 Inírida r. Col.
Inis Ireland see Ennis
Inis Córthaidh Ireland see Enniscorthy
147 B5 Inishark i. Ireland
147 B5 Inishbofin i. Ireland
147 F2 Inishbofin i. Ireland
147 C6 Inisheer i. Ireland
147 B4 Inishkea North i. Ireland
147 B4 Inishkea South i. Ireland
147 C6 Inishmaan i. Ireland
147 C6 Inishmore i. Ireland
147 E4 Inishmurray i. Ireland
147 H2 Inishowen pen. Ireland
147 I2 Inishowen Head Ireland
147 H2 Inishtrahull i. Ireland
147 H2 Inishtrahull Sound sea chan. Ireland
147 B5 Inishturk i. Ireland
107 P4 Injgan Sum Nei Mongol China
210 C2 Injibara Eth.
85 I8 Injune Qld Austr.
120 K5 Inkardar'ya Kazakh.
151 I3 Inkberrow Worcestershire, England U.K.
176 G5 Inke Hungary
206 D2 I-n-Kerchef well Mali
85 H4 Inkerman Qld Austr.
137 M9 Inkerman Ukr.
222 C3 Inklin B.C. Can.
222 C3 Inklin r. B.C. Can.
123 I3 Inkylap Turkm.
81 H9 Inland Kaikoura Range mts South I. N.Z.
Inland Sea Japan see Seto-naikai
233 K5 Inlet NY U.S.A.
206 E2 I-n-Milach well Mali
222 H4 Inn r. Europe
121 L2 Innaanganeq c. Greenland
103 I13 Innai Japan
82 H2 Innamincka S.A. Austr.
82 H2 Innamincka Regional Reserve nature res. S.A. Austr.
140 M3 Inndyr Norway
146 G11 Innellan Argyll and Bute, Scotland U.K.
178 A5 Innerbraz Austria
217 □2a Inner Islands Seychelles
146 J11 Innerleithen Scottish Borders, Scotland U.K.
Inner Mongolia aut. reg. China see Nei Mongol Zizhiqu
173 O4 Innernzell Ger.
Inner Port Shelter b. H.K. China see Sai Kung Hoi
146 E8 Inner Sound sea chan. Scotland U.K.
190 E2 Innertkirchen Switz.
178 F6 Innervillgraten Austria
82 F6 Innes National Park S.A. Austr.
140 M3 Innhavet Norway
195 □ In-Nieżfa, Ras pt Malta
173 K5 Inning am Ammersee Ger.
85 K4 Innisfail Qld Austr.
222 H4 Innisfail Alta Can.
147 E9 Innishannon Ireland
147 I4 Inniskeen Ireland
100 F4 Innokent'yevka Rus. Fed.
103 K12 Innoshima Japan
178 D5 Innsbruck Austria
178 D5 Innsbruck airport Austria
224 E1 Innuksuak r. Que. Can.
179 H3 Innviertel reg. Austria
147 G5 Inny r. Ireland
147 B9 Inny r. Ireland
104 B9 Ino Japan
93 D3 Inobonto Sulawesi Indon.
256 B3 Inocência Brazil
104 E2 Inokuchi Japan
208 C5 Inongo Dem. Rep. Congo
209 B6 Inoni Congo
250 C5 Inonias Peru
199 L3 İnönü Turkey
250 D1 Inosu Col.
Inoucdjouac Que. Can. see Inukjuak
206 E2 I-n-Ouchef well Mali
205 F5 I-n-Ouzzal, Oued watercourse Alg.
173 H3 Inovec mt. Slovakia
175 I4 Inowłódz Pol.
175 H3 Inowrocław Pol.
129 E2 Inozemtsevo Rus. Fed.
252 D4 Inquisivi Bol.
190 C1 Ins Switz.
205 F4 In Salah Alg.
135 I5 Insar Rus. Fed.
146 K8 Insch Aberdeenshire, Scotland U.K.
87 B8 Inscription, Cape W.A. Austr.
96 C6 Insein Myanmar
170 J3 Insel Usedom park Ger.
171 K3 Inski Park Krajobrazowy Pol.
174 D2 Ińsko Pol.
174 D2 Ińsko, Jezioro l. Pol.
157 M6 Insming France
173 J5 In Sokki, Oued watercourse Alg.
205 F3 Insterburg Rus. Fed. see Chernyakhovsk
129 H5 İnstitut Azer.
138 E7 Instruch r. Rus. Fed.
197 P6 Însurăţei Romania
244 G6 Insurgente José María Morelos y Pavón, Parque Nacional nat. park Mex.
213 E3 Insuza r. Zimbabwe
134 M2 Inta Rus. Fed.
207 G2 I-n-Tabakat well Niger
206 E2 I-n-Tadéra well Niger
207 H2 I-n-Tadrof well Niger
205 G4 In Takoufi, Oued watercourse Alg.
207 F2 I-n-Talak well Mali
206 E2 I-n-Tassit well Mali
207 F2 I-n-Tebezas Mali
207 F2 I-n-Tefiniti well Mali
207 F2 I-n-Téguift well Mali
207 F3 I-n-Tékélit well Mali
207 F3 I-n-Tekoret well Mali
207 F2 I-n-Telli well Mali
207 F2 I-n-Témeguí well Mali
261 F4 Intendente Alvear Arg.
199 H2 İntepe Turkey
Interamna Italy see Teramo
190 D2 Interlaken Switz.
226 A1 International Falls MN U.S.A.
236 E1 International Peace Garden tourist site Can./U.S.A.
113 M6 Interview Island Andaman & Nicobar Is India
124 D8 Intich'o Eth.
206 E3 I-n-Tillit Mali
197 O5 Întorsura Buzăului Romania
207 F2 I-n-Touft well Mali
237 H11 Intracoastal Waterway canal TX U.S.A.
190 G4 Introbio Italy
134 H2 Intsy Rus. Fed.
213 F3 Intundhla Zimbabwe
250 C5 Intutu Peru
105 M4 Inubō-zaki pt Japan
103 I13 Inukai Japan
224 E1 Inukjuak Que. Can.
259 C9 Inútil, Bahía b. Chile
220 E3 Inuvik N.W.T. Can.
252 B2 Inuya r. Peru
104 E5 Inuyama Japan
134 L4 In'va r. Rus. Fed.
147 F3 Inver Ireland
146 E7 Inveralligin Highland, Scotland U.K.
146 M7 Inverallochy Aberdeenshire, Scotland U.K.
147 D6 Inveran Ireland
146 F10 Inveraray Argyll and Bute, Scotland U.K.
146 K9 Inverarity Angus, Scotland U.K.
146 G10 Inverarnan Argyll and Bute, Scotland U.K.
147 F3 Inver Bay Ireland
146 L9 Inverbervie Aberdeenshire, Scotland U.K.
81 C13 Invercargill South I. N.Z.
146 G7 Invercassley Highland, Scotland U.K.
146 G11 Inverclyde admin. div. Scotland U.K.
83 M3 Inverell N.S.W. Austr.
146 I9 Inverey Aberdeenshire, Scotland U.K.
146 G8 Invergarry Highland, Scotland U.K.
146 H7 Invergordon Highland, Scotland U.K.
146 F10 Inverinan Argyll and Bute, Scotland U.K.
146 K9 Inverkeilor Angus, Scotland U.K.
146 J10 Inverkeithing Fife, Scotland U.K.
146 F6 Inverkirkaig Highland, Scotland U.K.
146 F7 Inverlael Highland, Scotland U.K.
85 H5 Inverleigh Qld Austr.
223 K5 Invermay Sask. Can.
146 G8 Invermoriston Highland, Scotland U.K.
225 I4 Inverness N.S. Can.
146 H8 Inverness Highland, Scotland U.K.
240 J3 Inverness CA U.S.A.
231 F11 Inverness FL U.S.A.
146 F10 Invernoaden Argyll and Bute, Scotland U.K.
146 G10 Inversnaid Stirling, Scotland U.K.
146 L8 Inverurie Aberdeenshire, Scotland U.K.
84 B4 Inverway N.T. Austr.
97 C8 Investigator Channel Myanmar
82 E5 Investigator Group is S.A. Austr.
265 K5 Investigator Ridge sea feature Indian Ocean
82 F6 Investigator Strait S.A. Austr.
115 M7 Invisible Bank sea feature Andaman & Nicobar Is India
232 G9 Inwood WV U.S.A.
215 M7 Inxu r. S. Africa
110 H1 Inya Rus. Fed.
Inyanga Zimbabwe see Nyanga
213 G3 Inyanga Mountains Zimbabwe
Inyanga National Park Zimbabwe see Nyanga National Park
213 G3 Inyangani mt. Zimbabwe
Inyati Zimbabwe see Nyathi
Inyazura Zimbabwe see Nyazura
240 O6 Inyokern CA U.S.A.
240 N4 Inyo Mountains CA U.S.A.
211 B6 Inyonga Tanz.
135 I5 Inza Rus. Fed.
105 L4 Inzai Japan
173 N6 Inzell Ger.
120 L4 Inzer Rus. Fed.
134 L5 Inzer r. Rus. Fed.
135 H5 Inzhavino Rus. Fed.
178 D5 Inzing Austria
158 E6 Inzinzac-Lochrist France
198 B3 Ioannina Greece
191 O3 Iôf di Montasio mt. Italy
103 □2 Iō-jima i. Kazan-rettō Japan
102 □H16 Iō-jima i. Japan
134 G2 Iokanga r. Rus. Fed.
237 H7 Iola KS U.S.A.
234 B2 Iola PA U.S.A.
226 E5 Iola WI U.S.A.
Iolotan' Turkm. see Yolöten
209 B9 Iona Angola
225 I4 Iona N.S. Can.
146 D10 Iona i. Scotland U.K.
209 B9 Iona, Parque Nacional do nat. park Angola
146 D10 Iona, Sound of sea chan. Scotland U.K.
146 D10 Iona Abbey tourist site Scotland U.K.
240 O3 Ione NV U.S.A.
238 F2 Ione WA U.S.A.
197 M6 Ionești Romania
226 I7 Ionia MI U.S.A.
198 A3 Ionia Nisia is Greece
Ionian Islands Greece see Ionia Nisia
198 A5 Ionian Sea Greece/Italy
Ionio prov. Italy see Taranto
105 L2 Iono Japan
131 P4 Iony, Ostrov i. Rus. Fed.
Iordan Uzbek. see Yordon
129 H4 Iori r. Georgia
199 G6 Ios i. Greece
Iō-shima i. Japan see Iō-jima
102 □F19 Iō-Tori-jima i. Nansei-shotō Japan
206 A2 Iouik Maur.
198 F5 Ioulis Kea Greece
236 J5 Iowa r. IA U.S.A.
236 I4 Iowa state U.S.A.
236 J5 Iowa City IA U.S.A.
236 I4 Iowa Falls IA U.S.A.
104 E2 Iō-zan hill Japan
136 I1 Ipa r. Belarus
244 B5 Ipala Guat.
211 B7 Ipala Tanz.
256 E2 Ipameri Brazil
256 C2 Ipameri Brazil
257 G3 Ipanema Brazil
254 F4 Ipanema r. Brazil
252 B2 Iparia Peru
257 F3 Ipatinga Brazil
135 H7 Ipatovo Rus. Fed.
255 C5 Ipaucu Brazil
226 D9 Ipava IL U.S.A.
198 B3 Ipeiros admin. reg. Greece
129 E6 İpek Geçidi pass Turkey
177 I4 Ipel' r. Slovakia
215 N3 Ipelegeng S. Africa
177 H4 Ipeľská pahorkatina mts Slovakia
173 I2 Iphofen Ger.
256 C3 Ipiaçu Brazil
250 B4 Ipiales Col.
255 F5 Ipiaú Brazil
254 F5 Ipirá Brazil
250 D5 Ipiranga Amazonas Brazil
251 F6 Ipiranga Amazonas Brazil
256 B6 Ipiranga Paraná Brazil
Ipiros admin. reg. Greece see Ipeiros
78 □4a Ipis i. Chuuk Micronesia
252 B1 Ipixuna Brazil
252 B1 Ipixuna r. Brazil
251 F6 Ipixuna r. Brazil
95 D2 Ipoh Malaysia
211 B6 Ipole Tanz.
177 H4 Ipoly r. Hungary
215 J5 Ipopeng S. Africa
256 B2 Iporá Brazil
256 C6 Iporanga Brazil
194 G10 Ippari r. Sicilia Italy
173 I2 Ippesheim Ger.
150 F7 Ipplepen Devon, England U.K.
208 D3 Ippy C.A.R.
199 H2 Ipsala Turkey
168 H4 Ipsheim Ger.
149 N7 Ipstones Staffordshire, England U.K.
85 N9 Ipswich Qld Austr.
246 □ Ipswich Jamaica
151 O3 Ipswich Suffolk, England U.K.
236 F3 Ipswich SD U.S.A.

Ipu to Jackson, Cape

327

254 E3 Ipu Brazil
256 C4 Ipuã Brazil
254 E3 Ipueiras Brazil
94 D6 Ipuh Sumatera Indon.
256 D5 Ipuiúna Brazil
254 E4 Ipupiara Brazil
139 O9 Iput' r. Rus. Fed.
137 K1 Iputs' r. Belarus
221 L3 Iqaluit Nunavut Can.
106 D8 Iqe Qinghai China
111 L7 Iqe He r. China
253 F3 Iquê r. Brazil
252 C5 Iquique Chile
Iquiri r. Brazil see Ituxi
250 C5 Iquitos Peru
208 D3 Ira Banda C.A.R.
102 □C22 Irabu-jima i. Nansei-shotō Japan
251 H3 Iracoubo Fr. Guiana
123 I8 Irafshān Iran
123 J8 Īrafshān reg. Iran
104 F6 Irago-misaki pt Japan
104 E6 Irago-suidō str. Japan
255 B8 Irai Brazil
85 M1 Irai Island P.N.G.
198 E1 Irakleia Greece
199 G6 Irakleia i. Greece
198 G7 Irakleio Kriti Greece
198 G7 Irakleiou, Kolpos b. Kriti Greece
Iráklia i. Greece see Irakleia
Iraklion Kriti Greece see Irakleio
261 G4 Irala Arg.
253 G6 Irala Para.
254 E5 Iramaia Brazil
122 F6 Iran country Asia
95 K4 Iran, Pegunungan mts Indon.
129 I6 Īrānābād Iran
114 G8 Iranamadu Tank resr Sri Lanka
156 G8 Irancy France
122 B3 Īrānshāh Iran
122 I8 Īrānshahr Iran
251 F2 Irapa Venez.
244 F5 Irapuato Mex.
127 K7 Iraq country Asia
205 G4 Irarrarene reg. Alg.
233 M4 Irasville VT U.S.A.
251 H5 Iratapuru r. Brazil
256 B6 Irati Brazil
183 R3 Irati r. Spain
177 K5 Iratoșu Romania
134 K2 Irayel' Rus. Fed.
242 □R13 Irazú, Volcán vol. Costa Rica
138 F4 Irbe r. Latvia
Irbes šaurums sea chan. Estonia/Latvia see Irbe Strait
138 F4 Irbe Strait Estonia/Latvia
Irbe väin sea chan. Estonia/Latvia see Irbe Strait
128 D6 Irbid Jordan
Irbil Iraq see Arbīl
130 H4 Irbit Rus. Fed.
151 K3 Irchester Northamptonshire, England U.K.
179 J4 Irdning Austria
137 K4 Irdyn' Ukr.
208 C5 Irebu Dem. Rep. Congo
254 E4 Irecê Brazil
177 H5 Iregszemcse Hungary
183 P4 Iregua r. Spain
208 C5 Ireko Dem. Rep. Congo
147 G5 Ireland country Europe
235 G1 Ireland Corners NY U.S.A.
231 □1 Ireland Island Bermuda
147 J6 Ireland's Eye i. Ireland
134 L4 Iren' r. Rus. Fed.
261 G6 Irene Arg.
81 B12 Irene, Mount South I. N.Z.
251 G4 Ireng r. Guyana/Venez.
256 A6 Iretama Brazil
129 F1 Irgakly Rus. Fed.
129 F4 Irganch'ai Georgia
199 K4 Irgıllı Turkey
120 I3 Irgiz Kazakh.
120 J3 Irgiz r. Kazakh.
192 D7 Irgoli Sardegna Italy
205 G3 Irharrhar, Oued watercourse Illizi/Tamanrasset Alg.
205 G5 Irharrhar, Oued watercourse Illizi/Tamanrasset Alg.
204 C3 Irherm Morocco
204 D3 Irhil M'Goun mt. Morocco
Iri S. Korea see Iksan
Irian, Teluk b. Papua Indon. see Cenderawasih, Teluk
Irian Barat prov. Indon. see Papua
Irian Jaya prov. Indon. see Papua
91 I7 Irian Jaya reg. Indon.
202 D6 Iriba Chad
251 G4 Iricoumé, Serra hills Brazil
122 B2 Īrī Dāgh mt. Iran
196 H5 Irig Vojvodina Serbia
92 D5 Iriga Luzon Phil.
160 F5 Irigny France
120 H2 Iriklinskiy Rus. Fed.
120 H2 Iriklinskoye Vodokhranilishche resr Rus. Fed.
211 B6 Iringa Tanz.
211 B7 Iringa admin. reg. Tanz.
114 E7 Irinjalakuda Kerala India
102 □A22 Iriomote-jima i. Nansei-shotō Japan
102 □A22 Iriomote Kokuritsu-kōen nat. park Nansei-shotō Japan
251 H5 Iriri r. Brazil
254 B4 Iriri Novo r. Brazil
145 E5 Irish Sea Ireland/U.K.
163 B9 Irissarry France
254 D2 Irituia Brazil
125 I2 'Irj well Saudi Arabia
Irkeshtam Kyrg. see Erkech-Tam
137 S8 Irkliyevskaya Rus. Fed.
137 L4 Irkliyiv Ukr.
98 H1 Irkutsk Rus. Fed.
98 H1 Irkutskaya Oblast' admin. div. Rus. Fed.
Irkutsk Oblast admin. div. Rus. Fed. see Irkutskaya Oblast'
173 N4 Irlbach Ger.
223 I4 Irma Alta Can.
226 E4 Irma WI U.S.A.
126 F4 Irmak Turkey
264 G2 Irminger Basin sea feature N. Atlantic Ocean
194 H10 Irminio r. Sicilia Italy
231 G8 Irmo SC U.S.A.
140 T4 Irnijärvi l. Fin.
208 C2 Iro, Lac l. Chad
158 H5 Irodouër France
158 B5 Iroise, Mer d' g. France
82 F5 Iron Baron S.A. Austr.
78 □6 Iron Bottom Sound sea chan. Solomon Is
227 K3 Iron Bridge Ont. Can.
150 H2 Ironbridge Telford and Wrekin, England U.K.
232 H5 Irondequoit NY U.S.A.
226 B2 Iron Junction MN U.S.A.
82 F5 Iron Knob S.A. Austr.
226 F4 Iron Mountain MI U.S.A.
241 S4 Iron Mountain mt. UT U.S.A.
147 F4 Iron Mountains hills Ireland
85 I2 Iron Range National Park Qld Austr.
226 F3 Iron River MI U.S.A.
226 C3 Iron River WI U.S.A.
237 J7 Ironton MO U.S.A.
232 C10 Ironton OH U.S.A.
226 D3 Ironwood MI U.S.A.
241 U9 Ironwood Forest National Monument nat. park AZ U.S.A.
233 J4 Iroquois Ont. Can.
226 G8 Iroquois r. IN U.S.A.
224 D3 Iroquois Falls Ont. Can.
92 E5 Irosin Luzon Phil.
105 I6 Irō-zaki pt Japan
Irpen' Ukr. see Irpin'
136 J3 Irpin' Ukr.
136 J3 Irpin' r. Ukr.
125 H9 Īrqah Yemen
195 □ Irqieqa, Ras i- pt Malta
195 □ Ir-Raħeb, Ras pt Malta
84 F6 Irramarne Aboriginal Land res. N.T. Austr.
195 □ Ir-Ramla b. Gozo Malta
96 B6 Irrawaddy admin. div. Myanmar
96 B7 Irrawaddy r. Myanmar
96 B7 Irrawaddy, Mouths of the Myanmar
172 A2 Irrel Ger.
172 B2 Irsch Ger.
178 H6 Irschen Austria
173 L6 Irschenberg Ger.
173 J6 Irsee Ger.
136 I3 Irsha r. Ukr.
123 P3 Irshad Pass Afgh./Pak.
136 H3 Irshans'k Ukr.
136 C5 Irshava Ukr.
193 Q6 Irsina Italy
143 M2 Irsta Sweden
134 J3 Irta Rus. Fed.
149 L4 Irthing r. England U.K.
151 K3 Irthlingborough Northamptonshire, England U.K.
121 M1 Irtysh r. Kazakh./Rus. Fed.
121 P1 Irtyshsk Kazakh.
Irtyshskoye Kazakh. see Irtyshsk
183 O7 Irueste Spain
105 J4 Iruma Japan
105 K4 Iruma-gawa r. Japan
208 F4 Irumu Dem. Rep. Congo
186 B1 Irun Spain
Iruña Spain see Pamplona
252 D4 Irupana Bol.
186 B1 Irurita Spain
183 R3 Irurozqui Spain
183 Q3 Irurtzun Spain
Irurzun Spain see Irurtzun
146 G11 Irvine North Ayrshire, Scotland U.K.
240 O8 Irvine CA U.S.A.
232 B11 Irvine KY U.S.A.
85 J4 Irvinebank Qld Austr.
146 G11 Irvine Bay Scotland U.K.
262 T2 Irvine Glacier Antarctica
147 G4 Irvinestown Northern Ireland U.K.
237 G9 Irving TX U.S.A.
87 C10 Irwin r. W.A. Austr.
231 F9 Irwinton GA U.S.A.
171 D6 Irxleben Ger.
207 G3 Isa Nigeria
124 F8 'Īsá, Ra's pt Yemen
85 L7 Isaac r. Qld Austr.
222 F4 Isaac Lake B.C. Can.
186 D2 Isaba Spain
236 E3 Isabel SD U.S.A.
92 D6 Isabela Negros Phil.
92 C8 Isabela Phil.
247 □1 Isabela Puerto Rico
246 H4 Isabela, Cabo c. Dom. Rep.
250 □ Isabela, Isla i. Islas Galápagos Ecuador
244 B4 Isabela, Isla i. Mex.
242 □Q11 Isabelia, Cordillera mts Nic.
226 C2 Isabella MN U.S.A.
86 I6 Isabella, Lake salt flat W.A. Austr.
226 J6 Isabella Indian Reservation res. MI U.S.A.
240 N6 Isabella Lake CA U.S.A.
226 G2 Isabelle, Point MI U.S.A.
247 □1 Isabel Segunda Puerto Rico
186 F3 Isábena r. Spain
199 K5 İsabey Turkey
129 E7 İsabey Dağı mt. Turkey
158 G6 Isac r. France
197 Q5 Isaccea Romania
130 J2 Isachenko, Ostrov i. Rus. Fed.
221 H2 Isachsen, Cape Nunavut Can.
140 □B1 Ísafjarðardjúp est. Iceland
140 □B1 Ísafjörður Iceland
116 F7 Isagarh Madh. Prad. India
103 H14 Isahaya Japan
123 K8 Isai Kalat Pak.
208 C5 Isaka Dem. Rep. Congo
123 N5 Isa Khel Pak.
134 H2 Isakogorka Rus. Fed.
139 Q1 Isakovo Leningradskaya Oblast' Rus. Fed.
139 R6 Isakovo Smolenskaya Oblast' Rus. Fed.
192 D7 Isalle r. Italy
197 L6 Ișalnița Romania
213 □J4 Isalo, Massif de l' mts Madag.
213 □J4 Isalo, Parc National de l' nat. park Madag.
250 D4 Isana r. Col.
208 D5 Isanga Dem. Rep. Congo
211 A7 Isangano National Park Zambia
207 G4 Isanlu Nigeria
205 G4 Isaouane-n-Tifernine des. Alg.
173 N4 Isar r. Ger.
191 K3 Isarco r. Italy
92 D5 Isarog, Mount Phil.
177 I4 Isaszeg Hungary
105 I4 Isawa Japan
156 D2 Isbergues France
146 □N1 Isbister Shetland, Scotland U.K.
146 □O2 Isbister Shetland, Scotland U.K.
Isca Newport, Wales U.K. see Caerleon
183 K6 Íscar Spain
252 D5 Iscayachi Bol.
199 L4 İscehisar Turkey
157 K7 Isches France
178 B5 Ischgl Austria
193 L6 Ischia Italy
193 L6 Ischia, Isola d' i. Italy
260 C2 Ischigualasto, Parque Provincial nat. park Arg.
193 P4 Ischitella Italy
86 H4 Isdell r. W.A. Austr.
156 D8 Isdes France
104 E7 Ise Japan
142 H6 Isefjord b. Denmark
105 J5 Isehara Japan
211 B6 Iseke Tanz.
178 G6 Isel r. Austria
178 G6 Iseltal val. Austria
173 M5 Isen Ger.
173 N5 Isen r. Ger.
157 J7 Is-en-Bassigny France
134 K4 Isenbayevo Rus. Fed.
169 K6 Isenbüttel Ger.
208 E4 Isengi Dem. Rep. Congo
102 □F19 Isen-zaki hd Nansei-shotō Japan
190 I4 Iseo Italy
190 I4 Iseo, Lago d' l. Italy
161 K6 Iseran, Col de l' pass France
161 H6 Isère dept France
161 F7 Isère r. France
251 H3 Isère, Pointe pt Fr. Guiana
169 E8 Iserlohn Ger.
169 I6 Isernhagen Ger.
193 M4 Isernia Italy
193 M4 Isernia prov. Italy
105 J3 Isesaki Japan
104 E7 Ise-shima Kokuritsu-kōen nat. park Japan
104 E6 Ise-wan b. Japan
207 F5 Iseyin Nigeria
Isfahan Iran see Eşfahān
121 M8 Isfana Kyrg.
Isfandaqeh Iran see Sangū'īyeh
123 N1 Isfara Tajik.
140 □ Isfjorden inlet Svalbard
140 □ Isfjord Radio Svalbard
129 G2 Ishcherskaya Rus. Fed.
134 L3 Isherim, Gora mt. Rus. Fed.
251 G4 Isherton Guyana
135 J5 Isheyevka Rus. Fed.
105 K3 Ishibashi Japan
104 D5 Ishibe Japan
102 S7 Ishidoriya Japan
102 □B22 Ishigaki Nansei-shotō Japan
102 □B22 Ishigaki-jima i. Nansei-shotō Japan
105 K3 Ishige Japan
102 S3 Ishikari Japan
102 S3 Ishikari-gawa r. Japan
102 R3 Ishikari-wan b. Japan
105 L1 Ishikawa Fukushima Japan
102 □1 Ishikawa Okinawa Japan
104 D3 Ishikawa pref. Japan
121 N1 Ishim r. Kazakh./Rus. Fed.
130 H4 Ishim Rus. Fed.
104 A8 I-shima i. Japan
120 G1 Ishimbay Rus. Fed.
102 S8 Ishinomaki Japan
105 L3 Ishioka Japan
103 K13 Ishizuchi-san mt. Japan
123 N3 Ishkoshim Tajik.
116 D1 Ishkuman Jammu and Kashmir
139 W4 Ishnya Rus. Fed.
226 G3 Ishpeming MI U.S.A.
Ishtikhon Uzbek. see Ishtixon
121 L8 Ishtixon Uzbek.
123 N3 Ishtragh Afgh.
117 L7 Ishurdi Bangl.
252 D3 Isiboro r. Bol.
252 D4 Isiboro Sécure, Parque Nacional nat. park Bol.
159 I4 Isigny-le-Buat France
159 I3 Isigny-sur-Mer France
199 L4 Işıklar Turkey
199 K4 Işıklı Turkey
199 K4 Işıklı Barajı resr Turkey
192 C8 Isili Sardegna Italy
130 I4 Isil'kul' Rus. Fed.
211 B6 Isimbira Tanz.
250 B5 Isinliví Ecuador
210 C4 Isiolo Kenya
215 O5 Isipingo S. Africa
208 E4 Isiro Dem. Rep. Congo
85 J8 Isisford Qld Austr.
140 □ Isispynten pt Svalbard
179 J8 Iška r. Slovenia
123 L3 Iskabad Canal Afgh.
123 N3 Iskan Afgh.
134 K2 Iskateley Rus. Fed.
İskele Cyprus see Trikomon
126 H5 İskenderun Turkey
126 G5 İskenderun Körfezi b. Turkey
126 G3 İskilip Turkey
Iski-Naukat Kyrg. see Eski-Nookat
120 E4 Iskine Kazakh.
120 E4 Iskininskiy Kazakh.
130 J4 Iskitim Rus. Fed.
139 W7 Iskra Rus. Fed.
137 M5 Iskrivka Kirovohrads'ka Oblast' Ukr.
137 O4 Iskrivka Poltavs'ka Oblast' Ukr.
197 M7 Iskŭr r. Bulg.
197 L8 Iskŭr, Yazovir resr Bulg.
210 F2 Iskushuban Somalia
222 D3 Iskut r. B.C. Can.
245 L7 Isla Mex.
146 J9 Isla r. Angus/Perth and Kinross, Scotland U.K.
258 C2 Isla, Salar de la salt flat Chile
261 I2 Isla Cabellos Uru.
184 E6 Isla Canela Spain
184 E6 Isla Cristina Spain
250 C2 Isla de Salamanca, Parque Nacional nat. park Col.
85 L8 Isla Gorge National Park Qld Austr.
126 H5 İslahiye Turkey
129 B5 İslâhiye Turkey
Islamabad Jammu and Kashmir see Anantnag
123 O5 Islamabad Pak.
259 B7 Isla Magdalena, Parque Nacional nat. park Chile
184 G6 Isla Mayor marsh Spain
184 G6 Isla Menor marsh Spain
123 N8 Islamgarh Pak.
123 N9 Islamkot Pak.
231 G13 Islamorada FL U.S.A.
117 J7 Islampur Bihar India
222 F2 Island r. N.W.T. Can.
Ísland country Europe see Iceland
92 B7 Island Bay Palawan Phil.
233 □Q2 Island Falls ME U.S.A.
82 F4 Island Lagoon salt flat S.A. Austr.
223 M4 Island Lake Man. Can.
223 M4 Island Lake l. Man. Can.
226 B2 Island Lake l. MN U.S.A.
147 K3 Island Magee pen. Northern Ireland U.K.
238 I4 Island Park ID U.S.A.
233 N4 Island Pond VT U.S.A.
80 I2 Islands, Bay of North I. N.Z.
182 C4 Islas Atlánticas de Galicia, Parque Nacional de las nature res. Spain
242 □Q9 Islas de Bahá, Parque Nacional nat. park Hond.
261 F3 Isla Verde Arg.
146 D11 Islay i. Scotland U.K.
146 D11 Islay, Sound of sea chan. Scotland U.K.
197 M7 Islaz Romania
162 G4 Isle France
162 D6 Isle r. France
151 M3 Isleham Cambridgeshire, England U.K.
150 D1 Isle of Anglesey admin. div. Wales U.K.
148 H5 Isle of Man i. Irish Sea
146 H13 Isle of Whithorn Dumfries and Galloway, Scotland U.K.
151 J6 Isle of Wight admin. div. England U.K.
232 I12 Isle of Wight VA U.S.A.
226 F2 Isle Royale National Park MI U.S.A.
156 H5 Isles-sur-Suippe France
260 B1 Islón Chile
247 □7 Islote Point Trin. and Tob.
252 C4 Isluga, Parque Nacional nat. park Chile
261 I3 Ismael Cortinas Uru.
Ismail Ukr. see Izmayil
Ismâ'ilîya Egypt see Al Ismā'īlīyah
Ismailly Azer. see İsmayıllı
173 L5 Ismaning Ger.
129 J5 İsmayıllı Azer.
129 J5 İsmayıllı Qoruğu nature res. Azer.
123 N2 Ismoili Somoní, Qullai mt. Tajik.
203 G3 Isnā Egypt
182 E9 Isna Port.
194 G8 Isnello Sicilia Italy
173 I6 Isny im Allgäu Ger.
213 □J4 Isoanala Madag.
104 E7 Isobe Japan
105 K5 Isogo Japan
141 P5 Isojoki Fin.
211 B7 Isoka Zambia
140 S3 Isokylä Fin.
140 Q5 Isokyrö Fin.
161 K8 Isola France
161 K8 Isola 2000 France
192 C3 Isolaccio-di-Fiumorbo Corse France
193 L2 Isola del Gran Sasso d'Italia Italy
191 K5 Isola della Scala Italy
194 E7 Isola delle Femmine Sicilia Italy
193 L4 Isola del Liri Italy
195 M6 Isola di Capo Rizzuto Italy
158 D6 Isole r. France
190 F6 Isole del Cantone Italy
186 H3 Isona Spain
191 P4 Isonzo r. Italy
211 A7 Isopa Tanz.
216 □3e Isora El Hierro Canary Is
213 □J4 Isorana Madag.
190 I5 Isorella Italy
140 S4 Iso-Syöte hill Fin.
161 D8 Ispagnac France
Ispahan Iran see Eşfahān
199 L5 Isparta Turkey
199 L5 Isparta prov. Turkey
197 O7 Isperikh Bulg.
194 H10 Ispica Sicilia Italy
194 H10 Ispica r. Sicilia Italy
123 J8 Ispikan Pak.
127 J3 İspir Turkey
Ispisar Tajik. see Khŭjand
123 L7 Isplinji Pak.
163 B9 Ispoure France
190 F4 Ispra Italy
129 C1 Ispravnaya Rus. Fed.
172 F4 Ispringen Ger.
128 C6 Israel country Asia
256 B2 Israelândia Brazil
87 G12 Israelite Bay W.A. Austr.
Isra'īl country Asia see Israel
Issa Croatia see Vis
135 I5 Issa Rus. Fed.
138 L5 Issa r. Rus. Fed.
161 J10 Issambres, Pointe des pt France
207 H5 Issanguele Cameroon
251 G3 Issano Guyana
205 G4 Issaouane, Erg des. Alg.
161 E7 Issarlès France
202 B6 Isséirom Chad
169 B7 Isselburg Ger.
157 N8 Issenheim France
104 F6 Isshiki Japan
206 D5 Issia Côte d'Ivoire
163 F6 Issigeac France
190 D4 Issime Italy
93 C3 Issimu Sulawesi Indon.
127 L8 Issin tourist site Iraq
185 P4 Isso Spain
190 D4 Issogne Italy
160 C5 Issoire France
161 I10 Issole r. France
207 F2 Issouanka well Mali
162 H2 Issoudun France
205 F5 Issoulane Erareine slope Alg.
169 B7 Issum Ger.
211 B6 Issuna Tanz.
160 G1 Is-sur-Tille France
Issyk-Ata Kyrg. see Ysyk-Ata
Issyk-Kul' Kyrg. see Balykchy
Issyk-Kul', Ozero salt l. Kyrg. see Ysyk-Köl
Issyk-Kul Oblast admin. div. Kyrg. see Ysyk-Köl
Issyk-Kul'skaya Oblast' admin. div. Kyrg. see Ysyk-Köl
160 D3 Issy-l'Évêque France
191 R7 Ist Croatia
191 R7 Ist i. Croatia
139 T8 Ista r. Rus. Fed.
124 D3 Işṭabl 'Antar Saudi Arabia
127 K6 Iṣṭablāt tourist site Iraq
123 M5 Īstādeh-ye Moqor, Āb-e l. Afgh.
177 J3 Istállós-kő hill Hungary
185 J7 Istán Spain
199 J1 İstanbul Turkey
199 J1 İstanbul prov. Turkey
199 K1 İstanbul Boğazı str. Turkey
151 M5 Istead Rise Kent, England U.K.
174 G6 Istebna Pol.
177 I2 Istebné Slovakia
176 F5 Isten dombja hill Hungary
122 C5 Īstgāh-e Eznā Iran
258 F3 Isthilart Arg.
198 E4 Istiaia Greece
123 P3 Istik r. Tajik.
129 G6 İstısu Azer.
250 B3 Istmina Col.
137 R2 Istobnoye Rus. Fed.
196 I8 Istok Kosovo Serbia
231 G12 Istokpoga, Lake FL U.S.A.
188 D3 Istra pen. Croatia
139 T6 Istra Rus. Fed.
161 F9 Istres France
Istria pen. Croatia see Istra
197 Q6 Istria Romania
197 O5 Istrița, Dealul hill Romania
163 B9 Isturits France
139 X7 Ist'ya r. Rus. Fed.
186 E3 Isuela r. Aragón Spain
183 R5 Isuela r. Spain
163 B11 Isuerre Spain
105 L5 Isumi Japan
105 L5 Isumi-gawa r. Japan
117 L8 Iswaripur Bangl.
215 O2 Iswepe S. Africa
120 G1 Isyangulovo Rus. Fed.
254 F4 Itabaianinha Brazil
257 G4 Itabapoana Brazil
257 G4 Itabapoana r. Brazil
256 C5 Itaberá Brazil
254 E5 Itaberaba Brazil
256 C2 Itaberaí Brazil
257 F3 Itabira Brazil
257 F4 Itabirito Brazil
251 F6 Itaboca Brazil
257 F5 Itaboraí Brazil
255 F5 Itabuna Brazil
254 C3 Itacaiuna r. Brazil
254 D4 Itacajá Brazil
257 F2 Itacambira Brazil
255 D5 Itacarambi Brazil
254 F5 Itacaré Brazil
253 H1 Itacayunas, Serra hills Brazil
251 G5 Itacoatiara Brazil
250 D6 Itacuaí r. Brazil
253 F6 Itacurubí del Rosario Para.
104 E4 Itadori Japan
254 E5 Itaetê Brazil
211 B6 Itaga Tanz.
Itagmatana Iran see Hamadān
257 H2 Itagmirim Brazil
257 G3 Itaguaçu Brazil
257 F5 Itaguaí Brazil
256 B5 Itaguajé Brazil
257 E4 Itaguara Brazil
252 C3 Itahuania Peru
256 C5 Itaí Brazil
254 E3 Itaim r. Brazil
255 C8 Itaiópolis Brazil
255 B8 Itaipu, Represa de resr Brazil
141 S6 Itäisen Suomenlahden kansallispuisto nat. park Fin.
251 G6 Itaituba Brazil
256 B3 Itajá Brazil
255 C8 Itajaí Brazil
256 C4 Itajobi Brazil
257 E5 Itajubá Brazil
255 F5 Itajuipe Brazil
100 A2 Itaka Rus. Fed.
117 J8 Itaki Jharkhand India
105 M4 Itako Japan
105 K3 Itakura Gunma Japan
105 H1 Itakura Niigata Japan
215 P3 Itala Game Reserve nature res. S. Africa
Italia country Europe see Italy
261 F4 Italó Arg.
188 E5 Italy country Europe
254 G3 Itamaracá, Ilha de i. Brazil
257 H2 Itamaraju Brazil
257 F2 Itamarandiba Brazil
254 D2 Itamataré Brazil
257 G3 Itambacuri Brazil
257 G3 Itambacuri r. Brazil
255 E5 Itambé Brazil
257 F3 Itambé, Pico de mt. Brazil
104 B6 Itami Japan
104 B6 Itami airport Japan
213 □I5 Itampolo Madag.
112 H6 Itanagar Arun. Prad. India
254 D5 Itanguari r. Brazil
256 D6 Itanhaém Brazil
257 E5 Itanhandu Brazil
251 F6 Itanhauã r. Brazil
257 G2 Itanhém Brazil
257 H2 Itanhém r. Brazil
257 G3 Itanhomi Brazil
251 H4 Itany r. Fr. Guiana/Suriname
257 G2 Itaobím Brazil
257 F4 Itaocara Brazil
254 C5 Itapaci Brazil
254 F2 Itapagé Brazil
256 C3 Itapajipe Brazil
251 F6 Itaparaná r. Brazil
254 F4 Itaparica, Represa de resr Brazil
257 H1 Itapebi Brazil
261 I2 Itapebí Uru.
257 E4 Itapecerica Brazil
257 G4 Itapemirim Brazil
257 G4 Itaperuna Brazil
255 E5 Itapetinga Brazil
256 C5 Itapetininga Brazil
256 C5 Itapeva Brazil
255 C9 Itapeva, Lago l. Brazil
251 G5 Itapi r. Brazil
254 E4 Itapicuru Brazil
254 F4 Itapicuru r. Brazil
254 D3 Itapicuru, Serra de hills Brazil
254 D2 Itapicuru Mirim Brazil
254 F4 Itapicuru Mirim r. Brazil
251 F6 Itapinima Brazil
254 F2 Itapipoca Brazil
256 D5 Itapira Brazil
251 G5 Itapiranga Brazil
256 B1 Itapirapuã Brazil
261 I1 Itapitocai Brazil
254 F3 Itapiúna Brazil
256 C4 Itápolis Brazil
254 F3 Itaporanga Paraíba Brazil
256 C5 Itaporanga São Paulo Brazil
255 C9 Itapuã Brazil
255 C5 Itapuranga Brazil
256 D5 Itaquaquecetuba Brazil
255 A9 Itaqui Brazil
257 G3 Itarana Brazil
257 G1 Itarantim Brazil
256 C6 Itararé Brazil
256 C5 Itararé r. Brazil
116 F8 Itarsi Madh. Prad. India
256 B3 Itarumã Brazil
140 T5 Itä-Suomi prov. Fin.
260 A5 Itata r. Chile
253 F7 Itati, Laguna l. Arg.
256 D5 Itatiba Brazil
256 C5 Itatinga Brazil
251 F6 Itatuba Brazil
251 I5 Itatupã Brazil
256 C2 Itauçu Brazil
254 E3 Itaueira r. Brazil
251 E5 Itaúna Amazonas Brazil
257 E4 Itaúna Minas Gerais Brazil
257 H3 Itaúnas Brazil
257 H3 Itaúnas r. Brazil
92 C1 Itbayat i. Phil.
222 E4 Itcha Ilgachuz Provincial Park B.C. Can.
222 H1 Itchen Lake N.W.T. Can.
252 C4 Ite Peru
198 D4 Itea Greece
208 F5 Itebero Dem. Rep. Congo
121 N1 Itemgen, Ozero l. Kazakh.
211 B6 Itende Tanz.
183 L4 Itero de la Vega Spain
211 C7 Itete Tanz.
162 E3 Iteuil France
209 E8 Itezhi-Tezhi Dam Zambia
Ithaca Greece see Ithaki
Ithaca i. Greece see Ithaki
226 J6 Ithaca MI U.S.A.
232 I6 Ithaca NY U.S.A.
198 B4 Ithaki Greece
198 B4 Ithaki i. Greece
198 B4 Ithakis, Steno sea chan. Greece
169 H6 Ith Hils ridge Ger.
128 F7 Ithrah Saudi Arabia
211 B6 Itigi Tanz.
221 M3 Itilleq Greenland
208 D4 Itimbiri r. Dem. Rep. Congo
257 G2 Itinga Brazil
255 B6 Itiquira Brazil
253 F4 Itiquira r. Brazil
256 D5 Itirapina Brazil
256 D4 Itirapuã Brazil
254 F4 Itiúba Brazil
254 F4 Itiúba, Serra de hills Brazil
258 E1 Itiyura r. Arg.
117 J7 Itkhari Jharkhand India
120 E3 Itmurinkol', Ozero l. Kazakh.
105 J6 Itō Japan
213 I2 Itoculo Moz.
105 G1 Itoigawa Japan
208 D5 Itoko Dem. Rep. Congo
102 □1 Itoman Okinawa Japan
156 B5 Iton r. France
213 □J4 Itongafeno mt. Madag.
Iton-Qälla Rus. Fed. see Itum-Kale
104 E5 Itonuki Japan
185 L7 Itrabo Spain
193 L5 Itri Italy
217 □3a Itsandzéni Njazidja Comoros
217 □3a Itsikoudi Njazidja Comoros
103 H14 Itsuki Japan
103 J12 Itsukushima i. Japan
205 G2 Ittel, Oued watercourse Alg.
192 B6 Ittireddu Sardegna Italy
192 B6 Ittiri Sardegna Italy
221 P2 Ittoqqortoormiit Greenland
165 F7 Ittre Belgium
256 D5 Itu Brazil
207 G5 Itu Nigeria
90 D4 Itu Abu Island S. China Sea
254 E5 Ituaçu Brazil
254 F5 Ituberá Brazil
252 C1 Itucumã r. Brazil
182 G8 Ituero de Azaba Spain
250 D6 Ituí r. Brazil
256 C3 Ituiutaba Brazil
209 E5 Itula Dem. Rep. Congo
211 B6 Itumba Tanz.
256 C3 Itumbiara Brazil
256 C3 Itumbiara, Barragem resr Brazil
129 G3 Itum-Kale Rus. Fed.
211 B7 Itungi Port Malawi
251 G3 Ituni Guyana
254 C3 Itupiranga Brazil
256 B3 Iturama Brazil
253 F6 Iturbe Para.
243 O8 Iturbide Campeche Mex.
245 H1 Iturbide Nuevo León Mex.
208 E4 Ituri r. Dem. Rep. Congo
99 Q3 Iturup, Ostrov i. Kuril'skiye O-va Rus. Fed.
257 E4 Itutinga Brazil
256 D4 Ituverava Brazil
252 D1 Ituxi r. Brazil
258 F2 Ituzaingo Arg.
Ityopia country Africa see Ethiopia
169 K11 Itz r. Ger.
168 I3 Itzehoe Ger.
168 J3 Itzstedt Ger.
250 D4 Iuaretê Brazil
194 H8 Iudica, Monte hill Sicilia Italy
237 K8 Iuka MS U.S.A.
131 T3 Iul'tin Rus. Fed.
213 H2 Iuluti Moz.
257 G4 Iúna Brazil
250 D4 Iutica Brazil
256 B6 Ivaí Brazil
256 A5 Ivaí r. Brazil
256 B6 Ivaiporã Brazil
213 □J4 Ivakoany mt. Madag.
140 S2 Ivalo Fin.
140 S2 Ivalojoki r. Fin.
176 F4 Iván Hungary
175 L6 Ivana Franka Ukr.
136 E1 Ivanava Belarus
176 F2 Ivančice Czech Rep.
188 F2 Ivanec Croatia
138 L2 Ivangorod Rus. Fed.
Ivangrad Montenegro see Berane
83 J5 Ivanhoe N.S.W. Austr.
86 J3 Ivanhoe W.A. Austr.
224 D3 Ivanhoe r. Ont. Can.
240 M5 Ivanhoe CA U.S.A.
236 G3 Ivanhoe MN U.S.A.
232 E12 Ivanhoe VA U.S.A.
223 J2 Ivanhoe Lake N.W.T. Can.
227 L1 Ivanhoe Lake Ont. Can.
188 F3 Ivanić-Grad Croatia
137 O2 Ivanino Rus. Fed.
139 X6 Ivanishchi Rus. Fed.
137 Q3 Ivanivka Kharkivs'ka Oblast' Ukr.
137 L7 Ivanivka Khersons'ka Oblast' Ukr.
137 N7 Ivanivka Khersons'ka Oblast' Ukr.
137 K4 Ivanivka Kyivs'ka Oblast' Ukr.
137 R5 Ivanivka Luhans'ka Oblast' Ukr.
136 J7 Ivanivka Odes'ka Oblast' Ukr.
137 M8 Ivanivka Respublika Krym Ukr.
177 L3 Ivanivka Zakarpats'ka Oblast' Ukr.
136 G5 Ivanivtsi Ukr.
196 I7 Ivanjica Serbia
176 G3 Ivanka pri Dunaji Slovakia
136 I3 Ivankiv Ukr.
188 G3 Ivankovo Croatia
139 U7 Ivan'kovo Rus. Fed.
139 X5 Ivan'kovskiy Rus. Fed.
139 T5 Ivan'kovskoye Vodokhranilishche resr Rus. Fed.
100 I4 Ivankovtsy Rus. Fed.
136 D5 Ivano-Frankivs'k Ukr.
136 D5 Ivano-Frankivs'ka Oblast' admin. div. Ukr.
Ivano-Frankivs'k Oblast admin. div. Ukr. see Ivano-Frankivs'ka Oblast'
136 C4 Ivano-Frankove Ukr.
Ivano-Frankovsk Ukr. see Ivano-Frankivs'k
Ivano-Frankovskaya Oblast' admin. div. Ukr. see Ivano-Frankivs'ka Oblast'
Ivano-Frankovsk Oblast admin. div. Ukr. see Ivano-Frankivs'ka Oblast'
136 H4 Ivanopil' Ukr.
137 O3 Ivano-Shyychyne Ukr.
Ivanovka Kazakh. see Kokzhayyk
100 E3 Ivanovka Amurskaya Oblast' Rus. Fed.
120 E1 Ivanovka Orenburgskaya Oblast' Rus. Fed.
Ivanovo Belarus see Ivanava
197 N7 Ivanovo tourist site Bulg.
139 X5 Ivanovo Ivanovskaya Oblast' Rus. Fed.
139 N5 Ivanovo Pskovskaya Oblast' Rus. Fed.
139 U3 Ivanovo Tverskaya Oblast' Rus. Fed.
Ivanovo Oblast admin. div. Rus. Fed. see Ivanovskaya Oblast'
137 R8 Ivanovskaya Rus. Fed.
139 Y4 Ivanovskaya Oblast' admin. div. Rus. Fed.
121 T2 Ivanovskiy Khrebet mts Kazakh.
137 N2 Ivanovskoye Kurskaya Oblast' Rus. Fed.
139 T8 Ivanovskoye Orlovskaya Oblast' Rus. Fed.
139 W5 Ivanovskoye Yaroslavskaya Oblast' Rus. Fed.
241 Q6 Ivanpah Lake CA U.S.A.
188 E2 Ivanšćica mts Croatia
179 O8 Ivanska Croatia
197 P7 Ivanski Bulg.
120 C1 Ivanteyevka Rus. Fed.
Ivantsevichi Belarus see Ivatsevichy
136 D3 Ivanychi Ukr.
137 L3 Ivanytsya Ukr.
213 □J4 Ivato Madag.
138 I9 Ivatsevichy Belarus
197 O9 Ivaylovgrad Bulg.
197 N9 Ivaylovgrad, Yazovir resr Bulg.
134 M3 Ivdel' Rus. Fed.
217 □3a Ivembeni Njazidja Comoros
151 K4 Iver Buckinghamshire, England U.K.
147 C9 Iveragh reg. Ireland
140 □ Iversenfjellet hill Svalbard
197 P5 Ivești Galați Romania
197 P4 Ivești Vaslui Romania
208 B5 Ivindo r. Gabon
151 K4 Ivinghoe Buckinghamshire, England U.K.
255 B7 Ivinheima Brazil
256 A5 Ivinheima r. Brazil
139 R1 Ivinskiy Razliv resr Rus. Fed.
253 H1 Iviti Brazil
221 N3 Ivittuut Greenland
Iviza i. Spain see Eivissa
137 P2 Ivnya Rus. Fed.
213 □J4 Ivohibe Madag.
256 B2 Ivolândia Brazil
252 D2 Ivón Bol.
232 I12 Ivor VA U.S.A.
Ivory Coast country Africa see Côte d'Ivoire
143 K5 Ivösjön l. Sweden
139 R8 Ivot Rus. Fed.
137 M2 Ivot Ukr.
137 M2 Ivotka r. Ukr.
190 D5 Ivrea Italy
199 I3 İvrindi Turkey
129 F3 Ivris Ugheltekhili pass Georgia
129 G4 Ivris Zegani plat. Georgia
156 B6 Ivry-la-Bataille France
156 D6 Ivry-sur-Seine France
Ivugivik Que. Can. see Ivujivik
221 K3 Ivujivik Que. Can.
211 B7 Ivuna Tanz.
220 E3 Ivvavik National Park Y.T. Can.
138 J8 Ivyanyets Belarus
150 E7 Ivybridge Devon, England U.K.
232 D10 Ivydale WV U.S.A.
104 B7 Iwade Japan
151 N5 Iwade Kent, England U.K.
105 K3 Iwafune Japan
105 K3 Iwai Japan
103 I13 Iwai-shima i. Japan
102 S7 Iwaizumi Japan
105 M1 Iwaki Japan
102 R6 Iwaki-san vol. Japan
103 J12 Iwakuni Japan
104 E5 Iwakura Japan
105 L3 Iwama Japan
103 J13 Iwamatsu Japan
102 S3 Iwamizawa Japan
104 F5 Iwamura Japan
105 H3 Iwamurada Japan
95 K4 Iwan r. Indon.
102 R4 Iwanai Japan
211 B7 Iwanda Tanz.
175 J5 Iwaniska Pol.
102 R8 Iwanuma Japan
102 Q6 Iwasaki Japan
105 L3 Iwase Japan
104 F2 Iwasehama Japan
105 I2 Iwasuge-yama vol. Japan
105 G6 Iwata Japan
104 B4 Iwataki Japan
102 S7 Iwate Japan
102 S7 Iwate pref. Japan
102 R7 Iwate-san vol. Japan
105 K4 Iwatsuki Japan
175 I6 Iwkowa Pol.
207 G5 Iwo Nigeria
84 D7 Iwupataka Aboriginal Land res. N.T. Austr.
138 I8 Iwye Belarus
245 L9 Ixaltepec Mex.
245 I7 Ixcamilpa Mex.
245 H7 Ixcateopan Mex.
245 M9 Ixhuatán Mex.
245 I5 Ixhuatlán Veracruz Mex.
245 K6 Ixhuatlán Veracruz Mex.
252 C3 Ixiamas Bol.
245 H5 Ixmiquilpán Mex.
215 O6 Ixopo S. Africa
245 J6 Ixtacamaxtitlán Mex.
243 M9 Ixtacomitán Mex.
244 F8 Ixtapa Guerrero Mex.
244 B5 Ixtapa Jalisco Mex.
244 F8 Ixtapa, Punta pt Mex.
245 H7 Ixtapan de la Sal Mex.
245 H6 Ixtlahuaca Mex.
244 D6 Ixtlahuacán Mex.
244 E5 Ixtlán Michoacán Mex.
244 C4 Ixtlán Nayarit Mex.
245 K8 Ixtlán Oaxaca Mex.
151 N3 Ixworth Suffolk, England U.K.
93 B8 Iya i. Indon.
98 G1 Iya r. Rus. Fed.
203 F6 Iyal Bakhit Sudan
211 B7 Iyayi Tanz.
129 B4 İyidere Turkey
İyirmi Altı Bakı Komissarı Azer. see Uzboy
103 J13 Iyo Japan
103 K13 Iyomishima Japan
103 J13 Iyo-nada b. Japan
197 L3 Iza r. Romania
177 H4 Iža Slovakia
242 □O10 Izabal Guat.
243 O10 Izabal, Lago de l. Guat.
183 R3 Izaga, Peña de mt. Spain
183 N2 Izalde r. Spain
243 O7 Izamal Mex.
243 M10 Izapa tourist site Mex.
102 S4 Izari-dake mt. Japan
183 O3 Izarra Spain
211 B6 Izazi Tanz.
134 H2 Izba Bol'shaya Bab'ya Rus. Fed.
197 M5 Izbășești hill Romania
129 I3 Izberbash Rus. Fed.
175 L5 Izbica Pol.
174 G3 Izbica Kujawska Pol.
183 Q3 Izco, Sierra de mts Spain
139 Q6 Izdeshkovo Rus. Fed.
161 G6 Izeaux France
182 G5 Izeda Port.
165 D7 Izegem Belgium
122 C6 Īzeh Iran
102 □E20 Izena-jima i. Nansei-shotō Japan
160 H4 Izernore France
161 G6 Izeron France
207 H2 Izgagane well Niger
123 O4 Izgal Pak.
134 K4 Izhevsk Rus. Fed.
139 X7 Izhevskoye Rus. Fed.
134 K2 Izhma Respublika Komi Rus. Fed.
Izhma Respublika Komi Rus. Fed. see Sosnogorsk
134 K2 Izhma r. Rus. Fed.
125 M4 Izkī Oman
Izmail Ukr. see Izmayil
139 U9 Izmalkovo Rus. Fed.
136 H8 Izmayil Ukr.
Izmeny, Proliv sea chan. Japan/Rus. Fed. see Notsuke-suidō
199 I4 İzmir Turkey
199 I4 İzmir prov. Turkey
199 H4 İzmir Körfezi g. Turkey
199 K2 İzmit Turkey
199 K2 İzmit Körfezi b. Turkey
180 E5 Izmorene Morocco
185 K6 Iznájar Spain
185 K6 Iznajar, Embalse de resr Spain
185 L6 Iznalloz Spain
199 K2 İznik Turkey
199 K2 İznik Gölü l. Turkey
139 S7 Iznoski Rus. Fed.
137 O2 Iznoskovo Rus. Fed.
161 J7 Izoard, Col d' pass France
Izobil'noye Rus. Fed. see Izobil'nyy
135 H7 Izobil'nyy Rus. Fed.
188 D3 Izola Slovenia
139 T5 Izoplit Rus. Fed.
253 E4 Izozog Bol.
253 E4 Izozog Bajo Bol.
128 E6 Izra' Syria
177 I5 Izsák Hungary
245 I6 Iztaccihuatl, Volcán vol. Mex.
245 I6 Iztaccihuatl-Popocatépetl, Parque Nacional nat. park Mex.
197 N9 Iztochni Rodopi mts Bulg.
245 I7 Izúcar de Matamoros Mex.
105 I6 Izu-hantō pen. Japan
103 G12 Izuhara Japan
104 E4 Izumi Fukui Japan
105 M2 Izumi Fukushima Japan
103 H14 Izumi Kagoshima Japan
105 J5 Izumi Kanagawa Japan
102 R8 Izumi Miyagi Japan
104 B7 Izumi Ōsaka Japan
104 B6 Izumiōtsu Japan
104 B7 Izumisano Japan
105 L1 Izumizaki Japan
103 J11 Izumo Japan
103 P9 Izumozaki Japan
105 I5 Izunagaoka Japan
266 E3 Izu-Ogasawara Trench sea feature N. Pacific Ocean
104 A5 Izushi Japan
105 J7 Izu-shotō is Japan
Izu-tobu vol. Japan see Amagi-san
130 J2 Izvestiy Tsentral'nogo Ispolnitel'nogo Komiteta, Ostrova Rus. Fed.
100 G4 Izvestkovyy Rus. Fed.
197 N6 Izvoarele Giurgiu Romania
197 M6 Izvoarele Olt Romania
197 O5 Izvoarele Prahova Romania
197 N6 Izvoru Romania
136 F3 Izyaslav Ukr.
134 L2 Iz"yayu Rus. Fed.
120 H5 Izyndy Kazakh.
137 Q4 Izyum Ukr.

J

141 S6 Jaala Fin.
138 K2 Jaama Estonia
124 G9 Ja'ar Yemen
140 R3 Jaatila Fin.
122 G4 Jaba watercourse Iran
183 P8 Jabaga Spain
191 R6 Jabalanac Croatia
123 M4 Jabal as Sirāj Afgh.
185 N5 Jabalcón mt. Spain
125 I4 Jabal Dab Saudi Arabia
185 K3 Jabalón r. Spain
187 C7 Jabaloyas Spain
116 G8 Jabalpur Madh. Prad. India
185 L4 Jabalquinto Spain
184 F2 Jabarriega hill Spain
124 E6 Jabbārah Fara Islands Saudi Arabia
165 D6 Jabbeke Belgium
128 F2 Jabbūl Syria
128 F3 Jabbūl, Sabkhat al salt flat Syria
170 G3 Jabel Ger.
84 D2 Jabiluka Aboriginal Land res. N.T. Austr.
125 N4 Jabir reg. Oman
84 D2 Jabiru N.T. Austr.
128 D3 Jablah Syria
191 Q5 Jablanac, Rt pt Croatia
188 F4 Jablanica Bos.-Herz.
197 J7 Jablanica r. Serbia
175 L4 Jabłoń Pol.
176 E1 Jablonec nad Nisou Czech Rep.
176 G3 Jablonica Slovakia
175 H6 Jabłonka Pol.
175 K3 Jabłonka Kościelna Pol.
175 I3 Jabłonna Pol.
175 K3 Jabłonna Lacka Pol.
175 K4 Jabłonna Pierwsza Pol.
176 D1 Jablonné v Podještědí Czech Rep.
175 H2 Jabłonowo Pomorskie Pol.
177 G2 Jablůnka Czech Rep.
177 H2 Jablunkov Czech Rep.
254 G4 Jaboatão Pernambuco Brazil
254 G4 Jaboatão Brazil
256 C4 Jaboticabal Brazil
257 F3 Jaboticatubas Brazil
161 F7 Jabron r. France
184 F5 Jabugo Spain
188 E4 Jabuka i. Croatia
196 I6 Jabuka Vojvodina Serbia
94 F5 Jabung, Tanjung pt Indon.
251 E6 Jaburu Brazil
251 G6 Jabuti Brazil
186 D2 Jaca Spain
245 H4 Jacala Mex.
243 N10 Jacaltenango Guat.
254 B5 Jacaré Mato Grosso Brazil
252 D2 Jacaré Rondônia Brazil
254 E4 Jacaré r. Brazil
251 F6 Jacaré r. Brazil
251 G6 Jacareacanga Brazil
257 D5 Jacareí Brazil
253 F2 Jacaretinga Brazil
256 C5 Jacarézinho Brazil
257 F4 Jaceaba Brazil
260 D2 Jáchal r. Arg.
173 L6 Jachen r. Ger.
173 K6 Jachenau Ger.
176 B1 Jáchymov Czech Rep.
255 B5 Jaciara Brazil
257 G2 Jacinto Brazil
261 F6 Jacinto Arauz Arg.
255 C9 Jacinto Machado Brazil
252 D2 Jaciparaná Brazil
252 D2 Jaciparaná r. Brazil
85 J3 Jack r. Qld Austr.
226 H1 Jackfish Ont. Can.
223 I4 Jackfish Lake Sask. Can.
227 P5 Jack Lake Ont. Can.
237 I9 Jack Lee, Lake resr AR U.S.A.
233 □O3 Jackman ME U.S.A.
232 A12 Jacksboro TN U.S.A.
237 F9 Jacksboro TX U.S.A.
85 L9 Jackson Qld Austr.
231 D10 Jackson AL U.S.A.
240 L3 Jackson CA U.S.A.
231 F9 Jackson GA U.S.A.
232 B11 Jackson KY U.S.A.
226 J7 Jackson MI U.S.A.
236 H4 Jackson MN U.S.A.
237 K7 Jackson MO U.S.A.
237 J9 Jackson MS U.S.A.
231 I7 Jackson NC U.S.A.
232 C9 Jackson OH U.S.A.
237 K8 Jackson TN U.S.A.
226 F6 Jackson WI U.S.A.
238 I5 Jackson WY U.S.A.
81 I7 Jackson, Cape South I. N.Z.

328
Jackson, Mount to Jiexiu

262 T2 Jackson, Mount Antarctica
81 C10 Jackson Bay South I. N.Z.
81 C10 Jackson Bay b. South I. N.Z.
81 C10 Jackson Head South I. N.Z.
Jackson Island Zemlya Frantsa-Iosifa Rus. Fed. see Dzheksona, Ostrov
238 I5 Jackson Lake WY U.S.A.
226 G5 Jacksonport WI U.S.A.
81 F9 Jacksons South I. N.Z.
225 J3 Jackson's Arm Nfld and Lab. Can.
231 E9 Jacksonville AL U.S.A.
237 I8 Jacksonville AR U.S.A.
231 G10 Jacksonville FL U.S.A.
236 J6 Jacksonville IL U.S.A.
234 B5 Jacksonville MD U.S.A.
231 I8 Jacksonville NC U.S.A.
232 C9 Jacksonville OH U.S.A.
237 H10 Jacksonville TX U.S.A.
231 G10 Jacksonville Beach FL U.S.A.
246 G4 Jacmel Haiti
93 E8 Jaco i. East Timor
123 M7 Jacobabad Pak.
254 E4 Jacobina Brazil
241 T5 Jacob Lake AZ U.S.A.
215 I5 Jacobsdal S. Africa
226 A2 Jacobson MN U.S.A.
81 D10 Jacobs River South I. N.Z.
234 B6 Jacobsville MD U.S.A.
234 B5 Jacobus PA U.S.A.
244 E6 Jacona Mex.
225 H3 Jacques-Cartier, Détroit de sea chan. Que. Can.
225 H3 Jacques Cartier, Mont mt. Que. Can.
Jacques Cartier Passage Que. Can. see Jacques-Cartier, Détroit de
225 H4 Jacquet River N.B. Can.
256 A3 Jacuba r. Brazil
256 D4 Jacuí Brazil
255 C9 Jacuí r. Brazil
254 F5 Jacuípe r. Brazil
250 D4 Jacumã r. Brazil
254 C3 Jacunda Brazil
251 I5 Jacundá r. Brazil
257 G3 Jacupemba Brazil
256 D6 Jacupiranga Brazil
250 D2 Jacura Venez.
188 G3 Jadar r. Bos.-Herz.
196 H6 Jadar r. Serbia
114 F4 Jadcherla Andhra Prad. India
114 H4 Jaddangi Andhra Prad. India
123 J9 Jaddi, Ras pt Pak.
168 F4 Jade r. Ger.
168 F3 Jade sea chan. Ger.
168 F4 Jadebusen b. Ger.
124 E6 Jadhdhānah Saudi Arabia
125 K7 Jādib Yemen
221 N3 J. A. D. Jensen Nunatakker nunataks Greenland
Jadotville Dem. Rep. Congo see Likasi
188 E3 Jadova r. Croatia
188 F3 Jadovnik mt. Bos.-Herz.
175 J3 Jadów Pol.
183 O7 Jadraque Spain
250 B6 Jaén Peru
92 C4 Jaen Luzon Phil.
185 L5 Jaén Spain
185 M4 Jaén prov. Spain
142 B3 Jæren reg. Norway
116 C9 Jafarabad Gujarat India
122 C2 Ja'farābād Ardabīl Iran
122 H3 Ja'farābād Khorāsān Iran
122 C4 Ja'farābād Qazvīn Iran
122 G5 Ja'fārn Iran
Jaffa Israel see Tel Aviv-Yafo
82 G7 Jaffa, Cape S.A. Austr.
114 F8 Jaffna Sri Lanka
233 M6 Jaffrey NH U.S.A.
128 E8 Jafr, Qā' al imp. l. Jordan
116 F4 Jagadhri Haryana India
138 I2 Jägala r. Estonia
114 E5 Jagalur Karnataka India
117 K9 Jagatsinghpur Orissa India
123 M4 Jagdalak Afgh.
114 H3 Jagdalpur Chhattisgarh India
107 S1 Jagdaqi Nei Mongol China
111 E13 Jagdishpur Uttar Prad. India
117 J7 Jagdispur Bihar India
179 M6 Jagerberg Austria
215 J5 Jagersfontein S. Africa
111 D10 Jaggang Xizang China
114 G4 Jaggayyapeta Andhra Prad. India
122 G8 Jaghīn Iran
122 H9 Jagīn watercourse Iran
122 H9 Jagīn, Ra's pt Iran
214 E5 Jagkolk Vloer salt pan S. Africa
196 J7 Jagodina Serbia
175 J2 Jagodne, Jezioro l. Pol.
174 D4 Jagodzin Pol.
Jagok Tso salt l. China see Urru Co
Jagsamka Sichuan China see Luding
172 G3 Jagst r. Ger.
172 G3 Jagsthausen Ger.
173 I3 Jagstzell Ger.
114 F3 Jagtial Andhra Prad. India
256 B5 Jaguapitã Brazil
258 G4 Jaguarão r. Brazil/Uru.
258 G4 Jaguarão Uru.
254 E4 Jaguarari Brazil
254 F3 Jaguaretama Brazil
255 B9 Jaguari Brazil
256 C6 Jaguariaíva Brazil
254 F3 Jaguaribe Brazil
254 F5 Jaguaripe Brazil
254 F3 Jaguaruana Brazil
258 C3 Jagüe Arg.
246 C2 Jagüey Grande Cuba
125 H2 Jahām, 'Irq des. Saudi Arabia
Jahanabad Bihar India see Jehanabad
122 C3 Jahān Dāgh mt. Iran
128 E9 Jahdānīyah, Wādī al watercourse Jordan
84 C1 Jahleel, Point N.T. Austr.
127 L9 Jahmah well Iraq
171 H8 Jahna r. Ger.
171 J5 Jahnsfelde Ger.
122 E7 Jahrom Iran
207 H3 Jahun Nigeria
122 H8 Jāhyad Iran
254 E3 Jaicós Brazil
114 C4 Jaigarh Mahar. India
93 E3 Jailolo Halmahera Indon.
93 F4 Jailolo, Selat sea chan. Maluku Indon.
Jailolo Gilolo i. Maluku Indon. see Halmahera
252 C4 Jaiña Chile
106 H9 Jainca Qinghai China
117 I6 Jainpur Uttar Prad. India
117 N7 Jaintiapur Bangl.
Jainzhug Xizang China see Gutang
116 E6 Jaipur Rajasthan India
116 H6 Jais Uttar Prad. India
116 C6 Jaisalmer Rajasthan India
116 E7 Jaisamand Lake India
116 H8 Jaisinghnagar Madh. Prad. India
116 E6 Jaitaran Rajasthan India
116 G9 Jaitgarh hill Mahar. India
116 G7 Jaitpur Uttar Prad. India
116 I5 Jajarkot Nepal
188 F3 Jajce Bos.-Herz.
Jajnagar state India see Orissa
117 K9 Jajpur Orissa India
176 F4 Ják Hungary
177 I5 Jakabszállás Hungary
117 M6 Jakar Bhutan
94 G8 Jakarta Jawa Indon.
222 C2 Jakes Corner Y.T. Can.
116 B8 Jakhan Gujarat India
202 D2 Jakharrah Libya
123 L6 Jakin mt. Afgh.
212 C3 Jakkalsberg Namibia
123 I8 Jakkī Kowr Iran
140 N3 Jäkkvik Sweden
116 E5 Jakliat Haryana India
Jako i. East Timor see Jaco
Jakobshavn Greenland see Ilulissat
140 Q5 Jakobstad Fin.
179 M8 Jakovlje Croatia
207 G5 Jakpa Nigeria
175 I3 Jaktorów Pol.
177 J2 Jakubany Slovakia
176 F3 Jakubov Slovakia
196 J9 Jakupica mts Macedonia
237 D9 Jal NM U.S.A.
244 C4 Jala Mex.
245 J6 Jalacingo Mex.
Jalaid Nei Mongol China see Inder
124 G3 Jalājil Saudi Arabia
123 N4 Jalālābād Afgh.
116 E4 Jalalabad Punjab India
116 F5 Jalalabad Uttar Prad. India
116 G6 Jalalabad Uttar Prad. India
121 O7 Jalal-Abad Kyrg.
121 O7 Jalal-Abad admin. div. Kyrg.
Jalal-Abad Oblast admin. div. Kyrg. see Jalal-Abad
203 F2 Jalālah al Baḩrīyah, Jabal plat. Egypt
116 D9 Jalalpur Gujarat India
117 I6 Jalalpur Uttar Prad. India
203 H2 Jalāmid, Ḥazm al ridge Saudi Arabia
125 N4 Ja'lān, Jabal mts Oman
187 C9 Jalance Spain
116 E4 Jalandhar Punjab India
94 □ Jalan Kayu Sing.
243 O10 Jalapa Guat.
243 M9 Jalapa Mex.
245 K6 Jalapa Mex.
242 □P11 Jalapa Nic.
245 K7 Jalapa de Díaz Mex.
245 L9 Jalapa del Marqués Mex.
123 P5 Jalapur Pak.
123 N7 Jalapur Pirwala Pak.
140 Q5 Jalasjärvi Fin.
116 G6 Jalaun Uttar Prad. India
127 L6 Jalawlā' Iraq
84 E3 Jalboi r. N.T. Austr.
244 B4 Jalcocotán Mex.
245 K6 Jalcomulco Mex.
123 L6 Jaldak Afgh.
117 L7 Jaldhaka r. Bangl.
114 E4 Jaldrug Karnataka India
256 B4 Jales Brazil
116 G6 Jalesar Uttar Prad. India
117 K9 Jaleshwar Orissa India
Jaleshwar Nepal see Jaleswar
117 J6 Jaleswar Nepal
116 E9 Jalgaon Mahar. India
165 I7 Jalhay Belgium
127 M8 Jalībah Iraq
160 D4 Jaligny-sur-Besbre France
207 H4 Jalingo Nigeria
244 C4 Jalisco Mex.
244 C6 Jalisco state Mex.
123 O4 Jalkot Pak.
122 G8 Jallābī Iran
159 J7 Jallais France
114 D3 Jalna Mahar. India
123 J8 Jālo Iran
78 □3b Jaloklab i. Majuro Marshall Is
187 E10 Jalón Spain
183 R5 Jalón r. Spain
183 P4 Jalón de Cameros Spain
116 D7 Jalore Rajasthan India
244 E4 Jalostotitlán Mex.
196 H6 Jalovik Serbia
175 L2 Jałówka Pol.
244 F5 Jalpa Guanajuato Mex.
244 D4 Jalpa Zacatecas Mex.
117 L6 Jalpaiguri W. Bengal India
245 H4 Jalpan Mex.
123 M4 Jalrez Afgh.
245 M8 Jaltepec r. Mex.
245 M8 Jaltipan Mex.
245 I4 Jaltocán Mex.
202 D2 Jālū Libya
202 D2 Jālū, Wāḩāt oasis Libya
Jalūlā Iraq see Jalawlā'
122 I4 Jām r. Iran
122 I4 Jām reg. Iran
250 A5 Jama Ecuador
210 D4 Jamaame Somalia
246 F3 Jamaica Cuba
246 □ Jamaica country West Indies
235 H3 Jamaica Bay NY U.S.A.
246 F4 Jamaica Channel Haiti/Jamaica
138 F3 Jämaja Estonia
123 L9 Jama Jamot Pak.
117 L7 Jamalpur Bangl.
117 K7 Jamalpur Bihar India
247 □9 Jamanota hill Aruba
251 G6 Jamanxim r. Brazil
245 K6 Jamapa r. Mex.
252 E2 Jamari Brazil
207 H4 Jamari Nigeria
110 F4 Jamati Xinjiang China
209 C8 Jamba Angola
94 E5 Jambi Sumatera Indon.
94 E5 Jambi prov. Indon.
215 O1 Jambila S. Africa
85 M8 Jambin Qld Austr.
116 D6 Jambo Rajasthan India
94 B2 Jamboaye r. Indon.
95 L1 Jambongan i. Malaysia
95 L5 Jambu Kalimantan Indon.
94 B2 Jambuair, Tanjung pt Indon.
116 D8 Jambusar Gujarat India
114 F3 Jamekunte Andhra Prad. India
170 D4 Jameln Ger.
84 F6 James watercourse N.T. Austr.
237 I7 James r. MO U.S.A.
236 G4 James r. ND/SD U.S.A.
232 I11 James r. VA U.S.A.
259 B7 James, Isla i. Chile
123 M9 Jamesabad Pak.
224 D2 James Bay Can.
235 G4 Jamesburg NJ U.S.A.
246 E1 James Cistern Eleuthera Bahamas
261 F3 James Craik Arg.
140 □ James I Land reg. Svalbard
James Island Islas Galápagos Ecuador see San Salvador, Isla
221 P2 Jameson Land reg. Greenland
87 I8 Jameson Range hills W.A. Austr.
81 C12 James Peak South I. N.Z.
84 D8 James Ranges mts N.T. Austr.
262 U2 James Ross Island Antarctica
221 I3 James Ross Strait Nunavut Can.
82 G5 Jamestown S.A. Austr.
Jamestown Ont. Can. see Wawa
147 H6 Jamestown Ireland
215 K7 Jamestown S. Africa
216 □2b Jamestown St Helena
240 L4 Jamestown CA U.S.A.
230 E7 Jamestown KY U.S.A.
236 F2 Jamestown ND U.S.A.
232 F6 Jamestown NY U.S.A.
232 B9 Jamestown OH U.S.A.
232 E7 Jamestown PA U.S.A.
231 E7 Jamestown TN U.S.A.
157 J5 Jametz France
175 H2 Jamielnik Pol.
141 Q6 Jämijärvi Fin.
185 L5 Jamilena Spain
245 J9 Jamiltepec Mex.
234 E4 Jamison PA U.S.A.
143 L5 Jämjö Sweden
114 D4 Jamkhandi Karnataka India
114 D3 Jamkhed Mahar. India
125 M4 Jammah Oman
114 F5 Jammalamadugu Andhra Prad. India
142 F4 Jammerbugten b. Denmark
116 E3 Jammu Jammu and Kashmir India
116 F2 Jammu and Kashmir terr. Asia
116 C8 Jamnagar Gujarat India
116 E9 Jamner Mahar. India
116 G7 Jamni r. India
143 M7 Jamno, Jezioro lag. Pol.
165 H9 Jamoigne Belgium
94 G8 Jampang Kulon Jawa Indon.
123 N7 Jampur Pak.
141 R6 Jämsä Fin.
203 G3 Jamsah Egypt
141 R6 Jämsänkoski Fin.
117 K8 Jamshedpur Jharkhand India
110 E6 Jamtai Xinjiang China
117 K8 Jamtara Jharkhand India
207 H5 Jamtari Nigeria
140 L5 Jämtland county Sweden
117 K7 Jamui Bihar India
95 L3 Jamuk, Gunung mt. Indon.
196 J5 Jamu Mare Romania
117 L7 Jamuna r. Bangl. alt. Dihang (India), alt. Yarlung Zangbo (China), conv. Brahmaputra
117 N6 Jamuna r. India
182 I4 Jamuz r. Spain
125 J2 Janā i. Saudi Arabia
210 E4 Janaale Somalia
128 E7 Janāb, Wādī al watercourse Jordan
141 R6 Janakkala Fin.
116 H8 Janakpur Chhattisgarh India
117 J6 Janakpur Nepal
257 F1 Janaúba Brazil
251 I4 Janaucú, Ilha i. Brazil
177 L3 Jánd Hungary
123 O5 Jand Pak.
256 B2 Jandaia Brazil
256 B5 Jandaia do Sul Brazil
122 F4 Jandaq Iran
129 G4 Jandari Georgia
173 P4 Jandelsbrunn Ger.
216 □3b Jandía hill Fuerteventura Canary Is
216 □3b Jandía, Península de pen. Fuerteventura Canary Is
216 □3b Jandía, Punta de pt Fuerteventura Canary Is
116 E4 Jandiala Punjab India
123 P6 Jandiala Pak.
216 □3b Jandía Playa Fuerteventura Canary Is
250 D5 Jandiatuba r. Brazil
123 N5 Jandola Pak.
208 D4 Jandongi Dem. Rep. Congo
85 M9 Jandowae Qld Austr.
185 K4 Jándula r. Spain
185 L4 Jándula, Embalse del resr Spain
185 M5 Jandulilla r. Spain
254 D5 Janeiro r. Brazil
240 L1 Janesville CA U.S.A.
226 E7 Janesville WI U.S.A.
94 F5 Jang, Tanjung pt Indon.
122 H4 Jangal Iran
213 G5 Jangamo Moz.
114 F4 Jangaon Andhra Prad. India
111 J11 Jangco Xizang China
Jangeldi Uzbek. see Jongeldi
116 G4 Jangi Hima. Prad. India
117 L7 Jangipur W. Bengal India
Jangnga Turkm. see Jaňňa
111 H10 Jangngai Ri mts Xizang China
111 H10 Jangngai Zangbo r. Xizang China
253 G5 Jango Brazil
121 N7 Jangy-Bazar Kyrg.
121 O7 Jangy-Jol Kyrg.
122 B2 Jānī Beyglū Iran
171 H6 Jänickendorf Ger.
123 N5 Jani Khel Pak.
174 G3 Janikowo Pol.
256 A6 Janiópolis Brazil
188 G3 Janja Bos.-Herz.
188 G3 Janja r. Bos.-Herz.
196 J8 Janjevo Kosovo Serbia
140 S3 Jänkälä Fin.
215 I3 Jan Kempdorp S. Africa
177 L4 Jánkmajtis Hungary
196 I7 Jankov Kamen mt. Serbia
175 H3 Janków Pol.
174 F3 Jankowo Dolne Pol.
132 C2 Jan Mayen i. Arctic Ocean
138 I4 Jānmuiža Latvia
122 E1 Jaňňa Turkm.
127 M7 Jannah Iraq
122 D4 Jannatābād Iran
182 G8 Jañona mt. Spain
242 E2 Janos Mex.
177 I5 Jánoshalma Hungary
176 G4 Jánosháza Hungary
176 G4 Jánossomorja Hungary
173 O3 Janovice nad Úhlavou Czech Rep.
175 L2 Janów Podlaskie Pol.
175 H5 Janów Śląskie Pol.
175 J4 Janowiec Pol.
175 I2 Janowiec Kościelny Pol.
174 F3 Janowiec Wielkopolski Pol.
175 K5 Janów Lubelski Pol.
175 I2 Janowo Pol.
175 L3 Janów Podlaski Pol.
223 I4 Jans Bay Sask. Can.
171 K7 Jänschwalde Ger.
214 I8 Jansenville S. Africa
251 I5 Jânua Coeli Brazil
255 D5 Januária Brazil
124 G1 Janūbī, Al Fulayj al watercourse Saudi Arabia
216 □3c Janubio, Laguna de l. Lanzarote Canary Is
128 B9 Janūb Sīnā' governorate Egypt
156 C7 Janville France
114 E3 Janwada Karnataka India
123 J9 Janzar mt. Pak.
158 I6 Janzé France
202 B1 Janzūr Libya
123 J8 Jaodar Pak.
116 E8 Jaora Madh. Prad. India
102 K12 Japan country Asia
101 H9 Japan, Sea of N. Pacific Ocean
Japan Alps National Park Japan see Chūbu-Sangaku Kokuritsu-kōen
266 E3 Japan Basin sea feature Sea of Japan
266 E3 Japan Trench sea feature N. Pacific Ocean
129 H4 Jap'aridze Georgia
242 □P10 Japón Hond.
168 F1 Japsand i. Ger.
251 E5 Japurá r. Caquetá Brazil
117 O7 Japvo Mount Nagaland India
242 □T14 Jaqué Panama
183 Q6 Jaraba Spain
246 H4 Jarabacoa Dom. Rep.
128 G2 Jarābulus Syria
174 F4 Jaraczewo Pol.
124 E6 Jarad Saudi Arabia
187 C9 Jarafuel Spain
256 C1 Jaraguá Brazil
255 C8 Jaraguá do Sul Brazil
255 B7 Jaraguari Brazil
182 I9 Jaraicejo Spain
182 I8 Jaraiz de la Vera Spain
244 F4 Jaral de Berrios Mex.
244 F5 Jaral del Progreso Mex.
117 O5 Jaram Arun. Prad. India
183 N8 Jarama r. Spain
259 D7 Jaramillo Arg.
182 I8 Jarandilla de la Vera Spain
128 D6 Jarash Jordan
251 H5 Jarauçu r. Brazil
143 M1 Järbo Sweden
Jarboesville MD U.S.A. see Lexington Park
175 L5 Jarczów Pol.
254 F3 Jardim Ceará Brazil
253 F5 Jardim Mato Grosso do Sul Brazil
185 O3 Jardín r. Spain
85 I1 Jardine River National Park Qld Austr.
246 D3 Jardines de la Reina, Archipiélago de los is Cuba
256 C3 Jardinésia Brazil
256 D4 Jardinópolis Brazil
162 A3 Jard-sur-Mer France
Jares r. Spain see Xares
143 N3 Järflotta naturreservat nature res. Sweden
106 G3 Jargalant Arhangay Mongolia
106 F3 Jargalant Bayanhongor Mongolia
106 B3 Jargalant Bayan-Ölgiy Mongolia
107 N3 Jargalant Dornod Mongolia
106 E4 Jargalant Govĭ-Altay Mongolia
Jargalant Hovd Mongolia see Hovd
106 I2 Jargalant Töv Mongolia
106 C3 Jargalant Hayrhan mt. Mongolia
107 K3 Jargalthaan Mongolia
156 D8 Jargeau France
251 I5 Jari r. Brazil
117 M7 Jaria Jhanjail Bangl.
170 H3 Jarmen Ger.
157 M7 Jarménil France
143 K1 Järna Dalarna Sweden
143 N2 Järna Stockholm Sweden
162 D4 Jarnac France
162 I3 Jarnages France
143 L3 Järnlunden l. Sweden
142 I2 Järnsjön l. Sweden
157 K5 Jarny France
175 K5 Jarocin Podkarpackie Pol.
174 F4 Jarocin Wielkopolskie Pol.
176 E1 Jaroměř Czech Rep.
176 E2 Jaroměřice nad Rokytnou Czech Rep.
176 F3 Jaroslavice Czech Rep.
175 K5 Jarosław Pol.
174 E1 Jarosławiec Pol.
176 E2 Jarošov nad Nežárkou Czech Rep.
177 K2 Jarovnice Slovakia
140 L5 Järpen Sweden
168 H1 Jarplund-Weding Ger.
121 L9 Jarqo'rg'o'n Uzbek.
Jarqŭrghon Uzbek. see Jarqo'rg'o'n
122 C6 Jarrāhi watercourse Iran
84 D6 Jarra Jarra Range hills N.T. Austr.
232 H12 Jarratt VA U.S.A.
234 C5 Jarrettsville MD U.S.A.
149 O4 Jarrow Tyne and Wear, England U.K.
106 I7 Jartai Nei Mongol China
106 I7 Jartai Yanchi salt l. Nei Mongol China
253 E2 Jarú Brazil
125 K7 Jarūb Yemen
Jarud Nei Mongol China see Lubei
196 I7 Jarut mt. Serbia
138 H3 Järvakandi Estonia
141 R6 Järvenpää Fin.
157 L6 Jarville-la-Malgrange France
75 I4 Jarvis Island terr. N. Pacific Ocean
140 M4 Järvsand Sweden
141 N6 Järvsö Sweden
117 I6 Jarwa Uttar Prad. India
159 K6 Jarzé France
116 C8 Jasdan Gujarat India
161 H10 Jas de Laure hill France
177 I3 Jasenie Slovakia
177 K3 Jasenov Slovakia
117 J8 Jashpurnagar Chhattisgarh India
174 D4 Jasień Lubuskie Pol.
174 F1 Jasień Pomorskie Pol.
175 J3 Jasienica Pol.
175 I4 Jasieniec Pol.
207 F5 Jasikan Ghana
175 J6 Jasiołka r. Pol.
175 K5 Jasionka Pol.
175 I5 Jasionna Pol.
175 L2 Jasionówka Pol.
122 G9 Jāsk Iran
122 G9 Jāsk-e Kohneh Iran
120 G6 Jasliq Uzbek.
175 J6 Jaśliska Pol.
175 J6 Jasło Pol.
177 G3 Jaslovské Bohunice Slovakia
138 I7 Jašlūnai Lith.
170 I1 Jasmund pen. Ger.
170 I1 Jasmund, Nationalpark nature res. Ger.
262 T2 Jason Peninsula Antarctica
177 J3 Jasov Slovakia
177 H4 Jásová Slovakia
222 G4 Jasper Alta Can.
231 D9 Jasper AL U.S.A.
237 I7 Jasper AR U.S.A.
231 F10 Jasper FL U.S.A.
231 E8 Jasper GA U.S.A.
230 D6 Jasper IN U.S.A.
232 H6 Jasper NY U.S.A.
232 B9 Jasper OH U.S.A.
231 E8 Jasper TN U.S.A.
237 I10 Jasper TX U.S.A.
222 G4 Jasper National Park Alta Can.
127 L7 Jaşşān Iraq
160 F5 Jassans-Riottier France
160 G4 Jasseron France
Jassy Romania see Iaşi
143 O7 Jastarnia Pol.
188 E3 Jastrebarsko Croatia
174 E2 Jastrowie Pol.
175 I4 Jastrząb Pol.
174 G1 Jastrzębia Góra Pol.
174 G6 Jastrzębie-Zdrój Pol.
175 K2 Jaświły Pol.
177 J4 Jászapáti Hungary
177 I4 Jászárokszállás Hungary
177 I4 Jászberény Hungary
177 I4 Jászboldogháza Hungary
177 I4 Jászfényszaru Hungary
177 J4 Jászkarajenő Hungary
177 J4 Jászkisér Hungary
177 J4 Jászladány Hungary
177 J4 Jász-Nagykun-Szolnok county Hungary
177 J4 Jászszentandrás Hungary
177 I5 Jászszentlászló Hungary
177 J4 Jásztelek Hungary
183 O2 Jata, Monte hill Spain
256 B2 Jataí Brazil
251 G5 Jatapu r. Brazil
185 L7 Jatar Spain
116 G7 Jatara Madh. Prad. India
114 D4 Jath Mahar. India
123 M9 Jati Pak.
95 H8 Jatibarang Jawa Indon.
246 D3 Jatibonico Cuba
94 G8 Jatiluhur, Waduk resr Jawa Indon.
Játiva Spain see Xátiva
95 H8 Jatiwangi Jawa Indon.
194 E7 Jato r. Sicilia Italy
254 B5 Jatobá Brazil
123 N7 Jatoi Pak.
123 K6 Jat Poti Afgh.
141 N6 Jättendal Sweden
253 E1 Jatuarana Brazil
170 I3 Jatzke Ger.
170 I3 Jatznick Ger.
256 C5 Jaú Brazil
251 F5 Jaú r. Brazil
163 I10 Jau, Col de pass France
251 F5 Jaú, Parque Nacional do nat. park Brazil
251 F5 Jauaperi r. Brazil
251 E3 Jaua Sarisariñama, Parque Nacional nat. park Venez.
246 F3 Jauco Cuba
252 B2 Jauja Peru
186 D5 Jaulín Spain
245 H2 Jaumave Mex.
160 K3 Jaun Switz.
251 F6 Jauna r. Brazil
138 K4 Jaunanna Latvia
158 H8 Jaunay r. France
162 E2 Jaunay-Clan France
138 I5 Jaunjelgava Latvia
138 I5 Jaunkalsnava Latvia
138 F5 Jaunlutriņi Latvia
138 G5 Jaunmārupe Latvia
138 J4 Jaunpiebalga Latvia
138 G5 Jaunpils Latvia
117 I7 Jaunpur Uttar Prad. India
179 K6 Jauntal val. Austria
256 B2 Jaupaci Brazil
161 B9 Jaur r. France
261 H4 Jauregui Arg.
186 C2 Jaurrieta Spain
255 B6 Jauru Brazil
253 F4 Jauru r. Brazil
161 J8 Jausiers France
Java i. Indon. see Jawa
114 F6 Javadi Hills India
Javaés r. Brazil see Formoso
254 C4 Javaés, Serra dos hills Brazil
129 E4 Javakhet'is K'edi hills Armenia/Georgia
187 D7 Javalambre mt. Spain
187 C7 Javalambre, Sierra de mts Spain
183 R8 Javalón mt. Spain
123 K4 Javand Afgh.
250 D6 Javari r. Brazil/Peru alt. Yavari
265 L5 Java Ridge sea feature Indian Ocean
107 M2 Javarthushuu Mongolia
Java Sea Indon. see Jawa, Laut
265 K5 Java Trench sea feature Indian Ocean
187 F10 Jávea-Xábia Spain
170 E5 Jävenitz Ger.
185 K6 Javerero mt. Spain
162 F4 Javerlhac-et-la-Chapelle-St-Robert France
186 C2 Javier Spain
259 B7 Javier, Isla i. Chile
261 I2 Javier de Viana Uru.
196 I7 Javor mts Serbia
176 E2 Javořice hill Czech Rep.
177 I3 Javorie mt. Slovakia
196 H7 Javorje mt. Serbia
176 G1 Javorník Czech Rep.
188 E2 Javornik mt. Slovenia
179 J8 Javorniki mts Slovenia
177 H2 Javorníky mts Slovakia
140 P4 Jävre Sweden
159 K5 Javron-les-Chapelles France
95 G9 Jawa i. Indon.
95 I7 Jawa, Laut sea Indon.
94 G8 Jawa Barat prov. Indon.
116 E7 Jawad Madh. Prad. India
116 C7 Jawai r. India
116 F4 Jawala Mukhi Hima. Prad. India
116 F9 Jawar Madh. Prad. India
95 H8 Jawa Tengah prov. Indon.
95 J8 Jawa Timur prov. Indon.
128 F2 Jawbān Bayk Syria
124 G8 Jawf, Wādī al watercourse Yemen
114 C3 Jawhar Mahar. India
210 E4 Jawhar Somalia
174 E4 Jawor Pol.
175 K6 Jawornik Polski Pol.
175 J4 Jawor Solecki Pol.
174 G6 Jaworze Pol.
175 H5 Jaworzno Pol.
175 H6 Jaworzyna mt. Pol.
174 E5 Jaworzyna Śląska Pol.
84 D3 Jawoyn Aboriginal Land res. N.T. Austr.
237 H7 Jay OK U.S.A.
91 I7 Jaya, Puncak mt. Papua Indon.
245 K8 Jayacatlán Mex.
114 C3 Jayakwadi Sagar l. India
250 B6 Jayanca Peru
117 L6 Jayanti W. Bengal India
91 J7 Jayapura Papua Indon.
128 D7 Jayb, Wādī al watercourse Israel/Jordan
185 L7 Jayena Spain
122 C6 Jāyezān Iran
128 C8 Jayfī, Wādī al watercourse Egypt
117 K6 Jaynagar Bihar India
117 L8 Jaynagar W. Bengal India
115 H3 Jaypur Orissa India
128 E5 Jayrūd Syria
237 E9 Jayton TX U.S.A.
247 □1 Jayuya Puerto Rico
162 E3 Jazeneuil France
175 K2 Jaziewo Pol.
125 L3 Jazīrat al Hamrā U.A.E.
122 D7 Jazīreh-ye Shīf Iran
243 I5 Jazminal Mex.
122 H8 Jaz Mūrīān, Hāmūn-e salt marsh Iran
122 C3 Jazvān Iran
128 D4 Jbail Lebanon
226 G8 J. C. Murphey Lake IN U.S.A.
128 D4 Jdaidet Ghazir Lebanon
204 C4 Jdiriya Western Sahara
241 Q6 Jean NV U.S.A.
237 J11 Jeanerette LA U.S.A.
222 F2 Jean Marie River N.W.T. Can.
225 H1 Jeannin, Lac l. Que. Can.
122 G7 Jebāl Bārez, Kūh-e mts Iran
207 G4 Jebba Nigeria
202 C2 Jebel Libya
196 J5 Jebel Romania
Jebel Turkm. see Jebel
122 F2 Jebel Turkm.
210 A2 Jebel, Bahr el r. Sudan/Uganda alt. Abiad, Bahr el, conv. White Nile
203 F5 Jebel Abyad Plateau Sudan
Jebel Ali U.A.E. see Mina Jebel Ali
203 G6 Jebel Dud Sudan
250 B6 Jeberos Peru
180 D5 Jebha Morocco
123 K8 Jebri Pak.
157 N7 Jebsheim France
94 F5 Jebus Indon.
146 K12 Jedburgh Scottish Borders, Scotland U.K.
Jeddah Makkah Saudi Arabia see Jiddah
225 K3 Jeddore Lake Nfld and Lab. Can.
189 B7 Jedeida Tunisia
175 K4 Jedlanka Pol.
175 J6 Jedlicze Pol.
174 E5 Jedlina-Zdrój Pol.
175 J4 Jedlińsk Pol.
175 J4 Jedlnia-Letnisko Pol.
175 J2 Jednorożec Pol.
175 I5 Jędrzejów Pol.
184 H7 Jédula Spain
175 K2 Jedwabne Pol.
175 I2 Jedwabno Pol.
170 D4 Jeetze r. Ger.
231 F8 Jefferson GA U.S.A.
236 H4 Jefferson IA U.S.A.
232 D12 Jefferson NC U.S.A.
232 E7 Jefferson OH U.S.A.
237 H9 Jefferson TX U.S.A.
226 F6 Jefferson WI U.S.A.
238 I4 Jefferson r. MT U.S.A.
240 P3 Jefferson, Mount NV U.S.A.
238 D4 Jefferson, Mount vol. OR U.S.A.
236 I6 Jefferson City MO U.S.A.
232 H10 Jeffersonton VA U.S.A.
231 F9 Jeffersonville GA U.S.A.
230 E6 Jeffersonville IN U.S.A.
232 B11 Jeffersonville KY U.S.A.
232 B9 Jeffersonville OH U.S.A.
232 D11 Jeffrey WV U.S.A.
215 I10 Jeffreys Bay S. Africa
207 G3 Jega Nigeria
163 E8 Jegun France
117 J7 Jehanabad Bihar India
168 G1 Jejsing Denmark
Jeju S. Korea see Cheju
138 I5 Jēkabpils Latvia
262 X2 Jelbart Ice Shelf Antarctica
174 F4 Jelcz-Laskowice Pol.
210 D2 Jeldēsa Eth.
177 H3 Jelenec Slovakia
174 D5 Jelenia Góra Pol.
175 K1 Jeleniewo Pol.
177 K1 Jeleniowski Park Krajobrazowy Pol.
191 Q5 Jelenje Croatia
111 I13 Jelep La pass China/India
175 H6 Jeleśnia Pol.
138 G5 Jelgava Latvia
177 G3 Jelka Slovakia
232 A12 Jellico TN U.S.A.
224 C3 Jellicoe Ont. Can.
80 I3 Jellicoe Channel North I. N.Z.
142 F6 Jelling Denmark
232 C8 Jelloway OH U.S.A.
168 K4 Jelmstorf Ger.
123 O3 Jelondí Kŭhistoni Badakhshon Tajik.
179 J7 Jelovica mt. Slovenia
122 B5 Jelow Gīr Iran
191 Q4 Jelšane Slovenia
177 J3 Jelšava Slovakia
193 N4 Jelsi Italy
94 F3 Jemaja i. Indon.
95 J9 Jember Jawa Indon.
169 K6 Jembke Ger.
165 G8 Jemeppe Belgium
239 K9 Jemez Pueblo NM U.S.A.
168 D4 Jemgum Ger.
174 G5 Jemielnica Pol.
174 E4 Jemielno Pol.
110 G3 Jeminay Xinjiang China
121 U4 Jeminay Kazakh.
207 H4 Jemma Bauchi Nigeria
207 H4 Jemma Kaduna Nigeria
176 E2 Jemnice Czech Rep.
95 L5 Jempang, Danau l. Indon.
171 E9 Jena Ger.
237 I10 Jena LA U.S.A.
178 E5 Jenbach Austria
211 B8 Jenda Malawi
205 H1 Jendouba Tunisia
189 B7 Jendouba admin. div. Tunisia
171 J10 Jeneč Czech Rep.
173 J6 Jengen Ger.
110 E5 Jengish Chokusu mt. China/Kyrg.
174 D2 Jenikowo Pol.
128 D6 Jenīn West Bank
251 F6 Jenipapo Brazil
232 D11 Jenkinjones WV U.S.A.
232 C11 Jenkins KY U.S.A.
234 F5 Jenkins NJ U.S.A.
234 E4 Jenkintown PA U.S.A.
111 H12 Jênlung Xizang China
Jenne Mali see Djenné
223 I5 Jenner Alta Can.
179 N6 Jennersdorf Austria
247 □2 Jennings Antigua and Barbuda
222 C3 Jennings r. B.C. Can.
237 I10 Jennings LA U.S.A.
223 L4 Jenpeg Man. Can.
241 W1 Jensen UT U.S.A.
95 I8 Jepara Jawa Indon.
83 I7 Jeparit Vic. Austr.
140 Q5 Jeppo Fin.
254 E5 Jequié Brazil
257 E2 Jequitaí Brazil
257 E2 Jequitaí r. Brazil
257 G2 Jequitinhonha Brazil
257 H1 Jequitinhonha r. Brazil
94 E3 Jerantut Malaysia
205 H2 Jerba, Île de i. Tunisia
210 A3 Jerbar Sudan
171 D6 Jerchel Ger.
244 G5 Jerécuaro Mex.
127 O9 Jereh Iran
246 F4 Jérémie Haiti
254 F4 Jeremoabo Brazil
210 D3 Jerer Shet' watercourse Eth.
95 L9 Jereweh Sumbawa Indon.
244 D3 Jerez Mex.
244 D3 Jerez r. Mex.
184 G7 Jerez de la Frontera Spain
185 M6 Jerez del Marquesado Spain
184 F4 Jerez de los Caballeros Spain
140 O4 Jerfojaur Sweden
140 R2 Jergol Norway
198 B3 Jergucat Albania
187 D8 Jérica Spain
85 K7 Jericho Qld Austr.
235 H3 Jericho NY U.S.A.
128 D7 Jericho West Bank
171 F5 Jerichow Ger.
205 H2 Jerid, Chott el salt l. Tunisia
95 I3 Jerijeh, Tanjung pt Malaysia
83 J6 Jerilderie N.S.W. Austr.
174 E4 Jerka Pol.
129 G6 Jermuk Armenia
234 D1 Jermyn PA U.S.A.
253 H3 Jeroaquara Brazil
241 T7 Jerome AZ U.S.A.
238 G5 Jerome ID U.S.A.
232 G8 Jerome PA U.S.A.
244 F7 Jerónimo Mex.
261 G2 Jeronimo Norte Arg.
87 E12 Jerramungup W.A. Austr.
123 M9 Jerruck Pak.
168 J3 Jersbek Ger.
158 G3 Jersey terr. Channel Is
233 K8 Jersey City NJ U.S.A.
227 Q8 Jersey Shore PA U.S.A.
236 J6 Jerseyville IL U.S.A.
182 I8 Jerte Spain
182 H9 Jerte r. Spain
254 E3 Jerumenha Brazil
128 D7 Jerusalem Israel/West Bank
80 J6 Jerusalem North I. N.Z.
83 M6 Jervis Bay Jervis Bay Austr.
83 M6 Jervis Bay b. Jervis Bay Austr.
83 M6 Jervis Bay Territory admin. div. Austr.
222 F5 Jervis Inlet B.C. Can.
84 E7 Jervois Range hills N.T. Austr.
169 K6 Jerxheim Ger.
178 C5 Jerzens Austria
174 E4 Jerzmanowa Pol.
192 D8 Jerzu Sardegna Italy
169 H9 Jesberg Ger.
176 C1 Jesenice Středočeský kraj Czech Rep.
176 D2 Jesenice Středočeský kraj Czech Rep.
188 E2 Jesenice Slovenia
176 B1 Jesenice, Vodní nádrž resr Czech Rep.
176 G1 Jeseník Czech Rep.
176 G1 Jeseníky park Czech Rep.
177 J3 Jesenské Slovakia
171 F6 Jeserig Brandenburg Ger.
171 G6 Jeserig Brandenburg Ger.
171 G8 Jesewitz Ger.
191 O8 Jesi Italy
170 L4 Jesionowo Pol.
222 F5 Jesmond B.C. Can.
191 N4 Jesolo Italy
Jesselton Sabah Malaysia see Kota Kinabalu
171 G7 Jessen Ger.
142 H1 Jessheim Norway
117 L8 Jessore Bangl.
234 B6 Jessup MD U.S.A.
168 I4 Jesteburg Ger.
176 D1 Ještěd mt. Czech Rep.
172 F6 Jestetten Ger.
Jesu Maria Island Admiralty Is P.N.G. see Rambutyo Island
231 G10 Jesup GA U.S.A.
245 M8 Jesús Carranza Mex.
261 E2 Jesús María Arg.
244 E4 Jesús María Aguascalientes Mex.
245 M9 Jesús María Chiapas Mex.
244 C3 Jesús María Mex.
244 C4 Jesús María r. Mex.
245 J1 Jesús María, Barra spit Mex.
244 G1 Jesús María de Aquirre Mex.
206 A4 Jeta, Ilha de i. Guinea-Bissau
116 C9 Jetalsar Gujarat India
Jethro tourist site Saudi Arabia see Maghā'ir Shu'ayb
121 R6 Jeti-Ögüz Kyrg.
236 F6 Jetmore KS U.S.A.
173 I5 Jettingen-Scheppach Ger.
173 K5 Jetzendorf Ger.
156 H3 Jeumont France
168 I2 Jevenstedt Ger.
168 E3 Jever Ger.
176 F2 Jevíčko Czech Rep.
176 F3 Jevišovice Czech Rep.
176 F3 Jevišovka r. Czech Rep.
142 G1 Jevnaker Norway
232 A7 Jewell OH U.S.A.
232 D11 Jewell Ridge VA U.S.A.
235 L1 Jewett City CT U.S.A.
Jewish Autonomous Oblast admin. div. Rus. Fed. see Yevreyskaya Avtonomnaya Oblast'
120 J8 Jeýhun Turkm.
Jeyhun Turkm. see Jeýhun
122 C4 Jeyḩūnābād Iran
173 O3 Jezerní Stěna mt. Ger.
174 G2 Jeżewo Kujawsko-Pomorskie Pol.
175 K2 Jeżewo Podlaskie Pol.
175 H2 Jeziorak, Jezioro l. Pol.
143 Q8 Jeziorany Pol.
175 J3 Jeziorka r. Pol.
174 G4 Jeziorsko, Jezioro l. Pol.
175 K4 Jeziorzany Pol.
175 H4 Jeżów Pol.
175 K5 Jeżowe Pol.
128 D5 Jezzine Lebanon
116 E8 Jhabua Madh. Prad. India
117 K7 Jha Jha Bihar India
116 F5 Jhajjar Haryana India
116 D6 Jhajju Rajasthan India
117 M8 Jhalakati Bangl.
116 F7 Jhalawar Rajasthan India
117 J8 Jhalida W. Bengal India
123 K8 Jhal Jhao Pak.
123 L7 Jhal Magsi Pak.
116 F7 Jhalrapatan Rajasthan India
123 O6 Jhang Pak.
117 K6 Jhanjharpur Bihar India
116 G7 Jhansi Uttar Prad. India
111 L13 Jhanzi r. India
117 K6 Jhapa Nepal
116 E8 Jharda Madh. Prad. India
117 K8 Jhargram W. Bengal India
117 K8 Jharia Jharkhand India
117 J8 Jharkhand state India
117 J9 Jharsuguda Orissa India
123 M7 Jhatpat Pak.
117 J6 Jhawani Nepal
116 D4 Jhelum r. India/Pak.
123 O5 Jhelum Pak.
117 L8 Jhenaidah Bangl.
Jhenaidaha Bangl. see Jhenaidah
168 E4 Jheringsfehn (Moormerland) Ger.
123 M9 Jhimpir Pak.
116 C8 Jhinjhuvada Gujarat India
117 J8 Jhinkpani Jharkhand India
123 N6 Jhok Bodo Pak.
123 M9 Jhudo Pak.
117 J7 Jhumritilaiya Jharkhand India
116 E5 Jhunjhunun Rajasthan India
116 H7 Jhusi Uttar Prad. India
108 F2 Jiachuan Sichuan China
Jiachuanzhen Sichuan China see Jiachuan
Jiading Jiangxi China see Xinfeng
109 M3 Jiading Shanghai China
109 I6 Jiahe Hunan China
108 D4 Jiajiang Sichuan China
108 F4 Jialing Jiang r. Sichuan China
Jialu Shaanxi China see Jiaxian
109 J2 Jialu He r. China
100 G5 Jiamusi Heilong. China
109 J5 Ji'an Jiangxi China
109 J5 Ji'an Jiangxi China
101 E8 Ji'an Jilin China
Jianchang Jiangxi China see Nancheng
107 P6 Jianchang Liaoning China
108 B5 Jianchuan Yunnan China
109 L4 Jiande Zhejiang China
108 G9 Jianfeng Hainan China
108 E4 Jiang'an Sichuan China
Jiangbei Chongqing China see Yubei
108 C7 Jiangcheng Yunnan China
108 D6 Jiangchuan Yunnan China
109 H6 Jiangcun Hunan China
109 L2 Jiangdu Jiangsu China
Jiange Sichuan China see Pu'an
108 G8 Jianghong Guangdong China
109 H6 Jianghua Hunan China
107 Q8 Jiangjiapo Shandong China
108 F5 Jiangjiehe Guizhou China
108 F4 Jiangjin Chongqing China
106 A4 Jiangjunmiao Xinjiang China
107 N8 Jiangjunmu Hebei China
106 E6 Jiangjuntai Gansu China
Jiangkou Guangdong China see Fengkai
108 G5 Jiangkou Guizhou China
108 F2 Jiangkou Shaanxi China
Jiangkou Sichuan China see Pingchang
109 K5 Jiangle Fujian China
Jiangling Hubei China see Jingzhou
108 E2 Jiangluozhen Gansu China
109 I7 Jiangmen Guangdong China
Jiangna Yunnan China see Yanshan
Jiangning Jiangsu China see Dongshan
109 L4 Jiangshan Zhejiang China
Jiangsi Guizhou China see Dejiang
109 L2 Jiangsu prov. China
106 I9 Jiangtaibu Ningxia China
109 J5 Jiangxi prov. China
109 J3 Jiangxia Hubei China
107 L9 Jiangxian Shanxi China
106 G8 Jiangxigou Qinghai China
109 M2 Jiangyan Jiangsu China
109 M3 Jiangyin Jiangsu China
109 H6 Jiangyong Hunan China
108 E3 Jiangyou Sichuan China
107 P8 Jiangyu Shandong China
111 G11 Jiangzhesongrong Xizang China
109 L2 Jianhu Jiangsu China
109 H8 Jian Jiang r. China
Jianjun Shaanxi China see Yongshou
108 C5 Jiankang Sichuan China
109 I4 Jianli Hubei China
109 K5 Jianning Fujian China
109 L5 Jian'ou Fujian China
107 P6 Jianping Liaoning China
107 P6 Jianping Liaoning China
107 O8 Jianqiao Hebei China
108 B2 Jianshe Qinghai China
Jianshe Sichuan China see Baiyü
108 G3 Jianshi Hubei China
108 D7 Jianshui Yunnan China
111 F9 Jianshui Hu l. Xizang China
108 E3 Jianxing Sichuan China
109 L5 Jianyang Fujian China
108 E3 Jianyang Sichuan China
108 D2 Jiaochang Sichuan China
Jiaochangba Sichuan China see Jiaochang
Jiaocheng Guangdong China see Jiaoling
107 M8 Jiaocheng Shanxi China
107 O7 Jiaohe Hebei China
100 E7 Jiaohe Jilin China
Jiaojiang Zhejiang China see Taizhou
107 L8 Jiaokou Shanxi China
Jiaokui Yunnan China see Yiliang
107 P8 Jiaolai He r. China
107 R5 Jiaolai He r. China
109 K6 Jiaoling Guangdong China
107 P9 Jiaonan Shandong China
109 L6 Jiaowei Fujian China
107 Q8 Jiaozhou Shandong China
107 Q8 Jiaozhou Wan b. China
107 M9 Jiaozuo Henan China
100 E7 Jiapigou Jilin China
106 D8 Jiarsu Qinghai China
108 C6 Jiasa Yunnan China
Jiashan Anhui China see Mingguang
110 C7 Jiashi Xinjiang China
111 H12 Jia Tsuo La pass Xizang China
109 I2 Jiaxian Henan China
107 L8 Jiaxian Shaanxi China
107 O9 Jiaxiang Shandong China
109 M3 Jiaxing Zhejiang China
Jiayi Taiwan see Chiai
100 G4 Jiayin Heilong. China
109 I4 Jiayu Hubei China
106 F7 Jiayuguan Gansu China
109 K7 Jiazi Guangdong China
197 L3 Jibou Romania
125 N5 Jibsh, Ra's c. Oman
Jībūtī country Africa see Djibouti
Jibuti Djibouti see Djibouti
239 K8 Jicarilla Apache Indian Reservation res. NM U.S.A.
245 I9 Jicayán Mex.
176 E1 Jičín Czech Rep.
124 D5 Jiddah Makkah Saudi Arabia
203 G2 Jiddī, Jabal al hill Egypt
117 O5 Jido Arun. Prad. India
100 G6 Jidong Heilong. China
109 K7 Jiedong Guangdong China
140 O2 Jiehkkevárri mt. Norway
Jiehu Shandong China see Yinan
109 J7 Jieshi Guangdong China
106 I9 Jieshipu Gansu China
109 J7 Jieshi Wan b. China
109 J2 Jieshou Anhui China
138 G7 Jiesia r. Lith.
109 J7 Jiexi Guangdong China
107 L8 Jiexiu Shanxi China

Kaeng Krachan National Park to Kangerlussuaq

330

97 D8 Kaeng Krachan National Park Thai.
80 H2 Kaeo North I. N.Z.
168 I1 Kær Denmark
101 E10 Kaesŏng N. Korea
126 H8 Kāf Saudi Arabia
Kafa Ukr. see Feodosiya
209 D7 Kafakumba Dem. Rep. Congo
Kafan Armenia see Kapan
207 H4 Kafanchan Nigeria
Kāfar Qal'eh Iran see Eslām Qal'eh
215 K5 Kafferrivier S. Africa
207 H3 Kaffin-Hausa Nigeria
215 J5 Kaffir r. S. Africa
206 B3 Kaffrine Senegal
208 E2 Kafia Kingi Sudan
93 F4 Kafiau i. Papua Indon.
198 F5 Kafireos, Steno sea chan. Greece
123 N4 Kafiristan reg. Pak.
Kafirnigan Tajik. see Kofarnihon
206 D4 Kafolo Côte d'Ivoire
203 F2 Kafr ash Shaykh Egypt
126 E8 Kafr ash Shaykh governorate Egypt
128 E3 Kafr Buhum Syria
202 E2 Kafret Rihama Egypt
128 E4 Kafrūn Bashūr Syria
210 B4 Kafu r. Uganda
209 F8 Kafue Zambia
209 F8 Kafue r. Zambia
209 E8 Kafue Flats marsh Zambia
209 E8 Kafue National Park Zambia
104 D3 Kaga Japan
120 G1 Kaga Rus. Fed.
208 C3 Kaga Bandoro C.A.R.
137 S6 Kagal'nik Rus. Fed.
137 S6 Kagal'nik r. Rus. Fed.
135 H7 Kagal'nitskaya Rus. Fed.
105 L1 Kagamiishi Japan
123 O4 Kagan Pak.
Kagan Uzbek. see Kogon
106 G9 Kagang Qinghai China
Kaganovich Rus. Fed. see Tovarkovskiy
Kaganovichabad Tajik. see Kolkhozobod
Kaganovichi Pervyye Ukr. see Polis'ke
Kagarlyk Ukr. see Kaharlyk
103 L12 Kagawa pref. Japan
227 L4 Kagawong Ont. Can.
140 P4 Kåge Sweden
211 A5 Kagera admin. reg. Tanz.
215 L2 Kagiso S. Africa
127 K3 Kağızman Turkey
203 F6 Kagmar Sudan
94 C5 Kagologolo Indon.
208 C2 Kagopal Chad
105 I5 Kagosaka-tōge pass Japan
103 H15 Kagoshima Japan
102 □H15 Kagoshima pref. Japan
103 H15 Kagoshima-wan b. Japan
Kagul Moldova see Cahul
122 G3 Kāhak Iran
122 C3 Kahak Qazvīn Iran
240 □E13 Kahakuloa HI U.S.A.
240 □B11 Kahala Point HI U.S.A.
240 □D12 Kahalu'u HI U.S.A.
211 B5 Kahama Tanz.
123 M7 Kahan Pak.
240 □D12 Kahana HI U.S.A.
136 J4 Kaharlyk Ukr.
93 E3 Kahatola i. Maluku Indon.
212 B4 Kahawero waterhole Namibia
95 K6 Kahayan r. Indon.
209 C6 Kahemba Dem. Rep. Congo
240 □C12 Kahe Point HI U.S.A.
81 B12 Kaherekoau Mountains South I. N.Z.
169 G10 Kahl r. Ger.
171 E9 Kahla Ger.
169 H10 Kahl am Main Ger.
222 F3 Kahntah B.C. Can.
Kahnu Iran see Kahnūj
122 G8 Kahnūj Kermān Iran
122 H6 Kahnūj Kermān Iran
206 C5 Kahnwia Liberia
80 H2 Kahoe North I. N.Z.
236 J5 Kahoka MO U.S.A.
104 E2 Kahoku-gata l. Japan
240 □E13 Kaho'olawe i. HI U.S.A.
130 D3 Kahperusvaarat mts Fin.
123 I8 Kahrād Iran
126 H5 Kahramanmaraş Turkey
123 N7 Kahror Pak.
126 I5 Kâhta Turkey
240 □F13 Kahuā HI U.S.A.
122 G4 Kahugish well Iran
80 □ Kahuitara Point Chatham Is S. Pacific Ocean
240 □D12 Kahuku HI U.S.A.
240 □C12 Kahuku Point HI U.S.A.
136 H8 Kahul, Ozero l. Ukr.
Kahulaui i. HI U.S.A. see Kaho'olawe
240 □E13 Kahului HI U.S.A.
122 H7 Kahūrak Iran
81 G8 Kahurangi National Park South I. N.Z.
80 G7 Kahurangi Point South I. N.Z.
123 O5 Kahuta Pak.
208 E5 Kahuzi-Biega, Parc National du nat. park Dem. Rep. Congo
91 H8 Kai, Kepulauan is Indon.
210 A3 Kaia r. Sudan
80 H2 Kaiaka North I. N.Z.
207 F4 Kaiama Nigeria
91 K8 Kaiapit P.N.G.
81 G10 Kaiapoi South I. N.Z.
241 T5 Kaibab AZ U.S.A.
241 T5 Kaibab Plateau AZ U.S.A.
106 E7 Kaibamardang Qinghai China
104 B5 Kaibara Japan
91 H8 Kai Besar i. Indon.
241 U5 Kaibito Plateau AZ U.S.A.
78 □6 Kaichui, Mount Guadalcanal Solomon Is
104 G4 Kaida Japan
110 H6 Kaidu He r. China
251 G3 Kaieteur Falls Guyana
107 N9 Kaifeng Henan China
107 N9 Kaifeng Henan China
80 H2 Kaihu North I. N.Z.
Kaihua Yunnan China see Wenshan
109 L4 Kaihua Zhejiang China
214 F5 Kaiingveld reg. S. Africa
108 F3 Kaijiang Sichuan China
91 H8 Kai Kecil i. Indon.
109 □J7 Kai Keung Leng H.K. China
80 H2 Kaikohe North I. N.Z.
81 H9 Kaikoura South I. N.Z.
81 H9 Kaikoura Peninsula South I. N.Z.
206 C4 Kailahun Sierra Leone
116 H5 Kailali Nepal
Kailas mt. Xizang China see Kangrinboqê Feng
117 N7 Kailashahar Tripura India
Kailas Range mts Xizang China see Gangdisê Shan
108 F5 Kaili Guizhou China
210 B3 Kailongong waterhole Kenya
107 Q5 Kailu Nei Mongol China
240 □D12 Kailua HI U.S.A.
240 □F14 Kailua-Kona HI U.S.A.
80 J4 Kaimai North I. N.Z.
80 J4 Kaimai-Mamaku Forest Park nature res. North I. N.Z.
80 J4 Kaimai Range hills North I. N.Z.
91 H7 Kaimana Papua Indon.
80 K5 Kaimanawa Forest Park nature res. North I. N.Z.
80 J6 Kaimanawa Mountains North I. N.Z.
108 A2 Kaimar Qinghai China
81 F9 Kaimata South I. N.Z.
116 G6 Kaimganj Uttar Prad. India
103 H15 Kaimon-dake hill Japan
116 H7 Kaimur Range hills India
138 F3 Käina Estonia
103 L13 Kainan Tokushima Japan
104 B7 Kainan Wakayama Japan
Kainda Kyrg. see Kayyngdy
96 B4 Kaing Myanmar
80 K5 Kaingaroa Forest North I. N.Z.
80 □ Kaingaroa Harbour b. Chatham Is S. Pacific Ocean
207 F3 Kaingiwa Nigeria
207 G4 Kainji Lake National Park Nigeria
207 G4 Kainji Lake National Park Nigeria
207 G4 Kainji Reservoir Nigeria
117 J9 Kaintaragarh Orissa India
140 Q3 Kainulasjärvi Sweden
80 I3 Kaipara Flats North I. N.Z.
80 I3 Kaipara Harbour North I. N.Z.
241 U4 Kaiparowits Plateau UT U.S.A.
109 I7 Kaiping Guangdong China
Kaiping Yunnan China see Dêqên
225 J2 Kaipokok Bay Nfld and Lab. Can.
Kaira Gujarat India see Kheda
80 K6 Kairakau Beach North I. N.Z.
140 S3 Kairala Fin.
116 F5 Kairana Uttar Prad. India
93 F5 Kairatu Seram Indon.
205 H2 Kairouan Tunisia
140 O2 Kaisepakte Sweden
178 F4 Kaisergebirge mts Austria
178 F4 Kaisergebirge nature res. Austria
172 D3 Kaiserslautern Ger.
263 F2 Kaiser Wilhelm II Land reg. Antarctica
100 F7 Kaishantun Jilin China
173 J4 Kaisheim Ger.
138 H7 Kaišiadorys Lith.
94 G6 Kait, Tanjung pt Indon.
103 J12 Kaita Japan
80 H2 Kaitaia North I. N.Z.
81 D13 Kaitangata South I. N.Z.
80 L5 Kaitawa North I. N.Z.
116 F8 Kaitha Madh. Prad. India
116 F5 Kaithal Haryana India
Kaitong Jilin China see Tongyu
140 P3 Kaitum Sweden
140 P3 Kaitumälven r. Sweden
93 E8 Kaiwatu Maluku Indon.
240 □D13 Kaiwi Channel HI U.S.A.
108 G3 Kaixian Chongqing China
108 F5 Kaiyang Guizhou China
107 S5 Kaiyuan Liaoning China
108 D7 Kaiyuan Yunnan China
Kaiyun Hunan China see Hengshan
104 E5 Kaizu Japan
104 B7 Kaizuka Japan
140 S4 Kajaani Fin.
84 H6 Kajabbi Qld Austr.
123 K5 Kajaki Afgh.
94 D3 Kajang Malaysia
123 N7 Kajanpur Pak.
85 L9 Kajarabie, Lake resr Qld Austr.
129 H6 K'ajaran Armenia
177 H5 Kajdacs Hungary
123 I8 Kajdar Iran
211 C5 Kajiado Kenya
105 H4 Kajikazawa Japan
103 H15 Kajiki Japan
208 E2 Kajok Sudan
210 A4 Kajo Kaji Sudan
176 D3 Kájov Czech Rep.
123 K5 Kajrān Afgh.
122 B3 Kaju Iran
83 J5 Kajuligah Nature Reserve N.S.W. Austr.
207 G4 Kajuru Nigeria
121 Q6 Kajy-Say Kyrg.
121 L1 Kak, Ozero salt l. Kazakh.
210 B2 Kaka Sudan
122 H3 Kaka Turkm.
95 M3 Kakaban i. Indon.
224 B3 Kakabeka Falls Ont. Can.
129 G4 Kakabet'i Georgia
93 C7 Kakabia i. Indon.
84 D2 Kakadu Aboriginal Land res. N.T. Austr.
84 D2 Kakadu National Park N.T. Austr.
223 M5 Kakagi Lake Ont. Can.
92 E8 Kakal r. Mindanao Phil.
93 A4 Kakali Sulawesi Barat Indon.
214 E4 Kakamas S. Africa
210 B4 Kakamega Kenya
104 E5 Kakamigahara Japan
209 A6 Kakamoéka Congo
115 M8 Kakana Andaman & Nicobar Is India
188 G3 Kakanj Bos.-Herz.
81 E12 Kakanui Mountains South I. N.Z.
123 L8 Kakar Pak.
207 H3 Kakarahil well Niger
80 I6 Kakaramea North I. N.Z.
80 J5 Kakaramea vol. North I. N.Z.
177 H5 Kakasd Hungary
206 C5 Kakata Liberia
80 J6 Kakatahi North I. N.Z.
117 O7 Kakching Manipur India
103 J12 Kake Japan
222 C3 Kake AK U.S.A.
105 H6 Kakegawa Japan
209 D6 Kakenge Dem. Rep. Congo
168 I4 Kakenstorf Ger.
170 D5 Kakerbeck Ger.
102 □G18 Kakeroma-jima i. Nansei-shotō Japan
211 B5 Kakesio Tanz.
129 C3 Kakhat'i Georgia
129 G3 Kakhet'is K'edi hills Georgia
Kakhi Azer. see Qax
129 H3 Kakhib Rus. Fed.
137 M7 Kakhovka Ukr.
137 M7 Kakhovs'ke Vodoskhovyshche resr Ukr.
122 H4 Kakht Iran
Kakhul Moldova see Cahul
122 D7 Kākī Iran
114 H4 Kakinada Andhra Prad. India
196 H8 Kakinjës, Maja e mt. Albania
222 G2 Kakisa N.W.T. Can.
222 G2 Kakisa r. N.W.T. Can.
222 G2 Kakisa Lake N.W.T. Can.
138 E5 Kākišķe Latvia
105 H1 Kakizaki Japan
209 C6 Kakobola Dem. Rep. Congo
104 A6 Kakogawa Japan
104 A6 Kako-gawa r. Japan
175 K4 Kąkolewnica Wschodnia Pol.
174 E4 Kąkolewo Pol.
211 A5 Kakonko Tanz.
106 B4 Kakpak Kuduk well Xinjiang China
206 E4 Kakpin Côte d'Ivoire
116 G6 Kakrala Uttar Prad. India
206 B4 Kakrima r. Guinea
119 L1 Kakshaal-Too mts China/Kyrg.
220 D2 Kaktovik AK U.S.A.
177 I4 Kakucs Hungary
102 R9 Kakuda Japan
210 B4 Kakuma Kenya
122 D6 Kakun Iran
95 J3 Kakus r. Malaysia
222 G4 Kakwa r. Alta Can.
222 F4 Kakwa Provincial Park B.C. Can.
222 G4 Kakwa Wildland Provincial Park Alta Can.
188 E3 Kal hill Croatia
177 J4 Kál Hungary
207 I3 Kala Nigeria
123 N6 Kala Pak.
211 A7 Kala Tanz.
205 H2 Kalaâ Kebira Tunisia
Kalaallit Nunaat terr. N. America see Greenland
123 N5 Kalabagh Pak.
93 D8 Kalabahi Indon.
Kalabak mt. Bulg./Greece see Radomir
Kalabáka Greece see Kalampaka
95 L2 Kalabakan Sabah Malaysia
Kalabákion Greece see Kalampaki
210 E2 Kalabaydh Togdheer Somalia
210 D2 Kalabaydh Woqooyi Galbeed Somalia
114 F4 Kalabgur Andhra Prad. India
82 H4 Kalabity S.A. Austr.
209 D8 Kalabo Zambia
135 H6 Kalach Rus. Fed.
123 L4 Kalacha Afgh.
210 C4 Kalacha Dida Kenya
135 H6 Kalach-na-Donu Rus. Fed.
96 A4 Kaladan r. India/Myanmar
224 E4 Kaladar Ont. Can.
114 D4 Kaladgi Karnataka India
93 B5 Kalaena r. Indon.
96 C3 Kalagwe Myanmar
212 D4 Kalahari Desert Africa
214 E1 Kalahari Gemsbok National Park S. Africa
240 □B12 Kalaheo HI U.S.A.
Kalaikhum Tajik. see Qal'aikhum
Kalai-Khumb Tajik. see Qal'aikhum
117 J6 Kalaiya Nepal
140 Q4 Kalajoki Fin.
140 Q4 Kalajoki r. Fin.
140 S1 Kalak Norway
197 O7 Kalakoch hill Bulg.
207 F4 Kalalé Benin
93 B4 Kalaliok Sulawesi Indon.
93 D1 Kalalusu i. Indon.
116 G9 Kalam Mahar. India
123 O4 Kalam Pak.
Kalámai Greece see Kalamata
198 D3 Kalamaki Greece
212 E4 Kalamare Botswana
198 D2 Kalamaria Greece
198 B3 Kalamas r. Greece
198 D5 Kalamata Greece
226 I7 Kalamazoo MI U.S.A.
226 H7 Kalamazoo r. MI U.S.A.
95 K7 Kalambau i. Indon.
114 E3 Kalamnuri Mahar. India
198 B4 Kalamos i. Greece
199 G6 Kalamos, Akrotirio pt Greece
198 C3 Kalampaka Greece
198 F1 Kalampaki Greece
137 M8 Kalamyts'ka Zatoka b. Ukr.
138 F3 Kalana Estonia
206 C4 Kalana Mali
111 C12 Kalanaur Haryana India
116 E4 Kalanaur Punjab India
137 M7 Kalanchak Ukr.
123 J7 Kalandi Pak.
Kalandula Angola see Calandula
210 B5 Kalangala Uganda
211 B6 Kalangali Tanz.
107 O1 Kalanguy Rus. Fed.
87 D11 Kalannie W.A. Austr.
202 D2 Kalanshiyū ar Ramlī al Kabīr, Sarīr des. Libya
116 E5 Kalanwali Haryana India
122 H8 Kālān Zīād Iran
93 B7 Kalao i. Indon.
240 □F14 Kalaoa HI U.S.A.
92 E8 Kalaong Mindanao Phil.
93 B7 Kalaotoa i. Indon.
114 F8 Kala Oya r. Sri Lanka
94 F5 Kalapa Indon.
240 □G14 Kalapana HI U.S.A.
122 I9 Kalar watercourse Iran
127 L6 Kalār Iraq
Kalarash Moldova see Călărași
139 S4 Kalashnikovo Rus. Fed.
96 F6 Kalasin Thai.
123 L5 Kalāt Afgh.
Kalāt Khorāsān Iran see Kabūd Gonbad
122 H9 Kalāt Sīstān va Balūchestān Iran
123 K9 Kalat Balochistan Pak.
123 L7 Kalat Balochistan Pak.
122 H4 Kalat, Kūh-e mt. Iran
123 I5 Kalata Barangak Afgh.
122 F3 Kalāteh-ye Molla Iran
240 □E12 Kalaupapa HI U.S.A.
135 I7 Kalaus r. Rus. Fed.
116 C8 Kalavad Gujarat India
198 D4 Kalavryta Greece
174 D3 Kaława Pol.
125 I8 Kalb, Ra's al c. Yemen
125 M3 Kalbā U.A.E.
129 H5 Kälbäcär Azer.
87 C9 Kalbarri W.A. Austr.
87 C9 Kalbarri National Park W.A. Austr.
214 C9 Kalbaskraal S. Africa
170 D5 Kalbe (Milde) Ger.
121 T3 Kalbinskiy Khrebet mts Kazakh.
122 H4 Kalbū Iran
179 J8 Kalce Slovenia
173 K2 Kalchreuth Ger.
137 Q6 Kal'chyk Ukr.
137 Q6 Kal'chyk r. Ukr.
176 G4 Káld Hungary
128 D2 Kaldırım Turkey
120 E3 Kaldygayty r. Kazakh.
199 K6 Kale Antalya Turkey
199 J5 Kale Denizli Turkey
129 A5 Kale Gümüşhane Turkey
129 A4 Kale r. Turkey
126 F3 Kalecik Turkey
93 C6 Kaledupa i. Indon.
169 J7 Kalefeld Ger.
96 C7 Kalegauk Island Myanmar
122 C3 Kaleh Sarai Iran
96 B5 Kaleindaung inlet Myanmar
210 B4 Kalekol Kenya
209 E6 Kalema Dem. Rep. Congo
209 F6 Kalemie Dem. Rep. Congo
96 B3 Kalemyo Myanmar
122 F4 Kāl-e Namak Iran
120 D3 Kalenoye Kazakh.
198 B3 Kalentzi Greece
188 G3 Kalesija Bos.-Herz.
174 G5 Kalety Pol.
140 U4 Kalevala Rus. Fed.
96 B3 Kalewa Myanmar
146 L11 Kale Water r. Scotland U.K.
122 B2 Kaleybar Iran
107 P1 Kalga Rus. Fed.
87 D13 Kalgan r. W.A. Austr.
Kalgan Hebei China see Zhangjiakou
114 D5 Kalghatgi Karnataka India
87 F11 Kalgoorlie W.A. Austr.
207 H3 Kalguéri Niger
122 H6 Kāl Gūsheh Iran
188 E3 Kali Croatia
116 H5 Kali r. India/Nepal
197 Q7 Kaliakra, Nos pt Bulg.
94 F7 Kalianda Sumatera Indon.
92 D6 Kalibo Panay Phil.
232 A8 Kalida OH U.S.A.
94 C6 Kaliet Indon.
123 M3 Kalifgan Afgh.
117 J6 Kali Gandaki r. Nepal
114 F5 Kaligiri Andhra Prad. India
Kalikata W. Bengal India see Kolkata
139 W9 Kalikino Rus. Fed.
208 E5 Kalima Dem. Rep. Congo
95 I6 Kalimantan reg. Indon.
95 I4 Kalimantan Barat prov. Indon.
95 K6 Kalimantan Selatan prov. Indon.
95 J5 Kalimantan Tengah prov. Indon.
95 L3 Kalimantan Timur prov. Indon.
177 G5 Kali-medence park Hungary
Kálimnos i. Greece see Kalymnos
117 L6 Kalimpang W. Bengal India
114 D5 Kalinadi r. India
116 H6 Kali Nadi r. India
211 B7 Kalinda Zambia
115 I3 Kalingapatnam Andhra Prad. India
Kalinin Kyrg. see Tash-Bashat
Kalinin Rus. Fed. see Tver'
Kalinin Turkm. see Boldumsaz
Kalininabad Tajik. see Kalininobod
Kalinin Adyndaky Tajik. see Cheshtebe
137 M8 Kalinine Ukr.
138 D7 Kaliningrad Rus. Fed.
Kaliningrad Oblast admin. div. Rus. Fed. see Kaliningradskaya Oblast'
138 E7 Kaliningradskaya Oblast' admin. div. Rus. Fed.
138 C7 Kaliningradskiy Zaliv b. Rus. Fed.
129 G4 Kalininkänd Azer.
Kalinino Armenia see Tashir
175 K1 Kalinino Kaliningradskaya Oblast' Rus. Fed.
134 H4 Kalinino Kostromskaya Oblast' Rus. Fed.
137 S8 Kalinino Krasnodarskiy Kray Rus. Fed.
121 O1 Kalinino Omskaya Oblast' Rus. Fed.
134 L4 Kalinino Permskaya Oblast' Rus. Fed.
123 M3 Kalininobod Tajik.
Kalininsk Moldova see Cupcina
135 I6 Kalininsk Rus. Fed.
135 G7 Kalininskaya Rus. Fed.
Kalininskaya Oblast' admin. div. Rus. Fed. see Tverskaya Oblast'
137 L6 Kalinins'ke Ukr.
116 E8 Kalinjara Rajasthan India
136 I1 Kalinkavichy Belarus
Kalinkovichi Belarus see Kalinkavichy
129 J6 Kalinovka Azer.
120 F3 Kalinovka Kazakh.
137 N2 Kalinovka Rus. Fed.
Kalinovka Ukr. see Kalynivka
129 G2 Kalinovskaya Rus. Fed.
129 H2 Kalinovskiy Rus. Fed.
174 G4 Kalinowa Pol.
175 K2 Kalinowo Pol.
210 B4 Kaliro Uganda
210 F2 Kalis Somalia
95 J9 Kalisat Jawa Indon.
Kalisch Pol. see Kalisz
114 E1 Kali Sindh r. India
174 G2 Kaliska Pol.
238 G2 Kalispell MT U.S.A.
176 D3 Kaliště hill Czech Rep.
174 G4 Kalisz Pol.
174 D2 Kalisz Pomorski Pol.
122 G7 Kalituyeh Iran
135 H6 Kalitva r. Rus. Fed.
211 A6 Kaliua Tanz.
116 H7 Kaliujar Uttar Prad. India
140 Q4 Kalix Sweden
140 Q4 Kalixälven r. Sweden
116 F4 Kalka Haryana India
137 Q6 Kalka r. Ukr.
179 J4 Kalkalpen, Nationalpark nat. park Austria
199 K6 Kalkan Turkey
129 B5 Kalkandere Turkey
169 B7 Kalkar Ger.
84 C4 Kalkaringi N.T. Austr.
226 I5 Kalkaska MI U.S.A.
212 C4 Kalkfeld Namibia
215 J5 Kalkfonteindam dam S. Africa
215 J5 Kalkfontein Dam Nature Reserve S. Africa
170 D3 Kalkhorst Ger.
114 G9 Kalkudah Sri Lanka
251 G3 Kalkuni Guyana
214 F4 Kalkwerf S. Africa
169 C9 Kall Ger.
114 F7 Kallakkurichchi Tamil Nadu India
82 F2 Kallakoopah Creek watercourse S.A. Austr.
140 N3 Kallaktjåkkå mt. Sweden
114 E3 Kallam Mahar. India
142 J3 Kållandsö i. Sweden
94 □ Kallang Sing.
94 □ Kallang r. Sing.
138 K3 Kallaste Estonia
140 S5 Kallavesi l. Fin.
140 L5 Kållberget Sweden
140 Q4 Kallfjärden b. Sweden
179 I3 Kallham Austria
198 D4 Kallidromo mts Greece
198 C3 Kallifoni Greece
143 L5 Kallinge Sweden
196 H9 Kallmet i Madh Albania
173 L3 Kallmünz Ger.
198 G5 Kalloni Tinos Greece
199 H3 Kallonis, Kolpos b. Lesvos Greece
177 K4 Kállósemjén Hungary
140 L5 Kallsjön l. Sweden
114 E4 Kallur Karnataka India
120 K4 Kalmakkyrgan watercourse Kazakh.
177 K4 Kálmánháza Hungary
121 T1 Kalmanka Rus. Fed.
143 M5 Kalmar Sweden
143 M4 Kalmar county Sweden
143 M4 Kalmarsund sea chan. Sweden
172 E3 Kalmit hill Ger.
137 Q6 Kal'mius r. Ukr.
165 F6 Kalmthout Belgium
165 F6 Kalmthoutse Heide Natuurreservaat nature res. Belgium
122 G3 Kalmūkh Qal'eh Iran
114 G9 Kalmunai Sri Lanka
Kalmykia aut. rep. Rus. Fed. see Kalmykiya-Khalm'g-Tangch, Respublika
135 I7 Kalmykiya-Khalm'g-Tangch, Respublika aut. rep. Rus. Fed.
Kalmykovo Kazakh. see Taypak
Kalmytskaya Avtonomnaya Oblast' aut. rep. Rus. Fed. see Kalmykiya-Khalm'g-Tangch, Respublika
117 I8 Kalnai Chhattisgarh India
177 H3 Kalná nad Hronom Slovakia
138 G5 Kalnciems Latvia
117 M7 Kalni r. Bangl.
188 F2 Kalnik mts Croatia
177 H5 Kalocsa Hungary
136 F2 Kalodnaye Belarus
240 □D13 Kalohi Channel HI U.S.A.
128 A3 Kalokhorio Cyprus
209 E6 Kaloko Dem. Rep. Congo
116 D8 Kalol Gujarat India
116 D8 Kalol Gujarat India
93 D2 Kaloma i. Indon.
209 E9 Kalomo Zambia
96 C3 Kalon Myanmar
222 E4 Kalone Peak B.C. Can.
93 E1 Kalongan Sulawesi Indon.
128 A4 Kalopanagiotis Cyprus
78 □6 Kalourat, Mount Malaita Solomon Is
122 B2 Kalow r. Iran
177 H5 Káloz Hungary
140 U3 Kalozhnoye, Ozero l. Rus. Fed.
116 G4 Kalpa Hima. Prad. India
198 B3 Kalpaki Greece
114 C7 Kalpeni atoll India
114 E7 Kalpetta Kerala India
116 G6 Kalpi Uttar Prad. India
110 D6 Kalpin Xinjiang China
114 F8 Kalpitiya Sri Lanka
Kalquduq Uzbek. see Ko'lquduq
127 M6 Kal Safīd Iran
178 G5 Kals am Großglockner Austria
179 L6 Kalsdorf bei Graz Austria
122 G3 Kāl-Shūr, Rūd-e r. Iran
116 F4 Kalsi Uttaranchal India
220 C3 Kaltag AK U.S.A.
138 I6 Kaltanėnai Lith.
134 K5 Kaltasy Rus. Fed.
190 G1 Kaltbrunn Switz.
178 E5 Kaltenbach Austria
168 I3 Kaltenkirchen Ger.
169 J9 Kaltennordheim Ger.
169 J9 Kaltensundheim Ger.
169 J9 Kaltenwestheim Ger.
138 F6 Kaltinėnai Lith.
84 B8 Kaltukatjara N.T. Austr.
207 H4 Kaltungo Nigeria
116 D5 Kalu Rajasthan India
114 C3 Kalu r. India
240 □E12 Kalua'aha HI U.S.A.
196 I6 Kaluđerica Serbia
139 T7 Kaluga Rus. Fed.
Kaluga Oblast admin. div. Rus. Fed. see Kaluzhskaya Oblast'
137 L6 Kaluha Ukr.
95 L7 Kalukalukuang i. Indon.
93 A5 Kaluku Sulawesi Barat Indon.
95 K3 Kalulong, Bukit mt. Malaysia
209 F8 Kalulushi Zambia
86 I3 Kalumburu W.A. Austr.
86 I3 Kalumburu Aboriginal Reserve W.A. Austr.
142 H6 Kalundborg Denmark
209 E7 Kalundwe Dem. Rep. Congo
95 L1 Kalupis Falls Malaysia
123 N5 Kalur Kot Pak.
136 D4 Kalush Ukr.
175 J3 Kałuszyn Pol.
114 F9 Kalutara Sri Lanka
139 S7 Kaluzhskaya Oblast' admin. div. Rus. Fed.
141 H6 Kalvåg Norway
116 E9 Kalvan Mahar. India
138 G7 Kalvarija Lith.
138 I7 Kalveliai Lith.
134 C3 Kälviä Fin.
141 S6 Kalvitsa Fin.
141 R6 Kalvola Fin.
175 I2 Kalwa, Jezioro l. Pol.
114 F4 Kalwakurti Andhra Prad. India
179 K5 Kalwang Austria
175 H6 Kalwaria Zebrzydowska Pol.
134 L3 Kal'ya Rus. Fed.
114 C3 Kalyan Mahar. India
114 E5 Kalyandurg Andhra Prad. India
114 E4 Kalyani Karnataka India
115 H3 Kalyansingapuram Orissa India
139 U4 Kalyazin Rus. Fed.
136 E2 Kalyena Belarus
199 H6 Kalymnos Greece
199 H5 Kalymnos i. Greece
136 J3 Kalynivka Kyivs'ka Oblast' Ukr.
137 O8 Kalynivka Respublika Krym Ukr.
136 H4 Kalynivka Vinnyts'ka Oblast' Ukr.
139 N6 Kalyshki Belarus
137 K3 Kalyta Ukr.
199 J6 Kalythies Rodos Greece
198 C4 Kalyvia Greece
207 H4 Kam Nigeria
209 E5 Kama Dem. Rep. Congo
96 B5 Kama Myanmar
134 K4 Kama Rus. Fed.
134 K4 Kama r. Rus. Fed.
105 K4 Kamagaya Japan
102 S7 Kamaishi Japan
103 □3 Kama-iwa i. Japan
105 K5 Kamakura Japan
251 G3 Kamakusa Guyana
206 B4 Kamakwie Sierra Leone
202 C4 Kamal Chad
114 F5 Kamalapuram Andhra Prad. India
123 O6 Kamalia Pak.
240 □E12 Kamalō HI U.S.A.
96 C6 Kamamaung Myanmar
116 F6 Kaman Rajasthan India
126 F4 Kaman Turkey
105 I4 Kamanashi-gawa r. Japan
105 H4 Kamanashi-yama mt. Japan
214 G9 Kamanassie r. S. Africa
214 G9 Kamanassieberg mts S. Africa
227 Q4 Kamaniskeg Lake Ont. Can.
212 B3 Kamanjab Namibia
78 □6 Kamaosi Sta Isabel Solomon Is
124 F8 Kamaran Yemen
124 F8 Kamarān i. Yemen
251 F3 Kamarang Guyana
Kamaran Island Yemen see Kamarān
123 L4 Kamard reg. Afgh.
138 H5 Kamarde Latvia
114 F3 Kamareddi Andhra Prad. India
198 C4 Kamares Dytiki Ellas Greece
198 F6 Kamares Sifnos Greece
251 G3 Kamaria Falls Guyana
129 G4 Kämärli Azer.
Kamarlu Armenia see Artashat
136 J2 Kamaryn Belarus
Kamashi Uzbek. see Qamashi
116 H7 Kamasin Uttar Prad. India
213 E3 Kamativi Zimbabwe
207 F4 Kamba Nigeria
96 D2 Kambaiti Myanmar
208 C3 Kamba Kota C.A.R.
87 F11 Kambalda W.A. Austr.
134 I1 Kambal'nitskiye Koshki, Ostrova is Rus. Fed.
114 E8 Kambam Tamil Nadu India
94 D5 Kambang Sumatera Indon.
95 H9 Kambangan i. Indon.
209 C6 Kamba-Poko Dem. Rep. Congo
Kambara i. Fiji see Kabara
Kambara Japan see Kanbara
110 E6 Kambardi Xinjiang China
134 K4 Kambarka Rus. Fed.
206 B4 Kambia Sierra Leone
Kambing, Pulau i. East Timor see Ataúro, Ilha de
86 □2 Kambling Island Cocos Is
Kambo-san mt. N. Korea see Kwanmo-bong
209 E7 Kambove Dem. Rep. Congo
93 B5 Kambuno, Bukit mt. Indon.
197 O7 Kamburovo Bulg.
202 E2 Kambūt Libya
131 R4 Kamchatka r. Rus. Fed.
131 Q4 Kamchatka, Poluostrov pen. Rus. Fed.
266 G2 Kamchatka Basin sea feature Bering Sea
Kamchatka Peninsula Rus. Fed. see Kamchatka, Poluostrov
131 R4 Kamchatskiy Proliv str. Rus. Fed.
131 R4 Kamchatskiy Zaliv b. Rus. Fed.
197 P7 Kamchiya r. Bulg.
197 P8 Kamchiyska Planina hills Bulg.
214 H3 Kamden S. Africa
123 N4 Kamdesh Afgh.
Kameia, Parque Nacional de nat. park Angola see Cameia, Parque Nacional da
120 C1 Kamelik r. Rus. Fed.
197 N7 Kamen Bulg.
169 E7 Kamen Ger.
131 K3 Kamen', Gory mts Rus. Fed.
209 E6 Kamende Dem. Rep. Congo
176 D3 Kamenec mt. Czech Rep.
Kamenets-Podol'skiy Ukr. see Kam"yanets'-Podil's'kyy
197 K7 Kamenica Serbia
177 J2 Kamenica Slovakia
176 E2 Kamenice nad Lipou Czech Rep.
171 J9 Kamenický Šenov Czech Rep.
177 H4 Kameničná Slovakia
177 H4 Kamenín Slovakia
126 A3 Kamenitsa mt. Bulg.
197 M7 Kamenitsa r. Bulg.
177 H6 Kamenjak hill Croatia
188 D3 Kamenjak, Rt pt Croatia
120 D2 Kamenka Kazakh.
Kamenka Moldova see Camenca
134 I2 Kamenka Arkhangel'skaya Oblast' Rus. Fed.
139 S7 Kamenka Kaluzhskaya Oblast' Rus. Fed.
138 M1 Kamenka Leningradskaya Oblast' Rus. Fed.
135 I5 Kamenka Penzenskaya Oblast' Rus. Fed.
100 J6 Kamenka Primorskiy Kray Rus. Fed.
139 P6 Kamenka Smolenskaya Oblast' Rus. Fed.
135 G6 Kamenka Voronezhskaya Oblast' Rus. Fed.
Kamenka Ukr. see Kam"yanka
Kamenka-Bugskaya Ukr. see Kam"yanka-Buz'ka
Kamenka-Shevchenkovskaya Ukr. see Kam"yanka
Kamen'-Kashirskiy Ukr. see Kamin'-Kashyrs'kyy
Kamenka-Strumilovskaya Ukr. see Kam"yanka-Buz'ka
139 U5 Kamenki Rus. Fed.
130 J4 Kamen'-na-Obi Rus. Fed.
134 G4 Kamenniki Rus. Fed.
138 M1 Kamennogorsk Rus. Fed.
129 B1 Kamennomostskiy Rus. Fed.
140 U4 Kamennoye, Ozero l. Rus. Fed.
176 D2 Kamenný Přívoz Czech Rep.
176 D3 Kamenný Újezd Czech Rep.
197 P8 Kameno Bulg.
137 T6 Kamenolomni Rus. Fed.
Kamenongue Angola see Camanongue
100 H6 Kamen'-Rybolov Rus. Fed.
135 I6 Kamenskiy Rus. Fed.
131 R3 Kamenskoye Koryakskiy Avtonomnyy Okrug Rus. Fed.
139 V9 Kamenskoye Lipetskaya Oblast' Rus. Fed.
Kamenskoye Ukr. see Dniprodzerzhyns'k
135 H6 Kamensk-Shakhtinskiy Rus. Fed.
130 H4 Kamensk-Ural'skiy Rus. Fed.
171 J8 Kamenz Ger.
104 C5 Kameoka Japan
210 B4 Kameramaido Uganda
170 F5 Kamern Ger.
146 F11 Kames Argyll and Bute, Scotland U.K.
139 X5 Kameshkovo Rus. Fed.
111 D11 Kamet mt. Xizang China
104 D6 Kameyama Japan
196 H9 Kamëz Albania
104 A5 Kami Hyōgo Japan
105 G5 Kami Nagano Japan
103 G12 Kamiagata Japan
238 F3 Kamiah ID U.S.A.
104 F2 Kamichi Japan
175 L4 Kamień Lubelskie Pol.
175 K5 Kamień Podkarpackie Pol.
175 I6 Kamienica Pol.
174 E3 Kamieniec Pol.
174 E5 Kamieniec Ząbkowicki Pol.
174 F2 Kamień Krajeński Pol.
175 J4 Kamienna r. Pol.
174 E5 Kamienna Gora Pol.
174 F5 Kamiennik Pol.
174 C2 Kamień Pomorski Pol.
175 H4 Kamieńsk Pol.
170 K5 Kamień Wielkie Pol.
214 C6 Kamiesberg S. Africa
214 C6 Kamiesberge mts S. Africa
214 B6 Kamieskroon S. Africa
105 K4 Kamifukuoka Japan
102 T3 Kamifurano Japan
104 D5 Kami-ishizu Japan
209 D6 Kamiji Dem. Rep. Congo
104 E6 Kami-jima i. Japan
102 T3 Kamikawa Hokkaidō Japan
105 J3 Kamikawa Saitama Japan
105 K2 Kamikawachi Japan
104 C7 Kamikitayama Japan
103 G15 Kami-Koshiki-jima i. Japan
105 I4 Kamikuishiki Japan
84 H5 Kamileroi Qld Austr.
223 K2 Kamilukuak Lake Nunavut Can.
209 E7 Kamina Dem. Rep. Congo
209 E7 Kamina Base Dem. Rep. Congo
104 C5 Kaminaka Japan
223 M2 Kaminak Lake Nunavut Can.
136 D2 Kamin'-Kashyrs'kyy Ukr.
104 F4 Kaminoho Japan
105 K3 Kaminokawa Japan
102 R5 Kaminokuni Japan
102 □G18 Kaminone-jima i. Nansei-shotō Japan
102 R8 Kaminoyama Japan
188 E2 Kaminške in Savinjske Alpe mts Slovenia
139 Y4 Kaminskiy Rus. Fed.
Kaminuriak Lake Nunavut Can. see Qamanirjuaq Lake
104 F3 Kamioka Japan
175 I3 Kamion Mazowieckie Pol.
175 I4 Kamion Mazowieckie Pol.
175 K4 Kamionka Pol.
199 I6 Kamiros Rodos Greece
104 D3 Kamishihi Japan
102 U3 Kamishihoro Japan
105 M4 Kamisu Japan
104 E3 Kami-taira Japan
104 F3 Kami-takara Japan
103 G12 Kamitsushima Japan
209 F5 Kamituga Dem. Rep. Congo
104 F5 Kami-yahagi Japan
102 □H16 Kamiyaku Japan
105 H3 Kamiyamada Japan
102 U2 Kamiyūbetsu Japan
117 O7 Kamjong Manipur India
121 N5 Kamkaly Kazakh.
117 K6 Kamla r. India
117 N6 Kamla r. India
121 U2 Kamlak Rus. Fed.
222 F5 Kamloops B.C. Can.
222 F5 Kamloops Lake B.C. Can.
173 I5 Kammel r. Ger.
214 I9 Kammiebos S. Africa
173 I5 Kammlach Ger.
Kammuri-jima i. Japan see Kanmuri-jima
Kammuri-yama mt. Japan see Kanmuri-yama
188 E2 Kamnik Slovenia
179 I7 Kamno Slovenia
Kamo Armenia see Gavarr
104 C6 Kamo Kyōto Japan
105 I6 Kamo Yamanashi Japan
80 I2 Kamo North I. N.Z.
203 H5 Kamob Sanha Sudan
104 A8 Kamoda-misaki pt Japan
102 R3 Kamoenai Japan
105 L5 Kamogawa Japan
103 L12 Kamojima Japan
123 P6 Kamoke Pak.
209 E6 Kamola Dem. Rep. Congo
211 A6 Kamonanira Tanz.
179 M3 Kamp r. Austria
169 E10 Kamp Ger.
94 F5 Kampa Indon.
210 B4 Kampala Uganda
198 F4 Kampanos, Akrotirio pt Andros Greece
94 E4 Kampar r. Indon.
94 D2 Kampar Malaysia
117 I8 Kampara Chhattisgarh India
138 F4 Kamparkalns hill Latvia
94 D4 Kamparkiri r. Indon.
168 F1 Kampen Ger.
164 I3 Kampen Neth.
209 E5 Kampene Dem. Rep. Congo
172 F4 Kämpfelbach Ger.
96 D6 Kamphaeng Phet Thai.
211 B6 Kampi Katoto Tanz.
175 I3 Kampinos Pol.
175 I3 Kampinoski Park Narodowy nat. park Pol.
114 E5 Kampli Karnataka India
169 C8 Kamp-Lintfort Ger.
103 G11 Kamp'o S. Korea
209 F7 Kampolombo, Lake Zambia
97 G9 Kâmpóng Cham Cambodia
97 G8 Kâmpóng Chhnăng Cambodia
97 G8 Kâmpóng Khleăng Cambodia
Kâmpóng Saôm Cambodia see Sihanoukville
97 G9 Kâmpóng Spœ Cambodia
97 G8 Kâmpóng Thum Cambodia
97 G9 Kâmpóng Trâbêk Cambodia
97 G9 Kâmpóng Tranch Cambodia
97 G9 Kâmpôt Cambodia
206 E4 Kampti Burkina
Kampuchea country Asia see Cambodia
91 H7 Kamrau, Teluk b. Papua Indon.
223 K5 Kamsack Sask. Can.
206 B4 Kamsar Guinea
171 D9 Kamsdorf Ger.
134 K3 Kamskiy Rus. Fed.
135 J5 Kamskoye Ust'ye Rus. Fed.
134 L4 Kamskoye Vodokhranilishche resr Rus. Fed.
210 D4 Kamsuuma Somalia
116 H9 Kamtha Mahar. India
223 K3 Kamuchawie Lake Man./Sask. Can.
102 T4 Kamui-dake mt. Japan
210 B4 Kamuli Uganda
209 E6 Kamungu Dem. Rep. Congo
177 J5 Kamut Hungary
210 A4 Kamwenge Uganda
136 G2 Kam"yane Rivnens'ka Oblast' Ukr.
137 N3 Kam"yane Sums'ka Oblast' Ukr.
136 F5 Kam"yanets'-Podil's'kyy Ukr.
137 L4 Kam"yanka Cherkas'ka Oblast' Ukr.
137 Q4 Kam"yanka Kharkivs'ka Oblast' Ukr.
137 L5 Kam"yanka r. Ukr.
136 D3 Kam"yanka-Buz'ka Ukr.
137 N6 Kam"yanka-Dniprovs'ka Ukr.
136 I8 Kam"yans'ke Odes'ka Oblast' Ukr.
137 O6 Kam"yans'ke Zaporiz'ka Oblast' Ukr.
138 G9 Kamyanyets Belarus
138 G9 Kamyanyuki Belarus
122 B4 Kāmyārān Iran
138 L6 Kamyen' Belarus
138 H8 Kamyenka Belarus
135 G7 Kamyshevatskaya Rus. Fed.
135 I6 Kamyshin Rus. Fed.
135 K5 Kamyshla Rus. Fed.
120 I4 Kamyshlybash Kazakh.
Kamyshnaya r. Rus. Fed./Ukr. see Komyshna
120 C3 Kamysh-Samarskiye Ozera lakes Kazakh.
Kamyslybas Kazakh. see Kamyshlybash
120 I4 Kamyslybas, Ozero l. Kazakh.
120 I2 Kamysty Kazakh.
120 C4 Kamyzyak Rus. Fed.
125 M2 Kamzar Oman
131 K4 Kan r. Rus. Fed.
210 A2 Kan Sudan
208 F4 Kana Dem. Rep. Congo
213 E3 Kana r. Zimbabwe
224 E2 Kanaaupscow r. Que. Can.
241 T4 Kanab UT U.S.A.
241 T5 Kanab Creek r. AZ U.S.A.
79 □7 Kanacea Taveuni Fiji
105 G5 Kanae Japan
220 A4 Kanaga Island AK U.S.A.
105 J5 Kanagawa pref. Japan
102 R6 Kanagi Japan
251 F3 Kanaima Falls Guyana
225 J2 Kanairiktok r. Nfld and Lab. Can.
123 L7 Kanak Pak.
114 E6 Kanakapura Karnataka India
179 I7 Kanal Slovenia
198 F5 Kanala Kythnos Greece
198 B3 Kanali Greece
198 B3 Kanallaki Greece
127 L7 Kan'ān Iraq
140 M4 Kanan Sweden
215 K2 Kanana S. Africa
209 D6 Kananga Dem. Rep. Congo
83 M5 Kanangra-Boyd National Park N.S.W. Austr.
Kanarak Orissa India see Konarka
241 S4 Kanarraville UT U.S.A.
214 B3 Kanas watercourse Namibia
105 L2 Kanasagō Japan
134 I5 Kanash Rus. Fed.
110 H2 Kanas Köl l. China
Kanathea Taveuni Fiji see Kanacea
134 K3 Kanava Rus. Fed.
95 K3 Kanawang, Bukit mt. Malaysia
232 C10 Kanawha r. WV U.S.A.
105 H6 Kanaya Shizuoka Japan
104 B7 Kanaya Wakayama Japan
104 F4 Kanayama Japan
121 S3 Kanayka Kazakh.
104 E2 Kanazawa Ishikawa Japan
105 K5 Kanazawa Kanagawa Japan
104 D3 Kanazu Japan
96 B3 Kanbalu Myanmar
105 I5 Kanbara Japan
97 D8 Kanchanaburi Thai.
Kanchanjanga mt. India/Nepal see Kangchenjunga
117 L6 Kanchenjunga Conservation Area nature res. Nepal
114 F6 Kanchipuram Tamil Nadu India
175 K6 Kańczuga Pol.
123 L6 Kand mt. Pak.
123 L7 Kanda Pak.
123 K6 Kandahār Afgh.
123 K6 Kandahār prov. Afgh.
114 E3 Kandahar Mahar. India
140 V3 Kandalaksha Rus. Fed.
134 F2 Kandalakshskiy Zaliv g. Rus. Fed.
209 C6 Kandale Dem. Rep. Congo
94 B3 Kandang Sumatera Indon.
95 K6 Kandangan Kalimantan Indon.
138 F4 Kandava Latvia
Kandavu i. Fiji see Kadavu
Kandavu Passage Fiji see Kadavu Passage
207 F4 Kandé Togo
172 E3 Kandel Ger.
172 E5 Kandel mt. Ger.
170 H2 Kandelin Ger.
190 D2 Kander r. Switz.
172 D6 Kandern Ger.
190 D3 Kandersteg Switz.
123 M7 Kandhkot Pak.
123 N4 Kandhura Pak.
207 F4 Kandi Benin
123 L7 Kandi Pak.
93 B3 Kandi, Tanjung pt Indon.
123 M8 Kandiaro Pak.
198 B4 Kandila Dytiki Ellas Greece
198 D5 Kandila Peloponnisos Greece
207 H3 Kandil Bouzou well Niger
129 E6 Kandil Dağı mt. Turkey
129 B6 Kandilli Turkey
199 L1 Kandıra Turkey
208 D3 Kandja C.A.R.
116 C8 Kandla Gujarat India
113 □1 Kandooma Fushi i. S. Male Maldives
83 L5 Kandos N.S.W. Austr.
115 J1 Kandra Jharkhand India
213 □J3 Kandreho Madag.
117 I8 Kandri Chhattisgarh India
91 K8 Kandrian New Britain P.N.G.
114 F5 Kandukur Andhra Prad. India
114 G9 Kandy Sri Lanka
120 G3 Kandyagash Kazakh.
232 G7 Kane PA U.S.A.
221 L2 Kane Bassin b. Greenland
122 E8 Kaneh watercourse Iran
202 B6 Kanem pref. Chad
240 □D12 Kāne'ohe HI U.S.A.
240 □D12 Kāne'ohe Bay HI U.S.A.
116 E7 Kanera Rajasthan India
123 L7 Kaneti Pak.
Kanev Ukr. see Kaniv
134 G2 Kanevka Rus. Fed.
135 G7 Kanevskaya Rus. Fed.
104 F5 Kaneyama Gifu Japan
103 R8 Kaneyama Yamagata Japan
191 P5 Kanfanar Croatia
206 B4 Kanfarande Guinea
123 I6 Kang Afgh.
212 D4 Kang Botswana
117 L9 Kanga r. Bangl.
221 M3 Kangaamiut Greenland
221 K2 Kangaarsussuaq c. Greenland
221 M3 Kangaatsiaq Greenland
206 C4 Kangaba Mali
126 H4 Kangal Turkey
131 N3 Kangalassy Rus. Fed.
122 E8 Kangān Būshehr Iran
122 G9 Kangān Hormozgan Iran
86 E6 Kangan Aboriginal Reserve W.A. Austr.
Kangandala, Parque Nacional de nat. park Angola see Cangandala, Parque Nacional de
94 D1 Kangar Malaysia
206 C4 Kangaré Mali
82 F6 Kangaroo Island S.A. Austr.
84 G4 Kangaroo Point Qld Austr.
251 G3 Kangaruma Guyana
141 R6 Kangasala Fin.
140 T5 Kangaslampi Fin.
141 S6 Kangasniemi Fin.
122 B4 Kangāvar Iran
114 E7 Kangayam Tamil Nadu India
107 N6 Kangbao Hebei China
117 L6 Kangchenjunga mt. India/Nepal
108 C3 Kangding Sichuan China
95 K8 Kangean, Kepulauan is Indon.
221 L3 Kangeeak Point Nunavut Can.
210 B3 Kangen r. Sudan
221 N3 Kangeq c. Greenland
221 M3 Kangerluarsoruseq Greenland
221 M3 Kangerlussuaq Greenland

Kangerlussuaq to Kastl
331

221 M2 **Kangerlussuaq** *inlet* Greenland
221 M3 **Kangerlussuaq** *inlet* Greenland
221 O3 **Kangerlussuaq** *inlet* Greenland
221 N3 **Kangerlussuatsiaq** *inlet* Greenland
221 M2 **Kangersuatsiaq** Greenland
221 P2 **Kangertittivaq** *sea chan.* Greenland
221 O3 **Kangertittivatsiaq** *inlet* Greenland
210 C4 **Kangetet** Kenya
101 E8 **Kanggye** N. Korea
221 P2 **Kangikajik** *c.* Greenland
221 N3 **Kangilinnguit** Greenland
Kangiqcliniq *Nunavut* Can. *see* **Rankin Inlet**
225 H1 **Kangiqsualujjuaq** *Que.* Can.
221 K3 **Kangiqsujuaq** *Que.* Can.
Kangiqtugaapik *Nunavut* Can. *see* **Clyde River**
221 K3 **Kangirsuk** *Que.* Can.
97 D10 **Kang Krung National Park** Thai.
106 H9 **Kangle** *Gansu* China
Kangle *Jiangxi* China *see* **Wanzai**
111 I12 **Kangmar** *Xizang* China
101 F10 **Kangnŭng** S. Korea
208 A4 **Kango** Gabon
103 □3 **Kangoku-iwa** *i.* Japan
140 Q3 **Kangos** Sweden
107 R5 **Kangping** *Liaoning* China
116 F3 **Kangra** *Hima. Prad.* India
117 P5 **Kangri Karpo Pass** China/India
111 E11 **Kangrinboqê Feng** *mt. Xizang* China
111 G10 **Kangro** *Xizang* China
Kangsangdobdê *Xizang* China *see* **Xainza**
92 C9 **Kang Tipayan Dakula** *i.* Phil.
111 K13 **Kangto** *mt.* China/India
111 G10 **Kangtog** *Xizang* China
108 E2 **Kangxian** *Gansu* China
111 G10 **Kangxiwar** *Xinjiang* China
96 B6 **Kangyidaung** Myanmar
116 G9 **Kanhan** *r.* India
117 I7 **Kanhar** *r. Jharkhand* India
114 E3 **Kanhargaon** *Mahar.* India
143 O2 **Kanholmsfjärden** *b.* Sweden
206 D4 **Kani** Côte d'Ivoire
122 F8 **Kānī** Iran
104 F5 **Kani** Japan
96 B3 **Kani** Myanmar
210 D4 **Kaniama** Dem. Rep. Congo
209 E6 **Kaniama, Réserve des Éléphants de** *nature res.* Dem. Rep. Congo
Kanibadam Tajik. *see* **Konibodom**
95 L1 **Kanibongan** *Sabah* Malaysia
104 E5 **Kanie** Japan
81 F9 **Kaniere** *South I.* N.Z.
81 F9 **Kaniere, Lake** *South I.* N.Z.
206 A3 **Kanifing** Gambia
113 □1 **Kanifinolhu** *i. N. Male* Maldives
114 F5 **Kanigiri** *Andhra Prad.* India
123 M5 **Kaniguram** Pak.
217 □3b **Kani-Kéli** Mayotte
134 I2 **Kanin, Poluostrov** *pen.* Rus. Fed.
134 H1 **Kanin Nos** Rus. Fed.
134 H1 **Kanin Nos, Mys** *c.* Rus. Fed.
134 H2 **Kaninskiy Bereg** *coastal area* Rus. Fed.
127 L5 **Kānī Rash** Iraq
178 A5 **Kanisfluh** *mt.* Austria
115 R5 **Kanita** Japan
137 K4 **Kaniv** Ukr.
82 H7 **Kaniva** *Vic.* Austr.
137 K3 **Kanivs'ke Vodoskhovyshche** *resr* Ukr.
116 G8 **Kaniwara** *Madh. Prad.* India
117 I5 **Kanjiroba** *mt.* Nepal
196 I4 **Kanjiža** *Vojvodina* Serbia
141 Q6 **Kankaanpää** Fin.
226 G8 **Kankakee** *IL* U.S.A.
226 F8 **Kankakee** *r. IL* U.S.A.
206 C4 **Kankan** Guinea
206 C4 **Kankan, Réserve Naturelle de** *nature res.* Guinea
116 H9 **Kanker** *Chhattisgarh* India
113 H9 **Kankesanturai** Sri Lanka
207 G3 **Kankiya** Nigeria
206 C3 **Kankossa** Maur.
92 D6 **Kanlaon, Mount** *vol.* Phil.
97 D9 **Kanmaw Kyun** *i.* Myanmar
104 B4 **Kanmuri-jima** *i.* Japan
104 D4 **Kanmuri-yama** *mt.* Japan
103 J12 **Kanmuri-yama** *mt.* Japan
116 E9 **Kannad** *Mahar.* India
105 J3 **Kanna-gawa** *r.* Japan
105 I5 **Kannami** Japan
230 D4 **Kannapolis** *NC* U.S.A.
116 G6 **Kannauj** *Uttar Prad.* India
171 D8 **Kannawurf** Ger.
114 E8 **Kanniyakumari** *Tamil Nadu* India
Kanniya Kumari *c.* India *see* **Comorin, Cape**
116 F8 **Kannod** *Madh. Prad.* India
140 R5 **Kannonkoski** Fin.
104 F1 **Kannon-zaki** *pt* Japan
Kannur *Kerala* India *see* **Cannanore**
140 Q5 **Kannus** Fin.
138 K1 **Kannuskoski** Fin.
93 D5 **Kano** *i.* Indon.
207 H3 **Kano** Nigeria
207 H3 **Kano** *r.* Nigeria
207 H4 **Kano** *state* Nigeria
105 I5 **Kano-gawa** *r.* Japan
247 □10 **Kanon, Punt** *pt* Curaçao Neth. Antilles
211 A8 **Kanona** Zambia
121 R2 **Kanonerka** Kazakh.
103 K12 **Kan'onji** Japan
214 F10 **Kanonpunt** *pt* S. Africa
116 E7 **Kanor** *Rajasthan* India
236 D6 **Kanorado** *KS* U.S.A.
241 T3 **Kanosh** *UT* U.S.A.
212 C3 **Kanovlei** Namibia
95 J3 **Kanowit** *Sarawak* Malaysia
103 H15 **Kanoya** Japan
183 O2 **Kanpantxua** Spain
116 H6 **Kanpur** *Uttar Prad.* India
123 M7 **Kanpur** Pak.
105 J3 **Kanra** Japan
123 L8 **Kanrach** *reg.* Pak.
104 B7 **Kansai** *airport* Japan
209 E8 **Kansanshi** Zambia
236 H6 **Kansas** *r. KS* U.S.A.
236 F6 **Kansas** *state* U.S.A.
236 H6 **Kansas City** *KS* U.S.A.
236 H6 **Kansas City** *MO* U.S.A.
209 E7 **Kansenia** Dem. Rep. Congo
131 K4 **Kansk** Rus. Fed.
110 B7 **Kansu** *Xinjiang* China
Kansu *prov.* China *see* **Gansu**
210 B3 **Kanta** *mt.* Eth.
141 S5 **Kantala** Fin.
97 D11 **Kantang** Thai.
128 B3 **Kantara** *hill* Cyprus
97 G7 **Kantaralak** Thai.
129 C6 **Kantarkaya** Turkey
129 B5 **Kantarlı** Turkey
183 O3 **Kantauri Mendilerroa** *mts* Spain
Kantavu *i.* Fiji *see* **Kadavu**
207 F3 **Kantchari** Burkina
135 G6 **Kantemirovka** Rus. Fed.
164 K2 **Kantens** Neth.
116 G5 **Kanth** *Uttar Prad.* India
117 K9 **Kanthi** *W. Bengal* India
117 J6 **Kanti** *Bihar* India
117 J9 **Kantilo** *Orissa* India
220 C3 **Kantishna** *r. AK* U.S.A.
111 B12 **Kantli** *r.* India
105 K4 **Kantō-heiya** *plain* Japan
77 I2 **Kanton** *atoll Phoenix Is* Kiribati
Kan-Too, Pik *mt.* Kazakh./Kyrg. *see* **Khan-Tengri, Pik**
105 H4 **Kanto-sanchi** *mts* Japan
84 D5 **Kanttaji Aboriginal Land** *res. N.T.* Austr.
96 C5 **Kantulong** Myanmar
147 E8 **Kanturk** Ireland
84 E5 **Kanturrpa Aboriginal Land** *res. N.T.* Austr.
122 F5 **Kanūgar** Iran
251 G4 **Kanuku Mountains** Guyana
105 K2 **Kanuma** Japan
211 A5 **Kanungu** Uganda
114 E5 **Kanur** *Andhra Prad.* India
212 C5 **Kanus** Namibia
91 J8 **Kanuwe** *r.* P.N.G.
Kanyakubja *Uttar Prad.* India *see* **Kannauj**
215 P1 **Kanyamazane** S. Africa
212 E5 **Kanye** Botswana
212 F2 **Kanyemba** Zimbabwe
139 Q6 **Kanyutino** Rus. Fed.
104 A5 **Kanzaki** Japan
93 E3 **Kao** *Halmahera* Indon.
207 G3 **Kao** Niger
79 □8 **Kao** *i.* Tonga
93 E3 **Kao, Teluk** *b. Halmahera* Indon.
109 M7 **Kaohsiung** Taiwan
97 F9 **Kaôh Tang** *i.* Cambodia
212 B3 **Kaokoveld** *plat.* Namibia
206 A3 **Kaolack** Senegal
78 □6 **Kaolo** *Sta Isabel* Solomon Is
209 F7 **Kaoma** *Northern* Zambia
209 E8 **Kaoma** *Western* Zambia
202 C5 **Kaortchi** *well* Chad
208 D3 **Kaouadja** C.A.R.
79 □8 **Kapa** *i. Vava'u Gp* Tonga
240 □B11 **Kapa'a** *HI* U.S.A.
240 □F13 **Kapa'au** *HI* U.S.A.
121 R5 **Kapal** Kazakh.
93 E4 **Kapalabuaya** *Maluku* Indon.
196 H8 **Kapa Moračka** *mt.* Montenegro
129 H6 **Kapan** Armenia
209 D7 **Kapanga** Dem. Rep. Congo
209 F6 **Kapangolo** Dem. Rep. Congo
Kapara Te Hau *l. South I.* N.Z. *see* **Grassmere, Lake**
198 E4 **Kaparelli** Greece
122 G8 **Kaparhā** Iran
136 H1 **Kapatkyevichy** Belarus
211 A7 **Kapatu** Zambia
121 Q6 **Kapchagay** Kazakh.
121 Q6 **Kapchagayskoye Vodokhranilishche** *resr* Kazakh.
210 B4 **Kapchorwa** Uganda
138 G8 **Kapčiamiestis** Lith.
Kap Dan Greenland *see* **Kulusuk**
164 E6 **Kapelle** Neth.
165 F6 **Kapellen** Belgium
198 E6 **Kapello, Akrotirio** *pt Kythira* Greece
143 P2 **Kapellskär** Sweden
Kapelskär Sweden *see* **Kapellskär**
210 B4 **Kapenguria** Kenya
179 L5 **Kapfenberg** Austria
179 K5 **Kapfenstein** Austria
199 I2 **Kapıdağı Yarımadası** *pen.* Turkey
117 M6 **Kapili** *r.* India
77 F1 **Kapingamarangi** *atoll* Micronesia
266 F5 **Kapingamarangi Rise** *sea feature* N. Pacific Ocean
199 L2 **Kapıorman Dağları** *mts* Turkey
123 M6 **Kapip** Pak.
208 F4 **Kapiri Mposhi** Zambia
123 M3 **Kāpīsā** *prov.* Afgh.
221 Q5 **Kapisillit** Greenland
224 D2 **Kapiskau** *r. Ont.* Can.
227 M2 **Kapiskong Lake** *Ont.* Can.
95 J3 **Kapit** *Sarawak* Malaysia
137 K5 **Kapitanivka** Ukr.
81 I7 **Kapiti Island** *North I.* N.Z.
251 H4 **Kapiting** Brazil
202 D5 **Kapka** *well* Chad
202 D6 **Kapka, Massif du** *mts* Chad
93 E5 **Kaplamada, Gunung** *mt. Buru* Indon.
122 F1 **Kaplankyr, Chink** *esc.* Turkm./Uzbek.
122 G1 **Kaplankyr Döwlet Gorugy** *nature res.* Turkm.
176 D3 **Kaplice** Czech Rep.
97 D10 **Kapoe** Thai.
208 B3 **Kapoeta** Sudan
177 J4 **Kápolna** Hungary
93 C8 **Kapondai, Tanjung** *pt Flores* Indon.
80 I6 **Kaponga** *North I.* N.Z.
211 B7 **Kaporo** Malawi
196 G4 **Kapos** *r.* Romania
177 G5 **Kaposfő** Hungary
177 H5 **Kaposszekcső** Hungary
177 G5 **Kaposvár** Hungary
123 J9 **Kappar** Pak.
172 C2 **Kappel** Ger.
179 J6 **Kappel am Krappfeld** Austria
172 D5 **Kappel-Grafenhausen** Ger.
168 I1 **Kappeln** Ger.
172 E4 **Kappelrodeck** Ger.
178 B5 **Kappl** Austria
116 E7 **Kapran** *Rajasthan* India
178 G5 **Kaprun** Austria
210 B4 **Kapsabet** Kenya
123 J8 **Kap Salt Swamp** Pak.
101 F8 **Kapsan** N. Korea
139 Q2 **Kapsha** *r.* Rus. Fed.
198 D5 **Kapsia** Greece
Kapsukas Lith. *see* **Marijampolė**
117 N8 **Kaptai** Bangl.
107 P2 **Kaptsegaytuy** Rus. Fed.
136 H1 **Kaptsevichy** Belarus
175 L2 **Kaptsyowka** Belarus
95 H5 **Kapuas** *r.* Indon.
95 K6 **Kapuas** *r.* Indon.
95 J4 **Kapuas Hulu, Pegunungan** *mts* Indon./Malaysia
82 G6 **Kapunda** *S.A.* Austr.
116 D6 **Kapuriya** *Rajasthan* India
116 E4 **Kapurthala** *Punjab* India
177 K2 **Kapušany** Slovakia
224 D3 **Kapuskasing** *Ont.* Can.
224 D3 **Kapuskasing** *r. Ont.* Can.
135 I6 **Kapustin Yar** Rus. Fed.
137 K3 **Kapustyntsi** *Kyivs'ka Oblast'* Ukr.
137 N3 **Kapustyntsi** *Sums'ka Oblast'* Ukr.
209 F7 **Kaputa** Zambia
122 H9 **Kapūtānī** Iran
83 M4 **Kaputar** *mt. N.S.W.* Austr.
210 B4 **Kaputir** Kenya
176 G4 **Kapuvár** Hungary
Kapydzhik, Gora *mt.* Armenia/Azer. *see* **Qazangödağ**
138 K8 **Kapyl'** Belarus
101 E10 **Kap'yŏng** S. Korea
139 P6 **Kapyrevshchina** Rus. Fed.
111 L11 **Ka Qu** *r. Xizang* China
116 H7 **Kara** *Uttar Prad.* India
134 N1 **Kara** *r.* Rus. Fed.
207 F4 **Kara** Togo
127 J4 **Kara** *r.* Turkey
199 K2 **Kara** *r.* Turkey
199 H4 **Kara Ada** *i.* Turkey
199 I6 **Kara Ada** *i.* Turkey
199 H3 **Karaağaç** Turkey
126 F4 **Karaali** Turkey
110 A7 **Kara Art Pass** *Xinjiang* China
Karaaul Kazakh. *see* **Karaul**
121 O6 **Kara-Balta** Kyrg.
120 J1 **Karabalyk** Kazakh.
139 V5 **Karabanovo** Rus. Fed.
121 O3 **Karabas** Kazakh.
120 E3 **Karabau** Kazakh.
120 F6 **Karabaur, Uval** *hills* Uzbek.
Karabekaul Turkm. *see* **Garabekewül**
129 C7 **Karabey** Turkey
199 I2 **Karabiga** Turkey
129 B6 **Karaboğa Dağları** *mts* Turkey
Kara-Bogaz-Gol Turkm. *see* **Garabogazköl**
Karaboynak Turkm. *see* **Ataýap**
129 I3 **Karabudakhkent** Rus. Fed.
126 F3 **Karabük** Turkey
121 R5 **Karabulak** *Almatinskaya Oblast'* Kazakh.
121 U4 **Karabulak** *Vostochnyy Kazakhstan* Kazakh.
129 F2 **Karabulak** Rus. Fed.
121 P3 **Karabulakskaya** Kazakh.
Karabura *Xinjiang* China *see* **Yumin**
199 J4 **Karaburç** Turkey
199 H4 **Karaburun** Turkey
120 I3 **Karabutak** Kazakh.
199 J2 **Karacabey** Turkey
126 F5 **Karacadağ** *mts* Turkey
199 I1 **Karacakılavuz** Turkey
126 D3 **Karacaköy** Turkey
127 I5 **Karacalı Dağ** *mt.* Turkey
128 A2 **Karaçal Tepe** *mt.* Turkey
199 L5 **Karacaören Barajı** *resr* Turkey
199 J5 **Karacasu** Turkey
199 L6 **Karaca Yarımadası** *pen.* Turkey
Karachay-Cherkess Republic *aut. rep.* Rus. Fed. *see* **Karachayevo-Cherkesskaya Respublika**
Karachayevo-Cherkesskaya A.S.S.R. *aut. rep.* Rus. Fed. *see* **Karachayevo-Cherkesskaya Respublika**
129 C2 **Karachayevo-Cherkesskaya Respublika** *aut. rep.* Rus. Fed.
129 C2 **Karachayevsk** Rus. Fed.
139 R8 **Karachev** Rus. Fed.
123 L9 **Karachi** Pak.
137 M6 **Karachunivs'ke Vodoskhovyshche** *resr* Ukr.
127 K4 **Karaçoban** Turkey
199 K6 **Karaçulha** Turkey
Karacurun Turkey *see* **Hilvan**
177 G5 **Karád** Hungary
114 D4 **Karad** *Mahar.* India
128 G2 **Kara Dağ** *hill* Turkey
199 H2 **Kara Dağ** *hill* Turkey
199 J2 **Kara Dağ** *hills* Turkey
126 F5 **Kara Dağ** *mt.* Turkey
121 O7 **Kara-Darya** *r.* Kyrg.
Kara-Dar'ya Uzbek. *see* **Payshanba**
Kara Deniz *sea* Asia/Europe *see* **Black Sea**
206 E4 **Karaga** Ghana
100 B2 **Karagan** Rus. Fed.
121 O3 **Karaganda** Kazakh.
121 O3 **Karagandinskaya Oblast'** *admin. div.* Kazakh.
129 G1 **Karagas** Rus. Fed.
121 Q5 **Karagash** Kazakh.
120 D2 **Karagay** Kazakh.
134 K4 **Karagay** Rus. Fed.
121 P3 **Karagayly** Kazakh.
121 U3 **Karagaylybulak** Kazakh.
122 F2 **Karagez** Turkm.
131 R4 **Karaginskiy, Ostrov** *i.* Rus. Fed.
120 D6 **Karagiye, Vpadina** *depr.* Kazakh.
117 K7 **Karagola** *Bihar* India
129 B6 **Karagöl Dağları** *mts* Turkey
121 T2 **Karaguzhikha** Kazakh.
211 A5 **Karagwe** Tanz.
197 P9 **Karahalil** Turkey
199 K4 **Karahallı** Turkey
126 G4 **Karahasanlı** Turkey
199 J5 **Karahisar** Turkey
134 L5 **Karaidel'** Rus. Fed.
114 F7 **Karaikal** *Pondicherry* India
114 F7 **Karaikkudi** *Tamil Nadu* India
121 U4 **Kara Irtysh** *r.* Kazakh.
126 G5 **Karaisalı** Turkey
95 L4 **Karaitan** *Kalimantan* Indon.
122 D4 **Karaj** Iran
Karak Jordan *see* **Al Karak**
Kara-Kala Turkm. *see* **Magtymguly**
Karakalli Turkey *see* **Özalp**
Karakalpakistan, Respublika *aut. rep.* Uzbek. *see* **Qoraqalpog'iston Respublikasi**
Karakalpakskaya Respublika *aut. rep.* Uzbek. *see* **Qoraqalpog'iston Respublikasi**
Karakalpakstan *aut. rep.* Uzbek. *see* **Qoraqalpog'iston Respublikasi**
129 C5 **Karakamış** Turkey
83 I7 **Kara Kara State Park** *nature res. Vic.* Austr.
Karakax *Xinjiang* China *see* **Moyu**
111 E7 **Karakax He** *r.* China
111 E9 **Karakax Shan** *mts Xinjiang* China
129 C5 **Karakaya** Turkey
129 D6 **Karakaya** *r.* Turkey
129 C6 **Karakaya Tepe** *mt.* Turkey
126 I5 **Karakeçi** Turkey
126 F4 **Karakeçili** Turkey
93 E1 **Karakelong** *i.* Indon.
111 E8 **Karaki** *Xinjiang* China
93 D2 **Karakitang** *i.* Indon.
Karaklis Armenia *see* **Vanadzor**
127 J4 **Karakoçan** Turkey
121 N1 **Karakoga** Kazakh.
Karakoin *salt l.* Kazakh. *see* **Karakoyyn, Ozero**
120 E3 **Karakol'** Kazakh.
121 O7 **Kara-Köl** Kyrg.
121 Q7 **Karakol** *Ysyk-Köl* Kyrg.
121 R6 **Karakol** *Ysyk-Köl* Kyrg.
Karakolka Kyrg. *see* **Karakol**
Karaköprü Turkey *see* **Karaçoban**
116 F2 **Karakoram Pass** China/Jammu and Kashmir
123 P3 **Karakoram Range** *mts* Asia
210 C2 **Kara K'orē** Eth.
206 B3 **Karakoro** *r.* Mali/Maur.
Karaköse *Ağrı* Turkey *see* **Ağrı**
128 D2 **Karaköse** *Hatay* Turkey
199 H3 **Karaköy** Turkey
129 I3 **Karakoysu** *r.* Rus. Fed.
129 F6 **Karakoyunlu** Turkey
121 M4 **Karakoyyn, Ozero** *salt l.* Kazakh.
Karakubbud Ukr. *see* **Komsomol's'ke**
Kara-Kuga Kazakh. *see* **Karakoga**
Kara Kul' Kyrg. *see* **Kara-Köl**
Karakul', Ozero *l.* Tajik. *see* **Qarokŭl**
Kara-Kul'dzha Kyrg. *see* **Kara-Kulja**
134 K4 **Karakulino** Rus. Fed.
121 O7 **Kara-Kulja** Kyrg.
120 J1 **Karakul'skoye** Rus. Fed.
121 R4 **Karakum** Kazakh.
120 E5 **Karakum, Peski** *des.* Kazakh.
Karakum Desert Kazakh. *see* **Karakum, Peski**
Karakum Desert Turkm. *see* **Garagum**
127 K3 **Karakurt** *Kars* Turkey
199 I3 **Karakurt** *Manisa* Turkey
199 L4 **Karakuş Dağı** *ridge* Turkey
212 C3 **Karakuwisa** Namibia
208 B1 **Karal** Chad
138 E3 **Karala** Estonia
87 E8 **Karalundi** *W.A.* Austr.
93 A5 **Karama** *r.* Indon.
Karamagay *Xinjiang* China *see* **Haramgai**
199 J3 **Karaman** *Balıkesir* Turkey
126 F5 **Karaman** *Karaman* Turkey
128 B1 **Karaman** *prov.* Turkey
199 L6 **Karamanbeyli Geçidi** *pass* Turkey
199 K5 **Karamanlı** Turkey
110 G4 **Karamay** *Xinjiang* China
123 O3 **Karambar Pass** Afgh./Pak.
95 L6 **Karambu** *Kalimantan* Indon.
81 G8 **Karamea** *South I.* N.Z.
81 G8 **Karamea** *r. South I.* N.Z.
81 F8 **Karamea Bight** *b. South I.* N.Z.
120 K2 **Karamendy** Kazakh.
95 K7 **Karamian** *i.* Indon.
199 L4 **Karamıkkaracaören** Turkey
111 G8 **Karamiran** *Xinjiang* China
111 G8 **Karamiran He** *r.* China
111 H8 **Karamiran Shankou** *pass Xinjiang* China
131 Q3 **Karamken** Rus. Fed.
199 K2 **Karamürsel** Turkey
175 K1 **Karamyshevo** *Kaliningradskaya Oblast'* Rus. Fed.
138 L4 **Karamyshevo** *Pskovskaya Oblast'* Rus. Fed.
123 N3 **Karan** *r.* Afgh.
Karan *state* Myanmar *see* **Kayin**
125 I2 **Karān** *i.* Saudi Arabia
251 G4 **Karanambo** Guyana
177 I3 **Karancsalja** Hungary
177 I3 **Karancskeszi** Hungary
177 I3 **Karancsság** Hungary
206 A3 **Karang** Senegal
93 A4 **Karang, Tanjung** *pt* Indon.
94 F6 **Karangagung** *Sumatera* Indon.
94 F7 **Karangan** *Sumatera* Indon.
81 D10 **Karangarua** *South I.* N.Z.
95 K9 **Karangasem** *Bali* Indon.
95 H9 **Karangbolong, Tanjung** *pt* Indon.
93 D2 **Karangetang** *vol.* Indon.
208 B4 **Karangoua** *r.* Congo
116 F9 **Karanja** *Mahar.* India
114 E3 **Karanja** *r.* India
116 H8 **Karanjia** *Madh. Prad.* India
117 J9 **Karanjia** *Orissa* India
116 D5 **Karanpura** *Rajasthan* India
121 Q1 **Karaoba** Kazakh.
199 I5 **Karaova** Turkey
199 K6 **Karaovabeli Geçidi** *pass* Turkey
121 P5 **Karaoy** *Almatinskaya Oblast'* Kazakh.
121 P5 **Karaoy** *Almatinskaya Oblast'* Kazakh.
197 P7 **Karapelit** Bulg.
128 E2 **Karapınar** *Gaziantep* Turkey
126 F5 **Karapınar** *Konya* Turkey
199 J3 **Karapürçek** *Balıkesir* Turkey
199 L2 **Karapürçek** *Sakarya* Turkey
110 C6 **Karaqi** *Xinjiang* China
212 C5 **Karas** *admin. reg.* Namibia
214 B3 **Karas** *mts* Namibia
129 A6 **Karasakal Dağları** *mts* Turkey
126 E3 **Karaşar** Turkey
111 F8 **Karasay** *Xinjiang* China
121 Q7 **Kara-Say** Kyrg.
212 C6 **Karasburg** Namibia
Kara Sea Rus. Fed. *see* **Karskoye More**
139 W5 **Karash** Rus. Fed.
121 P2 **Karashoky** Kazakh.
188 G3 **Karašica** *r.* Croatia
177 H6 **Karasica** *r.* Hungary/Romania
137 N8 **Karasivka** *r.* Ukr.
Kárášjohka *Finnmark* Norway *see* **Karasjok**
140 R2 **Kárášjohka** *r.* Norway
140 R2 **Karasjok** *Finnmark* Norway
Karasjokka *r.* Norway *see* **Kárášjohka**
121 P2 **Karasor** Kazakh.
121 M1 **Karasor, Ozero** *l.* Kazakh.
121 P2 **Karasor, Ozero** *salt l.* Kazakh.
121 P3 **Karasor, Ozero** *salt l.* Kazakh.
Kara Strait Rus. Fed. *see* **Karskiye Vorota, Proliv**
104 E6 **Karasu** Japan
121 P4 **Karasu** *Karagandinskaya Oblast'* Kazakh.
120 J2 **Karasu** *Kostanayskaya Oblast'* Kazakh.
120 K1 **Karasu** *Kostanayskaya Oblast'* Kazakh.
121 P1 **Karasu** *r.* Kazakh.
128 E2 **Karasu** *r.* Syria/Turkey
Karasu *Bitlis* Turkey *see* **Hizan**
199 L1 **Karasu** *Sakarya* Turkey
127 K4 **Karasu** *r.* Turkey
Karasubazar Ukr. *see* **Bilohirs'k**
105 J3 **Karasu-gawa** *r.* Japan
121 R1 **Karasuk** Rus. Fed.
136 H8 **Karasulak** *r.* Ukr.
121 O7 **Kara-Suu** Kyrg.
105 L2 **Karasuyama** Japan
136 E2 **Karasyn** Ukr.
122 I4 **Karāt** Iran
129 H3 **Karata** Rus. Fed.
121 U4 **Karatal** Kazakh.
126 G5 **Karataş** *Adana* Turkey
128 E2 **Karataş** *Hatay* Turkey
199 J4 **Karatas** Turkey
Karataş Burnu *hd* Turkey *see* **Fener Burnu**
121 N6 **Karatau** Kazakh.
121 L5 **Karatau, Khrebet** *mts* Kazakh.
134 M1 **Karatayka** Rus. Fed.
128 A2 **Karatepe** Turkey
97 D9 **Karathuri** Myanmar
114 F8 **Karativu** *i.* Sri Lanka
140 O3 **Karatj** *l.* Sweden
120 E3 **Karatobe** Kazakh.
120 H4 **Karatobe, Mys** *pt* Kazakh.
120 H3 **Karatogay** Kazakh.
121 Q4 **Karatol** *r.* Kazakh.
120 J1 **Karatomarskoye Vodokhranilishche** *resr* Kazakh.
120 E4 **Karaton** Kazakh.
140 O3 **Karats** Sweden
103 G13 **Karatsu** Japan
93 E1 **Karatung** *i.* Indon.
106 A3 **Karatüngü** *Xinjiang* China
120 H4 **Karatup, Poluostrov** *pen.* Kazakh.
120 K2 **Kara-Turgay** *r.* Kazakh.
121 R3 **Karaul** Kazakh.
116 F6 **Karauli** *Rajasthan* India
Karaulkel'dy Kazakh. *see* **Bayganin**
127 K3 **Karaurgan** Turkey
Karavan Kyrg. *see* **Kerben**
198 D6 **Karavas** *Kythira* Greece
196 H10 **Karavastasë, Gjiri i** *b.* Albania
196 H10 **Karavastasë, Laguna e** *lag.* Albania
136 J1 **Karavatsichy** Belarus
139 Y4 **Karavayevo** Rus. Fed.
198 E6 **Karavia** *i.* Greece
199 H7 **Karavonisia** *i.* Greece
128 A3 **Karavostasi** Cyprus
198 E7 **Karavoutas, Akra** *pt Kriti* Greece
208 D4 **Karawa** Dem. Rep. Congo
94 G8 **Karawang** *Jawa* Indon.
179 J6 **Karawanken** *mts* Austria
Karaxahar *r.* China *see* **Kaidu He**
129 D6 **Karayazı** Turkey
128 E2 **Karayılan** Turkey
110 E6 **Karayulgan** *Xinjiang* China
121 N3 **Karazhal** Kazakh.
120 D5 **Karazhanbas** Kazakh.
121 O4 **Karazhingil** Kazakh.
127 L7 **Karbalā'** Iraq
127 K7 **Karbalā'** *governorate* Iraq
169 G10 **Karben** Ger.
170 F4 **Karbow-Vietlübbe** Ger.
121 P3 **Karbushevka** Kazakh.
168 I1 **Karby** Ger.
177 J4 **Karcag** Hungary
177 K3 **Karcsa** Hungary
175 J3 **Karczew** Pol.
175 K4 **Karczmiska** Pol.
197 Q7 **Kardam** Bulg.
199 I6 **Kardamaina** *Kos* Greece
198 D6 **Kardamyli** Greece
179 K1 **Kardašova Řečice** Czech Rep.
Kardeljevo Croatia *see* **Ploče**
169 D10 **Karden** Ger.
Kardhaámaina *Kos* Greece *see* **Kardamaina**
Kardhítsa Greece *see* **Karditsa**
198 G6 **Kardiotissa** *i.* Greece
140 Q3 **Kardis** Sweden
198 C3 **Karditsa** Greece
138 F3 **Kärdla** Estonia
177 J5 **Kardos** Hungary
179 O4 **Kardos-ér** *r.* Hungary
177 J5 **Kardoskút** Hungary
139 P7 **Kardymovo** Rus. Fed.
129 F2 **Kardzhin** Rus. Fed.
215 K4 **Karee** S. Africa
214 F6 **Kareeberge** *mts* S. Africa
214 G6 **Kareebospoort** *pass* S. Africa
214 I9 **Kareedouw** S. Africa
180 D5 **Kareha, Jebel** *mt.* Morocco
203 F5 **Kareima** Sudan
129 E4 **K'areli** Georgia
116 G8 **Kareli** *Madh. Prad.* India
Karelia *aut. rep.* Rus. Fed. *see* **Kareliya, Respublika**
138 J8 **Karelichy** Belarus
134 F3 **Kareliya, Respublika** *aut. rep.* Rus. Fed.
Karel'skaya A.S.S.R. *aut. rep.* Rus. Fed. *see* **Kareliya, Respublika**
134 F2 **Karel'skiy Bereg** *coastal area* Rus. Fed.
211 A6 **Karema** *Rukwa* Tanz.
Karen *state* Myanmar *see* **Kayin**
99 K1 **Karenga** *r.* Rus. Fed.
116 G7 **Karera** *Madh. Prad.* India
140 Q2 **Karesuando** Sweden
122 I8 **Kārevāndar** Iran
80 I4 **Karewa** *i. North I.* N.Z.
80 K4 **Karewa Island** *North I.* N.Z.
123 I5 **Karez Dasht** Afgh.
120 F2 **Kargala** Rus. Fed.
129 H2 **Kargalinskaya** Rus. Fed.
Kargalinski Rus. Fed. *see* **Kargalinskaya**
120 G2 **Kargalinskoye** Kazakh.
121 P3 **Kargaly** Kazakh.
127 J4 **Kargapazarı Dağları** *mts* Turkey
Karghalik *Xinjiang* China *see* **Yecheng**
126 G3 **Kargı** Turkey
116 F3 **Kargiakh** Jammu and Kashmir
116 F2 **Kargil** Jammu and Kashmir
Kargilik *Xinjiang* China *see* **Yecheng**
128 C2 **Kargıpınarı** Turkey
134 G3 **Kargopol'** Rus. Fed.
174 D3 **Kargowa** Pol.
122 G8 **Kargūshkī** Iran
116 G6 **Karhal** *Uttar Prad.* India
207 H4 **Kari** Nigeria
204 D2 **Karia Ba Mohammed** Morocco
122 G8 **Karīān** Iran
137 U1 **Karian** Rus. Fed.
198 E2 **Kariani** Greece
181 E5 **Kariat-Arkmane** Morocco
213 F3 **Kariba** Zimbabwe
209 E9 **Kariba, Lake** *resr* Zambia/Zimbabwe
209 F9 **Kariba Dam** Zambia/Zimbabwe
102 Q4 **Kariba-yama** *vol.* Japan
212 B4 **Karibib** Namibia
214 H9 **Kariega** *r.* S. Africa
125 I7 **Karīf Salāsil** *well* Yemen
140 R2 **Karigasniemi** Fin.
138 J1 **Karijärvi** *l.* Fin.
87 E7 **Karijini National Park** *W.A.* Austr.
80 H1 **Karikari, Cape** *North I.* N.Z.
122 F5 **Karīmābād** Iran
95 H5 **Karimata** *i.* Indon.
95 H5 **Karimata, Pulau-pulau** *is* Indon.
95 H5 **Karimata, Selat** *str.* Indon.
117 N7 **Karimganj** *Assam* India
122 D4 **Karim Khanch** Iran
114 F3 **Karimnagar** *Andhra Prad.* India
94 E4 **Karimun Besar** *i.* Indon.
95 I7 **Karimunjawa** *i.* Indon.
95 I7 **Karimunjawa, Pulau-pulau** *is* Indon.
210 E2 **Karin** Somalia
141 Q6 **Karinainen** Fin.
199 J5 **Karınçalı Dağı** *mts* Turkey
141 L5 **Käringsjön** Sweden
215 P1 **Karino** S. Africa
80 I4 **Karioi** *hill North I.* N.Z.
141 Q6 **Karis** Fin.
211 A5 **Karisimbi, Mont** *vol.* Rwanda
Káristos Greece *see* **Karystos**
122 G5 **Karit** Iran
198 D2 **Karitsa** Greece
104 E6 **Kariya** Japan
213 E3 **Kariyangwe** Zimbabwe
Karjaa Fin. *see* **Karis**
138 G1 **Karjalohja** Fin.
116 D8 **Karjan** *Gujarat* India
114 D3 **Karjat** *Mahar.* India
117 K8 **Karkai** *r. Jharkhand* India
114 D6 **Karkal** *Karnataka* India
114 D4 **Karkamb** *Mahar.* India
214 B6 **Karkams** S. Africa
121 P3 **Karkaralinsk** Kazakh.
92 E9 **Karkaralong, Kepulauan** *is* Indon.
91 K7 **Karkar Island** P.N.G.
122 D5 **Karkas, Kūh-e** *mts* Iran
123 L8 **Karkh** Pak.
122 B6 **Karkheh, Rūdkhāneh-ye** *r.* Iran
137 L8 **Karkinits'ka Zatoka** *g.* Ukr.
141 R6 **Karkkila** Fin.
141 R6 **Kärkölä** Fin.
Karkonoski Park Narodowy *nat. park* Czech Rep./Pol. *see* **Krkonošský narodní park**
174 D5 **Karkonoski Park Narodowy** *nat. park* Pol.
138 I3 **Karksi-Nuia** Estonia
124 C3 **Karkūmā, Ra's** *hd* Saudi Arabia
123 N5 **Karlachi** Pak.
84 D5 **Karlantijpa North Aboriginal Land** *res. N.T.* Austr.
84 D6 **Karlantijpa South Aboriginal Land** *res. N.T.* Austr.
138 D2 **Karlby** *Åland* Fin.
143 N1 **Karlholmsbruk** Sweden
129 C5 **Karlı** Turkey
117 I8 **Karlidi** *Chhattisgarh* India
106 D5 **Karlik Shan** *mts Xinjiang* China
174 D1 **Karlino** Pol.
127 J4 **Karlıova** Turkey
137 O4 **Karlivka** Ukr.
129 E6 **Karlıyayla** Turkey
123 O3 **Karl Marks, Qullai** *mt.* Tajik.
Karl-Marx-Stadt Ger. *see* **Chemnitz**
Karlo-Libknekhtovsk Ukr. *see* **Soledar**
188 E3 **Karlovac** Croatia
176 B1 **Karlovarský kraj** *admin. reg.* Czech Rep.
199 H5 **Karlovasi** *Samos* Greece
176 G1 **Karlovice** Czech Rep.
Karlovka Ukr. *see* **Karlivka**
197 M8 **Karlovo** Bulg.
176 B1 **Karlovy Vary** Czech Rep.
172 F4 **Karlsbad** Ger.
141 M6 **Karlsberg** Sweden
143 K3 **Karlsborg** Sweden
170 I3 **Karlsburg** Ger.
Karlsburg Romania *see* **Alba Iulia**
172 F3 **Karlsdorf-Neuthard** Ger.
173 K5 **Karlsfeld** Ger.
170 I2 **Karlshagen** Ger.
143 K5 **Karlshamn** Sweden
168 H4 **Karlshöfen** Ger.
173 K4 **Karlshuld** Ger.
143 K2 **Karlskoga** Sweden
173 K4 **Karlskron** Ger.
143 L5 **Karlskrona** Sweden
143 N4 **Karlsöarna** *i.* Sweden
172 E3 **Karlsruhe** Ger.
172 F4 **Karlsruhe** *admin. reg.* Ger.
142 J2 **Karlstad** Sweden
236 G1 **Karlstad** *MN* U.S.A.
172 H2 **Karlstadt** Ger.
169 H10 **Karlstein am Main** Ger.
179 L2 **Karlstein an der Thaya** Austria
179 M3 **Karlstetten** Austria
220 C4 **Karluk** *AK* U.S.A.
140 □ **Karl XII Øyane** *i.* Svalbard
123 L3 **Karlyk** Turkm.
139 N8 **Karma** Belarus
207 F3 **Karma** Niger
202 C6 **Karma, Ouadi** *watercourse* Chad
129 F3 **Karmadon** Rus. Fed.
114 D3 **Karmala** *Mahar.* India
139 R6 **Karmanovo** Rus. Fed.
140 O3 **Karmas** Sweden
128 D6 **Karmel, Har** *hill* Israel
Karmir Armenia *see* **Chambarak**
Karmona Spain *see* **Córdoba**
142 B2 **Karmøy** *i.* Norway
123 O7 **Karmpur** Pak.
117 N8 **Karnafuli Reservoir** Bangl.
116 F5 **Karnal** *Haryana* India
116 H5 **Karnali** *r.* Nepal
136 J7 **Karnaliyivka** Ukr.
117 M8 **Karnaphuli** *r.* Bangl.
116 G4 **Karnaprayag** *Uttaranchal* India
114 D5 **Karnataka** *state* India
137 N5 **Karnaukhivka** Ukr.
237 G11 **Karnes City** *TX* U.S.A.
174 D1 **Karnice** Pol.
175 I3 **Karniewo** Pol.
178 G6 **Karnische Alpen** *mts* Austria
197 O8 **Karnobat** Bulg.
179 I6 **Kärnten** *land* Austria
123 K8 **Karodi** Pak.
213 F3 **Karoi** Zimbabwe
191 P5 **Karojba** Croatia
96 C7 **Karokpi** Myanmar
111 J12 **Karo La** *pass Xizang* China
177 H2 **Karolinka** Czech Rep.
93 B7 **Karompalompo** *i.* Indon.
117 O7 **Karong** *Manipur* India
211 B7 **Karonga** Malawi
87 G11 **Karonie** *W.A.* Austr.
121 Q7 **Karool-Döbö** Kyrg.
Karool-Tëbë Kyrg. *see* **Karool-Döbö**
214 G8 **Karoo National Park** S. Africa
82 G6 **Karoonda** *S.A.* Austr.
123 N6 **Karor** Pak.
203 H5 **Karora** Eritrea
Káros *i.* Greece *see* **Keros**
93 A4 **Karossa** *Sulawesi Barat* Indon.
95 M9 **Karossa, Tanjung** *pt Sumba* Indon.
199 H1 **Karoti** Greece
206 E2 **Karouassa** *well* Mali
202 D6 **Karoub** Chad
198 A3 **Karousades** *Kerkyra* Greece
170 F3 **Karow** *Mecklenburg-Vorpommern* Ger.
171 F6 **Karow** *Sachsen-Anhalt* Ger.
174 D5 **Karpacz** Pol.
128 C3 **Karpasia** *pen.* Cyprus
Karpas Peninsula Cyprus *see* **Karpasia**
199 I7 **Karpathos** *Karpathos* Greece
199 I7 **Karpathos** *i.* Greece
199 I6 **Karpathou, Steno** *sea chan.* Greece
136 D5 **Karpats'kiy** *nat. park* Ukr.
Karpaty *mts* Europe *see* **Carpathian Mountains**
198 C4 **Karpenisi** Greece
Karpilovka Belarus *see* **Aktsyabrski**
134 M4 **Karpinsk** Rus. Fed.
134 I2 **Karpogory** Rus. Fed.
137 L1 **Karpovychi** Ukr.
199 I5 **Karpuzlu** *Aydın* Turkey
199 H2 **Karpuzlu** *Edirne* Turkey
136 J3 **Karpylivka** *Chernihivs'ka Oblast'* Ukr.
137 M3 **Karpylivka** *Chernihivs'ka Oblast'* Ukr.
136 G2 **Karpylivka** *Rivnens'ka Oblast'* Ukr.
86 D6 **Karratha** *W.A.* Austr.
Karrats Fjord *inlet* Greenland *see* **Nuugaatsiaap Imaa**
170 E4 **Karrenzin** Ger.
122 D7 **Karrī** Iran
215 L6 **Karringmelkspruit** S. Africa
Karroo *plat.* S. Africa *see* **Great Karoo**
87 E10 **Karroun Hill Nature Reserve** *W.A.* Austr.
123 J4 **Karrukh** Afgh.
Karrychirla Turkm. *see* **Garryçyrla**
127 K3 **Kars** Turkey
129 E5 **Kars** *prov.* Turkey
129 E5 **Kars** *r.* Turkey
121 L4 **Karsakpay** Kazakh.
140 R5 **Kärsämäki** Fin.
138 K5 **Kārsava** Latvia
171 E8 **Karsdorf** Ger.
Karshi *Qashqadaryo* Uzbek. *see* **Qarshi**
129 C4 **Karşıköy** Turkey
174 F2 **Karsin** Pol.
199 J2 **Karşıyaka** *Balıkesir* Turkey
199 I4 **Karşıyaka** *İzmir* Turkey
117 L6 **Karsiyang** *W. Bengal* India
130 G3 **Karskiye Vorota, Proliv** *str.* Rus. Fed.
170 L5 **Karsko** Pol.
130 I2 **Karskoye More** *sea* Rus. Fed.
170 E4 **Karstädt** *Brandenburg* Ger.
170 D4 **Karstädt** *Mecklenburg-Vorpommern* Ger.
134 D3 **Karstula** Fin.
135 I5 **Karsun** Rus. Fed.
177 I4 **Kartal** Hungary
199 K2 **Kartal** Turkey
217 □3a **Kartala** *vol. Njazidja* Comoros
217 □3a **Kartala, Forêt du** *for. Njazidja* Comoros
120 I1 **Kartaly** Rus. Fed.
116 E4 **Kartarpur** *Punjab* India
139 O6 **Kartashevichi** Rus. Fed.
139 O6 **Kartavshchina** Rus. Fed.
134 K2 **Kartayel'** Rus. Fed.
138 E6 **Kartena** Lith.
232 G7 **Karthaus** *PA* U.S.A.
178 G6 **Kartitsch** Austria
178 G6 **Kartitscher Sattel** *pass* Austria
129 F3 **K'art'lis K'edi** *hills* Georgia
Kartsa Rus. Fed. *see* **Oktyabr'skoye**
139 N5 **Kartsevo** Rus. Fed.
198 F4 **Kartsino, Akrotirio** *pt Skyros* Greece
140 S5 **Karttula** Fin.
251 G3 **Kartuni** Guyana
143 O7 **Kartuzy** Pol.
209 F8 **Karubwe** Zambia
105 I3 **Karuizawa** Japan
122 H7 **Karūk** Iran
102 S6 **Karumai** Japan
85 H4 **Karumba** *Qld* Austr.
122 D6 **Karun, Kūh-e** *hill* Iran
122 C6 **Kārūn, Rūd-e** *r.* Iran
114 E8 **Karunagapalli** *Kerala* India
140 Q3 **Karungi** Sweden
210 B5 **Karungu** Kenya
93 A8 **Karuni** *Sumba* Indon.
86 I4 **Karunjie** *W.A.* Austr.
142 F5 **Karup** Denmark
142 F5 **Karup** *r.* Denmark
114 F7 **Karur** *Tamil Nadu* India
211 A5 **Karuzi** Burundi
114 F6 **Karvetnagar** *Andhra Prad.* India
141 Q5 **Karvia** Fin.
177 H2 **Karviná** Czech Rep.
136 H3 **Karvynivka** Ukr.
114 D5 **Karwar** *Karnataka* India
178 D5 **Karwendelgebirge** *mts* Austria
178 D5 **Karwendelgebirge** *nature res.* Austria
116 H7 **Karwi** *Uttar Prad.* India
175 J2 **Karwica** Pol.
170 D4 **Karwitz** Ger.
198 B4 **Karya** *Lefkada* Greece
Karyagino Azer. *see* **Füzuli**
198 F2 **Karyes** Greece
99 J1 **Karymskoye** Rus. Fed.
120 E6 **Karynzharyk, Peski** *des.* Kazakh.
198 F4 **Karystos** Greece
137 N2 **Karyzh** Rus. Fed.
202 E6 **Kas** Sudan
199 K6 **Kaş** Turkey
114 C3 **Kasa** *Mahar.* India
Kasaba Turkey *see* **Turgutlu**
211 A7 **Kasaba Lodge** Zambia
224 B2 **Kasabonika** *Ont.* Can.
224 B2 **Kasabonika Lake** *Ont.* Can.
211 A6 **Kasacasia** Tanz.
104 G3 **Kasaga-dake** *mt.* Japan
104 C6 **Kasagi** Japan
104 F4 **Kasagi-yama** *mt.* Japan
104 F5 **Kasahara** Japan
209 C5 **Kasaï** *r.* Dem. Rep. Congo
104 A6 **Kasai** Japan
209 D6 **Kasaï, Plateau du** Dem. Rep. Congo
209 D6 **Kasaï-Occidental** *prov.* Dem. Rep. Congo
209 E6 **Kasaï-Oriental** *prov.* Dem. Rep. Congo
209 D7 **Kasaji** Dem. Rep. Congo
105 J3 **Kasakake** Japan
105 L3 **Kasama** Japan
211 A7 **Kasama** Zambia
104 E5 **Kasamatsu** Japan
Kasan Uzbek. *see* **Koson**
211 A5 **Kasana** Tanz.
212 E3 **Kasane** Botswana
211 A7 **Kasanga** Tanz.
209 B6 **Kasangulu** Dem. Rep. Congo
209 F8 **Kasanka National Park** Zambia
104 D3 **Kasano-misaki** *pt* Japan
Kasansay Uzbek. *see* **Kosonsoy**
209 C6 **Kasanza** Dem. Rep. Congo
203 H5 **Kasar, Ras** *pt* Sudan
114 D6 **Kasaragod** *Kerala* India
102 □G18 **Kasarai-zaki** *hd Nansei-shotō* Japan
138 G3 **Kasari** *r.* Estonia
138 L6 **Kasary** Belarus
100 G4 **Kasatkino** Rus. Fed.
104 D6 **Kasatori-yama** *hill* Japan
223 K2 **Kasba Lake** Can.
204 D2 **Kasba Tadla** Morocco
142 E5 **Kås Bredning** *b.* Denmark
103 H15 **Kaseda** Japan
176 C2 **Kasejovice** Czech Rep.
209 E8 **Kasempa** Zambia
171 D10 **Kasendorf** Ger.
209 D7 **Kasenga** *Katanga* Dem. Rep. Congo
209 F7 **Kasenga** *Katanga* Dem. Rep. Congo
208 F4 **Kasenye** Dem. Rep. Congo
208 E5 **Kasese** Dem. Rep. Congo
210 A4 **Kasese** Uganda
Kasevo Rus. Fed. *see* **Neftekamsk**
116 G6 **Kasganj** *Uttar Prad.* India
108 B3 **Kasha** *Xizang* China
210 D5 **Kasha** *waterhole* Kenya
224 B3 **Kashabowie** *Ont.* Can.
239 K9 **Kasha-Katuwe Tent Rocks National Monument** *nat. park NM* U.S.A.
122 D5 **Kāshān** Iran
135 H6 **Kashary** Rus. Fed.
224 D2 **Kashechewan** *Ont.* Can.
Kashgar *Xinjiang* China *see* **Kashi**
110 C7 **Kashi** *Xinjiang* China
104 C6 **Kashiba** Japan
104 C7 **Kashihara** Japan
105 M4 **Kashima** *Ibaraki* Japan
104 E2 **Kashima** *Ishikawa* Japan
103 H13 **Kashima** *Saga* Japan
105 M3 **Kashima-nada** *b.* Japan
104 G2 **Kashimayaria-dake** *mt.* Japan
104 F4 **Kashimo** Japan
139 U4 **Kashin** Rus. Fed.
139 U4 **Kashinka** *r.* Rus. Fed.
209 F7 **Kashiobwe** Dem. Rep. Congo
116 G5 **Kashipur** *Uttaranchal* India
139 V7 **Kashira** Rus. Fed.
139 V7 **Kashirka** *r.* Rus. Fed.
137 S2 **Kashirskoye** Rus. Fed.
209 F8 **Kashitu** Zambia
105 K4 **Kashiwa** Japan
104 C6 **Kashiwara** Japan
103 P9 **Kashiwazaki** Japan
Kashkadar'ya *r.* Uzbek. *see* **Qashqadaryo**
Kashkadarya Oblast *admin. div.* Uzbek. *see* **Qashqadaryo**
121 O5 **Kashkanteniz** Kazakh.
134 G2 **Kashkarantsy** Rus. Fed.
Kashken-Teniz Kazakh. *see* **Kashkanteniz**
129 E2 **Kashkhatau** Rus. Fed.
122 F6 **Kashku'iyeh** Iran
139 O6 **Kashkurino** Rus. Fed.
137 P6 **Kashlahach** *r.* Ukr.
122 H4 **Kāshmar** Iran
Kashmir *terr.* Asia *see* **Jammu and Kashmir**
116 E2 **Kashmir, Vale of** *reg.* India
123 M7 **Kashmor** Pak.
123 N4 **Kashmund** *reg.* Afgh.
137 M9 **Kashtany** Ukr.
209 E6 **Kashyukulu** Dem. Rep. Congo
Kasi *Uttar Prad.* India *see* **Varanasi**
117 I6 **Kasia** *Uttar Prad.* India
123 N4 **Kasigar** Afgh.
139 Q8 **Kasilovo** Rus. Fed.
93 A4 **Kasimbar** *Sulawesi* Indon.
199 M5 **Kasımlar** Turkey
135 H5 **Kasimov** Rus. Fed.
179 N8 **Kašina** Croatia
208 F4 **Kasingi** Dem. Rep. Congo
93 E4 **Kasiruta** *i. Maluku* Indon.
177 I5 **Kaskantyú** Hungary
236 K7 **Kaskaskia** *r. IL* U.S.A.
223 N3 **Kaskattama** *r. Man.* Can.
121 Q6 **Kaskelen** Kazakh.
141 P5 **Kaskinen** Fin.
Kas Klong *i.* Cambodia *see* **Kŏng, Kaôh**
Kaskö Fin. *see* **Kaskinen**
122 E1 **Kaskyrbulak Yuzhnyy, Gora** *hill* Turkm.
222 G5 **Kaslo** *B.C.* Can.
223 K3 **Kasmere Lake** *Man.* Can.
139 R6 **Kasnya** *r.* Rus. Fed.
209 F7 **Kasomeno** Dem. Rep. Congo
95 J5 **Kasongan** *Kalimantan* Indon.
209 E6 **Kasongo** Dem. Rep. Congo
209 C6 **Kasongo-Lunda** Dem. Rep. Congo
209 C6 **Kasongo Lunda Falls** Angola/Dem. Rep. Congo
209 E6 **Kasonguele** Dem. Rep. Congo
199 H7 **Kasos** *i.* Greece
199 I7 **Kasou, Steno** *sea chan.* Greece
176 C2 **Kašperské Hory** Czech Rep.
129 F4 **Kaspi** Georgia
Kaspīy Mangy Oypaty *lowland* Kazakh./Rus. Fed. *see* **Prikaspiyskaya Nizmennost'**
129 I3 **Kaspiysk** Rus. Fed.
Kaspiyskiy Rus. Fed. *see* **Lagan'**
Kaspiyskoye More *l.* Asia/Europe *see* **Caspian Sea**
139 O7 **Kasplya** Rus. Fed.
139 N6 **Kasplya** *r.* Rus. Fed.
116 E8 **Kasrawad** *Madh. Prad.* India
Kasrik Turkey *see* **Gürpınar**
129 H4 **Kasristsqali** Georgia
Kassa Slovakia *see* **Košice**
138 F3 **Kassaare laht** *b.* Estonia
203 H6 **Kassala** Sudan
203 G6 **Kassala** *state* Sudan
198 E3 **Kassandras, Akrotirio** *pt* Greece
198 E2 **Kassandras, Kolpos** *b.* Greece
198 E2 **Kassandras Chersonisos** *pen.* Greece
198 E2 **Kassandreia** Greece
168 K2 **Kasseedorf** Ger.
169 I8 **Kassel** Ger.
169 H8 **Kassel** *admin. reg.* Ger.
205 H2 **Kasserine** Tunisia
Kassinga Angola *see* **Cassinga**
226 B5 **Kasson** *MN* U.S.A.
207 H3 **Kassouloua** *well* Niger
123 I9 **Kastag** Pak.
126 F3 **Kastamonu** Turkey
169 D10 **Kastellaun** Ger.
199 G7 **Kastelli** *Kriti* Greece
Kastéllion *Kriti* Greece *see* **Kissamos**
Kastellorizon *i.* Greece *see* **Megisti**
199 I7 **Kastelo, Akrotirio** *pt Karpathos* Greece
165 G6 **Kasterlee** Belgium
173 L3 **Kastl** *Bayern* Ger.
173 N5 **Kastl** *Bayern* Ger.

Kęsowo to Kilmaurs
333

174 F2 Kęsowo Pol.
165 G6 Kessel Belgium
173 J4 Kessel r. Ger.
165 J6 Kessel Neth.
151 P3 Kessingland Suffolk, England U.K.
199 K2 Kestel Bursa Turkey
Kestel Bursa Turkey see Gürsu
199 L5 Kestel Gölü l. Turkey
215 M4 Kestell S. Africa
140 U4 Kesten'ga Rus. Fed.
140 S4 Kestilä Fin.
227 O5 Keswick Ont. Can.
149 K4 Keswick Cumbria, England U.K.
176 G5 Keszthely Hungary
176 G5 Keszthelyihegység park Hungary
130 J4 Ket' r. Rus. Fed.
207 F5 Keta Ghana
94 D6 Ketahun Sumatera Indon.
94 □ Ketam, Pulau i. Sing.
95 J8 Ketapang Jawa Indon.
95 I5 Ketapang Kalimantan Indon.
220 E4 Ketchikan AK U.S.A.
238 G5 Ketchum ID U.S.A.
262 T2 Ketchum Glacier Antarctica
177 K5 Kétegyháza Hungary
207 E5 Kete Krachi Ghana
164 I3 Ketelmeer l. Neth.
176 G5 Kéthely Hungary
111 J10 Ketian Qinghai China
123 L9 Keti Bandar Pak.
121 S6 Ketmen', Khrebet mts China/Kazakh.
207 F5 Kétou Benin
137 L6 Ketrysanivka Ukr.
143 R7 Kętrzyn Pol.
177 J5 Kétsoprony Hungary
208 B4 Ketta Congo
207 I5 Kétté Cameroon
168 E5 Kettenkamp Ger.
151 K3 Kettering Northamptonshire, England U.K.
232 A9 Kettering OH U.S.A.
173 I5 Kettershausen Ger.
170 E1 Kettinge Denmark
222 G5 Kettle r. B.C. Can.
226 B4 Kettle r. MN U.S.A.
232 H7 Kettle Creek r. PA U.S.A.
238 E2 Kettle Falls WA U.S.A.
240 M5 Kettleman City CA U.S.A.
226 B3 Kettle River MN U.S.A.
238 E2 Kettle River Range mts WA U.S.A.
146 K4 Kettletoft Orkney, Scotland U.K.
149 M5 Kettlewell North Yorkshire, England U.K.
95 I4 Ketungau r. Indon.
175 H6 Kęty Pol.
171 H8 Ketzerbach r. Ger.
171 G6 Ketzin Ger.
232 H6 Keuka NY U.S.A.
232 H6 Keuka Lake NY U.S.A.
169 K8 Keula Ger.
Keumgang, Mount N. Korea see Kumgang-san
Keumsang, Mount N. Korea see Kumgang-san
206 A2 Keur Massène Maur.
141 R5 Keurusselkä l. Fin.
141 R5 Keuruu Fin.
179 J6 Keutschach am See Austria
179 J6 Keutscharcher See l. Austria
169 B7 Kevelaer Ger.
177 K5 Kevermes Hungary
140 S2 Kevo Fin.
140 S2 Kevon luonnonpuisto nature res. Fin.
246 G3 Kew Turks and Caicos Is
226 E8 Kewanee IL U.S.A.
93 C8 Kewapante Flores Indon.
226 F6 Kewaskum WI U.S.A.
226 G5 Kewaunee WI U.S.A.
226 F3 Keweenaw Bay MI U.S.A.
226 F3 Keweenaw Bay b. MI U.S.A.
226 F2 Keweenaw Peninsula MI U.S.A.
226 G2 Keweenaw Point MI U.S.A.
150 G5 Kewstoke North Somerset, England U.K.
147 F4 Key, Lough l. Ireland
210 B3 Keyala Sudan
236 F4 Keya Paha r. NE U.S.A.
224 D4 Key Harbour Ont. Can.
110 F5 Keyi Xinjiang China
107 R1 Keyihe Nei Mongol China
149 Q6 Keyingham East Riding of Yorkshire, England U.K.
231 G13 Key Largo FL U.S.A.
231 G13 Key Largo National Marine Sanctuary nature res. FL U.S.A.
84 B3 Keyling Inlet N.T. Austr.
122 E3 Keymir Turkm.
Keymir Turkm. see Keymir
150 G5 Keynsham Bath and North East Somerset, England U.K.
232 G9 Keyser WV U.S.A.
232 F9 Keysers Ridge MD U.S.A.
237 G7 Keystone Lake OK U.S.A.
227 O9 Keystone Lake PA U.S.A.
241 U10 Keystone Peak AZ U.S.A.
232 G11 Keysville VA U.S.A.
236 I6 Keytesville MO U.S.A.
122 C4 Keytū Iran
134 G2 Keyvy, Vozvyshennost' hills Rus. Fed.
231 G13 Key West FL U.S.A.
151 J2 Keyworth Nottinghamshire, England U.K.
134 K4 Kez Rus. Fed.
233 □O5 Kezar Falls ME U.S.A.
213 F4 Kezi Zimbabwe
177 J2 Kežmarok Slovakia
215 K3 Kgakala S. Africa
212 D5 Kgalagadi admin. dist. Botswana
214 F1 Kgalagadi Transfrontier Park nat. park Botswana/S. Africa
212 E5 Kgatleng admin. dist. Botswana
215 K3 Kgotsong S. Africa
215 M4 Kgubetswana S. Africa
128 E5 Khabab Syria
122 F6 Khabar Iran
134 K2 Khabarikha Rus. Fed.
100 I4 Khabarovsk Rus. Fed.
100 I3 Khabarovskiy Kray admin. div. Rus. Fed.
Khabarovsk Kray admin. div. Rus. Fed. see Khabarovskiy Kray
121 R1 Khabary Rus. Fed.
124 G7 Khabb, Wādī watercourse Yemen
125 N4 Khabbah, Ra's al pt Oman
129 C1 Khabez Rus. Fed.
Khabis Iran see Shahdād
123 J4 Khabody Pass Afgh.
175 M3 Khabovichy Belarus
122 G7 Khabr Iran
124 E4 Khabrā al'Arn salt pan Saudi Arabia
128 H7 Khabrah Sāfiyah hill Saudi Arabia
118 E2 Khābūr, Nahr al r. Syria
Khachmas Azer. see Xaçmaz
116 E8 Khachrod Madh. Prad. India
125 N4 Khadar, Jabal mt. Oman
124 F7 Khaḑāran Saudi Arabia
208 E2 Khadari watercourse Sudan
124 F1 Khadd, Wādī al watercourse Saudi Arabia
127 N8 Khādeyn Iran
139 O8 Khadun' Belarus
129 A1 Khadyzhensk Rus. Fed.
129 I3 Khadzhalmakhi Rus. Fed.
197 L9 Khadzhidimovo Bulg.
122 G2 Khadzhiolen Turkm.
136 J7 Khadzhybeys'kyy Lyman l. Ukr.
175 M2 Khadziloni Belarus
124 H3 Khafs Banbān well Saudi Arabia
125 H4 Khafs Daghrah Saudi Arabia
122 E7 Khāftar Iran
116 H7 Khaga Uttar Prad. India
117 K7 Khagaria Bihar India
117 J7 Khagaul Bihar India
117 M8 Khagrachari Bangl.
Khagrachchari Bangl. see Khagrachari
116 H9 Khairagarh Chhattisgarh India
111 C13 Khairagarh Uttar Prad. India
123 N7 Khairgarh Pak.
116 H5 Khairigarh Uttar Prad. India
123 O7 Khairpur Pak.
123 M8 Khairpur Pak.
116 D8 Khairwara Rajasthan India
129 D3 Khaishi Georgia
122 D6 Khāīz, Kūh-e mt. Iran
123 K3 Khaja Du Koh hill Afgh.
123 M5 Khajuri Kach Pak.
98 F1 Khakasiya, Respublika aut. rep. Rus. Fed.
Khakassia aut. rep. Rus. Fed. see Khakasiya, Respublika
Khakasskaya A.S.S.R. aut. rep. Rus. Fed. see Khakasiya, Respublika
123 M4 Khāk-e Jabbar Afgh.
129 G3 Khakhalgi, Gora mt. Rus. Fed.
212 D5 Khakhea Botswana
123 K6 Khak-rēz Afgh.
123 K6 Khakriz reg. Afgh.
129 I3 Khalagork r. Rus. Fed.
122 D4 Khalajestan reg. Iran
129 H4 Khalakhurkats, Pereval pass Rus. Fed.
138 M6 Khalamyer"ye Belarus
129 E3 Khalatsa, Mt'a Georgia/Rus. Fed.
116 F2 Khalatse Jammu and Kashmir
122 E5 Khalidabad Iran
123 L6 Khalifat mt. Pak.
117 I6 Khalilabad Uttar Prad. India
122 H4 Khalilabad Iran
122 E8 Khalīlī Iran
120 H2 Khalilovo Rus. Fed.
123 J1 Khalkabad Turkm.
122 C3 Khalkhāl Iran
Khálki i. Greece see Chalki
129 G3 Khal-Kiloy Rus. Fed.
Khalkís Greece see Chalkida
115 I3 Khallikot Orissa India
134 N2 Khal'mer-Yu Rus. Fed.
138 L7 Khalopyenichy Belarus
Khalqobod Uzbek. see Xalqobod
117 J6 Khalte Nepal
Khalturin Rus. Fed. see Orlov
129 H2 Khamamatyurt Rus. Fed.
106 H1 Khamar-Daban, Khrebet mts Rus. Fed.
116 H8 Khamaria Madh. Prad. India
116 B8 Khambhaliya Gujarat India
116 D8 Khambhat Gujarat India
114 B3 Khambhat, Gulf of India
116 F9 Khamgaon Mahar. India
122 F8 Khamīr Iran
124 F7 Khamir Yemen
213 F4 Khami Ruins National Monument tourist site Zimbabwe
124 F6 Khamis Mushayṭ Saudi Arabia
120 D4 Khamit Yergaliyev Kazakh.
96 G5 Khamkkeut Laos
124 H2 Khamma well Saudi Arabia
114 G4 Khammam Andhra Prad. India
131 N3 Khampa Rus. Fed.
96 B3 Khampat Myanmar
131 M3 Khamra Rus. Fed.
128 A8 Khamsah Egypt
122 C4 Khamseh reg. Iran
129 B1 Khamyshki Rus. Fed.
Khamza Uzbek. see Hamza
123 M5 Khan Afgh.
96 F5 Khan, Nam r. Laos
123 M3 Khānābād Afgh.
127 K7 Khān al Baghdādī Iraq
127 L7 Khān al Maḩāwīl Iraq
127 L7 Khān al Mashāhidah Iraq
127 L7 Khān al Muşallá Iraq
114 D5 Khanapur Karnataka India
114 D4 Khanapur Mahar. India
122 A3 Khānaqāh Iran
127 L8 Khān ar Raḩbah Iraq
127 L4 Khanasur Pass Iran/Turkey
122 F3 Khān Bāgh Iran
Khanbalik Beijing China see Beijing
122 A3 Khānch Iran
83 L7 Khancoban N.S.W. Austr.
106 C1 Khandagayty Rus. Fed.
114 D4 Khandala Mahar. India
116 E6 Khandela Rajasthan India
123 O3 Khandud Afgh.
116 F9 Khandwa Madh. Prad. India
131 O3 Khandyga Rus. Fed.
122 E6 Khāneh Khowreh Iran
123 N6 Khanewal Pak.
123 N7 Khangarh Pak.
Khan Hung Vietnam see Soc Trăng
131 N4 Khani Rus. Fed.
Khaniá Kriti Greece see Chania
116 G7 Khaniadhana Madh. Prad. India
139 T7 Khanino Rus. Fed.
122 E7 Khānī Yek Iran
127 L7 Khān Jadwal Iraq
100 H6 Khanka, Lake China/Rus. Fed.
Khanka, Ozero l. China/Rus. Fed. see Khanka, Lake
Khankendi Azer. see Xankändi
Khanki Uzbek. see Xonqa
116 F4 Khanna Punjab India
128 E6 Khannā, Qā' salt pan Jordan
205 G4 Khannfoussa hill Alg.
134 M2 Khanovey Rus. Fed.
123 N7 Khanpur Pak.
Khān Ruḩābah Iraq see Khān ar Raḩbah
128 E3 Khān Shaykhūn Syria
210 E2 Khansiir, Raas pt Somalia
129 A1 Khanskaya Rus. Fed.
137 R7 Khanskoye, Ozero salt l. Rus. Fed.
121 O5 Khantau Kazakh.
131 K3 Khantayskoye, Ozero l. Rus. Fed.
130 J3 Khantayskoye Vodokhranilishche resr Rus. Fed.
121 S6 Khan-Tengri, Pik mt. Kazakh./Kyrg.
130 H3 Khanty-Mansiysk Rus. Fed.
134 M3 Khanty-Mansiyskiy Avtonomnyy Okrug-Yugra admin. div. Rus. Fed.
128 C7 Khān Yūnis Gaza
97 E8 Khao Ang Rua Nai Wildlife Reserve nature res. Thai.
97 D11 Khao Banthat Wildlife Reserve nature res. Thai.
97 D10 Khao Chum Thong Thai.
97 D7 Khaoen Si Nakarin National Park Thai.
97 D7 Khao Laem National Park Thai.
96 D7 Khao Laem Reservoir Thai.
97 D10 Khao Luang National Park Thai.
97 D11 Khao Pu-Khao Ya National Park Thai.
97 F8 Khao Soi Dao Wildlife Reserve nature res. Thai.
97 D10 Khao Sok National Park Thai.
97 E7 Khao Yai National Park Thai.
116 G9 Khapa Mahar. India
116 F2 Khapalu Jammu and Kashmir
107 M2 Khapcheranga Rus. Fed.
116 H5 Khaptad National Park Nepal
120 B4 Kharabali Rus. Fed.
129 E3 Kharagauli Georgia
117 K7 Kharagdiha Jharkhand India
116 C8 Kharaghoda Gujarat India
117 K7 Kharagpur Bihar India
117 K8 Kharagpur W. Bengal India
122 G3 Kharakī Iran
122 H8 Khārān r. Iran
123 K7 Kharan Pak.
107 O2 Kharanor Rus. Fed.
Kharari Rajasthan India see Abu Road
175 M3 Kharava Belarus
114 D3 Kharda Mahar. India
114 C3 Khardi Mahar. India
116 F2 Khardung La pass Jammu and Kashmir
123 I4 Kharez Ilias Afgh.
127 M8 Kharfiyah Iraq
100 H2 Kharga r. Rus. Fed.
Kharga Oasis Egypt see Khārijah, Wāḩāt al
116 G7 Khargapur Madh. Prad. India
Khārg Island Iran see Khārk
122 D7 Khārg Islands Iran
116 E9 Khargon Madh. Prad. India
116 E7 Khari r. Rajasthan India
123 O9 Khari r. Rajasthan India
123 O5 Kharian Pak.
117 I9 Khariar Orissa India
203 F3 Khārijah, Wāḩāt al oasis Egypt
128 B8 Kharīm, Jabal hill Egypt
129 E3 Kharist'vala Georgia
122 D7 Khārk i. Iran
116 H9 Kharkhara r. India
116 F5 Kharkhauda Haryana India
Kharkiv r. Rus. Fed./Ukr. see Khar'kov
137 P4 Kharkiv Ukr.
Kharkiv Oblast admin. div. Ukr. see Kharkivs'ka Oblast'
137 P4 Kharkivs'ka Oblast' admin. div. Ukr.
137 P3 Khar'kov r. Rus. Fed./Ukr.
Khar'kov Ukr. see Kharkiv
Kharkov Oblast admin. div. Ukr. see Kharkivs'ka Oblast'
Khar'kovskaya Oblast' admin. div. Ukr. see Kharkivs'ka Oblast'
122 E6 Khār Kūh mt. Iran
134 G1 Kharlovka Rus. Fed.
134 E3 Kharlu Rus. Fed.
125 K9 Kharmah, Ghubbat b. Suquṭrā Yemen
116 F2 Kharmang Jammu and Kashmir
197 N9 Kharmanli Bulg.
116 H9 Kharora Chhattisgarh India
123 M5 Kharoti reg. Afgh.
134 H4 Kharovsk Rus. Fed.
100 J3 Kharpin r. Rus. Fed.
122 D4 Khar Rūd r. Iran
117 J8 Kharsawan Jharkhand India
117 I8 Kharsia Chhattisgarh India
117 M6 Kharteng Arun. Prad. India
203 G6 Khartoum Sudan
203 G6 Khartoum state Sudan
203 G6 Khartoum North Sudan
137 R5 Khartsyz'k Ukr.
Kharuf, Ra's mt. Israel see Ḩarif, Har
134 L2 Kharutoyuvom Rus. Fed.
123 M5 Kharwar reg. Afgh.
125 L2 Khasab, Khor b. Oman
129 E2 Khasan'ya Rus. Fed.
129 D2 Khasaut Rus. Fed.
129 H2 Khasavyurt Rus. Fed.
123 J6 Khash Afgh.
123 I7 Khāsh Iran
123 J6 Khāsh, Dasht-e des. Afgh.
130 H3 Khashgort Rus. Fed.
203 G6 Khashm el Girba Sudan
210 B1 Khashm el Girba Dam Sudan
124 C2 Khashm Şana' Saudi Arabia
123 I6 Khash Rūd r. Afgh.
129 B2 Khashup'sa Georgia
129 E4 Khashuri Georgia
117 M7 Khasi Hills Meghalaya India
197 N9 Khaskovo Bulg.
124 D2 Khatam, Jabal al hill Saudi Arabia
131 L2 Khatanga Rus. Fed.
131 L2 Khatanga r. Rus. Fed.
Khatanga, Gulf of Rus. Fed. see Khatangskiy Zaliv
131 L2 Khatangskiy Zaliv b. Rus. Fed.
134 L2 Khatayakha Rus. Fed.
116 F8 Khategaon Madh. Prad. India
123 N3 Khatinza Pass Pak.
123 M3 Khatlon admin. div. Tajik.
Khatlon Oblast admin. div. Tajik. see Khatlon
124 G6 Khaṭmah, Banī reg. Saudi Arabia
125 M3 Khatmat al Malāha Oman
129 F2 Khatuley Rus. Fed.
122 F6 Khātūnābād Iran
131 S3 Khatyrka Rus. Fed.
137 S2 Khava r. Rus. Fed.
123 M4 Khāvāk, Khowtal-e pass Afgh.
116 B8 Khavda Gujarat India
129 E4 Khavet'i Georgia
125 L9 Khawlaf, Ra's pt Suquṭrā Yemen
125 M3 Khawr Fakkan U.A.E.
125 K6 Khawr Shiban well Saudi Arabia
96 C7 Khawsa Myanmar
124 E6 Khawsh Saudi Arabia
215 J7 Khayamnandi S. Africa
124 D3 Khaybar Al Madīnah Saudi Arabia
124 F6 Khaybar 'Asīr Saudi Arabia
121 N8 Khaydarken Kyrg.
214 C10 Khayelitsha S. Africa
134 L1 Khaypudyrskaya Guba b. Rus. Fed.
Khazarasp Uzbek. see Hazorasp
129 H3 Khebda Rus. Fed.
114 C3 Khed Mahar. India
114 C4 Khed Mahar. India
116 D8 Kheda Gujarat India
116 D7 Khedbrahma Gujarat India
122 H4 Khedrī Iran
Khefa Israel see Ḩefa
213 G4 Khehuene, Ponta pt Moz.
96 B1 Khela Arun. Prad. India
116 H5 Khela Uttaranchal India
117 J8 Khelari Jharkhand India
141 U6 Khelyulya Rus. Fed.
180 D5 Khemis Beni Arous Morocco
205 F1 Khemis Miliana Alg.
204 D2 Khemisset Morocco
204 C2 Khemis Zemamra Morocco
96 G6 Khemmarat Thai.
205 G2 Khenchela Alg.
204 D2 Khenifra Morocco
123 M4 Khenjan Afgh.
116 D8 Kheralu Gujarat India
122 E7 Kherāmeh Iran
122 E8 Kherreh Iran
122 D6 Khersan r. Iran
137 L7 Kherson Ukr.
137 M9 Khersones, Mys pt Ukr.
Kherson Oblast admin. div. Ukr. see Khersons'ka Oblast'
137 M7 Khersons'ka Oblast' admin. div. Ukr.
Khersonskaya Oblast' admin. div. Ukr. see Khersons'ka Oblast'
96 H6 Khe Sanh Vietnam
123 M4 Khesh Afgh.
122 D7 Khesht Iran
131 L2 Kheta r. Rus. Fed.
139 N1 Kheynyasensari, Ostrov i. Rus. Fed.
122 F7 Kheyrābād Iran
122 E3 Khezerābād Iran
97 E7 Khiaw, Khao mt. Thai.
117 J9 Khiching Orissa India
124 G5 Khidā, Jabal hill Saudi Arabia
129 F4 Khidist'avi Georgia
116 F7 Khilchipur Madh. Prad. India
Khiliomódhion Greece see Chiliomodi
107 L1 Khilok Rus. Fed.
107 J1 Khilok r. Rus. Fed.
Khimadhítis, Límni l. Greece see Cheimaditida, Limni
139 U6 Khimki Rus. Fed.
100 G4 Khingansk Rus. Fed.
100 F4 Khinganskiy Zapovednik nature res. Rus. Fed.
123 N9 Khinsar Pak.
116 C6 Khinyan Rajasthan India
Khíos i. Greece see Chios
Khios Strait Greece see Chios Strait
128 F3 Khirbat Isrīyah Syria
116 F8 Khirkiya Madh. Prad. India
197 M8 Khisarya Bulg.
139 P7 Khislavichi Rus. Fed.
111 D9 Khitai Dawan pass Aksai Chin
129 I4 Khiv Rus. Fed.
Khiwa Uzbek. see Xiva
122 B2 Khīyāv Iran
138 M1 Khiytola Rus. Fed.
139 R6 Khlepen' Rus. Fed.
139 W9 Khlevnoye Rus. Fed.
175 L5 Khlivchany Ukr.
97 E8 Khlong, Mae r. Thai.
97 D10 Khlong Saeng Wildlife Reserve nature res. Thai.
96 D6 Khlong Wang Chao National Park Thai.
97 F8 Khlung Thai.
139 R1 Khmelezero Rus. Fed.
139 V9 Khmelinets Rus. Fed.
139 Q6 Khmelita Rus. Fed.
137 M3 Khmeliv Ukr.
Khmel'nik Ukr. see Khmil'nyk
Khmel'nitskaya Oblast' admin. div. Ukr. see Khmel'nyts'ka Oblast'
Khmel'nitskiy Ukr. see Khmel'nyts'kyy
Khmelnitskiy Oblast admin. div. Ukr. see Khmel'nyts'ka Oblast'
136 G4 Khmel'nyts'ka Oblast' admin. div. Ukr.
136 F4 Khmel'nyts'kyy Ukr.
Khmelnytskyy Oblast admin. div. Ukr. see Khmel'nyts'ka Oblast'
137 K5 Khmel'ove Ukr.
Khmer Republic country Asia see Cambodia
180 D5 Khmes, Jebel mt. Morocco
136 G4 Khmil'nyk Ukr.
175 L3 Khmyelyeva Belarus
129 G6 Khndzorut Armenia
97 G10 Khoai, Hon i. Vietnam
120 F2 Khobda Kazakh.
129 C3 Khobi r. Georgia
139 X8 Khobotovo Rus. Fed.
175 M5 Khobultova Ukr.
122 G5 Khodā Āfarīd spring Iran
129 H6 Khodā Āfarīn Iran
138 I8 Khodarawtsy Belarus
139 O8 Khodasy Belarus
136 D4 Khodoriv Ukr.
136 I3 Khodorkiv Ukr.
129 B1 Khodz' Rus. Fed.
Khodzhal, Gora mt. Georgia see Khojali, Mt'a
Khodzhavend Azer. see Xocavänd
Khodzhent Tajik. see Khŭjand
Khodzheyli Qoraqalpog'iston Respublikasi Uzbek. see Xo'jayli
Khodzhorni Georgia see Khojorni
136 I8 Khodzhyder r. Ukr.
208 E3 Khogali Sudan
129 C3 Khojali, Mt'a Georgia
Khojand Tajik. see Khŭjand
129 F4 Khojorni Georgia
139 U2 Khokhlovo Rus. Fed.
135 G6 Khokhol'skiy Rus. Fed.
123 N9 Khokhropar Pak.
116 F3 Khoksar Hima. Prad. India
116 F9 Kholapur Mahar. India
137 R3 Kholkhol-Trostyanka Rus. Fed.
123 L3 Kholm Afgh.
Kholm Pol. see Chełm
139 O4 Kholm Novgorodskaya Oblast' Rus. Fed.
139 O6 Kholm Smolenskaya Oblast' Rus. Fed.
139 O6 Kholm Smolenskaya Oblast' Rus. Fed.
139 R9 Kholmechi Rus. Fed.
177 L3 Kholmets' Ukr.
134 H2 Kholmogory Rus. Fed.
100 L5 Kholmsk Sakhalin Rus. Fed.
137 R9 Kholmskiy Rus. Fed.
137 L2 Kholmy Ukr.
136 J1 Kholmyech Belarus
139 Q6 Kholm-Zhirkovskiy Rus. Fed.
Kholon Israel see Ḩolon
139 P3 Kholova r. Rus. Fed.
106 H1 Kholtoson Rus. Fed.
121 U2 Kholzun, Khrebet mts Kazakh./Rus. Fed.
122 C3 Khoman Iran
129 I6 Khomārlū Iran
212 C4 Khomas admin. reg. Namibia
212 B4 Khomas Highland hills Namibia
122 D5 Khomeyn Iran
122 D5 Khomeynīshahr Iran
136 G3 Khomora r. Ukr.
175 N3 Khomsk Belarus
137 M3 Khomutets' Ukr.
137 R6 Khomutove Ukr.
137 N2 Khomutovka Rus. Fed.
139 U9 Khomutovo Rus. Fed.
Khong, Mae Nam r. Myanmar see Salween
129 D3 Khoni Georgia
122 E8 Khonj Iran
122 E8 Khonj, Kūh-e mts Iran
96 F6 Khon Kaen Thai.
Khon Kriel Cambodia see Phumĭ Kon Kriel
Khonobod Uzbek. see Xonobod
Khonqa Uzbek. see Xonqa
117 O6 Khonsa Arun. Prad. India
131 P3 Khonuu Rus. Fed.
135 H6 Khoper r. Rus. Fed.
129 D3 Khop'uri Georgia
100 I5 Khor Rus. Fed.
100 I5 Khor r. Rus. Fed.
Khóra Greece see Chora
122 F4 Khorāsān, Chāh-e well Iran
122 H5 Khorāsān-e Janūbī prov. Iran
122 G4 Khorāsān-e Razavī prov. Iran
122 G3 Khorāsān-e Shemālī prov. Iran
96 F6 Khorat Plateau Thai.
Khorazm Wiloyati admin. div. Uzbek. see Xorazm
134 L2 Khoreyver Rus. Fed.
Khorezm Oblast admin. div. Uzbek. see Xorazm
99 I1 Khorinsk Rus. Fed.
212 B4 Khorixas Namibia
137 M7 Khorly Ukr.
122 D7 Khormūj, Kūh-e mt. Iran
Khorog Tajik. see Khorugh
100 H6 Khorol Rus. Fed.
137 M4 Khorol Ukr.
137 M4 Khorol r. Ukr.
137 P5 Khoroshe Ukr.
121 R1 Khorosheye Rus. Fed.
122 B2 Khoroslū Dāgh hills Iran
136 E4 Khorostkiv Ukr.
122 C5 Khorramābād Iran
122 C3 Khorram Darreh Iran
122 C6 Khorramshahr Iran
123 N3 Khorugh Tajik.
137 M3 Khoruzhivka Ukr.
134 L2 Khosedayu r. Rus. Fed.
122 H5 Khosf Iran
135 I7 Khosheutovo Rus. Fed.
122 C6 Khosravī Iran
129 F5 Khosrovi Argelanots' nature res. Armenia
122 C6 Khosrowābād Iran
127 L6 Khosrowvī Iran
Khost prov. Afgh. see Khowst
123 L6 Khost Pak.
129 A2 Khosta Rus. Fed.
122 F7 Khosūyeh Iran
116 F5 Khot Haryana India
Khotan Xinjiang China see Hotan
117 K6 Khotang Nepal
175 M4 Khoteshiv Ukr.
139 T9 Khotetovo Rus. Fed.
137 P4 Khotimlya r. Ukr.
137 N2 Khotin' Ukr.
139 S8 Khot'kovo Kaluzhskaya Oblast' Rus. Fed.
139 U5 Khot'kovo Moskovskaya Oblast' Rus. Fed.
137 O3 Khotmyzhsk Rus. Fed.
139 Q8 Khotsimsk Belarus
137 K4 Khots'ky Ukr.
136 F5 Khotyn Ukr.
139 S8 Khotynets Rus. Fed.
204 D2 Khouribga Morocco
123 M2 Khovaling Tajik.
117 M7 Khowai Tripura India
Khowos Uzbek. see Xovos
122 E6 Khowrjān Iran
122 F5 Khowrnag, Kūh-e mt. Iran
123 M5 Khowst Afgh.
123 M5 Khowst prov. Afgh.
123 M5 Khowst reg. Afgh./Pak.
116 B2 Khowt-e Ashrow Afgh.
100 M3 Khoye Rus. Fed.
136 I2 Khoyniki Belarus
127 K3 Khozap'ini, Tba l. Georgia
124 F9 Khozor Anghar Djibouti
97 E8 Khram, Ko i. Thai.
137 T2 Khrenovoye Rus. Fed.
137 L4 Khrestyteleve Ukr.
96 A4 Khreum Myanmar
117 M6 Khri r. India
Khrisoúpolis Greece see Chrysoupoli
134 I3 Khristoforovo Rus. Fed.
131 P2 Khroma r. Rus. Fed.
120 H2 Khromtau Kazakh.
117 O6 Khru r. India
Khrushchev Ukr. see Svitlovods'k
139 X7 Khrushchevo Rus. Fed.
100 I6 Khrustalnyy Rus. Fed.
Khrysokhou Bay Cyprus see Chrysochou Bay
137 M6 Khrystoforivka Dnipropetrovs'ka Oblast' Ukr.
137 L6 Khrystoforivka Mykolayivs'ka Oblast' Ukr.
136 I5 Khrystynivka Ukr.
123 O5 Khuar Pak.
215 M5 Khubelu r. Lesotho
129 I4 Khuchni Rus. Fed.
Khudat Azer. see Xudat
122 F2 Khudayberdy Turkm.
123 L8 Khude Hills Pak.
123 P6 Khudian Pak.
125 I7 Khuḑrah, Wādī r. Yemen
212 E4 Khudumelapye Botswana
Khudzhand Tajik. see Khŭjand
124 H4 Khufaysah, Khashm al hill Saudi Arabia
124 G3 Khuff Saudi Arabia
Khugiana Afgh. see Pirzada
123 L6 Khugiani Afgh.
122 I9 Khūh Lab, Ra's pt Iran
214 F2 Khuis Botswana
123 M1 Khŭjand Tajik.
Khŭjand admin. div. Tajik. see Soghd
Khŭjayli Uzbek. see Xo'jayli
97 G7 Khu Khan Thai.
137 N3 Khukhra Ukr.
124 D4 Khulays Saudi Arabia
116 E9 Khuldabad Mahar. India
134 M2 Khulga r. Rus. Fed.
134 M3 Khulimsunt Rus. Fed.
123 L3 Khulm r. Afgh.
117 L8 Khulna Bangl.
117 L8 Khulna admin. div. Bangl.
215 K2 Khuma S. Africa
129 F2 Khumalag Rus. Fed.
97 G9 Khŭm Batheay Cambodia
128 F4 Khunayzīr, Jabal al mts Syria
203 F6 Khuneiqa watercourse Sudan
122 H5 Khūnīk Bālā Iran
Khūnīnshahr Iran see Khorramshahr
116 E1 Khunjerab National Park Jammu and Kashmir
116 E1 Khunjerab Pass China/Jammu and Kashmir
122 D5 Khunsar Iran
117 J8 Khunti Jharkhand India
96 C5 Khun Yuam Thai.
129 H3 Khunzakh Rus. Fed.
139 X8 Khupta r. Rus. Fed.
122 H4 Khūr Iran
122 H5 Khur Iran
116 G7 Khurai Madh. Prad. India
122 F8 Khūran sea chan. Iran
125 I3 Khurayş Saudi Arabia
124 G6 Khurb, Banī hills Saudi Arabia
117 J9 Khurda Orissa India
202 E6 Khureit Sudan
Khuria Tank resr Chhattisgarh India see Maniari Tank
116 F5 Khurja Uttar Prad. India
123 J5 Khurmalik Afgh.
100 J3 Khurmuli Rus. Fed.
127 K8 Khurr, Wādī al watercourse Saudi Arabia
122 E7 Khūrrāb Iran
122 F4 Khurz Iran
129 D2 Khurzuk Rus. Fed.
123 O5 Khushab Pak.
123 N5 Khushalgarh Pak.
122 C3 Khūshāvar Iran
122 H6 Khushk Rud Iran
128 E9 Khushshah, Wādī al watercourse Jordan/Saudi Arabia
122 F3 Khush Yailaq hill Iran
123 J5 Khuspas Afgh.
136 C5 Khust Ukr.
138 L8 Khutar Belarus
116 H9 Khutgaon Mahar. India
128 A8 Khutmīyah, Mamarr al pass Egypt
135 H7 Khutorskoy Rus. Fed.
212 E4 Khutse Game Reserve nature res. Botswana
215 L2 Khutsong S. Africa
100 K4 Khutu r. Rus. Fed.
203 F6 Khuwei Sudan
123 L8 Khuzdar Pak.
122 C6 Khūzestān prov. Iran
122 I4 Khvāf reg. Iran
122 B2 Khvājeh Iran
122 I6 Khvājeh Dow Chāhī Iran
123 M3 Khvājeh Ghār Afgh.
120 C1 Khvalynsk Rus. Fed.
129 E3 Khvanchkara Georgia
122 F7 Khvānsār Iran
139 S6 Khvashchevka Rus. Fed.
139 S8 Khvastovichi Rus. Fed.
122 F6 Khvodrān Iran
122 F5 Khvor Iran
122 G4 Khvord Nārvan Iran
122 D7 Khvormūj Iran
139 X9 Khvorostyanka Lipetskaya Oblast' Rus. Fed.
120 C1 Khvorostyanka Samarskaya Oblast' Rus. Fed.
122 B3 Khvosh Maqām Iran
139 N6 Khvoshna Belarus
122 A2 Khvoy Iran
139 R3 Khvoynaya Rus. Fed.
100 E1 Khvoynyy Rus. Fed.
97 D8 Khwae Noi r. Thai.
123 N3 Khwahan Afgh.
123 J6 Khwaja Ali Afgh.
123 L6 Khwaja Amran mt. Pak.
123 N3 Khwaja Muhammad Range mts Afgh.
123 N4 Khyber Pass Afgh./Pak.
Khynchest' Moldova see Hînceşti
Khynchesty Moldova see Hînceşti
175 K6 Khyriv Ukr.
Khyrov Ukr. see Khyriv
Khyzy Azer. see Xızı
129 H3 Khzanor r. Rus. Fed.
78 □6 Kia Sta Isabel Solomon Is
122 H9 Kīā'ī Iran
83 M6 Kiama N.S.W. Austr.
92 E8 Kiamba Mindanao Phil.
209 F6 Kiambi Dem. Rep. Congo
234 F1 Kiamesha Lake NY U.S.A.
237 H9 Kiamichi r. OK U.S.A.
Kiangsi prov. China see Jiangxi
Kiangsu prov. China see Jiangsu
206 B3 Kiang West National Park Gambia
Kianly Turkm. see Tarta
140 T4 Kiantajärvi l. Fin.
116 G3 Kiari Jammu and Kashmir
122 E3 Kīāseh Iran
221 M2 Kiatassuaq i. Greenland
198 D4 Kiato Greece
142 E5 Kibæk Denmark
211 C6 Kibaha Tanz.
209 B6 Kibala Angola
210 A4 Kibale Uganda
208 F4 Kibali r. Dem. Rep. Congo
209 B6 Kibambi Dem. Rep. Congo
209 B5 Kibangou Congo
211 B5 Kibara Tanz.
209 E7 Kibara, Monts mts Dem. Rep. Congo
211 B7 Kibau Tanz.
92 E8 Kibawe Mindanao Phil.
211 C6 Kibaya Tanz.
211 C6 Kiberashi Tanz.
211 C6 Kiberege Tanz.
104 B7 Kibi Japan
209 C6 Kibinga Dem. Rep. Congo
210 A4 Kiboga Uganda
209 E5 Kibombo Dem. Rep. Congo
211 A5 Kibondo Tanz.
Kibray Uzbek. see Qibray
210 C3 Kibre Mengist Eth.
Kibris country Asia see Cyprus
211 A5 Kibungo Rwanda
211 A5 Kibuye Rwanda
211 A6 Kibwesa Tanz.
151 K2 Kibworth Harcourt Leicestershire, England U.K.
196 I9 Kičevo Macedonia
202 C5 Kichi-Kichi well Chad
134 I4 Kichmengskiy Gorodok Rus. Fed.
210 A5 Kichwamba Uganda
122 F2 Kiçi Balkan Daglary hill Turkm.
129 I5 Kiçik Dähnä Azer.
222 G5 Kicking Horse Pass Alta/B.C. Can.
207 F2 Kidal Mali
207 F2 Kidal admin. reg. Mali
211 C6 Kidatu Tanz.
211 C6 Kidayi Tanz.
150 H3 Kidderminster Worcestershire, England U.K.
215 L9 Kidd's Beach S. Africa
210 B4 Kidepo Valley National Park Uganda
211 C6 Kidete Tanz.
206 B3 Kidira Senegal
151 J4 Kidlington Oxfordshire, England U.K.
116 G3 Kidmang Jammu and Kashmir
80 L6 Kidnappers, Cape North I. N.Z.
179 M7 Kidričevo Slovenia
149 M7 Kidsgrove Staffordshire, England U.K.
211 C6 Kidugallo Tanz.
95 J3 Kidurong, Tanjung pt Malaysia
124 E6 Kidwat at A'waj Saudi Arabia
150 D4 Kidwelly Carmarthenshire, Wales U.K.
169 F10 Kiedrich Ger.
173 M6 Kiefersfelden Ger.
174 E3 Kiekrz Pol.
168 J2 Kiel Ger.
226 F6 Kiel WI U.S.A.
Kiel Canal Ger. see Nord-Ostsee-Kanal
175 I5 Kielce Pol.
175 J3 Kiełczew Pol.
174 G4 Kiełczygłów Pol.
149 L3 Kielder Water resr England U.K.
165 F6 Kieldrecht Belgium
168 K2 Kieler Bucht b. Ger.
168 J2 Kieler Förde g. Ger.
206 E3 Kiembara Burkina
175 H3 Kiemozia Pol.
173 M5 Kienberg Ger.
209 E7 Kienge Dem. Rep. Congo
169 E8 Kierspe Ger.
169 J9 Kieselbach Ger.
78 □6 Kieta P.N.G.
174 G5 Kietrz Pol.
170 K5 Kietz Ger.
Kīev Kazakh. see Kiyevka
Kiev Ukr. see Kyiv
Kiev Oblast admin. div. Ukr. see Kyivs'ka Oblast'
206 C2 Kiffa Maur.
198 E4 Kifisia Greece
198 E4 Kifisos r. Greece
127 L6 Kifrī Iraq
209 C6 Kifwanzondo Dem. Rep. Congo
211 A5 Kigali Rwanda
127 J4 Kiğı Turkey
225 I1 Kiglapait Mountains Nfld and Lab. Can.
206 D4 Kignan Mali
211 A6 Kigoma Tanz.
211 A6 Kigoma admin. reg. Tanz.
211 A6 Kigosi r. Tanz.
211 B6 Kigwe Tanz.
95 J5 Kihambatang Kalimantan Indon.
240 □E13 Kīhei HI U.S.A.
80 J5 Kihikihi North I. N.Z.
140 Q3 Kihlanki Fin.
141 Q5 Kihniö Fin.
138 G3 Kihnu i. Estonia
240 □F14 Kīholo HI U.S.A.
104 C8 Kii-hantō pen. Japan
140 U5 Kiihtelysvaara Fin.
121 O4 Kiik Kazakh.
138 G1 Kiikala Fin.
141 Q6 Kiikoinen Fin.
140 R4 Kiiminki Fin.
104 D7 Kii-Nagashima Japan
103 H15 Kiire Japan
104 C8 Kii-sanchi mts Japan
140 R3 Kiistala Fin.
104 A8 Kii-suidō sea chan. Japan
191 Q6 Kijac, Rt pt Croatia
175 I5 Kije Pol.
174 G2 Kijewo Królewskie Pol.
105 H2 Kijimadaira Japan
103 I14 Kijo Japan
211 C6 Kijungu Well Tanz.
102 □G18 Kikai Nansei-shotō Japan
102 □H18 Kikai-jima i. Nansei-shotō Japan
138 M2 Kikerino Rus. Fed.
196 I5 Kikinda Vojvodina Serbia
123 J9 Kikki Pak.
Kikládhes is Greece see Kyklades
134 I4 Kiknur Rus. Fed.
175 H3 Kikół Pol.
102 R5 Kikonai Japan
209 E7 Kikondja Dem. Rep. Congo
209 C6 Kikongo Dem. Rep. Congo
91 J8 Kikori P.N.G.
91 J8 Kikori r. P.N.G.
174 D2 Kikorze Pol.
103 H14 Kikuchi Japan
105 H6 Kikugawa Japan
135 H6 Kikvidze Rus. Fed.
209 C6 Kikwit Dem. Rep. Congo
142 F3 Kil Norway
142 J2 Kil Sweden
143 N3 Kilaån r. Sweden
141 N6 Kilafors Sweden
114 F8 Kilakkarai Tamil Nadu India
122 E4 Kīlan Iran
116 F3 Kilar Hima. Prad. India
240 □B11 Kilauea HI U.S.A.
240 □F14 Kilauea Crater HI U.S.A.
179 L3 Kilb Austria
147 C7 Kilbaha Ireland
147 H6 Kilbeggan Ireland
147 F8 Kilbeheny Ireland
147 H6 Kilberry Kildare Ireland
147 I5 Kilberry Meath Ireland
146 E11 Kilberry Argyll and Bute, Scotland U.K.
148 H2 Kilbirnie North Ayrshire, Scotland U.K.
140 L3 Kilboghamn Norway
93 G5 Kilbon Seram Indon.
140 N2 Kilbotn Norway
146 F12 Kilbrannan Sound sea chan. Scotland U.K.
147 J6 Kilbride Meath Ireland
148 E7 Kilbride Wicklow Ireland
147 J7 Kilbride Wicklow Ireland
146 F10 Kilbride Argyll and Bute, Scotland U.K.
147 E9 Kilbrittain Ireland
147 E3 Kilcar Ireland
147 H6 Kilcavan Ireland
172 F7 Kilchberg Switz.
137 O5 Kil'chen' r. Ukr.
146 E12 Kilchenzie Argyll and Bute, Scotland U.K.
146 D9 Kilchoan Highland, Scotland U.K.
146 F10 Kilchrenan Argyll and Bute, Scotland U.K.
101 F8 Kilchu N. Korea
147 I6 Kilcock Ireland
147 E6 Kilcolgan Ireland
147 E9 Kilcolman Ireland
147 G8 Kilcommon Ireland
147 F6 Kilconnell Ireland
147 H4 Kilconney Ireland
147 J6 Kilcoole Ireland
147 G6 Kilcormac Ireland
85 N9 Kilcoy Qld Austr.
146 G11 Kilcreggan Argyll and Bute, Scotland U.K.
147 F6 Kilcrow r. Ireland
147 I6 Kilcullen Ireland
147 I5 Kildalkey Ireland
147 I6 Kildare Ireland
147 I6 Kildare county Ireland
140 V2 Kil'dinstroy Rus. Fed.
146 F12 Kildonan North Ayrshire, Scotland U.K.
213 F3 Kildonan Zimbabwe
147 F8 Kildorrery Ireland
147 I3 Kildress Northern Ireland U.K.
134 I4 Kilemary Rus. Fed.
209 C6 Kilembe Dem. Rep. Congo
209 E6 Kileo Dem. Rep. Congo
147 D7 Kilfenora Ireland
146 F11 Kilfinan Argyll and Bute, Scotland U.K.
147 F8 Kilfinnane Ireland
150 C4 Kilgetty Pembrokeshire, Wales U.K.
147 F6 Kilglass Galway Ireland
147 F5 Kilglass Roscommon Ireland
147 F5 Kilglass Lough l. Ireland
147 C8 Kilgobnet Ireland
237 H9 Kilgore TX U.S.A.
84 E4 Kilgour r. N.T. Austr.
149 Q5 Kilham East Riding of Yorkshire, England U.K.
149 M2 Kilham Northumberland, England U.K.
Kilia Ukr. see Kiliya
205 H5 Kilian, Erg des. Alg.
209 F5 Kiliba Dem. Rep. Congo
207 F4 Kilibo Benin
199 L5 Kılıç Turkey
129 C5 Kılıçkaya Turkey
129 A5 Kılıçlı Turkey
211 C5 Kilifi Kenya
111 B8 Kilik Pass Xinjiang China
211 C5 Kilimanjaro admin. reg. Tanz.
211 C5 Kilimanjaro vol. Tanz.
211 C5 Kilimanjaro National Park Tanz.
211 B6 Kilimatinde Tanz.
77 F2 Kilinailau Islands P.N.G.
211 C6 Kilindoni Tanz.
138 H3 Kilingi-Nõmme Estonia
126 H5 Kilis Turkey
128 F2 Kilis prov. Turkey
136 I8 Kiliya Ukr.
148 D8 Kilkea Ireland
147 C7 Kilkee Ireland
147 K4 Kilkeel Northern Ireland U.K.
147 E5 Kilkelly Ireland
147 H7 Kilkenny Ireland
147 H7 Kilkenny county Ireland
147 E5 Kilkerrin Ireland
150 D6 Kilkhampton Cornwall, England U.K.
147 D8 Kilkinlea Ireland
198 D2 Kilkis Greece
85 N9 Kilkivan Qld Austr.
147 I6 Kill Kildare Ireland
147 H8 Kill Waterford Ireland
147 C9 Killabunane Ireland
148 B5 Killadeas Northern Ireland U.K.
147 D7 Killadysert Ireland
148 E3 Killagan Bridge Northern Ireland U.K.
147 D4 Killala Ireland
147 D4 Killala Bay Ireland
226 H1 Killala Lake Ont. Can.
147 F7 Killaloe Ireland
227 Q4 Killaloe Station Ont. Can.
223 I4 Killam Alta Can.
147 H8 Killamerry Ireland
147 I7 Killann Ireland
147 C7 Killard Ireland
84 C4 Killarney N.T. Austr.
83 N3 Killarney Qld Austr.
224 D4 Killarney Ont. Can.
147 D8 Killarney Ireland
231 □2 Killarney, Lake New Prov. Bahamas
147 C9 Killarney National Park Ireland
227 M3 Killarney Provincial Park Ont. Can.
147 D6 Killarone Ireland
147 C5 Killary Harbour b. Ireland
148 C7 Killaskillen Ireland
147 E8 Killavullen Ireland
147 G9 Killeagh Cork Ireland
146 E11 Killean Argyll and Bute, Scotland U.K.
147 C6 Killeany Ireland
146 H10 Killearn Stirling, Scotland U.K.
237 G10 Killeen TX U.S.A.
147 H6 Killeigh Ireland
147 G3 Killen Northern Ireland U.K.
147 I7 Killerrig Ireland
147 G4 Killeshandra Ireland
129 D5 Kılı Dağ mt. Turkey
146 I9 Killiecrankie Perth and Kinross, Scotland U.K.
199 J4 Killik Turkey
147 D7 Killimer Ireland
147 F6 Killimor Ireland
146 H10 Killin Stirling, Scotland U.K.
147 D7 Killinaboy Ireland
147 K4 Killinchy Northern Ireland U.K.
Killinek Island Nfld and Lab./Nunavut Can. see Killiniq Island
140 F3 Killinge Sweden
149 N3 Killingworth Tyne and Wear, England U.K.
235 J2 Killingworth CT U.S.A.
Killíni mt. Greece see Kyllini
225 H1 Killiniq Que. Can.
225 H1 Killiniq Island Nfld and Lab./Nunavut Can.
141 Q5 Killinkoski Fin.
147 C8 Killorglin Ireland
147 J6 Killough Ireland
147 K4 Killough Northern Ireland U.K.
148 C6 Killucan Ireland
146 E9 Killundine Highland, Scotland U.K.
147 I8 Killurin Ireland
147 F3 Killybegs Ireland
147 H3 Killyclogher Northern Ireland U.K.
147 H5 Killyconnan Ireland
147 G3 Killygordon Ireland
147 I4 Killylea Northern Ireland U.K.
148 E7 Kilmacanogue Ireland
148 H2 Kilmacolm Inverclyde, Scotland U.K.
147 G2 Kilmacrenan Ireland
147 H8 Kilmacthomas Ireland
147 H8 Kilmaganny Ireland
147 D5 Kilmaine Ireland
147 D7 Kilmaley Ireland
146 F9 Kilmalieu Highland, Scotland U.K.
147 E8 Kilmallock Ireland
146 D7 Kilmaluag Highland, Scotland U.K.
147 H7 Kilmanagh Ireland
146 H11 Kilmarnock East Ayrshire, Scotland U.K.
233 I11 Kilmarnock VA U.S.A.
146 F10 Kilmartin Argyll and Bute, Scotland U.K.
148 H2 Kilmaurs East Ayrshire, Scotland U.K.

Kilmeague to Klepacze

334

148 D7 Kilmeague Ireland
147 C5 Kilmeena Ireland
146 F10 Kilmelford Argyll and Bute, Scotland U.K.
134 J4 Kil'mez' Rus. Fed.
134 J4 Kil'mez' r. Rus. Fed.
147 J7 Kilmichael Point Ireland
150 F6 Kilmington Devon, England U.K.
147 E9 Kilmona Ireland
83 J7 Kilmore Vic. Austr.
147 E7 Kilmore Clare Ireland
147 I8 Kilmore Wexford Ireland
147 I8 Kilmore Quay Ireland
147 D8 Kilmorna Ireland
146 E11 Kilmory Argyll and Bute, Scotland U.K.
146 D8 Kilmory Highland, Scotland U.K.
147 E7 Kilmurry Ireland
148 D8 Kilmyshall Ireland
147 H5 Kilnaleck Ireland
147 J7 Kilnamanagh Ireland
146 D9 Kilninian Argyll and Bute, Scotland U.K.
146 E10 Kilninver Argyll and Bute, Scotland U.K.
147 E5 Kilnock Ireland
146 D10 Kiloran Argyll and Bute, Scotland U.K.
211 C6 Kilosa Tanz.
140 P2 Kilpisjärvi Fin.
140 R4 Kilpua Fin.
147 I7 Kilquiggin Ireland
147 I3 Kilrea Northern Ireland U.K.
147 F3 Kilrean Ireland
147 F6 Kilreekill Ireland
147 C6 Kilronan Ireland
147 G3 Kilross Donegal Ireland
147 F8 Kilross Tipperary Ireland
147 D7 Kilrush Ireland
147 E5 Kilsallagh Ireland
148 E6 Kilsaran Ireland
147 I5 Kilskeer Ireland
148 B5 Kilskeery Northern Ireland U.K.
146 H11 Kilsyth North Lanarkshire, Scotland U.K.
114 C7 Kiltan atoll India
147 E6 Kiltartan Ireland
147 I7 Kiltealy Ireland
148 D7 Kilteel Ireland
147 E5 Kiltimagh Ireland
147 I7 Kiltogan Ireland
147 F6 Kiltoom Ireland
147 E6 Kiltullagh Ireland
137 P7 Kil'tychchya r. Ukr.
148 A5 Kiltyclogher Ireland
209 F7 Kilwa Dem. Rep. Congo
211 C7 Kilwa Kivinje Tanz.
211 C7 Kilwa Masoko Tanz.
147 K3 Kilwaughter Northern Ireland U.K.
146 G11 Kilwinning North Ayrshire, Scotland U.K.
147 F8 Kilworth Ireland
Kilyazi Azer. see Giläzi
208 B2 Kim Chad
116 D9 Kim r. India
237 D7 Kim CO U.S.A.
211 C7 Kimambi Tanz.
95 K2 Kimanis, Teluk b. Malaysia
82 F5 Kimba S.A. Austr.
209 B5 Kimba Congo
236 D5 Kimball NE U.S.A.
232 C7 Kimball OH U.S.A.
91 L8 Kimbe New Britain P.N.G.
222 H5 Kimberley B.C. Can.
215 I4 Kimberley S. Africa
151 O2 Kimberley Norfolk, England U.K.
86 H4 Kimberley Downs W.A. Austr.
86 I4 Kimberley Plateau W.A. Austr.
87 E9 Kimberley Range hills W.A. Austr.
234 D4 Kimberton PA U.S.A.
206 D4 Kimbirila-Sud Côte d'Ivoire
151 L3 Kimbolton Cambridgeshire, England U.K.
101 F8 Kimch'aek N. Korea
101 F10 Kimch'ŏn S. Korea
101 F11 Kimhae S. Korea
Kími Greece see Kymi
141 Q6 Kimito Fin.
105 K5 Kimitsu Japan
101 E11 Kimje S. Korea
221 L3 Kimmirut Nunavut Can.
102 R4 Kimobetsu Japan
198 F6 Kimolos i. Greece
198 F6 Kimolou-Sifnou, Steno sea chan. Greece
209 B6 Kimongo Congo
139 V8 Kimovsk Rus. Fed.
209 E6 Kimpanga Dem. Rep. Congo
209 B6 Kimpangu Dem. Rep. Congo
206 D3 Kimparana Mali
232 C11 Kimper KY U.S.A.
209 B6 Kimpese Dem. Rep. Congo
209 B6 Kimpila Congo
209 B6 Kimpoko Dem. Rep. Congo
Kimpoku-san mt. Japan see Kinpoku-san
151 L4 Kimpton Hertfordshire, England U.K.
139 U5 Kimry Rus. Fed.
222 E4 Kimsquit B.C. Can.
143 L3 Kimstad Sweden
209 B6 Kimvula Dem. Rep. Congo
134 I2 Kimzha Rus. Fed.
102 □1 Kin Okinawa Japan
102 □1 Kina Okinawa Japan
95 L1 Kinabalu, Gunung mt. Sabah Malaysia
95 L1 Kinabalu National Park Malaysia
95 L2 Kinabatangan r. Malaysia
95 M2 Kinabatangan, Kuala r. mouth Malaysia
199 K2 Kınalıada i. Turkey
211 C6 Kinango Kenya
199 H6 Kinaros i. Greece
95 L2 Kinarut Sabah Malaysia
105 H2 Kinasa Japan
175 M6 Kinashiv Ukr.
222 D3 Kinaskan Lake B.C. Can.
222 G4 Kinbasket Lake B.C. Can.
Kinbirila Côte d'Ivoire see Kimbirila-Sud
146 I6 Kinbrace Highland, Scotland U.K.
137 K7 Kinburns'ka Kosa spit Ukr.
223 J5 Kincaid Sask. Can.
224 D4 Kincardine Ont. Can.
149 J1 Kincardine Fife, Scotland U.K.
146 K8 Kincardine O'Neil Aberdeenshire, Scotland U.K.
96 D1 Kinchang Myanmar
83 I5 Kinchega National Park N.S.W. Austr.
222 D4 Kincolith B.C. Can.
146 I8 Kincraig Highland, Scotland U.K.
177 H4 Kincses Hungary
209 E7 Kinda Dem. Rep. Congo
209 B5 Kindamba Congo
96 B3 Kindat Myanmar
179 L4 Kindberg Austria
227 L6 Kinde MI U.S.A.
209 B6 Kindeje Angola
171 D8 Kindelbrück Ger.
209 E7 Kindele Dem. Rep. Congo
209 C6 Kindembe Dem. Rep. Congo
237 I10 Kinder LA U.S.A.
169 D10 Kinderbeuern Ger.
164 G5 Kinderdijk Neth.
149 N7 Kinder Scout hill England U.K.
223 I5 Kindersley Sask. Can.
206 B4 Kindia Guinea
173 K4 Kinding Ger.
209 C5 Kindongo-Mbe Dem. Rep. Congo
137 N2 Kindrativka Ukr.
172 D3 Kindsbach Ger.
209 E5 Kindu Dem. Rep. Congo
135 J5 Kinel' Rus. Fed.
120 D1 Kinel'-Cherkasy Rus. Fed.
134 H4 Kineshma Rus. Fed.
151 I4 Kineton Gloucestershire, England U.K.
84 D1 King r. N.T. Austr.
84 D3 King r. N.T. Austr.
86 J3 King r. W.A. Austr.
259 B7 King, Canal sea chan. Chile
87 F8 King, Lake salt flat W.A. Austr.
232 I11 King and Queen Courthouse VA U.S.A.
209 B6 Kinganga Dem. Rep. Congo
85 M9 Kingaroy Qld Austr.
147 F3 Kingarrow Ireland
146 F11 Kingarth Argyll and Bute, Scotland U.K.
221 H2 King Christian Island Nunavut Can.
240 K5 King City CA U.S.A.
222 E5 Kingcome r. B.C. Can.
84 G8 King Creek watercourse Qld Austr.
86 I3 King Edward r. W.A. Austr.
157 N8 Kingersheim France
233 □O4 Kingfield ME U.S.A.
237 G8 Kingfisher OK U.S.A.
232 H10 King George VA U.S.A.
259 E8 King George Bay Falkland Is
262 U2 King George Island Antarctica
224 E1 King George Islands Nunavut Can.
King George Islands Arch. des Tuamotu Fr. Polynesia see Roi Georges, Îles du
87 E13 King George Sound b. W.A. Austr.
251 F3 King George VI Falls Guyana
263 A2 King Haakon VII Sea Southern Ocean
86 G7 King Hill W.A. Austr.
146 J10 Kinghorn Fife, Scotland U.K.
146 F8 Kingie r. Scotland U.K.
209 B6 Kingimbi Dem. Rep. Congo
138 L2 Kingisepp Rus. Fed.
83 I8 King Island Tas. Austr.
222 E4 King Island B.C. Can.
King Island Myanmar see Kadan Kyun
Kingisseppa Estonia see Kuressaare
227 O1 King Kirkland Ont. Can.
83 J7 Kinglake National Park Vic. Austr.
263 F2 King Leopold and Queen Astrid Coast Antarctica
86 H4 King Leopold Range National Park W.A. Austr.
86 H4 King Leopold Ranges hills W.A. Austr.
241 R6 Kingman AZ U.S.A.
237 F7 Kingman KS U.S.A.
233 □Q3 Kingman ME U.S.A.
75 I3 Kingman Reef N. Pacific Ocean
222 D3 King Mountain B.C. Can.
237 D10 King Mountain hill TX U.S.A.
Kingnait Nunavut Can. see Cape Dorset
234 E4 King of Prussia PA U.S.A.
209 E5 Kingombe Mbali Dem. Rep. Congo
209 C6 Kingondji Dem. Rep. Congo
82 E4 Kingoonya S.A. Austr.
262 S1 King Peak Antarctica
262 R2 King Peninsula Antarctica
82 □2 King Point Lord Howe I. Austr.
123 M6 Kingri Pak.
147 H7 Kings r. Ireland
240 L5 Kings r. CA U.S.A.
238 E6 Kings r. NV U.S.A.
146 K10 Kingsbarns Fife, Scotland U.K.
150 E7 Kingsbridge Devon, England U.K.
240 M5 Kingsburg CA U.S.A.
151 I2 Kingsbury Warwickshire, England U.K.
150 G6 Kingsbury Episcopi Somerset, England U.K.
84 C8 Kings Canyon N.T. Austr.
240 N5 Kings Canyon National Park CA U.S.A.
151 J5 Kingsclere Hampshire, England U.K.
82 F6 Kingscote S.A. Austr.
235 H3 Kings County county NY U.S.A.
147 I5 Kingscourt Ireland
151 O5 Kingsdown Kent, England U.K.
80 I4 Kingseat North I. N.Z.
262 U2 King Sejong research stn Antarctica
226 F4 Kingsford MI U.S.A.
146 H10 Kingshouse Stirling, Scotland U.K.
150 E7 Kingskerswell Devon, England U.K.
231 G10 Kingsland GA U.S.A.
226 I9 Kingsland IN U.S.A.
151 L4 Kings Langley Hertfordshire, England U.K.
215 O3 Kingsley S. Africa
149 N7 Kingsley Staffordshire, England U.K.
226 I5 Kingsley MI U.S.A.
151 M2 King's Lynn Norfolk, England U.K.
77 H2 Kingsmill Group is Gilbert Is Kiribati
151 N5 Kingsnorth Kent, England U.K.
86 G4 King Sound b. W.A. Austr.
235 I3 Kings Park NY U.S.A.
238 I6 Kings Peak UT U.S.A.
232 C12 Kingsport TN U.S.A.
151 J3 King's Sutton Northamptonshire, England U.K.
150 E6 Kingsteignton Devon, England U.K.
150 G4 Kingsthorne Herefordshire, England U.K.
83 K10 Kingston Tas. Austr.
224 E4 Kingston Ont. Can.
246 □ Kingston Jamaica
82 □1 Kingston Norfolk I.
81 C12 Kingston South I. N.Z.
146 J7 Kingston Moray, Scotland U.K.
233 O7 Kingston MA U.S.A.
236 H6 Kingston MO U.S.A.
233 K7 Kingston NY U.S.A.
232 C9 Kingston OH U.S.A.
234 D2 Kingston PA U.S.A.
231 E8 Kingston TN U.S.A.
232 D11 Kingston WV U.S.A.
151 J4 Kingston Bagpuize Oxfordshire, England U.K.
150 G3 Kingstone Herefordshire, England U.K.
241 Q6 Kingston Peak CA U.S.A.
150 G5 Kingston Seymour North Somerset, England U.K.
82 G7 Kingston South East S.A. Austr.
149 Q6 Kingston upon Hull Kingston upon Hull, England U.K.
149 Q6 Kingston upon Hull admin. div. England U.K.
151 L5 Kingston upon Thames Greater London, England U.K.
247 □3 Kingstown St Vincent
231 H9 Kingstree SC U.S.A.
234 C6 Kingsville MD U.S.A.
237 G12 Kingsville TX U.S.A.
150 E7 Kingswear Devon, England U.K.
150 G5 Kingswood South Gloucestershire, England U.K.
151 L5 Kingswood Surrey, England U.K.
151 J5 Kings Worthy Hampshire, England U.K.
150 F3 Kington Herefordshire, England U.K.
209 C6 Kingungi Dem. Rep. Congo
225 I1 Kingurutik r. Nfld and Lab. Can.
146 H8 Kingussie Highland, Scotland U.K.
232 H11 King William VA U.S.A.
221 I3 King William Island Nunavut Can.
206 C5 King William's Town Liberia
Kingwilliamstown Ireland see Ballydesmond
215 L8 King William's Town S. Africa
237 H11 Kingwood TX U.S.A.
232 F9 Kingwood WV U.S.A.
209 F7 Kiniama Dem. Rep. Congo
199 K6 Kınık Antalya Turkey
199 I3 Kınık İzmir Turkey
215 M6 Kinirapoort S. Africa
223 J4 Kinistino Sask. Can.
137 O6 Kinka r. Ukr.
209 B6 Kinkala Congo
102 S8 Kinka-san i. Japan
80 J5 Kinleith North I. N.Z.
81 C11 Kinloch South I. N.Z.
146 D8 Kinloch Highland, Scotland U.K.
146 F6 Kinlochbervie Highland, Scotland U.K.
146 F9 Kinlocheil Highland, Scotland U.K.
146 F7 Kinlochewe Highland, Scotland U.K.
146 F8 Kinloch Hourn Highland, Scotland U.K.
146 G9 Kinlochleven Highland, Scotland U.K.
146 H9 Kinloch Rannoch Perth and Kinross, Scotland U.K.
146 I7 Kinloss Moray, Scotland U.K.
147 F4 Kinlough Ireland
96 B5 Kinmaw Myanmar
150 E1 Kinmel Bay Conwy, Wales U.K.
Kinmen Taiwan see Chinmen
102 □1 Kin-misaki pt Okinawa Japan
227 P5 Kinmount Ont. Can.
142 I4 Kinna Sweden
147 C5 Kinnadoohy Ireland
81 D10 Kinnaird, Mount South I. N.Z.
114 G4 Kinnarasani r. India
140 S1 Kinnarodden pt Norway
147 H6 Kinnegad Ireland
235 G2 Kinnelon NJ U.S.A.
128 D6 Kinneret, Yam l. Israel
142 J3 Kinneviken b. Sweden
147 G6 Kinnitty Ireland
114 G8 Kinniyai Sri Lanka
140 R5 Kinnula Fin.
224 D2 Kinoje r. Ont. Can.
104 B7 Kino-kawa r. Japan
104 D5 Kinomoto Japan
223 K3 Kinoosao Sask. Can.
104 A4 Kinosaki Japan
102 P8 Kinpoku-san mt. Japan
165 I6 Kinrooi Belgium
215 N2 Kinross S. Africa
146 J10 Kinross Perth and Kinross, Scotland U.K.
147 E9 Kinsale Ireland
232 I10 Kinsale VA U.S.A.
142 C1 Kinsarvik Norway
209 C6 Kinsele Dem. Rep. Congo
209 B6 Kinshasa Dem. Rep. Congo
209 C6 Kinshasa mun. Dem. Rep. Congo
137 P6 Kins'ki Rozdory Ukr.
237 F7 Kinsley KS U.S.A.
232 E7 Kinsman OH U.S.A.
231 I8 Kinston NC U.S.A.
138 E6 Kintai Lith.
206 E4 Kintampo Ghana
209 B6 Kintata Dem. Rep. Congo
151 J5 Kintbury West Berkshire, England U.K.
234 E3 Kintersville PA U.S.A.
206 C4 Kintinian Guinea
93 C4 Kintom Sulawesi Indon.
95 K6 Kintop Kalimantan Indon.
84 B7 Kintore N.T. Austr.
146 L8 Kintore Aberdeenshire, Scotland U.K.
82 C2 Kintore, Mount S.A. Austr.
86 J7 Kintore Range hills N.T. Austr.
146 D11 Kintour Argyll and Bute, Scotland U.K.
129 D4 Kintrishis Nakrdzali nature res. Georgia
146 E11 Kintyre pen. Scotland U.K.
96 B3 Kin-U Myanmar
105 L4 Kinu-gawa r. Japan
105 J2 Kinunuma-yama mt. Japan
224 D2 Kinushseo r. Ont. Can.
222 H4 Kinuso Alta Can.
147 E6 Kinvara Ireland
147 C6 Kinvarra Ireland
150 H3 Kinver Staffordshire, England U.K.
102 □1 Kin-wan b. Okinawa Japan
114 F3 Kinwat Mahar. India
211 B6 Kinyangiri Tanz.
210 B4 Kinyeti mt. Sudan
120 G3 Kinzhaly Kazakh.
172 D4 Kinzig r. Ger.
169 G10 Kinzig r. Ger.
211 B6 Kiomboi Tanz.
129 E3 Kion-Khokh, Gora mt. Rus. Fed.
227 P3 Kiosk Ont. Can.
239 L7 Kiowa CO U.S.A.
237 F7 Kiowa KS U.S.A.
238 L6 Kiowa Creek r. CO U.S.A.
223 K4 Kipahigan Lake Man./Sask. Can.
240 □E13 Kīpahulu HI U.S.A.
Kiparissía Greece see Kyparissia
224 E4 Kipawa, Lac l. Que. Can.
110 C6 Kipchak Pass Xinjiang China
134 G4 Kipelovo Rus. Fed.
211 B6 Kipembawe Tanz.
138 M2 Kipen' Rus. Fed.
211 B7 Kipengere Range mts Tanz.
173 K4 Kipfenberg Ger.
211 A6 Kipili Tanz.
211 D5 Kipini Kenya
223 K5 Kipling Sask. Can.
Kipling Station Sask. Can. see Kipling
149 O6 Kippax West Yorkshire, England U.K.
190 D3 Kippel Switz.
146 H10 Kippen Stirling, Scotland U.K.
172 D5 Kippenheim Ger.
147 J6 Kippure hill Ireland
121 T1 Kiprino Rus. Fed.
134 I4 Kipshenga Rus. Fed.
137 K2 Kipti Ukr.
233 J11 Kiptopeke VA U.S.A.
Kipungo Angola see Quipungo
209 E7 Kipushi Dem. Rep. Congo
209 F8 Kipushia Dem. Rep. Congo
104 F6 Kira Japan
129 B6 Kıraçtepe Turkey
117 I7 Kirakat Uttar Prad. India
78 □6 Kirakira San Cristobal Solomon Is
140 T2 Kirakkajärvi Fin.
177 J3 Királd Hungary
177 G5 Királyegyháza Hungary
177 J5 Királyhegyes Hungary
199 H4 Kiran Dağları hills Turkey
114 G3 Kirandul Chhattisgarh India
206 C3 Kirané Mali
213 □J3 Kiranomena Madag.
128 B2 Kıravga Turkey
138 M8 Kirawsk Belarus
199 J4 Kiraz Turkey
138 G3 Kirbla Estonia
237 I10 Kirbyville TX U.S.A.
173 N6 Kirchanschöring Ger.
172 F3 Kirchardt Ger.
178 H6 Kirchbach Austria
179 M6 Kirchbach in Steiermark Austria
173 O4 Kirchberg Bayern Ger.
171 G9 Kirchberg Sachsen Ger.
190 D1 Kirchberg Bern Switz.
190 G1 Kirchberg St Gallen Switz.
172 C2 Kirchberg (Hunsrück) Ger.
179 M3 Kirchberg am Wagram Austria
179 L2 Kirchberg am Walde Austria
179 M4 Kirchberg am Wechsel Austria
173 I5 Kirchberg an der Iller Ger.
172 H3 Kirchberg an der Jagst Ger.
179 L3 Kirchberg an der Pielach Austria
179 M6 Kirchberg an der Raab Austria
178 F5 Kirchberg in Tirol Austria
178 F4 Kirchbichl Austria
169 I7 Kirchbrak Ger.
170 D3 Kirchdorf Mecklenburg-Vorpommern Ger.
168 G5 Kirchdorf Niedersachsen Ger.
173 N5 Kirchdorf am Inn Ger.
173 L5 Kirchdorf an der Amper Ger.
179 J4 Kirchdorf an der Krems Austria
173 O4 Kirchdorf im Wald Ger.
178 F4 Kirchdorf in Tirol Austria
173 K2 Kirchehrenbach Ger.
169 E9 Kirchen (Sieg) Ger.
171 E10 Kirchenlamitz Ger.
173 L2 Kirchenpingarten Ger.
173 K2 Kirchensittenbach Ger.
172 G4 Kirchentellinsfurt Ger.
173 L2 Kirchenthumbach Ger.
169 G9 Kirchhain Ger.
169 K8 Kirchheilingen Ger.
172 H2 Kirchheim Bayern Ger.
169 I9 Kirchheim Hessen Ger.
172 G3 Kirchheim am Neckar Ger.
173 L5 Kirchheim bei München Ger.
172 E2 Kirchheim-Bolanden Ger.
173 I5 Kirchheim in Schwaben Ger.
172 G4 Kirchheim unter Teck Ger.
169 F8 Kirchhundem Ger.
170 D4 Kirch Jesar Ger.
169 K10 Kirchlauter Ger.
168 H5 Kirchlinteln Ger.
170 E3 Kirch Mulsow Ger.
169 H6 Kirchohsen (Emmerthal) Ger.
173 N4 Kirchroth Ger.
179 N4 Kirchschlag in der Buckligen Welt Austria
168 G5 Kirchseelte Ger.
168 H4 Kirchtimke Ger.
168 H4 Kirchwalsede Ger.
173 N5 Kirchweidach Ger.
168 G4 Kirchwistedt Ger.
169 J8 Kirchworbis Ger.
172 D6 Kirchzarten Ger.
172 G2 Kirchzell Ger.
147 K4 Kircubbin Northern Ireland U.K.
129 E5 Kırdamı Turkey
202 C5 Kirdimi Chad
129 C5 Kireçli Geçidi pass Turkey
Kirehesjävri Fin. see Kirakkajärvi
131 L4 Kirensk Rus. Fed.
Kirey watercourse Kazakh. see Kerey
Kirey, Ozero salt l. Kazakh. see Kerey, Ozero
139 U8 Kireyevsk Rus. Fed.
139 S8 Kireykovo Rus. Fed.
Kirghizia country Asia see Kyrgyzstan
121 O6 Kirghiz Range mts Asia
120 F1 Kirgiz-Miyaki Rus. Fed.
Kirgizskaya S.S.R. country Asia see Kyrgyzstan
Kirgizskiy Khrebet mts Asia see Kirghiz Range
Kirgizstan country Asia see Kyrgyzstan
208 C5 Kiri Dem. Rep. Congo
Kíria Greece see Kyrgia
Kiriákion Greece see Kyriaki
77 J2 Kiribati country Pacific Ocean
210 E2 Kiridh Somalia
105 H3 Kiriga-mine mt. Japan
127 J3 Kırık Turkey
126 H5 Kırıkhan Turkey
126 F4 Kırıkkale Turkey
106 B4 Kirikkuduk Xinjiang China
80 I2 Kirikopuni North I. N.Z.
139 V2 Kirillov Rus. Fed.
100 M5 Kirillovo Sakhalin Rus. Fed.
138 M1 Kirillovskoye Rus. Fed.
Kirin Jilin China see Jilin
Kirin prov. China see Jilin
114 G9 Kirinda Sri Lanka
210 C5 Kirinyaga mt. Kenya
123 N6 Kiri Shamozai Pak.
139 P2 Kirishi Rus. Fed.
102 □H15 Kirishima-Yaku Kokuritsu-kōen nat. park Japan
103 H15 Kirishima-yama vol. Japan
267 I5 Kiritimati atoll Kiribati
Kiriwina Islands P.N.G. see Trobriand Islands
199 L3 Kırka Turkey
199 I3 Kırkağaç Turkey
146 I13 Kirkbean Dumfries and Galloway, Scotland U.K.
149 K4 Kirkbride Cumbria, England U.K.
122 B3 Kirk Bulāg Dāgi mt. Iran
149 N6 Kirkburton West Yorkshire, England U.K.
149 L7 Kirkby Merseyside, England U.K.
149 O7 Kirkby in Ashfield Nottinghamshire, England U.K.
149 L5 Kirkby Lonsdale Cumbria, England U.K.
149 N5 Kirkby Malzeard North Yorkshire, England U.K.
149 P5 Kirkbymoorside North Yorkshire, England U.K.
149 M5 Kirkby Stephen Cumbria, England U.K.
149 L4 Kirkby Thore Cumbria, England U.K.
146 J10 Kirkcaldy Fife, Scotland U.K.
146 F13 Kirkcolm Dumfries and Galloway, Scotland U.K.
146 I12 Kirkconnel Dumfries and Galloway, Scotland U.K.
146 G13 Kirkcowan Dumfries and Galloway, Scotland U.K.
146 H13 Kirkcudbright Dumfries and Galloway, Scotland U.K.
148 I4 Kirkcudbright Bay Scotland U.K.
172 C3 Kirkel-Neuhäusel Ger.
142 I1 Kirkenær Norway
140 U2 Kirkenes Norway
227 P5 Kirkfield Ont. Can.
149 L6 Kirkham Lancashire, England U.K.
146 H13 Kirkinner Dumfries and Galloway, Scotland U.K.
146 H11 Kirkintilloch East Dunbartonshire, Scotland U.K.
141 R6 Kirkkonummi Fin.
241 T7 Kirkland AZ U.S.A.
226 F7 Kirkland IL U.S.A.
224 D3 Kirkland Lake Ont. Can.
129 A6 Kırklar Dağı mt. Turkey
129 B5 Kırklar Dağı mt. Turkey
126 C3 Kırklareli Turkey
199 I1 Kırklareli prov. Turkey
197 P9 Kırklareli Barajı resr Turkey
149 O5 Kirklevington Stockton-on-Tees, England U.K.
146 J11 Kirkliston Edinburgh, Scotland U.K.
81 E11 Kirkliston Range mts South I. N.Z.
148 H5 Kirk Michael Isle of Man
146 I9 Kirkmichael Perth and Kinross, Scotland U.K.
146 G12 Kirkmichael South Ayrshire, Scotland U.K.
146 I11 Kirkmuirhill South Lanarkshire, Scotland U.K.
138 K1 Kirkonmaanselkä b. Fin.
195 □ Kirkop Malta
149 L4 Kirkoswald Cumbria, England U.K.
146 G12 Kirkoswald South Ayrshire, Scotland U.K.
197 N9 Kirkovo Bulg.
129 C7 Kırköy Turkey
263 L1 Kirkpatrick, Mount Antarctica
146 J12 Kirkpatrick-Fleming Dumfries and Galloway, Scotland U.K.
149 O6 Kirk Sandall South Yorkshire, England U.K.
236 I5 Kirksville MO U.S.A.
148 F1 Kirkton Argyll and Bute, Scotland U.K.
146 L8 Kirkton of Durris Aberdeenshire, Scotland U.K.
146 K9 Kirkton of Menmuir Angus, Scotland U.K.
146 L8 Kirktown of Auchterless Aberdeenshire, Scotland U.K.
146 K7 Kirktown of Deskford Moray, Scotland U.K.
127 L6 Kirkūk Iraq
146 K5 Kirkwall Orkney, Scotland U.K.
215 J9 Kirkwood S. Africa
234 D5 Kirkwood DE U.S.A.
234 C5 Kirkwood PA U.S.A.
149 M2 Kirk Yetholm Scottish Borders, Scotland U.K.
Kirman Iran see Kermān
126 E3 Kırmır r. Turkey
129 A6 Kırmızıköprü Turkey
172 C2 Kirn Ger.
Kırobası Turkey see Mağara
Kīrov Kazakh. see Balpyk Bi
Kirov Kyrg. see Kyzyl-Adyr
139 R7 Kirov Kaluzhskaya Oblast' Rus. Fed.
134 J4 Kirov Kirovskaya Oblast' Rus. Fed.
Kirova, Zaliv b. Azer. see Qızılağac Körfäzi
Kirovabad Azer. see Gäncä
Kirovabad Tajik. see Panj
Kirovakan Armenia see Vanadzor
137 Q5 Kirove Donets'ka Oblast' Ukr.
137 M5 Kirove Kirovohrads'ka Oblast' Ukr.
137 O6 Kirove Zaporiz'ka Oblast' Ukr.
120 E2 Kirovo Kazakh.
Kirovo Donets'ka Oblast' Ukr. see Kirove
Kirovo Kirovohrads'ka Oblast' Ukr. see Kirovohrad
Kirovo Uzbek. see Beshariq
Kirov Oblast admin. div. Rus. Fed. see Kirovskaya Oblast'
134 J4 Kirovo-Chepetsk Rus. Fed.
Kirovo-Chepetskiy Rus. Fed. see Kirovo-Chepetsk
Kirovograd Ukr. see Kirovohrad
Kirovograd Oblast admin. div. Ukr. see Kirovohrads'ka Oblast'
Kirovogradskaya Oblast' admin. div. Ukr. see Kirovohrads'ka Oblast'
137 L5 Kirovohrad Ukr.
Kirovohrad Oblast admin. div. Ukr. see Kirovohrads'ka Oblast'
136 L5 Kirovohrads'ka Oblast' admin. div. Ukr.
129 J7 Kirovsk Azer.
139 N2 Kirovsk Leningradskaya Oblast' Rus. Fed.
134 F2 Kirovsk Murmanskaya Oblast' Rus. Fed.
Kirovsk Turkm. see Badabaýhan
137 Q4 Kirovs'k Donets'ka Oblast' Ukr.
137 R5 Kirovs'k Luhans'ka Oblast' Ukr.
137 T7 Kirovskaya Rus. Fed.
134 J4 Kirovskaya Oblast' admin. div. Rus. Fed.
137 N5 Kirovs'ke Dnipropetrovs'ka Oblast' Ukr.
137 R5 Kirovs'ke Donets'ka Oblast' Ukr.
137 M8 Kirovs'ke Respublika Krym Ukr.
137 O8 Kirovs'ke Respublika Krym Ukr.
Kirovskiy Kazakh. see Balpyk Bi
120 C5 Kirovskiy Astrakhanskaya Oblast' Rus. Fed.
137 P2 Kirovskiy Kurskaya Oblast' Rus. Fed.
100 H6 Kirovskiy Primorskiy Kray Rus. Fed.
Kirovskoye Kyrg. see Kyzyl-Adyr
Kirovskoye Dnipropetrovs'ka Oblast' Ukr. see Kirovs'ke
Kirovskoye Donets'ka Oblast' Ukr. see Kirovs'ke
Kirovskoye Respublika Krym Ukr. see Kirovs'ke
Kırpaşa pen. Cyprus see Karpasia
137 R8 Kirpili r. Rus. Fed.
122 G2 Kirpili Turkm.
137 S8 Kirpil'skaya Rus. Fed.
137 R8 Kirpil'skiy Liman marsh Rus. Fed.
146 J9 Kirriemuir Angus, Scotland U.K.
134 K4 Kirs Rus. Fed.
135 H5 Kirsanov Rus. Fed.
120 E2 Kirsanovo Kazakh.
172 C2 Kirschweiler Ger.
126 G4 Kırşehir Turkey
175 L1 Kirsna r. Lith.
207 F3 Kirtachi Niger
123 L9 Kirthar National Park Pak.
123 L8 Kirthar Range mts Pak.
151 J4 Kirtlington Oxfordshire, England U.K.
151 L2 Kirton Lincolnshire, England U.K.
151 O3 Kirton Suffolk, England U.K.
149 P7 Kirton in Lindsey North Lincolnshire, England U.K.
169 H9 Kirtorf Ger.
129 D3 Kirts'khi Georgia
140 P3 Kiruna Sweden
211 A5 Kirundo Burundi
208 E5 Kirundu Dem. Rep. Congo
262 X2 Kirwan Escarpment Antarctica
135 I5 Kirya Rus. Fed.
105 J3 Kiryū Japan
139 V5 Kirzhach Rus. Fed.
143 L4 Kisa Sweden
102 Q7 Kisakata Japan
211 C6 Kisaki Tanz.
Kisama, Parque Nacional de nat. park Angola see Quiçama, Parque Nacional do
208 E4 Kisangani Dem. Rep. Congo
211 C6 Kisangire Tanz.
209 C6 Kisantete Dem. Rep. Congo
177 L3 Kisar Hungary
93 E8 Kisar i. Maluku Indon.
94 C3 Kisaran Sumatera Indon.
211 C6 Kisarawe Tanz.
105 K5 Kisarazu Japan
128 G1 Kısas Turkey
176 G5 Kis-Balaton park Hungary
177 H4 Kisbér Hungary
104 D7 Kisei Japan
98 E1 Kiselevsk Rus. Fed.
188 G4 Kiseljak Bos.-Herz.
139 P1 Kisel'nya Rus. Fed.
100 K3 Kisel'ovka Rus. Fed.
211 B6 Kisere Tanz.
177 J3 Kisgyőr Hungary
122 F8 Kish i. Iran
117 K6 Kishanganj Bihar India
116 G7 Kishangarh Madh. Prad. India
116 C6 Kishangarh Rajasthan India
116 E6 Kishangarh Rajasthan India
116 D2 Kishen Ganga r. India/Pak.
207 F4 Kishi Nigeria
104 B7 Kishigawa Japan
104 B7 Kishi-gawa r. Japan
121 N1 Kishi-Karoy, Ozero salt l. Kazakh.
102 □I16 Kishika-zaki pt Japan
Kishinev Moldova see Chişinău
Kishiözen r. Kazakh./Rus. Fed. see Malyy Uzen'
104 B7 Kishiwada Japan
121 O1 Kishkenekol' Kazakh.
117 M7 Kishoreganj Bangl.
146 E8 Kishorn, Loch inlet Scotland U.K.
116 E3 Kishtwar Jammu and Kashmir
211 A6 Kisi Tanz.
175 H2 Kisielice Pol.
175 K2 Kisielnica Pol.
211 B6 Kisigo r. Tanz.
211 A5 Kisiguru Rwanda
210 B5 Kisii Kenya
211 C6 Kisiju Tanz.
129 E5 Kısır Dağı mt. Turkey
220 A4 Kiska Island AK U.S.A.
223 L4 Kiskittogisu Lake Man. Can.
223 L4 Kiskitto Lake Man. Can.
141 Q6 Kisko Fin.
177 J4 Kisköre Hungary
177 J4 Kiskörei-Víztároló resr Hungary
177 I5 Kiskőrös Hungary
177 I5 Kiskunfélegyháza Hungary
177 I5 Kiskunhalas Hungary
177 I4 Kiskunlacháza Hungary
177 I5 Kiskunmajsa Hungary
177 I4 Kiskunság reg. Hungary
177 I4 Kiskunsági nat. park Hungary
177 H5 Kisláng Hungary
177 K4 Kisléta Hungary
177 G4 Kislőd Hungary
129 D2 Kislovodsk Rus. Fed.
137 S7 Kislyakovskaya Rus. Fed.
210 D5 Kismaayo Somalia
177 K4 Kismarja Hungary
Kismayu Somalia see Kismaayo
105 G4 Kiso Japan
104 G4 Kisofukushima Japan
104 E5 Kisogawa Japan
104 E5 Kiso-gawa r. Japan
105 I5 Kiso-gawa r. Japan
211 A5 Kisoro Uganda
104 E5 Kisosaki Japan
105 F5 Kiso-sanmyaku mts Japan
209 F5 Kisosi Burundi
179 K7 Kisovec Slovenia
222 E4 Kispiox B.C. Can.
222 E4 Kispiox r. B.C. Can.
198 E7 Kissamos Kriti Greece
198 E7 Kissamou, Kolpos b. Kriti Greece
Kisseraing Island Myanmar see Kanmaw Kyun
206 C4 Kissidougou Guinea
231 G11 Kissimmee FL U.S.A.
231 G12 Kissimmee r. FL U.S.A.
231 G12 Kissimmee, Lake FL U.S.A.
173 J5 Kissing Ger.
223 K4 Kississing Lake Man. Can.
172 H6 Kißlegg Ger.
202 E4 Kissu, Jebel mt. Sudan
177 I5 Kisszállás Hungary
172 H2 Kist Ger.
188 E4 Kistanje Croatia
177 I5 Kistelek Hungary
135 H5 Kistendey Rus. Fed.
223 M4 Kistigan Lake Man. Can.
Kistna r. India see Krishna
177 J3 Kistokaj Hungary
140 R1 Kistrand Norway
177 J4 Kisújszállás Hungary
103 J11 Kisuki Japan
210 B5 Kisumu Kenya
177 L3 Kisvárda Hungary
Kisykkamys Kazakh. see Dzhangala
174 F3 Kiszkowo Pol.
177 J5 Kiszombor Hungary
210 A3 Kit r. Sudan
104 B6 Kita Hyōgo Japan
104 C5 Kita Kyōto Japan
206 C3 Kita Mali
Kitab Uzbek. see Kitob
99 N6 Kita-Daitō-jima i. Japan
104 E5 Kitagata Japan
103 I14 Kitagawa Japan
102 Q4 Kitahiyama Japan
105 M2 Kitaibaraki Japan
103 □2 Kita-Iō-jima vol. Kazan-rettō Japan
104 A7 Kitajima Japan
102 S7 Kitakami Japan
102 S7 Kitakami-gawa r. Japan
102 Q9 Kitakata Fukushima Japan
103 I14 Kitakata Miyazaki Japan
103 H13 Kita-Kyūshū Japan
210 B4 Kitale Kenya
102 U3 Kitami Japan
105 H3 Kitamimaki Japan
102 T2 Kitami-sanchi mts Japan
105 K3 Kitamoto Japan
209 E6 Kitanda Dem. Rep. Congo
103 □3 Kitano-hana c. Iō-jima Japan
105 J3 Kitatachibana Japan
105 M3 Kitaura Ibaraki Japan
103 I14 Kitaura Miyazaki Japan
105 M4 Kita-ura l. Japan
104 C8 Kitayama Japan
104 C8 Kitayama-gawa r. Japan
236 D6 Kit Carson CO U.S.A.
224 D5 Kitchener Ont. Can.
224 E3 Kitchigama r. Que. Can.
209 E6 Kiteba Dem. Rep. Congo
140 U5 Kitee Fin.
209 F6 Kitendwe Dem. Rep. Congo
210 B4 Kitgum Uganda
Kíthira i. Greece see Kythira
Kíthnos i. Greece see Kythnos
Kíthnou, Stenón sea chan. Greece see Kythnou, Steno
Kiti, Cape Cyprus see Kition, Cape
222 D4 Kitimat B.C. Can.
140 S3 Kitinen r. Fin.
128 B4 Kition, Cape Cyprus
Kitiou, Akra c. Cyprus see Kition, Cape
222 D4 Kitkatla B.C. Can.
222 E4 Kitlope Heritage Conservancy Provincial Park B.C. Can.
121 L8 Kitob Uzbek.
139 Y5 Kitovo Rus. Fed.
198 F6 Kitriani i. Greece
140 V2 Kitsa Rus. Fed.
222 D4 Kitsault B.C. Can.
223 I4 Kitscoty Alta Can.
136 E5 Kitsman' Ukr.
103 I13 Kitsuki Japan
105 L2 Kitsuregawa Japan
232 F8 Kittanning PA U.S.A.
234 F3 Kittatinny Mountains hills NJ U.S.A.
233 □O5 Kittery ME U.S.A.
140 R3 Kittilä Fin.
105 M1 Kittoya-yama hill Japan
179 P3 Kittsee Austria
114 D5 Kittur Karnataka India
231 J7 Kitty Hawk NC U.S.A.
211 C5 Kitui Kenya
211 C5 Kitumbeine vol. Tanz.
211 C7 Kitumbini Tanz.
211 B6 Kitunda Tanz.
222 D4 Kitwanga B.C. Can.
209 F8 Kitwe Zambia
178 F5 Kitzbühel Austria
178 F5 Kitzbüheler Alpen mts Austria
178 F5 Kitzbüheler Horn mt. Austria
179 L6 Kitzeck im Sausal Austria
171 F8 Kitzen Ger.
173 I2 Kitzingen Ger.
171 G8 Kitzscher Ger.
178 G5 Kitzsteinhorn mt. Austria
211 C5 Kiu Kenya
175 H5 Kiucze Pol.
141 Q6 Kiukainen Fin.
96 D5 Kiu Lom Reservoir Thai.
91 J8 Kiunga P.N.G.
211 D5 Kiunga Marine National Reserve nature res. Kenya
140 S5 Kiuruvesi Fin.
140 R4 Kivalo ridge Fin.
198 D5 Kiveri Greece
139 T4 Kiverichi Rus. Fed.
136 E3 Kivertsi Ukr.
140 R5 Kivijärvi Fin.
138 K1 Kivijärvi l. Fin.
140 R5 Kivijärvi l. Fin.
143 K6 Kivik Sweden
140 Q2 Kivilompolo Norway
138 J2 Kiviõli Estonia
140 U5 Kivivaara Fin.
138 H3 Kivi-Vigala Estonia
137 Q4 Kivsharivka Ukr.
208 F5 Kivu, Lake Dem. Rep. Congo/Rwanda
104 C8 Kiwa Japan
209 C7 Kiwaba N'zogi Angola
91 J8 Kiwai Island P.N.G.
211 C7 Kiwawa Tanz.
86 I7 Kiwirrkurra Aboriginal Reserve W.A. Austr.
175 I1 Kiwity Pol.
121 M3 Kiyakty, Ozero salt l. Kazakh.
102 □1 Kiyan Okinawa Japan
102 □1 Kiyan-zaki c. Okinawa Japan
124 E6 Kiyāt Saudi Arabia
Kiyev Ukr. see Kyiv
121 N2 Kiyevka Kazakh.
Kiyevskaya Oblast' admin. div. Ukr. see Kyivs'ka Oblast'
139 T6 Kiyevskiy Rus. Fed.
Kiyevskoye Vodokhranilishche resr Ukr. see Kyyivs'ke Vodoskhovyshche
197 Q9 Kıyıköy Turkey
121 L2 Kiyma Kazakh.
104 F3 Kiyomi Japan
105 L5 Kiyosumi-yama hill Japan
105 I1 Kiyotsu-gawa r. Japan
134 L4 Kizel Rus. Fed.
134 I3 Kizema Rus. Fed.
107 K1 Kizha Rus. Fed.
134 F3 Kizhi, Ostrov i. Rus. Fed.
209 E7 Kiziba-Baluba, Réserve de nature res. Dem. Rep. Congo
211 B6 Kizigo Game Reserve nature res. Tanz.
199 L4 Kızık Turkey
110 F6 Kizil Xinjiang China
128 B2 Kızılalan Turkey
110 C7 Kizilawat Xinjiang China
128 B2 Kızılca Turkey
199 K5 Kızılcadağ Turkey
199 K6 Kızılca Dağ mt. Turkey
126 F3 Kızılcahamam Turkey
199 L3 Kızılcaören Turkey
199 K4 Kızılcasöğüt Turkey
129 E6 Kızılcaziyaret Dağı mt. Turkey
129 A7 Kızılcık Turkey
129 B6 Kızılçubuk Turkey
128 C1 Kızıldağ mt. Turkey
128 B2 Kızıldağ mt. Turkey
126 I4 Kızıl Dağı mt. Turkey
126 F3 Kızılırmak Turkey
126 G3 Kızılırmak r. Turkey
199 L5 Kızılkaya Turkey
199 L4 Kızılören Afyon Turkey
126 F5 Kızılören Konya Turkey
120 H1 Kizil'skoye Rus. Fed.
137 Q8 Kiziltashskiy Liman lag. Rus. Fed.
127 J5 Kızıltepe Turkey
128 A1 Kızılyaka Karaman Turkey
199 J5 Kızılyaka Muğla Turkey
129 H2 Kizilyurt Rus. Fed.
211 C6 Kizimkazi, Ras pt Tanz.
128 C2 Kızkalesi Turkey
129 H2 Kizlyar Respublika Dagestan Rus. Fed.
129 F2 Kizlyar Respublika Severnaya Osetiya-Alaniya Rus. Fed.
129 H1 Kizlyarskiy Zaliv b. Rus. Fed.
134 J4 Kizner Rus. Fed.
104 C6 Kizu Japan
104 C6 Kizu-gawa r. Japan
Kizyl-Arbat Turkm. see Serdar
Kizyl-Atrek Turkm. see Etrek
111 D9 Kizyl Jilga Aksai Chin
142 F5 Kjellerup Denmark
141 K6 Kjemmoen Norway
140 M3 Kjerringøy Norway
140 S1 Kjøllefjord Norway
140 N2 Kjøpsvik Norway
214 G9 Klaarstroom S. Africa
164 F5 Klaaswaal Neth.
176 C2 Klabava r. Czech Rep.
143 J1 Klacken hill Sweden
177 H3 Kľačno Slovakia
188 G3 Kladanj Bos.-Herz.
170 E5 Kläden Ger.
176 D1 Kladno Czech Rep.
197 K6 Kladovo Serbia
176 B2 Kladruby Czech Rep.
95 L2 Klagan Sabah Malaysia
179 J6 Klagenfurt Austria
191 Q2 Klagenfurt airport Austria
241 W6 Klagetoh AZ U.S.A.
138 E6 Klaipėda Lith.
175 I6 Kłaj Pol.
177 H3 Kľak mt. Slovakia
177 I2 Kľak mt. Slovakia
Klaksvig Faroe Is see Klaksvík
144 D1 Klaksvík Faroe Is
238 B6 Klamath CA U.S.A.
238 B6 Klamath r. CA U.S.A.
238 D5 Klamath Falls OR U.S.A.
238 C6 Klamath Mountains CA U.S.A.
143 N2 Klämmingen l. Sweden
95 L4 Klampo Kalimantan Indon.
191 Q5 Klana Croatia
94 D3 Klang Malaysia
174 E1 Kłanino Pol.
179 M7 Klanjec Croatia
168 G1 Klanxbüll Ger.
222 D3 Klappan r. B.C. Can.
142 J2 Klarälven r. Sweden
140 N5 Klärke Sweden
177 H3 Klasov Slovakia
142 I2 Klässbol Sweden
176 C1 Klášterec nad Ohří Czech Rep.
95 I8 Klaten Jawa Indon.
176 C2 Klatovy Czech Rep.
179 J4 Klaus an der Pyhrnbahn Austria
171 H6 Klausdorf Brandenburg Ger.
170 H2 Klausdorf Mecklenburg-Vorpommern Ger.
168 J2 Klausdorf Schleswig-Holstein Ger.
172 B2 Klausen Ger.
179 N3 Klausen Leopoldsdorf Austria
136 J3 Klavdiyevo-Tarasove Ukr.
142 H4 Klåverön naturreservat nature res. Sweden
214 C7 Klawer S. Africa
220 E4 Klawock AK U.S.A.
164 K3 Klazienaveen Neth.
206 C5 Kle Liberia
179 H6 Kleblach-Lind Austria
174 E2 Klębowiec Pol.
234 E3 Klecknersville PA U.S.A.
174 F3 Kłecko Pol.
174 G3 Kleczew Pol.
222 E5 Kleena Kleene B.C. Can.
128 C3 Kleides Islands Cyprus
179 H5 Kleinarl Austria
214 F4 Kleinbegin S. Africa
168 D5 Klein Berßen Ger.
172 C3 Kleinblittersdorf Ger.
247 □8 Klein Bonaire i. Neth. Antilles
170 I3 Klein Bünzow Ger.
247 □10 Klein Curaçao i. Neth. Antilles
214 D7 Klein Doring r. S. Africa
171 H7 Kleine Elster r. Ger.
140 J5 Kleinegga mt. Norway
173 N4 Kleine Laaber r. Ger.
173 K4 Kleine Paar r. Ger.
170 I2 Kleiner Jasmunder Bodden b. Ger.
178 D5 Kleiner Solstein mt. Austria
171 J7 Kleine Spree r. Ger.
173 M4 Kleine Vils r. Ger.
234 C4 Kleinfeltersville PA U.S.A.
172 G2 Kleinheubach Ger.
171 E8 Kleinjena Ger.
212 C5 Klein Karas Namibia
171 G6 Klein Kreutz Ger.
179 K5 Kleinlobming Austria
171 H6 Kleinmachnow Ger.
214 D10 Kleinmond S. Africa
168 I3 Klein Nordende Ger.
172 G1 Kleinostheim Ger.
171 E7 Kleinpaschleben Ger.
215 I9 Kleinpoort S. Africa
179 K4 Kleinreifling Austria
172 H2 Kleinrinderfeld Ger.
214 E9 Klein Roggeveldberge mts S. Africa
168 J3 Klein Rönnau Ger.
179 K6 Klein Sankt Paul Austria
214 B5 Kleinsee S. Africa
170 G4 Kleinseenplatte Neustrelitz park Ger.
214 F9 Klein Swartberg mt. S. Africa
215 K4 Klein-Vet r. S. Africa
172 G2 Kleinwallstadt Ger.
171 D6 Klein Wanzleben Ger.
169 K6 Kleinwinnigstedt (Winnigstedt) Ger.
179 M4 Kleinzell Austria
198 D5 Kleitoria Greece
175 L3 Klejniki Pol.
188 F3 Klekovača mt. Bos.-Herz.
136 H5 Klembivka Ukr.
222 D4 Klemtu B.C. Can.
176 B2 Klenčí pod Čerchovem Czech Rep.
174 D4 Klenica Pol.
177 I3 Klenovec Slovakia
176 G2 Klenovice na Hané Czech Rep.
177 I3 Klenovský Vepor mt. Slovakia
175 L2 Kleosin Pol.
175 L2 Klepacze Pol.

137 T3	Klepovka Rus. Fed.
142 B3	Kleppe Norway
142 F2	Kleppestø Norway
174 D3	Klępsk Pol.
137 N8	Klepy Pol.
215 K2	Klerksdorp S. Africa
215 L2	Klerkskraal S. Africa
136 F2	Klesiv Ukr.
175 L3	Kleszczele Pol.
139 Q8	Kleszczów Pol.
137 H4	Kletnya Rus. Fed.
	Kletsk Belarus see Klyetsk
135 H6	Kletskaya Rus. Fed.
	Kletskiy Rus. Fed.
172 E6	Klettgau reg. Ger./Switz.
171 I7	Klettwitz Ger.
136 E3	Klevan' Ukr.
169 B7	Kleve Ger.
137 M2	Kleven' r. Rus. Fed.
107 O1	Klichaw Belarus
	Klichka Rus. Fed.
	Kleidos Islands Cyprus see Kleides Islands
171 F7	Klieken Ger.
170 F5	Klietz Ger.
139 U4	Klimavichy Belarus
137 K1	Klimawka Belarus
197 P7	Kliment Bulg.
177 H2	Klimkovice Czech Rep.
134 J4	Klimkovka Rus. Fed.
175 J5	Klimontów Małopolskie Pol.
175 J5	Klimontów Świętokrzyskie Pol.
	Klimovichi Belarus see Klimavichy
135 F5	Klimovo Rus. Fed.
139 U6	Klimovo Rus. Fed.
139 W1	Klimovskaya Rus. Fed.
139 R7	Klimov Zavod Rus. Fed.
144 M4	Klimpfjäll Sweden
139 T5	Klin Rus. Fed.
134 L4	Klin Slovakia
177 I2	Klina Kosovo Serbia
196 I8	Klinaklini r. B.C. Can.
92 E9	Kling Mindanao Phil.
171 I9	Klingenberg Ger.
172 G2	Klingenberg am Main Ger.
171 F10	Klingenthal Ger.
234 B3	Klingerstown PA U.S.A.
95 I4	Klingkang, Banjaran mts Indon./Malaysia
170 G4	Klink Ger.
176 C1	Klínovec mt. Czech Rep.
135 T5	Klintsi Rus. Fed.
	Klintsovka Rus. Fed.
143 O4	Klintehamn Gotland Sweden
120 C2	Klintsovka Rus. Fed.
139 P9	Klintsy Rus. Fed.
215 N3	Klip r. S. Africa
214 D10	Klipdale S. Africa
215 J9	Klipfontein S. Africa
168 H1	Kliplev Denmark
142 J5	Klippan Sweden
214 I9	Klipplaat S. Africa
215 O1	Klipskool S. Africa
188 H4	Klis Croatia
139 V7	Klishino Moskovskaya Oblast' Rus. Fed.
139 Q2	Klishino Novgorodskaya Oblast' Rus. Fed.
197 K8	Klisura Serbia
142 E4	Klitmøller Denmark
	Klitória Greece see Kleitoria
171 K8	Klitten Ger.
168 G1	Klixbüll Ger.
177 I6	Kljajićevo Vojvodina Serbia
188 F3	Ključ Bos.-Herz.
176 F3	Klobouky Czech Rep.
174 G5	Kłobuck Pol.
174 G5	Kłobucko Pol.
170 L5	Klockow Ger.
174 G3	Kłodawa Lubuskie Pol.
174 E3	Kłodawa Wielkopolskie Pol.
174 E5	Kłodzko Pol.
142 H1	Kløfta Norway
175 H5	Klomnice Pol.
222 C3	Klondike Gold Rush National Historical Park nat. park AK U.S.A.
174 G4	Klonowa Pol.
138 H2	Klooga Estonia
164 K4	Kloosterhaar Neth.
165 F6	Kloosterzande Neth.
197 J3	Klopot mt. Slovakia
196 I9	Klos Albania
179 N8	Kloštar Ivanić Croatia
210 H5	Kloštar Podravski Croatia
170 H5	Klosterfelde Ger.
171 E8	Klosterhäseler Ger.
173 J5	Klösterle Austria
173 J5	Klosterlechfeld Ger.
170 G3	Klostermansfeld Ger.
173 N6	Klosterneuburg Austria
190 H2	Klosters Switz.
171 J8	Klosterwasser r. Ger.
171 H6	Kloster Zinna Ger.
172 F7	Kloten Switz.
170 D10	Klötze (Altmark) Ger.
169 D5	Kloten Switz.
222 A2	Kluane Game Sanctuary nature res. Y.T. Can.
222 B2	Kluane Lake Y.T. Can.
222 B2	Kluane National Park Y.T. Can.
95 I6	Kluang Malaysia see Keluang
174 G5	Kluczbork Pol.
175 H5	Kluczewsko Pol.
	Klukhori Pass pass Georgia/Rus. Fed. see Klukhorskiy, Pereval pass
129 C2	Klukhori Ugheltekhili pass Georgia/Rus. Fed.
	Klukhorskiy, Pereval pass Georgia/Rus. Fed.
175 H4	Kluki Pol.
135 F6	Klukvenka Rus. Fed.
220 E4	Klukwan AK U.S.A.
95 L6	Klumpang, Teluk b. Indon.
164 G5	Klundert Neth.
175 J4	Klukuchów Pol.
168 D5	Klupro Pak.
176 F2	Klušov Slovakia
175 K2	Klusy Pol.
138 G4	Klvov mt. Rus. Fed.
178 I4	Klwów Pol.
138 L6	Klyastitsy Belarus
142 J4	Klyaz'ma r. Belarus
135 K5	Klyavlino Rus. Fed.
139 Z5	Klyaz'ma r. Rus. Fed.
138 J8	Klyetsk Belarus
137 G7	Klymivka Ukr.
135 K5	Klyosovo Ukr.
137 M2	Klyshky Ukr.
131 R4	Klyuchevskaya, Sopka vol. Rus. Fed.
100 E4	Klyuchi Altayskiy Kray Rus. Fed.
131 R4	Klyuchi Kamchatskiy Oblast' Rus. Fed.
131 R4	Klyuchi Amurskaya Oblast' Rus. Fed.
78 □6	Kmagha Sta Isabel Solomon Is
142 D3	Knaben Norway
81 C13	Knapdale South I. N.Z.
146 E11	Knapdale reg. Scotland U.K.
232 A5	Knapp Mount Hill WI U.S.A.
142 J3	Knared Sweden
149 O5	Knaresborough North Yorkshire, England U.K.
143 K1	Knästen hill Sweden
149 O5	Knayton North Yorkshire, England U.K.
151 L4	Knebworth Hertfordshire, England U.K.
223 H4	Knee Lake Man. Can.
223 J4	Knee Lake Sask. Can.
168 H2	Kneesebeck Ger.
168 K1	Kneese Ger.
171 L10	Kneebur Ger.
196 I7	Knić Serbia

236 E2	Knife r. ND U.S.A.
226 C3	Knife River MN U.S.A.
222 E5	Knight Inlet B.C. Can.
150 F3	Knighton Powys, Wales U.K.
240 K3	Knights Landing CA U.S.A.
188 F3	Knin Croatia
143 K5	Knislinge Sweden
179 K5	Knittelfeld Austria
172 F3	Knittlingen Ger.
143 N2	Knivsta Sweden
176 D3	Knížecí stolec mt. Czech Rep.
179 N8	Knjaževac Serbia
197 K7	Knjaževac Serbia
87 C10	Knob Head W.A. Austr.
	Knob Lake Nfld and Lab. Can. see Schefferville
86 J3	Knob Peak hill W.A. Austr.
147 D7	Knock Clare Ireland
147 E5	Knock Mayo Ireland
146 E10	Knock Argyll and Bute, Scotland U.K.
147 D9	Knockaboy hill Ireland
147 G9	Knockacummer hill Ireland
147 E4	Knockalongy hill Ireland
147 D7	Knockalough Ireland
148 E8	Knockananna Ireland
146 J3	Knockaphuca Moray, Scotland U.K.
147 D8	Knockanefune Ireland
147 K2	Knockban Highland, Scotland U.K.
147 J7	Knockbrandon Ireland
147 J5	Knockbridge Ireland
147 G7	Knockbrit Ireland
147 F5	Knockcroghery Ireland
146 K7	Knock Hill Scotland U.K.
147 E5	Knock International airport Ireland
147 J2	Knocklayd hill Northern Ireland U.K.
147 F8	Knocklong Ireland
147 F8	Knockmealdown Mountains hills Ireland
147 D4	Knockmore Ireland
147 D8	Knockmoyle Ireland
147 D8	Knocknabul Ireland
148 E3	Knocknacarry Northern Ireland U.K.
147 D8	Knocknagree Ireland
147 F9	Knocknaskagh hill Ireland
147 F9	Knockraha Ireland
146 K4	Knocks Ireland
210 B2	Knokke-Heist Belgium
170 H3	Knorrendorf Ger.
198 G2	Knossos tourist site Greece
	Knossós, Kríti Greece see Knosos
149 O6	Knottingley West Yorkshire, England U.K.
151 I3	Knowle West Midlands, England U.K.
262 T2	Knowles, Cape Antarctica
233 □Q2	Knowles Corner ME U.S.A.
233 M3	Knowlton Que. Can.
230 D5	Knox IN U.S.A.
234 C7	Knox PA U.S.A.
222 C4	Knox, Cape B.C. Can.
226 B9	Knox Atoll Kiribati see Tarawa
263 G2	Knox City MO U.S.A.
231 F9	Knox Coast Antarctica
236 I5	Knoxville GA U.S.A.
231 F8	Knoxville IA U.S.A.
236 I4	Knoxville TN U.S.A.
146 E8	Knoydart mts Scotland U.K.
150 F3	Knucklas Powys, Wales U.K.
221 L2	Knud Rasmussen Land reg. Greenland
169 H9	Knüllgebirge hills Ger.
169 H8	Knüllwald-Remsfeld Ger.
174 G5	Knurów Pol.
149 M7	Knutsford Cheshire, England U.K.
134 L5	Knyaginino Rus. Fed.
138 K7	Knyazha Belarus
100 I4	Knyaze-Bolkonskaye Rus. Fed.
137 M6	Knyazhychi Ukr.
138 L5	Knyaze-Hryhorivka Ukr.
139 T4	Knyazevo Rus. Fed.
138 L3	Knyazhikha r. Rus. Fed.
139 N7	Knyazhytsy Belarus
214 H10	Knysna S. Africa
175 K2	Knyszyn Pol.
100 J5	Ko, Gora mt. Rus. Fed.
208 F2	Koabib Chad
211 C6	Koani Tanz.
92 D6	Kobar Gamat Que. Can. see Quaqtaq
	Koa Valley watercourse S. Africa
94 G6	Koba Indon.
179 L6	Kobansko mts Slovenia
179 J7	Kobarid Slovenia
103 H15	Kobayashi Japan
140 T2	Kobbfoss Norway
93 E3	Kobe Halmahera Indon.
137 N4	Kōbe Japan
142 I6	Kobelyaky Ukr.
122 D6	Kobenhavn Japan
206 C3	København Maur.
179 K5	Kobenz Austria
179 H3	Koberbaumer Wald for. Austria
179 N4	Kobernaust Austria
93 F5	Kobi Seram Indon.
207 I4	Kobin Nigeria
175 H4	Kobiele Wielkie Pol.
174 G5	Kobierzyce Pol.
102 □G17	Kōbi-shō i. Nansei-shotō Japan
208 C2	Koblagué Chad
169 E10	Koblenz Ger.
137 K7	Koblevo Ukr.
210 C1	K'obo Eth.
117 O6	Kobo Uganda
210 A4	Kobo Uganda
100 H2	Kobozha r. Rus. Fed.
139 T3	Kobozha r. Rus. Fed.
134 J4	Kobra r. Rus. Fed.
222 A2	Kobrin Belarus see Kobryn
222 A2	Kobroör i. Indon.
170 E3	Kobryn Belarus
136 E1	Kobryn Belarus
105 H4	Kobuchizawa Japan
220 C3	Kobuk Valley National Park AK U.S.A.
129 C4	K'obulet'i Georgia
105 I4	Kobushiga-take mt. Japan
131 N3	Kobyay Rus. Fed.
179 N3	Kobyla Góra Pol.
137 □3	Kobylanka Rus. Fed.
136 D5	Kobylets'ka Polyana Ukr.
176 F3	Kobylí Czech Rep.
175 K2	Kobylin Pol.
175 K3	Kobylin-Borzymy Pol.
175 J3	Kobylnica Pol.
139 V1	Kobyłniki Pol.
122 I9	Koca r. Turkey
176 D2	Kocaafsar r. Turkey
199 I2	Kocaali Turkey
199 N3	Kocaaliler Turkey
199 N4	Kocabaş Turkey
78 □6	Koca Dağ mt. Turkey
81 C13	Kocael Turkey see İzmit
199 M5	Kocaeli prov. Turkey
199 K1	Kocaeli Yarımadası pen. Turkey
197 K9	Kočani Macedonia
199 L5	Koçarlı Turkey
199 I5	Kocasu r. Turkey
199 K4	Kocasu r. Turkey
128 F1	Koçatepe Turkey
136 G6	Koçbaşı Tepe mt. Turkey
106 H9	Koçé Gansu China
196 I5	Koçé Serbia
188 E3	Kočerin Bos.-Herz.
191 N4	Kočevska Reka Slovenia
121 P7	Kočevje Slovenia
101 E11	Koch' Jang S. Korea
174 G5	Kochanowice Pol.
117 J6	Koch Bihar W. Bengal India
173 K6	Kocheln Ger.
172 G3	Kocher r. Ger.

137 O5	Kocherezhky Ukr.
197 L8	Kocherinovo Bulg.
134 K4	Kochetovka Rus. Fed.
137 P2	Kochetovka Rus. Fed.
134 K4	Kochevo Rus. Fed.
	Kochi Kerala India see Cochin
103 K13	Kōchi Japan
103 K13	Kōchi pref. Japan
245 I8	Kochihuehuetlán Mex.
102 □1	Kochinda Okinawa Japan
120 I1	Kochkar' Rus. Fed.
121 P6	Kochkor Kyrg.
	Kochkorka Kyrg. see Kochkor
134 I5	Kochkurovo Rus. Fed.
134 M2	Kochmes Rus. Fed.
129 F1	Kochubey Rus. Fed.
198 F4	Kochylas hill Skyros Greece
175 K4	Kock Pol.
129 C3	Koçkaya Turkey
128 F1	Koçkoru Turkey
129 E5	Koçkurtlu Turkey
170 D5	Köckte Ger.
177 G3	Kočovce Slovakia
177 H4	Kocs Hungary
177 I4	Kocsér Hungary
177 H5	Kocsola Hungary
114 D5	Kod Karnataka India
134 K3	Kodachdikost Rus. Fed.
114 E7	Kodaikanal Tamil Nadu India
105 J4	Kodaira Japan
102 □G17	Kodakara-jima i. Nansei-shotō Japan
136 J3	Kodaky Ukr.
115 I3	Kodala Orissa India
105 J3	Kodama Japan
121 O7	Kodari Nepal
117 J7	Kodarma Jharkhand India
138 K3	Kodavere Estonia
175 L4	Kodeń Pol.
104 A6	Kodera Japan
171 K8	Kodersdorf Ger.
220 C4	Kodiak AK U.S.A.
220 C4	Kodiak Island AK U.S.A.
134 G3	Kodino Rus. Fed.
130 E1	Koditz Ger.
171 E10	Köditz Ger.
114 F7	Kodiyakkarai Tamil Nadu India
176 G4	Kōd r. Hungary
210 B2	Kodok Sudan
102 H5	Kodomari Japan
102 C3	Kodomari-misaki pt Japan
129 C3	Kodori r. Georgia
129 C3	Kodors K'edi hills Georgia
136 I3	Kodra Ukr.
175 H4	Kodrąb Pol.
114 E5	Kodumaru r. Andhra Prad. India
136 I5	Kodyma Ukr.
197 N9	Kodzhaele mt. Bulg./Greece
	Kodzhori Georgia see Kojori
214 E8	Koedoesberg mts S. Africa
214 G5	Koegas S. Africa
214 B5	Koegrabie S. Africa
	Koeho-jangsak S. Africa
	Kök-Janggak
111 C8	Koekange Neth.
210 B2	Koekelare Belgium
214 C7	Koekenaap S. Africa
165 E6	Koeweacht Neth.
241 S8	Kofa Mountains AZ U.S.A.
241 R8	Kofa National Wildlife Refuge nature res. AZ U.S.A.
123 M2	Kofarnihon Tajik.
123 M3	Kofarnihon r. Tajik.
197 P9	Kofçaz Turkey
173 M4	Koffachfen Ger.
215 J4	Koffiefontein S. Africa
198 G8	Kofinas mt. Kriti Greece
179 L5	Köflach Austria
206 E5	Koforidua Ghana
103 K11	Kōfu Tottori Japan
105 J4	Kōfu Yamanashi Japan
105 K3	Koga Japan
197 N9	Kogăǐonceanu airport Romania
224 E1	Kogaluc r. Que. Can.
224 E1	Kogaluc, Baie de b. Que. Can.
225 I1	Kogaluk r. Nfld and Lab. Can.
85 M9	Kogan Qld Austr.
142 I6	Køge Denmark
142 I6	Køge Bugt b. Denmark
134 L3	Kogel' r. Rus. Fed.
207 G4	Kogi state Nigeria
120 K8	Koghuf Austria
206 D3	Kogoni Mali
103 H12	Kōgushi Japan
177 G4	Kogyl'nicheny Moldova see Cogâlniceni
81 I6	Kōhaihai pt South I. N.Z.
123 N9	Kohalūen Pak.
123 L8	Kohan Pak.
123 N5	Kohat Pak.
123 K4	Kohestānāt Afgh.
122 D6	Kohgilūyeh va Būyer Aḥmad prov. Iran
117 O7	Kohīla India
117 M6	Kohima Nagaland India
81 G5	Kohimarama South I. N.Z.
78 □5	Kohinggo i. New Georgia Is Solomon Is
123 O4	Kohistan reg. Pak.
173 M2	Kohlberg Ger.
171 J6	Köhlen Ger.
262 W5	Kohler Range mts Antarctica
241 U7	Kohls Ranch AZ U.S.A.
123 M7	Kohlu Pak.
122 F4	Kohneh ‘Omar Iran
202 D5	Kohouro well Chad
206 B3	Koidern Y.T. Can.
208 C5	Koidagu Senegal
177 H4	Koidula Estonia
199 I4	Koihoa r. India
209 D5	Koilkuntla Andhra Prad. India
208 E4	Koilvesi l. Fin.
210 B3	Koin N. Korea
240 □1	Ko'ina Coll Fin.
140 T5	Koivu Fin.
101 F11	Kŏje-do i. S. Korea
173 J2	Kojetín Czech Rep.
122 I9	Kōji-ra r. Turkey
87 D12	Kojonup W.A. Austr.
122 F4	Kojūr Iran
116 N6	Kok, Nam Mae r. Thai.
104 D6	Kōka Japan
233 □P3	Koka r. Japan
105 I4	Kokai-gawa r. Japan
114 E7	Kokala India
173 O4	Kokava nad Rimavicou Slovakia
104 B7	Kokawa Japan
121 P7	Kök-Aygyr Kyrg.

123 M3	Kokcha r. Afgh.
	Kokchetav Kazakh. see Kokshetau
141 Q6	Kokemäki Fin.
212 C6	Kokerboom Namibia
96 D5	Ko Kha Thai.
138 M7	Kokhanava Belarus
139 V5	Kokhma Rus. Fed.
206 B3	Koki Senegal
120 □1	Kokkaï Japan
114 G8	Kokkala Sri Lanka
199 K6	Kokkino Nero Greece
140 Q5	Kokkola Fin.
110 H4	Kok Kuduk well Xinjiang China
138 I5	Koknese Latvia
207 G5	Koko Edo Nigeria
207 G4	Koko Kebbi Nigeria
134 K1	Kokofata Mali
240 □D12	Koko Head HI U.S.A.
206 D5	Kokolo-Pozo Côte d'Ivoire
206 C3	Kokoma IN U.S.A.
212 D6	Kokong Botswana
103 I13	Kokonoe Japan
139 U6	Kokorevka Rus. Fed.
139 U6	Kokorevo Rus. Fed.
207 C3	Kokosa Eth.
139 U6	Kokoshkino Rus. Fed.
215 L2	Kokosi S. Africa
206 B4	Kokou mt. Guinea
121 T3	Kokpekti Kazakh.
179 J7	Kokra r. Slovenia
121 T3	Kokrica Slovenia
101 E9	Koksan N. Korea
121 M6	Kokshaal-Tau, Khrebet mts China/Kyrg. see Kakshaal-Too
134 I4	Koksharka Rus. Fed.
121 M1	Kokshetau Kazakh.
165 C6	Koksijde Belgium
225 G1	Koksoak r. Que. Can.
215 N6	Kokstad S. Africa
121 Q5	Koksu Almatinskaya Oblast' Kazakh.
121 R5	Koksu Kazakh.
121 M7	Koksu Yuzhnyy Kazakhstan Kazakh.
121 O7	Koktal Kazakh.
121 R4	Kokterek Almatinskaya Oblast' Kazakh.
120 C3	Kokterek Zapadnyy Kazakhstan Kazakh.
121 Q2	Koktobe Kazakh.
106 A3	Koktokay Xinjiang China Fuyun
120 G3	Koktubek Kazakh.
175 H4	Kokuba r. Rus. Fed.
103 H15	Kokubu Japan
105 K3	Kokubunji Japan
105 I4	Kokūshiga-take mt. Japan
105 I4	Kokūyo Xinjiang China
106 B3	Kok-Yangak Kyrg.
	Kök-Jangak
121 S6	Kokzhayyk Kazakh.
140 V2	Kola r. Rus. Fed.
140 V2	Kola r. Rus. Fed.
93 B6	Kolaï r. see Sabari
117 J9	Kolabira Orissa India
123 L8	Kolachi r. Pak.
175 H4	Kolaczyce Pol.
174 E2	Kołacz Pol.
174 E3	Kolaczkowo Pol.
175 J6	Kolaczyce Pol.
124 C9	Kola Diba Eth.
117 K8	Kolaghat W. Bengal India
116 E2	Kolahoï mt. Jammu and Kashmir
206 C4	Kolahun Liberia
93 B6	Kolaka Sulawesi Indon.
95 H3	Kołaki Kościelne Pol.
92 D7	Kolambugan Mindanao Phil.
93 B3	Kolam Timor Indon.
114 C3	Kolar Chhattisgarh India
114 E7	Kolar Karnataka India
114 F6	Kolar Gold Fields Karnataka India
140 Q3	Kolari r. Pak.
	Kolarovgrad Bulg. see Shumen
177 G4	Kolárovo Slovakia
140 L5	Kolåsen Sweden
196 H8	Kolašin Montenegro
196 I6	Kolašinac Serbia
170 K4	Kolbano Timor Indon.
140 K3	Kolbano Timor Indon.
93 D4	Kolbano Timor Indon.
214 B5	Kolberg Pol. see Kołobrzeg
173 M6	Kolbermoor Ger.
175 I3	Kolbiel Pol.
210 C1	Kolbio Kenya
142 H1	Kolbotn Norway
174 G1	Kolbudy Górne Pol.
175 J5	Kolbuszowa Pol.
131 M3	Kolchanovo Rus. Fed.
139 R9	Kol'chugino Rus. Fed.
139 V5	Kol'chukyne Ukr.
136 E5	Kol'chyne Ukr.
197 L3	Kölcse Hungary
175 K3	Kolczygłowy Pol.
174 D3	Kolczyn Pol.
206 B3	Kolda Senegal
208 C3	Kolda reg. Senegal
142 E5	Kolding Denmark
138 M1	Kole Kasaï-Oriental Dem. Rep. Congo
208 E4	Kole Orientale Dem. Rep. Congo
139 Q3	Kolemukanka Rus. Fed.
179 R9	Kolendo Sakhalin Rus. Fed.
100 M1	Koledale mt. Hi U.S.A.
100 P4	Kolendo Sakhalin Rus. Fed.
177 H5	Kőlesd Hungary
138 J4	Kolga-Jaani Estonia
134 L1	Kolguyev, Ostrov i. Rus. Fed.
114 D4	Kolhan reg. Jharkhand India
114 D4	Kolhapur Mahar. India
93 C7	Kolimba S. Africa
93 D6	Kolimba Indon.
206 E5	Kolinba C.A.R.
209 C6	Kolinbo Tanz.
206 D3	Kolia i. Indon.
	Koliba r. Guinea/Guinea-Bissau
140 O3	Kolima i. Rus. Fed.
216 E1	Kolima l. Fin.
92 □	Kolima Czech Rep.
134 J3	Kolin r. India
179 I8	Kolin Slovenia
94 F6	Kolín i. Indon.
208 D3	Kolinga C.A.R.
221 P2	Komi, Respublika aut. rep. Rus. Fed.
179 N7	Komin Croatia
132 H4	Kominato Japan
102 R6	Kominato Japan
123 M3	Kominternivs'ke Ukr.
171 J7	Komiža Croatia
188 F4	Komjatice Slovakia
177 H3	Komjatná Slovakia
173 O4	Komló Hungary
173 O4	Komlóská Hungary
211 A6	Kommadagga S. Africa
214 B3	Kommandokraal S. Africa
95 L4	Kommunarsk Ukr. see Alchevs'k
214 C10	Kommetjie S. Africa
215 L5	Kommissiepoort S. Africa
214 B6	Kommuna Turkm.
104 C6	Kommunarka Rus. Fed.
140 □E1	Kópasker Iceland

175 I2	Kolno Warmińsko-Mazurskie Pol.
209 B6	Kolo Dem. Rep. Congo
174 G3	Koło Pol.
211 B6	Kolo Tanz.
240 □B12	Kōloa HI U.S.A.
139 Y5	Kolobrzeg Pol.
174 D2	Kołobrzeg Pol.
206 B3	Kolochau Ukr.
136 C5	Kolochava Ukr.
139 U2	Kolodenskoye, Ozero l. Rus. Fed.
137 S2	Kolodeznyy Rus. Fed.
136 E4	Kolodne Côte d'Ivoire
137 G3	Kolodne Côte d'Ivoire
137 O4	Kolodyazne Ukr.
210 D2	Kolofgi Sudan
134 I4	Kologriv Rus. Fed.
206 C3	Kolokani Mali
134 K1	Kolokolkova, Guba b. Rus. Fed.
137 O4	Kolomak Ukr.
134 N4	Kolomak Ukr.
78 □6	Kolombangara i. New Georgia Is Solomon Is
199 G1	Kolomea Ukr. see Kolomyya
137 L5	Kolomna Rus. Fed.
177 I5	Kolomyagivka Ukr.
139 V6	Kolomyagi Rus. Fed.
209 D6	Kolomonyi Dem. Rep. Congo
136 E5	Kolomyya Ukr.
136 D4	Kolomyya see Kolomyya
93 B5	Kolonedale Sulawesi Indon.
79 □8	Kolonga Tongatapu Tonga
128 A4	Koloni Cyprus
196 H10	Kolonja Albania
212 D5	Kolonkwane Botswana
139 Y4	Kolodno Sulawesi Indon.
134 F2	Kolp'skiy Poluostrov pen. Rus. Fed.
143 M2	Kolsnaren l. Sweden
143 L2	Kolsva Sweden
141 M6	Kölsvallen Sweden
177 H3	Kolta Slovakia
137 N4	Kol'tsove Ukr.
120 D1	Koltubanovskiy Rus. Fed.
196 I6	Kolubara r. Serbia
203 I6	Koluli Eritrea
175 H4	Koluszki Pol.
137 P4	Kolvenbach Ger.
123 K8	Kolva r. Pak.
114 D4	Kolva r. Rus. Fed.
131 O1	Kolva r. Rus. Fed.
140 R1	Kolvik Norway
134 K2	Kolvitskoye, Ozero l. Rus. Fed.
131 Q3	Kolwezi Dem. Rep. Congo
131 P3	Kolyma r. Rus. Fed.
	Kolyma Lowland Rus. Fed. see Kolymskaya Nizmennost'
100 J3	Kolymskaya Nizmennost' lowland Rus. Fed.
131 P3	Kolymskiy, Khrebet mts Rus. Fed.
135 I5	Kolyshley Rus. Fed.
135 I5	Kolyshleyka r. Rus. Fed.
137 P6	Kolyuchino Rus. Fed.
137 N4	Kolyvan' Rus. Fed.
197 N9	Komadugu-gana watercourse Nigeria
105 J3	Komae Japan
105 G4	Komaga-dake mt. Japan
105 J1	Komagane Japan
102 F4	Komaga-take mt. Japan
214 B5	Komaggas S. Africa
214 B5	Komaggas Mountains S. Africa
140 U1	Komagvær Norway
104 U5	Komaki Japan
96 D7	Komandnaya, Gora mt. Rus. Fed.
85 J4	Komandorskiye Ostrova is Rus. Fed.
227 R3	Komandiaronk, Lac l. Que. Can.
130 H3	Komárica r. Montenegro
176 C2	Komárno Czech Rep.
177 H4	Komárno Slovakia
177 H4	Komárom Hungary
177 H4	Komárom-Esztergom county Hungary
176 C2	Komarov Czech Rep.
138 M1	Komarovo Leningradskaya Oblast' Rus. Fed.
139 Q3	Komarovo Novgorodskaya Oblast' Rus. Fed.
136 C2	Komarów-Osada Pol.
177 H4	Komárváros Hungary
207 I3	Komba Nigeria
214 C5	Kombani S. Africa
134 G2	Komba i. Indon.
206 E3	Komba Dem. Rep. Congo
78 □4	Komba i. Indon.
206 E3	Kombane Tanz.
206 A6	Kombo Eth.
92 □	Kombissiri Burkina
140 F6	Kolima r. Rus. Fed.
179 I8	Komen Slovenia
94 F6	Komering r. Indon.
92 □	Komfane Indon.
208 E4	Komga S. Africa
221 O3	Komi, Respublika aut. rep. Rus. Fed.
142 F4	Kolind Denmark

142 F2	Kongsberg Norway
140 T1	Kongsfjord Norway
140 □	Kongsøya i. Svalbard
142 I1	Kongsvinger Norway
110 B7	Kongur Shan mt. Xinjiang China
211 C6	Kongwa Tanz.
221 P2	Kong Wilhelm Land reg. Greenland
123 N1	Konibodom Tajik.
176 F2	Konice Czech Rep.
175 H5	Koniecpol Pol.
172 H2	Königsbach Ger.
	Königsberg Rus. Fed. see Kaliningrad
169 K10	Königsberg in Bayern Ger.
171 E6	Königsborn Ger.
173 I4	Königsbronn Ger.
169 I9	Königsbrück Ger.
171 I6	Königsbrunn Ger.
174 G4	Königsdorf Ger.
173 K6	Königsdorf Ger.
171 D9	Königsee Ger.
173 K2	Königsfeld Ger.
172 E5	Königsfeld im Schwarzwald Ger.
171 H6	Königsgraben r. Ger.
171 K8	Königshain Ger.
171 I8	Königshofen Ger.
	Königslutter am Elm Ger. see Chorzów
169 K6	Königslutter am Elm Ger.
173 K4	Königsmoos Ger.
173 N6	Königssee Ger.
173 L2	Königstein Bayern Ger.
171 J9	Königstein Sachsen Ger.
173 N6	Königssee l. Ger.
169 J9	Königswartha Ger.
169 D9	Königswiesen Austria
170 H4	Königs Wusterhausen Ger.
	Königswinter Uzbek. see Konimex
120 K7	Konimex
174 G3	Konin Pol.
198 G1	Konispolis r. Greece
196 I9	Konitsa Greece
171 E9	Könitz Ger.
190 C2	Köniz Switz.
188 F4	Konj mt. Bos.-Herz.
188 G4	Konjic Bos.-Herz.
188 H4	Konjsko mts Bos.-Herz.
140 Q2	Könkämäeno r. Fin./Sweden
212 C6	Konkiep watercourse Namibia
139 W9	Kon'-Kolodez' Rus. Fed.
207 G4	Konkwesso Nigeria
206 E3	Konna Mali
212 D12	Konnarock VA U.S.A.
171 F10	Konnersreuth Ger.
140 S5	Konnevesi Fin.
141 S6	Könnu Estonia
206 E5	Konongo Ghana
137 C3	Kononovka Ukr.
177 I1	Konopiska Pol.
175 I2	Konopki Pol.
174 E4	Konopnica Pol.
174 G4	Konoradze Pol.
134 H3	Konosha Rus. Fed.
105 M3	Kōnosu Japan
136 I2	Konotop Ukr.
174 D2	Konotop Pol.
100 E4	Konstantinovka Rus. Fed.
	Konstantinovka Donets'ka Oblast' Ukr. see Kostyantynivka
	Konstantinovka Kherson'ska Oblast' Ukr. see Kostyantynivka
137 O6	Konstantinovka Zaporiz'ka Oblast' Ukr. see Kostyantynivka
139 V5	Konstantinovo Rus. Fed.
135 H7	Konstantinovsk Rus. Fed.
139 W4	Konstantinovskiy Rus. Fed.
176 C2	Konstantinovy Lázně Czech Rep.
172 G6	Konstanz Ger.
175 H3	Konstantynów Pol.
175 H4	Konstantynów Łódzki Pol.
123 I8	Kont Iran
207 G4	Kontagora Nigeria
207 I5	Kontcha Cameroon
96 C4	Kontha Myanmar
140 T4	Kontiolahti Fin.
140 T5	Kontiomäki Fin.
207 J4	Kontoor Belarus
97 H7	Kon Tum Vietnam
99 I8	Kon Tum, Cao Nguyên plat. Vietnam
199 M2	Konuk see Kyiv
134 H2	Konushin, Mys pt Rus. Fed.
199 L5	Konya Turkey
127 F4	Konya prov. Turkey
169 J7	Konz Ger.
137 O2	Konyshevka Rus. Fed.
121 N1	Konyukhovo Kazakh.
139 X3	Konzovo Rus. Fed.
175 L4	Koń r. Pol.
222 H5	Koocanusa, Lake resr Can./U.S.A.
87 F10	Kookynie W.A. Austr.
86 G3	Koolan Island W.A. Austr.
240 □D12	Ko'olau Range mts HI U.S.A.
87 D7	Kooline W.A. Austr.
84 F3	Koolivoo, Lake salt flat Qld Austr.
82 F3	Kooloonong Vic. Austr.
85 J6	Koolyanobbing W.A. Austr.
83 J6	Koondrook Vic. Austr.
86 I5	Koongie Park Aboriginal Reserve W.A. Austr.
84 A6	Koonibba S.A. Austr.
82 G5	Koonya Tas. Austr.
232 G9	Koon Lake PA U.S.A.
214 E3	Koopan-Suid S. Africa
82 H5	Koorawatha N.S.W. Austr.
87 D11	Koorda W.A. Austr.
138 I3	Koorküla Estonia
170 H3	Koos i. Ger.
138 K3	Koosa Estonia
222 G4	Kootenay r. Can./U.S.A.
222 G5	Kootenay Lake B.C. Can.
222 G5	Kootenay National Park B.C. Can.
83 M4	Kootingal N.S.W. Austr.
214 E7	Kootjieskolk S. Africa
164 I4	Kootwijkerbroek Neth.
140 □E1	Kópasker Iceland

Kresna to Kustanay
337

197 L9 Kresna Bulg.
179 K7 Kresnice Slovenia
172 H6 Kressbronn am Bodensee Ger.
131 T3 Kresta, Zaliv g. Rus. Fed.
198 C5 Krestena Greece
131 O3 Krest-Khal'dzhayy Rus. Fed.
134 K2 Krestovka Rus. Fed.
139 P3 Kresttsy Rus. Fed.
139 U6 Kresty Moskovskaya Oblast' Rus. Fed.
139 O6 Kresty Pskovskaya Oblast' Rus. Fed.
139 V8 Kresty Tul'skaya Oblast' Rus. Fed.
131 M3 Krestyakh Rus. Fed.
138 E6 Kretinga Lith.
171 F8 Kretzschau Ger.
173 L6 Kreuth Ger.
169 B9 Kreuzau Ger.
178 H6 Kreuzeck mt. Austria
178 G6 Kreuzeck Gruppe mts Austria
178 E5 Kreuzjoch mt. Austria
190 G1 Kreuzlingen Switz.
169 E9 Kreuztal Ger.
172 H2 Kreuzwertheim Ger.
138 J7 Kreva Belarus
207 H6 Kribi Cameroon
Krichev Belarus see Krychaw
197 M8 Krichim Bulg.
179 M4 Krieglach Austria
190 D1 Kriegstetten Switz.
215 N2 Kriel S. Africa
170 H3 Krien Ger.
190 E1 Kriens Switz.
138 E5 Krievukalns hill Latvia
198 F4 Krieza Greece
198 C4 Krikellos Greece
Krikovo Moldova see Cricova
100 M6 Kril'on, Mys c. Sakhalin Rus. Fed.
179 J8 Krim mt. Slovenia
208 B2 Krim-Krim Chad
178 F5 Krimmler Wasserfälle waterfall Austria
164 G5 Krimpen aan de IJssel Neth.
176 E1 Křinec Czech Rep.
198 F1 Krinides Greece
198 E7 Krios, Akrotirio pt Kriti Greece
Kripka r. Rus. Fed./Ukr. see Krepkaya
179 I4 Krippenstein mt. Austria
114 E4 Krishna Andhra Prad. India
114 G4 Krishna r. India
114 G5 Krishna, Mouths of the India
114 F6 Krishnagiri Tamil Nadu India
117 M6 Krishnai r. India
117 L8 Krishnanagar W. Bengal India
114 E6 Krishnaraja Sagara l. India
114 E6 Krishnarajpet Karnataka India
143 M4 Kristdala Sweden
Kristiania Norway see Oslo
142 D3 Kristiansand Norway
143 K5 Kristianstad Sweden
140 I5 Kristiansund Norway
Kristiinankaupunki Länsi-Suomi Fin. see Kristinestad
143 K2 Kristinehamn Sweden
141 P5 Kristinestad Fin.
Kristinopol' Ukr. see Chervonohrad
198 F8 Kriti admin. reg. Greece
198 F7 Kriti i. Kriti Greece
198 G6 Kritiko Pelagos sea Greece
170 F2 Kritzmow Ger.
138 G6 Kriūkai Lith.
Kriulyany Moldova see Criuleni
139 W7 Kriusha Rus. Fed.
Kriushi Kazakh. see Arshaly
196 I7 Krivača mt. Serbia
188 G3 Krivaja r. Bos.-Herz.
177 I6 Krivaja r. Serbia
139 W6 Krivandino Rus. Fed.
197 K8 Kriva Palanka Macedonia
197 J8 Kriva Reka r. Macedonia
137 S3 Krivaya Polyana Rus. Fed.
137 Q2 Krivets Rus. Fed.
191 R5 Krivi Put Croatia
196 J9 Krivogaštani Macedonia
176 C2 Křivoklátská vrchovina hills Czech Rep.
139 P8 Krivoles Rus. Fed.
139 W8 Krivopolyan'ye Rus. Fed.
135 H6 Krivorozh'ye Rus. Fed.
134 F2 Krivoy Porog Rus. Fed.
Krivoy Rog Ukr. see Kryvyy Rih
191 P5 Kriz, Rt pt Croatia
176 F2 Křižanov Czech Rep.
188 F2 Križevci Croatia
188 G3 Krk mt. Bos.-Herz.
188 E3 Krk Croatia
188 E3 Krk i. Croatia
188 E4 Krka r. Croatia
179 K8 Krka Slovenia
188 E3 Krka r. Slovenia
176 E1 Krkonoše mts Czech Rep.
174 D5 Krkonošský narodní park nat. park Czech Rep./Pol.
179 I7 Krn mt. Slovenia
191 Q6 Krnica Croatia
196 I6 Krnjača Serbia
177 G1 Krnov Czech Rep.
174 E4 Krobia Pol.
175 H5 Kroczyce Pol.
142 F1 Krøderen Norway
142 F1 Krøderen l. Norway
171 H8 Krögis Ger.
206 D5 Krohnwodoke Liberia
Krokeaí Greece see Krokees
198 D6 Krokees Greece
143 M3 Krokek Sweden
140 U1 Kroknes Norway
140 M5 Krokom Sweden
97 J14 Krokong Sarawak Malaysia
143 O7 Krokowa Pol.
140 □C1 Króksfjarðarnes Iceland
140 J5 Krokstadøra Norway
140 M3 Krokstranda Norway
137 M2 Krolevets' Ukr.
Królewska Huta Pol. see Chorzów
175 L2 Królowy Most Pol.
171 E9 Krölpa Ger.
215 I10 Krom r. S. Africa
139 S9 Kroma r. Rus. Fed.
215 N1 Kromdraai S. Africa
176 G2 Kroměříž Czech Rep.
164 G3 Krommenie Neth.
177 J3 Krompachy Slovakia
171 D9 Kromsdorf Ger.
139 S9 Kromy Rus. Fed.
171 D10 Kronach Ger.
172 F3 Kronau Ger.
169 F10 Kronberg im Taunus Ger.
142 E2 Kronfjell hill Norway
97 F9 Krŏng Kaôh Kŏng Cambodia
117 O5 Kronli Arun. Prad. India
143 K5 Kronoberg county Sweden
140 Q5 Kronoby Fin.
131 R4 Kronotskiy Poluostrov pen. Rus. Fed.
131 R4 Kronotskiy Zaliv b. Rus. Fed.
131 R4 Kronotskoye Ozero l. Rus. Fed.
221 P1 Kronprins Christian Land reg. Greenland
221 O3 Kronprins Frederik Bjerge nunataks Greenland
168 G3 Kronprinzenkoog Ger.
168 J2 Kronshagen Ger.
138 M2 Kronshtadt Rus. Fed.
Kronstadt Romania see Braşov
Kronstadt Rus. Fed. see Kronshtadt
179 J3 Kronstorf Austria
96 D7 Kronwa Myanmar
215 L3 Kroonstad S. Africa
179 J7 Kropa Slovenia
170 E2 Kröpelin Ger.
135 H7 Kropotkin Rus. Fed.
168 I2 Kropp Ger.
142 I3 Kroppefjäll hills Sweden
171 D7 Kroppenstedt Ger.
171 G7 Kropstädt Ger.
136 I3 Kropyvnya Ukr.
175 I6 Krościenko nad Dunajcem Pol.
170 I2 Kröslin Ger.
175 L1 Krosna Lith.
174 F4 Krośnice Pol.
175 H3 Krośniewice Pol.
175 J6 Krosno Pol.
174 D3 Krosno Odrzańskie Pol.
171 E9 Krossen Ger.
142 E2 Krossen Norway
171 F8 Krostitz Ger.
174 E4 Krotoszyce Pol.
174 F4 Krotoszyn Pol.
179 M5 Krottendorf Austria
237 J10 Krotz Springs LA U.S.A.
176 F2 Krouna Czech Rep.
198 F7 Krousonas Kriti Greece
172 C2 Kröv Ger.
95 H8 Kroya Jawa Indon.
191 Q5 Kršan Croatia
188 E3 Krško Slovenia
196 I8 Krstača mt. Montenegro
174 F3 Kruchowo Pol.
170 E5 Krüden Ger.
169 D10 Kruft Ger.
215 K4 Krugerdrifdam resr S. Africa
215 P1 Kruger National Park S. Africa
215 L2 Krugersdorp S. Africa
100 I4 Kruglikovo Rus. Fed.
129 D1 Kruglolesskoye Rus. Fed.
Kruglyakov Rus. Fed. see Oktyabr'skiy
138 M7 Kruhlaye Belarus
94 E7 Krui Sumatera Indon.
214 F8 Kruidfontein S. Africa
165 F6 Kruiningen Neth.
215 I10 Kruisfontein S. Africa
165 E7 Kruishoutem Belgium
196 H9 Krujë Albania
175 L6 Krukenychi Ukr.
175 J1 Kruklanki Pol.
175 J2 Krukowo Pol.
179 N4 Krumbach Austria
173 I5 Krumbach (Schwaben) Ger.
196 I8 Krumë Albania
168 K3 Krummesse Ger.
197 N9 Krumovgrad Bulg.
171 E8 Krumpa (Geiseltal) Ger.
179 J6 Krumpendorf am Wörther See Austria
173 K6 Krün Ger.
Krungkao Thai. see Ayutthaya
Krung Thep Thai. see Bangkok
138 G5 Kruoja r. Lith.
Krupa Bos.-Herz. see Bosanska Krupa
Krupa na Uni Bos.-Herz. see Bosanska Krupa
196 H6 Krupanj Serbia
175 N2 Krupava Belarus
175 L4 Krupe Pol.
137 N2 Krupets Rus. Fed.
177 I3 Krupina Slovakia
177 H3 Krupinica r. Slovakia
177 I3 Krupinská planina plat. Slovakia
176 C1 Krupka Czech Rep.
138 M7 Krupki Belarus
137 L4 Krupodernytsi Ukr.
137 L5 Krups'ke Ukr.
174 G5 Krupski Młyn Pol.
168 H1 Kruså Denmark
196 J7 Kruševac Serbia
196 J9 Kruševo Macedonia
176 B1 Krušné hory mts Czech Rep.
177 H3 Krušovce Slovakia
138 J5 Krustkalnu rezervāts nature res. Latvia
174 E3 Kruszewo Pol.
174 G3 Kruszwica Pol.
174 F1 Kruszyna Pomorskie Pol.
175 H5 Kruszyna Śląskie Pol.
174 F2 Kruszyńskie, Jezioro l. Pol.
137 S2 Krutchenskaya Baygora Rus. Fed.
137 K7 Krutoyarka Ukr.
139 U9 Krutoye Orlovskaya Oblast' Rus. Fed.
139 O6 Krutoye Smolenskaya Oblast' Rus. Fed.
137 L2 Kruty Ukr.
177 K2 Kružlov Slovakia
220 E4 Kruzof Island AK U.S.A.
138 M6 Krybinka r. Belarus
139 O8 Krychaw Belarus
196 I8 Kryezi Albania
199 H6 Krykello, Akrotirio pt Greece
136 F3 Kryliv Ukr.
264 H4 Krylov Seamount sea feature N. Atlantic Ocean
137 S7 Krylovskaya Krasnodarskiy Kray Rus. Fed.
137 S7 Krylovskaya Krasnodarskiy Kray Rus. Fed.
175 M5 Kryłów Pol.
Krym' aut. rep. Ukr. see Krym, Respublika
Krym' pen. Ukr. see Kryms'kyy Pivostriv
137 N8 Krym, Respublika aut. rep. Ukr.
129 D1 Krymgireyevskoye Rus. Fed.
175 M4 Krymne Ukr.
135 G7 Krymsk Rus. Fed.
Krymskaya Rus. Fed. see Krymsk
137 R5 Kryms'ke Ukr.
137 N9 Kryms'ki Hori mts Ukr.
137 N8 Kryms'kyy Pivostriv pen. Ukr.
137 N9 Kryms'kyy Zapovidnyk nature res. Ukr.
175 I6 Krynica Pol.
143 P7 Krynica Morska Pol.
174 F5 Krynka r. Pol.
137 R6 Krynka r. Ukr.
139 N6 Krynki Belarus
175 L2 Krynki Pol.
137 N5 Krynychky Dnipropetrovs'ka Oblast' Ukr.
137 K6 Krynychky Mykolayivs'ka Oblast' Ukr.
137 R5 Krynychna Ukr.
137 N6 Krynychuvate Ukr.
175 K2 Krypno Kościelne Pol.
121 P5 Krypsalo Kazakh.
171 H10 Kryry Czech Rep.
137 L2 Krysky Ukr.
Krystynopol Ukr. see Chervonohrad
137 R9 Kryukovskoye Vodokhranilishche resr Rus. Fed.
137 R6 Kryva Kosa spit Ukr.
137 L4 Kryva Ruda Ukr.
136 I4 Kryvchunka Ukr.
136 J6 Kryve Ozero Ukr.
138 K7 Kryvichy Belarus
137 M6 Kryvyy Rih Ukr.
136 H5 Kryzhopil' Ukr.
174 G5 Krzanowice Pol.
175 K4 Krzczonów-Wójtostwo Pol.
174 D2 Krzęcin Pol.
174 E4 Krzelów Pol.
174 G5 Krzepice Pol.
174 E4 Krzepielów Pol.
175 K3 Krzesk-Królowa Niwa Pol.
175 K5 Krzeszów Pol.
175 H5 Krzeszowice Pol.
174 D3 Krzeszyce Pol.
175 H5 Krzętów Pol.
175 L3 Krzna r. Pol.
175 K4 Krzna Południowa r. Pol.
174 G3 Krzymów Wielkopolskie Pol.
170 J5 Krzymów Zachodniopomorskie Pol.
175 I2 Krzynowłoga Mała Pol.
174 D4 Krzystkowice Pol.
175 K6 Krzywcza Pol.
175 K4 Krzywda Pol.
174 E4 Krzywiń Pol.
170 J4 Krzywin Pol.
175 L4 Krzywowierzba Pol.
175 H3 Krzyżanów Pol.
174 G6 Krzyżanowice Pol.
174 E3 Krzyż Wielkopolski Pol.
205 E3 Ksabi Alg.
129 F4 Ksani r. Georgia
205 F2 Ksar Chellala Alg.
205 F2 Ksar el Boukhari Alg.
205 F2 Ksar el Hirane Alg.
204 D2 Ksar el Kebir Morocco
Ksar-es-Souk Morocco see Er Rachidia
180 D5 Ksar Sghir Morocco
136 J3 Ksaverivka Ukr.
134 K3 Ksenofontova Rus. Fed.
139 U9 Kshen' r. Rus. Fed.
135 G6 Kshenskiy Rus. Fed.
176 F1 Książański Park Krajobrazowy Pol.
175 H2 Książki Pol.
175 I5 Książ Wielki Pol.
174 F3 Książ Wielkopolski Pol.
175 K5 Księżpol Pol.
205 E2 Ksour, Monts des mts Alg.
205 H2 Ksour, Monts des mts Tunisia
205 H2 Ksour Essaf Tunisia
134 I4 Kstovo Rus. Fed.
139 S8 Ktsyn' Rus. Fed.
125 H2 Kū', Jabal al hill Saudi Arabia
202 E6 Ku, Wadi el watercourse Sudan
94 C1 Kuah Malaysia
Kuaidamao Jilin China see Tonghua
95 K2 Kuala Belait Brunei
Kuala Dungun Malaysia see Dungun
95 I6 Kualajelai Kalimantan Indon.
94 D2 Kuala Kangsar Malaysia
95 K6 Kualakapuas Kalimantan Indon.
94 E2 Kuala Kerai Malaysia
95 J5 Kualakuayan Kalimantan Indon.
94 D3 Kuala Kubu Baharu Malaysia
95 J5 Kualakurun Kalimantan Indon.
94 B2 Kualalangsa Sumatera Indon.
94 D2 Kuala Lipis Malaysia
94 D3 Kuala Lumpur Malaysia
94 D1 Kuala Nerang Malaysia
95 J6 Kualapembuang Kalimantan Indon.
95 K2 Kuala Penyu Sabah Malaysia
94 E3 Kuala Pilah Malaysia
240 □D12 Kualapu'u HI U.S.A.
94 E3 Kuala Rompin Malaysia
95 J6 Kualasampit Indon.
94 D3 Kuala Selangor Malaysia
94 D2 Kuala Sepetang Malaysia
94 C2 Kualasimpang Sumatera Indon.
94 E2 Kuala Terengganu Malaysia
94 E5 Kualatungal Sumatera Indon.
95 L2 Kuamut Sabah Malaysia
95 L2 Kuamut r. Malaysia
107 P6 Kuancheng Hebei China
101 D8 Kuandian Liaoning China
Kuangyuan Yunnan China see Yiliang
109 M7 Kuanshan Taiwan
94 E3 Kuantan Malaysia
80 J3 Kuaotunu North I. N.Z.
Kuba Azer. see Quba
129 E2 Kuba Rus. Fed.
129 I3 Kubachi Rus. Fed.
129 C2 Kuban' r. Rus. Fed.
129 A1 Kubanskaya Rus. Fed.
129 D1 Kubanskoye Vodokhranilishche resr Rus. Fed.
127 I6 Kubār Dayr az Zawr Syria
127 I6 Kubār Dayr az Zawr Syria
125 M4 Kubārah Oman
138 G3 Kübassaare poolsaar pen. Estonia
128 F3 Kubaybāt Syria
127 K7 Kubaysah Iraq
140 O5 Kubbe Sweden
208 D2 Kubbum Sudan
177 J5 Kübekháza Hungary
134 G4 Kubenskoye, Ozero l. Rus. Fed.
Kuberle Rus. Fed. see Krasnoarmeyskiy
105 H1 Kubiki Japan
139 T6 Kubinka Rus. Fed.
170 H2 Kubitzer Bodden b. Ger.
190 H2 Küblis Switz.
136 I5 Kublych r. Ukr.
134 J5 Kubnya r. Rus. Fed.
103 K13 Kubokawa Japan
197 O7 Kubrat Bulg.
139 V5 Kubrinsk Rus. Fed.
95 K9 Kubu Bali Indon.
95 H5 Kubu Kalimantan Indon.
95 K3 Kubuang Kalimantan Indon.
107 N1 Kubukhay Rus. Fed.
95 K4 Kubumesaäi Kalimantan Indon.
102 □22 Kubura Nansei-shotō Japan
197 J6 Kučevo Serbia
116 E6 Kuchaman Rajasthan India
134 H2 Kuchema Rus. Fed.
172 H4 Kuchen Ger.
116 E6 Kuchera Rajasthan India
137 N2 Kucherivka Ukr.
95 I4 Kuching Sarawak Malaysia
102 □H16 Kuchino-Erabu-shima i. Japan
102 □G17 Kuchino-shima i. Nansei-shotō Japan
103 H14 Kuchinotsu Japan
178 H4 Kuchl Austria
121 R1 Kuchukskoye, Ozero salt l. Rus. Fed.
136 I7 Kuchurhan r. Ukr.
Kucing Sarawak Malaysia see Kuching
175 H4 Kuciny Pol.
175 L1 Kučiūnai Lith.
170 J3 Kückelsberg hill Ger.
198 A2 Kuçovë Albania
129 F6 Küçük Ağrı Dağı mt. Turkey
128 E2 Küçükdalyan Turkey
199 L5 Küçükköy Antalya Turkey
199 H3 Küçükköy Balıkesir Turkey
199 H3 Küçükkuyu Turkey
199 H2 Küçükmenderes r. Turkey
199 I5 Küçükmenderes r. Turkey
175 I2 Kuczbork-Osada Pol.
116 C8 Kuda Gujarat India
114 D4 Kudachi Karnataka India
113 □1 Kuda Finolhu i. S. Male Maldives
102 □1 Kudaka-jima i. Okinawa Japan
114 C5 Kudal Mahar. India
113 □1 Kudalhi i. N. Male Maldives
103 I13 Kudamatsu Japan
95 I5 Kudangan Kalimantan Indon.
94 E4 Kudap Sumatera Indon.
107 J1 Kudara-Somon Rus. Fed.
Kudarebe pt Aruba see Cudarebe
95 L1 Kudat Sabah Malaysia
124 E6 Kudayd Saudi Arabia
168 J3 Kuddewörde Ger.
138 L4 Kudev r. Rus. Fed.
138 M5 Kudever' Rus. Fed.
138 F7 Kudirkos Naumiestis Lith.
114 E5 Kudligi Karnataka India
174 E5 Kudowa-Zdrój Pol.
104 C7 Kudoyama Japan
114 D6 Kudremukh mt. Karnataka India
139 S7 Kudrinskaya Rus. Fed.
139 S8 Kudryavets Rus. Fed.
137 K6 Kudryavtsivka Ukr.
207 G4 Kudu Nigeria
95 I8 Kudus Jawa Indon.
134 K4 Kudymkar Rus. Fed.
109 N6 Kueishan Tao i. Taiwan
Kūfah Iraq see Al Kūfah
93 G5 Kufar Seram Indon.
178 F4 Kufstein Austria
221 J3 Kugaaruk Nunavut Can.
121 R5 Kugaly Kazakh.
134 I4 Kugesi Rus. Fed.
137 S7 Kugey Rus. Fed.
111 I11 Kugka Lhai Xizang China
220 G3 Kugluktuk Nunavut Can.
220 E3 Kugmallit Bay N.W.T. Can.
137 S7 Kugo-Eya r. Rus. Fed.
106 F9 Kugri Qinghai China
135 H7 Kugul'ta Rus. Fed.
104 F3 Kuguno Japan
122 G9 Kūh, Ra's-al- pt Iran
123 J8 Kūhak Iran
173 K5 Kühbach Ger.
170 F4 Kuhbier Ger.
122 G6 Kūhbonān Iran
122 B5 Kūhdasht Iran
122 G8 Kūhestak Iran
170 D5 Kuhfelde Ger.
122 C3 Kūhīn Iran
122 I8 Kūhīrī Iran
123 O3 Kŭhistoni Badakhshon aut. rep. Tajik.
170 E3 Kuhlen Ger.
170 E2 Kühlung park Ger.
170 E2 Kühlungsborn, Ostseebad Ger.
140 T4 Kuhmo Fin.
141 R6 Kuhmoinen Fin.
169 J9 Kühndorf Ger.
122 E5 Kūhpāyeh Iran
122 G6 Kūhpāyeh mt. Iran
122 H8 Kūhrān, Kūh-e mt. Iran
122 D6 Kūhrang r. Iran
171 G8 Kühren Ger.
168 G3 Kührstedt Ger.
170 F3 Kuhs Ger.
168 G4 Kuhstedt Ger.
97 D8 Kui Buri Thai.
127 P5 Kuidzhuk Turkm.
107 S2 Kuile He r. China
138 I2 Kuimetsa Estonia
164 I3 Kuinre Neth.
212 C5 Kuis Namibia
212 B4 Kuiseb watercourse Namibia
109 J7 Kuitan Guangdong China
209 C8 Kuito Angola
Kuitun Xinjiang China see Kuytun
222 C3 Kuiu Island AK U.S.A.
140 R4 Kuivaniemi Fin.
138 G3 Kuivastu Estonia
138 J5 Kuja r. Latvia
174 G4 Kujakowice Dolne Pol.
117 K9 Kujang Orissa India
101 E9 Kujang N. Korea
174 G2 Kujawsko-Pomorskie prov. Pol.
102 S6 Kuji Japan
105 M3 Kuji-gawa r. Japan
105 L4 Kujikuri Japan
102 S6 Kuji-wan b. Japan
105 L5 Kujūkuri-hama coastal area Japan
103 I13 Kujū-san vol. Japan
122 D6 Kukālār, Kūh-e hill Iran
100 H4 Kukan Rus. Fed.
100 H4 Kukan r. Rus. Fed.
227 L1 Kukatush Ont. Can.
207 I3 Kukawa Nigeria
87 E12 Kukerin W.A. Austr.
196 I8 Kukës Albania
136 E2 Kukhits'ka Volya Ukr.
105 K3 Kuki Japan
105 L4 Kukizaki Japan
104 D7 Kuki-zaki pt Japan
140 R4 Kukkola Fin.
175 I2 Kuklin Pol.
174 F4 Kuklinów Pol.
179 N5 Kukmirn Austria
134 J4 Kukmor Rus. Fed.
134 G4 Kukoboy Rus. Fed.
138 K2 Kukruse Estonia
116 E8 Kukshi Madh. Prad. India
78 □6 Kukudu New Georgia Is Solomon Is
240 □F13 Kukuihaele HI U.S.A.
206 B4 Kukuna Sierra Leone
114 G4 Kukunuru Andhra Prad. India
94 E4 Kukup Malaysia
122 H2 Kükürtli Turkm.
95 K6 Kukusan, Gunung hill Indon.
134 L4 Kukushtan Rus. Fed.
122 F8 Kūl r. Iran
197 K7 Kula Bulg.
Kula r. Moldova see Cula
207 G5 Kula Nigeria
196 H5 Kula Vojvodina Serbia
196 H8 Kula mt. Montenegro
199 J4 Kula Turkey
94 C4 Kulabu, Gunung mt. Indon.
123 N6 Kulachi Pak.
139 P9 Kulagi Rus. Fed.
120 D3 Kulagino Kazakh.
117 M5 Kula Kangri mt. Bhutan
124 E5 Kulākh Saudi Arabia
210 C4 Kulal, Mount Kenya
120 D5 Kulaly, Ostrov i. Kazakh.
121 O6 Kulan Kazakh.
121 P7 Kulanak Kyrg.
120 H4 Kulandy Kazakh.
123 J9 Kulaneh reg. Pak.
121 M2 Kulanotpes watercourse Kazakh.
123 K7 Kulao r. Pak.
131 O2 Kular Rus. Fed.
92 C8 Kulassein i. Phil.
95 L4 Kulat, Gunung mt. Indon.
138 G7 Kulautuva Lith.
93 A4 Kulawi Sulawesi Indon.
203 F4 Kulb Sudan
137 N2 Kul'baki Rus. Fed.
138 E5 Kuldīga Latvia
Kuldja Xinjiang China see Yining
100 G4 Kul'dur Rus. Fed.
212 D4 Kule Botswana
135 H5 Kulebaki Rus. Fed.
97 G8 Kulen Cambodia
199 L5 Kuleönü Turkey
139 U9 Kuleshi Rus. Fed.
137 S6 Kuleshovka Rus. Fed.
175 K2 Kulesze Pol.
175 K2 Kulesze Kościelne Pol.
120 I1 Kulevchinskoye Rus. Fed.
Kulevi Georgia see Qulevi
84 D8 Kulgera N.T. Austr.
120 G1 Kulgunino Rus. Fed.
129 I3 Kuli Rus. Fed.
138 E6 Kuliai Lith.
134 K4 Kuligi Rus. Fed.
121 R6 Kulikovka Kazakh.
134 I3 Kulikovo Arkhangel'skaya Oblast' Rus. Fed.
139 W9 Kulikovo Lipetskaya Oblast' Rus. Fed.
94 D2 Kulim Malaysia
87 E12 Kulin W.A. Austr.
114 F7 Kulittalai Tamil Nadu India
87 D11 Kulja W.A. Austr.
83 J4 Kulkyne watercourse N.S.W. Austr.
141 Q6 Kullaa Fin.
138 H3 Kullamaa Estonia
142 I5 Kullen pt Sweden
169 J8 Küllstedt Ger.
116 F4 Kullu Hima. Prad. India
173 L2 Kulmain Ger.
171 D10 Kulmbach Ger.
123 M3 Kŭlob Tajik.
139 Q3 Kulotino Rus. Fed.
134 H3 Kuloy Rus. Fed.
134 H2 Kuloy r. Rus. Fed.
127 J4 Kulp Turkey
82 F6 Kulpara S.A. Austr.
234 C3 Kulpmont PA U.S.A.
120 F4 Kul'sary Kazakh.
208 F2 Kulshabi Sudan
172 H2 Külsheim Ger.
177 G5 Külső-Somogy reg. Hungary
126 F4 Kulu Turkey
199 L5 Kulübe Tepe mt. Turkey
121 R1 Kulunda Rus. Fed.
121 R1 Kulunda r. Rus. Fed.
121 P1 Kulundinskaya Step' plain Kazakh./Rus. Fed.
121 R1 Kulundinskoye, Ozero salt l. Rus. Fed.
221 O3 Kulusuk Greenland
107 N1 Kulusutay Rus. Fed.
122 F6 Kūlvand Iran
83 I6 Kulwin Vic. Austr.
Kulyab Tajik. see Kŭlob
136 D4 Kulykiv Ukr.
137 K2 Kulykivka Ukr.
103 J13 Kuma Japan
129 H1 Kuma r. Rus. Fed.
140 U3 Kuma r. Rus. Fed.
175 I1 Kumachevo Rus. Fed.
137 R6 Kumachove Ukr.
105 J3 Kumagaya Japan
95 I6 Kumai Kalimantan Indon.
95 I6 Kumai, Teluk b. Indon.
102 Q4 Kumaishi Japan
120 I2 Kumak Rus. Fed.
120 H2 Kumak r. Rus. Fed.
251 G4 Kumaka Guyana
107 M1 Kumakhta Rus. Fed.
199 L4 Kumalar Dağı mts Turkey
103 H14 Kumamoto Japan
103 H14 Kumamoto pref. Japan
104 D8 Kumano Japan
104 C8 Kumanogawa Japan
197 J8 Kumanovo Macedonia
81 F9 Kumara South I. N.Z.
100 E3 Kumara Rus. Fed.
81 F9 Kumara Junction South I. N.Z.
117 L8 Kumarkhali Bangl.
206 E5 Kumasi Ghana
215 M7 Ku-Mayima S. Africa
Kumayri Armenia see Gyumri
207 H5 Kumba Cameroon
199 I2 Kumbağ Turkey
114 F7 Kumbakonam Tamil Nadu India
179 M5 Kumberg Austria
199 L3 Kümbet Turkey
114 C4 Kumbharli Ghat mt. Mahar. India
116 H5 Kumbher Nepal
114 D6 Kumbla Kerala India
207 H5 Kumbo Cameroon
138 F5 Kumbri Latvia
212 D4 Kumchuru Botswana
Kum-Dag Turkm. see Gumdag
124 G5 Kumdah Saudi Arabia
199 L4 Kumdanlı Turkey
103 K11 Kume Japan
102 □D20 Kume-jima i. Nansei-shotō Japan
122 E4 Kumel well Iran
134 J4 Kumeny Rus. Fed.
120 F1 Kumertau Rus. Fed.
101 E11 Kŭm-gang r. S. Korea
101 F9 Kumgang-san mt. N. Korea
117 M6 Kumguri Assam India
111 C11 Kumharsain Hima. Prad. India
173 M4 Kumhausen Ger.
116 F6 Kumher Rajasthan India
101 F11 Kŭmho-gang r. S. Korea
101 F10 Kumi S. Korea
210 B4 Kumi Uganda
104 A4 Kumihama Japan
104 A4 Kumihama-wan l. Japan
207 I4 Kumishe Nigeria
104 C6 Kumiyama Japan
199 H3 Kumkale Turkey
110 J6 Kum Kuduk well Xinjiang China
143 L2 Kumla Sweden
141 P6 Kumlinge Åland Fin.
128 E2 Kumlu Turkey
199 L6 Kumluca Turkey
170 D4 Kummer Ger.
170 G3 Kummerow Ger.
170 G3 Kummerower See l. Ger.
173 L3 Kümmersbruck Ger.
171 H6 Kummersdorf-Alexanderdorf Ger.
171 H6 Kummersdorf Gut Ger.
207 H4 Kumo Nigeria
101 E11 Kŭmŏ-do i. S. Korea
121 L4 Kumola watercourse Kazakh.
96 C2 Kumon Range mts Myanmar
105 I4 Kumotori-yama mt. Japan
104 E6 Kumozu-gawa r. Japan
191 P6 Kumpare, Rt pt Croatia
96 F6 Kumphawapi Thai.
140 R3 Kumputunturi hill Fin.
179 M7 Kumrovec Croatia
214 D4 Kums Namibia
114 D5 Kumta Karnataka India
129 I2 Kumtorkala Rus. Fed.
208 E4 Kumu Dem. Rep. Congo
240 □G14 Kumukahi, Cape HI U.S.A.
129 I3 Kumukh Rus. Fed.
Kumul Xinjiang China see Hami
117 I9 Kumund Orissa India
129 E4 Kumurdo Georgia
110 I5 Kümüx Xinjiang China
Kumylzhenskaya Rus. Fed. see Kumylzhenskiy
135 H6 Kumylzhenskiy Rus. Fed.
121 N6 Kumyshtag, Pik mt. Kyrg.
96 C5 Kun r. Myanmar
177 I5 Kunadacs Hungary
177 K5 Kunágota Hungary
87 G7 Kunanaggi Well W.A. Austr.
123 N4 Kunar prov. Afgh.
123 N4 Kunar r. Afgh.
100 O6 Kunashir, Ostrov i. Kuril'skiye O-va Rus. Fed.
Kunashirskiy Proliv sea chan. Japan/Rus. Fed. see Nemuro-kaikyō
177 I5 Kunbaja Hungary
177 I5 Kunbaracs Hungary
129 G1 Kun'bator Rus. Fed.
96 C3 Kunchaung Myanmar
209 E5 Kunda Dem. Rep. Congo
138 J2 Kunda Estonia
138 J2 Kunda r. Estonia
116 H7 Kunda Uttar Prad. India
209 C7 Kunda-dia-Baze Angola
138 J2 Kunda laht b. Estonia
114 D6 Kundapura Karnataka India
123 M5 Kundar r. Afgh./Pak.
209 E7 Kundelungu, Parc National de nat. park Dem. Rep. Congo
209 E7 Kundelungu Ouest, Parc National de nat. park Dem. Rep. Congo
114 D5 Kundgol Karnataka India
123 N5 Kundian Pak.
178 E5 Kundl Austria
116 C9 Kundla Gujarat India
137 T6 Kundryuch'ya r. Rus. Fed./Ukr.
94 E4 Kundur i. Indon.
123 M3 Kunduz Afgh.
123 M3 Kunduz prov. Afgh.
209 A9 Kunene r. Angola/Namibia alt. Cunene
212 B3 Kunene admin. reg. Namibia
Künes Xinjiang China see Xinyuan
110 F5 Künes Chang Xinjiang China
110 E5 Künes He r. China
110 G5 Künes Linchang Xinjiang China
177 I5 Kunfehértó Hungary
142 H4 Kungälv Sweden
106 E1 Kungar-Tuk Rus. Fed.
121 Q6 Kungei Alatau mts Kazakh./Kyrg.
Kunggar Xizang China see Maizhokunggar
222 D4 Kunghit Island B.C. Can.
Küngöy Ala-Too mts Kazakh./Kyrg. see Kungei Alatau
143 N2 Kungsängen Sweden
142 I4 Kungsbacka Sweden
142 H3 Kungshamn Sweden
143 M2 Kungsör Sweden
208 C4 Kungu Dem. Rep. Congo
Kungur mt. Xinjiang China see Kongur Shan
134 L4 Kungur Rus. Fed.
96 B6 Kungyangon Myanmar
177 J4 Kunhegyes Hungary
157 O7 Kunheim France
108 B8 Kunhing Myanmar
114 F3 Kuni r. India
105 I2 Kuni Japan
174 E4 Kunice Pol.
122 H8 Kūnīch Iran
Kunicha Moldova see Cunicea
Kunié i. New Caledonia see Pins, Île des
114 E6 Kunigai Karnataka India
104 D3 Kunimi-dake hill Japan
103 I14 Kunimi-dake mt. Japan
177 G2 Kunín Czech Rep.
138 K2 Kuningaküla Estonia
95 H8 Kuningan Jawa Indon.
174 G5 Kuniów Pol.
103 I13 Kunisaki Japan
117 J9 Kunjabar Orissa India
234 E3 Kunkletown PA U.S.A.
116 C9 Kunlavav Gujarat India
96 D3 Kunlong Myanmar
117 L7 Kunlui r. India/Nepal
106 C9 Kunlun Shan mts China
106 D9 Kunlun Shankou pass Qinghai China
177 J4 Kunmadaras Hungary
108 D6 Kunming Yunnan China
86 H3 Kunmunya Aboriginal Reserve W.A. Austr.
116 F6 Kuno r. India
176 G2 Kunovice Czech Rep.
175 J5 Kunów Pol.
171 K6 Kunowice Pol.
174 F4 Kunowo Pol.
144 D1 Kunoy i. Faroe Is
177 I4 Kunpeszér Hungary
170 D5 Kunrau Ger.
101 E11 Kunsan S. Korea
109 M3 Kunshan Jiangsu China
176 F2 Kunštát Czech Rep.
177 I5 Kunszállás Hungary
177 J5 Kunszentmárton Hungary
177 I4 Kunszentmiklós Hungary
209 D5 Kuntshankoie Dem. Rep. Congo
86 J3 Kununurra W.A. Austr.
223 L2 Kunwak r. Nunavut Can.
116 G6 Kunwari r. India
139 N5 Kun'ya Rus. Fed.
139 O4 Kun'ya r. Rus. Fed.
Kunyang Henan China see Yexian
Kunyang Yunnan China see Jinning
Kunyang Zhejiang China see Pingyang
Kunya-Urgench Turkm. see Köneürgenç
137 Q4 Kun'ye Ukr.
107 Q8 Kunyu Shan mts China
176 E2 Kunžak Czech Rep.
169 I9 Künzell Ger.
172 H3 Künzelsau Ger.
171 D8 Künzels-Berg hill Ger.
173 O4 Künzing Ger.
209 C5 Kunzulu Dem. Rep. Congo
109 M4 Kuocang Shan mts China
140 T3 Kuolayarvi Rus. Fed.
141 S6 Kuolimo l. Fin.
140 S5 Kuopio Fin.
141 R6 Kuorevesi Fin.
140 T3 Kuosku Fin.
174 F5 Kup Pol.
188 F3 Kupa r. Croatia/Slovenia
93 C9 Kupang Timor Indon.
93 C9 Kupang, Teluk b. Timor Indon.
139 V5 Kupanskoye Rus. Fed.
117 K9 Kupari Orissa India
Kupchino Moldova see Cupcina
171 E10 Kupferberg Ger.
172 H3 Kupferzell Ger.
137 Q3 Kupino Rus. Fed.
138 H6 Kupiškis Lith.
191 R5 Kupjak Croatia
199 K2 Küplü Turkey
172 E4 Kuppenheim Ger.
138 K4 Kuprava Latvia
222 C3 Kupreanof AK U.S.A.
220 E4 Kupreanof Island AK U.S.A.
220 C4 Kupreanof Point AK U.S.A.
139 Y6 Kupreyevo Rus. Fed.
171 D10 Küps Ger.
139 N5 Kupuy Rus. Fed.
116 E2 Kupwara Jammu and Kashmir
137 Q4 Kup"yans'k Ukr.
137 Q4 Kup"yans'k-Vuzlovyy Ukr.
136 D3 Kupychiv Ukr.
110 F6 Kuqa Xinjiang China
129 H5 Kür Azer.
129 K6 Kür r. Azer.
100 I4 Kur r. Rus. Fed.
129 G4 Kura r. Turkey/Georgia
129 G1 Kura r. Rus. Fed.
87 D8 Kurabuka r. W.A. Austr.
121 O6 Kuragaty Kazakh.
207 H4 Kuragwi Nigeria
103 J12 Kurahashi-jima i. Japan
104 F3 Kurai-yama mt. Japan
129 H5 Küräkçay r. Azer.
129 I4 Kurakh Rus. Fed.
137 Q6 Kurakhove Ukr.
Kurakhovo Ukr. see Kurakhove
Kurakhovstroy Ukr. see Kurakhove
Kura kurk sea chan. Estonia/Latvia see Irbe Strait
124 E3 Kuramā, Ḥarrat lava field Saudi Arabia
104 C5 Kurama-yama hill Japan
85 J4 Kuranda Qld Austr.
122 H8 Kūrān Dap Iran
120 G2 Kurashasayskiy Kazakh.
103 K12 Kurashiki Japan
116 I8 Kurasia Chhattisgarh India
86 I5 Kura Soak well W.A. Austr.
125 I2 Kurayn i. Saudi Arabia
103 K11 Kurayoshi Japan
106 A1 Kurayskiy Khrebet mts Rus. Fed.
139 W4 Kurba Rus. Fed.
199 K2 Kurban Dağı mt. Turkey
137 R2 Kurbatovo Rus. Fed.
100 F4 Kurbin He r. China
196 I4 Kurca r. Romania
129 H2 Kurchaloy Rus. Fed.
137 Q8 Kurchanskiy Liman salt l. Rus. Fed.
135 F6 Kurchatov Rus. Fed.
121 T3 Kurchum Kazakh.
121 T3 Kurchum r. Kazakh.
129 I5 Kürd Azer.
177 H5 Kurd Hungary
129 J5 Kürdämir Azer.
121 P6 Kurday Kazakh.
122 E7 Kür Deh Iran
122 F8 Kürdeh Iran
129 K7 Kür Dili pt Azer.
114 D3 Kurduvadi Mahar. India
197 N9 Kŭrdzhali Bulg.
129 B2 Kurdzhinovo Rus. Fed.
103 J12 Kure Japan
126 F3 Küre Turkey
75 G1 Kure Atoll HI U.S.A.
138 F3 Kuressaare Estonia
138 M3 Kureya r. Rus. Fed.
130 J3 Kureyskoye Vodokhranilishche resr Rus. Fed.
Kurgal'dzhino Kazakh. see Korgalzhyn
130 H4 Kurgan Rus. Fed.
135 H7 Kurganinsk Rus. Fed.
Kurgannaya Rus. Fed. see Kurganinsk
Kurgantyube Tajik. see Qŭrghonteppa
Kurgasyn Kazakh. see Korgasyn
116 G9 Kurhad Mahar. India
123 N3 Kuri Afgh.
116 C6 Kuri Rajasthan India
77 H1 Kuria is Gilbert Is Kiribati
Kuria Muria Bay Oman see Ḥalāniyāt, Khalīj al
Kuria Muria Islands Oman see Ḥalāniyāt, Juzur al
84 H6 Kuridala Qld Austr.
117 L7 Kurigram Bangl.
105 K5 Kurihama Japan
105 K3 Kurihashi Japan
140 Q5 Kurikka Fin.
102 R8 Kurikoma-yama vol. Japan
266 E2 Kuril Basin sea feature Sea of Okhotsk
196 H8 Kurile, Mal mt. Albania
Kuril Islands Rus. Fed. see Kuril'skiye Ostrova
120 C2 Kurilovka Rus. Fed.
99 Q2 Kuril'sk Kuril'skiye O-va Rus. Fed.
99 Q2 Kuril'skiye Ostrova is Rus. Fed.
266 E3 Kuril Trench sea feature N. Pacific Ocean
176 F2 Kuřim Czech Rep.
177 K2 Kurima Slovakia
105 L4 Kurimoto Japan
103 H15 Kurino Japan
129 A1 Kurinskaya Rus. Fed.
102 S3 Kuriyama Hokkaidō Japan
105 K2 Kuriyama Tochigi Japan
Kurkçü Turkey see Sarıkavak
139 V8 Kurkino Rus. Fed.
87 I7 Kurlkuta Aboriginal Reserve W.A. Austr.
139 X6 Kurlovskiy Rus. Fed.
120 D1 Kurmanayevka Rus. Fed.
Kurmashkino Kazakh. see Kurchum
138 H5 Kurmene Latvia
210 B2 Kurmuk Sudan
173 I2 Kürnach Ger.
172 F3 Kürnbach Ger.
136 H3 Kurne Ukr.
114 E5 Kurnool Andhra Prad. India
105 L2 Kurobane Japan
104 F2 Kurobe Japan
104 F2 Kurobe-gawa r. Japan
104 G2 Kurobe-ko resr Japan
104 B5 Kurodashō Japan
105 G2 Kurohime-yama mt. Japan
105 J3 Kurohone Japan
105 I1 Kurohume-yama hill Japan
102 R6 Kuroishi Japan
105 L2 Kuroiso Japan
102 R4 Kuromatsunai Japan
203 F4 Kuror, Jebel mt. Sudan
171 I9 Kurort Bad Gottleuba Ger.
171 I9 Kurort-Berggießhübel Ger.
169 J9 Kurort Brotterode Ger.
137 P8 Kurortne Ukr.
171 G10 Kurort Oberwiesenthal Ger.
169 J9 Kurort Schmalkalden Ger.
169 K9 Kurort Steinbach-Hallenberg Ger.
137 O6 Kuroshany r. Ukr.
102 □B22 Kuro-shima i. Nansei-shotō Japan
104 B7 Kuro-shima i. Japan
102 □G16 Kuro-shima i. Japan
104 D6 Kuroso-yama mt. Japan
100 E1 Kurovskiy Rus. Fed.
139 T7 Kurovskoy Rus. Fed.
139 V6 Kurovskoye Rus. Fed.
175 M6 Kurovychi Ukr.
81 E11 Kurow South I. N.Z.
175 K4 Kurów Pol.
175 H4 Kurowice Pol.
123 N5 Kurram r. Afgh./Pak.
123 N5 Kurram Pak.
83 M5 Kurri Kurri N.S.W. Austr.
129 D1 Kursavka Rus. Fed.
117 K7 Kursela Bihar India
138 F5 Kuršėnai Lith.
124 F4 Kursh, Jabal hill Saudi Arabia
Kürshim Kazakh. see Kurchum
Kurshskiy Zaliv b. Lith./Rus. Fed. see Courland Lagoon
138 J9 Kurshynavichy Belarus
138 F5 Kursīši Latvia
Kuršių marios b. Lith./Rus. Fed. see Courland Lagoon
138 D6 Kuršių neringos nacionalinis parkas nat. park Lith.
135 G6 Kursk Rus. Fed.
129 F1 Kurskaya Rus. Fed.
135 G6 Kurskaya Oblast' admin. div. Rus. Fed.
Kurskiy Zaliv b. Lith./Rus. Fed. see Courland Lagoon
Kursk Oblast admin. div. Rus. Fed. see Kurskaya Oblast'
137 O2 Kurskoye Vodokhranilishche resr Rus. Fed.
196 J7 Kuršumlija Serbia
126 F3 Kurşunlu Turkey
127 J5 Kurtalan Turkey
199 H1 Kurtbey Turkey
Kürti r. Kazakh. see Kurtty
240 □F14 Kurtistown HI U.S.A.
129 F4 K'urt'lari Georgia
199 J6 Kurtoğlu Burnu pt Turkey
128 D2 Kurtpınar Turkey
128 D1 Kurttepe Turkey
121 Q5 Kurtty r. Kazakh.
Kurty r. Kazakh. see Kurtty
183 C2 Kurtzea Spain
141 Q6 Kuru Fin.
Kurú r. Greece see Kompsatos
117 J8 Kuru Jharkhand India
208 E2 Kuru watercourse Sudan
206 C4 Kurubonla Sierra Leone
126 F3 Kurucaşile Turkey
129 B7 Kurucu Geçidi pass Turkey
116 H9 Kurud Chhattisgarh India
199 L2 Kurudere Turkey
116 F5 Kurukshetra Haryana India
110 H6 Kuruktag mts China
214 H3 Kuruman S. Africa
214 E2 Kuruman watercourse S. Africa
214 H3 Kuruman Hills S. Africa
103 H13 Kurume Japan
99 J1 Kurumkan Rus. Fed.
210 B3 Kurun r. Sudan
84 E6 Kurundi watercourse N.T. Austr.
114 D4 Kurundvad Mahar. India
114 G9 Kurunegala Sri Lanka
107 O1 Kurunzulay Rus. Fed.
115 H3 Kurupam Andhra Prad. India
251 G3 Kurupukari Guyana
203 F4 Kurush, Jebel hills Sudan
121 T2 Kur'ya Altayskiy Kray Rus. Fed.
134 L3 Kur'ya Respublika Komi Rus. Fed.
137 R4 Kuryachivka Ukr.
120 D6 Kuryk Kazakh.
175 M2 Kurylavichy Belarus
137 N5 Kurylivka Ukr.
175 K5 Kuryłówka Pol.
103 G11 Kuryongp'o S. Korea
175 H5 Kurzelów Pol.
175 I4 Kurzeszyn Pol.
175 H2 Kurzętnik Pol.
199 I5 Kuşadası Turkey
199 I5 Kuşadası Körfezi b. Turkey
Kusaie atoll Micronesia see Kosrae
128 E2 Kuşalanı Turkey
Kusary Azer. see Qusar
105 I2 Kusatsu Gunma Japan
104 C5 Kusatsu Shiga Japan
222 B2 Kusawa Lake Y.T. Can.
128 D2 Kuşcenneti nature res. Turkey
199 I2 Kuşcenneti Milli Parkı nat. park Turkey
103 K11 Kuse Japan
172 C2 Kusel Ger.
170 D5 Kusey Ger.
199 I2 Kuş Gölü l. Turkey
116 E8 Kushalgarh Rajasthan India
139 T4 Kushalino Rus. Fed.
122 G4 Kūshank Iran
135 G7 Kushchevskaya Rus. Fed.
207 G4 Kusheriki Nigeria
102 □1 Kushi Okinawa Japan
104 E6 Kushida-gawa r. Japan
105 H4 Kushigata Japan
104 F5 Kushihara Japan
103 H15 Kushikino Japan
103 I15 Kushima Japan
103 M13 Kushimoto Japan
102 V4 Kushiro Japan
102 V3 Kushiro-Shitsugen Kokuritsu-kōen nat. park Japan
Kushka Turkm. see Serhetabat
122 B5 Kūshkī Iran
134 I3 Kushkopola Rus. Fed.
120 K1 Kushmurun Kazakh.
120 K1 Kushmurun, Ozero salt l. Kazakh.
134 K5 Kushnarenkovo Rus. Fed.
114 E5 Kushtagi Karnataka India
117 L8 Kushtia Bangl.
122 H7 Kushtih Iran
139 T1 Kushtozero, Ozero l. Rus. Fed.
137 O6 Kushuhum Ukr.
106 J7 Kushui He r. China
120 D2 Kushum Kazakh.
120 D3 Kushum r. Kazakh.
128 B2 Kuskan Turkey
220 B3 Kuskokwim r. AK U.S.A.
220 B4 Kuskokwim Bay AK U.S.A.
220 C3 Kuskokwim Mountains AK U.S.A.
139 S6 Kuskovo Rus. Fed.
Kuşluyan Turkey see Gölköy
190 F1 Küsnacht Switz.
101 D9 Kusŏng N. Korea
129 E2 Kusparty Rus. Fed.
102 V3 Kussharo-ko l. Japan
190 E1 Küssnacht Switz.
Kustanay Kazakh. see Kostanay

Kustanay Oblast to Lagganulva

338

Kustanay Oblast *admin. div.* Kazakh. *see* **Kostanayskaya Oblast'**
141 P6 **Kustavi** Fin.
170 D5 **Küsten** Ger.
Küstence Romania *see* **Constanța**
168 E4 **Küstenkanal** *canal* Ger.
172 G4 **Kusterdingen** Ger.
Kustia Bangl. *see* **Kushtia**
136 G4 **Kustivtsi** Ukr.
93 E3 **Kusu** *Halmahera* Indon.
104 E6 **Kusu** Japan
199 K4 **Kuşu** Turkey
129 H4 **Kusur** Rus. Fed.
122 C6 **Kut** Iran
97 F9 **Kut, Ko** *i.* Thai.
95 K9 **Kuta** *Bali* Indon.
94 B2 **Kutabagok** *Sumatera* Indon.
122 C6 **Kūt 'Abdollāh** Iran
94 B3 **Kutacane** *Sumatera* Indon.
199 K3 **Kütahya** Turkey
199 K3 **Kütahya** *prov.* Turkey
95 L4 **Kutai, Taman Nasional** *nat. park* Indon.
129 A1 **Kutais** Rus. Fed.
129 D3 **K'ut'aisi** Georgia
Kut-al-Imara Iraq *see* **Al Kūt**
129 H1 **Kutan** Rus. Fed.
Kutaraja *Sumatera* Indon. *see* **Banda Aceh**
80 L5 **Kutarere** *North I.* N.Z.
177 K4 **Kutas-főcsatorna** *canal* Hungary
Kutch, Gulf of *Gujarat* India *see* **Kachchh, Gulf of**
Kutch, Rann of *marsh* India *see* **Kachchh, Rann of**
102 R4 **Kutchan** Japan
127 N7 **Kūt-e Gapu** *tourist site* Iran
168 H4 **Kutenholz** Ger.
137 R6 **Kuteynykove** Ukr.
188 F3 **Kutina** Croatia
188 F3 **Kutjevo** Croatia
96 C3 **Kutkai** Myanmar
215 K3 **Kutlwanong** S. Africa
176 E2 **Kutná Hora** Czech Rep.
175 H3 **Kutno** Pol.
114 G3 **Kutru** *Chhattisgarh* India
104 C5 **Kutsuki** Japan
140 Q2 **Kuttainen** Sweden
208 C5 **Kutu** Dem. Rep. Congo
117 M9 **Kutubdia Channel** *inlet* Bangl.
117 M9 **Kutubdia Island** Bangl.
210 D4 **Kutulo, Lagh** *watercourse* Kenya/Somalia
202 E6 **Kutum** Sudan
Kutuzov Moldova *see* **Ialoveni**
176 G3 **Kúty** Slovakia
136 F3 **Kuty** Ukr.
173 J5 **Kutzenhausen** Ger.
234 D3 **Kutztown** *PA* U.S.A.
220 G2 **Kuujjua** *r. N.W.T.* Can.
225 G1 **Kuujjuaq** *Que.* Can.
224 E2 **Kuujjuarapik** *Que.* Can.
165 D7 **Kuurne** Belgium
140 R3 **Kuusajoki** Fin.
138 I2 **Kuusalu** Estonia
140 T4 **Kuusamo** Fin.
141 S6 **Kuusankoski** Fin.
138 G1 **Kuusjoki** Fin.
138 J3 **Kuutse mägi** *hill* Estonia
134 K4 **Kuva** Rus. Fed.
120 G2 **Kuvandyk** Rus. Fed.
209 C8 **Kuvango** Angola
139 R4 **Kuvshinovo** Rus. Fed.
Kuwaé *i.* Vanuatu *see* **Tongoa**
127 M9 **Kuwait** *country* Asia
Kuwait Kuwait *see* **Al Kuwayt**
127 M9 **Kuwait Jun** *b.* Kuwait
Kuwajleen *atoll* Marshall Is *see* **Kwajalein**
104 E5 **Kuwana** Japan
134 H2 **Kuya** Rus. Fed.
122 E6 **Kuyān** Iran
Kūybyshev Kazakh. *see* **Novoishimskiy**
130 I4 **Kuybyshev** *Novosibirskaya Oblast'* Rus. Fed.
Kuybyshev *Respublika Tatarstan* Rus. Fed. *see* **Bolgar**
Kuybyshev *Samarskaya Oblast'* Rus. Fed. *see* **Samara**
137 Q6 **Kuybysheve** *Donets'ka Oblast'* Ukr.
137 P6 **Kuybysheve** *Zaporiz'ka Oblast'* Ukr.
Kuybyshevka-Vostochnaya Rus. Fed. *see* **Belogorsk**
Kuybyshevo Kazakh. *see* **Zhyngyldy**
137 R6 **Kuybyshevo** Rus. Fed.
Kuybyshevskaya Oblast' *admin. div.* Rus. Fed. *see* **Samarskaya Oblast'**
135 J5 **Kuybyshevskoye Vodokhranilishche** *resr* Rus. Fed.
123 J3 **Kuybyshew Adyndaky** Turkm.
134 K4 **Kuyeda** Rus. Fed.
122 B2 **Kūyeh** Iran
107 L7 **Kuye He** *r.* China
121 P5 **Kuygan** Kazakh.
106 C5 **Küysu** *Xinjiang* China
110 G4 **Kuytun** *Xinjiang* China
110 F4 **Kuytun He** *r.* China
199 J5 **Kuyucak** Turkey
120 K2 **Kuyukkol', Ozero** *salt l.* Kazakh.
137 N7 **Kuyuktuk, Ostriv** *i.* Ukr.
128 C2 **Kuyuluk** Turkey
110 H1 **Kuyus** Rus. Fed.
242 □R10 **Kuyu Tingni** Nic.
251 G4 **Kuyuwini** *r.* Guyana
139 N1 **Kuyvozi** Rus. Fed.
104 E4 **Kuze** Japan
137 Q4 **Kuzemivka** Ukr.
137 N3 **Kuzemyn** Ukr.
134 J4 **Kuzhener** Rus. Fed.
139 Q4 **Kuzhenkino** Rus. Fed.
129 B1 **Kuzhorskaya** Rus. Fed.
138 G6 **Kužiai** Lith.
Kuzik'end Armenia *see* **Garrnarrich**
139 V2 **Kuzino** Rus. Fed.
177 K3 **Kuzmice** Slovakia
175 K6 **Kuźmina** Pol.
139 Q7 **Kuz'minichi** Rus. Fed.
139 W7 **Kuz'minskoye** Rus. Fed.
139 N1 **Kuz'molovskiy** Rus. Fed.
138 M1 **Kuznechnoye** Rus. Fed.
120 B1 **Kuznetsk** Rus. Fed.
100 K5 **Kuznetsovo** Rus. Fed.
136 E2 **Kuznetsovs'k** Ukr.
174 G5 **Kuźnia Raciborska** Pol.
175 L2 **Kuźnica** Pol.
174 E3 **Kuźnica Czarnkowska** Pol.
134 G2 **Kuzomen'** Rus. Fed.
135 I5 **Kuzovatovo** Rus. Fed.
139 V8 **Kuzovka** Rus. Fed.
102 S6 **Kuzumaki** Japan
104 D3 **Kuzuryū-gawa** *r.* Japan
104 E4 **Kuzuryū-ko** *resr* Japan
105 K3 **Kuzuu** Japan
140 P1 **Kvænangen** *sea chan.* Norway
142 G6 **Kværndrup** Denmark
168 H1 **Kværs** Denmark
140 O2 **Kvaløya** *i.* Norway
140 Q1 **Kvaløya** *i.* Norway
140 Q1 **Kvalsund** Norway
140 □ **Kvalvågen** *b.* Svalbard
Kvareli Georgia *see* **Qvareli**
120 H1 **Kvarkeno** Rus. Fed.
141 M6 **Kvarnberg** Sweden
188 E3 **Kvarner** *g.* Croatia
188 E3 **Kvarnerić** *sea chan.* Croatia
176 G2 **Kvasice** Czech Rep.
136 D5 **Kvasy** Ukr.
175 N3 **Kvasyevichy** Belarus
136 F3 **Kvasyliv** Ukr.
129 D2 **K'veda Marghi** Georgia
129 D4 **K'veda Nasakirali** Georgia
138 E6 **Kvėdarna** Lith.
142 F2 **Kvelde** Norway
129 G3 **K'vemo Alvani** Georgia
129 C2 **K'vemo Azhara** Georgia
129 G4 **K'vemo Bodbe** Georgia
129 F4 **K'vemo Bolnisi** Georgia
129 E4 **K'vemo Boshuri** Georgia
K'vemo-Marghi Georgia *see* **K'veda Marghi**
140 J5 **Kvenvær** Norway
220 C4 **Kvichak Bay** *AK* U.S.A.
142 D3 **Kvifjorden** *l.* Norway
140 N3 **Kvikkjokk** Sweden
143 L4 **Kvillsfors** Sweden
142 C3 **Kvinesdal** Norway
142 C3 **Kvinlog** Norway
141 N5 **Kvissleby** Sweden
141 I6 **Kvitanosi** *mt.* Norway
141 I5 **Kvitegga** *mt.* Norway
142 E2 **Kviteseid** Norway
140 □ **Kvitøya** *i.* Svalbard
142 B2 **Kvitsøy** Norway
209 C5 **Kwa** *r.* Dem. Rep. Congo
165 H6 **Kwaadmechelen** Belgium
Kwabhaca S. Africa *see* **Mount Frere**
215 O2 **Kwachibukhulu** S. Africa
222 E3 **Kwadacha Wilderness Provincial Park** *B.C.* Can.
215 N2 **KwaDela** S. Africa
Kwadelen *atoll* Marshall Is *see* **Kwajalein**
211 A6 **Kwaga** Tanz.
215 N1 **KwaGuqa** S. Africa
109 □J7 **Kwai Tau Leng** *hill H.K.* China
78 □3a **Kwajalein** *atoll* Marshall Is
78 □3a **Kwajalein** *i.* Marshall Is
78 □3a **Kwajalein Lagoon** *Kwajalein* Marshall Is
251 H3 **Kwakoegron** Suriname
251 G3 **Kwakwani** Guyana
215 L3 **Kwakwatsi** S. Africa
94 C3 **Kwala** *Sumatera* Indon.
211 C6 **Kwale** Kenya
207 G5 **Kwale** Nigeria
215 O5 **KwaMashu** S. Africa
215 Q4 **KwaMbonambi** S. Africa
206 E5 **Kwame Danso** Ghana
215 M1 **KwaMhlanga** S. Africa
209 C5 **Kwamouth** Dem. Rep. Congo
211 B6 **Kwa Mtoro** Tanz.
93 C3 **Kwandang** *Sulawesi* Indon.
209 E6 **Kwanga** Dem. Rep. Congo
Kwangchow *Guangdong* China *see* **Guangzhou**
101 E11 **Kwangju** S. Korea
209 C5 **Kwango** *r.* Dem. Rep. Congo *alt.* **Cuango (Angola)**
Kwangsi Chuang Autonomous Region *aut. reg.* China *see* **Guangxi Zhuangzu Zizhiqu**
Kwangtung *prov.* China *see* **Guangdong**
211 C6 **Kwangwazi** Tanz.
210 B4 **Kwania, Lake** Uganda
101 F8 **Kwanmo-bong** *mt.* N. Korea
215 J9 **Kwanobuhle** S. Africa
215 J8 **KwaNojoli** S. Africa
215 K9 **Kwanonqubela** S. Africa
215 I7 **KwaNonzame** S. Africa
Kwanza *r.* Angola *see* **Cuanza**
215 L8 **Kwa-Pita** S. Africa
207 F4 **Kwara** *state* Nigeria
215 O2 **KwaThandeka** S. Africa
215 K8 **Kwatinidubu** S. Africa
215 N2 **KwaZamokuhle** S. Africa
214 I8 **KwaZamukucinga** S. Africa
215 I7 **Kwazamuxolo** S. Africa
215 N2 **KwaZanele** S. Africa
215 O4 **KwaZulu-Natal** *prov.* S. Africa
Kweichow *prov.* China *see* **Guizhou**
Kweiyang *Guizhou* China *see* **Guiyang**
213 F3 **Kwekwe** Zimbabwe
215 O1 **Kwena Dam** S. Africa
212 E4 **Kweneng** *admin. dist.* Botswana
209 C6 **Kwenge** *r.* Dem. Rep. Congo
224 D3 **Kwetabohigan** *r. Ont.* Can.
215 L6 **Kwezi-Naledi** S. Africa
207 G4 **Kwiambana** Nigeria
174 G2 **Kwidzyn** Pol.
220 B4 **Kwigillingok** *AK* U.S.A.
124 D9 **Kwīhā** Eth.
91 K8 **Kwikila** P.N.G.
174 E3 **Kwilcz** Pol.
209 C5 **Kwilu** *r.* Angola/Dem. Rep. Congo
87 C12 **Kwinana** *W.A.* Austr.
174 D4 **Kwisa** *r.* Pol.
251 G4 **Kwitaro** *r.* Guyana
109 □J7 **Kwo Chau Kwan To** *is H.K.* China
91 H7 **Kwoka** *mt. Papua* Indon.
208 E3 **Kwoungo, Mont** *mt.* C.A.R.
109 □J7 **Kwun Tong** *H.K.* China
208 C2 **Kyabé** Chad
96 B3 **Kyabin** Myanmar
85 I9 **Kyabra** *Qld* Austr.
85 I8 **Kyabra** *watercourse Qld* Austr.
83 J7 **Kyabram** *Vic.* Austr.
96 B4 **Kyadet** Myanmar
96 B6 **Kyaiklat** Myanmar
96 C6 **Kyaikto** Myanmar
96 D6 **Kya-in Seikkyi** Myanmar
106 J1 **Kyakhta** Rus. Fed.
83 I6 **Kyalite** *N.S.W.* Austr.
82 E5 **Kyancutta** *S.A.* Austr.
134 G2 **Kyanda** Rus. Fed.
96 B5 **Kyangin** *Irrawaddy* Myanmar
96 C5 **Kyangin** *Mandalay* Myanmar
111 L11 **Kyangngoin** *Xizang* China
96 C5 **Kyaukhnyat** Myanmar
96 C5 **Kyaukkyi** Myanmar
96 C3 **Kyaukmaw** Myanmar
96 C3 **Kyaukme** Myanmar
96 B3 **Kyaukmyaung** Myanmar
96 B4 **Kyaukpadaung** Myanmar
96 A5 **Kyaukpyu** Myanmar
96 C4 **Kyaukse** Myanmar
96 C6 **Kyauktan** Myanmar
96 A4 **Kyauktaw** Myanmar
96 B4 **Kyaukyit** Myanmar
96 B6 **Kyaunggon** Myanmar
138 F7 **Kybartai** Lith.
83 L7 **Kybeyan Range** *mts N.S.W.* Austr.
82 H7 **Kybybolite** *S.A.* Austr.
96 H3 **Ky Cung, Sông** *r.* Vietnam
81 E12 **Kyeburn** *South I.* N.Z.
96 D6 **Kyeikdon** Myanmar
96 B6 **Kyeintali** Myanmar
211 B7 **Kyela** Tanz.
116 F3 **Kyelang** *Hima. Prad.* India
210 A4 **Kyenjojo** Uganda
206 E5 **Kyeraa** Ghana
96 C5 **Kyidaunggan** Myanmar
106 G8 **Kyikug** *Qinghai* China
207 E4 **Kyinderi** Ghana
136 J3 **Kyiv** Ukr.
136 J3 **Kyivs'ka Oblast'** *admin. div.* Ukr.
176 G2 **Kyjov** Czech Rep.
198 G5 **Kyklades** *dept* Greece
126 B5 **Kyklades** *is* Greece
223 I5 **Kyle** *Sask.* Can.
149 O5 **Kyle** *r. England* U.K.
146 E8 **Kyleakin** *Highland, Scotland* U.K.
146 E8 **Kyle of Lochalsh** *Highland, Scotland* U.K.
146 H6 **Kyle of Tongue** *inlet Scotland* U.K.
146 E8 **Kylerhea** *Highland, Scotland* U.K.
146 F11 **Kyles of Bute** *sea chan. Scotland* U.K.
146 C7 **Kyles Scalpay** *Western Isles, Scotland* U.K.
146 F6 **Kylestrome** *Highland, Scotland* U.K.
169 C11 **Kyll** *r.* Ger.
169 C10 **Kyllburg** Ger.
198 C5 **Kyllini** Greece
198 D5 **Kyllini** *mt.* Greece
198 C5 **Kyllinis, Akrotirio** *pt* Greece
141 Q6 **Kylmäkoski** Fin.
198 F4 **Kymi** Greece
138 J1 **Kymijoki** *r.* Fin.
198 F4 **Kymis, Akrotirio** *pt* Greece
142 I2 **Kymmen** *l.* Sweden
83 J7 **Kyneton** *Vic.* Austr.
142 I1 **Kynna** *r.* Norway
176 B1 **Kynšperk nad Ohří** Czech Rep.
85 H6 **Kynuna** *Qld* Austr.
102 □1 **Kyoda** *Okinawa* Japan
210 B4 **Kyoga, Lake** Uganda
104 E3 **Kyōga-dake** *mt.* Japan
105 G4 **Kyōga-dake** *mt.* Japan
104 B4 **Kyōga-misaki** *pt* Japan
83 N3 **Kyogle** *N.S.W.* Austr.
208 F2 **Kyom** *watercourse* Sudan
105 K5 **Kyonan** Japan
96 D6 **Kyondo** Myanmar
85 J6 **Kyong** *Qld* Austr.
96 C4 **Kyong** Myanmar
101 D10 **Kyŏnggi-man** *b.* S. Korea
101 F11 **Kyŏngju** S. Korea
101 F11 **Kyongju National Park** S. Korea
96 B6 **Kyonpyaw** Myanmar
104 C6 **Kyōtanabe** Japan
104 C6 **Kyōto** Japan
104 B5 **Kyōto** *pref.* Japan
102 R7 **Kyōwa** *Akita* Japan
105 L3 **Kyōwa** *Ibaraki* Japan
198 C5 **Kyparissia** Greece
198 C5 **Kyparissiakos Kolpos** *b.* Greece
Kypros *country* Asia *see* **Cyprus**
121 M2 **Kypshak, Ozero** *salt l.* Kazakh.
107 M2 **Kyra** Rus. Fed.
198 F3 **Kyra Panagia** *i.* Greece
Kyrenia Cyprus *see* **Keryneia**
Kyrenia Mountains Cyprus *see* **Pentadaktylos Range**
198 F1 **Kyrgia** Greece
121 P7 **Kyrgyzstan** *country* Asia
136 I8 **Kyrhyzh-Kytay** *r.* Ukr.
198 D4 **Kyriaki** Greece
170 F5 **Kyritz** Ger.
170 G4 **Kyritz-Ruppiner Heide** *park* Ger.
142 C2 **Kyrkjenuten** *mt.* Norway
120 D3 **Kyrkopa** Kazakh.
140 J5 **Kyrksæterøra** Norway
136 H5 **Kyrnasivka** Ukr.
136 I8 **Kyrnychky** Ukr.
134 L2 **Kyrta** Rus. Fed.
134 L4 **Kyr'ya** Rus. Fed.
137 O3 **Kyrykivka** Ukr.
137 O7 **Kyrylivka** Ukr.
137 P4 **Kyseli** Ukr.
136 E5 **Kyseliv** Ukr.
137 K2 **Kyselivka** Ukr.
136 G2 **Kyshyy** Ukr.
134 I2 **Kyssa** Rus. Fed.
177 I2 **Kysuce** *park* Slovakia
177 H2 **Kysucké Nové Mesto** Slovakia
131 O3 **Kytalyktakh** Rus. Fed.
136 I8 **Kytay, Ozero** *l.* Ukr.
137 N5 **Kytayhorod** Ukr.
198 D6 **Kythira** *Kythira* Greece
198 D6 **Kythira** *i.* Greece
198 F5 **Kythnos** *i.* Greece
198 F5 **Kythnou, Steno** *sea chan.* Greece
128 B3 **Kythrea** Cyprus
134 L4 **Kytlym** Rus. Fed.
Kyumyush-Tak, Pik *mt.* Kyrg. *see* **Kumyshtag, Pik**
111 E11 **Kyunglung** *Xizang* China
96 D7 **Kyungyaung** Myanmar
96 B3 **Kyunhla** Myanmar
222 E5 **Kyuquot** *B.C.* Can.
Kyurdamir Azer. *see* **Kürdämir**
120 G5 **Kyushe** Kazakh.
103 I15 **Kyūshū** *i.* Japan
266 E4 **Kyushu-Palau Ridge** *sea feature* N. Pacific Ocean
103 I14 **Kyūshū-sanchi** *mts* Japan
197 K8 **Kyustendil** Bulg.
96 C5 **Kywebwe** Myanmar
83 K6 **Kywong** *N.S.W.* Austr.
Kyyev Ukr. *see* **Kyiv**
Kyyiv Ukr. *see* **Kyiv**
136 J3 **Kyyivs'ke Vodoskhovyshche** *resr* Ukr.
140 R5 **Kyyjärvi** Fin.
141 S6 **Kyyvesi** *l.* Fin.
120 E5 **Kyzan** Kazakh.
129 E2 **Kyzburun Tretiy** Rus. Fed.
Kyzyl Moldova *see* **Ștefan Vodă**
98 F1 **Kyzyl** Rus. Fed.
121 N6 **Kyzyl-Adyr** Kyrg.
121 R5 **Kyzylagash** Kazakh.
Kyzyl-Art, Pereval *pass* Kyrg./Tajik. *see* **Kyzylart Pass**
123 O2 **Kyzylart Pass** Kyrg./Tajik.
121 O5 **Kyzylbelen, Gora** *hill* Kazakh.
Kyzyl-Burun Azer. *see* **Siyäzän**
121 M3 **Kyzyldyykan** Kazakh.
121 T4 **Kyzylkesek** Kazakh.
Kyzylkesken Kazakh. *see* **Kyzylkesek**
106 A1 **Kyzyl-Khaya** Rus. Fed.
Kyzyl-Kiya Kyrg. *see* **Kyzyl-Kyya**
120 E3 **Kyzylkoga** Kazakh.
120 I3 **Kyzylkol', Ozero** *l.* Kazakh.
Kyzylkum, Peski *des.* Kazakh./Uzbek. *see* **Kyzylkum Desert**
120 K6 **Kyzylkum Desert** Kazakh./Uzbek.
121 O7 **Kyzyl-Kyya** Kyrg.
98 F1 **Kyzyl-Mazhalyk** Rus. Fed.
120 K5 **Kyzylorda** Kazakh.
Kyzyl-Orda Oblast *admin. div.* Kazakh. *see* **Kyzylordinskaya Oblast'**
120 J5 **Kyzylordinskaya Oblast'** *admin. div.* Kazakh.
120 K5 **Kyzylordinskoye Vodokhranilishche** *resr* Kazakh.
Kyzylrabot Tajik. *see* **Qizilrabot**
120 E6 **Kyzylsay** Kazakh.
121 Q6 **Kyzyl-Suu** Kyrg.
121 N8 **Kyzyl-Suu** *r.* Kyrg.
121 P2 **Kyzyltas** Kazakh.
121 O4 **Kyzyltau** Kazakh.
120 K3 **Kyzyluy** Kazakh.
120 D5 **Kyzylysor** Kazakh.
120 F2 **Kyzylzhar** Kazakh.
121 M3 **Kyzylzhar** Kazakh.
Kzyl-Dzhar Kazakh. *see* **Kyzylzhar**
Kzyl-Orda Kazakh. *see* **Kyzylorda**
Kzyltu Kazakh. *see* **Kishkenekol'**
129 L1 **Kzyl-Uzen** Kazakh.

L

179 N2 **Laa an der Thaya** Austria
173 L3 **Laaber** Ger.
169 D10 **Laacher See** *l.* Ger.
261 E6 **La Adela** Arg.
170 F3 **Laage** Ger.
138 H2 **Laagri** Estonia
242 D6 **La Aguja** Mex.
182 H7 **La Alberca** *Castilla y León* Spain
187 C12 **La Alberca** *Murcia* Spain
183 P9 **La Alberca de Záncara** Spain
182 G8 **La Alberguería de Argañán** Spain
184 F3 **La Albuera** Spain
183 O7 **La Alcarria** *reg.* Spain
183 J8 **La Aldehuela** Spain
184 G6 **La Algaba** Spain
183 J8 **La Aliseda de Tormes** Spain
187 C12 **La Aljorra** Spain
183 P9 **La Almarcha** Spain
186 E4 **La Almolda** Spain
183 R6 **La Almunia de Doña Godina** Spain
260 E6 **La Amarga, Laguna** *l.* Arg.
242 □R13 **La Amistad, Parque Internacional** *nat. park* Costa Rica/Panama
216 □3b **La Ampuyenta** *Fuerteventura* Canary Is
243 M10 **La Angostura, Presa de** *resr* Mex.
134 D1 **Laanila** Fin.
138 K3 **Lääniste** Estonia
210 F2 **Laanle** *well* Somalia
260 D1 **La Antigua, Salina** *salt pan* Arg.
184 E6 **La Antilla** Spain
244 E3 **La Ardilla, Cerro** *mt.* Mex.
261 I5 **La Argentina, Laguna** *l.* Arg.
179 I4 **Laarkirchen** Austria
182 J6 **La Armuña** *reg.* Spain
165 E6 **Laarne** Belgium
210 F3 **Laas Aano** Somalia
210 E2 **Laascaanood** Somalia
210 F2 **Laas Dawaco** Somalia
210 F2 **Laasgoray** Somalia
170 E4 **Laaslich** Ger.
260 E5 **La Asturiana** Arg.
251 F2 **La Asunción** Venez.
182 F9 **La Atalaya de Santiago** *hill* Spain
169 I6 **Laatzen** Ger.
240 □D12 **La'au Point** *HI* U.S.A.
190 G2 **Laax** Switz.
204 B4 **Laâyoune** Western Sahara
187 C12 **La Azohía** Spain
196 J8 **Lab** *r.* Serbia
129 B2 **Laba** *r.* Rus. Fed.
242 H3 **La Babia** Mex.
159 J5 **La Baconnière** France
225 G3 **La Baie** *Que.* Can.
183 K7 **Labajos** Spain
93 C8 **Labala** Indon.
160 I5 **La Balme-de-Sillingy** France
258 D2 **La Banda** Arg.
244 B1 **La Bandera, Cerro** *mt.* Mex.
182 I4 **La Bañeza** Spain
95 J3 **Labang** *Sarawak* Malaysia
138 I6 **Labanoras** Lith.
Labao *Guangxi* China *see* **Liujiang**
244 E5 **La Barca** Mex.
238 I5 **La Barge** *WY* U.S.A.
158 G8 **La Barre-de-Monts** France
159 M4 **La Barre-en-Ouche** France
163 E9 **La Barthe-de-Neste** France
163 F9 **Labarthe-Rivière** France
79 □7 **Labasa** *Vanua Levu* Fiji
156 E2 **La Bassée** France
163 B9 **La Bastide-Clairence** France
163 H9 **Labastide-d'Anjou** France
163 D8 **Labastide-d'Armagnac** France
163 H9 **La Bastide-de Bousignac** France
163 G9 **La Bastide-de-Sérou** France
161 H9 **La Bastide-des-Jourdans** France
163 I7 **La Bastide-l'Évêque** France
163 H6 **Labastide-Murat** France
161 D7 **La Bastide-Puylaurent** France
161 B10 **Labastide-Rouairoux** France
163 G8 **Labastide-St-Pierre** France
163 H10 **La Bastide-sur-l'Hers** France
160 I5 **La Bâthie** France
161 I7 **La Bâtie-Neuve** France
217 □3b **Labattoir** Mayotte
163 C8 **Labatut** France
163 E8 **Labatut-Rivière** France
158 G7 **La Baule-Escoublac** France
131 K2 **Labaz, Ozero** *l.* Rus. Fed.
134 K2 **Labazhskoye** Rus. Fed.
159 M5 **La Bazoche-Gouet** France
159 L5 **La Bazoge** France
190 A2 **L'Abbaye** Switz.
176 D1 **Labe** *r.* Czech Rep. *alt.* **Elbe (Germany)**
206 B4 **Labé** Guinea
161 F7 **La Bégude-de-Mazenc** France
163 E8 **Labéjan** France
224 F4 **Labelle** *Que.* Can.
231 G12 **La Belle** *FL* U.S.A.
93 C5 **Labengke** *i.* Indon.
163 B8 **Labenne** France
161 I7 **La Bérarde** France
222 C2 **Laberge, Lake** *Y.T.* Can.
160 G2 **Labergement-lès-Seurre** France
261 F6 **Laberinto, Punta** *pt* Arg.
158 G7 **La Bernerie-en-Retz** France
190 C2 **La Berra** *mt.* Switz.
173 M4 **Laberweinting** Ger.
190 E5 **La Bessa, Riserva Naturale** *nature res.* Italy
95 K2 **Labi** Brunei
183 R3 **Labia, Sierra de** *mts* Spain
95 M2 **Labian, Tanjung** *pt* Malaysia
222 F3 **La Biche** *r. N.W.T.* Can.
223 H4 **La Biche, Lac** *l. Alta* Can.
188 E3 **Labin** Croatia
129 B1 **Labinsk** Rus. Fed.
160 H5 **La Biolle** France
94 E3 **Labis** Malaysia
186 G5 **La Bisbal de Falset** Spain
186 H5 **La Bisbal del Penedès** Spain
186 L4 **La Bisbal d'Empordà** Spain
174 F3 **Łabiszyn** Pol.
242 D3 **La Biznaga** Mex.
161 E8 **Lablachère** France
261 G2 **La Blanca, Laguna** *l.* Arg.
261 F6 **La Blanca Grande Laguna** *l.* Arg.
92 D4 **Labo** *Luzon* Phil.
93 C4 **Labobo** *i.* Indon.
129 E3 **Laboda, Gora** *mt.* Georgia/Rus. Fed.
183 O6 **La Bodera** *mt.* Spain
168 J2 **Laboe** Ger.
245 H2 **La Bolsa** Mex.
261 I2 **La Bolsa** Uru.
156 B6 **La Bonneville-sur-Iton** France
242 G4 **La Boquilla** Mex.
212 C4 **Labora** Namibia
261 F3 **Laborde** Arg.
177 K3 **Laborec** *r.* Slovakia
247 □3 **Laborie** St Lucia
87 E8 **Labouchere, Mount** *hill W.A.* Austr.
128 E4 **Laboué** Lebanon
158 I5 **La Bouëxière** France
261 I2 **Labougle** Arg.
163 C7 **Labouheyre** France
161 H10 **La Bouilladisse** France
261 F4 **Laboulaye** Arg.
160 B5 **La Bourboule** France
163 A9 **Labourd** *reg.* France
158 H4 **La Boussac** France
163 I8 **Laboutarie** France
183 J6 **La Bóveda de Toro** Spain
175 I6 **Łabowa** Pol.
225 I2 **Labrador** *reg. Nfld and Lab.* Can.
225 H2 **Labrador City** *Nfld and Lab.* Can.
221 M3 **Labrador Sea** Can./Greenland
Labrang *Gansu* China *see* **Xiahe**
250 C3 **Labranzagrande** Col.
261 G2 **La Brava** Arg.
261 F3 **La Brava, Laguna** *l.* Arg.
252 D1 **Lábrea** Brazil
250 A6 **La Brea** Peru
247 □7 **La Brea** Trin. and Tob.
163 C6 **La Brède** France
161 I8 **La Bréole** France
157 M7 **La Bresse** France
160 H5 **La Bridoire** France
163 C7 **Labrit** France
157 N7 **La Broque** France
158 I7 **La Bruffière** France
163 I8 **Labruguière** France
184 A2 **Labrujeira** Port.
159 J8 **L'Absie** France
95 K2 **Labuan** Malaysia
95 K2 **Labuan** *i.* Malaysia
95 K2 **Labuan** *state* Malaysia
93 B4 **Labuanbajo** *Sulawesi* Indon.
Labudalin *Nei Mongol* China *see* **Ergun**
244 D7 **La Bufa, Cerro** *mt.* Mex.
94 F8 **Labuhan** *Jawa* Indon.
93 A8 **Labuhanbajo** *Flores* Indon.
94 D3 **Labuhanbilik** *Sumatera* Indon.
94 B3 **Labuhanhaji** *Sumatera* Indon.
94 F7 **Labuhanmeringgai** *Sumatera* Indon.
94 C3 **Labuhanruku** *Sumatera* Indon.
161 H6 **La Buisse** France
95 L2 **Labuk** *r.* Malaysia
95 L1 **Labuk, Teluk** *b.* Malaysia
93 E4 **Labuna** *Maluku* Indon.
175 L5 **Łabunie** Pol.
183 N3 **La Bureba** *reg.* Spain
156 E8 **La Bussière** France
96 B6 **Labutta** Myanmar
143 N1 **Läby** Sweden
82 E4 **Labyrinth, Lake** *salt flat S.A.* Austr.
223 J2 **Labyrinth Lake** *N.W.T.* Can.
130 H3 **Labytnangi** Rus. Fed.
196 H9 **Laç** Albania
202 B6 **Lac** *pref.* Chad
187 K8 **La Cabaneta** Spain
261 G2 **La Cabral** Arg.
183 M7 **La Cabrera** Spain
242 G5 **La Cadena** Mex.
161 H10 **La Cadière-d'Azur** France
159 J8 **La Caillère-St-Hilaire** France
185 M6 **Lacalahorra** Spain
261 H2 **La Calandria** Arg.
185 L2 **La Calderina** *mt.* Spain
260 E2 **La Calera** Arg.
216 □3a **La Calera** *La Gomera* Canary Is
260 B3 **La Calera** Chile
216 □3c **La Caleta** *Lanzarote* Canary Is
192 D6 **La Caletta** *Sardegna* Italy
225 I3 **Lac Allard** *Que.* Can.
La Calle Alg. *see* **El Kala**
161 B7 **Lacalm** France
161 E9 **La Calmette** France
183 J9 **La Calzada de Oropesa** Spain
183 O2 **La Campa** Spain
185 I5 **La Campana** Spain
260 B3 **La Campana, Parque Nacional** *nat. park* Chile
185 O7 **La Cañada de San Urbano** Spain
186 E6 **La Cañada de Verich** Spain
162 B6 **Lacanau** France
162 B6 **Lacanau, Étang de** *l.* France
162 B5 **Lacanau-Océan** France
160 F2 **Lacanche** France
243 N9 **Lacandón, Parque Nacional** *nat. park* Guat.
La Cañiza Spain *see* **A Cañiza**
161 C8 **La Canourgue** France
243 N9 **Lacantún** *r.* Mex.
156 G4 **La Capelle** France
161 B7 **Lacapelle-Barrès** France
163 H6 **Lacapelle-Marival** France
163 I6 **Lacapelle-Viescamp** France
261 H2 **La Capila** Arg.
184 F3 **Lácara** *r.* Spain
196 H5 **Laćarak** *Vojvodina* Serbia
182 G1 **La Caridad** Spain
261 F3 **La Carlota** Arg.
92 D6 **La Carlota** *Negros* Phil.
185 J5 **La Carlota** Spain
185 L4 **La Carolina** Spain
163 B9 **Lacarre** France
161 B9 **Lacaune** France
161 B9 **Lacaune, Monts de** *mts* France
183 M2 **La Cavada** Spain
161 C8 **La Cavalerie** France
163 H6 **Lacave** France
163 J8 **Lacaze** France
233 □Q1 **Lac-Baker** *N.B.* Can.
Laccadive, Minicoy and Amindivi Islands *union terr.* India *see* **Lakshadweep**
114 C7 **Laccadive Islands** India
193 L6 **Lacco Ameno** Italy
223 L5 **Lac du Bonnet** *Man.* Can.
226 E4 **Lac du Flambeau** *WI* U.S.A.
149 Q6 **Laceby** *North East Lincolnshire, England* U.K.
Lacedaemon Greece *see* **Sparti**
193 O5 **Lacedonia** Italy
242 □P10 **La Ceiba** Hond.
186 K4 **La Cellera de Ter** Spain
159 M7 **La Celle-St-Avant** France
156 D6 **La Celle-St-Cloud** France
La Cenia Spain *see* **La Sènia**
82 G7 **Lacepede Bay** *S.A.* Austr.
86 G4 **Lacepede Islands** *W.A.* Austr.
183 N3 **La Cerca** Spain
La Cerdaña *reg.* Spain *see* **Cerdanya**
186 E6 **La Cerollera** Spain
191 J2 **Laces** Italy
261 F3 **La Cesira** Arg.
225 G4 **Lac-Etchemin** *Que.* Can.
234 C1 **Laceyville** *PA* U.S.A.
233 □O2 **Lac Frontière** *Que.* Can.
134 G3 **Lacha, Ozero** *l.* Rus. Fed.
161 D6 **La Chaise-Dieu** France
158 I8 **La Chaize-le-Vicomte** France
161 I6 **La Chambre** France
160 B4 **La Chapelaude** France
157 J4 **La Chapelle** France
162 G5 **La Chapelle-Aubareil** France
157 L7 **La Chapelle-aux-Bois** France
162 H6 **La Chapelle-aux-Saints** France
160 J4 **La Chapelle-d'Abondance** France
159 K6 **La Chapelle-d'Aligné** France
159 K4 **La Chapelle-d'Andaine** France
159 P7 **La Chapelle-d'Angillon** France
158 H5 **La Chapelle-des-Fougeretz** France
158 G7 **La-Chapelle-des-Marais** France
161 I7 **La Chapelle-en-Valgaudémar** France
161 G7 **La Chapelle-en-Vercors** France
156 E7 **La Chapelle-la-Reine** France
161 C6 **La Chapelle-Laurent** France
160 C2 **La Chapelle-St-André** France
159 K8 **La Chapelle-St-Laurent** France
156 H7 **La Chapelle-St-Luc** France
156 C8 **La Chapelle-St-Mesmin** France
160 H2 **La Chapelle-St-Quillain** France
159 P7 **La Chapelle-St-Ursin** France
161 E7 **Lachapelle-sous-Aubenas** France
158 H7 **La Chapelle-sur-Erdre** France
160 C2 **La Charité-sur-Loire** France
159 M6 **La Chartre-sur-le-Loir** France
162 C2 **La Châtaigneraie** France
162 H2 **La Châtre** France
162 G3 **La Châtre-Langlin** France
157 I8 **La Chaume** France
157 K5 **Lachaussée, Étang de** *l.* France
159 N6 **La Chaussée-St-Victor** France
156 I6 **La Chaussée-sur-Marne** France
190 B1 **La Chaux-de-Fonds** Switz.
160 H3 **La Chaux-du-Dombief** France
117 L6 **Lachen** *Sikkim* India
190 F1 **Lachen** Switz.
168 J5 **Lachendorf** Ger.
161 J9 **Lachens, Montagne de** *mt.* France
172 E3 **Lachen-Speyerdorf** Ger.
156 I5 **La Cheppe** France
158 H7 **La Chevrolière** France
158 F5 **La Chèze** France
227 K4 **Lachine** *MI* U.S.A.
137 Q2 **Lachinovo** Rus. Fed.
83 I6 **Lachlan** *r. N.S.W.* Austr.
250 C5 **La Chorrera** Col.
242 □T13 **La Chorrera** Panama
175 K2 **Lachowo** Pol.
168 J5 **Lachte** *r.* Ger.
117 L6 **Lachung** *Sikkim* India
224 F4 **Lachute** *Que.* Can.
138 J6 **Lāči** Latvia
183 Q8 **La Cierva** Spain
129 H6 **Laçın** Azer.
161 H10 **La Ciotat** France
183 K5 **La Cisterniga** Spain
244 B2 **La Ciudad** Mex.
225 I2 **Lac Joseph-Atikonak Wilderness Reserve** *Nfld and Lab.* Can.
175 H3 **Łąck** Pol.
148 B4 **Lack** *Northern Ireland* U.K.
143 N3 **Lacka naturreservat** *nature res.* Sweden
232 G6 **Lackawanna** *NY* U.S.A.
234 D2 **Lackawanna** *r. PA* U.S.A.
234 D2 **Lackawanna County** *county PA* U.S.A.
234 F2 **Lackawaxen** *r. PA* U.S.A.
175 I6 **Łącko** Pol.
223 I4 **Lac La Biche** *Alta* Can.
Lac la Martre *N.W.T.* Can. *see* **Wha Ti**
223 J4 **Lac La Ronge Provincial Park** *Sask.* Can.
160 E4 **La Clayette** France
208 B4 **Lac Lobeke, Réserve du** *res.* Cameroon
160 I5 **La Clusaz** France
161 H7 **La Cluse** France
160 I3 **La Cluse-et-Mijoux** France
225 G4 **Lac-Mégantic** *Que.* Can.
258 D2 **La Cocha** Arg.
150 H5 **Lacock** *Wiltshire, England* U.K.
184 E2 **La Codosera** Spain
186 G5 **La Cogulla** *mt.* Spain
261 G5 **La Colina** Arg.
183 J3 **La Collada** *pass* Spain
233 L3 **Lacolle** *Que.* Can.
161 K9 **La Colle-sur-Loup** France
245 H3 **La Colmena, Sierra** *mts* Mex.
242 D3 **La Colorada** *Sonora* Mex.
244 E2 **La Colorada** *Zacatecas* Mex.
222 H4 **Lacombe** *Alta* Can.
226 E8 **Lacon** *IL* U.S.A.
245 I2 **La Concepción** Mex.
242 □R13 **La Concepción** Panama
183 M2 **La Concha** Spain
243 M9 **La Concordia** Mex.
161 J8 **La Condamine-Châtelard** France
192 C8 **Laconi** *Sardegna* Italy
233 N5 **Laconia** *NH* U.S.A.
260 C3 **La Consulta** Arg.
261 G5 **La Copeta** Arg.
161 C9 **La Coquillade** *hill* France
162 F4 **La Coquille** France
223 I4 **La Corey** *Alta* Can.
227 Q1 **La Corne** *Que.* Can.
185 I4 **La Coronada** *Andalucía* Spain
184 H3 **La Coronada** *Extremadura* Spain
La Coruña Spain *see* **A Coruña**
La Coruña *prov.* Spain *see* **A Coruña**
161 G9 **Lacoste** France
161 G6 **La Côte-St-André** France
162 B3 **La-Couarde-sur-Mer** France
162 E4 **La Couronne** France
163 G10 **Lacourt** France
162 I4 **La Courtine** France
156 B6 **La Couture-Boussey** France
161 C9 **La Couvertoirade** France
246 □ **Lacovia** Jamaica
163 C9 **Lacq** France
161 I10 **La Crau** France
162 D3 **La Crèche** France
247 □8 **Lacre Punt** *pt Bonaire* Neth. Antilles
226 C6 **La Crescent** *MN* U.S.A.
222 G3 **La Crete** *Alta* Can.
186 G6 **La Creu de Santos** *hill* Spain
261 H2 **La Criolla** *Entre Ríos* Arg.
261 G2 **La Criolla** *Santa Fé* Arg.
226 C1 **La Croix, Lac** *l.* Can./U.S.A.
161 B7 **Lacroix-Barrez** France
159 I5 **La Croixille** France
156 E5 **Lacroix-St-Ouen** France
161 J10 **La Croix-Valmer** France
236 F6 **La Crosse** *KS* U.S.A.
232 G12 **La Crosse** *VA* U.S.A.
226 C6 **La Crosse** *WI* U.S.A.
163 I8 **Lacrouzette** France
260 E3 **La Cruz** *Córdoba* Arg.
258 F3 **La Cruz** *Corrientes* Arg.
250 B4 **La Cruz** Col.
242 □Q12 **La Cruz** Costa Rica
242 G4 **La Cruz** *Chihuahua* Mex.
242 F6 **La Cruz** *Sinaloa* Mex.
245 H1 **La Cruz** *Tamaulipas* Mex.
245 J2 **La Cruz** *Tamaulipas* Mex.
242 □Q11 **La Cruz** Nic.
261 I3 **La Cruz** Uru.
244 F8 **La Cruz, Cerro** *mt.* Mex.
244 B6 **La Cruz de Loreto** Mex.
242 H3 **La Cuesta** *Coahuila* Mex.
244 C5 **La Cuesta** *Jalisco* Mex.
260 E2 **La Cumbre** Arg.
184 H2 **La Cumbre** Spain
Lacunza Spain *see* **Lakuntza**
239 K11 **La Curva** Mex.
236 H6 **La Cygne** *KS* U.S.A.
175 J4 **Łączany** Pol.
175 I5 **Łączna** Pol.
174 F5 **Łącznik** Pol.
175 K5 **Łada** *r.* Pol.
94 F8 **Lada, Teluk** *b.* Indon.
257 G2 **Ladainha** Brazil
116 F2 **Ladakh** *reg.* Jammu and Kashmir
116 F2 **Ladakh Range** *mts* India
137 L3 **Ladan** Ukr.
94 C1 **Ladang, Ko** *i.* Thai.
177 I4 **Ladánybene** Hungary
169 E6 **Ladbergen** Ger.
177 H2 **Ladce** Slovakia
226 E8 **Ladd** *IL* U.S.A.
174 F3 **Lądek** Pol.
174 E5 **Lądek-Zdrój** Pol.
168 H1 **Ladelund** Ger.
246 B3 **La Demajagua** Cuba
243 N10 **La Democracia** Guat.
172 F3 **Ladenburg** Ger.
247 □2 **La Désirade** *i.* Guadeloupe
146 E8 **Ladhar Bheinn** *mt. Scotland* U.K.
162 G4 **Ladignac-le-Long** France
217 □2a **La Digue** *i. Inner Islands* Seychelles
126 G3 **Ladik** Turkey
179 K6 **Ladinger Spitz** *mt.* Austria
163 J6 **Ladinhac** France
214 F9 **Ladismith** S. Africa
192 I4 **Ladispoli** Italy
260 B3 **La Disputada** Chile
123 I7 **Lādīz** Iran
116 E6 **Ladnun** *Rajasthan* India
182 F9 **Ladoeiro** Port.
Ladoga, Lake Rus. Fed. *see* **Ladozhskoye Ozero**
190 A3 **La Dôle** *mt.* Switz.
156 E7 **Ladon** France
198 C5 **Ladonas** *r.* Greece
108 G6 **Ladong** *Guangxi* China
260 D3 **La Dormida** Arg.
139 O1 **Ladozhskoye Ozero** *l.* Rus. Fed.
182 E2 **Ladra** *r.* Spain
259 A8 **Ladrillero, Canal** *sea chan.* Chile
Ladrones *terr.* N. Pacific Ocean *see* **Northern Mariana Islands**
242 □R14 **Ladrones, Islas** *is* Panama
117 N6 **Ladu** *mt. Arun. Prad.* India
222 A2 **Ladue** *r.* Can./U.S.A.
260 D6 **La Dulce, Laguna** *l.* Arg.
242 E3 **La Dura** Mex.
138 D7 **Ladushkin** Rus. Fed.
134 F3 **Ladva** Rus. Fed.
134 F3 **Ladva-Vetka** Rus. Fed.
116 F5 **Ladwa** *Haryana* India
221 J2 **Lady Ann Strait** *Nunavut* Can.
146 J10 **Ladybank** *Fife, Scotland* U.K.
83 L9 **Lady Barron** *Tas.* Austr.
149 N7 **Ladybower Reservoir** *England* U.K.
215 L5 **Ladybrand** S. Africa
227 N2 **Lady Evelyn Lake** *Ont.* Can.
215 L7 **Lady Frere** S. Africa
215 L6 **Lady Grey** S. Africa
136 G4 **Ladyhy** Ukr.
148 H2 **Lady Isle** *i. Scotland* U.K.
146 L11 **Ladykirk** *Scottish Borders, Scotland* U.K.
263 L2 **Lady Newnes Bay** Antarctica
146 L7 **Ladysford** *Aberdeenshire, Scotland* U.K.
222 F5 **Ladysmith** *B.C.* Can.
215 N4 **Ladysmith** S. Africa
226 C4 **Ladysmith** *WI* U.S.A.
121 M2 **Ladyzhenka** Kazakh.
136 I5 **Ladyzhyn** Ukr.
136 J5 **Ladyzhynka** Ukr.
Ladzhanurges Georgia *see* **Lajanurpekhi**
175 H4 **Ładzice** Pol.
170 K3 **Ładzin** Pol.
91 K8 **Lae** P.N.G.
261 G3 **La Emilia** Arg.
97 F8 **Laem Ngop** Thai.
143 L5 **Läen** *l.* Sweden
245 H5 **La Encarnación** Mex.
187 D10 **La Encina** Spain
250 E2 **La Encrucijada** Venez.
169 D6 **Laer** Ger.
183 J3 **La Ercina** Spain
141 I6 **Lærdalsøyri** Norway
192 B6 **Laerru** *Sardegna* Italy
La Escala Spain *see* **L'Escala**
244 E1 **La Escalera** Mex.
245 H1 **La Escondida** Mex.
261 H2 **La Esmeralda** *Entre Ríos* Arg.
258 D3 **La Esmeralda** *Santiago del Estero* Arg.
253 E5 **La Esmeralda** Bol.
251 E4 **La Esmeralda** Venez.
142 H4 **Læsø** *i.* Denmark
142 G4 **Læsø Rende** *sea chan.* Denmark
260 D5 **La Esperanza** Arg.
252 D3 **La Esperanza** *Beni* Bol.
253 E3 **La Esperanza** *Santa Cruz* Bol.
216 □3a **La Esperanza** *Tenerife* Canary Is
242 □O10 **La Esperanza** Hond.
182 H2 **La Espina** Spain
260 E3 **La Esquina** Arg.
245 H5 **La Estancia, Cerro** *mt.* Mex.
260 D5 **La Estrella** Arg.
252 E4 **La Estrella** Bol.
260 B4 **La Estrella** Chile
183 J9 **La Estrella** Spain
138 J3 **Laeva** Estonia
161 C6 **La Fageolle, Col de** *pass* France
260 E2 **La Falda** Arg.
161 G9 **La Fare-les-Oliviers** France
226 D6 **La Farge** *WI* U.S.A.
233 J4 **La Fargeville** *NY* U.S.A.
161 I10 **La Farlède** France
210 E2 **Lafaruug** Somalia
186 F5 **La Fatarrella** Spain
161 H7 **La Faurie** France
162 B3 **La Faute-sur-Mer** France
Lafayette Alg. *see* **Bougaa**
231 E9 **La Fayette** *AL* U.S.A.
240 J4 **Lafayette** *CA* U.S.A.
238 L7 **Lafayette** *CO* U.S.A.
231 E8 **La Fayette** *GA* U.S.A.
230 D5 **Lafayette** *IN* U.S.A.
237 I10 **Lafayette** *LA* U.S.A.
234 F2 **Lafayette** *NJ* U.S.A.
232 B9 **Lafayette** *OH* U.S.A.
231 D7 **Lafayette** *TN* U.S.A.
217 □1b **Lafayette, Pointe** *pt* Mauritius
246 A2 **Lafé** Cuba
245 I1 **La Fe del Golfo** Mex.
185 P2 **La Felipa** Spain
156 F4 **La Fère** France
217 □1a **La Ferme** *Rodrigues I.* Mauritius
158 I8 **La Ferrière** France
159 J4 **La Ferrière-aux-Etangs** France
227 P1 **Laferté** *Que.* Can.
222 G2 **Laferte** *r. N.W.T.* Can.
156 D7 **La Ferté-Alais** France
159 M5 **La Ferté-Bernard** France
159 M4 **La Ferté-Frênel** France
156 F6 **La Ferté-Gaucher** France
159 O7 **La Ferté-Imbault** France
156 F8 **La Ferté-Loupièrre** France
159 K4 **La Ferté-Macé** France
156 F5 **La-Ferté-Milon** France
156 C8 **La Ferté-St-Aubin** France
156 C8 **La Ferté-St-Cyr** France
156 F6 **La Ferté-sous-Jouarre** France
157 K8 **Laferté-sur-Amance** France
157 I7 **Laferté-sur-Aube** France
159 M4 **La Férte-Vidame** France
156 B8 **La Ferté-Villeneuil** France
125 J3 **Laffān, Ra's** *pt* Qatar
207 H4 **Lafia** Nigeria
207 G4 **Lafiagi** Nigeria
163 E9 **Lafitole** France
224 E3 **Laflamme** *r. Que.* Can.
223 J5 **Lafleche** *Sask.* Can.
159 K6 **La Flèche** France
245 H4 **La Florida** Mex.
162 B3 **La Flotte** France
179 N5 **Lafnitz** Austria
179 N6 **Lafnitz** *r.* Austria
78 □5 **La Foa** New Caledonia
232 A12 **La Follette** *TN* U.S.A.
217 □1c **La Fontaine** Réunion
226 I9 **La Fontaine** *IN* U.S.A.
159 L6 **La Fontaine-St-Martin** France
187 D10 **La Font de la Figuera** Spain
227 P2 **Laforce** *Que.* Can.
163 E6 **La Force** France
227 M2 **Laforest** *Ont.* Can.
225 G2 **La Forest, Lac** *l. Que.* Can.
158 D6 **La Forêt-Fouesnant** France
159 J8 **La Forêt-sur-Sèvre** France
225 F2 **Laforge** *Que.* Can.
225 F2 **Laforge** *r. Que.* Can.
157 M7 **La Forge** France
186 F2 **Lafortunada** Spain
La Fouce, Pointe *pt Rodrigues I.* Mauritius *see* **La Fouche, Pointe**
217 □1a **La Fouche, Pointe** *pt Rodrigues I.* Mauritius
163 I7 **La Fouillade** France
160 E5 **La Fouillouse** France
237 J11 **Lafourche, Bayou** *r. LA* U.S.A.
161 J8 **La Foux-d'Allos** France
163 G7 **Lafrançaise** France
156 I4 **La Francheville** France
261 F2 **La Francia** Arg.
182 G7 **La Fregeneda** Spain
159 L5 **La Fresnaye-sur-Chédouat** France
157 N6 **Lafrimbolle** France
183 P8 **La Frontera** Spain
122 F8 **Lāft** Iran
182 H7 **La Fuente de San Esteban** Spain
115 M9 **Laful** *Andaman & Nicobar Is* India
186 H4 **La Fuliola** Spain
158 G6 **La Gacilly** France
186 F6 **La Galera** Spain
205 H1 **La Galite** *i.* Tunisia
258 E3 **La Gallareta** Arg.
242 G5 **La Gallega** Mex.
256 D3 **Lagamar** Brazil
120 B5 **Lagan'** Rus. Fed.
143 I5 **Lagan** *r.* Sweden
147 K3 **Lagan** *r. Northern Ireland* U.K.
198 B5 **Lagana, Kolpos** *b. Zakynthos* Greece
207 I3 **Lagané** *well* Niger
161 I10 **La Garde** France
161 F8 **La Garde-Adhémar** France
161 I10 **La Garde-Freinet** France
163 G9 **Lagardelle-sur-Lèze** France
182 F5 **Lagarelhos** Port.
182 E8 **Lagares da Beira** Port.
185 K4 **La Garganta** Spain
245 I4 **La Garita** Mex.
158 H8 **La Garnache** France
186 J4 **La Garriga** Spain
163 I8 **Lagarrigue** France
184 G3 **La Garrovilla** Spain
183 J9 **Lagartera** Spain
254 F4 **Lagarto** Brazil
256 A5 **Lagarto, Serra do** *hills* Brazil
159 I8 **La Gaubretière** France
148 E3 **Lagavara** *Northern Ireland* U.K.
206 B3 **Lagbar** Senegal
207 I4 **Lagdo, Lac de** *l.* Cameroon
169 C6 **Lage** *Niedersachsen* Ger.
169 G7 **Lage** *Nordrhein-Westfalen* Ger.
165 H6 **Lage Mierde** Neth.
142 E1 **Lågen** *r.* Norway
142 G2 **Lågen** *r.* Norway
168 I3 **Lägerdorf** Ger.
164 H4 **Lage Vaart** *canal* Neth.
146 F12 **Lagg** *North Ayrshire, Scotland* U.K.
146 G8 **Laggan** *Highland, Scotland* U.K.
146 H8 **Laggan** *Highland, Scotland* U.K.
146 G9 **Laggan, Loch** *l. Scotland* U.K.
148 E2 **Laggan Bay** *Scotland* U.K.
146 D10 **Lagganulva** *Argyll and Bute, Scotland* U.K.

Laghey to Lansford
339

147 F3 Laghey Ireland
123 N4 Laghmān prov. Afgh.
205 F2 Laghouat Alg.
147 E6 Laghtgeorge Ireland
174 E5 Łagiewniki Pol.
260 E3 La Gilda Arg.
185 P2 La Gineta Spain
198 E2 Lagkadas Greece
111 G10 Lagkor Co salt l. China
158 H2 La Glacerie France
250 C2 La Gloria Col.
245 M9 La Gloria Chiapas Mex.
237 F12 La Gloria Nuevo León Mex.
160 G5 Lagnieu France
156 E6 Lagny-sur-Marne France
193 Q9 Lago Italy
Lago prov. Moz. see Niassa
216 □1b Lagoa São Miguel Azores
182 G6 Lagoa Bragança Port.
184 C6 Lagoa Faro Port.
182 G6 Lagoaça Port.
257 E4 Lagoa da Prata Brazil
216 □1b Lagoa do Fogo nature res. São Miguel Azores
257 E4 Lagoa Dourada Brazil
256 D3 Lagoa Formosa Brazil
250 B4 Lago Agrio Ecuador
257 F3 Lagoa Santa Brazil
255 C9 Lagoa Vermelha Brazil
259 B7 Lago Belgrano Arg.
259 C8 Lago Cardiel Arg.
254 D3 Lago da Pedra Brazil
129 H4 Lagodekhi Georgia
129 H4 Lagodekhis Nakrdzali nature res. Georgia
182 G4 Lago del Sanabria, Parque Natural del nature res. Spain
192 I3 Lago di Vico, Riserva Naturale nature res. Italy
187 L8 Lago Menor Spain
216 □3a La Gomera i. Canary Is
243 N10 La Gomera Guat.
193 P7 Lagonegro Italy
95 H3 Lagong i. Indon.
92 D5 Lagonoy Gulf Luzon Phil.
84 G4 Lagoon Creek r. Qld Austr.
Lagoon Island atoll Arch. des Tuamotu Fr. Polynesia see Tematangi
259 C7 Lago Posadas Arg.
163 C9 Lagor France
162 D5 Lagorce Aquitaine France
161 E8 Lagorce Rhône-Alpes France
262 O1 La Gorce Mountains Antarctica
162 B3 Lagord France
186 I5 La Gornal Spain
198 G1 Lagos Greece
244 E4 Lagos r. Mex.
207 F5 Lagos Nigeria
207 F5 Lagos state Nigeria
184 B6 Lagos Port.
211 A6 Lagosa Tanz.
191 M6 Lagosanto Italy
244 F4 Lagos de Moreno Mex.
253 E2 Lago Verde Brazil
259 B8 Lago Viedma Arg.
174 D3 Łagów Lubuskie Pol.
175 J5 Łagów Świętokrzyskie Pol.
171 L6 Łagowski Park Krajobrazowy Pol.
140 □ Lågøya i. Svalbard
183 O3 Lagrán Spain
184 G5 La Granada de Riotinto Spain
186 G5 La Granadella Spain
160 F5 La Grand-Croix France
224 E2 La Grande r. Que. Can.
238 E4 La Grande OR U.S.A.
224 E2 La Grande 2, Réservoir resr Que. Can.
224 F2 La Grande 3, Réservoir resr Que. Can.
224 F2 La Grande 4, Réservoir resr Que. Can.
161 E8 La Grande-Combe France
225 I3 La Grande Île i. Que. Can.
161 E9 La Grande-Motte France
86 F5 La Grange W.A. Austr.
240 L4 La Grange CA U.S.A.
231 E9 La Grange GA U.S.A.
230 E5 Lagrange IN U.S.A.
230 E6 La Grange KY U.S.A.
233 □Q3 La Grange ME U.S.A.
237 G11 La Grange TX U.S.A.
86 F5 Lagrange Bay W.A. Austr.
235 H1 Lagrangeville NY U.S.A.
186 F5 La Granja d'Escarp Spain
185 I4 La Granjuela Spain
251 F3 La Gran Sabana plat. Venez.
161 B10 Lagrasse France
161 I6 La Grave France
250 D2 La Grita Venez.
225 G4 La Guadeloupe Que. Can.
250 E2 La Guaira Venez.
250 C2 La Guajira dept Col.
216 □3a La Guancha Tenerife Canary Is
184 H3 La Guarda Spain
258 D3 La Guardia Arg.
258 C2 La Guardia Chile
183 N9 La Guardia Castilla-La Mancha Spain
La Guardia Galicia Spain see A Guarda
183 O3 Laguardia Spain
185 L5 La Guardia de Jaén Spain
186 E3 Laguarta Spain
La Gudiña Spain see A Gudiña
162 H5 Laguenne France
163 H7 Laguépie France
158 I6 La Guerche-de-Bretagne France
160 B3 La Guerche-sur-l'Aubois France
158 G8 La Guérinière France
160 E3 La Guiche France
161 B7 Laguiole France
244 B1 La Guitarra Mex.
247 □10 Lagún Curaçao Neth. Antilles
255 C9 Laguna Brazil
239 K9 Laguna NM U.S.A.
251 I5 Laguna, Ilha da i. Brazil
242 D6 Laguna, Picacho de la mt. Mex.
261 F5 Laguna Alsina Arg.
240 O8 Laguna Beach CA U.S.A.
260 B6 Laguna Blanca, Parque Nacional nat. park Arg.
182 I4 Laguna Dalga Spain
241 R9 Laguna Dam AZ/CA U.S.A.
183 K5 Laguna de Duero Spain
260 B5 Laguna de Laja, Parque Nacional nat. park Chile
182 I4 Laguna de Negrillos Spain
242 □R11 Laguna de Perlas Nic.
245 K7 Laguna de Temascal, Parque Natural nature res. Mex.
259 C8 Laguna Grande Arg.
243 N10 Laguna Lachua, Parque Nacional nat. park Guat.
241 P9 Laguna Mountains CA U.S.A.
242 B4 Laguna Ojo de Liebre, Parque Natural de la nature res. Mex.
261 G2 Laguna Paiva Arg.
252 C5 Lagunas Chile
250 C6 Lagunas Peru
259 B7 Laguna San Rafael, Parque Nacional nat. park Chile
245 L7 Lagunas de Catemaco, Parque Natural nature res. Mex.
245 J10 Lagunas de Chacahua, Parque Nacional nat. park Mex.
243 N9 Lagunas de Montebello, Parque Nacional nat. park Mex.
185 N2 Lagunas de Ruidera park Spain
245 H6 Lagunas de Zempoala, Parque Nacional nat. park Mex.
258 E2 Laguna Yema Arg.
191 K2 Lagundo Italy
245 H5 Lagunilla Mex.
182 I8 Lagunilla Spain
252 E4 Lagunillas Bol.
244 F8 Lagunillas Guerrero Mex.
245 H4 Lagunillas San Luis Potosí Mex.
250 D2 Lagunillas Venez.
107 S2 Laha Heilong. China
184 H3 La Haba Spain
246 B2 La Habana Cuba
240 O8 La Habra CA U.S.A.
95 M2 Lahad Datu Sabah Malaysia
95 M2 Lahad Datu, Teluk b. Malaysia
240 □E13 Lahaina HI U.S.A.
116 G6 Lahar Madh. Prad. India
147 D4 Lahardaun Ireland
226 D9 La Harpe IL U.S.A.
116 H6 Laharpur Uttar Prad. India
234 E4 Lahaska PA U.S.A.
94 E6 Lahat Sumatera Indon.
158 H3 La Haye-du-Puits France
158 I4 La Haye-Pesnel France
168 E5 Lähden Ger.
96 B1 Lahe Myanmar
138 I2 Lahemaa rahvuspark nat. park Estonia
138 H2 Lahepera laht b. Estonia
260 D4 La Herradura Arg.
260 B2 La Herradura Chile
245 J8 La Herradura Mex.
185 O3 La Herrera Spain
94 B4 Lahewa Indon.
157 J6 Laheycourt France
129 J5 Lahıc Azer.
261 H2 La Hierra Arg.
260 E2 La Higuera Arg.
187 C10 La Higuera Spain
124 G9 Laḩij Yemen
124 G9 Laḩij governorate Yemen
118 F2 Lāhījān Iran
240 □C12 Lahilahi Point HI U.S.A.
147 D7 Lahinch Ireland
182 I5 La Hiniesta Spain
136 E1 Lahishyn Belarus
168 E5 Lahn Ger.
169 E10 Lahn r. Ger.
169 G9 Lahnau Ger.
179 L4 Lahnsattel pass Austria
169 E10 Lahnstein Ger.
169 G9 Lahntal-Goßfelden Ger.
142 J5 Laholm Sweden
142 I5 Laholmsbukten b. Sweden
179 N7 Lahonci Slovenia
244 D1 La Honda Mex.
240 M2 Lahontan Reservoir NV U.S.A.
183 J8 La Horcajada Spain
123 P6 Lahore Pak.
245 M8 La Horqueta Mex.
251 F3 La Horqueta Venez.
183 M5 La Horra Spain
217 □1c La Houssaye, Cap c. Réunion
138 K7 Lahoysk Belarus
172 D5 Lahr (Schwarzwald) Ger.
123 M7 Lahri Pak.
141 R6 Lahti Fin.
250 A6 La Huaca Peru
244 F7 La Huacana Mex.
244 C6 La Huerta Mex.
208 C2 Laï Chad
109 L2 Lai'an Anhui China
Laibach Slovenia see Ljubljana
108 G7 Laibin Guangxi China
117 K9 Laichanpur Orissa India
172 H5 Laichingen Ger.
146 E7 Laide Highland, Scotland U.K.
85 N9 Laidley Qld Austr.
146 G9 Laidon, Loch l. Scotland U.K.
240 □D12 Lā'ie HI U.S.A.
240 □D12 Lā'ie Point HI U.S.A.
108 G4 Laifeng Hubei China
156 I4 Laifour France
159 M4 L'Aigle France
183 K8 La Iglesuela Spain
186 E7 La Iglesuela del Cid Spain
156 H8 Laignes France
190 E8 Laigueglia Italy
162 B3 L'Aiguillon-sur-Mer France
140 Q5 Laihia Fin.
96 C4 Lai-hka Myanmar
96 C4 Lai-Hsak Myanmar
141 T6 Laikko Fin.
129 D3 Laila, Mt'a Georgia
156 C8 Lailly-en-Val France
78 □5 Laimbélé, Mount hill Vanuatu
157 J6 Laimont France
198 E3 Laimos, Akrotirio pt Greece
190 G4 Lainate Italy
214 E9 Laingsburg S. Africa
227 J7 Laingsburg MI U.S.A.
140 Q3 Lainioälven r. Sweden
179 L2 Lainsitz r. Austria
232 A10 Lair KY U.S.A.
234 B2 Lairdsville PA U.S.A.
146 H6 Lairg Highland, Scotland U.K.
185 N5 La Iruela Spain
94 E6 Lais Sumatera Indon.
92 E8 Lais Mindanao Phil.
246 C2 La Isabela Cuba
140 N4 Laisälven r. Sweden
134 J5 Laishevo Rus. Fed.
107 O7 Laishui Hebei China
250 B3 La Isla Col.
216 □3f La Isleta pen. Gran Canaria Canary Is
161 B8 Laissac France
140 N3 Laisvall Sweden
141 P6 Laitila Fin.
129 C4 Lait'uri Georgia
211 C6 Laivera well Tanz.
191 K3 Laives Italy
107 O8 Laiwu Shandong China
93 E4 Laiwui Maluku Indon.
107 Q8 Laixi Shandong China
107 Q8 Laiyang Shandong China
107 N7 Laiyuan Hebei China
159 K3 Laize r. France
107 P8 Laizhou Shandong China
107 P8 Laizhou Wan b. China
159 K3 Laizon r. France
260 B5 Laja, Laguna de l. Chile
245 I5 La Jabonera Mex.
250 C2 La Jagua Col.
84 C5 Lajamanu N.T. Austr.
186 F6 La Jana Spain
129 D3 Lajanurpekhi Georgia
183 K9 La Jara reg. Spain
216 □3b Lajares Fuerteventura Canary Is
162 B3 La Jarrie France
191 J9 Lajatico Italy
161 I8 La Javie France
255 B9 Lajeado Brazil
254 F4 Lajedo Brazil
256 D6 Laje dos Santos i. Brazil
182 G8 Lajeosa Guarda Port.
182 E7 Lajeosa Viseu Port.
182 F7 Lajeosa do Mondego Port.
216 □1a Lajes Terceira Azores
255 C8 Lajes Brazil
216 □1c Lajes do Pico Pico Azores
257 G4 Lajinha Brazil
196 I6 Lajkovac Serbia
162 G3 La Jonchère-St-Maurice France
186 K3 La Jonquera Spain
177 H5 Lajoskomárom Hungary
177 I4 Lajosmizse Hungary
245 N10 La Jova, Laguna l. Mex.
242 F4 La Joya Chihuahua Mex.
244 D2 La Joya Durango Mex.
252 C4 La Joya Peru
250 B5 La Joya de los Sachas Ecuador
176 G4 Lajta r. Austria/Hungary
159 J7 La Jumellière France
La Junquera Spain see La Jonquera
253 E3 La Junta Bol.
242 F3 La Junta Mex.
236 D7 La Junta CO U.S.A.
116 C8 Lakadiya Gujarat India
139 X7 Lakash Rus. Fed.
124 E6 Lakathah Saudi Arabia
213 □K3 Lakato Madag.
140 P3 Lakaträsk Sweden
232 B11 Lake KY U.S.A.
238 I4 Lake WY U.S.A.
80 J7 Lake Alice North I. N.Z.
236 F4 Lake Andes SD U.S.A.
234 E2 Lake Ariel PA U.S.A.
237 I10 Lake Arthur LA U.S.A.
83 I7 Lake Bolac Vic. Austr.
231 F10 Lake Butler FL U.S.A.
83 K5 Lake Cargelligo N.S.W. Austr.
235 H2 Lake Carmel NY U.S.A.
237 I10 Lake Charles LA U.S.A.
237 J8 Lake City AR U.S.A.
239 K8 Lake City CO U.S.A.
231 F10 Lake City FL U.S.A.
236 H4 Lake City IA U.S.A.
226 I5 Lake City MI U.S.A.
226 B5 Lake City MN U.S.A.
231 H9 Lake City SC U.S.A.
220 C3 Lake Clark National Park and Preserve AK U.S.A.
233 K4 Lake Clear NY U.S.A.
81 F10 Lake Coleridge South I. N.Z.
222 E5 Lake Cowichan B.C. Can.
137 R6 Lakedemonovka Rus. Fed.
149 K5 Lake District National Park England U.K.
83 J7 Lake Eildon State Park nature res. Vic. Austr.
227 M2 Lake Evelyn-Smoothwater Provincial Park Ont. Can.
82 F3 Lake Eyre National Park S.A. Austr.
81 J8 Lake Ferry North I. N.Z.
85 J3 Lakefield Qld Austr.
224 E4 Lakefield Ont. Can.
85 J3 Lakefield National Park Qld Austr.
241 W1 Lake Fork r. CO U.S.A.
82 G4 Lake Frome Regional Reserve nature res. S.A. Austr.
82 E4 Lake Gardner National Park S.A. Austr.
226 F7 Lake Geneva WI U.S.A.
233 L5 Lake George NY U.S.A.
82 F5 Lake Gilles Conservation Park nature res. S.A. Austr.
87 E12 Lake Grace W.A. Austr.
86 I6 Lake Gregory Aboriginal Reserve W.A. Austr.
Lake Harbour Nunavut Can. see Kimmirut
241 R7 Lake Havasu City AZ U.S.A.
235 G3 Lake Hiawatha NJ U.S.A.
234 F3 Lake Hopatcong NJ U.S.A.
235 G4 Lakehurst NJ U.S.A.
240 N6 Lake Isabella CA U.S.A.
237 H11 Lake Jackson TX U.S.A.
87 E12 Lake King W.A. Austr.
87 E12 Lake King Nature Reserve W.A. Austr.
85 J3 Lakeland Qld Austr.
231 G12 Lakeland FL U.S.A.
231 F10 Lakeland GA U.S.A.
234 F3 Lake Lenape NJ U.S.A.
226 F2 Lake Linden MI U.S.A.
222 G5 Lake Louise Alta Can.
84 B6 Lake Mackay Aboriginal Land res. N.T. Austr.
87 E12 Lake Magenta Nature Reserve W.A. Austr.
211 B5 Lake Manyara National Park Tanz.
210 A5 Lake Mburo National Park Uganda
241 R5 Lake Mead National Recreation Area park AZ U.S.A.
236 I4 Lake Mills IA U.S.A.
84 F6 Lake Nash N.T. Austr.
151 N3 Lakenheath Suffolk, England U.K.
238 C4 Lake Oswego OR U.S.A.
81 □4 Lakepa Niue
81 D10 Lake Paringa South I. N.Z.
234 F5 Lake Pine NJ U.S.A.
231 G12 Lake Placid FL U.S.A.
233 L4 Lake Placid NY U.S.A.
233 K5 Lake Pleasant NY U.S.A.
240 J2 Lakeport CA U.S.A.
227 L6 Lakeport MI U.S.A.
237 J9 Lake Providence LA U.S.A.
240 M1 Lake Range mts NV U.S.A.
224 D2 Lake River Ont. Can.
235 G4 Lake Riviera NJ U.S.A.
227 P4 Lake St Peter Ont. Can.
83 L7 Lakes Entrance Vic. Austr.
240 M4 Lakeshore CA U.S.A.
234 C6 Lake Shore MD U.S.A.
241 W7 Lakeside AZ U.S.A.
240 P9 Lakeside CA U.S.A.
235 I1 Lakeside CT U.S.A.
235 G2 Lakeside NJ U.S.A.
235 H3 Lake Success NY U.S.A.
81 G9 Lake Sumner Forest Park nature res. South I. N.Z.
226 J2 Lake Superior Provincial Park Ont. Can.
83 M6 Lake Tabourie N.S.W. Austr.
81 E11 Lake Tekapo South I. N.Z.
235 G3 Lake Telemark NJ U.S.A.
82 F4 Lake Torrens National Park S.A. Austr.
236 G3 Lake Traverse (Sisseton) Indian Reservation res. ND/SD U.S.A.
232 G6 Lake View NY U.S.A.
232 B8 Lakeview OH U.S.A.
238 D5 Lakeview OR U.S.A.
237 J9 Lake Village AR U.S.A.
226 A5 Lakeville MN U.S.A.
231 G12 Lake Wales FL U.S.A.
238 L7 Lakewood CO U.S.A.
235 G4 Lakewood NJ U.S.A.
232 F6 Lakewood NY U.S.A.
232 D7 Lakewood OH U.S.A.
226 F4 Lakewood WI U.S.A.
116 C6 Lakha Rajasthan India
Lakha Nevre Rus. Fed. see Meken-Yurt
141 U6 Lakhdenpokh'ya Rus. Fed.
116 F7 Lakheri Rajasthan India
116 H6 Lakhimpur Uttar Prad. India
117 N7 Lakhipur Assam India
117 K7 Lakhisarai Bihar India
128 C7 Lakhish r. Israel
116 G8 Lakhnadon Madh. Prad. India
116 B8 Lakhpat Gujarat India
116 C8 Lakhtar Gujarat India
117 O6 Lakhuti Nagaland India
139 N8 Lakhva r. Belarus
129 I5 Läki Azer.
174 F2 Łąkie Pol.
236 E7 Lakin KS U.S.A.
139 W5 Lakinsk Rus. Fed.
Lakinskiy Rus. Fed. see Lakinsk
177 I5 Lakitelek Hungary
224 D2 Lakitusaki r. Ont. Can.
129 G2 Lakkha-Nevre Rus. Fed.
123 N5 Lakki Pak.
199 G2 Lakkoma Samothraki Greece
93 B8 Lakohembi Sumba Indon.
198 D6 Lakonikos Kolpos b. Greece
93 F8 Lakor i. Maluku Indon.
175 H2 Łąkorz Pol.
206 D5 Lakota Côte d'Ivoire
236 F1 Lakota ND U.S.A.
140 S1 Laksefjorden sea chan. Norway
140 R1 Lakselv Norway
140 L4 Laksfors Norway
Lakshadweep is India see Laccadive Islands
114 C7 Lakshadweep union terr. India
117 M8 Laksham Bangl.
114 F3 Lakshettipet Andhra Prad. India
114 D5 Lakshmeshwar Karnataka India
117 L8 Lakshmikantapur W. Bengal India
138 J9 Laktyshy Vodaskhovishcha resr Belarus
183 P3 Lakuntza Spain
92 D8 Lala Mindanao Phil.
117 N7 Lalaghat Assam India
211 B5 Lalago Tanz.
261 F3 La Laguna Arg.
244 B3 La Lagunita Mex.
260 A5 La Laja Chile
245 J4 La Laja Mex.
244 F5 La Laja r. Mex.
123 P5 Lala Musa Pak.
245 L8 Lalana r. Mex.
185 I6 La Lantejuela Spain
184 F4 La Lapa Spain
213 F3 Lalapanzi Zimbabwe
197 O9 Lalapaşa Turkey
208 A4 Lalara Gabon
213 H2 Lalaua Moz.
186 G5 L'Albagés Spain
116 H9 Lalbara Madh. Prad. India
161 K6 L'Albaron mt. France
163 H7 Lalbenque France
187 E9 L'Albufera l. Spain
187 E7 L'Alcora Spain
187 D9 L'Alcudia Spain
78 □6 Lale New Georgia Is Solomon Is
160 I5 La Léchère France
85 L7 Laleham Qld Austr.
122 G7 Lāleh Zār, Kūh-e mt. Iran
170 F3 Lalendorf Ger.
251 F2 La Leona Venez.
150 E4 Laleston Bridgend, Wales U.K.
161 E7 Lalevade-d'Ardèche France
187 E10 L'Alfàs del Pi Spain
117 J7 Lalganj Bihar India
116 I7 Lalganj Uttar Prad. India
114 F7 Lalgudi Tamil Nadu India
122 C5 Lālī Iran
210 C1 Lalībela Eth.
250 A5 La Libertad Ecuador
243 O11 La Libertad El Salvador
243 N9 La Libertad Guat.
245 I1 La Libertad Mex.
242 □Q11 La Libertad Nic.
252 A2 La Libertad dept Peru
260 B3 La Ligua Chile
Laligyugh Armenia see Vazashen
93 E7 Laliki Maluku Indon.
93 C5 Lalimboee Sulawesi Indon.
100 E6 Lalin Heilong. China
182 D3 Lalín Spain
163 F6 Lalinde France
185 I8 La Línea de la Concepción Spain
100 D6 Lalin He r. China
116 G7 Lalitpur Uttar Prad. India
Lalitpur Nepal see Patan
161 B10 La Livinière France
261 H3 La Llave Arg.
161 H7 Lalley France
92 C2 Lal-Lo Luzon Phil.
121 L9 Lalmikor Uzbek.
117 L7 Lalmonirhat Bangl.
93 B6 Laloa Sulawesi Indon.
223 I3 La Loche Sask. Can.
223 I3 La Loche, Lac l. Sask. Can.
252 D5 La Loma Bol.
78 □2 Lalomanu Samoa
161 I10 La Londe-les-Maures France
183 M3 La Lora reg. Spain
183 N3 La Losa reg. Spain
163 E9 Laloubère France
261 H4 La Louisa Arg.
156 B7 La Loupe France
161 F6 Lalouvesc France
165 F8 La Louvière Belgium
177 L3 Lalove Ukr.
160 H2 La Loye France
161 I6 L'Alpe-d'Huez France
116 B8 Lalpur Gujarat India
134 I3 Lal'sk Rus. Fed.
116 F6 Lalsot Rajasthan India
178 D6 L'Altissima mt. Austria/Italy
186 E4 Lalueza Spain
93 E4 Laluin i. Maluku Indon.
185 I5 La Luisiana Spain
111 H12 Lalung La pass Xizang China
163 C8 Laluque France
244 E2 La Luz Mex.
173 O3 Lam Ger.
117 N9 Lama Bangl.
193 M3 Lama Italy
250 C4 La Macarena, Parque Nacional nat. park Col.
160 C3 La Machine France
192 C5 La Maddalena Sardegna Italy
107 S3 Lamadian Heilong. China
Lamadianzi Heilong. China see Lamadian
95 L2 Lamag Sabah Malaysia
182 I3 La Magdalena Spain
163 F7 Lamagistère France
96 C7 Lamaing Myanmar
93 C8 Lamakera Indon.
225 G4 La Malbaie Que. Can.
161 C8 La Malène France
245 I6 La Malinche, Parque Nacional nat. park Mex.
245 I6 La Malinche, Volcán vol. Mex.
161 C9 Lamalou-les-Bains France
96 H7 Lamam Laos
191 J7 Lama Mocogno Italy
242 H5 La Mancha Mex.
185 N2 La Mancha reg. Spain
La Manche str. France/U.K. see English Channel
190 C5 La Mandria, Parco Regionale park Italy
187 D12 La Manga del Mar Menor Spain
185 P5 La Manilla hill Spain
161 G9 Lamanon France
78 □5 Lamap Vanuatu
242 G2 La Máquina Mex.
236 D6 Lamar CO U.S.A.
237 H7 Lamar MO U.S.A.
160 C2 La Marche France
157 K7 Lamarche France
160 G2 Lamarche-sur-Saône France
122 E8 Lamard Iran
160 F1 Lamargelle France
192 C8 La Marmora, Punta mt. Sardegna Italy
260 D4 La Maroma Arg.
260 E6 Lamarque Arg.
237 H11 La Marque TX U.S.A.
261 G5 La Martinetas Arg.
222 G2 La Martre, Lac l. N.W.T. Can.
260 E4 La Maruja Arg.
182 C7 Lamas Port.
128 C2 Lamas r. Turkey
182 E6 Lamas de Olo Port.
242 □P10 La Masica Hond.
186 I2 La Massana Andorra
161 F7 Lamastre France
183 L9 La Mata Spain
186 E6 La Mata de los Olmos Spain
216 □3a La Matanza de Acentejo Tenerife Canary Is
183 M6 La Matilla Spain
225 F4 La Mauricie, Parc National de nat. park Que. Can.
107 L6 Lamawan Nei Mongol China
246 F3 La Maya Cuba
179 I3 Lambach Austria
158 F5 Lamballe France
208 A5 Lambaréné Gabon
257 E4 Lambari Brazil
Lambasa Fiji see Labasa
93 B6 Lambasina i. Indon.
250 B6 Lambayeque Peru
250 B6 Lambayeque dept Peru
147 K6 Lambay Island Ireland
95 K5 Lambeng Kalimantan Indon.
151 M5 Lamberhurst Kent, England U.K.
156 F2 Lambersart France
260 B1 Lambert Chile
Lambert atoll Marshall Is see Ailinglaplap
86 D6 Lambert, Cape W.A. Austr.
263 E2 Lambert Glacier Antarctica
214 C8 Lambert's Bay S. Africa
234 F4 Lambertville NJ U.S.A.
161 G9 Lambesc France
227 M7 Lambeth Ont. Can.
116 E4 Lambi Punjab India
78 □6 Lambi Guadalcanal Solomon Is
82 E2 Lambina S.A. Austr.
174 F5 Łambinowice Pol.
141 M6 Lamborn Sweden
151 I4 Lambourn West Berkshire, England U.K.
151 I4 Lambourn Downs hills England U.K.
172 E3 Lambrecht (Pfalz) Ger.
156 F3 Lambres-lez-Douai France
190 H5 Lambro r. Italy
147 B9 Lamb's Head Ireland
172 E2 Lambsheim Ger.
94 B3 Lame Sumatera Indon.
238 K4 Lame Deer MT U.S.A.
190 E5 Lame del Sesia, Parco Naturale nature res. Italy
182 E6 Lamego Port.
161 I6 La Meije mt. France
158 I6 La Meilleraye-de-Bretagne France
182 F7 Lameiras Port.
252 B3 La Mejorada Peru
78 □5 Lamen Bay Vanuatu
247 □2 Lamentin Guadeloupe
225 H4 Lamèque, Île i. N.B. Can.
258 D3 La Merced Arg.
252 B2 La Merced Peru
173 J5 Lamerdingen Ger.
82 H6 Lameroo S.A. Austr.
193 L4 La Merta mt. Italy
250 C3 La Mesa Col.
245 H9 La Mesa Mex.
240 O9 La Mesa CA U.S.A.
237 E9 Lamesa TX U.S.A.
149 N4 Lamesley Tyne and Wear, England U.K.
186 G6 L'Ametlla de Mar Spain
193 Q10 Lamezia Italy
204 A5 Lamhar Touil, Sabkhet imp. l. Western Sahara
198 D4 Lamia Greece
183 O2 Lamiako Spain
92 F8 Lamigan Point Mindanao Phil.
159 L5 La Milesse France
179 L5 Laming r. Austria
83 N3 Lamington National Park Qld Austr.
122 C2 Lamir Iran
244 E7 La Mira Mex.
240 N8 La Mirada CA U.S.A.
242 D3 La Misa Mex.
240 P9 La Misión Mex.
92 D8 Lamitan Phil.
93 G4 Lamlam Papua Indon.
78 □1 Lamlam, Mount hill Guam
146 F11 Lamlash North Ayrshire, Scotland U.K.
109 □J7 Lamma Island H.K. China
215 N1 Lammerkop S. Africa
146 K11 Lammer Law hill Scotland U.K.
81 D12 Lammerlaw Range mts South I. N.Z.
81 D12 Lammerlaw Top mt. South I. N.Z.
146 K11 Lammermuir Hills Scotland U.K.
143 K4 Lammhult Sweden
141 R6 Lammi Fin.
138 K3 Lammijärv lake channel Estonia/Rus. Fed.
97 F7 Lam Nang Rong Reservoir Thai.
226 E8 La Moille IL U.S.A.
233 L4 Lamoille r. VT U.S.A.
226 D9 La Moine r. IL U.S.A.
185 N7 La Mojonera Spain
161 I10 La Môle France
191 L3 Lamon Italy
92 C4 Lamon Bay Phil.
191 M6 Lamone r. Italy
95 J8 Lamongan Jawa Indon.
163 E10 La Mongie France
236 I5 Lamoni IA U.S.A.
160 D5 La Monnerie-le-Montel France
240 N6 Lamont CA U.S.A.
238 K5 Lamont WY U.S.A.
194 H9 La Montagna hill Italy
158 H7 La Montagne France
217 □1c La Montagne Réunion
163 F7 Lamontjoie France
163 E6 Lamonzie-St-Martin France
260 D4 La Mora Arg.
242 H4 La Mora Mex.
245 H4 La Morena Mex.
242 G3 La Morita Chihuahua Mex.
237 D11 La Morita Coahuila Mex.
156 D5 Lamorlaye France
260 B3 La Mostaza Chile
161 C6 Lamothe France
162 A2 La Mothe-Achard France
163 G7 Lamothe-Capdeville France
163 G6 Lamothe-Cassel France
163 E6 Lamothe-Landerron France
162 D3 La Mothe-St-Héray France
91 K5 Lamotrek atoll Micronesia
227 P1 La Motte Que. Can.
161 J9 La Motte France
159 P6 Lamotte-Beuvron France
161 G8 La Motte-Chalancon France
161 H7 La Motte-d'Aveillans France
161 I8 La Motte-du-Caire France
160 H5 La Motte-Servolex France
236 F2 La Moure ND U.S.A.
260 B3 Lampa Chile
252 C3 Lampa Peru
245 H1 Lampacitos Mex.
96 D5 Lampang Thai.
96 F6 Lam Pao Reservoir Thai.
237 F10 Lampasas TX U.S.A.
237 G10 Lampasas r. TX U.S.A.
158 A5 Lampaul France
158 C5 Lampaul-Guimilau France
158 B5 Lampaul-Plouarzel France
243 I4 Lampazos Mex.
189 D8 Lampedusa, Isola di i. Sicilia Italy
142 F2 Lampeland Norway
172 E2 Lampertheim Ger.
171 I8 Lampertswalde Ger.
150 D3 Lampeter Ceredigion, Wales U.K.
234 C5 Lampeter PA U.S.A.
96 D5 Lamphun Thai.
151 K3 Lamport Northamptonshire, England U.K.
134 I2 Lampozhnya Rus. Fed.
178 G4 Lamprechtshausen Austria
Lampsacus Turkey see Lâpseki
94 F7 Lampung prov. Indon.
94 F7 Lampung, Teluk b. Indon.
171 J7 Lamsfeld-Groß Liebitz Ger.
139 V9 Lamskoye Rus. Fed.
169 J7 Lamspringe Ger.
168 H3 Lamstedt Ger.
116 H8 Lamta Madh. Prad. India
109 □J7 Lam Tin H.K. China
211 D5 Lamu Kenya
96 B5 Lamu Myanmar
183 K5 La Mudarra Spain
186 C4 La Muela Spain
185 M4 La Muela hill Spain
187 C8 La Muela mt. Spain
186 L3 La Muga r. Spain
183 L7 La Mujer Muerta hill Spain
161 H7 La Mure France
160 E4 Lamure-sur-Azergues France
85 I7 Lana Qld Austr.
191 K2 Lana Italy
260 E4 La Nacional Arg.
240 □D13 Lāna'i i. HI U.S.A.
240 □E13 Lāna'i City HI U.S.A.
186 E4 Lanaja Spain
165 I7 Lanaken Belgium
92 E8 Lanao, Lake Mindanao Phil.
161 E7 Lanarce France
227 R4 Lanark Ont. Can.
146 I11 Lanark South Lanarkshire, Scotland U.K.
226 E7 Lanark IL U.S.A.
95 L2 Lanas Sabah Malaysia
184 F5 La Nava Spain
183 K9 La Nava de Ricomalillo Spain
184 G2 La Nava de Santiago Spain
129 I5 Länbaran Azer.
97 D9 Lanbi Kyun i. Myanmar
92 D7 Lanboyan Point Mindanao Phil.
108 B7 Lancang Yunnan China
90 A1 Lancang Jiang r. Xizang China
108 C8 Lancang Jiang r. China alt. Mènam Khong (Laos/Thai.) conv. Mekong
149 L6 Lancashire admin. div. England U.K.
149 K7 Lancashire Plain England U.K.
233 K3 Lancaster Ont. Can.
149 L5 Lancaster Lancashire, England U.K.
240 N7 Lancaster CA U.S.A.
230 E7 Lancaster KY U.S.A.
236 I5 Lancaster MO U.S.A.
233 N4 Lancaster NH U.S.A.
232 G6 Lancaster NY U.S.A.
232 C9 Lancaster OH U.S.A.
234 C4 Lancaster PA U.S.A.
231 G8 Lancaster SC U.S.A.
232 I11 Lancaster VA U.S.A.
236 J4 Lancaster WI U.S.A.
149 L6 Lancaster Canal England U.K.
234 C4 Lancaster County county PA U.S.A.
221 J2 Lancaster Sound str. Nunavut Can.
247 □6 Lance aux Épines Grenada
87 C11 Lancelin W.A. Austr.
87 C11 Lancelin Island W.A. Austr.
149 N4 Lanchester Durham, England U.K.
129 D3 Lanch'khut'i Georgia
193 M3 Lanciano Italy
183 P3 Lanciego Spain
259 B5 Lanco Chile
107 Q8 Lancun Shandong China
175 K5 Łańcut Pol.
190 A3 Lancy Switz.
245 H4 Landa de Matamoros Mex.
95 H5 Landak r. Indon.
Landana Angola see Cacongo
173 N4 Landau an der Isar Ger.
172 E3 Landau in der Pfalz Ger.
178 C5 Landeck Austria
158 B4 Landéda France
184 B3 Landeira Port.
158 D5 Landeleau France
165 H7 Landen Belgium
84 C6 Lander watercourse N.T. Austr.
238 J5 Lander WY U.S.A.
158 C5 Landerneau France
157 N6 Landersheim France
163 C8 Landes dept France
163 C6 Landes reg. France
168 H5 Landesbergen Ger.
163 C7 Landes de Gascogne, Parc Naturel Régional des nature res. France
158 F6 Landes de Lanvaux reg. France
158 F5 Landes du Mené reg. France
261 F3 Landeta Arg.
187 C8 Landete Spain
158 E6 Landévant France
158 C5 Landévennec France
115 M6 Landfall Island Andaman & Nicobar Is India
165 J7 Landgraaf Neth.
151 O4 Landguard Point England U.K.
168 G3 Land Hadeln reg. Ger.
123 L9 Landhi Pak.
123 J6 Landi Barechi Afgh.
94 D5 Landik, Gunung mt. Indon.
123 N4 Landi Kotal Pak.
182 D6 Landim Port.
234 F3 Landing NJ U.S.A.
156 H7 Landion r. France
163 D6 Landiras France
223 I4 Landis Sask. Can.
234 C4 Landisville PA U.S.A.
158 C4 Landivisiau France
159 I5 Landivy France
168 H3 Land Kehdingen reg. Ger.
170 D2 Landkirchen auf Fehmarn Ger.
209 F8 Landless Corner Zambia
140 M5 Landögssjön l. Sweden
226 E3 Land O' Lakes WI U.S.A.
169 J7 Landolfshausen Ger.
140 M5 Landön Sweden
87 D8 Landor W.A. Austr.
150 E4 Landore Swansea, Wales U.K.
161 D7 Landos France
190 H2 Landquart Switz.
190 H2 Landquart r. Switz.
156 G3 Landrecies France
157 K5 Landres France
157 J5 Landres-et-St-Georges France
227 Q1 Landrienne Que. Can.
182 E1 Landro r. Spain
Landrove r. Spain see Landro
231 F8 Landrum SC U.S.A.
160 J5 Landry France
171 F7 Landsberg Ger.
Landsberg Pol. see Gorzów Wielkopolski
173 J5 Landsberg am Lech Ger.
81 D10 Landsborough r. South I. N.Z.
85 J7 Landsborough Creek watercourse Qld Austr.
169 C11 Landscheid Ger.
150 □ Land's End pt England U.K.
173 M4 Landshut Ger.
143 K4 Landsjön l. Sweden
142 I6 Landskrona Sweden
164 G4 Landsmeer Neth.
172 D3 Landstuhl Ger.
158 C5 Landudec France
168 G3 Land Wursten reg. Ger.
197 L5 La Nedei mt. Romania
261 H5 La Negra Arg.
252 C5 La Negra Chile
87 D12 Lane Pool Reserve nature res. W.A. Austr.
147 G5 Lanesborough Ireland
158 E6 Lanester France
231 E9 Lanett AL U.S.A.
159 M4 La Neuve-Lyre France
190 C1 La Neuveville Switz.
157 I5 La Neuville-au-Pont France
157 J5 Laneuville-sur-Meuse France
Lanfeng Henan China see Lankao
96 C1 Lang, Nam r. Myanmar
142 F5 Langå Denmark
183 K6 Langa Spain
97 H9 La Nga, Sông r. Vietnam
129 J5 Längäbiz Silsiläsi hills Azer.
111 E11 La'nga Co l. China
183 N5 Langa de Duero Spain
Langadhás Greece see Lagkadas
117 N7 Langai r. India
140 M5 Långan r. Sweden
108 G2 Langao Shaanxi China
123 O3 Langar Badakhshān Afgh.
123 I5 Langar Farāh Afgh.
123 M4 Langar Parwān Afgh.
122 I4 Langar Iran
121 L7 Langar Navoiy Uzbek.
121 L8 Langar Qashqadaryo Uzbek.
93 C6 Langara Sulawesi Indon.
222 C4 Langara Island B.C. Can.
143 L5 Långasjö Sweden
179 M2 Langau Austria
146 C6 Langavat, Loch l. Western Isles, Scotland U.K.
168 I1 Langballig Ger.
214 G4 Langberg mts S. Africa
236 F1 Langdon ND U.S.A.
82 □3 Langdon Point S. Pacific Ocean
173 O3 Langdorf Ger.
161 C6 Langeac France
162 E1 Langeais France
214 C9 Langebaan S. Africa
170 F1 Langebæk Denmark
214 D9 Langeberg mts S. Africa
164 G3 Langedijk Neth.
214 I2 Langehorn S. Africa
142 G6 Langeland i. Denmark
142 G7 Langelands Bælt str. Denmark
141 R6 Längelmäki Fin.
134 D3 Längelmävesi l. Fin.
169 K7 Langeln Ger.
169 J7 Langelsheim Ger.
165 C7 Langemark Belgium
172 F2 Langen Hessen Ger.
168 D5 Langen Niedersachsen Ger.
168 G3 Langen Niedersachsen Ger.
173 J4 Langenaltheim Ger.
172 H6 Langenargen Ger.
173 I5 Langenau Ger.
169 F9 Langenaubach Ger.
173 L5 Langenbach Ger.
178 A4 Langen bei Bregenz Austria
169 F7 Langenberg Ger.
171 F9 Langenbernsdorf Ger.
223 K5 Langenburg Sask. Can.
172 H3 Langenburg Ger.
171 E8 Langendorf Ger.
178 A5 Langenegg Austria
171 E8 Langeneichstädt Ger.
172 G5 Langenenslingen Ger.
178 C5 Längenfeld Austria
169 C8 Langenfeld (Rheinland) Ger.
169 I6 Langenhagen Ger.
169 E9 Langenhahn Ger.
168 G1 Langenhorn Ger.
171 G9 Langenleuba-Niederhain Ger.
179 M3 Langenlois Austria
172 D2 Langenlonsheim Ger.
173 K4 Langenmosen Ger.
171 H7 Langennaundorf Ger.
173 J5 Langenneufnach Ger.
171 E9 Langenorla Ger.
173 L5 Langenpreising Ger.
169 H10 Langenselbold Ger.
173 K2 Langensendelbach Ger.
169 K7 Langenstein Ger.
190 D1 Langenthal Switz.
179 M4 Langenwang Austria
171 E6 Langenweddingen Ger.
171 F9 Langenwetzendorf Ger.
173 J3 Langenzenn Ger.
179 N3 Langenzersdorf Austria
168 D3 Langeoog Ger.
168 E3 Langeoog i. Ger.
130 I3 Langepas Rus. Fed.
142 G4 Langerak sea chan. Denmark
170 I5 Langer Berg hill Ger.
173 J5 Langerringen Ger.
171 H6 Langerwisch Ger.
142 G6 Langeskov Denmark
142 F2 Langesund Norway
142 B2 Langevåg Norway
217 □1c Langevin, Pointe de pt Réunion
169 K9 Langewiesen Ger.
107 O7 Langfang Hebei China
141 L5 Långfjallets naturreservat nature res. Sweden
151 L3 Langford Bedfordshire, England U.K.
173 I3 Langfurth Ger.
94 D4 Langgam Sumatera Indon.
94 D4 Langgapayung Sumatera Indon.
111 K12 Langgar Xizang China
169 G10 Langgöns Ger.
170 F3 Langhagen Ger.
223 J4 Langham Sask. Can.
151 K2 Langham Rutland, England U.K.
142 J4 Länghem Sweden
190 I6 Langhirano Italy
215 K9 Langholm S. Africa
146 K12 Langholm Dumfries and Galloway, Scotland U.K.
142 H1 Langholsberget hill Norway
234 F4 Langhorne PA U.S.A.
140 □C1 Langjökull ice cap Iceland
94 B2 Langka Sumatera Indon.
94 C1 Langkawi i. Malaysia
93 D6 Langkesi, Kepulauan is Indon.
97 D10 Lang Kha Toek, Khao mt. Thai.
96 C4 Langkho Myanmar
214 E4 Langklip S. Africa
95 L1 Langkon Sabah Malaysia
227 S1 Langlade Que. Can.
226 F4 Langlade WI U.S.A.
222 F5 Langley B.C. Can.
232 C11 Langley KY U.S.A.
168 J5 Langlingen Ger.
85 K9 Langlo watercourse Qld Austr.
85 J9 Langlo Crossing Qld Austr.
Langmusi Gansu China see Dagcanglhamo
190 D2 Langnau Switz.
168 L1 Langø Denmark
161 D7 Langogne France
163 D6 Langoiran France
163 D6 Langon France
96 H6 Langong, Xé r. Laos
158 D5 Langonnet France
140 M2 Langøya i. Norway
150 G5 Langport Somerset, England U.K.
111 D11 Langqên Zangbo r. China
109 L5 Langqi Fujian China
173 M4 Langquaid Ger.
182 I2 Langreo Spain
157 J8 Langres France
157 I8 Langres, Plateau de France
111 D8 Langru Xinjiang China
94 B2 Langsa Sumatera Indon.
94 C2 Langsa, Teluk b. Indon.
179 K2 Langschlag Austria
140 N5 Långsele Sweden
107 J6 Langshan Nei Mongol China
107 J6 Lang Shan mts China
143 M1 Långshyttan Sweden
140 P2 Langslett Norway
96 H4 Lang Son Vietnam
149 M5 Langstrothdale Chase hills England U.K.
172 B2 Langsur Ger.
207 H4 Langtang Nigeria
117 J5 Langtang National Park Nepal
96 C1 Langtao Myanmar
117 N7 Langting Assam India
149 Q5 Langtoft East Riding of Yorkshire, England U.K.
107 Q3 Langtoutun Nei Mongol China
140 P4 Långträsk Sweden
237 E11 Langtry TX U.S.A.
Languan Shaanxi China see Lantian
163 H9 Languedoc reg. France
161 A11 Languedoc-Roussillon admin. reg. France
158 F5 Langueux France
261 H5 Langueyú Arg.
Languiaru r. Brazil see Iquê
158 E6 Languidic France
183 N6 Languilla Spain
259 C6 Languiñeo Arg.
169 J8 Langula Ger.
95 M9 Langundu, Tanjung pt Sumbawa Indon.
134 C2 Långvattnet Sweden
143 L2 Långvattnet l. Sweden
141 N6 Långvinds bruk Sweden
168 F3 Langwarden (Butjadingen) Ger.
149 L4 Langwathby Cumbria, England U.K.
168 H5 Langwedel Niedersachsen Ger.
168 I2 Langwedel Schleswig-Holstein Ger.
173 J5 Langweid am Lech Ger.
107 N7 Langya Shan mt. Hebei China
108 F3 Langzhong Sichuan China
182 C5 Lanheses Port.
158 C4 Lanhouarneau France
227 O2 Laniel Que. Can.
175 H3 Łanięta Pol.
223 J5 Lanigan Sask. Can.
240 □D12 Lanikai HI U.S.A.
259 C5 Lanín, Parque Nacional nat. park Arg.
259 C5 Lanín, Volcán vol. Arg./Chile
150 C7 Lanivet Cornwall, England U.K.
136 F4 Lanivtsi Ukr.
95 I4 Lanjak, Bukit mt. Malaysia
185 M7 Lanjarón Spain
116 H9 Lanji Madh. Prad. India
Lanka country Asia see Sri Lanka
113 □1 Lankanfinolhu i. N. Male Maldives
Lankanfushifinolu i. N. Male Maldives see Lankanfinolhu
107 N9 Lankao Henan China
129 J7 Länkäran Azer.
129 J7 Länkäran r. Azer.
109 □I7 Lan Kok Tsui pt H.K. China
252 C3 Lanlacuni Bajo Peru
158 F4 Lanloup France
158 D4 Lanmeur France
179 L6 Lannach Austria
163 E9 Lannemezan France
163 E9 Lannemezan, Plateau de France
163 E8 Lannepax France
158 B4 Lannilis France
158 E4 Lannion France
158 D4 Lannion, Baie de b. France
224 F4 L'Annonciation Que. Can.
156 F2 Lannoy France
161 B6 Lanobre France
160 D3 La Nocle-Maulaix France
186 I5 L'Anoia r. Spain
235 G5 Lanoka Harbor NJ U.S.A.
253 E3 La Noria Bol.
244 A2 La Noria Mex.
162 G5 Lanouaille France
108 B5 Lanping Yunnan China
178 D5 Lans Austria
161 H7 Lans, Montagne de mts France
161 E9 Lansargues France
234 E4 Lansdale PA U.S.A.
234 B6 Lansdowne MD U.S.A.
226 F3 L'Anse MI U.S.A.
170 G3 Lansen Ger.
225 G3 L'Anse-St-Jean Que. Can.
234 D3 Lansford PA U.S.A.

Lazise to Lesmahagow
341

191 J5 Lazise Italy
175 J4 Łaziska Pol.
176 E1 Lázně Bělohrad Czech Rep.
176 E1 Lázně Bohdaneč Czech Rep.
176 B1 Lázně Kynžvart Czech Rep.
261 H3 Lazo Arg.
100 H7 Lazo Primorskiy Kray Rus. Fed.
131 O3 Lazo Respublika Sakha (Yakutiya) Rus. Fed.
149 L4 Lazonby Cumbria, England U.K.
237 E11 La Zorra watercourse Mex.
Lazovsk Moldova see Sîngerei
177 L4 Lazuri Romania
177 L5 Lazuri de Beiuş Romania
137 L7 Lazurne Ukr.
175 H5 Łazy Pol.
261 H5 Lazzarino Arg.
190 G6 Lazzaro, Monte hill Italy
148 E2 Leacan, Rubha nan pt Scotland U.K.
97 F8 Leach Cambodia
226 J2 Leach Island Ont. Can.
234 C4 Leacock PA U.S.A.
220 H5 Lead SD U.S.A.
146 J11 Leadburn Midlothian, Scotland U.K.
149 P7 Leadenham Lincolnshire, England U.K.
223 I5 Leader Sask. Can.
234 B5 Leader Heights PA U.S.A.
146 K11 Leader Water r. Scotland U.K.
149 N4 Leadgate Durham, England U.K.
146 I12 Leadhills South Lanarkshire, Scotland U.K.
83 L5 Leadville N.S.W. Austr.
239 K7 Leadville CO U.S.A.
237 K10 Leaf r. MS U.S.A.
Leaf Bay Que. Can. see Tasiujaq
223 K3 Leaf Rapids Man. Can.
262 Q2 Leahy, Cape Antarctica
86 I4 Leake, Mount hill W.A. Austr.
237 K10 Leakesville MS U.S.A.
237 F11 Leakey TX U.S.A.
Leaksville NC U.S.A. see Eden
86 D6 Leal, Mount hill W.A. Austr.
258 D2 Leales Arg.
224 D5 Leamington Ont. Can.
151 I3 Leamington Spa, Royal Warwickshire, England U.K.
109 J5 Le'an Jiangxi China
215 M2 Leandra S. Africa
261 G4 Leandro N. Alem Buenos Aires Arg.
258 G2 Leandro N. Alem Misiones Arg.
147 C8 Leane, Lough l. Ireland
213 □J2 Leanja Madag.
177 I4 Leányfalu Hungary
147 D9 Leap Ireland
86 C7 Learmonth W.A. Austr.
149 Q7 Leasingham Lincolnshire, England U.K.
151 L5 Leatherhead Surrey, England U.K.
165 F8 L'Eau d'Heure l. Belgium
165 F8 L'Eau d'Heure r. Belgium
Leava Wallis and Futuna Is see Sigave
149 P5 Leavening North Yorkshire, England U.K.
236 H6 Leavenworth KS U.S.A.
238 D3 Leavenworth WA U.S.A.
240 M3 Leavitt Peak CA U.S.A.
140 S2 Leavvajohka Norway
143 N7 Łeba Pol.
174 F1 Łeba r. Pol.
174 G1 Łeba r. Pol.
172 B3 Lebach Ger.
92 E8 Lebak Mindanao Phil.
215 J3 Lebaleng S. Africa
208 A5 Lébamba Gabon
197 J8 Lebane Serbia
128 D5 Lebanon country Asia
230 D5 Lebanon IN U.S.A.
236 F6 Lebanon KS U.S.A.
230 E7 Lebanon KY U.S.A.
237 I7 Lebanon MO U.S.A.
233 M5 Lebanon NH U.S.A.
234 F3 Lebanon NJ U.S.A.
232 A9 Lebanon OH U.S.A.
238 C4 Lebanon OR U.S.A.
227 R9 Lebanon PA U.S.A.
231 D7 Lebanon TN U.S.A.
232 C12 Lebanon VA U.S.A.
234 C4 Lebanon County county PA U.S.A.
157 L5 Le Ban-St-Martin France
123 I1 Lebap Turkm.
123 J2 Lebap admin. div. Turkm.
Lebap Oblast admin. div. Turkm. see Lebap
163 K10 Le Barcarès France
163 C6 Le Barp France
165 F6 Lebbeke Belgium
Lebda tourist site Libya see Leptis Magna
161 E7 Le Béage France
161 H10 Le Beausset France
240 N7 Lebec CA U.S.A.
159 M3 Le Bec-Hellouin France
Lebedin Ukr. see Lebedyn
139 W8 Lebedyan' Rus. Fed.
137 N3 Lebedyn Ukr.
224 E3 Lebel-sur-Quévillon Que. Can.
171 E7 Lebendorf Ger.
159 J4 Le Bény-Bocage France
176 G4 Lébénymiklós Hungary
163 I8 Le Bez France
156 C3 Lebiez France
210 E3 Lebiolali well Eth.
160 J4 Le Biot France
162 G2 Le Blanc France
161 D8 Le Bleymard France
174 G1 Łebno Pol.
208 D3 Lebo Dem. Rep. Congo
93 C6 Lebo Sulawesi Indon.
215 M2 Lebohang S. Africa
160 F5 Le Bois-d'Oingt France
162 B3 Le Bois-Plage-en-Ré France
Lebomboberge hills Moz. see Lebombo Mountains
215 Q2 Lebombo Mountains hills Moz.
117 L6 Lebong W. Bengal India
161 K8 Le Boréon France
143 N7 Lębork Pol.
163 J10 Le Boulou France
159 J8 Le Boupère France
163 H6 Le Bourg France
161 I6 Le Bourg-d'Oisans France
160 H5 Le Bourget-du-Lac France
159 J5 Le Bourgneuf-la-Forêt France
163 C6 Le Bouscat France
161 C9 Le Bousquet-d'Orb France
213 F5 Lebowakgomo S. Africa
168 J2 Lebrade Ger.
160 E3 Le Breuil Bourgogne France
156 G6 Le Breuil Champagne-Ardenne France
160 J5 Le Brévent mt. France
184 G7 Lebrija Spain
179 M6 Lebring-Sankt Margarethen Austria
163 E8 Le Brouilh-Monbert France
217 □1c Le Brûlé Réunion
161 I8 Le Brusquet France
143 N7 Łebsko, Jezioro lag. Pol.
258 B5 Lebu Chile
182 F5 Lebução Port.
163 F6 Le Bugue France
161 C7 Le Buisson France
163 F6 Le Buisson-de-Cadouin France
171 K6 Lebus Ger.
171 H7 Lebusa Ger.
162 C2 Le Busseau France
137 O4 Leb"yazhe Ukr.
137 R8 Lebyazhiy, Liman l. Rus. Fed.
Lebyazh'ye Kazakh. see Akku
134 J4 Lebyazh'ye Kirovskaya Oblast' Rus. Fed.
138 M2 Lebyazh'ye Leningradskaya Oblast' Rus. Fed.
139 V9 Lebyazh'ye Lipetskaya Oblast' Rus. Fed.
182 C6 Leça da Palmeira Port.
182 C6 Leça do Bailio Port.
Le Caire Egypt see Al Qāhirah
163 I10 Lecamp, Plateau de France
161 K9 Le Cannet France
161 I10 Le Cannet-des-Maures France
158 B5 Le Cap c. France
247 □3 Le Carbet Martinique
147 F5 Lecarrow Ireland
161 H10 Le Castellet France
156 G3 Le Cateau-Cambrésis France
156 F3 Le Catelet France
161 C9 Le Caylar France
161 B7 Le Cayrol France
195 O3 Lecce Italy
195 O3 Lecce prov. Italy
190 G4 Lecco Italy
190 G4 Lecco prov. Italy
190 G4 Lecco, Lago di l. Italy
236 I3 Le Center MN U.S.A.
186 D5 Lécera Spain
178 B5 Lech Austria
178 C4 Lech r. Austria/Ger.
198 C5 Lechaina Greece
161 E6 Le Chambon-Feugerolles France
161 E6 Le Chambon-sur-Lignon France
109 I6 Lechang Guangdong China
178 C5 Lechaschau Austria
190 B2 Le Chasseron mt. Switz.
162 B4 Le Château-d'Oléron France
160 I5 Le Châtelard France
159 P8 Le Châtelet France
156 E6 Le Châtelet-en-Brie France
173 J6 Lechbruck Ger.
156 H6 Le Chêne France
156 I4 Le Chesne France
160 J4 Le Cheval Blanc mt. France
161 I6 Le Cheval Noir mt. France
161 E7 Le Cheylard France
161 H6 Le Cheylas France
197 M3 Lechința Romania
197 M4 Lechința r. Romania
129 D3 Lech'khumis K'edi hills Georgia
151 I4 Lechlade Gloucestershire, England U.K.
178 B5 Lechtal val. Austria
178 B5 Lechtaler Alpen mts Austria
169 F6 Lechtingen (Wallenhorst) Ger.
186 D4 Leciñena Spain
168 G1 Leck Ger.
147 F4 Leckaun Ireland
146 F7 Leckmelm Highland, Scotland U.K.
161 C9 Le Clapier France
161 D8 Le Collet-de-Dèze France
237 I10 Lecompte LA U.S.A.
158 B5 Le Conquet France
161 I6 Le Corbier France
160 E4 Le Coteau France
156 C5 Le Coudray-St-Germer France
158 I5 Lécousse France
161 D9 Le Crès France
160 E3 Le Creusot France
185 L7 Lecrín Spain
158 F7 Le Croisic France
156 C3 Le Crotoy France
163 F8 Lectoure France
175 K4 Łęczna Pol.
175 H3 Łęczyca Pol.
174 F1 Łęczyce Pol.
168 D4 Leda r. Ger.
146 F10 Ledaig Argyll and Bute, Scotland U.K.
185 P2 Ledaña Spain
183 O7 Ledanca Spain
94 E3 Ledang, Gunung mt. Malaysia
188 F2 Ledava r. Slovenia
151 K4 Ledburn Buckinghamshire, England U.K.
150 H3 Ledbury Herefordshire, England U.K.
165 E7 Lede Belgium
163 F7 Lède r. France
176 E2 Ledeč nad Sázavou Czech Rep.
165 D7 Ledegem Belgium
134 I4 Ledengskoye Rus. Fed.
176 D3 Ledenice Czech Rep.
163 I7 Lédergues France
182 I6 Ledesma Spain
163 C9 Ledeuix France
161 D7 Le Devès mt. France
247 □3 Le Diamant Martinique
209 C5 Lediba Dem. Rep. Congo
161 E9 Lédignan France
183 K4 Ledigos Spain
134 J2 Ledkovo Rus. Fed.
146 G6 Ledmore Highland, Scotland U.K.
134 F2 Ledmozero Rus. Fed.
177 H2 Lednica Slovakia
176 F3 Lednice Czech Rep.
95 H4 Ledo Kalimantan Indon.
108 G9 Ledong Hainan China
96 I5 Ledong Hainan China
160 D4 Le Donjon France
162 G3 Le Dorat France
Ledosus France see Lezoux
182 I8 Ledrada Spain
178 C8 Ledro, Lago di l. Italy
106 H8 Ledu Qinghai China
222 H4 Leduc Alta Can.
161 H8 Le Duffre mt. France
131 S3 Ledyanaya, Gora mt. Rus. Fed.
174 E2 Lędyczek Pol.
174 D1 Lędzin Pol.
175 H5 Lędziny Pol.
147 F9 Lee r. Ireland
149 L6 Lee Lancashire, England U.K.
233 L6 Lee MA U.S.A.
233 □Q3 Lee ME U.S.A.
232 F8 Leechburg PA U.S.A.
236 H2 Leech Lake MN U.S.A.
236 H2 Leech Lake Indian Reservation res. MN U.S.A.
149 N6 Leeds West Yorkshire, England U.K.
149 N6 Leeds Bradford International airport England U.K.
150 B7 Leedstown Cornwall, England U.K.
164 J2 Leek Neth.
149 M7 Leek Staffordshire, England U.K.
87 C10 Leeman W.A. Austr.
149 N5 Leeming North Yorkshire, England U.K.
150 D7 Lee Moor Devon, England U.K.
147 C5 Leenane Ireland
165 I6 Leende Neth.
164 J2 Leens Neth.
151 J6 Lee-on-the-Solent Hampshire, England U.K.
232 F7 Leeper PA U.S.A.
168 D4 Leer (Ostfriesland) Ger.
164 H5 Leerdam Neth.
164 H4 Leersum Neth.
163 C10 Lées-Athas France
231 G11 Leesburg FL U.S.A.
231 E10 Leesburg GA U.S.A.
232 A10 Leesburg KY U.S.A.
234 F6 Leesburg NJ U.S.A.
232 B9 Leesburg OH U.S.A.
232 H9 Leesburg VA U.S.A.
169 H5 Leese Ger.
234 D4 Leesport PA U.S.A.
236 H6 Lees Summit MO U.S.A.
87 F8 Lee Steere Range hills W.A. Austr.
81 G10 Leeston South I. N.Z.
237 I10 Leesville LA U.S.A.
232 F11 Leesville Lake VA U.S.A.
83 K6 Leeton N.S.W. Austr.
215 K3 Leeudoringstad S. Africa
214 F8 Leeu-Gamka S. Africa
215 J4 Leeukop mt. S. Africa
215 L5 Leeurivierdam l. S. Africa
214 F8 Leeuw r. S. Africa
164 I2 Leeuwarden Neth.
87 C13 Leeuwin, Cape W.A. Austr.
87 C12 Leeuwin-Naturaliste National Park W.A. Austr.
240 M4 Lee Vining CA U.S.A.
247 K4 Leeward Islands Caribbean Sea
Leeward Islands Arch. de la Société Fr. Polynesia see Sous le Vent, Îles
170 D3 Leezen Mecklenburg-Vorpommern Ger.
168 J3 Leezen Schleswig-Holstein Ger.
158 C5 Le Faou France
158 E5 Le Faouët France
163 G9 Le Fauga France
197 N7 Lefedzha r. Bulg.
158 H8 Le Fenouiller France
156 D1 Leffrinckoucke France
208 B5 Léfini, Réserve de Chasse de la nature res. Congo
128 A3 Lefka Cyprus
198 B4 Lefkada Lefkada Greece
198 B4 Lefkada i. Greece
198 E7 Lefka Ori mts Kriti Greece
Lefkás Lefkada Greece see Lefkada
Lefke Cyprus see Lefka
198 B3 Lefkimmi Kerkyra Greece
Lefkoniko Cyprus see Lefkonikon
128 B3 Lefkonikon Cyprus
198 E4 Lefkonisia i. Greece
Lefkoşa Cyprus see Lefkosia
128 B3 Lefkosia Cyprus
163 E6 Le Fleix France
158 C4 Le Folgoët France
156 F3 Leforest France
163 G9 Le Fossat France
163 G9 Le Fousseret France
247 □3 Le François Martinique
225 G1 Lefroy r. Que. Can.
87 G11 Lefroy, Lake salt flat W.A. Austr.
161 J8 Le Fugeret France
159 I7 Le Fuilet France
175 J5 Łęg r. Pol.
78 □3a Legan i. Kwajalein Marshall Is
183 M8 Leganés Spain
183 O8 Leganiel Spain
224 C3 Legarde r. Ont. Can.
92 D5 Legaspi Luzon Phil.
173 I6 Legau Ger.
156 B7 Le Gault-St-Denis France
156 G6 Le Gault-Soigny France
186 A1 Legazpi Spain
170 E5 Legde Ger.
169 D6 Legden Ger.
158 H8 Legé France
163 B6 Lège-Cap-Ferret France
86 D6 Legendre Island W.A. Austr.
159 J5 Le Genest-St-Isle France
83 K9 Legges Tor mt. Tas. Austr.
240 I2 Leggett CA U.S.A.
147 G3 Leggs Northern Ireland U.K.
Leghorn Italy see Livorno
175 I3 Legionowo Pol.
165 I9 Léglise Belgium
191 K5 Legnago Italy
190 F4 Legnano Italy
174 E4 Legnica Pol.
174 E4 Legnickie Pole Pol.
190 G3 Legnone, Monte mt. Italy
Legohli N.W.T. Can. see Norman Wells
162 E4 Le Gond-Pontouvre France
247 □2 Le Gosier Guadeloupe
174 G1 Łęgowo Pol.
179 O7 Legrad Croatia
240 L4 Le Grand CA U.S.A.
87 F13 Le Grand, Cape W.A. Austr.
217 □1c Le Grand Bénare mt. Réunion
160 I5 Le Grand-Bornand France
162 H3 Le Grand-Bourg France
161 J8 Le Grand Coyer mt. France
160 H4 Le Grand Crêt d'Eau mt. France
161 G6 Le Grand-Lemps France
159 L6 Le Grand-Lucé France
160 J5 Le Grand Mont mt. France
159 M8 Le Grand-Pressigny France
156 B5 Le Grand-Quevilly France
161 G6 Le Grand-Serre France
160 I3 Le Grand Taureau mt. France
161 H7 Le Grand Veymont mt. France
161 E9 Le Grau-du-Roi France
217 □1c Le Gros Morne mt. Réunion
159 M3 Le Gros Theil France
161 H6 Le Gua France
252 C5 Leguena Chile
158 E4 Léguer r. France
163 G8 Léguevin France
208 E4 Leguga Dem. Rep. Congo
261 H2 Leguizamón Arg.
84 B3 Legune N.T. Austr.
183 O3 Legutiano Spain
208 E4 Legwe r. Dem. Rep. Congo
96 C4 Le-gya Myanmar
116 F2 Leh Jammu and Kashmir
157 J8 Le Haut du Sec hill France
159 L2 Le Havre France
168 H2 Lehe Ger.
171 D10 Lehesten Ger.
241 U1 Lehi UT U.S.A.
234 E3 Lehigh r. PA U.S.A.
234 D3 Lehigh County county PA U.S.A.
234 D3 Lehighton PA U.S.A.
197 O6 Lehliu-Gară Romania
215 M6 Lehlohonolo S. Africa
261 G2 Lehmann Arg.
169 D10 Lehmen Ger.
168 J2 Lehmkuhlen Ger.
171 F9 Lehndorf Ger.
176 G3 Lehnice Slovakia
171 G6 Lehnin Ger.
170 H5 Lehnitz Ger.
157 N7 Le Hohwald France
158 G5 Léhon France
159 K5 Le Horps France
177 G3 Lehota Slovakia
163 D8 Le Houga France
173 J3 Lehrberg Ger.
169 K6 Lehre Ger.
169 I6 Lehrte Ger.
170 D4 Lehsen Ger.
140 Q5 Lehtimäki Fin.
240 □A11 Lehua i. HI U.S.A.
212 D4 Lehututu Botswana
192 B7 Lei Sardegna Italy
123 N6 Leiah Pak.
198 D4 Leianokladi Greece
172 G5 Leibertingen Ger.
173 M4 Leiblfing Ger.
179 M6 Leibnitz Austria
108 D4 Leibo Sichuan China
171 I6 Leibsch Ger.
151 J2 Leicester Leicester, England U.K.
151 J2 Leicester admin. div. England U.K.
151 K2 Leicestershire admin. div. England U.K.
84 G4 Leichhardt r. Qld Austr.
84 G5 Leichhardt Falls Qld Austr.
85 K6 Leichhardt Range mts Qld Austr.
169 D8 Leichlingen (Rheinland) Ger.
164 G4 Leiden Neth.
164 G4 Leiderdorp Neth.
164 F4 Leidschendam Neth.
165 E6 Leie r. Belgium
138 J3 Leie Estonia
169 J6 Leiferde Ger.
82 G3 Leigh watercourse S.A. Austr.
80 I3 Leigh North I. N.Z.
149 L7 Leigh Greater Manchester, England U.K.
150 H3 Leigh Worcestershire, England U.K.
82 G4 Leigh Creek S.A. Austr.
147 I7 Leighlinbridge Ireland
151 K4 Leighton Buzzard Bedfordshire, England U.K.
141 I6 Leikanger Norway
96 C5 Leiktho Myanmar
172 F3 Leimen Ger.
164 G4 Leimuiden Neth.
173 K3 Leinburg Ger.
169 I5 Leine r. Ger.
169 J8 Leinefelde Ger.
172 G4 Leinfelden-Echterdingen Ger.
190 D5 Leinì Italy
87 F10 Leinster W.A. Austr.
147 I6 Leinster reg. Ireland
147 I7 Leinster, Mount hill Ireland
172 H4 Leinzell Ger.
183 O2 Leioa Spain
138 G7 Leipalingis Lith.
173 I5 Leipheim Ger.
140 P3 Leipojärvi Sweden
234 D6 Leipsic DE U.S.A.
232 B7 Leipsic OH U.S.A.
234 E6 Leipsic r. DE U.S.A.
199 H5 Leipsoi i. Greece
171 F8 Leipzig Ger.
171 G8 Leipzig admin. reg. Ger.
171 F8 Leipzig-Halle airport Ger.
140 J5 Leira Møre og Romsdal Norway
141 J6 Leira Oppland Norway
182 D4 Leirado Spain
140 M3 Leiranger Norway
160 C6 Leiranoux mt. France
140 Q1 Leirbotn Norway
182 C9 Leiria Port.
182 C9 Leiria admin. dist. Port.
182 D4 Leiro Spain
182 C8 Leirosa Port.
142 B2 Leirvik Norway
178 G6 Leisach Austria
179 N2 Leiser Berge park Austria
108 G5 Leishan Guizhou China
109 I5 Lei Shui r. China
138 F3 Leisi Estonia
84 B7 Leisler, Mount hill N.T. Austr.
82 C3 Leisler Hills S.A. Austr.
171 G8 Leisnig Ger.
151 P3 Leiston Suffolk, England U.K.
182 H3 Leitariegos, Puerto de pass Spain
230 D7 Leitchfield KY U.S.A.
149 K2 Leith Edinburgh, Scotland U.K.
179 O4 Leithagebirge hills Austria
81 G10 Leithfield South I. N.Z.
151 L5 Leith Hill England U.K.
147 F4 Leitrim county Ireland
186 B1 Leitza Spain
173 L6 Leitzach r. Ger.
171 E6 Leitzkau Ger.
141 S6 Leivonmäki Fin.
172 B2 Leiwen Ger.
147 J6 Leixlip Ireland
Leiyang Anhui China see Wangjiang
109 I5 Leiyang Hunan China
108 H8 Leizhou Guangdong China
108 G8 Leizhou Bandao pen. China
108 H8 Leizhou Wan b. China
143 K1 Lejberget hill Sweden
164 G5 Lek r. Neth.
140 K4 Leka Norway
140 K4 Leka i. Norway
208 B5 Lékana Congo
177 L3 Lekárovce Slovakia
208 D5 Lekatero Dem. Rep. Congo
175 H6 Łękawica Pol.
205 H1 Le Kef Tunisia
189 B8 Le Kef admin. div. Tunisia
183 P2 Lekeitio Spain
208 B5 Lékéti r. Congo
215 K9 Lekfontein S. Africa
Lekhainá Greece see Lechaina
206 C2 Lekhcheb Maur.
139 N6 Lekhovo Rus. Fed.
208 B5 Lékila Gabon
93 D4 Lekitobi Maluku Indon.
214 B5 Lekkersing S. Africa
174 C4 Łęknica Pol.
206 C3 Léko Mali
140 L2 Lekoes Norway
207 I6 Lékoli-Pandaka, Réserve de Faune de la nature res. Congo
208 B5 Lékoni Gabon
209 B5 Lékoumou admin. reg. Congo
174 D2 Lekowo Pol.
143 L1 Leksand Sweden
Lek'suiri Georgia see Lentekhi
93 E5 Leksula Buru Indon.
Leksura Georgia see Lentekhi
140 K5 Leksvik Norway
186 B1 Lekunberri Spain
93 F3 Lelai, Tanjung pt Halmahera Indon.
247 □3 Le Lamentin Martinique
140 L3 Leland Norway
226 F8 Leland IL U.S.A.
226 I4 Leland MI U.S.A.
237 J9 Leland MS U.S.A.
142 I2 Lelång l. Sweden
162 C3 Le Langon France
162 G5 Le Lardin-St-Lazare France
161 I8 Le Lauzet-Ubaye France
161 I10 Le Lavandou France
259 C6 Leleque Arg.
177 L3 Leles Slovakia
177 L6 Lelese Romania
136 H2 Leleta Ukr.
163 C8 Le Leuy France
Leli Guangxi China see Tianlin
78 □6 Leli i. Solomon Is
175 H3 Lelice Pol.
188 G4 Lelija mt. Bos.-Herz.
107 O8 Leling Shandong China
93 G5 Lelinta Papua Indon.
159 J6 Le Lion-d'Angers France
175 J2 Lelis Pol.
175 I1 Lelkowo Pol.
190 B1 Le Locle Switz.
93 C8 Lelogama Timor Indon.
158 I7 Le Loroux-Bottereau France
247 □3 Le Lorrain Martinique
206 B4 Lélouma Guinea
159 J6 Le Louroux-Béconnais France
175 H5 Lelów Pol.
161 I10 Le Luc France
159 L6 Le Lude France
161 B6 Le Luguet mt. France
251 H3 Lelydorp Suriname
164 H3 Lelystad Neth.
259 D9 Le Maire, Estrecho de sea chan. Arg.
161 C7 Le Malzieu-Ville France
190 A3 Léman, Lac l. France/Switz.
159 L5 Le Mans France
247 □3 Le Marin Martinique
157 N8 Le Markstein France
236 G4 Le Mars IA U.S.A.
161 E8 Le Martinet France
163 E7 Le Mas-d'Agenais France
163 G9 Le Mas-d'Azil France
210 D3 Lema Shilindi Eth.
163 J8 Le Masnau-Massuguiès France
161 C8 Le Massegros France
160 D4 Le Mayet-de-Montagne France
262 T2 LeMay Range mts Antarctica
159 J7 Le May-sur-Èvre France
179 I2 Lembach im Mühlkreis Austria
211 C6 Lembai well Tanz.
95 L9 Lembar Lombok Indon.
93 D3 Lembeh i. Indon.
165 E6 Lembeke Belgium
157 N5 Lemberg France
172 D3 Lemberg Ger.
172 F5 Lemberg mt. Ger.
Lemberg Ukr. see L'viv
163 D9 Lembeye France
163 G7 Lemboulas r. France
163 F6 Lembras France
168 F5 Lembruch Ger.
95 L3 Lembu Kalimantan Indon.
94 B2 Lembu, Gunung mt. Indon.
95 L2 Lembubut Kalimantan Indon.
Lemdiyya Alg. see Médéa
256 D5 Leme Brazil
164 J4 Lemele Neth.
164 J4 Lemelerveld Neth.
159 L4 Le Mêle-sur-Sarthe France
210 E3 Lemem Bar YeWha Gudgwad well Eth.
159 L4 Le Merlerault France
161 G7 Le Merlu Rocher mt. France
177 K3 Lemešany Slovakia
139 O6 Lemeshi Rus. Fed.
137 K1 Lemeshivka Ukr.
156 H6 Le Mesnil-sur-Oger France
128 B4 Lemesos Cyprus
169 F6 Lemförde Ger.
169 G6 Lemgo Ger.
238 H4 Lemhi r. ID U.S.A.
238 H4 Lemhi Range mts ID U.S.A.
141 S6 Lemi Fin.
174 C3 Lemierzyce Pol.
221 L3 Lemieux Islands Nunavut Can.
141 P6 Lemland Åland Fin.
140 R2 Lemmenjoen kansallispuisto nat. park Fin.
164 I3 Lemmer Neth.
236 D3 Lemmon SD U.S.A.
241 V9 Lemmon, Mount AZ U.S.A.
Lemnos i. Greece see Limnos
214 E9 Lemoenshoek S. Africa
159 J3 Le Molay-Littry France
160 I4 Le Môle mt. France
190 C2 Le Moleson mt. Switz.
246 G4 Le Môle St-Nicolas Haiti
161 C7 Le Monastier France
161 D7 Le Monastier-sur-Gazeille France
240 M5 Lemoncove CA U.S.A.
161 J7 Le Monêtier-les-Bains France
240 O9 Lemon Grove CA U.S.A.
226 F8 Lemont IL U.S.A.
78 □5 Le Mont-Dore New Caledonia
160 C4 Le Montet France
158 H4 Le Mont-St-Michel tourist site France
240 M5 Lemoore CA U.S.A.
217 □1b Le Morne Brabant pen. Mauritius
247 □3 Le Morne-Rouge Martinique
78 □4a Lemotol Bay Chuuk Micronesia
247 □2 Le Moule Guadeloupe
161 D7 Le Moure de la Gardille mt. France
161 I7 Le Mourre Froid mt. France
225 G1 Le Moyne, Lac l. Que. Can.
141 Q6 Lempäälä Fin.
160 C5 Lempdes Auvergne France
161 C6 Lempdes Auvergne France
96 A4 Lemro r. Myanmar
134 L3 Lemtybozh Rus. Fed.
95 H4 Lemukutan i. Indon.
193 Q5 Le Murge hills Italy
161 J10 Le Muy France
134 M2 Lemva r. Rus. Fed.
142 E5 Lemvig Denmark
168 G4 Lemwerder Ger.
147 G8 Lemybrien Ireland
96 B6 Lemyethna Myanmar
134 L3 Lem'yu r. Rus. Fed.
142 G1 Lena Norway
182 C9 Lena r. Port.
131 N3 Lena r. Rus. Fed.
226 E7 Lena IL U.S.A.
226 F5 Lena WI U.S.A.
147 D4 Lenadoon Point Ireland
78 □5 Lénakel Vanuatu
95 L9 Lenangguar Sumbawa Indon.
179 M6 Lenart Slovenia
138 E5 Lēnas Latvia
177 J6 Lenauheim Romania
162 E2 Lencloître France
254 E2 Lençóis Maranhenses, Parque Nacional dos nat. park Brazil
256 C5 Lençóis Paulista Brazil
163 D7 Lencouacq France
178 H5 Lend Austria
208 F4 Lenda r. Dem. Rep. Congo
177 J2 Lendak Slovakia
188 F2 Lendava Slovenia
122 D6 Lendeh Iran
165 D7 Lendelede Belgium
134 E3 Lendery Rus. Fed.
191 L5 Lendinara Italy
179 H6 Lendorf Austria
148 C6 Lene, Lough l. Ireland
176 C1 Lenešice Czech Rep.
159 M3 Le Neubourg France
178 H3 Lengau Oberösterreich Austria
178 G5 Lengau Salzburg Austria
122 H7 Lengbarūt Iran
173 M5 Lengdorf Ger.
169 J6 Lengede Ger.
171 H9 Lengefeld Ger.
171 F9 Lengenfeld Ger.
169 J8 Lengenfeld unterm Stein Ger.
173 J6 Lengenwang Ger.
121 M6 Lenger Kazakh.
168 E5 Lengerich Niedersachsen Ger.
169 E6 Lengerich Nordrhein-Westfalen Ger.
173 L6 Lenggries Ger.
110 K7 Lenghuzhen Qinghai China
106 G7 Lenglong Ling mts China
190 C1 Lengnau Switz.
208 C5 Lengoué r. Congo
109 H5 Lengshuijiang Hunan China
109 H5 Lengshuitan Hunan China
260 B2 Lengua de Vaca, Punta pt Chile
211 B8 Lengwe National Park Malawi
177 G5 Lengyeltóti Hungary
151 N5 Lenham Kent, England U.K.
234 D3 Lenhartsville PA U.S.A.
143 L5 Lenhovda Sweden
192 B9 Leni r. Italy
129 H5 Lenin Azer.
Lenīn Kazakh. see Kazygurt
123 M2 Lenin Tajik.
Lenin, Qullai mt. Kyrg./Tajik. see Lenin Peak
129 F2 Lenina, Kanal canal Rus. Fed.
Lenina, Pik mt. Kyrg./Tajik. see Lenin Peak
Leninabad Tajik. see Khŭjand
Leninabad Oblast admin. div. Tajik. see Soghd
Leninakan Armenia see Gyumri
Lenin Atyndagy Choku mt. Kyrg./Tajik. see Lenin Peak
137 L6 Lenine Mykolayivs'ka Oblast' Ukr.
137 O8 Lenine Respublika Krym Ukr.
157 M6 Léning France
Leningori Georgia see Akhalgori
Leningrad Rus. Fed. see Sankt-Peterburg
123 N2 Leningrad Tajik.
Leningrad Oblast admin. div. Rus. Fed. see Leningradskaya Oblast'
135 G7 Leningradskaya Rus. Fed.
139 P2 Leningradskaya Oblast' admin. div. Rus. Fed.
131 S3 Leningradskiy Rus. Fed.
Leningradskiy Tajik. see Leningrad
137 K2 Leninivka Ukr.
129 I3 Leninkent Rus. Fed.
100 I6 Lenino Rus. Fed.
Lenino Ukr. see Lenine
Leninobod Tajik. see Khŭjand
Leninobod Uzbek. see Qanliko'l
Lenīnogor Kazakh. see Leninogorsk
121 T2 Leninogorsk Kazakh.
135 K5 Leninogorsk Rus. Fed.
121 O8 Lenin Peak Kyrg./Tajik.
121 N6 Leninpol' Kyrg.
Leninsk Kazakh. see Baykonyr
135 I6 Leninsk Rus. Fed.
Leninsk Turkm. see Akdepe
Leninsk Uzbek. see Asaka
137 N6 Lenins'ke Dnipropetrovs'ka Oblast' Ukr.
137 N8 Lenins'ke Respublika Krym Ukr.
137 O8 Lenins'ke Respublika Krym Ukr.
120 G3 Leninskiy Kazakh.
139 U7 Leninskiy Rus. Fed.
130 J4 Leninsk-Kuznetskiy Rus. Fed.
Leninskoye Yuzhnyy Kazakhstan Kazakh. see Kazygurt
120 C3 Leninskoye Zapadnyy Kazakhstan Kazakh.
134 I4 Leninskoye Kirovskaya Oblast' Rus. Fed.
100 H5 Leninskoye Yevreyskaya Avtonomnaya Oblast' Rus. Fed.
163 D7 Le Nizan France
190 C3 Lenk Switz.
136 G4 Lenkivtsi Ukr.
Lenkoran' Azer. see Länkäran
86 H4 Lennard r. W.A. Austr.
169 I7 Lenne Ger.
169 D8 Lenne r. Ger.
169 F8 Lennestadt Ger.
172 G4 Lenningen Ger.
259 D9 Lennox, Isla i. Chile
263 L1 Lennox-King Glacier Antarctica
146 H11 Lennoxtown East Dunbartonshire, Scotland U.K.
190 I5 Leno Italy
231 G8 Lenoir NC U.S.A.
231 E8 Lenoir City TN U.S.A.
190 B1 Le Noirmont Switz.
193 K5 Lenola Italy
232 C11 Lenore WV U.S.A.
223 J4 Lenore Lake Sask. Can.
156 G3 Le Nouvion-en-Thiérache France
233 L6 Lenox MA U.S.A.
165 E7 Lens Belgium
156 E3 Lens France
168 K2 Lensahn Ger.
131 M3 Lensk Rus. Fed.
160 G4 Lent France
164 I5 Lent Neth.
129 D3 Lentekhi Georgia
168 I3 Lentföhrden Ger.
176 F5 Lenti Hungary
191 M3 Lentiai Italy
173 K4 Lenting Ger.
195 I9 Lentini Sicilia Italy
195 I9 Lentini r. Sicilia Italy
140 T4 Lentua l. Fin.
Lentvaravas Lith. see Lentvaris
138 I7 Lentvaris Lith.
139 T3 Lent'yevo Rus. Fed.
240 O7 Lenwood CA U.S.A.
97 D9 Lenya Myanmar
190 E1 Lenzburg Switz.
170 D4 Lenzen Ger.
179 I4 Lenzing Austria
172 E6 Lenzkirch Ger.
206 E4 Léo Burkina
191 J7 Leo r. Italy
179 I6 Leoben Kärnten Austria
179 L5 Leoben Steiermark Austria
179 N3 Leobendorf Austria
179 N4 Leobersdorf Austria
Leodhais, Eilean i. Scotland U.K. see Lewis, Isle of
246 G4 Léogane Haiti
178 G5 Leogang Austria
178 G5 Leoganger Steinberge mts Austria
163 C6 Léognan France
93 B3 Leok Sulawesi Indon.
236 F3 Leola SD U.S.A.
150 G3 Leominster Herefordshire, England U.K.
233 N6 Leominster MA U.S.A.
163 B8 Léon France
244 F4 León Mex.
242 □P11 León Nic.
182 I3 León Spain
182 I3 León prov. Spain
236 I5 Leon IA U.S.A.
237 G10 Leon r. TX U.S.A.
163 B8 Léon, Étang de l. France
184 G8 León, Isla de i. Spain
182 G4 León, Montes de mts Spain
237 G9 Leonard TX U.S.A.
193 I4 Leonardo da Vinci airport Italy
232 I10 Leonardtown MD U.S.A.
212 C4 Leonardville Namibia
Leonarisso Cyprus see Leonarisson
128 C3 Leonarisson Cyprus
243 P7 Leona Vicario Mex.
172 G4 Leonberg Ger.
161 G7 Léoncel France
Leondárion Greece see Leontari
179 J3 Leonding Austria
78 □2 Leone American Samoa
190 E3 Leone, Monte mt. Italy/Switz.
261 F3 Leones Arg.
193 J2 Leonessa Italy
194 G8 Leonforte Sicilia Italy
83 J8 Leongatha Vic. Austr.
192 G2 Leoni, Monte hill Italy
198 D5 Leonidio Greece
100 M4 Leonidovo Sakhalin Rus. Fed.
87 F10 Leonora W.A. Austr.
198 D3 Leontari Greece
117 M6 Leopani Bhutan
86 I5 Leopold r. W.A. Austr.
232 E9 Leopold WV U.S.A.
86 H5 Leopold Downs W.A. Austr.
86 H4 Leopold Downs Aboriginal Reserve W.A. Austr.
Léopold II, Lac l. Dem. Rep. Congo see Mai-Ndombe, Lac
257 F4 Leopoldina Brazil
256 C2 Leopoldo de Bulhões Brazil
165 H6 Leopoldsburg Belgium
179 O3 Leopoldsdorf im Marchfelde Austria
170 I3 Leopoldshagen Ger.
169 G6 Leopoldshöhe Ger.
172 D5 Leopoldskanal canal Ger.
Léopoldville Dem. Rep. Congo see Kinshasa
236 E6 Leoti KS U.S.A.
136 H7 Leova Moldova
223 J4 Leoville Sask. Can.
Leovo Moldova see Leova
158 E7 Le Palais France
162 G4 Le Palais-sur-Vienne France
158 I7 Le Pallet France
94 G6 Lepar i. Indon.
156 D3 Le Parcq France
163 F7 Le Passage France
156 G7 Le Pavillon-Ste-Julie France
260 B3 Lepe Chile
184 E6 Lepe Spain
161 F6 Le Péage-de-Roussillon France
162 H2 Le Pêchereau France
Lepel' Belarus see Lyepyel'
158 H7 Le Pellerin France
198 C4 Lepenou Greece
161 H7 Le Périer France
163 J11 Le Perthus France
159 I5 Le Pertre France
156 B5 Le Petit-Quevilly France
213 E4 Lephalale S. Africa
212 E4 Lephepe Botswana
215 J6 Lephoi S. Africa
162 C6 Le Pian-Médoc France
159 L4 Le Pin-au-Haras France
156 H6 L'Épine Champagne-Ardenne France
161 H8 L'Épine Provence-Alpes-Côte d'Azur France
109 K4 Leping Jiangxi China
159 M5 Le Pin-la-Garenne France
217 □1c Le Piton Réunion
162 E5 Le Pizou France
163 G9 Le Plan France
156 E5 Le Plessis-Belleville France
134 M3 Lep'lya r. Rus. Fed.
161 H8 Le Poët France
188 F2 Lepoglava Croatia
159 O8 Le Poinçonnet France
158 H8 Le Poiré-sur-Vie France
160 H5 Le Pont-de-Beauvoisin France
161 H6 Le Pont-de-Claix France
161 D8 Le Pont-de-Monvert France
161 F9 Le Pontet France
190 E3 Lepontine, Alpi mts Italy/Switz.
195 M3 Leporano Italy
163 B6 Le Porge France
163 B6 Le Porge-Océan France
217 □1c Le Port Réunion
156 C2 Le Portel France
196 I7 Leposavić Kosovo Serbia
217 □1b Le Pouce hill Mauritius
161 D9 Le Pouget France
158 D6 Le Pouldu France
158 G7 Le Pouliguen France
161 F7 Le Pouzin France
140 R5 Leppävesi Fin.
140 S5 Leppävirta Fin.
161 I10 Le Pradet France
225 H4 Lepreau, Point N.B. Can.
247 □3 Le Prêcheur Martinique
Lepsa Kazakh. see Lepsy
Lepsa r. Kazakh. see Lepsy
177 H4 Lepsény Hungary
Lepsi Kazakh. see Lepsinsk
121 S5 Lepsinsk Kazakh.
121 R4 Lepsy Kazakh.
121 R4 Lepsy r. Kazakh.
202 B1 Leptis Magna tourist site Libya
198 D2 Leptokarya Greece
156 C7 Le Puiset France
161 D6 Le Puy-en-Velay France
159 K7 Le Puy-Notre-Dame France
161 G9 Le Puy-Ste-Réparade France
206 B2 Leqceïba Maur.
156 G3 Le Quesnoy France
206 D4 Léraba r. Burkina/Côte d'Ivoire
156 E6 Le Raincy France
213 E4 Lerala Botswana
163 H10 Léran France
215 L4 Leratswana S. Africa
194 F8 Lercara Friddi Sicilia Italy
83 J7 Lerderderg State Park nature res. Vic. Austr.
245 L7 Lerdo Mex.
208 B2 Léré Chad
160 B2 Léré France
206 D3 Léré Mali
207 H4 Lere Nigeria
93 A4 Lereh, Tanjung pt Indon.
158 C5 Le Relecq-Kerhuon France
182 C4 Lérez r. Spain
158 H5 Le Rheu France
190 H7 Lerici Italy
250 D5 Lérida Col.
Lérida Spain see Lleida
Lérida prov. Cataluña Spain see Lleida
129 J7 Lerik Azer.
183 Q4 Lerín Spain
161 K9 Lérins, Îles de is France
243 N8 Lerma Mex.
244 E5 Lerma r. Mex.
183 M4 Lerma Spain
245 H6 Lerma de Vilada Mex.
163 D7 Lerm-et Musset France
129 D1 Lermontov Rus. Fed.
100 I5 Lermontovka Rus. Fed.
Lermontovskiy Rus. Fed. see Lermontov
178 C5 Lermoos Austria
192 C6 Lerno, Monte mt. Italy
247 □3 Le Robert Martinique
160 J5 Le Roignais mt. France
199 H5 Leros i. Greece
163 I6 Le Rouget France
157 K6 Lérouville France
226 F9 Le Roy IL U.S.A.
226 B6 Le Roy MN U.S.A.
232 H6 Le Roy NY U.S.A.
234 B1 Leroy PA U.S.A.
224 F1 Le Roy, Lac l. Que. Can.
161 C8 Le Rozier France
157 L7 Lerrain France
190 E7 Lerrone r. Italy
142 I4 Lerum Sweden
160 J2 Le Russey France
146 □N2 Lerwick Shetland, Scotland U.K.
208 E2 Ler Zerai well Sudan
163 F10 Lés Spain
190 F4 Lesa Italy
160 H5 Les Abrets France
247 □2 Les Abymes Guadeloupe
178 G6 Lesachtal val. Austria
161 J9 Les Adrets-de-l'Estérel France
186 J4 Les Agudes mt. Spain
160 B2 Les Aix-d'Angillon France
186 B1 Lesaka Spain
163 J11 Les Albères reg. France
160 B5 Les Ancizes-Comps France
156 B5 Les Andelys France
161 F9 Les Angles Languedoc-Roussillon France
163 I10 Les Angles Languedoc-Roussillon France
247 □3 Les Anses-d'Arlets Martinique
159 L4 Le Sap France
161 I10 Les Arcs Provence-Alpes-Côte d'Azur France
160 J5 Les Arcs Rhône-Alpes France
159 J8 Les Aubiers France
161 J8 Le Sauze-Super-Sauze France
186 G4 Les Avellanes Spain
160 H5 Les Avenières France
217 □1c Les Avirons Réunion
161 D8 Les Bondons France
156 D8 Les Bordes France
163 G9 Les Bordes-sur-Arize France
186 G4 Les Borges Blanques Spain
186 H5 Les Borges del Camp Spain
Lesbos i. Greece see Lesvos
160 H4 Les Bouchoux France
190 B1 Les Brenets Switz.
149 N3 Lesbury Northumberland, England U.K.
163 H10 Les Cabannes France
186 L3 L'Escala Spain
161 I8 L'Escale France
217 □1b L'Escalier Mauritius
163 I9 Les Cammazes France
163 D9 Lescar France
161 K9 L'Escarène France
160 J4 Les Carroz-d'Arâches France
186 G6 Les Cases d'Alcanar Spain
246 G4 Les Cayes Haiti
179 J7 Lesce Slovenia
159 K5 Les Coëvrons hills France
158 C6 Lesconil France
160 J5 Les Contamines-Montjoie France
160 J4 Les Cornettes de Bise mts France/Switz.
187 F7 Les Coves de Vinromà Spain
163 I8 Lescure-d'Albigeois France
161 I6 Les Deux-Alpes France
190 C3 Les Diablerets Switz.
190 C3 Les Diablerets mts Switz.
208 D4 Lese r. Dem. Rep. Congo
195 L5 Lese r. Italy
161 H6 Les Échelles France
158 H3 Les Écréhou is Channel Is
162 D5 Les Églisottes-et-Chalaures France
161 J8 Le Seignus-d'Allos France
158 H6 Le Sel-de-Bretagne France
163 C7 Le Sen France
176 G5 Lesencetomaj Hungary
190 A2 Le Sentier Switz.
157 K5 Les Éparges France
159 J8 Les Epesses France
186 I2 Les Escaldes Andorra
225 G3 Les Escoumins Que. Can.
160 G3 Les Essards-Taignevaux France
158 I8 Les Essarts France
233 □Q1 Les Étroits Que. Can.
186 H3 La Seu d'Urgell Spain
163 G6 Les Eyzies-de-Tayac-Sireuil France
160 J2 Les Fins France
157 L7 Les Forges France
160 I3 Les Fourgs France
160 J4 Les Gets France
108 D4 Leshan Sichuan China
157 I4 Les Hautes-Rivières France
137 P2 Leshchinka r. Rus. Fed.
162 B2 Les Herbiers France
Leshou Hebei China see Xianxian
160 J5 Les Houches France
134 I2 Leshukonskoye Rus. Fed.
129 D3 Lesichine Georgia
179 M7 Lesično Slovenia
156 E6 Lésigny France
190 G6 Lesima, Monte mt. Italy
193 O4 Lesina Italy
193 O4 Lesina, Lago di lag. Italy
161 J10 Les Issambres France
141 J5 Lesja Norway
143 K2 Lesjöfors Sweden
163 G6 Les Junies France
161 I6 Les Karellis France
129 E2 Lesken Rus. Fed.
Leskhimstroy Ukr. see Syeverodonets'k
175 K6 Lesko Pol.
197 J8 Leskovac Serbia
198 B2 Leskovik Albania
263 F2 Leskov Island Antarctica
137 L4 Les'ky Ukr.
159 I8 Les Landes-Genusson France
162 E5 Les Lèches France
161 H10 Les Lecques France
146 J10 Leslie Fife, Scotland U.K.
226 J7 Leslie MI U.S.A.
158 I8 Les Lucs-sur-Boulogne France
146 I11 Lesmahagow South Lanarkshire, Scotland U.K.

Les Maillys to Linosa, Isola di

342

160 G2 Les Maillys France
247 □2 Les Mangles Guadeloupe
160 I6 Les Marches France
160 C5 Les Martres-de-Veyre France
161 D9 Les Matelles France
159 J7 Les Mauges reg. France
156 I4 Les Mazures France
225 H3 Les Méchins Que. Can.
186 L3 Les Medes is Spain
161 H8 Les Mées France
161 J6 Les Menuires France
158 G4 Les Minquiers is Channel Is
161 I8 Les Monges mt. France
156 H7 Lesmont France
156 C6 Les Mureaux France
177 G2 Lešná Czech Rep.
174 D4 Leśna Pol.
175 L3 Leśna r. Pol.
158 C4 Lesneven France
174 G5 Leśnica Pol.
174 D4 Leśniów Wielki Pol.
156 H7 Les Noës-près-Troyes France
134 K4 Lesnoy Kirovskaya Oblast' Rus. Fed.
Lesnoy Murmanskaya Oblast' Rus. Fed. see Umba
139 X7 Lesnoy Ryazanskaya Oblast' Rus. Fed.
139 O6 Lesnoy Smolenskaya Oblast' Rus. Fed.
138 L1 Lesnoy, Ostrov i. Rus. Fed.
139 S3 Lesnoye Rus. Fed.
134 K4 Lesnyye Polyany Rus. Fed.
100 M4 Lesogorsk Sakhalin Rus. Fed.
138 L1 Lesogorskiy Rus. Fed.
161 F7 Les Ollières-sur-Eyrieux France
100 I5 Lesopil'noye Rus. Fed.
161 J7 Les Orres France
131 K4 Lesosibirsk Rus. Fed.
215 M5 Lesotho country Africa
215 M5 Lesotho Highlands Water Project Lesotho
100 H6 Lesozavodsk Rus. Fed.
162 C5 Lesparre-Médoc France
162 D5 Les Peintures France
161 G10 Les Pennes-Mirabeau France
217 □2b L'Espérance Mahé Seychelles
77 I5 L'Espérance Rock i. N.Z.
163 B8 Lesperon France
156 H5 Les Petites-Loges France
197 L3 Lespezi hill Romania
158 H2 Les Pieux France
161 C10 Lespignan France
186 F6 L'Espina mt. Spain
163 J9 Lespinassière France
160 I3 Les Planches-en-Montagne France
186 H5 L'Espluga Calba Spain
186 H5 L'Espluga de Francolí Spain
162 C1 Les Ponts-de-Cé France
190 B1 Les Ponts-de-Martel Switz.
186 J3 Les Preses Spain
163 F9 Lespugue France
156 H8 Les Riceys France
159 K7 Les Rosiers-sur-Loire France
160 I4 Les Rousses France
162 A3 Les Sables-d'Olonne France
179 I5 Lessach Austria
161 E8 Les Salles-du-Gardon France
158 H3 Lessay France
165 G8 Lesse r. Belgium
165 H8 Lesse et Lomme, Parc Naturel de nature res. Belgium
158 E4 Les Sept-Îles is France
247 J7 Lesser Antilles is Caribbean Sea
129 D4 Lesser Caucasus mts Asia
116 F4 Lesser Himalaya mts India/Nepal
Lesser Khingan Mountains China see Xiao Hinggan Ling
222 H4 Lesser Slave Lake Alta Can.
222 H4 Lesser Slave Lake Provincial Park Alta Can.
90 E8 Lesser Sunda Islands Indon.
125 L2 Lesser Tunb i. The Gulf
156 G7 Les Sièges France
165 E7 Lessines Belgium
215 K5 Lessingskop mt. S. Africa
191 J4 Lessini, Monti mts Italy
217 □2a Les Sœurs is Inner Islands Seychelles
158 H7 Les Sorinières France
163 D9 Lestelle-Bétharram France
232 D11 Lester WV U.S.A.
161 C6 Les Ternes France
156 C5 Les Thilliers-en-Vexin France
161 J8 Les Thuiles France
140 R5 Lestijärvi Fin.
140 Q4 Lestijoki r. Fin.
161 B8 Lestrade France
158 D4 Les Triagoz is France
217 □1c Les Trois Bassins Réunion
247 □3 Les Trois-Îlets Martinique
159 L7 Les Trois-Moutiers France
208 E3 Les Trois Rivieres C.A.R.
161 B7 Les Trucs d'Aubrac mt. France
177 L5 Leşu, Lacul l. Romania
86 I2 Lesueur Island W.A. Austr.
156 D6 Les Ulis France
95 K4 Lesung, Bukit mt. Indon.
161 E8 Les Vans France
161 C8 Les Vignes France
199 G3 Lesvos i. Greece
174 D2 Leszczyn Pol.
175 K4 Leszkowice Pol.
175 I3 Leszno Mazowieckie Pol.
174 E4 Leszno Wielkopolskie Pol.
174 D4 Leszno Górne Pol.
161 H6 Le Taillefer mt. France
186 E2 Le Taillon mt. Spain
159 K8 Le Tallud France
143 K2 Letälven r. Sweden
217 □1c Le Tampon Réunion
161 E7 Le Tanargue mt. France
177 K4 Létavértes Hungary
151 L4 Letchworth Garden City Hertfordshire, England U.K.
163 B6 Le Teich France
161 F7 Le Teil France
159 J4 Le Teilleul France
160 E2 Le Télégraphe hill France
163 C6 Le Temple France
176 F5 Letenye Hungary
116 F7 Leteri Madh. Prad. India
96 A3 Letha Range mts Myanmar
222 H5 Lethbridge Alta Can.
225 K3 Lethbridge Nfld and Lab. Can.
168 F4 Lethe r. Ger.
159 M5 Le Theil France
158 I6 Le-Theil-de-Bretagne France
251 G4 Lethem Guyana
151 O2 Letheringsett Norfolk, England U.K.
157 M8 Le Thillot France
157 M7 Le Tholy France
161 I10 Le Thoronet France
93 E8 Leti i. Maluku Indon.
93 E8 Leti, Kepulauan is Maluku Indon.
250 D6 Leticia Col.
107 P7 Leting Hebei China
193 M5 Letino Italy
214 G8 Letjiesbos S. Africa
177 H4 Letkés Hungary
215 L1 Letlhabile S. Africa
212 E4 Letlhakane Botswana
212 E5 Letlhakeng Botswana
134 F2 Letnerechenskiy Rus. Fed.
134 G2 Letniy Navolok Rus. Fed.
93 F8 Letoda Maluku Indon.
191 M2 Le Tofane mt. Italy
195 I8 Letoianni Sicilia Italy
179 O1 Letonice Czech Rep.
156 C2 Le Touquet-Paris-Plage France
161 C9 Le Tour d'Arre hill France
161 H6 Le Touvet France
176 F2 Letovice Czech Rep.
96 B6 Letpadan Myanmar
156 B3 Le Tréport France
161 B8 Le Truel France
141 M6 Letsbo Sweden
170 J5 Letschin Ger.
97 D9 Letsok-aw Kyun i. Myanmar
215 J2 Letsopa S. Africa
207 I5 Letta Cameroon
Lette Island Vava'u Gp Tonga see Late
142 I1 Letten l. Sweden
148 B5 Letterbreen Northern Ireland U.K.
147 C6 Lettercallow Ireland
147 C9 Letterfinish Ireland
147 C5 Letterfrack Ireland
147 G3 Letterkenny Ireland
150 C4 Letterston Pembrokeshire, Wales U.K.
94 F3 Letung Indon.
185 O4 Letur Spain
163 C7 Le Tuzan France
93 F7 Letwurung Maluku Indon.
135 H6 Letyazhevka Rus. Fed.
136 G4 Letychiv Ukr.
Lëtzebuerg country Europe see Luxembourg
171 D6 Letzlingen Ger.
197 M6 Leu Romania
209 D7 Léua Angola
171 H8 Leuben Ger.
171 D8 Leubingen Ger.
163 I9 Leuc France
Leucas Lefkada Greece see Lefkada
163 K10 Leucate France
163 K10 Leucate, Cap c. France
163 K10 Leucate, Étang de l. France
146 K10 Leuchars Fife, Scotland U.K.
173 M2 Leuchtenberg Ger.
170 I5 Leuenberg Ger.
157 I8 Leuglay France
190 D3 Leuk Switz.
Leukas Lefkada Greece see Lefkada
190 D3 Leukerbad Switz.
146 D6 Leumrabhagh Western Isles, Scotland U.K.
169 F9 Leun Ger.
109 □J7 Leung Shuen Wan Chau i. H.K. China
134 H2 Leunovo Rus. Fed.
241 V6 Leupp AZ U.S.A.
85 L7 Leura Qld Austr.
164 H4 Leusden Neth.
94 B3 Leuser, Gunung mt. Indon.
178 D5 Leutasch Austria
173 K7 Leutascher Dreitorspitze mt. Ger.
171 D9 Leutenberg Ger.
173 I3 Leutershausen Ger.
169 D10 Leutesdorf Ger.
173 I6 Leutkirch im Allgäu Ger.
179 L6 Leutschach Austria
165 G7 Leuven Belgium
165 E7 Leuze-en-Hainaut Belgium
161 I10 Le Val France
157 L8 Le Val-d'Ajol France
157 J8 Le Vallinot-Longeau-Percey France
158 I4 Le Val-St-Père France
198 A2 Levan Albania
241 U2 Levan UT U.S.A.
140 K5 Levanger Norway
161 I10 Levant, Île du i. France
190 F7 Levante, Riviera di coastal area Italy
190 H7 Levanto Italy
194 C8 Levanzo Sicilia Italy
194 C7 Levanzo, Isola di i. Sicilia Italy
129 I3 Levashi Rus. Fed.
247 □3 Le Vauclin Martinique
137 S2 Levaya Rossosh' Rus. Fed.
176 G4 Levél Hungary
237 D9 Levelland TX U.S.A.
81 F11 Levels South I. N.Z.
149 Q6 Leven East Riding of Yorkshire, England U.K.
146 K10 Leven Fife, Scotland U.K.
146 F9 Leven, Loch inlet Scotland U.K.
146 J10 Leven, Loch l. Scotland U.K.
161 K9 Levens France
149 L5 Levens Cumbria, England U.K.
190 F3 Leventina, Valle val. Switz.
146 □N3 Levenwick Shetland, Scotland U.K.
86 G4 Lévêque, Cape W.A. Austr.
80 □ L'Eveque, Cape Chatham Is S. Pacific Ocean
195 O3 Leverano Italy
146 B7 Leverburgh Western Isles, Scotland U.K.
162 B4 Le-Verdon-sur-Mer France
226 J4 Levering MI U.S.A.
169 C8 Leverkusen Ger.
222 G1 Lever Lake N.W.T. Can.
163 H9 Le Vernet France
Leverville Dem. Rep. Congo see Lusanga
156 B7 Lèves France
159 P8 Levet France
161 B8 Lévézou mts France
177 H3 Levice Slovakia
191 K3 Levico Terme Italy
198 D5 Levidi Greece
192 C4 Levie Corse France
160 I3 Levier France
161 D9 Le Vigan France
163 G8 Lévignac France
163 E6 Lévignac-de-Guyanne France
163 B7 Lévignacq France
191 M9 Le Ville Italy
80 J7 Levin North I. N.Z.
225 G4 Lévis Que. Can.
199 H6 Levitha i. Greece
Levittown NJ U.S.A. see Willingboro
235 H3 Levittown NY U.S.A.
234 F4 Levittown PA U.S.A.
158 H4 Le-Vivier-sur-Mer France
197 O9 Levka Bulg.
Levkás i. Greece see Lefkada
Levkímmi Kerkyra Greece see Lefkimmi
177 J2 Levoča Slovakia
177 J2 Levočské vrchy mts Slovakia
162 H2 Levroux France
197 N7 Levski Bulg.
Levskigrad Bulg. see Karlovo
139 W8 Lev Tolstoy Rus. Fed.
79 □7a Levuka Ovalau Fiji
138 H6 Lėvuo r. Lith.
158 I2 Lévy, Cap c. France
93 A8 Lewa Sumba Indon.
96 C5 Lewe Myanmar
151 M6 Lewes East Sussex, England U.K.
233 J10 Lewes DE U.S.A.
174 F5 Lewin Brzeski Pol.
241 X4 Lewis CO U.S.A.
237 F7 Lewis KS U.S.A.
238 C4 Lewis r. WA U.S.A.
146 C6 Lewis, Isle of i. Scotland U.K.
84 D7 Lewis, Lake salt flat N.T. Austr.
234 B4 Lewisberry PA U.S.A.
232 A9 Lewisburg OH U.S.A.
227 R9 Lewisburg PA U.S.A.
231 D8 Lewisburg TN U.S.A.
232 E11 Lewisburg WV U.S.A.
222 D3 Lewis Cass, Mount Can./U.S.A.
225 J3 Lewis Hills Nfld and Lab. Can.
115 M6 Lewis Inlet Andaman & Nicobar Is India
81 G9 Lewis Pass South I. N.Z.
81 G9 Lewis Pass National Reserve nature res. South I. N.Z.
225 K3 Lewisporte Nfld and Lab. Can.
86 J6 Lewis Range hills W.A. Austr.
238 G2 Lewis Range mts MT U.S.A.
231 D8 Lewis Smith, Lake AL U.S.A.
238 F3 Lewiston ID U.S.A.
233 □O4 Lewiston ME U.S.A.
227 J5 Lewiston MI U.S.A.
226 C6 Lewiston MN U.S.A.
232 F5 Lewiston NY U.S.A.
226 D9 Lewistown IL U.S.A.
226 C9 Lewistown MO U.S.A.
238 J3 Lewistown MT U.S.A.
232 H8 Lewistown PA U.S.A.
237 I9 Lewisville AR U.S.A.
232 D9 Lewisville OH U.S.A.
170 E4 Lewitz park Ger.
93 C8 Lewoleba Indon.
93 C8 Lewotobi, Gunung vol. Flores Indon.
231 F9 Lexington GA U.S.A.
226 F9 Lexington IL U.S.A.
230 E6 Lexington KY U.S.A.
227 L6 Lexington MI U.S.A.
236 I6 Lexington MO U.S.A.
237 J9 Lexington MS U.S.A.
231 G8 Lexington NC U.S.A.
236 F5 Lexington NE U.S.A.
232 C8 Lexington OH U.S.A.
231 G9 Lexington SC U.S.A.
237 K8 Lexington TN U.S.A.
232 F11 Lexington VA U.S.A.
232 I10 Lexington Park MD U.S.A.
149 N5 Leyburn North Yorkshire, England U.K.
Leyden Neth. see Leiden
108 F6 Leye Guangxi China
122 B3 Leyla Dāgh mt. Iran
149 L6 Leyland Lancashire, England U.K.
163 H6 Leyme France
151 N5 Leysdown-on-Sea Kent, England U.K.
190 C3 Leysin Switz.
92 E6 Leyte i. Phil.
92 E6 Leyte Gulf Phil.
190 C3 Leytron Switz.
163 G10 Lez r. France
183 P4 Leza r. Spain
175 K5 Leżajsk Pol.
250 E2 Lezama Venez.
161 E8 Lézan France
158 E4 Lézardrieux France
163 G9 Lézat-sur-Lèze France
162 D3 Lezay France
163 G9 Lèze r. France
196 H9 Lezhë Albania
108 E3 Lezhi Sichuan China
139 X5 Lezhnevo Rus. Fed.
161 B10 Lézignan-Corbières France
175 H2 Leźno Pol.
160 C5 Lezoux France
185 O3 Lezuza Spain
185 O2 Lezuza r. Spain
175 H4 Lgota Wielka Pol.
135 F6 L'gov Rus. Fed.
111 H12 Lhagoi Kangri mt. Xizang China
146 J7 Lhanbryde Moray, Scotland U.K.
Lhari Xizang China see Si'erdingka
111 K11 Lhari Xizang China
87 B8 Lharidon Bight b. W.A. Austr.
111 J10 Lharigarbo Xizang China
111 J12 Lhasa Xizang China
111 J12 Lhasa He r. China
111 K12 Lhasoi Xizang China
108 A3 Lhatog Xizang China
156 D6 L'Hay-les-Roses France
111 H12 Lhazê Xizang China
111 L11 Lhazê Xizang China
179 J1 Lhenice Czech Rep.
163 G9 Lherm France
162 C2 L'Hermenault France
158 H5 L'Hermitage France
113 □1 Lhohifushi i. N. Male Maldives
94 A2 Lhokkruet Sumatera Indon.
94 B2 Lhokseumawe Sumatera Indon.
94 B2 Lhoksukon Sumatera Indon.
111 J11 Lhomar Xizang China
163 G7 L'Honor-de-Cos France
111 L11 Lhorong Xizang China
163 G7 L'Hospitalet France
186 G6 L'Hospitalet de l'Infant Spain
186 J5 L'Hospitalet de Llobregat Spain
161 C9 L'Hospitalet-du-Larzac France
163 H10 L'Hospitalet-près-l'Andorre France
186 G6 L'Hostal del Alls Spain
162 B3 L'Houmeau France
137 N8 L'hovs'ke Ukr.
111 J12 Lhozhag Xizang China
160 H5 Lhuis France
159 J5 L'Huisserie France
156 H6 Lhuître France
117 M6 Lhuntshi Bhutan
Lhünzê Xizang China see Xingba
111 K12 Lhünzê Xizang China
96 D5 Li, Mae r. Thai.
199 H6 Liadi i. Greece
129 F3 Liakhvis Nakrdzali nature res. Georgia
198 D4 Liakoura mt. Greece
192 B3 Liamone r. Corse France
247 □2 Liamuiga, Mount vol. St Kitts and Nevis
109 K6 Liancheng Fujian China
Liancheng Guizhou China see Qinglong
Liancheng Yunnan China see Guangnan
156 D5 Liancourt France
101 G10 Liancourt Rocks i. N. Pacific Ocean
156 C2 Liane r. France
Lianfeng Fujian China see Liancheng
93 C4 Liang Sulawesi Indon.
92 F7 Lianga Mindanao Phil.
92 F7 Lianga Bay Mindanao Phil.
107 M6 Liangcheng Nei Mongol China
108 F2 Liangdang Gansu China
111 J11 Liangdaohe Xizang China
108 H6 Liangfeng Guangxi China
108 G4 Lianghe Chongqing China
108 B6 Lianghe Yunnan China
Lianghekou Chongqing China see Lianghe
108 E2 Lianghekou Gansu China
108 D3 Lianghekou Sichuan China
Liangjiayoufang Shanxi China see Youyu
108 F3 Liangping Chongqing China
95 K4 Liangpran, Bukit mt. Indon.
Liangshan Chongqing China see Liangping
96 D2 Liang Shan mt. Myanmar
Liangshi Hunan China see Shaodong
108 H8 Liangtian Guangxi China
94 D3 Liang Timur, Gunung mt. Malaysia
108 D6 Liangwang Shan mts Yunnan China
107 K8 Liangzhen Shaanxi China
Liangzhou Gansu China see Wuwei
109 J3 Liangzi Hu l. China
Lianhe Chongqing China see Qianjiang
109 I5 Lianhua Jiangxi China
109 J7 Lianhua Shan mts China
109 L5 Lianjiang Fujian China
108 H8 Lianjiang Guangdong China
Lianjiang Jiangxi China see Xingguo
108 F6 Lian Jiang r. China
109 I6 Lianjiangkou Guangdong China
109 I6 Liannan Guangdong China
109 J6 Lianping Guangdong China
Lianran Yunnan China see Anning
109 I6 Lianshan Guangdong China
107 Q6 Lianshan Liaoning China
Liant, Cape i. Thai. see Samae San, Laem
Liantang Jiangxi China see Nanchang
109 H3 Liantuo Hubei China
Lianxian Guangdong China see Lianzhou
100 C2 Lianyin Heilong. China
109 H5 Lianyuan Hunan China
107 P9 Lianyungang Jiangsu China
109 I6 Lianzhou Guangdong China
Lianzhou Guangxi China see Hepu
100 G6 Lianzhushan Heilong. China
107 N8 Liaocheng Shandong China
107 R6 Liaodong Bandao pen. China
107 Q6 Liaodong Wan b. China
106 C5 Liaodun Xinjiang China
106 C5 Liaodunzhan Xinjiang China
Liaogao Guizhou China see Songtao
107 R6 Liao He r. China
107 R6 Liaoning prov. China
107 R6 Liaoyang Liaoning China
100 D7 Liaoyuan Jilin China
107 R6 Liaozhong Liaoning China
198 A3 Liapades Kerkyra Greece
123 N5 Liaqatabad Pak.
222 F2 Liard r. Can.
222 F2 Liard Highway N.W.T. Can.
222 E2 Liard Plateau Y.T. Can.
222 E3 Liard River B.C. Can.
123 L9 Liari Pak.
156 H4 Liart France
94 G6 Liat i. Indon.
146 F7 Liathach mt. Scotland U.K.
143 K5 Liatorp Sweden
Liban country Asia see Lebanon
176 E1 Libáň Czech Rep.
128 E4 Liban, Jebel mts Lebanon
261 G5 Líbano Arg.
250 C3 Líbano Col.
185 I7 Líbar, Sierra de mts Spain
Libau Latvia see Liepāja
146 I11 Libberton South Lanarkshire, Scotland U.K.
238 G2 Libby MT U.S.A.
176 C1 Libčeves Czech Rep.
171 J10 Libčice nad Vltavou Czech Rep.
208 C4 Libenge Dem. Rep. Congo
175 I2 Liberadz Pol.
237 E7 Liberal KS U.S.A.
257 E5 Liberdade Brazil
254 B4 Liberdade r. Brazil
252 C1 Liberdade r. Brazil
176 E1 Liberec Czech Rep.
176 E1 Liberecký kraj admin. reg. Czech Rep.
206 C5 Liberia country Africa
242 □Q12 Liberia Costa Rica
247 □2 Liberta Antigua and Barbuda
261 I2 Libertad Arg.
261 I4 Libertad Uru.
250 D2 Libertad Venez.
258 D1 Libertador General San Martin Arg.
260 E3 Libertador General San Martín Arg.
215 L4 Libertase S. Africa
230 E6 Liberty IN U.S.A.
230 E7 Liberty KY U.S.A.
233 □P4 Liberty ME U.S.A.
236 H6 Liberty MO U.S.A.
233 K7 Liberty NY U.S.A.
234 A1 Liberty PA U.S.A.
237 H10 Liberty TX U.S.A.
232 A7 Liberty Center OH U.S.A.
234 B6 Liberty Lake MD U.S.A.
226 G7 Libertyville IL U.S.A.
171 J9 Liběšice Czech Rep.
175 H5 Libiąż Pol.
176 E1 Libice nad Cidlinou Czech Rep.
165 H9 Libin Belgium
176 D3 Libín mt. Czech Rep.
176 G2 Libina Czech Rep.
92 D5 Libmanan Luzon Phil.
128 B8 Libnī, Jabal hill Egypt
108 F6 Libo Guizhou China
93 F4 Libobo, Tanjung pt Halmahera Indon.
171 J10 Libochovice Czech Rep.
215 N7 Libode S. Africa
198 B2 Libohovë Albania
210 D4 Liboi Kenya
209 D8 Libonda Zambia
97 D11 Libong, Ko i. Thai.
215 M4 Libono Lesotho
260 E3 Liborio Luna Arg.
171 J9 Libouchec Czech Rep.
163 D6 Libourne France
86 H7 Libral Well W.A. Austr.
165 H9 Libramont Belgium
196 I9 Librazhd Albania
242 D3 Libre, Sierra mts Mex.
245 J6 Libres Mex.
208 A4 Libreville Gabon
187 C12 Librilla Spain
187 C7 Libros Spain
92 E8 Libuganon r. Mindanao Phil.
202 C3 Libya country Africa
202 E3 Libyan Desert Egypt/Libya
202 E2 Libyan Plateau Egypt
260 A4 Licantén Chile
194 F9 Licata Sicilia Italy
190 I7 Licciana Nardi Italy
127 J4 Lice Turkey
193 J3 Licenza Italy
183 N6 Liceras Spain
169 G9 Lich Ger.
198 D4 Lichas pen. Greece
Licheng Fujian China see Xianyou
Licheng Guangxi China see Lipu
107 O8 Licheng Shandong China
107 M8 Licheng Shanxi China
80 J5 Lichfield North I. N.Z.
151 I2 Lichfield Staffordshire, England U.K.
211 B8 Lichinga Moz.
177 G1 Lichnov Czech Rep.
174 G1 Lichnowy Pol.
171 D9 Lichte Ger.
172 E4 Lichtenau Baden-Württemberg Ger.
173 J3 Lichtenau Bayern Ger.
169 G7 Lichtenau Nordrhein-Westfalen Ger.
179 L2 Lichtenau im Waldviertel Austria
171 E10 Lichtenberg Bayern Ger.
171 H9 Lichtenberg Sachsen Ger.
215 K2 Lichtenburg S. Africa
171 D10 Lichtenfels Ger.
171 G9 Lichtenstein Ger.
164 K5 Lichtenvoorde Neth.
179 N4 Lichtenwörth Austria
170 I5 Lichterfelde Ger.
165 D6 Lichtervelde Belgium
108 G3 Lichuan Hubei China
109 K5 Lichuan Jiangxi China
213 H3 Liciro Moz.
232 A9 Licking r. KY U.S.A.
188 E3 Lički Osik Croatia
194 H9 Licodia Eubea Sicilia Italy
193 N7 Licosa, Isola i. Italy
163 C9 Licq-Athérey France
156 C2 Licques France
Licun Shandong China see Laoshan
139 S2 Lid' r. Rus. Fed.
138 I8 Lida Belarus
142 J3 Lidan r. Sweden
149 L3 Liddel Water r. England/Scotland U.K.
146 K12 Liddesdale val. Scotland U.K.
215 K8 Liddleton S. Africa
177 H2 Lidečko Czech Rep.
142 J5 Lidhult Sweden
143 O2 Lidingö Sweden
208 C4 Lidjombo C.A.R.
142 J3 Lidköping Sweden
191 M5 Lido Italy
191 M7 Lido Adriano Italy
191 M7 Lido di Classe Italy
193 J5 Lido di Foce Verde Italy
191 N4 Lido di Jesolo Italy
195 L3 Lido di Metaponto Italy
193 I4 Lido di Ostia Italy
193 P4 Lido di Siponto Italy
191 M6 Lido di Spina Italy
140 M4 Lidsjöberg Sweden
138 K5 Lidumnieki Latvia
175 H2 Lidzbark Pol.
143 Q7 Lidzbark Warmiński Pol.
179 K2 Liebenau Austria
169 H8 Liebenau Hessen Ger.
168 H5 Liebenau Niedersachsen Ger.
215 M3 Liebenbergs Vlei r. S. Africa
169 J6 Liebenburg Ger.
179 J6 Liebenfels Austria
170 H5 Liebenwalde Ger.
171 J7 Lieberose Ger.
171 F8 Liebertwolkwitz Ger.
84 C7 Liebig, Mount N.T. Austr.
196 J5 Liebling Romania
179 L6 Lieboch Austria
171 I9 Liebstadt Ger.
172 H7 Liechtenstein country Europe
183 R3 Liédena Spain
165 I7 Liège Belgium
165 I8 Liège prov. Belgium
Liegnitz Pol. see Legnica
140 U5 Lieksa Fin.
138 K5 Lielais Ludzas l. Latvia
138 H4 Lielupe r. Latvia
138 H5 Lielvārde Latvia
164 H5 Liempde Neth.
140 N5 Lien Sweden
164 I5 Lienden Neth.
169 E6 Lienen Ger.
97 I9 Liên Nghia Vietnam
97 I8 Liên Sơn Vietnam
178 G6 Lienz Austria
138 E5 Liepāja Latvia
Liepaya Latvia see Liepāja
170 I5 Liepe Ger.
170 H3 Liepen Ger.
170 J3 Liepgarten Ger.
138 K4 Liepna Latvia
175 M1 Lieponys Lith.
165 G6 Lier Belgium
160 E2 Liernais France
165 I8 Lierneux Belgium
Lierre Belgium see Lier
177 I2 Liesek Slovakia
172 C2 Lieser Ger.
164 I5 Lieshout Neth.
178 L5 Liesing r. Austria
138 G1 Liesjärven kansallispuisto nat. park Fin.
165 I6 Liessel Neth.
156 G4 Liesse-Notre-Dame France
190 C1 Liestal Switz.
177 H3 Liešťany Slovakia
138 F1 Lieto Fin.
185 P3 Liétor Spain
Lietuva country Europe see Lithuania
141 S6 Lietvesi l. Fin.
159 M3 Lieurey France
159 L3 Lieuvin reg. France
141 S5 Lievestuore Fin.
156 E3 Liévin France
224 F4 Lièvre r. Que. Can.
179 J4 Liezen Austria
93 E4 Lifamatola i. Indon.
208 D4 Lifanga Dem. Rep. Congo
148 E7 Liffey r. Ireland
157 K7 Liffol-le-Grand France
147 H3 Lifford Ireland
158 H5 Liffré France
259 C6 Lifi Mahuida mt. Arg.
78 □5 Lifou i. Îles Loyauté New Caledonia
150 D6 Lifton Devon, England U.K.
Lifu i. Îles Loyauté New Caledonia see Lifou
Lifudzin Rus. Fed. see Rudnyy
79 □8 Lifuka i. Tonga
92 D5 Ligao Luzon Phil.
163 E7 Ligardes France
208 D4 Ligasa Dem. Rep. Congo
138 I4 Līgatne Latvia
87 G10 Lightfoot Lake salt flat W.A. Austr.
243 P9 Lighthouse Reef Belize
83 K3 Lightning Ridge N.S.W. Austr.
234 C2 Lightstreet PA U.S.A.
179 L6 Ligist Austria
191 O4 Lignano Pineta Italy
191 O4 Lignano Sabbiadoro Italy
158 I7 Ligné France
158 H8 Ligneron r. France
165 J8 Ligneuville Belgium
159 P8 Lignières France
160 D5 Lignon r. France
161 E6 Lignon r. France
157 J6 Ligny-en-Barrois France
156 G8 Ligny-le-Châtel France
156 C8 Ligny-le-Ribault France
190 I7 Ligonchio Italy
213 H3 Ligonha r. Moz.
226 I8 Ligonier IN U.S.A.
232 F8 Ligonier PA U.S.A.
Ligoúrion Greece see Asklipieio
175 H3 Ligowo Pol.
260 B3 Ligua, Bahía de la b. Chile
82 E6 Liguanea Island S.A. Austr.
159 M7 Ligueil France
162 E2 Ligugé France
242 D5 Ligui Mex.
Ligure, Mar sea France/Italy see Ligurian Sea
190 F7 Liguria admin. reg. Italy
188 B4 Ligurian Sea France/Italy
Ligurienne, Mer sea France/Italy see Ligurian Sea
241 R9 Ligurta AZ U.S.A.
81 □4 Liha Point Niue
91 L7 Lihir Group is P.N.G.
142 E5 Lihme Denmark
85 M4 Lihou Reef and Cays Coral Sea Is Terr. Austr.
240 □B11 Līhu'e HI U.S.A.
260 E5 Lihuel Calel, Parque Nacional nat. park Arg.
138 G3 Lihula Estonia
Liidli Kue N.W.T. Can. see Fort Simpson
Liivi laht b. Estonia/Latvia see Riga, Gulf of
195 □ Lija Malta
185 O6 Lijar Spain
185 I7 Líjar, Sierra de mts Spain
108 C5 Lijiang Yunnan China
Lijiang Yunnan China see Yuanjiang
96 J2 Li Jiang r. China
109 J3 Lijiazhai Henan China
96 F5 Lik, Nam r. Laos
188 E3 Lika reg. Croatia
122 D6 Līkak Iran
208 C4 Likala Dem. Rep. Congo
209 E7 Likasi Dem. Rep. Congo
208 D4 Likati Dem. Rep. Congo
208 E4 Likati r. Dem. Rep. Congo
222 F4 Likely B.C. Can.
Likhachevo Ukr. see Pervomays'kyy
Likhachyovo Ukr. see Pervomays'kyy
Likhás pen. Greece see Lichas
139 S4 Likhoslavl' Rus. Fed.
137 T5 Likhovskoy Rus. Fed.
208 D4 Likimi Dem. Rep. Congo
139 V6 Likino-Dulevo Rus. Fed.
Likisia East Timor see Liquiçá
116 I9 Likma Chhattisgarh India
208 D5 Likolia Dem. Rep. Congo
208 C4 Likouala admin. reg. Congo
208 C5 Likouala r. Congo
208 C5 Likouala aux Herbes r. Congo
143 N3 Likstammen l. Sweden
95 H4 Liku Kalimantan Indon.
95 K2 Liku Sarawak Malaysia
81 □4 Liku Niue
93 D3 Likupang Sulawesi Indon.
134 H4 Likurga Rus. Fed.
79 □7a Likuri Harbour b. Viti Levu Fiji
159 L7 L'Île-Bouchard France
192 B2 L'Île-Rousse Corse France
179 M3 Lilienfeld Austria
168 G4 Lilienthal Ger.
109 I5 Liling Hunan China
138 J1 Liljendal Fin.
123 O5 Lilla Pak.
142 I3 Lilla Edet Sweden
140 P3 Lilla Luleälven r. Sweden
140 N4 Lillblaiken hill Sweden
165 G6 Lille Belgium
156 F2 Lille France
142 F6 Lille Bælt sea chan. Denmark
159 M2 Lillebonne France
141 K6 Lillehammer Norway
156 D2 Lillers France
142 E3 Lillesand Norway
150 H2 Lilleshall Telford and Wrekin, England U.K.
142 H2 Lillestrøm Norway
226 I6 Lilley MI U.S.A.
87 I9 Lillian, Point hill W.A. Austr.
263 L2 Lillie Glacier Antarctica
146 K11 Lilliesleaf Scottish Borders, Scotland U.K.
231 H8 Lillington NC U.S.A.
183 N9 Lillo Spain
222 F5 Lillooet B.C. Can.
222 F5 Lillooet r. B.C. Can.
222 F5 Lillooet Range mts B.C. Can.
208 E5 Lilo r. Dem. Rep. Congo
117 N7 Lilong Manipur India
211 B8 Lilongwe Malawi
258 E2 Lilo Viejo Arg.
92 D7 Liloy Mindanao Phil.
226 F4 Lily WI U.S.A.
82 G5 Lilydale S.A. Austr.
83 K9 Lilydale Tas. Austr.
196 H7 Lim r. Montenegro/Serbia
261 H4 Lima Arg.
191 J7 Lima r. Italy
253 F5 Lima Para.
252 A3 Lima Peru
252 A2 Lima dept Peru
226 C9 Lima IL U.S.A.
238 H4 Lima MT U.S.A.
232 H6 Lima NY U.S.A.
232 A8 Lima OH U.S.A.
251 F4 Limaão Brazil
260 B3 Limache Chile
257 F4 Lima Duarte Brazil
160 C5 Limagne reg. France
125 M3 Līmah Oman
Lima Islands Guangdong China see Wanshan Qundao
120 B5 Liman Rus. Fed.
178 F7 Limana Italy
175 I6 Limanowa Pol.
93 E7 Limar Maluku Indon.
260 B2 Limarí r. Chile
94 F4 Limas Indon.
92 E7 Limasawa i. Phil.
Limassol Cyprus see Lemesos
147 I2 Limavady Northern Ireland U.K.
260 D6 Limay r. Arg.
156 C5 Limay France
260 D5 Limay Mahuida Arg.
172 G3 Limbach Baden-Württemberg Ger.
172 B3 Limbach Saarland Ger.
171 F9 Limbach Sachsen Ger.
171 G9 Limbach-Oberfrohna Ger.
195 J6 Limbadi Italy
95 K2 Limbang Sarawak Malaysia
95 K2 Limbang r. Sarawak Malaysia
252 C3 Limbani Peru
192 C6 Limbara, Monte mts Sardegna Italy
138 H4 Limbaži Latvia
116 C8 Limbdi Gujarat India
207 H5 Limbe Cameroon
211 B8 Limbe Malawi
93 C3 Limboto Sulawesi Indon.
93 C3 Limboto, Danau l. Indon.
165 I7 Limbourg Belgium
213 H3 Limbuè Moz.
93 A6 Limbung Sulawesi Indon.
95 K6 Limbungan Kalimantan Indon.
84 B4 Limbunya N.T. Austr.
165 H6 Limburg prov. Belgium
165 I6 Limburg prov. Neth.
169 F10 Limburg an der Lahn Ger.
172 E3 Limburgerhof Ger.
94 □ Lim Chu Kang Sing.
94 □ Lim Chu Kang hill Sing.
214 H4 Lime Acres S. Africa
141 L6 Limedsforsen Sweden
81 C13 Limehills South I. N.Z.
256 D5 Limeira Brazil
149 K1 Limekilns Fife, Scotland U.K.
198 F2 Limenaria Thasos Greece
199 G7 Limenas Chersonisou Kriti Greece
147 E7 Limerick Ireland
147 E8 Limerick county Ireland
226 B6 Lime Springs IA U.S.A.
233 □R2 Limestone ME U.S.A.
223 L4 Limestone Point Man. Can.
142 E5 Limfjorden sea chan. Denmark
182 D5 Limia r. Spain
140 L4 Limingen Norway
140 L4 Limingen l. Norway
233 □O5 Limington ME U.S.A.
140 R4 Liminka Fin.
142 J4 Limmared Sweden
164 G3 Limmen Neth.
84 F3 Limmen Bight b. N.T. Austr.
84 E3 Limmen Bight River r. N.T. Austr.
198 E4 Limni Greece
199 G3 Limnos i. Greece
254 G3 Limoeiro Brazil
233 J3 Limoges Ont. Can.
162 G4 Limoges France
163 H7 Limogne, Causse de hills France
163 H7 Limogne-en-Quercy France
242 □Q10 Limón Hond.
236 D6 Limon CO U.S.A.
217 □1a Limon, Mount hill Rodrigues I. Mauritius
190 D7 Limone Piemonte Italy
250 B4 Limones Ecuador
160 F5 Limonest France
191 J4 Limone sul Garda Italy
184 F3 Limonetes r. Spain
126 G5 Limonlu Turkey
Limonum France see Poitiers
252 D3 Limoquije Bol.
193 N4 Limosano Italy
162 H4 Limousin admin. reg. France
162 H4 Limousin, Monts du hills France
162 G4 Limousin, Plateaux du France
163 I9 Limoux France
213 F4 Limpopo prov. S. Africa
213 G5 Limpopo r. S. Africa/Zimbabwe
213 F4 Limpopo National Park S. Africa
108 H6 Limu Guangxi China
79 □8 Limu atoll Tonga
81 □4 Limufuafua Point Niue
209 D8 Limulunga Zambia
140 Q3 Linaälven r. Sweden
124 F1 Līnah Saudi Arabia
215 M5 Linakeng Lesotho
140 U2 Linakhamari Rus. Fed.
Lin'an Yunnan China see Jianshui
109 L3 Lin'an Zhejiang China
92 E8 Linao Bay Mindanao Phil.
92 B6 Linapacan i. Phil.
92 B6 Linapacan Strait Phil.
162 H4 Linards France
260 B4 Linares Chile
243 J5 Linares Mex.
185 L4 Linares Spain
183 M5 Linares, Embalse de resr Spain
187 D7 Linares de Mora Spain
182 I7 Linares de Riofrío Spain
192 B9 Linas, Monte mt. Sardegna Italy
190 G5 Linate airport Italy
95 K3 Linau Balui plat. Malaysia
108 C7 Lincang Yunnan China
165 H7 Lincent Belgium
Lincheng Hainan China see Lingao
Lincheng Hunan China see Huitong
Linchuan Jiangxi China see Fuzhou
262 R1 Linck Nunataks nunataks Antarctica
261 G4 Lincoln Arg.
81 G10 Lincoln South I. N.Z.
149 P7 Lincoln Lincolnshire, England U.K.
240 K3 Lincoln CA U.S.A.
234 E7 Lincoln DE U.S.A.
230 C5 Lincoln IL U.S.A.
236 F6 Lincoln KS U.S.A.
233 □Q3 Lincoln ME U.S.A.
227 K5 Lincoln MI U.S.A.
236 G5 Lincoln NE U.S.A.
233 N4 Lincoln NH U.S.A.
234 C4 Lincoln PA U.S.A.
238 B4 Lincoln City OR U.S.A.
90 D3 Lincoln Island Paracel Is
82 E6 Lincoln National Park S.A. Austr.
232 B6 Lincoln Park MI U.S.A.
221 N1 Lincoln Sea Can./Greenland
149 Q7 Lincolnshire admin. div. England U.K.
149 Q7 Lincolnshire Wolds hills England U.K.
231 F9 Lincolnton GA U.S.A.
234 D5 Lincoln University PA U.S.A.
235 G4 Lincroft NJ U.S.A.
254 E5 Linda, Serra hills Brazil
84 G7 Linda Creek watercourse Qld Austr.
144 J1 Lindas Norway
171 F6 Lindau Sachsen-Anhalt Ger.
168 I1 Lindau Schleswig-Holstein Ger.
172 H6 Lindau (Bodensee) Ger.
164 I3 Linde r. Neth.
168 K1 Lindelse Denmark
85 L6 Lindeman Group is Qld Austr.
222 H5 Linden Alta Can.
169 G9 Linden Hessen Ger.
168 H2 Linden Schleswig-Holstein Ger.
251 G3 Linden Guyana
231 D9 Linden AL U.S.A.
240 K3 Linden CA U.S.A.
232 B6 Linden MI U.S.A.
235 G3 Linden NJ U.S.A.
231 D8 Linden TN U.S.A.
237 H9 Linden TX U.S.A.
170 F4 Lindenberg Brandenburg Ger.
170 I5 Lindenberg Brandenburg Ger.
171 J6 Lindenberg Brandenburg Ger.
172 H6 Lindenberg im Allgäu Ger.
172 F2 Lindenfels Ger.
226 B2 Linden Grove MN U.S.A.
Lindenow Fjord inlet Greenland see Kangerlussuatsiaq
234 F5 Lindenwold NJ U.S.A.
168 E5 Lindern (Oldenburg) Ger.
143 L2 Lindesberg Sweden
142 D3 Lindesnes c. Norway
168 H1 Lindewitt Ger.
151 L5 Lindfield West Sussex, England U.K.
169 H6 Lindhorst Ger.
Líndhos Rodos Greece see Lindos
208 E4 Lindi r. Dem. Rep. Congo
211 C7 Lindi Tanz.
211 C7 Lindi admin. reg. Tanz.
107 S3 Lindian Heilong. China
Lindisfarne i. England U.K. see Holy Island
81 D11 Lindis Peak South I. N.Z.
169 D8 Lindlar Ger.
215 L3 Lindley S. Africa
256 D5 Lindóia Brazil
142 I4 Lindome Sweden
107 P5 Lindong Nei Mongol China
199 J6 Lindos Rodos Greece
182 D5 Lindoso Port.
170 G5 Lindow Ger.
157 M6 Lindre, Étang de l. France
233 □R2 Lindsay N.B. Can.
224 E4 Lindsay Ont. Can.
240 M5 Lindsay CA U.S.A.
238 L3 Lindsay MT U.S.A.
87 F9 Lindsay Gordon Lagoon salt flat W.A. Austr.
236 G6 Lindsborg KS U.S.A.
143 M5 Lindsdal Sweden
232 E11 Lindside WV U.S.A.
170 E5 Lindstedt Ger.
Lindum Lincolnshire, England U.K. see Lincoln
168 I5 Lindwedel Ger.
176 C2 Líně Czech Rep.
234 B5 Lineboro MD U.S.A.
266 I5 Line Islands S. Pacific Ocean
234 E4 Line Lexington PA U.S.A.
137 O1 Linets Rus. Fed.
107 L8 Linfen Shanxi China
234 D4 Linfield PA U.S.A.
151 M5 Linford Thurrock, England U.K.
146 F8 Ling r. Scotland U.K.
114 H4 Lingamparti Andhra Prad. India
114 D6 Linganamakki Reservoir India
108 G9 Lingao Hainan China
161 D8 Lingas, Montagne du mt. France
92 C3 Lingayen Luzon Phil.
92 C3 Lingayen Gulf Luzon Phil.
107 L9 Lingbao Henan China
109 K2 Lingbi Anhui China
Lingcheng Anhui China see Lingbi
Lingcheng Guangxi China see Lingshan
Lingcheng Hainan China see Lingshui
Lingcheng Shandong China see Lingxian
108 H6 Lingchuan Guangxi China
107 M9 Lingchuan Shanxi China
215 K8 Lingelethu S. Africa
215 J8 Lingelihle S. Africa
168 D5 Lingen (Ems) Ger.
178 A5 Lingenau Austria
172 E3 Lingenfeld Ger.
151 L5 Lingfield Surrey, England U.K.
94 F5 Lingga i. Indon.
95 I4 Lingga Sarawak Malaysia
94 F5 Lingga, Kepulauan is Indon.
111 I10 Linggo Co l. Xizang China
107 Q6 Linghai Liaoning China
92 F8 Lingig Mindanao Phil.
95 L1 Lingkabau Sabah Malaysia
95 L3 Lingkas Kalimantan Indon.
238 L5 Lingle WY U.S.A.
234 B4 Linglestown PA U.S.A.
84 G4 Lingnoonganee Island Qld Austr.
157 O6 Lingolsheim France
208 D4 Lingomo Dem. Rep. Congo
107 N7 Lingqiu Shanxi China
108 G7 Lingshan Guangxi China
107 Q9 Lingshan Wan b. China
117 L6 Lingshi Bhutan
107 L8 Lingshi Shanxi China
108 G9 Lingshui Hainan China
108 G9 Lingshui Wan b. China
114 E4 Lingsugur Karnataka India
107 J9 Lingtai Gansu China
195 I8 Linguaglossa Sicilia Italy
206 B3 Linguère Senegal
108 H6 Lingui Guangxi China
192 C3 Linguizzetta Corse France
151 O2 Lingwood Norfolk, England U.K.
Lingxi Hunan China see Yongshun
Lingxian Hunan China see Yanling
107 O8 Lingxian Shandong China
109 J3 Lingxiang Hubei China
Lingyang Hunan China see Cili
107 P6 Lingyuan Liaoning China
108 F6 Lingyun Guangxi China
108 A4 Lingza Xizang China
Lingzhi Bhutan see Lingshi
111 D9 Lingzi Tang reg. Aksai Chin
109 M4 Linhai Zhejiang China
257 G3 Linhares Brazil
182 F7 Linhares Port.
107 J6 Linhe Nei Mongol China
96 B2 Linhpa Myanmar
174 F1 Linia Pol.
81 D11 Linidis Valley South I. N.Z.
233 □O2 Linière Que. Can.
174 G1 Liniewo Pol.
Linjiang Fujian China see Shanghang
108 E2 Linjiang Gansu China
101 E8 Linjiang Jilin China
Linjiang Sichuan China see Cangxi
172 E3 Linkenheim-Hochstetten Ger.
143 L3 Linköping Sweden
100 G6 Linkou Heilong. China
146 J5 Linksness Orkney, Scotland U.K.
138 G5 Linkuva Lith.
109 H4 Linli Hunan China
146 I11 Linlithgow West Lothian, Scotland U.K.
107 M8 Linlü Shan mt. Henan China
Linmingguan Hebei China see Yongnian
236 J6 Linn MO U.S.A.
237 F12 Linn TX U.S.A.
240 J1 Linn, Mount CA U.S.A.
141 T5 Linnansaaren kansallispuisto nat. park Fin.
142 H2 Linnekleppen hill Norway
233 □R2 Linneus ME U.S.A.
150 B4 Linney Head Wales U.K.
146 E9 Linnhe, Loch inlet Scotland U.K.
169 B9 Linnich Ger.
189 D8 Linosa, Isola di i. Sicilia Italy

Linova to Loire et de l'Allier, Plaines de la
343

138 H9 Linova Belarus
138 K4 Linovo Rus. Fed.
170 G4 Linow Ger.
96 C4 Linpo Myanmar
107 N8 Linqing Shandong China
Linru Henan China see Ruzhou
107 M9 Linruzhen Henan China
256 C4 Lins Brazil
206 B4 Linsan Guinea
168 H5 Linsburg Ger.
108 F3 Linshui Sichuan China
246 □ Linstead Jamaica
213 □J5 Linta r. Madag.
93 A8 Lintah, Selat sea chan. Indon.
106 H9 Lintan Gansu China
106 H9 Lintao Gansu China
190 G1 Linth r. Switz.
190 G2 Linthal Switz.
171 G6 Linthe Ger.
234 B6 Linthicum Heights MD U.S.A.
168 G3 Lintig Ger.
80 J7 Linton North I. N.Z.
151 M3 Linton Cambridgeshire, England U.K.
236 E2 Linton ND U.S.A.
107 K9 Lintong Shaanxi China
186 C2 Lintzoain Spain
170 G5 Linum Ger.
234 F6 Linwood NJ U.S.A.
109 I6 Linwu Hunan China
163 B8 Linxe France
107 P5 Linxi Nei Mongol China
106 H9 Linxia Gansu China
106 H9 Linxia Gansu China
Linxian Henan China see Linzhou
107 L8 Linxian Shanxi China
109 I4 Linxiang Hunan China
212 E3 Linyanti r. Botswana/Namibia
212 D3 Linyanti Swamp Namibia
107 O8 Linyi Shandong China
107 P9 Linyi Shandong China
107 L9 Linyi Shanxi China
109 J2 Linying Henan China
186 G4 Linyola Spain
108 F1 Linyou Shaanxi China
179 J3 Linz Austria
169 D9 Linz am Rhein Ger.
106 G7 Linze Gansu China
172 G6 Linzgau reg. Ger.
107 M8 Linzhou Henan China
136 D2 Lioboml' Ukr.
213 H2 Lioma Moz.
95 K3 Lio Matoh Sarawak Malaysia
161 D11 Lion, Golfe du g. France
246 □ Lionel Town Jamaica
193 O6 Lioni Italy
Lions, Gulf of France see Lion, Golfe du
222 F5 Lions Bay B.C. Can.
213 F3 Lions Den Zimbabwe
227 M5 Lion's Head Ont. Can.
159 K3 Lion-sur-Mer France
93 E7 Lioppa Maluku Indon.
163 F6 Liorac-sur-Louyre France
202 B6 Lioua Chad
208 B4 Liouesso Congo
92 C5 Lipa Luzon Phil.
175 I2 Lipa Pol.
93 D2 Lipang i. Indon.
177 J2 Lipany Slovakia
194 H7 Lipari Isole Lipari Italy
194 H7 Lipari, Isola i. Isole Lipari Italy
194 H6 Lipari, Isole is Italy
94 D4 Lipatkain Sumatera Indon.
138 K6 Lipawki Belarus
136 F5 Lipcani Moldova
175 H4 Lipce Reymontowskie Pol.
140 T5 Liperi Fin.
139 W9 Lipetsk Rus. Fed.
139 V9 Lipetskaya Oblast' admin. div. Rus. Fed.
Lipetsk Oblast admin. div. Rus. Fed. see Lipetskaya Oblast'
252 D5 Lipez, Cordillera de mts Bol.
151 K5 Liphook Hampshire, England U.K.
174 C2 Lipiany Pol.
139 U1 Lipin Bor Rus. Fed.
108 G5 Liping Guizhou China
175 J6 Lipinki Pol.
174 D4 Lipinki Łużyckie Pol.
139 U8 Lipitsy Rus. Fed.
174 F2 Lipka Pol.
Lipkany Moldova see Lipcani
139 U8 Lipki Rus. Fed.
174 D3 Lipki Wielkie Pol.
196 J8 Lipljan Kosovo Serbia
139 Q2 Lipnaya Gorka Rus. Fed.
175 H2 Lipnica Kujawsko-Pomorskie Pol.
174 F2 Lipnica Pomorskie Pol.
175 I6 Lipnica Murowana Pol.
175 J5 Lipnik Pol.
175 H6 Lipnika Wielka Pol.
177 G2 Lipník nad Bečvou Czech Rep.
175 H3 Lipno Kujawsko-Pomorskie Pol.
174 E4 Lipno Wielkopolskie Pol.
176 D3 Lipno, Vodní nádrž resr Czech Rep.
163 C7 Liposthey France
197 J4 Lipova Romania
177 L6 Lipovei, Dealurile hills Romania
135 I6 Lipovka Volgogradskaya Oblast' Rus. Fed.
137 T3 Lipovka Voronezhskaya Oblast' Rus. Fed.
197 L6 Lipovu Romania
175 J2 Lipowiec Pol.
169 C7 Lippe r. Ger.
164 J2 Lippenhuizen Neth.
169 I7 Lippoldsberg (Wahlsburg) Ger.
169 F7 Lippstadt Ger.
237 E7 Lipscomb TX U.S.A.
175 L2 Lipsk Pol.
175 J4 Lipsko Pol.
Lipsoí i. Greece see Leipsoi
177 G2 Liptál Czech Rep.
116 H4 Lipti Lekh pass Nepal
207 F3 Liptougou Burkina
177 I2 Liptovská Kokava Slovakia
177 I2 Liptovská Mara, Vodná nádrž resr Slovakia
177 I3 Liptovská Osada Slovakia
177 J3 Liptovská Teplička Slovakia
177 I2 Liptovský Hrádok Slovakia
177 I2 Liptovský Mikuláš Slovakia
83 J8 Liptrap, Cape Vic. Austr.
139 R6 Liptsy Rus. Fed.
108 H6 Lipu Guangxi China
195 M5 Lipuda r. Italy
174 F1 Lipusz Pol.
93 D8 Liquiçá East Timor
Liquissa East Timor see Liquiçá
210 B4 Lira Uganda
93 D7 Liran i. Maluku Indon.
208 C5 Liranga Congo
159 I7 Liré France
182 B3 Lires, Ría de b. Spain
193 L5 Liri r. Italy
210 A2 Liri, Jebel el mt. Sudan
190 G3 Liro r. Italy
93 E2 Lirung Sulawesi Indon.
196 I9 Lis Albania
197 M5 Lisa Romania
147 E5 Lisacul Ireland
120 J1 Lisakovsk Kazakh.
208 D4 Lisala Dem. Rep. Congo
247 □7 Lisas Bay Trin. and Tob.
148 F4 Lisbane Northern Ireland U.K.
147 G4 Lisbellaw Northern Ireland U.K.
184 A3 Lisboa Port.
184 A2 Lisboa admin. dist. Port.
Lisbon Port. see Lisboa
226 F8 Lisbon IL U.S.A.
234 A6 Lisbon MD U.S.A.
233 □O4 Lisbon ME U.S.A.
236 G2 Lisbon ND U.S.A.
233 N4 Lisbon NH U.S.A.
232 E8 Lisbon OH U.S.A.
233 □O5 Lisbon Falls ME U.S.A.
147 J3 Lisburn Northern Ireland U.K.
195 I6 Lisca Blanca, Isola i. Isole Lipari Italy
147 D7 Liscannor Ireland
147 D7 Liscannor Bay Ireland
147 C5 Liscarney Ireland
147 E8 Liscarroll Ireland
192 C5 Liscia r. Sardegna Italy
192 C5 Liscia, Lago di l. Sardegna Italy
192 C7 Liscoi r. Italy
225 I4 Liscomb Game Sanctuary nature res. N.S. Can.
147 D6 Lisdoonvarna Ireland
147 H5 Lisduff Ireland
197 K9 Lisec mt. Macedonia
142 H5 Liseleje Denmark
147 F7 Lisgarode Ireland
147 F9 Lisgoold Ireland
Lishan Shaanxi China see Lintong
109 M6 Lishan Taiwan
136 H3 Lishchyn Ukr.
108 C6 Lishe Jiang r. Yunnan China
Lishi Jiangxi China see Dingnan
107 L8 Lishi Shanxi China
122 D6 Līshtar-e Bālā Iran
100 D7 Lishu Jilin China
109 L3 Lishui Jiangsu China
109 L4 Lishui Zhejiang China
108 H4 Li Shui r. China
175 J5 Lisia Góra Pol.
75 H2 Lisianski Island HI U.S.A.
Lisichansk Ukr. see Lysychans'k
174 F5 Lisięcice Pol.
159 L3 Lisieux France
139 N1 Lisiy Nos Rus. Fed.
143 K1 Lisjön l. Sweden
150 D7 Liskeard Cornwall, England U.K.
135 G6 Liski Rus. Fed.
177 I2 Lisková Slovakia
162 F5 Lisle France
147 I3 Lislea Northern Ireland U.K.
156 D5 L'Isle-Adam France
160 G5 L'Isle-d'Abeau France
163 E8 L'Isle-de-Noé France
162 E4 L'Isle-d'Espagnac France
163 F9 L'Isle-en-Dodon France
163 G8 L'Isle-Jourdain Midi-Pyrénées France
162 F3 L'Isle-Jourdain Poitou-Charentes France
161 G9 L'Isle-sur-la-Sorgue France
160 J2 L'Isle-sur-le-Doubs France
160 E1 L'Isle-sur-Serein France
163 H8 Lisle-sur-Tarn France
83 N3 Lismore N.S.W. Austr.
81 F10 Lismore South I. N.Z.
147 G8 Lismore Ireland
146 E10 Lismore i. Scotland U.K.
147 E7 Lisnagry Ireland
147 H8 Lisnakill Ireland
147 I3 Lisnamuck Northern Ireland U.K.
147 G4 Lisnarrick Northern Ireland U.K.
147 H4 Lisnaskea Northern Ireland U.K.
136 I7 Lisne Ukr.
192 G3 L'Isolotto i. Italy
160 H2 Lison r. France
176 D2 Lišov Czech Rep.
147 E9 Lispatrick Ireland
147 B8 Lispole Ireland
147 G8 Lisronagh Ireland
148 C6 Lisryan Ireland
128 G7 Liss mt. Saudi Arabia
151 K5 Liss Hampshire, England U.K.
Lissa Croatia see Vis
Lissa Pol. see Leszno
163 H6 Lissac-et-Mouret France
148 D4 Lissan Northern Ireland U.K.
164 G4 Lisse Neth.
147 C8 Lisselton Ireland
169 C10 Lissendorf Ger.
205 H2 Lisseri, Oued watercourse Tunisia
142 J1 Lisskogsbrändan Sweden
190 G4 Lissone Italy
199 G2 Lissos r. Greece
147 D7 Lissycasey Ireland
168 F1 List Ger.
142 C3 Lista pen. Norway
142 C3 Listafjorden b. Norway
143 L6 Listed Bornholm Denmark
263 K1 Lister, Mount Antarctica
147 H8 Listerlin Ireland
148 F5 Listooder Northern Ireland U.K.
84 G8 Listore watercourse Qld Austr.
224 D5 Listowel Ont. Can.
147 D8 Listowel Ireland
85 J8 Listowel Downs Qld Austr.
162 C5 Listrac-Médoc France
121 U3 Listvyaga, Khrebet mts Kazakh./Rus. Fed.
174 H4 Liswarta r. Pol.
150 G4 Liswerry Newport, Wales U.K.
175 H5 Liszki Pol.
174 F2 Liszkowo Pol.
140 M5 Lit Sweden
108 G7 Litang Guangxi China
108 C3 Litang Sichuan China
108 C4 Litang Qu r. Sichuan China
251 H4 Litani r. Fr. Guiana/Suriname
128 D5 Lîtâni, Nahr el r. Lebanon
177 I3 Litava Slovakia
176 D2 Litavka r. Czech Rep.
240 L1 Litchfield CA U.S.A.
235 I1 Litchfield CT U.S.A.
236 K6 Litchfield IL U.S.A.
226 J7 Litchfield MI U.S.A.
236 H3 Litchfield MN U.S.A.
232 C7 Litchfield OH U.S.A.
234 I1 Litchfield County county CT U.S.A.
211 D7 Litembe Tanz.
138 K4 Litene Latvia
177 G4 Litér Hungary
163 B7 Lit-et-Mixe France
164 H5 Lith Neth.
124 E5 Līth, Wādī al watercourse Saudi Arabia
149 L7 Litherland Merseyside, England U.K.
83 M5 Lithgow N.S.W. Austr.
198 F8 Lithino, Akrotirio pt Kriti Greece
138 G6 Lithuania country Europe
188 E2 Litija Slovenia
227 R9 Lititz PA U.S.A.
177 I3 Litke Hungary
131 T2 Litke, Mys c. Rus. Fed.
198 D2 Litochoro Greece
176 D1 Litoměřice Czech Rep.
176 F2 Litomyšl Czech Rep.
184 B1 Litoral reg. Port.
176 G2 Litovel Czech Rep.
100 I4 Litovko Rus. Fed.
Litovskaya S.S.R. country Europe see Lithuania
179 L2 Litschau Austria
190 E1 Littau Switz.
237 I10 Little r. LA U.S.A.
237 I9 Little r. OK U.S.A.
237 G10 Little r. TX U.S.A.
231 I12 Little Abaco i. Bahamas
224 D3 Little Abitibi r. Ont. Can.
224 D3 Little Abitibi Lake Ont. Can.
Little Aden Yemen see 'Adan aş Şughrá
115 M7 Little Andaman i. Andaman & Nicobar Is India
Little Ararat mt. Turkey see Küçük Ağrı Dağı
236 G7 Little Arkansas r. KS U.S.A.
231 H12 Little Bahama Bank sea feature Bahamas
80 J3 Little Barrier i. North I. N.Z.
185 □ Little Bay Gibraltar
226 G4 Little Bay de Noc MI U.S.A.
Little Belt sea chan. Denmark see Lille Bælt
238 I3 Little Belt Mountains MT U.S.A.
238 K4 Little Bighorn r. MT U.S.A.
Little Bitter Lake Egypt see Murrah aş Şughrá, Al Buḩayrah al
236 G6 Little Blue r. KS U.S.A.
149 M6 Littleborough Greater Manchester, England U.K.
222 H5 Little Bow r. Alta Can.
222 H2 Little Buffalo r. N.W.T. Can.
246 C4 Little Cayman i. Cayman Is
223 M3 Little Churchill r. Man. Can.
151 O4 Little Clacton Essex, England U.K.
97 A8 Little Coco Island Cocos Is
146 D10 Little Colonsay i. Scotland U.K.
241 U5 Little Colorado r. AZ U.S.A.
151 M6 Little Common East Sussex, England U.K.
234 E6 Little Creek DE U.S.A.
241 T4 Little Creek Peak UT U.S.A.
148 H2 Little Cumbrae i. Scotland U.K.
224 D4 Little Current Ont. Can.
224 C3 Little Current r. Ont. Can.
150 E6 Little Dart r. England U.K.
150 H4 Littledean Gloucestershire, England U.K.
82 H7 Little Desert National Park Vic. Austr.
151 M3 Little Downham Cambridgeshire, England U.K.
235 G5 Little Egg Harbor inlet NJ U.S.A.
246 F2 Little Exuma i. Bahamas
236 H3 Little Falls MN U.S.A.
233 K5 Little Falls NY U.S.A.
146 H7 Littleferry Highland, Scotland U.K.
241 S5 Littlefield AZ U.S.A.
237 D9 Littlefield TX U.S.A.
215 K9 Little Fish r. S. Africa
226 A1 Little Fork MN U.S.A.
226 A1 Little Fork r. MN U.S.A.
222 F5 Little Fort B.C. Can.
Little Ganges atoll Cook Is see Rakahanga
234 D3 Little Gap PA U.S.A.
223 M4 Little Grand Rapids Man. Can.
240 K2 Little Grass Valley Reservoir CA U.S.A.
151 K6 Littlehampton West Sussex, England U.K.
246 G3 Little Inagua Island Bahamas
232 D9 Little Kanawha r. WV U.S.A.
214 C3 Little Karas Berg plat. Namibia
214 E9 Little Karoo plat. S. Africa
240 O6 Little Lake CA U.S.A.
146 F7 Little Loch Broom inlet Scotland U.K.
Little Mecatina r. Nfld and Lab./Que. Can. see Petit Mécatina
Little Mecatina Island Que. Can. see Petit Mécatina, Île du
232 A9 Little Miami r. OH U.S.A.
146 I7 Littlemill Highland, Scotland U.K.
146 B7 Little Minch sea chan. Scotland U.K.
151 K4 Little Missenden Buckinghamshire, England U.K.
236 D2 Little Missouri r. ND U.S.A.
151 J4 Littlemore Oxfordshire, England U.K.
232 D9 Little Muskingum r. OH U.S.A.
115 M9 Little Nicobar i. Andaman & Nicobar Is India
151 O4 Little Oakley Essex, England U.K.
215 N1 Little Olifants r. S. Africa
151 M3 Little Ouse r. England U.K.
123 P3 Little Pamir mts Afgh.
235 K2 Little Peconic Bay NY U.S.A.
226 H1 Little Pic r. Ont. Can.
234 A2 Little Pine Creek r. PA U.S.A.
234 A5 Little Pipe Creek r. MD U.S.A.
151 M3 Littleport Cambridgeshire, England U.K.
238 L4 Little Powder r. MT U.S.A.
222 D2 Little Rancheria r. B.C. Can.
116 C8 Little Rann marsh Gujarat India
237 J8 Little Red r. AR U.S.A.
222 H3 Little Red River Alta Can.
81 G10 Little River South I. N.Z.
231 H9 Little River SC U.S.A.
237 I8 Little Rock AR U.S.A.
240 O7 Littlerock CA U.S.A.
226 H6 Little Sable Point MI U.S.A.
223 M4 Little Sachigo Lake Ont. Can.
222 C2 Little Salmon Lake Y.T. Can.
241 T4 Little Salt Lake UT U.S.A.
87 E7 Little Sandy Desert W.A. Austr.
246 F1 Little San Salvador i. Bahamas
236 G5 Little Sioux r. IA U.S.A.
220 A4 Little Sitkin Island AK U.S.A.
222 G4 Little Smoky Alta Can.
222 G4 Little Smoky r. Alta Can.
238 J6 Little Snake r. CO U.S.A.
231 □1 Little Sound b. Bermuda
151 N6 Littlestone-on-Sea Kent, England U.K.
234 A5 Littlestown PA U.S.A.
Little Tibet reg. Jammu and Kashmir see Ladakh
247 □5 Little Tobago i. Trin. and Tob.
148 B8 Littleton Ireland
151 J5 Littleton Hampshire, England U.K.
226 D9 Littleton IL U.S.A.
233 N4 Littleton NH U.S.A.
232 E9 Littleton WV U.S.A.
226 I4 Little Traverse Bay MI U.S.A.
233 K4 Little Tupper Lake NY U.S.A.
226 B1 Little Turtle Lake Ont. Can.
232 G6 Little Valley NY U.S.A.
236 K7 Little Wabash r. IL U.S.A.
81 G8 Little Wanganui South I. N.Z.
236 E4 Little White r. SD U.S.A.
237 G9 Little Wichita r. TX U.S.A.
238 J5 Little Wind r. WY U.S.A.
238 G5 Little Wood r. ID U.S.A.
Little Zab r. Iraq see Zāb aş Şaghīr, Nahr az
143 S1 Littoinen Fin.
207 H5 Littoral prov. Cameroon
260 B4 Litueche Chile
211 B8 Litunde Moz.
222 B3 Lituya Bay AK U.S.A.
176 C1 Litvínov Czech Rep.
136 H4 Lityn Ukr.
173 K2 Litzendorf Ger.
138 H3 Liu Estonia
Liu'an Anhui China see Lu'an
108 F2 Liuba Shaanxi China
175 L1 Liubavas Lith.
96 I2 Liucheng Guangxi China
109 L4 Liucheng Zhejiang China
109 M7 Liuchiu Yü i. Taiwan
108 F5 Liuchong He r. Guizhou China
Liuchow Guangxi China see Liuzhou
Liudu Guangdong China see Yun'an
175 L1 Liudvinavas Lith.
107 R8 Liugong Dao i. China
107 Q6 Liugu He r. China
100 D7 Liuhe Jilin China
107 P6 Liu He r. China
107 R6 Liu He r. China
109 N4 Liuheng Dao i. China
109 H3 Liujiachang Hubei China
108 G6 Liujiang Guangxi China
Liujiaxia Gansu China see Yongjing
106 H9 Liujiaxia Shuiku resr Gansu China
100 E5 Liukesong Heilong. China
108 B6 Liuku Yunnan China
Liulin Gansu China see Jonê
107 L8 Liulin Shanxi China
Liupai Guangxi China see Tian'e
106 J9 Liupan Shan mts China
Liupanshui Guizhou China see Lupanshui
213 H2 Liupo Moz.
107 O9 Liuquan Jiangsu China
242 □P11 Liure Hond.
106 C5 Liushuquan Xinjiang China
209 D8 Liuwa Plain Zambia
209 D8 Liuwa Plain National Park Zambia
109 I4 Liuyang Hunan China
109 I4 Liuyang He r. China
110 L6 Liuyuan Gansu China
107 S1 Liuzhan Heilong. China
Liuzhangzhen Shanxi China see Yuanqu
108 G6 Liuzhou Guangxi China
177 K5 Livada Arad Romania
197 L3 Livada Satu Mare Romania
199 G5 Livada, Akrotirio pt Tinos Greece
198 D4 Livadeia Greece
198 C2 Livadero Greece
198 D2 Livadi Greece
198 E1 Livadia Greece
100 H7 Livadiya Rus. Fed.
198 E4 Livanates Greece
138 J5 Līvāni Latvia
188 F3 Livanjsko Polje plain Bos.-Herz.
159 L3 Livarot France
138 G5 Livbērze Latvia
137 R3 Livenka Rus. Fed.
191 M4 Livenza r. Italy
240 K2 Live Oak CA U.S.A.
231 F10 Live Oak FL U.S.A.
157 L6 Liverdun France
86 H5 Liveringa W.A. Austr.
240 K4 Livermore CA U.S.A.
239 L11 Livermore, Mount TX U.S.A.
233 □O4 Livermore Falls ME U.S.A.
163 H6 Livernon France
83 M5 Liverpool N.S.W. Austr.
84 E2 Liverpool r. N.T. Austr.
225 H4 Liverpool N.S. Can.
149 L7 Liverpool Merseyside, England U.K.
233 I5 Liverpool NY U.S.A.
234 B3 Liverpool PA U.S.A.
221 K2 Liverpool, Cape Nunavut Can.
220 E3 Liverpool Bay N.W.T. Can.
149 K7 Liverpool Bay England U.K.
83 M4 Liverpool Plains N.S.W. Austr.
83 L4 Liverpool Range mts N.S.W. Austr.
149 N6 Liversedge West Yorkshire, England U.K.
192 G3 Lividonia, Punta pt Italy
190 I2 Livigno Italy
243 O10 Livingston Guat.
146 I11 Livingston West Lothian, Scotland U.K.
237 K9 Livingston AL U.S.A.
240 L4 Livingston CA U.S.A.
232 A11 Livingston KY U.S.A.
237 J10 Livingston LA U.S.A.
238 I4 Livingston MT U.S.A.
235 G3 Livingston NJ U.S.A.
237 H10 Livingston TX U.S.A.
237 H10 Livingston, Lake TX U.S.A.
209 E9 Livingstone Zambia
211 B7 Livingstone Mountains Tanz.
211 B7 Livingstonia Malawi
262 T2 Livingston Island Antarctica
233 K7 Livingston Manor NY U.S.A.
81 C11 Livingston Mountains South I. N.Z.
188 F4 Livno Bos.-Herz.
139 U9 Livny Rus. Fed.
140 U4 Livo r. Rus. Fed.
191 R4 Livold Slovenia
227 K7 Livonia MI U.S.A.
232 H6 Livonia NY U.S.A.
190 I8 Livorno Italy
190 J9 Livorno prov. Italy
190 E5 Livorno Ferraris Italy
160 D6 Livradois, Monts du mts France
160 D5 Livradois Forez, Parc Naturel Régional du nature res. France
216 □1b Livramento São Miguel Azores
254 E5 Livramento do Brumado Brazil
161 F7 Livron-sur-Drôme France
175 J3 Liw Pol.
125 M3 Liwā Oman
128 E6 Liwā', Wādī al watercourse Syria
211 C7 Liwale Tanz.
211 C7 Liwale Juu Tanz.
175 J3 Liwiec r. Pol.
211 B8 Liwonde Malawi
211 B8 Liwonde National Park Malawi
Liwu Hebei China see Lixian
106 I9 Lixian Gansu China
107 N7 Lixian Hebei China
109 H4 Lixian Hunan China
108 D3 Lixian Sichuan China
109 K2 Lixin Anhui China
157 M5 Lixing-lès-St-Avold France
198 B4 Lixouri Kefallonia Greece
Lixus Morocco see Larache
Liyang Anhui China see Hexian
Liyang Hunan China see Lixian
109 L3 Liyang Jiangsu China
Liyuan Hunan China see Sangzhi
182 C9 Liz r. Port.
150 B8 Lizard Cornwall, England U.K.
254 D4 Lizarda Brazil
85 J3 Lizard Island Qld Austr.
150 B8 Lizard Point England U.K.
Lizarra Spain see Estella
183 P3 Lizarraga Spain
232 D10 Lizemores WV U.S.A.
137 S3 Lizinovka Rus. Fed.
108 D4 Liziping Sichuan China
162 E5 Lizonne r. France
156 F5 Lizy-sur-Ourcq France
195 O3 Lizzanello Italy
195 M3 Lizzano Italy
196 I6 Ljig Serbia
142 D2 Ljomsnuten mt. Norway
188 F3 Ljubija Bos.-Herz.
196 H7 Ljubišnja mts Bos.-Herz./Montenergo
188 E2 Ljubljana Slovenia
179 J7 Ljubljana airport Slovenia
179 K7 Ljubljanica r. Slovenia
196 H6 Ljubovija Serbia
188 F4 Ljubuški Bos.-Herz.
143 O4 Ljugarn Gotland Sweden
140 N5 Ljungå Sweden
141 N5 Ljungan r. Sweden
141 N5 Ljungaverk Sweden
143 J5 Ljungby Sweden
143 M5 Ljungbyån r. Sweden
140 L5 Ljungdalen Sweden
143 L3 Ljungsbro Sweden
142 H3 Ljungskile Sweden
141 N6 Ljusdal Sweden
143 L3 Ljusfallshammar Sweden
142 J1 Ljusnan r. Sweden
141 N6 Ljusnan r. Sweden
141 N6 Ljusne Sweden
188 F2 Ljutomer Slovenia
186 K4 Llagostera Spain
260 B6 Llaima, Volcán vol. Chile
261 G2 Llambí Campbell Arg.
150 D2 Llanaelhaearn Gwynedd, Wales U.K.
Llanandras Wales U.K. see Presteigne
150 F2 Llanarmon Dyffryn Ceiriog Wrexham, Wales U.K.
150 D3 Llanarth Ceredigion, Wales U.K.
150 D4 Llanarthney Carmarthenshire, Wales U.K.
150 F1 Llanasa Flintshire, Wales U.K.
150 D3 Llanbadarn Fawr Ceredigion, Wales U.K.
150 D1 Llanbadrig Isle of Anglesey, Wales U.K.
Llanbedr Ceredigion, Wales U.K. see Lampeter
150 D2 Llanbedr Gwynedd, Wales U.K.
150 D2 Llanbedrog Gwynedd, Wales U.K.
Llanbedr Pont Steffan Wales U.K. see Lampeter
150 D1 Llanberis Gwynedd, Wales U.K.
150 F3 Llanbister Powys, Wales U.K.
150 E2 Llanbryn-mair Powys, Wales U.K.
186 L3 Llançà Spain
260 C4 Llancanelo, Laguna l. Arg.
260 C4 Llancanelo, Salina salt flat Arg.
150 D2 Llandanwg Gwynedd, Wales U.K.
150 D4 Llanddarog Carmarthenshire, Wales U.K.
150 D1 Llanddeiniolen Gwynedd, Wales U.K.
150 E2 Llandderfel Gwynedd, Wales U.K.
150 C4 Llanddowror Carmarthenshire, Wales U.K.
150 E4 Llandeilo Carmarthenshire, Wales U.K.
150 G4 Llandinabo Herefordshire, England U.K.
150 F3 Llandinam Powys, Wales U.K.
150 C4 Llandissilio Pembrokeshire, Wales U.K.
150 E4 Llandovery Carmarthenshire, Wales U.K.
150 F2 Llandrillo Denbighshire, Wales U.K.
150 F3 Llandrindod Wells Powys, Wales U.K.
150 E1 Llandudno Conwy, Wales U.K.
Llandudoch Wales U.K. see St Dogmaels
150 D1 Llandwrog Gwynedd, Wales U.K.
150 D4 Llandybie Carmarthenshire, Wales U.K.
150 D3 Llandysul Ceredigion, Wales U.K.
150 D4 Llanegwad Carmarthenshire, Wales U.K.
150 D1 Llaneilian Isle of Anglesey, Wales U.K.
150 D4 Llanelli Carmarthenshire, Wales U.K.
150 E2 Llanelltyd Gwynedd, Wales U.K.
150 F4 Llanelly Monmouthshire, Wales U.K.
Llanelwy Denbighshire, Wales U.K. see St Asaph
Llanelwy Wales U.K. see St Asaph
183 K2 Llanes Spain
150 D1 Llanfaelog Isle of Anglesey, Wales U.K.
150 F2 Llanfair Caereinion Powys, Wales U.K.
150 E1 Llanfairfechan Conwy, Wales U.K.
150 D1 Llanfairpwllgwyngyll Isle of Anglesey, Wales U.K.
150 E1 Llanfair Talhaiarn Conwy, Wales U.K.
Llanfair-ym-Muallt Wales U.K. see Builth Wells
150 C1 Llanfair-yn-neubwll Isle of Anglesey, Wales U.K.
150 D3 Llanfarian Ceredigion, Wales U.K.
150 D3 Llanfihangel-ar-arth Carmarthenshire, Wales U.K.
150 F2 Llanfyllin Powys, Wales U.K.
150 F1 Llanfynydd Flintshire, Wales U.K.
150 F2 Llangadfan Powys, Wales U.K.
150 E4 Llangadog Carmarthenshire, Wales U.K.
150 D1 Llangefni Isle of Anglesey, Wales U.K.
150 D3 Llangeler Carmarthenshire, Wales U.K.
150 D2 Llangelynin Gwynedd, Wales U.K.
150 D4 Llangendeirne Carmarthenshire, Wales U.K.
150 E1 Llangernyw Conwy, Wales U.K.
150 D1 Llangoed Isle of Anglesey, Wales U.K.
150 F2 Llangollen Denbighshire, Wales U.K.
150 D3 Llangrannog Ceredigion, Wales U.K.
150 D1 Llangristiolus Isle of Anglesey, Wales U.K.
150 D4 Llangunnor Carmarthenshire, Wales U.K.
150 E3 Llangurig Powys, Wales U.K.
150 C4 Llangwm Pembrokeshire, Wales U.K.
150 F4 Llangynidr Powys, Wales U.K.
150 F4 Llanharan Rhondda Cynon Taff, Wales U.K.
150 E3 Llanidloes Powys, Wales U.K.
150 D3 Llanilar Ceredigion, Wales U.K.
150 F4 Llanishen Cardiff, Wales U.K.
150 F2 Llanllwchaiarn Powys, Wales U.K.
150 D1 Llanllyfni Gwynedd, Wales U.K.
150 D1 Llannerch-y-medd Isle of Anglesey, Wales U.K.
150 D4 Llannon Carmarthenshire, Wales U.K.
150 D3 Llan-non Ceredigion, Wales U.K.
150 D2 Llannor Gwynedd, Wales U.K.
242 D2 Llano Mex.
237 F10 Llano TX U.S.A.
237 F10 Llano r. TX U.S.A.
237 D9 Llano Estacado plain NM/TX U.S.A.
244 B2 Llano Grande Durango Mex.
244 B3 Llano Grande Nayarit Mex.
250 D3 Llanos plain Col./Venez.
260 D2 Llanos, Sierra de los mts Arg.
259 B6 Llanquihue, Lago l. Chile
150 F2 Llanrhaeadr-ym-Mochnant Powys, Wales U.K.
150 D4 Llanrhidian Swansea, Wales U.K.
150 D3 Llanrhystud Ceredigion, Wales U.K.
150 D1 Llanrug Gwynedd, Wales U.K.
150 F4 Llanrumney Cardiff, Wales U.K.
150 E1 Llanrwst Conwy, Wales U.K.
Llansá Spain see Llançà
150 E1 Llansanffraid Glan Conwy Conwy, Wales U.K.
150 E1 Llansannan Conwy, Wales U.K.
150 D3 Llansawel Carmarthenshire, Wales U.K.
150 D4 Llansteffan Carmarthenshire, Wales U.K.
Llanstephan Carmarthenshire, Wales U.K. see Llansteffan
150 F4 Llanthony Monmouthshire, Wales U.K.
150 F4 Llantilio Pertholey Monmouthshire, Wales U.K.
150 G4 Llantrisant Monmouthshire, Wales U.K.
150 F4 Llantrisant Rhondda Cynon Taff, Wales U.K.
150 F5 Llantwit Major Vale of Glamorgan, Wales U.K.
150 E2 Llanuwchllyn Gwynedd, Wales U.K.
150 F2 Llanwddyn Powys, Wales U.K.
150 D3 Llanwenog Ceredigion, Wales U.K.
150 D1 Llanwnda Gwynedd, Wales U.K.
150 F2 Llanwnog Powys, Wales U.K.
150 E4 Llanwrda Carmarthenshire, Wales U.K.
150 E3 Llanwrtyd Wells Powys, Wales U.K.
150 D3 Llanybydder Carmarthenshire, Wales U.K.
Llanymddyfri Carmarthenshire, Wales U.K. see Llandovery
150 C1 Llanynghenedl Isle of Anglesey, Wales U.K.
150 D2 Llanystumdwy Gwynedd, Wales U.K.
186 G5 Llardecans Spain
252 A2 Llata Peru
187 E9 Llaurí Spain
186 H2 Llavorsí Spain
150 F1 Llay Wrexham, Wales U.K.
260 B3 Llay-Llay Chile
187 K9 Llebeig, Es Cap des c. Spain
150 E3 Lledrod Ceredigion, Wales U.K.
186 G4 Lleida Spain
186 H3 Lleida prov. Cataluña Spain
187 H10 Llentrisca, Cap c. Spain
184 G4 Llera Spain
245 H2 Llera de Canales Mex.
184 G4 Llerena Spain
150 C2 Lleyn Peninsula Wales U.K.
252 C4 Llica Bol.
187 D8 Lliria Spain
186 I3 Llívia Spain
186 H4 Llobregós r. Spain
183 O2 Llodio Spain
260 B3 Llolleo Chile
186 I5 Llorenç del Penedès Spain
186 K4 Lloret de Mar Spain
198 A2 Llorgara nat. park Albania
187 D9 Llosa de Ranes Spain
187 K8 Lloseta Spain
85 I2 Lloyd Bay Qld Austr.
222 E3 Lloyd George, Mount B.C. Can.
235 I3 Lloyd Harbor NY U.S.A.
223 I3 Lloyd Lake Sask. Can.
223 I4 Lloydminster Alta Can.
187 L8 Llubí Spain
Lluchmayor Spain see Llucmajor
187 K9 Llucmajor Spain
246 □ Lluidas Vale Jamaica
252 C6 Llullaillaco, Parque Nacional nat. park Chile
252 C6 Llullaillaco, Volcán vol. Chile
Llyn Tegid l. Wales U.K. see Bala Lake
150 F3 Llyswen Powys, Wales U.K.
174 G2 Lniano Pol.
165 C7 Lo Belgium
Lo i. Vanuatu see Loh
96 G4 Lô, Sông r. China/Vietnam
252 C5 Loa r. Chile
241 U3 Loa UT U.S.A.
95 K3 Loagan Bunut National Park Malaysia
95 L5 Loakulu Kalimantan Indon.
256 A5 Loanda Brazil
146 J11 Loanhead Midlothian, Scotland U.K.
190 E7 Loano Italy
146 G11 Loans South Ayrshire, Scotland U.K.
186 D3 Loarre Spain
92 E7 Loay Bohol Phil.
139 S5 Lob' r. Rus. Fed.
175 M5 Lobachivka Ukr.
215 P2 Lobamba Swaziland
134 J4 Loban' r. Rus. Fed.
139 V8 Lobanovo Rus. Fed.
93 C5 Lobata Sulawesi Indon.
185 K6 Lobatejo mt. Spain
212 E5 Lobatse Botswana
171 K8 Löbau Ger.
208 C3 Lobaye pref. C.A.R.
208 C4 Lobaye r. C.A.R.
161 K7 Lobbie, Cima delle mt. Italy
171 E7 Löbejün Ger.
171 G8 Löbenberg hill Ger.
186 C3 Lobera de Onsella Spain
261 H6 Loberia Arg.
174 D2 Łobez Pol.
92 E6 Lobi, Mount vol. Phil.
78 □3b Lobikaere i. Majuro Marshall Is
164 J5 Lobith Neth.
209 B8 Lobito Angola
250 A6 Lobitos Peru
170 G2 Löbnitz Mecklenburg-Vorpommern Ger.
171 F7 Löbnitz Sachsen Ger.
139 U5 Lobnya Rus. Fed.
208 C5 Loboko Congo
180 C3 Lobón Spain
261 H4 Lobos Arg.
216 □3b Lobos i. Canary Is
185 O5 Lobos mt. Spain
242 C3 Lobos, Cabo c. Mex.
242 D4 Lobos, Isla i. Mex.
245 J4 Lobos, Isla de i. Mex.
260 A4 Lobos, Punta de pt Chile
246 E2 Lobos Cay i. Cuba
250 A6 Lobos de Afuera, Islas is Peru
250 A6 Lobos de Tierra, Isla i. Peru
Lobositz Czech Rep. see Lovosice
137 N5 Loboykivka Ukr.
171 F8 Lobstädt Ger.
171 F6 Loburg Ger.
81 G10 Loburn South I. N.Z.
174 F2 Łobżenica Pol.
190 C5 Locana Italy
190 F3 Locarno Switz.
96 H4 Lôc Binh Vietnam
169 H6 Loccum (Rehburg-Loccum) Ger.
192 D8 Loceri Sardegna Italy
146 G9 Lochaber reg. Scotland U.K.
146 E9 Lochailort Highland, Scotland U.K.
146 E9 Lochaline Highland, Scotland U.K.
227 J1 Lochalsh Ont. Can.
146 F13 Lochans Dumfries and Galloway, Scotland U.K.
146 I12 Locharbriggs Dumfries and Galloway, Scotland U.K.
178 A4 Lochau Austria
109 □J7 Lo Chau i. H.K. China
146 F10 Lochawe Argyll and Bute, Scotland U.K.
146 H10 Lochay r. Scotland U.K.
Loch Baghasdail Western Isles, Scotland U.K. see Lochboisdale
146 B8 Lochboisdale Western Isles, Scotland U.K.
146 E10 Lochbuie Argyll and Bute, Scotland U.K.
146 E8 Lochcarron Highland, Scotland U.K.
146 E10 Lochdon Argyll and Bute, Scotland U.K.
146 H10 Lochearnhead Stirling, Scotland U.K.
164 J4 Lochem Neth.
178 H3 Lochen Austria
146 H8 Lochend Highland, Scotland U.K.
85 I8 Lochern National Park Qld Austr.
162 F1 Loches France
Loch Garman Ireland see Wexford
146 J10 Lochgelly Fife, Scotland U.K.
146 F10 Lochgilphead Argyll and Bute, Scotland U.K.
146 G10 Lochgoilhead Argyll and Bute, Scotland U.K.
81 C13 Lochiel South I. N.Z.
215 O2 Lochiel S. Africa
209 E8 Lochinvar National Park Zambia
146 F6 Lochinver Highland, Scotland U.K.
146 G10 Loch Lomond 1 Trossachs National Park Scotland U.K.
146 J12 Lochmaben Dumfries and Galloway, Scotland U.K.
146 B7 Lochmaddy Western Isles, Scotland U.K.
81 C11 Lochnagar l. South I. N.Z.
146 J9 Lochnagar mt. Scotland U.K.
Loch na Madadh Western Isles, Scotland U.K. see Lochmaddy
176 C2 Lochovice Czech Rep.
175 J3 Łochów Pol.
146 F11 Lochranza North Ayrshire, Scotland U.K.
234 B6 Loch Raven Reservoir MD U.S.A.
165 E6 Lochristi Belgium
238 G3 Lochsa r. ID U.S.A.
146 B8 Loch Sgioport Western Isles, Scotland U.K.
146 G11 Lochwinnoch Renfrewshire, Scotland U.K.
146 G9 Lochy, Loch l. Scotland U.K.
82 E5 Lock S.A. Austr.
232 C9 Lockbourne OH U.S.A.
232 I6 Locke NY U.S.A.
240 K3 Lockeford CA U.S.A.
179 N5 Lockenhaus Austria
146 J12 Lockerbie Dumfries and Galloway, Scotland U.K.
86 C6 Locker Point W.A. Austr.
83 K6 Lockhart N.S.W. Austr.
237 G11 Lockhart TX U.S.A.
85 I2 Lockhart River Qld Austr.
85 I2 Lockhart River Aboriginal Reserve Qld Austr.
232 H7 Lock Haven PA U.S.A.
150 G5 Locking North Somerset, England U.K.
170 J4 Löcknitz Ger.
170 D4 Löcknitz r. Ger.
232 G5 Lockport NY U.S.A.
151 J6 Locks Heath Hampshire, England U.K.
149 P5 Lockton North Yorkshire, England U.K.
158 E7 Locmaria France
158 B5 Locmaria-Plouzané France
158 F6 Locmariaquer France
158 F6 Locminé France
158 E6 Locmiquélic France
97 H9 Lôc Ninh Vietnam
158 E6 Locoal-Mendon France
193 P5 Locone r. Italy
195 M2 Locorotondo Italy
158 D4 Locquirec France
195 K7 Locri Italy
158 C5 Locronan France
158 C6 Loctudy France
192 D7 Loculi Sardegna Italy
252 C4 Locumba r. Peru
235 G4 Locust NJ U.S.A.
235 H3 Locust Valley NY U.S.A.
128 C7 Lod Israel
171 E7 Lödderitz Ger.
170 J2 Loddin Ger.
150 E7 Loddiswell Devon, England U.K.
83 I6 Loddon r. Vic. Austr.
151 O2 Loddon Norfolk, England U.K.
192 D6 Lodè Sardegna Italy
138 I4 Lode Latvia
244 B5 Lo de Marcos Mex.
176 D1 Loděnice Czech Rep.
171 E8 Lodersleben Ger.
161 C9 Lodève France
139 Q1 Lodeynoye Pole Rus. Fed.
222 B3 Lodge, Mount Can./U.S.A.
223 I5 Lodge Creek r. Can./U.S.A.
238 K4 Lodge Grass MT U.S.A.
236 D5 Lodgepole Creek r. WY U.S.A.
116 G9 Lodhikheda Madh. Prad. India
123 N7 Lodhran Pak.
190 H5 Lodi Italy
190 H5 Lodi prov. Italy
240 K3 Lodi CA U.S.A.
235 G3 Lodi NJ U.S.A.
232 C7 Lodi OH U.S.A.
226 E6 Lodi WI U.S.A.
140 M3 Løding Norway
140 M2 Lødingen Norway
190 G5 Lodi Vecchio Italy
209 D5 Lodja Dem. Rep. Congo
Lodomeria Rus. Fed. see Vladimir
79 □7a Lodoni Viti Levu Fiji
183 P4 Lodosa Spain
183 Q5 Lodosa, Canal de Spain
116 C8 Lodrani Gujarat India
210 B4 Lodwar Kenya
175 H6 Łodygowice Pol.
175 H4 Łódź Pol.
175 H4 Łódzkie prov. Pol.
183 N8 Loeches Spain
96 E6 Loei Thai.
164 J4 Loenen Gelderland Neth.
164 H4 Loenen Utrecht Neth.
215 J9 Loerie S. Africa
214 D6 Loeriesfontein S. Africa
169 D10 Löf Ger.
178 G4 Lofer Austria
172 E6 Löffingen Ger.
140 L2 Lofoten is Norway
141 L5 Lofsdalen Sweden
215 J6 Lofter S. Africa
149 P4 Loftus Redcar and Cleveland, England U.K.
87 E8 Lofty Range hills W.A. Austr.
210 B4 Lofusa Sudan
135 H6 Log Rus. Fed.
179 I7 Log Slovenia
207 F3 Loga Niger
214 I1 Logageng S. Africa
146 H12 Logan East Ayrshire, Scotland U.K.
236 H5 Logan IA U.S.A.
237 D8 Logan NM U.S.A.
232 C9 Logan OH U.S.A.
238 I6 Logan UT U.S.A.
232 D11 Logan WV U.S.A.
222 A2 Logan, Mount Y.T. Can.
238 D2 Logan, Mount WA U.S.A.
85 K6 Logan Creek r. Qld Austr.
236 G5 Logan Creek r. NE U.S.A.
241 R5 Logandale NV U.S.A.
222 F5 Logan Lake B.C. Can.
222 D2 Logan Mountains N.W.T./Y.T. Can.
230 D5 Logansport IN U.S.A.
237 I10 Logansport LA U.S.A.
234 B5 Loganville PA U.S.A.
188 E3 Logatec Slovenia
140 O4 Lögda Sweden
140 O5 Lögdeälven r. Sweden
209 B6 Loge r. Angola
150 H2 Loggerheads Staffordshire, England U.K.
142 D3 Logna r. Norway
158 H7 Logne r. France
208 B1 Logone r. Africa
207 I4 Logone Birni Cameroon
208 B2 Logone Occidental pref. Chad
208 C2 Logone Oriental pref. Chad
206 D5 Logoualé Côte d'Ivoire
106 G9 Logpung Qinghai China
197 L6 Logreşti Romania
156 B7 Logron France
183 P4 Logroño Spain
185 I2 Logrosán Spain
142 F5 Løgstør Denmark
117 N7 Logtak Lake India
192 B6 Logudoro reg. Sardegna Italy
142 E6 Løgumkloster Denmark
78 □5 Loh i. Vanuatu
142 G6 Lohals Denmark
117 J8 Lohardaga Jharkhand India
116 E5 Loharu Haryana India
214 H4 Lohatlha S. Africa
116 D6 Lohawat Rajasthan India
173 O3 Lohberg Ger.
158 H6 Lohéac France
168 H2 Lohe-Rickelshof Ger.
169 I8 Lohfelden Ger.
Lohifushi i. N. Male Maldives see Lhohifushi
Lohil r. China/India see Zayü Qu
141 T6 Lohilahti Fin.
140 R3 Lohiniva Fin.
141 R6 Lohja Fin.
138 G1 Lohjanjärvi l. Fin.
169 D9 Lohmar Ger.
170 I1 Lohme Ger.
170 F3 Lohmen Mecklenburg-Vorpommern Ger.
171 J9 Lohmen Sachsen Ger.
169 F9 Löhnberg Ger.
169 G6 Löhne Ger.
168 F5 Lohne (Oldenburg) Ger.
179 H3 Lohnsburg am Kobernaußerwald Austria
172 H2 Lohr r. Ger.
169 G9 Lohra Ger.
172 H2 Lohr am Main Ger.
171 J8 Lohsa Ger.
140 Q4 Lohtaja Fin.
138 K3 Lohusuu Estonia
96 E4 Loi, Nam r. Myanmar alt. Nanlei He (China)
191 K7 Loiano Italy
173 M4 Loiching Ger.
159 J6 Loigné-sur-Mayenne France
156 C7 Loigny-la-Bataille France
96 C5 Loikaw Myanmar
96 C5 Loi Lan mt. Myanmar/Thai.
208 D5 Loile r. Dem. Rep. Congo
96 C4 Loi-lem Myanmar
96 D3 Loi Lun Myanmar
141 Q6 Loimaa Fin.
138 F1 Loimaan kunta Fin.
138 F1 Loimijoki r. Fin.
156 E7 Loing r. France
96 C2 Loipyet Hills Myanmar
156 B7 Loir r. France
159 L6 Loir, Les Vaux du val. France
159 J6 Loiré France
160 E5 Loire dept France
159 G7 Loire r. France
160 C3 Loire, Canal latéral à la France
160 E5 Loire, Gorges de la France
156 C8 Loire, Val de val. France
158 G7 Loire-Atlantique dept France
160 C3 Loire et de l'Allier, Plaines de la plain France

Luala to Lyuban'
345

213 H3 Luala r. Moz.
209 B6 Luali Dem. Rep. Congo
240 □C12 Lualualei HI U.S.A.
211 B8 Luambe National Park Zambia
209 E8 Luampa Zambia
209 E8 Luampa r. Zambia
109 K3 Lu'an Anhui China
246 □ Luana Point Jamaica
96 F4 Luân Châu Vietnam
109 H2 Luanchuan Henan China
182 I1 Luanco Spain
209 B7 Luanda Angola
209 B7 Luanda prov. Angola
209 C7 Luando Angola
209 C7 Luando r. Angola
209 C7 Luando, Reserva Natural Integral do nature res. Angola
93 F8 Luang i. Maluku Indon.
96 F6 Luang, Huai r. Thai.
97 D10 Luang, Khao mt. Thai.
97 E11 Luang, Thale lag. Thai.
209 D8 Luanginga r. Zambia
78 □6 Luangiua i. Solomon Is
Luang Nam Tha Laos see Louangnamtha
Luang Phrabang, Thiu Khao mts Laos/Thai. see Luang Prabang Range
Luang Prabang Laos see Louangphabang
108 C10 Luang Prabang Range mts Laos/Thai.
209 C7 Luangue Angola
209 D8 Luanguinga r. Angola
209 F8 Luangwa Zambia
211 A8 Luangwa r. Zambia
106 C9 Luanhaizi Qinghai China
107 P7 Luan He r. China
107 P7 Luannan Hebei China
251 G6 Lua Nova Brazil
107 O6 Luanping Hebei China
209 F8 Luanshya Zambia
260 E5 Luan Toro Arg.
107 P7 Luanxian Hebei China
209 F7 Luanza Dem. Rep. Congo
Luanzhou Hebei China see Luanxian
Luao Angola see Luau
209 F7 Luapula r. Dem. Rep. Congo/Zambia
209 F7 Luapula prov. Zambia
Luar i. Cocos Is see Horsburgh Island
95 J4 Luar, Danau l. Indon.
182 G1 Luarca Spain
209 D7 Luashi Dem. Rep. Congo
209 D8 Luatamba Angola
211 C8 Luatize r. Moz.
209 D7 Luau Angola
207 H6 Luba Equat. Guinea
175 L5 Lubaczów Pol.
175 K5 Lubaczówka r. Pol.
209 C7 Lubalo Angola
174 D4 Lubań Pol.
138 J5 Lubāna Latvia
138 J5 Lubānas ezers l. Latvia
92 C5 Lubang Phil.
92 C5 Lubang i. Phil.
92 B5 Lubang Islands Phil.
209 B8 Lubango Angola
174 C2 Lubanowo Pol.
209 E6 Lubao Dem. Rep. Congo
171 F6 Lübars Ger.
175 K4 Lubartów Pol.
174 E3 Lubasz Pol.
175 H2 Lubawa Pol.
174 E5 Lubawka Pol.
169 G6 Lübbecke Ger.
165 G7 Lubbeek Belgium
171 I7 Lübben Ger.
171 I7 Lübbenau Ger.
214 D5 Lubbeskolk salt pan S. Africa
237 E9 Lubbock TX U.S.A.
170 D5 Lübbow Ger.
174 C2 Lubczyna Pol.
233 □S4 Lubec ME U.S.A.
168 K3 Lübeck Ger.
232 D9 Lubeck WV U.S.A.
168 K2 Lübecker Bucht b. Ger.
209 E6 Lubefu Dem. Rep. Congo
107 Q4 Lubei Nei Mongol China
177 I2 Ľubeľa Slovakia
175 K4 Lubelska, Wyżyna hills Pol.
175 K4 Lubelskie prov. Pol.
Lüben Pol. see Lubin
176 C1 Lubenec Czech Rep.
175 J6 Lubenia Pol.
177 J3 Lubeník Slovakia
120 F2 Lubenka Kazakh.
208 F5 Lubero Dem. Rep. Congo
161 G9 Lubéron, Montagne du ridge France
161 G9 Lubéron, Parc Naturel Régional du nature res. France
162 G5 Lubersac France
170 D4 Lübesse Ger.
182 G4 Lubián Spain
174 G2 Łubianka Pol.
174 E4 Lubiąż Pol.
92 C6 Lubic i. Phil.
177 J2 Ľubica r. Slovakia
174 G2 Lubichowo Pol.
174 G2 Lubicz Dolny Pol.
174 D2 Lubie, Jezioro l. Pol.
174 D4 Lubięcin Pol.
175 H6 Lubień Pol.
175 G3 Lubienka r. Pol.
175 H3 Lubień Kujawski Pol.
174 D2 Lubieszewo Pol.
174 G2 Lubiewo Pol.
174 E4 Lubin Pol.
167 H3 Lubiń Pol.
209 F5 Lubirizi Dem. Rep. Congo
215 L7 Lubisi Dam resr S. Africa
174 C3 Lubiszyn Pol.
175 K4 Lublin Pol.
174 G5 Lubliniec Pol.
170 I2 Lubmin Ger.
Lubnān country Asia see Lebanon
174 F2 Lubnia Pol.
174 G5 Łubniany Pol.
174 G4 Łubnice Łódzkie Pol.
175 J5 Łubnice Świętokrzyskie Pol.
174 D3 Lubniewice Pol.
175 H3 Łubno Łódzkie Pol.
174 F1 Łubno Pomorskie Pol.
174 E2 Lubno Pol.
137 M3 Lubny Ukr.
95 I4 Lubok Antu Sarawak Malaysia
215 P2 Lubombo admin. dist. Swaziland
175 I1 Lubomino Pol.
174 E3 Luboń Pol.
140 U5 Lubosalma Rus. Fed.
177 K2 Ľubotice Slovakia
177 J2 Ľubotín Slovakia
170 E3 Lübow Ger.
175 H2 Lubowidz Pol.
174 F3 Łubowo Wielkopolskie Pol.
174 E2 Łubowo Zachodniopomorskie Pol.
174 G3 Lubraniec Pol.
185 O6 Lubrín Spain
174 D3 Lubrza Lubuskie Pol.
174 F5 Lubrza Opolskie Pol.
174 C4 Lubsko Pol.
170 D3 Lübstorf Ger.
174 G3 Lubstów Pol.
174 F5 Lubsza Pol.
174 C4 Lubsza r. Pol.
170 D4 Lübtheen Ger.
92 C3 Lubuagan Luzon Phil.
209 E6 Lububu Dem. Rep. Congo
209 E7 Lubudi Dem. Rep. Congo
209 E7 Lubudi r. Dem. Rep. Congo
94 F6 Lubukbalang Sumatera Indon.
94 E6 Lubuklinggau Sumatera Indon.
94 C3 Lubukpakam Sumatera Indon.
94 D4 Lubuksikaping Sumatera Indon.
209 E7 Lubumbashi Dem. Rep. Congo
209 E6 Lubunda Dem. Rep. Congo
209 E8 Lubungu Zambia
174 D3 Lubuskie prov. Pol.
174 C3 Lubuskie, Pojezierze reg. Pol.
209 D9 Lubuta Zambia
208 E5 Lubutu Dem. Rep. Congo
208 E5 Lubutu r. Dem. Rep. Congo
209 F7 Lubwe Zambia
176 B1 Luby Czech Rep.
139 S9 Lubyanki Rus. Fed.
175 L5 Lubycza Królewska Pol.
170 F4 Lübz Ger.
161 D7 Luc Languedoc-Roussillon France
163 J7 Luc Midi-Pyrénées France
185 O6 Lucainena de las Torres Spain
209 B7 Lucala Angola
227 M6 Lucan Ont. Can.
147 J6 Lucan Ireland
252 B3 Lucanas Peru
177 L5 Lucani Romania
196 I7 Lučani Serbia
222 A2 Lucania, Mount Y.T. Can.
111 L8 Lücaoshan Qinghai China
209 D7 Lucapa Angola
185 O6 Lúcar Spain
185 O6 Lúcar mt. Spain
185 N6 Lúcar, Sierra de mts Spain
261 H2 Lucas r. Arg.
253 G3 Lucas Brazil
261 H3 Lucas González Arg.
261 H2 Lucas Sur Arg.
232 C10 Lucasville OH U.S.A.
231 H12 Lucaya Gd Bahama Bahamas
159 N7 Luçay-le-Mâle France
190 J8 Lucca Italy
190 J8 Lucca prov. Italy
236 G2 Lucca ND U.S.A.
194 E8 Lucca Sicula Sicilia Italy
192 C2 Lucciana Corse France
156 B7 Lucé France
179 K7 Luče Slovenia
246 □ Lucea Jamaica
146 G13 Luce Bay Scotland U.K.
237 K10 Lucedale MS U.S.A.
256 B4 Lucélia Brazil
92 C5 Lucena Luzon Phil.
185 K6 Lucena Spain
187 E7 Lucena, Riu r. Spain
185 L5 Lucena, Sierra de mts Spain
186 C4 Lucena de Jalón Spain
187 E7 Lucena del Cid Spain
160 C3 Lucenay-lès-Aix France
160 E2 Lucenay-l'Évêque France
161 G7 Luc-en-Diois France
177 I3 Lučenec Slovakia
186 C4 Luceni Spain
193 O4 Lucera Italy
161 K9 Lucéram France
252 C3 Lucerna Peru
Lucerne Switz. see Luzern
240 J2 Lucerne CA U.S.A.
240 P7 Lucerne Valley CA U.S.A.
242 F2 Lucero Mex.
157 K6 Lucey France
177 I3 Lucfalva Hungary
136 H2 Luchanky Ukr.
138 K6 Luchay Belarus
100 I5 Luchegorsk Rus. Fed.
129 I4 Luchek Rus. Fed.
Lucheng Guangxi China see Luchuan
107 M8 Lucheng Shanxi China
Lucheng Sichuan China see Kangding
159 L6 Luché-Pringé France
211 C7 Lucheringo r. Moz.
156 D3 Lucheux France
139 W5 Luchki Rus. Fed.
139 N7 Luchosa r. Belarus
170 D5 Lüchow Ger.
108 H7 Luchuan Guangxi China
108 D7 Lüchun Yunnan China
156 D4 Luchy France
185 K3 Luciana Spain
175 H4 Luciąża r. Pol.
175 H3 Lucień Pol.
191 L9 Lucignano Italy
188 D3 Lucija Slovenia
182 H4 Lucillo de Somoza Spain
85 K5 Lucinda Qld Austr.
82 H7 Lucindale S.A. Austr.
179 J7 Lučine Slovenia
245 H3 Lucio Vázquez Mex.
93 E6 Lucipara, Kepulauan is Maluku Indon.
209 B8 Lucira Angola
193 N4 Lucito Italy
197 P6 Luciu Romania
Łuck Ukr. see Luts'k
226 B4 Luck WI U.S.A.
171 F8 Lucka Ger.
171 I7 Luckau Ger.
Luckeesarai Bihar India see Lakhisarai
171 H6 Luckenwalde Ger.
215 I5 Luckhoff S. Africa
227 M6 Lucknow Ont. Can.
116 H6 Lucknow Uttar Prad. India
170 E5 Lückstedt Ger.
191 K2 Luco, Monte mt. Italy
193 K4 Luco dei Marsi Italy
162 B3 Luçon France
108 H3 Lücongpo Hubei China
163 C9 Lucq-de-Béarn France
246 F3 Lucrecia, Cabo c. Cuba
159 K3 Luc-sur-Mer France
209 B6 Lucunga Angola
209 D8 Lucusse Angola
84 F7 Lucy Creek N.T. Austr.
160 D1 Lucy-le-Bois France
Lüda Liaoning China see Dalian
134 G2 Luda Rus. Fed.
146 B8 Ludag Western Isles, Scotland U.K.
197 P7 Luda Kamchiya r. Bulg.
188 F2 Ludbreg Croatia
169 E8 Lüdenscheid Ger.
168 K5 Lüder Ger.
171 E5 Lüderitz Ger.
212 B5 Lüderitz Namibia
168 K3 Lüdersdorf Ger.
178 A5 Ludesch Austria
211 B7 Ludewa Tanz.
151 I5 Ludgershall Wiltshire, England U.K.
150 A7 Ludgvan Cornwall, England U.K.
116 E4 Ludhiana Punjab India
108 D5 Ludian Yunnan China
108 D4 Luding Sichuan China
169 D7 Lüdinghausen Ger.
226 H6 Ludington MI U.S.A.
235 H1 Ludingtonville NY U.S.A.
234 F6 Ludlam Bay NJ U.S.A.
150 G3 Ludlow Shropshire, England U.K.
241 P7 Ludlow CA U.S.A.
233 M5 Ludlow VT U.S.A.
179 J6 Ludmannsdorf Austria
197 O7 Ludogorie reg. Bulg.
197 O7 Ludogorsko Plato plat. Bulg.
138 M3 Ludoni Rus. Fed.
162 C6 Ludon-Médoc France
231 G10 Ludowici GA U.S.A.
157 L6 Ludres France
197 M4 Luduș Romania
143 L1 Ludvika Sweden
173 K3 Ludwig-Donau-Main-Kanal canal Ger.
169 I9 Ludwigsau-Friedlos Ger.
172 G4 Ludwigsburg Ger.
171 L8 Ludwigsdorf Ger.
171 H6 Ludwigsfelde Ger.
172 G6 Ludwigshafen Ger.
172 E3 Ludwigshafen am Rhein Ger.
170 D4 Ludwigslust Ger.
170 D4 Ludwigsluster Kanal canal Ger.
Ludwigsort Rus. Fed. see Ladushkin
171 D10 Ludwigsstadt Ger.
175 K4 Ludwin Pol.
138 K5 Ludza Latvia
163 C7 Lüe France
209 D6 Luebo Dem. Rep. Congo
209 E5 Lueki Dem. Rep. Congo
209 E5 Lueki r. Dem. Rep. Congo
182 H6 Luelmo Spain
209 F5 Luemba Dem. Rep. Congo
209 F8 Luembe Zambia
209 C7 Luena Angola
209 E7 Luena Dem. Rep. Congo
209 F7 Luena Zambia
209 D8 Luena r. Zambia
209 D8 Luena Flats plain Zambia
209 D9 Luengé, Coutada Pública do nature res. Angola
209 D9 Luengue r. Angola
213 G3 Luenha r. Moz./Zimbabwe
251 F3 Luepa Venez.
169 I7 Lüerdissen Ger.
186 C3 Luesia Spain
108 F2 Lüeyang Shaanxi China
109 J7 Lufeng Guangdong China
Lufeng Hunan China see Xupu
108 D6 Lufeng Yunnan China
209 B6 Lufico Angola
209 E7 Lufira r. Dem. Rep. Congo
209 E7 Lufira, Lac de retenue de la resr Dem. Rep. Congo
237 H10 Lufkin TX U.S.A.
Lufu Yunnan China see Shilin
211 A7 Lufubu r. Zambia
196 J6 Lug r. Serbia
138 M3 Luga Rus. Fed.
138 L2 Luga r. Rus. Fed.
190 F3 Lugano Switz.
190 F4 Lugano, Lago di l. Italy/Switz.
Lugano, Lake Italy/Switz. see Lugano, Lago di
Lugansk Ukr. see Luhans'k
Luganskaya Oblast' admin. div. Ukr. see Luhans'ka Oblast'
Lugansk Oblast admin. div. Ukr. see Luhans'ka Oblast'
78 □5 Luganville Vanuatu
177 L4 Lugașu de Jos Romania
171 G9 Lugau Ger.
169 H7 Lügde Ger.
Lugdunum France see Lyon
213 H3 Lugela Moz.
213 H3 Lugela r. Moz.
213 H1 Lugenda r. Moz.
150 G3 Lugg r. Wales U.K.
81 D11 Luggate South I. N.Z.
111 J11 Luggudontsen mt. Xizang China
210 D2 Lughaye Somalia
163 C7 Luglon France
193 I2 Lugnano in Teverina Italy
147 J7 Lugnaquilla hill Ireland
160 F4 Lugny France
160 E4 Lugny-lès-Charolles France
191 L7 Lugo Italy
182 E2 Lugo Spain
182 F3 Lugo prov. Spain
192 C3 Lugo-di-Nazza Corse France
197 J5 Lugoj Romania
182 I2 Lugones Spain
162 D6 Lugon-et-l'Île-du-Carnay France
163 C7 Lugos France
139 U5 Lugovaya Rus. Fed.
Lugovaya Proleyka Rus. Fed. see Primorsk
121 O6 Lugovoy Kazakh.
160 J4 Lugrin France
185 M6 Lugros Spain
108 D4 Lugu Sichuan China
111 G10 Lugu Xizang China
92 C9 Lugus i. Phil.
136 D3 Luha r. Ukr.
177 G2 Luhačovice Czech Rep.
137 S5 Luhan' r. Ukr.
137 S5 Luhanchyk r. Ukr.
141 R6 Luhanka Fin.
137 S5 Luhans'k Ukr.
137 S4 Luhans'ka Oblast' admin. div. Ukr.
137 N8 Luhans'ke Ukr.
Luhansk Oblast admin. div. Ukr. see Luhans'ka Oblast'
139 N6 Luhawskiya Belarus
169 H6 Luhden Ger.
109 J7 Luhe Guangdong China
109 L2 Luhe Jiangsu China
107 K8 Lu He r. China
168 J4 Luhe r. Ger.
173 M2 Luhe-Wildenau Ger.
128 E6 Luḩfī, Wādī watercourse Jordan
107 P3 Luhin Sum Nei Mongol China
Luhit r. China/India see Zayü Qu
96 B1 Luhit r. India
170 I2 Lühmannsdorf Ger.
211 C7 Luhombero Tanz.
137 O8 Luhove Ukr.
140 U5 Luhtapohja Fin.
Luhua Sichuan China see Heishui
108 C3 Luhuo Sichuan China
136 H2 Luhyny Ukr.
209 D7 Luia Angola
209 D6 Luia r. Angola
213 G3 Luia r. Moz.
209 D9 Luiana Angola
209 D9 Luiana r. Angola
209 D9 Luiana, Coutada Pública do nature res. Angola
197 O6 Luica Romania
146 G7 Luichart, Loch l. Scotland U.K.
Luichow Peninsula China see Leizhou Bandao
213 G4 Luido Moz.
Luik Belgium see Liège
208 D5 Luilaka r. Dem. Rep. Congo
Luimbale Angola see Londuimbali
Luimneach Ireland see Limerick
146 E10 Luing i. Scotland U.K.
146 E10 Luing, Sound of sea chan. Scotland U.K.
190 F4 Luino Italy
182 E4 Luintra Spain
209 D8 Luio r. Angola
140 S3 Luiro r. Fin.
156 B7 Luisant France
254 E2 Luís Correia Brazil
241 P9 Luis Echeverría Álvarez Mex.
254 F3 Luís Gomes Brazil
209 E7 Luishia Dem. Rep. Congo
242 G3 Luis L. León, Presa resr Mex.
244 D1 Luis Moya Durango Mex.
244 E3 Luis Moya Zacatecas Mex.
247 □1 Luis Peña, Cayo de i. Puerto Rico
262 V1 Luitpold Coast Antarctica
244 G7 Luivanos Mex.
209 D6 Luiza Dem. Rep. Congo
209 E6 Luizi Dem. Rep. Congo
261 H4 Luján Buenos Aires Arg.
260 E3 Luján San Luis Arg.
261 H4 Lujan r. Arg.
260 C3 Luján de Cuyo Arg.
109 K3 Lujiang Anhui China
106 I9 Lüjing Gansu China
137 M3 Luka Ukr.
100 H2 Lukachek Rus. Fed.
177 G3 Lukáčovce Slovakia
176 F4 Lukácsháza Hungary
209 B6 Lukala Dem. Rep. Congo
209 C6 Lukanga Dem. Rep. Congo
209 E8 Lukanga Swamps Zambia
Lukapa Angola see Lucapa
137 N6 Lukasheve Ukr.
188 G3 Lukavac Bos.-Herz.
175 L5 Łukawiec Pol.
87 D9 Luke, Mount hill W.A. Austr.
209 E7 Lukenga, Lac l. Dem. Rep. Congo
209 C5 Lukenie r. Dem. Rep. Congo
147 H8 Lukeswell Ireland
241 T10 Lukeville AZ U.S.A.
134 H4 Lukh Rus. Fed.
134 H4 Lukh r. Rus. Fed.
139 W7 Lukhovitsy Rus. Fed.
197 M9 Lŭki Bulg.
139 R1 Lukinskaya Rus. Fed.
136 D2 Lukiv Ukr.
109 □J7 Luk Keng H.K. China
208 C5 Lukolela Équateur Dem. Rep. Congo
209 E6 Lukolela Kasaï-Oriental Dem. Rep. Congo
138 M7 Lukomskaye, Vozyera l. Belarus
Lukou Hunan China see Zhuzhou
188 G3 Lukovac r. Bos.-Herz.
198 A3 Lukovë Albania
197 M7 Lukovit Bulg.
139 R5 Lukovnikovo Rus. Fed.
191 R6 Lukovo Croatia
175 K4 Łuków Pol.
175 K3 Łukowisko Pol.
135 I5 Lukoyanov Rus. Fed.
110 I5 Lükqün Xinjiang China
93 C4 Luksagu Sulawesi Indon.
138 G7 Lukšiai Lith.
209 E6 Lukuga r. Dem. Rep. Congo
209 B6 Lukula Dem. Rep. Congo
211 C7 Lukuledi Tanz.
209 D8 Lukulu Zambia
211 B7 Lukumburu Tanz.
209 C6 Lukuni Dem. Rep. Congo
209 F8 Lukusashi r. Zambia
211 B8 Lukusuzi National Park Zambia
136 C4 Luky Ukr.
209 D5 Lula r. Dem. Rep. Congo
192 C7 Lula Sardegna Italy
140 Q4 Luleå Sweden
140 Q4 Luleälven r. Sweden
199 I1 Lüleburgaz Turkey
258 D2 Lules Arg.
108 D6 Luliang Yunnan China
107 L8 Lüliang Shan mts China
209 F6 Lulimba Dem. Rep. Congo
237 G11 Luling TX U.S.A.
147 I6 Lullymore Ireland
107 P7 Lulong Hebei China
208 C4 Lulonga Dem. Rep. Congo
208 C4 Lulonga r. Dem. Rep. Congo
208 D4 Lulu r. Dem. Rep. Congo
Luluabourg Dem. Rep. Congo see Kananga
111 G12 Lülung Xizang China
87 D9 Lulworth, Mount hill W.A. Austr.
78 □2 Luma American Samoa
209 C7 Luma Cassai Angola
111 H11 Lumachomo Xizang China
260 A6 Lumaco Chile
209 D8 Lumai Angola
95 J9 Lumajang Jawa Indon.
111 E9 Lumajangdong Co salt l. China
209 E5 Lumana Dem. Rep. Congo
138 F3 Lümanda Estonia
127 M7 Lümär Iran
Lumbala Moxico Angola see Lumbala Kaquengue
Lumbala Moxico Angola see Lumbala N'guimbo
209 D8 Lumbala Kaquengue Angola
209 D8 Lumbala N'guimbo Angola
211 A6 Lumbe Tanz.
209 D9 Lumbe r. Zambia
231 H8 Lumber r. SC U.S.A.
231 H8 Lumberton NC U.S.A.
209 C6 Lumbi Dem. Rep. Congo
183 R3 Lumbier Spain
95 L2 Lumbis Kalimantan Indon.
213 I2 Lumbo Moz.
182 G7 Lumbrales Spain
183 O4 Lumbreras Spain
156 D2 Lumbres France
117 N7 Lumding Assam India
211 B7 Lumecha Tanz.
190 I4 Lumezzane Italy
91 J7 Lumi P.N.G.
140 R4 Lumijoki Fin.
197 Q6 Lumina Romania
257 E4 Luminárias Brazil
192 B2 Lumio Corse France
143 O4 Lummelunda Gotland Sweden
165 H7 Lummen Belgium
96 D5 Lum-nan-pai Wildlife Reserve nature res. Thai.
141 P6 Lumparland Åland Fin.
138 D1 Lumparn b. Fin.
146 K8 Lumphanan Aberdeenshire, Scotland U.K.
97 H8 Lumphăt Cambodia
186 C4 Lumpiaque Spain
231 E9 Lumpkin GA U.S.A.
223 J5 Lumsden Sask. Can.
81 C12 Lumsden South I. N.Z.
94 D2 Lumut Malaysia
95 K5 Lumut, Gunung mt. Indon.
94 F6 Lumut, Tanjung pt Indon.
209 E7 Lumwana Zambia
191 R6 Lun Croatia
106 I3 Lün Mongolia
191 R6 Lun, Rt pt Croatia
92 C3 Luna Luzon Phil.
186 D3 Luna Spain
184 H8 Luna hill Spain
182 I4 Luna r. Spain
241 X8 Luna NM U.S.A.
209 D8 Lunache Angola
156 E7 Lunain r. France
192 B8 Lunamatrona Sardegna Italy
146 L9 Lunan Bay Scotland U.K.
108 D5 Lunan Shan mts Sichuan China
227 K8 Luna Pier MI U.S.A.
161 C9 Lunas France
116 D8 Lunavada Gujarat India
124 C3 Lunayyir, Ḩarrat lava field Saudi Arabia
177 L5 Lunca Bihor Romania
197 M7 Lunca Teleorman Romania
197 N4 Lunca Bradului Romania
177 L6 Lunca Cernii de Jos Romania
197 M3 Lunca Ilvei Romania
146 J10 Luncarty Perth and Kinross, Scotland U.K.
197 M6 Luncavăț r. Romania
177 L5 Luncoiu de Jos Romania
123 M8 Lund Pak.
142 J6 Lund Sweden
241 Q3 Lund NV U.S.A.
241 S3 Lund UT U.S.A.
209 C7 Lunda Norte prov. Angola
223 L5 Lundar Man. Can.
209 D7 Lunda Sul prov. Angola
211 B8 Lundazi Zambia
222 H5 Lundbreck Alta Can.
168 K1 Lundby Denmark
142 E6 Lunde Denmark
168 H2 Lunden Ger.
142 C3 Lundevatn l. Norway
Lundi r. Zimbabwe see Runde
146 K10 Lundin Links Fife, Scotland U.K.
226 F5 Lunds WI U.S.A.
143 K2 Lundsfjärden l. Sweden
95 H4 Lundu Sarawak Malaysia
211 B7 Lundu Tanz.
150 C5 Lundy i. England U.K.
168 G3 Lune r. Ger.
149 L5 Lune r. England U.K.
169 B10 Lünebach Ger.
215 O3 Luneberg S. Africa
168 J4 Lüneburg Ger.
168 J4 Lüneburger Heide reg. Ger.
168 I4 Lüneburger Heide, Naturpark nature res. Ger.
161 E9 Lunel France
161 K6 Lunella, Punta mt. Italy
161 E9 Lunel-Viel France
169 E7 Lünen Ger.
232 G12 Lunenburg VA U.S.A.
178 A5 Lünersee l. Austria
159 P8 Lunery France
168 G4 Lunestedt Ger.
157 L6 Lunéville France
213 I2 Lunga Moz.
209 E8 Lunga r. Zambia
179 H5 Lungau r. source Austria
190 E2 Lungern Switz.
78 □6 Lungga Guadalcanal Solomon Is
111 F11 Lunggar Xizang China
111 F11 Lunggar Shan mts Xizang China
206 B4 Lungi Sierra Leone
109 □I7 Lung Kwu Chau i. H.K. China
Lungleh Mizoram India see Lunglei
117 N8 Lunglei Mizoram India
111 H11 Lungmari mt. Xizang China
111 E9 Lungmu Co salt l. China
193 J3 Lungo, Lago l. Italy
193 Q8 Lungro Italy
209 D8 Lungué-Bungo r. Angola
209 D8 Lungwebungu r. Zambia
117 I5 Lunh Nepal
116 D6 Luni Rajasthan India
116 C7 Luni r. India
123 N6 Luni r. Pak.
Luninets Belarus see Luninyets
240 N3 Luning NV U.S.A.
135 I5 Lunino Rus. Fed.
136 F1 Luninyets Belarus
163 G8 L'Union France
116 D5 Lunkaransar Rajasthan India
116 D5 Lunkha Rajasthan India
123 O3 Lunkho mt. Afgh./Pak.
140 S3 Lunkkaus Fin.
138 H8 Lunna Belarus
146 □N2 Lunna Ness hd Scotland U.K.
169 D6 Lünne Ger.
85 M1 Lunn Island P.N.G.
170 J5 Lunow Ger.
206 B4 Lunsar Sierra Leone
209 F8 Lunsemfwa r. Zambia
213 F5 Lunsklip S. Africa
110 G6 Luntai Xinjiang China
164 I4 Lunteren Neth.
198 B2 Lunxhërisë, Mali i ridge Albania
95 L9 Lunyuk Sumbawa Indon.
171 G9 Lunzenau Ger.
211 A7 Lunzua Zambia
100 G5 Luobei Heilong. China
110 I7 Luobuzhuang Xinjiang China
Luocheng Fujian China see Hui'an
106 F7 Luocheng Gansu China
108 G6 Luocheng Guangxi China
107 K9 Luochuan Shaanxi China
108 F6 Luodian Guizhou China
109 H7 Luoding Guangdong China
140 R4 Luodonselkä sea chan. Fin.
108 H8 Luodou Sha i. China
192 C5 Luogosanto Sardegna Italy
109 J2 Luohe Henan China
107 M9 Luo He r. Henan China
107 L9 Luo He r. Shaanxi China
108 E3 Luojiang Sichuan China
108 H8 Luo Jiang r. China
107 P9 Luoma Hu l. China
107 L9 Luonan Shaanxi China
107 L9 Luoning Henan China
141 S6 Luonteri l. Fin.
108 E6 Luoping Yunnan China
141 R6 Luopioinen Fin.
109 J2 Luoshan Henan China
109 J3 Luotian Hubei China
106 E6 Luotuoquan Gansu China
140 T1 Luovttejohka Norway
109 I5 Luoxiao Shan mts China
Luoxiong Yunnan China see Luoping
Luoyang Guangdong China see Boluo
107 M9 Luoyang Henan China
Luoyang Zhejiang China see Taishun
109 L5 Luoyuan Fujian China
209 B6 Luozi Dem. Rep. Congo
100 G7 Luozigou Jilin China
211 B7 Lupa Market Tanz.
213 E3 Lupane Zimbabwe
108 E5 Lupanshui Guizhou China
95 I4 Lupar r. Malaysia
143 N7 Łupawa r. Pol.
173 L3 Lupburg Ger.
184 D2 Lupe r. Port.
197 N4 Lupeni Harghita Romania
197 L5 Lupeni Hunedoara Romania
246 H4 Luperón Dom. Rep.
172 F5 Lupfen hill Ger.
163 E8 Lupiac France
211 B7 Lupilichi Moz.
186 D3 Lupiñén Spain
185 L5 Lupión Spain
209 C8 Lupire Angola
211 C7 Lupiro Tanz.
175 K6 Łupków Pol.
191 Q5 Lupoglav Croatia
92 F8 Lupon Mindanao Phil.
170 L5 Łupowo Pol.
171 G8 Luppa Ger.
157 L6 Luppy France
241 W6 Lupton AZ U.S.A.
134 K3 Lup'ya r. Rus. Fed.
Luqiao Sichuan China see Luding
106 H9 Luqu Gansu China
Lu Qu r. China see Tao He
107 N7 Luquan Hebei China
108 D6 Luquan Yunnan China
185 K5 Luque Spain
209 C7 Luquembo Angola
247 □1 Luquillo Puerto Rico
247 □1 Luquillo, Sierra de mts Puerto Rico
192 C6 Luras Sardegna Italy
122 A3 Lūrā Shīrīn Iran
226 C9 Luray MO U.S.A.
232 G10 Luray VA U.S.A.
163 C9 Lurbe-St-Christau France
160 B3 Lurcy-Lévis France
157 L8 Lure France
161 H8 Lure, Montagne de mt. France
161 H8 Lure, Sommet de mt. France
211 C8 Lureco r. Moz.
209 C7 Luremo Angola
146 F6 Lurgainn, Loch l. Scotland U.K.
147 J4 Lurgan Northern Ireland U.K.
122 H5 Lūrg-e Shotorān salt pan Iran
192 C2 Luri Corse France
210 A3 Luri r. Sudan
252 D4 Luribay Bol.
252 A3 Lurín Peru
213 I2 Lúrio Moz.
213 I2 Lurio r. Moz.
213 I2 Lúrio, Baía do b. Moz.
140 L3 Lurøy Norway
161 H9 Lurs France
159 P7 Lury-sur-Arnon France
142 C2 Lusaheia park Norway
211 A5 Lusahunga Tanz.
209 F6 Lusaka Dem. Rep. Congo
209 F8 Lusaka Zambia
209 F8 Lusaka prov. Zambia
209 D6 Lusambo Dem. Rep. Congo
91 L8 Lusancay Islands and Reefs P.N.G.
209 C6 Lusanga Dem. Rep. Congo
209 E6 Lusangi Dem. Rep. Congo
129 F6 Lusashogh Armenia
194 G2 Lusciano Italy
223 I4 Luseland Sask. Can.
209 F7 Lusenga Plain National Park Zambia
190 C6 Luserna San Giovanni Italy
211 C7 Lusewa Tanz.
86 I4 Lush, Mount hill W.A. Austr.
108 D3 Lushan Sichuan China
Lushar Qinghai China see Huangzhong
107 L9 Lushi Henan China
196 H10 Lushnjë Albania
211 C6 Lushoto Tanz.
100 E7 Lushuihe Jilin China
107 Q7 Lüshun Liaoning China
109 M2 Lüsi Jiangsu China
95 I8 Lusi r. Indon.
162 E3 Lusignan France
160 C3 Lusigny France
156 H7 Lusigny-sur-Barse France
215 N7 Lusikisiki S. Africa
82 □3 Lusitania Bay S. Pacific Ocean
211 A8 Lusiwasi Zambia
147 J5 Lusk Ireland
238 L5 Lusk WY U.S.A.
161 H7 Lus-la-Croix-Haute France
Luso Angola see Luena
182 D8 Luso Port.
146 G10 Luss Argyll and Bute, Scotland U.K.
162 D6 Lussac France
162 F3 Lussac-les-Châteaux France
162 G3 Lussac-les-Églises France
148 F2 Lussa Loch l. Scotland U.K.
161 E8 Lussan France
256 B4 Lussanvira Brazil
168 J5 Lüßberg hill Ger.
170 F3 Lüssow Ger.
209 B7 Lussusso Angola
146 C7 Lusta Highland, Scotland U.K.
172 E3 Lustadt Ger.
190 H1 Lustenau Austria
215 P2 Lusushwana r. Swaziland
Lusutufu r. Africa see Usutu
175 H3 Luszyn Pol.
Lut, Bahrat salt l. Asia see Dead Sea
122 H6 Lut, Dasht-e des. Iran
191 L2 Lutago Italy
Lutai Tianjin China see Ninghe
109 M7 Lü Tao i. Taiwan
168 K4 Lütau Ger.
256 B5 Lutécia Brazil
209 D8 Lutembo Angola
143 Q8 Luterskie, Jezioro l. Pol.
Lutetia France see Paris
122 H7 Lūt-e Zangī Aḩmad des. Iran
226 I5 Luther MI U.S.A.
227 N6 Luther Lake Ont. Can.
232 G7 Luthersburg PA U.S.A.
171 G7 Lutherstadt Wittenberg Ger.
208 F5 Lutiba Dem. Rep. Congo
176 G2 Lutín Czech Rep.
168 K2 Lütjenburg Ger.
168 J3 Lütjensee Ger.
175 H3 Lutocin Pol.
175 H4 Lutomiersk Pol.
151 L4 Luton Luton, England U.K.
151 L4 Luton admin. div. England U.K.
95 K2 Lutong Sarawak Malaysia
213 F3 Lutope r. Zimbabwe
175 K6 Lutowiska Pol.
175 I1 Lutry Pol.
223 I2 Łutselk'e N.W.T. Can.
209 E6 Lutshi Dem. Rep. Congo
136 E3 Luts'k Ukr.
169 J7 Lutter am Barenberge Ger.
157 N8 Lutterbach France
151 J3 Lutterworth Leicestershire, England U.K.
214 G8 Luttig S. Africa
Lutto r. Fin./Rus. Fed. see Lotta
209 D8 Lutuai Angola
137 S5 Lutuhyne Ukr.
174 G4 Lututów Pol.
174 F3 Lutynia r. Pol.
231 F11 Lutz FL U.S.A.
171 F8 Lützen Ger.
169 D10 Lutzerath Ger.
173 J4 Lutzingen Ger.
179 O5 Lutzmannsburg Austria
170 D3 Lützow Ger.
263 C2 Lützow-Holm Bay Antarctica
214 E4 Lutzputs S. Africa
171 F8 Lützschena Ger.
214 C7 Lutzville S. Africa
92 C9 Luuk Phil.
141 S6 Luumäki Fin.
210 D4 Luuq Somalia
140 S3 Luusua Fin.
209 B6 Luvaka Dem. Rep. Congo
215 P2 Luve Swaziland
231 D10 Luverne AL U.S.A.
236 G4 Luverne MN U.S.A.
141 P6 Luvia Fin.
209 B6 Luvo Angola
140 U4 Luvozero Rus. Fed.
209 E6 Luvua r. Dem. Rep. Congo
209 D8 Luvuei Angola
213 F4 Luvuvhu r. S. Africa
211 B8 Luwawa Malawi
211 C7 Luwegu r. Tanz.
210 B4 Luwero Uganda
209 F7 Luwingu Zambia
93 F3 Luwo i. Maluku Indon.
95 I5 Luwuhuyu Kalimantan Indon.
93 C4 Luwuk Sulawesi Indon.
160 G2 Lux France
165 H8 Luxembourg prov. Belgium
165 J9 Luxembourg country Europe
165 J9 Luxembourg Lux.
165 J9 Luxembourg admin. dist. Lux.
Luxemburg country Europe see Luxembourg
226 G5 Luxemburg WI U.S.A.
163 B9 Luxe-Sumberraute France
157 L8 Luxeuil-les-Bains France
163 C7 Luxey France
109 J5 Luxi Jiangxi China
108 B6 Luxi Yunnan China
108 D6 Luxi Yunnan China
108 E4 Luxian Sichuan China
215 J7 Luxolweni S. Africa
Luxor Egypt see Al Uqşur
150 C7 Luxulyan Cornwall, England U.K.
163 B8 Luy r. France
Luyang Sichuan China see Lushan
107 L7 Luya Shan mts China
163 C8 Luy de Béarn r. France
163 C8 Luy de France r. France
182 H4 Luyego de Somoza Spain
109 J2 Luyi Henan China
165 H6 Luyksgestel Neth.
159 M7 Luynes France
Luyuan Shaanxi China see Gaoling
257 E3 Luz Brazil
184 E4 Luz Évora Port.
184 B6 Luz Faro Port.
184 D6 Luz Faro Port.
182 H5 Luz hill Port.
134 I3 Luza Rus. Fed.
134 I3 Luza r. Rus. Fed.
134 L2 Luza r. Rus. Fed.
183 P7 Luzaga Spain
156 D5 Luzarches France
163 D10 Luz-Ardiden France
176 F2 Luže Czech Rep.
163 G7 Luzech France
176 D1 Lužec nad Vltavou Czech Rep.
190 E1 Luzern Switz.
190 E1 Luzern canton Switz.
234 D2 Luzerne PA U.S.A.
234 C2 Luzerne County county PA U.S.A.
139 T7 Luzha r. Rus. Fed.
108 G6 Luzhai Guangxi China
108 B6 Luzhang Yunnan China
108 E5 Luzhi Guizhou China
108 E4 Luzhou Sichuan China
184 C5 Luzianes Port.
256 D2 Luziânia Brazil
176 D1 Lužické hory mts Czech Rep.
254 E2 Luzilândia Brazil
174 G1 Luzino Pol.
183 L2 Luzmela Spain
176 C1 Lužná Czech Rep.
175 J6 Łużna Pol.
138 E4 Lūžņas Latvia
176 D2 Lužnice r. Czech Rep.
92 D4 Luzon i. Phil.
183 P6 Luzón Spain
92 C1 Luzon Strait Phil.
163 E10 Luz-St-Sauveur France
160 D3 Luzy France
174 G4 Łużyca r. Pol.
191 J6 Luzzara Italy
193 Q9 Luzzi Italy
136 G1 L'va r. Ukr.
136 D4 L'viv Ukr.
Lviv Oblast admin. div. Ukr. see L'vivs'ka Oblast'
136 D3 L'vivs'ka Oblast' admin. div. Ukr.
L'vov Ukr. see L'viv
Lvov Oblast admin. div. Ukr. see L'vivs'ka Oblast'
L'vovskaya Oblast' admin. div. Ukr. see L'vivs'ka Oblast'
139 U6 L'vovskiy Rus. Fed.
129 I2 L'vovskiy Pervyy Rus. Fed.
Lwów Ukr. see L'viv
174 E3 Lwówek Pol.
174 D4 Lwówek Śląski Pol.
136 G5 Lyadova r. Ukr.
139 O7 Lyady Belarus
138 L3 Lyady Rus. Fed.
138 J8 Lyakhavichy Belarus
Lyakhovichi Belarus see Lyakhavichy
131 P2 Lyakhovskiye Ostrova is Novosibirskiye O-va Rus. Fed.
137 L1 Lyalichi Rus. Fed.
81 B12 Lyall, Mount South I. N.Z.
Lyallpur Pak. see Faisalabad
Lyal'mikar Uzbek. see Lalmikor
135 I5 Lyambir' Rus. Fed.
134 L4 Lyamino Rus. Fed.
134 G2 Lyamtsa Rus. Fed.
Lyangar Navoiy Uzbek. see Langar
Lyangar Qashqadaryo Uzbek. see Langar
134 M3 Lyapin r. Rus. Fed.
137 L4 Lyashivka Ukr.
141 U6 Lyaskelya Rus. Fed.
197 N7 Lyaskovets Bulg.
138 I9 Lyasnaya Belarus
138 G9 Lyasnaya r. Belarus
175 L3 Lyasnaya Lyevaya r. Belarus
177 L3 Lybokhora Ukr.
146 J6 Lybster Highland, Scotland U.K.
175 M4 Lybytiv Ukr.
170 H4 Lychen Ger.
170 H4 Lychen-Boitzenberg park Ger.
137 O4 Lychkove Ukr.
139 P4 Lychkovo Rus. Fed.
Lyck Pol. see Ełk
140 O4 Lycksele Sweden
234 A2 Lycoming County county PA U.S.A.
234 A2 Lycoming Creek r. PA U.S.A.
Lycopolis Egypt see Asyūţ
151 N6 Lydd Kent, England U.K.
Lydda Israel see Lod
262 W2 Lyddan Island Antarctica
213 F5 Lydenburg S. Africa
150 D6 Lydford Devon, England U.K.
199 I4 Lydia reg. Turkey
150 G4 Lydney Gloucestershire, England U.K.
175 I3 Łydynia r. Pol.
138 I8 Lyebyada r. Belarus
136 H2 Lyel'chytsy Belarus
240 M4 Lyell, Mount CA U.S.A.
84 C7 Lyell Brown, Mount hill N.T. Austr.
222 D4 Lyell Island B.C. Can.
81 G8 Lyell Range mts South I. N.Z.
137 K1 Lyenina Belarus
175 M3 Lyeninski Belarus
138 L7 Lyepyel' Belarus
231 □2 Lyford Cay New Prov. Bahamas
142 I4 Lygnern l. Sweden
138 G5 Lygumai Lith.
137 P4 Lyhivka Ukr.
227 R9 Lykens PA U.S.A.
137 K2 Lykhachiv Ukr.
137 M5 Lykhivka Ukr.
139 Q3 Lykoshino Rus. Fed.
214 I3 Lykso S. Africa
226 B6 Lyle MN U.S.A.
136 I8 Lyman Ukr.
238 I6 Lyman WY U.S.A.
137 P4 Lyman, Ozero l. Ukr.
136 I7 Lymans'ke Ukr.
150 G6 Lyme Bay England U.K.
150 G6 Lyme Regis Dorset, England U.K.
151 O5 Lyminge Kent, England U.K.
151 I6 Lymington Hampshire, England U.K.
149 M7 Lymm Warrington, England U.K.
151 O5 Lympne Kent, England U.K.
150 F6 Lympstone Devon, England U.K.
143 R7 Łyna r. Pol.
232 C12 Lynch KY U.S.A.
231 D8 Lynchburg TN U.S.A.
232 F11 Lynchburg VA U.S.A.
231 H9 Lynches r. SC U.S.A.
232 F11 Lynch Station VA U.S.A.
233 □O4 Lynchville ME U.S.A.
85 I4 Lynd r. Qld Austr.
238 C2 Lynden WA U.S.A.
85 J5 Lyndhurst Qld Austr.
82 G4 Lyndhurst S.A. Austr.
151 I6 Lyndhurst Hampshire, England U.K.
87 C7 Lyndon W.A. Austr.
87 B7 Lyndon r. W.A. Austr.
236 H6 Lyndon KS U.S.A.
226 E6 Lyndon Station WI U.S.A.
232 G5 Lyndonville NY U.S.A.
233 M4 Lyndonville VT U.S.A.
149 K4 Lyne r. England U.K.
151 I4 Lyneham Wiltshire, England U.K.
149 N3 Lynemouth Northumberland, England U.K.
146 J5 Lyness Orkney, Scotland U.K.
142 E5 Lyngby nature res. Denmark
142 D3 Lyngdal Norway
140 P2 Lyngen sea chan. Norway
140 P2 Lyngseidet Norway
150 D7 Lynher r. England U.K.
86 F3 Lynher Reef W.A. Austr.
150 E5 Lynmouth Devon, England U.K.
Lynn Norfolk, England U.K. see King's Lynn
233 O6 Lynn MA U.S.A.
222 C3 Lynn Canal sea chan. AK U.S.A.
241 T2 Lynndyl UT U.S.A.
231 E10 Lynn Haven FL U.S.A.
223 K3 Lynn Lake Man. Can.
137 N2 Lynove Ukr.
137 L3 Lynovytsya Ukr.
87 C10 Lynton W.A. Austr.
150 E5 Lynton Devon, England U.K.
138 J6 Lyntupy Belarus
223 J2 Lynx Lake N.W.T. Can.
226 C6 Lynxville WI U.S.A.
160 F5 Lyon France
Lyon airport France see Satolas
146 I9 Lyon r. Scotland U.K.
146 G9 Lyon, Loch l. Scotland U.K.
233 L4 Lyon Mountain NY U.S.A.
160 F5 Lyonnais, Monts du hills France
82 D4 Lyons S.A. Austr.
87 C8 Lyons r. W.A. Austr.
Lyons France see Lyon
231 F9 Lyons GA U.S.A.
236 F6 Lyons KS U.S.A.
232 I5 Lyons NY U.S.A.
233 J5 Lyons Falls NY U.S.A.
156 B5 Lyons-la-Forêt France
235 I2 Lyons Plain CT U.S.A.
234 D4 Lyon Station PA U.S.A.
139 N6 Lyozna Belarus
136 E3 Lypa r. Ukr.
136 H2 Lypnyky Ukr.
137 M3 Lypova Dolyna Ukr.
136 I4 Lypovets' Ukr.
137 P3 Lyptsi Ukr.
77 F2 Lyra Reef P.N.G.
156 F2 Lys r. France
190 D4 Lys r. Italy
168 J1 Lysabild Denmark
177 H2 Lysá hora mt. Czech Rep.
137 K5 Lysa Hora Ukr.
171 K10 Lysá nad Labem Czech Rep.
177 H2 Lysá pod Makytou Slovakia
175 J2 Łyse Pol.
142 C2 Lysefjorden inlet Norway
142 C2 Lysekammen mt. Norway
142 H3 Lysekil Sweden
139 P9 Lyshchichi Rus. Fed.
175 L3 Lyshchytsy Belarus
128 B3 Lysi Cyprus
175 I5 Łysica hill Pol.
176 F2 Lysice Czech Rep.
198 C4 Lysimacheia, Limni l. Greece
175 M3 Lyskava Belarus
139 N6 Lys'kava Belarus
174 G5 Lyski Pol.
134 I4 Lyskovo Rus. Fed.
137 S6 Lysogorka Rus. Fed.
174 G2 Łysomice Pol.
96 I7 Ly Sơn, Đao i. Vietnam
190 C1 Lyss Switz.
142 G5 Lystrup Denmark
134 L4 Lys'va Rus. Fed.
142 J1 Lysvik Sweden
136 J4 Lysyanka Ukr.
137 R5 Lysychans'k Ukr.
135 I6 Lysyye Gory Rus. Fed.
175 H4 Łyszkowice Pol.
150 H6 Lytchett Matravers Dorset, England U.K.
150 H6 Lytchett Minster Dorset, England U.K.
146 J5 Lyth Highland, Scotland U.K.
149 K6 Lytham St Anne's Lancashire, England U.K.
139 U6 Lytkarino Rus. Fed.
175 M5 Lytovezh Ukr.
81 G10 Lyttelton South I. N.Z.
81 G10 Lyttelton Harbour South I. N.Z.
222 F5 Lytton B.C. Can.
138 L9 Lyuban' Belarus
139 O2 Lyuban' Rus. Fed.

Lyubanskaye Vodaskhovishcha to Majholi

346

138 L9 Lyubanskaye Vodaskhovishcha resr Belarus
136 G4 Lyubar Ukr.
136 J6 Lyubashivka Ukr.
139 N7 Lyubavichi Rus. Fed.
137 O1 Lyubazh Rus. Fed.
138 J8 Lyubcha Belarus
136 J2 Lyubech Ukr.
139 U6 Lyubertsy Rus. Fed.
136 E2 Lyubeshiv Ukr.
134 H4 Lyubim Rus. Fed.
197 O9 Lyubimets Bulg.
137 O2 Lyubimovka Kurskaya Oblast' Rus. Fed.
139 V8 Lyubimovka Tul'skaya Oblast' Rus. Fed.
138 I9 Lyubishchytsy Belarus
139 R3 Lyubitovo Rus. Fed.
175 I1 Lyublino Rus. Fed.
175 M4 Lyublynets' Ukr.
139 R8 Lyubokhna Rus. Fed.
175 M4 Lyubokhyny Ukr.
137 L6 Lyubomyrivka Ukr.
137 O2 Lyubostan' Rus. Fed.
Lyubotin Ukr. see Lyubotyn
137 O4 Lyubotyn Ukr.
138 K8 Lyubyacha Belarus
137 P6 Lyubymivka Ukr.
175 L6 Lyubyntsi Ukr.
139 Q3 Lyubytino Rus. Fed.
139 R8 Lyudinovo Rus. Fed.
139 Q1 Lyugovichi Rus. Fed.
197 P8 Lyulyakovo Bulg.
134 I4 Lyunda r. Rus. Fed.
138 J9 Lyusina Belarus
137 O3 Lyutivka Ukr.
134 L2 Lyzha r. Rus. Fed.
137 R4 Lyzyne Ukr.
138 L4 Lzha r. Rus. Fed.

M

96 D3 Ma r. Myanmar
96 E4 Ma, Nam r. Laos
96 G5 Ma, Sông r. Vietnam
113 □1 Maabadi i. N. Male Maldives
Maafushi i. S. Male Maldives see Mafushi
240 □E13 Ma'alaea HI U.S.A.
114 C10 Maalhosmadulu Atoll Maldives
147 C5 Maam Ireland
Maamakundhoo i. N. Male Maldives see Makunudhoo
209 E9 Maamba Zambia
147 C6 Maam Cross Ireland
207 H6 Ma'an Cameroon
128 D8 Ma'ān Jordan
Maan Turkey see Nusratiye
140 S5 Maaninka Fin.
140 T3 Maaninkavaara Fin.
140 T5 Maanselkä Fin.
109 L3 Ma'anshan Anhui China
106 H2 Maanyt Bulgan Mongolia
107 J3 Maanyt Töv Mongolia
138 I2 Maardu Estonia
165 I6 Maarheeze Neth.
Maarianhamina Åland Fin. see Mariehamn
124 G6 Ma'āriḍ, Banī des. Saudi Arabia
164 H4 Maarn Neth.
128 E2 Ma'arrat al Ikhwān Syria
128 E3 Ma'arrat an Nu'mān Syria
164 H4 Maarssen Neth.
164 H4 Maarssenbroek Neth.
164 H4 Maartensdijk Neth.
164 G5 Maas r. Neth. alt. Meuse (Belgium/France)
147 F3 Maas Ireland
165 I6 Maasbracht Neth.
165 J6 Maasbree Neth.
164 G5 Maasdam Neth.
165 I6 Maaseik Belgium
92 E6 Maasin Leyte Phil.
164 F5 Maasland Neth.
165 I7 Maasmechelen Belgium
169 A8 Maas-Schwalm-Nette nat. park Ger./Neth.
164 F5 Maassluis Neth.
165 I7 Maastricht Neth.
83 K10 Maatsuyker Group is Tas. Austr.
Maba Guangdong China see Qujiang
109 L2 Maba Jiangsu China
93 F3 Maba Halmahera Indon.
202 D6 Maba, Ouadi watercourse Chad
215 K1 Mabaalstad North West S. Africa
215 K1 Mabaalstad North West S. Africa
212 E3 Mababe Depression Botswana
92 C4 Mabalacat Luzon Phil.
213 G4 Mabalane Moz.
208 F4 Mabana Dem. Rep. Congo
208 A5 Mabanda Gabon
124 G8 Ma'bar Yemen
251 G2 Mabaruma Guyana
Mabating Yunnan China see Hongshan
96 C3 Mabein Myanmar
82 E3 Mabel Creek S.A. Austr.
86 I4 Mabel Downs W.A. Austr.
224 B3 Mabella Ont. Can.
222 G5 Mabel Lake B.C. Can.
227 R5 Maberly Ont. Can.
108 D4 Mabian Sichuan China
111 H12 Mabja Xizang China
149 R7 Mablethorpe Lincolnshire, England U.K.
160 E4 Mably France
215 M1 Mabopane S. Africa
213 G4 Mabote Moz.
225 I4 Mabou N.S. Can.
128 D8 Mabrak, Jabal mt. Jordan
206 E2 Mabroûk well Mali
202 B4 Mabrous well Niger
212 D5 Mabuasehube Game Reserve nature res. Botswana
92 C1 Mabudis i. Phil.
214 I1 Mabule Botswana
102 □1 Mabuni Okinawa Japan
202 D3 Ma'būs Yūsuf oasis Libya
212 D5 Mabutsane Botswana
259 B7 Macá, Monte mt. Chile
261 F5 Macachín Arg.
87 D8 Macadam Plains W.A. Austr.
84 B3 Macadam Range hills N.T. Austr.
257 G5 Macaé Brazil
185 O6 Macael Spain
129 C4 Maçahel Geçidi pass Turkey
254 G3 Macaíba Brazil
92 E7 Macajalar Bay Mindanao Phil.
254 E5 Macajuba Brazil
211 B8 Macaloge Moz.
221 H3 MacAlpine Lake Nunavut Can.
224 E3 Macamic Que. Can.
Macan, Kepulauan atolls Indon. see Taka'Bonerate, Kepulauan
213 G4 Macandze Moz.
215 Q1 Macaneta, Ponta de pt Moz.
186 K3 Maçanet de Cabrenys Spain
109 I7 Macao Macao China
182 E9 Mação Port.
251 I4 Macapá Amapá Brazil
252 D2 Macapá Amazonas Brazil
Macar Turkey see Gebiz
250 B6 Macará Ecuador
242 □S14 Macaracas Panama
255 E5 Macarani Brazil
250 C4 Macarena, Cordillera mts Col.
251 F2 Macareo, Caño r. Venez.
83 I8 Macarthur Vic. Austr.
250 B5 Macas Ecuador
182 G6 Maçãs r. Port./Spain
Macassar Sulawesi Indon. see Makassar
Macassar Strait Indon. see Makassar, Selat
187 D9 Macastre Spain
213 H3 Macatanja Moz.
254 F3 Macau Brazil
162 C5 Macau France
252 C2 Macauã r. Brazil
254 C4 Macaúba Brazil
254 E5 Macaúbas Brazil
77 I5 Macauley Island N.Z.
250 C4 Macayari Col.
210 F2 Macbar, Raas pt Somalia
259 F8 Macbride Head Falkland Is
190 F3 Maccagno Italy
213 G5 Maccaretane Moz.
195 I8 Macchia r. Sicilia Italy
193 M4 Macchiagodena Italy
231 F10 Macclenny FL U.S.A.
149 M7 Macclesfield Cheshire, England U.K.
90 D3 Macclesfield Bank sea feature S. China Sea
224 B3 Macdiarmid Ont. Can.
86 J7 Macdonald, Lake salt flat W.A. Austr.
84 C7 Macdonnell Ranges mts N.T. Austr.
223 M4 MacDowell Lake Ont. Can.
146 L7 Macduff Aberdeenshire, Scotland U.K.
177 K5 Macea Romania
182 E4 Maceda Spain
261 I5 Macedo Arg.
182 G5 Macedo de Cavaleiros Port.
Macedon country Europe see Macedonia
197 J9 Macedonia country Europe
235 I1 Macedonia CT U.S.A.
254 G4 Maceió Brazil
254 F3 Maceio, Ponta da pt Brazil
182 F7 Maceira Guarda Port.
182 C9 Maceira Leiria Port.
179 M7 Macelj Croatia
206 C4 Macenta Guinea
191 O9 Macerata Italy
191 O9 Macerata prov. Italy
191 M8 Macerata Feltria Italy
82 F5 Macfarlane, Lake salt flat S.A. Austr.
147 C9 Macgillycuddy's Reeks mts Ireland
148 E4 MacGregor's Corner Northern Ireland U.K.
123 L7 Mach Pak.
131 M3 Macha Rus. Fed.
257 G2 Machacalis Brazil
252 D4 Machacamarca Bol.
250 B5 Machachi Ecuador
253 E2 Machadinho r. Brazil
257 E4 Machado Brazil
215 O1 Machadodorp S. Africa
184 E4 Machados Port.
209 E8 Machai Zambia
213 G4 Machaila Moz.
211 C5 Machakos Kenya
250 B5 Machala Ecuador
260 B4 Machali Chile
Machali Qinghai China see Madoi
95 J4 Machan Sarawak Malaysia
78 □1 Machanao, Mount hill Guam
213 G4 Machanga Moz.
253 E5 Macharetí Bol.
210 B2 Machar Marshes Sudan
84 G8 Machattie, Lake salt flat Qld Austr.
215 Q1 Machatuine Moz.
156 I5 Machault France
Machaze Moz. see Chitobe
158 H8 Machecoul France
165 F7 Machelen Belgium
150 F4 Machen Caerphilly, Wales U.K.
109 J3 Macheng Hubei China
157 M5 Macheren France
114 F4 Macherla Andhra Prad. India
171 G8 Machern Ger.
185 K2 Machero mt. Spain
226 E7 Machesney Park IL U.S.A.
117 K9 Machhagan Orissa India
116 F4 Machhiwara Punjab India
116 I7 Machhlishahr Uttar Prad. India
233 □R4 Machias ME U.S.A.
232 G6 Machias NY U.S.A.
233 □Q2 Machias r. ME U.S.A.
233 □R4 Machias Bay ME U.S.A.
184 □ Machico Madeira
105 J4 Machida Japan
114 G4 Machilipatnam Andhra Prad. India
211 B8 Machinga Malawi
250 C2 Machiques Venez.
146 D11 Machir Bay Scotland U.K.
Machiwara Punjab India see Machhiwara
123 I9 Māch Kowr Iran
239 L10 Macho, Arroyo del watercourse NM U.S.A.
245 N7 Machona, Laguna lag. Mex.
146 E12 Machrihanish Argyll and Bute, Scotland U.K.
137 N4 Machukhy Ukr.
252 B3 Machu Picchu tourist site Peru
252 D3 Machupo r. Bol.
150 E2 Machynlleth Powys, Wales U.K.
213 G5 Macia Moz.
Macias Nguema i. Equat. Guinea see Bioco
175 J4 Maciejowice Pol.
261 G3 Maciel Arg.
197 Q5 Măcin Romania
192 C2 Macinaggio Corse France
83 M3 Macintyre r. N.S.W. Austr.
83 M3 Macintyre Brook r. Qld Austr.
252 B3 Macizo de Tocate mts Peru
241 X2 Mack CO U.S.A.
129 A5 Maçka Turkey
85 L6 Mackay Qld Austr.
223 I3 MacKay r. Alta Can.
238 H4 Mackay ID U.S.A.
86 J7 Mackay, Lake salt flat W.A. Austr.
223 I2 MacKay Lake N.W.T. Can.
262 O1 Mackay Mountains Antarctica
172 D3 Mackenbach Ger.
169 K7 Mackenrode Ger.
85 L7 Mackenzie r. Qld Austr.
222 F4 Mackenzie B.C. Can.
226 F1 Mackenzie Ont. Can.
222 E1 Mackenzie r. N.W.T. Can.
Mackenzie Guyana see Linden
Mackenzie atoll Micronesia see Ulithi
263 E2 Mackenzie Bay Antarctica
220 E3 Mackenzie Bay Y.T. Can.
222 G2 Mackenzie Bison Sanctuary nature res. N.W.T. Can.
222 G2 Mackenzie Highway N.W.T. Can.
221 G2 Mackenzie King Island N.W.T. Can.
222 C1 Mackenzie Mountains N.W.T./Y.T. Can.
Mackillop, Lake salt flat Qld Austr. see Yamma Yamma, Lake
226 I4 Mackinac, Straits of lake channel MI U.S.A.
226 J4 Mackinac Island MI U.S.A.
226 E9 Mackinaw r. IL U.S.A.
226 J4 Mackinaw City MI U.S.A.
223 I4 Macklin Sask. Can.
179 N6 Mačkovci Slovenia
83 N4 Macksville N.S.W. Austr.
85 H7 Mackunda Creek watercourse Qld Austr.
83 N3 Maclean N.S.W. Austr.
215 L8 Macleantown S. Africa
215 M7 Maclear S. Africa
83 N4 Macleay r. N.S.W. Austr.
MacLeod Alta Can. see Fort Macleod
87 B8 MacLeod, Lake imp. l. W.A. Austr.
Macleod's Table South hill Scotland U.K. see Healabhal Bheag
222 C2 Macmillan r. Y.T. Can.
222 D2 Macmillan Pass Y.T. Can.
147 G4 Macnean Lower, Lough l. Northern Ireland U.K.
147 G4 Macnean Upper, Lough l. Ireland/U.K.
213 G4 Maçobere Moz.
209 C6 Macocola Angola
226 D9 Macomb IL U.S.A.
192 B7 Macomer Sardegna Italy
211 D8 Macomia Moz.
160 F4 Mâcon France
231 F9 Macon GA U.S.A.
236 I6 Macon MO U.S.A.
237 K9 Macon MS U.S.A.
232 B10 Macon OH U.S.A.
237 J10 Macon, Bayou r. LA U.S.A.
209 D8 Macondo Angola
160 F4 Mâconnais reg. France
235 G2 Macopin NJ U.S.A.
213 G3 Macossa Moz.
183 J7 Macotera Spain
223 K3 Macoun Lake Sask. Can.
213 G4 Macovane Moz.
Macpherson Robertson Land reg. Antarctica see Mac. Robertson Land
83 K4 Macquarie r. N.S.W. Austr.
83 K9 Macquarie r. Tas. Austr.
83 M5 Macquarie, Lake b. N.S.W. Austr.
83 J10 Macquarie Harbour Tas. Austr.
82 □3 Macquarie Island S. Pacific Ocean
83 K4 Macquarie Marshes N.S.W. Austr.
83 L5 Macquarie Mountain N.S.W. Austr.
266 F9 Macquarie Ridge sea feature S. Pacific Ocean
81 E12 Macraes Flat South I. N.Z.
94 □ MacRitchie Reservoir Sing.
263 E2 Mac. Robertson Land reg. Antarctica
147 E9 Macroom Ireland
243 N9 Mactún Mex.
250 D4 Macú Brazil
190 D4 Macugnaga Italy
245 K8 Macuiltianguis Mex.
250 D1 Macuira, Parque Nacional nat. park Col.
250 C4 Macuje Col.
196 I9 Macukull Albania
82 E2 Macumba S.A. Austr.
82 F2 Macumba watercourse S.A. Austr.
234 D3 Macungie PA U.S.A.
254 F4 Macururé Brazil
252 C3 Macusani Peru
243 M9 Macuspana Mex.
242 E4 Macuzari, Presa resr Mex.
213 H3 Macuze Moz.
233 □Q3 Macwahoc ME U.S.A.
177 K3 Mád Hungary
128 D7 Mādabā Jordan
215 O3 Madadeni S. Africa
123 K7 Madagan Pak.
213 □ Madagascar i. Africa
265 H6 Madagascar Basin sea feature Indian Ocean
265 G7 Madagascar Ridge sea feature Indian Ocean
129 H5 Madagiz Azer.
207 I4 Madagli Nigeria
124 C2 Madā'in Şāliḥ Saudi Arabia
114 E6 Madakasira Andhra Prad. India
92 □ Madalai Palau
216 □1c Madalena Pico Azores
254 F3 Madalena Brazil
202 B4 Madama Niger
197 M9 Madan Bulg.
122 H3 Ma'dan Iran
208 C2 Madana Chad
202 C5 Madana well Chad
114 F6 Madanapalle Andhra Prad. India
91 K8 Madang P.N.G.
116 G7 Madaora Uttar Prad. India
207 G3 Madaoua Niger
197 P7 Madara Bulg.
177 I5 Madaras Hungary
197 J4 Mădăraş Romania
117 M8 Madaripur Bangl.
207 G3 Madarounfa Niger
Madaw Turkm. see Madaw
122 F2 Madaw Turkm.
227 Q4 Madawaska Ont. Can.
224 E4 Madawaska r. Ont. Can.
233 □Q1 Madawaska ME U.S.A.
96 C3 Madaya Myanmar
192 C5 Maddalena, Isola i. Sardegna Italy
195 I9 Maddalena, Penisola della pen. Sicilia Italy
192 C9 Maddalena Spiaggia Sardegna Italy
193 M5 Maddaloni Italy
114 G3 Madded Chhattisgarh India
114 E6 Maddur Karnataka India
164 G5 Made Neth.
208 F3 Madeir Sudan
251 G5 Madeira r. Brazil
184 □ Madeira terr. N. Atlantic Ocean
184 □ Madeira, Arquipélago da is N. Atlantic Ocean
Madeira, Arquipélago da terr. N. Atlantic Ocean see Madeira
184 □ Madeira, Ilha da i. Madeira
184 □ Madeira, Parque Natural de nature res. Madeira
Madeira Islands N. Atlantic Ocean see Madeira, Arquipélago da
253 E2 Madeirinha r. Brazil
225 I4 Madeleine, Îles de la is Que. Can.
160 D4 Madeleine, Monts de la mts France
150 H2 Madeley Staffordshire, England U.K.
150 H2 Madeley Telford and Wrekin, England U.K.
236 H3 Madelia MN U.S.A.
226 D3 Madeline Island WI U.S.A.
208 C2 Madel Ouèï Chad
126 I4 Maden Turkey
121 R4 Madeniyet Kazakh.
188 B2 Mäder Austria
242 E3 Madera Mex.
185 N4 Madera r. Spain
240 L5 Madera CA U.S.A.
183 K5 Maderano r. Spain
178 B5 Madererspitze mt. Austria
183 M6 Maderuelo Spain
140 S3 Madetkoski Fin.
114 C5 Madgaon Goa India
217 □2a Madge Rocks is Inner Islands Seychelles
210 D1 Madgoul Djibouti
116 C9 Madhavpur Gujarat India
117 K7 Madhepura Bihar India
111 E13 Madhoganj Uttar Prad. India
117 K6 Madhubani Bihar India
114 E6 Madhugiri Karnataka India
117 K7 Madhupur Jharkhand India
116 G8 Madhya Pradesh state India
95 J4 Madi, Dataran Tinggi plat. Indon.
211 B7 Madibira Tanz.
215 J2 Madibogo S. Africa
252 D3 Madidi r. Bol.
82 F3 Madigan Gulf salt flat S.A. Austr.
114 D6 Madikeri Karnataka India
237 G8 Madill OK U.S.A.
209 B6 Madimba Angola
209 B6 Madimba Dem. Rep. Congo
206 D4 Madinani Côte d'Ivoire
124 F8 Madīnat al 'Abīd Yemen
124 G9 Madīnat ash Sha'b Yemen
128 G3 Madīnat ath Thawrah Syria
157 K6 Madine, Lac de l. France
209 A6 Madingo-Kayes Congo
209 B6 Madingou Congo
207 I4 Madingrin Cameroon
163 D8 Madiran France
213 □J3 Madirovalo Madag.
231 D8 Madison AL U.S.A.
235 J2 Madison CT U.S.A.
231 F10 Madison FL U.S.A.
231 F9 Madison GA U.S.A.
230 E6 Madison IN U.S.A.
233 □P4 Madison ME U.S.A.
236 G3 Madison MN U.S.A.
236 G5 Madison NE U.S.A.
235 G3 Madison NJ U.S.A.
232 D7 Madison OH U.S.A.
236 G3 Madison SD U.S.A.
232 G10 Madison VA U.S.A.
226 E6 Madison WI U.S.A.
232 D10 Madison WV U.S.A.
238 I4 Madison r. MT U.S.A.
232 F11 Madison Heights VA U.S.A.
230 D7 Madisonville KY U.S.A.
231 E8 Madisonville TN U.S.A.
237 H10 Madisonville TX U.S.A.
93 B9 Madita Sumba Indon.
95 I8 Madiun Jawa Indon.
208 B4 Madjingo Gabon
205 I4 Madjūl Libya
150 G3 Madley Herefordshire, England U.K.
87 G8 Madley, Mount hill W.A. Austr.
138 I5 Madliena Latvia
Madnishkevi Rus. Fed. see Uchkulan
208 F4 Mado Dem. Rep. Congo
224 E4 Madoc Ont. Can.
177 H5 Madocsa Hungary
210 C4 Mado Gashi Kenya
106 F9 Madoi Qinghai China
157 L6 Madon r. France
138 J5 Madona Latvia
212 D4 Madongo Pan salt pan Botswana
194 F8 Madonie mts Sicilia Italy
234 B5 Madonna MD U.S.A.
191 J3 Madonna di Campiglio Italy
116 C7 Madpura Rajasthan India
199 H3 Madra Dağı mts Turkey
124 D5 Madrakah Saudi Arabia
125 M6 Madrakah, Ra's c. Oman
Madras Tamil Nadu India see Chennai
Madras state India see Tamil Nadu
238 D4 Madras OR U.S.A.
129 J5 Mädräsä Azer.
245 J1 Madre, Laguna lag. Mex.
237 G12 Madre, Laguna lag. TX U.S.A.
Madre, Sierra mts Mex. see Madre de Chiapas, Sierra
92 C3 Madre, Sierra mt. Luzon Phil.
245 N9 Madre de Chiapas, Sierra mts Mex.
257 E4 Madre de Deus de Minas Brazil
252 C2 Madre de Dios dept Peru
259 B8 Madre de Dios, Isla i. Chile
244 F7 Madre del Sur, Sierra mts Mex.
208 F3 Madreggi Sudan
244 B1 Madre Occidental, Sierra mts Mex.
244 F1 Madre Oriental, Sierra mts Mex.
163 I10 Madrès, Pic de mt. France
92 E7 Madrid Mindanao Phil.
183 M8 Madrid Spain
183 M7 Madrid aut. comm. Spain
92 D6 Madridejos Phil.
185 L2 Madridejos Spain
183 K6 Madrigal de las Altas Torres Spain
183 J8 Madrigal de la Vera Spain
183 M4 Madrigal del Monte Spain
184 H2 Madrigalejo Spain
185 P2 Madrigueras Spain
178 A6 Madrisahorn mt. Austria/Switz.
143 L4 Madroken l. Sweden
150 □ Madron Cornwall, England U.K.
185 K4 Madrona, Sierra mts Spain
184 H2 Madroñera Spain
185 P3 Madroño mt. Spain
246 C2 Madruga Cuba
202 B3 Madrūsah Libya
93 B7 Madu i. Indon.
113 □1 Madu i. S. Male Maldives
209 B6 Maduda Dem. Rep. Congo
115 H4 Madugula Andhra Prad. India
87 I11 Madura W.A. Austr.
95 J8 Madura i. Indon.
95 J8 Madura, Selat sea chan. Indon.
114 F8 Madurai Tamil Nadu India
114 F6 Madurantakam Tamil Nadu India
122 F6 Madvār, Kūh-e mt. Iran
116 H7 Madwas Madh. Prad. India
123 O4 Madyan Pak.
211 B6 Madyo Tanz.
129 I3 Madzhalis Rus. Fed.
197 N9 Madzharovo Bulg.
213 F3 Madziwadzido Zimbabwe
213 F3 Madziwa Mine Zimbabwe
191 M3 Maè r. Italy
Maé i. Vanuatu see Émaé
105 J3 Maebashi Japan
96 D5 Mae Chang Reservoir Thai.
96 C5 Mae Hong Son Thai.
102 □1 Mae-jima i. Okinawa Japan
93 C3 Maelang Sulawesi Indon.
158 E5 Maël-Carhaix France
142 E2 Mælefjell mt. Norway
186 F5 Maella Spain
183 K7 Maello Spain
150 C4 Maenclochog Pembrokeshire, Wales U.K.
96 D5 Mae Ngat Reservoir Thai.
150 E2 Maentwrog Gwynedd, Wales U.K.
193 K4 Maenza Italy
96 D6 Mae Ping National Park Thai.
96 D6 Mae Ramat Thai.
96 D5 Mae Rim Thai.
197 K3 Măerişte Romania
96 D4 Mae Sai Thai.
96 C5 Mae Sariang Thai.
96 D6 Mae Sot Thai.
150 E4 Maesteg Bridgend, Wales U.K.
246 E4 Maestra, Sierra mts Cuba
185 I6 Maestre hill Spain
92 C5 Maestre de Campo i. Phil.
191 L9 Maestro, Canale canal Italy
96 D5 Mae Suai Thai.
96 D6 Mae Tuen Wildlife Reserve nature res. Thai.
213 □J3 Maevatanana Madag.
78 □5 Maéwo i. Vanuatu
96 D7 Mae Wong National Park Thai.
96 E5 Mae Yom National Park Thai.
183 P3 Maeztu Spain
93 E3 Mafa Halmahera Indon.
217 □1c Mafaté, Cirque de vol. crater Réunion
223 K4 Mafeking Man. Can.
Mafeking S. Africa see Mafikeng
215 L5 Mafeteng Lesotho
83 K7 Maffra Vic. Austr.
211 C7 Mafia Channel Tanz.
211 C6 Mafia Island Tanz.
215 J1 Mafikeng S. Africa
211 B7 Mafinga Tanz.
255 C8 Mafra Brazil
184 A3 Mafra Port.
Mafraq Jordan see Al Mafraq
254 E4 Mafrense Brazil
213 F3 Mafungabusi Plateau Zimbabwe
113 □1 Mafushi i. S. Male Maldives
215 O6 Magabeni S. Africa
184 H3 Magacela hill Spain
131 Q4 Magadan Rus. Fed.
211 C5 Magadi Kenya
213 G4 Magaiza Moz.
161 C10 Magalas France
215 L1 Magaliesberg mts S. Africa
215 L1 Magaliesburg S. Africa
Magallanes Chile see Punta Arenas
92 D5 Magallanes Luzon Phil.
259 C9 Magallanes, Estrecho de sea chan. Chile
246 E2 Magallanes Bank sea feature Bahamas
259 B9 Magallanes y Antártica Chilena admin. reg. Chile
183 R5 Magallón Spain
187 K8 Magalluf Spain
183 P5 Magaña Spain
147 I7 Maganey Ireland
250 C2 Magangue Col.
126 F5 Mağara Turkey
129 E5 Mağara tourist site Turkey
128 A2 Mağara Dağı mt. Turkey
128 G2 Mağarali Turkey
129 J4 Magaramkent Rus. Fed.
207 H3 Magaria Niger
102 □1 Magari-zaki pt Okinawa Japan
Magas Iran see Zābolī
129 F2 Magas Rus. Fed.
92 C3 Magat r. Luzon Phil.
183 L5 Magaz Spain
237 I8 Magazine Mountain hill AR U.S.A.
194 E9 Magazzolo r. Sicilia Italy
208 D4 Magbakele Dem. Rep. Congo
206 C4 Magburaka Sierra Leone
100 D2 Magdagachi Rus. Fed.
171 D9 Magdala Ger.
261 I4 Magdalena Arg.
252 D3 Magdalena Bol.
250 C2 Magdalena dept Col.
250 C2 Magdalena r. Col.
242 C4 Magdalena Baja California Sur Mex.
242 D2 Magdalena Sonora Mex.
242 D2 Magdalena r. Mex.
239 K9 Magdalena NM U.S.A.
250 B3 Magdalena, Bahía b. Col.
242 D5 Magdalena, Bahía b. Mex.
259 B7 Magdalena, Isla i. Chile
242 C5 Magdalena, Isla i. Mex.
187 C10 Magdalena, Sierra de la mts Spain
245 J7 Magdalena Cuayucatepec Mex.
Magdalena Island Fr. Polynesia see Fatu Hiva
95 L2 Magdaline, Gunung mt. Malaysia
171 E6 Magdeburg Ger.
171 F6 Magdeburgerforth Ger.
85 M4 Magdelaine Cays atoll Coral Sea Is Terr. Austr.
237 K10 Magee MS U.S.A.
95 I8 Magelang Jawa Indon.
Magellan, Strait of Chile see Magallanes, Estrecho de
266 E4 Magellan Seamounts sea feature N. Pacific Ocean
190 F5 Magenta Italy
87 E12 Magenta, Lake salt flat W.A. Austr.
140 R1 Magerøya i. Norway
163 B8 Magescq France
102 □H16 Mage-shima i. Japan
177 L4 Măgeşti Romania
190 F3 Maggia Switz.
190 F3 Maggia r. Switz.
261 F3 Maggiolo Arg.
190 G6 Maggiorasca, Monte mt. Italy
192 I1 Maggiore, Isola i. Italy
190 F4 Maggiore, Lago l. Italy
Maggiore, Lake Italy see Maggiore, Lago
192 D6 Maggiore, Monte hill Sardegna Italy
193 M5 Maggiore, Monte mt. Italy
246 □ Maggotty Jamaica
203 F2 Maghāghah Egypt
128 C10 Maghā'ir Shu'ayb tourist site Saudi Arabia
206 B3 Maghama Maur.
147 C9 Maghanlawaun Ireland
128 B8 Maghārah, Jabal hill Egypt
Magharee Islands Ireland see The Seven Hogs
147 E3 Maghera Ireland
147 I3 Maghera Northern Ireland U.K.
147 I3 Magherafelt Northern Ireland U.K.
148 E5 Magheralin Northern Ireland U.K.
147 H3 Magheramason Northern Ireland U.K.
147 I3 Maghery Northern Ireland U.K.
204 E2 Maghnia Alg.
123 J4 Maghor Afgh.
149 L6 Maghull Merseyside, England U.K.
148 D3 Magilligan Northern Ireland U.K.
147 I2 Magilligan Point Northern Ireland U.K.
185 M5 Mágina mt. Spain
185 L5 Mágina, Sierra mts Spain
211 B7 Magingo Tanz.
192 I1 Magione Italy
195 L5 Magisano Italy
245 I3 Magiscatzín Mex.
Magitang Qinghai China see Jainca
Magiyan Tajik. see Moghiyon
188 G3 Maglaj Bos.-Herz.
160 J4 Magland France
197 L6 Maglavit Romania
193 K3 Magliano de'Marsi Italy
192 G2 Magliano in Toscana Italy
193 I3 Magliano Sabina Italy
195 O3 Maglie Italy
177 I4 Maglód Hungary
241 U8 Magma AZ U.S.A.
162 G3 Magnac-Laval France
162 E4 Magnac-sur-Touvre France
194 C10 Magna Grande hill Italy
195 I8 Magna Grande mt. Sicilia Italy
162 C3 Magné France
263 D2 Magnet Bay Antarctica
85 K5 Magnetic Island Qld Austr.
85 K5 Magnetic Passage Qld Austr.
134 F1 Magnetity Rus. Fed.
157 M7 Magnières France
195 I9 Magnisi, Penisola pen. Sicilia Italy
139 S9 Magnitnyy Rus. Fed.
120 H1 Magnitogorsk Rus. Fed.
237 I9 Magnolia AR U.S.A.
234 E6 Magnolia DE U.S.A.
234 C6 Magnolia MD U.S.A.
237 J10 Magnolia MS U.S.A.
142 I2 Magnor Norway
175 J4 Magnuszew Pol.
160 C3 Magny-Cours France
156 C5 Magny-en-Vexin France
100 L2 Mago Rus. Fed.
177 H5 Mágocs Hungary
177 J5 Mágocs-ér r. Hungary
213 F2 Màgoé Moz.
225 F4 Magog Que. Can.
211 C6 Magole Tanz.
192 B7 Magomadas Sardegna Italy
210 C3 Mago National Park Eth.
Magosa Cyprus see Ammochostos
209 E8 Magoye Zambia
245 J4 Magozal Mex.
225 H3 Magpie Que. Can.
224 C4 Magpie r. Ont. Can.
225 H3 Magpie r. Que. Can.
225 H3 Magpie, Lac l. Que. Can.
225 H3 Magpie-Ouest r. Que. Can.
190 H7 Magra r. Italy
222 H5 Magrath Alta Can.
187 E9 Magre r. Spain
240 O4 Magruder Mountain NV U.S.A.
203 F6 Magrur Sudan
202 E5 Magrur, Wadi watercourse Sudan
206 B2 Magṭa' Laḥjar Maur.
122 G2 Magtymguly Turkm.
211 B5 Magu Tanz.
122 G5 Magu, Chashmeh-ye well Iran
100 J2 Magu, Khrebet mts Rus. Fed.
108 E7 Maguan Yunnan China
254 C2 Maguarinho, Cabo c. Brazil
213 G5 Magude Moz.
215 P3 Magudu S. Africa
182 E6 Magueija Port.
242 H4 Magueyal Mex.
216 □3c Máguez Lanzarote Canary Is
184 H4 Maguilla Spain
147 H4 Maguiresbridge Northern Ireland U.K.
207 I3 Magumeri Nigeria
233 □R3 Magundy N.B. Can.
213 F3 Magunge Zimbabwe
117 L8 Magura Bangl.
177 H3 Magura mt. Slovakia
136 G6 Măgura, Dealul hill Moldova
197 K3 Măgura Mare, Vârful hill Romania
197 K5 Măgurii, Vârful mt. Romania
223 M2 Maguse Lake Nunavut Can.
215 L8 Magwali S. Africa
Magway Myanmar see Magwe
Magway admin. div. Myanmar see Magwe
96 B4 Magwe Myanmar
96 B4 Magwe admin. div. Myanmar
210 B3 Magwe Sudan
212 D3 Magweqqana watercourse Botswana
177 K4 Magy Hungary
177 G5 Magyaratád Hungary
177 H6 Magyarbóly Hungary
Magyarkanizsa Vojvodina Serbia see Kanjiža
Magyar Köztársaság country Europe see Hungary
177 H5 Magyarszék Hungary
96 A4 Magyichaung Myanmar
122 A3 Mahābād Iran
114 C4 Mahabaleshwar Mahar. India
213 □J3 Mahabe Madag.
116 J6 Mahabharat Range mts Nepal
213 □J4 Mahabo Toliara Madag.
213 □J4 Mahabo Toliara Madag.
213 □J4 Mahaboboka Madag.
114 C3 Mahad Mahar. India
210 E4 Mahaddayweyne Somalia
116 F8 Mahadeo Hills Madh. Prad. India
114 G3 Mahadeopur Andhra Prad. India
79 □9a Mahaena Tahiti Fr. Polynesia
232 G8 Mahaffey PA U.S.A.
208 F4 Mahagi Dem. Rep. Congo
208 F4 Mahagi Port Dem. Rep. Congo
111 L7 Mahai Qinghai China
251 G3 Mahaicony Guyana
213 □J2 Mahajamba r. Madag.
116 D5 Mahajan Rajasthan India
213 □J2 Mahajanga Madag.
213 □J3 Mahajanga prov. Madag.
95 L5 Mahakam r. Indon.
213 E4 Mahalapye Botswana
211 A6 Mahale Mountains National Park Tanz.
213 □K2 Mahalevona Madag.
122 D5 Mahallāt Iran
116 F5 Maham Haryana India
122 G6 Māhān Iran
117 K9 Mahanadi r. India
213 □K3 Mahanoro Madag.
234 C3 Mahanoy City PA U.S.A.
234 B3 Mahanoy Creek r. PA U.S.A.
234 B3 Mahantango Creek r. PA U.S.A.
114 G9 Maha Oya Sri Lanka
117 J6 Maharajganj Bihar India
116 H6 Maharajganj Uttar Prad. India
117 I6 Maharajganj Uttar Prad. India
116 G7 Maharajpur Madh. Prad. India
114 D3 Maharashtra state India
124 B2 Mahārish, Ra's pt Saudi Arabia
122 E7 Mahārlū, Daryācheh-ye salt l. Iran
116 I9 Mahasamund Chhattisgarh India
96 F6 Maha Sarakham Thai.
213 □J5 Mahatalaky Madag.
128 E7 Maḥaṭṭat Ḍab'ah Jordan
247 □2 Mahaut Dominica
213 □J2 Mahavavy r. Madag.
213 □K3 Mahavelona Madag.
114 G8 Mahaweli Ganga r. Sri Lanka
213 □J3 Mahazoma Madag.
203 F6 Mahbub Sudan
114 G4 Mahbubabad Andhra Prad. India
114 E4 Mahbubnagar Andhra Prad. India
124 E4 Mahd adh Dhahab Saudi Arabia
125 L3 Maḥḍah Oman
137 N5 Mahdalynivka Dnipropetrovs'ka Oblast' Ukr.
137 M7 Mahdalynivka Khersons'ka Oblast' Ukr.
205 F2 Mahdia Alg.
251 G3 Mahdia Guyana
205 H2 Mahdia Tunisia
106 I9 Mahe Gansu China
114 D7 Mahe Pondicherry India
217 □2b Mahé i. Inner Islands Seychelles
217 □1b Mahébourg Mauritius
148 F5 Mahee Island Northern Ireland U.K.
117 L7 Mahendraganj Meghalaya India
116 F5 Mahendragarh Haryana India
115 I3 Mahendragiri mt. Orissa India
211 C7 Mahenge Tanz.
81 E12 Maheno South I. N.Z.
175 L5 Maheriv Ukr.
116 D8 Mahesana Gujarat India
116 E8 Maheshwar Madh. Prad. India
125 L9 Maḥfirhīn Suquṭrā Yemen
116 G6 Mahgawan Madh. Prad. India
116 D8 Mahi r. Rajasthan India
122 H7 Māhī watercourse Iran
80 L6 Mahia North I. N.Z.
80 L6 Mahia Peninsula North I. N.Z.
182 H5 Mahíde Spain
78 □6 Mahige Island Solomon Is
139 N8 Mahilyow Belarus
Mahilyow Oblast admin. div. Belarus see Mahilyowskaya Voblasts'
139 N8 Mahilyowskaya Voblasts' admin. div. Belarus
114 C3 Mahim Mahar. India
207 G5 Mahin Nigeria
79 □9a Mahina Tahiti Fr. Polynesia
206 C3 Mahina Mali
81 E9 Mahinapua, Lake South I. N.Z.
81 D12 Mahinerangi, Lake South I. N.Z.
116 G3 Mahiya Jammu and Kashmir
114 G9 Mahiyangana Sri Lanka
122 E6 Mah Jān Iran
140 L4 Mahkene mt. Sweden
215 P4 Mahlabatini S. Africa
96 B4 Mahlaing Myanmar
215 P3 Mahlangasi S. Africa
215 L4 Mahlatswetsa S. Africa
172 D5 Mahlberg Ger.
171 H6 Mahlow Ger.
170 D5 Mahlsdorf Ger.
171 E6 Mahlwinkel Ger.
116 H6 Mahmudabad Uttar Prad. India
122 E3 Mahmudabad Iran
123 M4 Maḥmūd-e Rāqī Afgh.
197 R5 Mahmudia Romania
199 H3 Mahmudiye Çanakkale Turkey
199 L3 Mahmudiye Eskişehir Turkey
128 A2 Mahmutlar Turkey
199 K1 Mahmutşevketpaşa Turkey
122 C4 Mahniān Iran
236 G2 Mahnomen MN U.S.A.
114 G9 Maho Sri Lanka
116 G7 Mahoba Uttar Prad. India
80 I5 Mahoenui North I. N.Z.
116 H6 Maholi Uttar Prad. India
186 □ Mahón Spain
225 H4 Mahone Bay N.S. Can.
212 D3 Mahongo Game Park nature res. Namibia
222 E1 Mahony Lake N.W.T. Can.
235 H2 Mahopac NY U.S.A.
235 H2 Mahopac Lake NY U.S.A.
185 P2 Mahora Spain
206 D3 Mahou Mali
208 C2 Mahoua Chad
125 J7 Mahrāt, Jabal mt. Yemen
125 J7 Mahrāt, Wādī r. Yemen
116 G7 Mahrauni Uttar Prad. India
Mähren reg. Czech Rep. see Morava
205 H2 Mahrès Tunisia
173 N2 Mähring Ger.
122 I5 Māhrūd Iran
Mahsana Gujarat India see Mahesana
111 L8 Mahuanggou Qinghai China
117 O8 Mahudaung mts Myanmar
240 □F13 Māhukona HI U.S.A.
117 N7 Mahur Assam India
114 E3 Mahur Mahar. India
207 G4 Mahuta Nigeria
211 C7 Mahuta Tanz.
116 C9 Mahuva Gujarat India
116 F6 Mahwa Rajasthan India
197 P9 Mahya Dağı mt. Turkey
122 D5 Mahyār Iran
93 E6 Mai i. Maluku Indon.
Mai i. Vanuatu see Émaé
78 □2 Maia American Samoa
216 □1b Maia São Miguel Azores
182 C6 Maia Port.
Maiaia Moz. see Nacala
186 G5 Maials Spain
77 H1 Maiana atoll Gilbert Is Kiribati
117 N7 Maibang Assam India
250 C2 Maicao Col.
224 E3 Maicasagi r. Que. Can.
224 E3 Maicasagi, Lac l. Que. Can.
160 J2 Maîche France
108 G8 Maichen Guangdong China
251 F6 Maici r. Brazil
251 H5 Maicuru r. Brazil
195 K6 Maida Italy
150 H5 Maiden Bradley Wiltshire, England U.K.
234 D4 Maiden Creek r. PA U.S.A.
151 K4 Maidenhead Windsor and Maidenhead, England U.K.
150 G6 Maiden Newton Dorset, England U.K.
226 B5 Maiden Rock WI U.S.A.
146 G12 Maidens South Ayrshire, Scotland U.K.
93 E3 Maidi Halmahera Indon.
223 I4 Maidstone Sask. Can.
151 N5 Maidstone Kent, England U.K.
207 I4 Maiduguri Nigeria
193 M3 Maiella, Parco Nazionale della nat. park Italy
190 H1 Maienfeld Switz.
195 K6 Maierato Italy
173 I6 Maierhöfen Ger.
197 M3 Maieru Romania
187 D10 Maigmó mt. Spain
156 E4 Maignelay-Montigny France
210 C3 Mai Gudo mt. Eth.
147 E7 Maigue r. Ireland
116 H7 Maihar Madh. Prad. India
104 D5 Maihara Japan
80 J5 Maihiihi North I. N.Z.
117 M8 Maijdi Bangl.
108 E1 Maiji Gansu China
108 F2 Maiji Shan mt. Gansu China
116 H8 Maikala Range hills Madh. Prad. India
172 E3 Maikammer Ger.
208 E4 Maiko r. Dem. Rep. Congo
208 E5 Maiko, Parc National de la nat. park Dem. Rep. Congo
117 I8 Mailan Hill mt. Chhattisgarh India
116 H5 Mailani Uttar Prad. India
208 B2 Maïlao Chad
94 C6 Maileppe Indon.
240 □C12 Mā'ili HI U.S.A.
163 D7 Maillas France
156 B6 Maillebois France
162 C3 Maillezais France
156 H6 Mailly-le-Camp France
160 D1 Mailly-le-Château France
156 E3 Mailly-Maillet France
123 O7 Mailsi Pak.
108 D2 Maima Gansu China
169 F10 Main r. Ger.
124 G7 Ma'īn tourist site Yemen
117 L6 Mainaguri W. Bengal India
198 D5 Mainalo mts Greece
172 G2 Mainaschaff Ger.
173 I2 Mainbernheim Ger.
225 K3 Main Brook Nfld and Lab. Can.
173 L4 Mainburg Ger.
224 D4 Main Channel lake channel Ont. Can.
114 E4 Maindargi Mahar. India
208 C5 Mai-Ndombe, Lac l. Dem. Rep. Congo
173 J2 Main-Donau-Kanal canal Ger.
227 R6 Main Duck Island Ont. Can.
159 J7 Maine r. France
159 K5 Maine reg. France
233 □P3 Maine state U.S.A.
233 □P5 Maine, Gulf of U.S.A.
159 K7 Maine-et-Loire dept France
250 C5 Mainé Hanari, Cerro hill Col.
207 I3 Maïné-Soroa Niger
96 C1 Maingkwan Myanmar
97 D8 Maingy Island Myanmar
147 I6 Mainham Ireland
172 H3 Mainhardt Ger.
92 E7 Mainit Mindanao Phil.
92 E7 Mainit, Lake Mindanao Phil.
108 B4 Mainkung Xizang China
146 J4 Mainland i. Orkney, Scotland U.K.
146 □N2 Mainland i. Shetland, Scotland U.K.
171 D10 Mainleus Ger.
111 L12 Mainling Xizang China
84 E3 Mainoru N.T. Austr.
84 E3 Mainoru r. N.T. Austr.
117 I8 Mainpat reg. Chhattisgarh India
116 G6 Mainpuri Uttar Prad. India
83 N3 Main Range National Park Qld Austr.
162 I3 Mainsat France
156 C6 Maintenon France
213 □J3 Maintirano Madag.
140 S4 Mainua Fin.
156 B7 Mainvilliers France
96 B3 Mainyaung Myanmar
169 F10 Mainz Ger.
206 □ Maio i. Cape Verde
191 O9 Maiolati Spontini Italy
184 B2 Maior r. Port.
182 C8 Maiorca Port.
182 C9 Maiorga Port.
194 H2 Maiori Italy
260 B3 Maipó r. Chile
260 C4 Maipó, Volcán vol. Chile
261 I5 Maipú Buenos Aires Arg.
260 C3 Maipú Mendoza Arg.
260 B3 Maipú Chile
250 E3 Maipures Col.
251 G3 Maipuri Landing Guyana
250 E2 Maiquetía Venez.
111 H12 Maiqu Zangbo r. Xizang China
190 D6 Maira r. Italy
184 H6 Mairena del Alcor Spain
254 E4 Mairi Brazil
256 D5 Mairiporã Brazil
256 C2 Mairipotaba Brazil
182 F5 Mairos mt. Spain
173 K5 Maisach Ger.
173 K5 Maisach r. Ger.
104 G6 Maisaka Japan
178 G5 Maishofen Austria
246 F3 Maisí Cuba
138 I7 Maišiagala Lith.
117 M9 Maiskhal Channel inlet Bangl.
117 M9 Maiskhal Island Bangl.
156 D6 Maisons-Laffitte France
179 M2 Maissau Austria
156 D7 Maisse France
165 H9 Maissin Belgium
Maitea i. Arch. de la Société Fr. Polynesia see Mehetia
173 M5 Maitenbeth Ger.
258 C3 Maitencillo Chile
213 E4 Maitengwe Botswana
117 K8 Maithon W. Bengal India
83 M5 Maitland N.S.W. Austr.
82 F6 Maitland S.A. Austr.
86 D6 Maitland r. W.A. Austr.
95 L2 Maitland, Banjaran mts Malaysia
87 F9 Maitland, Lake salt flat W.A. Austr.
263 A2 Maitri research stn Antarctica
Maiwo i. Vanuatu see Maéwo
84 E3 Maiwok r. N.T. Austr.
84 B4 Maiyu, Mount hill N.T. Austr.
242 □R11 Maíz, Islas del is Nic.
111 J12 Maizhokunggar Xizang China
156 G6 Maizières-la-Grande-Paroisse France
157 L5 Maizières-lès-Metz France
104 B5 Maizuru Japan
184 H7 Majaceite r. Spain
183 M8 Majadahonda Spain
182 I9 Majadas de Tiétar Spain
196 H8 Maja Jezercë mt. Albania
114 E3 Majalgaon Mahar. India
251 F4 Majari r. Brazil
125 I8 Majdaḥah Yemen
175 J5 Majdan Królewski Pol.
175 L5 Majdan Niepryski Pol.
197 J6 Majdanpek Serbia
128 D5 Majdel Aanjar tourist site Lebanon
257 F5 Majé Brazil
93 A5 Majene Sulawesi Barat Indon.
188 G3 Majevica mts Bos.-Herz.
116 H7 Majhgawan Madh. Prad. India
116 G8 Majholi Madh. Prad. India

125 J4 Majḫūd well Saudi Arabia
107 O7 Majia He r. China
109 H7 Majiang Guangxi China
108 F5 Majiang Guizhou China
Majiawan Ningxia China see Huinong
100 D3 Majiazi Nei Mongol China
207 F3 Majibo well Mali
Majōl country N. Pacific Ocean see Marshall Islands
244 F2 Majoma Mex.
216 □3a Majona, Punta pt La Gomera Canary Is
187 K8 Major, Puig mt. Spain
Majorca i. Spain see Mallorca
82 □3 Major Lake S. Pacific Ocean
Mājro atoll Marshall Is see Majuro
177 H6 Majs Hungary
179 M7 Majšperk Slovenia
117 N6 Majuli Island India
Majunga Madag. see Mahajanga
252 D1 Majuriã Brazil
78 □3b Majuro atoll Marshall Is
78 □3b Majuro Lagoon Majuro Marshall Is
215 K4 Majwemasweu S. Africa
206 B3 Maka Senegal
78 □6 Maka Malaita Solomon Is
209 B5 Makabana Congo
105 L3 Makabe Japan
177 H4 Makád Hungary
129 H3 Makadzhoy Rus. Fed.
240 □C12 Mākaha HI U.S.A.
240 □B12 Makahū'ena Point HI U.S.A.
207 H6 Makak Cameroon
209 B5 Makaka Congo
208 E5 Makalado Dem. Rep. Congo
93 A5 Makale Sulawesi Indon.
93 D2 Makalehi i. Indon.
117 K6 Makalu mt. China/Nepal
117 K6 Makalu Barun National Park Nepal
211 A6 Makamba Burundi
121 T4 Makanchi Kazakh.
Makane Rus. Fed. see Meken-Yurt
211 B8 Makanjila Malawi
116 H6 Makanpur Uttar Prad. India
211 C6 Makanya Tanz.
208 C4 Makanza Dem. Rep. Congo
240 □D12 Makapu'u Head HI U.S.A.
213 □J3 Makaraingo Madag.
81 C13 Makarewa South I. N.Z.
207 I3 Makari Cameroon
134 J3 Makar-Ib Rus. Fed.
134 L2 Makarikha Rus. Fed.
Makari Mountain National Park Tanz. see Mahale Mountains National Park
136 I3 Makariv Ukr.
81 D11 Makarora r. South I. N.Z.
100 M4 Makarov Sakhalin Rus. Fed.
268 M1 Makarov Basin sea feature Arctic Ocean
136 B5 Makarove Ukr.
135 H5 Makarovo Rus. Fed.
188 F4 Makarska Croatia
123 N5 Makarwal Pak.
134 J4 Makar'ye Rus. Fed.
134 H4 Makar'yev Rus. Fed.
211 A7 Makasa Zambia
93 A6 Makassar Sulawesi Indon.
93 A3 Makassar, Selat str. Indon.
120 E4 Makat Kazakh.
215 Q3 Makatini Flats lowland S. Africa
96 C1 Makaw Myanmar
240 □E13 Makawao HI U.S.A.
213 □J4 Makay, Massif du mts Madag.
Makedonija country Europe see Macedonia
81 □4 Makefu Niue
215 K4 Makeleketla S. Africa
92 □ Makelulu hill Palau
79 □9 Makemo atoll Arch. des Tuamotu Fr. Polynesia
206 B4 Makeni Sierra Leone
211 B7 Makete Tanz.
Makeyevka Ukr. see Makiyivka
212 E4 Makgadikgadi depr. Botswana
212 E4 Makgadikgadi Pans National Park Botswana
129 I3 Makhachkala Rus. Fed.
123 N5 Makhad Pak.
213 F4 Makhado S. Africa
215 L6 Makhaleng r. Lesotho
120 D4 Makhambet Kazakh.
124 F3 Makhāmīr, Jabal al hill Saudi Arabia
Makharadze Georgia see Ozurget'i
128 A8 Makhāzin, Kathīb al des. Egypt
215 N5 Makheka mt. Lesotho
128 G3 Makhfar al Ḩammām Syria
122 I3 Makhmaldepe Turkm.
129 G1 Makhmud-Mekteb Rus. Fed.
127 K6 Makhmūr Iraq
138 M4 Makhnovka Rus. Fed.
121 M1 Makhorovka Kazakh.
114 E4 Makhtal Andhra Prad. India
105 H1 Maki Japan
93 E3 Makian vol. Maluku Indon.
105 I2 Makihata-yama mt. Japan
81 F11 Makikihi South I. N.Z.
Makima atoll Arch. des Tuamotu Fr. Polynesia see Makemo
Makin atoll Kiribati see Butaritari
211 C5 Makindu Kenya
104 D5 Makino Japan
121 N1 Makinsk Kazakh.
221 J2 Makinson Inlet Nunavut Can.
105 I4 Makioka Japan
Makira i. Solomon Is see San Cristobal
136 F5 Makiv Ukr.
137 K3 Makiyivka Chernihivs'ka Oblast' Ukr.
137 Q5 Makiyivka Donets'ka Oblast' Ukr.
124 D5 Makkah Saudi Arabia
124 E5 Makkah prov. Saudi Arabia
140 U1 Makkaurhalvøya Naturreservat nature res. Norway
225 J2 Makkovik Nfld and Lab. Can.
225 J2 Makkovik, Cape Nfld and Lab. Can.
164 H2 Makkum Neth.
139 R7 Maklaki Rus. Fed.
188 F4 Makljen pass Bos.-Herz.
177 J5 Makó Hungary
206 B3 Mako Senegal
251 G4 Makoa, Serra hills Brazil
79 □7 Makogai i. Fiji
208 B4 Makokou Gabon
215 K2 Makokskraal S. Africa
211 C7 Makonde Plateau Tanz.
Makongai i. Fiji see Makogai
211 B7 Makongolosi Tanz.
212 D5 Makopong Botswana
129 A2 Makopse Rus. Fed.
208 F4 Makoro Dem. Rep. Congo
213 G3 Makosa Zimbabwe
208 C5 Makotipoko Congo
80 K7 Makotuku North I. N.Z.
208 B5 Makoua Congo
209 B5 Makoubi Congo
177 H2 Makov Slovakia
188 E3 Makovnik mt. Croatia
175 I4 Maków Pol.
174 F2 Mąkowarsko Pol.
175 J3 Maków Mazowiecki Pol.
175 H6 Maków Podhalański Pol.
199 G6 Makra i. Greece
198 D4 Makrakomi Greece
122 I8 Makran reg. Iran/Pak.
116 E6 Makrana Rajasthan India
123 J9 Makran Coast Range mts Pak.
175 M4 Makrany Belarus
114 G3 Makri Chhattisgarh India
199 H5 Makronisi i. Greece
198 F5 Makronisos i. Greece
198 D2 Makrygialos Kentriki Makedonia Greece
199 G7 Makrygialos Kriti Greece
139 S4 Maksatikha Rus. Fed.
116 F8 Maksi Madh. Prad. India
100 J5 Maksimovka Rus. Fed.
123 J7 Maksotag Iran
116 F8 Maksudangarh Madh. Prad. India
129 H5 Maksudlu Azer.
174 G2 Maksymilianowo Pol.
122 A2 Mākū Iran
102 U4 Makubetsu Japan
117 O6 Makum Assam India
211 B7 Makumbako Tanz.
209 D6 Makumbi Dem. Rep. Congo
Makundu i. N. Male Maldives see Makunudhoo
211 C6 Makunduchi Tanz.
109 L7 Makung Taiwan
211 B7 Makungu Tanz.
211 C7 Makunguwiro Tanz.
113 □1 Makunudhoo i. N. Male Maldives
103 H15 Makurazaki Japan
207 H5 Makurdi Nigeria
80 J7 Makuri North I. N.Z.
210 D4 Makuungo Somalia
122 E7 Makūyeh Iran
211 C5 Makuyuni Tanz.
215 J3 Makwassie S. Africa
213 F3 Makwiro Zimbabwe
117 L6 Mal W. Bengal India
252 A3 Mala Peru
Mala Ireland see Mallow
Mala i. Solomon Is see Malaita
185 L6 Malá Spain
140 O4 Malå Sweden
242 □S14 Mala, Punta pt Panama
185 I8 Mala, Punta pt Spain
84 C6 Mala Aboriginal Land res. N.T. Austr.
128 A9 Mal'ab, Ra's pt Egypt
92 E8 Malabang Mindanao Phil.
82 □2 Malabar b. Lord Howe I. Austr.
114 D6 Malabar Coast India
137 N6 Mala Bilozerka Ukr.
207 H6 Malabo Equat. Guinea
177 I5 Mala Bosna Vojvodina Serbia
261 I4 Mal Abrigo Uru.
92 A7 Malabuñgan Palawan Phil.
Malaca Spain see Málaga
257 F2 Malacacheta Brazil
Malacca Malaysia see Melaka
Malacca state Malaysia see Melaka
94 C2 Malacca, Strait of Indon./Malaysia
176 G3 Malacky Slovakia
238 H6 Malad r. ID U.S.A.
238 H5 Malad City ID U.S.A.
137 L3 Mala Divytsya Ukr.
138 J7 Maladzyechna Belarus
177 H2 Malá Fatra mts Slovakia
177 I2 Malá Fatra nat. park Slovakia
185 K7 Málaga Spain
185 J7 Málaga prov. Spain
234 E5 Malaga NJ U.S.A.
239 L10 Malaga NM U.S.A.
232 D9 Malaga OH U.S.A.
185 J7 Málaga, Montes de mts Spain
211 A6 Malagarasi r. Burundi/Tanz.
211 A6 Malagarasi Tanz.
185 L2 Malagón Spain
184 E5 Malagon r. Spain
183 L7 Malagón, Sierra de mts Spain
93 B8 Malahar Sumba Indon.
147 J6 Malahide Ireland
213 □J4 Malaimbandy Madag.
174 D2 Mała Ina r. Pol.
78 □6 Malaita i. Solomon Is
95 M9 Malaka mt. Sumbawa Indon.
92 □ Malakal Palau
210 A2 Malakal Sudan
92 □ Malakal Passage Palau
188 E3 Mala Kapela mts Croatia
79 □7a Malake i. Fiji
116 H5 Malakheti Nepal
188 E3 Mala Kladuša Bos.-Herz.
84 C2 Malak Malak Aboriginal Land res. N.T. Austr.
78 □6 Malakobi Island Solomon Is
78 □5 Malakula i. Vanuatu
123 O5 Malakwal Pak.
191 L6 Malalbergo Italy
137 M6 Mala Lepetykha Ukr.
251 G3 Malali Guyana
93 B5 Malamala Sulawesi Indon.
92 C8 Malamaui i. Phil.
191 M5 Malamocco Italy
136 E3 Mala Moshchanytsya Ukr.
92 B6 Malampaya Sound sea chan. Palawan Phil.
123 K9 Malan, Ras pt Pak.
92 B7 Malanao i. Phil.
157 J5 Malancourt France
184 G7 Malandar, Punta de pt Spain
95 J8 Malang Jawa Indon.
213 H2 Malanga Moz.
211 B7 Malangali Tanz.
Malangana Nepal see Malangwa
Malange Angola see Malanje
140 O2 Malangseidet Norway
117 J6 Malangwa Nepal
92 D8 Malanipa i. Phil.
209 C7 Malanje Angola
209 C7 Malanje prov. Angola
174 G4 Malanów Pol.
158 G6 Malansac France
92 B7 Malanut Bay Palawan Phil.
207 F4 Malanville Benin
260 D2 Malanzán Arg.
260 D2 Malanzán, Sierra de mts Arg.
137 N4 Mala Pereshchepyna Ukr.
114 E7 Malappuram Kerala India
143 N2 Mälaren l. Sweden
260 C4 Malargüe Arg.
251 H4 Malaripo Brazil
224 E3 Malartic Que. Can.
227 P1 Malartic, Lac l. Que. Can.
136 D2 Malaryta Belarus
176 E1 Malá Skála Czech Rep.
93 A6 Malasoro, Teluk b. Indon.
259 D7 Malaspina Arg.
222 A3 Malaspina Glacier AK U.S.A.
222 E5 Malaspina Strait B.C. Can.
179 O7 Mala Subotica Croatia
95 J6 Malatayur, Tanjung pt Indon.
137 O5 Mala Ternivka r. Ukr.
126 I4 Malatya Turkey
161 G8 Malaucène France
156 B4 Malaunay France
163 D8 Malaussanne France
116 E4 Malaut Punjab India
114 E6 Malavalli Karnataka India
251 H4 Malavate Fr. Guiana
122 B5 Malāvī Iran
136 J4 Mala Vil'shanka Ukr.
137 K5 Mala Vyska Ukr.
207 H3 Malawa Niger
95 L1 Malawali i. Malaysia
174 F3 Mała Wełna r. Pol.
211 B7 Malawi country Africa
Malawi, Lake Africa see Nyasa, Lake
Malawi National Park Zambia see Nyika National Park
203 H6 Malawiya Sudan
140 P5 Malax Fin.
Malaya pen. Malaysia see Malaysia, Semenanjung
129 H1 Malaya Areshevka Rus. Fed.
138 G8 Malaya Byerastavitsa Belarus
134 K2 Malaya Pera Rus. Fed.
139 P3 Malaya Vishera Rus. Fed.
92 E7 Malaybalay Mindanao Phil.
122 C4 Malāyer Iran
156 F7 Malay-le-Grand France
85 L4 Malay Reef Coral Sea Is Terr. Austr.
121 Q5 Malay Sary Kazakh.
94 H3 Malaysia country Asia
94 E3 Malaysia, Semenanjung pen. Malaysia
127 K4 Malazgirt Turkey
225 G4 Malbaie r. Que. Can.
260 B5 Malbarco, Laguna l. Arg.
207 G3 Malbaza Niger
84 H6 Malbon Qld Austr.
175 H1 Malbork Pol.
172 B2 Malborn Ger.
161 C7 Malbouzon France
258 E3 Malbrán Arg.
160 I3 Malbuisson France
182 F8 Malcata, Serra de mts Port.
191 J4 Malcesine Italy
137 T4 Mal'chevskaya Rus. Fed.
170 G3 Malchin Ger.
170 G3 Malchiner See l. Ger.
170 F4 Malchow Ger.
177 K3 Malčice Slovakia
184 H4 Malcocinado Spain
87 F10 Malcolm W.A. Austr.
87 G12 Malcolm, Point W.A. Austr.
Malcolm Inlet Oman see Ghazira, Ghubbat al
146 D10 Malcolm's Point Scotland U.K.
177 K2 Malcov Slovakia
174 E4 Malczyce Pol.
117 L7 Maldah W. Bengal India
165 D6 Maldegem Belgium
164 I5 Malden Neth.
237 K7 Malden MO U.S.A.
267 I6 Malden Island Kiribati
186 G2 Malditos, Montes mts Spain
192 A8 Mal di Ventre, Isola di i. Sardegna Italy
113 D10 Maldives country Indian Ocean
83 J7 Maldon Vic. Austr.
151 N4 Maldon Essex, England U.K.
258 G4 Maldonado Uru.
245 I9 Maldonado, Punta pt Mex.
175 H2 Małdyty Pol.
217 □3a Male Njazidja Comoros
191 J3 Malè Italy
113 □1 Male N. Male Maldives
96 C3 Male Myanmar
206 C4 Maléa Guinea
198 E6 Maleas, Akrotirio pt Greece
113 □1 Male Atoll Maldives
215 J4 Malebogo S. Africa
174 E1 Malechowo Pol.
114 E3 Malegaon Mahar. India
116 E9 Malegaon Mahar. India
213 H3 Malei Moz.
183 Q5 Maleján Spain
210 A3 Malek Sudan
122 E5 Malek, Chāh-e well Iran
176 G3 Malé Karpaty hills Slovakia
176 G3 Malé Karpaty park Slovakia
215 M6 Malekgonyane Wildlife Reserve nature res. S. Africa
122 F6 Malek Mīrzā, Chāh-e well Iran
122 I7 Malek Sīāh, Kūh-e mt. Afgh.
208 E5 Malela Maniema Dem. Rep. Congo
209 E6 Malela Maniema Dem. Rep. Congo
209 B6 Malélé Congo
209 B6 Malele Dem. Rep. Congo
213 H2 Malema Moz.
209 E7 Malemba Nkulu Dem. Rep. Congo
161 G8 Malemort-du-Comtat France
162 H5 Malemort-sur-Corrèze France
207 G4 Malendo watercourse Nigeria
168 K2 Malente Ger.
215 N1 Maleoskop S. Africa
143 L5 Målerås Sweden
116 E4 Maler Kotla Punjab India
190 F3 Malesco Italy
197 K9 Maleševske Planine mts Bulg./Macedonia
156 D7 Malesherbes France
198 E4 Malesina Greece
Malesso' Guam see Merizo
123 L5 Mālestān Afgh.
158 G6 Malestroit France
107 K1 Maleta Rus. Fed.
194 H8 Maletto Sicilia Italy
78 □6 Malevangga Choiseul Solomon Is
139 V8 Malevka Rus. Fed.
194 H6 Malfa Isole Lipari Italy
214 E10 Malgas S. Africa
173 N4 Malgersdorf Ger.
129 F2 Malgobek Rus. Fed.
140 N4 Malgomaj l. Sweden
186 K4 Malgrat de Mar Spain
202 E6 Malha Sudan
254 E5 Malhada Brazil
182 H5 Malhadas Port.
124 H3 Malham Saudi Arabia
116 E7 Malhargarh Madh. Prad. India
238 F4 Malheur r. OR U.S.A.
217 □1b Malheureux, Cape Mauritius
238 E5 Malheur Lake OR U.S.A.
238 E5 Malheur National Wildlife Refuge nature res. OR U.S.A.
206 D3 Mali country Africa
208 E5 Mali Dem. Rep. Congo
206 B3 Mali Guinea
199 G7 Malia Kriti Greece
198 D4 Maliakos Kolpos b. Greece
100 G4 Malian Heilong. China
93 D8 Maliana East Timor
107 J9 Malian He r. China
106 D6 Malianjing Gansu China
106 G7 Malianjing Gansu China
215 M5 Malibamatso r. Lesotho
240 N7 Malibu CA U.S.A.
159 K6 Malicorne-sur-Sarthe France
92 D8 Maligay Bay Mindanao Phil.
156 G8 Maligny France
111 E13 Malihabad Uttar Prad. India
96 C2 Mali Hka r. Myanmar
177 I6 Mali Iđoš Vojvodina Serbia
161 I8 Malijai France
123 M5 Malikdin Afgh.
123 J7 Malik Naro mt. Pak.
93 C4 Maliku Sulawesi Indon.
97 D8 Mali Kyun i. Myanmar
93 B5 Malili Sulawesi Indon.
143 L4 Målilla Sweden
188 E3 Mali Lošinj Croatia
260 C1 Malimán de Abajo Arg.
209 F6 Malimba, Monts mts Dem. Rep. Congo
175 L6 Mali Mokryany Ukr.
94 G8 Malimping Jawa Indon.
147 H2 Malin Ireland
Malin Ukr. see Malyn
136 E1 Malinavka Belarus
147 E3 Malin Beg Ireland
211 D5 Malindi Kenya
213 E3 Malindi Zimbabwe
177 I3 Málinec Slovakia
Malines Belgium see Mechelen
107 J8 Maling Gansu China
208 B5 Malinga Gabon
147 H2 Malin Head Ireland
197 O3 Mălini Romania
147 E3 Malin More Ireland
93 A6 Malino Sulawesi Indon.
139 V6 Malino Rus. Fed.
93 B3 Malino, Gunung mt. Indon.
79 □8a Malinoa i. Tonga
121 N2 Malinovka Kazakh.
100 H6 Malinovka r. Rus. Fed.
121 R2 Malinovoye Ozero Rus. Fed.
191 R5 Malinska Croatia
211 C7 Malinyi Tanz.
199 G7 Malion, Kolpos b. Kriti Greece
108 E7 Malipo Yunnan China
198 B2 Maliq Albania
188 E3 Mali Raginac mt. Croatia
196 I8 Malit, Qafa e pass Albania
92 E8 Malita Mindanao Phil.
92 E6 Malitbog Leyte Phil.
97 D9 Maliwun Myanmar
116 C8 Maliya Gujarat India
137 L6 Maliyivka Ukr.
196 H6 Mali Zvornik Serbia
129 E2 Malka Rus. Fed.
129 F2 Malka r. Rus. Fed.
122 B5 Malkaili Iran
210 D3 Malka Mari Kenya
114 G3 Malkangiri Orissa India
114 C4 Malkapur Mahar. India
116 F9 Malkapur Mahar. India
199 H2 Malkara Turkey
138 J9 Mal'kavichy Belarus
107 K1 Malkhanskiy Khrebet mts Rus. Fed.
175 K3 Małkinia Górna Pol.
197 P9 Malko Tŭrnovo Bulg.
83 L7 Mallacoota Vic. Austr.
83 L7 Mallacoota Inlet b. Vic. Austr.
146 E9 Mallaig Highland, Scotland U.K.
202 D5 Mallanga well Chad
116 C7 Mallani reg. India
203 F3 Mallawī Egypt
83 I6 Mallee Cliffs National Park N.S.W. Austr.
161 G9 Mallemort France
183 R5 Mallén Spain
170 D3 Mallentin Ger.
190 H3 Mallero r. Italy
173 M4 Mallersdorf Ger.
223 L1 Mallery Lake Nunavut Can.
191 J2 Malles Venosta Italy
255 C8 Mallét Brazil
Mallia Kriti Greece see Malia
170 D4 Malliß Ger.
178 H6 Mallnitz Austria
260 B4 Malloa Chile
187 K8 Mallorca i. Spain
147 E8 Mallow Ireland
86 H7 Mallowa Well W.A. Austr.
150 D1 Malltraeth Bay Wales U.K.
150 E2 Mallwyd Gwynedd, Wales U.K.
140 K4 Malm Norway
123 J5 Malman Rūd r. Afgh.
140 P3 Malmberget Sweden
165 J8 Malmédy Belgium
214 C9 Malmesbury S. Africa
150 H4 Malmesbury Wiltshire, England U.K.
143 M2 Malmköping Sweden
142 J6 Malmö Sweden
247 □8 Malmok hd Bonaire Neth. Antilles
142 J6 Malmö-Sturup airport Sweden
143 L3 Malmslätt Sweden
134 J4 Malmyzh Rus. Fed.
190 F4 Malnate Italy
93 E1 Malo i. Indon.
191 K4 Malo Italy
78 □5 Malo i. Vanuatu
139 T9 Maloarkhangel'sk Rus. Fed.
251 F5 Maloca Amazonas Brazil
251 H4 Maloca Pará Brazil
253 E3 Maloca Salamaim Brazil
196 J6 Malo Crniće Serbia
175 I5 Małogoszcz Pol.
79 □7a Malolo i. Fiji
79 □7a Malolo Barrier Reef Fiji
92 C4 Malolos Luzon Phil.
215 P2 Malolotja Nature Reserve Swaziland
215 P3 Maloma Swaziland
211 B8 Malombe, Lake Malawi
174 D4 Małomice Pol.
211 B8 Malomo Malawi
137 N5 Malomykhaylivka Dnipropetrovs'ka Oblast' Ukr.
137 P5 Malomykhaylivka Dnipropetrovs'ka Oblast' Ukr.
183 Q5 Malón Spain
190 D5 Malone r. Italy
233 K4 Malone NY U.S.A.
108 D6 Malong Yunnan China
209 D7 Malonga Dem. Rep. Congo
212 B2 Malongo Angola
190 I3 Malonno Italy
176 D3 Malonty Czech Rep.
175 I5 Małopolska, Wyżyna hills Pol.
175 I6 Małopolskie prov. Pol.
137 N9 Malorichens'ke Ukr.
Malorita Belarus see Malaryta
134 G3 Maloshuyka Rus. Fed.
188 F4 Malovan pass Bos.-Herz.
197 K6 Malovăț Romania
Malovata Moldova see Molovata
213 F2 Malowera Moz.
141 H6 Måløy Norway
139 T6 Maloyaroslavets Rus. Fed.
139 S9 Maloye Bobrovo Rus. Fed.
139 T2 Maloye Borisovo Rus. Fed.
175 I1 Maloye-Lugovoye Rus. Fed.
134 J2 Malozemel'skaya Tundra lowland Rus. Fed.
216 □3d Malpaises La Palma Canary Is
182 G7 Malpartida Port.
184 G2 Malpartida de Cáceres Spain
184 H3 Malpartida de la Serena Spain
182 H9 Malpartida de Plasencia Spain
149 L7 Malpas Cheshire, England U.K.
150 F4 Malpas Newport, Wales U.K.
216 □3e Malpaso mt. El Hierro Canary Is
244 E3 Malpaso Mex.
267 N5 Malpelo, Isla de i. N. Pacific Ocean
182 H1 Mal Perro, Punta pt Spain
182 C2 Malpica Spain
183 K9 Malpica de Tajo Spain
182 F9 Malpica do Tejo Port.
138 H4 Mālpils Latvia
114 E4 Malprabha r. India
116 E6 Malpura Rajasthan India
172 E4 Malsch Ger.
176 D3 Malše r. Czech Rep.
169 I8 Malsfeld Ger.
114 D4 Malsiras Mahar. India
179 I6 Malta Austria
189 E8 Malta country Europe
138 K5 Malta Latvia
138 K5 Malta r. Latvia
195 □ Malta i. Malta
182 F7 Malta Port.
238 H5 Malta ID U.S.A.
238 K2 Malta MT U.S.A.
212 C5 Maltahöhe Namibia
207 I3 Maltam Cameroon
149 O7 Maltby South Yorkshire, England U.K.
149 R7 Maltby le Marsh Lincolnshire, England U.K.
172 D5 Malterdingen Ger.
172 E7 Malters Switz.
140 T3 Maltion luonnonpuisto nature res. Fin.
149 P5 Malton North Yorkshire, England U.K.
78 □2 Malua Samoa
183 Q6 Maluenda Spain
Maluera Moz. see Malowera
Malukken is Indon. see Maluku
209 B6 Maluku Dem. Rep. Congo
93 E4 Maluku is Indon.
93 E3 Maluku is Indon.
93 F5 Maluku prov. Indon.
93 D4 Maluku, Laut sea Indon.
93 E4 Maluku Utara prov. Indon.
128 E5 Ma'lūlā, Jabal mts Syria
197 K4 Malului, Vârful hill Romania
207 G4 Malumfashi Nigeria
209 E9 Malundano Zambia
209 D8 Malundo Angola
143 J1 Malung Sweden
174 D3 Małuszów Pol.
175 H5 Maluszyn Pol.
215 M5 Maluti Mountains Lesotho
78 □6 Malu'u Malaita Solomon Is
206 E4 Maluwe Ghana
183 J5 Malva Spain
190 F3 Malvaglia Switz.
114 C4 Malvan Mahar. India
Malvasia Greece see Monemvasia
184 A3 Malveira Port.
246 □ Malvern Jamaica
246 □ Malvern hill Jamaica
Malvern Worcestershire, England U.K. see Great Malvern
237 I8 Malvern AR U.S.A.
232 D8 Malvern OH U.S.A.
Malvérnia Moz. see Chicualacuala
150 H3 Malvern Link Worcestershire, England U.K.
Malvinas, Islas terr. S. Atlantic Ocean see Falkland Islands
116 F8 Malwa reg. Madh. Prad. India
210 A2 Malwal Sudan
171 J7 Malxe r. Ger.
177 H4 Malý Dunaj r. Slovakia
175 M3 Malyech Belarus
177 K3 Malý Horeš Slovakia
177 J3 Mályi Hungary
131 M3 Malykay Rus. Fed.
136 I3 Malyn Ukr.
137 P4 Malynivka Ukr.
136 F2 Malyns'k Ukr.
175 K2 Mały Płock Pol.
138 L1 Malyy, Ostrov i. Rus. Fed.
131 R3 Malyy Anyuy r. Rus. Fed.
177 L3 Malyy Bereznyy Ukr.
135 I7 Malyye Derbety Rus. Fed.
Malyye Kotyuzhany Moldova see Cotiujenii Mici
139 X4 Malyye Soli Rus. Fed.
135 J5 Malyy Irgiz r. Rus. Fed.
Malyy Kavkaz mts Asia see Lesser Caucasus
107 J1 Malyy Kunaley Rus. Fed.
131 P2 Malyy Lyakhovskiy, Ostrov i. Novosibirskiye O-va Rus. Fed.
136 F2 Malyy Stydyn Ukr.
131 L2 Malyy Taymyr, Ostrov i. Rus. Fed.
138 J2 Malyy Tyuters, Ostrov i. Estonia
120 C3 Malyy Uzen' r. Kazakh./Rus. Fed.
129 C1 Malyy Zelenchuk r. Rus. Fed.
131 P3 Mama r. Rus. Fed.
134 J5 Mamadysh Rus. Fed.
215 M3 Mamafubedu S. Africa
215 L4 Mamahabane S. Africa
79 □7 Mamanuca-i-Cake Group is Fiji
Mamanutha-i-Thake Group is Fiji see Mamanuca-i-Cake Group
80 H2 Mamaranui North I. N.Z.
235 H3 Mamaroneck NY U.S.A.
93 A5 Mamasa Sulawesi Barat Indon.
123 K6 Mamatān Nāvar l. Afgh.
122 C6 Māmātīn Iran
111 K11 Mamba Xizang China
Mamba Japan see Manba
92 B8 Mambahenauhan i. Phil.
254 D5 Mambai Brazil
92 E7 Mambajao Phil.
207 I5 Mambal Cameroon
211 B6 Mambali Tanz.
208 F4 Mambasa Dem. Rep. Congo
208 C4 Mambéré r. C.A.R.
208 B3 Mambéré-Kadéï pref. C.A.R.
93 A5 Mambi Sulawesi Barat Indon.
207 H5 Mambila Mountains Cameroon/Nigeria
208 C4 Mambili r. Congo
206 B4 Mambolo Sierra Leone
256 A6 Mamborê Brazil
183 M5 Mambrilla de Castejón Spain
211 D5 Mambrui Kenya
92 C5 Mamburao Mindoro Phil.
129 J3 Mamedkala Rus. Fed.
217 □2a Mamelle i. Inner Islands Seychelles
215 M1 Mamelodi S. Africa
159 L5 Mamers France
207 H5 Mamfe Cameroon
251 F6 Mamiá Brazil
251 F6 Mamiá, Lago l. Brazil
212 D3 Mamili National Park Namibia
252 C5 Mamiña Chile
250 E5 Mamirauá, Reserve de Desenvolvimento Sustentával nature res. Brazil
160 I2 Mamirolle France
129 E3 Mamison Pass Georgia/Rus. Fed.
117 N8 Mamit Mizoram India
121 M1 Mamlyutka Kazakh.
129 H6 Mämmädbäyli Azer.
173 K5 Mammendorf Ger.
173 N4 Mamming Ger.
195 K7 Mammola Italy
241 V9 Mammoth AZ U.S.A.
230 D7 Mammoth Cave National Park KY U.S.A.
240 N4 Mammoth Lakes CA U.S.A.
240 M4 Mammoth Reservoir CA U.S.A.
192 C7 Mamoiada Sardegna Italy
246 F8 Mamonal Col.
192 C6 Mamone Sardegna Italy
138 C7 Mamonovo Kaliningradskaya Oblast' Rus. Fed.
139 W8 Mamonovo Ryazanskaya Oblast' Rus. Fed.
121 S1 Mamontovo Rus. Fed.
234 F6 Mamora NJ U.S.A.
252 D2 Mamoré r. Bol./Brazil
250 E5 Mamori Brazil
251 F5 Mamori, Lago l. Brazil
252 D1 Mamoriá Brazil
206 B4 Mamou Guinea
217 □3b Mamoudzou Mayotte
Mamoutsou Mayotte see Mamoudzou
213 □J3 Mampikony Madag.
206 E5 Mampong Ghana
214 C9 Mamre S. Africa
175 J1 Mamry, Jezioro l. Pol.
93 A5 Mamuju Sulawesi Barat Indon.
125 L6 Ma'mūl Oman
122 D4 Māmūnīyeh Iran
212 D4 Mamuno Botswana
196 H9 Mamuras Albania
102 R8 Mamurogawa Japan
Mamutzu Mayotte see Mamoudzou
120 H2 Mamyt Kazakh.
206 D5 Man Côte d'Ivoire
114 D4 Man r. India
116 G3 Man Jammu and Kashmir
232 D11 Man WV U.S.A.
148 H5 Man, Isle of i. Irish Sea
79 □7a Mana i. Fiji
251 H3 Mana Fr. Guiana
177 H3 Maňa Slovakia
240 □B11 Mānā HI U.S.A.
250 C2 Mana Bárbara Venez.
250 B5 Manabí prov. Ecuador
250 C3 Manacacias r. Col.
251 F5 Manacapuru Brazil
187 L8 Manacor Spain
216 □1c Manadas São Jorge Azores
93 D3 Manado Sulawesi Indon.
93 D3 Manadotua i. Indon.
165 F8 Manage Belgium
242 □P11 Managua Nic.
242 □P11 Managua, Lago de l. Nic.
125 M4 Manaḩ Oman
235 G5 Manahawkin Bay NJ U.S.A.
80 I6 Manaia North I. N.Z.
213 □J4 Manakara Madag.
80 J7 Manakau North I. N.Z.
81 H9 Manakau mt. South I. N.Z.
124 F8 Manākhah Yemen
116 F3 Manali Hima. Prad. India
Manama Bahrain see Al Manāmah
114 F8 Manamadurai Tamil Nadu India
213 □J3 Manambaho r. Madag.
213 □J4 Manambondro Madag.
114 F7 Manamelkudi Tamil Nadu India
91 K7 Manam Island P.N.G.
251 F2 Manamo, Caño r. Venez.
92 C6 Manamoc i. Phil.
240 □D12 Mānana i. HI U.S.A.
213 □J4 Mananantañana r. Madag.
213 □J4 Mananara r. Madag.
213 □K3 Mananara, Parc National de nat. park Madag.
213 □K3 Mananara Avaratra Madag.
83 I6 Manangatang Vic. Austr.
84 F4 Manangoora N.T. Austr.
213 □K4 Mananjary Madag.
213 □J5 Manankoliva Madag.
206 D4 Manankoro Mali
206 C3 Manantali, Lac de l. Mali
114 E7 Manantavadi Kerala India
213 □J5 Manantenina Madag.
244 C6 Manantlán, Sierra mts Mex.
78 □6 Manaoba Island Solomon Is
111 D11 Mana Pass China/India
213 F3 Mana Pools National Park Zimbabwe
81 B12 Manapouri South I. N.Z.
81 B12 Manapouri, Lake South I. N.Z.
114 F7 Manapparai Tamil Nadu India
213 □J3 Manarantsandry Madag.
183 O2 Mañaria Spain
110 H4 Manas Xinjiang China
117 M6 Manas r. India
142 J1 Månäs Sweden
121 N6 Manas, Gora mt. Uzbek.
116 E7 Manasa Madh. Prad. India
129 I3 Manasaul Rus. Fed.
110 G4 Manas He r. China
110 H4 Manas Hu l. China
125 K4 Manāşīr reg. U.A.E.
129 I3 Manaskent Rus. Fed.
117 J5 Manaslu mt. Nepal
117 J5 Manaslu Conservation Area nature res. Nepal
235 G4 Manasquan NJ U.S.A.
235 G4 Manasquan r. NJ U.S.A.
232 H10 Manassas VA U.S.A.
Manastir Macedonia see Bitola
177 L6 Mănăştiur Romania
117 M6 Manas Wildlife Sanctuary nature res. Bhutan
93 D8 Manatang Indon.
247 □1 Manatí Puerto Rico
247 □1 Manati, Río Grande de r. Puerto Rico
216 □2b Manati Bay St Helena
105 J5 Manatsuru Japan
93 D8 Manatuto East Timor
96 A5 Man-aung Myanmar
96 A5 Man-aung Kyun i. Myanmar
251 F5 Manaus Brazil
126 E5 Manavgat Turkey
226 F5 Manawa WI U.S.A.
116 E8 Manawar Madh. Prad. India
80 J4 Manawaru North I. N.Z.
202 E6 Manawashei Sudan
80 J7 Manawatu r. North I. N.Z.
80 J6 Manawatu-Wanganui admin. reg. North I. N.Z.
92 F8 Manay Mindanao Phil.
139 T8 Manayenki Rus. Fed.
105 J5 Manazuru-misaki pt Japan
105 I3 Manba Japan
117 K8 Manbazar W. Bengal India
128 F2 Manbij Syria
149 R7 Manby Lincolnshire, England U.K.
159 K5 Mancelles, Alpes hills France
226 I5 Mancelona MI U.S.A.
183 J7 Mancera de Abajo Spain
114 C3 Manchar Mahar. India
185 L5 Mancha Real Spain
158 I4 Manche dept France
246 □ Manchester parish Jamaica
149 M7 Manchester Greater Manchester, England U.K.
233 M7 Manchester CT U.S.A.
236 J4 Manchester IA U.S.A.
232 B11 Manchester KY U.S.A.
234 B5 Manchester MD U.S.A.
227 J7 Manchester MI U.S.A.
233 N6 Manchester NH U.S.A.
232 B10 Manchester OH U.S.A.
234 B4 Manchester PA U.S.A.
231 D8 Manchester TN U.S.A.
233 L5 Manchester VT U.S.A.
123 L8 Manchhar Lake Pak.
173 K4 Manching Ger.
246 □ Manchioneal Jamaica
184 G3 Manchita Spain
Manchuria reg. Heilong. China see Dongbei
192 H2 Manciano Italy
163 E8 Manciet France
126 H4 Mancılık Turkey
199 I3 Mancınık Dağı mts Turkey
239 J8 Mancos CO U.S.A.
241 X5 Mancos r. CO U.S.A.
123 J8 Mand Pak.
122 D7 Mand, Rūd-e r. Iran
117 L7 Manda Bangl.
211 B7 Manda Malawi
211 B6 Manda Tanz.
208 E2 Manda, Jebel mt. Sudan
208 C2 Manda, Parc National de nat. park Chad
213 □J4 Mandabe Madag.
256 A5 Mandaguaçu Brazil
256 B5 Mandaguari Brazil
94 E5 Mandah Sumatera Indon.
94 □ Mandai Sing.
123 I5 Mandal Afgh.
116 C8 Mandal Gujarat India
116 E7 Mandal Rajasthan India
106 H2 Mandal Bulgan Mongolia
106 J2 Mandal Töv Mongolia
142 D3 Mandal Norway
91 J7 Mandala, Puncak mt. Papua Indon.
96 C4 Mandalay Myanmar
96 B4 Mandalay admin. div. Myanmar
Mandale Myanmar see Mandalay
Mandale admin. div. Myanmar see Mandalay
92 D6 Mandalgan, Mount vol. Phil.
116 E7 Mandalgarh Rajasthan India
106 J4 Mandalgovĭ Mongolia
127 L7 Mandalī Iraq
142 D3 Mandalselva r. Norway
107 M5 Mandalt Nei Mongol China
107 M4 Mandalt Sum Nei Mongol China
236 E2 Mandan ND U.S.A.
195 I7 Mandanici Sicilia Italy
92 D5 Mandaon Masbate Phil.
207 H3 Mandaoua Soumounti well Niger
114 F8 Mandapam Tamil Nadu India
93 A5 Mandar, Teluk b. Indon.
192 C8 Mandas Sardegna Italy
195 L5 Mandatoriccio Italy
116 C8 Mandav Hills Gujarat India
123 P7 Mandawa Rajasthan India
183 O7 Mandayona Spain
160 F4 Mandé, Mont de hill France
Mandeghughusu i. New Georgia Is Solomon Is see Simbo
172 C3 Mandelbachtal-Ormesheim Ger.
161 J9 Mandelieu-la-Napoule France
190 G4 Mandello del Lario Italy
182 D2 Mandeo r. Spain
210 D4 Mandera Kenya
241 T3 Manderfield UT U.S.A.
169 C10 Manderscheid Ger.
160 J2 Mandeure France
246 □ Mandeville Jamaica
81 C12 Mandeville South I. N.Z.
116 C6 Mandha Rajasthan India
210 E2 Mandheera Somalia
Mandhoúdhíon Greece see Mantoudi
116 F4 Mandi Hima. Prad. India
206 D3 Mandiakui Mali
206 C4 Mandiana Guinea
94 E2 Mandi Angin, Gunung mt. Malaysia
123 O6 Mandi Burewala Pak.
Mandidzuzure Zimbabwe see Chimanimani
213 G3 Mandié Moz.
213 G2 Mandimba Moz.
206 C3 Manding, Monts mts Mali
245 K6 Mandinga Grande, Laguna l. Mex.
93 E4 Mandioli i. Maluku Indon.
261 H2 Mandiso ví Arg.
208 A5 Mandji Gabon
116 H8 Mandla Madh. Prad. India
177 L3 Mándok Hungary
116 D6 Mandor Rajasthan India
95 H4 Mandor Kalimantan Indon.
95 H4 Mandor, Cagar Alam nature res. Indon.
86 F5 Mandora W.A. Austr.
84 C2 Mandorah N.T. Austr.
208 F3 Mandoro Dem. Rep. Congo
213 □J3 Mandoro Madag.
207 F4 Mandouri Togo
198 E4 Mandra Greece
116 F6 Mandrael Rajasthan India
199 I6 Mandraki Greece
213 □J5 Mandrare r. Madag.
Mandrenska r. Bulg. see Sredetska Reka
157 J7 Mandres-en-Barrois France
213 □K2 Mandritsara Madag.
213 □J4 Mandrosonoro Madag.
137 R3 Mandrovo Rus. Fed.
116 E7 Mandsaur Madh. Prad. India
161 E9 Manduel France
95 L3 Mandul i. Indon.
87 C12 Mandurah W.A. Austr.
195 N3 Manduria Italy
116 B8 Mandvi Gujarat India
116 D9 Mandvi Gujarat India
114 E6 Mandya Karnataka India
217 □3a Mandza Njazidja Comoros
163 F9 Mane Midi-Pyrénées France
161 H9 Mane Provence-Alpes-Côte d'Azur France
142 E2 Måne r. Norway
151 M3 Manea Cambridgeshire, England U.K.
169 K9 Manebach Ger.
116 C9 Manekwara Gujarat India
122 G3 Maneli Iran
78 □1 Manell Point Guam
116 I8 Manendragarh Chhattisgarh India
117 J7 Maner Bihar India
114 F3 Maner r. India
190 I5 Manerbio Italy
211 C6 Maneromango Tanz.
183 Q3 Mañeru Spain
122 B5 Manesht Kūh mt. Iran
197 N6 Mănești Romania
176 C2 Manětín Czech Rep.
Maneva Madag. see Mahaboboka
136 E2 Manevychi Ukr.
203 F3 Manfalūţ Egypt
193 P4 Manfredonia Italy
193 Q4 Manfredonia, Golfo di g. Italy
254 E5 Manga Brazil
206 E4 Manga Burkina
254 D4 Mangabeiras, Serra das hills Brazil
209 B6 Manga Grande Angola
209 C6 Mangai Dem. Rep. Congo
209 C5 Mangai, Réserve de Faune des Hippopotames de nature res. Dem. Rep. Congo
81 □2 Mangaia i. Cook Is
80 J5 Mangakino North I. N.Z.
114 G4 Mangalagiri Andhra Prad. India
117 N6 Mangaldai Assam India
197 Q7 Mangalia Romania
202 C6 Mangalmé Chad
114 D6 Mangalore Karnataka India
123 M4 Mangalpur Afgh.
114 D4 Mangalvedha Mahar. India
81 H9 Mangamaunu South I. N.Z.
80 I6 Mangamingi North I. N.Z.
80 H2 Mangamuka North I. N.Z.
182 I5 Manganeses de la Lampreana Spain
182 I4 Manganeses de la Polvorosa Spain
208 D4 Mangania Dem. Rep. Congo
80 H2 Manganui r. North I. N.Z.
114 C3 Mangaon Mahar. India
114 G3 Mangapet Andhra Prad. India
80 G7 Mangarakau South I. N.Z.
257 E5 Mangaratiba Brazil
79 □9 Mangareva i. Arch. des Tuamotu Fr. Polynesia
Mangareva Islands Arch. des Tuamotu Fr. Polynesia see Gambier, Îles
80 J7 Mangatainoka North I. N.Z.
80 J4 Mangatawhiri North I. N.Z.
215 K5 Mangaung S. Africa
116 H7 Mangawan Madh. Prad. India
80 J6 Mangaweka North I. N.Z.
80 K6 Mangaweka mt. North I. N.Z.
80 I3 Mangawhai North I. N.Z.
Mangde Chhu r. Bhutan see Trongsa Chhu
Ma'ngê Gansu China see Luqu
Mangea i. Cook Is see Mangaia
209 E6 Mangembe Dem. Rep. Congo
141 H6 Manger Norway
80 □ Mangere Island Chatham Is S. Pacific Ocean
147 D9 Mangerton Mountain hill Ireland
173 M6 Mangfall r. Ger.
173 L6 Mangfallgebirge mts Ger.
95 H6 Manggar Indon.
78 □6 Manggautu Rennell Solomon Is
Mangghyshlaq Kazakh. see Mangystau
Mangghystaū Kazakh. see Mangystau
Mangghystaū Oblysy admin. div. Kazakh. see Mangistauskaya Oblast'
Mangghyt Uzbek. see Mang'it
Manghit Uzbek. see Mang'it
157 K5 Mangiennes France
78 □1 Mangilao Guam
120 D5 Mangistau, Gory hills Kazakh.
120 F6 Mangistauskaya Oblast' admin. div. Kazakh.
120 I6 Mang'it Uzbek.
95 M4 Mangkalihat, Tanjung pt Indon.
95 K6 Mangkutup r. Indon.
96 D1 Mangkyi Myanmar
123 O5 Mangla Pak.
250 B4 Manglares, Punta pt Col.
129 F4 Manglisi Georgia
111 J8 Mangnai Qinghai China
111 J7 Mangnai Zhen Qinghai China
213 □K2 Mangoaka Madag.
211 B8 Mangochi Malawi
206 D4 Mangodara Burkina
213 □I4 Mangoky r. Toliara Madag.
213 □J4 Mangoky r. Toliara Madag.
93 D4 Mangole i. Indon.
93 D5 Mangole, Selat sea chan. Indon.
114 D4 Mangoli Karnataka India
213 □I4 Mangolovolo Madag.
208 E5 Mangombe Dem. Rep. Congo
80 H2 Mangonui North I. N.Z.
213 □K3 Mangoro r. Madag.
150 G5 Mangotsfield South Gloucestershire, England U.K.
Mangqystaū Shyghanaghy b. Kazakh. see Mangyshlakskiy Zaliv
Mangra Qinghai China see Guinan
116 C9 Mangrol Gujarat India
116 F7 Mangrol Rajasthan India
231 H12 Mangrove Cay i. Bahamas
116 F9 Mangrul Mahar. India
182 E7 Mangualde Port.
250 D5 Manguari Brazil
123 L7 Manguchar Pak.
208 D2 Mangueigne Chad
258 G4 Mangueira, Lago l. Brazil
255 B8 Mangueirinha Brazil
205 H5 Manguéni, Plateau du Niger
100 C3 Mangui Nei Mongol China
254 F4 Manguinha, Pontal do pt Brazil
Mangula Zimbabwe see Mhangura
242 □P10 Mangulile Hond.
237 F8 Mangum OK U.S.A.
254 D2 Mangunça, Ilha i. Brazil
93 E1 Mangupung i. Indon.
208 F4 Manguredjipa Dem. Rep. Congo
107 M2 Mangut Rus. Fed.
Mangyshlak Kazakh. see Mangystau
120 D5 Mangyshlak, Poluostrov pen. Kazakh.
Mangyshlak Oblast admin. div. Kazakh. see Mangistauskaya Oblast'
Mangyshlakskaya Oblast' admin. div. Kazakh. see Mangistauskaya Oblast'
120 D5 Mangyshlakskiy Zaliv b. Kazakh.
120 D6 Mangystau Kazakh.
Manhan Hovd Mongolia see Tögrög
106 F1 Manhan Hövsgöl Mongolia
179 M2 Manhartsberg hill Austria
236 G6 Manhattan KS U.S.A.
240 N8 Manhattan Beach CA U.S.A.
165 I8 Manhay Belgium
234 C4 Manheim PA U.S.A.
213 G5 Manhica Moz.
215 Q2 Manhoca Moz.
257 F4 Manhuaçu Brazil
257 G3 Manhuaçu r. Brazil
157 K5 Manhuelles France
257 G4 Manhumirim Brazil
202 B6 Mani Chad
202 C5 Mani well Chad
111 H9 Mani Xizang China
250 C3 Mani Col.

Marknesse to Maule
349

164 I3 Marknesse Neth.
171 F10 Markneukirchen Ger.
177 G4 Márkó Hungary
108 C2 Markog Qu r. Sichuan China
198 E5 Markopoulo Greece
208 C3 Markounda C.A.R.
179 O8 Markovac Trojstveni Croatia
131 S3 Markovo Chukotskiy Avtonomnyy Okrug Rus. Fed.
139 X4 Markovo Ivanovskaya Oblast' Rus. Fed.
137 N2 Markovo Kurskaya Oblast' Rus. Fed.
207 F3 Markoye Burkina
171 F8 Markranstädt Ger.
120 B2 Marks Rus. Fed.
237 J8 Marks MS U.S.A.
234 F3 Marksboro NJ U.S.A.
151 N4 Marks Tey Essex, England U.K.
169 J9 Marksuhl Ger.
237 I10 Marksville LA U.S.A.
179 N5 Markt Allhau Austria
173 I3 Marktbergel Ger.
173 J3 Markt Berolzheim Ger.
173 I2 Markt Bibart Ger.
173 I2 Marktbreit Ger.
173 J3 Markt Erlbach Ger.
179 M5 Markt Hartmannsdorf Austria
172 H2 Marktheidenfeld Ger.
173 K5 Markt Indersdorf Ger.
173 N5 Marktl Ger.
171 E10 Marktleugast Ger.
171 F10 Marktleuthen Ger.
173 J6 Marktoberdorf Ger.
173 I4 Marktoffingen Ger.
222 E5 Marktosis B.C. Can.
179 N4 Markt Piesting Austria
173 M1 Marktredwitz Ger.
173 I6 Markt Rettenbach Ger.
171 D10 Marktrodach Ger.
179 J3 Markt Sankt Florian Austria
179 N4 Markt Sankt Martin Austria
173 O6 Marktschellenberg Ger.
173 L5 Markt Schwaben Ger.
173 I2 Marktseft Ger.
173 J5 Markt Wald Ger.
179 N8 Markusevec Croatia
175 K4 Markuszów Pol.
151 L4 Markyate Hertfordshire, England U.K.
169 D7 Marl Ger.
82 D2 Marla S.A. Austr.
87 D10 Marlandy Hill W.A. Austr.
234 E6 Marlboro NJ U.S.A.
235 G4 Marlboro NJ U.S.A.
235 H1 Marlboro NY U.S.A.
85 L7 Marlborough Qld Austr.
81 H8 Marlborough admin. reg. South I. N.Z.
151 I5 Marlborough Wiltshire, England U.K.
235 K1 Marlborough CT U.S.A.
233 N6 Marlborough MA U.S.A.
233 M6 Marlborough NH U.S.A.
151 I5 Marlborough Downs hills England U.K.
150 E7 Marldon Devon, England U.K.
156 G4 Marle France
191 K2 Marlengo Italy
157 O6 Marlenheim France
191 P6 Marlera, Rt pt Croatia
227 K6 Marlette MI U.S.A.
161 E6 Marlhes France
160 G4 Marlieux France
237 G10 Marlin TX U.S.A.
232 E10 Marlinton WV U.S.A.
171 D9 Marlishausen Ger.
83 L7 Marlo Vic. Austr.
214 E10 Marloth Nature Reserve S. Africa
170 G2 Marlow Ger.
151 K4 Marlow Buckinghamshire, England U.K.
234 F5 Marlton NJ U.S.A.
157 L5 Marly Lorraine France
156 G3 Marly Nord-Pas-de-Calais France
190 C2 Marly Switz.
156 E5 Marly-la-Ville France
114 C5 Marmagao Goa India
160 E3 Marmagne Bourgogne France
159 P7 Marmagne Centre France
163 E6 Marmande France
199 I2 Marmara Turkey
Marmara, Sea of g. Turkey see Marmara Denizi
199 I2 Marmara Adası i. Turkey
199 J2 Marmara Denizi g. Turkey
199 I2 Marmaraereğlisi Turkey
199 J4 Marmara Gölü l. Turkey
202 E2 Marmarica reg. Libya
199 J6 Marmaris Turkey
199 H4 Marmaro Chios Greece
236 D2 Marmarth ND U.S.A.
111 F10 Marmê Xizang China
184 D4 Marmelar Port.
184 B2 Marmeleira Port.
184 B6 Marmelete Port.
251 F6 Marmelos r. Brazil
232 D10 Marmet WV U.S.A.
87 F10 Marmion, Lake salt l. W.A. Austr.
224 B3 Marmion Lake Ont. Can.
191 J5 Marmirolo Italy
244 A2 Mármol Mex.
191 L3 Marmolada mt. Italy
185 K4 Marmolejo Spain
190 D4 Marmore r. Italy
157 N6 Marmoutier France
160 H2 Marnay France
160 J4 Marnaz France
156 H5 Marne dept France
156 D6 Marne r. France
168 H3 Marne Ger.
157 J8 Marne, Source de la France
157 J7 Marne à la Saône, Canal de la France
157 M6 Marne au Rhin, Canal de la France
156 E6 Marne-la-Vallée France
129 F4 Marneuli Georgia
172 E2 Marnheim Ger.
150 H6 Marnhull Dorset, England U.K.
170 E4 Marnitz Ger.
117 O6 Marniu Arun. Prad. India
83 I7 Marnoo Vic. Austr.
208 C2 Maro Chad
213 □K2 Maroambihy Madag.
213 □K2 Maroantsetra Madag.
257 H2 Maroba r. Brazil
213 □J4 Marofandilia Madag.
194 G9 Maroglio r. Sicilia Italy
79 □9 Marokau atoll Arch. des Tuamotu Fr. Polynesia
80 I5 Marokopa North I. N.Z.
116 F2 Marol Jammu and Kashmir
123 O7 Marol Pak.
213 □K4 Marolambo Madag.
169 K10 Maroldsweisach Ger.
159 L5 Marolles-les-Braults France
213 □K2 Maromandia Madag.
156 B5 Maromme France
213 □K2 Maromokotro mt. Madag.
213 F3 Marondera Zimbabwe
251 H3 Maroni r. Fr. Guiana
162 H5 Maronne r. France
85 N9 Maroochydore Qld Austr.
87 C7 Maroonah W.A. Austr.
239 K7 Maroon Peak CO U.S.A.
246 □ Maroon Town Jamaica
93 A6 Maros Sulawesi Indon.
93 A6 Maros r. Indon.
196 I4 Maros r. Hungary
213 □K3 Maroseranana Madag.
177 J5 Maros-Körös Köze plain Hungary
177 J5 Maroslele Hungary
191 L4 Marostica Italy
Marosvásárhely Romania see Târgu Mureș
213 □K3 Marotandrano Madag.
79 □9 Marotiri is Îs Australes Fr. Polynesia
80 I2 Marotiri Islands North I. N.Z.
213 □K2 Marotolana Madag.
207 I4 Maroua Cameroon
158 F5 Maroué France
251 F5 Marova Brazil
213 □K2 Marovato Antsiraňana Madag.
213 □J5 Marovato Toliara Madag.
213 □J3 Marovoay Mahajanga Madag.
213 □K3 Marovoay Toamasina Madag.
213 □J3 Marovoay Atsimo Madag.
93 B4 Marowali Sulawesi Indon.
251 H3 Marowijne r. Suriname
175 I2 Maróz, Jezioro l. Pol.
172 C3 Marpingen Ger.
149 M7 Marple Greater Manchester, England U.K.
127 J6 Marqādah Syria
Marqakōl l. Kazakh. see Markakol', Ozero
215 L4 Marquard S. Africa
173 M6 Marquartstein Ger.
245 I9 Marquelia Mex.
156 C3 Marquenterre reg. France
183 O6 Marquesado de Berlanga reg. Spain
Marquesas Islands Fr. Polynesia see Marquises, Îles
231 F13 Marquesas Keys is FL U.S.A.
257 F5 Marquês de Valença Brazil
226 G3 Marquette MI U.S.A.
237 G10 Marquez TX U.S.A.
256 A6 Marquinho Brazil
156 F3 Marquion France
247 □3 Marquis, Cap c. St Lucia
156 C2 Marquise France
79 □9 Marquises, Îles is Fr. Polynesia
163 I10 Marquixanes France
83 I4 Marra N.S.W. Austr.
83 K4 Marra r. N.S.W. Austr.
202 E6 Marra, Jebel mt. Sudan
202 E6 Marra, Jebel plat. Sudan
84 E3 Marra Aboriginal Land res. N.T. Austr.
213 H3 Marracua Moz.
213 G5 Marracuene Moz.
191 L7 Marradi Italy
124 E7 Marrāk i. Saudi Arabia
204 D3 Marrakech Morocco
Marrakesh Morocco see Marrakech
124 E6 Marrān Saudi Arabia
140 R3 Marraskoski Fin.
83 J9 Marrawah Tas. Austr.
82 G3 Marree S.A. Austr.
237 J11 Marrero LA U.S.A.
213 G3 Marromeu Moz.
213 G3 Marromeu, Reserva de nature res. Moz.
245 H1 Marroquin Mex.
192 B8 Marrubiu Sardegna Italy
164 I2 Marrum Neth.
211 C8 Marrupa Moz.
82 D2 Marryat S.A. Austr.
161 A6 Mars r. France
232 E8 Mars PA U.S.A.
203 G3 Marsá al 'Alam Egypt
202 C2 Marsa al Burayqah Libya
181 E5 Marsa-Ben-Mehidi Alg.
210 C4 Marsabit Kenya
210 C4 Marsabit National Reserve nature res. Kenya
160 D6 Marsac-en-Livradois France
158 H6 Marsac-sur-Don France
203 H5 Marsa Darur Sudan
203 H4 Marsa Delwein Sudan
190 G6 Marsaglia Italy
124 B3 Marsá Iljī Egypt
157 M6 Marsal France
194 C8 Marsala Sicilia Italy
195 □ Marsalforn Gozo Malta
124 C5 Marsa Mar'ob Sudan
202 E2 Marsá Maṭrūḥ Egypt
160 F2 Marsannay-la-Côte France
161 F7 Marsanne France
203 H4 Marsa Oseif Sudan
124 C5 Marsa Salak Sudan
124 C5 Marsa Shin'ab Sudan
Marsaskala Malta see Wied Il-Għajn
206 B3 Marsassoum Senegal
124 B3 Marsá Ṭunḍubah Egypt
195 □ Marsaxlokk Malta
195 □ Marsaxlokk, Il-Bajja ta' b. Malta
246 E2 Mars Bay Andros Bahamas
216 □2a Mars Bay b. Ascension S. Atlantic Ocean
169 G8 Marsberg Ger.
168 J4 Marschacht Ger.
193 I2 Marsciano Italy
83 K5 Marsden N.S.W. Austr.
223 I4 Marsden Sask. Can.
149 N6 Marsden West Yorkshire, England U.K.
80 I2 Marsden Point N.Z.
164 G3 Marsdiep sea chan. Neth.
161 D10 Marseillan France
161 G10 Marseille France
Marseille airport France see Provence
161 F9 Marseille au Rhône, Canal de France
156 C4 Marseille-en-Beauvaisis France
Marseilles France see Marseille
226 F8 Marseilles IL U.S.A.
252 D3 Marsella Bol.
140 M4 Marsfjället mt. Sweden
128 C10 Marshah, Jabal mt. Saudi Arabia
84 F7 Marshall watercourse N.T. Austr.
223 I4 Marshall Sask. Can.
237 I8 Marshall AR U.S.A.
230 D6 Marshall IL U.S.A.
226 J7 Marshall MI U.S.A.
236 H3 Marshall MN U.S.A.
236 I6 Marshall MO U.S.A.
231 F8 Marshall NC U.S.A.
237 H9 Marshall TX U.S.A.
232 H10 Marshall VA U.S.A.
266 F5 Marshall Islands country N. Pacific Ocean
234 E2 Marshalls Creek PA U.S.A.
234 D5 Marshallton DE U.S.A.
236 I4 Marshalltown IA U.S.A.
234 D4 Marsh Creek Lake PA U.S.A.
150 H5 Marshfield South Gloucestershire, England U.K.
237 I7 Marshfield MO U.S.A.
226 D5 Marshfield WI U.S.A.
231 I12 Marsh Harbour Bahamas
233 □R2 Mars Hill ME U.S.A.
237 J11 Marsh Island LA U.S.A.
222 C2 Marsh Lake Y.T. Can.
222 C2 Marsh Lake l. Y.T. Can.
223 M3 Marsh Point Man. Can.
122 C3 Marshūn Iran
161 E9 Marsillargues France
238 F5 Marsing ID U.S.A.
149 O4 Marske-by-the-Sea Redcar and Cleveland, England U.K.
157 K5 Mars-la-Tour France
156 I6 Marson France
163 I8 Marssac-sur-Tarn France
143 N2 Märsta Sweden
142 G7 Marstal Denmark
168 K1 Marstal Bugt b. Denmark
190 G1 Märstetten Switz.
151 J4 Marston Oxfordshire, England U.K.
150 G6 Marston Magna Somerset, England U.K.
151 K3 Marston Moretaine Bedfordshire, England U.K.
78 □3a Marsugalt i. Kwajalein Marshall Is
117 J6 Marsyangdi r. Nepal
234 D7 Marsyhope r. MD U.S.A.
192 H2 Marta Italy
192 H3 Marta r. Italy
Martaban, Gulf of Myanmar see Mottama, Gulf of
192 H2 Martana, Isola i. Italy
95 L1 Martanai Besar i. Malaysia
195 O3 Martano Italy
193 J2 Martano, Monte mt. Italy
207 I5 Martap Cameroon
95 K6 Martapura Kalimantan Indon.
94 F7 Martapura Sumatera Indon.
207 I3 Marte Nigeria
162 H6 Martel France
232 C8 Martel OH U.S.A.
162 G6 Martel, Causse de hills France
165 I9 Martelange Belgium
191 M4 Martellago Italy
191 J2 Martello Italy
177 J5 Mártély Hungary
177 J5 Mártélyi park Hungary
224 E4 Marten River Ont. Can.
223 J4 Martensville Sask. Can.
243 J4 Marte R. Gómez, Presa resr Mex.
187 D9 Martés mt. Spain
187 C9 Martés, Serra mts Spain
168 H5 Martfeld Ger.
177 J4 Martfű Hungary
151 P2 Martham Norfolk, England U.K.
233 O7 Martha's Vineyard i. MA U.S.A.
162 E4 Marthon France
246 E3 Martí Cuba
182 H8 Martiago Spain
191 O3 Martignacco Italy
193 I3 Martignano, Lago di l. Italy
163 C6 Martignas-sur-Jalle France
159 K7 Martigné-Briand France
158 I6 Martigné-Ferchaud France
159 J5 Martigné-sur-Mayenne France
190 C3 Martigny Switz.
160 E3 Martigny-le-Comte France
157 K7 Martigny-les-Bains France
157 K7 Martigny-les-Gerbonvaux France
161 G10 Martigues France
183 K7 Martiherrero Spain
185 I9 Martil Morocco
163 C6 Martillac France
184 D6 Martim Longo Port.
Martim Vaz, Ilhas is S. Atlantic Ocean see Martin Vaz, Ilhas
222 F2 Martin r. N.W.T. Can.
177 H2 Martin Slovakia
186 E5 Martín r. Spain
236 E4 Martin SD U.S.A.
146 F7 Martin, Isle i. Scotland U.K.
231 E9 Martin, Lake AL U.S.A.
195 M2 Martina Franca Italy
81 J8 Martinborough North I. N.Z.
182 D9 Martinchel Port.
261 H4 Martín Chico Uru.
261 H5 Martín Colman Arg.
185 J6 Martín de la Jara Spain
260 D4 Martín de Loyola Arg.
182 H7 Martín de Yeltes Spain
190 H4 Martinengo Italy
186 I3 Martinet Spain
245 J5 Martínez Mex.
240 J3 Martinez CA U.S.A.
231 F9 Martinez GA U.S.A.
241 R9 Martinez Lake AZ U.S.A.
169 J8 Martinfeld Ger.
182 C9 Martingança Port.
261 H4 Martín García, Isla i. Arg.
185 K4 Martín Gonzalo, Embalse de resr Spain
257 E3 Martinho Campos Brazil
247 □3 Martinique terr. West Indies
247 □2 Martinique Passage Dominica/Martinique
183 K6 Martín Muñoz de las Posadas Spain
198 E4 Martino Greece
256 B5 Martinópolis Brazil
262 Q2 Martin Peninsula Antarctica
182 I2 Martinporra Spain
81 B11 Martins Bay South I. N.Z.
179 L3 Martinsberg Austria
232 C8 Martinsburg OH U.S.A.
232 G8 Martinsburg PA U.S.A.
232 H9 Martinsburg WV U.S.A.
191 Q6 Martinšćica Croatia
234 E3 Martins Creek PA U.S.A.
234 D1 Martins Creek r. PA U.S.A.
232 E8 Martins Ferry OH U.S.A.
193 L2 Martinsicuro Italy
147 F8 Martinstown Ireland
230 D6 Martinsville IN U.S.A.
232 F12 Martinsville VA U.S.A.
264 H7 Martin Vaz, Ilhas is S. Atlantic Ocean
Martin Vaz Islands S. Atlantic Ocean see Martin Vaz, Ilhas
192 B6 Martis Sardegna Italy
159 N8 Martizay France
151 O3 Martlesham Suffolk, England U.K.
150 H3 Martley Worcestershire, England U.K.
150 G6 Martock Somerset, England U.K.
Martök Kazakh. see Martuk
111 E11 Martoli Uttaranchal India
80 J7 Marton North I. N.Z.
177 H4 Martonvásar Hungary
186 I5 Martorell Spain
185 L5 Martos Spain
163 G9 Martres-Tolosane France
140 T3 Martti Fin.
141 Q6 Marttila Fin.
120 G2 Martuk Kazakh.
129 G5 Martuni Armenia
129 D3 Martvili Georgia
137 L3 Martynivka Ukr.
136 I2 Martynovychi Ukr.
106 H9 Maru Gansu China
207 G3 Maru Nigeria
123 J4 Maruchak Afgh.
95 K2 Marudi Sarawak Malaysia
95 L1 Marudu, Teluk b. Malaysia
123 L6 Maruf Afgh.
103 K12 Marugame Japan
183 L7 Marugán Spain
195 N3 Maruggio Italy
81 G8 Maruia r. South I. N.Z.
254 F4 Maruim Brazil
129 C2 Marukhis Ugheltekhili pass Georgia/Rus. Fed.
105 H3 Maruko Japan
83 L6 Marulan N.S.W. Austr.
261 F2 Marull Arg.
164 J2 Marum Neth.
78 □5 Marum, Mount vol. Vanuatu
122 C6 Mārūn r. Iran
209 D9 Marunga Angola
104 D3 Maruoka Japan
121 U1 Marushka Rus. Fed.
116 C6 Marusthali reg. India
175 J4 Maruszów Mazowieckie Pol.
175 J5 Maruszów Świętokrzyskie Pol.
79 □9 Marutea (Nord) atoll Arch. des Tuamotu Fr. Polynesia
79 □9 Marutea (Sud) atoll Arch. des Tuamotu Fr. Polynesia
86 I7 Maruwa Aboriginal Reserve W.A. Austr.
210 B3 Maruwa Hills Sudan
105 K5 Maruyama Japan
104 A4 Maruyama-gawa r. Japan
184 E2 Marvão Port.
122 F6 Marvast Iran
122 E7 Marv Dasht Iran
161 C7 Marvejols France
87 E11 Marvel Loch W.A. Austr.
157 J5 Marville France
241 U3 Marvine, Mount UT U.S.A.
116 D7 Marwar Junction Rajasthan India
223 I4 Marwayne Alta Can.
173 J4 Marxheim Ger.
Marxwalde Ger. see Neuhardenberg
172 E4 Marxzell Ger.
84 C2 Mary r. N.T. Austr.
85 N8 Mary r. Qld Austr.
86 I5 Mary r. W.A. Austr.
123 I3 Mary Turkm.
122 J3 Mary admin. div. Turkm.
208 E2 Maryal Bai Sudan
137 N8 Mar"yanivka Respublika Krym Ukr.
175 M5 Mar"yanivka Volyns'ka Oblast' Ukr.
137 P6 Mar"yanivka Zaporiz'ka Oblast' Ukr.
136 G3 Mar"yanivka Zhytomyrs'ka Oblast' Ukr.
137 R8 Mar'yanskaya Rus. Fed.
Mary A.S.S.R. aut. rep. Rus. Fed. see Mariy El, Respublika
146 G7 Marybank Highland, Scotland U.K.
85 N8 Maryborough Qld Austr.
83 I7 Maryborough Vic. Austr.
214 G5 Marydale S. Africa
234 D6 Marydel MD U.S.A.
120 C1 Mar'yevka Rus. Fed.
146 □N2 Maryfield Shetland, Scotland U.K.
223 J2 Mary Frances Lake N.W.T. Can.
137 Q6 Mar"yinka Ukr.
Maryino Rus. Fed. see Pristen'
137 P8 Mar"yivka Respublika Krym Ukr.
137 N6 Mar"yivka Zaporiz'ka Oblast' Ukr.
146 K9 Marykirk Aberdeenshire, Scotland U.K.
223 K2 Mary Lake N.W.T. Can.
234 B7 Maryland state U.S.A.
234 B5 Maryland Line MD U.S.A.
136 E5 Marynychi Ukr.
Mary Oblast admin. div. Turkm. see Mary
146 J8 Marypark Moray, Scotland U.K.
149 K4 Maryport Cumbria, England U.K.
225 K2 Mary's Harbour Nfld and Lab. Can.
225 K4 Marystown Nfld and Lab. Can.
241 T3 Marysvale UT U.S.A.
83 J7 Marysville Vic. Austr.
225 H4 Marysville N.B. Can.
240 K2 Marysville CA U.S.A.
236 G6 Marysville KS U.S.A.
227 L7 Marysville MI U.S.A.
232 B8 Marysville OH U.S.A.
234 B4 Marysville PA U.S.A.
238 C2 Marysville WA U.S.A.
84 E8 Maryvale N.T. Austr.
85 J5 Maryvale Qld Austr.
236 H5 Maryville MO U.S.A.
231 F8 Maryville TN U.S.A.
146 K8 Marywell Aberdeenshire, Scotland U.K.
191 K7 Marzabotto Italy
256 C2 Marzagão Brazil
171 G6 Marzahna Ger.
171 G5 Marzahne Ger.
195 I10 Marzamemi Sicilia Italy
158 G6 Marzan France
191 L7 Marzeno r. Italy
173 L5 Marzling Ger.
250 B3 Marzo, Cabo c. Col.
160 C3 Marzy France
183 M3 Masa Spain
242 □P12 Masachapa Nic.
128 D7 Masada tourist site Israel
Más Afuera i. S. Pacific Ocean see Alejandro Selkirk, Isla
210 E4 Masagaweyn Somalia
243 N10 Masagua Guat.
211 C7 Masaguro Tanz.
122 F6 Masāhūn, Kūh-e mt. Iran
211 B5 Masai Mara National Reserve nature res. Kenya
192 B9 Masainas Sardegna Italy
211 C6 Masai Steppe plain Tanz.
210 A5 Masaka Uganda
215 K7 Masakhane S. Africa
211 C6 Masaki Tanz.
212 D4 Masalanyane Pan salt pan Botswana
187 D9 Masalavés Spain
95 K7 Masalembu Besar i. Indon.
95 K7 Masalembu Kecil i. Indon.
129 J6 Masallı Azer.
93 B5 Masamba Sulawesi Indon.
93 B5 Masamba mt. Indon.
101 F11 Masan S. Korea
137 N9 Masandra Ukr.
93 E7 Masapun Maluku Indon.
124 F7 Masāqif i. Saudi Arabia
211 C7 Masasi Tanz.
242 □P12 Masatepe Nic.
Más á Tierra i. S. Pacific Ocean see Robinson Crusoe, Isla
253 E4 Masavi Bol.
242 □P12 Masaya Nic.
242 □P12 Masaya, Volcán vol. Nic.
92 D5 Masbate Masbate Phil.
92 D5 Masbate i. Phil.
163 I9 Mas-Cabardès France
195 I8 Mascali Sicilia Italy
195 I8 Mascalucia Sicilia Italy
205 F2 Mascara Alg.
183 M9 Mascaraque Spain
265 H6 Mascarene Basin sea feature Indian Ocean
265 H6 Mascarene Plain sea feature Indian Ocean
265 H5 Mascarene Ridge sea feature Indian Ocean
182 F5 Mascarenhas Port.
245 J4 Mascareõs Mex.
260 D2 Mascasín Arg.
260 D2 Mascasín, Salinas de salt pan Arg.
193 P6 Maschito Italy
163 G6 Masclat France
244 C5 Mascota Mex.
244 B5 Mascota r. Mex.
230 K3 Mascouche Que. Can.
186 E3 Mascún r. Spain
186 F6 Mas de Barberans Spain
186 E6 Mas de las Matas Spain
183 P7 Masegosa Spain
185 O3 Masegoso Spain
183 O7 Masegoso de Tajuña Spain
96 B3 Masein Myanmar
95 L3 Ma Sekatok b. Indon.
93 F8 Masela Maluku Indon.
93 F8 Masela i. Maluku Indon.
172 H5 Maselheim Ger.
210 B4 Maseno Kenya
93 C5 Masepe i. Indon.
190 E3 Masera Italy
178 F8 Maserada sul Piave Italy
227 R1 Masères, Lac l. Que. Can.
215 L5 Maseru Lesotho
157 M8 Masevaux France
141 H6 Masfjorden Norway
163 G8 Mas-Grenier France
Mashaba Zimbabwe see Mashava
124 C3 Mashābih i. Saudi Arabia
215 M5 Mashai Lesotho
209 D6 Mashala Dem. Rep. Congo
149 N5 Masham North Yorkshire, England U.K.
108 G7 Mashan Guangxi China
213 F4 Mashava Zimbabwe
116 F2 Masherbrum mt. Jammu and Kashmir
137 L1 Masheve Ukr.
122 H3 Mashhad Iran
116 E6 Mashi r. India
102 S3 Mashike Japan
105 L3 Mashiko Japan
122 B2 Mashīrān Iran
137 N4 Mashivka Ukr.
123 J7 Mashkel, Hamun-i- salt flat Pak.
123 J8 Mashket r. Pak.
123 J7 Mashki Chah Pak.
123 J8 Māshkīd r. Iran
213 F3 Mashonaland Central prov. Zimbabwe
213 F3 Mashonaland East prov. Zimbabwe
213 F3 Mashonaland West prov. Zimbabwe
Mashtagi Azer. see Maştağa
140 Q2 Masi Norway
242 E4 Masiáca Mex.
209 C5 Masia-Mbia Dem. Rep. Congo
215 L7 Masibambane S. Africa
182 D4 Maside Spain
125 J8 Masīlah, Wādī al watercourse Yemen
215 K4 Masilo S. Africa
209 C6 Masi-Manimba Dem. Rep. Congo
93 A4 Masimbu Sulawesi Barat Indon.
210 A4 Masindi Uganda
92 B4 Masinloc Luzon Phil.
190 H3 Masino r. Italy
214 H7 Masinyusane S. Africa
Masira, Gulf of Oman see Maşīrah, Khalīj
Masira Channel Oman see Maşīrah, Tur'at
125 N5 Maşīrah, Jazīrat i. Oman
125 N6 Maşīrah, Khalīj b. Oman
125 N5 Maşīrah, Tur'at sea chan. Oman
Masira Island Oman see Maşīrah, Jazīrat
129 F5 Masis Armenia
252 B2 Masisea Peru
208 F5 Masisi Dem. Rep. Congo
191 L6 Masi Torello Italy
93 G5 Masiwang r. Seram Indon.
215 M4 Masjaing S. Africa
122 C6 Masjed Soleymān Iran
147 D5 Mask, Lough l. Ireland
125 I1 Maskān i. Kuwait
118 E7 Maskan, Raas pt Somalia
128 G2 Maskanah Syria
122 H8 Maskūtān Iran
163 C9 Maslacq France
177 K5 Maşloc Romania
137 P3 Maslova Pristan' Rus. Fed.
137 S2 Maslovka Rus. Fed.
175 H4 Masłowice Pol.
123 K7 Maslti Pak.
182 F1 Masma r. Spain
125 I8 Maşna'ah Yemen
191 L3 Maso r. Italy
213 □K2 Masoala, Parc National de nat. park Madag.
213 □K2 Masoala, Saikanosy pen. Madag.
213 □K2 Masoala, Tanjona c. Madag.
93 F5 Masohi Seram Indon.
226 J7 Mason MI U.S.A.
232 A9 Mason OH U.S.A.
237 F10 Mason TX U.S.A.
226 C3 Mason WI U.S.A.
232 C9 Mason WV U.S.A.
87 E9 Mason, Lake salt flat W.A. Austr.
81 B13 Mason Bay Stewart I. N.Z.
236 I4 Mason City IA U.S.A.
226 E9 Mason City IL U.S.A.
190 F6 Masone Italy
247 □5 Mason Hall Trin. and Tob.
93 D4 Masoni i. Indon.
81 G9 Masons Flat South I. N.Z.
232 F9 Masontown PA U.S.A.
232 F9 Masontown WV U.S.A.
216 □3f Maspalomas Gran Canaria Canary Is
216 □3f Maspalomas, Punta de pt Gran Canaria Canary Is
125 N4 Masqaṭ Oman
125 N4 Masqaṭ governorate Oman
125 M3 Masqaṭ reg. Oman
209 B5 Massa Congo
190 I7 Massa Italy
233 M6 Massachusetts state U.S.A.
233 O6 Massachusetts Bay MA U.S.A.
190 I8 Massaciuccoli, Lago di l. Italy
241 X1 Massadona CO U.S.A.
190 H7 Massa e Carrara prov. Italy
191 M6 Massa Fiscaglia Italy
195 M2 Massafra Italy
202 B6 Massaguet Chad
161 C8 Mas-St-Chély France
202 B6 Massakory Chad
208 C2 Massalassef Chad
191 L7 Massa Lombarda Italy
193 M6 Massa Lubrense Italy
187 E8 Massamagrell Spain
192 F1 Massa Marittimo Italy
193 J2 Massa Martana Italy
213 G2 Massamba Moz.
255 B9 Massambará Brazil
208 A5 Massana Gabon
213 G4 Massangena Moz.
209 C7 Massango Angola
213 G2 Massangulo Moz.
235 I3 Massapequa NY U.S.A.
254 E4 Massaroca Brazil
190 I8 Massarosa Italy
163 G10 Massat France
209 C6 Massau Angola
203 H6 Massawa Eritrea
203 H5 Massawa Channel Eritrea
159 O7 Massay France
169 J10 Maßbach Ger.
171 I7 Massen Ger.
233 K4 Massena NY U.S.A.
208 C2 Massenya Chad
162 H4 Masseret France
195 M2 Masseria Risana hill Italy
222 C4 Masset B.C. Can.
222 C4 Masset Inlet B.C. Can.
163 F9 Masseube France
224 D4 Massey Ont. Can.
234 D6 Massey MD U.S.A.
161 C6 Massiac France
209 D7 Massibi Angola
193 L5 Massico, Monte hill Italy
232 C9 Massieville OH U.S.A.
161 C6 Massif Central mts France
206 D4 Massigui Mali
Massilia France see Marseille
232 D8 Massillon OH U.S.A.
190 E7 Massimino Italy
206 D3 Massina Mali
173 N5 Massing Ger.
213 G4 Massinga Moz.
213 G4 Massingir Moz.
227 S4 Masson Que. Can.
192 F2 Massoncello, Monte hill Italy
263 G2 Masson Island Antarctica
156 D6 Massy France
129 K5 Maştağa Azer.
190 E4 Mastallone, Parco Naturale nature res. Italy
123 M2 Mastchoh Tajik.
169 D10 Mastershausen Ger.
81 J7 Masterton North I. N.Z.
235 J3 Mastic NY U.S.A.
235 J3 Mastic Beach NY U.S.A.
246 E1 Mastic Point Andros Bahamas
224 F4 Mastigouche, Réserve Faunique de nature res. Que. Can.
192 D8 Mastixi, Punta su pt Sardegna Italy
144 J1 Mastrevik Norway
123 O3 Mastuj Pak.
123 L7 Mastung Pak.
124 D4 Mastūrah Saudi Arabia
138 H8 Masty Belarus
192 A9 Masua Sardegna Italy
103 I12 Masuda Japan
105 H4 Masuho Japan
209 D6 Masuika Dem. Rep. Congo
Masuku Gabon see Franceville
122 C3 Masuleh Iran
Masulipatam Andhra Prad. India see Machilipatnam
192 B8 Masullas Sardegna Italy
Masuna i. American Samoa see Tutuila
94 D6 Masurai, Bukit mt. Indon.
213 F4 Masvingo Zimbabwe
213 F4 Masvingo prov. Zimbabwe
211 B5 Maswa Tanz.
211 B5 Maswe Game Reserve nature res. Tanz.
128 E3 Maşyāf Syria
136 C2 Masyevichy Belarus
174 C3 Maszewo Lubuskie Pol.
174 F1 Maszewo Pomorskie Pol.
174 D2 Maszewo Zachodniopomorskie Pol.
196 H9 Mat r. Albania
96 G5 Mat, Nam r. Laos
217 □1c Mât, Rivière du r. Réunion
96 C1 Mata Myanmar
80 M4 Mata r. North I. N.Z.
251 E3 Mata, Serranía de mts Venez.
259 C8 Mata Amarilla Arg.
209 D8 Mataba Zambia
210 E3 Matabaan Somalia
213 E3 Matabeleland North prov. Zimbabwe
213 F4 Matabeleland South prov. Zimbabwe
117 L6 Matabhanga W. Bengal India
183 M6 Matabuena Spain
184 G3 Matachel r. Spain
224 D4 Matachewan Ont. Can.
242 F3 Matachic Mex.
209 B6 Matadi Dem. Rep. Congo
237 E8 Matador TX U.S.A.
186 J4 Matagalls mt. Spain
242 □Q11 Matagalpa Nic.
224 E3 Matagami Que. Can.
224 E3 Matagami, Lac l. Que. Can.
237 G11 Matagorda TX U.S.A.
237 G11 Matagorda Island TX U.S.A.
254 F4 Mata Grande Brazil
80 J6 Matahiwi North I. N.Z.
79 □9a Mataiea Tahiti Fr. Polynesia
Mataigou Ningxia China see Taole
94 G3 Matak i. Indon.
121 P3 Matak Kazakh.
80 K4 Matakana Island North I. N.Z.
80 M4 Matakaoa Point North I. N.Z.
81 G8 Matakitaki South I. N.Z.
209 B8 Matala Angola
184 F6 Matalascañas Spain
114 G9 Matale Sri Lanka
183 P5 Matalebreras Spain
214 I4 Matalenq S. Africa
124 E2 Maṭāli', Jabal hill Saudi Arabia
183 J4 Matallana de Valmadrigal Spain
206 B3 Matam Senegal
183 O5 Matamala de Almazán Spain
80 J4 Matamata North I. N.Z.
214 E1 Mata-Mata S. Africa
80 K7 Matamau North I. N.Z.
207 H3 Matamey Niger
234 F2 Matamoras PA U.S.A.
243 N8 Matamoros Campeche Mex.
237 C12 Matamoros Chihuahua Mex.
242 H5 Matamoros Coahuila Mex.
245 L8 Matamoros Oaxaca Mex.
243 K5 Matamoros Tamaulipas Mex.
183 L3 Matamorosa Spain
206 B2 Ma'ta Moûlana well Maur.
182 C9 Mata Mourisca Port.
93 B5 Matana, Danau l. Indon.
92 D8 Matanal Point Phil.
202 D4 Ma'ṭan as Sārah well Libya
202 D4 Ma'ṭan Bishrah well Libya
260 B2 Matancilla Chile
211 C7 Matandu r. Tanz.
225 H3 Matane Que. Can.
225 H3 Matane, Réserve Faunique de nature res. Que. Can.
251 F2 Mata Negra Venez.
213 □J4 Matanga Madag.
80 J4 Matangi North I. N.Z.
207 G3 Matankari Niger
123 N5 Matanui Pak.
246 C2 Matanzas Cuba
260 C5 Matanzilla, Pampa de la plain Arg.
256 C4 Matão Brazil
254 C4 Matão, Serra do hills Brazil
261 I2 Mataojo Uru.
242 □R13 Matapalo, Cabo c. Costa Rica
Matapan, Cape pt Greece see Tainaro, Akrotirio
174 G5 Mata Panew r. Pol.
225 H3 Matapédia, Lac l. Que. Can.
81 □4 Mata Point Niue
183 L3 Mataporquera Spain
183 K6 Matapozuelos Spain
260 A4 Mataquito r. Chile
125 H2 Maṭār well Saudi Arabia
258 E3 Matará Arg.
114 G10 Matara Sri Lanka
198 C4 Mataragka Greece
95 L9 Mataram Lombok Indon.
Matarānga Greece see Mataragka
252 B4 Matarani Peru
84 D3 Mataranka N.T. Austr.
93 C5 Matarape, Teluk b. Indon.
128 A9 Matārimah, Ra's pt Egypt
92 E6 Matarinao Bay Samar Phil.
204 E2 Matarka Morocco
186 J4 Mataró Spain
80 J6 Mataroa North I. N.Z.
93 C5 Matarombea r. Indon.
196 I7 Mataruška Banja Serbia
216 □3b Matas Blancas Fuerteventura Canary Is
95 K7 Matasiri i. Indon.
203 F5 Matassi well Sudan
211 C6 Matassi Tanz.
215 M6 Matatiele S. Africa
116 G7 Matatila Dam India
78 □2 Matatula, Cape American Samoa
80 I6 Matau North I. N.Z.
81 C13 Mataura South I. N.Z.
81 C13 Mataura r. South I. N.Z.
78 □2 Matautu Samoa
77 I3 Matā'utu Wallis and Futuna Is
79 □9a Matavai, Baie de b. Tahiti Fr. Polynesia
78 □2 Matavanu, Mount vol. crater Samoa
81 □3 Matavera Rarotonga Cook Is
80 L5 Matawai North I. N.Z.
80 H2 Matawaia North I. N.Z.
235 G4 Matawan NJ U.S.A.
230 K2 Matawin r. Que. Can.
121 R5 Matay Kazakh.
125 J3 Maṭbakh, Ra's al pt Qatar
Matcha Tajik. see Mastchoh
227 Q1 Matchi-Manitou, Lac l. Que. Can.
96 G5 Mat Con, Hon i. Vietnam
253 E3 Mategua Bol.
244 G2 Matehuala Mex.
197 M4 Matei Romania
208 C2 Matékaga Chad
213 F4 Mateke Hills Zimbabwe
191 O9 Matelica Italy
247 □7 Matelot Trin. and Tob.
211 C7 Matemanga Tanz.
80 I6 Matemateaonga Range hills North I. N.Z.
209 C9 Matende Angola
213 G2 Matenge Moz.
195 L2 Matera Italy
193 R7 Matera prov. Italy
191 Q4 Materija Slovenia
193 M5 Matese, Lago del l. Italy
193 M5 Matese, Monti del mts Italy
177 L4 Mátészalka Hungary
212 E3 Matetsi Zimbabwe
205 H1 Mateur Tunisia
257 E3 Mateus Leme Brazil
232 C11 Matewan WV U.S.A.
162 D4 Matha France
116 C6 Mathaji Rajasthan India
160 J2 Mathay France
224 D3 Matheson Ont. Can.
233 I11 Mathews VA U.S.A.
190 D5 Mathi Italy
232 G10 Mathias WV U.S.A.
113 □1 Mathidahura i. N. Male Maldives
237 G11 Mathis TX U.S.A.
83 J6 Mathoura N.S.W. Austr.
198 A3 Mathraki i. Greece
116 F6 Mathura Uttar Prad. India
217 □1a Mathurin Bay Rodrigues I. Mauritius
116 E8 Mathwar Madh. Prad. India
92 F8 Mati Mindanao Phil.
207 F3 Matiacoali Burkina
117 L6 Matiali W. Bengal India
109 I5 Matianxu Hunan China
123 M9 Matiari Pak.
257 F4 Matias Barbosa Brazil
254 E5 Matias Cardoso Brazil
245 L9 Matías Romero Mex.
213 I2 Matibane Moz.
158 G4 Matignon France
156 F4 Matigny France
225 H2 Matimekosh Que. Can.
116 I8 Matin Chhattisgarh India
242 □R12 Matina Costa Rica
224 D4 Matinenda Lake Ont. Can.
233 □Q5 Matinicus Island ME U.S.A.
195 O3 Matino Italy
79 □9a Matiti Tahiti Fr. Polynesia
108 D2 Matizi Sichuan China
214 E9 Matjiesfontein S. Africa
129 D3 Mat'khoji Georgia
117 L9 Matla r. India
123 M9 Matli Pak.
149 N7 Matlock Derbyshire, England U.K.
149 N7 Matlock Bath Derbyshire, England U.K.
215 L3 Matlwangtlwang S. Africa
203 G6 Matna Sudan
251 E3 Mato r. Venez.
251 E3 Mato, Cerro mt. Venez.
232 D11 Matoaka WV U.S.A.
213 F4 Matobo Hills Zimbabwe
213 F4 Matobo National Park Zimbabwe
253 F3 Mato Grosso Brazil
256 A2 Mato Grosso state Brazil
254 B5 Mato Grosso, Planalto do plat. Brazil
256 A4 Mato Grosso do Sul state Brazil
213 G5 Matola Moz.
213 G3 Matondo Moz.
211 B8 Matope Malawi
Matopo Hills Zimbabwe see Matobo Hills
Matoriki i. Fiji see Moturiki
216 □3b Matorral, Punta del pt Fuerteventura Canary Is
252 D3 Matos r. Bol.
182 C6 Matosinhos Port.
Matou Guangxi China see Pingguo
160 E4 Matour France
257 E3 Matozinhos Brazil
177 I4 Mátra mts Hungary
177 J4 Mátraballa Hungary
125 N4 Maṭraḥ Oman
177 J4 Matrai park Hungary
142 I1 Matrand Norway
177 I3 Mátraterenye Hungary
177 I4 Mátraverebély Hungary
178 D5 Matrei am Brenner Austria
178 G5 Matrei in Osttirol Austria
214 D9 Matroosberg S. Africa
214 D9 Matroosberg mt. S. Africa
215 K1 Matrooster S. Africa
206 B5 Matru Sierra Leone
126 C8 Maṭrūḥ governorate Egypt
147 I5 Matry Ireland
138 G3 Matsalu laht b. Estonia
138 G3 Matsalu riiklik looduskaitseala nature res. Estonia
214 G4 Matsap S. Africa
129 A2 Matsesta Rus. Fed.
213 □J4 Matsiatra r. Madag.
215 L5 Matsieng Lesotho
212 E4 Matsitama Botswana
211 F8 Matsoandakana Madag.
104 C6 Matsubara Japan
105 J5 Matsuda Japan
105 I1 Matsudai Japan
105 K4 Matsudo Japan
103 K11 Matsue Japan
105 I3 Matsuida Japan
105 G3 Matsukawa Nagano Japan
105 G4 Matsukawa Nagano Japan
102 R5 Matsumae Japan
105 G3 Matsumoto Japan
103 J13 Matsuno Japan
105 I1 Matsunoyama Japan
105 L4 Matsuo Japan
104 D3 Matsuoka Japan
104 E6 Matsusaka Japan
105 H2 Matsushiro Japan
109 M5 Matsu Tao i. Taiwan
103 G13 Matsuura Japan
103 J13 Matsuyama Japan
105 I6 Matsuzaki Japan
190 G2 Matt Switz.
224 D3 Mattagami r. Ont. Can.
157 L7 Mattaincourt France
261 E4 Mattaldi Arg.
231 I8 Mattamuskeet, Lake NC U.S.A.
224 E4 Mattawa Ont. Can.
233 □Q3 Mattawamkeag ME U.S.A.
190 D4 Matterhorn mt. Italy/Switz.
238 G6 Matterhorn mt. NV U.S.A.
179 N4 Mattersburg Austria
190 D3 Mattertal val. Switz.
Matthew atoll Gilbert Is Kiribati see Marakei
77 H4 Matthew Island S. Pacific Ocean
231 G8 Matthews NC U.S.A.
210 C4 Matthews Peak Kenya
251 F3 Matthews Ridge Guyana
246 G3 Matthew Town Gt Inagua Bahamas
125 K4 Maṭṭī, Sabkhat salt pan Saudi Arabia
178 H3 Mattighofen Austria
193 Q4 Mattinata Italy
151 O2 Mattishall Norfolk, England U.K.
235 J3 Mattituck NY U.S.A.
140 L5 Mattmar Sweden
104 E2 Mattō Japan
236 K6 Mattoon IL U.S.A.
178 H4 Mattsee Austria
178 H4 Mattsee l. Austria
141 M6 Mattsmyra Sweden
140 P4 Måttsund Sweden
Matturai Sri Lanka see Matara
95 I3 Matu Sarawak Malaysia
252 A2 Matucana Peru
114 G9 Matugama Sri Lanka
175 M1 Matuizos Lith.
79 □7 Matuku i. Fiji
191 Q5 Matulji Croatia
209 C8 Matumbo Angola
Matun Afgh. see Khowst
247 □7 Matura Trin. and Tob.
247 □7 Matura Bay Trin. and Tob.
251 F2 Maturín Venez.
251 F3 Maturuca Brazil
213 F3 Matusadona National Park Zimbabwe
183 P5 Matute mt. Spain
257 E3 Matutina Brazil
93 D1 Matutuang i. Indon.
92 E8 Matutum, Mount vol. Phil.
134 L1 Matveyev, Ostrov i. Rus. Fed.
120 E1 Matveyevka Rus. Fed.
137 R6 Matveyev Kurgan Rus. Fed.
137 K6 Matviyivka Mykolayivs'ka Oblast' Ukr.
137 O6 Matviyivka Zaporiz'ka Oblast' Ukr.
215 L4 Matwabeng S. Africa
183 O2 Matxitxako, Cabo c. Spain
Maty Island P.N.G. see Wuvulu Island
137 S1 Matyra r. Rus. Fed.
139 W9 Matyrskiy Rus. Fed.
139 W9 Matyrskoye Vodokhranilishche resr Rus. Fed.
138 L6 Matyryna Belarus
135 I6 Matyshevo Rus. Fed.
116 G6 Mau Madh. Prad. India
116 H7 Mau Uttar Prad. India
213 H2 Maúa Moz.
116 H7 Mau Aimma Uttar Prad. India
186 G2 Maubermé, Pic de mt. France/Spain
156 H4 Maubert-Fontaine France
156 G3 Maubeuge France
115 N4 Maubin Myanmar
96 C2 Ma-ubin Myanmar
163 E9 Maubourguet France
162 B5 Maubuisson France
146 H11 Mauchline East Ayrshire, Scotland U.K.
146 L7 Maud Aberdeenshire, Scotland U.K.
87 B7 Maud, Point W.A. Austr.
116 H7 Maudaha Uttar Prad. India
83 J6 Maude N.S.W. Austr.
264 J10 Maud Seamount sea feature S. Atlantic Ocean
Mau-é-ele Moz. see Marão
179 N3 Mauerbach Austria
178 H3 Mauerkirchen Austria
173 L4 Mauern Ger.
173 J6 Mauerstetten Ger.
251 G5 Maués Brazil
251 G5 Maués r. Brazil
Mauga Afi mt. Samoa see Afi, Mount
116 H7 Mauganj Madh. Prad. India
148 I5 Maughold Isle of Man
148 I5 Maughold Head Isle of Man
91 K2 Maug Islands N. Mariana Is
161 E9 Mauguio France
240 □E13 Maui i. HI U.S.A.
81 □2 Mauke i. Cook Is
96 B3 Maukkadaw Myanmar
172 F4 Maulbronn Ger.
157 O8 Maulburg Ger.
162 H4 Maulde r. France
151 L3 Maulden Bedfordshire, England U.K.
260 B4 Maule Chile
260 A4 Maule admin. reg. Chile

Maule to Mella

350

260 A4 Maule r. Chile
260 B5 Maule, Lago del l. Chile
162 C2 Mauléon France
163 F10 Mauléon-Barousse France
163 D8 Mauléon-d'Armagnac France
163 C9 Mauléon-Licharre France
159 J7 Maulévrier France
259 B6 Maullín Chile
147 D4 Maumakeogh hill Ireland
80 J4 Maumaupaki hill North I. N.Z.
232 B7 Maumee OH U.S.A.
232 B7 Maumee r. OH U.S.A.
232 B7 Maumee Bay MI/OH U.S.A.
93 C8 Maumere Flores Indon.
147 C5 Maumturk Mountains hills Ireland
212 D3 Maun Botswana
247 □1 Maunabo Puerto Rico
240 □F14 Mauna Kea vol. HI U.S.A.
240 □D12 Mauna Loa HI U.S.A.
240 □F14 Mauna Loa vol. HI U.S.A.
240 □D12 Maunalua Bay HI U.S.A.
117 I7 Maunath Bhanjan Uttar Prad. India
213 E4 Maunatlala Botswana
116 G9 Maunda Mahar. India
80 K6 Maungaharuru Range mts North I. N.Z.
80 L5 Maungahaumi mt. North I. N.Z.
80 L5 Maungapohatu mt. North I. N.Z.
80 I6 Maungarau hill North I. N.Z.
80 K5 Maungataniwha mt. North I. N.Z.
80 I2 Maungatapere North I. N.Z.
80 I3 Maungaturoto North I. N.Z.
96 A4 Maungdaw Myanmar
97 C7 Maungmagan Islands Myanmar
97 D7 Maungmagon Myanmar
220 F3 Maunoir, Lac l. N.W.T. Can.
79 □9 Maupihaa atoll Arch. de la Société Fr. Polynesia
238 D4 Maupin OR U.S.A.
142 G1 Maura Norway
116 G7 Mau Ranipur Uttar Prad. India
116 H6 Maurawan Uttar Prad. India
161 I8 Maure, Col de pass France
158 H6 Maure-de-Bretagne France
163 J11 Maureillas-las-Illas France
162 E6 Maurens France
237 J10 Maurepas, Lake LA U.S.A.
161 I10 Maures, Massif des hills France
252 C4 Mauri r. Bol.
163 D6 Mauriac Aquitaine France
162 I5 Mauriac Auvergne France
Maurice country Indian Ocean see Mauritius
234 E6 Maurice r. NJ U.S.A.
82 C3 Maurice, Lake salt flat S.A. Austr.
234 F6 Mauricetown NJ U.S.A.
161 I6 Maurienne reg. France
164 H5 Maurik Neth.
204 C6 Mauritania country Africa
Mauritanie country Africa see Mauritania
217 □1b Mauritius country Indian Ocean
193 N4 Mauro, Monte mt. Italy
158 G5 Mauron France
163 G7 Mauroux France
163 I6 Maurs France
163 J10 Maury France
234 B3 Mausdale PA U.S.A.
161 F9 Maussanne-les-Alpilles France
226 D6 Mauston WI U.S.A.
174 F1 Mausz, Jezioro l. Pol.
179 M3 Mautern an der Donau Austria
179 I5 Mauterndorf Austria
179 K5 Mautern in Steiermark Austria
173 P4 Mauth Ger.
179 K3 Mauthausen Austria
178 H6 Mauthen Austria
Mauti i. Cook Is see Mauke
157 K6 Mauvages France
161 F6 Mauves France
163 F8 Mauvezin France
190 C3 Mauvoisin Switz.
162 C3 Mauzé-sur-le-Mignon France
208 E4 Mava Dem. Rep. Congo
251 E4 Mavaca r. Venez.
211 C8 Mavago Moz.
77 I3 Mavana Fiji
213 G4 Mavanza Moz.
140 N3 Mavasjaure l. Sweden
209 C9 Mavengue Angola
199 L6 Mavikent Turkey
209 D8 Mavinga Angola
246 □ Mavis Bank Jamaica
232 C11 Mavisdale VA U.S.A.
146 □N2 Mavis Grind isth. Scotland U.K.
213 G3 Mavita Moz.
193 L2 Mavone r. Italy
199 H6 Mavria i. Greece
198 C2 Mavrodendri Greece
199 G6 Mavropetra, Akrotirio pt Greece
198 E2 Mavrothalassa Greece
196 I9 Mavrovo nat. park Macedonia
213 G4 Mavume Moz.
215 L7 Mavuya S. Africa
95 J4 Mawa, Bukit mt. Indon.
109 □J7 Ma Wan i. H.K. China
124 H4 Māwān, Khashm hill Saudi Arabia
116 F5 Mawana Uttar Prad. India
209 C6 Mawanga Dem. Rep. Congo
93 C6 Mawasangka Sulawesi Indon.
96 C5 Mawchi Myanmar
97 D9 Mawdaung Pass Myanmar/Thai.
109 L5 Mawei Fujian China
80 M5 Mawhai Point North I. N.Z.
81 F9 Mawheraiti South I. N.Z.
Māwheranui r. South I. N.Z. see Grey
96 C2 Mawhun Myanmar
124 G9 Māwiyah Yemen
128 D7 Mawjib, Wādī al r. Jordan
96 D6 Mawkhi Myanmar
96 C4 Mawkmai Myanmar
96 B3 Mawlaik Myanmar
96 C6 Mawlamyaing Myanmar
96 B6 Mawlamyainggyun Myanmar
Mawlamyine Myanmar see Mawlamyaing
150 B7 Mawnan Cornwall, England U.K.
117 M7 Mawphlang Meghalaya India
124 E2 Mawqaq Saudi Arabia
203 I6 Mawshij Yemen
263 E2 Mawson research stn Antarctica
263 E2 Mawson Coast Antarctica
263 E2 Mawson Escarpment Antarctica
263 K2 Mawson Peninsula Antarctica
97 D9 Maw Taung mt. Myanmar
124 F9 Mawza Yemen
236 E2 Max ND U.S.A.
210 E3 Maxaas Somalia
258 D3 Maxán Arg.
234 D3 Maxatawny PA U.S.A.
243 O7 Maxcanú Mex.
158 G6 Maxent France
222 F3 Maxhamish Lake B.C. Can.
173 M3 Maxhütte-Haidhof Ger.
192 B9 Maxia, Punta mt. Sardegna Italy
182 E9 Maxieira Port.
261 G3 Máximo Paz Arg.
197 P5 Măxineni Romania
213 G4 Maxixe Moz.
140 Q5 Maxmo Fin.
169 E9 Maxsain Ger.
233 K3 Maxville Ont. Can.
80 I6 Maxwell North I. N.Z.
85 I6 Maxwelton Qld Austr.
86 G4 May r. W.A. Austr.
146 K10 May, Isle of i. Scotland U.K.
208 C3 Maya Chad
108 D2 Maya Gansu China
95 H5 Maya i. Indon.
131 O3 Maya r. Rus. Fed.
137 N4 Mayachka Ukr.
135 K5 Mayachnyy Rus. Fed.
246 G2 Mayaguana i. Bahamas
246 G2 Mayaguana Passage Bahamas
247 □1 Mayagüez Puerto Rico
247 □1 Mayagüez, Bahía de b. Puerto Rico
207 G3 Mayahi Niger
100 J4 Mayak Rus. Fed.
120 F2 Mayak Rus. Fed.
Mayakovskiy Georgia see Baghdat'i
123 N3 Mayakovskiy, Qullai mt. Tajik.
Mayakovskogo, Pik mt. Tajik. see Mayakovskiy, Qullai
175 K1 Mayakovskoye Rus. Fed.
121 M6 Mayakum Kazakh.
136 H5 Mayaky Ukr.
209 C6 Mayala Dem. Rep. Congo
93 G4 Mayalibit, Teluk b. Papua Indon.
Mayals Spain see Maials
209 B5 Mayama Congo
209 C6 Mayamba Dem. Rep. Congo
122 F3 Mayamey Iran
243 O9 Maya Mountains Belize/Guat.
Mayan Gansu China see Mayanhe
108 G5 Mayang Hunan China
106 I9 Mayanhe Gansu China
Mayaqum Kazakh. see Mayakum
146 J9 Mayar hill Scotland U.K.
246 F3 Mayarí Cuba
247 □7 Mayaro county Trin. and Tob.
247 □7 Mayaro Bay Trin. and Tob.
104 B6 Maya-san hill Japan
102 Q8 Maya-san mt. Japan
238 J6 Maybell CO U.S.A.
232 D11 Maybeury WV U.S.A.
146 G12 Maybole South Ayrshire, Scotland U.K.
235 G2 Maybrook NY U.S.A.
210 C1 Maych'ew Eth.
246 □ May Day Mountains hills Jamaica
83 K10 Maydena Tas. Austr.
210 E2 Maydh Somalia
Maydos Turkey see Eceabat
169 D10 Mayen Ger.
159 J5 Mayenne France
159 J5 Mayenne dept France
159 J7 Mayenne r. France
241 T7 Mayer AZ U.S.A.
111 H10 Mayêr Kangri mt. Xizang China
237 J9 Mayersville MS U.S.A.
222 H4 Mayerthorpe Alta Can.
159 L6 Mayet France
125 H8 Mayfa'ah Yemen
81 F10 Mayfield South I. N.Z.
149 N7 Mayfield Staffordshire, England U.K.
237 K7 Mayfield KY U.S.A.
234 D1 Mayfield PA U.S.A.
241 U2 Mayfield UT U.S.A.
106 H3 Mayhan Mongolia
239 L10 Mayhill NM U.S.A.
100 F6 Mayi He r. China
121 P2 Maykain Kazakh.
121 Q4 Maykamys Kazakh.
123 M2 Maykhura Tajik.
129 B1 Maykop Rus. Fed.
134 K4 Maykor Rus. Fed.
Maylibash Kazakh. see Maylybas
121 O7 Mayluu-Suu Kyrg.
120 J5 Maylybas Kazakh.
Mayly-Say Kyrg. see Mayluu-Suu
121 U1 Mayma Rus. Fed.
121 N6 Maymak Kazakh.
244 B1 Maymorita Mex.
98 F1 Mayna Respublika Khakasiya Rus. Fed.
135 I5 Mayna Ul'yanovskaya Oblast' Rus. Fed.
231 F7 Maynardville TN U.S.A.
85 H7 Mayne watercourse Qld Austr.
114 D4 Mayni Mahar. India
227 Q4 Maynooth Ont. Can.
147 I6 Maynooth Ireland
222 C2 Mayo Y.T. Can.
239 J13 Mayo r. Mex.
252 A1 Mayo r. Peru
147 D5 Mayo Ireland
147 D5 Mayo county Ireland
231 F10 Mayo FL U.S.A.
234 B7 Mayo MD U.S.A.
207 I4 Mayo Alim Cameroon
207 I4 Mayo-Belwa Nigeria
147 J4 Mayobridge Northern Ireland U.K.
207 H5 Mayo Darlé Cameroon
208 B2 Mayo-Kebbi pref. Chad
208 B5 Mayoko Congo
208 D5 Mayoko Dem. Rep. Congo
222 C2 Mayo Lake Y.T. Can.
Mayo Landing Y.T. Can. see Mayo
208 B3 Mayo Lara C.A.R.
92 D5 Mayon vol. Luzon Phil.
183 O8 Mayor r. Spain
183 Q4 Mayor r. Spain
183 M2 Mayor, Cabo c. Spain
Mayor, Puig mt. Spain see Major, Puig
261 F6 Mayor Buratovich Arg.
183 J4 Mayorga Spain
80 K4 Mayor Island North I. N.Z.
253 E4 Mayor Pablo Lagerenza Para.
217 □3b Mayotte terr. Africa
246 □ May Pen Jamaica
Mayqayyng Kazakh. see Maykain
92 C2 Mayraira Point Luzon Phil.
247 □3 Mayreau i. St Vincent
161 E7 Mayres France
163 H9 Mayreville France
178 E5 Mayrhofen Austria
128 D7 Maysah, Tall al mt. Jordan
127 M8 Maysān governorate Iraq
169 D9 Mayschoss Ger.
175 I1 Mayskaya r. Rus. Fed.
137 N8 Mays'ke Ukr.
100 F2 Mayskiy Amurskaya Oblast' Rus. Fed.
137 P3 Mayskiy Belgorodskaya Oblast' Rus. Fed.
129 F2 Mayskiy Kabardino-Balkarskaya Respublika Rus. Fed.
134 K4 Mayskiy Permskaya Oblast' Rus. Fed.
137 T6 Mayskiy Rostovskaya Oblast' Rus. Fed.
121 R2 Mayskoye Kazakh.
234 F6 Mays Landing NJ U.S.A.
223 J3 Mayson Lake Sask. Can.
232 B10 Maysville KY U.S.A.
236 H6 Maysville MO U.S.A.
Maytag Xinjiang China see Dushanzi
93 E3 Mayu i. Maluku Indon.
96 A4 Mayu r. Myanmar
210 B4 Mayuge Uganda
209 A5 Mayumba Gabon
111 F11 Mayum La pass Xizang China
114 F7 Mayuram Tamil Nadu India
227 K6 Mayville MI U.S.A.
236 G2 Mayville ND U.S.A.
232 F6 Mayville NY U.S.A.
236 E5 Maywood NE U.S.A.
131 O3 Mayya Rus. Fed.
261 F5 Maza Arg.
139 T2 Maza Rus. Fed.
209 E8 Mazabuka Zambia
Mazaca Turkey see Kayseri
Mazagan Morocco see El Jadida
251 I5 Mazagão Brazil
251 I5 Mazagão Velho Brazil
184 F6 Mazagón Spain
156 I5 Mazagran France
138 H5 Maza Jugla r. Latvia
186 F5 Mazaleón Spain
163 I9 Mazamet France
244 D6 Mazamitla Mex.
161 G8 Mazan France
250 C5 Mazán Peru
122 D3 Māzandarān prov. Iran
161 E7 Mazan-l'Abbaye France
209 D7 Mazao Dem. Rep. Congo
244 F1 Mazapil Mex.
111 C8 Mazar Xinjiang China
128 D7 Mazār Jordan
125 N4 Mazāra Oman
194 D8 Mazara, Val di reg. Sicilia Italy
194 D8 Mazara del Vallo Sicilia Italy
183 L9 Mazarambroz Spain
123 L3 Mazār-e Sharīf Afgh.
183 P7 Mazarete Spain
194 D8 Mazaro r. Sicilia Italy
259 D7 Mazarredo Arg.
187 C12 Mazarrón Spain
187 C13 Mazarrón, Golfo de b. Spain
110 E7 Mazartag Xinjiang China
110 D7 Mazartag mt. Xinjiang China
251 G3 Mazaruni r. Guyana
242 D3 Mazatán Mex.
245 K7 Mazateca, Sierra mts Mex.
243 N10 Mazatenango Guat.
244 A2 Mazatlán Mex.
241 U7 Mazatzal Peak AZ U.S.A.
122 G8 Mazāvī watercourse Iran
159 K7 Mazé France
104 F4 Maze Japan
104 F4 Maze-gawa r. Japan
138 F5 Mažeikiai Lith.
207 H2 Mazelet well Niger
234 B3 Mazeppa PA U.S.A.
215 M8 Mazeppa Bay S. Africa
211 C5 Mazeras Kenya
163 H9 Mazères France
163 D9 Mazerolles France
161 E6 Mazet-St-Voy France
163 G6 Mazeyrolles France
129 A6 Mazgirt Turkey
124 F2 Maẓhūr, 'Irq al des. Saudi Arabia
199 I5 Mazı Turkey
138 K5 Mazīča r. Latvia
232 C10 Mazie KY U.S.A.
162 D2 Mazières-en-Gâtine France
125 M4 Mazīm Oman
209 C6 Mazinda Dem. Rep. Congo
138 F4 Mazirbe Latvia
216 □3d Mazo La Palma Canary Is
242 D3 Mazocahui Mex.
252 C4 Mazocruz Peru
Mazoe Zimbabwe see Mazowe
226 E6 Mazomanie WI U.S.A.
209 E6 Mazomeno Dem. Rep. Congo
211 C6 Mazomora Tanz.
106 E6 Mazong Shan mt. Gansu China
106 D6 Mazong Shan mts China
183 M3 Mazorra, Puerto de la pass Spain
213 F3 Mazowe Zimbabwe
213 G3 Mazowe r. Zimbabwe
175 I3 Mazowiecka, Nizina reg. Pol.
175 I4 Mazowiecka, Nizina reg. Pol.
175 J3 Mazowieckie prov. Pol.
136 A1 Mazowiecki Park Krajobrazowy Pol.
122 C3 Mazr'eh Iran
203 F6 Mazrub well Sudan
138 I4 Mazsalaca Latvia
122 C5 Māzū Iran
213 F4 Mazunga Zimbabwe
175 I2 Mazurskie, Pojezierze reg. Pol.
167 J2 Mazurski Park Krajobrazowy Pol.
175 J1 Mazurskiy Kanal canal Pol./Rus. Fed.
136 I1 Mazyr Belarus
136 I1 Mazyrskaye Hrada ridge Belarus
190 I4 Mazzano Italy
193 I3 Mazzano Romano Italy
194 G9 Mazzarino Sicilia Italy
194 H9 Mazzarrone Sicilia Italy
178 B7 Mazzo di Valtellina Italy
205 H2 Mazzouna Tunisia
207 H5 Mba Cameroon
Mba Viti Levu Fiji see Ba
215 P2 Mbabane Swaziland
206 B3 Mbacké Senegal
208 C4 Mbaéré r. C.A.R.
206 B2 Mbagne Maur.
206 D5 Mbahiakro Côte d'Ivoire
208 C4 Mbaïki C.A.R.
207 I5 Mbakaou Cameroon
207 I5 Mbakaou, Lac de l. Cameroon
209 C5 Mbala Dem. Rep. Congo
211 A7 Mbala Zambia
213 F4 Mbalabala Zimbabwe
207 I6 Mbalam Cameroon
210 B4 Mbale Uganda
207 H6 Mbalmayo Cameroon
78 □6 Mbalo Guadalcanal Solomon Is
207 H5 Mbam r. Cameroon
207 I7 Mbama Congo
211 B7 Mbamba Bay Tanz.
208 C5 Mbandaka Dem. Rep. Congo
207 H5 Mbandjok Cameroon
208 B4 Mbandza Congo
207 I5 Mbang Adamaoua Cameroon
207 I6 Mbang Est Cameroon
207 H5 Mbanga Cameroon
78 □6 Mbanika i. Solomon Is
209 B6 M'banza Congo Angola
209 B6 Mbanza-Ngungu Dem. Rep. Congo
206 B3 Mbar Senegal
211 C7 Mbarangandu Tanz.
210 A5 Mbarara Uganda
208 D3 Mbari r. C.A.R.
211 C7 Mbarika Mountains Tanz.
215 Q3 Mbaswana S. Africa
208 C4 Mbata C.A.R.
211 A7 Mbati Zambia
Mbatiki i. Fiji see Batiki
Mbau i. Fiji see Bau
78 □6 Mbava i. New Georgia Is Solomon Is
207 I5 Mbé Cameroon
209 B5 Mbé Congo
211 B8 Mbemba Moz.
213 F3 Mbembesi Zimbabwe
211 C7 Mbemkuru r. Tanz.
Mbengga i. Fiji see Beqa
207 H5 Mbengwi Cameroon
217 □3a Mbéni Njazidja Comoros
206 D4 Mbenqué Côte d'Ivoire
213 F4 Mberengwa Zimbabwe
209 F7 Mbereshi Zambia
211 B7 Mbeya Tanz.
211 B7 Mbeya admin. reg. Tanz.
207 I5 Mbi r. Cameroon
208 C3 Mbi r. C.A.R.
208 A5 Mbigou Gabon
208 A5 Mbilapé Gabon
208 F3 Mbili Sudan
196 H8 Mbilqethit, Maja e mt. Albania
208 B5 Mbinda Congo
211 B7 Mbinga Tanz.
207 H6 Mbini Equat. Guinea
207 H6 Mbini r. Equat. Guinea
78 □6 Mbita'ama Malaita Solomon Is
208 D3 Mbiyi C.A.R.
213 F4 Mbizi Zimbabwe
211 A7 Mbizi Mountains Tanz.
208 C2 Mbo C.A.R.
208 E3 Mboki C.A.R.
208 D3 Mboli Dem. Rep. Congo
Mbolompo Point S. Africa see Mncwasa Point
208 B4 Mbomo Congo
208 D3 Mbomou pref. C.A.R.
208 D3 Mbomou r. C.A.R./Dem. Rep. Congo
208 B5 Mbon Congo
206 A3 Mboro Senegal
78 □6 Mborokua i. Solomon Is
207 H5 Mbouda Cameroon
206 B3 Mboun Senegal
206 A3 Mbour Senegal
206 B2 Mbout Maur.
209 E8 Mbowela Zambia
211 B7 Mbozi Tanz.
208 C3 Mbrès C.A.R.
198 A2 Mbrostar Albania
Mbua Vanua Levu Fiji see Bua
209 D6 Mbuji-Mayi Dem. Rep. Congo
78 □6 Mbulo i. New Georgia Is Solomon Is
211 B5 Mbulu Tanz.
215 P2 Mbuluzana r. Swaziland
215 Q2 Mbuluzi r. Swaziland
211 B7 Mbura Tanz.
258 F3 Mburucuyá Arg.
78 □6 Mburuku New Georgia Is Solomon Is
Mbutha Vanua Levu Fiji see Buca
215 P2 Mbutini Hills Swaziland
211 C6 Mbuyuni Tanz.
211 C6 Mbwewe Tanz.
225 H4 McAdam N.B. Can.
234 D3 McAdoo PA U.S.A.
234 F2 McAfee NJ U.S.A.
237 H8 McAlester OK U.S.A.
234 A3 McAlisterville PA U.S.A.
237 F12 McAllen TX U.S.A.
226 G4 McAllister WI U.S.A.
84 F3 McArthur r. N.T. Austr.
232 C9 McArthur OH U.S.A.
227 Q4 McArthur Mills Ont. Can.
222 C2 McArthur Wildlife Sanctuary nature res. Y.T. Can.
226 I5 McBain MI U.S.A.
222 F4 McBride B.C. Can.
238 F4 McCall ID U.S.A.
237 D10 McCamey TX U.S.A.
238 H5 McCammon ID U.S.A.
223 J2 McCann Lake N.W.T. Can.
226 F4 McCaslin Mountain hill WI U.S.A.
222 D4 McCauley Island B.C. Can.
263 K1 McClintock, Mount Antarctica
221 H2 McClintock Channel Nunavut Can.
86 I5 McClintock Range hills W.A. Austr.
84 D1 McCluer Island N.T. Austr.
232 B7 McClure OH U.S.A.
232 H8 McClure PA U.S.A.
240 L4 McClure, Lake CA U.S.A.
220 G2 McClure Strait N.W.T. Can.
236 E2 McClusky ND U.S.A.
237 J10 McComb MS U.S.A.
232 B7 McComb OH U.S.A.
236 E5 McConaughy, Lake NE U.S.A.
232 H9 McConnellsburg PA U.S.A.
232 D9 McConnelsville OH U.S.A.
236 E5 McCook NE U.S.A.
231 F9 McCormick SC U.S.A.
232 E11 McCoy VA U.S.A.
222 H2 McCrea r. N.W.T. Can.
223 L5 McCreary Man. Can.
241 Q6 McCullough Range mts NV U.S.A.
232 B8 McCutchenville OH U.S.A.
222 D3 McDame B.C. Can.
238 F6 McDermitt NV U.S.A.
232 B10 McDermott OH U.S.A.
265 I8 McDonald Islands Indian Ocean
238 H3 McDonald Peak MT U.S.A.
82 G3 McDonnell Creek watercourse S.A. Austr.
231 E9 McDonough GA U.S.A.
84 E5 McDouall Range hills N.T. Austr.
214 A5 McDougall's Bay S. Africa
241 U8 McDowell Peak AZ U.S.A.
234 B2 McEwensville PA U.S.A.
240 M6 McFarland CA U.S.A.
226 E6 McFarland WI U.S.A.
223 J3 McFarlane r. Sask. Can.
81 D10 McFarlane, Mount South I. N.Z.
241 R2 McGill NV U.S.A.
225 H4 McGivney N.B. Can.
220 C3 McGrath AK U.S.A.
226 A3 McGrath MN U.S.A.
222 F4 McGregor r. B.C. Can.
214 D9 McGregor S. Africa
226 A3 McGregor MN U.S.A.
222 H5 McGregor, Lake Alta Can.
227 M3 McGregor Bay Ont. Can.
85 I9 McGregor Range hills Qld Austr.
238 G4 McGuire, Mount ID U.S.A.
129 F3 Mchadijvari Georgia
204 D4 Mcherrah reg. Alg.
211 C7 Mchinga Tanz.
211 B8 Mchinji Malawi
85 I3 McIlwraith Range hills Qld Austr.
223 M4 McInnes Lake Ont. Can.
236 E3 McIntosh SD U.S.A.
86 G7 McKay Range hills W.A. Austr.
77 I2 McKean i. Phoenix Is Kiribati
232 A11 McKee KY U.S.A.
234 F6 McKee NJ U.S.A.
232 F8 McKeesport PA U.S.A.
232 E8 McKees Rocks PA U.S.A.
232 H12 McKenney VA U.S.A.
237 K7 McKenzie TN U.S.A.
238 C4 McKenzie r. OR U.S.A.
81 C11 McKerrow, Lake South I. N.Z.
85 H6 McKinlay Qld Austr.
85 H6 McKinlay r. Qld Austr.
220 C3 McKinley, Mount AK U.S.A.
237 G9 McKinney TX U.S.A.
240 M6 McKittrick CA U.S.A.
236 E3 McLaughlin SD U.S.A.
226 E9 McLean IL U.S.A.
234 A7 McLean VA U.S.A.
236 K6 McLeansboro IL U.S.A.
222 G4 McLennan Alta Can.
222 H4 McLeod r. Alta Can.
223 I2 McLeod Bay N.W.T. Can.
222 F4 McLeod Lake B.C. Can.
97 D9 McLeod's Island Myanmar
86 □1 McMicken Point Christmas I.
84 D8 McMinns Creek watercourse N.T. Austr.
238 C4 McMinnville OR U.S.A.
231 E8 McMinnville TN U.S.A.
263 L1 McMurdo research stn Antarctica
263 L1 McMurdo Sound b. Antarctica
241 W7 McNary AZ U.S.A.
226 E4 McNaughton WI U.S.A.
McNaughton Lake B.C. Can. see Kinbasket Lake
241 W10 McNeal AZ U.S.A.
225 H2 McPhadyen r. Nfld and Lab. Can.
236 G6 McPherson KS U.S.A.
83 N3 McPherson Range mts N.S.W. Austr.
222 B2 McQuesten r. Y.T. Can.
231 F9 McRae GA U.S.A.
232 C11 McRoberts KY U.S.A.
234 A5 McSherrystown PA U.S.A.
147 E3 McSwynes Bay Ireland
220 G3 McTavish Arm b. N.W.T. Can.
232 H8 McVeytown PA U.S.A.
222 F1 McVicar Arm b. N.W.T. Can.
232 E9 McWhorter WV U.S.A.
139 P3 Mda r. Rus. Fed.
215 L8 Mdantsane S. Africa
205 G1 M'Daourouch Alg.
217 □3a Mde Njazidja Comoros
195 □ Mdina Malta
180 D5 Mdiq Morocco
97 I8 M'Đrak Vietnam
96 G5 Mê, Hon i. Vietnam
241 R5 Mead, Lake resr NV U.S.A.
235 H2 Mead Corners NY U.S.A.
237 E7 Meade KS U.S.A.
220 C2 Meade r. AK U.S.A.
87 C9 Meadow W.A. Austr.
236 D3 Meadow SD U.S.A.
241 T3 Meadow UT U.S.A.
232 E11 Meadow Bridge WV U.S.A.
223 I4 Meadow Lake Sask. Can.
223 I4 Meadow Lake Provincial Park Sask. Can.
241 R5 Meadow Valley Wash r. NV U.S.A.
232 D12 Meadowview VA U.S.A.
237 J10 Meadville MS U.S.A.
232 E7 Meadville PA U.S.A.
227 N5 Meaford Ont. Can.
102 V3 Meaken-dake vol. Japan
146 B6 Mealasta Island Scotland U.K.
146 G8 Meal Fuar-mhonaidh hill Scotland U.K.
182 D8 Mealhada Port.
146 B6 Mealisval hill Scotland U.K.
146 H9 Meall Chuaich hill Scotland U.K.
146 G8 Meall Dubh hill Scotland U.K.
149 K4 Mealsgate Cumbria, England U.K.
225 J2 Mealy Mountains Nfld and Lab. Can.
192 C8 Meana Sardo Sardegna Italy
85 L9 Meandarra Qld Austr.
222 G3 Meander River Alta Can.
150 G5 Meare Somerset, England U.K.
93 D1 Meares i. Indon.
151 I2 Mease r. England U.K.
151 I2 Measham Leicestershire, England U.K.
147 I5 Meath county Ireland
161 H6 Méaudre, Roche de mt. France
160 B3 Meaulne France
156 E4 Méaulte France
156 E6 Meaux France
163 G7 Meauzac France
209 B6 Mebridege r. Angola
117 O5 Mebu Arun. Prad. India
95 K9 Mebulu, Tanjung pt Indon.
213 G2 Mecanhelas Moz.
244 B4 Mecatán Mex.
Mecca Saudi Arabia see Makkah
241 P8 Mecca CA U.S.A.
232 E7 Mecca OH U.S.A.
233 □O4 Mechanic Falls ME U.S.A.
232 B8 Mechanicsburg OH U.S.A.
234 A4 Mechanicsburg PA U.S.A.
232 E11 Mechanicsburg VA U.S.A.
232 H11 Mechanicsville VA U.S.A.
233 L6 Mechanicville NY U.S.A.
210 D2 Mechāra Eth.
165 F6 Mechelen Belgium
165 I7 Mechelen Neth.
Mecherchar i. Palau see Eil Malk
205 E2 Mecheria Alg.
169 C9 Mechernich Ger.
135 H7 Mechetinskaya Rus. Fed.
202 B6 Mechiméré Chad
261 G4 Mechita Arg.
197 N8 Mechka r. Bulg.
261 H6 Mechongue Arg.
174 D2 Mechowo Pol.
168 J4 Mechtersen Ger.
169 K9 Mechterstädt Ger.
199 H2 Mecidiye Edirne Turkey
199 I4 Mecidiye Manisa Turkey
176 C2 Měčín Czech Rep.
185 M7 Mecina-Bombarón Spain
174 E4 Męcinka Pol.
126 G3 Mecitözü Turkey
172 H6 Meckenbeuren Ger.
169 D9 Meckenheim Ger.
172 F3 Meckesheim Ger.
170 D2 Mecklenburger Bucht b. Ger.
170 D3 Mecklenburgische Seenplatte reg. Ger.
170 G3 Mecklenburg-Vorpommern land Ger.
Mecklenburg - West Pomerania land Ger. see Mecklenburg-Vorpommern
183 N7 Meco Spain
213 H2 Meconta Moz.
235 K3 Mecox Bay NY U.S.A.
177 H5 Mecsek mts Hungary
177 H5 Mecseknádasd Hungary
213 H2 Mecubúri Moz.
213 I2 Mecubúri r. Moz.
213 I2 Mecúfi Moz.
211 C8 Mecula Moz.
86 G4 Meda r. W.A. Austr.
182 F7 Meda Port.
182 E4 Meda mt. Spain
114 F3 Medak Andhra Prad. India
94 C3 Medan Sumatera Indon.
95 L9 Medang i. Indon.
260 E2 Medano Arg.
261 F6 Médanos Buenos Aires Arg.
261 H3 Médanos Entre Ríos Arg.
259 D8 Medanosa, Punta pt Arg.
250 D2 Médanos de Coro, Parque Nacional nat. park Venez.
226 H8 Medaryville IN U.S.A.
182 D6 Medas Port.
114 G8 Medawachchiya Sri Lanka
114 F4 Medchal Andhra Prad. India
172 D2 Meddersheim Ger.
164 K4 Meddo Neth.
233 □R3 Meddybemps Lake ME U.S.A.
190 F5 Mede Italy
205 F1 Médéa Alg.
169 G8 Medebach Ger.
257 G2 Medeiros Neto Brazil
182 F8 Medelim Port.
250 C3 Medellín Col.
184 H3 Medellín Spain
168 G3 Medem r. Ger.
164 H3 Medemblik Neth.
149 P7 Meden r. England U.K.
205 H2 Medenine Tunisia
Medenitsa Ukr. see Medenychi
136 C4 Medenychi Ukr.
124 E8 Meder Eritrea
206 B2 Mederdra Maur.
190 I6 Medesano Italy
233 M8 Medford NY U.S.A.
237 G7 Medford OK U.S.A.
238 C5 Medford OR U.S.A.
226 D4 Medford WI U.S.A.
234 F5 Medford Lakes NJ U.S.A.
197 Q6 Medgidia Romania
177 J5 Medgyesbodzás Hungary
177 K5 Medgyesegyháza Hungary
113 □1 Medhufinolhu i. N. Male Maldives
234 E5 Media PA U.S.A.
206 E2 Mediadilet well Mali
260 D4 Media Luna Arg.
242 □R10 Media Luna, Arrecife de la rf Hond.
186 D5 Mediana Spain
185 P7 Media Naranja, Punta de la pt Spain
186 F3 Mediano, Embalse de resr Spain
197 M4 Mediaș Romania
238 F3 Medical Lake WA U.S.A.
191 L7 Medicina Italy
238 K6 Medicine Bow WY U.S.A.
238 K6 Medicine Bow r. WY U.S.A.
238 K6 Medicine Bow Mountains WY U.S.A.
238 K6 Medicine Bow Peak WY U.S.A.
223 I5 Medicine Hat Alta Can.
238 L2 Medicine Lake MT U.S.A.
237 F7 Medicine Lodge KS U.S.A.
257 G2 Medina Brazil
250 C3 Medina Col.
Medina Al Madīnah Saudi Arabia see Al Madīnah
236 F2 Medina ND U.S.A.
232 G5 Medina NY U.S.A.
232 D7 Medina OH U.S.A.
237 G11 Medina r. TX U.S.A.
183 P6 Medinaceli Spain
184 G4 Medina de las Torres Spain
183 K6 Medina del Campo Spain
183 N3 Medina de Pomar Spain
183 J5 Medina de Rioseco Spain
206 B3 Medina Gounas Senegal
237 F11 Medina Lake TX U.S.A.
184 H8 Medina-Sidonia Spain
217 □1b Medine Mauritius
117 K8 Medinipur W. Bengal India
192 B8 Medio-Campidano prov. Italy
Mediolanum Italy see Milano
162 C4 Médis France
132 F7 Mediterranean Sea
161 D9 Méditerranée airport France
208 E4 Medje Dem. Rep. Congo
205 F2 Medjedel Alg.
189 A7 Medjerda, Monts de la mts Alg.
176 G2 Medlov Czech Rep.
120 G2 Mednogorsk Rus. Fed.
139 S5 Mednoye Rus. Fed.
131 R4 Mednyy, Ostrov i. Rus. Fed.
162 B5 Médoc reg. France
111 L12 Mêdog Xizang China
191 K6 Medolla Italy
236 D2 Medora ND U.S.A.
208 A4 Médouneu Gabon
175 I1 Medovoye Rus. Fed.
260 C3 Medrano Arg.
175 I5 Mędrzechów Pol.
223 I4 Medstead Sask. Can.
151 J5 Medstead Hampshire, England U.K.
Medu Kongkar Xizang China see Maizhokunggar
191 P6 Medulin Croatia
179 N7 Međumurje reg. Croatia
191 N4 Meduna r. Italy
191 N3 Meduno Italy
Meduro atoll Marshall Is see Majuro
197 J8 Medveđa Serbia
137 M8 Medvedeve Ukr.
134 I4 Medvedevo Rus. Fed.
135 H6 Medveditsa r. Rus. Fed.
137 N8 Medvedivka Ukr.
188 E3 Medvednica mts Croatia
134 J4 Medvedok Rus. Fed.
137 S8 Medvedovskaya Rus. Fed.
138 F6 Medvėgalio kalnis hill Lith.
137 P2 Medvenka Rus. Fed.
131 R2 Medvezh'i, Ostrova is Rus. Fed.
134 F3 Medvezh'yegorsk Rus. Fed.
179 J7 Medvode Slovenia
151 N5 Medway admin. div. England U.K.
151 M5 Medway r. England U.K.
86 □1 Medwin Point Christmas I.
175 K6 Medyka Pol.
139 S7 Medyn' Rus. Fed.
136 G4 Medzhybizh Ukr.
177 K2 Medzilaborce Slovakia
87 C9 Meeberrie W.A. Austr.
164 K2 Meeden Neth.
169 K10 Meeder Ger.
87 E9 Meekatharra W.A. Austr.
238 K6 Meeker CO U.S.A.
232 B8 Meeker OH U.S.A.
240 L2 Meeks Bay CA U.S.A.
210 F2 Meeladeen Somalia
214 I8 Meelberg mt. S. Africa
147 F6 Meelick Ireland
225 J3 Meelpaeg Reservoir Nfld and Lab. Can.
147 F3 Meenacross Ireland
147 F3 Meenanarwa Ireland
147 F3 Meentullynagarn Ireland
165 G6 Meer Belgium
171 F9 Meerane Ger.
138 K3 Meerapalu Estonia
169 H6 Meerbeck Ger.
169 C8 Meerbusch Ger.
165 H6 Meerhout Belgium
164 G5 Meerkerk Neth.
165 G6 Meerle Belgium
164 J5 Meerlo Neth.
172 G6 Meersburg Ger.
165 I7 Meerssen Neth.
113 □1 Meerufenfushi i. N. Male Maldives
116 F5 Meerut Uttar Prad. India
163 B8 Mées France
238 J4 Meeteetse WY U.S.A.
Me'etia i. Arch. de la Société Fr. Polynesia see Mehetia
165 D6 Meetkerke Belgium
165 I6 Meeuwen Belgium
140 N2 Mefjordvær Norway
210 C3 Mēga Eth.
94 D6 Mega i. Indon.
210 C3 Mega Escarpment Eth./Kenya
198 C3 Megala Kalyvia Greece
198 E2 Megali Panagia Greece
210 D3 Megalo Eth.
199 I6 Megalo Chorio Greece
198 D5 Megalopoli Greece
199 H5 Megalos Anthropofagos i. Greece
198 B4 Meganisi i. Greece
225 G4 Mégantic, Lac l. Que. Can.
198 E4 Megara Greece
164 I5 Megen Neth.
160 J5 Megève France
210 C2 Megezez mt. Eth.
117 M7 Meghalaya state India
117 K9 Meghasani mt. Orissa India
117 M8 Meghna r. Bangl.
129 H7 Meghri Armenia
Meghrut Armenia see Gugark'
122 G2 Megin Turkm.
130 I3 Megion Rus. Fed.
227 S1 Mégiscane, Lac l. Que. Can.
199 K6 Megisti i. Greece
139 R3 Megletsy Rus. Fed.
139 S3 Meglino, Ozero l. Rus. Fed.
139 S1 Megra r. Rus. Fed.
139 Q1 Megrega Rus. Fed.
Megri Armenia see Meghri
139 Q1 Megrozero Rus. Fed.
Megrut Armenia see Gugark'
197 K5 Mehadica Romania
165 H7 Mehaigne r. Belgium
205 F2 Mehaïguène, Oued watercourse Alg.
140 S1 Mehamn Norway
137 O9 Mehanom, Mys pt Ukr.
123 L8 Mehar Pak.
87 E7 Meharry, Mount W.A. Austr.
Mehdia Tunisia see Mahdia
122 B4 Mehdīkhān Iran
122 E4 Mehdīshahr Iran
168 H3 Mehe r. Ger.
143 N1 Mehedeby Sweden
205 F4 Mehedjibat, Erg des. Alg.
116 F9 Mehekar Mahar. India
117 L8 Meherpur Bangl.
232 G11 Meherrin VA U.S.A.
232 I12 Meherrin r. VA U.S.A.
79 □9 Mehetia i. Arch. de la Société Fr. Polynesia
116 E8 Mehidpur Madh. Prad. India
167 J5 Méhkerék Hungary
171 F9 Mehltheuer Ger.
236 J6 Mehlville MO U.S.A.
116 D8 Mehmadabad Gujarat India
117 I6 Mehndawal Uttar Prad. India
234 C1 Mehoopany PA U.S.A.
122 B2 Mehrābān Iran
122 F8 Mehrān Iran
122 F8 Mehrān watercourse Iran
127 M7 Mehrān Iraq
169 C10 Mehren Ger.
172 B2 Mehring Ger.
171 E7 Mehringen Ger.
179 H3 Mehrnbach Austria
172 H5 Mehrstetten Ger.
123 N4 Mehtar Lām Afgh.
162 I1 Mehun-sur-Yèvre France
256 C3 Meia Ponte r. Brazil
Meicheng Anhui China see Qianshan
Meicheng Fujian China see Minqing
109 H4 Meichengzhen Hunan China
108 E1 Meichuan Gansu China
207 I5 Meidougou Cameroon
150 D4 Meidrim Carmarthenshire, Wales U.K.
207 I5 Meiganga Cameroon
148 E5 Meigh Northern Ireland U.K.
221 I2 Meighen Island Nunavut Can.
146 J9 Meigle Perth and Kinross, Scotland U.K.
108 D4 Meigu Sichuan China
100 D7 Meihekou Jilin China
104 F4 Meihō Japan
165 I6 Meijel Neth.
164 F4 Meijendel nature res. Neth.
Meijiang Jiangxi China see Ningdu
109 J6 Mei Jiang r. China
109 J6 Meikeng Guangdong China
222 G3 Meikle r. Alta Can.
148 I1 Meikle Bin hill Scotland U.K.
148 G2 Meikle Kilmory Argyll and Bute, Scotland U.K.
146 J9 Meikleour Perth and Kinross, Scotland U.K.
146 K11 Meikle Says Law hill Scotland U.K.
96 B4 Meiktila Myanmar
190 F1 Meilen Switz.
163 C8 Meilhan France
163 E6 Meilhan-sur-Garonne France
Meilin Jiangxi China see Ganxian
158 H5 Meillac France
160 A3 Meillant France
160 J4 Meillerie France
222 E2 Meilleur r. N.W.T. Can.
108 H8 Meilu Guangdong China
182 F8 Meimoa Port.
190 F4 Meina Italy
169 K6 Meine Ger.
169 J6 Meinersen Ger.
169 E8 Meinerzhagen Ger.
178 A5 Meiningen Austria
169 J9 Meiningen Ger.
182 F2 Meira Spain
182 F2 Meira, Serra de mts Spain
190 E2 Meiringen Switz.
214 G9 Meiringspoort pass S. Africa
146 D9 Meirleach, Rubha nam pt Scotland U.K.
171 D7 Meisdorf Ger.
172 D2 Meisenheim Ger.
Meishan Anhui China see Jinzhai
108 D3 Meishan Sichuan China
171 H8 Meißen Ger.
168 I5 Meißendorf Ger.
172 D5 Meißenheim Ger.
169 I8 Meißner hill Ger.
169 I8 Meißner-Kaufunger Wald, Naturpark nature res. Ger.
222 D2 Meister r. Y.T. Can.
108 F5 Meitan Guizhou China
173 J4 Meitingen Ger.
105 K3 Meiwa Gunma Japan
104 E6 Meiwa Mie Japan
165 H9 Meix-devant-Virton Belgium
100 F5 Meixi Heilong. China
Meixian Guangdong China see Meizhou
109 J6 Meixian Guangdong China
107 J9 Meixian Shaanxi China
Meixing Sichuan China see Xiaojin
109 K6 Meizhou Guangdong China
116 F7 Mej r. India
116 I7 Meja Uttar Prad. India
161 E7 Méjan, Sommet de mt. France
204 D5 Mejaouda well Maur.
78 □3a Mejatto i. Kwajalein Marshall Is
161 C8 Méjean, Causse plat. France
189 B7 Mejez el Bab Tunisia
258 D3 Mejicana mt. Arg.
252 C5 Mejillones Chile
252 C5 Mejillones del Sur, Bahía de b. Chile
183 K8 Mejorada Spain
183 N8 Mejorada del Campo Spain
203 G5 Mekadio well Sudan
208 B4 Mékambo Gabon
199 L2 Mekece Turkey
210 C1 Mek'elē Eth.
129 G2 Meken-Yurt Rus. Fed.
205 F4 Mekerrhane, Sebkha salt pan Alg.
139 Q1 Mekhbaza Rus. Fed.
206 A3 Mékhé Senegal
129 H3 Mekhel'ta Rus. Fed.
123 M6 Mekhtar Pak.
210 C2 Mekī Eth.
179 K7 Mekinje Slovenia
207 F5 Mekkaw Nigeria
204 D2 Meknès Morocco
97 G9 Mekong r. Asia
alt. Lancang Jiang (China)
alt. Mènam Khong (Laos/Thai.)
97 H10 Mekong, Mouths of the Vietnam
129 D3 Mek'vena Georgia
191 M3 Mel Italy
208 D2 Méla, Mont hill C.A.R.
260 B4 Melado r. Chile
205 G3 Melah, Oued el watercourse Alg.
94 E3 Melaka Malaysia
94 E3 Melaka state Malaysia
95 K2 Melalap Sabah Malaysia
94 F5 Melalo, Tanjung pt Indon.
193 O6 Melandro r. Italy
266 F6 Melanesia is Oceania
266 F5 Melanesian Basin sea feature Pacific Ocean
140 □B1 Melar Iceland
191 K5 Melara Italy
95 I4 Melawi r. Indon.
160 E4 Melay Bourgogne France
157 K8 Melay Champagne-Ardenne France
159 J7 Melay Pays de la Loire France
190 E6 Melazzo Italy
168 J4 Melbeck Ger.
151 M3 Melbourn Cambridgeshire, England U.K.
83 J7 Melbourne Vic. Austr.
151 J2 Melbourne Derbyshire, England U.K.
237 J7 Melbourne AR U.S.A.
231 G11 Melbourne FL U.S.A.
140 M2 Melbu Norway
146 □M2 Melby Shetland, Scotland U.K.
140 □ Melchers, Kapp c. Svalbard
259 B7 Melchor, Isla i. Chile
243 O9 Melchor de Mencos Guat.
243 I5 Melchor Ocampo Mex.
170 I5 Melchow Ger.
140 J5 Meldal Norway
191 M7 Meldola Italy
168 H2 Meldorf Ger.
232 B12 Meldrum KY U.S.A.
224 D4 Meldrum Bay Ont. Can.
190 F7 Mele Italy
190 E8 Mele, Capo c. Italy
139 T4 Melech r. Rus. Fed.
190 G5 Melegnano Italy
176 G4 Meleg-víz r. Hungary
92 □ Melekeiok Palau
Melekess Rus. Fed. see Dimitrovgrad
134 K4 Melekhina Rus. Fed.
139 Y5 Melekhovo Rus. Fed.
137 Q7 Melekyne Ukr.
216 □3f Melenara Gran Canaria Canary Is
196 I5 Melenci Vojvodina Serbia
126 G4 Melendiz Dağı mt. Turkey
195 O3 Melendugno Italy
135 H5 Melenki Rus. Fed.
158 H5 Melesse France
Melet Turkey see Mesudiye
120 F1 Meleuz Rus. Fed.
225 G1 Mélèzes, Rivière aux r. Que. Can.
193 L4 Melfa r. Italy
233 J11 Melfa VA U.S.A.
208 C2 Melfi Chad
193 P6 Melfi Italy
223 J4 Melfort Sask. Can.
251 I5 Melgaço Brazil
182 D4 Melgaço Port.
183 M9 Melgar r. Spain
183 J4 Melgar de Arriba Spain
183 L4 Melgar de Fernamental Spain
182 H5 Melgar de Tera Spain
158 D6 Melgven France
140 K5 Melhus Norway
223 M2 Meliadine Lake Nunavut Can.
95 I5 Meliau Kalimantan Indon.
165 J6 Melick Neth.
195 K7 Melicucco Italy
182 E3 Melide Spain
184 B4 Melides Port.
198 C5 Meligalas Greece
129 E5 Melikköyü Turkey
93 C4 Melilis i. Indon.
181 E5 Melilla N. Africa
195 I9 Melilli Sicilia Italy
259 B7 Melimoyu, Monte mt. Chile
81 D11 Melina, Mount South I. N.Z.
261 G3 Melincué Arg.
261 G3 Melincué, Laguna l. Arg.
95 L5 Melintang, Danau l. Indon.
137 O5 Melioratyvne Ukr.
260 B6 Melipeuco Chile
260 B3 Melipilla Chile
157 M8 Mélisey France
164 E5 Meliskerke Neth.
195 M5 Melissa Italy
223 K5 Melita Man. Can.
Melitene Turkey see Malatya
198 C2 Meliti Greece
195 J8 Melito r. Italy
195 J8 Melito di Porto Salvo Italy
137 O7 Melitopol' Ukr.
179 L3 Melk Austria
179 L3 Melk r. Austria
215 I8 Melk r. S. Africa
210 C3 Melka Guba Eth.
214 B5 Melkbospunt pt S. Africa
214 C9 Melkbosstrand S. Africa
150 H5 Melksham Wiltshire, England U.K.
190 I5 Mella r. Italy

Mellac to Midlothian
351

158 D6 Mellac France
140 R3 Mellakoski Fin.
142 J2 Mellanfryken l. Sweden
140 O5 Mellansel Sweden
141 M5 Mellansjö Sweden
140 O4 Mellanström Sweden
178 A5 Mellau Austria
165 E6 Melle Belgium
162 D3 Melle France
169 F6 Melle Ger.
170 E4 Mellen Ger.
226 D3 Mellen WI U.S.A.
168 I5 Mellendorf (Wedemark) Ger.
171 H6 Mellensee Ger.
142 I3 Mellerud Sweden
236 F3 Mellette SD U.S.A.
Mellid Spain see Melide
195 □ Mellieħa Malta
195 □ Mellieħa, Il-Bajja tal- b. Malta
168 K5 Mellin Ger.
171 D9 Mellingen Ger.
168 G5 Mellinghausen Ger.
202 E6 Mellit Sudan
259 B8 Mellizo Sur, Cerro mt. Chile
263 E2 Mellor Glacier Antarctica
180 D5 Mellousa Morocco
169 J10 Mellrichstadt Ger.
150 E4 Mellte r. Wales U.K.
78 □3a Mellu i. Kwajalein Marshall Is
168 F3 Mellum i. Ger.
78 □3a Mellu Passage Kwajalein Marshall Is
202 C6 Melmele watercourse Chad
149 L4 Melmerby Cumbria, England U.K.
215 P4 Melmoth S. Africa
100 I6 Mel'nichoye Rus. Fed.
176 D1 Mělník Czech Rep.
138 M1 Mel'nikovo Rus. Fed.
137 N8 Mel'nychne Ukr.
137 O4 Mel'nykove Ukr.
136 F5 Mel'nytsya-Podil's'ka Ukr.
261 F4 Melo Arg.
208 A4 Melo Gabon
258 G4 Melo Uru.
213 H2 Meloco Moz.
215 K4 Meloding S. Africa
93 B8 Melolo Sumba Indon.
182 D4 Melón Spain
207 H5 Mélong Cameroon
129 M2 Melovoy, Mys pt Kazakh.
Melovoye Ukr. see Milove
220 C3 Melozitna r. AK U.S.A.
158 E6 Melrand France
182 D6 Melres Port.
205 G2 Melrhir, Chott salt l. Alg.
87 F9 Melrose W.A. Austr.
146 K11 Melrose Scottish Borders, Scotland U.K.
236 H3 Melrose MN U.S.A.
190 G1 Mels Switz.
169 D10 Melsbach Ger.
168 J2 Melsdorf Ger.
Melsetter Zimbabwe see Chimanimani
149 N5 Melsonby North Yorkshire, England U.K.
169 I8 Melsungen Ger.
Melta, Mount Malaysia see Tawai, Bukit
140 R3 Meltaus Fin.
149 N6 Meltham West Yorkshire, England U.K.
83 J7 Melton Vic. Austr.
151 O3 Melton Suffolk, England U.K.
151 K2 Melton Mowbray Leicestershire, England U.K.
95 I4 Meluan Sarawak Malaysia
211 C8 Meluco Moz.
156 E6 Melun France
114 F7 Melur Tamil Nadu India
210 B2 Melut Sudan
146 E7 Melvaig Highland, Scotland U.K.
146 I5 Melvich Highland, Scotland U.K.
223 K5 Melville Sask. Can.
85 J3 Melville, Cape Qld Austr.
Melville, Cape Dominica see Capucin, Cape
92 A8 Melville, Cape Phil.
225 J2 Melville, Lake Nfld and Lab. Can.
84 F2 Melville Bay N.T. Austr.
Melville Bugt b. Greenland see Qimusseriarsuaq
84 C1 Melville Island N.T. Austr.
221 H2 Melville Island N.W.T./Nunavut Can.
221 J3 Melville Peninsula Nunavut Can.
226 F9 Melvin IL U.S.A.
147 F4 Melvin, Lough l. Ireland/U.K.
177 I5 Mélykút Hungary
190 G5 Melzo Italy
198 A2 Memaliaj Albania
111 F9 Mêmar Co salt l. China
213 I2 Memba Moz.
213 I2 Memba, Baía de b. Moz.
91 I7 Memberamo r. Papua Indon.
93 A8 Memboro Sumba Indon.
160 H1 Membrey France
185 M3 Membrilla Spain
182 F9 Membrío Spain
Memel Lith. see Klaipėda
215 N3 Memel S. Africa
138 H5 Mēmele r. Latvia
138 J6 Memiakalnis hill Lith.
173 J2 Memmelsdorf Ger.
173 I6 Memmingen Ger.
173 I6 Memmingerberg Ger.
156 I5 Mémorial Américain tourist site France
95 H4 Mempawah Kalimantan Indon.
126 E9 Memphis tourist site Egypt
227 L7 Memphis MI U.S.A.
236 I5 Memphis MO U.S.A.
237 J8 Memphis TN U.S.A.
237 E8 Memphis TX U.S.A.
233 M3 Memphrémagog, Lac l. Que. Can.
146 L7 Memsie Aberdeenshire, Scotland U.K.
102 T4 Memuro-dake mt. Japan
210 C3 Mena Eth.
93 D8 Mena Timor Indon.
137 L2 Mena Ukr.
137 L2 Mena r. Ukr.
237 H8 Mena AR U.S.A.
213 □J4 Menabe mts Madag.
261 I3 Menafra Uru.
190 G3 Menaggio Italy
191 K5 Menago r. Italy
150 D1 Menai Bridge Isle of Anglesey, Wales U.K.
150 D1 Menai Strait Wales U.K.
207 F3 Ménaka Mali
164 I2 Menaldum Neth.
97 G7 Mènam Khong r. Laos/Thai. alt. Lancang Jiang (China) conv. Mekong
93 D4 Menanga Maluku Indon.
213 □J5 Menarandra r. Madag.
237 F10 Menard TX U.S.A.
156 B8 Menars France
183 L9 Menasalbas Spain
224 B4 Menasha WI U.S.A.
160 B4 Menat France
191 M6 Menata Italy
157 J6 Menaucourt France
185 M5 Mencal mt. Spain
259 C6 Mencué Arg.
103 H14 Menda Japan
94 G6 Mendanau i. Indon.
257 F3 Mendanha Brazil
116 C9 Mendarda Gujarat India
94 G4 Mendarik i. Indon.
186 B1 Mendaur mt. Spain
183 P4 Mendavia Spain
95 J6 Mendawai Kalimantan Indon.
95 J6 Mendawai r. Indon.
161 D7 Mende France
210 C3 Mendebo mts Eth.
203 H6 Mendefera Eritrea
122 C3 Mendejīn Iran
268 M1 Mendeleyev Ridge sea feature Arctic Ocean
134 K5 Mendeleyevsk Rus. Fed.
169 E8 Menden (Sauerland) Ger.
237 K10 Mendenhall MS U.S.A.
220 B4 Mendenhall, Cape AK U.S.A.
222 C3 Mendenhall Glacier AK U.S.A.
199 I4 Menderes Turkey
121 L2 Mendesh Kazakh.
243 J5 Méndez Tamaulipas Mex.
245 I3 Méndez Veracruz Mex.
92 C4 Mendez-Nuñez Luzon Phil.
234 F3 Mendham NJ U.S.A.
210 B2 Mendī Eth.
91 J8 Mendi P.N.G.
183 Q3 Mendigorría Spain
150 G5 Mendip Hills England U.K.
163 C9 Menditte France
240 I2 Mendocino CA U.S.A.
238 B6 Mendocino, Cape CA U.S.A.
240 I2 Mendocino, Lake CA U.S.A.
194 F8 Mendola r. Sicilia Italy
194 F9 Mendola r. Sicilia Italy
226 I7 Mendon MI U.S.A.
83 L4 Mendooran N.S.W. Austr.
240 L5 Mendota CA U.S.A.
226 E8 Mendota IL U.S.A.
226 E6 Mendota, Lake WI U.S.A.
260 C3 Mendoza Arg.
260 C4 Mendoza prov. Arg.
260 C3 Mendoza r. Arg.
252 D4 Mendoza Bol.
261 I4 Mendoza Uru.
190 F4 Mendrisio Switz.
87 F12 Mends, Lake salt flat W.A. Austr.
158 G5 Ménéac France
250 D2 Mene de Mauroa Venez.
190 H6 Menegosa, Monte mt. Italy
246 H9 Mene Grande Venez.
199 I4 Menemen Turkey
165 D7 Menen Belgium
161 G9 Ménerbes France
162 E5 Ménesplet France
160 E2 Ménessaire France
161 B6 Menet France
159 P7 Menetou-Salon France
158 E4 Menez Bré hill France
158 C5 Menez Hom hill France
194 D8 Menfi Sicilia Italy
183 J8 Menga, Puerto de pass Spain
192 B10 Menga, Punta pt Sardegna Italy
95 K1 Mengalum i. Malaysia
107 J9 Mengba Gansu China
108 C7 Mengban Yunnan China
109 K2 Mengcheng Anhui China
Mengdong Yunnan China see Cangyuan
172 G5 Mengen Ger.
126 F3 Mengen Turkey
169 F9 Mengerskirchen Ger.
179 K7 Mengeš Slovenia
234 B5 Menges Mills PA U.S.A.
94 F7 Menggala Sumatera Indon.
108 C8 Menghai Yunnan China
185 L5 Mengíbar Spain
121 L1 Mengisor, Ozero salt l. Kazakh.
95 K6 Mengkatip Kalimantan Indon.
95 I4 Mengkiang r. Indon.
173 M4 Mengkofen Ger.
93 B5 Mengkoka, Gunung mt. Indon.
108 C8 Mengla Yunnan China
Menglang Yunnan China see Lancang
108 B7 Menglian Yunnan China
Menglie Yunnan China see Jiangcheng
Mengmeng Yunnan China see Shuangjiang
207 H6 Mengong Cameroon
108 H6 Mengshan Guangxi China
Mengsuo Yunnan China see Ximeng
Mengxian Henan China see Mengzhou
Mengyang Sichuan China see Mingshan
107 O9 Mengyin Shandong China
107 M9 Mengzhou Henan China
108 D7 Mengzi Yunnan China
150 D7 Menheniot Cornwall, England U.K.
162 D3 Ménigoute France
225 H2 Menihek Nfld and Lab. Can.
225 H2 Menihek Lakes Nfld and Lab. Can.
157 K6 Ménil-la-Tour France
157 M7 Ménil-sur-Belvitte France
Menin Belgium see Menen
179 O1 Měnín Czech Rep.
179 K7 Menina mts Slovenia
83 I5 Menindee N.S.W. Austr.
83 I5 Menindee, Lake N.S.W. Austr.
83 I5 Menindee Aboriginal Reserve N.S.W. Austr.
82 G6 Meningie S.A. Austr.
122 C4 Menjān Iran
131 N3 Menkere Rus. Fed.
147 D6 Menlough Ireland
124 D9 Menna r. Eth.
156 D6 Mennecy France
159 O7 Mennetou-sur-Cher France
253 F5 Mennonite Colony res. Para.
226 G4 Menominee MI U.S.A.
226 G4 Menominee r. WI U.S.A.
226 F4 Menominee Indian Reservation res. WI U.S.A.
226 F6 Menomonee Falls WI U.S.A.
226 C5 Menomonie WI U.S.A.
209 C8 Menongue Angola
187 D12 Menor, Mar lag. Spain
186 □ Menorca i. Spain
186 □ Menorca, Cap c. Spain
160 C2 Menou France
204 E3 Menouarar Alg.
161 H7 Mens France
95 L3 Mensalong Kalimantan Indon.
162 F5 Mensignac France
168 E5 Menslage Ger.
149 N6 Menston West Yorkshire, England U.K.
Mentakab Malaysia see Mentekab
193 J3 Mentana Italy
92 A9 Mentapok mt. Malaysia
95 L3 Mentarang r. Indon.
94 C6 Mentawai, Kepulauan is Indon.
94 D6 Mentawai, Selat sea chan. Indon.
95 J6 Mentaya r. Indon.
182 F5 Mente r. Port./Spain
146 H10 Menteith, Lake of Scotland U.K.
94 E3 Mentekab Malaysia
87 C12 Mentelle, Cape W.A. Austr.
169 K8 Menteroda Ger.
199 L4 Menteş Turkey
160 I5 Menthon-St-Bernard France
184 E4 Mentiras hill Port.
185 O4 Mentiras mt. Spain
241 X6 Mentmore NM U.S.A.
94 F6 Mentok Indon.
161 L9 Menton France
237 D10 Mentone TX U.S.A.
232 D7 Mentor OH U.S.A.
183 L8 Méntrida Spain
95 J6 Mentuba r. Indon.
Menufia governorate Egypt see Minūfīyah
95 J5 Menukung Kalimantan Indon.
105 J3 Menuma Japan
95 K2 Menumbok Sabah Malaysia
93 B3 Menunu Sulawesi Indon.
95 L4 Menyapa, Gunung mt. Indon.
106 G8 Menyuan Qinghai China
107 K2 Menza Rus. Fed.
107 K1 Menza r. Rus. Fed.
205 H1 Menzel Bourguiba Tunisia
126 H5 Menzelet Barajı resr Turkey
134 K5 Menzelinsk Rus. Fed.
189 C7 Menzel Temime Tunisia
87 F10 Menzies W.A. Austr.
263 E2 Menzies, Mount Antarctica
190 E1 Menznau Switz.
212 B5 Meobbaai b. Namibia
159 N8 Méobecq France
191 M4 Meolo Italy
242 G3 Meoqui Mex.
161 H10 Méounes-les-Montrieux France
209 B6 Mepala Angola
129 D4 Mep'istsqaro, Mt'a Georgia
211 B8 Meponda Moz.
164 J3 Meppel Neth.
168 D5 Meppen Ger.
213 G4 Mepuze Moz.
215 L4 Meqheleng S. Africa
253 E3 Mequéns r. Brazil
186 F5 Mequinenza Spain
186 F5 Mequinenza, Embalse de resr Spain
226 G6 Mequon WI U.S.A.
156 C8 Mer France
190 G3 Mera r. Italy
188 E3 Merag Croatia
95 L4 Merah Kalimantan Indon.
94 G7 Merak Jawa Indon.
140 K5 Meråker Norway
82 D3 Meramangye, Lake salt flat S.A. Austr.
236 J6 Meramec r. MO U.S.A.
191 K2 Merano Italy
95 I8 Merapi, Gunung vol. Jawa Indon.
95 K9 Merapi, Gunung vol. Jawa Indon.
163 D8 Méraq France
251 F3 Merari, Serra mt. Brazil
225 K4 Merasheen Nfld and Lab. Can.
140 P3 Merasjärvi Sweden
190 G4 Merate Italy
212 E4 Meratswe r. Botswana
95 K6 Meratus, Pegunungan mts Indon.
91 J8 Merauke Papua Indon.
94 E4 Merbau Sumatera Indon.
83 I6 Merbein Vic. Austr.
165 F8 Merbes-le-Château Belgium
Merca Somalia see Marka
183 N2 Mercadillo Spain
129 B6 Mercan Turkey
129 A6 Mercan Dağları mts Turkey
161 J8 Mercantour, Parc National du nat. park France
191 M9 Mercatale Italy
191 M8 Mercatello sul Metauro Italy
191 N8 Mercatino Conca Italy
193 N6 Mercato San Severino Italy
191 M8 Mercato Saraceno Italy
240 L4 Merced CA U.S.A.
240 L4 Merced r. CA U.S.A.
260 B2 Mercedario, Cerro mt. Arg.
245 K9 Merced del Potrero Mex.
261 H4 Mercedes Buenos Aires Arg.
258 F3 Mercedes Corrientes Arg.
261 H3 Mercedes Uru.
216 □3a Mercedes, Monte de las hill Tenerife Canary Is
258 C3 Merceditas Chile
233 □P4 Mercer ME U.S.A.
232 A8 Mercer OH U.S.A.
232 E7 Mercer PA U.S.A.
226 D3 Mercer WI U.S.A.
234 F4 Mercer County county NJ U.S.A.
232 H9 Mercersburg PA U.S.A.
234 F4 Mercerville NJ U.S.A.
252 C2 Mercês Acre Brazil
257 F4 Mercês Minas Gerais Brazil
173 J5 Merching Ger.
165 F7 Merchtem Belgium
252 C2 Mercier Bol.
128 D1 Mercimek Turkey
162 H5 Mercœur France
193 N6 Mercogliano Italy
163 G7 Mercuès France
160 F3 Mercurey France
160 I5 Mercury France
241 Q5 Mercury NV U.S.A.
80 J3 Mercury Bay North I. N.Z.
80 J3 Mercury Islands North I. N.Z.
163 H10 Mercus-Garrabet France
221 L3 Mercy, Cape Nunavut Can.
Merdenik Turkey see Göle
172 D5 Merdingen Ger.
204 D2 Merdja Zerga, Réserve de nature res. Morocco
158 G5 Merdrignac France
165 E7 Mere Belgium
150 H5 Mere Wiltshire, England U.K.
159 P7 Méreau France
233 N5 Meredith NH U.S.A.
259 E9 Meredith, Cape Falkland Is
237 E8 Meredith, Lake TX U.S.A.
205 F4 Meredoua Alg.
210 E4 Mereeg Somalia
137 P4 Merefa Ukr.
78 □5 Mere Lava i. Vanuatu
165 E7 Merelbeke Belgium
138 K4 Meremäe Estonia
80 J4 Meremere North I. N.Z.
140 P5 Merenkurkku str. Fin./Sweden
163 H10 Mérens-les-Vals France
85 I2 Merepah Aboriginal Holding res. Qld Austr.
156 D7 Méréville France
139 T2 Merezha Rus. Fed.
202 E5 Merga Oasis Sudan
120 D3 Mergenevo Kazakh.
190 E4 Mergozzo Italy
Mergui Myanmar see Myeik
Mergui Archipelago is Myanmar see Myeik Kyunzu
197 R5 Merhei, Lacul l. Romania
192 C2 Meria Corse France
82 H6 Meribah S.A. Austr.
161 J6 Méribel-les-Allues France
199 H1 Meriç Turkey
199 H2 Meriç r. Turkey alt. Evros (Greece) alt. Maritsa (Bulgaria)
198 F5 Merichas Kythnos Greece
156 E3 Méricourt France
243 O7 Mérida Mex.
184 G3 Mérida Spain
250 D2 Mérida Venez.
250 D2 Mérida state Venez.
250 D3 Mérida, Cordillera de mts Venez.
151 I3 Meriden West Midlands, England U.K.
233 M7 Meriden CT U.S.A.
237 K9 Meridian MS U.S.A.
237 G10 Meridian TX U.S.A.
261 F4 Meridiano Arg.
163 C6 Mérignac France
140 R4 Merijärvi Fin.
141 P6 Merikarvia Fin.
83 L7 Merimbula N.S.W. Austr.
176 E2 Měřín Czech Rep.
Merín, Laguna l. Brazil/Uru. see Mirim, Lagoa
160 A5 Mérinchal France
85 L6 Merinda Qld Austr.
161 G9 Mérindol France
215 L2 Merindol S. Africa
173 J5 Mering Ger.
207 I4 Meringa Nigeria
82 H6 Meringur Vic. Austr.
261 I3 Merinos Uru.
91 H6 Merir i. Palau
251 H4 Merirumã Brazil
95 J3 Merit Sarawak Malaysia
85 K8 Merivale r. Qld Austr.
78 □1 Merizo Guam
177 L4 Mérk Hungary
121 O6 Merke Kazakh.
237 E9 Merkel TX U.S.A.
179 M6 Merkendorf Austria
173 J3 Merkendorf Ger.
138 H7 Merkinė Lith.
176 C2 Merklín Czech Rep.
172 H4 Merklingen Ger.
165 G6 Merksplas Belgium
175 M1 Merkys r. Lith.
191 K5 Merlara Italy
Merlav i. Vanuatu see Mere Lava
158 E6 Merlevenez France
94 □ Merlimau, Pulau reg. Sing.
162 I4 Merlines France
260 E3 Merlo Arg.
137 N4 Merlo r. Ukr.
85 I2 Merluna Qld Austr.
86 E4 Mermaid Reef W.A. Austr.
177 G5 Mernye Hungary
182 D2 Mero r. Spain
87 G10 Merolia W.A. Austr.
186 J3 Merolla, Coll de pass Spain
128 D6 Meron, Har mt. Israel
197 J7 Merošina Serbia
203 F5 Merowe Sudan
87 E11 Merredin W.A. Austr.
157 K7 Merrey France
226 I8 Merriam IN U.S.A.
146 H12 Merrick hill Scotland U.K.
227 S5 Merrickville Ont. Can.
227 J6 Merrill MI U.S.A.
226 E4 Merrill WI U.S.A.
222 E2 Merrill, Mount Y.T. Can.
226 D5 Merrillan WI U.S.A.
230 D5 Merrillville IN U.S.A.
214 H7 Merriman S. Africa
236 E4 Merriman NE U.S.A.
150 G6 Merriott Somerset, England U.K.
222 F5 Merritt B.C. Can.
231 G11 Merritt Island FL U.S.A.
231 G11 Merritt Island National Wildlife Refuge nature res. FL U.S.A.
83 M5 Merriwa N.S.W. Austr.
83 L4 Merrygoen N.S.W. Austr.
203 I6 Mersa Fatma Eritrea
203 H5 Mersa Gulbub Eritrea
203 H5 Mersa Teklay Eritrea
165 J9 Mersch Lux.
171 H8 Merschwitz Ger.
192 G1 Merse r. Italy
151 N4 Mersea Island England U.K.
171 E8 Merseburg (Saale) Ger.
149 L7 Mersey est. England U.K.
149 K6 Merseyside admin. div. England U.K.
126 G5 Mersin Turkey
129 A4 Mersin Trabzon Turkey
128 B2 Mersin prov. Turkey
199 I5 Mersinbeleni Turkey
94 E3 Mersing Malaysia
95 J3 Mersing, Bukit mt. Malaysia
210 E3 Mersin Galgalo Eth.
156 B3 Mers-les-Bains France
138 G4 Mērsrags Latvia
138 G4 Mērsrags pt Latvia
116 E6 Merta Rajasthan India
116 D6 Merta Road Rajasthan India
165 J9 Mertert Lux.
172 B2 Mertesdorf Ger.
150 F4 Merthyr Tydfil Merthyr Tydfil, Wales U.K.
150 F4 Merthyr Tydfil admin. div. Wales U.K.
210 C4 Merti Kenya
173 J4 Mertingen Ger.
210 C4 Merti Plateau Kenya
169 D10 Mertloch Ger.
184 D5 Mértola Port.
184 D5 Mértola, Serra de hills Port.
205 G4 Mertoutek Alg.
120 E5 Mertvyy Kultuk, Sor dry lake Kazakh.
263 J2 Mertz Glacier Antarctica
263 J2 Mertz Glacier Tongue Antarctica
237 E10 Mertzon TX U.S.A.
234 D3 Mertztown PA U.S.A.
157 O6 Mertzwiller France
156 D5 Méru France
210 C4 Meru Kenya
211 C5 Meru vol. Tanz.
95 J9 Meru Betiri, Taman Nasional nat. park Indon.
182 D4 Merufe Port.
123 J7 Merui Pak.
210 C4 Meru National Park Kenya
95 L2 Merutai Sabah Malaysia
Merv Turkm. see Mary
160 G3 Mervans France
162 C2 Mervent France
163 G8 Merville Midi-Pyrénées France
156 E2 Merville Nord-Pas-de-Calais France
159 K3 Merville-Franceville-Plage France
214 F8 Merweville S. Africa
Merya Turkey see Veliköy
156 G6 Méry-sur-Seine France
169 E6 Merzen Ger.
126 G3 Merzifon Turkey
172 B3 Merzig Ger.
262 T2 Merz Peninsula Antarctica
93 F3 Mesa Halmahera Indon.
215 K2 Mesa S. Africa
183 Q6 Mesa r. Spain
241 U8 Mesa AZ U.S.A.
239 L10 Mesa NM U.S.A.
226 B2 Mesabi Range hills MN U.S.A.
250 D2 Mesa Bolívar Venez.
195 N2 Mesagne Italy
222 H1 Mesa Lake N.W.T. Can.
94 F4 Mesanak i. Indon.
158 I7 Mésanger France
182 E6 Mesão Frio Port.
239 J8 Mesa Verde National Park CO U.S.A.
239 L10 Mescalero Apache Indian Reservation res. NM U.S.A.
169 F8 Meschede Ger.
162 C4 Meschers-sur-Gironde France
129 B5 Mescit Dağları mts Turkey
140 N4 Meselefors Sweden
78 □4a Meseong i. Chuuk Micronesia
210 C1 Mesfinto Eth.
224 F3 Mesgouez, Lac l. Que. Can.
156 G7 Mesgrigny France
134 J5 Mesha r. Rus. Fed.
139 S7 Meshchovsk Rus. Fed.
Meshed Iran see Mashhad
122 H3 Meshkān Iran
122 F2 Meshkhed Turkm.
135 H6 Meshkovskaya Rus. Fed.
234 C1 Meshoppen PA U.S.A.
234 C1 Meshoppen Creek r. PA U.S.A.
208 F2 Meshra'er Req Sudan
226 I5 Mesick MI U.S.A.
188 F4 Mesihovina Bos.-Herz.
195 J6 Mesima r. Italy
198 E2 Mesimeri Greece
129 C4 Meskhet'is K'edi hills Georgia
204 D3 Meski Morocco
159 J6 Meslay-du-Maine France
160 H3 Mesnay France
190 G3 Mesocco Switz.
191 M6 Mesola Italy
198 C4 Mesolongi Greece
Mesolóngion Greece see Mesolongi
198 C4 Mesolongiou, Limnothalassa lag. Greece
Mesón del Viente Spain see O Mesón do Vento
195 L5 Mesoraca Italy
172 G2 Mespelbrunn Ger.
158 G7 Mesquer France
257 F3 Mesquita Brazil
241 R5 Mesquite NV U.S.A.
237 G9 Mesquite TX U.S.A.
241 Q6 Mesquite Lake CA U.S.A.
205 F2 Messaad Alg.
158 H6 Messac France
202 A3 Messak Mellet hills Libya
211 D7 Messalo r. Moz.
207 I6 Messaména Cameroon
Messana Sicilia Italy see Messina
165 I9 Messancy Belgium
163 B8 Messanges France
205 E4 Messaoud, Oued watercourse Alg.
198 F7 Messaras, Kolpos b. Kriti Greece
170 E5 Meßdorf Ger.
159 J4 Messei France
160 B5 Messeix France
184 C5 Messejana Port.
172 F2 Messel Ger.
259 B8 Messier, Canal sea chan. Chile
195 J7 Messina Sicilia Italy
194 G8 Messina prov. Sicilia Italy
Messina, Strait of Italy see Messina, Stretta di
195 J7 Messina, Stretta di str. Italy
157 J4 Messincourt France
227 R3 Messines Que. Can.
169 D6 Messingen Ger.
149 P6 Messingham North Lincolnshire, England U.K.
198 D5 Messini Greece
198 D6 Messiniakos Kolpos b. Greece
172 G6 Meßkirch Ger.
140 L5 Messlingen Sweden
172 F5 Meßstetten Ger.
197 M9 Mesta r. Bulg.
185 N3 Mesta r. Spain
199 G4 Mesta, Akrotirio pt Chios Greece
185 K3 Mestanza Spain
197 N3 Mestecănişului, Obcina ridge Romania
176 E1 Městec Králové Czech Rep.
Mestghanem Alg. see Mostaganem
129 D2 Mestia Georgia
170 E3 Mestlin Ger.
177 G1 Město Albrechtice Czech Rep.
173 O2 Město Touškov Czech Rep.
191 M5 Mestre Italy
126 H3 Mesudiye Turkey
94 F7 Mesuji r. Indon.
160 B2 Mesves-sur-Loire France
160 E3 Mesvres France
160 E3 Mesvrin r. France
250 C4 Meta dept Col.
250 E3 Meta r. Col./Venez.
193 M6 Meta Italy
225 G3 Métabetchouan Que. Can.
160 I3 Métabief France
227 M2 Metagama Ont. Can.
221 L3 Meta Incognita Peninsula Nunavut Can.
237 J11 Metairie LA U.S.A.
197 K4 Metaliferi, Munţii mts Romania
196 H7 Metalika pass Bos.-Herz./Montenegro
191 J9 Metallifere, Colline mts Italy
139 N2 Metallostroy Rus. Fed.
226 E9 Metamora IL U.S.A.
258 D2 Metán Arg.
210 C2 Metanara Eth.
95 K6 Metangai Kalimantan Indon.
211 B8 Metangula Moz.
243 O10 Metapán El Salvador
213 H2 Metarica Moz.
191 O8 Metauro r. Italy
225 H4 Meteghan N.S. Can.
169 D6 Metelen Ger.
138 G7 Metelys l. Lith.
210 C1 Metema Eth.
213 G2 Metengobalame Moz.
198 C3 Meteora tourist site Greece
85 L8 Meteor Creek r. Qld Austr.
151 O3 Metfield Suffolk, England U.K.
198 E5 Methanon, Chersonisos pen. Greece
198 E5 Methanon, Steno sea chan. Greece
149 Q7 Metheringham Lincolnshire, England U.K.
146 L8 Methlick Aberdeenshire, Scotland U.K.
198 C6 Methoni Greece
233 N6 Methuen MA U.S.A.
86 H3 Methuen, Mount hill W.A. Austr.
81 F10 Methven South I. N.Z.
146 I10 Methven Perth and Kinross, Scotland U.K.
151 N2 Methwold Norfolk, England U.K.
261 F4 Metileo Arg.
224 B3 Metionga Lake Ont. Can.
188 F4 Metković Croatia
222 D4 Metlakatla AK U.S.A.
245 J5 Metlaltoyuca Mex.
205 H2 Metlaoui Tunisia
245 I8 Metlatonoc Mex.
188 E3 Metlika Slovenia
205 G2 Metlili, Oued watercourse Alg.
179 J6 Metnitz Austria
179 J6 Metnitz r. Austria
213 H2 Metoro Moz.
195 K6 Metramo r. Italy
94 F7 Metro Sumatera Indon.
237 K7 Metropolis IL U.S.A.
Metsada tourist site Israel see Masada
140 T4 Metsäkylä Fin.
170 G3 Metschow Ger.
164 J2 Metslawier Neth.
198 C3 Metsovo Greece
173 N4 Metten Ger.
172 A2 Mettendorf Ger.
173 M5 Mettenheim Ger.
231 F9 Metter GA U.S.A.
179 M6 Mettersdorf am Saßbach Austria
165 G8 Mettet Belgium
169 E6 Mettingen Ger.
172 B3 Mettlach Ger.
240 N6 Mettler CA U.S.A.
179 H3 Mettmach Austria
169 C8 Mettmann Ger.
159 M7 Mettray France
114 E7 Mettuppalaiyam Tamil Nadu India
114 E7 Mettur Tamil Nadu India
210 B2 Metu Eth.
235 G3 Metuchen NJ U.S.A.
176 E1 Metuje r. Czech Rep.
211 D7 Metundo, Ilha i. Moz.
157 L5 Metz France
157 N7 Metzeral France
157 L5 Metzervisse France
172 G4 Metzingen Ger.
245 I5 Metzquititlán Mex.
158 H5 Meu r. France
169 E10 Meudt Ger.
94 B2 Meulaboh Sumatera Indon.
156 C5 Meulan France
165 D7 Meulebeke Belgium
156 C8 Meung-sur-Loire France
94 B2 Meureudu Sumatera Indon.
160 F3 Meursault France
157 L6 Meurthe r. France
157 L6 Meurthe-et-Moselle dept France
157 J5 Meuse dept France
165 I6 Meuse r. Belgium/France alt. Maas (Neth.)
171 F8 Meuselwitz Ger.
162 G4 Meuzac France
160 G3 Meuzin r. France
150 C7 Mevagissey Cornwall, England U.K.
108 D2 Mêwa Sichuan China
149 O7 Mexborough South Yorkshire, England U.K.
245 H8 Mexcala Mex.
244 B4 Mexcaltitán Mex.
237 G10 Mexia TX U.S.A.
251 I4 Mexiana, Ilha i. Brazil
242 B1 Mexicali Mex.
241 W4 Mexican Hat UT U.S.A.
242 F3 Mexicanos, Lago de los l. Mex.
241 W5 Mexican Water AZ U.S.A.
242 B2 Mexico country Central America
245 H6 México Mex.
245 H6 México state Mex.
233 □O4 Mexico ME U.S.A.
236 J6 Mexico MO U.S.A.
233 I5 Mexico NY U.S.A.
229 G6 Mexico, Gulf of Mex./U.S.A.
Mexico City Mex. see México
184 B6 Mexilhoeira Grande Port.
160 G5 Meximieux France
244 F3 Mexquitic Mex.
146 J5 Mey Highland, Scotland U.K.
122 E5 Meybod Iran
122 F7 Meydān Eyn ol Baqar-e Gel Iran
122 H9 Meydanī, Ra's-e pt Iran
123 M4 Meydān Shahr Afgh.
170 F4 Meyenburg Ger.
222 C4 Meyers Chuck AK U.S.A.
232 F9 Meyersdale PA U.S.A.
215 M2 Meyerton S. Africa
199 L2 Meyitler Geçidi pass Turkey
161 H6 Meylan France
162 I4 Meymac France
123 K4 Meymaneh Afgh.
122 D5 Meymeh Iran
131 S3 Meynypil'gyno Rus. Fed.
207 H6 Meyo Centre Cameroon
161 H9 Meyrargues France
161 H10 Meyreuil France
161 J8 Meyronnes France
161 C8 Meyrueis France
162 H5 Meyssac France
161 F7 Meysse France
160 I5 Meythet France
160 F5 Meyzieu France
96 C2 Meza Myanmar
Mezada tourist site Israel see Masada
186 C5 Mezalocha, Embalse de resr Spain
182 G8 Mezas mt. Spain
245 H8 Mezcala r. Mex.
243 M9 Mezcalapa Mex.
243 M8 Mezcalapa r. Mex.
197 L7 Mezdra Bulg.
161 D10 Mèze France
161 I9 Mézel France
134 I2 Mezen' Rus. Fed.
134 I2 Mezen' r. Rus. Fed.
161 E7 Mézenc, Mont mt. France
134 H2 Mezenskaya Guba b. Rus. Fed.
160 G4 Mézériat France
139 O6 Mezha r. Rus. Fed.
98 E1 Mezhdurechensk Kemerovskaya Oblast' Rus. Fed.
134 J3 Mezhdurechensk Respublika Komi Rus. Fed.
130 H4 Mezhdurechenskiy Rus. Fed.
Mezhdurechnye Rus. Fed. see Shali
130 G2 Mezhdusharskiy, Ostrov i. Novaya Zemlya Rus. Fed.
137 P5 Mezhova Ukr.
120 H1 Mezhozernyy Rus. Fed.
137 N3 Mezhyrich Ukr.
176 C1 Meziboří Czech Rep.
179 K6 Mežica Slovenia
159 K3 Mézidon-Canon France
159 N8 Mézières-en-Brenne France
162 F3 Mézières-sur-Issoire France
161 E7 Mézilhac France
156 F8 Mézilles France
176 F1 Meziměstí Czech Rep.
163 E7 Mézin France
139 X6 Mezinovskiy Rus. Fed.
182 E7 Mezio Port.
128 C2 Mezitli Turkey
177 K5 Mezőberény Hungary
177 J4 Mezőcsát Hungary
177 H5 Mezőfalva Hungary
177 K5 Mezőgyán Hungary
177 J5 Mezőhegyes Hungary
177 J4 Mezőkeresztes Hungary
177 H5 Mezőkomárom Hungary
177 J5 Mezőkovácsháza Hungary
177 J4 Mezőkövesd Hungary
177 G4 Mezőörs Hungary
163 B7 Mézos France
177 J4 Mezőszemere Hungary
177 H5 Mezőszilas Hungary
177 J4 Mezőtárkány Hungary
177 J5 Mezőtúr Hungary
186 D6 Mezquita de Jarque Spain
244 C2 Mezquital Mex.
244 B4 Mezquital r. Mex.
244 D4 Mezquital del Oro Mex.
244 D3 Mezquitic Mex.
128 F2 Mezraaköy Turkey
138 K5 Mežvidi Latvia
191 J3 Mezzana Italy
190 G7 Mezzanego Italy
191 L3 Mezzano Italy
191 K3 Mezzocorona Italy
194 E8 Mezzojuso Sicilia Italy
190 G3 Mezzola, Lago di l. Italy
190 H3 Mezzoldo Italy
191 K3 Mezzolombardo Italy
207 H6 Mfou Cameroon
209 B6 Mfouati Congo
211 A8 Mfuwe Zambia
100 M3 Mgachi Sakhalin Rus. Fed.
195 □ Mġarr Gozo Malta
195 □ Mġarr Malta
207 G5 Mgbidi Nigeria
139 P8 Mglin Rus. Fed.
215 M7 Mgwali r. S. Africa
146 D11 Mhàil, Rubh' a' pt Scotland U.K.
213 F3 Mhangura Zimbabwe
184 H9 Mharhar, Oued r. Morocco
114 D4 Mhasvad Mahar. India
215 P2 Mhlambanyatsi Swaziland
215 P3 Mhlosheni Swaziland
215 P2 Mhlume Swaziland
215 N1 Mhluzi S. Africa
146 H8 Mhòr, Loch l. Scotland U.K.
116 E8 Mhow Madh. Prad. India
96 A4 Mi r. Myanmar
Miabhaig Scotland U.K. see Miavaig
245 H7 Miacatlan Mex.
175 L5 Miączyn Pol.
245 K9 Miahuatlán Mex.
245 K9 Miahuatlán, Sierra de mts Mex.
184 H2 Miajadas Spain
162 F4 Mialet France
174 E3 Miały Pol.
208 C2 Miaméré C.A.R.
241 V8 Miami AZ U.S.A.
231 G13 Miami FL U.S.A.
237 H7 Miami OK U.S.A.
237 E8 Miami TX U.S.A.
Miami Zimbabwe see Mwami
231 G13 Miami Beach FL U.S.A.
232 A9 Miamisburg OH U.S.A.
122 G3 Miānābād Iran
123 J8 Mianaz Pak.
106 F9 Miancaowan Qinghai China
123 O6 Mian Chanmun Pak.
107 L9 Mianchi Henan China
122 E4 Mīāndarreh Iran
122 G3 Mīāndasht Iran
122 H4 Mīāndehī Iran
122 B3 Mīāndowāb Iran
213 □J3 Miandrivazo Madag.
107 Q2 Mianduhe Nei Mongol China
122 B3 Mīāneh Iran
92 F9 Miangas i. Phil.
123 L9 Miani Hor b. Pak.
123 K5 Mianjoi Afgh.
123 N4 Mian Kalai Pak.
122 E3 Mīān Kāleh, Shebh-e Jazīreh-ye pen. Iran
108 C5 Mianmian Shan mts Sichuan/Yunnan China
108 D4 Mianning Sichuan China
123 N5 Mianwali Pak.
108 F2 Mianxian Shaanxi China
Mianyang Hubei China see Xiantao
Mianyang Shaanxi China see Mianxian
108 E3 Mianyang Sichuan China
108 E3 Mianzhu Sichuan China
101 B10 Miao Dao i. China
107 Q8 Miaodao Liedao is China
110 F4 Miao'ergou Xinjiang China
Miaogao Zhejiang China see Suichang
109 M6 Miaoli Taiwan
213 □J3 Miarinarivo Madag.
105 G2 Miasa Japan
130 H4 Miass Rus. Fed.
174 F2 Miasteckzo Krajeńskie Pol.
174 E1 Miastko Pol.
175 J4 Miastków Kościelny Pol.
175 J2 Miastkowo Pol.
146 C6 Miavaig Western Isles, Scotland U.K.
104 E3 Miboro-ko l. Japan
105 K3 Mibu Japan
105 G4 Mibu-gawa r. Japan
252 C5 Mica, Cerro de mt. Chile
222 G4 Mica Creek B.C. Can.
261 G6 Micaela Cascallares Arg.
241 V9 Mica Mountain AZ U.S.A.
108 F2 Micang Shan mts China
213 H3 Micaune Moz.
134 J2 Michaichmon' Rus. Fed.
177 K3 Michaľany Slovakia
177 I3 Michalová Slovakia
177 K3 Michalovce Slovakia
175 I5 Michałów Pol.
175 J4 Michałów Górny Pol.
175 H5 Michałowice Małopolskie Pol.
174 F5 Michałowice Opolskie Pol.
175 L2 Michałowo Pol.
223 I4 Michel Sask. Can.
171 D10 Michelau in Oberfranken Ger.
172 H3 Michelbach an der Bilz Ger.
179 J6 Micheldorf Austria
179 J4 Micheldorf in Oberösterreich Austria
172 H3 Michelfeld Ger.
220 D5 Michelson, Mount AK U.S.A.
172 G2 Michelstadt Ger.
171 H6 Michendorf Ger.
Micheng Yunnan China see Midu
247 I4 Miches Dom. Rep.
226 F3 Michigamme Lake MI U.S.A.
226 F3 Michigamme Reservoir MI U.S.A.
236 K2 Michigan state U.S.A.
226 G6 Michigan, Lake MI/WI U.S.A.
230 D5 Michigan City IN U.S.A.
208 B2 Michika Nigeria
114 G3 Michinberi Chhattisgarh India
224 C4 Michipicoten Bay Ont. Can.
224 C4 Michipicoten Island Ont. Can.
224 C4 Michipicoten River Ont. Can.
244 E7 Michoacán state Mex.
175 K4 Michów Pol.
Michurin Bulg. see Tsarevo
135 H5 Michurinsk Rus. Fed.
149 M4 Mickleton Durham, England U.K.
151 I3 Mickleton Gloucestershire, England U.K.
242 □Q11 Mico r. Nic.
245 H3 Micos Mex.
247 □3 Micoud St Lucia
266 E5 Micronesia is Pacific Ocean
91 L6 Micronesia, Federated States of country N. Pacific Ocean
197 K3 Micula Romania
95 G3 Midai i. Indon.
207 G2 Midal well Niger
223 K5 Midale Sask. Can.
264 F4 Mid-Atlantic Ridge sea feature Atlantic Ocean
146 K4 Midbea Orkney, Scotland U.K.
165 H6 Middelbeers Neth.
214 D8 Middelberg Pass S. Africa
164 E5 Middelburg Neth.
215 J7 Middelburg Eastern Cape S. Africa
215 N1 Middelburg Mpumalanga S. Africa
142 F6 Middelfart Denmark
164 F5 Middelharnis Neth.
165 C6 Middelkerke Belgium
214 E7 Middelpos S. Africa
164 K2 Middelstum Neth.
213 E5 Middelwit S. Africa
164 G3 Middenbeemster Neth.
164 H3 Middenmeer Neth.
238 D6 Middle Alkali Lake CA U.S.A.
267 M5 Middle America Trench sea feature N. Pacific Ocean
115 M6 Middle Andaman i. Andaman & Nicobar Is India
Middle Atlas mts Morocco see Moyen Atlas
151 J4 Middle Barton Oxfordshire, England U.K.
225 J3 Middle Bay Que. Can.
82 □2 Middle Beach b. Lord Howe I. Austr.
233 O7 Middleboro MA U.S.A.
230 G6 Middlebourne WV U.S.A.
227 Q9 Middleburg PA U.S.A.
232 H10 Middleburg VA U.S.A.
233 K6 Middleburgh NY U.S.A.
235 I1 Middlebury CT U.S.A.
226 I8 Middlebury IN U.S.A.
233 L4 Middlebury VT U.S.A.
246 H3 Middle Caicos i. Turks and Caicos Is
237 E10 Middle Concho r. TX U.S.A.
Middle Congo country Africa see Congo
85 H4 Middle Creek r. Qld Austr.
234 E2 Middle Creek r. PA U.S.A.
235 J1 Middlefield CT U.S.A.
235 J1 Middle Haddam CT U.S.A.
149 N5 Middleham North Yorkshire, England U.K.
185 □ Middle Hill Gibraltar
235 G1 Middle Hope NY U.S.A.
216 □2c Middle Island i. Tristan da Cunha S. Atlantic Ocean
235 J3 Middle Island NY U.S.A.
236 G5 Middle Loup r. NE U.S.A.
150 H6 Middlemarsh Dorset, England U.K.
85 L7 Middlemount Qld Austr.
86 □1 Middle Point Christmas I.
232 C9 Middleport OH U.S.A.
234 C3 Middleport PA U.S.A.
236 I5 Middle Raccoon r. IA U.S.A.
149 Q7 Middle Rasen Lincolnshire, England U.K.
225 K3 Middle Ridge Wildlife Reserve nature res. Nfld and Lab. Can.
234 C6 Middle River MD U.S.A.
232 B12 Middlesboro KY U.S.A.
149 O4 Middlesbrough Middlesbrough, England U.K.
149 O4 Middlesbrough admin. div. England U.K.
243 O9 Middlesex Belize
246 □ Middlesex reg. Jamaica
232 H6 Middlesex NY U.S.A.
234 A4 Middlesex PA U.S.A.
235 J1 Middlesex County county CT U.S.A.
235 G4 Middlesex County county NJ U.S.A.
149 N5 Middlesmoor North Yorkshire, England U.K.
Middle Strait Andaman & Nicobar Is India see Andaman Strait
85 H7 Middleton Qld Austr.
225 H4 Middleton N.S. Can.
215 J8 Middleton S. Africa
149 M6 Middleton Greater Manchester, England U.K.
151 M2 Middleton Norfolk, England U.K.
232 A5 Middleton MI U.S.A.
226 E6 Middleton WI U.S.A.
151 J3 Middleton Cheney Northamptonshire, England U.K.
149 M4 Middleton in Teesdale Durham, England U.K.
151 K6 Middleton-on-Sea West Sussex, England U.K.
149 P6 Middleton-on-the-Wolds East Riding of Yorkshire, England U.K.
77 F4 Middleton Reef Austr.
151 J4 Middleton Stoney Oxfordshire, England U.K.
147 I4 Middletown Northern Ireland U.K.
240 J3 Middletown CA U.S.A.
235 J1 Middletown CT U.S.A.
234 D6 Middletown DE U.S.A.
232 H9 Middletown MD U.S.A.
235 G4 Middletown NJ U.S.A.
233 K7 Middletown NY U.S.A.
232 A9 Middletown OH U.S.A.
227 R9 Middletown PA U.S.A.
232 G9 Middletown VA U.S.A.
226 I7 Middleville MI U.S.A.
233 K5 Middleville NY U.S.A.
149 M7 Middlewich Cheshire, England U.K.
81 C12 Mid Dome mt. South I. N.Z.
204 D2 Midelt Morocco
80 I6 Midhirst North I. N.Z.
210 E2 Midhisho well Somalia
151 K6 Midhurst West Sussex, England U.K.
124 F7 Mīdī Yemen
163 I9 Midi, Canal du France
163 E10 Midi de Bigorre, Pic du mt. France
163 D10 Midi d'Ossau, Pic du mt. France
265 J5 Mid-Indian Basin sea feature Indian Ocean
265 I6 Mid-Indian Ridge sea feature Indian Ocean
161 A8 Midi-Pyrénées admin. reg. France
224 E4 Midland Ont. Can.
241 R8 Midland CA U.S.A.
227 J6 Midland MI U.S.A.
236 E3 Midland SD U.S.A.
237 E9 Midland TX U.S.A.
87 C11 Midland Junction W.A. Austr.
213 F3 Midlands prov. Zimbabwe
147 F9 Midleton Ireland
146 J11 Midlothian admin. div. Scotland U.K.
237 G9 Midlothian TX U.S.A.

Column 1

232 H11 Midlothian VA U.S.A.
168 G3 Midlum Ger.
215 O5 Midmar Nature Reserve S. Africa
227 M5 Midnapore W. Bengal India see Medinipur
213 □J4 Midongy Atsimo Madag.
105 K4 Midori Japan
103 H14 Midori-gawa r. Japan
163 C8 Midou r. France
163 C8 Midouze r. France
266 F4 Mid-Pacific Mountains sea feature N. Pacific Ocean
215 M1 Midrand S. Africa
92 E8 Midsayap Mindanao Phil.
150 H5 Midsomer Norton Bath and North East Somerset, England U.K.
140 I5 Midsund Norway
108 C6 Midu Yunnan China
113 □2 Midu i. Addu Atoll Maldives
238 F4 Midvale ID U.S.A.
241 U1 Midway Oman see Thamarīt
75 H2 Midway Is. N. Pacific Ocean
87 G7 Midway Well W.A. Austr.
238 K5 Midwest WY U.S.A.
238 K5 Midwest City OK U.S.A.
164 L2 Midwolda Neth.
124 B2 Midyan reg. Saudi Arabia
127 J5 Midyat Turkey
Midye Turkey see Kıyıköy
146 □N1 Mid Yell Shetland, Scotland U.K.
197 K7 Midzhur mt. Bulg./Yugo.
103 I14 Mie Japan
104 D7 Mie pref. Japan
175 I5 Miechów Pol.
177 L1 Mieczka r. Pol.
178 D5 Mieders Austria
183 R6 Miedes Spain
174 C2 Miedwie, Jezioro i. Pol.
175 I5 Miedziana Góra r. Pol.
174 D3 Miedzichowo Pol.
175 K3 Miedzna Pol.
175 H6 Miedzna Pol.
174 G5 Miedzno Pol.
174 F4 Miedzybórz Pol.
174 D3 Miedzychód Pol.
174 E5 Miedzylesie Pol.
175 K4 Miedzyrzec Podlaski Pol.
174 D3 Miedzyrzecz Pol.
167 I3 Miedzyrzecza Warty i Widawki, Park Krajobrazowy Pol.
174 C2 Miedzyzdroje Pol.
141 S6 Miehikkälä Fin.
169 E10 Miehlen Ger.
175 J6 Miejsce Piastowe Pol.
174 E4 Miejska Górka Pol.
174 E4 Miékinie Pol.
163 E9 Miélan France
161 G8 Miélandre, Montagne de mt. France
175 J5 Mielec Pol.
170 K4 Mielęcin Pol.
174 F3 Mieleszyn Pol.
168 J2 Mielkendorf Ger.
175 L3 Mielnik Pol.
174 E1 Mielno Pol.
211 C7 Miembwe Tanz.
178 D5 Mieming Austria
178 C5 Mieminger Gebirge mts Austria
175 G3 Mień r. Pol.
143 K5 Miena i. Sweden
83 K9 Miena Tas. Austr.
209 C9 Mienga Angola
209 F8 Mienga Zambia
109 N6 Mienhua Yü i. Taiwan
183 M2 Miera r. Spain
140 S2 Mieraslompolo Fin.
Mieraslvuoppal Fin. see Mieraslompolo
197 N4 Miercurea-Ciuc Romania
182 I2 Mieres Spain
Mieres del Camín Spain see Mieres
Mieres del Camino Spain see Mieres
165 I6 Mierlo Neth.
140 Q2 Mierojávri Norway
174 E5 Mieroszów Pol.
163 H6 Miers r. France
244 C2 Mier y Noriega Mex.
175 I5 Mierzawa r. Pol.
170 J4 Mierzyn Pol.
172 C3 Miesau Ger.
173 L6 Miesbach Ger.
173 G3 Miescisko Pol.
173 D3 Miesenbach Ger.
210 D2 Mi'ēso Eth.
171 D6 Mieste Ger.
171 D6 Miesterhorst Ger.
173 F3 Mieszkowice Pol.
174 C3 Mieszkowice Pol.
172 H5 Mietingen Ger.
141 P6 Mietoinen Fin.
160 J4 Mieussy France
182 G6 Mieza Spain
124 E6 Mifah Saudi Arabia
232 C8 Mifflin OH U.S.A.
227 Q9 Mifflinburg PA U.S.A.
232 H8 Mifflintown PA U.S.A.
234 C2 Mifflinville PA U.S.A.
111 □J2 Mifune-zaki pt Japan
106 J9 Migang Shan mt. China
Gansu/Ningxia China
215 J2 Migdol S. Africa
156 G8 Migennes France
122 H6 Mighān Iran
117 O5 Miging Arun. Prad. India
191 L6 Migiondo Italy
190 I8 Migliarino-San Rossore-Massaciuccoli, Parco Naturale di nature res. Italy
191 L6 Migliaro Italy
195 K2 Miglionico Italy
162 E2 Mignaloux-Beauvoir France
193 L5 Mignano Monte Lungo Italy
192 H3 Mignone r. Italy
160 I3 Mignovillard France
111 J10 Migriggyangzham Co i. Qinghai China
225 H3 Miguasha, Parc de nature res. N.B. Can.
245 K7 Miguel Alemán Mex.
245 K7 Miguel Alemán, Presa resr Mex.
254 E3 Miguel Alves Brazil
244 D1 Miguel Auza Mex.
254 E4 Miguel Calmon Brazil
242 □S13 Miguel de la Borda Panama
245 K8 Miguel de la Madrid, Presa resr Mex.
183 N9 Miguel Esteban Spain
261 I4 Miguelete Uru.
245 H3 Miguel Hidalgo Mex.
242 E4 Miguel Hidalgo, Presa resr Mex.
257 F3 Miguel Pereira Brazil
261 F5 Miguel Riglos Arg.
185 L3 Miguelturra Spain
138 M6 Miguhino Rus. Fed.
96 B5 Migyaunye Myanmar
197 N6 Mihăileşti Romania
176 G5 Mihald Hungary
199 L2 Mihalgazi Turkey
176 G4 Mihályi Hungary
103 M14 Mihama Aichi Japan
104 B4 Mihama Fukui Japan
104 D8 Mihama Japan
103 K12 Mihara Hiroshima Japan
104 A7 Mihara Hyōgo Japan
105 J6 Mihara-yama vol. Japan
107 P8 Mi He r. China
Mihijam W. Bengal India see Chittaranjan
117 K8 Mihijam Jharkhand India
114 C8 Mihintale Sri Lanka
169 J8 Mihla Ger.
105 L4 Miho Japan
103 K11 Miho-wan b. Japan
211 C7 Mihumo Chini Tanz.
183 K8 Mijares r. Spain
187 D7 Mijares r. Spain
185 J7 Mijas Spain
185 J7 Mijas mt. Spain
164 G4 Mijdrecht Neth.
105 J1 Mijōga-take mt. Japan
160 I4 Mijoux France

Column 2

102 S3 Mikasa Japan
136 G1 Mikashevichy Belarus
104 C4 Mikata Japan
104 C4 Mikata-ko i. Japan
104 C4 Mikawa Japan
104 F6 Mikawa-wan b. Japan
104 F6 Mikawa-wan Kokutei-kōen park Japan
177 K4 Mikepércs Hungary
Mikhailovka Rus. Fed. see Paneyevo
139 W6 Mikhalevo Rus. Fed.
138 U7 Mikhalki Belarus
138 K8 Mikhanavichy Belarus
Mikha Tskhakaia Georgia see Senaki
87 D11 Mikhaylov Georgia
84 C1 Mikhaylov Rus. Fed.
84 E2 Mikhaylov Rus. Fed.
87 D11 Mikhaylov Rus. Fed.
192 B7 Mikhaylov Italy
114 H9 Mikhaylovgrad Bulg. see Montana
139 W7 Mikhaylov Rus. Fed.
121 Q1 Mikhaylovka Pavlodarskaya Oblast' Kazakh.
100 F4 Mikhaylovka Zhambylskaya Oblast' Kazakh. see Sarykemer
100 A3 Mikhaylovka Amurskaya Oblast' Rus. Fed.
137 O1 Mikhaylovka Chitinskaya Oblast' Rus. Fed.
100 H7 Mikhaylovka Kurskaya Oblast' Rus. Fed.
135 H6 Mikhaylovka Primorskiy Kray Rus. Fed.
226 B9 Mikhaylovka Tul'skaya Oblast' Rus. Fed.
187 D9 Mikhaylovka Volgogradskaya Oblast' Rus. Fed.
137 T4 Mikhaylovka Kimovsk
78 □5 Mikhaylovka Volgogradskaya Oblast' Rus. Fed.
121 R2 Mikhaylovka Altayskiy Kray Rus. Fed.
Malinovoye Ozero
121 R2 Mikhaylovka Altayskiy Kray Rus. Fed.
Mikhaylovka Rus. Fed. see Shpakovskoye
263 F2 Mikhaylov Island Antarctica
139 U6 Mikhnevo Rus. Fed.
128 C9 Mikhrot Timna Israel
104 A6 Miki Japan
224 B3 Mikines tourist site Greece see Mycenae
231 G9 Mikir Hills India
117 N6 Mikir Hills India
104 D8 Mikkeli Fin.
141 S6 Mikkeli Fin.
141 S6 Mikkelin mlk Fin.
222 H3 Mikkwa r. Alta Can.
179 M6 Miklavž Slovenia
174 G5 Mikoláw Pol.
263 F2 Mikolajki Pomorskie Pol.
174 G1 Mikolówka Pol.
198 E1 Mikropoli Greece
174 F4 Mikro Vermio Greece
171 J9 Mikulasovice Czech Rep.
134 I2 Mikulkin, Mys c. Rus. Fed.
176 F3 Mikulov Czech Rep.
178 G1 Mikulovice Czech Rep.
211 C6 Mikumi Tanz.
211 C6 Mikumi National Park Tanz.
104 E6 Mikuni Japan
104 E6 Mikuni-sanmyaku mts Japan
105 I2 Mikuni-yama mt. Japan
105 I4 Mikura-jima i. Japan
205 G1 Mila Alg.
236 I3 Miladhunmadulu Atoll Maldives
114 C9 Miladhunmadulu Atoll Maldives
254 F3 Milagres Brazil
260 E2 Milagro Arg.
250 B5 Milagro Ecuador
183 M5 Milagros Spain
175 I1 Milakowo Pol.
116 H4 Milam Uttaranchal India
Milan Italy see Milano
227 K7 Milan MI U.S.A.
236 I5 Milan MO U.S.A.
232 C7 Milan OH U.S.A.
209 C7 Milando Angola
209 C7 Milando, Reserva Especial do nature res. Angola
82 G6 Milang S.A. Austr.
213 G3 Milanga Madag.
190 G5 Milano Italy
190 G5 Milano prov. Italy
190 F4 Milano (Malpensa) airport Italy
213 □K2 Milanoa Madag.
191 M7 Milano Marittima Italy
175 K4 Milanów Pol.
175 I3 Milanówek Pol.
191 E11 Milanville PA U.S.A.
197 M4 Milaş Turkey
199 I5 Milas Turkey
136 G2 Milashavichy Belarus
138 P8 Milašavichy Rus. Fed.
138 I9 Milavidy Belarus
195 I7 Milazzo Sicilia Italy
195 I7 Milazzo, Capo di c. Sicilia Italy
195 I7 Milazzo, Golfo di b. Sicilia Italy
236 G3 Milbank SD U.S.A.
150 H6 Milborne Port Somerset, England U.K.
150 H6 Milborne St Andrew Dorset, England U.K.
233 □R4 Milbridge ME U.S.A.
170 E5 Milde r. Ger.
151 N3 Mildenhall Suffolk, England U.K.
227 R8 Mildred PA U.S.A.
168 H2 Mildstedt Ger.
83 I6 Mildura Vic. Austr.
108 B6 Mile Yunnan China
235 H2 Milé Eth.
148 F4 Milebush Northern Ireland U.K.
151 N4 Mile End Essex, England U.K.
151 G5 Miléepol Pol.
177 D9 Milejczyce Pol.
183 Q6 Milejewo Pol.
175 I1 Milejów Pol.
194 F9 Milena Sicilia Italy
85 M9 Miles Qld Austr.
232 H8 Milesburg PA U.S.A.
238 L3 Miles City MT U.S.A.
210 D2 Mile Serdo Reserve nature res. Eth.
176 C1 Miletín Czech Rep.
147 F7 Milestone Ireland
171 P3 Miletín Ger.
193 M5 Miletto, Monte mt. Italy
87 D9 Milford W.A. Austr.
176 D2 Milevsko Czech Rep.
149 M2 Milfield Northumberland, England U.K.
184 D5 Milfontes Port.
147 E8 Milford Cork Ireland
147 D3 Milford Donegal Ireland
151 K5 Milford Surrey, England U.K.
235 I2 Milford CT U.S.A.
233 □R4 Milford DE U.S.A.
232 B12 Milford IL U.S.A.
233 N6 Milford MA U.S.A.
231 J10 Milford MD U.S.A.
234 C5 Milford MI U.S.A.
233 O4 Milford NE U.S.A.
233 N5 Milford NH U.S.A.
234 E5 Milford NJ U.S.A.
232 D7 Milford OH U.S.A.
232 H8 Milford PA U.S.A.
238 F6 Milford UT U.S.A.
232 B10 Milford VA U.S.A.
150 B4 Milford Haven Pembrokeshire, Wales U.K.
236 G6 Milford Lake KS U.S.A.

Column 3

151 I6 Milford on Sea Hampshire, England U.K.
81 B11 Milford Sound South I. N.Z.
81 B11 Milford Sound inlet South I. N.Z.
234 E4 Milford Square PA U.S.A.
85 H5 Milgarra Qld Austr.
87 E8 Milgun W.A. Austr.
Milh, Bahr al Iraq see Razāzah, Buhayrat ar
182 G5 Milicz Pol.
161 E9 Milhaud France
174 F4 Milicz r. Pol.
84 C1 Milikapiti N.T. Austr.
84 D1 Milikapiti N.T. Austr.
84 E2 Milingimbi N.T. Austr.
78 □5 Milii Vanuatu
192 B7 Militello Sardegna Italy
194 H9 Militello in Val di Catania Sicilia Italy
158 B5 Milizac France
179 M7 Miljana Croatia
238 K2 Milk r. MT U.S.A.
203 F5 Milk, Wadi el watercourse Sudan
171 J8 Milkel Ger.
175 J2 Miłki Pol.
226 G6 Milwaukee WI U.S.A.
174 E4 Milewko Pol.
233 H5 Milk River Alta Can.
164 I5 Mill Neth.
146 Millaa Millaa Qld Austr.
226 B9 Millard MO U.S.A.
187 D9 Millares Spain
169 K10 Millars New Prov. Bahamas
161 C8 Millau France
175 I5 Millaville r. Pol.
150 D7 Millbrook Cornwall, England U.K.
231 D9 Millbrook AL U.S.A.
233 L7 Millbrook NY U.S.A.
147 I7 Mill Buie Hill Scotland U.K.
224 C5 Mill City OR U.S.A.
232 F10 Mill Creek WV U.S.A.
240 J1 Mill Creek r. PA U.S.A.
234 C5 Mill Creek r. PA U.S.A.
235 J1 Milldale CT U.S.A.
231 F9 Milledgeville GA U.S.A.
226 C5 Milledgeville IL U.S.A.
236 I2 Mille Lacs lakes MN U.S.A.
224 B3 Mille Lacs, Lac des I. Ont. Can.
231 G9 Mille Lacs Lac des I. Ont. Can.
227 M4 Miller Peak AZ U.S.A.
135 H6 Millerovo Rus. Fed.
241 V10 Miller Peak AZ U.S.A.
227 J4 Millersburg MI U.S.A.
232 D9 Millersburg OH U.S.A.
227 R9 Millersburg PA U.S.A.
232 I11 Millers Creek NC U.S.A.
233 M6 Millers Falls MA U.S.A.
81 D12 Millers Flat South I. N.Z.
234 C9 Millersport OH U.S.A.
234 B6 Millersville MD U.S.A.
234 C5 Millersville PA U.S.A.
233 L7 Millerton NY U.S.A.
240 M4 Millerton Lake CA U.S.A.
234 D4 Mill Point Scotland U.K.
162 H4 Millevaches France
162 H4 Millevaches, Plateau de France
147 I4 Millford Northern Ireland U.K.
85 J2 Millard Antarctica
232 H7 Mill Hall PA U.S.A.
234 F5 Millhurst NJ U.S.A.
82 H7 Millicent S.A. Austr.
157 J7 Millières France
86 H5 Millijiddie Aboriginal Reserve W.A. Austr.
164 J5 Millingen aan de Rijn Neth.
234 D6 Millington MD U.S.A.
227 K6 Millington MI U.S.A.
237 K8 Millington TN U.S.A.
281 Mill Inlet Antarctica
262 □2 Mill Island Antarctica
252 C5 Millit, Cerro mt. Bol.
263 G2 Mill Island Antarctica
221 K3 Mill Island Nunavut Can.
147 K3 Millisle Northern Ireland U.K.
258 G4 Millmerran Qld Austr.
234 A3 Millmont PA U.S.A.
149 K5 Millom Cumbria, England U.K.
146 G11 Millport North Ayrshire, Scotland U.K.
234 F2 Millrift PA U.S.A.
233 J10 Millsboro DE U.S.A.
85 I7 Mills Creek watercourse Qld Austr.
222 F2 Mills Lake N.W.T. Can.
179 I6 Millstatt Austria
179 I6 Millstätter See I. Austria
226 D5 Millston WI U.S.A.
232 C11 Millstone WV U.S.A.
232 D10 Millstone WV U.S.A.
234 F3 Millstone r. NJ U.S.A.
86 D6 Millstream r. W.A. Austr.
86 D6 Millstream-Chichester National Park W.A. Austr.
147 D5 Millstreet Ireland
225 H2 Milltown N.B. Can.
147 E4 Milltown Cavan Ireland
147 E5 Milltown Galway Ireland
147 B7 Milltown Kerry Ireland
148 D7 Milltown Kildare Ireland
147 I4 Milltown Northern Ireland U.K.
147 D7 Milltown Malbay Ireland
146 K8 Milltown of Kildrummy Aberdeenshire, Scotland U.K.
146 K7 Milltown of Rothiemay Moray, Scotland U.K.
85 H5 Millungera Qld Austr.
215 K1 Millvale S. Africa
240 J4 Mill Valley CA U.S.A.
233 □R2 Millville N.B. Can.
126 I5 Millville MA U.S.A.
148 E5 Millville PA U.S.A.
235 H2 Millwood AR U.S.A.
257 D7 Millwood Lake AR U.S.A.
156 I7 Milly-la-Forêt France
160 F4 Milly-Lamartine France
87 D9 Milly Milly W.A. Austr.
183 O8 Milmarcos Spain
170 I4 Milmersdorf Ger.
175 I7 Milmorot Belgium
146 J10 Milnathort Perth and Kinross, Scotland U.K.
146 I10 Milngavie East Dunbartonshire, Scotland U.K.
149 M6 Milnrow Greater Manchester, England U.K.
149 L5 Milnthorpe Cumbria, England U.K.
206 C4 Milo r. Guinea
195 I8 Milo Sicilia Italy
233 O3 Milo ME U.S.A.
174 E2 Miłocice Pol.
100 I7 Milogradovo Rus. Fed.
191 O5 Miloli'i HI U.S.A.
240 □F14 Miloli'i HI U.S.A.
260 E6 Milos i. Greece
199 H6 Milos i. Greece
226 B7 Milton IA U.S.A.
237 F9 Milton FL U.S.A.
174 F3 Mitoslaw Pol.
204 D1 Mitoud well Alg.
146 C8 Milovaig Highland, Scotland U.K.
191 K6 Milovice Czech Rep.
137 T4 Milove Ukr.
171 K10 Milovice Czech Rep.
171 F5 Milow Brandenburg Ger.
170 F4 Milow Mecklenburg-Vorpommern Ger.
175 H6 Miłówka Pol.
161 B10 Milpa r. Italy
240 K4 Milpitas CA U.S.A.
232 H8 Milroy PA U.S.A.

Column 4

173 N3 Miltach Ger.
172 G2 Miltenberg Ger.
227 O6 Milton Ont. Can.
81 D13 Milton South I. N.Z.
146 G3 Milton Highland, Scotland U.K.
146 I9 Milton Perth and Kinross, Scotland U.K.
233 J10 Milton DE U.S.A.
231 D10 Milton FL U.S.A.
233 □O5 Milton NH U.S.A.
233 H4 Milton VT U.S.A.
234 B2 Milton PA U.S.A.
233 L4 Milton VT U.S.A.
232 C10 Milton WV U.S.A.
150 D6 Milton Abbot Devon, England U.K.
238 E4 Milton-Freewater OR U.S.A.
151 K3 Milton Keynes Milton Keynes, England U.K.
151 K3 Milton Keynes admin. div. England U.K.
170 H2 Miltzow Ger.
109 I4 Miluo Hunan China
227 N6 Milverton Ont. Can.
150 F5 Milverton Somerset, England U.K.
226 G6 Milwaukee WI U.S.A.
264 E4 Milwaukee Deep sea feature Caribbean Sea
120 I3 Mily Kazakh.
121 P3 Milybulakk Kazakh.
135 H6 Milyutinskaya Rus. Fed.
169 C10 Milz Ger.
163 C6 Milz r. Ger.
208 C4 Mimbelly Congo
239 K10 Mimbres watercourse NM U.S.A.
183 N2 Mimetiz Spain
82 D2 Mimili S.A. Austr.
114 F8 Mimisal Tamil Nadu India
163 B7 Mimizan France
163 B7 Mimizan-Plage France
176 D1 Mimoň Czech Rep.
208 A5 Mimongo Gabon
257 G4 Mimoso do Sul Brazil
103 L11 Mimuro-yama mt. Japan
243 I4 Mina r. Mex.
240 N3 Mina NV U.S.A.
238 L4 Mina NV U.S.A.
252 C3 Mina, Nevada mt. Peru
125 I1 Mīnā' 'Abd Allāh Kuwait
122 D8 Mināb Iran
122 D8 Mināb r. Iran
123 M6 Mina Bazar Pak.
104 B8 Minabe Japan
104 B8 Minabe-gawa r. Japan
260 C2 Mina Clavero Arg.
254 C5 Minaçu Brazil
184 E5 Mina de São Domingos Port.
223 L4 Minago r. Man. Can.
93 B3 Minahasa, Semenanjung pen. Indon.
Minahasa Peninsula Indon. see Minahasa, Semenanjung
125 I3 Mina Jebel Ali U.A.E.
105 I2 Minakami Japan
232 D8 Minaker B.C. Can. see Prophet River
128 F2 Minakh Syria
223 M5 Minaki Ont. Can.
104 D6 Minakuchi Japan
208 D4 Minami Côte d'Ivoire
104 J4 Minami Japan
84 E3 Minamata Japan
103 C14 Minamata Japan
105 J5 Minami-Arupusu Kokuritsu-kōen nat. park Japan
105 K6 Minami-Bōsō Kokutei-kōen park Japan
99 N6 Minamichita Japan
104 C4 Minami-Daitō-jima i. Japan
109 L5 Minami Japan
84 D1 Minami-Iō-jima vol. Kazan-rettō Japan
105 I6 Minamiizu Japan
105 J3 Minami-kawara Japan
105 L3 Minamiōminami Japan
105 L2 Minamiasu Japan
105 H5 Minamishima-gun Japan
105 I3 Min'an Hunan China see Longshan
104 D6 Minano Japan
146 F10 Minard Argyll and Bute, Scotland U.K.
105 J3 Minas Cuba
93 H3 Minas Sumatera Indon.
255 D5 Minas Uru.
243 O10 Minas, Sierra de las mts Guat.
127 N9 Mīnā' Sa'ūd Kuwait
225 H4 Minas Basin b. N.S. Can.
236 F1 Minas Channel N.S. Can.
246 D2 Minas de Corrales Uru.
87 C7 Minas de Matahambre Cuba
184 F5 Minas de Riotinto Spain
256 D3 Minas Gerais state Brazil
257 F2 Minas Novas Brazil
185 P4 Minateda Spain
245 M7 Minatitlán Colima Mex.
245 N9 Minatitlán Veracruz Mex.
103 □2 Minatogawa Japan
96 B4 Minbu Myanmar
96 A4 Minbya Myanmar
123 D6 Minchinábad Pak.
259 B9 Minchinmávida vol. Chile
146 J11 Minch Moor hill Scotland U.K.
191 J5 Mincio r. Italy
129 H6 Mincivan Azer.
92 E8 Mindanao i. Phil.
92 E8 Mindanao r. Mindanao Phil.
82 H6 Mindarie S.A. Austr.
96 A4 Mindat Sakan Myanmar
192 I1 Mindel r. Ger.
173 I5 Mindelheim Ger.
206 □ Mindelo Cape Verde
182 C6 Mindelo Port.
172 E3 Mindelstetten Ger.
227 R4 Minden Ont. Can.
168 H3 Minden Ger.
237 E9 Minden LA U.S.A.
236 F5 Minden NE U.S.A.
240 O2 Minden NV U.S.A.
227 L6 Minden City MI U.S.A.

Column 5

172 E3 Minfeld Ger.
111 F8 Minfeng Xinjiang China
209 E7 Minga Dem. Rep. Congo
211 A8 Minga Zambia
129 I5 Mingäçevir Azer.
129 I5 Mingäçevir Su Anbarı
208 D3 Mingan C.A.R.
225 I3 Mingan, Îles de is Que. Can.
193 O7 Mingardo r. Italy
82 H5 Mingary S.A. Austr.
120 J6 Mingbulak Uzbek.
Mingçevir Uzbek.
Mingçaurskoye Vodokhranilishche resr Azer.
see Mingäçevir Su Anbarı
85 K5 Mingela Qld Austr.
87 C10 Mingenew W.A. Austr.
84 F6 Mingera Creek watercourse Qld Austr.
Mingfeng Hubei China see Yuan'an
109 L2 Mingguang Anhui China
96 B3 Mingin Myanmar
96 B3 Mingin Range mts Myanmar
148 C6 Mingulay i. Scotland U.K.
96 A9 Mingun Myanmar
213 I2 Mingxi Moz.
109 K5 Mingxi Fujian China
Mingshan Chongqing China see Fengdu
108 D3 Mingshan Sichuan China
110 E5 Mingshui Gansu China
100 D5 Mingshui Heilong. China
111 B8 Mingteke Xinjiang China
186 C6 Mínguez, Puerto de pass Spain
146 A9 Mingulay i. Scotland U.K.
96 A3 Mingun Myanmar
109 K5 Mingxi Fujian China
108 E7 Mingxin Hebei China see Weixian
111 B8 Mingzhou Shaanxi China see Suide
110 E5 Minhe Jiangxi China see Jinxian
112 J4 Minhe Qinghai China
96 B5 Minhla Magwe Myanmar
96 B6 Minhla Pegu Myanmar
182 D5 Minho reg. Port.
109 L5 Minhou Fujian China
158 H4 Minhou r. W.A. Austr.
260 E2 Miniac-Morvan France
191 J5 Minico, Parco del park Italy
87 D7 Minilya r. W.A. Austr.
87 D7 Minilya W.A. Austr.
184 D3 Minilla, Embalse de la resr Spain
87 G10 Minilya, Lake salt flat W.A. Austr.
238 G5 Minidoka Internment National Monument nat. park ID U.S.A.
223 L4 Minago r. Man. Can.
179 N6 Minihof-Liebau Austria
138 E6 Minija r. Lith.
184 G5 Minilla, Embalse de la resr Spain
163 I6 Minion-de-Guyenne France
179 N6 Minihof-Liebau Austria
123 N5 Minin Shah Pak.
123 N5 Minin Shah Pak.
110 I7 Miran Xinjiang China
260 A5 Minian Côte d'Ivoire
208 D4 Minianka Côte d'Ivoire
224 B3 Miniss Lake Ont. Can.
183 P6 Ministra r. Spain
183 O6 Ministra, Sierra mts Spain
240 I1 Ministkaya Rus. Fed.
139 R1 Minjan Sichuan China see Mabian
108 E4 Min Jiang r. Sichuan China
109 L5 Min Jiang r. China
84 D1 Minjilang N.T. Austr.
168 D2 Minkädär Azer.
Min-Kush Kyrg. see Ming-Kush
106 C2 Minle Gansu China
207 G4 Minna Nigeria
261 I1 Minna Bluff pt Antarctica
102 □1 Minna-jima i. Okinawa Japan
102 □B22 Minna-shima i. Okinawa Japan
141 M6 Minne Sweden
226 G5 Minneapolis KS U.S.A.
236 G6 Minneapolis MN U.S.A.
223 L5 Minnedosa Man. Can.
232 F10 Minnehaha Springs WV U.S.A.
237 I6 Minnesota r. MN U.S.A.
236 I3 Minnesota state U.S.A.
236 G2 Minnesota City MN U.S.A.
236 F1 Minnewaukan ND U.S.A.
87 C7 Min-ngan Myanmar
111 I8 Minningaff Dumfries and Galloway, Scotland U.K.
82 E5 Minnipa S.A. Austr.
85 J6 Minnitaki Lake Ont. Can.
104 E4 Mino Japan
104 E4 Mino r. Port./Spain
105 H5 Minobu Japan
105 H5 Minobu-san mt. Japan
104 D4 Mino-Mikawa-kōgen reg. Japan
261 H2 Miñones Arg.
90 G1 Minong WI U.S.A.
226 B6 Minonk IL U.S.A.
168 I6 Minor, Isola i. Italy
192 I1 Minore Japan
105 L3 Minori Japan
161 F7 Minot France
123 I7 Minot ND U.S.A.
95 M2 Minqār, Ghadīr imp. l. Syria
109 L5 Minqing Fujian China
183 O2 Minquadale DE U.S.A.
107 N9 Minquan Henan China
106 B3 Minsen Ger.
108 D7 Min Shan mts Sichuan China
96 B2 Minsin Myanmar
138 K9 Minsk Belarus
138 K9 Minskaya Oblast' admin. div. Belarus see Minskaya Voblasts'
138 K9 Minskaya Voblasts' admin. div. Belarus
175 J3 Mińsk Mazowiecki Pol.
138 K9 Minsk Oblast admin. div. Belarus see Minskaya Voblasts'
150 G5 Minsterley Shropshire, England U.K.
207 I5 Minta Cameroon
108 D7 Mintaka Pass China/Jammu and Kashmir
110 I4 Mintang Qinghai China
146 M7 Mintlaw Aberdeenshire, Scotland U.K.
256 B2 Minturno Brazil
193 L5 Minturno Italy
191 O1 Minturno Italy see Minturno
122 F3 Mīnūdasht Iran
122 C5 Minūf Egypt
125 J3 Minūr Egypt
126 C7 Minrah Egypt
191 J5 Minturo mts Spain
121 I1 Minusinsk Rus. Fed.
208 B4 Minvoul Gabon
109 J5 Minxian Gansu China
108 D3 Minya Konka mt. Sichuan China see Gongga Shan

Column 6

134 L5 Minyar Rus. Fed.
83 J7 Minyip Vic. Austr.
96 B3 Minywa Myanmar
117 P6 Minzong Arun. Prad. India
227 J5 Mio MI U.S.A.
196 I2 Mionica Serbia
160 F5 Mionnay France
160 F5 Mions France
84 G8 Mipia, Lake salt flat Qld Austr.
110 H5 Miquan Xinjiang China
224 E3 Miquelon Que. Can.
225 J4 Miquelon i. St Pierre and Miquelon
245 H2 Miquihuana Mex.
138 J8 Mir Belarus
183 C5 Mira r. Col.
191 M5 Mira Italy
182 C8 Mira Port.
184 B5 Mira r. Port.
183 R9 Mira r. Spain
182 H5 Mira, Sierra de mts Spain
161 I9 Mira France
233 K3 Mirabel Que. Can.
163 G7 Mirabel France
257 F2 Mirabela Brazil
161 G8 Mirabel-aux-Baronnies France
194 G9 Mirabella Imbaccari Sicilia Italy
257 F4 Miracema Brazil
108 D3 Miracema do Norte Brazil
254 C4 Miracema do Tocantins Brazil
254 C4 Mirada Hills CA U.S.A.
Miracema do Tocantins Brazil
La Mirada
182 H2 Mira de Aire Port.
256 A5 Mirador Brazil
243 O9 Mirador-Dos Lagunos-Río Azul, Parque Nacional nat. park Guat.
257 F4 Miradouro Brazil
250 C2 Miraflores Boyacá Col.
250 C4 Miraflores Guaviare Col.
242 E6 Miraflores Mex.
183 N7 Miraflores de la Sierra Spain
127 J7 Mīrah, Wādī al watercourse Iraq/Saudi Arabia
257 F4 Miraí Brazil
114 D4 Miraj Mahar. India
260 E5 Miramar Buenos Aires Arg.
261 F2 Miramar Córdoba Arg.
238 G5 Miramar, Canal sea chan. Chile
243 N9 Miramar Lago I. Mex.
191 M1 Miramare Italy
161 G9 Miramas France
162 C5 Mirambeau France
186 E6 Mirambel Spain
225 H4 Miramichi N.B. Can.
225 H4 Miramichi Bay N.B. Can.
163 B6 Miramont-de-Guyenne France
163 D8 Miramont-Sensacq France
123 N5 Miran Shah Pak.
110 I7 Miran Xinjiang China
250 D5 Miña Col.
261 F5 Miranda Arg.
253 F4 Miranda Brazil
240 I1 Miranda Moz. see Macaloge
250 B3 Miranda Moz.
250 D2 Miranda Venez.
87 F9 Miranda, Lake salt flat W.A. Austr.
183 O3 Miranda de Arga Spain
183 O3 Miranda de Ebro Spain
182 D8 Miranda do Castañar Spain
182 E6 Miranda do Corvo Port.
182 G5 Miranda do Douro Port.
163 E8 Mirande France
182 E6 Mirandela Port.
182 F6 Mirandela Port.
191 J5 Mirandola Italy
256 B5 Mirandópolis Brazil
256 C6 Mirante Brazil
256 D6 Mirante, Serra do hills Brazil
256 B5 Mirante do Paranapanema Brazil
261 H3 Mira Pampa Arg.
255 F5 Mirapinima Brazil
198 B2 Miraka Albania
103 J12 Mirasaka Japan
182 G3 Mirassol Brazil
256 B5 Mirassol Brazil
123 M4 Mir Bacheh Kowt Afgh.
129 H5 Mir-Bashir Azer. see Tärtär
125 I7 Mirbāt Oman
129 J6 Mirbāt Azer.
175 L5 Mircze Pol.
151 J5 Mirear Island Egypt see Murayt, Jazīrat
246 C3 Mirebalais Haiti
160 G2 Mirebeau Bourgogne France
162 E2 Mirebeau Poitou-Charentes France
157 J7 Mirecourt France
202 B4 Miré́éné Chad
163 G9 Miremont France
178 H1 Mirem Slovenia
161 B8 Mirepoix France
179 M8 Mirna r. Croatia
232 C8 Mireši Albania
150 G3 Mitcheldean Gloucestershire, England U.K.

Column 7

183 J7 Mirueña de los Infanzones Spain
213 F2 Miruro Moz.
101 F11 Miryang S. Korea
122 E5 Mīrzā, Chāh-e well Iran
Mirzachirla Turkm. see Gulistan
117 I7 Mirzapur Uttar Prad. India
175 J4 Misa r. Pol.
191 O8 Misa i. Italy
105 L4 Misaka Japan
103 J13 Misaki Japan
104 B7 Misaki Japan
105 G5 Misaki Japan
103 O13 Misaki Japan
111 F7 Misaki Xinjiang China
191 N8 Misano Adriatico Italy
245 K6 Misantla Mex.
104 D6 Misato Gunma Japan
105 G3 Misato Nagano Japan
105 L3 Misato Saitama Japan
102 □1 Misato Okinawa Japan
103 J3 Misato Saitama Japan
105 K4 Misato Saitama Japan
105 G3 Misato Shimane Japan
105 K4 Misato Wakayama Japan
102 S6 Misawa Japan
223 K4 Misaw Lake Sask. Can.
177 K5 Mişca Romania
105 L3 Miscano r. Italy
190 D3 Mischabel mt. Switz.
179 N5 Mischendorf Austria
106 C2 Miscou Island N.B. Can.
224 B3 Miseheww r. Ont. Can.
193 M2 Miseno, Capo c. Italy
195 L9 Mishawaka r. Sicilia Italy
226 H5 Mishawaka IN U.S.A.
139 N6 Mishawaka Rus. Fed.
226 I1 Mishbishu Lake Ont. Can.
226 G5 Mishicot WI U.S.A.
105 I5 Mishima Japan
103 I12 M-shina i. Japan
103 □5 Mishino Rus. Fed.
124 G5 Mishlah, Khashm hill Saudi Arabia
129 I4 Mishesh Rus. Fed.
117 O5 Mishmi Hills India
139 M5 Mishukovo Rus. Fed.
134 K2 Mishvan' r. Rus. Fed.
194 E7 Misilmeri Sicilia Italy
88 E1 Misima Island P.N.G.
258 G2 Misiones prov. Arg.
153 A9 Misiones, Sierra de hills Arg.
128 D2 Misis Dağ hills Turkey
175 I5 Miske Hungary
242 □R10 Miskitos, Cayos is Nic.
242 □R10 Miskitos, Costa de coastal area Nic.
177 J4 Miskolc Hungary
179 J5 Mislinja Slovenia
188 E2 Mislinja r. Slovenia
94 D4 Mismā, Jibāl al mts Saudi Arabia
124 G5 Mismā, Tall al hill Jordan
251 H4 Misni, Nevado mt. Peru
159 H6 Mison France
93 G4 Misool i. Papua Indon.
234 B2 Misquamicut RI U.S.A.
235 L2 Misrātah Libya
116 H6 Misrikh Uttar Prad. India
227 J1 Missanabie Ont. Can.
158 I7 Missillac France
224 D3 Missinaibi r. Ont. Can.
224 D3 Missinaibi Lake Ont. Can.
85 H4 Mission TX U.S.A.
236 D4 Mission SD U.S.A.
240 O8 Mission Beach Qld Austr.
240 O8 Mission Viejo CA U.S.A.
206 B3 Missira Senegal
224 C2 Missisa Lake Ont. Can.
224 D4 Missisicabi r. Que. Can.
227 N7 Mississagi r. Ont. Can.
227 N8 Mississauga Ont. Can.
226 J6 Mississinewa Lake IN U.S.A.
237 K10 Mississippi r. U.S.A.
237 K9 Mississippi state U.S.A.
237 K11 Mississippi Delta LA U.S.A.
227 R4 Mississippi Lake Ont. Can.
237 K10 Mississippi Sound sea chan. U.S.A.
238 E3 Missoula MT U.S.A.
236 J4 Missour Morocco
236 J5 Missouri state U.S.A.
236 I2 Missouri r. U.S.A.
227 K1 Mistake Creek N.T. Austr.
225 G2 Mistanipisipou r. Que. Can.
225 G2 Mistassibi r. Que. Can.
225 F2 Mistassini Que. Can.
225 F2 Mistassini r. Que. Can.
225 J13 Mistassini, Lac I. Que. Can.
225 I2 Mistassini Lake Nfld and Lab. Can.
179 O2 Mistelbach Austria
173 J6 Mistelgau Ger.
191 B11 Mistelbach Sicilia Italy
143 M3 Misterhults nature res. Sweden
151 N2 Misterton Nottinghamshire, England U.K.
246 B4 Misteriosa Bank sea feature Caribbean Sea
149 P7 Misterton Nottinghamshire, England U.K.
194 H10 Misterbianco Sicilia Italy
194 H9 Mistretta Sicilia Italy
220 D2 Misty Fiords National Monument Wilderness nat. park AK U.S.A.
223 H3 Misty Lake Man. Can.
103 I12 Misumi Japan
191 M2 Misurata Libya see Mişrātah
181 Misurina Italy
140 M3 Misvær Norway
104 D6 Mita, Punta de pt Mex.
104 E6 Mitake Gifu Japan
105 I3 Mitake Nagano Japan
105 K3 Mitake Tokyo Japan
251 G3 Mitaraca hill Suriname
250 D2 Mitatib Sudan
150 H4 Mitcheldean Gloucestershire, England U.K.
224 C4 Mitchell r. Qld Austr.
85 I3 Mitchell Qld Austr.
83 K7 Mitchell r. Vic. Austr.
227 K8 Mitchell IN U.S.A.
226 E8 Mitchell IN U.S.A.
236 F4 Mitchell NE U.S.A.
238 C4 Mitchell OR U.S.A.
236 G4 Mitchell SD U.S.A.
85 I4 Mitchell r. Qld Austr.
85 J4 Mitchell, Lake Qld Austr.

Mitchell, Lake to Monroe
353

226 I5 Mitchell, Lake MI U.S.A.
231 F8 Mitchell, Mount NC U.S.A.
85 I3 Mitchell and Alice Rivers National Park Qld Austr.
Mitchell Island Cook Is see Nassau
Mitchell Island atoll Tuvalu see Nukulaelae
84 C1 Mitchell Point N.T. Austr.
84 E2 Mitchell Range hills N.T. Austr.
83 K7 Mitchell River National Park Vic. Austr.
214 D9 Mitchells Pass S. Africa
232 F10 Mitchelltown VA U.S.A.
147 F8 Mitchelstown Ireland
203 F2 Mīt Ghamr Egypt
116 B8 Mithapur Gujarat India
123 O5 Mitha Tiwano Pak.
123 M9 Mithi Pak.
Míthimna Greece see Mithymna
123 M9 Mithrani Can canal Pak.
123 M8 Mithrau Pak.
199 H3 Mithymna Greece
93 F3 Miti i. Maluku Indon.
81 □2 Mitiaro i. Cook Is
Mitiero i. Cook Is see Mitiaro
Mitilíni Lesvos Greece see Mytilini
139 Q7 Mitishkino Rus. Fed.
80 H3 Mititai North I. N.Z.
222 C3 Mitkof Island AK U.S.A.
245 K9 Mitla Mex.
104 F6 Mito Aichi Japan
105 L3 Mito Ibaraki Japan
103 I12 Mitō Japan
211 C7 Mitole Tanz.
105 I4 Mitomi Japan
211 B7 Mitomoni Tanz.
140 □ Mitra, Kapp c. Svalbard
80 J7 Mitre mt. North I. N.Z.
259 D9 Mitre, Península pen. Arg.
77 H3 Mitre Island Solomon Is
81 B11 Mitre Peak South I. N.Z.
135 G6 Mitrofanovka Rus. Fed.
Mitrovica Kosovo Serbia see Kosovska Mitrovica
156 E6 Mitry-Mory France
217 □3a Mitsamiouli Njazidja Comoros
198 B3 Mitsikeli mt. Greece
213 □J3 Mitsinjo Madag.
Mits'iwa Eritrea see Massawa
217 □3a Mitsoudjé Njazidja Comoros
104 D7 Mitsue Japan
102 T4 Mitsuishi Japan
105 K3 Mitsukaidō Japan
103 P9 Mitsuke Japan
104 G3 Mitsumatarenge-dake mt. Japan
103 G12 Mitsushima Japan
105 I4 Mitsutōge-yama mt. Japan
83 M6 Mittagong N.S.W. Austr.
83 K7 Mitta Mitta Vic. Austr.
178 C6 Mittelberg Tirol Austria
178 B5 Mittelberg Vorarlberg Austria
173 J3 Mittelberg hill Ger.
172 H5 Mittelbiberach Ger.
171 E7 Mittelelbe park Ger.
173 J3 Mittelfranken admin. reg. Ger.
171 D8 Mittelhausen Ger.
169 I10 Mittelkalbach Ger.
190 C2 Mittelland reg. Switz.
169 F6 Mittellandkanal canal Ger.
169 I10 Mittelsinn Ger.
173 N6 Mittelspitze mt. Ger.
173 K7 Mittenwald Ger.
170 I4 Mittenwalde Brandenburg Ger.
171 I6 Mittenwalde Brandenburg Ger.
179 L4 Mitterbach am Erlaufsee Austria
179 H3 Mitterding Austria
179 M4 Mitterdorf im Mürztal Austria
173 N4 Mitterfels Ger.
157 M6 Mittersheim France
178 F5 Mittersill Austria
173 N5 Mitterskirchen Ger.
173 M2 Mitterteich Ger.
140 I5 Mittet Norway
Mittimatalik Nunavut Can. see Pond Inlet
143 M5 Mittlands skogen reg. Öland Sweden
171 E9 Mittleres Saaletal park Ger.
171 G9 Mittweida Ger.
250 D4 Mitú Col.
250 D4 Mituas Col.
209 E7 Mitumba, Chaîne des mts Dem. Rep. Congo
208 F5 Mitumba, Monts mts Dem. Rep. Congo
209 E7 Mitwaba Dem. Rep. Congo
171 D10 Mitwitz Ger.
208 A4 Mitzic Gabon
Miughalaigh i. Scotland U.K. see Mingulay
105 K5 Miura Japan
105 K5 Miura-hantō pen. Japan
135 G7 Mius r. Rus. Fed.
137 R6 Miusskiy Liman est. Rus. Fed.
137 R5 Miusyns'k Ukr.
105 M1 Miwa Fukushima Japan
105 L2 Miwa Ibaraki Japan
104 B5 Miwa Kyōto Japan
Mixian Henan China see Xinmi
245 I7 Mixteco r. Mex.
244 C5 Mixtlán Mex.
104 F3 Miya Japan
105 G4 Miyada Japan
105 J5 Miyagase-ko resr Japan
104 F3 Miyagawa Gifu Japan
104 D7 Miyagawa Mie Japan
104 E6 Miya-gawa r. Japan
104 F3 Miya-gawa r. Japan
102 □1 Miyagi Okinawa Japan
102 R8 Miyagi pref. Japan
102 □1 Miyagusuku-jima i. Okinawa Japan
124 F3 Miyah, Wādī al watercourse Saudi Arabia
126 I6 Miyāh, Wādī al watercourse Syria
103 J12 Miyajima Japan
105 K7 Miyake-jima i. Japan
102 S7 Miyako Japan
102 R9 Miyakoji Japan
102 □C22 Miyako-jima i. Nansei-shotō Japan
103 I15 Miyakonojō Japan
102 □B22 Miyako-rettō is Japan
102 S7 Miyako-wan b. Japan
120 E3 Miyaly Kazakh.
104 D3 Miyama Fukui Japan
104 E4 Miyama Gifu Japan
104 C5 Miyama Kyōto Japan
104 D7 Miyama Mie Japan
104 B8 Miyama Wakayama Japan
105 K4 Miyamae Japan
Miyang Yunnan China see Mile
116 B9 Miyani Gujarat India
103 H15 Miyanojō Japan
102 □H16 Miyanoura-dake mt. Japan
104 D4 Miyazaki Fukui Japan
103 I15 Miyazaki Miyazaki Japan
103 I14 Miyazaki pref. Japan
104 B4 Miyazu Japan
104 B4 Miyazu-wan b. Japan
108 D5 Miyi Sichuan China
104 F5 Miyoshi Aichi Japan
105 K5 Miyoshi Chiba Japan
103 J12 Miyoshi Hiroshima Japan
105 H3 Miyota Japan
107 O6 Miyun Beijing China
107 O6 Miyun Shuiku resr China
123 L5 Mīzāni Afgh.
210 B3 Mīzan Teferī Eth.
Mizar Turkey see Karakeçi
202 B2 Mizdah Libya
147 C10 Mizen Head Ireland
147 J7 Mizen Head Ireland
138 I9 Mizhevichy Belarus
136 C5 Mizhhir"ya Ukr.
107 L8 Mizhi Shaanxi China
197 O5 Mizil Romania
197 L7 Miziya Bulg.
136 F3 Mizoch Ukr.
195 L4 Mizofato r. Italy
Mizo Hills state India see Mizoram
117 N8 Mizoram state India
234 F6 Mizpah NJ U.S.A.
128 C8 Mizpe Ramon Israel
252 D4 Mizque Bol.
252 D4 Mizque r. Bol.
105 I4 Mizugaki-yama mt. Japan
104 F2 Mizuhashi Japan
104 B5 Mizuho Kyōto Japan
105 J4 Mizuho Tōkyō Japan
104 F5 Mizunami Japan
105 K3 Mizuno-gawa r. Japan
102 S7 Mizusawa Japan
140 M3 Mjelde Norway
143 L3 Mjölby Sweden
141 I6 Mjølfell Norway
142 G2 Mjøndalen Norway
142 I4 Mjörn l. Sweden
142 G1 Mjøsa l. Norway
215 N7 Mkambati S. Africa
215 O7 Mkambati Nature Reserve S. Africa
211 C6 Mkata Tanz.
211 C6 Mkata Plain Tanz.
215 P2 Mkhaya Game Reserve nature res. Swaziland
215 P2 Mkhondvo r. Swaziland
211 C6 Mkoani Tanz.
211 C6 Mkokotoni Tanz.
211 C6 Mkomazi Tanz.
211 C5 Mkomazi Game Reserve nature res. Tanz.
211 C6 Mkujani Tanz.
211 C6 Mkumbi, Ras pt Tanz.
Mkumvura Zimbabwe see Mukumbura
211 C7 Mkunja Tanz.
211 C6 Mkuranga Tanz.
211 B6 Mkurusi Tanz.
209 F8 Mkushi Zambia
215 Q3 Mkuze S. Africa
215 Q3 Mkuze r. S. Africa
215 Q3 Mkuzi Game Reserve nature res. S. Africa
176 D1 Mladá Boleslav Czech Rep.
176 D2 Mladá Vožice Czech Rep.
176 E1 Mladé Buky Czech Rep.
196 I6 Mladenovac Serbia
197 J8 Mlado Nagoričane Macedonia
211 A6 Mlala Hills Tanz.
211 C6 Mlandizi Tanz.
211 B7 Mlangali Tanz.
215 Q2 Mlaula r. Swaziland
196 J6 Mlava r. Serbia
175 I2 Mława Pol.
175 I3 Mławka r. Pol.
215 Q2 Mlawula Nature Reserve Swaziland
215 P2 Mlilwane Nature Reserve Swaziland
217 □3b Mlima Bénara hill Mayotte
217 □3b Mlima Choungui hill Mayotte
188 F4 Mljet i. Croatia
188 F4 Mljet nat. park Croatia
188 F4 Mljetski Kanal sea chan. Croatia
137 P2 Mlodat' r. Rus. Fed.
175 I3 Młodzieszyn Pol.
211 C7 Mlowoka Tanz.
215 P1 Mlumati r. S. Africa
215 K7 Mlungisi S. Africa
175 H1 Młynary Pol.
175 J3 Młynarze Pol.
136 E3 Mlyniv Ukr.
175 M6 Mlynys'ka Ukr.
215 J1 Mmabatho S. Africa
213 E4 Mmadinare Botswana
212 E4 Mmamabula Botswana
212 E4 Mmashoro Botswana
212 E5 Mmathethe Botswana
215 N8 Mncwasa Point S. Africa
176 D2 Mnichovice Czech Rep.
176 D1 Mnichovo Hradiště Czech Rep.
175 I5 Mnichów Pol.
198 B4 Mnimati mt. Lefkada Greece
175 I4 Mniów Pol.
177 J3 Mníšek nad Hnilcom Slovakia
175 J4 Mniszew Pol.
175 I4 Mniszków Pol.
215 P2 Mnjoli Dam Swaziland
100 K1 Mnogovershinnyy Rus. Fed.
141 H6 Mo Norway
252 B1 Moa r. Brazil
246 F3 Moa Cuba
93 F8 Moa i. Maluku Indon.
128 D7 Moab reg. Jordan
241 W3 Moab UT U.S.A.
208 A5 Moabi Gabon
252 C1 Moaco r. Brazil
91 J9 Moa Island Qld Austr.
79 □7 Moala i. Fiji
122 F4 Mo'allemān Iran
213 G5 Moamba Moz.
81 F9 Moana South I. N.Z.
182 C4 Moaña Spain
208 B5 Moanda Gabon
241 R5 Moapa NV U.S.A.
147 G6 Moate Ireland
213 G3 Moatize Moz.
209 F6 Moba Dem. Rep. Congo
105 L5 Mobara Japan
122 E7 Mobārakābād Iran
122 D5 Mobārakeh Eşfahān Iran
122 F7 Mobārakeh Yazd Iran
208 D3 Mobaye C.A.R.
Mobayembongo Dem. Rep. Congo see Mobayi-Mbongo
208 D3 Mobayi-Mbongo Dem. Rep. Congo
149 M7 Mobberley Cheshire, England U.K.
208 C4 Mobeka Dem. Rep. Congo
236 I6 Moberly MO U.S.A.
222 F4 Moberly Lake B.C. Can.
226 I1 Mobert Ont. Can.
231 C10 Mobile AL U.S.A.
241 T8 Mobile AZ U.S.A.
237 K10 Mobile Bay AL U.S.A.
231 D10 Mobile Point AL U.S.A.
85 J9 Moble watercourse Qld Austr.
92 D5 Mobo Masbate Phil.
236 E3 Mobridge SD U.S.A.
Mobutu, Lake Dem. Rep. Congo/Uganda see Albert, Lake
Mobutu Sese Seko, Lake Dem. Rep. Congo/Uganda see Albert, Lake
246 H4 Moca Dom. Rep.
128 B2 Moca Geçidi pass Turkey
254 C2 Mocajuba Brazil
213 H2 Moçambicano, Planalto plat. Moz.
Moçambique country Africa see Mozambique
213 I2 Moçambique Moz.
213 I2 Mocambo, Porto b. Moz.
Moçâmedes Angola see Namibe
216 □3e Mocanal El Hierro Canary Is
234 C2 Mocanaqua PA U.S.A.
184 B2 Moçarria Port.
240 L4 Moccasin CA U.S.A.
232 C12 Moccasin Gap VA U.S.A.
96 G4 Môc Châu Vietnam
183 M9 Mocejón Spain
177 G3 Močenok Slovakia
139 U6 Mocha r. Rus. Fed.
Mocha Yemen see Al Mukhā
258 B5 Mocha, Isla i. Chile
183 Q6 Mochales Spain
78 □4a Mochenap sea chan. Chuuk Micronesia
242 E5 Mochicahui Mex.
139 V7 Mochily Rus. Fed.
251 E2 Mochirma, Parque Nacional nat. park Venez.
105 H3 Mochizuki Japan
246 □ Mocho Mountains Jamaica
78 □4a Mochonap sea chan. Chuuk Micronesia
175 H3 Mochowo Pol.
212 E5 Mochudi Botswana
174 E3 Mochy Pol.
211 D7 Mocimboa da Praia Moz.
211 C7 Mocimboa do Rovuma Moz.
197 M4 Mociu Romania
143 K2 Möckeln l. Sweden
143 K5 Möckeln l. Sweden
171 E6 Möckern Ger.
171 F6 Möckern-Magdeburger Forst park Ger.
172 G3 Möckmühl Ger.
171 G7 Mockrehna Ger.
231 G8 Mocksville NC U.S.A.
185 L6 Moclín Spain
185 K7 Moclinejo Spain
250 E5 Mocó r. Brazil
250 B4 Mocoa Col.
256 D4 Mococa Brazil
213 G4 Mocoduene Moz.
261 I2 Mocoretá r. Arg.
242 F5 Mocorito Mex.
242 F2 Moctezuma Chihuahua Mex.
244 F3 Moctezuma San Luis Potosí Mex.
242 E3 Moctezuma Sonora Mex.
245 I4 Moctezuma r. Mex.
239 J12 Moctezuma r. Mex.
213 H3 Mocuba Moz.
109 I7 Mocun Guangdong China
161 J6 Modane France
116 D8 Modasa Gujarat India
165 H8 Modave Belgium
150 E7 Modbury Devon, England U.K.
215 I5 Modder r. S. Africa
214 I5 Modderivier S. Africa
123 P6 Model Town Pak.
191 J6 Modena Italy
191 J7 Modena prov. Italy
235 G1 Modena NY U.S.A.
234 D5 Modena PA U.S.A.
241 S4 Modena UT U.S.A.
157 O6 Moder r. France
260 E4 Modestino Pizarro Arg.
240 L4 Modesto CA U.S.A.
194 H10 Modica Sicilia Italy
191 L7 Modigliana Italy
213 F5 Modimolle S. Africa
194 D8 Modione r. Sicilia Italy
175 K5 Modliborzyce Pol.
179 N3 Mödling Austria
175 I4 Modliszewice Pol.
192 B7 Modolo Sardegna Italy
107 K3 Modot Mongolia
176 G3 Modra Slovakia
179 L6 Modriach Austria
188 G3 Modriča Bos.-Herz.
176 F2 Modřice Czech Rep.
179 J6 Mödringberg mt. Austria
177 I3 Modrý Kameň Slovakia
195 L1 Modugno Italy
83 K8 Moe Vic. Austr.
213 H3 Moebase Moz.
80 J3 Moehau hill North I. N.Z.
158 D6 Moëlan-sur-Mer France
150 F1 Moel Famau hill Wales U.K.
150 D1 Moelfre Isle of Anglesey, Wales U.K.
150 F2 Moel Sych hill Wales U.K.
141 K6 Moelv Norway
215 L4 Moemaneng S. Africa
209 D6 Moembe Dem. Rep. Congo
Moen i. Chuuk Micronesia see Weno
140 O2 Moen Norway
191 L3 Moena Italy
251 H3 Moengo Suriname
241 U5 Moenkopi AZ U.S.A.
241 U6 Moenkopi Wash r. AZ U.S.A.
81 E12 Moeraki Point South I. N.Z.
165 E6 Moerbeke Belgium
80 I2 Moerewa North I. N.Z.
164 H5 Moergestel Neth.
165 D6 Moerkerke Belgium
Moero, Lake Dem. Rep. Congo/Zambia see Mweru, Lake
169 C8 Moers Ger.
190 G3 Moesa r. Switz.
214 G3 Moeswal S. Africa
78 □6 Moetambe, Mount Choiseul Solomon Is
146 J12 Moffat Dumfries and Galloway, Scotland U.K.
182 G5 Mofreita Port.
177 L4 Moftin Romania
116 E4 Moga Punjab India
Mogadishu Somalia see Muqdisho
Mogador Morocco see Essaouira
182 G6 Mogadouro Port.
182 G6 Mogadouro, Serra de mts Port.
213 F4 Mogalakwena r. S. Africa
208 C4 Mogalo Dem. Rep. Congo
114 G4 Mogalturra Andhra Prad. India
102 Q8 Mogami-gawa r. Japan
216 □3f Mogán Gran Canaria Canary Is
208 E4 Mogandjo Dem. Rep. Congo
213 F5 Moganyaka S. Africa
110 L7 Mogao Ku Gansu China
124 C8 Mogareb watercourse Eritrea
96 C2 Mogaung Myanmar
100 H3 Mogdy Rus. Fed.
147 F9 Mogeely Ireland
170 F5 Mögelin Ger.
168 G1 Møgeltønder Denmark
179 N6 Mogersdorf Austria
205 G2 Moggar Alg.
191 O3 Moggio Udinese Italy
172 H4 Mögglingen Ger.
123 L2 Moghiyon Tajik.
205 E2 Moghrar-Foukani Alg.
175 I4 Mogielnica Pol.
175 I6 Mogielnica mt. Pol.
256 D5 Mogi-Guaçu Brazil
196 J9 Mogila Macedonia
175 H6 Mogilany Pol.
Mogilev Belarus see Mahilyow
Mogilev Oblast admin. div. Belarus see Mahilyowskaya Voblasts'
Mogilev Podol'skiy Ukr. see Mohyliv Podil's'kyy
Mogilevskaya Oblast' admin. div. Belarus see Mahilyowskaya Voblasts'
174 E3 Mogilnica r. Pol.
174 F3 Mogilno Pol.
256 D5 Mogi-Mirim Brazil
213 I2 Mogincual Moz.
257 H2 Mogiquiçaba Brazil
191 J6 Moglia Italy
191 O9 Mogliano Italy
191 M4 Mogliano Veneto Italy
172 G4 Möglingen Ger.
260 C2 Mogna Arg.
100 A2 Mogocha Rus. Fed.
139 T4 Mogocha r. Rus. Fed.
205 H1 Mogod mts Tunisia
212 E5 Mogoditshane Botswana
182 D8 Mogofores Port.
210 A2 Mogogh Sudan
96 C3 Mogok Myanmar
241 U7 Mogollon Plateau AZ U.S.A.
185 M4 Mogón Spain
Mogontiacum Ger. see Mainz
210 D3 Mogor Eth.
192 B8 Mogorella Sardegna Italy
192 B8 Mogoro Sardegna Italy
192 B8 Mogoro r. Sardegna Italy
197 P3 Mogoşeşti Romania
261 I6 Mogotes, Punta pt Arg.
175 I3 Mogowo Pol.
107 N1 Mogoytuy Rus. Fed.
208 B2 Mogroum Chad
184 F6 Moguer Spain
107 R3 Moguqi Nei Mongol China
213 F4 Mogwadi S. Africa
215 L1 Mogwase S. Africa
177 I4 Mogyoród Hungary
177 H6 Mohács Hungary
80 L6 Mohaka r. North I. N.Z.
116 H9 Mohala Chhattisgarh India
215 M5 Mohale Dam Lesotho
215 L6 Mohale's Hoek Lesotho
236 E1 Mohall ND U.S.A.
122 H4 Mohammad Iran
Moḩammadābād Iran see Darreh Gaz
205 F2 Mohammadia Alg.
Mohammad Reza Shah Pahlavi Dam resr Iran see Dez, Sadd-e
116 H5 Mohan r. India/Nepal
116 F7 Mohana Madh. Prad. India
117 M7 Mohanganj Bangl.
116 G9 Mohari Mahar. India
185 P4 Moharque Spain
241 R6 Mohave, Lake NV U.S.A.
241 R7 Mohave Mountains AZ U.S.A.
226 F2 Mohawk MI U.S.A.
233 L6 Mohawk r. NY U.S.A.
241 S9 Mohawk Mountains AZ U.S.A.
116 H7 Mohdra Madh. Prad. India
100 C2 Mohe Heilong. China
141 N6 Mohed Sweden
143 K4 Moheda Sweden
182 H8 Mohedas de Granadilla Spain
235 K2 Mohegan CT U.S.A.
235 H2 Mohegan Lake NY U.S.A.
Mohéli i. Comoros see Mwali
176 F2 Mohelnice Czech Rep.
176 F2 Mohelno Czech Rep.
212 D3 Mohembo Botswana
123 M8 Mohenjo Daro tourist site Pak.
147 D7 Moher, Cliffs of Ireland
183 N7 Mohernando Spain
147 H7 Mohil Ireland
137 P6 Mohila Bel'mak, Hora hill Ukr.
147 G5 Mohill Ireland
140 U5 Möhkö Fin.
215 L2 Mohlakeng S. Africa
171 F7 Möhlau Ger.
140 □ Mohn, Kapp c. Svalbard
169 E8 Möhne r. Ger.
169 F8 Möhnetalsperre resr Ger.
234 C4 Mohnton PA U.S.A.
96 C2 Mohnyin Myanmar
252 C3 Moho Peru
114 D4 Mohol Mahar. India
241 S7 Mohon Peak AZ U.S.A.
177 I4 Mohora Hungary
171 H9 Mohorn Ger.
217 □3a Mohoro Njazidja Comoros
211 C7 Mohoro Tanz.
116 G8 Mohpani Madh. Prad. India
173 J2 Möhrendorf Ger.
168 I1 Mohrkirch Ger.
234 D4 Mohrsville PA U.S.A.
136 G5 Mohyliv Podil's'kyy Ukr.
136 F3 Mohylyany Ukr.
142 C3 Moi Rogaland Norway
142 D3 Moi Vest-Agder Norway
186 J4 Moià Spain
194 H1 Moiano Italy
146 E9 Moidart reg. Scotland U.K.
212 E4 Moijabana Botswana
182 E7 Moimenta da Beira Port.
111 E11 Moincêr Xizang China
111 J12 Moinda Xizang China
117 M6 Moindawang Arun. Prad. India
78 □5 Moindou New Caledonia
159 I7 Moine r. France
213 G5 Moine Moz.
197 O4 Moineşti Romania
160 E5 Moingt France
Moinkum des. Kazakh. see Moyynkum, Peski
Mointy Kazakh. see Moyynty
147 J4 Moira Northern Ireland U.K.
251 I5 Moiraba Brazil
Moírai Kriti Greece see Moires
140 M3 Mo i Rana Norway
117 N7 Moirang Manipur India
160 H4 Moirans-en-Montagne France
163 F7 Moirax France
198 F7 Moires Kriti Greece
138 I3 Mõisaküla Estonia
168 I4 Moisburg Ger.
158 I6 Moisdon-la-Rivière France
197 M3 Moisei Romania
261 G2 Moisés Ville Arg.
225 H3 Moisie Que. Can.
225 H3 Moisie r. Que. Can.
156 E4 Moislains France
163 G7 Moissac France
161 I9 Moissac-Bellevue France
208 C2 Moïssala Chad
160 H2 Moissey France
192 C3 Moïta Corse France
182 D8 Moita Aveiro Port.
184 B3 Moita Setúbal Port.
251 E3 Moitaco Venez.
187 D10 Moixent-Mogente Spain
143 O2 Möja i. Sweden
185 P6 Mojácar Spain
183 K6 Mojados Spain
240 N6 Mojave CA U.S.A.
240 O7 Mojave r. CA U.S.A.
240 O6 Mojave Desert CA U.S.A.
108 C7 Mojiang Yunnan China
256 D5 Moji das Cruzes Brazil
256 C4 Moji-Guaçu r. Brazil
103 H13 Mojikō Japan
185 L3 Mojina mt. Spain
196 H8 Mojkovac Montenegro
252 D5 Mojo Bol.
210 C2 Mojo Eth.
95 J8 Mojokerto Jawa Indon.
185 M6 Mojón Alto mt. Spain
183 P9 Mojón Alto mt. Spain
258 D2 Mojones, Cerro mt. Arg.
252 D3 Mojos, Llanos de plain Bol.
210 D3 Mojo Shet' r. Eth.
252 D4 Mojotoro Bol.
179 I7 Mojstrana Slovenia
254 C2 Moju Brazil
105 L3 Mōka Japan
217 □1b Moka Mauritius
80 J5 Mokai North I. N.Z.
117 J7 Mokama Bihar India
209 F8 Mokambo Dem. Rep. Congo
240 □D12 Mōkapu Peninsula HI U.S.A.
208 D4 Mokaria Dem. Rep. Congo
80 I5 Mokau North I. N.Z.
80 I5 Mokau r. North I. N.Z.
208 B4 Mokéko Congo
240 K3 Mokelumne r. CA U.S.A.
240 K3 Mokelumne Aqueduct canal CA U.S.A.
122 F7 Mokh, Gowd-e l. Iran
215 M5 Mokhoabong Pass Lesotho
215 N5 Mokhotlong Lesotho
139 T9 Mokhovoye Rus. Fed.
131 N3 Mokhsogollokh Rus. Fed.
122 H5 Mokhtārān Iran
209 F6 Mokimbo Dem. Rep. Congo
81 B14 Mokinui Island Stewart I. N.Z.
136 G3 Mokiyivtsi Ukr.
205 H2 Moknine Tunisia
175 K3 Mokobody Pol.
Mokogai i. Fiji see Makogai
80 J2 Mokohinau Islands North I. N.Z.
117 O6 Mokokchung Nagaland India
207 I4 Mokolo Cameroon
213 E4 Mokolo r. S. Africa
213 F5 Mokopane S. Africa
81 D13 Mokoreta South I. N.Z.
81 D13 Mokoreta hill South I. N.Z.
81 C13 Mokotua South I. N.Z.
101 E11 Mokp'o S. Korea
196 I8 Mokra Gora mts Montenegro/Serbia
137 K5 Mokra Kalyhirka Ukr.
177 K3 Mokrance Slovakia
175 J2 Mokre, Jezioro l. Pol.
196 I5 Mokrin Vojvodina Serbia
137 P6 Mokri Yaly r. Ukr.
179 L8 Mokronog Slovenia
120 B2 Mokrous Rus. Fed.
139 S6 Mokroye Moskovskaya Oblast' Rus. Fed.
139 T8 Mokroye Tul'skaya Oblast' Rus. Fed.
135 H5 Moksha r. Rus. Fed.
135 I5 Mokshan Rus. Fed.
Môktama Myanmar see Mottama
240 □D12 Moku 'Āuia i. HI U.S.A.
240 □C12 Mokulē'ia HI U.S.A.
240 □D12 Moku Lua is HI U.S.A.
Mokundurra Rajasthan India see Mukandwara
Mokvin Pershotravnevoye Ukr. see Mokvyn
136 F3 Mokvyn Ukr.
207 G4 Mokwa Nigeria
215 L3 Mokwallo S. Africa
165 H6 Mol Belgium
177 J6 Mol Vojvodina Serbia
187 J8 Mola, Cap de sa c. Spain
186 E7 Mola de Ares mt. Spain
195 M1 Mola di Bari Italy
Molaly Kazakh. see Mulaly
163 H9 Molandier France
245 I5 Molango Mex.
198 D6 Molaoi Greece
192 D6 Molara, Isola i. Sardegna Italy
190 F6 Molare Italy
191 R7 Molat Croatia
188 E3 Molat i. Croatia
187 C10 Molatón mt. Spain
168 E5 Molbergen Ger.
179 J6 Mölbling Austria
150 F1 Mold Flintshire, Wales U.K.
121 R2 Moldary Kazakh.
177 J3 Moldava nad Bodvou Slovakia
Moldavia country Europe see Moldova
Moldavskaya S.S.R. country Europe see Moldova
140 I5 Molde Norway
140 I5 Moldefjorden inlet Norway
140 M3 Moldjord Norway
136 H7 Moldova country Europe
197 O4 Moldova r. Romania
197 J6 Moldova Nouă Romania
197 M5 Moldoveanu, Vârful mt. Romania
197 M2 Moldovei, Podişul plat. Romania
136 G6 Moldovei Centrale, Podişul plat. Moldova
136 G6 Moldovei de Nord, Cîmpia lowland Moldova
136 G5 Moldovei de Nord, Podişul plat. Moldova
136 H7 Moldovei de Sud, Cîmpia plain Moldova
197 N3 Moldoviţa Romania
129 A2 Moldovka Rus. Fed.
211 B7 Mole Tanz.
150 E6 Mole r. England U.K.
108 A6 Mole Chaung r. Myanmar
182 C5 Moledo Viana do Castelo Port.
182 E7 Moledo Viseu Port.
225 H4 Molega Lake N.S. Can.
208 D3 Molegbe Dem. Rep. Congo
182 D7 Molelos Port.
215 M3 Molen r. S. Africa
206 E4 Mole National Park Ghana
165 F7 Molenbeek-St-Jean Belgium
158 B5 Molène, Île de i. France
212 E5 Molepolole Botswana
149 Q6 Molescroft East Riding of Yorkshire, England U.K.
156 H8 Molesmes France
138 I6 Molėtai Lith.
193 R5 Molfetta Italy
168 J2 Molfsee Ger.
140 O5 Moliden Sweden
163 G7 Molières Midi-Pyrénées France
163 H6 Molières Midi-Pyrénées France
161 E8 Molières-sur-Cèze France
163 B8 Moliets-et-Maa France
260 C3 Molina Arg.
260 B4 Molina Chile
193 L3 Molina Aterno Italy
183 Q7 Molina de Aragón Spain
187 C11 Molina de Segura Spain
191 J4 Molina di Ledro Italy
193 N5 Molinara Italy
182 H3 Molinaseca Spain
236 J5 Moline IL U.S.A.
237 G7 Moline KS U.S.A.
191 L6 Molinella Italy
161 J7 Molines-en-Queyras France
160 D4 Molinet France
160 H4 Molinges France
185 O4 Molinicos Spain
191 L2 Molini di Tures Italy
231 D10 Molino FL U.S.A.
234 C3 Molino PA U.S.A.
186 E3 Molino de Villobas Spain
261 G3 Molino Doll Arg.
258 D2 Molinos Arg.
186 E6 Molinos Spain
184 G3 Molinos de Matachel, Embalse de los resr Spain
186 J5 Molins de Rei Spain
209 F7 Moliro Dem. Rep. Congo
193 N4 Molise admin. reg. Italy
193 P7 Moliterno Italy
163 I10 Molitg-les-Bains France
177 L5 Moliviş mt. Romania
171 F8 Mölkau Ger.
143 J2 Molkom Sweden
178 H6 Möll r. Austria
192 A5 Molla, Capo c. Sardegna Italy
122 C4 Mollā Bodāgh Iran
120 F8 Mollagara Turkm.
129 J5 Mollakänd Azer.
129 B6 Mollaömer Turkey
142 F6 Møllebjerg hill Denmark
183 L2 Molledo Spain
140 Q2 Mollejos hill Norway
117 O7 Mol Len mt. Nagaland India
170 H4 Möllenbeck Ger.
252 C4 Mollendo Peru
170 G3 Möllenhagen Ger.
87 D11 Mollerin, Lake salt flat W.A. Austr.
186 G4 Mollerussa Spain
160 D4 Molles France
186 J4 Mollet del Vallès Spain
156 D4 Molliens-Dreuil France
185 J6 Mollina Spain
190 G1 Mollis Switz.
179 J4 Molln Austria
170 H3 Mölln Mecklenburg-Vorpommern Ger.
168 K3 Mölln Schleswig-Holstein Ger.
186 J3 Molló Spain
178 G5 Mölltal val. Austria
143 K3 Mölltorp Sweden
142 I4 Mölnlycke Sweden
240 □B11 Moloa'a HI U.S.A.
137 O6 Molochans'k Ukr.
137 O7 Molochna r. Ukr.
137 M8 Molochne Ukr.
134 G4 Molochnoye Rus. Fed.
134 F1 Molochnyy Rus. Fed.
137 O7 Molochnyy Lyman inlet Ukr.
Molodechno Belarus see Maladzyechna
137 L5 Molodizhne Kirovohrads'ka Oblast' Ukr.
137 N9 Molodizhne Respublika Krym Ukr.
139 P8 Molod'kovo Rus. Fed.
206 D3 Molodo Mali
121 N1 Molodogvardeyskoye Kazakh.
139 Q5 Molodoy Tud Rus. Fed.
139 U3 Mologa r. Rus. Fed.
240 □D12 Moloka'i i. HI U.S.A.
139 T3 Molokovo Rus. Fed.
134 J4 Moloma r. Rus. Fed.
161 C6 Molompize France
83 L5 Molong N.S.W. Austr.
212 D6 Molopo watercourse Botswana/S. Africa
214 I1 Moloporivier Botswana
198 D4 Molos Greece
Molotov Rus. Fed. see Perm'
Molotovo Rus. Fed. see Oktyabr'skoye
Molotovsk Kyrg. see Kayyngdy
Molotovsk Arkhangel'skaya Oblast' Rus. Fed. see Severodvinsk
Molotovsk Kirovskaya Oblast' Rus. Fed. see Nolinsk
207 I6 Moloundou Cameroon
136 I6 Molovata Moldova
209 D6 Molowaie Dem. Rep. Congo
160 F1 Moloy France
169 K8 Molschleben Ger.
157 N6 Molsheim France
223 L5 Molson Man. Can.
223 L4 Molson Lake Man. Can.
215 K7 Molteno S. Africa
214 G8 Moltenopass pass S. Africa
192 C3 Moltifao Corse France
91 H8 Molu i. Indon.
Moluccas is Indon. see Maluku
Molucca Sea Indon. see Maluku, Laut
183 R10 Moluengo mt. Spain
213 H2 Molumbo Moz.
191 J3 Molveno Italy
191 J3 Molveno, Lago di l. Italy
139 P4 Molvotitsy Rus. Fed.
209 E7 Molwe Dem. Rep. Congo
208 D5 Moma Dem. Rep. Congo
213 H3 Moma Moz.
244 D4 Momax Mex.
83 I4 Momba N.S.W. Austr.
254 F3 Mombaça Brazil
190 E6 Mombaldone Italy
211 C5 Mombasa Kenya
184 C4 Mombeja Port.
183 J8 Mombeltrán Spain
208 C4 Mombenzélé Dem. Rep. Congo
190 E6 Mombercelli Italy
Mombetsu Hokkaidō Japan see Monbetsu
117 N7 Mombi New Manipur India
208 C5 Momboyo r. Dem. Rep. Congo
169 H10 Mömbris Ger.
256 A3 Mombuca, Serra da hills Brazil
182 H4 Mombuey Spain
197 N9 Momchilgrad Bulg.
124 E7 Momed i. Saudi Arabia
Momeik Myanmar see Mong Mit
226 G8 Momence IL U.S.A.
125 L9 Momi, Ra's pt Suquţrā Yemen
184 H8 Momia, Sierra mts Spain
165 F8 Momignies Belgium
242 □P11 Momotombo, Volcán vol. Nic.
104 B7 Momoyama Japan
92 D5 Mompog Passage Phil.
208 D4 Mompono Dem. Rep. Congo
250 C2 Mompós Col.
131 P3 Momskiy Khrebet mts Rus. Fed.
163 C8 Momuy France
142 I6 Møn i. Denmark
117 O6 Mon Nagaland India
96 C6 Mon state Myanmar
241 U2 Mona UT U.S.A.
247 J4 Mona, Isla i. Puerto Rico
185 L7 Mona, Punta de la pt Spain
232 E8 Monaca PA U.S.A.
146 A7 Monach, Sound of sea chan. Scotland U.K.
185 L6 Monachil Spain
185 L6 Monachil r. Spain
146 A7 Monach Islands Scotland U.K.
192 C4 Monacia-d'Aullène Corse France
161 K9 Monaco country Europe
264 H4 Monaco Basin sea feature N. Atlantic Ocean
146 G8 Monadhliath Mountains Scotland U.K.
251 F2 Monagas state Venez.
147 I4 Monaghan Ireland
147 I4 Monaghan county Ireland
237 D10 Monahans TX U.S.A.
147 J7 Monamolin Ireland
247 I4 Mona Passage Dom. Rep./Puerto Rico
213 I2 Monapo Moz.
209 C7 Mona Quimbundo Angola
146 F8 Monar, Loch l. Scotland U.K.
222 E5 Monarch Mountain B.C. Can.
239 K7 Monarch Pass CO U.S.A.
241 U2 Mona Reservoir UT U.S.A.
222 G5 Monashee Mountains B.C. Can.
195 L7 Monasterace Italy
147 H6 Monasterevin Ireland
192 C9 Monastir Sardegna Italy
Monastir Macedonia see Bitola
205 H2 Monastir Tunisia
175 M6 Monastyrets' Ukr.
Monastyrishche Ukr. see Monastyryshche
139 O7 Monastyrshchina Rus. Fed.
136 I5 Monastyryshche Ukr.
136 E4 Monastyrys'ka Ukr.
207 H5 Monatélé Cameroon
81 E11 Monavale South I. N.Z.
79 □7a Monavatu mt. Viti Levu Fiji
147 G8 Monavullagh Mountains hills Ireland
163 F6 Monbahus France
163 E6 Monbazillac France
163 G8 Monbéqui France
102 T4 Monbetsu Hokkaidō Japan
102 U2 Monbetsu Hokkaidō Japan
207 I4 Monboré Cameroon
163 G8 Monbrun France
187 E8 Moncada Spain
190 D5 Moncalieri Italy
190 E5 Moncalvo Italy
182 G4 Moncalvo mt. Spain
182 D4 Monção Port.
184 D6 Moncarapacho Port.
163 E7 Moncaut France
183 Q5 Moncayo, Sierra del mts Spain
159 L6 Moncé-en-Belin France
157 L6 Moncel-sur-Seille France
190 E2 Mönch mt. Switz.
140 V3 Monchegorsk Rus. Fed.
169 B8 Mönchengladbach Ger.
179 O4 Mönchhof Austria
190 I7 Monchio delle Corti Italy
184 B6 Monchique Port.
184 B6 Monchique, Serra de mts Port.
173 J4 Mönchsdeggingen Ger.
247 □3 Monchy St Lucia
231 G9 Moncks Corner SC U.S.A.
163 F7 Monclar France
163 H8 Monclar-de-Quercy France
243 I4 Monclova Mex.
187 E8 Moncofa Spain
158 F5 Moncontour Bretagne France
159 K8 Moncontour Poitou-Charentes France
225 G3 Moncouche, Lac l. Que. Can.
159 J8 Moncoutant France
163 E7 Moncrabeau France
225 H4 Moncton N.B. Can.
185 J7 Monda Spain
255 B8 Mondai Brazil
182 D4 Mondariz Spain
182 D4 Mondariz-Balneario Spain
163 G9 Mondavezan France
191 N8 Mondavio Italy
182 C8 Mondego r. Port.
182 C8 Mondego, Cabo c. Port.
183 N8 Mondéjar Spain
194 E7 Mondello Sicilia Italy
159 K3 Mondeville France
208 D4 Mondimbi Dem. Rep. Congo
182 E6 Mondim de Basto Port.
208 D4 Mondjamboli Dem. Rep. Congo
215 O3 Mondlo S. Africa
202 B6 Mondo Chad
191 O8 Mondolfo Italy
182 F2 Mondoñedo Spain
165 J9 Mondorf-les-Bains Lux.
159 M6 Mondoubleau France
190 D7 Mondovì Italy
226 C5 Mondovi WI U.S.A.
161 F8 Mondragon France
193 L5 Mondragone Italy
179 H4 Mondsee Austria
179 H4 Mondsee l. Austria
211 C5 Monduli Tanz.
187 E9 Mondúver hill Spain
246 □ Moneague Jamaica
177 L5 Moneasa Romania
162 H4 Monédières, Massif des hills France
226 G8 Monee IL U.S.A.
147 E6 Moneen Ireland
190 G7 Moneglia Italy
186 E4 Monegrillo Spain
186 D4 Monegros, Canal de Spain
163 C9 Monein France
198 E6 Monemvasia Greece
100 L5 Moneron, Ostrov i. Rus. Fed.
232 F8 Monessen PA U.S.A.
184 G4 Monesterio Spain
161 H7 Monestier-de-Clermont France
163 I7 Monestiés France
227 S1 Monet Que. Can.
232 F11 Moneta VA U.S.A.
238 K5 Moneta WY U.S.A.
156 G8 Monéteau France
237 I7 Monett MO U.S.A.
186 D5 Moneva, Embalse de resr Spain
147 G7 Moneygall Ireland
146 D13 Moneyglass Northern Ireland U.K.
147 I3 Moneymore Northern Ireland U.K.
148 D4 Moneyneany Northern Ireland U.K.
148 F4 Moneyreagh Northern Ireland U.K.
191 P4 Monfalcone Italy
193 N6 Monfecorvino Rovella Italy
163 F6 Monflanquin France
250 D4 Monfort Col.
163 F8 Monfort France
184 E2 Monforte Port.
182 F9 Monforte da Beira Port.
190 D6 Monforte d'Alba Italy
187 D11 Monforte del Cid Spain
182 E3 Monforte de Lemos Spain
186 D5 Monforte de Moyuela Spain
182 G8 Monfortinho Port.
184 C3 Monfurado hill Port.
184 C3 Monfurado, Serra de mts Port.
209 E7 Monga Katanga Dem. Rep. Congo
208 D3 Monga Orientale Dem. Rep. Congo
256 D6 Mongaguá Brazil
208 C4 Mongala r. Dem. Rep. Congo
210 A3 Mongalla Sudan
117 M6 Mongar Bhutan
234 F2 Mongaup r. NY U.S.A.
234 F1 Mongaup Valley NY U.S.A.
208 F4 Mongbwalu Dem. Rep. Congo
96 H4 Mông Cai Vietnam
209 D5 Mongemputu Dem. Rep. Congo
87 D10 Mongers Lake salt flat W.A. Austr.
78 □6 Mongga New Georgia Is Solomon Is
107 P2 Monggon Qulu Nei Mongol China
96 D4 Mong Hai Myanmar
96 D4 Mong Hang Myanmar
191 K7 Monghidoro Italy
108 C8 Mong Hkan Myanmar
96 D4 Mong Hkok Myanmar
96 D4 Mong Hpayak Myanmar
96 D4 Mong Hsat Myanmar
96 C4 Mong Hsawk Myanmar
96 D4 Mong Hsu Myanmar
Monghyr Bihar India see Munger
96 C4 Mong Kung Myanmar
96 D5 Mong Kyawt Myanmar
117 L8 Mongla Bangl.
96 E4 Mong La Myanmar
96 C4 Mong Lang Myanmar
96 E4 Mong Lin Myanmar
96 E4 Mong Loi Myanmar
96 C3 Mong Long Myanmar
96 D4 Mong Ma Myanmar
96 C5 Mong Mau Myanmar
96 C3 Mong Mit Myanmar
96 C4 Mong Nai Myanmar
96 D4 Mong Nawng Myanmar
202 C6 Mongo Chad
Mongó hill Spain see Montgó
106 H3 Mongolia country Asia
Mongolküre Xinjiang China see Zhaosu
Mongol Uls country Asia see Mongolia
207 H6 Mongomo Equat. Guinea
86 I3 Mongona, Mount hill W.A. Austr.
207 I3 Mongonu Nigeria
123 O4 Mongora Pak.
202 D6 Mongororo Chad
208 C4 Mongoumba C.A.R.
146 L9 Mongour hill Scotland U.K.
96 D4 Mong Pan Myanmar
96 D3 Mong Pat Myanmar
96 D3 Mong Pawk Myanmar
96 D4 Mong Ping Myanmar
96 D4 Mong Pu Myanmar
96 D4 Mong Pu-awn Myanmar
190 E4 Mongrando Italy
244 E8 Mongrove, Punta pt Mex.
96 D3 Mong Si Myanmar
108 B8 Mong Ton Myanmar
96 D4 Mong Tum Myanmar
108 A7 Mong Tung Myanmar
209 D8 Mongu Zambia
209 B9 Mongua Angola
206 B2 Mônguel Maur.
191 M2 Monguelfo Italy
96 E4 Mong Un Myanmar
96 D3 Mong Yai Myanmar
96 D4 Mong Yang Myanmar
96 D4 Mong Yawn Myanmar
96 E4 Mong Yawng Myanmar
96 C3 Mong Yu Myanmar
106 H3 Mönhbulag Mongolia
233 □P5 Monhegan Island ME U.S.A.
173 J4 Monheim Ger.
106 B3 Mönh Hayrhan Uul mt. Mongolia
146 I12 Moniaive Dumfries and Galloway, Scotland U.K.
226 E4 Monico WI U.S.A.
161 G8 Monieux France
146 K10 Monifieth Angus, Scotland U.K.
261 G2 Monigotes Arg.
148 C6 Monilea Ireland
250 C3 Moniquirá Col.
161 D7 Monistrol-d'Allier France
186 I4 Monistrol de Montserrat Spain
161 E6 Monistrol-sur-Loire France
240 P3 Monitor Mountain NV U.S.A.
240 P3 Monitor Range mts NV U.S.A.
250 B2 Moñitos Col.
122 E6 Monj Iran
183 P9 Monje, Sierra del mts Spain
257 E3 Monjolos Brazil
122 F2 Monjukly Turkm.
168 J2 Mönkeberg Ger.
211 B8 Monkey Bay Malawi
87 B8 Monkey Mia W.A. Austr.
175 K2 Mońki Pol.
84 H8 Monkira Qld Austr.
222 F4 Monkman Provincial Park B.C. Can.
150 D6 Monkokehampton Devon, England U.K.
208 D5 Monkoto Dem. Rep. Congo
151 N3 Monks Eleigh Suffolk, England U.K.
227 M6 Monkton Ont. Can.
234 B5 Monkton MD U.S.A.
163 F9 Monléon-Magnoac France
187 E7 Monlleó, Riu r. Spain
150 G4 Monmouth Monmouthshire, Wales U.K.
240 M5 Monmouth CA U.S.A.
236 J5 Monmouth IL U.S.A.
235 G4 Monmouth County county NJ U.S.A.
234 F4 Monmouth Junction NJ U.S.A.
222 F5 Monmouth Mountain B.C. Can.
150 G4 Monmouthshire admin. div. Wales U.K.
159 M6 Monnaie France
232 B8 Monnett OH U.S.A.
164 H4 Monnickendam Neth.
150 G4 Monnow r. England/Wales U.K.
207 F5 Mono r. Togo
242 □R12 Mono, Punta del pt Nic.
78 □6 Mono Island Solomon Is
177 K3 Monok Hungary
240 N3 Mono Lake CA U.S.A.
199 I6 Monolithos Rodos Greece
233 P7 Monomoy Island MA U.S.A.
226 H9 Monon IN U.S.A.
226 C6 Monona IA U.S.A.
232 F8 Monongahela r. PA U.S.A.
195 M2 Monopoli Italy
177 I4 Monor Hungary
247 □7 Monos Island Trin. and Tob.
177 K4 Monostorpályi Hungary
202 D5 Monou Chad
187 D11 Monóvar Spain
Monover Spain see Monóvar
81 B12 Monowai, Lake South I. N.Z.
163 F6 Monpazier France
183 R3 Monreal Spain
185 N2 Monreal r. Spain
186 C6 Monreal del Campo Spain
194 E7 Monreale Sicilia Italy
146 G13 Monreith Dumfries and Galloway, Scotland U.K.
231 F9 Monroe GA U.S.A.
236 I5 Monroe IA U.S.A.
237 I9 Monroe LA U.S.A.
227 K8 Monroe MI U.S.A.
231 G8 Monroe NC U.S.A.
234 F2 Monroe NJ U.S.A.
235 G2 Monroe NY U.S.A.
241 T3 Monroe UT U.S.A.
232 F11 Monroe VA U.S.A.

Monroe to Morrill

354

238 D3 Monroe WA U.S.A.
226 E7 Monroe WI U.S.A.
226 E5 Monroe Center WI U.S.A.
236 J6 Monroe City MO U.S.A.
234 E2 Monroe County county PA U.S.A.
230 D6 Monroe Lake IN U.S.A.
227 R8 Monroeton PA U.S.A.
231 D10 Monroeville AL U.S.A.
226 J9 Monroeville IN U.S.A.
234 E5 Monroeville NJ U.S.A.
232 C7 Monroeville OH U.S.A.
206 C5 Monrovia Liberia
182 H9 Monroy Spain
186 E6 Monroyo Spain
165 E8 Mons Belgium
161 B9 Mons Languedoc-Roussillon France
161 J9 Mons Provence-Alpes-Côte d'Azur France
261 I5 Monsalvo Arg.
193 L2 Monsampolo del Tronto Italy
182 F8 Monsanto Port.
257 H3 Monsarás, Ponta de pt Brazil
184 E4 Monsaraz Port.
169 B9 Monschau Ger.
162 F5 Monsec France
163 D9 Monségur Aquitaine France
163 E6 Monségur Aquitaine France
191 L5 Monselice Italy
163 F7 Monsempron-Libos France
156 F2 Mons-en-Barœul France
235 G2 Monsey NY U.S.A.
172 F4 Mönsheim Ger.
172 E2 Monsheim Ger.
142 I7 Møns Klint cliff Denmark
160 F4 Monsols France
233 □P3 Monson ME U.S.A.
164 F4 Monster Neth.
143 M4 Mönsterås Sweden
191 J8 Monsummano Terme Italy
190 D6 Monta Italy
169 E10 Montabaur Ger.
187 E10 Montaberner Spain
163 K9 Montady France
178 A5 Montafon val. Austria
161 C10 Montagnac France
191 K5 Montagnana Italy
162 D6 Montagne France
213 □K2 Montagne d'Ambre, Parc National de la nat. park Madag.
156 G5 Montagne de Reims, Parc Naturel Régional de la nature res. France
160 H2 Montagney France
161 C9 Montagnol France
160 E4 Montagny France
162 E5 Montagrier France
214 E9 Montagu S. Africa
225 I4 Montague P.E.I. Can.
234 F2 Montague NJ U.S.A.
237 G9 Montague TX U.S.A.
220 D3 Montague Island AK U.S.A.
87 E9 Montague Range hills W.A. Austr.
86 H3 Montague Sound b. W.A. Austr.
249 G7 Montagu Island S. Sandwich Is
Montagu Island Vanuatu see Nguna
158 I8 Montaigu France
163 G7 Montaigu-de-Quercy France
160 B4 Montaigut France
163 G8 Montaigut-sur-Save France
191 J8 Montaione Italy
95 K5 Montalat r. Indon.
186 D6 Montalbán Spain
185 J5 Montalbán de Córdoba Spain
195 I7 Montalbano Elicona Sicilia Italy
195 L3 Montalbano Jonico Italy
183 O9 Montalbo Spain
192 G1 Montalcino Italy
191 K8 Montale Italy
182 E5 Montalegre Port.
160 G5 Montalieu-Vercieu France
162 B5 Montalivet-les-Bains France
194 E9 Montallegro Sicilia Italy
195 J7 Montalto mt. Italy
193 L2 Montalto delle Marche Italy
192 H3 Montalto di Castro Italy
192 H3 Montalto Marina Italy
193 Q9 Montalto Uffugo Italy
182 E9 Montalvão Port.
250 B5 Montalvo Ecuador
240 M7 Montalvo CA U.S.A.
182 I5 Montamarta Spain
197 L7 Montana Bulg.
190 C3 Montana Switz.
238 J3 Montana state U.S.A.
216 □3c Montaña Clara i. Canary Is
242 □P10 Montaña de Comayagua, Parque Nacional nat. park Hond.
243 O10 Montaña de Cusuco, Parque Nacional nat. park Hond.
242 □P10 Montaña de Yoro nat. park Hond.
Montañana Spain see Puente de Montañana
242 □Q10 Montañas de Colón mts Hond.
184 G2 Montánchez hill Spain
184 G2 Montánchez, Sierra de mts Spain
234 B3 Montandon PA U.S.A.
187 D7 Montanejos Spain
163 D9 Montaner France
257 G3 Montanha Brazil
251 H4 Montanhas do Tumucumaque, Parque Nacional nat. park Brazil
193 O7 Montano Antilia Italy
163 H8 Montans France
193 M4 Montaquila Italy
184 C2 Montargil Port.
184 C2 Montargil, Barragem de resr Port.
156 E8 Montargis France
163 H8 Montastruc-la-Conseillère France
156 D5 Montataire France
163 G7 Montauban France
158 G5 Montauban-de-Bretagne France
163 I9 Montaud, Pic de mt. France
159 J5 Montaudin France
233 N7 Montauk NY U.S.A.
235 L2 Montauk, Lake b. NY U.S.A.
233 N7 Montauk Point NY U.S.A.
163 F6 Montauriol France
161 J9 Montauroux France
163 C8 Montaut Aquitaine France
163 D9 Montaut Aquitaine France
163 H9 Montaut Midi-Pyrénées France
163 F8 Montaut-les-Crénaux France
215 M4 Mont-aux-Sources mt. Lesotho
163 F7 Montayral France
193 M4 Montazzoli Italy
160 E1 Montbard France
160 H2 Montbarrey France
163 G8 Montbartier France
163 I7 Montbazens France
161 D9 Montbazin France
159 M7 Montbazon France
160 J1 Montbéliard France
160 I3 Montbenoît France
163 F9 Montbernard France
163 G7 Montbeton France
161 C10 Montblanc France
186 H5 Montblanc Spain
Montblanch Spain see Montblanc
217 □1b Mont Blanche Mauritius
160 J5 Mont Blanc Tunnel France/Italy
161 F7 Montboucher-sur-Jabron France
160 I2 Montbozon France
186 H5 Montbrió del Camp Spain
160 E5 Montbrison France
162 F4 Montbron France
163 H6 Montbrun France
161 G8 Montbrun-les-Bains France
232 D11 Montcalm WV U.S.A.
163 E6 Montcaret France
156 C2 Montcavrel France
160 E3 Montceau-les-Mines France
160 E3 Montcenis France
161 J6 Mont Cenis, Lac du l. France
160 E3 Montchanin France
235 G3 Montclair NJ U.S.A.
156 H4 Montcornet France
156 E8 Montcresson France
163 G7 Montcuq France
156 I4 Montcy-Notre-Dame France
161 D9 Montdardier France
161 J7 Mont-Dauphin France
163 D8 Mont-de-Marsan France
156 E4 Montdidier France
160 B5 Mont-Dore France
261 F5 Monte, Laguna del l. Arg.
193 P8 Montea mt. Italy
252 D4 Monteagudo Bol.
183 Q5 Monteagudo Spain
183 Q9 Monteagudo de las Salinas Spain
183 P6 Monteagudo de las Vicarías Spain
260 A5 Monte Águila Chile
245 K8 Monte Alban tourist site Mex.
251 H5 Monte Alegre Brazil
256 B2 Monte Alegre r. Brazil
254 D5 Monte Alegre de Goiás Brazil
187 C10 Montealegre del Castillo Spain
256 C3 Monte Alegre de Minas Brazil
256 C4 Monte Alto Brazil
256 C4 Monte Aprazível Brazil
255 E5 Monte Azul Brazil
256 C4 Monte Azul Paulista Brazil
224 F4 Montebello Que. Can.
250 C6 Monte Bello Peru
195 J8 Montebello Ionico Italy
86 C6 Montebello Islands W.A. Austr.
191 K5 Montebello Vicentino Italy
191 M4 Montebelluna Italy
158 I3 Montebourg France
190 G6 Montebruno Italy
261 F3 Monte Buey Arg.
191 N8 Montecalvo in Foglia Italy
258 G2 Montecarlo Arg.
161 K9 Monte-Carlo Monaco
256 D3 Monte Carmelo Brazil
261 I2 Monte Caseros Arg.
191 O9 Montecassiano Italy
193 I2 Monte Castello di Vibio Italy
193 I2 Montecastrilli Italy
191 J8 Montecatini Terme Italy
191 J9 Montecatini Val di Cecina Italy
191 N8 Montecchio Italy
190 I6 Montecchio Emilia Italy
191 K4 Montecchio Maggiore Italy
163 G8 Montech France
190 E5 Montechiaro d'Asti Italy
184 C6 Montechoro Port.
193 N4 Montecilfone Italy
240 M7 Montecito CA U.S.A.
182 E9 Monte Claro Port.
260 D4 Monte Comán Arg.
182 D6 Monte Córdova Port.
193 N7 Montecorice Italy
191 K3 Monte Corno, Parco Naturale nature res. Italy
193 Q7 Monte Cotugna, Lago di l. Italy
191 N3 Montecreale Valcellina Italy
191 J7 Montecreto Italy
246 H4 Monte Cristi Dom. Rep.
246 H4 Monte Cristi nat. park Dom. Rep.
250 A5 Montecristi Ecuador
261 F2 Monte Cristo Arg.
253 E3 Monte Cristo Bol.
213 E4 Monte Cristo S. Africa
192 E3 Montecristo, Isola di i. Italy
191 N9 Monte Cucco, Parco Naturale Regionale del park Italy
184 D2 Monte da Pedra Port.
184 C5 Monte da Rocha, Barragem do resr Port.
182 F4 Montederramo Spain
259 C9 Monte Dinero Arg.
193 M6 Monte di Procida Italy
191 M8 Montedoglio, Lago di l. Italy
184 D4 Monte do Trigo Port.
251 H5 Monte Dourado Brazil
244 D3 Monte Escobedo Mex.
193 N6 Montefalcione Italy
193 J2 Montefalco Italy
193 N4 Montefalcone Italy
193 O5 Montefalcone di Val Fortore Italy
191 L8 Monte Falterona, Campigna e delle Foreste Casentinesi, Parco Nazionale del nat. park Italy
191 O9 Montefano Italy
191 N8 Montefelcino Italy
191 M8 Montefeltro reg. Italy
192 I2 Montefiascone Italy
184 C6 Monte Figo, Serra de mts Port.
193 L1 Montefiore dell'Aso Italy
191 J7 Montefiorino Italy
193 N6 Monteforte Irpino Italy
193 K2 Montefortino Italy
193 J2 Montefranco Italy
185 K6 Montefrío Spain
195 L3 Montegiordano Italy
193 L1 Montegiorgio Italy
246 □ Montego Bay Jamaica
246 □ Montego Bay b. Jamaica
184 E6 Monte Gordo Port.
191 P9 Montegranaro Italy
261 H4 Monte Grande Arg.
163 E9 Montégut-Arros France
261 G6 Monte Hermoso Arg.
182 H8 Montehermoso Spain
195 M3 Monteiasi Italy
163 H7 Monteils France
254 F3 Monteiro Brazil
216 □1c Monteiros, Ponta dos pt São Jorge Azores
185 I7 Montejaque Spain
185 M5 Montejícar Spain
84 C4 Montejinnie N.T. Austr.
183 M6 Montejo de la Sierra Spain
184 A2 Montejunto, Serra de hill Port.
191 N8 Montelabbate Italy
193 K4 Montelanico Italy
184 A3 Montelavar Port.
160 B5 Montel-de-Gelat France
259 C8 Monte León Arg.
193 O5 Monteleone di Puglia Italy
193 J2 Monteleone di Spoleto Italy
192 I2 Monteleone d'Orvieto Italy
192 B7 Monteleone Rocca Doria Sardegna Italy
193 J3 Monteleone Sabino Italy
194 E7 Montelepre Sicilia Italy
250 C2 Monte Libano Col.
193 J3 Montelibretti Italy
161 G7 Montélier France
161 F7 Montélimar France
253 F5 Monte Lindo r. Para.
193 O6 Montella Italy
184 H6 Montellano Spain
226 E6 Montello WI U.S.A.
163 G9 Montels France
191 K8 Montelupo Fiorentino Italy
191 P9 Montelupone Italy
194 F8 Montemaggiore Belsito Sicilia Italy
261 F3 Monte Maíz Arg.
193 O6 Montemarano Italy
191 O8 Montemarciano Italy
185 O3 Montemayon r. Spain
185 J5 Montemayor Spain
259 D7 Montemayor, Meseta de plat. Arg.
183 L5 Montemayor de Pililla Spain
162 F4 Montemboeuf France
195 M2 Montemesola Italy
193 P5 Montemilone Italy
184 G4 Montemolín Spain
193 K2 Montemonaco Italy
243 J5 Montemorelos Mex.
184 C3 Montemor-o-Novo Port.
182 C8 Montemor-o-Velho Port.
191 K8 Montemurlo Italy
182 D6 Montemuro, Serra de mts Port.
193 P7 Montemurro Italy
159 J5 Montenay France
162 D5 Montendre France
196 H8 Montenegro country Europe
183 O4 Montenegro de Cameros Spain
193 N4 Montenero di Bisaccia Italy
193 M3 Montenerodomo Italy
195 M3 Monteparano Italy
257 H2 Monte Pascoal, Parque Nacional de nat. park Brazil
260 B2 Monte Patria Chile
247 I4 Monte Plata Dom. Rep.
191 O8 Monte Porzio Italy
193 L2 Monteprandone Italy
211 C8 Montepuez Moz.
211 D8 Montepuez r. Moz.
192 H1 Montepulciano Italy
192 H1 Montepulciano, Lago di l. Italy
258 E2 Monte Quemado Arg.
158 F6 Monterblanc France
191 M9 Monterchi Italy
182 C9 Monte Real Port.
193 K2 Montereale Italy
156 E7 Montereau-fault-Yonne France
182 C9 Monte Redondo Port.
191 K7 Monterenzio Italy
Monterey Mex. see Monterrey
240 K5 Monterey CA U.S.A.
232 F10 Monterey VA U.S.A.
240 J5 Monterey Bay CA U.S.A.
240 J5 Monterey Bay National Marine Sanctuary nature res. CA U.S.A.
250 C2 Montería Col.
191 K9 Monteriggioni Italy
253 E4 Montero Bol.
193 M4 Monteroduni Italy
192 H3 Monte Romano Italy
191 K9 Monteroni d'Arbia Italy
195 O3 Monteroni di Lecce Italy
251 F3 Monte Roraima, Parque Nacional do nat. park Brazil
258 D2 Monteros Arg.
193 I3 Monterosi Italy
190 H7 Monterosso al Mare Italy
194 H9 Monterosso Almo Sicilia Italy
195 K6 Monterosso Calabro Italy
193 J3 Monterotondo Italy
192 F1 Monterotondo Marittimo Italy
182 F5 Monterrei Spain
241 Q9 Monterrey Baja California Mex.
243 I5 Monterrey Nuevo León Mex.
182 E3 Monterroso Spain
185 I3 Monterrubio de la Serena Spain
193 L1 Monterubbiano Italy
187 D10 Montesa Spain
254 D3 Montes Altos Brazil
193 K5 Monte San Biagio Italy
193 L4 Monte San Giovanni Campano Italy
238 C3 Montesano WA U.S.A.
195 O4 Montesano Salentino Italy
193 P7 Montesano sulla Marcellana Italy
191 L9 Monte San Savino Italy
191 M9 Monte Santa Maria Tiberina Italy
193 P4 Monte Sant'Angelo Italy
254 F4 Monte Santo Brazil
256 D4 Monte Santo de Minas Brazil
192 D7 Monte Santu, Capo di c. Sardegna Italy
193 N5 Montesarchio Italy
195 L2 Montescaglioso Italy
257 F2 Montes Claros Brazil
183 K8 Montesclaros Spain
191 J9 Montescudaio Italy
261 F6 Montes de Oca Arg.
191 J7 Montese Italy
193 M2 Montesilvano Italy
163 G7 Montesquieu France
163 G9 Montesquieu-Volvestre France
163 E8 Montesquiou France
163 F8 Montestruc-sur-Gers France
193 J1 Monte Subasio, Parco Naturale Regionale del park Italy
184 C5 Montes Velhos Port.
161 F8 Monteux France
194 D8 Montevago Sicilia Italy
191 L8 Montevarchi Italy
192 B8 Montevecchia Sardegna Italy
261 G2 Monte Vera Arg.
193 P5 Monteverde Italy
261 I4 Montevideo Uru.
261 I4 Montevideo dept Uru.
236 H3 Montevideo MN U.S.A.
184 B4 Montevil Port.
239 K8 Monte Vista CO U.S.A.
182 G5 Montezinho, Parque Natural de nature res. Port.
236 I5 Montezuma IA U.S.A.
237 E7 Montezuma KS U.S.A.
241 W4 Montezuma Creek UT U.S.A.
241 W4 Montezuma Creek r. CO U.S.A.
240 O4 Montezuma Peak NV U.S.A.
163 H6 Montfaucon Midi-Pyrénées France
159 I7 Montfaucon Pays de la Loire France
157 J5 Montfaucon-d'Argonne France
161 E6 Montfaucon-en-Velay France
163 F8 Montferran-Savès France
161 I9 Montferrat France
163 H10 Montferrier France
164 G4 Montfoort Neth.
163 C9 Montfort Aquitaine France
158 H5 Montfort Bretagne France
163 C8 Montfort-en-Chalosse France
156 C6 Montfort-l'Amaury France
159 L5 Montfort-le-Gesnois France
159 M3 Montfort-sur-Risle France
182 I9 Montfragüe, Parque Natural de nature res. Spain
186 G4 Montgai Spain
163 E9 Montgaillard Midi-Pyrénées France
163 F8 Montgaillard Midi-Pyrénées France
163 H10 Montgaillard Midi-Pyrénées France
161 J7 Montgenèvre France
161 J7 Montgenèvre, Col de pass France
156 D6 Montgeron France
163 H9 Montgiscard France
159 O8 Montgivray France
187 F10 Montgó hill Spain
186 L3 Montgó, Cala b. Spain
150 F2 Montgomery Powys, Wales U.K.
231 D9 Montgomery AL U.S.A.
235 G1 Montgomery NY U.S.A.
232 A9 Montgomery OH U.S.A.
227 R8 Montgomery PA U.S.A.
232 D10 Montgomery WV U.S.A.
236 J6 Montgomery City MO U.S.A.
234 A6 Montgomery County county MD U.S.A.
234 E4 Montgomery County county PA U.S.A.
86 G3 Montgomery Islands W.A. Austr.
162 D5 Montguyon France
156 I4 Monthermé France
190 B3 Monthey Switz.
156 I5 Monthois France
157 K7 Monthureux-sur-Saône France
192 C6 Monti Sardegna Italy
191 N4 Monticano r. Italy
190 H5 Monticelli d'Ongina Italy
192 B2 Monticello Corse France
237 J9 Monticello AR U.S.A.
231 F10 Monticello FL U.S.A.
231 F9 Monticello GA U.S.A.
236 K5 Monticello IL U.S.A.
230 D5 Monticello IN U.S.A.
230 E7 Monticello KY U.S.A.
233 □R2 Monticello ME U.S.A.
236 I3 Monticello MN U.S.A.
236 J5 Monticello MO U.S.A.
237 J10 Monticello MS U.S.A.
234 F1 Monticello NY U.S.A.
241 W4 Monticello UT U.S.A.
226 E7 Monticello WI U.S.A.
190 I5 Montichiari Italy
192 G1 Monticiano Italy
185 N3 Montiel Spain
261 H2 Montiel, Cuchilla de hills Arg.
159 O8 Montierchaume France
156 I7 Montier-en-Der France
192 G1 Montieri Italy
157 J6 Montiers-sur-Saulx France
162 G5 Montignac France
165 F8 Montignies-le-Tilleul Belgium
190 I7 Montignoso Italy
157 M6 Montigny France
227 Q1 Montigny, Lac de l. Que. Can.
156 G8 Montigny-la-Resie France
157 J7 Montigny-le-Roi France
157 L5 Montigny-lès-Metz France
160 G1 Montigny-Mornay-Villeneuve-sur-Vingeanne France
157 I8 Montigny-sur-Aube France
184 B3 Montijo Port.
184 F3 Montijo Spain
185 J5 Montilla Spain
185 L5 Montillana Spain
209 B8 Montipa Angola
163 I7 Montirat France
193 K2 Monti Sibillini, Parco Nazionale dei nat. park Italy
193 K4 Monti Simbruini, Parco Naturale Regionale dei nature res. Italy
256 B2 Montividiu Brazil
159 L2 Montivilliers France
185 M4 Montizón Spain
185 M4 Montizón r. Spain
161 B8 Montjaux France
159 J5 Montjean France
159 J7 Montjean-sur-Loire France
225 G3 Mont-Joli Que. Can.
190 D4 Montjovet Italy
163 J9 Montlaur France
224 F4 Mont-Laurier Que. Can.
156 D6 Montlhéry France
162 D5 Montlieu-la-Garde France
225 H3 Mont Louis Que. Can.
163 I10 Mont-Louis France
159 M7 Montlouis-sur-Loire France
160 B4 Montluçon France
160 G5 Montluel France
221 K5 Montmagny Que. Can.
160 B4 Montmarault France
158 H4 Montmartin-sur-Mer France
157 J4 Montmédy France
160 I5 Montmélian France
160 F4 Montmerle-sur-Saône France
161 F7 Montmeyran France
161 I9 Montmeyan France
156 G6 Montmirail Champagne-Ardenne France
159 M5 Montmirail Pays de la Loire France
160 H2 Montmirey-le-Château France
162 E5 Montmoreau-St-Cybard France
226 G9 Montmorenci IN U.S.A.
230 L2 Montmorency Que. Can.
162 F3 Montmorillon France
161 H8 Montmorin France
160 H3 Montmorot France
156 G6 Montmort-Lucy France
186 K4 Montnegre de Llevant hill Spain
85 M8 Monto Qld Austr.
158 G7 Montoir-de-Bretagne France
159 M6 Montoire-sur-le-Loir France
156 F6 Montois slope France
161 F7 Montoison France
184 D3 Montoito Port.
163 I9 Montolieu France
183 R6 Montón Spain
191 M9 Montone Italy
191 M7 Montone r. Italy
193 J3 Montopoli di Sabina Italy
193 L2 Montorio al Vomano Italy
185 K4 Montoro Spain
185 L4 Montoro r. Spain
185 K3 Montoro, Embalse de resr Spain
163 C9 Montory France
234 B2 Montour County county PA U.S.A.
232 I6 Montour Falls NY U.S.A.
159 J8 Montournais France
227 R8 Montoursville PA U.S.A.
206 D5 Mont Peko, Parc National du nat. park Côte d'Ivoire
246 □ Montpelier Jamaica
238 I5 Montpelier ID U.S.A.
226 I9 Montpelier IN U.S.A.
232 A7 Montpelier OH U.S.A.
233 M4 Montpelier VT U.S.A.
161 D9 Montpellier France
161 B7 Montpeyroux France
163 F7 Montpezat France
163 F9 Montpézat France
163 G7 Montpezat-de-Quercy France
161 E7 Montpezat-sous-Bauzon France
162 E5 Montpon-Ménestérol France
160 G3 Montpont-en-Bresse France
159 N6 Mont-près-Chambord France
Montreal Que. Can. see Montréal
224 F4 Montréal Que. Can.
224 C4 Montreal r. Ont. Can.
224 E4 Montreal r. Ont. Can.
160 E1 Montréal Bourgogne France
163 I9 Montréal Languedoc-Roussillon France
163 E8 Montréal Midi-Pyrénées France
226 D3 Montreal WI U.S.A.
226 J2 Montreal Island Ont. Can.
160 H4 Montréal-la-Cluse France
223 J4 Montreal Lake Sask. Can.
223 J4 Montreal Lake l. Sask. Can.
224 F4 Montréal-Mirabel airport Que. Can.
224 C4 Montreal River Ont. Can.
224 F4 Montréal-Trudeau airport Que. Can.
163 I8 Montredon-Labessonnié France
161 E6 Montregard France
163 F9 Montréjeau France
159 N7 Montrésor France
192 B7 Montresta Sardegna Italy
160 G3 Montret France
156 D6 Montreuil Île-de-France France
156 C3 Montreuil Nord-Pas-de-Calais France
159 K7 Montreuil-Bellay France
159 J6 Montreuil-Juigné France
190 B3 Montreux Switz.
159 I7 Montrevault France
160 G4 Montrevel-en-Bresse France
159 N7 Montrichard France
163 H7 Montricoux France
160 J4 Montriond France
161 C7 Montrodat France
161 B9 Montrodre mt. France
186 G5 Mont-roig del Camp Spain
160 H3 Montrond France
160 E5 Montrond-les-Bains France
214 E2 Montrose well S. Africa
146 L9 Montrose Angus, Scotland U.K.
239 K7 Montrose CO U.S.A.
227 K6 Montrose MI U.S.A.
235 H2 Montrose NY U.S.A.
233 J7 Montrose PA U.S.A.
232 F9 Montrose WV U.S.A.
232 I10 Montross VA U.S.A.
187 D9 Montroy Spain
161 B8 Montrozier France
162 F1 Monts France
156 B5 Mont-St-Aignan France
160 E2 Mont-St-Jean France
157 K4 Mont-St-Martin France
158 H4 Mont-St-Michel, Baie du b. France
156 G8 Mont-St-Sulpice France
160 E3 Mont-St-Vincent France
163 I6 Montsalvy France
206 D5 Mont Sangbé, Parc National du nat. park Côte d'Ivoire
186 G5 Montsant r. Spain
160 E2 Montsauche-les-Settons France
163 F9 Montsaunès France
186 G3 Montsec, Serra del mts Spain
163 H10 Montségur France
186 J4 Montseny Spain
186 J4 Montseny, Parc Natural de nature res. Spain
247 □2 Montserrat terr. West Indies
159 L7 Montsoreau France
163 C8 Montsoué France
160 H3 Mont-sous-Vaudrey France
159 L8 Monts-sur-Guesnes France
Mont St-Michel tourist site France see Le Mont-St-Michel
159 J5 Montsûrs France
156 H7 Montsuzain France
187 K8 Montuïri Spain
242 □R14 Montuosa, Isla i. Panama
185 J6 Monturque Spain
232 F11 Montvale VA U.S.A.
163 H6 Montvalent France
225 G2 Montviel, Lac l. Que. Can.
156 B4 Montville France
235 K2 Montville CT U.S.A.
165 I7 Montzen Belgium
157 J5 Montzéville France
237 D9 Monument Draw watercourse NM/TX U.S.A.
241 V5 Monument Valley reg. AZ U.S.A.
208 D4 Monveda Dem. Rep. Congo
215 K3 Monyakeng S. Africa
96 B3 Monywa Myanmar
190 G4 Monza Italy
209 E9 Monze Zambia
Monze, Cape pt Pak. see Muari, Ras
172 C2 Monzelfeld Ger.
104 E1 Monzen Japan
172 D2 Monzingen Ger.
252 A2 Monzón Peru
186 F4 Monzón Spain
183 L4 Monzón de Campos Spain
235 K1 Moodus CT U.S.A.
235 K1 Moodus Reservoir CT U.S.A.
215 O4 Mooi r. KwaZulu-Natal S. Africa
215 K2 Mooi r. North West S. Africa
215 O5 Mooirivier S. Africa
164 I5 Mook Neth.
212 E4 Mookane Botswana
82 G3 Moolawatana S.A. Austr.
82 H3 Moomba S.A. Austr.
83 L3 Moomin Creek r. N.S.W. Austr.
84 G7 Moonah Creek watercourse Qld Austr.
82 E4 Moonaree S.A. Austr.
83 M4 Moonbi Range mts N.S.W. Austr.
147 H8 Mooncoin Ireland
84 H8 Moonda Lake salt flat Qld Austr.
147 I7 Moone Ireland
85 M9 Moonie Qld Austr.
83 L3 Moonie r. N.S.W./Qld Austr.
82 F6 Moonta S.A. Austr.
87 D11 Moora W.A. Austr.
85 H8 Mooraberree Qld Austr.
171 E10 Moorbad Lobenstein Ger.
238 L4 Moorcroft WY U.S.A.
215 M6 Moordenaarsnek pass S. Africa
168 D4 Moordorf (Südbrookmerland) Ger.
164 G5 Moordrecht Neth.
87 C11 Moore r. W.A. Austr.
238 J3 Moore MT U.S.A.
87 D10 Moore, Lake salt flat W.A. Austr.
79 □9a Moorea i. Fr. Polynesia
263 K1 Moore Embayment b. Antarctica
232 G9 Moorefield WV U.S.A.
231 G12 Moore Haven FL U.S.A.
149 P6 Moorends South Yorkshire, England U.K.
173 K5 Moorenweis Ger.
85 L4 Moore Reef Coral Sea Is Terr. Austr.
233 N4 Moore Reservoir NH/VT U.S.A.
87 C11 Moore River National Park W.A. Austr.
261 F4 Moores Arg.
234 B3 Mooresburg PA U.S.A.
246 E1 Moores Island Bahamas
233 □R3 Moores Mills N.B. Can.
234 F5 Moorestown NJ U.S.A.
246 □ Moore Town Jamaica
148 E4 Moorfields Northern Ireland U.K.
146 J11 Moorfoot Hills Scotland U.K.
236 G2 Moorhead MN U.S.A.
83 I5 Moornanyah Lake imp. l. N.S.W. Austr.
82 H6 Moorook S.A. Austr.
84 E1 Mooroongga Island N.T. Austr.
83 J7 Mooroopna Vic. Austr.
240 N7 Moorpark CA U.S.A.
214 C9 Moorreesburg S. Africa
85 J6 Moorrinya National Park Qld Austr.
165 D7 Moorslede Belgium
168 E3 Moorweg Ger.
172 F6 Moos Baden-Württemberg Ger.
173 N4 Moos Bayern Ger.
173 M2 Moosbach Ger.
179 J6 Moosburg Austria
173 L5 Moosburg an der Isar Ger.
224 D3 Moose r. Ont. Can.
224 D3 Moose Factory Ont. Can.
233 □P3 Moosehead Lake ME U.S.A.
223 J5 Moose Jaw Sask. Can.
223 J5 Moose Jaw r. Sask. Can.
226 B3 Moose Lake MN U.S.A.
233 □O4 Mooselookmeguntic Lake ME U.S.A.
223 K5 Moose Mountain Creek r. Sask. Can.
178 G5 Mooserboden, Stausee resr Austria
224 D3 Moose River Ont. Can.
233 N4 Moosilauke, Mount NH U.S.A.
173 L5 Moosinning Ger.
179 L6 Mooskirchen Austria
223 K5 Moosomin Sask. Can.
224 D3 Moosonee Ont. Can.
173 N4 Moosthenning Ger.
83 I4 Mootwingee National Park N.S.W. Austr.
213 F4 Mopane S. Africa
213 G3 Mopeia Moz.
Mopelia atoll Arch. de la Société Fr. Polynesia see Maupihaa
212 E4 Mopipi Botswana
206 D3 Mopti Mali
206 E3 Mopti admin. reg. Mali
210 B1 Moqatta Sudan
123 L5 Moqor Afgh.
252 C4 Moquegua Peru
252 C4 Moquegua dept Peru
261 H4 Moquehuá Arg.
177 H4 Mór Hungary
207 I4 Mora Cameroon
184 C3 Mora Port.
183 M9 Mora Spain
141 M6 Mora Sweden
226 A4 Mora MN U.S.A.
239 L9 Mora NM U.S.A.
239 L9 Mora r. NM U.S.A.
260 B4 Mora, Cerro mt. Arg./Chile
196 H8 Morača r. Montenegro
138 K9 Morach r. Belarus
123 L7 Morad r. Pak.
116 G5 Moradabad Uttar Prad. India
252 C1 Morada Nova Amazonas Brazil
254 F3 Morada Nova Ceará Brazil
257 E3 Morada Nova de Minas Brazil
186 G5 Móra d'Ebre Spain
187 D7 Mora de Rubielos Spain
183 M5 Moradillo de Roa Spain
129 J6 Morādlū Iran
213 □J3 Morafenobe Madag.
175 H2 Morąg Pol.
177 I5 Mórahalom Hungary
223 J1 Moraine Lake N.W.T. Can.
187 F10 Moraira, Punta de pt Spain
182 G5 Morais Port.
186 G5 Móra la Nova Spain
185 L3 Moral de Calatrava Spain
259 B7 Moraleda, Canal sea chan. Chile
185 L6 Moraleda de Zafayona Spain
182 G8 Moraleja Spain
182 I6 Moraleja del Vino Spain
182 I6 Moraleja de Sayago Spain
242 □O10 Morales Guat.
185 O7 Morales r. Spain
182 I6 Morales del Vino Spain
183 J5 Morales de Toro Spain
182 I5 Morales de Valverde Spain
182 H6 Moralina Spain
114 E4 Moram Mahar. India
213 □K3 Moramanga Madag.
226 J4 Moran MI U.S.A.
238 I5 Moran WY U.S.A.
85 L6 Moranbah Qld Austr.
116 G4 Morang Hima. Prad. India
Morang Nepal see Biratnagar
256 A3 Morangas Brazil
117 O6 Moranhat Assam India
129 J6 Moranlı Azer.
193 Q8 Morano Calabro Italy
190 E5 Morano sul Po Italy
246 □ Morant Bay Jamaica
246 F5 Morant Cays is Jamaica
246 □ Morant Point Jamaica
114 F6 Morappur Tamil Nadu India
146 E9 Morar Highland, Scotland U.K.
146 E9 Morar hills Scotland U.K.
146 E9 Morar, Loch l. Scotland U.K.
116 G3 Morari, Tso l. Jammu and Kashmir
142 I5 Mörarp Sweden
182 F1 Morás, Punta de pt Spain
182 H7 Morasverdes Spain
183 R6 Morata de Jalón Spain
183 N8 Morata de Tajuña Spain
185 P4 Moratalla Spain
114 F9 Moratuwa Sri Lanka
176 F2 Morava reg. Czech Rep.
179 O3 Morava r. Europe alt. March (Austria)
191 R4 Morava Slovenia
179 O1 Moravany Czech Rep.
177 K3 Moravany Slovakia
213 □K2 Moravato Madag.
179 K8 Moravče Slovenia
122 F3 Moraveh Tappeh Iran
Moravia reg. Czech Rep. see Morava
232 I6 Moravia NY U.S.A.
196 I7 Moravica r. Serbia
197 J7 Moravica r. Serbia
177 G2 Moravice r. Czech Rep.
177 H2 Morávka Czech Rep.
176 E3 Moravská Dyje r. Czech Rep.
179 P2 Moravská Nová Ves Czech Rep.
176 F2 Moravská Třebová Czech Rep.
176 E2 Moravské Budějovice Czech Rep.
177 H2 Moravskoslezské Beskydy mts Czech Rep.
177 H2 Moravskoslezský kraj admin. reg. Czech Rep.
176 G2 Moravský Beroun Czech Rep.
Moravský Ján Slovakia see Moravský Svätý Ján
176 F2 Moravský Kras park Czech Rep.
179 N1 Moravský Krumlov Czech Rep.
176 G3 Moravský Písek Czech Rep.
176 G3 Moravský Svätý Ján Slovakia
87 C10 Morawa W.A. Austr.
251 G2 Morawhanna Guyana
175 I5 Morawica Pol.
146 J7 Moray admin. div. Scotland U.K.
85 K6 Moray Downs Qld Austr.
146 H7 Moray Firth b. Scotland U.K.
84 C3 Moray Range hills N.T. Austr.
172 C2 Morbach Ger.
190 H3 Morbegno Italy
116 C8 Morbi Gujarat India
160 I3 Morbier France
158 F6 Morbihan dept France
179 O4 Mörbisch am See Austria
143 M5 Mörbylånga Öland Sweden
163 C7 Morcenx France
195 O4 Morciano di Leuca Italy
191 N8 Morciano di Romagna Italy
244 C1 Morcillo Mex.
193 N5 Morcone Italy
100 B3 Mordaga Nei Mongol China
127 L5 Mor Dağı mt. Turkey
158 H5 Mordelles France
223 L5 Morden Man. Can.
199 H4 Mordoğan Turkey
Mordovia aut. rep. Rus. Fed. see Mordoviya, Respublika
135 I5 Mordoviya, Respublika aut. rep. Rus. Fed.
135 H5 Mordoviya Zapovednik nature res. Rus. Fed.
135 H5 Mordovo Rus. Fed.
Mordovskaya A.S.S.R. aut. rep. Rus. Fed. see Mordoviya, Respublika
139 V7 Mordves Rus. Fed.
Mordvinia aut. rep. Rus. Fed. see Mordoviya, Respublika
137 O7 Mordvynivka Ukr.
175 K3 Mordy Pol.
146 G6 More, Loch l. Highland, Scotland U.K.
146 I6 More, Loch l. Highland, Scotland U.K.
158 F6 Moréac France
184 D5 Moreanes Port.
236 E3 Moreau r. SD U.S.A.
236 D3 Moreau, South Fork r. SD U.S.A.
146 L11 Morebattle Scottish Borders, Scotland U.K.
149 L5 Morecambe Lancashire, England U.K.
149 K5 Morecambe Bay England U.K.
182 I2 Moreda Spain
183 P3 Moreda Spain
83 L3 Moree N.S.W. Austr.
156 B8 Morée France
91 J8 Morehead P.N.G.
232 B10 Morehead KY U.S.A.
231 I8 Morehead City NC U.S.A.
251 F5 Moreira Brazil
182 D6 Moreira do Rei Port.
116 F6 Morel r. India
190 E3 Mörel Switz.
250 C4 Morelia Col.
244 F6 Morelia Mex.
85 I7 Morella Qld Austr.
186 E6 Morella Spain
194 G9 Morello r. Sicilia Italy
244 E3 Morelos Mex.
245 I7 Morelos state Mex.
245 J7 Morelos Cañada Mex.
212 D3 Moremi Wildlife Reserve nature res. Botswana
116 G6 Morena Madh. Prad. India
184 G5 Morena, Sierra mts Spain
241 W8 Morenci AZ U.S.A.
227 J8 Morenci MI U.S.A.
197 N6 Moreni Romania
261 H4 Moreno Arg.
242 D3 Moreno Mex.
240 O8 Moreno Valley CA U.S.A.
183 P3 Morentín Spain
140 I5 Møre og Romsdal county Norway
253 F2 Morerú r. Brazil
182 I5 Moreruela de Tábara Spain
192 B6 Mores Sardegna Italy
220 E4 Moresby, Mount B.C. Can.
222 C4 Moresby Island B.C. Can.
149 J4 Moresby Parks Cumbria, England U.K.
160 G5 Morestel France
85 N9 Moreton Bay Qld Austr.
150 E6 Moretonhampstead Devon, England U.K.
151 I4 Moreton-in-Marsh Gloucestershire, England U.K.
85 N9 Moreton Island Qld Austr.
150 G2 Moreton Say Shropshire, England U.K.
156 E7 Moret-sur-Loing France
190 D6 Moretta Italy
156 D4 Moreuil France
134 L1 Moreyu r. Rus. Fed.
160 I3 Morez France
150 C2 Morfa Nefyn Gwynedd, Wales U.K.
190 H6 Morfasso Italy
172 F2 Mörfelden Ger.
198 C2 Morfi Greece
128 A3 Morfou Cyprus
128 A3 Morfou Bay Cyprus
140 R2 Morgam-Viibus hill Fin.
82 G6 Morgan S.A. Austr.
231 E10 Morgan GA U.S.A.
232 A10 Morgan KY U.S.A.
240 N4 Morgan, Mount CA U.S.A.
237 J11 Morgan City LA U.S.A.
230 D7 Morganfield KY U.S.A.
240 K4 Morgan Hill CA U.S.A.
231 G8 Morganton NC U.S.A.
230 D7 Morgantown KY U.S.A.
234 D4 Morgantown PA U.S.A.
232 F9 Morgantown WV U.S.A.
235 G4 Morganville NJ U.S.A.
158 B5 Morgat France
184 B5 Morgavel, Barragem de resr Port.
215 N2 Morgenzon S. Africa
190 B2 Morges Switz.
190 C4 Morgex Italy
123 M4 Morgh, Kowtal-e pass Afgh.
122 E6 Morghāb Iran
157 M6 Morhange France
117 J7 Morhar r. India
106 B5 Mori Xinjiang China
191 J4 Mori Italy
102 R4 Mori Hokkaidō Japan
105 G6 Mori Shizuoka Japan
247 □5 Moriah Trin. and Tob.
241 R2 Moriah, Mount NV U.S.A.
239 L9 Moriarty NM U.S.A.
83 J3 Moriarty's Range hills Qld Austr.
206 C4 Moribaya Guinea
149 K4 Moricambe b. England U.K.
222 E4 Morice Lake B.C. Can.
222 E4 Moricetown B.C. Can.
123 O3 Morich Pak.
250 D4 Morichal Col.
235 J3 Moriches Bay NY U.S.A.
193 J3 Moricone Italy
138 F4 Moricsalas rezervāts nature res. Latvia
156 E5 Morienval France
117 N6 Morigaon Assam India
104 C6 Moriguchi Japan
215 L5 Morija Lesotho
207 G3 Moriki Nigeria
185 J6 Moriles Spain
Morin Dawa Nei Mongol China see Nirji
188 G4 Morine pass Bos.-Herz.
169 I7 Moringen Ger.
193 K4 Morino Italy
139 N4 Morino Rus. Fed.
102 S7 Morioka Japan
213 G3 Morire Moz.
242 E3 Moris Mex.
197 O3 Morişca r. Romania
83 M5 Morisset N.S.W. Austr.
146 G8 Moriston r. Scotland U.K.
245 H3 Morita Mex.
171 I8 Moritzburg Ger.
105 K4 Moriya Japan
104 D5 Moriyama Japan
102 R6 Moriyoshi Japan
102 R7 Moriyoshi-zan vol. Japan
140 Q3 Morjärv Sweden
123 J7 Morjen r. Pak.
134 J4 Morki Rus. Fed.
139 T4 Morkiny Gory Rus. Fed.
163 D9 Morlaàs France
158 D4 Morlaix France
158 D4 Morlaix, Baie de b. France
163 C8 Morlanne France
165 F8 Morlanwelz Belgium
172 F2 Mörlenbach Ger.
222 H5 Morley Alta Can.
157 J6 Morley France
149 N6 Morley West Yorkshire, England U.K.
138 M9 Mormal' Belarus
193 Q8 Mormanno Italy
156 E6 Mormant France
161 G8 Mormoiron France
241 U7 Mormon Lake AZ U.S.A.
Mormugao Goa India see Marmagao
160 E5 Mornand France
160 F5 Mornant France
161 F8 Mornas France
247 □2 Morne-à-l'Eau Guadeloupe
247 □2 Morne Constant hill Guadeloupe
247 □ Morne Diablotin National Park Dominica
247 □2 Morne Diablotins vol. Dominica
247 □2 Morne Macaque vol. Dominica
190 F6 Mornese Italy
217 □2b Morne Seychellois hill Mahé Seychelles
247 □2 Morne Trois Pitons National Park Dominica
85 H8 Morney Qld Austr.
85 H8 Morney watercourse Qld Austr.
259 B8 Mornington, Isla i. Chile
264 D9 Mornington Abyssal Plain sea feature S. Atlantic Ocean
84 G4 Mornington Island Qld Austr.
83 J8 Mornington Peninsula National Park Vic. Austr.
198 C4 Mornos r. Greece
173 K4 Mörnsheim Ger.
123 L8 Moro Pak.
238 D4 Moro OR U.S.A.
183 P9 Moro, Cerro mts Spain
187 C11 Moro, Rambla del r. Spain
91 K8 Morobe P.N.G.
204 D3 Morocco country Africa
226 G9 Morocco IN U.S.A.
136 E2 Morochne Ukr.
237 I9 Moro Creek r. AR U.S.A.
211 C6 Morogoro Tanz.
211 C7 Morogoro admin. reg. Tanz.
92 D8 Moro Gulf Phil.
215 K5 Morojaneng S. Africa
214 H2 Morokweng S. Africa
244 F5 Moroleón Mex.
193 K4 Morolo Italy
93 D7 Moromaho i. Indon.
213 □I4 Morombe Madag.
252 D4 Moromoro Bol.
259 E6 Morón Arg.
246 D2 Morón Cuba
245 J3 Morón Mex.
106 G2 Mörön Mongolia
190 C1 Moron mt. Switz.
247 I8 Morón Venez.
250 B5 Morona Ecuador
250 B6 Morona r. Peru
250 B5 Morona-Santiago prov. Ecuador
213 □J4 Morondava Madag.
183 P6 Morón de Almazán Spain
185 I6 Morón de la Frontera Spain
206 D4 Morondo Côte d'Ivoire
244 D4 Morone, Sierra mts Mex.
240 P7 Morongo Valley CA U.S.A.
217 □3a Moroni Njazidja Comoros
241 U2 Moroni UT U.S.A.
Moron Us He r. Qinghai China see Tongtian He
183 Q6 Moros Spain
183 L6 Moros r. Spain
192 C3 Morosaglia Corse France
93 F2 Morotai i. Maluku Indon.
93 E2 Morotai, Selat sea chan. Maluku Indon.
210 B4 Moroto Uganda
210 B4 Moroto, Mount Uganda
103 I14 Morotsuka Japan
196 H5 Morović Vojvodina Serbia
247 □1 Morovis Puerto Rico
81 B12 Morowai South I. N.Z.
93 B4 Morowali, Cagar Alam nature res. Indon.
139 N2 Morozova Rus. Fed.
137 S3 Morozovka Rus. Fed.
139 X5 Morozovo Rus. Fed.
135 H6 Morozovsk Rus. Fed.
190 D7 Morozzo Italy
254 E4 Morpara Brazil
227 M7 Morpeth Ont. Can.
149 N3 Morpeth Northumberland, England U.K.
Morphou Cyprus see Morfou
172 G2 Morre r. Ger.
186 I3 Morreres, Puig de les mt. Spain
256 C6 Morretes Brazil
232 A11 Morrill KY U.S.A.
236 D4 Morrill NE U.S.A.

Morrilton to Muhos

355

237 I8 Morrilton AR U.S.A.
222 H5 Morrin Alta Can.
256 C2 Morrinhos Brazil
80 J4 Morrinsville North I. N.Z.
223 L5 Morris Man. Can.
226 F8 Morris IL U.S.A.
236 H3 Morris MN U.S.A.
227 Q8 Morris PA U.S.A.
233 J4 Morrisburg Ont. Can.
234 F3 Morris County county NJ U.S.A.
221 O1 Morris Jesup, Kap c. Greenland
261 F3 Morrison Arg.
226 E8 Morrison IL U.S.A.
81 E12 Morrisons South I. N.Z.
235 G3 Morris Plains NJ U.S.A.
234 B1 Morris Run PA U.S.A.
150 E4 Morriston Swansea, Wales U.K.
241 T8 Morristown AZ U.S.A.
235 G3 Morristown NJ U.S.A.
233 J4 Morristown NY U.S.A.
231 F7 Morristown TN U.S.A.
233 J6 Morrisville NY U.S.A.
234 F4 Morrisville PA U.S.A.
233 M4 Morrisville VT U.S.A.
85 H4 Morr Morr Aboriginal Holding res. Qld Austr.
257 E2 Morro Brazil
192 D5 Morro, Monte hill Italy
258 C2 Morro, Punta pt Chile
256 C4 Morro Agudo Brazil
240 L6 Morro Bay CA U.S.A.
257 H3 Morro d'Anta Brazil
185 J3 Morro del Águila hill Spain
244 F8 Morro de Papanoa hd Mex.
244 F8 Morro de Petatlán hd Mex.
254 E4 Morro do Chapéu Brazil
257 G4 Morro do Coco Brazil
253 G2 Morro do Sinal hills Brazil
245 L9 Morro Mazatán Mex.
193 L3 Morrone, Monte mt. Italy
254 D2 Morros Brazil
250 C2 Morrosquillo, Golfo de b. Col.
191 P9 Morrovalle Italy
213 G3 Morrumbala Moz.
213 G4 Morrumbene Moz.
142 E5 Mors reg. Denmark
169 E9 Morsbach Ger.
172 F2 Morsberg hill Ger.
169 I8 Morschen Ger.
223 J5 Morse Sask. Can.
237 E7 Morse TX U.S.A.
226 D3 Morse WI U.S.A.
263 I2 Morse, Cape Antarctica
135 H5 Morshanka Rus. Fed.
Morshansk Rus. Fed. see Morshanka
136 C4 Morshyn Ukr.
116 G9 Morsi Mahar. India
129 I1 Morskaya Chapura, Ostrov i. Rus. Fed.
134 F3 Morskaya Masel'ga Rus. Fed.
137 N9 Mors'ke Ukr.
171 D6 Morsleben Ger.
168 H5 Morsum Ger.
140 M3 Mørsvikbotn Norway
84 H7 Mort watercourse Qld Austr.
223 I2 Mort, Lac du l. N.W.T. Can.
157 L6 Mortagne r. France
159 M4 Mortagne-au-Perche France
162 C5 Mortagne-sur-Gironde France
162 C1 Mortagne-sur-Sèvre France
182 D8 Mortágua Port.
159 J4 Mortain France
190 F5 Mortara Italy
160 H2 Morte r. France
160 J2 Morteau France
159 K4 Morteaux-Coulibœuf France
150 D5 Morte Bay England U.K.
156 E5 Mortefontaine France
191 O4 Mortegliano Italy
150 D5 Mortehoe Devon, England U.K.
195 J7 Mortelle Sicilia Italy
261 G2 Morteros Arg.
244 E1 Morteros Mex.
257 E4 Mortes, Rio das r. Brazil
254 C4 Mortes, Rio das r. Brazil
215 J8 Mortimer S. Africa
151 J5 Mortimer West Berkshire, England U.K.
246 F2 Mortimer's Long I. Bahamas
150 G3 Mortimer's Cross Herefordshire, England U.K.
223 J5 Mortlach Sask. Can.
83 I8 Mortlake Vic. Austr.
266 F5 Mortlock Islands Micronesia
Mortlock Islands P.N.G. see Takuu Islands
151 L2 Morton Lincolnshire, England U.K.
149 P7 Morton Lincolnshire, England U.K.
226 E9 Morton IL U.S.A.
237 D9 Morton TX U.S.A.
238 C3 Morton WA U.S.A.
83 M6 Morton National Park N.S.W. Austr.
192 D5 Mortorio, Isola i. Sardegna Italy
159 L4 Mortrée France
178 G6 Mörtschach Austria
165 F6 Mortsel Belgium
247 □7 Moruga Trin. and Tob.
247 □7 Moruga Point Trin. and Tob.
83 K6 Morundah N.S.W. Austr.
210 B4 Morungole mt. Uganda
213 E4 Morupule Botswana
Moruroa atoll Arch. des Tuamotu Fr. Polynesia see Mururoa
83 M6 Moruya N.S.W. Austr.
160 D2 Morvan hills France
160 E2 Morvan, Parc Naturel Régional du nature res. France
85 K9 Morven Qld Austr.
81 F11 Morven South I. N.Z.
146 J8 Morven hill Aberdeenshire, Scotland U.K.
146 I6 Morven hill Highland, Scotland U.K.
146 E9 Morvern reg. Scotland U.K.
Morvi Gujarat India see Morbi
150 H2 Morville Shropshire, England U.K.
116 C7 Morwara Gujarat India
83 K8 Morwell Vic. Austr.
150 C6 Morwenstow Cornwall, England U.K.
139 O1 Mor'ye Rus. Fed.
174 C3 Moryń Pol.
174 G2 Morzeszczyn Pol.
134 H2 Morzhovets, Ostrov i. Rus. Fed.
160 J4 Morzine France
139 R7 Mosal'sk Rus. Fed.
136 G5 Moșana Moldova
172 G3 Mosbach Ger.
149 O7 Mosborough South Yorkshire, England U.K.
238 K3 Mosby MT U.S.A.
187 I9 Moscarter, Punta des pt Spain
184 A3 Moscavide Port.
191 Q5 Mošćenička Draga Croatia
191 L8 Moscia r. Italy
193 L2 Mosciano Sant'Angelo Italy
Moscow Rus. Fed. see Moskva
238 F3 Moscow ID U.S.A.
234 D2 Moscow PA U.S.A.
Moscow Oblast admin. div. Rus. Fed. see Moskovskaya Oblast'
263 I2 Moscow University Ice Shelf Antarctica
171 F9 Mosel Ger.
169 E10 Mosel r. Ger.
212 D5 Moselebe watercourse Botswana
232 H11 Moseley VA U.S.A.
157 M5 Moselle dept France
157 L5 Moselle r. France
171 E6 Möser Ger.
240 O1 Moses, Mount NV U.S.A.
238 E3 Moses Lake WA U.S.A.
212 E4 Mosetse Botswana
134 I2 Moseyevo Rus. Fed.
81 E12 Mosgiel South I. N.Z.
232 G7 Moshannon PA U.S.A.
214 G2 Moshaweng watercourse S. Africa
138 K2 Moshchnyy, Ostrov i. Rus. Fed.
139 R3 Moshenskoye Rus. Fed.
227 J1 Mosher Ont. Can.
122 F7 Moshgān Iran
207 G4 Moshi r. Nigeria
211 C5 Moshi Tanz.
137 K4 Moshny Ukr.
134 K2 Mosh'yuga Rus. Fed.
174 E3 Mosina Pol.
226 E5 Mosinee WI U.S.A.
Mosi-oa-Tunya National Park Zimbabwe see Victoria Falls National Park
215 I2 Mosita S. Africa
140 L4 Mosjøen Norway
100 M2 Moskal'vo Sakhalin Rus. Fed.
140 P2 Moskánjáisi mt. Norway
140 L3 Moskenesøy i. Norway
140 L3 Moskenestraumen sea chan. Norway
175 H5 Moskorzew Pol.
140 O4 Moskosel Sweden
139 V6 Moskovskaya Oblast' admin. div. Rus. Fed.
Moskovskiy Uzbek. see Shahrihon
137 S2 Moskovskoye Rus. Fed.
139 U6 Moskva Rus. Fed.
139 V6 Moskva r. Rus. Fed.
123 M3 Moskva Tajik.
139 U5 Moskvy, Kanal imeni canal Rus. Fed.
177 G6 Moslavna Podravska Croatia
260 D3 Mosmota Arg.
197 P4 Moșna Romania
177 K6 Moșnița Nouă Romania
78 □5 Moso i. Vanuatu
191 K2 Moso in Passiria Italy
176 G4 Mosonmagyaróvár Hungary
188 F4 Mosor mts Croatia
177 H3 Mošovce Slovakia
137 P4 Mos'panove Ukr.
137 R6 Mospyne Ukr.
250 B4 Mosquera Col.
239 L9 Mosquero NM U.S.A.
187 E7 Mosqueruela Spain
242 □R10 Mosquitia reg. Hond.
247 □1 Mosquito Puerto Rico
232 E7 Mosquito Creek Lake OH U.S.A.
223 K2 Mosquito Lake N.W.T. Can.
242 □S13 Mosquitos, Golfo de los b. Panama
142 G2 Moss Norway
208 C5 Mossaka Congo
Mossâmedes Angola see Namibe
256 B2 Mossâmedes Brazil
146 K8 Mossat Aberdeenshire, Scotland U.K.
81 C12 Mossburn South I. N.Z.
Mosselbaai S. Africa see Mossel Bay
214 G10 Mossel Bay S. Africa
214 G10 Mossel Bay b. S. Africa
209 B5 Mossendjo Congo
163 I10 Mosset France
83 J5 Mossgiel N.S.W. Austr.
215 N1 Mossiesdal S. Africa
172 G5 Mössingen Ger.
148 F4 Mossley Northern Ireland U.K.
85 J4 Mossman Qld Austr.
142 F5 Mossø l. Denmark
187 H9 Mossons, Cap des c. Spain
254 F3 Mossoró Brazil
147 J2 Moss-side Northern Ireland U.K.
146 J7 Mosstodloch Moray, Scotland U.K.
213 I2 Mossuril Moz.
83 M6 Moss Vale N.S.W. Austr.
223 K4 Mossy r. Sask. Can.
197 N9 Most Bulg.
176 C1 Most Czech Rep.
195 □ Mosta Malta
122 F5 Moștafaabad Iran
205 F2 Mostaganem Alg.
188 F4 Mostar Bos.-Herz.
255 C9 Mostardas Brazil
184 D5 Mosteiro Beja Port.
182 E9 Mosteiro Castelo Branco Port.
182 F2 Mosteiro Galicia Spain
216 □1b Mosteiros São Miguel Azores
197 N6 Moșteni Romania
197 O6 Mostiștea r. Romania
175 I2 Mostkowo Warmińsko-Mazurskie Pol.
174 D3 Mostkowo Zachodniopomorskie Pol.
179 I7 Most na Soči Slovenia
183 M8 Móstoles Spain
223 I4 Mostoos Hills Sask. Can.
136 J6 Mostove Ukr.
129 B1 Mostovskoy Rus. Fed.
175 J3 Mostówka Pol.
Mosty Belarus see Masty
175 L4 Mosty Pol.
95 M2 Mostyn Sabah Malaysia
136 C4 Mostys'ka Ukr.
175 L6 Mostys'ka Druha Ukr.
212 E4 Mosu Botswana
Mosul Iraq see Al Mawșil
110 H4 Mosuowan Xinjiang China
142 E2 Møsvatn Austfjell park Norway
142 E2 Møsvatnet l. Norway
140 K5 Mosvik Norway
175 M4 Mosyr Ukr.
175 H4 Moszczenica Pol.
210 C2 Mot'a Eth.
78 □5 Mota i. Vanuatu
208 C4 Motaba r. Congo
185 N2 Mota del Cuervo Spain
183 J5 Mota del Marqués Spain
243 O10 Motagua r. Guat.
108 B6 Motai Myanmar
136 E1 Motal' Belarus
143 L3 Motala Sweden
78 □5 Mota Lava i. Vanuatu
174 F1 Motarzyno Pol.
213 G5 Motaze Moz.
197 O3 Moțca Romania
105 L2 Motegi Japan
208 C4 Motenge-Boma Dem. Rep. Congo
215 M4 Moteng Pass Lesotho
213 F5 Motetema S. Africa
116 G7 Moth Uttar Prad. India
146 I11 Motherwell North Lanarkshire, Scotland U.K.
214 H3 Mothibistad S. Africa
198 E6 Mothonaio, Akrotirio pt Kythira Greece
93 E3 Moti i. Maluku Indon.
101 C8 Motian Ling hill Liaoning China
190 B2 Môtiers Switz.
117 J6 Motihari Bihar India
185 I3 Motilla hill Spain
183 Q9 Motilla del Palancar Spain
80 K4 Motiti Island North I. N.Z.
143 J2 Motjärnshyttan Sweden
213 F4 Motloutse r. Botswana
102 □1 Motobu Okinawa Japan
102 □1 Motobu-hantō pen. Okinawa Japan
251 E3 Motocurunya Venez.
212 D5 Motokwe Botswana
105 L4 Motono Japan
183 Q7 Motos Spain
104 E5 Motosu Japan
105 I5 Motosu-ko l. Japan
140 V2 Motovskiy Zaliv sea chan. Rus. Fed.
191 P5 Motovun Croatia
103 □3 Moto-yama hill Iō-jima Japan
102 S8 Motoyoshi Japan
243 M10 Motozintla Mex.
185 L7 Motril Spain
197 K6 Motru Romania
197 L6 Motru r. Romania
215 L1 Motshikiri S. Africa
214 I5 Motswedimosa S. Africa
236 D2 Mott ND U.S.A.
96 C6 Mottama Myanmar
96 C6 Mottama, Gulf of Myanmar
193 O4 Motta Montecorvino Italy
195 J7 Motta San Giovanni Italy
190 F5 Motta Visconti Italy
169 I10 Motten Ger.
173 J4 Möttingen Ger.
252 D7 Motto Botello Arg.
195 M2 Mottola Italy
81 H8 Motueka South I. N.Z.
81 □1 Motu Fakataga i. Tokelau
Motuhora Island North I. N.Z. see Moutohora Island
Motu Ihupuku i. N.Z. see Campbell Island
79 □9 Motu Iti i. Fr. Polynesia
Motuiti i. Fr. Polynesia see Motu Iti
81 G10 Motukarara South I. N.Z.
243 O7 Motul Mex.
81 H10 Motunau Island South I. N.Z.
79 □9 Motu One atoll Arch. de la Société Fr. Polynesia
79 □9 Motu One i. Fr. Polynesia
81 G8 Motupiko South I. N.Z.
80 G7 Motupipi South I. N.Z.
79 □7a Moturiki i. Fiji
80 H1 Motutangi North I. N.Z.
81 □3 Motutapu i. Rarotonga Cook Is
178 C5 Mötz Austria
142 G5 Mou Denmark
208 C4 Mouali Gbangba Congo
96 G5 Mouan, Nam r. Laos
207 H6 Mouanko Cameroon
161 J9 Mouans-Sartoux France
Mouaskar Alg. see Mascara
263 L2 Moubray Bay Antarctica
225 G3 Mouchalagane r. Que. Can.
159 I8 Mouchamps France
163 E8 Mouchan France
160 H3 Mouchard France
161 C7 Mouchet, Mont mt. France
246 H3 Mouchoir Bank sea feature Turks and Caicos Is
246 H3 Mouchoir Passage Turks and Caicos Is
182 E6 Mouçós Port.
108 C6 Mouding Yunnan China
206 B2 Moudjéria Maur.
190 B2 Moudon Switz.
198 G3 Moudros Limnos Greece
208 C2 Moufa Chad
208 A5 Mougalaba, Réserve de la nature res. Gabon
161 K9 Mougins France
206 B2 Mougri well Maur.
141 Q6 Mouhijärvi Fin.
206 E4 Mouhoun r. Africa alt. Volta Noire, conv. Black Volta
208 A5 Mouila Gabon
205 E4 Mouilah well Alg.
159 J8 Mouilleron-en-Pareds France
208 D3 Mouka C.A.R.
207 I3 Moul well Niger
83 J6 Moulamein N.S.W. Austr.
83 I6 Moulamein Creek r. N.S.W. Austr.
163 I7 Moularès France
Moulavibazar Bangl. see Moulvibazar
159 J5 Moulay France
247 □3 Moule à Chique, Cape St Lucia
209 A5 Moulèngui Binza Gabon
206 D2 Moulentâr well Mali
163 F6 Mouleydier France
210 D1 Moulhoulé Djibouti
159 L7 Mouliherne France
163 H9 Moulin-Neuf France
160 C3 Moulins France
160 D3 Moulins-Engilbert France
159 L4 Moulins-la-Marche France
163 G10 Moulis France
162 C5 Moulis-en-Médoc France
162 F3 Moulismes France
163 D9 Moulle de Jaut, Pic du mt. France
Moulmein Myanmar see Mawlamyaing
204 E2 Moulouya, Oued r. Morocco
151 L6 Moulsecoomb Brighton and Hove, England U.K.
159 K3 Moult France
151 L2 Moulton Lincolnshire, England U.K.
151 K3 Moulton Northamptonshire, England U.K.
151 M3 Moulton Suffolk, England U.K.
231 D8 Moulton AL U.S.A.
262 P1 Moulton, Mount Antarctica
233 N5 Moultonborough NH U.S.A.
231 F10 Moultrie GA U.S.A.
231 H9 Moultrie, Lake SC U.S.A.
117 M7 Moulvibazar Bangl.
Moumolu-Naunitu i. Solomon Is see San Jorge
208 B5 Mounana Gabon
237 K7 Mound City IL U.S.A.
236 H6 Mound City KS U.S.A.
236 H5 Mound City MO U.S.A.
236 E3 Mound City SD U.S.A.
208 C2 Moundou Chad
232 E9 Moundsville WV U.S.A.
231 D9 Moundville AL U.S.A.
208 B5 Moungoundou-Sud Congo
161 J8 Mounier, Mont mt. France
198 B4 Mounta, Akrotirio pt Kefallonia Greece
198 B4 Mounta, Akrotirio pt Greece
116 D7 Mount Abu Rajasthan India
234 C4 Mount Aetna PA U.S.A.
239 K9 Mountainair NM U.S.A.
150 F4 Mountain Ash Rhondda Cynon Taff, Wales U.K.
231 D9 Mountain Brook AL U.S.A.
232 D12 Mountain City TN U.S.A.
237 I7 Mountain Grove MO U.S.A.
237 I7 Mountain Home AR U.S.A.
238 G5 Mountain Home ID U.S.A.
234 E2 Mountainhome PA U.S.A.
241 V1 Mountain Home UT U.S.A.
226 B2 Mountain Iron MN U.S.A.
232 F9 Mountain Lake Park MD U.S.A.
235 G3 Mountain Lakes NJ U.S.A.
241 Q6 Mountain Pass CA U.S.A.
234 D2 Mountain Top PA U.S.A.
237 I8 Mountain View AR U.S.A.
240 J4 Mountain View CA U.S.A.
240 □F14 Mountain View HI U.S.A.
220 B3 Mountain Village AK U.S.A.
215 J8 Mountain Zebra National Park S. Africa
234 A6 Mount Airy MD U.S.A.
232 E12 Mount Airy NC U.S.A.
86 G4 Mount Anderson Aboriginal Reserve W.A. Austr.
82 H7 Mount Arapiles-Tooan State Park nature res. Vic. Austr.
234 F3 Mount Arlington NJ U.S.A.
81 C11 Mount Aspiring National Park South I. N.Z.
222 H5 Mount Assiniboine Provincial Park B.C. Can.
87 D8 Mount Augustus W.A. Austr.
215 N6 Mount Ayliff S. Africa
236 H5 Mount Ayr IA U.S.A.
240 O7 Mount Baldy CA U.S.A.
82 G6 Mount Barker S.A. Austr.
87 D13 Mount Barker W.A. Austr.
86 H4 Mount Barnett W.A. Austr.
86 I4 Mount Barnett Aboriginal Reserve W.A. Austr.
83 K7 Mount Beauty Vic. Austr.
147 F6 Mount Bellew Ireland
146 J11 Mountbenger Scottish Borders, Scotland U.K.
80 J7 Mount Bruce North I. N.Z.
227 M7 Mount Brydges Ont. Can.
83 K7 Mount Buffalo National Park Vic. Austr.
85 J4 Mount Carbine Qld Austr.
233 □S1 Mount Carleton Provincial Park N.B. Can.
230 D6 Mount Carmel IL U.S.A.
234 C3 Mount Carmel PA U.S.A.
232 C12 Mount Carmel TN U.S.A.
241 T4 Mount Carmel Junction UT U.S.A.
226 E7 Mount Carroll IL U.S.A.
84 D8 Mount Cavenagh N.T. Austr.
147 F3 Mountcharles Ireland
87 D8 Mount Clere W.A. Austr.
147 D8 Mountcollins Ireland
Mount Cook South I. N.Z. see Aoraki
85 K6 Mount Coolon Qld Austr.
215 N6 Mount Currie Nature Reserve S. Africa
213 F3 Mount Darwin Zimbabwe
84 D7 Mount Denison N.T. Austr.
233 □Q4 Mount Desert Island ME U.S.A.
82 E4 Mount Eba S.A. Austr.
84 D8 Mount Ebenezer N.T. Austr.
82 H8 Mount Eccles National Park Vic. Austr.
222 C3 Mount Edgecumbe AK U.S.A.
222 D3 Mount Edziza Provincial Park B.C. Can.
237 H10 Mount Enterprise TX U.S.A.
226 I9 Mount Etna IN U.S.A.
148 C4 Mountfield Northern Ireland U.K.
83 K10 Mount Field National Park Tas. Austr.
215 M6 Mount Fletcher S. Africa
224 D5 Mount Forest Ont. Can.
87 D13 Mount Frankland National Park W.A. Austr.
215 M6 Mount Frere S. Africa
82 H7 Mount Gambier S.A. Austr.
85 J4 Mount Garnet Qld Austr.
232 C11 Mount Gay WV U.S.A.
232 C8 Mount Gilead OH U.S.A.
91 J8 Mount Hagen P.N.G.
148 C4 Mount Hamilton Northern Ireland U.K.
234 F5 Mount Holly NJ U.S.A.
234 A4 Mount Holly Springs PA U.S.A.
83 J5 Mount Hope N.S.W. Austr.
82 E6 Mount Hope S.A. Austr.
232 D11 Mount Hope WV U.S.A.
226 E6 Mount Horeb WI U.S.A.
86 H4 Mount House W.A. Austr.
85 I9 Mount Howitt Qld Austr.
81 F10 Mount Hutt South I. N.Z.
237 I8 Mount Ida AR U.S.A.
84 G6 Mount Isa Qld Austr.
232 G10 Mount Jackson VA U.S.A.
87 D8 Mount James Aboriginal Reserve W.A. Austr.
232 G7 Mount Jewett PA U.S.A.
147 H3 Mountjoy Northern Ireland U.K.
147 I3 Mountjoy Northern Ireland U.K.
234 B4 Mount Joy PA U.S.A.
83 M4 Mount Kaputar National Park N.S.W. Austr.
87 F9 Mount Keith W.A. Austr.
210 C5 Mount Kenya National Park Kenya
235 H2 Mount Kisco NY U.S.A.
85 M7 Mount Larcom Qld Austr.
232 E8 Mount Lebanon PA U.S.A.
82 G6 Mount Lofty Range mts S.A. Austr.
227 N2 Mount MacDonald Ont. Can.
87 D10 Mount Magnet W.A. Austr.
83 I5 Mount Manara N.S.W. Austr.
87 E10 Mount Manning Nature Reserve W.A. Austr.
80 K4 Mount Maunganui North I. N.Z.
Mount McKinley National Park AK U.S.A. see Denali National Park and Preserve
240 L1 Mount Meadows Reservoir CA U.S.A.
147 H6 Mountmellick Ireland
85 J4 Mount Molloy Qld Austr.
215 L6 Mount Moorosi Lesotho
85 M7 Mount Morgan Qld Austr.
226 E7 Mount Morris IL U.S.A.
227 K6 Mount Morris MI U.S.A.
232 H6 Mount Morris NY U.S.A.
83 I4 Mount Murchison N.S.W. Austr.
232 E10 Mount Nebo WV U.S.A.
147 J4 Mount Norris Northern Ireland U.K.
147 H5 Mount Nugent Ireland
232 A10 Mount Olivet KY U.S.A.
232 B9 Mount Orab OH U.S.A.
225 K4 Mount Pearl Nfld and Lab. Can.
234 D4 Mount Penn PA U.S.A.
85 M8 Mount Perry Qld Austr.
86 I5 Mount Pierre Aboriginal Reserve W.A. Austr.
81 D11 Mount Pisa South I. N.Z.
82 G6 Mount Pleasant S.A. Austr.
231 □2 Mount Pleasant New Prov. Bahamas
225 H4 Mount Pleasant P.E.I. Can.
236 J5 Mount Pleasant IA U.S.A.
226 J6 Mount Pleasant MI U.S.A.
232 F8 Mount Pleasant PA U.S.A.
231 H9 Mount Pleasant SC U.S.A.
237 H9 Mount Pleasant TX U.S.A.
241 U2 Mount Pleasant UT U.S.A.
234 A3 Mount Pleasant Mills PA U.S.A.
234 E2 Mount Pocono PA U.S.A.
234 B7 Mount Rainier MD U.S.A.
238 D3 Mount Rainier National Park WA U.S.A.
147 H6 Mountrath Ireland
82 G5 Mount Remarkable National Park S.A. Austr.
222 G5 Mount Revelstoke National Park B.C. Can.
81 H8 Mount Richmond Forest Park nature res. South I. N.Z.
222 G4 Mount Robson Provincial Park B.C. Can.
232 D12 Mount Rogers National Recreation Area park VA U.S.A.
214 I4 Mount Rupert S. Africa
238 C3 Mount St Helens National Volcanic Monument nat. park WA U.S.A.
234 F3 Mount Salem NJ U.S.A.
84 C4 Mount Sanford N.T. Austr.
150 B7 Mount's Bay England U.K.
147 F7 Mountshannon Ireland
238 C6 Mount Shasta CA U.S.A.
81 F10 Mount Somers South I. N.Z.
151 J2 Mountsorrel Leicestershire, England U.K.
236 J6 Mount Sterling IL U.S.A.
232 B10 Mount Sterling KY U.S.A.
232 B9 Mount Sterling OH U.S.A.
214 I9 Mount Stewart S. Africa
232 F9 Mount Storm WV U.S.A.
85 J5 Mount Surprise Qld Austr.
84 E7 Mount Swan N.T. Austr.
147 F5 Mount Talbot Ireland
232 H8 Mount Union PA U.S.A.
233 J6 Mount Upton NY U.S.A.
87 E8 Mount Vernon W.A. Austr.
237 K10 Mount Vernon AL U.S.A.
231 F9 Mount Vernon GA U.S.A.
236 K6 Mount Vernon IL U.S.A.
230 D7 Mount Vernon IN U.S.A.
232 A11 Mount Vernon KY U.S.A.
237 I7 Mount Vernon MO U.S.A.
235 H3 Mount Vernon NY U.S.A.
232 C8 Mount Vernon OH U.S.A.
237 H9 Mount Vernon TX U.S.A.
238 C2 Mount Vernon WA U.S.A.
234 C4 Mountville PA U.S.A.
84 D7 Mount Wedge N.T. Austr.
82 E5 Mount Wedge S.A. Austr.
86 D6 Mount Welcome Aboriginal Reserve W.A. Austr.
83 L9 Mount William National Park Tas. Austr.
82 E2 Mount Willoughby S.A. Austr.
234 B4 Mount Wolf PA U.S.A.
234 B7 Mount Zion MD U.S.A.
85 L8 Moura Qld Austr.
251 F5 Moura Brazil
252 B1 Moura r. Brazil
184 E4 Moura Port.
184 E4 Mourão Port.
208 D2 Mouraya Chad
202 D5 Mourdi, Dépression du depr. Chad
206 D3 Mourdiah Mali
182 D5 Moure Port.
163 C9 Mourenx France
161 F9 Mouriès France
182 D7 Mourisca do Vouga Port.
182 D9 Mouriscas Port.
156 H5 Mourmelon-le-Grand France
148 C4 Mourne r. Northern Ireland U.K.
147 J4 Mourne Mountains hills Northern Ireland U.K.
217 □1c Mourouvin, Forêt reg. Réunion
161 I9 Mourre de Chanier mt. France
161 G9 Mourre Nègre mt. France
198 G3 Mourtzeflos, Akrotirio pt Limnos Greece
146 □N2 Mousa i. Scotland U.K.
165 D7 Mouscron Belgium
165 D7 Mouscron dept Belgium
208 C2 Mousgougou Chad
232 C11 Mousie KY U.S.A.
161 E9 Moussac France
208 C2 Moussafoyo Chad
161 B10 Moussan France
157 N7 Moussey France
202 C5 Mousso well Chad
202 C6 Moussoro Chad
163 I9 Moussoulens France
160 C2 Moussy France
158 E4 Moustéru France
163 C7 Moustey France
161 I9 Moustiers-Ste-Marie France
209 B5 Moutamba Congo
160 I3 Mouthe France
160 G3 Mouthier-en-Bresse France
160 I2 Mouthier-Haute-Pierre France
162 E4 Mouthiers-sur-Boëme France
232 D12 Mouth of Wilson VA U.S.A.
163 J10 Mouthoumet France
190 C1 Moutier Switz.
162 I3 Moutier-d'Ahun France
160 J6 Moûtiers France
162 B3 Moutiers-les-Mauxfaits France
179 O1 Moutnice Czech Rep.
80 K4 Moutohora Island North I. N.Z.
93 B3 Moutong Sulawesi Indon.
207 I4 Moutourwa Cameroon
161 B10 Moux France
160 E2 Moux-en-Morvan France
156 D5 Mouy France
205 F4 Mouydir, Monts du plat. Alg.
209 B5 Mouyondzi Congo
198 C3 Mouzaki Greece
202 B6 Mouzarak Chad
157 J5 Mouzay France
157 J4 Mouzon France
157 K7 Mouzon r. France
242 E3 Movas Mex.
122 C6 Moveyleh Iran
197 P5 Movila Miresii Romania
197 M6 Movileni Romania
147 H2 Moville Ireland
86 G4 Mowanjum Aboriginal Reserve W.A. Austr.
85 M9 Mowbullan, Mount Qld Austr.
138 I8 Mowchadz' Belarus
146 L9 Mowtie Aberdeenshire, Scotland U.K.
232 C9 Moxahala OH U.S.A.
246 E1 Moxey Town Andros Bahamas
209 C8 Moxico prov. Angola
233 □P3 Moxie, Lake ME U.S.A.
147 D4 Moy r. Ireland
146 H8 Moy Highland, Scotland U.K.
147 I4 Moy Northern Ireland U.K.
216 □3f Moya Gran Canaria Canary Is
217 □3 Moya Nzwani Comoros
187 C8 Moya Castilla-La Mancha Spain
Moya Cataluña Spain see Moià
244 D4 Moyahua Mex.
210 C4 Moyale Eth.
206 B4 Moyamba Sierra Leone
147 B5 Moyard Ireland
147 D6 Moycullen Ireland
156 F4 Moy-de-l'Aisne France
204 D2 Moyen Atlas mts Morocco
208 C2 Moyen-Chari pref. Chad
Moyen Congo country Africa see Congo
215 L6 Moyeni Lesotho
157 M7 Moyenmoutier France
217 □2b Moyenne, Île i. Inner Islands Seychelles
206 B4 Moyenne-Guinée admin. reg. Guinea
156 C3 Moyenneville France
208 A5 Moyen-Ogooué prov. Gabon
147 I5 Moyer hill Ireland
157 L5 Moyeuvre-Grande France
147 I4 Moygashel Northern Ireland U.K.
147 D4 Moylaw Ireland
148 C6 Moylett Ireland
147 E6 Moylough Ireland
139 S8 Moylovo Rus. Fed.
147 I5 Moynalty Ireland
Moynaq Uzbek. see Mo'ynoq
147 G5 Moyne Ireland
120 H6 Mo'ynoq Uzbek.
209 E5 Moyo Dem. Rep. Congo
95 L9 Moyo i. Indon.
210 A4 Moyo Uganda
250 B6 Moyobamba Peru
148 D4 Moyola r. Northern Ireland U.K.
211 A6 Moyowosi r. Tanz.
140 M2 Møysalen mt. Norway
202 C6 Moyto Chad
111 D8 Moyu Xinjiang China
210 C4 Moyum waterhole Kenya
147 I6 Moyvalley Ireland
147 D7 Moyvane Ireland
148 B6 Moyvore Ireland
148 B7 Moyvoughly Ireland
121 O5 Moyynkum Kazakh.
121 O6 Moyynkum Kazakh.
121 L4 Moyynkum, Peski des. Kazakh.
121 M5 Moyynkum, Peski des. Kazakh.
121 O4 Moyynty Kazakh.
160 C5 Mozac France
213 G4 Mozambique country Africa
213 I4 Mozambique Channel Africa
265 G6 Mozambique Ridge sea feature Indian Ocean
182 I7 Mozárbez Spain
129 F2 Mozdok Rus. Fed.
122 I3 Mozdūrān Iran
232 B11 Mozelle KY U.S.A.
182 E7 Mozelos Port.
137 P4 Mozh r. Ukr.
138 M7 Mozha r. Belarus
137 S5 Mozhayevka Rus. Fed.
139 T6 Mozhaysk Rus. Fed.
134 K4 Mozhga Rus. Fed.
122 I4 Mozhnābād Iran
108 A2 Mozhong Qinghai China
179 K7 Mozirje Slovenia
179 K7 Mozirske planine mts Slovenia
96 B3 Mozo Myanmar
137 L4 Mozoliyivka Ukr.
183 L6 Mozoncillo Spain
177 G5 Mozsgó Hungary
Mozyr' Belarus see Mazyr
175 J1 Mozyr' Rus. Fed.
206 A3 Mpal Senegal
211 A6 Mpanda Tanz.
212 E3 Mpandamatenga Botswana
211 A7 Mpande Zambia
208 B5 Mpé Congo
215 O3 Mpemvana S. Africa
206 D3 Mpessoba Mali
215 M8 Mpetu S. Africa
210 B4 Mpigi Uganda
211 A7 Mpika Zambia
215 K8 Mpofu Game Reserve nature res. S. Africa
208 C3 Mpoko r. C.A.R.
215 O5 Mpolweni S. Africa
209 F8 Mpongwe Zambia
209 F7 Mporokoso Zambia
215 Q4 Mposa S. Africa
208 C5 Mpouya Congo
211 A7 Mpui Tanz.
211 A7 Mpulungu Zambia
215 O5 Mpumalanga S. Africa
215 N2 Mpumalanga prov. S. Africa
211 C6 Mpwapwa Tanz.
195 □ Mqabba Malta
215 M7 Mqanduli S. Africa
Mqinvartsveri mt. Georgia/Rus. Fed. see Kazbek
175 J2 Mrągowo Pol.
173 N3 Mrákov Czech Rep.
135 L5 Mrakovo Rus. Fed.
96 A4 Mrauk-U Myanmar
Mrewa Zimbabwe see Murehwa
188 E3 Mrežnica r. Croatia
188 F3 Mrkonjić-Grad Bos.-Herz.
191 R5 Mrkopalj Croatia
174 F2 Mrocza Pol.
174 F4 Mroczeń Pol.
175 I4 Mroczków Pol.
175 H2 Mroczno Pol.
175 H3 Mroga r. Pol.
175 J3 Mrozy Pol.
137 K2 Mryn Ukr.
205 H2 M'Saken Tunisia
211 C6 Msambweni Kenya
211 C6 Msata Tanz.
174 E1 Mścice Pol.
176 D1 Mšeno Czech Rep.
138 M2 Mshinskaya Rus. Fed.
205 G2 M'Sila Alg.
139 R4 Msta Rus. Fed.
139 O3 Msta r. Rus. Fed.
139 P3 Mstinskiy Most Rus. Fed.
Mstislavl' Belarus see Mstsislaw
175 H5 Mstów Pol.
139 O7 Mstsislaw Belarus
215 Q3 Msunduze r. S. Africa
175 I6 Mszana Dolna Pol.
175 I4 Mszczonów Pol.
211 A6 Mtakuja Tanz.
211 C7 Mtama Tanz.
129 G3 Mt'at'ushet'is Nakrdzali nature res. Georgia
210 B4 Mtelo Kenya
211 B6 Mtera Reservoir Tanz.
Mtoko Zimbabwe see Mutoko
215 P4 Mtonjaneni S. Africa
Mtorashanga Zimbabwe see Mutorashanga
217 □3b Mtsamboro Mayotte
217 □3b Mtsangamouji Mayotte
139 T8 Mtsensk Rus. Fed.
129 F4 Mts'khet'a Georgia
213 G6 Mtubatuba S. Africa
211 C7 Mtukula Tanz.
215 P4 Mtunzini S. Africa
211 D7 Mtwara Tanz.
211 C7 Mtwara admin. reg. Tanz.
96 B4 Mu r. Myanmar
184 C6 Mu hill Port.
79 □8a Mu'a Tongatapu Tonga
Mu'āb, Jibāl reg. Jordan see Moab
211 C8 Muaguide Moz.
213 G2 Mualadzi Moz.
213 H3 Mualama Moz.
254 C2 Muana Brazil
209 B6 Muanda Dem. Rep. Congo
96 G4 Muang Ham Laos
96 F4 Muang Hiam Laos
96 G6 Muang Hinboun Laos
96 E5 Muang Hôngsa Laos
108 D8 Muang Hounxianghoung Laos
96 F5 Muang Kao Laos
96 E5 Muang Khi Laos
97 G7 Muang Khôngxédôn Laos
96 G7 Muang Khôngxédôn Laos
96 F4 Muang Khoua Laos
96 G5 Muang Mok Laos
96 F4 Muang Ngoy Laos
96 H6 Muang Nong Laos
96 E3 Muang Ou Nua Laos
96 E5 Muang Pakbeng Laos
96 E4 Muang Paktha Laos
96 G6 Muang Phalan Laos
96 E5 Muang Phiang Laos
96 H6 Muang Phin Laos
96 F5 Muang Phôn-Hông Laos
96 G7 Muang Sam Sip Thai.
96 E4 Muang Sing Laos
96 G6 Muang Songkhon Laos
96 F5 Muang Soum Laos
96 F5 Muang Souy Laos
96 E5 Muang Thadua Laos
Muang Thai country Asia see Thailand
96 F4 Muang Va Laos
96 F5 Muang Vangviang Laos
96 F4 Muang Xon Laos
213 G3 Muanza Moz.
94 E3 Muar Malaysia
94 E3 Muar r. Malaysia
95 K2 Muara Brunei
95 L4 Muaraancalong Kalimantan Indon.
95 L4 Muaraatap Kalimantan Indon.
94 E6 Muarabeliti Sumatera Indon.
94 E5 Muarabulian Sumatera Indon.
94 E5 Muarabungo Sumatera Indon.
94 F7 Muaradua Sumatera Indon.
94 E6 Muaraenim Sumatera Indon.
95 K5 Muarainu Kalimantan Indon.
95 L5 Muarajawa Kalimantan Indon.
95 L5 Muarakaman Kalimantan Indon.
95 L4 Muara Kaman Sedulang, Cagar Alam nature res. Kalimantan Indon.
94 D5 Muaralabuh Sumatera Indon.
94 E6 Muaralakitan Sumatera Indon.
95 K5 Muaralaung Kalimantan Indon.
95 L4 Muaralesan Kalimantan Indon.
95 L4 Muaramayang Kalimantan Indon.
95 L4 Muaranawai Kalimantan Indon.
94 E6 Muararupit Sumatera Indon.
94 E5 Muarasabak Sumatera Indon.
94 C5 Muarasiberut Indon.
94 C4 Muarasipongi Sumatera Indon.
94 C4 Muarasoma Sumatera Indon.
95 M4 Muaras Reef Indon.
94 E5 Muaratebo Sumatera Indon.
94 E5 Muaratembesi Sumatera Indon.
95 K5 Muarateweh Kalimantan Indon.
Muara Tuang Sarawak Malaysia see Kota Samarahan
95 L4 Muarawahau Kalimantan Indon.
93 E4 Muari i. Maluku Indon.
123 L9 Muari, Ras pt Pak.
213 H2 Muatua Moz.
125 I2 Mu'ayqil, Khashm al hill Saudi Arabia
116 E4 Muazzam Punjab India
128 D9 Mubārak, Jabal mt. Jordan/Saudi Arabia
117 I6 Mubarakpur Uttar Prad. India
Mubarek Uzbek. see Muborak
127 J9 Mubarraz well Saudi Arabia
210 A4 Mubende Uganda
207 I4 Mubi Nigeria
120 K8 Muborak Uzbek.
94 G3 Mubur i. Indon.
209 B6 Mucaba Angola
209 B6 Mucaba, Serra mts Angola
251 G5 Mucajá Brazil
251 F4 Mucajaí r. Brazil
251 F4 Mucajaí, Serra do mts Brazil
225 H1 Mucalic r. Que. Can.
213 F2 Mucanha r. Moz.
196 I7 Mučanj mt. Serbia
86 F6 Muccan W.A. Austr.
193 K1 Muccia Italy
169 D9 Much Ger.
175 H6 Mucharz Pol.
87 C11 Muchea W.A. Austr.
171 E8 Mücheln (Geiseltal) Ger.
Mucheng Henan China see Wuzhi
100 B2 Muchikan Rus. Fed.
211 A8 Muchinga Escarpment Zambia
253 E4 Muchiri Bol.
135 H6 Muchkapskiy Rus. Fed.
134 J2 Muchkas Rus. Fed.
170 E4 Muchow Ger.
175 I6 Muchówka Pol.
108 D4 Muchuan Sichuan China
150 G2 Much Wenlock Shropshire, England U.K.
183 K5 Mucientes Spain
146 D9 Muck i. Scotland U.K.
171 K8 Mücka Ger.
85 L9 Muckadilla Qld Austr.
84 D5 Muckaty Aboriginal Land res. N.T. Austr.
169 H9 Mücke Große-Eichen Ger.
169 H9 Mücke-Nieder-Ohmen Ger.
147 F2 Muckish Mountain hill Ireland
146 □O1 Muckle Flugga i. Scotland U.K.
146 □N2 Muckle Roe i. Scotland U.K.
148 D5 Muckno Lake Ireland
250 D3 Muco r. Col.
211 D8 Mucojo Moz.
209 D7 Muconda Angola
195 K5 Mucone r. Italy
209 B9 Mucope Angola
177 H5 Mucsi-hegy hill Hungary
177 J3 Múcsony Hungary
213 H3 Mucubela Moz.
213 H3 Mucúbi Moz.
251 F5 Mucucuaú r. Brazil
251 E6 Mucuim r. Brazil
213 F3 Mucumbura Moz.
209 C9 Mucundi Angola
209 C8 Mucunha Angola
213 H3 Mucupia Moz.
126 G4 Mucur Turkey
251 F5 Mucura Brazil
257 H3 Mucuri Brazil
257 H3 Mucuri r. Brazil
257 G3 Mucurici Brazil
250 D5 Mucuripe Brazil
254 F2 Mucuripe, Ponta de pt Brazil
209 D9 Mucusso, Coutada Pública do nature res. Angola
209 D7 Mucussueje Angola
216 □3b Muda hill Fuerteventura Canary Is
94 D2 Muda r. Malaysia
114 D6 Mudabidri Karnataka India
Mudan Shandong China see Heze
100 F6 Mudanjiang Heilong. China
100 F5 Mudan Jiang r. China
100 E7 Mudan Ling mts China
199 J2 Mudanya Turkey
172 G2 Mudau Ger.
127 M9 Mudayrah Kuwait
128 E7 Mudaysīsāt, Jabal al hill Jordan
114 E4 Muddebihal Karnataka India
140 O3 Muddus nationalpark nat. park Sweden
241 R5 Muddy r. NV U.S.A.
237 H9 Muddy Boggy Creek r. OK U.S.A.
234 C5 Muddy Creek r. PA U.S.A.
241 V3 Muddy Creek r. UT U.S.A.
238 K5 Muddy Gap pass WY U.S.A.
241 R5 Muddy Peak NV U.S.A.
234 C5 Muddy Run Reservoir PA U.S.A.
122 H5 Mūd-e Dahanāb Iran
215 O4 Muden S. Africa
168 J5 Müden (Aller) Ger.
168 J5 Müden (Örtze) Ger.
169 E9 Mudersbach Ger.
114 E5 Mudgal Karnataka India
83 L5 Mudgee N.S.W. Austr.
114 D4 Mudhol Karnataka India
114 D6 Mudigere Karnataka India
223 J3 Mudjatik r. Sask. Can.
114 E3 Mudkhed Mahar. India
116 E4 Mudki Punjab India
240 O4 Mud Lake NV U.S.A.
96 C6 Mudon Myanmar
Mudraya country Africa see Egypt
210 E3 Mudug admin. reg. Somalia
211 B5 Mudukani Tanz.
212 D3 Mudumu National Park Namibia
199 M2 Mudurnu Turkey
199 L2 Mudurnu r. Turkey
134 G3 Mud'yuga Rus. Fed.
213 H2 Muecate Moz.
211 C7 Mueda Moz.
186 C5 Muel Spain
183 M4 Muela de Quintanilla hill Spain
182 I5 Muelas del Pan Spain
86 I5 Mueller Range hills W.A. Austr.
213 G2 Muende Moz.
245 M9 Muerto, Mar lag. Mex.
246 C1 Muertos Cays is Bahamas
125 I1 Mufattah, Khawr b. Saudi Arabia
147 H2 Muff Ireland
203 G4 Muftah well Sudan
134 I2 Muftyuga Rus. Fed.
209 F8 Mufulira Zambia
209 E8 Mufumbwe Zambia
109 J4 Mufu Shan mts China
182 H6 Muga de Sayago Spain
225 H4 Mugaguadavic Lake N.B. Can.
129 J5 Muğan Azer.
129 J6 Muğan Düzü lowland Azer.
129 H4 Muğanlı Azer.
182 D2 Mugardos Spain
184 B2 Muge Port.
184 B2 Muge r. Port.
213 H3 Mugeba Moz.
104 E4 Mugegawa Japan
171 H8 Mügeln Sachsen Ger.
171 H7 Mügeln Sachsen-Anhalt Ger.
172 E4 Muggensturm Ger.
191 P4 Muggia Italy
Mughalbhin Pak. see Jati
117 I7 Mughal Sarai Uttar Prad. India
122 E5 Mūghār Iran
126 H9 Mughayrā' Saudi Arabia
124 G3 Mughayrā' well Saudi Arabia
125 L6 Mughshin Oman
123 N2 Mughsu r. Tajik.
104 F4 Mugi Gifu Japan
103 L13 Mugi Tokushima Japan
Mugia Spain see Muxía
209 F6 Mugila, Monts mts Dem. Rep. Congo
199 J5 Muğla Turkey
199 J5 Muğla prov. Turkey
120 H3 Mugodzharskoye Kazakh.
120 H4 Mugodzhary, Gory mts Kazakh.
106 C9 Mug Qu r. Qinghai China
163 C8 Mugron France
211 C8 Muguia Moz.
116 H5 Mugu Karnali r. Nepal
211 B5 Mugumu Tanz.
106 B1 Mugur-Aksy Rus. Fed.
111 L10 Mugxung Qinghai China
128 G4 Mūḩ, Sabkhat imp. l. Syria
208 E2 Muhagiriya Sudan
Muhala Xinjiang China see Yutian
209 F6 Muhala Dem. Rep. Congo
203 G3 Muḩammad, Ra's pt Egypt
117 I7 Muhammadabad Uttar Prad. India
123 M8 Muhammad Ashraf Pak.
203 H4 Muhammad Qol Sudan
Muhammarah Iran see Khorramshahr
106 F8 Muhar Qinghai China
128 C8 Muhashsham, Wādī al watercourse Egypt
124 G4 Muḩayriqah Saudi Arabia
128 E9 Muḩaysh, Wādī al watercourse Jordan
128 H2 Muhaysin Syria
211 C6 Muheza Tanz.
172 F4 Mühlacker Ger.
171 G7 Mühlanger Ger.
170 I3 Mühlbach r. Ger.
171 H8 Mühlberg Brandenburg Ger.
169 K9 Mühlberg Thüringen Ger.
179 H6 Mühldorf Austria
173 N5 Mühldorf am Inn Ger.
179 K5 Mühlen Austria
170 G2 Mühlen hill Ger.
170 H5 Mühlenbeck Ger.
170 D3 Mühlen-Eichsen Ger.
172 F3 Mühlhausen Baden-Württemberg Ger.
173 K3 Mühlhausen Bayern Ger.
169 J8 Mühlhausen (Thüringen) Ger.
169 G10 Mühlheim am Main Ger.
172 F5 Mühlheim an der Donau Ger.
263 A2 Mühlig-Hofmann Mountains Antarctica
172 G6 Mühlingen Ger.
171 E9 Mühltroff Ger.
179 J2 Mühlviertel reg. Austria
140 R4 Muhos Fin.

128 E3 Muḥradah Syria
173 J3 Muhr am See Ger.
123 L7 Muhri Pak.
138 G3 Muhu i. Estonia
211 B7 Muhulu Dem. Rep. Congo
213 H2 Muhula Moz.
208 C5 Muhulu Dem. Rep. Congo
210 B3 Mui Eth.
Mui Bai Bung c. Vietnam see Ca Mau, Mui
164 H4 Muiden Neth.
156 B5 Muié Angola
211 C7 Muidumbe Moz.
232 D11 Muié Angola
105 I1 Muika Japan
93 F4 Muiliýk i. Maluku Indon.
Muineachán Ireland see Monaghan
147 I7 Muine Bheag Ireland
182 E5 Muiños Spain
226 J7 Muir MI U.S.A.
234 B3 Muir PA U.S.A.
146 K9 Muirdrum Angus, Scotland U.K.
222 B3 Muir Glacier Can./U.S.A.
146 J10 Muirhead Angus, Scotland U.K.
146 H11 Muirkirk East Ayrshire, Scotland U.K.
146 D6 Muirneag hill Scotland U.K.
146 K8 Muir of Fowlis Aberdeenshire, Scotland U.K.
146 H7 Muir of Ord Highland, Scotland U.K.
250 B4 Muisne Ecuador
213 H2 Muite Moz.
156 C5 Muizon France
122 F4 Müjän, Chāh-e well Iran
243 P7 Mujeres, Isla i. Mex.
111 D8 Muji Xinjiang China
95 J3 Mujong r. Malaysia
101 E10 Muju S. Korea
251 H5 Mujuí Joboti Brazil
122 B2 Mujumbar Iran
Mukačevo Ukr. see Mukacheve
136 B5 Mukachevo Ukr.
Mukachevo Ukr. see Mukacheve
95 J3 Mukah Sarawak Malaysia
95 J3 Mukah r. Malaysia
116 E6 Mukalla Yemen see Al Mukallā
116 F7 Mukandwara Rajasthan India
209 D6 Mukanga Dem. Rep. Congo
125 I5 Mukassir, Bani des. Saudi Arabia
102 S4 Mukawa Hokkaidō Japan
105 H4 Mukawa Yamanashi Japan
102 S4 Mu-kawa r. Japan
203 H4 Mukawwar, Gezirat i. Sudan
96 G6 Mukdahan Thai.
Mukden Liaoning China see Shenyang
116 E4 Mukerian Punjab India
92 □ Mukery Palau
224 C2 Muketei r. Ont. Can.
210 C2 Muke T'uri Eth.
175 L3 Mukhavets r. Belarus
100 J4 Mukhen Rus. Fed.
100 E2 Mukhino Rus. Fed.
107 K1 Mukhorshibir' Rus. Fed.
Mukhtuya Rus. Fed. see Lensk
129 F6 Mükhnor Iran
122 G5 Mükik, Chashmeh-ye spring Iran
87 E11 Mukinbudin W.A. Austr.
104 C6 Mukō Japan
97 F9 Mu Ko Chang Marine National Park Thai.
103 □2 Mukō-jima i. Japan
103 □2 Mukojima-rettō is Japan
94 D6 Mukomuko Sumatera Indon.
210 B4 Mukono Uganda
209 F7 Mukoshi Zambia
123 K3 Mukry Turkm.
Muksu r. Tajik. see Mughsu
117 I5 Muktinath Nepal
116 F4 Muktsar Punjab India
209 F8 Mukuku Zambia
213 F3 Mukumbura Zimbabwe
209 F7 Mukunsa Zambia
120 F4 Mukur Atyrauskaya Oblast' Kazakh.
121 S2 Mukur Vostochnyy Kazakhstan Kazakh.
223 L4 Mukutawa r. Man. Can.
226 F7 Mukwonago WI U.S.A.
116 G9 Mul Mahar. India
114 D3 Mula r. Pak.
123 □7 Mula r. Pak.
187 C11 Mula Spain
185 Q4 Mula r. Spain
Mulaku atoll Maldives see Mulaku Atoll
113 D11 Mulaku Atoll Maldives
121 R5 Mulaly Kazakh.
100 F6 Mulan Heilong. China
92 D5 Mulanay Luzon Phil.
211 B8 Mulanje Malawi
213 G2 Mulanje, Mount Malawi
82 F3 Mulapula, Lake salt flat S.A. Austr.
192 C8 Mulargia, Lago l. Sardegna Italy
242 E3 Mulatos Mex.
242 CU13 Mula-tupo Panama
124 G2 Mulaykh Saudi Arabia
128 Q9 Mulayh salt pan Saudi Arabia
125 I2 Mulaykah Saudi Arabia
128 B8 Mulayz, Wādī al watercourse Egypt
190 H7 Mulazzo Italy
114 F6 Mulbagal Karnataka India
151 O2 Mulbarton Norfolk, England U.K.
116 F2 Mulbekh Jammu and Kashmir
146 J7 Mulben Moray, Scotland U.K.
237 H8 Mulberry AR U.S.A.
220 C3 Mulchatna r. AK U.S.A.
260 A5 Mulchén Chile
171 H9 Mulde Ger.
171 F7 Mulde r. Ger.
171 F7 Muldenstein Ger.
211 A5 Muleba Tanz.
238 L6 Mule Creek WY U.S.A.
242 C4 Mulegé Mex.
211 A7 Mulekatembo Zambia
93 B8 Mules i. Indon.
237 D8 Muleshoe TX U.S.A.
213 H3 Mulevala Moz.
172 H3 Mulfingen Ger.
57 B7 Mulga Downs W.A. Austr.
84 C8 Mulga Park N.T. Austr.
82 E4 Mulgathrogie S.A. Austr.
185 M6 Mulhacén mt. Spain
Mulhouse
169 C8 Mülheim an der Ruhr Ger.
169 D10 Mülheim-Kärlich Ger.
157 N8 Mulhouse France
108 C5 Muli Sichuan China
Muli Rus. Fed. see Vysokogornyy
78 □2 Mulifanua Samoa
113 □7 Mulikatu i. Addu Atoll Maldives
116 G8 Mulila Gujarat India
211 B7 Mulilansolo Zambia
100 G6 Muling Heilong. China
100 F6 Muling r. Heilong. China
100 H6 Muling He r. China
78 □2 Mulitapu'ili, Cape Samoa
179 K8 Muljava Slovenia
146 E10 Mull i. Scotland U.K.
146 E10 Mull, Sound of sea chan. Scotland U.K.
122 C3 Mulla Ali Iran
210 E2 Mullaaxe Beyle Somalia
148 D6 Mullagh Cavan Ireland
147 C5 Mullagh Clare Ireland
147 C5 Mullagh Mayo Ireland
147 I6 Mullagh Meath Ireland
147 D8 Mullaghareirk Ireland
147 D8 Mullaghareirk Mountains hills Ireland
147 H3 Mullaghcarn hill Northern Ireland U.K.
147 J6 Mullaghcleevaun hill Ireland

147 H3 Mullaghcloga hill Northern Ireland U.K.
147 F4 Mullaghmore Ireland
114 G8 Mullaittivu Sri Lanka
83 L4 Mullaley N.S.W. Austr.
147 I4 Mullan Ireland
147 G4 Mullan Northern Ireland U.K.
146 F8 Mullardoch, Loch i. Scotland U.K.
147 K4 Mullartown Northern Ireland U.K.
236 E4 Mullen NE U.S.A.
83 K4 Mullengudgery N.S.W. Austr.
232 D11 Mullens WV U.S.A.
84 E7 Muller watercourse N.T. Austr.
95 J4 Muller, Pegunungan mts Indon.
226 J4 Mullett Lake MI U.S.A.
87 C10 Mullewa W.A. Austr.
146 K5 Mull Head Orkney, Scotland U.K.
172 D6 Müllheim Ger.
234 G5 Mullica r. NJ U.S.A.
234 E5 Mullica Hill NJ U.S.A.
84 G8 Mulligan watercourse Qld Austr.
147 H8 Mullinavat Ireland
147 H5 Mullingar Ireland
231 H8 Mullins SC U.S.A.
150 B7 Mullion Cornwall, England U.K.
83 L5 Mullion Creek N.S.W. Austr.
146 E12 Mull of Galloway c. Scotland U.K.
146 D11 Mull of Oa hd Scotland U.K.
135 J5 Mullovka Rus. Fed.
171 J6 Müllrose Ger.
143 J4 Mullsjö Sweden
138 F3 Mullutu salt l. Estonia
209 E9 Mulobezi Zambia
209 B8 Mulondo Angola
209 D9 Mulonga Plain Zambia
209 E6 Mulongo Dem. Rep. Congo
147 C5 Mulroy Ireland
147 G2 Mulroy Bay Ireland
159 L6 Mulsanne France
114 C3 Mulshi Lake India
116 G9 Multai Madh. Prad. India
123 I8 Multān Iran
123 N6 Multan Pak.
114 K5 Multia Fin.
209 F7 Multien reg. France
95 K2 Mulu, Gunung mt. Malaysia
114 I3 Mulug Andhra Prad. India
209 E7 Mulumbe, Monts mts Dem. Rep. Congo
83 I5 Mulurulu Lake N.S.W. Austr.
208 D4 Mulumba Dem. Rep. Congo
208 E2 Mumallah Sudan
122 I9 Mumallah Iran
114 C3 Mumbai India
209 D8 Mumbeji Zambia
83 L5 Mumbil N.S.W. Austr.
150 E4 Mumbles Head Wales U.K.
209 B7 Mumbondo Angola
209 C8 Mumbué Angola
209 E8 Mumbwa Zambia
211 C6 Mumbu Tanz.
209 E7 Mume Dem. Rep. Congo
Muminabad Tajik. see Leningrad
Mŭ'minobod Tajik. see Leningrad
97 D11 Mümliswil Switz.
209 D6 Mumoma Dem. Rep. Congo
120 B5 Mumra r. Rus. Fed.
192 A9 Mumullonis, Punta volt Italy
96 G7 Mun, Mae Nam r. Thai.
93 C6 Muna i. Indon.
243 O7 Muna Mex.
131 N3 Muna r. Rus. Fed.
123 N9 Munabao Pak.
140 OC1 Munaðarnes Iceland
114 F4 Munagala Andhra Prad. India
110 H13 Munakata Japan
183 J7 Munana Spain
114 C3 Munayjah, Jabal mts Egypt/Sudan
120 F4 Munaýly Kazakh.
114 F4 Munaýshy Kazakh.
171 E10 Münchberg Ger.
171 J5 Müncheberg Ger.
173 L5 München Ger.
München airport Ger. see Franz Josef Strauss
171 E9 Münchebernsdorf Ger.
190 C1 Münchenbuchsee Ger.
Mönchengladbach Ger. see Mönchengladbach
169 G9 Münchhausen Ger.
250 B4 Munchique, Parque Nacional nat. park Col.
222 E3 Muncho Lake B.C. Can.
222 E3 Muncho Lake Provincial Park B.C. Can.
101 E9 Munch'ŏn N. Korea
173 L4 Münchsmünster Ger.
173 J2 Münchsteinach Ger.
172 D3 Münchweiler an der Rodalb Ger.
190 C1 Münchwilen Switz.
230 E5 Muncie IN U.S.A.
84 G8 Muncoonie West, Lake salt flat Qld Austr.
227 R8 Muncy PA U.S.A.
234 B2 Muncy Creek r. PA U.S.A.
234 B2 Muncy Valley PA U.S.A.
209 D6 Munda Angola
123 N6 Munda Pak.
78 □6 Munda New Georgia Is Solomon Is
183 O2 Mundaka Spain
114 F9 Mundel Lake Sri Lanka
207 H5 Mundemba Cameroon
178 H3 Munderfing Austria
172 H5 Munderkingen Ger.
151 O2 Mundesley Norfolk, England U.K.
151 N2 Mundford Norfolk, England U.K.
87 B7 Mundiwindi W.A. Austr.
85 H5 Mundjura Creek r. Qld Austr.
185 P4 Mundo r. Spain
197 O6 Mundoldsheim France
254 E4 Mundo Novo Brazil
116 B8 Mundra Gujarat India
87 I11 Mundrabilla W.A. Austr.
241 U1 Munds Park AZ U.S.A.
185 M8 Mundúbbera Qld Austr.
116 D6 Mundwa Rajasthan India
183 J6 Munebrega Spain
185 O2 Munera Spain
114 G4 Munéru r. India
230 E7 Munfordville KY U.S.A.
85 H9 Mungallala Qld Austr.
83 K3 Mungallala Creek r. Qld Austr.
85 J4 Mungana Qld Austr.
116 G7 Mungaoli Madh. Prad. India
86 E6 Mungaroona Range Nature Reserve W.A. Austr.
208 F4 Mungbere Dem. Rep. Congo
116 H8 Munger Chhattisgarh India
117 K7 Munger Bihar India
227 K6 Mungeranie S.A. Austr.
82 G3 Mungeranie S.A. Austr.
Mu Ngiki i. Solomon Is see Bellona
97 H8 Mungilli Aboriginal Reserve W.A. Austr.
95 H4 Mungindi N.S.W. Austr.
179 M6 Mungkung Madh. Prad. India
84 E6 Mungi Aboriginal Land res. N.T. Austr.
209 C8 Mungo Angola
83 I5 Mungo, Lake Brazil
196 I4 Mungo National Park N.S.W. Austr.
147 E7 Mungret Ireland
209 C9 Munguba Angola
211 A7 Munhango Angola
209 B8 Munhino Angola
256 D5 Munhoz Brazil

183 J7 Muñico Spain
182 G2 Muniellos, Reserva Natural Integral de nature res. Spain
186 D5 Muniesa Spain
183 P4 Munilla Spain
226 H3 Munising MI U.S.A.
257 G4 Muniz Freire Brazil
116 C8 Munjpur Gujarat India
197 Q4 Munjani Romania
190 D1 Münnerstadt Ger.
208 C4 Munkebo Dem. Rep. Congo
138 H5 Munkebo Norway
142 H4 Munkedal Sweden
140 M5 Munkfors Sweden
142 J2 Munkfors Sweden
165 E7 Munkzwalm Belgium
146 H7 Munlochy Highland, Scotland U.K.
169 J10 Munningen Ger.
173 J4 Munningen Ger.
80 □ Munning Point Chatham Is S. Pacific Ocean
183 K7 Muñogalindo Spain
83 L9 Munro, Mount Tas. Austr.
117 J8 Munro r. Jharkhand India
190 E1 Müri Aargau Switz.
190 C2 Müri Switz.
127 J3 Müri Switz.
95 I8 Muria, Gunung mt. Indon.
257 F4 Muriaé Brazil
183 J7 Murias de Paredes Spain
209 D7 Muriege Angola
95 H4 Murih, Pulau i. Indon.
102 U3 Murii-dake mt. Japan
226 E1 Murillo Ont. Can.
185 O5 Murillo el Fruto Spain
170 G4 Müritz l. Ger.
170 H4 Müritz, Nationalpark nat. park Ger.
170 D4 Müritz-Elde-Wasserstraße r. Ger.
170 G4 Müritz Seenpark nature res. Ger.
80 L5 Muriwai North I. N.Z.
117 C7 Murjek Sweden
192 G1 Murlo Italy
140 W2 Murmansk Rus. Fed.
Murmanskaya Oblast' admin. div. Rus. Fed.
140 V2 Murmanskaya Oblast' admin. div. Rus. Fed.
140 V2 Murmansk Oblast admin. div. Rus. Fed.
156 C5 Murnau am Staffelsee Ger.
147 I8 Murntown Ireland
104 D7 Muro Japan
157 M5 Muro Port.
183 M2 Muro r. Spain
192 B4 Muro, Capo di c. Corse France
104 D6 Muro-Akame-Aoyama Kokutei-kōen park Japan
117 I5 Murol Nepal
160 B5 Murol France
195 O3 Muro Leccese Italy
137 L4 Muravýeva r. Ukr.
194 H5 Muro Lucano Italy
104 A8 Murom Rus. Fed.
102 S4 Muroran Japan
183 B2 Muros Spain
183 B2 Muros e Noia, Ría de est. Spain
103 L13 Muroto Japan
104 A8 Muroto-zaki pt Japan
175 M5 Murovane Ukr.
137 L4 Murovani Kurylivtsi Ukr.
137 L4 Murovaný Slisisasi hills Ukr.
174 F5 Murów Pol.
209 F8 Murowa Gosliná Pol.
173 M3 Murrch r. Ger.
182 E9 Muradie r. Port.
199 I4 Muradiye Manisa Turkey
127 K4 Muradiye Van Turkey
114 C7 Murafa r. Ukr.
104 □3 Murai, Tanjong pt Sing.
102 Q3 Murakami Japan
176 F5 Murakeresztúr Hungary
259 B8 Murallón, Cerro mt. Chile
114 C3 Muramya Burundi
177 J3 Murán Slovakia
177 J3 Murán r. Slovakia
210 C5 Murang'a Kenya
191 M5 Murano Italy
177 I3 Muránska planina park Slovakia
103 L11 Muraoka Japan
182 E2 Muras Spain
134 I4 Murashi Rus. Fed.
160 F4 Murasson France
176 F5 Murat France
161 D6 Murat r. Turkey
127 I4 Murat r. Turkey
127 C7 Muratgören Turkey
199 K4 Murato Corse France
161 B8 Murat-sur-Vèbre France
178 H4 Murau Austria
175 M3 Murava Belarus
172 H4 Murava Sardegna Italy
240 O8 Muravera Italy
102 H8 Muravera Japan
124 C3 Muray, Jabal mt. Saudi Arabia
209 K7 Murayr, Jazirat i. Egypt
202 E2 Muraysah, Ra's al pt Libya
127 K3 Murazzano Italy
213 H2 Murça Port.
183 Q4 Murchante Spain
122 D5 Murch Khvort Iran
170 I3 Murchin Ger.
83 J7 Murchison watercourse W.A. Austr.
81 G8 Murchison South I. N.Z.
263 I2 Murchison, Mount Antarctica
190 C2 Murchison, Mount hill
83 K3 Murchison, Mount N.Z.
81 F10 Murchison, Mount South I. N.Z.
210 A4 Murchison Falls National Park Uganda
224 B3 Murchison Mountains South I. N.Z.
81 B12 Murchison Mountains South I. N.Z.
84 E6 Murchison Range hills N.T.
210 B4 Murchison Range hills Kenya
204 H2 Murchison Moz.
179 L7 Murci Port.
161 B7 Mur-de-Barrez France
158 F5 Mür-de-Bretagne France
234 E4 Murderkill r. DE U.S.A.
161 B7 Mur-de-Sologne France
186 C4 Murdo SD U.S.A.
225 H4 Murdochville Que. Can.
240 □ Mure Japan
141 O3 Mureck Austria
140 G3 Murefte Turkey
251 I5 Mureji Nigeria
213 F3 Murehwa Zimbabwe
184 E3 Mureș r. Romania
161 C10 Mureș-lès-Mauleon France
124 D4 Murwani, Wādī watercourse Saudi Arabia
193 L6 Muravera Moz.
161 G9 Muret France
180 D5 Murehwa Zimbabwe
234 H8 Murfreesboro NC U.S.A.
231 I7 Murfreesboro NC U.S.A.
231 D8 Murfreesboro TN U.S.A.
172 E4 Murg r. Ger.
172 E5 Murg r. Ger.

Murgab Tajik. see Murghob
202 B3 Murgab Turkm. see Murgap
202 B3 Murgap r. Turkm. see Murgap
84 D1 Murgenella Creek r. N.T. Austr.
197 Q4 Murgeni Romania
208 C4 Murgeni Switz.
138 H5 Mūsa i. Lith.
alt. Mūsa (Latvia)
141 R8 Mūsa r. Latvia
alt. Mūsa (Lith.)
124 A1 Mūsa, Jabal mt. Egypt
122 C6 Mūsa, Khowr-e b. Iran
124 F9 Musa Ali Terara vol. Africa
117 K8 Musabani Jharkhand India
128 C2 Musabeyli Turkey
124 E6 Muşabih Saudi Arabia
123 M8 Musa Khel Bazar Pak.
197 L8 Musala mt. Bulg.
94 C4 Musala i. Indon.
128 C2 Musalı Turkey
101 F7 Musan N. Korea
125 M3 Musandam admin. reg. Oman
125 M2 Musandam Peninsula Oman/U.A.E.
123 K5 Musa Qala Afgh.
123 K5 Mūsā Qal'eh, Rūd-e r. Afgh.
105 K4 Musashino Japan
124 G9 Musayir Yemen
202 E6 Musbat well Sudan
150 F6 Musbury Devon, England U.K.
236 J3 Muscoda WI U.S.A.
234 E3 Musconetcong r. NJ U.S.A.
233 □P5 Musconus Bay ME U.S.A.
138 H7 Musė r. Lith.
192 B9 Musei Sardegna Italy
85 I3 Musgrave Qld Austr.
84 C2 Musgrave, Mount South I. N.Z.
225 K3 Musgrave Harbour Nfld and Lab. Can.
82 C2 Musgrave Ranges mts S.A. Austr.
256 D4 Musial r. Brazil
213 G4 Musiamana Moz.
117 H7 Musina S. Africa
241 U2 Musinia Peak UT U.S.A.
137 L4 Musiyivka Ukr.
114 D5 Musiri Tamil Nadu India
222 F2 Muskeg r. N.W.T. Can.
233 O7 Musket Channel MA U.S.A.
226 H6 Muskegon r. MI U.S.A.
226 H6 Muskegon Heights MI U.S.A.
226 H6 Muskegon River Alta Can.
232 A9 Muskingum r. OH U.S.A.
237 H8 Muskogee OK U.S.A.
224 E4 Muskoka Ont. Can.
224 E4 Muskoka, Lake Ont. Can.
222 I3 Muskwa r. B.C. Can.
123 L6 Muslimbagh Pak.
Muslim-Croat Federation aut. div. Bos.-Herz. see Federacija Bosna i Hercegovina
128 F2 Muslimiyah Syria
125 I4 Muslyumovo Rus. Fed.
203 G5 Musmar Sudan
209 F8 Musofu Zambia
211 B6 Musoma Tanz.
209 B6 Musombe Dem. Rep. Congo
225 I3 Musquaro, Lac l. Que. Can.
225 I3 Musquaro, Lac l. Que. Can.
209 D8 Mussaca Angola
209 D8 Mussacossa Angola
91 K7 Mussau Island P.N.G.
146 J11 Musselburgh East Lothian, Scotland U.K.
164 K3 Musselkanaal Neth.
238 K3 Musselshell r. MT U.S.A.
209 C8 Musserra Angola
209 B6 Mussera Angola
190 D1 Mussidan France
191 K8 Mussomeli Sicilia Italy
165 I9 Musson Belgium
114 C3 Mussoorie Uttaranchal India
209 D8 Mussuma Angola
115 H6 Mussuma r. Angola
87 J8 Mussy-sur-Seine France
226 H5 Mustafabad Uttar Prad. India
116 G6 Mustafabad Uttar Prad. India
199 J2 Mustafakemalpaşa Turkey
210 E3 Mustahîl Eth.
138 J3 Mustajärvi Estonia
138 I1 Mustamaa i. Fin.
138 J3 Mustasaari Fin.
138 K1 Mustijõgi r. Estonia
138 J3 Mustla Estonia
138 J3 Mustvee Estonia
101 B8 Musu-dan pt N. Korea
129 G4 Müsüslü Azer.
175 I6 Muszaki Pol.
175 I6 Muszyna Pol.
203 F3 Mūţ Egypt
126 E5 Mut Turkey
179 L6 Muta Slovenia
126 I5 Mutalau Niue
81 □ Muta, Lago di l. Italy
254 F5 Mutá, Ponta do pt Brazil
81 □ Mutalau Niue
209 D8 Mutanda Zambia
140 T4 Mutanda Moz.
252 C2 Mutare Zimbabwe
Mutarjim, Khashm hill
127 M8 Mutayr reg. Saudi Arabia
209 B8 Mutenge Dem. Rep. Congo
134 H2 Muteta Dem. Rep. Congo
180 Q3 Mutis, Gunung mt. Timor Indon.
92 □ Muti Oman
183 Q3 Mutilva Baja Spain
257 N4 Mutirikwi r. Zimbabwe
250 B7 Mutis Col.
213 I5 Mutis, Gunung mt. Timor Indon.
139 T4 Mutnyy Materik Rus. Fed.
213 I3 Mutoko Zimbabwe
85 K2 Mutomba Zimbabwe
213 H3 Mutton r. Rus. Fed.
209 B7 Mutoray Rus. Fed.
193 N6 Mutsamudu Comoros
102 R4 Mutsu Japan
85 J4 Mutsu-wan b. Japan
102 R5 Mutsu-wan b. Japan

179 M4 Mürzsteg Austria
178 B5 Mutters Austria
172 E3 Mutterstadt Ger.
82 □2 Mutton Bird Island Lord Howe I. Austr.
81 C13 Muttonbird Islands Stewart I. N.Z.
Muttonbird Islands N.Z. see Titi Islands
147 C7 Mutton Island Ireland
114 G5 Muttukuru Andhra Prad. India
114 F7 Muttupet Tamil Nadu India
213 H2 Mutuali Moz.
257 G3 Mutum Brazil
256 C2 Mutum Brazil
207 H4 Mutum Biu Cameroon
252 D2 Mutumparaná Brazil
209 C6 Mutungu-Tari Dem. Rep. Congo
254 C5 Mutunópolis Brazil
114 G8 Mutur Sri Lanka
187 E11 Mutxamel Spain
137 M2 Mutyn Ukr.
157 N6 Mutzig France
209 B7 Muxaluando Angola
199 B6 Muxía Spain
207 H4 Muxima Angola
134 F3 Muya Rus. Fed.
192 □2 Muyezerskiy Rus. Fed.
211 A5 Muyinga Burundi
209 C6 Muyumba Dem. Rep. Congo
108 B3 Muyuping Hubei China
123 O4 Muzaffarabad Pak.
123 N6 Muzaffargarh Pak.
116 F5 Muzaffarnagar Uttar Prad. India
117 K7 Muzaffarpur Bihar India
213 G4 Muzamane Moz.
256 D4 Muzambinho Brazil
213 F2 Muzarabani Zimbabwe
213 F2 Muze Moz.
129 F2 Muzhichi Rus. Fed.
158 G3 Muzillac France
111 M8 Muzo Col.
229 B4 Muzon, Cape AK U.S.A.
243 I4 Múzquiz Mex.
111 F9 Muztag mt. Xinjiang China
111 H8 Muz Tag mt. Xinjiang China
110 B7 Muztagata mt. Xinjiang China
207 D7 Mushenge Dem. Rep. Congo
209 C5 Mushie Dem. Rep. Congo
137 M5 Mushin Nigeria
114 F4 Musi r. India
94 F6 Musi r. Indon.
196 J9 Musica mt. Macedonia
163 B6 Musson Mountain AZ U.S.A.
117 I5 Muskodol Nepal
191 H5 Musile di Piave Italy
196 J4 Musina S. Africa

137 Q5 Mykolayivka Donets'ka Oblast' Ukr.
137 P5 Mykolayivka Kharkivs'ka Oblast' Ukr.
137 N6 Mykolayivka Khersons'ka Oblast' Ukr.
136 J6 Mykolayivka Odes'ka Oblast' Ukr.
136 J8 Mykolayivka Odes'ka Oblast' Ukr.
137 P6 Mykolayivka Zaporiz'ka Oblast' Ukr.
136 I7 Mykolayivka-Novorosiys'ka Ukr.
Mykolayivs'ka Oblast' admin. div. Ukr. see Mykolayivs'ka Oblast'
137 L6 Mykolo-Hulak Ukr.
199 G5 Mykonos i. Greece
199 G5 Mykonos i. Greece
136 E4 Mykulyntsi Ukr.
175 M5 Mykytychi Ukr.
134 J2 Myla Rus. Fed.
134 J2 Myla Rus. Fed.
Mylae Sicilia Italy see Milazzo
Mylasa Turkey see Milas
171 F9 Myllykoski Fin.
138 J1 Myllykoski Fin.
150 B7 Mylor Cornwall, England U.K.
Mymensing Bangl. see Mymensingh
117 M7 Mymensingh Bangl.
138 E1 Mynämäki Fin.
141 Q6 Mynämäki Fin.
121 O5 Mynaral Kazakh.
214 H6 Mynfontein S. Africa
Myngaral Kazakh. see Mynaral
105 I3 Myōgi Japan
105 I3 Myōgi-Arafune-Saku-kōen Kokutei-kōen park Japan
104 A6 Myōgi-san mt. Japan
105 H2 Myōkō-yama hill Japan
105 H2 Myōkō Japan
105 H2 Myōkō-kōgen Japan
160 N2 Myon France
101 F8 Myŏnggan N. Korea
138 K6 Myory Belarus
94 B4 Myothit Myanmar
103 Q15 Myōzin-sho i. Japan
103 R15 Myōzin-sho i. Japan
97 H9 My Phươc Vietnam
Myrdalsjökull ice cap
140 □C2 Myrdalssandur sand area Iceland
140 M2 Myre Nordland Norway
140 M2 Myre Nordland Norway
137 M4 Myrhorod Ukr.
198 C5 Myrina Limnos Greece
140 N2 Myrlandshaugen Norway
223 I4 Myrnam Alta Can.
136 H5 Myrne Odes'ka Oblast' Ukr.
136 H5 Myrne Khersons'ka Oblast' Ukr.
137 O7 Myrne Kyiv's'ka Oblast' Ukr.
175 M5 Myrne Zaporiz'ka Oblast' Ukr.
137 P4 Myrnivka Kharkivs'ka Ukr.
136 J3 Myronivka Kyïv's'ka Oblast' Ukr.
136 G3 Myropil' Ukr.
137 N6 Myropillya Ukr.
141 R6 Myrskylä Fin.
231 E10 Myrtle Beach SC U.S.A.
238 B5 Myrtle Creek OR U.S.A.
83 K7 Myrtleford Vic. Austr.
238 B5 Myrtle Point OR U.S.A.
198 E6 Mytros Pelagos sea Greece
121 M7 Myrzakent Kazakh.
142 I4 Mysen Norway
148 D8 Myshall Ireland
138 I9 Myshanka r. Belarus
138 V4 Myshkin Rus. Fed.
Myshkino Rus. Fed. see Myshkin
136 J4 Myshako Rus. Fed.
174 C3 Myśla r. Pol.
Mysłą Lazareva Rus. Fed. see Lazarev
140 O3 Myślenice Pol.
174 C3 Myśliborskie, Jezioro l. Pol.
174 C3 Myślibórz Pol.
175 H6 Myslowice Pol.
96 I4 Mysłowice Pol.
114 E6 My Son tourist site Vietnam
114 E6 Mysore Karnataka India
Mysore state India see Karnataka
137 N8 Mysovsk Rus. Fed.
Babushkin
131 T3 Mys Shmidta Rus. Fed.
136 G3 Mystic CT U.S.A.
235 K2 Mystic Islands NJ U.S.A.
134 K3 Mysy Rus. Fed.
175 H1 Myszewo Pol.
175 I5 Myszków Pol.
175 I5 Myszyniec Pol.
96 I7 Mỹ Tho Vietnam
198 D2 Mytikas mt. Greece
Mytilene i. Greece see Lesvos
199 H5 Mytilini Greece
199 H5 Mytilini Samos Greece
126 C4 Mytilini Strait Greece/Turkey
139 U6 Mytishchi Rus. Fed.
177 I3 Mýtna Slovakia
177 I1 Mýtne Ludany Slovakia
140 □C2 Mýtô Czech Rep.
241 V1 Myton UT U.S.A.
129 J3 Mytrofanivka Ukr.
129 J3 Myuregi Rus. Fed.
140 □C1 Mývatn l. Iceland
Mývatn-Laxá nature res. Iceland
140 □E1 Mývatnssörae̅fi lava field Iceland
134 K3 Myyeldino Rus. Fed.
Myylybulak Kazakh. see Milybulak
205 F4 M'Zab, Vallée du tourist site Alg.
215 K7 Mzamomhle S. Africa
211 C6 Mže r. Czech Rep.
211 B6 Mzimba Malawi
213 F4 Mzimvubu r. S. Africa
211 B7 Mzuzu Malawi
129 A2 Mzymta r. Rus. Fed.

N

96 F3 Na, Nam r. China/Vietnam
173 M3 Naab r. Ger.
Naâl Jibilji Hu.S.A.
240 □F14 Nāʻālehu HI U.S.A.
208 F2 Naalga Rus. Fed.
205 F2 Naama Alg.
141 Q6 Naantali Fin.
164 H4 Naarden Neth.
141 R6 Naarva Fin.
159 In Machlande Austria
141 T4 Naas Ireland
141 S6 Näätämö Fin.
141 S6 Näätämä Fin.
94 C2 Naba Myanmar
211 B5 Nababeep S. Africa
117 L7 Nabadwip W. Bengal India see Navadwip
129 C3 Nabakevi Georgia
124 D6 Nabao r. Port.
Nabarangpur Orissa India
104 C4 Nabari Japan
104 C4 Nabari-gawa r. Japan
87 B9 Nabas Panay Phil.
128 D5 Nabatîyé et Tahta Lebanon
82 □1 Nabberu, Lake salt flat W.A. Austr.
87 M3 Nabburg Ger.
206 E4 Naberá, Réserve Partielle de nature res. Burkina
211 C6 Naberera Tanz.
137 R2 Naberezhnoye Rus. Fed.

Naberezhnyye Chelny to Naşīb
357

134 K5 Naberezhnyye Chelny Rus. Fed.
120 A2 Naberezhnyy Uvekh Rus. Fed.
205 H1 Nabeul Tunisia
189 C7 Nabeul admin. div. Tunisia
116 F4 Nabha Punjab India
129 H5 Näbiağalı Azer.
253 F5 Nabileque r. Brazil
117 J7 Nabinagar Bihar India
91 I7 Nabire Papua Indon.
128 D5 Nabi Younés, Ras en pt Lebanon
128 D6 Nāblus West Bank
206 E4 Nabolo Ghana
213 F5 Naboomspruit S. Africa
79 □7a Naboutini Viti Levu Fiji
79 □7 Nabouwalu Vanua Levu Fiji
177 L3 Nábrád Hungary
97 D7 Nabule Myanmar
243 M8 Nacajuca Mex.
213 I2 Nacala Moz.
245 K8 Nacaltepec Mex.
242 □P11 Nacaome Hond.
213 H2 Nacaroa Moz.
252 D2 Nacebe Bol.
176 D2 Načeradec Czech Rep.
138 H7 Nacha Belarus
138 L7 Nacha r. Belarus
120 C4 Nachalovo Rus. Fed.
238 D3 Naches WA U.S.A.
225 H1 Nachicapau, Lac l. Que. Can.
211 C7 Nachingwea Tanz.
116 C6 Nachna Rajasthan India
176 F1 Náchod Czech Rep.
115 M7 Nachuge Andaman & Nicobar Is India
79 □7a Nacilau Point Viti Levu Fiji
260 A5 Nacimiento Chile
185 N6 Nacimiento Spain
185 N7 Nacimiento r. Spain
240 L6 Nacimiento Reservoir CA U.S.A.
170 G5 Nackel Ger.
172 E2 Nackenheim Ger.
237 H10 Nacogdoches TX U.S.A.
242 E2 Nacozari de García Mex.
175 I3 Nacpolsk Pol.
260 D4 Nacuñan Arg.
Nada Hainan China see Danzhou
105 H1 Nadachi Japan
222 C2 Nadaleen r. Y.T. Can.
79 □7a Nadarivatu Viti Levu Fiji
174 E2 Nadarzyce Pol.
176 F5 Nádasd Hungary
177 H4 Nádasdladány Hungary
116 F6 Nadbai Rajasthan India
151 I5 Nadder r. England U.K.
137 L7 Naddnipryans'ke Ukr.
Nådendal Fin. see Naantali
120 J1 Nadezhdinka Kazakh.
Nadezhdinskiy Kazakh. see Nadezhdinka
100 H4 Nadezhdinskoye Rus. Fed.
79 □7a Nadi Viti Levu Fiji
124 A6 Nadi Sudan
116 D8 Nadiad Gujarat India
79 □7a Nadi Bay Viti Levu Fiji
122 F6 Nadīk Iran
196 I4 Nădlac Romania
143 O7 Nadmorski Park Krajobrazowy Pol.
177 J1 Nadnidziański Park Krajobrazowy Pol.
116 D7 Nadol Rajasthan India
204 E2 Nador Morocco
180 E5 Nador prov. Morocco
139 R1 Nadporozh'ye Rus. Fed.
125 J4 Nadqān, Qalamat well Saudi Arabia
197 K5 Nădrag Romania
79 □7a Nadrau Plateau Viti Levu Fiji
129 G2 Nadterechnaya Rus. Fed.
177 K4 Nádudvar Hungary
195 □ Nadur Gozo Malta
195 □ Nadur hill Malta
79 □7 Naduri Vanua Levu Fiji
122 E5 Nadūshan Iran
136 D5 Nadvirna Ukr.
Nadvornaya Ukr. see Nadvirna
130 I3 Nadym Rus. Fed.
116 E7 Naenwa Rajasthan India
142 H6 Næstved Denmark
117 N9 Naf r. Bangl./Myanmar
128 C9 Nafas, Ra's an mt. Egypt
190 G1 Näfels Switz.
149 Q5 Nafferton East Riding of Yorkshire, England U.K.
128 C8 Nafḩa, Har hill Israel
198 C4 Nafpaktos Greece
198 D5 Nafplio Greece
Naft r. Iraq see Nafţ, Āb
127 L7 Nafţ, Āb r. Iraq
129 H5 Naftalan Azer.
122 C6 Naft-e Safīd Iran
Naft-e Shāh Iran see Naft Shahr
122 A4 Naft Shahr Iran
202 A2 Nafūsah, Jabal hills Libya
124 F3 Nafy Saudi Arabia
111 J10 Nag, Co l. China
104 B7 Naga Japan
92 D5 Naga Luzon Phil.
224 C3 Nagagami r. Ont. Can.
224 C3 Nagagami Lake Ont. Can.
103 J13 Nagahama Ehime Japan
104 D5 Nagahama Shiga Japan
117 O6 Naga Hills India
Naga Hills state India see Nagaland
102 R8 Nagai Japan
105 I5 Nagaizumi Japan
104 F5 Nagakute Japan
117 O6 Nagaland state India
83 J7 Nagambie Vic. Austr.
102 □1 Nagannu-jima i. Okinawa Japan
105 H2 Nagano Japan
105 G3 Nagano pref. Japan
105 I2 Naganohara Japan
105 L1 Naganuma Japan
103 P9 Nagaoka Japan
104 C6 Nagaokakyō Japan
117 N6 Nagaon Assam India
Nagapatam Tamil Nadu India see Nagapattinam
114 F7 Nagapattinam Tamil Nadu India
117 L7 Nagar r. Bangl./India
116 F3 Nagar Hima. Prad. India
114 D6 Nagar Karnataka India
116 F6 Nagar Rajasthan India
105 L5 Nagara Japan
206 C3 Nagara Mali
104 E5 Nagara-gawa r. Japan
114 G3 Nagaram Andhra Prad. India
105 K4 Nagareyama Japan
114 F4 Nagarjuna Sagar Reservoir India
114 F4 Nagar Karnul Andhra Prad. India
242 □P11 Nagarote Nic.
123 N9 Nagar Parkar Pak.
111 J12 Nagarzê Xizang China
105 H4 Nagasaka Japan
103 G14 Nagasaki Japan
103 G13 Nagasaki pref. Japan
103 H14 Nagashima Kagoshima Japan
104 E5 Nagashima Mie Japan
103 H14 Naga-shima i. Japan
103 J13 Naga-shima i. Japan
105 H3 Nagato Nagano Japan
103 I12 Nagato Yamaguchi Japan
105 J3 Nagatoro Japan
116 D6 Nagaur Rajasthan India
115 H3 Nagavali r. India
104 G3 Nagawa Japan
116 G9 Nagbhir Mahar. India
116 E8 Nagda Madh. Prad. India
173 L2 Nagel Ger.
164 I3 Nagele Neth.
114 E8 Nagercoil Tamil Nadu India
123 K8 Nagha Kalat Pak.
116 G5 Nagina Uttar Prad. India
122 G4 Nagineh Iran
111 L13 Naginimara Nagaland India
104 G4 Nagiso Japan
111 M11 Nagjog Xizang China
147 E8 Nagles Mountains hills Ireland
175 I5 Nagłowice Pol.
116 H5 Nagma Nepal
102 □1 Nago Okinawa Japan
116 H7 Nagod Madh. Prad. India
172 F4 Nagold Ger.
172 F4 Nagold r. Ger.
Nagong Chu r. China see Parlung Zangbo
183 R3 Nagore Spain
Nagorno-Karabakh aut. reg. Azer. see Dağlıq Qarabağ
131 N4 Nagornyy Rus. Fed.
Nagornyy Karabakh aut. reg. Azer. see Dağlıq Qarabağ
134 J4 Nagorsk Rus. Fed.
139 V5 Nagor'ye Rus. Fed.
191 J4 Nago-Torbole Italy
102 □1 Nago-wan b. Okinawa Japan
104 E5 Nagoya Japan
116 G9 Nagpur Mahar. India
111 K11 Nagqu Xizang China
111 K11 Nag Qu r. Xizang China
247 □2 Nag's Head pt St Kitts and Nevis
141 P6 Nagu Fin.
247 I4 Nagua Dom. Rep.
247 □1 Naguabo Puerto Rico
92 E5 Nagumbuaya Point Phil.
130 F1 Nagurskoye Zemlya Frantsa-Iosifa Rus. Fed.
129 D1 Nagutskoye Rus. Fed.
176 G5 Nagyatád Hungary
177 G5 Nagybajom Hungary
177 J5 Nagybánhegyes Hungary
177 H5 Nagybaracska Hungary
Nagybecskerek Vojvodina Serbia see Zrenjanin
177 G5 Nagybereki Fehérvíz nature res. Hungary
177 H5 Nagyberény Hungary
177 H5 Nagyberki Hungary
176 F4 Nagycenk Hungary
177 J4 Nagycsécs Hungary
177 K4 Nagycserkesz Hungary
177 L3 Nagydobos Hungary
177 H5 Nagydorog Hungary
177 L4 Nagyecsed Hungary
Nagyenyed Romania see Aiud
177 J4 Nagyfüged Hungary
177 K3 Nagyhalász Hungary
177 H6 Nagyharsány Hungary
177 K4 Nagyhegyes Hungary
177 H4 Nagyigmánd Hungary
177 J4 Nagyiván Hungary
177 K4 Nagykálló Hungary
177 K5 Nagykamarás Hungary
176 F5 Nagykanizsa Hungary
176 F5 Nagykapornak Hungary
177 H5 Nagykarácsony Hungary
177 I4 Nagykáta Hungary
177 K4 Nagykereki Hungary
177 H5 Nagykónyi Hungary
177 I4 Nagykőrös Hungary
177 H4 Nagykovácsi Hungary
177 J5 Nagykunság reg. Hungary
177 J4 Nagykunsági Öntöző Főcsatorna canal Hungary
177 J5 Nagylak Hungary
177 I3 Nagylóc Hungary
176 F4 Nagylózs Hungary
177 J5 Nagymágocs Hungary
177 H5 Nagymányok Hungary
177 H4 Nagymaros Hungary
177 K3 Nagy-Milic hill Hungary/Slovakia
177 H6 Nagynyárád Hungary
177 I4 Nagyoroszi Hungary
177 K4 Nagyrábé Hungary
176 G5 Nagyrécse Hungary
177 K5 Nagy-sárrét reg. Hungary
176 G4 Nagysimonyi Hungary
177 J5 Nagyszénás Hungary
177 G4 Nagyszentjános Hungary
177 H5 Nagyszokoly Hungary
177 I4 Nagytarcsa Hungary
177 J5 Nagytőke Hungary
177 K4 Nagy-Vadas-tó l. Hungary
Nagyvárad Romania see Oradea
177 L3 Nagyvarsány Hungary
177 G5 Nagyvázsony Hungary
177 H5 Nagyvenyim Hungary
138 K3 Naha Estonia
102 □1 Naha Okinawa Japan
116 F4 Nahan Hima. Prad. India
123 J8 Nahang r. Iran/Pak.
222 F2 Nahanni Butte N.W.T. Can.
222 E2 Nahanni National Park Reserve N.W.T. Can.
222 F2 Nahanni Range mts N.W.T. Can.
128 D6 Naharāyim Jordan
103 L13 Nahari Japan
128 D5 Nahariyya Israel
183 P8 Naharros Spain
122 C4 Nahāvand Iran
168 J3 Nahe Ger.
172 D2 Nahe r. Ger.
Na h-Eileanan an Iar admin. div. Scotland U.K. see Western Isles
205 F4 N'Ahnet, Adrar mts Alg.
78 □5 Nahoï, Cap c. Vanuatu
159 O7 Nahon r. France
124 D2 Nahr, Jabal hill Saudi Arabia
168 K4 Nahrendorf Ger.
244 F6 Nahuatzen Mex.
259 C6 Nahuel Huapí Arg.
259 C6 Nahuel Huapí, Parque Nacional nat. park Arg.
260 D4 Nahuel Mapá Arg.
259 D6 Nahuel Niyeu Arg.
261 I5 Nahuel Rucá Arg.
123 J8 Nāhūg Iran
231 F10 Nahunta GA U.S.A.
123 L3 Naibabad Afgh.
92 C4 Naic Luzon Phil.
242 G4 Naica Mex.
260 E5 Naicó Arg.
211 C6 Naidor well Tanz.
96 C1 Nai Ga Myanmar
79 □7a Naigani i. Fiji
106 D9 Naij Tal Qinghai China
202 C3 Nā'ikah, Qarārat an depr. Libya
93 C8 Naikliu Timor Indon.
222 C4 Naikoon Provincial Park B.C. Can.
171 E10 Naila Ger.
163 H9 Nailloux France
150 G5 Nailsea North Somerset, England U.K.
150 H4 Nailsworth Gloucestershire, England U.K.
111 K12 Nailung Xizang China
203 G6 Na'ima Sudan
Naiman Qi Nei Mongol China see Daqin Tal
106 B4 Naimin Shuiquan well Xinjiang China
225 I1 Nain Nfld and Lab. Can.
122 E5 Nā'īn Iran
116 H7 Naina Uttar Prad. India
Naingani i. Fiji see Naigani
116 G5 Nainital Uttaranchal India
116 H8 Nainpur Madh. Prad. India
159 L8 Naintré France
213 H3 Naiopué Moz.
79 □7 Nairai i. Fiji
79 □9a Nairiri Tahiti Fr. Polynesia
146 I7 Nairn Highland, Scotland U.K.
146 I7 Nairn r. Scotland U.K.
227 M3 Nairn Centre Ont. Can.
211 C5 Nairobi Kenya
138 H2 Naissaar i. Estonia
Naissus Serbia see Niš
210 C5 Naivasha Kenya
157 J6 Naives-Rosières France
158 F6 Naizin France
100 E7 Naizishan Jilin China
163 H7 Najac France
Najaf Iraq see An Najaf
122 D5 Najafābād Iran
125 H3 Na'jān Saudi Arabia
246 E3 Najasa r. Cuba
124 E2 Najd reg. Saudi Arabia
183 O4 Nájera Spain
183 O3 Najerilla r. Spain
203 G3 Naj' Ḩammādī Egypt
107 R2 Naji Nei Mongol China
116 G5 Najibabad Uttar Prad. India
183 P6 Nájima r. Spain
101 G7 Najin N. Korea
Najitun Nei Mongol China see Naji
125 J2 Najmah Saudi Arabia
124 G7 Najrān Saudi Arabia
124 G6 Najrān prov. Saudi Arabia
124 G7 Najrān, Wādī watercourse Saudi Arabia
104 A5 Naka Hyōgo Japan
105 L3 Naka Ibaraki Japan
113 □1 Nakachchaafushi i. N. Male Maldives
103 G14 Nakadōri-shima i. Japan
96 G6 Na Kae Thai.
105 G4 Nakagawa Nagano Japan
104 A8 Nakagawa Tokushima Japan
103 L13 Naka-gawa r. Japan
105 M3 Naka-gawa r. Japan
105 H2 Nakagō Japan
102 □1 Nakagusuku Okinawa Japan
102 □1 Nakagusuku-wan b. Okinawa Japan
Nakahchaafushi i. N. Male Maldives see Nakachchaafushi
104 C8 Nakahechi Japan
105 J5 Nakai Japan
105 J6 Nakaizu Japan
105 L1 Nakajima Fukushima Japan
104 E1 Nakajima Ishikawa Japan
103 J13 Naka-jima i. Japan
105 H2 Nakajō Japan
105 H5 Nakakawane Japan
240 □E12 Nākālele Point HI U.S.A.
103 H13 Nakama Japan
206 E4 Nakambé watercourse Burkina alt. Nakanbe, alt. Volta Blanche, conv. White Volta
105 I4 Nakamichi Japan
105 M3 Nakaminato Japan
103 J14 Nakamura Japan
131 L3 Nakanno Rus. Fed.
105 H2 Nakano Japan
105 I2 Nakanojō Japan
102 □G17 Nakano-shima i. Nansei-shotō Japan
103 K10 Nakano-shima i. Japan
105 J1 Nakano-take mt. Japan
102 □1 Nakaoshi Okinawa Japan
211 C7 Nakapanya Tanz.
210 B4 Nakapiripirit Uganda
102 R6 Nakasato Aomori Japan
105 I3 Nakasato Gunma Japan
105 I1 Nakasato Niigata Japan
102 U4 Nakasatsunai Japan
102 R7 Nakasen Japan
102 V3 Nakashibetsu Japan
210 B4 Nakasongola Uganda
Nakatchafushi i. N. Male Maldives see Nakachchaafushi
105 H5 Nakatomi Japan
102 T2 Nakatonbetsu-chō hill Japan
103 I13 Nakatsu Ōita Japan
104 B8 Nakatsu Wakayama Japan
104 G5 Nakatsugawa Japan
105 I2 Nakatsu-gawa r. Japan
113 □1 Nakatuku Fushi i. N. Male Maldives
203 H5 Nakfa Eritrea
203 H5 Nakfa Wildlife Reserve nature res. Eritrea
Nakhichevan' Azer. see Naxçıvan
Nakhichevan' aut. reg. Azer. see Naxçıvan
203 G2 Nakhl Egypt
122 E8 Nakhl-e Taqī Iran
100 H7 Nakhodka Rus. Fed.
117 N6 Nakhola Assam India
97 E7 Nakhon Nayok Thai.
97 E8 Nakhon Pathom Thai.
96 G6 Nakhon Phanom Thai.
97 F7 Nakhon Ratchasima Thai.
96 E7 Nakhon Sawan Thai.
97 D10 Nakhon Si Thammarat Thai.
96 E6 Nakhon Thai Thai.
Nakhrachi Rus. Fed. see Kondinskoye
116 B8 Nakhtarana Gujarat India
224 C3 Nakina Ont. Can.
222 C3 Nakina r. B.C. Can.
129 D3 Nakip'u Georgia
174 F1 Nakla Pol.
124 E5 Nakl an Nīlah Saudi Arabia
176 G2 Náklo Czech Rep.
175 H5 Nakło Pol.
179 J7 Naklo Slovenia
174 F2 Nakło nad Notecią Pol.
220 C4 Naknek AK U.S.A.
116 E4 Nakodar Punjab India
103 □2 Nakōdo-jima i. Japan
175 J1 Nakomiady Pol.
211 B7 Nakonde Zambia
214 D4 Nakop Namibia
79 □7a Nakorokula Viti Levu Fiji
105 M2 Nakoso Japan
138 G5 Nākotne Latvia
177 J6 Nakovo Vojvodina Serbia
207 E4 Nakpanduri Ghana
129 D2 Nakra, Ugheltekhili pass Georgia/Rus. Fed.
142 H7 Nakskov Denmark
168 L1 Nakskov Fjord inlet Denmark
140 M5 Näkten l. Sweden
101 F11 Naktong-gang r. S. Korea
210 C5 Nakuru Kenya
222 G5 Nakusp B.C. Can.
123 L8 Nal Pak.
123 K8 Nal r. Pak.
208 E4 Nala Dem. Rep. Congo
96 C3 Na-lang Myanmar
107 J3 Nalayh Mongolia
213 G5 Nalázi Moz.
172 B3 Nalbach Ger.
117 M6 Nalbari Assam India
129 E2 Nal'chik Rus. Fed.
183 P4 Nalda Spain
114 E4 Naldurg Mahar. India
175 K4 Nałęczów Pol.
177 J3 Nálepkovo Slovakia
206 E4 Nalerigu Ghana
114 F4 Nalgonda Andhra Prad. India
117 K7 Nalhati W. Bengal India
117 M7 Nalitabari Bangl.
116 B8 Naliya Gujarat India
116 F8 Nalkhera Madh. Prad. India
114 F5 Nallamala Hills India
162 B3 Nalliers France
199 M2 Nallıhan Turkey
121 M1 Nalobino Kazakh.
209 D8 Nalolo Zambia
182 H2 Nalón r. Spain
210 B4 Nalubaale Dam Uganda
202 A2 Nālūt Libya
176 C2 Nalžovské Hory Czech Rep.
93 F5 Namaa, Tanjung pt Seram Indon.
213 G5 Namaacha Moz.
213 H2 Namacala Moz.
79 □7 Namacu Fiji
209 B9 Namacunde Angola
213 H3 Namacurra Moz.
83 L6 Namadgi National Park N.S.W. Austr.
215 M3 Namahadi S. Africa
92 □ Namai Bay Palau
122 D4 Namak, Daryācheh-ye salt flat Iran
122 G4 Namak, Kavīr-e salt flat Iran
122 C4 Namak-e Mīqhān, Kavīr-e salt flat Iran
122 F6 Nāmakī watercourse Iran
114 F7 Namakkal Tamil Nadu India
122 I5 Namakzar Afgh.
122 H6 Namakzar-e Shadad salt flat Iran
94 G6 Namang Indon.
211 C5 Namanga Kenya
121 N7 Namangan Uzbek.
121 N7 Namangan admin. div. Uzbek.
Namangan Oblast admin. div. Uzbek. see Namangan
Namangan Wiloyati admin. div. Uzbek. see Namangan
211 A6 Namanyere Tanz.
213 H2 Namapa Moz.
213 H2 Namaponda Moz.
214 A4 Namaqualand reg. S. Africa
214 B6 Namaqua National Park S. Africa
213 H2 Namarrói Moz.
210 B4 Namasale Uganda
122 A3 Namashīr Iran
91 L7 Namatanai New Ireland P.N.G.
Namathu Fiji see Namacu
209 B7 Namba Angola
209 E8 Nambala Zambia
211 C7 Nambiranji Tanz.
117 N7 Nambol Manipur India
172 C2 Namborn Ger.
85 N9 Nambour Qld Austr.
Namboutini Viti Levu Fiji see Naboutini
Nambouwalu Vanua Levu Fiji see Nabouwalu
183 M9 Nambroca Spain
Nambu Japan see Nanbu
83 N4 Nambucca Heads N.S.W. Austr.
87 C11 Nambung National Park W.A. Austr.
97 G10 Năm Căn Vietnam
Namcha Barwa mt. Xizang China see Namjagbarwa Feng
117 K6 Namche Bazar Nepal
111 J11 Namco Xizang China
111 J11 Nam Co salt l. China
122 D6 Namdagūn Iran
140 L4 Namdalen val. Norway
140 K4 Namdalseid Norway
96 H4 Nam Đinh Vietnam
143 O2 Nämdö i. Sweden
143 O2 Nämdöfjärden b. Sweden
97 G10 Nam Du, Quân Đao i. Vietnam
105 J3 Namegawa Japan
226 C4 Namekagon r. WI U.S.A.
92 □ Namelakl Passage Palau
Namen Belgium see Namur
104 F2 Namerikawa Japan
176 F2 Náměšť nad Oslavou Czech Rep.
177 I2 Námestovo Slovakia
213 H2 Nametil Moz.
223 K4 Namew Lake Man./Sask. Can.
101 D9 Nam-gang r. N. Korea
101 E11 Namhae-do i. S. Korea
96 C3 Namhkan Myanmar
96 C3 Namhsan Myanmar
104 G5 Namiai Japan
213 H2 Namialo Moz.
212 B5 Namib Desert Namibia
209 B8 Namibe Angola
209 B8 Namibe prov. Angola
209 B8 Namibe, Reserva de nature res. Angola
212 B4 Namibia country Africa
264 J8 Namibia Abyssal Plain sea feature N. Atlantic Ocean
212 B5 Namib-Naukluft Game Park nature res. Namibia
211 C7 Namichiga Tanz.
213 H2 Namicunde Moz.
213 H3 Namidobe Moz.
102 R9 Namie Japan
214 D5 Namies S. Africa
122 C2 Namīn Iran
213 H2 Namina Moz.
211 B8 Namitete Malawi
111 L12 Namjagbarwa Feng mt. Xizang China
111 J12 Namka Xizang China
96 C3 Namlan Myanmar
96 C3 Namlang r. Myanmar
93 E5 Namlea Buru Indon.
111 I12 Namling Xizang China
96 E6 Nam Nao National Park Thai.
96 G5 Nam Neun r. Laos
96 F5 Nam Ngum Reservoir Laos
111 H11 Namoding Xizang China
83 L4 Namoi r. N.S.W. Austr.
105 I3 Namoku Japan
91 K5 Namonuito atoll Micronesia
209 E5 Namoya Dem. Rep. Congo
222 G3 Nampa Alta Can.
116 H4 Nampa mt. Nepal
238 F5 Nampa ID U.S.A.
206 D3 Nampala Mali
96 E6 Nam Pat Thai.
213 H3 Nampevo Moz.
96 F6 Nam Phong Thai.
96 F6 Nam Phung Reservoir Thai.
101 D9 Namp'o N. Korea
213 I2 Nampuecha Moz.
213 H2 Nampula Moz.
213 H2 Nampula prov. Moz.
93 E5 Namrole Buru Indon.
117 O6 Namrup Assam India
117 O6 Namsai Arun. Prad. India
96 C2 Namsai Myanmar
96 C4 Namsang Myanmar
140 K4 Namsfjorden sea chan. Norway
109 □J7 Nam She Tsim hill H.K. China
140 K4 Namsos Norway
140 L4 Namsskogan Norway
207 I4 Namtari Nigeria
96 C2 Namti Myanmar
96 C5 Namtok Myanmar
97 D7 Nam Tok Thai.
96 E6 Namtok Chattakan National Park Thai.
96 D5 Namtok Mae Surin National Park Thai.
96 D3 Namton Myanmar
131 N3 Namtsy Rus. Fed.
96 C3 Namtu Myanmar
222 E5 Namu B.C. Can.
Namuka i. Tonga see Nomuka
81 □4 Namukulu Niue
213 H2 Namuli, Monte mt. Moz.
213 H2 Namuno Moz.
165 G8 Namur Belgium
165 G8 Namur prov. Belgium
212 C3 Namutoni Namibia
209 E8 Namwala Zambia
211 B8 Namwera Malawi
101 E11 Namwŏn S. Korea
96 C1 Namya Ra Myanmar
90 D4 Namyit Island S. China Sea
174 F4 Namysłów Pol.
96 E5 Nan Thai.
96 E7 Nan, Mae Nam r. Thai.
207 I5 Nana Cameroon
208 B3 Nana r. C.A.R.
177 H4 Nána Slovakia
208 C3 Nana Bakassa C.A.R.
208 C3 Nana Barya r. C.A.R./Chad
208 C3 Nana-Grébizi pref. C.A.R.
222 F5 Nanaimo B.C. Can.
105 L3 Nanakai Japan
240 □C12 Nānākuli HI U.S.A.
208 B3 Nana-Mambéré pref. C.A.R.
109 L6 Nan'an Fujian China
Nan'an Jiangxi China see Dayu
85 N9 Nanango Qld Austr.
212 C5 Nananib Plateau Namibia
79 □7a Nananu-i-Ra i. Fiji
104 E1 Nanao Japan
104 E1 Nanao-wan b. Japan
104 E2 Nanatsuka Japan
103 N9 Nanatsu-shima i. Japan
250 C5 Nanay r. Peru
Nanbai Guizhou China see Zunyi
111 L8 Nanbaxian Qinghai China
Nanbin Chongqing China see Shizhu
108 F3 Nanbu Sichuan China
105 H5 Nanbu Japan
260 B4 Nancagua Chile
159 P7 Nançay France
100 F5 Nancha Heilong. China
109 J4 Nanchang Jiangxi China
109 J4 Nanchang Jiangxi China
Nanchangshan Shandong China see Changdao
109 K5 Nancheng Jiangxi China
245 M7 Nanchital Mex.
108 F3 Nanchong Sichuan China
108 F4 Nanchuan Chongqing China
183 O3 Nanclares de la Oca Spain
253 E5 Ñancorainza Bol.
115 M9 Nancowry i. Andaman & Nicobar Is India
107 M9 Nancun Henan China
Nancun Shanxi China see Zezhou
222 E4 Nancut B.C. Can.
157 L6 Nancy France
81 B12 Nancy Sound inlet South I. N.Z.
116 H4 Nanda Devi mt. Uttaranchal India
116 H4 Nanda Kot mt. Uttaranchal India
108 F6 Nandan Guangxi China
104 A7 Nandan Japan
Nandarivatu Viti Levu Fiji see Nadarivatu
114 E3 Nanded Mahar. India
Nander Mahar. India see Nanded
83 M4 Nandewar Range mts N.S.W. Austr.
116 E9 Nandgaon Mahar. India
Nandi Fiji see Nadi
213 F4 Nandi Zimbabwe
Nandi Bay Viti Levu Fiji see Nadi Bay
114 G4 Nandigama Andhra Prad. India
114 F5 Nandikotkur Andhra Prad. India
108 B7 Nanding He r. Yunnan China
116 D9 Nandod Gujarat India
Nandrau Plateau Viti Levu Fiji see Nadrau Plateau
165 H7 Nandrin Belgium
261 G2 Ñanducita Arg.
108 H8 Nandu Jiang r. China
116 F9 Nandura Mahar. India
116 E9 Nandurbar Mahar. India
Nanduri Vanua Levu Fiji see Naduri
114 F5 Nandyal Andhra Prad. India
197 P5 Năneşti Romania
109 H7 Nanfeng Guangdong China
109 K5 Nanfeng Jiangxi China
111 K12 Nang Xizang China
211 C7 Nangade Moz.
207 I5 Nanga Eboko Cameroon
95 J4 Nangahbunut Kalimantan Indon.
95 I5 Nangah Dedai Kalimantan Indon.
95 J4 Nangahembaloh Kalimantan Indon.
95 I4 Nangahkantuk Kalimantan Indon.
95 J5 Nangahkemangai Kalimantan Indon.
95 I4 Nangahketungau Kalimantan Indon.
95 I5 Nangahmau Kalimantan Indon.
95 I4 Nangah Merakai Kalimantan Indon.
95 I5 Nangahpinoh Kalimantan Indon.
95 J4 Nangahsuruk Kalimantan Indon.
95 J4 Nangahtempuai Kalimantan Indon.
84 E2 Nangalala N.T. Austr.
92 C6 Nangalao i. Phil.
211 C7 Nanganga Tanz.
100 F7 Nangang Shan mts China
116 E2 Nanga Parbat mt. Jammu and Kashmir
123 N4 Nangarhār prov. Afgh.
95 I5 Nangataman Kalimantan Indon.
95 I5 Nangatayap Kalimantan Indon.
207 F5 Nangbéto, Retenue de resr Togo
106 G8 Nangdoi Qinghai China
97 D9 Nangin Myanmar
156 F6 Nangis France
116 H4 Nangling Uttaranchal India
101 E8 Nangnim N. Korea
101 E8 Nangnim-sanmaek mts N. Korea
105 K1 Nangō Fukushima Japan
103 I15 Nangō Miyazaki Japan
107 N8 Nangong Hebei China
108 A2 Nangqên Qinghai China
107 K7 Nangsin Sum Nei Mongol China
211 C7 Nangulangwa Tanz.
114 E8 Nanguneri Tamil Nadu India
109 I7 Nanhai Guangdong China
107 N8 Nanhe Hebei China
110 L7 Nanhu Gansu China
106 F7 Nanhua Gansu China
108 C6 Nanhua Yunnan China
109 M3 Nanhui Shanghai China
123 M5 Nani Afgh.
221 J2 Nanisivik Nunavut Can.
114 E6 Nanjangud Karnataka India
108 G5 Nanjia Guizhou China
108 C6 Nanjian Yunnan China
108 F2 Nanjiang Sichuan China
Nanjie Guangdong China see Guangning
109 K6 Nanjing Fujian China
109 L2 Nanjing Jiangsu China
109 M5 Nanji Shan i. China
104 D4 Nanjō Japan
108 B7 Nanka Jiang r. Yunnan China
109 J6 Nankang Jiangxi China
Nankang Jiangxi China see Xingzi
Nanking Jiangsu China see Nanjing
103 K13 Nankoku Japan
209 C9 Nankova Angola
108 B8 Nanlan He r. Yunnan China
78 □4b Nanlaud hill Pohnpei Micronesia
107 N8 Nanle Henan China
108 B8 Nanlei He r. Yunnan China alt. Loi, Nam (Myanmar)
109 L3 Nanling Anhui China
109 H6 Nan Ling mts China
108 G8 Nanliu Jiang r. China
Nanlong Sichuan China see Nanbu
Nanma Shandong China see Yiyuan
Nanmulingzue Xizang China see Namling
87 E9 Nannine W.A. Austr.
108 G7 Nanning Guangxi China
107 K8 Nanniwan Shaanxi China
104 E5 Nannō Japan
87 C12 Nannup W.A. Austr.
96 E5 Na Noi Thai.
221 N3 Nanortalik Greenland
Nanouki atoll Gilbert Is Kiribati see Nonouti
Nanouti atoll Gilbert Is Kiribati see Nonouti
108 F6 Nanpan Jiang r. China
116 H6 Nanpara Uttar Prad. India
107 O7 Nanpi Hebei China
107 Q6 Nanpiao Liaoning China
109 L5 Nanping Fujian China
Nanpu Fujian China see Pucheng
109 L5 Nanpu Xi r. China
Nanqiao Shanghai China see Fengxian
109 L6 Nanri Dao i. China
183 L2 Nansa r. Spain
210 C3 Nansebo Eth.
104 E7 Nansei Japan
102 □B22 Nansei-shotō is Japan
Nansei-shotō Trench sea feature N. Pacific Ocean see Ryukyu Trench
268 B1 Nansen Basin sea feature Arctic Ocean
209 E8 Nansenga Zambia
221 N1 Nansen Land reg. Greenland
221 I1 Nansen Sound sea chan. Nunavut Can.
Nansha Yunnan China see Yuanyang
90 E4 Nanshan Island S. China Sea
106 D8 Nanshankou Qinghai China
106 C5 Nanshankou Xinjiang China
Nansha Qundao is S. China Sea see Spratly Islands
211 B5 Nansio Tanz.
161 H10 Nans-les-Pins France
161 C8 Nant France
116 E7 Nanta Rajasthan India
105 L2 Nantai-san hill Japan
105 J2 Nantai-san mt. Japan
82 G4 Nantawarrina Aboriginal Land res. S.A. Austr.
150 F4 Nant Bran r. Wales U.K.
213 H3 Nante Moz.
156 D6 Nanterre France
158 H7 Nantes France
158 G6 Nantes à Brest, Canal de France
162 A1 Nantes Atlantique airport France
156 E5 Nanteuil-le-Haudouin France
114 G8 Nanthi Kadal lag. Sri Lanka
162 G3 Nantiat France
224 D5 Nanticoke Ont. Can.
233 J10 Nanticoke MD U.S.A.
234 C2 Nanticoke PA U.S.A.
233 J10 Nanticoke r. MD U.S.A.
104 E7 Nantō Japan
222 H5 Nanton Alta Can.
109 M3 Nantong Jiangsu China
Nantong Jiangsu China see Tongzhou
109 □I7 Nantou Guangdong China
109 M7 Nant'ou Taiwan
160 H4 Nantua France
233 O7 Nantucket MA U.S.A.
233 P7 Nantucket Island MA U.S.A.
233 O7 Nantucket Sound g. MA U.S.A.
211 C8 Nantulo Moz.
149 L7 Nantwich Cheshire, England U.K.
150 F4 Nantyglo Blaenau Gwent, Wales U.K.
232 G8 Nanty Glo PA U.S.A.
150 E3 Nant-y-moch Reservoir Wales U.K.
235 G2 Nanuet NY U.S.A.
79 □7a Nanukuloa Viti Levu Fiji
Nanumaga i. Tuvalu see Nanumanga
77 H2 Nanumanga i. Tuvalu
77 H2 Nanumea atoll Tuvalu
257 G2 Nanuque Brazil
93 E1 Nanusa, Kepulauan is Indon.
87 C7 Nanutarra Roadhouse W.A. Austr.
Nanwai Sichuan China see Daxian
108 E4 Nanxi Sichuan China
109 I4 Nanxian Hunan China
109 J6 Nanxiong Guangdong China
109 M5 Nanyandang Shan mt. Zhejiang China
109 I2 Nanyang Henan China
102 R8 Nanyō Japan
210 C5 Nanyuki Kenya
Nan Yunhe canal China see Da Yunhe
107 S6 Nanzamu Liaoning China
109 H3 Nanzhang Hubei China
Nanzhao Fujian China see Zhao'an
109 I2 Nanzhao Henan China
Nanzheng Shaanxi China see Zhoujiaping
Nanzhou Hunan China see Nanxian
123 N4 Nao Afgh.
187 F10 Nao, Cabo de la c. Spain
225 G2 Naococane, Lac l. Que. Can.
117 L7 Naogaon Bangl.
123 M9 Naokot Pak.
100 I5 Naoli He r. China
245 K6 Naolinco Mex.
122 I5 Naomid, Dasht-e des. Afgh./Iran
95 J3 Naong, Bukit mt. Malaysia
116 E3 Naoshera Jammu and Kashmir
198 D2 Naousa Kentriki Makedonia Greece
198 G5 Naousa Paros Greece
240 J3 Napa CA U.S.A.
233 □S2 Napadogan N.B. Can.
213 H2 Napaha Moz.
220 C3 Napaimiut AK U.S.A.
210 B4 Napak mt. Uganda
220 G3 Napaktulik Lake Nunavut Can.
261 H5 Napaleofú Arg.
224 E4 Napanee Ont. Can.
235 G1 Napanoch NY U.S.A.
116 D6 Napasar Rajasthan India
220 B3 Napaskiak AK U.S.A.
221 M3 Napasoq Greenland
226 F8 Naperville IL U.S.A.
190 D1 Napf mt. Switz.
80 K6 Napier North I. N.Z.
214 D10 Napier S. Africa
86 I2 Napier Broome Bay W.A. Austr.
263 D2 Napier Mountains Antarctica
84 E2 Napier Peninsula N.T. Austr.
86 H4 Napier Range hills W.A. Austr.
233 L3 Napierville Que. Can.
175 I2 Napiwoda Pol.
177 K4 Napkor Hungary
Naples Italy see Napoli
231 G12 Naples FL U.S.A.
233 □O5 Naples ME U.S.A.
232 H6 Naples NY U.S.A.
241 W1 Naples UT U.S.A.
108 E7 Napo Guangxi China
250 B5 Napo prov. Ecuador
250 C5 Napo r. Ecuador
194 D8 Napola Sicilia Italy
236 F2 Napoleon ND U.S.A.
232 A7 Napoleon OH U.S.A.
216 □2b Napoleon's Tomb tourist site St Helena
237 J11 Napoleonville LA U.S.A.
193 M6 Napoli Italy
193 M6 Napoli prov. Italy
193 M6 Napoli, Golfo di b. Italy
261 F6 Naposta Arg.
261 F6 Naposta r. Arg.
161 J9 Napoule, Golfe de la b. France
226 I8 Nappanee IN U.S.A.
84 D7 Napperby N.T. Austr.
122 A3 Naqadeh Iran
128 A9 Naqb Māliḩah mt. Egypt
128 H3 Naqīb Mustajidd Syria
122 C4 Naqqash Iran
124 G8 Naqūb Yemen
187 E8 Náquera Spain
116 B8 Nara Gujarat India
104 C6 Nara Japan
104 C7 Nara pref. Japan
206 D3 Nara Mali
139 U7 Nara r. Rus. Fed.
138 J7 Narach Belarus
138 J7 Narach r. Belarus
138 J7 Narach, Vozyera l. Belarus
82 H7 Naracoorte S.A. Austr.
83 K5 Naradhan N.S.W. Austr.
176 F4 Nárai Hungary
105 G3 Narai-gawa r. Japan
117 L8 Narail Bangl.
116 E6 Naraina Rajasthan India
114 G3 Narainpur Chhattisgarh India
105 G4 Narakawa Japan
117 K6 Naralua Bihar India
107 M2 Naranbulag Dornod Mongolia
106 C2 Naranbulag Uvs Mongolia
123 N4 Narang Afgh.
250 B5 Naranjal Ecuador
250 C6 Naranjal Peru
247 □1 Naranjito Puerto Rico
245 J4 Naranjos Mex.
106 E5 Naran Sebstein Bulag spring Gansu China
103 G14 Narao Japan
122 D5 Naraq Iran
115 I3 Narasannapeta Andhra Prad. India
114 G4 Narasapatnam, Point India
114 G4 Narasapur Andhra Prad. India
114 G4 Narasaraopet Andhra Prad. India
105 L4 Narashino Japan
117 J9 Narasinghapur Orissa India
107 M2 Narasun Rus. Fed.
110 G5 Narat Xinjiang China
97 E11 Narathiwat Thai.
110 F5 Narat Shan mts China
237 D8 Nara Visa NM U.S.A.
117 M8 Narayanganj Bangl.
116 H8 Narayanganj Madh. Prad. India
114 D3 Narayangaon Mahar. India
114 E4 Narayanpet Andhra Prad. India
175 M6 Narayiv Ukr.
175 M6 Narayivka r. Ukr.
123 N4 Naray Kelay Afgh.
Narbada r. India see Narmada
150 C4 Narberth Pembrokeshire, Wales U.K.
Narbo France see Narbonne
192 B7 Narbolia Sardegna Italy
161 C10 Narbonne France
161 C10 Narbonne-Plage France
151 J2 Narborough Leicestershire, England U.K.
151 N2 Narborough Norfolk, England U.K.
Narborough Island Islas Galápagos Ecuador see Fernandina, Isla
141 K5 Narbuvoll Norway
192 B9 Narcao Sardegna Italy
182 H1 Narcea r. Spain
115 N6 Narcondam Island Andaman & Nicobar Is India
160 C2 Narcy France
122 F3 Nardin Iran
195 O3 Nardò Italy
261 G2 Nare Arg.
123 M6 Narechi r. Pak.
114 D5 Naregal Karnataka India
87 E12 Narembeen W.A. Austr.
116 G4 Narendranagar Uttaranchal India
264 E4 Nares Abyssal Plain sea feature S. Atlantic Ocean
264 E4 Nares Deep sea feature N. Atlantic Ocean
221 K2 Nares Strait Can./Greenland
129 H5 Nareştar Azer.
87 H11 Naretha W.A. Austr.
175 L3 Narew Pol.
175 I3 Narew r. Pol.
175 L3 Narewka Pol.
175 L3 Narewka r. Pol.
123 L7 Nari r. Pak.
117 M8 Naria Bangl.
212 C5 Narib Namibia
175 I2 Narie, Jezioro l. Pol.
214 B6 Nariep S. Africa
182 C2 Nariga, Punta pt Spain
129 J7 Närimanabad Azer.
129 J5 Närimankänd Azer.
120 B4 Narimanov Rus. Fed.
123 M3 Narin Afgh.
123 M3 Narin reg. Afgh.
107 L7 Narin Nei Mongol China
126 I5 Narince Turkey
111 K8 Narin Gol watercourse China
250 B4 Nariño dept Col.
105 L4 Narita Japan
105 L4 Narita airport Japan
104 B4 Nariu-misaki pt Japan
247 □7 Nariva county Trin. and Tob.
247 □7 Nariva Swamp Trin. and Tob.
103 K12 Nariwa Japan
242 D4 Narizon, Punta pt Mex.
116 F4 Narkanda Hima. Prad. India
111 G13 Narkatiaganj Bihar India
140 S3 Narkaus Fin.
140 Q3 Narken Sweden
116 G9 Narkher Mahar. India
139 Y6 Narma r. Rus. Fed.
116 D9 Narmada r. India
129 C5 Narman Turkey
116 F5 Narnaul Haryana India
193 J2 Narni Italy
Narnia Italy see Narni
194 F9 Naro Sicilia Italy
194 F9 Naro r. Sicilia Italy
134 M2 Narodnaya, Gora mt. Rus. Fed.
136 I2 Narodychi Ukr.
139 T6 Naro-Fominsk Rus. Fed.
79 □7 Naroi Fiji
211 B5 Narok Kenya
83 M7 Narooma N.S.W. Austr.
135 H5 Narovchat Rus. Fed.
136 I2 Narowlya Belarus
141 P5 Närpes Fin.
83 L4 Narrabri N.S.W. Austr.
233 N7 Narragansett Bay RI U.S.A.
83 K3 Narran r. N.S.W. Austr.
83 K6 Narrandera N.S.W. Austr.
83 K3 Narran Lake N.S.W. Austr.
87 D12 Narrogin W.A. Austr.
83 L5 Narromine N.S.W. Austr.
163 B8 Narrosse France
223 J4 Narrow Hills Provincial Park Sask. Can.
232 E11 Narrows VA U.S.A.
234 E1 Narrowsburg NY U.S.A.
221 N3 Narsalik Greenland
114 F3 Narsapur Andhra Prad. India
221 N3 Narsaq Greenland
221 N3 Narsarsuaq Greenland
171 G8 Narsdorf Ger.
117 M8 Narsingdi Bangl.
116 F8 Narsinghgarh Madh. Prad. India
116 G8 Narsinghpur Madh. Prad. India
115 H4 Narsipatnam Andhra Prad. India
107 N5 Nart Nei Mongol China
106 I2 Nart Mongolia
179 O8 Narta Croatia
198 A2 Nartë Albania
129 E2 Nartkala Rus. Fed.
161 J10 Nartuby r. France
102 R8 Naruko Japan
105 I5 Narusawa Japan
103 F14 Naru-shima i. Japan
175 I3 Naruszewo Pol.
105 L4 Narutō Japan
104 A7 Naruto Japan
104 A7 Naruto-kaikyō sea chan. Japan
138 L2 Narva Estonia
138 L2 Narva r. Estonia/Rus. Fed.
138 K2 Narva Bay Estonia/Rus. Fed.
92 C3 Narvacan Luzon Phil.
138 L2 Narva-Jõesuu Estonia
Narva laht b. Estonia/Rus. Fed. see Narva Bay
138 L2 Narva Reservoir Estonia/Rus. Fed.
140 N2 Narvik Norway
Narvskiy Zaliv b. Estonia/Rus. Fed. see Narva Bay
Narvskoye Vodokhranilishche resr Estonia/Rus. Fed. see Narva Reservoir
116 F5 Narwana Haryana India
116 F7 Narwar Madh. Prad. India
167 K2 Narwiański Park Krajobrazowy Pol.
84 D7 Narwietooma N.T. Austr.
84 F4 Narwinbi Aboriginal Land res. N.T. Austr.
134 K2 Nar'yan-Mar Rus. Fed.
121 U3 Narymskiy Khrebet mts Kazakh.
121 P7 Naryn Kyrg.
121 P7 Naryn admin. div. Kyrg.
121 O7 Naryn r. Kyrg./Uzbek.
106 D1 Naryn Rus. Fed.
121 S6 Narynkol Kazakh.
Naryn Oblast admin. div. Kyrg. see Naryn
Narynqol Kazakh. see Narynkol
Narynskaya Oblast' admin. div. Kyrg. see Naryn
139 S9 Naryshkino Rus. Fed.
190 D6 Narzole Italy
140 N5 Näsåker Sweden
197 M3 Năsăud Romania
176 E2 Nasavrky Czech Rep.
161 C7 Nasbinals France
143 M5 Näsby Öland Sweden
254 D4 Nascentes do Rio Parnaíba, Parque Nacional das nat. park Brazil
260 E3 Naschel Arg.
81 E12 Naseby South I. N.Z.
116 D9 Nashik Mahar. India
226 B7 Nashua IA U.S.A.
233 N6 Nashua NH U.S.A.
143 M2 Näshultasjön l. Sweden
237 I9 Nashville AR U.S.A.
231 F10 Nashville GA U.S.A.
236 K6 Nashville IL U.S.A.
231 I8 Nashville NC U.S.A.
232 C8 Nashville OH U.S.A.
234 B5 Nashville PA U.S.A.
231 D7 Nashville TN U.S.A.
226 A2 Nashwauk MN U.S.A.
206 E4 Nasia Ghana
126 H7 Naşīb Syria

Našice to Neuse

358

188 G3 Našice Croatia
175 I3 Nasielsk Pol.
141 Q6 Näsijärvi l. Fin.
Nasik Mahar. India see Nashik
79 □7a Nasilai Reef Fiji
95 I4 Nasilat Kalimantan Indon.
123 M7 Nasir Pak.
210 B2 Nasir Sudan
203 G4 Nāṣir, Buḥayrat resr Egypt
Nasirabad Bangl. see Mymensingh
116 E6 Nasirabad Rajasthan India
123 M7 Nasirabad Pak.
Nāṣirīyah Iraq see An Nāṣirīyah
225 I2 Naskaupi r. Nfld and Lab. Can.
202 B2 Nasmah Libya
117 J7 Nasmganj Bihar India
143 M3 Näsnaren l. Sweden
194 H7 Naso Sicilia Italy
194 H7 Naso r. Sicilia Italy
209 E7 Nasondoye Dem. Rep. Congo
226 D5 Nasonville WI U.S.A.
79 □7 Nasorolevu mt. Vanua Levu Fiji
Nasosnyy Azer. see Hacı Zeynalabdin
122 G5 Nasqenj Iran
203 F2 Naṣr Egypt
122 D4 Naṣrābād Eṣfahān Iran
122 H4 Naṣrābād Khorāsān Iran
Nasratabad Iran see Zābol
122 H8 Naṣrī Iran
122 B5 Naṣrīān-e Pā'īn Iran
222 D4 Nass r. B.C. Can.
207 G4 Nassarawa Nigeria
207 H4 Nassarawa state Nigeria
85 H3 Nassau r. Qld Austr.
246 E1 Nassau New Prov. Bahamas
81 □2 Nassau i. Cook Is
169 E10 Nassau Rheinland-Pfalz Ger.
171 I9 Nassau Sachsen Ger.
233 L6 Nassau NY U.S.A.
169 E10 Nassau, Naturpark nature res. Ger.
235 H3 Nassau County county NY U.S.A.
233 J11 Nassawadox VA U.S.A.
170 H5 Nassenheide Ger.
Nasser, Lake resr Egypt see Nāṣir, Buḥayrat
178 C5 Nassereith Austria
206 E4 Nassian Côte d'Ivoire
143 K4 Nässjö Sweden
165 H8 Nassogne Belgium
221 M3 Nassuttooq inlet Greenland
224 E1 Nastapoca r. Que. Can.
224 E1 Nastapoka Islands Nunavut Can.
169 E10 Nastätten Ger.
138 I1 Nastola Fin.
105 L1 Nasu Japan
105 K1 Nasu-dake vol. Japan
92 C4 Nasugbu Luzon Phil.
175 K4 Nasutów Pol.
139 N5 Nasva Rus. Fed.
139 N5 Nasva r. Rus. Fed.
141 N6 Näsviken Sweden
177 H4 Naszály Hungary
212 E4 Nata Botswana
212 E4 Nata watercourse Botswana/Zimbabwe
93 E5 Nataboti Buru Indon.
253 E1 Natal Amazonas Brazil
254 G3 Natal Rio Grande do Norte Brazil
94 C4 Natal Sumatera Indon.
Natal prov. S. Africa see KwaZulu-Natal
265 G7 Natal Basin sea feature Indian Ocean
234 C3 Natalie PA U.S.A.
122 D5 Naṭanz Iran
104 C5 Natashō Japan
225 I3 Natashquan Que. Can.
225 I3 Natashquan r. Nfld and Lab./Que. Can.
81 □1 Na Taulaga i. Tokelau
237 J10 Natchez MS U.S.A.
237 I10 Natchitoches LA U.S.A.
149 M5 Nateby Cumbria, England U.K.
174 D3 Natecka, Puszcza for. Pol.
190 D3 Naters Switz.
79 □7 Natewa Bay Vanua Levu Fiji
83 J7 Nathalia Vic. Austr.
116 E4 Nathana Punjab India
84 E3 Nathan River N.T. Austr.
116 D7 Nathdwara Rajasthan India
Nathilau Point Viti Levu Fiji see Nacilau Point
140 □ Nathorst Land reg. Svalbard
186 □ Nati, Punta pt Spain
207 F4 Natiaboani Burkina
243 I5 Natillas Mex.
240 O9 National City CA U.S.A.
80 J6 National Park North I. N.Z.
212 B4 National West Coast Tourist Recreation Area park Namibia
191 O4 Natisone r. Italy
207 F4 Natitingou Benin
242 B4 Natividad, Isla i. Mex.
257 G4 Natividade Rio de Janeiro Brazil
254 D4 Natividade Tocantins Brazil
97 C7 Natkyizin Myanmar
222 D2 Natla r. N.W.T. Can.
96 B4 Natmauk Myanmar
96 B4 Natogyi Myanmar
239 J12 Nátora Mex.
117 L7 Natore Bangl.
102 R8 Natori Japan
211 C5 Natron, Lake salt l. Tanz.
105 M1 Natsui-gawa r. Japan
138 G9 Natsyyanal'ny Park Byelavyezhskaya Pushcha Belarus
136 G2 Natsyyanal'ny Park Prypyatski nature res. Belarus
83 M6 Nattai National Park N.S.W. Austr.
96 B5 Nattalin Myanmar
114 F7 Nattam Tamil Nadu India
143 O3 Nåttarö i. Sweden
96 C5 Nattaung mt. Myanmar
140 P3 Nattavaara Sweden
140 P3 Nattavaara by Sweden
179 I3 Natternback Austria
173 I4 Nattheim Ger.
122 I4 Na'tū Iran
79 □7 Natua Vanua Levu Fiji
225 I2 Natuashish Nfld and Lab. Can.
137 Q9 Natukhayevskaya Rus. Fed.
95 G2 Natuna, Kepulauan is Indon.
95 H2 Natuna Besar i. Indon.
232 F11 Natural Bridge VA U.S.A.
241 V4 Natural Bridges National Monument nat. park UT U.S.A.
87 C12 Naturaliste, Cape W.A. Austr.
87 A8 Naturaliste Channel W.A. Austr.
265 L7 Naturaliste Plateau sea feature Indian Ocean
214 H9 Nature's Valley S. Africa
241 X3 Naturita CO U.S.A.
191 J2 Naturno Italy
Nau Tajik. see Nov
226 I3 Naubinway MI U.S.A.
163 I7 Naucelle France
162 I6 Naucelles France
212 C4 Nauchas Namibia
111 F10 Nau Co l. Xizang China
178 C6 Nauders Austria
214 I8 Naudesberg Pass S. Africa
213 H2 Nauela Moz.
170 G5 Nauen Ger.
171 E7 Nauendorf Ger.
235 I2 Naugatuck CT U.S.A.
235 I2 Naugatuck r. CT U.S.A.
172 E2 Nauheim Ger.
123 L6 Nau Hissar Pak.
Naujaat Nunavut Can. see Repulse Bay
162 B5 Naujac-sur-Mer France
92 C5 Naujan Mindoro Phil.
138 F5 Naujoji Akmenė Lith.
116 D6 Naukh Rajasthan India
147 J5 Naul Ireland
209 B9 Naulila Angola
169 H8 Naumburg (Hessen) Ger.
171 E8 Naumburg (Saale) Ger.
171 H8 Naundorf Sachsen Ger.
171 H9 Naundorf Sachsen Ger.
96 C6 Naunglon Myanmar
96 C5 Naungpale Myanmar
128 D7 Na'ūr Jordan
169 E9 Nauroth Ger.
123 K7 Nauroz Kalat Pak.
129 G2 Naurskaya Rus. Fed.
77 G2 Nauru i. Nauru
77 G2 Nauru country S. Pacific Ocean
123 M8 Naushahro Firoz Pak.
123 M8 Naushara Pak.
106 J1 Naushki Rus. Fed.
79 □7a Nausori Viti Levu Fiji
161 D7 Naussac, Barrage de dam France
141 H6 Naustdal Norway
250 C6 Nauta Peru
Nautaca Uzbek. see Qarshi
117 I6 Nautanwa Uttar Prad. India
214 B2 Naute Dam Namibia
245 K5 Nautla Mex.
140 T2 Nautsi Rus. Fed.
226 C9 Nauvoo IL U.S.A.
123 K5 Nauzad Afgh.
208 E4 Nava r. Dem. Rep. Congo
243 I3 Nava Mex.
183 J2 Nava Spain
Navabad Tajik. see Novobod
183 J8 Navacepeda de Tormes Spain
183 M7 Navacerrada, Puerto de pass Spain
183 L7 Navacerreda Spain
185 L7 Navachica mt. Spain
182 I8 Navaconcejo Spain
183 K7 Nava de Arévalo Spain
183 L6 Nava de la Asunción Spain
183 J6 Nava del Rey Spain
183 J7 Nava de Sotrobal Spain
138 K6 Navadrutsk Belarus
117 L8 Navadwip W. Bengal India
183 M6 Navafría Spain
183 L9 Navahermosa Spain
129 K5 Navahı Azer.
138 I8 Navahrudak Belarus
138 I8 Navahrudskaye Wzvyshsha hills Belarus
187 E8 Navajas Spain
239 K8 Navajo r. CO U.S.A.
241 W6 Navajo Indian Reservation res. AZ U.S.A.
239 K8 Navajo Lake NM U.S.A.
241 V4 Navajo Mountain UT U.S.A.
183 J4 Navajos hill Spain
92 E6 Naval Phil.
186 F3 Naval Spain
183 L8 Navalagamella Spain
183 O5 Navalcaballo Spain
183 J8 Navalcán Spain
183 J8 Navalcán, Embalse de resr Spain
183 L8 Navalcarnero Spain
183 O5 Navalero Spain
183 L6 Navalmanzano Spain
183 K8 Navalmoral Spain
183 K7 Navalmoral, Puerto de pass Spain
182 I9 Navalmoral de la Mata Spain
183 J8 Navalonguilla Spain
183 K8 Navalosa Spain
183 L7 Navalperal de Pinares Spain
185 J2 Navalpino Spain
183 K8 Navaluenga Spain
183 J9 Navalvillar de Ibor Spain
185 I2 Navalvillar de Pela Spain
183 K8 Navamorcuende Spain
147 I5 Navan Ireland
Navangar Gujarat India see Jamnagar
138 L6 Navapolatsk Belarus
123 L5 Nāvar, Dasht-e depr. Afgh.
186 I4 Navarcles Spain
186 C2 Navardún Spain
131 S3 Navarin, Mys c. Rus. Fed.
259 D9 Navarino, Isla i. Chile
183 Q3 Navarra aut. comm. Spain
83 I7 Navarre Vic. Austr.
Navarre aut. comm. Spain see Navarra
182 H7 Navarredonda de la Rinconada Spain
163 C9 Navarrenx France
187 D9 Navarrés Spain
183 O4 Navarrete Spain
261 H4 Navarro Arg.
250 C6 Navarro Peru
240 I2 Navarro r. CA U.S.A.
186 I4 Navàs Spain
163 D10 Navasa Spain
186 C2 Navascués Spain
185 J1 Navas de Estrena Spain
182 G9 Navas del Madroño Spain
183 L8 Navas del Rey Spain
183 L6 Navas de Oro Spain
185 M4 Navas de San Juan Spain
182 G8 Navasfrías Spain
134 H5 Navashino Rus. Fed.
237 G10 Navasota TX U.S.A.
237 G10 Navasota r. TX U.S.A.
246 F4 Navassa Island terr. West Indies
136 H1 Navasyolki Belarus
186 K3 Navata Spain
183 K8 Navatalgordo Spain
138 I8 Navayel'nya Belarus
190 I4 Nave Italy
184 B6 Nave Port.
182 B3 Nave, Cabo da c. Spain
182 F4 Navea r. Spain
182 G7 Nave de Haver Port.
148 E2 Nave Island Scotland U.K.
193 L3 Navelli Italy
160 I1 Navenne France
146 H5 Naver r. Scotland U.K.
146 H6 Naver, Loch l. Scotland U.K.
184 C6 Nave Redonda Port.
142 H3 Naverstad Sweden
162 H5 Naves France
186 I4 Navès Spain
139 U9 Navesnoye Rus. Fed.
138 H3 Navesti r. Estonia
247 □7 Navet Trin. and Tob.
185 I1 Navezuelas Spain
260 D4 Navia Arg.
182 G1 Navia Spain
182 G1 Navia r. Spain
182 G1 Navia, Ría de inlet Spain
116 B9 Navibandar Gujarat India
260 B3 Navidad Chile
237 G11 Navidad r. TX U.S.A.
247 I3 Navidad Bank sea feature Caribbean Sea
190 G5 Naviglio di Pavia canal Italy
190 G5 Naviglio Grande canal Italy
160 G3 Navilly France
114 C3 Navi Mumbai Mahar. India
255 B7 Naviraí Brazil
79 □7 Naviti i. Fiji
136 E2 Naviz Ukr.
116 C8 Navlakhi Gujarat India
139 R9 Navlya Rus. Fed.
139 R9 Navlya r. Rus. Fed.
197 Q6 Năvodari Romania
120 K7 Navoiy Uzbek.
120 J7 Navoiy admin. div. Uzbek.
242 E4 Navojoa Mex.
242 F5 Navolato Mex.
79 □7 Navotuvotu hill Vanua Levu Fiji
Navoy Oblast admin. div. Uzbek. see Navoiy
Návpaktos Greece see Nafpaktos
Návplion Greece see Nafplio
143 L5 Nävragöl Sweden
142 C3 Navrestad hill Norway
206 E4 Navrongo Ghana
Navşar Turkey see Şemdinli
116 D9 Navsari Gujarat India
79 □7a Navua Viti Levu Fiji
79 □7a Navua r. Viti Levu Fiji
79 □7a Navula rf Fiji
116 E6 Nawa Rajasthan India
128 E6 Nawá Syria
117 L7 Nawabganj Bangl.
98 D6 Nawabganj Uttar Prad. India
111 F13 Nawabganj Uttar Prad. India
123 M8 Nawabshah Pak.
117 J7 Nawada Bihar India
117 I9 Nawagaon Chhattisgarh India
123 L5 Nāwah Afgh.
117 J6 Nawakot Nepal
123 N7 Nawakot Pak.
116 E6 Nawalgarh Rajasthan India
123 N6 Nawan Kot Pak.
111 C11 Nawanshahr Punjab India
124 F5 Nawāṣīf, Ḥarrat lava field Saudi Arabia
96 C3 Nawnghkio Myanmar
96 D3 Nawngleng Myanmar
Nawoiy Uzbek. see Navoiy
Nawoiy Wiloyati admin. div. Uzbek. see Navoiy
175 I6 Nawojowa Pol.
125 L7 Naws, Ra's c. Oman
129 G6 Naxçıvan Azer.
129 G6 Naxçıvan aut. reg. Azer.
129 G6 Naxçıvançay r. Azer.
108 E4 Naxi Sichuan China
199 G5 Naxos Naxos Greece
199 G5 Naxos i. Greece
250 B4 Naya Col.
111 K10 Nayag Xizang China
117 J9 Nayagarh Orissa India
123 L4 Nayak Afgh.
244 C3 Nayar Mex.
244 C3 Nayarit state Mex.
122 G5 Nāy Band, Kūh-e mt. Iran
163 D9 Nay-Bourdettes France
137 N8 Nayd'onivka Ukr.
125 J6 Nayfah oasis Saudi Arabia
108 E5 Nayong Guizhou China
102 T2 Nayoro Japan
96 C5 Naypyidaw Myanmar
125 K9 Nayt Suquṭrā Yemen
211 B8 Nayuchi Malawi
114 F6 Nayudupeta Andhra Prad. India
124 D1 Nayyāl, Wādī watercourse Saudi Arabia
116 F8 Nazarabad Madh. Prad. India
250 E4 Nazare Amazonas Brazil
251 H6 Nazaré Brazil
254 E3 Nazare Piauí Brazil
182 B9 Nazaré Port.
242 H5 Nazareno Mex.
114 E8 Nazareth Tamil Nadu India
Nazareth Israel see Naẕerat
234 E3 Nazareth PA U.S.A.
256 C2 Nazário Brazil
242 G5 Nazas Mex.
242 G5 Nazas r. Mex.
252 B3 Nazca Peru
267 N7 Nazca Ridge sea feature S. Pacific Ocean
102 □G18 Naze Nansei-shotō Japan
151 M4 Nazeing Essex, England U.K.
159 M7 Nazelles-Négron France
128 D6 Naẕerat Israel
122 C5 Nazian Iran
122 A2 Nāzīk Iran
122 I7 Nāzīl Iran
199 J5 Nazilli Turkey
123 L9 Nazimabad Pak.
127 I4 Nazımiye Turkey
206 E4 Nazinon r. Burkina conv. Red Volta
117 O6 Nazira Assam India
117 M8 Nazir Hat Bangl.
129 I5 Näzirli Azer.
139 O2 Naziya Rus. Fed.
222 F4 Nazko B.C. Can.
222 F4 Nazko r. B.C. Can.
122 A3 Nāzlū r. Iran
129 F2 Nazran' Rus. Fed.
210 C2 Nazrēt Eth.
125 M4 Nazwá Oman
130 I4 Nazyvayevsk Rus. Fed.
206 B2 Nbâk Maur.
206 D2 Nbeïket Dlîm well Maur.
215 J9 Ncanaha S. Africa
209 F7 Nchelenge Zambia
Ncheu Malawi see Ntcheu
212 D4 Ncojane Botswana
215 L7 Ncora S. Africa
207 H6 Ncue Equat. Guinea
206 C2 Ndaghma Barké well Maur.
211 B6 Ndala Tanz.
209 B7 N'dalatando Angola
207 F4 Ndali Benin
208 D3 Ndanda C.A.R.
213 F4 Ndanga Zimbabwe
93 C9 Ndao i. Indon.
211 B6 Ndareda Tanz.
208 B5 Ndekabalandji Gabon
208 D2 Ndélé C.A.R.
207 I5 Ndélélé Cameroon
208 A5 Ndendé Gabon
Ndende i. Santa Cruz Is Solomon Is see Ndeni
78 □6 Ndeni i. Santa Cruz Is Solomon Is
207 H5 Ndikiniméki Cameroon
208 B3 Ndim C.A.R.
209 A5 Ndindi Gabon
206 B3 Ndioum Guènt Senegal
N'Djamena Chad see Ndjamena
202 B6 Ndjamena Chad
208 D3 Ndji r. C.A.R.
207 H5 Ndjim r. Cameroon
208 A5 Ndjolé Gabon
Ndjouani i. Comoros see Nzwani
208 B5 Ndjounou Gabon
206 B3 Ndofane Senegal
208 A5 Ndogo, Lagune lag. Gabon
Ndoi i. Fiji see Doi
207 I5 Ndok Cameroon
209 F8 Ndola Zambia
206 D4 Ndorola Burkina
210 C4 Ndoto mt. Kenya
208 A5 Ndougou Gabon
208 D3 Ndoukou C.A.R.
208 C3 Ndoumbou C.A.R.
78 □6 Ndovele New Georgia Is Solomon Is
78 □6 Nduindui Solomon Is
Nduke i. New Georgia Is Solomon Is see Kolombangara
211 C7 Ndumbwe Tanz.
215 Q2 Ndumu S. Africa
215 Q2 Ndumu Game Reserve nature res. Moz.
208 F4 Nduye Dem. Rep. Congo
215 O5 Ndwedwe S. Africa
162 D4 Né r. France
96 G5 Ne, Hon i. Vietnam
163 E10 Né, Mont mt. France
198 G7 Nea Alikarnassos Kriti Greece
198 D3 Nea Anchialos Greece
198 E2 Nea Apollonia Greece
198 E4 Nea Artaki Greece
85 K9 Neabul Creek r. Qld Austr.
198 E5 Nea Epidavros Greece
198 C5 Nea Figaleia Greece
104 D3 Neagari Japan
147 J3 Neagh, Lough l. Northern Ireland U.K.
238 B2 Neah Bay WA U.S.A.
197 N6 Neajlov r. Romania
198 E2 Nea Kallikrateia Greece
198 F2 Nea Karvali Greece
147 D5 Neale Ireland
84 C8 Neale, Lake salt flat N.T. Austr.
87 H10 Neale Junction Nature Reserve W.A. Austr.
82 F3 Neales watercourse S.A. Austr.
198 E4 Nea Liosia Greece
198 E4 Nea Makri Greece
199 H4 Nea Monu tourist site Greece
198 E2 Nea Moudania Greece
197 O3 Neamț r. Romania
198 F2 Nea Peramos Greece
198 C2 Neapoli Dytiki Makedonia Greece
199 G7 Neapoli Kriti Greece
198 E6 Neapoli Peloponnisos Greece
Neapolis Italy see Napoli
198 E2 Nea Roda Greece
149 L5 Near Sawrey Cumbria, England U.K.
198 D2 Nea Santa Greece
Néa Stíra Greece see Nea Styra
198 F4 Nea Styra Greece
150 E4 Neath Neath Port Talbot, Wales U.K.
150 E4 Neath r. Wales U.K.
150 E4 Neath Port Talbot admin. div. Wales U.K.
198 E1 Nea Zichni Greece
104 G5 Neba Japan
210 A4 Nebbi Uganda
192 C2 Nebbio reg. Corse France
206 E4 Nebbou Burkina
168 F1 Nebel Ger.
173 I7 Nebelhorn mt. Ger.
110 E5 Nebesnaya, Gora mt. Xinjiang China
163 I10 Nébias France
83 K3 Nebine Creek r. Qld Austr.
85 L6 Nebo Qld Austr.
241 U2 Nebo, Mount UT U.S.A.
139 Q2 Nebolchi Rus. Fed.
163 F9 Nébouzan reg. France
171 E8 Nebra (Unstrut) Ger.
236 E5 Nebraska state U.S.A.
236 H5 Nebraska City NE U.S.A.
183 M5 Nebreda Spain
194 G8 Nebrodi, Monti mts Sicilia Italy
139 W5 Nebyloye Rus. Fed.
245 J5 Necaxa r. Mex.
226 D5 Necedah WI U.S.A.
226 D5 Necedah National Wildlife Refuge nature res. WI U.S.A.
176 E1 Nechanice Czech Rep.
137 K7 Nechayane Ukr.
139 X6 Nechayevskaya Rus. Fed.
137 L5 Nechayivka Ukr.
237 I11 Neches r. TX U.S.A.
250 C2 Nechí r. Col.
210 C3 Nechisar National Park Eth.
185 M7 Nechite r. Spain
171 H10 Nechranice, Vodní nádrž resr Czech Rep.
172 E2 Neckar r. Ger.
172 F3 Neckarbischofsheim Ger.
172 F3 Neckargemünd Ger.
172 F3 Neckarsteinach Ger.
172 G3 Neckarsulm Ger.
172 G3 Neckartal-Odenwald, Naturpark nature res. Ger.
75 H2 Necker Island HI U.S.A.
261 H6 Necochea Arg.
250 B2 Necoclí Col.
151 N2 Necton Norfolk, England U.K.
198 C5 Neda r. Greece
182 D2 Neda Spain
136 J2 Nedanchychi Ukr.
177 H2 Nedašov Czech Rep.
170 H3 Neddemin Ger.
202 C6 Nédéley Chad
197 N9 Nedelino Bulg.
188 F2 Nedelišće Croatia
139 T7 Nedel'noye Rus. Fed.
Nederland country Europe see Netherlands
Nederlandse Antillen terr. West Indies see Netherlands Antilles
164 H4 Nederlangbroek Neth.
164 H5 Neder Rijn r. Neth.
170 E1 Neder Vindinge Denmark
165 I6 Nederweert Neth.
Nédha r. Greece see Neda
175 M1 Nedingis l. Lith.
171 F6 Nedlitz Ger.
225 F1 Nedlouc, Lac l. Que. Can.
Nedluk Lake Que. Can. see Nedlouc, Lac
136 F5 Nedoboyivtsi Ukr.
111 J12 Nêdong Xizang China
140 P2 Nedre Soppero Sweden
142 F2 Nedre Tokke l. Norway
137 M3 Nedryhayliv Ukr.
142 B2 Nedstrand Norway
142 B2 Nedstrandsfjorden sea chan. Norway
208 F4 Neduka r. Dem. Rep. Congo
176 F2 Nedvědice Czech Rep.
174 G5 Nędza Pol.
105 I2 Neeba-san mt. Japan
164 K4 Neede Neth.
233 N6 Needham MA U.S.A.
151 O3 Needham Market Suffolk, England U.K.
151 L3 Needingworth Cambridgeshire, England U.K.
241 R7 Needles CA U.S.A.
232 G9 Needmore PA U.S.A.
116 E7 Neemuch Madh. Prad. India
226 F5 Neenah WI U.S.A.
223 L5 Neepawa Man. Can.
165 J6 Neer Neth.
221 J2 Neergaard Lake Nunavut Can.
164 H5 Neerijnen Neth.
168 D4 Neermoor Ger.
165 I6 Neeroeteren Belgium
165 H6 Neerpelt Belgium
142 E5 Nees Sund sea chan. Denmark
168 K4 Neetze Ger.
210 C2 Nefas Mewch'a Eth.
234 D3 Neffs PA U.S.A.
234 C4 Neffsville PA U.S.A.
205 G2 Nefta Tunisia
129 K6 Neftçala Azer.
129 L5 Neft Daşları Azer.
Neftechala Azer. see Uzboy
Neftechala Azer. see Neftçala
129 A1 Neftegorsk Krasnodarskiy Kray Rus. Fed.
100 M2 Neftegorsk Sakhalin Rus. Fed.
120 D1 Neftegorsk Samarskaya Oblast' Rus. Fed.
134 K4 Neftekamsk Rus. Fed.
129 F1 Neftekumsk Rus. Fed.
190 F1 Neftenbach Switz.
130 I3 Nefteyugansk Rus. Fed.
Neftezavodsk Turkm. see Seýdi
Neftyanyye Kamni Azer. see Neft Daşları
150 C2 Nefyn Gwynedd, Wales U.K.
189 B7 Nefza Tunisia
210 E3 Negada Weyn well Eth.
209 B6 Negage Angola
206 C3 Négala Mali
122 G7 Negār Iran
95 K9 Negara Bali Indon.
95 K6 Negara Kalimantan Indon.
95 K6 Negara r. Indon.
226 G3 Negaunee MI U.S.A.
210 C3 Negēlē Oromīya Eth.
210 C3 Negēlē Oromīya Eth.
94 E3 Negeri Sembilan state Malaysia
128 D8 Negev des. Israel
209 B8 Negola Angola
211 C7 Negomane Moz.
114 F9 Negombo Sri Lanka
197 K6 Negotin Serbia
196 I9 Negotino Macedonia
197 K9 Negotino Macedonia
252 A2 Negra, Cordillera mts Peru
258 G4 Negra, Lago l. Uru.
182 H4 Negra, Peña mt. Spain
250 A6 Negra, Punta pt Peru
257 F3 Negra, Serra mts Brazil
253 E3 Negra, Serranía de mts Bol.
96 B7 Negrais, Cape Myanmar
191 J4 Negrar Italy
185 N5 Negratín, Embalse de resr Spain
163 H11 Negre, Pic mt. Andorra
183 O6 Negredo Spain
182 C3 Negreira Spain
252 C4 Negreiros Chile
163 H7 Nègrepelisse France
197 P4 Negrești Romania
197 L3 Negrești-Oaș Romania
260 A5 Negrete Chile
187 D12 Negrete, Cabo c. Spain
84 B4 Negri r. N.T. Austr.
197 O4 Negri Romania
140 □ Negribreen glacier Svalbard
246 □ Negril Jamaica
205 G2 Négrine Alg.
Negri Sembilan state Malaysia see Negeri Sembilan
250 A6 Negritos Peru
260 D6 Negro r. Arg.
253 F4 Negro r. Brazil
253 F6 Negro r. Para.
251 G5 Negro r. S. America
182 H4 Negro r. Spain
261 H3 Negro r. Uru.
261 I3 Negro r. Uru.
180 D5 Negro, Cabo c. Morocco
Negroponte i. Greece see Evvoia
92 D7 Negros i. Phil.
197 Q7 Negru Vodă Romania
238 C4 Nehalem r. OR U.S.A.
122 C4 Nehavand Iran
122 I6 Nehbandān Iran
107 S2 Nehe Heilong. China
197 O5 Nehoiu Romania
209 C9 Nehone Angola
79 □8 Neiafu Vava'u Gp Tonga
246 H4 Neiba Dom. Rep.
157 L5 Neid Française r. France
106 I9 Neiguanying Gansu China
108 E4 Neijiang Sichuan China
183 N4 Neila, Sierra de mts Spain
223 I4 Neilburg Sask. Can.
214 E4 Neilersdrif S. Africa
115 M7 Neill Island Andaman & Nicobar Is India
226 D5 Neillsville WI U.S.A.
107 H6 Nei Mongol Zizhiqu aut. reg. China
171 D7 Neinstedt Ger.
107 N8 Neiqiu Hebei China
171 K6 Neiße r. Ger./Pol.
250 C4 Neiva Col.
182 C5 Neiva r. Port.
190 E6 Neive Italy
109 H2 Neixiang Henan China
244 E7 Neixpa r. Mex.
223 L3 Nejanilini Lake Man. Can.
245 L9 Nejapa Mex.
Nejd reg. Saudi Arabia see Najd
176 B1 Nejdek Czech Rep.
122 E3 Neka Iran
122 E3 Neka r. Iran
210 C2 Nek'emtē Eth.
135 H6 Nekhayevskaya Rus. Fed.
Nekhayevskiy Rus. Fed. see Nekhayevskaya
137 L2 Nekhayivka Ukr.
174 F3 Nekla Pol.
139 X6 Neklyudovo Rus. Fed.
117 L7 Nekmarad Bangl.
104 A4 Neko-zaki pt Japan
136 H4 Nekrasove Ukr.
135 I6 Nekrasovo Rus. Fed.
139 U5 Nekrasovskiy Rus. Fed.
139 X4 Nekrasovskoye Rus. Fed.
142 H6 Nekselø i. Denmark
143 L6 Neksø Bornholm Denmark
183 N3 Nela r. Spain
114 E6 Nelamangala Karnataka India
116 G4 Nelang Hima. Prad. India
182 E7 Nelas Port.
142 E3 Nelaug l. Norway
139 U2 Nelazskoye Rus. Fed.
85 I6 Nelia Qld Austr.
139 P5 Nelidovo Rus. Fed.
236 G4 Neligh NE U.S.A.
131 O4 Nel'kan Khabarovskiy Kray Rus. Fed.
131 P3 Nel'kan Respublika Sakha (Yakutiya) Rus. Fed.
78 □3a Nell i. Kwajalein Marshall Is
227 N1 Nellie Lake Ont. Can.
140 T2 Nellim Fin.
172 H4 Nellingen Ger.
114 F5 Nellore Andhra Prad. India
78 □3a Nell Passage Kwajalein Marshall Is
128 H2 Nelluz watercourse Turkey
100 K5 Nel'ma Rus. Fed.
215 O1 Nelshoogte pass S. Africa
261 G2 Nelson Arg.
222 G5 Nelson B.C. Can.
223 M3 Nelson r. Man. Can.
81 H8 Nelson South I. N.Z.
81 H8 Nelson admin. reg. South I. N.Z.
149 M6 Nelson Lancashire, England U.K.
241 S6 Nelson AZ U.S.A.
236 F5 Nelson NE U.S.A.
241 R6 Nelson NV U.S.A.
226 B5 Nelson WI U.S.A.
82 H8 Nelson, Cape Vic. Austr.
259 B8 Nelson, Estrecho str. Chile
83 N5 Nelson Bay N.S.W. Austr.
81 F9 Nelson Creek South I. N.Z.
222 F3 Nelson Forks B.C. Can.
223 L4 Nelson House Man. Can.
233 J11 Nelsonia VA U.S.A.
81 G9 Nelson Lakes National Park South I. N.Z.
235 H2 Nelsonville NY U.S.A.
214 H8 Nelspoort S. Africa
215 O1 Nelspruit S. Africa
134 K3 Nem r. Rus. Fed.
206 D2 Néma Maur.
134 J4 Nema Rus. Fed.
226 B3 Nemadji r. MN U.S.A.
Neman r. Belarus/Lith. see Nyoman
138 F6 Neman Rus. Fed.
alt. Nemunas (Lith.)
alt. Nyoman (Belarus)
138 F6 Neman r. Rus. Fed.
122 H7 Ne'matābād Iran
Nemausus France see Nîmes
78 □6 Nembao Santa Cruz Is Solomon Is
207 G5 Nembe Nigeria
190 H4 Nembro Italy
177 I3 Nemce Slovakia
134 H4 Nemda r. Rus. Fed.
198 D5 Nemea Greece
134 K3 Nemed Rus. Fed.
227 K2 Nemegos Ont. Can.
227 K1 Nemegosenda Lake Ont. Can.
138 I7 Nemenčine Lith.
205 G2 Nementcha, Monts des mts Alg.
198 B2 Nëmerçkë, Mal ridge Albania
176 G4 Nemesszalók Hungary
176 G5 Nemesvid Hungary
177 H5 Németkér Hungary
Nemetocenna France see Arras
140 U2 Nemetskiy, Mys c. Rus. Fed.
Nemirov Ukr. see Nemyriv
224 E3 Nemiscau r. Que. Can.
224 E3 Nemiscau, Lac l. Que. Can.
136 J3 Nemishayeve Ukr.
107 S2 Nemor He r. China
Nemours Alg. see Ghazaouet
156 E7 Nemours France
127 K4 Nemrut Dağı mt. Turkey
171 E8 Nemsdorf-Göhrendorf Ger.
177 H3 Nemšová Slovakia
100 I4 Nemta r. Rus. Fed.
175 M1 Nemunaitis Lith.
138 E6 Nemunas r. Lith.
alt. Neman (Rus. Fed.)
alt. Nyoman (Belarus)
138 H5 Nemunėlio Radviliškis Lith.
138 I5 Nemunėlis r. Lith.
102 W3 Nemuro Japan
102 W3 Nemuro-hantō pen. Japan
102 W3 Nemuro-kaikyō sea chan. Japan/Rus. Fed.
102 W3 Nemuro-wan b. Japan
136 C3 Nemyriv L'vivs'ka Oblast' Ukr.
136 H5 Nemyriv Vinnyts'ka Oblast' Ukr.
136 G4 Nemyryntsi Ukr.
147 F7 Nenagh Ireland
100 D4 Nenan Heilong. China
220 D3 Nenana AK U.S.A.
139 U7 Nenashevo Rus. Fed.
190 C3 Nendaz Switz.
151 M2 Nene r. England U.K.
Nenets Autonomous Okrug admin. div. Rus. Fed. see Nenetskiy Avtonomnyy Okrug
134 K2 Nenetskiy Avtonomnyy Okrug admin. div. Rus. Fed.
177 I3 Nenince Slovakia
107 S2 Nenjiang Heilong. China
107 S4 Nen Jiang r. China
168 D3 Nenndorf Ger.
170 G5 Nennhausen Ger.
173 K3 Nennslingen Ger.
134 G2 Nenoksa Rus. Fed.
169 I8 Nentershausen Hessen Ger.
169 E10 Nentershausen Rheinland-Pfalz Ger.
149 M4 Nenthead Cumbria, England U.K.
178 A5 Nenzing Austria
104 E4 Neo Japan
198 D2 Neo Agioneri Greece
78 □4a Neoch atoll Chuuk Micronesia
198 F2 Neo Erasmio Greece
104 E5 Neo-gawa r. Japan
Neokhórion Greece see Oichalia
241 V1 Neola UT U.S.A.
146 J4 Neolithic Orkney tourist site Scotland U.K.
198 D3 Neo Monastiri Greece
192 B7 Neoneli Sardegna Italy
Néon Karlovásion Samos Greece see Karlovasi
226 F5 Neopit WI U.S.A.
237 H7 Neosho MO U.S.A.
237 H7 Neosho r. KS U.S.A.
198 E2 Neos Marmaras Greece
161 I10 Néoules France
186 F2 Néouvielle, Pic de mt. France
163 E10 Néouvielle, Réserve Naturelle de nature res. France
116 I5 Nepal country Asia
116 H5 Nepalganj Nepal
116 H6 Nepalganj Road Uttar Prad. India
116 F9 Nepanagar Madh. Prad. India
224 F4 Nepean Ont. Can.
82 □1 Nepean Island Norfolk I.
241 U2 Nephi UT U.S.A.
147 D4 Nephin hill Ireland
147 C4 Nephin Beg Range hills Ireland
193 I3 Nepi Italy
221 L5 Nepisiguit r. N.B. Can.
176 C2 Nepomuk Czech Rep.
139 V8 Nepryadva r. Rus. Fed.
235 G4 Neptune City NJ U.S.A.
82 F6 Neptune Islands S.A. Austr.
175 G3 Ner r. Pol.
193 I3 Nera r. Italy
163 E7 Nérac France
114 C3 Neral Mahar. India
85 N9 Nerang Qld Austr.
176 D1 Neratovice Czech Rep.
177 J6 Nerău Romania
138 H7 Neravai Lith.
171 G8 Nerchau Ger.
99 K1 Nerchinsk Rus. Fed.
100 A3 Nerchinskiy Zavod Rus. Fed.
162 D4 Nercillac France
192 D7 Nercone, Monte su mt. Italy
134 K4 Nerdva Rus. Fed.
162 D4 Néré France
197 O5 Nereju Romania
139 X4 Nerekhta Rus. Fed.
173 I4 Neresheim Ger.
225 G2 Néret, Lac l. Que. Can.
138 I5 Nereta Latvia
193 L2 Nereto Italy
188 F4 Neretva r. Bos.-Herz./Croatia
175 L4 Neretva r. Ukr.
188 F4 Neretvanski Kanal sea chan. Croatia
191 Q6 Nerezine Croatia
116 G9 Neri Mahar. India
111 J11 Nêri Pünco l. Xizang China
209 D8 Neriquinha Angola
138 G7 Neris r. Lith.
160 B4 Néris-les-Bains France
185 L7 Nerja Spain
220 C4 Nerka, Lake AK U.S.A.
139 X5 Nerl' Ivanovskaya Oblast' Rus. Fed.
139 V4 Nerl' Tverskaya Oblast' Rus. Fed.
139 U4 Nerl' r. Rus. Fed.
139 W4 Nero, Ozero l. Rus. Fed.
134 M3 Nerokhi Rus. Fed.
160 E5 Néronde France
160 B3 Nérondes France
256 C2 Nerópolis Brazil
169 C10 Neroth Ger.
137 S3 Nerovnovka Rus. Fed.
134 L2 Neroyka, Gora mt. Rus. Fed.
116 F9 Ner Pinglai Mahar. India
185 O4 Nerpio Spain
162 E4 Nersac France
173 I5 Nersingen Ger.
136 J7 Nerubays'ke Ukr.
139 T9 Neruch' r. Rus. Fed.
139 Q9 Nerussa r. Rus. Fed.
184 F5 Nerva Spain
191 M4 Nervesa della Battaglia Italy
160 E5 Nervieux France
183 O2 Nervión r. Spain
190 D4 Nery, Monte mt. Italy
131 N4 Neryungri Rus. Fed.
164 I2 Nes Neth.
142 F1 Nes Norway
134 I2 Nes' Rus. Fed.
134 I2 Nes' r. Rus. Fed.
122 G7 Nesā' Iran
122 D3 Nesa' Iran
142 F1 Nesbyen Norway
171 J8 Neschwitz Ger.
234 F5 Nesco NJ U.S.A.
234 C2 Nescopeck PA U.S.A.
234 C2 Nescopeck Creek r. PA U.S.A.
197 P8 Nesebŭr Bulg.
247 □4 Nesfield Barbados
142 C2 Nes Flaten Norway
234 F4 Neshaminy Creek r. PA U.S.A.
140 □G1 Neskaupstaður Iceland
156 E4 Nesle France
177 H2 Nesluša Slovakia
140 L3 Nesna Norway
136 G3 Nesolon' Ukr.
176 G2 Nesovice Czech Rep.
161 F8 Nesque r. France
234 D3 Nesquehoning PA U.S.A.
114 D4 Nesri Mahar. India
146 H8 Ness r. Scotland U.K.
146 G8 Ness, Loch l. Scotland U.K.
192 B2 Nessa Corse France
236 F6 Ness City KS U.S.A.
168 D3 Nesse Ger.
169 J9 Nesse r. Ger.
222 C3 Nesselrode, Mount Can./U.S.A.
173 J6 Nesselwang Ger.
190 G1 Nesslau Switz.
163 F9 Neste r. France
138 F7 Nesterov Rus. Fed.
Nesterov Ukr. see Zhovkva
139 Q7 Nestery Rus. Fed.
149 K7 Neston Cheshire, England U.K.
247 □7 Nestor Trin. and Tob.
193 I2 Nestore r. Italy
191 M9 Nestore r. Italy
223 M5 Nestor Falls Ont. Can.
226 F3 Nestoria MI U.S.A.
198 F2 Nestos r. Greece
142 E2 Nesvatn l. Norway
Nesvizh Belarus see Nyasvizh
128 C6 Netanya Israel
117 J8 Netarhat Jharkhand India
234 F3 Netcong NJ U.S.A.
169 H7 Nethe r. Ger.
164 I3 Netherlands country Europe
247 I7 Netherlands Antilles terr. West Indies
146 L8 Netherley Aberdeenshire, Scotland U.K.
150 F5 Nether Stowey Somerset, England U.K.
149 M3 Netherton Northumberland, England U.K.
146 I8 Nethy Bridge Highland, Scotland U.K.
213 H2 Netia Moz.
136 F3 Netishyn Ukr.
195 M5 Neto r. Italy
176 D2 Netolice Czech Rep.
169 F9 Netphen Ger.
169 J8 Netra (Ringgau) Ger.
117 M7 Netrakona Bangl.
116 D9 Netrang Gujarat India
190 G1 Netstal Switz.
157 I6 Nettancourt France
169 C10 Nettersheim Ger.
169 B8 Nettetal Ger.
221 K3 Nettilling Lake Nunavut Can.
226 A1 Nett Lake MN U.S.A.
149 Q7 Nettleham Lincolnshire, England U.K.
193 J5 Nettuno Italy
171 F9 Netzschkau Ger.
173 M2 Neualbenreuth Ger.
169 G10 Neu-Anspach Ger.
210 B3 Neubari r. Sudan
168 I1 Neuberend Ger.
179 M4 Neuberg an der Mürz Austria
173 M6 Neubeuern Ger.
173 L5 Neubiberg Ger.
168 D5 Neubörger Ger.
159 M3 Neubourg, Campagne du reg. France
170 H3 Neubrandenburg Ger.
168 G5 Neubruchhausen Ger.
172 H2 Neubrunn Ger.
170 E2 Neubukow Ger.
172 F4 Neubulach Ger.
173 O4 Neuburg am Inn Ger.
172 E4 Neuburg am Rhein Ger.
173 K4 Neuburg an der Donau Ger.
173 I5 Neuburg an der Kammel Ger.
170 E3 Neuburg-Steinhausen Ger.
171 H8 Neuburxdorf Ger.
190 B2 Neuchâtel Switz.
190 B1 Neuchâtel canton Switz.
190 B2 Neuchâtel, Lac de l. Switz.
168 K4 Neu Darchau Ger.
169 K9 Neudietendorf Ger.
179 N4 Neudorf Austria
171 G10 Neudorf Ger.
171 E10 Neudrossenfeld Ger.
172 F4 Neuenbürg Ger.
172 D6 Neuenburg am Rhein Ger.
173 J3 Neuendettelsau Ger.
171 I6 Neuendorfer See l. Ger.
170 J5 Neuenhagen Ger.
170 I5 Neuenhagen Berlin Ger.
169 C6 Neuenhaus Ger.
172 E7 Neuenhof Switz.
190 E1 Neuenkirch Switz.
170 H1 Neuenkirchen Mecklenburg-Vorpommern Ger.
170 H2 Neuenkirchen Mecklenburg-Vorpommern Ger.
168 G3 Neuenkirchen Niedersachsen Ger.
168 G4 Neuenkirchen Niedersachsen Ger.
168 G5 Neuenkirchen Niedersachsen Ger.
168 I4 Neuenkirchen Niedersachsen Ger.
169 E6 Neuenkirchen Niedersachsen Ger.
169 D6 Neuenkirchen Nordrhein-Westfalen Ger.
168 H2 Neuenkirchen Schleswig-Holstein Ger.
169 F5 Neuenkirchen (Oldenburg) Ger.
169 D9 Neuenkirchen-Seelscheid Ger.
169 E8 Neuenrade Ger.
172 G3 Neuenstadt am Kocher Ger.
172 H3 Neuenstein Ger.
168 G3 Neuenwalde Ger.
169 B10 Neuerburg Ger.
173 L5 Neufahrn bei Freising Ger.
173 M4 Neufahrn in Niederbayern Ger.
157 O7 Neuf-Brisach France
165 H9 Neufchâteau Belgium
157 K7 Neufchâteau France
156 B4 Neufchâtel-en-Bray France
159 L5 Neufchâtel-en-Saosnois France
156 C2 Neufchâtel-Hardelot France
156 H5 Neufchâtel-sur-Aisne France
168 H3 Neufeld Ger.
179 N4 Neufeld an der Leitha Austria
179 J3 Neufelden Austria
172 G4 Neuffen Ger.
157 I4 Neufmanil France
172 G5 Neufra Ger.
171 E7 Neugattersleben Ger.
171 K9 Neugersdorf Ger.
170 H4 Neuglobsow Ger.
170 J5 Neuhardenberg Ger.
168 E3 Neuharlingersiel Ger.
179 K6 Neuhaus Kärnten Austria
179 L4 Neuhaus Niederösterreich Austria
168 K4 Neuhaus (Elbe) Ger.
168 H3 Neuhaus (Oste) Ger.
173 O5 Neuhaus am Inn Ger.
179 N6 Neuhaus am Klausenbach Austria
171 D9 Neuhaus am Rennweg Ger.
173 L2 Neuhaus an der Pegnitz Ger.
172 F4 Neuhausen Baden-Württemberg Ger.
171 H9 Neuhausen Sachsen Ger.
Neuhausen Rus. Fed. see Gur'yevsk
190 F1 Neuhausen Switz.
172 F6 Neuhausen ob Eck Ger.
171 D10 Neuhaus-Schierschnitz Ger.
169 I10 Neuhof Ger.
173 J3 Neuhof an der Zenn Ger.
179 J3 Neuhofen an der Krems Austria
179 K3 Neuhofen an der Ybbs Austria
159 M6 Neuillé-Pont-Pierre France
160 D2 Neuilly France
156 D5 Neuilly-en-Thelle France
160 C4 Neuilly-le-Réal France
157 J8 Neuilly-l'Évêque France
156 F5 Neuilly-St-Front France
156 D6 Neuilly-sur-Seine France
169 G10 Neu-Isenburg Ger.
170 G3 Neukalen Ger.
170 D4 Neu Kaliß Ger.
168 E4 Neukamperfehn Ger.
171 F8 Neukieritzsch Ger.
172 H6 Neukirch Baden-Württemberg Ger.
171 J8 Neukirch Sachsen Ger.
169 H9 Neukirchen Hessen Ger.
171 F9 Neukirchen Sachsen Ger.
171 G9 Neukirchen Sachsen Ger.
170 D2 Neukirchen Schleswig-Holstein Ger.
168 G1 Neukirchen Schleswig-Holstein Ger.
178 F5 Neukirchen am Großvenediger Austria
178 H3 Neukirchen an der Enknach Austria
179 I3 Neukirchen an der Vöckla Austria
173 M3 Neukirchen-Balbini Ger.
173 L2 Neukirchen bei Sulzbach-Rosenberg Ger.
173 O4 Neukirchen vorm Wald Ger.
170 E3 Neukloster Ger.
Neukuhren Rus. Fed. see Pionerskiy
168 D4 Neulehe Ger.
179 M3 Neulengbach Austria
173 I4 Neuler Ger.
170 J5 Neulewin Ger.
160 E5 Neulise France
186 K3 Neulós, Puig mt. Spain
171 I6 Neu Lübbenau Ger.
172 B2 Neumagen Ger.
171 F9 Neumark Sachsen Ger.
171 D8 Neumark Thüringen Ger.
178 H4 Neumarkt am Wallersee Austria
179 J3 Neumarkt im Mühlkreis Austria
173 K3 Neumarkt in der Oberpfalz Ger.
179 J5 Neumarkt in Steiermark Austria
173 N5 Neumarkt-Sankt Veit Ger.
262 X2 Neumayer research stn Antarctica
168 I2 Neumünster Ger.
96 G5 Neun, Nam r. Laos
173 M3 Neunburg vorm Wald Ger.
171 F9 Neundorf Ger.
159 O6 Neung-sur-Beuvron France
190 F1 Neunkirch Switz.
179 N4 Neunkirchen Austria
169 F9 Neunkirchen Nordrhein-Westfalen Ger.
172 C3 Neunkirchen Saarland Ger.
173 K2 Neunkirchen am Sand Ger.
173 N5 Neuötting Ger.
171 J7 Neupetershain Ger.
179 L2 Neupölla Austria
260 C6 Neuquén Arg.
260 C6 Neuquén prov. Arg.
260 D6 Neuquén r. Arg.
173 P4 Neureichenau Ger.
173 K5 Neuried Ger.
170 G5 Neuruppin Ger.
171 K8 Neusalza-Spremberg Ger.
Neu Sandez Pol. see Nowy Sącz
173 J5 Neusäß Ger.
173 O4 Neuschönau Ger.
231 I8 Neuse r. NC U.S.A.

171 G6	Neuseddin Ger.	150 F3	Newbridge on Wye Powys, Wales U.K.
179 O4	Neusiedl am See Austria		
179 O4	Neusiedler See l.	232 E8	New Brighton PA U.S.A.
	Austria/Hungary	91 K8	New Britain i. P.N.G.
179 O4	Neusiedler See Seewinkel,	225 J1	New Britain CT U.S.A.
	Nationalpark nat. park Austria	234 E4	New Britain PA U.S.A.
173 L2	Neusorg Ger.	266 F6	New Britain Trench
169 C8	Neuss Ger.		sea feature Pacific Ocean
161 B6	Neussargues-Moissac France	246 □	New Broughton Jamaica
172 E6	Neustadt Baden-	225 H4	New Brunswick prov. Can.
	Württemberg Ger.	233 K8	New Brunswick NJ U.S.A.
170 F5	Neustadt Brandenburg Ger.	226 H8	New Buffalo MI U.S.A.
171 E9	Neustadt Thüringen Ger.	234 B4	New Buffalo PA U.S.A.
169 K7	Neustadt (Harz) Ger.	147 H3	New Buildings Northern
169 H9	Neustadt Ger.		Ireland U.K.
170 D9	Neustadt (Wied) Ger.	232 H8	Newburg PA U.S.A.
173 L2	Neustadt am Kulm Ger.	227 R5	Newburgh Ont. Can.
169 K9	Neustadt am Rennsteig Ger.	146 L8	Newburgh Aberdeenshire,
169 H5	Neustadt an der Rübenberge Ger.		Scotland U.K.
173 J2	Neustadt an der Aisch Ger.	146 J10	Newburgh Fife, Scotland U.K.
173 L4	Neustadt an der Hardt Ger.	146 J12	Newburgh Scottish Borders,
	see Neustadt an der		Scotland U.K.
	Weinstraße	233 K7	Newburgh NY U.S.A.
173 M2	Neustadt an der Waldnaab Ger.	151 J5	Newbury West Berkshire,
172 E3	Neustadt an der Weinstraße		England U.K.
	Ger.		Newbury admin. div. England
171 D10	Neustadt bei Coburg Ger.	233 O6	Newburyport MA U.S.A.
170 E4	Neustadt-Glewe Ger.	207 G4	New Bussa Nigeria
168 K2	Neustadt in Holstein Ger.	149 L5	Newby Bridge Cumbria,
171 J8	Neustadt in Sachsen Ger.		England U.K.
178 D5	Neustift im Stubaital Austria	146 L7	New Byth Aberdeenshire,
170 H4	Neustrelitz Ger.		Scotland U.K.
173 M4	Neutraubling Ger.	146 G13	New Luce Dumfries and
173 I5	Neu-Ulm Ger.		Galloway, Scotland U.K.
161 B7	Neuvéglise France	150 □	Newlyn Cornwall, England U.K.
157 L6	Neuves-Maisons France	78 □5	New Caledonia terr.
162 E5	Neuvic Aquitaine France		S. Pacific Ocean
162 I5	Neuvic Limousin France	147 K7	New Machar Aberdeenshire,
162 I5	Neuvic, Barrage de dam		Scotland U.K.
	France	237 K7	New Madrid MO U.S.A.
156 D7	Neuville-aux-Bois France	87 E7	Newman W.A. Austr.
159 L8	Neuville-de-Poitou France	80 J7	Newman North I. N.Z.
160 G4	Neuville-les-Dames France	240 K4	Newman CA U.S.A.
156 B4	Neuville-lès-Dieppe France	87 E7	Newman, Mount W.A. Austr.
160 F5	Neuville-sur-Saône France	262 O1	Newman Island Antarctica
159 I5	Neuville-sur-Sarthe France	234 C4	Newmanstown PA U.S.A.
157 J5	Neuvy-en-Argonne France	224 E4	Newmarket Ont. Can.
159 D3	Neuvy-Grandchamp France	246 □	Newmarket Jamaica
159 M6	Neuvy-le-Roi France	147 D8	Newmarket Cork Ireland
159 O8	Neuvy-Pailloux France	147 H8	Newmarket Kilkenny Ireland
159 C8	Neuvy-St-Sépulchre France	147 M3	Newmarket Suffolk,
159 G7	Neuvy-Sautour France		England U.K.
159 P7	Neuvy-sur-Barangeon France	147 J6	Newmarket Western Isles,
171 D6	Neuwegersleben Ger.		Scotland U.K.
172 F4	Neuweiler r. Ger.	146 D6	Newmarket Western Isles,
168 G3	Neuwerk i. Ger.		Scotland U.K.
169 D10	Neuwied Ger.	233 □O5	Newmarket NH U.S.A.
168 I5	Neuwittenbek Ger.	232 G10	New Market VA U.S.A.
168 I4	Neu Wulmstorf Ger.	147 E5	Newmarket-on-Fergus
171 G9	Neuwürschnitz Ger.		Ireland
171 J7	Neu Zauche Ger.	232 E9	New Martinsville WV U.S.A.
171 K6	Neuzelle Ger.	238 F4	New Meadows ID U.S.A.
171 I6	Neu Zittau Ger.	239 L9	New Mexico state U.S.A.
130 N2	Neva r. Rus. Fed.	232 A9	New Milford OH U.S.A.
161 J6	Névache France	235 I1	New Milford CT U.S.A.
236 I4	Nevada IA U.S.A.	233 J7	New Milford PA U.S.A.
237 H7	Nevada MO U.S.A.	234 F4	Newmill Moray, Scotland U.K.
240 O2	Nevada state U.S.A.	149 M7	New Mills Derbyshire,
258 O2	Nevada, Sierra mt. Arg.		England U.K.
185 M6	Nevada, Sierra mt. Spain	146 H11	Newmilns East Ayrshire,
185 M6	Nevada, Sierra nature res.		Scotland U.K.
	Spain	151 I6	New Milton Hampshire,
240 K1	Nevada, Sierra mts CA U.S.A.		England U.K.
240 K2	Nevada City CA U.S.A.	151 O4	New Mistley Essex,
260 C4	Nevado, Cerro mt. Arg.		England U.K.
260 C5	Nevado, Sierra del mts Arg.	232 B9	New Moorefield OH U.S.A.
244 D6	Nevado de Colima, Parque	236 G2	New Moorefield OH U.S.A.
	Nacional nat. park Mex.	232 B9	Newnan GA U.S.A.
245 H6	Nevado de Toluca, Parque	150 H4	Newnham Gloucestershire,
	Nacional nat. park Mex.		England U.K.
245 H6	Nevado de Toluca, Volcán	87 D11	New Norcia W.A. Austr.
	vol. Mex.	83 K10	New Norfolk Tas. Austr.
185 I4	Névalo r. Spain	237 J11	New Orleans LA U.S.A.
114 D3	Nevasa Mahar. India	234 A5	New Oxford PA U.S.A.
128 C7	Nevatim Israel	233 K7	New Paltz NY U.S.A.
137 N1	Nevdol'sk Rus. Fed. see	232 A9	New Paris OH U.S.A.
	Kirovsk	233 J11	New Philadelphia OH U.S.A.
209 B8	Neve, Serra da mts Angola	234 C3	New Philadelphia PA U.S.A.
176 D2	Neveklov Czech Rep.	146 L7	New Pitsligo Aberdeenshire,
138 M5	Nevel' Rus. Fed.		Scotland U.K.
138 M6	Nevel', Ozero r. Rus. Fed.	80 I6	New Plymouth North I. N.Z.
165 E6	Nevele Belgium	150 C6	New Polzeath Cornwall,
100 L5	Nevel'sk Sakhalin Rus. Fed.		England U.K.
183 O7	Nevera mt. Spain	246 □	Newport Jamaica
120 B1	Neverkino Rus. Fed.	147 H7	Newport Mayo Ireland
150 C3	Nevers France	147 J7	Newport Tipperary Ireland
138 H7	Neveronys Lith.	151 M4	Newport Essex, England U.K.
160 C2	Nevers France	217 □1c	Newport Highland,
234 F2	Neversink r. NY U.S.A.		Scotland U.K.
83 K4	Neversink r. N.S.W. Austr.	151 J6	Newport Isle of Wight,
257 F5	Neves Brazil		England U.K.
191 L2	Neves, Lago di l. Italy	150 F4	Newport Newport, Wales U.K.
188 G4	Nevesinje Bos.-Herz.	150 C3	Newport Pembrokeshire,
158 D6	Névez France		Wales U.K.
158 I5	Nevèrès r. Lith.	151 J6	Newport Isle of Wight,
181 B10	Névian France		England U.K.
195 O3	Néviano Italy	150 H2	Newport Telford and Wrekin,
159 M2	Néville France		England U.K.
129 C1	Nevinnomyssk Rus. Fed.	150 G4	Newport admin. div.
247 □7	Nevis i. St Kitts and Nevis		Wales U.K.
146 E8	Nevis, Loch inlet Scotland U.K.	237 J8	Newport AR U.S.A.
247 □7	Nevis Peak hill	230 D5	Newport DE U.S.A.
	St Kitts and Nevis	236 J2	Newport IN U.S.A.
126 G4	Nevşehir Turkey	233 □O4	Newport ME U.S.A.
100 H6	Nevskoye Rus. Fed.	227 K8	Newport MI U.S.A.
232 D1	New r. WV U.S.A.	233 M5	Newport NH U.S.A.
146 I13	New Abbey Dumfries and	234 E6	Newport NJ U.S.A.
	Galloway, Scotland U.K.	238 A4	Newport OR U.S.A.
146 L7	New Aberdour Aberdeenshire,	234 A4	Newport PA U.S.A.
	Scotland U.K.	231 N7	Newport TN U.S.A.
151 L5	New Addington Greater	231 F8	Newport TN U.S.A.
	London, England U.K.	232 G8	Newport VA U.S.A.
222 D4	New Aiyansh B.C. Can.	233 M4	Newport VT U.S.A.
211 C7	Newala Tanz.	238 F2	Newport WA U.S.A.
230 E6	New Albany IN U.S.A.	150 C3	Newport Bay Wales U.K.
237 K8	New Albany MS U.S.A.	240 O8	Newport Beach CA U.S.A.
234 C1	New Albany PA U.S.A.	232 H11	Newport News VA U.S.A.
226 F4	Newald WI U.S.A.	151 K3	Newport-on-Tay Fife,
151 J5	New Alresford Hampshire,		Scotland U.K.
	England U.K.	151 K3	Newport Pagnell Milton
251 G3	New Amsterdam Guyana		Keynes, England U.K.
83 K3	New Angledool N.S.W. Austr.	231 F11	New Port Richey FL U.S.A.
215 P5	Newark S. Africa	147 I3	Newport Trench Northern
240 J4	Newark CA U.S.A.		Ireland U.K.
234 D5	Newark DE U.S.A.	235 H3	New Richmond Que. Can.
233 K8	Newark NJ U.S.A.	232 A10	New Richmond OH U.S.A.
232 H5	Newark NY U.S.A.	226 B4	New Richmond WI U.S.A.
233 I8	Newark OH U.S.A.	241 T8	New River AZ U.S.A.
233 K8	Newark NJ U.S.A.	96 D5	Ngai Thai.
241 Q2	Newark Lake NV U.S.A.	207 I5	Ngaoundal Cameroon
149 P7	Newark-on-Trent	207 I5	Ngaoundéré Cameroon
	Nottinghamshire, England U.K.	80 J5	Ngapuke North I. N.Z.
227 R7	New Augusta MS U.S.A.	211 B7	Ngara Malawi
226 I6	Newaygo MI U.S.A.	92 □	Ngaras Sumatera Indon.
233 O7	New Bedford MA U.S.A.	92 □	Ngardmau Palau
238 C4	New Berlin WI U.S.A.	92 □	Ngardmau Bay Palau
234 D4	New Berlin PA U.S.A.	92 □	Ngaregur i. Palau
231 I8	New Bern NC U.S.A.	92 □	Ngariungs i. Palau
226 I3	Newberry MI U.S.A.	82 H6	Ngarkat Conservation Park
231 G8	Newberry SC U.S.A.		nature res. S.A. Austr.
238 D5	Newberry Oregon, U.S.A.		
240 P7	Newberry Springs CA U.S.A.	233 M7	New Haven CT U.S.A.
148 F1	New Bethlehem PA U.S.A.	226 I8	New Haven IN U.S.A.
234 A2	New Bethlehem PA U.S.A.	227 L7	New Haven MI U.S.A.
179 N3	Newbiggin-by-the-Sea	232 D10	New Haven WV U.S.A.
	Northumberland, England U.K.	235 G2	New Haven County county
146 I11	Newbigging South Lanarkshire,		CT U.S.A.
	Scotland U.K.	222 E4	New Hazelton B.C. Can.
246 F1	New Bight Cat I. Bahamas		New Hebrides country
147 H7	Newbliss Ireland		S. Pacific Ocean see Vanuatu
147 G9	New Bloomfield PA U.S.A.	266 G7	New Hebrides Trench
232 C10	New Boston OH U.S.A.		sea feature Pacific Ocean
237 H9	New Boston TX U.S.A.	237 F11	New Hogan Reservoir
237 F11	New Braunfels TX U.S.A.		CA U.S.A.
147 G5	Newbridge Galway Ireland		New Holland country Oceania
147 I7	Newbridge Kildare Ireland		see Australia
147 E7	Newbridge Limerick Ireland	234 C4	New Holland PA U.S.A.
150 F4	Newbridge Caerphilly,	226 F6	New Holstein WI U.S.A.
	Wales U.K.	234 F4	New Hope PA U.S.A.

Nil Kowtal to North Siberian Lowland

360

123 L4 **Nīl Kowtal** *pass* Afgh.
257 F5 **Nilópolis** Brazil
117 L7 **Nilphamari** Bangl.
140 T5 **Nilsiä** Fin.
245 M9 **Niltepec** Mex.
199 J2 **Nilüfer** *r.* Turkey
157 L5 **Nilvange** France
142 F6 **Nim** Denmark
103 J11 **Nima** Japan
Nimach *Madh. Prad.* India *see* **Neemuch**
116 E6 **Nimaj** *Rajasthan* India
100 H3 **Niman** *r.* Rus. Fed.
Nimba, Monts *mts* Africa *see* **Nimba, Mount**
206 C5 **Nimba, Mount** *mts* Africa
116 E7 **Nimbahera** *Rajasthan* India
114 D4 **Nimbal** *Karnataka* India
86 G7 **Nimberra Well** *W.A.* Austr.
Nimbhera *Rajasthan* India *see* **Nimbahera**
100 J2 **Nimelen** *r.* Rus. Fed.
161 E9 **Nîmes** France
191 O3 **Nimis** Italy
116 E6 **Nimka Thana** *Rajasthan* India
83 L7 **Nimmitabel** *N.S.W.* Austr.
199 I6 **Nimos** *i.* Greece
222 E5 **Nimpkish** *r.* *B.C.* Can.
263 K1 **Nimrod Glacier** Antarctica
123 J6 **Nīmrūz** *prov.* Afgh.
116 F2 **Nimu** Jammu and Kashmir
210 B4 **Nimule** Sudan
210 B4 **Nimule National Park** Sudan
Nimwegen Neth. *see* **Nijmegen**
138 K3 **Nina** Estonia
78 □3a **Ninai** *i.* *Kwajalein* Marshall Is
127 K6 **Nīnawá** *governorate* Iraq
127 K5 **Nīnawá** *tourist site* Iraq
209 D8 **Ninda** Angola
211 B7 **Nindai** Tanz.
83 L3 **Nindigully** *Qld* Austr.
168 H2 **Nindorf** Ger.
114 C8 **Nine Degree Channel** India
Nine Islands P.N.G. *see* **Kilinailau Islands**
Ninemile Bar *Dumfries and Galloway, Scotland* U.K. *see* **Crocketford**
83 I4 **Nine Mile Lake** *salt flat N.S.W.* Austr.
241 P2 **Ninemile Peak** *NV* U.S.A.
Ninepin Group *is H.K.* China *see* **Kwo Chau Kwan To**
265 J7 **Ninetyeast Ridge** *sea feature* Indian Ocean
83 K8 **Ninety Mile Beach** *Vic.* Austr.
80 G1 **Ninety Mile Beach** *North I.* N.Z.
Nineveh *tourist site* Iraq *see* **Nīnawá**
259 D6 **Ninfas, Punta** *pt* Arg.
151 M6 **Ninfield** *East Sussex, England* U.K.
87 B7 **Ningaloo Marine Park** *nature res. W.A.* Austr.
100 F6 **Ning'an** *Heilong.* China
109 M4 **Ningbo** *Zhejiang* China
107 P6 **Ningcheng** *Nei Mongol* China
109 L5 **Ningde** *Fujian* China
109 J5 **Ningdu** *Jiangxi* China
Ning'er *Yunnan* China *see* **Pu'er**
109 L3 **Ningguo** *Anhui* China
109 M4 **Ninghai** *Zhejiang* China
107 O7 **Ninghe** *Tianjin* China
Ninghsia Hui Autonomous Region *aut. reg.* China *see* **Ningxia Huizu Zizhiqu**
109 K5 **Ninghua** *Fujian* China
207 H4 **Ningi** Nigeria
117 O5 **Ninging** *Arun. Prad.* India
108 B3 **Ningjing Shan** *mts Xizang* China
108 C5 **Ninglang** *Yunnan* China
107 N9 **Ningling** *Henan* China
108 F7 **Ningming** *Guangxi* China
108 D5 **Ningnan** *Sichuan* China
108 F2 **Ningqiang** *Shaanxi* China
108 G2 **Ningshan** *Shaanxi* China
107 M7 **Ningwu** *Shanxi* China
Ningxia *aut. reg.* China *see* **Ningxia Huizu Zizhiqu**
106 I8 **Ningxia Huizu Zizhiqu** *aut. reg.* China
107 J9 **Ningxian** *Gansu* China
109 I4 **Ningxiang** *Hunan* China
107 O9 **Ningyang** *Shandong* China
109 H6 **Ningyuan** *Hunan* China
Ningzhou *Yunnan* China *see* **Huaning**
96 H4 **Ninh Binh** Vietnam
97 I8 **Ninh Hoa** Vietnam
97 I9 **Ninh Sơn** Vietnam
260 A5 **Ninhue** Chile
91 J7 **Ninigo Group** *atolls* P.N.G.
263 J2 **Ninnis Glacier** Antarctica
263 K2 **Ninnis Glacier Tongue** Antarctica
184 H8 **Niño, Sierra del** *mts* Spain
102 S6 **Ninohe** Japan
105 J5 **Ninomiya** *Kanagawa* Japan
105 K3 **Ninomiya** *Tochigi* Japan
129 E4 **Ninotsminda** Georgia
165 F7 **Ninove** Belgium
259 B7 **Ninualac, Canal** *sea chan.* Chile
129 E1 **Niny** Rus. Fed.
253 G5 **Nioaque** Brazil
236 F4 **Niobrara** *r.* *NE* U.S.A.
221 Q2 **Nioghalvfjerdsfjorden** *inlet* Greenland
208 F4 **Nioka** Dem. Rep. Congo
208 C5 **Nioki** Dem. Rep. Congo
116 O6 **Nioko** *Arun. Prad.* India
206 B3 **Niokolo Koba, Parc National du** *nat. park* Senegal
206 D3 **Niono** Mali
206 C3 **Nioro** Mali
206 B3 **Nioro du Rip** Senegal
162 D3 **Niort** France
206 D3 **Nioût** *well* Maur.
91 J8 **Nipa** P.N.G.
114 D4 **Nipani** *Karnataka* India
93 C5 **Nipanipa, Tanjung** *pt* Indon.
260 A5 **Ñipas** Chile
223 J4 **Nipawin** *Sask.* Can.
116 E9 **Niphad** *Mahar.* India
224 B3 **Nipigon** *Ont.* Can.
236 K1 **Nipigon** *r.* *Ont.* Can.
224 B3 **Nipigon, Lake** *Ont.* Can.
224 C3 **Nipigon Bay** *Ont.* Can.
213 H3 **Nipiodi** Moz.
225 I2 **Nipishish Lake** *Nfld and Lab.* Can.
227 O3 **Nipissing** *Ont.* Can.
224 E4 **Nipissing, Lake** *Ont.* Can.
240 L6 **Nipomo** *CA* U.S.A.
Nippon *country* Asia *see* **Japan**
Nippon Hai *sea* N. Pacific Ocean *see* **Japan, Sea of**
127 L7 **Nippur** *tourist site* Iraq
241 Q6 **Nipton** *CA* U.S.A.
254 C5 **Niquelândia** Brazil
260 B5 **Niquen** Chile
246 E3 **Niquero** Cuba
260 C2 **Niquivil** Arg.
122 B2 **Nir** *Ardabīl* Iran
122 F6 **Nir** *Yazd* Iran
114 D4 **Nira** *r.* India
105 H4 **Nirasaki** Japan
105 I5 **Nirayama** Japan
260 A4 **Nirivilo** Chile
107 S2 **Nirji** *Nei Mongol* China
114 F3 **Nirmal** *Andhra Prad.* India
117 K6 **Nirmali** *Bihar* India
114 E3 **Nirmal Range** *hills* India
138 K5 **Nirzas** *l.* Latvia
197 J7 **Niš** Serbia
182 E9 **Nisa** Port.
182 E9 **Nisa** *r.* Port.
122 E9 **Nisāb** Yemen
124 H3 **Nisāh, Wādī** *watercourse* Saudi Arabia
197 J7 **Nišava** *r.* Serbia
146 K11 **Nisbet** *Scottish Borders, Scotland* U.K.
194 G9 **Niscemi** *Sicilia* Italy
102 R4 **Niseko** Japan
111 G10 **Nishan** *Xizang* China
Nīshāpūr Iran *see* **Neyshābūr**
138 L6 **Nishcha** *r.* Belarus
108 H4 **Nishi** *Hunan* China
104 D5 **Nishiazai** Japan
102 W3 **Nishibetsu-gawa** *r.* Japan
105 L1 **Nishigō** Japan
105 I6 **Nishiizu** Japan
103 H15 **Nishikata** *Kagoshima* Japan
105 K3 **Nishikata** *Tochigi* Japan
105 I4 **Nishikatsura** Japan
102 R8 **Nishikawa** Japan
104 B5 **Nishi-maizuru** Japan
105 K2 **Nishinasuno** Japan
104 B6 **Nishinomiya** Japan
102 □H16 **Nishino-omote** Japan
103 K10 **Nishino-shima** *i.* Japan
103 □2 **Nishino-shima** *vol.* Japan
104 F6 **Nishio** Japan
103 G14 **Nishi-Sonogi-hantō** *pen.* Japan
103 G12 **Nishi-suidō** *sea chan.* Japan/S. Korea
104 A6 **Nishiwaki** Japan
104 C7 **Nishiyoshino** Japan
254 G3 **Nísia Floresta** Brazil
Nisibis Turkey *see* **Nusaybin**
104 E5 **Nisiharu** Japan
103 I14 **Nisi-mera** Japan
Nísiros *i.* Greece *see* **Nisyros**
140 S4 **Niskanselkä** *l.* Fin.
233 L6 **Niskayuna** *NY* U.S.A.
224 B1 **Niskibi** *r.* *Ont.* Can.
175 K5 **Nisko** Pol.
222 B2 **Nisling** *r.* *Y.T.* Can.
165 G8 **Nismes** Belgium
165 G8 **Nismes, Forêt de** *for.* Belgium
136 H6 **Nisporeni** Moldova
142 I5 **Nissan** *r.* Sweden
161 C10 **Nissan-lez-Enserune** France
142 E2 **Nisser** *l.* Norway
104 F5 **Nisshin** Japan
194 G8 **Nissoria** *Sicilia* Italy
142 E5 **Nissum Bredning** *b.* Denmark
164 I5 **Nistelrode** Neth.
136 J7 **Nistru** *r.* Moldova *alt.* **Dnister (Ukraine),** *conv.* **Dniester**
136 I6 **Nistrului Inferior, Cîmpia** *lowland* Moldova
222 C2 **Nisutlin** *r.* *Y.T.* Can.
199 I6 **Nisyros** *i.* Greece
103 K11 **Nita** Japan
125 I2 **Niţā** Saudi Arabia
103 G12 **Nita-wan** *b.* Japan
225 G2 **Nitchequon** *Que.* Can.
Nitendi *i.* *Santa Cruz Is* Solomon Is *see* **Ndeni**
257 F5 **Niterói** Brazil
146 I12 **Nith** *r.* *Scotland* U.K.
146 I12 **Nithsdale** *val. Scotland* U.K.
93 D8 **Nitibe** East Timor
119 L3 **Niti Pass** *Xizang* China
84 D3 **Nitmiluk National Park** *N.T.* Austr.
177 H3 **Nitra** Slovakia
177 H4 **Nitra** *r.* Slovakia
177 H3 **Nitrianske Pravno** Slovakia
177 H3 **Nitriansky kraj** *admin. reg.* Slovakia
232 D10 **Nitro** *WV* U.S.A.
156 G8 **Nitry** France
105 J3 **Nitta** Japan
142 G1 **Nittedal** Norway
172 A2 **Nittel** Ger.
173 M3 **Nittenau** Ger.
173 L3 **Nittendorf** Ger.
Niua *i.* Vanuatu *see* **Aniwa**
77 I3 **Niuafo'ou** *i.* Tonga
Niuafu *i.* Tonga *see* **Niuafo'ou**
77 I3 **Niuatoputopu** *i.* Tonga
79 □8a **Niu 'Aunofo** *cliff Tongatapu* Tonga
110 K7 **Niubiziliang** *Qinghai* China
81 □4 **Niue** *terr.* S. Pacific Ocean
Niujing *Yunnan* China *see* **Binchuan**
77 H3 **Niulakita** *i.* Tuvalu
108 D5 **Niulan Jiang** *r.* *Yunnan* China
240 □F13 **Niuli'i** *HI* U.S.A.
94 E5 **Niur, Pulau** *i.* Indon.
Niushan *Jiangsu* China *see* **Donghai**
77 H2 **Niutao** *i.* Tuvalu
109 L3 **Niutoushan** *Anhui* China
107 R6 **Niuzhuang** *Liaoning* China
140 R5 **Nivala** Fin.
140 V3 **Nivastroy** Rus. Fed.
85 K8 **Nive** *watercourse Qld* Austr.
163 B9 **Nive** *r.* France
85 K8 **Nive Downs** *Qld* Austr.
165 F7 **Nivelles** Belgium
175 I1 **Nivenskoye** Rus. Fed.
160 C2 **Nivernais** *reg.* France
160 D2 **Nivernais, Canal du** France
158 G6 **Nivillac** France
156 D5 **Nivillers** France
139 P8 **Nivnoye** Rus. Fed.
160 G5 **Nivolas-Vermelle** France
134 K3 **Nivshera** Rus. Fed.
140 V3 **Nivskiy** Rus. Fed.
116 E6 **Niwai** *Rajasthan* India
116 G7 **Niwari** *Madh. Prad.* India
116 H8 **Niwas** *Madh. Prad.* India
175 J5 **Niwiska** Pol.
157 J5 **Nixéville-Blercourt** France
Nixia *Sichuan* China *see* **Sêrxü**
240 M2 **Nixon** *NV* U.S.A.
Niya *Xinjiang* China *see* **Minfeng**
111 F8 **Niya He** *r.* China
129 J4 **Niyazoba** Azer.
95 H4 **Niyut, Gunung** *mt.* Indon.
139 S2 **Niz** Rus. Fed.
105 K4 **Niza** Japan
114 F3 **Nizamabad** *Andhra Prad.* India
114 G5 **Nizampatnam** *Andhra Prad.* India
114 E3 **Nizam Sagar** *l.* India
176 D2 **Nižbor** Czech Rep.
122 G2 **Nizh Aydere** Turkm.
134 I4 **Nizhegorodskaya Oblast'** *admin. div.* Rus. Fed.
131 L4 **Nizhneangarsk** Rus. Fed.
137 Q9 **Nizhnebakanskiy** Rus. Fed.
135 G6 **Nizhnedevitsk** Rus. Fed.
121 U1 **Nizhnekamenka** Rus. Fed.
134 J5 **Nizhnekamsk** Rus. Fed.
134 K5 **Nizhnekamskoye Vodokhranilishche** *resr* Rus. Fed.
131 R3 **Nizhnekolymsk** Rus. Fed.
139 Q1 **Nizhne-Svirskiy Zapovednik** *nature res.* Rus. Fed.
100 K3 **Nizhnetambovskoye** Rus. Fed.
98 G1 **Nizhneudinsk** Rus. Fed.
130 I3 **Nizhnevartovsk** Rus. Fed.
Nizhnevolzhsk Rus. Fed. *see* **Narimanov**
131 O2 **Nizhneyansk** Rus. Fed.
139 P9 **Nizhneye** Rus. Fed.
107 O1 **Nizhneye Giryunino** Rus. Fed.
134 L4 **Nizhni Irginski** Rus. Fed.
135 I6 **Nizhniy Baskunchak** Rus. Fed.
134 K2 **Nizhniy Bugayevo** Rus. Fed.
129 E2 **Nizhniy Chegem** Rus. Fed.
135 H6 **Nizhniy Chir** Rus. Fed.
129 I3 **Nizhniy Dzhengutay** Rus. Fed.
121 O3 **Nizhniye Kayrakty** Kazakh.
Nizhniye Kresty Rus. Fed. *see* **Cherskiy**
Nizhniye Ustriki Pol. *see* **Ustrzyki Dolne**
137 S3 **Nizhniy Karabut** Rus. Fed.
137 T3 **Nizhniy Kislyay** Rus. Fed.
129 F2 **Nizhniy Kurp** Rus. Fed.
135 H5 **Nizhniy Lomov** Rus. Fed.
137 T3 **Nizhniy Mamon** Rus. Fed.
134 H4 **Nizhniy Novgorod** Rus. Fed.
Nizhniy Novgorod Oblast *admin. div.* Rus. Fed. *see* **Nizhegorodskaya Oblast'**
134 K3 **Nizhniy Odes** Rus. Fed.
137 R3 **Nizhniy Ol'shan** Rus. Fed.
Nizhniy Pyandzh Tajik. *see* **Panji Poyon**
130 G4 **Nizhniy Tagil** Rus. Fed.
107 N1 **Nizhniy Tsasuchey** Rus. Fed.
134 I4 **Nizhniy Yenangsk** Rus. Fed.
134 J2 **Nizhnyaya Kamenka** Rus. Fed.
134 I2 **Nizhnyaya Mola** Rus. Fed.
134 K3 **Nizhnyaya Omra** Rus. Fed.
134 I2 **Nizhnyaya Pesha** Rus. Fed.
140 V3 **Nizhnyaya Pirenga, Ozero** *l.* Rus. Fed.
131 K4 **Nizhnyaya Poyma** Rus. Fed.
121 R1 **Nizhnyaya Suyetka** Rus. Fed.
129 C2 **Nizhnyaya Teberda** Rus. Fed.
131 J3 **Nizhnyaya Tunguska** *r.* Rus. Fed.
130 G4 **Nizhnyaya Tura** Rus. Fed.
137 R2 **Nizhnyaya Veduga** Rus. Fed.
134 H2 **Nizhnyaya Zolotitsa** Rus. Fed.
137 K2 **Nizhyn** Ukr.
126 H5 **Nizip** Turkey
139 N6 **Nizkabor"ye** Belarus
177 K2 **Nízke Beskydy** *hills* Slovakia
177 I3 **Nízke Tatry** *mts* Slovakia
177 I3 **Nízke Tatry** *nat. park* Slovakia
100 I7 **Nizmennyy, Mys** *pt* Rus. Fed.
177 J3 **Nižná Slaná** Slovakia
177 K3 **Nižný Hrušov** Slovakia
177 K3 **Nižný Žipov** Slovakia
Nizwā Oman *see* **Nazwá**
Nizza France *see* **Nice**
195 I8 **Nizza di Sicilia** *Sicilia* Italy
190 E6 **Nizza Monferrato** Italy
217 □3a **Njazidja** *i.* Comoros
196 G8 **Njegoš** *mts* Montenegro
Njellim Fin. *see* **Nellim**
213 F4 **Njesuthi** *mt.* Lesotho/S. Africa
211 C7 **Njinjo** Tanz.
191 R5 **Njivice** Croatia
209 E9 **Njoko** *r.* Zambia
211 B7 **Njombe** Tanz.
211 B6 **Njombe** *r.* Tanz.
78 □6 **Njoroveto** *New Georgia Is* Solomon Is
141 N5 **Njurundabommen** Sweden
141 N6 **Njutånger** Sweden
Nkai Zimbabwe *see* **Nkayi**
207 H5 **Nkambe** Cameroon
215 P4 **Nkandla** S. Africa
211 A6 **Nkasi** Tanz.
206 E5 **Nkawkaw** Ghana
213 F3 **Nkayi** Zimbabwe
206 D2 **Nkhaïlé** *well* Maur.
211 B7 **Nkhata Bay** Malawi
211 B8 **Nkhotakota** Malawi
211 B8 **Nkhotakota Game Reserve** *nature res.* Malawi
208 A4 **Nkolabona** Gabon
207 H5 **Nkomfap** Nigeria
208 A5 **Nkomi, Lagune** *lag.* Gabon
211 A6 **Nkondwe** Tanz.
207 H5 **Nkongsamba** Cameroon
206 E5 **Nkoranza** Ghana
207 I5 **Nkoteng** Cameroon
215 L6 **Nkululeko** S. Africa
211 A6 **Nkundi** Tanz.
211 A6 **Nkungwi** Tanz.
212 C3 **Nkurenkuru** Namibia
210 A4 **Nkusi** *r.* Uganda
215 P4 **Nkwalini** S. Africa
207 F4 **Nkwanta** Ghana
215 K9 **Nkwenkwezi** S. Africa
96 C2 **Nmai Hka** *r.* Myanmar
117 P6 **Noa Dihing** *r.* India
163 D7 **Noaillan** France
156 D5 **Noailles** France
163 A10 **Noain** Spain
117 M8 **Noakhali** Bangl.
191 M4 **Noale** Italy
185 L5 **Noalejo** Spain
117 J8 **Noamundi** *Jharkhand* India
164 J2 **Noardburgum** Neth.
190 C5 **Noasca** Italy
220 B3 **Noatak** *r.* *AK* U.S.A.
220 C3 **Noatak National Preserve** *nature res. AK* U.S.A.
148 D6 **Nobber** Ireland
103 I14 **Nobeoka** Japan
171 F9 **Nobitz** Ger.
183 N9 **Noblejas** Spain
230 D5 **Noblesville** *IN* U.S.A.
215 L7 **Nobokwe** S. Africa
102 S4 **Noboribetsu** Japan
253 F3 **Nobres** Brazil
85 I9 **Noccundra** *Qld* Austr.
159 M5 **Nocé** France
191 K3 **Noce** *r.* Italy
193 P8 **Noce** *r.* Italy
182 H3 **Noceda** Spain
193 N6 **Nocera Inferiore** Italy
193 Q9 **Nocera Terinese** Italy
193 J1 **Nocera Umbra** Italy
190 I6 **Noceto** Italy
244 E4 **Nochistlán** Mex.
245 J8 **Nochixtlán** Mex.
179 K3 **Nöchling** Austria
195 M2 **Noci** Italy
175 M1 **Nočia** *r.* Belarus/Lith.
195 O3 **Nociglia** Italy
234 E4 **Nockamixon Lake** *PA* U.S.A.
85 I9 **Nockatunga** *Qld* Austr.
83 J3 **Nocoleche Nature Reserve** *N.S.W.* Austr.
237 G9 **Nocona** *TX* U.S.A.
105 K4 **Noda** Japan
104 B4 **Nodagawa** Japan
259 D8 **Nodales, Bahía de los** *b.* Arg.
236 H6 **Nodaway** *r.* *MO* U.S.A.
142 D3 **Nodeland** Norway
160 I2 **Nods** France
163 G9 **Noé** France
253 E3 **Noel Kempff Mercado, Parque Nacional** *nat. park* Bol.
224 D4 **Noelville** *Ont.* Can.
214 E3 **Noenieput** S. Africa
193 Q7 **Noepoli** Italy
168 J2 **Noer** Ger.
261 F3 **Noetinger** Arg.
156 E3 **Nœux-les-Mines** France
183 L9 **Noez** Spain
183 L9 **Noez, Pico de** *mt.* Spain
183 N3 **Nofuentes** Spain
242 D2 **Nogales** Mex.
184 F3 **Nogales** Spain
239 I11 **Nogales** *AZ* U.S.A.
129 F2 **Nogamirzin-Yurt** Rus. Fed.
191 K5 **Nogara** Italy
163 D8 **Nogaro** France
174 H1 **Nogat** *r.* Pol.
103 H13 **Nōgata** Japan
Nogaysk Ukr. *see* **Prymors'ke**
129 H1 **Nogayskaya Step'** *reg.* Rus. Fed.
120 F3 **Nogayty** Kazakh.
157 J7 **Nogent** France
159 L5 **Nogent-le-Bernard** France
156 C6 **Nogent-le-Roi** France
159 M5 **Nogent-le-Rotrou** France
156 H7 **Nogent-sur-Aube** France
156 D6 **Nogent-sur-Marne** France
156 D5 **Nogent-sur-Oise** France
156 G7 **Nogent-sur-Seine** France
156 E8 **Nogent-sur-Vernisson** France
105 K3 **Nogi** Japan
131 K3 **Noginsk** *Evenkiyskiy Avtonomnyy Okrug* Rus. Fed.
139 V6 **Noginsk** *Moskovskaya Oblast'* Rus. Fed.
100 M3 **Nogliki** *Sakhalin* Rus. Fed.
85 M8 **Nogo** *r.* *Qld* Austr.
85 L7 **Nogoa** *r.* *Qld* Austr.
104 E4 **Nōgōhaku-san** *mt.* Japan
106 I7 **Nogon Toli** *Nei Mongol* China
261 H3 **Nogoyá** Arg.
261 H3 **Nogoya** *r.* Arg.
177 I4 **Nógrád** Hungary
177 I4 **Nógrád** *county* Hungary
183 O6 **Nograles** Spain
104 G3 **Noguchigorō-dake** *mt.* Japan
182 G5 **Nogueira, Serra de** *mts* Port.
186 G4 **Noguera** *reg.* Spain
183 Q8 **Noguera de Albarracín** Spain
163 C9 **Noguères** France
187 D7 **Nogueruelas** Spain
160 B2 **Nohain** *r.* France
243 O8 **Nohalal** Mex.
159 O8 **Nohant-Vic** France
116 E5 **Nohar** *Rajasthan* India
163 I10 **Nohèdes, Réserve Naturelle de** *nature res.* France
102 S6 **Noheji** Japan
172 C2 **Nohfelden** Ger.
163 G8 **Nohic** France
240 □B11 **Nohili Point** *HI* U.S.A.
106 D7 **Nohoit** *Qinghai* China
122 G2 **Nohur** Turkm.
182 C3 **Noia** Spain
195 L1 **Noicattaro** Italy
116 F5 **Noida** *Uttar Prad.* India
160 I1 **Noidans-lès-Vesoul** France
163 F8 **Noilhan** France
161 C8 **Noir, Causse** *plat.* France
227 R4 **Noire** *r.* *Que.* Can.
163 I9 **Noire, Montagne** *mts* France
180 E5 **Noire, Pointe** *pt* Morocco
158 D5 **Noires, Montagnes** *hills* France
160 D5 **Noirétable** France
158 G8 **Noirmoutier, Île de** *i.* France
158 G7 **Noirmoutier-en-l'Île** France
157 L5 **Noisseville** France
183 M2 **Noja** Spain
105 K6 **Nojima-zaki** *c.* Japan
105 H2 **Nojiri-ko** *l.* Japan
104 B7 **Nokami** Japan
232 H10 **Nokesville** *VA* U.S.A.
116 D6 **Nokha** *Rajasthan* India
123 J9 **Nokhbur** Pak.
122 I8 **Nokhowch, Kūh-e** *mt.* Iran
141 Q6 **Nokia** Fin.
Nökis Uzbek. *see* **Nukus**
123 J7 **Nok Kundi** Pak.
223 J5 **Nokomis** *Sask.* Can.
223 K3 **Nokomis Lake** *Sask.* Can.
202 B6 **Nokou** Chad
117 M7 **Nokrek Peak** *Meghalaya* India
142 I4 **Nol** Sweden
208 C4 **Nola** C.A.R.
194 H2 **Nola** Italy
160 F3 **Nolay** France
190 E7 **Noli** Italy
190 E7 **Noli, Capo di** *c.* Italy
231 F7 **Nolichucky** *r.* *TN* U.S.A.
134 J4 **Nolinsk** Rus. Fed.
214 G9 **Noll** S. Africa
144 D1 **Nólsoy** *i.* Faroe Is
103 H15 **Noma-misaki** *pt* Japan
233 O7 **No Mans Land** *i.* *MA* U.S.A.
183 L8 **Nombela** Spain
244 C2 **Nombre de Dios** Mex.
220 B3 **Nome** *AK* U.S.A.
179 J7 **Nomenj** Slovenia
157 L6 **Nomeny** France
157 L7 **Nomexy** France
106 I5 **Nomgon** Mongolia
106 E8 **Nomhon** *Qinghai* China
106 D8 **Nomhon He** *r.* *Qinghai* China
107 S2 **Nomin Gol** *r.* China
Nomoi Islands Micronesia *see* **Mortlock Islands**
215 K7 **Nomonde** S. Africa
78 □4a **Nomoneas** *is Chuuk* Micronesia
103 G14 **Nomo-zaki** *pt* Japan
106 I1 **Nomto** Rus. Fed.
104 G3 **Nomugi-tōge** *pass* Japan
77 I4 **Nomuka** Tonga
79 □8 **Nomuka** *i.* Tonga
79 □8 **Nomuka Group** *is* Tonga
79 □8 **Nomuka Iki** *i.* Tonga
91 L5 **Nomwin** *atoll* Micronesia
134 H4 **Nomzha** Rus. Fed.
223 I2 **Nonacho Lake** *N.W.T.* Can.
156 B6 **Nonancourt** France
159 L4 **Nonant-le-Pin** France
191 K6 **Nonantola** Italy
186 F5 **Nonaspe** Spain
215 O4 **Nondweni** S. Africa
156 D5 **Nonette** *r.* France
100 D6 **Nong'an** *Jilin* China
96 G5 **Nông Hèt** Laos
97 F7 **Nong Hong** Thai.
Nonghui *Sichuan* China *see* **Guang'an**
117 M7 **Nongkha** *Meghalaya* India
96 F6 **Nong Khai** Thai.
215 P3 **Nongoma** S. Africa
117 M7 **Nongpoh** *Meghalaya* India
117 M7 **Nongstoin** *Meghalaya* India
161 E7 **Nonières** France
172 D5 **Nonnenweier** Ger.
Nonni *r.* China *see* **Nen Jiang**
82 F5 **Nonning** *S.A.* Austr.
172 B2 **Nonnweiler** Ger.
250 B5 **Nono** Ecuador
255 B8 **Nonoai** Brazil
242 F4 **Nonoava** Mex.
104 E2 **Nonoichi** Japan
77 H2 **Nonouti** *atoll Gilbert Is* Kiribati
260 A5 **Nonquén** Chile
101 E10 **Nonsan** S. Korea
231 □1 **Nonsuch Island** Bermuda
97 E8 **Nonthaburi** Thai.
162 F4 **Nontron** France
192 C2 **Nonza** *Corse* France
214 I6 **Nonzwakazi** S. Africa
138 J3 **Nõo** Estonia
87 D9 **Nookawarra** *W.A.* Austr.
82 F2 **Noolyeanna Lake** *salt flat S.A.* Austr.
84 C2 **Noonamah** *N.T.* Austr.
87 E10 **Noondie, Lake** *salt flat W.A.* Austr.
86 H5 **Noonkanbah** *W.A.* Austr.
86 H5 **Noonkanbah Aboriginal Reserve** *W.A.* Austr.
83 H4 **Noonthorangee Range** *hills N.S.W.* Austr.
85 J9 **Noorama Creek** *watercourse Qld* Austr.
164 E5 **Noordbeveland** *i.* Neth.
164 H5 **Noord-Brabant** *prov.* Neth.
164 K2 **Noordbroek-Uiterburen** Neth.
164 G3 **Noorderhaaks** *i.* Neth.
164 G3 **Noord-Holland** *prov.* Neth.
164 G3 **Noordhollands Duinreservaat** *nature res.* Neth.
215 P1 **Noordkaap** S. Africa
214 C8 **Noordkuil** S. Africa
214 B4 **Noordoewer** Namibia
164 I3 **Noordoost Polder** Neth.
247 □10 **Noordpunt** *pt Curaçao* Neth. Antilles
164 F4 **Noordwijk aan Zee** Neth.
164 F4 **Noordwijk-Binnen** Neth.
164 G4 **Noordwijkerhout** Neth.
164 J3 **Noordwolde** Neth.
141 P6 **Noormarkku** Fin.
220 B3 **Noorvik** *AK* U.S.A.
85 N9 **Noosa Heads** *Qld* Austr.
164 F4 **Nootdorp** Neth.
222 E5 **Nootka Island** *B.C.* Can.
245 J9 **Nopala** Mex.
245 K7 **Nopaltepec** Mex.
223 M5 **Nopiming Provincial Park** *Man.* Can.
260 D2 **Noqueves** Arg.
209 B6 **Nóqui** Angola
193 M3 **Nora** *r.* Italy
100 F3 **Nora** *r.* Rus. Fed.
143 L2 **Nora** Sweden
192 B7 **Noragugume** *Sardegna* Italy
123 M2 **Norak** Tajik.
123 M2 **Norak, Obanbori** *resr* Tajik.
Norakert Armenia *see* **Baghramyan**
92 E8 **Norala** *Mindanao* Phil.
224 E3 **Noranda** *Que.* Can.
Nor-Bayazet Armenia *see* **Gavarr**
143 L1 **Norberg** Sweden
261 H4 **Norberto de la Riestra** Arg.
111 G11 **Norcang** *Xizang* China
193 K2 **Norcia** Italy
233 □Q3 **Norcross** *ME* U.S.A.
207 I4 **Nord** *prov.* Cameroon
156 F3 **Nord** *dept* France
Nord Greenland *see* **Station Nord**
156 F3 **Nord, Canal du** France
217 □3a **Nord, Pointe** *pt Njazidja* Comoros
217 □3b **Nord, Récif du** *rf* Mayotte
140 □ **Nordaustlandet** *i.* Svalbard
142 F6 **Nordborg** Denmark
143 K6 **Nord-Bornholm** *nature res. Bornholm* Denmark
140 Q2 **Nordbotn** Norway
142 G6 **Nordby** Denmark
168 D3 **Norddeich** Ger.
168 F1 **Norddorf** Ger.
222 G4 **Nordegg** *Alta* Can.
168 D3 **Norden** Ger.
173 J4 **Nordendorf** Ger.
168 F4 **Nordenham** Ger.
131 K2 **Nordenshel'da, Arkhipelag** *is* Rus. Fed.
222 B2 **Nordenskiold** *r.* *Y.T.* Can.
140 □ **Nordenskiøld Land** *reg.* Svalbard
Nordenskjold Archipelago *is* Rus. Fed. *see* **Nordenshel'da, Arkhipelag**
168 G2 **Norder Hever** *sea chan.* Ger.
168 D3 **Norderland** *reg.* Ger.
168 D3 **Norderney** Ger.
168 D3 **Norderney** *i.* Ger.
168 F1 **Norderoogsand** *i.* Ger.
168 J3 **Norderstedt** Ger.
216 □1b **Nordeste** *São Miguel* Azores
216 □1b **Nordestinho** *São Miguel* Azores
140 U1 **Nordfjord** Norway
141 H6 **Nordfjord** *reg.* Norway
141 H6 **Nordfjordeid** Norway
140 □ **Nordfjorden** *inlet* Svalbard
140 M3 **Nordfold** Norway
168 F1 **Nordfriesische Inseln** *is* Ger.
168 G1 **Nordfriesland** *reg.* Ger.
171 D6 **Nordgermersleben** Ger.
171 E10 **Nordhalben** Ger.
168 H2 **Nordhastedt** Ger.
169 K8 **Nordhausen** Ger.
172 G3 **Nordheim** Ger.
168 G3 **Nordholz** Ger.
169 D6 **Nordhorn** Ger.
142 B2 **Nordhuglo** Norway
140 O5 **Nordingrå naturreservat** *nature res.* Sweden
142 F5 **Nordjylland** *county* Denmark
Nord Kap *c.* Iceland *see* **Horn**
140 R1 **Nordkapp** *c.* Norway
140 S1 **Nordkinnhalvøya** *i.* Norway
169 E7 **Nordkirchen** Ger.
208 F5 **Nord-Kivu** *prov.* Dem. Rep. Congo
140 O1 **Nordkvaløy** *i.* Norway
140 M3 **Nordland** *county* Norway
168 G3 **Nordleda** Ger.
140 L4 **Nordli** Norway
173 M2 **Nördlicher Oberpfälzer Wald** *park* Ger.
169 K7 **Nördliches Harzvorland** *park* Ger.
173 I4 **Nördlingen** Ger.
140 O5 **Nordmaling** Sweden
142 D1 **Nordmannslågen** *l.* Norway
140 P2 **Nordmannvik** Norway
168 G1 **Nordmarsch-Langeness** *i.* Ger.
221 O2 **Nord- og Østgrønland, Nationalparken i** *nat. park* Greenland
168 H2 **Nord-Ostsee-Kanal** *canal* Ger.
207 H5 **Nord-Ouest** *prov.* Cameroon
130 A3 **Norðoyar** *i.* Faroe Is
156 E3 **Nord-Pas-de-Calais** *admin. reg.* France
156 F3 **Nord-Pas-de-Calais, Parc Naturel Régional du** *nature res.* France
172 D2 **Nordpfälzer Bergland** *reg.* Ger.
Nordre Strømfjord *inlet* Greenland *see* **Nassuttooq**
169 D8 **Nordrhein-Westfalen** *land* Ger.
169 I6 **Nordstemmen** Ger.
168 G1 **Nordstrand** *pen.* Ger.
168 G1 **Nordstrandischmoor** *i.* Ger.
140 L4 **Nord-Trøndelag** *county* Norway
140 □D1 **Norðurland eystra** *constituency* Iceland
140 □C1 **Norðurland vestra** *constituency* Iceland
131 M2 **Nordvik** Rus. Fed.
140 J5 **Nordvika** Norway
169 D6 **Nordwalde** Ger.
147 I8 **Nore** *r.* Ireland
163 I9 **Nore, Pic de** *mt.* France
Noreg *country* Europe *see* **Norway**
138 G7 **Noreikiškės** Lith.
182 I2 **Noreña** Spain
142 F1 **Noresund** Norway
186 L3 **Norfeu, Cap de** *c.* Spain
151 N2 **Norfolk** *admin. div. England* U.K.
236 G4 **Norfolk** *NE* U.S.A.
233 K4 **Norfolk** *NY* U.S.A.
233 I12 **Norfolk** *VA* U.S.A.
82 □1 **Norfolk Island** *terr.* S. Pacific Ocean
266 G7 **Norfolk Island Ridge** *sea feature* Tasman Sea
237 I7 **Norfork Lake** *AR* U.S.A.
164 J2 **Norg** Neth.
Norge *country* Europe *see* **Norway**
149 M2 **Norham** *Northumberland, England* U.K.
142 C1 **Norheimsund** Norway
252 C5 **Noria** Chile
244 F3 **Noria de Ángeles** Mex.
244 E1 **Norias** Mex.
104 G3 **Norikura-dake** *vol.* Japan
130 J3 **Noril'sk** Rus. Fed.
137 M1 **Norino** Rus. Fed.
111 I12 **Norkyung** *Xizang* China
227 P5 **Norland** *Ont.* Can.
193 J4 **Norma** Italy
234 E6 **Norma** *NJ* U.S.A.
111 I10 **Norma Co** *l.* *Xizang* China
226 F9 **Normal** *IL* U.S.A.
85 H4 **Norman** *r.* *Qld* Austr.
237 G8 **Norman** *OK* U.S.A.
231 G8 **Norman, Lake** *resr NC* U.S.A.
85 J3 **Normanby** *r.* *Qld* Austr.
80 I6 **Normanby** *North I.* N.Z.
91 L8 **Normanby Island** P.N.G.
85 M7 **Normanby Range** *hills Qld* Austr.
Normandes, Îles *is* English Chan. *see* **Channel Islands**
251 G4 **Normandia** Brazil
159 J4 **Normandie** *reg.* France
159 J4 **Normandie, Collines de** *hills* France
159 K5 **Normandie-Maine, Parc Naturel Régional** *nature res.* France
215 N3 **Normandien** S. Africa
Normandy *reg.* France *see* **Normandie**
85 H4 **Normanton** *Qld* Austr.
149 O6 **Normanton** *West Yorkshire, England* U.K.
82 G6 **Normanville** *S.A.* Austr.
222 E1 **Norman Wells** *N.W.T.* Can.
227 O1 **Normétal** *Que.* Can.
87 D13 **Nornalup** *W.A.* Austr.
78 □6 **Noro** *New Georgia Is* Solomon Is
242 F4 **Norogachic** Mex.
160 I1 **Noroy-le-Bourg** France
223 K5 **Norquay** *Sask.* Can.
260 B5 **Norquín** Arg.
259 C6 **Ñorquinco** Arg.
143 L1 **Norra Barken** *l.* Sweden
143 N2 **Norra Björkfjärden** *b.* Sweden
140 P4 **Norra Bredåker** Sweden
140 P5 **Norra gloppet** *b.* Fin.
140 M4 **Norråker** Sweden
140 P5 **Norra Kvarken** *str.* Fin./Sweden
143 O2 **Norra Ljusterö** *i.* Sweden
140 O3 **Norrbotten** *county* Sweden
142 F5 **Nørreå** *r.* Denmark
142 H7 **Nørre Alslev** Denmark
168 L1 **Nørreballe** Denmark
142 G6 **Nørre Lyndelse** Denmark
142 E6 **Nørre Nebel** Denmark
156 D2 **Norrent-Fontes** France
142 F6 **Nørre Snede** Denmark
140 P4 **Norrfjärden** Sweden
143 K1 **Norr Hörken** *l.* Sweden
143 L4 **Norrhult-Klavreström** Sweden
232 B12 **Norris Lake** *TN* U.S.A.
234 E4 **Norristown** *PA* U.S.A.
143 M3 **Norrköping** Sweden
141 N6 **Norrsundet** Sweden
143 O2 **Norrtälje** Sweden
87 F12 **Norseman** *W.A.* Austr.
80 K7 **Norsewood** *North I.* N.Z.
142 F2 **Norsjø** *l.* Norway
140 O4 **Norsjö** Sweden
100 F2 **Norsk** Rus. Fed.
221 Q2 **Norske Øer** *is* Greenland
78 □5 **Norsup** Vanuatu
251 I4 **Norte, Cabo** *c.* Brazil
251 I4 **Norte, Canal do** *sea chan.* Brazil
247 □1 **Norte, Cayo** *i.* Puerto Rico
261 I5 **Norte, Punta** *pt* Arg.
259 C8 **Norte, Punta** *pt* Arg.
259 E6 **Norte, Punta** *pt* Arg.
216 □3e **Norte, Punta** *pt El Hierro* Canary Is
253 F2 **Norte, Serra do** *hills* Brazil
261 E2 **Norte, Sierra de** *mts* Arg.
250 C2 **Norte de Santander** *dept* Col.
216 □1c **Norte Grande** *São Jorge* Azores
253 F3 **Nortelândia** Brazil
169 I7 **Nörten-Hardenberg** Ger.
216 □1c **Norte Pequeno** *São Jorge* Azores
263 L2 **North, Cape** Antarctica
225 I4 **North, Cape** *N.S.* Can.
233 L6 **North Adams** *MA* U.S.A.
149 O5 **Northallerton** *North Yorkshire, England* U.K.
87 D11 **Northam** *W.A.* Austr.
150 D5 **Northam** *Devon, England* U.K.
218 **North America** *continent*
233 □R3 **North Amity** *ME* U.S.A.
87 C10 **Northampton** *W.A.* Austr.
151 K3 **Northampton** *Northamptonshire, England* U.K.
233 M6 **Northampton** *MA* U.S.A.
234 E3 **Northampton** *PA* U.S.A.
234 E3 **Northampton County** *county PA* U.S.A.
85 J8 **Northampton Downs** *Qld* Austr.
151 K3 **Northamptonshire** *admin. div. England* U.K.
115 M6 **North Andaman** *i.* *Andaman & Nicobar Is* India
232 H11 **North Anna** *r.* *VA* U.S.A.
233 □P4 **North Anson** *ME* U.S.A.
222 H2 **North Arm** *b.* *N.W.T.* Can.
225 I1 **North Aulatsivik Island** *Nfld and Lab.* Can.
265 L5 **North Australian Basin** *sea feature* Indian Ocean
146 G11 **North Ayrshire** *admin. div. Scotland* U.K.
151 J6 **North Baddesley** *Hampshire, England* U.K.
92 A7 **North Balabac Strait** Phil.
232 B7 **North Baltimore** *OH* U.S.A.
223 I4 **North Battleford** *Sask.* Can.
224 E4 **North Bay** *Ont.* Can.
224 E1 **North Belcher Islands** *Nunavut* Can.
238 B5 **North Bend** *OR* U.S.A.
232 H7 **North Bend** *PA* U.S.A.
233 L6 **North Bennington** *VT* U.S.A.
235 G3 **North Bergen** *NJ* U.S.A.
146 K10 **North Berwick** *East Lothian, Scotland* U.K.
233 □O5 **North Berwick** *ME* U.S.A.
North Borneo *state* Malaysia *see* **Sabah**
237 G10 **North Bosque** *r.* *TX* U.S.A.
83 J4 **North Bourke** *N.S.W.* Austr.
227 K6 **North Branch** *MI* U.S.A.
226 B4 **North Branch** *MN* U.S.A.
234 F3 **North Branch** *NJ* U.S.A.
235 J2 **North Branford** *CT* U.S.A.
246 H3 **North Caicos** *i.* Turks and Caicos Is
237 H8 **North Canadian** *r.* *OK* U.S.A.
225 H4 **North Cape** *c.* *P.E.I.* Can.
North Cape *c.* Norway *see* **Nordkapp**
80 H1 **North Cape** *c.* *North I.* N.Z.
259 □ **North Cape** *c.* S. Georgia
226 F7 **North Cape** *WI* U.S.A.
220 A4 **North Cape** *c.* *AK* U.S.A.
234 F7 **North Cape May** *NJ* U.S.A.
224 B2 **North Caribou Lake** *Ont.* Can.
231 H7 **North Carolina** *state* U.S.A.
238 D2 **North Cascades National Park** *WA* U.S.A.
234 E3 **North Catasauqua** *PA* U.S.A.
149 P6 **North Cave** *East Riding of Yorkshire, England* U.K.
231 □2 **North Cay** *i.* *New Prov.* Bahamas
86 I7 **North Central Aboriginal Reserve** *W.A.* Austr.
224 D4 **North Channel** *lake channel Ont.* Can.
146 D12 **North Channel** *Northern Ireland/Scotland* U.K.
231 H9 **North Charleston** *SC* U.S.A.
150 H5 **North Cheriton** *Somerset, England* U.K.
238 K4 **North Cheyenne Indian Reservation** *res. MT* U.S.A.
87 D13 **Northcliffe** *W.A.* Austr.
263 G2 **Northcliffe Glacier** Antarctica
232 G6 **North Collins** *NY* U.S.A.
237 E10 **North Concho** *r.* *TX* U.S.A.
233 □N4 **North Conway** *NH* U.S.A.
North Cousin Islet *i.* *Inner Islands* Seychelles *see* **Cousin**
222 F5 **North Cowichan** *B.C.* Can.
149 N5 **North Cowton** *North Yorkshire, England* U.K.
233 L5 **North Creek** *NY* U.S.A.
236 E2 **North Dakota** *state* U.S.A.
146 D6 **North Dell** *Western Isles, Scotland* U.K.
150 G6 **North Dorset Downs** *hills England* U.K.
151 K5 **North Downs** *hills England* U.K.
149 P6 **North Duffield** *North Yorkshire, England* U.K.
213 E4 **North-East** *admin. dist.* Botswana
234 D5 **North East** *MD* U.S.A.
232 F6 **North East** *PA* U.S.A.
216 □2a **North East Bay** *Ascension* S. Atlantic Ocean
85 N3 **North East Cay** *rf Coral Sea Is Terr.* Austr.
210 D4 **North Eastern** *prov.* Kenya
North-East Frontier Agency *state* India *see* **Arunachal Pradesh**
149 Q6 **North East Lincolnshire** *admin. div. England* U.K.
267 I4 **Northeast Pacific Basin** *sea feature* Pacific Ocean
246 G2 **Northeast Point** *Acklins I.* Bahamas
246 G3 **Northeast Point** *Gt Inagua* Bahamas
86 □1 **North East Point** Christmas I.
246 □ **Northeast Point** Jamaica
246 E1 **Northeast Providence Channel** Bahamas
240 O6 **North Edwards** *CA* U.S.A.
169 I7 **Northeim** Ger.
151 N2 **North Elmham** *Norfolk, England* U.K.
231 J13 **North End Point** Bahamas
92 □ **North Entrance** *sea chan.* Palau
206 E4 **Northern** *admin. reg.* Ghana
211 B7 **Northern** *admin. reg.* Malawi
206 C4 **Northern** *prov.* Sierra Leone
203 F4 **Northern** *state* Sudan
209 F7 **Northern** *prov.* Zambia
Northern Aegean *admin. reg.* Greece *see* **Voreio Aigaio**
123 O3 **Northern Areas** *admin. div.* Pak.
208 E2 **Northern Bahr el Ghazal** *state* Sudan
214 D5 **Northern Cape** *prov.* S. Africa
81 □2 **Northern Cook Islands** Cook Is
202 E5 **Northern Darfur** *state* Sudan
Northern Donets *r.* Rus. Fed. *see* **Severskiy Donets**
Northern Dvina *r.* Rus. Fed. *see* **Severnaya Dvina**
223 L3 **Northern Indian Lake** *Man.* Can.
147 I3 **Northern Ireland** *prov.* U.K.
203 F6 **Northern Kordofan** *state* Sudan
77 I3 **Northern Lau Group** *is* Fiji
224 B3 **Northern Light Lake** *Ont.* Can.
91 J3 **Northern Mariana Islands** *terr.* N. Pacific Ocean
Northern Pindus Mountains Greece *see* **Voreia Pindos**
86 □1 **Northern Plateau** Christmas I.
247 □7 **Northern Range** *hills* Trin. and Tob.
Northern Rhodesia *country* Africa *see* **Zambia**
222 E3 **Northern Rocky Mountains Provincial Park** *nat. park B.C.* Can.
Northern Sporades *is* Greece *see* **Voreies Sporades**
84 D4 **Northern Territory** *admin. div.* Austr.
Northern Transvaal *prov.* S. Africa *see* **Limpopo**
146 L9 **North Esk** *r.* *Angus, Scotland* U.K.
236 J6 **North Fabius** *r.* *MO* U.S.A.
149 P6 **North Ferriby** *East Riding of Yorkshire, England* U.K.
233 M6 **Northfield** *MA* U.S.A.
226 A5 **Northfield** *MN* U.S.A.
234 F6 **Northfield** *NJ* U.S.A.
233 M4 **Northfield** *VT* U.S.A.
226 C5 **Northfield** *WI* U.S.A.
151 M5 **Northfleet** *Kent, England* U.K.
235 J2 **Northford** *CT* U.S.A.
151 O5 **North Foreland** *c. England* U.K.
240 M4 **North Fork** *CA* U.S.A.
226 I4 **North Fox Island** *MI* U.S.A.
235 K1 **North Franklin** *CT* U.S.A.
224 D3 **North French** *r.* *Ont.* Can.
247 □2 **North Friar's Bay** St Kitts and Nevis
North Frisian Islands Ger. *see* **Nordfriesische Inseln**
221 K2 **North Geomagnetic Pole** *Nunavut* Can.
149 P5 **North Grimston** *North Yorkshire, England* U.K.
235 J2 **North Haven** *CT* U.S.A.
233 □S4 **North Head** *N.B.* Can.
80 I3 **North Head** *hd North I.* N.Z.
82 □3 **North Head** *hd* S. Pacific Ocean
223 L2 **North Henik Lake** *Nunavut* Can.
233 L4 **North Hero** *VT* U.S.A.
240 K3 **North Highlands** *CA* U.S.A.
210 C4 **North Horr** Kenya
233 L5 **North Hudson** *NY* U.S.A.
149 P7 **North Hykeham** *Lincolnshire, England* U.K.
151 L3 **Northill** *Bedfordshire, England* U.K.
84 F3 **North Island** *N.T.* Austr.
87 B10 **North Island** *W.A.* Austr.
114 C7 **North Island** India
80 H5 **North Island** N.Z.
92 C1 **North Island** Phil.
217 □2a **North Island** *Inner Islands* Seychelles
92 C7 **North Islet** *rf* Phil.
241 V6 **North Jadito Canyon** *gorge AZ* U.S.A.
226 H8 **North Judson** *IN* U.S.A.
North Kazakhstan Oblast *admin. div.* Kazakh. *see* **Severnyy Kazakhstan**
86 □2 **North Keeling Island** Cocos Is
85 J3 **North Kennedy** *r.* *Qld* Austr.
146 H7 **North Kessock** *Highland, Scotland* U.K.
232 E7 **North Kingsville** *OH* U.S.A.
223 M3 **North Knife** *r.* *Man.* Can.
223 L3 **North Knife Lake** *Man.* Can.
117 I7 **North Koel** *r.* *Jharkhand* India
241 U9 **North Komelik** *AZ* U.S.A.
101 E8 **North Korea** *country* Asia
117 O6 **North Lakhimpur** *Assam* India
146 I11 **North Lanarkshire** *admin. div. Scotland* U.K.
80 I2 **Northland** *admin. reg. North I.* N.Z.
North Land *is* Rus. Fed. *see* **Severnaya Zemlya**
80 H2 **Northland Forest Park** *nature res. North I.* N.Z.
241 Q5 **North Las Vegas** *NV* U.S.A.
151 I4 **Northleach** *Gloucestershire, England* U.K.
226 H8 **North Liberty** *IN* U.S.A.
232 E8 **North Lima** *OH* U.S.A.
149 P6 **North Lincolnshire** *admin. div. England* U.K.
237 I8 **North Little Rock** *AR* U.S.A.
236 F5 **North Loup** *r.* *NE* U.S.A.
211 B7 **North Luangwa National Park** Zambia
222 C2 **North Macmillan** *r.* *Y.T.* Can.
235 J2 **North Madison** *CT* U.S.A.
221 F1 **North Magnetic Pole** Arctic Ocean
113 □1 **North Male Atoll** Maldives
239 K7 **North Mam Peak** *CO* U.S.A.
226 I9 **North Manchester** *IN* U.S.A.
226 H4 **North Manitou Island** *MI* U.S.A.
232 A10 **North Middletown** *KY* U.S.A.
150 E5 **North Molton** *Devon, England* U.K.
223 K4 **North Moose Lake** *Man.* Can.
234 C2 **North Mountain** *mts PA* U.S.A.
86 C6 **North Muiron Island** *W.A.* Austr.
222 F2 **North Nahanni** *r.* *N.W.T.* Can.
246 □ **North Negril Point** Jamaica
227 M8 **North Olmsted** *OH* U.S.A.
236 H2 **Northome** *MN* U.S.A.
North Ossetia *aut. rep.* Rus. Fed. *see* **Severnaya Osetiya-Alaniya, Respublika**
240 N4 **North Palisade** *mt.* *CA* U.S.A.
236 E5 **North Platte** *NE* U.S.A.
236 E5 **North Platte** *r.* *NE* U.S.A.
87 C11 **North Point** *W.A.* Austr.
247 □4 **North Point** Barbados
North Point *H.K.* China *see* **Tsat Tsze Mui**
216 □2a **North Point** *Ascension* S. Atlantic Ocean
216 □2c **North Point** *Tristan da Cunha* S. Atlantic Ocean
217 □2b **North Point** *Mahé* Seychelles
268 A1 **North Pole** *POLE* Arctic Ocean
231 D9 **Northport** *AL* U.S.A.
231 F12 **North Port** *FL* U.S.A.
226 I4 **Northport** *MI* U.S.A.
149 K1 **North Queensferry** *Fife, Scotland* U.K.
115 M6 **North Reef Island** *Andaman & Nicobar Is* India
North Rhine - Westphalia *land* Ger. *see* **Nordrhein-Westfalen**
241 T5 **North Rim** *AZ* U.S.A.
225 I4 **North River Bridge** *N.S.* Can.
82 □2 **North Rock** *i.* *Lord Howe I.* Austr.
146 □N1 **North Roe** *Shetland, Scotland* U.K.
North Rona *i.* *Western Isles, Scotland* U.K. *see* **Rona**
146 L4 **North Ronaldsay** *i. Scotland* U.K.
146 L4 **North Ronaldsay Firth** *sea chan. Scotland* U.K.
238 C4 **North Santiam** *r.* *OR* U.S.A.
222 J4 **North Saskatchewan** *r.* *Alta/Sask.* Can.
241 R2 **North Schell Peak** *NV* U.S.A.
144 H3 **North Sea** *sea* Europe
235 K3 **North Sea** *NY* U.S.A.
223 L3 **North Seal** *r.* *Man.* Can.
115 M7 **North Sentinel Island** *Andaman & Nicobar Is* India
149 O3 **North Shields** *Tyne and Wear, England* U.K.
223 L5 **North Shoal Lake** *Man.* Can.
240 O2 **North Shoshone Peak** *NV* U.S.A.
North Siberian Lowland Rus. Fed. *see* **Severo-Sibirskaya Nizmennost'**

North Simlipal National Park to Nurrai Lakes
361

117 K9 North Simlipal National Park India
North Sinai governorate Egypt see Shamāl Sīnā'
220 D3 North Slope plain AK U.S.A.
149 R7 North Somercotes Lincolnshire, England U.K.
150 G5 North Somerset admin. div. England U.K.
147 C6 North Sound sea chan. Ireland
223 M4 North Spirit Lake Ont. Can.
85 N9 North Stradbroke Island Qld Austr.
233 N4 North Stratford NH U.S.A.
149 N2 North Sunderland Northumberland, England U.K.
80 I5 North Taranaki Bight b. North I. N.Z.
222 F5 North Thompson r. B.C. Can.
149 Q7 North Thoresby Lincolnshire, England U.K.
146 B7 Northton Western Isles, Scotland U.K.
232 G5 North Tonawanda NY U.S.A.
81 B14 North Trap rf South I. N.Z.
233 M4 North Troy VT U.S.A.
233 O6 North Truro MA U.S.A.
94 □ North Tuas Basin dock Sing.
224 E2 North Twin Island Nunavut Can.
225 K3 North Twin Lake Nfld and Lab. Can.
149 M4 North Tyne r. England U.K.
92 C8 North Ubian i. Phil.
146 M7 North Ugie r. Scotland U.K.
146 B7 North Uist i. Scotland U.K.
149 L3 Northumberland admin. div. England U.K.
234 B3 Northumberland PA U.S.A.
234 B3 Northumberland County county PA U.S.A.
85 M6 Northumberland Isles Qld Austr.
149 M3 Northumberland National Park England U.K.
225 H4 Northumberland Strait Can.
238 C5 North Umpqua r. OR U.S.A.
222 F5 North Vancouver B.C. Can.
92 B6 North Verde i. Phil.
233 K5 Northville NY U.S.A.
222 H3 North Wabasca Lake Alta Can.
234 E4 North Wales PA U.S.A.
151 O2 North Walsham Norfolk, England U.K.
233 □O4 North Waterford ME U.S.A.
151 M4 North Weald Bassett Essex, England U.K.
215 J2 North West prov. S. Africa
264 F1 Northwest Atlantic Mid-Ocean Channel N. Atlantic Ocean
North West Bay Mahé Seychelles see Beau Vallon, Baie
247 □2 North West Bluff c. Montserrat
86 C6 North West Cape W.A. Austr.
235 K1 North Westchester CT U.S.A.
209 D8 North-Western prov. Zambia
123 N5 North West Frontier prov. Pak.
North West Nelson Forest Park nat. park South I. N.Z. see Kahurangi National Park
266 F3 Northwest Pacific Basin sea feature N. Pacific Ocean
86 □1 North West Point Christmas I.
246 D1 Northwest Providence Channel Bahamas
225 J2 North West River Nfld and Lab. Can.
222 J2 Northwest Territories admin. div. Can.
149 L7 Northwich Cheshire, England U.K.
237 F9 North Wichita r. TX U.S.A.
234 F6 North Wildwood NJ U.S.A.
235 K1 North Windham CT U.S.A.
233 □O5 North Windham ME U.S.A.
268 N1 Northwind Ridge sea feature Arctic Ocean
149 O7 North Wingfield Derbyshire, England U.K.
151 J6 Northwood Isle of Wight, England U.K.
236 I4 Northwood IA U.S.A.
236 G2 Northwood ND U.S.A.
233 N5 Northwood NH U.S.A.
226 C4 Northwoods Beach WI U.S.A.
227 O6 North York Ont. Can.
149 P5 North York Moors moorland England U.K.
149 P5 North York Moors National Park England U.K.
149 N5 North Yorkshire admin. div. England U.K.
168 E4 Nortmoor Ger.
225 H4 Norton N.B. Can.
149 P5 Norton North Yorkshire, England U.K.
151 N3 Norton Suffolk, England U.K.
236 F6 Norton KS U.S.A.
232 C12 Norton VA U.S.A.
233 M4 Norton VT U.S.A.
213 F3 Norton Zimbabwe
149 N8 Norton Canes Staffordshire, England U.K.
Norton de Matos Angola see Balombo
150 F5 Norton Fitzwarren Somerset, England U.K.
226 H6 Norton Shores MI U.S.A.
220 B3 Norton Sound sea chan. AK U.S.A.
168 I2 Nortorf Ger.
168 E5 Nortrup Ger.
158 H7 Nort-sur-Erdre France
261 G4 Norumbega Arg.
262 X2 Norvegia, Cape Antarctica
235 I2 Norwalk CT U.S.A.
232 C7 Norwalk OH U.S.A.
226 D6 Norwalk WI U.S.A.
235 I2 Norwalk r. CT U.S.A.
141 K5 Norway country Europe
233 □O4 Norway ME U.S.A.
227 R4 Norway Bay Que. Can.
223 L4 Norway House Man. Can.
264 I1 Norwegian Basin sea feature N. Atlantic Ocean
221 I2 Norwegian Bay Nunavut Can.
264 J1 Norwegian Sea N. Atlantic Ocean
227 N7 Norwich Ont. Can.
151 O2 Norwich Norfolk, England U.K.
233 M7 Norwich CT U.S.A.
233 J6 Norwich NY U.S.A.
146 □O1 Norwick Shetland, Scotland U.K.
233 N6 Norwood MA U.S.A.
231 G8 Norwood NC U.S.A.
233 K4 Norwood NY U.S.A.
232 A9 Norwood OH U.S.A.
92 C4 Norzagaray Luzon Phil.
105 M4 Nosaka Japan
102 W3 Nosapu-misaki pt Japan
104 B6 Nose Japan
104 C7 Nosegawa Japan
223 I1 Nose Lake Nunavut Can.
102 S1 Noshappu-misaki hd Japan
102 R6 Noshiro Japan
134 J3 Noshul' Rus. Fed.
137 K3 Nosivka Ukr.
136 G5 Noskivtsi Ukr.
134 I4 Noskovo Rus. Fed.
214 E2 Nosop watercourse Botswana alt. Nossob (Namibia/S. Africa)
134 K1 Nosovaya Rus. Fed.
Nosovka Ukr. see Nosivka
122 H7 Noşratābād Iran
146 □N2 Noss, Isle of i. Scotland U.K.
142 I3 Nossan r. Sweden
184 C3 Nossa Senhora da Boa Fé Port.
252 B1 Nossa Senhora da Glória Brazil
184 D1 Nossa Senhora da Graça de Póvoa e Meadas Port.
184 D3 Nossa Senhora da Graça do Divor Port.
184 D4 Nossa Senhora das Neves Port.
184 C4 Nossa Senhora da Torega Port.
184 D3 Nossa Senhora de Machede Port.
253 F3 Nossa Senhora do Livramento Brazil
216 □1b Nossa Senhora dos Remédios São Miguel Azores
142 I3 Nossebro Sweden
171 H8 Nossen Ger.
170 G3 Nossendorf Ger.
170 F3 Nossentiner Hütte Ger.
146 J6 Noss Head Scotland U.K.
214 E2 Nossob watercourse Namibia/S. Africa alt. Nosop (Botswana)
214 E1 Nossob Camp S. Africa
206 D3 Nossombougou Mali
213 □K4 Nosy Varika Madag.
176 G4 Noszlop Hungary
177 J4 Noszvaj Hungary
140 U2 Nota r. Fin./Rus. Fed.
Notabile Malta see Mdina
225 I1 Notakwanon r. Nfld and Lab. Can.
193 L2 Notaresco Italy
241 S2 Notch Peak UT U.S.A.
174 D3 Noteć r. Pol.
174 F2 Notecki, Kanał canal Pol.
198 C3 Notia Pindos mts Greece
222 G3 Notikewin r. Alta Can.
177 I4 Nőtincs Hungary
198 H6 Notio Aigaio admin. reg. Greece
Nótion Aiyaíon admin. reg. Greece see Notio Aigaio
198 E4 Notios Evvoïkos Kolpos sea chan. Greece
198 B3 Notio Steno Kerkyras sea chan. Greece
138 E2 Nötö Fin.
195 I10 Noto Sicilia Italy
104 F1 Noto Japan
195 I10 Noto, Golfo di g. Sicilia Italy
142 F2 Notodden Norway
104 D5 Notogawa Japan
104 E1 Noto-hantō pen. Japan
104 E1 Noto-hantō Kokutei-kōen park Japan
104 F1 Notojima Japan
104 F1 Noto-jima i. Japan
102 V2 Notoro-ko l. Japan
179 J8 Notranje Gorice Slovenia
225 G4 Notre Dame, Monts mts Que. Can.
225 K3 Notre Dame Bay Nfld and Lab. Can.
159 M3 Notre-Dame-de-Gravenchon France
Notre-Dame-de-Koartac Que. Can. see Quaqtaq
227 S4 Notre-Dame-de-la-Salette Que. Can.
158 G8 Notre-Dame-de-Monts France
158 H8 Notre-Dame-de-Riez France
162 F5 Notre-Dame-de-Sanilhac France
233 □N3 Notre-Dame-des-Bois Que. Can.
159 M7 Notre-Dame-d'Oé France
227 S3 Notre-Dame-du-Laus Que. Can.
227 O2 Notre-Dame-du-Nord Que. Can.
179 I6 Nötsch im Gailtal Austria
207 F5 Notsé Togo
103 I13 Notsu Japan
102 W3 Notsuke-saki pt Japan
102 W3 Notsuke-suidō sea chan. Japan/Rus. Fed.
227 N5 Nottawasaga Bay Ont. Can.
224 E3 Nottaway r. Que. Can.
168 I4 Nottensdorf Ger.
151 J2 Nottingham Nottingham, England U.K.
151 J2 Nottingham admin. div. England U.K.
234 C5 Nottingham PA U.S.A.
151 J2 Nottingham East Midlands airport England U.K.
221 K3 Nottingham Island Nunavut Can.
215 O5 Nottingham Road S. Africa
149 P7 Nottinghamshire admin. div. England U.K.
232 G11 Nottoway VA U.S.A.
232 I12 Nottoway r. VA U.S.A.
169 D7 Nottuln Ger.
223 J5 Notukeu Creek r. Sask. Can.
105 G1 Nou Japan
208 C4 Nouabalé-Ndoki, Parc National nat. park Congo
204 A5 Nouâdhibou Maur.
204 A5 Nouâdhibou, Râs c. Maur.
206 B2 Nouakchott Maur.
206 D2 Noual well Maur.
206 A2 Nouâmghâr Maur.
159 P6 Nouan-le-Fuzelier France
159 N7 Nouans-les-Fontaines France
157 J5 Nouart France
96 H7 Nouei Vietnam
206 B2 Noueïch well Maur.
78 □5 Nouméa New Caledonia
207 H5 Noun r. Cameroon
206 E3 Nouna Burkina
146 J4 Noup Head Scotland U.K.
215 I7 Noupoort S. Africa
215 M4 Noupoortsnek pass S. Africa
140 T3 Nousu Fin.
Nouveau-Comptoir Que. Can. see Wemindji
Nouvelle Anvers Dem. Rep. Congo see Makanza
78 □5 Nouvelle Calédonie i. S. Pacific Ocean
Nouvelle Calédonie terr. S. Pacific Ocean see New Caledonia
Nouvelles Hébrides country S. Pacific Ocean see Vanuatu
156 C3 Nouvion France
158 H5 Nouvoitou France
159 M6 Nouzilly France
156 I4 Nouzonville France
123 M1 Nov Tajik.
138 G2 Nõva Estonia
176 F5 Nova Hungary
257 G4 Nova Almeida Brazil
254 C5 Nova América Brazil
256 A5 Nova Andradina Brazil
137 R4 Nova Astrakhan' Ukr.
256 C3 Nova Aurora Brazil
Novabad Tajik. see Novobod
177 H3 Nová Baňa Slovakia
136 H3 Nova Borova Ukr.
176 E2 Nová Bystřice Czech Rep.
209 B6 Nova Caipemba Angola
256 A6 Nova Cantu Brazil
Nova Chaves Angola see Muconda
197 L5 Novaci Romania
196 I5 Nova Crnja Vojvodina Serbia
254 G3 Nova Cruz Brazil
177 H3 Nová Dubnica Slovakia
257 F3 Nova Era Brazil
Nova Esperança Angola see Buengas
256 A5 Nova Esperança Brazil
191 M8 Novafeltria Italy
Nova Freixa Moz. see Cuamba
257 F5 Nova Friburgo Brazil
Nova Gaia Angola see Cambundi-Catembo
Nova Goa Goa India see Panaji
213 G4 Nova Golegã Moz.
188 D3 Nova Gorica Slovenia
188 F3 Nova Gradiška Croatia
256 C4 Nova Granada Brazil
137 M4 Nova Haleshchyna Ukr.
257 F5 Nova Iguaçu Brazil
137 M7 Nova Kakhovka Ukr.
137 M6 Nova Kam"yanka Ukr.
177 H3 Nováky Slovakia
160 H5 Novalaise France
186 E3 Novales Spain
191 L3 Nova Levante Italy
257 F3 Nova Lima Brazil
Nova Lisboa Angola see Huambo
191 R6 Novalja Croatia
256 A5 Nova Londrina Brazil
177 J2 Nová Ľubovňa Slovakia
138 M7 Novalukoml' Belarus
213 G4 Nova Mambone Moz.
137 M7 Nova Mayachka Ukr.
213 H3 Nova Nabúri Moz.
137 K6 Nova Odesa Ukr.
176 E1 Nová Paka Czech Rep.
137 O4 Nova Parafiyivka Ukr.
251 F4 Nova Paraiso Brazil
196 I6 Nova Pazova Vojvodina Serbia
254 E4 Nova Pilão Arcado Brazil
256 D3 Nova Ponte Brazil
256 D3 Nova Ponte, Represa resr Minas Gerais Brazil
255 D6 Nova Ponte, Represa resr Brazil
137 L5 Nova Praha Ukr.
190 F5 Novara Italy
190 E3 Novara prov. Italy
195 I7 Novara di Sicilia Sicilia Italy
254 E4 Nova Remanso Brazil
256 D4 Nova Resende Brazil
171 G10 Nová Role Czech Rep.
254 D5 Nova Roma Brazil
254 E3 Nova Russas Brazil
225 H5 Nova Scotia prov. Can.
254 E4 Nova Sento Sé Brazil
257 E3 Nova Serrana Brazil
Nova Sintra Angola see Catabola
195 L3 Nova Siri Italy
137 N2 Nova Sloboda Ukr.
254 F4 Nova Soure Brazil
190 G3 Novate Mezzola Italy
240 J3 Novato CA U.S.A.
188 F3 Nova Topola Bos.-Herz.
134 I3 Novator Rus. Fed.
136 G5 Nova Ushytsya Ukr.
213 G3 Nova Vandúzi Moz.
196 H7 Nova Varoš Serbia
179 J8 Nova Vas Slovenia
179 L1 Nová Včelnice Czech Rep.
257 G3 Nova Venécia Brazil
171 L10 Nová Ves Czech Rep.
257 H2 Nova Viçosa Brazil
250 E5 Nova Vida Amazonas Brazil
253 E2 Nova Vida Rondônia Brazil
137 O4 Nova Vodolaha Ukr.
254 B5 Nova Xavantino Brazil
137 T2 Novaya Chigla Rus. Fed.
Novaya Kakhovka Ukr. see Nova Kakhovka
137 T3 Novaya Kalitva Rus. Fed.
120 C3 Novaya Kazanka Kazakh.
139 P1 Novaya Ladoga Rus. Fed.
Novaya Odessa Ukr. see Nova Odesa
Novaya Pismyanka Rus. Fed. see Leninogorsk
131 P2 Novaya Sibir', Ostrov i. Novosibirskiye O-va Rus. Fed.
137 S2 Novaya Usman' Rus. Fed.
100 J4 Novaya Ussura Rus. Fed.
Novaya Volodaga Ukr. see Nova Vodolaha
136 J2 Novaya Yolcha Belarus
130 G2 Novaya Zemlya is Rus. Fed.
Novaya Zhizn Rus. Fed. see Kazinka
197 O8 Nova Zagora Bulg.
137 L7 Nova Zbur"yivka Ukr.
137 L5 Nove Ukr.
176 D3 Nové Hrady Czech Rep.
187 D11 Novelda Spain
191 J6 Novellara Italy
176 F1 Nové Město nad Metuj Czech Rep.
177 G3 Nové Mesto nad Váhom Slovakia
176 F2 Nové Město na Moravé Czech Rep.
175 K6 Nove Misto Ukr.
176 F3 Nové Mlýny, Vodní nádrž resr Czech Rep.
176 B6 Noventa di Piave Italy
191 L5 Noventa Vicentina Italy
161 F9 Noves France
183 L8 Novés Spain
171 G10 Nové Sedlo Czech Rep.
171 I10 Nové Strašecí Czech Rep.
177 H4 Nové Zámky Slovakia
Novgorod Rus. Fed. see Velikiy Novgorod
138 L4 Novgorodka Rus. Fed.
Novgorod Oblast admin. div. Rus. Fed. see Novgorodskaya Oblast'
Novgorod-Severskiy Ukr. see Novhorod-Sivers'kyy
139 P3 Novgorodskaya Oblast' admin. div. Rus. Fed.
Novgorod-Volynskiy Ukr. see Novohrad-Volyns'kyy
Novgradets Bulg. see Suvorovo
137 L5 Novhorodka Ukr.
137 O7 Novhorodkivka Ukr.
137 M2 Novhorod-Sivers'kyy Ukr.
137 Q5 Novhorods'ke Ukr.
227 K7 Novi MI U.S.A.
196 I5 Novi Bečej Vojvodina Serbia
136 H2 Novi Bilokorovychi Ukr.
137 K2 Novi Borovychi Ukr.
136 E2 Novi Chervyshcha Ukr.
121 S1 Novichikha Rus. Fed.
191 J6 Novi di Modena Italy
183 P5 Noviergas Spain
Novi Grad Bos.-Herz. see Bosanski Novi
191 P5 Novigrad Croatia
176 F5 Novigrad Podravski Croatia
197 L8 Novi Iskŭr Bulg.
177 J5 Novi Kneževac Vojvodina Serbia
100 M5 Novikovo Sakhalin Rus. Fed.
196 I5 Novi Kozarci Vojvodina Serbia
Novi Kritsim Bulg. see Stamboliyski
190 F6 Novi Ligure Italy
160 I2 Novillars France
165 G7 Noville Belgium
244 B3 Novillero Mex.
188 F2 Novi Marof Croatia
137 L2 Novi Mlyny Ukr.
156 H4 Novion-Porcien France
197 P7 Novi Pazar Bulg.
196 I7 Novi Pazar Serbia
196 H5 Novi Sad Vojvodina Serbia
137 N4 Novi Sanzhary Ukr.
175 M6 Novi Strilyshcha Ukr.
188 F3 Novi Travnik Bos.-Herz.
188 E3 Novi Vinodolski Croatia
139 Y5 Novki Rus. Fed.
251 I4 Novo, Lago l. Brazil
100 M5 Novoaleksandropov Sakhalin Rus. Fed.
137 R3 Novoaleksandrovka Rus. Fed.
135 H7 Novoaleksandrovsk Rus. Fed.
139 R7 Novoaleksandrovskiy Rus. Fed.
Novoalekseyevka Kazakh. see Khobda
98 D1 Novoaltaysk Rus. Fed.
137 R6 Novoamvrosiyivs'ke Ukr.
137 N8 Novoandriyivka Ukr.
135 H6 Novoanninskiy Rus. Fed.
251 F6 Novo Aripuanã Brazil
136 J5 Novoarkhanhel's'k Ukr.
137 S5 Novoaydar Ukr.
137 R6 Novoazovs'k Ukr.
137 S7 Novobataysk Rus. Fed.
137 S4 Novobelaya Rus. Fed.
196 I6 Novo Beograd Serbia
137 S8 Novobeysugskaya Rus. Fed.
137 S4 Novobila Ukr.
129 I2 Novobiryuzyak Rus. Fed.
123 M2 Novobod Tajik.
123 N2 Novobod Tajik.
Novobogatinsk Kazakh. see Khamit Yergaliyev
137 O6 Novobohdanivka Ukr.
137 R4 Novoborove Ukr.
100 F4 Novobureyskiy Rus. Fed.
134 I4 Novocheboksarsk Rus. Fed.
135 J5 Novocheremshansk Rus. Fed.
135 H7 Novocherkassk Rus. Fed.
100 H6 Novochuguyevka Rus. Fed.
257 G2 Novo Cruzeiro Brazil
137 N7 Novodanylivka Ukr.
137 R7 Novoderevyankovskaya Rus. Fed.
136 G5 Novodnistrovs'k Ukr.
121 O2 Novodolinka Kazakh.
137 Q5 Novodonets'ke Ukr.
107 M1 Novodoroninskoye Rus. Fed.
137 R5 Novodruzhes'k Ukr.
139 R6 Novodugino Rus. Fed.
134 H2 Novodvinsk Rus. Fed.
Novoekonomicheskoye Ukr. see Dymytrov
136 I4 Novofastiv Ukr.
137 K7 Novofedorivka Ukr.
100 E3 Novogeorgiyevka Rus. Fed.
139 S9 Novognezdilovo Rus. Fed.
Novogroznenskiy Rus. Fed. see Oyskhara
Novogrudok Belarus see Navahrudak
139 U7 Novogurovskiy Rus. Fed.
255 C9 Novo Hamburgo Brazil
137 O6 Novohorivka Ukr.
256 C4 Novo Horizonte Brazil
137 L6 Novohradivka Ukr.
176 D3 Novohradské hory mts Czech Rep.
136 G3 Novohrad-Volyns'kyy Ukr.
137 Q5 Novohrodivka Ukr.
137 N7 Novohryhorivka Ukr.
121 L1 Novoishimskiy Kazakh.
137 N6 Novoivanivka Dnipropetrovs'ka Oblast' Ukr.
137 R6 Novoivanivka Donets'ka Oblast' Ukr.
137 M8 Novoivanivka Respublika Krym Ukr.
137 O5 Novoivankivka Ukr.
129 G5 Novoivanovka Azer.
120 H1 Novokaolinovyy Rus. Fed.
129 I3 Novokayakent Rus. Fed.
Novokazalinsk Kazakh. see Ayteke Bi
135 H6 Novokhopersk Rus. Fed.
138 M6 Novokhovansk Rus. Fed.
100 F3 Novokiyevskiy Uval Rus. Fed.
137 K6 Novokostyantynivka Mykolayivs'ka Oblast' Ukr.
137 O7 Novokostyantynivka Zaporiz'ka Oblast' Ukr.
137 K5 Novokrasne Ukr.
137 R4 Novokrasnyanka Ukr.
137 N8 Novokryms'ke Ukr.
135 H7 Novokubansk Rus. Fed.
Novokubanskiy Rus. Fed. see Novokubansk
120 C1 Novokuybyshevsk Rus. Fed.
130 J4 Novokuznetsk Rus. Fed.
137 M7 Novokyyivka Ukr.
129 H2 Novolakskoye Rus. Fed.
263 A2 Novolazarevskaya research stn Antarctica
137 S8 Novoleushkovskaya Rus. Fed.
Novolukoml' Belarus see Novalukoml'
139 V8 Novol'vovsk Rus. Fed.
137 S8 Novomalorossiyskaya Rus. Fed.
251 E5 Novo Marapi Brazil
121 O2 Novomarkovka Kazakh.
137 N5 Novomar"yivka Ukr.
137 T3 Novomelovatka Rus. Fed.
188 E3 Novo Mesto Slovenia
139 W7 Novomichurinsk Rus. Fed.
135 G7 Novomikhaylovskiy Rus. Fed.
196 I5 Novo Miloševo Vojvodina Serbia
137 R7 Novominskaya Rus. Fed.
Novomirgorod Ukr. see Novomyrhorod
139 V7 Novomoskovsk Rus. Fed.
137 O5 Novomoskovs'k Ukr.
175 I1 Novomoskovskiy Rus. Fed.
252 C1 Novo Mundo Brazil
137 N7 Novomykhaylivka Ukr.
137 R4 Novomykil's'ke Ukr.
137 N5 Novomykolayivka Dnipropetrovs'ka Oblast' Ukr.
137 L7 Novomykolayivka Khersons'ka Oblast' Ukr.
137 N7 Novomykolayivka Khersons'ka Oblast' Ukr.
136 I8 Novomykolayivka Odes'ka Oblast' Ukr.
137 O6 Novomykolayivka Zaporiz'ka Oblast' Ukr.
137 K5 Novomyrhorod Ukr.
137 M7 Novonatalivka Ukr.
Novonazyvayevka Rus. Fed. see Nazyvayevsk
121 N6 Novonikolayevka Kazakh.
Novonikolayevsk Rus. Fed. see Novosibirsk
137 R8 Novonikolayevskaya Rus. Fed.
135 H6 Novonikolayevskiy Rus. Fed.
135 I6 Novonikol'skoye Rus. Fed.
137 N7 Novooleksandrivka Ukr.
137 N7 Novooleksiyivka Ukr.
251 G5 Novo Olinda do Norte Brazil
177 I6 Novo Orahovo Vojvodina Serbia
254 E3 Novo Oriente Brazil
120 H2 Novoorsk Rus. Fed.
137 L3 Novoorzhyts'ke Ukr.
137 M8 Novoozerne Ukr.
136 H2 Novoozeryanka Ukr.
254 E3 Novo Parnarama Brazil
Novopashiyskiy Rus. Fed. see Gornozavodsk
137 P5 Novopavlivka Dnipropetrovs'ka Oblast' Ukr.
136 J6 Novopavlivka Mykolayivs'ka Oblast' Ukr.
107 K1 Novopavlovka Rus. Fed.
129 E2 Novopavlovsk Rus. Fed.
Novopavlovskaya Rus. Fed. see Novopavlovsk
137 N4 Novopetrivka Ukr.
137 N5 Novopidkryazh Ukr.
120 K1 Novopokrovka Kostanayskaya Oblast' Kazakh.
121 L1 Novopokrovka Severnyy Kazakhstan Kazakh.
121 S2 Novopokrovka Vostochnyy Kazakhstan Kazakh.
100 I6 Novopokrovka Primorskiy Kray Rus. Fed.
137 T1 Novopokrovka Tambovskaya Oblast' Rus. Fed.
137 N5 Novopokrovka Ukr.
135 H7 Novopokrovskaya Rus. Fed.
Novopolotsk Belarus see Navapolatsk
137 L6 Novopoltavka Mykolayivs'ka Oblast' Ukr.
137 P6 Novopoltavka Zaporiz'ka Oblast' Ukr.
139 W8 Novopolyan'ye Rus. Fed.
137 S4 Novopskov Ukr.
Novo Redondo Angola see Sumbe
120 C2 Novorepnoye Rus. Fed.
100 F2 Novorossiyka Rus. Fed.
135 G7 Novorossiysk Rus. Fed.
Novorossiyskiy Kazakh. see Akzhar
137 S8 Novorozhdestvenskaya Rus. Fed.
121 N2 Novorybinka Akmolinskaya Oblast' Kazakh.
121 L1 Novorybinka Severnyy Kazakhstan Kazakh.
131 L2 Novorybnaya Rus. Fed.
138 M4 Novorzhev Rus. Fed.
136 I6 Novosamarka Ukr.
129 G5 Novosaratovka Azer.
171 I9 Novosedlice Czech Rep.
176 F3 Novosedly Czech Rep.
106 J1 Novoselenginsk Rus. Fed.
129 E1 Novoselitskoye Rus. Fed.
136 I6 Novoselivka Ukr.
137 M8 Novoselivs'ke Ukr.
139 V7 Novoselki Moskovskaya Oblast' Rus. Fed.
139 O6 Novoselki Tverskaya Oblast' Rus. Fed.
197 K9 Novo Selo Macedonia
175 I1 Novoselovo Kaliningradskaya Oblast' Rus. Fed.
139 W5 Novoselovo Vladimirskaya Oblast' Rus. Fed.
Novoselskoye Rus. Fed. see Achkhoy-Martan
138 L3 Novosel'ye Rus. Fed.
136 F5 Novoselytsya Ukr.
120 E1 Novosergiyevka Rus. Fed.
135 G7 Novoshakhtinsk Rus. Fed.
100 H6 Novoshakhtinskiy Rus. Fed.
137 R7 Novoshcherbinovskaya Rus. Fed.
135 J5 Novosheshminsk Rus. Fed.
130 J4 Novosibirsk Rus. Fed.
131 P2 Novosibirskiye Ostrova is Rus. Fed.
139 U9 Novosil' Rus. Fed.
137 L8 Novosil's'ke Ukr.
137 R2 Novosil'skoye Rus. Fed.
137 L7 Novosofiyivka Ukr.
139 N5 Novosokol'niki Rus. Fed.
137 P7 Novospas'ke Ukr.
120 B1 Novospasskoye Rus. Fed.
175 J1 Novostroyevo Rus. Fed.
137 S5 Novosvitlivka Ukr.
177 I2 Novoť Slovakia
129 I1 Novoterechnoye Rus. Fed.
137 R8 Novotitarovskaya Rus. Fed.
100 G4 Novotroichkoye Rus. Fed.
120 H2 Novotroitsk Rus. Fed.
Novotroitskoye Kazakh. see Tole Bi
139 Q8 Novotroitskoye Rus. Fed.
137 Q5 Novotroyits'ke Donets'ka Oblast' Ukr.
137 Q6 Novotroyits'ke Donets'ka Oblast' Ukr.
137 N7 Novotroyits'ke Khersons'ka Oblast' Ukr.
137 O6 Novotroyits'ke Zaporiz'ka Oblast' Ukr.
Novoukrainka Kirovohrads'ka Oblast' Ukr. see Novoukrayinka
Novoukrainka Rivnens'ka Oblast' Ukr. see Novoukrayinka
137 K5 Novoukrayinka Kirovohrads'ka Oblast' Ukr.
136 E3 Novoukrayinka Rivnens'ka Oblast' Ukr.
120 G2 Novoural'sk Rus. Fed.
120 C2 Novouzensk Rus. Fed.
121 P1 Novovarshavka Rus. Fed.
137 O7 Novovasylivka Zaporiz'ka Oblast' Ukr.
137 P7 Novovasylivka Zaporiz'ka Oblast' Ukr.
188 F2 Novo Virje Croatia
136 D3 Novovolyns'k Ukr.
135 G6 Novovoronezh Rus. Fed.
Novovoronezhskiy Rus. Fed. see Novovoronezh
137 M6 Novovorontsovka Ukr.
100 E2 Novo-Voskresenovka Rus. Fed.
137 M6 Novovoskresens'ke Ukr.
121 R6 Novovoznesenovka Kyrg.
137 O5 Novov"yazivs'ke Ukr.
137 N1 Novoyamskoye Rus. Fed.
136 C4 Novoyavorivs'ke Ukr.
139 W9 Novoye Dubovoye Rus. Fed.
121 S2 Novoyegor'yevskoye Rus. Fed.
139 X5 Novoye Leushino Rus. Fed.
139 T5 Novozavidovskiy Rus. Fed.
134 J2 Novozhilovskaya Rus. Fed.
136 I4 Novozhyvotiv Ukr.
139 O9 Novozybkov Rus. Fed.
188 F3 Novska Croatia
136 J1 Novy Barsuk Belarus
139 N6 Novy Boletsk Belarus
176 D1 Nový Bor Czech Rep.
176 E1 Nový Bydžov Czech Rep.
139 N8 Novy Bykhaw Belarus
156 H4 Novy-Chevrières France
175 M2 Novy Dvor Hrodzyenskaya Voblasts' Belarus
138 H9 Novy Dvor Hrodzyenskaya Voblasts' Belarus
Novyj Cholmogory Rus. Fed. see Arkhangel'sk
Novyj Holmogory Rus. Fed. see Arkhangel'sk
177 G2 Nový Jičín Czech Rep.
176 G2 Nový Malín Czech Rep.
Novyy Afon Georgia see Akhali Ap'oni
138 K6 Novyya Kruki Belarus
138 L7 Novyya Valosavichy Belarus
139 N8 Novyya Zhuravichy Belarus
134 K2 Novyy Bor Rus. Fed.
Novyy Bug Ukr. see Novyy Buh
137 L6 Novyy Buh Ukr.
137 K3 Novyy Bykiv Ukr.
Novyy Donbass Ukr. see Dymytrov
175 M5 Novyy Dvir Ukr.
Novyye Aneny Moldova see Anenii Noi
Novyye Belokorovichi Ukr. see Novi Bilokorovychi
120 B1 Novyye Burasy Rus. Fed.
139 Q9 Novyye Ivaytenki Rus. Fed.
Novyye Petushki Rus. Fed. see Petushki
138 K4 Novyy Izborsk Rus. Fed.
Novyy Kholmogory Rus. Fed. see Arkhangel'sk
Novyy Margelan Uzbek. see Farg'ona
137 O4 Novyy Merchyk Ukr.
139 V4 Novyy Nekouz Rus. Fed.
135 G6 Novyy Oskol Rus. Fed.
130 I3 Novyy Port Rus. Fed.
137 L1 Novyy Ropsk Rus. Fed.
136 D4 Novyy Rozdil Ukr.
139 T8 Novyy Sinets Rus. Fed.
137 M5 Novyystarodub Ukr.
137 R6 Novyy Svit Donets'ka Oblast' Ukr.
137 N9 Novyy Svit Respublika Krym Ukr.
129 I2 Novyy Terek r. Rus. Fed.
134 J4 Novyy Tor'yal Rus. Fed.
130 I3 Novyy Urengoy Rus. Fed.
100 H3 Novyy Urgal Rus. Fed.
Novyy Uzen' Kazakh. see Zhanaozen
175 M5 Novyy Vytkiv Ukr.
175 M6 Novyy Yarychiv Ukr.
134 K5 Novyy Zay Rus. Fed.
176 G3 Nový Život Slovakia
122 F6 Now Iran
175 H4 Nowa Brzeźnica Pol.
175 L2 Nowa Chodorówka Pol.
175 J5 Nowa Dęba Pol.
174 G1 Nowa Karczma Pol.
174 E5 Nowa Ruda Pol.
175 K5 Nowa Sarzyna Pol.
175 J5 Nowa Słupia Pol.
174 D4 Nowa Sól Pol.
237 H7 Nowata OK U.S.A.
171 L6 Nowa Wieś Pol.
175 K2 Nowa Wieś Ełcka Pol.
174 F1 Nowa Wieś Lęborskie Pol.
174 G3 Nowa Wieś Wielka Pol.
175 L2 Nowa Wola Pol.
175 J4 Nowa Wola Gołębiowska Pol.
122 C4 Nowbarān Iran
122 H5 Now Deh Iran
122 D4 Now Dezh Iran
122 C3 Nowdī Iran
174 G2 Nowe Pol.
175 I5 Nowe Brzesko Pol.
174 C2 Nowe Czarnowo Pol.
174 D4 Nowe Miasteczko Pol.
175 I3 Nowe Miasto Pol.
175 H2 Nowe Miasto Lubawskie Pol.
175 I4 Nowe Miasto nad Pilicą Pol.
147 D9 Nowen Hill Ireland
175 H3 Nowe Ostrowy Pol.
175 K3 Nowe Piekuty Pol.
174 F4 Nowe Skalmierzyce Pol.
174 C2 Nowe Warpno Pol.
122 D4 Nowfel low Shātow Qom Iran
122 E5 Now Gombad Iran
Nowgong Assam India see Nagaon
116 G7 Nowgong Madh. Prad. India
175 K2 Nowinka Pol.
127 N4 Nowjeh Deh Iran
122 F3 Now Kharegan Iran
223 K2 Nowleye Lake Nunavut Can.
175 K4 Nowodwór Pol.
174 D2 Nowogard Pol.
175 J2 Nowogród Pol.
174 D4 Nowogród Bobrzański Pol.
174 D3 Nowogródek Pomorski Pol.
174 D4 Nowogrodziec Pol.
238 K4 Nowood r. WY U.S.A.
Noworadomsk Pol. see Radomsko
175 L3 Nowosady Pol.
175 K6 Nowosielce Pol.
175 K5 Nowosielec Pol.
175 H4 Nowosolna Pol.
83 M6 Nowra N.S.W. Austr.
122 C2 Nowshahr Iran
122 D3 Nowshahr Iran
123 O4 Nowshera Pak.
122 B4 Nowsūd Iran
223 L2 Nowyak Lake Nunavut Can.
175 K3 Nowy Bartków Pol.
175 H3 Nowy Duninów Pol.
174 F2 Nowy Dwór Kujawsko-Pomorskie Pol.
175 L2 Nowy Dwór Podlaskie Pol.
143 P7 Nowy Dwór Gdański Pol.
175 I3 Nowy Dwór Mazowiecki Pol.
175 I5 Nowy Korczyn Pol.
175 L5 Nowy Lubliniec Pol.
175 I6 Nowy Sącz Pol.
143 P7 Nowy Staw Pol.
175 I6 Nowy Targ Pol.
174 E3 Nowy Tomyśl Pol.
175 J6 Nowy Żmigród Pol.
227 R8 Noxen PA U.S.A.
237 K9 Noxubee National Wildlife Refuge nature res. MS U.S.A.
96 G6 Noy, Xé r. Laos
Noya Cataluña Spain see Sant Sadurní d'Anoia
Noya Galicia Spain see Noia
130 I3 Noyabr'sk Rus. Fed.
158 G6 Noyal-Muzillac France
158 F6 Noyalo France
158 F5 Noyal-Pontivy France
159 L6 Noyant France
159 K7 Noyant-la-Plaine France
161 H6 Noyarey France
127 Q5 Noyek Iran
129 G4 Noyemberyan Armenia
159 K6 Noyen-sur-Sarthe France
156 G8 Noyers France
159 N7 Noyers-sur-Cher France
161 H8 Noyers-sur-Jabron France
222 C4 Noyes Island AK U.S.A.
114 E7 Noyil r. India
156 E4 Noyon France
105 H2 Nozawaonsen-mura Japan
158 H6 Nozay France
175 K6 Nozdrzec Pol.
160 I3 Nozeroy France
129 H2 Nozhay-Yurt Rus. Fed.
215 J6 Nozizwe S. Africa
178 B8 Nozza r. Italy
210 B4 Npitamaiong mt. Kenya
215 O6 Nqabeni S. Africa
215 L8 Nqamakwe S. Africa
215 O4 Nqutu S. Africa
129 H7 Nrnadzor Armenia
208 B5 Nsa Congo
211 A8 Nsalamu Zambia
208 C5 Nsambi Dem. Rep. Congo
211 B8 Nsanje Malawi
206 E5 Nsawam Ghana
211 A7 Nseluka Zambia
207 H6 Nsoc Equat. Guinea
215 P3 Nsoko Swaziland
209 F7 Nsombo Zambia
208 C5 Nsondia Dem. Rep. Congo
207 G5 Nsukka Nigeria
Nsumbu National Park Zambia see Sumbu National Park
204 B5 Ntalfa well Maur.
209 E8 Ntambu Zambia
208 C5 Ntandembele Dem. Rep. Congo
211 B8 Ntcheu Malawi
211 B8 Ntchisi Malawi
207 H6 Ntem r. Cameroon
215 L3 Ntha S. Africa
215 M2 Nthorwane S. Africa
215 M7 Ntibane S. Africa
202 B6 Ntiona Chad
198 F4 Ntoro, Kavo pt Greece
210 A4 Ntoroko Uganda
208 A4 Ntoum Gabon
217 □3a Ntsamouéni Njazidja Comoros
215 N3 Ntshingwayo Dam S. Africa
217 □3a Ntsoudjini Njazidja Comoros
207 H5 Ntui Cameroon
211 A5 Ntungamo Uganda
212 E4 Ntwetwe Pan salt pan Botswana
215 M7 Ntywenka S. Africa
159 J7 Nuaillé France
162 C3 Nuaillé-d'Aunis France
Nuanetsi r. Zimbabwe see Mwenezi
93 D3 Nuangan Sulawesi Indon.
234 D2 Nuangola PA U.S.A.
117 I9 Nuapara Orissa India
125 L4 Nu'aym reg. Oman
203 F4 Nuba, Lake resr Sudan
210 A2 Nuba Mountains Sudan
168 I2 Nübbel Ger.
245 K9 Nube Flan, Cerro mt. Mex.
168 I1 Nübel Ger.
203 G4 Nubian Desert Sudan
140 Q2 Nubivarri hill Norway
260 A5 Ñuble r. Chile
182 I1 Nubledo Spain
116 F2 Nubra r. India
79 □7 Nubu Vanua Levu Fiji
197 K4 Nucet Romania
241 X3 Nucla CO U.S.A.
107 L5 Nüden Mongolia
171 G7 Nudersdorf Ger.
169 J10 Nüdlingen Ger.
139 T5 Nudol' Rus. Fed.
175 M4 Nudyzhe Ukr.
237 G12 Nueces r. TX U.S.A.
159 J8 Nueil-sur-Argent France
223 L2 Nueltin Lake Man./Nunavut Can.
165 I6 Nuenen Neth.
186 E3 Nueno Spain
183 K2 Nueva Spain
259 D9 Nueva, Isla i. Chile
250 C6 Nueva Alejandría Peru
242 □O10 Nueva Arcadia Hond.
260 C3 Nueva California Arg.
185 K5 Nueva-Carteya Spain
237 F12 Nueva Ciudad Guerrero Mex.
260 D4 Nueva Constitución Arg.
260 E3 Nueva Escocia Arg.
251 E2 Nueva Esparta state Venez.
250 D2 Nueva Florida Venez.
260 E4 Nueva Galia Arg.
253 F5 Nueva Germania Para.
246 B3 Nueva Gerona Cuba
259 D9 Nueva Harberton Arg.
261 I4 Nueva Helvecia Uru.
260 A6 Nueva Imperial Chile
244 E6 Nueva Italia de Ruiz Mex.
184 G7 Nueva Jarilla Spain
259 C7 Nueva Lubecka Arg.
242 □O10 Nueva Ocotepeque Hond.
261 H3 Nueva Palmira Uru.
258 E2 Nueva Población Arg.
245 I3 Nueva Polonia Mex.
243 I4 Nueva Rosita Mex.
243 O11 Nueva San Salvador El Salvador
Nueva Tabarca i. Spain see Plana, Isla
245 I1 Nueva Villa de Padilla Mex.
Nueve de Julio Arg. see 9 de Julio
246 E3 Nuevitas Cuba
243 N7 Nuevo, Cayo i. Mex.
259 D6 Nuevo, Golfo g. Arg.
261 I3 Nuevo Berlín Uru.
242 F2 Nuevo Casas Grandes Mex.
242 G5 Nuevo Ideal Mex.
243 J4 Nuevo Laredo Mex.
241 Q9 Nuevo León Mex.
244 G1 Nuevo León state Mex.
251 F2 Nuevo Mamo Venez.
245 H3 Nuevo-Morelos Mex.
244 C2 Nuevo Pilares Mex.
250 C5 Nuevo Rocatuerte Ecuador
244 F4 Nuevo Valle de Moreno Mex.
124 G4 Nufayyid Şabḩah des. Saudi Arabia
106 D2 Nuga Mongolia
210 F2 Nugaal admin. reg. Somalia
210 F3 Nugaal watercourse Somalia
85 L8 Nuga Nuga, Lake Qld Austr.
81 D13 Nugget Point South I. N.Z.
82 □3 Nuggetts Point S. Pacific Ocean
192 C6 Nughedu di San Nicolò Sardegna Italy
139 T8 Nugr' r. Rus. Fed.
114 E6 Nugu r. India
77 F2 Nuguria Islands P.N.G.
123 J9 Nuh, Ras pt Pak.
80 L6 Nuhaka North I. N.Z.
199 L4 Nuhköy Turkey
77 H2 Nui atoll Tuvalu
Nui Con Voi r. Vietnam see Hông, Sông
138 L1 Nuijamaa Fin.
159 J6 Nuillé-sur-Vicoin France
96 I7 Nui Thanh Vietnam
96 H7 Nui Ti On mt. Vietnam
156 H8 Nuits France
160 F2 Nuits-St-Georges France
Nu Jiang r. Myanmar see Salween
104 F6 Nukata Japan
82 E5 Nukey Bluff hill S.A. Austr.
Nukha Azer. see Şäki
78 □6 Nukiki Choiseul Solomon Is
122 E5 Nūklok, Chāh-e well Iran
79 □8a Nuku i. Tonga
79 □8a Nuku'alofa Tongatapu Tonga
77 H2 Nukufetau atoll Tuvalu
79 □9 Nuku Hiva i. Fr. Polynesia
Nukuhiva i. Fr. Polynesia see Nuku Hiva
77 H2 Nukulaelae atoll Tuvalu
Nukulailai atoll Tuvalu see Nukulaelae
77 F2 Nukumanu Islands P.N.G.
Nukunau i. Gilbert Is Kiribati see Nikunau
Nukunono atoll Tokelau see Nukunonu
81 □1 Nukunonu Tokelau
81 □1 Nukunonu atoll Tokelau
120 H6 Nukus Uzbek.
164 H5 Nuland Neth.
220 C3 Nulato AK U.S.A.
192 C7 Nule Sardegna Italy
187 E8 Nules Spain
86 F6 Nullagine W.A. Austr.
86 F6 Nullagine r. W.A. Austr.
82 C4 Nullarbor S.A. Austr.
82 C4 Nullarbor National Park S.A. Austr.
82 B4 Nullarbor Plain S.A. Austr.
82 C4 Nullarbor Regional Reserve park S.A. Austr.
224 E1 Nuluarniavik, Lac l. Que. Can.
107 P6 Nulu'erhu Shan mts China
192 B6 Nulvi Sardegna Italy
91 I7 Num i. Papua Indon.
117 K6 Num Nepal
83 J3 Numalla, Lake salt flat Qld Austr.
207 I4 Numan Nigeria
124 B2 Nu'mān i. Saudi Arabia
191 P8 Numana Italy
92 E7 Numancia Phil.
164 F5 Numansdorp Neth.
105 J2 Numata Gunma Japan
102 S3 Numata Hokkaidō Japan
208 E3 Numatinna watercourse Sudan
105 I5 Numazu Japan
215 P1 Numbi Gate S. Africa
Numbu Vanua Levu Fiji see Nubu
84 E3 Numbulwar N.T. Austr.
142 F1 Numedal val. Norway
91 H7 Numfoor i. Papua Indon.
100 E5 Numin He r. China
212 C3 Numkaub Namibia
141 Q6 Nummi Fin.
83 J7 Numurkah Vic. Austr.
225 I2 Nunaksaluk Island Nfld and Lab. Can.
221 N3 Nunakuluut i. Greenland
221 N3 Nunap Isua c. Greenland
Nunarsuit i. Greenland see Nunakuluut
224 E1 Nunavik reg. Que. Can.
223 L2 Nunavut admin. div. Can.
250 C3 Nunchía Col.
171 H8 Nünchritz Ger.
209 F5 Nunda Dem. Rep. Congo
232 H6 Nunda NY U.S.A.
83 M4 Nundle N.S.W. Austr.
151 J2 Nuneaton Warwickshire, England U.K.
87 E11 Nungarin W.A. Austr.
117 N7 Nungba Manipur India
223 M5 Nungesser Lake Ont. Can.
107 P4 Nungnain Sum Nei Mongol China
213 H2 Nungo Moz.
211 C6 Nungwi, Ras pt Tanz.
220 B4 Nunivak Island AK U.S.A.
117 J9 Nunkapasi Orissa India
172 B3 Nunkirchen Ger.
116 F3 Nunkun mt. Jammu and Kashmir
131 T3 Nunligran Rus. Fed.
187 H9 Nunó, Cap c. Spain
252 C3 Nuñoa Peru
182 H8 Nuñomoral Spain
171 H6 Nunsdorf Ger.
164 I4 Nunspeet Neth.
95 L3 Nunukan i. Indon.
Nuojiang Sichuan China see Tongjiang
192 C7 Nuoro Sardegna Italy
192 C7 Nuoro prov. Sardegna Italy
Nuorttijoki r. Rus. Fed. see Nota
78 □6 Nupani i. Santa Cruz Is Solomon Is
122 F6 Nūq Iran
202 C4 Nuqayy, Jabal mts Libya
124 E3 Nuqrah Saudi Arabia
203 G3 Nuqruş, Jabal mt. Egypt
250 B3 Nuquí Col.
111 E8 Nur Xinjiang China
122 E3 Nur r. Iran
175 K3 Nur Pol.
121 Q6 Nura Almatinskaya Oblast' Kazakh.
121 P3 Nura Kazakh.
121 M2 Nura r. Kazakh.
122 D6 Nūrābād Iran
122 C4 Nūrābād Iran
192 C8 Nuragus Sardegna Italy
Nurakita i. Tuvalu see Niulakita
192 C8 Nurallao Sardegna Italy
192 C9 Nuraminis Sardegna Italy
Nurata Uzbek. see Nurota
128 E1 Nurdağı Turkey
126 G5 Nur Dağları mts Turkey
190 H5 Nure r. Italy
192 B8 Nureci Sardegna Italy
Nurek Tajik. see Norak
Nurek Reservoir Tajik. see Norak, Obanbori
Nurekskoye Vodokhranilishche resr Tajik. see Norak, Obanbori
Nuremberg Ger. see Nürnberg
234 C3 Nuremberg PA U.S.A.
123 N4 Nūrestān prov. Afgh.
123 N4 Nūrestān reg. Afgh.
123 N4 Nūr Gal Afgh.
242 E3 Nuri Mex.
203 G5 Nuri Sudan
95 H5 Nuri, Teluk b. Indon.
193 K3 Nuria, Monte mt. Italy
Nuristan prov. Afgh. see Nūrestān
116 F2 Nurla Jammu and Kashmir
135 J5 Nurlat Rus. Fed.
134 J5 Nurlaty Rus. Fed.
140 T5 Nurmes Fin.
141 R6 Nurmijärvi Fin.
140 Q5 Nurmo Fin.
173 K3 Nürnberg Ger.
148 D8 Nurney Carlow Ireland
148 D7 Nurney Kildare Ireland
121 L8 Nurobad Uzbek.
120 K7 Nurota Uzbek.
121 L7 Nurota tizmasi mts Uzbek.
123 N6 Nurpur Pak.
82 C3 Nurrai Lakes salt flat S.A. Austr.

Nurri to Okeene

362

192 C8 Nurri Sardegna Italy
83 K4 Nurri, Mount hill N.S.W. Austr.
140 L4 Nursfjellet mt. Norway
Nursia Italy see Norcia
138 F3 Nurste Estonia
172 G4 Nürtingen Ger.
111 K8 Nur Turu Qinghai China
175 K3 Nurzec r. Pol.
175 L3 Nurzec-Stacja Pol.
190 C4 Nus Italy
95 H8 Nusa Kambaran, Cagar Alam nature res. Jawa Indon.
93 F5 Nusa Laut i. Maluku Indon.
95 L9 Nusa Tenggara Barat prov. Indon.
93 B8 Nusa Tenggara Timur prov. Indon.
127 J5 Nusaybin Turkey
193 O6 Nusco Italy
93 G4 Nusela, Kepulauan is Papua Indon.
197 K3 Nuşfalău Romania
108 B5 Nu Shan mts China
104 A7 Nu-shima i. Japan
123 L7 Nushki Pak.
172 F5 Nusplingen Ger.
128 G2 Nusratiye Turkey
179 J4 Nußbach Austria
173 N6 Nußdorf Ger.
173 M6 Nußdorf am Inn Ger.
178 G6 Nußdorf-Debant Austria
168 K3 Nusse Ger.
225 I1 Nutak Nfld and Lab. Can.
223 L2 Nutarawit Lake Nunavut Can.
165 I7 Nuth Neth.
171 H6 Nuthe r. Ger.
151 L5 Nuthurst West Sussex, England U.K.
235 G3 Nutley NJ U.S.A.
241 W8 Nutrioso AZ U.S.A.
123 M7 Nuttal Pak.
147 J3 Nutt's Corner Northern Ireland U.K.
84 E3 Nutwood Downs N.T. Austr.
221 M2 Nuugaatsiaap Imaa inlet Greenland
221 M2 Nuugaatsiaq Greenland
221 M3 Nuuk Greenland
138 H1 Nuuksion kansallispuisto nat. park Fin.
140 S3 Nuupas Fin.
79 □9a Nuupere, Pointe pt Moorea Fr. Polynesia
221 M2 Nuussuaq Greenland
221 M2 Nuussuaq pen. Greenland
78 □2 Nu'uuli American Samoa
117 I5 Nuwakot Nepal
125 L3 Nuway Oman
203 G2 Nuwaybi' al Muzayyinah Egypt
214 H9 Nuwekloof pass S. Africa
214 C7 Nuwerus S. Africa
214 F8 Nuweveldberge mts S. Africa
244 G8 Nuxco Mex.
192 B9 Nuxis Sardegna Italy
175 M4 Nuyno Ukr.
87 D13 Nuyts, Point W.A. Austr.
82 D5 Nuyts Archipelago is S.A. Austr.
82 D5 Nuyts Archipelago Conservation Park nature res. S.A. Austr.
87 H12 Nuytsland Nature Reserve W.A. Austr.
128 H3 Nuzayzah reg. Syria
178 A5 Nüziders Austria
114 G4 Nuzvid Andhra Prad. India
207 H5 Nwa Cameroon
212 E3 Nxai Pan National Park Botswana
212 D3 Nxaunxau Botswana
95 K4 Nyaän, Bukit hill Indon.
207 H6 Nyabessan Cameroon
87 E12 Nyabing W.A. Austr.
233 L7 Nyack NY U.S.A.
130 H3 Nyagan' Rus. Fed.
Nyagquka Sichuan China see Yajiang
Nyagrong Sichuan China see Xinlong
211 B6 Nyahua Tanz.
210 C4 Nyahururu Kenya
83 I6 Nyah West Vic. Austr.
111 K12 Nyaimai Xizang China
111 J11 Nyainqêntanglha Feng mt. Xizang China
111 J12 Nyainqêntanglha Shan mts Xizang China
111 K10 Nyainrong Xizang China
211 A5 Nyakahanga Tanz.
211 A5 Nyakahura Kagera Tanz.
211 A6 Nyaka Kangaga Tanz.
211 B5 Nyakaliro Tanz.
215 K3 Nyakallong S. Africa
211 A5 Nyakanazi Tanz.
140 O5 Nyåker Sweden
Nyakh Rus. Fed. see Nyagan'
138 I9 Nyakhachava Belarus
206 E5 Nyakrom Ghana
134 M3 Nyaksimvol' Rus. Fed.
202 E6 Nyala Sudan
Nyalam Xizang China see Congdü
140 □ Ny-Ålesund Svalbard
209 F8 Nyama Zambia
213 F3 Nyamandhiovu Zimbabwe
213 G3 Nyamapanda Zimbabwe
211 B5 Nyambiti Tanz.
211 A5 Nyamirembe Kagera Tanz.
208 E2 Nyamlell Sudan
211 C7 Nyamtumbo Tanz.
175 N3 Nyamyerzha Belarus
Nyande Zimbabwe see Masvingo
134 H3 Nyandoma Rus. Fed.
134 G3 Nyandomskiy Vozvyshennost' hills Rus. Fed.
208 A5 Nyanga Congo
209 A5 Nyanga Gabon
209 A5 Nyanga prov. Gabon
213 G3 Nyanga Zimbabwe
213 G3 Nyanga National Park Zimbabwe
111 K11 Nyangbo Xizang China
111 I12 Nyang Qu r. China
111 L12 Nyang Qu r. China
206 E4 Nyankpala Ghana
211 A5 Nyanza Rwanda
211 A6 Nyanza-Lac Burundi
95 L4 Nyapa, Gunung mt. Indon.
210 B3 Nyapongeth Sudan
116 G4 Nyar r. India
176 G4 Nyárád Hungary
222 H2 Nyarling r. N.W.T. Can.
177 I5 Nyárlőrinc Hungary
177 I4 Nyársapát Hungary
211 A5 Nyarugumba Rwanda
211 B7 Nyasa, Lake Africa
Nyasaland country Africa see Malawi
134 K2 Nyashabozh Rus. Fed.
138 J8 Nyasvizh Belarus
213 F3 Nyathi Zimbabwe
96 C6 Nyaunglebin Myanmar
96 B4 Nyaungu Myanmar
134 M3 Nyays r. Rus. Fed.
213 G3 Nyazura Zimbabwe
168 I1 Nybøl Nor b. Denmark
142 G6 Nyborg Denmark
140 T1 Nyborg Norway
140 Q4 Nyborg Sweden
143 L5 Nybro Sweden
177 H2 Nýdek Czech Rep.
221 M1 Nyeboe Land reg. Greenland
138 K8 Nyeharelaye Belarus
111 J12 Nyêmo Xizang China
Nyenchen Tanglha Range mts Xizang China see Nyainqêntanglha Shan
210 C5 Nyeri Kenya
210 B2 Nyerol Sudan
138 M6 Nyeshcharda, Vozyera l. Belarus
140 □ Ny-Friesland reg. Svalbard
143 K1 Nyhammar Sweden
111 H9 Nyi, Co l. Xizang China
211 B7 Nyika National Park Zambia
211 B7 Nyika Plateau Malawi
111 H11 Nyima Xizang China
111 K11 Nyima Xizang China
211 A8 Nyimba Zambia
111 L12 Nyingchi Xizang China
111 J11 Nyingzhong Xizang China
Nyinma Gansu China see Maqu
177 L4 Nyírábrány Hungary
177 K4 Nyíracsád Hungary
176 G4 Nyirád Hungary
177 K4 Nyíradony Hungary
211 A5 Nyiragongo vol. Dem. Rep. Congo
177 L4 Nyírbátor Hungary
177 L4 Nyírbéltek Hungary
177 L4 Nyírbogát Hungary
177 K3 Nyírbogdány Hungary
177 L4 Nyírcsászári Hungary
177 K4 Nyíregyháza Hungary
177 K4 Nyírgelse Hungary
211 C5 Nyiri Desert Kenya
177 L4 Nyírlugos Hungary
177 K4 Nyírmártonfalva Hungary
177 K4 Nyírmihálydi Hungary
177 K3 Nyírtelek Hungary
177 K3 Nyírtét Hungary
177 K3 Nyírtura Hungary
210 C4 Nyiru, Mount Kenya
177 L4 Nyírvasvári Hungary
140 Q5 Nykarleby Fin.
142 H7 Nykøbing Denmark
142 E5 Nykøbing Mors Denmark
142 H6 Nykøbing Sjælland Denmark
143 N3 Nyköping Sweden
143 K2 Nykroppa Sweden
143 N2 Nykvarn Sweden
134 B3 Nyland Sweden
83 K5 Nymagee N.S.W. Austr.
83 N3 Nymboida N.S.W. Austr.
83 N3 Nymboida National Park N.S.W. Austr.
176 E1 Nymburk Czech Rep.
142 E6 Nymindegab Denmark
143 N3 Nynäshamn Sweden
83 K4 Nyngan N.S.W. Austr.
111 F11 Nyogzê Xizang China
105 K2 Nyohō-san mt. Japan
159 J6 Nyoiseau France
215 M8 Nyokana S. Africa
138 G8 Nyoman r. Belarus alt. Neman (Rus. Fed.) alt. Nemunas (Lith.)
138 I8 Nyomanskaya Nizina lowland Belarus
190 A3 Nyon Switz.
207 H6 Nyong r. Cameroon
161 G8 Nyons France
170 F1 Nyord i. Denmark
170 E1 Nyråd Denmark
176 C2 Nýřany Czech Rep.
134 L3 Nyrob Rus. Fed.
176 C2 Nýrsko Czech Rep.
140 T2 Nyrud Norway
174 F5 Nysa Pol.
174 F5 Nysa Kłodzka r. Pol.
142 I2 Nysäter Sweden
140 L5 Nysätern Sweden
100 M3 Nysh Sakhalin Rus. Fed.
142 I2 Nysockensjön l. Sweden
238 F5 Nyssa OR U.S.A.
Nystad Fin. see Uusikaupunki
142 H7 Nysted Denmark
134 J3 Nyuchpas Rus. Fed.
102 Q7 Nyūdō-zaki pt Japan
105 H4 Nyūgasa-yama mt. Japan
177 K4 Nyugati-főcsatorna canal Hungary
104 F3 Nyūkawa Japan
134 I3 Nyukhcha Rus. Fed.
134 I3 Nyuksenitsa Rus. Fed.
177 G4 Nyúl Hungary
209 F6 Nyunzu Dem. Rep. Congo
131 M3 Nyurba Rus. Fed.
134 J3 Nyuvchim Rus. Fed.
131 M3 Nyuya Rus. Fed.
131 M3 Nyuya r. Rus. Fed.
104 G2 Nyūzen Japan
137 M8 Nyva Ukr.
100 M1 Nyvrovo Rus. Fed.
175 M5 Nyvytsi Ukr.
100 M2 Nyyskiy Zaliv lag. Sakhalin Rus. Fed.
136 B4 Nyzhankovychi Ukr.
137 N7 Nyzhni Sirohozy Ukr.
137 N7 Nyzhni Torhayi Ukr.
136 C5 Nyzhni Vorota Ukr.
136 C5 Nyzhniy Bystryy Ukr.
137 S5 Nyzhniy Nahol'chyk Ukr.
137 N8 Nyzhn'ohirs'kyy Ukr.
137 R4 Nyzhnya Dubanka Ukr.
137 N3 Nyzhnya Syrovatka Ukr.
137 O5 Nyzhnya Tersa r. Ukr.
177 M2 Nyzhnya Vysots'ke Ukr.
177 L2 Nyzhnya Yablun'ka Ukr.
137 N3 Nyzy Ukr.
208 D3 Nzako C.A.R.
209 A5 Nzambi Congo
208 F3 Nzara Sudan
206 C4 Nzébéla Guinea
211 B6 Nzega Tanz.
206 C5 Nzérékoré Guinea
209 B6 N'zeto Angola
206 D5 Nzi r. Côte d'Ivoire
209 E7 Nzilo, Lac l. Dem. Rep. Congo
209 E5 Nzingu Dem. Rep. Congo
206 D5 Nzo r. Côte d'Ivoire
206 D5 N'Zo, Réserve de Faune du nature res. Côte d'Ivoire
209 B6 Nzobe Dem. Rep. Congo
210 B4 Nzoia r. Kenya
208 F4 Nzoro r. Dem. Rep. Congo
217 □3 Nzwani i. Comoros

O

236 F4 Oacoma SD U.S.A.
151 J2 Oadby Leicestershire, England U.K.
236 E3 Oahe, Lake SD U.S.A.
240 □D12 O'ahu i. HI U.S.A.
Oaitupu i. Tuvalu see Vaitupu
82 H5 Oakbank S.A. Austr.
233 O7 Oak Bluffs MA U.S.A.
241 T2 Oak City UT U.S.A.
226 G7 Oak Creek WI U.S.A.
240 L4 Oakdale CA U.S.A.
235 K2 Oakdale CT U.S.A.
237 I10 Oakdale LA U.S.A.
235 I3 Oakdale NY U.S.A.
150 H2 Oakengates Telford and Wrekin, England U.K.
236 F2 Oakes ND U.S.A.
85 M9 Oakey Qld Austr.
232 G5 Oakfield NY U.S.A.
234 F4 Oakford PA U.S.A.
237 J9 Oak Grove LA U.S.A.
226 J5 Oak Grove MI U.S.A.
151 K2 Oakham Rutland, England U.K.
232 B7 Oak Harbor OH U.S.A.
238 C2 Oak Harbor WA U.S.A.
232 C10 Oak Hill OH U.S.A.
232 D11 Oak Hill WV U.S.A.
240 M4 Oakhurst CA U.S.A.
235 G4 Oakhurst NJ U.S.A.
226 D3 Oak Island WI U.S.A.
240 L7 Oak Knolls CA U.S.A.
223 K5 Oak Lake Man. Can.
240 J4 Oakland CA U.S.A.
232 F9 Oakland MD U.S.A.
233 □P4 Oakland ME U.S.A.
236 G5 Oakland NE U.S.A.
235 G2 Oakland NJ U.S.A.
238 C5 Oakland OR U.S.A.
240 J4 Oakland airport CA U.S.A.
230 D6 Oakland City IN U.S.A.
83 K6 Oaklands N.S.W. Austr.
226 G8 Oak Lawn IL U.S.A.
151 K3 Oakley Bedfordshire, England U.K.
151 J4 Oakley Buckinghamshire, England U.K.
146 I10 Oakley Fife, Scotland U.K.
151 J5 Oakley Hampshire, England U.K.
236 E6 Oakley KS U.S.A.
227 J6 Oakley MI U.S.A.
232 F8 Oakmont PA U.S.A.
86 F6 Oakover r. W.A. Austr.
226 G8 Oak Park IL U.S.A.
235 G2 Oak Ridge NJ U.S.A.
238 C5 Oakridge OR U.S.A.
231 E7 Oak Ridge TN U.S.A.
234 E4 Oaks PA U.S.A.
234 F5 Oak Shade NJ U.S.A.
80 H6 Oakura North I. N.Z.
82 H5 Oakvale S.A. Austr.
240 M7 Oak View CA U.S.A.
224 E5 Oakville Ont. Can.
235 I1 Oakville CT U.S.A.
232 A7 Oakwood OH U.S.A.
232 A9 Oakwood OH U.S.A.
234 D5 Oakwood Beach NJ U.S.A.
81 E12 Oamaru South I. N.Z.
105 L4 Ōamishirasato Japan
80 H6 Oaonui North I. N.Z.
105 M3 Ōarai Japan
81 H9 Oaro South I. N.Z.
182 C4 O Arrabal Spain
103 J12 Ōasa Japan
105 K3 Ōashi-gawa r. Japan
240 O4 Oasis CA U.S.A.
238 G6 Oasis NV U.S.A.
197 L2 Oaşului, Munţii mts Romania
Oates Coast reg. Antarctica see Oates Land
263 K2 Oates Land reg. Antarctica
83 K10 Oatlands Tas. Austr.
214 I8 Oatlands S. Africa
245 K8 Oaxaca Mex.
245 K8 Oaxaca state Mex.
121 M1 Ob' r. Rus. Fed.
Ob, Gulf of sea chan. Rus. Fed. see Obskaya Guba
224 C3 Oba Ont. Can.
Oba i. Vanuatu see Aoba
Obaghan r. Kazakh. see Ubagan
104 C7 Obako-dake mt. Japan
128 A2 Obaköy Turkey
138 M6 Obal' Vitsyebskaya Voblasts' Belarus
138 M6 Obal' Vitsyebskaya Voblasts' Belarus
138 M6 Obal' canal Belarus
207 H5 Obala Cameroon
227 J1 Oba Lake Ont. Can.
104 C5 Obama Japan
104 C4 Obama-wan b. Japan
207 H5 Oban Nigeria
146 F10 Oban Argyll and Bute, Scotland U.K.
102 R8 Obanazawa Japan
207 H5 Oban Hills mt. Nigeria
104 F5 Obara Japan
182 G4 O Barco Spain
183 N3 Obarenes, Montes mts Spain
197 P4 Obârşeni, Dealul hill Romania
104 E6 Obata Japan
129 D5 Obayayla Turkey
Obbia Somalia see Hobyo
140 P5 Obbola Sweden
197 N3 Obcina Mare ridge Romania
179 K5 Obdach Austria
164 G3 Obdam Neth.
Obdorsk Rus. Fed. see Salekhard
176 C2 Obecnice Czech Rep.
Óbecse Vojvodina Serbia see Bečej
222 G4 Obed Alta Can.
185 J4 Obejo Spain
129 A5 Öbektaş Turkey
138 I6 Obeliai Lith.
175 L1 Obelija l. Lith.
81 D12 Obelisk mt. South I. N.Z.
258 G2 Oberá Arg.
179 L5 Oberaich Austria
178 H4 Oberalm Austria
190 F2 Oberalpstock mt. Switz.
173 K6 Oberammergau Ger.
173 J3 Oberasbach Ger.
173 K6 Oberau Ger.
173 M6 Oberaudorf Ger.
169 H9 Oberaula Ger.
173 L6 Oberbayern admin. reg. Ger.
172 F3 Oberderdingen Ger.
173 L5 Oberding Ger.
169 J8 Oberdorla Ger.
178 G6 Oberdrauburg Austria
172 F5 Obere Donau park Ger.
190 H1 Oberegg Switz.
169 J10 Oberelsbach Ger.
190 H2 Ober Engadin reg. Switz.
190 E1 Oberentfelden Switz.
173 N3 Oberer Bayerischer Wald park Ger.
171 E9 Obere Saale park Ger.
172 H6 Oberessendorf Ger.
171 G10 Oberes Westerzgebirge park Ger.
169 D10 Oberfell Ger.
171 D11 Oberfranken admin. reg. Ger.
169 J6 Oberg (Lahstedt) Ger.
190 D1 Obergösgen Switz.
179 M3 Ober-Grafendorf Austria
173 K5 Obergriesbach Ger.
173 I6 Obergünzburg Ger.
178 D6 Obergurgl Austria
171 J8 Obergurig Ger.
179 L6 Oberhaag Austria
173 L5 Oberhaching Ger.
173 J2 Oberhaid Ger.
172 E5 Oberharmersbach Ger.
173 K4 Oberhausen Bayern Ger.
169 C8 Oberhausen Nordrhein-Westfalen Ger.
169 K9 Oberhof Ger.
190 D2 Oberhofen Switz.
178 D5 Oberhofen im Inntal Austria
157 O6 Oberhoffen-sur-Moder France
178 B4 Oberjochpass pass Austria/Ger.
172 E4 Oberkirch Ger.
173 I4 Oberkochen Ger.
171 E10 Oberkotzau Ger.
168 D5 Oberlangen Ger.
171 J8 Oberlausitz reg. Ger.
171 J8 Oberlausitzer Bergland park Ger.
171 J8 Oberlichtenau Ger.
178 G6 Oberlienz Austria
236 E6 Oberlin KS U.S.A.
237 I10 Oberlin LA U.S.A.
232 C7 Oberlin OH U.S.A.
172 H5 Obermarchtal Ger.
169 J9 Obermaßfeld-Grimmenthal Ger.
172 D2 Obermoschel Ger.
157 N7 Obernai France
179 H3 Obernberg am Inn Austria
172 G2 Obernburg am Main Ger.
173 J4 Oberndorf am Lech Ger.
172 F5 Oberndorf am Neckar Ger.
179 L3 Oberndorf an der Melk Austria
178 G4 Oberndorf bei Salzburg Austria
179 J3 Oberneukirchen Austria
169 J7 Obernfeld Ger.
172 F5 Obernheim Ger.
172 D3 Obernheim-Kirchenarnbach Ger.
169 H6 Obernkirchen Ger.
173 P4 Obernzell Ger.
173 I3 Obernzenn Ger.
171 K9 Oberoderwitz Ger.
172 E2 Ober-Olm Ger.
83 L5 Oberon N.S.W. Austr.
173 J6 Oberostendorf Ger.
179 I3 Oberösterreich land Austria
173 L2 Oberpfalz admin. reg. Ger.
173 M2 Oberpfälzer Wald mts Ger.
176 B2 Oberpfälzer Wald park Ger.
173 L5 Oberpframmern Ger.
179 O4 Oberpullendorf Austria
172 F2 Ober-Ramstadt Ger.
172 H6 Oberreute Ger.
172 D6 Oberried Ger.
173 I5 Oberrieden Ger.
190 H1 Oberriet Switz.
171 D8 Oberröblingen Ger.
172 F2 Ober-Roden Ger.
171 D8 Oberroßla Ger.
172 H3 Oberrot Ger.
172 D5 Oberrotweil Ger.
173 L5 Oberschleißheim Ger.
173 N4 Oberschneiding Ger.
171 H9 Oberschöna Ger.
179 N5 Oberschützen Austria
179 O3 Obersiebenbrunn Austria
190 E1 Obersiggenthal Switz.
169 I10 Obersinn Ger.
172 H3 Obersontheim Ger.
169 K8 Oberspier Ger.
172 H5 Oberstadion Ger.
173 I6 Oberstaufen Ger.
173 I7 Oberstdorf Ger.
172 G3 Oberstenfeld Ger.
173 M5 Obertaufkirchen Ger.
172 G6 Oberteuringen Ger.
172 C2 Oberthal Ger.
169 I10 Oberthulba Ger.
178 G6 Obertilliach Austria
173 M4 Obertraubling Ger.
173 K2 Obertrubach Ger.
178 H4 Obertrum am See Austria
178 H4 Obertrumer See l. Austria
169 G10 Obertshausen Ger.
136 E5 Obertyn Ukr.
170 I4 Oberueckersee l. Ger.
169 G10 Oberursel (Taunus) Ger.
178 H6 Obervellach Austria
173 M3 Oberviechtach Ger.
190 E2 Oberwald Switz.
169 H7 Oberwälder Land reg. Ger.
179 N4 Oberwaltersdorf Austria
179 N5 Oberwart Austria
169 E10 Oberwesel Ger.
179 M3 Oberwölbling Austria
172 E5 Oberwolfach Ger.
179 J5 Oberwölz Austria
137 N2 Obesta r. Rus. Fed.
171 E8 Obhausen Ger.
93 E4 Obi i. Maluku Indon.
207 H4 Obi Nigeria
93 E4 Obi, Kepulauan is Maluku Indon.
93 E4 Obi, Selat sea chan. Maluku Indon.
251 H5 Óbidos Brazil
184 A2 Óbidos Port.
184 A2 Óbidos, Lagoa de lag. Port.
123 M2 Obigarm Tajik.
102 U4 Obihiro Japan
93 E4 Obilatu i. Maluku Indon.
196 J8 Obilić Kosovo Serbia
135 I7 Obil'noye Rus. Fed.
173 M5 Obing Ger.
237 K7 Obion r. TN U.S.A.
102 S2 Obira Japan
250 D2 Obispos Venez.
261 F2 Obispo Trejo Arg.
Obitochnaya Kosa spit Ukr. see Obytichna Kosa
105 K5 Obitsu-gawa r. Japan
162 G5 Objat France
174 F1 Objazda Pol.
175 M4 Oblapy Ukr.
179 I5 Öblarn Austria
135 H6 Oblivskaya Rus. Fed.
100 G4 Obluch'ye Rus. Fed.
139 T6 Obninsk Rus. Fed.
208 E3 Obo C.A.R.
106 G8 Obo Qinghai China
214 E3 Obobogorap S. Africa
210 D2 Obock Djibouti
136 I5 Obodivka Ukr.
101 F8 Ŏbŏk N. Korea
208 E5 Obokote Dem. Rep. Congo
110 K7 Obo Liang Qinghai China
207 G5 Obolo Nigeria
182 F4 O Bolo Spain
137 L4 Obolon' Ukr.
186 D6 Obón Spain
95 K2 Obong, Gunung mt. Malaysia
177 K3 Oborín Slovakia
174 E3 Oborniki Pol.
174 E4 Oborniki Śląskie Pol.
208 B5 Obouya Congo
135 G6 Oboyan' Rus. Fed.
134 H3 Obozerskiy Rus. Fed.
117 I7 Obra Uttar Prad. India
174 D3 Obra r. Pol.
258 F3 Obrage Arg.
242 E4 Obregón, Presa resr Mex.
223 K2 Obre Lake N.W.T. Can.
196 I6 Obrenovac Serbia
238 C5 O'Brien OR U.S.A.
172 G3 Obrigheim Ger.
172 E2 Obrigheim (Pfalz) Ger.
Obringa r. Switz. see Aare
176 C1 Obrnice Czech Rep.
197 Q7 Obrochishte Bulg.
191 Q4 Obrov Slovenia
174 G3 Obrowo Pol.
126 F4 Obruk Turkey
174 E4 Obry, Kanał canal Pol.
175 J3 Obryte Pol.
174 E3 Obrzycko Pol.
82 D3 Observatory Hill S.A. Austr.
222 D4 Observatory Inlet B.C. Can.
82 □2 Observatory Rock i. Lord Howe I. Austr.
139 P6 Obsha r. Rus. Fed.
120 D2 Obshchiy Syrt hills Rus. Fed.
130 I3 Obskaya Guba sea chan. Rus. Fed.
175 K5 Obsza Pol.
137 M2 Obtove Ukr.
104 E5 Ōbu Japan
206 E5 Obuasi Ghana
207 H5 Obubra Nigeria
188 G3 Obudovac Bos.-Herz.
207 H5 Obudu Nigeria
136 J3 Obukhiv Ukr.
Obukhov Ukr. see Obukhiv
139 V6 Obukhovo Rus. Fed.
105 H2 Obuse Japan
134 K4 Obva r. Rus. Fed.
190 E2 Obwalden canton Switz.
134 J3 Ob"yachevo Rus. Fed.
137 P7 Obytichna Kosa spit Ukr.
137 O7 Obytichna Zakota b. Ukr.
182 F2 O Cádavo Spain
231 F11 Ocala FL U.S.A.
182 C5 O Calvario Spain
242 E3 Ocampo Chihuahua Mex.
242 H4 Ocampo Coahuila Mex.
244 F4 Ocampo Guanajuato Mex.
245 H3 Ocampo Tamaulipas Mex.
182 D2 O Campo da Feira Spain
250 C2 Ocaña Col.
192 B4 Ocana Corse France
252 B3 Ocaña Peru
183 N9 Ocaña Spain
183 N9 Ocaña, Mesa de plat. Spain
182 D4 O Carballiño Spain
182 D4 O Castelo Spain
182 D3 O Castro Spain
182 E3 O Castro de Ferreira Spain
191 L6 Occhiobello Italy
193 N4 Occhito, Lago di l. Italy
252 C4 Occidental, Cordillera mts Chile
250 B4 Occidental, Cordillera mts Col.
252 C4 Occidental, Cordillera mts Peru
190 F5 Occimiano Italy
232 H10 Occoquan VA U.S.A.
232 D11 Oceana WV U.S.A.
235 I3 Ocean Beach NY U.S.A.
222 B3 Ocean Cape AK U.S.A.
246 D1 Ocean Cay i. Bahamas
233 J10 Ocean City MD U.S.A.
234 F6 Ocean City NJ U.S.A.
235 G5 Ocean County county NJ U.S.A.
222 E4 Ocean Falls B.C. Can.
235 G5 Ocean Gate NJ U.S.A.
235 G4 Ocean Grove NJ U.S.A.
74 Oceania continent
Ocean Island Kiribati see Banaba
Ocean Island atoll HI U.S.A. see Kure Atoll
240 L6 Oceano CA U.S.A.
240 O8 Oceanside CA U.S.A.
237 K10 Ocean Springs MS U.S.A.
234 F6 Ocean View NJ U.S.A.
235 G6 Oceanville NJ U.S.A.
183 N6 Ocejón mt. Spain
78 □4a Ocha i. Chuuk Micronesia
78 □4a Ocha, Mochun sea chan. Chuuk Micronesia
186 C2 Ochagavía Spain
137 K7 Ochakiv Ukr.
129 C3 Och'amch'ire Georgia
182 E2 O Chao Spain
134 K4 Ocher Rus. Fed.
136 I4 Ocheretnya Ukr.
137 O6 Ocheretuvate Ukr.
157 K6 Ochey France
198 F4 Ochi mt. Greece
103 J11 Ōchi Japan
102 W3 Ochiishi-misaki pt Japan
146 I10 Ochil Hills Scotland U.K.
146 H12 Ochiltree East Ayrshire, Scotland U.K.
137 M1 Ochkyne Ukr.
231 E11 Ochlockonee r. GA U.S.A.
175 H3 Ochnia r. Pol.
168 E4 Ocholt Ger.
246 □ Ocho Rios Jamaica
Ochrida, Lake Albania/Macedonia see Ohrid, Lake
173 I2 Ochsenfurt Ger.
172 H5 Ochsenhausen Ger.
169 D10 Ochtendung Ger.
171 D6 Ochtmersleben Ger.
169 D6 Ochtrup Ger.
231 F10 Ocilla GA U.S.A.
141 N6 Ockelbo Sweden
168 G1 Ockholm Ger.
146 E9 Ockle Highland, Scotland U.K.
197 N4 Ocland Romania
231 F10 Ocmulgee r. GA U.S.A.
197 L4 Ocna Mureş Romania
197 M5 Ocna Sibiului Romania
136 G5 Ocniţa Moldova
197 N4 Ocolaşul Mare, Vârful mt. Romania
252 B4 Ocoña Peru
231 F9 Oconee, Lake resr GA U.S.A.
85 I6 O'Connell Creek r. Qld Austr.
226 F6 Oconomowoc WI U.S.A.
226 G5 Oconto WI U.S.A.
226 F5 Oconto Falls WI U.S.A.
182 C4 O Convento Spain
182 F3 O Corgo Spain
242 E5 Ocoroni Mex.
252 C3 Ocoruro Peru
243 M10 Ocos Guat.
243 M9 Ocosingo Mex.
242 □P11 Ocotal Nic.
245 K9 Ocotepec Mex.
244 E5 Ocotlán Jalisco Mex.
245 K9 Ocotlán Oaxaca Mex.
177 I3 Očová Slovakia
243 M9 Ocozocoautla Mex.
182 E9 Ocreza r. Port.
177 I4 Ócsa Hungary
177 I4 Ocsai park Hungary
177 H5 Őcsény Hungary
177 J5 Öcsöd Hungary
158 H2 Octeville France
159 L2 Octeville-sur-Mer France
October Revolution Island Severnaya Zemlya Rus. Fed. see Oktyabr'skoy Revolyutsii, Ostrov
234 C5 Octoraro Creek r. MD U.S.A.
234 C5 Octoraro Lake PA U.S.A.
242 □S14 Ocú Panama
213 H2 Ocua Moz.
245 H7 Ocuilan de Arteaga Mex.
247 J8 Ocumare del Tuy Venez.
252 D4 Ocurí Bol.
174 G2 Ocypel Pol.
206 E5 Oda Ghana
103 J11 Ōda Japan
203 H4 Oda, Jebel mt. Sudan
128 E2 Odabaşı Turkey
140 □E1 Ódáðahraun lava field Iceland
101 F8 Ŏdaejin N. Korea
101 F10 Odae-san National Park S. Korea
104 D7 Ōdai Japan
104 D7 Ōdaigahara-zan mt. Japan
104 G4 Odaira-tōge pass Japan
102 R9 Odaka Japan
226 D3 Odanah WI U.S.A.
102 R6 Ōdate Japan
105 J5 Odawara Japan
142 C1 Odda Norway
142 G6 Odder Denmark
146 □O1 Oddsta Shetland, Scotland U.K.
184 D4 Odearce r. Port.
184 B6 Odeceixe Port.
223 L3 Odei r. Man. Can.
184 E6 Odeleite Port.
184 E6 Odeleite r. Port.
226 F8 Odell IL U.S.A.
184 C6 Odelouca r. Port.
173 K5 Odelzhausen Ger.
237 G12 Odem TX U.S.A.
184 B5 Odemira Port.
199 I4 Ödemiş Turkey
186 I4 Òdena Spain
Ödenburg Hungary see Sopron
215 K3 Odendaalsrus S. Africa
143 L2 Odensbacken Sweden
142 G6 Odense Denmark
142 G6 Odense Fjord b. Denmark
234 B6 Odenton MD U.S.A.
172 F2 Odenwald reg. Ger.
174 C2 Oder r. Ger. alt. Odra (Poland)
169 I7 Oder r. Ger.
170 J5 Oderberg Ger.
170 J5 Oderbruch reg. Ger.
170 J2 Oderbucht b. Ger.
170 J3 Oderhaff b. Ger.
170 H5 Oder-Havel-Kanal canal Ger.
171 I6 Oderin Ger.
172 D2 Odernheim am Glan Ger.
191 M4 Oderzo Italy
136 J7 Odesa Ukr.
134 K3 Odesdino Rus. Fed.
143 K3 Ödeshog Sweden
136 I6 Odes'ka Oblast' admin. div. Ukr.
Odessa Ukr. see Odesa
234 D6 Odessa DE U.S.A.
237 D10 Odessa TX U.S.A.
238 E3 Odessa WA U.S.A.
Odessa Oblast admin. div. Ukr. see Odes'ka Oblast'
Odesskaya Oblast' admin. div. Ukr. see Odes'ka Oblast'
121 O1 Odesskoye Rus. Fed.
Odessus Bulg. see Varna
158 C6 Odet r. France
203 H5 Odi watercourse Sudan
184 B6 Odiáxere Port.
184 F6 Odiel r. Spain
206 D4 Odienné Côte d'Ivoire
151 K5 Odiham Hampshire, England U.K.
164 H4 Odijk Neth.
208 A5 Odimba Gabon
139 U6 Odintsovo Rus. Fed.
184 C4 Odivelas Beja Port.
184 A3 Odivelas Lisboa Port.
184 C4 Odivelas r. Port.
184 C4 Odivelas, Barragem de resr Port.
197 P5 Odobeşti Romania
197 O5 Odobeştilor, Măgura hill Romania
174 F4 Odolanów Pol.
171 J10 Odolena Voda Czech Rep.
262 T2 Odom Inlet Antarctica
159 K3 Odon r. France
183 Q7 Odón Spain
97 G9 Ŏdôngk Cambodia
164 K3 Odoorn Neth.
197 N4 Odorheiu Secuiesc Romania
139 T8 Odoyev Rus. Fed.
174 C2 Odra r. Pol. alt. Oder (Germany)
183 L4 Odra r. Spain
137 N7 Odradivka Ukr.
177 G2 Odry Czech Rep.
175 I4 Odrzywół Pol.
196 H5 Odžaci Vojvodina Serbia
208 B4 Odzala, Parc National d' nat. park Congo
213 G3 Odzi Zimbabwe
213 G3 Odzi r. Zimbabwe
104 B5 Ōe Japan
Oea Libya see Ţarābulus
169 K6 Oebisfelde Ger.
169 I7 Oedelsheim (Oberweser) Ger.
171 H9 Oederan Ger.
168 H3 Oederquart Ger.
103 G11 Oedong S. Korea
164 I5 Oeffelt Neth.
164 G4 Oegstgeest Neth.
254 E3 Oeiras Brazil
184 A3 Oeiras Port.
184 D5 Oeiras r. Port.
169 F7 Oelde Ger.
168 I3 Oelixdorf Ger.
236 D4 Oelrichs SD U.S.A.
171 F10 Oelsnitz Sachsen Ger.
171 G9 Oelsnitz Sachsen Ger.
236 J4 Oelwein IA U.S.A.
164 J4 Oene Neth.
84 D2 Oenpelli N.T. Austr.
190 D1 Oensingen Switz.
168 H4 Oerel Ger.
168 J3 Oering Ger.
169 J10 Oerlenbach Ger.
169 G7 Oerlinghausen Ger.
Oesel i. Estonia see Hiiumaa
165 I9 Oesling hills Lux.
165 F6 Oesterdam barrage Neth.
258 E2 Oetling Arg.
171 E9 Oettersdorf Ger.
173 J4 Oettingen in Bayern Ger.
178 C5 Oetz Austria
168 K4 Oetzen Ger.
225 F2 Oeufs, Lac des l. Que. Can.
168 H1 Oeversee Ger.
104 B5 Ōe-yama hill Japan
163 B8 Œyreluy France
127 J3 Of Turkey
238 L3 O'Fallon r. MT U.S.A.
193 Q5 Ofanto r. Italy
128 C7 Ofaqim Israel
193 L3 Ofena Italy
207 G4 Offa Nigeria
147 G6 Offaly county Ireland
190 H5 Offanengo Italy
157 M8 Offemont France
169 G10 Offenbach am Main Ger.
172 E3 Offenbach an der Queich Ger.
173 N4 Offenberg Ger.
172 D5 Offenburg Ger.
179 I4 Offensee l. Austria
140 M5 Offerdal Sweden
193 L2 Offida Italy
173 I5 Offingen Ger.
156 B4 Offranville France
199 H6 Ofidoussa i. Greece
79 □8 Ofolanga atoll Tonga
182 D3 O Forte Spain
140 N2 Ofotfjorden sea chan. Norway
172 G5 Ofterdingen Ger.
78 □2 Ofu i. American Samoa
102 S7 Ōfunato Japan
95 K4 Oga r. Indon.
102 Q7 Oga Japan
102 R7 Ogachi Japan
105 K1 Oga-dake mt. Japan
210 E3 Ogadēn reg. Eth.
102 Q7 Oga-hantō pen. Japan
104 E5 Ōgaki Japan
236 E5 Ogallala NE U.S.A.
94 F6 Ogan r. Indon.
105 J3 Ogano Japan
105 H6 Ogasa Japan
103 □2 Ogasawara-shotō is N. Pacific Ocean
227 P2 Ogascanane, Lac l. Que. Can.
105 H1 Ōgata Japan
105 H3 Ōga-tō mt. Japan
105 M1 Ogawa Fukushima Japan
105 L3 Ogawa Ibaraki Japan
105 L2 Ogawa Ibaraki Japan
105 G2 Ogawa Nagano Japan
105 J3 Ogawa Saitama Japan
105 L2 Ōgawa Japan
102 R8 Ōgawara Japan
102 S6 Ogawara-ko l. Japan
207 G4 Ogbomosho Nigeria
Ogbomoso Nigeria see Ogbomosho
236 H4 Ogden IA U.S.A.
238 I6 Ogden UT U.S.A.
222 C3 Ogden, Mount B.C. Can.
234 F2 Ogdensburg NJ U.S.A.
233 J4 Ogdensburg NY U.S.A.
231 G10 Ogeechee r. GA U.S.A.
226 D4 Ogema WI U.S.A.
168 E3 Ogenbargen Ger.
156 H6 Oger France
163 C9 Ogeu-les-Bains France
157 M6 Ogéviller France
190 G4 Oggiono Italy
116 D7 Oghna Rajasthan India
78 □6 Ogho Choiseul Solomon Is
103 P9 Ogi Japan
224 C4 Ogidaki Ont. Can.
220 E3 Ogilvie r. Y.T. Can.
220 D3 Ogilvie Mountains Y.T. Can.
102 □1 Ogimi Okinawa Japan
129 D6 Oğlaksuyu Turkey
122 F2 Oglanly Turkm.
204 E5 'Oglât el Khnâchîch well Mali
204 D4 Oglat Sbot well Alg.
192 D8 Ogliastra prov. Sardegna Italy
192 D8 Ogliastra reg. Sardegna Italy
192 D8 Ogliastra, Isola dell' i. Sardegna Italy
192 C2 Ogliastro Corse France
194 H9 Ogliastro, Lago di l. Sicilia Italy
190 J5 Oglio r. Italy
100 K2 Oglongi Rus. Fed.
85 L7 Ogmore Qld Austr.
150 E5 Ogmore Vale of Glamorgan, Wales U.K.
150 E4 Ogmore Vale Bridgend, Wales U.K.
160 G2 Ognon r. France
Oğnut Turkey see Göynük
105 J3 Ōgo Japan
93 B3 Ogoamas, Gunung mt. Indon.
105 J4 Ogōchi-damu dam Japan
100 H2 Ogodzha Rus. Fed.
207 H5 Ogoja Nigeria
224 C3 Ogoki r. Ont. Can.
224 C3 Ogoki Lake Ont. Can.
224 B3 Ogoki Reservoir Ont. Can.
100 M5 Ogon'ki Rus. Fed.
183 O2 Ogoño, Cabo c. Spain
208 A5 Ogooué r. Gabon
208 B5 Ogooué-Ivindo prov. Gabon
208 B5 Ogooué-Lolo prov. Gabon
208 A5 Ogooué-Maritime prov. Gabon
103 I12 Ogōri Japan
100 F1 Ogoron Rus. Fed.
105 J4 Ogose Japan
197 L7 Ogosta r. Bulg.
207 F5 Ogou r. Togo
87 D11 O'Grady, Lake salt flat W.A. Austr.
197 K9 Ograždеn mts Bulg./Macedonia
Ograzhden mts Bulg./Macedonia see Ograždеn
138 H5 Ogre Latvia
138 H5 Ogre r. Latvia
175 J3 Ogrodniki Pol.
175 H5 Ogrodzieniec Pol.
171 J7 Ogrosen Ger.
182 C4 O Grove Spain
104 E5 Ōguchi Japan
139 V5 Ogudnevo Rus. Fed.
204 E4 Oguîlet Merzoug well Mali
188 E3 Ogulin Croatia
207 F5 Ogun state Nigeria
105 I1 Oguni Japan
233 □O5 Ogunquit ME U.S.A.
122 E2 Ogurjaly Adasy i. Turkm.
129 I4 Oğuz Azer.
129 I1 Oguzer Rus. Fed.
177 K5 Ohaba Lungă Romania
207 G5 Ohafia Nigeria
81 B12 Ohai South I. N.Z.
80 J6 Ohakune North I. N.Z.
210 E3 Ohale well Somalia
185 N6 Ohanes Spain
205 H3 Ohanet Alg.
212 C3 Ohangwena admin. reg. Namibia
105 L5 Ōhara Japan
102 S5 Ōhata Japan
80 J7 Ohau North I. N.Z.
81 E11 Ohau r. South I. N.Z.
81 D11 Ohau, Lake South I. N.Z.
80 J4 Ohaupo North I. N.Z.
Ohcejohka Fin. see Utsjoki
168 E4 Ohe r. Ger.
173 O4 Ohe r. Ger.
Ohétéroah i. Îs Australes Fr. Polynesia see Rurutu
165 H8 Ohey Belgium
252 C5 O'Higgins Chile
260 B4 O'Higgins admin. reg. Chile
259 B8 O'Higgins, Lago l. Chile
80 J4 Ohinewai North I. N.Z.
226 E8 Ohio IL U.S.A.
236 K7 Ohio r. OH/WV U.S.A.
232 C8 Ohio state U.S.A.
232 A8 Ohio City OH U.S.A.
262 Q1 Ohio Range mts Antarctica
235 G1 Ohioville NY U.S.A.
105 K3 Ōhira Japan
105 I5 Ōhito Japan
80 L4 Ohiwa Harbour North I. N.Z.
137 O4 Ohiyivka Ukr.
172 D5 Ohlsbach Ger.
179 I4 Ohlsdorf Austria
173 K6 Ohlstadt Ger.
169 G9 Ohm r. Ger.
138 J3 Õhne r. Estonia
169 D6 Ohne Ger.
172 F6 Öhningen Ger.
79 □8 'Ohonua Tonga
80 L4 Ohope North I. N.Z.
177 G3 Ohrady Slovakia
169 K9 Ohrdruf Ger.
176 D1 Ohře r. Czech Rep.
171 E6 Ohre r. Ger.
196 I9 Ohrid Macedonia
196 I9 Ohrid, Lake Albania/Macedonia
Ohridsko Ezero l. Albania/Macedonia see Ohrid, Lake
213 F5 Ohrigstad S. Africa
172 G3 Öhringen Ger.
Ohrit, Liqeni i l. Albania/Macedonia see Ohrid, Lake
169 K6 Ohrum Ger.
80 I5 Ohura North I. N.Z.
104 C5 Ōi Fukui Japan
105 J5 Ōi Kanagawa Japan
182 C7 Oiã Port.
251 I4 Oiapoque Brazil
186 B1 Oiartzun Spain
250 C3 Oiba Col.
146 G8 Oich r. Scotland U.K.
146 G8 Oich, Loch l. Scotland U.K.
198 C3 Oichalia Greece
113 □1 Oidhuni i. S. Male Maldives
111 K12 Oiga Xizang China
105 H6 Ōigawa Japan
104 C5 Ōi-gawa r. Japan
105 H6 Ōi-gawa r. Japan
146 C9 Oigh-sgeir is Scotland U.K.
156 E3 Oignies France
160 H4 Oignin r. France
182 D4 O Igrexario Spain
140 R4 Oijärvi Fin.
164 H5 Oijen Neth.
Oik Kazakh. see Uyuk
232 F7 Oil City PA U.S.A.
240 M6 Oildale CA U.S.A.
108 C4 Oilê Sichuan China
147 I8 Oilgate Ireland
147 F3 Oily r. Ireland
182 F5 Oímbra Spain
183 P3 Oion Spain
108 B4 Oi Qu r. Xizang China
102 S6 Oirase-gawa r. Japan
182 D3 O Irixo Spain
159 K8 Oiron France
164 H5 Oirschot Neth.
161 H6 Oisans reg. France
156 D5 Oise dept France
156 D6 Oise r. France
156 F5 Oise à l'Aisne, Canal de l' France
163 B6 Oiseaux, Île aux i. France
206 A2 Oiseaux du Djoudj, Parc National des nat. park Senegal
160 H2 Oiselay-et-Grachaux France
156 C4 Oisemont France
105 J5 Ōiso Japan
159 J5 Oisseau France
156 B5 Oissel France
164 H5 Oisterwijk Neth.
247 □4 Oistins Barbados
103 I13 Ōita Japan
103 I13 Ōita pref. Japan
182 C4 Oitavén r. Spain
198 D4 Oiti mt. Greece
198 D4 Oitis, Ethnikos Drymos nat. park Greece
197 O4 Oituz r. Romania
198 D6 Oitylo Greece
202 C4 Oiuru well Libya
102 S4 Oiwake Japan
159 Q7 Oizon France
105 J3 Ōizumi Gunma Japan
105 H4 Ōizumi Yamanashi Japan
104 E3 Oizuruga-dake mt. Japan
143 N3 Öja i. Sweden
240 M7 Ojai CA U.S.A.
185 L3 Ojailén r. Spain
Ojalava i. Samoa see 'Upolu
138 K2 Ojamaa r. Estonia
143 M1 Öjaren l. Sweden
175 H5 Ojcowski Park Narodowy nat. park Pol.
141 L6 Öje Sweden
261 E4 Ojeda Arg.
185 J7 Ojén Spain
104 C6 Ōji Japan
103 F13 Ojika-jima i. Japan
242 G3 Ojinaga Mex.
245 K7 Ojitlán Mex.
105 I1 Ojiya Japan
207 G5 Ojobo Nigeria
244 E3 Ojocaliente Mex.
239 K8 Ojo Caliente NM U.S.A.
260 E2 Ojo de Agua Arg.
244 G5 Ojo de Agua Mex.
242 F3 Ojo de Laguna Mex.
242 B4 Ojo de Liebre, Lago b. Mex.
185 L2 Ojos del Guadiana lakes Spain
258 C2 Ojos del Salado, Nevado mt. Arg./Chile
183 R7 Ojos Negros Spain
175 I3 Ojrzeń Pol.
207 H5 Oju Nigeria
244 F4 Ojuelos de Jalisco Mex.
141 M6 Öjung Sweden
207 G5 Oka Nigeria
139 W7 Oka r. Rus. Fed.
105 J3 Okabe Saitama Japan
105 H6 Okabe Shizuoka Japan
212 C4 Okahandja Namibia
Okahu b. South I. N.Z. see Jackson Bay
80 J5 Okahukura North I. N.Z.
80 H2 Okaihau North I. N.Z.
81 H10 Okains Bay South I. N.Z.
81 H10 Okains Bay b. South I. N.Z.
207 F4 Okaka Nigeria
212 C4 Okakarara Namibia
225 I1 Okak Islands Nfld and Lab. Can.
175 H2 Okalewo Pol.
222 G5 Okanagan Falls B.C. Can.
222 G5 Okanagan Lake B.C. Can.
114 G9 Okanda Sri Lanka
238 E2 Okanogan WA U.S.A.
238 E2 Okanogan r. WA U.S.A.
238 D2 Okanogan Range mts WA U.S.A.
177 K5 Okány Hungary
208 E4 Okapi, Parc National de la nat. park Dem. Rep. Congo
212 C4 Okaputa Namibia
123 O6 Okara Pak.
81 E10 Okarito Lagoon South I. N.Z.
80 H6 Okato North I. N.Z.
212 B3 Okaukuejo Namibia
212 D3 Okavango r. Botswana/Namibia
212 C3 Okavango admin. reg. Namibia
212 D3 Okavango Delta swamp Botswana
103 H13 Ōkawa Japan
104 A5 Ōkawachi Japan
80 □ Okawa Point Chatham Is S. Pacific Ocean
105 H3 Okaya Japan
103 K12 Okayama Japan
103 K12 Okayama pref. Japan
104 F6 Okazaki Japan
129 B5 Okçular Dağı mt. Turkey
231 G12 Okeechobee FL U.S.A.
231 G12 Okeechobee, Lake FL U.S.A.
237 F7 Okeene OK U.S.A.

Okefenokee National Wildlife Refuge and Wilderness to Orbais-l'Abbaye

363

231 F10 Okefenokee National Wildlife Refuge and Wilderness nature res. GA U.S.A.
231 F10 Okefenokee Swamp GA U.S.A.
105 K3 Okegawa Japan
150 D6 Okehampton Devon, England U.K.
207 F4 Oke-Iho Nigeria
237 G8 Okemah OK U.S.A.
150 D6 Okement r. England U.K.
207 G5 Okene Nigeria
169 J5 Oker r. Ger.
102 U3 Oketo Japan
116 B8 Okha Gujarat India
100 M2 Okha Sakhalin Rus. Fed.
Okhadunga Nepal see Okhaldhunga
117 K6 Okhaldhunga Nepal
134 K4 Okhansk Rus. Fed.
116 G4 Okhimath Uttaranchal India
100 M1 Okhinskiy Peresheyek isth. Rus. Fed.
Ókhi Óros mt. Greece see Ochi
137 P2 Okhochevka Rus. Fed.
139 V4 Okhotino Rus. Fed.
131 P4 Okhotka r. Rus. Fed.
137 M8 Okhotnykove Ukr.
131 P4 Okhotsk Rus. Fed.
102 V2 Okhotsk, Sea of Japan/Rus. Fed.
Okhotskoye More sea Japan/Rus. Fed. see Okhotsk, Sea of
137 O7 Okhrimivka Ukr.
Okhthonià Greece see Oktonia
137 N3 Okhtyrka Ukr.
139 P5 Okhvat Rus. Fed.
214 B5 Okiep S. Africa
102 □1 Okinawa Okinawa Japan
102 □1 Okinawa i. Japan
102 □ Okinawa pref. Japan
Okinawa-guntō is Japan see Okinawa-shotō
102 □D20 Okinawa-shotō is Japan
99 N7 Okino-Daitō-jima i. Japan
102 □F19 Okinoerabu-jima i. Nansei-shotō Japan
104 B7 Okino-shima i. Japan
103 H12 Okino-shima i. Japan
103 J14 Okino-shima i. Japan
99 O7 Okino-Tori-shima i. Japan
103 J10 Oki-shotō is Japan
99 N4 Oki-shotō is Japan
207 G5 Okitipupa Nigeria
96 B6 Okkan Myanmar
237 G8 Oklahoma state U.S.A.
237 G8 Oklahoma City OK U.S.A.
231 G11 Oklawaha r. FL U.S.A.
237 G8 Okmulgee OK U.S.A.
177 L3 Okna r. Slovakia
Oknitsa Moldova see Ocnița
203 H4 Oko, Wadi watercourse Sudan
177 G4 Okoč Slovakia
207 H5 Okola Cameroon
237 K8 Okolona MS U.S.A.
232 A7 Okolona OH U.S.A.
212 B4 Okombahe Namibia
208 B5 Okondja Gabon
174 E2 Okonek Pol.
175 L4 Okopy Pol.
177 G6 Okor r. Hungary
222 H5 Okotoks Alta Can.
212 A3 Okotusu well Namibia
139 P7 Okovskiy Les for. Rus. Fed.
208 B5 Okoyo Congo
121 S4 Okpety, Gora mt. Kazakh.
176 E2 Okříšky Czech Rep.
176 E2 Okrouhlice Czech Rep.
175 K4 Okrzeja Pol.
175 I5 Oksa Pol.
142 E6 Oksbøl Denmark
140 Q1 Øksfjord Norway
139 X7 Okskiy Zapovednik nature res. Rus. Fed.
134 G3 Oksovskiy Rus. Fed.
140 M3 Oksskolten mt. Norway
Oktemberyan Armenia see Armavir
198 F4 Oktonia Greece
122 E1 Oktumgum des. Turkm.
96 C5 Oktwin Myanmar
Oktyabr' Aktyubinskaya Oblast' Kazakh. see Kandyagash
139 U4 Oktyabr' Rus. Fed.
Oktyabr'sk Kazakh. see Kandyagash
120 C1 Oktyabr'sk Rus. Fed.
Oktyabr'skaya Belarus see Aktsyabrskaya
137 S7 Oktyabr'skaya Rus. Fed.
Oktyabr'skiy Homyel'skaya Voblasts' Belarus see Aktsyabrski
Oktyabr'skiy Vitsyebskaya Voblasts' Belarus see Aktsyabrski
120 J1 Oktyabr'skiy Kazakh.
100 F2 Oktyabr'skiy Amurskaya Oblast' Rus. Fed.
100 F2 Oktyabr'skiy Amurskaya Oblast' Rus. Fed.
134 H3 Oktyabr'skiy Arkhangel'skaya Oblast' Rus. Fed.
137 P3 Oktyabr'skiy Belgorodskaya Oblast' Rus. Fed.
139 X4 Oktyabr'skiy Ivanovskaya Oblast' Rus. Fed.
139 T7 Oktyabr'skiy Kaluzhskaya Oblast' Rus. Fed.
131 Q4 Oktyabr'skiy Kamchatskaya Oblast' Rus. Fed.
137 R8 Oktyabr'skiy Krasnodarskiy Kray Rus. Fed.
134 F2 Oktyabr'skiy Murmanskaya Oblast' Rus. Fed.
Oktyabr'skiy Respublika Adygeya Rus. Fed. see Takhtamukay
135 K5 Oktyabr'skiy Respublika Bashkortostan Rus. Fed.
137 S6 Oktyabr'skiy Rostovskaya Oblast' Rus. Fed.
139 V7 Oktyabr'skiy Ryazanskaya Oblast' Rus. Fed.
139 W8 Oktyabr'skiy Ryazanskaya Oblast' Rus. Fed.
134 L4 Oktyabr'skiy Sverdlovskaya Oblast' Rus. Fed.
135 H7 Oktyabr'skiy Volgogradskaya Oblast' Rus. Fed.
120 K1 Oktyabr'skoye Kazakh.
120 J1 Oktyabr'skoye Chelyabinskaya Oblast' Rus. Fed.
130 H3 Oktyabr'skoye Khanty-Mansiyskiy Avtonomnyy Okrug Rus. Fed.
139 W9 Oktyabr'skoye Lipetskaya Oblast' Rus. Fed.
120 F1 Oktyabr'skoye Orenburgskaya Oblast' Rus. Fed.
129 F2 Oktyabr'skoye Respublika Severnaya Osetiya-Alaniya Rus. Fed.
100 G5 Oktyabr'skoye Yevreyskaya Avtonomnaya Oblast' Rus. Fed.
131 K2 Oktyabr'skoy Revolyutsii, Ostrov i. Severnaya Zemlya Rus. Fed.
102 □1 Oku Okinawa Japan
188 F3 Okučani Croatia
104 E3 Okuchi Japan
103 H14 Ōkuchi Japan
139 Q3 Okulovka Rus. Fed.
129 C3 Ok'umi Georgia
Okureshi Georgia see Oqureshi
81 C10 Okuru South I. N.Z.
104 G4 Oku-sangai-dake mt. Japan
102 Q4 Okushiri-kaikyō sea chan. Japan
102 Q4 Okushiri-tō i. Japan
207 F4 Okuta Nigeria
105 J1 Okutadami-ko resr Japan
105 J4 Okutama Japan
105 J4 Okutama-ko l. Japan
104 B4 Okutango-hantō pen. Japan
105 J2 Okutone-ko resr Japan
104 G4 Ōkuwa Japan
212 E4 Okwa watercourse Botswana
131 Q4 Ola Rus. Fed.
237 I8 Ola AR U.S.A.
261 F3 Olaeta Arg.
140 □B1 Ólafsvík Iceland
186 B2 Olague Spain
113 □1 Olahali i. N. Male Maldives
138 G5 Olaine Latvia
114 F6 Olakkur Tamil Nadu India
182 D9 Olalhas Port.
161 I7 Olan, Pic d' mt. France
240 N5 Olancha CA U.S.A.
240 N5 Olancha Peak CA U.S.A.
242 □P10 Olanchito Hond.
141 K7 Öland i. Sweden
143 N4 Ölands norra udde pt Öland Sweden
143 N5 Ölands sodra udde pt Öland Sweden
140 U3 Olanga Rus. Fed.
161 B9 Olargues France
177 K5 Olari Romania
82 H5 Olary S.A. Austr.
82 H5 Olary watercourse S.A. Austr.
261 G4 Olascoaga Arg.
177 K3 Olaszliszka Hungary
236 H6 Olathe KS U.S.A.
117 E4 Olavakod Kerala India
261 G5 Olavarría Arg.
183 Q3 Olave Spain
140 □ Olav V Land reg. Svalbard
174 F5 Oława Pol.
183 P3 Olazti Spain
187 D7 Olba Spain
179 N5 Olbendorf Austria
171 H9 Olbernhau Ger.
171 H9 Olbersdorf Ger.
171 D8 Olbersleben Ger.
192 C6 Olbia Sardegna Italy
192 C6 Olbia, Golfo di b. Sardegna Italy
192 C6 Olbia-Tempio prov. Sardegna Italy
175 K5 Olbięcin Pol.
176 D2 Olbramovice Czech Rep.
177 K5 Olcea Romania
129 D4 Ölçek Turkey
129 C6 Ölçekli Turkey
131 P3 Ol'chan Rus. Fed.
173 F5 Olching Ger.
232 G5 Olcott NY U.S.A.
129 E5 Ölçülü Turkey
246 D2 Old Bahama Channel Bahamas/Cuba
151 J5 Old Basing Hampshire, England U.K.
114 G3 Old Bastar Chhattisgarh India
235 G4 Old Bridge NJ U.S.A.
150 H2 Old Bridge West Midlands, England U.K.
147 H5 Oldcastle Ireland
86 H5 Old Cherrabun W.A. Austr.
150 E1 Old Colwyn Conwy, Wales U.K.
85 H7 Old Cork Qld Austr.
220 E3 Old Crow Y.T. Can.
146 G12 Old Dailly South Ayrshire, Scotland U.K.
203 F5 Old Dongola Sudan
164 J3 Oldeberkoop Neth.
164 I4 Oldebroek Neth.
164 J2 Oldehove Neth.
141 H6 Oldeide Norway
164 I3 Oldemarkt Neth.
168 F4 Oldenbrok Ger.
168 F4 Oldenburg Ger.
168 K3 Oldenburg in Holstein Ger.
168 H3 Oldendorf Ger.
168 K4 Oldendorf (Luhe) Ger.
168 G2 Oldenswort Ger.
164 K4 Oldenzaal Neth.
140 P2 Olderdalen Norway
151 O4 Old Felixstowe Suffolk, England U.K.
87 F12 Oldfield r. W.A. Austr.
233 K5 Old Forge NY U.S.A.
234 G2 Old Forge PA U.S.A.
232 B7 Old Fort OH U.S.A.
231 □2 Old Fort Point New Prov. Bahamas
247 □2 Old Fort Point Montserrat
87 E9 Old Gidgee W.A. Austr.
149 M6 Oldham Greater Manchester, England U.K.
246 □ Old Harbour Jamaica
246 □ Old Harbour Bay Jamaica
147 E9 Old Head of Kinsale Ireland
171 D8 Oldisleben Ger.
150 H5 Oldland South Gloucestershire, England U.K.
149 R7 Old Leake Lincolnshire, England U.K.
235 K2 Old Lyme CT U.S.A.
220 G5 Oldman r. Alta Can.
235 E5 Oldman's Creek r. NJ U.S.A.
146 L8 Oldmeldrum Aberdeenshire, Scotland U.K.
209 F8 Old Mkushi Zambia
215 N7 Old Morley S. Africa
235 L2 Old Mystic CT U.S.A.
233 □O5 Old Orchard Beach ME U.S.A.
221 N3 Old Perlican Nfld and Lab. Can.
240 M6 Old River CA U.S.A.
247 □2 Old Road Antigua and Barbuda
147 I8 Old Ross Ireland
222 H5 Olds Alta Can.
235 K2 Old Saybrook CT U.S.A.
233 □O4 Old Speck Mountain ME U.S.A.
168 F1 Oldsum Ger.
147 J5 Oldtown Ireland
149 L5 Old Town Cumbria, England U.K.
232 C10 Oldtown KY U.S.A.
233 □Q4 Old Town ME U.S.A.
211 B5 Olduvai Gorge tourist site Tanz.
232 D8 Old Washington OH U.S.A.
234 F5 Oldwick NJ U.S.A.
223 J5 Old Wives Lake Sask. Can.
241 Q7 Old Woman Mountains CA U.S.A.
106 G2 Öldziyt Arhangay Mongolia
107 K4 Öldziyt Dornogovĭ Mongolia
232 G6 Olean NY U.S.A.
175 K1 Olecko Pol.
182 F9 Oledo Port.
178 D4 Oleggio Italy
182 E9 Oleiros Port.
131 N3 Olekma r. Rus. Fed.
131 M3 Olekminsk Rus. Fed.
137 L2 Oleksandriivka Chernihivs'ka Oblast' Ukr.
137 P6 Oleksandrivka Dnipropetrovs'ka Oblast' Ukr.
137 P5 Oleksandrivka Donets'ka Oblast' Ukr.
137 Q3 Oleksandrivka Kharkivs'ka Oblast' Ukr.
137 K5 Oleksandrivka Kirovohrads'ka Oblast' Ukr.
137 L5 Oleksandrivka Kirovohrads'ka Oblast' Ukr.
137 K6 Oleksandrivka Mykolayivs'ka Oblast' Ukr.
137 L7 Oleksandrivka Mykolayivs'ka Oblast' Ukr.
137 N8 Oleksandrivka Respublika Krym Ukr.
137 O7 Oleksandrivka Zaporiz'ka Oblast' Ukr.
Oleksandrivs'k Ukr. see Zaporizhzhya
137 M5 Oleksandriya Kirovohrads'ka Oblast' Ukr.
136 F3 Oleksandriya Rivnens'ka Oblast' Ukr.
137 Q5 Oleksiyevo-Druzhkivka Ukr.
137 M7 Oleksiyivka Khersons'ka Oblast' Ukr.
137 R4 Oleksiyivka Luhans'ka Oblast' Ukr.
137 M8 Oleksiyivka Respublika Krym Ukr.
134 I2 Olema Rus. Fed.
165 G6 Olen Belgium
182 B2 Ølen Norway
134 F1 Olenegorsk Rus. Fed.
131 M3 Olenek Rus. Fed.
131 M2 Olenek r. Rus. Fed.
Olenek Bay Rus. Fed. see Olenekskiy Zaliv
131 N2 Olenekskiy Zaliv b. Rus. Fed.
Ölengti r. Kazakh. see Olenti
139 Q5 Olenino Rus. Fed.
134 F2 Olenitsa Rus. Fed.
137 Q6 Olenivka Ukr.
Olenivs'ki Kar"yery Ukr. see Dokuchayevs'k
130 I2 Oleniy, Ostrov i. Rus. Fed.
120 E3 Olenti r. Kazakh.
121 P1 Olenti r. Kazakh.
107 N1 Olentuy Rus. Fed.
Olenya Rus. Fed. see Olenegorsk
162 B4 Oléron, Île d' i. France
186 I4 Olesa de Montserrat Spain
Oleshky Ukr. see Tsyurupyns'k
137 K2 Oleshnya Chernihivs'ka Oblast' Ukr.
137 N3 Oleshnya Sums'ka Oblast' Ukr.
136 D4 Oles'ko Ukr.
174 F4 Oleśnica Dolnośląskie Pol.
175 J5 Oleśnica Świętokrzyskie Pol.
175 I5 Olesno Małopolskie Pol.
174 G5 Olesno Opolskie Pol.
175 L5 Oleszyce Pol.
162 C1 Olette France
163 I10 Olette France
95 L9 Olet Tongo mt. Sumbawa Indon.
136 G2 Olevs'k Ukr.
236 D2 Oley PA U.S.A.
169 D7 Olfen Ger.
140 M3 Ølfjellet mt. Norway
100 I7 Ol'ga Rus. Fed.
224 E3 Olga, Lac l. Que. Can.
84 C8 Olga, Mount N.T. Austr.
131 J5 Olgastretet str. Svalbard
190 G4 Olginate Italy
137 R9 Ol'ginka Rus. Fed.
186 F3 Ol'ginsk Rus. Fed.
100 H2 Ol'ginsk Rus. Fed.
137 R8 Ol'ginskaya Krasnodarskiy Kray Rus. Fed.
137 S6 Ol'ginskaya Rostovskaya Oblast' Rus. Fed.
Olginskoye Rus. Fed. see Kochubeyevskoye
106 A2 Ölgiy Mongolia
146 I6 Olgrinmore Highland, Scotland U.K.
184 A2 Olhalvo Port.
184 D6 Olhão Port.
184 A1 Olhava Fin.
184 D6 Olho Marinho Port.
257 F2 Olhos d'Agua Brazil
113 □1 Olhuveli i. S. Male Maldives
84 C8 Olia Chain mts N.T. Austr.
186 H3 Oliana Spain
186 H3 Oliana, Embassament d' resr Spain
183 M9 Olías del Rey Spain
191 R7 Olib Croatia
188 E3 Olib i. Croatia
192 C7 Oliena Sardegna Italy
192 C7 Oliena r. Sardegna Italy
186 D5 Oliete Spain
212 C5 Olifants watercourse Namibia
214 C7 Olifants r. Western Cape S. Africa
214 F9 Olifants r. Western Cape S. Africa
213 F4 Olifants r. S. Africa
214 D4 Olifantshoek S. Africa
214 C8 Olifantsrivierberge mts S. Africa
193 N7 Oligastro Marina Italy
91 K5 Olimarao atoll Micronesia
Olimbos hill Cyprus see Olympos
Olimbos mt. Greece see Mytikas
256 C4 Olímpia Brazil
199 L6 Olimpos Beydağları Milli Parkı nat. park Turkey
259 D5 Olinalá Mex.
255 G5 Olinda Brazil
213 H3 Olinda, Ponta pt Moz.
85 J1 Olinda Entrance sea chan. Qld Austr.
213 H3 Olinga Moz.
141 M6 Olingsjövallen Sweden
85 I6 Olio Qld Austr.
186 H4 Oliola Spain
Öli Qoltyq Sory dry lake Kazakh. see Mertvyy Kultuk, Sor
Olisipo Port. see Lisboa
183 Q4 Olite Spain
261 F3 Oliva Arg.
193 Q9 Oliva r. Italy
187 E10 Oliva Spain
186 D4 Oliva hill Spain
183 Q4 Oliva, Cordillera de mts Arg./Chile
258 C3 Oliva, Cordillera de mts Arg./Chile
184 F4 Oliva de la Frontera Spain
184 G3 Oliva de Mérida Spain
182 C6 Olival Port.
260 C2 Olivares, Cerro de mt. Arg./Chile
183 P9 Olivares de Júcar Spain
232 B10 Olive Hill KY U.S.A.
231 C1 Olivehurst CA U.S.A.
182 B3 Oliveira Brazil
257 E4 Oliveira Brazil
182 D7 Oliveira de Azeméis Port.
182 D7 Oliveira de Frades Port.
182 D7 Oliveira do Bairro Port.
182 E8 Oliveira do Conde Port.
182 C6 Oliveira do Douro Port.
182 E8 Oliveira do Hospital Port.
254 E5 Oliveira dos Brejinhos Brazil
Olivença Moz. see Lupilichi
184 E5 Olivença-a-Nova Angola see Capunda Cavilongo
193 P5 Oliveto r. Italy
184 E4 Olivenza r. Port./Spain
184 E3 Olivenza Spain
184 E3 Olivenza, Llanos de plain Spain
222 G5 Oliver B.C. Can.
195 I7 Oliveri Sicilia Italy
236 E4 Oliver Springs TN U.S.A.
223 L4 Oliver Lake Sask. Can.
221 K3 Oliveros Arg.
156 C8 Olivet France
226 J7 Olivet MI U.S.A.
236 G4 Olivet SD U.S.A.
193 Q6 Olivetto Citra Italy
193 Q6 Oliveto Lucano Italy
236 H3 Olivia MN U.S.A.
81 C11 Olivine Range mts South I. N.Z.
190 F2 Olivone Switz.
136 E4 Oliyiv Ukr.
107 J7 Oljoq Nei Mongol China
149 F3 Oljoq Wells Tanz.
141 I6 Øljuvatnet l. Norway
145 I5 Ol'ka Rus. Fed.
177 K2 Olka Slovakia
177 K3 Olka r. Slovakia
210 C5 Ol Kalou Kenya
Ol'kayat Kazakh. see Ul'kayak
135 H5 Ol'khi Rus. Fed.
135 G6 Ol'khovatka Rus. Fed.
139 W8 Ol'khovets Rus. Fed.
135 H5 Ol'khovka Rus. Fed.
175 H5 Olkusz Pol.
146 □N1 Ollaberry Shetland, Scotland U.K.
252 C5 Ollachea Peru
258 C5 Ollagüe Chile
252 D6 Ollagüe, Volcán vol. Bol.
151 Q5 Ollastu r. Italy
192 C7 Ollerton Nottinghamshire, England U.K.
149 O7 Olliergues France
160 D5 Ollioules France
161 H10 Ollita, Cordillera de mts Arg./Chile
260 B2 Ollitas mt. Arg.
260 B2 Ollo Spain
183 Q3 Öllölä Fin.
140 U5 Ollombo Congo
129 C6 Ollon Switz.
209 B5 Olmaliq Uzbek.
190 B3 Olmedilla de Roa Spain
121 M7 Olmedo Sardegna Italy
183 M5 Olmedo Spain
192 A6 Olmeta-di-Tuda Corse France
183 K6 Olmeto Corse France
192 C2 Olmo al Brembo Italy
261 F4 Olmos Arg.
250 B6 Olmos Peru
183 L3 Olmos de Ojeda Spain
Olmütz Czech Rep. see Olomouc
151 K3 Olney Milton Keynes, England U.K.
236 K6 Olney IL U.S.A.
234 A6 Olney MD U.S.A.
237 F9 Olney TX U.S.A.
187 D8 Olocau Spain
186 E6 Olocau del Rey Spain
100 A3 Olochi Rus. Fed.
143 K5 Olofström Sweden
121 L1 Ol'oinka Kazakh.
225 I3 Olomane r. Que. Can.
78 □6 Olomburi Malaita Solomon Is
176 G2 Olomouc Czech Rep.
176 G2 Olomoucký kraj admin. reg. Czech Rep.
190 G5 Olona r. Italy
139 P1 Olonets Rus. Fed.
139 Q1 Olonetskaya Vozvyshennost' hills Rus. Fed.
92 C4 Olongapo Luzon Phil.
95 K5 Olongliko Kalimantan Indon.
139 P1 Olonka r. Rus. Fed.
162 A2 Olonne-sur-Mer France
161 B10 Olonzac France
163 C9 Oloron-Ste-Marie France
78 □2 Olosega i. American Samoa
Olosega atoll American Samoa see Swains Island
186 J3 Olot Spain
120 J8 Olot Uzbek.
171 G10 Olovi Czech Rep.
188 G3 Olovo Bos.-Herz.
107 N1 Olovyannaya Rus. Fed.
240 □E13 Olowalu HI U.S.A.
Oloy, Qatorkŭhi mts Asia see Alai Range
116 D9 Olpad Gujarat India
260 D2 Olpas Arg.
169 E8 Olpe Ger.
178 E5 Olperer mt. Austria
138 M8 Ol'sa r. Belarus
176 F2 Olšany Czech Rep.
176 G2 Olšany u Prostějova Czech Rep.
142 J2 Olsätter Sweden
177 G2 Olšava r. Czech Rep.
177 J4 Olšava r. Slovakia
169 E8 Olsberg Ger.
176 F2 Olše r. Czech Rep.
139 O7 Ol'sha Rus. Fed.
137 Q2 Ol'shanka Rus. Fed.
137 K6 Ol'shans'ke Ukr.
164 J4 Olst Neth.
175 K3 Olszanka Mazowieckie Pol.
175 F6 Olszanka Opolskie Pol.
175 K6 Olszany Pol.
175 J2 Olszewka Pol.
175 J2 Olszewo-Borki Pol.
175 J2 Olszówka Pol.
175 H5 Olsztyn Śląskie Pol.
175 I2 Olsztyn Warmińsko-Mazurskie Pol.
175 I2 Olsztynek Pol.
175 L3 Olszyn Pol.
174 D4 Olszyna Pol.
177 M7 Olt r. Romania
260 D2 Olta Arg.
259 C6 Olte, Sierra de mts Arg.
142 C3 Oltedal Norway
190 D1 Olten Switz.
177 O6 Oltenița Romania
177 M6 Olteț r. Romania
176 P6 Oltina Romania
120 H6 Oltinko'l Uzbek.
Oltinkŭl Uzbek. see Oltinko'l
123 M1 Oltintopkan Tajik.
127 J3 Oltu Turkey
129 C5 Oltu r. Turkey
109 M8 Oluan Pi c. Taiwan
113 □1 Olugiri i. N. Male Maldives
129 D5 Oluklu Turkey
185 O6 Olula del Río Spain
129 D5 Olur Turkey
92 D8 Olutanga i. Phil.
183 Q5 Olvega Spain
186 F3 Olvena Spain
185 I7 Olvera Spain
150 G4 Olveston South Gloucestershire, England U.K.
Ol'viopol' Ukr. see Pervomays'k
136 E3 Olyka Ukr.
139 V9 Olym r. Rus. Fed.
Olymbos hill Cyprus see Olympos
198 C5 Olympia tourist site Greece
238 C3 Olympia WA U.S.A.
198 E2 Olympiada Greece
238 C3 Olympic National Park WA U.S.A.
128 B3 Olympos hill Cyprus
199 L6 Olympos tourist site Turkey
198 D2 Olympou, Ethnikos Drymos nat. park Greece
Olympus, Mount Greece see Mytikas
238 C3 Olympus, Mount WA U.S.A.
137 R2 Olymskiy Rus. Fed.
234 D2 Olyphant PA U.S.A.
137 K2 Olyshivka Ukr.
131 R3 Olyutorskiy Rus. Fed.
131 S4 Olyutorskiy, Mys c. Rus. Fed.
131 R4 Olyutorskiy Zaliv b. Rus. Fed.
192 C7 Olzai Sardegna Italy
Olzheras Rus. Fed. see Mezhdurechensk
111 F10 Om r. Rus. Fed.
105 J4 Ōma Japan
134 I2 Oma r. Rus. Fed.
105 G3 Ōmachi Japan
105 H6 Omaezaki Japan
105 H6 Omae-zaki pt Japan
147 H3 Omagh Northern Ireland U.K.
250 C6 Omaguas Peru
236 H5 Omaha NE U.S.A.
236 G4 Omaha Indian Reservation res. NE U.S.A.
212 C4 Omaheke admin. reg. Namibia
80 K7 Omakere North I. N.Z.
129 G3 Omalo Georgia
129 G3 Omalo Georgia
100 J2 Omal'skiy Khrebet mts Rus. Fed.
114 F7 Omalur Tamil Nadu India
105 J3 Ōmama Japan
125 K6 Oman country Asia
125 M3 Oman, Gulf of Asia
212 B3 Omangambo Namibia
80 H2 Omapere, Lake North I. N.Z.
81 D11 Omarama South I. N.Z.
197 O8 Omarchevo Bulg.
123 N7 Omarkot Pak.
188 F3 Omarska Bos.-Herz.
212 B4 Omaruru Namibia
252 A3 Omas Peru
212 B3 Omatako watercourse Namibia
252 C4 Omate Peru
212 C4 Omatjette Namibia
214 G1 Omawewozonyanda Botswana
102 R5 Ōma-zaki c. Japan
Omba i. Vanuatu see Aoba
93 D8 Ombai, Selat sea chan. Indon.
Ombalantu Namibia see Uutapi
208 C3 Ombella-Mpoko pref. C.A.R.
150 H3 Ombersley Worcestershire, England U.K.
207 H5 Ombessa Cameroon
Ombetsu Japan see Onbetsu
212 B3 Ombika waterhole Namibia
94 B4 Ombolata Indon.
208 A5 Omboué Gabon
190 E2 Ombrone r. Italy
111 H11 Ombu Xizang China
260 C5 Ombúes de Lavalle Uru.
129 C5 Omcalı Turkey
214 H6 Omdraaisvlei S. Africa
203 G6 Omdurman Sudan
105 J4 Ōme Japan
245 K7 Omealca Mex.
147 J4 Omeath Ireland
138 K3 Omedu Estonia
190 E4 Omegna Italy
137 M4 Omel'nyk Poltavs'ka Oblast' Ukr.
137 O6 Omel'nyk Zaporiz'ka Oblast' Ukr.
137 N8 Omelyanivka Ukr.
202 D5 Omena well Chad
83 K7 Omeo Vic. Austr.
232 B4 Omer MI U.S.A.
199 K3 Ömerler Turkey
182 D2 O Mesón do Vento Spain
162 C3 Omessa Corse France
242 □Q12 Ometepe, Isla de i. Nic.
245 I9 Ometepec Mex.
147 B5 Omey Island Ireland
96 D6 Omgoy Wildlife Reserve nature res. Thai.
203 H6 Om Hajēr Eritrea
105 H3 Ōmi Japan
105 G1 Ōmi Niigata Japan
105 G4 Ōmi Shiga Japan
122 C6 Omīdīyeh Iran
105 M4 Omigawa Japan
104 D5 Ōmihachiman Japan
81 G10 Omihi South I. N.Z.
Omilo Georgia see Omalo
222 E3 Omineca Mountains B.C. Can.
222 E4 Omineca Provincial Park B.C. Can.
188 F4 Omiš Croatia
191 R5 Omišalj Croatia
103 I12 Ōmi-shima i. Japan
212 C4 Omitara Namibia
245 H8 Omitlán r. Mex.
105 L2 Ōmiya Ibaraki Japan
104 B4 Ōmiya Kyōto Japan
104 D7 Ōmiya Mie Japan
105 K4 Ōmiya Saitama Japan
222 C3 Ommaney, Cape AK U.S.A.
142 E6 Omme r. Denmark
168 J1 Ommel Denmark
164 J3 Ommen Neth.
106 D3 Ömnögovĭ prov. Mongolia
192 C7 Omodeo, Lago l. Sardegna Italy
105 K3 Ōmoi-gawa r. Japan
207 G5 Omoku Nigeria
198 D3 Omolio Greece
131 R3 Omolon Rus. Fed.
131 Q3 Omolon r. Rus. Fed.
210 B3 Omo National Park Eth.
102 R7 Omono-gawa r. Japan
156 I4 Omont France
102 R7 Omori Japan
182 C3 O Mosteiro Galicia Spain
102 I1 Omotegō Japan
105 L1 Omo Wenz r. Eth.
209 B9 Ompupa Angola
226 F5 Omro WI U.S.A.
130 I4 Omsk Rus. Fed.
131 Q3 Omsukchan Rus. Fed.
102 T2 Ōmu Japan
96 D3 O-mu Myanmar
197 N5 Omu, Vârful mt. Romania
102 O4 Ōmu-Aran Nigeria
175 J2 Omulew r. Pol.
175 I2 Omulew, Jezioro l. Pol.
207 G5 Omuo-Ekiti Nigeria
103 G14 Ōmura Japan
238 F4 Ōmura-wan b. Japan
105 J6 Ōmuro-yama hill Japan
105 I5 Ōmuro-yama mt. Japan
105 J4 Ōmuro-yama mt. Japan
197 O7 Omurtag Bulg.
212 B3 Omusati admin. reg. Namibia
103 H13 Ōmuta Japan
134 K4 Omutninsk Rus. Fed.
183 N3 Oña Spain
102 S8 Onagawa Japan
147 C6 Onaght Ireland
80 K5 Onakuri, Lake North I. N.Z.
226 C6 Onalaska WI U.S.A.
226 C6 Onaman Lake Ont. Can.
226 C6 Onamia MN U.S.A.
78 □4a Onamue i. Chuuk Micronesia
233 J11 Onancock VA U.S.A.
93 A5 Onang Sulawesi Barat Indon.
208 A5 Onangué, Lac l. Gabon
192 C7 Onani Sardegna Italy
192 H2 Onano Italy
224 D4 Onaping Lake Ont. Can.
226 F9 Onarga IL U.S.A.
225 G3 Onatchiway, Lac l. Que. Can.
183 P2 Oñati Spain
242 E3 Onavas Mex.
236 G4 Onawa IA U.S.A.
227 J4 Onaway MI U.S.A.
102 U4 Onbetsu Japan
97 C7 Onbingwin Myanmar
183 P5 Oncala Spain
183 P5 Oncala, Puerto de pass Spain
261 F2 Oncativo Arg.
148 I5 Onchan Isle of Man
209 B9 Oncócua Angola
129 C6 Öncül Turkey
187 E8 Onda Spain
Ondal W. Bengal India see Andal
212 B3 Ondangwa Namibia
187 F10 Ondara Spain
183 P2 Ondarroa Spain
177 K3 Ondava r. Slovakia
214 E6 Onderstedorings S. Africa
209 B9 Ondjiva Angola
207 G5 Ondo Nigeria
207 G5 Ondo state Nigeria
107 L3 Öndörhaan Mongolia
107 Q4 Ondor Had Nei Mongol China
107 M2 Öndörhushuu Mongolia
106 A3 Ondorkara Xinjiang China
106 I6 Ondor Mod Nei Mongol China
107 M5 Ondor Sum Nei Mongol China
134 F3 Ondozero Rus. Fed.
162 E3 Ondres France
214 D4 One Botswana
113 D11 One and a Half Degree Channel Maldives
85 J3 One and a Half Mile Opening sea chan. Qld Austr.
One Arm Point W.A. Austr. see Bardi
235 L1 Oneco CT U.S.A.
134 G3 Onega Rus. Fed.
134 G3 Onega r. Rus. Fed.
Onega, Lake Rus. Fed. see Onezhskoye Ozero
Onega Bay g. Rus. Fed. see Onezhskaya Guba
190 E8 Oneglia Italy
One Hundred and Fifty Mile House B.C. Can. see 150 Mile House
One Hundred Mile House B.C. Can. see 100 Mile House
233 J5 Oneida NY U.S.A.
234 C3 Oneida PA U.S.A.
233 J5 Oneida Lake NY U.S.A.
236 F4 O'Neill NE U.S.A.
80 G7 Onekaka South I. N.Z.
226 H5 Onekama MI U.S.A.
131 Q5 Onekotan, Ostrov i. Kuril'skiye O-va Rus. Fed.
78 □3a Onemak i. Kwajalein Marshall Is
231 D9 Oneonta AL U.S.A.
233 J6 Oneonta NY U.S.A.
78 □6 Onepusu Malaita Solomon Is
80 □3 Oneroa i. Rarotonga Cook Is
80 J3 Oneroa North I. N.Z.
163 B7 Onesse-et-Laharie France
197 O4 Onești Romania
161 B8 Onet-le-Château France
79 □8a Oneval i. Tonga
134 F2 Onezhskaya Guba g. Rus. Fed.
139 S1 Onezhskiy Kanal canal Rus. Fed.
130 E3 Onezhskoye Ozero l. Rus. Fed.
134 F3 Onezhskoye Ozero l. Rus. Fed.
117 I9 Ong r. India
208 B5 Onga Gabon
212 B3 Ongandjera Namibia
80 K6 Ongaonga North I. N.Z.
97 G10 Ông Đốc, Sông r. Vietnam
209 E6 Ongeri Dem. Rep. Congo
214 H5 Ongers watercourse S. Africa
87 E12 Ongerup W.A. Austr.
106 H4 Ongi Dundgovĭ Mongolia
106 H3 Ongi Övörhangay Mongolia
106 H4 Ongiyn Gol r. Mongolia
101 D10 Ongjin N. Korea
161 H8 Ongles France
Ongniud Qi Nei Mongol China see Wudan
114 G5 Ongole Andhra Prad. India
106 H3 Ongon Mongolia
208 C5 Ongonyi Congo
Ongtüstik Qazaqstan Oblysy admin. div. Kazakh. see Yuzhnyy Kazakhstan
110 H1 Onguday Rus. Fed.
129 E3 Oni Georgia
146 F9 Onich Highland, Scotland U.K.
236 E3 Onida SD U.S.A.
192 D7 Onifai Sardegna Italy
192 C7 Oniferi Sardegna Italy
105 J3 Onishi Japan
187 D10 Onil Spain
213 □14 Onilahy r. Madag.
225 G3 Onistagane, Lac l. Que. Can.
207 G5 Onitsha Nigeria
212 C4 Onjati Mountain Namibia
Onjiva Angola see Ondjiva
105 L5 Onjuku Japan
140 U5 Onkamo Fin.
140 S5 Onkivesi l. Fin.
102 □1 Onna Okinawa Japan
102 □1 Onna-dake hill Okinawa Japan
156 G3 Onnaing France
78 □4a Onnang i. Chuuk Micronesia
131 O3 Onnes Rus. Fed.
79 □7 Ono i. Fiji
104 D4 Ōno Fukui Japan
105 M1 Ōno Fukushima Japan
104 E5 Ōno Gifu Japan
102 R5 Ōno Hokkaidō Japan
104 A6 Ōno Hyōgo Japan
234 B4 Ono PA U.S.A.
103 I13 Onoda Japan
105 J7 Onohara-jima i. Japan
103 Q12 Ono-i-Lau i. Fiji
103 H13 Onojō Japan
103 K12 Onomichi Japan
Onon atoll Micronesia see Namonuito
107 L2 Onon Mongolia
107 N1 Onon Rus. Fed.
107 M2 Onon Gol r. Mongolia
100 M3 Onor Rus. Fed.
100 M3 Onor, Gora mt. Sakhalin Rus. Fed.
77 H2 Onotoa atoll Gilbert Is Kiribati
182 C4 Ons, Illa de i. Spain
103 G11 Onsan S. Korea
214 D4 Onseepkans S. Africa
186 C2 Onsella r. Spain
170 E1 Onslev Denmark
86 C6 Onslow W.A. Austr.
81 D12 Onslow, Lake South I. N.Z.
231 I8 Onslow Bay NC U.S.A.
100 F7 Onsong N. Korea
172 F5 Onstmettingen Ger.
164 L2 Onstwedde Neth.
104 F4 Ontake-san vol. Japan
185 P3 Ontalafia, Laguna de l. Spain
223 N5 Ontario prov. Can.
240 O7 Ontario CA U.S.A.
238 F4 Ontario OR U.S.A.
226 D6 Ontario WI U.S.A.
227 Q6 Ontario, Lake Can./U.S.A.
234 D4 Ontelaunee, Lake PA U.S.A.
Onteniente Spain see Ontinyent
186 F4 Ontiñena Spain
187 D10 Ontinyent Spain
140 T4 Ontojärvi l. Fin.
226 E3 Ontonagon MI U.S.A.
78 □6 Ontong Java Atoll Solomon Is
187 C10 Ontur Spain
137 M5 Onufriyivka Ukr.
175 M1 Onuškis Lith.
Onutu atoll Gilbert Is Kiribati see Onotoa
251 H3 Onverwacht Suriname
240 N6 Onyx CA U.S.A.
160 M6 Onzain France
182 I3 Onzonilla Spain
163 E10 Oô, Lac d' l. France
212 B3 Oodnadatta S.A. Austr.
82 E2 Oodweyne Somalia
105 G2 Ōoka Japan
240 □F13 'Ō'ōkala HI U.S.A.
147 F7 Oola Ireland
82 C4 Ooldea S.A. Austr.
82 C4 Ooldea Range hills S.A. Austr.
237 H7 Oologah Lake resr OK U.S.A.
164 F5 Ooltgensplaat Neth.
86 I3 Oombulgurri Aboriginal Reserve W.A. Austr.
86 I3 Oombulgurri W.A. Austr.
84 F6 Oorindi Qld Austr.
85 H6 Oorindi Qld Austr.
Oos-Londen S. Africa see East London
165 E6 Oostakker Belgium
231 E8 Oostanaula r. GA U.S.A.
165 D6 Oostburg Neth.
165 C6 Oostende Belgium
164 I4 Oostendorp Neth.
164 I5 Oosterbeek Neth.
164 G2 Oosterend Neth.
164 J3 Oosterhesselen Neth.
164 G5 Oosterhout Neth.
164 F5 Oosterland Neth.
164 E5 Oosterschelde est. Neth.
164 E5 Oosterscheldekering barrage Neth.
164 J3 Oosterwolde Neth.
165 F7 Oosterzele Belgium
157 J1 Oostham Belgium
164 G3 Oosthuizen Neth.
165 G6 Oostmalle Belgium
165 E6 Oostkamp Belgium
165 E6 Oost-Souburg Neth.
164 H4 Oostvaardersplassen nature res. Neth.
165 E7 Oost-Vlaanderen prov. Belgium
165 C7 Oostvleteren Belgium
164 H2 Oost-Vlieland Neth.
164 F5 Oostvoorne Neth.
164 G4 Ootacamund Tamil Nadu India see Udagamandalam
164 K4 Ootmarsum Neth.
222 E4 Ootsa Lake B.C. Can.
222 E4 Ootsa Lake l. B.C. Can.
240 □C12 'Ōpae'ula r. HI U.S.A.
244 E1 Opal Mex.
208 E5 Opala Dem. Rep. Congo
174 E3 Opalenica Pol.
174 G2 Opalenie Pol.
177 L4 Opályi Hungary
81 I5 Oparau North I. N.Z.
81 J7 Opari North I. N.Z.
210 B4 Opari Sudan
134 J4 Oparino Rus. Fed.
Oparo i. Is Australes Fr. Polynesia see Rapa
224 D3 Opasatika r. Ont. Can.
224 D3 Opasatika Lake Ont. Can.
223 M4 Opasquia Ont. Can.
223 M4 Opasquia Provincial Park Ont. Can.
224 F3 Opataca, Lac l. Que. Can.
188 E3 Opatija Croatia
176 F2 Opatov Czech Rep.
176 E1 Opatovice nad Labem Czech Rep.
174 G5 Opatów Śląskie Pol.
175 J5 Opatów Świętokrzyskie Pol.
174 G4 Opatów Wielkopolskie Pol.
174 G4 Opatówek Pol.
175 I5 Opatowiec Pol.
175 J5 Opatówka r. Pol.
176 G2 Opava Czech Rep.
177 G1 Opava r. Czech Rep.
182 D4 O Pazo Spain
182 D2 O Pazo de Irixoa Spain
139 R3 Opechenskiy Posad Rus. Fed.
182 D3 O Pedrouzo Spain
164 J2 Opeinde Neth.
162 D2 Opel hill Ger.
231 E9 Opelika AL U.S.A.
237 I10 Opelousas LA U.S.A.
164 J2 Opende Neth.
261 H4 Open Door Arg.
224 E4 Opeongo Lake Ont. Can.
172 H6 Opfenbach Ger.
172 F7 Opfikon Switz.
165 I6 Opglabbeek Belgium
238 K2 Opheim MT U.S.A.
164 I5 Opheusden Neth.
227 K3 Ophir Ont. Can.
81 D12 Ophir South I. N.Z.
94 D4 Ophir, Gunung vol. Indon.
193 L4 Opi Italy
208 E4 Opienge Dem. Rep. Congo
81 F11 Opihi r. South I. N.Z.
240 □G14 Opihikao HI U.S.A.
80 J7 Opiki North I. N.Z.
93 F5 Opin Seram Indon.
224 E2 Opinaca r. Que. Can.
224 E2 Opinaca, Réservoir resr Que. Can.
224 D2 Opinnagau r. Ont. Can.
161 J9 Opio France
127 L7 Opis tourist site Iraq
225 G2 Opiscotéo, Lac l. Que. Can.
137 N4 Opishnya Ukr.
164 I5 Opleo Neth.
179 L7 Oplotnica Slovenia
179 L7 Oplotnica r. Slovenia
96 D5 Op Luang National Park Thai.
164 G3 Opmeer Neth.
207 G5 Opobo Nigeria
138 L5 Opochka Rus. Fed.
176 F1 Opočno Czech Rep.
252 D4 Opoco Bol.
225 H2 Opocopa, Lac l. Que. Can.
175 I4 Opoczno Pol.
242 D3 Opodepe Mex.
165 I6 Opoeteren Belgium
174 F5 Opole Pol.
175 J4 Opole Lubelskie Pol.
174 F5 Opolskie prov. Pol.
80 H2 Opononi North I. N.Z.
136 C5 Oporets' Ukr.
182 C4 O Porriño Spain
Oporto Port. see Porto
80 L5 Opotiki North I. N.Z.
163 J10 Opoul-Périllos France
196 I5 Opovo Vojvodina Serbia
231 D10 Opp AL U.S.A.
171 K8 Oppach Ger.
102 S8 Oppa-wan b. Japan
140 J5 Oppdal Norway
191 K5 Oppeano Italy
141 H6 Oppedal Norway
Oppeln Pol. see Opole
172 E5 Oppenau Ger.
172 E2 Oppenheim Ger.
172 G4 Oppenweiler Ger.
193 P6 Oppido Lucano Italy
195 J7 Oppido Mamertina Italy
171 F7 Oppin Ger.
142 G1 Oppkuven hill Norway
141 J6 Oppland county Norway
179 K4 Opponitz Austria
238 F3 Opportunity WA U.S.A.
171 E9 Oppurg Ger.
197 L6 Oprișor Romania
191 P5 Oprtalj Croatia
197 M6 Optași-Măgura Romania
237 E7 Optima Lake OK U.S.A.
80 I2 Opua North I. N.Z.
80 I4 Opuatia North I. N.Z.
80 K6 Opunake North I. N.Z.
79 □3a Opunohu, Baie d' b. Moorea Fr. Polynesia
177 J5 Ópusztaszer Hungary
212 B3 Opuwo Namibia
165 F7 Opwijk Belgium
120 I4 Opytnoye Kazakh.
120 K6 Oqbaytal Uzbek.
120 H6 Oqqal'a Uzbek.
Oqqal"a Uzbek. see Oqqal'a
123 P2 Oqsu r. Tajik.
120 K8 Oqtosh Uzbek.
236 J5 Oquawka IL U.S.A.
242 D2 Oquitoa Mex.
233 □O4 Oquossoc ME U.S.A.
129 D3 Oqureshi Georgia
177 L4 Ór Hungary
120 H2 Or' r. Rus. Fed.
160 I3 Or, Le Mont d' mt. France
192 I2 Ora Italy
105 J3 Ōra Japan
140 P1 Øra Norway
142 G2 Øra nature res. Norway
163 C9 Orabs France
246 □ Oracabessa Jamaica
241 V9 Oracle AZ U.S.A.
184 E3 Orada Port.
197 J3 Oradea Romania
162 F4 Oradour-sur-Glane France
162 F4 Oradour-sur-Vayres France
196 I8 Orahovac Kosovo Serbia
188 F3 Orahovica Croatia
116 G7 Orai Uttar Prad. India
241 V6 Oraibi AZ U.S.A.
241 V6 Oraibi Wash watercourse AZ U.S.A.
160 G3 Orain r. France
161 H9 Oraison France
140 R3 Orajärvi Fin.
Oral Kazakh. see Ural'sk
205 E2 Oran Alg.
258 D1 Orán Arg.
136 J2 Orane Ukr.
97 H8 O Rang Cambodia
117 N6 Orang Assam India
101 E8 Orang N. Korea
83 L5 Orange N.S.W. Austr.
161 F8 Orange France
212 C6 Orange r. Namibia/S. Africa
240 O8 Orange CA U.S.A.
235 I2 Orange CT U.S.A.
237 I10 Orange TX U.S.A.
232 G10 Orange VA U.S.A.
251 I3 Orange, Cabo c. Brazil
235 H2 Orangeburg NY U.S.A.
231 G9 Orangeburg SC U.S.A.
246 D1 Orange Cay i. Bahamas
236 G4 Orange City IA U.S.A.
264 J8 Orange Cone sea feature S. Atlantic Ocean
235 G2 Orange County county NY U.S.A.
240 M5 Orange Cove CA U.S.A.
Orange Free State prov. S. Africa see Free State
235 G1 Orange Lake NY U.S.A.
231 G10 Orange Park FL U.S.A.
240 K3 Orangevale CA U.S.A.
224 D5 Orangeville Ont. Can.
234 C2 Orangeville PA U.S.A.
241 U2 Orangeville UT U.S.A.
243 G8 Orange Walk Belize
206 A4 Orango, Ilha de i. Guinea-Bissau
192 C7 Orani Sardegna Italy
92 C4 Orani Luzon Phil.
171 F7 Oranienbaum Ger.
170 H5 Oranienburg Ger.
Oranje r. Namibia/S. Africa see Orange
251 H4 Oranje Gebergte hills Suriname
164 K3 Oranjekanaal canal Neth.
212 C6 Oranjemund Namibia
214 I5 Oranjerivier S. Africa
247 □9 Oranjestad Aruba
247 □2 Oranjestad St Eustatius Neth. Antilles
215 M2 Oranjeville S. Africa
147 E6 Oranmore Ireland
87 J7 Orantjugurr, Lake salt flat W.A. Austr.
135 I7 Oranzherei Rus. Fed.
212 E4 Orapa Botswana
188 H3 Orašje Bos.-Herz.
184 F6 Oraque r. Spain
81 F11 Orari r. South I. N.Z.
92 E5 Oras Samar Phil.
188 F3 Orašac Bos.-Herz.
92 E5 Oras Bay Samar Phil.
197 K5 Orăștie Romania
197 L5 Orăștioara de Sus Romania
Orașul Stalin Romania see Brașov
136 I4 Orativ Ukr.
78 □6 Orava P.N.G.
177 I2 Orava r. Slovakia
177 I2 Orava, Vodná nádrž resr Slovakia
140 Q5 Oravais Fin.
197 J5 Oravița Romania
177 I2 Oravská Lesná Slovakia
177 I2 Oravská Magura mts Slovakia
177 I2 Oravská Polhora Slovakia
81 B13 Orawia South I. N.Z.
161 B9 Orb r. France
190 F6 Orba r. Italy
187 E10 Orba Spain
182 C5 Orbacém Port.
111 E9 Orba Co China
142 G6 Ørbæk Denmark
156 G6 Orbais-l'Abbaye France

Orbara to Ouegoa

364

186 C2 Orbara Spain
190 D5 Orbassano Italy
190 B2 Orbe Switz.
190 B2 Orbe r. Switz.
197 N6 Orbeasca Romania
159 L3 Orbec France
192 G3 Orbetello Italy
192 G3 Orbetello, Laguna di lag. Italy
157 N7 Orbey France
163 J9 Orbieu r. France
182 I5 Orbigo r. Spain
232 H8 Orbisonia PA U.S.A.
83 L7 Orbost Vic. Austr.
143 N1 Örbyhus Sweden
182 F8 Orca Port.
262 V2 Orcadas research stn S. Orkney Is Antarctica
185 O5 Orce Spain
185 N4 Orcera Spain
160 J2 Orchamps-Vennes France
234 B6 Orchard Beach MD U.S.A.
241 X2 Orchard Mesa CO U.S.A.
116 G7 Orchha Madh. Prad. India
156 F3 Orchies France
251 E2 Orchila, Isla i. Venez.
216 □3e Orchilla, Punta pt El Hierro Canary Is
198 D4 Orchomenos Greece
175 H4 Orchów Pol.
174 G3 Orchowo Pol.
146 F10 Orchy r. Scotland U.K.
192 G2 Orcia r. Italy
191 N8 Orciano di Pesaro Italy
161 I7 Orcières France
160 B5 Orcival France
190 D5 Orco r. Italy
129 I5 Orconikidze Azer.
129 I6 Orconikidze Azer.
252 B2 Orcotuna Peru
240 L7 Orcutt CA U.S.A.
86 J3 Ord r. W.A. Austr.
236 F5 Ord NE U.S.A.
86 H4 Ord, Mount hill W.A. Austr.
Orda Kazakh. see Urda
134 L4 Orda Rus. Fed.
163 E8 Ordan-Larroque France
Órdenes Spain see Ordes
241 T4 Orderville UT U.S.A.
182 D2 Ordes Spain
186 F2 Ordesa-Monte Perdido, Parque Nacional nat. park Spain
186 I2 Ordino Andorra
240 P7 Ord Mountain CA U.S.A.
193 P5 Ordona Italy
183 P3 Ordoñana Spain
261 F3 Ordoñez Arg.
107 L7 Ordos Nei Mongol China
86 J4 Ord River Dam W.A. Austr.
86 J3 Ord River Nature Reserve W.A. Austr.
Ordu Hatay Turkey see Yayladağı
126 H3 Ordu Ordu Turkey
129 H7 Ordubad Azer.
185 L6 Orduña mt. Spain
183 N2 Ordunte, Montes de mts Spain
236 D6 Ordway CO U.S.A.
Ordzhonikidze Georgia see Kharagauli
Ordzhonikidze Kazakh. see Denisovka
Ordzhonikidze Rus. Fed. see Vladikavkaz
137 M5 Ordzhonikidze Dnipropetrovs'ka Oblast' Ukr.
137 N6 Ordzhonikidze Dnipropetrovs'ka Oblast' Ukr.
Ordzhonikidzeabad Tajik. see Kofarnihon
Ordzhonikidzevskaya Rus. Fed. see Sleptsovskaya
129 C2 Ordzhonikidzevskiy Rus. Fed.
207 G5 Ore Nigeria
183 Q7 Orea Spain
182 D2 O Real Spain
251 G3 Orealla Guyana
141 M6 Oreälven r. Sweden
140 O5 Öreälven r. Sweden
240 N1 Oreana NV U.S.A.
78 □3a Oreba i. Kwajalein Marshall Is
141 L6 Örebäcken Sweden
143 L2 Örebro Sweden
143 K2 Örebro county Sweden
176 F2 Ořechov Czech Rep.
139 M3 Oredezh r. Rus. Fed.
234 D3 Orefield PA U.S.A.
177 H4 Öreg-Futóné hill Hungary
177 G5 Öreglak Hungary
226 E7 Oregon IL U.S.A.
236 H6 Oregon MO U.S.A.
232 B7 Oregon OH U.S.A.
226 E7 Oregon WI U.S.A.
238 D5 Oregon state U.S.A.
238 C4 Oregon City OR U.S.A.
143 O1 Öregrund Sweden
143 O1 Öregrundsgrepen b. Sweden
170 E1 Orehoved Denmark
Orekhi-Vydritsa Belarus see Arekhawsk
Orekhov Ukr. see Orikhiv
Orekhova Belarus see Arekhava
139 V6 Orekhovo-Zuyevo Rus. Fed.
Orekhovsk Belarus see Arekhawsk
139 T9 Orel Orlovskaya Oblast' Rus. Fed.
134 L4 Orel Permskaya Oblast' Rus. Fed.
137 N5 Orel' r. Ukr.
100 K1 Orel, Gora mt. Rus. Fed.
100 K2 Orel', Ozero l. Rus. Fed.
197 L9 Orelek mt. Bulg.
250 B5 Orellana prov. Ecuador
250 C6 Orellana Peru
185 I2 Orellana, Embalse de resr Spain
184 H2 Orellana la Vieja Spain
Orel Oblast admin. div. Rus. Fed. see Orlovskaya Oblast'
241 U1 Orem UT U.S.A.
Ore Mountains Czech Rep./Ger. see Erzgebirge
199 I5 Ören Muğla Turkey
199 K6 Ören Muğla Turkey
120 F2 Orenburg Rus. Fed.
Orenburg Oblast admin. div. Rus. Fed. see Orenburgskaya Oblast'
120 D2 Orenburgskaya Oblast' admin. div. Rus. Fed.
129 B5 Örence Turkey
199 K3 Örencik Turkey
172 B2 Orenhofen Ger.
261 H6 Orense Arg.
Orense Spain see Ourense
Orense prov. Galicia Spain see Ourense
Oreón, Dhíavlos sea chan. Greece see Oreon, Diavlos
198 D4 Oreon, Diavlos sea chan. Greece
Oreor Palau see Koror
Oreor i. Palau see Koror
81 B13 Orepuki South I. N.Z.
136 G3 Orepy Ukr.
186 C3 Orés Spain
197 N7 Oresh Bulg.
142 I4 Öresjön l. Sweden
142 H3 Öreskilsälven r. Sweden
199 H1 Orestiada Greece
Orestiás Greece see Orestiada
142 I6 Öresund str. Denmark/Sweden
Oretana, Cordillera mts Spain see Toledo, Montes de
81 C13 Oreti r. South I. N.Z.
80 I3 Orewa North I. N.Z.
165 H7 Oreye Belgium
207 G2 Orfane well Niger
198 E2 Orfanou, Kolpos b. Greece
83 K10 Orford Tas. Austr.
151 P3 Orford Suffolk, England U.K.
85 I1 Orford Bay Qld Austr.
151 P3 Orford Ness hd England U.K.
Orgañá Spain see Organyà
251 H3 Organabo Fr. Guiana
216 □3a Órganos, Punta de los pt La Gomera Canary Is
241 T9 Organ Pipe Cactus National Monument nat. park AZ U.S.A.
186 H3 Organyà Spain
183 M9 Orgaz Spain
156 D6 Orge r. France
160 H3 Orgelet France
156 C7 Orgères-en-Beauce France
Orgeyev Moldova see Orhei
191 K5 Orgiano Italy
106 F2 Orgil Mongolia
185 M7 Orgiva Spain
161 G9 Orgon France
107 M5 Orgon Tal Nei Mongol China
192 C7 Orgosolo Sardegna Italy
177 I5 Orgovány Hungary
177 I5 Orgoványi park Hungary
139 X5 Orgtrud Rus. Fed.
123 M5 Orgūn Afgh.
177 I3 Őrhalom Hungary
199 J3 Orhaneli Turkey
199 K2 Orhangazi Turkey
199 J6 Orhaniye Turkey
199 I3 Orhanlar Turkey
136 H6 Orhei Moldova
106 J1 Orhon Gol r. Mongolia
106 I2 Orhontuul Mongolia
186 C2 Orhy, Pic d' mt. France/Spain
195 N3 Oria Italy
185 O6 Oria Spain
186 A1 Oria r. Spain
182 C4 O Rial Spain
182 D4 O Ribeiro reg. Spain
215 O6 Oribi Gorge Nature Reserve S. Africa
134 J4 Orichi Rus. Fed.
233 □R3 Orient ME U.S.A.
235 K2 Orient NY U.S.A.
156 H7 Orient, Lac d' resr France
245 J6 Oriental Mex.
181 E5 Oriental prov. Morocco
252 D4 Oriental, Cordillera mts Bol.
250 C3 Oriental, Cordillera mts Col.
252 C3 Oriental, Cordillera mts Peru
208 E4 Orientale prov. Dem. Rep. Congo
261 G6 Oriente Arg.
252 D2 Oriente Rondônia Brazil
256 B5 Oriente São Paulo Brazil
235 K2 Orient Island NY U.S.A.
156 H4 Origny-en-Thiérache France
156 G7 Origny-le-Sec France
156 F4 Origny-Ste-Benoîte France
187 D11 Orihuela Spain
137 O6 Orikhiv Ukr.
198 A2 Orikum Albania
137 O4 Oril' r. Ukr.
137 P5 Oril'ka Ukr.
137 O5 Oril'ka r. Ukr.
224 E4 Orillia Ont. Can.
141 R6 Orimattila Fin.
238 L5 Orin WY U.S.A.
251 F3 Orinduik Falls Brazil/Guyana
251 F2 Orinoco r. Col./Venez.
251 F2 Orinoco Delta Venez.
186 A1 Orio Spain
184 D4 Oriola Port.
234 A2 Oriole PA U.S.A.
195 K3 Oriolo Italy
192 I3 Oriolo Romano Italy
141 Q6 Oripää Fin.
233 J5 Oriskany NY U.S.A.
117 J9 Orissa state India
138 G3 Orissaare Estonia
186 J4 Oristà Spain
192 B8 Oristano Sardegna Italy
192 B8 Oristano prov. Sardegna Italy
192 B8 Oristano, Golfo di b. Sardegna Italy
147 I5 Oristown Ireland
176 F5 Őriszentpéter Hungary
175 L6 Oriv Ukr.
141 R6 Orivesi Fin.
140 T5 Orivesi l. Fin.
251 H5 Oriximiná Brazil
245 J7 Orizaba Mex.
245 J6 Orizaba, Pico de vol. Mex.
245 I4 Orizatlán Mex.
256 C2 Orizona Brazil
Orjonikidze Georgia see Kharagauli
Orjonikidzeobod Tajik. see Kofarnihon
142 J5 Örkelljunga Sweden
177 I4 Örkény Hungary
Orkhey Moldova see Orhei
Orkhomenós Greece see Orchomenos
106 H3 Orkhon Valley tourist site Mongolia
215 K2 Orkney S. Africa
146 K5 Orkney admin. div. Scotland U.K.
144 F2 Orkney Islands Scotland U.K.
175 L3 Orla Pol.
174 E4 Orla r. Pol.
174 F2 Orla r. Pol.
237 D10 Orla TX U.S.A.
171 E9 Orlamünde Ger.
240 J2 Orland CA U.S.A.
256 D4 Orlândia Brazil
231 G11 Orlando FL U.S.A.
175 L3 Orlanka r. Pol.
255 C9 Orleaes Brazil
156 C7 Orléanais reg. France
156 C8 Orléans France
233 P7 Orleans MA U.S.A.
233 M4 Orleans VT U.S.A.
156 E7 Orléans, Canal d' France
225 G4 Orléans, Île d' i. Que. Can.
156 D8 Orléans, Val d' val. France
Orléansville Alg. see Chlef
163 E9 Orleix France
143 K3 Orlen l. Sweden
176 E1 Orlice r. Czech Rep.
177 I1 Orlich Gniazd, Park Krajobrazowy Pol.
176 F1 Orlické hory mts Czech Rep.
176 F1 Orlické hory park Czech Rep.
99 G1 Orlik Rus. Fed.
176 D2 Orlik, Vodní nádrž resr Czech Rep.
137 L2 Orlivka Chernihivs'ka Oblast' Ukr.
137 P7 Orlivka Zaporiz'ka Oblast' Ukr.
137 M8 Orlivs'ke Ukr.
188 F3 Orljava r. Croatia
134 J4 Orlov Rus. Fed.
177 H2 Orlová Czech Rep.
120 C2 Orlov Gay Rus. Fed.
137 T2 Orlovka Rus. Fed.
135 G6 Orlovo Rus. Fed.
139 T9 Orlovskaya Oblast' admin. div. Rus. Fed.
135 H7 Orlovskiy Rus. Fed.
137 O6 Orlyans'ke Ukr.
137 N5 Orlyk Ukr.
137 M9 Orlyne Ukr.
138 I5 Ormaņkalns hill Latvia
177 G6 Ormánság reg. Hungary
123 K9 Ormara Pak.
123 K9 Ormara, Ras hd Pak.
190 D7 Ormea Italy
177 J5 Örménykút Hungary
151 P2 Ormesby St Margaret Norfolk, England U.K.
Ormília Greece see Ormylia
223 J5 Ormiston Sask. Can.
149 L2 Ormiston East Lothian, Scotland U.K.
92 E6 Ormoc Leyte Phil.
80 L5 Ormond North I. N.Z.
231 G11 Ormond Beach FL U.S.A.
179 N7 Ormož Slovenia
149 L6 Ormskirk Lancashire, England U.K.
233 L3 Ormstown Que. Can.
198 E2 Ormylia Greece
123 L8 Ornach Pak.
186 E3 Orna de Gállego Spain
157 I6 Ornain r. France
161 B10 Ornaisons France
160 I2 Ornans France
190 E4 Ornavasso Italy
173 J3 Ornbau Ger.
159 L4 Orne dept France
159 K3 Orne r. France
159 L5 Orne r. France
140 L3 Ørnes Norway
143 Q7 Orneta Pol.
143 O2 Ornö i. Sweden
163 H10 Ornolac-Ussat-les-Bains France
140 O5 Örnsköldsvik Sweden
138 F2 Örö i. Fin.
101 E8 Oro N. Korea
Oro r. Spain see Ouro
192 C3 Oro, Monte d' mt. Corse France
252 E3 Orobayaya Bol.
190 H3 Orobie, Alpi mts Italy
254 F4 Orocó Brazil
250 D3 Orocué Col.
206 D4 Orodara Burkina
Orodzholari Georgia see Orojolari
186 D2 Oroel, Peña de mt. Spain
238 F3 Orofino ID U.S.A.
106 G4 Orog Nuur salt l. Mongolia
240 O7 Oro Grande CA U.S.A.
239 K10 Orogrande NM U.S.A.
79 □9a Orohena mt. Tahiti Fr. Polynesia
129 E4 Orojolari Georgia
Orol Dengizi salt l. Kazakh./Uzbek. see Aral Sea
191 L5 Orolo r. Italy
196 H5 Orom Vojvodina Serbia
210 C2 Oromīya admin. reg. Eth.
225 H4 Oromocto N.B. Can.
225 H4 Oromocto Lake N.B. Can.
128 D8 Oron Israel
207 H5 Oron Nigeria
77 I2 Orona atoll Phoenix Is Kiribati
190 B2 Oron-la-Ville Switz.
233 □Q4 Orono ME U.S.A.
251 G4 Oronoque Guyana
251 G4 Oronoque r. Guyana
186 B1 Oronoz Spain
146 D10 Oronsay i. Scotland U.K.
175 I4 Orońsko Pol.
128 E4 Orontes r. Asia alt. 'Āṣī (Lebanon), alt. Asi (Turkey), alt. 'Āṣī, Nahr al (Syria)
190 D4 Oropa Italy
250 C2 Orope Venez.
244 F7 Oropeo Mex.
183 J9 Oropesa Castilla-La Mancha Spain
187 F7 Oropesa, Cabo de c. Spain
187 F7 Oropesa del Mar Valencia Spain
247 □7 Oropuche r. Trin. and Tob.
Oroqen Zizhiqi Nei Mongol China see Alihe
92 D7 Oroquieta Mindanao Phil.
183 Q3 Ororbia Spain
254 F3 Orós Brazil
254 F3 Orós, Açude resr Brazil
192 D7 Orosei Sardegna Italy
192 D7 Orosei, Golfo di b. Sardegna Italy
177 J5 Orosháza Hungary
179 M8 Oroslavje Croatia
177 H4 Oroszlány Hungary
192 C7 Orotelli Sardegna Italy
78 □1 Orote Peninsula Guam
131 Q3 Orotukan Rus. Fed.
241 V9 Oro Valley AZ U.S.A.
240 K2 Oroville CA U.S.A.
238 E2 Oroville WA U.S.A.
240 K2 Oroville, Lake resr CA U.S.A.
161 H8 Orpierre France
107 Q2 Orqohan Nei Mongol China
226 B1 Orr MN U.S.A.
186 C1 Orreaga Navarra Spain
149 L6 Orrell Greater Manchester, England U.K.
192 B9 Orri, Monte hill Italy
186 H3 Orri, Tossal de l' mt. Spain
146 H7 Orrin r. Scotland U.K.
146 G7 Orrin Reservoir Scotland U.K.
186 D6 Orrios Spain
142 H1 Orrkjølen hill Norway
192 C8 Orroli Sardegna Italy
82 G5 Orroroo S.A. Austr.
232 D8 Orrville OH U.S.A.
141 M6 Orsa Sweden
193 O5 Orsara di Puglia Italy
156 D6 Orsay France
176 F5 Őrség reg. Hungary
176 F5 Őrségi Tájvédelmi Körzet nature res. Hungary
162 H3 Orsennes France
139 N7 Orsha Belarus
139 T5 Orsha Rus. Fed.
134 I4 Orshanka Rus. Fed.
190 C5 Orsiera-Rocciavrè, Parco Naturale nature res. Italy
190 C3 Orsières Switz.
141 N6 Orsjön l. Sweden
120 H2 Orsk Rus. Fed.
170 E1 Ørslev Denmark
193 M3 Orsogna Italy
193 P8 Orsomarso Italy
197 K6 Orşova Romania
140 I5 Ørsta Norway
143 N2 Örsundaån r. Sweden
143 N2 Örsundsbro Sweden
190 E4 Orta, Lago d' l. Italy
199 J6 Ortaca Turkey
129 B4 Ortaköy Turkey
193 P5 Orta Nova Italy
128 B2 Orta Toroslar plat. Turkey
129 G1 Orta-Tyube Rus. Fed.
193 I3 Orte Italy
182 E1 Ortegal, Cabo c. Spain
250 C4 Orteguaza r. Col.
172 D5 Ortenau reg. Ger.
172 D5 Ortenberg Baden-Württemberg Ger.
169 H10 Ortenberg Hessen Ger.
173 O4 Ortenburg Ger.
179 O3 Orth an der Donau Austria
163 C9 Orthez France
141 L5 Ortholmen Sweden
184 H3 Ortiga r. Spain
183 O4 Ortigosa Spain
256 B6 Ortigueira Brazil
182 E1 Ortigueira Spain
182 E1 Ortigueira, Ría de inlet Spain
191 L2 Ortisei Italy
196 J5 Ortişoara Romania
242 D3 Ortiz Mex.
250 E2 Ortíz Venez.
191 J2 Ortles mt. Italy
247 □7 Ortoire r. Trin. and Tob.
192 B4 Ortolo r. Corse France
149 L5 Orton Cumbria, England U.K.
193 M3 Ortona Italy
151 L2 Orton Longueville Peterborough, England U.K.
227 K7 Ortonville MI U.S.A.
236 G3 Ortonville MN U.S.A.
Ortospana Afgh. see Kābul
121 P6 Orto-Tokoy Kyrg.
190 E7 Ortovera Italy
171 I8 Ortrand Ger.
140 O4 Örträsk Sweden
193 L4 Ortucchio Italy
192 B7 Ortueri Sardegna Italy
Örtülü Turkey see Şenkaya
168 I5 Örtze r. Ger.
138 K2 Oru Estonia
92 □ Orukuizu i. Palau
131 N3 Orulgan, Khrebet mts Rus. Fed.
212 C4 Orumbo Namibia
206 D5 Orumbo Boka hill Côte d'Ivoire
122 A3 Orūmīyeh Iran
122 A3 Orūmīyeh, Daryācheh-ye salt l. Iran
192 C7 Orune Sardegna Italy
252 D4 Oruro Bol.
252 D4 Oruro dept Bol.
183 N8 Orusco Spain
142 H3 Orust i. Sweden
123 L5 Orūzgān Afgh.
159 P8 Orval France
182 E8 Orvalho Port.
158 H7 Orvault France
192 I2 Orvieto Italy
262 T1 Orville Coast Antarctica
198 E1 Orvilos mts Greece
193 J3 Orvinio Italy
140 □ Orvin Land reg. Svalbard
151 O3 Orwell l. England U.K.
232 E7 Orwell OH U.S.A.
233 L5 Orwell VT U.S.A.
234 C3 Orwigsburg PA U.S.A.
107 O2 Orxon Gol r. China
197 L7 Oryakhovo Bulg.
136 F5 Orynyn Ukr.
Oryol Rus. Fed. see Orel
175 J3 Orz r. Pol.
174 F3 Orzechowo Pol.
174 G5 Orzesze Pol.
175 L3 Orzeszkowo Pol.
136 F3 Orzhiv Ukr.
137 L4 Orzhytsya Ukr.
137 L4 Orzhytsya r. Ukr.
190 H5 Orzinuovi Italy
216 □3c Orzola Lanzarote Canary Is
175 J3 Orzyc r. Pol.
175 J2 Orzyny Pol.
175 J2 Orzysz Pol.
175 K2 Orzysz, Jezioro l. Pol.
140 K5 Os Norway
138 J5 Oša r. Latvia
175 G2 Osa r. Pol.
134 K4 Osa Rus. Fed.
242 □R13 Osa, Península de pen. Costa Rica
183 O9 Osa de Vega Spain
226 B6 Osage IA U.S.A.
232 E9 Osage WV U.S.A.
238 L4 Osage WY U.S.A.
236 I6 Osage r. MO U.S.A.
236 H6 Osage City KS U.S.A.
104 F4 Osaka Japan
104 B6 Ōsaka Japan
104 B6 Ōsaka pref. Japan
121 O2 Osakarovka Kazakh.
104 C7 Ōsakasayama Japan
104 B7 Ōsaka-wan b. Japan
190 H7 Osaro, Monte mt. Italy
256 D5 Osasco Brazil
104 F2 Ōsawano Japan
236 H6 Osawatomie KS U.S.A.
236 M1 Osawin r. Ont. Can.
149 O6 Osbaldwick York, England U.K.
182 E4 Os Blancos Spain
215 P4 Osborn S. Africa
236 F6 Osborne KS U.S.A.
172 B2 Osburg Ger.
172 B2 Osburger Hochwald mts Ger.
142 F6 Øsby Denmark
143 J5 Osby Sweden
177 H2 Oščadnica Slovakia
251 H4 Oscar Fr. Guiana
140 □ Oscar II Land reg. Svalbard
86 H4 Oscar Range hills W.A. Austr.
235 H2 Oscawana Corners NY U.S.A.
237 J8 Osceola AR U.S.A.
236 I5 Osceola IA U.S.A.
236 I6 Osceola MO U.S.A.
236 G5 Osceola NE U.S.A.
226 B4 Osceola WI U.S.A.
171 H8 Oschatz Ger.
171 D6 Oschersleben (Bode) Ger.
192 C6 Oschiri Sardegna Italy
227 K5 Oscoda MI U.S.A.
182 C3 Os Dices Spain
168 J2 Osdorf Ger.
196 H6 Osečina Serbia
182 C5 O Seixo Spain
183 J2 Oseja de Sajambre Spain
173 P2 Osek Plzeňský kraj Czech Rep.
171 I9 Osek Ústecký kraj Czech Rep.
Ösel i. Estonia see Hiiumaa
141 K6 Osensjøen l. Norway
186 D4 Osera Spain
137 T3 Osered' r. Rus. Fed.
174 E4 Osetno Pol.
103 G14 Ōseto Japan
139 V7 Osetr r. Rus. Fed.
103 F14 Ōse-zaki pt Japan
105 I5 Ōse-zaki pt Japan
224 F4 Osgoode Ont. Can.
238 F6 Osgood Mountains NV U.S.A.
121 O7 Osh Kyrg.
121 O7 Osh admin. div. Kyrg.
212 B3 Oshakati Namibia
Oshamambe Japan see Oshamanbe
102 R4 Oshamanbe Japan
212 B3 Oshana admin. reg. Namibia
224 E5 Oshawa Ont. Can.
102 S8 Oshika Japan
105 H4 Ōshika Japan
102 S8 Oshika-hantō pen. Japan
212 B3 Oshikango Namibia
212 C3 Oshikoto admin. reg. Namibia
212 B3 Oshikuku Namibia
105 I1 Ōshima Niigata Japan
105 J6 Ōshima Tōkyō Japan
104 F2 Ōshima Toyama Japan
104 D3 Ō-shima i. Japan
102 Q5 Ō-shima i. Japan
105 J6 Ō-shima i. Japan
103 M13 Ō-shima i. Japan
102 Q4 Oshima-hantō pen. Japan
104 E2 Oshimizu Japan
207 G4 Oshin r. Nigeria
105 I5 Oshino Japan
212 C3 Oshivelo Namibia
236 D5 Oshkosh NE U.S.A.
226 F5 Oshkosh WI U.S.A.
134 L2 Oshkur'ya Rus. Fed.
Oshmyany Belarus see Ashmyany
122 A3 Oshnovīyeh Iran
Osh Oblast admin. div. Kyrg. see Osh
207 G5 Oshogbo Nigeria
134 M2 Oshper Rus. Fed.
Oshskaya Oblast' admin. div. Kyrg. see Osh
122 C5 Oshtorān Kūh mt. Iran
127 N7 Oshtorīnān Iran
207 G5 Oshun state Nigeria
134 M2 Oshvor Rus. Fed.
209 C5 Oshwe Dem. Rep. Congo
177 H4 Ősi Hungary
197 M6 Osica de Sus Romania
192 C6 Osidda Sardegna Italy
174 G2 Osie Pol.
174 G3 Osięciny Pol.
174 G2 Osieczna Pomorskie Pol.
174 E4 Osieczna Wielkopolskie Pol.
174 D4 Osiecznica Pol.
175 H2 Osiek Kujawsko-Pomorskie Pol.
174 G2 Osiek Pomorskie Pol.
175 J5 Osiek Świętokrzyskie Pol.
175 J6 Osiek Jasielski Pol.
190 E7 Osiglia Italy
188 G3 Osijek Croatia
197 M8 Osikovitsa Bulg.
222 E3 Osilinka r. B.C. Can.
192 B6 Osilo Sardegna Italy
191 O9 Osimo Italy
174 D2 Osina Pol.
192 C8 Osini Sardegna Italy
107 K1 Osinovka Rus. Fed.
175 K4 Osiny Pol.
196 J6 Osipaonica Serbia
Osipenko Ukr. see Berdyans'k
Osipovichi Belarus see Asipovichy
212 C4 Osire Namibia
116 D6 Osiyan Rajasthan India
215 O3 Osizweni S. Africa
174 G4 Osjaków Pol.
188 F3 Osječenica mts Bos.-Herz.
134 A3 Ösjön l. Sweden
236 I5 Oskaloosa IA U.S.A.
236 H6 Oskaloosa KS U.S.A.
143 M4 Oskarshamn Sweden
142 I5 Oskarström Sweden
227 S1 Oskélanéo Que. Can.
Öskemen Kazakh. see Ust'-Kamenogorsk
137 Q4 Oskil r. Ukr. alt. Oskol (Rus. Fed.)
135 G6 Oskol r. Rus. Fed. alt. Oskil (Ukraine)
171 L10 Oskořínek Czech Rep.
177 H4 Öskü Hungary
139 O2 Oskuya r. Rus. Fed.
177 H3 Osľany Slovakia
176 F2 Oslava r. Czech Rep.
176 F2 Oslavany Czech Rep.
175 K6 Osława r. Pol.
176 G4 Osli Hungary
142 G2 Oslo Norway
Oslo airport Norway see Gardermoen
142 G2 Oslo county Norway
92 D7 Oslob Cebu Phil.
142 G2 Oslofjorden sea chan. Norway
169 K6 Osloß Ger.
183 N3 Osma Spain
114 E3 Osmanabad Mahar. India
126 G3 Osmancık Turkey
199 K2 Osmaneli Turkey
126 H5 Osmaniye Turkey
128 E1 Osmaniye prov. Turkey
114 F3 Osmannagar Andhra Prad. India
138 M2 Os'mino Rus. Fed.
143 N3 Ösmo Sweden
175 H3 Osmolin Pol.
138 G2 Osmussaar i. Estonia
169 F6 Osnabrück Ger.
Osnaburg atoll Arch. des Tuamotu Fr. Polynesia see Mururoa
Osnaburgh Fife, Scotland U.K. see Dairsie
174 C3 Osno Lubuskie Pol.
156 D5 Osny France
208 E5 Oso r. Dem. Rep. Congo
183 L7 Oso mt. Spain
177 G1 Osoblaha Czech Rep.
Osogbo Nigeria see Oshogbo
190 F3 Osogna Switz.
197 K8 Osogovska Planina mts Bulg./Macedonia
137 M6 Osokorivka Ukr.
191 O3 Osoppo Italy
191 Q6 Osor Croatia
188 E3 Osor hill Croatia
191 Q6 Osor, Rt pt Croatia
177 L4 Oşorhei Romania
255 C9 Osório Brazil
259 B6 Osorno Chile
183 L4 Osorno Spain
137 M2 Osota r. Ukr.
175 K1 Osowa Pol.
175 J3 Osownica r. Pol.
222 G5 Osoyoos B.C. Can.
142 B1 Osøyri Norway
192 C4 Ospédale, Forêt de l' for. Corse France
250 D2 Ospino Venez.
85 K2 Osprey Reef Coral Sea Is Terr. Austr.
164 I5 Oss Neth.
180 C3 Ossa hill Port.
83 K9 Ossa, Mount Tas. Austr.
184 D3 Ossa, Serra de hills Port.
185 N3 Ossa de Montiel Spain
191 J3 Ossana Italy
163 D10 Ossau, Vallée d' val. France
163 E7 Osse r. France
207 G5 Osse r. Nigeria
163 C9 Osse-en-Aspe France
163 H11 Osséja France
165 F6 Ossendrecht Neth.
226 C5 Osseo WI U.S.A.
163 B9 Ossès France
149 N6 Ossett West Yorkshire, England U.K.
192 B6 Ossi Sardegna Italy
179 I6 Ossiach Austria
179 I6 Ossiacher See l. Austria
226 C6 Ossian IA U.S.A.
227 K5 Ossineke MI U.S.A.
235 H2 Ossining NY U.S.A.
233 □N5 Ossipee NH U.S.A.
233 □N5 Ossipee Lake NH U.S.A.
225 H2 Ossokmanuan Lake Nfld and Lab. Can.
131 R4 Ossora Rus. Fed.
93 E8 Ossu East Timor
163 D9 Ossun France
137 M4 Ostap"ye Ukr.
139 S6 Ostashevo Rus. Fed.
139 Q4 Ostashkov Rus. Fed.
174 G1 Ostaszewo Pol.
169 E6 Ostbevern Ger.
141 L6 Østby Norway
168 H3 Oste r. Ger.
168 D3 Osteel Ger.
191 L6 Ostellato Italy
168 H3 Osten Ger.
Ostend Belgium see Oostende
261 I5 Ostende Arg.
Ostende Belgium see Oostende
168 H2 Ostenfeld (Husum) Ger.
139 P7 Oster Rus. Fed.
139 P8 Oster r. Rus. Fed.
136 J3 Oster Ukr.
142 E5 Øster Agger Denmark
173 O4 Osterbach r. Ger.
170 E5 Osterburg (Altmark) Ger.
172 G3 Osterburken Ger.
168 I2 Osterby Ger.
143 N1 Österbybruk Sweden
143 L4 Österbymo Sweden
169 F6 Ostercappeln Ger.
141 L6 Österdalälven l. Sweden
143 M1 Österfärnebo Sweden
171 E8 Osterfeld Ger.
143 L3 Östergotland county Sweden
171 E8 Osterhausen Ger.
168 G2 Osterhever Ger.
173 O4 Osterhofen Ger.
168 H1 Øster Højst Denmark
168 G4 Osterholz-Scharmbeck Ger.
142 G5 Øster Hurup Denmark
178 G3 Ostermiething Austria
190 C2 Ostermundigen Switz.
171 F7 Osternienburg Ger.
179 I6 Osternig mt. Austria/Italy
169 J7 Osterode am Harz Ger.
Österreich country Europe see Austria
168 I2 Osterrönfeld Ger.
140 M5 Östersund Sweden
170 E1 Øster Ulslev Denmark
143 N1 Östervåla Sweden
142 G4 Østervrå Denmark
168 D5 Osterwald Ger.
171 E6 Osterweddingen Ger.
169 K7 Osterwieck Ger.
171 I9 Osterzgebirge park Ger.
142 C1 Østese Norway
172 G4 Ostfildern Ger.
142 H2 Østfold county Norway
168 D3 Ostfriesische Inseln is Ger.
168 E4 Ostfriesland reg. Ger.
168 E4 Ostgroßefehn (Großefehn) Ger.
143 O1 Östhammar Sweden
169 J10 Ostheim vor der Rhön Ger.
172 E2 Osthofen Ger.
193 I4 Ostia Italy
190 I5 Ostiano Italy
191 K5 Ostiglia Italy
183 Q3 Ostiz Spain
136 G2 Ostky Ukr.
173 N6 Östliche Chiemgauer Alpen nature res. Ger.
178 D5 Östliche Karwendelspitze mt. Austria/Ger.
142 I1 Östmark Sweden
177 J6 Ostojićevo Vojvodina Serbia
179 O1 Ostopovice Czech Rep.
172 G6 Ostrach Ger.
172 G5 Ostrach r. Ger.
140 P5 Östra gloppet b. Fin.
140 P5 Östra Kvarken str. Fin./Sweden
143 L4 Östra Lägern l. Sweden
142 I4 Östra Nedsjön l. Sweden
142 J6 Östra Ringsjön l. Sweden
142 I2 Östra Silen l. Sweden
171 H8 Ostrau Sachsen Ger.
171 F7 Ostrau Sachsen-Anhalt Ger.
177 H2 Ostrava Czech Rep.
177 H2 Ostravice Czech Rep.
177 I3 Ostredok mt. Slovakia
168 E4 Ostrhauderfehn Ger.
172 F3 Östringen Ger.
171 K8 Ostritz Ger.
175 H2 Ostróda Pol.
135 G6 Ostrogozhsk Rus. Fed.
136 F3 Ostroh Ukr.
196 J7 Oštro Koplje mt. Serbia
175 J2 Ostrołęka Pol.
174 G2 Ostromecko Pol.
176 E1 Ostroměř Czech Rep.
174 E3 Ostroróg Pol.
176 B1 Ostrov Czech Rep.
197 P6 Ostrov Constanța Romania
197 Q6 Ostrov Tulcea Romania
138 L4 Ostrov Rus. Fed.
Ostrovets Pol. see Ostrowiec Świętokrzyski
137 N8 Ostrovs'ke Ukr.
134 H4 Ostrovskoye Rus. Fed.
175 J5 Ostrów Pol.
Ostrow Pol. see Ostrów Wielkopolski
174 G4 Ostrówek Łódzkie Pol.
175 K4 Ostrówek Lubelskie Pol.
174 D2 Ostrowice Pol.
Ostrowiec Świętokrzyskie Pol. see Ostrowiec Świętokrzyski
174 E1 Ostrowiec Zachodniopomorskie Pol.
175 J5 Ostrowiec Świętokrzyski Pol.
175 H2 Ostrowite Kujawsko-Pomorskie Pol.
174 G3 Ostrowite Wielkopolskie Pol.
175 K4 Ostrów Lubelski Pol.
175 J3 Ostrów Mazowiecka Pol.
174 G3 Ostrowo Kujawsko-Pomorskie Pol.
Ostrowo Wielkopolskie Pol. see Ostrów Wielkopolski
174 F4 Ostrów Wielkopolski Pol.
175 H5 Ostrowy nad Okszą Pol.
175 J4 Ostrożeń Pol.
174 F4 Ostrzeszów Pol.
168 J3 Oststeinbek Ger.
178 F6 Osttirol reg. Austria
244 D7 Ostula Mex.
195 N2 Ostuni Italy
157 O6 Ostwald France
139 R4 Osuga r. Rus. Fed.
139 R5 Osuga r. Rus. Fed.
105 G6 Ōsuka Japan
227 S2 O'Sullivan, Lac l. Que. Can.
224 C3 O'Sullivan Lake Ont. Can.
198 A2 Osum r. Albania
197 M7 Osŭm r. Bulg.
103 H16 Ōsumi-hantō pen. Japan
103 H16 Ōsumi-kaikyō sea chan. Japan
102 □H16 Ōsumi-shotō is Japan
Osun state Nigeria see Oshun
185 I6 Osuna Spain
256 B4 Osvaldo Cruz Brazil
149 O5 Oswaldkirk North Yorkshire, England U.K.
149 M6 Oswaldtwistle Lancashire, England U.K.
226 F8 Oswego IL U.S.A.
237 H7 Oswego KS U.S.A.
232 I5 Oswego NY U.S.A.
235 F5 Oswego r. NJ U.S.A.
232 I5 Oswego r. NY U.S.A.
150 F2 Oswestry Shropshire, England U.K.
175 H5 Oświęcim Pol.
138 L5 Osyno Rus. Fed.
137 P7 Osypenko Ukr.
192 B3 Ota Corse France
104 D4 Ota Japan
105 J3 Ōta Japan
184 B2 Ota Port.
184 B2 Ota r. Port.
81 D12 Otago admin. reg. South I. N.Z.
81 E12 Otago Peninsula South I. N.Z.
Otahiti i. Fr. Polynesia see Tahiti
80 J6 Otairi North I. N.Z.
104 G4 Ōtake Japan
102 □G17 O-take vol. Nansei-shotō Japan
102 □G17 O-take vol. Nansei-shotō Japan
105 J4 Ōtake-san mt. Japan
105 L5 Ōtaki Chiba Japan
105 I4 Ōtaki Saitama Japan
80 J7 Otaki North I. N.Z.
81 C12 Otama South I. N.Z.
80 K6 Otamauri North I. N.Z.
120 K6 O'tamurot Uzbek.
121 P6 Otar Kazakh.
105 G2 Otari Japan
102 R3 Otaru Japan
176 G2 Otaslavice Czech Rep.
81 C13 Otatara South I. N.Z.
245 K7 Otatitlán Mex.
81 B13 Otautau South I. N.Z.
176 D2 Otava r. Czech Rep.
141 S6 Otava Fin.
250 B4 Otavalo Ecuador
212 C3 Otavi Namibia
105 L2 Ōtawara Japan
209 B9 Otchinjau Angola
Otdia atoll Marshall Is see Wotje
121 Q6 Otegen Batyr Kazakh.
183 Q3 Oteiza Spain
81 E11 Otekaieke South I. N.Z.
225 G1 Otelnuc, Lac l. Que. Can.
197 K5 Oţelu Roşu Romania
81 E11 Otematata South I. N.Z.
128 E2 Ötençay Turkey
138 J3 Otepää Estonia
138 J3 Otepää kõrgustik hills Estonia
140 O2 Oteren Norway
182 H5 Otero de Bodas Spain
183 L7 Otero de Herreros Spain
239 J13 Oteros r. Mex.
198 B2 Oteševo Macedonia
175 I5 Otfinów Pol.
151 M5 Otford Kent, England U.K.
106 E3 Otgon Tenger Uul mt. Mongolia
157 J4 Othain r. France
156 F7 Othe, Forêt d' for. France
238 E3 Othello WA U.S.A.
198 A3 Othonoi i. Greece
198 D3 Othrys mt. Greece
207 F4 Oti r. Ghana/Togo
93 A4 Oti Sulawesi Indon.
207 F4 Oti, Réserve de Faune de l' nature res. Togo
177 G2 Otice Czech Rep.
172 E4 Ötigheim Ger.
215 P5 Otimati S. Africa
244 B1 Otinapa Mex.
81 F9 Otira South I. N.Z.
236 D5 Otis CO U.S.A.
233 I6 Otisco Lake NY U.S.A.
225 G3 Otish, Monts hills Que. Can.
172 F4 Ötisheim Ger.
234 F2 Otisville NY U.S.A.
185 L7 Otívar Spain
212 C4 Otjinene Namibia
212 B3 Otjitambi Namibia
212 C4 Otjiwarongo Namibia
212 C4 Otjosondu Namibia
212 B3 Otjovasandu waterhole Namibia
212 C4 Otjozondjupa admin. reg. Namibia
151 O3 Otley Suffolk, England U.K.
149 N6 Otley West Yorkshire, England U.K.
129 A6 Otlukbeli Turkey
129 A6 Otlukbeli Dağları mts Turkey
174 F5 Otmuchów Pol.
141 K6 Otnes Norway
179 O1 Otnice Czech Rep.
104 C7 Ōto Japan
102 R5 Otobe Japan
102 R4 Otobe-dake mt. Japan
188 E3 Otočac Croatia
102 U4 Otofuke Japan
Otog Qi Nei Mongol China see Ulan
102 T2 Otoineppu Japan
188 G3 Otok Croatia
188 F3 Otoka Bos.-Herz.
80 L5 Otoko North I. N.Z.
207 F4 Otola Benin
80 I2 Otonga North I. N.Z.
210 A2 Otoro, Jebel mt. Sudan
80 J5 Otorohanga North I. N.Z.
174 E3 Otorowo Pol.
224 B3 Otoskwin r. Ont. Can.
103 □2 Otōto-jima i. Ogasawara-shotō Japan
182 C4 O Toural Spain
104 F6 Otowa Japan
103 K13 Ōtoyo Japan
120 D5 Otpan, Gora hill Kazakh.
Otpor Rus. Fed. see Zabaykal'sk
142 E3 Otra r. Norway
247 □10 Otrabanda Curaçao Neth. Antilles
139 T8 Otradinskiy Rus. Fed.
129 C1 Otradnaya Rus. Fed.
139 N2 Otradnoye Leningradskaya Oblast' Rus. Fed.
Otradnoye Samarskaya Oblast' Rus. Fed. see Otradnyy
139 N1 Otradnoye, Ozero l. Rus. Fed.
120 D1 Otradnyy Rus. Fed.
195 O3 Otranto Italy
195 P2 Otranto, Strait of Albania/Italy
193 I3 Otricoli Italy
Otrogovo Rus. Fed. see Stepnoye
177 G2 Otrokovice Czech Rep.
131 S3 Otrozhnyy Rus. Fed.
179 L4 Ötscher-Tormäuer nature res. Austria
226 I7 Otsego MI U.S.A.
233 K6 Otsego Lake NY U.S.A.
105 M2 Ōtsu Ibaraki Japan
104 C5 Ōtsu Shiga Japan
102 S7 Ōtsuchi Japan
105 I4 Ōtsuki Japan
141 J6 Otta Norway
192 C7 Ottana Sardegna Italy
157 L5 Ottange France
224 F4 Ottawa Ont. Can.
224 F4 Ottawa r. Ont./Que. Can.
226 F8 Ottawa IL U.S.A.
236 H6 Ottawa KS U.S.A.
232 A7 Ottawa OH U.S.A.
224 D1 Ottawa Islands Nunavut Can.
171 I8 Ottendorf-Okrilla Ger.
172 D5 Ottenheim Ger.
172 E4 Ottenhöfen im Schwarzwald Ger.
179 L3 Ottenschlag Austria
179 J3 Ottensheim Austria
169 H7 Ottenstein Ger.
179 L2 Ottenstein Stausee resr Austria
168 I4 Otter Ger.
150 F6 Otter r. England U.K.
172 D3 Otterbach Ger.
172 D2 Otterberg Ger.
149 M3 Otterburn Northumberland, England U.K.
146 F10 Otter Ferry Argyll and Bute, Scotland U.K.
173 L6 Otterfing Ger.
226 H1 Otter Island Ont. Can.
223 J4 Otter Lake Sask. Can.
164 I4 Otterlo Neth.
168 G3 Otterndorf Ger.
224 D3 Otter Rapids Ont. Can.
168 H4 Ottersberg Ger.
142 J3 Otterstad Sweden
172 E4 Ottersweier Ger.
146 □N1 Otterswick Shetland, Scotland U.K.
142 G6 Otterup Denmark
171 G8 Otterwisch Ger.
150 D6 Ottery r. England U.K.
150 F6 Ottery St Mary Devon, England U.K.
177 G4 Öttevény Hungary
165 G7 Ottignies Belgium
192 D6 Ottiolo, Punta d' pt Sardegna Italy
157 O8 Ottmarsheim France
179 I3 Ottnang am Hausruck Austria
143 M1 Ottnaren l. Sweden
173 I6 Ottobeuren Ger.
173 L5 Ottobrunn Ger.
221 J1 Otto Fiord inlet Nunavut Can.
177 I5 Öttömös Hungary
190 G6 Ottone Italy
215 J2 Ottosdal S. Africa
215 J1 Ottoshoop S. Africa
169 H9 Ottrau Ger.
121 P7 Ottuk Kyrg.
236 I5 Ottumwa IA U.S.A.
172 C3 Ottweiler Ger.
207 G5 Otukpa Nigeria
207 H5 Otukpo Nigeria
245 I6 Otumba Mex.
252 D4 Otuyo Bol.
250 B6 Otuzco Peru
Otvazhniy Rus. Fed. see Zhigulevsk
232 B10 Otway OH U.S.A.
259 B9 Otway, Bahía b. Chile
83 I8 Otway, Cape Vic. Austr.
259 C9 Otway, Seno b. Chile
83 I8 Otway National Park Vic. Austr.
83 I8 Otway Range mts Vic. Austr.
175 J3 Otwock Pol.
183 O2 Otxandio Spain
174 D4 Otyń Pol.
136 D5 Otyniya Ukr.
173 N4 Otzing Ger.
178 C5 Ötztal val. Austria
178 C6 Ötztaler Alpen mts Austria
96 F4 Ou, Nam r. Laos
207 H3 Ouacha Niger
237 J10 Ouachita r. AR U.S.A.
237 I8 Ouachita, Lake AR U.S.A.
228 H4 Ouachita Mountains AR/OK U.S.A.
237 H8 Ouachita Mountains AR/OK U.S.A.
204 C5 Ouadâne Maur.
208 D2 Ouadda C.A.R.
202 D6 Ouaddaï pref. Chad
207 G1 Ouadjinkarem well Niger
206 B2 Ouâd Nâga Maur.
206 C3 Ouadou watercourse Maur.
206 E3 Ouagadougou Burkina
206 E3 Ouahigouya Burkina
Ouahran Alg. see Oran
208 D3 Ouaka pref. C.A.R.
208 C3 Ouaka r. C.A.R.
206 D2 Oualâta Maur.
207 F4 Oualé r. Burkina
206 C3 Oualia Mali
207 F3 Ouallam Niger
205 F4 Ouallene Alg.
251 I3 Ouanary Fr. Guiana
202 C5 Ouanazein well Chad
208 D2 Ouanda-Djailé C.A.R.
208 C3 Ouandago C.A.R.
208 D2 Ouandja Haute-Kotto C.A.R.
208 D2 Ouandja Vakaga C.A.R.
208 D2 Ouandja-Vakaga, Réserve de Faune de la nature res. C.A.R.
208 E3 Ouando C.A.R.
208 D3 Ouango C.A.R.
206 D4 Ouangolodougou Côte d'Ivoire
207 G3 Ouani Kalaoua well Niger
160 C1 Ouanne France
251 H4 Ouaqui Fr. Guiana
208 E3 Ouara r. C.A.R.
207 F4 Ouargaye Burkina
205 G3 Ouargla Alg.
207 F2 Ouarissibitil well Mali
207 F2 Ouaritoufoulout well Mali
204 C3 Ouarkziz, Jbel ridge Alg./Morocco
Ouarogou Burkina see Ouargaye
156 C7 Ouarville France
204 D3 Ouarzazate Morocco
207 F3 Ouatagouna Mali
Oubangui r. C.A.R./Dem. Rep. Congo see Ubangi
212 E7 Oubergpas pass S. Africa
182 C7 Ouca Port.
160 G2 Ouche r. France
104 D7 Ōuchiyama Japan
156 B8 Oucques France
104 C7 Ouda Japan
164 F5 Oud-Beijerland Neth.
164 E5 Ouddorp Neth.
164 J2 Oudega Neth.
164 I3 Oudehaske Neth.
206 E2 Oudeïka well Mali
164 I3 Oudemirdum Neth.
165 E7 Oudenaarde Belgium
164 G5 Oudenbosch Neth.
165 D6 Oudenburg Belgium
164 L2 Oude Pekela Neth.
164 G4 Oude Rijn r. Neth.
164 G4 Ouderkerk aan de Amstel Neth.
164 G2 Oudeschild Neth.
164 F5 Oude-Tonge Neth.
164 G4 Oudewater Neth.
164 F5 Oud-Gastel Neth.
158 I7 Oudon France
159 J6 Oudon r. France
214 G9 Oudtshoorn S. Africa
165 G6 Oud-Turnhout Belgium
165 D6 Oudzele Belgium
180 D5 Oued Laou Morocco
204 D2 Oued Zem Morocco
78 □5 Ouegoa New Caledonia

Ouela to Palos, Cabo de
365

217 □3a Ouela Njazidja Comoros
206 D4 Ouéléssébougou Mali
207 F3 Ouella Niger
207 F5 Ouémé r. Benin
78 □5 Ouen i. New Caledonia
206 E4 Ouessa Burkina
158 A5 Ouessant, Île d' i. France
207 F4 Ouèssè Benin
208 C4 Ouesso Congo
207 H5 Ouest prov. Cameroon
225 H3 Ouest, Pointe de l' pt Que. Can.
204 D2 Ouezzane Morocco
165 H8 Ouffet Belgium
147 H4 Oughter, Lough l. Ireland
147 D6 Oughterard Ireland
204 D3 Ougnat, Jbel mt. Morocco
160 H2 Ougney France
104 A6 Ougo-gawa r. Japan
184 E2 Ouguela Port.
105 I3 Ougura-yama mt. Japan
208 C3 Ouham pref. C.A.R.
208 C2 Ouham r. C.A.R./Chad
208 C3 Ouham-Pendé pref. C.A.R.
207 F5 Ouidah Benin
206 E2 Ouinardene Mali
242 E4 Ouiriego Mex.
159 K3 Ouistreham France
206 D2 Oujâf well Maur.
204 E2 Oujda Morocco
206 B2 Oujeft Maur.
204 C3 Oulad Teïma Morocco
140 H2 Oulainen Fin.
140 T3 Oulangan kansallispuisto nat. park Fin.
156 F5 Oulchy-le-Château France
165 J8 Oulder Belgium
206 C3 Ould Yenjé Maur.
205 G2 Ouled Djellal Alg.
205 F2 Ouled Naïl, Monts des mts Alg.
205 F3 Ouled Saïd well Alg.
207 I5 Ouli Cameroon
160 F5 Oullins France
204 D2 Oulmès Morocco
151 P3 Oulton Suffolk, England U.K.
140 R4 Oulu Fin.
140 S4 Oulu prov. Fin.
140 S4 Oulujärvi l. Fin.
140 R4 Oulujoki r. Fin.
140 R4 Oulunsalo Fin.
190 B5 Oulx Italy
202 D6 Oum-Chalouba Chad
206 D5 Oumé Côte d'Ivoire
205 G2 Oum el Bouaghi Alg.
205 H6 Oum-Hadjer Chad
204 C5 Oumm ed Droûs Guebli, Sebkhet salt flat Maur.
204 C4 Oumm ed Droûs Telli, Sebkha salt flat Maur.
205 D4 Oumm el A'sel well Mali
205 G4 Ounane, Djebel mt. Alg.
204 C3 Ounara Morocco
140 R3 Ounasjoki r. Fin.
151 L3 Oundle Northamptonshire, England U.K.
223 K5 Oungre Sask. Can.
205 D5 Ounianga Kébir Chad
202 D5 Ounianga Sérir Chad
207 I2 Ounissoui well Niger
208 C3 Ouogo C.A.R.
165 I7 Oupeye Belgium
165 J9 Our r. Lux.
199 H4 Oura, Akrotirio pt Chios Greece
198 E2 Ouranoupoli Greece
102 □1 Oura-wan b. Okinawa Japan
237 K5 Ouray CO U.S.A.
241 W1 Ouray UT U.S.A.
156 H7 Ource r. France
156 F5 Ourcq r. France
206 C4 Ouré Kaba Guinea
254 D2 Ourém Brazil
182 E4 Ourense Spain
182 F4 Ourense prov. Galicia Spain
254 E3 Ouricuri Brazil
256 C5 Ourinhos Brazil
202 D5 Ourini Chad
184 C5 Ourique Port.
254 D4 Ouro Brazil
254 D4 Ouro r. Brazil
182 F1 Ouro r. Spain
215 G2 Ouro, Ponta do pt Moz.
257 F4 Ouro Branco Brazil
256 D5 Ouro Fino Brazil
182 E1 Ourol Spain
257 F4 Ouro Preto Brazil
160 D2 Ouroux-en-Morvan France
160 F3 Ouroux-sur-Saône France
165 I7 Ourthe r. Belgium
159 M2 Ourville-en-Caux France
151 M6 Ouse r. East Sussex, England U.K.
149 P6 Ouse r. England U.K.
163 G10 Oust France
158 G6 Oust r. France
206 B4 Outamba Kilimi National Park Sierra Leone
184 B3 Outão Port.
225 G3 Outardes r. Que. Can.
225 G3 Outardes Quatre, Réservoir resr Que. Can.
156 D7 Outarville France
204 E2 Outat Oulad el Haj Morocco
206 D2 Outeïd Arkâs well Mali
182 G5 Outeiro Bragança Port.
182 C5 Outeiro Viana do Castelo Port.
182 E2 Outeiro de Rei Spain
182 F5 Outeiro Seco Port.
214 G9 Outeniekwaberge mts S. Africa
146 B7 Outer Hebrides is Scotland U.K.
226 D2 Outer Island WI U.S.A.
100 G2 Outer Mongolia country Asia see Mongolia
240 N8 Outer Santa Barbara Channel CA U.S.A.
206 C2 Outfene well Maur.
212 C4 Outjo Namibia
223 J5 Outlook Sask. Can.
134 E3 Outokumpu Fin.
182 E4 Outomuro Spain
205 G5 Outoul Alg.
81 E12 Outram South I. N.Z.
156 C2 Outreau France
146 □O2 Out Skerries is Scotland U.K.
151 M2 Outwell Norfolk, England U.K.
78 □5 Ouvéa atoll Îles Loyauté New Caledonia
161 B10 Ouveillan France
161 F8 Ouvèze r. France
109 I6 Ouyanghai Shuiku resr China
83 I6 Ouyen Vic. Austr.
151 K3 Ouzel r. England U.K.
156 C8 Ouzouer-le-Marché France
156 D8 Ouzouer-sur-Loire France
191 I3 Ova r. Turkey
192 C4 Ovace, Punta d' mt. Corse France
126 F5 Ovacık İçel Turkey
126 I4 Ovacık Tunceli Turkey
199 M5 Ovacık Dağı mt. Turkey
190 C4 Ovada Italy
199 I5 Ovaeymiri Turkey
199 K6 Ova Gölü l. Turkey
199 J4 Ovakent Turkey
129 D7 Ovakışla Turkey
199 I5 Ovakışlacık Turkey
199 K6 Ovaköy Turkey
234 A2 Oval PA U.S.A.
79 □7a Ovalau i. Fiji
260 B2 Ovalle Chile
212 B3 Ovamboland reg. Namibia
208 B4 Ovan Gabon
182 C7 Ovar Port.
191 N3 Ovaro Italy
78 □6 Ovau i. Solomon Is
260 E3 Oveja mt. Arg.
250 C2 Ovejas Col.
260 D4 Ovejería Arg.
168 F4 Ovelgönne Ger.
207 I6 Oveng Cameroon
207 H6 Oveng Equat. Guinea
83 K7 Ovens r. Vic. Austr.
147 C9 Ovens Ireland
169 D9 Overath Ger.
146 K4 Overbister Orkney, Scotland U.K.
164 L4 Overdinkel Neth.
140 Q2 Øvergard Norway
140 K4 Overhalla Norway
165 G7 Overijse Belgium
164 K4 Overijssel prov. Neth.
164 J4 Overijssels Kanaal canal Neth.
140 Q3 Överkalix Sweden
87 C9 Overlander Roadhouse W.A. Austr.
236 H6 Overland Park KS U.S.A.
234 B6 Overlea MD U.S.A.
164 I5 Overloon Neth.
140 P5 Övermark Fin.
260 B4 Overo, Volcán vol. Arg.
165 H6 Overpelt Belgium
151 I2 Overseal Derbyshire, England U.K.
151 J5 Overton Hampshire, England U.K.
150 G2 Overton Wrexham, Wales U.K.
241 R5 Overton NV U.S.A.
237 H9 Overton TX U.S.A.
140 Q3 Övertorneå Sweden
146 I11 Overtown North Lanarkshire, Scotland U.K.
143 M4 Överum Sweden
140 M3 Överuman l. Sweden
164 G4 Overveen Neth.
151 I5 Over Wallop Hampshire, England U.K.
190 E3 Ovesca r. Italy
165 E6 Ovezande Neth.
182 E1 O Vicedo Spain
236 D5 Ovid CO U.S.A.
226 J6 Ovid MI U.S.A.
232 I6 Ovid NY U.S.A.
136 J7 Ovidiopol' Ukr.
197 Q6 Ovidiu Romania
182 I2 Oviedo Spain
182 H2 Oviedo prov. Spain
190 E6 Oviglio Italy
193 L3 Ovindoli Italy
139 T3 Ovinishchenskaya Vozvyshennost' hills Rus. Fed.
138 E4 Ovišrags hd Latvia
215 J6 Oviston Nature Reserve S. Africa
120 J7 Ovminzatov tog'lari hills Uzbek.
195 N3 Ovo, Punta dell' pt Italy
192 C7 Ovodda Sardegna Italy
106 E2 Övögdiy Mongolia
Ovolau i. Fiji see Ovalau
107 M4 Ovoot Mongolia
106 H4 Övörhangay prov. Mongolia
140 R2 Øvre Anárjohka Nasjonalpark nat. park Norway
141 I6 Øvre Årdal Norway
140 O2 Øvre Dividal Nasjonalpark nat. park Norway
140 K5 Øvre Forra nature res. Norway
142 J2 Övre Fryken l. Sweden
142 I2 Övre Gla l. Sweden
142 D1 Øvre Hein l. Norway
140 T2 Øvre Pasvik Nasjonalpark nat. park Norway
141 K6 Øvre Rendal Norway
140 P2 Övre Soppero Sweden
136 H2 Ovruch Ukr.
100 E2 Ovsyanka Rus. Fed.
106 H3 Övt Mongolia
80 K7 Owahanga North I. N.Z.
81 D13 Owaka South I. N.Z.
226 D1 Owakonze Ont. Can.
208 B5 Owando Congo
102 R6 Ōwani Japan
Owa Rafa i. Solomon Is see Santa Ana
104 F5 Owariasahi Japan
Owa Riki i. Solomon Is see Santa Catalina
232 I6 Owasco Lake NY U.S.A.
104 D7 Owase Japan
104 D7 Owase-wan b. Japan
237 H7 Owasso OK U.S.A.
236 I3 Owatonna MN U.S.A.
123 J4 Owbeh Afgh.
175 J4 Owczarnia Pol.
233 I6 Owego NY U.S.A.
147 H5 Owel, Lough l. Ireland
172 G4 Owen Ger.
81 G8 Owen, Mount South I. N.Z.
207 G5 Owena Nigeria
147 E4 Owenbeg Ireland
214 H4 Owendale S. Africa
147 C4 Owenduff r. Ireland
80 □ Owenga Chatham Is S. Pacific Ocean
147 C4 Oweniny r. Ireland
97 D9 Owen Island Myanmar
147 C4 Owenmore r. Ireland
147 H3 Owenreagh r. Northern Ireland U.K.
81 G8 Owen River South I. N.Z.
240 O5 Owens r. CA U.S.A.
230 D7 Owensboro KY U.S.A.
240 O5 Owens Lake CA U.S.A.
224 D4 Owen Sound Ont. Can.
227 N5 Owen Sound inlet Ont. Can.
84 D7 Owen Springs N.T. Austr.
91 K8 Owen Stanley Range mts P.N.G.
236 J6 Owensville MO U.S.A.
232 A9 Owensville OH U.S.A.
230 E6 Owenton KY U.S.A.
207 G5 Owerri Nigeria
147 F2 Owey Island Ireland
80 J6 Owhango North I. N.Z.
222 E5 Owikeno Lake B.C. Can.
172 G6 Owingen Ger.
232 I10 Owings MD U.S.A.
234 B6 Owings Mills MD U.S.A.
232 B10 Owingsville KY U.S.A.
223 M3 Owl r. Man. Can.
238 J5 Owl Creek r. WY U.S.A.
233 □P4 Owls Head ME U.S.A.
Owminzatow Toghi hills Uzbek. see Ovminzatov tog'lari
207 G5 Owo Nigeria
227 J7 Owosso MI U.S.A.
Owrtyn Wales U.K. see Overton
168 I2 Owschlag Ger.
238 F6 Owyhee NV U.S.A.
238 F5 Owyhee r. OR U.S.A.
238 F5 Owyhee Mountains ID U.S.A.
238 F5 Owyhee North Fork r. ID U.S.A.
238 F5 Owyhee South Fork r. ID U.S.A.
252 B2 Oxapampa Peru
140 □E1 Öxarfjörður b. Iceland
223 K5 Oxbow Sask. Can.
236 E1 Ox Creek r. ND U.S.A.
143 N3 Oxelösund Sweden
149 N6 Oxenhope West Yorkshire, England U.K.
81 G10 Oxford South I. N.Z.
151 J4 Oxford Oxfordshire, England U.K.
235 I2 Oxford CT U.S.A.
233 N6 Oxford MA U.S.A.
233 □O4 Oxford ME U.S.A.
227 K7 Oxford MI U.S.A.
237 K8 Oxford MS U.S.A.
231 H7 Oxford NC U.S.A.
234 F3 Oxford NJ U.S.A.
233 J6 Oxford NY U.S.A.
232 A9 Oxford OH U.S.A.
234 D5 Oxford PA U.S.A.
226 E6 Oxford WI U.S.A.
85 L6 Oxford Downs Qld Austr.
223 M4 Oxford House Man. Can.
223 M4 Oxford Lake Man. Can.
151 J4 Oxfordshire admin. div. England U.K.
142 J6 Oxie Sweden
243 O7 Oxkutzcab Mex.
83 J6 Oxley N.S.W. Austr.
83 M4 Oxleys Peak N.S.W. Austr.
83 N4 Oxley Wild Rivers National Park N.S.W. Austr.
Ox Mountains hills Ireland see Slieve Gamph
240 M7 Oxnard CA U.S.A.
151 L5 Oxshott Surrey, England U.K.
151 M5 Oxted Surrey, England U.K.
146 K11 Oxton Scottish Borders, Scotland U.K.
227 P4 Oxtongue Lake Ont. Can.
Oxus r. Asia see Amudar'ya
198 F4 Oxylithos Greece
95 I3 Oya Sarawak Malaysia
95 I3 Oya r. Malaysia
140 L? Øya Norway
104 E2 Oyabe Japan
104 F2 Oyabe-gawa r. Japan
105 I5 Oyama Shizuoka Japan
105 K3 Oyama Tochigi Japan
104 F2 Ōyama Japan
105 J5 Ō-yama mt. Japan
105 K7 Ō-yama vol. Japan
104 D6 Ōyamada Japan
104 C6 Ōyamazaki Japan
183 L2 Oyambre, Cabo de c. Spain
251 I3 Oyapock r. Brazil/Fr. Guiana
251 I3 Oyapock, Baie d' b. Fr. Guiana
121 T4 Oychilik Kazakh.
208 A4 Oyem Gabon
223 I5 Oyen Alta Can.
156 D2 Oye-Plage France
142 H2 Øyeren l. Norway
106 E3 Oygon Mongolia
146 H7 Oykel r. Scotland U.K.
146 G7 Oykel Bridge Highland, Scotland U.K.
173 I6 Oy-Mittelberg Ger.
131 P3 Oymyakon Rus. Fed.
208 B5 Oyo Congo
207 F5 Oyo Nigeria
207 F5 Oyo state Nigeria
203 H4 Oyo Sudan
104 C7 Ōyodo Japan
252 A2 Oyón Peru
160 H4 Oyonnax France
120 K7 Oyoqog'itma botig'i depr. Uzbek.
120 K7 Oyoqquduq Uzbek.
Oysangur Rus. Fed. see Oyskhara
Oyshilik Kazakh. see Oychilik
129 H2 Oyskhara Rus. Fed.
214 I10 Oyster Bay S. Africa
235 H3 Oyster Bay NY U.S.A.
235 G6 Oyster Creek NJ U.S.A.
96 A4 Oyster Island Myanmar
114 D5 Oyster Rocks is India
121 O6 Oytal Kazakh.
121 P7 Oy-Tal Kyrg.
168 H4 Oyten Ger.
111 E8 Oytograk Xinjiang China
128 A2 Oyukludağı mt. Turkey
Oyyl Kazakh. see Uil
Oyyq Kazakh. see Uyuk
182 D2 Oza Spain
183 P3 Ozaeta Spain
102 T7 Ō-zaki pt Japan
127 L4 Özalp Turkey
92 D7 Ozamiz Mindanao Phil.
156 B7 Ozanne r. France
231 E10 Ozark AL U.S.A.
237 I8 Ozark AR U.S.A.
237 I7 Ozark MO U.S.A.
237 I7 Ozark Plateau MO U.S.A.
236 I6 Ozarks, Lake of the MO U.S.A.
175 J5 Ożarów Pol.
175 H5 Ożarowice Pol.
175 I3 Ożarów Mazowiecki Pol.
122 G4 Ozbagū Iran
179 L6 Ožbalt Slovenia
199 I5 Özbaşı Turkey
Ozbekiston country Asia see Uzbekistan
177 J3 Ózd Hungary
177 I3 Ožďany Slovakia
129 C5 Özdere Erzurum Turkey
199 I5 Özdere İzmir Turkey
129 C7 Özdilek Turkey
Özen Kazakh. see Kyzylsay
175 J6 Ożenna Pol.
139 R2 Ozerevo Rus. Fed.
139 Q7 Ozerishche Rus. Fed.
136 H8 Ozerne Odes'ka Oblast' Ukr.
136 E2 Ozerne Volyns'ka Oblast' Ukr.
136 H3 Ozerne Zhytomyrs'ka Oblast' Ukr.
139 T6 Ozerninskoye Vodokhranilishche resr Rus. Fed.
131 Q4 Ozernovskiy Rus. Fed.
120 J1 Ozernoye Kazakh.
120 D2 Ozernoye Rus. Fed.
Ozernyy Karagandinskaya Oblast' Kazakh. see Shashubay
Ozernyy Kostanayskaya Oblast' Kazakh. see Ozernoye
139 X4 Ozernyy Ivanovskaya Oblast' Rus. Fed.
120 I2 Ozernyy Orenburgskaya Oblast' Rus. Fed.
139 P6 Ozernyy Smolenskaya Oblast' Rus. Fed.
121 U1 Ozero Petrovskoye Rus. Fed.
198 C4 Ozeros, Limni l. Greece
100 L2 Ozerpakh Rus. Fed.
138 F7 Ozersk Rus. Fed.
100 M5 Ozerskiy Sakhalin Rus. Fed.
139 V7 Ozery Rus. Fed.
100 F3 Ozeryane Rus. Fed.
137 L3 Ozeryany Ukr.
121 O7 Özgön Kyrg.
139 V7 Ozherel'ye Rus. Fed.
131 Q3 Ozhogina r. Rus. Fed.
192 C6 Ozieri Sardegna Italy
174 G5 Ozimek Pol.
120 C2 Ozinki Rus. Fed.
129 B6 Özlüce Barajı resr Turkey
156 E6 Ozoir-la-Ferrière France
138 G5 Ozolnieki Latvia
237 E10 Ozona TX U.S.A.
177 H5 Ozora Hungary
175 H4 Ozorków Pol.
207 G5 Ozoro Nigeria
103 J13 Ōzu Ehime Japan
103 H14 Ōzu Kumamoto Japan
103 I12 Ozuki Japan
245 J4 Ozuluama Mex.
245 I6 Ozumba de Alzate Mex.
129 D4 Ozurget'i Georgia
128 A1 Özyurt Dağı mts Turkey
175 M5 Ozyutychi Ukr.
191 K7 Ozzano dell'Emilia Italy
190 E5 Ozzano Monferrato Italy

P

206 E4 Pâ Burkina
140 R4 Paakkola Fin.
165 H6 Paal Belgium
78 □5 Paama i. Vanuatu
221 N3 Paamiut Greenland
Pa-an Myanmar see Hpa-an
Paanopa i. Kiribati see Banaba
214 C9 Paarl S. Africa
138 J2 Paasvere Estonia
78 □4a Paata i. Chuuk Micronesia
Paatsjoki r. Europe see Patsoyoki
240 □F13 Pa'auilo HI U.S.A.
Pabaigh i. Western Isles, Scotland U.K. see Pabbay
Pabail Uarach Scotland U.K. see Upper Bayble
214 F4 Paballelo S. Africa
101 F8 P'abal-li N. Korea
146 B7 Pabbay i. Western Isles, Scotland U.K.
146 A9 Pabbay i. Western Isles, Scotland U.K.
244 E3 Pabeilón de Arteaga Mex.
260 B2 Pabellón Chile
175 H4 Pabianice Pol.
Pabianitz Pol. see Pabianice
192 B8 Pabillonis Sardegna Italy
245 H1 Pablillo r. Mex.
261 H5 Pablo Acosta Arg.
117 L7 Pabna Bangl.
179 K3 Pabneukirchen Austria
138 I7 Pabradė Lith.
123 L8 Pab Range mts Pak.
158 E4 Pabu France
252 D2 Pacaás, Serra dos hills Brazil
253 E2 Pacaás Novos, Parque Nacional nat. park Brazil
256 B4 Pacaembu Brazil
252 D2 Pacahuaras r. Bol.
254 F3 Pacajus Brazil
214 G10 Pacaltsdorp S. Africa
175 J5 Pacanów Pol.
252 B3 Pacapausa Peru
Pacaraimã, Serra mts S. America see Pakaraima Mountains
252 B3 Pacarán Peru
250 B6 Pacasmayo Peru
254 F2 Pacatuba Brazil
250 C6 Pacaya r. Peru
243 N10 Pacaya, Volcán de vol. Guat.
250 C6 Pacaya Samiria, Reserva Nacional nature res. Peru
158 H5 Pacé France
194 D8 Paceco Sicilia Italy
260 C2 Pachaco Arg.
114 F7 Pachaimalai Hills India
235 L1 Pachaug Pond l. CT U.S.A.
242 E2 Pacheco Chihuahua Mex.
244 E1 Pacheco Zacatecas Mex.
199 G6 Pacheia i. Greece
135 H5 Pachelma Rus. Fed.
252 C4 Pachía Peru
134 I3 Pachikha Rus. Fed.
195 I10 Pachino Sicilia Italy
252 B2 Pachitea r. Peru
252 A1 Pachiza Peru
116 G8 Pachmarhi Madh. Prad. India
198 F1 Pachni Greece
116 F8 Pachor Madh. Prad. India
116 E9 Pachora Mahar. India
116 D7 Pachpadra Rajasthan India
116 D7 Pachpadra Salt Depot Rajasthan India
245 I5 Pachuca Mex.
192 I1 Paciano Italy
240 J4 Pacifica CA U.S.A.
267 I9 Pacific-Antarctic Ridge sea feature Pacific Ocean
240 K5 Pacific Grove CA U.S.A.
266 Pacific Ocean
222 E5 Pacific Rim National Park B.C. Can.
92 E6 Pacijan i. Phil.
177 K3 Pácin Hungary
95 K8 Pacinan, Tanjung pt Indon.
196 H5 Pačir Vojvodina Serbia
95 I9 Pacitan Jawa Indon.
179 K6 Pack Austria
83 H4 Packsaddle N.S.W. Austr.
179 K6 Packsattel pass Austria
182 D6 Pacos de Ferreira Port.
176 E2 Pacov Czech Rep.
251 H5 Pacoval Brazil
176 G5 Pacsa Hungary
257 E2 Pacuí r. Brazil
177 K2 Pacutová hill Slovakia
175 H3 Pacyna Pol.
156 B5 Pacy-sur-Eure France
174 F5 Paczków Pol.
92 E8 Padada Mindanao Phil.
93 C5 Padalere Sulawesi Indon.
Padali Rus. Fed. see Amursk
93 B6 Padamarang i. Indon.
116 D5 Padampur Rajasthan India
116 B8 Padana Gujarat India
95 H5 Padang Kalimantan Indon.
93 B7 Padang Sulawesi Indon.
94 D5 Padang Sumatera Indon.
94 E4 Padang i. Indon.
94 E3 Padang Endau Malaysia
95 L5 Padang Luwai, Cagar Alam nature res. Kalimantan Indon.
94 D5 Padangpanjang Sumatera Indon.
94 C4 Padangsidimpuan Sumatera Indon.
95 H5 Padangtikar Kalimantan Indon.
95 H5 Padangtikar i. Indon.
134 F3 Padany Rus. Fed.
138 H9 Padarosk Belarus
129 J5 Padarqışlaq Azer.
95 K2 Padas r. Malaysia
141 R6 Padasjoki Fin.
122 C5 Padatha, Kūh-e mt. Iran
251 E5 Padauiri r. Brazil
96 B5 Padaung Myanmar
168 H1 Padborg Denmark
151 K4 Padbury Buckinghamshire, England U.K.
252 D5 Padcaya Bol.
83 J5 Paddington N.S.W. Austr.
215 O6 Paddock S. Africa
151 M5 Paddock Wood Kent, England U.K.
93 C5 Padeabesar i. Indon.
177 J6 Padej Vojvodina Serbia
232 E9 Paden City WV U.S.A.
169 G7 Paderborn Ger.
184 C6 Paderne Faro Port.
182 D4 Paderne Viana do Castelo Port.
182 E4 Paderne de Allariz Spain
210 B4 Pader Palwo Uganda
197 K5 Padeșu, Vârful mt. Romania
175 J5 Padew Narodowa Pol.
96 C3 Padibyu Myanmar
149 M6 Padiham Lancashire, England U.K.
252 D4 Padilla Bol.
197 P6 Padina Romania
196 I5 Padina Vojvodina Serbia
196 I6 Padinska Skela Serbia
163 H6 Padirac France
140 N3 Padjelanta nationalpark nat. park Sweden
139 O8 Padluzhzha Belarus
117 L8 Padma r. Bangl. alt. Ganga, conv. Ganges
114 E8 Padmanabhapuram Tamil Nadu India
116 H9 Padmapur Mahar. India
182 G4 Padornelo, Portilla del pass Spain
157 M7 Padoux France
191 L5 Padova Italy
191 L5 Padova prov. Italy
116 D8 Padra Gujarat India
117 J6 Padrauna Uttar Prad. India
184 F5 Padre Caro hill Spain
237 G12 Padre Island TX U.S.A.
237 G12 Padre Island National Seashore nature res. TX U.S.A.
257 G2 Padre Paraíso Brazil
192 B7 Padria Sardegna Italy
192 B3 Padro, Monte mt. Corse France
182 C3 Padrón Spain
215 K9 Padrone, Cape S. Africa
192 D6 Padru Sardegna Italy
150 C6 Padstow Cornwall, England U.K.
138 K6 Padsvillye Belarus
82 H7 Padthaway S.A. Austr.
115 H3 Padua Orissa India
Padua Italy see Padova
237 K7 Paducah KY U.S.A.
237 E8 Paducah TX U.S.A.
185 L6 Padul Spain
193 P7 Padula Italy
193 N5 Paduli Italy
116 F3 Padum Jammu and Kashmir
197 K4 Pădurea Craiului, Munții mts Romania
79 □9a Paea Tahiti Fr. Polynesia
101 F8 Paegam N. Korea
81 I7 Paekakariki North I. N.Z.
Paektu-san mt. China/N. Korea see Baotou Shan
101 D10 Paengnyŏng-do i. S. Korea
81 D12 Paerau South I. N.Z.
80 J4 Paeroa North I. N.Z.
80 K5 Paeroa hill North I. N.Z.
190 C6 Paesana Italy
191 M4 Paese Italy
195 H3 Paestum tourist site Italy
92 C4 Paete Luzon Phil.
128 A4 Pafos Cyprus
128 A4 Pafos airport Cyprus
213 F4 Pafuri Moz.
188 E3 Pag Croatia
188 E3 Pag i. Croatia
93 C8 Paga Flores Indon.
134 M2 Paga r. Rus. Fed.
251 H6 Paga Conta Brazil
95 G8 Pagadenbaru Jawa Indon.
92 D8 Pagadian Mindanao Phil.
94 D6 Pagai Selatan i. Indon.
94 D6 Pagai Utara i. Indon.
Pagalu i. Equat. Guinea see Annobón
91 K3 Pagan i. N. Mariana Is
191 K3 Paganella mt. Italy
193 K3 Paganica Italy
192 G2 Paganico Italy
260 D2 Paganzo Arg.
94 E6 Pagaralam Sumatera Indon.
198 D3 Pagasitikos Kolpos b. Greece
95 J6 Pagatan Kalimantan Indon.
95 K6 Pagatan Kalimantan Indon.
241 U5 Page AZ U.S.A.
86 H4 Page, Mount hill W.A. Austr.
138 E6 Pagėgiai Lith.
94 F6 Pagerdewa Sumatera Indon.
259 □ Paget, Mount S. Georgia
85 N5 Paget Cay rf Coral Sea Is Terr. Austr.
151 K6 Pagham West Sussex, England U.K.
123 M4 Paghman mt. Afgh.
138 H6 Pagiriai Kaunas Lith.
138 I7 Pagiriai Vilnius Lith.
192 I2 Paglia r. Italy
193 M3 Paglieta Italy
157 L6 Pagny-sur-Moselle France
78 □1 Pago Bay Guam
261 H1 Pago Largo Arg.
Pagon i. N. Mariana Is see Pagan
78 □2 Pago Pago American Samoa
239 K8 Pagosa Springs CO U.S.A.
207 F4 Pagouda Togo
Paggên Qinghai China see Gadê
111 I13 Pagri Xizang China
247 □2 Pagua Bay Dominica
224 C3 Pagwachuan r. Ont. Can.
224 C3 Pagwa River Ont. Can.
240 □F14 Pāhala HI U.S.A.
94 E3 Pahang r. Malaysia
94 E3 Pahang state Malaysia
116 F6 Pahari Rajasthan India
117 L7 Paharpur tourist site Bangl.
123 N5 Paharpur Pak.
95 H4 Pahauman Kalimantan Indon.
81 B13 Pahia Point South I. N.Z.
80 J7 Pahiatua North I. N.Z.
173 K6 Pähl Ger.
Pahlavī Dezh Iran see Āq Qal'eh
168 H2 Pahlen Ger.
116 E2 Pahlgam Jammu and Kashmir
240 □G14 Pāhoa HI U.S.A.
231 G12 Pahokee FL U.S.A.
136 F1 Pahost Vodaskhovishcha resr Belarus
116 H7 Pahra Uttar Prad. India
123 I4 Pahra Kariz Afgh.
241 Q4 Pahranagat Range mts NV U.S.A.
138 G8 Pahranichny Belarus
241 Q5 Pahrump NV U.S.A.
116 G6 Pahuj r. India
240 P4 Pahute Mesa plat. NV U.S.A.
96 D5 Pai Thai.
240 □E13 Paia HI U.S.A.
253 F4 Paiaguás Brazil
182 C8 Paião Port.
240 K5 Paicines CA U.S.A.
138 I3 Paide Estonia
150 E7 Paignton Torbay, England U.K.
80 I2 Paihia North I. N.Z.
260 B2 Paihuano Chile
250 B6 Paiján Peru
141 R6 Päijänne l. Fin.
207 G4 Paiko Nigeria
111 G12 Paikü Co l. China
252 D4 Paila r. Bol.
260 A6 Pailahueque Chile
116 H7 Pailani Uttar Prad. India
163 G9 Pailhès France
97 F8 Pailin Cambodia
259 B6 Paillaco Chile
240 □E13 Pailolo Channel HI U.S.A.
158 G7 Paimbœuf France
141 Q6 Paimio Fin.
138 F1 Paimionselkä b. Fin.
158 E4 Paimpol France
158 G5 Paimpont France
158 G6 Paimpont, Forêt de for. France
94 D5 Painan Sumatera Indon.
114 E8 Painavu Kerala India
260 B3 Paine Chile
259 B8 Paine, Cerro mt. Chile
257 E3 Paineiras Brazil
255 C8 Painel Brazil
226 F2 Painesdale MI U.S.A.
232 D7 Painesville OH U.S.A.
257 E4 Pains Brazil
150 H4 Painswick Gloucestershire, England U.K.
241 U5 Painted Desert AZ U.S.A.
241 S8 Painted Rock Dam AZ U.S.A.
173 L4 Painten Ger.
Paint Hills Que. Can. see Wemindji
223 L4 Paint Lake Man. Can.
223 L4 Paint Lake Provincial Recreation Park Man. Can.
237 F10 Paint Rock TX U.S.A.
232 C11 Paintsville KY U.S.A.
250 C3 Paipa Col.
116 H9 Pairi r. India
227 M5 Paisley Ont. Can.
146 H11 Paisley Renfrewshire, Scotland U.K.
183 P2 País Vasco aut. comm. Spain
78 □5 Paita New Caledonia
250 A6 Paita Peru
95 L1 Paitan, Teluk b. Malaysia
114 D3 Paithan Mahar. India
109 M4 Paitou Zhejiang China
182 D6 Paiva r. Port.
Paiva Couceiro Angola see Quipungo
243 N9 Paixban Mex.
109 I3 Paizhou Hubei China
140 Q3 Pajala Sweden
250 A5 Paján Ecuador
245 M7 Pajapán Mex.
216 □3b Pájara Fuerteventura Canary Is
182 I2 Pajares, Puerto de pass Spain
250 C3 Pajarito Col.
183 Q9 Pajarón Spain
183 Q9 Pajaroncillo Spain
258 C3 Pájaros, Islotes Chile
174 G4 Pajęczno Pol.
176 F5 Páka Hungary
94 E2 Paka Malaysia
93 F3 Pakal i. Maluku Indon.
114 F6 Pakala Andhra Prad. India
Pakanbaru Sumatera Indon. see Pekanbaru
115 N2 Pakangyi Myanmar
138 G6 Pakapė Lith.
251 F4 Pakaraima Mountains S. America
224 B3 Pakashkan Lake Ont. Can.
117 K7 Pakaur Jharkhand India
80 G7 Pakawau South I. N.Z.
101 D9 Pakch'ŏn N. Korea
224 D4 Pakesley Ont. Can.
131 R3 Pakhachi Rus. Fed.
120 G3 Pakhar' Kazakh.
Pakhiá i. Greece see Pacheia
Pákhni Greece see Pachni
Pakhoi Guangxi China see Beihai
139 U7 Pakhomovo Rus. Fed.
123 K7 Pakistan country Asia
109 □J7 Pak Ka Shan hill H.K. China
94 C3 Pakkat Sumatera Indon.
188 E3 Paklenica nat. park Croatia
193 Q1 Pakleni Otoci is Croatia
Paknampho Thai. see Nakhon Sawan
176 G5 Pakod Hungary
96 B4 Pakokku Myanmar
174 G3 Pakość Pol.
174 G3 Pakoskie, Jezioro l. Pol.
174 F4 Pakosław Pol.
188 E4 Pakoštane Croatia
80 H2 Pakotai North I. N.Z.
223 I5 Pakowki Lake imp. l. Alta Can.
177 H4 Pákozd Hungary
123 O6 Pakpattan Pak.
97 E10 Pak Phanang Thai.
97 E11 Pak Phayun Thai.
188 F3 Pakra r. Croatia
188 F3 Pakrac Croatia
138 G6 Pakruojis Lith.
177 H5 Paks Hungary
Pakse Laos see Pakxé
109 □J7 Pak Tai To Yan mt. H.K. China
109 □J7 Pak Tam Chung H.K. China
97 F7 Pak Thong Chai Thai.
123 M5 Paktīā prov. Afgh.
123 M5 Paktīkā prov. Afgh.
95 J3 Paku r. Malaysia
94 G6 Paku, Tanjung pt Indon.
93 B5 Pakue Sulawesi Indon.
136 J2 Pakul' Ukr.
223 M5 Pakwash Lake Ont. Can.
96 F5 Pakxan Laos
96 G7 Pakxé Laos
96 F4 Pakxeng Laos
Pal Senegal see Mpal
208 B2 Pala Chad
97 D8 Pala Myanmar
94 G8 Palabuhanratu Jawa Indon.
94 F8 Palabuhanratu, Teluk b. Indon.
261 G2 Palacios Arg.
252 D3 Palacios Bol.
183 K6 Palacios de Goda Spain
183 N5 Palacios de la Sierra Spain
182 H3 Palacios del Sil Spain
182 G4 Palacios de Sanabria Spain
178 E7 Pala di San Martino mt. Italy
161 H6 Paladru, Lac de l. France
Palaestinia reg. Asia see Palestine
186 L4 Palafrugell Spain
195 L2 Palagianello Italy
195 M2 Palagiano Italy
194 H9 Palagonia Sicilia Italy
188 F4 Palagruža i. Croatia
191 J8 Palaia Italy
198 E5 Palaia Fokaia Greece
128 B4 Palaichori Cyprus
199 H7 Palaikastro Kriti Greece
198 E7 Palaiochora Kriti Greece
Palaiókastron Kriti Greece see Palaikastro
198 B4 Palairos Greece
156 D6 Palaiseau France
Palakkat Kerala India see Palghat
117 J9 Pala Laharha Orissa India
115 M7 Palalankwe Andaman & Nicobar Is India
212 D4 Palamakoloi Botswana
198 D3 Palamas Greece
93 E4 Palamea Maluku Indon.
186 L4 Palamós Spain
116 F3 Palam Pur Hima. Prad. India
117 J8 Palamu Jharkhand India
116 D6 Palana Rajasthan India
131 Q4 Palana Rus. Fed.
92 D3 Palanan Luzon Phil.
92 D3 Palanan Point Luzon Phil.
187 E8 Palancia, Riu r. Spain
129 B6 Palandöken Dağları mts Turkey
116 H9 Palandur Mahar. India
138 E6 Palanga Lith.
127 M6 Palangān Iran
122 I6 Palangān, Kūh-e mts Iran
161 B8 Palanges, Montagne des mts France
95 J6 Palangkaraya Kalimantan Indon.
114 E7 Palani Tamil Nadu India
116 D7 Palanpur Gujarat India
93 A6 Palanro Sulawesi Indon.
123 K8 Palantak Pak.
190 I7 Palanzano Italy
92 E5 Palapag Samar Phil.
213 E4 Palapye Botswana
114 G6 Palar r. India
123 O4 Palas Pak.
93 B3 Palasa Sulawesi Indon.
117 M6 Palasbari Assam India
182 E3 Palas de Rei Spain
138 L6 Palata r. Belarus
193 N4 Palata Italy
131 Q3 Palatka Rus. Fed.
231 G11 Palatka FL U.S.A.
192 C5 Palau Sardegna Italy
92 □ Palau country N. Pacific Ocean
93 G6 Palau Hatta i. Maluku Indon.
92 D2 Palaui i. Phil.
92 B4 Palauig Luzon Phil.
91 H5 Palau Islands Palau
97 D8 Palauk Myanmar
78 □2 Palauli Bay Samoa
94 F7 Palausekopong, Tanjung pt Indon.
266 D5 Palau Trench sea feature N. Pacific Ocean
176 F3 Pálava park Czech Rep.
161 D9 Palavas-les-Flots France
97 D8 Palaw Myanmar
92 A7 Palawan i. Phil.
92 A7 Palawan Passage str. Phil.
266 C5 Palawan Trough sea feature N. Pacific Ocean
92 C4 Palayan Luzon Phil.
114 E8 Palayankottai Tamil Nadu India
183 L7 Palazuelos de Eresma Spain
192 B3 Palazzo, Punta pt Corse France
194 E8 Palazzo Adriano Sicilia Italy
194 H9 Palazzolo Acreide Sicilia Italy
190 H4 Palazzolo sull'Oglio Italy
193 Q6 Palazzo San Gervasio Italy
114 G4 Palchal Lake India
179 M6 Paldau Austria
138 H2 Paldiski Estonia
188 G4 Pale Bos.-Herz.
96 B4 Pale Myanmar
134 H4 Palekh Rus. Fed.
Palekhori Cyprus see Palaichori
93 B3 Paleleh Sulawesi Indon.
94 F6 Palembang Sumatera Indon.
261 G4 Palemón Huergo Arg.
259 B6 Palena Aisén Chile
259 C6 Palena Los Lagos Chile
193 M4 Palena Italy
183 K4 Palencia Spain
183 K4 Palencia prov. Spain
185 J6 Palenciana Spain
243 M9 Palenque Mex.
183 L4 Palenzuela Spain
258 D2 Palermo Arg.
194 E7 Palermo Sicilia Italy
194 F8 Palermo prov. Sicilia Italy
194 E7 Palermo, Golfo di b. Sicilia Italy
128 D6 Palestine reg. Asia
237 H10 Palestine TX U.S.A.
193 J4 Palestrina Italy
96 A4 Paletwa Myanmar
100 M3 Palevo Rus. Fed.
123 M6 Palezgir Chauki Pak.
177 H5 Pálfa Hungary
114 C3 Palghar Mahar. India
114 E7 Palghat Kerala India
87 C7 Palgrave, Mount hill W.A. Austr.
212 B4 Palgrave Point Namibia
182 C7 Palhaça Port.
177 K3 Pálháza Hungary
255 C8 Palhoca Brazil
116 H8 Pali Madh. Prad. India
114 C3 Pali Mahar. India
116 D7 Pali Rajasthan India
193 K4 Paliano Italy
95 K8 Paliat i. Indon.
177 I5 Palić Vojvodina Serbia
196 H4 Palićko Jezero l. Serbia
138 L7 Palik Belarus
78 □4b Palikir Pohnpei Micronesia
78 □4b Palikir Passage Pohnpei Micronesia
92 E8 Palimbang Mindanao Phil.
160 E3 Palinges France
193 O7 Palinuro Italy
193 O7 Palinuro, Capo c. Italy
198 E3 Paliouri Greece
198 E3 Paliouri, Akrotirio pt Greece
156 G7 Palis France
239 J7 Palisade CO U.S.A.
165 H9 Paliseul Belgium
116 C9 Palitana Gujarat India
138 G3 Palivere Estonia
195 K8 Palizzi Italy
140 O3 Palja hill Sweden
140 T4 Paljakka hill Fin.
141 R6 Pälkäne Fin.
114 F8 Palk Bay Sri Lanka
138 L4 Palkino Rus. Fed.
140 S2 Palkisoja Fin.
115 H3 Palkohda Andhra Prad. India
114 F6 Palkonda Range mts India
117 J8 Palkot Jharkhand India
177 H2 Palkovice Czech Rep.
114 F8 Palk Strait India/Sri Lanka
Palla Bianca mt. Austria/Italy see Weißkugel
114 E7 Palladani Tamil Nadu India
195 L5 Pallagorio Italy
252 B3 Pallapalla mt. Peru
184 G4 Pallarés Spain
186 H3 Pallaresa r. Spain
186 G3 Pallaresa, Noguera r. Spain
147 F7 Pallas Green Ireland
140 Q2 Pallas ja Ounastunturin kansallispuisto nat. park Fin.
147 E7 Pallaskenry Ireland
120 B2 Pallasovka Rus. Fed.
114 G6 Pallavaram Tamil Nadu India
114 G4 Palleru r. India
196 H9 Pallës, Bishti i pt Albania
173 N5 Palling Ger.
87 E13 Pallinup r. W.A. Austr.
210 B4 Pallisa Uganda
81 J8 Palliser, Cape North I. N.Z.
79 □9 Palliser, Îles is Arch. des Tuamotu Fr. Polynesia
81 J8 Palliser Bay North I. N.Z.
192 A7 Pallosu, Cala su b. Sardegna Italy
116 E5 Pallu Rajasthan India
158 H8 Palluau France
159 N8 Palluau-sur-Indre France
254 D5 Palma r. Brazil
117 K8 Palma W. Bengal India
211 D7 Palma Moz.
184 B4 Palma Port.
187 K8 Palma, Badia de b. Spain
192 A8 Palma, Porto b. Sardegna Italy
193 N6 Palma Campania Italy
183 O6 Pálmaces, Embalse de resr Spain
185 I5 Palma del Río Spain
187 K8 Palma de Mallorca Spain
194 F9 Palma di Montechiaro Sicilia Italy
192 A6 Palmadula Sardegna Italy
114 F6 Palmaner Andhra Prad. India
191 O4 Palmanova Italy
187 K8 Palmanova Spain
244 F3 Palma Pegada Mex.
258 G4 Palmar, Punta del pt Uru.
244 G7 Palmar Chico Mex.
252 D2 Palmares Acre Brazil
254 G4 Palmares Pernambuco Brazil
255 C9 Palmares do Sul Brazil
190 H7 Palmaria, Isola i. Italy
250 D3 Palmarito Venez.
193 J6 Palmarola, Isola i. Italy
227 O1 Palmarolle Que. Can.
242 □R13 Palmar Sur Costa Rica
255 C8 Palmas Paraná Brazil
254 C4 Palmas Tocantins Brazil
206 D5 Palmas, Cape Liberia
192 B10 Palmas, Golfo di b. Sardegna Italy
245 K6 Palma Sola Mex.
247 I8 Palma Sola Venez.
246 F3 Palma Soriano Cuba
182 D7 Palmaz Port.
231 G12 Palm Bay FL U.S.A.
231 G11 Palm Coast FL U.S.A.
240 N7 Palmdale CA U.S.A.
241 P8 Palm Desert CA U.S.A.
256 C6 Palmeira Brazil
182 D5 Palmeira Port.
255 B8 Palmeira das Missões Brazil
254 F4 Palmeira dos Índios Brazil
254 E3 Palmeirais Brazil
254 D5 Palmeiras r. Brazil
256 C2 Palmeiras de Goiás Brazil
209 B7 Palmeirinhas, Ponta das pt Angola
184 B3 Palmela Port.
262 T2 Palmer research stn Antarctica
85 I4 Palmer r. Qld Austr.
84 D8 Palmer watercourse N.T. Austr.
220 D3 Palmer AK U.S.A.
262 T2 Palmer Land reg. Antarctica
234 B7 Palmer Park MD U.S.A.
Palmerston N.T. Austr. see Darwin
84 C2 Palmerston N.T. Austr.
227 N6 Palmerston Ont. Can.
81 □2 Palmerston atoll Cook Is
81 E12 Palmerston South I. N.Z.
147 J6 Palmerston Ireland
85 L6 Palmerston, Cape Qld Austr.
80 J7 Palmerston North North I. N.Z.
234 D3 Palmerton PA U.S.A.
85 J3 Palmerville Qld Austr.
231 F12 Palmetto FL U.S.A.
247 □2 Palmetto Point Antigua and Barbuda
231 I13 Palmetto Point Bahamas
195 J7 Palmi Italy
245 H2 Palmillas Mex.
260 C3 Palmira Arg.
250 B4 Palmira Col.
246 C2 Palmira Cuba
125 L3 Palm Islands tourist site U.A.E.
256 A6 Palmital Paraná Brazil
256 B5 Palmital São Paulo Brazil
261 I3 Palmitas Uru.
Palmnicken Rus. Fed. see Yantarnyy
184 I8 Palmones r. Spain
177 I5 Pálmonostora Hungary
240 P8 Palm Springs CA U.S.A.
85 L8 Palm Tree Creek r. Qld Austr.
84 D8 Palm Valley N.T. Austr.
Palmyra Syria see Tadmur
236 J6 Palmyra MO U.S.A.
234 E4 Palmyra NJ U.S.A.
232 H5 Palmyra NY U.S.A.
227 R9 Palmyra PA U.S.A.
232 G11 Palmyra VA U.S.A.
75 I3 Palmyra Atoll N. Pacific Ocean
117 K9 Palmyras Point India
146 I13 Palnackie Dumfries and Galloway, Scotland U.K.
192 C4 Palneca Corse France
114 E7 Palni Hills India
134 K3 Pal'niki Rus. Fed.
92 E6 Palo Leyte Phil.
192 C4 Palo, Étang de lag. Corse France
182 G2 Palo, Puerto del pass Spain
244 E4 Palo Alto Aguascalientes Mex.
245 H1 Palo Alto Tamaulipas Mex.
240 J4 Palo Alto CA U.S.A.
258 D2 Palo Blanco Arg.
243 I4 Palo Blanco Mex.
250 B3 Palo de las Letras Col.
195 L1 Palo del Colle Italy
237 E8 Palo Duro watercourse TX U.S.A.
95 I3 Paloh Sarawak Malaysia
210 B2 Paloich Sudan
140 Q2 Palojärvi Fin.
140 Q2 Palojoensuu Fin.
140 S2 Palomaa Fin.
252 C3 Palomani mt. Peru
186 D6 Palomar de Arroyos Spain
245 L8 Palomares Mex.
184 G6 Palomares del Río Spain
240 P8 Palomar Mountain CA U.S.A.
184 G3 Palomas Spain
184 H8 Palomas, Punta pt Spain
193 M3 Palombaro Italy
183 L2 Palombera, Embalse de mts Spain
183 L2 Palombera, Puerto de pass Spain
194 I10 Palombieri r. Sicilia Italy
183 P8 Palomera Spain
186 C6 Palomera, Sierra mts Spain
183 O9 Palomeras del Campo Spain
184 G3 Palomilas r. Spain
250 C2 Palomino Col.
258 D2 Palomitas Arg.
193 O6 Palomonte Italy
191 K4 Palòn, Cima mt. Italy
114 G4 Paloncha Andhra Prad. India
237 F9 Palo Pinto TX U.S.A.
93 B5 Palopo Sulawesi Indon.
187 D12 Palos, Cabo de c. Spain

258 F2 Palo Santo Arg.
184 F6 Palos de la Frontera Spain
247 □7 Palo Seco Trin. and Tob.
123 O4 Palosi Pak.
238 F3 Palouse r. WA U.S.A.
241 R8 Palo Verde CA U.S.A.
242 □Q12 Palo Verde, Parque Nacional nat. park Costa Rica
141 Q6 Palovesi l. Fin.
252 B3 Palpa Ica Peru
252 A2 Palpa Lima Peru
85 H8 Palparara Qld Austr.
93 E5 Palpetu, Tanjung pt Buru Indon.
260 B3 Palquico Chile
186 L4 Pals Spain
116 D9 Palsana Gujarat India
140 S4 Paltamo Fin.
140 S4 Paltaselkä l. Fin.
138 L1 Pal'tsevo Rus. Fed.
139 R8 Pal'tso Rus. Fed.
93 A4 Palu Sulawesi Indon.
93 B8 Palu i. Indon.
93 A4 Palu r. Indon.
127 I4 Palu Turkey
92 C5 Paluan Mindoro Phil.
92 C5 Paluan Bay Mindoro Phil.
195 L4 Paludi Italy
163 B8 Palue r. France
159 M2 Paluel France
191 O2 Paluzza Italy
123 K2 Pal'vart Turkm.
116 F5 Palwal Haryana India
Palwancha Andhra Prad. India see Paloncha
130 H3 Pal'yanovo Rus. Fed.
138 I7 Palyatskishki Belarus
131 S3 Palyavaam r. Rus. Fed.
Palyeskaya Nizina marsh Belarus/Ukr. see Pripet Marshes
138 M9 Palyessye Homyel'skaya Voblasts' Belarus
139 O8 Palyessye Homyel'skaya Voblasts' Belarus
172 A2 Palzem Ger.
179 P3 Pama Austria
207 F4 Pama Burkina
208 C3 Pama r. C.A.R.
207 F4 Pama, Réserve Partielle de nature res. Burkina
83 I5 Pamamaroo Lake N.S.W. Austr.
93 C9 Pamana i. Indon.
93 C8 Pamana Besar i. Indon.
217 □3b Pamandzi Mayotte
95 G8 Pamanukan Jawa Indon.
217 □3b Pamanzi, Récif rf Mayotte
250 D5 Pamar Col.
129 F5 P'ambaki Lerrnashght'a mts Armenia
114 F8 Pamban Channel India
213 G4 Pambarra Moz.
93 A3 Pambero Sulawesi Indon.
83 L7 Pambula N.S.W. Austr.
179 L6 Pameče Slovenia
95 J8 Pamekasan Jawa Indon.
95 G8 Pameungpeuk Jawa Indon.
199 H3 Pamfylla Lesvos Greece
179 O4 Pamhagen Austria
174 E3 Pamiątkowo Pol.
114 E5 Pamidi Andhra Prad. India
163 H9 Pamiers France
123 O3 Pamir r. Afgh./Tajik.
121 O8 Pamir mts Asia
231 I8 Pamlico r. NC U.S.A.
231 I8 Pamlico Sound sea chan. NC U.S.A.
225 G3 Pamouscachiou, Lac l. Que. Can.
252 C5 Pampa Chile
237 E8 Pampa TX U.S.A.
259 C7 Pampa Chica Arg.
252 B3 Pampachiri Peru
258 E2 Pampa de Infierno Arg.
252 D4 Pampa Grande Bol.
93 B6 Pampanua Sulawesi Indon.
190 D7 Pamparato Italy
261 E5 Pampas reg. Arg.
252 B3 Pampas Peru
252 B3 Pampas r. Peru
163 I7 Pampelonne France
Pampeluna Spain see Pamplona
214 I3 Pampierstad S. Africa
182 D8 Pampilhosa Port.
182 E8 Pampilhosa da Serra Port.
217 □1b Pamplemousses Mauritius
183 M4 Pampliega Spain
232 G11 Pamplin VA U.S.A.
250 C3 Pamplona Col.
92 D7 Pamplona Negros Phil.
183 Q3 Pamplona Spain
170 D3 Pampow Ger.
162 D3 Pamproux France
95 L6 Pamukan, Teluk b. Indon.
199 I3 Pamukçu Turkey
126 D5 Pamukkale Turkey
199 L2 Pamukova Turkey
232 I11 Pamunkey r. VA U.S.A.
198 B3 Pamvotida, Limni l. Greece
116 G2 Pamzal Jammu and Kashmir
182 I5 Pan, Tierra del reg. Spain
208 B5 Pana Gabon
236 K6 Pana IL U.S.A.
243 O7 Panabá Mex.
92 E8 Panabo Mindanao Phil.
92 D8 Panabutan Bay Mindanao Phil.
241 R4 Panaca NV U.S.A.
198 C4 Panachaïko mts Greece
224 D4 Panache, Lake Ont. Can.
197 N3 Panaci Romania
85 N1 Panaeati Island P.N.G.
116 H8 Panagar Madh. Prad. India
198 F2 Panagia i. Thasos Greece
114 F4 Panagiri Andhra Prad. India
92 B7 Panagtaran Point Palawan Phil.
197 M8 Panagyurishte Bulg.
94 F8 Panaitan i. Indon.
198 C4 Panaitolio Greece
114 C5 Panaji Goa India
246 C9 Panama country Central America
242 □T13 Panamá Panama
242 □T13 Panamá, Bahía de b. Panama
242 □T13 Panamá, Canal de Panama
242 □T14 Panamá, Golfo de g. Panama
Panama, Gulf of Panama see Panamá, Golfo de
Panama City Panama see Panamá
231 E10 Panama City FL U.S.A.
116 F2 Panamik Jammu and Kashmir
240 O5 Panamint Range mts CA U.S.A.
240 O5 Panamint Valley CA U.S.A.
95 H8 Pananjung Pangandaran, Taman Wisata nat. park Indon.
252 A2 Panao Peru
92 E7 Panaon i. Phil.
85 N1 Panapompom Island P.N.G.
117 L7 Panar r. India
195 I6 Panarea, Isola i. Isole Lipari Italy
95 H3 Panarik Indon.
191 K6 Panaro r. Italy
95 J8 Panarukan Jawa Indon.
163 F9 Panassac France
92 D6 Panay i. Phil.
140 T3 Panayarvi Natsional'nyy Park nat. park Rus. Fed.
92 D6 Panay Gulf Phil.
Panayía i. Thasos Greece see Panagia
162 G4 Panazol France
215 O2 Panbult S. Africa
241 Q3 Pancake Range mts NV U.S.A.
190 D6 Pancalieri Italy
257 G3 Pancas Brazil
196 I6 Pančevo Vojvodina Serbia
117 L6 Panchagarh Bangl.
116 G7 Panchamnagar Madh. Prad. India
137 K5 Pancheve Ukr.
109 M6 Panch'iao Taiwan
116 F4 Panchkula Haryana India
95 K4 Pancingapan, Bukit mt. Indon.
197 P5 Panciu Romania
183 N3 Pancorbo Spain
197 J4 Pâncota Romania
186 C6 Pancrudo Spain
186 C6 Pancrudo r. Spain
Pancsova Vojvodina Serbia see Pančevo
94 C3 Pancurbatu Sumatera Indon.
213 G5 Panda Moz.
116 H9 Pandada Chhattisgarh India
92 D6 Pandan Panay Phil.
92 E4 Pandan Phil.
94 □ Pandan, Selat str. Sing.
92 C6 Pandan Bay Panay Phil.
95 K5 Pandang Kalimantan Indon.
86 □2 Pandang, Pulu i. Cocos Is
94 □ Pandan Reservoir Sing.
116 H8 Pandaria Chhattisgarh India
116 H8 Pandatarai Chhattisgarh India
114 E6 Pandavapura Karnataka India
258 C2 Pan de Azúcar Chile
92 D6 Pan de Azucar i. Phil.
258 C2 Pan de Azúcar, Parque Nacional nat. park Chile
94 G8 Pandeglang Jawa Indon.
255 D5 Pandeiros r. Brazil
138 I5 Pandėlys Lith.
116 F9 Pandhana Madh. Prad. India
114 D4 Pandharpur Mahar. India
116 G9 Pandhurna Madh. Prad. India
82 G2 Pandie Pandie S.A. Austr.
190 H5 Pandino Italy
252 D2 Pando dept Bol.
261 J4 Pando Uru.
Pandokrátor hill Kerkyra Greece see Pantokratoras
242 □R13 Pandora Costa Rica
232 B8 Pandora OH U.S.A.
85 J1 Pandora Entrance sea chan. Qld Austr.
142 F4 Pandrup Denmark
150 G4 Pandy Monmouthshire, Wales U.K.
177 G4 Pándzsa r. Hungary
78 □5 Pané, Mont mt. New Caledonia
Paneas Syria see Bāniyās
194 I9 Panebianco r. Sicilia Italy
253 E2 Panelas Brazil
183 K2 Panes Spain
191 L3 Paneveggio-Pale di San Martino, Parco Naturale nature res. Italy
138 H6 Panevėžys Lith.
139 X5 Paneyevo Rus. Fed.
Panfilov Kazakh. see Zharkent
139 Y5 Panfilovo Ivanovskaya Oblast' Rus. Fed.
135 H6 Panfilovo Volgogradskaya Oblast' Rus. Fed.
137 K3 Panfyly Ukr.
96 D4 Pang, Nam r. Myanmar
208 E4 Panga Dem. Rep. Congo
138 F3 Pangai Estonia
79 □8 Pangai Tonga
114 F4 Pangal Andhra Prad. India
114 F4 Pangal Andhra Prad. India
209 B5 Pangala Congo
95 H8 Pangandaran Jawa Indon.
211 C6 Pangani Tanz.
211 C6 Pangani r. Tanz.
92 E5 Pañganiban Phil.
207 I5 Pangar r. Cameroon
207 I5 Pangar Djerem, Réserve du nature res. Cameroon
151 J5 Pangbourne West Berkshire, England U.K.
157 L5 Pange France
93 A4 Pangean Sulawesi Barat Indon.
78 □6 Panggoe Choiseul Solomon Is
96 D3 Panghsang Myanmar
209 E5 Pangi Dem. Rep. Congo
123 P4 Pangi Range mts Pak.
107 N6 Pangjiabu Hebei China
95 J8 Pangkah, Tanjung pt Indon.
93 A6 Pangkajene Sulawesi Indon.
95 I6 Pangkalanbuun Kalimantan Indon.
94 C3 Pangkalanlunang Sumatera Indon.
94 C2 Pangkalansusu Sumatera Indon.
94 E2 Pangkal Kalong Malaysia
94 G6 Pangkalpinang Indon.
93 C4 Pangkalsiang, Tanjung pt Indon.
96 C2 Panglang Myanmar
92 D7 Panglao i. Phil.
223 J5 Pangman Sask. Can.
221 L3 Pangnirtung Nunavut Can.
209 B7 Pango Aluquém Angola
130 I3 Pangody Rus. Fed.
208 D3 Pangonda C.A.R.
Pangong Tso salt l. China/Jammu and Kashmir see Bangong Co
94 G8 Pangrango vol. Indon.
97 F7 Pang Sida National Park Thai.
94 □ Pang Sua, Sungai r. Sing.
96 C4 Pangtara Myanmar
100 D2 Pangu He r. China
259 B5 Panguipulli Chile
241 T4 Panguitch UT U.S.A.
95 I6 Pangujon, Tanjung pt Indon.
78 □6 Panguna P.N.G.
80 H2 Panguru North I. N.Z.
94 C3 Pangururan Sumatera Indon.
92 C8 Pangutaran i. Phil.
92 C8 Pangutaran Group is Phil.
237 E8 Panhandle TX U.S.A.
260 B4 Paniahue Chile
209 F6 Pania-Mwanga Dem. Rep. Congo
192 I1 Panicale Italy
260 B4 Panimávida Chile
116 D8 Pani Mines Gujarat India
244 F6 Panindícuaro Mex.
139 R5 Panino Tverskaya Oblast' Rus. Fed.
135 H6 Panino Voronezhskaya Oblast' Rus. Fed.
139 T1 Paninskaya Rus. Fed.
116 F5 Panipat Haryana India
123 L7 Panir Pak.
160 E5 Panissières France
92 B7 Panitan Palawan Phil.
245 J9 Panixtlahuaca Mex.
186 C5 Paniza Spain
139 N7 Panizowye Belarus
123 M3 Panj r. Afgh./Tajik.
123 M3 Panj Tajik.
123 L4 Panjāb Afgh.
123 L2 Panjakent Tajik.
94 F7 Panjang Sumatera Indon.
95 H3 Panjang i. Indon.
95 M3 Panjang i. Indon.
94 □ Panjang, Bukit Sing.
94 E4 Panjang, Selat sea chan. Indon.
163 D8 Panjas France
122 B5 Panjbarār Iran
123 K8 Panjgur Pak.
116 E9 Panjhra r. India
Panjim Goa India see Panaji
Panjin Liaoning China see Panshan
123 M3 Panji Poyon Tajik.
123 N4 Panjkora r. Pak.
123 N7 Panjnad r. Pak.
123 N7 Panjnad Barrage Pak.
123 M4 Panjshir reg. Afgh.
140 U5 Pankakoski Fin.
168 K2 Panker Ger.
174 G5 Panki Pol.
139 O3 Pankovka Rus. Fed.
207 H4 Pankshin Nigeria
Panlian Sichuan China see Miyi
100 G7 Pan Ling mts China
Panlong Henan China see Queshan
98 D7 Panna Madh. Prad. India
86 D4 Pannawonica W.A. Austr.
156 E7 Pannes France
160 D2 Pannesière-Chaumard, Barrage de dam France
193 O5 Panni Italy
165 I6 Panningen Neth.
177 G4 Pannonhalma Hungary
123 M8 Pano Aqil Pak.
184 C5 Panóias Port.
128 B4 Pano Lefkara Cyprus
95 I5 Panopah Kalimantan Indon.
Panoplis Egypt see Akhmīm
256 B4 Panorama Brazil
Panormus Sicilia Italy see Palermo
114 F7 Panruti Tamil Nadu India
171 J8 Panschwitz-Kuckau Ger.
107 R6 Panshan Liaoning China
100 E7 Panshi Jilin China
Panshui Guizhou China see Pu'an
122 F4 Pansu, Chāh-e well Iran
151 N4 Pant r. England U.K.
95 L6 Pantai Kalimantan Indon.
94 D5 Pantaicermin, Gunung mt. Indon.
253 F4 Pantanal reg. S. America
253 F4 Pantanal Matogrossense, Parque Nacional do nat. park Brazil
96 B6 Pantanaw Myanmar
241 V10 Pantano AZ U.S.A.
93 D8 Pantar i. Indon.
137 L5 Pantayivka Ukr.
Pantelaria Sicilia Italy see Pantelleria
137 Q5 Panteleymonivka Ukr.
194 B10 Pantelleria Sicilia Italy
194 C10 Pantelleria, Isola di i. Sicilia Italy
93 D8 Pante Macassar East Timor
Pantemakassar East Timor see Pante Macassar
245 J5 Pantepec r. Mex.
96 B3 Pantha Myanmar
116 E8 Panth Piploda Madh. Prad. India
Panticapaeum Ukr. see Kerch
186 E2 Panticosa Spain
86 H4 Pantijan Aboriginal Reserve W.A. Austr.
183 M8 Pantoja Spain
198 A3 Pantokratoras hill Kerkyra Greece
86 J4 Panton r. W.A. Austr.
94 B2 Pantonlabu Sumatera Indon.
82 F2 Pantoowarinna, Lake salt flat S.A. Austr.
186 F5 Pantorrillas hill Spain
92 E8 Pantukan Mindanao Phil.
150 F3 Pant-y-dwr Powys, Wales U.K.
209 C5 Panu Dem. Rep. Congo
93 B3 Panua, Cagar Alam nature res. Indon.
244 B2 Pánuco Sinaloa Mex.
245 I3 Pánuco Veracruz Mex.
245 J3 Pánuco r. Mex.
244 C1 Pánuco de Coronado Mex.
116 G7 Panwari Uttar Prad. India
108 E6 Panxian Guizhou China
96 G2 Panxian Guizhou China
109 I7 Panyu Guangdong China
137 P5 Panyutyne Ukr.
179 I8 Panzano, Golfo di b. Italy
108 C5 Panzhihua Sichuan China
209 C6 Panzi Dem. Rep. Congo
243 O10 Panzos Guat.
251 E2 Pao r. Venez.
80 K7 Paoanui Point North I. N.Z.
254 F4 Pão de Açúcar Brazil
193 Q9 Paola Italy
236 H6 Paola KS U.S.A.
230 D6 Paoli IN U.S.A.
234 E4 Paoli PA U.S.A.
192 C5 Paoloni, Serra hill Italy
93 F5 Paoni Seram Indon.
239 K7 Paonia CO U.S.A.
79 □9a Paopao Moorea Fr. Polynesia
Paopao, Baie de b. Moorea Fr. Polynesia see Cook, Baie de
208 C3 Paoua C.A.R.
97 F8 Paôy Pêt Cambodia
Pap Uzbek. see Pop
176 G4 Pápa Hungary
240 □F14 Pāpā HI U.S.A.
193 P7 Papa, Monte del mt. Italy
240 □F14 Pāpa'aloa HI U.S.A.
198 D6 Papadianika Greece
Papagaio r. Brazil see Sauêruiná
257 E3 Papagaios Minas Gerais Brazil
253 E2 Papagaios Rondônia Brazil
245 H9 Papagayo r. Mex.
216 □3c Papagayo, Punta del pt Lanzarote Canary Is
260 D2 Papagayos Arg.
114 F5 Papagni r. India
240 □F14 Pāpa'ikou HI U.S.A.
80 I4 Papakura North I. N.Z.
250 B5 Papallacta Ecuador
245 L7 Papaloapan r. Mex.
80 K4 Papamoa Beach North I. N.Z.
114 E8 Papanasam Tamil Nadu India
114 F7 Papanasam Tamil Nadu India
244 F8 Papanoa Mex.
245 J5 Papantla Mex.
250 C6 Papa Playa Peru
95 K2 Papar Sabah Malaysia
79 □9a Papara Tahiti Fr. Polynesia
115 H3 Paparhahandi Orissa India
80 I3 Paparoa North I. N.Z.
81 F9 Paparoa National Park South I. N.Z.
81 F9 Paparoa Range mts South I. N.Z.
199 G5 Papas, Akrotirio pt Ikaria Greece
193 P8 Papasidero Italy
146 □M2 Papa Stour i. Scotland U.K.
146 K4 Papa Stronsay i. Scotland U.K.
177 G4 Pápateszér Hungary
80 I3 Papatoetoe North I. N.Z.
81 D13 Papatowai South I. N.Z.
79 □9a Papawa Tahiti Fr. Polynesia
146 K4 Papa Westray i. Scotland U.K.
Papay i. Scotland U.K. see Papa Westray
79 □9a Papeete Tahiti Fr. Polynesia
168 D4 Papenburg Ger.
170 F2 Papendorf Ger.
214 C7 Papendorp S. Africa
164 G5 Papendrecht Neth.
79 □9a Papenoo Tahiti Fr. Polynesia
79 □9a Papenoo r. Tahiti Fr. Polynesia
79 □9a Papetoai Moorea Fr. Polynesia
Papetoai, Baie de b. Moorea Fr. Polynesia see Opunohu, Baie d'
Paphos Cyprus see Pafos
Paphus Cyprus see Pafos
239 K12 Papigochic r. Mex.
197 N9 Papikio mt. Bulg./Greece
138 F5 Papilė Lith.
236 G5 Papillion NE U.S.A.
177 L2 Papín Slovakia
224 F4 Papineau-Labelle, Réserve Faunique de nature res. Que. Can.
233 J3 Papineauville Que. Can.
197 P8 Papiya hill Bulg.
177 H4 Papkeszi Hungary
241 Q4 Papoose Lake NV U.S.A.
258 C2 Paposo Chile
174 G2 Papowo Biskupie Pol.
173 J4 Pappenheim Ger.
175 K3 Paprotnia Pol.
146 D11 Paps of Jura hills Scotland U.K.
93 F4 Papua prov. Indon.
91 J8 Papua, Gulf of P.N.G.
78 □6 Papua New Guinea country Oceania
260 B3 Papudo Chile
84 C7 Papunya N.T. Austr.
151 L3 Papworth Everard Cambridgeshire, England U.K.
150 C7 Par Cornwall, England U.K.
257 E3 Pará r. Brazil
251 I5 Pará state Brazil
93 D2 Para i. Indon.
135 H5 Para r. Rus. Fed.
254 C2 Pará, Rio do r. Brazil
87 D7 Paraburdoo W.A. Austr.
177 I2 Paráč mt. Slovakia
92 D4 Paracale Luzon Phil.
257 F5 Paracambi Brazil
252 A3 Paracas Peru
252 A3 Paracas, Península pen. Peru
256 D2 Paracatu Brazil
256 D2 Paracatu r. Brazil
257 E2 Paracatu r. Brazil
90 D3 Paracel Islands S. China Sea
175 N2 Parachany Belarus
82 G4 Parachilna S.A. Austr.
123 N5 Parachinar Pak.
244 E6 Paracho Mex.
196 J7 Paraćin Serbia
244 G5 Parácuaro Guanajuato Mex.
244 E6 Parácuaro Michoacán Mex.
183 Q9 Paracuellos Spain
254 F2 Paracuru Brazil
177 J4 Parád Hungary
182 F7 Parada Port.
252 B3 Parada, Punta pt Peru
182 D7 Parada de Ester Port.
182 E6 Parada de Pinhão Port.
183 J6 Parada de Rubiales Spain
182 E4 Parada de Sil Spain
185 I6 Paradas Spain
198 D5 Paradeisia Greece
182 E5 Paradela Vila Real Port.
182 E6 Paradela Viseu Port.
182 F3 Paradela Spain
182 E6 Paradela de Guiães Port.
257 E3 Pará de Minas Brazil
247 □9 Paradera Aruba
224 E3 Paradis Que. Can.
225 J2 Paradise r. Nfld and Lab. Can.
251 G3 Paradise Guyana
240 K2 Paradise CA U.S.A.
226 I3 Paradise MI U.S.A.
241 Q5 Paradise NV U.S.A.
222 H2 Paradise Gardens N.W.T. Can.
223 I4 Paradise Hill Sask. Can.
231 □2 Paradise Island New Prov. Bahamas
240 O3 Paradise Peak NV U.S.A.
225 J2 Paradise River Nfld and Lab. Can.
241 U8 Paradise Valley AZ U.S.A.
238 F6 Paradise Valley NV U.S.A.
95 M9 Parado Sumbawa Indon.
117 K9 Paradwip Orissa India
175 I4 Paradyż Pol.
Paraetonium Egypt see Marsá Maţrūḩ
137 L3 Parafiyivka Ukr.
138 K7 Paraf"yanava Belarus
129 G6 Parağaçay Azer.
254 D2 Paragominas Brazil
237 J7 Paragould AR U.S.A.
253 E3 Paragua r. Bol.
Paragua i. Phil. see Palawan
251 F3 Paragua r. Venez.
257 E4 Paraguaçu Brazil
256 B5 Paraguaçu Paulista Brazil
253 F5 Paraguai r. Brazil
250 D2 Paraguáipoa Venez.
246 I7 Paraguaná, Península de pen. Venez.
253 F6 Paraguarí Para.
258 F2 Paraguay r. Arg./Para.
253 F5 Paraguay country S. America
123 J8 Parahadab Pak.
123 J8 Paraíba r. Brazil
254 F3 Paraíba state Brazil
257 F5 Paraíba do Sul Brazil
257 G4 Paraíba do Sul r. Brazil
257 E5 Paraibuna Brazil
Parainen Fin. see Pargas
256 A3 Paraíso Brazil
243 M8 Paraíso Campeche Mex.
243 M8 Paraíso Tabasco Mex.
245 N8 Paraíso Tabasco Mex.
254 C4 Paraíso do Norte Brazil
257 E5 Paraisópolis Brazil
140 P3 Parakka Sweden
207 F4 Parakou Benin
82 F4 Parakylia S.A. Austr.
115 I3 Paralakhemundi Orissa India
198 D6 Paralia Peloponnisos Greece
198 D4 Paralia Saranti Sterea Ellas Greece
114 G3 Paralkot Chhattisgarh India
Paramagudi Tamil Nadu India see Paramakkudi
114 F8 Paramakkudi Tamil Nadu India
251 H3 Paramaribo Suriname
158 H4 Paramé France
183 K7 Paramera, Puerto de la pass Spain
183 J8 Paramera, Sierra de la mts Spain
250 C3 Paramillo mt. Col.
250 B3 Paramillo, Parque Nacional nat. park Col.
260 C3 Paramillos, Sierra de los mts Arg.
182 G5 Parâmio Port.
254 E5 Paramirim Brazil
254 E4 Paramirim r. Brazil
182 E3 Páramo hill Spain
182 H3 Páramo del Sil Spain
183 M3 Páramo de Masa, Puerto del pass Spain
182 I4 Páramo Leonés reg. Spain
252 A2 Paramonga Peru
139 U8 Paramonovo Rus. Fed.
182 C7 Paramos Port.
235 G3 Paramus NJ U.S.A.
131 Q4 Paramushir, Ostrov i. Kuril'skiye O-va Rus. Fed.
198 B3 Paramythia Greece
128 D8 Paran watercourse Israel
261 G2 Paraná Arg.
254 D5 Paraná Brazil
254 C5 Paraná r. Brazil
256 B6 Paraná state Brazil
261 H4 Paraná r. S. America
261 H4 Paraná, Delta del Arg.
255 C8 Paranaguá Brazil
256 C6 Paranaguá, Baía de b. Brazil
256 B3 Paranaíba Brazil
256 B4 Paranaíba r. Brazil
261 H3 Paraná Ibicuy r. Arg.
256 B3 Paranaiguara Brazil
253 F2 Paranaita r. Brazil
256 A5 Paranapanema r. Brazil
256 B6 Paranapiacaba, Serra mts Brazil
250 B6 Paranapura Peru
251 E5 Paranari Brazil
256 A5 Paranavaí Brazil
122 D4 Parandak Iran
95 I7 Parang i. Indon.
92 C9 Parang Phil.
114 G8 Parangi Aru r. Sri Lanka
116 F3 Parangipettai Tamil Nadu India
116 F3 Parang Pass Hima. Prad. India
197 L5 Parângul Mare, Vârful mt. Romania
182 E8 Paranhos Port.
114 G8 Paranthan Sri Lanka
116 D8 Parantij Gujarat India
257 E3 Paraopeba Brazil
257 E3 Paraopeba r. Brazil
185 L6 Parapanda mt. Spain
93 E3 Parapara Halmahera Indon.
127 L6 Pārāpāra Iraq
81 I7 Paraparaumu North I. N.Z.
198 E6 Parapola i. Greece
256 B4 Parapuã Brazil
250 E3 Paraque, Cerro mt. Venez.
140 P2 Paras Norway
123 O4 Paras Pak.
199 I7 Paraspori, Akrotirio pt Greece
192 B4 Parata, Pointe de la pt Corse France
257 E5 Parati Brazil
254 E5 Paratinga Brazil
82 G5 Paratoo S.A. Austr.
127 M6 Parāū, Kūh-e mt. Iraq
254 C3 Parauapebas r. Brazil
251 H5 Parauaquara, Serra hill Brazil
251 G6 Parauarí r. Brazil
129 I3 Paraulozen' r. Rus. Fed.
256 B2 Paraúna Brazil
160 E4 Paray-le-Monial France
116 F7 Parbati r. India
117 L7 Parbatipur Bangl.
114 E3 Parbhani Mahar. India
149 L6 Parbold Lancashire, England U.K.
247 □1 Parcelas Martorell Puerto Rico
187 E10 Parcent Spain
159 K6 Parcé-sur-Sarthe France
216 □3f Parchel, Punta del pt Gran Canaria Canary Is
171 F6 Parchen Ger.
121 L1 Parchevka Kazakh.
170 E4 Parchim Ger.
127 O6 Parchīn Iran
226 I7 Parchment MI U.S.A.
177 K3 Parchovany Slovakia
174 D4 Parchów Pol.
174 F1 Parchowo Pol.
175 J2 Parciaki Pol.
162 E5 Parcoul France
175 K4 Parczew Pol.
184 E3 Pardais Port.
240 L3 Pardee Reservoir CA U.S.A.
226 E6 Pardeeville WI U.S.A.
163 C9 Pardies France
182 C7 Pardilhó Port.
197 Q5 Pardina Romania
261 H5 Pardo Arg.
256 A4 Pardo r. Brazil
256 C4 Pardo r. Brazil
256 C6 Pardo r. Brazil
255 D5 Pardo r. Brazil
255 F5 Pardo r. Brazil
86 E6 Pardoo W.A. Austr.
183 Q6 Pardos, Sierra de mts Spain
176 E1 Pardubice Czech Rep.
176 F2 Pardubický kraj admin. reg. Czech Rep.
95 J8 Pare Jawa Indon.
Parece Vela i. Japan see Okino-Tori-shima
138 H8 Parechcha Belarus
111 D10 Pare Chu r. China
253 F3 Parecis Brazil
253 F3 Parecis r. Brazil
253 E2 Parecis, Serra dos hills Brazil
182 D6 Paredes Port.
182 C5 Paredes de Coura Port.
183 K4 Paredes de Nava Spain
260 C3 Pareditas Arg.
245 N9 Paredón Chiapas Mex.
243 I5 Paredón Coahuila Mex.
260 B4 Paredones Chile
122 A2 Pareh Iran
183 O7 Pareja Spain
161 B8 Pareloup, Lac de l. France
78 □4a Parem i. Chuuk Micronesia
81 I8 Paremata North I. N.Z.
78 □4b Parempei i. Pohnpei Micronesia
162 C6 Parempuyre France
114 D3 Parenda Mahar. India
80 G1 Parengarenga Harbour North I. N.Z.
95 J6 Parenggean Kalimantan Indon.
224 F4 Parent Que. Can.
224 E3 Parent, Lac l. Que. Can.
195 K5 Parenti Italy
163 B7 Parentis-en-Born France
81 F11 Pareora South I. N.Z.
93 A6 Parepare Sulawesi Indon.
260 E4 Parera Arg.
186 J4 Parets del Vallès Spain
171 E6 Parey Ger.
134 H4 Parfen'yevo Rus. Fed.
139 O4 Parfino Rus. Fed.
198 B3 Parga Greece
141 Q6 Pargas Fin.
195 J6 Parghelia Italy
114 E4 Pargi Andhra Prad. India
157 I6 Pargny-sur-Saulx France
184 □ Pargo, Ponta do pt Madeira
139 N1 Pargolovo Rus. Fed.
247 □2 Parham Antigua and Barbuda
252 D4 Paria Bol.
241 U5 Paria r. AZ/UT U.S.A.
247 □7 Paria, Gulf of Trin. and Tob./Venez.
251 F2 Paria, Península de pen. Venez.
94 D5 Pariaman Sumatera Indon.
241 T5 Paria Plateau AZ U.S.A.
251 F6 Paricatuba Brazil
244 E6 Paricutín, Volcán vol. Mex.
242 □R13 Parida, Isla i. Panama
93 B4 Parigi Sulawesi Indon.
159 L6 Parigné-l'Évêque France
177 H5 Pári-hegy hill Hungary
141 T6 Parikkala Fin.
115 I3 Parikud Islands India
Parima r. Brazil see Uatatás
251 E4 Parima, Serra mts Brazil
251 E4 Parima-Tapirapecó, Parque Nacional nat. park Venez.
250 C6 Parinari Peru
250 A6 Pariñas, Punta pt Peru
82 H6 Paringa S.A. Austr.
178 A8 Parino r. Italy
251 G5 Parintins Brazil
227 N6 Paris Ont. Can.
156 D6 Paris France
237 I8 Paris AR U.S.A.
238 I5 Paris ID U.S.A.
230 D6 Paris IL U.S.A.
232 A10 Paris KY U.S.A.
233 □O4 Paris ME U.S.A.
236 I6 Paris MO U.S.A.
237 K7 Paris TN U.S.A.
237 H9 Paris TX U.S.A.
156 E5 Paris (Charles de Gaulle) airport France
156 D6 Paris (Orly) airport France
153 Paris area map France
233 I5 Parish NY U.S.A.
226 J3 Parisienne, Île i. Ont. Can.
163 H7 Parisot Midi-Pyrénées France
163 H8 Parisot Midi-Pyrénées France
94 D2 Parit Buntar Malaysia
122 F7 Pārīz Iran
120 I1 Parizh Rus. Fed.
122 I9 Pārk Iran
236 G1 Park r. ND U.S.A.
208 E3 Parka Dem. Rep. Congo
140 Q3 Parkajoki Sweden
114 F3 Parkal Andhra Prad. India
141 Q5 Parkano Fin.
225 J2 Parke Lake Nfld and Lab. Can.
121 M7 Parkent Uzbek.
241 R7 Parker AZ U.S.A.
236 C6 Parker CO U.S.A.
236 G4 Parker SD U.S.A.
Parker, Mount hill H.K. China see Pak Ka Shan
241 R7 Parker Dam CA U.S.A.
223 M2 Parker Lake Nunavut Can.
87 E12 Parker Range hills W.A. Austr.
232 D9 Parkersburg WV U.S.A.
83 L5 Parkes N.S.W. Austr.
234 D5 Parkesburg PA U.S.A.
226 D4 Park Falls WI U.S.A.
226 G8 Park Forest IL U.S.A.
Parkhar Tajik. see Farkhor
227 M6 Parkhill Ont. Can.
137 S5 Parkhomenko Ukr.
137 O3 Parkhomivka Ukr.
227 K3 Parkinson Ont. Can.
232 D7 Parkman OH U.S.A.
147 C9 Parknasilla Ireland
236 H2 Park Rapids MN U.S.A.
233 J11 Parksley VA U.S.A.
173 M2 Parkstein Ger.
173 N4 Parkstetten Ger.
236 G4 Parkston SD U.S.A.
222 E5 Parksville B.C. Can.
116 F2 Parkutta Jammu and Kashmir
238 H6 Park Valley UT U.S.A.
234 B6 Parkville MD U.S.A.
183 M8 Parla Spain
Parlakimedi Orissa India see Paralakhemundi
115 I3 Parla Kimedi Orissa India
163 I6 Parlan France
247 □5 Parlatuvier Trin. and Tob.
114 E3 Parli Vaijnath Mahar. India
108 A3 Parlung Zangbo r. China
190 I6 Parma Italy
190 I6 Parma prov. Italy
190 I6 Parma r. Italy
134 L2 Parma Rus. Fed.
238 F5 Parma ID U.S.A.
226 J7 Parma MI U.S.A.
232 D7 Parma OH U.S.A.
251 E3 Parmana Venez.
163 A9 Parme airport France
254 D4 Parnaguá Brazil
254 E2 Parnaíba Brazil
254 B4 Parnaíba r. Brazil
254 D4 Parnaibinha r. Brazil
254 E3 Parnarama Brazil
198 D4 Parnassou, Ethnikos Drymos nat. park Greece
81 H9 Parnassus South I. N.Z.
Parnassus, Mount Greece see Liakoura
82 F6 Parndana S.A. Austr.
179 O4 Parndorf Austria
114 D3 Parner Mahar. India
198 E4 Parnithas, Ethnikos Drymos nat. park Greece
198 D5 Parnonas mts Greece
138 H3 Pärnu Estonia
138 H3 Pärnu r. Estonia
138 H3 Pärnu-Jaagupi Estonia
138 H3 Pärnu laht b. Estonia
117 L6 Paro Bhutan
81 F9 Paroa South I. N.Z.
198 G5 Paroikia Paros Greece
138 H1 Parola Fin.
156 F7 Paron France
Parona Turkey see Fındık
83 I4 Paroo watercourse Qld Austr.
83 I4 Paroo Channel watercourse N.S.W. Austr.
83 I4 Paroo-Darling National Park N.S.W. Austr.
123 I4 Paropamisus mts Afgh.
93 A5 Paroreang, Bukit mt. Indon.
198 G5 Paros i. Greece
246 □ Parottee Point Jamaica
214 C9 Parow S. Africa
171 L8 Parowa Pol.
241 T4 Parowan UT U.S.A.
161 J8 Parpaillon mts France
82 H6 Parrakie S.A. Austr.
260 B5 Parral Chile
237 C12 Parral r. Mex.
83 M5 Parramatta N.S.W. Austr.
233 J11 Parramore Island VA U.S.A.
242 H5 Parras Mex.
261 I5 Parravicini Arg.
150 F5 Parrett r. England U.K.
183 J8 Parrillas Spain
226 E4 Parrish WI U.S.A.
242 □Q13 Parrita Costa Rica
225 H4 Parrsboro N.S. Can.
220 F2 Parry, Cape N.W.T. Can.
Parry, Kap c. Greenland see Kangaarsussuaq
224 F1 Parry, Lac l. Que. Can.
221 J3 Parry Bay Nunavut Can.
221 G2 Parry Channel Nunavut Can.
Parry Island Cook Is see Mauke
221 G2 Parry Islands Nunavut Can.
86 J3 Parry Lagoons Nature Reserve W.A. Austr.
247 □7 Parrylands Trin. and Tob.
86 C7 Parry Range hills W.A. Austr.
224 D4 Parry Sound Ont. Can.
234 D3 Parryville PA U.S.A.
Pars prov. Iran see Fārs
117 J7 Parsa Bihar India
Parsa prov. Iran see Fārs
129 I6 Pārsābād Iran
168 K5 Parsau Ger.
117 J6 Parsa Wildlife Reserve nature res. Nepal
173 L3 Parsberg Ger.
174 E2 Parsęcko Pol.
178 B5 Parseierspitze mt. Austria
174 D1 Parsęta r. Pol.
236 D2 Parshall ND U.S.A.
235 G3 Parsippany NJ U.S.A.
241 R3 Parsnip Peak NV U.S.A.
237 H7 Parsons KS U.S.A.
232 F9 Parsons WV U.S.A.
84 E2 Parsons Range hills N.T. Austr.
170 J5 Parstein Ger.
170 I5 Parsteiner See l. Ger.
111 J11 Parta Xizang China
114 C4 Partabgarh Mahar. India
114 G3 Partabpur Chhattisgarh India
117 I8 Partabpur Chhattisgarh India
140 S2 Partakko Fin.
185 O6 Partaloa Spain
129 I6 Par Talū Iran
194 D8 Partanna Sicilia Italy
140 N3 Pårte mt. Sweden
178 B6 Partenen Austria
169 I10 Partenstein Ger.
162 D2 Parthenay France
242 D5 Partida, Isla i. Mex.
192 B3 Partinello Corse France
149 M7 Partington Greater Manchester, England U.K.
194 E7 Partinico Sicilia Italy
100 H7 Partizansk Rus. Fed.
177 I2 Partizánska Ľupča Slovakia
177 H3 Partizánske Slovakia
149 R7 Partney Lincolnshire, England U.K.
149 J4 Parton Cumbria, England U.K.
224 D3 Partridge r. Ont. Can.
147 D5 Partry Ireland
138 K3 Partsi Estonia
129 D3 P'arts'khanaqanevi Georgia
137 N7 Partyzany Ukr.
251 H5 Paru r. Brazil
251 E3 Parú, Serranía mts Venez.
123 I8 Pārūd Iran
251 G5 Paru de Oeste r. Brazil
114 E7 Parur Kerala India
137 K7 Parutyne Ukr.
122 G5 Parvāreh Iran
115 H3 Parvatipuram Andhra Prad. India
116 E6 Parvatsar Rajasthan India
123 M4 Parwān prov. Afgh.
111 F11 Paryang Xizang China
138 M9 Parychy Belarus
143 L5 Påryd Sweden
121 U3 Parygino Kazakh.
215 L2 Parys S. Africa
175 J4 Parysów Pol.
175 H4 Parzęczew Pol.
183 M2 Pas r. Spain
122 E5 Pās, Chāh well Iran
138 K8 Pasachnaye Belarus
126 F4 Pas Dağı mt. Turkey
240 N7 Pasadena CA U.S.A.
234 B6 Pasadena MD U.S.A.
237 H11 Pasadena TX U.S.A.
250 A5 Pasado, Cabo c. Ecuador
186 B1 Pasai Donibane Spain
250 B5 Pasaje Ecuador
Pasajes de San Juan Spain see Pasai Donibane
96 E7 Pa Sak, Mae Nam r. Thai.
129 D5 Paşalı Turkey
199 I2 Paşalimanı Adası i. Turkey
116 I8 Pasan Chhattisgarh India
129 F3 P'asanauri Georgia
96 D5 Pa Sang Thai.
93 A4 Pasangkayu Sulawesi Barat Indon.
94 D6 Pasarbantal Sumatera Indon.
127 P8 Pasargadae tourist site Iran
94 D6 Pasarseblat Sumatera Indon.
94 E7 Pasarseluma Sumatera Indon.
93 C6 Pasarwajo Sulawesi Indon.
96 C5 Pasawng Myanmar
224 F3 Pascagama r. Que. Can.
237 K10 Pascagoula MS U.S.A.
237 K10 Pascagoula r. MS U.S.A.
227 Q1 Pascalis Que. Can.
197 O3 Paşcani Romania
179 J3 Pasching Austria
252 B2 Pasco dept Peru
238 E3 Pasco WA U.S.A.
233 N7 Pascoag RI U.S.A.
257 H2 Pascoal, Monte hill Brazil
85 I2 Pascoe r. Qld Austr.
84 C4 Pascoe Inlet Qld Austr.
248 C5 Pascua, Isla de i. S. Pacific Ocean
92 D5 Pascual Phil.
156 D2 Pas-de-Calais dept France
Pas de Calais str. France/U.K. see Dover, Strait of
156 D3 Pas-en-Artois France
170 J3 Pasewalk Ger.
223 J3 Pasfield Lake Sask. Can.
139 Q1 Pasha Rus. Fed.
139 P1 Pasha r. Rus. Fed.
100 G4 Pashkovo Rus. Fed.
137 S8 Pashkovskiy Rus. Fed.
139 R1 Pashozero Rus. Fed.
123 J4 Pashtun Zarghun Afgh.
122 H7 Pashū'īyeh Iran
191 O3 Pasiàn di Prato Italy
178 G8 Pasiano di Pordenone Italy
175 J3 Pasieki Pol.
92 C4 Pasig Luzon Phil.
96 C1 Pasi Ga Myanmar
93 D2 Pasige i. Indon.
117 O5 Pasighat Arun. Prad. India
127 J4 Pasinler Turkey
94 □ Pasir Gudang Malaysia
95 J9 Pasirian Jawa Indon.
94 □ Pasir Laba, Tanjong pt Sing.
94 E1 Pasir Mas Malaysia
94 D4 Pasirpangarayan Sumatera Indon.
94 □ Pasir Panjang Sing.
94 □ Pasir Panjang hill Sing.
94 E2 Pasir Putih Malaysia
93 B7 Pasitelu, Pulau-pulau is Indon.
143 M4 Påskallavik Sweden
Paskevicha, Zaliv l. Kazakh. see Shevchenko, Zaliv
191 R6 Paški Kanal sea chan. Croatia
177 H2 Paskov Czech Rep.
123 I8 Paskūh Iran
143 P7 Pasłęk Pol.
143 P7 Pasłęka r. Pol.
87 G12 Pasley, Cape W.A. Austr.
129 D5 Paslı Geçidi pass Turkey
188 E4 Pašman i. Croatia
82 G4 Pasmore watercourse S.A. Austr.
123 J9 Pasni Pak.
243 N9 Paso Caballos Guat.
250 E2 Paso de Caballo Venez.
259 C6 Paso de Indios Arg.
261 H2 Paso de la Laguna Arg.
245 J5 Paso del Correo Mex.
259 C6 Paso del Limay Arg.
245 K6 Paso del Macho Mex.
260 D5 Paso de los Algarrobos Arg.
260 C6 Paso de los Indios Arg.
261 I1 Paso de los Libres Arg.
261 I3 Paso de los Toros Uru.
261 I3 Paso del Palmar, Lago Artificial de resr Uru.
245 N8 Paso del Rosario Mex.
259 C6 Paso del Sapo Arg.
245 K6 Paso de Ovejas Mex.
253 F6 Paso de Patria Para.
237 D11 Paso de San Antonio Chihuahua Mex.
244 G3 Paso de San Antonio San Luis Potosí Mex.
260 E3 Paso Grande Arg.
96 B4 Pasok Myanmar
242 □Q10 Paso Real Hond.
259 C7 Paso Río Mayo Arg.
240 L6 Paso Robles CA U.S.A.
223 K4 Pasquia Hills Sask. Can.
123 P5 Pasrur Pak.
233 □Q3 Passadumkeag ME U.S.A.
226 F1 Passage Island MI U.S.A.
254 E3 Passagem Franca Brazil
147 F9 Passage West Ireland
235 G3 Passaic NJ U.S.A.
235 G3 Passaic r. NJ U.S.A.
235 G2 Passaic County county NJ U.S.A.
179 M5 Passail Austria
159 J4 Passais France
217 □3b Passamainti Mayotte
257 E5 Passa Quatro Brazil
257 E4 Passa Tempo Brazil
173 O4 Passau Ger.
157 L8 Passavant-la-Rochère France
92 D6 Passi Panay Phil.
192 I1 Passignano sul Trasimeno Italy
191 K2 Passirio r. Italy
255 B9 Passo Fundo Brazil
258 G2 Passo Fundo, Barragem do resr Brazil
255 B9 Passo Real, Barragem resr Brazil
256 D4 Passos Brazil
170 J4 Passow Ger.
160 J5 Passy France
138 J6 Pastavy Belarus
250 B5 Pastaza prov. Ecuador
250 B6 Pastaza r. Peru
261 F4 Pasteur Arg.
250 B4 Pasto Col.
253 E1 Pasto Grande Brazil
241 W5 Pastora Peak AZ U.S.A.
245 I4 Pastoría Mex.
245 J10 Pastoria, Laguna l. Mex.
182 F2 Pastoriza Spain
244 F5 Pastor Ortiz Mex.
254 D3 Pastos Bons Brazil
183 O8 Pastrana Spain
116 E1 Pasu Jammu and Kashmir
92 C2 Pasuquin Luzon Phil.
Pasur Turkey see Kulp
95 J8 Pasuruan Jawa Indon.
138 H5 Pasvalys Lith.
Pasvikelva r. Europe see Patsoyoki
175 I2 Pasym Pol.
174 E4 Paszowice Pol.
177 I4 Pásztó Hungary
252 C3 Pata Bol.
208 D2 Pata C.A.R.
92 C9 Pata i. Phil.
206 B3 Pata Senegal
177 G3 Pata Slovakia
259 C8 Patagonia reg. Arg.
241 V10 Patagonia AZ U.S.A.
182 C9 Pataias Port.
111 J14 Patakata Assam India
Pataliputra Bihar India see Patna
244 E6 Patambán Mex.
Patan Gujarat India see Somnath
116 D8 Patan Gujarat India
117 J7 Patan Jharkhand India
116 G8 Patan Madh. Prad. India
114 C4 Patan Mahar. India
117 J6 Patan Nepal
123 O4 Patan Pak.
114 F4 Patancheru Andhra Prad. India
123 K8 Patandar, Koh-i- mt. Pak.
93 F3 Patani Halmahera Indon.
207 G5 Patani Nigeria
116 G9 Patan Saongi Mahar. India
234 B6 Patapsco r. MD U.S.A.
234 B6 Patapsco, South Branch r. MD U.S.A.
116 F5 Pataudi Haryana India
Patavium Italy see Padova
258 E2 Patay Arg.
156 C7 Patay France
83 I6 Patchewollock Vic. Austr.
235 I3 Patchogue NY U.S.A.
150 G4 Patchway South Gloucestershire, England U.K.
80 I6 Patea North I. N.Z.
Patea inlet South I. N.Z. see Doubtful Sound
80 I6 Patea r. North I. N.Z.
207 G4 Pategi Nigeria
211 D5 Pate Island Kenya
149 N5 Pateley Bridge North Yorkshire, England U.K.
215 I9 Patensie S. Africa
179 I6 Patergassen Austria
187 E8 Paterna Spain
184 G6 Paterna del Campo Spain
184 H7 Paterna de Rivera Spain
179 I6 Paternion Austria
193 P7 Paterno Italy
194 H8 Paternò Sicilia Italy
193 O6 Paternopoli Italy
214 B8 Paternoster S. Africa
173 N3 Petersdorf Ger.
83 M5 Paterson N.S.W. Austr.
83 K3 Paterson r. Qld Austr.
215 J9 Paterson S. Africa
233 K8 Paterson NJ U.S.A.
81 B13 Paterson Inlet Stewart I. N.Z.
86 G6 Paterson Range hills W.A. Austr.
117 I8 Pathalgaon Chhattisgarh India
111 L13 Pathalipam Assam India
122 G8 Pathān Iran
114 E8 Pathanamthitta Kerala India
116 E3 Pathankot Punjab India
116 G8 Pathari Madh. Prad. India
116 G8 Patharia Madh. Prad. India
Pathein Myanmar see Bassein
116 F6 Pathena Rajasthan India
238 K5 Pathfinder Reservoir WY U.S.A.
97 D9 Pathiu Thai.
114 E3 Pathri Mahar. India
97 E8 Pathum Thani Thai.

Pati to Perechyn
367

250 E5 Pati r. Brazil
116 E9 Pati Madh. Prad. India
95 I8 Pati Jawa Indon.
250 B4 Patía r. Col.
116 F4 Patiala Punjab India
247 □1 Patillas Puerto Rico
247 □1 Patillas, Puerto b. Puerto Rico
93 E4 Patinti, Selat sea chan. Maluku Indon.
78 □1 Pati Point Guam
93 B6 Patiro, Tanjung pt Indon.
198 E3 Patitiri Greece
252 A2 Pativilca r. Peru
96 B1 Patkai Bum mts India/Myanmar
111 H8 Patkaklik Xinjiang China
199 K6 Patlangıç Turkey
199 H5 Patmos i. Greece
117 J7 Patna Bihar India
146 H12 Patna East Ayrshire, Scotland U.K.
117 I9 Patnagarh Orissa India
92 D4 Patnanongan i. Phil.
127 K4 Patnos Turkey
174 G4 Pątnów Pol.
259 B7 Pato, Cerro mt. Chile
255 B8 Pato Branco Brazil
114 D3 Patoda Mahar. India
230 D6 Patoka r. IN U.S.A.
131 M4 Patomskoye Nagor'ye mts Rus. Fed.
116 H4 Paton Uttaranchal India
140 S2 Patoniva Fin.
198 A2 Patos Albania
254 F3 Patos Paraíba Brazil
254 E3 Patos Piauí Brazil
247 □7 Patos, Isla i. Venez.
255 C9 Patos, Lagoa dos l. Brazil
261 F2 Patos, Laguna de los l. Arg.
260 C2 Patos, Río de los r. Arg.
256 D3 Patos de Minas Brazil
260 D2 Patquía Arg.
198 C4 Patra Greece
Patrae Greece see Patra
Pátrai Greece see Patra
198 C4 Patraïkos Kolpos b. Greece
134 H2 Patrakeyevka Rus. Fed.
Patras Greece see Patra
117 K8 Patrasaer W. Bengal India
117 J8 Patratu Jharkhand India
140 □B1 Patreksfjörður Iceland
116 C8 Patri Gujarat India
195 I7 Patri r. Sicilia Italy
81 H8 Patriarch, Mount South I. N.Z.
193 K4 Patrica Italy
84 C6 Patricia, Mount hill N.T. Austr.
259 B8 Patricio Lynch, Isla i. Chile
148 H5 Patrick Isle of Man
85 J7 Patrick Creek watercourse Qld Austr.
232 E12 Patrick Springs VA U.S.A.
147 E7 Patrickswell Ireland
256 C3 Patrimônio Brazil
192 C2 Patrimonio Corse France
149 R6 Patrington East Riding of Yorkshire, England U.K.
256 D3 Patrocínio Brazil
177 K3 Pátroha Hungary
122 H4 Paṭrū Iran
178 D5 Patscherkofel mt. Austria
134 E1 Patsoyoki r. Europe
192 C6 Pattada Sardegna Italy
114 D4 Pattadakal tourist site Karnataka India
114 E8 Pattanapuram Kerala India
97 E11 Pattani Thai.
97 E11 Pattani, Mae Nam r. Thai.
97 E8 Pattaya Thai.
233 □Q3 Patten ME U.S.A.
234 E3 Pattenburg NJ U.S.A.
169 I6 Pattensen Ger.
149 L4 Patterdale Cumbria, England U.K.
240 K4 Patterson CA U.S.A.
237 J11 Patterson LA U.S.A.
235 H1 Patterson NY U.S.A.
232 G9 Patterson r. WV U.S.A.
222 C1 Patterson, Mount Y.T. Can.
226 I4 Patterson, Point MI U.S.A.
240 M5 Patterson Mountain CA U.S.A.
Patteson Passage Vanuatu see Lolvavana, Passage
116 I7 Patti Uttar Prad. India
93 E8 Patti Maluku Indon.
194 H7 Patti Sicilia Italy
140 R4 Pattijoki Fin.
140 P2 Pättikkä Fin.
114 E5 Pattikonda Andhra Prad. India
150 H2 Pattingham Staffordshire, England U.K.
80 □ Pattisson, Cape Chatham Is S. Pacific Ocean
114 F7 Pattukkottai Tamil Nadu India
222 D3 Pattullo, Mount B.C. Can.
254 F3 Patu Brazil
117 M8 Patuakhali Bangl.
223 J4 Patuanak Sask. Can.
242 □Q10 Patuca r. Hond.
242 □Q10 Patuca, Punta pt Hond.
242 □Q10 Patucas, Parque Nacional nat. park Hond.
197 K6 Pătulele Romania
116 F9 Patur Mahar. India
165 E8 Pâturages Belgium
80 J6 Patutu mt. North I. N.Z.
232 I10 Patuxent r. MD U.S.A.
262 S1 Patuxent Range mts Antarctica
140 U5 Patvinsuon kansallispuisto nat. park Fin.
177 H4 Páty Hungary
244 F6 Pátzcuaro Mex.
244 F6 Patzcuaro, Laguna de l. Mex.
163 D9 Pau France
Pau airport France see Pyrénées
257 H2 Pau Brasil, Parque Nacional do nat. park Brazil
252 B3 Paucarbamba Peru
252 B2 Paucartambo Peru
Paucartambo r. Peru see Yavero
254 C3 Pau d'Arco Brazil
253 H1 Pau d'Arco r. Brazil
179 M3 Paudorf Austria
117 L6 Pauhunri mt. China/India
163 F8 Pauilhac France
162 C5 Pauillac France
252 D1 Pauini Brazil
252 D1 Pauiní r. Brazil
251 F5 Pauini r. Brazil
96 B4 Pauk Myanmar
96 B5 Paukkaung Myanmar
96 A4 Pauktaw Myanmar
182 E8 Paul Port.
191 O2 Paularo Italy
220 F3 Paulatuk N.W.T. Can.
241 T7 Paulden AZ U.S.A.
237 K9 Paulding MS U.S.A.
232 A7 Paulding OH U.S.A.
263 I2 Paulding Bay Antarctica
161 B6 Paulhac France
161 C7 Paulhac-en-Margeride France
161 D6 Paulhaguet France
161 C9 Paulhan France
256 B4 Paulicéia Brazil
192 B7 Paulilatino Sardegna Italy
170 G5 Paulinenaue Ger.
163 I8 Paulinet France
234 E3 Paulins Kill r. NJ U.S.A.
Paulis Dem. Rep. Congo see Isiro
197 J4 Păuliș Romania
225 I1 Paul Island Nfld and Lab. Can.
254 G3 Paulista Brazil
254 E4 Paulistana Brazil
236 H4 Paullina IA U.S.A.
254 F4 Paulo Afonso Brazil
256 C4 Paulo de Faria Brazil
215 O3 Paulpietersburg S. Africa
186 F6 Paüls Spain
237 G8 Pauls Valley OK U.S.A.
150 G5 Paulton Bath and North East Somerset, England U.K.
158 H8 Paulx France
Paum i. Vanuatu see Paama
Paumotu, Îles is Fr. Polynesia see Tuamotu, Archipel des
260 E3 Paunero Arg.
197 P4 Păunești Romania
96 C6 Paung Myanmar
96 B2 Paungbyin Myanmar
96 B5 Paungde Myanmar
116 G9 Pauni Mahar. India
234 E2 Paupack PA U.S.A.
116 G4 Pauri Uttaranchal India
171 F9 Pausa Ger.
252 B3 Pausa Peru
250 D3 Pauto r. Col.
140 N4 Pauträsk Sweden
156 I5 Pauvres France
240 □E13 Pa'uwela HI U.S.A.
114 E5 Pavagada Karnataka India
257 G2 Pavão Brazil
250 B3 Pavarandocito Col.
134 L4 Pavda Rus. Fed.
122 B4 Pāveh Iran
139 W8 Pavelets Rus. Fed.
190 G5 Pavia Italy
190 G5 Pavia prov. Italy
184 C3 Pavia Port.
182 D8 Pavia r. Port.
191 O4 Pavia di Udine Italy
187 E8 Pavías Spain
163 F8 Pavie France
232 G6 Pavilion NY U.S.A.
156 A4 Pavilly France
138 E5 Pāvilosta Latvia
134 I4 Pavino Rus. Fed.
138 F7 Pavištyčio kalnas hill Lith.
175 M4 Pavitstsye Belarus
197 N7 Pavlikeni Bulg.
139 Q7 Pavlinovo Rus. Fed.
136 I6 Pavlivka Odes'ka Oblast' Ukr.
137 N2 Pavlivka Sums'ka Oblast' Ukr.
136 D3 Pavlivka Volyns'ka Oblast' Ukr.
121 Q1 Pavlodar Kazakh.
Pavlodar Oblast admin. div. Kazakh. see Pavlodarskaya Oblast'
Pavlodar Oblysy admin. div. Kazakh. see Pavlodarskaya Oblast'
121 Q1 Pavlodarskaya Oblast' admin. div. Kazakh.
220 B4 Pavlof Volcano AK U.S.A.
Pavlograd Ukr. see Pavlohrad
121 O1 Pavlogradka Rus. Fed.
137 O5 Pavlohrad Ukr.
137 N6 Pavlopillya Ukr.
177 L3 Pavlovce nad Uhom Slovakia
121 O2 Pavlovka Akmolinskaya Oblast' Kazakh.
120 J1 Pavlovka Kostanayskaya Oblast' Kazakh.
134 L5 Pavlovka Respublika Bashkortostan Rus. Fed.
120 B1 Pavlovka Ul'yanovskaya Oblast' Rus. Fed.
134 H5 Pavlovo Rus. Fed.
121 T1 Pavlovsk Altayskiy Kray Rus. Fed.
139 N2 Pavlovsk Leningradskaya Oblast' Rus. Fed.
135 H6 Pavlovsk Voronezhskaya Oblast' Rus. Fed.
135 G7 Pavlovskaya Rus. Fed.
120 J1 Pavlovskiy Kazakh.
139 V6 Pavlovskiy Posad Rus. Fed.
139 X5 Pavlovskoye Rus. Fed.
134 L5 Pavlovskoye Vodokhranilishche resr Rus. Fed.
137 M5 Pavlysh Ukr.
191 J7 Pavullo nel Frignano Italy
78 □6 Pavuvu i. Solomon Is
138 M3 Pavy Rus. Fed.
78 □6 Pawa Solomon Is
108 B5 Pawahku Myanmar
116 H7 Pawai Madh. Prad. India
95 H5 Pawan r. Indon.
80 H2 Pawarenga North I. N.Z.
116 H5 Pawayan Uttar Prad. India
235 L2 Pawcatuck CT U.S.A.
171 G5 Päwesin Ger.
237 G7 Pawhuska OK U.S.A.
139 P8 Pawlavichy Belarus
235 H1 Pawling NY U.S.A.
174 F2 Pawłówek Pol.
174 G6 Pawłowice Śląskie Pol.
174 E4 Pawłowice Wielkopolskie Pol.
174 G5 Pawłowiczki Pol.
96 C5 Pawn r. Myanmar
237 G7 Pawnee OK U.S.A.
236 F6 Pawnee r. KS U.S.A.
236 G5 Pawnee City NE U.S.A.
174 G5 Pawonków Pol.
226 I7 Paw Paw MI U.S.A.
232 G9 Paw Paw WV U.S.A.
233 N7 Pawtucket RI U.S.A.
84 D6 Pawu Aboriginal Land res. N.T. Austr.
97 D8 Pawut Myanmar
182 F3 Paxaro mt. Spain
199 H7 Paximada i. Greece
198 F7 Paximadia i. Greece
234 B3 Paxinos PA U.S.A.
198 B3 Paxoi i. Greece
220 D3 Paxson AK U.S.A.
121 O7 Paxtaobod Uzbek.
146 L11 Paxton Scottish Borders, Scotland U.K.
226 F9 Paxton IL U.S.A.
236 E5 Paxton NE U.S.A.
234 B4 Paxtonia PA U.S.A.
234 A3 Paxtonville PA U.S.A.
93 E3 Payahe Halmahera Indon.
94 D5 Payakumbuh Sumatera Indon.
94 □ Paya Lebar Sing.
114 D6 Payaswani r. India
140 □ Payer, Kapp c. Svalbard
179 M4 Payerbach Austria
190 B2 Payerne Switz.
238 F4 Payette ID U.S.A.
238 F4 Payette r. ID U.S.A.
134 M1 Pay-Khoy, Khrebet hills Rus. Fed.
184 E5 Paymogo Spain
Payne Que. Can. see Kangirsuk
232 A7 Payne OH U.S.A.
224 F1 Payne, Lac l. Que. Can.
240 K1 Paynes Creek CA U.S.A.
87 D10 Payne's Find W.A. Austr.
83 K7 Paynesville Vic. Austr.
236 H3 Paynesville MN U.S.A.
184 F4 Payo, Sierra hills Spain
163 G6 Payrac France
163 I8 Payrin-Augmontel France
261 H3 Paysandú Uru.
261 I3 Paysandú dept Uru.
163 A9 Pays Basque reg. France
159 L3 Pays d'Auge reg. France
163 B7 Pays de Born reg. France
156 B4 Pays de Bray reg. France
159 M2 Pays de Caux reg. France
162 B1 Pays de la Loire admin. reg. France
158 B5 Pays de Léon reg. France
158 G7 Pays de Retz reg. France
163 I10 Pays de Sault reg. France
156 G7 Pays d'Othe reg. France
159 M4 Pays d'Ouche reg. France
121 L7 Payshanba Uzbek.
241 U7 Payson AZ U.S.A.
260 C5 Payún, Cerro vol. Arg.
95 J3 Payung, Tanjung pt Malaysia
260 C5 Payún Matrú, Altiplanicie del plat. Arg.
258 C5 Payún Matrú, Volcán vol. Arg.
134 N2 Payyer, Gora mt. Rus. Fed.
162 G5 Payzac France
Payzawat Xinjiang China see Jiashi
254 C4 Paz, Rio da r. Brazil
127 J3 Pazar Turkey
126 H5 Pazarcık Turkey
197 M8 Pazardzhik Bulg.
199 I2 Pazarköy Turkey
199 K4 Pazarlar Turkey
199 K3 Pazaryeri Turkey
129 B5 Pazaryolu Turkey
250 D3 Paz de Ariporo Col.
250 C3 Paz de Río Col.
188 D3 Pazin Croatia
163 J10 Paziols France
252 D4 Pazña Bol.
178 B5 Paznauntal val. Austria
182 C4 Pazos Spain
122 G4 Pazūk Iran
139 O2 Pchevzha r. Rus. Fed.
175 H6 Pcim Pol.
197 J9 Pčinja r. Macedonia
97 D8 Pe Myanmar
79 □8a Pea Tongatapu Tonga
256 A5 Peabiru Brazil
236 G6 Peabody KS U.S.A.
233 O6 Peabody MA U.S.A.
222 I3 Peace r. Alta/B.C. Can.
231 F12 Peace r. FL U.S.A.
151 L6 Peacehaven East Sussex, England U.K.
223 H3 Peace Point Alta Can.
222 G3 Peace River Alta Can.
232 D11 Peach Creek WV U.S.A.
222 G5 Peachland B.C. Can.
241 S6 Peach Springs AZ U.S.A.
223 I1 Peacock Hills Nunavut Can.
251 F3 Peaima Falls Guyana
231 J8 Pea Island National Wildlife Refuge nature res. NC U.S.A.
87 F12 Peak Charles hill W.A. Austr.
87 F12 Peak Charles National Park W.A. Austr.
149 N7 Peak District National Park England U.K.
82 F3 Peake watercourse S.A. Austr.
233 □Q2 Peaked Mountain hill ME U.S.A.
83 L5 Peak Hill N.S.W. Austr.
87 E8 Peak Hill W.A. Austr.
240 M7 Peak Mountain CA U.S.A.
85 L7 Peak Range hills Qld Austr.
185 M5 Peal de Becerro Spain
241 W3 Peale, Mount UT U.S.A.
241 W10 Pearce AZ U.S.A.
84 B3 Pearce Point N.T. Austr.
182 E3 Peares, Encoro dos resr Spain
232 E11 Pearisburg VA U.S.A.
226 F1 Pearl Ont. Can.
237 K10 Pearl r. MS U.S.A.
75 H1 Pearl and Hermes Atoll HI U.S.A.
240 □D12 Pearl City HI U.S.A.
240 □C13 Pearl Harbor inlet HI U.S.A.
Pearl River r. Guangdong China see Zhu Jiang
235 G2 Pearl River NY U.S.A.
237 F11 Pearsall TX U.S.A.
261 G3 Pearson Arg.
231 F10 Pearson GA U.S.A.
226 E4 Pearson WI U.S.A.
82 E5 Pearson Islands S.A. Austr.
215 J8 Pearston S. Africa
221 I2 Peary Channel Nunavut Can.
221 O1 Peary Land reg. Greenland
237 F8 Pease r. TX U.S.A.
150 H5 Peasedown St John Bath and North East Somerset, England U.K.
158 G6 Péaule France
226 F3 Peavy Falls Reservoir MI U.S.A.
86 D6 Peawah r. W.A. Austr.
224 C2 Peawanuck Ont. Can.
213 H3 Pebane Moz.
250 D5 Pebas Peru
259 F8 Pebble Island Falkland Is
209 D6 Pebeangu Dem. Rep. Congo
93 B4 Pebengko Sulawesi Indon.
161 D6 Pébrac France
196 I8 Peć Kosovo Serbia
237 F10 Pecan Bayou r. TX U.S.A.
257 F3 Peçanha Brazil
237 I11 Pecan Island LA U.S.A.
256 C6 Peças, Ilha das i. Brazil
226 E7 Pecatonica IL U.S.A.
190 F3 Peccia Switz.
191 J8 Peccioli Italy
177 I4 Pécel Hungary
140 U2 Pecha r. Rus. Fed.
140 U2 Pechenga Rus. Fed.
140 U2 Pechenga r. Rus. Fed.
137 P4 Pechenihy Ukr.
139 R1 Pechenitsy Rus. Fed.
137 P4 Pecheniz'ke Vodoskhovyshche resr Ukr.
139 W7 Pecherniki Rus. Fed.
139 P7 Pechersk Rus. Fed.
216 □3c Pechiguera, Punta pt Lanzarote Canary Is
185 O7 Pechina Spain
134 L2 Pechora Rus. Fed.
134 K1 Pechora r. Rus. Fed.
Pechora Sea Rus. Fed. see Pechorskoye More
134 L3 Pechoro-Ilyiskiy Zapovednik nature res. Rus. Fed.
134 K1 Pechorskaya Guba b. Rus. Fed.
134 K1 Pechorskoye More sea Rus. Fed.
138 K4 Pechory Rus. Fed.
140 □ Pechuel Løsche, Kapp c. Svalbard
196 J4 Pecica Romania
197 Q7 Pecineaga Romania
206 A4 Pecixe, Ilha de i. Guinea-Bissau
227 L6 Peck MI U.S.A.
222 E3 Peck, Mount B.C. Can.
234 E2 Pecks Pond PA U.S.A.
176 E1 Pečky Czech Rep.
174 E4 Pecław Pol.
97 H8 Pe Cô, Krông r. Vietnam
192 F2 Pecora r. Italy
192 A9 Pecora, Capo c. Sardegna Italy
237 D10 Pecos TX U.S.A.
237 E11 Pecos r. NM/TX U.S.A.
165 D7 Pecq Belgium
177 H5 Pécs Hungary
177 H5 Pécsvárad Hungary
174 G4 Pęczniew Pol.
242 □S14 Pedasí Panama
193 L1 Pedaso Italy
114 F3 Pedda Vagu r. India
114 F4 Peddavagu r. India
83 K10 Pedder, Lake Tas. Austr.
215 L9 Peddie S. Africa
138 K4 Pededze Latvia
138 J5 Pededze r. Latvia
250 A4 Pedernales Ecuador
246 H4 Pedernales Haiti
239 K12 Pedernales Mex.
237 F10 Pedernales r. TX U.S.A.
251 F2 Pedernales Venez.
258 C2 Pedernales, Salar de salt flat Chile
256 C5 Pederneiras Brazil
191 L4 Pederobba Italy
140 Q5 Pedersöre Fin.
209 B9 Pediva Angola
93 E3 Pediwang Halmahera Indon.
138 J3 Pedja r. Estonia
257 G1 Pedra Azul Brazil
206 □ Pedra Badejo Santiago Cape Verde
182 D5 Pedrada mt. Port.
182 F3 Pedrafita do Cebreiro Spain
182 C6 Pedra Furada Port.
183 K6 Pedrajas de San Esteban Spain
187 D8 Pedralba Spain
182 G4 Pedralba de la Pradería Spain
206 □ Pedra Lume Cape Verde
254 C5 Pedra Preta, Serra da mts Brazil
254 B3 Pedras r. Brazil
254 D5 Pedras r. Brazil
182 E8 Pedras Lavradas pass Port.
253 E3 Pedras Negras Brazil
242 □R13 Pedregal Panama
250 D2 Pedregal Venez.
187 F10 Pedreguer Spain
256 D4 Pedregulho Brazil
254 D2 Pedreiras Maranhão Brazil
256 D5 Pedreiras São Paulo Brazil
185 J6 Pedrera Spain
187 D11 Pedrera, Embalse de la resr Spain
186 J4 Pedres, Serrat de les hill Spain
242 H5 Pedriceña Mex.
234 E5 Pedricktown NJ U.S.A.
183 N5 Pedro r. Spain
114 G8 Pedro, Point Sri Lanka
185 K5 Pedro Abad Spain
254 C4 Pedro Afonso Brazil
245 I4 Pedro Antonio de los Santos Mex.
254 F3 Pedro Avelino Brazil
246 D5 Pedro Bank sea feature Jamaica
256 D6 Pedro Barros Brazil
183 K8 Pedro Bernardo Spain
246 E5 Pedro Cays is Jamaica
185 J4 Pedroche Spain
250 D4 Pedro Chico Col.
251 I4 Pedro de Freitas Brazil
252 C5 Pedro de Valdivia Chile
261 H2 Pedro Díaz Colodrero Arg.
244 G5 Pedro Escobedo Mex.
184 D4 Pedrógão Beja Port.
182 F8 Pedrógão Castelo Branco Port.
182 C9 Pedrógão Leiria Port.
182 D9 Pedrógão Grande Port.
182 D9 Pedrógão Pequeno Port.
255 B6 Pedro Gomes Brazil
184 H2 Pedro Gómez mt. Spain
254 E3 Pedro II Brazil
250 E4 Pedro II, Ilha reg. Brazil/Venez.
253 G5 Pedro Juan Caballero Para.
257 E3 Pedro Leopoldo Brazil
261 F6 Pedro Luro Arg.
185 M5 Pedro-Martínez Spain
185 N2 Pedro Muñoz Spain
258 G3 Pedro Osório Brazil
246 □ Pedro Point Jamaica
186 I3 Pedrós, Puig mt. Spain
183 M2 Pedrosa Spain
183 L4 Pedrosa del Príncipe Spain
182 I7 Pedrosillo de los Aires Spain
182 C6 Pedroso Port.
183 O4 Pedroso Spain
256 D6 Pedro Toledo Brazil
163 H10 Pédrous, Pic mt. France
182 C3 Pedrouzos Spain
192 B6 Pedruso, Monte hill Italy
82 H6 Peebinga S.A. Austr.
146 J11 Peebles Scottish Borders, Scotland U.K.
232 B10 Peebles OH U.S.A.
86 C6 Peedamulla W.A. Austr.
86 C6 Peedamulla Aboriginal Reserve W.A. Austr.
231 H9 Pee Dee r. SC U.S.A.
233 L7 Peekskill NY U.S.A.
220 E3 Peel r. Y.T. Can.
148 H5 Peel Isle of Man
81 F10 Peel, Mount South I. N.Z.
87 C12 Peel Inlet W.A. Austr.
170 I3 Peene r. Ger.
170 I2 Peenemünde Ger.
170 I3 Peenestrom sea chan. Ger.
165 H6 Peer Belgium
140 P2 Peera Fin.
82 G2 Peera Peera Poolanna Lake salt flat S.A. Austr.
222 H3 Peerless Lake Alta Can.
222 H3 Peerless Lake l. Alta Can.
222 G4 Peers Alta Can.
182 F8 Pega Port.
161 C9 Pégairolles-de-l'Escalette France
81 G10 Pegasus Bay South I. N.Z.
171 F8 Pegau Ger.
179 L5 Peggau Austria
190 F7 Pegli Italy
193 P7 Peglio r. Italy
173 L2 Pegnitz Ger.
173 J3 Pegnitz r. Ger.
184 C2 Pego Port.
187 E10 Pego Spain
184 C4 Pego do Altar, Barragem do resr Port.
184 B3 Pegões Port.
174 E4 Pęgów Pol.
96 C6 Pegu Myanmar
96 B5 Pegu admin. div. Myanmar
187 J8 Peguera Spain
93 B5 Pegunungan Latimojong nature res. Indon.
93 B5 Pegunungan Peruhumpenai nature res. Indon.
96 B5 Pegu Yoma mts Myanmar
151 O5 Pegwell Bay England U.K.
134 J3 Pegysh Rus. Fed.
199 H1 Pehlivanköy Turkey
207 F4 Péhonko Benin
116 F5 Pehowa Haryana India
261 G4 Pehuajó Arg.
261 G6 Pehuén-Có Arg.
109 M7 Peikang Taiwan
158 G6 Peillac France
161 K9 Peille France
146 D8 Peinchorran Highland, Scotland U.K.
252 C5 Peine Chile
169 J6 Peine Ger.
259 B8 Peineta, Cerro mt. Arg.
116 D9 Peint Mahar. India
191 J3 Peio Italy
161 H8 Peipin France
Peipsi järv l. Estonia/Rus. Fed. see Peipus, Lake
138 K3 Peipus, Lake Estonia/Rus. Fed.
161 K9 Peïra-Cava France
198 E5 Peiraias Greece
160 J5 Peisey-Nancroix France
Pei Shan mts China see Bei Shan
171 E7 Peißen Sachsen-Anhalt Ger.
171 F7 Peißen Sachsen-Anhalt Ger.
173 K6 Peißenberg Ger.
173 J6 Peiting Ger.
171 J7 Peitz Ger.
254 C5 Peixe Brazil
256 B4 Peixe r. Brazil
256 C2 Peixe r. Brazil
254 C5 Peixe r. Brazil
256 A2 Peixe, Rio do r. Brazil
257 F5 Peixes r. Brazil
253 F2 Peixes r. Brazil
107 O9 Peixian Jiangsu China
Peixian Jiangsu China see Pizhou
256 D4 Peixoto, Represa resr Brazil
254 B4 Peixoto de Azevedo Brazil
253 G2 Peixoto de Azevedo r. Brazil
164 K2 Peize Neth.
94 G4 Pejantan i. Indon.
Peje Kosovo Serbia see Peć
197 J6 Pek r. Serbia
215 L4 Peka Lesotho
93 A5 Pekabata Sulawesi Indon.
95 H8 Pekalongan Jawa Indon.
94 E3 Pekan Malaysia
94 D4 Pekanbaru Sumatera Indon.
225 H2 Pékans, Rivière aux r. Que. Can.
139 X8 Pekhlets Rus. Fed.
207 F5 Peki Ghana
226 E9 Pekin IL U.S.A.
Peking Beijing China see Beijing
139 Q8 Peklino Rus. Fed.
183 N6 Pela, Sierra de mts Spain
94 D3 Pelabuhan Klang Malaysia
259 C7 Pelada, Pampa hills Arg.
187 C8 Pelado mt. Spain
189 D8 Pelagie, Isole is Sicilia Italy
191 L8 Pelago Italy
196 J9 Pelagonija plain Macedonia
183 K8 Pelahustán Spain
95 K6 Pelaihari Kalimantan Indon.
96 E4 Pelalawan Sumatera Indon.
95 H5 Pelapis i. Indon.
260 B4 Pelarco Chile
182 C9 Pelariga Port.
182 H7 Pelarrodríguez Spain
198 D4 Pelasgia Greece
Pelasyía Greece see Pelasgia
161 J8 Pelat, Mont mt. France
215 M4 Pelatsoeu mt. Lesotho
78 □6 Pelau i. Solomon Is
95 L4 Pelawanbesar Kalimantan Indon.
174 D2 Pełczyce Pol.
197 K5 Peleaga, Vârful mt. Romania
183 J6 Peleagonzalo Spain
252 C3 Pelechuco Bol.
138 J5 Pelēči Latvia
247 □3 Pelée, Montagne vol. Martinique
224 D5 Pelee Island Ont. Can.
224 D5 Pelee Point Ont. Can.
193 Q1 Pelegrin, Rt pt Croatia
92 □ Peleliu i. Palau
93 C4 Peleng i. Indon.
93 C4 Peleng, Selat sea chan. Indon.
93 C4 Peleng, Teluk b. Indon.
134 J3 Peles Rus. Fed.
176 E2 Pelhřimov Czech Rep.
220 E4 Pelican AK U.S.A.
85 I4 Pelican Creek r. Qld Austr.
223 K4 Pelican Lake l. Man. Can.
226 E4 Pelican Lake WI U.S.A.
226 B1 Pelican Lake l. MN U.S.A.
223 K4 Pelican Narrows Sask. Can.
216 □3a Peligro, Punta del pt La Gomera Canary Is
185 L6 Peligros Spain
136 G6 Pelinia Moldova
161 G9 Pélissanne France
196 J10 Pelister mt. Macedonia
196 J10 Pelister nat. park Macedonia
188 F4 Pelješac pen. Croatia
140 S3 Pelkosenniemi Fin.
214 D5 Pella S. Africa
226 A1 Pelland MN U.S.A.
195 J7 Pellaro Italy
223 I1 Pellatt Lake N.W.T. Can.
231 D9 Pell City AL U.S.A.
261 F5 Pellegrini Arg.
260 D6 Pellegrini, Lago l. Arg.
190 H6 Pellegrino Parmense Italy
163 E6 Pellegrue France
91 J7 Pelleluhu Islands P.N.G.
177 H5 Pellérd Hungary
191 M5 Pellestrina Italy
159 N8 Pellevoisin France
190 D6 Pellice r. Italy
178 C7 Pellizzano Italy
140 Q3 Pello Fin.
226 J4 Pellston MI U.S.A.
260 A4 Pelluhue Chile
168 G1 Pellworm i. Ger.
222 B2 Pelly r. Y.T. Can.
Pelly Bay Nunavut Can. see Kugaaruk
222 B2 Pelly Crossing Y.T. Can.
222 C2 Pelly Mountains Y.T. Can.
169 C10 Pelm Ger.
178 F7 Pelmo, Monte mt. Italy
185 I2 Peloche Spain
95 M8 Pelokang is Indon.
Peloponnese admin. reg. Greece see Peloponnisos
Peloponnesus admin. reg. Greece see Peloponnisos
198 D5 Peloponnisos admin. reg. Greece
198 D5 Peloponnisos pen. Greece
195 H8 Peloritani, Monti mts Sicilia Italy
195 J7 Peloro, Capo c. Sicilia Italy
81 H8 Pelorus Sound sea chan. South I. N.Z.
258 G3 Pelotas Brazil
255 C8 Pelotas, Rio das r. Brazil
197 M7 Pelovo Bulg.
174 G2 Pelplin Pol.
151 I2 Pelsall West Midlands, England U.K.
87 B10 Pelsart Group is W.A. Austr.
170 I3 Pelsin Ger.
140 R2 Peltovuoma Fin.
128 A7 Pelusium tourist site Egypt
Pelusium, Bay of Egypt see Ṭīnah, Khalīj aṭ
161 F6 Pélussin France
161 I7 Pelvoux France
161 I7 Pelvoux, Massif du mts France
161 I7 Pelvoux, Mont mt. France
177 J4 Pély Hungary
150 C7 Pelynt Cornwall, England U.K.
227 K2 Pemache r. Ont. Can.
233 □Q3 Pemadumcook Lake ME U.S.A.
95 H8 Pemalang Jawa Indon.
95 H4 Pemangkat Kalimantan Indon.
95 L5 Pemarung, Pulau i. Indon.
94 C3 Pematangsiantar Sumatera Indon.
213 I2 Pemba Moz.
209 E9 Pemba Zambia
211 D8 Pemba, Baía de b. Moz.
211 C6 Pemba Channel Tanz.
211 C6 Pemba Island Tanz.
211 C6 Pemba North admin. reg. Tanz.
211 C6 Pemba South admin. reg. Tanz.
87 C13 Pemberton W.A. Austr.
222 F5 Pemberton B.C. Can.
234 F5 Pemberton NJ U.S.A.
222 H4 Pembina r. Alta Can.
236 G1 Pembina ND U.S.A.
236 G1 Pembina r. ND U.S.A.
226 G4 Pembine WI U.S.A.
150 D4 Pembrey Carmarthenshire, Wales U.K.
150 G3 Pembridge Herefordshire, England U.K.
224 E4 Pembroke Ont. Can.
150 C4 Pembroke Pembrokeshire, Wales U.K.
231 G9 Pembroke GA U.S.A.
233 □R4 Pembroke ME U.S.A.
259 F8 Pembroke, Cape Falkland Is
81 B11 Pembroke, Mount South I. N.Z.
150 C4 Pembroke Dock Pembrokeshire, Wales U.K.
231 G12 Pembroke Pines FL U.S.A.
150 C4 Pembrokeshire admin. div. Wales U.K.
150 B4 Pembrokeshire Coast National Park Wales U.K.
95 J6 Pembuanghulu Kalimantan Indon.
151 M5 Pembury Kent, England U.K.
260 B5 Pemehue, Cordillera de mts Chile
173 N3 Pemfling Ger.
95 I5 Pemuar Kalimantan Indon.
260 A5 Pemuco Chile
114 C3 Pen Mahar. India
96 A4 Pen r. Myanmar
137 O2 Pena r. Rus. Fed.
186 D3 Peña, Embalse de la resr Spain
252 D5 Pena Barrosa Bol.
260 B2 Peña Blanca Chile
183 O3 Peñacerrada Spain
182 D8 Penacova Port.
182 H8 Peña de Francia, Sierra de la mts Spain
184 F2 Peña del Águila, Embalse de la resr Spain
182 D6 Penafiel Port.
183 L5 Peñafiel Spain
185 I5 Peñaflor Spain
183 K5 Peñaflor de Hornija Spain
183 M2 Peñagos Spain
247 □7 Penal Trin. and Tob.
183 K2 Peña Labra, Sierra de mts Spain
183 M7 Peñalara mt. Spain
186 E5 Peñalba Spain
182 G4 Peñalba de Santiago tourist site Spain
183 P7 Peñalén Spain
150 C4 Penally Pembrokeshire, Wales U.K.
185 I3 Peñalsordo Spain
182 E7 Penalva do Castelo Port.
182 F8 Penamacor Port.
Penambo Range mts Malaysia see Tama Abu, Banjaran
245 H4 Pemamiller Mex.
95 L2 Penampang Sabah Malaysia
245 H2 Peña Nevada, Cerro mt. Mex.
Penang state Malaysia see Pinang
256 B4 Penápolis Brazil
183 J7 Peñaranda de Bracamonte Spain
183 N5 Peñaranda de Duero Spain
234 E3 Pen Argyl PA U.S.A.
83 I6 Penarie N.S.W. Austr.
Penarlâg Wales U.K. see Hawarden
186 D7 Peñarroya mt. Spain
185 M2 Peñarroya, Embalse de resr Spain
185 I4 Peñarroya-Pueblonuevo Spain
185 O4 Peñarrubia Spain
150 F5 Penarth Vale of Glamorgan, Wales U.K.
182 I1 Peñas, Cabo de c. Spain
259 B7 Penas, Golfo de g. Chile
247 □7 Peñas, Punta pt Venez.
183 L2 Peña Sagra, Sierra mts Spain
260 D5 Peñas Blancas Arg.
242 □Q12 Peñas Blancas Nic.
239 L10 Peñasco watercourse NM U.S.A.
185 O3 Peñascosa Spain
183 M5 Peñas de Cervera hills Spain
185 P3 Peñas de San Pedro Spain
94 A2 Penasi, Pulau i. Indon.
182 I6 Peñausende Spain
150 D3 Penbryn Ceredigion, Wales U.K.
177 I4 Penc Hungary
150 D3 Pencader Carmarthenshire, Wales U.K.
146 K11 Pencaitland East Lothian, Scotland U.K.
116 G9 Pench r. India
Pencheng Jiangxi China see Ruichang
263 F2 Penck, Cape Antarctica
150 F4 Pencoed Bridgend, Wales U.K.
208 C3 Pendé r. C.A.R.
150 □ Pendeen Cornwall, England U.K.
206 C4 Pendembu Eastern Sierra Leone
206 B4 Pendembu Northern Sierra Leone
236 G4 Pender NE U.S.A.
86 G4 Pender Bay W.A. Austr.
86 G4 Pender Bay Aboriginal Reserve W.A. Austr.
199 K2 Pendik Turkey
182 E7 Pendilhe Port.
150 C4 Pendine Carmarthenshire, Wales U.K.
207 F4 Pendjari, Parc National de la nat. park Benin
149 M6 Pendle Hill England U.K.
238 E4 Pendleton OR U.S.A.
222 E4 Pendleton Bay B.C. Can.
94 E6 Pendopo Sumatera Indon.
238 F2 Pend Oreille r. WA U.S.A.
238 F2 Pend Oreille Lake ID U.S.A.
116 H8 Pendra Chhattisgarh India
116 H8 Pendra Road Chhattisgarh India
114 C4 Penduv Mahar. India
Pendzhikent Tajik. see Panjakent
95 H5 Penebangan i. Indon.
182 D5 Peneda, Serra da mts Port.
182 D5 Peneda Gerês, Parque Nacional da nat. park Port.
184 D5 Penedo Gordo Port.
182 F7 Penedono Port.
182 D8 Penela Port.
209 F6 Pene-Mende Dem. Rep. Congo
207 F4 Pénessoulou Benin
158 G7 Pénestin France
177 L4 Penészlek Hungary
227 O5 Penetanguishene Ont. Can.
232 G7 Penfield PA U.S.A.
Penfro Pembrokeshire, Wales U.K. see Pembroke
108 F3 Peng'an Sichuan China
114 F3 Penganga r. India
109 □J7 Peng Chau i. H.K. China
109 N6 P'engchia Yü i. Taiwan
209 E6 Penge Dem. Rep. Congo
109 L7 P'enghu Ch'üntao is Taiwan
P'enghu Liehtao is Taiwan see P'enghu Ch'üntao
109 L7 P'enghu Tao i. Taiwan
95 H4 Pengiki i. Indon.
226 A2 Pengilly MN U.S.A.
94 D2 Pengkalan Hulu Malaysia
94 □ Peng Kang hill Sing.
107 Q8 Penglai Shandong China
108 D3 Pengshan Sichuan China
108 G4 Pengshui Chongqing China
94 □ Peng Siang, Sungai r. Sing.
96 A4 Pengwa Myanmar
108 E3 Pengxi Sichuan China
Pengxian Sichuan China see Pengzhou
109 K4 Pengze Jiangxi China
108 D3 Pengzhou Sichuan China
255 C8 Penha Brazil
182 F8 Penha Garcia Port.
213 G3 Penhalonga Zimbabwe
182 D9 Penhascoso Port.
158 B5 Penhir, Pointe de pt France
215 K7 Penhoek Pass S. Africa
232 F12 Penhook VA U.S.A.
184 A2 Peniche Port.
146 J11 Penicuik Midlothian, Scotland U.K.
95 K9 Penida i. Indon.
171 G9 Penig Ger.
134 F3 Peninga Rus. Fed.
Peninsular Malaysia Malaysia see Malaysia, Semenanjung
146 E12 Peninver Argyll and Bute, Scotland U.K.
187 F7 Peñíscola Spain
149 N6 Penistone South Yorkshire, England U.K.
254 D4 Penitente, Serra do hills Brazil
207 H5 Penja Cameroon
244 F5 Penjamo Mex.
127 L6 Pēnjwīn Iraq
149 L7 Penketh Warrington, England U.K.
139 X5 Penkino Rus. Fed.
150 H2 Penkridge Staffordshire, England U.K.
170 J4 Penkun Ger.
150 G2 Penley Wrexham, Wales U.K.
156 B4 Penly France
158 C6 Penmarch France
158 C6 Penmarch, Pointe de pt France
Penn PA U.S.A. see Penn Hills
193 N3 Penna, Punta della pt Italy
193 I3 Penna in Teverina Italy
163 I9 Pennautier France
163 H7 Penne France
193 L3 Penne Italy
195 N2 Penne, Punta pt Italy
163 F7 Penne-d'Agenais France
263 L2 Pennell Coast Antarctica
114 G5 Penner r. India
82 F6 Penneshaw S.A. Austr.
233 □S3 Pennfield N.B. Can.
234 D3 Penn Forest Reservoir PA U.S.A.
232 F8 Penn Hills PA U.S.A.
160 K5 Pennine, Alpi mts Italy/Switz.
Pennine Alps mts Italy/Switz. see Pennine, Alpi
149 M5 Pennines hills England U.K.
215 O6 Pennington S. Africa
234 F4 Pennington NJ U.S.A.
232 B12 Pennington Gap VA U.S.A.
193 J1 Pennino, Monte mt. Italy
232 E9 Pennsboro WV U.S.A.
234 E4 Pennsburg PA U.S.A.
234 A3 Penns Creek PA U.S.A.
234 B3 Penns Creek r. PA U.S.A.
234 E5 Penns Grove NJ U.S.A.
234 D5 Pennsville NJ U.S.A.
227 P8 Pennsylvania state U.S.A.
247 □2 Pennville Dominica
232 H6 Penn Yan NY U.S.A.
146 D10 Pennyghael Argyll and Bute, Scotland U.K.
221 L3 Penny Icecap Nunavut Can.
263 K1 Penny Point Antarctica
234 F5 Penny Pot NJ U.S.A.
139 P5 Peno Rus. Fed.
233 □Q4 Penobscot r. ME U.S.A.
233 □Q4 Penobscot Bay ME U.S.A.
82 H7 Penola S.A. Austr.
242 G5 Peñón Blanco Mex.
187 F10 Peñón de Ifach pt Spain
82 D4 Penong S.A. Austr.
242 □S13 Penonomé Panama
150 D3 Penrhiw-pâl Ceredigion, Wales U.K.
81 □2 Penrhyn atoll Cook Is
267 I6 Penrhyn Basin sea feature Pacific Ocean
150 E1 Penrhyn Bay Conwy, Wales U.K.
150 D2 Penrhyndeudraeth Gwynedd, Wales U.K.
150 C2 Penrhyn Mawr pt Wales U.K.
83 M5 Penrith N.S.W. Austr.
149 L4 Penrith Cumbria, England U.K.
150 B7 Penryn Cornwall, England U.K.
231 D10 Pensacola FL U.S.A.
231 D10 Pensacola Bay FL U.S.A.
262 T1 Pensacola Mountains Antarctica
253 E3 Pensamiento Bol.
122 C2 Pensär Azer.
226 G5 Pensaukee WI U.S.A.
83 I7 Penshurst Vic. Austr.
95 L2 Pensiangan Sabah Malaysia
116 F3 Pensi La pass Jammu and Kashmir
150 D6 Pensilva Cornwall, England U.K.
128 B3 Pentadaktylos Range mts Cyprus
192 C3 Penta-di-Casinca Corse France
115 H4 Pentakota Andhra Prad. India
198 C2 Pentalofos Greece
86 I3 Pentecost r. W.A. Austr.
78 □5 Pentecost Island Vanuatu
225 H3 Pentecôte r. Que. Can.
Pentecôte, Île i. Vanuatu see Pentecost Island
197 O5 Penteleu, Vârful mt. Romania
158 F5 Penthièvre reg. France
222 G5 Penticton B.C. Can.
186 □ Pentinat, Punta pt Spain
150 D1 Pentir Gwynedd, Wales U.K.
150 B6 Pentire Point England U.K.
85 J6 Pentland Qld Austr.
146 J5 Pentland Firth sea chan. Scotland U.K.
146 I11 Pentland Hills Scotland U.K.
173 M4 Pentling Ger.
150 D1 Pentraeth Isle of Anglesey, Wales U.K.
150 E1 Pentrefoelas Conwy, Wales U.K.
226 H6 Pentwater MI U.S.A.
94 F5 Penuba Indon.
94 F6 Penuguan Sumatera Indon.
114 E5 Penukonda Andhra Prad. India
94 E2 Penunjuk, Tanjung pt Malaysia
158 E4 Penvénan France
96 C5 Penwegon Myanmar
149 L6 Penwortham Lancashire, England U.K.
137 O2 Peny Rus. Fed.
187 E7 Penyagolosa mt. Spain
150 F3 Penybont Powys, Wales U.K.
Pen-y-Bont ar Ogwr Bridgend, Wales U.K. see Bridgend
Pen-y-bont ar Ogwr Wales U.K. see Bridgend
150 F2 Penybontfawr Powys, Wales U.K.
150 E4 Pen-y-fai Bridgend, Wales U.K.
150 E2 Penygadair hill Wales U.K.
149 M5 Pen-y-Ghent hill England U.K.
150 D1 Penygroes Gwynedd, Wales U.K.
223 J2 Penylan Lake N.W.T. Can.
93 E6 Penyu, Kepulauan is Maluku Indon.
150 F4 Penywaun Rhondda Cynon Taff, Wales U.K.
135 I5 Penza Rus. Fed.
150 □ Penzance Cornwall, England U.K.
Penza Oblast admin. div. Rus. Fed. see Penzenskaya Oblast'
173 K6 Penzberg Ger.
135 I5 Penzenskaya Oblast' admin. div. Rus. Fed.
131 R3 Penzhinskaya Guba b. Rus. Fed.
173 J5 Penzing Ger.
170 H4 Penzlin Ger.
161 J8 Péone France
238 J2 Peoples Creek r. MT U.S.A.
241 T8 Peoria AZ U.S.A.
226 E9 Peoria IL U.S.A.
226 E9 Peoria Heights IL U.S.A.
240 □F14 Pepe'ekeo HI U.S.A.
206 B4 Pepel Sierra Leone
170 E2 Pepelow Ger.
261 I2 Pepe Nuñez Uru.
210 B3 Peper Sudan
Peper, Teluk b. Indon. see Lada, Teluk
161 B10 Pépieux France
165 F7 Pepingen Belgium
165 I7 Pepinster Belgium
174 F4 Pępowo Pol.
215 N4 Pepworth S. Africa
196 H9 Peqin Albania
235 G3 Pequannock NJ U.S.A.
182 H4 Peque Spain
234 C5 Pequea PA U.S.A.
234 C5 Pequea Creek r. PA U.S.A.
242 C4 Pequeña, Punta pt Mex.
234 E3 Pequest r. NJ U.S.A.
257 E3 Pequi Brazil
177 G4 Pér Hungary
184 C6 Pêra Port.
198 D4 Perachora Greece
114 G9 Peradeniya Sri Lanka
85 H2 Pera Head Qld Austr.
97 E12 Perai Malaysia
182 E9 Perais Port.
251 F3 Peraitepuy Venez.
94 C2 Perak i. Malaysia
94 D2 Perak r. Malaysia
94 D2 Perak state Malaysia
186 L3 Peralada Spain
183 J9 Peraleda de la Mata Spain
184 H4 Peraleda del Zaucejo Spain
186 C7 Peralejos Spain
186 D6 Perales del Alfambra Spain
182 G8 Perales del Puerto Spain
261 G6 Peralta Arg.
183 Q4 Peralta Spain
186 E4 Peralta de Alcofea Spain
186 F4 Peralta de la Sal Spain
186 E3 Peraltilla Spain
184 D6 Peralva Port.
183 P7 Peralveche Spain
198 F7 Perama Kriti Greece
114 F7 Perambalur Tamil Nadu India
140 R4 Perämeren kansallispuisto nat. park Fin.
211 B7 Peramiho Tanz.
186 H3 Peramola Spain
184 E5 Peramora r. Spain
94 E5 Peranap Sumatera Indon.
140 S3 Perä-Posio Fin.
178 F7 Perarolo di Cadore Italy
225 H3 Percé Que. Can.
159 L4 Perche, Collines du hills France
179 N3 Perchtoldsdorf Austria
86 H6 Percival Lakes salt flat W.A. Austr.
158 I4 Percy France
233 N4 Percy NH U.S.A.
85 M6 Percy Isles Qld Austr.
227 Q5 Percy Reach l. Ont. Can.
192 C8 Perdasdefogu Sardegna Italy
192 B9 Perdaxius Sardegna Italy
215 N3 Perdekop S. Africa
214 H9 Perdepoort pass S. Africa
261 H3 Perdices Arg.
183 P5 Perdices, Sierra de mts Spain
254 D4 Perdida r. Brazil
261 H5 Perdido r. Arg.
253 F5 Perdido r. Brazil
186 F2 Perdido, Monte mt. Spain
193 O7 Perdifumo Italy
186 D4 Perdiguera Spain
186 G2 Perdiguère, Pic mt. France/Spain
198 B3 Perdika Greece
234 B4 Perdix PA U.S.A.
256 D3 Perdizes Brazil
257 E4 Perdões Brazil
225 G3 Perdu, Lac l. Que. Can.
185 O5 Perea mt. Spain
136 F2 Perebrody Ukr.
136 B5 Perechyn Ukr.

Peredel to Piesport

368

139 S6 Peredel Kaluzhskaya Oblast' Rus. Fed.
139 X6 Peredel Vladimirskaya Oblast' Rus. Fed.
182 G6 Peredo Port.
130 H3 Peregrebnoye Rus. Fed.
177 J5 Peregu Mare Romania
136 D5 Perehins'ke Ukr.
250 C3 Pereira Col.
256 B4 Pereira Barreto Brazil
Pereira de Eça Angola see Ondjiva
184 C6 Pereiras Port.
254 F3 Pereiro Brazil
180 C4 Pereiro Port.
182 E1 Pereiro Spain
182 E4 Pereiro de Aguiar Spain
183 Q6 Perejiles r. Spain
139 O3 Perekhoda r. Rus. Fed.
137 M3 Perekopivka Ukr.
137 M8 Perekops'ka Zatoka b. Ukr.
135 H6 Perelazovskiy Rus. Fed.
139 O8 Perelazy Rus. Fed.
137 T2 Pereleshinskiy Rus. Fed.
120 D2 Perelyub Rus. Fed.
226 H6 Pere Marquette r. MI U.S.A.
120 D2 Peremetnoye Kazakh.
137 P4 Peremoha Kharkivs'ka Oblast' Ukr.
137 K3 Peremoha Kyivs'ka Oblast' Ukr.
114 C7 Peremul Par rf India
139 T7 Peremyshl' Rus. Fed.
136 D4 Peremyshlyany Ukr.
252 B2 Perené r. Peru
87 D10 Perenjori W.A. Austr.
182 I6 Pereruela Spain
136 H6 Peresecina Moldova
137 O4 Pereshchepyne Ukr.
139 V5 Pereslavl'-Zalesskiy Rus. Fed.
139 V5 Pereslavskiy Natsional'nyy Park nat. park Rus. Fed.
175 M5 Perespa Ukr.
179 O4 Pereszteg Hungary
191 K8 Peretola airport Italy
197 N6 Peretu Romania
137 R5 Pereval's'k Ukr.
137 L3 Perevid r. Ukr.
120 F2 Perevolotskiy Rus. Fed.
134 I5 Perevoz Rus. Fed.
100 I5 Pereyaslavka Rus. Fed.
Pereyaslav-Khmel'nitskiy Ukr. see Pereyaslav-Khmel'nyts'kyy
137 K3 Pereyaslav-Khmel'nyts'kyy Ukr.
261 G3 Pérez Arg.
258 C2 Pérez Chile
192 B6 Perfugas Sardegna Italy
179 K3 Perg Austria
261 G3 Pergamino Arg.
199 L6 Perge tourist site Turkey
191 L9 Pergine Valdarno Italy
191 K3 Pergine Valsugana Italy
191 N8 Pergola Italy
136 G2 Perha Ukr.
94 E2 Perhentian Besar, Pulau i. Malaysia
140 R5 Perho Fin.
196 I4 Periam Romania
185 K7 Periana Spain
244 E6 Peribán de Ramos Mex.
225 F3 Péribonka r. Que. Can.
225 G3 Péribonka, Lac l. Que. Can.
258 D2 Perico Arg.
244 B3 Pericos Nayarit Mex.
242 F5 Pericos Sinaloa Mex.
241 V8 Peridot AZ U.S.A.
197 P4 Perieni Romania
158 I3 Périers France
162 B3 Périgny France
162 F6 Périgord reg. France
162 F5 Périgord Blanc reg. France
163 F6 Périgord Noir reg. France
251 I5 Perigoso, Canal sea chan. Brazil
162 F5 Périgueux France
250 C2 Perijá, Parque Nacional nat. park Venez.
250 C2 Perija, Sierra de mts Venez.
182 I5 Perilla de Castro Spain
Perim Island Yemen see Barīm
177 K3 Perín-Chym Slovakia
94 E1 Peringat Malaysia
197 R5 Periprava Romania
197 P6 Perişoru Romania
198 E3 Peristera i. Greece
198 E4 Peristeri Greece
129 A7 Peri Suyu r. Turkey
197 R6 Periteasca-Gura Portiţei nature res. Romania
259 C7 Perito Moreno Arg.
259 B7 Perito Moreno, Parque Nacional nat. park Arg.
114 E7 Perivar r. India
198 B3 Perivoli Kerkyra Greece
198 F7 Perivolia Kriti Greece
177 J4 Perje r. Hungary
234 E4 Perkasie PA U.S.A.
94 F5 Perkat, Tanjung pt Indon.
177 H4 Perkáta Hungary
234 E4 Perkiomen Creek r. PA U.S.A.
172 A3 Perl Ger.
242 □T13 Perlas, Archipiélago de las is Panama
242 □R11 Perlas, Laguna de lag. Nic.
242 □R11 Perlas, Punta de pt Nic.
173 M3 Perlbach r. Ger.
170 E4 Perleberg Ger.
175 K3 Perlejewo Pol.
173 O4 Perlesreut Ger.
137 R2 Perlevka Rus. Fed.
94 D1 Perlis state Malaysia
175 M1 Perloja Lith.
175 J1 Perły Pol.
134 L4 Perm' Rus. Fed.
191 Q5 Permani Croatia
134 I4 Permas Rus. Fed.
198 B2 Përmet Albania
134 K4 Permskiy Kray admin. div. Rus. Fed.
191 R7 Permuda Croatia
188 E3 Permuda i. Croatia
138 J1 Pernå Fin.
Pernambuco Brazil see Recife
254 F4 Pernambuco state Brazil
264 H6 Pernambuco Plain sea feature S. Atlantic Ocean
160 F2 Pernand-Vergelesses France
176 C2 Pernarec Czech Rep.
184 C5 Perna Seca, Barragem da resr Port.
191 Q6 Pernat, Rt pt Croatia
82 F4 Pernatty Lagoon salt flat S.A. Austr.
179 L5 Pernegg an der Mur Austria
114 C5 Pernem Goa India
179 N2 Pernersdorf Austria
184 B2 Pernes Port.
161 G9 Pernes-les-Fontaines France
198 F1 Perni Greece
197 L8 Pernik Bulg.
141 Q6 Perniö Fin.
179 M4 Pernitz Austria
Pernov Estonia see Pärnu
190 G4 Pero Italy
184 C4 Peroguarda Port.
256 A2 Perolândia Brazil
161 D9 Pérols France
160 H4 Péron France
87 B8 Peron, Cape W.A. Austr.
87 C12 Peron, Point W.A. Austr.
84 C2 Peron Islands N.T. Austr.
160 G4 Péronnas France
156 E4 Péronne France
87 B8 Peron Peninsula W.A. Austr.
190 C6 Perosa Argentina Italy
245 J6 Perote Mex.
160 G5 Pérouges France
182 F8 Pero Viseu Port.
83 M6 Perpendicular, Point N.S.W. Austr.
163 J10 Perpignan France
260 A6 Perquenco Chile
260 B4 Perquilauquén r. Chile
260 D5 Perra, Salitral de la salt pan Arg.
150 B7 Perranporth Cornwall, England U.K.
150 B7 Perranzabuloe Cornwall, England U.K.
160 E3 Perrecy-les-Forges France
Perrégaux Alg. see Mohammadia
160 E4 Perreux France
160 H3 Perrigny France
240 O8 Perris CA U.S.A.
184 G7 Perro, Punta del pt Spain
157 J8 Perrogney-les-Fontaines France
154 C2 Perros-Guirec France
233 L3 Perrot, Île i. Que. Can.
140 S2 Perrum-Äbmir Fin.
226 J2 Perry Ont. Can.
231 F10 Perry FL U.S.A.
231 F9 Perry GA U.S.A.
236 H5 Perry IA U.S.A.
233 □R4 Perry ME U.S.A.
227 J7 Perry MI U.S.A.
237 G7 Perry OK U.S.A.
234 A4 Perry County county PA U.S.A.
234 C6 Perry Hall MD U.S.A.
234 C6 Perryman MD U.S.A.
263 G2 Perrymennyy, Cape Antarctica
232 B7 Perrysburg OH U.S.A.
237 E7 Perryton TX U.S.A.
237 I8 Perryville AR U.S.A.
234 C5 Perryville MD U.S.A.
163 I6 Pers France
129 E4 P'ersa Georgia
156 D5 Persan France
129 D3 P'ersat'i Georgia
179 L3 Persenbeug Austria
122 E7 Persepolis tourist site Iran
253 E3 Perseverancia Bol.
143 N2 Pershagen Sweden
137 M5 Pershe Travnya Dnipropetrovs'ka Oblast' Ukr.
137 O5 Pershe Travnya Dnipropetrovs'ka Oblast' Ukr.
Pershnotravnevoye Ukr. see Pershotravens'k
150 H3 Pershore Worcestershire, England U.K.
137 P5 Pershotravens'k Ukr.
137 Q6 Pershotravneve Donets'ka Oblast' Ukr.
137 Q4 Pershotravneve Kharkivs'ka Oblast' Ukr.
137 L7 Pershotravneve Mykolayivs'ka Oblast' Ukr.
136 H2 Pershotravneve Zhytomyrs'ka Oblast' Ukr.
Pershotravnevoye Ukr. see Mokvyn
Persia country Asia see Iran
Persian Gulf Asia see The Gulf
Persis prov. Iran see Fārs
143 M4 Persnäs Öland Sweden
143 N3 Persö naturreservat nature res. Sweden
142 J5 Perstorp Sweden
126 I4 Pertek Turkey
83 K9 Perth Tas. Austr.
87 C11 Perth W.A. Austr.
224 E4 Perth Ont. Can.
146 J10 Perth Perth and Kinross, Scotland U.K.
235 G3 Perth Amboy NJ U.S.A.
146 H9 Perth and Kinross admin. div. Scotland U.K.
225 H4 Perth-Andover N.B. Can.
265 L6 Perth Basin sea feature Indian Ocean
156 H5 Perthes Champagne-Ardenne France
156 E7 Perthes Île-de-France France
156 I6 Perthois reg. France
163 J11 Perthus, Col du pass France/Spain
134 G2 Pertominsk Rus. Fed.
141 Q6 Pertteli Fin.
161 H9 Pertuis France
162 A3 Pertuis Breton sea chan. France
162 A3 Pertuis d'Antioche sea chan. France
141 S6 Pertunmaa Fin.
186 E3 Pertusa Spain
192 C5 Pertusato, Capo c. Corse France
261 E5 Perú Arg.
252 D3 Perú Bol.
Peru atoll Gilbert Is Kiribati see Beru
252 B2 Peru country S. America
226 E8 Peru IL U.S.A.
230 D5 Peru IN U.S.A.
233 L4 Peru NY U.S.A.
267 M7 Peru Basin sea feature S. Pacific Ocean
171 I10 Peruc Czech Rep.
267 N6 Peru-Chile Trench sea feature S. Pacific Ocean
188 F4 Perućko Jezero l. Croatia
193 I1 Perugia Italy
191 M9 Perugia prov. Italy
258 F3 Perugorría Arg.
256 D6 Peruíbe Brazil
114 E5 Peruru Andhra Prad. India
197 M8 Perushtitsa Bulg.
Perusia Italy see Perugia
165 E7 Péruwelz Belgium
129 C1 Pervaya Sinyukha Rus. Fed.
159 L5 Pervenchères France
165 C6 Pervijze Belgium
137 O1 Pervoavgustovskiy Rus. Fed.
136 I7 Pervomaisc Moldova
121 P6 Pervomay Kyrg.
121 N2 Pervomayka Kazakh.
135 H5 Pervomaysk Rus. Fed.
137 R5 Pervomays'k Luhans'ka Oblast' Ukr.
136 J5 Pervomays'k Mykolayivs'ka Oblast' Ukr.
138 L3 Pervomayskaya Rus. Fed.
137 L6 Pervomays'ke Mykolayivs'ka Oblast' Ukr.
137 M8 Pervomays'ke Respublika Krym Ukr.
121 T2 Pervomayskiy Kazakh.
Pervomayskiy Kyrg. see Pervomay
Pervomayskiy Arkhangel'skaya Oblast' Rus. Fed. see Novodvinsk
120 F2 Pervomayskiy Orenburgskaya Oblast' Rus. Fed.
139 P7 Pervomayskiy Smolenskaya Oblast' Rus. Fed.
139 X8 Pervomayskiy Tambovskaya Oblast' Rus. Fed.
139 U7 Pervomayskiy Tul'skaya Oblast' Rus. Fed.
Pervomayskoye Kyrg. see Pervomay
138 M1 Pervomayskoye Leningradskaya Oblast' Rus. Fed.
129 I3 Pervomayskoye Respublika Dagestan Rus. Fed.
100 M4 Pervomayskoye Sakhalinskaya Oblast' Rus. Fed.
137 P4 Pervomays'kyy Ukr.
131 R3 Pervorechenskiy Rus. Fed.
165 G7 Perwez Belgium
139 R3 Pes' Rus. Fed.
139 S2 Pes' r. Rus. Fed.
191 K8 Pesa r. Italy
183 M3 Pesadas de Burgos Spain
95 I5 Pesaguan Kalimantan Indon.
95 I6 Pesaguan r. Indon.
191 N8 Pesaro Italy
191 N8 Pesaro e Urbino prov. Italy
240 J4 Pescadero CA U.S.A.
Pescadores is Taiwan see P'enghu Ch'üntao
252 B4 Pescadores, Punta pt Peru
190 I8 Pescaglia Italy
191 J5 Pescantina Italy
193 M3 Pescara Italy
193 L3 Pescara prov. Italy
193 M3 Pescara r. Italy
197 J6 Pescari Romania
193 L4 Pescasseroli Italy
160 C5 Peschadoires France
135 H7 Peschanokopskoye Rus. Fed.
Peschanoye Rus. Fed. see Yashkul'
120 D6 Peschanyy, Mys pt Kazakh.
193 Q4 Peschici Italy
191 J8 Pescia Italy
193 L3 Pescina Italy
193 M4 Pescocostanzo Italy
193 M4 Pescolanciano Italy
193 O6 Pescopagano Italy
193 M4 Pescopennataro Italy
193 K3 Pescorocchiano Italy
193 N5 Pesco Sannita Italy
242 □S14 Pesé Panama
216 □3b Pesebre, Punta pt Fuerteventura Canary Is
94 □ Pesek, Pulau i. Sing.
94 □ Pesek Kechil, Pulau i. Sing.
190 B2 Peseux Switz.
134 I2 Pesha r. Rus. Fed.
123 I5 Peshanjan Afgh.
123 N4 Peshawar Pak.
196 I9 Peshkopi Albania
137 S7 Peshkovo Rus. Fed.
Peshnyye, Ostrova is Kazakh. see Bol'shiye Peshnyye, Ostrova
197 M8 Peshtera Bulg.
226 G4 Peshtigo WI U.S.A.
226 G5 Peshtigo r. WI U.S.A.
190 D7 Pesio r. Italy
121 L1 Peski Kazakh.
139 V6 Peski Moskovskaya Oblast' Rus. Fed.
135 H6 Peski Voronezhskaya Oblast' Rus. Fed.
123 J2 Peski Turkm.
134 K4 Peskovka Rus. Fed.
160 H2 Pesmes France
188 E2 Pesnica Slovenia
139 W3 Pesochnoye Rus. Fed.
139 Q8 Pesochnya Rus. Fed.
182 E6 Peso da Régua Port.
242 □P11 Pespire Hond.
254 F4 Pesqueira Brazil
242 D3 Pesqueira Mex.
183 L5 Pesquera de Duero Spain
163 C6 Pessac France
163 F8 Pessan France
164 J3 Pesse Neth.
170 G5 Pessin Ger.
177 I4 Pest county Hungary
139 S3 Pestovo Rus. Fed.
120 C1 Pestravka Rus. Fed.
134 H4 Pestyaki Rus. Fed.
183 L2 Pesués Spain
134 L1 Pesyakov, Ostrov i. Rus. Fed.
244 E8 Petacalco, Bahía de b. Mex.
193 N3 Petacciato Italy
128 C6 Petah Tiqwa Israel
141 R5 Petäjävesi Fin.
93 F3 Petak, Tanjung pt Halmahera Indon.
198 C6 Petalidi Greece
198 F4 Petalioi i. Greece
198 F4 Petalion, Kolpos sea chan. Greece
240 J3 Petaluma CA U.S.A.
165 I9 Pétange Lux.
95 K5 Petangis Kalimantan Indon.
250 E2 Petare Venez.
198 C3 Petas Greece
244 F8 Petatlán Mex.
211 A8 Petauke Zambia
227 S3 Petawaga, Lac l. Que. Can.
227 Q4 Petawawa Ont. Can.
243 O9 Petén Itzá, Lago l. Guat.
226 E5 Petenwell Lake WI U.S.A.
179 O7 Peteranec Croatia
224 D3 Peterbell Ont. Can.
82 G5 Peterborough S.A. Austr.
83 I8 Peterborough Vic. Austr.
224 E4 Peterborough Ont. Can.
151 L2 Peterborough Peterborough, England U.K.
151 L2 Peterborough admin. div. England U.K.
233 N6 Peterborough NH U.S.A.
146 L8 Peterculter Aberdeen, Scotland U.K.
146 M7 Peterhead Aberdeenshire, Scotland U.K.
177 I4 Péteri Hungary
262 R2 Peter I Island Antarctica
Peter I Øy i. Antarctica see Peter I Island
177 I5 Péteri-tó l. Hungary
223 M2 Peter Lake Nunavut Can.
149 O4 Peterlee Durham, England U.K.
222 H5 Peter Lougheed Provincial Park B.C. Can.
84 C8 Petermann Aboriginal Land res. N.T./W.A. Austr.
221 P2 Petermann Bjerg nunatak Greenland
84 B8 Petermann Ranges mts N.T. Austr.
260 B4 Peteroa, Volcán vol. Chile
223 I4 Peter Pond Lake Sask. Can.
225 G1 Peters, Lac l. Que. Can.
173 J3 Petersaurach Ger.
169 I9 Petersberg Ger.
215 I8 Petersburg S. Africa
220 E4 Petersburg AK U.S.A.
236 K6 Petersburg IL U.S.A.
230 D6 Petersburg IN U.S.A.
234 F6 Petersburg NJ U.S.A.
233 L6 Petersburg NY U.S.A.
232 E8 Petersburg OH U.S.A.
232 H11 Petersburg VA U.S.A.
232 F10 Petersburg WV U.S.A.
173 K4 Petersdorf Ger.
170 D2 Petersdorf auf Fehmarn Ger.
151 K5 Petersfield Hampshire, England U.K.
171 J6 Petershagen Brandenburg Ger.
169 G6 Petershagen Nordrhein-Westfalen Ger.
173 K5 Petershausen Ger.
251 G3 Peters Mine Guyana
232 E11 Peterstown WV U.S.A.
220 C3 Petersville AK U.S.A.
147 E6 Peterswell Ireland
Peter the Great Bay Rus. Fed. see Petra Velikogo, Zaliv
Pétervárad Vojvodina Serbia see Petrovaradin
177 J3 Pétervására Hungary
Peterwardein Vojvodina Serbia see Petrovaradin
114 D4 Peth Mahar. India
195 L5 Petilia Policastro Italy
186 C3 Petilla de Aragón Spain
182 F4 Petín Spain
Petit Atlas mts Morocco see Anti Atlas
247 □2 Petit-Bourg Guadeloupe
247 □2 Petit-Canal Guadeloupe
225 H4 Petitcodiac N.B. Can.
159 N3 Petit-Couronne France
247 □2 Petit Cul de Sac Marin b. Guadeloupe
161 E10 Petite Camargue reg. France
162 H3 Petite Creuse r. France
217 □1c Petite-Île Réunion
163 C7 Petite Leyre r. France
247 □3 Petite Martinique i. Grenada
157 M5 Petite-Rosselle France
159 P7 Petite Sauldre r. France
165 J9 Petite Suisse Luxembourgeoise reg. Lux.
217 □3b Petite Terre i. Mayotte
246 G4 Petit-Goâve Haiti
Petitjean Morocco see Sidi Kacem
159 I8 Petit Lay r. France
208 A5 Petit-Loango, Réserve de nature res. Gabon
158 I7 Petit Maine r. France
233 □R4 Petit Manan Point ME U.S.A.
158 I7 Petit-Mars France
225 I3 Petit Mécatina r. Nfld and Lab./Que. Can.
221 M4 Petit Mécatina r. Que. Can.
225 J3 Petit Mécatina, Île du i. Que. Can.
157 M6 Petitmont France
156 F6 Petit Morin r. France
160 G3 Petit-Noir France
222 F2 Petitot r. Alta/B.C. Can.
161 E10 Petit Rhône r. France
160 J5 Petit St-Bernard, Col du pass France
139 W7 Petkino Rus. Fed.
140 S3 Petkula Fin.
171 H7 Petkus Ger.
116 D8 Petlad Gujarat India
245 J7 Petlalcingo Mex.
116 E8 Petlawad Madh. Prad. India
177 L3 Petneháza Hungary
243 O7 Peto Mex.
177 I4 Petőfibánya Hungary
177 I5 Petőfiszállás Hungary
260 B3 Petorca Chile
226 J4 Petoskey MI U.S.A.
128 D8 Petra tourist site Jordan
187 L8 Petra Spain
195 J7 Petrace r. Italy
194 G8 Petralia-Soprana Sicilia Italy
194 G8 Petralia-Sottana Sicilia Italy
262 P1 Petras, Mount Antarctica
100 G7 Petra Velikogo, Zaliv b. Rus. Fed.
227 Q6 Petre, Point Ont. Can.
80 □ Petre Bay Chatham Is S. Pacific Ocean
Petrel Valencia Spain see Petrer
193 L5 Petrella, Monte mt. Italy
193 K3 Petrella Salto Italy
193 N4 Petrella Tifernina Italy
187 D11 Petrer Spain
177 L4 Petreşti Romania
192 B4 Petreto-Bicchisano Corse France
191 N8 Petriano Italy
197 L9 Petrich Bulg.
78 □5 Petrie, Récif rf New Caledonia
241 W6 Petrified Forest National Park AZ U.S.A.
188 G3 Petrijevci Croatia
Petrikau Pol. see Piotrków Trybunalski
Petrikov Belarus see Pyetrykaw
197 L5 Petrila Romania
188 F3 Petrinja Croatia
177 L5 Petriş Romania
193 L1 Petritoli Italy
137 N7 Petrivka Khersons'ka Oblast' Ukr.
136 J7 Petrivka Odes'ka Oblast' Ukr.
137 Q6 Petrivs'ke Ukr.
137 M4 Petrivtsi Ukr.
258 C3 Petro, Cerro de mt. Chile
Petroaleksandrovsk Uzbek. see To'rtko'l
138 M2 Petrodvorets Rus. Fed.
Petrograd Rus. Fed. see Sankt-Peterburg
Petrokov Pol. see Piotrków Trybunalski
Petrokrepost' Rus. Fed. see Shlissel'burg
139 O1 Petrokrepost', Bukhta b. Rus. Fed.
185 P3 Pétrola Spain
254 F4 Petrolândia Brazil
250 C2 Petrólea Col.
227 L7 Petrolia Ont. Can.
240 H1 Petrolia CA U.S.A.
250 E5 Petrolina Amazonas Brazil
254 E4 Petrolina Pernambuco Brazil
256 C2 Petrolina de Goiás Brazil
Petromaryevka Ukr. see Pervomays'k
198 C2 Petron, Limni l. Greece
195 L5 Petronà Italy
Petropavl Kazakh. see Petropavlovsk
137 P5 Petropavlivka Ukr.
121 S5 Petropavlovka Kazakh.
100 E2 Petropavlovka Amurskaya Oblast' Rus. Fed.
106 I1 Petropavlovka Respublika Buryatiya Rus. Fed.
135 H6 Petropavlovka Voronezhskaya Oblast' Rus. Fed.
121 M1 Petropavlovsk Kazakh.
Petropavlovsk Rus. Fed. see Petropavlovsk-Kamchatskiy
131 Q4 Petropavlovsk-Kamchatskiy Rus. Fed.
121 U1 Petropavlovskoye Rus. Fed.
257 F5 Petrópolis Brazil
197 L5 Petroşani Romania
194 D8 Petrosino Sicilia Italy
176 G3 Petrov Czech Rep.
Petrovac Bos.-Herz. see Bosanski Petrovac
196 J6 Petrovac Serbia
177 K3 Petrovany Slovakia
196 H5 Petrovaradin Vojvodina Serbia
137 M5 Petrove Ukr.
176 D2 Petrovice Czech Rep.
139 P8 Petrovichi Rus. Fed.
121 M1 Petrovka Kazakh.
120 A1 Petrovsk Rus. Fed.
135 G7 Petrovskaya Rus. Fed.
137 R5 Petrovs'ke Ukr.
139 X5 Petrovskiy Rus. Fed.
139 T5 Petrovskoye Moskovskaya Oblast' Rus. Fed.
120 G1 Petrovskoye Respublika Bashkortostan Rus. Fed.
Petrovskoye Stavropol'skiy Kray Rus. Fed. see Svetlograd
139 X9 Petrovskoye Tambovskaya Oblast' Rus. Fed.
139 W4 Petrovskoye Yaroslavskaya Oblast' Rus. Fed.
107 K1 Petrovsk-Zabaykal'skiy Rus. Fed.
135 I6 Petrov Val Rus. Fed.
134 F3 Petrozavodsk Rus. Fed.
197 M3 Petru Rareş Romania
215 J5 Petrusburg S. Africa
136 G6 Petruşeni Moldova
215 M3 Petrus Steyn S. Africa
214 I6 Petrusville S. Africa
177 H2 Petřvald Czech Rep.
137 N5 Petrykivka Ukr.
Petsamo Rus. Fed. see Pechenga
215 M3 Petsana S. Africa
Pettau Slovenia see Ptuj
164 G3 Petten Neth.
173 M3 Pettendorf Ger.
147 G3 Pettigo Northern Ireland U.K.
195 L5 Pettinascura, Monte mt. Italy
194 G8 Pettineo Sicilia Italy
173 N6 Petting Ger.
178 B5 Pettneu am Arlberg Austria
193 L4 Pettorano sul Gizio Italy
191 L3 Pettorina r. Italy
130 H4 Petukhovo Rus. Fed.
139 W6 Petushki Rus. Fed.
151 K6 Petworth West Sussex, England U.K.
178 G6 Petzeck mt. Austria
179 I3 Peuerbach Austria
94 B2 Peuetsagu, Gunung vol. Indon.
162 D5 Peujard France
260 B4 Peumo Chile
140 S3 Peurasuvanto Fin.
94 B2 Peureula Sumatera Indon.
131 S3 Pevek Rus. Fed.
151 M6 Pevensey East Sussex, England U.K.
151 M6 Pevensey Levels lowland England U.K.
190 D7 Peveragno Italy
151 I5 Pewsey Wiltshire, England U.K.
151 I5 Pewsey, Vale of val. England U.K.
168 D4 Pewsum (Krummhörn) Ger.
157 M7 Pexonne France
111 K10 Pêxung Xizang China
122 H9 Pey Beshk Iran
161 J9 Peymeinade France
161 C10 Peyne r. France
161 H10 Peynier France
122 G4 Pey Ostān Iran
161 H10 Peypin France
261 G3 Peyrano Arg.
162 H4 Peyrat-le-Château France
163 B8 Peyrehorade France
161 C8 Peyreleau France
162 I4 Peyrelevade France
163 E10 Peyresourde, Col de pass France
190 D8 Peyrevieille, Mont mt. Italy
161 B10 Peyriac-de-Mer France
163 J9 Peyriac-Minervois France
160 H5 Peyrieu France
161 G6 Peyrins France
161 H9 Peyrolles-en-Provence France
161 H8 Peyruis France
163 E8 Peyrusse-Grande France
163 I6 Peyrusse-le-Roc France
134 I2 Peza r. Rus. Fed.
161 C10 Pézenas France
174 D2 Pęzino Pol.
176 G3 Pezinok Slovakia
123 N5 Pezu Pak.
163 F6 Pezuls France
173 M4 Pfaffenberg Ger.
171 J6 Pfaffendorf Ger.
173 I5 Pfaffenhausen Ger.
173 L4 Pfaffenhofen an der Ilm Ger.
173 I5 Pfaffenhofen an der Roth Ger.
157 O6 Pfaffenhoffen France
179 M4 Pfaffensattel pass Austria
172 D6 Pfaffenweiler Ger.
190 F1 Pfäffikon Schwyz Switz.
190 F1 Pfäffikon Zürich Switz.
173 M5 Pfaffing Ger.
172 D3 Pfälzer Wald hills Ger.
172 D3 Pfälzer Wald park Ger.
169 E10 Pfalzfeld Ger.
172 F4 Pfalzgrafenweiler Ger.
173 N5 Pfarrkirchen Ger.
169 K10 Pfarrweisach Ger.
178 H5 Pfarrwerfen Austria
173 M4 Pfatter Ger.
172 G3 Pfedelbach Ger.
173 L4 Pfeffenhausen Ger.
178 C4 Pflach Austria
178 D5 Pfons Austria
173 L4 Pförring Ger.
173 J6 Pforzen Ger.
172 F4 Pforzheim Ger.
173 M3 Pfreimd Ger.
173 M2 Pfreimd r. Ger.
172 G5 Pfronstetten Ger.
173 J6 Pfronten Ger.
172 G6 Pfullendorf Ger.
172 G5 Pfullingen Ger.
178 C6 Pfunds Austria
172 F2 Pfungstadt Ger.
190 F1 Pfyn Switz.
96 F4 Phac Mo, Phu mt. Vietnam
213 F5 Phagameng Limpopo S. Africa
116 E4 Phagwara Punjab India
215 K4 Phahameng Free State S. Africa
213 F4 Phalaborwa S. Africa
123 O5 Phalia Pak.
116 D6 Phalodi Rajasthan India
157 N6 Phalsbourg France
116 C6 Phalsund Rajasthan India
114 D4 Phaltan Mahar. India
117 L6 Phalut Peak India/Nepal
97 E10 Phangan, Ko i. Thai.
96 E6 Phang Hoei, San Khao mts Thai.
97 D10 Phangnga Thai.
96 F3 Phăng Xi Păng mt. Vietnam
97 G7 Phanom Dong Rak, Thiu Khao mts Cambodia/Thai.
97 I9 Phan Rang-Thap Cham Vietnam
97 I9 Phan Ri Cửa Vietnam
97 I9 Phan Thiêt Vietnam
97 I9 Phan Thiêt, Vinh b. Vietnam
116 G6 Phaphund Uttar Prad. India
117 K6 Phaplu Nepal
148 E3 Pharis Northern Ireland U.K.
96 H4 Phat Diêm Vietnam
97 E11 Phatthalung Thai.
96 D5 Phayao Thai.
96 E7 Phayuhakhiri Thai.
117 O7 Phek Nagaland India
84 E3 Phelp r. N.T. Austr.
232 H6 Phelps NY U.S.A.
226 E3 Phelps WI U.S.A.
223 K3 Phelps Lake Sask. Can.
96 F6 Phen Thai.
232 G11 Phenix VA U.S.A.
231 E9 Phenix City AL U.S.A.
214 G1 Phephane watercourse S. Africa
97 D8 Phet Buri Thai.
96 E6 Phetchabun Thai.
97 G7 Phiafai Laos
96 E6 Phichai Thai.
96 E6 Phichit Thai.
Philadelphia Jordan see 'Ammān
214 C9 Philadelphia S. Africa
Philadelphia Turkey see Alaşehir
237 K9 Philadelphia MS U.S.A.
233 J4 Philadelphia NY U.S.A.
234 E5 Philadelphia PA U.S.A.
234 E5 Philadelphia County county PA U.S.A.
203 G4 Philae tourist site Egypt
Philip atoll Arch. des Tuamotu Fr. Polynesia see Makemo
236 E3 Philip SD U.S.A.
Philip Atoll Micronesia see Sorol
82 □1 Philip Island Norfolk I.
Philippeville Alg. see Skikda
165 G8 Philippeville Belgium
232 E9 Philippi WV U.S.A.
84 G8 Philippi, Lake salt flat Qld Austr.
165 E6 Philippine Neth.
266 D4 Philippine Basin sea feature N. Pacific Ocean
92 D4 Philippines country Asia
90 F3 Philippine Sea N. Pacific Ocean
266 D4 Philippine Trench sea feature N. Pacific Ocean
215 J6 Philippolis S. Africa
215 J6 Philippolis Road S. Africa
Philippopolis Bulg. see Plovdiv
172 E3 Philippsburg Ger.
173 P4 Philippsreut Ger.
169 J9 Philippsthal (Werra) Ger.
247 L4 Philipsburg St Maarten Neth. Antilles
238 H3 Philipsburg MT U.S.A.
232 G8 Philipsburg PA U.S.A.
164 F5 Philipsdam barrage Neth.
220 D3 Philip Smith Mountains AK U.S.A.
214 I6 Philipstown S. Africa
83 J8 Phillip Island Vic. Austr.
82 □2 Phillip Point Lord Howe I. Austr.
87 F12 Phillips r. W.A. Austr.
233 □O4 Phillips ME U.S.A.
226 D4 Phillips WI U.S.A.
222 E5 Phillips Arm B.C. Can.
236 F6 Phillipsburg KS U.S.A.
234 E3 Phillipsburg NJ U.S.A.
221 J1 Phillips Inlet Nunavut Can.
82 E3 Phillipson, Lake salt flat S.A. Austr.
86 H4 Phillips Range hills W.A. Austr.
232 F8 Phillipston PA U.S.A.
233 L6 Philmont NY U.S.A.
Philomelium Turkey see Akşehir
232 E12 Philpott Reservoir VA U.S.A.
96 G7 Phimun Mangsahan Thai.
215 L3 Phiritona S. Africa
96 E6 Phitsanulok Thai.
226 E4 Phlox WI U.S.A.
Phnom Penh Cambodia see Phnum Pénh
97 G9 Phnum Pénh Cambodia
97 E11 Pho, Laem pt Thai.
96 G5 Phô Châu Vietnam
233 K6 Phoenicia NY U.S.A.
217 □1b Phoenix Mauritius
241 T8 Phoenix AZ U.S.A.
233 I5 Phoenix NY U.S.A.
Phoenix Island Phoenix Is Kiribati see Rawaki
77 I2 Phoenix Islands Kiribati
234 D4 Phoenixville PA U.S.A.
215 N2 Phola S. Africa
96 G3 Phô Lu Vietnam
215 L3 Phomolong S. Africa
96 F7 Phon Thai.
96 H6 Phong Nha Vietnam
96 F4 Phôngsali Laos
Phong Saly Laos see Phôngsali
96 F3 Phong Thô Vietnam
96 F5 Phon Phisai Thai.
96 F6 Phon Thong Thai.
83 I8 Phoques Bay Tas. Austr.
84 H6 Phosphate Hill Qld Austr.
116 F2 Photaksur Jammu and Kashmir
96 E5 Phrae Thai.
Phra Nakhon Si Ayutthaya Thai. see Ayutthaya
96 D5 Phrao Thai.
97 D10 Phra Saeng Thai.
97 D10 Phra Thong, Ko i. Thai.
96 E6 Phrom Phiram Thai.
97 F9 Phsar Ream Cambodia
96 H6 Phu Bai Vietnam
97 G7 Phuchong-Nayoi National Park Thai.
Phu Cuong Vietnam see Thu Dâu Môt
96 G4 Phuc Yên Vietnam
212 E4 Phuduhudu Botswana
117 L6 Phuentsholing Bhutan
97 D11 Phuket Thai.
97 D11 Phuket, Ko i. Thai.
96 E6 Phu-khieo Wildlife Reserve nature res. Thai.
117 J9 Phulbani Orissa India
123 L8 Phulji Pak.
96 H6 Phu Lôc Vietnam
97 G10 Phu Lôc Vietnam
116 I7 Phulpur Uttar Prad. India
96 E6 Phu Luang National Park Thai.
96 G4 Phu Ly Vietnam
97 F8 Phumĭ Bânhchok Kon Cambodia
97 G8 Phumĭ Chhlong Cambodia
97 G9 Phumĭ Chhuk Cambodia
97 G7 Phumĭ Kâmpóng Srâlau Cambodia
97 G8 Phumĭ Kâmpóng Trâlach Cambodia
97 F9 Phumĭ Kaôh Kŏng Cambodia
97 F8 Phumĭ Kiliěk Cambodia
97 F7 Phumĭ Kon Kriel Cambodia
97 F8 Phumĭ Koŭk Kduŏch Cambodia
97 G8 Phumĭ Mlu Prey Cambodia
97 F8 Phumĭ Prâmaôy Cambodia
97 G8 Phumĭ Prêk Kak Cambodia
97 F7 Phumĭ Sâmraông Cambodia
97 G8 Phumĭ Thalabârĭvăt Cambodia
97 G8 Phumĭ Toêng Cambodia
97 G9 Phumĭ Trâm Kak Cambodia
97 F7 Phumĭ Trom Cambodia
97 F9 Phumĭ Veal Renh Cambodia
97 I7 Phu My Vietnam
97 G10 Phung Hiêp Vietnam
Phuntsholing Bhutan see Phuentsholing
97 H9 Phươc Bưu Vietnam
97 H9 Phươc Hai Vietnam
97 G10 Phươc Long Vietnam
96 F6 Phu Phan National Park Thai.
97 F9 Phu Quôc, Đao i. Vietnam
97 I9 Phu Quy, Đao i. Vietnam
215 M4 Phuthaditjhaba S. Africa
96 G4 Phu Tho Vietnam
Phu Vinh Vietnam see Tra Vinh
96 F6 Phu Wiang Thai.
96 G4 Phu Yên Vietnam
96 C5 Phyu Myanmar
163 J10 Pia France
87 D9 Pia Aboriginal Reserve W.A. Austr.
95 J4 Piabung, Gunung mt. Indon.
254 D3 Piaca Brazil
256 B4 Piacatu Brazil
190 H5 Piacenza Italy
190 H6 Piacenza prov. Italy
225 G3 Piacouadie, Lac l. Que. Can.
190 I5 Piadena Italy
224 E2 Piagochioui r. Que. Can.
94 E4 Piai, Tanjung pt Malaysia
261 G3 Piamonte Arg.
83 L4 Pian r. N.S.W. Austr.
192 B3 Piana Corse France
192 A6 Piana, Isola i. Sardegna Italy
192 A9 Piana, Isola i. Sardegna Italy
190 E7 Piana Crixia Italy
194 E8 Piana degli Albanesi Sicilia Italy
193 K3 Piana del Fucino plain Italy
194 H9 Piana di Catania plain Sicilia Italy
192 H2 Piancastagnaio Italy
191 M8 Piandimeleto Italy
193 M3 Pianella Italy
190 G6 Pianello Val Tidone Italy
83 I6 Piangil Vic. Austr.
107 L7 Pianguan Shanxi China
96 D1 Pianma Yunnan China
191 K7 Piano del Voglio Italy
191 K7 Pianoro Italy
192 E2 Pianosa Italy
192 E2 Pianosa, Isola i. Italy
193 P3 Pianosa, Isole is Italy
192 C5 Pianotolli-Caldarello Corse France
192 H2 Piansano Italy
247 □7 Piarco airport Trin. and Tob.
184 E4 Pias Port.
182 G4 Pias, Embalse de resr Spain
175 J3 Piaseczno Mazowieckie Pol.
174 C2 Piaseczno Zachodniopomorskie Pol.
174 C3 Piasek Pol.
175 K4 Piaski Lubelskie Pol.
174 F4 Piaski Wielkopolskie Pol.
254 F4 Piassabussu Brazil
175 I3 Piastów Pol.
254 E5 Piatã Brazil
175 H3 Piątek Pol.
175 K2 Piątnica Poduchowna Pol.
197 N7 Piatra Romania
197 O4 Piatra Neamţ Romania
197 M6 Piatra Olt Romania
197 O4 Piatra Şoimului Romania
163 E10 Piau-Engaly France
254 E3 Piauí r. Brazil
254 E3 Piauí state Brazil
254 E4 Piauí, Serra de hills Brazil
191 N4 Piave r. Italy
244 A2 Piaxtla r. Mex.
190 I7 Piazza al Serchio Italy
194 G9 Piazza Armerina Sicilia Italy
190 H4 Piazza Brembana Italy
190 H4 Piazzatorre Italy
190 I3 Piazzi, Cima de' mt. Italy
259 B8 Piazzi, Isla i. Chile
191 L4 Piazzola sul Brenta Italy
210 B2 Pibor r. Sudan
210 B3 Pibor Post Sudan
163 G8 Pibrac France
224 C3 Pic r. Ont. Can.
252 C5 Pica Chile
241 U9 Picacho AZ U.S.A.
244 B3 Picachos Mex.
242 B3 Picachos, Cerro dos mt. Mex.
191 Q5 Pićan Croatia
187 C8 Picaracho mt. Spain
156 E4 Picardie admin. reg. France
156 C4 Picardie reg. France
Picardy reg. France see Picardie
187 E9 Picassent Spain
158 I3 Picauville France
237 K10 Picayune MS U.S.A.
191 L2 Picco della Croce mt. Italy
161 K6 Piccolo, Lago l. Italy
243 N8 Pich Mex.
260 B5 Pichachén, Paso pass Arg./Chile
242 F3 Picháchic Mex.
258 D1 Pichanal Arg.
260 B2 Pichasca Chile
170 D4 Picher Ger.
260 C3 Pichi Ciego Arg.
260 B3 Pichidanguí Chile
260 A4 Pichilemu Chile
242 D5 Pichilingue Mex.
260 E6 Pichi Mahuida Arg.
250 B5 Pichincha prov. Ecuador
179 I3 Pichl bei Wels Austria
116 G7 Pichor Madh. Prad. India
243 M9 Pichucalco Mex.
226 H1 Pic Island Ont. Can.
232 E10 Pickens WV U.S.A.
226 C1 Pickerel Lake Ont. Can.
227 O6 Pickering Ont. Can.
149 P5 Pickering North Yorkshire, England U.K.
149 P5 Pickering, Vale of val. England U.K.
251 G3 Pickersgill Guyana
227 J3 Pickford MI U.S.A.
246 C3 Pickle Bank sea feature Caribbean Sea
224 B3 Pickle Lake Ont. Can.
216 □1c Pico i. Azores
216 □1c Pico mt. Pico Azores
193 L5 Pico Italy
183 J8 Pico, Puerto del pass Spain
242 □P10 Pico Bonito, Parque Nacional nat. park Hond.
192 D9 Picocca r. Italy
251 E4 Pico da Neblina, Parque Nacional do nat. park Brazil
245 J6 Pico de Orizaba, Parque Nacional nat. park Mex.
244 E6 Pico de Tancítaro, Parque Nacional nat. park Mex.
216 □1c Pico Gorda vol. Faial Azores
185 K2 Picón Spain
254 E3 Picos Brazil
182 C5 Picos, Punta dos pt Spain
183 K2 Picos de Europa, Parque Nacional de los nat. park Spain
250 B6 Picota Peru
182 C6 Picoto Port.
259 D7 Pico Truncado Arg.
156 D4 Picquigny France
226 H1 Pic River Ont. Can.
83 M6 Picton N.S.W. Austr.
224 E5 Picton Ont. Can.
81 I8 Picton South I. N.Z.
83 K10 Picton, Mount Tas. Austr.
225 I4 Pictou N.S. Can.
222 H5 Picture Butte Alta Can.
226 H3 Pictured Rocks National Lakeshore nature res. MI U.S.A.
234 B2 Picture Rocks PA U.S.A.
247 □1 Picua, Punta pt Puerto Rico
254 F3 Picuí Brazil
260 C6 Picún Leufú Arg.
260 C6 Picún Leufú r. Arg.
123 J9 Pidarak Pak.
175 M5 Pidberezzya Ukr.
175 L6 Pidbuzh Ukr.
150 H6 Piddle r. England U.K.
150 H6 Piddletrenthide Dorset, England U.K.
136 E4 Pidhaytsi Ukr.
136 J5 Pidhorodna Ukr.
137 O5 Pidhorodne Ukr.
175 L6 Pidhorodtsi Ukr.
173 N6 Piding Ger.
217 □3a Pidjani Njazidja Comoros
136 E4 Pidkamin' Ukr.
137 L5 Pidlisne Ukr.
139 R1 Pid'ma Rus. Fed.
114 G9 Pidurutalagala mt. Sri Lanka
136 F4 Pidvolochys'k Ukr.
136 J5 Pidvysoke Ukr.
174 G3 Piechcin Pol.
174 D5 Piechowice Pol.
175 J2 Piecki Pol.
174 E2 Piecnik Pol.
216 □1c Piedade Pico Azores
256 D5 Piedade Brazil
184 B6 Piedade, Ponta da pt Port.
260 C2 Pie de Palo, Sierra mts Arg.
192 C3 Piedicorte-di-Gaggio Corse France
192 C3 Piedicroce Corse France
193 J2 Piediluco, Lago di l. Italy
195 I8 Piedimonte Etneo Sicilia Italy
193 M5 Piedimonte Matese Italy
190 E3 Piedimulera Italy
Piedmont admin. reg. Italy see Piemonte
231 E9 Piedmont AL U.S.A.
237 J7 Piedmont MO U.S.A.
232 D8 Piedmont OH U.S.A.
232 D8 Piedmont Lake OH U.S.A.
183 Q6 Piedra r. Spain
184 F3 Piedra Aguda, Embalse de resr Spain
185 K2 Piedrabuena Spain
259 C6 Piedra de Águila Arg.
245 J8 Piedra de Olla, Cerro mt. Mex.
Piedrafita Spain see Pedrafita do Cebreiro
182 F3 Piedrafita, Porto de pass Spain
182 H3 Piedrafita de Babia Spain
183 J8 Piedrahita Spain
183 K8 Piedralaves Spain
184 E6 Piedras, Embalse de resr Spain
261 I4 Piedras, Punta pt Arg.
252 C3 Piedras, Río de las r. Peru
182 G9 Piedras Albas Spain
182 I1 Piedras Blancas Spain
240 K6 Piedras Blancas Point CA U.S.A.
183 L2 Piedrasluengas, Puerto de pass Spain
243 N9 Piedras Negras Guat.
243 I3 Piedras Negras Coahuila Mex.
245 K7 Piedras Negras Veracruz Mex.
261 I3 Piedra Sola Uru.
261 F4 Piedritas Arg.
192 I2 Piegaro Italy
162 F4 Piégut-Pluviers France
226 E1 Pie Island Ont. Can.
174 G5 Piekary Śląskie Pol.
170 I1 Piekberg hill Ger.
175 I5 Piekoszów Pol.
140 S5 Pieksämäki Fin.
207 E3 Piéla Burkina
179 L3 Pielach r. Austria
140 S5 Pielavesi Fin.
140 S5 Pielavesi l. Fin.
174 D4 Pielgrzymka Pol.
140 T5 Pielinen l. Fin.
140 N3 Pieljekaise nationalpark nat. park Sweden
161 F10 Piémanson, Plage de coastal area France
190 D6 Piemonte admin. reg. Italy
215 M1 Pienaarsrivier S. Africa
174 E2 Pieniężnica Pol.
143 Q7 Pieniężno Pol.
175 I6 Pieniński Park Narodowy nat. park Pol.
177 J2 Pieninský nat. park Slovakia
174 E1 Pieńkowo Pol.
157 K5 Piennes France
174 D4 Pieńsk Pol.
192 H1 Pienza Italy
186 I4 Piera Spain
236 G4 Pierce NE U.S.A.
223 M4 Pierce Lake Man./Ont. Can.
223 I4 Pierceland Sask. Can.
226 I8 Pierceton IN U.S.A.
261 H6 Pieres Arg.
198 D2 Pieria mts Greece
146 K4 Pierowall Orkney, Scotland U.K.
236 E3 Pierre SD U.S.A.
237 J10 Pierre, Bayou r. MS U.S.A.
237 I10 Pierre Bayou r. LA U.S.A.
162 G4 Pierre-Buffière France
161 H7 Pierre-Châtel France
160 G3 Pierre-de-Bresse France
161 I10 Pierrefeu-du-Var France
163 D10 Pierrefitte-Nestalas France
157 J6 Pierrefitte-sur-Aire France
160 D4 Pierrefitte-sur-Loire France
156 E5 Pierrefonds France
160 J2 Pierrefontaine-les-Varans France
161 B7 Pierrefort France
161 F8 Pierrelatte France
157 K5 Pierrepont France
156 C6 Pierres France
160 D5 Pierre-sur-Haute mt. France
161 H9 Pierrevert France
247 □7 Pierreville Trin. and Tob.
217 □1a Pierrot Island Rodrigues I. Mauritius
156 G5 Pierry France
164 F5 Piershil Neth.
175 I5 Pierzchnica Pol.
171 D9 Piesau Ger.
178 G5 Piesendorf Austria
140 N3 Pieskehaure l. Sweden
174 D3 Pieski Pol.
172 B2 Piesport Ger.

177 G3 Piešťany Slovakia
175 I1 Pieszkowo Pol.
174 E5 Pieszyce Pol.
217 □1b Pieter Both hill Mauritius
215 O5 Pietermaritzburg S. Africa
Pietersaari Fin. see Jakobstad
Pietersburg Limpopo S. Africa see Polokwane
214 I2 Piet Plessis S. Africa
193 M4 Pietrabbondante Italy
193 N4 Pietracatella Italy
192 C2 Pietracorbara Corse France
192 C3 Pietra-di-Verde Corse France
193 P6 Pietragalla Italy
192 C2 Pietralba Corse France
190 E7 Pietra Ligure Italy
191 M9 Pietralunga Italy
193 M5 Pietramelara Italy
193 O4 Pietramontecorvino Italy
194 G9 Pietraperzia Sicilia Italy
190 C7 Pietraporzio Italy
190 I8 Pietrasanta Italy
195 K6 Pietra Spada, Passo di pass Italy
193 N6 Pietrastornina Italy
193 M5 Pietravairano Italy
193 N5 Pietrelcina Italy
215 O3 Piet Retief S. Africa
177 L5 Pietroasa Bihor Romania
177 L6 Pietroasa Timiș Romania
192 B4 Pietrosella Corse France
197 M3 Pietrosu, Vârful mt. Romania
197 N3 Pietrosu, Vârful mt. Romania
197 M3 Pietrosul Mare nature res. Romania
174 G5 Pietrowice Wielkie Pol.
191 M3 Pieve d'Alpago Italy
190 F5 Pieve del Cairo Italy
178 C8 Pieve di Bono Italy
191 M3 Pieve di Cadore Italy
191 M3 Pieve di Cadore, Lago di l. Italy
191 K6 Pieve di Cento Italy
191 M4 Pieve di Soligo Italy
190 D7 Pieve di Teco Italy
193 K1 Pievefavera, Lago di l. Italy
191 J7 Pievepelago Italy
191 M8 Pieve Santo Stefano Italy
193 K1 Pieve Torina Italy
190 E3 Pieve Vergonte Italy
156 F7 Piffonds France
224 B3 Pigeon r. Can./U.S.A.
227 K6 Pigeon MI U.S.A.
227 L8 Pigeon Bay Ont. Can.
81 G10 Pigeon Bay South I. N.Z.
246 □ Pigeon Island Jamaica
222 H4 Pigeon Lake Alta Can.
247 □3 Pigeon Point St Lucia
247 □5 Pigeon Point Trin. and Tob.
226 E1 Pigeon River MN U.S.A.
232 F11 Pigg r. VA U.S.A.
237 J7 Piggott AR U.S.A.
215 P1 Pigg's Peak Swaziland
193 K4 Piglio Italy
190 D8 Pigna Italy
161 D9 Pignan France
161 I10 Pignans France
193 L5 Pignataro Interamna Italy
194 G1 Pignataro Maggiore Italy
193 P6 Pignola Italy
198 C3 Pigon Aoou, Limni l. Greece
Pigs, Bay of Cuba see Cochinos, Bahía de
261 F5 Pigüé Arg.
245 H4 Piguicas mt. Mex.
80 I3 Piha North I. N.Z.
80 H6 Pihama North I. N.Z.
116 H6 Pihani Uttar Prad. India
79 □8a Piha Passage Tonga
109 K2 Pi He r. China
Pihkva järv l. Estonia/Rus. Fed. see Pskov, Lake
141 T6 Pihlajavesi l. Fin.
141 P6 Pihlava Fin.
140 R5 Pihtipudas Fin.
244 D6 Pihuamo Mex.
138 F1 Piikkiö Fin.
140 R4 Piippola Fin.
138 K3 Piirissaar i. Estonia
138 H2 Piirsalu Estonia
140 T4 Piispajärvi Fin.
78 □4a Piis-Panewu i. Chuuk Micronesia
Piji Sichuan China see Puge
243 M10 Pijijiapan Mex.
164 F4 Pijnacker Neth.
139 R2 Pikalevo Rus. Fed.
138 J3 Pikasilla Estonia
232 G6 Pike NY U.S.A.
232 D9 Pike WV U.S.A.
227 M5 Pike Bay Ont. Can.
234 E2 Pike County county PA U.S.A.
91 K5 Pikelot i. Micronesia
234 C2 Pikes Creek Reservoir PA U.S.A.
239 L7 Pikes Peak CO U.S.A.
234 B6 Pikesville MD U.S.A.
214 C8 Piketberg S. Africa
232 B9 Piketon OH U.S.A.
232 C11 Pikeville KY U.S.A.
231 E8 Pikeville TN U.S.A.
Pikihatiti b. Stewart I. N.Z. see Port Pegasus
Pikirakatahi mt. South I. N.Z. see Earnslaw, Mount
164 I2 Pikmeer l. Neth.
107 R7 Pikou Liaoning China
208 C4 Pikounda Congo
261 H5 Pila Arg.
191 M6 Pila Italy
174 E2 Piła Pol.
187 C11 Pila mt. Spain
97 C9 Pila, Kyun i. Myanmar
261 I5 Pila, Laguna de l. Arg.
187 C11 Pila, Sierra de la mts Spain
258 F2 Pilagá r. Arg.
215 L1 Pilanesberg National Park S. Africa
116 E5 Pilani Rajasthan India
261 H4 Pilar Buenos Aires Arg.
261 F2 Pilar Córdoba Arg.
261 G2 Pilar Santa Fé Arg.
253 F6 Pilar Para.
92 F7 Pilar Phil.
259 B9 Pilar, Cabo c. Chile
254 C5 Pilar de Goiás Brazil
187 D12 Pilar de la Horadada Spain
187 I10 Pilar de la Mola Spain
256 D5 Pilar do Sul Brazil
92 C8 Pilas i. Phil.
184 G6 Pilas Spain
92 C8 Pilas Channel Phil.
161 F6 Pilat, Mont mt. France
161 F6 Pilat, Parc Naturel Régional du nature res. France
190 E2 Pilatus mt. Switz.
175 J4 Pilawa Pol.
174 E2 Piława r. Pol.
174 E5 Piława Górna Pol.
252 D5 Pilaya r. Bol.
259 C6 Pilcaniyeu Arg.
174 D5 Pilchowice, Jezioro l. Pol.
170 J3 Pilchowo Pol.
253 F6 Pilcomayo r. Bol./Para.
174 E2 Pile, Jezioro l. Pol.
Pilenkovo Georgia see Gant'iadi
114 F6 Piler Andhra Prad. India
187 E10 Piles Spain
Pili Kos Greece see Pyli
92 D5 Pili Luzon Phil.
252 D5 Pili, Cerro mt. Chile
138 I6 Piliakalnis hill Lith.
116 E5 Pilibangan Rajasthan India
116 G5 Pilibhit Uttar Prad. India
175 H5 Pilica Pol.
175 J4 Pilica r. Pol.
Pilipinas country Asia see Philippines
177 I4 Pilis Hungary
177 H4 Pilis hill Hungary
177 H4 Piliscsév Hungary
177 H4 Pilisi park Hungary
177 H4 Pilisszentiván Hungary
177 H4 Pilisszentkereszt Hungary
177 H4 Pilisvörösvár Hungary
178 E5 Pill Austria
149 K5 Pillar hill England U.K.
216 □2a Pillar Bay Ascension S. Atlantic Ocean
Pillau Rus. Fed. see Baltiysk
252 C3 Pillcopata Peru
178 G4 Pillersee l. Austria
83 L4 Pilliga N.S.W. Austr.
149 L6 Pilling Lancashire, England U.K.
261 G3 Pillo, Isla del i. Arg.
234 B3 Pillow PA U.S.A.
240 J2 Pillsbury, Lake CA U.S.A.
134 I5 Pil'na Rus. Fed.
137 P3 Pil'na Ukr.
137 P3 Pil'na r. Ukr.
150 G4 Pilning South Gloucestershire, England U.K.
134 L1 Pil'nya, Ozero l. Rus. Fed.
256 D2 Pilões, Serra dos mts Brazil
246 E4 Pilón Cuba
183 J2 Piloña r. Spain
Pílos Greece see Pylos
223 I2 Pilot Lake N.W.T. Can.
244 B5 Piloto Mex.
261 H2 Piloto Ávila Arg.
Piloto Juan Fernández i. S. Pacific Ocean see Alejandro Selkirk, Isla
240 O3 Pilot Peak NV U.S.A.
220 C4 Pilot Point AK U.S.A.
238 E4 Pilot Rock OR U.S.A.
220 B3 Pilot Station AK U.S.A.
237 K11 Pilottown LA U.S.A.
173 L3 Pilsach Ger.
Pilsen Czech Rep. see Plzeň
226 G5 Pilsen WI U.S.A.
175 H6 Pilsko mt. Pol.
173 N4 Pilsting Ger.
138 E4 Piltene Latvia
123 N9 Pilu Pak.
177 K5 Pilu Romania
96 C5 Pilu, Nam r. Myanmar
138 G7 Pilvė r. Lith.
138 G7 Pilviškiai Lith.
100 M3 Pil'vo Rus. Fed.
175 J6 Pilzno Pol.
241 W9 Pima AZ U.S.A.
253 E2 Pimenta Bueno Brazil
192 C9 Pimentel Sardegna Italy
116 E9 Pimpalner Mahar. India
150 H6 Pimperne Dorset, England U.K.
116 D9 Pimpri Gujarat India
208 D4 Pimu Dem. Rep. Congo
116 G3 Pin r. India
96 B4 Pin r. Myanmar
136 F1 Pina r. Belarus
186 D5 Pina Spain
187 D7 Pina mt. Spain
186 D4 Pina, Embalse de resr Spain
241 S10 Pinacate, Cerro del mt. Mex.
183 L5 Piña de Esgueva Spain
116 G6 Pinahat Uttar Prad. India
241 V9 Pinaleno Mountains AZ U.S.A.
92 C5 Pinamalayan Mindoro Phil.
261 I5 Pinamar Arg.
Pinang Malaysia see George Town
94 D2 Pinang i. Malaysia
94 D2 Pinang state Malaysia
95 L2 Pinangah Sabah Malaysia
185 I7 Pinar mt. Spain
187 L8 Pinar, Cap des c. Spain
185 O4 Pinar, Puerto del pass Spain
126 H4 Pınarbaşı Turkey
246 B2 Pinar del Río Cuba
126 C3 Pinarhisar Turkey
199 I5 Pınarköy Turkey
129 A7 Pınarlar Turkey
129 E6 Pınarlı Turkey
250 B5 Piñas Ecuador
190 C6 Pinasca Italy
90 F3 Pinatubo, Mount vol. Phil.
177 H5 Pincehely Hungary
151 L2 Pinchbeck Lincolnshire, England U.K.
222 H5 Pincher Creek Alta Can.
236 K6 Pinckneyville IL U.S.A.
159 J4 Pinçon, Mont hill France
227 K6 Pinconning MI U.S.A.
Pîncota Romania see Pâncota
175 I5 Pińczów Pol.
254 B5 Pindaíba Brazil
257 E5 Pindamonhangaba Brazil
87 C10 Pindar W.A. Austr.
116 G4 Pindar r. India
254 D2 Pindaré r. Brazil
254 D2 Pindaré Mirim Brazil
123 O5 Pind Dadan Khay Pak.
Píndhos Óros mts Greece see Pindos
123 O6 Pindi Bhattian Pak.
123 O5 Pindi Gheb Pak.
254 C2 Pindobal Brazil
198 B3 Pindos mts Greece
198 C3 Pindou, Ethnikos Drymos nat. park Greece
116 H8 Pindrei Madh. Prad. India
Pindus Mountains Greece see Pindos
116 D7 Pindwara Rajasthan India
82 H5 Pine watercourse N.S.W. Austr.
226 I5 Pine r. MI U.S.A.
226 J6 Pine r. MI U.S.A.
226 D6 Pine r. WI U.S.A.
226 F4 Pine r. WI U.S.A.
225 K4 Pine, Cape Nfld and Lab. Can.
237 I8 Pine Bluff AR U.S.A.
238 L6 Pine Bluffs WY U.S.A.
235 G1 Pine Bush NY U.S.A.
226 B4 Pine City MN U.S.A.
84 C2 Pine Creek N.T. Austr.
232 H7 Pine Creek r. PA U.S.A.
241 P1 Pine Creek watercourse NV U.S.A.
240 L3 Pinecrest CA U.S.A.
183 O8 Pineda de Cigüela Spain
183 N4 Pineda de la Sierra Spain
186 K4 Pineda de Mar Spain
238 J5 Pinedale WY U.S.A.
223 L5 Pine Dock Man. Can.
223 L5 Pine Falls Man. Can.
239 E8 Pine Flat Lake CA U.S.A.
134 H2 Pinega Rus. Fed.
134 H2 Pinega r. Rus. Fed.
87 C9 Pinegrove W.A. Austr.
232 A10 Pine Grove KY U.S.A.
227 R9 Pine Grove PA U.S.A.
232 E9 Pine Grove WV U.S.A.
84 D7 Pine Hill N.T. Austr.
234 F5 Pine Hill NJ U.S.A.
231 G11 Pine Hills FL U.S.A.
223 J4 Pinehouse Lake Sask. Can.
223 J4 Pinehouse Lake l. Sask. Can.
234 C6 Pinehurst MD U.S.A.
224 B2 Pineimuta r. Ont. Can.
198 D3 Pineios r. Greece
198 C5 Pineiou, Techniti Limni resr Greece
226 B5 Pine Island MN U.S.A.
235 G2 Pine Island NY U.S.A.
262 R2 Pine Island Bay Antarctica
262 R1 Pine Island Glacier Antarctica
231 F12 Pine Islands FL U.S.A.
231 G13 Pine Islands FL U.S.A.
182 G5 Pinela Port.
237 I10 Pineland TX U.S.A.
183 L5 Piñel de Abajo Spain
222 F4 Pine Le Moray Provincial Park B.C. Can.
81 D12 Pinelheugh mt. South I. N.Z.
231 F12 Pinellas Park FL U.S.A.
240 K6 Pine Mountain CA U.S.A.
241 S7 Pine Peak AZ U.S.A.
222 H2 Pine Point N.W.T. Can.
222 H2 Pine Point pt N.W.T. Can.
261 I3 Piñera Uru.
240 M4 Pineridge CA U.S.A.
236 D4 Pine Ridge SD U.S.A.
236 D4 Pine Ridge Indian Reservation res. SD U.S.A.
190 C6 Pinerolo Italy
198 F2 Pines, Akrotirio pt Greece
Pines, Isle of i. Cuba see Juventud, Isla de la
Pines, Isle of i. New Caledonia see Pins, Île des
237 H9 Pines, Lake o' the TX U.S.A.
190 F4 Pinet di Appiano Tradate, Parco del park Italy
193 M2 Pineto Italy
241 W7 Pinetop AZ U.S.A.
215 O5 Pinetown S. Africa
163 E6 Pineuilh France
227 R7 Pine Valley NY U.S.A.
232 B12 Pineville KY U.S.A.
237 I10 Pineville LA U.S.A.
234 E4 Pineville PA U.S.A.
232 D11 Pineville WV U.S.A.
156 H7 Piney France
96 E7 Ping, Mae Nam r. Thai.
116 D1 Pingal Jammu and Kashmir
106 H8 Ping'an Qinghai China
Ping'anyi Qinghai China see Ping'an
87 E12 Pingaring W.A. Austr.
108 F5 Pingba Guizhou China
108 D7 Pingbian Yunnan China
108 F3 Pingchang Sichuan China
108 C5 Pingchuan Sichuan China
107 P9 Ping Dao i. China
107 M8 Pingding Shanxi China
Pingdingbu Hebei China see Guyuan
109 I2 Pingdingshan Henan China
Pingdong Taiwan see P'ingtung
Pingdu Jiangxi China see Anfu
107 P8 Pingdu Shandong China
87 D12 Pingelly W.A. Austr.
100 D7 Pinggang Liaoning China
179 N5 Pinggau Austria
107 O6 Pinggu Beijing China
108 F7 Pingguo Guangxi China
109 J7 Pinghai Guangdong China
109 K6 Pinghe Fujian China
Pinghu Guizhou China see Pingtang
109 M3 Pinghu Zhejiang China
109 I4 Pingjiang Hunan China
108 H6 Pingle Guangxi China
108 G2 Pingli Shaanxi China
106 J9 Pingliang Gansu China
107 L9 Pinglu Shanxi China
106 J7 Pingluo Ningxia China
106 J7 Pingluozhan Ningxia China
Pingma Guangxi China see Tiandong
109 L5 Pingnan Fujian China
108 H7 Pingnan Guangxi China
107 J9 Pingquan Gansu China
107 P6 Pingquan Hebei China
87 E12 Pingrup W.A. Austr.
Pingshan Guangdong China see Huidong
107 N7 Pingshan Hebei China
108 E4 Pingshan Sichuan China
Pingshan Yunnan China see Luquan
109 I6 Pingshi Guangdong China
Pingshu Hebei China see Daicheng
109 L6 Pingtan Fujian China
Pingtan Dao i. China see Haitan Dao
108 F6 Pingtang Guizhou China
109 M7 P'ingtung Taiwan
108 E2 Pingwu Sichuan China
Pingxi Guizhou China see Yuping
Pingxiang Gansu China see Tongwei
108 F7 Pingxiang Guangxi China
109 I5 Pingxiang Jiangxi China
107 S2 Pingyang Heilong. China
109 M5 Pingyang Zhejiang China
107 M8 Pingyao Shanxi China
107 O9 Pingyi Shandong China
107 O8 Pingyin Shandong China
109 J2 Pingyu Henan China
109 J6 Pingyuan Guangdong China
107 O8 Pingyuan Shandong China
Pingyuan Yunnan China see Yingjiang
108 D7 Pingyuanjie Yunnan China
108 G6 Pingzhai Guizhou China
256 D5 Pinhal Brazil
184 B3 Pinhal Novo Port.
182 E6 Pinhão Port.
254 D2 Pinheiro Brazil
182 D6 Pinheiro Porto Port.
184 B4 Pinheiro Setúbal Port.
258 G3 Pinheiro Machado Brazil
257 G3 Pinheiros Brazil
182 F7 Pinhel Port.
150 F6 Pinhoe Devon, England U.K.
251 E6 Pinhuã r. Brazil
94 C4 Pini i. Indon.
185 N3 Pinilla r. Spain
183 M7 Pinilla, Embalse de resr Spain
183 Q7 Pinilla de Molina Spain
183 J5 Pinilla de Toro Spain
Piniós r. Greece see Pineios
87 C12 Pinjarra W.A. Austr.
87 G11 Pinjin W.A. Austr.
87 G11 Pinjin Aboriginal Reserve W.A. Austr.
179 N5 Pinkafeld Austria
82 E5 Pinkawilinie Conservation Park nature res. S.A. Austr.
84 B3 Pinkerton Range hills N.T. Austr.
222 F3 Pink Mountain B.C. Can.
96 C4 Pinlaung Myanmar
96 B2 Pinlebu Myanmar
81 H8 Pinnacle mt. South I. N.Z.
232 G9 Pinnacle hill VA/WV U.S.A.
240 K5 Pinnacles National Monument nat. park CA U.S.A.
82 H6 Pinnaroo S.A. Austr.
168 I3 Pinnau r. Ger.
168 I3 Pinneberg Ger.
171 K7 Pinnow Ger.
192 C2 Pino Corse France
182 H5 Pino Spain
183 K3 Pino del Río Spain
182 H8 Pinofranqueado Spain
95 I5 Pinoh r. Indon.
161 C6 Pinols France
240 O7 Pinon Hills CA U.S.A.
182 D3 Piñor Spain
244 F3 Pinos Mex.
186 I4 Pinós hill Spain
Pinos, Isla de i. Cuba see Juventud, Isla de la
240 M7 Pinos, Mount CA U.S.A.
187 C11 Pinoso Spain
183 O7 Pinoso mt. Spain
185 L6 Pinos-Puente Spain
245 I9 Pinotepa Nacional Mex.
93 A5 Pinrang Sulawesi Indon.
93 B5 Pinrang Sulawesi Indon.
217 □2b Pins, Anse aux b. Mahé Seychelles
78 □5 Pins, Île des i. New Caledonia
227 M7 Pins, Pointe aux pt Ont. Can.
163 H6 Pinsac France
179 I4 Pinsdorf Austria
136 F1 Pinsk Belarus
183 R4 Pinsoro Spain
250 □ Pinta, Isla i. Islas Galápagos Ecuador
241 S9 Pinta, Sierra hill AZ U.S.A.
239 L9 Pintada Creek watercourse NM U.S.A.
261 I2 Pintado Grande Uru.
252 C5 Pintados Chile
186 C2 Pintano Spain
95 L2 Pintasan Sabah Malaysia
183 M8 Pinto Spain
241 S4 Pintura UT U.S.A.
192 C6 Pinu, Monte hill Italy
146 G12 Pinwherry South Ayrshire, Scotland U.K.
191 N3 Pinzano al Tagliamento Italy
178 F5 Pinzgau val. Austria
182 F7 Pinzio Port.
191 J3 Pinzolo Italy
191 N8 Piobbico Italy
241 R4 Pioche NV U.S.A.
209 E6 Piodi Dem. Rep. Congo
78 □6 Pio Island Solomon Is
254 E3 Pio IX Brazil
161 F8 Piolenc France
190 G5 Pioltello Italy
193 M2 Piomba r. Italy
192 F2 Piombino Italy
192 E2 Piombino, Canale di sea chan. Italy
191 L4 Piombino Dese Italy
232 A7 Pioneer OH U.S.A.
238 H4 Pioneer Mountains MT U.S.A.
131 K2 Pioner, Ostrov i. Severnaya Zemlya Rus. Fed.
138 D7 Pionerskiy Kaliningradskaya Oblast' Rus. Fed.
130 H3 Pionerskiy Khanty-Mansiyskiy Avtonomnyy Okrug Rus. Fed.
175 J4 Pionki Pol.
160 B4 Pionsat France
80 J5 Piopio North I. N.Z.
Piopiotahi inlet South I. N.Z. see Milford Sound
193 J1 Pioraco Italy
251 F5 Piorini r. Brazil
251 F5 Piorini, Lago l. Brazil
190 C6 Piossasco Italy
174 E4 Piotrkowice Pol.
174 G3 Piotrków Kujawski Pol.
175 H4 Piotrków Trybunalski Pol.
191 M5 Piove di Sacco Italy
191 K4 Piovene Rocchette Italy
190 G3 Pioverna r. Italy
122 I8 Pīp Iran
100 F7 Pipa Dingzi mt. China
258 D3 Pipanaco, Salar de salt flat Arg.
116 D6 Pipar Rajasthan India
116 D6 Pipar Road Rajasthan India
198 F3 Piperi i. Greece
240 O4 Piper Peak NV U.S.A.
234 E4 Pipersville PA U.S.A.
223 K5 Pipestone Man. Can.
224 B2 Pipestone r. Ont. Can.
236 G4 Pipestone MN U.S.A.
197 O3 Pipirig Romania
80 J6 Pipiriki North I. N.Z.
116 E5 Pipli Haryana India
225 G3 Pipmuacan, Réservoir resr Que. Can.
86 E6 Pippingarra Aboriginal Reserve W.A. Austr.
116 H9 Pipraud Chhattisgarh India
158 H6 Pipriac France
Piqan Xinjiang China see Shanshan
110 E6 Piqanlik Xinjiang China
232 A8 Piqua OH U.S.A.
163 F9 Pique r. France
183 O4 Piqueras, Puerto de pass Spain
254 F3 Piquet Carneiro Brazil
257 E5 Piquete Brazil
256 A6 Piquiri r. Brazil
253 G4 Piquiri r. Brazil
177 L4 Pir Romania
256 D5 Piracaia Brazil
256 C2 Piracanjuba Brazil
256 C3 Piracanjuba r. Brazil
256 D5 Piracicaba Brazil
256 C5 Piracicaba r. Brazil
257 F3 Piracicaba r. Brazil
256 D4 Piraçununga Brazil
254 E2 Piracuruca Brazil
79 □9a Pirae Tahiti Fr. Polynesia
Piraeus Greece see Peiraias
256 C6 Piraí do Sul Brazil
Piráievs Greece see Peiraias
194 H7 Piraino Sicilia Italy
256 C5 Piraju Brazil
256 C3 Pirajuba Brazil
256 C4 Pirajuí Brazil
129 L5 Pirallahı Adası Azer.
191 P4 Piran Slovenia
258 F2 Pirané Arg.
257 F4 Piranga Brazil
257 F4 Piranga r. Brazil
257 E5 Piranguinho Brazil
254 F4 Piranhas Alagoas Brazil
251 F6 Piranhas Amazonas Brazil
256 B2 Piranhas Goiás Brazil
256 B2 Piranhas r. Brazil
254 F3 Piranhas r. Brazil
254 D2 Pirapemas Brazil
253 E1 Pirapetinga Amazonas Brazil
257 F4 Pirapetinga Minas Gerais Brazil
256 A5 Pirapó r. Brazil
257 E2 Pirapora Brazil
256 B5 Pirapozinho Brazil
253 F4 Piraputangas Brazil
256 C6 Piraquara Brazil
251 G4 Pirara Guyana
258 G4 Pirarajá Uru.
117 J6 Pirari Nepal
258 G3 Piratini Brazil
256 C5 Piratininga Brazil
225 G3 Piraube, Lac l. Que. Can.
116 F7 Pirawa Rajasthan India
129 I5 Piräzä Azer.
151 K5 Pirbright Surrey, England U.K.
Pirchevan Azer. see Zängilan
175 M1 Pirčiupiai Lith.
259 C6 Pire Mahuida, Sierra mts Arg.
256 C1 Pirenópolis Brazil
256 C2 Pires do Rio Brazil
117 L7 Pirganj Bangl.
Pírgos Greece see Pyrgos
197 N7 Pirgovo Bulg.
158 F7 Piriac-sur-Mer France
80 J5 Piriaka North I. N.Z.
258 G4 Piriápolis Uru.
177 L4 Piricse Hungary
197 L9 Pirin mts Bulg.
197 L9 Pirin nat. park Bulg.
254 E3 Piripiri Brazil
138 H2 Pirita r. Estonia
250 D2 Píritu Falcón Venez.
250 D2 Píritu Portuguesa Venez.
253 F4 Pirizal Brazil
179 L5 Pirka Austria
141 Q6 Pirkkala Fin.
123 I6 Pir Kundil Afgh.
Pirlerkondu Turkey see Taşkent
172 D3 Pirmasens Ger.
114 E8 Pirmed Kerala India
122 G5 Pīr Morāl spring Iran
171 I9 Pirna Ger.
146 F11 Pirnmill North Ayrshire, Scotland U.K.
117 L8 Pirojpur Bangl.
183 K6 Pirón r. Spain
80 J4 Pirongia North I. N.Z.
80 J4 Pirongia vol. North I. N.Z.
80 J4 Pirongia Forest Park nature res. North I. N.Z.
139 Q3 Piros, Ozero l. Rus. Fed.
197 K7 Pirot Serbia
261 G5 Pirovano Arg.
117 K7 Pirpainti Bihar India
116 E3 Pir Panjal Pass Jammu and Kashmir
116 D2 Pir Panjal Range mts India/Pak.
127 K4 Pirrasit Dağ hill Turkey
129 K6 Pirsaat Azer.
129 J5 Pirsaatçay r. Azer.
177 I5 Pirtó Hungary
140 O3 Pirttivuopio Sweden
93 F5 Piru Seram Indon.
93 F5 Piru, Teluk b. Seram Indon.
Pir'yakh, Gora mt. Tajik. see Piryakh, Kŭhi
123 M2 Piryakh, Kŭhi mt. Tajik.
Piryatin Ukr. see Pyryatyn
Piryetós Greece see Pyrgetos
Piryíon Chios Greece see Pyrgi
123 K6 Pirzada Afgh.
190 I8 Pisa Italy
191 J9 Pisa prov. Italy
175 J2 Pisa r. Pol.
252 C3 Pisac Peru
Pisae Italy see Pisa
252 C4 Pisagua Chile
78 □4a Pisamwe i. Chuuk Micronesia
93 F4 Pisang i. Maluku Indon.
162 C4 Pisany France
78 □4a Pisar i. Chuuk Micronesia
81 D11 Pisa Range mts South I. N.Z.
95 M1 Pisau, Tanjung pt Malaysia
Pisaurum Italy see Pesaro
250 C3 Pisba, Parque Nacional nat. park Col.
235 F3 Piscataway NJ U.S.A.
179 M5 Pischelsdorf in der Steiermark Austria
177 K6 Pișchia Romania
193 O7 Pisciotta Italy
252 A3 Pisco Peru
252 A3 Pisco r. Peru
260 B2 Pisco Elqui Chile
177 L4 Pișcolt Romania
179 M7 Pišece Slovenia
233 K5 Piseco Lake NY U.S.A.
176 D2 Písek Czech Rep.
81 B12 Pisgah, Mount South I. N.Z.
81 E12 Pisgah, Mount South I. N.Z.
122 F5 Pish Iran
Pisha Sichuan China see Ningnan
111 D8 Pishan Xinjiang China
136 C2 Pishcha Ukr.
136 I5 Pishchana Ukr.
137 K4 Pishchane Ukr.
136 H5 Pishchanka Ukr.
137 M8 Pishchanyy, Mys pt Ukr.
123 I8 Pīshīn Iran
123 L6 Pishin Pak.
123 K7 Pishin Lora r. Pak.
123 I9 Pishkan, Ras pt Pak.
Pishpek Kyrg. see Bishkek
120 G9 Pīsh Qal'eh Iran
175 I3 Pisia r. Pol.
126 E5 Pisidia reg. Turkey
93 B6 Pising Sulawesi Indon.
241 T9 Pisinimo AZ U.S.A.
78 □4a Pisininin i. Chuuk Micronesia
121 M7 Piskent Uzbek.
136 I3 Piskivka Ukr.
137 Q4 Pisky Kharkivs'ka Oblast' Ukr.
137 S4 Pisky Luhans'ka Oblast' Ukr.
240 L6 Pismo Beach CA U.S.A.
253 E3 Piso Firme Bol.
190 I4 Pisogne Italy
138 E7 Pissa r. Rus. Fed.
258 C2 Pissis, Cerro mt. Arg.
163 C7 Pissos France
140 U4 Pista r. Rus. Fed.
243 O7 Pisté Mex.
195 L3 Pisticci Italy
191 J8 Pistoia Italy
191 J8 Pistoia prov. Italy
Pistoriae Italy see Pistoia
139 X4 Pistsovo Rus. Fed.
183 K5 Pisuerga r. Spain
175 J2 Pisz Pol.
175 L4 Piszczac Pol.
238 C6 Pit r. CA U.S.A.
206 B4 Pita Guinea
225 H2 Pitaga Nfld and Lab. Can.
243 N8 Pital Mex.
250 B4 Pitalito Col.
256 B6 Pitanga Brazil
256 C4 Pitangueiras Brazil
257 E3 Pitangui Brazil
116 C8 Pitar Gujarat India
83 I6 Pitarpunga Lake imp. l. N.S.W. Austr.
186 D6 Pitarque Spain
267 K7 Pitcairn Island S. Pacific Ocean
206 B3 Pitche Guinea-Bissau
247 □7 Pitch Lake Trin. and Tob.
140 P4 Piteå Sweden
140 P4 Piteälven r. Sweden
191 J7 Piteglio Italy
135 H5 Pitelino Rus. Fed.
120 B2 Piterka Rus. Fed.
197 M6 Pitești Romania
87 D11 Pithara W.A. Austr.
156 D7 Pithiviers France
116 H5 Pithoragarh Uttaranchal India
78 □1 Piti Guam
123 L9 Pitiani Creek inlet Pak.
192 H2 Pitigliano Italy
116 G8 Pitihra Madh. Prad. India
183 Q4 Pitillas Spain
163 A11 Pitillas, Laguna de l. Spain
242 C2 Pitiquito Mex.
134 E3 Pitkyaranta Rus. Fed.
146 I9 Pitlochry Perth and Kinross, Scotland U.K.
234 E5 Pitman NJ U.S.A.
146 L8 Pitmedden Aberdeenshire, Scotland U.K.
150 F6 Pitminster Somerset, England U.K.
207 I4 Pitoa Cameroon
188 F3 Pitomača Croatia
217 □1c Piton de la Fournaise vol. Réunion
217 □1b Piton de la Petite Rivière Noire hill Mauritius
217 □1c Piton des Neiges mt. Réunion
Pitong Sichuan China see Pixian
156 B5 Pîtres France
185 M7 Pitres Spain
260 A6 Pitrufquén Chile
215 J1 Pitsane Siding Botswana
179 L6 Pitschgau Austria
215 M5 Pitseng Lesotho
151 K3 Pitsford Reservoir England U.K.
151 K4 Pitstone Buckinghamshire, England U.K.
Pitsunda Georgia see Bichvint'a
151 J5 Pitt Hampshire, England U.K.
165 D7 Pittem Belgium
179 N4 Pitten Austria
146 H7 Pittentrail Highland, Scotland U.K.
146 K10 Pittenweem Fife, Scotland U.K.
114 C7 Pitti i. India
114 C7 Pitti Sand Bank sea feature India
222 D4 Pitt Island B.C. Can.
80 □ Pitt Island Chatham Is S. Pacific Ocean
Pitt Islands Santa Cruz Is Solomon Is see Vanikoro Islands
237 K9 Pittsboro MS U.S.A.
231 H8 Pittsboro NC U.S.A.
240 K3 Pittsburg CA U.S.A.
237 H7 Pittsburg KS U.S.A.
233 N3 Pittsburg NH U.S.A.
237 H9 Pittsburg TX U.S.A.
232 F8 Pittsburgh PA U.S.A.
236 J6 Pittsfield IL U.S.A.
233 L6 Pittsfield MA U.S.A.
233 □P4 Pittsfield ME U.S.A.
233 N5 Pittsfield NH U.S.A.
233 M5 Pittsfield VT U.S.A.
234 D2 Pittston PA U.S.A.
233 □P3 Pittston Farm ME U.S.A.
80 □ Pitt Strait Chatham Is S. Pacific Ocean
226 D5 Pittsville WI U.S.A.
85 M9 Pittsworth Qld Austr.
84 G7 Pituri Creek watercourse Qld Austr.
177 J5 Pitvaros Hungary
223 L2 Pitz Lake Nunavut Can.
178 C5 Pitztal val. Austria
254 C4 Pium Brazil
257 E4 Piumhí Brazil
250 A6 Piura Peru
250 A6 Piura dept Peru
138 K4 Piusa r. Estonia
241 Q7 Piute Mountains CA U.S.A.
240 N6 Piute Peak CA U.S.A.
117 I5 Piuthan Nepal
224 D3 Pivabiska r. Ont. Can.
175 M1 Pivašiūnai Lith.
136 K7 Pivdennyy Buh r. Ukr.
250 C2 Pivijay Col.
188 E3 Pivka Slovenia
191 Q4 Pivka r. Slovenia
137 N8 Pivnichno-Kryms'kyy Kanal canal Ukr.
175 I6 Piwniczna-Zdrój Pol.
111 D8 Pixa Xinjiang China
Pixariá mt. Greece see Pyxaria
108 D3 Pixian Sichuan China
240 M6 Pixley CA U.S.A.
243 N8 Pixoyal Mex.
252 C4 Pizacoma Peru
185 J7 Pizarra Spain
190 H3 Piz Bernina mt. Italy/Switz.
178 E6 Piz Boè mt. Italy
178 B6 Piz Buin mt. Austria/Switz.
190 G2 Piz d'Anarosa mt. Switz.
190 H3 Piz Duan mt. Switz.
190 H2 Piz Ela mt. Switz.
134 J4 Pizhanka Rus. Fed.
207 G4 Pizhi Nigeria
134 I4 Pizhma Rus. Fed.
134 J4 Pizhma r. Rus. Fed.
134 K2 Pizhma r. Rus. Fed.
107 P9 Pizhou Jiangsu China
190 H2 Piz Kesch mt. Switz.
190 F2 Piz Medel mt. Switz.
190 G2 Pizol mt. Switz.
190 I2 Piz Pisoc mt. Switz.
190 H3 Piz Platta mt. Switz.
190 H3 Piz Varuna mt. Italy/Switz.
190 H5 Pizzighettone Italy
195 K6 Pizzo Italy
193 M4 Pizzoferrato Italy
193 K3 Pizzoli Italy
193 J3 Pizzuto, Monte mt. Italy
92 □ Pkulagalid Point Palau
92 □ Pkulagasemieg pt Palau
92 □ Pkulngril pt Palau
92 □ Pkurengei pt Palau
170 F3 Plaaz Ger.
158 C4 Plabennec France
160 L5 Place Moulin, Lago di l. Italy
225 K4 Placentia Nfld and Lab. Can.
Placentia Italy see Piacenza
225 K4 Placentia Bay Nfld and Lab. Can.
92 D6 Placer Masbate Phil.
92 E7 Placer Mindanao Phil.
240 L3 Placerville CA U.S.A.
239 J7 Placerville CO U.S.A.
246 D2 Placetas Cuba
252 D2 Plácido de Castro Brazil
260 B3 Placilla Chile
190 C2 Plaffeien Switz.
169 D10 Plaidt Ger.
97 F7 Plai Mat, Lam r. Thai.
159 P7 Plaimpied-Givaudins France
237 I9 Plain Dealing LA U.S.A.
209 A5 Plaine Ouanga, Réserve de la nature res. Gabon
157 N7 Plainfaing France
235 L1 Plainfield CT U.S.A.
230 D6 Plainfield IN U.S.A.
235 G3 Plainfield NJ U.S.A.
233 M4 Plainfield VT U.S.A.
226 E5 Plainfield WI U.S.A.
237 E7 Plains KS U.S.A.
237 D9 Plains TX U.S.A.
234 F4 Plainsboro NJ U.S.A.
158 F5 Plaintel France
226 B5 Plainview MN U.S.A.
236 G4 Plainview NE U.S.A.
235 I3 Plainview NY U.S.A.
237 E8 Plainview TX U.S.A.
235 J1 Plainville CT U.S.A.
236 F6 Plainville KS U.S.A.
226 I7 Plainwell MI U.S.A.
163 E8 Plaisance France
246 G4 Plaisance Haiti
163 G8 Plaisance-du-Touch France
156 C6 Plaisir France
233 N6 Plaistow NH U.S.A.
94 F6 Plaju Sumatera Indon.
199 G2 Plaka Limnos Greece
199 H7 Plaka, Akrotirio pt Kriti Greece
128 C3 Plakoti, Cape Cyprus
95 L9 Plampang Sumbawa Indon.
176 B2 Planá Czech Rep.
187 E11 Plana, Isla i. Spain
187 K9 Plana, Sa Punta pt Spain
246 G2 Plana Cays is Bahamas
240 L4 Planada CA U.S.A.
256 D1 Planaltina Brazil
171 L10 Plaňany Czech Rep.
157 M8 Plancher-Bas France
157 M8 Plancher-les-Mines France
260 Planchón, Paso del pass Arg.
Planchón, Portezuelo del pass Arg. see Planchón, Paso del
158 G4 Plancoët France
156 G6 Plancy-l'Abbaye France
245 J6 Plan de Arroyos Mex.
244 F4 Plan de Ayala Mex.
244 C4 Plan de Barrancas Mex.
161 G7 Plan-de-Baux France
161 G10 Plan-de-Cuques France
245 K6 Plan de las Hayas Mex.
161 J10 Plan-de-la-Tour France
196 J5 Plandište Vojvodina Serbia
161 F9 Plan-d'Orgon France
171 F6 Plane r. Ger.
217 □2b Planeau, Montagne plat. Mahé Seychelles
173 K5 Planegg Ger.
163 I11 Planès France
161 B7 Planèze reg. France
176 C2 Plánice Czech Rep.
161 G10 Planier, Île de i. France
191 Q5 Planik mt. Croatia
179 J8 Planina Postojna Slovenia
179 L7 Planina Šentjur pri Celju Slovenia
173 K2 Plankenfels Ger.
236 F4 Plankinton SD U.S.A.
226 F8 Plano IL U.S.A.
237 G9 Plano TX U.S.A.
261 I1 Plano Alto Brazil
178 C5 Plansee l. Austria
246 □ Plantain Garden r. Jamaica
260 B3 Planta Los Queltehues Chile
216 □2b Plantation House St Helena
163 G9 Plantaurel, Montagnes du hills France
231 F12 Plant City FL U.S.A.
235 J1 Plantsville CT U.S.A.
256 C4 Planura Brazil
237 J10 Plaquemine LA U.S.A.
182 H8 Plasencia Spain
186 C4 Plasencia, Llano de plain Spain
186 D3 Plasencia del Monte Spain
175 L2 Płaska Pol.
188 E3 Plaški Croatia
196 J9 Plasnica Macedonia
120 I1 Plast Rus. Fed.
241 Q9 Plaster City CA U.S.A.
225 H4 Plaster Rock N.B. Can.
215 P1 Plaston S. Africa
177 H3 Plášťovce Slovakia
100 J6 Plastun Rus. Fed.
129 A2 Plastunka Rus. Fed.
137 S8 Plastunovskaya Rus. Fed.
176 C2 Plasy Czech Rep.
196 G8 Platamon, Rt pt Montenegro
192 A6 Platamona Lido Sardegna Italy
198 D3 Platamonas Greece
252 C4 Platanal Peru
194 E9 Platani r. Sicilia Italy
195 K5 Platania Italy
198 E3 Platanias Greece
245 L9 Platanillo Mex.
198 F4 Platanistos Greece
198 C5 Platanos Greece
214 C6 Platbakkies S. Africa
215 N4 Platberg mt. S. Africa
170 E3 Plate Ger.
207 G4 Plateau state Nigeria
165 I8 Plateau des Tailles, Réserves Domaniales du nature res. Belgium
208 B5 Plateaux admin. reg. Congo
138 E5 Plateliai Lith.
140 □ Platen, Kapp c. Svalbard
168 K5 Platendorf (Sassenburg) Ger.
244 E2 Plateros Mex.
214 E9 Plathuis S. Africa
195 K7 Platì Italy
196 H6 Platičevo Vojvodina Serbia
Platíkambos Greece see Platykampos
240 J1 Platina CA U.S.A.
220 B4 Platinum AK U.S.A.
186 L4 Platja d'Aro Spain
137 S8 Platnirovskaya Rus. Fed.
250 C2 Plato Col.
258 C2 Plato de Sopa Chile
245 I4 Platón Sánchez Mex.
215 N3 Platrand S. Africa
236 H6 Platte r. MO U.S.A.
236 H5 Platte r. NE U.S.A.
236 H6 Platte City MO U.S.A.
217 □2 Platte Island Seychelles
235 G1 Plattekill NY U.S.A.
179 K3 Plattenberg hill Austria
238 L6 Platteville CO U.S.A.
236 J4 Platteville WI U.S.A.
173 N4 Plattling Ger.
233 L4 Plattsburgh NY U.S.A.
236 H5 Plattsmouth NE U.S.A.
198 D2 Platy Greece
198 D3 Platykampos Greece
170 F4 Plau Ger.
169 K9 Plaue Ger.
171 F9 Plauen Ger.
170 F4 Plauer See l. Ger.
196 H8 Plav Montenegro
136 G2 Plav r. Ukr.
139 U8 Plava r. Rus. Fed.
176 G3 Plavecký Mikuláš Slovakia
179 P3 Plavecký Štvrtok Slovakia
138 I5 Pļaviņas Latvia
137 T1 Plavitsa r. Rus. Fed.
188 E3 Plavnik i. Croatia
139 U8 Plavsk Rus. Fed.
244 E8 Playa Azul Mex.
216 □3c Playa Blanca Lanzarote Canary Is
216 □3b Playa Blanca coastal area Fuerteventura Canary Is
261 I6 Playa Chapadmalal Arg.
244 D7 Playa Corrida de San Juan, Punta pt Mex.
216 □3b Playa de Barlovento coastal area Fuerteventura Canary Is
184 F6 Playa de Castilla coastal area Spain
247 □1 Playa de Fajardo Puerto Rico
216 □3a Playa de las Americas Tenerife Canary Is
243 P7 Playa del Carmen Mex.
181 □ Playa del Inglés Gran Canaria Canary Is
216 □3b Playa de Sotavento coastal area Fuerteventura Canary Is
245 L7 Playa Hermosa Mex.
261 I4 Playa Pascaul Uru.
250 A5 Playas Ecuador
245 N8 Playas r. Mex.
216 □3b Playas de Corralejo coastal area Fuerteventura Canary Is
245 L8 Playa Vicente Mex.
84 F5 Playford watercourse N.T. Austr.
223 L4 Playgreen Lake Man. Can.
97 I8 Plây Ku Vietnam
242 E5 Playón Mex.
250 C2 Playones de Santa Ana l. Col.
183 O2 Plaza Spain
162 G5 Plazac France
185 J3 Plaza del Judío mt. Spain
260 C6 Plaza Huincul Arg.
175 L5 Płazów Pol.
241 T8 Pleasant, Lake AZ U.S.A.
233 □S3 Pleasant, Mount hill N.B. Can.
233 P7 Pleasant Bay MA U.S.A.
234 D3 Pleasant Corners PA U.S.A.
235 G4 Pleasant Grove NJ U.S.A.
241 U1 Pleasant Grove UT U.S.A.
240 J4 Pleasant Hill CA U.S.A.
232 A8 Pleasant Hill OH U.S.A.
240 K4 Pleasanton CA U.S.A.
237 F11 Pleasanton TX U.S.A.
81 F11 Pleasant Point South I. N.Z.
235 H1 Pleasant Valley NY U.S.A.
234 D5 Pleasantville DE U.S.A.
234 F6 Pleasantville NJ U.S.A.
235 H2 Pleasantville NY U.S.A.
234 B5 Pleaseant Hill PA U.S.A.
149 O7 Pleasley Derbyshire, England U.K.
235 K2 Pleasure Beach CT U.S.A.
234 B5 Pleasureville PA U.S.A.
162 I5 Pleaux France
173 K2 Plech Ger.
176 C3 Plechý mt. Czech Rep.
175 H3 Plecka Dąbrowa Pol.
158 F5 Plédran France
158 E4 Pléhédel France
97 H7 Plei Doch Vietnam
95 K6 Pleihari Martapura, Suaka Margasatwa nature res. Indon.
95 K7 Pleihari Tanah, Suaka Margasatwa nature res. Kalimantan Indon.
97 H7 Plei Kân Vietnam
158 H4 Pleine-Fougères France
173 J3 Pleinfeld Ger.
173 N5 Pleiskirchen Ger.
171 G9 Pleiße Ger.
171 F8 Pleiße r. Ger.
137 S1 Plekhanovo Rus. Fed.
158 G5 Plélan-le-Grand France
158 G5 Plélan-le-Petit France
158 F4 Plélo France
158 F5 Plémet France
158 G5 Plénée-Jugon France
158 F4 Pléneuf-Val-André France
84 F8 Plenty watercourse N.T. Austr.
80 K4 Plenty, Bay of g. North I. N.Z.
238 L2 Plentywood MT U.S.A.
183 O2 Plentzia Spain
158 F4 Plérin France
139 Y4 Ples Rus. Fed.
179 L5 Pleschkogel mt. Austria
158 F6 Plescop France
177 L5 Pleșcuța Romania
134 H3 Plesetsk Rus. Fed.
120 E1 Pleshanovo Rus. Fed.
Pleshchentsy Belarus see Plyeshchanitsy
139 V5 Pleshcheyevo, Ozero l. Rus. Fed.
177 J3 Plešivec Slovakia
179 K7 Plešivec mt. Slovenia
158 G4 Pleslin-Trigavou France
176 B1 Plesná Czech Rep.
139 S2 Pleso Rus. Fed.
169 J9 Pleß hill Ger.
171 I8 Plessa Ger.
158 H6 Plessé France
158 D4 Plestin-les-Grèves France
174 F4 Pleszew Pol.
137 K5 Pletenyy Tashlyk Ukr.
188 F3 Pleternica Croatia
225 G3 Plétipi, Lac l. Que. Can.
169 E8 Plettenberg Ger.
214 H10 Plettenberg Bay S. Africa
179 K5 Pletzen mt. Austria
158 E4 Pleubian France
158 H4 Pleudihen-sur-Rance France
159 M8 Pleumartin France
158 D4 Pleumeur-Bodou France
156 G6 Pleurs France
158 G4 Pleurtuit France
158 C6 Pleuven France
197 M7 Pleven Bulg.
Plevna Bulg. see Pleven
177 H2 Plevník-Drienové Slovakia
158 D5 Pleyben France
158 D4 Pleyber-Christ France
173 M2 Pleystein Ger.
187 C12 Pliego Spain
173 L5 Pliening Ger.
95 K3 Plieran r. Malaysia
177 I3 Pliešovce Slovakia
163 F8 Plieux France
191 J2 Plima r. Italy
138 F5 Plinkšių ežeras l. Lith.
174 C3 Pliszka r. Pol.
196 D6 Plitvička Jezera nat. park Croatia
188 E3 Plješevica mts Croatia
196 H7 Pljevlja Montenegro
192 B6 Ploaghe Sardegna Italy
158 C6 Plobannalec France
157 O7 Plobsheim France
188 F4 Ploče Croatia
172 G4 Plochingen Ger.
175 K1 Płociczno Pol.
175 H3 Płock Pol.
178 G6 Plöckenpass pass Austria/Italy
146 E8 Plockton Highland, Scotland U.K.
188 F4 Pločno mt. Bos.-Herz.
139 N1 Plodovoye Rus. Fed.
158 E6 Ploemeur France
158 F6 Ploeren France
158 G6 Ploërmel France
Ploești Romania see Ploiești
158 F5 Plœuc-sur-Lié France
158 C6 Plogastel-St-Germain France
158 C5 Plogonnec France
170 H1 Plogshagen Ger.
197 O6 Ploiești Romania
199 H4 Plomari Lesvos Greece
161 B6 Plomb du Cantal mt. France
157 L8 Plombières-les-Bains France
158 C6 Plomelin France
158 C6 Plomeur France
191 Q5 Plomin Croatia
158 C5 Plomodiern France
244 B2 Plomosas Mex.

Plön to Porecatu

370

168 J2 Plön Ger.
174 D2 Płoń, Jezioro l. Pol.
158 C6 Plonéour-Lanvern France
158 D5 Plonévez-du-Faou France
158 C5 Plonevez-Porzay France
174 C2 Płonia r. Pol.
175 I3 Płonka r. Pol.
175 I3 Płońsk Pol.
197 K3 Plopiş Romania
175 H1 Płoskinia Pol.
139 O5 Ploskosh' Rus. Fed.
Ploskoye Rus. Fed. see Stanovoye
175 I2 Płośnica Pol.
173 M2 Plößberg Ger.
139 R1 Plotichino Rus. Fed.
136 F1 Plotnitsa Belarus
174 D2 Płoty Pol.
171 G6 Plötzin Ger.
171 E6 Plötzky Ger.
158 F4 Plouagat France
158 E4 Plouaret France
158 B5 Plouarzel France
158 E6 Plouay France
158 G4 Ploubalay France
158 E4 Ploubazlanec France
158 E4 Ploubezre France
176 D1 Ploučnice r. Czech Rep.
158 B4 Ploudalmézeau France
158 C4 Ploudaniel France
158 C5 Ploudiry France
158 C5 Plouédern France
158 D4 Plouénan France
158 C4 Plouescat France
158 F4 Plouézec France
158 F5 Ploufragan France
158 D4 Plougasnou France
158 C5 Plougastel-Daoulas France
158 B5 Plougonvelin France
158 D4 Plougonven France
158 E5 Plougonver France
158 E4 Plougrescant France
158 F5 Plouguenast France
158 B4 Plouguerneau France
158 E5 Plouguernével France
158 E4 Plouguiel France
158 B4 Plouguin France
158 F4 Plouha France
158 E6 Plouharnel France
158 C5 Plouhinec Bretagne France
158 E6 Plouhinec Bretagne France
158 D4 Plouigneau France
158 E4 Ploumagoar France
158 D4 Ploumilliau France
158 C4 Plounévez-Lochrist France
158 E4 Plounévez-Moëdec France
158 E5 Plounévez-Quintin France
158 E5 Plouray France
158 D4 Plourin-lès-Morlaix France
158 C4 Plouvien France
158 C4 Plouvorn France
158 D5 Plouyé France
158 B5 Plouzané France
158 C4 Plouzévédé France
197 M8 Plovdiv Bulg.
226 E5 Plover WI U.S.A.
226 E5 Plover r. WI U.S.A.
109 □J7 Plover Cove Reservoir H.K. China
158 C6 Plozévet France
Plozk Pol. see Płock
147 G3 Pluck Ireland
234 F3 Pluckemin NJ U.S.A.
172 H4 Plüderhausen Ger.
158 C6 Pluguffan France
232 F8 Plum PA U.S.A.
147 H3 Plumbridge Northern Ireland U.K.
223 L5 Plum Coulee Man. Can.
158 F6 Plumelec France
158 F6 Pluméliau France
158 F6 Plumergat France
235 K2 Plum Island NY U.S.A.
238 F3 Plummer ID U.S.A.
87 H10 Plumridge Lakes salt flat W.A. Austr.
87 H10 Plumridge Lakes Nature Reserve W.A. Austr.
234 E4 Plumsteadville PA U.S.A.
213 E4 Plumtree Zimbabwe
138 E6 Plungė Lith.
175 K1 Pluszkiejmy Pol.
175 I2 Pluszne, Jezioro l. Pol.
242 E3 Plutarco Elís Calles, Presa resr Mex.
225 G2 Pluto, Lac l. Que. Can.
158 E6 Pluvigner France
196 G7 Plužine Montenegro
174 G2 Płużnica Pol.
158 E4 Pluzunet France
150 D3 Plwmp Ceredigion, Wales U.K.
138 K7 Plyeshchanitsy Belarus
96 D6 Ply Huey Wati, Khao mt. Myanmar/Thai.
150 D7 Plym r. England U.K.
247 □2 Plymouth Montserrat
247 □5 Plymouth Trin. and Tob.
150 D7 Plymouth Plymouth, England U.K.
150 D7 Plymouth admin. div. England U.K.
240 L3 Plymouth CA U.S.A.
235 I1 Plymouth CT U.S.A.
226 D9 Plymouth IL U.S.A.
230 D5 Plymouth IN U.S.A.
233 O7 Plymouth MA U.S.A.
231 I8 Plymouth NC U.S.A.
233 N5 Plymouth NH U.S.A.
234 D2 Plymouth PA U.S.A.
226 G6 Plymouth WI U.S.A.
233 O7 Plymouth Bay MA U.S.A.
150 D7 Plympton Plymouth, England U.K.
150 D7 Plymstock Plymouth, England U.K.
150 E3 Plynlimon hill Wales U.K.
136 I4 Plyskiv Ukr.
137 L2 Plysky Ukr.
138 M3 Plyussa Rus. Fed.
138 L2 Plyussa r. Rus. Fed.
176 C2 Plzeň Czech Rep.
176 C2 Plzeňský kraj admin. reg. Czech Rep.
84 E8 Pmere Nyente Aboriginal Land res. N.T. Austr.
175 J3 Pniewo Pol.
175 I4 Pniewy Mazowieckie Pol.
174 E3 Pniewy Wielkopolskie Pol.
206 E4 Pô Burkina
191 M5 Po r. Italy
206 E4 Pô, Parc National de nat. park Burkina
95 I4 Po, Tanjung pt Malaysia
242 □Q12 Poás, Volcán vol. Costa Rica
93 C4 Poat i. Indon.
207 F5 Pobè Benin
131 P3 Pobeda, Gora mt. Rus. Fed.
264 P10 Pobeda Ice Island Antarctica
Pobeda Peak China/Kyrg. see Jengish Chokusu
177 G3 Pobedím Slovakia
100 M4 Pobedino Sakhalin Rus. Fed.
Pobedinskiy Rus. Fed. see Zarechnyy
Pobedy, Pik mt. China/Kyrg. see Jengish Chokusu
176 B2 Poběžovice Czech Rep.
174 F3 Pobiedziska Pol.
170 K2 Pobierowo Pol.
175 K3 Pobikry Pol.
260 B4 Población Chile
182 I4 Pobladura del Valle Spain
261 H4 Poblet Arg.
186 H5 Poblet tourist site Spain
185 L3 Poblete Spain
174 F1 Pobłocie Pol.
186 G5 Poboleda Spain
216 □3c Pobre, Punta de pt Canary Is
174 D2 Pobrzeże reg. Pol.
174 F1 Pobrzeże Koszalińskie reg. Pol.
136 J5 Pobuz'ke Ukr.
137 N8 Pobyedne Ukr.
232 D10 Poca WV U.S.A.
237 J7 Pocahontas AR U.S.A.
236 H4 Pocahontas IA U.S.A.
232 D10 Pocatalico r. WV U.S.A.
238 H5 Pocatello ID U.S.A.
176 E2 Počátky Czech Rep.
184 B3 Poceirão Port.
210 B3 Pochala Sudan
136 E3 Pochayiv Ukr.
139 Q9 Pochep Rus. Fed.
135 I5 Pochinki Rus. Fed.
139 P7 Pochinok Smolenskaya Oblast' Rus. Fed.
139 R4 Pochinok Tverskaya Oblast' Rus. Fed.
179 L3 Pöchlarn Austria
260 E2 Pocho, Sierra de mts Arg.
245 K10 Pochutla Mex.
185 O3 Pocicos, Puerto de los pass Spain
260 A5 Pocillas Chile
95 M2 Pock, Gunung hill Malaysia
171 H9 Pockau Ger.
173 K6 Pöcking Ger.
173 O5 Pocking Ger.
149 P6 Pocklington East Riding of Yorkshire, England U.K.
254 E5 Poções Brazil
257 E4 Poço Fundo Brazil
177 L5 Pocola Romania
233 J10 Pocomoke City MD U.S.A.
233 J11 Pocomoke Sound b. MD/VA U.S.A.
252 D4 Pocona Bol.
253 F4 Poconé Brazil
234 D2 Pocono Mountains hills PA U.S.A.
234 E2 Pocono Pines PA U.S.A.
234 E2 Pocono Summit PA U.S.A.
93 B8 Poco Ranakah vol. Flores Indon.
256 D4 Poços de Caldas Brazil
257 G3 Pocrane Brazil
177 K4 Pocsaj Hungary
175 H5 Poczesna Pol.
139 N5 Podberez'ye Rus. Fed.
177 I2 Podbiel Slovakia
176 C1 Podbořany Czech Rep.
138 L4 Podborov'ye Rus. Fed.
179 I7 Podbrdo Slovenia
179 M7 Podčetrtek Slovenia
134 L3 Podcher'ye Rus. Fed.
134 L3 Podcher'ye r. Rus. Fed.
174 G4 Poddębice Pol.
139 O4 Poddor'ye Rus. Fed.
176 E1 Poděbrady Czech Rep.
175 I6 Podegrodzie Pol.
171 K6 Podelzig Ger.
163 D6 Podensac France
190 H7 Podenzana Italy
190 H6 Podenzano Italy
179 O4 Podersdorf am See Austria
174 E2 Podgaje Pol.
197 J7 Podgorac Serbia
135 G6 Podgorenskiy Rus. Fed.
196 H8 Podgorica Montenegro
179 K7 Podgorica Slovenia
198 B2 Podgorie Albania
129 E1 Podgornaya Rus. Fed.
130 J4 Podgornoye Rus. Fed.
191 Q4 Podgrad Slovenia
177 L3 Podhoroď Slovakia
114 F5 Podile Andhra Prad. India
191 M5 Po di Levante r. Italy
179 O2 Podivín Czech Rep.
131 K3 Podkamennaya Tunguska Rus. Fed.
131 K3 Podkamennaya Tunguska r. Rus. Fed.
175 K6 Podkarpackie prov. Pol.
139 V7 Podkhozheye Rus. Fed.
197 N9 Podkova Bulg.
175 I3 Podkowa Leśna Pol.
179 L7 Podkum Slovenia
129 E1 Podkumok r. Rus. Fed.
175 K2 Podlaska, Nizina lowland Pol.
175 K2 Podlaskie prov. Pol.
179 M7 Podlehnik Slovenia
120 B2 Podlesnoye Rus. Fed.
179 K7 Podlipoglav Slovenia
179 I8 Podnanos Slovenia
250 B6 Podocarpus, Parque Nacional nat. park Ecuador
197 O4 Podoleni Romania
179 O1 Podolí Czech Rep.
139 U6 Podol'sk Rus. Fed.
206 B2 Podor Senegal
175 M6 Podorozhnye Ukr.
139 O6 Podosinki Rus. Fed.
137 N7 Podove Ukr.
139 X4 Podozerskiy Rus. Fed.
139 R1 Podporozh'ye Rus. Fed.
176 F5 Podravina reg. Croatia
176 G5 Podravske Sesvete Croatia
179 M7 Podsreda Slovenia
179 K8 Podtabor Slovenia
179 O7 Podturen Croatia
196 J8 Podujevo Kosovo Serbia
175 H6 Podwilk Pol.
176 E3 Podyjí park Czech Rep.
134 H3 Podyuga Rus. Fed.
137 N1 Podyvot'ye Rus. Fed.
134 J3 Podz' Rus. Fed.
170 D2 Poel i. Ger.
164 F4 Poeldijk Neth.
84 F8 Poeppel Corner salt flat N.T. Austr.
Poetovio Slovenia see Ptuj
214 D5 Pofadder S. Africa
193 K4 Pofi Italy
227 M3 Pogamasing Ont. Can.
139 Q9 Pogar Rus. Fed.
170 H2 Poggendorf Ger.
179 J6 Poggersdorf Austria
195 O3 Poggiardo Italy
191 K9 Poggibonsi Italy
192 F2 Poggio Ballone hill Italy
193 J2 Poggio Bustone Italy
192 G3 Poggio del Leccio hill Italy
192 G1 Poggio di Montieri mt. Italy
193 J2 Poggiodomo Italy
193 O4 Poggio Imperiale Italy
192 G2 Poggio Lecci hill Italy
192 C3 Poggio-Mezzana Corse France
193 J3 Poggio Mirteto Italy
193 J3 Poggio Moiano Italy
192 F2 Poggio Peroni hill Italy
193 L3 Poggio Picenze Italy
194 E8 Poggioreale Sicilia Italy
191 L6 Poggio Renatico Italy
193 Q6 Poggiorsini Italy
191 K6 Poggio Rusco Italy
179 L3 Pöggstall Austria
196 I8 Pogled mt. Montenegro/Serbia
192 A7 Poglina, Punta di pt Sardegna Italy
156 H6 Pogny France
198 B3 Pogoniani Greece
139 R5 Pogoreloye-Gorodishche Rus. Fed.
174 F4 Pogorzela Pol.
174 F1 Pogorzelice Pol.
137 Q2 Pogozheye Rus. Fed.
196 I10 Pogradec Albania
100 G6 Pogranichnyy Rus. Fed.
Pogrebishche Ukr. see Pohrebyshche
175 H1 Pogrodzie Pol.
253 G4 Poguba r. Brazil
93 C4 Poh Sulawesi Indon.
Po Hai g. China see Bo Hai
101 F10 P'ohang S. Korea
141 Q6 Pohja Fin.
169 H6 Pohle Ger.
191 R7 Pohlibski Kanal sea chan. Croatia
78 □4b Pohnpei atoll Micronesia
177 J3 Pohorelá Slovakia
176 F3 Pohořelice Czech Rep.
179 L7 Pohorje mts Slovenia
177 H3 Pohranice Slovakia
136 J3 Pohreby Kyivs'ka Oblast' Ukr.
137 M4 Pohreby Poltavs'ka Oblast' Ukr.
136 I4 Pohrebyshche Ukr.
116 F7 Pohri Madh. Prad. India
177 H3 Pohronská pahorkatina mts Slovakia
117 O7 Poi Manipur India
190 I3 Poia r. Italy
197 L7 Poiana Mare Romania
197 K5 Poiana Ruscă, Munții mts Romania
197 N3 Poiana Stampei Romania
177 L5 Poiana Vadului Romania
197 P4 Poienești Romania
177 L5 Poieni Romania
197 M3 Poienile de Sub Munte Romania
197 L4 Poienița, Vârful mt. Romania
93 D3 Poigar Sulawesi Indon.
156 E8 Poilly-lez-Gien France
135 H5 Poim Rus. Fed.
156 H8 Poinçon-lès-Larrey France
232 A10 Poindexter KY U.S.A.
77 G4 Poindimié New Caledonia
78 □5 Poindimié r. New Caledonia
173 L5 Poing Ger.
263 H2 Poinsett, Cape Antarctica
240 I3 Point Arena CA U.S.A.
237 J11 Point au Fer Island LA U.S.A.
222 C3 Point Baker AK U.S.A.
227 S3 Point-Comfort Que. Can.
237 K11 Pointe a la Hache LA U.S.A.
247 □7 Pointe-à-Pierre Trin. and Tob.
247 □2 Pointe-à-Pitre Guadeloupe
227 N4 Pointe au Baril Station Ont. Can.
226 J4 Pointe Aux Pins MI U.S.A.
247 □2 Pointe Michel Dominica
209 A6 Pointe-Noire Congo
247 □2 Pointe-Noire Guadeloupe
160 J5 Pointe Percée mt. France
247 □7 Point Fortin Trin. and Tob.
220 B3 Point Hope AK U.S.A.
186 G1 Pointis-Inard France
82 E5 Point Kenny S.A. Austr.
222 H1 Point Lake N.W.T. Can.
232 F9 Point Marion PA U.S.A.
232 H9 Point of Rocks MD U.S.A.
238 J6 Point of Rocks WY U.S.A.
227 L8 Point Pelee National Park Ont. Can.
233 K8 Point Pleasant NJ U.S.A.
232 C10 Point Pleasant WV U.S.A.
235 G4 Point Pleasant Beach NJ U.S.A.
240 J3 Point Reyes National Seashore nature res. CA U.S.A.
87 G10 Point Salvation Aboriginal Reserve W.A. Austr.
76 B4 Point Samson W.A. Austr.
190 D6 Poirino Italy
160 C2 Poiseux France
134 K5 Poisevo Rus. Fed.
81 B11 Poison Bay South I. N.Z.
227 S4 Poisson Blanc, Lac du l. Que. Can.
86 E5 Poissonnier Point W.A. Austr.
157 J7 Poissons France
156 D6 Poissy France
160 I5 Poisy France
162 E2 Poitiers France
162 E2 Poitou reg. France
162 E3 Poitou, Plaines et Seuil du plain France
162 D3 Poitou-Charentes admin. reg. France
217 □2 Poivre Atoll Seychelles
156 C4 Poix-de-Picardie France
156 I4 Poix-Terron France
179 M8 Pojatno Croatia
167 I2 Pojezierza Iławskiego, Park Krajobrazowy Pol.
136 C2 Pojezierze Łęczyńskie, Park Krajobrazowy Pol.
252 D4 Pojo Bol.
254 F5 Pojuca Brazil
240 □C12 Pōka'ī Bay HI U.S.A.
123 O4 Pokal Pak.
116 C6 Pokaran Rajasthan India
176 F5 Pókaszepetk Hungary
83 L3 Pokataroo N.S.W. Austr.
139 N9 Pokats' r. Belarus
134 L3 Pokcha Rus. Fed.
80 J4 Pokeno North I. N.Z.
117 I5 Pokhara Nepal
120 E1 Pokhvistnevo Rus. Fed.
251 H3 Pokigron Suriname
140 R2 Pokka Fin.
Pok Liu Chau i. H.K. China see Lamma Island
179 I7 Pokljuka reg. Slovenia
208 E4 Poko Dem. Rep. Congo
174 F5 Pokój Pol.
129 F1 Pokoynoye Rus. Fed.
123 L9 Pokran Pak.
139 S6 Pokrov Smolenskaya Oblast' Rus. Fed.
139 W6 Pokrov Vladimirskaya Oblast' Rus. Fed.
129 J6 Pokrovka Azer.
121 M2 Pokrovka Kazakh.
121 N6 Pokrovka Talas Kyrg.
Pokrovka Ysyk-Köl Kyrg. see Kyzyl-Suu
100 B2 Pokrovka Chitinskaya Oblast' Rus. Fed.
139 T5 Pokrovka Moskovskaya Oblast' Rus. Fed.
120 E2 Pokrovka Orenburgskaya Oblast' Rus. Fed.
100 G7 Pokrovka Primorskiy Kray Rus. Fed.
Pokrovka Yevreyskaya Avtonomnaya Oblast' Rus. Fed. see Priamurskiy
137 K6 Pokrovka Mykolayivs'ka Oblast' Ukr.
137 K7 Pokrovka Mykolayivs'ka Oblast' Ukr.
137 O3 Pokrovka Sums'ka Oblast' Ukr.
137 U1 Pokrovo-Marfino Rus. Fed.
131 N3 Pokrovsk Respublika Sakha (Yakutiya) Rus. Fed.
Pokrovsk Saratovskaya Oblast' Rus. Fed. see Engel's
137 N6 Pokrovs'ke Dnipropetrovs'ka Oblast' Ukr.
137 R4 Pokrovs'ke Luhans'ka Oblast' Ukr.
139 V9 Pokrovskoye Lipetskaya Oblast' Rus. Fed.
139 T9 Pokrovskoye Orlovskaya Oblast' Rus. Fed.
135 G7 Pokrovskoye Rostovskaya Oblast' Rus. Fed.
134 L3 Pokrovsk-Ural'skiy Rus. Fed.
175 L4 Pokrówka Pol.
139 Y4 Poksha r. Rus. Fed.
134 I3 Pokshen'ga r. Rus. Fed.
116 D8 Pol Gujarat India
139 X6 Pol' r. Rus. Fed.
Pola Croatia see Pula
92 C5 Pola Mindoro Phil.
139 O4 Pola Rus. Fed.
139 O4 Pola r. Rus. Fed.
241 V6 Polacca AZ U.S.A.
241 V6 Polacca Wash watercourse AZ U.S.A.
185 P7 Polacra, Punta de la pt Spain
182 G2 Pola de Allande Spain
182 I2 Pola de Laviana Spain
182 I2 Pola de Lena Spain
182 I2 Pola de Siero Spain
182 H2 Pola de Somiedo Spain
157 L8 Polaincourt-et-Clairefontaine France
174 E3 Połajewo Pol.
123 I9 Polān Iran
183 L9 Polán Spain
177 I3 Poľana mt. Slovakia
177 I3 Poľana mt. Slovakia
177 I3 Poľana park Slovakia
175 H3 Poland country Europe
233 J5 Poland NY U.S.A.
232 E7 Poland OH U.S.A.
174 E5 Polanica-Zdrój Pol.
175 J5 Połaniec Pol.
174 E1 Polanów Pol.
224 D2 Polar Bear Provincial Park Ont. Can.
262 V1 Polar Plateau Antarctica
263 E2 Polar Times Glacier Antarctica
128 F2 Polatbey Turkey
Polathane Turkey see Akçaabat
126 F4 Polatlı Turkey
138 L6 Polatsk Belarus
138 L6 Polatskaya Nizina lowland Belarus
114 G4 Polavaram Andhra Prad. India
134 L4 Polazna Rus. Fed.
169 D10 Polch Ger.
260 B5 Polcura Chile
174 G1 Połczyno Pol.
174 E2 Połczyn Zdrój Pol.
134 I3 Poldarsa Rus. Fed.
122 A2 Pol Dasht Iran
123 M5 Pol-e 'Alam Afgh.
93 G5 Polee i. Papua Indon.
122 E7 Pol-e Fāsā Iran
151 M6 Polegate East Sussex, England U.K.
123 I3 Pol-e Khatum Iran
123 M4 Pol-e Khomrī Afgh.
186 E4 Poleñino Spain
176 D1 Polepy Czech Rep.
122 E3 Pol-e Safid Iran
191 L6 Polesella Italy
191 K6 Polesine reg. Italy
191 M6 Polesine, Isola di i. Italy
175 L4 Poleski Park Narodowy nat. park Pol.
138 E7 Polessk Rus. Fed.
151 I2 Polesworth Warwickshire, England U.K.
Poles'ye marsh Belarus/Ukr. see Pripet Marshes
137 U2 Poletayevo Rus. Fed.
137 P2 Polevaya Rus. Fed.
93 A5 Polewali Sulawesi Barat Indon.
114 G9 Polgahawela Sri Lanka
177 K4 Polgár Hungary
179 J7 Polhograjsko Hribovje mts Slovenia
207 I4 Poli Cameroon
107 P9 Poli Shandong China
Poli Cyprus see Polis
195 K6 Polia Italy
Políaigos i. Greece see Polyaigos
175 H6 Polica mt. Pol.
198 B2 Poliçan Albania
262 T3 Policarpo Arg.
193 P8 Policastro, Golfo di b. Italy
174 C2 Police Pol.
217 □2b Police, Pointe pt Mahé Seychelles
176 F1 Police nad Metuj Czech Rep.
199 H3 Polichnitos Lesvos Greece
176 F2 Polička Czech Rep.
195 L3 Policoro Italy
175 J4 Policzna Pol.
Polídhrosos Greece see Polydrosos
183 M3 Polientes Spain
161 D6 Polignac France
195 M2 Polignano a Mare Italy
160 H3 Poligny France
Políkastron Greece see Polykastro
Polikhnítos Lesvos Greece see Polichnitos
197 N7 Polikrayshte Bulg.
92 C4 Polillo i. Phil.
92 D4 Polillo Islands Phil.
92 C4 Polillo Strait Phil.
128 A3 Polis Cyprus
136 I2 Polis'ke Kyivs'ka Oblast' Ukr.
136 F3 Polis'ke Rivnens'ka Oblast' Ukr.
136 H3 Polis'ke Zhytomyrs'ka Oblast' Ukr.
136 H2 Polis'kyy Zapovidnyk nature res. Ukr.
156 H7 Polisot France
139 O3 Polist' r. Rus. Fed.
195 K7 Polistena Italy
139 N4 Polisto, Ozero l. Rus. Fed.
137 S6 Politotdel'skoye Rus. Fed.
134 J2 Politovo Rus. Fed.
168 J3 Pölitz Ger.
139 V7 Polivanovo Rus. Fed.
Políyiros Greece see Polygyros
194 G8 Polizzi Generosa Sicilia Italy
179 J7 Poljane Slovenia
179 M7 Poljčane Slovenia
232 F7 Polk PA U.S.A.
138 J5 Polkorona Latvia
174 E4 Polkowice Pol.
193 O6 Polla Italy
114 E7 Pollachi Tamil Nadu India
Pollard Islands HI U.S.A. see Gardner Pinnacles
179 M5 Pöllau Austria
179 M5 Pöllauberg Austria
179 M5 Pöllauer Tal nature res. Austria
169 H7 Polle Ger.
171 E7 Polleben Ger.
187 L8 Pollença Spain
187 L8 Pollença, Badia de b. Spain
173 K4 Pollenfeld Ger.
Pollensa Spain see Pollença
169 H6 Pollhagen Ger.
160 G4 Polliat France
193 O7 Pollica Italy
194 G8 Pollina Sicilia Italy
194 G7 Pollina r. Sicilia Italy
173 K6 Polling Bayern Ger.
173 N5 Polling Bayern Ger.
193 Q8 Pollino, Monte mt. Italy
193 Q8 Pollino, Parco Nazionale del nat. park Italy
170 E5 Pollitz Ger.
146 E9 Polloch Highland, Scotland U.K.
92 D8 Polloc Harbour b. Mindanao Phil.
240 L3 Pollock Pines CA U.S.A.
87 G13 Pollock Reef W.A. Austr.
80 I4 Pollok North I. N.Z.
183 J6 Pollos Spain
81 C11 Pollux mt. South I. N.Z.
140 S1 Polmak Norway
161 B7 Polminhac France
146 I11 Polmont Falkirk, Scotland U.K.
176 E2 Polná Czech Rep.
137 P2 Polnaya r. Rus. Fed.
174 F2 Polnica Pol.
130 H3 Polnovat Rus. Fed.
140 T4 Polo Fin.
226 E8 Polo IL U.S.A.
79 □8a Polo'a i. Tonga
Poloat atoll Micronesia see Puluwat
Pologi Ukr. see Polohy
137 P6 Polohy Ukr.
213 F4 Polokwane Limpopo S. Africa
134 J4 Polom Rus. Fed.
139 P4 Polomet' r. Rus. Fed.
92 E8 Polomoloc Mindanao Phil.
114 G9 Polonnaruwa Sri Lanka
136 G3 Polonne Ukr.
Polonnoye Ukr. see Polonne
185 M7 Polopos Spain
179 O6 Pölöske Hungary
139 S7 Polotnyanyy Zavod Rus. Fed.
Polotsk Belarus see Polatsk
Polovinka Rus. Fed. see Ugleural'skiy
197 L5 Polovragi Romania
260 B3 Polpaico Chile
150 C7 Polperro Cornwall, England U.K.
179 K5 Pöls Austria
179 K5 Pöls r. Austria
164 G5 Polsbroek Neth.
173 J4 Polsingen Ger.
Polska country Europe see Poland
179 M7 Polskava r. Slovenia
197 N7 Polski Trŭmbesh Bulg.
238 G3 Polson MT U.S.A.
134 H2 Polta r. Rus. Fed.
177 I3 Poltár Slovakia
137 N4 Poltava Ukr.
Poltava Oblast admin. div. Ukr. see Poltavs'ka Oblast'
121 N1 Poltavka Omskaya Oblast' Rus. Fed.
100 G6 Poltavka Primorskiy Kray Rus. Fed.
137 Q5 Poltavka Donets'ka Oblast' Ukr.
137 L5 Poltavka Kirovohrads'ka Oblast' Ukr.
137 P6 Poltavka Zaporiz'ka Oblast' Ukr.
137 M4 Poltavs'ka Oblast' admin. div. Ukr.
135 G7 Poltavskaya Rus. Fed.
Poltavskaya Oblast' admin. div. Ukr. see Poltavs'ka Oblast'
Poltoratsk Turkm. see Aşgabat
138 I3 Põltsamaa Estonia
138 J3 Põltsamaa r. Estonia
121 M1 Poludino Kazakh.
136 C3 Południoworoztoczański Park Krajobrazowy Pol.
174 D3 Połupin Pol.
114 F6 Polur Tamil Nadu India
176 D3 Poluška hill Czech Rep.
138 K3 Põlva Estonia
239 K9 Polvadera NM U.S.A.
260 C3 Polvaredos Arg.
191 O8 Polverigi Italy
192 I1 Polvese, Isola i. Italy
140 T5 Polvijärvi Fin.
243 N8 Polvoxal Mex.
146 L11 Polwarth Scottish Borders, Scotland U.K.
139 W6 Polya r. Rus. Fed.
198 F6 Polyaigos i. Greece
136 B5 Polyana Ukr.
Polyanovgrad Bulg. see Karnobat
138 M1 Polyany Rus. Fed.
Polyarnoye Rus. Fed. see Russkoye Ust'ye
131 S3 Polyarnyy Chukotskiy Avtonomnyy Okrug Rus. Fed.
140 V2 Polyarnyy Murmanskaya Oblast' Rus. Fed.
140 V3 Polyarnyye Zori Rus. Fed.
134 M2 Polyarnyy Ural mts Rus. Fed.
198 D4 Polydrosos Greece
198 E2 Polygyros Greece
198 F6 Polyialgou-Folegandrou, Steno sea chan. Greece
198 D2 Polykastro Greece
266 H6 Polynesia is Oceania
Polynésie Française terr. S. Pacific Ocean see French Polynesia
175 N4 Polytsi Ukr.
179 L7 Polzela Slovenia
171 F9 Pölzig Ger.
194 E8 Poma, Lago l. Sicilia Italy
252 A2 Pomabamba Peru
81 D13 Pomahaka r. South I. N.Z.
250 B6 Pomahuaca Peru
183 M2 Pomaluengo Spain
258 D3 Pomán Arg.
191 J9 Pomarance Italy
184 D5 Pomarão Port.
163 C8 Pomarez France
195 L2 Pomarico Italy
141 Q6 Pomarkku Fin.
177 I4 Pomáz Hungary
257 F4 Pomba r. Brazil
251 H5 Pombal Pará Brazil
254 F3 Pombal Paraíba Brazil
182 F6 Pombal Bragança Port.
182 C9 Pombal Leiria Port.
251 F6 Pombas r. Brazil
206 □ Pombas Cape Verde
256 A4 Pombo r. Brazil
161 G10 Pomègues, Île i. France
213 G4 Pomene Moz.
183 Q5 Pomer Spain
174 C1 Pomeranian Bay Pol.
215 O4 Pomeroy S. Africa
147 I3 Pomeroy Northern Ireland U.K.
232 C9 Pomeroy OH U.S.A.
234 D5 Pomeroy PA U.S.A.
238 F3 Pomeroy WA U.S.A.
177 L5 Pomezeu Romania
176 F2 Pomezí Czech Rep.
193 J4 Pomezia Italy
214 H1 Pomfret S. Africa
137 K5 Pomichna Ukr.
175 I3 Pomiechówek Pol.
91 L8 Pomio New Britain P.N.G.
160 F2 Pommard France
158 E4 Pommerit-Jaudy France
173 J2 Pommersfelden Ger.
140 S3 Pomokaira reg. Fin.
85 N9 Pomona Qld Austr.
243 O9 Pomona Belize
212 B5 Pomona Namibia
240 O7 Pomona CA U.S.A.
234 F6 Pomona NJ U.S.A.
260 E6 Pomono Arg.
197 P8 Pomorie Bulg.
174 F1 Pomorskie prov. Pol.
174 F2 Pomorskie, Pojezierze reg. Pol.
134 F2 Pomorskiy Bereg coastal area Rus. Fed.
134 J1 Pomorskiy Proliv sea chan. Rus. Fed.
174 D3 Pomorsko Pol.
191 L6 Po Morto di Primaro watercourse Italy
128 A3 Pomos Point Cyprus
Pomo Tso l. China see Puma Yumco
Pomou, Akra pt Cyprus see Pomos Point
134 K3 Pomozdino Rus. Fed.
111 K11 Pompain Xizang China
162 D2 Pompaire France
193 N6 Pompei Italy
256 B5 Pompéia Brazil
257 E3 Pompéu Brazil
157 L6 Pompey France
100 G4 Pompeyevka Rus. Fed.
238 K3 Pompeys Pillar National Monument nat. park MT U.S.A.
161 D9 Pompignan France
235 G2 Pompton Lakes NJ U.S.A.
174 F1 Pomysk Mały Pol.
Ponape atoll Micronesia see Pohnpei
223 M4 Ponask Lake Ont. Can.
134 I4 Ponazyrevo Rus. Fed.
236 G4 Ponca NE U.S.A.
237 G7 Ponca City OK U.S.A.
247 □1 Ponce Puerto Rico
231 G13 Ponce de Leon Bay FL U.S.A.
239 K7 Poncha Springs CO U.S.A.
224 E3 Poncheville, Lac l. Que. Can.
160 G4 Poncin France
244 E5 Poncitlán Mex.
86 H3 Pond, Cape W.A. Austr.
114 D5 Ponda Goa India
237 G7 Pond Creek OK U.S.A.
234 F2 Pond Eddy NY U.S.A.
151 L2 Pondersbridge Cambridgeshire, England U.K.
114 F7 Pondicherry Pondicherry India
114 F7 Pondicherry union terr. India
Pondichéry Pondicherry India see Pondicherry
221 K2 Pond Inlet Nunavut Can.
215 N7 Pondoland reg. S. Africa
179 H3 Pöndorf Austria
225 K2 Ponds, Island of Nfld and Lab. Can.
Ponds Bay Nunavut Can. see Pond Inlet
97 H7 Pơ Ne, Đak r. Vietnam
242 □P11 Poneloya Nic.
190 D8 Ponente, Riviera di coastal area Italy
78 □5 Ponérihouen New Caledonia
78 □4a Pones i. Chuuk Micronesia
137 S9 Ponezhukay Rus. Fed.
182 G3 Ponferrada Spain
80 K4 Pongakawa North I. N.Z.
208 A4 Pongara, Pointe pt Gabon
80 K7 Pongaroa North I. N.Z.
179 H5 Pongau val. Austria
117 O6 Pong-Chaa Arun. Prad. India
111 L11 Pongda Xizang China
208 E3 Pongo watercourse Sudan
250 B6 Pongo de Manseriche gorge Peru
215 P3 Pongola S. Africa
215 Q2 Pongola r. S. Africa
215 P3 Pongolapoort Dam l. S. Africa
215 P3 Pongolapoort Public Resort Nature Reserve S. Africa
206 E4 Pong Tamale Ghana
175 K4 Poniatowa Pol.
175 H2 Poniatowo Pol.
174 E4 Poniec Pol.
93 C3 Poniki, Gunung mt. Indon.
177 I3 Poniky Slovakia
93 B4 Ponindilisa, Tanjung pt Indon.
136 G3 Poninka Ukr.
177 H3 Ponitrie park Slovakia
171 F9 Ponitz Ger.
139 O6 Ponizov'ye Rus. Fed.
96 A4 Ponnagyun Myanmar
114 F7 Ponnaivar r. India
114 D6 Ponnampet Karnataka India
114 D7 Ponnani Kerala India
114 D7 Ponnani r. India
114 G6 Ponneri Tamil Nadu India
96 B3 Ponnyadaung Range mts Myanmar
222 H4 Ponoka Alta Can.
120 F1 Ponomarevka Rus. Fed.
137 L2 Ponornytsya Ukr.
95 I8 Ponorogo Jawa Indon.
134 H2 Ponoy Rus. Fed.
134 H2 Ponoy r. Rus. Fed.
225 G1 Pons r. Que. Can.
162 C4 Pons France
Pons Spain see Ponts
191 J8 Ponsacco Italy
92 E6 Ponson i. Phil.
182 F9 Ponsul r. Port.
160 E2 Pont, Lac de l. France
184 □ Ponta Madeira
165 F7 Pont-à-Celles Belgium
163 D9 Pontacq France
216 □1b Ponta Delgada São Miguel Azores
184 □ Ponta Delgada Madeira
254 C2 Ponta de Pedras Brazil
184 □ Ponta do Pargo Madeira
206 □ Ponta do Sol Cape Verde
184 □ Ponta do Sol Madeira
216 □1b Ponta Garça São Miguel Azores
256 B6 Ponta Grossa Brazil
160 G2 Pontailler-sur-Saône France
161 G7 Pontaix France
256 C4 Pontal Brazil
257 H3 Pontal do Ipiranga Brazil
256 C2 Pontalina Brazil
156 F2 Pont-à-Marcq France
157 L6 Pont-à-Mousson France
261 G5 Pontant Arg.
254 C3 Pontão Brazil
253 G5 Ponta Porã Brazil
150 E4 Pontardawe Neath Port Talbot, Wales U.K.
150 D4 Pontarddulais Swansea, Wales U.K.
Pontardulais Swansea, Wales U.K. see Pontarddulais
Pontarfynach Ceredigion, Wales U.K. see Devil's Bridge
162 H4 Pontarion France
160 I3 Pontarlier France
191 K8 Pontassieve Italy
158 I4 Pontaubault France
159 M3 Pont-Audemer France
160 B5 Pontaumur France
158 D6 Pont-Aven France
224 E3 Pontax r. Que. Can.
190 D5 Pont-Canavese Italy
161 I6 Pontcharra France
237 J10 Pontchartrain, Lake LA U.S.A.
158 G7 Pontchâteau France
158 C5 Pont-Croix France
160 G4 Pont-d'Ain France
158 C5 Pont-de-Buis-lès-Quimerch France
160 G5 Pont-de-Chéruy France
163 I8 Pont-de-Larn France
161 F6 Pont-de-l'Isère France
165 G8 Pont-de-Loup Belgium
160 H3 Pont-de-Poitte France
160 J2 Pont-de-Roide France
161 B8 Pont-de-Salars France
186 G3 Pont de Suert Spain
160 F4 Pont-de-Vaux France
160 F4 Pont-de-Veyle France
161 D8 Pont-d'Hérault France
159 K4 Pont-d'Ouilly France
163 F7 Pont-du-Casse France
160 C5 Pont-du-Château France
161 F9 Pont du Gard tourist site France
160 H3 Pont-du-Navoy France
193 N5 Ponte Italy
182 D6 Ponte Port.
254 D4 Ponte Alta do Norte Brazil
182 E2 Ponte Aranga Spain
182 D4 Ponteareas Spain
191 O2 Pontebba Italy
256 A2 Ponte Branca Brazil
182 D4 Ponte Caldelas Spain
182 C2 Ponteceso Spain
190 C6 Pontechianale Italy
193 L5 Pontecorvo Italy
190 F6 Pontecurone Italy
182 D5 Ponte da Barca Port.
190 E8 Pontedassio Italy
182 C5 Ponte de Lima Port.
190 H6 Ponte dell'Olio Italy
253 F3 Ponte de Pedra Brazil
191 J8 Pontedera Italy
184 C2 Ponte de Sor Port.
182 D2 Pontedeume Spain
182 C8 Ponte de Vagos Port.
178 C7 Ponte di Legno Italy
191 M4 Ponte di Piave Italy
255 B6 Ponte do Rio Verde Brazil
184 A2 Ponte do Rol Port.
256 D3 Ponte Firme Brazil
149 O6 Pontefract West Yorkshire, England U.K.
191 L2 Ponte Gardena Italy
223 J5 Ponteix Sask. Can.
149 N3 Ponteland Northumberland, England U.K.
193 N5 Pontelandolfo Italy
192 C3 Ponte-Leccia Corse France
191 M5 Pontelongo Italy
191 M3 Ponte nelle Alpi Italy
190 H4 Ponte Nossa Italy
257 F4 Ponte Nova Brazil
191 K3 Ponte Nova Italy
161 G6 Pont-en-Royans France
190 H5 Pontenure Italy
163 B7 Pontenx-les-Forges France
150 E3 Ponterwyd Ceredigion, Wales U.K.
184 B3 Pontes Port.
191 L5 Ponte San Nicolò Italy
190 H4 Ponte San Pietro Italy
150 G2 Pontesbury Shropshire, England U.K.
178 F7 Pontesei, Lago di l. Italy
253 F3 Pontes-e-Lacerda Brazil
182 C3 Ponte Valga Spain
182 C4 Pontevedra Spain
182 D4 Pontevedra prov. Spain
182 C4 Pontevedra, Ría de est. Spain
184 B2 Pontével Port.
160 F5 Pont-Évêque France
190 I5 Pontevico Italy
159 I4 Pont-Farcy France
156 H5 Pontfaverger-Moronvilliers France
160 B5 Pontgibaud France
159 I3 Pont-Hébert France
Ponthierville Dem. Rep. Congo see Ubundu
156 C3 Ponthieu reg. France
226 F9 Pontiac IL U.S.A.
227 K7 Pontiac MI U.S.A.
Pontiae is Italy see Ponziane, Isole
95 H5 Pontianak Kalimantan Indon.
156 G8 Pontigny France
Pontine Islands is Italy see Ponziane, Isole
193 K5 Pontinia Italy
158 F5 Pontivy France
158 C6 Pont-l'Abbé France
162 C4 Pont-l'Abbé-d'Arnoult France
157 I7 Pont-la-Ville France
160 I2 Pont-les-Moulins France
159 L3 Pont-l'Évêque France
159 N7 Pontlevoy France
159 I5 Pontmain France
257 G3 Pontões Capixabas, Parque Nacional dos nat. park Brazil
251 H4 Pontoetoe Suriname
156 D5 Pontoise France
87 G10 Ponton watercourse W.A. Austr.
223 L4 Ponton Man. Can.
183 J2 Pontón, Puerto del pass Spain
185 N4 Pontones Spain
163 C8 Pontonx-sur-l'Adour France
147 D5 Pontoon Ireland
158 H4 Pontorson France
129 D4 Pontos Mucha Nakrdzali nature res. Georgia
237 K8 Pontotoc MS U.S.A.
158 H5 Pont-Péan France
156 E5 Pontpoint France
190 H7 Pontremoli Italy
190 H3 Pontresina Switz.
150 E3 Pontrhydfendigaid Ceredigion, Wales U.K.
158 E4 Pontrieux France
150 G4 Pontrilas Herefordshire, England U.K.
186 H4 Ponts Spain
156 H7 Pont-Ste-Marie France
156 E5 Pont-Ste-Maxence France
161 F8 Pont-St-Esprit France
190 D4 Pont-St-Martin Italy
158 E6 Pont-Scorff France
150 F4 Pontsticill Reservoir Wales U.K.
156 G6 Pont-sur-Seine France
156 F7 Pont-sur-Yonne France
159 L6 Pontvallain France
150 D4 Pontyberem Carmarthenshire, Wales U.K.
227 P5 Pontypool Ont. Can.
150 F4 Pontypool Torfaen, Wales U.K.
150 F4 Pontypridd Rhondda Cynon Taff, Wales U.K.
80 J3 Ponui Island North I. N.Z.
137 R8 Ponura r. Rus. Fed.
137 L1 Ponurovka Rus. Fed.
139 P8 Ponyatovka Rus. Fed.
139 T9 Ponyri Rus. Fed.
193 J6 Ponza Italy
193 J6 Ponza, Isola di i. Italy
193 J6 Ponziane, Isole is Italy
190 E6 Ponzone Italy
190 E4 Ponzone r. Italy
82 E5 Poochera S.A. Austr.
209 B5 Pool admin. reg. Congo
149 N6 Pool West Yorkshire, England U.K.
81 D12 Poolburn Reservoir South I. N.Z.
247 □7 Poole Trin. and Tob.
151 I6 Poole Poole, England U.K.
151 I6 Poole admin. div. England U.K.
151 I6 Poole Bay England U.K.
146 E7 Poolewe Highland, Scotland U.K.
149 L4 Pooley Bridge Cumbria, England U.K.
82 F2 Poolowanna Lake salt flat S.A. Austr.
Poona Mahar. India see Pune
83 I5 Pooncarie N.S.W. Austr.
87 D9 Poondarrie, Mount hill W.A. Austr.
83 J4 Poopelloe Lake N.S.W. Austr.
252 D4 Poopó Bol.
252 D4 Poopó, Lago de l. Bol.
80 I2 Poor Knights Islands North I. N.Z.
121 N7 Pop Uzbek.
246 B9 Popa, Isla i. Panama
96 B4 Popa Mountain Myanmar
137 R5 Popasna Ukr.
Popasnaya Ukr. see Popasna
137 O5 Popasne Dnipropetrovs'ka Oblast' Ukr.
137 Q4 Popasne Kharkivs'ka Oblast' Ukr.
250 B4 Popayán Col.
138 E4 Pope Latvia
137 M5 Popel'naste Ukr.
165 C7 Poperinge Belgium
232 I10 Popes Creek MD U.S.A.
174 F5 Popielów Pol.
131 L2 Popigay r. Rus. Fed.
136 I4 Popil'nya Ukr.
83 H5 Popilta Lake imp. l. N.S.W. Austr.
83 H5 Popio Lake N.S.W. Austr.
137 M3 Popivka Ukr.
223 L4 Poplar r. Man. Can.
222 G2 Poplar r. N.W.T. Can.
238 L2 Poplar MT U.S.A.
226 C3 Poplar WI U.S.A.
238 L2 Poplar r. MT U.S.A.
238 L2 Poplar, West Fork r. MT U.S.A.
237 J7 Poplar Bluff MO U.S.A.
232 E12 Poplar Camp VA U.S.A.
232 B10 Poplar Plains KY U.S.A.
237 K10 Poplarville MS U.S.A.
139 X8 Poplevino Rus. Fed.
139 W8 Poplevinskiy Rus. Fed.
245 I6 Popocatépetl, Volcán vol. Mex.
95 I9 Popoh Jawa Indon.
209 C6 Popokabaka Dem. Rep. Congo
193 L3 Popoli Italy
78 □6 Popomanaseu, Mount Guadalcanal Solomon Is
91 K8 Popondetta P.N.G.
188 F3 Popovača Croatia
Popovichskaya Rus. Fed. see Kalininskaya
139 U2 Popovka Rus. Fed.
197 O7 Popovo Bulg.
188 F4 Popovo Polje plain Bos.-Herz.
197 O8 Popovska Reka r. Bulg.
175 H3 Popów Łódzkie Pol.
174 G4 Popów Śląskie Pol.
173 L3 Poppberg hill Ger.
169 K7 Poppenberg hill Ger.
169 J10 Poppenhausen Ger.
169 I10 Poppenhausen (Wasserkuppe) Ger.
173 L3 Poppenricht Ger.
191 L8 Poppi Italy
175 I6 Poprad r. Pol.
177 J2 Poprad Slovakia
177 J2 Popradzki Park Krajobrazowy Pol.
177 J3 Poproč Slovakia
243 O9 Poptún Guat.
192 E2 Populonia Italy
129 C1 Poputnaya Rus. Fed.
235 K2 Poquetanuck CT U.S.A.
252 D5 Poquis, Nevado de mt. Chile
235 K2 Poquonock Bridge CT U.S.A.
233 I11 Poquoson VA U.S.A.
175 L5 Por r. Pol.
175 H6 Porąbka Pol.
175 H5 Poraj Pol.
123 L9 Porali r. Pak.
80 K7 Porangahau North I. N.Z.
254 C5 Porangatu Brazil
138 H9 Porazava Belarus
116 B9 Porbandar Gujarat India
191 J8 Porcari Italy
123 J5 Por Chaman Afgh.
222 D4 Porcher Island B.C. Can.
191 N4 Porcia Italy
156 H4 Porcien reg. France
257 F4 Porciúncula Brazil
252 D4 Porco Bol.
177 L4 Porcsalma Hungary
185 K5 Porcuna Spain
220 D3 Porcupine r. Can./U.S.A.
225 J2 Porcupine, Cape Nfld and Lab. Can.
264 H2 Porcupine Abyssal Plain sea feature N. Atlantic Ocean
85 J6 Porcupine Creek r. Qld Austr.
238 K2 Porcupine Creek r. MT U.S.A.
85 J6 Porcupine Gorge National Park Qld Austr.
223 K4 Porcupine Hills Man./Sask. Can.
226 E3 Porcupine Mountains MI U.S.A.
223 K4 Porcupine Plain Sask. Can.
223 K4 Porcupine Provincial Forest nature res. Sask. Can.
191 N4 Pordenone Italy
191 N3 Pordenone prov. Italy
158 F4 Pordic France
197 M7 Pordim Bulg.
250 D3 Pore Col.
188 D3 Poreč Croatia
256 B5 Porecatu Brazil

Presa to Punjab

372

182 D9 Presa Port.
244 G3 Presa de Guadalupe Mex.
243 I3 Presa de la Amistad, Parque Natural nature res. Mex.
161 E7 Présailles France
160 J5 Pre-St-Didier Italy
191 J3 Presanella, Cima mt. Italy
243 I5 Presa San Antonio Mex.
Prescelly Mts hills Wales U.K. see Preseli, Mynydd
149 L7 Prescot Merseyside, England U.K.
224 F4 Prescott Ont. Can.
237 I9 Prescott AR U.S.A.
241 T7 Prescott AZ U.S.A.
226 B5 Prescott WI U.S.A.
237 P1 Prescott Valley AZ U.S.A.
150 C4 Preseli, Mynydd hills Wales U.K.
81 A13 Preservation Inlet South I. N.Z.
197 J8 Preševo Serbia
236 E4 Presho SD U.S.A.
195 O4 Presicce Italy
258 F2 Presidencia Roca Arg.
258 E2 Presidencia Roque Sáenz Peña Arg.
256 C5 Presidente Alves Brazil
256 B5 Presidente Bernardes Brazil
258 F2 Presidente de la Plaza Arg.
254 D3 Presidente Dutra Brazil
262 U2 Presidente Eduardo Frei research stn Antarctica
256 A4 Presidente Epitácio Brazil
253 E2 Presidente Hermes Brazil
Presidente Juan Perón prov. Arg. see Chaco
257 E3 Presidente Juscelino Brazil
256 D3 Presidente Olegário Brazil
256 B5 Presidente Prudente Brazil
256 B4 Presidente Venceslau Brazil
246 A2 Presidio r. Mex.
239 L12 Presidio TX U.S.A.
Preslav Bulg. see Veliki Preslav
121 L1 Presnovka Kazakh.
190 I4 Presolana, Pizzo della mt. Italy
177 K3 Prešov Slovakia
177 K2 Prešovský kraj admin. reg. Slovakia
198 C2 Prespa, Lake Europe
Prespansko Ezero l. Europe see Prespa, Lake
198 C2 Prespes nat. park Greece
Prespës, Liqeni i l. Europe see Prespa, Lake
233 □Q2 Presque Isle ME U.S.A.
227 K4 Presque Isle MI U.S.A.
226 E3 Presque Isle WI U.S.A.
226 G3 Presque Isle Point MI U.S.A.
162 F3 Pressac France
173 L2 Pressath Ger.
179 N3 Pressbaum Austria
Pressburg Slovakia see Bratislava
171 E10 Presseck Ger.
179 H6 Pressegger See l. Austria
171 G7 Pressel Ger.
171 D10 Pressig Ger.
150 F1 Prestatyn Denbighshire, Wales U.K.
149 M7 Prestbury Cheshire, England U.K.
150 H4 Prestbury Gloucestershire, England U.K.
206 E5 Prestea Ghana
142 H3 Prestebakke Norway
150 F3 Presteigne Powys, Wales U.K.
176 C2 Preštice Czech Rep.
150 H6 Preston Dorset, England U.K.
149 Q6 Preston East Riding of Yorkshire, England U.K.
149 L6 Preston Lancashire, England U.K.
146 L11 Preston Scottish Borders, Scotland U.K.
231 E9 Preston GA U.S.A.
238 I5 Preston ID U.S.A.
233 J10 Preston MD U.S.A.
226 B6 Preston MN U.S.A.
237 I7 Preston MO U.S.A.
86 D6 Preston, Cape W.A. Austr.
149 L2 Prestonpans East Lothian, Scotland U.K.
232 C11 Prestonsburg KY U.S.A.
262 N1 Prestrud Inlet Antarctica
149 M6 Prestwich Greater Manchester, England U.K.
146 G12 Prestwick South Ayrshire, Scotland U.K.
256 B3 Preto r. Brazil
256 C4 Preto r. Brazil
256 D2 Preto r. Brazil
253 E2 Preto r. Brazil
254 E4 Preto r. Brazil
251 E5 Preto r. Brazil
251 F5 Preto r. Brazil
215 M1 Pretoria S. Africa
Pretoria-Witwatersrand-Vereeniging prov. S. Africa see Gauteng
171 G7 Prettin Ger.
234 B5 Prettyboy Lake MD U.S.A.
173 K2 Pretzfeld Ger.
170 D5 Pretzier Ger.
171 G7 Pretzsch Ger.
171 F7 Pretzschendorf Ger.
159 M8 Preuilly-sur-Claise France
Preussisch-Eylau Rus. Fed. see Bagrationovsk
169 G6 Preußisch Oldendorf Ger.
Preußisch Stargard Pol. see Starogard Gdański
179 K6 Prevalje Slovenia
161 D7 Prévenchères France
162 I3 Préveranges France
198 B4 Preveza Greece
97 G9 Prey Vêng Cambodia
179 K7 Prežganje Slovenia
191 R4 Prezid Croatia
157 J7 Prez-sous-Lafauche France
178 D8 Priafora, Monte mt. Italy
100 I4 Priamurskiy Rus. Fed.
120 J4 Priaral'skiye Karakumy, Peski des. Kazakh.
182 G3 Priaranza del Bierzo Spain
107 P1 Priargunsk Rus. Fed.
137 R8 Priazovskaya Rus. Fed.
177 H4 Pribeta Slovakia
176 F3 Příbice Czech Rep.
220 A4 Pribilof Islands AK U.S.A.
188 F3 Pribinić Bos.-Herz.
179 N7 Pribislavec Croatia
196 H7 Priboj Serbia
177 H2 Příbor Czech Rep.
170 G4 Priborn Ger.
176 D2 Příbram Czech Rep.
175 I1 Pribreznoye Rus. Fed.
176 E2 Příbyslav Czech Rep.
84 C3 Price r. N.T. Austr.
225 G3 Price Que. Can.
232 F12 Price NC U.S.A.
241 V2 Price UT U.S.A.
241 V2 Price r. UT U.S.A.
222 D4 Price Island B.C. Can.
138 E6 Prichaly Rus. Fed.
237 K10 Prichard AL U.S.A.
232 C10 Prichard WV U.S.A.
173 I2 Prichsenstadt Ger.
247 □6 Prickly Point Grenada
183 P8 Priego Spain
185 K6 Priego de Córdoba Spain
138 E5 Priekule Latvia
138 E6 Priekulė Lith.
138 I4 Priekuļi Latvia
138 G7 Prienai Kaunas Lith.
138 I7 Prienai Vilnius Lith.
173 M6 Prien am Chiemsee Ger.
171 I6 Prieros Ger.
214 G5 Prieska S. Africa
214 G5 Prieskapoort pass S. Africa
171 G8 Prießnitz Sachsen Ger.
171 E8 Prießnitz Sachsen-Anhalt Ger.
171 I8 Priestewitz Ger.
Priestholm i. Wales U.K. see Puffin Island
238 F2 Priest Lake ID U.S.A.
246 □ Priestman's River Jamaica
183 K2 Prieta, Peña mt. Spain
185 J7 Prieta, Sierra mt. Spain
185 M3 Prieto hill Spain
176 G3 Prievaly Slovakia
177 H3 Prievidza Slovakia
170 F4 Prignitz reg. Ger.
139 Q8 Prigor'ye Rus. Fed.
188 F3 Prijedor Bos.-Herz.
196 H7 Prijepolje Serbia
120 A5 Prikaspiyskaya Nizmennost' lowland Kazakh./Rus. Fed.
206 E5 Prikro Côte d'Ivoire
137 R8 Prikubanskaya Nizmennost' lowland Rus. Fed.
197 J9 Prilep Macedonia
Priluki Ukr. see Pryluky
187 H10 Prima, Punta pt Spain
252 D2 Primavera Bol.
254 B5 Primavera do Leste Brazil
176 B2 Přimda Czech Rep.
254 E2 Primeira Cruz Brazil
158 D4 Primel, Pointe de pt France
261 F2 Primero r. Arg.
246 D3 Primero de Enero Cuba
236 H4 Primghar IA U.S.A.
191 L4 Primolano Italy
175 I1 Primorsk Kaliningradskaya Oblast' Rus. Fed.
138 L1 Primorsk Leningradskaya Oblast' Rus. Fed.
135 I6 Primorsk Volgogradskaya Oblast' Rus. Fed.
Primorsk Ukr. see Prymors'k
100 G7 Primorskiy Rus. Fed.
100 I6 Primorskiy Kray admin. div. Rus. Fed.
135 G7 Primorsko-Akhtarsk Rus. Fed.
Primorskoye Ukr. see Prymors'ke
242 A1 Primo Tapia Mex.
222 B2 Primrose r. Y.T. Can.
223 I4 Primrose Lake Alta/Sask. Can.
172 B3 Prims r. Ger.
223 J4 Prince Albert Sask. Can.
214 G9 Prince Albert S. Africa
263 K1 Prince Albert Mountains Antarctica
223 J4 Prince Albert National Park Sask. Can.
220 G2 Prince Albert Peninsula N.W.T. Can.
214 F8 Prince Albert Road S. Africa
220 G2 Prince Albert Sound sea chan. N.W.T. Can.
220 F2 Prince Alfred, Cape N.W.T. Can.
214 D9 Prince Alfred Hamlet S. Africa
221 K3 Prince Charles Island Nunavut Can.
263 E2 Prince Charles Mountains Antarctica
225 I4 Prince Edward Island prov. Can.
265 G8 Prince Edward Islands Indian Ocean
227 R6 Prince Edward Point Ont. Can.
232 I10 Prince Frederick MD U.S.A.
86 H3 Prince Frederick Harbour W.A. Austr.
222 F4 Prince George B.C. Can.
234 B7 Prince George's County county MD U.S.A.
221 H2 Prince Gustaf Adolf Sea Nunavut Can.
263 C2 Prince Harald Coast Antarctica
220 B3 Prince of Wales, Cape AK U.S.A.
85 I1 Prince of Wales Island Qld Austr.
221 I2 Prince of Wales Island Nunavut Can.
220 E4 Prince of Wales Island AK U.S.A.
220 G2 Prince of Wales Strait N.W.T. Can.
220 G2 Prince Patrick Island N.W.T. Can.
86 H3 Prince Regent r. W.A. Austr.
221 I2 Prince Regent Inlet sea chan. Nunavut Can.
86 H3 Prince Regent Nature Reserve W.A. Austr.
222 D4 Prince Rupert B.C. Can.
247 □2 Prince Rupert Bay Dominica
151 K4 Princes Risborough Buckinghamshire, England U.K.
233 J10 Princess Anne MD U.S.A.
263 A2 Princess Astrid Coast Antarctica
85 I3 Princess Charlotte Bay Qld Austr.
263 F2 Princess Elizabeth Land reg. Antarctica
223 L1 Princess Mary Lake Nunavut Can.
86 H3 Princess May Range hills W.A. Austr.
81 B12 Princess Mountains South I. N.Z.
263 B2 Princess Ragnhild Coast Antarctica
87 F8 Princess Range hills W.A. Austr.
222 D4 Princess Royal Island B.C. Can.
247 □7 Prince's Town Trin. and Tob.
151 J3 Princethorpe Warwickshire, England U.K.
222 F5 Princeton B.C. Can.
240 J2 Princeton CA U.S.A.
226 E8 Princeton IL U.S.A.
230 D6 Princeton IN U.S.A.
230 D7 Princeton KY U.S.A.
233 □R3 Princeton ME U.S.A.
226 B5 Princeton MO U.S.A.
234 F4 Princeton NJ U.S.A.
226 E6 Princeton WI U.S.A.
232 D11 Princeton WV U.S.A.
234 F4 Princeton Junction NJ U.S.A.
150 E6 Princetown Devon, England U.K.
233 □R3 Prince William N.B. Can.
82 □2 Prince William Henry Bay Lord Howe I. Austr.
220 D3 Prince William Sound b. AK U.S.A.
207 G6 Príncipe i. São Tomé and Príncipe
238 D4 Prineville OR U.S.A.
198 F2 Prinos Thasos Greece
164 G5 Prinsenbeek Neth.
Prins Harald Kyst coastal area Antarctica see Prince Harald Coast
140 □ Prins Karls Forland i. Svalbard
137 Q3 Printseva Rus. Fed.
242 □R11 Prinzapolca Nic.
168 G5 Prinzhöfte Ger.
195 I9 Priolo Gargallo Sicilia Italy
82 □3 Prion Lake S. Pacific Ocean
182 D1 Prior, Cabo c. Spain
182 D2 Priorio Grande, Cabo c. Spain
183 K3 Prioro Spain
Priozernyy Kazakh. see Tugyl
139 N1 Priozersk Rus. Fed.
Priozyorsk Rus. Fed. see Priozersk
136 J2 Pripet r. Belarus/Ukr. alt. Pryp"yat' (Ukraine), alt. Prypyats' (Belarus)
136 D2 Pripet Marshes Belarus/Ukr.
111 K14 Priphema Nagaland India
134 L2 Pripolyarnyy Ural mts Rus. Fed.
197 P4 Priponeşti Romania
140 U2 Prirechnyy Rus. Fed.
197 P3 Prisăcani Romania
188 F3 Priseka hill Croatia
197 M3 Prislop, Pasul pass Romania
176 E1 Příšovice Czech Rep.
162 G2 Prissac France
160 F4 Prissé France
Pristan' Przheval'sk Kyrg. see Przheval'sk Pristany
137 P2 Pristen' Rus. Fed.
196 J8 Priština Kosovo Serbia
116 G7 Prithvipur Madh. Prad. India
173 J5 Prittriching Ger.
171 F6 Pritzerbe Ger.
170 D4 Pritzier Ger.
170 F4 Pritzwalk Ger.
161 F7 Privas France
170 H5 Priverno Italy
188 E3 Privlaka Croatia
139 S6 Privokzal'nyy Rus. Fed.
137 R7 Privol'naya Rus. Fed.
139 Y4 Privolzhsk Rus. Fed.
135 I6 Privolzhskaya Vozvyshennost' hills Rus. Fed.
135 I6 Privolzhskiy Rus. Fed.
120 A2 Privolzhskoye Rus. Fed.
120 C1 Privolzh'ye Rus. Fed.
135 H7 Privutnoye Rus. Fed.
196 I8 Prizren Kosovo Serbia
194 E8 Prizzi Sicilia Italy
188 F3 Prnjavor Bos.-Herz.
182 G3 Proaza Spain
197 K8 Probištip Macedonia
95 J8 Probolinggo Jawa Indon.
168 J2 Probsteierhagen Ger.
171 D9 Probstzella Ger.
150 C7 Probus Cornwall, England U.K.
190 F2 Proceno Italy
174 E4 Prochowice Pol.
193 M6 Procida Italy
193 M6 Procida, Isola di i. Italy
226 B3 Proctor MN U.S.A.
233 L5 Proctor VT U.S.A.
232 C10 Proctorville OH U.S.A.
114 F5 Proddatur Andhra Prad. India
182 E9 Proença-a-Nova Port.
182 F8 Proença-a-Velha Port.
171 F8 Profen Ger.
251 H3 Professor van Blommestein Meer resr Suriname
165 G8 Profondeville Belgium
191 J5 Progno r. Italy
261 G2 Progreso Arg.
243 I4 Progreso Coahuila Mex.
245 H5 Progreso Hidalgo Mex.
245 K9 Progreso Oaxaca Mex.
243 O7 Progreso Yucatán Mex.
244 D2 Progreso Zacatecas Mex.
262 F2 Progress research stn Antarctica
100 F4 Progress Rus. Fed.
252 C2 Progresso Brazil
170 H2 Prohn Ger.
238 C6 Project City CA U.S.A.
175 I1 Prokhladnaya r. Rus. Fed.
129 F2 Prokhladnyy Rus. Fed.
137 P2 Prokhorovka Rus. Fed.
137 L2 Prokhory Ukr.
196 H8 Prokletije mts Albania/Yugo.
168 F3 Prökoldt Ger.
130 J4 Prokop'yevsk Rus. Fed.
197 J7 Prokuplje Serbia
139 O3 Proletariy Rus. Fed.
135 H7 Proletarsk Rus. Fed.
Proletarskaya Rus. Fed. see Proletarsk
137 O3 Proletarskiy Rus. Fed.
Prome Myanmar see Pyè
234 E2 Promised Land Lake PA U.S.A.
253 G4 Promissão Mato Grosso do Sul Brazil
256 C4 Promissão São Paulo Brazil
256 C4 Promissão, Represa resr Brazil
175 I4 Promna Pol.
193 P4 Promontorio del Gargano plat. Italy
234 E1 Prompton PA U.S.A.
234 E1 Prompton Lake PA U.S.A.
134 H4 Pronino Rus. Fed.
169 E10 Pronsfeld Ger.
139 W7 Pronsk Rus. Fed.
168 J3 Pronstorf Ger.
139 O8 Pronya r. Belarus
222 F3 Prophet r. B.C. Can.
222 F3 Prophet River B.C. Can.
226 E8 Prophetstown IL U.S.A.
254 F4 Propriá Brazil
192 B4 Propriano Corse France
170 I2 Prorer Wiek b. Ger.
129 H1 Prorva r. Rus. Fed.
120 C3 Proryvnoye Rus. Fed.
176 F2 Prosek Czech Rep.
171 I8 Prösen Ger.
179 N6 Prosenjakovci Slovenia
146 K9 Prosen Water r. Scotland U.K.
85 L6 Proserpine Qld Austr.
138 L6 Proshkava Belarus
Proskurov Ukr. see Khmel'nyts'kyy
199 G2 Proskynites Greece
174 F3 Prosna r. Pol.
198 D1 Prosotsani Greece
235 J1 Prospect CT U.S.A.
233 J5 Prospect NY U.S.A.
232 B8 Prospect OH U.S.A.
238 C5 Prospect OR U.S.A.
232 E8 Prospect PA U.S.A.
235 G4 Prospect Plains NJ U.S.A.
246 □ Prospect Point Jamaica
92 E7 Prosperidad Mindanao Phil.
148 D7 Prosperous Ireland
216 □2b Prosperous Bay St Helena
196 G6 Prosperous Bay St Helena
216 □2b Prosser WA U.S.A.
176 G2 Prostějov Czech Rep.
175 K2 Prostki Pol.
85 M9 Proston Qld Austr.
121 O3 Prostornoye Kazakh.
134 K2 Prosunduy Rus. Fed.
137 O4 Prosyane Ukr.
174 F5 Prószków Pol.
175 I5 Proszowice Pol.
175 I4 Proszówki Pol.
214 E10 Protem S. Africa
198 C5 Proti i. Greece
176 F2 Protivanov Czech Rep.
176 D2 Protivín Czech Rep.
176 G2 Protivka r. Czech Rep.
137 P4 Protopopivka Ukr.
136 J3 Protsiv Ukr.
139 T6 Protva Rus. Fed.
139 U7 Protva r. Rus. Fed.
175 J2 Protviny Rus. Fed.
170 I5 Prötzel Ger.
197 P7 Provadiya Bulg.
Prøven Greenland see Kangersuatsiaq
184 B5 Provença Port.
161 G9 Provence airport France
161 I9 Provence-Alpes-Côte d'Azur admin. reg. France
157 N7 Provenchères-sur-Fave France
Providence MD U.S.A. see Annapolis
233 N7 Providence RI U.S.A.
81 A13 Providence, Cape South I. N.Z.
217 □2 Providence Atoll Seychelles
227 L4 Providence Bay Ont. Can.
250 B5 Providencia Ecuador
246 C7 Providencia, Isla de i. Caribbean Sea
253 E2 Providência, Serra de hills Brazil
246 G3 Providenciales Island Turks and Caicos Is
131 T3 Provideniya Rus. Fed.
85 I2 Providential Channel Qld Austr.
233 O6 Provincetown MA U.S.A.
250 C3 Provincia Col.
156 F6 Provins France
241 U1 Provo UT U.S.A.
223 I4 Provost Alta Can.
188 F4 Prozor Bos.-Herz.
139 U3 Prozorovo Rus. Fed.
196 I9 Prrenjas Albania
206 E4 Pru r. Ghana
134 K3 Prub r. Rus. Fed.
137 L8 Prubiynyy, Mys pt Ukr.
156 H5 Prucy France
256 B6 Prudentópolis Brazil
149 N4 Prudhoe Northumberland, England U.K.
220 D2 Prudhoe Bay AK U.S.A.
85 L6 Prudhoe Island Qld Austr.
137 N8 Prudki Ukr.
139 P7 Prudki Rus. Fed.
174 F5 Prudnik Pol.
137 P3 Prudyanka Ukr.
138 L6 Prudzinki Belarus
177 K3 Prügy Hungary
171 K10 Průhonice Czech Rep.
169 B10 Prüm Ger.
169 B11 Prüm r. Ger.
185 I7 Pruna Spain
197 M6 Prundeni Romania
197 O6 Prundu Romania
197 M3 Prundu Bârgăului Romania
Prundu Bârgăului Romania see Prundu Bârgăului
192 C3 Prunelli-di-Fiumorbo Corse France
163 I6 Prunet France
161 I7 Prunières France
159 O7 Pruniers-en-Sologne France
232 E9 Pruntytown WV U.S.A.
Prusa Turkey see Bursa
179 O2 Prušánky Czech Rep.
Prushkov Pol. see Pruszków
174 E4 Prusice Pol.
177 G2 Prusinovice Czech Rep.
174 G2 Pruszcz Pol.
143 O7 Pruszcz Gdański Pol.
175 I3 Pruszków Pol.
136 H8 Prut r. Europe
173 M6 Prutting Ger.
178 C5 Prutz Austria
138 H9 Pruzhany Belarus
177 O9 Pruzhinki Rus. Fed.
139 R2 Pružina Slovakia
179 I8 Prvačina Slovenia
188 E3 Prvić i. Croatia
137 O2 Pryamitsyno Rus. Fed.
137 O6 Pryazovs'ka Vysochyna hills Ukr.
137 O7 Pryazovs'ke Ukr.
137 L6 Prychornomors'ka Nyzovyna lowland Ukr.
263 F2 Prydz Bay Antarctica
129 D2 Pryelbrusskiy Natsional'nyy Park nat. park Rus. Fed.
137 Q3 Prykolotne Ukr.
137 L3 Pryluky Ukr.
137 P7 Prymors'k Ukr.
Prymors'ke Donets'ka Oblast' Ukr. see Sartana
137 M7 Prymors'ke Khersons'ka Oblast' Ukr.
136 I8 Prymors'ke Odes'ka Oblast' Ukr.
137 O6 Prymors'ke Zaporiz'ka Oblast' Ukr.
137 O8 Prymors'kyy Ukr.
237 H7 Pryor OK U.S.A.
136 J2 Pryp"yat' Ukr.
136 J2 Pryp"yat' r. Ukr. alt. Prypyats' (Belarus), conv. Pripet
136 H1 Prypyats' r. Belarus alt. Pryp"yat' (Ukraine), conv. Pripet
138 K6 Prypyernaye Belarus
137 R4 Pryvillya Ukr.
137 L6 Pryvil'ne Ukr.
137 O8 Pryvitne Respublika Krym Ukr.
136 D3 Pryvitne Volyns'ka Oblast' Ukr.
137 M5 Pryyutivka Ukr.
174 F3 Przasnysz Pol.
174 F2 Przechlewo Pol.
175 H5 Przeciszów Pol.
175 J5 Przecław Pol.
177 I1 Przedborski Park Krajobrazowy Pol.
175 H4 Przedbórz Pol.
174 D2 Przedecz Pol.
174 E2 Przelewice Pol.
167 H3 Przemęcki Park Krajobrazowy Pol.
174 D4 Przemków Pol.
177 I1 Przemsza r. Pol.
175 K6 Przemyśl Pol.
175 K1 Przerośl Pol.
175 K3 Przesmyki Pol.
175 L5 Przeworsk Pol.
175 L4 Przewłoka Pol.
174 F5 Przeworno Pol.
175 K5 Przeworsk Pol.
175 I2 Przewóz Pol.
174 C4 Przeździatka Pol.
175 K3 Przeździęk Wielki Pol.
175 H2 Przezmark Pol.
Przheval'sk Kyrg. see Karakol
100 H7 Przheval'skogo, Gory mts Rus. Fed.
139 O6 Przheval'skoye Rus. Fed.
121 R6 Przheval'sk Pristany Kyrg.
174 G1 Przodkowo Pol.
174 C2 Przybiernów Pol.
175 I3 Przyborowice Pol.
174 G3 Przybranowo Pol.
174 D3 Przygodzice Pol.
174 G4 Przykona Pol.
175 H5 Przyrów Pol.
175 J5 Przyrwa r. Pol.
174 G5 Przystajń Pol.
175 I4 Przysucha Pol.
174 G3 Przytoczna Pol.
175 K4 Przytoczno Pol.
175 K2 Przytuły Pol.
175 I4 Przytyk Pol.
174 G1 Przywidz Pol.
198 E4 Psachna Greece
Psakhná Greece see Psachna
198 F6 Psalidi, Akrotirio pt Milos Greece
199 G4 Psara Greece
199 G4 Psara i. Greece
198 F3 Psathoura i. Greece
129 B1 Psebay Rus. Fed.
129 F2 Psedakh Rus. Fed.
129 A1 Psekups r. Rus. Fed.
Psel r. Rus. Fed./Ukr. see Ps'ol
137 P2 Pselets Rus. Fed.
199 I6 Pserimos i. Greece
137 R9 Pshada Rus. Fed.
129 A1 Pshekha r. Rus. Fed.
137 Q8 Pshenychne Ukr.
129 A1 Pshish r. Rus. Fed.
Pskent Uzbek. see Piskent
129 B2 P'skhu Georgia
129 C2 P'skhus Nakrdzali nature res. Georgia
138 K3 Pskov Rus. Fed.
138 K3 Pskov, Lake Estonia/Rus. Fed.
138 L4 Pskova r. Rus. Fed.
Pskov Oblast admin. div. Rus. Fed. see Pskovskaya Oblast'
138 M4 Pskovskaya Oblast' admin. div. Rus. Fed.
Pskovskoye Ozero l. Estonia/Rus. Fed. see Pskov, Lake
137 O2 Ps'ol r. Rus. Fed./Ukr.
188 F3 Psunj mts Croatia
129 E2 Psynodakh Rus. Fed.
174 D3 Pszczew Pol.
167 G2 Pszczewski Park Krajobrazowy Pol.
174 G1 Pszczółki Pol.
175 H4 Pszczonów Pol.
174 G6 Pszczyna Pol.
139 V8 Ptan' r. Rus. Fed.
198 D3 Pteleos Greece
Ptich' Belarus see Ptsich
198 C2 Ptolemaïda Greece
Ptolemais Israel see 'Akko
136 H1 Ptsich Belarus
138 L9 Ptsich r. Belarus
188 E2 Ptuj Slovenia
179 M7 Ptujsko jezero l. Slovenia
136 E3 Ptycha Ukr.
94 E6 Pu r. Indon.
260 A6 Púa Chile
96 E5 Pua Thai.
94 □ Puaka hill Sing.
240 □F14 Puakō HI U.S.A.
261 F5 Puán Arg.
108 E6 Pu'an Guizhou China
108 E3 Pu'an Sichuan China
78 □2 Pu'apu'a Samoa
78 □2 Puava, Cape Samoa
96 I3 Pubei Guangxi China
160 J4 Publier France
250 B6 Pucacaca Peru
250 C5 Pucacuro Peru
250 C5 Pucacuro r. Peru
250 B6 Pucalá Peru
252 B2 Pucallpa Peru
252 D4 Pucará Bol.
252 C3 Pucara Peru
252 C4 Pucarani Bol.
Pucarevo Bos.-Herz. see Novi Travnik
250 D5 Puca Urco Peru
178 H4 Puch bei Hallein Austria
179 M4 Puchberg am Schneeberg Austria
109 L5 Pucheng Fujian China
107 K9 Pucheng Shaanxi China
134 H4 Puchezh Rus. Fed.
173 K5 Puchheim Ger.
101 E10 Puch'ŏn S. Korea
177 H2 Púchov Slovakia
260 C2 Puchuzúh Arg.
197 N5 Pucioasa Romania
92 C6 Pucio Point Panay Phil.
143 O7 Puck Pol.
143 O7 Pucka, Zatoka b. Pol.
147 F7 Puckaun Ireland
87 D8 Puckford, Mount hill W.A. Austr.
187 E8 Puçol Spain
260 B6 Pucón Chile
Pudai watercourse Afgh. see Dor
122 F5 Pūdanū Iran
140 S4 Pudasjärvi Fin.
150 H6 Puddletown Dorset, England U.K.
169 E9 Puderbach Ger.
95 L6 Pudi Kalimantan Indon.
215 I3 Pudimoe S. Africa
108 E5 Puding Guizhou China
109 M3 Pudong Shanghai China
Pudong airport Shanghai China
109 M3 Pudong airport China
134 G3 Pudozh Rus. Fed.
149 N6 Pudsey West Yorkshire, England U.K.
Pudu Hubei China see Suizhou
Puduchcheri Pondicherry India see Pondicherry
114 F7 Pudukkottai Tamil Nadu India
245 J5 Puebillo Mex.
241 Q9 Puebla Baja California Mex.
245 I6 Puebla Puebla Mex.
245 I7 Puebla state Mex.
261 G2 Puebla Brugo Arg.
186 D5 Puebla de Albortón Spain
185 I3 Puebla de Alcocer Spain
186 D4 Puebla de Alfindén Spain
183 O9 Puebla de Almenara Spain
183 N7 Puebla de Beleña Spain
185 O5 Puebla de Don Fadrique Spain
185 J2 Puebla de Don Rodrigo Spain
184 E5 Puebla de Guzmán Spain
184 F3 Puebla de la Calzada Spain
184 G3 Puebla de la Reina Spain
183 J2 Puebla de Lillo Spain
184 G4 Puebla del Maestre Spain
183 N3 Puebla del Príncipe Spain
184 G5 Puebla del Prior Spain
183 K2 Puebla de Obando Spain
182 G4 Puebla de Sanabria Spain
184 G4 Puebla de Sancho Pérez Spain
Puebla de San Julián Spain see A Pobra de San Xiao
187 C7 Puebla de San Miguel Spain
182 H7 Puebla de Yeltes Spain
Puebla de Zaragoza Mex. see Puebla
246 F8 Pueblito Col.
239 L7 Pueblo CO U.S.A.
261 H2 Pueblo Arrúa Arg.
258 C2 Pueblo Hundido Chile
261 F3 Pueblo Italiano Arg.
261 E3 Pueblo Libertador Arg.
261 G2 Pueblo Marini Arg.
244 B2 Pueblo Nuevo Mex.
242 □P11 Pueblo Nuevo Nic.
250 E4 Pueblo Viejo Col.
245 J3 Pueblo Viejo, Laguna de lag. Mex.
242 D4 Pueblo Yaqui Mex.
161 B8 Puech del Pal mt. France
163 I7 Puech de Rouet hill France
260 E6 Puelches Arg.
260 D5 Puelén Arg.
260 B3 Puente Alto Chile
Puenteareas Spain see Ponteareas
Puente Caldelas Spain see Ponte Caldelas
244 D2 Puente de Camotlán Mex.
182 G4 Puente de Domingo Flórez Spain
185 N4 Puente de Génave Spain
245 H7 Puente de Ixtla Mex.
182 I8 Puente del Congosto Spain
260 C3 Puente del Inca Arg.
186 G3 Puente de Montañana Spain
183 L2 Puente de San Miguel Spain
185 J6 Puente-Genil Spain
185 I8 Puente la Reina Spain
183 L2 Puentenansa Spain
185 J4 Puente Nuevo, Embalse de resr Spain
185 P5 Puentes, Embalse de resr Spain
Puentes de García Rodríguez Spain see As Pontes de García Rodríguez
183 M6 Puentes Viejas, Embalse de resr Spain
250 D2 Puente Torres Venez.
183 M2 Puente Viesgo Spain
108 C7 Pu'er Yunnan China
247 □1 Puerca, Punta pt Puerto Rico
241 V7 Puerco watercourse AZ U.S.A.
239 K9 Puerco watercourse NM U.S.A.
252 C3 Puerto Acosta Bol.
259 B7 Puerto Aisén Chile
253 E3 Puerto Alegre Bol.
259 C3 Puerto Alejandría Bol.
250 D5 Puerto Alfonso Col.
250 B6 Puerto America Peru
243 K10 Puerto Ángel Mex.
245 K10 Puerto Ángel Mex.
259 D5 Puerto Antequera Para.
245 N10 Puerto Arista Mex.
242 □R13 Puerto Armuelles Panama
250 B4 Puerto Asís Col.
250 E3 Puerto Ayacucho Venez.
250 □ Puerto Ayora Islas Galápagos Ecuador
259 B7 Puerto Bajo Pisagua Chile
250 □ Puerto Baquerizo Moreno Islas Galápagos Ecuador
242 □O10 Puerto Barrios Guat.
261 F6 Puerto Belgrano Arg.
250 C2 Puerto Bermejo Arg.
250 C3 Puerto Berrío Col.
250 D2 Puerto Boyacá Col.
250 D2 Puerto Cabello Venez.
242 □R10 Puerto Cabezas Nic.
242 □R10 Puerto Cabo Gracias á Dios Nic.
250 E3 Puerto Carreño Col.
253 F5 Puerto Casado Para.
252 D3 Puerto Cavinas Bol.
253 F5 Puerto Cerpera Peru
252 C2 Puerto Ceticayo Peru
257 B7 Puerto Chacabuco Chile
250 B6 Puerto Chicama Peru
259 B7 Puerto Cisnes Chile
259 C8 Puerto Coig Arg.
250 D3 Puerto Colombia Col.
261 F3 Puerto Constanza Arg.
250 D5 Puerto Córdoba Col.
242 □R13 Puerto Cortés Costa Rica
242 □P10 Puerto Cortés Hond.
242 D5 Puerto Cortés Mex.
250 C4 Puerto Cuemaní Col.
250 D2 Puerto Cumarebo Venez.
182 I8 Puerto de Béjar Spain
Puerto de Cabras Fuerteventura Canary Is see Puerto del Rosario
250 A5 Puerto de Cayo Ecuador
252 C3 Puerto Definitivo Peru
247 L8 Puerto de Hierro Venez.
216 □3a Puerto de la Cruz Canary Is
216 □3a Puerto de la Cruz Tenerife Canary Is
216 □3e Puerto de la Estaca El Hierro Canary Is
244 G2 Puerto del Aire Mex.
216 □3b Puerto de la Peña Fuerteventura Canary Is
Puerto de la Selva Spain see El Port de la Selva
216 □3c Puerto del Carmen Lanzarote Canary Is
244 G8 Puerto del Gallo Mex.
245 H3 Puerto del Higuerón Mex.
242 C2 Puerto de Lobos Mex.
244 B2 Puerto de Los Ángeles, Parque Natural nature res. Mex.
245 I1 Puerto de los Ébanos Mex.
216 □3b Puerto del Rosario Fuerteventura Canary Is
Puerto del Son Galicia Spain see Porto do Son
Puerto do Son Galicia Spain see Porto do Son
187 C12 Puerto de Mazarrón Spain
243 P7 Puerto de Morelos Mex.
250 D2 Puerto de Nutrias Venez.
244 G4 Puerto de Palmas Mex.
244 G1 Puerto de Pastores Mex.
Puerto de Pollensa Spain see Port de Pollença
185 I1 Puerto de San Vicente Spain
Puerto de Sóller Spain see Port de Sóller
245 J10 Puerto Escondido Mex.
250 D1 Puerto Estrella Col.
250 B6 Puerto Eten Peru
259 B5 Puerto Flamenco Chile
258 C2 Puerto Francisco de Orellana Orellana Ecuador see Coca
253 E3 Puerto Frey Bol.
261 F6 Puerto Galván Arg.
252 D3 Puerto Génova Bol.
252 D4 Puerto Grether Bol.
253 F5 Puerto Guaraní Para.
259 D9 Puerto Harberton Arg.
252 C3 Puerto Heath Bol.
250 C4 Puerto Huitoto Col.
261 H3 Puerto Ibicuy Arg.
252 B2 Puerto Inca Peru
259 B7 Puerto Ingeniero Ibáñez Chile
261 F6 Puerto Ingeniero White Arg.
250 D4 Puerto Inírida Col.
258 E1 Puerto Irigoyen Arg.
253 F4 Puerto Isabel Bol.
242 □Q12 Puerto Jesús Costa Rica
243 P7 Puerto Juárez Mex.
247 K8 Puerto La Cruz Venez.
258 E1 Puerto La Paz Arg.
185 M2 Puerto Lápice Spain
186 F2 Puértolas Spain
250 C5 Puerto Leguízamo Col.
242 □R10 Puerto Lempira Hond.
253 E3 Puerto Libertad Mex.
242 □R12 Puerto Limón Costa Rica
185 K3 Puertollano Spain
259 D6 Puerto Lobos Arg.
250 D2 Puerto Lopez Col.
250 C3 Puerto López Col.
250 A5 Puerto López Ecuador
185 P5 Puerto Lumbreras Spain
243 M10 Puerto Madero Mex.
259 D6 Puerto Madryn Arg.
250 C6 Puerto Magdalena Mex.
252 C3 Puerto Maldonado Peru
252 D3 Puerto Mamoré Bol.
246 E3 Puerto Manatí Cuba
250 A6 Puerto Máncora Peru
253 F5 Puerto María Auxiliadora Para.
Puerto Marmarín Spain see Portomarín
252 D3 Puerto Marquez Bol.
259 B6 Puerto Melinka Chile
250 C4 Puerto Mercedes Col.
Puerto México Mex. see Coatzacoalcos
253 F5 Puerto Mihanovich Para.
187 E7 Puertomingalvo Spain
250 E3 Puerto Miranda Venez.
259 B6 Puerto Montt Chile
242 □P11 Puerto Morazán Nic.
250 B6 Puerto Morín Peru
216 □3d Puerto Naos La Palma Canary Is
259 B8 Puerto Natales Chile
250 D3 Puerto Nuevo Col.
250 C3 Puerto Olaya Col.
251 F2 Puerto Ordaz Venez.
250 C4 Puerto Ospina Col.
246 E3 Puerto Padre Cuba
250 E3 Puerto Páez Venez.
252 D3 Puerto Pando Bol.
250 B5 Puerto Pardo Peru
252 D2 Puerto Pariamanu Peru
242 C2 Puerto Peñasco Mex.
253 F5 Puerto Pinasco Para.
259 D6 Puerto Pirámides Arg.
251 E2 Puerto Píritu Venez.
250 C5 Puerto Pizarro Col.
246 H4 Puerto Plata Dom. Rep.
252 B2 Puerto Portillo Peru
252 B2 Puerto Prado Peru
Puerto Presidente Stroessner Para. see Ciudad del Este
92 B7 Puerto Princesa Palawan Phil.
242 □Q13 Puerto Quepos Costa Rica
242 N11 Puerto Quetzal Guat.
243 N8 Puerto Real Mex.
184 G7 Puerto Real Spain
258 G2 Puerto Rico Arg.
252 D2 Puerto Rico Bol.
216 □3f Puerto Rico Gran Canaria Canary Is
250 C4 Puerto Rico Col.
247 □1 Puerto Rico terr. West Indies
264 E4 Puerto Rico Trench sea feature Caribbean Sea
261 H3 Puerto Ruiz Arg.
259 B5 Puerto Saavedra Chile
255 C5 Puerto Salgar Col.
Puerto Sama Cuba see Samá
250 D5 Puerto San Agustín Peru
259 B7 Puerto San Carlos Chile
242 □P11 Puerto Sandino Nic.
243 N11 Puerto San José Guat.
259 C8 Puerto Santa Cruz Arg.
253 F5 Puerto Sastre Para.
253 E3 Puerto Saucedo Bol.
Puerto de Beseite mts Spain see Ports de Beseit
182 G7 Puerto Seguro Spain
184 H7 Puerto Serrano Spain
252 D3 Puerto Siles Bol.
250 D5 Puerto Socorro Peru
Puerto Somoza Nic. see Puerto Sandino
253 F4 Puerto Suárez Bol.
252 A2 Puerto Supe Peru
252 C2 Puerto Tahuantisuyo Peru
250 D3 Puerto Tejado Col.
250 B5 Puerto Tunigrama Peru
250 B4 Puerto Umbría Col.
259 E6 Puerto Valdés Arg.
244 B5 Puerto Vallarta Mex.
259 B6 Puerto Varas Chile
250 □ Puerto Velasco Ibarra Islas Galápagos Ecuador
252 B2 Puerto Victoria Peru
250 □ Puerto Villamil Islas Galápagos Ecuador
253 E3 Puerto Villazón Bol.
259 D7 Puerto Visser Arg.
250 C3 Puerto Wilches Col.
259 C9 Puerto Yartou Chile
261 H2 Puerto Yeruá Arg.
250 C5 Puerto Arturo Peru
260 D6 Puerto Sánchez Arg.
79 □9a Pueu Tahiti Fr. Polynesia
183 Q3 Pueyo Spain
191 L2 Puez-Odle, Parco Naturale nature res. Italy
150 D1 Puffin Island Wales U.K.
254 F4 Puga Brazil
120 C1 Pugachev Rus. Fed.
134 K4 Pugachevo Rus. Fed.
116 D5 Pugal Rajasthan India
211 C8 Puga Puga, Ilha i. Moz.
108 D5 Puge Sichuan China
95 J9 Puger Jawa Indon.
161 J10 Puget-sur-Argens France
161 J9 Puget-Théniers France
161 I10 Puget-Ville France
234 D4 Pughtown PA U.S.A.
193 P5 Puglia admin. reg. Italy
193 I2 Puglia r. Italy
162 C5 Pugnac France
193 Q4 Pugnochiuso Italy
225 I4 Pugwash N.S. Can.
80 L5 Puha North I. N.Z.
122 F8 Pūhāl-e Khamīr, Kūh-e mts Iran
107 J9 Pu He r. China
Puhiwaero c. Stewart I. N.Z. see South West Cape
138 J3 Puhja Estonia
197 L5 Pui Romania
161 B10 Puichéric France
197 P5 Puiești Romania
187 E8 Puig Spain
186 I3 Puigcerdà Spain
186 J3 Puigmal mt. France/Spain
186 I4 Puig-reig Spain
186 G4 Puigverd de Lleida Spain
161 I9 Puimoisson France
109 □I7 Pui O Wan b. H.K. China
160 B2 Puisaye reg. France
156 D7 Puiseaux France
156 E3 Puisieux France
163 D6 Puisseguin France
161 C10 Puisserguier France
156 H6 Puits r. France
202 C6 Puits 29 well Chad
202 C6 Puits 30 well Chad
163 I10 Puivert France
92 F8 Pujada Bay Mindanao Phil.
161 F8 Pujaut France
206 C5 Pujehun Sierra Leone
Puji Shaanxi China see Wugong
109 L4 Pujiang Zhejiang China
163 E9 Pujo France
163 D6 Pujols Aquitaine France
163 F7 Pujols Aquitaine France
81 E11 Pukaki, Lake South I. N.Z.
177 H3 Pukanec Slovakia
101 E10 Puk'an-san National Park S. Korea
81 □2 Pukapuka atoll Cook Is
79 □9 Pukapuka atoll Arch. des Tuamotu Fr. Polynesia
79 □9 Pukarua atoll Arch. des Tuamotu Fr. Polynesia
226 I1 Pukaskwa r. Ont. Can.
224 C3 Pukaskwa National Park Ont. Can.
223 K4 Pukatawagan Man. Can.
101 D8 Pukchin N. Korea
101 G7 Pukch'ŏng N. Korea
196 H8 Pukë Albania
80 M4 Pukeamaru hill North I. N.Z.
80 I5 Pukearuhe North I. N.Z.
80 K6 Pukehoi North I. N.Z.
80 K6 Pukehou North I. N.Z.
80 H1 Pukenui North I. N.Z.
80 J6 Pukeokahu North I. N.Z.
81 E12 Pukerangi South I. N.Z.
81 D13 Pukerau South I. N.Z.
80 J6 Pukeroa North I. N.Z.
81 I8 Pukerua Bay North I. N.Z.
81 G10 Puketeraki Range mts South I. N.Z.
80 K6 Puketitiri North I. N.Z.
80 L4 Puketoetoe mt. North I. N.Z.
80 K7 Puketoi Range hills North I. N.Z.
80 J5 Puketutu North I. N.Z.
81 F12 Pukeuri Junction South I. N.Z.
139 O6 Pukhnovo Rus. Fed.
137 S3 Pukhovo Rus. Fed.
141 R6 Pukkila Fin.
134 K3 Puksib Rus. Fed.
134 H3 Puksoozero Rus. Fed.
101 E8 Puksubaek-san mt. N. Korea
188 D3 Pula Croatia
191 P6 Pula airport Croatia
192 C9 Pula Sardegna Italy
192 C10 Pula, Capo di c. Sardegna Italy
252 D5 Pulacayo Bol.
107 R7 Pulandian Liaoning China
107 Q7 Pulandian Wan b. China
92 E8 Pulangi r. Mindanao Phil.
95 K6 Pulangpisau Kalimantan Indon.
91 K5 Pulap atoll Micronesia
252 C6 Pular, Cerro mt. Chile
93 B7 Pulasi i. Indon.
233 I5 Pulaski NY U.S.A.
231 D8 Pulaski TN U.S.A.
232 E11 Pulaski VA U.S.A.
226 F5 Pulaski WI U.S.A.
91 I8 Pulau r. Papua Indon.
94 E5 Pulaubiajang Sumatera Indon.
95 J4 Pulaumajang Kalimantan Indon.
Pulau Pinang state Malaysia see Pinang
175 J4 Puławy Pol.
151 K6 Pulborough West Sussex, England U.K.
191 O3 Pulfero Italy
116 G9 Pulgaon Mahar. India
183 L9 Pulgar Spain
169 G8 Pulheim Ger.
114 G6 Pulicat Tamil Nadu India
114 G6 Pulicat Lake inlet India
160 F3 Puligny-Montrachet France
114 F5 Pulivendla Andhra Prad. India
141 R2 Puljo Fin.
179 M2 Pulkau Austria
179 N2 Pulkau r. Austria
140 R4 Pulkkila Fin.
173 I5 Pullach im Isartal Ger.
238 F3 Pullman WA U.S.A.
252 B3 Pullo Peru
92 C3 Pulog, Mount Luzon Phil.
140 V2 Pulozero Rus. Fed.
185 P6 Pulpí Spain
245 M8 Pulpito, Punta pt Mex.
195 M3 Pulsano Italy
171 H8 Pulsen Ger.
171 J8 Pulsnitz Ger.
171 I8 Pulsnitz r. Ger.
175 J3 Pułtusk Pol.
109 F8 Pulu Xinjiang China
127 I4 Pülümür Turkey
91 K5 Pulusuk atoll Micronesia
93 E1 Pulutan Sulawesi Indon.
91 K5 Puluwat atoll Micronesia
157 N8 Pulversheim France
116 E3 Pulwama Jammu and Kashmir
211 B6 Puma Tanz.
259 B6 Pumalín, Parque nat. park Chile
260 B4 Pumanque Chile
111 J12 Puma Yumco l. China
Pumiao Guangxi China see Yongning
238 L3 Pumpkin Creek r. MT U.S.A.
150 E3 Pumsaint Carmarthenshire, Wales U.K.
258 E2 Puna Arg.
250 A5 Puná, Isla i. Ecuador
79 □9a Punaauia Tahiti Fr. Polynesia
79 □9a Punaauia, Pointe pt Tahiti Fr. Polynesia
81 F9 Punakaiki South I. N.Z.
117 L6 Punakha Bhutan
240 □F14 Punalu'u HI U.S.A.
79 □9a Punaruu r. Tahiti Fr. Polynesia
191 R5 Punat Croatia
252 D4 Punata Bol.
120 E5 Punch Pak.
222 F4 Punchaw B.C. Can.
213 F4 Punda Maria S. Africa
116 F5 Pundri Haryana India
114 C3 Pune Mahar. India
114 F6 Punganuru Andhra Prad. India
94 □ Punggol Sing.
94 □ Punggol, Sungai r. Sing.
209 B7 Pungo Andongo Angola
101 F8 P'ungsan N. Korea
213 G3 Púngoè r. Moz.
191 J2 Puni r. Italy
208 E5 Punia Dem. Rep. Congo
175 M1 Punia Lith.
258 C3 Punilla, Cordillera de la mts Chile
109 K7 Puning Guangdong China
260 B2 Punitaqui Chile
116 E4 Punjab state India

Punjab to Quatre Bornes

373

123 N6 Punjab prov. Pak.
141 T6 Punkaharju Fin.
116 F2 Punmah Glacier China/Jammu and Kashmir
252 C3 Puno Peru
252 C3 Puno dept Peru
117 J7 Punpun r. India
175 L1 Puńsk Pol.
247 □1 Punta, Cerro de mt. Puerto Rico
192 F2 Punta Ala Italy
261 F6 Punta Alta Arg.
259 C9 Punta Arenas Chile
250 D2 Punta Cardón Venez.
252 C4 Punta de Bombón Peru
258 C3 Punta de Diaz Chile
260 C4 Punta del Agua Arg.
258 G4 Punta del Este Uru.
259 E6 Punta Delgada Arg.
260 D2 Punta de los Llanos Arg.
244 B5 Punta de Mita Mex.
260 C3 Punta de Vacas Arg.
242 □O9 Punta Gorda Belize
216 □3d Puntagorda La Palma Canary Is
242 □R12 Punta Gorda Nic.
231 F12 Punta Gorda FL U.S.A.
261 I4 Punta Indio Arg.
191 Q6 Punta Križa Croatia
216 □3d Puntallana La Palma Canary Is
260 D4 Puntana, Travesía des. Arg.
252 C6 Punta Negra, Salar salt flat Chile
259 E6 Punta Norte Arg.
242 B3 Punta Prieta Mex.
242 □Q12 Puntarenas Costa Rica
191 M5 Punta Sabbioni Italy
247 □1 Punta Santiago Puerto Rico
252 D5 Puntas Negras, Cerro mt. Chile
184 F6 Punta Umbría Spain
245 K5 Puntilla Aldama Mex.
250 D2 Punto Fijo Venez.
186 E3 Puntón de Guara mt. Spain
232 G8 Punxsutawney PA U.S.A.
140 S4 Puokio Fin.
140 S4 Puolanka Fin.
140 P3 Puoltikasvaara Sweden
Puqi Hubei China see Chibi
252 B3 Puquio Peru
252 C4 Puquios Chile
130 I3 Pur r. Rus. Fed.
250 B4 Puracé, Parque Nacional nat. park Col.
114 D3 Purandhar Mahar. India
116 H5 Puranpur Uttar Prad. India
91 J8 Purari r. P.N.G.
179 O4 Purbach am Neusiedler See Austria
95 H8 Purbalingga Jawa Indon.
150 H6 Purbeck, Isle of pen. England U.K.
237 G8 Purcell OK U.S.A.
222 G5 Purcell Mountains B.C. Can.
232 H9 Purcellville VA U.S.A.
185 O6 Purchena Spain
185 L6 Purchil Spain
111 E9 Pur Co l. China
82 E4 Pureba Conservation Park nature res. S.A. Austr.
138 I2 Purekkari neem pt Estonia
258 B5 Purén Chile
80 J5 Pureora Forest Park nature res. North I. N.Z.
244 E6 Purépero Mex.
151 M5 Purfleet Thurrock, England U.K.
111 G10 Purgadala Xizang China
237 D6 Purgatoire r. CO U.S.A.
173 J5 Pürgen Ger.
179 L3 Purgstall an der Erlauf Austria
209 B6 Puri Angola
115 I3 Puri Orissa India
244 C6 Purificación Mex.
245 I2 Purificación r. Mex.
150 G5 Puriton Somerset, England U.K.
179 N3 Purkersdorf Austria
151 L5 Purley Greater London, England U.K.
151 J5 Purley on Thames West Berkshire, England U.K.
164 G3 Purmerend Neth.
114 E3 Purna Mahar. India
114 E3 Purna r. Mahar. India
116 F9 Purna r. Mahar. India
117 L7 Purnabhaba r. India
114 C4 Purnagad Mahar. India
82 C2 Purndu Saltpan salt flat S.A. Austr.
Purnea Bihar India see Purnia
117 K7 Purnia Bihar India
86 J4 Purnululu National Park W.A. Austr.
259 B6 Purranque Chile
Pursat Cambodia see Poŭthĭsăt
151 I4 Purton Wiltshire, England U.K.
221 K3 Purtuniq Que. Can.
244 F5 Puruandiro Mex.
244 F6 Puruarán Mex.
250 D5 Puruê r. Brazil
183 Q5 Purujosa Spain
95 K5 Purukcahu Kalimantan Indon.
117 K8 Puruliya W. Bengal India
185 M6 Purullena Spain
251 F5 Purus r. Peru
141 T6 Puruvesi l. Fin.
237 K10 Purvis MS U.S.A.
197 N8 Pŭrvomay Bulg.
116 H6 Purwa Uttar Prad. India
94 G8 Purwakarta Jawa Indon.
95 I8 Purwareja Jawa Indon.
95 I8 Purwodadi Jawa Indon.
95 H8 Purwokerto Jawa Indon.
101 F7 Puryŏng N. Korea
114 E3 Pus r. India
117 J7 Pusa Bihar India
138 K5 Pusa Latvia
95 J4 Pusa Sarawak Malaysia
183 K9 Pusa r. Spain
114 E3 Pusad Mahar. India
101 F11 Pusan S. Korea
92 F8 Pusan Point Mindanao Phil.
95 I4 Pusatdamai Kalimantan Indon.
173 J2 Puschendorf Ger.
171 J8 Puschwitz Ger.
233 □Q4 Pushaw Lake ME U.S.A.
136 J3 Pushcha-Vodytsya Ukr.
139 U7 Pushchino Rus. Fed.
139 I3 Pushemskiy Rus. Fed.
116 E6 Pushkar Rajasthan India
139 N2 Pushkin Rus. Fed.
Pushkino Azer. see Biläsuvar
120 B2 Pushkino Rus. Fed.
100 M5 Pushkinskaya, Gora mt. Sakhalin Rus. Fed.
138 L4 Pushkinskiye Gory Rus. Fed.
186 D3 Pusilibro mt. Spain
177 K4 Püspökladány Hungary
138 K2 Püssi Estonia
176 H2 Pustá Polom Czech Rep.
191 L2 Pusteria, Val val. Italy
176 F8 Pustertal val. Austria
179 J5 Pusterwald Austria
177 G3 Pustě Úľany Slovakia
196 G8 Pusti Lisac mt. Montenegro
176 G2 Pustiměř Czech Rep.
137 C4 Pustomyty Ukr.
138 M5 Pustoshka Rus. Fed.
136 J4 Pustovity Ukr.
138 G1 Pusula Fin.
117 L9 Pusur r. Bangl.
175 I4 Puszcza Mariańska Pol.
167 K2 Puszczy Knyszyńskiej, Park Krajobrazowy Pol.
174 E3 Puszczykowo Pol.
177 M1 Puszczy Solskiej, Park Krajobrazowy Pol.
177 J4 Pusztakocsi mocsarak nature res. Hungary
177 G5 Pusztakovácsi Hungary
177 I5 Pusztamérges Hungary
177 I4 Pusztamonostor Hungary
177 I4 Pusztaszabolcs Hungary
177 I3 Pusztaszer Hungary
177 J5 Pusztaszeri park Hungary
177 I4 Pusztavacs Hungary
177 H4 Pusztavám Hungary
260 B3 Putaendo Chile
223 K3 Putahow Lake Man. Can.
93 D8 Putain Timor Indon.
159 K4 Putanges-Pont-Écrepin France
96 C1 Putao Myanmar
80 J5 Putaruru North I. N.Z.
170 H2 Putbus Ger.
Puteoli Italy see Pozzuoli
95 K8 Puteran i. Indon.
80 L5 Putere North I. N.Z.
134 L2 Puteyets Rus. Fed.
122 I8 Puthak Iran
Puthein Myanmar see Bassein
109 L6 Putian Fujian China
192 A6 Putifigari Sardegna Italy
195 M2 Putignano Italy
134 I4 Putilovo Rus. Fed.
139 T9 Putimets Rus. Fed.
252 C3 Putina Peru
Puting Jiangxi China see De'an
95 I6 Puting, Tanjung pt Indon.
121 U3 Putintsevo Kazakh.
245 J8 Putla Mex.
123 L6 Putla Khan Afgh.
170 F4 Putlitz Ger.
197 O5 Putna r. Romania
233 N7 Putnam CT U.S.A.
235 H2 Putnam County county NY U.S.A.
235 H2 Putnam Valley NY U.S.A.
233 M6 Putney VT U.S.A.
177 J3 Putnok Hungary
108 B4 Pütog Xizang China
Putoi i. H.K. China see Po Toi
131 K3 Putorana, Gory mts Rus. Fed.
94 D3 Putrajaya Malaysia
252 C4 Putre Chile
214 F5 Putsonderwater S. Africa
114 F8 Puttalam Sri Lanka
114 F8 Puttalam Lagoon Sri Lanka
165 G6 Putte Belgium
165 F6 Putte Neth.
157 M5 Puttelange-aux-Lacs France
164 I4 Putten Neth.
170 D1 Puttgarden Ger.
172 B3 Püttlingen Ger.
114 D6 Puttur Karnataka India
260 A4 Putú Chile
209 C6 Putubumba Dem. Rep. Congo
250 C4 Putumayo dept Col.
250 D5 Putumayo r. Col.
126 I4 Pütürge Turkey
95 J4 Putusibau Kalimantan Indon.
135 H5 Putyatino Rus. Fed.
136 E6 Putyla Ukr.
136 H2 Putylovychi Ukr.
137 M2 Putyvl' Ukr.
170 I3 Putzar Ger.
171 J8 Putzkau Ger.
240 □F14 Pu'uanahulu HI U.S.A.
240 □E13 Pu'ukoli'i HI U.S.A.
141 S6 Puula l. Fin.
141 T6 Puumala Fin.
165 F6 Puurs Belgium
240 □A12 Pu'uwai HI U.S.A.
221 K3 Puvirnituq Que. Can.
107 L8 Puxian Shanxi China
238 C3 Puyallup WA U.S.A.
107 N9 Puyang Henan China
Puyang Zhejiang China see Pujiang
163 H6 Puybrun France
163 F8 Puycasquier France
159 J8 Puy Crapaud hill France
160 C5 Puy-de-Dôme dept France
160 B5 Puy de Dôme mt. France
163 H9 Puy de Faucher hill France
161 G7 Puy de la Gagère mt. France
160 D5 Puy de Montoncel mt. France
160 B5 Puy de Sancy mt. France
162 H3 Puy des Trois-Cornes hill France
259 C6 Puyehue, Parque Nacional nat. park Chile
259 C6 Puyel Arg.
163 I8 Puygouzon France
161 B6 Puy Griou mt. France
161 I6 Puy Gris mt. France
160 C5 Puy-Guillaume France
163 H7 Puylaroque France
163 I8 Puylaurens France
163 G6 Puy-l'Évêque France
161 B6 Puy Mary mt. France
163 F9 Puymaurin France
163 F7 Puymirol France
163 H10 Puymorens, Col de pass France
162 E4 Puymoyen France
250 B5 Puyo Ecuador
163 C8 Puyôo France
161 I7 Puy-St-Vincent France
81 A13 Puysegur Point South I. N.Z.
123 I6 Puzak, Hāmūn-e marsh Afgh.
134 K3 Puzla Rus. Fed.
Puzol Valencia Spain see Puçol
211 C6 Pwani admin. reg. Tanz.
78 □4b Pwel Weite Pohnpei Micronesia
209 F7 Pweto Dem. Rep. Congo
150 D2 Pwllheli Gwynedd, Wales U.K.
78 □4b Pwok Pohnpei Micronesia
134 G2 Pyalitsa Rus. Fed.
134 F3 Pyal'ma Rus. Fed.
96 B5 Pyalo Myanmar
96 B7 Pyamalaw r. Myanmar
Pyandzh r. Afgh./Tajik. see Panj
Pyandzh Khatlon Tajik. see Dŭstí
Pyandzh Khatlon Tajik. see Panj
Pyanskiy Perevoz Rus. Fed. see Perevoz
134 L3 Pyanteg Rus. Fed.
140 U3 Pyaozero, Ozero l. Rus. Fed.
140 U4 Pyaozerskiy Rus. Fed.
96 B6 Pyapon Myanmar
130 J2 Pyasina r. Rus. Fed.
130 J3 Pyasino, Ozero l. Rus. Fed.
130 J2 Pyasinskiy Zaliv b. Rus. Fed.
197 M8 Pyasŭchnik r. Bulg.
175 I1 Pyatidorozhnoye Rus. Fed.
129 E1 Pyatigorsk Rus. Fed.
Pyatikhatka Ukr. see P"yatykhatka
Pyatikhatki Ukr. see P"yatykhatky
Pyatimar Kazakh. see Pyatimarskoye
120 D3 Pyatimarskoye Kazakh.
139 N1 Pyatirech'ye Rus. Fed.
136 H3 P"yatka Ukr.
137 Q3 Pyatnitskoye Rus. Fed.
139 T7 Pyatovskiy Rus. Fed.
137 N8 P"yatykhatka Ukr.
137 M5 P"yatykhatky Ukr.
96 C5 Pyaunglaung r. Myanmar
96 C4 Pyawbwe Myanmar
139 S1 Pyazhelka Rus. Fed.
139 S1 Pyazhozero, Ozero l. Rus. Fed.
134 K4 Pychas Rus. Fed.
96 B5 Pyè Myanmar
81 D13 Pye, Mount hill South I. N.Z.
175 L3 Pyelishcha Belarus
138 I8 Pyershamayski Belarus
138 H8 Pyeski Belarus
80 K4 Pyes Pa North I. N.Z.
136 H1 Pyetrykaw Belarus
115 M9 Pygmalion Point Andaman & Nicobar Is India
138 G1 Pyhäjärvi l. Fin.
141 Q6 Pyhäjärvi l. Fin.
140 R5 Pyhäjärvi l. Fin.
140 R5 Pyhäjärvi l. Fin.
141 S6 Pyhäjärvi l. Fin.
141 U6 Pyhäjärvi l. Fin.
140 R4 Pyhäjoki Fin.
140 R4 Pyhäjoki r. Fin.
138 K1 Pyhältö Fin.
140 S4 Pyhäntä Fin.
141 P6 Pyhäranta Fin.
140 R5 Pyhäsalmi Fin.
140 T5 Pyhäselkä Fin.
140 T5 Pyhäselkä l. Fin.
140 S3 Pyhätunturin kansallispuisto nat. park Fin.
179 M3 Pyhra Austria
141 S6 Pyhtää Fin.
Pyin Myanmar see Pyè
96 B3 Pyingaing Myanmar
96 C5 Pyinmana Myanmar
96 C3 Pyin-U-Lwin Myanmar
163 B6 Pyla-sur-Mer France
150 E4 Pyle Bridgend, Wales U.K.
199 I6 Pyli Kos Greece
198 C3 Pyli Thessalia Greece
130 J3 Pyl'karamo Rus. Fed.
140 R5 Pylkönmäki Fin.
198 C6 Pylos Greece
136 G3 Pylypovychi Ukr.
232 E7 Pymatuning Reservoir PA U.S.A.
101 D9 Pyŏksŏng N. Korea
101 D8 Pyŏktong N. Korea
101 E9 P'yŏnggang N. Korea
101 E9 P'yŏngsan N. Korea
101 D9 P'yŏngsong N. Korea
101 E10 P'yŏngt'aek S. Korea
101 D9 P'yŏngyang N. Korea
101 E11 Pyŏnsan Bando National Park S. Korea
178 F4 Pyramidenspitze mt. Austria
83 J7 Pyramid Hill Vic. Austr.
80 □ Pyramid Island Chatham Is S. Pacific Ocean
87 F12 Pyramid Lake salt flat W.A. Austr.
240 M1 Pyramid Lake NV U.S.A.
240 M1 Pyramid Lake Indian Reservation res. NV U.S.A.
216 □2a Pyramid Point Ascension S. Atlantic Ocean
226 I5 Pyramid Point MI U.S.A.
240 M2 Pyramid Range mts NV U.S.A.
126 E9 Pyramids of Giza tourist site Egypt
173 K3 Pyrbaum Ger.
186 J3 Pyrenees mts Europe
163 D9 Pyrénées airport France
163 C9 Pyrénées-Atlantiques dept France
186 D2 Pyrénées Occidentales, Parc National des nat. park France/Spain
163 J10 Pyrénées-Orientales dept France
198 D3 Pyrgetos Greece
199 G4 Pyrgi Chios Greece
198 C5 Pyrgos Greece
136 I3 Pyrizhky Ukr.
137 M4 Pyrohy Ukr.
198 B2 Pyrsogianni Greece
86 D6 Pyrton, Mount hill W.A. Austr.
137 L3 Pyryatyn Ukr.
174 C2 Pyrzyce Pol.
134 I4 Pyshchug Rus. Fed.
137 N8 Pyshkine Ukr.
138 L7 Pyshna Belarus
174 G5 Pyskowice Pol.
137 O5 Pys'menne Ukr.
174 G4 Pyszna r. Pol.
175 K5 Pysznica Pol.
138 K4 Pytalovo Rus. Fed.
227 R3 Pythonga, Lac l. Que. Can.
198 E4 Pyxaria mt. Greece

Q

124 D2 Qā', Wādī al watercourse Saudi Arabia
126 H6 Qaa Lebanon
221 L2 Qaanaaq Greenland
129 I5 Qäbälä Azer.
128 D6 Qabātiya West Bank
125 L4 Qābil Oman
129 H4 Qabırrı r. Azer.
111 L12 Qabnag Xizang China
Qabqa Qinghai China see Gonghe
125 I7 Qabr Hūd Oman
Qabyrgha r. Kazakh. see Kabyrga
Qacentina Alg. see Constantine
129 F4 Qach'aghani Georgia
215 M6 Qacha's Nek Lesotho
129 J4 Qäçräş Azer.
122 H3 Qadamgāli Iran
124 F6 Qaḍḍā Saudi Arabia
123 J4 Qādes Afgh.
124 D4 Qaḍīmah Saudi Arabia
127 L6 Qādir Karam Iraq
127 K6 Qādisīyah, Sadd dam Iraq
Qadisiyah Dam Iraq see Qādisīyah, Sadd
125 K9 Qādub Suquṭrā Yemen
122 I6 Qa'emabad Iran
122 D7 Qā'emiyeh Iran
198 B2 Qafzez Albania
107 P2 Qagan Nei Mongol China
106 J6 Qagan Ders Nei Mongol China
107 K7 Qagan Nur Nei Mongol China
107 M5 Qagan Nur Nei Mongol China
107 N5 Qagan Nur Nei Mongol China
106 F8 Qagan Nur Qinghai China
110 H5 Qagan Nur Xinjiang China
107 S4 Qagan Nur l. China
107 N5 Qagan Nur resr China
107 L4 Qagan Obo Nei Mongol China
107 P3 Qagan Qulut Nei Mongol China
107 M5 Qagan Teg Nei Mongol China
106 D9 Qagan Tohoi Qinghai China
Qagan Us Qinghai China see Dulan
106 E8 Qagan Us He r. China
108 B2 Qagca Sichuan China
Qagchêng Sichuan China see Xiangcheng
Qahar Youyi Houqi Nei Mongol China see Bayan Qagan
Qahar Youyi Qianqi Nei Mongol China see Togrog Ul
Qahar Youyi Zhongqi Nei Mongol China see Hobor
124 F3 Qahd, Wādī watercourse Saudi Arabia
124 G6 Qahr, Jibāl al hills Saudi Arabia
129 I6 Qährämanlı Azer.
Qahremānshahr Iran see Kermānshāh
124 F5 Qaḥṭān reg. Saudi Arabia
106 D8 Qaidam He r. China
111 K8 Qaidam Pendi basin China
106 D8 Qaidam Shan mts Qinghai China
Qaidar Qinghai China see Cêtar
111 I10 Qainaqangma Xizang China
123 K4 Qaisar Afgh.
123 K3 Qaisar r. Afgh.
111 E8 Qakar Xinjiang China
195 □ Qala Gozo Malta
205 G2 Qal'a Beni Hammad tourist site Alg.
215 M3 Qalabotjha S. Africa
127 L5 Qalā Diza Iraq
203 G6 Qala'en Nahl Sudan
123 M4 Qalagai Afgh.
123 N2 Qal'aikhum Tajik.
123 J5 Qala Jamal Afgh.
125 K5 Qalamat Abū Shafrah Saudi Arabia
Qalamshia Georgia see Gant'iadi
125 K9 Qalansīyah Suquṭrā Yemen
123 L4 Qala Shinia Takht Afgh.
127 P9 Qalāt Iran
124 B2 Qal'at al Azlam Saudi Arabia
128 E4 Qal'at al Ḥiṣn Syria
128 E4 Qal'at al Ḥiṣn tourist site Syria
128 D3 Qal'at al Marqab tourist site Syria
124 C2 Qal'at al Mu'aẓẓam Saudi Arabia
128 D5 Qal'at ash Shaqīf tourist site Lebanon
124 F5 Qal'at Bīshah Saudi Arabia
128 G3 Qal'at Muqaybirah, Jabal mt. Syria
127 M8 Qal'at Ṣāliḥ Iraq
127 M8 Qal'at Sukkar Iraq
123 J4 Qala Vali Afgh.
Qalbī Zhotasy mts Kazakh. see Kalbinskiy Khrebet
122 F3 Qal'eh Iran
122 A2 Qal'eh Dāgh mt. Iran
123 I4 Qal'eh Tirpul Afgh.
123 K6 Qal'eh-ye Bost Afgh.
123 I6 Qal'eh-ye Fatḥ Afgh.
122 G8 Qal'eh-ye Ganj Iran
123 J4 Qal'eh-ye Now Afgh.
127 N7 Qal'eh-ye Now Iran
122 H5 Qal'eh-ye Shūrak well Iran
106 I8 Qalgar Nei Mongol China
125 N4 Qalhāt Oman
127 L9 Qalīb Bāqūr well Iraq
224 F1 Qalluviartuuq, Lac l. Que. Can.
128 C6 Qalqīlya West Bank
Qalqutan Kazakh. see Koluton
203 F2 Qalyūb Egypt
126 E8 Qalyūbīyah governorate Egypt
106 F9 Qamalung Qinghai China
223 M2 Qamanirjuaq Lake Nunavut Can.
Qamanittuaq Nunavut Can. see Baker Lake
125 K7 Qamar, Ghubbat al b. Yemen
125 K7 Qamar, Jabal al mts Oman
129 I4 Qämärvan Azer.
121 L8 Qamashi Uzbek.
123 M8 Qambar Pak.
122 B4 Qāmchīān Iran
108 A3 Qamdo Xizang China
79 □7 Qamea i. Fiji
124 E6 Qam Hadīl Saudi Arabia
202 C2 Qamīnis Libya
195 □ Qammieħ, Il-Ponta tal- pt Malta
123 M6 Qamruddin Karez Pak.
122 D5 Qamṣar Iran
Qamystybas Kazakh. see Kamyshlybash
128 E6 Qanawāt Syria
125 L7 Qanawt Oman
Qandahar Afgh. see Kandahār
210 F2 Qandala Somalia
122 B2 Qandarānbāshī, Kūh-e mt. Iran
Qandyaghash Kazakh. see Kandyagash
107 N5 Qangdin Sum Nei Mongol China
111 E10 Qangdoi Xizang China
111 D11 Qangzê Xizang China
120 H6 Qanliko'l Uzbek.
Qapal Kazakh. see Kapal
122 F3 Qapan Iran
110 E5 Qapqal Xinjiang China
Qapshagay Kazakh. see Kapchagay
Qapshagay Bögeni resr Kazakh. see Kapchagayskoye Vodokhranilishche
Qaq Köli salt l. Kazakh. see Kak, Ozero
221 N3 Qaqortoq Greenland
125 K7 Qarā', Jabal al mts Oman
Qara Āghach r. Iran see Mand, Rūd-e
128 D5 Qaraaoun Lebanon
123 I4 Qarabagh Afgh.
129 H5 Qarabağ Silsiläsi hills Azer.
129 G6 Qarabağ Yaylası plat. Armenia/Azer.
Qarabas Kazakh. see Karabas
Qarabaū Kazakh. see Karabau
Qarabulaq Kazakh. see Karabulak
Qarabutaq Kazakh. see Karabutak
129 J6 Qaraçala Azer.
127 K6 Qarachōq, Jabal mts Iraq
129 J6 Qaradonlu Azer.
Qara Ertis r. China/Kazakh. see Ertix He
Qaraghandy Kazakh. see Karaganda
Qaraghandy Oblysy admin. div. Kazakh. see Karagandinskaya Oblast'
Qaraghayly Kazakh. see Karagayly
126 C9 Qārah Egypt
127 J9 Qārah Saudi Arabia
124 G6 Qārah, Jabal al hill Saudi Arabia
123 M5 Qarah Bāgh Ghaznī Afgh.
123 M4 Qarah Bāgh Kābul Afgh.
Qarah Tappah Iraq see Qara Tepe
110 C7 Qarak Xinjiang China
Qaraköl Kazakh. see Karakol'
129 G5 Qaralar Azer.
129 J5 Qaramäryam Azer.
122 B3 Qaranqu r. Iran
Qaraoy Kazakh. see Karaoy
Qara Özek Uzbek. see Qorao'zak
Qaraqalpaqstan Respublikasy aut. rep. Uzbek. see Qoraqalpog'iston Respublikasi
Qaraqoyyn Köli salt l. Kazakh. see Karakoyyn, Ozero
Qaraqozha Kazakh. see Karaguzhikha
Qaraqum des. Kazakh. see Karakum, Peski
Qaraqum des. Turkm. see Garagum
122 F3 Qara Quzi Iran
Qarasor Köli l. Kazakh. see Karasor, Ozero
129 J5 Qarasu Azer.
129 I5 Qarasu r. Azer.
129 I6 Qarasu r. Azer.
Qarasū Kazakh. see Karasu
129 K6 Qarasu Adası i. Azer.
Qara Şū Chāy r. Syria/Turkey see Karasu
123 K4 Qara Tarai mt. Afgh.
Qarataū Kazakh. see Karatau
Qarataū Zhotasy mts Kazakh. see Karatau, Khrebet
127 L6 Qara Tepe Iraq
127 N5 Qara Tikan Iran
Qaratöbe Kazakh. see Karatobe
Qaratoghay Kazakh. see Karatogay
Qaratomar Bögeni resr Kazakh. see Karatomarskoye Vodokhranilishche
Qaraton Kazakh. see Karaton
Qaraūyl Kazakh. see Karaul
129 H5 Qarayeri Azer.
Qarazhal Kazakh. see Karazhal
210 F2 Qardho Somalia
208 F2 Qardud Sudan
129 I6 Qareh Āghāj Iran
122 B3 Qar'eh Aqāj Iran
122 D4 Qareh Chāy r. Iran
122 A2 Qareh Dāgh mt. Iran
122 B2 Qareh Dāgh mts Iran
122 B3 Qareh Dāsh, Kūh-e mt. Iran
129 F6 Qareh Khāj Iran
122 E4 Qareh Qāch, Kūh-e mts Iran
122 B2 Qareh Sū r. Iran
122 I3 Qareh Tekān Turkm.
129 G7 Qareh Ẓīā' od Dīn Iran
106 D8 Qarhan Qinghai China
Qarkilik Xinjiang China see Ruoqiang
203 G2 Qarn al Kabsh, Jabal mt. Egypt
125 K3 Qarnayn i. U.A.E.
124 E5 Qarnayṭ, Jabal hill Saudi Arabia
120 K8 Qarnobcho'l cho'li plain Uzbek.
123 O2 Qarokŭl l. Tajik.
Qarqan Xinjiang China see Qiemo
110 H7 Qarqan He r. China
Qarqaraly Kazakh. see Karkaralinsk
129 I6 Qarqarçay r. Azer.
110 E6 Qarqi Xinjiang China
110 G6 Qarqi Xinjiang China
120 F9 Qārqi Iran
123 L3 Qarqīn Afgh.
198 B2 Qarrit, Qafa e pass Albania
Qarsaqbay Kazakh. see Karsakpay
120 K8 Qarshi Qashqadaryo Uzbek.
120 K8 Qarshi cho'li plain Uzbek.
Qarshi Chŭli plain Uzbek. see Qarshi cho'li
128 D4 Qartaba Lebanon
127 N9 Qārūh, Jazīrat i. Kuwait
203 F2 Qārūn, Birkat l. Egypt
124 G6 Qaryat al Fāw tourist site Saudi Arabia
125 H2 Qaryat al Ulyā Saudi Arabia
125 H2 Qaryat as Sufla Saudi Arabia
122 F3 Qāsam, Kūh-e mt. Iran
122 G5 Qasamī Iran
123 J4 Qasa Murg mts Afgh.
117 K7 Qasba Bihar India
125 M4 Qaşbīyat al Burayk Oman
122 G4 Qāsemābād Khorāsān Iran
122 H3 Qāsemābād Khorāsān Iran
121 L8 Qashqadaryo admin. div. Uzbek.
123 K2 Qashqadaryo r. Uzbek.
Qashqadaryo Wiloyati admin. div. Uzbek. see Qashqadaryo
122 D6 Qash Qai reg. Iran
Qashqantengiz Kazakh. see Kashkanteniz
221 M3 Qasigiannguit Greenland
124 F2 Qasīm reg. Saudi Arabia
Qaskelen Kazakh. see Kaskelen
107 L6 Qasq Nei Mongol China
128 D8 Qaşr ad Dayr, Jabal mt. Jordan
128 E7 Qaşr al Azraq Jordan
202 E3 Qaşr al Farāfirah Egypt
128 F4 Qasr al Ḥayr tourist site Syria
128 E7 Qaşr al Kharānah Jordan
127 K7 Qasr al Khubbāz Iraq
128 E7 Qaşr 'Amrah tourist site Jordan
127 N9 Qaşr aş Şabīyah Kuwait
202 C2 Qaşr Bū Hādī Libya
128 F6 Qaşr Burqu' tourist site Jordan
122 I8 Qaşr-e Qand Iran
127 L6 Qaşr-e Shīrīn Iran
124 G5 Qaşr Ḥimām Saudi Arabia
202 B3 Qaşr Larocu Libya
221 N3 Qassimiut Greenland
124 G9 Qa'ṭabah Yemen
128 E5 Qaṭanā Syria
125 J3 Qatar country Asia
119 H5 Qatār, Jabal hill Oman
122 G3 Qatlish Iran
128 E2 Qaṭmah Syria
203 F2 Qaṭrānī, Jabal esc. Egypt
122 F7 Qaṭrūyeh Iran
128 F7 Qaṭṭāfī, Wādī al watercourse Jordan
Qattara Depression Egypt see Qaṭṭārah, Munkhafaḍ al
202 E2 Qaṭṭārah, Munkhafaḍ al depr. Egypt
202 E2 Qaṭṭārah, Ra's esc. Egypt
128 E4 Qaṭṭīnah, Buḥayrat resr Syria
Qausuittuq Nunavut Can. see Resolute
122 G6 Qavāmābād Iran
129 H4 Qax Azer.
110 F5 Qaxi Xinjiang China
122 H5 Qāyen Iran
Qayghy Kazakh. see Kayga
Qaynar Kazakh. see Kaynar
Qayraqty Kazakh. see Nizhniye Kayrakty
123 M1 Qayroqqum Tajik.
123 N1 Qayroqqum, Obanbori resr Tajik.
129 H4 Qaysa Georgia
128 E7 Qaysīyah, Qā' al imp. l. Jordan
124 A2 Qaysūm, Juzur is Egypt
111 K12 Qayü Xizang China
127 K6 Qayyārah Iraq
Qazaly Kazakh. see Kazalinsk
129 H6 Qazangödağ mt. Armenia/Azer.
129 H6 Qazanzämi Azer.
Qazaq Shyghanaghy b. Kazakh. see Kazakhskiy Zaliv
Qazaqstan country Asia see Kazakhstan
129 G4 Qazax Azer.
129 F3 Qazbegi Georgia
123 M8 Qazi Ahmad Pak.
129 J5 Qazımämmäd Azer.
122 C3 Qazvīn Iran
122 C3 Qazvīn prov. Iran
Qazyqurt Kazakh. see Kazygurt
110 G6 Qedir Xinjiang China
106 G5 Qeh Nei Mongol China
Qeisûm Islands Egypt see Qaysūm, Juzur
198 B2 Qelqëzës, Mali i mt. Albania
129 E3 Qemult'a Georgia
Qena Qinā Egypt see Qinā
221 M3 Qeqertarsuaq Greenland
221 M3 Qeqertarsuaq i. Greenland
221 M3 Qeqertarsuatsiaat Greenland
221 M2 Qeqertarsuatsiaq i. Greenland
221 M3 Qeqertarsuup Tunua b. Greenland
122 B4 Qeshlāq Iran
122 D4 Qeshlāq-e Ḥoseyn Iran
122 G8 Qeshm Iran
122 G8 Qeshm i. Iran
122 C3 Qeydār Iran
122 F7 Qeyşar, Chāh-e well Iran
123 K5 Qeyşār, Kūh-e mt. Afgh.
122 C3 Qezel Owzan, Rūdkhāneh-ye r. Iran
129 G6 Qezel Qeshlāq Iran
128 C8 Qeẓi'ot Israel
107 P7 Qian'an Hebei China
107 S4 Qian'an Jilin China
Qiancheng Hunan China see Hongjiang
Qiandaohu Zhejiang China see Chun'an
Qianfo Dong Gansu China see Mogao Ku
110 F6 Qianfodong Xinjiang China
100 D6 Qianguozhen Jilin China
107 P9 Qiangwei He r. China
107 J9 Qian He r. China
108 G4 Qianjiang Chongqing China
109 I3 Qianjiang Hubei China
100 H5 Qianjin Heilong. China
100 F6 Qianjin Jilin China
108 C3 Qianning Sichuan China
107 R4 Qianqihao Jilin China
109 K3 Qianshan Anhui China
107 R6 Qian Shan mts China
110 G4 Qianshanlaoba Xinjiang China
264 R4 Qiansuo Zhejiang China
108 D4 Qianwei Sichuan China
108 F5 Qianxi Guizhou China
107 P6 Qianxi Hebei China
107 K9 Qianxian Shaanxi China
108 H5 Qianyang Hunan China
107 J9 Qianyang Shaanxi China
Qianyou Shaanxi China see Zhashui
Qiaocheng Anhui China see Bozhou
107 M7 Qiaocun Shanxi China
108 D5 Qiaojia Yunnan China
Qiaoshan Shaanxi China see Huangling
Qiaotou Qinghai China see Datong
Qiaowa Sichuan China see Muli
106 E6 Qiaowan Gansu China
Qiaozhuang Sichuan China see Qingchuan
122 A2 Qīās Iran
124 G2 Qibā' Saudi Arabia
215 L5 Qibing S. Africa
121 M7 Qibray Uzbek.
109 J3 Qichun Hubei China
109 I5 Qidong Hunan China
109 M3 Qidong Jiangsu China
111 G7 Qiemo Xinjiang China
107 O8 Qihe Shandong China
107 N9 Qi He r. China
108 F4 Qijiang Chongqing China
106 B5 Qijiaojing Xinjiang China
221 L3 Qikiqtarjuaq Nunavut Can.
106 B5 Qiktim Xinjiang China
123 L6 Qila Abdullah Pak.
123 J8 Qila Ladgasht Pak.
107 O6 Qilaotu Shan mts China
123 I7 Qila Safed Pak.
123 M6 Qila Saifullah Pak.
Qili Anhui China see Shitai
106 G7 Qilian Qinghai China
106 F7 Qilian Shan mt. China
106 E7 Qilian Shan mts China
110 L6 Qilizhen Gansu China
221 O3 Qillak i. Greenland
Qīma Kazakh. see Kiyma
110 F6 Qiman Xinjiang China
111 J8 Qiman Tag mts China
109 K4 Qimen Anhui China
221 L2 Qimusseriarsuaq b. Greenland
203 G3 Qinā Qinā Egypt
124 A3 Qinā governorate Egypt
203 G3 Qinā, Wādī watercourse Egypt
125 I7 Qināb, Wādī r. Yemen
106 I9 Qin'an Gansu China
Qincheng Jiangxi China see Nanfeng
106 D5 Qincheng Xinjiang China
100 E5 Qing'an Heilong. China
Qingaq Nunavut Can. see Bathurst Inlet
Qingcheng Gansu China see Qingyang
101 C8 Qingchengzi Liaoning China
108 E2 Qingchuan Sichuan China
107 Q8 Qingdao Shandong China
100 E5 Qinggang Heilong. China
Qinggil Xinjiang China see Qinghe
111 G8 Qinggilik Xinjiang China
108 H4 Qingguandu Hunan China
106 E8 Qinghai prov. China
106 G8 Qinghai Hu salt l. Qinghai China
106 F8 Qinghai Nanshan mts China
107 N8 Qinghe Hebei China
100 F5 Qinghe Heilong. China
106 B3 Qinghe Xinjiang China
100 C7 Qing He r. China
101 D8 Qinghecheng Liaoning China
Qinghua Henan China see Bo'ai
107 L8 Qingjian Shaanxi China
Qingjiang Jiangsu China see Huai'an
Qingjiang Jiangxi China see Zhangshu
108 H3 Qing Jiang r. China
Qingkou Jiangsu China see Ganyu
108 H9 Qinglan Hainan China
109 K5 Qingliu Fujian China
108 E6 Qinglong Guizhou China
107 P6 Qinglong Hebei China
107 P7 Qinglong He r. China
111 J11 Qinglung Xizang China
96 I4 Qingping Guangdong China
109 M3 Qingpu Shanghai China
Qingquan Hubei China see Xishui
Qingshan Heilong. China see Wudalianchi
108 D4 Qingshen Sichuan China
106 G8 Qingshizui Qinghai China
Qingshui Gansu China see Qingshuipu
106 J9 Qingshui Gansu China
107 L7 Qingshuihe Nei Mongol China
108 A2 Qingshuihe Qinghai China
110 E4 Qingshuihezi Xinjiang China
110 H5 Qingshuihezi Xinjiang China
108 B5 Qingshuilang Shan mts Yunnan China
106 F7 Qingshuipu Gansu China
109 M4 Qingtian Zhejiang China
106 J7 Qingtongxia Ningxia China
107 O7 Qingxian Hebei China
109 I7 Qingxin Guangdong China
107 M8 Qingxu Shanxi China
109 K3 Qingyang Anhui China
107 J8 Qingyang Gansu China
Qingyang Jiangsu China see Sihong
Qingyuan Gansu China see Weiyuan
109 I7 Qingyuan Guangdong China
Qingyuan Guangxi China see Yizhou
100 D7 Qingyuan Liaoning China
Qingyuan Shanxi China see Qingxu
109 L5 Qingyuan Zhejiang China
107 O8 Qingyun Shandong China
111 G10 Qingzang Gaoyuan plat. Xizang China
108 F5 Qingzhen Guizhou China
Qingzhou Hebei China see Qingxian
109 H3 Qingzhou Hubei China
107 P8 Qingzhou Shandong China
107 M9 Qin He r. China
107 P7 Qinhuangdao Hebei China
Qinjiang Jiangxi China see Shicheng
108 F2 Qin Ling mts China
Qinshan Heilong. China see Wudalianchi
107 M9 Qinshui Shanxi China
Qinting Jiangxi China see Lianhua
107 M8 Qinxian Shanxi China
107 M9 Qinyang Henan China
107 M8 Qinyuan Shanxi China
108 G8 Qinzhou Guangxi China
108 G8 Qinzhou Wan b. China
108 H9 Qionghai Hainan China
Qiongjiexue Xizang China see Qonggyai
108 D3 Qionglai Sichuan China
108 D3 Qionglai Shan mts Sichuan China
108 H9 Qiongshan Hainan China
Qiongxi Sichuan China see Hongyuan
108 G9 Qiongzhong Hainan China
108 G9 Qiongzhou Haixia str. China
129 H4 Qıpçaq Azer.
106 E7 Qiping Gansu China
107 R3 Qiqihar Heilong. China
110 I5 Qiquanhu Xinjiang China
122 E7 Qīr Fārs Iran
122 C5 Qīr Lorestān Iran
111 E8 Qira Xinjiang China
129 H6 Qırmızı Bazar Azer.
129 H5 Qırmızı Samux Azer.
129 J6 Qırmızıkänd Azer.
128 C7 Qiryat Gat Israel
128 D5 Qiryat Shemona Israel
108 G8 Qisha Guangxi China
Qishan Anhui China see Qimen
107 J9 Qishan Shaanxi China
125 J8 Qishn Yemen
128 D6 Qishon r. Israel
124 E5 Qishrān i. Saudi Arabia
126 H8 Qitab ash Shāmah vol. crater Saudi Arabia
110 I5 Qitai Xinjiang China
100 G6 Qitaihe Heilong. China
125 L7 Qitbīt, Wādī r. Oman
108 E6 Qiubei Yunnan China
109 J4 Qiujin Jiangxi China
107 Q8 Qixia Shandong China
107 N9 Qixian Henan China
107 N9 Qixian Henan China
107 M8 Qixian Shanxi China
100 H5 Qixing He r. China
100 D4 Qixingpao Heilong. China
109 H5 Qiyang Hunan China
106 J8 Qiying Ningxia China
108 B4 Qizhong Xizang China
109 H9 Qizhou Liedao i. China
129 K6 Qızılağac Körfäzi b. Azer.
129 K6 Qızılağaç Qoruğu nature res. Azer.
Qizil-Art, Aghbai pass Kyrg./Tajik. see Kyzylart Pass
123 I4 Qizil Bulak Afgh.
129 K5 Qızıldaş Azer.
123 P3 Qizilrabot Tajik.
120 J7 Qizilravot Uzbek.
120 H6 Qizketkan Uzbek.
Qizqetkan Uzbek. see Qizketkan
122 E4 Qobād, Chāh-e well Iran
215 M8 Qoboqobo S. Africa
129 K5 Qobustan Azer.
129 K5 Qobustan Qoruğu nature res. Azer.
Qoghaly Kazakh. see Kugaly
107 O4 Qog Ul Nei Mongol China
106 G9 Qoigargoinba Qinghai China
106 F8 Qoijê Qinghai China
122 B3 Qojūr Iran
215 M8 Qolora Mouth S. Africa
110 I5 Qoltag mts China
122 D4 Qom Iran
122 D4 Qom prov. Iran
Qomdo Xizang China see Qumdo
Qomishēh Iran see Shahrezā
Qomolangma Feng mt. China/Nepal see Everest, Mount
129 J4 Qonaqkänd Azer.
111 J12 Qonggyai Xizang China
120 H6 Qo'ng'irot Uzbek.
107 K6 Qongj Nei Mongol China
110 H6 Qongkol Xinjiang China
111 F9 Qong Muztag mt. Xinjiang/Xizang China
Qongrat Uzbek. see Qo'ng'irot
Qongyrat Karagandinskaya Oblast' Kazakh. see Kounradskiy
Qongyrat Karagandinskaya Oblast' Kazakh. see Konyrat
Qongyröleng Kazakh. see Konyrolen
106 F8 Qonj Qinghai China
Qonystanū Kazakh. see Konystanu
210 F3 Qooriga Neegro b. Somalia
221 M3 Qoornoq Greenland
Qoqek Xinjiang China see Tacheng
215 K7 Qoqodala S. Africa
121 N7 Qo'qon Farg'ona Uzbek.
Qoradaryo r. Kyrg. see Kara-Darya
Qoraghaty Kazakh. see Kuragaty
120 H6 Qorajar Uzbek.
120 J8 Qorako'l Buxoro Uzbek.
120 J8 Qorako'l Buxoro Uzbek.
120 H6 Qorao'zak Uzbek.
Qoraqalpoghiston Uzbek. see Qoraqalpog'iston
Qoraqalpoghiston Respublikasi aut. rep. Uzbek. see Qoraqalpog'iston Respublikasi
120 G5 Qoraqalpog'iston Uzbek.
120 H6 Qoraqalpog'iston Respublikasi aut. rep. Uzbek.
120 K7 Qoraqata botig'i depr. Uzbek.
Qoraŭzak Uzbek. see Qorao'zak
Qorday Kazakh. see Kurday
Qorghalzhyn Kazakh. see Korgalzhyn
195 □ Qormi Malta
128 E4 Qornet es Saouda mt. Lebanon
129 E3 Qornisi Georgia
120 K8 Qorovulbozor Uzbek.
Qorowulbozor Uzbek. see Qorovulbozor
122 D3 Qoroy, Gardaneh-ye pass Iran
122 B4 Qorveh Iran
129 I5 Qoşaqovaq Azer.
120 I7 Qo'shko'pir Uzbek.
Qoshqar Kazakh. see Koshkar
121 L7 Qo'shrabot Uzbek.
127 K5 Qosh Tepe Iraq
129 H5 Qoşqarçay r. Azer.
Qosshaghyl Kazakh. see Koschagyl
Qostanay Kazakh. see Kostanay
Qostanay Oblysy admin. div. Kazakh. see Kostanayskaya Oblast'
122 G8 Qoṭbābād Iran
122 A2 Qoṭūr Iran
128 E4 Qoubaiyat Lebanon
129 G5 Qovlar Azer.
Qowowuyag mt. China/Nepal see Cho Oyu
Qozhaköl l. Kazakh. see Kozhakol', Ozero
123 N3 Qozideh Kŭhistoni Badakhshon Tajik.
120 H6 Qozonketkan Uzbek.
120 H6 Qozoqdaryo Uzbek.
195 □ Qrejten, Il-Ponta tal- pt Malta
195 □ Qrendi Malta
233 M6 Quabbin Reservoir MA U.S.A.
222 E5 Quadra Island B.C. Can.
182 G8 Quadrazais Port.
193 M4 Quadri Italy
255 C9 Quadros, Lago dos l. Brazil
214 E7 Quaggasfontein Poort pass S. Africa
146 I9 Quaich r. Scotland U.K.
123 N5 Quaidabad Pak.
240 O6 Quail Mountains CA U.S.A.
87 D12 Quairading W.A. Austr.
168 E5 Quakenbrück Ger.
235 K2 Quaker Hill CT U.S.A.
234 F3 Quakertown NJ U.S.A.
234 E4 Quakertown PA U.S.A.
234 C3 Qualake PA U.S.A.
125 I2 Qualay'ah, Ra's al pt Saudi Arabia
193 M6 Qualiano Italy
83 I6 Quambatook Vic. Austr.
83 K4 Quambone N.S.W. Austr.
84 H6 Quamby Qld Austr.
237 F8 Quanah TX U.S.A.
107 L9 Quanbao Shan mt. Henan China
Quan Dao Hoang Sa is S. China Sea see Paracel Islands
Quan Dao Truong Sa is S. China Sea see Spratly Islands
96 H4 Quang Ha Vietnam
96 I7 Quang Ngai Vietnam
96 H6 Quang Tri Vietnam
96 H4 Quang Yên Vietnam
109 J2 Quan He r. China
96 G4 Quan Hoa Vietnam
Quanjiang Jiangxi China see Suichuan
Quan Long Vietnam see Ca Mau
109 J6 Quannan Jiangxi China
Quan Phu Quoc i. Vietnam see Phu Quôc, Đao
109 K5 Quanshang Fujian China
116 G2 Quanshuigou Aksai Chin
150 F5 Quantock Hills England U.K.
Quanwan H.K. China see Tsuen Wan
109 L6 Quanzhou Fujian China
109 H6 Quanzhou Guangxi China
223 K5 Qu'Appelle Sask. Can.
223 K5 Qu'Appelle r. Man./Sask. Can.
221 L3 Quaqtaq Que. Can.
255 A9 Quaraí Brazil
261 I2 Quaraí r. Brazil
165 E8 Quaregnon Belgium
209 C7 Quarenta Angola
146 □N2 Quarff Shetland, Scotland U.K.
190 F6 Quargnento Italy
142 F7 Quarnbek Ger.
190 E4 Quarona Italy
191 J8 Quarrata Italy
160 D2 Quarré-les-Tombes France
109 □J7 Quarry Bay H.K. China
81 D13 Quarry Hills South I. N.Z.
234 C5 Quarryville PA U.S.A.
184 C6 Quarteira Port.
187 E8 Quartell Spain
190 G1 Quarten Switz.
217 □1c Quartier-Français Réunion
217 □1b Quartier Militaire Mauritius
191 M8 Quarto, Lago di l. Italy
192 C9 Quartu Sant'Elena Sardegna Italy
241 P4 Quartzite Mountain NV U.S.A.
241 R8 Quartzsite AZ U.S.A.
256 B5 Quatá Brazil
247 □3 Quatre, Isle á i. St Vincent
217 □1b Quatre Bornes Mauritius

Rance to Renoster
375

158 G5 **Rance** *r.* France
161 B9 **Rance** *r.* France
256 B5 **Rancharia** Brazil
222 D2 **Rancheria** *Y.T.* Can.
222 D2 **Rancheria** *r. Y.T.* Can.
238 K4 **Ranchester** *WY* U.S.A.
117 J8 **Ranchi** *Jharkhand* India
240 K3 **Rancho Cordova** *CA* U.S.A.
253 F2 **Rancho de Caçados Tapiúnas** Brazil
244 E2 **Rancho Grande** Mex.
245 J2 **Rancho Nuevo** Mex.
261 H4 **Ranchos** Arg.
239 L8 **Ranchos de Taos** *NM* U.S.A.
259 B6 **Ranco, Lago** *l.* Chile
234 F5 **Rancocas Creek, North Branch** *r. NJ* U.S.A.
234 F5 **Rancocas Woods** *NJ* U.S.A.
83 K6 **Rand** *N.S.W.* Austr.
232 D10 **Rand** *WV* U.S.A.
215 P4 **Randalhurst** S. Africa
234 B6 **Randallstown** *MD* U.S.A.
147 J3 **Randalstown** *Northern Ireland* U.K.
160 C4 **Randan** France
194 H8 **Randazzo** *Sicilia* Italy
215 L2 **Randburg** S. Africa
179 K3 **Randegg** Austria
142 G5 **Randers** Denmark
172 H2 **Randersacker** Ger.
215 L2 **Randfontein** S. Africa
140 O3 **Randijaure** *l.* Sweden
233 N6 **Randolph** *MA* U.S.A.
233 □P4 **Randolph** *ME* U.S.A.
232 G6 **Randolph** *NY* U.S.A.
238 I6 **Randolph** *UT* U.S.A.
233 M5 **Randolph** *VT* U.S.A.
159 M4 **Randonnai** France
170 J3 **Randow** *r.* Ger.
240 O6 **Randsburg** *CA* U.S.A.
142 G1 **Randsfjorden** *l.* Norway
141 L5 **Randsjö** Sweden
141 J6 **Randsverk** Norway
215 M2 **Randvaal** S. Africa
140 Q4 **Råneå** Sweden
206 B3 **Ranérou** Senegal
159 K4 **Rânes** France
81 E12 **Ranfurly** *South I.* N.Z.
117 O6 **Ranga** *r.* India
97 E11 **Rangae** Thai.
117 N8 **Rangamati** Bangl.
117 N6 **Rangapara** *Assam* India
93 A5 **Rangas, Tanjung** *pt* Indon.
93 A5 **Rangasa, Tanjung** *pt* Indon.
80 □ **Rangatira Island** *Chatham Is* S. Pacific Ocean
80 H1 **Rangaunu Bay** *North I.* N.Z.
233 □O4 **Rangeley** *ME* U.S.A.
233 □O3 **Rangeley Lake** *ME* U.S.A.
241 X1 **Rangely** *CO* U.S.A.
172 F5 **Rangendingen** Ger.
224 D4 **Ranger Lake** *Ont.* Can.
227 K3 **Ranger Lake** *l. Ont.* Can.
178 G6 **Rangersdorf** Austria
116 H9 **Rangi** *Mahar.* India
117 M6 **Rangia** *Assam* India
Rangiauria *i. Chatham Is* S. Pacific Ocean *see* **Pitt Island**
81 G10 **Rangiora** *South I.* N.Z.
80 L4 **Rangipoua** *mt. North I.* N.Z.
79 □9 **Rangiroa** *atoll Arch. des Tuamotu* Fr. Polynesia
80 K5 **Rangitaiki** *North I.* N.Z.
80 K4 **Rangitaiki** *r. North I.* N.Z.
81 F11 **Rangitata** *South I.* N.Z.
81 F11 **Rangitata** *r. South I.* N.Z.
80 J7 **Rangitikei** *r. North I.* N.Z.
80 H7 **Rangitoto Islands** *South I.* N.Z.
80 J6 **Rangiwaea Junction** *North I.* N.Z.
80 J6 **Rangiwahia** *North I.* N.Z.
94 G8 **Rangkasbitung** *Jawa* Indon.
117 O5 **Rangku** *Arun. Prad.* India
123 P2 **Rangkŭl** Tajik.
Rangôn Myanmar *see* **Yangôn**
Rangôn *admin. div.* Myanmar *see* **Yangôn**
Rangoon Myanmar *see* **Yangôn**
Rangoon *admin. div.* Myanmar *see* **Yangôn**
96 C6 **Rangoon** *r.* Myanmar
117 L7 **Rangpur** Bangl.
123 N6 **Rangpur** Pak.
94 E4 **Rangsang** *i.* Indon.
171 H6 **Rangsdorf** Ger.
96 B1 **Rangse** Myanmar
108 D2 **Rangtag** *Gansu* China
182 E7 **Ranhados** Port.
116 D7 **Rani** *Rajasthan* India
116 E5 **Rania** *Haryana* India
114 D5 **Ranibennur** *Karnataka* India
226 A1 **Ranier City** *MN* U.S.A.
117 K8 **Raniganj** *W. Bengal* India
117 I8 **Ranijula Peak** *Chhattisgarh* India
116 G5 **Ranikhet** *Uttaranchal* India
123 M8 **Ranipur** Pak.
171 E9 **Ranis** Ger.
116 D7 **Raniwara** *Rajasthan* India
175 J5 **Ranizów** Pol.
117 I7 **Ranka** *Jharkhand* India
84 F6 **Ranken** *watercourse N.T.* Austr.
237 E10 **Rankin** *TX* U.S.A.
223 M2 **Rankin Inlet** *Nunavut* Can.
223 M2 **Rankin Inlet** *inlet Nunavut* Can.
83 K5 **Rankin's Springs** *N.S.W.* Austr.
Rankovićevo Serbia *see* **Kraljevo**
178 A5 **Rankweil** Austria
138 K3 **Ranna** Estonia
85 M8 **Rannes** *Qld* Austr.
120 E2 **Ranneye** Rus. Fed.
146 H9 **Rannoch, Loch** *l. Scotland* U.K.
146 G9 **Rannoch Moor** *moorland Scotland* U.K.
146 G9 **Rannoch Station** *Perth and Kinross, Scotland* U.K.
138 J3 **Rannu** Estonia
207 H4 **Rano** Nigeria
143 O3 **Ränö** *i.* Sweden
78 □6 **Rano, Mount** *New Georgia Is* Solomon Is
213 □J3 **Ranobe** *r.* Madag.
213 □J4 **Ranohira** Madag.
213 □K3 **Ranomafana** Madag.
213 □J5 **Ranomatana** Madag.
213 □J4 **Ranomena** Madag.
78 □5 **Ranon** Vanuatu
97 D10 **Ranong** Thai.
78 □6 **Ranongga** *i. New Georgia Is* Solomon Is
213 □J5 **Ranopiso** Madag.
97 E11 **Ranot** Thai.
213 □J4 **Ranotsara Avaratra** Madag.
139 X7 **Ranova** *r.* Rus. Fed.
116 C8 **Ranpur** *Gujarat* India
260 C5 **Ranquilcó, Salitral** *salt pan* Arg.
260 C5 **Ranquil del Norte** Arg.
123 M6 **Ranrkan** Pak.
127 N7 **Rānsa** Iran
169 E10 **Ransbach-Baumbach** Ger.
142 I1 **Ransby** Sweden
91 H7 **Ransiki** *Papua* Indon.
149 O7 **Ranskill** *Nottinghamshire, England* U.K.
226 F8 **Ransom** *IL* U.S.A.
234 D2 **Ransom** *PA* U.S.A.
165 G6 **Ranst** Belgium
140 S2 **Ranta** Fin.
213 □K2 **Rantabe** Madag.
141 T5 **Rantasalmi** Fin.
95 K6 **Rantau** *Kalimantan* Indon.
94 E4 **Rantau** *i.* Indon.
94 D4 **Rantaukampar** *Sumatera* Indon.
95 J5 **Rantaupanjang** *Kalimantan* Indon.
95 L3 **Rantaupanjang** *Kalimantan* Indon.
94 C3 **Rantauprapat** *Sumatera* Indon.
95 J5 **Rantaupulut** *Kalimantan* Indon.
93 B5 **Rantemario, Gunung** *mt.* Indon.
179 J5 **Ranten** Austria
93 A5 **Rantepao** *Sulawesi* Indon.
226 F9 **Rantoul** *IL* U.S.A.
168 H2 **Rantrum** Ger.
139 R5 **Rantsevo** Rus. Fed.
140 R4 **Rantsila** Fin.
168 F1 **Rantum** Ger.
140 S4 **Ranua** Fin.
142 F5 **Ranum** Denmark
196 H9 **Ranxë** Albania
127 L5 **Ŗānya** Iraq
124 F5 **Ranyah, Wādī** *watercourse* Saudi Arabia
96 G5 **Rao Go** *mt.* Laos/Vietnam
100 H5 **Raohe** *Heilong.* China
157 M7 **Raon-l'Étape** France
191 K4 **Raossi** Italy
77 I4 **Raoul Island** N.Z.
79 □9 **Rapa** *i. Îs Australes* Fr. Polynesia
140 O3 **Rapaälven** *r.* Sweden
Rapa-iti *i. Îs Australes* Fr. Polynesia *see* **Rapa**
190 G7 **Rapallo** Italy
Rapa Nui *i.* S. Pacific Ocean *see* **Pascua, Isla de**
116 C8 **Rapar** *Gujarat* India
122 H9 **Rapch** *watercourse* Iran
260 B3 **Rapel** Chile
260 B3 **Rapel** *r.* Chile
260 B4 **Rapel, Embalse** *resr* Chile
148 B7 **Rapemills** Ireland
221 L3 **Raper, Cape** *Nunavut* Can.
147 G3 **Raphoe** Ireland
171 K6 **Rapice** Pol.
232 H10 **Rapidan** *r. VA* U.S.A.
82 G6 **Rapid Bay** *S.A.* Austr.
236 D3 **Rapid City** *SD* U.S.A.
227 P2 **Rapide-Deux** *Que.* Can.
227 P2 **Rapide-Sept** *Que.* Can.
193 L4 **Rapido** *r.* Italy
226 H4 **Rapid River** *MI* U.S.A.
138 K3 **Räpina** Estonia
252 D2 **Rapirrān** *r.* Brazil
138 H3 **Rapla** Estonia
191 L9 **Rapolano Terme** Italy
193 P6 **Rapolla** Italy
184 B2 **Raposa** Port.
176 G1 **Rapotín** Czech Rep.
182 F8 **Rapoula do Côa** Port.
232 I11 **Rappahannock** *r. VA* U.S.A.
93 A5 **Rappang** *Sulawesi* Indon.
169 K7 **Rappbodetalstausee** *resr* Ger.
172 F7 **Rapperswil** Switz.
179 L2 **Rappottenstein** Austria
116 I6 **Rapti** *r.* India
81 □3 **Rapua Passage** *Rarotonga* Cook Is
252 D3 **Rapulo** *r.* Bol.
114 F5 **Rapur** *Andhra Prad.* India
116 B8 **Rapur** *Gujarat* India
92 E5 **Rapurapu** *i.* Phil.
Raqqa Syria *see* **Ar Raqqah**
233 K4 **Raquette** *r. NY* U.S.A.
233 K5 **Raquette Lake** *NY* U.S.A.
84 F1 **Raragala Island** *N.T.* Austr.
116 I5 **Rara National Park** Nepal
156 E5 **Raray** France
234 F3 **Raritan, South Branch** *r. NJ* U.S.A.
235 G4 **Raritan Bay** *NJ* U.S.A.
79 □9 **Raroia** *atoll Arch. des Tuamotu* Fr. Polynesia
190 D3 **Raron** Switz.
81 □3 **Rarotonga** *i.* Cook Is
116 E6 **Ras** *Rajasthan* India
191 Q5 **Raša** Croatia
188 E3 **Raša** *r.* Croatia
92 B7 **Rasa** *i.* Phil.
259 E6 **Rasa, Punta** *pt* Arg.
125 M6 **Ra's ad Daqm** Oman
125 N4 **Ra's al Ḩadd** Oman
202 E2 **Ra's al Ḩikmah** Egypt
Ras al Khaimah U.A.E. *see* **Ra's al Khaymah**
125 L3 **Ra's al Khaymah** U.A.E.
125 I1 **Ra's al Mish āb** Saudi Arabia
124 F4 **Raşan, Jabal** *hill* Saudi Arabia
128 D8 **Ra's an Naqb** Jordan
128 E4 **Ras Ba'albek** Lebanon
216 □3a **Rasca, Punta de la** *pt Tenerife* Canary Is
183 M7 **Rascafría** Spain
Râşcani Moldova *see* **Rîşcani**
171 G9 **Raschau** Ger.
210 C1 **Ras Dejen** *mt.* Eth.
169 I9 **Rasdorf** Ger.
138 G6 **Raseiniai** Lith.
205 E2 **Râs el Ma** Alg.
206 D2 **Râs el Mâ** Mali
113 □1 **Rasfaree** *i. N. Male* Maldives
203 G2 **Ra's Ghārib** Egypt
106 B3 **Rashaant** *Bayan-Ölgiy* Mongolia
106 J4 **Rashaant** *Dundgovĭ* Mongolia
210 A2 **Rashad** Sudan
147 J3 **Rasharkin** *Northern Ireland* U.K.
147 G3 **Rashedoge** Ireland
203 F2 **Rashīd** Egypt
125 K4 **Rāshid** *reg.* Saudi Arabia
123 L6 **Rashid Qala** Afgh.
137 M3 **Rashivka** Ukr.
122 F4 **Rashm** Iran
215 L1 **Rashoop** S. Africa
125 H8 **Rashshah** Yemen
122 C3 **Rasht** Iran
179 K8 **Rašica** Slovenia
138 K3 **Rasina** Estonia
196 J7 **Rasina** *r.* Serbia
183 N2 **Rasines** Spain
179 O7 **Rasinja** Croatia
141 M5 **Råsjö** Sweden
123 I8 **Rāsk** Iran
196 I7 **Raška** Serbia
111 B8 **Raskam** *mts* China
181 E5 **Ras Kebdana** Morocco
123 K7 **Ras Koh** *mt.* Pak.
123 K7 **Raskoh** *mts* Pak.
177 H2 **Raškovice** Czech Rep.
177 K2 **Raslavice** Slovakia
128 A9 **Ra's Matārimah** Egypt
124 B2 **Ra's Muḩammad National Park** Egypt
221 I3 **Rasmussen Basin** *sea feature Nunavut* Can.
139 O7 **Rasna** *Mahilyowskaya Voblasts'* Belarus
138 M7 **Rasna** *Vitsyebskaya Voblasts'* Belarus
197 N5 **Râşnov** Romania
206 □ **Raso** *i.* Cape Verde
259 D7 **Raso, Cabo** *c.* Arg.
254 F4 **Raso da Catarina** *hills* Brazil
87 H10 **Rason Lake** *salt flat W.A.* Austr.
138 L6 **Rasony** Belarus
197 P6 **Rasova** Romania
197 L7 **Rasovo** Bulg.
171 L9 **Raspenava** Czech Rep.
186 G5 **Rasquera** Spain
117 I7 **Rasra** *Uttar Prad.* India
124 C2 **Ra's Sāq, Jabal** *hill* Saudi Arabia
125 J8 **Ra's Sharwayn** *c.* Yemen
217 □3b **Rassi Douamounyo** *c.* Mayotte
125 M5 **Ra's Şirāb** Oman
189 C7 **Rass Jebel** Tunisia
135 H5 **Rasskazovo** Rus. Fed.
197 L7 **Rast** Romania
139 N8 **Rasta** *r.* Belarus
125 J2 **Ras Tannūrah** Saudi Arabia
172 E4 **Rastatt** Ger.
168 E5 **Rastdorf** Ger.
142 F5 **Råsted** Denmark
168 F4 **Rastede** Ger.
171 D8 **Rastenberg** Ger.
179 L2 **Rastenfeld** Austria
178 E5 **Rastkogel** *mt.* Austria
Rastorguyevo Rus. Fed. *see* **Vidnoye**
170 D4 **Rastow** Ger.
183 J6 **Rasueros** Spain
123 O5 **Rasul** Pak.
142 C3 **Rasvåg** Norway
143 L2 **Råsvalen** *l.* Sweden
174 F4 **Raszków** Pol.
137 P2 **Rat'** *r.* Rus. Fed.
80 J6 **Rata** *North I.* N.Z.
Ratae *Leicester, England* U.K. *see* **Leicester**
94 F7 **Ratai, Gunung** *mt.* Indon.
138 K8 **Ratamka** Belarus
215 M2 **Ratanda** S. Africa
116 E7 **Ratangarh** *Madh. Prad.* India
116 E5 **Ratangarh** *Rajasthan* India
116 I8 **Ratanpur** *Chhattisgarh* India
116 D9 **Ratanpur** *Gujarat* India
141 M5 **Rätansbyn** Sweden
175 L3 **Rataychytsy** Belarus
97 D8 **Rat Buri** Thai.
139 W8 **Ratchino** *Lipetskaya Oblast'* Rus. Fed.
120 F1 **Ratchino** *Orenburgskaya Oblast'* Rus. Fed.
179 I6 **Rateče** Slovenia
168 K3 **Ratekau** Ger.
214 C7 **Ratelfontein** S. Africa
182 C6 **Rates** Port.
116 G7 **Rath** *Uttar Prad.* India
148 B7 **Rath** Ireland
147 I6 **Rathangan** Ireland
236 I5 **Rathbun Lake** *IA* U.S.A.
147 F6 **Rathcabban** Ireland
147 G5 **Rathconrath** Ireland
147 E8 **Rathcool** Ireland
147 J6 **Rathcoole** Ireland
147 F8 **Rathcormac** Ireland
148 D8 **Rathdangan** Ireland
147 G7 **Rathdowney** Ireland
147 J7 **Rathdrum** Ireland
96 A4 **Rathedaung** Myanmar
170 F5 **Rathenow** Ger.
170 F5 **Rathenower Wald- und Seengebiet** *park* Ger.
150 A1 **Rathfarnham** Ireland
147 J4 **Rathfriland** *Northern Ireland* U.K.
146 J10 **Rathillet** *Fife, Scotland* U.K.
147 E7 **Rathkeale** Ireland
147 G8 **Rathkeevin** Ireland
147 D4 **Rathlackan** Ireland
147 D4 **Rathlee** Ireland
147 J2 **Rathlin Island** *Northern Ireland* U.K.
147 E3 **Rathlin O'Birne Island** Ireland
147 E8 **Rathluirc** Ireland
147 I6 **Rathmolyon** Ireland
147 D8 **Rathmore** Ireland
147 G2 **Rathmullan** Ireland
123 L9 **Rath Nath** Pak.
147 J7 **Rathnew** Ireland
146 J11 **Ratho** *Edinburgh, Scotland* U.K.
147 G5 **Rathowen** Ireland
Ratibor Pol. *see* **Racibórz**
169 C8 **Ratingen** Ger.
Ratisbon Ger. *see* **Regensburg**
188 E2 **Ratitovec** *mt.* Slovenia
116 E5 **Ratiya** *Haryana* India
128 E9 **Raţīyah, Wādī** *watercourse* Jordan
177 K3 **Rátka** Hungary
223 L3 **Rat Lake** *Man.* Can.
116 E8 **Ratlam** *Madh. Prad.* India
114 C4 **Ratnagiri** *Mahar.* India
114 G9 **Ratnapura** Sri Lanka
136 D2 **Ratne** Ukr.
Ratno Ukr. *see* **Ratne**
148 E6 **Ratoath** Ireland
123 M8 **Rato Dero** Pak.
239 L8 **Raton** *NM* U.S.A.
161 G10 **Ratonneau, Île** *i.* France
169 K10 **Rattelsdorf** Ger.
179 M5 **Ratten** Austria
140 R3 **Rattosjärvi** Fin.
146 J9 **Rattray** *Perth and Kinross, Scotland* U.K.
146 M7 **Rattray Head** *Scotland* U.K.
141 M6 **Rättvik** Sweden
222 C3 **Ratz, Mount** *B.C.* Can.
168 K3 **Ratzeburg** Ger.
168 K3 **Ratzeburger See** *l.* Ger.
171 D6 **Rätzlingen** Ger.
93 F2 **Rau** *i. Maluku* Indon.
94 D3 **Raub** Malaysia
169 E9 **Raubach** Ger.
173 M6 **Raubling** Ger.
261 H5 **Rauch** Arg.
234 A2 **Rauchtown** *PA* U.S.A.
260 B4 **Rauco** Chile
157 I4 **Raucourt-et-Flaba** France
245 N8 **Raudales de Malpaso** Mex.
140 □B1 **Rauðamýri** Iceland
140 S3 **Raudanjoki** *r.* Fin.
197 K5 **Râu de Mori** Romania
127 M9 **Raudhatain** Kuwait
138 I3 **Raudna** *r.* Estonia
138 G7 **Raudondvaris** Lith.
171 J6 **Rauen** Ger.
172 F3 **Rauenberg** Ger.
171 D10 **Rauenstein** Ger.
140 □F1 **Raufarhöfn** Iceland
138 L1 **Rauha** Fin.
173 J2 **Rauhe Ebrach** *r.* Ger.
80 L4 **Raukokore** *North I.* N.Z.
80 M4 **Raukumara** *mt. North I.* N.Z.
80 L4 **Raukumara Forest Park** *nature res. North I.* N.Z.
80 L5 **Raukumara Range** *mts North I.* N.Z.
117 I9 **Raul** *r.* India
161 B7 **Raulhac** France
257 F4 **Raul Soares** Brazil
141 P6 **Rauma** Fin.
81 I7 **Raumati** *North I.* N.Z.
138 I4 **Rauna** Latvia
151 K3 **Raunds** *Northamptonshire, England* U.K.
80 J6 **Raurimu** *North I.* N.Z.
178 G5 **Rauris** Austria
117 J8 **Raurkela** *Orissa* India
Rauschen Rus. Fed. *see* **Svetlogorsk**
169 G9 **Rauschenberg** Ger.
102 W2 **Rausu** Japan
102 W2 **Rausu-dake** *mt.* Japan
136 I6 **Răut** *r.* Moldova
191 N3 **Raut, Monte** *mt.* Italy
140 S5 **Rautalampi** Fin.
140 T5 **Rautavaara** Fin.
171 F10 **Rautenkranz** Ger.
141 T6 **Rautjärvi** Fin.
Rauza *Mahar.* India *see* **Khuldabad**
163 D6 **Rauzan** France
79 □9 **Ravahere** *atoll Arch. des Tuamotu* Fr. Polynesia
122 I8 **Rāvak** Iran
238 G3 **Ravalli** *MT* U.S.A.
122 G8 **Rāvang** Iran
122 B4 **Ravānsar** Iran
194 F9 **Ravanusa** *Sicilia* Italy
122 G6 **Rāvar** Iran
136 C3 **Rava-Rus'ka** Ukr.
121 N8 **Ravat** Kyrg.
193 N6 **Ravello** Italy
165 G6 **Ravels** Belgium
179 M2 **Ravelsbach** Austria
143 L5 **Rävemåla** Sweden
233 L6 **Ravena** *NY* U.S.A.
149 K5 **Ravenglass** *Cumbria, England* U.K.
191 M7 **Ravenna** Italy
191 M7 **Ravenna** *prov.* Italy
236 F5 **Ravenna** *NE* U.S.A.
232 D7 **Ravenna** *OH* U.S.A.
234 E4 **Raven Rock** *NJ* U.S.A.
85 J8 **Ravensbourne Creek** *watercourse Qld* Austr.
172 H6 **Ravensburg** Ger.
148 E5 **Ravensdale** Ireland
85 J4 **Ravenshoe** *Qld* Austr.
164 I5 **Ravenstein** Neth.
87 F12 **Ravensthorpe** *W.A.* Austr.
149 M5 **Ravenstonedale** *Cumbria, England* U.K.
85 K6 **Ravenswood** *Qld* Austr.
232 D10 **Ravenswood** *WV* U.S.A.
116 F9 **Raver** *Mahar.* India
123 N6 **Ravi** *r.* Pak.
161 B9 **Raviège, Lac de la** *l.* France
156 H8 **Ravières** France
234 C3 **Ravine** *PA* U.S.A.
188 E3 **Ravna Gora** Croatia
188 F3 **Ravna Gora** *hill* Croatia
179 L7 **Ravne** Slovenia
179 K6 **Ravne na Koroškem** Slovenia
120 H6 **Ravshan** Uzbek.
168 H1 **Ravsted** Denmark
93 B6 **Rawa Aopa Watumohai, Taman Nasional** *nat. park* Indon.
127 J6 **Rāwah** Iraq
128 A10 **Rawāhimī, Ra's** *pt* Egypt
203 G5 **Rawai** *well* Sudan
77 I2 **Rawaki** *i. Phoenix Is* Kiribati
123 O5 **Rawala Kot** Pak.
123 O5 **Rawalpindi** Pak.
222 H1 **Rawalpindi Lake** *N.W.T.* Can.
175 I4 **Rawa Mazowiecka** Pol.
127 L5 **Ŗawāndiz** Iraq
94 E6 **Rawas** *r.* Indon.
116 E5 **Rawatsar** *Rajasthan* India
149 P6 **Rawcliffe** *East Riding of Yorkshire, England* U.K.
149 O6 **Rawcliffe** *York, England* U.K.
124 G8 **Rawḑah** Yemen
128 F10 **Rawghah** *watercourse* Saudi Arabia
227 L3 **Rawhide Lake** *Ont.* Can.
94 C1 **Rawi, Ko** *i.* Thai.
174 E4 **Rawicz** Pol.
175 I3 **Rawka** *r.* Pol.
87 H11 **Rawlinna** *W.A.* Austr.
238 K6 **Rawlins** *WY* U.S.A.
87 I8 **Rawlinson, Mount** *hill W.A.* Austr.
87 J8 **Rawlinson Range** *hills W.A.* Austr.
149 O7 **Rawmarsh** *South Yorkshire, England* U.K.
123 J2 **Rawnina** Turkm.
Rawnina Turkm. *see* **Rawnina**
261 G4 **Rawson** *Buenos Aires* Arg.
259 D6 **Rawson** *Chubut* Arg.
262 N1 **Rawson Mountains** Antarctica
214 D9 **Rawsonville** S. Africa
149 M6 **Rawtenstall** *Lancashire, England* U.K.
108 A4 **Rawu** *Xizang* China
179 M4 **Raxalpe** *mts* Austria
117 J6 **Raxaul** *Bihar* India
226 A1 **Ray** *MN* U.S.A.
225 J4 **Ray, Cape** *Nfld and Lab.* Can.
95 I5 **Raya, Bukit** *mt. Kalimantan* Indon.
95 J5 **Raya, Bukit** *mt. Kalimantan* Indon.
114 F5 **Rayachoti** *Andhra Prad.* India
114 E5 **Rayadurg** *Andhra Prad.* India
115 H3 **Rayagada** *Orissa* India
128 E5 **Rayak** Lebanon
123 O3 **Rayan** Pak.
100 F4 **Raychikhinsk** Rus. Fed.
139 T3 **Rayda** Rus. Fed.
124 G8 **Raydah** Yemen
125 I7 **Raydah, Wādīar** *r.* Yemen
122 G7 **Rāyen** Iran
240 M7 **Rayes Peak** *CA* U.S.A.
120 F1 **Rayevskiy** Rus. Fed.
137 K4 **Rayhorod** Ukr.
137 S5 **Rayhorodka** Ukr.
137 Q5 **Rayhorodok** Ukr.
151 N4 **Rayleigh** *Essex, England* U.K.
222 H5 **Raymond** *Alta* Can.
233 N5 **Raymond** *NH* U.S.A.
238 C3 **Raymond** *WA* U.S.A.
83 M5 **Raymond Terrace** *N.S.W.* Austr.
237 G12 **Raymondville** *TX* U.S.A.
223 J5 **Raymore** *Sask.* Can.
117 K8 **Rayna** *W. Bengal* India
151 N4 **Rayne** *Essex, England* U.K.
263 D2 **Rayner Glacier** Antarctica
161 I10 **Rayol-Canadel-sur-Mer** France
245 H4 **Rayón** Mex.
244 G6 **Rayón, Parque Nacional** *nat. park* Mex.
243 I5 **Rayones** Mex.
97 E8 **Rayong** Thai.
137 L4 **Rayozero** Ukr.
237 G9 **Ray Roberts, Lake** *TX* U.S.A.
232 G8 **Raystown Lake** *PA* U.S.A.
125 K7 **Raysūt** Oman
128 F10 **Rayth al Khayl** *watercourse* Saudi Arabia
215 M1 **Rayton** S. Africa
111 L11 **Rayü** *Xizang* China
237 J9 **Rayville** *LA* U.S.A.
124 D4 **Rayyis** Saudi Arabia
158 B5 **Raz, Pointe du** *pt* France
162 F5 **Razac-sur-l'Isle** France
115 H3 **Razam** *Andhra Prad.* India
122 C4 **Razan** Iran
122 C5 **Rāzān** Iran
123 N5 **Razani** Pak.
197 J7 **Ražanj** Serbia
127 K7 **Razāzah, Buḩayrat ar** *l.* Iraq
Razdan Armenia *see* **Hrazdan**
Razdel'naya Ukr. *see* **Rozdil'na**
100 G7 **Razdol'noye** Rus. Fed.
129 H1 **Razdol'ye** Rus. Fed.
179 J8 **Razdrto** Slovenia
138 J9 **Razdzyalavichy** Belarus
122 C5 **Razeh** Iran
162 G3 **Razès** France
163 I9 **Razès** *reg.* France
197 O7 **Razgrad** Bulg.
175 M2 **Razhanka** Belarus
111 J11 **Razhêng Zangbo** *r. Xizang* China
197 Q6 **Razim, Lacul** *lag.* Romania
197 L9 **Razlog** Bulg.
138 K5 **Rāznas** *l.* Latvia
177 H3 **Ráztočno** Slovakia
137 P3 **Razumnoye** Rus. Fed.
Raz"yezd 3km Rus. Fed. *see* **Novyy Urgal**
192 C5 **Razzoli, Isola** *i. Sardegna* Italy
232 D11 **R. D. Bailey Lake** *WV* U.S.A.
162 B3 **Ré, Île de** *i.* France
147 E6 **Rea, Lough** *l.* Ireland
150 G3 **Rea Brook** *r. England* U.K.
246 □ **Reading** Jamaica
151 K5 **Reading** *Reading, England* U.K.
151 K5 **Reading** *admin. div. England* U.K.
226 J8 **Reading** *MI* U.S.A.
232 A9 **Reading** *OH* U.S.A.
234 D4 **Reading** *PA* U.S.A.
234 F3 **Readington** *NJ* U.S.A.
233 M6 **Readsboro** *VT* U.S.A.
226 D6 **Readstown** *WI* U.S.A.
147 I5 **Reaghstown** Ireland
215 K1 **Reagile** S. Africa
254 F4 **Real** *r.* Brazil
261 H5 **Real Audiencia** Arg.
260 D4 **Real de Padre** Arg.
195 N2 **Reale, Canale** *r.* Italy
192 A5 **Reale, Rada della** *b. Sardegna* Italy
185 I8 **Reales** *mt.* Spain
261 E4 **Realicó** Arg.
163 I8 **Réalmont** France
194 E9 **Realmonte** *Sicilia* Italy
163 G7 **Réalville** France
234 C4 **Reamstown** *PA* U.S.A.
97 F8 **Reăng Kesei** Cambodia
79 □9 **Reao** *atoll Arch. des Tuamotu* Fr. Polynesia
243 I4 **Reata** Mex.
Reate Italy *see* **Rieti**
163 E7 **Réaup** France
234 F4 **Reaville** *NJ* U.S.A.
146 I5 **Reay** *Highland, Scotland* U.K.
205 H3 **Rebaa** Alg.
156 F6 **Rebais** France
140 O1 **Rebbenesøya** *i.* Norway
87 G10 **Rebecca, Lake** *salt flat W.A.* Austr.
165 F7 **Rebecq** Belgium
163 D9 **Rébénacq** France
163 I10 **Rébenty** *r.* France
222 G1 **Rebesca Lake** *N.W.T.* Can.
Rebiana Sand Sea *des.* Libya *see* **Rabyānah, Ramlat**
185 K4 **Rebollera** *mt.* Spain
183 M6 **Rebollo** Spain
183 O6 **Rebollosa de Jadraque** Spain
140 U5 **Reboly** Rus. Fed.
182 F5 **Rebordelo** Port.
182 D2 **Rebordelo** Spain
210 E3 **Rebrebti Dhubo** *well* Eth.
121 T1 **Rebrikha** Rus. Fed.
102 R1 **Rebun-suidō** *sea chan.* Japan
102 R1 **Rebun-tō** *i.* Japan
261 G5 **Recalde** Arg.
194 G1 **Recale** Italy
191 P9 **Recanati** Italy
197 J5 **Recaş** Romania
183 M8 **Recas** Spain
190 G7 **Recco** Italy
136 H6 **Recea** Moldova
147 C6 **Recess** Ireland
157 I8 **Recey-sur-Ource** France
139 O5 **Rechane** Rus. Fed.
87 G13 **Recherche, Archipelago of the** *is W.A.* Austr.
87 G13 **Recherche Archipelago Nature Reserve** *W.A.* Austr.
157 M6 **Réchicourt-le-Château** France
Rechitsa Belarus *see* **Rechytsa**
170 G4 **Rechlin** Ger.
123 O6 **Rechna Doab** *lowland* Pak.
179 N5 **Rechnitz** Austria
165 J8 **Recht** Belgium
172 H2 **Rechtenbach** Ger.
168 D3 **Rechtsupweg** Ger.
136 F2 **Rechytsa** *Brestskaya Voblasts'* Belarus
136 J1 **Rechytsa** *Homyel'skaya Voblasts'* Belarus
179 L7 **Rečica** Slovenia
254 G4 **Recife** Brazil
215 J10 **Recife, Cape** S. Africa
217 □2a **Récifs, Île aux** *i. Inner Islands* Seychelles
260 B5 **Recinto** Chile
169 E6 **Recke** Ger.
190 E3 **Reckingen** Switz.
169 D7 **Recklinghausen** Ger.
170 F2 **Recknitz** *r.* Ger.
191 K4 **Recoaro Terme** Italy
258 F3 **Reconquista** Arg.
161 G7 **Recoubeau-Jansac** France
161 B8 **Recoules-Prévinquières** France
262 V1 **Recovery Glacier** Antarctica
253 F2 **Recreio** *Mato Grosso* Brazil
257 F4 **Recreio** *Minas Gerais* Brazil
258 D3 **Recreo** *Catamarca* Arg.
261 G2 **Recreo** *Santa Fé* Arg.
177 J4 **Recsk** Hungary
232 B10 **Rectorville** *KY* U.S.A.
183 O6 **Recuerda** Spain
174 D2 **Recz** Pol.
175 H4 **Ręczno** Pol.
85 I4 **Red** *r. Qld* Austr.
222 E3 **Red** *r. B.C.* Can.
223 L5 **Red** *r.* Can./U.S.A.
237 J10 **Red** *r.* U.S.A.
237 F8 **Red, North Fork** *r. OK* U.S.A.
174 G1 **Reda** Pol.
174 G1 **Reda** *r.* Pol.
94 E2 **Redang** *i.* Malaysia
165 I9 **Redange** Lux.
235 G4 **Red Bank** *NJ* U.S.A.
231 E8 **Red Bank** *TN* U.S.A.
Red Basin *Sichuan* China *see* **Sichuan Pendi**
225 J3 **Red Bay** *Nfld and Lab.* Can.
223 J4 **Redberry Lake** *Sask.* Can.
87 E8 **Red Bluff** *hill W.A.* Austr.
240 J1 **Red Bluff** *CA* U.S.A.
237 D10 **Red Bluff Lake** *TX* U.S.A.
151 L4 **Redbourn** *Hertfordshire, England* U.K.
241 T6 **Red Butte** *mt. AZ* U.S.A.
149 O4 **Redcar** *Redcar and Cleveland, England* U.K.
149 O4 **Redcar and Cleveland** *admin. div. England* U.K.
148 C3 **Redcastle** Ireland
223 I5 **Redcliff** *Alta* Can.
226 D3 **Red Cliff** *WI* U.S.A.
213 F3 **Redcliff** Zimbabwe
150 G5 **Redcliff Bay** *North Somerset, England* U.K.
85 N9 **Redcliffe** *Qld* Austr.
87 F10 **Redcliffe, Mount** *hill W.A.* Austr.
83 I6 **Red Cliffs** *Vic.* Austr.
236 F5 **Red Cloud** *NE* U.S.A.
147 J7 **Redcross** Ireland
222 H4 **Red Deer** *Alta* Can.
222 I5 **Red Deer** *r. Alta/Sask.* Can.
223 K4 **Red Deer** *r. Man./Sask.* Can.
223 K4 **Red Deer Lake** *Man.* Can.
170 E2 **Reddelich** Ger.
215 K5 **Reddersburg** S. Africa
238 C6 **Redding** *CA* U.S.A.
235 I2 **Redding** *CT* U.S.A.
235 I2 **Redding Ridge** *CT* U.S.A.
151 I3 **Redditch** *Worcestershire, England* U.K.
149 M3 **Rede** *r. England* U.K.
222 H3 **Red Earth Creek** *Alta* Can.
170 D4 **Redefin** Ger.
214 C8 **Redelinghuys** S. Africa
254 C3 **Redenção** *Pará* Brazil
254 D4 **Redenção** *Piauí* Brazil
158 E6 **Rédené** France
161 E9 **Redessan** France
205 H2 **Redeyef** Tunisia
236 F3 **Redfield** *SD* U.S.A.
146 K9 **Redford** *Angus, Scotland* U.K.
222 B2 **Red Granite Mountain** *Y.T.* Can.
247 □7 **Redhead** Trin. and Tob.
82 G5 **Redhill** *S.A.* Austr.
151 L5 **Redhill** *Surrey, England* U.K.
234 E4 **Red Hill** *PA* U.S.A.
147 H4 **Redhills** Ireland
237 F7 **Red Hills** *KS* U.S.A.
233 L7 **Red Hook** *NY* U.S.A.
176 F5 **Rédics** Hungary
111 I12 **Red Idol Gorge** China
225 J3 **Red Indian Lake** *Nfld and Lab.* Can.
157 N6 **Réding** France
Redingen Lux. *see* **Redange**
182 C8 **Redinha** Port.
230 E5 **Redkey** *IN* U.S.A.
139 T5 **Redkino** Rus. Fed.
222 G2 **Redknife** *r. N.W.T.* Can.
223 M5 **Red Lake** *Ont.* Can.
223 M5 **Red Lake** *l. Ont.* Can.
241 T6 **Red Lake** *AZ* U.S.A.
236 H2 **Red Lake** *MN* U.S.A.
236 G2 **Red Lake** *r. MN* U.S.A.
236 G2 **Red Lake Falls** *MN* U.S.A.
236 H1 **Red Lake Indian Reservation** *res. MN* U.S.A.
236 H1 **Red Lakes** *MN* U.S.A.
240 O7 **Redlands** *CA* U.S.A.
234 F5 **Red Lion** *NJ* U.S.A.
234 B5 **Red Lion** *PA* U.S.A.
238 J4 **Red Lodge** *MT* U.S.A.
151 I6 **Redlynch** *Wiltshire, England* U.K.
80 J3 **Red Mercury Island** *North I.* N.Z.
238 D4 **Redmond** *OR* U.S.A.
241 U2 **Redmond** *UT* U.S.A.
173 J2 **Rednitz** *r.* Ger.
173 K3 **Rednitzhembach** Ger.
236 H5 **Red Oak** *IA* U.S.A.
235 H1 **Red Oaks Mill** *NY* U.S.A.
210 C5 **Redojari** *waterhole* Kenya
158 G6 **Redon** France
247 □2 **Redonda** *i.* Antigua and Barbuda
182 C4 **Redondela** Spain
182 E5 **Redondelo** Port.
184 D3 **Redondo** Port.
240 N8 **Redondo Beach** *CA* U.S.A.
238 H3 **Red Peak** *MT* U.S.A.
146 E7 **Red Point** *Highland, Scotland* U.K.
Red River *r.* Vietnam *see* **Hông, Sông**
Red River, Mouths of the Vietnam *see* **Hong, Mouths of the**
224 B3 **Red Rock** *Ont.* Can.
241 U9 **Red Rock** *AZ* U.S.A.
227 R8 **Red Rock** *PA* U.S.A.
238 H4 **Red Rock** *r. MT* U.S.A.
222 H1 **Redrock Lake** *N.W.T.* Can.
87 I12 **Red Rocks Point** *W.A.* Austr.
150 C4 **Red Roses** *Carmarthenshire, Wales* U.K.
150 B7 **Redruth** *Cornwall, England* U.K.
124 B2 **Red Sea** Africa/Asia
203 G5 **Red Sea** *state* Sudan
222 F4 **Redstone** *B.C.* Can.
222 E1 **Redstone** *r. N.W.T.* Can.
227 M1 **Redstone** *r. Ont.* Can.
223 M4 **Red Sucker Lake** *Man.* Can.
164 I2 **Reduzum** Neth.
206 E4 **Red Volta** *r.* Burkina/Ghana *alt.* **Nazinon (Burkina)**
238 L2 **Redwater** *r. MT* U.S.A.
240 I1 **Redway** *CA* U.S.A.
150 D1 **Red Wharf Bay** *Wales* U.K.
236 E5 **Red Willow Creek** *r. NE* U.S.A.
225 J2 **Red Wine** *r. Nfld and Lab.* Can.
226 B5 **Red Wing** *MN* U.S.A.
171 D10 **Redwitz an der Rodach** Ger.
240 J4 **Redwood City** *CA* U.S.A.
236 H3 **Redwood Falls** *MN* U.S.A.
238 B6 **Redwood National Park** *CA* U.S.A.
240 I2 **Redwood Valley** *CA* U.S.A.
175 H5 **Rędziny** Pol.
147 G5 **Ree, Lough** *l.* Ireland
226 I6 **Reed City** *MI* U.S.A.
223 K4 **Reed Lake** *Man.* Can.
240 M5 **Reedley** *CA* U.S.A.
235 G6 **Reeds Bay** *NJ* U.S.A.
226 E6 **Reedsburg** *WI* U.S.A.
238 B5 **Reedsport** *OR* U.S.A.
232 D9 **Reedsville** *OH* U.S.A.
232 H8 **Reedsville** *PA* U.S.A.
233 I11 **Reedville** *VA* U.S.A.
232 D10 **Reedy** *WV* U.S.A.
85 J7 **Reedy Creek** *watercourse Qld* Austr.
262 P1 **Reedy Glacier** Antarctica
Reef Islands Vanuatu *see* **Rowa**
81 F9 **Reefton** *South I.* N.Z.
147 E7 **Reens** Ireland
151 O2 **Reepham** *Norfolk, England* U.K.
169 B7 **Rees** Ger.
227 K6 **Reese** *MI* U.S.A.
240 P1 **Reese** *r. NV* U.S.A.
168 H4 **Reeßum** Ger.
170 E4 **Reetz** *Brandenburg* Ger.
171 F6 **Reetz** *Brandenburg* Ger.
164 G4 **Reeuwijksebrug** Neth.
126 I4 **Refahiye** Turkey
182 C5 **Refóios do Lima** Port.
237 K9 **Reform** *AL* U.S.A.
243 M9 **Reforma** *Chiapas* Mex.
245 M9 **Reforma** *Oaxaca* Mex.
234 C5 **Refton** *PA* U.S.A.
237 G11 **Refugio** *TX* U.S.A.
174 D1 **Rega** *r.* Pol.
182 D6 **Regadas** Port.
244 F8 **Regaditos** Mex.
187 E8 **Regajo, Embalse del** *resr* Spain
194 H8 **Regalbuto** *Sicilia* Italy
186 E5 **Regallo** *r.* Spain
179 I4 **Regau** Austria
173 O4 **Regen** Ger.
173 M3 **Regen** *r.* Ger.
257 H3 **Regência** Brazil
173 M3 **Regensburg** Ger.
190 E1 **Regensdorf** Switz.
173 M3 **Regenstauf** Ger.
256 B5 **Regente Feijó** Brazil
205 F4 **Reggane** Alg.
164 J3 **Regge** *r.* Neth.
191 L8 **Reggello** Italy
Reggio *Calabria* Italy *see* **Reggio di Calabria**
Reggio *Emilia-Romagna* Italy *see* **Reggio nell'Emilia**
195 J7 **Reggio di Calabria** Italy
195 K7 **Reggio di Calabria** *prov.* Italy
Reggio Emilia Italy *see* **Reggio nell'Emilia**
191 J6 **Reggio nell'Emilia** Italy
191 J6 **Reggio nell'Emilia** *prov.* Italy
197 M4 **Reghin** Romania
123 K5 **Regi** Afgh.
193 L6 **Regi Lagni** *canal* Italy
175 I3 **Regimin** Pol.
223 J5 **Regina** *Sask.* Can.
251 H3 **Régina** Fr. Guiana
123 K6 **Registān** *reg.* Afgh.
256 D6 **Registro** Brazil
256 B1 **Registro do Araguaia** Brazil
Regium Lepidum Italy *see* **Reggio nell'Emilia**
171 F10 **Regnitzlosau** Ger.
160 E5 **Régny** France
117 O5 **Regong** *Arun. Prad.* India
140 U4 **Regozero** Rus. Fed.
182 C4 **Reguengo** Spain
184 D4 **Reguengos de Monsaraz** Port.
158 F6 **Réguiny** France
171 F10 **Rehau** Ger.
169 H6 **Rehburg (Rehburg-Loccum)** Ger.
168 F5 **Rehden** Ger.
116 G8 **Rehli** *Madh. Prad.* India
173 J5 **Rehling** Ger.
172 B3 **Rehlingen-Siersburg** Ger.
171 I9 **Řehlovice** Czech Rep.
170 D3 **Rehna** Ger.
212 C4 **Rehoboth** Namibia
233 J10 **Rehoboth Bay** *DE* U.S.A.
233 J10 **Rehoboth Beach** *DE* U.S.A.
157 K4 **Réhon** France
128 C7 **Rehovot** Israel
Reïbell Alg. *see* **Ksar Chellala**
171 F7 **Reibitz** Ger.
173 J2 **Reiche Ebrach** *r.* Ger.
172 F2 **Reichelsheim (Odenwald)** Ger.
169 G10 **Reichelsheim (Wetterau)** Ger.
172 G6 **Reichenau** Ger.
179 M4 **Reichenau an der Rax** Austria
172 F2 **Reichenbach** *Hessen* Ger.
171 F9 **Reichenbach** *Sachsen* Ger.
190 D2 **Reichenbach** Switz.
171 K8 **Reichenbach (Oberlausitz)** Ger.
172 H2 **Reichenberg** Ger.
179 K5 **Reichenfels** Austria
169 J8 **Reichensachsen (Wehretal)** Ger.
173 K2 **Reichenschwand** Ger.
178 F5 **Reichenspitze** *mt.* Austria
179 J2 **Reichenthal** Austria
173 L5 **Reichertshausen** Ger.
173 M5 **Reichertsheim** Ger.
173 K4 **Reichertshofen** Ger.
173 J6 **Reichling** Ger.
171 D9 **Reichmannsdorf** Ger.
172 H2 **Reicholzheim** Ger.
179 J4 **Reichraming** Austria
157 O6 **Reichshoffen** France
157 O6 **Reichstett** France
87 J11 **Reid** *W.A.* Austr.
190 D1 **Reiden** Switz.
146 E7 **Reidh, Rubha** *pt Scotland* U.K.
231 F9 **Reidsville** *GA* U.S.A.
231 H7 **Reidsville** *NC* U.S.A.
182 G7 **Reigada** Port.
151 L5 **Reigate** *Surrey, England* U.K.
162 C5 **Reignac** France
160 I4 **Reignier** France
169 D10 **Reil** Ger.
241 V9 **Reiley Peak** *AZ* U.S.A.
163 G6 **Reilhaguet** France
172 F3 **Reilingen** Ger.
161 H9 **Reillanne** France
183 Q9 **Reillo** Spain
156 H5 **Reims** France
184 H4 **Reina** Spain
259 B9 **Reina Adelaida, Archipiélago de la** *is* Chile
190 E1 **Reinach** *Aargau* Switz.
190 D1 **Reinach** *Basellandschaft* Switz.
142 C2 **Reinaknuten** *hill* Norway
168 J3 **Reinbek** Ger.
170 H2 **Reinberg** Ger.
223 K4 **Reindeer** *r. Sask.* Can.
223 L4 **Reindeer Island** *Man.* Can.
223 K3 **Reindeer Lake** *Man./Sask.* Can.
140 L3 **Reine** Norway
232 D9 **Reinersville** *OH* U.S.A.
141 J6 **Reineskarvet** *mt.* Norway
168 J3 **Reinfeld (Holstein)** Ger.
80 G1 **Reinga, Cape** *North I.* N.Z.
169 H7 **Reinhardswald** *mts* Ger.
172 F2 **Reinheim** Ger.
234 C4 **Reinholds** *PA* U.S.A.
183 L3 **Reinosa** Spain
160 E4 **Reins** *r.* France
171 G7 **Reinsdorf** *Sachsen-Anhalt* Ger.
171 D8 **Reinsdorf** *Thüringen* Ger.
172 B2 **Reinsfeld** Ger.
142 C2 **Reinsnosi** *mt.* Norway
140 □B1 **Reipholsfjöll** *hill* Iceland
Reirson Island *atoll* Cook Is *see* **Rakahanga**
140 Q2 **Reisa Nasjonalpark** *nat. park* Norway
173 N4 **Reisbach** Ger.
173 N5 **Reischach** Ger.
140 R5 **Reisjärvi** Fin.
169 G9 **Reiskirchen** Ger.
234 B6 **Reisterstown** *MD* U.S.A.
194 G8 **Reitano** *Sicilia* Italy
164 J2 **Reitdiep** *r.* Neth.
173 M6 **Reit im Winkl** Ger.
215 M3 **Reitz** S. Africa
215 L3 **Reitzburg** S. Africa
138 H3 **Reiu** *r.* Estonia
214 I3 **Reivilo** S. Africa
210 A3 **Rejaf** Sudan
143 L3 **Rejmyre** Sweden
175 L4 **Rejowiec** Pol.
175 L4 **Rejowiec Fabryczny** Pol.
179 O7 **Reka** Croatia
191 Q5 **Reka** *r.* Slovenia
114 G4 **Rekapalle** *Andhra Prad.* India
169 D7 **Reken** Ger.
123 L7 **Rekgwash** Pak.
164 K4 **Rekken** Neth.
175 M5 **Reklynets'** Ukr.
Rekohua *i. Chatham Is* S. Pacific Ocean *see* **Chatham Island**
196 J7 **Rekovac** Serbia
175 M6 **Rekshyn** Ukr.
142 E1 **Reksjåeggi** *mt.* Norway
138 G6 **Rėkyvos ežeras** *l.* Lith.
223 I2 **Reliance** *N.W.T.* Can.
194 H10 **Religione, Punta** *pt Sicilia* Italy
184 C5 **Relíquias** Port.
205 F2 **Relizane** Alg.
242 G4 **Rellano** Mex.
187 E10 **Relleu** Spain
115 H4 **Relli** *Andhra Prad.* India
168 I3 **Rellingen** Ger.
216 □1b **Relva** *São Miguel* Azores
177 I5 **Rém** Hungary
205 H2 **Remada** Tunisia
169 D9 **Remagen** Ger.
159 M5 **Rémalard** France
82 G5 **Remarkable, Mount** *hill S.A.* Austr.
95 I8 **Rembang** *Jawa* Indon.
157 J6 **Rembercourt-Sommaisne** France
171 D9 **Remda** Ger.
261 F5 **Remecó** Arg.
216 □1b **Remédios** *São Miguel* Azores
250 C3 **Remedios** Col.
246 D2 **Remedios** Cuba
244 A1 **Remedios** Mex.
243 O11 **Remedios, Punta** *pt* El Salvador
182 B3 **Remedios, Punta dos** *pt* Spain
205 H3 **Remel el Abiod** *des.* Tunisia
168 E4 **Remels (Uplengen)** Ger.
138 L5 **Remennikovo** Rus. Fed.
236 I2 **Remer** *MN* U.S.A.
122 H8 **Remeshk** Iran
140 S5 **Remeskylä** Fin.
177 L5 **Remetea** Romania
177 K6 **Remetea Mare** Romania
197 L3 **Remeţi** Romania
179 N7 **Remetinec** Croatia
Remi France *see* **Reims**
165 J9 **Remich** Lux.
165 H7 **Remicourt** Belgium
157 I4 **Remilly-Aillicourt** France
232 H10 **Remington** *VA* U.S.A.
251 H3 **Rémire** Fr. Guiana
217 □2 **Rémire** *i.* Seychelles
157 M7 **Remiremont** France
169 K6 **Remlingen** Ger.
238 D2 **Remmel Mountain** *WA* U.S.A.
186 C4 **Remolinos** Spain
157 L7 **Remoncourt** France
135 H7 **Remontnoye** Rus. Fed.
165 I8 **Remouchamps** Belgium
161 F9 **Remoulins** France
94 F4 **Rempang** *i.* Indon.
217 □1c **Remparts, Rivière des** *r.* Réunion
170 G3 **Remplin** Ger.
171 E9 **Remptendorf** Ger.
172 G4 **Rems** *r.* Ger.
169 D8 **Remscheid** Ger.
178 B7 **Remulo** *r.* Italy
158 F6 **Remungol** France
226 I6 **Remus** *MI* U.S.A.
161 G8 **Rémuzat** France
141 K6 **Rena** Norway
141 K6 **Rena** *r.* Norway
184 H2 **Rena** Spain
227 K1 **Renabie** *Ont.* Can.
161 G6 **Renage** France
260 A5 **Renaico** Chile
160 D4 **Renaison** France
Renaix Belgium *see* **Ronse**
96 D1 **Renam** Myanmar
114 E3 **Renapur** *Mahar.* India
159 I6 **Renazé** France
260 E3 **Renca** Arg.
172 E4 **Renchen** Ger.
213 F4 **Renco** Zimbabwe
Rende *Yunnan* China *see* **Xundian**
193 Q9 **Rende** Italy
236 K6 **Rend Lake** *IL* U.S.A.
78 □6 **Rendova** *i. New Georgia Is* Solomon Is
168 I2 **Rendsburg** Ger.
183 M2 **Renedo** *Cantabria* Spain
183 K5 **Renedo** *Castilla y León* Spain
183 K4 **Renedo de la Vega** Spain
225 G3 **René-Levasseur, Île** *i. Que.* Can.
190 B2 **Renens** Switz.
164 E5 **Renesse** Neth.
225 K4 **Renews** *Nfld and Lab.* Can.
224 E4 **Renfrew** *Ont.* Can.
146 H11 **Renfrew** *Renfrewshire, Scotland* U.K.
146 G11 **Renfrewshire** *admin. div. Scotland* U.K.
117 J9 **Rengali Reservoir** *Orissa* India
94 E5 **Rengat** *Sumatera* Indon.
260 B4 **Rengo** Chile
169 D9 **Rengsdorf** Ger.
169 I8 **Rengshausen (Knüllwald)** Ger.
108 G2 **Ren He** *r.* China
109 J3 **Renheji** *Henan* China
Renhou *Hebei* China *see* **Tangxian**
109 I6 **Renhua** *Guangdong* China
108 F5 **Renhuai** *Guizhou* China
136 H8 **Reni** Ukr.
232 E11 **Renick** *WV* U.S.A.
114 F6 **Renigunta** *Andhra Prad.* India
146 C7 **Renish Point** *Scotland* U.K.
168 D5 **Renkenberge** Ger.
138 H1 **Renko** Fin.
164 I5 **Renkum** Neth.
Renland *reg.* Greenland *see* **Tuttut Nunaat**
82 H6 **Renmark** *S.A.* Austr.
194 H10 **Renna** *r. Sicilia* Italy
169 K6 **Rennau** Ger.
78 □6 **Rennell** *i.* Solomon Is
259 B8 **Rennell, Islas** *is* Chile
169 F9 **Rennerod** Ger.
84 D5 **Renner Springs** *N.T.* Austr.
173 K4 **Rennertshofen** Ger.
158 H5 **Rennes** France
158 H5 **Rennes, Bassin de** *basin* France
163 I10 **Rennes-les-Bains** France
142 B2 **Rennesøy** *i.* Norway
263 K2 **Rennick Glacier** Antarctica
223 M5 **Rennie** *Man.* Can.
223 J2 **Rennie Lake** *N.W.T.* Can.
172 F4 **Renningen** Ger.
149 N3 **Rennington** *Northumberland, England* U.K.
179 I5 **Rennweg** Austria
191 M6 **Reno** *r.* Italy
226 C6 **Reno** *MN* U.S.A.
240 M2 **Reno** *NV* U.S.A.
191 K2 **Renòn** Italy
192 C3 **Rénoso, Monte** *mt. Corse* France
215 K2 **Renoster** *r.* S. Africa
214 E7 **Renoster** *watercourse* S. Africa

Renosterkop to Rivière-au-Renard

376

214 G8 Renosterkop S. Africa
215 K2 Renosterspruit S. Africa
232 H7 Renovo PA U.S.A.
107 O7 Renqiu Hebei China
168 H1 Rens Denmark
108 E4 Renshou Sichuan China
174 F5 Reńska Wieś Opolskie Pol.
174 G5 Reńska Wieś Opolskie Pol.
230 D5 Rensselaer IN U.S.A.
233 L6 Rensselaer NY U.S.A.
164 I4 Renswoude Neth.
Rentería Spain see Errenteria
198 C3 Rentina Greece
140 O4 Rentjärn Sweden
238 C3 Renton WA U.S.A.
169 K10 Rentweinsdorf Ger.
117 I7 Renukut Uttar Prad. India
156 I4 Renwez France
81 H8 Renwick South I. N.Z.
139 U3 Renya r. Rus. Fed.
170 D3 Renzow Ger.
206 E3 Réo Burkina
93 B8 Reo Flores Indon.
251 G5 Repartimento Brazil
176 F4 Répce r. Hungary
176 G4 Répcelak Hungary
213 G4 Repembe r. Moz.
123 J2 Repetek Turkm.
123 J2 Repetek Döwlet Gorugy nature res. Turkm.
139 P6 Repino Rus. Fed.
175 K3 Repki Pol.
160 F4 Replonges France
140 R2 Repokaira reg. Fin.
138 M2 Repolka Rus. Fed.
80 K5 Reporoa North I. N.Z.
141 P6 Reposaari Fin.
170 F2 Reppelin Ger.
168 J4 Reppenstedt Ger.
232 B7 Republic OH U.S.A.
238 E2 Republic WA U.S.A.
236 G6 Republican r. NE U.S.A.
236 E5 Republican, South Fork r. NE U.S.A.
188 F3 Republika Srpska aut. div. Bos.-Herz.
161 E6 République, Col de la pass France
85 L6 Repulse Bay b. Qld Austr.
221 J3 Repulse Bay Nunavut Can.
140 R1 Repvåg Norway
135 G6 Rep'yevka Rus. Fed.
195 □ Requa, Il-Ponta ta' pt Gozo Malta
183 L3 Requejada, Embalse de resr Spain
182 G4 Requejo Spain
250 C6 Requena Peru
183 O6 Requena Spain
260 B4 Requinoa Chile
163 J7 Réquista France
78 □6 Rere Guadalcanal Solomon Is
170 E2 Rerik, Ostseebad Ger.
254 E3 Reriutaba Brazil
127 K4 Reşadiye Turkey
Reşadiye Bolu Turkey see Yeniçağa
126 H3 Reşadiye Tokat Turkey
199 I6 Reşadiye Yarımadası pen. Turkey
94 F7 Resag, Gunung mt. Indon.
191 L4 Resana Italy
197 J6 Resava r. Serbia
197 J6 Resavica Serbia
146 K9 Rescobie Angus, Scotland U.K.
196 J9 Resen Macedonia
257 E5 Resende Brazil
182 E6 Resende Port.
256 B6 Reserva Brazil
239 J10 Reserve NM U.S.A.
139 T5 Reshetnikovo Rus. Fed.
137 N4 Reshetylivka Ukr.
109 H4 Reshi Hunan China
106 G8 Reshui Qinghai China
191 J2 Resia, Lago di l. Italy
178 C6 Resia, Passo di pass Austria/Italy
234 E2 Resica Falls PA U.S.A.
258 F2 Resistencia Arg.
197 J5 Reşiţa Romania
174 D2 Resko Pol.
174 D1 Resko Przymorskie, Jezioro lag. Pol.
221 I2 Resolute Nunavut Can.
221 L3 Resolution Island Nunavut Can.
81 A12 Resolution Island South I. N.Z.
150 E4 Resolven Neath Port Talbot, Wales U.K.
146 B6 Resort, Loch inlet Scotland U.K.
183 K3 Respenda de la Peña Spain
257 G3 Resplendor Brazil
139 S7 Ressa r. Rus. Fed.
251 G5 Ressaca Brazil
215 P1 Ressano Garcia S. Africa
139 S8 Resseta r. Rus. Fed.
156 E4 Ressons-sur-Matz France
252 B2 Restauração Brazil
161 J8 Restefond, Col de pass France
196 I9 Restelica Kosovo Serbia
233 □S1 Restigouche r. N.B. Can.
180 D5 Restinga Morocco
216 □3e Restinga, Punta de la pt El Hierro Canary Is
257 E5 Restinga de Marambaia coastal area Brazil
255 B9 Restinga Seca Brazil
250 C3 Restrepo Col.
Resülayn Turkey see Ceylanpınar
194 G8 Resuttano Sicilia Italy
137 M2 Ret' r. Ukr.
243 N10 Retalhuleu Guat.
184 H3 Retamal Spain
260 C3 Retamito Arg.
94 □ Retan Laut, Pulau i. Sing.
182 E9 Retaxo Port.
205 G2 Retem, Oued er watercourse Alg.
260 B3 Retén Atalaya Chile
260 A4 Retén Llico Chile
197 K5 Retezat, Parcul Naţional nat. park Romania
149 P7 Retford Nottinghamshire, England U.K.
156 H4 Rethel France
168 H5 Rethem (Aller) Ger.
Réthimnon Kriti Greece see Rethymno
156 E5 Rethondes France
198 F7 Rethymno Kriti Greece
165 H6 Retie Belgium
183 N7 Retiendas Spain
158 I6 Retiers France
184 G3 Retín r. Spain
250 B5 Retiro Chile
191 K4 Retje Slovenia
177 K3 Rétköz reg. Hungary
182 H7 Retortillo Spain
183 L3 Retortillo tourist site Spain
185 I5 Retortillo, Embalse de resr Spain
183 O6 Retortillo de Soria Spain
161 E6 Retournac France
85 I8 Retreat Qld Austr.
177 I4 Rétság Hungary
173 I6 Rettenberg Ger.
186 C6 Retuerta mt. Spain
185 K2 Retuerta del Bullaque Spain
179 M2 Retz Austria
171 F6 Reuden Sachsen-Anhalt Ger.
171 F8 Reuden Sachsen-Anhalt Ger.
159 P7 Reuilly France
260 A5 Reunión Chile
217 □1c Réunion terr. Indian Ocean
169 K10 Reurieth Ger.
186 H5 Reus Spain
94 B3 Reusam, Pulau i. Indon.
165 H6 Reusel Neth.
165 H5 Reusel r. Neth.
190 E1 Reuss r. Switz.
173 N5 Reut Ger.
Reut r. Moldova see Răut
137 O2 Reut r. Rus. Fed.
167 J5 Reute Ger.
136 D6 Reutel Moldova
170 G3 Reuterstadt Stavenhagen Ger.
173 M2 Reuth bei Erbendorf Ger.
172 G5 Reutlingen Ger.
139 U6 Reutov Rus. Fed.
178 C5 Reutte Austria
165 J6 Reuver Neth.
123 N3 Revak Afgh.
Reval Estonia see Tallinn
134 F2 Revda Rus. Fed.
241 P4 Reveille Peak NV U.S.A.
Revel Estonia see Tallinn
163 I9 Revel France
117 J7 Revelganj Bihar India
192 B2 Revellata, Pointe de la pt Corse France
190 C6 Revello Italy
222 G5 Revelstoke B.C. Can.
245 I3 Reventadero Mex.
250 A6 Reventazón Peru
234 E3 Revere PA U.S.A.
160 G5 Revermont reg. France
161 H8 Revest-du-Bion France
177 G5 Révfülöp Hungary
213 H2 Rèvia Moz.
197 P6 Reviga Romania
197 P6 Reviga r. Romania
157 I6 Revigny-sur-Ornain France
183 L3 Revilla de Collazos Spain
183 M4 Revilla del Campo Spain
228 D7 Revillagigedo, Islas is Mex.
220 E4 Revillagigedo Island AK U.S.A.
156 I4 Revin France
191 M4 Revine-Lago Italy
128 C7 Revivim Israel
139 R9 Revna r. Rus. Fed.
176 D2 Řevnice Czech Rep.
176 C1 Řevničov Czech Rep.
191 K3 Revò Italy
185 O4 Revolcadores mt. Spain
Revolyutsii, Pik mt. Tajik. see Revolyutsiya, Qullai
123 O2 Revolyutsiya, Qullai mt. Tajik.
140 N2 Revsnes Norway
177 J3 Revúca Slovakia
213 G3 Revuè r. Moz.
139 U7 Revyakino Rus. Fed.
79 □7a Rewa r. Viti Levu Fiji
116 H7 Rewa Madh. Prad. India
81 J8 Rewa hill North I. N.Z.
174 D1 Rewal Pol.
116 F5 Rewari Haryana India
262 S2 Rex, Mount Antarctica
238 I5 Rexburg ID U.S.A.
225 H4 Rexton N.B. Can.
242 □T13 Rey, Isla del i. Panama
136 H3 Reya Ukr.
207 I4 Rey Bouba Cameroon
151 P3 Reydon Suffolk, England U.K.
252 D3 Reyes Bol.
216 □3e Reyes, Bahía de los b. El Hierro Canary Is
240 I3 Reyes, Point CA U.S.A.
250 B4 Reyes, Punta pt Col.
128 E2 Reyhanlı Turkey
140 □B2 Reykir Iceland
140 □B2 Reykjanes constituency Iceland
264 G2 Reykjanes Ridge sea feature N. Atlantic Ocean
140 □B2 Reykjanestá pt Iceland
140 □C1 Reykjavík Iceland
84 C2 Reynolds r. N.T. Austr.
232 C9 Reynoldsburg OH U.S.A.
84 D7 Reynolds Range mts N.T. Austr.
243 J4 Reynosa Mex.
160 F5 Reyrieux France
160 F4 Reyssouze r. France
122 E5 Rezā Iran
122 D5 Rezā, Kūh-e hill Iran
122 E6 Reẕā'ābād Iran
Reẕā'īyeh Iran see Orūmīyeh
Reẕā'īyeh, Daryācheh-ye salt l. Iran see Orūmīyeh, Daryācheh-ye
158 H7 Rezé France
138 K5 Rēzekne Latvia
138 K5 Rēzekne r. Latvia
176 G5 Rezi Hungary
136 H6 Rezina Moldova
188 E3 Rezinjski vrh mt. Slovenia
196 E4 Rezovska Reka r. Bulg./Turkey
123 I7 Rezvān Iran
Reẕvāndeh Iran see Reẕvānshahr
122 C3 Reẕvānshahr Iran
190 I4 Rezzato Italy
190 D7 Rezzo Italy
190 G6 Rezzoaglio Italy
R. F. Magón Mex. see Ricardo Flores Magón
197 K6 Rgotina Serbia
168 H4 Rhade Ger.
Rhaeadr Gwy Wales U.K. see Rhayader
205 F3 Rharbi, Oued el watercourse Alg.
190 H1 Rhätikon mts Switz.
172 C2 Rhaunen Ger.
150 E3 Rhayader Powys, Wales U.K.
169 F7 Rheda-Wiedenbrück Ger.
169 C7 Rhede Ger.
168 D4 Rhede (Ems) Ger.
169 I6 Rheden Ger.
234 B4 Rheems PA U.S.A.
Rhegium Italy see Reggio di Calabria
150 D3 Rheidol r. Wales U.K.
Rheims France see Reims
168 B7 Rhein r. Ger. alt. Rhin (France), conv. Rhine
172 D4 Rheinau Ger.
169 C9 Rheinbach Ger.
169 C7 Rheinberg Ger.
172 D2 Rheinböllen Ger.
169 D9 Rheinbreitbach Ger.
169 D10 Rheinbrohl Ger.
169 D6 Rheine Ger.
190 H1 Rheineck Switz.
190 D1 Rheinfelden Switz.
172 D6 Rheinfelden (Baden) Ger.
169 E10 Rheingaugebirge hills Ger.
169 B10 Rheinisches Schiefergebirge hills Ger.
169 D11 Rheinland-Pfalz land Ger.
169 C8 Rhein-Ruhr airport Ger.
170 G4 Rheinsberg Ger.
172 E4 Rheinstetten Ger.
169 F10 Rhein-Taunus, Naturpark nature res. Ger.
190 E2 Rheinwaldhorn mt. Switz.
169 D9 Rhein-Westerwald, Naturpark nature res. Ger.
172 E3 Rheinzabern Ger.
190 C4 Rhêmes-Notre-Dame Italy
190 C4 Rhêmes-St-Georges Italy
204 D3 Rhemilès well Alg.
164 I5 Rhenen Neth.
169 E10 Rhens Ger.
204 D3 Rheris, Oued watercourse Morocco
146 G6 Rhiconich Highland, Scotland U.K.
157 P6 Rhin r. France alt. Rhein (Germany), conv. Rhine
170 G4 Rhin r. Ger.
157 O7 Rhinau France
168 B7 Rhine r. Europe alt. Rhein (Germany), alt. Rhin (France)
233 L7 Rhinebeck NY U.S.A.
226 E4 Rhinelander WI U.S.A.
Rhineland-Palatinate land Ger. see Rheinland-Pfalz
170 G5 Rhinkanal canal Ger.
170 G5 Rhinluch marsh Ger.
146 H12 Rhinns of Kells hills Scotland U.K.
210 A4 Rhino Camp Uganda
170 F5 Rhinow Ger.
170 F5 Rhinower Berge hills Ger.
204 C3 Rhir, Cap c. Morocco
165 G7 Rhisnes Belgium
Rhiwabon Wales U.K. see Ruabon
190 G4 Rho Italy
246 □ Rhoades, Point Jamaica
147 H6 Rhode Ireland
233 N7 Rhode Island state U.S.A.
169 H8 Rhoden (Diemelstadt) Ger.
Rhodes Rodos Greece see Rodos
Rhodes i. Greece see Rodos
Rhodesia country Africa see Zimbabwe
Rhodes Inyanga National Park Zimbabwe see Nyanga National Park
Rhodes Matopos National Park Zimbabwe see Matobo National Park
238 G3 Rhodes Peak ID U.S.A.
197 L9 Rhodope Mountains Bulg./Greece
Rhodus i. Greece see Rodos
169 I10 Rhön mts Ger.
150 F4 Rhondda reg. Wales U.K.
150 F4 Rhondda Cynon Taff admin. div. Wales U.K.
160 F5 Rhône dept France
161 F9 Rhône r. France/Switz.
161 G6 Rhône-Alpes admin. reg. France
161 E9 Rhône à Sète, Canal du France
157 N8 Rhône au Rhin, Canal du France
150 F5 Rhoose Vale of Glamorgan, Wales U.K.
173 M6 Rhordorf Ger.
150 E4 Rhos Neath Port Talbot, Wales U.K.
150 F1 Rhosllanerchrugog Wrexham, Wales U.K.
150 E1 Rhôs-on-Sea Conwy, Wales U.K.
150 E5 Rhossili Swansea, Wales U.K.
205 G2 Rhoufi Alg.
148 H1 Rhu Argyll and Bute, Scotland U.K.
Rhube, Oasis of Syria see Rubbah
150 F1 Rhuddlan Denbighshire, Wales U.K.
161 A6 Rhue r. France
Rhum i. Scotland U.K. see Rum
169 J7 Rhumspringe Ger.
Rhuthun Denbighshire, Wales U.K. see Ruthin
158 F6 Rhuys, Presqu'île de pen. France
Rhydaman Carmarthenshire, Wales U.K. see Ammanford
150 F1 Rhyl Denbighshire, Wales U.K.
150 F4 Rhymney Caerphilly, Wales U.K.
146 K8 Rhynie Aberdeenshire, Scotland U.K.
207 H6 Riaba Equat. Guinea
195 K7 Riace Italy
254 D3 Riachão Brazil
254 D4 Riachão das Neves Brazil
257 G3 Riacho Brazil
254 E5 Riacho de Santana Brazil
257 F1 Riacho dos Machados Brazil
259 E6 Riachos, Islas de los is Arg.
184 D6 Ria Formosa, Parque Natural da nature res. Port.
183 N6 Riaguas r. Spain
158 I6 Riaillé France
Rialb de Noguera Spain see Rialp
255 C5 Rialma Brazil
186 H3 Rialp Spain
186 H4 Rialp, Pantà de resr Spain
240 O7 Rialto CA U.S.A.
95 I5 Riam Kalimantan Indon.
117 N6 Riang Arun. Prad. India
208 F2 Riangnom Sudan
Rianjo Galicia Spain see Rianxo
193 J3 Riano Italy
183 K3 Riaño Spain
183 J3 Riaño, Embalse de resr Spain
253 H3 Rianópolis Brazil
161 H9 Rians France
183 N9 Riansáres r. Spain
158 E6 Riantec France
182 C3 Rianxo Spain
116 E3 Riasi Jammu and Kashmir
94 E4 Riau prov. Indon.
94 F4 Riau, Kepulauan is Indon.
190 C2 Riaz Switz.
183 N6 Riaza Spain
183 M5 Riaza r. Spain
183 M2 Riba Spain
182 D4 Ribadavia Spain
182 G4 Ribadelago Spain
182 F1 Ribadeo Spain
182 F1 Ribadeo, Ría del inlet Spain
183 P7 Riba de Saelices Spain
183 J2 Ribadesella Spain
183 Q4 Ribaforada Spain
183 P4 Ribafrecha Spain
186 G4 Ribagorçana, Noguera r. Spain
186 F5 Riba-roja, Pantà de resr Spain
186 F5 Riba-roja d'Ebre Spain
Ribas de Fresser Spain see Ribes de Freser
255 B7 Ribas do Rio Pardo Brazil
123 M3 Ribat Afgh.
184 C2 Ribatejo reg. Port.
213 H2 Ribáuè Moz.
169 K6 Ribbesbüttel Ger.
149 L6 Ribble r. England U.K.
149 M5 Ribblesdale val. England U.K.
142 E6 Ribe Denmark
142 E6 Ribe county Denmark
157 N7 Ribeauvillé France
156 E4 Ribécourt-Dreslincourt France
256 C6 Ribeira Brazil
256 D6 Ribeira r. Brazil
182 E2 Ribeira, Encoro da resr Spain
184 □ Ribeira Brava Madeira
184 □ Ribeira da Janela Madeira
182 E5 Ribeira de Pena Port.
216 □1b Ribeira Grande São Miguel Azores
252 D2 Ribeirão Brazil
182 C6 Ribeirão Port.
256 C6 Ribeirão Branco Brazil
257 E3 Ribeirão das Neves Brazil
256 B5 Ribeirão do Pinhal Brazil
256 D4 Ribeirão Preto Brazil
216 □1c Ribeiras Pico Azores
216 □1c Ribeira Seca São Jorge Azores
216 □1b Ribeira Seca São Miguel Azores
216 □1c Ribeirinha Faial Azores
216 □1c Ribeirinha Pico Azores
216 □1a Ribeirinha Terceira Azores
156 F4 Ribemont France
194 E8 Ribera Sicilia Italy
162 E5 Ribérac France
184 G3 Ribera del Fresno Spain
252 D2 Riberalta Bol.
183 Q4 Ribera Navarra reg. Spain
187 E7 Ribesalbes Spain
186 J3 Ribes de Freser Spain
161 H8 Ribiers France
177 L5 Ribiţa Romania
179 L6 Ribnica Radlje Ob Dravi Slovenia
188 E3 Ribnica Ribnica Slovenia
136 I6 Rîbniţa Moldova
170 F2 Ribnitz-Damgarten Ger.
197 L9 Ribnovo Bulg.
100 L2 Ribnovsk Rus. Fed.
183 N6 Ribota Spain
252 C5 Rica Aventura Chile
195 J6 Ricadi Italy
179 N1 Říčany Jihomoravský kraj Czech Rep.
176 D2 Říčany Středočeský kraj Czech Rep.
242 F3 Ricardo Flores Magón Mex.
149 P5 Riccal r. England U.K.
193 N5 Riccia Italy
191 M9 Riccio Italy
191 N7 Riccione Italy
190 H7 Riccò del Golfo di Spezia Italy
241 R7 Rice CA U.S.A.
232 G11 Rice VA U.S.A.
227 L2 Rice Lake l. Ont. Can.
224 E4 Rice Lake l. Ont. Can.
226 C4 Rice Lake WI U.S.A.
226 A3 Rice Lake l. MN U.S.A.
226 B6 Riceville IA U.S.A.
232 C11 Riceville KY U.S.A.
157 L6 Richardménil France
215 Q4 Richards Bay S. Africa
263 L1 Richards Inlet Antarctica
220 E3 Richards Island N.W.T. Can.
223 I3 Richardson r. Alta Can.
222 G1 Richardson Island N.W.T. Can.
233 □O4 Richardson Lakes ME U.S.A.
220 E3 Richardson Mountains N.W.T. Can.
81 C11 Richardson Mountains South I. N.Z.
206 B2 Richard Toll Senegal
217 □1b Riche en Eau Mauritius
164 H2 Richel i. Neth.
233 L3 Richelieu Que. Can.
162 E1 Richelieu France
234 A3 Richfield PA U.S.A.
241 T3 Richfield UT U.S.A.
233 K6 Richfield Springs NY U.S.A.
233 I6 Richford NY U.S.A.
233 M3 Richford VT U.S.A.
240 M6 Richgrove CA U.S.A.
147 I4 Richhill Northern Ireland U.K.
225 H4 Richibucto N.B. Can.
223 I4 Rich Lake Alta Can.
234 F6 Richland NJ U.S.A.
234 C4 Richland PA U.S.A.
238 E3 Richland WA U.S.A.
226 D6 Richland Center WI U.S.A.
232 D11 Richlands VA U.S.A.
234 E4 Richlandtown PA U.S.A.
83 M5 Richmond N.S.W. Austr.
85 I5 Richmond Qld Austr.
227 S4 Richmond Ont. Can.
225 F4 Richmond Que. Can.
246 □ Richmond Jamaica
81 H8 Richmond South I. N.Z.
215 O5 Richmond KwaZulu-Natal S. Africa
214 H7 Richmond Northern Cape S. Africa
149 N5 Richmond North Yorkshire, England U.K.
240 J4 Richmond CA U.S.A.
226 F7 Richmond IL U.S.A.
230 E6 Richmond IN U.S.A.
232 A11 Richmond KY U.S.A.
233 □P4 Richmond ME U.S.A.
227 L7 Richmond MI U.S.A.
237 H5 Richmond TX U.S.A.
232 H11 Richmond VA U.S.A.
233 M4 Richmond VT U.S.A.
81 H8 Richmond, Mount South I. N.Z.
235 G3 Richmond County county NY U.S.A.
232 C9 Richmond Dale OH U.S.A.
224 E5 Richmond Hill Ont. Can.
231 G10 Richmond Hill GA U.S.A.
247 □3 Richmond Peak St Vincent
83 N3 Richmond Range hills N.S.W. Austr.
81 H8 Richmond Range mts South I. N.Z.
233 K6 Richmondville NY U.S.A.
111 H11 Richoi Xizang China
170 G2 Richtenberg Ger.
214 B4 Richtersveld National Park S. Africa
172 F7 Richterswil Switz.
237 K10 Richton MS U.S.A.
177 K2 Richvald Slovakia
240 K2 Richvale CA U.S.A.
232 B8 Richwood OH U.S.A.
232 E10 Richwood WV U.S.A.
193 O6 Ricigliano Italy
172 D6 Rickenbach Ger.
151 N3 Rickinghall Suffolk, England U.K.
140 P4 Rickleån r. Sweden
168 J2 Rickling Ger.
151 L4 Rickmansworth Hertfordshire, England U.K.
183 R5 Ricla Spain
182 I5 Ricobayo, Embalse de resr Spain
Ricomagus France see Riom
177 K3 Ricse Hungary
263 E2 Riddell Nunataks nunataks Antarctica
Ridder Kazakh. see Leninogorsk
164 G5 Ridderkerk Neth.
190 C3 Riddes Switz.
232 G8 Riddlesburg PA U.S.A.
227 S4 Rideau r. Ont. Can.
224 E4 Rideau Lakes Ont. Can.
234 B6 Riderwood MD U.S.A.
224 C3 Ridge r. Ont. Can.
235 J3 Ridge NY U.S.A.
240 O6 Ridgecrest CA U.S.A.
235 I2 Ridgefield CT U.S.A.
235 G3 Ridgefield NJ U.S.A.
237 J9 Ridgeland MS U.S.A.
231 G9 Ridgeland SC U.S.A.
226 C4 Ridgeland WI U.S.A.
234 D7 Ridgely MD U.S.A.
227 M7 Ridgetown Ont. Can.
226 C6 Ridgeway IA U.S.A.
235 G4 Ridgeway NJ U.S.A.
232 F12 Ridgeway VA U.S.A.
235 G3 Ridgewood NJ U.S.A.
232 G7 Ridgway PA U.S.A.
177 I6 Riđica Vojvodina Serbia
146 M13 Riding Mill Northumberland, England U.K.
223 K5 Riding Mountain National Park Man. Can.
86 E6 Ridley r. W.A. Austr.
215 K3 Riebeeckstad S. Africa
214 C9 Riebeek-Kasteel S. Africa
215 K9 Riebeek-Oos S. Africa
214 C9 Riebeek-Wes S. Africa
140 N3 Riebnes l. Sweden
250 D2 Riecito Venez.
158 D6 Riec-sur-Belon France
173 K5 Ried Ger.
190 E3 Ried Switz.
173 I7 Riedbergerhorn mt. Ger.
168 G5 Riede Ger.
173 L3 Rieden Ger.
173 L4 Riedenburg Ger.
173 M6 Riedering Ger.
179 H3 Ried im Innkreis Austria
178 C5 Ried im Oberinntal Austria
178 E5 Ried im Zillertal Austria
179 K3 Ried in der Riedmark Austria
157 N8 Riedisheim France
172 G5 Riedlingen Ger.
172 B3 Riegelsberg Ger.
179 M5 Riegersburg Austria
234 E3 Riegleisville PA U.S.A.
184 H7 Riego, Canal de Spain
182 I4 Riego de la Vega Spain
190 D1 Riehen Switz.
215 K1 Riekertsdam S. Africa
172 F6 Rielasingen-Worblingen Ger.
182 I3 Riello Spain
183 L9 Rielves Spain
165 I7 Riemst Belgium
169 I10 Rieneck Ger.
177 L5 Rieni Romania
191 L2 Rienza r. Italy
140 P2 Rieppesgai'sa mt. Norway
168 K2 Riepsdorf Ger.
171 H8 Riesa Ger.
259 B9 Riesco, Isla i. Chile
168 I1 Rieseby Ger.
194 G9 Riesi Sicilia Italy
169 F6 Rieste Ger.
171 D8 Riestedt Ger.
214 H5 Riet r. S. Africa
214 E7 Riet watercourse S. Africa
138 E6 Rietavas Lith.
169 F7 Rietberg Ger.
214 H8 Rietbron S. Africa
214 E2 Rietfontein S. Africa
170 J3 Rieth Ger.
165 H6 Riethoven Neth.
214 F10 Riethuiskraal S. Africa
193 J3 Rieti Italy
193 J3 Rieti prov. Italy
215 N3 Rietkuil S. Africa
214 C6 Rietpoort S. Africa
171 K8 Rietschen Ger.
214 E6 Riet se Vloer salt pan S. Africa
215 O5 Rietvlei S. Africa
215 M1 Rietvlei Nature Reserve S. Africa
178 D5 Rietz Austria
163 G9 Rieumes France
163 I7 Rieupeyroux France
161 C7 Rieutort-de-Randon France
158 G6 Rieux Bretagne France
163 G9 Rieux Midi-Pyrénées France
163 J9 Rieux-Minervois France
161 I9 Riez France
128 E6 Rifā'ī, Tall mt. Jordan/Syria
256 D4 Rifaina Brazil
Rifeng Jiangxi China see Lichuan
178 H4 Rifflkopf mt. Austria
191 K2 Rifiano Italy
239 K7 Rifle CO U.S.A.
210 B4 Rift Valley prov. Kenya
Rift Valley Lakes National Park Eth. see Abijatta-Shalla National Park
111 L12 Riga Arun. Prad. India
138 H5 Rīga Latvia
138 G4 Riga, Gulf of Estonia/Latvia
207 G4 Rigacikun Nigeria
111 H10 Rigain Pünco l. Xizang China
198 D3 Rigaio Greece
122 H7 Rīgān Iran
Rīgas jūras līcis b. Estonia/Latvia see Riga, Gulf of
233 K3 Rigaud Que. Can.
161 J9 Rigaud France
238 I5 Rigby ID U.S.A.
238 F4 Riggins ID U.S.A.
160 K3 Riggisberg Switz.
146 E11 Righ Mòr, Loch l. Scotland U.K.
190 F1 Rigi mts Switz.
190 H5 Riglio r. Italy
122 H8 Rīg Matī Iran
163 I7 Rignac France
193 I3 Rignano Flaminio Italy
193 P4 Rignano Garganico Italy
191 K8 Rignano sull'Arno Italy
156 G7 Rigny-le-Ferron France
160 E3 Rigny-sur-Arroux France
159 L7 Rigny-Ussé France
225 J2 Rigolet Nfld and Lab. Can.
202 B6 Rig-Rig Chad
146 I11 Rigside South Lanarkshire, Scotland U.K.
183 R4 Riguel r. Spain
124 D6 Rīḥ, Gezirat er i. Sudan
124 D6 Rīḥ, Gezirat er i. Sudan
113 □1 Rihiveli i. S. Male Maldives
Riia laht b. Estonia/Latvia see Riga, Gulf of
141 R6 Riihimäki Fin.
140 S3 Riipi Fin.
262 W2 Riiser-Larsen Ice Shelf Antarctica
138 H2 Riisipere Estonia
140 T3 Riisitunturin kansallispuisto nat. park Fin.
242 B1 Riito Mex.
207 G4 Rijau Nigeria
188 E3 Riječki Zaliv b. Croatia
188 E3 Rijeka Croatia
191 R5 Rijeka airport Croatia
164 G5 Rijen Neth.
165 G6 Rijkevorsel Belgium
164 G4 Rijnsaterwoude Neth.
164 F4 Rijnsburg Neth.
140 □ Rijpfjorden inlet Svalbard
164 G5 Rijsbergen Neth.
164 K4 Rijssen Neth.
164 F4 Rijswijk Neth.
136 C5 Rika r. Ukr.
124 G4 Rikā, Wādī ar watercourse Saudi Arabia
94 B2 Rikitgaib Sumatera Indon.
117 O5 Rikor Arun. Prad. India
140 O2 Riksgränsen Sweden
102 U3 Rikubetsu Japan
102 T7 Rikuchū-kaigan Kokuritsu-kōen nat. park Japan
102 S7 Rikuzen-takata Japan
197 L8 Rila Bulg.
197 L8 Rila mts Bulg.
111 G12 Rila Xizang China
238 E5 Riley OR U.S.A.
232 G10 Rileyville VA U.S.A.
162 G4 Rilhac-Rancon France
165 F6 Rilland Neth.
159 L7 Rillé France
160 F5 Rillieux-la-Pape France
241 U9 Rillito AZ U.S.A.
186 D6 Rillo Spain
183 Q7 Rillo de Gallo Spain
156 H5 Rilly-la-Montagne France
207 G3 Rima watercourse Niger/Nigeria
124 F2 Rimah, Wādī al watercourse Saudi Arabia
79 □9 Rimatara i. Îs Australes Fr. Polynesia
Rimatera i. Îs Australes Fr. Polynesia see Rimatara
94 F6 Rimau, Pulau i. Indon.
157 J7 Rimaucourt France
177 J3 Rimava r. Slovakia
177 I3 Rimavská Baňa Slovakia
177 J3 Rimavská Seč Slovakia
177 J3 Rimavská Sobota Slovakia
173 N3 Rimbach Bayern Ger.
172 F2 Rimbach Hessen Ger.
222 H4 Rimbey Alta Can.
143 O2 Rimbo Sweden
232 F7 Rimersburg PA U.S.A.
197 L4 Rimetea Romania
143 L3 Rimforsa Sweden
191 N7 Rimini Italy
191 M7 Rimini prov. Italy
Rîmnicu Sărat Romania see Râmnicu Sărat
Rîmnicu Vîlcea Romania see Râmnicu Vâlcea
116 F2 Rimo Glacier Jammu and Kashmir
156 I4 Rimogne France
163 G10 Rimont France
225 G3 Rimouski Que. Can.
225 G3 Rimouski, Réserve Faunique de nature res. Que. Can.
172 H2 Rimpar Ger.
179 L7 Rimske Toplice Slovenia
173 M6 Rimsting Ger.
81 J8 Rimutaka Forest Park nature res. North I. N.Z.
111 I12 Rinbung Xizang China
93 A8 Rinca i. Indon.
256 C4 Rincão Brazil
173 O4 Rinchnach Ger.
258 D2 Rincón Arg.
Rincon Morocco see Mdiq
247 □8 Rincón Bonaire Neth. Antilles
247 □1 Rincón Puerto Rico
247 □1 Rincón, Bahía de b. Puerto Rico
252 D6 Rincón, Cerro del mt. Chile
258 D1 Rinconada Arg.
245 K6 Rinconada Mex.
185 J2 Rinconada, Sierra de la mts Spain
187 C7 Rincón de Ademuz reg. Spain
261 I3 Rincón de Cololó Uru.
260 C4 Rincón del Atuel Arg.
185 K7 Rincón de la Victoria Spain
261 I3 Rincón del Bonete, Lago Artificial de resr Uru.
260 C5 Rincón de los Sauces Arg.
261 I4 Rincón del Pino Uru.
261 I3 Rincón de Palacio Uru.
244 E3 Rincón de Romos Mex.
183 Q4 Rincón de Soto Spain
116 H7 Rind r. India
138 E4 Rinda r. Latvia
140 J5 Rindal Norway
117 L5 Rindü Xizang China
198 G5 Rineia i. Greece
194 H6 Rinella Isole Lipari Italy
232 E11 Riner VA U.S.A.
83 K9 Ringarooma Bay Tas. Austr.
143 M3 Ringarum Sweden
116 E6 Ringas Rajasthan India
147 F9 Ringaskiddy Ireland
142 G6 Ringe Denmark
168 C5 Ringe Ger.
141 K6 Ringebu Norway
190 G2 Ringelspitz mt. Switz.
170 I4 Ringenwalde Ger.
231 E8 Ringgold GA U.S.A.
96 D1 Ringhkung Myanmar
207 H3 Ringim Nigeria
142 E5 Ringkøbing Denmark
142 E5 Ringkøbing county Denmark
142 E6 Ringkøbing Fjord lag. Denmark
151 O2 Ringland Norfolk, England U.K.
171 D8 Ringleben Ger.
151 M6 Ringmer East Sussex, England U.K.
234 F4 Ringoes NJ U.S.A.
148 D3 Ringsend Northern Ireland U.K.
142 H6 Ringsted Denmark
111 F11 Ringtor Xizang China
140 O2 Ringvassøya i. Norway
147 G8 Ringville Ireland
151 I6 Ringwood Hampshire, England U.K.
233 K7 Ringwood NJ U.S.A.
Rinia i. Greece see Rineia
168 I1 Rinkenæs Denmark
146 J8 Rinloan Aberdeenshire, Scotland U.K.
178 E5 Rinn Austria
146 D11 Rinns of Islay pen. Scotland U.K.
146 D11 Rinns Point Scotland U.K.
256 B4 Rinópolis Brazil
169 H6 Rinteln Ger.
196 F5 Rinya r. Romania
226 E6 Rio WI U.S.A.
252 A1 Río Abiseo, Parque Nacional nat. park Peru
253 F4 Rio Alegre Brazil
255 C8 Rio Azul Brazil
250 B5 Riobamba Ecuador
257 G3 Rio Bananal Brazil
260 B3 Río Blanco Chile
239 K7 Rio Blanco CO U.S.A.
257 F5 Rio Bonito Brazil
252 D2 Rio Branco Brazil
Rio Branco state Brazil see Roraima
251 F4 Rio Branco, Parque Nacional do nat. park Brazil
256 C6 Rio Branco do Sul Brazil
242 H3 Río Bravo, Parque Internacional del nat. park Mex.
255 B7 Rio Brilhante Brazil
259 B6 Río Bueno Chile
246 □ Rio Bueno Jamaica
182 D5 Rio Caldo Port.
251 F2 Río Caribe Venez.
257 F4 Rio Casca Brazil
260 E2 Rio Ceballos Arg.
259 C8 Río Chico Arg.
251 E2 Río Chico Venez.
257 E5 Rio Claro Rio de Janeiro Brazil
256 D5 Rio Claro São Paulo Brazil
247 □7 Rio Claro Trin. and Tob.
247 I9 Río Claro Venez.
246 □ Rio Cobre r. Jamaica
261 E6 Río Colorado Arg.
250 B5 Río Corrientes Ecuador
260 E3 Río Cuarto Arg.
213 G4 Rio das Pedras Moz.
257 F5 Rio de Janeiro Brazil
257 F4 Rio de Janeiro state Brazil
242 □S14 Río de Jesús Panama
238 B6 Rio Dell CA U.S.A.
260 E3 Río de Los Sauces Arg.
182 F7 Rio de Mel Port.
184 C5 Rio de Moinhos Beja Port.
184 D5 Rio de Moinhos Évora Port.
184 C4 Rio de Moinhos Setúbal Port.
182 G5 Rio de Onor Port.
204 A5 Río de Oro, Bahía de b. Western Sahara
187 C7 Riodeva r. Spain
191 L2 Rio di Pusteria Italy
257 F4 Rio Doce Brazil
255 C8 Rio do Sul Brazil
182 E5 Rio Douro Port.
254 G4 Rio Formoso Brazil
242 □R12 Río Frío Costa Rica
183 K7 Riofrío Spain
182 H5 Riofrío de Aliste Spain
183 N6 Riofrío de Riaza Spain
259 C8 Río Gallegos Arg.
185 K7 Ríogordo Spain
259 D9 Río Grande Arg.
252 D5 Río Grande Bol.
258 G4 Rio Grande Brazil
246 □ Rio Grande r. Jamaica
245 J10 Río Grande Oaxaca Mex.
244 D2 Río Grande Zacatecas Mex.
243 K5 Rio Grande r. Mex./U.S.A. alt. Bravo del Norte, Río
247 □1 Rio Grande Puerto Rico
234 F6 Rio Grande NJ U.S.A.
258 C2 Río Grande, Salar de salt flat Arg.
237 F12 Rio Grande City TX U.S.A.
247 □1 Río Grande de Loiza, Embalse resr Puerto Rico
254 F3 Rio Grande do Norte state Brazil
255 B9 Rio Grande do Sul state Brazil
264 G8 Rio Grande Rise sea feature S. Atlantic Ocean
250 C2 Ríohacha Col.
242 □S13 Río Hato Panama
258 D2 Río Hondo, Embalse resr Arg.
250 B6 Rioja Peru
185 O7 Rioja Spain
243 O7 Río Lagartos Mex.
254 G4 Rio Largo Brazil
192 B8 Riola Sardo Sardegna Italy
182 H9 Riolobos Spain
245 K7 Río Lodo Mex.
191 L7 Riolo Terme Italy
161 B9 Riols France
160 C5 Riom France
190 H7 Riomaggiore Italy
184 B2 Rio Maior Port.
260 B4 Río Malo Chile
253 G3 Rio Manso, Represa do resr Brazil
192 E2 Rio Marina Italy
182 C6 Rio Mau Port.
161 B6 Riom-ès-Montagnes France
246 □ Rio Minho r. Jamaica
258 E2 Río Muerto Arg.
252 D4 Río Mulatos Bol.
207 H6 Río Muni reg. Equat. Guinea
163 C8 Rion-des-Landes France
260 D6 Río Negro prov. Arg.
255 C8 Rio Negro Brazil
259 B6 Río Negro Chile
261 I3 Río Negro dept Uru.
182 H4 Rionegro del Puente Spain
193 P6 Rionero in Vulture Italy
193 M4 Rionero Sannitico Italy
129 C3 Rioni r. Georgia
257 F4 Rio Novo Brazil
257 G4 Rio Novo do Sul Brazil
163 D6 Rions France
181 E3 Riópar Spain
261 H3 Río Paranacito Arg.
255 E5 Rio Pardo de Minas Brazil
246 □ Rio Pedro r. Jamaica
242 □Q10 Río Plátano, Reserva Biósfera del nature res. Hond.
257 F4 Rio Pomba Brazil
257 F5 Rio Preto Brazil
256 D2 Rio Preto, Serra do hills Brazil
261 F2 Río Primero Arg.
239 K9 Rio Rancho NM U.S.A.
160 E4 Riorges France
241 V10 Rio Rico AZ U.S.A.
182 F5 Ríos Spain
182 I3 Rioseco de Tapia Spain
261 F2 Río Segundo Arg.
183 M7 Riosequillo, Embalse de resr Spain
250 B3 Ríosucio Col.
261 H3 Río Tala Arg.
261 E3 Río Tercero Arg.
260 E3 Río Tercero, Embalse resr Arg.
250 B5 Río Tigre Ecuador
254 G3 Rio Tinto Brazil
246 I8 Río Tocuyo Venez.
182 F5 Rio Torto Port.
92 A7 Rio Tuba Palawan Phil.
161 G10 Riou, Île de i. France
223 J3 Riou Lake Sask. Can.
256 B2 Rio Verde Brazil
259 C9 Río Verde Chile
250 B4 Rioverde Ecuador
190 D6 Rioverde r. Italy
243 O8 Río Verde Quintana Roo Mex.
245 H4 Río Verde San Luis Potosí Mex.
255 B6 Rio Verde de Mato Grosso Brazil
257 F3 Rio Vermelho Brazil
240 K3 Rio Vista CA U.S.A.
160 I2 Rioz France
252 D2 Riozinho Amazonas Brazil
253 E2 Riozinho Rondônia Brazil
250 E5 Riozinho r. Brazil
253 F4 Riozinho r. Brazil
190 B5 Ripa r. Italy
192 E2 Ripalti, Punta dei pt Italy
196 I6 Ripanj Serbia
191 J9 Riparbella Italy
193 J3 Ripa Sottile, Lago di l. Italy
193 L2 Ripatransone Italy
140 P3 Ripats Sweden
191 O8 Ripe Italy
193 K4 Ripi Italy
193 O7 Ripiti r. Italy
137 K2 Ripky Ukr.
149 O7 Ripley Derbyshire, England U.K.
149 N5 Ripley North Yorkshire, England U.K.
237 K8 Ripley MS U.S.A.
232 F6 Ripley NY U.S.A.
232 B10 Ripley OH U.S.A.
237 K8 Ripley TN U.S.A.
232 D10 Ripley WV U.S.A.
186 J3 Ripoll Spain
186 J3 Ripolles reg. Spain
149 N5 Ripon North Yorkshire, England U.K.
240 K4 Ripon CA U.S.A.
226 F6 Ripon WI U.S.A.
195 I8 Riposto Sicilia Italy
150 H3 Ripple Worcestershire, England U.K.
149 N6 Ripponden West Yorkshire, England U.K.
164 I5 Rips Neth.
117 M6 Ripu Assam India
157 N7 Riquewihr France
123 O4 Risalpur Pak.
128 B8 Rīsān 'Unayzah hill Egypt
250 C3 Risaralda dept Col.
141 M6 Risarven Sweden
208 E5 Risasi Dem. Rep. Congo
140 M4 Risbäck Sweden
150 F4 Risca Caerphilly, Wales U.K.
136 G6 Rîşcani Moldova
163 D8 Riscle France
260 C4 Risco Plateado mt. Arg.
140 M4 Risede Sweden
142 F5 Risgårde Bredning b. Denmark
124 G3 Rishā, Wādī ar watercourse Saudi Arabia
116 G4 Rishikesh Uttaranchal India
102 R1 Rishiri-Rebun-Sarobetsu Kokuritsu-kōen nat. park Japan
102 S1 Rishiri-tō i. Japan
100 L6 Rishiri-zan vol. Japan
128 C7 Rishon Le Ẕiyyon Israel
123 J8 Rish Pish Iran
149 M6 Rishton Lancashire, England U.K.
230 E6 Rising Sun IN U.S.A.
234 C5 Rising Sun MD U.S.A.
159 L3 Risle r. France
188 E3 Risnjak nat. park Croatia
Rîşnov Romania see Râşnov
237 I8 Rison AR U.S.A.
142 F3 Risør Norway
156 D6 Ris-Orangis France
160 I3 Risoux, Mont mt. France
140 M2 Risøyhamn Norway
172 H5 Riß r. Ger.
140 J5 Rissa Norway
160 I4 Risse r. France
80 K6 Rissington North I. N.Z.
141 S6 Ristiina Fin.
140 T4 Ristijärvi Fin.
140 U2 Ristikent Rus. Fed.
111 D10 Risum Xizang China
168 G1 Risum-Lindholm Ger.
95 K4 Ritan r. Indon.
111 K12 Ritang Xizang China
138 H5 Rītausma Latvia
214 I5 Ritchie S. Africa
115 M6 Ritchie's Archipelago is Andaman & Nicobar Is India
78 □1 Ritidian Point Guam
209 C9 Rito Angola
129 B2 Ritsa Georgia
262 X2 Ritscher Upland mts Antarctica
140 N3 Ritsem Sweden
129 B2 Ritsis Nakrdzali nature res. Georgia
240 M4 Ritter, Mount CA U.S.A.
168 G4 Ritterhude Ger.
169 B10 Rittersdorf Ger.
171 G10 Rittersgrün Ger.
104 C5 Rittō Japan
183 P5 Rituerto r. Spain
138 K5 Rītupe r. Latvia
238 E3 Ritzville WA U.S.A.
186 H5 Riudoms Spain
136 H4 Riv r. Ukr.
138 E5 Rīva r. Latvia
159 K3 Riva Bella France
261 F4 Rivadavia Buenos Aires Arg.
260 C3 Rivadavia Mendoza Arg.
258 E2 Rivadavia Salta Arg.
260 B1 Rivadavia Chile
191 J4 Riva del Garda Italy
178 B8 Riva di Solto Italy
191 M2 Riva di Tures Italy
140 □ Rivalensundet str. Svalbard
190 D8 Riva Ligure Italy
190 G6 Rivanazzano Italy
239 K12 Riva Palacio Mex.
190 F7 Rivardo Ligure Italy
190 D5 Rivarolo Canavese Italy
190 I5 Rivarolo Mantovano Italy
261 H4 Rivas Arg.
242 □Q12 Rivas Nic.
261 I2 Rivas Uru.
122 H4 Rīvash Iran
183 N8 Rivas-Vaciamadrid Spain
160 F5 Rive-de-Gier France
162 B3 Rivedoux-Plage France
193 P7 Rivello Italy
261 F5 Rivera Arg.
255 B9 Rivera Uru.
206 C5 River Cess Liberia
240 M5 Riverdale CA U.S.A.
226 B5 River Falls WI U.S.A.
233 M8 Riverhead NY U.S.A.
223 J5 Riverhurst Sask. Can.
87 F10 Riverina W.A. Austr.
83 J6 Riverina reg. N.S.W. Austr.
259 B7 Rivero, Isla i. Chile
207 G5 Rivers state Nigeria
81 C12 Riversdale South I. N.Z.
214 F10 Riversdale S. Africa
81 K8 Riversdale Beach North I. N.Z.
81 F11 Riverside South I. N.Z.
215 N6 Riverside S. Africa
240 O8 Riverside CA U.S.A.
234 F4 Riverside NJ U.S.A.
234 B3 Riverside PA U.S.A.
222 E5 Rivers Inlet B.C. Can.
84 G5 Riversleigh Qld Austr.
147 F4 Riverstown Sligo Ireland
147 G6 Riverstown Tipperary Ireland
223 L5 Riverton Man. Can.
81 C13 Riverton South I. N.Z.
214 I4 Riverton S. Africa
234 E4 Riverton NJ U.S.A.
241 U1 Riverton UT U.S.A.
232 G10 Riverton VA U.S.A.
238 J5 Riverton WY U.S.A.
225 H4 Riverview N.B. Can.
215 Q4 River View S. Africa
235 G4 Riverwood NJ U.S.A.
156 D4 Rivery France
161 H6 Rives France
163 J10 Rivesaltes France
232 E9 Rivesville WV U.S.A.
234 B6 Riviera Beach MD U.S.A.
235 G4 Riviera Beach NJ U.S.A.
225 H3 Rivière-au-Renard Que. Can.

Rivière Bleue to Rossoszyca

377

225 G4 Rivière Bleue Que. Can.
217 □1c Rivière d'Abord, Pointe pt Réunion
217 □1b Rivière des Anguilles Mauritius
225 G4 Rivière-du-Loup Que. Can.
217 □1b Rivière-du Rempart Mauritius
225 H3 Rivière-Pentecôte Que. Can.
225 H3 Rivière-Pigou Que. Can.
247 □3 Rivière-Pilote Martinique
247 □3 Rivière-Salée Martinique
161 C8 Rivière-sur-Tarn France
214 D10 Riviersonderend S. Africa
214 D10 Riviersonderend Mountains S. Africa
191 O4 Rivignano Italy
137 K5 Rivne Kirovohrads'ka Oblast' Ukr.
137 N8 Rivne Respublika Krym Ukr.
136 F3 Rivne Rivnens'ka Oblast' Ukr.
136 G5 Rivne Vinnyts'ka Oblast' Ukr.
136 F2 Rivnens'ka Oblast' admin. div. Ukr.
Rivne Oblast admin. div. Ukr. see Rivnens'ka Oblast'
193 J2 Rivodutri Italy
190 D5 Rivoli Italy
215 O1 Rivulets S. Africa
209 D9 Rivungo Angola
81 G8 Riwaka South I. N.Z.
108 A3 Riwoqê Xizang China
165 G7 Rixensart Belgium
157 N8 Rixheim France
Riyadh Saudi Arabia see Ar Riyāḍ
125 I8 Riyan Yemen
106 G8 Riyue Shankou pass Qinghai China
122 F4 Riza well Iran
92 C4 Rizal Luzon Phil.
127 J3 Rize Turkey
129 B4 Rize prov. Turkey
107 P9 Rizhao Shandong China
Rizhao Shandong China see Donggang
245 M9 Rizo de Oro Mex.
Rizokarpaso Cyprus see Rizokarpason
128 C3 Rizokarpason Cyprus
198 D3 Rizomylos Greece
122 G5 Rīzū well Iran
122 G6 Rīzū'īyeh Iran
182 B4 Rizzanese r. Corse France
195 J7 Rizziconi Italy
194 G9 Rizzuto r. Sicilia Italy
195 M6 Rizzuto, Capo c. Italy
142 E2 Rjukan Norway
142 D2 Rjuvbrokkene mt. Norway
206 B2 Rkîz Maur.
231 E9 R. L. Harris Reservoir AL U.S.A.
191 L6 Ro Italy
142 G1 Roa Norway
185 M5 Roa Spain
82 □2 Roach Island Lord Howe I. Austr.
241 Q6 Roach Lake NV U.S.A.
151 K3 Roade Northamptonshire, England U.K.
150 D6 Roadford Reservoir England U.K.
232 C9 Roads OH U.S.A.
146 J5 Roadside Highland, Scotland U.K.
247 K4 Road Town Virgin Is (U.K.)
163 D7 Roaillan France
140 K4 Roan Norway
241 W2 Roan Cliffs ridge UT U.S.A.
146 K12 Roan Fell hill Scotland U.K.
160 E4 Roannais reg. France
160 E4 Roanne France
160 E4 Roanne à Digoin, Canal de France
231 E9 Roanoke AL U.S.A.
226 E9 Roanoke IL U.S.A.
232 F11 Roanoke VA U.S.A.
232 I12 Roanoke r. NC U.S.A.
232 H12 Roanoke Rapids NC U.S.A.
231 I7 Roanoke Island NC U.S.A.
241 W2 Roan Plateau UT U.S.A.
234 E11 Roaring Branch PA U.S.A.
147 C10 Roaringwater Bay Ireland
190 I3 Roasco r. Italy
242 □P9 Roatán Hond.
150 F5 Roath Cardiff, Wales U.K.
134 C3 Röbäck Sweden
123 J6 Robāt r. Afgh.
122 G6 Robāt Iran
122 G5 Robāt-e Ābgarm Iran
122 G5 Robāt-e Khān Iran
122 F6 Robāt-e Shahr-e Bābak Iran
124 D3 Robāt-e Sorkh Afgh.
122 D5 Robāte Tork Iran
122 H3 Robāt-e Ţoroq Iran
122 D2 Robāt Karīm Iran
122 H4 Robāt-Sang Iran
122 I4 Robat Thana Pak.
237 G4 Robb Alta Can.
214 C9 Robben Island S. Africa
83 J9 Robbins Island Tas. Austr.
231 F8 Robbinsville NC U.S.A.
234 F4 Robbinsville NJ U.S.A.
195 F5 Robbio Italy
82 G7 Robe S.A. Austr.
86 C6 Robe r. W.A. Austr.
210 C3 Robē Eth.
147 D5 Robe r. Ireland
87 H4 Robe, Mount hill N.S.W. Austr.
190 I5 Robecco d'Oglio Italy
170 G4 Röbel Ger.
225 I3 Robe Noire, Lac de la l. Que. Can.
157 J6 Robert-Espagne France
263 D2 Robert Glacier Antarctica
237 E10 Robert Lee TX U.S.A.
146 K12 Roberton Scottish Borders, Scotland U.K.
146 I11 Roberton South Lanarkshire, Scotland U.K.
261 F4 Roberts Arg.
238 H5 Roberts ID U.S.A.
83 N3 Roberts, Mount Qld Austr.
232 D10 Robertsburg WV U.S.A.
263 K2 Roberts Butte mt. Antarctica
241 P2 Roberts Creek Mountain NV U.S.A.
140 P4 Robertsfors Sweden
117 I7 Robertsganj Uttar Prad. India
237 H8 Robert S. Kerr Reservoir OK U.S.A.
85 I5 Robertson r. Qld Austr.
214 D9 Robertson S. Africa
225 J3 Robertson, Lac l. Que. Can.
263 L2 Robertson Bay Antarctica
262 U2 Robertson Island Antarctica
81 I8 Robertson Point South I. N.Z.
87 F7 Robertson Range hills W.A. Austr.
206 C5 Robertsport Liberia
82 G5 Robertstown S.A. Austr.
Robert Williams Angola see Caála
225 F3 Roberval Que. Can.
221 L1 Robeson Channel Can./Greenland
234 C4 Robesonia PA U.S.A.
161 E8 Robiac-Rochessadoule France
149 P5 Robin Hood's Bay North Yorkshire, England U.K.
Robin's Nest hill H.K. China see Hung Fa Leng
84 F4 Robinson r. N.T. Austr.
86 H4 Robinson r. W.A. Austr.
222 C2 Robinson Y.T. Can.
230 D6 Robinson IL U.S.A.
232 A10 Robinson KY U.S.A.
85 I8 Robinson Creek r. Qld Austr.
252 □ Robinson Crusoe, Isla i. S. Pacific Ocean
87 E8 Robinson Range hills W.A. Austr.
84 F4 Robinson River N.T. Austr.
83 I6 Robinvale Vic. Austr.
161 G9 Robion France
185 O3 Robledo Spain
183 L7 Robledo de Chavela Spain
183 K9 Robledo del Mazo Spain
182 I9 Robledollano Spain
183 J3 Robles de la Valcueva Spain
250 C2 Robles La Paz Col.
223 K5 Roblin Man. Can.
171 E8 Röblingen am See Ger.
182 I7 Robliza de Cojos Spain
253 F4 Robore Bol.
183 M6 Robregordo Spain
186 E4 Robres Spain
183 P4 Robres del Castillo Spain
78 □6 Rob Roy i. Solomon Is
223 I5 Robsart Sask. Can.
222 G4 Robson, Mount B.C. Can.
237 G12 Robstown TX U.S.A.
237 E9 Roby TX U.S.A.
191 Q5 Roč Croatia
184 A3 Roca, Cabo da c. Port.
Roçadas Angola see Xangongo
186 H5 Rocafort de Queralt Spain
163 H6 Rocamadour France
261 H3 Rocamora Arg.
228 D7 Roca Partida, Isla i. Mex.
245 L7 Roca Partida, Punta pt Mex.
250 □ Roca Redonda i. Islas Galápagos Ecuador
242 B5 Rocas Alijos is Mex.
195 O3 Roca Vecchia Italy
161 F9 Rocbaron France
190 I5 Roccabianca Italy
194 E8 Roccabruna, Bastimento mt. Sicilia Italy
193 O7 Roccadaspide Italy
193 L5 Rocca d'Evandro Italy
193 K3 Rocca di Cambio Italy
193 L3 Rocca di Mezzo Italy
195 L5 Rocca di Neto Italy
193 J4 Rocca di Papa Italy
190 H5 Roccafranca Italy
193 O7 Roccagloriosa Italy
193 L5 Rocca Imperiale Italy
190 C7 Rocca la Meia mt. Italy
192 H2 Roccalbegna Italy
195 I8 Roccalumera Sicilia Italy
193 M4 Roccamandolfi Italy
193 J4 Rocca Massima Italy
194 E8 Roccamena Sicilia Italy
193 L5 Roccamonfina Italy
193 M3 Roccamontepiano Italy
193 Q7 Roccanova Italy
194 F8 Roccapalumba Sicilia Italy
193 L5 Rocca Pia Italy
193 M4 Roccaraso Italy
191 L7 Rocca San Casciano Italy
193 M3 Rocca San Giovanni Italy
193 L4 Roccasecca Italy
193 K5 Roccasecca dei Volsci Italy
193 J3 Rocca Sinibalda Italy
192 G1 Roccastrada Italy
190 C7 Roccavione Italy
195 K7 Roccella Ionica Italy
193 O5 Rocchetta Sant'Antonio Italy
186 K3 Roc de France mt. France/Spain
161 B9 Roc de Layre mt. France
161 B9 Roc de Montalet mt. France
160 J4 Roc d'Enfer mt. France
158 D5 Roc de Toullaëron hill France
151 I2 Rocester Staffordshire, England U.K.
258 G4 Rocha Uru.
149 M6 Rochdale Greater Manchester, England U.K.
150 C7 Roche Cornwall, England U.K.
184 G8 Roche, Cabo c. Spain
161 J7 Rochebrune, Grand Pic de mt. France
162 F4 Rochechouart France
159 M7 Rochecorbon France
255 B6 Rochedo Brazil
165 H8 Rochefort Belgium
162 C4 Rochefort France
225 F1 Rochefort, Lac l. Que. Can.
158 G6 Rochefort-en-Terre France
160 B5 Rochefort-Montagne France
160 H2 Rochefort-sur-Nenon France
134 H3 Rochegda Rus. Fed.
161 F8 Rocheguide France
165 H9 Rochehaut Belgium
161 E6 Roche-la-Molière France
160 I2 Roche-lez-Beaupré France
226 E8 Rochelle IL U.S.A.
161 F7 Rochemaure France
217 □1b Roches, Plaine des plain Mauritius
157 J7 Roches-Bettaincourt France
158 H8 Rocheservière France
83 J7 Rochester Vic. Austr.
151 N5 Rochester Medway, England U.K.
149 M3 Rochester Northumberland, England U.K.
230 D5 Rochester IN U.S.A.
227 K7 Rochester MI U.S.A.
226 B5 Rochester MN U.S.A.
233 □O5 Rochester NH U.S.A.
233 H5 Rochester NY U.S.A.
147 H8 Rochestown Ireland
157 J8 Rochetaillée France
151 N4 Rochford Essex, England U.K.
147 H6 Rochfortbridge Ireland
156 F2 Rochin France
171 G8 Rochlitz Ger.
158 D5 Roc'h Trévezel hill France
184 F6 Rociana del Condado Spain
184 G7 Rocina r. Spain
179 I7 Ročinj Slovenia
222 E2 Rock r. Y.T. Can.
150 H3 Rock Worcestershire, England U.K.
226 G3 Rock MI U.S.A.
236 G4 Rock r. IA U.S.A.
226 D8 Rock r. IL U.S.A.
144 □ Rockall i. N. Atlantic Ocean
264 H2 Rockall Bank sea feature N. Atlantic Ocean
81 D12 Rock and Pillar Range mts South I. N.Z.
164 F5 Rockanje Neth.
222 E5 Rock Bay B.C. Can.
146 I13 Rockcliffe Dumfries and Galloway, Scotland U.K.
147 H4 Rockcorry Ireland
232 E7 Rock Creek OH U.S.A.
238 K2 Rock Creek r. MT U.S.A.
234 A5 Rock Creek r. PA U.S.A.
236 B6 Rockdale MD U.S.A.
237 G10 Rockdale TX U.S.A.
237 I11 Rockefeller National Wildlife Refuge nature res. LA U.S.A.
262 O1 Rockefeller Plateau Antarctica
169 G10 Rockenberg Ger.
172 D2 Rockenhausen Ger.
235 J1 Rockfall CT U.S.A.
231 D9 Rockford AL U.S.A.
226 E7 Rockford IL U.S.A.
226 I6 Rockford MI U.S.A.
232 A8 Rockford OH U.S.A.
223 J5 Rockglen Sask. Can.
236 I2 Rock Glen PA U.S.A.
234 C3 Rock Glen PA U.S.A.
234 C6 Rock Hall MD U.S.A.
85 M7 Rockhampton Qld Austr.
84 E5 Rockhampton Downs N.T. Austr.
226 F1 Rock Harbor MI U.S.A.
147 E8 Rockhill Ireland
234 F1 Rock Hill NY U.S.A.
231 G8 Rock Hill SC U.S.A.
87 C12 Rockingham W.A. Austr.
151 K2 Rockingham Northamptonshire, England U.K.
231 H8 Rockingham NC U.S.A.
85 K5 Rockingham Bay Qld Austr.
151 K2 Rockingham Forest England U.K.
223 H1 Rockinghorse Lake Nunavut Can.
233 M3 Rock Island Que. Can.
236 G4 Rock Island IL U.S.A.
236 F1 Rocklake ND U.S.A.
233 J3 Rockland Ont. Can.
233 O6 Rockland MA U.S.A.
233 □P4 Rockland ME U.S.A.
226 E3 Rockland MI U.S.A.
235 G2 Rockland County county NY U.S.A.
83 I7 Rocklands Reservoir Vic. Austr.
87 D7 Rocklea W.A. Austr.
240 K3 Rocklin CA U.S.A.
222 H1 Rocknest Lake N.W.T. Can.
171 G8 Röcknitz Ger.
241 W5 Rock Point AZ U.S.A.
230 D7 Rockport IN U.S.A.
233 O6 Rockport MA U.S.A.
237 G12 Rockport TX U.S.A.
238 E2 Rockport WA U.S.A.
232 D9 Rockport WV U.S.A.
236 G4 Rock Rapids IA U.S.A.
238 L6 Rock River WY U.S.A.
246 E1 Rock Sound Eleuthera Bahamas
238 K3 Rock Springs MT U.S.A.
237 E11 Rocksprings TX U.S.A.
238 J6 Rock Springs WY U.S.A.
251 G3 Rockstone Guyana
226 E7 Rockton IL U.S.A.
230 D6 Rockville IN U.S.A.
234 A6 Rockville MD U.S.A.
235 L1 Rockville RI U.S.A.
235 H3 Rockville Centre NY U.S.A.
237 G9 Rockwall TX U.S.A.
236 H4 Rockwell City IA U.S.A.
150 F6 Rockwell Green Somerset, England U.K.
233 □P3 Rockwood ME U.S.A.
227 K7 Rockwood MI U.S.A.
232 F9 Rockwood PA U.S.A.
238 J2 Rocky Boy's Indian Reservation res. MT U.S.A.
222 H5 Rockyford Alta Can.
236 D6 Rocky Ford CO U.S.A.
232 B9 Rocky Fork Lake OH U.S.A.
87 D13 Rocky Gully W.A. Austr.
225 J3 Rocky Harbour Nfld and Lab. Can.
235 J1 Rocky Hill CT U.S.A.
232 C10 Rocky Hill OH U.S.A.
223 M2 Rocky Island Lake Ont. Can.
222 G3 Rocky Lane Alta Can.
231 I8 Rocky Mount NC U.S.A.
232 F12 Rocky Mount VA U.S.A.
222 H4 Rocky Mountain House Alta Can.
238 L6 Rocky Mountain National Park CO U.S.A.
228 E2 Rocky Mountains CO U.S.A.
222 G4 Rocky Mountains Forest Reserve nature res. Alta Can.
246 □ Rocky Point Jamaica
246 □ Rocky Point pt Jamaica
212 B3 Rocky Point pt Namibia
82 □1 Rocky Point pt Norfolk I.
156 F5 Rocourt-St-Martin France
156 I4 Rocroi France
171 D10 Rodach r. Ger.
171 E10 Rodach Ger.
169 K10 Rodach bei Coburg Ger.
186 F5 Roda de Bara Spain
186 J4 Roda de Ter Spain
172 D3 Rodalben Ger.
168 H4 Rodau r. Ger.
142 E1 Rødberg Norway
150 H4 Rodborough Gloucestershire, England U.K.
168 L1 Rødby Denmark
142 H7 Rødbyhavn Denmark
225 K3 Roddickton Nfld and Lab. Can.
142 F7 Rødding Sønderjylland Denmark
142 F5 Rødding Viborg Denmark
215 N6 Rode S. Africa
143 L5 Rödeby Sweden
147 M7 Rode Heath Cheshire, England U.K.
182 E3 Rodeiro Spain
142 F6 Rødekro Denmark
146 C7 Rodel Western Isles, Scotland U.K.
186 E3 Rodellar Spain
161 B7 Rodelle France
164 J2 Roden Neth.
150 G2 Roden r. England U.K.
183 R7 Rödenas Spain
168 F4 Rodenkirchen (Stadland) Ger.
171 D10 Rödental Ger.
242 C2 Rodeo Arg.
242 G5 Rodeo Mex.
239 I11 Rodeo NM U.S.A.
87 D9 Roderick r. W.A. Austr.
168 H5 Rodewald Ger.
171 F9 Rodewisch Ger.
161 B8 Rodez France
169 G9 Rodheim-Bieber Ger.
Rodholivos Greece see Rodolivos
Rodhópolis Greece see Rodopoli
Rodhos i. Greece see Rodos
Ródhos Greece see Rodos
179 I7 Rodica mt. Slovenia
193 P4 Rodi Garganico Italy
173 N3 Roding Ger.
121 S1 Rodino Rus. Fed.
137 S6 Rodionovo-Nesvetayskaya Rus. Fed.
143 N1 Rödjebro Sweden
123 K8 Rodkhan Pak.
171 F7 Rodleben Ger.
140 M3 Rødlia Norway
197 N3 Rodna Romania
197 M3 Rodnei, Munţii mts Romania
80 I3 Rodney, Cape North I. N.Z.
150 G5 Rodney Stoke Somerset, England U.K.
234 D6 Rodney Village DE U.S.A.
Rodnichok Rus. Fed. see Rodnichok
135 H6 Rodnichok Rus. Fed.
120 H2 Rodnikovka Kazakh.
139 P8 Rodnya Belarus
139 R5 Rodnya Rus. Fed.
137 L5 Rodnykivka Ukr.
184 J4 Rodó, Puig mt. Spain
242 A2 Rodolfo Sanchez Toboada Mex.
198 E2 Rodolivos Greece
196 H9 Rodonit, Kepi i pt Albania
Rodopi Planina mts Bulg./Greece see Rhodope Mountains
198 E1 Rodopoli Greece
198 E7 Rodopos Kriti Greece
199 J6 Rodos Rodos Greece
199 J6 Rodos i. Greece
Rodosto Turkey see Tekirdağ
138 K4 Rodovoye Rus. Fed.
140 L3 Rødøya i. Norway
250 C6 Rodrigues Peru
217 □1a Rodrigues Island Mauritius
261 I4 Rodriguez Uru.
170 E1 Rødsand sea feature Denmark
140 J2 Rødsand Norway
142 E1 Rødungen l. Norway
86 H3 Roe r. W.A. Austr.
147 G3 Roe r. Northern Ireland U.K.
148 D3 Roe r. Northern Ireland U.K.
87 G11 Roe, Lake salt flat W.A. Austr.
234 F4 Roebling NJ U.S.A.
86 D6 Roebourne W.A. Austr.
86 G5 Roebuck Bay W.A. Austr.
215 F5 Roedtan S. Africa
191 K3 Roèn, Monte mt. Italy
86 E6 Roe Plains W.A. Austr.
165 I6 Roermond Neth.
165 C7 Roesbrugge-Haringe Belgium
165 D7 Roeselare Belgium
221 J3 Roes Welcome Sound sea chan. Nunavut Can.
169 B9 Roetgen Ger.
193 O7 Rofrano Italy
Rogachev Belarus see Rahachow
137 S2 Rogachevka Rus. Fed.
139 U5 Rogachevo Rus. Fed.
253 D2 Rogagua, Laguna l. Bol.
142 C2 Rogaland county Norway
188 E2 Rogaška Slatina Slovenia
174 F4 Rogatec Slovenia
151 K5 Rogate West Sussex, England U.K.
179 M7 Rogatica Bos.-Herz.
188 G4 Rogatin Ukr. see Rohatyn
171 E6 Rogätz Ger.
142 E1 Rogden l. Norway
227 P2 Roger, Lac l. Que. Can.
222 G6 Rogers B.C. Can.
237 H7 Rogers AR U.S.A.
232 D12 Rogers, Mount VA U.S.A.
227 K4 Rogers City MI U.S.A.
240 O8 Rogers Lake CA U.S.A.
232 G5 Rogerson ID U.S.A.
232 C12 Rogersville TN U.S.A.
232 B12 Rogersville TN U.S.A.
224 E2 Roggan r. Que. Can.
224 E2 Roggan, Lac l. Que. Can.
165 I6 Roggel Neth.
173 I5 Roggenburg Ger.
170 D3 Roggendorf Ger.
170 G4 Roggentin Ger.
267 N8 Roggeveen Basin sea feature S. Pacific Ocean
214 E8 Roggeveld plat. S. Africa
214 E8 Roggeveldberge esc. S. Africa
193 Q8 Roggiano Gravina Italy
Roghadal Scotland U.K. see Rodel
Roghadal Western Isles, Scotland U.K. see Rodel
195 J7 Roghudi Italy
184 B6 Rogil Port.
162 F3 Rogliano Corse France
193 F5 Rogliano Italy
195 J8 Roglio r. Italy
161 G10 Rognac France
140 M3 Rognan Norway
139 Q8 Rognedino Rus. Fed.
161 G9 Rognes France
168 K4 Rögnitz r. Ger.
157 J7 Rognon r. France
170 I9 Rognonas France
137 R7 Rogonaya, Punta mt. Italy
137 R8 Rogovatoye Rus. Fed.
175 H4 Rogovskaya Rus. Fed.
174 F3 Rogów Pol.
Rogowo Kujawsko-Pomorskie Pol.
175 H3 Rogowo Kujawsko-Pomorskie Pol.
174 E4 Rogoźnica Pol.
175 K3 Rogoźniczka Pol.
176 G4 Rogóźno Pol.
174 F3 Rogoźno Pol.
143 L1 Rogsjön l. Sweden
141 N6 Rogsta Sweden
238 B5 Rogue r. OR U.S.A.
78 □3b Roguron i. Majuro Marshall Is
115 J3 Roguszyn Pol.
136 G3 Roha Mahar. India
158 F5 Rohachiv Ukr.
137 P4 Rohan France
176 G3 Rohan' Ukr.
136 D4 Rohatec Czech Rep.
116 D7 Rohatyn Ukr.
78 □6 Rohera Rajasthan India
137 K2 Rohinari Malaita Solomon Is
171 D10 Rohizky Ukr.
170 E4 Röhlingen Ger.
170 F4 Rohlsdorf Brandenburg Ger.
240 J3 Rohlsdorf Brandenburg Ger.
177 L3 Rohnert Park CA U.S.A.
176 G3 Rohod Hungary
176 G3 Rohovce Slovakia
173 L4 Rohrau Austria
179 I2 Rohrbach Ger.
Rohrbach in Oberösterreich Austria
157 N5 Rohrbach-lès-Bitche France
170 D5 Rohrberg Ger.
173 L4 Rohr in Niederbayern Ger.
123 M8 Rohri Sangar Pak.
173 N5 Röhrmoos Ger.
173 P4 Röhrnbach Ger.
168 H5 Rohrsen Ger.
118 D8 Rohtak Haryana India
138 G3 Rohuküla Estonia
96 F6 Roi Et Thai.
161 F6 Roiffieux France
187 D12 Roig, Cabo c. Spain
187 I9 Roig, Cap c. Spain
78 □ Roi Georges, Îles du is Arch. des Tuamotu Fr. Polynesia
78 □3a Roi-Namur i. Kwajalein Marshall Is
141 R6 Roine l. Fin.
117 O5 Roing Arun. Prad. India
141 E9 Rois-Bheinn hill Scotland U.K.
156 F4 Roisel France
156 E6 Roissy-en-Brie France
183 L2 Roiz Spain
138 G4 Roja Latvia
216 □3a Roja, Punta pt Tenerife Canary Is
187 I10 Roja, Punta pt Spain
187 O11 Rojales Spain
261 G4 Rojas Arg.
142 I1 Röjdåfors Sweden
174 G3 Rojewo Pol.
123 M7 Rojhan Pak.
245 J4 Rojo, Cabo c. Mex.
247 □1 Rojo, Cabo c. Puerto Rico
252 D3 Rojo Aguado, Laguna l. Bol.
94 D4 Rokan r. Indon.
85 I2 Rokeby Qld Austr.
85 I2 Rokeby National Park Qld Austr.
78 □6 Rokera Solomon Is
175 H6 Rokiciny Pol.
175 K6 Rokietnica Podkarpackie Pol.
174 E3 Rokietnica Wielkopolskie Pol.
138 H6 Rokiškis Lith.
135 I6 Rokitnoye Rus. Fed.
102 S6 Rokkasho Japan
103 O9 Rokkō-zaki pt Japan
142 D3 Røkland Norway
143 M3 Rökland Norway
143 M4 Roknäs Sweden
177 H3 Rokoš mt. Slovakia
105 H3 Rokugo Japan
105 H3 Rokuriga-hara plain Japan
104 E2 Rokusei Japan
176 C2 Rokycany Czech Rep.
136 E3 Rokytne Ukr.
176 F2 Rokytná r. Czech Rep.
136 G3 Rokytne Kyivs'ka Oblast' Ukr.
136 G2 Rokytne Rivnens'ka Oblast' Ukr.
176 G2 Rokytnice Czech Rep.
111 I9 Rola Co l. Xizang China
111 I9 Rolagang Xizang China
111 I9 Rola Kangri mt. Xizang China
157 J8 Rolampont France
256 B5 Rolândia Brazil
111 I5 Rolas, Ilha das i. São Tomé and Príncipe
261 G3 Roldán Arg.
164 K3 Rolde Neth.
253 E2 Rolim de Moura Brazil
241 S9 Roll AZ U.S.A.
236 J7 Rolla MO U.S.A.
236 F1 Rolla ND U.S.A.
142 F1 Rollag Norway
182 I7 Rollán Spain
190 A3 Rolle Switz.
151 P2 Rollesby Norfolk, England U.K.
85 L8 Rolleston Qld Austr.
81 G10 Rolleston South I. N.Z.
81 F9 Rolleston, Mount South I. N.Z.
81 F10 Rolleston Range mts South I. N.Z.
227 O2 Rollet Que. Can.
246 F2 Rolleville Gt Exuma Bahamas
237 J9 Rolling Fork MS U.S.A.
233 G3 Rollins MT U.S.A.
233 □O5 Rollinsford NH U.S.A.
206 E3 Rollo Burkina
227 G3 Rolphton Ont. Can.
140 M5 Rolvenes Norway
140 R1 Rolvsøya i. Norway
162 E3 Rom France
170 E4 Rom Ger.
210 B4 Rom mt. Uganda
85 J3 Roma Qld Austr.
193 J4 Roma Italy
193 J4 Roma prov. Italy
215 L5 Roma Lesotho
197 O3 Roma Romania
143 P4 Roma Gotland Sweden
237 F12 Roma TX U.S.A.
Roma, Pulau i. Maluku Indon. see Romang, Pulau
190 E4 Romagnano Sesia Italy
158 I5 Romagné France
81 D13 Romahapa South I. N.Z.
231 H9 Romain, Cape SC U.S.A.
225 I3 Romaine r. Que. Can.
190 A2 Romainmôtier Switz.
197 O4 Roman Romania
151 N4 Roman r. England U.K.
192 B7 Romana Sardegna Italy
197 K4 Română, Câmpia plain Romania
197 L6 Romanaţilor, Câmpia plain Romania
149 O5 Romanby North Yorkshire, England U.K.
161 H6 Romanche r. France
264 H6 Romanche Gap sea feature S. Atlantic Ocean
234 C7 Romancoke MD U.S.A.
160 F4 Romanèche-Thorins France
225 H1 Romanet, Lac l. Que. Can.
93 E7 Romang, Pulau i. Maluku Indon.
197 M4 Romania country Europe
183 O6 Romanillos de Atienza Spain
175 M6 Romaniv Ukr.
137 N9 Roman-Kosh mt. Ukr.
146 J11 Romannobridge Scottish Borders, Scotland U.K.
260 D2 Romano, Cayo i. Cuba
191 L4 Romano d'Ezzelino Italy
190 H4 Romano di Lombardia Italy
183 O7 Romanones Spain
Romanovka Moldova see Basarabeasca
99 J1 Romanovka Respublika Buryatiya Rus. Fed.
135 H6 Romanovka Saratovskaya Oblast' Rus. Fed.
121 S1 Romanovo Rus. Fed.
174 E3 Romanowo Pol.
190 G1 Romanshorn Switz.
161 G6 Romans-sur-Isère France
220 B3 Romanzof, Cape AK U.S.A.
251 F5 Romão Brazil
158 I5 Romazy France
157 L5 Rombas France
195 K6 Rombiolo Italy
92 D5 Romblon Phil.
92 D5 Romblon i. Phil.
92 D5 Romblon Passage Phil.
Rombo, Ilhéus do is Cape Verde see Secos, Ilhéus
Rome Italy see Roma
231 E8 Rome GA U.S.A.
226 E9 Rome IL U.S.A.
233 □P4 Rome ME U.S.A.
233 J5 Rome NY U.S.A.
160 F3 Rome Château, Mont de hill France
226 I8 Rome City IN U.S.A.
184 B2 Romeira Port.
137 M3 Romen r. Ukr.
239 K8 Romeo CO U.S.A.
227 K7 Romeo MI U.S.A.
172 H4 Römerstein hill Ger.
182 F5 Romeu Port.
151 M4 Romford Greater London, England U.K.
169 K10 Römhild Ger.
158 H5 Romillé France
156 B5 Romilly-sur-Andelle France
156 G6 Romilly-sur-Seine France
123 M2 Romit Tajik.
244 F5 Romita Mex.
120 K8 Romitan Uzbek.
169 C8 Rommerskirchen Ger.
232 G9 Romney WV U.S.A.
151 N5 Romney Marsh reg. England U.K.
137 M3 Romny Ukr.
142 E6 Rømø i. Denmark
137 M4 Romodan Ukr.
135 I5 Romodanovo Rus. Fed.
190 B2 Romont Switz.
78 □4a Romonum i. Chuuk Micronesia
162 H1 Romorantin-Lanthenay France
94 E3 Rompin r. Malaysia
140 T5 Romppala Fin.
169 H9 Romrod Ger.
151 J6 Romsey Hampshire, England U.K.
142 H2 Rømskog Norway
150 H3 Romsley Worcestershire, England U.K.
95 M9 Romu mt. Sumbawa Indon.
197 M3 Romuli Romania
227 K7 Romulus MI U.S.A.
114 D5 Ron Karnataka India
96 H5 Ron Vietnam
96 H5 Ron, Mui hd Vietnam
146 F7 Rona i. Highland, Scotland U.K.
146 E4 Rona i. Western Isles, Scotland U.K.
Ronaigh i. Scotland U.K. see Ronay
146 □N1 Ronas Hill Scotland U.K.
146 B8 Ronay i. Scotland U.K.
191 M4 Roncade Italy
182 E1 Roncadoira, Punta pt Spain
256 A6 Roncador Brazil
254 B5 Roncador, Serra do hills Brazil
246 C7 Roncador Cay i. Caribbean Sea
78 □6 Roncador Reef Solomon Is
186 D2 Roncal Spain
186 C2 Roncal, Valle del val. Spain
178 D7 Roncegno Italy
156 F3 Ronce-les-Bains France
Roncesvalles Navarra Spain see Orreaga
232 E11 Ronceverte WV U.S.A.
157 M8 Ronchamp France
191 O4 Ronchi dei Legionari Italy
192 I3 Ronciglione Italy
191 M7 Ronco r. Italy
190 D5 Ronco Canavese Italy
191 J4 Roncone Italy
190 F6 Ronco Scrivia Italy
156 F2 Roncq France
182 C2 Roncudo, Punta pt Spain
185 I7 Ronda Spain
185 I7 Ronda, Serranía de mts Spain
185 J7 Ronda, Serranía de nature res. Spain
253 E3 Ronda das Salinas Brazil
142 F1 Rondane Nasjonalpark nat. park Norway
142 F1 Rondane Nasjonalpark nat. park Norway
263 B5 Rønde Denmark
247 □6 Ronde i. Grenada
190 D5 Rondissone Italy
256 A5 Rondon Brazil
254 E4 Rondon Col.
252 E2 Rondônia state Brazil
255 B6 Rondonópolis Brazil
233 K7 Rondout Reservoir NY U.S.A.
Ronda Jammu and Kashmir
112 E6 Rong'an Guangxi China
108 B3 Rongbaca Sichuan China
108 E4 Rongchang Chongqing China
Rongcheng Anhui China see Qingyang
Rongcheng Guangxi China see Rongxian
Rongcheng Hubei China see Jianli
107 R8 Rongcheng Shandong China
107 R8 Rongcheng Wan b. China
111 K5 Rong Chu r. China
266 G6 Rongelap atoll Marshall Is
108 G6 Rongjiang Guizhou China
Rongjiang Jiangxi China see Nankang
108 G7 Rong Jiang r. China
Rongjiawan Hunan China see Yueyang
96 A3 Rongklang Range mts Myanmar
Rongmei Hubei China see Hefeng
108 G6 Rongshui Guangxi China
Rongwo Qinghai China see Tongren
108 H7 Rongxian Guangxi China
108 E4 Rongxian Sichuan China
Rongzhag Sichuan China see Danba
79 □9a Roniu mt. Tahiti Fr. Polynesia
Rönlap atoll Marshall Is see Rongelap
143 K6 Rønne Bornholm Denmark
171 F9 Ronneburg Ger.
143 L5 Ronneby Sweden
262 S2 Ronne Entrance str. Antarctica
262 T1 Ronne Ice Shelf Antarctica
169 I6 Ronnenberg Ger.
140 L5 Rönnöfors Sweden
86 D6 Ronsard Island W.A. Austr.
176 G3 Ronsberg Ger.
165 E7 Ronse Belgium
169 F8 Ronshausen Ger.
254 B5 Ronuro r. Brazil
147 F6 Rooaun Ireland
215 N2 Roodebank S. Africa
164 K2 Roodeschool Neth.
215 M4 Rooiberg mt. Free State S. Africa
214 F9 Rooiberg mt. Western Cape S. Africa
214 F5 Rooibergdam l. S. Africa
214 E8 Rooikloof pass S. Africa
214 E5 Rooikraal S. Africa
215 L3 Rooiwal S. Africa
Rooke Island P.N.G. see Umboi
216 □2c Rookery Point Tristan da Cunha S. Atlantic Ocean
86 E6 Rookh Aboriginal Reserve W.A. Austr.
147 C5 Roonah Quay Ireland
116 F5 Roorkee Uttaranchal India
215 N4 Roosboom S. Africa
164 F5 Roosendaal Neth.
241 U8 Roosevelt AZ U.S.A.
235 G4 Roosevelt NJ U.S.A.
241 W1 Roosevelt UT U.S.A.
222 E3 Roosevelt, Mount B.C. Can.
235 G5 Roosevelt City NJ U.S.A.
262 N1 Roosevelt Island Antarctica
147 G5 Roosky Leitrim Ireland
147 E5 Roosky Mayo Ireland
138 I2 Roosna-Alliku Estonia
215 N1 Roossenekal S. Africa
222 F2 Root r. N.W.T. Can.
226 C6 Root r. MN U.S.A.
175 J6 Ropa Pol.
175 J6 Ropa r. Pol.
138 H5 Ropaži Latvia
175 J5 Ropczyce Pol.
84 E3 Roper r. N.T. Austr.
84 E3 Roper Bar N.T. Austr.
84 E3 Roper Bar Aboriginal Land res. N.T. Austr.
85 L7 Roper Creek r. Qld Austr.
182 I4 Roperuelos del Páramo Spain
84 E3 Roper Valley N.T. Austr.
175 K6 Ropienka Pol.
140 P2 Ropinsalmi Fin.
178 C5 Roppen Austria
161 K8 Roquebillière France
161 C9 Roquebrun France
161 K9 Roquebrune-Cap-Martin France
161 J10 Roquebrune-sur-Argens France
163 F7 Roquecor France
163 I8 Roquecourbe France
216 □3c Roque del Este i. Canary Is
216 □3d Roque de los Muchachos vol. La Palma Canary Is
163 D7 Roquefort France
161 B9 Roquefort-sur-Soulzon France
161 F8 Roquemaure France
261 H4 Roque Pérez Arg.
161 K9 Roquesteron France
186 G6 Roquetas Spain
185 N7 Roquetas de Mar Spain
161 H10 Roquevaire France
251 F4 Roraima state Brazil
251 F3 Roraima, Mount Guyana
142 E3 Rore i. Norway
116 E5 Rori Punjab India
Ro Ro Reef Fiji see Malolo Barrier Reef
140 K5 Røros Norway
190 H1 Rorschach Switz.
142 H6 Rørvig Denmark
140 K4 Rørvik Norway
175 M2 Ros' Belarus
138 H8 Ros' r. Belarus
136 K4 Ros' r. Ukr.
175 J2 Roś, Jezioro l. Pol.
165 I4 Rosà Italy
246 G3 Rosa, Lake Gt Inagua Bahamas
190 D4 Rosa, Monte mt. Italy/Switz.
242 E4 Rosa, Punta pt Mex.
174 D4 Rosablanche mt. Switz.
216 □1c Rosais São Jorge Azores
216 □1c Rosais, Ponta dos pt São Jorge Azores
182 C5 Rosal, Val do reg. Spain
184 E5 Rosal de la Frontera Spain
242 G3 Rosales Mex.
238 F3 Rosalia WA U.S.A.
247 □2 Rosalie Bay Dominica
246 C5 Rosalind Bank sea feature Caribbean Sea
240 N7 Rosamond CA U.S.A.
240 N7 Rosamond Lake CA U.S.A.
244 B3 Rosamorada Mex.
256 A5 Rosana Brazil
178 B5 Rosanna r. Austria
161 G8 Rosans France
147 G2 Rosapenna Ireland
258 D1 Rosario Jujuy Arg.
261 G3 Rosario Santa Fé Arg.
254 D2 Rosario Brazil
252 D6 Rosario Chile
242 B2 Rosario Baja California Mex.
242 E3 Rosario Coahuila Mex.
244 B3 Rosario Sinaloa Mex.
242 E4 Rosario Sonora Mex.
244 F1 Rosario Zacatecas Mex.
253 F6 Rosario Para.
92 C3 Rosario Luzon Phil.
92 C5 Rosario Luzon Phil.
184 C5 Rosário Port.
261 I4 Rosario Uru.
251 C2 Rosario Venez.
250 C2 Rosario, Cayo del i. Cuba
246 C3 Rosario Bank sea feature Caribbean Sea
246 A4 Rosario de la Frontera Arg.
258 D2 Rosario de Lerma Arg.
261 H3 Rosario del Tala Arg.
260 D2 Rosario del Tama Arg.
255 B9 Rosário do Sul Brazil
253 E3 Rosario Oeste Brazil
242 A1 Rosarito Baja California Mex.
242 B3 Rosarito Baja California Mex.
242 D4 Rosarito Baja California Sur Mex.
183 J8 Rosarito, Embalse de resr Spain
195 J7 Rosarno Italy
Rosas Spain see Roses
Rosas, Golfo de b. Spain see Roses, Golf de
137 K4 Rosava r. Ukr.
169 G10 Rosbach vor der Höhe Ger.
147 E3 Rosbeg Ireland
147 I8 Rosbercon Ireland
158 B5 Roscanvel France
168 K5 Rosche Ger.
178 D5 Röschitz Austria
179 M2 Rościszewo Pol.
175 H3 Rościszewo Pol.
226 E7 Roscoe IL U.S.A.
158 D4 Roscoff France
147 F5 Roscommon Ireland
147 F5 Roscommon county Ireland
226 J5 Roscommon MI U.S.A.
147 G7 Roscrea Ireland
169 I8 Rosdorf Ger.
84 E3 Rose r. N.T. Austr.
193 Q9 Rose Italy
240 M2 Rose, Mount NV U.S.A.
247 □2 Roseau Dominica
236 H1 Roseau MN U.S.A.
236 H1 Roseau r. MN U.S.A.
217 □1b Rose Belle Mauritius
149 O4 Roseberry Topping hill England U.K.
84 G8 Roseberth Qld Austr.
83 J9 Rosebery Tas. Austr.
225 J4 Rose Blanche Nfld and Lab. Can.
222 H5 Rosebud r. Alta Can.
238 K3 Rosebud MT U.S.A.
238 K3 Rosebud Creek r. MT U.S.A.
236 E4 Rosebud Indian Reservation res. SD U.S.A.
238 C5 Roseburg OR U.S.A.
227 J5 Rose City MI U.S.A.
226 B6 Rose Creek MN U.S.A.
85 M8 Rosedale Qld Austr.
83 K8 Rosedale Vic. Austr.
234 B6 Rosedale MD U.S.A.
237 J9 Rosedale MS U.S.A.
149 P5 Rosedale Abbey North Yorkshire, England U.K.
214 G8 Rosedene S. Africa
165 G8 Rosée Belgium
179 J6 Rosegg Austria
251 G3 Rosehall Guyana
246 □ Rose Hall Jamaica
146 L7 Rosehearty Aberdeenshire, Scotland U.K.
217 □1b Rose Hill Mauritius
210 B2 Roseires Reservoir Sudan
75 H4 Rose Island atoll American Samoa
231 □2 Rose Island Bahamas
160 J5 Roselend, Barrage de dam France
235 G3 Roselle NJ U.S.A.
146 H7 Rosemarkie Highland, Scotland U.K.
86 D6 Rosemary Island W.A. Austr.
147 H6 Rosenallis Ireland
237 H11 Rosenberg TX U.S.A.
142 C2 Rosendal Norway
215 L4 Rosendal S. Africa
226 F6 Rosendale WI U.S.A.
146 K5 Rose Ness hd Scotland U.K.
172 F5 Rosenfeld Ger.
168 I4 Rosengarten Ger.
234 E6 Rosenhayn NJ U.S.A.
173 M6 Rosenheim Ger.
179 I6 Rosenkock mt. Austria
170 H3 Rosenow Ger.
179 J6 Rosental val. Austria
169 G9 Rosenthal Ger.
241 W8 Rose Peak AZ U.S.A.
222 D4 Rose Point B.C. Can.
143 N2 Roserberg Sweden
186 L3 Roses Spain
186 L3 Roses, Golf de b. Spain
234 E3 Roseto PA U.S.A.
193 P5 Roseto Capo Spulico Italy
193 M2 Roseto degli Abruzzi Italy
193 O5 Roseto Valfortore Italy
223 J5 Rosetown Sask. Can.
Rosetta Egypt see Rashīd
85 K6 Rosetta Creek r. Qld Austr.
223 K4 Rose Valley Sask. Can.
240 K3 Roseville CA U.S.A.
236 J5 Roseville IL U.S.A.
227 L7 Roseville MI U.S.A.
232 C9 Roseville OH U.S.A.
146 J11 Rosewell Midlothian, Scotland U.K.
85 N9 Rosewood Qld Austr.
232 B8 Rosewood OH U.S.A.
139 W6 Roshal' Rus. Fed.
138 M1 Roshchino Leningradskaya Oblast' Rus. Fed.
129 G1 Roshchino Stavropol'skiy Kray Rus. Fed.
137 N8 Roshchyne Ukr.
157 N6 Rosheim France
122 H4 Roshkhvār Iran
129 G2 Roshni-Chu Rus. Fed.
226 E5 Rosholt WI U.S.A.
212 C5 Rosh Pinah Namibia
Roshtkala Tajik. see Roshtqal'a
123 N3 Roshtqal'a Tajik.
146 E9 Roshven Highland, Scotland U.K.
185 □ Rosia Gibraltar
177 L5 Roşia Romania
185 □ Rosia Bay Gibraltar
176 F2 Rosice Czech Rep.
161 D6 Rosières France
156 E4 Rosières-en-Santerre France
156 H7 Rosières-près-Troyes France
190 I9 Rosignano Marittimo Italy
86 C6 Rosily Island W.A. Austr.
197 M3 Rosiana Slovakia
197 P6 Roşiori Romania
197 N6 Roşiori de Vede Romania
138 K6 Rositsa Belarus
197 P7 Rositsa Bulg.
197 N7 Rositsa r. Bulg.
171 F8 Rositz Ger.
147 E4 Roskeeragh Point Ireland
146 C8 Roskhill Highland, Scotland U.K.
142 I6 Roskilde Denmark
142 I6 Roskilde county Denmark
173 E3 Roskilde county Denmark
198 A2 Roskovec Albania
171 G6 Roskow Ger.
241 U9 Roskruge Mountains AZ U.S.A.
171 E10 Röslau Ger.
171 F10 Röslau r. Ger.
139 P8 Roslavl' Rus. Fed.
146 J11 Roslin Midlothian, Scotland U.K.
140 V2 Roslyakovo Rus. Fed.
134 I6 Roslyatino Rus. Fed.
164 H5 Rosmalen Neth.
182 F9 Rosmaninhal Port.
215 J7 Rosmead S. Africa
147 C5 Rosmuck Ireland
174 E1 Rosnowo Pol.
191 M5 Rosolina Italy
191 M5 Rosolina Mare Italy
194 H10 Rosolini Sicilia Italy
197 J9 Rosoman Macedonia
156 F7 Rosoy France
178 F5 Rospitze mt. Austria/Italy
158 D6 Rosporden France
169 D9 Rösrath Ger.
83 K10 Ross Tas. Austr.
222 C2 Ross r. Y.T. Can.
81 E9 Ross South I. N.Z.
81 J8 Ross, Mount hill North I. N.Z.
195 J5 Rossano Italy
191 L4 Rossano Veneto Italy
147 E3 Rossan Point Ireland
182 D5 Rossas Port.
147 C6 Rossaveel Ireland
173 N4 Roßbach Bayern Ger.
171 E8 Roßbach Sachsen-Anhalt Ger.
237 K9 Ross Barnett Reservoir MS U.S.A.
225 H2 Ross Bay Junction Nfld and Lab. Can.
147 D9 Rossbrin Ireland
147 D6 Rosscahill Ireland
147 D9 Ross Carbery Ireland
147 F4 Rosscor Northern Ireland U.K.
262 N2 Ross Dependency Antarctica
172 F2 Roßdorf Ger.
227 O4 Rosseau, Lake Ont. Can.
91 L9 Rossel Island P.N.G.
186 F6 Rossell Spain
186 G4 Rosselló Spain
191 J7 Rossenno r. Italy
147 F2 Rosses Bay Ireland
147 E4 Rosses Point Ireland
150 G1 Rossett Wrexham, Wales U.K.
173 J6 Roßhaupten Ger.
86 □1 Ross Hill Christmas I.
263 M1 Ross Ice Shelf Antarctica
191 J4 Rossiglione Italy
156 H9 Rossignol Belgium
224 F2 Rossignol, Lac l. Que. Can.
225 H4 Rossignol, Lake N.S. Can.
212 B4 Rössing Namibia
169 I6 Rössing (Nordstemmen) Ger.
149 O7 Rossington South Yorkshire, England U.K.
147 F4 Rossinver Ireland
184 C2 Rossio ao Sul do Tejo Port.
263 L1 Ross Island Antarctica
Ross Island Myanmar see Daung Kyun
87 G12 Rossiter Bay W.A. Austr.
Rossiyskaya Sovetskaya Federativnaya Sotsialisticheskaya Respublika country Asia/Europe see Russian Federation
142 D2 Rosskreppfjorden l. Norway
171 D8 Roßla Ger.
222 G5 Rossland B.C. Can.
147 J8 Rosslare Ireland
147 J8 Rosslare Harbour Ireland
147 J8 Rosslare Point Ireland
171 F7 Roßlau Ger.
147 H4 Rosslea Northern Ireland U.K.
171 D8 Roßleben Ger.
179 J4 Roßleithen Austria
227 O5 Rossmore Ont. Can.
147 F3 Rossnowlagh Ireland
206 B2 Rosso Maur.
192 B3 Rosso, Capo c. Corse France
140 N5 Rossön Sweden
150 G4 Ross-on-Wye Herefordshire, England U.K.
Rossony Belarus see Rasony
135 G6 Rossosh' Rus. Fed.
175 L4 Rossosz Pol.
174 G4 Rossoszyca Pol.

Column 1

215 L7 Rossouw S. Africa
170 G4 Rossow Ger.
222 C2 Rossport Ont. Can.
84 E7 Ross River N.T. Austr.
222 C2 Ross River Y.T. Can.
263 L1 Ross Sea Antarctica
173 J3 Roßtal Ger.
164 H5 Rossum Neth.
140 M4 Rossvatnet l. Norway
226 C6 Rossville IA U.S.A.
226 G9 Rossville IL U.S.A.
226 H9 Rossville IN U.S.A.
226 A5 Rossville PA U.S.A.
171 H8 Roßwein Ger.
222 D4 Rosswood B.C. Can.
127 L5 Röst Iraq
140 L3 Røst Norway
123 M3 Rostāq Afgh.
122 F7 Rostāq Iran
122 E8 Rostāq Hormozgan Iran
174 E3 Rostarzevo Rus. Fed.
223 J4 Rosthern Sask. Can.
170 F2 Rostock Ger.
140 P2 Rostonsölkä ridge Sweden
137 T2 Rostoshi Rus. Fed.
139 W4 Rostov Rus. Fed.
135 G7 Rostov-na-Donu Rus. Fed.
Rostov Oblast admin. div. Rus. Fed. see Rostovskaya Oblast'
Rostov-on-Don Rus. Fed. see Rostov-na-Donu
135 H7 Rostovskaya Oblast' admin. div. Rus. Fed.
215 J2 Rostratavile S. Africa
158 E5 Rostrenen France
147 J4 Rostrevor Northern Ireland U.K.
122 F7 Rostujärvi l. Sweden
147 C5 Rosturk Ireland
140 M3 Rosvik Norway
140 P4 Rosvik Sweden
231 E9 Roswell GA U.S.A.
239 L10 Roswell NM U.S.A.
149 K1 Rosyth Fife, Scotland U.K.
177 J5 Röszke Hungary
172 H5 Rot r. Ger.
91 K4 Rota i. N. Mariana Is
184 G7 Rota Spain
172 H6 Rotach r. Ger.
193 O9 Rota Greca Italy
173 I3 Rot am See Ger.
173 I5 Rot an der Rot Ger.
171 G10 Rotava Czech Rep.
Rotch Island Gilbert Is Kiribati see Tamana
93 C9 Rote i. Indon.
193 N4 Rotello Italy
168 H4 Rotenburg (Wümme) Ger.
169 I8 Rotenburg an der Fulda Ger.
171 D10 Roter Main r. Ger.
178 A5 Rote Wand mt. Austria
Rot-Front Ukr. see Dobropillya
179 H5 Rotgülden Austria
173 K3 Roth Ger.
173 I5 Roth r. Ger.
173 K3 Roth r. Ger.
171 F8 Rötha Ger.
169 F9 Rothaargebirge hills Ger.
149 N3 Rothbury Northumberland U.K.
149 N3 Rothbury Forest England U.K.
173 K3 Röthenbach an der Pegnitz Ger.
172 F2 Rothenbach Ger.
172 G2 Rothenbuch Ger.
171 E7 Rothenburg Ger.
171 K8 Rothenburg (Oberlausitz) Ger.
173 I3 Rothenburg ob der Tauber Ger.
158 H4 Rothéneuf France
172 H2 Rothenfels Ger.
171 E9 Rothenstein Ger.
151 K6 Rother r. England U.K.
262 T2 Rothera research stn Antarctica
151 M5 Rotherfield East Sussex, England U.K.
81 G9 Rotherham South I. N.Z.
149 O7 Rotherham South Yorkshire, England U.K.
146 J7 Rothes Moray, Scotland U.K.
146 F11 Rothesay Argyll and Bute, Scotland U.K.
165 H7 Rotheux-Rimière Belgium
146 K4 Rothiesholm Orkney, Scotland U.K.
173 I2 Röthlein Ger.
172 D7 Rothrist Switz.
226 E5 Rothschild WI U.S.A.
262 T2 Rothschild Island Antarctica
234 C4 Rothsville PA U.S.A.
151 K3 Rothwell Northamptonshire, England U.K.
149 O6 Rothwell West Yorkshire, England U.K.
169 I8 Rothwesten (Fuldatal) Ger.
93 C9 Roti i. Indon.
Roti, Selat sea chan. Indon. see Rote
Rotja, Punta pt Spain see Roja, Punta
83 J5 Roto N.S.W. Austr.
80 J6 Rotoaira, Lake North I. N.Z.
80 K5 Rotoehu, Lake North I. N.Z.
80 K5 Rotoiti, Lake North I. N.Z.
81 G8 Rotoiti, Lake South I. N.Z.
80 K5 Rotoma, Lake North I. N.Z.
Rotomagus France see Rouen
80 K5 Rotomanu, Lake North I. N.Z.
81 F9 Rotomanu South I. N.Z.
193 Q8 Rotonda Italy
195 L3 Rotondella Italy
192 C3 Rotondo, Monte mt. Corse France
190 E2 Rotondo, Pizzo mt. Switz.
81 G8 Rotoroa, Lake South I. N.Z.
80 K5 Rotorua North I. N.Z.
80 K5 Rotorua, Lake North I. N.Z.
231 H7 Rotselaar Belgium
165 G7 Rotsethorn mt. Austria
178 G6 Rott Ger.
173 J6 Rott Ger.
173 O5 Rott r. Ger.
173 L4 Rott r. Ger.
173 I3 Rottach-Egern Ger.
173 M6 Rott an der Inn Ger.
157 L6 Rotte r. France
172 H5 Rottenacker Ger.
173 J2 Röttenbach Bayern Ger.
173 K3 Röttenbach Bayern Ger.
173 O9 Rottenbach Ger.
173 J6 Rottenbuch Ger.
172 F5 Rottenburg am Neckar Ger.
173 M4 Rottenburg an der Laaber Ger.
173 I2 Rottendorf Ger.
179 J4 Rottenmann Austria
179 J5 Rottenmanner Tauern mts Austria
164 G5 Rotterdam Neth.
233 L6 Rotterdam NY U.S.A.
144 J2 Rottnan hill U.K.
173 O5 Rottmünster Ger.
151 L6 Rottingdean Brighton and Hove, England U.K.
172 H2 Rottingham Ger.
169 K7 Rottleberode Ger.
146 I2 Rottnen i. Sweden
143 L5 Rottnen l. Sweden
187 H4 Rottnest Island W.A. Austr.
190 H5 Rottofreno Italy
164 J1 Rottumeroog i. Neth.
164 J1 Rottumerplaat i. Neth.
172 F5 Rottweil Ger.
77 H3 Rotuma i. Fiji
197 M7 Rotunda Romania
140 M5 Rötviken Sweden
173 N3 Rötz Ger.
158 H7 Rouans France
156 F1 Roubion r. France
186 I2 Rouch, Mont mt. France/Spain
160 D4 Rouchain, Barrage du dam France
176 F2 Roudnice nad Labem Czech Rep.
156 B5 Rouen France
163 I7 Rouergue reg. France

Column 2

157 N8 Rouffach France
175 J3 Roúffiac France
162 F5 Rouffignac France
138 J4 Rouge Estonia
158 I6 Rougé France
224 F4 Rouge, Point Trin. and Tob.
Rouge-Matawin, Réserve Faunique nature res. Que. Can.
160 I2 Rougemont France
157 M8 Rougemont-le-Château France
81 D12 Rough Ridge South I. N.Z.
151 O2 Roughton Norfolk, England U.K.
147 C9 Roughty r. Ireland
162 E4 Rougnac France
202 A4 Roui, Oued er watercourse Alg.
162 D4 Rouillac France
162 E3 Rouillé France
161 C9 Roujan France
160 I2 Roulans France
Roulers Belgium see Roeselare
232 G7 Roulette PA U.S.A.
84 D7 Roulpmaulpma Aboriginal Land res. N.T. Austr.
162 F4 Roumazières-Loubert France
159 M3 Roumois reg. France
161 I9 Roumoules France
225 G2 Roundeyed Lake Que. Can.
232 B8 Roundhead OH U.S.A.
149 O5 Round Hill England U.K.
83 K5 Round Hill Nature Reserve N.S.W. Austr.
217 □1b Round Island Mauritius
224 E4 Round Lake Ont. Can.
83 N4 Round Mountain mt. N.S.W. Austr.
240 O3 Round Mountain NV U.S.A.
241 W5 Round Rock AZ U.S.A.
237 G10 Round Rock TX U.S.A.
234 B3 Roundstone Ireland
234 E3 Round Top hill PA U.S.A.
238 J3 Roundup MT U.S.A.
234 F3 Round Valley Reservoir NJ U.S.A.
151 I5 Roundway Wiltshire, England U.K.
148 E7 Roundwood Ireland
251 H3 Roura Fr. Guiana
190 C5 Roure Italy
149 L2 Rousay i. Scotland U.K.
233 L4 Rouses Point NY U.S.A.
176 F2 Rousínov Czech Rep.
148 C4 Rousky Northern Ireland U.K.
161 H10 Rousset France
161 G7 Rousset, Col de pass France
161 G9 Roussillon Provence-Alpes-Côte d'Azur France
155 G4 Roussillon Rhône-Alpes France
163 J10 Roussillon reg. France
161 E8 Rousson France
Routh Bank sea feature Phil. see Seahorse Bank
159 M3 Routot France
164 J3 Rouveen Neth.
159 K4 Rouvre r. France
159 F5 Rouvres France
156 I4 Rouvroy-sur-Audry France
161 J10 Roux, Cap c. France
215 K6 Rouxville S. Africa
160 D2 Rouy France
224 E3 Rouyn-Noranda Que. Can.
Rouyuanchengzi Gansu China see Huachi
140 R3 Rovaniemi Fin.
190 E5 Rovasenda r. Italy
190 I4 Rovato Italy
190 G6 Rovegno Italy
Roven'ki Ukr. see Roven'ky
137 S5 Roven'ky Ukr.
Rovenskaya Oblast' admin. div. Ukr. see Rivnens'ka Oblast'
191 J5 Roverbella Italy
190 G3 Roverè della Luna Italy
191 K4 Roverè Veronese Italy
170 F2 Rövershagen Ger.
258 E2 Roversi Arg.
193 J3 Roviano Italy
97 G8 Rôviĕng Tbong Cambodia
191 L5 Rovigo prov. Italy
191 L5 Rovigo Italy
188 D3 Rovinj Croatia
176 G3 Rovinka Slovakia
179 O8 Rovišće Croatia
Rovno Ukr. see Rivne
Rovno Oblast admin. div. Ukr. see Rivnens'ka Oblast'
138 L3 Rovnoye Pskovskaya Oblast' Rus. Fed.
120 B2 Rovnoye Saratovskaya Oblast' Rus. Fed.
174 C3 Rów Pol.
78 □5 Rowa Vanuatu
151 M7 Rowde Wiltshire, England U.K.
83 L3 Rowena N.S.W. Austr.
234 F2 Rowland PA U.S.A.
232 F9 Rowlesburg WV U.S.A.
91 J4 Rowley Island Nunavut Can.
86 E4 Rowley Shoals sea feature W.A. Austr.
138 M6 Rownaye Belarus
Równe Ukr. see Rivne
174 E4 Rów Polski r. Pol.
232 C8 Rowsburg OH U.S.A.
92 C3 Roxas Luzon Phil.
92 D7 Roxas Mindanao Phil.
121 S2 Roxas Mindoro Phil.
92 B6 Roxas Palawan Phil.
92 D6 Roxas Panay Phil.
231 I8 Roxboro NC U.S.A.
81 D12 Roxburgh South I. N.Z.
81 H8 Roxburgh Island Cook Is Rarotonga
235 I1 Roxbury CT U.S.A.
235 I1 Roxbury Falls CT U.S.A.
82 F4 Roxby Downs S.A. Austr.
143 J3 Roxen l. Sweden
184 C5 Roxo r. Port.
184 C5 Roxo, Barragem do resr Port.
151 I4 Roxton Bedfordshire, England U.K.
85 H7 Roy r. Qld Austr.
241 Q1 Roy r. Scotland U.K.
238 J5 Roy MT U.S.A.
239 L8 Roya r. France/Italy
147 H6 Royal Canal Ireland
226 H9 Royal Center IN U.S.A.
117 J6 Royal Chitwan National Park Nepal
151 M3 Royale, Isle i. MI U.S.A.
215 M4 Royal Natal National Park S. Africa
227 K7 Royal Oak MI U.S.A.
263 K1 Royal Society Range mts Antarctica
116 H5 Royal Sukla Phanta Wildlife Reserve nature res. Nepal
234 B4 Royalton PA U.S.A.
226 F2 Royalton WI U.S.A.
162 B4 Royan France
161 G6 Roybon France
151 N2 Roydon Norfolk, England U.K.
151 L3 Roydon Norfolk, England U.K.
156 E4 Roye France
159 O6 Royère-de-Vassivière France
149 O6 Royston Hertfordshire, England U.K.
149 N6 Royston South Yorkshire, England U.K.
149 N6 Royton Greater Manchester, England U.K.

Column 3

183 O9 Rozalén del Monte Spain
175 J3 Rozanki Pol.
196 H6 Rožanj hill Serbia
174 D3 Rożanki Pol.
182 H3 Rozas, Embalse de las resr Spain
156 E6 Rozay-en-Brie France
176 E1 Rožďalovice Czech Rep.
175 M6 Rozdil Ukr.
136 J7 Rozdol'ne Ukr.
137 R6 Rozdol'ne Donets'ka Oblast' Ukr.
136 G7 Rozdol'ne Respublika Krym Ukr.
137 O5 Rozdory Ukr.
174 F4 Rozdrażew Pol.
164 G3 Rozenburg Neth.
164 I4 Rozendaal Neth.
121 N2 Rozhdestvenka Kazakh.
139 T5 Rozhdestvenka Tverskaya Oblast' Rus. Fed.
139 U4 Rozhdestveno Yaroslavskaya Oblast' Rus. Fed.
134 I4 Rozhdestvenskoye Rus. Fed.
139 Q4 Rozhdestvo Rus. Fed.
129 B2 Rozhki Rus. Fed.
137 N1 Rozhkovychi Rus. Fed.
137 L3 Rozhnivka Ukr.
136 J3 Rozhnyativ Ukr.
177 I1 Rozhnyatov Ukr.
136 E5 Rozhyshche Ukr.
197 M8 Rozino Bulg.
137 Q6 Rozivka Ukr.
176 C2 Rožmitál pod Třemšínem Czech Rep.
177 J3 Rožňava Slovakia
174 Q3 Rožniatow Pol.
177 H2 Rožnov pod Radhoštěm Czech Rep.
176 I6 Roznowo Pol.
174 E3 Rozoga r. Pol.
175 J2 Rozogi Pol.
156 H4 Rozoy-sur-Serre France
175 H4 Rozprza Pol.
137 P4 Rozsochy Ukr.
175 L5 Roztocze reg. Pol.
175 I6 Roztoczański Park Narodowy nat. park Pol.
175 I6 Roztoka Wielka Pol.
171 I10 Roztoky Středočeský kraj Czech Rep.
171 J10 Roztoky Středočeský kraj Czech Rep.
122 D5 Rozveh Iran
190 G5 Rozzano Italy
196 H9 Rrëshen Albania
196 H9 Rrogozhinë Albania
135 H5 Rtishchevo Rus. Fed.
182 D2 Ru Spain
182 E7 Rua Port.
93 A8 Rua, Tanjung pt Sumba Indon.
212 B3 Ruacana Namibia
211 B6 Ruaha National Park Tanz.
80 K6 Ruahine Forest Park nature res. North I. N.Z.
80 J7 Ruahine Range mts North I. N.Z.
80 I2 Ruakaka North I. N.Z.
147 E7 Ruan Ireland
Ruanda country Africa see Rwanda
93 D2 Ruang i. Indon.
80 J6 Ruapehu, Mount vol. North I. N.Z.
81 E9 Ruapuke South I. N.Z.
80 M4 Ruatoria North I. N.Z.
159 I3 Ruaudin France
203 G6 Rufa'a Sudan
205 D3 Ruaba Belarus
139 N9 Rub' al Khālī des. Saudi Arabia
162 E3 Rúban Slovakia
148 C3 Rubane Northern Ireland U.K.
137 N7 Rubanivka Ukr.
191 L5 Rubano Italy
138 L6 Rubashki Belarus
125 I3 Rubayd reg. Saudi Arabia
211 C7 Rubeho Mountains Tanz.
169 K8 Rubeland Ger.
257 F2 Rubelita Brazil
183 R4 Rubena Spain
109 M2 Rubeshibe Japan
171 H9 Rübezahl Ger.
249 F2 Rubezhnoye Ukr. see
102 U3 Rubeznoye Japan

Column 4

172 H4 Rudersberg Ger.
172 N5 Rudersdorf Austria
177 I6 Rüdersdorf Berlin Ger.
169 J7 Rüdershausen Ger.
173 O4 Ruderting Ger.
140 I4 Rude Selo Ukr.
174 E4 Rudgwick West Sussex, England U.K.
196 H7 Rudina pass Montenegro
138 H7 Rūdiškės Lith.
169 K9 Rüdisleben Ger.
173 L3 Rudivka Chernihivs'ka Oblast' Ukr.
137 R4 Rudivka Luhans'ka Oblast' Ukr.
175 K3 Rudka Pol.
175 K3 Rudka r. Pol.
175 L6 Rudki Pol.
171 J10 Rudná Czech Rep.
174 D4 Rudna Pol.
197 K6 Rudna Glava Serbia
174 E4 Rudna Wielka Pol.
100 I6 Rudnaya Pristan' Primorskiy Kray Rus. Fed.
100 I7 Rudnaya Pristan' Primorskiy Kray Rus. Fed.
136 C4 Rudnya Ukr.
177 I1 Rudnica Pol.
134 K2 Rudnichnyy Rus. Fed.
174 G5 Rudnik Pol.
174 G4 Rudnik Pol.
211 A5 Rudnik Ingichka Uzbek. see Ingichka
175 K5 Rudnik nad Sadem Podkarpackie Pol.
175 I10 Rüdnitz Ger.
175 M3 Rudnya Belarus
139 O7 Rudnya Smolenskaya Oblast' Rus. Fed.
139 O5 Rudnya Tverskaya Oblast' Rus. Fed.
135 I6 Rudnya Volgogradskaya Oblast' Rus. Fed.
136 I5 Rudnya-Ivanivs'ka Ukr.
175 L6 Rudnyky Ukr.
136 I5 Rudnytsya Ukr.
120 I6 Rudnyy Kazakh.
181 □ Rudolf, Lake salt l. Eth./Kenya see Turkana, Lake
130 G1 Rudol'fa, Ostrov i. Zemlya Frantsa-Iosifa Rus. Fed.
260 C4 Rudolfo Iselín Arg.
179 K2 Rudolfov Czech Rep.
182 B2 Rudolph Island Zemlya Frantsa-Iosifa Rus. Fed. see Rudol'fa, Ostrov
171 D9 Rudolstadt Ger.
109 M2 Rudong Jiangsu China
109 M9 Rudozem Bulg.
183 M3 Rudrón r. Spain
183 M3 Rudrón resr Spain
122 D3 Rūdsar Iran
142 E2 Rudsgrend Norway
185 E9 Rudston East Riding of Yorkshire, England U.K.
141 T6 Rudyard MI U.S.A.
174 F5 Rudziczka Pol.
138 G6 Rudzyensk Belarus
138 G5 Ruds Spain
184 F7 Ruecas r. Spain
237 D7 Rueda Spain
169 D6 Rueil-Malmaison France
232 M2 Ruel Ont. Can.
Ruen mt. Macedonia see Rujen
183 L2 Ruente Spain
213 G3 Ruenya r. Zimbabwe
178 D5 Ruetz r. Austria
161 E8 Ruffec Poitou-Charentes France
160 G2 Ruffey-lès-Echirey France
161 G9 Ruffieu-sur-Seille France
160 H4 Ruffieu France
160 H5 Ruffieux France
149 L6 Rufford Lancashire, England U.K.
224 E3 Rufino Arg.
232 E11 Rufino Arg.
206 A3 Rufisque Senegal
209 F8 Rufunsa Zambia
138 K4 Rugāji Latvia
109 M2 Rugao Jiangsu China
151 J3 Rugby Warwickshire, England U.K.
236 E1 Rugby ND U.S.A.
151 J3 Rugby Staffordshire, England U.K.
170 H2 Rügen i. Ger.
170 H1 Rügen, Naturpark nature res. Ger.
222 E5 Rugged Mountain B.C. Can.
203 F5 Ruggiwa well Sudan
173 J3 Rugles France
191 Q5 Rugvica Croatia
212 B5 Ruhango Tanz.
125 I3 Ruḥayyat al Ḩamr'ā' waterhole Saudi Arabia
126 H7 Rubhah oasis Syria
169 K6 Rühen Ger.
211 A5 Ruhengeri Rwanda
191 I8 Ruhland Ger.
173 N4 Ruhmannsfelden Ger.
169 J8 Rühn Ger.
138 J3 Ruhnu i. Estonia
138 C4 Ruhner Berge hills Ger.
169 J8 Ruhr r. Ger.
173 O5 Ruhstorf an der Rott Ger.
169 E7 Ruhudji r. Tanz.
114 G4 Ruhuna National Park Sri Lanka
147 D5 Rush Ireland
151 L2 Rush West Midlands, England U.K.
107 Q8 Rushan Shandong China
123 M3 Rushan Tajik. see Rushon
185 N3 Rushanskiy Khrebet mts Tajik. see Rushon, Qatorkŭhi
236 D6 Rushden Northamptonshire, England U.K.
226 K3 Rushford MN U.S.A.
151 O3 Rushmere St Andrew Suffolk, England U.K.
117 O5 Rushon Arun. Prad. India
123 N3 Rushon Tajik.
123 N3 Rushon, Qatorkŭhi mts Tajik.
232 F3 Rushville IL U.S.A.
236 C4 Rushville IN U.S.A.
236 D5 Rushville NE U.S.A.
232 A8 Rushville OH U.S.A.
83 I7 Rushworth Vic. Austr.
174 E1 Rusiec Pol.
175 I4 Rusinowo Pol.
237 H10 Rusk TX U.S.A.
134 K4 Rusk Rus. Fed.
145 L4 Ruskele Sweden
196 H5 Ruski Krstur Vojvodina Serbia
231 F12 Ruskin FL U.S.A.
149 O7 Rusko Fin.
177 K3 Ruská Slovakia
211 C5 Rusolaïta r. Latvia
211 A5 Rusovce Slovakia
137 V3 Rusovce Slovakia
150 E4 Ruspidge Gloucestershire, England U.K.
142 F3 Russ, Mont mt. France
141 T6 Russ r. Rus. Fed.

Column 5

122 H5 Rūm Iran
146 D9 Rum Jordan see Ramm
236 I3 Rum r. MN U.S.A.
Rum, Jebel mts Jordan see Ramm, Jabal
146 D9 Rum, Sound of sea chan. Scotland U.K.
207 G3 Ruma Nigeria
196 H5 Ruma Vojvodina Serbia
124 F9 Rumādah Yemen
125 J4 Rumāh Saudi Arabia
210 B5 Ruma National Park Kenya
Rumania country Asia/Europe see Romania
124 F7 Rumayn i. Saudi Arabia
93 D3 Rumbai Sulawesi Indon.
208 F3 Rumbek Sudan
185 L4 Rumblar r. Spain
185 L4 Rumblar, Embalse del resr Spain
176 D1 Rumburk Czech Rep.
246 F2 Rum Cay i. Bahamas
165 J10 Rumelange Lux.
165 D7 Rumeln Ger.
233 O4 Rumford ME U.S.A.
143 O7 Rumia Pol.
156 H4 Rumigny France
164 G7 Rumilly France
177 I1 Rumin Ukr.
170 F6 Rümlang Switz.
128 G5 Rummānah hill Syria
147 C7 Rumney Cardiff, Wales U.K.
103 S3 Rumoi Japan
211 A5 Rumonge Burundi
157 J6 Rumont France
211 B7 Rumphi Malawi
234 B4 Rumson NJ U.S.A.
154 H4 Rumst Belgium
210 C4 Rumuruti Kenya
93 F6 Run i. Maluku Indon.
184 A2 Runa Port.
147 J2 Runabay Head Northern Ireland U.K.
109 J2 Runan Henan China
81 F9 Runanga South I. N.Z.
80 L4 Runaway, Cape North I. N.Z.
246 □ Runaway Bay Jamaica
149 L7 Runcorn Halton, England U.K.
197 L3 Runcu Romania
197 J4 Runcu Romania
213 G4 Runde r. Zimbabwe
212 B4 Rundu Namibia
143 M6 Rundvik Sweden
140 O5 Rundvik Sweden
97 F9 Rŭng, Kaôh i. Cambodia
95 J6 Rungan r. Indon.
208 E4 Rungu Dem. Rep. Congo
211 B6 Rungwa Rukwa Tanz.
211 A6 Rungwa Singida Tanz.
211 A6 Rungwa r. Tanz.
211 B6 Rungwa Game Reserve nature res. Tanz.
109 K2 Runhe r. Henan China
122 I9 Rūniz-e Bālā Iran
169 F10 Runkel Ger.
143 O2 Runmarö i. Sweden
240 O7 Running Springs CA U.S.A.
237 E9 Running Water watercourse NM/TX U.S.A.
146 H11 Runtha mt. Mhd. Prad. India
116 F7 Ruokolahti Fin.
141 T6 Ruoms France
161 E8 Ruovesi Fin.
141 R6 Rupa Croatia
191 Q5 Rupa Arun. Prad. India
117 N6 Rupat i. Indon.
94 D4 Rupea Romania
197 N4 Rupert r. Que. Can.
238 H6 Rupert ID U.S.A.
232 E11 Rupert WV U.S.A.
224 E3 Rupert Bay Que. Can.
262 O1 Rupert Coast Antarctica
85 I6 Rupert Creek r. Qld Austr.
116 C6 Rupnagar Punjab India
116 E6 Rupnarayan r. India
216 C7 Ruponda Tanz.
170 G3 Ruppiner See l. Ger.
179 L3 Ruprechtshofen Austria
116 F3 Rupshu reg. India
157 M8 Rupt-sur-Moselle France
124 E6 Ruqayțah, Wādī ar watercourse Israel
232 D12 Rural Retreat VA U.S.A.
252 D3 Rurrenabaque Bol.
169 B9 Rurstausee resr Ger.
79 □7 Rurutu i. Is Australes Fr. Polynesia
79 □7 Rurutu i. Is Australes Fr. Polynesia
197 R9 Rus Romania
185 N3 Rus r. Spain
Rusaddir N. Africa see Melilla
125 K3 Ruwais U.A.E.

Column 6

221 I2 Russell Island Nunavut Can.
78 □6 Russell Islands Solomon Is
223 K3 Russell Lake Man. Can.
222 H2 Russell Lake N.W.T. Can.
223 J3 Russell Lake Sask. Can.
231 D8 Russellville AL U.S.A.
230 D9 Russellville AR U.S.A.
230 D7 Russellville KY U.S.A.
232 B10 Russellville OH U.S.A.
234 D5 Russellville PA U.S.A.
172 L1 Rüsselsheim Ger.
191 M7 Russi Italy
Russia country Asia/Europe see Russian Federation
130 F4 Russian Federation country Asia/Europe
Russian Soviet Federal Socialist Republic country Asia/Europe see Russian Federation
121 O1 Russkaya-Polyana Rus. Fed.
135 H6 Russkaya Zhuravka Rus. Fed.
139 H9 Russki Brod Rus. Fed.
120 B1 Russkiy Kameshkir Rus. Fed.
134 K1 Russkiy Zavorot, Poluostrov pen. Rus. Fed.
139 F2 Russkoye Smolenskaya Oblast' Rus. Fed.
129 F2 Russkoye Stavropol'skiy Kray Rus. Fed.
131 P2 Russkoye Ust'ye Rus. Fed.
129 O4 Rust Austria
129 G3 Rüstäm Äliyev Azer.
231 F12 Rustburg VA U.S.A.
215 M1 Rust de Winter S. Africa
215 M1 Rust de Winter Nature Reserve S. Africa
142 D3 Rustfjellheii mt. Norway
215 K5 Rustfontein Dam l. S. Africa
215 L3 Rustig S. Africa
151 L5 Rustington West Sussex, England U.K.
237 I9 Ruston LA U.S.A.
129 J4 Rustov Azer.
159 F1 Rustrel France
174 D4 Ruszów Pol.
137 T6 Rut' r. Rus. Fed.
213 G3 Ruta r. Zimbabwe
93 D6 Ruteng Flores Indon.
140 O5 Rutengu r. Burundi
97 P4 Rutenga Zimbabwe
172 F4 Rutesheim Ger.
148 A4 Ruth NV U.S.A.
240 Q2 Ruth NV U.S.A.
169 F8 Rüthen Ger.
227 K7 Ruther Glen VA U.S.A.
232 H7 Rutherford NJ U.S.A.
231 D8 Rutherfordton NC U.S.A.
83 I7 Rutherglen Vic. Austr.
227 O3 Rutherglen South Lanarkshire, Scotland U.K.
146 H11 Ruthin Denbighshire, Wales U.K.
116 F7 Ruthiyai Mdh. Prad. India
190 F1 Rüti Switz.
191 M1 Rutigliano Italy
193 O7 Rutino Italy
151 K5 Rutka r. Pol.
175 K1 Rutka-Tartak Pol.
175 K2 Rutki-Kossaki Pol.
151 K2 Rutland admin. div. England U.K.
233 M5 Rutland VT U.S.A.
115 M7 Rutland Island Andaman & Nicobar Is India
85 H5 Rutland Plains Qld Austr.
151 K2 Rutland Water resr England U.K.
232 B12 Rutledge TN U.S.A.
223 I2 Rutledge Lake N.W.T. Can.
111 H12 Rutog Xizang China
111 D10 Rutog Xizang China
111 D10 Rutog Xizang China
208 F5 Rutshuru Dem. Rep. Congo
164 I3 Rutten Neth.
227 N3 Rutter Ont. Can.
129 I4 Rutul Rus. Fed.
164 J4 Ruurlo Neth.
138 M3 Ruusa Estonia
140 T5 Ruvaslahti Fin.
193 P6 Ruvo del Monte Italy
191 M1 Ruvo di Puglia Italy
140 U3 Ruvozero, Ozero l. Rus. Fed.
211 C8 Ruvu Tanz. see Pangani
211 D7 Ruvuma r. Moz./Tanz.
216 B8 Ruvuma admin. reg. Tanz.
124 G3 Ruwaydah Saudi Arabia
125 N5 Ruways, Ra's ar c. Oman
128 F6 Ruwayshid, Wādī watercourse Jordan
124 C9 Ruweis U.A.E.
125 K3 Ruweiji pt Saudi Arabia
125 K3 Ruweis U.A.E.
210 D5 Ruwenzori National Park Uganda see Queen Elizabeth National Park
160 G5 Ruy France
213 G3 Ruya r. Zimbabwe
122 D3 Ruyan Iran
191 L6 Ruyigi Burundi
108 E6 Ruynes-en-Margeride France
150 D2 Ruyton-XI-Towns Shropshire, England U.K.
109 I6 Ruyuan Guangdong China
121 L1 Ruzayevka Kazakh.
134 G4 Ruzayevka Rus. Fed.
138 M9 Ruzhany Belarus
197 R9 Ruzhintsi Bulg.
111 H10 Ruzhou Henan China
109 M9 Ruzomberok Slovakia
190 F2 Ruza Rus. Fed.
211 A5 Rwanda country Africa
208 F5 Rwenzori mts Dem. Rep. Congo/Uganda see Rwenzori Mountains
210 A4 Rwenzori Mountains National Park Uganda
111 K6 Ry Denmark
142 F5 Ryä r. Denmark
142 F4 Ryät r. Iran

Column 7

134 F3 Rybreka Rus. Fed.
175 H2 Rychliki Pol.
176 F1 Rychnov nad Kněžnou Czech Rep.
171 L9 Rychnov u Jablonce nad Nisou Czech Rep.
175 L9 Rychtal Pol.
174 F3 Rychwał Pol.
170 F2 Ryck r. Ger.
222 G4 Rycroft Alta Can.
175 J4 Ryczywół Mazowieckie Pol.
175 H3 Ryczywół Wielkopolskie Pol.
143 K5 Ryd Sweden
262 S2 Rydberg Peninsula Antarctica
151 J6 Ryde Isle of Wight, England U.K.
136 E4 Rydomyl' Ukr.
174 E5 Rydułtowy Pol.
151 K6 Rye East Sussex, England U.K.
151 N6 Rye r. England U.K.
235 P5 Rye r. England U.K.
235 H3 Rye NY U.S.A.
151 N6 Rye Bay England U.K.
233 G5 Rye Beach NH U.S.A.
238 J5 Ryegate MT U.S.A.
240 N1 Rye Patch CA U.S.A.
240 N1 Rye Patch Reservoir NV U.S.A.
159 J3 Ryes France
175 J6 Ryglice Pol.
175 J2 Ryhall Rutland, England U.K.
174 G2 Ryjewo Pol.
136 G3 Rykhal's'ke Ukr.
Rykovo Ukr. see Yenakiyeve
175 M5 Ryki Pol.
175 M1 Ryłkiai Lith.
135 F6 Ryl'sk Rus. Fed.
83 L5 Rylstone N.S.W. Austr.
175 J6 Rymanów Pol.
174 D3 Rýmařov Czech Rep.
175 M2 Rymättylä Fin.
143 R8 Ryn Pol.
175 H1 Rynarzewo Pol.
134 G1 Rynda Rus. Fed.
120 C4 Ryn-Peski des. Kazakh.
175 J2 Ryńsk Pol.
175 J2 Ryńskie, Jezioro l. Pol.
104 D4 Ryōgami-san mt. Japan
104 E4 Ryōhaku-sanchi mts Japan
Ryōju Liaoning China see Lüshun
105 I3 Ryōkami Japan
102 S7 Ryōri-zaki pt Japan
105 H6 Ryōtsu Japan
175 H2 Rypin Pol.
Rypnaya Moldova see Ripcani
137 O1 Ryshkovo Rus. Fed.
141 H6 Rysjedal Norway
168 D4 Rysum (Krummhörn) Ger.
177 H2 Rysy mt. Pol.
175 I6 Rytel Pol.
143 K6 Rytterknægten hill Bornholm Denmark
138 H1 Ryttylä Fin.
103 □5 Ryūgasaki Japan
104 D5 Ryūga-dake mt. Japan
105 L4 Ryūgasaki Japan
104 B8 Ryūjin Japan
139 P9 Ryukhovo Rus. Fed.
Ryukyu Islands Japan see Nansei-shotō
Ryukyu-rettō is Japan see Nansei-shotō
266 D4 Ryukyu Trench sea feature N. Pacific Ocean
104 D5 Ryō Shiga Japan
104 D5 Ryō Yamanashi Japan
105 H5 Ryūsō-san mt. Japan
104 B8 Ryūyō Japan
139 W2 Ryzhikovo Rus. Fed.
141 F6 Rysjedal Norway
175 H2 Rzhanka Belarus
139 W7 Ryzhkawka Belarus
175 J3 Rzadza r. Pol.
175 I3 Rząśnia Pol.
188 G4 Rzav r. Bos.-Herz.
174 E5 Rzeczenica Pol.
175 H3 Rzeczyca Łódzkie Pol.
175 K4 Rzeczyca Lubelskie Pol.
175 H3 Rzejowice Pol.
175 L5 Rzepiennik Strzyżewski Pol.
175 H3 Rzepin Pol.
175 L5 Rzerzęczyce Pol.
175 I5 Rzeszkowo Pol.
175 K6 Rzeszów Pol.
175 H2 Rzgów Pierwszy Pol.
135 G5 Rzhaksa Rus. Fed.
135 F5 Rzhev Rus. Fed.
137 P1 Rzhyshchiv Ukr.
175 L3 Rzoły Pol.

S

122 G4 Sa'ābād Iran
210 E4 Saacow Somalia
128 E9 Sa'ādah al Barṣā' pass Saudi Arabia
122 E6 Sa'ādatābād Fārs Iran
214 F7 Sa'ādatābād Hormozgan Iran
170 F2 Saal Ger.
173 L4 Saalach r. Ger.
173 O6 Saal an der Donau Ger.
169 J10 Saal an der Saale Ger.
171 L1 Saalbach r. Ger.
135 I5 Saalbach r. Ger.
138 H9 Saalburg Ger.
179 R9 Saaldorf Ger.
171 F8 Saale r. Ger.
171 E10 Saalburg Ger.
173 N6 Saaldorf Ger.
177 I2 Saalfeld Ger.
178 F5 Saalfelden am Steinernen Meer Austria
210 A4 Saamba K'e N.W.T. Can. see Trout Lake
151 T6 Sääre France
190 C2 Saâne r. Switz.
154 C3 Saanen Switz.
222 F5 Saanich B.C. Can.
Saarbrücken Ger. see Saarland
172 B2 Saarbrücken Ger.
172 B2 Saarburg Ger.
138 E3 Saare Estonia
138 E3 Saaremaa i. Estonia
140 Q4 Saari Fin.
175 N4 Saari-Hunsrück, Naturpark nature res. Ger.
141 T6 Saarijärvi Fin.
140 R2 Saari-Kämä Fin.
140 S3 Saarikoski Fin.
140 S3 Saaristomeri Fin. see Skärgårdshavets nationalpark
140 R2 Saarivaara Fin.
172 B2 Saarland admin. reg. Ger.
172 B2 Saarland Ger.
138 E3 Saarlouis Ger.
172 B2 Saarwellingen Ger.
190 D3 Saas Fee Switz.
190 D3 Saas Grund Switz.
203 G6 Sa'ata Sudan
Sa'ata Sudan
129 J6 Saatli Azer.
Saatly Azer. see Saatli
261 K4 Saatse Estonia
261 G2 Saavedra Buenos Aires Arg.
261 G2 Saavedra Santa Fé Arg.

Saba to St-Ghislain
379

247 L5 Saba i. Neth. Antilles
124 C1 Saba, Wādī watercourse Saudi Arabia
128 A8 Saba'ah Egypt
128 F5 Sab' Ābār Syria
169 I7 Sababurg Ger.
196 H6 Šabac Serbia
186 J4 Sabadell Spain
206 C4 Sabadou Baranama Guinea
104 D4 Sabae Japan
211 A6 Sabagusi Tanz.
95 L2 Sabah state Malaysia
94 D3 Sabak Malaysia
211 D5 Sabaki r. Kenya
122 B2 Sabalan, Kūhhā-ye mts Iran
93 A7 Sabalana i. Indon.
93 A7 Sabalana, Kepulauan is Indon.
116 F6 Sabalgarh Madh. Prad. India
251 E2 Saban Venez.
246 C2 Sabana, Archipiélago de is Cuba
247 I4 Sabana de la Mar Dom. Rep.
242 □P11 Sabanagrande Hond.
247 □1 Sabana Grande Puerto Rico
250 C2 Sabanalarga Col.
Sabaneta Aruba see Savaneta
246 H4 Sabaneta Dom. Rep.
246 I8 Sabaneta Venez.
94 A2 Sabang Aceh Indon.
93 A3 Sabang Sulawesi Indon.
93 B5 Sabang Sulawesi Indon.
250 C5 Sabano Col.
126 F3 Şabanözü Turkey
197 O3 Săbăoani Romania
257 F3 Sabará Brazil
163 G9 Sabarat France
114 G4 Sabari r. India
116 D8 Sabarmati r. Gujarat India
93 A7 Sabaru i. Indon.
128 D6 Sabastiya West Bank
124 G8 Sab'atayn, Ramlat as des. Yemen
193 N5 Sabato r. Italy
193 K5 Sabaudia Italy
193 K5 Sabaudia, Lago di lag. Italy
252 C4 Sabaya Bol.
124 E6 Şabāyā i. Saudi Arabia
129 C3 Sabazho Georgia
190 I6 Sabbionetta Italy
214 H7 Sabelo S. Africa
210 C4 Sabena Desert Kenya
123 I6 Sāberi, Hāmūn-e marsh Afgh.
183 J3 Sabero Spain
128 E6 Şabḩā Jordan
202 B3 Sabhā Libya
124 G4 Şabḩā' Saudi Arabia
116 B8 Sabhrai Gujarat India
116 F5 Sabi r. India
Sabi r. Moz./Zimbabwe see Save
213 G5 Sabie Moz.
215 Q1 Sabie r. Moz./S. Africa
213 F5 Sabie S. Africa
126 D3 Sabiha Gökçen airport Turkey
138 F4 Sabile Latvia
232 B9 Sabina OH U.S.A.
242 F2 Sabinal Mex.
246 E3 Sabinal, Cayo i. Cuba
186 E2 Sabiñánigo Spain
185 N7 Sabinar, Punta pt Spain
185 N7 Sabinar, Punta del mt. Spain
243 I4 Sabinas Mex.
237 E12 Sabinas r. Mex.
237 F12 Sabinas r. Mex.
243 I4 Sabinas Hidalgo Mex.
237 I11 Sabine r. LA/TX U.S.A.
237 I11 Sabine Lake LA/TX U.S.A.
140 □ Sabine Land reg. Svalbard
237 I11 Sabine National Wildlife Refuge nature res. LA U.S.A.
237 I11 Sabine Pass TX U.S.A.
193 J3 Sabini, Monti mts Italy
257 F3 Sabinópolis Brazil
216 □3e Sabinosa El Hierro Canary Is
177 K2 Sabinov Slovakia
185 M4 Sabiote Spain
129 J5 Sabir Azer.
129 J5 Sabirabad Azer.
92 C5 Sablayan Mindoro Phil.
225 H5 Sable, Cape N.S. Can.
231 G13 Sable, Cape FL U.S.A.
78 □5 Sable, Île de i. New Caledonia
225 H2 Sable, Lac du l. Que. Can.
225 G2 Sable, Rivière du r. Que. Can.
217 □3b Sable Blanc, Récif du rf Mayotte
225 J5 Sable Island N.S. Can.
217 □1a Sables, Île aux i. Rodrigues I. Mauritius
227 L3 Sables, River aux r. Ont. Can.
158 G4 Sables-d'Or-les-Pins France
159 K6 Sablé-sur-Sarthe France
161 G8 Sablet France
161 E7 Sablières France
129 E1 Sablinskoye Rus. Fed.
161 F10 Sablon, Pointe du pt France
161 F6 Sablons France
122 G6 Sablū'īyeh Iran
254 F3 Saboeiro Brazil
184 C5 Sabóia Port.
207 H3 Sabon Kafi Niger
182 F6 Sabor r. Port.
206 E3 Sabou Burkina
227 Q2 Sabourin, Lac l. Que. Can.
202 B1 Sabrātah Libya
163 C7 Sabres France
263 H2 Sabrina Coast Antarctica
182 E6 Sabrosa Port.
92 C1 Sabtang i. Phil.
129 G3 Sabue Georgia
182 F8 Sabugal Port.
184 C3 Sabugueiro Évora Port.
182 E8 Sabugueiro Guarda Port.
93 B4 Sabulu Sulawesi Indon.
129 K5 Sabunçu Azer.
199 L3 Sabuncu Turkey
95 K8 Sabunten i. Indon.
105 I2 Saburyū-yama mt. Japan
124 F7 Şabyā Saudi Arabia
Sabzawar Afgh. see Shīndand
122 G3 Sabzevār Iran
Sabzvārān Iran see Jīroft
197 N4 Saca, Vârful mt. Romania
252 D4 Sacaba Bol.
252 D4 Sacaca Bol.
177 L4 Săcădat Romania
177 K6 Săcălaz Romania
197 R6 Sacalinul Mare, Insula i. Romania
259 C6 Sacanana, Pampa plain Arg.
233 K5 Sacandaga r. NY U.S.A.
209 C6 Sacandica Angola
187 D8 Sacañet Spain
261 F2 Sacanta Arg.
177 L4 Săcăşeni Romania
241 U8 Sacaton AZ U.S.A.
184 A3 Sacavém Port.
190 D7 Saccarel, Mont mt. France/Italy
236 H4 Sac City IA U.S.A.
193 L4 Sacco r. Italy
183 P7 Sacecorbo Spain
183 O8 Sacedón Spain
197 N5 Săcele Braşov Romania
197 Q6 Săcele Constanţa Romania
197 N6 Săceni Romania
185 J3 Saceruela Spain
129 D6 Saç Geçidi pass Turkey
209 C8 Sachanga Angola
223 N4 Sachigo r. Ont. Can.
223 M4 Sachigo Lake Ont. Can.
116 D9 Sachin Gujarat India
129 E3 Sach'khere Georgia
101 F11 Sach'on S. Korea
116 F3 Sach Pass Hima. Prad. India
190 E2 Sachseln Switz.
171 H8 Sachsen land Ger.
171 E6 Sachsen-Anhalt land Ger.
173 J3 Sachsen bei Ansbach Ger.
169 G8 Sachsenberg (Lichtenfels) Ger.
169 K10 Sachsenbrunn Ger.
179 H6 Sachsenburg Austria
169 H6 Sachsenhagen Ger.
169 H8 Sachsenhausen (Waldeck) Ger.
172 G4 Sachsenheim Ger.
220 F2 Sachs Harbour N.W.T. Can.
171 J9 Sächsische Schweiz park Ger.
171 J9 Sächsische Schweiz, Nationalpark nat. park Ger.
191 M4 Sacile Italy
Sacirsuyu r. Syria/Turkey see Sājūr, Nahr
233 I5 Sackets Harbor NY U.S.A.
169 G9 Sackpfeife hill Ger.
225 H4 Sackville N.B. Can.
233 □O5 Saco ME U.S.A.
238 K2 Saco MT U.S.A.
92 D8 Sacol i. Phil.
177 K6 Sacoşu Turcesc Romania
160 G1 Sacquenay France
183 M5 Sacramenia Spain
256 D3 Sacramento Brazil
240 K3 Sacramento CA U.S.A.
240 K3 Sacramento r. CA U.S.A.
252 A1 Sacramento, Pampa del plain Peru
239 K9 Sacramento Mountains NM U.S.A.
240 J1 Sacramento Valley CA U.S.A.
185 M7 Sacratif, Cabo c. Spain
253 F3 Sacre r. Brazil
187 I10 Sa Creu, Punta de pt Spain
149 N4 Sacriston Durham, England U.K.
193 I3 Sacrofano Italy
197 K3 Săcueni Romania
177 L5 Săcuieu Romania
253 F3 Sacuriuiná r. Brazil
243 O8 Sacxán Mex.
217 □3b Sada Mayotte
215 K8 Sada S. Africa
182 D2 Sada Spain
163 B10 Sada Spain
183 R4 Sádaba Spain
116 G6 Sadabad Uttar Prad. India
122 D7 Sa'dābād Iran
Sá da Bandeira Angola see Lubango
128 E4 Şadad Syria
124 F7 Şa'dah Yemen
124 F7 Şa'dah governorate Yemen
192 C8 Sadali Sardegna Italy
103 J13 Sada-misaki pt Japan
93 A5 Sadang r. Indon.
211 C6 Sadani Tanz.
97 E11 Sadao Thai.
125 I8 Şadārah Yemen
129 F6 Sädäräk Azer.
114 E4 Sadaseopet Andhra Prad. India
123 N5 Sadda Pak.
128 E7 Sadd as Sultānī Jordan
127 L7 Saddat al Hindīyah Iraq
146 E11 Saddell Argyll and Bute, Scotland U.K.
215 P1 Saddleback pass S. Africa
Saddleback hill England U.K. see Blencathra
237 D8 Saddleback Mesa mt. NM U.S.A.
85 J3 Saddle Hill Qld Austr.
81 H8 Saddle Hill mt. South I. N.Z.
Saddle Island Vanuatu see Mota Lava
115 M6 Saddle Peak hill Andaman & Nicobar Is India
97 G9 Sa Đec Vietnam
125 L7 Sadḩ Oman
116 F4 Sadhaura Haryana India
247 □7 Sadhoowa Trin. and Tob.
210 B2 Sadī Eth.
122 H9 Sadīj watercourse Iran
123 N7 Sadiqabad Pak.
129 G4 Sadıqlı Azer.
117 O6 Sadiya Assam India
124 D5 Sa'dīya Saudi Arabia
127 M7 Sa'dīyah, Hawr as imp. l. Iraq
125 L3 Sa'diyyat i. U.A.E.
213 □K2 Sadjoavato Madag.
122 G3 Sad-Kharv Iran
174 F2 Sadki Pol.
175 I4 Sadkowice Pol.
174 E2 Sadkowo Pol.
174 G2 Sadlinki Pol.
184 B4 Sado r. Port.
102 P9 Sadoga-shima i. Japan
184 B5 Sado Morgavel, Canal do Port.
127 L2 Sadon Rus. Fed.
95 I4 Sadong r. Malaysia
192 C6 Sa Donna, Pico mt. Italy
137 N8 Sadove Ukr.
175 J1 Sadovoye Kaliningradskaya Oblast' Rus. Fed.
135 I7 Sadovoye Respublika Kalmykiya-Khalm'g-Tangch Rus. Fed.
137 T2 Sadovoye Voronezhskaya Oblast' Rus. Fed.
175 J5 Sadowie Pol.
175 J3 Sadowne Pol.
187 J8 Sa Dragonera i. Spain
114 G6 Sadras Tamil Nadu India
116 D7 Sadri Rajasthan India
234 D5 Sadsburyville PA U.S.A.
171 K10 Sadská Czech Rep.
116 E5 Sadulshahar Rajasthan India
124 H3 Sādūs Saudi Arabia
128 C7 Sadūt Egypt
142 G4 Sæby Denmark
168 G1 Sæd Denmark
232 E7 Saegertown PA U.S.A.
183 O9 Saelices Spain
183 P7 Saelices de la Sal Spain
183 J3 Saelices del Rio Spain
183 J4 Saelices de Mayorga Spain
Saena Julia Italy see Siena
169 E6 Saerbeck Ger.
165 I9 Saeul Lux.
Safad Israel see Ẕefat
Safâga Island Egypt see Safājah, Jazīrat
203 G3 Safājah, Jazīrat i. Egypt
206 E3 Safané Burkina
184 E4 Safara Port.
Šafárikovo Slovakia see Tornaľa
129 I6 Şafarlū Iran
122 E6 Safāshahr Iran
78 □2 Safata Bay Samoa
127 M8 Safayal Maqūf well Iraq
123 N2 Safed Khirs mts Afgh.
123 K4 Safed Koh mts Afgh.
123 N4 Safed Koh mts Afgh./Pak.
125 I1 Saffānīyah, Ra's as pt Saudi Arabia
142 I2 Säffle Sweden
241 W9 Safford AZ U.S.A.
158 H6 Saffré France
151 M3 Saffron Walden Essex, England U.K.
Safi Jordan see Aş Şāfī
204 C2 Safi Morocco
122 G3 Safiabad Iran
122 D3 Safīd r. Iran
122 G5 Safīd, Chashmeh-ye spring Iran
123 K3 Safīd, Daryā-ye r. Afgh.
122 E4 Safīd Ab Iran
122 I6 Safidabeh Iran
122 E7 Safīdār, Kūh-e mt. Iran
122 C5 Safid Dasht Iran
Safīd Kūh mts Afgh. see Paropamisus
122 I4 Safīd Sagak Iran
124 H8 Sāfir Yemen
257 G3 Safiras, Serra das mts Brazil
128 E4 Şāfītā Syria
134 J2 Safonovo Arkhangel'skaya Oblast' Rus. Fed.
134 F1 Safonovo Murmanskaya Oblast' Rus. Fed.
139 Q6 Safonovo Smolenskaya Oblast' Rus. Fed.
78 □2 Safotu Samoa
124 F2 Safrā' al Asyāḩ esc. Saudi Arabia
124 G2 Safrā' as Sark esc. Saudi Arabia
126 F3 Safranbolu Turkey
78 □2 Safune Samoa
125 I2 Şafwa Saudi Arabia
127 M8 Safwān Iraq
177 L4 Sâg Romania
196 J5 Şag Romania
111 G12 Saga Xizang China
103 K13 Saga Kōchi Japan
103 H13 Saga Saga Japan
103 H13 Saga pref. Japan
120 J3 Saga Kostanayskaya Oblast' Kazakh.
120 K2 Saga Kostanayskaya Oblast' Kazakh.
102 R8 Sagae Japan
96 B4 Sagaing Myanmar
96 B3 Sagaing admin. div. Myanmar
Sagala Mali see Séguéla
192 B7 Sagama Sardegna Italy
105 J4 Sagamihara Japan
105 J4 Sagamiko Japan
105 J6 Sagami-nada g. Japan
105 J5 Sagami-wan b. Japan
232 F8 Sagamore PA U.S.A.
Sagamu Nigeria see Shagamu
227 L1 Saganash Lake Ont. Can.
103 I13 Saganoseki Japan
97 D8 Saganthit Kyun i. Myanmar
114 D5 Sagar Karnataka India
114 E4 Sagar Karnataka India
116 G8 Sagar Madh. Prad. India
105 H6 Sagara Japan
170 I1 Sagard Ger.
Sagaredzho Georgia see Sagarejo
129 G4 Sagarejo Georgia
117 M8 Sagaria Bangl.
117 L9 Sagar Island India
Sagarmatha mt. China/Nepal see Everest, Mount
117 K6 Sagarmatha National Park Nepal
131 N2 Sagastyr Rus. Fed.
117 J6 Sagauli Bihar India
220 D2 Sagavanirktok r. AK U.S.A.
168 F5 Sage Ger.
238 I6 Sage WY U.S.A.
238 I2 Sage Creek r. MT U.S.A.
143 K1 Sågen Sweden
147 J6 Saggart Ireland
140 N3 Saggat l. Sweden
128 C8 Saggi, Har mt. Israel
122 F5 Saghand Iran
123 J5 Saghar Afgh.
235 K3 Sag Harbor NY U.S.A.
Saghyz Kazakh. see Sagiz
114 F5 Sagileru r. India
227 K6 Saginaw MI U.S.A.
226 B3 Saginaw MN U.S.A.
227 K6 Saginaw Bay MI U.S.A.
199 J3 Sağırlar Turkey
193 L3 Sagittario r. Italy
120 E4 Sagiz Atyrauskaya Oblast' Kazakh.
120 F3 Sagiz Atyrauskaya Oblast' Kazakh.
Sagiz r. Kazakh. see Sagyz
199 I2 Sağlamtaş Turkey
129 J7 Şağlasär Azer.
206 C5 Sagleipie Liberia
225 I1 Saglek Bay Nfld and Lab. Can.
Saglouc Que. Can. see Salluit
106 B1 Sagly Rus. Fed.
192 B3 Sagone Corse France
192 B3 Sagone, Golfe de b. Corse France
185 N5 Sagra mt. Spain
260 B4 Sagrada Familia Chile
184 B6 Sagres Port.
184 B7 Sagres, Ponta de pt Port.
106 E4 Sagsay watercourse Mongolia
116 E8 Sagthale Rajasthan India
93 C8 Sagu Indon.
96 B4 Sagu Myanmar
177 K5 Şagu Romania
239 K7 Saguache CO U.S.A.
239 L8 Saguache Creek r. CO U.S.A.
246 F3 Sagua de Tánamo Cuba
246 C2 Sagua la Grande Cuba
241 V9 Saguaro National Park AZ U.S.A.
225 G3 Saguenay r. Que. Can.
94 G8 Saguling, Waduk resr Jawa Indon.
Sagunt Spain see Sagunto
187 E8 Sagunto Spain
Saguntum Spain see Sagunto
137 S3 Saguny Rus. Fed.
142 B2 Sagvåg Norway
116 E8 Sagwara Rajasthan India
160 G3 Sagy France
120 D5 Sagyndyk, Mys pt Kazakh.
120 E4 Sagyz r. Kazakh.
128 E7 Saḩāb Jordan
116 G5 Sahabab Uttar Prad. India
122 C2 Şahağac Azer.
245 I6 Sahagún Mex.
183 J4 Sahagún Spain
141 R6 Sahalahti Fin.
151 N2 Saham Toney Norfolk, England U.K.
122 B3 Sahand, Kūh-e mt. Iran
129 D5 Sahandöken Turkey
204 G6 Sahara des. Africa
Saharan Atlas mts Alg. see Atlas Saharien
116 F5 Saharanpur Uttar Prad. India
86 G6 Sahara Well W.A. Austr.
117 K7 Saharsa Bihar India
116 G5 Sahaswan Uttar Prad. India
122 F4 Sahat, Kūh-e hill Iran
117 J7 Sahatwar Uttar Prad. India
213 □K4 Sahavato Madag.
125 I4 Sahbā', Wādī as watercourse Saudi Arabia
129 G6 Şahbuz Azer.
129 G5 Şahdağ Silsiläsi hills Armenia/Azer.
206 C3 Sahel reg. Africa
124 D7 Sahel prov. Eritrea
206 E3 Sahel, Réserve Partielle du nature res. Burkina
117 K7 Sahibganj Jharkhand India
123 O6 Sahiwal Punjab Pak.
123 O6 Sahiwal Punjab Pak.
122 H5 Sahlābād Iran
124 D2 Sahl al Maţrān Saudi Arabia
124 E5 Sahl Rakbah plain Saudi Arabia
125 M3 Şaḩm Oman
122 B4 Şaḩneh Iran
127 L8 Şaḩrā al Ḩijārah reg. Iraq
Sahu Qinghai China see Zadoi
93 E3 Sahu Halmahera Indon.
242 E3 Sahuaripa Mex.
241 V10 Sahuarita AZ U.S.A.
244 E5 Sahuayo Mex.
186 F2 Sahun Spain
161 G8 Sahune France
137 L4 Sahunivka Ukr.
124 E3 Şāḩūq reg. Saudi Arabia
124 F3 Şāḩūq, Wādī watercourse Saudi Arabia
97 I7 Sa Huynh Vietnam
129 C6 Şahvelet Dağları mts Turkey
177 H3 Šahy Slovakia
Sahyadri mts India see Western Ghats
116 E9 Sahyadriparvat Range hills India
128 E3 Şahyūn tourist site Syria
116 I7 Sai r. India
91 J8 Saibai Island Qld Austr.
97 E11 Sai Buri Thai.
97 E11 Sai Buri, Mae Nam r. Thai.
205 F2 Saïda Alg.
128 D5 Saïda Lebanon
97 F8 Sai Dao Tai, Khao mt. Thai.
125 M4 Sa'id Bin Sahrān Oman
123 J8 Sa'īdī Iran
181 E5 Saïdia Morocco
Sa'īdīyeh Iran see Solţānīyeh
117 L7 Saidpur Bangl.
117 I7 Saidpur Uttar Prad. India
123 O4 Saidu Pak.
104 E2 Sai-gawa r. Japan
105 H2 Sai-gawa r. Japan
146 B7 Saighdinis Western Isles, Scotland U.K.
162 I5 Saignes France
161 G9 Saignon France
103 K10 Saigō Japan
Saigon Vietnam see Hô Chi Minh
117 N8 Saiha Mizoram India
107 M5 Saihan Tal Nei Mongol China
106 G6 Saihan Toroi Nei Mongol China
140 T3 Saija Fin.
103 K13 Saijō Japan
103 G13 Saikai Kokuritsu-kōen nat. park Japan
103 I14 Saiki Japan
103 I14 Saiki-wan b. Japan
109 □J7 Sai Kung H.K. China
109 □J7 Sai Kung Hoi b. H.K. China
116 E8 Sailana Madh. Prad. India
163 I11 Saillagouse-Llo France
161 G7 Saillans France
162 F4 Saillat-sur-Vienne France
93 G4 Sailolof Papua Indon.
160 D5 Sail-sous-Couzan France
141 T6 Saimaa l. Fin.
141 T6 Saimaankanava r. Fin.
126 H4 Saimbeyli Turkey
244 D2 Sain Alto Mex.
160 C3 Saincaize-Meauce France
123 I7 Saindak Pak.
122 B3 Sa'īndezh Iran
Sa'īn Qal'eh Iran see Sa'īndezh
206 C3 Saïnsoubou Senegal
156 G4 Sains-Richaumont France
236 K7 Saint r. IL U.S.A.
146 L11 St Abbs Scottish Borders, Scotland U.K.
185 □ St Abb's Head Gibraltar
146 L11 St Abb's Head Scotland U.K.
156 D3 St-Acheul France
161 B9 St-Affrique France
161 B8 St-Affrique, Causse de plat. France
160 D3 St-Agnan Bourgogne France
160 E2 St-Agnan Bourgogne France
161 G7 St-Agnan-en-Vercors France
162 C4 St-Agnant France
162 H3 St-Agnant-de-Versillat France
150 B7 St Agnes Cornwall, England U.K.
150 □ St Agnes i. England U.K.
161 E6 St-Agrève France
162 G1 St-Aignan France
159 I6 St-Aignan-sur-Roë France
162 D5 St-Aigulin France
160 F4 St-Albain France
158 F4 St-Alban France
161 F6 St-Alban-d'Ay France
160 H5 St-Alban-Leysse France
225 K4 St Alban's Nfld and Lab. Can.
151 L4 St Albans Hertfordshire, England U.K.
233 L4 St Albans VT U.S.A.
232 D10 St Albans WV U.S.A.
St Alban's Head England U.K. see St Aldhelm's Head
161 C7 St-Alban-sur-Limagnole France
222 H4 St Albert Alta Can.
150 H6 St Aldhelm's Head England U.K.
159 J3 St-Amand France
160 C1 St-Amand-en-Puisaye France
156 F3 St-Amand-les-Eaux France
159 N6 St-Amand-Longpré France
160 B3 St-Amand-Montrond France
156 I6 St-Amand-sur-Fion France
161 C7 St-Amans France
161 B7 St-Amans-des-Cots France
163 I9 St-Amans-Soult France
162 E4 St-Amant-de-Boixe France
160 D5 St-Amant-Roche-Savine France
160 C5 St-Amant-Tallende France
157 N8 St-Amarin France
225 G3 St-Ambroise Que. Can.
161 E8 St-Ambroix France
160 G4 St-Amour France
161 F9 St-Andiol France
163 J10 St-André Languedoc-Roussillon France
161 K9 St-André Provence-Alpes-Côte d'Azur France
217 □1b St-André Mauritius
217 □1c St-André Réunion
St-André, Cap pt Madag. see Vilanandro, Tanjona
156 B6 St-André, Plaine de plain France
160 F5 St-André-de-Corcy France
161 E8 St-André-de-Cruzières France
162 D6 St-André-de-Cubzac France
156 B6 St-André-de-l'Eure France
161 J7 St-André-d'Embrun France
161 D9 St-André-de-Sangonis France
163 B8 St-André-de-Seignanx France
161 D8 St-André-de-Valborgne France
160 D2 St-André-en-Morvan France
160 H5 St-André-le-Gaz France
161 J9 St-André-les-Alpes France
156 H7 St-André-les-Vergers France
246 □ St Andrew parish Jamaica
247 □7 St Andrew county Trin. and Tob.
233 □R3 St Andrews N.B. Can.
81 F11 St Andrews South I. N.Z.
146 K10 St Andrews Fife, Scotland U.K.
231 G10 St Andrew Sound inlet GA U.S.A.
162 I4 St-Angel France
246 □ St Ann parish Jamaica
158 G2 St Anne Channel Is
226 G8 St Anne IL U.S.A.
246 □ St Ann's Bay Jamaica
150 B4 St Ann's Head Wales U.K.
226 B6 St Ansgar IA U.S.A.
160 D5 St-Anthème France
225 K3 St Anthony Nfld and Lab. Can.
238 I5 St Anthony ID U.S.A.
128 A10 St Anthony, Monastery of tourist site Egypt
163 H7 St-Antonin-Noble-Val France
159 O8 St-Août France
160 G2 St-Apollinaire France
161 D6 St-Arcons-d'Allier France
83 I7 St Arnaud Vic. Austr.
81 G8 St Arnaud South I. N.Z.
81 G9 St Arnaud Range mts South I. N.Z.
156 C6 St-Arnoult-en-Yvelines France
150 F1 St Asaph Denbighshire, Wales U.K.
84 C1 St Asaph Bay N.T. Austr.
162 F5 St-Astier Aquitaine France
163 E6 St-Astier Aquitaine France
150 F5 St Athan Vale of Glamorgan, Wales U.K.
161 J9 St-Auban France
161 G8 St-Auban-sur-l'Ouvèze France
160 G2 St-Aubin France
156 F8 St-Aubin-Château-Neuf France
158 H5 St-Aubin-d'Aubigné France
158 I5 St-Aubin-du-Cormier France
156 B5 St-Aubin-lès-Elbeuf France
159 K3 St-Aubin-sur-Mer France
225 J3 St-Augustin Que. Can.
225 J3 St Augustin r. Nfld and Lab./Que. Can.
231 G11 St Augustine FL U.S.A.
162 E5 St-Aulaye France
150 C7 St Austell Cornwall, England U.K.
150 C7 St Austell Bay England U.K.
158 F6 St-Avé France
159 M7 St-Avertin France
157 M5 St-Avold France
156 C8 St-Ay France
161 J10 St-Aygulf France
160 H5 St-Baldoph France
225 J3 St Barbe Nfld and Lab. Can.
225 F4 St-Barthélemy Que. Can.
247 L5 St-Barthélemy i. West Indies
163 H10 St-Barthélemy, Pic de mt. France
163 E6 St-Barthélemy-d'Agenais France
159 K7 St-Barthélemy-d'Anjou France
162 E5 St-Barthélemy-de-Bellegarde France
161 F6 St-Barthélemy-de-Vals France
81 D11 St Bathans South I. N.Z.
81 D11 St Bathans, Mount South I. N.Z.
161 D9 St-Bauzille-de-Putois France
163 F10 St-Béat France
161 B8 St-Beauzély France
149 J5 St Bees Cumbria, England U.K.
149 J4 St Bees Head England U.K.
160 C2 St-Benin-d'Azy France
163 I9 St-Benoît Languedoc-Roussillon France
162 E2 St-Benoît Poitou-Charentes France
217 □1c St-Benoît Réunion
163 I7 St-Benoît-de-Carmaux France
162 G3 St-Benoît-du-Sault France
156 D8 St-Benoît-sur-Loire France
81 H9 St Bernard mt. South I. N.Z.
160 H5 St-Béron France
159 J5 St-Berthevin France
163 F9 St-Bertrand-de-Comminges France
190 B1 St-Blaise Switz.
157 N7 St-Blaise-la-Roche France
157 J7 St-Blin-Semilly France
160 F3 St-Boil France
162 F3 St-Bonnet-de-Bellac France
160 E4 St-Bonnet-de-Joux France
160 E4 St-Bonnet-des-Bruyères France
161 I7 St-Bonnet-en-Champsaur France
161 E6 St-Bonnet-le-Château France
161 E6 St-Bonnet-le-Froid France
162 C5 St-Bonnet-sur-Gironde France
160 E2 St-Brancher France
159 M7 St-Branchs France
158 G3 St Brelade Channel Is
158 G7 St-Brevin-les-Pins France
158 G4 St-Briac-sur-Mer France
150 G4 St Briavels Gloucestershire, England U.K.
156 H5 St-Brice-Courcelles France
158 I5 St-Brice-en-Coglès France
150 B4 St Brides Pembrokeshire, Wales U.K.
150 B4 St Bride's Bay Wales U.K.
150 E5 St Brides Major Vale of Glamorgan, Wales U.K.
158 F4 St-Brieuc France
158 F4 St-Brieuc, Baie de b. France
156 G8 St-Bris-le-Vineux France
160 E2 St-Brisson France
157 I8 St-Broing-les-Moines France
158 H4 St-Broladre France
150 □ St Buryan Cornwall, England U.K.
159 M6 St-Calais France
161 G9 St-Cannat France
158 G4 St-Cast-le-Guildo France
224 E5 St Catharines Ont. Can.
246 □ St Catherine parish Jamaica
128 B10 St Catherine, Monastery of tourist site Egypt
247 □6 St Catherine, Mount hill Grenada
225 K4 St Catherine's Nfld and Lab. Can.
231 G10 St Catherines Island GA U.S.A.
231 □1 St Catherine's Point Bermuda
151 J6 St Catherine's Point England U.K.
163 H6 St-Céré France
190 A3 St-Cergue Switz.
160 I4 St-Cergues France
162 I5 St-Cernin France
233 L3 St-Césaire Que. Can.
161 J7 St-Chaffrey France
163 G6 St-Chamarand France
161 G9 St-Chamas France
161 F6 St-Chamond France
161 E9 St-Chaptes France
227 N3 St Charles Ont. Can.
238 I5 St Charles ID U.S.A.
232 I10 St Charles MD U.S.A.
227 J6 St Charles MI U.S.A.
226 B6 St Charles MN U.S.A.
236 J6 St Charles MO U.S.A.
160 G5 St-Chef France
161 C7 St-Chély-d'Apcher France
161 B7 St-Chély-d'Aubrac France
161 B10 St-Chinian France
161 G8 St-Christol France
161 E8 St-Christol-lès-Alès France
162 C5 St-Christoly-de-Blaye France
162 C5 St-Christoly-Médoc France
160 K5 St-Christophe Italy
158 H8 St-Christophe-du-Ligneron France
159 O7 St-Christophe-en-Bazelle France
160 E4 St-Christophe-en-Brionnais France
162 C5 St-Ciers-sur-Gironde France
161 E7 St-Cirgues-en-Montagne France
163 H7 St-Cirq-Lapopie France
224 D5 St Clair r. Can./U.S.A.
227 L7 St Clair MI U.S.A.
234 C3 St Clair PA U.S.A.
227 L7 St Clair, Lake Can./U.S.A.
161 F6 St-Clair-du-Rhône France
156 C5 St-Clair-sur-Epte France
159 I3 St-Clair-sur-l'Elle France
232 E8 St Clairsville OH U.S.A.
163 F8 St-Clar France
162 E4 St-Claud France
160 H4 St-Claude France
247 □2 St-Claude Guadeloupe
150 D4 St Clears Carmarthenshire, Wales U.K.
158 G3 St Clement Channel Is
156 F7 St-Clément Bourgogne France
162 H5 St-Clément Limousin France
157 M6 St-Clément Lorraine France
161 D9 St-Clément de-Rivière France
231 G11 St Cloud FL U.S.A.
236 H3 St Cloud MN U.S.A.
225 G3 St-Coeur-de-Marie Que. Can.
150 C7 St Columb Major Cornwall, England U.K.
146 M7 St Combs Aberdeenshire, Scotland U.K.
163 I6 St-Constant France
159 L5 St-Cosme-en-Vairais France
162 F5 St-Crépin-de-Richemont France
163 C8 St-Cricq-Chalosse France
221 L5 St Croix r. Can./U.S.A.
226 B4 St Croix r. WI U.S.A.
247 K5 St Croix i. Virgin Is (U.S.A.)
226 B4 St Croix Falls WI U.S.A.
163 G6 St-Cyprien Aquitaine France
163 K10 St-Cyprien Languedoc-Roussillon France
163 G7 St-Cyprien Midi-Pyrénées France
156 D6 St-Cyr-l'École France
162 F1 St-Cyr-sur-Loire France
161 H10 St-Cyr-sur-Mer France
156 F6 St-Cyr-sur-Morin France
161 J8 St-Dalmas-le-Selvage France
225 G4 St-Damien-de-Buckland Que. Can.
247 □7 St David county Trin. and Tob.
241 V10 St David AZ U.S.A.
226 D9 St David IL U.S.A.
150 B4 St David's Pembrokeshire, Wales U.K.
150 B4 St David's Head Wales U.K.
231 □1 St David's Island Bermuda
150 B7 St Day Cornwall, England U.K.
156 D6 St-Denis Île-de-France France
163 I9 St-Denis Languedoc-Roussillon France
217 □1c St-Denis Réunion
159 K6 St-Denis-d'Anjou France
159 J5 St-Denis-de-Gastines France
162 H2 St-Denis-de-Jouhet France
162 B3 St-Denis-d'Oléron France
159 K5 St-Denis-d'Orques France
St-Denis-du-Sig Alg. see Sig
160 G5 St-Denis-en-Bugey France
160 G4 St-Denis-lès-Bourg France
150 C7 St Dennis Cornwall, England U.K.
158 G4 St-Denoual France
160 F3 St-Désert France
161 E6 St-Didier-en-Velay France
160 F4 St-Didier-sur-Chalaronne France
160 D5 St-Didier-sur-Rochefort France
157 M7 St-Dié France
160 C5 St-Dier-d'Auvergne France
157 I6 St-Dizier France
162 H3 St-Dizier-Leyrenne France
150 C3 St Dogmaels Pembrokeshire, Wales U.K.
158 G6 St-Dolay France
158 H5 St-Domineuc France
St-Domingue country West Indies see Haiti
161 F6 St-Donat-sur-l'Herbasse France
159 P7 St-Doulchard France
159 L2 Ste-Adresse France
162 F6 Ste-Alvère France
223 L5 Sainte Anne Man. Can.
247 □2 Ste-Anne Guadeloupe
247 □3 Ste-Anne Martinique
217 □1c Ste-Anne Réunion
217 □2b Ste-Anne i. Seychelles
222 H4 Sainte Anne, Lac l. Alta Can.
225 H3 Ste-Anne, Lac l. Que. Can.
158 F6 Ste-Anne-d'Auray France
225 G4 Ste-Anne-de-Beaupré Que. Can.
233 □Q1 Ste-Anne-de-Madawaska N.B. Can.
225 G3 Ste-Anne-de-Portneuf Que. Can.
225 H3 Ste-Anne-des-Monts Que. Can.
227 S3 Ste-Anne-du-Lac Que. Can.
161 H10 Ste-Baume, Chaîne de la mts France
163 E6 Ste-Bazeille France
233 □O2 Ste-Camille-de-Lellis Que. Can.
208 A5 Ste-Catherine, Pointe pt Gabon
161 F8 Ste-Cécile-les-Vignes France
160 G3 Ste-Croix Bourgogne France
161 G7 Ste-Croix Rhône-Alpes France
190 B2 Ste-Croix Switz.
161 I9 Ste-Croix, Barrage de dam France
161 I9 Ste-Croix, Lac de l. France
163 G9 Ste-Croix-Volvestre France
224 F4 Ste-Émélie-de-l'Énergie Que. Can.
163 C9 Ste-Engrâce France
161 C8 Ste-Énimie France
161 B8 Ste-Eulalie d'Olt France
163 B7 Ste-Eulalie-en-Born France
162 H3 Ste-Feyre France
161 C6 Ste-Florine France
162 H5 Ste-Fortunade France
163 G9 Ste-Foy-de-Peyrolières France
163 E6 Ste-Foy-la-Grande France
160 E5 Ste-Foy-l'Argentière France
160 F5 Ste-Foy-lès-Lyon France
160 J5 Ste-Foy-Tarentaise France
159 L4 Ste-Gauburge-Ste-Colombe France
162 B3 Ste-Gemme-la-Plaine France
156 D5 Ste-Geneviève France
236 J7 Sainte Genevieve MO U.S.A.
161 B7 Ste-Geneviève-sur-Argence France
161 H6 St-Égrève France
162 C6 Ste-Hélène France
162 B2 Ste-Hermine France
233 □O2 Ste-Justine Que. Can.
233 □P1 St-Éleuthère Que. Can.
220 D4 St Elias, Cape AK U.S.A.
222 A2 St Elias, Mount AK U.S.A.
222 A2 St Elias Mountains Y.T. Can.
251 H3 St-Élie Fr. Guiana
163 F7 Ste-Livrade-sur-Lot France
163 G9 St-Élix-le-Château France
163 E9 St-Élix-Theux France
246 □ St Elizabeth parish Jamaica
159 P7 Ste-Lizaigne France
160 B4 St-Éloy-les-Mines France
247 □3 Ste-Luce Martinique
192 C4 Ste-Lucie-de-Tallano Corse France
225 H3 Ste-Marguerite r. Que. Can.
225 H3 Sainte-Marguerite 3 resr Que. Can.
157 M7 Ste-Marguerite France
225 G4 Ste-Marie Que. Can.
161 B7 Ste-Marie Auvergne France
163 K10 Ste-Marie Languedoc-Roussillon France
247 □3 Ste-Marie Martinique
217 □1c Ste-Marie Réunion
Ste-Marie, Cap c. Madag. see Vohimena, Tanjona
Sainte-Marie, Île i. Madag. see Boraha, Nosy
157 N7 Ste-Marie-aux-Mines France
159 M7 Ste-Maure, Plateau de France
163 E7 Ste-Maure-de-Peyriac France
162 F1 Ste-Maure-de-Touraine France
161 J10 Ste-Maxime France
157 I5 Ste-Menehould France
158 I3 Ste-Mère-Église France
160 E3 St-Émiland France
163 D6 St-Émilion France
150 C6 St Endellion Cornwall, England U.K.
150 C7 St Enoder Cornwall, England U.K.
162 G5 Ste-Orse France
158 H7 Ste-Pazanne France
159 K8 Ste-Radegonde France
156 G4 St-Erme-Outre-et-Ramecourt France
247 □2 Ste-Rose Guadeloupe
217 □1c Ste-Rose Réunion
Ste-Rose-du-Dégelé Que. Can. see Dégelis
223 L5 Sainte Rose du Lac Man. Can.
150 B7 St Erth Cornwall, England U.K.
162 C4 Saintes France
247 □2 Saintes, Îles des is Guadeloupe
160 F2 Ste-Sabine France
156 H7 Ste-Savine France
Ste-Scholastique Que. Can. see Mirabel
162 I3 Ste-Sévère-sur-Indre France
161 E6 Ste-Sigolène France
247 □3 St-Esprit Martinique
163 B9 St-Esteben France
162 C5 St-Estèphe France
163 J10 St-Estève France
159 K5 Ste-Suzanne France
217 □1c Ste-Suzanne Réunion
233 L3 Ste-Thérèse Que. Can.
222 F1 Sainte Thérèse, Lac l. N.W.T. Can.
161 E6 St-Étienne France
162 I6 St-Étienne-Cantalès France
163 B9 St-Étienne-de-Baïgorry France
161 H6 St-Étienne-de-Crossey France
161 E7 St-Étienne-de-Fontbellon France
162 H3 St-Étienne-de-Fursac France
161 D7 St-Étienne-de-Lugdarès France
158 H7 St-Étienne-de-Montluc France
161 G6 St-Étienne-de-St-Geoirs France
161 J8 St-Étienne-de-Tinée France
163 G7 St-Étienne-de-Tulmont France
160 G4 St-Étienne-du-Bois France
156 B5 St-Étienne-du-Rouvray France
161 H7 St-Étienne-en-Dévoluy France
161 H8 St-Étienne-les-Orgues France
157 M7 St-Étienne-lès-Remiremont France
161 D8 St-Étienne-Vallée-Française France
161 H9 Ste-Tulle France
233 K3 St Eugene Ont. Can.
233 □Q1 St-Eusèbe Que. Can.
233 L3 St-Eustache Que. Can.
158 C6 St-Évarzec France
156 G8 Ste-Vertu France
161 H9 Ste-Victoire, Montagne mt. France
225 G3 St-Fabien Que. Can.
215 O6 St Faith's S. Africa
160 C1 St-Fargeau France
225 F3 St-Félicien Que. Can.
161 F6 St-Félicien France
227 P1 St-Félix-de-Dalquier Que. Can.
163 H9 St-Félix-Lauragais France
146 M7 St Fergus Aberdeenshire, Scotland U.K.
163 E6 St-Ferme France
147 K4 Saintfield Northern Ireland U.K.
146 H10 St Fillans Perth and Kinross, Scotland U.K.
157 L7 St-Firmin Lorraine France
161 I7 St-Firmin Provence-Alpes-Côte d'Azur France
156 G7 St-Flavy France
192 C2 St-Florent Corse France
192 C2 St-Florent, Golfe de b. Corse France
162 B2 St-Florent-des-Bois France
156 G7 St-Florentin France
159 I7 St-Florent-le-Vieil France
162 I2 St-Florent-sur-Cher France
208 D2 St Floris, Parc National nat. park C.A.R.
161 C6 St-Flour France
159 N8 St-Flovier France
160 F5 St-Fons France
162 C5 St-Fort-sur-Gironde France
163 F9 St-Frajou France
237 J10 St Francesville LA U.S.A.
233 □Q1 St Francis r. Can./U.S.A.
236 E6 St Francis KS U.S.A.
233 □Q1 St Francis ME U.S.A.
237 J8 St Francis r. AR/MO U.S.A.
215 I10 St Francis, Cape S. Africa
215 J10 St Francis Bay S. Africa
82 D5 St Francis Isles S.A. Austr.
225 F4 St-François r. Que. Can.
247 □2 St-François Guadeloupe
217 □2 St François i. Seychelles
225 G4 St-François, Lac l. Que. Can.
161 I6 St-François-Longchamp France
233 □Q2 St Froid Lake ME U.S.A.
161 E7 St-Front France
162 E5 St-Front-de-Pradoux France
159 I8 St-Fulgent France
160 E5 St-Galmier France
159 L3 St-Gatien-des-Bois France
163 F9 St-Gaudens France
162 G2 St-Gaultier France
233 □O3 St-Gédéon Que. Can.
163 D8 St-Gein France
161 D9 St-Gély-du-Fesc France
161 E6 St-Genest-Malifaux France
160 F3 St-Gengoux-le-National France
161 E9 St-Geniès-de-Malgoirès France
161 I8 St-Geniez France
161 B8 St-Geniez-d'Olt France
162 C5 St-Genis-de-Saintonge France
163 J10 St-Génis-des-Fontaines France
160 F5 St-Genis-Laval France
160 I4 St-Genis-Pouilly France
160 H5 St-Genix-sur-Guiers France
150 C6 St Gennys Cornwall, England U.K.
159 N8 St-Genou France
161 H6 St-Geoire-en-Valdaine France
83 L3 St George Qld Austr.
85 J4 St George r. Qld Austr.
231 □1 St George Bermuda
225 H4 St George N.B. Can.
247 □7 St George county Trin. and Tob.
220 B4 St George AK U.S.A.
231 G9 St George SC U.S.A.
241 S4 St George UT U.S.A.
91 L7 St George, Cape New Ireland P.N.G.
238 B6 St George, Point CA U.S.A.
83 M6 St George Head A.C.T. Austr.
220 B4 St George Island AK U.S.A.
231 E11 St George Island FL U.S.A.
86 H5 St George Range hills W.A. Austr.
225 J3 St George's Nfld and Lab. Can.
225 G4 St-Georges Que. Can.
251 I4 St-Georges Fr. Guiana
247 □6 St George's Grenada
234 D5 St Georges DE U.S.A.
225 J3 St George's Bay Nfld and Lab. Can.
225 I4 St George's Bay N.S. Can.
159 J5 St-Georges-Buttavent France
243 P9 St George's Cay i. Belize
115 M9 St George's Channel Andaman & Nicobar Is India
91 L7 St George's Channel P.N.G.
147 J9 St George's Channel Ireland/U.K.
161 D6 St-Georges-d'Aurac France
161 H6 St-Georges-de-Commiers France
162 C4 St-Georges-de-Didonne France
161 B8 St-Georges-de-Luzençon France
160 B5 St-Georges-de-Mons France
158 I8 St-Georges-de-Montaigu France
160 F4 St-Georges-de-Reneins France
159 J4 St-Georges-des-Groseillers France
160 G5 St-Georges-d'Espéranche France
162 B4 St-Georges-d'Oléron France
159 M3 St-Georges-du-Vièvre France
160 D5 St-Georges-en-Couzan France
231 □1 St George's Harbour b. Bermuda
231 □1 St George's Island Bermuda
159 L8 St-Georges-lès-Baillargeaux France
156 G8 St-Georges-sur-Baulche France
159 N7 St-Georges-sur-Cher France
156 B7 St-Georges-sur-Eure France
159 J7 St-Georges-sur-Loire France
163 B8 St-Geours-de-Maremne France
160 D4 St-Gérand-le-Puy France
226 E4 St Germain WI U.S.A.
160 C3 St-Germain-Chassenay France
161 D8 St-Germain-de-Calberte France
159 M5 St-Germain-de-la-Coudre France
160 C4 St-Germain-des-Fossés France
162 C5 St-Germain-d'Esteuil France
163 G6 St-Germain-du-Bel-Air France
160 G3 St-Germain-du-Bois France
159 L5 St-Germain-du-Corbéis France
160 F3 St-Germain-du-Plain France
162 I1 St-Germain-du-Puy France
161 C8 St-Germain-du-Teil France
156 D6 St-Germain-en-Laye France
160 E5 St-Germain-Laval France
161 C6 St-Germain-Lembron France
162 G4 St-Germain-les-Belles France
160 D4 St-Germain-Lespinasse France
162 H5 St-Germain-les-Vergnes France
161 D6 St-Germain-l'Herm France
150 D7 St Germans Cornwall, England U.K.
163 D8 St-Germé France
156 C5 St-Germer-de-Fly France
158 G8 St-Gervais Pays de la Loire France
161 G6 St-Gervais Rhône-Alpes France
160 B4 St-Gervais-d'Auvergne France
159 N6 St-Gervais-la-Forêt France
160 J5 St-Gervais-les-Bains France
159 L8 St-Gervais-les-Trois-Clochers France
161 C9 St-Gervais-sur-Mare France
163 H7 St-Géry France
165 E8 St-Ghislain Belgium

Salem to San Francisco
381

236 K6 Salem IL U.S.A.
230 D6 Salem IN U.S.A.
233 O6 Salem MA U.S.A.
237 J7 Salem MO U.S.A.
234 E5 Salem NJ U.S.A.
233 L5 Salem NY U.S.A.
232 E8 Salem OH U.S.A.
238 C4 Salem OR U.S.A.
236 G4 Salem SD U.S.A.
241 U1 Salem UT U.S.A.
232 E11 Salem VA U.S.A.
232 E9 Salem WV U.S.A.
234 D5 Salem r. NJ U.S.A.
234 E5 Salem County county NJ U.S.A.
194 D8 Salemi Sicilia Italy
141 L6 Sälen Sweden
143 K5 Salen l. Sweden
146 E9 Salen Argyll and Bute, Scotland U.K.
146 E9 Salen Highland, Scotland U.K.
161 I9 Salernes France
193 N6 Salerno Italy
193 O7 Salerno prov. Italy
193 N7 Salerno, Golfo di g. Italy
Salernum Italy see Salerno
162 I5 Salers France
256 D4 Sales Oliveira Brazil
257 E5 Salesópolis Brazil
151 N4 Sales Point England U.K.
161 D7 Salettes France
156 D4 Saleux France
160 I4 Salève mt. France
149 M7 Salford Greater Manchester, England U.K.
151 L5 Salfords Surrey, England U.K.
251 F5 Salgada Brazil
254 F4 Salgado Brazil
254 F3 Salgado r. Brazil
177 I3 Salgótarján Hungary
254 F4 Salgueiro Brazil
182 E9 Salgueiro Port.
182 F5 Salgueiros Port.
261 F4 Salguero Arg.
151 O2 Salhouse Norfolk, England U.K.
142 B1 Salhus Norway
137 N8 Salhyr r. Ukr.
205 E4 Sali Alg.
123 I6 Salian Afgh.
93 E2 Salibabu i. Indon.
Salibea Trin. and Tob. see Salybia
195 N3 Salice Salentino Italy
190 E7 Saliceto Italy
194 H8 Salici, Monte mt. Sicilia Italy
239 L7 Salida CO U.S.A.
138 G5 Saliena Latvia
163 C9 Salies-de-Béarn France
163 F9 Salies-du-Salat France
162 G6 Salignac-Eyvignes France
199 J4 Salihli Turkey
138 K9 Salihorsk Belarus
138 K9 Salihorskaye Vodaskhovishcha resr Belarus
206 B3 Salikénié Senegal
186 C4 Salillas de Jalón Spain
211 B8 Salima Malawi
95 L3 Salimbatu Kalimantan Indon.
182 G2 Salime, Encoro de resr Spain
209 D7 Salimi Dem. Rep. Congo
211 C8 Salimo Moz.
96 B4 Salin Myanmar
236 G6 Salina KS U.S.A.
241 U3 Salina UT U.S.A.
195 □ Salina, Il-Bajja tas- b. Malta
194 H6 Salina, Isola i. Isole Lipari Italy
245 L9 Salina Cruz Mex.
246 F2 Salina Point Acklins I. Bahamas
257 F2 Salinas Brazil
250 A5 Salinas Ecuador
244 F3 Salinas San Luis Potosí Mex.
245 L7 Salinas Veracruz Mex.
237 F13 Salinas r. Mex.
247 □1 Salinas Puerto Rico
182 I1 Salinas Asturias Spain
187 D10 Salinas Valencia Spain
240 K5 Salinas CA U.S.A.
240 K5 Salinas r. CA U.S.A.
Salinas, Cabo de c. Spain see Salines, Cap de ses
260 D2 Salinas, Pampa de las salt pan Arg.
209 B8 Salinas, Ponta das pt Angola
216 □3d Salinas, Punta pt La Palma Canary Is
246 H4 Salinas, Punta pt Dom. Rep.
252 D4 Salinas de Garci Mendoza Bol.
183 Q8 Salinas del Manzano Spain
183 Q3 Salinas de Pamplona Spain
183 L3 Salinas de Pisuerga Spain
186 F2 Salinas de Sín Spain
239 K10 Salinas Peak NM U.S.A.
161 F10 Salin-de-Giraud France
161 E8 Salindres France
193 M2 Saline r. Italy
193 Q5 Saline salt marsh Italy
149 J1 Saline Fife, Scotland U.K.
227 K7 Saline MI U.S.A.
237 I9 Saline r. AR U.S.A.
236 G6 Saline r. KS U.S.A.
247 □7 Saline Bay Trin. and Tob.
191 J9 Saline di Volterra Italy
193 L2 Salinello r. Italy
187 L9 Salines, Cap de ses c. Spain
247 □6 Salines, Point Grenada
240 O5 Saline Valley depr. CA U.S.A.
232 E8 Salineville OH U.S.A.
96 B4 Salingyi Myanmar
254 D2 Salinópolis Brazil
252 A2 Salinosó Lachay, Punta pt Peru
162 I5 Salins France
160 H3 Salins-les-Bains France
184 C6 Salir Port.
151 I5 Salisbury Wiltshire, England U.K.
233 J10 Salisbury MD U.S.A.
231 G8 Salisbury NC U.S.A.
232 F9 Salisbury PA U.S.A.
Salisbury Zimbabwe see Harare
221 K3 Salisbury Island Nunavut Can.
235 G2 Salisbury Mills NY U.S.A.
151 H5 Salisbury Plain England U.K.
197 L5 Săliște Romania
197 M3 Săliștea de Sus Romania
194 F9 Salito r. Sicilia Italy
244 E3 Salitral de Carrera Mex.
254 E4 Salitre r. Brazil
177 H4 Salka Slovakia
128 E6 Şalkhad Syria
117 J9 Salki r. India
128 F1 Salkım Turkey
136 I5 Sal'kove Ukr.
140 T3 Salla Fin.
234 A2 Salladasburg PA U.S.A.
160 J5 Sallanches France
206 B4 Sallatouk, Pointe pt Guinea
186 I4 Sallent Spain
186 E2 Sallent de Gállego Spain
163 C6 Salles France
161 B8 Salles-Curan France
162 D4 Salles-d'Angles France
161 C10 Salles-d'Aude France
163 J7 Salles-la-Source France
163 H9 Salles-sur-l'Hers France
171 I7 Sallgast Ger.
142 E5 Salling reg. Denmark
179 L3 Sallingberg Austria
147 I6 Sallins Ireland
Salliq Nunavut Can. see Coral Harbour
261 F5 Salliqueló Arg.
237 H8 Sallisaw OK U.S.A.
203 H5 Sallom Sudan
221 K3 Salluit Que. Can.
202 E2 Sallum, Khalīj as b. Egypt
116 I5 Sallyana Nepal
147 F7 Sallypark Ireland
165 I8 Salm r. Belgium
128 E3 Salmá Syria
129 B5 Salmankas Geçidi pass Turkey
122 A2 Salmās Iran
183 P7 Salmerón Spain
183 O7 Salmeroncillos de Abajo Spain
134 E3 Salmi Rus. Fed.
140 T3 Salmivaara Fin.
222 G5 Salmo B.C. Can.
238 H4 Salmon ID U.S.A.
235 K2 Salmon r. CT U.S.A.
238 F4 Salmon r. ID U.S.A.
238 G4 Salmon, Middle Fork r. ID U.S.A.
222 G5 Salmon Arm B.C. Can.
238 G5 Salmon Falls Creek r. ID/NV U.S.A.
87 F12 Salmon Gums W.A. Austr.
Salmonhurst N.B. Can. see New Denmark
233 J5 Salmon Reservoir NY U.S.A.
238 G4 Salmon River Mountains ID U.S.A.
214 D10 Salmonsdam Nature Reserve S. Africa
183 J7 Salmoral Spain
172 B2 Salmtal Ger.
140 U2 Sal'nyye Tundry, Khrebet mts Rus. Fed.
208 C4 Salo C.A.R.
141 Q6 Salo Fin.
191 J4 Salò Italy
134 J4 Salobelyak Rus. Fed.
185 N3 Salobre Spain
185 L7 Salobreña Spain
140 R4 Saloinen Fin.
241 S8 Salome AZ U.S.A.
247 □3 Salomon, Cap c. Martinique
156 H6 Salon France
160 H1 Salon r. France
116 H6 Salon Uttar Prad. India
161 G9 Salon-de-Provence France
208 D5 Salonga r. Dem. Rep. Congo
208 D5 Salonga Nord, Parc National de la nat. park Dem. Rep. Congo
208 D5 Salonga Sud, Parc National de la nat. park Dem. Rep. Congo
Salonica Greece see Thessaloniki
Salonika Greece see Thessaloniki
197 J4 Salonta Romania
Salop admin. div. England U.K. see Shropshire
182 F9 Salor r. Spain
184 G2 Salor, Embalse de resr Spain
186 H2 Salòria, Pic de mt. Spain
184 E2 Salorino Spain
160 F3 Salornay-sur-Guye France
191 K3 Salorno Italy
186 H5 Salou Spain
186 H5 Salou, Cap de c. Spain
156 D4 Salouël France
206 A3 Saloum watercourse Senegal
179 N6 Šalovci Slovenia
141 R6 Salpausselkä reg. Fin.
140 □ Salpynten pt Svalbard
128 E2 Salqīn Syria
206 □ Sal Rei Cape Verde
147 C5 Salruck Ireland
260 E2 Salsacate Arg.
140 K4 Salsbruket Norway
Salses, Étang de l. France see Leucate, Étang de
163 J10 Salses-le-Château France
135 H7 Sal'sk Rus. Fed.
194 F9 Salso r. Sicilia Italy
194 H8 Salso r. Sicilia Italy
193 P4 Salsola r. Italy
190 H6 Salsomaggiore Terme Italy
Salt Jordan see As Salţ
214 H9 Salt watercourse S. Africa
186 K4 Salt Spain
241 T8 Salt r. AZ U.S.A.
236 J6 Salt r. MO U.S.A.
238 I5 Salt r. WY U.S.A.
258 D2 Salta Arg.
258 D2 Salta prov. Arg.
149 N6 Saltaire West Yorkshire, England U.K.
235 I3 Saltaire NY U.S.A.
139 R9 Saltanovka Rus. Fed.
191 N8 Saltara Italy
150 D7 Saltash Cornwall, England U.K.
149 P4 Saltburn-by-the-Sea Redcar and Cleveland, England U.K.
231 □2 Salt Cay i. New Prov. Bahamas
146 G11 Saltcoats North Ayrshire, Scotland U.K.
232 C9 Salt Creek r. OH U.S.A.
151 L6 Saltdean Brighton and Hove, England U.K.
147 I8 Saltee Islands Ireland
184 G6 Salteras Spain
222 E5 Saltery Bay B.C. Can.
140 M3 Saltfjellet Svartisen Nasjonalpark nat. park Norway
140 L3 Saltfjorden sea chan. Norway
239 L11 Salt Flat TX U.S.A.
150 H5 Saltford Bath and North East Somerset, England U.K.
237 F7 Salt Fork r. KS U.S.A.
237 G7 Salt Fork Arkansas r. KS U.S.A.
237 E9 Salt Fork Brazos r. TX U.S.A.
232 D8 Salt Fork Lake OH U.S.A.
237 F8 Salt Fork Red r. OK U.S.A.
147 D6 Salthill Ireland
243 I5 Saltillo Mex.
Salt Island Vanuatu see Loh
116 E6 Salt Lake salt l. India
214 I5 Salt Lake S. Africa
238 I6 Salt Lake City UT U.S.A.
232 B10 Salt Lick KY U.S.A.
241 S2 Salt Marsh Lake salt l. UT U.S.A.
150 G1 Saltney Flintshire, Wales U.K.
261 G4 Salto Arg.
256 D5 Salto Brazil
193 J3 Salto r. Italy
182 E5 Salto Port.
261 I2 Salto Uru.
261 I2 Salto dept Uru.
193 K3 Salto, Lago del l. Italy
257 H2 Salto da Divisa Brazil
243 M9 Salto de Agua Chiapas Mex.
245 H3 Salto de Agua San Luis Potosí Mex.
260 C4 Saltode Las Rosas Arg.
253 G6 Salto del Guairá Para.
192 C8 Salto di Quirra reg. Sardegna Italy
261 G3 Salto Grande Arg.
256 C5 Salto Grande Brazil
244 A1 Salto Grande Mex.
261 I2 Salto Grande, Embalse de resr Uru.
241 P8 Salton City CA U.S.A.
241 Q8 Salton Sea salt l. CA U.S.A.
206 E5 Saltpond Ghana
223 H2 Salt River N.W.T. Can.
Saltrou Haiti see Belle-Anse
143 O2 Saltsjöbaden Sweden
141 P6 Saltvik Åland Fin.
232 D12 Saltville VA U.S.A.
81 E10 Saltwater Lagoon South I. N.Z.
139 W8 Saltyki Rus. Fed.
78 □2 Saluafata Samoa
231 G8 Saluda SC U.S.A.
232 I11 Saluda VA U.S.A.
231 F8 Saluda r. SC U.S.A.
191 N8 Saludecio Italy
93 C4 Saluebesar i. Indon.
93 C5 Saluekecil i. Indon.
93 C4 Salue Timpaus, Selat sea chan. Indon.
190 E5 Saluggia Italy
116 E7 Salumbar Rajasthan India
122 G3 Saluq, Kūh-e mt. Iran
115 H3 Salur Andhra Prad. India
190 E5 Salussola Italy
190 C6 Saluzzo Italy
129 H6 Şälvä Azer.
183 R8 Salvacañete Spain
184 D5 Salvada Port.
183 N3 Sálvada, Sierra mts Spain
260 E2 Salvador Arg.
254 F5 Salvador Brazil
182 F8 Salvador Port.
237 J11 Salvador, Lake LA U.S.A.
258 E1 Salvador Mazza Arg.
163 H8 Salvagnac France
184 F3 Salvaleón Spain
254 C2 Salvaterra Brazil
184 B2 Salvaterra de Magos Port.
182 G9 Salvaterra do Extremo Port.
244 G5 Salvatierra Mex.
183 P3 Salvatierra Spain
184 F4 Salvatierra de los Barros Spain
184 G2 Salvatierra de Santiago Spain
241 V3 Salvation Creek r. UT U.S.A.
195 O4 Salve Italy
163 G6 Salviac France
182 B4 Sálvora, Illa de i. Spain
125 J3 Salwah Saudi Arabia
125 J3 Salwah, Dawḩat b. Qatar/Saudi Arabia
108 B6 Salween r. China
96 C6 Salween r. Myanmar
129 D6 Salyamaç Turkey
129 J6 Salyan Azer.
Sal'yany Azer. see Salyan
247 □7 Salybia Trin. and Tob.
232 B11 Salyersville KY U.S.A.
179 K4 Salza r. Austria
178 G3 Salzach r. Austria/Ger.
179 I4 Salza-Stausee resr Austria
169 D6 Salzbergen Ger.
212 C5 Salzbrunn Namibia
178 H4 Salzburg Austria
178 H5 Salzburg land Austria
169 J6 Salzgitter Ger.
168 J4 Salzhausen Ger.
169 I6 Salzhemmendorf Ger.
179 I4 Salzkammergut reg. Austria
169 G7 Salzkotten Ger.
171 E7 Salzmünde Ger.
170 D5 Salzwedel Ger.
168 K5 Salzwedel-Diesdorf park Ger.
173 O4 Salzweg Ger.
208 A4 Sam Gabon
116 C6 Sam Rajasthan India
96 G5 Sam, Nam r. Laos/Vietnam
246 F3 Samá Cuba
174 E3 Sama r. Pol.
Šamac Bos.-Herz. see Bosanski Šamac
125 N4 Şamad Oman
163 D8 Samadet France
97 E8 Samae San, Laem i. Thai.
106 D1 Samagaltay Rus. Fed.
124 G1 Samāh well Saudi Arabia
Samaida Iran see Someydeh
252 E4 Samaipata Bol.
111 F10 Samaixung Xizang China
94 F5 Samak, Tanjung pt Indon.
206 C3 Samakoulou Mali
92 E8 Samal i. Phil.
78 □2 Samalae'ulu Samoa
94 B2 Samalanga Sumatera Indon.
95 H4 Samalantan Kalimantan Indon.
242 F2 Samalayuca Mex.
92 C9 Samales Group is Phil.
114 H4 Samalkot Andhra Prad. India
203 F2 Samālūţ Egypt
247 I4 Samaná Dom. Rep.
116 F4 Samana Punjab India
247 I4 Samaná, Cabo c. Dom. Rep.
246 G2 Samana Cay i. Bahamas
Samanala mt. Sri Lanka see Sri Pada
126 G5 Samandağı Turkey
123 L3 Samangān prov. Afgh.
122 I4 Samangān Iran
102 T4 Samani Japan
250 B4 Samaniego Col.
199 J2 Samanlı Dağları mts Turkey
203 F2 Samannūd Egypt
225 F3 Samaqua r. Que. Can.
Samar Kazakh. see Samarskoye
92 E6 Samar i. Phil.
120 D1 Samara Rus. Fed.
120 D1 Samara r. Rus. Fed.
137 O5 Samara r. Ukr.
Samarahan Sarawak Malaysia see Sri Aman
91 L9 Samarai P.N.G.
Samara Oblast admin. div. Rus. Fed. see Samarskaya Oblast'
190 F4 Samarate Italy
100 K5 Samarga Rus. Fed.
250 E3 Samariapo Venez.
198 E7 Samarias, Ethnikos Drymos nat. park Greece
179 O8 Samarica Croatia
95 L5 Samarinda Kalimantan Indon.
121 O3 Samarka Karagandinskaya Oblast' Kazakh.
100 I6 Samarka Rus. Fed.
Samarkand Uzbek. see Samarqand
Samarkand, Pik mt. Tajik. see Samarqand, Qullai
Samarkand Oblast admin. div. Uzbek. see Samarqand
Samarobriva France see Amiens
121 L8 Samarqand Uzbek.
121 L8 Samarqand admin. div. Uzbek.
123 M2 Samarqand, Qullai mt. Tajik.
Samarqand Wiloyati admin. div. Uzbek. see Samarqand
127 K6 Sāmarrā' Iraq
92 E6 Samar Sea g. Phil.
120 C1 Samarskaya Oblast' admin. div. Rus. Fed.
121 T3 Samarskoye Vostochnyy Kazakhstan Kazakh.
137 S7 Samarskoye Rus. Fed.
136 D2 Samary Ukr.
107 N4 Samarz Nei Mongol China
123 N7 Samasata Pak.
192 B9 Samassi Sardegna Italy
117 J7 Samastipur Bihar India
163 F9 Samatan France
93 G4 Samate Papua Indon.
192 C9 Samatzai Sardegna Italy
251 F6 Samaúma Brazil
129 J5 Şamaxı Azer.
208 D4 Samba Équateur Dem. Rep. Congo
209 E6 Samba Maniema Dem. Rep. Congo
95 J5 Samba r. Indon.
116 E3 Samba Jammu and Kashmir
209 B7 Samba Cajú Angola
182 G6 Sambade Port.
254 D3 Sambaiba Brazil
206 B3 Sambaïlo Guinea
95 L4 Sambaliung mts Indon.
117 I9 Sambalpur Orissa India
95 I6 Sambar, Tanjung pt Indon.
95 H4 Sambas Kalimantan Indon.
Sambat Ukr. see Kyiv
177 L5 Sâmbăta Romania
213 □K2 Sambava Madag.
137 S6 Sambek Rostovskaya Oblast' Rus. Fed.
137 S6 Sambek Rostovskaya Oblast' Rus. Fed.
Sambe-san vol. Japan see Sanbe-san
117 M6 Sambha Arun. Prad. India
116 G5 Sambhal Uttar Prad. India
116 E6 Sambhar Rajasthan India
116 E6 Sambhar Lake India
193 Q10 Sambiase Italy
93 C4 Sambiat Sulawesi Indon.
136 C4 Sambir Ukr.
95 M4 Sambit i. Indon.
209 C8 Sambo Angola
93 A5 Sambo Sulawesi Barat Indon.
183 L6 Samboal Spain
95 L5 Samboja Kalimantan Indon.
97 H8 Sâmbor Cambodia
Sambor Ukr. see Sambir
97 H8 Sâmbor Dam Cambodia
261 I4 Samborombón r. Arg.
261 I4 Samborombón, Bahía b. Arg.
175 J5 Samborzec Pol.
165 F8 Sambre r. Belgium/France
Sambu Japan see Sanbu
194 E8 Sambuca di Sicilia Sicilia Italy
191 K7 Sambuca Pistoiese Italy
161 K8 Sambuco Italy
194 G8 Sambughetti, Monte mt. Sicilia Italy
101 F10 Samch'ŏk S. Korea
Samch'ŏnp'o S. Korea see Sach'on
118 E2 Samdi Dag mt. Turkey
190 H2 Samedan Switz.
105 M1 Samegawa Japan
96 B4 Sameikkon Myanmar
182 F8 Sameiro Port.
156 C2 Samer France
169 D6 Samern Ger.
129 E3 Samerts'khle, Mt'a Georgia
183 J2 Sames Spain
139 X4 Samet' Rus. Fed.
97 E8 Samet, Ko i. Thai.
209 F7 Samfya Zambia
125 K9 Samḩah i. Yemen
125 L7 Samḩān, Jabal mts Oman
136 I4 Samhorodok Kyivs'ka Oblast' Ukr.
136 H4 Samhorodok Vinnyts'ka Oblast' Ukr.
198 B4 Sami Kefallonia Greece
116 C8 Sami Gujarat India
123 J8 Sami Pak.
93 C3 Samia, Tanjung pt Indon.
182 G5 Samil Port.
124 F2 Samīrah Saudi Arabia
182 H5 Samir de los Caños Spain
250 C6 Samiria r. Peru
Samirum Iran see Yazd-e Khvāst
124 F7 Sāmitah Saudi Arabia
137 N6 Samiylivka Ukr.
105 H2 Samizu Japan
101 F8 Samjiyŏn N. Korea
108 A3 Samka Xizang China
129 E3 Samkhret' Oset'i reg. Georgia
129 H5 Şämkir Azer.
129 H5 Şämkirçay r. Azer.
128 F1 Samköy Turkey
199 I3 Şamlı Turkey
195 L2 Sammichele di Bari Italy
124 C3 Samnah oasis Saudi Arabia
190 I2 Samnaun Switz.
178 B5 Samnaungruppe mts Austria
Sam Neua Laos see Xam Nua
202 B3 Samnū Libya
182 D3 Samo r. Spain
78 □2 Samoa country S. Pacific Ocean
266 H7 Samoa Basin sea feature Pacific Ocean
Samoa i Sisifo country S. Pacific Ocean see Samoa
260 B2 Samo Alto Chile
188 E3 Samobor Croatia
179 M8 Samoborska Gora hills Croatia
134 H3 Samoded Rus. Fed.
160 J4 Samoëns France
191 K6 Samoggia r. Italy
197 L8 Samokov Bulg.
190 G3 Samolaco Italy
136 F4 Samoluskivtsi Ukr.
138 K3 Samolva Rus. Fed.
184 B3 Samora Correia Port.
176 G3 Šamorín Slovakia
199 H5 Samos Samos Greece
199 H5 Samos i. Greece
182 F3 Samos Spain
94 C3 Samosir i. Indon.
Samothrace i. Greece see Samothraki
199 G2 Samothraki Samothraki Greece
199 G2 Samothraki i. Greece
197 N7 Samovodene Bulg.
135 H6 Samoylovka Rus. Fed.
206 E5 Sampa Côte d'Ivoire
260 E3 Sampacho Arg.
93 A5 Sampaga Sulawesi Barat Indon.
95 J8 Sampang Jawa Indon.
186 E5 Samper de Calanda Spain
190 C6 Sampeyre Italy
194 H10 Sampieri Sicilia Italy
157 K6 Sampigny France
95 J6 Sampit Kalimantan Indon.
95 J6 Sampit r. Indon.
95 J6 Sampit, Teluk b. Indon.
93 C6 Sampolawa Sulawesi Indon.
135 H5 Sampur Rus. Fed.
209 E7 Sampwe Dem. Rep. Congo
97 G7 Samran, Huai r. Thai.
237 H10 Sam Rayburn Reservoir TX U.S.A.
206 E5 Samreboe Ghana
138 L3 Samro, Ozero l. Rus. Fed.
Samrong Cambodia see Phumĭ Sâmraông
111 F11 Samsang Xizang China
96 F4 Sam Sao, Phou mts Laos/Vietnam
142 J4 Sämsjön l. Sweden
142 G6 Samsø i. Denmark
142 G6 Samsø Bælt sea chan. Denmark
96 G5 Sâm Sơn Vietnam
177 L4 Şamşud Romania
126 H3 Samsun Turkey
171 E6 Samswegen Ger.
121 Q6 Samsy Kazakh.
170 H2 Samtens Ger.
116 G7 Samthar Uttar Prad. India
129 D3 Samtredia Georgia
84 E5 Samuel, Mount hill N.T. Austr.
192 B8 Samugheo Sardegna Italy
97 E10 Samui, Ko i. Thai.
105 J5 Samukawa Japan
94 □ Samulun, Pulau i. Sing.
123 O6 Samundri Pak.
129 J4 Samur Azer.
129 J4 Samur r. Azer./Rus. Fed.
129 J4 Samur-Abşeron Kanalı canal Azer.
Samutlu Turkey see Temelli
97 E8 Samut Prakan Thai.
97 E8 Samut Sakhon Thai.
97 E8 Samut Songkhram Thai.
111 J12 Samyai Xizang China
206 D3 San Mali
175 J5 San r. Pol.
96 F5 San, Phou mt. Laos
97 H8 San, Tônlé r. Cambodia
188 F3 Sana r. Bos.-Herz.
124 G8 Şan'ā' Yemen
124 G8 Şan'ā' governorate Yemen
210 E2 Sanaag admin. reg. Somalia
182 H4 Sanabria reg. Spain
105 H3 Sanada Japan
183 Q4 San Adrián Spain
182 C2 San Adrián, Cabo c. Spain
262 X2 Sanae IV research stn Antarctica
207 H6 Sanaga r. Cameroon
104 F5 Sanage Japan
116 G7 Sanagir Madh. Prad. India
San Agostín FL U.S.A. see St Augustine
260 E2 San Agustín Arg.
216 □3f San Agustín Gran Canaria Canary Is
250 B4 San Agustín Col.
92 F8 San Agustin, Cape Mindanao Phil.
250 B4 San Agustín, Parque Arqueológico tourist site Col.
183 M7 San Agustín de Guadalix Spain
146 D11 Sanaigmore Argyll and Bute, Scotland U.K.
220 B4 Sanak Island AK U.S.A.
124 G4 Sanām Saudi Arabia
182 D4 San Amaro Spain
252 A6 San Ambrosio, Isla i. Islas de los Desventurados S. Pacific Ocean
93 D5 Sanana Maluku Indon.
122 B4 Sanandaj Iran
206 D3 Sanando Mali
240 L3 San Andreas CA U.S.A.
177 K6 Sânandrei Romania
252 D3 San Andrés Bol.
250 C3 San Andrés Col.
243 O9 San Andrés Guat.
92 E5 San Andres Phil.
246 C7 San Andrés, Isla de i. Caribbean Sea
185 L4 San Andrés, Sierra de mts Spain
261 H4 San Andrés de Giles Arg.
182 I3 San Andrés del Rabanedo Spain
244 D6 San Andrés Ixtlán Mex.
239 K10 San Andres Mountains NM U.S.A.
245 L7 San Andrés Tuxtla Mex.
246 F8 San Ángel Col.
237 E10 San Angelo TX U.S.A.
206 D3 Sanankoroba Mali
240 J4 San Anselmo CA U.S.A.
182 G2 San Antolín Spain
244 G4 San Antón de los Martinez Mex.
258 D3 San Antonio Catamarca Arg.
260 D3 San Antonio San Luis Arg.
242 □O9 San Antonio Belize
252 D3 San Antonio Bol.
258 C2 San Antonio Atacama Chile
260 B3 San Antonio Valparaíso Chile
242 □P10 San Antonio Hond.
244 G2 San Antonio San Luis Potosí Mex.
245 H2 San Antonio Tamaulipas Mex.
250 C5 San Antonio Peru
92 C4 San Antonio Luzon Phil.
187 C8 San Antonio Spain
261 I2 San Antonio Uru.
239 K10 San Antonio NM U.S.A.
237 F11 San Antonio TX U.S.A.
240 L6 San Antonio r. CA U.S.A.
237 G11 San Antonio r. TX U.S.A.
247 L8 San Antonio Venez.
261 I5 San Antonio, Cabo c. Arg.
246 A3 San Antonio, Cabo c. Cuba
187 F10 San Antonio, Cabo de c. Spain
240 O7 San Antonio, Mount CA U.S.A.
183 K2 San Antonio, Punta de pt Spain
92 A7 San Antonio Bay Palawan Phil.
261 H4 San Antonio de Areco Arg.
250 D3 San Antonio de Caparo Venez.
247 L8 San Antonio del Golfo Venez.
242 A2 San Antonio del Mar Mex.
258 D2 San Antonio de los Cobres Arg.
242 □P10 San Antonio de Oriente Hond.
207 G7 San Antonio de Palé Equat. Guinea
251 E2 San Antonio de Tamanaco Venez.
245 H5 San Antonio Escabedo Mex.
259 D6 San Antonio Este Arg.
245 I2 San Antonio Nogalar Mex.
259 D6 San Antonio Oeste Arg.
245 I3 San Antonio Rayón Mex.
240 L6 San Antonio Reservoir CA U.S.A.
245 H4 San Antonio Tancoyol Mex.
161 H10 Sanary-sur-Mer France
183 O3 San Asensio Spain
78 □4a Sanat i. Chuuk Micronesia
234 D4 Sanatoga PA U.S.A.
261 H6 San Augustín Arg.
260 D2 San Augustín de Valle Fértil Arg.
237 H10 San Augustine TX U.S.A.
125 N4 Sanāw Oman
125 J7 Sanaw Yemen
116 F8 Sanawad Madh. Prad. India
123 N6 Sanawan Pak.
245 K9 San Baltasar Loxicha Mex.
244 G3 San Bartolo Mex.
216 □3c San Bartolomé Lanzarote Canary Is
183 K9 San Bartolomé de las Abiertas Spain
184 E6 San Bartolomé de la Torre Spain
183 K7 San Bartolomé de Pinares Spain
216 □3f San Bartolomé de Tirajana Gran Canaria Canary Is
193 O5 San Bartolomeo in Galdo Italy
245 H6 San Bartolo Morelos Mex.
245 I5 San Bartolo Tutotepec Mex.
260 E3 San Basilio Arg.
192 C8 San Basilio Sardegna Italy
San Baudillo de Llobregat Cataluña Spain see Sant Boi de Llobregat
193 L2 San Benedetto del Tronto Italy
191 J5 San Benedetto Po Italy
228 D7 San Benedicto, Isla i. Mex.
243 O9 San Benito Guat.
185 J3 San Benito Spain
237 G12 San Benito TX U.S.A.
240 K5 San Benito r. CA U.S.A.
184 E3 San Benito de la Contienda Spain
240 L5 San Benito Mountain CA U.S.A.
240 O7 San Bernardino CA U.S.A.
190 G3 San Bernardino, Passo di pass Switz.
241 O7 San Bernardino Mountains CA U.S.A.
92 E5 San Bernardino Strait Phil.
261 I5 San Bernardo Arg.
260 B3 San Bernardo Chile
242 G5 San Bernardo Mex.
244 B2 San Bernardo de Milipas Chico Mex.
103 J11 Sanbe-san vol. Japan
191 M4 San Biagio di Callalta Italy
194 F8 San Biago Platani Sicilia Italy
258 D3 San Blas Arg.
244 B4 San Blas Nayarit Mex.
242 E4 San Blas Sinaloa Mex.
242 □T13 San Blas, Archipiélago de is Panama
231 E11 San Blas, Cape FL U.S.A.
242 □T13 San Blas, Cordillera de mts Panama
195 □ San Blas, Il-Bajja ta' b. Gozo Malta
191 K5 San Bonifacio Italy
252 D3 San Borja Bol.
236 H4 Sanborn IA U.S.A.
233 □N5 Sanbornville NH U.S.A.
Sanbu Guangdong China see Kaiping
105 L4 Sanbu Japan
243 I4 San Buenaventura Mex.
213 G3 Sança Moz.
191 M2 San Candido Italy
186 E4 San Caprasio hill Spain
260 E2 San Carlos Córdoba Arg.
260 C3 San Carlos Mendoza Arg.
258 D2 San Carlos Salta Arg.
260 B5 San Carlos Chile
San Carlos Equat. Guinea see Luba
243 I3 San Carlos Coahuila Mex.
245 I1 San Carlos Tamaulipas Mex.
242 □Q12 San Carlos Nic.
253 F5 San Carlos Para.
253 F5 San Carlos r. Para.
92 C4 San Carlos Luzon Phil.
92 D6 San Carlos Negros Phil.
258 G4 San Carlos Uru.
241 V8 San Carlos AZ U.S.A.
250 E4 San Carlos Amazonas Venez.
250 E3 San Carlos Apure Venez.
250 D2 San Carlos Cojedes Venez.
261 G2 San Carlos Centro Arg.
259 C6 San Carlos de Bariloche Arg.
261 G5 San Carlos de Bolívar Arg.
San Carlos de la Rápita Spain see Sant Carles de la Ràpita
185 M3 San Carlos del Valle Spain
250 D2 San Carlos del Zulia Venez.
241 V8 San Carlos Indian Reservation res. AZ U.S.A.
241 V8 San Carlos Lake AZ U.S.A.
261 G2 San Carlos Sur Arg.
192 H2 San Casciano dei Bagni Italy
191 K8 San Casciano in Val di Pesa Italy
195 O3 San Cataldo Puglia Italy
194 F9 San Cataldo Sicilia Italy
261 H6 San Cayetano Arg.
182 I5 San Cebrián de Castro Spain
San Celoni Spain see Sant Celoni
160 B2 Sancergues France
160 B2 Sancerre France
160 B2 Sancerrois, Collines du hills France
195 O3 San Cesario di Lecce Italy
160 J2 Sancey-le-Grand France
106 I9 Sancha Gansu China
107 L7 Sancha Shanxi China
Sanchahe Jilin China see Fuyu
108 F5 Sancha He r. Guizhou China
110 D7 Sanchakou Xinjiang China
156 C7 Sancheville France
245 N7 Sánchez Magallanes Mex.
116 F8 Sanchi Madh. Prad. India
183 K7 Sanchidrián Spain
96 F4 San Chien Pau mt. Laos
244 F7 Sanchiqueo Mex.
193 Q6 San Chirico Nuovo Italy
193 Q7 San Chirico Raparo Italy
184 E6 Sancho, Embalse de resr Spain
116 C7 Sanchor Rajasthan India
107 L8 Sanchuan He r. China
134 I4 Sanchursk Rus. Fed.
182 E4 San Cibráo das Viñas Spain
194 E8 San Cipirello Sicilia Italy
193 M6 San Cipriano d'Aversa Italy
245 H4 San Ciro de Acosta Mex.
260 B4 San Clemente Chile
185 O2 San Clemente Spain
240 O8 San Clemente CA U.S.A.
185 N5 San Clemente, Embalse de resr Spain
261 I5 San Clemente del Tuyú Arg.
240 N9 San Clemente Island CA U.S.A.
Sanclêr Wales U.K. see St Clears
182 F4 San Clodio Spain
160 B3 Sancoins France
92 F7 Sanco Point Mindanao Phil.
258 F2 San Cosme Arg.
182 F1 San Cosme Spain
193 Q7 San Costantino Albanese Italy
191 O8 San Costanzo Italy
243 N10 San Crisóbal Verapez Guat.
261 G2 San Cristóbal Arg.
252 D5 San Cristóbal Potosí Bol.
253 E3 San Cristóbal Santa Cruz Bol.
250 C5 San Cristóbal Col.
246 H4 San Cristóbal Dom. Rep.
245 I5 San Cristóbal Hidalgo Mex.
244 F4 San Cristóbal Jalisco Mex.
78 □6 San Cristobal i. Solomon Is
250 C3 San Cristóbal Venez.
250 □ San Cristóbal, Isla i. Islas Galápagos Ecuador
242 □P11 San Cristóbal, Volcán vol. Nic.
San Cristóbal de Cea Spain see Cea
182 I4 San Cristóbal de Entreviñas Spain
244 D4 San Cristóbal de la Barranca Mex.
216 □3a San Cristóbal de la Laguna Tenerife Canary Is
243 M9 San Cristóbal de las Casas Mex.
183 K6 San Cristóbal de la Vega Spain
241 S9 San Cristobal Wash watercourse AZ U.S.A.
193 P6 San Croce, Monte mt. Italy
184 G8 Sancti Petri, Isla i. Spain
261 F3 Sancti Spíritu Arg.
246 D3 Sancti Spíritus Cuba
246 D3 Sancti Spíritus prov. Cuba
182 H7 Sancti-Spíritus Spain
185 I3 Sancti-Spíritus Spain
157 K5 Sancy France
142 C2 Sand Norway
215 K4 Sand r. Free State S. Africa
213 F4 Sand r. Limpopo S. Africa
104 B6 Sanda Japan
100 I7 Sandagou Rus. Fed.
95 I5 Sandai Kalimantan Indon.
146 E12 Sanda Island Scotland U.K.
95 M2 Sandakan Sabah Malaysia
95 M2 Sandakan, Pelabuhan inlet Malaysia
117 L6 Sandakphu Peak Sikkim India
183 N2 Sandamendi Spain
190 E6 San Damiano d'Asti Italy
190 C7 San Damiano Macra Italy
169 K11 Sand am Main Ger.
97 H8 Sândăn Cambodia
141 I6 Sandane Norway
178 H7 San Daniele del Friuli Italy
190 I5 San Daniele Po Italy
197 L9 Sandanski Bulg.
Sandaohezi Xinjiang China see Shawan
206 C3 Sandaré Mali
170 F5 Sandau Ger.
146 L4 Sanday i. Scotland U.K.
146 K4 Sanday Sound sea chan. Scotland U.K.
149 M7 Sandbach Cheshire, England U.K.
169 J10 Sandberg Ger.
214 C8 Sandberg S. Africa
168 L1 Sandby Denmark
114 C7 Sand Cay rf India
140 L4 Sanddøla r. Norway
168 F4 Sande Ger.
141 H6 Sande Sogn og Fjordane Norway
142 G2 Sande Vestfold Norway
182 D6 Sande Port.
142 G2 Sandefjord Norway
142 G2 Sandefjord (Torp) airport Norway
142 B2 Sandeid Norway
82 □3 Sandell Bay S. Pacific Ocean
140 P2 Sandelva Norway
195 K4 San Demetrio Corone Italy
193 L3 San Demetrio ne Vestini Italy
263 D2 Sandercock Nunataks nunataks Antarctica
241 W6 Sanders AZ U.S.A.
171 F7 Sandersdorf Ger.
169 I8 Sandershausen (Niestetal) Ger.
171 E7 Sandersleben Ger.
237 D10 Sanderson TX U.S.A.
231 F9 Sandersville GA U.S.A.
168 J3 Sandesneben Ger.
86 F5 Sandfire Roadhouse W.A. Austr.
142 D2 Sandfloeggi mt. Norway
232 E10 Sand Fork WV U.S.A.
146 K4 Sandgarth Orkney, Scotland U.K.
172 F3 Sandhausen Ger.
146 G13 Sandhead Dumfries and Galloway, Scotland U.K.
236 G2 Sand Hill r. MN U.S.A.
236 D5 Sand Hills NE U.S.A.
140 M3 Sandhornøy i. Norway
151 K5 Sandhurst Bracknell Forest, England U.K.
116 H6 Sandi Uttar Prad. India
252 C3 Sandia Peru
182 E4 Sandiás Spain
242 G3 San Diego Chihuahua Mex.
239 J11 San Diego Chihuahua Mex.
244 G4 San Diego Guanajuato Mex.
240 O9 San Diego CA U.S.A.
237 F12 San Diego TX U.S.A.
259 D9 San Diego, Cabo c. Arg.
242 E2 San Diego, Sierra mts Mex.
245 H6 San Diego Alcalá Mex.
251 E2 San Diego de Cabrutica Venez.
245 H3 San Dieguito Mex.
199 L4 Sandıklı Turkey
116 H6 Sandila Uttar Prad. India
231 □2 Sandilands Village New Prov. Bahamas
156 D8 Sandillon France
87 C8 Sandiman, Mount hill W.A. Austr.
195 □ San Dimitri, Il-Ponta ta' pt Gozo Malta
94 D6 Sanding i. Indon.
245 M9 San Dionisio del Mar Mex.
226 D3 Sand Island WI U.S.A.
134 L2 Sandivey r. Rus. Fed.
170 I5 Sandkrug Ger.
179 K2 Sandl Austria
224 C4 Sand Lake Ont. Can.
223 M5 Sand Lake l. Ont. Can.
142 B3 Sandnes Norway
146 □M2 Sandness Shetland, Scotland U.K.
140 L3 Sandnessjøen Norway
Sandø i. Faroe Is see Sandoy
182 H7 Sando Spain
209 D7 Sandoa Dem. Rep. Congo
175 J5 Sandomierska, Kotlina basin Pol.
175 J5 Sandomierz Pol.
197 N4 Sândominic Romania
193 O3 San Domino, Isola i. Italy
250 B4 Sandoná Col.
195 N3 San Donaci Italy
191 N4 San Donà di Piave Italy
195 O3 San Donato di Lecce Italy
193 Q8 San Donato di Ninea Italy
190 G5 San Donato Milanese Italy
193 L4 San Donato Val di Comino Italy
177 J5 Sándorfalva Hungary
84 F6 Sandover watercourse N.T. Austr.
139 T3 Sandovo Rus. Fed.
263 G2 Sandow, Mount Antarctica
Sandoway Myanmar see Thandwè
151 J6 Sandown Isle of Wight, England U.K.
214 C10 Sandown Bay S. Africa
144 D1 Sandoy i. Faroe Is
140 I5 Sandøy Norway
150 D7 Sandplace Cornwall, England U.K.
238 F2 Sandpoint ID U.S.A.
146 B9 Sandray i. Scotland U.K.
151 L4 Sandridge Hertfordshire, England U.K.
84 G8 Sandringham Qld Austr.
215 P2 Sand River Reservoir Swaziland
176 G6 Šandrovac Croatia
140 N4 Sandsele Sweden
149 P4 Sandsend North Yorkshire, England U.K.
222 D4 Sandspit B.C. Can.
237 G7 Sand Springs OK U.S.A.
240 N2 Sand Springs Salt Flat NV U.S.A.
215 K3 Sandspruit r. S. Africa
168 G4 Sandstedt Ger.
232 H11 Sandston VA U.S.A.
87 E9 Sandstone W.A. Austr.
226 B3 Sandstone MN U.S.A.
240 N7 Sandstone Peak hill CA U.S.A.
241 T9 Sand Tank Mountains AZ U.S.A.
215 M2 Sandton S. Africa
234 E3 Sandts Eddy PA U.S.A.
108 F6 Sandu Guizhou China
109 I6 Sandu Hunan China
114 E5 Sandur Karnataka India
227 L6 Sandusky MI U.S.A.
232 C7 Sandusky OH U.S.A.
232 C7 Sandusky Bay OH U.S.A.
214 C7 Sandveld mts S. Africa
215 J3 Sandveld Nature Reserve S. Africa
214 B2 Sandverhaar Namibia
142 G2 Sandvika Akershus Norway
140 L5 Sandvika Nord-Trøndelag Norway
143 M1 Sandviken Sweden
214 I9 Sandvlakte S. Africa
151 O5 Sandwich Kent, England U.K.
233 O7 Sandwich MA U.S.A.
225 J2 Sandwich Bay Nfld and Lab. Can.
212 B4 Sandwich Bay Namibia
Sandwich Island Vanuatu see Éfaté
Sandwich Islands N. Pacific Ocean see Hawai'ian Islands
117 M8 Sandwip Bangl.
117 M8 Sandwip Channel Bangl.
151 L3 Sandy Bedfordshire, England U.K.
238 I6 Sandy UT U.S.A.
233 □P4 Sandy r. ME U.S.A.
223 K4 Sandy Bay Sask. Can.
185 □ Sandy Bay b. Gibraltar
246 □ Sandy Bay Jamaica
80 I2 Sandy Bay b. North I. N.Z.
82 □3 Sandy Bay b. S. Pacific Ocean
216 □2b Sandy Bay b. St Helena
87 G12 Sandy Bight b. W.A. Austr.
85 N8 Sandy Cape Qld Austr.
83 J9 Sandy Cape Tas. Austr.
84 G5 Sandy Creek r. Qld Austr.
148 H5 Sandygate Isle of Man
235 I2 Sandy Hook CT U.S.A.
232 B10 Sandy Hook KY U.S.A.
235 G4 Sandy Hook pt NJ U.S.A.
86 F3 Sandy Island W.A. Austr.
Sandy Island Rodrigues I. Mauritius see Sables, Île aux
123 J3 Sandykgaçy Turkm.
123 J2 Sandykly Gumy des. Turkm.
222 H4 Sandy Lake Alta Can.
223 M4 Sandy Lake Ont. Can.
223 M4 Sandy Lake l. Ont. Can.
216 □2c Sandy Point Tristan da Cunha S. Atlantic Ocean
247 □2 Sandy Point Town St Kitts and Nevis
231 E9 Sandy Springs GA U.S.A.
232 D10 Sandyville WV U.S.A.
160 G3 Sâne r. France
165 I9 Sanem Lux.
182 I3 San Emiliano Spain
261 G4 San Enrique Arg.
253 F6 San Estanislao Para.
242 □Q10 San Esteban Hond.
245 J3 San Esteban Mex.
242 C3 San Esteban, Isla i. Mex.
245 J6 San Esteban Cuautempan Mex.
183 N5 San Esteban de Gormaz Spain
182 I7 San Esteban de la Sierra Spain
260 B5 San Fabián de Alico Chile
193 P6 San Fele Italy
193 M5 San Felice a Cancello Italy
193 K5 San Felice Circeo Italy
182 G7 San Felices de los Gallegos Spain
191 K6 San Felice sul Panaro Italy
260 B3 San Felipe Chile
242 B2 San Felipe Baja California Mex.
242 F4 San Felipe Chihuahua Mex.
244 F4 San Felipe Guanajuato Mex.
183 Q8 San Felipe mt. Spain
250 D2 San Felipe Venez.
246 B3 San Felipe, Cayos de is Cuba
241 Q8 San Felipe Creek watercourse CA U.S.A.
244 E1 San Felipe de Teyra Mex.
244 E1 San Felipe Nuevo Mercurio Mex.
245 K8 San Felipe Usila Mex.
San Feliú de Guíxols Spain see Sant Feliu de Guíxols
San Feliú de Pallarols Spain see Sant Feliu de Pallerols
San Feliú Sasssera Spain see Sant Feliu Sasserra
252 A6 San Félix, Isla i. Islas de los Desventurados S. Pacific Ocean
195 J7 San Ferdinando Italy
193 Q5 San Ferdinando di Puglia Italy
261 H4 San Fernando Arg.
260 B4 San Fernando Chile
242 B3 San Fernando Baja California Mex.
243 J5 San Fernando Tamaulipas Mex.
92 C3 San Fernando Luzon Phil.
92 C4 San Fernando Luzon Phil.
184 G8 San Fernando Spain
247 □7 San Fernando Trin. and Tob.
240 N7 San Fernando CA U.S.A.
250 E3 San Fernando de Apure Venez.
250 E3 San Fernando de Atabapo Venez.
183 M8 San Fernando de Henares Spain
193 Q9 San Fili Italy
195 I7 San Filippo del Mela Sicilia Italy
182 F6 Sanfins do Douro Port.
141 L5 Sånfjället nationalpark nat. park Sweden
87 C9 Sanford r. W.A. Austr.
231 G11 Sanford FL U.S.A.
233 □O5 Sanford ME U.S.A.
226 J6 Sanford MI U.S.A.
231 H8 Sanford NC U.S.A.
247 □7 San Francique Trin. and Tob.
261 F2 San Francisco Arg.

San Francisco to Santa Cesarea Terme
382

252 D3 San Francisco Bol.
244 F2 San Francisco San Luis Potosí Mex.
245 H3 San Francisco San Luis Potosí Mex.
242 C2 San Francisco Sonora Mex.
240 J4 San Francisco CA U.S.A.
239 J10 San Francisco r. NM U.S.A.
246 H8 San Francisco Venez.
250 A4 San Francisco, Cabo de c. Ecuador
258 C2 San Francisco, Paso de pass Arg.
242 C4 San Francisco, Sierra mts Mex.
240 J4 San Francisco Bay inlet CA U.S.A.
245 K10 San Francisco Cozoaltepec Mex.
261 G6 San Francisco de Bellocq Arg.
242 G4 San Francisco de Conchos Mex.
258 E3 San Francisco del Chañar Arg.
260 D3 San Francisco del Monte de Oro Arg.
242 G4 San Francisco del Oro Mex.
253 E5 San Francisco del Parapetí Bol.
244 F4 San Francisco del Rincón Mex.
246 H4 San Francisco de Macorís Dom. Rep.
260 B3 San Francisco de Mostazal Chile
259 D8 San Francisco de Paula, Cabo c. Arg.
245 I2 San Francisco el Alto Mex.
242 □O11 San Francisco Gotera El Salvador
187 H10 San Francisco Javier Spain
194 H7 San Fratello Sicilia Italy
190 C6 Sanfront Italy
209 B7 Sanga Angola
209 F6 Sanga Dem. Rep. Congo
260 B3 San Gabriel Chile
250 B4 San Gabriel Ecuador
242 C3 San Gabriel, Punta pt Mex.
245 J7 San Gabriel Chilac Mex.
240 N7 San Gabriel Mountains CA U.S.A.
129 K5 Sängäçal Burnu pt Azer.
Sangachaly Azer. see Sangaçal
94 F6 Sangaigerong Sumatera Indon.
108 B3 Sang'ngain Xizang China
182 D8 Sangalhos Port.
252 A3 San Gallan, Isla i. Peru
114 F5 Sangam Andhra Prad. India
114 C4 Sangameshwar Mahar. India
114 D3 Sangamner Mahar. India
236 J5 Sangamon r. IL U.S.A.
123 K5 Sangan Afgh.
123 K4 Sangan Khorāsān Iran
122 I4 Sangan Iran
123 I7 Sangān Sīstān va Balūchestān Iran
123 L7 Sangan Pak.
123 K5 Sangān, Kūh-e mt. Afgh.
123 N6 Sangar r. Pak.
131 N3 Sangar Rus. Fed.
183 L7 Sangarcía Spain
206 B4 Sangaréa Guinea
114 F4 Sangareddi Andhra Prad. India
206 B4 Sangarédi Guinea
116 E5 Sangaria Rajasthan India
95 E8 Sangasanga Kalimantan Indon.
92 B9 Sanga Sanga i. Phil.
Sangasso Mali see Zangasso
138 J4 Sangaste Estonia
208 A5 Sangatanga Gabon
156 C2 Sangatte France
192 B8 San Gavino Monreale Sardegna Italy
250 B5 Sangay, Parque Nacional nat. park Ecuador
250 B5 Sangay, Volcán vol. Ecuador
111 K11 Sangba Xizang China
141 M5 Sångbäcken Sweden
122 H4 Sang Bast Iran
207 I5 Sangbé Cameroon
92 C8 Sangboy Islands Phil.
123 L5 Sangbur Afgh.
93 A8 Sangeang i. Indon.
106 I6 Sangejing Nei Mongol China
193 J2 San Gemini Italy
261 G3 San Genaro Arg.
Sangenjo Galicia Spain see Sanxenxo
195 O2 San Gennaro, Capo c. Italy
197 M4 Sângeorgiu de Pădure Romania
197 M3 Sângeorz-Băi Romania
106 B5 Sangequanzi Xinjiang China
197 M4 Sângeru Romania
240 M5 Sanger CA U.S.A.
Sângera Moldova see Sîngera
Sângerei Moldova see Sîngerei
233 J6 Sangerfield NY U.S.A.
171 D8 Sangerhausen Ger.
261 F6 San German Arg.
247 □1 San Germán Puerto Rico
161 K7 San Germano Chisone Italy
260 D3 San Gerónimo Arg.
Sang-e Sar Iran see Mehdīshahr
107 N6 Sanggan He r. China
95 M9 Sanggar, Teluk b. Sumbawa Indon.
95 I4 Sanggau Kalimantan Indon.
95 H4 Sanggauledo Kalimantan Indon.
93 D2 Sanggeluhang i. Indon.
107 R8 Sanggou Wan b. China
207 F4 Sangha Burkina
208 B4 Sangha admin. reg. Congo
208 C5 Sangha r. Congo
208 C4 Sangha-Mbaéré pref. C.A.R.
123 M8 Sanghar Pak.
191 K2 San Giacomo, Cima mt. Italy
190 I2 San Giacomo, Lago di l. Italy
250 C3 San Gil Col.
106 D1 Sangilen, Nagor'ye mts Rus. Fed.
195 □ San Ġiljan Malta
191 K9 San Gimignano Italy
123 K5 Sangīn Afgh.
183 R7 San Ginés mt. Spain
193 K1 San Ginesio Italy
193 L5 San Giorgio a Liri Italy
191 N3 San Giorgio della Richinvelda Italy
191 O4 San Giorgio di Nogaro Italy
191 K6 San Giorgio di Piano Italy
195 M3 San Giorgio Ionico Italy
193 N5 San Giorgio la Molara Italy
195 K3 San Giorgio Lucano Italy
193 O7 San Giovanni a Piro Italy
190 H4 San Giovanni Bianco Italy
192 H1 San Giovanni d'Asso Italy
194 F8 San Giovanni Gemini Sicilia Italy
193 K4 San Giovanni Incarico Italy
191 K6 San Giovanni in Croce Italy
195 L5 San Giovanni in Fiore Italy
191 K6 San Giovanni in Persiceto Italy
191 K5 San Giovanni Lupatoto Italy
193 P4 San Giovanni Rotondo Italy
192 B9 San Giovanni Suergiu Sardegna Italy
193 M3 San Giovanni Teatino Italy
191 L8 San Giovanni Valdarno Italy
116 E9 Sangir Mahar. India
93 D2 Sangir i. Indon.
93 D2 Sangir, Kepulauan is Indon.
195 K2 San Giuliano, Lago di l. Italy
190 I8 San Giuliano Terme Italy
194 E8 San Giuseppe Jato Sicilia Italy
194 H2 San Giuseppe Vesuviano Italy
191 M8 San Giustino Italy
106 I3 Sangiyn Dalay Mongolia
106 F2 Sangiyn Dalay Nuur salt l. Mongolia
101 F10 Sangju S. Korea
95 J7 Sangkapura Jawa Indon.
93 A6 Sangkarang, Kepulauan is Indon.
97 F8 Sângke, Stœng r. Cambodia
97 D7 Sangkha Buri Thai.
95 M4 Sangkulirang Kalimantan Indon.
95 M4 Sangkulirang, Teluk b. Indon.
123 O6 Sangla Pak.
114 D4 Sangli Mahar. India
123 N3 Sanglich Afgh.
183 K2 San Glorio, Puerto de pass Spain
207 H6 Sangmélima Cameroon
116 G4 Sangnam Hima. Prad. India
111 K12 Sangngagqoiling Xizang China
213 F4 Sango Zimbabwe
116 F7 Sangod Rajasthan India
191 L8 San Godenzo Italy
114 D4 Sangole Mahar. India
187 C12 Sangonera r. Spain
240 P7 San Gorgonio Mountain CA U.S.A.
190 F2 San Gottardo, Passo del pass Switz.
93 F2 Sangowo Maluku Indon.
Sangpi Sichuan China see Xiangcheng
108 A4 Sang Qu r. Xizang China
239 K7 Sangre de Cristo Range mts CO U.S.A.
261 F4 San Gregorio Arg.
260 B5 San Gregorio Chile
261 I3 San Gregorio Uru.
258 G4 San Gregorio de Polanca Uru.
193 O6 San Gregorio Magno Italy
193 N5 San Gregorio Matese Italy
247 □7 Sangre Grande Trin. and Tob.
183 K9 Sangrera r. Spain
111 K12 Sangri Xizang China
193 N3 Sangro r. Italy
175 L1 Sangrūda Lith.
108 B2 Sangruma Qinghai China
116 E4 Sangrur Punjab India
111 H12 Sangsang Xizang China
117 M8 Sangu r. Bangl.
222 H4 Sangudo Alta Can.
252 F4 Sangue r. Brazil
183 R3 Sangüesa Spain
190 G5 San Guiliano Milanese Italy
261 G2 San Guillermo Arg.
258 C3 San Guillermo, Parque Nacional nat. park Arg.
186 H4 San Guim de Freixenet Spain
192 B4 Sanguinaires, Îles i. Corse France
163 B7 Sanguinet France
191 K5 Sanguinetto Italy
122 G7 Sang-ū'īyeh Iran
261 H2 San Gustavo Arg.
123 N2 Sangvor Tajik.
Sangyuan Hebei China see Wuqiao
108 H4 Sangzhi Hunan China
206 D4 Sanhala Côte d'Ivoire
Sanhe Guizhou China see Sandu
107 Q1 Sanhe Nei Mongol China
109 K3 Sanhezhen Anhui China
242 D5 San Hilario Mex.
San Hilario Sacalm Spain see Sant Hilari Sacalm
242 B4 San Hipólito, Punta pt Mex.
203 F2 Sanhūr Egypt
231 F12 Sanibel Island FL U.S.A.
261 H5 San Ignacio Arg.
243 O9 San Ignacio Belize
252 D3 San Ignacio Beni Bol.
253 E4 San Ignacio Santa Cruz Bol.
253 E4 San Ignacio Santa Cruz Bol.
242 B4 San Ignacio Baja California Mex.
242 C4 San Ignacio Baja California Sur Mex.
244 A2 San Ignacio Sinaloa Mex.
242 D2 San Ignacio Sonora Mex.
253 F6 San Ignacio Para.
250 B6 San Ignacio Peru
242 C4 San Ignacio, Laguna l. Mex.
224 E1 Sanikiluaq Nunavut Can.
183 M7 San Ildefonso Spain
92 D3 San Ildefonso Peninsula Luzon Phil.
104 A4 Sanin-kaigan Kokuritsu-kōen nat. park Japan
215 N5 Sanipas pass S. Africa
Sanirajak Nunavut Can. see Hall Beach
193 O2 San Isidro Arg.
245 K10 San Isidro Oaxaca Mex.
245 I1 San Isidro Tamaulipas Mex.
244 E1 San Isidro Zacatecas Mex.
183 J2 San Isidro, Puerto de pass Spain
245 L10 San Isidro Chacalapa Mex.
245 K10 San Isidro del Palmar Mex.
197 M3 Sanislău Romania
170 F2 Sanitz Ger.
202 C3 Sāniyat al Fawākhir well Libya
250 C2 San Jacinto Col.
92 D5 San Jacinto Masbate Phil.
240 P8 San Jacinto CA U.S.A.
240 P8 San Jacinto Peak CA U.S.A.
117 K8 Sanjai r. Jharkhand India
183 P2 San Jaime Arg.
261 H2 San Javier Arg.
252 D3 San Javier Beni Bol.
253 E4 San Javier Santa Cruz Bol.
245 H5 San Javier Mex.
187 D12 San Javier Spain
261 H3 San Javier Uru.
260 B4 San Javier de Loncomilla Chile
123 M6 Sanjawi Pak.
122 C3 Sanjbod Iran
244 G8 San Jerónimo Guerrero Mex.
244 D2 San Jerónimo Zacatecas Mex.
252 B1 San Jerónimo Peru
245 K9 San Jerónimo Taviche Mex.
Sanjiang Guangdong China see Liannan
108 G6 Sanjiang Guangxi China
Sanjiang Guizhou China see Jinping
107 R5 Sanjiangkou Liaoning China
Sanjiaocheng Qinghai China see Haiyan
108 H4 Sanjiaoping Hunan China
109 M4 Sanjie Zhejiang China
103 P9 Sanjō Japan
252 D3 San Joaquín Bol.
245 H5 San Joaquín Mex.
253 F5 San Joaquín Para.
240 L5 San Joaquin CA U.S.A.
240 L5 San Joaquin r. CA U.S.A.
240 L4 San Joaquin Valley CA U.S.A.
237 D8 San Jon NM U.S.A.
186 F6 San Jordi Spain
260 D3 San Jorge San Luis Arg.
261 G2 San Jorge Santa Fé Arg.
78 □6 San Jorge i. Solomon Is
259 D7 San Jorge, Golfo de g. Arg.
San Jorge, Golfo de g. Spain see Sant Jordi, Golf de
184 E3 San Jorge de Alor Spain
260 C3 San José Arg.
250 D4 San José Col.
242 □Q13 San José Costa Rica
244 G1 San José Mex.
92 C4 San Jose Luzon Phil.
92 C5 San Jose Mindoro Phil.
92 C5 San Jose Mindoro Phil.
185 O7 San José Andalucía Spain
261 I4 San José dept Uru.
261 I4 San José Uru.
240 K4 San Jose CA U.S.A.
239 L9 San Jose NM U.S.A.
239 K9 San Jose watercourse NM U.S.A.
250 E2 San José Venez.
259 D7 San José, Cabo c. Arg.
261 I2 San José, Cuchilla de hills Uru.
259 D6 San José, Golfo g. Arg.
242 D5 San José, Isla i. Mex.
260 B3 San José, Volcán vol. Chile
246 G6 San José Allende Mex.
243 N8 San José Carpizo Mex.
244 G4 San José de Alburquerque Mex.
251 F2 San José de Amacuro Venez.
242 F3 San José de Bavicora Mex.
92 C6 San José de Buenavista Panay Phil.
253 E4 San José de Chiquitos Bol.
244 D2 San José de Comondú Mex.
261 H2 San José de Feliciano Arg.
244 G3 San José de Gallinas Mex.
244 E3 San José de Gracia Mex.
242 C4 San José de Gracia Baja California Sur Mex.
244 D6 San José de Gracia Michoacán Mex.
242 F4 San José de Gracia Sinaloa Mex.
242 D3 San José de Gracia Sonora Mex.
247 K9 San José de Guaribe Venez.
260 C2 San Jose de Jáchal Arg.
242 E5 San Joséde la Brecha Mex.
261 F2 San José de la Dormida Arg.
261 G3 San José de la Esquina Arg.
259 B5 San José de la Mariquina Chile
244 D7 San José de la Montaña Mex.
260 E2 San José de las Salinas Arg.
258 E2 San José del Boquerón Arg.
242 E6 San José del Cabo Mex.
250 C4 San José del Guaviare Col.
260 E3 San José del Morro Arg.
245 J9 San José del Progreso Mex.
184 H7 San José del Valle Spain
260 B3 San José de Maipó Chile
261 I4 San José de Mayo Uru.
246 H4 San José de Ocoa Dom. Rep.
250 D3 San José de Ocuné Col.
239 I12 San José de Primas Mex.
244 G1 San José de Raíces Mex.
244 D1 San José de Reyes Mex.
244 G4 San José Iturbide Mex.
111 D8 Sanju Xinjiang China
260 C2 San Juan Arg.
260 C2 San Juan prov. Arg.
253 E4 San Juan Bol.
216 □3a San Juan Tenerife Canary Is
250 B2 San Juan Col.
250 B3 San Juan r. Col.
242 □R12 San Juan r. Costa Rica/Nic.
246 C3 San Juan mt. Cuba
246 H4 San Juan Dom. Rep.
242 F4 San Juan Chihuahua Mex.
243 I4 San Juan Coahuila Mex.
244 E2 San Juan Zacatecas Mex.
244 E4 San Juan r. Mex.
245 L7 San Juan r. Mex.
252 B3 San Juan Peru
92 E6 San Juan Leyte Phil.
92 F7 San Juan Mindanao Phil.
247 □1 San Juan Puerto Rico
183 O2 San Juan Spain
184 G3 San Juan r. Spain
247 □7 San Juan Trin. and Tob.
240 L6 San Juan r. CA U.S.A.
241 V4 San Juan r. UT U.S.A.
251 E3 San Juan Venez.
247 □1 San Juan, Bahía de b. Puerto Rico
259 E9 San Juan, Cabo c. Arg.
207 H6 San Juan, Cabo c. Equat. Guinea
183 L8 San Juan, Embalse de resr Spain
242 □O11 San Juan, Punta pt El Salvador
185 I7 San Juan, Sierra de hills Spain
245 J8 San Juan Achiutla Mex.
253 F6 San Juan Bautista Para.
252 □ San Juan Bautista S. Pacific Ocean
240 K5 San Juan Bautista CA U.S.A.
245 I9 San Juan Bautista lo de Soto Mex.
245 J8 San Juan Bautista Suchitepec Mex.
245 K7 San Juan Bautista Tuxtepec Mex.
240 O8 San Juan Capistrano CA U.S.A.
242 □P10 San Juancito Hond.
245 I8 San Juan de Abajo Mex.
187 E11 San Juan de Alicante Spain
184 G6 San Juan de Aznalfarache Spain
250 C2 San Juan de Cesar Col.
244 E1 San Juan de Guadalupe Mex.
246 F8 San Juan de Guía, Cabo de c. Col.
259 B6 San Juan dela Costa Chile
186 D3 San Juan de la Peña, Sierra de mts Spain
245 H6 San Juan de las Huertas Mex.
242 □R12 San Juan del Norte Nic.
242 □R12 San Juan del Norte, Bahía de b. Nic.
250 D2 San Juan de los Cayos Venez.
244 E4 San Juan de los Lagos Mex.
250 E2 San Juan de los Morros Venez.
244 D4 San Juan de los Potreros Mex.
184 F6 San Juan del Puerto Spain
242 G5 San Juan del Río Durango Mex.
245 I8 San Juan del Río Oaxaca Mex.
245 H5 San Juan del Río Querétaro Mex.
242 □Q12 San Juan del Sur Nic.
259 E9 San Juan de Salvamento Arg.
242 C4 San Juan Evangelista Mex.
245 J8 San Juanico, Punta pt Mex.
238 C2 San Juan Islands WA U.S.A.
242 F4 San Juanito Mex.
244 A4 San Juanito, Isla i. Mex.
245 J7 San Juan Ixcaquixtla Mex.
243 N10 San Juan Ixcoy Guat.
245 L8 San Juan Lachixila Mex.
245 J8 San Juan Mazatlán Mex.
245 K9 San Juan Mixtepec Mex.
239 K8 San Juan Mountains CO U.S.A.
245 K8 San Juan Tepeuxila Mex.
246 B8 San Juan y Martínez Cuba
109 M4 Sanju He watercourse China
259 D8 San Julián Arg.
244 E4 San Julián Mex.
186 D6 San Just mt. Spain
261 G2 San Justo Arg.
182 H4 San Justo de la Vega Spain
96 C4 Sanka Myanmar
206 C4 Sankanbiaiwa mt. Sierra Leone
206 C4 Sankarani r. Côte d'Ivoire/Guinea
114 E8 Sankarankovil Tamil Nadu India
114 D4 Sankeshwar Karnataka India
117 J8 Sankh r. Jharkhand India
122 G3 Sankhās Iran
116 E5 Sankhu Rajasthan India
Sankosh r. Bhutan see Sunkosh Chhu
116 I9 Sankra Chhattisgarh India
116 C6 Sankra Rajasthan India
179 M4 Sankt Aegyd am Neuwalde Austria
179 K6 Sankt Andrä Austria
179 O4 Sankt Andrä am Zicksee Austria
169 K7 Sankt Andreasberg Ger.
179 M6 Sankt Anna am Aigen Austria
178 B5 Sankt Anton am Arlberg Austria
179 L4 Sankt Anton an der Jeßnitz Austria
169 D9 Sankt Augustin Ger.
172 E6 Sankt Blasien Ger.
171 G9 Sankt Egidien Ger.
179 K4 Sankt Gallen Austria
190 G1 Sankt Gallen Switz.
190 G1 Sankt Gallen canton Switz.
178 A5 Sankt Gallenkirch Austria
171 E9 Sankt Gangloff Ger.
179 J6 Sankt Georgen am Längsee Austria
179 K3 Sankt Georgen am Walde Austria
179 J3 Sankt Georgen an der Gusen Austria
179 H4 Sankt Georgen im Attergau Austria
179 K6 Sankt Georgen im Lavanttal Austria
172 E5 Sankt Georgen im Schwarzwald Ger.
179 H4 Sankt Gilgen Austria
169 E10 Sankt Goar Ger.
169 E10 Sankt Goarshausen Ger.
Sankt Gotthard Hungary see Szentgotthárd
172 C3 Sankt Ingbert Ger.
179 J6 Sankt Jakob im Rosental Austria
179 M5 Sankt Jakob im Walde Austria
178 F6 Sankt Jakob in Defereggen Austria
179 J5 Sankt Johann am Tauern Austria
178 H5 Sankt Johann im Pongau Austria
179 L6 Sankt Johann im Saggautal Austria
178 G6 Sankt Johann im Walde Austria
178 F4 Sankt Johann in Tirol Austria
172 D2 Sankt Julian Ger.
179 K6 Sankt Kanzian am Klopeiner See Austria
179 J5 Sankt Lambrecht Austria
179 L3 Sankt Leonhard am Forst Austria
179 M2 Sankt Leonhard am Hornerwald Austria
178 C5 Sankt Leonhard im Pitztal Austria
179 H4 Sankt Lorenz Austria
178 H6 Sankt Lorenzen im Gitschtal Austria
178 G6 Sankt Lorenzen im Lesachtal Austria
179 L5 Sankt Lorenzen im Mürztal Austria
179 J5 Sankt Lorenzen ob Murau Austria
179 L5 Sankt Marein im Mürztal Austria
179 J6 Sankt Margareten im Rosental Austria
168 H3 Sankt Margarethen Ger.
179 M5 Sankt Margarethen an der Raab Austria
179 K5 Sankt Margarethen bei Knittelfeld Austria
179 O4 Sankt Margarethen im Burgenland Austria
172 E5 Sankt Märgen Ger.
179 J3 Sankt Marien Austria
179 I3 Sankt Marienkirchen an der Polsenz Austria
179 K2 Sankt Martin Niederösterreich Austria
179 H5 Sankt Martin Salzburg Austria
179 N6 Sankt Martin an der Raab Austria
179 J3 Sankt Martin im Mühlkreis Austria
179 L6 Sankt Martin im Sulmtal Austria
179 N5 Sankt Michael im Burgenland Austria
179 I5 Sankt Michael im Lungau Austria
179 L5 Sankt Michael in Obersteiermark Austria
168 H3 Sankt Michaelisdonn Ger.
190 H2 Sankt Moritz Switz.
190 D3 Sankt Niklaus Switz.
179 L6 Sankt Nikolai im Sausal Austria
179 J5 Sankt Nikolai im Sölktal Austria
179 K2 Sankt Oswald bei Freistadt Austria
179 L6 Sankt Oswald ob Eibiswald Austria
173 O4 Sankt Oswald-Riedlhütte Ger.
179 J4 Sankt Pankraz Austria
178 G3 Sankt Pantaleon Austria
179 K6 Sankt Paul im Lavanttal Austria
172 E5 Sankt Peter Ger.
178 H3 Sankt Peter am Hart Austria
179 J5 Sankt Peter am Kammersberg Austria
179 M6 Sankt Peter am Ottersbach Austria
139 N2 Sankt-Peterburg Rus. Fed.
179 L5 Sankt Peter-Freienstein Austria
179 L6 Sankt Peter im Sulmtal Austria
179 K3 Sankt Peter in der Au Austria
168 G2 Sankt Peter-Ording Ger.
Sankt Petersburg Rus. Fed. see Sankt-Peterburg
179 M3 Sankt Pölten Austria
178 G3 Sankt Radegund Austria
179 M5 Sankt Ruprecht an der Raab Austria
179 K6 Sankt Stefan Austria
179 I6 Sankt Stefan im Gailtal Austria
179 M6 Sankt Stefan im Rosental Austria
179 K5 Sankt Stefan ob Leoben Austria
179 L6 Sankt Stefan ob Stainz Austria
178 G4 Sankt Ulrich am Pillersee Austria
179 J3 Sankt Ulrich bei Steyr Austria
179 J6 Sankt Urban Austria
179 K3 Sankt Valentin Austria
179 M6 Sankt Veit am Vogau Austria
179 J6 Sankt Veit an der Glan Austria
179 M3 Sankt Veit an der Gölsen Austria
178 H5 Sankt Veit im Pongau Austria
178 F6 Sankt Veit in Defereggen Austria
172 C3 Sankt Wendel Ger.
173 M5 Sankt Wolfgang Ger.
179 H4 Sankt Wolfgang im Salzkammergut Austria
116 F2 Sanku Jammu and Kashmir
209 D6 Sankuru r. Dem. Rep. Congo
195 □ San Lawrenz Gozo Malta
253 F5 San Lázaro Para.
242 C5 San Lázaro, Cabo c. Mex.
242 E6 San Lázaro, Sierra de mts Mex.
191 K7 San Lazzaro di Savena Italy
240 J4 San Leandro CA U.S.A.
191 M8 San Leo Italy
194 F8 San Leonardo r. Sicilia Italy
183 N5 San Leonardo de Yagüe Spain
191 K2 San Leonardo in Passiria Italy
126 I5 Şanlıurfa Turkey
128 H1 Şanlıurfa prov. Turkey
258 F3 San Lorenzo Corrientes Arg.
261 G3 San Lorenzo Santa Fé Arg.
252 D3 San Lorenzo Beni Bol.
252 D2 San Lorenzo Pando Bol.
252 D5 San Lorenzo Tarija Bol.
250 B4 San Lorenzo Ecuador
242 □P11 San Lorenzo Hond.
195 J8 San Lorenzo Italy
242 F3 San Lorenzo Mex.
252 C2 San Lorenzo Peru
183 O4 San Lorenzo mt. Spain
250 A5 San Lorenzo, Cabo c. Ecuador
192 D9 San Lorenzo, Capo c. Sardegna Italy
259 B7 San Lorenzo, Cerro mt. Arg./Chile
242 C3 San Lorenzo, Isla i. Mex.
252 A3 San Lorenzo, Isla i. Peru
190 D8 San Lorenzo al Mare Italy
193 Q8 San Lorenzo Bellizzi Italy
245 K8 San Lorenzo Cacaotepec Mex.
185 L4 San Lorenzo de Calatrava Spain
183 L7 San Lorenzo de El Escorial Spain
183 P9 San Lorenzo de la Parrilla Spain
San Lorenzo de Morunys Spain see Sant Llorenç de Morunys
191 L2 San Lorenzo di Sebato Italy
191 N8 San Lorenzo in Campo Italy
192 H2 San Lorenzo Nuovo Italy
195 K7 San Luca Italy
184 G7 Sanlúcar de Barrameda Spain
184 E6 Sanlúcar de Guadiana Spain
184 G6 Sanlúcar la Mayor Spain
252 D5 San Lucas Bol.
242 C4 San Lucas Baja California Sur Mex.
242 E6 San Lucas Baja California Sur Mex.
244 G7 San Lucas Michoacán Mex.
242 E6 San Lucas, Cabo c. Mex.
250 C3 San Lucas, Serranía de mts Col.
193 Q9 San Lucido Italy
260 D3 San Luis Arg.
260 D3 San Luis prov. Arg.
252 D2 San Luis Brazil
246 F3 San Luis Cuba
243 O9 San Luis Guat.
244 G8 San Luis Guerrero Mex.
245 M8 San Luis Veracruz Mex.
250 C5 San Luis Peru
241 R9 San Luis AZ U.S.A.
241 U9 San Luis AZ U.S.A.
239 L8 San Luis CO U.S.A.
250 D2 San Luis Venez.
242 B3 San Luis, Isla i. Mex.
241 R9 San Luis, Mesa de plat. Mex.
260 D3 San Luis, Sierra de mts Arg.
245 I9 San Luis Acatlán Mex.
245 K9 San Luis Amatlán Mex.
244 G4 San Luis de la Paz Mex.
258 F2 San Luis del Palmar Arg.
242 D5 San Luis Gonzaga Mex.
244 D5 San Luisito Mex.
240 L6 San Luis Obispo CA U.S.A.
240 L6 San Luis Obispo Bay CA U.S.A.
242 □O10 San Luis Pajón Hond.
244 G3 San Luis Potosí Mex.
244 G3 San Luis Potosí state Mex.
240 K4 San Luis Reservoir CA U.S.A.
242 B1 San Luis Río Colorado Mex.
192 B8 Sanluri Sardegna Italy
191 M2 San Maddalena Vallalta Italy
182 E4 San Mamede, Serra do mts Spain
183 K4 San Mamés de Campos Spain
193 Q9 San Mango d'Aquino Italy
261 H5 San Manuel Arg.
260 B3 San Manuel Chile
241 V9 San Manuel AZ U.S.A.
191 O8 San Marcello Italy
191 J7 San Marcello Pistoiese Italy
244 D5 San Marcial, Punta pt Mex.
192 A8 San Marco, Capo c. Sardegna Italy
194 E9 San Marco, Capo c. Sicilia Italy
193 Q8 San Marco Argentano Italy
194 H7 San Marco d'Alunzio Sicilia Italy
193 N5 San Marco dei Cavoti Italy
193 P4 San Marco in Lamis Italy
260 B2 San Marcos Chile
250 C2 San Marcos Col.
243 N10 San Marcos Guat.
242 □P11 San Marcos Hond.
245 H9 San Marcos Guerrero Mex.
244 C5 San Marcos Jalisco Mex.
252 A1 San Marcos Peru
182 D2 San Marcos Spain
240 O8 San Marcos CA U.S.A.
237 G11 San Marcos TX U.S.A.
237 G11 San Marcos r. TX U.S.A.
242 C4 San Marcos, Isla i. Mex.
191 M8 San Marino country Europe
191 M8 San Marino San Marino
262 T2 San Martín research stn Antarctica
258 D3 San Martín Catamarca Arg.
260 C3 San Martín Mendoza Arg.
253 E3 San Martín r. Bol.
245 I6 San Martín Mex.
252 A1 San Martín dept Peru
177 K4 Sânmartin Romania
186 A1 San Martin Spain
187 F10 San Martín, Cabo de c. Spain
259 B8 San Martín, Lago l. Arg./Chile
245 L7 San Martín, Volcán vol. Mex.
245 I4 San Martín Chalchicuautla Mex.
244 D4 San Martín de Bolaños Mex.
183 M8 San Martín de la Vega Spain
183 J8 San Martín de la Vega del Alberche Spain
259 C6 San Martín de los Andes Arg.
183 J8 San Martín del Pimpollar Spain
183 L9 San Martín de Montalbán Spain
183 K9 San Martín de Pusa Spain
183 Q3 San Martín de Unx Spain
183 L8 San Martín de Valdeiglesias Spain
244 D5 San Martín Hidalgo Mex.
191 K5 San Martino Buon Albergo Italy
191 L3 San Martino di Castrozza Italy
192 C2 San-Martino-di-Lota Corse France
191 L4 San Martino di Lupari Italy
191 L5 San Martino di Venezze Italy
191 L2 San Martino in Badia Italy
191 K2 San Martino in Passiria Italy
193 O4 San Martino in Pensilis Italy
250 D5 San Mateo Peru
San Mateo Spain see Sant Mateu
240 J4 San Mateo CA U.S.A.
251 E2 San Mateo Venez.
186 D4 San Mateo de Gállego Spain
243 N10 San Mateo Ixtatán Guat.
252 D4 San Matías Bol.
259 D6 San Matías, Golfo g. Arg.
250 E2 San Mauricio Venez.
194 G8 San Mauro Castelverde Sicilia Italy
193 Q7 San Mauro Forte Italy
191 M7 San Mauro Pascoli Italy
190 D5 San Mauro Torinese Italy
109 M4 Sanmen Zhejiang China
193 P4 San Menaio Italy
109 M4 Sanmen Wan b. China
107 L9 Sanmenxia Henan China
191 N4 San Michele al Tagliamento Italy
190 D7 San Michele Mondovì Italy
195 N2 San Michele Salentino Italy
258 F3 San Miguel Corrientes Arg.
260 D3 San Miguel San Juan Arg.
253 E4 San Miguel Bol.
252 E3 San Miguel r. Bol.
250 C4 San Miguel r. Col.
242 □O11 San Miguel El Salvador
244 B3 San Miguel Mex.
242 □T13 San Miguel Panama
252 B3 San Miguel Peru
92 C5 San Miguel Luzon Phil.
San Miguel Spain see Sant Miquel de Balansat
240 L6 San Miguel CA U.S.A.
239 J7 San Miguel r. CO U.S.A.
251 E2 San Miguel Venez.
92 D5 San Miguel Bay Luzon Phil.
245 K9 San Miguel Coatlán Mex.
216 □3a San Miguel de Abona Tenerife Canary Is
244 G5 San Miguel de Allende Mex.
183 L6 San Miguel de Arroyo Spain
183 M6 San Miguel de Bernuy Spain
244 B1 San Miguel de Cruces Mex.
244 G5 San Miguel Deheti Mex.
242 D3 San Miguel de Horcasitas r. Mex.
252 D3 San Miguel de Huachi Bol.
244 C5 San Miguel de la Sierra Mex.
261 H4 San Miguel del Monte Arg.
245 K10 San Miguel del Puerto Mex.
187 D12 San Miguel de Salinas Spain
258 D2 San Miguel de Tucumán Arg.
254 C5 San Miguel do Araguaia Brazil
244 E4 San Miguel el Alto Mex.
240 L7 San Miguel Island CA U.S.A.
92 B8 San Miguel Islands Phil.
244 G2 San Miguelito Mex.
242 □T13 San Miguelito Panama
244 G5 San Miguel Octopan Mex.
245 K9 San Miguel Sola de Vega Mex.
245 H8 San Miguel Tecuixiapan Mex.
183 N4 San Millán mt. Spain
183 O4 San Millán de la Cogolla Spain
109 K5 Sanming Fujian China
191 J8 San Miniato Italy
175 J5 Sanna r. Pol.
104 B5 Sannan Japan
92 C4 San Narciso Luzon Phil.
215 K5 Sannaspos S. Africa
195 □ Sannat Gozo Malta
190 F5 Sannazzaro de'Burgondi Italy
114 D5 Sanndatti Karnataka India
Sanndraigh i. Scotland U.K. see Sandray
123 L7 Sanni Pak.
195 L2 Sannicandro di Bari Italy
193 P4 Sannicandro Garganico Italy
195 O3 Sannicola Italy
193 P3 San Nicola, Isole is Italy
195 L5 San Nicola dell'Alto Italy
192 C3 San-Nicolao Corse France
260 A5 San Nicolás Chile
245 I9 San Nicolás Guerrero Mex.
245 I1 San Nicolás Tamaulipas Mex.
244 B6 San Nicolás r. Mex.
250 B6 San Nicolás Peru
92 C3 San Nicolas Luzon Phil.
252 B3 San Nicolás, Bahía b. Peru
244 G5 San Nicolás de los Agustinos Mex.
261 G3 San Nicolás de los Arroyos Arg.
242 G5 San Nicolás del Presidio Mex.
184 H4 San Nicolás del Puerto Spain
216 □3f San Nicolás de Tolentino Gran Canaria Canary Is
239 E10 San Nicolas Island CA U.S.A.
244 G3 San Nicolás Tolentino Mex.
196 I4 Sânnicolau Mare Romania
191 L6 San Nicolò Italy
192 B8 San Nicolò d'Arcidano Sardegna Italy
192 C9 San Nicolò Gerrei Sardegna Italy
215 J2 Sannieshof S. Africa
175 H3 Sanniki Pol.
193 N4 Sannio, Monti del mts Italy
206 C5 Sanniquellie Liberia
102 S6 Sannohe Japan
105 K3 Sano Japan
258 D3 Sañogasta, Sierra de mts Arg.
175 K6 Sanok Pol.
250 C2 San Onofre Col.
259 D9 San Pablo Arg.
252 D5 San Pablo Potosí Bol.
253 E3 San Pablo Santa Cruz Bol.
253 E3 San Pablo r. Bol.
250 D3 San Pablo Col.
245 H5 San Pablo Mex.
92 C4 San Pablo Luzon Phil.
240 J4 San Pablo CA U.S.A.
183 L9 San Pablo de los Montes Spain
San Pablo de Manta Ecuador see Manta
191 K2 San Pancrazio Italy
195 N3 San Pancrazio Salentino Italy
178 B8 San Paolo, Isola i. Italy
193 O4 San Paolo di Civitate Italy
195 □ San Pawl, Gżejjer ta' is Malta
195 □ San Pawl il-Baħar Malta
195 □ San Pawl-il-Baħar, Il-Bajja ta' b. Malta
261 H3 San Pedro Buenos Aires Arg.
258 D2 San Pedro Catamarca Arg.
260 E2 San Pedro Córdoba Arg.
258 D2 San Pedro Jujuy Arg.
258 G2 San Pedro Misiones Arg.
243 P9 San Pedro Belize
252 D3 San Pedro Beni Bol.
253 E4 San Pedro Santa Cruz Bol.
252 D4 San Pedro r. Bol.
260 B3 San Pedro Santiago Chile
260 B3 San Pedro Valparaíso Chile
206 D5 San-Pédro Côte d'Ivoire
246 D3 San Pedro r. Cuba
242 D6 San Pedro Baja California Sur Mex.
242 F3 San Pedro Chihuahua Mex.
244 B4 San Pedro r. Mex.
239 L12 San Pedro r. Mex.
252 C2 San Pedro Peru
92 C5 San Pedro Mindoro Phil.
185 O3 San Pedro Spain
261 I4 San Pedro Uru.
241 V9 San Pedro watercourse AZ U.S.A.
242 □R13 San Pedro, Punta pt Costa Rica
184 E1 San Pedro, Sierra de mts Spain
244 F4 San Pedro Almoloyan Mex.
244 C4 San Pedro Analco Mex.
245 K9 San Pedro Apóstol Mex.
243 N10 San Pedro Carchá Guat.
240 N8 San Pedro Channel CA U.S.A.
185 J8 San Pedro de Alcántara Spain
250 D3 San Pedro de Arimena Col.
252 C5 San Pedro de Atacama Chile
182 H4 San Pedro de Ceque Spain
239 I12 San Pedro de la Cueva Mex.
183 K7 San Pedro del Arroyo Spain
242 H5 San Pedro de las Colonias Mex.
183 J5 San Pedro de Latarce Spain
250 B6 San Pedro de Lloc Peru
253 F6 San Pedro del Paraná Para.
187 D12 San Pedro del Pinatar Spain
183 M2 San Pedro del Romeral Spain
247 I4 San Pedro de Macorís Dom. Rep.
182 I7 San Pedro de Rozados Spain
253 F6 San Pedro de Ycuamandyyú Para.
245 K9 San Pedro el Alto Mex.
242 D3 San Pedro el Saucito Mex.
183 P4 San Pedro Manrique Spain
242 B2 San Pedro Martir, Parque Nacional nat. park Mex.
245 J10 San Pedro Mixtepec Mex.
242 □O10 San Pedro Sula Hond.
177 J5 Sânpetru Mare Romania
191 K8 San Piero a Sieve Italy
195 H7 San Piero Patti Sicilia Italy
195 I6 San Pietro Isole Lipari Italy
192 A9 San Pietro, Isola di i. Sardegna Italy
178 G6 San Pietro di Cadore Italy
191 J4 San Pietro in Cariano Italy
191 K6 San Pietro in Casale Italy
195 O3 San Pietro Vernotico Italy
241 U2 San Pitch r. UT U.S.A.
190 I6 San Polo d'Enza Italy
191 K6 San Prospero Italy
106 G7 Sanpu Gansu China
129 K5 Sanqaçal Azer.
146 I12 Sanquhar Dumfries and Galloway, Scotland U.K.
250 B4 Sanquianga, Parque Nacional nat. park Col.
186 F4 San Quílez mt. Spain
242 A2 San Quintín, Cabo c. Mex.
192 H1 San Quirico d'Orcia Italy
260 C4 San Rafael Arg.
253 E4 San Rafael Bol.
260 B4 San Rafael Chile
250 D3 San Rafael Col.
244 F2 San Rafael San Luis Potosí Mex.
245 K5 San Rafael Veracruz Mex.
240 J4 San Rafael CA U.S.A.
241 V3 San Rafael r. UT U.S.A.
250 D2 San Rafael Venez.
San Rafael del Moján Venez. see San Rafael
242 □P11 San Rafael del Norte Nic.
186 F6 San Rafael del Río Spain
247 I4 San Rafael del Yuma Dom. Rep.
241 V3 San Rafael Knob mt. UT U.S.A.
240 L7 San Rafael Mountains CA U.S.A.
185 J5 San Rafael Navallana, Embalse de resr Spain
260 D2 San Ramón Arg.
252 D3 San Ramón Beni Bol.
253 E4 San Ramón Santa Cruz Bol.
245 I2 San Ramón Mex.
261 J4 San Ramón Uru.
109 K6 Sanrao Guangdong China
190 D8 San Remo Italy
235 I3 San Remo NY U.S.A.
102 S7 Sanriku Japan
237 E11 San Rodrigo watercourse Mex.
261 G6 San Román Arg.
182 F3 San Román Spain
250 D1 San Román, Cabo c. Venez.
183 K4 San Román de la Cuba Spain
183 K8 San Román de los Montes Spain
185 I8 San Roque Andalucía Spain
182 C2 San Roque Galicia Spain
182 D4 San Roque Galicia Spain
242 B4 San Roque, Punta pt Mex.
193 O7 San Rufo Italy
237 F10 San Saba TX U.S.A.
237 F10 San Saba r. TX U.S.A.
163 I6 Sansac-de-Marmiesse France
San Sadurniño Spain see Avenida do Marqués de Figueroa
260 E2 San Salano Arg.
245 J6 San Salavador el Seco Mex.
206 B4 Sansalé Guinea
261 H2 San Salvador Arg.
246 F1 San Salvador i. Bahamas
243 O11 San Salvador El Salvador
245 H1 San Salvador Mex.
250 D5 San Salvador Peru
261 H3 San Salvador r. Uru.
250 □ San Salvador, Isla i. Islas Galápagos Ecuador
183 L3 San Salvador de Cantamunda Spain
258 D2 San Salvador de Jujuy Arg.
192 A8 San Salvatore Sardegna Italy
190 F6 San Salvatore Monferrato Italy
193 M5 San Salvatore Telesino Italy
193 N3 San Salvo Italy
207 F3 Sansané Haoussa Niger
207 F4 Sansanné-Mango Togo
259 C9 San Sebastián Arg.
244 C5 San Sebastián Mex.
247 □1 San Sebastián Puerto Rico
182 D3 San Sebastián hill Spain
259 C9 San Sebastián, Bahía de b. Arg.
182 G4 San Sebastián, Embalse de resr Spain
216 □3a San Sebastián de la Gomera La Gomera Canary Is
183 M7 San Sebastián de los Reyes Spain
245 K9 San Sebastián Río Hondo Mex.
245 J7 San Sebastián Zinacatepec Mex.
190 I6 San Secondo Parmense Italy
191 M8 Sansepolcro Italy
192 H3 San Severa Italy
193 Q7 San Severino Lucano Italy
191 O9 San Severino Marche Italy
193 O4 San Severo Italy
109 M5 Sansha Fujian China
252 C2 San Silvestre Bol.
250 D2 San Silvestre Venez.
241 W9 San Simon AZ U.S.A.
188 F3 Sanski Most Bos.-Herz.
183 P3 Sansol Spain
80 J7 Sanson North I. N.Z.
Sansoral Islands Palau see Sonsorol Islands
193 Q8 San Sosti Italy
192 C9 San Sperate Sardegna Italy
195 L1 San Spirito Italy
247 □2 Sans Toucher mt. Guadeloupe
108 G5 Sansui Guizhou China
252 A2 Santa Peru
252 A2 Santa r. Peru
256 C4 Santa Adélia Brazil
184 G2 Santa Amalia Spain
243 O9 Santa Amelia Guat.
261 I2 Santa Ana Entre Ríos Arg.
258 D2 Santa Ana Tucumán Arg.
252 D3 Santa Ana La Paz Bol.
253 E4 Santa Ana Santa Cruz Bol.
253 F4 Santa Ana Santa Cruz Bol.
243 O10 Santa Ana El Salvador
78 □1 Santa Ana Guam
245 H6 Santa Ana México Mex.
244 G1 Santa Ana Nuevo León Mex.
242 D2 Santa Ana Sonora Mex.
78 □6 Santa Ana i. Solomon Is
185 P3 Santa Ana Spain
183 L8 Santa Ana hill Spain
240 O8 Santa Ana CA U.S.A.
186 G4 Santa Ana, Embassament de resr Spain
183 K9 Santa Ana de Pusa Spain
252 D3 Santa Ana de Yacuma Bol.
261 H3 Santa Anita Arg.
242 E6 Santa Anita Baja California Sur Mex.
244 D5 Santa Anita Jalisco Mex.
237 F10 Santa Anna TX U.S.A.
216 □1a Santa Bárbara Terceira Azores
253 F3 Santa Bárbara Mato Grosso Brazil
257 F3 Santa Bárbara Minas Gerais Brazil
260 A5 Santa Bárbara Chile
Santa Bárbara Cuba see La Demajagua
242 □O10 Santa Bárbara Hond.
242 G4 Santa Bárbara Chihuahua Mex.
244 E4 Santa Bárbara Jalisco Mex.
186 G6 Santa Bàrbara Spain
187 C10 Santa Bárbara mt. Spain
185 N6 Santa Bárbara mt. Spain
240 M7 Santa Barbara CA U.S.A.
250 E4 Santa Bárbara Amazonas Venez.
250 D3 Santa Bárbara Barinas Venez.
257 H2 Santa Bárbara, Ilha i. Brazil
216 □1a Santa Bárbara, Serra de vol. Terceira Azores
255 B7 Santa Bárbara, Serra de hills Brazil
240 L7 Santa Barbara Channel CA U.S.A.
184 E5 Santa Bárbara de Casa Spain
184 D5 Santa Bárbara de Padrões Port.
256 D5 Santa Bárbara d'Oeste Brazil
255 B9 Santa Bárbara do Sul Brazil
240 M8 Santa Barbara Island CA U.S.A.
261 I3 Santa Bernardina Uru.
216 □3f Santa Brígida Gran Canaria Canary Is
183 Q4 Santacara Spain
260 E3 Santa Catalina Arg.
258 C2 Santa Catalina Chile
242 □S13 Santa Catalina Panama
78 □6 Santa Catalina i. Solomon Is
251 F2 Santa Catalina Venez.
240 O9 Santa Catalina, Gulf of CA U.S.A.
242 D5 Santa Catalina, Isla i. Mex.
182 C2 Santa Catalina de Armada Spain
240 N8 Santa Catalina Island CA U.S.A.
255 C8 Santa Catarina state Brazil
242 B3 Santa Catarina Baja California Mex.
243 I5 Santa Catarina Nuevo León Mex.
245 H4 Santa Catarina San Luis Potosí Mex.
245 I9 Santa Catarina r. Mex.
247 □10 Santa Catarina Curaçao Neth. Antilles
184 C4 Santa Catarina Port.
255 C8 Santa Catarina, Ilha de i. Brazil
195 L6 Santa Caterina dello Ionio Italy
192 B7 Santa Caterina di Pittinuri Sardegna Italy
245 J9 Santa Catarina Juquila Mex.
194 G8 Santa Caterina Villarmosa Sicilia Italy
195 O3 Santa Cesarea Terme Italy

Santa Cilia de Jaca to São Vicente
383

186 D2 Santa Cilia de Jaca Spain
260 A5 Santa Clara Chile
250 D5 Santa Clara Col.
246 D2 Santa Clara Cuba
242 F3 Santa Clara *Chihuahua* Mex.
244 D1 Santa Clara *Durango* Mex.
241 P10 Santa Clara *r.* Mex.
239 K12 Santa Clara *r.* Mex.
240 K4 Santa Clara *CA* U.S.A.
241 S4 Santa Clara *UT* U.S.A.
240 M7 Santa Clara *r. CA* U.S.A.
184 C5 Santa Clara, Barragem de *resr* Port.
252 □ Santa Clara, Isla *i.* S. Pacific Ocean
184 C6 Santa Clara-a-Nova Port.
184 C5 Santa Clara-a-Velha Port.
261 G2 Santa Clara de Buena Vista Arg.
184 D5 Santa Clara de Louredo Port.
261 G2 Santa Clara de Saguier Arg.
240 N7 Santa Clarita *CA* U.S.A.
250 C5 Santa Clotilde Peru
186 K4 Santa Coloma de Farners Spain
186 J5 Santa Coloma de Gramanet Spain
186 H4 Santa Coloma de Queralt Spain
182 H4 Santa Colomba de Somoza Spain
183 J3 Santa Columba de Curueño Spain
Santa Comba Angola *see* Waku-Kungo
182 D8 Santa Comba Dão Port.
182 G5 Santa Comba de Rossas Port.
186 K4 Santa Cristina d'Aro Spain
182 I4 Santa Cristina de la Polvorosa Spain
195 I9 Santa Croce, Capo *c. Sicilia* Italy
194 H10 Santa Croce Camerina *Sicilia* Italy
193 N5 Santa Croce del Sannio Italy
193 O4 Santa Croce di Magliano Italy
191 J8 Santa Croce sull'Arno Italy
261 E2 Santa Cruz Arg.
259 C8 Santa Cruz *prov.* Arg.
259 C8 Santa Cruz *r.* Arg.
247 □9 Santa Cruz Aruba
253 E4 Santa Cruz Bol.
253 E4 Santa Cruz *dept* Bol.
250 D5 Santa Cruz *Amazonas* Brazil
257 G3 Santa Cruz *Espírito Santo* Brazil
251 H5 Santa Cruz *Pará* Brazil
251 I5 Santa Cruz *Pará* Brazil
254 G3 Santa Cruz *Rio Grande do Norte* Brazil
260 B4 Santa Cruz Chile
242 □Q12 Santa Cruz Costa Rica
246 □ Santa Cruz Jamaica
184 □ Santa Cruz Madeira
244 B4 Santa Cruz *Nayarit* Mex.
244 B4 Santa Cruz *Nayarit* Mex.
242 D2 Santa Cruz *Sonora* Mex.
250 C6 Santa Cruz Peru
92 B4 Santa Cruz *Luzon* Phil.
92 C3 Santa Cruz *Luzon* Phil.
92 C4 Santa Cruz *Luzon* Phil.
184 A2 Santa Cruz Port.
183 Q6 Santa Cruz *mt.* Spain
240 J5 Santa Cruz *CA* U.S.A.
241 T8 Santa Cruz *watercourse AZ* U.S.A.
250 D2 Santa Cruz Venez.
250 □ Santa Cruz, Isla *i. Islas Galápagos* Ecuador
242 D5 Santa Cruz, Isla *i.* Mex.
259 C8 Santa Cruz, Puerto *inlet* Arg.
183 Q6 Santa Cruz, Sierra de *mts* Spain
243 N10 Santa Cruz Barillas Guat.
257 H2 Santa Cruz Cabrália Brazil
256 D4 Santa Cruz das Palmeiras Brazil
182 D7 Santa Cruz da Tapa Port.
183 M2 Santa Cruz de Bezana Spain
183 P3 Santa Cruz de Campézo Spain
256 C2 Santa Cruz de Goiás Brazil
216 □3d Santa Cruz de la Palma *La Palma* Canary Is
163 C10 Santa Cruz de la Serós Spain
244 D5 Santa Cruz de las Flores Mex.
184 H2 Santa Cruz de la Sierra Spain
183 N9 Santa Cruz de la Zarza Spain
243 N10 Santa Cruz del Quiché Guat.
183 L8 Santa Cruz del Retamar Spain
246 E3 Santa Cruz del Sur Cuba
187 C8 Santa Cruz de Moya Spain
185 M3 Santa Cruz de Mudela Spain
216 □3a Santa Cruz de Tenerife *Tenerife* Canary Is
242 □P10 Santa Cruz de Yojoa Hond.
256 C5 Santa Cruz do Rio Pardo Brazil
255 B9 Santa Cruz do Sul Brazil
245 K10 Santa Cruz Huatulco Mex.
240 M7 Santa Cruz Island *CA* U.S.A.
78 □6 Santa Cruz Islands Solomon Is
246 □ Santa Cruz Mountains *hills* Jamaica
183 K2 Santa de Enol, Peña *mt.* Spain
192 B9 Santadi *Sardegna* Italy
193 P8 Santa Domenica Talao Italy
194 H8 Santa Domenica Vittoria *Sicilia* Italy
257 F3 Santa Efigênia de Minas Brazil
261 G5 Santa Elena *Buenos Aires* Arg.
261 F2 Santa Elena *Córdoba* Arg.
261 H2 Santa Elena *Entre Ríos* Arg.
252 D5 Santa Elena Bol.
250 C6 Santa Elena Peru
185 L4 Santa Elena Spain
251 F3 Santa Elena Venez.
242 □Q12 Santa Elena, Cabo *c.* Costa Rica
250 A5 Santa Elena, Punta *pt* Ecuador
182 I4 Santa Elena de Jamuz Spain
261 F4 Santa Eleonora Arg.
194 F9 Santa Elisabetta *Sicilia* Italy
185 J5 Santaella Spain
183 P4 Santa Engracia Spain
256 D4 Santa Eudóxia Brazil
261 F3 Santa Eufemia Arg.
185 J3 Santa Eufemia Spain
193 Q10 Santa Eufemia, Golfo di *g.* Italy
Santa Eugenia *Galicia* Spain *see* Santa Uxía de Ribeira
243 I3 Santa Eulalia Mex.
184 E2 Santa Eulália Port.
186 C6 Santa Eulalia *Aragón* Spain
182 I2 Santa Eulalia *Asturias* Spain
183 J2 Santa Eulalia *Asturias* Spain
187 I10 Santa Eulalia del Río Spain
182 F2 Santa Eulalia de Oscos Spain
186 J4 Santa Eulàlia de Riuprimer Spain
261 G2 Santa Fé Arg.
261 G2 Santa Fé *prov.* Arg.
246 B3 Santa Fé Cuba
242 □S13 Santa Fé Panama
92 C5 Santa Fe Phil.
185 L6 Santa Fé Spain
239 L9 Santa Fe *NM* U.S.A.
250 □ Santa Fé, Isla *i. Islas Galápagos* Ecuador
Santa Fé de Bogotá Col. *see* Bogotá
257 E2 Santa Fé de Minas Brazil
256 B4 Santa Fé do Sul Brazil
254 D4 Santa Filomena Brazil
192 H2 Santa Fiora Italy
193 N5 Sant'Agata de'Goti Italy
195 K7 Sant'Agata del Bianco Italy
193 P8 Sant'Agata di Esaro Italy
194 H7 Sant'Agata di Militello *Sicilia* Italy
193 O5 Sant'Agata di Puglia Italy
191 M8 Sant'Agata Feltria Italy
242 G4 Santa Gertrudis Mex.
192 B8 Santa Giusta *Sardegna* Italy
192 B8 Santa Giusta, Stagno di *l. Sardegna* Italy
191 M3 Santa Giustina Italy
191 K6 Sant'Agostino Italy
254 D2 Santa Helena Brazil
256 B2 Santa Helena de Goiás Brazil
108 E3 Santai *Sichuan* China
110 E4 Santai *Xinjiang* China
110 I4 Santai *Xinjiang* China
108 C5 Santai *Yunnan* China
254 F5 Santa Inês *Bahia* Brazil
254 D2 Santa Inês *Maranhão* Brazil
245 K9 Santa Ines Mex.
259 B9 Santa Inés, Isla *i.* Chile
184 D5 Santa Iria Port.
260 D5 Santa Isabel *La Pampa* Arg.
261 G3 Santa Isabel *Santa Fé* Arg.
252 D5 Santa Isabel Bol.
253 E3 Santa Isabel Brazil
250 B5 Santa Isabel Ecuador
Santa Isabel Equat. Guinea *see* Malabo
245 N9 Santa Isabel Mex.
250 C6 Santa Isabel Peru
247 □1 Santa Isabel Puerto Rico
78 □6 Santa Isabel *i.* Solomon Is
254 E2 Santa Isabel, Ilha Grande de *i.* Brazil
242 B2 Santa Isabel, Sierra *mts* Mex.
252 B4 Santa Isabel de Sihuas Peru
256 A5 Santa Isabel do Ivaí Brazil
260 A5 Santa Juana Chile
256 D3 Santa Juliana Brazil
184 C2 Santa Justa Port.
247 □10 Santa Krus *Curaçao* Neth. Antilles
191 M6 Sant'Alberto Italy
182 F5 Santalha Port.
186 F3 Santa Liestra y San Quílez Spain
116 C8 Santalpur *Gujarat* India
191 J9 Santa Luce Italy
261 G3 Santa Lucia Arg.
252 C5 Santa Lucia Chile
Santa Lucía Cuba *see* Rafael Freyre
250 B5 Santa Lucía Ecuador
243 N10 Santa Lucia Guat.
192 D6 Santa Lucia *Sardegna* Italy
261 I4 Santa Lucia Uru.
261 I4 Santa Lucia *r.* Uru.
185 K6 Santa Lucía, Cerro de *mt.* Spain
261 F3 Santa Lucia, Lago *l.* Arg.
244 C3 Santa Lucia de la Sierra Mex.
195 I7 Santa Lucia del Mela *Sicilia* Italy
182 C3 Santa Lucía de Moraña Spain
216 □3f Santa Lucía de Tirajana *Gran Canaria* Canary Is
240 K5 Santa Lucia Range *mts CA* U.S.A.
261 G5 Santa Luisa Arg.
216 □1c Santa Luzia *Pico* Azores
254 D3 Santa Luzia *Maranhão* Brazil
254 F3 Santa Luzia *Paraíba* Brazil
206 □ Santa Luzia *i.* Cape Verde
184 C5 Santa Luzia *Beja* Port.
184 D6 Santa Luzia *Faro* Port.
261 F4 Santa Magdalena Arg.
187 F7 Santa Magdalena de Pulpís Spain
192 C5 Santa-Manza, Golfe de *b. Corse* France
197 P3 Santa Mare Romania
187 L8 Santa Margalida Spain
186 I4 Santa Margarida de Montbui Spain
184 C4 Santa Margarida do Sádão Port.
258 E3 Santa Margarita Arg.
240 L6 Santa Margarita *CA* U.S.A.
242 D5 Santa Margarita, Isla *i.* Mex.
194 E8 Santa Margherita di Belice *Sicilia* Italy
190 G7 Santa Margherita Ligure Italy
258 D2 Santa María Arg.
216 □1 Santa Maria *i.* Azores
252 E3 Santa María Bol.
251 F5 Santa Maria *Amazonas* Brazil
251 G5 Santa Maria *Amazonas* Brazil
251 H5 Santa Maria *Pará* Brazil
255 B9 Santa Maria *Rio Grande do Sul* Brazil
258 G3 Santa Maria *r.* Brazil
206 □ Santa Maria Cape Verde
243 N8 Santa María Mex.
242 F2 Santa María *r.* Mex.
244 H4 Santa María *r.* Mex.
186 D3 Santa María Spain
187 D8 Santa María *mt.* Spain
184 G6 Santa María *r.* Spain
190 I2 Santa Maria Switz.
240 L7 Santa Maria *CA* U.S.A.
241 S7 Santa Maria *r. AZ* U.S.A.
250 E3 Santa María Venez.
258 G4 Santa María, Cabo *c.* Uru.
213 G5 Santa Maria, Cabo de *c.* Moz.
184 D7 Santa Maria, Cabo de *c.* Port.
231 J14 Santa Maria, Cape Bahamas
246 D2 Santa María, Cayo *i.* Cuba
255 D5 Santa Maria, Chapadão de *hills* Brazil
258 B5 Santa María, Isla *i.* Chile
250 □ Santa María, Isla *i. Islas Galápagos* Ecuador
192 C5 Santa Maria, Isola *i. Sardegna* Italy
252 B3 Santa María, Punta *pt* Peru
254 D5 Santa Maria, Serra de *hills* Brazil
260 C5 Santa María, Volcán *vol.* Arg.
245 H6 Santa María Ajoloapan Mex.
193 M5 Santa Maria Capua Vetere Italy
254 F4 Santa Maria da Boa Vista Brazil
182 C7 Santa Maria da Feira Port.
254 C4 Santa Maria das Barreiras Brazil
256 C5 Santa Maria da Serra Brazil
254 D5 Santa Maria da Vitória Brazil
183 M2 Santa María de Cayón Spain
242 F4 Santa María de Cuevas Mex.
245 H3 Santa María de Guadalupe Mex.
216 □3f Santa María de Guía *Gran Canaria* Canary Is
244 C3 Santa María de Huazamota Mex.
183 P6 Santa María de Huertas Spain
251 E2 Santa María de Ipire Venez.
183 J7 Santa María del Berrocal Spain
183 M4 Santa María del Campo Spain
183 P9 Santa María del Campo Rus Spain
193 P8 Santa Maria del Cedro Italy
190 G6 Santa Maria della Versa Italy
245 J7 Santa María del Monte Mex.
242 G5 Santa María del Oro Mex.
244 C4 Santa María del Oro Mex.
182 I4 Santa María del Páramo Spain
244 F2 Santa María del Refugio Mex.
244 G4 Santa María del Río Mex.
183 P7 Santa María del Val Spain
185 P6 Santa María de Nieva Spain
185 O5 Santa María de Nieva, Puerto de *pass* Spain
193 N7 Santa Maria di Castellabate Italy
195 O4 Santa Maria di Leuca, Capo *c.* Italy
194 H8 Santa Maria di Licodia *Sicilia* Italy
192 C2 Santa-Maria-di-Lota *Corse* France
191 M4 Santa Maria di Sala Italy
257 G2 Santa Maria do Salto Brazil
257 F3 Santa Maria do Suaçuí Brazil
245 L9 Santa María Ecatepec Mex.
245 K10 Santa María Huatulco Mex.
78 □5 Santa Maria Island Vanuatu
245 J8 Santa María Ixcatlán Mex.
183 L6 Santa María la Real de Nieva Spain
257 F4 Santa Maria Madalena Brazil
190 E3 Santa Maria Maggiore Italy
241 T7 Santa Maria Mountains *AZ* U.S.A.
192 D8 Santa Maria Navarrese *Sardegna* Italy
190 G3 Santa Maria Rezzonico Italy
192 B4 Santa-Maria-Siché *Corse* France
245 K8 Santa María Tlalixtac Mex.
245 J9 Santa María Zaniza Mex.
245 K9 Santa María Zoquitlán Mex.
193 P7 Santa Marina Italy
182 I3 Santa Marina del Rey Spain
194 H6 Santa Marina Salina *Isole Lipari* Italy
192 H3 Santa Marinella Italy
250 C2 Santa Marta Col.
185 O2 Santa Marta *Castilla-La Mancha* Spain
184 F3 Santa Marta *Extremadura* Spain
209 B8 Santa Marta, Cabo de *c.* Angola
Santa Marta, Serra de *mts* Brazil *see* Divisões, Serra das
182 I7 Santa Marta de Tormes Spain
255 C9 Santa Marta Grande, Cabo de *c.* Brazil
245 M7 Santa Martha, Cerro *mt.* Mex.
Santa Maura *i.* Greece *see* Lefkada
192 B2 Sant'Ambroggio *Corse* France
240 N7 Santa Monica *CA* U.S.A.
239 H13 Santa Monica, Pico *mt.* Mex.
240 N8 Santa Monica Bay *CA* U.S.A.
240 N7 Santa Monica Mountains National Recreation Area *park CA* U.S.A.
95 L5 Santan *Kalimantan* Indon.
250 E4 Santana *Amazonas* Brazil
254 E5 Santana *Bahia* Brazil
256 B3 Santana *r.* Brazil
184 □ Santana Madeira
182 C8 Santana *Coimbra* Port.
184 D4 Santana *Évora* Port.
184 A4 Santana *Setúbal* Port.
197 J4 Sântana Romania
255 B9 Santana da Boa Vista Brazil
184 C5 Santana da Serra Port.
184 D5 Santana de Cambas Port.
254 E2 Santana do Acarau Brazil
254 C4 Santana do Araguaia Brazil
184 C3 Santana do Campo Port.
254 F3 Santana do Cariri Brazil
255 B9 Santana do Livramento Brazil
184 C3 Santana do Mato Port.
257 F3 Santana do Paraíso Brazil
194 G2 Sant'Anastasia Italy
193 J2 Sant'Anatolia di Narco Italy
250 B4 Santander Col.
250 C3 Santander *dept* Col.
183 M2 Santander Spain
183 L2 Santander *prov.* Spain
183 M2 Santander, Bahía de *b.* Spain
195 N3 Sant'Andrea, Isola *i.* Italy
195 L6 Sant'Andrea Apostolo dello Ionio Italy
192 C9 Sant'Andrea Frius *Sardegna* Italy
177 K4 Sântandrei Romania
240 K4 Santa Nella *CA* U.S.A.
195 K6 Sant'Angelo Italy
193 N5 Sant'Angelo a Cupola Italy
193 O7 Sant'Angelo a Fasanella Italy
193 O6 Sant'Angelo dei Lombardi Italy
191 N8 Sant'Angelo in Lizzola Italy
191 M8 Sant'Angelo in Vado Italy
190 G5 Sant'Angelo Lodigiano Italy
106 C4 Santanghu *Xinjiang* China
Santanilla, Islas *is* Caribbean Sea *see* Cignes, Islas del
194 D8 Santa Ninfa *Sicilia* Italy
241 U8 Santan Mountain *hill AZ* U.S.A.
257 G5 Sant'Anna, Ilha de *i.* Brazil
192 B9 Sant'Anna Arresi *Sardegna* Italy
192 A9 Sant'Antioco *Sardegna* Italy
192 A9 Sant'Antioco, Isola di *i. Sardegna* Italy
187 H10 Sant Antoni de Portmany Spain
192 C6 Sant'Antonio di Gallura *Sardegna* Italy
192 A8 Sant'Antonio di Santadi *Sardegna* Italy
Santañy Spain *see* Santanyí
187 L9 Santanyí Spain
183 L8 Santa Olalla Spain
182 G8 Santa Olalla *hill* Spain
186 I5 Santa Oliva Spain
184 G5 Santa Ollala del Cala Spain
195 I9 Santa Panagia, Capo *c. Sicilia* Italy
186 K3 Santa Pau Spain
240 M7 Santa Paula *CA* U.S.A.
115 H3 Santapilly *Andhra Prad.* India
187 D11 Santa Pola Spain
187 E11 Santa Pola, Cabo de *c.* Spain
241 U2 Santaquin *UT* U.S.A.
254 E3 Santa Quitéria Brazil
182 E7 Santar Port.
193 Q7 Sant'Arcangelo Italy
191 M7 Santarcangelo di Romagna Italy
261 F4 Santa Regina Arg.
251 H5 Santarém Brazil
184 B2 Santarém Port.
184 B2 Santarém *admin. dist.* Port.
246 D2 Santaren Channel Bahamas
253 F1 Santa Rita *Mato Grosso* Brazil
254 G3 Santa Rita *Paraíba* Brazil
250 C4 Santa Rita Col.
78 □1 Santa Rita Guam
243 I4 Santa Rita *Coahuila* Mex.
244 G1 Santa Rita *Nuevo León* Mex.
250 E2 Santa Rita *Guárico* Venez.
246 H8 Santa Rita *Zulia* Venez.
254 D4 Santa Rita de Cassia Brazil
256 A2 Santa Rita do Araguaia Brazil
256 A4 Santa Rita do Pardo Brazil
257 E5 Santa Rita do Sapucaí Brazil
250 D5 Santa Rita do Weil Brazil
258 F3 Santa Rosa *Corrientes* Arg.
261 E5 Santa Rosa *La Pampa* Arg.
260 C3 Santa Rosa *Mendoza* Arg.
259 D6 Santa Rosa *Río Negro* Arg.
258 D2 Santa Rosa *Salta* Arg.
252 D3 Santa Rosa Bol.
252 C2 Santa Rosa *Acre* Brazil
255 B8 Santa Rosa *Rio Grande do Sul* Brazil
250 D4 Santa Rosa Col.
250 B5 Santa Rosa Ecuador
244 G6 Santa Rosa *Michoacán* Mex.
244 G1 Santa Rosa *Nuevo León* Mex.
243 O8 Santa Rosa *Quintana Roo* Mex.
245 I4 Santa Rosa *San Luis Potosí* Mex.
245 J1 Santa Rosa *Tamaulipas* Mex.
253 F6 Santa Rosa Para.
250 C5 Santa Rosa *Loreto* Peru
252 C3 Santa Rosa *Puno* Peru
261 I4 Santa Rosa Uru.
240 J3 Santa Rosa *CA* U.S.A.
239 L9 Santa Rosa *NM* U.S.A.
250 E4 Santa Rosa *Amazonas* Venez.
251 E2 Santa Rosa *Anzoátegui* Venez.
250 E3 Santa Rosa *Apure* Venez.
78 □1 Santa Rosa, Mount Guam
241 P8 Santa Rosa and San Jacinto Mountains National Monument *nat. park CA* U.S.A.
242 □O10 Santa Rosa de Copán Hond.
253 E4 Santa Rosa de la Roca Bol.
260 E3 Santa Rosa del Conlara Arg.
253 E4 Santa Rosa del Palmar Bol.
261 F2 Santa Rosa del Río Primero Arg.
250 C3 Santa Rosa de Osos Col.
250 B4 Santa Rosa de Sucumbio Ecuador
252 D3 Santa Rosa de Vigo Bol.
256 D4 Santa Rosa de Viterbo Brazil
240 L8 Santa Rosa Island *CA* U.S.A.
244 G5 Santa Rosa Jauregui Mex.
242 C4 Santa Rosalía Mex.
241 P8 Santa Rosa Mountains *CA* U.S.A.
238 F6 Santa Rosa Range *mts NV* U.S.A.
241 T8 Santa Rosa Wash *watercourse AZ* U.S.A.
193 O7 Sant'Arsenio Italy
195 L5 Santa Severina Italy
183 J4 Santas Martas Spain
191 L8 Santa Sofia Italy
184 C3 Santa Sofia Port.
184 D3 Santa Susana *Évora* Port.
184 C4 Santa Susana *Setúbal* Port.
258 E2 Santa Sylvina Arg.
261 G3 Santa Teresa Arg.
84 E8 Santa Teresa *N.T.* Austr.
257 G3 Santa Teresa Brazil
254 C4 Santa Teresa *r.* Brazil
244 C1 Santa Teresa *Durango* Mex.
244 C3 Santa Teresa *Nayarit* Mex.
243 K5 Santa Teresa *Tamaulipas* Mex.
247 J8 Santa Teresa Venez.
182 I7 Santa Teresa, Embalse de *resr* Spain
Santa Teresa Aboriginal Land *res. N.T.* Austr. *see* Ltyentye Apurte Aboriginal Land
192 C5 Santa Teresa di Gallura *Sardegna* Italy
195 I8 Santa Teresa di Riva *Sicilia* Italy
261 I5 Santa Teresita Arg.
254 C4 Santa Terezinha Brazil
177 L4 Santău Romania
216 □3a Santa Úrsula *Tenerife* Canary Is
182 C3 Santa Uxía de Ribeira *Galicia* Spain
195 I8 Santa Venerina *Sicilia* Italy
256 B3 Santa Vitória Brazil
184 C5 Santa Vitória Port.
184 D3 Santa Vitória do Ameixial Port.
258 G4 Santa Vitória do Palmar Brazil
192 C8 Santa Vittoria, Monte *mt. Sardegna* Italy
240 L7 Santa Ynez *r. CA* U.S.A.
Santa Ysabel *i.* Solomon Is *see* Santa Isabel
186 K4 Sant Benet *mt.* Spain
186 J5 Sant Boi de Llobregat Spain
186 G6 Sant Carles de la Ràpita Spain
186 J4 Sant Celoni Spain
186 J5 Sant Cugat del Vallès Spain
158 C4 Santec France
240 P9 Santee *CA* U.S.A.
231 H9 Santee *r. SC* U.S.A.
193 L2 Sant'Egidio alla Vibrata Italy
192 C9 Sant'Elia, Capo *c. Sardegna* Italy
193 N4 Sant'Elia a Pianisi Italy
193 L4 Sant Elia Fiumerapido Italy
187 J8 Sant Elm Spain
242 A2 San Telmo Mex.
184 F5 San Telmo Spain
191 P9 Sant'Elpidio a Mare Italy
192 D6 San Teodoro *Sardegna* Italy
189 F5 Santeramo in Colle Italy
191 L6 Santerno *r.* Italy
156 D4 Santerre *reg.* France
183 K3 Santervás de la Vega Spain
186 H5 Santes Creus Spain
195 J7 Sant'Eufemia d'Aspromonte Italy
186 L4 Sant Feliu de Guíxols Spain
186 K3 Sant Feliu de Pallerols Spain
186 J4 Sant Feliu Sasserra Spain
190 E5 Santhià Italy
186 K4 Sant Hilari Sacalm Spain
186 J3 Sant Hipòlit de Voltregà Spain
255 B9 Santiago Brazil
206 □ Santiago *i.* Cape Verde
260 B3 Santiago Chile
260 B3 Santiago *admin. reg.* Chile
246 H4 Santiago Dom. Rep.
242 E6 Santiago *Baja California Sur* Mex.
244 C6 Santiago *Colima* Mex.
243 I5 Santiago *Nuevo León* Mex.
244 B1 Santiago *r.* Mex.
242 □S13 Santiago Panama
253 F6 Santiago Para.
252 B3 Santiago Peru
250 B6 Santiago *r.* Peru
92 C3 Santiago *Luzon* Phil.
259 B8 Santiago, Cabo *c.* Chile
242 □S13 Santiago, Cerro *mt.* Panama
244 B4 Santiago, Río Grande de *r.* Mex.
253 F4 Santiago, Sierra de *hills* Bol.
245 L9 Santiago Astata Mex.
182 F9 Santiago de Alcántara Spain
185 K5 Santiago de Calatrava Spain
250 B6 Santiago de Cao Peru
Santiago de Carbajo Spain *see* Santiago de Alcántara
182 C3 Santiago de Compostela Spain
182 D4 Santiago de Covelo Spain
246 F3 Santiago de Cuba Cuba
185 N4 Santiago de la Espada Spain
245 J5 Santiago de la Peña Mex.
187 D12 Santiago de la Ribera Spain
182 H9 Santiago del Campo Spain
258 D2 Santiago del Estero Arg.
261 F1 Santiago del Estero *prov.* Arg.
Santiago de los Caballeros Dom. Rep. *see* Santiago
216 □3a Santiago del Teide *Tenerife* Canary Is
250 B5 Santiago de Méndez Ecuador
252 C3 Santiago de Pacaguaras Bol.
184 B4 Santiago do Cacém Port.
184 C3 Santiago do Escoural Port.
244 B4 Santiago Ixcuintla Mex.
245 J9 Santiago Ixtayutla Mex.
245 I8 Santiago Juxtlahuaca Mex.
245 J9 Santiago Minas Mex.
245 J8 Santiago Mitlatengo Mex.
240 O8 Santiago Peak *CA* U.S.A.
261 F2 Santiago Temple Arg.
245 L8 Santiago Tutla Mex.
245 L7 Santiago Tuxtla Mex.
261 I4 Santiago Vazquez Uru.
244 C1 Santiaguillo, Laguna de *l.* Mex.
182 I8 Santibáñez de Béjar Spain
183 K3 Santibáñez de la Peña Spain
182 I7 Santibáñez de la Sierra Spain
182 H4 Santibáñez de Vidriales Spain
182 H8 Santibáñez el Bajo Spain
183 M4 Santibáñez Zarzaguda Spain
244 F1 San Tiburcio Mex.
93 B3 Santigi *Sulawesi* Indon.
93 B3 Santiki, Tanjung *pt* Indon.
190 I6 Sant'Ilario d'Enza Italy
183 L2 Santillana Spain
183 M7 Santillana, Embalse de *resr* Spain
250 D2 San Timoteo Venez.
184 G6 Santiponce Spain
Santipur *W. Bengal* India *see* Shantipur
190 G1 Säntis *mt.* Switz.
185 M4 Santisteban del Puerto Spain
183 K6 Santiuste de San Juan Bautista Spain
182 I6 Santiz Spain
186 □ Sant Jaime Mediterráneo Spain
186 G6 Sant Jaume d'Enveja Spain
186 □ Sant Joan Spain
187 I9 Sant Joan de Labritja Spain
186 J3 Sant Joan de les Abadesses Spain
186 I4 Sant Joan de Vilatorrada Spain
186 G6 Sant Jordi, Golf de *g.* Spain
187 H10 Sant Josep de sa Talaia *Illes Balears* Spain
186 I3 Sant Julià de Lòria Andorra
186 I3 Sant Llorenç de Morunys Spain
186 I4 Sant Llorenç de Munt, Parc Natural del *nature res.* Spain
187 L8 Sant Llorenç des Cardassar Spain
186 □ Sant Lluís Spain
186 I4 Sant Martí de Tous Spain
186 I5 Sant Martí Sarroca Spain
186 F7 Sant Mateu Spain
187 H9 Sant Miquel de Balansat Spain
104 A5 Santō *Hyōgo* Japan
104 D5 Santō *Shiga* Japan
184 E3 Santo Aleixo Port.
184 E4 Santo Aleixo da Restauração Port.
216 □1c Santo Amaro *Pico* Azores
216 □1c Santo Amaro *São Jorge* Azores
254 F5 Santo Amaro Brazil
257 G4 Santo Amaro de Campos Brazil
256 B4 Santo Anastácio Brazil
256 A4 Santo Anastácio *r.* Brazil
256 D5 Santo André Brazil
184 B4 Santo André Port.
184 B4 Santo André, Lagoa de *lag.* Port.
255 B9 Santo Angelo Brazil
216 □1c Santo Antão *São Jorge* Azores
206 □ Santo Antão *i.* Cape Verde
182 C3 Santo Antoniño Spain
216 □1c Santo António *Pico* Azores
216 □1b Santo António *São Miguel* Azores
251 F5 Santo Antônio *Amazonas* Brazil
254 D3 Santo Antônio *Maranhão* Brazil
254 G3 Santo Antônio *Rio Grande do Norte* Brazil
257 F3 Santo Antônio *r.* Brazil
207 G6 Santo António São Tomé and Príncipe
257 H2 Santo Antônio, Ponta *pt* Brazil
256 B2 Santo Antônio da Barra Brazil
251 H5 Santo Antônio da Cachoeira Brazil
256 B5 Santo Antônio da Platina Brazil
254 F5 Santo Antônio de Jesus Brazil
253 F3 Santo Antônio de Leverger Brazil
257 F4 Santo Antônio de Pádua Brazil
257 E4 Santo Antônio do Amparo Brazil
250 E5 Santo Antônio do Içá Brazil
257 G2 Santo Antônio do Jacinto Brazil
257 E4 Santo Antônio do Monte Brazil
256 D2 Santo Antônio do Rio Verde Brazil
184 A3 Santo António dos Cavaleiros Port.
Santo António do Zaire Angola *see* Soyo
253 F4 Santo Corazón Bol.
191 M3 Santo Croce, Lago di *l.* Italy
261 I5 Santo Domingo Arg.
260 B3 Santo Domingo Chile
246 C2 Santo Domingo Cuba
246 I4 Santo Domingo Dom. Rep.
243 O10 Santo Domingo Guat.
242 B3 Santo Domingo *Baja California* Mex.
242 D5 Santo Domingo *Baja California Sur* Mex.
245 M9 Santo Domingo *Oaxaca* Mex.
244 F2 Santo Domingo *San Luis Potosí* Mex.
245 K7 Santo Domingo *r.* Mex.
242 □Q11 Santo Domingo Nic.
252 C3 Santo Domingo Peru
186 D3 Santo Domingo *mt.* Spain
Santo Domingo *country* West Indies *see* Dominican Republic
Santo Domingo de Garafía *La Palma* Canary Is *see* Garafía
183 O4 Santo Domingo de la Calzada Spain
245 K10 Santo Domingo de Morelos Mex.
183 N5 Santo Domingo de Silos Spain
245 K9 Santo Domingo Ozolotepec Mex.
245 L9 Santo Domingo Petapa Mex.
239 K9 Santo Domingo Pueblo *NM* U.S.A.
245 L9 Santo Domingo Tehuantepec Mex.
257 G4 Santo Eduardo Brazil
184 D6 Santo Estêvão *Faro* Port.
184 B3 Santo Estêvão *Santarém* Port.
182 F4 Santo Estevo, Encoro de *resr* Spain
80 J7 Santoft *North I.* N.Z.
257 E3 Santo Hipólito Brazil
254 E4 Santo Inácio *Bahia* Brazil
256 B5 Santo Inácio *Paraná* Brazil
184 B3 Santo Isidro de Pegões Port.
251 E2 San Tomé Venez.
187 C11 Santomera Spain
187 C11 Santomera, Embalse de *resr* Spain
193 L2 Sant Omero Italy
183 N2 Santoña Spain
100 E7 Santong He *r.* China
92 E6 Santo Niño *i.* Phil.
195 K6 Sant'Onofrio Italy
194 H9 Santo Pietro *Sicilia* Italy
192 C2 Santo-Pietro-di-Tenda *Corse* France
192 C3 Santo-Pietro-di-Venaco *Corse* France
199 G6 Santorini *i.* Greece
256 D5 Santos Brazil
185 I4 Santos, Sierra de los *hills* Spain
257 F4 Santos Dumont Brazil
252 D2 Santos Mercado Bol.
264 F7 Santos Plateau *sea feature* S. Atlantic Ocean
190 E6 Santo Stefano Belbo Italy
191 N2 Santo Stefano di Cadore Italy
194 G7 Santo Stefano di Camastra *Sicilia* Italy
190 H7 Santo Stefano di Magra Italy
194 E8 Santo Stefano Quisquina *Sicilia* Italy
191 N4 Santo Stino di Livenza Italy
182 D6 Santo Tirso Port.
239 K12 Santo Tomás *Chihuahua* Mex.
239 H11 Santo Tomás *Sonora* Mex.
242 □P11 Santo Tomás Nic.
252 B3 Santo Tomás Peru
258 F3 Santo Tomé *Corrientes* Arg.
261 G2 Santo Tomé *Santa Fé* Arg.
185 M4 Santo Tomé Spain
182 I5 Santovenia Spain
186 I5 Sant Pere de Ribes Spain
186 J3 Sant Pere de Torelló Spain
186 L3 Sant Pere Pescador Spain
164 G4 Santpoort Neth.
186 J3 Sant Privat d'en Bas Spain
186 I5 Sant Quintí de Mediona Spain
116 D8 Santrampur *Gujarat* India
186 I5 Sant Sadurní d'Anoia Spain
187 L9 Sant Salvador, Puig de *hill* Spain
182 I2 Santullano Spain
192 B7 Santu Lussurgiu *Sardegna* Italy
195 □ San Tumas, Il-Bajja ta' *b.* Malta
Santurce *País Vasco* Spain *see* Santurtzi
183 O4 Santurde Spain
183 N2 Santurtzi Spain
186 I4 Sant Vincenç de Castellet Spain
241 S5 Sanup Plateau *AZ* U.S.A.
259 B7 San Valentín, Cerro *mt.* Chile
178 F8 San Vendemiano Italy
192 B7 San Vero Milis *Sardegna* Italy
261 G2 San Vicente Arg.
252 D5 San Vicente Bol.
260 B4 San Vicente Chile
242 □O11 San Vicente El Salvador
242 A2 San Vicente *Baja California* Mex.
244 G1 San Vicente *San Luis Potosí* Mex.
92 D2 San Vicente *Luzon* Phil.
183 K8 San Vicente, Sierra de *mts* Spain
184 E2 San Vicente de Alcántara Spain
183 P3 San Vicente de Arana Spain
252 A3 San Vicente de Cañete Peru
San Vicente de Castellet Spain *see* Sant Vincenç de Castellet
183 L2 San Vicente de la Barquera Spain
183 O3 San Vicente de la Sonsierra Spain
250 C4 San Vicente del Caguán Col.
187 D11 San Vicente del Raspeig Spain
183 K6 San Vicente de Palacio Spain
183 M2 San Vicente de Toranzo Spain
245 I4 San Vicente Tancuayalab Mex.
182 C3 San Vicenzo Spain
191 O9 San Vicino, Monte *mt.* Italy
261 H2 San Victor Arg.
160 E3 Sanvignes-les-Mines France
244 G8 San Vincente de Benitez Mex.
195 I6 San Vincenzo *Isole Lipari* Italy
192 F1 San Vincenzo *Toscana* Italy
182 H5 San Vitero Spain
192 D9 San Vito *Sardegna* Italy
194 D7 San Vito, Capo *c. Sicilia* Italy
195 M3 San Vito, Capo *c.* Italy
191 N4 San Vito al Tagliamento Italy
193 M3 San Vito Chietino Italy
195 N2 San Vito dei Normanni Italy
191 M3 San Vito di Cadore Italy
194 D7 San Vito lo Capo *Sicilia* Italy
193 J4 San Vito Romano Italy
195 K6 San Vito sullo Ionio Italy
105 K3 Sanwa *Ibaraki* Japan
105 H1 Sanwa *Niigata* Japan
116 E8 Sanwer *Madh. Prad.* India
182 C4 Sanxenxo Spain
108 G9 Sanya *Hainan* China
250 D4 San Yanaro Col.
213 F3 Sanyati *r.* Zimbabwe
107 K9 Sanyuan *Shaanxi* China
123 J3 S. A. Nyýazow Adyndaky Turkm.
193 P7 Sanza Italy
209 C6 Sanza Pombo Angola
182 I6 Sanzoles Spain
96 F5 Sao, Phou *mt.* Laos
184 C6 São Barnabé Port.
216 □1a São Bartolomeu *Terceira* Azores
256 D2 São Bartolomeu *r.* Brazil
184 D2 São Bartolomeu Port.
184 B4 São Bartolomeu da Serra Port.
184 C6 São Bartolomeu de Messines Port.
254 E3 São Benedito Brazil
216 □1a São Bento *Terceira* Azores
252 D1 São Bento *Amazonas* Brazil
254 D2 São Bento *Maranhão* Brazil
251 F4 São Bento *Roraima* Brazil
256 B6 São Bento do Amparo Brazil
254 G3 São Bento do Norte Brazil
254 E2 São Bernardo Brazil
256 D5 São Bernardo do Campo Brazil
253 F7 São Borja Brazil
184 D5 São Brás Port.
184 D6 São Brás de Alportel Port.
184 C4 São Brás do Regedouro Port.
216 □1c São Caetano *Pico* Azores
252 D2 São Carlos *Rondônia* Brazil
253 E2 São Carlos *Rondônia* Brazil
255 B8 São Carlos *Santa Catarina* Brazil
256 D5 São Carlos *São Paulo* Brazil
182 E6 São Cosmado Port.
184 C4 São Cristóvão Port.
184 B4 São Cristóvão *r.* Port.
254 D5 São Desidério Brazil
254 D5 São Domingos Brazil
256 A4 São Domingos *r.* Brazil
256 B3 São Domingos *r.* Brazil
184 B5 São Domingos Port.
257 G3 São Domingos do Norte Brazil
184 C2 São Facundo Port.
257 E1 São Felipe, Serra de *hills* Brazil
254 F5 São Félix *Bahia* Brazil
254 C4 São Félix *Mato Grosso* Brazil
251 I6 São Félix *Pará* Brazil
182 C6 São Félix da Marinha Port.
257 G4 São Fidélis Brazil
206 □ São Filipe Cape Verde
252 C2 São Francisco *Acre* Brazil
251 F6 São Francisco *Amazonas* Brazil
257 E1 São Francisco *Minas Gerais* Brazil
257 E1 São Francisco *r.* Brazil
252 D2 São Francisco *r.* Brazil
255 C8 São Francisco, Ilha de *i.* Brazil
184 B4 São Francisco da Serra Port.
255 B9 São Francisco de Assis Brazil
256 C1 São Francisco de Goiás Brazil
255 C9 São Francisco de Paula Brazil
256 C3 São Francisco de Sales Brazil
254 E3 São Francisco do Maranhão Brazil
255 C8 São Francisco do Sul Brazil
255 B9 São Gabriel Brazil
257 G3 São Gabriel da Palha Brazil
184 C3 São Geraldo Port.
257 F5 São Gonçalo Brazil
257 E3 São Gonçalo do Abaeté Brazil
257 E3 São Gonçalo do Pará Brazil
257 E4 São Gonçalo do Sapucaí Brazil
257 E3 São Gotardo Brazil
184 D3 São Gregório Port.
211 B7 Sao Hill Tanz.
182 C7 São Jacinto Port.
256 B5 São Jerônimo da Serra Brazil
216 □1c São João *Pico* Azores
250 E5 São João Brazil
254 D2 São João, Ilhas de *is* Brazil
253 E2 São João, Serra de *hills* Brazil
254 D5 São João da Aliança Brazil
257 G4 São João da Barra Brazil
256 D4 São João da Boa Vista Brazil
182 D7 São João da Madeira Port.
182 F6 São João da Pesqueira Port.
257 E1 São João da Ponte Brazil
256 B4 São João das Duas Pontas Brazil
257 E4 São João del Rei Brazil
257 F5 São João de Meriti Brazil
182 E7 São João de Tarouca Port.
254 C3 São João do Araguaia Brazil
256 A5 São João do Caiuá Brazil
182 D8 São João do Campo Port.
254 F3 São João do Cariri Brazil
255 E5 São João do Paraíso Brazil
254 E4 São João do Piauí Brazil
184 D5 São João dos Caldeireiros Port.
254 E3 São João dos Patos Brazil
209 B8 São João do Sul Angola
257 F3 São João Evangelista Brazil
257 F4 São João Nepomuceno Brazil
250 E4 São Joaquim *Amazonas* Brazil
255 C9 São Joaquim *Santa Catarina* Brazil
256 D4 São Joaquim da Barra Brazil
216 □1c São Jorge *i.* Azores
184 □ São Jorge Madeira
216 □1c São Jorge, Canal de *sea chan.* Azores
São Jorge da Mina Ghana *see* Elmina
256 A5 São Jorge do Ivaí Brazil
250 E5 São José *Amazonas* Brazil
255 C8 São José *Santa Catarina* Brazil
256 D4 São José da Boa Vista Brazil
184 C2 São José da Lamarosa Port.
251 F4 São José do Anauá Brazil
257 E5 São José do Barreiro Brazil
254 F3 São José do Belmonte Brazil
257 G4 São José do Calçado Brazil
257 G3 São José do Divino Brazil
254 F3 São José do Egito Brazil
257 F3 São José do Jacurí Brazil
258 G4 São José do Norte Brazil
254 E3 São José do Peixe Brazil
256 D4 São José do Rio Pardo Brazil
256 C4 São José do Rio Preto Brazil
257 E5 São José dos Campos Brazil
256 B4 São José dos Dourados *r.* Brazil
255 C8 São José dos Pinhais Brazil
182 F5 São Julião de Montenegro Port.
253 G4 São Lourenço *Mato Grosso* Brazil
257 E5 São Lourenço *Minas Gerais* Brazil
253 F4 São Lourenço *r.* Brazil
253 F4 São Lourenço, Pantanal de *marsh* Brazil
184 □ São Lourenço, Ponta de *pt* Madeira
184 D3 São Lourenço de Mamporcão Port.
258 H3 São Lourenço do Sul Brazil
209 C7 São Lucas Angola
254 D2 São Luís Brazil
251 G6 São Luís Brazil
184 B5 São Luís Port.
252 D1 São Luís de Cassianã Brazil
256 B2 São Luís de Montes Belos Brazil
257 E5 São Luís do Paraitinga Brazil
254 G4 São Luís do Quitunde Brazil
255 B9 São Luís Gonzaga Brazil
184 E2 São Mamede, Serra de *mts* Port.
184 C4 São Mamede do Sádão Port.
184 D4 São Manços Port.
256 C5 São Manuel Brazil
250 E4 São Marceline Brazil
256 D3 São Marcos *r.* Brazil
254 D2 São Marcos, Baía de *b.* Brazil
184 D5 São Marcos da Ataboeira Port.
184 C6 São Marcos da Serra Port.
184 D4 São Marcos do Campo Port.
251 G6 São Martinho Brazil
182 D8 São Martinho da Cortiça Port.
184 C5 São Martinho das Amoreiras Port.
182 H5 São Martinho de Angueira Port.
182 B9 São Martinho do Porto Port.
216 □1c São Mateus *Pico* Azores
216 □1a São Mateus *Terceira* Azores
257 H3 São Mateus Brazil
257 H3 São Mateus *r.* Brazil
255 C8 São Mateus do Sul Brazil
184 D4 São Matias Port.
216 □1b São Miguel *i.* Azores
256 D2 São Miguel *r.* Brazil
182 E9 São Miguel *hill* Port.
256 D5 São Miguel Arcanjo Brazil
255 B9 São Miguel das Missões *tourist site* Brazil
182 F8 São Miguel de Acha Port.
184 D3 São Miguel de Machede Port.
184 C2 São Miguel de Rio Torto Port.
184 D5 São Miguel do Pinheiro Port.
254 E3 São Miguel do Tapuio Brazil
247 I4 Saona, Isla *i.* Dom. Rep.
191 N9 Saonda *r.* Italy
217 □3a Saondzou *mt. Njazidja* Comoros
160 I2 Saône France
157 L7 Saône *r.* France
160 F3 Saône-et-Loire *dept* France
116 G9 Saoner *Mahar.* India
São Nicolau Angola *see* Bentiaba
253 G7 São Nicolau Brazil
206 □ São Nicolau *i.* Cape Verde
256 D5 São Paulo Brazil
256 C5 São Paulo *state* Brazil
250 D5 São Paulo de Olivença Brazil
251 G6 São Pedro *Amazonas* Brazil
256 B3 São Pedro *Mato Grosso do Sul* Brazil
253 E2 São Pedro *Rondônia* Brazil
256 D5 São Pedro *São Paulo* Brazil
257 F5 São Pedro da Aldeia Brazil
184 A2 São Pedro da Cadeira Port.
182 F5 São Pedro de Agostem Port.
182 B9 São Pedro de Muel Port.
184 D6 São Pedro de Solis Port.
184 E4 São Pedro do Corval Port.
252 D2 São Pedro do Desterro Brazil
256 B5 São Pedro do Ivaí Brazil
255 B9 São Pedro do Sul Brazil
182 D7 São Pedro do Sul Port.
264 H5 São Pedro e São Paulo *is* N. Atlantic Ocean
São Pires *r.* Brazil *see* Teles Pires
254 D3 São Raimundo das Mangabeiras Brazil
254 E4 São Raimundo Nonato Brazil
161 L9 Saorge France
104 E5 Saori Japan
250 E6 São Romão *Amazonas* Brazil
257 E2 São Romão *Minas Gerais* Brazil
184 E3 São Romão *Évora* Port.
182 E8 São Romão *Guarda* Port.
184 C4 São Romão do Sado Port.
216 □1c São Roque *Pico* Azores
256 D5 São Roque Brazil
256 D4 São Roque de Minas Brazil
São Salvador Angola *see* M'banza Congo
São Salvador do Congo Angola *see* M'banza Congo
216 □1a São Sebastião *Terceira* Azores
252 C1 São Sebastião *Amazonas* Brazil
251 H6 São Sebastião *Pará* Brazil
253 E2 São Sebastião *Rondônia* Brazil
257 E5 São Sebastião *São Paulo* Brazil
257 E5 São Sebastião, Ilha do *i.* Brazil
256 B5 São Sebastião da Amoreira Brazil
251 I5 São Sebastião da Boa Vista Brazil
251 F6 São Sebastião de Tapuru Brazil
256 D4 São Sebastião do Paraíso Brazil
255 B9 São Sepé Brazil
182 C8 São Silvestre Port.
253 F5 São Simão *Mato Grosso do Sul* Brazil
256 B3 São Simão *Minas Gerais* Brazil
256 D4 São Simão *São Paulo* Brazil
256 B3 São Simão, Barragem de *resr* Brazil
256 C3 São Simão, Represa de *resr* Brazil
93 E3 Sao-Siu *Maluku* Indon.
184 B5 São Teotónio Port.
257 E4 São Tiago Brazil
São Tiago *i.* Cape Verde *see* Santiago
207 G6 São Tomé São Tomé and Príncipe
207 G6 São Tomé *i.* São Tomé and Príncipe
257 G5 São Tomé, Cabo de *c.* Brazil
207 G6 São Tomé, Pico de *mt.* São Tomé and Príncipe
207 G6 São Tomé and Príncipe *country* Africa
184 B3 São Torcato *hill* Port.
161 G7 Saou France
204 E3 Saoura, Oued *watercourse* Alg.
256 D5 São Vicente Brazil
206 □ São Vicente *i.* Cape Verde
184 □ São Vicente Madeira
184 E3 São Vicente *Portalegre* Port.
182 F5 São Vicente *Vila Real* Port.

São Vicente, Cabo de to Schnaitsee

384

184 B6 São Vicente, Cabo de c. Port.
182 E8 São Vicente da Beira Port.
254 D2 São Vicente Ferrer Brazil
177 K4 Sáp Hungary
Sápai Greece see Sapes
94 C5 Sapako Indon.
184 E6 Sapal de Castro Marim e Vila Real de Santo António, Reserva Natural do nature res. Spain
252 B3 Sapallanga Peru
199 L2 Sapanca Turkey
199 L2 Sapanca Gölü l. Turkey
254 D4 Sapão r. Brazil
122 H1 Saparmyrat Türkmenbaşy Turkm.
93 F5 Saparua Maluku Indon.
93 F5 Saparua i. Maluku Indon.
151 J2 Sapcote Leicestershire, England U.K.
93 A8 Sape, Selat sea chan. Indon.
95 M9 Sape, Teluk b. Sumbawa Indon.
207 G5 Sapele Nigeria
199 G1 Sapes Greece
199 K3 Şaphane Turkey
192 C6 Sa Pianedda, Monte hill Italy
198 C6 Sapienza i. Greece
242 □T14 Sapo, Serranía del mts Panama
187 L8 Sa Pobla Spain
195 I7 Saponara Sicilia Italy
206 C5 Sapo National Park Liberia
256 B5 Sapopema Brazil
138 G8 Sapotskin Belarus
206 E4 Sapouy Burkina
139 X8 Sapozhok Rus. Fed.
236 F5 Sappa Creek r. NE U.S.A.
191 N2 Sappada Italy
231 □1 Sapphire Bay Bermuda
102 S3 Sapporo Japan
117 L9 Saptamukhi r. India
256 C4 Sapucai r. Brazil
257 E4 Sapucai r. Brazil
251 G5 Sapucaia Brazil
95 K8 Sapudi i. Indon.
237 G7 Sapulpa OK U.S.A.
95 J8 Sapulu Jawa Indon.
95 L2 Sapulut Sabah Malaysia
124 F2 Sāq, Jabal hill Saudi Arabia
122 H5 Sāqī Iran
221 M2 Saqqaq Greenland
122 B3 Saqqez Iran
124 F7 Saqr Saudi Arabia
129 D3 Saqulia Georgia
117 L7 Sara Bangl.
122 B3 Sarā Iran
122 B3 Sarāb Āžarbāyjān-e Sharqī Iran
122 H5 Sarāb Khorāsān Iran
127 M7 Sarābe Meymeh Iran
128 B9 Sarābīṭ al Khādim tourist site Egypt
97 E7 Sara Buri Thai.
140 Q1 Saraby Norway
251 G5 Saracá, Lago l. Brazil
195 L4 Saraceno r. Italy
194 D7 Saraceno, Punta del pt Sicilia Italy
179 N7 Saračinec Croatia
116 C9 Saradiya Gujarat India
202 C6 Saraf Doungous Chad
Saragossa Spain see Zaragoza
123 I3 Saragt Turkm.
250 B5 Saraguro Ecuador
123 L5 Sarai Afgh.
135 H5 Sarai Rus. Fed.
117 J8 Saraikela Jharkhand India
123 O6 Sarai Sidhu Pak.
140 S4 Säräisniemi Fin.
188 G4 Sarajevo Bos.-Herz.
85 L7 Saraji Qld Austr.
123 I3 Sarakhs Iran
198 E4 Sarakiniko, Akrotirio pt Greece
198 F4 Sarakino i. Greece
120 G2 Saraktash Rus. Fed.
237 K10 Saraland AL U.S.A.
120 F3 Saralzhin Kazakh.
117 O7 Saramati mt. India/Myanmar
250 B6 Sarameriza Peru
163 F8 Saramon France
156 C8 Saran France
121 O3 Saran' Kazakh.
95 I5 Saran, Gunung mt. Indon.
233 L4 Saranac r. NY U.S.A.
233 K4 Saranac Lake NY U.S.A.
177 K4 Sáránd Hungary
198 B3 Sarandë Albania
256 B5 Sarandi Paraná Brazil
255 B8 Sarandi Rio Grande do Sul Brazil
Sarandib country Asia see Sri Lanka
258 G4 Sarandí del Yí Uru.
261 I3 Sarandí de Navarro Uru.
261 I3 Sarandí Grande Uru.
92 E9 Sarangani i. Phil.
92 E9 Sarangani Bay Mindanao Phil.
92 E9 Sarangani Islands Phil.
92 E9 Sarangani Strait Phil.
117 I9 Sarangarh Chhattisgarh India
116 F8 Sarangpur Madh. Prad. India
135 I5 Saransk Rus. Fed.
Sara-Ostrov Azer. see Närimanabad
207 H4 Sara Peak Nigeria
96 D5 Saraphi Thai.
134 K4 Sarapul Rus. Fed.
128 E3 Sarāqib Syria
231 F12 Sarasota FL U.S.A.
116 C8 Saraswati r. Gujarat India
136 H7 Sărata r. Moldova
197 O6 Sărata r. Romania
136 I7 Sarata Ukr.
136 I8 Sarata r. Ukr.
136 H6 Sărătenii Vechi Moldova
240 J4 Saratoga CA U.S.A.
238 K6 Saratoga WY U.S.A.
233 L5 Saratoga Lake NY U.S.A.
233 L5 Saratoga Springs NY U.S.A.
95 I4 Saratok Sarawak Malaysia
120 A2 Saratov Rus. Fed.
Saratov Oblast admin. div. Rus. Fed. see Saratovskaya Oblast'
129 A1 Saratovskaya Rus. Fed.
120 B2 Saratovskaya Oblast' admin. div. Rus. Fed.
120 B1 Saratovskoye Vodokhranilishche resr Rus. Fed.
199 G3 Saratsina, Akrotirio pt Lesvos Greece
123 J8 Saravan Iran
92 D6 Saravia Negros Phil.
97 D8 Sarawa r. Myanmar
95 I4 Sarawak state Malaysia
129 K5 Saray Azer.
126 C3 Saray Turkey
206 C4 Saraya Guinea
206 C3 Saraya Senegal
128 D3 Şarāyā Syria
199 K4 Saraycık Turkey
199 J5 Sarayköy Turkey
199 I2 Saraylar Turkey
126 F4 Sarayönü Turkey
123 I8 Sarbāz Iran
123 I9 Sarbāz r. Iran
123 I8 Sarbāz reg. Iran
197 N6 Sârbeni Romania
117 M6 Sarbhang Bhutan
177 L4 Sârbi Romania
122 H5 Sarbīsheh Iran
177 H5 Sárbogárd Hungary
174 F1 Sarbsko, Jezioro lag. Pol.
106 A3 Sarbulak Xinjiang China
191 J4 Sarca r. Italy
178 C7 Sarca di Genova r. Italy
156 D6 Sarcelles France
122 C3 Sarcham Iran
129 F4 Sarch'apet Armenia
192 B8 Sarcidano reg. Sardegna Italy
258 C3 Sarco Chile
111 E12 Sarda r. India/Nepal
116 H5 Sarda r. Nepal
123 N3 Sard Āb pass Afgh.
123 I8 Sardāb Iran
184 B5 Sardão, Cabo c. Port.
192 B8 Sardara Sardegna Italy
116 E8 Sardarpur Madh. Prad. India
116 E5 Sardarshahr Rajasthan India
122 A3 Sar Dasht Iran
122 C5 Sardasht Khūzestān Iran
122 D6 Sardasht Khūzestān Iran
192 C7 Sardegna admin. reg. Italy
192 A7 Sardegna i. Sardegna Italy
Sardica Bulg. see Sofiya
176 G3 Šardice Czech Rep.
216 □3f Sardina Gran Canaria Canary Is
216 □3f Sardina, Punta de pt Gran Canaria Canary Is
250 C2 Sardinata Col.
242 □Q12 Sardinia Costa Rica
Sardinia i. Sardegna Italy see Sardegna
185 L4 Sardinilla r. Spain
237 K8 Sardis MS U.S.A.
232 E9 Sardis WV U.S.A.
237 K8 Sardis Lake resr MS U.S.A.
182 D9 Sardoal Port.
127 M5 Sardrūd Iran
163 A9 Sare France
125 J3 Sareb, Rās as pt U.A.E.
123 L4 Sar-e Būm Afgh.
140 N3 Sareks nationalpark nat. park Sweden
140 N3 Sarektjåkkå mt. Sweden
95 K5 Sarempaka, Gunung mt. Indon.
187 K8 S'Arenal Spain
191 K2 Sarentino Italy
123 K3 Sar-e Pol Afgh.
123 L4 Sar-e Pol Afgh.
123 L3 Sar-e Pol prov. Afgh.
127 L6 Sar-e Pol-e Žahāb Iran
Sar Eskandar Iran see Hashtrud
190 C4 Sareva r. Italy
122 F6 Sare Yazd Iran
123 O2 Sarez, Kŭli l. Tajik.
Sarezskoye Ozero l. Tajik. see Sarez, Kŭli
190 G1 Sargans Switz.
264 E4 Sargasso Sea Atlantic Ocean
250 C5 Sargentu Loros Peru
123 O5 Sargodha Pak.
208 C2 Sarh Chad
122 I7 Sarhad reg. Iran
206 D4 Sarhala Côte d'Ivoire
204 D3 Sarhro, Jbel mt. Morocco
122 E3 Sārī Iran
199 I7 Saria i. Karpathos Greece
242 D2 Sáric Mex.
199 L2 Sarıcakaya Turkey
129 B7 Sarıcan Turkey
197 Q6 Sarichioi Romania
129 E6 Sarıçiçek Dağı mt. Turkey
192 B3 Sari-d'Orcino Corse France
182 I3 Sariegos Spain
91 K3 Sarigan i. N. Mariana Is
129 C5 Sarıgöl Artvin Turkey
199 J4 Sarıgöl Manisa Turkey
199 M5 Sarıidris Turkey
127 K3 Sarıkamış Turkey
128 B2 Sarıkavak Turkey
95 I3 Sarikei Sarawak Malaysia
199 I5 Sarıkemer Turkey
199 I2 Sarıköy Turkey
Sarikŭl, Qatorkŭhi mts China/Tajik. see Sarykol Range
116 G7 Sarila Uttar Prad. India
94 □ Sarimbun Reservoir Sing.
85 L6 Sarina Qld Austr.
186 E4 Sariñena Spain
210 D4 Sarinleev Somalia
Sarıoğlan Turkey see Belören
129 D6 Sarıpınar Turkey
122 F3 Sāri Qamīsh Iran
Sariqamish Kuli salt l. Turkm./Uzbek. see Sarykamyshskoye Ozero
202 C4 Sarīr Tibesti des. Libya
202 D3 Sarir Water Wells Field Libya
117 L7 Sarishabari Bangl.
129 B4 Sarısu Turkey
129 J5 Sarısu Gölü l. Azer.
237 G12 Sarita TX U.S.A.
128 A2 Sarıveliler Turkey
101 D9 Sariwŏn N. Korea
129 I6 Sarıxanlı Azer.
199 M2 Sarıyar Turkey
199 K1 Sarıyer Turkey
126 H4 Sarız Turkey
158 G3 Sark i. Channel Is
177 K5 Sarkad Hungary
177 K5 Sarkadkeresztúr Hungary
121 R5 Sarkand Kazakh.
116 C6 Sarkari Tala Rajasthan India
177 H4 Sárkeresztes Hungary
177 H4 Sárkeresztúr Hungary
126 E4 Şarkikaraağaç Turkey
141 Q6 Särkisalo Fin.
126 H4 Şarkışla Turkey
199 I2 Şarköy Turkey
123 L7 Sarlath Range mts Afgh./Pak.
163 G6 Sarlat-la-Canéda France
122 F2 Şarlawuk Turkm.
179 I2 Sarleinsbach Austria
162 F5 Sarliac-sur-l'Isle France
129 E2 Sarmakovo Rus. Fed.
123 K5 Sarmalan Afgh.
134 K5 Sarmanovo Rus. Fed.
197 K3 Şărmăşag Romania
197 M4 Sărmaşu Romania
195 K3 Sarmento r. Italy
91 I7 Sarmi Papua Indon.
259 C7 Sarmiento Arg.
141 L6 Särna Sweden
182 E9 Sarnadas do Ródão Port.
175 K3 Sarnaki Pol.
193 K1 Sarnano Italy
138 E4 Sārnate Latvia
117 I7 Sarnath Uttar Prad. India
122 B5 Sarneh Iran
190 E2 Sarnen Switz.
190 E2 Sarner See l. Switz.
Sarni Madh. Prad. India see Amla
224 D5 Sarnia Ont. Can.
190 H4 Sarnico Italy
193 N6 Sarno Italy
174 E4 Sarnowa Pol.
136 F2 Sarny Ukr.
93 B5 Saroako Sulawesi Indon.
139 S3 Sarogozha r. Rus. Fed.
94 E6 Sarolangun Sumatera Indon.
102 U2 Saroma-ko l. Japan
226 C4 Sarona WI U.S.A.
198 E5 Saronikos Kolpos g. Greece
190 G4 Saronno Italy
177 H4 Sárosd Hungary
199 H2 Saros Körfezi b. Turkey
177 K3 Sárospatak Hungary
116 D7 Sarotra Gujarat India
135 H5 Sarova Rus. Fed.
177 H3 Šarovce Slovakia
170 H3 Sarow Ger.
123 M4 Sarowbī Afgh.
135 I6 Sarpa, Ozero l. Rus. Fed.
135 I7 Sarpa, Ozero l. Rus. Fed.
Sarpan i. N. Mariana Is see Rota
92 □ Sar Passage Palau
196 I9 Šar Planina mts Macedonia/Yugo.
142 H2 Sarpsborg Norway
Sarqant Kazakh. see Sarkand
192 C9 Sarrabus reg. Sardegna Italy
183 M4 Sarracín Spain
186 H5 Sarral Spain
157 N6 Sarralbe France
163 C9 Sarrance France
163 E10 Sarrancolin France
161 B7 Sarrans, Barrage de dam France
182 E5 Sarraquinhos Port.
161 F6 Sarras France
157 N5 Sarre r. France
190 C4 Sarre Italy
151 O5 Sarre Kent, England U.K.
Sarreal Spain see Sarral
182 E4 Sarreaus Spain
157 N6 Sarre Blanche r. France
157 N6 Sarrebourg France
157 N5 Sarreguemines France
177 H4 Sarreti park Hungary
177 K4 Sárrétudvari Hungary
157 N6 Sarre-Union France
182 F3 Sarria Spain
186 K3 Sarrià de Ter Spain
161 F8 Sarrians France
187 D7 Sarrión Spain
206 D3 Sarro Mali
186 G5 Sarroca de Lleida Spain
192 C9 Sarròch Sardegna Italy
179 O4 Sarród Hungary
192 B3 Sarrola-Carcopino Corse France
163 D8 Sarron France
156 H6 Sarry France
134 L4 Sars Rus. Fed.
191 M8 Sarsina Italy
162 I4 Sarssonne r. France
169 I6 Sarstedt Ger.
177 H5 Sárszentágota Hungary
177 H4 Sárszentmihály Hungary
165 I7 Sart Belgium
183 P4 Sartaguda Spain
137 Q6 Sartana Ukr.
123 N8 Sartanahu Pak.
192 H2 Sarteano Italy
192 B4 Sartène Corse France
159 L6 Sarthe dept France
159 J6 Sarthe r. France
198 E2 Sarti Greece
129 G4 Sart'ichala Georgia
158 I4 Sartilly France
138 E6 Sartininkai Lith.
106 A3 Sartokay Xinjiang China
Sartu Heilong. China see Daqing
177 J4 Sarud Hungary
122 D4 Sarud, Rūdkhāneh-ye r. Iran
102 T4 Saru-gawa r. Japan
199 I4 Saruhanlı Turkey
192 C7 Sarule Sardegna Italy
123 L8 Saruna Pak.
123 L8 Saruna r. Pak.
116 D5 Sarupsar Rajasthan India
122 C4 Saruq Iran
129 F6 Şärur Azer.
123 J6 Saru Tara tourist site Afgh.
125 O2 Sarvāb Iran
122 B4 Sarvābād Iran
Sarvani Georgia see Marneuli
176 F4 Sárvár Hungary
122 E7 Sarvestān Iran
186 E2 Sarvisé Spain
196 G4 Sárvíz r. Romania
177 H5 Sárvíz-malomcsatorna canal Hungary
116 E6 Sarwar Rajasthan India
114 C3 Sarya r. India
121 M7 Saryagash Kazakh.
138 K6 Sar"yanka r. Belarus/Latvia
120 I4 Sarybasat Kazakh.
121 O7 Sary-Bulak Kyrg.
Sarydhaz r. Kyrg. see Sary-Jaz
Sarydzhas Kazakh. see Saryzhaz
Sarygamysh Köli salt l. Turkm./Uzbek. see Sarykamyshskoye Ozero
Sary-Ishikotrau, Peski des. Kazakh. see Saryyesik-Atyrau, Peski
121 R6 Sary-Jaz r. Kyrg.
120 E5 Sarykamys Atyrauskaya Oblast' Kazakh.
121 L3 Sarykamys Karagandinskaya Oblast' Kazakh.
122 G1 Sarykamyshskoye Ozero salt l. Turkm./Uzbek.
121 N6 Sarykemer Kazakh.
121 P2 Sarykiyak Kazakh.
120 K1 Sarykol' Kazakh.
123 P2 Sarykol Range mts China/Tajik.
121 P5 Sarykomey Kazakh.
120 K2 Sarymoyyn, Ozero salt l. Kazakh.
121 R5 Saryozek Kazakh.
Saryqamys Kazakh. see Sarykamys
121 O4 Saryshagan Kazakh.
121 L5 Sarysu watercourse Kazakh.
129 H2 Sarysu Rus. Fed.
120 D5 Sarytash Kazakh.
121 O8 Sary-Tash Kyrg.
121 Q7 Saryter, Gora mt. Kyrg.
120 D2 Saryumir Kazakh.
123 J3 Saryýazy Suw Howdany resr Turkm.
121 P5 Saryyesik-Atyrau, Peski des. Kazakh.
Saryzhal Kazakh. see Sarzhal
121 R6 Saryzhaz Kazakh.
190 H7 Sarzana Italy
158 F6 Sarzeau France
182 E9 Sarzedas Port.
120 D6 Sarzha Kazakh.
121 R3 Sarzhal Kazakh.
241 U10 Sasabe AZ U.S.A.
210 D2 Sasabeneh Eth.
94 C4 Sasak Sumatera Indon.
183 L4 Sasamón Spain
78 □6 Sasamungga Choiseul Solomon Is
93 A8 Sasar, Tanjung pt Sumba Indon.
117 J7 Sasaram Bihar India
78 □6 Sasari, Mount Sta Isabel Solomon Is
104 B5 Sasayama Japan
172 D5 Sasbach Baden-Württemberg Ger.
172 E4 Sasbach Baden-Württemberg Ger.
172 E4 Sasbachwalden Ger.
137 L3 Saschnivka Ukr.
177 H5 Sásd Hungary
103 G13 Sasebo Japan
175 I2 Sasek Wielki, Jezioro l. Pol.
105 K3 Sashima Japan
137 L5 Sasivka Ukr.
223 J4 Saskatchewan prov. Can.
223 K4 Saskatchewan r. Man./Sask. Can.
222 J5 Saskatchewan Landing Provincial Park Sask. Can.
223 J4 Saskatoon Sask. Can.
131 M2 Saskylakh Rus. Fed.
242 □Q11 Saslaya mt. Nic.
242 □Q11 Saslaya, Parque Nacional nat. park Nic.
136 I1 Sasnovy Bor Belarus
215 L2 Sasolburg S. Africa
135 H5 Sasovo Rus. Fed.
222 H2 Sass r. N.W.T. Can.
234 D6 Sassafras MD U.S.A.
206 D5 Sassandra Côte d'Ivoire
206 D5 Sassandra r. Côte d'Ivoire
193 P7 Sassano Italy
192 B6 Sassari Sardegna Italy
192 B6 Sassari prov. Sardegna Italy
190 E7 Sassello Italy
170 H2 Sassen Ger.
161 H6 Sassenage France
169 F7 Sassenberg Ger.
164 G4 Sassenheim Neth.
192 F1 Sassetta Italy
170 I1 Sassnitz Ger.
191 M8 Sassocorvaro Italy
190 G3 Sasso della Paglia mt. Switz.
191 K7 Sasso di Castro mt. Italy
191 N9 Sassoferrato Italy
191 L2 Sasso Lungo mt. Italy
191 K7 Sasso Marconi Italy
191 L2 Sass Rigais mt. Italy
206 C5 Sass Town Liberia
191 J6 Sassuolo Italy
186 E5 Sástago Spain
176 G3 Šaštín-Stráže Slovakia
121 N6 Sastobe Kazakh.
261 G2 Sastre Arg.
114 D3 Sasvad Mahar. India
165 E6 Sas Van Gent Neth.
137 K7 Sasyk r. Ukr.
137 M8 Sasyk, Ozero l. Ukr.
121 S4 Sasykkol', Ozero l. Kazakh.
135 I7 Sasykoli Rus. Fed.
Sasyqköl l. Kazakh. see Sasykkol', Ozero
206 C3 Satadougou Mali
Satahual i. Micronesia see Satawal
206 D5 Satama-Sokoura Côte d'Ivoire
103 H16 Sata-misaki c. Japan
116 E9 Satana Mahar. India
136 F4 Sataniv Ukr.
182 E7 Satão Port.
78 □2 Satapuala Samoa
114 D4 Satara Mahar. India
213 F5 Satara S. Africa
78 □2 Sataua Samoa
91 K5 Satawal i. Micronesia
Sätbaev Kazakh. see Satpayev
196 J5 Satchinez Romania
208 D3 Satéma C.A.R.
95 L8 Satengar i. Indon.
143 L1 Säter Sweden
242 F4 Satevó Mex.
239 K13 Satevo r. Mex.
240 M7 Saticoy CA U.S.A.
140 O3 Satihaure l. Sweden
231 G10 Satilla r. GA U.S.A.
161 F6 Satillieu France
135 H5 Satinka Rus. Fed.
252 B2 Satipo Peru
206 D4 Satiri Burkina
Satırlar Turkey see Yeşilova
130 G4 Satka Rus. Fed.
117 N9 Satkania Bangl.
129 E4 Sat'khe Georgia
117 L8 Satkhira Bangl.
Satluj r. India/Pak. see Sutlej
114 F3 Satmala Range hills India
116 H7 Satna Madh. Prad. India
160 G5 Satolas airport France
105 L2 Satomi Japan
95 L9 Satonda i. Indon.
177 K3 Sátoraljaújhely Hungary
188 E3 Satorina mt. Croatia
170 E3 Satow Ger.
121 L3 Satpayev Karagandinskaya Oblast' Kazakh.
121 L4 Satpayev Karagandinskaya Oblast' Kazakh.
116 E9 Satpura Range mts India
193 P6 Satriano di Lucania Italy
138 F6 Šatrijos kalnis hill Lith.
168 I1 Satrup Ger.
103 H15 Satsuma-hantō pen. Japan
102 U4 Satsunai-gawa r. Japan
97 E8 Sattahip Thai.
140 S3 Sattanen Fin.
105 K3 Satte Japan
178 A5 Satteins Austria
173 I3 Satteldorf Ger.
114 G4 Sattenapalle Andhra Prad. India
96 B5 Satthwa Myanmar
116 F2 Satti Jammu and Kashmir
179 J3 Sattledt Austria
179 J6 Sattnitz reg. Austria
95 K6 Satui Kalimantan Indon.
197 K3 Satu Mare Romania
177 L4 Satu Mare county Romania
97 E11 Satun Thai.
102 □F18 Satunan-shotō is Japan
78 □2 Satupa'itea Samoa
261 F2 Saturnino M. Laspiur Arg.
116 F8 Satwas Madh. Prad. India
186 J4 Sau, Pantà de resr Spain
179 K6 Saualpe mts Austria
142 C2 Sauanuten mt. Norway
95 K8 Saubi i. Indon.
163 B8 Saubusse France
177 L4 Săuca Romania
183 O6 Saúca Spain
163 C6 Saucats France
261 H2 Sauce Arg.
261 G6 Sauce r. Arg.
237 E13 Sauceda Mex.
241 T9 Sauceda Mountains AZ U.S.A.
261 H2 Sauce de Luna Arg.
261 I2 Saucedo Uru.
182 G6 Saucelle, Embalse de resr Port./Spain
242 G3 Saucillo Mex.
161 C9 Sauclières France
142 C2 Sauda Norway
121 M6 Saudakent Kazakh.
140 □D1 Sauðárkrókur Iceland
118 E5 Saudi Arabia country Asia
138 H2 Saue Estonia
168 I4 Sauensiek Ger.
157 P6 Sauer r. France
173 L6 Sauerlach Ger.
169 E8 Sauerland reg. Ger.
253 F3 Sauêruiná r. Brazil
92 E8 Saug r. Mindanao Phil.
138 H3 Sauga r. Estonia
226 H7 Saugatuck MI U.S.A.
235 I2 Saugatuck Reservoir CT U.S.A.
224 D4 Saugeen r. Ont. Can.
233 L6 Saugerties NY U.S.A.
149 L7 Saughall Cheshire, England U.K.
163 C7 Saugnacq-et-Muret France
161 D7 Saugues France
Sāūjbolāgh Iran see Mahābād
258 D2 Saujil Arg.
162 C4 Saujon France
138 I5 Saukas ezers l. Latvia
236 H3 Sauk Center MN U.S.A.
226 E6 Sauk City WI U.S.A.
251 H4 Saül Fr. Guiana
147 K4 Saul Northern Ireland U.K.
163 G10 Saula, Port de pass Spain
142 E2 Sauland Norway
161 F7 Saulce-sur-Rhône France
157 M7 Saulcy-sur-Meurthe France
172 G6 Sauldorf Ger.
162 G1 Sauldre r. France
172 H5 Saulgau Ger.
162 F3 Saulgé France
173 K6 Saulgrub Ger.
172 E2 Saulheim Ger.
160 E2 Saulieu France
138 H4 Saulkrasti Latvia
157 L6 Saulnois reg. France
161 G8 Sault France
163 C8 Sault-de-Navailles France
156 H5 Sault-lès-Rethel France
224 C4 Sault Sainte Marie Ont. Can.
227 J3 Sault Sainte Marie MI U.S.A.
157 L8 Saulx France
157 I6 Saulx r. France
157 M8 Saulxures-sur-Moselotte France
160 B3 Saulzais-le-Potier France
121 M1 Saumalkol' Kazakh.
85 N6 Saumarez Reef Coral Sea Is Terr. Austr.
91 H8 Saumlakki Maluku Indon.
163 B6 Saumos France
162 D1 Saumur France
159 K7 Saumurois reg. France
140 S3 Saunavaara Fin.
84 C2 Saunders, Mount hill N.T. Austr.
262 O1 Saunders Coast Antarctica
150 C4 Saundersfoot Pembrokeshire, Wales U.K.
259 E8 Saunders Island Falkland Is
249 G7 Saunders Island S. Sandwich Is
226 F9 Saunemin IL U.S.A.
97 D10 Saung Thai.
96 C2 Saungka Myanmar
233 J5 Sauquoit NY U.S.A.
121 U4 Saur, Khrebet mts China/Kazakh.
120 D5 Saura Kazakh.
163 H10 Saurat France
138 H5 Saurieši Latvia
209 D7 Saurimo Angola
191 N3 Sauris Italy
191 N3 Sauris, Lago di l. Italy
193 Q7 Sauro r. Italy
179 L6 Sausal hills Austria
240 J4 Sausalito CA U.S.A.
116 G9 Sausar Madh. Prad. India
161 G10 Sausset-les-Pins France
160 F2 Saussy France
93 B4 Sausu Sulawesi Indon.
209 C7 Sautar Angola
178 C5 Sautens Austria
163 D6 Sauternes France
247 □6 Sauteurs Grenada
158 H7 Sautron France
163 D9 Sauvagnon France
161 D9 Sauve France
161 C8 Sauveterre, Causse de plat. France
163 C9 Sauveterre-de-Béarn France
163 D6 Sauveterre-de-Guyenne France
163 I7 Sauveterre-de Rouergue France
163 G6 Sauveterre-la-Lémance France
162 H4 Sauviat-sur-Vige France
160 C3 Sauvigny-les-Bois France
141 Q6 Sauvo Fin.
164 K2 Sauwerd Neth.
160 C5 Sauxillanges France
260 A4 Sauzal Maule Chile
260 B4 Sauzal O'Higgins Chile
244 C1 Sauz de Arriba Mex.
163 G7 Sauzet France
162 E3 Sauzé-Vaussais France
158 E7 Sauzon France
167 J6 Sava r. Europe
242 □P10 Savá Hond.
195 N3 Sava Italy
179 K7 Sava Slovenia
234 B6 Savage MD U.S.A.
83 J9 Savage River Tas. Austr.
78 □2 Savai'i i. Samoa
135 H6 Savala r. Rus. Fed.
207 F5 Savalou Benin
Savanat Iran see Eşṭahbān
225 G3 Savane r. Que. Can.
213 G3 Savane Moz.
247 □9 Savaneta Aruba
236 J4 Savanna IL U.S.A.
231 G9 Savannah GA U.S.A.
236 H6 Savannah MO U.S.A.
232 C8 Savannah OH U.S.A.
237 K8 Savannah TN U.S.A.
231 G9 Savannah r. GA/SC U.S.A.
246 E1 Savannah Sound Eleuthera Bahamas
96 G6 Savannakhét Laos
246 □ Savanna-la-Mar Jamaica
226 D1 Savanne Ont. Can.
224 B3 Savant Lake Ont. Can.
224 B3 Savant Lake l. Ont. Can.
Savantvadi Mahar. India see Vadi
114 D5 Savanur Karnataka India
140 P5 Sävar Sweden
197 K4 Săvârşin Romania
140 P4 Sävast Sweden
199 I3 Savaştepe Turkey
179 N7 Savci Slovenia
207 F4 Savè Benin
163 G8 Save r. France
213 G4 Save Moz.
213 G4 Save r. Moz./Zimbabwe
122 D4 Sāveh Iran
195 L5 Savelli Italy
206 E4 Savelugu Ghana
191 K7 Savena r. Italy
158 H7 Savenay France
197 O3 Săveni Romania
163 H9 Saverdun France
251 G3 Saveretik Guyana
157 N6 Saverne France
140 T5 Saviaho Fin.
156 G7 Savières France
190 D6 Savigliano Italy
162 F5 Savignac-les-Églises France
193 O5 Savignano Irpino Italy
191 M7 Savignano sul Rubicone Italy
159 L5 Savigné-l'Évêque France
160 E5 Savigneux France
160 B2 Savigny-en-Sancerre France
160 F2 Savigny-lès-Beaune France
159 M6 Savigny-sur-Braye France
156 D6 Savigny-sur-Orge France
161 I7 Savines-le-Lac France
197 O4 Săvineşti Romania
139 O8 Savinichy Belarus
188 E2 Savinja r. Slovenia
120 B2 Savinka Rus. Fed.
139 Y5 Savino Rus. Fed.
134 L3 Savinobor Rus. Fed.
134 H3 Savinskiy Rus. Fed.
139 W6 Savinskoye Rus. Fed.
191 M7 Savio r. Italy
141 S6 Savitaipale Fin.
114 C3 Savitri r. India
143 N2 Sävja Sweden
199 L5 Savköy Turkey
196 H8 Šavnik Montenegro
78 □6 Savo i. Solomon Is
190 H2 Savognin Switz.
193 P6 Savoia di Lucania Italy
160 J6 Savoie dept France
160 I4 Savoie reg. France
156 H8 Savoisy France
190 E7 Savona Italy
190 E7 Savona prov. Italy
193 L5 Savone r. Italy
141 T6 Savonlinna Fin.
140 T5 Savonranta Fin.
220 A3 Savoonga AK U.S.A.
Savoy reg. France see Savoie
139 Q1 Savozero, Ozero l. Rus. Fed.
136 J5 Savran' Ukr.
136 J5 Savranka r. Ukr.
127 K3 Şavşat Turkey
143 K4 Sävsjö Sweden
93 B9 Savu i. Indon.
191 O5 Savudrija Croatia
188 D3 Savudrija, Rt pt Croatia
140 T3 Savukoski Fin.
127 J5 Savur Turkey
79 □7 Savusavu Vanua Levu Fiji
79 □7 Savusavu Bay Vanua Levu Fiji
Savu Sea Indon. see Sawu, Laut
212 E3 Savute r. Botswana
212 E3 Savuti Botswana
193 Q9 Savuto r. Italy
107 P1 Savvo-Borzya Rus. Fed.
137 L2 Savynky Ukr.
137 Q4 Savyntsi Ukr.
96 B4 Saw Myanmar
94 D5 Sawahlunto Sumatera Indon.
93 F5 Sawai, Teluk b. Seram Indon.
116 F7 Sawai Madhopur Rajasthan India
79 □7 Sawaleke Fiji
95 K5 Sawan Kalimantan Indon.
96 C1 Sawan Myanmar
96 D6 Sawankhalok Thai.
116 E7 Sawar Rajasthan India
105 M4 Sawara Japan
103 P9 Sawasaki-bana pt Japan
102 P9 Sawata Japan
239 K7 Sawatch Range mts CO U.S.A.
151 M4 Sawbridgeworth Hertfordshire, England U.K.
202 B2 Sawdā', Jabal as hills Libya
147 H3 Sawel Mountain hill Northern Ireland U.K.
203 F3 Sawhāj Sawhāj Egypt
97 D9 Sawi, Ao b. Thai.
175 L4 Sawin Pol.
206 E4 Sawla Ghana
213 F3 Sawmills Zimbabwe
96 C3 Sawn Yunnan China
125 M6 Şawqirah, Ghubbat b. Oman
125 M6 Şawqirah, Ra's c. Oman
Şawqirah Bay Oman see Şawqirah, Ghubbat
151 M3 Sawston Cambridgeshire, England U.K.
83 N4 Sawtell N.S.W. Austr.
226 C2 Sawtooth Mountains hills MN U.S.A.
238 G4 Sawtooth Range mts ID U.S.A.
238 D2 Sawtooth Range mts WA U.S.A.
151 L3 Sawtry Cambridgeshire, England U.K.
93 B9 Sawu Indon.
Sawu i. Indon. see Savu
93 B8 Sawu, Laut sea Indon.
187 D10 Sax Spain
146 □O1 Saxa Vord hill Scotland U.K.
85 H5 Saxby r. Qld Austr.
179 K3 Saxen Austria
149 P7 Saxilby Lincolnshire, England U.K.
222 D4 Saxman AK U.S.A.
151 O3 Saxmundham Suffolk, England U.K.
140 M4 Saxnäs Sweden
190 C3 Saxon Switz.
Saxony land Ger. see Sachsen
Saxony-Anhalt land Ger. see Sachsen-Anhalt
151 O2 Saxthorpe Norfolk, England U.K.
232 A12 Saxton KY U.S.A.
232 G8 Saxton PA U.S.A.
206 D3 Say Mali
207 F3 Say Niger
108 C2 Saya Sichuan China
104 E5 Saya Japan
128 D3 Şāyā Syria
Sayabouri Laos see Xaignabouli
93 F3 Sayafi i. Maluku Indon.
182 H6 Sayago reg. Spain
121 Q4 Sayak Kazakh.
114 F8 Sayalkudi Tamil Nadu India
207 I3 Sayam well Niger
105 J4 Sayama Japan
252 A2 Sayán Peru
93 F3 Sayang i. Papua Indon.
98 F1 Sayano-Shushenskoye Vodokhranilishche resr Rus. Fed.
Sayaq Kazakh. see Sayak
123 J2 Saýat Turkm.
183 O8 Sayatón Spain
243 N9 Sayaxché Guat.
171 H9 Sayda Ger.
Sayda Lebanon see Saïda
162 D6 Saye r. France
122 F6 Sāyen Iran
128 D1 Saygeçit Turkey
123 L4 Sayghān Afgh.
124 G7 Şayḩ well Yemen
125 M5 Şayḩ al Aḩmar reg. Oman
125 J8 Sayḩūt Yemen
129 H6 Şayıflı Azer.
108 D5 Sayingpan Yunnan China
120 B3 Saykhin Kazakh.
210 D2 Saylac Somalia
Saylan country Asia see Sri Lanka
234 E3 Saylorsburg PA U.S.A.
110 I2 Saylyugem, Khrebet mts Rus. Fed.
107 L4 Saynshand Mongolia
106 D3 Sayn-Ust Mongolia
Sayot Turkm. see Saýat
Say-Ötesh Kazakh. see Say-Utes
128 F5 Şayqal, Baḩr imp. l. Syria
Şayqyn Kazakh. see Saykhin
110 E4 Sayram Hu salt l. China
121 N6 Sayramskiy, Pik mt. Uzbek.
237 F8 Sayre OK U.S.A.
227 R8 Sayre PA U.S.A.
235 G4 Sayreville NJ U.S.A.
123 L3 Sayrob Uzbek.
106 D5 Saysu Xinjiang China
244 D6 Sayula Jalisco Mex.
245 M8 Sayula Veracruz Mex.
244 D6 Sayula, Laguna de imp. l. Mex.
125 I7 Say'ūn Yemen
120 E5 Say-Utes Kazakh.
235 I3 Sayville NY U.S.A.
222 E5 Sayward B.C. Can.
125 M6 Sayy well Oman
Sayyod Turkm. see Saýat
198 A2 Sazan i. Albania
176 D2 Sázava r. Czech Rep.
120 C4 Sazdy Kazakh.
134 L4 Sazhino Rus. Fed.
137 P3 Sazhnoye Rus. Fed.
217 □3b Sazile, Pointe pt Mayotte
123 O4 Sazin Pak.
139 S2 Sazonovo Rus. Fed.
Saztöbe Kazakh. see Sastobe
205 E3 Sbaa Alg.
205 H2 Sbeitla Tunisia
87 F12 Scaddan W.A. Austr.
158 D5 Scaër France
193 M3 Scafa Italy
149 K5 Scafell Pike hill England U.K.
234 B6 Scaggsville MD U.S.A.
194 G9 Scala, Monte della hill Italy
146 D10 Scalasaig Argyll and Bute, Scotland U.K.
149 Q5 Scalby North Yorkshire, England U.K.
149 K2 Scald Law hill Scotland U.K.
193 P8 Scalea Italy
193 P8 Scalea, Capo c. Italy
195 I7 Scaletta Zanclea Sicilia Italy
146 □N2 Scalloway Shetland, Scotland U.K.
Scalpaigh, Eilean i. Western Isles, Scotland U.K. see Scalpay
146 E8 Scalpay i. Highland, Scotland U.K.
146 C7 Scalpay i. Western Isles, Scotland U.K.
147 H2 Scalp Mountain hill Ireland
83 L9 Scamander Tas. Austr.
161 E9 Scamandre, Étang de lag. France
220 B3 Scammon Bay AK U.S.A.
149 P7 Scampton Lincolnshire, England U.K.
195 L5 Scandale Italy
193 K2 Scandarello, Lago di l. Italy
191 J6 Scandiano Italy
191 K8 Scandicci Italy
193 J3 Scandriglia Italy
Scania reg. Sweden see Skåne
193 L4 Scanno Italy
193 L4 Scanno, Lago di l. Italy
192 B7 Scano di Montiferro Sardegna Italy
192 G2 Scansano Italy
197 P6 Scânteia Romania
195 L3 Scanzano Jonico Italy
146 K5 Scapa Orkney, Scotland U.K.
146 J5 Scapa Flow inlet Scotland U.K.
146 I6 Scaraben hill Scotland U.K.
146 E10 Scarba i. Scotland U.K.
224 E5 Scarborough Ont. Can.
247 □5 Scarborough Trin. and Tob.
149 Q5 Scarborough North Yorkshire, England U.K.
90 E3 Scarborough Shoal sea feature S. China Sea
232 D11 Scarbro WV U.S.A.
191 M6 Scardovari Italy
81 G9 Scargill South I. N.Z.
147 B9 Scariff Island Ireland
146 C9 Scarinish Argyll and Bute, Scotland U.K.
149 L6 Scarisbrick Lancashire, England U.K.
234 D4 Scarlets Mill PA U.S.A.
192 F2 Scarlino Italy
146 B6 Scarp i. Scotland U.K.
Scarpanto i. Greece see Karpathos
156 F2 Scarpe r. France
191 K8 Scarperia Italy
147 E7 Scarriff Ireland
235 H2 Scarsdale NY U.S.A.
147 J4 Scarva Northern Ireland U.K.
225 J4 Scaterie Island N.S. Can.
194 B10 Scauri Sicilia Italy
146 D8 Scavaig, Loch b. Scotland U.K.
179 N6 Ščavnica r. Slovenia
94 G1 Scawfell Shoal sea feature S. China Sea
82 E5 Sceale Bay S.A. Austr.
188 F4 Šćedro i. Croatia
193 N3 Scerni Italy
157 K8 Scey-sur-Saône-et-St-Albin France
172 G2 Schaafheim Ger.
168 I1 Schaalby Ger.
168 K4 Schaale r. Ger.
168 K3 Schaalsee l. Ger.
168 K3 Schaalsee park Ger.
172 H7 Schaan Liechtenstein
164 I4 Schaarsbergen Neth.
168 I2 Schacht-Audorf Ger.
234 C4 Schaefferstown PA U.S.A.
165 F7 Schaerbeek Belgium
165 J7 Schaesberg Neth.
190 F1 Schaffhausen Switz.
190 F1 Schaffhausen canton Switz.
168 H1 Schafflund Ger.
168 H2 Schafstedt Ger.
173 K6 Schäftlarn Ger.
164 G3 Schagen Neth.
164 G3 Schagerbrug Neth.
164 I5 Schaijk Neth.
212 C5 Schakalskuppe Namibia
178 H3 Schalchen Austria
171 D10 Schalkau Ger.
164 J4 Schalkhaar Neth.
169 E8 Schalksmühle Ger.
172 D6 Schallstadt Ger.
190 G1 Schänis Switz.
122 I6 Schao watercourse Afgh./Iran
169 E6 Schapen Ger.
170 H1 Schaprode Ger.
168 K2 Scharbeutz Ger.
179 H2 Schardenberg Austria
179 H3 Schärding Austria
178 H5 Schareck mt. Austria
164 E5 Scharendijke Neth.
178 E4 Scharfreiter mt. Austria/Ger.
168 F3 Scharhörn sea feature Ger.
171 J6 Scharmützelsee l. Ger.
168 K4 Scharnebeck Ger.
164 I2 Scharnegoutum Neth.
178 D5 Scharnitz Austria
179 I4 Scharnstein Austria
168 E4 Scharrel (Oldenburg) Ger.
169 C10 Scharteberg hill Ger.
164 H3 Scharwoude Neth.
168 K2 Schashagen Ger.
179 O4 Schattendorf Austria
226 F7 Schaumburg IL U.S.A.
173 I2 Schebheim Ger.
173 M6 Schechen Ger.
169 I8 Scheden Ger.
164 K2 Scheemda Neth.
172 G5 Scheer Ger.
168 H4 Scheeßel Ger.
178 H4 Scheffau am Tennengebirge Austria
178 F4 Scheffau am Wilden Kaiser Austria
225 H2 Schefferville Nfld and Lab. Can.
172 G3 Schefflenz Ger.
191 N9 Scheggia e Pascelupo Italy
193 J2 Scheggino Italy
179 L3 Scheibbs Austria
179 N4 Scheiblingkirchen Austria
172 H6 Scheidegg Ger.
179 J5 Scheifling Austria
173 I2 Scheinfeld Ger.
172 H5 Schelklingen Ger.
241 R3 Schell Creek Range mts NV U.S.A.
165 F6 Schelle Belgium
169 J6 Schellerten Ger.
168 J2 Schellhorn Ger.
232 G8 Schellsburg PA U.S.A.
240 J3 Schellville CA U.S.A.
172 H5 Schemmerhofen Ger.
233 L6 Schenectady NY U.S.A.
168 H2 Schenefeld Schleswig-Holstein Ger.
168 I3 Schenefeld Schleswig-Holstein Ger.
179 J2 Schenkenfelden Austria
172 E5 Schenkenzell Ger.
169 I9 Schenklengsfeld Ger.
169 C7 Schermbeck Ger.
171 E6 Schermen Ger.
164 G3 Schermerhorn Neth.
169 K8 Schernberg Ger.
173 K4 Schernfeld Ger.
165 G7 Scherpenheuvel Belgium
164 H4 Scherpenzeel Neth.
237 F11 Schertz TX U.S.A.
157 N7 Scherwiller France
190 G1 Scherzingen Switz.
178 A5 Schesaplana mt. Austria/Switz.
173 K2 Scheßlitz Ger.
173 K5 Scheyern Ger.
191 M3 Schiara, Monte mt. Italy
193 M4 Schiavi di Abruzzo Italy
164 F5 Schiedam Neth.
169 H7 Schieder-Schwalenberg Ger.
179 J6 Schiefling am See Austria
146 H9 Schiehallion mt. Scotland U.K.
165 J9 Schieren Lux.
169 K7 Schierke Ger.
173 M4 Schierling Ger.
164 J2 Schiermonnikoog Neth.
164 J1 Schiermonnikoog i. Neth.
164 J1 Schiermonnikoog Nationaal Park nat. park Neth.
190 H2 Schiers Switz.
168 G3 Schiffdorf Ger.
172 E3 Schifferstadt Ger.
165 J9 Schifflange Lux.
172 C3 Schiffweiler Ger.
164 H5 Schijndel Neth.
165 G6 Schilde Belgium
168 K4 Schilde r. Ger.
164 K2 Schildmeer l. Neth.
170 H5 Schildow Ger.
164 K2 Schildwolde-Hellum Neth.
172 B2 Schillingen Ger.
173 I3 Schillingsfürst Ger.
190 I3 Schilpario Italy
172 E5 Schiltach Ger.
173 K5 Schiltberg Ger.
157 O6 Schiltigheim France
198 E4 Schimatari Greece
165 I7 Schinnen Neth.
165 I7 Schinveld Neth.
191 K4 Schio Italy
164 J4 Schipbeek r. Neth.
164 G4 Schiphol airport Neth.
171 I7 Schipkau Ger.
157 N7 Schirmeck France
173 M2 Schirmitz Ger.
171 F10 Schirnding Ger.
197 P3 Schitu Duca Romania
198 C6 Schiza i. Greece
171 F8 Schkeuditz Ger.
171 E8 Schkölen Ger.
171 G7 Schköna Ger.
171 E8 Schkopau Ger.
171 I7 Schlabendorf Ger.
169 K6 Schladen Ger.
179 I5 Schladming Austria
179 I5 Schladminger Tauern mts Austria
168 K3 Schlagsdorf Ger.
169 G7 Schlangen Ger.
169 F10 Schlangenbad Ger.
171 D6 Schlanstedt Ger.
173 M6 Schleching Ger.
178 E5 Schlegeisspeicher l. Austria
168 J1 Schlei r. Ger.
169 B9 Schleiden Ger.
171 K7 Schleife Ger.
179 N3 Schleinbach Austria
190 E1 Schleitheim Switz.
171 E9 Schleiz Ger.
171 G9 Schlema Ger.
171 I6 Schlepzig Ger.
Schlesien reg. Europe see Silesia
168 I1 Schleswig Ger.
168 I2 Schleswig-Holstein land Ger.
168 G2 Schleswig-Holsteinisches Wattenmeer, Nationalpark nat. park Ger.
171 G9 Schlettau Ger.
169 K9 Schleusingen Ger.
171 H7 Schlieben Ger.
172 D6 Schliengen Ger.
172 H6 Schlier Ger.
179 J4 Schlierbach Austria
190 E1 Schlieren Switz.
173 L6 Schliersee Ger.
173 L6 Schliersee l. Ger.
178 A5 Schlins Austria
178 E5 Schlitters Austria
169 I9 Schlitz Ger.
169 G7 Schloss Holte-Stukenbrock Ger.
190 D2 Schlosswil Switz.
169 K8 Schlotheim Ger.
172 E6 Schluchsee Ger.
172 E6 Schluchsee l. Ger.
157 N7 Schlucht, Col de la pass France
169 I10 Schlüchtern Ger.
Schlüsselburg Rus. Fed. see Shlissel'burg
173 J2 Schlüsselfeld Ger.
168 I3 Schmalfeld Ger.
169 F8 Schmallenberg Ger.
172 B3 Schmelz Ger.
173 M3 Schmidgaden Ger.
173 L3 Schmidmühlen Ger.
Schmidt Island Rus. Fed. see Shmidta, Ostrov
214 I4 Schmidtsdrif S. Africa
171 I9 Schmiedeberg Ger.
178 E5 Schmirn Austria
178 G5 Schmittenhöhe mt. Austria
170 J4 Schmölln Brandenburg Ger.
171 F9 Schmölln Thüringen Ger.
173 L2 Schnabelwaid Ger.
170 E4 Schnackenburg Ger.
173 M5 Schnaitsee Ger.

Sennybridge to Shargorod

386

150 E4 **Sennybridge** *Powys, Wales* U.K.
177 I3 **Senohrad** Slovakia
156 F7 **Sénonais** *reg.* France
156 B6 **Senonches** France
157 M7 **Senones** France
192 C8 **Senorbì** *Sardegna* Italy
163 H8 **Senouillac** France
161 C6 **Senouire** *r.* France
179 L7 **Senovo** Slovenia
179 J8 **Senožeče** Slovenia
215 L6 **Senqu** *r.* Lesotho
156 F7 **Sens** France
158 H5 **Sens-de-Bretagne** France
156 F3 **Sensée, Canal de la** *r.* France
242 □O11 **Sensuntepeque** El Salvador
196 I5 **Senta** *Vojvodina* Serbia
121 T3 **Sentas** Kazakh.
163 F10 **Sentein** France
163 G10 **Sentenac-d'Oust** France
186 G3 **Senterada** Spain
179 M6 **Šentilj** Slovenia
241 S9 **Sentinel** *AZ* U.S.A.
193 N4 **Sentinella, Colle della** *hill* Italy
222 F4 **Sentinel Peak** *B.C.* Can.
262 S1 **Sentinel Range** *mts* Antarctica
Sentinum Italy *see* Sassoferrato
244 B4 **Sentispac** Mex.
179 L8 **Šentjernej** Slovenia
179 L7 **Šentjur pri Celju** Slovenia
94 □ **Sentosa** *i.* Sing.
157 I5 **Senuc** France
95 L4 **Senyiur** *Kalimantan* Indon.
177 K4 **Sényő** Hungary
129 C5 **Senyurt** Turkey
127 J5 **Şenyurt** Turkey
103 I12 **Senzaki** Japan
103 J14 **Sen-zaki** *pt* Japan
171 I6 **Senzig** Ger.
Seo de Urgell Spain *see* **La Seu d'Urgell**
190 E1 **Seon** Switz.
116 I9 **Seonath** *r.* India
116 G6 **Seondha** *Madh. Prad.* India
116 G8 **Seoni** *Madh. Prad.* India
116 G8 **Seoni Chhapara** *Madh. Prad.* India
116 F8 **Seoni-Malwa** *Madh. Prad.* India
117 I9 **Seorinarayan** *Chhattisgarh* India
Seoul S. Korea *see* **Sŏul**
163 F7 **Séoune** *r.* France
95 K8 **Sepanjang** *i.* Indon.
80 G7 **Separation Point** *South I.* N.Z.
86 G7 **Separation Well** *W.A.* Austr.
122 B4 **Separ Shāhābād** Iran
95 L4 **Sepasu** *Kalimantan* Indon.
252 D1 **Sepatini** *r.* Brazil
95 I4 **Sepauk** *Kalimantan* Indon.
257 E5 **Sepetiba, Baía de** *b.* Brazil
91 J7 **Sepik** *r.* P.N.G.
95 M4 **Sepinang** *Kalimantan* Indon.
95 K3 **Seping** *r.* Malaysia
193 N5 **Sepino** Italy
101 E9 **Sep'o** N. Korea
174 F2 **Sępólno Krajeńskie** Pol.
174 E2 **Sępolno Wielkie** Pol.
117 O6 **Sepon** *Assam* India
253 F3 **Sepotuba** *r.* Brazil
117 N6 **Seppa** *Arun. Prad.* India
160 K1 **Seppois-le-Bas** France
197 J4 **Şepreuş** Romania
160 B3 **Septaine** *reg.* France
161 G10 **Septèmes-les-Vallons** France
156 E6 **Septeuil** France
163 H7 **Septfonds** France
225 H3 **Sept-Îles** *Que.* Can.
158 E4 **Sept-Îles, Réserve Naturelle des** *nature res.* France
225 H3 **Sept-Îles-Port-Cartier, Réserve Faunique de** *nature res. Que.* Can.
160 H4 **Septmoncel** France
182 H7 **Sepulcro-Hilario** Spain
183 M6 **Sepúlveda** Spain
212 D3 **Sepupa** Botswana
94 F7 **Seputih** *r.* Indon.
191 N3 **Sequals** Italy
231 E8 **Sequatchie** *r. TN* U.S.A.
261 I2 **Sequeira** Uru.
182 F4 **Sequeiros, Embalse de** *resr* Spain
182 H7 **Sequeros** Spain
183 J5 **Sequillo** *r.* Spain
240 N5 **Sequoia National Park** *CA* U.S.A.
124 D8 **Serae** *prov.* Eritrea
129 B6 **Şerafettin Dağları** *mts* Turkey
135 H6 **Serafimovich** Rus. Fed.
156 H4 **Seraincourt** France
165 I7 **Seraing** Belgium
Sêraitang *Qinghai* China *see* **Baima**
93 F5 **Seram** *i. Maluku* Indon.
93 G5 **Seram, Laut** *sea* Indon.
160 H5 **Séran** *r.* France
94 G8 **Serang** *Jawa* Indon.
94 □ **Serangoon, Pulau** *i.* Sing.
94 □ **Serangoon, Sungai** *r.* Sing.
94 □ **Serangoon Harbour** *b.* Sing.
161 D9 **Séranne, Montagne de la** *ridge* France
161 J9 **Séranon** France
94 □ **Serapong, Mount** *hill* Sing.
95 H3 **Serasan** *i.* Indon.
95 H3 **Serasan, Selat** *sea chan.* Indon.
190 I8 **Seravezza** Italy
93 A8 **Seraya** *i.* Indon.
95 H3 **Seraya** *i.* Indon.
94 □ **Seraya, Pulau** *reg.* Sing.
196 I6 **Serbia** *country* Europe
111 I10 **Sêrbug Co** *l. Xizang* China
136 G4 **Serbynivtsi** Ukr.
111 L11 **Sêrca** *Xizang* China
129 B6 **Serçeli Dağı** *mts* Turkey
117 N8 **Serchhip** *Mizoram* India
191 I8 **Serchio** *r.* Italy
122 G2 **Serdar** Turkm.
192 C9 **Serdiana** *Sardegna* Italy
Serdica Bulg. *see* **Sofiya**
210 D2 **Serdo** Eth.
135 I5 **Serdoba** *r.* Rus. Fed.
135 I5 **Serdobsk** Rus. Fed.
134 K3 **Serebryanka** Rus. Fed.
137 M8 **Serebryanka** Ukr.
121 T3 **Serebryansk** Kazakh.
137 L8 **Serebryanyye Prudy** Rus. Fed.
177 G3 **Sereď** Slovakia
139 S6 **Sereda** *Moskovskaya Oblast'* Rus. Fed.
139 X4 **Sereda** *Yaroslavskaya Oblast'* Rus. Fed.
139 S7 **Seredeyskiy** Rus. Fed.
138 L3 **Seredka** Rus. Fed.
139 W6 **Serednikovo** Rus. Fed.
136 J7 **Seredniy Kuyal'nyk** *r.* Ukr.
206 C4 **Sérédou** Guinea
137 N1 **Seredyna-Buda** Rus. Fed.
136 B5 **Seredyne** Ukr.
126 F4 **Şereflikoçhisar** Turkey
177 H4 **Seregélyes** Hungary
190 G4 **Seregno** Italy
162 G4 **Sérelhac** France
156 G8 **Serein** *r.* France
94 G3 **Seremban** Malaysia
185 I3 **Serena, Embalse de la** *resr* Spain
211 B5 **Serengeti National Park** Tanz.
211 B5 **Serengeti Plain** Tanz.
209 F8 **Serenje** Zambia
158 F6 **Sérent** France
210 B4 **Serere** Uganda
136 E5 **Seret** *r.* Ukr.
134 H5 **Serezha** *r.* Rus. Fed.
139 N5 **Serezha** *r.* Rus. Fed.
178 C5 **Serfaus** Austria
134 L4 **Ser'ga** Rus. Fed.
134 I5 **Sergach** Rus. Fed.
139 X5 **Sergeikha** Rus. Fed.
107 N2 **Sergelen** *Dornod* Mongolia
107 L3 **Sergelen** *Sühbaatar* Mongolia
197 P9 **Sergen** Turkey
121 M2 **Sergeyevka** *Akmolinskaya Oblast'* Kazakh.
121 L1 **Sergeyevka** *Severnyy Kazakhstan* Kazakh.
137 S3 **Sergeyevka** Rus. Fed.
156 F7 **Sergines** France
130 H3 **Sergino** Rus. Fed.
254 F4 **Sergipe** *state* Brazil
139 V5 **Sergiyev Posad** Rus. Fed.
135 J5 **Sergiyevsk** Rus. Fed.
Sergiyevskiy Rus. Fed. *see* **Fakel**
139 V8 **Sergiyevskoye** *Lipetskaya Oblast'* Rus. Fed.
139 U9 **Sergiyevskoye** *Orlovskaya Oblast'* Rus. Fed.
190 H5 **Sergnano** Italy
Sergo Ukr. *see* **Stakhanov**
129 I3 **Sergokala** Rus. Fed.
106 F8 **Serh** *Qinghai* China
123 J4 **Serhetabat** Turkm.
137 L3 **Serhiyivka** *Chernihivs'ka Oblast'* Ukr.
137 N7 **Serhiyivka** *Khersons'ka Oblast'* Ukr.
136 J6 **Serhiyivka** *Odes'ka Oblast'* Ukr.
136 J7 **Serhiyivka** *Odes'ka Oblast'* Ukr.
137 N2 **Serhiyivka** *Sums'ka Oblast'* Ukr.
95 K2 **Seria** Brunei
95 I4 **Serian** *Sarawak* Malaysia
190 H4 **Seriate** Italy
94 G7 **Seribu, Kepulauan** *is* Indon.
94 C3 **Seribudolok** *Sumatera* Indon.
156 C5 **Sérifontaine** France
198 F5 **Serifos** *Serifos* Greece
198 F5 **Serifos** *i.* Greece
198 F5 **Serifou, Steno** *sea chan.* Greece
161 C10 **Sérignan** France
161 F8 **Sérignan-du-Comtat** France
225 G2 **Sérigny** *r. Que.* Can.
225 G2 **Sérigny, Lac** *l. Que.* Can.
199 M6 **Serik** Turkey
110 C7 **Serikbuya** *Xinjiang* China
93 E5 **Serikkembelo** *Seram* Indon.
190 H4 **Serina** Italy
213 □J3 **Sèrinama** Madag.
251 I6 **Seringa, Serra da** *hills* Brazil
86 G2 **Seringapatam Reef** *W.A.* Austr.
199 K5 **Serinhisar** Turkey
129 C7 **Serinova** Turkey
128 E2 **Serinyol** Turkey
193 K5 **Serio** *r.* Italy
190 H5 **Serio, Parco del** *park* Italy
Sêrkang *Xizang* China *see* **Nyainrong**
136 E2 **Serkhiv** Ukr.
205 G5 **Serkout** *mt.* Alg.
Serle *atoll Arch. des Tuamotu* Fr. Polynesia *see* **Pukarua**
156 D7 **Sermaises** France
157 I6 **Sermaize-les-Bains** France
192 C3 **Sermano** *Corse* France
93 F8 **Sermata** *i. Maluku* Indon.
93 F8 **Sermata, Kepulauan** *is Maluku* Indon.
197 K9 **Sermenin** Macedonia
221 L2 **Sermersuaq** *glacier* Greenland
221 M2 **Sermersuaq** *glacier* Greenland
191 K6 **Sermide** Italy
160 C3 **Sermoise-sur-Loire** France
193 K4 **Sermoneta** Italy
160 F3 **Sermoyer** France
138 I4 **Sērmūkši** Latvia
182 F7 **Sernancelhe** Port.
177 L3 **Serne** *r.* Ukr.
175 K4 **Serniki** Pol.
171 F7 **Serno** Ger.
135 J5 **Sernovodsk** Rus. Fed.
134 J4 **Sernur** Rus. Fed.
136 F2 **Sernyky** Ukr.
Sernyy Zavod Turkm. *see* **Kükürtli**
174 G2 **Serock** *Kujawsko-Pomorskie* Pol.
175 J3 **Serock** *Mazowieckie* Pol.
Sero Colorado Aruba *see* **Seroe Colorado**
261 G3 **Serodino** Arg.
247 □9 **Seroe Colorado** Aruba
135 I7 **Seroglazka** Rus. Fed.
183 P5 **Serón** Spain
185 P6 **Serón de Nájima** Spain
183 L7 **Serones, Embalse de** *resr* Spain
212 D3 **Seronga** Botswana
164 E5 **Serooskerke** Neth.
186 F5 **Seròs** Spain
205 G4 **Serouenout** *well* Alg.
130 H4 **Serov** Rus. Fed.
212 E4 **Serowe** Botswana
184 D5 **Serpa** Port.
Serpa Pinto Angola *see* **Menongue**
225 G3 **Serpent** *r. Que.* Can.
206 C3 **Serpent, Vallée du** *watercourse* Mali
192 D9 **Serpentara, Isola** *i. Sardegna* Italy
87 C12 **Serpentine** *r. W.A.* Austr.
82 B3 **Serpentine Lakes** *salt flat SA* Austr.
249 M9 **Serpent's Mouth** *sea chan.* Trin. and Tob./Venez.
139 S7 **Serpeysk** Rus. Fed.
182 D8 **Serpins** Port.
187 E10 **Serpis** *r.* Spain
136 I7 **Serpneve** Ukr.
139 U7 **Serpukhov** Rus. Fed.
157 K8 **Serqueux** France
159 M3 **Serquigny** France
257 G4 **Serra** Brazil
192 A6 **Serra** *r.* Italy
187 E8 **Serra** Spain
193 O4 **Serracapriola** Italy
183 K6 **Serrada** Spain
257 E5 **Serra da Bocaina, Parque Nacional da** *nat. park* Brazil
256 D4 **Serra da Canastra, Parque Nacional da** *nat. park* Brazil
254 E4 **Serra da Capivara, Parque Nacional da** *nat. park* Brazil
252 D2 **Serra da Cutia, Parque Nacional** *nat. park* Brazil
182 E8 **Serra da Estrela, Parque Natural da** *nature res.* Port.
254 C5 **Serra da Mesa, Represa** *resr* Brazil
251 F4 **Serra da Mociade, Parque Nacional da** *nat. park* Brazil
254 E4 **Serra das Confusões, Parque Nacional da** *nat. park* Brazil
191 O8 **Serra de' Conti** Italy
193 Q6 **Serra del Corvo, Lago di** *l.* Italy
180 C3 **Serra de São Mamede, Parque Natural da** *nature res.* Port.
194 F9 **Serradifalco** *Sicilia* Italy
192 B4 **Serra-di-Ferro** *Corse* France
182 H9 **Serradilla** Spain
182 H7 **Serradilla del Arroyo** Spain
252 B2 **Serra do Divisor, Parque Nacional da** *nat. park* Brazil
251 H4 **Serra do Navio** Brazil
257 G2 **Serra dos Aimorés** Brazil
256 D3 **Serra do Salitre** Brazil
Serrai Greece *see* **Serres**
192 B9 **Serramanna** *Sardegna* Italy
191 J7 **Serramazzoni** Italy
256 D4 **Serrana** Brazil
246 C6 **Serrana Bank** *sea feature* Caribbean Sea
251 E4 **Serrania de la Neblina, Parque Nacional** *nat. park* Venez.
246 D6 **Serranilla Bank** *sea feature* Caribbean Sea
183 K8 **Serranillos** Spain
261 F4 **Serrano** Arg.
259 B8 **Serrano** *i.* Chile
256 A3 **Serranópolis** Brazil
Serrapinha, Ilha *i.* Brazil *see* **Queimada, Ilha**
190 F6 **Serra Riccò** Italy
195 K6 **Serra San Bruno** Italy
191 O9 **Serra San Quirico** Italy
182 C9 **Serras de Aire e Candeeiros, Parque Natural das** *nature res.* Port.
254 F3 **Serra Talhada** Brazil
191 M8 **Serravalle** San Marino
193 J1 **Serravalle di Chienti** Italy
190 F6 **Serravalle Scrivia** Italy
156 F4 **Serre** *r.* France
193 O6 **Serre** Italy
160 H2 **Serre, Massif de la** *hills* France
161 J7 **Serre-Chevalier** France
182 I9 **Serrejón** Spain
192 B9 **Serrenti** *Sardegna* Italy
161 I8 **Serre-Ponçon, Lac de** *l.* France
Serrera, Pic de la *mt.* Andorra *see* **Serrère, Pic de**
186 I2 **Serrère, Pic de** *mt.* Andorra
161 H8 **Serres** France
198 E1 **Serres** Greece
160 D9 **Serres-Castet** France
216 □1a **Serreta** *Terceira* Azores
260 E2 **Serrezuela** Arg.
192 C8 **Serri** *Sardegna* Italy
192 B3 **Serriera** *Corse* France
160 G5 **Serrières-de-Briord** France
161 F6 **Serrières** France
172 B2 **Serrig** Ger.
254 F4 **Serrinha** Brazil
255 F4 **Serrita** Brazil
257 F3 **Sêrro** Brazil
183 M7 **Serrota** *mt.* Spain
162 E4 **Sers** France
189 B7 **Sers** Tunisia
195 L5 **Sersale** Italy
162 D5 **Sersa** Spain
182 D8 **Sertã** Port.
254 F4 **Sertânia** Brazil
256 B5 **Sertanópolis** Brazil
256 A3 **Sertão de Camapuã** *reg.* Brazil
256 D4 **Sertãozinho** Brazil
108 C2 **Sêrtar** *Sichuan* China
128 B2 **Sertavul Geçidi** *pass* Turkey
207 H5 **Serti** Nigeria
139 N1 **Sertolovo** Rus. Fed.
93 G7 **Serua** *vol. Maluku* Indon.
94 C2 **Seruai** *Sumatera* Indon.
95 H5 **Serui** *Papua* Indon.
213 E4 **Serule** Botswana
95 H5 **Seruna** *i.* Indon.
95 J6 **Seruyan** *r.* Indon.
138 K7 **Servach** *r.* Belarus
157 M8 **Servance** France
161 C7 **Serverette** France
198 D2 **Servia** Greece
161 C10 **Servian** France
193 K1 **Servigliano** Italy
158 I5 **Servon-sur-Vilaine** France
160 J5 **Servoz** France
93 E8 **Serwaru** *Maluku* Indon.
109 D9 **Sêrwolungwa** *Qinghai* China
108 C3 **Sêrxü** *Sichuan* China
156 H4 **Sery** France
Serytisi *i. Limnos* Greece *see* **Sideritis**
186 E4 **Sesa** Spain
95 L3 **Sesayap** *Kalimantan* Indon.
95 L3 **Sesayap** *r.* Indon.
208 E4 **Sese** Dem. Rep. Congo
203 F4 **Sese** Sudan
224 B3 **Seseganaga Lake** *Ont.* Can.
227 N1 **Sesekinika** *Ont.* Can.
Sesel *country* Indian Ocean *see* **Seychelles**
183 M8 **Seseña** Spain
93 E4 **Sesepe** *Maluku* Indon.
212 B3 **Sesfontein** Namibia
114 F5 **Seshachalam Hills** India
139 Q8 **Seshcha** Rus. Fed.
209 E9 **Sesheke** Zambia
190 F5 **Sesia** *r.* Italy
209 E9 **Sesimbra** Port.
140 Q4 **Seskar Furö** *i.* Sweden
199 I6 **Seskilo** *i.* Greece
183 P4 **Sesma** Spain
102 □1 **Sesoko** *Okinawa* Japan
102 □1 **Sesoko-jima** *i. Okinawa* Japan
114 B6 **Sesostris Bank** *sea feature* India
187 H10 **S'Espalmador** *i.* Spain
187 H10 **S'Espardell** *i.* Spain
209 D8 **Sessa** Angola
193 L5 **Sessa Aurunca** Italy
193 O7 **Sessa Cilento** Italy
187 L9 **Ses Salines** Spain
190 E4 **Sessera** *r.* Italy
190 E4 **Seßlach** Ger.
190 H7 **Sesta Godano** Italy
187 K9 **S'Estanyol de Migjorn** Spain
183 N3 **Sestao** Spain
191 M8 **Sestino** Italy
191 M2 **Sesto** Italy
190 H5 **Sesto al Reghena** Italy
190 F4 **Sesto Calende** Italy
193 M5 **Sesto Campano** Italy
191 K8 **Sesto Fiorentino** Italy
175 L1 **Šėtokai** Lith.
193 O1 **Sestola** Italy
190 G4 **Sesto San Giovanni** Italy
139 U5 **Sestra** *r.* Rus. Fed.
190 B6 **Sestriere** Italy
190 G5 **Sestri Levante** Italy
139 M1 **Sestroretsk** Rus. Fed.
188 E3 **Sestrunj** *i.* Croatia
192 C9 **Sestu** *Sardegna* Italy
138 F6 **Šešupė** *r.* Lith./Rus. Fed.
188 F3 **Sesvete** Croatia
186 G4 **Set** France
96 H7 **Set, Phou** *mt.* Laos
102 F6 **Setana** Japan
235 I3 **Setauket** *NY* U.S.A.
161 D10 **Sète** France
258 D3 **Sete Barras** Brazil
136 I6 **Šetekšna** *r.* Lith.
257 E3 **Sete Lagoas** Brazil
185 I7 **Setenil** Spain
140 O2 **Setermoen** Norway
140 O2 **Setesdal** *val.* Norway
102 □G18 **Setouchi** *Nansei-shotō* Japan
168 J3 **Seth** Ger.
Seti Georgia *see* **Mestia**
116 H5 **Seti** *r.* Nepal
116 F5 **Seti** *r.* Nepal
Setia Italy *see* **Sezze**
205 G1 **Sétif** Alg.
183 Q7 **Setiles** Spain
203 G6 **Setit** *r.* Africa
104 F5 **Seto** Japan
103 F4 **Seto-naikai** *sea* Japan
104 A7 **Seto-naikai Kokuritsu-kōen** *nat. park* Japan
96 B6 **Setsan** Myanmar
191 K7 **Setta** *r.* Italy
205 E2 **Settat** Morocco
208 B5 **Setté Cama** Gabon
190 E5 **Sette Fratelli, Monte dei** *mt. Sardegna* Italy
190 E7 **Settepani, Monte** *mt.* Italy
190 D5 **Settimo Torinese** Italy
190 D4 **Settimo Vittone** Italy
149 M5 **Settle** *North Yorkshire, England* U.K.
84 G4 **Settlement Creek** *r. Qld* Austr.
216 □2c **Settlement of Edinburgh** *Tristan da Cunha* S. Atlantic Ocean
160 E2 **Settons, Lac des** *l.* France
257 F2 **Setúbal** *r.* Brazil
184 B3 **Setúbal** Port.
184 B3 **Setúbal** *admin. dist.* Port.
184 B3 **Setúbal, Baía de** *b.* Port.
261 G2 **Setúbal, Laguna** *l.* Arg.
257 F2 **Setubinha** Brazil
Seu *i.* Vanuatu *see* **Hiu**
173 L3 **Seubersdorf in der Oberpfalz** Ger.
162 C4 **Seudre** *r.* France
162 C4 **Seugne** *r.* France
192 C8 **Seui** *Sardegna* Italy
156 J7 **Seuil-d'Argonne** France
223 M5 **Seul, Lac** *l. Ont.* Can.
226 I4 **Seul Choix Point** *MI* U.S.A.
94 A2 **Seulimeum** *Sumatera* Indon.
169 J7 **Seulingen** Ger.
159 K3 **Seulles** *r.* France
192 C8 **Seulo** *Sardegna* Italy
160 G3 **Seurre** France
137 N1 **Sev** *r.* Rus. Fed.
186 J4 **Seva** Spain
129 F5 **Sevan** Armenia
Sevan, Lake Armenia *see* **Sevana Lich**
Sevan, Ozero *l.* Armenia *see* **Sevana Lich**
129 G5 **Sevana Lich** *l.* Armenia
252 D4 **Sevaruyo** Bol.
137 M9 **Sevastopol'** Ukr.
149 P5 **Seven** *r. England* U.K.
147 E9 **Seven Heads** Ireland
Seven Islands *Que.* Can. *see* **Sept-Îles**
225 I1 **Seven Islands Bay** *Nfld and Lab.* Can.
87 D7 **Seven Mile Creek** *r. W.A.* Austr.
215 O5 **Sevenoaks** S. Africa
151 M5 **Sevenoaks** *Kent, England* U.K.
150 E4 **Seven Sisters** *Neath Port Talbot, Wales* U.K.
150 □ **Seven Stones** *is England* U.K.
85 M8 **Seventeen Seventy** *Qld* Austr.
Seventy Mile House *B.C.* Can. *see* **70 Mile House**
165 J6 **Sevenum** Neth.
234 B5 **Seven Valleys** *PA* U.S.A.
182 E6 **Sever** Port.
161 C8 **Sévérac-le-Château** France
162 D7 **Sever do Vouga** Port.
176 F6 **Severin** Croatia
255 B9 **Severino Ribeiro** Brazil
139 V6 **Severka** *r.* Rus. Fed.
83 M3 **Severn** *r. N.S.W.* Austr.
224 C2 **Severn** *r. Ont.* Can.
81 H9 **Severn** *mt. South I.* N.Z.
214 G2 **Severn** S. Africa
150 H4 **Severn** *r. England/Wales* U.K.
234 B6 **Severn** *MD* U.S.A.
234 H12 **Severn** *NC* U.S.A.
234 C7 **Severn** *r. MD* U.S.A.
234 B6 **Severna Park** *MD* U.S.A.
134 H2 **Severnaya Dvina** *r.* Rus. Fed.
134 L3 **Severnaya Mylva** *r.* Rus. Fed.
129 F2 **Severnaya Osetiya-Alaniya, Respublika** *aut. rep.* Rus. Fed.
130 H3 **Severnaya Sos'va** *r.* Rus. Fed.
131 L1 **Severnaya Zemlya** *is* Rus. Fed.
150 G4 **Severn Beach** *South Gloucestershire, England* U.K.
224 B2 **Severn Lake** *Ont.* Can.
135 K5 **Severnoye** Rus. Fed.
224 B2 **Severn River Provincial Park** *Ont.* Can.
137 P3 **Severnyy** *Belgorodskaya Oblast'* Rus. Fed.
139 U5 **Severnyy** *Moskovskaya Oblast'* Rus. Fed.
134 J1 **Severnyy** *Nenetskiy Avtonomnyy Okrug* Rus. Fed.
134 N2 **Severnyy** *Respublika Komi* Rus. Fed.
175 H1 **Severnyy, Mys** *pt* Rus. Fed.
100 L1 **Severnyy, Zaliv** *b.* Rus. Fed.
131 S3 **Severnyy Anyuyskiy Khrebet** *mts* Rus. Fed.
122 E2 **Severnyy Chink Ustyurta** *esc.* Kazakh.
138 L1 **Severnyy Berezovyy, Ostrov** *i.* Rus. Fed.
120 G4 **Severnyy Chink Ustyurta** *esc.* Kazakh.
121 M1 **Severnyy Kazakhstan** *admin. div.* Kazakh.
134 K4 **Severnyy Kommunar** Rus. Fed.
129 C2 **Severnyy Priyut** Rus. Fed.
Severnyy Suchan Rus. Fed. *see* **Uglekamensk**
134 L3 **Severnyy Ural** *mts* Rus. Fed.
99 I1 **Severobaykal'sk** Rus. Fed.
131 M4 **Severo-Baykal'skoye Nagor'ye** *mts* Rus. Fed.
110 H1 **Severo-Chuyskiy Khrebet** *mts* Rus. Fed.
Severodonetsk Ukr. *see* **Syeverodonets'k**
134 G2 **Severodvinsk** Rus. Fed.
Severo-Kazakhstanskaya Oblast' *admin. div.* Kazakh. *see* **Severnyy Kazakhstan**
131 Q4 **Severo-Kuril'sk** *Kuril'skiye O-va* Rus. Fed.
140 V2 **Severomorsk** Rus. Fed.
134 G3 **Severoonezhsk** Rus. Fed.
Severo-Osetinskaya A.S.S.R. *aut. rep.* Rus. Fed. *see* **Severnaya Osetiya-Alaniya, Respublika**
129 F3 **Severo-Osetinskiy Zapovednik** *nature res.* Rus. Fed.
100 M2 **Severo-Sakhalinskaya Ravnina** *plain* Rus. Fed.
131 L2 **Severo-Sibirskaya Nizmennost'** *lowland* Rus. Fed.
134 L3 **Severoural'sk** Rus. Fed.
131 K3 **Severo-Yeniseyskiy** Rus. Fed.
139 V7 **Severo-Zadonsk** Rus. Fed.
Seversk Ukr. *see* **Sivers'k**
135 G7 **Severskaya** Rus. Fed.
137 S7 **Severskiy Donets** *r.* Rus. Fed.
135 H7 **Severskiy Donets** *r.* Ukr. *see* **Sivers'kyy Donets'**
158 I3 **Sèves** *r.* France
155 I4 **Seveso** Italy
190 G5 **Seveso** *r.* Italy
179 K1 **Ševětín** Czech Rep.
140 T2 **Sevettijärvi** Fin.
160 J5 **Sevi, Col de** *pass* France
241 T3 **Sevier** *UT* U.S.A.
241 T2 **Sevier** *r. UT* U.S.A.
241 U2 **Sevier Bridge Reservoir** *UT* U.S.A.
241 T2 **Sevier Desert** *UT* U.S.A.
241 S3 **Sevier Lake** *UT* U.S.A.
231 F8 **Sevierville** *TN* U.S.A.
158 G5 **Sévignac** France
163 D9 **Sévignacq** France
156 H4 **Sévigny-Waleppe** France
250 C3 **Sevilla** Col.
184 H6 **Sevilla** Spain
184 H5 **Sevilla** *prov.* Spain
183 L8 **Sevilla la Nueva** Spain
Sevilla Spain *see* **Seville**
183 K9 **Sevilleja de la Jara** Spain
261 I5 **Sevingé** Arg.
197 N7 **Sevlievo** Bulg.
Sevlyush Ukr. *see* **Vynohradiv**
188 E2 **Sevnica** Slovenia
185 K6 **Sevojno** Serbia
162 A1 **Sèvre Nantaise** *r.* France
162 B3 **Sèvre Niortaise** *r.* France
160 I5 **Sévrier** France
160 G3 **Sevron** *r.* France
139 P8 **Sevsk** Rus. Fed.
116 E3 **Sêwa** *Xizang* China *see* **Sêwa**
111 I10 **Sêwa** *Xizang* China
114 D3 **Sewand** *r.* India
116 E5 **Sewani** *Haryana* India
220 D3 **Seward** *AK* U.S.A.
226 E7 **Seward** *IL* U.S.A.
225 D5 **Seward** *NE* U.S.A.
232 F8 **Seward** *PA* U.S.A.
262 T2 **Seward Mountains** Antarctica
220 B3 **Seward Peninsula** *AK* U.S.A.
260 B4 **Sewell** Chile
234 E5 **Sewell** *NJ* U.S.A.
222 C4 **Sewell Inlet** *B.C.* Can.
172 D5 **Sexau** Ger.
Sexi Spain *see* **Almuñécar**
222 G4 **Sexsmith** *Alta* Can.
242 G4 **Sextín** Mex.
242 G5 **Sextín** *r.* Mex.
105 J5 **Seya** Japan
Seyah Band Koh *mts* Afgh.
123 J5 **Seyakha** Rus. Fed.
130 I2 **Seybaplaya** Mex.
243 N8 **Seychelles** *country* Indian Ocean
217 □2 **Seyches** France
163 E6 **Seyda** Ger.
171 G7 **Seydi** *r.* Turkey
199 M3 **Seydi** Turkm.
123 J2 **Seydişehir** Turkey
126 E5 **Seyðisfjörður** Iceland
140 □F1 **Seye** *r.* France
163 H8 **Seyfe Gölü** *salt flat* Turkey
126 G8 **Seyhan** Turkey *see* **Adana**
126 G5 **Seyhan** *r.* Turkey
128 D1 **Seyhan Barajı** *resr* Turkey
129 H5 **Seyidlär** Azer.
199 L3 **Seyitgazi** Turkey
199 K3 **Seyitömer** Turkey
137 Q2 **Seym** Rus. Fed.
137 N2 **Seym** *r.* Rus. Fed./Ukr.
131 Q3 **Seymchan** Rus. Fed.
199 J1 **Seymen** Turkey
83 J7 **Seymour** *Vic.* Austr.
215 K8 **Seymour** S. Africa
235 I2 **Seymour** *CT* U.S.A.
230 E6 **Seymour** *IN* U.S.A.
237 F9 **Seymour** *TX* U.S.A.
222 E5 **Seymour Inlet** *B.C.* Can.
84 D8 **Seymour Range** *mts N.T.* Austr.
161 I8 **Seyne** France
161 E8 **Seynes** France
160 I5 **Seynod** France
Seypan *i.* N. Mariana Is *see* **Saipan**
160 H5 **Seyssel** France
163 G8 **Seysses** France
160 F5 **Seysseuel** France
160 H6 **Seyssins** France
197 P9 **Seytan** *r.* Turkey
123 M4 **Seyyedābād** Afgh.
188 D3 **Sežana** Slovenia
156 G6 **Sézanne** France
215 O6 **Sezela** S. Africa
139 R6 **Sezha** *r.* Rus. Fed.
176 D2 **Sezimovo Ústí** Czech Rep.
193 K5 **Sezze** Italy
198 G7 **Sfaka** *Kriti* Greece
197 N5 **Sfântu Gheorghe** *Covasna* Romania
197 R6 **Sfântu Gheorghe** *Tulcea* Romania
197 R5 **Sfântu Gheorghe, Braţul** *watercourse* Romania
197 R6 **Sfântu Gheorghe-Palade-Perişor** *nature res.* Romania
205 H2 **Sfax** Tunisia
198 D2 **Sfendami** Greece
192 D8 **Sferracavallo, Capo** *c. Sardegna* Italy
198 D2 **Sfikias, Limni** *resr* Greece
Sfintu Gheorghe Romania *see* **Sfântu Gheorghe**
Sgiersch Pol. *see* **Zgierz**
146 D6 **Sgiogarstaigh** *Western Isles, Scotland* U.K.
146 F7 **Sgurr Ruadh** *hill Scotland* U.K.
164 G4 **'s-Gravendeel** Neth.
164 F4 **'s-Gravenhage** Neth.
165 E6 **'s-Gravenpolder** Neth.
165 I7 **'s-Gravenvoeren** Belgium
164 F5 **'s-Gravenzande** Neth.
193 K4 **Sgurgola** Italy
146 F8 **Sgurr a' Chaorachain** *mt. Scotland* U.K.
146 D8 **Sgurr a' Choire Ghlais** *mt. Scotland* U.K.
146 G8 **Sgurr Alasdair** *hill Scotland* U.K.
146 G7 **Sgurr a' Mhuilinn** *hill Scotland* U.K.
146 F9 **Sgurr Dhomhnuill** *hill Scotland* U.K.
146 F8 **Sgurr Fhuaran** *mt. Scotland* U.K.
146 E7 **Sgurr Mhòr** *hill Scotland* U.K.
146 F7 **Sgurr Mòr** *mt. Scotland* U.K.
146 F8 **Sgurr na Ciche** *mt. Scotland* U.K.
129 G2 **Shaami-Yurt** Rus. Fed.
107 K9 **Shaanxi** *prov.* China
Shaartuz Tajik. *see* **Shahrtuz**
125 I3 **Sha'b, Jabal ash** *hills* Saudi Arabia
Shaba *prov.* Dem. Rep. Congo *see* **Katanga**
123 L7 **Shaban** Pak.
Shabani Zimbabwe *see* **Zvishavane**
137 R9 **Shabanovskoye** Rus. Fed.
Shabbaz Uzbek. *see* **Beruniy**
210 E4 **Shabeellaha Dhexe** *admin. reg.* Somalia
210 D4 **Shabeellaha Hoose** *admin. reg.* Somalia
135 G7 **Shabel'sk** Rus. Fed.
122 A2 **Shabestar** Iran
197 Q7 **Shabla** Bulg.
197 Q7 **Shabla, Nos** *pt* Bulg.
139 S9 **Shablykino** Rus. Fed.
225 H2 **Shabogamo Lake** *Nfld and Lab.* Can.
208 E5 **Shabunda** Dem. Rep. Congo
124 H8 **Shabwah** Yemen
124 H8 **Shabwah** *governorate* Yemen
110 C7 **Shache** *Xinjiang* China
Shacheng *Hebei* China *see* **Huailai**
263 L1 **Shackleton Coast** Antarctica
263 M1 **Shackleton Glacier** Antarctica
263 G2 **Shackleton Ice Shelf** Antarctica
262 V1 **Shackleton Range** *mts* Antarctica
124 E5 **Shadād** Saudi Arabia
123 L8 **Shadadkot** Pak.
108 G4 **Shadaogou** *Hubei* China
96 C5 **Shadaw** Myanmar
232 C9 **Shade** *OH* U.S.A.
122 C6 **Shādegān** Iran
234 D2 **Shades Glen** *PA* U.S.A.
122 L7 **Shadihar** Pak.
122 E7 **Shādkām** *watercourse* Iran
130 H4 **Shadrinsk** Rus. Fed.
Shadwan Island Egypt *see* **Shākir, Jazīrat**
232 G10 **Shadwell** *VA* U.S.A.
235 C4 **Shady Grove** *OR* U.S.A.
234 B7 **Shady Side** *MD* U.S.A.
232 D11 **Shady Spring** *WV* U.S.A.
226 H9 **Shafer, Lake** *IN* U.S.A.
263 K2 **Shafer Peak** Antarctica
122 G3 **Shafi'abad** Iran
Shafirkan Uzbek. *see* **Shofirkon**
120 F1 **Shafranovo** Rus. Fed.
Shafrikan Uzbek. *see* **Shofirkon**
240 M6 **Shafter** *CA* U.S.A.
150 H5 **Shaftesbury** *Dorset, England* U.K.
81 E12 **Shag** *r. South I.* N.Z.
224 C2 **Shagamu** *r. Ont.* Can.
207 F5 **Shagamu** Nigeria
120 G4 **Shagan** *watercourse* Kazakh.
121 R2 **Shagan** *watercourse* Kazakh.
107 L7 **Shagedu** *Nei Mongol* China
220 C3 **Shageluk** *AK* U.S.A.
124 C2 **Shaghab** *oasis* Saudi Arabia
Shaghan Kazakh. *see* **Chagan**
Shaghyray Üstirti *plat.* Kazakh. *see* **Shagyray, Plato**
Shag'irlik Uzbek.
120 H6 **Shaglyteniz, Ozero** *l.* Kazakh.
121 N1 **Shag Point** *South I.* N.Z.
81 E12 **Shag Rocks** *is* S. Georgia
249 G7 **Shagyray, Plato** *plat.* Kazakh.
120 G4 **Shahabad** *Andhra Prad.* India
114 F4 **Shahabad** *Haryana* India
116 E3 **Shahabad** *Karnataka* India
114 E4 **Shahabad** *Rajasthan* India
116 F7 **Shahabad** *Uttar Prad.* India
116 H6 **Shāhābād** *Āzarbāyjān-e Gharbī* Iran *see* **Showt**
122 G7 **Shāhābād** *Kermān* Iran
Shāhābād *Kermānshāh* Iran *see* **Eslāmābād-e Gharb**
116 E9 **Shahada** *Mahar.* India
94 D3 **Shah Alam** Malaysia
123 J8 **Shahana** Pak.
114 D5 **Shahapur** *Karnataka* India
114 D5 **Shahapur** *Mahar.* India
123 M5 **Shahbā'** Syria
128 E6 **Shahbandar** Pak.
123 L9 **Shahbanu Farah Dam** Iran
123 K8 **Shahbaz Kalat** Pak.
117 M8 **Shahbazpur** *sea chan.* Bangl.
123 L9 **Shahbeg** Pak.
123 L9 **Shah Bilawal** Pak.
122 G6 **Shahdād** Iran
123 M9 **Shahdadpur** Pak.
116 H8 **Shahdol** *Madh. Prad.* India
123 P6 **Shahdura** Pak.
108 G3 **Shahe** *Chongqing* China
107 P8 **Shahe** *Shandong* China
107 N8 **Sha He** *r.* China
Shahe *Jiangxi* China *see* **Jiujiang**
Shahepu *Gansu* China *see* **Linze**
Shahezhen *Gansu* China *see* **Linze**
Shahezhen *Jiangxi* China *see* **Jiujiang**
123 L4 **Shah Fuladi** *mt.* Afgh.
117 I6 **Shahganj** *Uttar Prad.* India
116 G7 **Shahgarh** *Madh. Prad.* India
116 B6 **Shahgarh** *Rajasthan* India
202 D1 **Shaḥḥāt** Libya
123 O6 **Shah Hussain** Pak.
123 J9 **Shahid, Ras** *pt* Pak.
Shāhīn Dezh Iran *see* **Sa'īndezh**
123 K7 **Shah Ismail** Afgh.
116 F5 **Shahjahanpur** *Rajasthan* India
116 G6 **Shahjahanpur** *Uttar Prad.* India
122 H3 **Shāh Jehān, Kūh-e** *mts* Iran
123 L5 **Shāh Jūy** Afgh.
122 H6 **Shāh Kūh** *mt.* Iran
127 P6 **Shahmirzād** Iran
107 Q6 **Shahmirzad** *Liaoning* China
Shāh Pasand Iran *see* **Āzād Shahr**
114 E4 **Shahpur** *Karnataka* India
116 F8 **Shahpur** *Madh. Prad.* India
116 F9 **Shahpur** *Madh. Prad.* India
116 G8 **Shahpur** *Madh. Prad.* India
116 H8 **Shahpur** *Madh. Prad.* India
Shāhpūr Iran *see* **Salmās**
123 M7 **Shahpur** *Balochistan* Pak.
123 O5 **Shahpur** *Punjab* Pak.
123 M8 **Shahpur** *Sindh* Pak.
116 G8 **Shahpura** *Madh. Prad.* India
116 H8 **Shahpura** *Madh. Prad.* India
116 E7 **Shahpura** *Rajasthan* India
125 J6 **Shahr** *oasis* Saudi Arabia
123 K4 **Shahrak** Afgh.
122 F7 **Shāhrakht** Iran
124 F6 **Shahrān** *reg.* Saudi Arabia
122 D5 **Shahr-e Bābak** Iran
122 F6 **Shahr-e Kord** Iran
122 I4 **Shahr-e Now** Iran
123 L6 **Shahr-e Şafā** Afgh.
122 D5 **Shahrezā** Iran
123 L6 **Shahrig** Pak.
121 O7 **Shahrihon** Uzbek.
121 L8 **Shahrisabz** Uzbek.
123 M2 **Shahriston** Tajik.
123 O2 **Shahr Rey** Iran
123 N7 **Shahr Sultan** Pak.
123 M3 **Shahrtuz** Tajik.
Shāhrūd Iran *see* **Emāmrūd**
122 C3 **Shāhrūd, Rūdkhāneh-ye** *r.* Iran
122 F4 **Shahrud Bustam** *reg.* Iran
122 H7 **Shāh Savārān, Kūh-e** *mts* Iran
Shāh Taqī Iran *see* **Emām Taqī**
123 K7 **Shah Umar** Pak.
123 M6 **Shaighalu** Pak.
123 M3 **Shaikh Husain** *mt.* Pak.
128 F4 **Sha'īr, Jabal** *mts* Syria
128 C9 **Sha'īrah, Jabal** *mt.* Egypt
117 M7 **Shaistaganj** Bangl.
125 I3 **Shaj'ah, Jabal** *hill* Saudi Arabia
116 F8 **Shajapur** *Madh. Prad.* India
101 D8 **Shajianzi** *Liaoning* China
104 C7 **Shakaga-dake** *mt.* Japan
122 B3 **Shakar Bolāghī** Iran
215 P5 **Shakaskraal** S. Africa
215 P5 **Shakaville** S. Africa
212 D3 **Shakawe** Botswana
224 B3 **Shakespeare Island** *Ont.* Can.
Shakh *Khatlon* Tajik. *see* **Shoh**
Shakhagach Azer. *see* **Şahağac**
Shakhbuz Azer. *see* **Şahbuz**
122 H5 **Shākhen** Iran
137 P3 **Shakhovo** Rus. Fed.
139 S5 **Shakhovskaya** Rus. Fed.
Shakhrisabz Uzbek. *see* **Shahrisabz**
Shakhristan Tajik. *see* **Shahriston**
124 E8 **Shakhs, Ras** *pt* Eritrea
137 R5 **Shakhtars'k** Ukr.
Shakhtersk Ukr. *see* **Shakhtars'k**
Shakhterskoye Ukr. *see* **Pershotravens'k**
121 O3 **Shakhtinsk** Kazakh.
120 H3 **Shakhty** Kazakh.
Shakhty *Respublika Buryatiya* Rus. Fed. *see* **Gusinoozersk**
135 H7 **Shakhty** *Rostovskaya Oblast'* Rus. Fed.
Shakhtyorsk Ukr. *see* **Shakhtars'k**
Shakhtyorskoye Ukr. *see* **Pershotravens'k**
134 I4 **Shakhun'ya** Rus. Fed.
207 F4 **Shaki** Nigeria
203 G3 **Shākir, Jazīrat** *i.* Egypt
236 I3 **Shakopee** *MN* U.S.A.
102 R3 **Shakotan-hantō** *pen.* Japan
102 R3 **Shakotan-misaki** *c.* Japan
109 K6 **Shakou** *Guangdong* China
202 A1 **Shakshūk** Libya
210 C3 **Shala Hāyk'** *l.* Eth.
134 H3 **Shalakusha** Rus. Fed.
122 D5 **Shalāmzār** Iran
109 H8 **Shalang** *Guangdong* China
129 I4 **Shalbuzdag, Gora** *mt.* Rus. Fed.
121 R2 **Shalday** Kazakh.
151 J6 **Shalfleet** *Isle of Wight, England* U.K.
151 K5 **Shalford** *Surrey, England* U.K.
121 N4 **Shalginskiy** Kazakh.
Shalgiya Kazakh. *see* **Shalginskiy**
129 G2 **Shali** Rus. Fed.
106 C8 **Shaliangzi** *Qinghai* China
125 I6 **Shalim** Oman
Shaliuhe *Qinghai* China *see* **Gangca**
116 G4 **Shalkar** *Hima. Prad.* India
120 H4 **Shalkar** *Aktyubinskaya Oblast'* Kazakh.
Shalkar Kazakh. *see* **Chelkar**
120 D2 **Shalkar, Ozero** *salt l.* Kazakh.
120 F2 **Shalkar Karashatau** *salt l.* Kazakh.
120 I2 **Shalkar-Yega-Kara, Ozero** *l.* Rus. Fed.
Shalqar *Aktyubinskaya Oblast'* Kazakh. *see* **Shalkar**
Shalqar *Zapadnyy Kazakhstan* Kazakh. *see* **Chelkar**
Shalqar Köli *salt l.* Kazakh. *see* **Shalkar, Ozero**
Shalqīya Kazakh. *see* **Shalginskiy**
122 D3 **Shaltrak** Iran
108 B3 **Shaluli Shan** *mts Sichuan* China
117 P5 **Shaluni** *mt. Arun. Prad.* India
134 L4 **Shalya** Rus. Fed.
122 J6 **Shalyhyne** Ukr.
119 H5 **Shām, Jabal** *mt.* Oman
211 B6 **Shama** *r.* Tanz.
128 A8 **Shamāl Sīnā'** *governorate* Egypt
123 L6 **Shamalzā'ī** Afgh.
134 L4 **Shamary** Rus. Fed.
124 F1 **Shāmat al Akbād** *des.* Saudi Arabia
223 M3 **Shamattawa** *Man.* Can.
224 C2 **Shamattawa** *r. Ont.* Can.
139 O7 **Shamava** Belarus
122 C5 **Shamīl** Iran
210 A3 **Shambe** Sudan
210 C2 **Shambu** Eth.
209 D6 **Shambuanda** Dem. Rep. Congo
109 □ **Sham Chun** *r. Guangdong/H.K.* China
116 E7 **Shamgarh** *Madh. Prad.* India
Shamgong Bhutan *see* **Shemgang**
122 G8 **Shamil** Iran
129 H4 **Shamil'kala** Rus. Fed.
125 I5 **Shamis** U.A.E.
129 I2 **Shamkhal** Rus. Fed.
Shamkhor Azer. *see* **Şämkir**
124 F2 **Shammar, Jabal** *reg.* Saudi Arabia
234 B3 **Shamokin** *PA* U.S.A.
234 B3 **Shamokin Dam** *PA* U.S.A.
136 Q1 **Shamrayivka** Ukr.
136 I4 **Shamrock** *TX* U.S.A.
237 E8 **Shamrock** *TX* U.S.A.
213 F3 **Shamva** Zimbabwe
215 K9 **Shamwari Game Reserve** *nature res.* S. Africa
96 D4 **Shan** *state* Myanmar
Shancheng *Fujian* China *see* **Nanjing**
Shancheng *Shandong* China *see* **Shanxian**
123 I6 **Shand** Afgh.
122 I7 **Shāndak** Iran
106 G7 **Shandan** *Gansu* China
106 G7 **Shandan He** *r. Gansu* China
107 O6 **Shandian He** *r.* China
122 H3 **Shandiz** Iran
107 Q8 **Shandong** *prov.* China
107 Q8 **Shandong Bandao** *pen.* China
137 K4 **Shandra** Ukr.
127 L7 **Shandrūkh** Iraq
123 O3 **Shandur Pass** Pak.
234 D4 **Shanesville** *PA* U.S.A.
213 F3 **Shangani** Zimbabwe
213 E3 **Shangani** *r.* Zimbabwe
108 B2 **Shang Boingor** *Qinghai* China
109 J2 **Shangcai** *Henan* China
108 G6 **Shangchao** *Guangxi* China
109 J3 **Shangcheng** *Henan* China
111 I12 **Shang Chu** *r.* China
109 I8 **Shangchuan Dao** *i. Guangdong* China
Shangchuankou *Qinghai* China *see* **Minhe**
107 M6 **Shangdu** *Nei Mongol* China
100 F5 **Shangganling** *Heilong.* China
109 J4 **Shanggao** *Jiangxi* China
109 M3 **Shanghai** *Shanghai* China
109 M3 **Shanghai** *mun.* China
109 K6 **Shanghang** *Fujian* China
109 M3 **Shanghe** *Shandong* China
101 D8 **Shanghekou** *Liaoning* China
Shangji *Henan* China *see* **Xichuan**
Shangjie *Yunnan* China *see* **Yangbi**
108 H2 **Shangjin** *Hubei* China
108 B2 **Shang Kongma** *Qinghai* China
107 Q1 **Shangkuli** *Nei Mongol* China
108 G2 **Shangluo** *Shaanxi* China
Shangmei *Hunan* China *see* **Xinhua**
108 H2 **Shangnan** *Shaanxi* China
209 D9 **Shangombo** Zambia
Shangpai *Anhui* China *see* **Feixi**
Shangpai *Yunnan* China *see* **Fugong**
Shangpaihe *Anhui* China *see* **Feixi**
107 N9 **Shangqiu** *Henan* China
109 K4 **Shangrao** *Jiangxi* China
110 F3 **Shangsanshilipu** *Xinjiang* China
109 J2 **Shangshui** *Henan* China
108 G7 **Shangsi** *Guangxi* China
Shangtang *Zhejiang* China *see* **Yongjia**
109 I6 **Shangyou** *Jiangxi* China
109 J6 **Shangyou Shuiku** *resr* China
109 M3 **Shangyu** *Zhejiang* China
108 A4 **Shang Zayü** *Xizang* China
100 F3 **Shangzhi** *Heilong.* China
108 G2 **Shangzhou** *Shaanxi* China *see* **Shangluo**
107 P6 **Shanhaiguan** *Hebei* China
Shanhe *Gansu* China *see* **Zhengning**
100 E6 **Shanhetun** *Heilong.* China
175 M3 **Shani** Belarus
207 I4 **Shani** Nigeria
129 F3 **Shani, Mt'a** *Georgia/Rus. Fed.*
151 J6 **Shanklin** *Isle of Wight, England* U.K.
108 G8 **Shankou** *Guangxi* China
109 H4 **Shankou** *Hunan* China
106 D5 **Shankou** *Xinjiang* China
80 J7 **Shannon** *North I.* N.Z.
147 E7 **Shannon** *airport* Ireland
147 E7 **Shannon** *est.* Ireland
147 F5 **Shannon** *r.* Ireland
215 K5 **Shannon** S. Africa
226 E7 **Shannon** *IL* U.S.A.
147 C7 **Shannon, Mouth of the** Ireland
87 D13 **Shannon National Park** *W.A.* Austr.
221 Q2 **Shannon Ø** *i.* Greenland
96 C4 **Shan Plateau** Myanmar
106 B5 **Shanshan** *Xinjiang* China
106 B5 **Shanshanzhan** *Xinjiang* China
Shansi *prov.* China *see* **Shanxi**
131 O4 **Shantarskiye Ostrova** *is* Rus. Fed.
109 □J7 **Shan Tei Tong** *hill H.K.* China
Shan Teng *hill H.K.* China *see* **Victoria Peak**
117 L8 **Shantipur** *W. Bengal* India
148 D5 **Shantonagh** Ireland
109 K7 **Shantou** *Guangdong* China
Shantung *prov.* China *see* **Shandong**
147 F4 **Shanvus** Ireland
109 J7 **Shanwei** *Guangdong* China
107 J5 **Shanxi** *prov.* China
107 O9 **Shanxian** *Shandong* China
139 S7 **Shanya** *r.* Rus. Fed.
108 G2 **Shanyang** *Shaanxi* China
107 M7 **Shanyin** *Shanxi* China
109 H5 **Shaodong** *Hunan* China
109 I6 **Shaoguan** *Guangdong* China
109 I5 **Shaoshan** *Hunan* China
109 K5 **Shaowu** *Fujian* China
109 M3 **Shaoxing** *Zhejiang* China
109 H5 **Shaoyang** *Hunan* China
109 H5 **Shaoyang** *Hunan* China
149 L4 **Shap** *Cumbria, England* U.K.
109 H8 **Shapa** *Guangdong* China
209 D6 **Shapembe** Dem. Rep. Congo
Shaping *Sichuan* China *see* **Ebian**
146 K4 **Shapinsay** *i. Scotland* U.K.
146 K4 **Shapinsay Sound** *sea chan. Scotland* U.K.
139 O2 **Shapki** Rus. Fed.
134 K2 **Shapkina** *r.* Rus. Fed.
137 L2 **Shapovalivka** Ukr.
139 R1 **Shapsha** Rus. Fed.
110 I1 **Shapshal'skiy Khrebet** *mts* Rus. Fed.
137 R9 **Shapsugskaya** Rus. Fed.
137 R9 **Shapsugskoye Vodokhranilishche** *resr* Rus. Fed.
138 M7 **Shapyalyevichy** Belarus
110 I4 **Shaqiuhe** *Xinjiang* China
202 E6 **Shaqq el Giefer, Wadi** *watercourse* Sudan
202 E6 **Shaqq el Khadir** Sudan
124 G3 **Shaqrā'** Saudi Arabia
110 F4 **Shaquanzi** *Xinjiang* China
121 S3 **Shar** Kazakh.
124 G3 **Shār, Jabal** *mt.* Saudi Arabia
127 K8 **Sharaf** *well* Iraq
202 E6 **Sharafa** Sudan
127 L4 **Sharaf-Khāneh** Iran
107 J1 **Sharalday** Rus. Fed.
123 M5 **Sharan** Afgh.
134 K5 **Sharan** Rus. Fed.
134 I4 **Sharanga** Rus. Fed.
123 M6 **Sharan Jogizai** Pak.
139 U6 **Sharapovo** Rus. Fed.
128 G2 **Sharaqraq** Syria
139 N6 **Sharashova** Belarus
128 B10 **Sharātīb, Ra's** *pt* Egypt
147 G5 **Sharavogue** Ireland
128 E10 **Sharawrā, Jabal** *hills* Saudi Arabia
128 E10 **Sharawrā', Qā'** *salt pan* Saudi Arabia
Sharbaqty Kazakh. *see* **Shcherbakty**
125 M7 **Sharbithāt, Ra's** *c.* Oman
106 C2 **Sharbulag** Mongolia
121 S1 **Sharchino** Rus. Fed.
121 T2 **Shardara** Kazakh.
Shardara Bögeni *resr* Kazakh./Uzbek. *see* **Chardarinskoye Vodokhranilishche**
123 P4 **Shardi** Pak.
106 D3 **Sharga** *Govĭ-Altay* Mongolia
106 F2 **Sharga** *Hövsgöl* Mongolia
Shargorod Ukr. *see* **Sharhorod**

121 L8 **Sharg‘un** Uzbek.
136 H5 **Sharhorod** Ukr.
106 I4 **Sharhulsan** Mongolia
Shari *r.* Cameroon/Chad *see* Chari
102 V3 **Shari** Japan
127 L6 **Shārī, Buḩayrat** *imp. l.* Iraq
102 V3 **Shari-dake** *vol.* Japan
128 F4 **Sharīfah** Syria
128 C10 **Sharīrah Pass** Egypt
137 O3 **Sharivka** *Kharkivs'ka Oblast'* Ukr.
137 R4 **Sharivka** *Luhans'ka Oblast'* Ukr.
129 E3 **Sharivtsek, Pereval** *pass* Georgia/Rus. Fed.
Sharjah U.A.E. *see* Ash Shāriqah
111 J12 **Sharka-leb La** *pass Xizang* China
134 K4 **Sharkan** Rus. Fed.
138 K6 **Sharkawshchyna** Belarus
87 B8 **Shark Bay** *W.A.* Austr.
92 B6 **Shark Fin Bay** *Palawan* Phil.
125 J8 **Sharkhāt** Yemen
85 K3 **Shark Reef** *Coral Sea Is Terr.* Austr.
235 G4 **Shark River Hills** *NJ* U.S.A.
Sharlawuk Turkm. *see* Şarlawuk
120 F1 **Sharlyk** Rus. Fed.
124 B1 **Sharmah** Saudi Arabia
203 G3 **Sharm ash Shaykh** Egypt
129 G2 **Sharo-Argun** *r.* Rus. Fed.
232 E7 **Sharon** *PA* U.S.A.
226 F7 **Sharon** *WI* U.S.A.
Sharon, Plain of Israel *see* **HaSharon**
236 E6 **Sharon Springs** *KS* U.S.A.
232 A9 **Sharonville** *OH* U.S.A.
129 G3 **Sharoy** Rus. Fed.
87 F12 **Sharpe, Lake** *salt flat W.A.* Austr.
223 M4 **Sharpe Lake** *Man.* Can.
150 H4 **Sharpness** *Gloucestershire, England* U.K.
Sharp Peak *hill H.K.* China *see* **Nam She Tsim**
232 H9 **Sharpsburg** *MD* U.S.A.
232 D9 **Sharpsburg** *OH* U.S.A.
Sharqat Iraq *see* **Ash Sharqāţ**
128 D5 **Sharqī, Jabal ash** *mts* Lebanon/Syria
120 H6 **Sharqiy Ustyurt Chink** *esc.* Uzbek.
123 P6 **Sharqpur** Pak.
234 C3 **Shartlesville** *PA* U.S.A.
Sharur Azer. *see* **Şărur**
106 E3 **Shar Us Gol** *r.* Mongolia
124 F2 **Shary** *well* Saudi Arabia
134 I4 **Shar'ya** Rus. Fed.
139 P2 **Shar'ya** *r.* Rus. Fed.
Sharyn Kazakh. *see* **Charyn**
207 G5 **Shasha** Nigeria
213 E4 **Shashe** Botswana
213 F4 **Shashe** *r.* Botswana/Zimbabwe
213 E4 **Shashe Dam** *resr* Botswana
210 C3 **Shashemenē** Eth.
Shashi *Hubei* China *see* **Jingzhou**
121 P4 **Shashubay** Kazakh.
238 C6 **Shasta, Mount** *vol. CA* U.S.A.
238 C6 **Shasta Lake** *CA* U.S.A.
137 R2 **Shatalovka** Rus. Fed.
139 P7 **Shatalovo** Rus. Fed.
109 □J7 **Sha Tau Kok Hoi** *inlet H.K.* China
202 B3 **Shāţi', Wādī ash** *watercourse* Libya
129 G3 **Shatili** Georgia
Shatilki Belarus *see* Svyetlahorsk
109 □J7 **Sha Tin** *H.K.* China
109 □J7 **Sha Tin Hoi** *b. H.K.* China
135 I5 **Shatki** Rus. Fed.
128 G3 **Shaţnat as Salmās, Wādī** *watercourse* Syria
109 □J7 **Sha Tong Hau Shan** *i. H.K.* China
127 L2 **Shatoy** Rus. Fed.
135 H5 **Shatsk** Rus. Fed.
136 C2 **Shats'k** Ukr.
136 C2 **Shats'k** *nat. park* Ukr.
122 D7 **Shaţţ, Ra's osh** *pt* Iran
122 C7 **Shaţţ al 'Arab** *r.* Iran/Iraq
127 M8 **Shaţţ al Gharrāf** *r.* Iraq
237 F7 **Shattuck** *OK* U.S.A.
139 W6 **Shatura** Rus. Fed.
139 W6 **Shaturtorf** Rus. Fed.
Shaubak Jordan *see* **Ash Shawbak**
Shāūildir Kazakh. *see* Shaul'der
121 M6 **Shaul'der** Kazakh.
223 I5 **Shaunavon** *Sask.* Can.
140 U5 **Shaverki** Rus. Fed.
240 M4 **Shaver Lake** *CA* U.S.A.
232 F10 **Shavers Fork** *r. WV* U.S.A.
129 G3 **Shavi Klde, Mt'a** Georgia/Rus. Fed.
149 M7 **Shavington** *Cheshire, England* U.K.
261 H5 **Shaw** Arg.
86 E6 **Shaw** *r. W.A.* Austr.
149 M6 **Shaw** *Greater Manchester, England* U.K.
110 G4 **Shawan** *Xinjiang* China
234 B6 **Shawan** *MD* U.S.A.
235 G1 **Shawangunk Kill** *r. NY* U.S.A.
235 F2 **Shawangunk Mountains** *hills NY* U.S.A.
226 F5 **Shawano** *WI* U.S.A.
226 F5 **Shawano Lake** *WI* U.S.A.
124 C2 **Shawāq** *well* Saudi Arabia
146 C6 **Shawbost** *Western Isles, Scotland* U.K.
232 A10 **Shawhan** *KY* U.S.A.
237 G8 **Shawnee** *OK* U.S.A.
238 L5 **Shawnee** *WY* U.S.A.
232 E11 **Shawsville** *VA* U.S.A.
109 L5 **Sha Xi** *r.* China
109 K5 **Shaxian** *Fujian* China
121 M6 **Shayan** Kazakh.
109 I3 **Shayang** *Hubei* China
124 C3 **Shaybārā** *i.* Saudi Arabia
131 R3 **Shayboveyem** *r.* Rus. Fed.
86 F6 **Shay Gap** *W.A.* Austr.
Shaykh, Jabal ash *mt.* Lebanon/Syria *see* **Hermon, Mount**
128 B10 **Shaykh, Wādī ash** *watercourse* Egypt
127 M7 **Shaykh Jūwī** Iraq
128 E6 **Shaykh Miskīn** Syria
127 M7 **Shaykh Sa'd** Iraq
139 R7 **Shaykovka** Rus. Fed.
137 P6 **Shaytanka** *r.* Ukr.
122 F6 **Shayţūr** Iran
128 E3 **Shayzar** Syria
122 C5 **Shāzand** Iran
110 L7 **Shazaoyuan** *Gansu* China
124 E2 **Shaẕāẕ, Jabal** *mt.* Saudi Arabia
123 O3 **Shazud** Tajik.
138 H8 **Shchara** *r.* Belarus
175 M3 **Shcharchova** Belarus
137 S5 **Shchastya** Ukr.
137 O9 **Shchebetovka** Ukr.
139 R9 **Shcheglovka** Rus. Fed.
139 U7 **Shchekino** Rus. Fed.
136 F3 **Shchekychyn** Ukr.
139 S7 **Shchelkanovo** Rus. Fed.
139 V6 **Shchelkovo** Rus. Fed.
134 K2 **Shchel'yayur** Rus. Fed.
Shcherbakov Rus. Fed. *see* **Rybinsk**
121 R1 **Shcherbakty** Kazakh.
137 K6 **Shcherbani** Ukr.
Shcherbinovka Ukr. *see* **Dzerzhyns'k**
134 G4 **Shchetinskoye** Rus. Fed.
135 G6 **Shchigry** Rus. Fed.
137 O8 **Shcholkine** Ukr.
138 K8 **Shchomyslitsa** Belarus
137 K2 **Shchors** Ukr.
137 N5 **Shchors'k** Ukr.
Shchuchin Belarus *see* Shchuchyn
121 N1 **Shchuchinsk** Kazakh.
137 T2 **Shchuch'ye** Rus. Fed.
138 H8 **Shchuchyn** Belarus
134 L2 **Shchuger** *r.* Rus. Fed.
136 C4 **Shchyrets'** Ukr.
138 L8 **Shchytkavichy** Belarus
251 G4 **Shea** Guyana
121 U2 **Shebalino** Rus. Fed.
226 D1 **Shebandowan Lakes** *Ont.* Can.
135 G6 **Shebekino** Rus. Fed.
123 K3 **Sheberghān** Afgh.
226 G6 **Sheboygan** *WI* U.S.A.
137 R9 **Shebsh** *r.* Rus. Fed.
207 H4 **Shebshi Mountains** Nigeria
100 L5 **Shebunino** *Sakhalin* Rus. Fed.
Shecheng *Hebei* China *see* Shexian
225 H4 **Shediac** *N.B.* Can.
222 E4 **Shedin Peak** *B.C.* Can.
129 B1 **Shedok** Rus. Fed.
147 H5 **Sheelin, Lough** *l.* Ireland
147 G2 **Sheep Haven** *b.* Ireland
215 O2 **Sheepmoor** S. Africa
241 Q5 **Sheep Peak** *NV* U.S.A.
164 J5 **'s-Heerenberg** Neth.
151 M4 **Sheering** *Essex, England* U.K.
151 N5 **Sheerness** *Kent, England* U.K.
225 I4 **Sheet Harbour** *N.S.* Can.
128 D6 **Shefar'am** Israel
81 G10 **Sheffield** *South I.* N.Z.
149 O7 **Sheffield** *South Yorkshire, England* U.K.
231 D8 **Sheffield** *AL* U.S.A.
226 E8 **Sheffield** *IL* U.S.A.
232 F7 **Sheffield** *PA* U.S.A.
237 E10 **Sheffield** *TX* U.S.A.
225 J3 **Sheffield Lake** *Nfld and Lab.* Can.
151 L3 **Shefford** *Bedfordshire, England* U.K.
123 K6 **Shegah** Afgh.
116 F9 **Shegaon** *Mahar.* India
134 J2 **Shegmas** Rus. Fed.
227 M4 **Sheguiandah** *Ont.* Can.
210 D3 **Shēh Husēn** Eth.
108 E3 **Shehong** *Sichuan* China
147 D9 **Shehy Mountains** *hills* Ireland
Sheikh, Jebel esh *mt.* Lebanon/Syria *see* **Hermon, Mount**
Sheikh Othman Yemen *see* **Ash Shaykh 'Uthman**
123 P6 **Sheikhupura** Pak.
224 C3 **Shekak** *r. Ont.* Can.
122 F5 **Shekār Āb** Iran
116 E6 **Shekhawati** *reg.* India
Shekhem West Bank *see* **Nāblus**
137 T1 **Shekhman'** Rus. Fed.
Sheki Azer. *see* **Şāki**
109 □I7 **Shekka Ch'ün-Tao** *is H.K.* China
109 □I7 **Shek Kwu Chau** *i. H.K.* China
109 □I7 **Shek Pik** *resr H.K.* China
Shek Pik Reservoir *H.K.* China *see* **Shek Pik**
134 G4 **Sheksna** Rus. Fed.
134 G4 **Sheksninskoye Vodokhranilishche** *resr* Rus. Fed.
109 □J7 **Shek Uk Shan** *mt. H.K.* China
111 K11 **Shela** *Xizang* China
121 T1 **Shelabolikha** Rus. Fed.
123 I7 **Shelag** *watercourse* Afgh./Iran
131 S2 **Shelagskiy, Mys** *pt* Rus. Fed.
232 C11 **Shelbiana** *KY* U.S.A.
236 I6 **Shelbina** *MO* U.S.A.
230 D6 **Shelburn** *IN* U.S.A.
225 H5 **Shelburne** *N.S.* Can.
227 N5 **Shelburne** *Ont.* Can.
85 I1 **Shelburne Bay** *Qld* Austr.
233 M6 **Shelburne Falls** *MA* U.S.A.
226 H6 **Shelby** *MI* U.S.A.
237 J9 **Shelby** *MS* U.S.A.
238 I2 **Shelby** *MT* U.S.A.
231 G8 **Shelby** *NC* U.S.A.
232 C8 **Shelby** *OH* U.S.A.
236 K6 **Shelbyville** *IL* U.S.A.
230 E6 **Shelbyville** *IN* U.S.A.
236 I6 **Shelbyville** *MO* U.S.A.
231 D8 **Shelbyville** *TN* U.S.A.
236 K6 **Shelbyville, Lake** *IL* U.S.A.
215 J9 **Sheldon** S. Africa
236 H4 **Sheldon** *IA* U.S.A.
226 G9 **Sheldon** *IL* U.S.A.
226 D4 **Sheldon** *WI* U.S.A.
238 E6 **Sheldon National Wildlife Refuge** *nature res. NV* U.S.A.
233 M4 **Sheldon Springs** *VT* U.S.A.
225 H3 **Sheldrake** *Que.* Can.
Shelek Kazakh. *see* **Chilik**
136 J6 **Shelekhove** Ukr.
131 Q3 **Shelikhova, Zaliv** *g.* Rus. Fed.
220 C4 **Shelikof Strait** *AK* U.S.A.
129 H2 **Shelkovskaya** Rus. Fed.
238 K4 **Shell** *WY* U.S.A.
146 C6 **Shell, Loch** *inlet Scotland* U.K.
223 J4 **Shellbrook** *Sask.* Can.
238 H5 **Shelley** *ID* U.S.A.
83 M6 **Shellharbour** *N.S.W.* Austr.
223 J4 **Shell Lake** *Sask.* Can.
226 C4 **Shell Lake** *WI* U.S.A.
87 I10 **Shell Lakes** *salt flat W.A.* Austr.
240 I1 **Shell Mountain** *CA* U.S.A.
138 N3 **Shelon'** *r.* Rus. Fed.
Shelter Bay *Que.* Can. *see* **Port-Cartier**
235 K2 **Shelter Island** *NY* U.S.A.
235 K2 **Shelter Island** *i. NY* U.S.A.
235 K2 **Shelter Island Heights** *NY* U.S.A.
235 K2 **Shelter Island Sound** *str. NY* U.S.A.
81 C14 **Shelter Point** *Stewart I.* N.Z.
235 I2 **Shelton** *CT* U.S.A.
238 C3 **Shelton** *WA* U.S.A.
134 F3 **Sheltozero** Rus. Fed.
Shelyakino Rus. Fed. *see* **Sovetskoye**
122 D3 **Shem** Iran
Shemakha Azer. *see* **Şamaxı**
207 H4 **Shemankar** *r.* Nigeria
139 R1 **Shemenichi** Rus. Fed.
117 M6 **Shemgang** Bhutan
129 D4 **Shemok'medi** Georgia
121 S2 **Shemonaikha** Kazakh.
134 J4 **Shemordan** Rus. Fed.
135 I5 **Shemursha** Rus. Fed.
135 I5 **Shemysheyka** Rus. Fed.
236 H5 **Shenandoah** *IA* U.S.A.
227 R9 **Shenandoah** *PA* U.S.A.
232 G10 **Shenandoah** *VA* U.S.A.
232 H9 **Shenandoah** *r. VA* U.S.A.
232 F10 **Shenandoah Mountains** *VA/WV* U.S.A.
232 G10 **Shenandoah National Park** *VA* U.S.A.
109 K7 **Shen'ao** *Guangdong* China
120 I3 **Shenbertal** Kazakh.
107 M7 **Shenchi** *Shanxi* China
207 H4 **Shendam** Nigeria
203 G5 **Shendi** Sudan
100 H5 **Shending Shan** *hill Heilong.* China
206 B5 **Shenge** Sierra Leone
121 Q5 **Shengel'dy** *Almatinskaya Oblast'* Kazakh.
120 I5 **Shengel'dy** *Kyzylordinskaya Oblast'* Kazakh.
Shenggeldy Kazakh. *see* Shengel'dy
196 H9 **Shëngjin** Albania
109 J3 **Shengli** *Hubei* China
110 H5 **Shengli Daban** *pass Xinjiang* China
Shengli Feng *mt.* China/Kyrg. *see* **Jengish Chokusu**
110 D6 **Shengli Qichang** *Xinjiang* China
110 E6 **Shengli Shibachang** *Xinjiang* China
Shengrenjian *Shanxi* China *see* **Pinglu**
109 N3 **Shengsi** *Zhejiang* China
109 N3 **Shengsi Liedao** *is* China
Shengxian *Zhejiang* China *see* Shengzhou
109 M4 **Shengzhou** *Zhejiang* China
101 C14 **Shenjiamen** *Zhejiang* China
196 H9 **Shënkoll** Albania
134 H3 **Shenkursk** Rus. Fed.
107 L7 **Shenmu** *Shaanxi* China
108 H3 **Shennongjia** *Hubei* China
109 J2 **Shenqiu** *Henan* China
100 F5 **Shenshu** *Heilong.* China
Shensi *prov.* China *see* Shaanxi
151 I2 **Shenstone** *Staffordshire, England* U.K.
135 J5 **Shentala** Rus. Fed.
87 G10 **Shenton, Mount** *hill W.A.* Austr.
Shenxian *Hebei* China *see* Shenzhou
107 N8 **Shenxian** *Shandong* China
107 R6 **Shenyang** *Liaoning* China
109 J7 **Shenzhen** *Guangdong* China
109 □I7 **Shenzhen Wan** *b. H.K.* China
107 N8 **Shenzhou** *Hebei* China
116 D7 **Sheoganj** *Rajasthan* India
116 F7 **Sheopur** *Madh. Prad.* India
262 P2 **Shepard Island** Antarctica
136 G3 **Shepetivka** Ukr.
Shepetovka Ukr. *see* Shepetivka
232 A5 **Shepherd** *MI* U.S.A.
78 □5 **Shepherd Islands** Vanuatu
83 J7 **Shepparton** *Vic.* Austr.
151 L5 **Shepperton** *Surrey, England* U.K.
151 N5 **Sheppey, Isle of** *i. England* U.K.
234 C3 **Sheppton** *PA* U.S.A.
151 J2 **Shepshed** *Leicestershire, England* U.K.
137 M1 **Sheptaky** Ukr.
150 G5 **Shepton Mallet** *Somerset, England* U.K.
137 O2 **Sheptukhovka** Rus. Fed.
109 I2 **Sheqi** *Henan* China
208 E2 **Sherab** Sudan
Sherabad Uzbek. *see* Sherobod
221 J2 **Sherard, Cape** *Nunavut* Can.
123 I5 **Sher Bakhsh** Afgh.
215 I7 **Sherborne** S. Africa
150 G6 **Sherborne** *Dorset, England* U.K.
151 J5 **Sherborne St John** *Hampshire, England* U.K.
206 B5 **Sherbro Island** Sierra Leone
225 I4 **Sherbrooke** *N.S.* Can.
225 G4 **Sherbrooke** *Que.* Can.
149 N4 **Sherburn** *Durham, England* U.K.
233 J6 **Sherburne** *NY* U.S.A.
149 O6 **Sherburn in Elmet** *North Yorkshire, England* U.K.
147 I5 **Shercock** Ireland
202 C4 **Sherda** *well* Chad
151 L5 **Shere** *Surrey, England* U.K.
203 G5 **Shereiq** Sudan
116 D6 **Shergarh** *Rajasthan* India
117 J7 **Sherghati** *Bihar* India
237 I8 **Sheridan** *AR* U.S.A.
238 K4 **Sheridan** *WY* U.S.A.
221 L1 **Sheridan, Cape** *Nunavut* Can.
149 O5 **Sheriff Hutton** *North Yorkshire, England* U.K.
82 E5 **Sheringa** *S.A.* Austr.
151 O2 **Sheringham** *Norfolk, England* U.K.
130 H3 **Sherkaly** Rus. Fed.
123 L7 **Sher Khan Qala** Afgh.
147 D10 **Sherkin Island** Ireland
86 D6 **Sherlock** *r. W.A.* Austr.
107 O1 **Sherlovaya Gora** Rus. Fed.
232 F6 **Sherman** *NY* U.S.A.
237 G9 **Sherman** *TX* U.S.A.
233 □Q3 **Sherman Mills** *ME* U.S.A.
241 Q1 **Sherman Mountain** *NV* U.S.A.
121 L9 **Sherobod** Uzbek.
139 O7 **Sherovichi** Rus. Fed.
117 M7 **Sherpur** *Dhaka* Bangl.
117 L7 **Sherpur** *Rajshahi* Bangl.
116 E1 **Sher Qila** Jammu and Kashmir
223 K4 **Sherridon** *Man.* Can.
150 H4 **Sherston** *Wiltshire, England* U.K.
114 E8 **Shertally** *Kerala* India
164 H5 **'s-Hertogenbosch** Neth.
232 A7 **Sherwood** *OH* U.S.A.
81 E10 **Sherwood Downs** *South I.* N.Z.
149 O7 **Sherwood Forest** *reg. England* U.K.
223 K2 **Sherwood Lake** *N.W.T.* Can.
100 F3 **Sheryshevo** Rus. Fed.
227 L4 **Sheshegwaning** *Ont.* Can.
122 G3 **Sheshtamad** Iran
222 D3 **Sheslay** *B.C.* Can.
222 C3 **Sheslay** *r. B.C.* Can.
134 J4 **Shestakovo** *Kirovskaya Oblast'* Rus. Fed.
137 T3 **Shestakovo** *Voronezhskaya Oblast'* Rus. Fed.
139 V4 **Shestikhino** Rus. Fed.
137 M6 **Shestirnya** Ukr.
236 H3 **Shetek, Lake** *MN* U.S.A.
223 L3 **Shethanei Lake** *Man.* Can.
146 □O2 **Shetland** *admin. div. Scotland* U.K.
144 G1 **Shetland Islands** *Scotland* U.K.
120 E5 **Shetpe** Kazakh.
235 K1 **Shetucket** *r. CT* U.S.A.
109 □J7 **Sheung Shui** *H.K.* China
109 □J7 **Sheung Sze Mun** *sea chan. H.K.* China
109 □J7 **Sheung Yue Ho** *r. H.K.* China
114 F7 **Shevaroy Hills** India
137 N5 **Shevchenkivka** Ukr.
Shevchenko Kazakh. *see* **Aktau**
120 I4 **Shevchenko, Zaliv** *l.* Kazakh.
137 K4 **Shevchenkove** *Cherkas'ka Oblast'* Ukr.
137 Q4 **Shevchenkove** *Kharkivs'ka Oblast'* Ukr.
137 M2 **Shevchen Kove** Ukr.
Shevchenkovo Ukr. *see* **Dolyns'ka**
114 D3 **Shevgaon** *Mahar.* India
100 H1 **Shevli** *r.* Rus. Fed.
210 B3 **Shewa Gīmīra** Eth.
109 L4 **Shexian** *Anhui* China
107 M8 **Shexian** *Hebei* China
131 M3 **Sheya** Rus. Fed.
109 M2 **Sheyang** *Jiangsu* China
134 H4 **Sheybukhta** Rus. Fed.
236 F2 **Sheyenne** *ND* U.S.A.
236 G2 **Sheyenne** *r. ND* U.S.A.
139 O5 **Sheykino** Rus. Fed.
127 O8 **Sheykkī** Iran
117 I5 **Shey Phoksundo National Park** Nepal
146 D7 **Shiant, Sound of** *str. Scotland* U.K.
146 D7 **Shiant Islands** *Scotland* U.K.
131 Q5 **Shiashkotan, Ostrov** *i. Kuril'skiye O-va* Rus. Fed.
227 K6 **Shiawassee** *r. MI* U.S.A.
105 I5 **Shibakawa** Japan
125 I8 **Shibām** Yemen
106 D6 **Shibandong Jing** *well* China
106 F6 **Shiban Jing** *well* China
106 E7 **Shibaocheng** *Gansu* China
123 M4 **Shībar, Kowtal-e** *pass* Afgh.
102 Q9 **Shibata** Japan
105 L4 **Shibayama** Japan
104 D3 **Shibayama-gata** *l.* Japan
100 D2 **Shibazhan** *Heilong.* China
102 T2 **Shibetsu** *Hokkaidō* Japan
102 W3 **Shibetsu** *Hokkaidō* Japan
203 F2 **Shibīn al Kawm** Egypt
108 G5 **Shibing** *Guizhou* China
224 B2 **Shibogama Lake** *Ont.* Can.
Shibotsu-jima *i. Kuril'skiye O-va* Rus. Fed. *see* **Zelenyy, Ostrov**
105 J3 **Shibukawa** Japan
103 I15 **Shibushi** Japan
103 I15 **Shibushi-wan** *b.* Japan
105 I2 **Shibu-tōge** *pass* Japan
105 J2 **Shibutsu-san** *mt.* Japan
Shicheng *Fujian* China *see* **Zhouning**
109 K5 **Shicheng** *Jiangxi* China
107 R7 **Shicheng Dao** *i.* China
105 H5 **Shichimen-zan** *mt.* Japan
102 S6 **Shichinohe** Japan
227 R8 **Shickshinny** *PA* U.S.A.
Shicun *Shanxi* China *see* **Xiangfen**
128 G7 **Shidād al Mismā'** *hill* Saudi Arabia
107 R8 **Shidao** *Shandong* China
107 R8 **Shidao Wan** *b.* China
121 P1 **Shiderti** *r.* Kazakh.
108 B6 **Shidian** *Yunnan* China
Shidian *Yunnan* China *see* **Changning**
103 L12 **Shido** Japan
Shidongsi *Gansu* China *see* **Gaolan**
123 N3 **Shidud** Afgh.
146 E9 **Shiel, Loch** *l. Scotland* U.K.
146 F8 **Shiel Bridge** *Highland, Scotland* U.K.
84 F2 **Shield, Cape** *N.T.* Austr.
146 E7 **Shieldaig** *Highland, Scotland* U.K.
149 J2 **Shieldhill** *Falkirk, Scotland* U.K.
Shīeli Kazakh. *see* **Chiili**
124 B1 **Shifa, Jabal ash** *mts* Saudi Arabia
108 E3 **Shifang** *Sichuan* China
150 H2 **Shifnal** *Shropshire, England* U.K.
105 G3 **Shiga** *Nagano* Japan
104 C5 **Shiga** *Shiga* Japan
104 C5 **Shiga** *pref.* Japan
116 E2 **Shigar** Jammu and Kashmir
104 D6 **Shigaraki** Japan
Shigatse *Xizang* China *see* **Xigazê**
114 D5 **Shiggaon** *Karnataka* India
110 L6 **Shigong** *Gansu* China
120 C1 **Shigony** Rus. Fed.
107 L6 **Shiguai** *Nei Mongol* China
Shiguaigou *Nei Mongol* China *see* **Shiguai**
125 K7 **Shiḩan** Yemen
125 K7 **Shiḩan, Wādīal** *r.* Oman
110 H4 **Shihezi** *Xinjiang* China
Shihkiachwang *Hebei* China *see* **Shijiazhuang**
210 E2 **Shiikh** Somalia
196 H9 **Shijak** Albania
Shijiao *Guangdong* China *see* **Fogang**
107 N7 **Shijiazhuang** *Hebei* China
109 L3 **Shijiu Hu** *l.* China
Shijiusuo *Shandong* China *see* **Rizhao**
104 E1 **Shika** Japan
102 R4 **Shikabe** Japan
224 B3 **Shikag Lake** *Ont.* Can.
108 G8 **Shikang** *Guangxi* China
123 J7 **Shikar** *r.* Pak.
114 D5 **Shikarpur** *Karnataka* India
123 M8 **Shikarpur** Pak.
109 I6 **Shikengkong** *mt. Guangdong* China
120 B1 **Shikhany** Rus. Fed.
105 K4 **Shiki** Japan
105 J7 **Shikine-jima** *i.* Japan
105 I4 **Shikishima** Japan
116 G6 **Shikohabad** *Uttar Prad.* India
103 K13 **Shikoku** *i.* Japan
103 J13 **Shikoku-sanchi** *mts* Japan
99 Q3 **Shikotan, Ostrov** *i. Kuril'skiye O-va* Rus. Fed.
Shikotan-tō *i. Kuril'skiye O-va* Rus. Fed. *see* **Shikotan, Ostrov**
102 S4 **Shikotsu** *vol.* Japan
102 R4 **Shikotsu-Tōya Kokuritsu-kōen** *nat. park* Japan
149 N3 **Shilbottle** *Northumberland, England* U.K.
120 H2 **Shil'da** Rus. Fed.
149 N4 **Shildon** *Durham, England* U.K.
134 I2 **Shilega** Rus. Fed.
107 P9 **Shilianghe Shuiku** *resr* China
117 L6 **Shiliguri** *W. Bengal* India
108 D6 **Shilin** *Yunnan* China
109 I3 **Shilipu** *Hubei* China
Shiliu *Hainan* China *see* **Changjiang**
116 G3 **Shilla** *mt.* Jammu and Kashmir
146 B7 **Shillay** *i. Scotland* U.K.
147 I7 **Shillelagh** Ireland
227 N1 **Shillington** *Ont.* Can.
234 D4 **Shillington** *PA* U.S.A.
128 C6 **Shillo** *r.* Israel
117 M7 **Shillong** *Meghalaya* India
120 C2 **Shil'naya Balka** Kazakh.
234 E6 **Shiloh** *NJ* U.S.A.
232 C8 **Shiloh** *OH* U.S.A.
107 L8 **Shilou** *Shanxi* China
135 H5 **Shilovo** *Ryazanskaya Oblast'* Rus. Fed.
139 V8 **Shilovo** *Tul'skaya Oblast'* Rus. Fed.
Shilüüstey Mongolia *see* **Balgatay**
104 E7 **Shima** Japan
105 I2 **Shima** *spring* Japan
103 H14 **Shimabara** Japan
103 H14 **Shimabara-wan** *b.* Japan
105 H6 **Shimada** Japan
104 D6 **Shimagahara** Japan
104 D7 **Shima-hantō** *pen.* Japan
102 R4 **Shimamaki** Japan
104 C6 **Shimamoto** Japan
103 J12 **Shimane** *pref.* Japan
103 J11 **Shimane-hantō** *pen.* Japan
100 E2 **Shimanovsk** Rus. Fed.
210 E2 **Shimbiris** *mt.* Somalia
210 D4 **Shimbirre** *waterhole* Kenya
109 H4 **Shimen** *Hunan* China
Shimen *Yunnan* China *see* **Yunlong**
108 D4 **Shimian** *Sichuan* China
104 D3 **Shimizu** *Fukui* Japan
102 T3 **Shimizu** *Hokkaidō* Japan
105 H5 **Shimizu** *Shizuoka* Japan
105 I5 **Shimizu** *Shizuoka* Japan
104 B7 **Shimizu** *Wakayama* Japan
116 F4 **Shimla** *Hima. Prad.* India
Shimminato Japan *see* **Shinminato**
104 F2 **Shimo** Japan
105 H5 **Shimobe** Japan
105 I6 **Shimoda** Japan
105 K3 **Shimodate** Japan
105 L4 **Shimofusa** Japan
114 D6 **Shimoga** *Karnataka* India
105 K1 **Shimogō** Japan
104 C7 **Shimoichi** Japan
105 G5 **Shimojō** Japan
102 T2 **Shimokawa** Japan
102 R5 **Shimokita-hantō** *pen.* Japan
104 C7 **Shimokitayama** Japan
103 G15 **Shimo-Koshiki-jima** *i.* Japan
211 C6 **Shimoni** Kenya
105 I3 **Shimonita** Japan
103 H13 **Shimonoseki** Japan
105 H3 **Shimosuwa** Japan
104 B7 **Shimotsu** Japan
105 K3 **Shimotsuma** Japan
104 F5 **Shimoyama** Japan
114 E6 **Shimsha** *r.* India
116 E1 **Shimshal** Jammu and Kashmir
139 N3 **Shimsk** Rus. Fed.
105 J3 **Shin** Japan
146 G6 **Shin, Loch** *l. Scotland* U.K.
Shināfīyah Iraq *see* **Ash Shanāfīyah**
Shinan *Guangxi* China *see* **Xingye**
105 H2 **Shinano** Japan
104 D5 **Shin-asahi** Japan
102 □H16 **Shin-dake** *vol.* Japan
123 J5 **Shīndand** Afgh.
151 K5 **Shinfield** *Wokingham, England* U.K.
209 F8 **Shingana** Dem. Rep. Congo
96 C1 **Shingbwiyang** Myanmar
96 C1 **Shing-gai** Myanmar
123 P3 **Shinghshal Pass** Pak.
232 G7 **Shinglehouse** *PA* U.S.A.
226 H3 **Shingleton** *MI* U.S.A.
Shing Mun Reservoir *H.K.* China *see* **Ngan Hei Shui Tong**
121 S4 **Shingozha** Kazakh.
103 N13 **Shingū** Japan
213 F4 **Shingwedzi** S. Africa
149 M7 **Shining Tor** *hill England* U.K.
227 M2 **Shining Tree** *Ont.* Can.
102 R8 **Shinjō** Japan
123 L6 **Shīnkāy** Afgh.
123 M5 **Shīnkay Ghar** *mts* Afgh.
104 F2 **Shinminato** Japan
103 I12 **Shinnan-yō** Japan
123 L6 **Shin Narai Thana** Afgh.
235 K3 **Shinnecock Bay** *NY* U.S.A.
146 H6 **Shinness Lodge** *Highland, Scotland* U.K.
232 E9 **Shinnston** *WV* U.S.A.
104 E6 **Shino-jima** *i.* Japan
105 H2 **Shinonoi** Japan
123 N4 **Shinpokh** Pak.
147 G7 **Shinrone** Ireland
104 E5 **Shinsei** Japan
128 E4 **Shinshār** Syria
104 F6 **Shinshiro** Japan
105 H2 **Shinshūshin** Japan
105 I3 **Shintō** Japan
102 T3 **Shintoku** Japan
105 L4 **Shintone** Japan
129 H6 **Shinuhayr** Armenia
211 B5 **Shinyanga** Tanz.
211 B5 **Shinyanga** *admin. reg.* Tanz.
104 E2 **Shio** Japan
105 K2 **Shiobara** Japan
102 S8 **Shiogama** Japan
105 G3 **Shiojiri** Japan
102 □B22 **Shiokawa** *Nansei-shotō* Japan
105 H4 **Shiomi-dake** *mt.* Japan
103 M13 **Shiono-misaki** *c.* Japan
105 K2 **Shioya** Japan
105 M1 **Shioya-zaki** *pt* Japan
105 I1 **Shiozawa** Japan
109 K3 **Shipai** *Anhui* China
233 K9 **Ship Bottom** *NJ* U.S.A.
246 E1 **Ship Chan Cay** *i.* Bahamas
197 N8 **Shipchenski Prokhod** *pass* Bulg.
139 V4 **Shipilovo** Rus. Fed.
108 D7 **Shiping** *Yunnan* China
111 D11 **Shipki Pass** China/India
151 K5 **Shiplake** *Oxfordshire, England* U.K.
149 N6 **Shipley** *West Yorkshire, England* U.K.
232 G11 **Shipman** *VA* U.S.A.
225 H4 **Shippegan** *N.B.* Can.
225 H4 **Shippegan Island** *N.B.* Can.
232 H8 **Shippensburg** *PA* U.S.A.
232 F7 **Shippenville** *PA* U.S.A.
104 E5 **Shippō** Japan
241 X5 **Shiprock** *NM* U.S.A.
241 X5 **Shiprock Peak** *NM* U.S.A.
151 I3 **Shipston on Stour** *Warwickshire, England* U.K.
149 O5 **Shipton** *North Yorkshire, England* U.K.
150 G2 **Shipton** *Shropshire, England* U.K.
151 I4 **Shipton-under-Wychwood** *Oxfordshire, England* U.K.
Shipu *Shaanxi* China *see* **Huanglong**
109 M4 **Shipu** *Zhejiang* China
131 R4 **Shipunskiy, Mys** *hd* Rus. Fed.
108 G5 **Shiqian** *Guizhou* China
Shiqiao *Guangdong* China *see* **Panyu**
Shiqizhen *Guangdong* China *see* **Zhongshan**
124 H7 **Shiqqat al Kharītah** *des.* Saudi Arabia
108 G2 **Shiquan** *Shaanxi* China
116 G3 **Shiquan He** *r.* China *conv.* **Indus**
Shiquanhe *Xizang* China *see* **Ali**
108 G2 **Shiquan Shuiku** *resr* China
124 F3 **Shi'r, Jabal** *hill* Saudi Arabia
146 F10 **Shira** *r. Scotland* U.K.
125 K3 **Shirā'awh** *i.* Qatar
122 C2 **Shīrābād** Iran
105 K6 **Shirahama** *Chiba* Japan
103 M13 **Shirahama** *Wakayama* Japan
104 D6 **Shirai-san** *hill* Japan
102 R5 **Shirakami-misaki** *pt* Japan
105 L1 **Shirakawa** *Fukushima* Japan
104 E3 **Shirakawa** *Gifu* Japan
104 F4 **Shirakawa** *Gifu* Japan
104 F3 **Shirake-mine** *mt.* Japan
105 L5 **Shirako** Japan
104 G5 **Shirakura-yama** *mt.* Japan
104 B7 **Shirama-yama** *hill* Japan
104 E3 **Shiramine** Japan
105 H4 **Shirane** Japan
105 H4 **Shirane-san** *mt.* Japan
105 I2 **Shirane-san** *mt.* Japan
105 J2 **Shirane-san** *vol.* Japan
102 V4 **Shiranuka** Japan
102 S4 **Shiraoi** Japan
105 J2 **Shirasawa** Japan
262 O1 **Shirase Coast** Antarctica
263 C2 **Shirase Glacier** Antarctica
102 U3 **Shirataki** Japan
211 B5 **Shirati** Tanz.
122 E7 **Shīrāz** Iran
126 E8 **Shirbīn** Egypt
211 B8 **Shire** *r.* Malawi
149 O7 **Shirebrook** *Derbyshire, England* U.K.
107 M4 **Shireet** Mongolia
122 B3 **Shīreh Jīn** Iran
150 G4 **Shirenewton** *Monmouthshire, Wales* U.K.
102 V3 **Shiretoko-hantō** *pen.* Japan
102 W2 **Shiretoko Kokuritsu-kōen** *nat. park* Japan
102 W2 **Shiretoko-misaki** *c.* Japan
123 K8 **Shireza** Pak.
121 M7 **Shirin** Uzbek.
123 L6 **Shirinab** *r.* Pak.
123 K3 **Shīrīn Tagāb** Afgh.
102 R5 **Shiriuchi** Japan
102 S5 **Shiriya-zaki** *c.* Japan
120 G4 **Shirkala** *reg.* Kazakh.
122 F6 **Shīr Kūh** *mt.* Iran
149 O7 **Shirland** *Derbyshire, England* U.K.
235 J3 **Shirley** *NY* U.S.A.
185 □ **Shirley Cove** *b.* Gibraltar
105 L4 **Shiroi** Japan
102 R9 **Shiroishi** Japan
105 G5 **Shirokura-yama** *mt.* Japan
102 Q9 **Shirone** Japan
207 G4 **Shiroro Reservoir** Nigeria
104 E4 **Shirotori** Japan
104 G2 **Shirouma-dake** *mt.* Japan
105 J4 **Shiroyama** Japan
116 E9 **Shirpur** *Mahar.* India
106 E5 **Shirten Holoy Gobi** *des.* China
122 G3 **Shīrvān** Iran
106 B5 **Shisanjianfang** *Xinjiang* China
100 D3 **Shisanzhan** *Heilong.* China
215 P3 **Shiselweni** *admin. dist.* Swaziland
220 B4 **Shishaldin Volcano** *AK* U.S.A.
Shisha Pangma *mt. Xizang* China *see* **Xixabangma Feng**
103 L13 **Shishikui** Japan
Shishkaya Armenia *see* **Geghamasar**
109 I4 **Shishou** *Hubei* China
105 L4 **Shisui** Japan
109 K3 **Shitai** *Anhui* China
109 I6 **Shitan** *Guangdong* China
109 M4 **Shitang** *Zhejiang* China
106 J7 **Shitanjing** *Ningxia* China
104 G5 **Shitara** Japan
203 I1 **Shithāthah** Iraq
100 D7 **Shitoukoumen Shuiku** *resr Jilin* China
116 C6 **Shiv** *Rajasthan* India
131 R4 **Shiveluch, Sopka** *vol.* Rus. Fed.
116 F7 **Shivpuri** *Madh. Prad.* India
128 C8 **Shivta** *tourist site* Israel
241 S4 **Shivwits** *UT* U.S.A.
241 S5 **Shivwits Plateau** *AZ* U.S.A.
123 N3 **Shiwal** *l.* Afgh.
107 K8 **Shiwan** *Shaanxi* China
108 F8 **Shiwan Dashan** *mts* China
96 H3 **Shiwan Dashan** *mts* China
211 A7 **Shiwa Ngandu** Zambia
109 J6 **Shixing** *Guangdong* China
108 H2 **Shiyan** *Hubei* China
108 G4 **Shizhu** *Chongqing* China
107 J9 **Shizi** *Gansu* China
Shizilu *Shandong* China *see* **Junan**
109 L3 **Shizipu** *Anhui* China
108 D6 **Shizong** *Yunnan* China
102 S8 **Shizugawa** Japan
106 J7 **Shizuishan** *Ningxia* China
106 J7 **Shizuishanzhan** *Ningxia* China
102 R7 **Shizukuishi** Japan
102 T4 **Shizunai** Japan
105 H6 **Shizuoka** Japan
105 H6 **Shizuoka** *pref.* Japan
196 I8 **Shkëlzenit, Maja e** *mt.* Albania
129 E3 **Shkhara** *mt.* Georgia/Rus. Fed.
136 C4 **Shklo** Ukr.
Shklov Belarus *see* **Shklow**
139 N7 **Shklow** Belarus
136 E3 **Shklyn'** Ukr.
129 E3 **Shk'meri** Georgia
196 H8 **Shkodër** Albania
Shkodrës, Liqeni i *l.* Albania/Montenegro *see* **Scutari, Lake**
196 H9 **Shkumbin** *r.* Albania
137 S7 **Shkurinskaya** Rus. Fed.
136 E2 **Shlapan'** Ukr.
139 R4 **Shlina** *r.* Rus. Fed.
139 Q4 **Shlino, Ozero** *l.* Rus. Fed.
139 O2 **Shlissel'burg** Rus. Fed.
131 K1 **Shmidta, Ostrov** *i.* Rus. Fed.
100 M1 **Shmidta, Poluostrov** *pen. Sakhalin* Rus. Fed.
138 L4 **Shmoylovo** Rus. Fed.
138 L6 **Sho, Vozyera** *l.* Belarus
83 L6 **Shoalhaven** *r. N.S.W.* Austr.
223 K5 **Shoal Lake** *Man.* Can.
223 K4 **Shoal Lake** *Sask.* Can.
230 D6 **Shoals** *IN* U.S.A.
85 M7 **Shoalwater Bay** *Qld* Austr.
103 K12 **Shōbara** Japan
103 L12 **Shōdo-shima** *i.* Japan
151 N4 **Shoeburyness** *Southend, England* U.K.
234 D3 **Shoemakersville** *PA* U.S.A.
120 K7 **Shofirkon** Uzbek.
104 F2 **Shōgawa** Japan
104 F2 **Shō-gawa** *r.* Japan
122 H3 **Shoghlābād** Iran
123 M3 **Shoh** *Khatlon* Tajik.
Shohi Pass Pak. *see* **Tal Pass**
234 F2 **Shohola** *PA* U.S.A.
102 S3 **Shokanbetsu-dake** *mt.* Japan
104 E3 **Shōkawa** Japan
102 U2 **Shokotsu-gawa** *r.* Japan
Shokpar Kazakh. *see* **Chokpar**
139 U1 **Shola** *r.* Rus. Fed.
121 M6 **Sholakkorgan** Kazakh.
120 K2 **Sholaksay** Kazakh.
Sholapur *Mahar.* India *see* **Solapur**
Sholaqorghan Kazakh. *see* Sholakkorgan
Sholaqsay Kazakh. *see* Sholaksay
86 C6 **Sholl Island** *W.A.* Austr.
134 F2 **Shomba** *r.* Rus. Fed.
120 H4 **Shomishkol'** Kazakh.
134 J3 **Shomvukva** Rus. Fed.
104 F2 **Shōmyō-gawa** *r.* Japan
146 E9 **Shona, Eilean** *i. Scotland* U.K.
264 J9 **Shona Ridge** *sea feature* S. Atlantic Ocean
117 M6 **Shongar** Bhutan
Shonzha Kazakh. *see* **Chundzha**
139 W4 **Shopsha** Rus. Fed.
148 E4 **Shoptown** *Northern Ireland* U.K.
120 G4 **Shoptykol'** *Aktyubinskaya Oblast'* Kazakh.
121 P2 **Shoptykol'** *Pavlodarskaya Oblast'* Kazakh.
Shoqpar Kazakh. *see* **Chokpar**
116 F3 **Shor** *Hima. Prad.* India
123 L7 **Shoran** Pak.
114 E7 **Shoranur** *Kerala* India
123 K9 **Shorap** Pak.
114 E4 **Shorapur** *Karnataka* India
123 K6 **Shorawak** *reg.* Afgh.
121 L9 **Sho'rchi** Uzbek.
235 G4 **Shore Acres** *NJ* U.S.A.
151 M5 **Shoreham** *Kent, England* U.K.
151 L6 **Shoreham-by-Sea** *West Sussex, England* U.K.
Shorghun Uzbek. *see* Sharg‘un
123 O6 **Shorkot** Pak.
122 G1 **Shorkozakhly, Solonchak** *salt flat* Turkm.
123 P2 **Shorkŭl** *l.* Tajik.
Shornaq Kazakh. *see* **Chernak**
212 D3 **Shorobe** Botswana
121 N2 **Shortandy** Kazakh.
123 L3 **Shor Tepe** Afgh.
78 □6 **Shortland Island** Solomon Is
78 □6 **Shortland Islands** Solomon Is
232 H6 **Shortsville** *NY* U.S.A.
Shosambetsu Japan *see* Shosanbetsu
102 S2 **Shosanbetsu** Japan
139 T5 **Shosha** *r.* Rus. Fed.
241 P6 **Shoshone** *CA* U.S.A.
238 G5 **Shoshone** *ID* U.S.A.
238 J4 **Shoshone** *r. WY* U.S.A.
238 I4 **Shoshone Lake** *WY* U.S.A.
240 O2 **Shoshone Mountains** *NV* U.S.A.
241 P5 **Shoshone Peak** *NV* U.S.A.
212 E4 **Shoshong** Botswana
238 J5 **Shoshoni** *WY* U.S.A.
137 M2 **Shostka** Ukr.
137 M2 **Shostka** *r.* Ukr.
151 O4 **Shotley Gate** *Suffolk, England* U.K.
122 F5 **Shotoran, Chashmeh-ye** *well* Iran
123 K4 **Shotor Khūn** *pass* Afgh.
150 F1 **Shotton** *Flintshire, Wales* U.K.
146 I11 **Shotts** *North Lanarkshire, Scotland* U.K.
Shouchun *Anhui* China *see* Shouxian
107 P8 **Shouguang** *Shandong* China
109 K2 **Shouxian** *Anhui* China
107 M8 **Shouyang** *Shanxi* China
108 G2 **Shouyang Shan** *mt. Shaanxi* China
105 J2 **Shōwa** Japan
203 G6 **Showak** Sudan
241 V7 **Show Low** *AZ* U.S.A.
129 F6 **Showt** Iran
134 I2 **Shoyna** Rus. Fed.
135 H7 **Shpakovskoye** Rus. Fed.
137 K4 **Shpola** Ukr.
136 H5 **Shpykiv** Ukr.
136 I3 **Shpyli** Ukr.
Shqipërisë, Republika e *country* Europe *see* **Albania**
137 L3 **Shramkivka** Ukr.
232 C8 **Shreve** *OH* U.S.A.
237 I9 **Shreveport** *LA* U.S.A.
150 G2 **Shrewsbury** *Shropshire, England* U.K.
235 G4 **Shrewsbury** *NJ* U.S.A.
234 B5 **Shrewsbury** *PA* U.S.A.
151 I5 **Shrewton** *Wiltshire, England* U.K.
148 F5 **Shrigley** *Northern Ireland* U.K.
114 D3 **Shrigonda** *Mahar.* India
Shri Lanka *country* Asia *see* **Sri Lanka**
116 C6 **Shri Mohangarh** *Rajasthan* India
117 L8 **Shrirampur** *W. Bengal* India
114 E6 **Shrirangapattana** *Karnataka* India
151 I4 **Shrivenham** *Oxfordshire, England* U.K.
150 G2 **Shropshire** *admin. div. England* U.K.
235 H2 **Shrub Oak** *NY* U.S.A.
Shtefan-Vode Moldova *see* **Ştefan Vodă**
196 I10 **Shtërmen** Albania
196 I8 **Shtiqën** Albania
137 M8 **Shtormove** Ukr.
121 O6 **Shu** Kazakh.
125 K9 **Shu'ab, Ghubbat** *b. Suquţrā* Yemen
125 K9 **Shu'ab, Ra's** *pt Suquţrā* Yemen
127 M8 **Shu'aiba** Iraq
108 D2 **Shuajingsi** *Sichuan* China
129 D4 **Shuakhevi** Georgia
108 C6 **Shuangbai** *Yunnan* China
Shuangcheng *Fujian* China *see* **Zherong**
100 E6 **Shuangcheng** *Heilong.* China
109 I3 **Shuanghe** *Hubei* China
108 F3 **Shuanghechang** *Sichuan* China
100 G4 **Shuanghedagang** *Heilong.* China
111 H10 **Shuanghu** *Xizang* China
Shuanghuyu *Shaanxi* China *see* **Zizhou**
Shuangjiang *Guizhou* China *see* **Jiangkou**
Shuangjiang *Hunan* China *see* **Tongdao**
108 B7 **Shuangjiang** *Yunnan* China
Shuangjiang *Yunnan* China *see* **Eshan**
107 R5 **Shuangliao** *Jilin* China
109 H6 **Shuangpai** *Hunan* China
107 P6 **Shuangshanzi** *Hebei* China
Shuangshipu *Shaanxi* China *see* **Fengxian**
100 D7 **Shuangyang** *Jilin* China
100 G5 **Shuangyashan** *Heilong.* China
Shuangzhong *Jiangxi* China *see* **Hukou**
125 J7 **Shu'ayt, Wādī** *r.* Yemen
120 G3 **Shubarkuduk** Kazakh.
120 G3 **Shubarshi** Kazakh.
128 G8 **Shubayḩ** *well* Saudi Arabia
124 F3 **Shubayrimah** Saudi Arabia
118 C3 **Shubrā al Khaymah** Egypt
124 G3 **Shubrāmīyāh** Saudi Arabia
124 F4 **Shubrāmīyāh** *well* Saudi Arabia
109 K3 **Shucheng** *Anhui* China
250 C6 **Shucushuyacu** Peru
110 B7 **Shufu** *Xinjiang* China
96 A2 **Shuganu** *Manipur* India
123 N3 **Shughnon, Qatorkŭhi** *mts* Tajik.
Shugnanskiy Khrebet *mts* Tajik. *see* **Shughnon, Qatorkŭhi**
139 R2 **Shugozero** Rus. Fed.
130 H3 **Shugur** Rus. Fed.
107 P9 **Shu He** *r.* China
Shuicheng *Guizhou* China *see* **Lupanshui**
Shuiding *Xinjiang* China *see* **Huocheng**
Shuidong *Guangdong* China *see* **Dianbai**
Shuihu *Anhui* China *see* **Changfeng**
109 L5 **Shuiji** *Fujian* China
Shuiji *Shandong* China *see* **Laixi**
108 E2 **Shuijing** *Sichuan* China
111 J10 **Shuijingkuang** *Qinghai* China
109 J7 **Shuikou** *Guangdong* China
109 H6 **Shuikou** *Hunan* China
108 F7 **Shuikouguan** *Guangxi* China
109 I5 **Shuikoushan** *Hunan* China
Shuiluocheng *Gansu* China *see* **Zhuanglang**
106 I8 **Shuiquan** *Gansu* China
106 G7 **Shuiquanzi** *Gansu* China
108 C5 **Shuituo He** *r. Sichuan* China
Shuizhai *Guangdong* China *see* **Wuhua**
111 J8 **Shuizhan** *Qinghai* China
123 N7 **Shujaabad** Pak.
100 E6 **Shulan** *Jilin* China
110 C7 **Shule** *Xinjiang* China
110 M6 **Shulehe** *Gansu* China
106 C6 **Shule He** *r.* China
106 E7 **Shule Nanshan** *mts* China
137 T1 **Shul'gino** Rus. Fed.
137 R4 **Shul'hynka** Ukr.
107 L6 **Shulinzhao** *Nei Mongol* China
Shul'mak Tajik. *see* **Novobod**
Shulu *Hebei* China *see* **Xinji**
139 O2 **Shum** Rus. Fed.
220 B4 **Shumagin Islands** *AK* U.S.A.
137 P2 **Shumakovo** Rus. Fed.
120 H6 **Shumanay** Uzbek.
102 T2 **Shumarinai-ko** *l.* Japan
212 E3 **Shumba** Zimbabwe
197 O7 **Shumen** Bulg.
197 O7 **Shumensko Plato** *nat. park* Bulg.
134 I5 **Shumerlya** Rus. Fed.
130 H4 **Shumikha** Rus. Fed.
138 M6 **Shumilina** Belarus
131 Q4 **Shumshu, Ostrov** *i. Kuril'skiye O-va* Rus. Fed.
136 F3 **Shums'k** Ukr.
139 P8 **Shumyachi** Rus. Fed.
121 O4 **Shunak, Gora** *mt.* Kazakh.
128 D7 **Shūnat Nimrīn** Jordan
109 I7 **Shunde** *Guangdong* China
139 X4 **Shunga** Rus. Fed.
220 C3 **Shungnak** *AK* U.S.A.
234 B1 **Shunk** *PA* U.S.A.
Shunling *Hunan* China *see* Ningyuan
129 I3 **Shunudag, Gora** *mt.* Rus. Fed.
107 O6 **Shunyi** *Beijing* China
108 F7 **Shuolong** *Guangxi* China
Shuoxian *Shanxi* China *see* Shuozhou
107 M7 **Shuozhou** *Shanxi* China
124 G7 **Shuqqat Najrān** *depr.* Saudi Arabia
124 G9 **Shuqrah** Yemen
122 E7 **Shūr** *r.* Iran
122 F7 **Shūr** *r.* Iran
122 I4 **Shūr** *r.* Iran
122 I6 **Shūr** *r.* Iran
122 E7 **Shūr** *watercourse* Iran
122 F6 **Shūr** *watercourse* Iran
122 F8 **Shūr** *watercourse* Iran
122 H5 **Shur** *watercourse* Iran
122 E4 **Shūr, Chāh-e** *well* Iran
122 G6 **Shūr, Rūd-e** *watercourse* Iran
122 D5 **Shūrāb** *Chahār Maḩāll va Bakhtīārī* Iran
122 D4 **Shūr Āb** Iran
122 G5 **Shūrāb** *Khorāsān* Iran
122 F5 **Shūrāb** *Yazd* Iran
122 F6 **Shūr Āb** *watercourse* Iran
Shurab Tajik. *see* **Shŭrob**
122 E5 **Shureghestan** Iran
129 I6 **Shurestān** Iran
122 H7 **Shūr Gaz** Iran
129 I6 **Shūr Gol** Iran
102 □1 **Shuri** *Okinawa* Japan
122 E6 **Shūrjestān** Iran
134 J4 **Shurma** Rus. Fed.
123 N1 **Shŭrob** Tajik.
122 I7 **Shūrū** Iran
213 F3 **Shurugwi** Zimbabwe
127 L8 **Shuruppak** *tourist site* Iraq
122 I6 **Shusf** Iran
122 C5 **Shūsh** Iran
Shusha Azer. *see* **Şuşa**
198 A2 **Shushicë** *r.* Albania
122 C5 **Shushtar** Iran
139 S6 **Shustikovo** Rus. Fed.
137 O2 **Shustovo** Rus. Fed.
222 G5 **Shuswap Lake** *B.C.* Can.
125 K4 **Shutfah, Qalamat** *well* Saudi Arabia
128 F7 **Shuwaysh, Tall ash** *hill* Jordan
139 Y5 **Shuya** *Ivanovskaya Oblast'* Rus. Fed.
134 F3 **Shuya** *Respublika Kareliya* Rus. Fed.
220 C4 **Shuyak Island** *AK* U.S.A.
107 P9 **Shuyang** *Jiangsu* China
134 H4 **Shuyskoye** Rus. Fed.
105 I6 **Shuzenji** Japan
139 U7 **Shvartsevskiy** Rus. Fed.
96 B5 **Shwebandaw** Myanmar
96 B3 **Shwebo** Myanmar
96 B5 **Shwedaung** Myanmar
96 B2 **Shwedwin** Myanmar
96 C6 **Shwegun** Myanmar
96 C6 **Shwegyin** Myanmar
96 B6 **Shwelaung** *r.* Myanmar
96 C3 **Shweli** *r.* Myanmar
96 C4 **Shwenyaung** Myanmar
96 C3 **Shweudaung** *mt.* Myanmar
136 F4 **Shybena** Ukr.
121 N5 **Shyganak** Kazakh.
Shyghanaq Kazakh. *see* Chiganak
Shyghys Qazaqstan Oblysy *admin. div.* Kazakh. *see* **Vostochnyy Kazakhstan**
Shyghys-Qongyrat Kazakh. *see* **Shygys Konyrat**
121 P4 **Shygys Konyrat** Kazakh.
121 M6 **Shymkent** Kazakh.
Shynggyrlaū Kazakh. *see* Chingirlau
Shyngqozha Kazakh. *see* Shingozha
116 E2 **Shyok** *r.* India
116 G2 **Shyok** Jammu and Kashmir
137 Q4 **Shypuvate** Ukr.
137 M6 **Shyroke** *Dnipropetrovs'ka Oblast'* Ukr.
137 N8 **Shyroke** *Respublika Krym* Ukr.

Shyroke to Sitamarhi

388

137 N5 Shyroke Zaporiz'ka Oblast' Ukr.
137 K6 Shyrokolanivka Ukr.
137 Q6 Shyrokyne Ukr.
137 O6 Shyrokyy Var Ukr.
136 J6 Shyryayeve Ukr.
137 N4 Shyshaky Ukr.
138 K8 Shyshchytsy Belarus
91 H8 Sia Maluku Indon.
Siabost Scotland U.K. see Shawbost
94 C4 Siabu Sumatera Indon.
116 F2 Siachen Glacier Jammu and Kashmir
161 J9 Siagne r. France
123 J8 Siahan Range mts Pak.
122 A2 Sīah Chashmeh Iran
123 L3 Siahgird Afgh.
123 K5 Siah Koh mts Afgh.
123 I8 Sīāh Kowr, Rūdkhāneh-ye watercourse Iran
122 I6 Sīāh Kūh l. Iran
122 E4 Sīāh Kūh mts Iran
94 E4 Siak r. Indon.
94 E4 Siak Sri Inderapura Sumatera Indon.
123 P5 Sialkot Pak.
Siam country Asia see Thailand
192 B8 Siamanna Sardegna Italy
Sian Shaanxi China see Xi'an
Sianhala Côte d'Ivoire see Sanhala
143 M7 Sianów Pol.
94 G3 Siantan i. Indon.
251 E4 Siapa r. Venez.
122 I7 Sīāreh Iran
92 F7 Siargao i. Phil.
233 P7 Siasconset MA U.S.A.
92 C9 Siasi Phil.
92 C9 Siasi i. Phil.
198 C2 Siatista Greece
92 D7 Siaton Negros Phil.
93 D2 Siau i. Indon.
138 G6 Šiauliai Lith.
209 F9 Siavonga Zambia
92 C1 Siayan i. Phil.
Siazan' Azer. see Siyäzän
123 J8 Sib Iran
125 N4 Sīb Oman
96 G7 Si Bai, Lam r. Thai.
122 C5 Sībak Iran
246 E3 Sibanicú Cuba
195 K4 Sibari Italy
Sibati Xinjiang China see Xibet
92 C6 Sibay i. Phil.
120 H1 Sibay Rus. Fed.
215 Q3 Sibayi, Lake S. Africa
263 L2 Sibbald, Cape Antarctica
169 I6 Sibbesse Ger.
141 R6 Sibbo Fin.
141 R6 Sibbofjärden b. Fin.
122 H5 Sīb Chāh Iran
188 E4 Šibenik Croatia
Siberia reg. Rus. Fed. see Sibir'
94 C5 Siberut i. Indon.
94 C5 Siberut, Selat sea chan. Indon.
94 C5 Siberut, Taman Nasional nat. park Indon.
123 L7 Sibi Pak.
91 J8 Sibidiri P.N.G.
94 A3 Sibigo Indon.
210 C4 Sibiloi National Park Kenya
71 G2 Sibir' reg. Rus. Fed.
100 H6 Sibirtsevo Rus. Fed.
130 I2 Sibiryakova, Ostrov i. Rus. Fed.
209 B5 Sibiti Congo
197 M5 Sibiu Romania
151 N4 Sible Hedingham Essex, England U.K.
236 H4 Sibley IA U.S.A.
93 B3 Siboa Sulawesi Indon.
94 C4 Sibolga Sumatera Indon.
94 C3 Siborongborong Sumatera Indon.
215 P2 Sibowe r. Swaziland
117 O6 Sibsagar Assam India
149 R7 Sibsey Lincolnshire, England U.K.
95 I3 Sibu Sarawak Malaysia
92 D8 Sibuco Mindanao Phil.
92 D8 Sibuco Bay Mindanao Phil.
92 D8 Sibuguey r. Mindanao Phil.
92 D8 Sibuguey Bay Mindanao Phil.
208 C3 Sibut C.A.R.
95 J2 Sibuti Sarawak Malaysia
92 B9 Sibutu i. Phil.
92 B9 Sibutu Passage Phil.
92 D5 Sibuyan i. Phil.
92 D5 Sibuyan Sea Phil.
197 L4 Sic Romania
222 G5 Sicamous B.C. Can.
92 C2 Sicapoo mt. Luzon Phil.
252 D4 Sicasica Bol.
92 D7 Sicayac Mindanao Phil.
Sicca Veneria Tunisia see Le Kef
82 G4 Siccus watercourse S.A. Austr.
122 E5 Si Chah Iran
Sicheng Anhui China see Sixian
Sicheng Guangxi China see Lingyun
97 D10 Sichon Thai.
108 D3 Sichuan prov. China
108 E4 Sichuan Pendi basin Sichuan China
161 H10 Sicié, Cap c. France
194 G8 Sicilia admin. reg. Italy
194 G7 Sicilia i. Italy
194 C9 Sicilian Channel Italy/Tunisia
Sicily i. Italy see Sicilia
174 E4 Siciny Pol.
234 F5 Sicklerville NJ U.S.A.
169 K6 Sickte Ger.
252 C3 Sicuani Peru
177 K5 Şicula Romania
194 E9 Siculiana Sicilia Italy
196 H5 Šid Vojvodina Serbia
177 I3 Šíd Slovakia
93 E3 Sidangoli Halmahera Indon.
150 F6 Sidbury Devon, England U.K.
164 K2 Siddeburen Neth.
116 D8 Siddhapur Gujarat India
Siddharthanagar Nepal see Bhairawa
114 F3 Siddipet Andhra Prad. India
141 P5 Sideby Fin.
93 A5 Sidenreng, Danau l. Indon.
140 O5 Sidensjö Sweden
206 D4 Sidéradougou Burkina
198 G2 Sideritis i. Limnos Greece
195 K7 Siderno Italy
199 H7 Sideros, Akrotirio pt Kriti Greece
214 G8 Sidesaviwa S. Africa
150 F6 Sidford Devon, England U.K.
123 O6 Sidhai Pak.
116 H6 Sidhauli Uttar Prad. India
116 H7 Sidhi Madh. Prad. India
Sidhirókastron Greece see Sidirokastro
Sidhpur Gujarat India see Siddhapur
205 F2 Sidi Aïssa Alg.
202 E2 Sīdī Barrānī Egypt
205 E2 Sidi Bel Abbès Alg.
204 C2 Sidi Bennour Morocco
Sidi Bou Sa'id Tunisia see Sidi Bouzid
205 H2 Sidi Bouzid Tunisia
205 H2 Sidi El Hani, Sebkhet de salt pan Tunisia
206 E2 Sidi el Mokhtâr well Mali
204 C3 Sidi Ifni Morocco
204 D2 Sidi Kacem Morocco
94 C3 Sidikalang Sumatera Indon.
205 G2 Sidi Khaled Alg.
205 E3 Sidi Mannsour well Alg.
204 B5 Sidi Mhamed well Western Sahara
205 G2 Sidi Okba Alg.
198 E1 Sidirokastro Greece
204 C2 Sidi-Smaïl Morocco
223 J2 Sid Lake N.W.T. Can.
146 J10 Sidlaw Hills Scotland U.K.
151 M6 Sidley East Sussex, England U.K.
262 P1 Sidley, Mount Antarctica
150 F6 Sidmouth Devon, England U.K.
85 I2 Sidmouth, Cape Qld Austr.
226 F3 Sidnaw MI U.S.A.
222 F5 Sidney B.C. Can.
236 H5 Sidney IA U.S.A.
238 L3 Sidney MT U.S.A.
236 D5 Sidney NE U.S.A.
233 J6 Sidney NY U.S.A.
232 A8 Sidney OH U.S.A.
231 F8 Sidney Lanier, Lake GA U.S.A.
214 I4 Sidney-on-Vaal S. Africa
206 D4 Sido Mali
93 B3 Sidoan Sulawesi Indon.
93 B3 Sidoan Sulawesi Indon.
95 J8 Sidoarjo Jawa Indon.
163 I8 Sidobre reg. France
96 B4 Sidoktaya Myanmar
Sidon Lebanon see Saïda
134 H4 Sidorovo Rus. Fed.
128 A9 Sidr, Ra's as pt Egypt
175 L2 Sidra r. Pol.
128 B10 Sidrī, Wādī watercourse Egypt
255 B7 Sidrolândia Brazil
215 P2 Sidvokodvo Swaziland
215 M7 Sidwadweni S. Africa
174 F5 Sidzina Pol.
140 Q2 Siebe Norway
140 Q2 Siebejokka r. Norway
164 J5 Siebengewald Neth.
171 H8 Siebenlehn Ger.
174 D4 Siecieborzyce Pol.
175 J4 Sieciechów Pol.
174 E2 Siecino, Jezioro l. Pol.
168 G5 Siedenburg Ger.
175 J5 Siedlanka Pol.
175 K3 Siedlce Pol.
174 E3 Siedlec Pol.
174 D2 Siedlice Pol.
174 D4 Siedlisko Lubuskie Pol.
174 E3 Siedlisko Wielkopolskie Pol.
175 L4 Siedliszcze Lubelskie Pol.
175 L4 Siedliszcze Lubelskie Pol.
169 D9 Sieg r. Ger.
169 D9 Siegburg Ger.
169 F9 Siegen Ger.
173 L4 Siegenburg Ger.
179 O4 Siegendorf im Burgenland Austria
179 N4 Sieggraben Austria
179 N3 Sieghartskirchen Austria
173 N6 Siegsdorf Ger.
168 J3 Siek Ger.
171 L8 Siekierczyn Pol.
175 L4 Sielec Pol.
177 I3 Sielnica Slovakia
171 J7 Sielow Ger.
175 L3 Siemianówka Pol.
175 L3 Siemianówka, Jezioro l. Pol.
175 K3 Siemiatycze Pol.
175 K4 Siemień Pol.
174 G4 Siemkowice Pol.
97 H7 Siĕmpang Cambodia
97 F8 Siĕmréab Cambodia
Siem Reap Cambodia see Siĕmréab
174 D1 Siemyśl Pol.
Si'en Guangxi China see Huanjiang
191 K9 Siena Italy
191 K9 Siena prov. Italy
175 K5 Sieniawa Pol.
158 I3 Sienne r. France
175 J3 Siennica Pol.
175 J4 Sienno Pol.
140 Q3 Sieppijärvi Fin.
175 H6 Siepraw Pol.
167 J3 Sieradowicki Park Krajobrazowy Pol.
174 G4 Sieradz Pol.
174 G5 Sieraków Śląskie Pol.
174 E3 Sieraków Wielkopolskie Pol.
175 H3 Sierakówek Pol.
174 F1 Sierakowice Pol.
167 H2 Sierakowski Park Krajobrazowy Pol.
157 L5 Sierck-les-Bains France
111 K11 Si'erdingka Xizang China
157 N8 Sierentz France
168 K2 Sierksdorf Ger.
174 E2 Siernczyno Pol.
179 N3 Sierndorf Austria
179 J3 Sierning Austria
179 M4 Sierningtal nature res. Austria
174 F4 Sieroszewice Pol.
175 H3 Sierpc Pol.
175 H3 Sierpienica r. Pol.
259 D6 Sierra, Punta pt Arg.
183 J2 Sierra, Punta de la pt Spain
246 H4 Sierra Bahoruco nat. park Dom. Rep.
239 L11 Sierra Blanca TX U.S.A.
185 I4 Sierra Boyer, Embalse de resr Spain
261 G5 Sierra Chica Arg.
259 D6 Sierra Colorada Arg.
185 N4 Sierra de Cazorla Segurla y las Villas park Spain
184 G2 Sierra de Fuentes Spain
250 D2 Sierra de la Culata nat. park Venez.
258 D4 Sierra de las Quijadas, Parque Nacional nat. park Arg.
Sierra del Gistral mts Spain see Xistral, Serra do
186 D3 Sierra de Luna Spain
185 J6 Sierra de Yeguas Spain
187 F7 Sierra Engarcerán Spain
259 D6 Sierra Grande Arg.
206 C4 Sierra Leone country Africa
264 H5 Sierra Leone Basin sea feature N. Atlantic Ocean
264 H5 Sierra Leone Rise sea feature N. Atlantic Ocean
240 L6 Sierra Madre Mountains CA U.S.A.
242 H4 Sierra Mojada Mex.
245 N9 Sierra Morena Mex.
250 D2 Sierra Nevada, Parque Nacional nat. park Venez.
250 C2 Sierra Nevada de Santa Marta, Parque Nacional nat. park Col.
261 G5 Sierras Bayas Arg.
240 L2 Sierraville CA U.S.A.
241 V10 Sierra Vista AZ U.S.A.
190 D3 Sierre Switz.
185 O6 Sierro Spain
185 O6 Sierro r. Spain
171 E7 Siersleben Ger.
138 F7 Siesartis r. Lith.
138 H6 Siesartis r. Lith.
187 D9 Siete Aguas Spain
183 J6 Siete Iglesias de Trabancos Spain
170 G4 Sietow Ger.
197 M3 Şieu Romania
197 M3 Şieu r. Romania
191 K8 Sieve r. Italy
170 F5 Sieversdorf Ger.
168 H1 Sieverstedt Ger.
140 R5 Sievi Fin.
175 H5 Siewierz Pol.
108 F7 Sifang Ling mts China
210 D1 Sīfenī Eth.
206 D5 Sifié Côte d'Ivoire
198 F5 Sifnos i. Greece
198 F5 Sifnou, Steno sea chan. Greece
205 E2 Sig Alg.
139 Q4 Sig, Ozero l. Rus. Fed.
125 K6 Sigani well Saudi Arabia
79 □7a Sigatoka Viti Levu Fiji
77 I3 Sigave Wallis and Futuna Is
161 B10 Sigean France
94 C5 Sigep, Tanjung pt Indon.
170 E4 Siggelkow Ger.
195 □ Siġġiewi Malta
149 Q6 Sigglesthorne East Riding of Yorkshire, England U.K.
221 M2 Sigguup Nunaa pen. Greenland
197 L3 Sighetu Marmaţiei Romania
197 M4 Sighişoara Romania
191 N9 Sigillo Italy
114 G9 Sigiriya Sri Lanka
129 J5 Sığırlı Azer.
94 □ Siglap Sing.
94 A2 Sigli Sumatera Indon.
140 □D1 Siglufjörður Iceland
92 D6 Sigma Panay Phil.
172 G5 Sigmaringen Ger.
172 G5 Sigmaringendorf Ger.
179 M2 Sigmundsherberg Austria
191 K8 Signa Italy
173 N3 Signalberg hill Ger.
165 J8 Signal de Botrange hill Belgium
161 H10 Signal de la Ste-Baume mt. France
161 C7 Signal de Mailhebiau mt. France
161 D7 Signal de Randon mt. France
160 F5 Signal de St-André hill France
162 G3 Signal de Sauvagnac hill France
162 H4 Signal du Pic hill France
159 K5 Signal du Viviers hill France
185 □ Signal Hill Gibraltar
241 R8 Signal Peak AZ U.S.A.
190 D2 Signau Switz.
161 H10 Signes France
156 H4 Signy-l'Abbaye France
156 H4 Signy-le-Petit France
215 M6 Sigoga S. Africa
162 D4 Sigogne France
94 C6 Sigoisooinan Indon.
163 E6 Sigoulès France
236 I5 Sigourney IA U.S.A.
264 C4 Sigsbee Deep sea feature G. of Mexico
143 N2 Sigtuna Sweden
243 P10 Siguatepeque Hond.
182 D3 Sigüeiro Spain
183 O6 Sigüenza Spain
163 H10 Siguer r. France
186 C2 Sigües Spain
206 C4 Siguiri Guinea
138 H4 Sigulda Latvia
241 U3 Sigurd UT U.S.A.
97 F9 Sihanoukville Cambodia
97 F9 Sihanoukville, Chhâk b. Cambodia
96 B3 Sihaung Myauk Myanmar
116 H9 Sihawa Chhattisgarh India
177 I2 Sihelné Slovakia
215 P1 Sihhoya Swaziland
190 F1 Sihlsee l. Switz.
109 L2 Sihong Jiangsu China
116 H8 Sihora Madh. Prad. India
116 G9 Sihora Mahar. India
Sihou Shandong China see Changdao
252 A2 Sihuas Peru
109 I7 Sihui Guangdong China
141 P6 Siikainen Fin.
140 R4 Siikajoki Fin.
140 R4 Siikajoki r. Fin.
140 S5 Siilinjärvi Fin.
Siipyy Fin. see Sideby
127 J5 Siirt Turkey
78 □4a Siis i. Chuuk Micronesia
123 M8 Sijawal Pak.
Sijjak Uzbek. see Sijjaq
121 N7 Sijjaq Uzbek.
165 D6 Sijsele Belgium
94 D5 Sijunjung Sumatera Indon.
116 B8 Sika Gujarat India
Sikaka Saudi Arabia see Sakākah
94 D6 Sikakap Indon.
116 F6 Sikandra Uttar Prad. India
116 G6 Sikandra Rao Uttar Prad. India
222 F3 Sikanni Chief B.C. Can.
222 F3 Sikanni Chief r. B.C. Can.
116 E6 Sikar Rajasthan India
123 M4 Sikaram mt. Afgh.
206 D4 Sikasso Mali
206 D4 Sikasso admin. reg. Mali
96 C3 Sikaw Myanmar
Sikéa Greece see Sykea
93 B6 Sikeli Sulawesi Indon.
177 H4 Sikenica r. Slovakia
237 K7 Sikeston MO U.S.A.
177 H5 Sík-hegy hill Hungary
100 H7 Sikhote-Alin' mts Rus. Fed.
100 J6 Sikhote-Alinskiy Zapovednik nature res. Rus. Fed.
198 G6 Sikinos i. Greece
188 G3 Sikirevci Croatia
117 L6 Sikkim state India
177 H6 Siklós Hungary
93 E3 Siko i. Maluku Indon.
209 D8 Sikongo Zambia
175 H3 Sikórz Pol.
140 N4 Siksjö Sweden
117 J6 Sikta Bihar India
107 R7 Sikuaishi Liaoning China
95 L1 Sikuati Sabah Malaysia
182 E4 Sil r. Spain
124 B2 Şila' i. Saudi Arabia
245 I8 Silacayoapan Mex.
92 E6 Silago Leyte Phil.
138 F6 Šilalė Lith.
191 J2 Silandro Italy
96 D5 Si Lanna National Park Thai.
192 B7 Silanus Sardegna Italy
244 F5 Silao Mex.
92 E5 Sila Point Samar Phil.
237 K10 Silas AL U.S.A.
114 F8 Silavatturai Sri Lanka
94 A2 Silawaih Agam vol. Indon.
92 D6 Silay Negros Phil.
191 R7 Silba Croatia
188 E3 Silba i. Croatia
191 R7 Silbanski Kanal sea chan. Croatia
168 H3 Silberberg hill Ger.
168 H1 Silberstedt Ger.
117 N7 Silchar Assam India
191 M4 Sile r. Italy
199 K1 Şile Turkey
151 J2 Sileby Leicestershire, England U.K.
149 K5 Silecroft Cumbria, England U.K.
138 J6 Silene Latvia
190 F2 Silenen Switz.
165 F8 Silenrieux Belgium
231 H8 Siler City NC U.S.A.
114 G4 Sileru r. India
185 N4 Siles Spain
174 E4 Silesia reg. Europe
205 G5 Silet Alg.
Sileti Kazakh. see Seletinskoye
121 O1 Sileti r. Kazakh.
121 O1 Siletiteniz, Ozero salt l. Kazakh.
158 E5 Silfiac France
Silgadi Nepal see Silgarhi
116 H5 Silgarhi Nepal
117 N6 Silghat Assam India
217 □2a Silhouette i. Inner Islands Seychelles
205 H1 Siliana Tunisia
189 B8 Siliana admin. div. Tunisia
126 F5 Silifke Turkey
192 B6 Siligo Sardegna Italy
Siliguri W. Bengal India see Shiliguri
209 E9 Sililo Zambia
177 K5 Şilindia Romania
111 I11 Siling Co salt l. China
116 F6 Silipur Madh. Prad. India
192 B9 Siliqua Sardegna Italy
192 B6 Silis r. Italy
78 □2 Silisili, Mount Samoa
Silistat Turkey see Bozkır
197 N6 Siliştea Romania
197 M6 Siliştea Nouă Romania
197 P6 Silistra Bulg.
Silistria Bulg. see Silistra
199 J1 Silivri Turkey
142 F2 Siljan Norway
141 M6 Siljan l. Sweden
143 K1 Siljansnäs Sweden
142 F5 Silkeborg Denmark
85 K4 Silkwood Qld Austr.
234 C2 Silkworth PA U.S.A.
178 D5 Sill r. Austria
187 E9 Silla Spain
138 K2 Sillamäe Estonia
190 I7 Sillano Italy
161 I9 Sillans-la-Cascade France
191 L6 Sillaro r. Italy
126 F5 Sille Turkey
182 D3 Silleda Spain
182 C4 Silleiro, Cabo c. Spain
159 K5 Sillé-le-Guillaume France
156 H5 Sillery France
206 E4 Silli Burkina
117 J8 Silli Jharkhand India
178 F6 Sillian Austria
116 E9 Sillod Mahar. India
158 E4 Sillon de Talbert pen. France
149 K4 Silloth Cumbria, England U.K.
174 E2 Silnowo Pol.
191 R5 Silo Croatia
237 H7 Siloam Springs AR U.S.A.
215 O2 Silobela S. Africa
184 F5 Silos de Calañas Spain
134 M2 Silovayakha r. Rus. Fed.
186 K4 Sils Spain
190 H3 Sils Switz.
237 H10 Silsbee TX U.S.A.
223 M4 Silsby Lake Man. Can.
149 N6 Silsden West Yorkshire, England U.K.
169 K7 Silstedt Ger.
140 S3 Siltaharju Fin.
138 J1 Siltakylä Fin.
202 B5 Siltou well Chad
95 H4 Siluas Kalimantan Indon.
123 I9 Sīlūp r. Iran
138 E6 Šilutė Lith.
215 O4 Silutshana S. Africa
138 G6 Šiluva Lith.
257 F5 Silva Jardim Brazil
127 J4 Silvan Turkey
256 C2 Silvânia Brazil
190 H3 Silvaplana Switz.
178 A7 Silvaplaner See l. Switz.
182 D6 Silvares Braga Port.
182 E8 Silvares Castelo Branco Port.
116 D9 Silvassa Dadra India
184 C3 Silveiras Port.
143 M4 Silverån r. Sweden
247 I3 Silver Bank sea feature Turks and Caicos Is
246 H3 Silver Bank Passage Turks and Caicos Is
226 C2 Silver Bay MN U.S.A.
222 B2 Silver City Y.T. Can.
239 J10 Silver City NM U.S.A.
240 M2 Silver City NV U.S.A.
232 F6 Silver Creek NY U.S.A.
241 V7 Silver Creek r. AZ U.S.A.
80 I3 Silverdale North I. N.Z.
149 L5 Silverdale Lancashire, England U.K.
234 E4 Silverdale PA U.S.A.
151 N4 Silver End Essex, England U.K.
80 J6 Silverhope North I. N.Z.
260 D3 Silverio, Laguna l. Arg.
226 F1 Silver Islet Ont. Can.
238 D5 Silver Lake OR U.S.A.
226 E5 Silver Lake WI U.S.A.
241 P6 Silver Lake l. CA U.S.A.
226 G3 Silver Lake l. MI U.S.A.
147 F7 Silvermine Mountains hills Ireland
147 F7 Silvermines Ireland
240 O4 Silver Peak Range mts NV U.S.A.
234 B7 Silver Spring MD U.S.A.
240 M2 Silver Springs NV U.S.A.
151 J3 Silverstone Northamptonshire, England U.K.
214 H4 Silver Streams S. Africa
222 E5 Silverthrone Mountain B.C. Can.
238 D2 Silvertip Mountain B.C. Can.
82 H4 Silverton N.S.W. Austr.
222 G5 Silverton B.C. Can.
150 F6 Silverton Devon, England U.K.
239 K8 Silverton CO U.S.A.
235 G4 Silverton NJ U.S.A.
237 E8 Silverton TX U.S.A.
227 L4 Silver Water Ont. Can.
251 G5 Silves Brazil
184 C6 Silves Port.
193 M2 Silvi Italy
250 B4 Silvia Col.
238 E5 Silvies r. OR U.S.A.
243 N8 Silvituc Mex.
190 I2 Silvretta Gruppe mts Switz.
178 B6 Silvrettahorn mt. Austria
129 J5 Şilyan Azer.
178 C5 Silz Austria
134 L5 Sim Rus. Fed.
134 L5 Sim r. Rus. Fed.
111 J11 Sima Xizang China
217 □3 Sima Nzwani Comoros
96 C2 Sima Myanmar
139 W5 Sima Rus. Fed.
192 B8 Simala Sardegna Italy
183 K5 Simancas Spain
177 K5 Şimand Romania
160 F3 Simandre France
136 H2 Simanichy Belarus
198 E2 Simantra Greece
108 C7 Simao Yunnan China
254 F4 Simão Dias Brazil
92 D5 Simara i. Phil.
251 F3 Simaraña Venez.
224 E4 Simàrd, Lac l. Que. Can.
127 M7 Şīmareh, Rūdkhāneh-ye r. Iran
117 J7 Simaria Jharkhand India
116 H7 Simaria Madh. Prad. India
117 K7 Simaria Ghat Bihar India
93 B3 Simatang i. Indon.
187 E9 Simat de la Valdigna Spain
199 J3 Simav Turkey
199 J3 Simav Dağları mts Turkey
111 E8 Simawat Xinjiang China
192 B8 Simaxis Sardegna Italy
124 E7 Sīmayr i. Saudi Arabia
208 D4 Simba Dem. Rep. Congo
173 N4 Simbach Ger.
173 O5 Simbach am Inn Ger.
195 K6 Simbario Italy
Simbirsk Rus. Fed. see Ul'yanovsk
78 □6 Simbo i. New Georgia Is Solomon Is
193 K4 Simbruini, Monti mts Italy
139 T6 Simbukhovo Rus. Fed.
224 D5 Simcoe Ont. Can.
224 E4 Simcoe, Lake Ont. Can.
117 J8 Simdega Jharkhand India
141 N6 Simeå Sweden
203 H6 Simēn mts Eth.
210 C1 Simēn Mountain National Park Eth.
197 N8 Simeonovgrad Bulg.
195 L6 Simeri r. Italy
197 L5 Simeria Romania
195 L6 Simeri-Crichi Italy
194 I9 Simeto r. Sicilia Italy
94 B3 Simeulue i. Indon.
137 N9 Simferopol' Ukr.
Sími i. Greece see Symi
177 L4 Şimian Romania
161 H9 Simiane-la-Rotonde France
116 H5 Simikot Nepal
97 C10 Similan, Ko i. Thai.
178 C6 Similaun mt. Austria/Italy
208 D3 Simindou C.A.R.
177 J2 Siminy mt. Slovakia
197 L9 Simitli Bulg.
240 N7 Simi Valley CA U.S.A.
Simla Hima. Prad. India see Shimla
239 L7 Simla CO U.S.A.
142 J5 Simlångsdalen Sweden
197 K3 Şimleu Silvaniei Romania
190 D2 Simme r. Switz.
173 K2 Simmelsdorf Ger.
190 C2 Simmental val. Switz.
169 B9 Simmerath Ger.
172 D2 Simmern (Hunsrück) Ger.
237 J10 Simmesport LA U.S.A.
246 F2 Simm's Long I. Bahamas
238 I3 Simms MT U.S.A.
231 □2 Simms Point New Prov. Bahamas
138 G7 Simnas Lith.
140 R4 Simo Fin.
140 S3 Simojärvi l. Fin.
244 E1 Simon Mex.
222 G4 Simonette r. Alta Can.
117 O5 Simong Arun. Prad. India
223 K4 Simonhouse Man. Can.
177 K3 Šimonka mt. Slovakia
232 E7 Simons OH U.S.A.
150 E5 Simonsbath Somerset, England U.K.
168 G2 Simonsberg Ger.
214 C10 Simon's Town S. Africa
164 J1 Simonszand i. Neth.
177 H5 Simontornya Hungary
241 W9 Simon Wash watercourse AZ U.S.A.
222 E5 Simoom Sound B.C. Can.
Simoon Sound B.C. Can. see Simoom Sound
163 F9 Simorre France
94 F5 Simpang Sumatera Indon.
95 L1 Simpang Mangayau, Tanjung pt Malaysia
165 I7 Simpelveld Neth.
254 E3 Simplício Mendes Brazil
190 E3 Simplon Switz.
190 E3 Simplon Pass Switz.
223 J5 Simpson Sask. Can.
238 I2 Simpson MT U.S.A.
234 E1 Simpson PA U.S.A.
84 F8 Simpson Desert N.T. Austr.
82 G2 Simpson Desert Conservation Park nature res. S.A. Austr.
84 G8 Simpson Desert National Park Qld Austr.
82 F2 Simpson Desert Regional Reserve nature res. S.A. Austr.
87 I9 Simpson Hill W.A. Austr.
226 G1 Simpson Island Ont. Can.
223 H2 Simpson Islands N.W.T. Can.
240 P2 Simpson Park Mountains NV U.S.A.
221 J3 Simpson Peninsula Nunavut Can.
234 B6 Simpsonville MD U.S.A.
231 F8 Simpsonville SC U.S.A.
117 J6 Simra Nepal
143 K6 Simrishamn Sweden
94 B5 Simuk i. Indon.
94 C5 Simulubek Indon.
95 I4 Simunjan Sarawak Malaysia
92 B9 Simunul i. Phil.
131 Q5 Simushir, Ostrov i. Kuril'skiye O-va Rus. Fed.
114 D4 Sina r. India
203 G2 Sīnā', Shibh Jazīrat pen. Egypt
94 B3 Sinabang Indon.
179 M5 Sinabelkirchen Austria
94 C3 Sinabung vol. Indon.
210 E3 Sina Dhaqa Somalia
Sinai pen. Egypt see Sīnā', Shibh Jazīrat
156 H5 Sinai, Mont hill France
Sinai, Mount Egypt see Mūsá, Jabal
197 N5 Sinaia Romania
Sinai al Janûbîya governorate Egypt see Janūb Sīnā'
Sinai ash Shamâlîya governorate Egypt see Shamāl Sīnā'
97 D7 Si Nakarin Reservoir Thai.
78 □6 Sinalanggu Malaita Solomon Is
244 A2 Sinaloa state Mex.
191 L9 Sinalunga Italy
250 D2 Sinamaica Venez.
Sinancha Rus. Fed. see Cheremshany
101 D9 Sinanju N. Korea
198 A3 Sinarades Kerkyra Greece
187 C8 Sinarcas Spain
202 A2 Sīnāwin Libya
209 E9 Sinazongwe Zambia
96 B5 Sinbaungwe Myanmar
96 C2 Sinbo Myanmar
96 B4 Sinbyugyun Myanmar
129 I5 Sincan Azer.
126 H4 Sincan Turkey
199 L4 Sincanlı Turkey
250 C2 Sincé Col.
250 C2 Sincelejo Col.
156 F4 Sinceny France
Sinchu Taiwan see T'aoyüan
231 F9 Sinclair, Lake GA U.S.A.
81 I8 Sinclair Head North I. N.Z.
222 F4 Sinclair Mills B.C. Can.
146 J5 Sinclair's Bay Scotland U.K.
254 E5 Sincora, Serra do hills Brazil
116 G6 Sind r. India
Sind prov. Pak. see Sindh
117 P4 Sinda Xizang China
100 J4 Sinda Rus. Fed.
211 A8 Sinda Zambia
142 G4 Sindal Denmark
92 D7 Sindañgan Mindanao Phil.
92 D7 Sindangan Bay Mindanao Phil.
94 G8 Sindangbarang Jawa Indon.
208 A5 Sindara Gabon
116 C7 Sindari Rajasthan India
93 B8 Sindeh, Teluk b. Flores Indon.
172 F4 Sindelfingen Ger.
114 E4 Sindgi Karnataka India
123 M9 Sindh prov. Pak.
114 E5 Sindhnur Karnataka India
Síndhos Greece see Sindos
117 J6 Sindhuli Garhi Nepal
Sindhulimadi Nepal see Sindhuli Garhi
138 H3 Sindi Estonia
116 G9 Sindi Mahar. India
192 B7 Sindia Sardegna Italy
245 J8 Sindihui Mex.
199 J3 Sındırgı Turkey
114 E3 Sindkhed Mahar. India
116 E9 Sindkheda Mahar. India
Sîndominic Romania see Sândominic
134 J3 Sindor Rus. Fed.
198 D2 Sindos Greece
206 D4 Sindou Burkina
114 E3 Sindphana r. India
117 K8 Sindri Jharkhand India
117 J8 Sindri Jharkhand India
123 N6 Sind Sagar Doab lowland Pak.
134 J4 Sinegor'ye Rus. Fed.
199 I2 Sinekçi Turkey
193 N3 Sinello r. Italy
Sinel'nikovo Ukr. see Synel'nykove
207 F4 Sinendé Benin
184 B5 Sines Port.
184 B5 Sines, Cabo de c. Port.
140 R3 Sinettä Fin.
187 L8 Sineu Spain
139 R8 Sinezerki Rus. Fed.
206 D5 Sinfra Côte d'Ivoire
96 D4 Sing Myanmar
203 G6 Singa Sudan
116 H5 Singahi Uttar Prad. India
96 C4 Singaing Myanmar
217 □3a Singani Njazidja Comoros
94 F4 Singapore country Asia
94 □ Singapore Sing.
94 □ Singapore r. Sing.
94 □ Singapore, Strait of Indon./Sing.
Singapura country Asia see Singapore
Singapura Sing. see Singapore
115 H3 Singapuru Orissa India
95 K9 Singaraja Bali Indon.
114 G4 Singareni Andhra Prad. India
Singatoka Viti Levu Fiji see Sigatoka
Singave Wallis and Futuna Is see Sigave
97 E7 Sing Buri Thai.
172 F6 Singen (Hohentwiel) Ger.
Sîngeorgiu de Pădure Romania see Sângeorgiu de Pădure
Sîngeorz-Băi Romania see Sângeorz-Băi
136 H7 Sîngera Moldova
136 H6 Sîngerei Moldova
110 I5 Singgimtay Xinjiang China
227 N5 Singhampton Ont. Can.
169 E10 Singhofen Ger.
211 B6 Singida Tanz.
211 B6 Singida admin. reg. Tanz.
Singidunum Serbia see Beograd
Singim Xinjiang China see Singgimtay
96 B2 Singkaling Hkamti Myanmar
93 B6 Singkang Sulawesi Indon.
94 D5 Singkarak Sumatera Indon.
95 H4 Singkawang Kalimantan Indon.
94 F5 Singkep i. Indon.
94 B3 Singkil Sumatera Indon.
94 C4 Singkuang Sumatera Indon.
83 M5 Singleton N.S.W. Austr.
84 E6 Singleton N.T. Austr.
84 C7 Singleton, Mount hill N.T. Austr.
87 D10 Singleton, Mount hill W.A. Austr.
143 O1 Singö i. Sweden
116 E7 Singoli Madh. Prad. India
96 B3 Singon Myanmar
Singora Thai. see Songkhla
Sin'gosan N. Korea see Kosan
207 F4 Singou, Réserve Totale du nature res. Burkina
117 M7 Singra Assam India
96 B3 Singu Myanmar
245 I6 Singuilucan Mex.
197 N6 Singureni Romania
116 H8 Singwara Madh. Prad. India
101 E9 Sin'gye N. Korea
124 G6 Sinḩ, Jabal hill Saudi Arabia
Sinhala country Asia see Sri Lanka
114 G9 Sinharaja Forest Reserve nature res. Sri Lanka
96 D2 Sinhkung Myanmar
101 E8 Sinhŭng N. Korea
192 B8 Sini Sardegna Italy
198 C2 Siniatsiko mt. Greece
178 D6 Sinigo r. Italy
92 C4 Siniloan Luzon Phil.
Sining Qinghai China see Xining
93 A4 Sinio, Gunung mt. Indon.
192 D6 Siniscola Sardegna Italy
197 N9 Sini Vrŭkh mt. Bulg.
137 R2 Siniye Lipyagi Rus. Fed.
120 I2 Siniy-Shikhan Rus. Fed.
188 F4 Sinj Croatia
93 B6 Sinjai Sulawesi Indon.
127 J5 Sinjār Iraq
127 J5 Sinjār, Jabal mt. Iraq
122 A3 Sīnji Iran
128 D6 Sinjil West Bank
203 H5 Sinkat Sudan
Sinkiang aut. reg. China see Xinjiang Uygur Zizhiqu
Sinkiang Uighur Autonomous Region aut. reg. China see Xinjiang Uygur Zizhiqu
147 E5 Sinking r. Ireland
232 B9 Sinking Spring OH U.S.A.
136 G1 Sinkyevichy Belarus
183 K6 Sinlabajos Spain
156 F3 Sin-le-Noble France
Sînmartin Romania see Sânmartin
101 D9 Sinmi-do i. N. Korea
169 F9 Sinn Ger.
169 I10 Sinn r. Ger.
192 C9 Sinnai Sardegna Italy
251 H3 Sinnamary Fr. Guiana
114 D3 Sinnar Mahar. India
128 A9 Sinn Bishr, Jabal hill Egypt
137 O3 Sinne Ukr.
Sinneh Iran see Sanandaj
232 G7 Sinnemahoning PA U.S.A.
193 R7 Sinni r. Italy
Sînnicolau Mare Romania see Sânnicolau Mare
Sinoia Zimbabwe see Chinhoyi
197 Q6 Sinoie, Lacul lag. Romania
138 J4 Sinole Latvia
253 G2 Sinop Brazil
126 G2 Sinop Turkey
Sinope Turkey see Sinop
195 J7 Sinopoli Italy
242 D2 Sinoquipe Mex.
101 E8 Sinp'a N. Korea
Sînpetru Mare Romania see Sânpetru Mare
101 F8 Sinp'o N. Korea
101 E9 Sinp'yŏng N. Korea
172 E7 Sins Switz.
101 E9 Sinsang N. Korea
172 F3 Sinsheim Ger.
95 I4 Sintang Kalimantan Indon.
247 □10 Sint Annabaai b. Curaçao Neth. Antilles
164 F5 Sint Annaland Neth.
164 I2 Sint Annaparochie Neth.
164 I5 Sint Anthonis Neth.
247 □10 Sint Christoffelberg hill Curaçao Neth. Antilles
177 K5 Sintea Mare Romania
177 L4 Şinteu Romania
247 □2 Sint Eustatius i. Neth. Antilles
165 F7 Sint-Genesius-Rode Belgium
165 F6 Sint-Gillis-Waas Belgium
165 H6 Sint-Huibrechts-Lille Belgium
164 I2 Sint Jacobiparochie Neth.
165 F6 Sint Jansteen Neth.
165 D6 Sint-Joris Belgium
165 G6 Sint-Katelijne-Waver Belgium
Sint Kruis Curaçao Neth. Antilles see Santa Krus
165 E6 Sint-Laureins Belgium
165 G6 Sint-Lenaarts Belgium
247 L4 Sint Maarten i. Neth. Antilles
164 F5 Sint Maartensdijk Neth.
165 E6 Sint-Margriete Belgium
165 E7 Sint-Maria-Lierde Belgium
165 E6 Sint-Martens-Latem Belgium
247 □10 Sint Michiel Curaçao Neth. Antilles
247 □9 Sint Nicolaas Aruba
164 I3 Sint Nicolaasga Neth.
165 F6 Sint-Niklaas Belgium
237 G11 Sinton TX U.S.A.
164 G3 Sint Pancras Neth.
164 F5 Sint Philipsland Neth.
165 F7 Sint-Pieters-Leeuw Belgium
184 A3 Sintra Port.
180 B3 Sintra-Cascais, Parque Natural de nature res. Port.
191 L7 Sintria r. Italy
139 T5 Sintsovo Rus. Fed.
165 H7 Sint-Truiden Belgium
247 □10 Sint Willebrordus Curaçao Neth. Antilles
250 C2 Sinú r. Col.
101 D8 Sinŭiju N. Korea
210 F2 Sinujiif Somalia
138 L4 Sinyaya r. Rus. Fed.
172 E4 Sinzheim Ger.
169 D9 Sinzig Ger.
173 M4 Sinzing Ger.
177 H5 Sió r. Romania
186 G4 Sió r. Spain
177 H5 Sióagárd Hungary
92 D8 Siocon Mindanao Phil.
177 H5 Siófok Hungary
209 D9 Sioma Zambia
209 D9 Sioma Ngwezi National Park Zambia
190 C3 Sion Switz.
146 F6 Sionascaig, Loch l. Scotland U.K.
129 G4 Sioni Georgia
147 H3 Sion Mills Northern Ireland U.K.
Sionmsheni Georgia see Sioni
221 K2 Siorapaluk Greenland
78 □6 Siota Solomon Is
160 C4 Sioule r. France
236 G4 Sioux Center IA U.S.A.
236 G4 Sioux City IA U.S.A.
236 G4 Sioux Falls SD U.S.A.
224 B3 Sioux Lookout Ont. Can.
243 N11 Sipacate Guat.
95 M2 Sipadan, Pulau i. Sabah Malaysia
92 D7 Sipalay Negros Phil.
188 F4 Šipan i. Croatia
95 I4 Sipang, Tanjung pt Malaysia
247 □7 Siparia Trin. and Tob.
96 C3 Sipein Myanmar
Siphaqeni S. Africa see Flagstaff
100 D7 Siping Jilin China
95 K2 Sipitang Sabah Malaysia
223 L4 Sipiwesk Man. Can.
223 L4 Sipiwesk Lake Man. Can.
262 P2 Siple, Mount Antarctica
262 N1 Siple Coast Antarctica
262 P2 Siple Island Antarctica
Sipolilo Zimbabwe see Guruve
Siponj Tajik. see Bartang
197 P3 Şipote Romania
188 F3 Šipovo Bos.-Herz.
172 G6 Sipplingen Ger.
237 K9 Sipsey r. AL U.S.A.
94 C6 Sipura i. Indon.
94 C6 Sipura, Selat sea chan. Indon.
128 A9 Siq, Wādī as watercourse Egypt
125 L9 Siqirah Suquṭrā Yemen
256 C5 Siqueira Campos Brazil
244 A2 Siqueiros Mex.
242 □Q11 Siquia r. Nic.
92 D7 Siquijor Phil.
92 D7 Siquijor i. Phil.
250 D2 Siquisique Venez.
123 M10 Sir r. Pak.
114 E6 Sira Karnataka India
142 C3 Sira Norway
142 C3 Sira r. Norway
125 L3 Şīr Abū Nu'āyr i. U.A.E.
161 I7 Sirac mt. France
97 E8 Si Racha Thai.
195 I9 Siracusa Sicilia Italy
195 I9 Siracusa prov. Sicilia Italy
Siraha Nepal see Sirha
117 L7 Sirajganj Bangl.
222 F4 Sir Alexander, Mount B.C. Can.
162 I6 Siran France
126 I3 Şiran Turkey
123 L9 Siranda Lake Pak.
116 H7 Sirathu Uttar Prad. India
207 F3 Sirba r. Burkina/Niger
128 B10 Sirbāl, Jabal mt. Egypt
125 K3 Şīr Banī Yās i. U.A.E.
Sircilla Andhra Prad. India see Sirsilla
127 N5 Sīrdān Iran
Sirdaryo r. Asia see Syrdar'ya
121 M7 Sirdaryo Uzbek.
121 M7 Sirdaryo admin. div. Uzbek.
Sirdaryo Wiloyati admin. div. Uzbek. see Sirdaryo
210 C2 Sīrē Oromīya Eth.
210 C2 Sīrē Oromīya Eth.
211 A6 Sire Tanz.
84 F3 Sir Edward Pellew Group is N.T. Austr.
226 B4 Siren WI U.S.A.
193 L3 Sirente, Monte mt. Italy
197 O3 Siret Romania
197 Q5 Siret r. Romania
Siret r. Ukr. see Seret
86 I2 Sir Graham Moore Islands W.A. Austr.
117 K6 Sirha Nepal
128 F7 Sirḩān, Wādī as watercourse Jordan/Saudi Arabia
197 J4 Şiria Romania
122 G8 Sīrīk Iran
95 I3 Sirik, Tanjung pt Malaysia
96 E6 Siri Kit Dam Thai.
142 F2 Sirikjerka hill Norway
Sirína i. Greece see Syrna
97 D10 Sirinat National Park Thai.
123 M6 Siritoi r. Pak.
122 F6 Sīrīz Iran
123 I9 Sīrjā Iran
222 E2 Sir James MacBrien, Mount N.W.T. Can.
122 F7 Sīrjān Iran
122 F7 Sīrjān salt flat Iran
82 F6 Sir Joseph Banks Group Conservation Park nature res. S.A. Austr.
140 R3 Sirkka Fin.
116 F4 Sirmaur Hima. Prad. India
221 K2 Sirmilik National Park Nunavut Can.
191 J5 Sirmione Italy
Sirmium Vojvodina Serbia see Sremska Mitrovica
116 H7 Sirmour Madh. Prad. India
Sirmur Hima. Prad. India see Sirmaur
190 G1 Sirnach Switz.
127 K5 Şırnak Turkey
140 T4 Sirniö Fin.
179 J6 Sirnitz Austria
160 I3 Sirod France
116 D7 Sirohi Rajasthan India
177 J4 Sirok Hungary
177 J2 Široké Slovakia
210 B4 Siroko Uganda
191 P8 Sirolo Italy
94 B4 Sirombu Indon.
114 G3 Sironcha Mahar. India
93 C4 Sirong Sulawesi Indon.
116 F7 Sironj Madh. Prad. India
191 L3 Siròr Italy
Síros i. Greece see Syros
138 M6 Sirotsina Belarus
204 D3 Siroua, Jbel mt. Morocco
114 F3 Sirpur Andhra Prad. India
124 G3 Sirr, Nafūd as des. Saudi Arabia
124 E6 Sirrayn i. Saudi Arabia
210 D3 Sirrei Eth.
240 N6 Sirretta Peak CA U.S.A.
122 F9 Sīrrī, Jazīreh-ye i. Iran
116 E5 Sirsa Haryana India
222 G5 Sir Sandford, Mount B.C. Can.
114 D5 Sirsi Karnataka India
116 F7 Sirsi Madh. Prad. India
116 G5 Sirsi Uttar Prad. India
114 F3 Sirsilla Andhra Prad. India
Sirte Libya see Surt
Sirte, Gulf of Libya see Surt, Khalīj
82 B2 Sir Thomas, Mount hill S.A. Austr.
185 I3 Siruela Spain
114 E5 Siruguppa Karnataka India
239 J12 Sirupa r. Mex.
114 D4 Sirur Karnataka India
114 D3 Sirur Mahar. India
138 G6 Sirutiškis Lith.
127 K4 Şirvan Turkey
129 I5 Şirvan Düzü lowland Azer.
122 B1 Şirvan Düzü plain Azer.
129 J4 Şirvanovka Azer.
129 K6 Şirvan Qoruğu nature res. Azer.
114 F5 Sirvel Andhra Prad. India
175 K1 Širvinta r. Lith.
138 H6 Širvintos Lith.
124 G8 Şirwāḩ Yemen
127 L6 Sīrwān r. Iraq
222 G4 Sir Wilfrid Laurier, Mount B.C. Can.
85 I2 Sir William Thompson Range hills Qld Austr.
122 H5 Siryan Iran
Sis Turkey see Kozan
123 L9 Sisa Creek inlet Pak.
188 F3 Sisak Croatia
96 G7 Sisaket Thai.
243 N7 Sisal Mex.
185 O2 Sisante Spain
182 C2 Sisargas, Illas is Spain
Siscia Croatia see Sisak
192 C2 Sisco Corse France
214 H3 Sishen S. Africa
106 J9 Sishilipu Gansu China
109 M5 Sishuang Liedao is China
129 H6 Sisian Armenia
129 G6 Sisiani Lerrnants'k pass Armenia/Azer.
206 E4 Sisili r. Ghana alt. Sissili (Burkina)
221 M3 Sisimiut Greenland
223 K4 Sisipuk Lake Man./Sask. Can.
226 F2 Siskiwit Bay MI U.S.A.
242 F4 Sisogúichic Mex.
97 F8 Sisŏphŏn Cambodia
240 L7 Sisquoc r. CA U.S.A.
190 D1 Sissach Switz.
236 G3 Sisseton SD U.S.A.
206 E4 Sissili r. Burkina alt. Sisili (Ghana)
233 □R1 Sisson Branch Reservoir N.B. Can.
156 G4 Sissonne France
232 D10 Sissonville WV U.S.A.
123 I6 Sīstān reg. Iran
122 I8 Sīstān va Balūchestān prov. Iran
177 K5 Şiştarovăţ Romania
226 G4 Sister Bay WI U.S.A.
161 H8 Sisteron France
115 M7 Sisters is Andaman & Nicobar Is India
238 D4 Sisters OR U.S.A.
216 □2a Sisters Peak hill Ascension S. Atlantic Ocean
232 E9 Sistersville WV U.S.A.
193 K5 Sisto r. Italy
178 D5 Sistrans Austria
122 H8 Sīt Iran
139 U3 Sit' r. Rus. Fed.
211 A6 Sitalike Tanz.
117 J6 Sitamarhi Bihar India

Sitamau to Sól
389

116 E8 Sitamau Madh. Prad. India
213 □J3 Sitampiky Madag.
92 B9 Sitangkai Phil.
175 L5 Sitaniec Pol.
116 H6 Sitapur Uttar Prad. India
176 F2 Šitbořice Czech Rep.
199 H7 Siteia Kriti Greece
215 P2 Siteki Swaziland
186 I5 Sitges Spain
198 E2 Sithonias, Chersonisos pen. Greece
Sitia Kriti Greece see Siteia
106 D5 Sitian Xinjiang China
213 G4 Sitila Moz.
96 H2 Siting Guizhou China
254 D5 Sítio da Abadia Brazil
254 E5 Sítio do Mato Brazil
187 E7 Sitjar, Embalse de resr Spain
220 E4 Sitka AK U.S.A.
175 I5 Sitkówka-Nowiny Pol.
116 H7 Sitlaha Madh. Prad. India
196 I8 Sitnica r. Serbia
177 H3 Sitno mt. Slovakia
138 M4 Sitnya r. Rus. Fed.
202 E2 Sitrah oasis Egypt
138 M6 Sitsyenyets Belarus
Sittang r. Myanmar see Sittaung
165 I7 Sittard Neth.
96 B2 Sittaung Myanmar
96 C6 Sittaung r. Myanmar
168 I4 Sittensen Ger.
172 G6 Sitter r. Ger.
179 K6 Sittersdorf Austria
215 L9 Sittingbourne S. Africa
151 N5 Sittingbourne Kent, England U.K.
Sittoung r. Myanmar see Sittaung
96 A4 Sittwe Myanmar
95 K8 Situbondo Jawa Indon.
171 D9 Sitzendorf Ger.
179 M2 Sitzendorf an der Schmida Austria
171 G8 Sitzenroda Ger.
109 □I7 Siu A Chau i. H.K. China
93 C6 Siumpu i. Indon.
78 □2 Si'umu Samoa
242 □Q11 Siuna Nic.
141 R6 Siuntio Fin.
192 C8 Siurgus Donigala Sardegna Italy
117 K8 Siuri W. Bengal India
134 K4 Siva Rus. Fed.
177 I6 Sivac Vojvodina Serbia
114 F8 Sivaganga Tamil Nadu India
114 E8 Sivakasi Tamil Nadu India
100 E2 Sivaki Rus. Fed.
122 E6 Sivand Iran
126 H4 Sivas Turkey
199 K4 Sivaslı Turkey
206 B3 Sivé Maur.
126 I5 Siverek Turkey
138 K5 Sivers l. Latvia
137 R5 Sivers'k Ukr.
139 N2 Siverskiy Rus. Fed.
Sivers'kyy Donets' r. Rus. Fed. see Severskiy Donets
137 S5 Sivers'kyy Donets' r. Ukr.
175 M6 Sivka-Voynylivs'ka Ukr.
134 M2 Sivomaskinskiy Rus. Fed.
126 I4 Sivrice Turkey
126 E4 Sivrihisar Turkey
165 F8 Sivry Belgium
157 J5 Sivry-sur-Meuse France
215 N2 Sivukile S. Africa
93 B5 Siwa Sulawesi Indon.
202 E2 Siwah Egypt
202 E2 Siwah, Wāḥāt oasis Egypt
116 F4 Siwalik Range mts India/Nepal
117 J6 Siwan Bihar India
116 D7 Siwana Rajasthan India
Siwa Oasis Egypt see Sīwah, Wāḥāt
129 H5 Şıxarx Azer.
247 □4 Six Cross Roads Barbados
161 H10 Six-Fours-les-Plages France
109 K2 Sixian Anhui China
226 I6 Six Lakes MI U.S.A.
147 E7 Sixmilebridge Ireland
147 H3 Sixmilecross Northern Ireland U.K.
160 J5 Sixt, Réserve Naturelle de nature res. France
160 J4 Sixt-Fer-à-Cheval France
215 N1 Siyabuswa S. Africa
129 H7 Siyah Rud Iran
Siyang Guangxi China see Shangsi
109 L2 Siyang Jiangsu China
215 M2 Siyathemba S. Africa
215 O1 Siyathuthuka S. Africa
129 K4 Siyäzän Azer.
107 K6 Siyitang Nei Mongol China
125 E1 Siyuni Iran
184 A2 Sizandro r. Port.
151 P3 Sizewell Suffolk, England U.K.
Siziwang Qi Nei Mongol China see Ulan Hua
158 C5 Sizun France
134 K2 Sizyabsk Rus. Fed.
142 H6 Sjælland i. Denmark
140 O3 Sjaunja naturreservat nature res. Sweden
196 I7 Sjenica Serbia
141 J6 Sjoa Norway
143 J6 Sjöbo Sweden
140 I5 Sjøholt Norway
140 L3 Sjona sea chan. Norway
140 M4 Sjoutnäset Sweden
140 N2 Sjøvegan Norway
140 P4 Sjulsmark Sweden
140 □ Sjuøyane is Svalbard
140 L5 Skäckerfjällen mts Sweden
196 H8 Skadarsko Jezero nat. park Montenegro
137 L7 Skadovs'k Ukr.
142 H6 Skælsør Denmark
142 E6 Skærbæk Denmark
221 Q2 Skærfjorden inlet Greenland
221 Q3 Skaftafell nat. park Iceland
140 □E1 Skaftafell nat. park Iceland
140 □E2 Skaftárós r. mouth Iceland
140 □D1 Skagafjörður inlet Iceland
140 □C1 Skagaheiði reg. Iceland
142 G4 Skagen Denmark
142 G4 Skagen nature res. Denmark
143 K3 Skagern l. Sweden
142 E4 Skagerrak str. Denmark/Norway
238 C2 Skagit r. WA U.S.A.
220 E5 Skagit Mountain B.C. Can.
220 E4 Skagway AK U.S.A.
140 R1 Skaidi Norway
140 I7 Skaidiškės Lith.
146 J4 Skaill Orkney, Scotland U.K.
146 K5 Skaill Orkney, Scotland U.K.
198 G4 Skala Notio Aigaio Greece
198 D6 Skala Peloponnisos Greece
175 H5 Skała Pol.
199 H3 Skala Kallonis Lesvos Greece
140 N2 Skaland Norway
136 F5 Skala-Podil's'ka Ukr.
142 I3 Skälderviken b. Sweden
171 K9 Skalice Czech Rep.
129 B1 Skalistyy Khrebet reg. Rus. Fed.
177 H2 Skalité Slovakia
140 J1 Skallelv Norway
140 N4 Skalmodal Sweden
176 B1 Skalná Czech Rep.
142 F5 Skals r. Denmark
137 M9 Skalyste Ukr.
142 F5 Skanderborg Denmark
142 J6 Skåne county Sweden
143 J6 Skåne reg. Sweden
232 I6 Skaneateles NY U.S.A.
233 I6 Skaneateles Lake NY U.S.A.
142 B2 Skånevik Norway
142 B2 Skånevikfjorden sea chan. Norway
140 N4 Skansholm Sweden
198 F3 Skantzoura i. Greece
174 D3 Skape Pol.
143 J3 Skara Sweden
146 J4 Skara Brae tourist site Orkney, Scotland U.K.
140 N2 Skarberget Norway
191 R7 Škarda i. Croatia
Skardarsko Jezero l. Albania/Montenegro see Scutari, Lake
85 I1 Skardon r. Qld Austr.
116 E2 Skardu Jammu and Kashmir
142 C2 Skare Norway
142 C3 Skåreheia mt. Norway
141 P7 Skärgårdshavets nationalpark nat. park Fin.
142 H4 Skärhamn Sweden
142 H1 Skarnes Norway
168 J1 Skarø i. Denmark
136 H2 Skarodnaye Belarus
143 N1 Skärplinge Sweden
141 L5 Skärsjövålen Sweden
141 J5 Skarstind mt. Norway
174 G1 Skarszewy Pol.
141 J5 Skarvedalseggen mt. Norway
140 N4 Skarvsjöby Sweden
175 J4 Skaryszew Pol.
136 F4 Skarzhyntsi Ukr.
175 I4 Skarżysko-Kamienna Pol.
142 I1 Skasberget hill Norway
142 I1 Skasen l. Norway
138 F6 Skaudvilė Lith.
140 P3 Skaulo Sweden
142 D1 Skaupsjøen-Hardangerjøkulen park Norway
142 E5 Skave Denmark
146 □O2 Skaw Shetland, Scotland U.K.
175 H5 Skawa r. Pol.
175 H6 Skawina Pol.
204 B4 Skaymat Western Sahara
143 O2 Skebobruk Sweden
143 J3 Skeda udde Sweden
143 O2 Skedviken l. Sweden
143 L2 Skedvisjön l. Sweden
222 D4 Skeena r. B.C. Can.
222 D3 Skeena Mountains B.C. Can.
149 R7 Skegness Lincolnshire, England U.K.
140 □E2 Skeiðarársandur sand area Iceland
146 □N2 Skeld Shetland, Scotland U.K.
146 □N2 Skelda Ness hd Scotland U.K.
168 I1 Skelde Denmark
212 B3 Skeleton Coast Game Park nature res. Namibia
140 P4 Skellefteå Sweden
140 P4 Skellefteälven r. Sweden
140 P4 Skelleftebukten b. Sweden
140 P4 Skelleftehamn Sweden
147 A9 Skellig Rocks is Ireland
149 L6 Skelmersdale Lancashire, England U.K.
146 G11 Skelmorlie North Ayrshire, Scotland U.K.
149 P4 Skelton Redcar and Cleveland, England U.K.
Skelton-in-Cleveland England U.K. see Skelton
150 G4 Skenfrith Monmouthshire, Wales U.K.
175 H3 Skępe Pol.
141 N5 Skeppshamn Sweden
214 G4 Skerpioenpunt S. Africa
146 H5 Skerray Highland, Scotland U.K.
147 J5 Skerries Ireland
150 E4 Sketty Swansea, Wales U.K.
136 B4 Skhidni Beskydy mts Pol./Ukr.
136 B4 Skhidni Karpaty mts Ukr.
175 L6 Skhidnytsya Ukr.
Skhimatárion Greece see Schimatari
205 H2 Skhira Tunisia
Skhiza i. Greece see Schiza
142 G2 Ski Norway
198 F3 Skiathos Greece
198 E3 Skiathos i. Greece
147 D9 Skibbereen Ireland
140 P2 Skibotn Norway
138 H8 Skidal' Belarus
148 K4 Skiddaw hill England U.K.
222 D4 Skidegate Mission B.C. Can.
Skidel' Belarus see Skidal'
234 C6 Skidmore MD U.S.A.
138 I6 Skiemonys Lith.
142 F2 Skien Norway
175 I4 Skierbieszów Pol.
175 I4 Skierniewice Pol.
141 P6 Skiftet sea chan. Fin.
205 G1 Skikda Alg.
138 K4 Šķilbēni Latvia
198 B5 Skinari, Akrotirio pt Zakynthos Greece
143 L2 Skinnskatteberg Sweden
116 F3 Skio Jammu and Kashmir
146 F11 Skipness Argyll and Bute, Scotland U.K.
234 E4 Skippack PA U.S.A.
149 Q6 Skipsea East Riding of Yorkshire, England U.K.
214 E10 Skipskop S. Africa
83 I7 Skipton Vic. Austr.
149 M6 Skipton North Yorkshire, England U.K.
234 C7 Skipton MD U.S.A.
149 Q6 Skirlaugh East Riding of Yorkshire, England U.K.
Skiropoula i. Greece see Skyropoula
Skíros i. Greece see Skyros
142 F5 Skive Denmark
175 K3 Skivy Duże Pol.
140 □E1 Skjálfandafljót r. Iceland
140 □E1 Skjálfandi b. Iceland
140 M3 Skjelatinden mt. Norway
140 L4 Skjellbreid Norway
142 G1 Skjellinhovde hill Norway
142 C1 Skjermene mt. Norway
140 P2 Skjerkeknuten hill Norway
142 E6 Skjern Denmark
142 E5 Skjern r. Denmark
140 K4 Skjern Norway
140 M3 Skjerstadfjorden inlet Norway
140 P1 Skjervøy Norway
141 I6 Skjolden Norway
168 J1 Skjoldnæs pen. Denmark
198 D3 Sklithro Greece
139 U4 Sknyatino Rus. Fed.
Skobelev Uzbek. see Farg'ona
121 O8 Skobeleva, Pik mt. Kyrg.
179 L8 Škocjan Slovenia
179 I8 Škocjanske Jame tourist site Slovenia
174 G6 Skoczów Pol.
215 J10 Skoenmakerskop S. Africa
178 E2 Škofja Loka Slovenia
179 K8 Škofljica Slovenia
176 N1 Skog Sweden
142 M1 Skoganvarri Norway
140 T2 Skogfoss Norway
140 Q2 Skoghall Sweden
143 L5 Skokholm Island Wales U.K.
150 B4 Skokholm Island Wales U.K.
174 F3 Skoki Pol.
226 G7 Skokie IL U.S.A.
120 I3 Skol' Kazakh.
136 C4 Skole Ukr.
143 L2 Sköllersta Sweden
136 L5 Skolyszyn Pol.
150 B4 Skomer Island Wales U.K.
174 G4 Skomlin Pol.
140 N4 Skomvær is Norway
215 K3 Skoonspruit r. S. Africa
198 E3 Skopelos Greece
198 E3 Skopelos i. Greece
199 G3 Skopelos i. Greece
198 G3 Skopia hill Limnos Greece
139 U4 Skopin Rus. Fed.
196 J9 Skopje Macedonia
Skoplje Macedonia see Skopje
144 D1 Skopunarfjørður sea chan. Faroe Is
174 G2 Skórcz Pol.
135 G6 Skorodnoye Rus. Fed.
175 K5 Skorogoszcz Pol.
174 F5 Skoroszyce Pol.
140 L4 Skorovatn Norway
140 J4 Skorpa i. Norway
142 F5 Skørping Denmark
175 K3 Skórzec Pol.
174 F3 Skorzęcińskie, Jezioro l. Pol.
198 F1 Skotoussa Greece
142 I2 Skotterud Norway
198 E3 Skoutari Greece
199 H3 Skoutaros Lesvos Greece
143 J3 Skövde Sweden
100 C2 Skovorodino Rus. Fed.
233 □P4 Skowhegan ME U.S.A.
142 F2 Skrimfjell hill Norway
138 I5 Skriveri Latvia
188 D2 Škrlatica mt. Slovenia
175 J2 Skroda r. Pol.
140 P3 Skröven Sweden
138 F5 Skrunda Latvia
175 H3 Skrwa r. Pol.
175 H2 Skrwilno Pol.
138 H7 Skrydlyeva Belarus
174 E2 Skrzatusz Pol.
175 G6 Skrzyczne mt. Pol.
175 I4 Skrzyńsko Pol.
175 J6 Skrzyszów Pol.
142 B2 Skudeneshavn Norway
215 K1 Skuinsdrif S. Africa
222 C2 Skukum, Mount Y.T. Can.
213 F5 Skukuza S. Africa
140 O5 Skuleskogens nationalpark nat. park Sweden
241 P5 Skull Peak NV U.S.A.
241 T7 Skull Valley AZ U.S.A.
214 B6 Skulpfonteinpunt pt S. Africa
174 G3 Skulsk Pol.
143 M2 Skultuna Sweden
236 J5 Skunk r. IA U.S.A.
138 E5 Skuodas Lith.
139 U7 Skuratovskiy Rus. Fed.
142 J6 Skurup Sweden
197 L7 Skŭt r. Bulg.
143 N1 Skutskär Sweden
140 M2 Skutvik Norway
144 D1 Skúvoy i. Faroe Is
136 D1 Skvaryava Ukr.
136 I4 Skvyra Ukr.
174 D3 Skwierzyna Pol.
146 E8 Skye i. Scotland U.K.
146 D8 Skye i. Scotland U.K.
142 C3 Skykula hill Norway
259 B9 Skyring, Seno b. Chile
198 F4 Skyropoula i. Greece
198 F4 Skyros Skyros Greece
198 F4 Skyros i. Greece
234 E2 Skytop PA U.S.A.
262 S1 Skytrain Ice Rise Antarctica
138 K6 Slabodka Belarus
175 J3 Słaboszów Pol.
234 C3 Slabtown PA U.S.A.
234 F4 Slack Woods NJ U.S.A.
Sláděčkovce Slovakia see Močenok
137 R7 Sladkiy, Liman salt l. Rus. Fed.
144 D1 Slættaratindur hill Faroe Is
142 H6 Slagelse Denmark
164 K3 Slagharen Neth.
140 O4 Slagnäs Sweden
149 M6 Slaidburn Lancashire, England U.K.
146 I11 Slamannan Falkirk, Scotland U.K.
95 H8 Slamet, Gunung vol. Indon.
177 J3 Slaná r. Slovakia
147 I5 Slane Ireland
177 K3 Slanec Slovakia
147 I8 Slaney r. Ireland
197 N5 Slănic Romania
177 Q4 Slănic r. Romania
197 O5 Slănic Moldova Romania
177 H3 Slanské vrchy mts Slovakia
138 L2 Slantsy Rus. Fed.
176 D1 Slaný Czech Rep.
179 I7 Slap Slovenia
138 G7 Šlapaberžė Lith.
176 G1 Šlapanice Czech Rep.
188 F4 Slapovi Krke nat. park Croatia
135 H6 Slashchevskaya Rus. Fed.
85 K5 Slashers Reefs Qld Austr.
Śląsk reg. Europe see Silesia
175 G5 Śląska, Nizina lowland Pol.
175 G5 Śląska, Wyżyna hills Pol.
175 G5 Śląskie prov. Pol.
234 E3 Slateford PA U.S.A.
234 F5 Slate Hill NY U.S.A.
224 C3 Slate Islands Ont. Can.
86 J5 Slatey watercourse W.A. Austr.
188 F3 Slatina Croatia
197 M6 Slatina Romania
177 I3 Slatina r. Slovakia
197 K3 Slatina-Timiş Romania
234 D3 Slatington PA U.S.A.
176 G2 Slatinice Czech Rep.
232 E10 Slaty Fork WV U.S.A.
137 P4 Slatyne Ukr.
139 J2 Slautnoye Rus. Fed.
181 I3 Slava Rus. Fed.
222 H2 Slave r. Alta/N.W.T. Can.
207 F5 Slave Coast Africa
222 H4 Slave Lake Alta Can.
222 H2 Slave Point N.W.T. Can.
Slavgorod Belarus see Slawharad
121 R1 Slavgorod Rus. Fed.
Slavgorod Ukr. see Slavhorod
137 O5 Slavhorod Dnipropetrovs'ka Oblast' Ukr.
137 O3 Slavhorod Sums'ka Oblast' Ukr.
177 G2 Slavičín Czech Rep.
197 K7 Slavinja Serbia
138 M4 Slavkovichi Rus. Fed.
176 G1 Slavkovský les for. Czech Rep.
176 F2 Slavkov u Brna Czech Rep.
191 P4 Slavnik mt. Slovenia
139 T5 Slavnoye Rus. Fed.
Slavonia reg. Croatia see Slavonija
176 E3 Slavonice Czech Rep.
188 F3 Slavonija reg. Croatia
Slavonska Požega Croatia see Požega
188 G3 Slavonski Brod Croatia
177 J3 Slavošovce Slovakia
138 E6 Slavsk Rus. Fed.
138 I5 Slavuta Ukr.
136 J2 Slavutych Ukr.
Slavyanka Kazakh. see Myrzakent
138 I4 Slavyanka Rus. Fed.
100 G7 Slavyanka Rus. Fed.
197 M7 Slavyanovo Bulg.
Slavyansk Ukr. see Slov"yans'k
Slavyanskaya Rus. Fed. see Slavyansk-na-Kubani
135 G7 Slavyansk-na-Kubani Rus. Fed.
174 E4 Sława Pol.
175 L4 Sławatycze Pol.
174 F2 Sławno Pol.
139 O5 Slawharad Belarus
174 F2 Sławianowskie Wielkie, Jezioro l. Pol.
143 M7 Sławno Pol.
143 O2 Sławoborze Pol.
174 E3 Sławskie, Jezioro l. Pol.
174 E4 Sławsko Pol.
236 E1 Slayton MN U.S.A.
149 Q7 Slea r. England U.K.
149 Q7 Sleaford Lincolnshire, England U.K.
82 E6 Sleaford Bay S.A. Austr.
147 B8 Slea Head Ireland
146 D8 Sleat pen. Scotland U.K.
146 E8 Sleat, Point of Scotland U.K.
146 E8 Sleat, Sound of sea chan. Scotland U.K.
223 J4 Sled Lake Sask. Can.
149 P5 Sledmere East Riding of Yorkshire, England U.K.
116 H8 Sleemanabad Madh. Prad. India
164 K3 Sleen Neth.
224 E1 Sleeper Islands Nunavut Can.
226 H5 Sleeping Bear Dunes National Lakeshore nature res. MI U.S.A.
226 G5 Sleeping Bear Point MI U.S.A.
109 □J7 Sleep Island H.K. China
164 G5 Sleeuwijk Neth.
149 P5 Sleights North Yorkshire, England U.K.
95 I8 Sleman Indon.
175 H6 Ślemień Pol.
129 G2 Sleptsovskaya Rus. Fed.
174 I3 Slesin Pol.
262 W1 Slessor Glacier Antarctica
175 E5 Ślęża hill Pol.
174 E4 Ślęża r. Pol.
176 F1 Ślężański Park Krajobrazowy Pol.
Slezsko reg. Europe see Silesia
177 I3 Sliač Slovakia
241 X3 Slick Rock CO U.S.A.
237 K10 Slidell LA U.S.A.
233 K7 Slide Mountain NY U.S.A.
141 J6 Slidre Norway
164 G5 Sliedrecht Neth.
195 □ Sliema Malta
147 B8 Slievanea hill Ireland
147 G4 Slieve Anierin hill Ireland
147 G7 Slieveardagh Hills Ireland
147 E6 Slieve Aughty Mountains hills Ireland
147 H4 Slieve Beagh hill Ireland/U.K.
147 E7 Slieve Bernagh hills Ireland
147 G7 Slieve Bloom Mountains hills Ireland
147 D7 Slievecallan hill Ireland
147 C4 Slieve Car hill Ireland
147 K4 Slieve Donard hill Northern Ireland U.K.
147 F7 Slievefelim Mountains hills Ireland
148 D4 Slieve Gallion hill Northern Ireland U.K.
147 D5 Slieve Gamph hills Ireland
147 E7 Slievekimalta hill Ireland
147 H3 Slievekirk hill Northern Ireland U.K.
147 B8 Slieve Mish Mountains hills Ireland
147 B9 Slieve Miskish Mountains hills Ireland
147 G4 Slievenakilla hill Ireland
147 G8 Slievenamon hill Ireland
148 B5 Slieve Rushen hill Northern Ireland U.K.
147 F3 Slieve Snaght hill Ireland
147 H2 Slieve Snaght hill Ireland
146 D8 Sligachan Highland, Scotland U.K.
Sligeach Ireland see Sligo
147 F4 Sligo Ireland
147 E4 Sligo county Ireland
232 F7 Sligo PA U.S.A.
147 E4 Sligo Bay Ireland
175 K2 Ślina r. Pol.
151 L5 Slinfold West Sussex, England U.K.
164 J4 Slinge r. Neth.
146 F7 Slioch hill Scotland U.K.
137 L4 Sliporid r. Ukr.
80 J4 Slipper Island North I. N.Z.
232 E7 Slippery Rock PA U.S.A.
143 O4 Slite Gotland Sweden
138 F4 Slīteres rezervāts nature res. Latvia
197 O8 Sliven Bulg.
197 I8 Slivnitsa Bulg.
197 O7 Slivo Pole Bulg.
174 G2 Śliwice Pol.
188 E3 Sljeme mt. Croatia
177 G3 Sľňava l. Slovakia
236 E4 Sloan NV U.S.A.
240 L2 Sloat CA U.S.A.
235 G2 Sloatsburg NY U.S.A.
136 I6 Slobidka Ukr.
134 I3 Sloboda Arkhangel'skaya Oblast' Rus. Fed.
Sloboda Respublika Komi Rus. Fed. see Ezhva
Sloboda Smolenskaya Oblast' Rus. Fed. see Przheval'skoye
135 H6 Sloboda Voronezhskaya Oblast' Rus. Fed.
137 M2 Sloboda Ukr.
134 J3 Slobodchikovo Rus. Fed.
139 R7 Slobodka Rus. Fed.
134 J4 Slobodskoy Rus. Fed.
Slobodzeya Moldova see Slobozia
136 I7 Slobozia Moldova
197 P6 Slobozia Romania
197 P5 Slobozia Bradului Romania
222 G5 Slocan B.C. Can.
162 G5 Slochteren Neth.
175 I5 Słomniki Pol.
138 I8 Slonim Belarus
137 Q3 Slonovka Rus. Fed.
174 D2 Słonowice Pol.
174 D2 Słońsk Pol.
164 G3 Slootdorp Neth.
164 I3 Sloten Neth.
164 I3 Slotermeer l. Neth.
151 K4 Slough Slough, England U.K.
151 K4 Slough admin. div. England U.K.
176 F2 Sloupnice Czech Rep.
137 M2 Slout Ukr.
177 I3 Slovakia country Europe
136 H2 Slovechna r. Ukr.
136 H2 Slovechne Ukr.
188 E2 Slovenia country Europe
Slovenija country Europe see Slovenia
188 E2 Slovenj Gradec Slovenia
188 E2 Slovenska Bistrica Slovenia
179 J8 Slovenske Konjice Slovenia
188 E2 Slovenske Gorice hills Slovenia
179 L7 Slovenske Konjice Slovenia
177 K3 Slovenské Nové Mesto Slovakia
177 I3 Slovenské Rudohorie mts Slovakia
Slovensko country Europe see Slovakia
177 J3 Slovenský kras mts Slovakia
177 J3 Slovenský kras park Slovakia
177 J3 Slovenský raj nat. park Slovakia
177 J3 Slovinky Slovakia
175 M6 Slovita Ukr.
137 P5 Slov"yans'k Ukr.
137 Q4 Slov"yanohirs'k Ukr.
137 R5 Slov"yanoserbs'k Ukr.
137 Q5 Slov"yans'k Ukr.
137 M8 Slov"yans'ke Ukr.
136 I2 Slovyechna r. Belarus
174 I3 Słowik Pol.
143 N7 Słowiński Park Narodowy nat. park Pol.
174 C3 Słubice Lubuskie Pol.
175 H3 Słubice Mazowieckie Pol.
138 K9 Sluch r. Belarus
136 F3 Sluch r. Ukr.
191 J2 Sluderno Italy
134 L4 Sludka Permskaya Oblast' Rus. Fed.
134 J4 Sludka Respublika Komi Rus. Fed.
165 D6 Sluis Neth.
165 E6 Sluiskil Neth.
176 D1 Šluknov Czech Rep.
176 D2 Slunečná hill Czech Rep.
97 H9 S'Lung, B'Nom mt. Vietnam
188 E3 Slunj Croatia
174 F3 Słupca Pol.
175 J5 Słupca Pol.
175 H4 Słupia Łódzkie Pol.
175 I5 Słupia Świętokrzyskie Pol.
175 J5 Słupia Świętokrzyskie Pol.
143 M7 Słupia r. Pol.
174 E3 Słupno Pol.
143 N7 Słupsk Pol.
143 L4 Slussfors Sweden
138 K5 Slutsk Belarus
138 F6 Šlyna r. Lith.
147 B6 Slyne Head Ireland
139 H8 Slyudyanka Rus. Fed.
98 H1 Slyudyanka Rus. Fed.
162 B2 Smagne r. France
146 K11 Smailholm Scottish Borders, Scotland U.K.
143 K4 Småland reg. Sweden
142 H6 Smålandsfarvandet sea chan. Denmark
143 K5 Smålandsstenar Sweden
151 J2 Smalley Derbyshire, England U.K.
233 □P5 Small Point ME U.S.A.
225 H2 Smallwood Reservoir Nfld and Lab. Can.
139 N6 Smalowka Belarus
175 M3 Smalyanitsa Belarus
138 L7 Smalyavichy Belarus
174 I3 Smardzewice Pol.
174 I3 Smardzewo Pol.
174 D2 Smardzko Pol.
132 Z2 Smarhon' Belarus
179 L8 Šmarje pri Jelšah Slovenia
179 M7 Šmarje pri Jelšah Slovenia
179 L8 Šmarjeta Slovenia
179 L7 Šmartinsko jezero l. Slovenia
223 J2 Smart Lake N.W.T. Can.
179 K7 Šmartno Mozirje Slovenia
179 L7 Šmartno Slovenj Gradec Slovenia
214 H6 Smartt Syndicate Dam resr S. Africa
162 E2 Smarves France
223 J4 Smeaton Sask. Can.
171 J10 Smečno Czech Rep.
176 D1 Smědá r. Czech Rep.
143 M5 Smedby Sweden
196 I6 Smederevo Serbia
196 I6 Smederevska Palanka Serbia
197 O5 Smeeni Romania
151 N5 Smeeth Kent, England U.K.
Smela Ukr. see Smila
140 U1 Smelror Norway
232 G7 Smethport PA U.S.A.
151 I3 Smethwick West Midlands, England U.K.
174 G2 Smętowo Graniczne Pol.
176 E1 Smidary Czech Rep.
175 M4 Smidyn Ukr.
174 E3 Śmigiel Pol.
137 K4 Smila Ukr.
138 L8 Smilavichy Belarus
164 J3 Smilde Neth.
137 M3 Smile Ukr.
136 G3 Smilka r. Ukr.
174 E2 Śmiłowo Pol.
138 I4 Smiltene Latvia
138 F5 Smiltiņu kalns hill Latvia
140 M2 Smines Norway
176 E1 Smiřice Czech Rep.
121 M1 Smirnovo Kazakh.
Smirnovskiy Kazakh. see Smirnovo
100 M4 Smirnykh Sakhalin Rus. Fed.
222 H4 Smith Alta Can.
238 I3 Smith r. MT U.S.A.
232 F12 Smith r. VA U.S.A.
220 F3 Smith Arm b. N.W.T. Can.
238 H3 Smith Bay AK U.S.A.
220 C2 Smith Bay AK U.S.A.
147 H4 Smithborough Ireland
236 F6 Smith Center KS U.S.A.
222 E4 Smithers B.C. Can.
222 E4 Smithers Landing B.C. Can.
215 K6 Smithfield S. Africa
231 H8 Smithfield NC U.S.A.
238 I6 Smithfield UT U.S.A.
232 I12 Smithfield VA U.S.A.
262 Q1 Smith Glacier Antarctica
262 T2 Smith Island Antarctica
221 K3 Smith Island Nunavut Can.
115 M6 Smith Island Andaman & Nicobar Is India
233 I10 Smith Island MD U.S.A.
233 J11 Smith Island VA U.S.A.
237 K7 Smithland KY U.S.A.
232 F11 Smith Mountain Lake VA U.S.A.
84 C1 Smith Point N.T. Austr.
222 E3 Smith River B.C. Can.
232 H9 Smithsburg MD U.S.A.
224 E4 Smiths Falls Ont. Can.
86 □1 Smithson Bight b. Christmas I.
221 K2 Smith Sound sea chan. Can./Greenland
83 J9 Smithton Tas. Austr.
83 N4 Smithtown N.S.W. Austr.
235 I3 Smithtown NY U.S.A.
235 G6 Smithville NJ U.S.A.
237 H8 Smithville OK U.S.A.
231 E8 Smithville TN U.S.A.
232 D9 Smithville WV U.S.A.
214 I9 Smitskraal S. Africa
177 J3 Smižany Slovakia
140 □F1 Smjörfjöll mts Iceland
240 M1 Smoke Creek Desert NV U.S.A.
222 G4 Smoky r. Alta Can.
82 D5 Smoky Bay S.A. Austr.
82 D5 Smoky Bay b. S.A. Austr.
83 N4 Smoky Cape N.S.W. Austr.
84 G7 Smoky Creek watercourse Qld Austr.
224 D3 Smoky Falls Ont. Can.
236 E6 Smoky Hill r. KS U.S.A.
236 E6 Smoky Hill, North Fork r. KS U.S.A.
228 G3 Smoky Hills KS U.S.A.
236 F6 Smoky Hills KS U.S.A.
223 H4 Smoky Lake Alta Can.
238 G5 Smoky Mountains ID U.S.A.
140 I5 Smøla i. Norway
174 F1 Smołdzino Pol.
120 C2 Smolenka Rus. Fed.
139 P7 Smolensk Rus. Fed.
139 Q7 Smolenskaya Oblast' admin. div. Rus. Fed.
Smolensk Oblast admin. div. Rus. Fed. see Smolenskaya Oblast'
139 P7 Smolensko-Moskovskaya Vozvyshennost' hills Rus. Fed.
121 U1 Smolenskoye Rus. Fed.
Smolevichi Belarus see Smalyavichy
174 F4 Smolice Pol.
198 B2 Smolikas mt. Greece
137 K5 Smoline Ukr.
143 J4 Smolmark Sweden
170 K5 Smolnica Pol.
177 J3 Smolník Slovakia
139 M9 Smolyany Belarus
100 H7 Smolyaninovo Rus. Fed.
224 D3 Smooth Rock Falls Ont. Can.
223 B3 Smoothrock Lake Ont. Can.
223 J4 Smoothstone Lake Sask. Can.
140 R1 Smørfjord Norway
Smorgon' Belarus see Smarhon'
139 P9 Smotrova Buda Rus. Fed.
136 F5 Smotrych Ukr.
137 L3 Smotryky Ukr.
176 G1 Smrk mt. Czech Rep.
171 L9 Smrk mt. Czech Rep.
137 P3 Smyach Ukr.
197 P7 Smyadovo Bulg.
142 J6 Smygehamn Sweden
142 F5 Smygehuk Sweden
175 I3 Smyków Pol.
262 S2 Smyley Island Antarctica
Smyrna Turkey see İzmir
234 D6 Smyrna DE U.S.A.
231 E9 Smyrna GA U.S.A.
231 D8 Smyrna TN U.S.A.
231 E8 Smyrna r. DE U.S.A.
233 □Q2 Smyrna Mills ME U.S.A.
259 B8 Smyth, Canal sea chan. Chile
140 □F1 Snæfell mt. Iceland
148 I5 Snæfell hill Isle of Man
140 □B1 Snæfellsjökull ice cap Iceland
140 □B1 Snæfellsnes pen. Iceland
222 A2 Snag Y.T. Can.
149 P5 Snainton North Yorkshire, England U.K.
149 O6 Snaith East Riding of Yorkshire, England U.K.
223 K4 Snake r. NE U.S.A.
238 E3 Snake r. U.S.A.
84 B3 Snake Creek r. N.T. Austr.
241 R2 Snake Range mts NV U.S.A.
222 F3 Snake River B.C. Can.
238 G5 Snake River Plain ID U.S.A.
Snap Point Andros Bahamas see Cistern Point
222 G2 Snare r. N.W.T. Can.
222 H1 Snare Lake N.W.T. Can.
223 J3 Snare Lake Sask. Can.
Snare Lakes N.W.T. Can. see Wekweti
77 G6 Snares Islands N.Z.
140 L4 Snåsa Norway
140 L4 Snåsavatn l. Norway
232 B12 Sneedville TN U.S.A.
164 I2 Sneek Neth.
164 I2 Sneekermeer l. Neth.
147 C9 Sneem Ireland
214 F8 Sneeuberg mts S. Africa
214 F8 Sneeuberge mts S. Africa
225 I2 Snegamook Lake Nfld and Lab. Can.
Snegurovka Ukr. see Tetiyiv
240 L4 Snelling CA U.S.A.
138 E5 Snēpele Latvia
151 N2 Snettisham Norfolk, England U.K.
178 H3 Snezhed' r. Rus. Fed.
130 J3 Snezhnogorsk Rus. Fed.
100 E1 Snezhnogorskiy Rus. Fed.
Snezhnoye Ukr. see Snizhne
176 E1 Sněžka mt. Czech Rep.
188 E3 Snežnik mt. Slovenia
175 J2 Śniadowo Pol.
175 J2 Śniardwy, Jezioro l. Pol.
Sniečkus Lith. see Visaginas
Sniežka mt. Czech Rep. see Sněžka
176 F1 Śnieżnicki Park Krajobrazowy Pol.
174 E5 Śnieżnik mt. Pol.
137 L6 Snihurivka Ukr.
177 L3 Snina Slovakia
151 I3 Snitterfield Warwickshire, England U.K.
137 M3 Snityn Ukr.
137 R5 Snizhne Ukr.
146 D7 Snizort, Loch b. Scotland U.K.
141 J5 Snøhetta mt. Norway
238 C3 Snohomish WA U.S.A.
142 C2 Snønuten mt. Norway
139 Q8 Snopot' r. Rus. Fed.
Snoul Cambodia see Snuŏl
137 K2 Snov r. Ukr.
137 P2 Snova r. Rus. Fed.
139 V9 Snova r. Rus. Fed.
Snovsk Ukr. see Shchors
138 J8 Snow Belarus
223 K2 Snowbird Lake N.W.T. Can.
222 G5 Snowcrest Mountain B.C. Can.
81 C12 Snowdon mt. South I. N.Z.
150 D1 Snowdon mt. Wales U.K.
150 E2 Snowdonia National Park Wales U.K.
Snowdrift N.W.T. Can. see Łutselk'e
223 I2 Snowdrift r. N.W.T. Can.
241 V7 Snowflake AZ U.S.A.
233 J10 Snow Hill MD U.S.A.
231 I8 Snow Hill NC U.S.A.
223 K4 Snow Lake Man. Can.
82 G5 Snowtown S.A. Austr.
238 H6 Snowville UT U.S.A.
83 L7 Snowy r. N.S.W./Vic. Austr.
233 K5 Snowy Mountain NY U.S.A.
83 K7 Snowy Mountains N.S.W. Austr.
83 L7 Snowy River National Park Vic. Austr.
200 L3 Snudy, Voyzera l. Belarus
246 G2 Snug Corner Acklins I. Bahamas
225 K2 Snug Harbour Nfld and Lab. Can.
227 N4 Snug Harbour Ont. Can.
97 H8 Snuŏl Cambodia
136 E5 Snyatyn Ukr.
237 F8 Snyder OK U.S.A.
237 E9 Snyder TX U.S.A.
234 A3 Snyder County county PA U.S.A.
234 D3 Snyders PA U.S.A.
214 E7 Snyderspoort pass S. Africa
139 T8 Snykhovo Rus. Fed.
136 H4 Snyvoda r. Ukr.
93 F5 Soabuwe Seram Indon.
213 □J3 Soahany Madag.
Soaigh i. Western Isles, Scotland U.K. see Soay
146 D10 Soa Island Scotland U.K.
182 D5 Soajo Port.
81 B12 Soaker, Mount South I. N.Z.
213 □J3 Soalala Madag.
182 D5 Soalhães Port.
182 D3 Soalheira Port.
182 F8 Soalheira Port.
213 □J4 Soamanonga Madag.
190 D5 Soana r. Italy
213 □K3 Soanierana-Ivongo Madag.
101 E11 Soan-kundo is S. Korea
191 M9 Soara r. Italy
250 C3 Soata Col.
191 K5 Soave Italy
213 □J3 Soavinandriana Madag.
146 D8 Soay i. Highland, Scotland U.K.
146 □1 Soay i. Western Isles, Scotland U.K.
136 I5 Sob r. Ukr.
207 H4 Soba Nigeria
101 E11 Sobaek-sanmaek mts S. Korea
101 F10 Sobaek-san National Park S. Korea
209 C8 Soba Matias Angola
203 F4 Sobat r. Sudan
105 H5 Sobatsubu-yama mt. Japan
182 E4 Sober Spain
176 D2 Soběslav Czech Rep.
91 J7 Sobger r. Papua Indon.
116 G8 Sobhapur Madh. Prad. India
136 C2 Sobibórski Park Krajobrazowy Pol.
139 X6 Sobinka Rus. Fed.
139 V6 Sobolevo Rus. Fed.
175 J4 Sobolew Pol.
104 G4 Sobo-san mt. Japan
175 J4 Sobota Pol.
179 L5 Soboth Austria
176 G1 Sobotín Czech Rep.
176 G3 Sobotište Slovakia
176 G1 Sobotka Czech Rep.
174 E5 Sobótka Dolnośląskie Pol.
175 J5 Sobótka Świętokrzyskie Pol.
174 F4 Sobótka Wielkopolskie Pol.
174 G1 Sobowidz Pol.
182 G3 Sobradelo Spain
256 D1 Sobradinho Brazil
254 E4 Sobradinho, Barragem de resr Brazil
254 E4 Sobrado Bahia Brazil
251 H6 Sobrado Pará Brazil
182 D4 Sobrado Galicia Spain
182 D4 Sobrado Galicia Spain
250 D7 Sobral Acre Brazil
254 E2 Sobral Ceará Brazil
182 D8 Sobral Port.
182 B8 Sobral da Adiça Port.
184 A2 Sobral de Monte Agraço Port.
182 D8 Sobral do Campo Port.
177 L3 Sobrance Slovakia
117 E8 Sobraon Punjab India
186 E3 Sobrarbe reg. Spain
182 D6 Sobreira Port.
182 D5 Sobreira Formosa Port.
183 N3 Sobrón, Embalse de resr Spain
104 E5 Sobue Japan
168 J1 Søby Denmark
137 M2 Sobych Ukr.
Soča r. Italy see Isonzo
179 I7 Soča Slovenia
188 D3 Soča r. Slovenia
191 P5 Sočerga Slovenia
175 I3 Sochaczew Pol.
175 L5 Sochi Rus. Fed.
129 A2 Sochi Rus. Fed.
175 I3 Sochocin Pol.
101 E10 Soch'on S. Korea
198 E2 Sochos Greece
79 □9 Société, Archipel de la is Fr. Polynesia
Society Islands Fr. Polynesia see Société, Archipel de la
177 K5 Socodor Romania
196 J6 Socol Romania
256 C2 Socompa Chile
177 L4 Socond Romania
Soconusco, Sierra de mts Mex. see Madre de Chiapas, Sierra
256 D5 Socorro Brazil
250 C3 Socorro Col.
239 K9 Socorro NM U.S.A.
228 D7 Socorro, Isla i. Mex.
250 B6 Socota Peru
Socotra i. Yemen see Suquṭrá
185 P4 Socovos Spain
97 H10 Soc Trăng Vietnam
185 N2 Socuéllamos Spain
240 O6 Soda Lake CA U.S.A.
241 P6 Soda Lake CA U.S.A.
140 S3 Sodankylä Fin.
111 D9 Soda Plains Aksai Chin China
116 G8 Sodarpur Madh. Prad. India
238 I5 Soda Springs ID U.S.A.
233 I10 Sodegaura Japan
143 M5 Söderåkra Sweden
143 L3 Söderbärke Sweden
143 O1 Söderboda Sweden
143 N1 Söderfors Sweden
141 N6 Söderhamn Sweden
143 M3 Söderköping Sweden
143 M2 Södermanland county Sweden
168 J4 Soderstorf Ger.
143 N2 Södertälje Sweden
203 F6 Sodiri Sudan
216 I4 Sodium S. Africa
210 C3 Sodo Eth.
143 L1 Södra Barken l. Sweden
143 N2 Södra Björkfjärden b. Sweden
143 M3 Södra Finnö i. Sweden
140 P5 Södra gloppet b. Fin.
141 O6 Södra Kvarken str. Fin./Sweden
143 L4 Södra Vi Sweden
179 K8 Sodražica Slovenia
232 H5 Sodus NY U.S.A.
215 Q3 Sodwana Bay S. Africa
215 Q3 Sodwana Bay National Park S. Africa
93 D8 Soë Timor Indon.
214 B6 Soebatsfontein S. Africa
215 F4 Soekmekaar S. Africa
138 F3 Soela väin sea chan. Estonia
Soerabaia Jawa Indon. see Surabaya
165 I6 Soerendonk Neth.
169 F7 Soest Ger.
164 H4 Soest Neth.
168 E4 Soeste r. Ger.
215 K4 Soetdoring Nature Reserve S. Africa
214 D10 Soetendalsvlei l. S. Africa
198 D3 Sofades Greece
83 L5 Sofala N.S.W. Austr.
213 G4 Sofala Moz.
213 G3 Sofala prov. Moz.
213 G4 Sofala, Baía de b. Moz.
Sofia Bulg. see Sofiya
213 □J2 Sofia r. Madag.
198 F5 Sofiko Greece
197 L8 Sofiya Bulg.
Sofiyevka Ukr. see Vil'nyans'k
137 M5 Sofiyivka Ukr.
100 H2 Sofiysk Khabarovskiy Kray Rus. Fed.
100 K3 Sofiysk Khabarovskiy Kray Rus. Fed.
140 U4 Sofporog Rus. Fed.
199 H6 Sofraña i. Greece
139 U5 Sofrino Rus. Fed.
177 K5 Şofronea Romania
128 A2 Şofta Kalesi tourist site Turkey
103 R17 Sōfu-gan i. Japan
111 K11 Sog Xizang China
250 C3 Sogamoso Col.
129 A5 Soğanlı Dağları mts Turkey
129 B5 Soğanlı Geçidi pass Turkey
110 H6 Sogat Xinjiang China
100 H3 Sogda Rus. Fed.
168 E5 Sögel Ger.
123 M2 Soghd admin. div. Tajik.
111 E9 Sogma Xizang China
111 D10 Sogmai Xizang China
142 D3 Søgne Norway
141 H6 Sognefjorden inlet Norway
141 I6 Sogn og Fjordane county Norway
131 N2 Sogo Rus. Fed.
92 E6 Sogod Leyte Phil.
92 E6 Sogod Bay Leyte Phil.
210 C4 Sogo Hills Kenya
202 B6 Sogolle well Chad
106 G5 Sogo Nur l. Nei Mongol China
111 K10 Sog Qu r. Xizang China
129 F6 Söğüksu Turkey
199 L2 Söğüt Turkey
199 J3 Söğütcük Turkey
199 K5 Söğüt Dağı mts Turkey
129 B7 Söğütlü Turkey
101 E12 Sögwip'o S. Korea
122 D5 Soh Iran
Sohāg Sawhāj Egypt see Sawhāj
116 G8 Sohagpur Madh. Prad. India
151 M3 Soham Cambridgeshire, England U.K.
123 N5 Sohan r. Pak.
91 L8 Sohano P.N.G.
Sohar Oman see Ṣuḥār
123 O5 Sohawa Pak.
165 H8 Soheit-Tinlot Belgium
117 I9 Sohela Orissa India
170 E6 Sohland am Rotstein Ger.
169 J6 Söhlde Ger.
116 F5 Sohna Haryana India
97 D7 Sohng Gwe, Khao hill Myanmar/Thai.
123 J8 Sohrag Pak.
172 C2 Sohren Ger.
156 H2 Soignes, Forêt de for. Belgium
165 F7 Soignies Belgium
108 A3 Soila Xizang China
177 L5 Şoimi Romania
160 H1 Soing France
159 O7 Soings-en-Sologne France
140 R5 Soini Fin.
169 H8 Soisberg hill Ger.
156 F5 Soissons France
260 D4 Soitue Arg.
156 G6 Soizy-aux-Bois France
103 K12 Soja Japan
116 D7 Sojat Rajasthan India
116 D7 Sojat Road Rajasthan India
175 K5 Sójkowa Pol.
92 D7 Sojoton Point Negros Phil.
179 O6 Sójtör Hungary
135 J5 Sok r. Rus. Fed.
105 K6 Sōka Japan
136 D3 Sokal' Ukr.
101 F9 Sokch'o S. Korea
199 I5 Söke Turkey
209 E7 Sokele Dem. Rep. Congo
107 L2 Sokhondo, Gora mt. Rus. Fed.
106 I1 Sokhor, Gora mt. Rus. Fed.
Sokhós Greece see Sochos
129 C2 Sokhumi Georgia
129 C3 Sokhumi-Babushara airport Georgia
Sokiryany Ukr. see Sokyryany
103 G11 Sokkuram Grotto tourist site S. Korea
142 F1 Sokna Norway
140 K5 Soknedal Norway
197 J7 Soko Banja Serbia
207 F4 Sokodé Togo
Soko Islands H.K. China see Shekka Ch'ün-Tao
100 M4 Sokol Sakhalin Rus. Fed.
134 H5 Sokol Vologodskaya Oblast' Rus. Fed.
188 G4 Sokolac Bos.-Herz.
175 L2 Sokolany Pol.
136 J4 Sokolivka Cherkas'ka Oblast' Ukr.
175 M5 Sokolivka L'vivs'ka Oblast' Ukr.
175 L2 Sokółka Pol.
175 K1 Sokółki Pol.
176 C1 Sokolnice Czech Rep.
139 V7 Sokol'niki Tul'skaya Oblast' Rus. Fed.
139 R5 Sokol'niki Tverskaya Oblast' Rus. Fed.
206 D3 Sokolo Mali
137 N7 Sokolohirne Ukr.
176 B1 Sokolov Czech Rep.
175 I4 Sokolov Balka Ukr.
179 O7 Sokolovac Croatia
121 M3 Sokolovka Kazakh.
137 Q1 Sokolovka Rus. Fed.
121 U1 Sokolovo Rus. Fed.
137 S6 Sokolovo-Kundryuchenskiy Rus. Fed.
175 K5 Sokołów Małopolski Pol.
175 K3 Sokołów Podlaski Pol.
140 U3 Sokolozero, Ozero l. Rus. Fed.
134 H4 Sokol'skoye Rus. Fed.
175 K3 Sokoły Pol.
206 A3 Sokone Senegal
177 G4 Sokorópátka Hungary
140 T2 Sokosti hill Fin.
207 G3 Sokoto Nigeria
207 G3 Sokoto r. Nigeria
207 G3 Sokoto state Nigeria
206 C4 Sokourala Guinea
136 G5 Sokyryany Ukr.
175 K5 Sól Pol.

Sola to Souto da Casa

390

261 H3 Sola Arg.
246 E3 Sola Cuba
209 E6 Sola Dem. Rep. Congo
175 H6 Soła r. Pol.
Sola i. Tonga see Ata
116 F4 Solan Hima. Prad. India
240 O9 Solana Beach CA U.S.A.
184 F3 Solana de los Barros Spain
185 K4 Solana del Pino Spain
183 K7 Solana de Rioalmar Spain
81 A13 Solander Island South I. N.Z.
142 F1 Sølandsfjellet mt. Norway
261 H5 Solanet Arg.
92 C3 Solano Luzon Phil.
250 E4 Solano Venez.
114 D4 Solapur Mahar. India
195 I9 Solarino Sicilia Italy
192 C4 Solaro Corse France
192 B8 Solarussa Sardegna Italy
Solas Scotland U.K. see Sollas
140 N5 Solberg Sweden
143 K4 Solberga Sweden
197 N3 Solca Romania
177 H3 Solčany Slovakia
179 K7 Solčava Slovenia
191 J2 Solda Italy
191 J2 Solda r. Italy
250 C5 Soldado Bartra Peru
136 H6 Şoldăneşti Moldova
129 E1 Soldato-Aleksandrovskoye Rus. Fed.
129 E2 Soldatskaya Rus. Fed.
178 D6 Sölden Austria
186 I2 Soldeu Andorra
233 □Q1 Soldier Pond ME U.S.A.
220 C3 Soldotna AK U.S.A.
174 G2 Solec Kujawski Pol.
175 I5 Solec-Zdrój Pol.
261 G2 Soledad Arg.
246 F8 Soledad Col.
240 K5 Soledad CA U.S.A.
251 F2 Soledad Venez.
245 K6 Soledad de Doblado Mex.
244 G3 Soledad Diez Gutierrez Mex.
250 D6 Soledade Amazonas Brazil
255 B9 Soledade Rio Grande do Sul Brazil
137 R5 Soledar Ukr.
192 C9 Soleminis Sardegna Italy
141 K6 Sølen mt. Norway
135 H7 Solenoye Rus. Fed.
192 C4 Solenzara Corse France
206 D3 Solenzo Burkina
191 L5 Solesino Italy
156 F3 Solesmes Nord-Pas-de-Calais France
159 K6 Solesmes Pays de la Loire France
195 O3 Soleto Italy
163 C7 Solférino France
191 J5 Solferino Italy
140 L3 Solfjellsjøen Norway
143 L4 Solgen l. Sweden
134 H3 Solginskiy Rus. Fed.
127 J4 Solhan Turkey
191 J6 Soliera Italy
134 H4 Soligalich Rus. Fed.
162 G4 Solignac France
190 H6 Solignano Italy
191 M4 Soligo r. Italy
Soligorsk Belarus see Salihorsk
151 I3 Solihull West Midlands, England U.K.
134 L4 Solikamsk Rus. Fed.
120 F2 Sol'-Iletsk Rus. Fed.
189 C7 Soliman Tunisia
243 P8 Solimón, Punta pt Mex.
175 K6 Solina Pol.
169 D8 Solingen Ger.
175 K6 Solinka r. Pol.
175 K6 Solińskie, Jezioro l. Pol.
244 G6 Solis Mex.
244 G5 Solís, Presa resr Mex.
250 C4 Solita Col.
250 D2 Solita Venez.
81 B12 Solitary, Mount South I. N.Z.
186 H5 Solivella Spain
Sol-Karmala Rus. Fed. see Severnoye
179 J5 Solker Tauern pass Austria
179 I5 Sölktäler nature res. Austria
178 F4 Söll Austria
192 B4 Sollacaro Corse France
129 J4 Şollar Azer.
146 B7 Sollas Western Isles, Scotland U.K.
142 I3 Sollebrunn Sweden
140 N5 Sollefteå Sweden
179 N4 Sollenau Austria
143 N2 Sollentuna Sweden
187 K8 Sóller Spain
141 M6 Sollerön Sweden
168 L1 Søllested Denmark
171 G7 Söllichau Ger.
161 I10 Solliès-Pont France
161 I10 Solliès-Ville France
169 H7 Solling hills Ger.
169 K6 Söllingen Ger.
169 K8 Sollstedt Ger.
169 F9 Solms Ger.
139 T5 Solnechnogorsk Rus. Fed.
100 C1 Solnechnyy Amurskaya Oblast' Rus. Fed.
100 J3 Solnechnyy Khabarovskiy Kray Rus. Fed.
Solnechnyy Khabarovskiy Kray Rus. Fed. see Gornyy
176 F1 Solnice Czech Rep.
137 P2 Solntsevo Rus. Fed.
93 C5 Solo r. Indon.
95 J8 Solo r. Indon.
136 F4 Solobkivtsi Ukr.
135 I6 Solodniki Rus. Fed.
193 N6 Solofra Italy
156 D8 Sologne reg. France
94 D5 Solok Sumatera Indon.
129 A2 Solokhaul Rus. Fed.
136 D3 Solokiya r. Ukr.
243 N10 Sololá Guat.
129 F1 Solomenskoye Rus. Fed.
163 F8 Solomiac France
136 F4 Solomna Ukr.
241 W9 Solomon AZ U.S.A.
236 G6 Solomon r. KS U.S.A.
236 F6 Solomon, North Fork r. KS U.S.A.
236 F6 Solomon, South Fork r. KS U.S.A.
78 □6 Solomon Islands country S. Pacific Ocean
91 L8 Solomon Sea P.N.G./Solomon Is
107 Q3 Solon Nei Mongol China
233 □P4 Solon ME U.S.A.
137 N6 Solona r. Ukr.
137 P5 Solona r. Ukr.
137 N5 Solone Ukr.
121 U2 Soloneshnoye Rus. Fed.
226 C3 Solon Springs WI U.S.A.
194 H1 Solopaca Italy
93 C8 Solor i. Indon.
93 C8 Solor, Kepulauan is Indon.
183 P6 Solorio, Sierra de mts Spain
183 M2 Solórzano Spain
183 K7 Solosancho Spain
139 W7 Solotcha Rus. Fed.
190 D1 Solothurn Switz.
190 D1 Solothurn canton Switz.
136 D5 Solotvyn Ukr.
134 F2 Solovetskiy Rus. Fed.
134 F2 Solovetskiye Ostrova is Rus. Fed.
134 I4 Solovetskoye Rus. Fed.
136 I3 Soloviyivka Ukr.
139 X8 Solovoye Rus. Fed.
175 M4 Solovychi Ukr.
139 P7 Solov'yevo Rus. Fed.
107 N2 Solov'yevsk Mongolia
100 D1 Solov'yevsk Rus. Fed.
157 H3 Solre-le-Château France
186 I4 Solsona Spain
177 I5 Solt Hungary
188 F4 Šolta i. Croatia
122 G7 Solţānābād Iran
122 H3 Soltānābād Khorāsān Iran
122 H4 Solţānābād Iran
122 D4 Soltānābād Tehrān Iran
123 J5 Soltān-e Bakva Afgh.
122 D7 Soltānī, Khowr-e b. Iran
127 N5 Solţānīyeh Iran
129 I6 Soltanlı Azer.
122 H3 Solţān Meydān Iran
122 B5 Solţanqolī Iran
168 I5 Soltau Ger.
168 K5 Soltendieck Ger.
177 I5 Solti-síkság reg. Hungary
121 V1 Solton Rus. Fed.
139 N3 Sol'tsy Rus. Fed.
177 I5 Soltszentimre Hungary
Soltüstik Qazaqstan Oblysy admin. div. Kazakh. see Severnyy Kazakhstan
177 I5 Soltvadkert Hungary
196 J9 Solunska Glava mt. Macedonia
160 F4 Solutré-Pouilly France
150 B4 Solva Pembrokeshire, Wales U.K.
150 B4 Solva r. Wales U.K.
240 L7 Solvang CA U.S.A.
233 I5 Solvay NY U.S.A.
143 K5 Sölvesborg Sweden
134 I3 Sol'vychegodsk Rus. Fed.
146 I13 Solway Firth est. Scotland U.K.
209 E8 Solwezi Zambia
102 R9 Sōma Japan
199 I3 Soma Turkey
213 F3 Somabhula Zimbabwe
Somabula Zimbabwe see Somabhula
156 F3 Somain France
210 E4 Somalia country Africa
265 H5 Somali Basin sea feature Indian Ocean
Somali Republic country Africa see Somalia
211 C7 Somanga Tanz.
207 E5 Somanya Ghana
Sombak'e N.W.T. Can. see Yellowknife
95 L3 Sombang, Gunung mt. Indon.
177 H5 Somberek Hungary
160 F2 Sombernon France
209 D7 Sombo Angola
196 H5 Sombor Vojvodina Serbia
169 H10 Somborn Ger.
165 G7 Sombreffe Belgium
244 D2 Sombrerete Mex.
247 L4 Sombrero i. Anguilla
259 C9 Sombrero Chile
115 M9 Sombrero Channel Andaman & Nicobar Is India
197 L3 Şomcuţa Mare Romania
116 D7 Somdari Rajasthan India
209 E6 Somene Dem. Rep. Congo
234 E5 Somerdale NJ U.S.A.
165 I6 Someren Neth.
141 Q6 Somero Fin.
231 □1 Somerset Bermuda
150 G5 Somerset admin. div. England U.K.
230 E7 Somerset KY U.S.A.
233 N7 Somerset MA U.S.A.
226 J7 Somerset MI U.S.A.
232 C9 Somerset OH U.S.A.
232 F9 Somerset PA U.S.A.
234 F3 Somerset County county NJ U.S.A.
215 J8 Somerset East S. Africa
231 □1 Somerset Island Bermuda
221 I2 Somerset Island Nunavut Can.
214 C10 Somerset West S. Africa
151 M3 Somersham Cambridgeshire, England U.K.
234 F6 Somers Point NJ U.S.A.
233 □O5 Somersworth NH U.S.A.
150 G5 Somerton Somerset, England U.K.
241 R9 Somerton AZ U.S.A.
138 J2 Sõmeru Estonia
234 F3 Somerville NJ U.S.A.
237 K8 Somerville TN U.S.A.
237 G10 Somerville Reservoir TX U.S.A.
197 K3 Someş r. Romania
80 □ Somes, Point Chatham Is S. Pacific Ocean
197 L4 Someşan, Podişul plat. Romania
197 L4 Someşu Cald r. Romania
197 L3 Someşul Mare r. Romania
197 K3 Someşului, Câmpia plain Romania
197 L3 Someşu Mic r. Romania
233 □Q4 Somesville ME U.S.A.
122 B5 Someydeh Iran
175 J3 Somianka Pol.
182 H2 Somiedo, Parque Natural de nature res. Spain
182 H2 Somiedo, Puerto de pass Spain
139 R2 Somino Rus. Fed.
174 F1 Sominy Pol.
215 Q4 Somkele S. Africa
176 G4 Somlóvásárhely Hungary
191 J5 Sommacampagna Italy
190 F4 Somma Lombardo Italy
190 D6 Sommariva del Bosco Italy
140 O2 Sommarøy Norway
194 F9 Sommatino Sicilia Italy
156 D4 Somme dept France
160 D3 Somme r. France
165 A8 Somme r. France
156 C3 Somme, Baie de la b. France
156 E4 Somme, Canal de la France
157 J5 Sommedieue France
165 H8 Somme-Leuze Belgium
143 K3 Sommen Sweden
143 L3 Sommen l. Sweden
156 I5 Sommepy-Tahure France
171 D8 Sömmerda Ger.
170 H5 Sommerfeld Ger.
171 D6 Sommersdorf Ger.
156 H5 Somme-Soude r. France
156 H6 Sommesous France
156 I5 Somme-Suippe France
225 G2 Sommet, Lac du l. Que. Can.
157 I7 Sommevoire France
161 E9 Sommières France
162 E3 Sommières-du-Clain France
116 C9 Somnath Gujarat India
176 G5 Somogy county Hungary
177 G5 Somogyapáti Hungary
177 G5 Somogyi-dombság reg. Hungary
177 G5 Somogyjád Hungary
177 G5 Somogysárd Hungary
176 G5 Somogyszentpál Hungary
176 G5 Somogyszob Hungary
226 F8 Somonauk IL U.S.A.
174 G1 Somonino Pol.
186 E3 Somontano reg. Spain
185 O6 Somontín Spain
183 M6 Somosierra mts Spain
183 M6 Somosierra, Puerto de pass Spain
79 □7 Somosomo Taveuni Fiji
242 □P11 Somotillo Nic.
242 □P11 Somoto Nic.
139 S9 Somovo Orlovskaya Oblast' Rus. Fed.
139 T8 Somovo Tul'skaya Oblast' Rus. Fed.
137 S2 Somovo Voronezhskaya Oblast' Rus. Fed.
115 I3 Sompeta Andhra Prad. India
174 G3 Sompolno Pol.
186 D2 Somport, Col du pass France/Spain
151 L6 Sompting West Sussex, England U.K.
156 H6 Sompuis France
197 J6 Šomrda hill Serbia
259 D6 Somuncurá, Mesa Volcánica de plat. Arg.
96 D1 Somutu Myanmar
114 D6 Somvarpet Karnataka India
165 F8 Somzée Belgium
117 J7 Son r. India
164 H5 Son Neth.
142 G2 Son Norway
191 J5 Sona Italy
242 □S14 Soná Panama
175 I3 Sona r. Pol.
Sonag Qinghai China see Zêkog
117 N6 Sonai r. India
117 N7 Sonai r. India
100 I3 Sonakh Rus. Fed.
116 F9 Sonala Mahar. India
121 N3 Sonaly Kazakh.
121 N3 Sonaly Kazakh.
117 K8 Sonamukhi W. Bengal India
117 I9 Sonapur Orissa India
117 O6 Sonari Assam India
190 C1 Sonceboz Switz.
101 D9 Sŏnch'ŏn N. Korea
183 M3 Soncillo Spain
190 H5 Soncino Italy
190 I3 Sondalo Italy
134 F3 Sondaly Rus. Fed.
142 F3 Søndeled Norway
142 E7 Sønderå r. Denmark
142 F7 Sønderborg Denmark
142 F6 Sønderjylland county Denmark
142 E6 Sønder Omme Denmark
169 K8 Sondershausen Ger.
142 G6 Søndersø Denmark
170 E1 Søndersø l. Denmark
142 F5 Sønderup Denmark
Søndre Strømfjord Greenland see Kangerlussuaq
Søndre Strømfjord inlet Greenland see Kangerlussuaq
Søndre Upernavik Greenland see Upernavik Kujalleq
190 H3 Sondrio Italy
190 H3 Sondrio prov. Italy
187 E8 Soneja Spain
114 E3 Sonepet Mahar. India
234 B2 Sonestown PA U.S.A.
208 A4 Song Gabon
95 J3 Song Sarawak Malaysia
207 I4 Song Nigeria
93 E4 Songa Maluku Indon.
116 C9 Songad Gujarat India
Songbai Hubei China see Shennongjia
109 J3 Songbu Hubei China
97 I8 Sông Câu Vietnam
Songcheng Fujian China see Xiapu
96 G4 Sông Đa, Hô resr Vietnam
211 B7 Songea Tanz.
156 C4 Songeons France
101 E8 Sŏnggan N. Korea
100 E7 Songhua Hu resr China
100 D6 Songhuajiang Jilin China
100 H5 Songhua Jiang r. China
Songjiachuan Shaanxi China see Wubu
100 F7 Songjiang Jilin China
109 M3 Songjiang Shanghai China
101 E7 Songjianghe Jilin China
Sŏngjin N. Korea see Kimch'aek
108 F4 Songkan Guizhou China
97 E11 Songkhla Thai.
96 G6 Songkhram, Mae Nam r. Thai.
121 P7 Songköl l. Kyrg.
107 P6 Song Ling mts China
96 D3 Songlong Myanmar
Songmai Sichuan China see Dêrong
108 D6 Songming Yunnan China
101 E10 Sŏngnam S. Korea
101 D9 Songnim N. Korea
101 E10 Songni-san National Park S. Korea
209 B6 Songo Angola
213 G2 Songo Moz.
209 B6 Songololo Bas-Congo Dem. Rep. Congo
Songololo Bas-Congo Dem. Rep. Congo see Mbanza-Ngungu
108 D2 Songpan Sichuan China
117 M7 Songsak Meghalaya India
101 E12 Sŏngsan S. Korea
106 H8 Songshan Gansu China
Songshan Guizhou China see Ziyun
107 M9 Song Shan mt. Henan China
108 G4 Songtao Guizhou China
109 L5 Songxi Fujian China
107 M9 Songxian Henan China
Songyang Yunnan China see Songming
Songyuan Fujian China see Songxi
100 D6 Songyuan Jilin China
109 H3 Songzi Hubei China
97 I9 Sơn Hai Vietnam
117 I8 Sonhat Chhattisgarh India
104 D6 Soni Japan
Sonid Youqi Nei Mongol China see Saihan Tal
Sonid Zuoqi Nei Mongol China see Mandalt
182 F5 Sonim Port.
116 F5 Sonipat Haryana India
116 F8 Sonkach Madh. Prad. India
134 D3 Sonkajärvi Fin.
Sonkël', Ozero l. Kyrg. see Songköl
139 U4 Sonkovo Rus. Fed.
96 F4 Sơn La Vietnam
123 L9 Sonmiani Pak.
123 L9 Sonmiani Bay Pak.
178 G5 Sonnblick mt. Austria
171 D10 Sonneberg Ger.
169 K9 Sonneborn Ger.
171 D10 Sonnefeld Ger.
178 F5 Sonnenjoch mt. Austria
171 I7 Sonnewalde Ger.
151 K4 Sonning Common Oxfordshire, England U.K.
193 K5 Sonnino Italy
178 A5 Sonntag Austria
179 K4 Sonntagberg Austria
257 E2 Sono r. Brazil
254 C4 Sono r. Brazil
104 B5 Sonobe Japan
241 T10 Sonoita Mex.
239 H11 Sonoita watercourse Mex.
241 V10 Sonoita AZ U.S.A.
240 J3 Sonoma CA U.S.A.
241 J3 Sonoma, Lake resr CA U.S.A.
215 L1 Sonop S. Africa
242 D3 Sonora r. Mex.
242 D3 Sonora state Mex.
240 L4 Sonora CA U.S.A.
237 E10 Sonora TX U.S.A.
241 T9 Sonoran Desert AZ U.S.A.
241 T9 Sonoran Desert National Monument nat. park AZ U.S.A.
240 M3 Sonora Peak CA U.S.A.
122 B4 Sonqor Iran
183 M9 Sonseca Spain
187 L8 Son Servera Spain
187 L8 Son Servera, Badia de b. Spain
175 I3 Sońsk Pol.
250 C3 Sonsón Col.
243 O11 Sonsonate El Salvador
91 H5 Sonsorol Islands Palau
214 G3 Sonstraal S. Africa
96 G4 Sơn Tây Vietnam
173 I5 Sontheim Ger.
173 I4 Sontheim an der Brenz Ger.
173 I6 Sonthofen Ger.
169 I8 Sontra Ger.
215 M7 Sonwabile S. Africa
137 O9 Sonyachna Dolyna Ukr.
216 □3c Sóo Lanzarote Canary Is
Soochow Jiangsu China see Suzhou
138 I2 Soodla r. Estonia
210 E2 Sool admin. div. Somalia
Soomaaliya country Africa see Somalia
172 D2 Soonwald mts Ger.
163 B8 Soorts-Hossegor France
261 I2 Sopas r. Uru.
186 G3 Sopeira Spain
231 F9 Soperton GA U.S.A.
161 K9 Sophia-Antipolis France
93 F2 Sopi, Tanjung pt Maluku Indon.
196 J9 Sopište Macedonia
208 E2 Sopo watercourse Sudan
197 M8 Sopot Bulg.
143 O7 Sopot Pol.
196 I6 Sopot Serbia
108 B10 Sop Prap Thai.
176 F4 Sopron Hungary
176 F4 Soproni park Hungary
176 F4 Sopronkövesd Hungary
121 O7 Sopu-Korgon Kyrg.
116 E2 Sopur Jammu and Kashmir
93 D3 Soputan, Gunung vol. Indon.
78 □4a Sopweru i. Chuuk Micronesia
78 □4a Sopweru, Mochun sea chan. Chuuk Micronesia
137 N2 Sopych Ukr.
163 I8 Sor r. France
184 C3 Sôr r. Port.
182 E1 Sor r. Spain
193 L4 Sora Italy
179 J7 Sora r. Slovenia
114 D5 Sorab Karnataka India
115 I3 Sorada Orissa India
191 L3 Soraga Italy
190 I6 Soragna Italy
141 N5 Söråker Sweden
101 F9 Sŏrak-san mt. S. Korea
101 F9 Sorak-san National Park S. Korea
192 H2 Sorano Italy
252 C4 Sorapa Peru
191 M3 Sorapis mt. Italy
140 L3 Sørarnøy Norway
252 C3 Sorata Bol.
207 I4 Sorau Nigeria
142 D3 Sør-Audnedal Norway
129 J5 Şorbaçı Azer.
185 O6 Sorbas Spain
183 N7 Sorbe r. Spain
146 H13 Sorbie Dumfries and Galloway, Scotland U.K.
190 I6 Sorbolo Italy
157 K6 Sorcy-St-Martin France
163 B8 Sorde-l'Abbaye France
163 C7 Sore France
163 J10 Sorède France
221 K5 Sorel Que. Can.
83 K10 Sorell Tas. Austr.
128 C7 Soreq r. Israel
190 H5 Soresina Italy
78 □6 Sorezaru Point New Georgia Is Solomon Is
163 I9 Sorèze France
143 M2 Sörfjärden l. Sweden
142 C1 Sørfjorden inlet Norway
169 K7 Sorge Ger.
168 H2 Sorge r. Ger.
162 F5 Sorges France
192 C7 Sorgono Sardegna Italy
161 F8 Sorgues France
161 B9 Sorgues r. France
128 C2 Sorgun İçel Turkey
126 G4 Sorgun Yozgat Turkey
128 C2 Sorgun r. Turkey
183 P5 Soria Spain
183 O5 Soria prov. Spain
261 H3 Soriano Uru.
261 I3 Soriano dept Uru.
195 K6 Soriano Calabro Italy
193 I3 Soriano nel Cimino Italy
182 I8 Sorihuela Spain
185 M4 Sorihuela del Gaudalimar Spain
94 C4 Sorikmarapi vol. Indon.
191 R6 Sorinj, Rt pt Croatia
146 D9 Sorisdale Argyll and Bute, Scotland U.K.
140 □ Sørkapp Land reg. Svalbard
130 C2 Sørkappøya i. Svalbard
122 F5 Sorkh, Kūh-e mts Iran
122 E4 Sorkheh Iran
128 A1 Sorkun Turkey
175 J2 Sorkwity Pol.
140 L3 Sørland Norway
140 L4 Sørli Norway
140 P5 Sörmjöle Sweden
156 I4 Sormonne r. France
148 I2 Sorn East Ayrshire, Scotland U.K.
162 I4 Sornac France
172 C7 Sorne r. Switz.
142 H6 Sorø Denmark
117 K9 Soro Orissa India
194 H8 Soro, Monte mt. Sicilia Italy
136 H5 Soroca Moldova
256 D5 Sorocaba Brazil
139 U8 Sorochinka Rus. Fed.
120 E1 Sorochinsk Rus. Fed.
Soroki Moldova see Soroca
121 U1 Sorokino Altayskiy Kray Rus. Fed.
138 M4 Sorokino Pskovskaya Oblast' Rus. Fed.
Sorokino Ukr. see Krasnodon
91 J5 Sorol atoll Micronesia
207 I4 Sorombéo Cameroon
93 G4 Sorong Papua Indon.
251 F4 Sororoca Brazil
138 L4 Sorot' r. Rus. Fed.
210 B4 Soroti Uganda
140 Q1 Sørøya i. Norway
140 Q1 Sørøysundet sea chan. Norway
Sorp Turkey see Reşadiye
169 E8 Sorpe Staubecken resr Ger.
192 B7 Sorradile Sardegna Italy
184 B2 Sorraia r. Port.
140 O2 Sørreisa Norway
193 M6 Sorrento Italy
140 S5 Sorsakoski Fin.
140 T3 Sorsatunturi hill Fin.
140 N4 Sorsele Sweden
192 B6 Sorso Sardegna Italy
92 E5 Sorsogon Luzon Phil.
129 J6 Şorsulu Azer.
186 H3 Sort Spain
141 U6 Sortavala Rus. Fed.
182 F8 Sortelha Port.
195 I9 Sortino Sicilia Italy
140 M2 Sortland Norway
134 J3 Sortopolovskaya Rus. Fed.
203 F5 Sortot Sudan
140 K5 Sør-Trøndelag county Norway
143 N2 Sorunda Sweden
168 I1 Sörup Ger.
140 P1 Sørvær Norway
140 L3 Sørvågen Norway
Sõrve väin sea chan. Estonia/Latvia see Irbe Strait
185 M7 Sorvilán Spain
163 E7 Sos France
101 E10 Sŏsan S. Korea
143 J5 Sösdala Sweden
186 C2 Sos del Rey Católico Spain
138 L3 Sosedno Rus. Fed.
139 S7 Sosenskiy Rus. Fed.
186 F4 Soses Spain
215 M1 Soshanguve S. Africa
175 M4 Soshychne Ukr.
194 E8 Sosio r. Sicilia Italy
139 S9 Soskovo Rus. Fed.
177 H4 Sóskút Hungary
139 V9 Sosna r. Rus. Fed.
260 C4 Sosneado mt. Arg.
174 E2 Sośnica Pol.
174 F4 Sośnie Pol.
136 D3 Sosnivka L'vivs'ka Oblast' Ukr.
137 M2 Sosnivka Sums'ka Oblast' Ukr.
136 E3 Sosnivka Ternopils'ka Oblast' Ukr.
174 F2 Sośno Pol.
134 K3 Sosnogorsk Rus. Fed.
136 G3 Sosnove Ukr.
121 R2 Sosnovka Kazakh.
121 O6 Sosnovka Kyrg.
134 I3 Sosnovka Arkhangel'skaya Oblast' Rus. Fed.
134 H2 Sosnovka Murmanskaya Oblast' Rus. Fed.
135 H5 Sosnovka Tambovskaya Oblast' Rus. Fed.
139 U3 Sosnovka Vologodskaya Oblast' Rus. Fed.
139 N1 Sosnovo Rus. Fed.
135 I5 Sosnovoborsk Rus. Fed.
99 J1 Sosnovo-Ozerskoye Rus. Fed.
134 F2 Sosnovyy Rus. Fed.
Sosnovyy Bor Belarus see Sasnovy Bor
138 M2 Sosnovyy Bor Rus. Fed.
175 L4 Sosnowica Pol.
175 H5 Sosnowiec Pol.
Sosnowitz Pol. see Sosnowiec
175 L4 Sosnówka Pol.
138 K9 Sosny Belarus
137 L2 Sosnytsya Ukr.
161 K9 Sospel France
208 B4 Sosso C.A.R.
163 F10 Sost France
179 L7 Šoštanj Slovenia
102 □1 Sosu Okinawa Japan
134 M3 Sos'va Khanty-Mansiyskiy Avtonomnyy Okrug Rus. Fed.
130 H4 Sos'va Sverdlovskaya Oblast' Rus. Fed.
137 S7 Sosyka r. Rus. Fed.
207 F4 Sota r. Benin
111 L11 Sotang Xizang China
260 B2 Sotaquí Chile
245 M7 Soteapan Mex.
252 D2 Sotério r. Brazil
184 F5 Sotiel Coronada Spain
184 I4 Sotillo r. Spain
183 K8 Sotillo de la Adrada Spain
183 O5 Sotillo del Rincón Spain
140 T4 Sotkamo Fin.
260 E2 Soto Arg.
247 □10 Soto Curaçao Neth. Antilles
182 H1 Soto Spain
182 I4 Soto de la Vega Spain
183 M7 Soto del Real Spain
182 I2 Soto de Ribera Spain
245 I2 Soto la Marina Mex.
245 J2 Soto La Marina r. Mex.
245 J1 Soto La Marina, Barra spit Mex.
186 D3 Sotonera, Embalse de resr Spain
183 M4 Sotopalacios Spain
183 P8 Sotos Spain
182 H8 Sotoserrano Spain
207 F4 Sotouboua Togo
182 I3 Soto y Amio Spain
183 K2 Sotres Spain
183 L3 Sotresgudo Spain
182 I2 Sotrondio Spain
137 R3 Sotsgorodok Rus. Fed.
Sotsgorodok Ukr. see Hirnyk
192 C4 Sotta Corse France
143 L2 Sottern l. Sweden
156 B5 Sotteville-lès-Rouen France
194 H8 Sotto di Troina r. Sicilia Italy
191 M5 Sottomarina Italy
168 H4 Sottrum Ger.
141 P6 Sottunga Åland Fin.
185 N2 Sotuélamos Spain
243 O7 Sotuta Mex.
156 I5 Souain-Perthes-lès-Hurlus France
163 I8 Soual France
208 B4 Souanké Congo
161 C9 Soubès France
206 D5 Soubré Côte d'Ivoire
81 H8 Soucis, Cape South I. N.Z.
156 F7 Soucy France
198 F7 Souda Kriti Greece
84 F6 Soudan N.T. Austr.
158 I6 Soudan France
198 F7 Soudas, Ormos b. Kriti Greece
234 E4 Souderton PA U.S.A.
Soúdha Kriti Greece see Souda
208 B2 Soudio Chad
163 F9 Soueich France
163 G10 Soueix France
159 P7 Souesmes France
157 O6 Soufflenheim France
199 H1 Soufli Greece
247 □2 Soufrière vol. Guadeloupe
247 □3 Soufrière St Lucia
247 □3 Soufrière vol. St Vincent
247 □2 Soufrière Hills Montserrat
206 B4 Souguéta Guinea
163 G6 Souillac France
217 □1b Souillac Mauritius
157 J5 Souilly France
205 G1 Souk Ahras Alg.
189 A7 Souk Ahras prov. Alg.
204 D2 Souk el Arbaâ du Rharb Morocco
180 D5 Souk el Had el Rharbia Morocco
180 D5 Souk-Khémis-des-Anjra Morocco
180 C5 Souk Khemis du Sahel Morocco
207 F3 Soukoukoutane Niger
129 B2 Souk'su, Konts'khi pt Georgia
180 D5 Souk Tleta Taghramet Morocco
180 D5 Souk-Tnine-de-Sidi-el-Yamani Morocco
101 E10 Sŏul S. Korea
206 B3 Soulabali Senegal
162 B4 Soulac-sur-Mer France
156 I7 Soulaines-Dhuys France
163 G10 Soulan France
163 J10 Soulatgé France
163 C9 Soule reg. France
159 J5 Soulgé-sur-Ouette France
158 H8 Soullans France
158 I3 Soulles r. France
157 O6 Soultz-sous-Forêts France
165 I7 Soumagne Belgium
163 D9 Soumoulou France
235 J3 Sound Beach NY U.S.A.
223 I4 Sounding Creek r. Alta Can.
Sounfat well Mali see Tessoûnfat
128 A4 Souni Cyprus
198 F5 Souniou, Ethnikos Drymos nat. park Greece
207 H2 Sountel well Niger
156 E7 Souppes-sur-Loing France
163 C8 Souprosse France
128 D5 Soûr Lebanon
159 J4 Sourdeval France
254 C2 Soure Brazil
182 C8 Soure Port.
223 K5 Souris Man. Can.
225 I4 Souris P.E.I. Can.
223 L5 Souris r. Sask. Can.
Souriya country Asia see Syria
163 I10 Sournia France
182 F7 Souro Pires Port.
206 C2 Souroumelli well Maur.
198 D3 Sourpi Greece
156 C7 Sours France
162 E5 Sourzac France
204 C3 Sous, Oued watercourse Morocco
254 F3 Sousa Brazil
182 C6 Sousa r. Port.
Sousa Lara Angola see Bocoio
163 I6 Sousceyrac France
251 I5 Sousel Brazil
184 D3 Sousel Port.
182 D8 Souselas Port.
217 □1c Sous le Vent reg. Réunion
79 □9 Sous le Vent, Îles is Arch. de la Société Fr. Polynesia
205 H2 Sousse Tunisia
163 B8 Soustons France
163 B8 Soustons, Étang de l. France
214 C7 Sout r. S. Africa
214 E4 Sout watercourse S. Africa
234 B7 South r. MD U.S.A.
South Africa country Africa see South Africa, Republic of
212 E6 South Africa, Republic of country Africa
84 D2 South Alligator r. N.T. Austr.
151 J3 Southam Warwickshire, England U.K.
235 G4 South Amboy NJ U.S.A.
248 South America continent
224 D4 Southampton Ont. Can.
151 J6 Southampton Southampton, England U.K.
151 J6 Southampton admin. div. England U.K.
233 M8 Southampton NY U.S.A.
221 J3 Southampton, Cape Nunavut Can.
223 O1 Southampton Island Nunavut Can.
151 J6 Southampton Water est. England U.K.
115 M7 South Andaman i. Andaman & Nicobar Is India
232 H11 South Anna r. VA U.S.A.
149 O7 South Anston South Yorkshire, England U.K.
235 G4 Southard NJ U.S.A.
225 I1 South Aulatsivik Island Nfld and Lab. Can.
82 D4 South Australia state Austr.
265 L7 South Australian Basin sea feature Indian Ocean
237 J8 Southaven MS U.S.A.
146 G12 South Ayrshire admin. div. Scotland U.K.
239 K10 South Baldy mt. NM U.S.A.
149 O4 South Bank Redcar and Cleveland, England U.K.
232 C7 South Bass Island OH U.S.A.
231 G12 South Bay FL U.S.A.
224 D4 South Baymouth Ont. Can.
230 D5 South Bend IN U.S.A.
238 C3 South Bend WA U.S.A.
151 N4 South Benfleet Essex, England U.K.
231 I13 South Bight sea chan. Bahamas
246 F2 South Bluff pt Acklins I. Bahamas
151 M5 Southborough Kent, England U.K.
232 G12 South Boston VA U.S.A.
150 E7 South Brent Devon, England U.K.
81 G10 Southbridge South I. N.Z.
233 M6 Southbridge MA U.S.A.
225 J3 South Brook Nfld and Lab. Can.
215 O6 Southbroom S. Africa
233 L4 South Burlington VT U.S.A.
81 F11 Southburn South I. N.Z.
235 I2 Southbury CT U.S.A.
234 E1 South Canaan PA U.S.A.
231 G8 South Carolina state U.S.A.
149 P6 South Cave East Riding of Yorkshire, England U.K.
151 I4 South Cerney Gloucestershire, England U.K.
150 G6 South Chard Somerset, England U.K.
232 B9 South Charleston OH U.S.A.
232 D10 South Charleston WV U.S.A.
90 E4 South China Sea N. Pacific Ocean
South Coast Town Qld Austr. see Gold Coast
South Cousin Islet i. Inner Islands Seychelles see Cousine
236 E3 South Dakota state U.S.A.
146 K12 Southdean Scottish Borders, Scotland U.K.
233 M6 South Deerfield MA U.S.A.
234 F6 South Dennis NJ U.S.A.
150 G6 South Dorset Downs hills England U.K.
151 L6 South Downs hills England U.K.
216 □2a South East Bay Ascension S. Atlantic Ocean
83 K10 South East Cape Tas. Austr.
83 L7 South East Forests National Park N.S.W. Austr.
265 J7 Southeast Indian Ridge sea feature Indian Ocean
South-East Island Inner Islands Seychelles see Suète, Île du
87 G13 South East Isles W.A. Austr.
267 L10 Southeast Pacific Basin sea feature S. Pacific Ocean
246 G3 Southeast Point Gt Inagua Bahamas
82 □3 South East Reef S. Pacific Ocean
82 □2 South East Rock i. Lord Howe I. Austr.
234 F5 South Egg Harbor NJ U.S.A.
223 K3 Southend Sask. Can.
146 E12 Southend Argyll and Bute, Scotland U.K.
151 N4 Southend admin. div. England U.K.
151 N4 Southend-on-Sea Southend, England U.K.
217 □1b South Entrance sea chan. Mauritius
212 E5 Southern admin. dist. Botswana
211 B8 Southern admin. reg. Malawi
206 B5 Southern prov. Sierra Leone
209 E9 Southern prov. Zambia
Southern Aegean admin. reg. Greece see Notio Aigaio
81 E10 Southern Alps mts South I. N.Z.
87 H9 Southern Central Aboriginal Reserve W.A. Austr.
81 □2 Southern Cook Islands Cook Is
87 E11 Southern Cross W.A. Austr.
208 E2 Southern Darfur state Sudan
223 L3 Southern Indian Lake Man. Can.
208 F2 Southern Kordofan state Sudan
77 I3 Southern Lau Group is Fiji
209 D9 Southern Lueti watercourse Angola/Zambia
208 F3 Southern National Park Sudan
262 R3 Southern Ocean OCEAN
231 H8 Southern Pines NC U.S.A.
Southern Rhodesia country Africa see Zimbabwe
249 G7 Southern Thule is S. Sandwich Is
146 G12 Southern Uplands hills Scotland U.K.
Southern Urals mts Rus. Fed. see Yuzhnyy Ural
239 K8 Southern Ute Indian Reservation res. CO U.S.A.
151 M2 Southery Norfolk, England U.K.
146 K9 South Esk r. Angus, Scotland U.K.
86 I5 South Esk Tableland reg. W.A. Austr.
223 J5 Southey Sask. Can.
215 L7 Southeyville S. Africa
236 J6 South Fabius r. MO U.S.A.
232 B6 Southfield MI U.S.A.
235 G2 Southfields NY U.S.A.
266 G7 South Fiji Basin sea feature S. Pacific Ocean
151 O5 South Foreland pt England U.K.
240 I1 South Fork CA U.S.A.
239 K8 South Fork CO U.S.A.
232 G8 South Fork PA U.S.A.
226 I4 South Fox Island MI U.S.A.
247 □2 South Friar's Bay St Kitts and Nevis
222 E5 Southgate r. B.C. Can.
151 L4 Southgate Greater London, England U.K.
263 H1 South Geomagnetic Pole Antarctica
249 G7 South Georgia terr. S. Atlantic Ocean
234 D1 South Gibson PA U.S.A.
226 E1 South Gillies Ont. Can.
235 J1 South Glastonbury CT U.S.A.
150 H4 South Gloucestershire admin. div. England U.K.
236 H6 South Grand r. MO U.S.A.
151 K6 South Harting West Sussex, England U.K.
117 M8 South Hatia Island Bangl.
226 H7 South Haven MI U.S.A.
151 K6 South Hayling Hampshire, England U.K.
80 I3 South Head North I. N.Z.
80 I3 South Head hd North I. N.Z.
223 L2 South Henik Lake Nunavut Can.
233 L4 South Hero VT U.S.A.
149 O4 South Hetton Durham, England U.K.
216 □2c South Hill hill Tristan da Cunha S. Atlantic Ocean
232 G12 South Hill VA U.S.A.
266 E3 South Honshu Ridge sea feature N. Pacific Ocean
210 C4 South Horr Kenya
223 L3 South Indian Lake Man. Can.
235 J1 Southington CT U.S.A.
86 □2 South Island Cocos Is
114 C7 South Island India
81 G11 South Island N.Z.
210 C4 South Island National Park Kenya
92 B7 South Islet rf Phil.
223 M5 South Junction Man. Can.
South Kazakhstan Oblast admin. div. Kazakh. see Yuzhnyy Kazakhstan
149 Q7 South Kelsey Lincolnshire, England U.K.
149 O6 South Kirkby West Yorkshire, England U.K.
211 C5 South Kitui National Reserve nature res. Kenya
117 J8 South Koel r. Jharkhand India
101 F11 South Korea country Asia
240 L3 South Lake Tahoe CA U.S.A.
146 I11 South Lanarkshire admin. div. Scotland U.K.
81 B12 Southland admin. reg. South I. N.Z.
151 N3 South Lopham Norfolk, England U.K.
236 F5 South Loup r. NE U.S.A.
211 A8 South Luangwa National Park Zambia
235 K2 South Lyme CT U.S.A.
222 C2 South Macmillan r. Y.T. Can.
263 J2 South Magnetic Pole Antarctica
113 □1 South Male Atoll Maldives
151 N4 Southminster Essex, England U.K.
150 E5 South Molton Devon, England U.K.
223 K4 South Moose Lake Man. Can.
234 A5 South Mountains hills PA U.S.A.
86 C6 South Muiron Island W.A. Austr.
222 D1 South Nahanni r. N.W.T. Can.
246 □ South Negril Point Jamaica
146 □N2 South Nesting Bay Scotland U.K.
233 J6 South New Berlin NY U.S.A.
151 M4 South Ockendon Thurrock, England U.K.
235 K2 Southold NY U.S.A.
264 G10 South Orkney Islands S. Atlantic Ocean
South Ossetia reg. Georgia see Samkhret' Oset'i
151 L4 South Oxhey Hertfordshire, England U.K.
235 I3 South Oyster Bay NY U.S.A.
233 □O4 South Paris ME U.S.A.
87 B9 South Passage W.A. Austr.
78 □3a South Passage Kwajalein Marshall Is
231 G11 South Patrick Shores FL U.S.A.
150 G6 South Petherton Somerset, England U.K.
235 G3 South Plainfield NJ U.S.A.
236 E5 South Platte r. CO U.S.A.
246 F2 South Point Long I. Bahamas
247 □4 South Point Barbados
86 □1 South Point Christmas I.
216 □2a South Point Ascension S. Atlantic Ocean
262 T1 South Pole POLE Antarctica
224 D3 South Porcupine Ont. Can.
85 N9 Southport Qld Austr.
83 K10 Southport Tas. Austr.
149 K6 Southport Merseyside, England U.K.
235 I2 Southport CT U.S.A.
231 H9 Southport NC U.S.A.
227 R7 Southport NY U.S.A.
233 □O5 South Portland ME U.S.A.
146 J11 South Queensferry Edinburgh, Scotland U.K.
82 □3 South Reef S. Pacific Ocean
227 O4 South River Ont. Can.
South Rona i. Highland, Scotland U.K. see Rona
146 K5 South Ronaldsay i. Scotland U.K.
233 M5 South Royalton VT U.S.A.
226 A5 South St Paul MN U.S.A.
264 H9 South Sandwich Islands S. Atlantic Ocean
264 H9 South Sandwich Trench sea feature S. Atlantic Ocean
240 J4 South San Francisco CA U.S.A.
223 J4 South Saskatchewan r. Alta/Sask. Can.
223 L3 South Seal r. Man. Can.
262 U2 South Shetland Islands Antarctica
264 E10 South Shetland Trough sea feature S. Atlantic Ocean
149 O3 South Shields Tyne and Wear, England U.K.
South Sinai governorate Egypt see Janūb Sīnā'
236 I5 South Skunk r. IA U.S.A.
266 F6 South Solomon Trench sea feature Pacific Ocean
147 D6 South Sound sea chan. Ireland
221 K3 South Spicer Island Nunavut Can.
234 E2 South Sterling PA U.S.A.
234 D3 South Tamaqua PA U.S.A.
80 I6 South Taranaki Bight b. North I. N.Z.
265 N8 South Tasman Rise sea feature Southern Ocean
241 U2 South Tent mt. UT U.S.A.
235 G5 South Toms River NJ U.S.A.
116 I7 South Tons r. India
241 V9 South Tucson AZ U.S.A.
210 B4 South Turkana Nature Reserve Kenya
224 E2 South Twin Island Nunavut Can.
225 K3 South Twin Lake Nfld and Lab. Can.
149 M4 South Tyne r. England U.K.
South Tyrol prov. Italy see Bolzano
146 B8 South Uist i. Scotland U.K.
238 C5 South Umpqua r. OR U.S.A.
146 J5 South Walls pen. Scotland U.K.
151 L5 Southwater West Sussex, England U.K.
149 P7 Southwell Nottinghamshire, England U.K.
84 G4 South Wellesley Islands Qld Austr.
South-West Africa country Africa see Namibia
231 □2 South West Bay New Prov. Bahamas
216 □2a South West Bay Ascension S. Atlantic Ocean
83 K10 South West Cape Tas. Austr.
81 B14 South West Cape Stewart I. N.Z.
85 N6 South West Cay rf Coral Sea Is Terr. Austr.
83 J9 Southwest Conservation Area nature res. Tas. Austr.
85 M1 South West Entrance sea chan. P.N.G.
233 □Q4 Southwest Harbor ME U.S.A.
265 G7 Southwest Indian Ridge sea feature Indian Ocean
85 L4 South West Island Coral Sea Is Terr. Austr.
83 K10 South West National Park Tas. Austr.
267 I8 Southwest Pacific Basin sea feature S. Pacific Ocean
South-West Peru Ridge sea feature S. Pacific Ocean see Nazca Ridge
246 □ South West Point Jamaica
216 □2b South West Point St Helena
246 D5 Southwest Rock i. Jamaica
83 N4 South West Rocks N.S.W. Austr.
226 I8 South Whitley IN U.S.A.
237 F9 South Wichita r. TX U.S.A.
150 H5 Southwick Wiltshire, England U.K.
232 C11 South Williamson KY U.S.A.
227 R8 South Williamsport PA U.S.A.
233 □O5 South Windham ME U.S.A.
151 P3 Southwold Suffolk, England U.K.
151 N4 South Woodham Ferrers Essex, England U.K.
85 M9 Southwood National Park Qld Austr.
151 M2 South Wootton Norfolk, England U.K.
149 O7 South Yorkshire admin. div. England U.K.
232 C9 South Zanesville OH U.S.A.
182 G8 Souto Guarda Port.
182 D9 Souto Santarém Port.
182 E3 Souto Spain
182 E8 Souto da Casa Port.

Soutpan to Stepanivka

391

215 K4 Soutpan S. Africa
213 F4 Soutpansberg mts S. Africa
204 B5 Souttouf, Adrar mts Western Sahara
160 C3 Souvigny France
142 C1 Sovarnuten mt. Norway
197 N4 Sovata Romania
197 O4 Soveja Romania
260 E4 Soven Arg.
195 L6 Soverato Italy
192 C3 Soveria Corse France
195 K5 Soveria Mannelli Italy
121 N7 Sovet Kyrg.
123 M2 Sovet Tajik.
Sovetabad Uzbek. see Xonobod
Sovetashen Armenia see Zangakatun
138 E6 Sovetsk Kaliningradskaya Oblast' Rus. Fed.
134 J4 Sovetsk Kirovskaya Oblast' Rus. Fed.
139 U8 Sovetsk Tul'skaya Oblast' Rus. Fed.
129 C1 Sovetskaya Krasnodarskiy Kray Rus. Fed.
129 F1 Sovetskaya Stavropol'skiy Kray Rus. Fed.
100 L4 Sovetskaya Gavan' Rus. Fed.
Sovetskiy Kyrg. see Sovet
130 H3 Sovetskiy Khanty-Mansiyskiy Avtonomnyy Okrug Rus. Fed.
138 L1 Sovetskiy Leningradskaya Oblast' Rus. Fed.
134 N2 Sovetskiy Respublika Komi Rus. Fed.
134 J4 Sovetskiy Respublika Mariy El Rus. Fed.
Sovetskiy Tajik. see Sovet
137 S3 Sovetskoye Belgorodskaya Oblast' Rus. Fed.
Sovetskoye Chechenskaya Respublika Rus. Fed. see Shatoy
Sovetskoye Kabardino-Balkarskaya Respublika Rus. Fed. see Kashkhatau
Sovetskoye Respublika Dagestan Rus. Fed. see Khebda
120 B2 Sovetskoye Saratovskaya Oblast' Rus. Fed.
Sovetskoye Stavropol'skiy Kray Rus. Fed. see Zelenokumsk
188 F4 Soviči Bos.-Herz.
191 K9 Sovicille Italy
134 H2 Sovpol'ye Rus. Fed.
137 N8 Sovyets'kyy Ukr.
212 E4 Sowa Botswana
108 B4 Sowa Sichuan China
105 K3 Sōwa Japan
212 E4 Sowa Pan salt pan Botswana
149 O5 Sowerby North Yorkshire, England U.K.
149 N6 Sowerby Bridge West Yorkshire, England U.K.
215 L2 Soweto S. Africa
174 C2 Sowno Zachodniopomorskie Pol.
174 E1 Sowno Zachodniopomorskie Pol.
123 N2 So'x Tajik.
Sōya-kaikyō str. Japan/Rus. Fed. see La Pérouse Strait
243 M9 Soyaló Mex.
102 S1 Sōya-misaki c. Japan
134 H2 Soyana r. Rus. Fed.
101 E9 Soyang-ho l. S. Korea
162 E4 Soyaux France
102 S1 Sōya-wan b. Japan
160 I2 Soye France
173 M5 Soyen Ger.
Soylan Armenia see Vayk'
134 J2 Soyma r. Rus. Fed.
209 B6 Soyo Angola
161 F7 Soyons France
242 E3 Soyopa Mex.
129 G5 Soyuqbulaq Azer.
Sozaq Kazakh. see Suzak
139 N9 Sozh r. Europe
134 K4 Sozimskiy Rus. Fed.
197 P8 Sozopol Bulg.
165 I8 Spa Belgium
262 T2 Spaatz Island Antarctica
172 D2 Spabrücken Ger.
195 I7 Spadafora Sicilia Italy
168 E5 Spahnharrenstätte Ger.
172 F5 Spaichingen Ger.
180 E2 Spain country Europe
Spalato Croatia see Split
Spalatum Croatia see Split
82 G5 Spalding S.A. Austr.
151 L2 Spalding Lincolnshire, England U.K.
176 C2 Spálené Poříčí Czech Rep.
173 J3 Spalt Ger.
169 I8 Spangenberg Ger.
150 E5 Span Head hill England U.K.
225 K4 Spaniard's Bay Nfld and Lab. Can.
224 D4 Spanish Ont. Can.
224 D4 Spanish r. Ont. Can.
241 U1 Spanish Fork UT U.S.A.
Spanish Guinea country Africa see Equatorial Guinea
Spanish Netherlands country Europe see Belgium
247 □2 Spanish Point pt Antigua and Barbuda
231 □1 Spanish Point pt Bermuda
145 C5 Spanish Point Ireland
Spanish Sahara terr. Africa see Western Sahara
246 □ Spanish Town Jamaica
246 E1 Spanish Wells Eleuthera Bahamas
170 I3 Spantekow Ger.
194 D7 Sparagio, Monte mt. Italy
193 M5 Sparanise Italy
192 C5 Spargi, Isola i. Sardegna Italy
240 M2 Sparks NV U.S.A.
232 C6 Sparlingville MI U.S.A.
234 F2 Sparrow Bush NY U.S.A.
Sparta Greece see Sparti
195 J7 Spartà Sicilia Italy
231 F9 Sparta GA U.S.A.
226 I6 Sparta MI U.S.A.
232 D12 Sparta NC U.S.A.
234 F2 Sparta NJ U.S.A.
231 E8 Sparta TN U.S.A.
226 D6 Sparta WI U.S.A.
231 G8 Spartanburg SC U.S.A.
232 F7 Spartansburg PA U.S.A.
180 D5 Spartel, Cap c. Morocco
198 D5 Sparti Greece
192 B10 Spartivento, Capo c. Sardegna Italy
195 K8 Spartivento, Capo c. Italy
222 H5 Sparwood B.C. Can.
139 R7 Spas-Demensk Rus. Fed.
137 O5 Spas'ke Ukr.
139 X6 Spas-Klepiki Rus. Fed.
137 P5 Spas'ko-Mykhaylivka Ukr.
137 M5 Spasove Ukr.
139 S6 Spass Rus. Fed.
135 H5 Spassk Rus. Fed.
134 F3 Spasskaya Guba Rus. Fed.
139 O3 Spasskaya Polist' Rus. Fed.
100 H6 Spassk-Dal'niy Rus. Fed.
121 M1 Spasskoye Kazakh.
139 T8 Spasskoye-Lutovinovo Rus. Fed.
139 X7 Spassk-Ryazanskiy Rus. Fed.
139 U5 Spas-Ugol Rus. Fed.
198 E7 Spatha, Akrotirio pt Kriti Greece
198 D6 Spathi, Akrotirio pt Kythira Greece
222 D3 Spatsizi Plateau Wilderness Provincial Park B.C. Can.
169 E10 Spay Ger.
146 G9 Spean Bridge Highland, Scotland U.K.
236 D3 Spearfish SD U.S.A.
237 E7 Spearman TX U.S.A.
195 O4 Specchia Italy
233 K5 Speculator NY U.S.A.
151 J5 Speen West Berkshire, England U.K.
190 G1 Speer mt. Switz.
223 J4 Speers Sask. Can.
216 □2b Speery Island St Helena
172 B2 Speicher Ger.
179 H5 Speicher Sameralm l. Austria
173 L2 Speichersdorf Ger.
247 □4 Speightstown Barbados
179 L5 Speikkogel mt. Austria
211 B5 Speke Gulf Tanz.
169 D6 Spelle Ger.
193 J2 Spello Italy
146 E10 Spelve, Loch inlet Scotland U.K.
Spence Bay Nunavut Can. see Taloyoak
236 H4 Spencer IA U.S.A.
238 H4 Spencer ID U.S.A.
230 D6 Spencer IN U.S.A.
233 N6 Spencer MA U.S.A.
236 F4 Spencer NE U.S.A.
227 R7 Spencer NY U.S.A.
232 E12 Spencer VA U.S.A.
232 D10 Spencer WV U.S.A.
82 F6 Spencer, Cape S.A. Austr.
222 B3 Spencer, Cape AK U.S.A.
220 B5 Spencer, Point AK U.S.A.
212 B5 Spencer Bay Namibia
82 F6 Spencer Gulf est. S.A. Austr.
233 □O3 Spencer Lake ME U.S.A.
84 B3 Spencer Range hills N.T. Austr.
84 D2 Spencer Range hills N.T. Austr.
222 F5 Spences Bridge B.C. Can.
169 F6 Spenge Ger.
149 N4 Spennymoor Durham, England U.K.
81 G9 Spenser Mountains South I. N.Z.
198 D4 Spercheios r. Greece
171 H6 Sperenberg Ger.
142 G1 Sperillen l. Norway
Sperkhiós r. Greece see Spercheios
194 G8 Sperlinga Sicilia Italy
193 K5 Sperlonga Italy
197 M3 Spermezeu Romania
192 A10 Sperone, Capo c. Sardegna Italy
147 H3 Sperrin Mountains hills Northern Ireland U.K.
232 G10 Sperryville VA U.S.A.
169 H11 Spessart reg. Ger.
234 C6 Spesutie Island MD U.S.A.
Spétsai i. Greece see Spetses
198 E5 Spetses Greece
198 E5 Spetses i. Greece
146 J7 Spey r. Scotland U.K.
146 J7 Spey Bay Moray, Scotland U.K.
172 E3 Speyer Ger.
247 □5 Speyside Trin. and Tob.
123 L7 Spezand Pak.
158 D5 Spézet France
193 Q8 Spezzano Albanese Italy
Spice Islands Indon. see Maluku
175 K4 Spiczyn Pol.
147 D6 Spiddal Ireland
173 O4 Spiegelau Ger.
168 E3 Spiekeroog Ger.
168 E3 Spiekeroog i. Ger.
179 K5 Spielberg bei Knittelfeld Austria
179 M6 Spielfeld Austria
172 C3 Spiesen-Elversberg Ger.
190 D2 Spiez Switz.
190 E6 Spigno Monferrato Italy
193 L5 Spigno Saturnia Italy
164 K2 Spijk Neth.
164 F5 Spijkenisse Neth.
129 A6 Spikör Geçidi pass Turkey
191 K6 Spilamberto Italy
199 I4 Spil Dağı Milli Parkı nat. park Turkey
198 F7 Spili Kriti Greece
191 N3 Spilimbergo Italy
195 J6 Spilinga Italy
149 R7 Spilsby Lincolnshire, England U.K.
193 Q6 Spinazzola Italy
123 L6 Spīn Būldak Afgh.
157 K5 Spincourt France
191 M5 Spinea Italy
193 L2 Spinetoli Italy
234 E4 Spinnerstown PA U.S.A.
195 □ Spinola, Ix-Xatt ta' b. Malta
193 P7 Spinoso Italy
123 M7 Spintangi Pak.
177 L4 Spinuș Romania
123 N5 Spinwam Pak.
215 N4 Spioenkop Dam Nature Reserve S. Africa
236 H4 Spirit Lake IA U.S.A.
238 F2 Spirit Lake ID U.S.A.
223 J4 Spiritwood Sask. Can.
139 R4 Spirovo Rus. Fed.
176 G6 Špišić-Bukovica Croatia
178 B6 Spiss Austria
177 J2 Spišská Belá Slovakia
177 J3 Spišská Nová Ves Slovakia
177 J2 Spišská Stará Ves Slovakia
177 J3 Spišské Podhradie Slovakia
177 J3 Spišské Vlachy Slovakia
177 J3 Spišský Hrad Slovakia
177 J2 Spišský Štvrtok Slovakia
129 F5 Spitak Armenia
179 J4 Spital am Pyhrn Austria
179 M4 Spital am Semmering Austria
116 G4 Spiti r. India
86 E6 Spit Point W.A. Austr.
140 □ Spitsbergen i. Svalbard
214 G9 Spitskop mt. S. Africa
215 J7 Spitskopvlei S. Africa
138 K3 Spitsyno Rus. Fed.
179 H6 Spittal an der Drau Austria
146 J9 Spittal of Glenshee Perth and Kinross, Scotland U.K.
231 □1 Spittal Pond Bermuda
179 L3 Spitz Austria
Spitzbergen i. Svalbard see Spitsbergen
178 G6 Spitzkofel mt. Austria
190 G1 Spitzmeilen mt. Switz.
137 R4 Spivakivka Ukr.
151 O2 Spixworth Norfolk, England U.K.
142 E5 Spjald Denmark
188 F4 Split Croatia
223 L3 Split Lake Man. Can.
223 L3 Split Lake l. Man. Can.
190 G2 Spluga, Passo dello pass Italy/Switz.
190 G2 Splügen Switz.
136 H4 Spodakhy Ukr.
179 J7 Spodnja Idrija Slovenia
179 M6 Spodnje Hoče Slovenia
168 K1 Spodsbjerg Denmark
149 O6 Spofforth North Yorkshire, England U.K.
238 F3 Spokane WA U.S.A.
238 E3 Spokane r. WA U.S.A.
238 E3 Spokane Indian Reservation res. WA U.S.A.
129 C1 Spokoynaya Rus. Fed.
190 I2 Spöl r. Italy
Spoletium Italy see Spoleto
193 J2 Spoleto Italy
193 M3 Spoltore Italy
191 J2 Spondigna Italy
165 H8 Spontin Belgium
226 D9 Spoon r. IL U.S.A.
226 C4 Spooner WI U.S.A.
171 F8 Spora Ger.
170 E4 Spornitz Ger.
234 C4 Sporting Hill PA U.S.A.
246 D4 Spot Bay Cayman Is
190 E7 Spotorno Italy
235 G4 Spotswood NJ U.S.A.
232 H10 Spotsylvania VA U.S.A.
238 L4 Spotted Horse WY U.S.A.
227 L3 Spragge Ont. Can.
238 D5 Sprague r. OR U.S.A.
172 H4 Spraitbach Ger.
168 K5 Sprakensehl Ger.
222 F4 Spranger, Mount B.C. Can.
90 D5 Spratly Island S. China Sea
90 D4 Spratly Islands S. China Sea
238 E4 Spray OR U.S.A.
226 F4 Spread Eagle WI U.S.A.
188 G3 Spreča r. Bos.-Herz.
171 H5 Spree r. Ger.
171 I6 Spreenhagen Ger.
171 J7 Spreewald park Ger.
171 I6 Spreewald reg. Ger.
172 E7 Spreitenbach Switz.
171 J7 Spremberg Ger.
172 D2 Sprendlingen Ger.
191 M4 Spresiano Italy
190 H3 Spriana Italy
165 I7 Sprimont Belgium
237 H7 Spring r. MO U.S.A.
227 L4 Spring Bay Ont. Can.
214 B5 Springbok S. Africa
234 D4 Spring City PA U.S.A.
241 U2 Spring City UT U.S.A.
84 F5 Spring Creek r. N.T. Austr.
85 H8 Spring Creek watercourse Qld Austr.
236 E5 Spring Creek r. NE U.S.A.
225 K3 Springdale Nfld and Lab. Can.
237 H7 Springdale AR U.S.A.
169 I6 Springe Ger.
239 L8 Springer NM U.S.A.
241 W7 Springerville AZ U.S.A.
81 F10 Springfield South I. N.Z.
147 G4 Springfield Northern Ireland U.K.
237 D7 Springfield CO U.S.A.
231 G9 Springfield GA U.S.A.
238 H5 Springfield ID U.S.A.
236 K6 Springfield IL U.S.A.
230 E7 Springfield KY U.S.A.
233 M6 Springfield MA U.S.A.
233 □Q3 Springfield ME U.S.A.
236 H3 Springfield MN U.S.A.
237 I7 Springfield MO U.S.A.
232 B9 Springfield OH U.S.A.
238 C4 Springfield OR U.S.A.
234 E5 Springfield PA U.S.A.
231 D7 Springfield TN U.S.A.
233 M5 Springfield VT U.S.A.
232 G9 Springfield WV U.S.A.
215 J6 Springfontein S. Africa
251 G3 Spring Garden Guyana
235 G1 Spring Glen NY U.S.A.
234 B3 Spring Glen PA U.S.A.
241 V2 Spring Glen UT U.S.A.
226 D6 Spring Green WI U.S.A.
226 C6 Spring Grove MN U.S.A.
234 B5 Spring Grove PA U.S.A.
232 I11 Spring Grove VA U.S.A.
225 H4 Springhill N.S. Can.
231 F11 Spring Hill FL U.S.A.
146 I12 Springholm Dumfries and Galloway, Scotland U.K.
222 F5 Springhouse B.C. Can.
226 H6 Spring Lake MI U.S.A.
235 G4 Spring Lake Heights NJ U.S.A.
241 Q5 Spring Mountains NV U.S.A.
226 J7 Springport MI U.S.A.
215 M2 Springs S. Africa
235 K2 Springs NY U.S.A.
81 G9 Springs Junction South I. N.Z.
85 L8 Springsure Qld Austr.
234 E5 Springton Reservoir PA U.S.A.
85 H7 Springvale Qld Austr.
215 K8 Spring Valley S. Africa
240 P9 Spring Valley CA U.S.A.
226 B6 Spring Valley MN U.S.A.
235 G2 Spring Valley NY U.S.A.
226 B5 Spring Valley WI U.S.A.
236 F4 Springview NE U.S.A.
240 N5 Springville CA U.S.A.
232 G6 Springville NY U.S.A.
234 D1 Springville PA U.S.A.
241 U1 Springville UT U.S.A.
232 H6 Springwater NY U.S.A.
149 Q6 Sproatley East Riding of Yorkshire, England U.K.
169 D8 Sprockhövel Ger.
151 O2 Sprowston Norfolk, England U.K.
222 H4 Spruce Grove Alta Can.
232 F10 Spruce Knob mt. WV U.S.A.
241 X3 Spruce Mountain CO U.S.A.
241 R1 Spruce Mountain NV U.S.A.
234 F3 Spruce Run Reservoir NJ U.S.A.
164 G5 Sprundel Neth.
234 B5 Spry PA U.S.A.
195 L4 Spulico, Capo c. Italy
149 R6 Spurn Head England U.K.
220 C5 Spurr, Mount vol. AK U.S.A.
222 F5 Spuzzum B.C. Can.
175 J2 Spychowo Pol.
222 F5 Squamish B.C. Can.
222 F5 Squamish r. B.C. Can.
233 N5 Squam Lake NH U.S.A.
233 □Q2 Squapan Lake ME U.S.A.
191 K5 Squaranto r. Italy
233 □Q1 Square Lake ME U.S.A.
195 L6 Squillace Italy
195 L6 Squillace, Golfo di g. Italy
195 O3 Squinzano Italy
232 D11 Squire WV U.S.A.
87 I9 Squires, Mount hill W.A. Austr.
95 I8 Sragen Jawa Indon.
196 I8 Srbica Kosovo Serbia
Srbija country Europe see Serbia
Srbinje Bos.-Herz. see Foča
Srbobran Bos.-Herz. see Donji Vakuf
196 H5 Srbobran Vojvodina Serbia
97 F9 Srê Âmběl Cambodia
197 P6 Srebărna tourist site Bulg.
188 G3 Srebrenica Bos.-Herz.
197 P8 Sredets Burgas Bulg.
Sredets Sofiya-Grad Bulg. see Sofiya
197 P8 Sredetska Reka r. Bulg.
131 Q4 Sredinnyy Khrebet mts Rus. Fed.
179 N7 Središče Slovenia
197 P7 Sredishte Bulg.
197 L8 Sredna Gora mts Bulg.
100 E3 Srednebelaya Rus. Fed.
131 Q3 Srednekolymsk Rus. Fed.
139 T7 Sredne-Russkaya Vozvyshennost' hills Rus. Fed.
131 M3 Sredne-Sibirskoye Ploskogor'ye plat. Rus. Fed.
140 U4 Sredneye Kuyto, Ozero l. Rus. Fed.
137 S2 Sredniy Ikorets Rus. Fed.
100 H3 Sredniy Urgal Rus. Fed.
191 Q5 Srednja Vrata, Kanal sea chan. Croatia
197 M8 Srednogorie Bulg.
135 I6 Srednyaya Akhtuba Rus. Fed.
97 H8 Sre Khtum Cambodia
174 F3 Śrem Pol.
196 H5 Srem reg. Serbia
196 H6 Sremska Mitrovica Vojvodina Serbia
97 G8 Srê Noy Cambodia
97 H8 Srêpok, Tônlé r. Cambodia
99 K1 Sretensk Rus. Fed.
95 I4 Sri Aman Sarawak Malaysia
137 L3 Sribne Ukr.
114 G6 Sriharikota Island India
114 F9 Sri Jayewardenepura Kotte Sri Lanka
115 I3 Srikakulam Andhra Prad. India
114 F6 Sri Kalahasti Andhra Prad. India
114 G9 Sri Lanka country Asia
116 E6 Sri Madhopur Rajasthan India
117 M7 Srimangal Bangl.
116 G4 Srinagar Uttaranchal India
116 E2 Srinagar Jammu and Kashmir
114 D6 Sringeri Karnataka India
114 G9 Sri Pada mt. Sri Lanka
114 F7 Srirangam Tamil Nadu India
114 F4 Srisailam Andhra Prad. India
114 E8 Srivaikuntam Tamil Nadu India
114 C3 Srivardhan Mahar. India
114 E8 Srivilliputtur Tamil Nadu India
188 F3 Srnetica mts Bos.-Herz.
188 G3 Srnice Bos.-Herz.
175 J1 Srockowo Pol.
174 E4 Środa Śląska Pol.
174 F3 Środa Wielkopolska Pol.
174 E3 Środkowy Kanał Obry canal Pol.
146 G8 Sròn a' Choire Ghairbh hill Scotland U.K.
121 U1 Srostki Rus. Fed.
196 I5 Srpska Crnja Vojvodina Serbia
Srpska Kostajnica Bos.-Herz. see Bosanska Kostajnica
Srpski Brod Bos.-Herz. see Bosanski Brod
196 I5 Srpski Itebej Vojvodina Serbia
115 H3 Srungavarapukota Andhra Prad. India
139 W9 Sselki Rus. Fed.
214 E3 Staansaam S. Africa
85 H4 Staaten r. Qld Austr.
85 I4 Staaten River National Park Qld Austr.
179 N2 Staatz Austria
140 R1 Stabbursdalen Nasjonalpark nat. park Norway
170 D2 Staberhuk c. Ger.
165 F6 Stabroek Belgium
Stabroek Guyana see Georgetown
176 C2 Stachy Czech Rep.
146 F6 Stac Pollaidh hill Scotland U.K.
Stac Polly hill Scotland U.K. see Stac Pollaidh
226 B4 Stacy MN U.S.A.
226 B6 Stacyville IA U.S.A.
168 H3 Stade Ger.
173 N6 Stadelhorn mt. Ger.
165 D7 Staden Belgium
168 K5 Stadensen Ger.
151 J4 Stadhampton Oxfordshire, England U.K.
Stadhlaigearraidh Scotland U.K. see Stilligarry
141 L6 Städjan-Nipfjällets naturreservat nature res. Sweden
179 I3 Stadl-Paura Austria
164 K3 Stadskanaal Neth.
164 K2 Stadskanaal canal Neth.
169 H9 Stadtallendorf Ger.
173 J5 Stadtbergen Ger.
169 H6 Stadthagen Ger.
171 D9 Stadtilm Ger.
169 C10 Stadtkyll Ger.
169 J10 Stadtlauringen Ger.
169 J9 Stadtlengsfeld Ger.
169 C7 Stadtlohn Ger.
169 I7 Stadtoldendorf Ger.
172 G2 Stadtprozelten Ger.
171 E9 Stadtroda Ger.
179 N5 Stadtschlaining Austria
171 E10 Stadtsteinach Ger.
168 H1 Stadum Ger.
190 F1 Stäfa Switz.
146 D10 Staffa i. Scotland U.K.
171 D10 Staffelberg hill Ger.
157 N8 Staffelfelden France
173 K6 Staffelsee l. Ger.
169 K10 Staffelstein Ger.
168 G5 Staffhorst Ger.
146 D7 Staffin Highland, Scotland U.K.
146 D7 Staffin Bay Scotland U.K.
191 O9 Staffolo Italy
190 G5 Staffora r. Italy
150 H2 Stafford Staffordshire, England U.K.
232 H10 Stafford VA U.S.A.
246 E1 Stafford Creek Andros Bahamas
150 H2 Staffordshire admin. div. England U.K.
215 N6 Stafford's Post S. Africa
233 M7 Stafford Springs CT U.S.A.
95 L6 Stagen Kalimantan Indon.
222 H2 Stagg Lake N.W.T. Can.
147 C4 Stags of Broad Haven is Ireland
173 P2 Štăhlavy Czech Rep.
232 F8 Stahlstown PA U.S.A.
171 H6 Stahnsdorf Ger.
179 K7 Stahovica Slovenia
138 H4 Staicele Latvia
172 H5 Staig Ger.
193 O4 Staina r. Italy
179 J4 Stainach Austria
149 N4 Staindrop Durham, England U.K.
151 K5 Staines Surrey, England U.K.
149 M5 Stainforth North Yorkshire, England U.K.
149 O6 Stainforth South Yorkshire, England U.K.
149 Q5 Staintondale North Yorkshire, England U.K.
157 J6 Stainville France
179 L6 Stainz Austria
195 K8 Staiti Italy
177 L3 Stakčín Slovakia
146 G11 Stake, Hill of Scotland U.K.
137 R5 Stakhanov Ukr.
137 M8 Stakhanovka Ukr.
Stakhanovo Rus. Fed. see Zhukovskiy
150 H6 Stalbridge Dorset, England U.K.
190 D3 Stalden Switz.
168 L1 Ståldyb sea chan. Denmark
151 P2 Stalham Norfolk, England U.K.
Stalin Bulg. see Varna
Stalinabad Tajik. see Dushanbe
Stalingrad Rus. Fed. see Volgograd
Stalingradskaya Oblast' admin. div. Rus. Fed. see Volgogradskaya Oblast'
Staliniri Georgia see Ts'khinvali
Stalino Ukr. see Donets'k
Stalino Uzbek. see Shahrihon
Stalinogorsk Rus. Fed. see Novomoskovsk
Stalinogród Pol. see Katowice
Stalinsk Rus. Fed. see Novokuznetsk
178 H6 Stall Austria
143 N2 Stallarholmen Sweden
179 L5 Stallhofen Austria
149 M5 Stalling Busk North Yorkshire, England U.K.
173 N3 Stallwang Ger.
175 K5 Stalowa Wola Pol.
197 O5 Stâlpu Romania
215 L9 Stalwart Point S. Africa
149 M7 Stalybridge Greater Manchester, England U.K.
197 M8 Stamboliyski Bulg.
85 I6 Stamford Qld Austr.
151 L2 Stamford Lincolnshire, England U.K.
233 L7 Stamford CT U.S.A.
233 K6 Stamford NY U.S.A.
237 F9 Stamford TX U.S.A.
149 P6 Stamford Bridge East Riding of Yorkshire, England U.K.
149 N3 Stamfordham Northumberland, England U.K.
171 E10 Stammbach Ger.
173 K4 Stammham Ger.
Stampalia i. Greece see Astypalaia
212 C5 Stampriet Namibia
178 C5 Stams Austria
173 N3 Stamsried Ger.
140 L2 Stamsund Norway
147 J5 Stamullen Ireland
232 G10 Stanardsville VA U.S.A.
236 H5 Stanberry MO U.S.A.
262 W1 Stancomb-Wills Glacier Antarctica
222 H5 Standard Alta Can.
164 G5 Standdaarbuiten Neth.
215 N2 Standerton S. Africa
236 E3 Standing Rock Indian Reservation res. ND/SD U.S.A.
149 L6 Standish Greater Manchester, England U.K.
227 K6 Standish MI U.S.A.
151 M4 Standon Hertfordshire, England U.K.
148 J2 Stane North Lanarkshire, Scotland U.K.
197 M6 Stănești Romania
241 U9 Stanfield AZ U.S.A.
214 D10 Stanford S. Africa
230 E7 Stanford KY U.S.A.
238 I3 Stanford MT U.S.A.
151 M4 Stanford-le-Hope Thurrock, England U.K.
143 O4 Stånga Gotland Sweden
143 M4 Stångån r. Sweden
140 T1 Stáŋganasčohkka hill Norway
215 P5 Stanger S. Africa
140 J5 Stangvikfjorden inlet Norway
151 N2 Stanhoe Norfolk, England U.K.
149 M4 Stanhope Durham, England U.K.
234 F3 Stanhope NJ U.S.A.
197 Q4 Stănilești Romania
175 K4 Stanin Pol.
196 H5 Stanišić Vojvodina Serbia
Stanislav Ivano-Frankivs'ka Oblast' Ukr. see Ivano-Frankivs'k
137 L7 Stanislav Khersons'ka Oblast' Ukr.
175 M5 Stanislavchyk Ukr.
175 J3 Stanisławów Pol.
197 N3 Stânișoarei, Munții mts Romania
179 I8 Štanjel Slovenia
Stanke Dimitrov Bulg. see Dupnitsa
176 C2 Staňkov Czech Rep.
83 J9 Stanley Tas. Austr.
233 □S2 Stanley N.B. Can.
109 □J7 Stanley H.K. China
259 F8 Stanley Falkland Is
149 N4 Stanley Durham, England U.K.
146 J10 Stanley Perth and Kinross, Scotland U.K.
238 G4 Stanley ID U.S.A.
236 D1 Stanley ND U.S.A.
232 G10 Stanley VA U.S.A.
226 D5 Stanley WI U.S.A.
Stanley, Chutes waterfall Dem. Rep. Congo see Boyoma, Chutes
84 C7 Stanley, Mount hill N.T. Austr.
83 J9 Stanley, Mount hill Tas. Austr.
Stanley, Mount Dem. Rep. Congo/Uganda see Margherita Peak
Stanley Falls Dem. Rep. Congo see Boyoma, Chutes
114 E7 Stanley Reservoir India
Stanleyville Dem. Rep. Congo see Kisangani
213 F4 Stanmore Zimbabwe
Stann Creek Belize see Dangriga
149 N3 Stannington Northumberland, England U.K.
174 D2 Stanomino Pol.
198 C4 Stanos Greece
139 V9 Stanovaya Rus. Fed.
139 W8 Stanovaya Ryasa r. Rus. Fed.
171 G10 Stanovice, Vodní nádrž resr Czech Rep.
139 V9 Stanovoye Rus. Fed.
131 M4 Stanovoye Nagor'ye mts Rus. Fed.
131 N4 Stanovoy Khrebet mts Rus. Fed.
139 T9 Stanovoy Kolodez' Rus. Fed.
178 E5 Stans Austria
190 E2 Stans Switz.
82 F6 Stansbury S.A. Austr.
86 J6 Stansmore Range hills W.A. Austr.
151 M4 Stansted Mountfitchet Essex, England U.K.
83 M3 Stanthorpe Qld Austr.
151 N3 Stanton Suffolk, England U.K.
234 D5 Stanton DE U.S.A.
232 B11 Stanton KY U.S.A.
226 I6 Stanton MI U.S.A.
236 E2 Stanton ND U.S.A.
236 G5 Stanton NE U.S.A.
237 E9 Stanton TX U.S.A.
139 V9 Stantsiya Babarykino Rus. Fed.
139 U8 Stantsiya Skuratovo Rus. Fed.
Stantsiya-Yakkabag Uzbek. see Yakkabog'
151 N4 Stanway Essex, England U.K.
137 S5 Stanychno-Luhans'ke Ukr.
178 C5 Stanzach Austria
179 M5 Stanz im Mürztal Austria
168 K4 Stapel Ger.
169 K7 Stapelburg Ger.
168 J3 Stapelfeld Ger.
164 J3 Staphorst Neth.
151 J2 Stapleford Nottinghamshire, England U.K.
151 N5 Staplehurst Kent, England U.K.
236 H2 Staples MN U.S.A.
236 E5 Stapleton NE U.S.A.
175 I4 Stąporków Pol.
85 J5 Star r. Qld Austr.
139 R8 Star' Rus. Fed.
137 K3 Stara Basan' Ukr.
177 H2 Stará Bystrica Slovakia
136 G3 Stara Chortoryya Ukr.
175 J4 Starachowice Pol.
176 D2 Stará Huť Czech Rep.
137 M1 Stara Huta Ukr.
174 G2 Stara Kiszewa Pol.
175 K3 Stara Kornica Pol.
136 H3 Stara Kotel'nya Ukr.
174 E2 Stara Łubianka Pol.
177 J2 Stará Ľubovňa Slovakia
177 I6 Stara Moravica Vojvodina Serbia
191 R6 Stara Novalja Croatia
176 E1 Stará Paka Czech Rep.
196 I6 Stara Pazova Vojvodina Serbia
197 K7 Stara Planina mts Bulg./Yugo.
179 O8 Stara Plošćica Croatia
170 J5 Stara Rudnica Pol.
175 K6 Stara Sil' Ukr.
177 G3 Stará Turá Slovakia
136 G5 Stara Ushytsya Ukr.
179 M8 Stara vas-Bizeljsko Slovenia
136 D2 Stara Vyzhivka Ukr.
175 K5 Stara Wieś Pol.
Staraya Barda Rus. Fed. see Krasnogorskoye
137 T2 Staraya Chigla Rus. Fed.
137 S3 Staraya Kalitva Rus. Fed.
120 B1 Staraya Kulatka Rus. Fed.
120 B2 Staraya Poltavka Rus. Fed.
139 O4 Staraya Russa Rus. Fed.
139 O5 Staraya Toropa Rus. Fed.
135 J5 Staraya Tumba Rus. Fed.
197 N8 Stara Zagora Bulg.
136 E5 Stara Zhadova Ukr.
267 I6 Starbuck Island Kiribati
137 P6 Starchenkove Ukr.
197 O5 Starchiojd Romania
237 J9 Star City AR U.S.A.
226 H9 Star City IN U.S.A.
85 J3 Starcke National Park Qld Austr.
150 F6 Starcross Devon, England U.K.
137 M8 Stare, Ozero l. Ukr.
174 G5 Stare Budkowice Pol.
179 M1 Stařeč Czech Rep.
174 C2 Stare Czarnowo Pol.
174 D2 Stare Dąbrowa Pol.
175 K2 Stare Dolistowo Pol.
175 K3 Stare Hołowczyce Pol.
171 J9 Staré Křečany Czech Rep.
174 D3 Stare Kurowo Pol.
176 F1 Staré Město Czech Rep.
174 G3 Stare Miasto Pol.
175 H1 Stare Pole Pol.
136 D4 Stare Selo Ukr.
174 E4 Stare Strącze Pol.
Stargard in Pommern Pol. see Stargard Szczeciński
174 D2 Stargard Szczeciński Pol.
177 I3 Star Huta Slovakia
191 R6 Starigrad Croatia
175 M4 Stari Koshary Ukr.
191 R4 Stari Log Slovenia
177 L2 Starina, Vodná nádrž resr Slovakia
136 J3 Stari Petrivtsi Ukr.
196 I7 Stari Ras and Sopoćani tourist site Serbia
191 Q4 Stari Trg Slovenia
139 R5 Staritsa Rus. Fed.
120 H3 Star Karabutak Kazakh.
231 F11 Starke FL U.S.A.
171 F9 Starkenberg Ger.
232 F11 Starkey VA U.S.A.
80 □ Star Keys is Chatham Is S. Pacific Ocean
139 X6 Starkovo Rus. Fed.
237 K9 Starkville MS U.S.A.
233 J4 Star Lake NY U.S.A.
Starling Inlet H.K. China see Sha Tau Kok Hoi
173 K6 Starnberg Ger.
173 K6 Starnberger See l. Ger.
110 F1 Staroaleyskoye Rus. Fed.
Starobel'sk Ukr. see Starobil's'k
137 R6 Starobesheve Ukr.
137 R6 Starobeshivs'ke Vodoskhovyshche resr Ukr.
137 R4 Starobil's'k Ukr.
138 K9 Starobin Belarus
137 O6 Starobohdanivka Ukr.
137 R7 Staroderevyankovskaya Rus. Fed.
139 P9 Starodub Rus. Fed.
174 D2 Starogard Pol.
174 G2 Starogard Gdański Pol.
129 H2 Starogladkovskaya Rus. Fed.
Starokonstantinov Ukr. see Starokostyantyniv
136 G4 Starokostyantyniv Ukr.
136 I7 Starokozache Ukr.
139 W7 Staroletovo Rus. Fed.
137 S8 Staroleushkovskaya Rus. Fed.
135 G7 Starominskaya Rus. Fed.
137 P6 Staromlynivka Ukr.
137 R8 Staronizhestebliyevskaya Rus. Fed.
197 P8 Staro Oryakhovo Bulg.
137 Q2 Starooskol'skoye Vodokhranilishche resr Rus. Fed.
197 M8 Starosel Bulg.
197 O7 Staro Selo Bulg.
139 X8 Staroseslavino Rus. Fed.
135 G7 Staroshcherbinovskaya Rus. Fed.
174 C4 Starosiedle Pol.
120 G1 Starosubkhangulovo Rus. Fed.
137 Q8 Starotitarovskaya Rus. Fed.
137 O4 Starovirivka Ukr.
175 H4 Starowa Góra Pol.
134 H4 Staroye Rus. Fed.
135 I5 Staroye Drozhzhanoye Rus. Fed.
139 Q6 Staroye Istomino Rus. Fed.
139 T5 Staroye Melkovo Rus. Fed.
139 T3 Staroye Sandovo Rus. Fed.
175 M3 Staroye Syalo Brestskaya Voblasts' Belarus
138 M6 Staroye Syalo Vitsyebskaya Voblasts' Belarus
135 H5 Staroyur'yevo Rus. Fed.
139 W7 Starozhilovo Rus. Fed.
175 H3 Staroźreby Pol.
240 N1 Star Peak NV U.S.A.
150 E7 Start Bay England U.K.
149 N4 Startforth Durham, England U.K.
150 E7 Start Point England U.K.
Starve Island Kiribati see Starbuck Island
175 H2 Stary Dzierzgoń Pol.
177 L1 Stary Dzików Pol.
177 G2 Starý Jičín Czech Rep.
174 D4 Stary Kisielin Pol.
175 H3 Stary Kobrzyniec Pol.
175 K5 Stary Majdan Pol.
138 K7 Starynki Belarus
138 M6 Starynovichy Belarus
176 C2 Starý Plzenec Czech Rep.
175 I6 Stary Sącz Pol.
177 J2 Starý Smokovec Slovakia
175 J3 Stary Szelków Pol.
175 H2 Stary Targ Pol.
177 H3 Starý Tekov Slovakia
137 P3 Starytsya Ukr.
175 K4 Stary Uścimów Pol.
138 L8 Staryya Darohi Belarus
136 E2 Staryy Chortoryys'k Ukr.
139 X5 Staryy Dvor Rus. Fed.
Staryye Dorogi Belarus see Staryya Darohi
137 K1 Staryye Yurkovichi Rus. Fed.
131 L2 Staryy Kayak Rus. Fed.
137 Q6 Staryy Krym Donets'ka Oblast' Ukr.
137 O8 Staryy Krym Respublika Krym Ukr.
129 E2 Staryy Lesken Rus. Fed.
130 I3 Staryy Nadym Rus. Fed.
136 E4 Staryy Oleksynets' Ukr.
135 G6 Staryy Oskol Rus. Fed.
136 G4 Staryy Ostropil' Ukr.
Staryy Salavan Rus. Fed. see Novocheremshansk
137 P3 Staryy Saltiv Ukr.
136 B4 Staryy Sambir Ukr.
Staryy Sambor Ukr. see Staryy Sambir
129 I2 Staryy Terek r. Rus. Fed.
174 G1 Starzyno Pol.
137 N4 Stasi Ukr.
171 E7 Staßfurt Ger.
175 J5 Staszów Pol.
232 H8 State College PA U.S.A.
237 K10 State Line MS U.S.A.
Staten Island Arg. see Estados, Isla de los
235 G3 Staten Island NY U.S.A.
231 F10 Statenville GA U.S.A.
231 G9 Statesboro GA U.S.A.
231 G8 Statesville NC U.S.A.
142 F2 Stathelle Norway
203 G4 Station No. 6 Sudan
203 G5 Station No. 10 Sudan
221 Q1 Station Nord Greenland
235 G3 Statue of Liberty tourist site NJ U.S.A.
179 L3 Statzberg hill Austria
179 M3 Statzendorf Austria
136 H6 Stăuceni Moldova
171 H8 Stauchitz Ger.
172 D6 Staufen im Breisgau Ger.
173 J5 Staufersberg hill Ger.
150 H4 Staunton Gloucestershire, England U.K.
232 F10 Staunton VA U.S.A.
171 I7 Staupitz Ger.
142 B3 Stavanger Norway
81 F10 Staveley South I. N.Z.
149 O7 Staveley Derbyshire, England U.K.
165 I8 Stavelot Belgium
164 F5 Stavenisse Neth.
142 G3 Stavern Norway
197 M7 Stavertsi Bulg.
136 J6 Stavkove Ukr.
175 M4 Stavky Ukr.
177 L3 Stavne Ukr.
164 H3 Stavoren Neth.
199 G5 Stavri, Akrotirio pt Naxos Greece
198 C5 Stavrodromi Greece
135 H7 Stavropol' Rus. Fed.
121 L1 Stavropolka Kazakh.
Stavropol Kray admin. div. Rus. Fed. see Stavropol'skiy Kray
Stavropol'-na-Volge Rus. Fed. see Tol'yatti
135 H7 Stavropol'skaya Vozvyshennost' hills Rus. Fed.
129 E1 Stavropol'skiy Kray admin. div. Rus. Fed.
198 D2 Stavros Kentriki Makedonia Greece
198 E2 Stavros Kentriki Makedonia Greece
198 F7 Stavros, Akrotirio pt Kriti Greece
198 F1 Stavroupoli Greece
170 K5 Staw Pol.
139 O9 Stawbun Belarus
83 I7 Stawell Vic. Austr.
85 I6 Stawell r. Qld Austr.
175 I2 Stawiguda Pol.
175 K2 Stawiski Pol.
174 G4 Stawiszyn Pol.
167 I3 Stawki, Park Krajobrazowy Pol.
149 Q5 Staxton North Yorkshire, England U.K.
139 S8 Stayki Rus. Fed.
136 J3 Stayky Ukr.
227 N5 Stayner Ont. Can.
238 C4 Stayton OR U.S.A.
215 N4 Steadville S. Africa
240 M2 Steamboat NV U.S.A.
238 K6 Steamboat Springs CO U.S.A.
175 I2 Stębark Pol.
220 B3 Stebbins AK U.S.A.
137 K4 Stebliv Ukr.
175 L6 Stebnyk Ukr.
195 L6 Steccato Italy
176 D2 Štěchovice Czech Rep.
170 F5 Stechow Ger.
190 F1 Steckborn Switz.
168 E3 Stedesdorf Ger.
171 E8 Stedten Ger.
164 K2 Stedum Neth.
178 B5 Steeg Austria
214 I3 Steekdorings S. Africa
224 C3 Steel r. Ont. Can.
236 F2 Steele ND U.S.A.
262 T2 Steele Island Antarctica
82 □1 Steel's Point Norfolk I.
234 B4 Steelton PA U.S.A.
236 J7 Steelville MO U.S.A.
222 G3 Steen r. Alta Can.
164 F5 Steenbergen Neth.
164 J4 Steenderen Neth.
215 O1 Steenkampsberge mts S. Africa
222 G3 Steen River Alta Can.
238 E5 Steens Mountain OR U.S.A.
Steenstrup Gletscher glacier Greenland see Sermersuaq
156 E2 Steenvoorde France
164 J3 Steenwijk Neth.
150 F5 Steep Holm i. England U.K.
149 R7 Steeping r. England U.K.
151 K4 Steeple Claydon Buckinghamshire, England U.K.
87 B9 Steep Point W.A. Austr.
149 N6 Steeton West Yorkshire, England U.K.
179 O8 Štefanje Croatia
176 G3 Štefanov Slovakia
198 D3 Stefanovikeio Greece
263 D2 Stefansson Bay Antarctica
221 H2 Stefansson Island Nunavut Can.
136 I7 Ștefan Vodă Moldova
197 P6 Ștefan Vodă Romania
190 D2 Steffisburg Switz.
139 V9 Stegalovka Rus. Fed.
173 J2 Stegaurath Ger.
142 I7 Stege Denmark
170 F1 Stege Bugt b. Denmark
171 E6 Stegelitz Ger.
170 F1 Stege Nor lag. Denmark
179 N5 Stegersbach Austria
164 J3 Steggerda Neth.
Stegi Swaziland see Siteki
175 H1 Stegny Pol.
139 O7 Stegrimovo Rus. Fed.
197 K4 Ștei Romania
179 L5 Steiermark land Austria
173 I2 Steigerwald mts Ger.
173 J2 Steigerwald park Ger.
215 P3 Steilrand S. Africa
168 H5 Steimbke Ger.
173 K3 Stein Ger.
165 I7 Stein Neth.
172 D6 Stein Switz.
172 E6 Steina r. Ger.
172 E5 Steinach Baden-Württemberg Ger.
173 N4 Steinach Bayern Ger.
171 D10 Steinach Thüringen Ger.
178 D5 Steinach am Brenner Austria
179 L3 Steinakirchen am Forst Austria
190 F1 Stein am Rhein Switz.
140 □D2 Steinar Iceland
168 G3 Steinau Ger.
169 H10 Steinau an der Straße Ger.
223 L5 Steinbach Man. Can.
171 H9 Steinbach Ger.
169 G10 Steinbach (Taunus) Ger.
179 I4 Steinbach am Attersee Austria
171 D10 Steinbach am Wald Ger.
179 J4 Steinbach an der Steyr Austria
173 M3 Steinberg Bayern Ger.
168 I1 Steinberg Schleswig-Holstein Ger.
168 I1 Steinbergkirche Ger.
168 J3 Steinburg Ger.
179 J6 Steindorf am Ossiacher See Austria
172 D6 Steinen Ger.
178 G4 Steinernes Meer mts Austria
178 H6 Steinfeld Austria
172 H2 Steinfeld Bayern Ger.
172 E3 Steinfeld Rheinland-Pfalz Ger.
168 F5 Steinfeld (Oldenburg) Ger.
165 I9 Steinfort Lux.
169 D6 Steinfurt Ger.
173 J6 Steingaden Ger.
170 G2 Steinhagen Mecklenburg-Vorpommern Ger.
169 F6 Steinhagen Nordrhein-Westfalen Ger.
212 C4 Steinhausen Namibia
171 D10 Steinheid Ger.
169 H7 Steinheim Ger.
173 I4 Steinheim am Albuch Ger.
172 G4 Steinheim an der Murr Ger.
171 J6 Steinhöfel Ger.
173 M5 Steinhöring Ger.
168 J5 Steinhorst Niedersachsen Ger.
168 J3 Steinhorst Schleswig-Holstein Ger.
169 H6 Steinhuder Meer l. Ger.
168 H5 Steinhuder Meer, Naturpark nature res. Ger.
171 J8 Steinigtwolmsdorf Ger.
168 I3 Steinkirchen Ger.
140 K4 Steinkjer Norway
169 G10 Steinkopf hill Ger.
214 B5 Steinkopf S. Africa
171 K6 Steinsdorf Ger.
173 I3 Steinsfeld Ger.
142 B1 Steinsland Norway
172 D3 Steinwenden Ger.
171 D10 Steinwiesen Ger.
172 F6 Steißlingen Ger.
214 H7 Stekaar S. Africa
165 F6 Stekene Belgium
191 K8 Stella r. Italy
191 O4 Stella r. Italy
215 I2 Stella S. Africa
246 F2 Stella Maris Long I. Bahamas
217 □1c Stella Matutina Réunion
168 J4 Stelle Ger.
214 C9 Stellenbosch S. Africa
164 F5 Stellendam Neth.
192 C2 Stello, Monte mt. Corse France
190 I3 Stelvio, Parco Nazionale dello nat. park Italy
190 I2 Stelvio, Passo dello pass Italy
168 I4 Stemmen Ger.
169 F6 Stemshorn Ger.
174 E5 Stěnava r. Pol.
157 J5 Stenay France
143 M4 Stenbo Sweden
170 E5 Stendal Ger.
138 F4 Stende Latvia
143 J4 Stengårdshultasjön l. Sweden
143 N2 Stenhamra Sweden
Stenhouse, Mount hill H.K. China see Shan Tei Tong
146 I10 Stenhousemuir Falkirk, Scotland U.K.
191 J3 Stenico Italy
142 I6 Stenløse Denmark
146 □M2 Stenness Shetland, Scotland U.K.
146 J4 Stenness, Loch of l. Scotland U.K.
198 D5 Steno Greece
173 O2 Štěnovice Czech Rep.
143 K6 Stenshuvuds nationalpark nat. park Sweden
142 I7 Stensved Denmark
146 K11 Stenton East Lothian, Scotland U.K.
140 N3 Stenudden Sweden
142 H3 Stenungsund Sweden
175 M5 Stenyatyn Ukr.
136 D3 Stenzharychi Ukr.
Steornabhagh Western Isles, Scotland U.K. see Stornoway
136 F2 Stepan' Ukr.
Stepanakert Azer. see Xankändi
129 F4 Step'anavan Armenia
137 L2 Stepanivka Chernihivs'ka Oblast' Ukr.
137 R6 Stepanivka Donets'ka Oblast' Ukr.
136 F3 Stepanivka Khmel'nyts'ka Oblast' Ukr.
137 N3 Stepanivka Sums'ka Oblast' Ukr.

Stepanivka Persha to Suigō-Tsukuba Kokutei-kōen

392

137 O7 **Stepanivka Persha** Ukr.
120 G2 **Stepanovka** Kazakh.
139 V6 **Stepanshchino** Rus. Fed.
139 T5 **Stepantsevo** Rus. Fed.
147 J6 **Stepaside** Ireland
168 K3 **Stepenitz** *r.* Ger.
173 M6 **Stephanskirchen** Ger.
173 N4 **Stephansposching** Ger.
236 G1 **Stephen** *MN* U.S.A.
83 I5 **Stephens** *watercourse N.S.W.* Austr.
80 H7 **Stephens, Cape** *South I.* N.Z.
234 F3 **Stephensburg** *NJ* U.S.A.
232 G9 **Stephens City** *VA* U.S.A.
83 H4 **Stephens Creek** *N.S.W.* Austr.
222 D4 **Stephens Island** *B.C.* Can.
223 M3 **Stephens Lake** *Man.* Can.
226 G4 **Stephenson** *MI* U.S.A.
262 T2 **Stephenson, Mount** Antarctica
225 J3 **Stephenville** *Nfld and Lab.* Can.
237 F9 **Stephenville** *TX* U.S.A.
137 R8 **Stepnaya** Rus. Fed.
137 M1 **Stepne** Ukr.
235 I2 **Stepney** *CT* U.S.A.
174 C2 **Stepnica** Pol.
121 O1 **Stepnogorsk** Kazakh.
137 O6 **Stepnohirs'k** Ukr.
121 O6 **Stepnoy** Kyrg.
Stepnoy Rus. Fed. *see* **Elista**
120 I1 **Stepnoye** *Chelyabinskaya Oblast'* Rus. Fed.
120 B2 **Stepnoye** *Saratovskaya Oblast'* Rus. Fed.
129 F1 **Stepnoye** *Stavropol'skiy Kray* Rus. Fed.
121 N1 **Stepnyak** Kazakh.
196 I6 **Stepojevac** Serbia
78 □2 **Steps Point** American Samoa
139 S5 **Stepurino** Rus. Fed.
175 K3 **Sterdyń-Osada** Pol.
198 E4 **Sterea Ellada** *admin. reg.* Greece
215 N4 **Sterkfontein Dam** *resr* S. Africa
215 L6 **Sterkspruit** S. Africa
215 K7 **Sterkstroom** S. Africa
175 J1 **Sterławki-Wielkie** Pol.
223 I1 **Sterlet Lake** *N.W.T.* Can.
120 F1 **Sterlibashevo** Rus. Fed.
214 F7 **Sterling** S. Africa
236 D5 **Sterling** *CO* U.S.A.
235 L1 **Sterling** *CT* U.S.A.
226 E8 **Sterling** *IL* U.S.A.
236 F6 **Sterling** *KS* U.S.A.
227 J5 **Sterling** *MI* U.S.A.
236 E2 **Sterling** *ND* U.S.A.
241 U2 **Sterling** *UT* U.S.A.
237 E10 **Sterling City** *TX* U.S.A.
227 K7 **Sterling Heights** *MI* U.S.A.
120 F1 **Sterlitamak** Rus. Fed.
191 P5 **Sterna** Croatia
198 D5 **Sterna** Greece
170 E3 **Sternberg** Ger.
176 G2 **Šternberk** Czech Rep.
168 I1 **Sterup** Ger.
161 F10 **Stes Maries, Golfe des** *b.* France
161 E10 **Stes-Maries-de-la-Mer** France
174 E3 **Stęszew** Pol.
176 D1 **Štětí** Czech Rep.
137 L4 **Stetsivka** Ukr.
137 N2 **Stets'kivka** Ukr.
172 G5 **Stetten am kalten Markt** Ger.
Stettin Pol. *see* **Szczecin**
Stettiner Haff *b.* Ger. *see* **Oderhaff**
238 H1 **Stettler** *Alta* Can.
232 E8 **Steubenville** *OH* U.S.A.
179 J6 **Steuerberg** Austria
171 F7 **Steutz** Ger.
151 L4 **Stevenage** *Hertfordshire, England* U.K.
80 G7 **Stevens, Mount** *South I.* N.Z.
238 D4 **Stevenson** *WA* U.S.A.
82 E2 **Stevenson Creek** *watercourse S.A.* Austr.
223 L4 **Stevenson Lake** *Man.* Can.
226 E5 **Stevens Point** *WI* U.S.A.
146 G11 **Stevenston** *North Ayrshire, Scotland* U.K.
220 D3 **Stevens Village** *AK* U.S.A.
234 C7 **Stevensville** *MD* U.S.A.
226 H7 **Stevensville** *MI* U.S.A.
227 R8 **Stevensville** *PA* U.S.A.
262 O1 **Steventon Island** Antarctica
142 I6 **Stevns Klint** *cliff* Denmark
85 I3 **Stewart** *r. Qld* Austr.
222 D4 **Stewart** *B.C.* Can.
222 B2 **Stewart** *r. Y.T.* Can.
240 U8 **Stewart** *NV* U.S.A.
84 E1 **Stewart, Cape** *N.T.* Austr.
259 C9 **Stewart, Isla** *i.* Chile
222 B2 **Stewart Crossing** *Y.T.* Can.
81 B14 **Stewart Island** N.Z.
81 B14 **Stewart Island** *nature res. Stewart I.* N.Z.
78 □6 **Stewart Islands** Solomon Is
221 J3 **Stewart Lake** *Nunavut* Can.
146 G11 **Stewarton** *East Ayrshire, Scotland* U.K.
240 I3 **Stewarts Point** *CA* U.S.A.
147 I3 **Stewartstown** *Northern Ireland* U.K.
234 B5 **Stewartstown** *PA* U.S.A.
246 □ **Stewart Town** Jamaica
223 J5 **Stewart Valley** *Sask.* Can.
226 B6 **Stewartville** *MN* U.S.A.
225 I4 **Stewiacke** *N.S.* Can.
168 H5 **Steyerberg** Ger.
151 L6 **Steyning** *West Sussex, England* U.K.
215 L3 **Steynrus** S. Africa
215 J7 **Steynsburg** S. Africa
179 J3 **Steyr** Austria
179 J4 **Steyr** *r.* Austria
179 J3 **Steyregg** Austria
214 I9 **Steytlerville** S. Africa
175 J4 **Stężyca** *Lubelskie* Pol.
174 F1 **Stężyca** *Pomorskie* Pol.
191 L8 **Stia** Italy
177 H3 **Štiavnické vrchy** *mts* Slovakia
177 H3 **Štiavnické vrchy** *park* Slovakia
177 H2 **Štiavnik** Slovakia
150 D6 **Stibb Cross** *Devon, England* U.K.
149 M2 **Stichill** *Scottish Borders, Scotland* U.K.
149 R7 **Stickney** *Lincolnshire, England* U.K.
169 K7 **Stiege** Ger.
164 I2 **Stiens** Neth.
191 L6 **Stienta** Italy
Stif Alg. *see* **Sétif**
237 H8 **Stigler** *OK* U.S.A.
193 Q7 **Stigliano** Italy
195 K7 **Stignano** Italy
143 M3 **Stigtomta** Sweden
222 C3 **Stikine** *r. B.C.* Can.
222 D3 **Stikine Plateau** *B.C.* Can.
222 C3 **Stikine Ranges** *mts B.C.* Can.
142 G2 **Stikkvasskollen** *hill* Norway
214 F10 **Stilbaai** S. Africa
214 F10 **Stilbaai** *b.* S. Africa
226 F5 **Stiles** *WI* U.S.A.
215 K2 **Stilfontein** S. Africa
Stilís Greece *see* **Stylida**
146 B8 **Stilligarry** *Western Isles, Scotland* U.K.
149 O5 **Stillington** *North Yorkshire, England* U.K.
234 C6 **Still Pond** *MD* U.S.A.
226 B4 **Stillwater** *MN* U.S.A.
237 G7 **Stillwater** *OK* U.S.A.
238 J4 **Stillwater** *r. MT* U.S.A.
240 N2 **Stillwater National Wildlife Refuge** *nature res. NV* U.S.A.
240 N2 **Stillwater Range** *mts NV* U.S.A.
195 K7 **Stilo** Italy
195 L7 **Stilo, Punta** *pt* Italy
188 F4 **Štilt** *mt.* Bos.-Herz.
151 L3 **Stilton** *Cambridgeshire, England* U.K.
237 H8 **Stilwell** *OK* U.S.A.
196 J8 **Štimlje** *Kosovo* Serbia
173 I3 **Stimpfach** Ger.
263 E2 **Stinear, Mount** Antarctica
197 Q3 **Stînga Nistrului** *reg.* Moldova
237 E8 **Stinnett** *TX* U.S.A.
192 A6 **Stintino** *Sardegna* Italy
193 O7 **Stio** Italy
197 K9 **Štip** Macedonia
188 E3 **Stipanov Grič** *mt.* Croatia
157 M5 **Stiring-Wendel** France
84 D6 **Stirling** *N.T.* Austr.
227 Q5 **Stirling** *Ont.* Can.
146 I10 **Stirling** *Stirling, Scotland* U.K.
146 H10 **Stirling** *admin. div. Scotland* U.K.
235 G3 **Stirling** *NJ* U.S.A.
87 D11 **Stirling, Mount** *hill W.A.* Austr.
84 B4 **Stirling Creek** *r. N.T.* Austr.
82 F5 **Stirling North** *S.A.* Austr.
87 D13 **Stirling Range** *mts W.A.* Austr.
87 D13 **Stirling Range National Park** *W.A.* Austr.
190 I6 **Stirone** *r.* Italy
232 C11 **Stirrat** *WV* U.S.A.
150 B7 **Stithians** *Cornwall, England* U.K.
177 J3 **Štítnik** Slovakia
227 S4 **Stittsville** *Ont.* Can.
176 F2 **Štíty** Czech Rep.
191 Q6 **Štivan** Croatia
191 L4 **Stizzon** *r.* Italy
140 Q1 **Stjernøya** *i.* Norway
140 K5 **Stjørdalshalsen** Norway
146 G9 **Stob Choire Claurigh** *mt. Scotland* U.K.
146 G9 **Stob Ghabhar** *mt. Scotland* U.K.
175 J6 **Stobnica** *r.* Pol.
174 F5 **Stobrawa** *r.* Pol.
176 C1 **Stochov** Czech Rep.
151 M4 **Stock** *Essex, England* U.K.
157 M6 **Stock, Étang du** *l.* France
172 G6 **Stockach** Ger.
151 J5 **Stockbridge** *Hampshire, England* U.K.
227 J7 **Stockbridge** *MI* U.S.A.
168 K3 **Stockelsdorf** Ger.
179 I6 **Stockenboi** Austria
179 N3 **Stockerau** Austria
234 E3 **Stockertown** *PA* U.S.A.
171 D10 **Stockheim** Ger.
143 O2 **Stockholm** Sweden
143 N2 **Stockholm** *county* Sweden
233 □Q1 **Stockholm** *ME* U.S.A.
235 F2 **Stockholm** *NJ* U.S.A.
190 D2 **Stockhorn** *mt.* Switz.
83 K6 **Stockinbingal** *N.S.W.* Austr.
179 M6 **Stocking** Austria
149 M7 **Stockport** *Greater Manchester, England* U.K.
149 N7 **Stocksbridge** *South Yorkshire, England* U.K.
168 H5 **Stöckse** Ger.
149 N4 **Stocksfield** *Northumberland, England* U.K.
149 M5 **Stocks Reservoir** *England* U.K.
264 G6 **Stocks Seamount** *sea feature* S. Atlantic Ocean
172 G2 **Stockstadt am Main** Ger.
172 E2 **Stockstadt am Rhein** Ger.
240 K4 **Stockton** *CA* U.S.A.
226 D7 **Stockton** *IL* U.S.A.
236 F6 **Stockton** *KS* U.S.A.
237 I7 **Stockton** *MO* U.S.A.
234 F4 **Stockton** *NJ* U.S.A.
241 T1 **Stockton** *UT* U.S.A.
149 L7 **Stockton Heath** *Warrington, England* U.K.
226 D3 **Stockton Island** *WI* U.S.A.
237 I7 **Stockton Lake** *MO* U.S.A.
149 O4 **Stockton-on-Tees** *Stockton-on-Tees, England* U.K.
149 O4 **Stockton-on-Tees** *admin. div. England* U.K.
237 D10 **Stockton Plateau** *TX* U.S.A.
233 □Q4 **Stockton Springs** *ME* U.S.A.
236 E5 **Stockville** *NE* U.S.A.
175 J3 **Stoczek** Pol.
175 J4 **Stoczek Łukowski** Pol.
176 C2 **Stod** Czech Rep.
141 N5 **Stöde** Sweden
139 P7 **Stodolishche** Rus. Fed.
97 G8 **Stœng Trêng** Cambodia
146 F6 **Stoer** *Highland, Scotland* U.K.
146 F6 **Stoer, Point of** *Scotland* U.K.
215 N1 **Stoffberg** S. Africa
196 I9 **Stogovo Planina** *mts* Macedonia
150 F5 **Stogursey** *Somerset, England* U.K.
179 M8 **Stojdraga** Croatia
179 M7 **Stojnci** Slovenia
151 K3 **Stoke Albany** *Northamptonshire, England* U.K.
151 O3 **Stoke Ash** *Suffolk, England* U.K.
151 N4 **Stoke-by-Nayland** *Suffolk, England* U.K.
151 O2 **Stoke Holy Cross** *Norfolk, England* U.K.
151 K4 **Stoke Mandeville** *Buckinghamshire, England* U.K.
151 K4 **Stokenchurch** *Buckinghamshire, England* U.K.
150 E7 **Stokenham** *Devon, England* U.K.
149 M7 **Stoke-on-Trent** *Stoke-on-Trent, England* U.K.
149 M7 **Stoke-on-Trent** *admin. div. England* U.K.
151 K4 **Stoke Poges** *Buckinghamshire, England* U.K.
150 H3 **Stoke Prior** *Worcestershire, England* U.K.
81 I8 **Stokes, Mount** *South I.* N.Z.
150 G3 **Stokesay** *Shropshire, England* U.K.
87 F12 **Stokes Inlet** *W.A.* Austr.
149 O5 **Stokesley** *North Yorkshire, England* U.K.
83 I9 **Stokes Point** *Tas.* Austr.
84 C4 **Stokes Range** *hills N.T.* Austr.
150 F6 **Stoke St Mary** *Somerset, England* U.K.
150 G6 **Stoke sub Hamdon** *Somerset, England* U.K.
81 I8 **Stokes Valley** *North I.* N.Z.
136 E2 **Stokhid** *r.* Ukr.
168 L1 **Stokkemarke** Denmark
140 □C2 **Stokkseyri** Iceland
140 L3 **Stokkvågen** Norway
140 M2 **Stokmarknes** Norway
176 E2 **Štoky** Czech Rep.
197 K6 **Stol** *mt.* Serbia
179 H7 **Stol** *mt.* Slovenia
188 F4 **Stolac** Bos.-Herz.
169 K7 **Stolberg (Harz) Kurort** Ger.
169 B9 **Stolberg (Rheinland)** Ger.
121 U2 **Stolboukha** *Vostochnyy Kazakhstan* Kazakh.
121 U3 **Stolboukha** *Vostochnyy Kazakhstan* Kazakh.
130 G2 **Stolbovoy** *Novaya Zemlya* Rus. Fed.
131 O2 **Stolbovoy, Ostrov** *i. Novosibirskiye O-va* Rus. Fed.
Stolbtsy Belarus *see* **Stowbtsy**
174 F2 **Stołczno** Pol.
177 J3 **Stolica** *mt.* Slovakia
188 G3 **Stolice** *hill* Bos.-Herz.
136 F2 **Stolin** Belarus
171 G9 **Stollberg** Ger.
168 F3 **Stollhamm (Butjadingen)** Ger.
174 G2 **Stolno** Pol.
Stolp Pol. *see* **Słupsk**
170 J5 **Stolpe** *Brandenburg* Ger.
168 J2 **Stolpe** *Schleswig-Holstein* Ger.
171 J8 **Stolpen** Ger.
141 I6 **Stolsheimen** *park* Norway
141 J6 **Stolsvatnet** *l.* Norway
216 □2c **Stoltenhoff Island** *Tristan da Cunha* S. Atlantic Ocean
164 G5 **Stolwijk** Neth.
169 H5 **Stolzenau** Ger.
214 B8 **Stompneusbaai** S. Africa
193 Q1 **Stončica, Rt** *pt* Croatia
150 H4 **Stone** *Gloucestershire, England* U.K.
151 M5 **Stone** *Kent, England* U.K.
150 H2 **Stone** *Staffordshire, England* U.K.
232 E7 **Stoneboro** *PA* U.S.A.
140 □ **Stonebreen** *glacier* Svalbard
224 E4 **Stonecliffe** *Ont.* Can.
Stonecutters' Island *pen. H.K.* China *see* **Ngong Shuen Chau**
236 D5 **Stoneham** *CO* U.S.A.
234 F6 **Stone Harbor** *NJ* U.S.A.
146 L9 **Stonehaven** *Aberdeenshire, Scotland* U.K.
85 I8 **Stonehenge** *Qld* Austr.
151 I5 **Stonehenge** *tourist site England* U.K.
150 H4 **Stonehouse** *Gloucestershire, England* U.K.
146 I11 **Stonehouse** *South Lanarkshire, Scotland* U.K.
226 C4 **Stone Lake** *WI* U.S.A.
222 E3 **Stone Mountain Provincial Park** *B.C.* Can.
233 K7 **Stone Ridge** *NY* U.S.A.
232 F12 **Stoneville** *NC* U.S.A.
223 L5 **Stonewall** *Man.* Can.
237 G8 **Stonewall** *OK* U.S.A.
227 O6 **Stoney Creek** *Ont.* Can.
234 D4 **Stoney Creek Mills** *PA* U.S.A.
147 H7 **Stoneyford** Ireland
146 G13 **Stoneykirk** *Dumfries and Galloway, Scotland* U.K.
227 L7 **Stoney Point** *Ont.* Can.
215 M7 **Stoneyride** S. Africa
142 B2 **Stong** Norway
144 J1 **Stongfjorden** Norway
235 L2 **Stonington** *CT* U.S.A.
233 □Q4 **Stonington** *ME* U.S.A.
211 C5 **Stony Athi** Kenya
146 □M3 **Stonybreck** *Shetland, Scotland* U.K.
235 I3 **Stony Brook** *NY* U.S.A.
234 B5 **Stony Brook** *PA* U.S.A.
235 J2 **Stony Creek** *CT* U.S.A.
232 H12 **Stony Creek** *VA* U.S.A.
240 J2 **Stony Gorge Reservoir** *CA* U.S.A.
246 □ **Stony Hill** Jamaica
216 □2c **Stonyhill Point** *Tristan da Cunha* S. Atlantic Ocean
223 L3 **Stony Lake** *Man.* Can.
222 H4 **Stony Plain** *Alta* Can.
233 I5 **Stony Point** *NY* U.S.A.
223 J3 **Stony Rapids** *Sask.* Can.
151 K3 **Stony Stratford** *Milton Keynes, England* U.K.
179 O4 **Stoob** Austria
224 D2 **Stooping** *r. Ont.* Can.
179 L8 **Stopiče** Slovenia
175 J1 **Stopki** Pol.
175 I5 **Stopnica** Pol.
168 H3 **Stör** *r.* Ger.
142 E5 **Stora** *r.* Denmark
143 L2 **Storå** Sweden
143 M5 **Stora Alvaret** *pen.* Sweden
143 M4 **Stora Askö** *i.* Sweden
142 I2 **Stora Bör** *l.* Sweden
142 I2 **Stora Gla** *l.* Sweden
142 I4 **Stora Horredssjön** *l.* Sweden
142 H3 **Stora Le** *l.* Sweden
140 O3 **Stora Lulevatten** *l.* Sweden
143 P2 **Stora Nassa naturreservat** *nature res.* Sweden
140 N3 **Stora Sjöfallets nationalpark** *nat. park* Sweden
140 O4 **Storavan** *l.* Sweden
141 L6 **Storbäcken** Sweden
141 K6 **Storbekkfjellet** *mt.* Norway
141 L6 **Storbo** Sweden
142 B2 **Stord** *i.* Norway
140 I5 **Stordal** Norway
141 K6 **Store** *mt.* Norway
179 L7 **Štore** Slovenia
142 G6 **Store Bælt** *sea chan.* Denmark
142 B1 **Storebø** Norway
170 F1 **Store Damme** Denmark
142 I6 **Store Heddinge** Denmark
141 J6 **Store Jukleeggi** *mt.* Norway
221 Q2 **Store Koldewey** *i.* Greenland
140 P2 **Store Lenangstind** *mt.* Norway
140 Q1 **Storelv** Norway
140 T1 **Store Molvik** Norway
143 J4 **Store Moss nationalpark** *nat. park* Sweden
140 K5 **Støren** Norway
142 D2 **Store Nup** *mt.* Norway
168 J1 **Store Rise** Denmark
142 B1 **Store Sotra** *i.* Norway
142 D2 **Store Urevatnet** *l.* Norway
143 N1 **Storfjärden** *l.* Sweden
140 S1 **Storfjordbotn** Norway
140 □ **Storfjorden** *sea chan.* Svalbard
143 K2 **Storfors** Sweden
140 M3 **Storforshei** Norway
179 I8 **Štorje** Slovenia
140 M4 **Storjola** Sweden
140 M3 **Storjord** Norway
140 N4 **Storjuktan** *l.* Sweden
142 D3 **Storkarshei** *hill* Norway
221 H2 **Storkerson Peninsula** *Nunavut* Can.
171 I6 **Storkow** Ger.
168 J3 **Stormarn** *reg.* Ger.
83 K10 **Storm Bay** *Tas.* Austr.
215 K7 **Stormberg** S. Africa
215 K6 **Stormberg** *mt.* S. Africa
215 K6 **Stormberg** *r.* S. Africa
215 K7 **Stormberge** *mts* S. Africa
236 H4 **Storm Lake** *IA* U.S.A.
214 H9 **Stormsrivier** S. Africa
193 P5 **Stornara** Italy
193 P5 **Stornarella** Italy
146 D6 **Stornoway** *Western Isles, Scotland* U.K.
191 J4 **Storo** Italy
143 O2 **Storö-Bockö-Lökaöns naturreservat** *nature res.* Sweden
140 □ **Storøya** *i.* Svalbard
139 P1 **Storozhenskiy, Mys** *pt* Rus. Fed.
134 K3 **Storozhevsk** Rus. Fed.
139 P1 **Storozhno** Rus. Fed.
136 E5 **Storozhynets'** Ukr.
151 L6 **Storrington** *West Sussex, England* U.K.
142 E2 **Stor-Roan** *mt.* Norway
233 M7 **Storrs** *CT* U.S.A.
140 N4 **Storseleby** Sweden
142 H1 **Storsjøen** *l.* Norway
143 M1 **Storsjön** *l.* Sweden
140 M5 **Storsjön** *l.* Sweden
143 N2 **Storsjön** *l.* Sweden
140 J5 **Storskarhø** *mt.* Norway
140 M4 **Storskog** Sweden
140 P2 **Storslett** Norway
142 G7 **Storstrøm** *county* Denmark
142 H7 **Storstrømmen** *sea chan.* Denmark
140 P4 **Storsund** Sweden
151 M4 **Stort** *r. England* U.K.
164 H2 **Stortemelk** *sea chan.* Neth.
140 N4 **Storuman** Sweden
140 N4 **Storuman** *l.* Sweden
140 L5 **Storvigelen** *mt.* Norway
143 M1 **Storvik** Sweden
140 N4 **Storvindeln** *l.* Sweden
142 G4 **Storvorde** Denmark
143 N2 **Storvreta** Sweden
238 K4 **Story** *WY* U.S.A.
196 I2 **Štós** Slovakia
259 B8 **Stosch, Isla** *i.* Chile
171 E8 **Stößen** Ger.
179 M3 **Stössing** Austria
151 L3 **Stotfold** *Bedfordshire, England* U.K.
173 J6 **Stötten am Auerberg** Ger.
171 D8 **Stotternheim** Ger.
234 C4 **Stouchsburg** *PA* U.S.A.
223 K5 **Stoughton** *Sask.* Can.
165 I8 **Stoumont** Belgium
97 G8 **Stoŭng, Stœng** *r.* Cambodia
150 I6 **Stour** *r. Dorset, England* U.K.
151 O4 **Stour** *r. Essex/Suffolk, England* U.K.
151 O5 **Stour** *r. Kent, England* U.K.
151 I3 **Stour** *r. Oxfordshire/Warwickshire, England* U.K.
150 H3 **Stourbridge** *West Midlands, England* U.K.
150 H3 **Stourport-on-Severn** *Worcestershire, England* U.K.
223 M4 **Stout Lake** *Ont.* Can.
146 K11 **Stow** *Scottish Borders, Scotland* U.K.
138 J8 **Stowbtsy** Belarus
234 D4 **Stowe** *PA* U.S.A.
174 F1 **Stowięcino** Pol.
151 N3 **Stowmarket** *Suffolk, England* U.K.
151 I4 **Stow-on-the-Wold** *Gloucestershire, England* U.K.
136 D3 **Stoyaniv** Ukr.
100 G2 **Stoyba** Rus. Fed.
175 K1 **Stożne** Pol.
191 M5 **Stra** Italy
171 G7 **Straach** Ger.
215 K1 **Straatsdrif** S. Africa
147 H3 **Strabane** *Northern Ireland* U.K.
175 L3 **Strabla** Pol.
146 K8 **Strachan** *Aberdeenshire, Scotland* U.K.
146 F10 **Strachur** *Argyll and Bute, Scotland* U.K.
175 M1 **Stračiūnai** Lith.
168 E4 **Strackholt (Großefehn)** Ger.
174 E2 **Strączno** Pol.
147 H6 **Stradbally** Ireland
151 O3 **Stradbroke** *Suffolk, England* U.K.
190 G5 **Stradella** Italy
179 M6 **Straden** Austria
151 N3 **Stradishall** *Suffolk, England* U.K.
147 H5 **Stradone** Ireland
151 M2 **Stradsett** *Norfolk, England* U.K.
169 B8 **Straelen** Ger.
83 J10 **Strahan** *Tas.* Austr.
241 U4 **Straight Cliffs** *ridge UT* U.S.A.
165 H9 **Straimont** Belgium
176 C2 **Strakonice** Czech Rep.
197 O8 **Straldzha** Bulg.
179 M5 **Strallegg** Austria
146 I9 **Straloch** *Perth and Kinross, Scotland* U.K.
170 H2 **Stralsund** Ger.
190 D5 **Strambino** Italy
165 I6 **Stramproy** Neth.
214 C10 **Strand** S. Africa
140 I5 **Stranda** Norway
142 D1 **Strandavatnet** *l.* Norway
168 J2 **Strande** Ger.
147 E4 **Strandhill** Ireland
231 H12 **Strangers Cay** *i.* Bahamas
147 K4 **Strangford** *Northern Ireland* U.K.
147 K4 **Strangford Lough** *inlet Northern Ireland* U.K.
143 N2 **Strängnäs** Sweden
193 K4 **Strangolagalli** Italy
84 D3 **Strangways** *r. N.T.* Austr.
84 E7 **Strangways Range** *mts N.T.* Austr.
177 G3 **Strání** Czech Rep.
147 J2 **Stranocum** *Northern Ireland* U.K.
147 G3 **Stranorlar** Ireland
146 F13 **Stranraer** *Dumfries and Galloway, Scotland* U.K.
194 D8 **Strasatti** *Sicilia* Italy
157 O6 **Strasbourg** France
170 I4 **Strasburg** Ger.
232 D8 **Strasburg** *OH* U.S.A.
234 C5 **Strasburg** *PA* U.S.A.
232 G10 **Strasburg** *VA* U.S.A.
136 H6 **Strășeni** Moldova
Strasheny Moldova *see* **Strășeni**
173 P2 **Strašice** Czech Rep.
172 G5 **Straßberg** *Baden-Württemberg* Ger.
171 D7 **Straßberg** *Sachsen-Anhalt* Ger.
179 J6 **Straßburg** Austria
Strassburg France *see* **Strasbourg**
165 J9 **Strassen** Lux.
179 L5 **Straßengel** Austria
169 E9 **Straßenhaus** Ger.
179 O3 **Strasshof an der Norbahn** Austria
173 N4 **Straßkirchen** Ger.
178 H4 **Straßwalchen** Austria
151 J5 **Stratfield Mortimer** *West Berkshire, England* U.K.
224 D5 **Stratford** *Ont.* Can.
80 I6 **Stratford** *North I.* N.Z.
147 I7 **Stratford** Ireland
240 M5 **Stratford** *CA* U.S.A.
235 I2 **Stratford** *CT* U.S.A.
237 D7 **Stratford** *TX* U.S.A.
226 D5 **Stratford** *WI* U.S.A.
151 I3 **Stratford-upon-Avon** *Warwickshire, England* U.K.
82 G6 **Strathalbyn** *S.A.* Austr.
146 H11 **Strathaven** *South Lanarkshire, Scotland* U.K.
148 I2 **Strathblane** *Stirling, Scotland* U.K.
146 K8 **Strathbogie** *reg. Scotland* U.K.
146 G7 **Strathcarron** *val. Scotland* U.K.
263 G2 **Strathcona, Mount** Antarctica
222 E5 **Strathcona Provincial Park** *B.C.* Can.
146 G7 **Strathconon** *val. Scotland* U.K.
146 H8 **Strath Dearn** *val. Scotland* U.K.
146 J8 **Strathdon** *Aberdeenshire, Scotland* U.K.
146 H10 **Strath Earn** *val. Scotland* U.K.
146 H6 **Strath Fleet** *val. Scotland* U.K.
146 G8 **Strathglass** *val. Scotland* U.K.
83 K10 **Strathgordon** *Tas.* Austr.
146 I6 **Strath Halladale** *val. Scotland* U.K.
222 H5 **Strathmore** *Alta* Can.
146 G5 **Strathmore** *r. Scotland* U.K.
240 M5 **Strathmore** *CA* U.S.A.
222 F4 **Strathnaver** *B.C.* Can.
146 H6 **Strathnaver** *val. Scotland* U.K.
146 I6 **Strath of Kildonan** *val. Scotland* U.K.
146 G7 **Strathpeffer** *Highland, Scotland* U.K.
227 M7 **Strathroy** *Ont.* Can.
146 I8 **Strathspey** *val. Scotland* U.K.
146 I9 **Strath Tay** *val. Scotland* U.K.
146 I5 **Strathy** *Highland, Scotland* U.K.
146 H5 **Strathy Point** *Scotland* U.K.
146 H10 **Strathyre** *Stirling, Scotland* U.K.
198 E2 **Stratoni** Greece
199 J5 **Stratonıkeıa** *tourist site* Turkey
198 C4 **Stratos** Greece
150 C6 **Stratton** *Cornwall, England* U.K.
233 □O3 **Stratton** *ME* U.S.A.
233 M5 **Stratton Mountain** *VT* U.S.A.
151 I4 **Stratton St Margaret** *Swindon, England* U.K.
173 N4 **Straubing** Ger.
140 M2 **Straume** Norway
140 M3 **Straumen** *Nordland* Norway
140 M3 **Straumen** *Nordland* Norway
140 □B1 **Straumnes** *pt* Iceland
171 J7 **Straupitz** Ger.
170 I5 **Strausberg** Ger.
169 K8 **Straußfurt** Ger.
234 C3 **Strausstown** *PA* U.S.A.
241 U7 **Strawberry** *AZ* U.S.A.
238 E4 **Strawberry Mountain** *OR* U.S.A.
241 U1 **Strawberry Reservoir** *UT* U.S.A.
175 I5 **Strawczyn** Pol.
226 F9 **Strawn** *IL* U.S.A.
197 K8 **Straža** *mt.* Macedonia
197 N7 **Strazhitsa** Bulg.
176 D2 **Stráž nad Nežárkou** Czech Rep.
171 L9 **Stráž nad Nisou** Czech Rep.
179 I2 **Strážný** Czech Rep.
176 C2 **Strážov** Czech Rep.
177 H3 **Strážov** *mt.* Slovakia
171 K9 **Stráž pod Ralskem** Czech Rep.
177 K3 **Strážske** Slovakia
82 E5 **Streaky Bay** *S.A.* Austr.
82 E5 **Streaky Bay** *b. S.A.* Austr.
147 G6 **Streamstown** Ireland
151 J4 **Streatley** *West Berkshire, England* U.K.
226 F8 **Streator** *IL* U.S.A.
176 D2 **Středočeský kraj** *admin. reg.* Czech Rep.
168 F4 **Streek** Ger.
150 G5 **Street** *Somerset, England* U.K.
197 L6 **Strehaia** Romania
171 H8 **Strehla** Ger.
197 L5 **Strei** *r.* Romania
87 G11 **Streich Mound** *hill W.A.* Austr.
177 H4 **Strekov** Slovakia
176 C2 **Střela** *r.* Czech Rep.
197 M8 **Strelcha** Bulg.
137 R1 **Strelets** Rus. Fed.
137 P3 **Streletskoye** Rus. Fed.
176 F2 **Střelice** Czech Rep.
137 R2 **Strelitsa** Rus. Fed.
131 Q3 **Strelka** Rus. Fed.
139 R1 **Strelkovo** Rus. Fed.
86 E6 **Strelley** *W.A.* Austr.
86 E6 **Strelley** *r. W.A.* Austr.
86 E6 **Strelley Aboriginal Reserve** *W.A.* Austr.
134 G2 **Strel'na** *r.* Rus. Fed.
179 N5 **Strem** Austria
191 J3 **Strembo** Italy
171 F5 **Stremme** *r.* Ger.
136 H3 **Stremyhorod** Ukr.
138 I4 **Strenči** Latvia
179 K3 **Strengberg** Austria
178 B5 **Strengen** Austria
149 O5 **Strensall** *York, England* U.K.
175 M5 **Streptiv** Ukr.
190 F4 **Stresa** Italy
149 M7 **Stretford** *Greater Manchester, England* U.K.
151 M3 **Stretham** *Cambridgeshire, England* U.K.
151 I2 **Stretton** *Staffordshire, England* U.K.
169 J10 **Streu** *r.* Ger.
169 K10 **Streufdorf** Ger.
144 D1 **Streymoy** *i.* Faroe Is
130 I3 **Strezhevoy** Rus. Fed.
176 B2 **Stříbro** Czech Rep.
146 L7 **Strichen** *Aberdeenshire, Scotland* U.K.
91 J8 **Strickland** *r.* P.N.G.
191 L3 **Strigno** Italy
179 N6 **Štrigova** Croatia
164 G5 **Strijen** Neth.
137 P3 **Strilechna** Ukr.
176 E2 **Strimilov** Czech Rep.
198 E1 **Strimoniko** Greece
Strimonikón Greece *see* **Strimoniko**
148 G2 **Striven, Loch** *inlet Scotland* U.K.
188 G3 **Strizivojna** Croatia
179 M8 **Strmec** Croatia
169 K7 **Ströbeck** Ger.
179 H4 **Strobl** Austria
259 E6 **Stroeder** Arg.
198 C5 **Strofades** *i.* Greece
173 L5 **Strogen** *r.* Ger.
137 M7 **Strohanivka** Ukr.
168 G5 **Ströhen** Ger.
136 H6 **Stroiești** Moldova
137 P3 **Stroitel'** Rus. Fed.
147 F5 **Strokestown** Ireland
170 I4 **Strom** *r.* Ger.
146 J5 **Stroma, Island of** *Scotland* U.K.
143 N1 **Strömaren** *l.* Sweden
141 N6 **Strömbacka** Sweden
172 D2 **Stromberg** Ger.
172 F3 **Stromberg-Heuchelberg, Naturpark** *nature res.* Ger.
195 I6 **Stromboli, Isola** *i. Isole Lipari* Italy
195 I6 **Strombolicchio, Isola** *i. Isole Lipari* Italy
146 E8 **Stromeferry** *Highland, Scotland* U.K.
259 □ **Stromness** S. Georgia
146 J5 **Stromness** *Orkney, Scotland* U.K.
141 N6 **Strömsbruk** Sweden
236 G5 **Stromsburg** *NE* U.S.A.
140 O2 **Strømsmoen** Norway
142 H3 **Strömstad** Sweden
140 M5 **Strömsund** Sweden
193 J3 **Stroncone** Italy
190 I5 **Strone** *r.* Italy
146 G11 **Strone** *Argyll and Bute, Scotland* U.K.
237 I9 **Strong** *AR* U.S.A.
195 M5 **Strongoli** Italy
232 D7 **Strongsville** *OH* U.S.A.
174 E5 **Stronie Śląskie** Pol.
146 K4 **Stronsay** *i. Scotland* U.K.
146 K4 **Stronsay Firth** *sea chan. Scotland* U.K.
179 N2 **Stronsdorf** Austria
146 E9 **Strontian** *Highland, Scotland* U.K.
177 K2 **Stropkov** Slovakia
176 D3 **Stropnice** *r.* Czech Rep.
190 E5 **Stroppiana** Italy
190 C6 **Stroppo** Italy
150 H4 **Stroud** *Gloucestershire, England* U.K.
83 M5 **Stroud Road** *N.S.W.* Austr.
234 E3 **Stroudsburg** *PA* U.S.A.
Stroyentsy Moldova *see* **Stroiești**
175 H6 **Stróża** Pol.
168 E4 **Strücklingen (Saterland)** Ger.
142 E5 **Struer** Denmark
196 I9 **Struga** Macedonia
174 F3 **Struga** *r.* Pol.
138 M3 **Strugi-Krasnyye** Rus. Fed.
139 P8 **Strugovskaya Buda** Rus. Fed.
214 E10 **Struis Bay** S. Africa
214 E10 **Struis Bay** *b.* S. Africa
147 H3 **Strule** *r. Northern Ireland* U.K.
173 J2 **Strullendorf** Ger.
197 L9 **Struma** *r.* Bulg.
150 B3 **Strumble Head** *Wales* U.K.
198 E1 **Strumeshnitsa** *r.* Bulg.
197 K9 **Strumica** Macedonia
197 K9 **Strumica** *r.* Macedonia
174 G6 **Strumień** Pol.
177 L3 **Strumkivka** Ukr.
139 V5 **Strunino** Rus. Fed.
179 J1 **Strunkovice nad Blanicí** Czech Rep.
169 J8 **Struth** Ger.
232 E7 **Struthers** *OH* U.S.A.
197 M8 **Stryama** *r.* Bulg.
214 H5 **Strydenburg** S. Africa
215 J2 **Strydpoort** S. Africa
175 H4 **Stryków** Pol.
198 E2 **Strymonas** *r.* Greece
141 I6 **Stryn** Norway
168 K1 **Strynø** *i.* Denmark
136 E5 **Strypa** *r.* Ukr.
136 J6 **Stryukove** Ukr.
136 C4 **Stryy** Ukr.
136 D4 **Stryy** *r.* Ukr.
136 H4 **Stryzhavka** Ukr.
174 F3 **Strzałkowo** Pol.
174 G5 **Strzebień** Pol.
175 I3 **Strzegocin** Pol.
174 E5 **Strzegom** Pol.
174 E4 **Strzegomka** *r.* Pol.
175 I3 **Strzegowo** Pol.
175 H3 **Strzelce** Pol.
174 D3 **Strzelce Krajeńskie** Pol.
174 G5 **Strzelce Opolskie** Pol.
175 H4 **Strzelce Wielkie** Pol.
84 D6 **Strzelecki, Mount** *hill N.T.* Austr.
82 G3 **Strzelecki Creek** *watercourse S.A.* Austr.
82 G3 **Strzelecki Regional Reserve** *nature res. S.A.* Austr.
174 F5 **Strzeleczki** Pol.
174 F5 **Strzelin** Pol.
174 G3 **Strzelno** Pol.
174 G1 **Strzepcz** Pol.
175 J6 **Strzyżów** Pol.
157 J8 **Sts-Geosmes** France
136 G1 **Stsvina** *r.* Belarus
85 M9 **Stuart** *r. Qld* Austr.
231 G12 **Stuart** *FL* U.S.A.
236 H5 **Stuart** *IA* U.S.A.
236 F4 **Stuart** *NE* U.S.A.
232 E12 **Stuart** *VA* U.S.A.
84 D7 **Stuart Bluff Range** *mts N.T.* Austr.
146 L7 **Stuartfield** *Aberdeenshire, Scotland* U.K.
222 E4 **Stuart Lake** *B.C.* Can.
81 B12 **Stuart Mountains** *South I.* N.Z.
82 E3 **Stuart Range** *hills S.A.* Austr.
232 F10 **Stuarts Draft** *VA* U.S.A.
178 D5 **Stubaier Alpen** *mts* Austria
178 D5 **Stubaital** *val.* Austria
179 K5 **Stubalpe** *mt.* Austria
168 H1 **Stubbæk** Denmark
170 F1 **Stubbekøbing** Denmark
168 G4 **Stubben** Ger.
170 I1 **Stubbenkammer** *hd* Ger.
86 □1 **Stubbings Point** Christmas I.
151 J6 **Stubbington** *Hampshire, England* U.K.
247 □3 **Stubbs** St Vincent
179 M5 **Stubenberg** Austria
196 J7 **Stubica** Serbia
196 I6 **Stubline** Serbia
175 K6 **Stubno** Pol.
Stuchka Latvia *see* **Aizkraukle**
174 D2 **Stuchowo** Pol.
Stučka Latvia *see* **Aizkraukle**
176 E2 **Studená** Czech Rep.
136 H5 **Studena** Ukr.
179 I2 **Studená Vltava** *r.* Czech Rep.
196 I7 **Studenica** *tourist site* Serbia
170 F5 **Stüdenitz** Ger.
177 H2 **Studénka** Czech Rep.
197 N9 **Studen Kladenets, Yazovir** *resr* Bulg.
137 Q1 **Studenoye** Rus. Fed.
136 G2 **Studenytsya** *r.* Ukr.
151 K4 **Studham** *Bedfordshire, England* U.K.
81 F11 **Studholme Junction** *South I.* N.Z.
176 G3 **Studienka** Slovakia
214 I9 **Studis** S. Africa
151 I6 **Studland** *Dorset, England* U.K.
151 I3 **Studley** *Warwickshire, England* U.K.
143 N3 **Studsvik** Sweden
134 B3 **Studsviken** Sweden
237 D11 **Study Butte** *TX* U.S.A.
174 F1 **Studzienice** Pol.
140 M5 **Stugun** Sweden
178 G5 **Stuhlfelden** Austria
172 E6 **Stühlingen** Ger.
136 J3 **Stuhna** *r.* Ukr.
168 G4 **Stuhr** Ger.
223 M4 **Stull Lake** *Man./Ont.* Can.
171 H6 **Stülpe** Ger.
197 N3 **Stulpicani** Romania
178 E5 **Stumm** Austria
223 L6 **Stump Lake** *ND* U.S.A.
Stung Treng Cambodia *see* **Stœng Trêng**
223 M4 **Stupart** *r. Man.* Can.
176 G3 **Stupava** Slovakia
139 V7 **Stupino** Rus. Fed.
193 Q1 **Stupišće, Rt** *pt* Croatia
175 I2 **Stupsk** Pol.
190 E5 **Stura** *r.* Italy
190 C5 **Stura di Ala** *r.* Italy
190 D6 **Stura di Demonte** *r.* Italy
161 K6 **Stura di Val Grande** *r.* Italy
190 C5 **Stura di Viù** *r.* Italy
263 K2 **Sturge Island** Antarctica
224 E4 **Sturgeon** *r. Ont.* Can.
223 J4 **Sturgeon** *r. Sask.* Can.
226 H4 **Sturgeon** *r. MI* U.S.A.
226 C1 **Sturgeon, Lake** *Ont.* Can.
223 L4 **Sturgeon Bay** *b. Man.* Can.
226 G5 **Sturgeon Bay** *WI* U.S.A.
226 J4 **Sturgeon Bay** *b. MI* U.S.A.
226 G5 **Sturgeon Bay Canal** *lake channel WI* U.S.A.
224 E4 **Sturgeon Falls** *Ont.* Can.
227 P5 **Sturgeon Lake** *Ont.* Can.
224 B3 **Sturgeon Lake** *Ont.* Can.
230 D7 **Sturgis** *KY* U.S.A.
226 I8 **Sturgis** *MI* U.S.A.
236 D3 **Sturgis** *SD* U.S.A.
190 G7 **Sturla** *r.* Italy
188 E3 **Šturlić** Bos.-Herz.
150 H6 **Sturminster Newton** *Dorset, England* U.K.
177 H4 **Štúrovo** Slovakia
151 O5 **Sturry** *Kent, England* U.K.
83 H3 **Sturt, Mount** *hill N.S.W.* Austr.
82 F6 **Sturt Bay** *S.A.* Austr.
86 J5 **Sturt Creek** *W.A.* Austr.
86 I5 **Sturt Creek** *watercourse W.A.* Austr.
226 G7 **Sturtevant** *WI* U.S.A.
83 H3 **Sturt National Park** *N.S.W.* Austr.
84 D4 **Sturt Plain** *N.T.* Austr.
82 H3 **Sturt Stony Desert** *Qld* Austr.
157 O5 **Sturzelbronn** France
215 L8 **Stutterheim** S. Africa
172 G4 **Stuttgart** Ger.
172 H3 **Stuttgart** *admin. reg.* Ger.
237 J8 **Stuttgart** *AR* U.S.A.
Stutthof Pol. *see* **Sztutowo**
169 K9 **Stützerbach** Ger.
136 G2 **Stvyha** *r.* Ukr.
140 □B1 **Stykkishólmur** Iceland
137 Q6 **Styla** Ukr.
198 D4 **Stylida** Greece
136 F1 **Styr** *r.* Belarus/Ukr.
Styria *land* Austria *see* **Steiermark**
257 G3 **Suaçuí Grande** *r.* Brazil
93 D8 **Suai** East Timor
95 J3 **Suai** *Sarawak* Malaysia
250 C3 **Suaita** Col.
203 H5 **Suakin** Sudan
124 D6 **Suakin Archipelago** *is* Sudan
203 H5 **Suakin Archipelago** *is* Sudan
209 D6 **Suana** Dem. Rep. Congo
183 L2 **Suances** Spain
109 M6 **Suao** Taiwan
242 E3 **Suaqui Grande** Mex.
203 H5 **Suara, Mount** Eritrea
261 G2 **Suardi** Arg.
250 B4 **Suárez** Col.
129 L1 **Suat** Kazakh.
251 E2 **Suata** Venez.
78 □6 **Suavanao** *Sta Isabel* Solomon Is
138 H6 **Subačius** Lith.
95 G8 **Subang** *Jawa* Indon.
117 M6 **Subankhata** *Assam* India
111 L13 **Subansiri** *r.* India
117 K9 **Subarnarekha** *r. W. Bengal* India
122 C4 **Sūbāshī** Iran
199 J1 **Subaşı** *İstanbul* Turkey
199 I4 **Subaşı** *İzmir* Turkey
193 J1 **Subasio, Monte** *mt.* Italy
138 I5 **Subate** Latvia
125 H2 **Subay** *reg.* Saudi Arabia
124 F4 **Subay, 'Irq** *des.* Saudi Arabia
126 I8 **Şubayḩah** Saudi Arabia
124 G9 **Şubayḩī** *reg.* Yemen
191 L8 **Subbiano** Italy
197 N4 **Subcetate** Romania
110 L7 **Subei** *Gansu* China
Subeita *tourist site* Israel *see* **Shivta**
179 H3 **Suben** Austria
193 K4 **Subiaco** Italy
95 H3 **Subi Besar** *i.* Indon.
95 H3 **Subi Kecil** *i.* Indon.
174 G1 **Subkowy** Pol.
237 E7 **Sublette** *KS* U.S.A.
196 H4 **Subotica** *Vojvodina* Serbia
203 I6 **Subucle** *mt.* Eritrea
211 B5 **Subugo** *mt.* Kenya
177 H2 **Sučany** Slovakia
162 H5 **Suc-au-May** *hill* France
234 F3 **Succasunna** *NJ* U.S.A.
240 N5 **Success, Lake** *CA* U.S.A.
190 I7 **Succiso, Alpi di** *mts* Italy
197 O3 **Suceava** Romania
197 N3 **Suceava** *r.* Romania
158 H7 **Sucé-sur-Erdre** France
175 H6 **Sucha Beskidzka** Pol.
175 H1 **Suchacz** Pol.
177 G3 **Suchá Loz** Czech Rep.
174 D2 **Suchań** Pol.
Suchan Rus. Fed. *see* **Partizansk**
100 H7 **Suchan** *r.* Rus. Fed.
176 E2 **Suchdol** Czech Rep.
176 D3 **Suchdol nad Lužnicí** Czech Rep.
175 I4 **Suchedniów** Pol.
167 J3 **Suchedniowsko-Oblęgorski Park Krajobrazowy** Pol.
190 A2 **Suchet, Mont** *mt.* Switz.
244 D2 **Suchil** Mex.
175 L2 **Suchowola** Pol.
175 K3 **Suchożebry** Pol.
247 □1 **Sucia, Bahía** *b.* Puerto Rico
187 D12 **Sucina** Spain
250 B3 **Sucio** *r.* Col.
197 M3 **Suciu de Sus** Romania
147 F6 **Suck** *r.* Ireland
227 N3 **Sucker Creek Landing** *Ont.* Can.
170 E4 **Suckow** Ger.
252 D4 **Sucre** Bol.
250 C2 **Sucre** *dept* Col.
251 F2 **Sucre** *state* Venez.
250 D3 **Sucuaro** Col.
250 B5 **Sucumbíos** *prov.* Ecuador
251 G6 **Sucunduri** *r.* Brazil
256 B4 **Sucuriú** *r.* Brazil
Suczawa Romania *see* **Suceava**
207 H6 **Sud** *prov.* Cameroon
78 □5 **Sud, Grand Récif du** *rf* New Caledonia
217 □3a **Sud, Pointe** *pt Njazidja* Comoros
217 □2b **Sud, Pointe du** *c. Mahé* Seychelles
217 □3b **Sud, Récif du** *rf* Mayotte
233 L3 **Sud, Rivière du** *r. Que.* Can.
139 U2 **Suda** Rus. Fed.
139 U2 **Suda** *r.* Rus. Fed.
137 N9 **Sudak** Ukr.
105 H4 **Sudama** Japan
203 F6 **Sudan** *country* Africa
134 H4 **Suday** Rus. Fed.
124 G3 **Sudayr** *reg.* Saudi Arabia
127 L8 **Sudayr, Sha'īb** *watercourse* Iraq
139 U9 **Sudbishchi** Rus. Fed.
120 E1 **Sud'bodarovka** Rus. Fed.
224 D4 **Sudbury** *Ont.* Can.
151 I2 **Sudbury** *Derbyshire, England* U.K.
151 N3 **Sudbury** *Suffolk, England* U.K.
210 A3 **Sudd** *swamp* Sudan
169 D6 **Suddendorf** Ger.
251 G3 **Suddie** Guyana
168 K4 **Sude** *r.* Ger.
168 G2 **Süden** Ger.
168 I1 **Süderbrarup** Ger.
168 J5 **Suderburg** Ger.
168 J4 **Südergellersen** Ger.
168 H2 **Süderhastedt** Ger.
168 G1 **Süderlügum** Ger.
168 G2 **Süderoog** *i.* Ger.
168 F2 **Süderoogsand** *i.* Ger.
168 H2 **Süderstapel** Ger.
Sudest Island P.N.G. *see* **Tagula Island**
Sudetenland *mts* Czech Rep./Pol. *see* **Sudety**
174 D5 **Sudety** *mts* Czech Rep./Pol.
168 G2 **Südfall** *i.* Ger.
139 R8 **Sudimir** Rus. Fed.
139 Y4 **Sudislavl'** Rus. Fed.
209 F5 **Sud-Kivu** *prov.* Dem. Rep. Congo
234 D6 **Sudlersville** *MD* U.S.A.
169 C7 **Südlohn** Ger.
168 D5 **Süd-Nord-Kanal** *canal* Ger.
184 B6 **Sudoeste Alentejano e Costa Vicentina, Parque Natural do** *nature res.* Port.
139 X6 **Sudogda** Rus. Fed.
139 X5 **Sudogda** *r.* Rus. Fed.
176 G3 **Sudoměřice** Czech Rep.
138 M4 **Sudomskiye Vysoty** *hills* Rus. Fed.
139 Q9 **Sudost'** *r.* Rus. Fed.
207 H5 **Sud-Ouest** *prov.* Cameroon
217 □1b **Sud Ouest, Pointe** *pt* Mauritius
136 C4 **Sudova Vyshnya** Ukr.
179 N7 **Sudovec** Croatia
203 G2 **Sudr** Egypt
Südtirol *prov.* Italy *see* **Bolzano**
129 I4 **Sudur** Azer.
129 B6 **Suduragı** Turkey
140 □B1 **Suðurland** *constituency* Iceland
130 A3 **Suðuroy** *i.* Faroe Is
144 D1 **Suðuroy** *i.* Faroe Is
144 D1 **Suðuroyarfjørður** *sea chan.* Faroe Is
168 G5 **Sudwalde** Ger.
137 O2 **Sudzha** Rus. Fed.
137 O2 **Sudzha** *r.* Rus. Fed.
208 F3 **Sue** *watercourse* Sudan
187 E9 **Sueca** Spain
197 M8 **Sŭedinenie** Bulg.
192 C8 **Suelli** *Sardegna* Italy
217 □2b **Suète, Île du** *i. Inner Islands* Seychelles
183 J2 **Sueva, Reserva Nacional de** *nature res.* Spain
156 B8 **Suèvres** France
231 □1 **Sue Wood Bay** Bermuda
Suez Egypt *see* **As Suways**
Suez, Gulf of Egypt *see* **Suways, Khalīj as**
Suez Bay Egypt *see* **Qulzum, Baḩr al**
Suez Canal Egypt *see* **Suways, Qanāt as**
124 E4 **Şufaynah** Saudi Arabia
235 G2 **Suffern** *NY* U.S.A.
151 N3 **Suffolk** *admin. div. England* U.K.
232 I12 **Suffolk** *VA* U.S.A.
235 J3 **Suffolk County** *county NY* U.S.A.
122 A2 **Sūfiān** Iran
Sufi-Kurgan Kyrg. *see* **Sopu-Korgon**
129 E3 **Sugan, Gora** *mt.* Rus. Fed.
226 E7 **Sugar** *r. WI* U.S.A.
226 F4 **Sugarbush Hill** *WI* U.S.A.
232 C9 **Sugar Grove** *OH* U.S.A.
235 G2 **Sugar Loaf** *NY* U.S.A.
147 C9 **Sugarloaf Mountain** *hill* Ireland
233 □O3 **Sugarloaf Mountain** *ME* U.S.A.
83 N5 **Sugarloaf Point** *N.S.W.* Austr.
216 □2b **Sugar Loaf Point** St Helena
234 D2 **Sugar Notch** *PA* U.S.A.
234 C1 **Sugar Run** *PA* U.S.A.
104 E7 **Suga-shima** *i.* Japan
92 F6 **Sugbuhan Point** Phil.
173 I2 **Sugenheim** Ger.
Süget *Xinjiang* China *see* **Sogat**
94 E4 **Sugi** *i.* Indon.
110 C7 **Sugun** *Xinjiang* China
95 L1 **Sugut** *r.* Malaysia
95 L1 **Sugut, Tanjung** *pt* Malaysia
197 N7 **Suhaia** Romania
110 K7 **Suhai Hu** *l. Qinghai* China
106 J6 **Suhai Obo** *Nei Mongol* China
106 I7 **Suhait** *Nei Mongol* China
Sūhāj Egypt *see* **Sawhāj**
179 K8 **Suha Krajina** *reg.* Slovenia
125 M3 **Şuḩār** Oman
197 O2 **Suharău** Romania
128 B8 **Suhaymī, Wādī as** *watercourse* Egypt
106 J1 **Sühbaatar** Mongolia
107 M3 **Sühbaatar** *prov.* Mongolia
114 C7 **Suheli Par** *i.* India
179 J8 **Suhi vrh** *mt.* Slovenia
169 K9 **Suhl** Ger.
168 K5 **Suhlendorf** Ger.
188 F3 **Suhopolje** Croatia
172 E7 **Suhr** Switz.
124 G4 **Suhul** *reg.* Saudi Arabia
125 K4 **Suhūl al Kidan** *plain* Saudi Arabia
206 E5 **Suhum** Ghana
199 L4 **Şuhut** Turkey
123 M7 **Sui** Pak.
97 D10 **Sui, Laem** *pt* Thai.
254 B4 **Suiá Missur** *r.* Brazil
Sui'an *Fujian* China *see* **Zhangpu**
100 G5 **Suibin** *Heilong.* China
109 L4 **Suichang** *Zhejiang* China
Suicheng *Fujian* China *see* **Jianning**
Suicheng *Guangdong* China *see* **Suixi**
109 J5 **Suichuan** *Jiangxi* China
Suid-Afrika *country* Africa *see* **South Africa, Republic of**
107 L8 **Suide** *Shaanxi* China
182 D3 **Suído, Serra do** *mts* Spain
Suidzhikurmsy Turkm. *see* **Madaw**
100 G6 **Suifenhe** *Heilong.* China
100 G7 **Suifen He** *r.* China
105 L2 **Suifu** Japan
116 C7 **Suigam** *Gujarat* India
104 C4 **Suigetsu-ko** *l.* Japan
105 L3 **Suigō-Tsukuba Kokutei-kōen** *park* Japan

Suihua to Syanno
393

100 E5 Suihua Heilong. China
108 D4 Suijiang Yunnan China
100 E5 Suileng Heilong. China
160 C2 Suilly-la-Tour France
146 F6 Suilven hill Scotland U.K.
108 H5 Suining Hunan China
109 K2 Suining Jiangsu China
108 E3 Suining Sichuan China
261 H4 Suipacha Arg.
252 D5 Suipacha Bol.
109 J2 Suiping Henan China
156 G5 Suippe r. France
156 I5 Suippes France
147 H8 Suir r. Ireland
Suisse country Europe see Switzerland
159 K4 Suisse Normande reg. France
104 C6 Suita Japan
129 L5 Suiti Burunu pt Azer.
234 B7 Suitland MD U.S.A.
109 K2 Suixi Anhui China
108 H8 Suixi Guangdong China
107 N9 Suixian Henan China
Suixian Hubei China see Suizhou
108 F5 Suiyang Guizhou China
107 N9 Suiyang Henan China
Suizhai Henan China see Xiangcheng
107 Q6 Suizhong Liaoning China
109 I3 Suizhou Hubei China
107 J5 Suj Nei Mongol China
116 E6 Sujangarh Rajasthan India
123 M9 Sujawal Pak.
Suk atoll Micronesia see Pulusuk
94 G8 Sukabumi Jawa Indon.
95 H5 Sukadana Kalimantan Indon.
94 F7 Sukadana Sumatera Indon.
95 H5 Sukadana, Teluk b. Indon.
105 L1 Sukagawa Japan
94 G8 Sukanegara Jawa Indon.
95 I6 Sukaraja Kalimantan Indon.
95 I6 Sukaramai Kalimantan Indon.
Sukarnapura Papua Indon. see Jayapura
Sukarno, Puntjak mt. Papua Indon. see Jaya, Puncak
95 M2 Sukau Sabah Malaysia
116 F7 Suket Rajasthan India
140 S5 Sukeva Fin.
100 H5 Sukhanovka Rus. Fed.
139 N8 Sukhary Belarus
139 S7 Sukhinichi Rus. Fed.
137 Q6 Sukhi Yaly r. Ukr.
175 M6 Sukhodil Ukr.
139 V8 Sukhodol'skiy Rus. Fed.
139 N1 Sukhodol'skoye, Ozero l. Rus. Fed.
139 S7 Sukhodrev r. Rus. Fed.
Sukhoivanovka Ukr. see Stepnohirs'k
129 G1 Sukhokumskiy Kanal canal Rus. Fed.
134 I3 Sukhona r. Rus. Fed.
96 D6 Sukhothai Thai.
100 E3 Sukhotino Rus. Fed.
139 S5 Sukhoverkovo Rus. Fed.
Sukhumi Georgia see Sokhumi
Sukhum-Kale Georgia see Sokhumi
137 Q5 Sukhyy Torets' r. Ukr.
137 K6 Sukhyy Yelanets' Ukr.
Sukkertoppen Greenland see Maniitsoq
134 F3 Sukkozero Rus. Fed.
123 M8 Sukkur Pak.
123 M8 Sukkur Barrage Pak.
114 G3 Sukma Chhattisgarh India
202 B2 Sūknah Libya
95 I8 Sukolilo Jawa Indon.
177 H5 Sükösd Hungary
170 E3 Sukow Ger.
100 J5 Sukpay Rus. Fed.
100 J5 Sukpay r. Rus. Fed.
116 D7 Sukri r. India
116 D7 Sukri r. India
139 R5 Sukromlya Rus. Fed.
139 T4 Sukromny Rus. Fed.
212 C4 Sukses Namibia
134 L4 Suksun Rus. Fed.
117 I9 Suktel r. India
103 J14 Sukumo Japan
103 J14 Sukumo-wan b. Japan
93 C8 Sukun i. Indon.
129 I6 Şükürbäyli Azer.
251 I5 Sul, Canal do sea chan. Brazil
257 F4 Sul, Pico do mt. Brazil
144 J1 Sula i. Norway
134 J2 Sula r. Rus. Fed.
137 L4 Sula r. Ukr.
93 D4 Sula, Kepulauan is Indon.
93 D5 Sulabesi i. Indon.
123 M6 Sulaiman Range mts Pak.
129 I2 Sulak Rus. Fed.
129 I2 Sulak r. Rus. Fed.
122 D6 Sūlār Iran
146 D4 Sula Sgeir i. Scotland U.K.
94 D5 Sulasih, Gunung vol. Indon.
95 L9 Sulat i. Indon.
92 E6 Sulat Samar Phil.
93 B5 Sulawesi i. Indon.
93 A5 Sulawesi Barat prov. Indon.
93 A6 Sulawesi Selatan prov. Indon.
93 B4 Sulawesi Tengah prov. Indon.
93 C6 Sulawesi Tenggara prov. Indon.
93 D3 Sulawesi Utara prov. Indon.
127 L6 Sulaymān Beg Iraq
Sulaymānīyah Iraq see As Sulaymānīyah
124 G5 Sulayyimah Saudi Arabia
Sulci Sardegna Italy see Sant'Antioco
Sulcis Sardegna Italy see Sant'Antioco
192 B9 Sulcis reg. Sardegna Italy
142 C2 Suldalsvatnet l. Norway
174 D3 Sulechów Pol.
174 D3 Sulęcin Pol.
174 F3 Sulęcinek Pol.
174 F1 Sulęczyno Pol.
122 D3 Suledeh Iran
207 G4 Suleja Nigeria
175 H4 Sulejów Pol.
175 J3 Sulejówek Pol.
175 H4 Sulejowskie, Jezioro l. Pol.
95 M4 Suleman, Teluk b. Indon.
192 D6 Su Lernu r. Italy
146 H4 Sule Skerry i. Scotland U.K.
146 G4 Sule Stack i. Scotland U.K.
126 H5 Süleymanlı Kahramanmaraş Turkey
199 I4 Süleymanlı Manisa Turkey
94 D5 Suliki Sumatera Indon.
174 D4 Sulików Pol.
206 C5 Sulima Sierra Leone
197 R5 Sulina Romania
197 R5 Sulina, Braţul watercourse Romania
168 G5 Sulingen Ger.
106 D8 Sulin Gol r. Qinghai China
140 N3 Suliskongen mt. Norway
174 D2 Suliszewo Pol.
140 N3 Sulitjelma Norway
141 T6 Sulkava Fin.
175 H6 Sułkowice Pol.
129 H2 Sulla-Chubutla r. Rus. Fed.
250 A6 Sullana Peru
147 E9 Sullane r. Ireland
199 K4 Süller Turkey
151 L6 Sullington West Sussex, England U.K.
236 K6 Sullivan IL U.S.A.
230 D6 Sullivan IN U.S.A.
236 J6 Sullivan MO U.S.A.
222 E5 Sullivan Bay B.C. Can.
234 F1 Sullivan County county NY U.S.A.
234 B2 Sullivan County county PA U.S.A.
Sullivan Island Myanmar see Lanbi Kyun
223 I5 Sullivan Lake Alta Can.
146 □N2 Sullom Voe inlet Scotland U.K.
233 □P1 Sully Que. Can.
160 E2 Sully France
150 F5 Sully Vale of Glamorgan, Wales U.K.
156 D8 Sully-sur-Loire France
179 M6 Sulm r. Austria
175 H4 Sulmierzyce Łódzkie Pol.
174 F4 Sulmierzyce Wielkopolskie Pol.
Sulmo Italy see Sulmona
193 L3 Sulmona Italy
158 F6 Sulniac France
78 □6 Sulofoloa Malaita Solomon Is
197 O9 Sülo ğlu Turkey
175 H5 Sułoszowa Pol.
174 F4 Sułów Dolnośląskie Pol.
175 K5 Sułów Lubelskie Pol.
237 I10 Sulphur LA U.S.A.
237 G8 Sulphur OK U.S.A.
237 H9 Sulphur r. TX U.S.A.
237 D9 Sulphur Draw watercourse TX U.S.A.
237 H9 Sulphur Springs TX U.S.A.
237 E9 Sulphur Springs Draw watercourse NM/TX U.S.A.
224 D4 Sultan Ont. Can.
202 D2 Sultan Libya
123 J7 Sultan, Koh-i- mts Pak.
Sultanabad Andhra Prad. India see Osmannagar
Sultanabad Iran see Arāk
199 K2 Sultanbeyli Turkey
199 M4 Sultandağı Turkey
126 F4 Sultanhanı Turkey
199 J5 Sultanhisar Turkey
199 H2 Sultaniça Turkey
Sultanıye Turkey see Karapınar
116 I6 Sultanpur Uttar Prad. India
123 I1 Sultansandzharskoye Vodokhranilishche resr Turkm.
129 D1 Sultanskoye Rus. Fed.
209 E6 Sulu Dem. Rep. Congo
92 E6 Suluan i. Phil.
92 D8 Sulu Archipelago is Phil.
126 F4 Sülüklü Turkey
121 M8 Sülüktü Kyrg.
117 N6 Sulung Arun. Prad. India
202 D1 Suluntah Libya
202 D2 Sulūq Libya
114 G6 Suluru Andhra Prad. India
266 C5 Sulu Sea N. Pacific Ocean
129 J5 Sulut Azer.
225 F1 Suluvvaulik, Lac l. Que. Can.
137 K3 Sulymivka Ukr.
Sulyukta Kyrg. see Sülüktü
178 A5 Sulz Austria
173 K3 Sulz r. Ger.
173 I3 Sulzach r. Ger.
172 F5 Sulz am Neckar Ger.
173 O4 Sulzbach r. Ger.
172 G2 Sulzbach am Main Ger.
172 G3 Sulzbach an der Murr Ger.
172 H4 Sulzbach-Laufen Ger.
173 L2 Sulzbach-Rosenberg Ger.
172 C3 Sulzbach/Saar Ger.
178 A4 Sulzberg Austria
173 I6 Sulzberg Ger.
262 N1 Sulzberger Bay Antarctica
172 D6 Sulzburg Ger.
169 K10 Sulzdorf an der Lederhecke Ger.
173 K5 Sulzemoos Ger.
172 F3 Sulzfeld Baden-Württemberg Ger.
169 J10 Sulzfeld Bayern Ger.
173 I2 Sulzheim Ger.
169 J10 Sulzthal Ger.
104 B6 Suma Japan
250 B5 Sumaco, Volcán vol. Ecuador
196 I6 Šumadija reg. Serbia
125 N4 Sumāil Oman
93 C3 Sumalata Sulawesi Indon.
210 D3 Sumalē admin. reg. Eth.
258 E3 Sumampa Arg.
95 L1 Sumangat, Tanjung pt Malaysia
250 C4 Sumapaz, Parque Nacional nat. park Col.
122 A5 Sūmār Iran
164 J2 Sumar Neth.
94 C3 Sumatera i. Indon.
94 D5 Sumatera Barat prov. Indon.
94 E6 Sumatera Selatan prov. Indon.
94 C3 Sumatera Utara prov. Indon.
Sumatra i. Indon. see Sumatera
253 E1 Sumaúma Brazil
176 C2 Šumava mts Czech Rep.
176 C2 Šumava nat. park Czech Rep.
78 □1 Sumay Guam
93 B8 Sumba i. Indon.
208 C4 Sumba, Île i. Dem. Rep. Congo
93 A8 Sumba, Selat sea chan. Indon.
122 F3 Sumbar r. Turkm.
93 A8 Sumbawa i. Indon.
95 L9 Sumbawabesar Sumbawa Indon.
211 A6 Sumbawanga Tanz.
252 C3 Sumbay Peru
209 B7 Sumbe Angola
94 D6 Sumbing, Gunung vol. Indon.
209 F7 Sumbu Zambia
209 F7 Sumbu National Park Zambia
146 □N3 Sumburgh Shetland, Scotland U.K.
146 □N3 Sumburgh Head Scotland U.K.
206 C5 Sumbuya Sierra Leone
134 J4 Sumchino Rus. Fed.
111 D9 Sumdo Aksai Chin
108 C4 Sumdo Sichuan China
222 C3 Sumdum AK U.S.A.
222 C3 Sumdum, Mount AK U.S.A.
254 F3 Sumé Brazil
179 N8 Šumećani Croatia
95 G8 Sumedang Jawa Indon.
122 C3 Sume'eh Sarā Iran
176 G5 Sümeg Hungary
208 E2 Sumeih Sudan
161 D9 Sumène France
95 J8 Sumenep Jawa Indon.
116 D7 Sumerpur Rajasthan India
Sumgait Azer. see Sumqayıt
177 J3 Šumiac Slovakia
103 R15 Sumisu-jima i. Japan
190 D1 Sumiswald Switz.
107 N2 Sümiyn Bulag Mongolia
102 □G18 Sumiyō Nansei-shotō Japan
127 K5 Summēl Iraq
224 B2 Summer Beaver Ont. Can.
149 N5 Summer Bridge North Yorkshire, England U.K.
212 C4 Summerdown Namibia
225 K3 Summerford Nfld and Lab. Can.
147 I6 Summerhill Ireland
226 H4 Summer Island MI U.S.A.
146 E6 Summer Isles Scotland U.K.
222 G5 Summerland B.C. Can.
225 I4 Summerside P.E.I. Can.
232 E10 Summersville WV U.S.A.
232 E10 Summersville Lake WV U.S.A.
231 E8 Summerville GA U.S.A.
231 G9 Summerville SC U.S.A.
80 K7 Summit hill North I. N.Z.
235 G3 Summit NJ U.S.A.
236 G3 Summit SD U.S.A.
234 D3 Summit Hill PA U.S.A.
222 E3 Summit Lake B.C. Can.
222 F4 Summit Lake B.C. Can.
241 P2 Summit Mountain NV U.S.A.
239 K8 Summit Peak CO U.S.A.
234 C3 Summit Station PA U.S.A.
179 M2 Šumná Czech Rep.
111 D9 Sumnal Aksai Chin
81 G10 Sumner South I. N.Z.
237 J9 Sumner MS U.S.A.
81 G9 Sumner, Lake South I. N.Z.
222 C3 Sumner Strait AK U.S.A.
105 J1 Sumon Japan
103 Q9 Sumon-dake mt. Japan
104 A7 Sumoto Japan
93 A6 Sumpangbinangae Sulawesi Indon.
176 F2 Šumperk Czech Rep.
96 C1 Sumprabum Myanmar
Sumpu Japan see Shizuoka
129 K5 Sumqayıt Azer.
129 K5 Sumqayıt r. Azer.
123 N8 Sumrahu Pak.
121 N7 Sumsar Kyrg.
137 M2 Sums'ka Oblast' admin. div. Ukr.
Sumskaya Oblast' admin. div. Ukr. see Sums'ka Oblast'
134 F2 Sumskiy Posad Rus. Fed.
168 K4 Sumte Ger.
231 G9 Sumter SC U.S.A.
116 F2 Sumur Jammu and Kashmir
176 G2 Šumvald Czech Rep.
190 F2 Sumvitg Switz.
111 E9 Sumxi Xizang China
137 N3 Sumy Ukr.
Sumy Oblast admin. div. Ukr. see Sums'ka Oblast'
108 A4 Sumzom Xizang China
238 I3 Sun r. MT U.S.A.
134 J4 Suna Rus. Fed.
102 S3 Sunagawa Japan
116 F7 Sunaj Madh. Prad. India
116 E4 Sunam Punjab India
117 M7 Sunamganj Bangl.
104 E5 Sunami Japan
106 F7 Sunan Gansu China
101 D9 Sunan N. Korea
146 E9 Sunart, Loch inlet Scotland U.K.
177 J2 Šuňava Slovakia
125 L4 Şunaynah Oman
186 B1 Sunbilla Spain
122 A4 Sunbula Kuh mts Iran
238 I2 Sunburst MT U.S.A.
83 J7 Sunbury Vic. Austr.
151 L5 Sunbury Surrey, England U.K.
232 C8 Sunbury OH U.S.A.
227 R9 Sunbury PA U.S.A.
261 G2 Sunchales Arg.
173 M4 Sünching Ger.
253 E6 Suncho Corral Arg.
101 D9 Sunch'ŏn N. Korea
101 E11 Sunch'ŏn S. Korea
215 L1 Sun City S. Africa
241 T8 Sun City AZ U.S.A.
240 O8 Sun City CA U.S.A.
233 N5 Suncook NH U.S.A.
177 L5 Şuncuiuş Romania
138 D1 Sund Åland Fin.
94 F8 Sunda, Selat str. Indon.
Sunda Kalapa Jawa Indon. see Jakarta
238 L4 Sundance WY U.S.A.
117 L9 Sundarbans coastal area Bangl./India
117 L9 Sundarbans National Park Bangl./India
117 J8 Sundargarh Orissa India
116 F4 Sundarnagar Hima. Prad. India
265 L4 Sunda Shelf sea feature Indian Ocean
Sunda Strait Indon. see Sunda, Selat
Sunda Trench sea feature Indian Ocean see Java Trench
214 J9 Sundays r. Eastern Cape S. Africa
215 O4 Sundays r. KwaZulu-Natal S. Africa
86 G4 Sunday Strait W.A. Austr.
261 F4 Sundblad Arg.
142 B2 Sunde Hordaland Norway
140 J5 Sunde Sør-Trøndelag Norway
149 O4 Sunderland Tyne and Wear, England U.K.
169 F8 Sundern (Sauerland) Ger.
160 K1 Sundgau reg. France
169 K8 Sundhausen Ger.
199 L3 Sündiken Dağları mts Turkey
209 B6 Sundi-Mamba Dem. Rep. Congo
222 H5 Sundre Alta Can.
224 E4 Sundridge Ont. Can.
142 F5 Sunds Denmark
142 E2 Sundsli Norway
141 N5 Sundsvall Sweden
129 J5 Sündü Azer.
215 P5 Sundumbili S. Africa
107 L2 Sunduyka Rus. Fed.
116 F7 Sunel Rajasthan India
211 C6 Sunga Tanz.
94 E4 Sungaiapit Sumatera Indon.
95 I4 Sungai Ayak Kalimantan Indon.
94 E4 Sungaiguntung Sumatera Indon.
94 E4 Sungaikabung Sumatera Indon.
95 H5 Sungaikakap Kalimantan Indon.
94 G5 Sungailiat Sumatera Indon.
94 D6 Sungaipenuh Sumatera Indon.
94 D2 Sungai Petani Malaysia
95 H4 Sungaipinyuh Kalimantan Indon.
94 G6 Sungaiselan Indon.
94 □ Sungai Tuas Basin dock Sing.
Sungari r. China see Songhua Jiang
94 □ Sungei Seletar Reservoir Sing.
93 A6 Sungguminasa Sulawesi Indon.
203 F6 Sungikai Sudan
Sungkiang Shanghai China see Songjiang
109 □J7 Sung Kong i. H.K. China
213 G3 Sungo Moz.
Sungqu Sichuan China see Songpan
94 F6 Sungsang Sumatera Indon.
129 D4 Süngülü Turkey
197 O8 Sungurlare Bulg.
126 G3 Sungurlu Turkey
192 B7 Suni Sardegna Italy
188 F3 Sunja Croatia
121 O5 Sunkar, Gora mt. Kazakh.
117 L7 Sunkosh Chhu r. Bhutan
117 K6 Sun Kosi r. Nepal
137 L4 Sunky Ukr.
169 J9 Sünna Ger.
142 C1 Sunndal Norway
140 J5 Sunndalsøra Norway
142 J2 Sunne Sweden
141 H6 Sunnfjord reg. Norway
151 K5 Sunninghill Windsor and Maidenhead, England U.K.
241 V2 Sunnyside UT U.S.A.
238 E3 Sunnyside WA U.S.A.
240 J4 Sunnyvale CA U.S.A.
105 K6 Suno-saki pt Japan
226 E6 Sun Prairie WI U.S.A.
253 F4 Sunsas, Sierra de hills Bol.
240 □C12 Sunset Beach HI U.S.A.
222 G4 Sunset House Alta Can.
Sunset Peak hill H.K. China see Tai Tung Shan
Sunshine Island H.K. China see Chau Kung To
131 M3 Suntar Rus. Fed.
123 J9 Suntsar Pak.
210 C2 Suntu Eth.
238 G5 Sun Valley ID U.S.A.
101 D10 Sunwi-do i. N. Korea
100 E4 Sunwu Heilong. China
206 E5 Sunyani Ghana
129 H2 Sunzha r. Rus. Fed.
140 T2 Suojanperä Fin.
140 R5 Suolahti Fin.
134 E2 Suolijärvet l. Fin.
Suoločielgi Fin. see Saariselkä
140 Q2 Suoluvuobmi Norway
141 S6 Suomenniemi Fin.
226 E1 Suomi Ont. Can.
Suomi country Europe see Finland
138 G1 Suomusjärvi Fin.
140 T4 Suomussalmi Fin.
103 I13 Suō-nada b. Japan
140 S5 Suonenjoki Fin.
97 G9 Suŏng Cambodia
96 F5 Suong r. Laos
140 S5 Suontee Fin.
140 S5 Suontienselkä l. Fin.
134 F3 Suoyarvi Rus. Fed.
Suozhen Shandong China see Huantai
114 D5 Supa Karnataka India
241 T5 Supai AZ U.S.A.
117 K6 Supaul Bihar India
163 F10 Superbagnères France
156 G6 Superbe r. France
160 B5 Superbesse France
161 H7 Superdévoluy France
241 U8 Superior AZ U.S.A.
238 G3 Superior MT U.S.A.
236 F5 Superior NE U.S.A.
226 B3 Superior WI U.S.A.
245 M9 Superior, Laguna lag. Mex.
226 G2 Superior, Lake Can./U.S.A.
191 J5 Superiore, Lago l. Italy
161 B6 Superlioran France
191 R6 Supertarska Draga Croatia
188 F4 Supetar Croatia
97 E7 Suphan Buri Thai.
127 K4 Süphan Dağı mt. Turkey
193 K4 Supino Italy
91 I7 Supiori i. Papua Indon.
137 K4 Supiy r. Ukr.
177 L4 Suplacu de Barcău Romania
139 R8 Suponevo Rus. Fed.
169 K6 Süpplingen Ger.
262 V1 Support Force Glacier Antarctica
175 L2 Supraśl Pol.
175 K2 Supraśl r. Pol.
129 C3 Sup'sa r. Georgia
101 D8 Supung N. Korea
177 L4 Supur Romania
124 G7 Sūq al Inān Yemen
124 E5 Sūq ar Rubū' Saudi Arabia
127 M8 Sūq ash Shuyūkh Iraq
109 L2 Suqian Jiangsu China
124 D3 Sūq Suwayq Saudi Arabia
125 L9 Suquṭrá i. Yemen
173 N6 Sur r. Ger.
206 E4 Sur r. Ghana
177 H4 Súr Hungary
125 N4 Şūr Oman
240 K5 Sur, Point CA U.S.A.
261 I5 Sur, Punta pt Arg.
135 I5 Sura Rus. Fed.
120 B1 Sura r. Rus. Fed.
129 K5 Şuraabad Azer.
123 L7 Surab Pak.
95 J8 Surabaya Jawa Indon.
123 K7 Surai Pak.
117 I8 Surajpur Chhattisgarh India
122 H9 Sūrak Iran
95 I8 Surakarta Jawa Indon.
93 A4 Suramana Sulawesi Indon.
197 M5 Şura Mare Romania
160 G4 Suran r. France
123 I8 Sūrān Iran
128 E3 Şūrān Syria
177 H3 Šurany Slovakia
210 D3 Surar Eth.
251 F6 Surára Brazil
85 L9 Surat Qld Austr.
116 D9 Surat Gujarat India
116 D5 Suratgarh Rajasthan India
97 D10 Surat Thani Thai.
175 K3 Suraż Pol.
139 N6 Surazh Belarus
139 P8 Surazh Rus. Fed.
173 N6 Surberg Ger.
85 K7 Surbiton Qld Austr.
195 O3 Surbo Italy
127 L6 Sūrdāsh Iraq
197 P5 Surdila-Greci Romania
197 L3 Surduc Romania
197 K8 Surdulica Serbia
172 B2 Sûre r. Ger./Lux.
165 I9 Sûre, Vallée de la val. Lux.
116 C8 Surendranagar Gujarat India
242 □R13 Suretka Costa Rica
240 L7 Surf CA U.S.A.
235 G5 Surf City NJ U.S.A.
151 L2 Surfleet Lincolnshire, England U.K.
116 D9 Surgana Mahar. India
162 C3 Surgères France
246 B2 Surgidero de Batabanó Cuba
130 I3 Surgut Rus. Fed.
164 J2 Surhuizum Neth.
Suri W. Bengal India see Siuri
186 I4 Súria Spain
114 F4 Suriapet Andhra Prad. India
103 □3 Suribachi-yama hill Iō-jima Japan
190 C4 Surier Italy
92 E7 Surigao Mindanao Phil.
92 E6 Surigao Strait Phil.
250 C4 Surimena Col.
97 F7 Surin Thai.
217 □1b Surinam Mauritius
Surinam country S. America see Suriname
251 G3 Suriname country S. America
251 H3 Suriname r. Suriname
97 C10 Surin Nua, Ko i. Thai.
250 D3 Suripá Venez.
127 P6 Surkhābād Iran
121 L9 Surkhandar'ya r. Uzbek.
Surkhandarya Oblast admin. div. Uzbek. see Surxondaryo
123 K6 Surkhduz Afgh.
116 H5 Surkhet Nepal
123 M2 Surkhob r. Tajik.
Surkhondaryo r. Uzbek. see Surkhandar'ya
Surkhondaryo Wiloyati admin. div. Uzbek. see Surxondaryo
122 E6 Surmāq Iran
156 G5 Surmelin r. France
127 J3 Sürmene Turkey
140 J5 Surnadalsøra Norway
197 N8 Sŭrnevo Bulg.
135 H6 Surovikino Rus. Fed.
222 C3 Surprise B.C. Can.
78 □5 Surprise, Île i. New Caledonia
222 C3 Surprise Lake B.C. Can.
124 F4 Surrah, Nafūd as des. Saudi Arabia
184 D2 Surrazala r. Port.
222 F5 Surrey B.C. Can.
246 □ Surrey reg. Jamaica
151 L5 Surrey admin. div. England U.K.
190 E1 Sursee Switz.
190 F2 Surselva reg. Switz.
137 N5 Surs'ko-Mykhaylivka Ukr.
135 I5 Surskoye Rus. Fed.
202 C2 Surt Libya
202 C2 Surt, Khalīj g. Libya
140 □C2 Surtsey i. Iceland
122 G8 Sūrū Hormozgan Iran
122 H9 Sūrū Sīstān va Balūchestān Iran
197 M5 Suru, Vârful mt. Romania
254 C2 Surubiú r. Brazil
126 I5 Suruç Turkey
210 E2 Surud, Raas pt Somalia
Surud Ad mt. Somalia see Shimbiris
105 H6 Suruga-wan b. Japan
94 E6 Surulangun Sumatera Indon.
251 F4 Surumú r. Brazil
92 F8 Surup Mindanao Phil.
156 E5 Survilliers France
168 E5 Surwold Ger.
121 L9 Surxondaryo admin. div. Uzbek.
Suryapet Andhra Prad. India see Suriapet
160 E5 Sury-le-Comtal France
158 F6 Surzur France
129 H6 Şuşa Azer.
142 H6 Suså r. Denmark
190 C5 Susa Italy
103 I12 Susa Japan
190 B5 Susa, Valle di val. Italy
188 F4 Sušac i. Croatia
Susah Tunisia see Sousse
191 Q6 Susak Croatia
188 E3 Susak i. Croatia
103 K13 Susaki Japan
103 M13 Susami Japan
Susamyr Kyrg. see Suusamyr
233 I11 Susan VA U.S.A.
122 C6 Sūsangerd Iran
100 L2 Susanino Khabarovskiy Kray Rus. Fed.
134 H4 Susanino Kostromskaya Oblast' Rus. Fed.
240 L1 Susanville CA U.S.A.
190 I2 Susch Switz.
136 G2 Suschany Ukr.
191 M4 Susegana Italy
126 I3 Suşehri Turkey
168 K2 Süsel Ger.
197 N7 Sushitsa Bulg.
107 L9 Sushui He r. China
176 C2 Sušice Czech Rep.
175 L5 Susiec Pol.
138 L5 Šuškova Latvia
116 F8 Susner Madh. Prad. India
97 D11 Suso Thai.
183 O4 Suso, Monasterio de tourist site Spain
105 H2 Susobana-gawa r. Japan
109 K3 Susong Anhui China
105 I5 Susono Japan
186 K4 Susqueda, Pantà de resr Spain
233 J7 Susquehanna PA U.S.A.
227 R9 Susquehanna r. PA U.S.A.
232 I8 Susquehanna, West Branch r. PA U.S.A.
258 D1 Susques Arg.
172 H4 Süßen Ger.
225 H4 Sussex N.B. Can.
234 F2 Sussex NJ U.S.A.
232 H12 Sussex VA U.S.A.
234 F2 Sussex County county NJ U.S.A.
168 G5 Süstedt Ger.
165 I6 Susteren Neth.
244 D3 Susticacán Mex.
191 K5 Sustinente Italy
168 D5 Sustrum Ger.
222 E3 Sustut Provincial Park B.C. Can.
93 B5 Susua Sulawesi Indon.
78 □6 Susubona Sta Isabel Solomon Is
78 □6 Susuka Choiseul Solomon Is
95 L2 Susul Sabah Malaysia
131 P3 Susuman Rus. Fed.
93 E2 Susupu Halmahera Indon.
199 J3 Susurluk Turkey
129 E5 Susuz Turkey
138 G6 Šušvė r. Lith.
175 H2 Susz Pol.
116 F3 Sutak Jammu and Kashmir
106 C3 Sutay Uul mt. Mongolia
199 L5 Sütçüler Turkey
194 F8 Sutera Sicilia Italy
83 M6 Sutherland N.S.W. Austr.
214 E8 Sutherland S. Africa
146 H6 Sutherland reg. Scotland U.K.
236 E5 Sutherland NE U.S.A.
232 H11 Sutherland VA U.S.A.
87 H9 Sutherland Range hills W.A. Austr.
188 G4 Sutjeska nat. park Bos.-Herz.
116 C5 Sutlej r. India/Pak.
138 G2 Sutlepa meri l. Estonia
128 B2 Sütlüce İçel Turkey
197 P9 Sütlüce Kırklareli Turkey
192 I3 Sutri Italy
240 K2 Sutter CA U.S.A.
240 L3 Sutter Creek CA U.S.A.
151 L2 Sutterton Lincolnshire, England U.K.
233 M3 Sutton Que. Can.
224 D2 Sutton r. Ont. Can.
81 E12 Sutton South I. N.Z.
151 M3 Sutton Cambridgeshire, England U.K.
236 G5 Sutton NE U.S.A.
232 E10 Sutton WV U.S.A.
151 M2 Sutton Bridge Lincolnshire, England U.K.
151 I2 Sutton Coldfield West Midlands, England U.K.
151 J4 Sutton Courtenay Oxfordshire, England U.K.
149 O7 Sutton in Ashfield Nottinghamshire, England U.K.
224 C2 Sutton Lake Ont. Can.
232 E10 Sutton Lake WV U.S.A.
149 O5 Sutton-on-the-Forest North Yorkshire, England U.K.
149 P7 Sutton on Trent Nottinghamshire, England U.K.
151 N5 Sutton Valence Kent, England U.K.
85 K6 Suttor r. Qld Austr.
102 R4 Suttsu Japan
220 C4 Sutwik Island AK U.S.A.
100 H3 Sutyr' r. Rus. Fed.
136 H4 Sutysky Ukr.
78 □6 Su'u Malaita Solomon Is
107 J4 Suugant Mongolia
78 □6 Su'uholo Solomon Is
215 J7 Suurberg mt. S. Africa
215 J9 Suurberg mts S. Africa
214 E10 Suurbraak S. Africa
138 I3 Suure-Jaani Estonia
138 F3 Suuremõisa Estonia
138 F3 Suur katel b. Estonia
138 G2 Suur-Pakri i. Estonia
138 I2 Suurpea Estonia
138 G3 Suur väin sea chan. Estonia
121 O6 Suusamyr Kyrg.
79 □7a Suva Viti Levu Fiji
Suvalki Pol. see Suwałki
196 I8 Suva Reka Kosovo Serbia
129 F6 Suveren Turkey
192 F1 Suvereto Italy
193 Q10 Suvero, Capo c. Italy
191 K7 Suviano, Lago di l. Italy
Suvorov atoll Cook Is see Suwarrow
136 H8 Suvorov Moldova
139 T7 Suvorov Rus. Fed.
137 M6 Suvorove Dnipropetrovs'ka Oblast' Ukr.
136 H8 Suvorove Odes'ka Oblast' Ukr.
197 P7 Suvorovo Bulg.
Suvorovo Moldova see Ştefan Vodă
129 D1 Suvorovskaya Rus. Fed.
137 M8 Suvorovs'ke Ukr.
105 H3 Suwa Japan
105 H3 Suwa-ko l. Japan
95 K5 Suwakong Kalimantan Indon.
175 K1 Suwałki Pol.
96 F7 Suwannaphum Thai.
231 F11 Suwannee r. FL U.S.A.
102 □G17 Suwanose-jima i. Nansei-shotō Japan
95 L4 Suwaran, Gunung mt. Indon.
81 □2 Suwarrow atoll Cook Is
128 D6 Suwaylih Jordan
127 L7 Suwayqīyah, Hawr as imp. l. Iraq
127 J8 Suwayr well Saudi Arabia
203 G2 Suways, Khalīj as g. Egypt
203 G2 Suways, Qanāt as canal Egypt
128 C10 Suweihil pt Saudi Arabia
Suweilih Jordan see Suwaylih
Suweis, Khalîg el g. Egypt see Suways, Khalīj as
101 E10 Suwŏn S. Korea
106 D7 Suxik Qinghai China
108 G7 Suxu Guangxi China
121 S3 Suykbulak Kazakh.
250 A6 Suyo Peru
Sūyqbulaq Kazakh. see Suykbulak
124 F9 Suyūl Ḥanīsh i. Yemen
129 I1 Suyutkina Kosa Rus. Fed.
129 I1 Suyutkina Kosa, Mys pt Rus. Fed.
120 E7 Suz, Mys pt Kazakh.
122 G8 Sūzā Iran
121 M5 Suzak Kazakh.
105 H2 Suzaka Japan
139 X5 Suzdal' Rus. Fed.
161 F8 Suze-la-Rousse France
137 N1 Suzemka Rus. Fed.
109 K2 Suzhou Anhui China
Suzhou Gansu China see Jiuquan
109 M3 Suzhou Jiangsu China
101 D8 Suzi He r. China
103 O9 Suzu Japan
104 E6 Suzuka Japan
104 E6 Suzuka-gawa r. Japan
104 D5 Suzuka Kokutei-kōen park Japan
104 D6 Suzuka-sanmyaku mts Japan
103 O9 Suzu-misaki pt Japan
191 J6 Suzzara Italy
141 M6 Svabensverk Sweden
140 S1 Sværholthalvøya pen. Norway
140 □ Svalbard terr. Arctic Ocean
197 O7 Svalenik Bulg.
142 H6 Svallerup Denmark
136 B5 Svalyava Ukr.
143 O2 Svanberga Sweden
129 D3 Svanet'is K'edi hills Georgia
143 K5 Svängsta Sweden
140 Q3 Svanstein Sweden
137 N2 Svapa r. Rus. Fed.
140 P3 Svappavaara Sweden
139 P4 Svapushcha Rus. Fed.
176 C3 Švarcenberský kanál canal Czech Rep.
143 L1 Svärdsjö Sweden
142 F2 Svarstad Norway
138 I1 Svarta r. Fin.
143 K2 Svartå Sweden
143 K2 Svartälven r. Sweden
143 J1 Svartån r. Sweden
143 M2 Svartån r. Sweden
140 Q3 Svartbyn Sweden
Svartenhuk Halvø pen. Greenland see Sigguup Nunaa
142 C2 Svartevatn l. Norway
140 P3 Svartlä Sweden
143 P2 Svartlögafjärden b. Sweden
136 F2 Svarytsevychi Ukr.
171 G10 Svatava Czech Rep.
144 J1 Svatjell hill Norway
179 P2 Svatobořice-Mistřín Czech Rep.
137 R4 Svatove Ukr.
177 K3 Svätuše Slovakia
176 G3 Svätý Jur Slovakia
177 H4 Svätý Peter Slovakia
97 G9 Svay Riĕng Cambodia
140 □ Sveagruva Svalbard
134 I4 Svecha Rus. Fed.
138 I6 Svėdasai Lith.
141 M5 Sveg Sweden
141 M5 Svegsjön l. Sweden
142 B2 Sveio Norway
138 J4 Sveķi Latvia
138 E6 Švėkšna Lith.
141 H6 Svelgen Norway
140 J5 Svellingen Norway
137 N1 Sven' Rus. Fed.
138 I6 Švenčionėliai Lith.
138 J6 Švenčionys Lith.
142 G6 Svendborg Denmark
142 J4 Svenljunga Sweden
140 □ Svenskøya i. Svalbard
140 M5 Svenstavik Sweden
175 L1 Šventežeris Lith.
138 H6 Šventoji r. Lith.
100 C2 Sverbeyevo Rus. Fed.
139 S6 Sverchkovo Rus. Fed.
135 I6 Sverdlovo Rus. Fed.
Sverdlovsk Rus. Fed. see Yekaterinburg
137 S5 Sverdlovs'k Ukr.
134 M4 Sverdlovskaya Oblast' admin. div. Rus. Fed.
Sverdlovsk Oblast admin. div. Rus. Fed. see Sverdlovskaya Oblast'
221 I2 Sverdrup Channel Nunavut Can.
221 I2 Sverdrup Islands Nunavut Can.
Sverige country Europe see Sweden
Švermovo Slovakia see Telgárt
137 M2 Svesa Ukr.
197 O7 Sveshtari, Tomb of tourist site Bulg.
188 E4 Sveta Andrija i. Croatia
179 O7 Sveta Marija Croatia
138 G5 Švėtė r. Lith.
191 R6 Sveti Damjan, Rt pt Croatia
191 R6 Sveti Grgur i. Croatia
Sveti Ivan Zelina Croatia see Zelina
188 F4 Sveti Jure mt. Croatia
197 J9 Sveti Nikole Macedonia
176 G1 Světlá Hora Czech Rep.
176 E2 Světlá nad Sázavou Czech Rep.
100 K5 Svetlaya Rus. Fed.
100 M4 Svetlodarskoye Sakhalin Rus. Fed.
Svetlogorsk Belarus see Svyetlahorsk
138 D7 Svetlogorsk Kaliningradskaya Oblast' Rus. Fed.
130 J3 Svetlogorsk Krasnoyarskiy Kray Rus. Fed.
135 H7 Svetlograd Rus. Fed.
134 K4 Svetlopolyansk Rus. Fed.
Svetlovodsk Ukr. see Svitlovods'k
138 D7 Svetlyy Kaliningradskaya Oblast' Rus. Fed.
120 I2 Svetlyy Orenburgskaya Oblast' Rus. Fed.
135 I6 Svetlyy Yar Rus. Fed.
138 L1 Svetogorsk Leningradskaya Oblast' Rus. Fed.
Svetogorsk Respublika Dagestan Rus. Fed. see Shamil'kala
Svetozarevo Serbia see Jagodina
196 H5 Svetozar Miletić Vojvodina Serbia
138 H4 Svētupe r. Latvia
191 P5 Svetvinčenat Croatia
140 □E1 Svíahnúkar vol. Iceland
136 D4 Svicha r. Ukr.
177 K2 Svidník Slovakia
176 C2 Švihov Czech Rep.
138 G3 Sviibi Estonia
188 F4 Svilaja mts Croatia
196 J6 Svilajnac Serbia
197 O9 Svilengrad Bulg.
197 K6 Svinecea Mare, Vârful mt. Romania
177 K2 Svinia Slovakia
177 H3 Svinná Slovakia
142 H6 Svinninge Denmark
Svinø i. Faroe Is see Svínoy
144 D1 Svínoy i. Faroe Is
138 J7 Svir Belarus
139 S1 Svir' r. Rus. Fed.
138 J7 Svir, Vozyera l. Belarus
139 P1 Sviritsa Rus. Fed.
139 P1 Svirskaya Guba b. Rus. Fed.
139 Q1 Svir'stroy Rus. Fed.
175 M6 Svirzh r. Ukr.
197 N7 Svishtov Bulg.
138 H8 Svislach Hrodzyenskaya Voblasts' Belarus
138 K8 Svislach Minskaya Voblasts' Belarus
175 M2 Svislach r. Belarus
138 L8 Svislach r. Belarus
138 L8 Svislach r. Belarus
Svisloch r. Belarus see Svislach
177 J2 Svit Slovakia
176 F3 Svitava r. Czech Rep.
176 F2 Svitavy Czech Rep.
137 R5 Svitlodars'k Ukr.
137 N5 Svitlohirs'ke Ukr.
137 M4 Svitlovods'k Ukr.
175 L4 Svityaz' Ukr.
190 I2 Svizzer, Parc Naziunal nat. park Switz.
Svizzera country Europe see Switzerland
138 E7 Svoboda Kaliningradskaya Oblast' Rus. Fed.
137 P2 Svoboda Kurskaya Oblast' Rus. Fed.
176 E1 Svoboda nad Úpou Czech Rep.
100 F3 Svobodnyy Rus. Fed.
129 E1 Svobody Rus. Fed.
197 L8 Svoge Bulg.
138 L6 Svol'nya r. Belarus
140 M2 Svolvær Norway
176 F2 Svratka Czech Rep.
176 F2 Svratka r. Czech Rep.
177 H2 Svrčinovec Slovakia
197 K7 Svrljig Serbia
197 K7 Svrljiške Planine mts Serbia
138 J7 Svyantsyanskiya Hrady hills Belarus
Svyatogorovskiy Rudnik Ukr. see Dobropillya
139 X6 Svyatoye, Ozero l. Rus. Fed.
134 J2 Svyatoy Nos, Mys c. Rus. Fed.
139 O9 Svyatsk Rus. Fed.
138 M9 Svyetlahorsk Belarus
137 M1 Svyha r. Ukr.
136 D3 Svynya r. Ukr.
136 F3 Svyten'ka r. Ukr.
123 O4 Swabi Pak.
151 I2 Swadlincote Derbyshire, England U.K.
215 J8 Swaershoek S. Africa
215 J8 Swaershoekpas pass S. Africa
151 N2 Swaffham Norfolk, England U.K.
85 N6 Swain Reefs Qld Austr.
231 F9 Swainsboro GA U.S.A.
77 I3 Swains Island atoll American Samoa
212 B4 Swakop watercourse Namibia
212 B4 Swakopmund Namibia
149 O5 Swale r. England U.K.
78 □6 Swallow Islands Santa Cruz Is Solomon Is
165 J6 Swalmen Neth.
114 E5 Swamihalli Karnataka India
225 G1 Swampy r. Que. Can.
87 C11 Swan r. W.A. Austr.
223 K4 Swan r. Man./Sask. Can.
224 D2 Swan r. Ont. Can.
148 C8 Swan Ireland
151 I6 Swanage Dorset, England U.K.
209 E7 Swana-Mume Dem. Rep. Congo
232 E10 Swandale WV U.S.A.
214 H9 Swanepoelspoort mt. S. Africa
83 I6 Swan Hill Vic. Austr.
222 H4 Swan Hills Alta Can.
Swan Islands see Cisne, Islas del
222 D4 Swan Lake l. B.C. Can.
223 K4 Swan Lake l. Man. Can.
234 F1 Swan Lake NY U.S.A.
236 H3 Swan Lake l. MN U.S.A.
151 M5 Swanley Kent, England U.K.
147 G4 Swanlinbar Ireland
81 G10 Swannanoa South I. N.Z.
231 I8 Swanquarter NC U.S.A.
231 I8 Swanquarter National Wildlife Refuge nature res. NC U.S.A.
82 G6 Swan Reach S.A. Austr.
223 K4 Swan River Man. Can.
226 A2 Swan River MN U.S.A.
148 D5 Swan's Cross Roads Ireland
83 L10 Swansea Tas. Austr.
150 E4 Swansea Swansea, Wales U.K.
150 E4 Swansea admin. div. Wales U.K.
150 E4 Swansea Bay Wales U.K.
233 □Q4 Swans Island ME U.S.A.
240 J4 Swanton CA U.S.A.
233 L4 Swanton VT U.S.A.
151 N2 Swanton Morley Norfolk, England U.K.
174 G1 Swarożyn Pol.
215 N6 Swartberg S. Africa
214 D10 Swartberg mt. S. Africa
214 F9 Swartbergpas pass S. Africa
214 B6 Swartdoorn r. S. Africa
234 E5 Swarthmore PA U.S.A.
215 L8 Swart Kei r. S. Africa
214 E6 Swartkolkvloer salt pan S. Africa
215 J9 Swartkops S. Africa
215 J9 Swartkops r. S. Africa
Swart Nossob watercourse Namibia see Black Nossob
215 K2 Swartplaas S. Africa
214 H4 Swartputs S. Africa
214 D2 Swartput se Pan salt pan Namibia
215 K1 Swartruggens S. Africa
215 K1 Swartruggens mts S. Africa
234 F2 Swartswood NJ U.S.A.
234 F2 Swartswood Lake NJ U.S.A.
215 P3 Swart Umfolozi S. Africa
227 K7 Swartz Creek MI U.S.A.
174 F3 Swarzędz Pol.
241 S2 Swasey Peak UT U.S.A.
227 N1 Swastika Ont. Can.
123 N4 Swat r. Pak.
234 B4 Swatara Creek r. PA U.S.A.
123 O4 Swat Kohistan reg. Pak.
Swatow Guangdong China see Shantou
148 D4 Swatragh Northern Ireland U.K.
151 I6 Sway Hampshire, England U.K.
215 P2 Swaziland country Africa
141 M6 Sweden country Europe
234 E5 Swedesboro NJ U.S.A.
84 G4 Sweers Island Qld Austr.
232 F11 Sweet Briar VA U.S.A.
238 C4 Sweet Home OR U.S.A.
232 E11 Sweet Springs WV U.S.A.
234 C2 Sweet Valley PA U.S.A.
237 E9 Sweetwater TX U.S.A.
238 K5 Sweetwater r. WY U.S.A.
238 J5 Sweetwater Station WY U.S.A.
214 E10 Swellendam S. Africa
215 L7 Swempoort S. Africa
175 I2 Świątki Pol.
174 G1 Świbno Pol.
175 J3 Świder r. Pol.
174 E5 Świdnica Dolnośląskie Pol.
174 D4 Świdnica Lubuskie Pol.
175 K4 Świdnik Pol.
174 D2 Świdwin Pol.
174 E5 Świebodzice Pol.
174 D3 Świebodzin Pol.
174 G2 Świecie Pol.
174 E4 Święciechowa Pol.
175 H2 Świecie nad Osą Pol.
171 K6 Świecko Pol.
175 H2 Świedziebnia Pol.
174 G2 Świekatowo Pol.
174 D5 Świeradów-Zdrój Pol.
175 I3 Świercze Pol.
174 F5 Świerczów Pol.
174 G5 Świerklaniec Pol.
174 D4 Świerzawa Pol.
174 E1 Świerzenko Pol.
174 C2 Świerzno Pol.
174 E1 Świeszyno Pol.
175 J2 Świętajno Warmińsko-Mazurskie Pol.
175 K1 Świętajno Warmińsko-Mazurskie Pol.
175 I5 Świętokrzyskie prov. Pol.
175 I5 Świętokrzyskie, Góry hills Pol.
175 I5 Świętokrzyski Park Narodowy nat. park Pol.
233 □O4 Swift r. ME U.S.A.
223 J5 Swift Current Sask. Can.
223 J5 Swiftcurrent Creek r. Sask. Can.
164 I3 Swifterbant Neth.
234 E2 Swiftwater PA U.S.A.
148 B4 Swilly r. Ireland
147 G2 Swilly, Lough inlet Ireland
151 I4 Swindon Swindon, England U.K.
151 I4 Swindon admin. div. England U.K.
149 P6 Swinefleet East Riding of Yorkshire, England U.K.
151 L2 Swineshead Lincolnshire, England U.K.
147 E5 Swinford Ireland
234 F1 Swinging Bridge Reservoir NY U.S.A.
174 G3 Świnice Warckie Pol.
215 J4 Swinkpan imp. l. S. Africa
175 H6 Świnna Pol.
174 C2 Świnoujście Pol.
146 L11 Swinton Scottish Borders, Scotland U.K.
149 O7 Swinton South Yorkshire, England U.K.
Swiss Confederation country Europe see Switzerland
Świstocz r. Belarus see Svislach
190 E2 Switzerland country Europe
Swnt Enlli sea chan. Wales U.K. see Bardsey Sound
174 C2 Swobnica Pol.
147 J6 Swords Ireland
85 H6 Swords Range hills Qld Austr.
174 F2 Swornegacie Pol.
234 D2 Swoyerville PA U.S.A.
138 M7 Syalyava, Vozyera l. Belarus
175 M3 Syalyets Brestskaya Voblasts' Belarus
139 N8 Syalyets Mahilyowskaya Voblasts' Belarus
138 H9 Syalyets Vodaskhovishcha resr Belarus
134 F3 Syamozero, Ozero l. Rus. Fed.
134 H3 Syamzha Rus. Fed.
117 I5 Syang Nepal
138 M7 Syanno Belarus

Syarednenemanskaya Nizina to Tamba

394

138 H8 **Syarednenemanskaya Nizina** *lowland* Belarus/Lith.
138 K8 **Syarhyeyevichy** Belarus
139 P1 **Syas'** *r.* Rus. Fed.
139 P1 **Syas'troy** Rus. Fed.
134 I4 **Syava** Rus. Fed.
147 B8 **Sybil Point** Ireland
215 M1 **Sybrandskraal** S. Africa
226 F8 **Sycamore** *IL* U.S.A.
174 E1 **Sycewice** Pol.
139 R6 **Sychevka** Rus. Fed.
139 T6 **Sychevo** Rus. Fed.
138 M8 **Sychkava** Belarus
174 F4 **Syców** Pol.
Sydenham *atoll Gilbert Is* Kiribati *see* **Nonouti**
83 M5 **Sydney** *N.S.W.* Austr.
225 I4 **Sydney** *N.S.* Can.
82 □1 **Sydney Bay** Norfolk I.
84 G4 **Sydney Island** *Qld* Austr.
Sydney Island *Phoenix Is* Kiribati *see* **Manra**
223 M5 **Sydney Lake** *Ont.* Can.
225 I4 **Sydney Mines** *N.S.* Can.
Sydzhak Uzbek. *see* **Sijjaq**
137 R6 **Syedove** Ukr.
128 A2 **Syedra** *tourist site* Turkey
137 R5 **Syeverne** Ukr.
137 R5 **Syeverodonets'k** Ukr.
168 G5 **Syke** Ger.
198 D6 **Sykea** Greece
234 B6 **Sykesville** *MD* U.S.A.
232 G7 **Sykesville** *PA* U.S.A.
198 E2 **Sykia** Greece
140 I5 **Sykkylven** Norway
134 J3 **Syktyvkar** Rus. Fed.
231 D9 **Sylacauga** *AL* U.S.A.
117 M7 **Sylhet** Bangl.
117 M7 **Sylhet** *admin. div.* Bangl.
134 H3 **Syloga** Rus. Fed.
168 F1 **Sylt** *i.* Ger.
168 F1 **Sylt-Ost** Ger.
134 L4 **Sylva** *r.* Rus. Fed.
231 F8 **Sylva** *NC* U.S.A.
87 E7 **Sylvania** *W.A.* Austr.
231 G9 **Sylvania** *GA* U.S.A.
232 B7 **Sylvania** *OH* U.S.A.
222 H4 **Sylvan Lake** *Alta* Can.
173 L6 **Sylvensteinsee** *l.* Ger.
231 F10 **Sylvester** *GA* U.S.A.
84 E5 **Sylvester, Lake** *salt flat N.T.* Austr.
222 E3 **Sylvia, Mount** *B.C.* Can.
199 I6 **Symi** Greece
199 I6 **Symi** *i.* Greece
146 I11 **Symington** *South Lanarkshire, Scotland* U.K.
137 N9 **Synapne** Ukr.
92 D5 **Syndicate** *Masbate* Phil.
137 O5 **Synel'nykove** Ukr.
120 E6 **Syngyrli, Mys** *pt* Kazakh.
127 P2 **Syngyrli, Mys** *pt* Kazakh.
137 N3 **Synivka** Ukr.
131 N4 **Synnagyn, Khrebet** *mts* Rus. Fed.
141 J6 **Synnfjell** *mt.* Norway
86 H4 **Synnott, Mount** *hill W.A.* Austr.
86 H4 **Synnott Range** *hills W.A.* Austr.
150 D3 **Synod Inn** *Ceredigion, Wales* U.K.
134 L2 **Synya** Rus. Fed.
134 N2 **Synya** *r.* Rus. Fed.
136 J5 **Synytsya** *r.* Ukr.
136 J5 **Synyukha** *r.* Ukr.
Synzhera Moldova *see* **Sîngerei**
Synzherey Moldova *see* **Sîngerei**
235 H3 **Syosset** *NY* U.S.A.
263 C2 **Syowa** *research stn* Antarctica
175 J2 **Sypniewo** *Mazowieckie* Pol.
174 E2 **Sypniewo** *Wielkopolskie* Pol.
Syracusae *Sicilia* Italy *see* **Siracusa**
Syracuse *Sicilia* Italy *see* **Siracusa**
236 E6 **Syracuse** *KS* U.S.A.
233 I5 **Syracuse** *NY* U.S.A.
171 F9 **Syrau** Ger.
121 I4 **Syrdar'ya** *r.* Asia
Syrdar'ya Uzbek. *see* **Sirdaryo**
Syrdarya Oblast *admin. div.* Uzbek. *see* **Sirdaryo**
Syrdaryinskiy Uzbek. *see* **Sirdaryo**
173 I4 **Syrgenstein** Ger.
126 I6 **Syria** *country* Asia
Syrian Desert Asia *see* **Bādiyat ash Shām**
199 H6 **Syrna** *i.* Greece
139 N5 **Syrokvashino** Rus. Fed.
198 F5 **Syros** *i.* Greece
139 W9 **Syrskiy** Rus. Fed.
141 R6 **Sysmä** Fin.
134 J3 **Sysola** *r.* Rus. Fed.
139 T2 **Sysoyevo** Rus. Fed.
151 J2 **Syston** *Leicestershire, England* U.K.
136 I5 **Sytkivtsi** Ukr.
134 J4 **Syumsi** Rus. Fed.
134 K5 **Syun** *r.* Rus. Fed.
100 L3 **Syurkum** Rus. Fed.
100 L3 **Syurkum, Mys** *pt* Rus. Fed.
137 O8 **Syvash, Zatoka** *lag.* Ukr.
137 N7 **Syvas'ke** Ukr.
141 T6 **Syyspohja** Fin.
137 M8 **Syzivka** Ukr.
120 C1 **Syzran'** Rus. Fed.
177 H4 **Szabadbattyán** Hungary
177 H4 **Szabadegyháza** Hungary
Szabadka *Vojvodina* Serbia *see* **Subotica**
177 K5 **Szabadkígyós** Hungary
177 K5 **Szabadkígyósi** *park* Hungary
177 I5 **Szabadszállás** Hungary
177 L3 **Szabolcs-Szatmár-Bereg** *county* Hungary
174 G4 **Szadek** Pol.
175 I6 **Szaflary** Pol.
177 J4 **Szajol** Hungary
177 H5 **Szakcs** Hungary
177 I5 **Szakmár** Hungary
177 H4 **Szákszend** Hungary
177 K3 **Szalaszend** Hungary
177 I5 **Szalkszentmárton** Hungary
177 J3 **Szalonna** Hungary
174 F2 **Szamocin** Pol.
177 L3 **Szamos** *r.* Hungary
177 L3 **Szamosszeg** Hungary
174 E3 **Szamotuły** Pol.
177 J1 **Szaniecki Park Krajobrazowy** Pol.
177 I5 **Szank** Hungary
176 G4 **Szany** Hungary
177 H4 **Szár** Hungary
177 J5 **Szárazér-Porgányi-főcsatorna** *canal* Hungary
177 J5 **Szarvas** Hungary
177 J4 **Szászberek** Hungary
177 H5 **Szászvár** Hungary
177 L3 **Szatmár-Beregi** *park* Hungary
177 L3 **Szatmárcseke** Hungary
177 J5 **Szatymaz** Hungary
177 H4 **Százhalombatta** Hungary
174 D3 **Szczaniec** Pol.
175 K6 **Szczawne** Pol.
175 I6 **Szczawnica** Pol.
174 E5 **Szczawno-Zdrój** Pol.
175 K5 **Szczebrzeszyn** Pol.
174 C2 **Szczecin** Pol.
174 E2 **Szczecinek** Pol.
174 C2 **Szczeciński, Zalew** *b.* Pol.
174 D2 **Szczecińskie** *reg.* Pol.
170 K4 **Szczeciński Park Krajobrazowy** Pol.
175 H5 **Szczekociny** Pol.
175 J2 **Szczepankowo** Pol.
175 H4 **Szczerców** Pol.
175 J5 **Szczucin** Pol.
175 K2 **Szczuczyn** Pol.
175 I1 **Szczurkowo** Pol.
175 I5 **Szczurowa** Pol.
175 H6 **Szczyrk** Pol.
174 E5 **Szczytna** Pol.
174 G4 **Szczytniki** Pol.
175 I2 **Szczytno** Pol.
174 F2 **Szczytno, Jezioro** *l.* Pol.
Szechwan *prov.* China *see* **Sichuan**
177 I3 **Szécsény** Hungary
177 H5 **Szederkény** Hungary
177 H5 **Szedres** Hungary
177 J5 **Szeged** Hungary
177 K4 **Szeghalom** Hungary
177 J5 **Szegvár** Hungary
177 H4 **Székesfehérvár** Hungary
177 J5 **Székkutas** Hungary
177 H5 **Szekszárd** Hungary
175 I2 **Szeląg Wielki, Jezioro** *l.* Pol.
174 G1 **Szemud** Pol.
177 I4 **Szendehely** Hungary
177 J3 **Szendrő** Hungary
177 J3 **Szendrőlád** Hungary
177 I4 **Szentendre** Hungary
177 J5 **Szentes** Hungary
176 F5 **Szentgotthárd** Hungary
176 F5 **Szentgyörgyvölgyi** *park* Hungary
177 J4 **Szentistván** Hungary
177 I5 **Szentkirály** Hungary
177 G5 **Szentlászló** Hungary
177 I4 **Szentlőrinckáta** Hungary
177 I4 **Szentmártonkáta** Hungary
177 G5 **Szentőrinc** Hungary
176 F4 **Szentpéterfa** Hungary
177 K4 **Szentpéterszeg** Hungary
176 F5 **Szepetnek** Hungary
175 K3 **Szepietowo** Pol.
177 H5 **Szeremle** Hungary
177 K3 **Szerencs** Hungary
177 K4 **Szerep** Hungary
175 J6 **Szerzyny** Pol.
175 K1 **Szeska Góra** *hill* Pol.
175 J2 **Szestno** Pol.
177 H4 **Szigetbecse** Hungary
177 H4 **Szigethalom** Hungary
177 I4 **Szigetszentmiklós** Hungary
177 H4 **Szigetújfalu** Hungary
177 G5 **Szigetvár** Hungary
176 G5 **Szigliget** Hungary
177 J4 **Szihalom** Hungary
177 J3 **Szikszó** Hungary
176 G4 **Szil** Hungary
177 J3 **Szilvásvárad** Hungary
174 F4 **Szkaradowo** Pol.
174 D5 **Szklarska Poręba** Pol.
174 E4 **Szklary Górne** Pol.
175 K6 **Szkło** *r.* Pol.
175 J2 **Szkwa** *r.* Pol.
174 E4 **Szlichtyngowa** Pol.
177 H4 **Szob** Hungary
177 J3 **Szögliget** Hungary
177 J4 **Szolnok** Hungary
177 G5 **Szőlősgyörök** Hungary
176 F4 **Szombathely** Hungary
177 J4 **Szomolya** Hungary
175 K5 **Szówsko** Pol.
174 D4 **Szprotawa** Pol.
174 D4 **Szprotawa** *r.* Pol.
175 I5 **Szreniawa** *r.* Pol.
176 E1 **Szrenica** *mt.* Czech Rep.
175 I2 **Szreńsk** Pol.
175 H2 **Szropy** Pol.
175 L2 **Sztabin** Pol.
Sztálinváros Hungary *see* **Dunaújváros**
175 H2 **Sztum** Pol.
175 H1 **Sztutowo** Pol.
174 F2 **Szubin** Pol.
177 I4 **Szűcsi** Hungary
175 L2 **Szudziałowo** Pol.
177 I3 **Szügy** Hungary
177 J3 **Szuhogy** Hungary
175 K3 **Szulborze Wielkie** Pol.
175 K3 **Szumowo** Pol.
177 I4 **Szurdokpüspöki** Hungary
175 I4 **Szydłowiec** Pol.
175 I2 **Szydłowo** *Mazowieckie* Pol.
174 E2 **Szydłowo** *Wielkopolskie* Pol.
175 J2 **Szymonka** Pol.
174 F4 **Szymonków** Pol.
174 G4 **Szynkielów** Pol.
175 L1 **Szypliszki** Pol.

T

206 D5 **Taabo, Lac de** *l.* Côte d'Ivoire
210 D2 **Taagga Duudka** *reg.* Somalia
81 □3 **Taakoka** *i. Rarotonga* Cook Is
92 C4 **Taal, Lake** *Luzon* Phil.
128 D5 **Taalabaya** Lebanon
79 □9a **Taapuna** *Tahiti* Fr. Polynesia
142 I6 **Taastrup** Denmark
177 H5 **Tab** Hungary
137 M9 **Tabachne** Ukr.
92 D5 **Tabaco** *Luzon* Phil.
122 H3 **Tabādkān** Iran
124 F2 **Tābah** Saudi Arabia
253 E2 **Tabajara** Brazil
177 H4 **Tabajd** Hungary
205 E5 **Tabakat** *well* Mali
95 K9 **Tabanan** *Bali* Indon.
183 L4 **Tabanera de Cerrato** Spain
95 L4 **Tabang** *Kalimantan* Indon.
95 K4 **Tabang** *r.* Indon.
215 N6 **Tabankulu** S. Africa
Ţabaqah *Ar Raqqah* Syria *see* **Madīnat ath Thawrah**
126 I6 **Ţabaqah** *Ar Raqqah* Syria
247 □7 **Tabaquite** Trin. and Tob.
182 I5 **Tábara** Spain
91 L7 **Tabar Islands** P.N.G.
189 B7 **Tabarka** Tunisia
169 K9 **Tabarz** Ger.
122 G5 **Ţabas** *Khorāsān* Iran
122 I5 **Ţabas** *Khorāsān* Iran
138 H2 **Tabasalu** Estonia
244 E4 **Tabasco** Mex.
245 N8 **Tabasco** *state* Mex.
122 G6 **Tabāsin** Iran
122 D7 **Tābask, Kūh-e** *mt.* Iran
250 D6 **Tabatinga** *Amazonas* Brazil
256 C4 **Tabatinga** *São Paulo* Brazil
254 D4 **Tabatinga, Serra da** *hills* Brazil
105 I4 **Tabayama** Japan
96 B3 **Tabayin** Myanmar
92 C3 **Tabayoo, Mount** *Luzon* Phil.
177 I5 **Tabdi** Hungary
202 B6 **Tabédé** *well* Chad
204 E3 **Tabelbala** Alg.
223 H5 **Taber** *Alta* Can.
205 G2 **Taberdga** Alg.
143 K4 **Taberg** *hill* Sweden
185 O6 **Tabernas** Spain
Tabernes de Valldigna Spain *see* **Tavernes de la Valldigna**
185 O6 **Taberno** Spain
96 C2 **Tabet, Nam** *r.* Myanmar
209 B7 **Tabi** Angola
111 G11 **Tabia Tsaka** *salt l.* China
78 □3a **Tabik** *i. Kwajalein* Marshall Is
78 □3a **Tabik Channel** *Kwajalein* Marshall Is
208 F4 **Tabili** Dem. Rep. Congo
95 M2 **Tabin Wildlife Reserve** *nature res.* Malaysia
94 E5 **Tabir** *r.* Indon.
77 H2 **Tabiteuea** *atoll Gilbert Is* Kiribati
138 J3 **Tabivere** Estonia
92 D5 **Tablas** *i.* Phil.
260 B2 **Tablas, Cabo** *c.* Chile
185 L2 **Tablas de Daimiel, Parque Nacional de las** *nat. park* Spain
92 C5 **Tablas Strait** Phil.
217 □1c **Table, Pointe de la** *pt* Réunion
214 C9 **Table Bay** S. Africa
80 L6 **Table Cape** *North I.* N.Z.
115 M6 **Table Islands** *Andaman & Nicobar Is* India
214 C9 **Table Mountain** *hill* S. Africa
92 B6 **Table Point** *Palawan* Phil.
237 I7 **Table Rock Reservoir** *MO* U.S.A.
207 F5 **Tabligbo** Togo
185 K3 **Tablillas** *r.* Spain
182 E3 **Taboada** Spain
251 F5 **Taboca** Brazil
251 G5 **Tabocal** Brazil
251 F6 **Tabocal** *r.* Brazil
253 G4 **Tabocó** *r.* Brazil
96 C1 **Tabong** Myanmar
176 D2 **Tábor** Czech Rep.
211 B6 **Tabora** Tanz.
211 B6 **Tabora** *admin. reg.* Tanz.
177 I4 **Táborfalva** Hungary
123 M1 **Taboshar** Tajik.
261 H2 **Tabossi** Arg.
Tabost *Scotland* U.K. *see* **Harbost**
206 D5 **Tabou** Côte d'Ivoire
207 F2 **Tabrichat** *well* Mali
122 B2 **Tabrīz** Iran
182 D8 **Tábua** Port.
182 E6 **Tabuaço** Port.
267 I5 **Tabuaeran** *atoll* Kiribati
183 Q5 **Tabuenca** Spain
124 C1 **Tabūk** Saudi Arabia
124 C2 **Tabūk** *prov.* Saudi Arabia
83 N3 **Tabulam** *N.S.W.* Austr.
93 C4 **Tabulan** *Sulawesi* Indon.
121 R1 **Tabuny** Rus. Fed.
193 N5 **Taburno, Monte** *mt.* Italy
94 C4 **Tabuyung** *Sumatera* Indon.
78 □5 **Tabwémasana** *hill* Vanuatu
78 □5 **Tabwémasana, Mount** Vanuatu
143 O2 **Täby** Sweden
177 H4 **Tác** Hungary
251 H5 **Tacaipu, Serra** *hills* Brazil
251 H4 **Tacalé** Brazil
244 F6 **Tacámbaro** Mex.
243 M10 **Tacaná, Volcán de** *vol.* Mex.
242 □U13 **Tacarcuna, Cerro** *mt.* Panama
179 J7 **Tacen** Slovenia
110 G4 **Tachakou** *Xinjiang* China
207 F2 **Tachdaït** *well* Mali
110 F3 **Tacheng** *Xinjiang* China
173 N5 **Tacherting** Ger.
103 G14 **Tachibana-wan** *b.* Japan
222 E4 **Tachie** *B.C.* Can.
105 J4 **Tachikawa** *Tōkyō* Japan
102 Q8 **Tachikawa** *Yamagata* Japan
173 N6 **Tachinger See** *l.* Ger.
250 C2 **Táchira** *state* Venez.
202 A3 **Tachiumet** *well* Libya
176 B2 **Tachov** Czech Rep.
195 L6 **Tacina** *r.* Italy
93 B6 **Tacipi** *Sulawesi* Indon.
251 F6 **Taciuã, Lago** *l.* Brazil
92 E6 **Tacloban** *Leyte* Phil.
250 D5 **Tacna** Col.
252 C4 **Tacna** Peru
252 C4 **Tacna** *dept* Peru
241 S9 **Tacna** *AZ* U.S.A.
238 C3 **Tacoma** *WA* U.S.A.
226 D2 **Taconite Harbor** *MN* U.S.A.
258 E2 **Taco Pozo** Arg.
216 □3a **Tacoronte** *Tenerife* Canary Is
258 G3 **Tacuarembó** Uru.
261 J3 **Tacuarembó** *dept* Uru.
261 G4 **Tacuari** Arg.
242 E3 **Tacupeto** Mex.
174 F4 **Taczanów Drugi** Pol.
103 Q9 **Tadami** Japan
103 Q9 **Tadami-gawa** *r.* Japan
192 B7 **Tadasuni** *Sardegna* Italy
149 O6 **Tadcaster** *North Yorkshire, England* U.K.
205 G5 **Tadeinte, Oued** *watercourse* Alg.
207 G3 **Tadélaka** *well* Niger
205 F3 **Tademaït, Plateau du** Alg.
78 □5 **Tadin** *Îles Loyauté* New Caledonia
205 H4 **Tadjentourt** *hill* Alg.
205 F5 **Tadjeraout, Oued** *watercourse* Alg.
Tadjikistan *country* Asia *see* **Tajikistan**
205 F4 **Tadjmout** Alg.
210 D2 **Tadjoura, Golfe de** *g.* Djibouti
210 D2 **Tadjourah** Djibouti
205 F2 **Tadjrouna** Alg.
151 J5 **Tadley** *Hampshire, England* U.K.
128 G4 **Tadmur** Syria
250 B3 **Tadó** Col.
104 E5 **Tado** Japan
101 E11 **Tadohae Haesang National Park** S. Korea
223 L3 **Tadoule Lake** *Man.* Can.
225 G3 **Tadoussac** *Que.* Can.
114 E5 **Tadpatri** *Andhra Prad.* India
205 H4 **Tadrart** *hills* Alg.
202 A3 **Tadrart Acacus** *tourist site* Libya
114 E3 **Tadwale** *Mahar.* India
151 L5 **Tadworth** *Surrey, England* U.K.
Tadzhikabad Tajik. *see* **Tojikobod**
Tadzhikskaya S.S.R. *country* Asia *see* **Tajikistan**
101 E10 **T'aean Haean National Park** S. Korea
101 E9 **T'aebaek-sanmaek** *mts* N. Korea/S. Korea
138 G3 **Taebla** Estonia
Taech'ŏn S. Korea *see* **Poryŏng**
101 D10 **Taech'ŏng-do** *i.* S. Korea
101 D9 **Taedong-gang** *r.* N. Korea
101 D10 **Taedong-man** *b.* N. Korea
101 F11 **Taegu** S. Korea
101 D11 **Taehŭksan-kundo** *is* S. Korea
101 E10 **Taejŏn** S. Korea
101 E12 **Taejŏng** S. Korea
101 F10 **T'aepaek** S. Korea
107 Q3 **Ta'erqi** *Nei Mongol* China
138 K3 **Taevaskoja** Estonia
150 D4 **Taf** *r. Wales* U.K.
77 I3 **Tafahi** *i.* Tonga
183 Q3 **Tafalla** Spain
205 H5 **Tafassasset, Oued** *watercourse* Alg./Niger
247 □10 **Tafelberg** *hill Curaçao* Neth. Antilles
215 J7 **Tafelberg** S. Africa
214 F8 **Tafelberg** *mt.* S. Africa
251 G4 **Tafelberg** *mt.* Suriname
251 G4 **Tafelberg, Natuurreservaat** *nature res.* Suriname
190 C2 **Tafers** Switz.
150 F4 **Taff** *r. Wales* U.K.
150 F4 **Taff's Well** *Cardiff, Wales* U.K.
Tafila Jordan *see* **Aţ Ţafīlah**
216 □3f **Tafira** *Gran Canaria* Canary Is
206 D4 **Tafiré** Côte d'Ivoire
258 D2 **Tafi Viejo** Arg.
141 I5 **Tafjord** Norway
204 C3 **Tafraoute** Morocco
122 C4 **Tafresh** Iran
122 F6 **Taft** Iran
240 M6 **Taft** *CA* U.S.A.
123 I7 **Taftān, Kūh-e** *mt.* Iran
128 E3 **Taftanāz** Syria
234 E2 **Tafton** *PA* U.S.A.
115 M9 **Tafwap** *Andaman & Nicobar Is* India
104 D5 **Taga** Japan
78 □2 **Taga** Samoa
186 J3 **Taga** *mt.* Spain
123 L5 **Tagāb** Afgh.
203 F5 **Tagab** Sudan
102 R8 **Tagajō** Japan
206 E2 **Tagânet Keyna** *well* Mali
135 G7 **Taganrog** Rus. Fed.
137 R7 **Taganrog, Gulf of** Rus. Fed./Ukr.
Taganrogskiy Zaliv *b.* Rus. Fed./Ukr. *see* **Taganrog, Gulf of**
206 C2 **Tagant** *admin. reg.* Maur.
122 G2 **Tagarev, Gora** *mt.* Iran/Turkm.
96 C3 **Tagaung** Myanmar
103 H13 **Tagawa** Japan
135 I5 **Tagay** Rus. Fed.
207 G2 **Tagaza** *well* Niger
92 D7 **Tagbilaran** *Bohol* Phil.
111 F10 **Tagchagpu Ri** *mt. Xizang* China
Tagdempt Alg. *see* **Tiaret**
190 D8 **Taggia** Italy
206 E3 **Taghin-Dassouri** Burkina
Tâghira Moldova *see* **Ţighira**
204 D4 **Taghmanant** *well* Mali
222 C2 **Tagish** *Y.T.* Can.
222 C3 **Tagish Lake** *B.C.* Can.
193 K3 **Tagliacozzo** Italy
191 O4 **Tagliamento** *r.* Italy
192 C3 **Taglio-Isolaccio** *Corse* France
156 H5 **Tagnon** France
205 E5 **Tagnout Chagguerett** *well* Mali
105 J1 **Tagokura-ko** *resr* Japan
92 E7 **Tagoloan** *r. Mindanao* Phil.
187 I9 **Tagomago, Illa de** *i.* Spain
206 D2 **Tagourâret** *well* Maur.
122 H1 **Tagta** Turkm.
123 J4 **Tagtabazar** Turkm.
256 C1 **Taguatinga** *Minas Gerais* Brazil
254 D5 **Taguatinga** *Tocantins* Brazil
104 B7 **Taguchi-zaki** *pt* Japan
92 C3 **Tagudin** *Luzon* Phil.
207 H2 **Taguedoufat** *well* Niger
Taguenout Haggueret *well* Mali *see* **Tagnout Chagguerett**
77 F3 **Tagula Island** P.N.G.
92 E8 **Tagum** *Mindanao* Phil.
184 B3 **Tagus** *r.* Port./Spain *alt.* **Tajo (Spain),** *alt.* **Tejo (Portugal)**
204 B4 **Tah, Sabkhat** *salt pan* Morocco
107 S3 **Taha** *Heilong.* China
222 G5 **Tahaetkun Mountain** *B.C.* Can.
185 O6 **Tahal** Spain
94 E2 **Tahan, Gunung** *mt.* Malaysia
204 D3 **Tahanaoute** Morocco
79 □9 **Tahanea** *atoll Arch. des Tuamotu* Fr. Polynesia
Tahanroz'ka Zatoka *b.* Rus. Fed./Ukr. *see* **Taganrog, Gulf of**
104 F6 **Tahara** Japan
80 H2 **Taharoa, Lake** *North I.* N.Z.
79 □9a **Taharuu** *r. Tahiti* Fr. Polynesia
205 G5 **Tahat, Mont** *mt.* Alg.
Tahaurawe *i. HI* U.S.A. *see* **Kaho'olawe**
243 O7 **Tahdzibichén** Mex.
100 D2 **Tahe** *Heilong.* China
80 H2 **Taheke** *North I.* N.Z.
138 K3 **Tähemaa** Estonia
122 G8 **Tāherū'ī** Iran
205 G5 **Tahifet** Alg.
147 C9 **Tahilla** Ireland
106 E4 **Tahilt** Mongolia
79 □9a **Tahiti** *i.* Fr. Polynesia
177 I4 **Tahitótfalu** Hungary
138 F2 **Tahkuna nina** *pt* Estonia
123 J7 **Tahlab** *r.* Iran/Pak.
123 J7 **Tahlab, Dasht-i-** *plain* Pak.
237 H8 **Tahlequah** *OK* U.S.A.
222 D3 **Tahltan** *B.C.* Can.
240 L2 **Tahoe, Lake** *CA* U.S.A.
240 L2 **Tahoe City** *CA* U.S.A.
220 H3 **Tahoe Lake** *Nunavut* Can.
240 L2 **Tahoe Vista** *CA* U.S.A.
237 E9 **Tahoka** *TX* U.S.A.
80 I6 **Tahora** *North I.* N.Z.
80 K5 **Tahorakuri** *North I.* N.Z.
207 G3 **Tahoua** Niger
207 G3 **Tahoua** *dept* Niger
122 G7 **Tahrūd** Iran
122 H7 **Tahrūd** *r.* Iran
96 D4 **Ta Hsai** Myanmar
222 E5 **Tahsis** *B.C.* Can.
203 F3 **Ţahţā** Egypt
199 K3 **Tahtaköprü** Turkey
199 L6 **Tahtali Dağ** *mt.* Turkey
222 E4 **Tahtsa Peak** *B.C.* Can.
252 D4 **Tahua** Bol.
252 D2 **Tahuamanú** *r.* Bol.
252 C2 **Tahuamanú** Peru
79 □9 **Tahuata** *i.* Fr. Polynesia
93 D2 **Tahulandang** *i.* Indon.
93 D2 **Tahuna** *Sulawesi* Indon.
206 D5 **Taï** Côte d'Ivoire
206 D5 **Taï, Parc National de** *nat. park* Côte d'Ivoire
117 L6 **Taiabpur** *Bihar* India
109 □I7 **Tai A Chau** *i. H.K.* China
107 R6 **Tai'an** *Liaoning* China
107 O8 **Tai'an** *Shandong* China
79 □9a **Taiarapu, Presqu'île de** *pen. Tahiti* Fr. Polynesia
81 E12 **Taiaroa Head** *South I.* N.Z.
107 K8 **Taibai** *Gansu* China
107 J9 **Taibai** *Shaanxi* China
108 F2 **Taibai Shan** *mt. Shaanxi* China
Taibei Taiwan *see* **T'aipei**
205 G2 **Taïbet** Alg.
185 O4 **Taibilla** *r.* Spain
187 C12 **Taibilla, Canal del** Spain
187 A11 **Taibilla, Embalse de** *resr* Spain
185 O4 **Taibilla, Sierra de** *mts* Spain
216 □3e **Taibique** *El Hierro* Canary Is
191 M3 **Taibòn Agordino** Italy
Taibus Qi *Nei Mongol* China *see* **Baochang**
109 M6 **T'aichung** Taiwan
Taidong Taiwan *see* **T'aitung**
105 L4 **Taiei** Japan
81 E13 **Taieri** *r. South I.* N.Z.
81 E12 **Taieri Ridge** *South I.* N.Z.
Taigong *Guizhou* China *see* **Taijiang**
107 M8 **Taigu** *Shanxi* China
107 M8 **Taihang Shan** *mts* China
107 N7 **Taihang Shan** *mts* China
80 J6 **Taihape** *North I.* N.Z.
109 J2 **Taihe** *Anhui* China
Taihe *Guangdong* China *see* **Qingxin**
109 J5 **Taihe** *Jiangxi* China
Taihe *Sichuan* China *see* **Shehong**
Taihezhen *Sichuan* China *see* **Shehong**
102 □1 **Taiho** *Okinawa* Japan
109 □J7 **Tai Ho Wan** *H.K.* China
109 K3 **Taihu** *Anhui* China
109 M3 **Tai Hu** *l.* China
107 M7 **Taihuai** *Shanxi* China
103 M13 **Taiji** Japan
108 G5 **Taijiang** *Guizhou* China
107 S3 **Taikang** *Heilong.* China
107 N9 **Taikang** *Henan* China
102 U4 **Taiki** Japan
96 B6 **Taikkyi** Myanmar
104 B4 **Taiko-yama** *hill* Japan
93 D8 **Tailaco** East Timor
107 R3 **Tailai** *Heilong.* China
109 □J7 **Tai Lam Chung Shui Tong** *resr H.K.* China
94 C5 **Taileleo** Indon.
82 G6 **Tailem Bend** *S.A.* Austr.
109 □J7 **Tai Long Wan** *b. H.K.* China
Tailuge Taiwan *see* **T'ailuko**
109 M6 **T'ailuko** Taiwan
258 G4 **Taim** Brazil
123 J5 **Taimani** *reg.* Afgh.
109 □J7 **Tai Mo Shan** *hill H.K.* China
206 E4 **Tain** *r.* Ghana
146 H7 **Tain** *Highland, Scotland* U.K.
109 M7 **T'ainan** Taiwan
198 D6 **Tainaro, Akrotirio** *pt* Greece
160 C1 **Taingy** France
161 F6 **Tain-l'Hermitage** France
157 M7 **Taintrux** France
109 □I7 **Tai O** *H.K.* China
191 K3 **Taio** Italy
257 F1 **Taiobeiras** Brazil
93 B4 **Taipa** *Sulawesi* Indon.
80 H2 **Taipa** *North I.* N.Z.
109 □J7 **Tai Pak Wan** *b. H.K.* China
141 T6 **Taipalsaari** Fin.
109 M6 **T'aipei** Taiwan
109 I7 **Taiping** *Guangdong* China
Taiping *Guangdong* China *see* **Shixing**
Taiping *Guangxi* China *see* **Chongzuo**
108 H7 **Taiping** *Guangxi* China
94 D2 **Taiping** Malaysia
107 R4 **Taipingchuan** *Jilin* China
107 Q3 **Taiping Ling** *mt. Nei Mongol* China
109 □J7 **Tai Po** *H.K.* China
109 □J7 **Tai Po Hoi** *b. H.K.* China
Tai Poutini National Park *South I.* N.Z. *see* **Westland National Park**
254 G3 **Taipu** Brazil
117 O6 **Taipudia** *Arun. Prad.* India
107 N9 **Taiqian** *Henan* China
102 □1 **Taira** *Okinawa* Japan
104 E3 **Taira** *Toyama* Japan
102 R5 **Tairadate-kaikyō** *sea chan.* Japan
102 □G17 **Taira-jima** *i. Nansei-shotō* Japan
Tairbeart *Western Isles, Scotland* U.K. *see* **Tarbert**
97 D10 **Tai Rom Yen National Park** Thai.
80 J4 **Tairua** *North I.* N.Z.
122 A4 **Tairuq** Iran
94 E7 **Tais** *Sumatera* Indon.
102 Q4 **Taisei** Japan
102 T3 **Taisetsu-zan** *mts* Japan
105 J2 **Taishaku-san** *mt.* Japan
109 I7 **Taishan** *Guangdong* China
109 □J7 **Tai Shek Mo** *hill H.K.* China
105 L1 **Taishin** Japan
109 L5 **Taishun** *Zhejiang* China
109 □I7 **Tai Siu Mo To** *is H.K.* China
179 I3 **Taiskirchen im Innkreis** Austria
156 H5 **Taissy** France
211 C5 **Taita Hills** Kenya
94 D6 **Taitaitanopo** *i.* Indon.
109 □J7 **Tai Tan Hoi Hap** *inlet H.K.* China
81 G10 **Taitanu** *South I.* N.Z.
259 B7 **Taitao, Península de** *pen.* Chile
259 B7 **Taitao, Punta** *pt* Chile
210 B4 **Taiti** *mt.* Kenya
109 □J7 **Tai To Yan** *mt. H.K.* China
105 L5 **Taitō-zaki** *pt* Japan
109 M7 **T'aitung** Taiwan
109 □I7 **Tai Tung Shan** *hill H.K.* China
109 M7 **T'aitung Shan** *mts* Taiwan
140 T4 **Taivalkoski** Fin.
140 R2 **Taivaskero** *hill* Fin.
141 P6 **Taivassalo** Fin.
109 M7 **Taiwan** *country* Asia
Taiwan Haixia *str.* China/Taiwan *see* **Taiwan Strait**
Taiwan Shan *mts* Taiwan *see* **Chungyang Shanmo**
109 L7 **Taiwan Strait** China/Taiwan
Taixian *Jiangsu* China *see* **Jiangyan**
109 M2 **Taixing** *Jiangsu* China
Taïyetos Óros *mts* Greece *see* **Taygetos**
107 M8 **Taiyuan** *Shanxi* China
107 L8 **Taiyue Shan** *mts* China
160 F3 **Taizé** France
111 K11 **Taizhao** *Xizang* China
Taizhong Taiwan *see* **T'aichung**
109 L2 **Taizhou** *Jiangsu* China
109 M4 **Taizhou** *Zhejiang* China
109 M4 **Taizhou Liedao** *i.* China
109 M4 **Taizhou Wan** *b.* China
101 D8 **Taizi He** *r.* China
124 F9 **Ta'izz** Yemen
124 F9 **Ta'izz** *governorate* Yemen
123 M8 **Tajal** Pak.
94 □ **Tajam, Tanjong** *pt* Sing.
243 N10 **Tajamulco, Volcán de** *vol.* Guat.
202 B3 **Tajarḥī** Libya
95 G6 **Tajem, Gunung** *hill* Indon.
122 D7 **Tāj-e Malekī** Iran
183 O7 **Tajera, Embalse de la** *resr* Spain
205 H2 **Tajerouine** Tunisia
123 N2 **Tajikistan** *country* Asia
105 K1 **Tajima** Japan
104 F5 **Tajimi** Japan
104 B7 **Tajiri** Japan
242 C2 **Tajitos** Mex.
116 G6 **Taj Mahal** *tourist site Uttar Prad.* India
180 D1 **Tajo** *r.* Spain *alt.* **Tejo (Portugal),** *conv.* **Tagus**
117 P5 **Tajobum** *Arun. Prad.* India
185 O2 **Tajo-Segura, Canal de Trasvase** Spain
117 J7 **Tajpur** *Bihar* India
127 O6 **Tajrīsh** Iran
252 D5 **Tajsara, Cordillera de** *mts* Bol.
183 M8 **Tajuña** *r.* Spain
202 B1 **Tājūra** Libya
96 D6 **Tak** Thai.
122 B3 **Takāb** Iran
210 D4 **Takabba** Kenya
93 B7 **Taka'Bonerate, Kepulauan** *atolls* Indon.
93 B7 **Taka Bonerate, Taman Nasional** *nat. park* Indon.
176 G4 **Takácsi** Hungary
208 D2 **Takadja** C.A.R.
105 G4 **Takagi** Japan
105 M2 **Takahagi** Japan
104 E6 **Takahama** *Aichi* Japan
104 C5 **Takahama** *Fukui* Japan
104 F3 **Takahara-gawa** *r.* Japan
103 K12 **Takahashi** Japan
262 Q1 **Takahe, Mount** Antarctica
104 B6 **Takaishi** Japan
104 E1 **Takaiwa-misaki** *pt* Japan
81 G7 **Takaka** *South I.* N.Z.
116 F9 **Takal** *Madh. Prad.* India
208 C2 **Takalaou** Chad
211 C6 **Takaloi** *well* Tanz.
205 G5 **Takalous, Oued** *watercourse* Alg.
251 G3 **Takama** Guyana
217 □2b **Takamaka** *Mahé* Seychelles
104 E2 **Takamatsu** *Ishikawa* Japan
103 L12 **Takamatsu** *Kagawa* Japan
104 D7 **Takami-yama** *mt.* Japan
103 I14 **Takamori** *Kumamoto* Japan
105 G4 **Takamori** *Nagano* Japan
103 I14 **Takanabe** Japan
104 F3 **Takane** *Gifu* Japan
105 H4 **Takane** *Yamanashi* Japan
105 K2 **Takanezawa** Japan
102 R6 **Takanosu** Japan
104 F2 **Takaoka** Japan
80 K7 **Takapau** *North I.* N.Z.
80 M5 **Takapau** *North I.* N.Z.
80 I3 **Takapuna** *North I.* N.Z.
102 □G17 **Takara-jima** *i. Nansei-shotō* Japan
104 B6 **Takarazuka** Japan
104 A6 **Takasago** Japan
105 J3 **Takasaki** Japan
104 D5 **Takashima** Japan
104 E3 **Takashōzu-yama** *mt.* Japan
104 E4 **Takasu** Japan
105 H2 **Takasuma-yama** *mt.* Japan
105 M2 **Takasuzu-san** *hill* Japan
105 H4 **Takatō** Japan
212 E5 **Takatokwane** Botswana
104 E4 **Takatomi** Japan
104 C7 **Takatori** Japan
212 D4 **Takatshwaane** Botswana
104 C6 **Takatsuki** *Ōsaka* Japan
104 D5 **Takatsuki** *Shiga* Japan
103 J13 **Takatsuki-yama** *mt.* Japan
251 G4 **Takatu** *r.* Brazil/Guyana
211 C5 **Takaungu** Kenya
96 D4 **Ta-Kaw** Myanmar
104 F3 **Takayama** *Gifu* Japan
105 I2 **Takayama** *Gunma* Japan
105 I1 **Takayanagi** Japan
97 E11 **Tak Bai** Thai.
104 D4 **Takefu** Japan
103 J12 **Takehara** Japan
151 M4 **Takeley** *Essex, England* U.K.
94 B2 **Takengon** *Sumatera* Indon.
104 A4 **Takeno** Japan
Takeo Cambodia *see* **Takêv**
103 H13 **Takeo** Japan
143 K3 **Tåkern** *l.* Sweden
143 K3 **Tåkern naturreservat** *nature res.* Sweden
105 H3 **Takeshi** Japan
102 □H16 **Take-shima** *i.* Japan
Take-shima *i.* N. Pacific Ocean *see* **Liancourt Rocks**
122 C3 **Takestān** Iran
209 C5 **Taketa** Dem. Rep. Congo
103 I14 **Taketa** Japan
104 E6 **Taketoyo** Japan
97 G9 **Takêv** Cambodia
123 M2 **Takfon** Tajik.
127 L9 **Takhādīd** *well* Iraq
123 M3 **Takhār** *prov.* Afgh.
116 H8 **Takhatpur** *Chhattisgarh* India
181 G5 **Takhemaret** Alg.
Takhiatash Uzbek. *see* **Taxiatosh**
222 C2 **Takhini** *r. Y.T.* Can.
222 C2 **Takhini Hotspring** *Y.T.* Can.
96 E7 **Ta Khli** Thai.
97 G9 **Ta Khmau** Cambodia
135 H7 **Takhta** Rus. Fed.
Takhta Turkm. *see* **Tagta**
Takhta-Bazar Turkm. *see* **Tagtabazar**
121 L1 **Takhtabrod** Kazakh.
137 R9 **Takhtamukay** Rus. Fed.
Takhtamukayskiy Rus. Fed. *see* **Takhtamukay**
122 C5 **Takht Apān, Kūh-e** *mt.* Iran
122 E7 **Takhteh** Iran
123 K6 **Takhteh Pol** Afgh.
127 P9 **Takht-e Jamshīd** *tourist site* Iran
122 D3 **Takht-e Soleymān** *mt.* Iran
123 N6 **Takht-i-Sulaiman** *mt.* Pak.
104 E7 **Taki** *Mie* Japan
103 J11 **Taki** *Shimane* Japan
207 H3 **Takiéta** Niger
Takijuq Lake *Nunavut* Can. *see* **Napaktulik Lake**
102 S3 **Takikawa** Japan
104 A6 **Takino** Japan
102 U2 **Takinoue** Japan
205 H4 **Takisset, Oued** *watercourse* Alg./Libya
95 K6 **Takisung** *Kalimantan* Indon.
81 B12 **Takitimu Mountains** *South I.* N.Z.
129 J6 **Täklä** Azer.
129 J6 **Täklä** Azer.
222 E4 **Takla Lake** *B.C.* Can.
222 E4 **Takla Landing** *B.C.* Can.
Takla Makan *des.* China *see* **Taklimakan Shamo**
Taklimakan Desert China *see* **Taklimakan Shamo**
110 E7 **Taklimakan Shamo** *des.* China
105 L4 **Tako** Japan
123 M2 **Takob** Tajik.
206 E5 **Takoradi** Ghana
80 H2 **Takou Bay** *North I.* N.Z.
111 K12 **Takpa Shiri** *mt. Xizang* China
177 I4 **Taksony** Hungary
177 K4 **Takta** *r.* Hungary
177 K3 **Taktaharkány** Hungary
177 K3 **Taktakenéz** Hungary
222 C3 **Taku** *B.C.* Can.
220 E4 **Taku** *r.* Can./U.S.A.
103 H13 **Taku** Japan
78 □6 **Takuan, Mount** P.N.G.
97 D10 **Takua Pa** Thai.
97 D10 **Takua Thung** Thai.
207 H5 **Takum** Nigeria
209 C6 **Takundi** Dem. Rep. Congo
81 □2 **Takutea** *i.* Cook Is
77 F2 **Takuu Islands** P.N.G.
78 □6 **Takwa** *Malaita* Solomon Is
137 P8 **Takyl, Mys** *pt* Ukr.
116 E8 **Tal** *Madh. Prad.* India
123 O4 **Tal** Pak.
244 D5 **Tala** Mex.
258 G4 **Tala** Uru.
260 C2 **Talacasto** Arg.
138 M7 **Talachyn** Belarus
123 O5 **Talagang** Pak.
260 B3 **Talagante** Chile
187 H10 **Talaiassa** *hill* Spain
114 F8 **Talaimannar** Sri Lanka
161 B10 **Talairan** France
162 B5 **Talais** France
116 D9 **Talaja** *Gujarat* India
100 G3 **Talakan** *Amurskaya Oblast'* Rus. Fed.
100 H4 **Talakan** *Khabarovskiy Kray* Rus. Fed.
116 C9 **Talala** *Gujarat* India
137 M3 **Talalayivka** Ukr.
242 □R13 **Talamanca, Cordillera de** *mts* Costa Rica
183 Q5 **Talamantes** Spain
190 H3 **Talamona** Italy
192 G2 **Talamone** Italy
260 D1 **Talampaya, Parque Nacional** *nat. park* Arg.
192 C7 **Talana** *Sardegna* Italy
100 G4 **Talandzha** Rus. Fed.
94 D6 **Talang, Gunung** *vol.* Indon.
94 F6 **Talangbatu** *Sumatera* Indon.
94 F6 **Talangbetutu** *Sumatera* Indon.
261 F2 **Tala Norte** Arg.
160 G2 **Talant** France
117 O6 **Talap** *Assam* India
250 A6 **Talara** Peru
Talar-i-Band *mts* Pak. *see* **Makran Coast Range**
186 G3 **Talarn, Embassament de** *resr* Spain
185 I2 **Talarrubias** Spain
121 M5 **Talas** *r.* Kazakh./Kyrg.
121 O6 **Talas** Kyrg.
121 N6 **Talas** *admin. div.* Kyrg.
121 N6 **Talas Ala-Too** *mts* Kyrg.
91 L8 **Talasea** *New Britain* P.N.G.
139 P7 **Talashkino** Rus. Fed.
Talas Oblast *admin. div.* Kyrg. *see* **Talas**
Talas Range *mts* Kyrg. *see* **Talas Ala-Too**
Talasskaya Oblast' *admin. div.* Kyrg. *see* **Talas**
Talasskiy Alatau, Khrebet *mts* Kyrg. *see* **Talas Ala-Too**
93 B4 **Talatakoh** *i.* Indon.
128 D8 **Tal'at al Jamā'ah, Rujm** *mt.* Jordan
207 G3 **Talata-Mafara** Nigeria
128 E4 **Ţal'at Mūsá** *mt.* Lebanon/Syria
93 E1 **Talaud, Kepulauan** *is* Indon.
182 H9 **Talaván** Spain
185 P3 **Talave, Embalse de** *resr* Spain
183 K9 **Talavera de la Reina** Spain
184 F3 **Talavera la Real** Spain
84 H5 **Talawanta** *Qld* Austr.
96 C2 **Talawgyi** Myanmar
131 Q3 **Talaya** Rus. Fed.
92 E8 **Talayan** *Mindanao* Phil.
187 B12 **Talayón** *hill* Spain
182 I9 **Talayuela** Spain
187 C8 **Talayuelas** Spain
183 P9 **Talayuelo** *mt.* Spain
116 G7 **Talbehat** *Uttar Prad.* India
128 E4 **Talbīsah** Syria
87 I9 **Talbot, Mount** *hill W.A.* Austr.
234 C7 **Talbot County** *county MD* U.S.A.
221 K2 **Talbot Inlet** *Nunavut* Can.
223 L4 **Talbot Lake** *Man.* Can.
231 E9 **Talbotton** *GA* U.S.A.
83 L5 **Talbragar** *r. N.S.W.* Austr.
260 B4 **Talca** Chile
260 B3 **Talca, Punta** *pt* Chile
258 B5 **Talcahuano** Chile
260 A5 **Talcamávida** Chile
117 J9 **Talcher** *Orissa* India
100 D2 **Taldan** Rus. Fed.
139 U5 **Taldom** Rus. Fed.
121 O8 **Taldyk, Pereval** *pass* Kyrg.
121 R5 **Taldykorgan** Kazakh.
Taldy-Kurgan Kazakh. *see* **Taldykorgan**
Taldyqorghan Kazakh. *see* **Taldykorgan**
121 M3 **Taldysay** Kazakh.
Taldysu Kyrg. *see* **Taldy-Suu**
121 R6 **Taldy-Suu** Kyrg.
245 K8 **Talea de Castro** Mex.
114 D3 **Talegaon** *Mahar.* India
114 F2 **Talegaon** *Mahar.* India
122 C5 **Taleh Zang** Iran
116 F8 **Talen** *Madh. Prad.* India
163 C6 **Talence** France
215 M8 **Taleni** S. Africa
158 H5 **Talensac** France
187 E8 **Tales** Spain
Tālesh *Gīlān* Iran *see* **Hashtpar**
122 C3 **Tālesh** *Gīlān* Iran
139 T2 **Talets, Ozero** *l.* Rus. Fed.
86 E6 **Talga** *r. W.A.* Austr.
121 Q6 **Talgar** Kazakh.
121 Q6 **Talgar, Pik** *mt.* Kazakh.
150 D3 **Talgarreg** *Ceredigion, Wales* U.K.
150 F4 **Talgarth** *Powys, Wales* U.K.
203 G5 **Talguharai** Sudan
182 D7 **Talhadas** Port.
124 F7 **Ţalḥah** Saudi Arabia
82 E5 **Talia** *S.A.* Austr.
93 D4 **Taliabu** *i.* Indon.
161 I8 **Taliard** France
92 E6 **Talibon** *Bohol* Phil.
150 E3 **Taliesin** *Ceredigion, Wales* U.K.
184 E3 **Táliga** Spain
114 E4 **Talikota** *Karnataka* India
92 E8 **Talikud** *i.* Phil.
Talimardzhan Uzbek. *see* **Tollimarjon**
129 E5 **T'alin** Armenia
107 S3 **Talin Hiag** *Heilong.* China
204 D3 **Taliouine** Morocco
114 D6 **Taliparamba** *Kerala* India
210 A3 **Tali Post** Sudan
92 D6 **Talisay** *Cebu* Phil.
95 M4 **Talisayan** *Kalimantan* Indon.
92 E7 **Talisayan** *Mindanao* Phil.
129 J7 **Talış Dağları** *mts* Azer./Iran
93 D3 **Talisei** *i.* Indon.
146 D8 **Talisker** *Highland, Scotland* U.K.
260 E3 **Talita** Arg.
134 I4 **Talitsa** *Kostromskaya Oblast'* Rus. Fed.
139 V9 **Talitsa** *Lipetskaya Oblast'* Rus. Fed.
137 T1 **Talitskiy Chamlyk** Rus. Fed.
95 L9 **Taliwang** *Sumbawa* Indon.
138 L8 **Tal'ka** Belarus
168 K3 **Talkau** Ger.
191 L8 **Talla** Italy
82 D4 **Tallacootra, Lake** *salt flat S.A.* Austr.
146 F7 **Talladale** *Highland, Scotland* U.K.
231 D9 **Talladega** *AL* U.S.A.
127 K5 **Tall 'Afar** Iraq
147 J6 **Tallaght** Ireland
231 E10 **Tallahassee** *FL* U.S.A.
128 G2 **Tall al Aḥmar** Syria
83 K7 **Tallangatta** *Vic.* Austr.
147 I5 **Tallanstown** Ireland
231 D9 **Tallapoosa** *r. AL* U.S.A.
82 D3 **Tallaringa Conservation Park** *nature res. S.A.* Austr.
231 E9 **Tallassee** *AL* U.S.A.
203 H5 **Talla Talla Seghir Island** Sudan
127 J5 **Tall Baydar** Syria
163 B8 **Taller** France
87 C10 **Tallering Peak** *hill W.A.* Austr.
234 D5 **Talleyville** *DE* U.S.A.
138 H2 **Tallinn** Estonia
138 H2 **Tallinna laht** *b.* Estonia
128 E4 **Tall Kalakh** Syria
127 K5 **Tall Kayf** Iraq
127 K5 **Tall Kūjik** Syria
232 D7 **Tallmadge** *OH* U.S.A.
160 I5 **Talloires** France
192 D3 **Tallone** *Corse* France
182 C3 **Tallós** Spain
147 F8 **Tallow** Ireland
237 J9 **Tallulah** *LA* U.S.A.
127 K5 **Tall 'Uwaynāt** Iraq
Tallymerjen Uzbek. *see* **Tollimarjon**
197 M5 **Tălmaciu** Romania
234 C4 **Talmage** *PA* U.S.A.
160 G2 **Talmay** France
204 C3 **Talmest** Morocco
251 H4 **Talmiã** Brazil
146 H5 **Talmine** *Highland, Scotland* U.K.
162 C4 **Talmont** France
162 A3 **Talmont-St-Hilaire** France
136 J5 **Tal'ne** Ukr.
Tal'noye Ukr. *see* **Tal'ne**
116 D8 **Talod** *Gujarat* India
116 E9 **Taloda** *Mahar.* India
208 F2 **Talodi** Sudan
78 □1 **Talofofo** Guam
78 □1 **Talofofo Bay** Guam
237 F7 **Taloga** *OK* U.S.A.
123 K9 **Taloi Range** *mts* Pak.
225 H2 **Talon, Lac** *l. Que.* Can.
96 D4 **Ta-long** Myanmar
123 M3 **Tāloqān** Afgh.
192 C7 **Talora** *r. Sardegna* Italy
263 K2 **Talos Dome** *ice feature* Antarctica
96 F4 **Ta Loung San** *mt.* Laos
137 M5 **Talova Balka** Ukr.
120 D2 **Talovaya** Kazakh.
135 H6 **Talovaya** Rus. Fed.
129 H1 **Talovka** Rus. Fed.
221 I3 **Taloyoak** *Nunavut* Can.
244 C5 **Talpa** Mex.
123 O4 **Tal Pass** Pak.
207 H3 **Talras** *well* Niger
195 M3 **Talsano** Italy
106 E4 **Talshand** Mongolia
138 F4 **Talsi** Latvia
122 I7 **Tal Sīyāh** Iran
171 K8 **Talsperre Quitzdorf Kollmer Höhen** *park* Ger.
258 C2 **Taltal** Chile
223 H2 **Taltson** *r. N.W.T.* Can.
175 J2 **Tałty, Jezioro** *l.* Pol.
111 L11 **Talu** *Xizang* China
94 C4 **Talu** *Sumatera* Indon.
93 C3 **Taludaa** *Sulawesi* Indon.
93 F5 **Taluti, Teluk** *b. Seram* Indon.
191 K3 **Talvera** *r.* Italy
140 Q1 **Talvik** Norway
83 L3 **Talwood** *Qld* Austr.
135 H6 **Taly** Rus. Fed.
136 J5 **Tal'yanky** Ukr.
83 I5 **Talyawalka** *r. N.S.W.* Austr.
Talyshskiye Gory *mts* Azer./Iran *see* **Talış Dağları**
134 K2 **Talyy** Rus. Fed.
105 J4 **Tama** Japan
183 K2 **Tama** Spain
95 K3 **Tama Abu, Banjaran** *mts* Malaysia
Tamabo Range *mts* Malaysia *see* **Tama Abu, Banjaran**
96 B3 **Tamadaw** Myanmar
105 K4 **Tama-gawa** *r.* Japan
102 □1 **Tamagusuku** *Okinawa* Japan
96 D1 **Tamai, Nam** *r.* Myanmar
183 N6 **Tamajón** Spain
81 □4 **Tamakautoga** Niue
105 L1 **Tamakawa** Japan
104 E7 **Tamaki** Japan
80 I3 **Tamaki Strait** *North I.* N.Z.
87 B9 **Tamala** *W.A.* Austr.
135 H5 **Tamala** Rus. Fed.
250 C2 **Tamalameque** Col.
206 E4 **Tamale** Ghana
207 F3 **Tamalelt** *well* Mali
95 J5 **Tamalung** *Kalimantan* Indon.
182 H7 **Tamames** Spain
105 J3 **Tamamura** Japan
103 H14 **Tamana** Japan
77 H2 **Tamana** *i. Gilbert Is* Kiribati
204 C3 **Tamanar** Morocco
261 H6 **Tamangueyú** Arg.
202 B3 **Tamanhint** Libya
206 D3 **Tamani** Mali
94 E2 **Taman Negara National Park** Malaysia
103 K12 **Tamano** Japan
205 G5 **Tamanrasset** Alg.
205 F5 **Tamanrasset, Oued** *watercourse* Alg.
96 B2 **Tamanthi** Myanmar
245 H4 **Tamapatz** Mex.
234 D3 **Tamaqua** *PA* U.S.A.
117 J8 **Tamar** *Jharkhand* India
Tamar Syria *see* **Tadmur**
150 D7 **Tamar** *r. England* U.K.
207 F2 **Tamaradant** *well* Mali
103 I14 **Tamarai** Japan
105 L3 **Tamari** Japan
217 □1b **Tamarin** Mauritius
247 L9 **Tamarindo** Venez.
186 F4 **Tamarite de Litera** Spain
252 C4 **Tamarugal, Pampa de** *plain* Chile
213 E4 **Tamasane** Botswana
207 G2 **Tamasgoï** *well* Niger
175 L4 **Tamashowka** Belarus
177 H5 **Tamási** Hungary
197 P4 **Tamași** Romania
245 H4 **Tamasopo** Mex.
Tamatave Madag. *see* **Toamasina**
105 L3 **Tamatsukuri** Japan
245 H3 **Tamaulipas** *state* Mex.
245 I2 **Tamaulipas, Sierra de** *mts* Mex.
210 C3 **Tama Wildlife Reserve** *nature res.* Eth.
102 S7 **Tamayama** Japan
242 F5 **Tamazula** *Durango* Mex.
244 D6 **Tamazula** *Jalisco* Mex.
245 J8 **Tamazulápam** Mex.
245 I4 **Tamazunchale** Mex.
Tamba Japan *see* **Tanba**

Tambach to Tavankut
395

210 B4 Tambach Kenya
169 K9 Tambach-Dietharz Ger.
206 B3 Tambacounda Senegal
Tamba-kōchi plat. Japan see Tanba-kōchi
93 B7 Tambalongang i. Indon.
95 I5 Tambangmunjul Kalimantan Indon.
94 E6 Tambangsawah Sumatera Indon.
215 P2 Tambankulu Swaziland
207 F3 Tambao Burkina
206 C3 Tambaoura, Falaise de esc. Mali
251 F6 Tambaqui Brazil
213 G3 Tambara Moz.
83 L4 Tambar Springs N.S.W. Austr.
256 D4 Tambau Brazil
207 G3 Tambawel Nigeria
93 B6 Tambea Sulawesi Indon.
94 G4 Tambelan, Kepulauan is Indon.
95 G4 Tambelan Besar i. Indon.
87 D13 Tambellup W.A. Austr.
260 C2 Tamberías Arg.
95 J8 Tamberu Jawa Indon.
260 C3 Tambillo, Cerro mt. Arg.
95 M2 Tambisan Sabah Malaysia
85 K8 Tambo Qld Austr.
83 K7 Tambo r. Vic. Austr.
252 C4 Tambo r. Peru
252 B3 Tambobamba Peru
252 A3 Tambo de Mora Peru
250 A6 Tambo Grande Peru
213 □I3 Tambohorano Madag.
93 B5 Tamboli Sulawesi Indon.
252 C3 Tambopata r. Peru
209 B9 Tambor Angola
242 G5 Tambor Mex.
95 L9 Tambora, Gunung vol. Sumbawa Indon.
261 I2 Tambores Uru.
254 E3 Tamboril Brazil
250 C5 Tamboryacu r. Peru
208 E3 Tamboura C.A.R.
135 H5 Tambov Rus. Fed.
129 E4 Tambovka Georgia
100 F3 Tambovka Rus. Fed.
Tambov Oblast admin. div. Rus. Fed. see Tambovskaya Oblast'
135 H5 Tambovskaya Oblast' admin. div. Rus. Fed.
182 C3 Tambre r. Spain
93 A3 Tambu, Teluk b. Indon.
95 M5 Tambulan Sulawesi Indon.
95 L2 Tambulanan, Bukit hill Malaysia
95 L2 Tambunan Sabah Malaysia
208 E3 Tambura Sudan
95 L1 Tambuyukon, Gunung mt. Malaysia
206 C2 Tâmchekkeṭ Maur.
120 G3 Tamdy Kazakh.
Tamdybulak Uzbek. see Tomdibuloq
250 D3 Tame Col.
182 D6 Tâmega r. Port.
259 C8 Tamel Aike Arg.
198 F5 Tamelos, Akrotirio pt Kea Greece
Tamenghest Alg. see Tamanrasset
117 N7 Tamenglong Manipur India
Tamerlanovka Kazakh. see Temirlanovka
207 G2 Tamesna reg. Niger
207 H2 Tamgak, Adrar mt. Niger
206 B3 Tamgué, Massif du mt. Guinea
116 G8 Tamia Madh. Prad. India
245 J4 Tamiahua Mex.
245 J4 Tamiahua, Laguna de lag. Mex.
231 G13 Tamiami Canal FL U.S.A.
94 C2 Tamiang r. Indon.
94 C2 Tamiang, Ujung pt Indon.
114 F7 Tamil Nadu state India
234 E2 Tamiment PA U.S.A.
95 K6 Taminglayang Kalimantan Indon.
190 G2 Tamins Switz.
106 H3 Tamirin Gol r. Mongolia
196 I6 Tamiš r. Serbia
254 B5 Tamitatoala r. Brazil
134 G2 Tamitsa Rus. Fed.
203 F2 Ţāmīyah Egypt
124 F3 Tamīyah, Jabal hill Saudi Arabia
207 H1 Tamjit well Niger
120 J3 Tamkamys Kazakh.
117 J6 Tamkuhi Uttar Prad. India
96 I7 Tam Ky Vietnam
204 E2 Tamlelt, Plaine de plain Morocco
117 K8 Tamluk W. Bengal India
172 G4 Tamm Ger.
193 N5 Tammaro r. Italy
223 K1 Tammarvi r. Nunavut Can.
138 G1 Tammela Etelä-Suomi Fin.
140 U4 Tammela Oulu Fin.
168 G1 Tammensiel Ger.
Tammerfors Fin. see Tampere
138 K1 Tammio i. Fin.
Tammisaaren Saariston Kansallispuisto nat. park Fin. see Ekenäskärgårds nationalpark
Tammisaari Fin. see Ekenäs
138 K3 Tammispää Estonia
143 N1 Tämnaren l. Sweden
196 I6 Tamnava r. Serbia
160 D2 Tamnay-en-Bazois France
182 E2 Támoga r. Spain
207 F3 Tamou Niger
207 F3 Tamou, Réserve Totale de Faune de nature res. Niger
231 F12 Tampa FL U.S.A.
231 F12 Tampa Bay FL U.S.A.
245 I4 Tampacán Mex.
245 I4 Tampamolón Mex.
94 F7 Tampang Sumatera Indon.
141 Q6 Tampere Fin.
245 J3 Tampico Mex.
245 J3 Tampico el Alto Mex.
94 E3 Tampin Malaysia
94 □ Tampines Sing.
94 □ Tampines, Sungai r. Sing.
93 C6 Tampo Sulawesi Indon.
97 I7 Tam Quan Vietnam
124 G5 Tamrah Saudi Arabia
107 O3 Tamsagbulag Mongolia
106 H6 Tamsag Muchang Nei Mongol China
138 J2 Tamsalu Estonia
250 C6 Tamshiyacu Peru
179 I5 Tamsweg Austria
96 B2 Tamu Myanmar
245 I4 Tamuín Mex.
78 □1 Tamuning Guam
117 K6 Tamur r. Nepal
185 J3 Tamurejo Spain
78 □4b Tamworohi Pohnpei Micronesia
83 M4 Tamworth N.S.W. Austr.
149 N8 Tamworth Staffordshire, England U.K.
121 Q3 Tan Kazakh.
Tana r. Fin./Norway see Tenojoki
210 D5 Tana r. Kenya
Tana Madag. see Antananarivo
Tana i. Vanuatu see Tanna
Tana, Lake Eth. see T'ana Hāyk'
103 M13 Tanabe Japan
256 C4 Tanabi Brazil
140 T1 Tana Bru Norway
140 T1 Tanafjorden inlet Norway
220 A4 Tanaga vol. AK U.S.A.
220 A4 Tanaga Island AK U.S.A.
193 O6 Tanagro r. Italy
105 L1 Tanagura Japan
95 H8 Tanah, Tanjung pt Indon.
210 C2 T'ana Hāyk' l. Eth.
94 C5 Tanahbala i. Indon.
95 L5 Tanahgrogot Kalimantan Indon.
93 B7 Tanahjampea i. Indon.
94 C5 Tanahmasa i. Indon.
95 L3 Tanahmerah Kalimantan Indon.
94 E2 Tanah Merah Malaysia
94 D4 Tanahputih Sumatera Indon.
94 D2 Tanah Rata Malaysia
93 A6 Tanakeke i. Indon.
116 H5 Tanakpur Uttaranchal India
93 A5 Tanambung Sulawesi Barat Indon.
84 B5 Tanami N.T. Austr.
84 C5 Tanami Desert N.T. Austr.
84 B6 Tanami Downs Aboriginal Land res. N.T. Austr.
97 H9 Tân An Vietnam
220 C3 Tanana AK U.S.A.
Tananarive Madag. see Antananarivo
213 □I4 Tanandava Madag.
125 I2 Tanāqīb, Ra's pt Saudi Arabia
190 F5 Tanaro r. Italy
150 F2 Tanat r. Wales U.K.
92 E6 Tanauan Leyte Phil.
192 D6 Tanaunella Sardegna Italy
79 □7a Tanavuso Point Viti Levu Fiji
104 B5 Tanba Japan
104 B5 Tanba-kōchi plat. Japan
85 H8 Tanbar Qld Austr.
107 P9 Tanbu Shandong China
159 L3 Tancarville France
Tancheng Fujian China see Pingtan
107 P9 Tancheng Shandong China
101 F8 Tanch'ŏn N. Korea
244 E6 Tancítaro Mex.
244 E6 Tancítaro, Cerro de mt. Mex.
245 N8 Tancochapa r. Mex.
206 E5 Tanda Côte d'Ivoire
116 E4 Tanda Punjab India
116 G5 Tanda Uttar Prad. India
117 I6 Tanda Uttar Prad. India
141 L6 Tandådalen Sweden
92 F7 Tandag Mindanao Phil.
197 P6 Ţăndărei Romania
209 C9 Tandaué Angola
95 L1 Tandek Sabah Malaysia
173 K5 Tandern Ger.
116 F3 Tandi Hima. Prad. India
261 H5 Tandil Arg.
261 H5 Tandil, Sierra del hills Arg.
208 C2 Tandjilé pref. Chad
123 M9 Tando Adam Pak.
123 M9 Tando Alahyar Pak.
123 M9 Tando Bago Pak.
123 M9 Tando Muhammmad Khan Pak.
83 I5 Tandou Lake imp. l. N.S.W. Austr.
147 J4 Tandragee Northern Ireland U.K.
141 M6 Tandsjöborg Sweden
92 C9 Tandubatu i. Phil.
116 H9 Tandula r. India
114 E4 Tandur Andhra Prad. India
114 F3 Tandur Andhra Prad. India
123 L7 Tanduri Pak.
80 K5 Taneatua North I. N.Z.
102 □H16 Tanega-shima i. Japan
102 S6 Taneichi Japan
96 D5 Tanen Taunggyi mts Thai.
93 E4 Taneti i. Maluku Indon.
175 K5 Tanew r. Pol.
234 A5 Taneytown MD U.S.A.
205 E5 Tanezrouft reg. Alg./Mali
205 E5 Tanezrouft Tan-Ahenet reg. Alg.
128 G5 Ţanf, Jabal aţ hill Syria
122 H9 Tang Iran
148 B6 Tang Ireland
122 H9 Tang, Ra's-e pt Iran
107 L1 Tanga Rus. Fed.
211 C6 Tanga Tanz.
211 C6 Tanga admin. reg. Tanz.
80 I3 Tangaehe North I. N.Z.
117 L7 Tangail Bangl.
213 □J4 Tangainony Madag.
91 L7 Tanga Islands P.N.G.
114 G9 Tangalla Sri Lanka
244 E6 Tangamandapio Mex.
244 E6 Tangancícuaro de Arista Mex.
Tanganyika country Africa see Tanzania
211 A6 Tanganyika, Lake Africa
122 F3 Tangar Iran
255 C8 Tangará Brazil
78 □6 Tangarare Guadalcanal Solomon Is
208 C2 Tangaray Chad
114 E8 Tangasseri Kerala India
108 D5 Tangdan Yunnan China
111 K11 Tangdê Xizang China
Tangdukou Hunan China see Shaoyang
127 P9 Tang-e Kalleh Iran
122 F3 Tangeli Iran
142 H1 Tangen Norway
263 D2 Tange Promontory hd Antarctica
204 D2 Tanger Morocco
180 D5 Tanger prov. Morocco
94 G8 Tangerang Jawa Indon.
171 E6 Tangerhütte Ger.
170 E5 Tangermünde Ger.
180 D5 Tanger-Tétouan prov. Morocco
122 H8 Tang-e Sarkheh Iran
106 F8 Tanggarma Qinghai China
111 J11 Tanggo Xizang China
108 D2 Tanggor Sichuan China
107 O7 Tanggu Tianjin China
106 C9 Tanggulashan Qinghai China
111 J10 Tanggula Shan mt. Qinghai/Xizang China
111 I10 Tanggula Shan mts Xizang China
111 J10 Tanggula Shankou pass Xizang China
111 G12 Tangguo Xizang China
107 O7 Tanghai Hebei China
109 I2 Tanghe Henan China
109 I2 Tang He r. China
123 N4 Tangi Pak.
Tangier Morocco see Tanger
233 I11 Tangier Island VA U.S.A.
80 J7 Tangimoana North I. N.Z.
93 B5 Tangkelemboko, Gunung mt. Indon.
94 F7 Tangkittebak, Gunung mt. Indon.
111 I13 Tang La pass Xizang China
96 A1 Tangla Assam India
108 B2 Tanglag Qinghai China
94 □ Tanglin Sing.
111 L11 Tangmai Xizang China
106 G9 Tangnag Qinghai China
104 B4 Tango Japan
85 J6 Tangorin Qld Austr.
111 H11 Tangra Yumco salt l. China
94 A2 Tangse Sumatera Indon.
Tangshan Guizhou China see Shiqian
107 P7 Tangshan Hebei China
168 J3 Tangstedt Ger.
Tangsyq Kazakh. see Tansyk
96 C3 Tangte mt. Myanmar
92 D7 Tangub Mindanao Phil.
92 D6 Tangub Negros Phil.
207 F4 Tanguieta Benin
108 H5 Tangwan Hunan China
100 F4 Tangwanghe Heilong. China
100 F5 Tangwang He r. China
107 N7 Tangxian Hebei China
109 I3 Tangxianzhen Hubei China
96 D3 Tang-yan Myanmar
108 G4 Tangyan He r. China
107 N9 Tangyin Henan China
100 F5 Tangyuan Heilong. China
254 E5 Tanhaçu Brazil
140 S3 Tanhua Fin.
245 J4 Tanhuijo, Arrecife rf Mex.
97 G9 Tani Cambodia
108 A3 Taniantaweng Shan mts Xizang China
105 I2 Tanigawa-dake mt. Japan
104 E4 Tanigumi Japan
91 H8 Tanimbar, Kepulauan is Indon.
160 J4 Taninges France
Taninthari Myanmar see Tenasserim
Tanintharyi Myanmar see Tenasserim
Tanintharyi admin. div. Myanmar see Tenasserim
Taninthayi Myanmar see Tenasserim
93 F5 Taniwel Seram Indon.
103 H15 Taniyama Japan
Tanjah Morocco see Tanger
92 D7 Tanjay Negros Phil.
106 H8 Tanjiajing Gansu China
Tanjore Tamil Nadu India see Thanjavur
95 K6 Tanjung Kalimantan Indon.
94 F5 Tanjung Sumatera Indon.
94 C3 Tanjungbalai Sumatera Indon.
94 E4 Tanjungbalai Sumatera Indon.
93 E5 Tanjungbaliha Maluku Indon.
95 M3 Tanjungbatu Kalimantan Indon.
94 E4 Tanjungbatu Sumatera Indon.
95 M4 Tanjungbuayabuaya, Pulau i. Indon.
94 E6 Tanjungenim Sumatera Indon.
95 L6 Tanjunggaru Kalimantan Indon.
Tanjungkarang-Telukbetung Sumatera Indon. see Bandar Lampung
95 G6 Tanjungpandan Indon.
94 F4 Tanjungpinang Indon.
94 C3 Tanjungpura Sumatera Indon.
95 J6 Tanjung Puting, Taman Nasional nat. park Indon.
94 F6 Tanjungraja Sumatera Indon.
95 L3 Tanjungredeb Kalimantan Indon.
95 H5 Tanjungsaleh i. Indon.
95 H5 Tanjungsatai Kalimantan Indon.
95 L3 Tanjungselor Kalimantan Indon.
123 N5 Tank Pak.
116 C8 Tankara Gujarat India
140 S2 Tankavaara Fin.
116 D9 Tankhala Gujarat India
106 I1 Tankhoy Rus. Fed.
116 G2 Tanktse Jammu and Kashmir
214 D8 Tankwa r. S. Africa
214 D8 Tankwa-Karoo National Park S. Africa
245 H4 Tanlacut Mex.
245 I4 Tanlajas Mex.
156 H8 Tanlay France
96 B5 Tanlwe r. Myanmar
173 N5 Tann Ger.
169 J9 Tann (Rhon) Ger.
171 E10 Tanna Ger.
78 □5 Tanna i. Vanuatu
146 K9 Tannadice Angus, Scotland U.K.
104 B5 Tannan Japan
141 L5 Tännäs Sweden
160 D2 Tannay Bourgogne France
157 I4 Tannay Champagne-Ardenne France
169 K7 Tanne Ger.
Tannenberg Pol. see Stębark
222 G5 Tanner, Mount B.C. Can.
161 J9 Tanneron France
234 E2 Tannersville PA U.S.A.
173 M2 Tännesberg Ger.
173 I4 Tannhausen Ger.
178 C5 Tannheim Austria
173 I6 Tannheim Ger.
178 B4 Tannheimer Gebirge mts Austria/Ger.
140 R4 Tannila Fin.
142 G4 Tannis Bugt b. Denmark
Tannoa i. Vanuatu see Tongoa
171 D9 Tannroda Ger.
85 M7 Tannum Sands Qld Austr.
106 B1 Tannu-Ola, Khrebet mts Rus. Fed.
Tannu Tuva aut. rep. Rus. Fed. see Tyva, Respublika
103 I15 Tano Japan
92 D7 Tañon Strait Phil.
116 C6 Tanot Rajasthan India
207 H3 Tanout Niger
174 C2 Tanowo Pol.
245 I4 Tanquian Mex.
117 I6 Tansen Nepal
109 M6 Tanshui Taiwan
206 D3 Tansilla Burkina
149 N7 Tansley Derbyshire, England U.K.
121 R4 Tansyk Kazakh.
203 F2 Ţanţā Egypt
96 C5 Tantabin Pegu Myanmar
96 B3 Tantabin Sagaing Myanmar
96 B6 Tantabin Yangôn Myanmar
204 C3 Tan-Tan Morocco
82 H7 Tantanoola S.A. Austr.
104 A5 Tantō Japan
157 L7 Tantonville France
170 J4 Tantow Ger.
245 I4 Tantoyuca Mex.
116 F6 Tantpur Uttar Prad. India
107 R3 Tantu Jilin China
114 G4 Tanuku Andhra Prad. India
105 K3 Tanuma Japan
84 E4 Tanumbirini N.T. Austr.
142 H3 Tanumshede Sweden
176 E1 Tanvald Czech Rep.
204 B5 Tanwakka, Sabkhat well Western Sahara
96 I3 Tanxu Guangxi China
137 R4 Tanyushivka Ukr.
211 B6 Tanzania country Africa
105 J5 Tanzawa-Ōyama Kokutei-kōen park Japan
222 D3 Tanzilla r. B.C. Can.
216 □3c Tao Lanzarote Canary Is
97 D9 Tao, Ko i. Thai.
Tao'an Jilin China see Taonan
Taobh Tuath Western Isles, Scotland U.K. see Northton
Taocheng Fujian China see Yongchun
Taocheng Guangdong China see Daxin
109 H6 Taochuan Hunan China
107 Q8 Taocun Shandong China
Taodeni Mali see Taoudenni
107 R4 Tao'er He r. China
106 H9 Tao He r. China
Taohong Hunan China see Longhui
Taohuajiang Hunan China see Taojiang
Taohuaping Hunan China see Longhui
109 I4 Taojiang Hunan China
Taolanaro Madag. see Tôlañaro
106 J7 Taole Ningxia China
107 R4 Taonan Jilin China
195 I8 Taormina Sicilia Italy
239 L8 Taos NM U.S.A.
207 F2 Taouârdeï well Mali
204 E5 Taoudenni Mali
204 D2 Taounate Morocco
205 E5 Taounnant well Mali
204 E2 Taourirt Morocco
204 D3 Taouz Morocco
109 K6 Taoxi Fujian China
Taoyang Gansu China see Lintao
109 H4 Taoyuan Hunan China
109 M6 T'aoyüan Taiwan
Taozhou Anhui China see Guangde
138 I2 Tapa Estonia
92 C9 Tapaan Passage Phil.
243 M10 Tapachula Mex.
78 □2 Tapaga Point Samoa
94 D2 Tapah Malaysia
251 H5 Tapajós r. Brazil
94 B3 Tapaktuan Sumatera Indon.
244 D6 Tapalpa Mex.
261 G5 Tapalqué Arg.
94 D6 Tapan Sumatera Indon.
Tapan Turkey see Mansurlu
251 H3 Tapanahoni r. Suriname
245 M9 Tapanatepec Mex.
94 C4 Tapanuli, Teluk b. Indon.
251 H5 Tapará, Ilha Grande do i. Brazil
251 H5 Tapara, Serra do hills Brazil
93 E4 Tapat i. Maluku Indon.
251 E6 Tapauá Brazil
251 E6 Tapauá r. Brazil
81 G8 Tapawera South I. N.Z.
255 B9 Tapera Rio Grande do Sul Brazil
251 F5 Tapera Roraima Brazil
259 C7 Tapera Chile
253 E3 Tapera Pesoe Brazil
254 F5 Taperoá Brazil
255 C9 Tapes Brazil
206 C5 Tapeta Liberia
173 J4 Tapfheim Ger.
116 D9 Tapi r. India
97 D10 Ta Pi, Mae Nam r. Thai.
253 F4 Tapia, Sierra de hills Bol.
182 G1 Tapia de Casariego Spain
259 C8 Tapi Aike Arg.
92 D8 Tapiantana i. Phil.
Tapiau Rus. Fed. see Gvardeysk
250 C6 Tapiche r. Peru
243 M9 Tapijulapa Mex.
95 I5 Tapinbini Kalimantan Indon.
177 J4 Tápió r. Hungary
177 I4 Tápióbicske Hungary
256 D2 Tapiocanga, Chapada do hills Brazil
177 I4 Tápiógyörgye Hungary
177 I4 Tápióság Hungary
177 I4 Tápiószecső Hungary
177 I4 Tápiószele Hungary
177 I4 Tápiószőlős Hungary
256 D3 Tapira Minas Gerais Brazil
256 A5 Tapira Paraná Brazil
254 D5 Tapiracanga Brazil
256 D5 Tapiraí Brazil
253 H2 Tapirapé r. Brazil
251 E4 Tapirapecó, Sierra mts Brazil/Venez.
253 F3 Tapirapuã Brazil
94 E2 Tapis, Gunung mt. Malaysia
242 E4 Tapisuelas Mex.
176 F4 Táplánszentkereszt Hungary
117 K6 Taplejung Nepal
109 □J7 Tap Mun Chau i. H.K. China
207 F3 Tapoa watercourse Burkina
208 B2 Tapol Chad
176 G5 Tapolca Hungary
96 D4 Ta-pom Myanmar
146 K8 Tap o' Noth hill Scotland U.K.
232 I11 Tappahannock VA U.S.A.
116 F5 Tappal Uttar Prad. India
95 M6 Tappalang Sulawesi Indon.
235 H2 Tappan NY U.S.A.
232 D8 Tappan Lake OH U.S.A.
122 D4 Tappeh, Kūh-e hill Iran
102 R5 Tappi-zaki pt Japan
129 H5 Tap Qaraqoyunlu Azer.
Taprobane country Asia see Sri Lanka
176 G5 Tapsony Hungary
100 B2 Taptugary Rus. Fed.
79 □8a Tapu, Motu i. Tonga
81 H8 Tapuaenuku mt. South I. N.Z.
92 C9 Tapul Phil.
92 C9 Tapul Group is Phil.
94 C4 Tapulonanjing mt. Indon.
94 D4 Tapung r. Indon.
251 F6 Tapurú Brazil
251 E5 Tapurucuara Brazil
78 □2 Taputapu, Cape American Samoa
Taputeouea atoll Gilbert Is Kiribati see Tabiteuea
124 G9 Taqar mt. Yemen
122 E6 Ţāqestān, Chāh-e well Iran
127 L6 Ţaqţaq Iraq
255 C9 Taquara Brazil
256 A1 Taquaral, Serra do hills Brazil
253 F4 Taquarí r. Brazil
253 F4 Taquarí, Pantanal do marsh Brazil
256 C4 Taquaritinga Brazil
256 C5 Taquarituba Brazil
256 A4 Taquaruçu r. Brazil
260 B5 Taquimilán Arg.
177 I4 Tar Hungary
147 G8 Tar r. Ireland
85 M9 Tara Qld Austr.
196 H7 Tara r. Montenegro
196 H7 Tara nat. park Montenegro
147 I5 Tara, Hill of Ireland
207 H4 Taraba r. Nigeria
207 H4 Taraba state Nigeria
256 B5 Tarabaí Brazil
252 D4 Tarabuco Bol.
202 B1 Ţarābulus Libya
183 N7 Taracena Spain
136 H8 Taraclia Moldova
252 C3 Taraco Peru
250 D4 Taracua Brazil
80 K6 Taradale North I. N.Z.
161 I10 Taradeau France
202 B3 Tarāghin Libya
123 N9 Tar Ahmad Rind Pak.
117 L6 Tarai reg. India
Taraíra r. Brazil see Traíra
252 E5 Tarairí Bol.
216 □3b Tarajalejo Fuerteventura Canary Is
95 L3 Tarakan Kalimantan Indon.
95 L3 Tarakan i. Indon.
123 L5 Tarakki reg. Afgh.
199 L2 Taraklı Turkey
Tarakliya Moldova see Taraclia
77 I3 Tarakua Fiji
102 X3 Taraku-shima i. Kuril'skiye O-va Rus. Fed.
83 L6 Taralga N.S.W. Austr.
102 □B22 Tarama-jima i. Nansei-shotō Japan
182 F2 Taramundi Spain
138 C7 Taran, Mys pt Rus. Fed.
116 F8 Tarana Madh. Prad. India
116 E5 Taranagar Rajasthan India
80 H6 Taranaki admin. reg. North I. N.Z.
80 I6 Taranaki, Mount vol. North I. N.Z.
183 N8 Tarancón Spain
137 L3 Tarandyntsi Ukr.
80 I2 Taranga Island North I. N.Z.
114 F7 Tarangambadi Tamil Nadu India
208 C2 Tarangara Chad
211 C6 Tarangire National Park Tanz.
Tarangul l. Kazakh. see Tarankol', Ozero
121 M1 Tarankol', Ozero l. Kazakh.
120 J1 Taranovskoye Kazakh.
146 B7 Taransay i. Scotland U.K.
195 M3 Taranto Italy
195 M2 Taranto prov. Italy
195 M3 Taranto, Golfo di g. Italy
176 G5 Tarany Hungary
252 C4 Tarapacá admin. reg. Chile
250 D5 Tarapacá Col.
78 □6 Tarapaina Malaita Solomon Is
250 B6 Tarapoto Peru
160 E5 Tarare France
261 I4 Tarariras Uru.
80 J7 Tararua Forest Park nature res. North I. N.Z.
81 J7 Tararua Range mts North I. N.Z.
Tarasaigh i. Scotland U.K. see Taransay
161 F9 Tarascon France
163 H10 Tarascon-sur-Ariège France
136 F5 Tarashany Ukr.
136 J4 Tarashcha Ukr.
122 G5 Tarasht Iran
137 M7 Tarasivka Khersons'ka Oblast' Ukr.
137 M7 Tarasivka Khersons'ka Oblast' Ukr.
137 L5 Tarasivka Kirovohrads'ka Oblast' Ukr.
137 R4 Tarasivka Luhans'ka Oblast' Ukr.
134 I2 Tarasovo Rus. Fed.
135 H6 Tarasovskiy Rus. Fed.
205 H4 Tarat Alg.
252 C4 Tarata Peru
252 C2 Tarauacá Brazil
250 D6 Tarauacá r. Brazil
79 □9a Taravao Tahiti Fr. Polynesia
79 □9a Taravao, Baie de b. Tahiti Fr. Polynesia
79 □9a Taravao, Isthme de isth. Tahiti Fr. Polynesia
191 P3 Taravisio, Foresta di Italy
192 B4 Taravo r. Corse France
77 H1 Tarawa atoll Kiribati
80 K6 Tarawera North I. N.Z.
80 K5 Tarawera, Lake North I. N.Z.
80 K5 Tarawera, Mount vol. North I. N.Z.
121 N6 Taraz Kazakh.
183 Q5 Tarazona Spain
185 P2 Tarazona de la Mancha Spain
121 S4 Tarbagatay Kazakh.
107 J1 Tarbagatay Rus. Fed.
121 S4 Tarbagatay, Khrebet mts Kazakh.
146 I7 Tarbat Ness pt Scotland U.K.
187 E10 Tárbena Spain
147 D7 Tarbert Ireland
146 E11 Tarbert Argyll and Bute, Scotland U.K.
146 F11 Tarbert Argyll and Bute, Scotland U.K.
146 C7 Tarbert Western Isles, Scotland U.K.
146 D11 Tarbert, Loch inlet Scotland U.K.
163 E9 Tarbes France
146 G10 Tarbet Argyll and Bute, Scotland U.K.
146 H11 Tarbolton South Ayrshire, Scotland U.K.
231 I8 Tarboro NC U.S.A.
177 L5 Tărcaia Romania
177 K3 Tarcal Hungary
177 L4 Tarcea Romania
191 O3 Tarcento Italy
82 E4 Tarcoola S.A. Austr.
83 K4 Tarcoon N.S.W. Austr.
82 D2 Tarcoonyinna watercourse S.A. Austr.
197 K5 Ţarcului, Munţii mts Romania
83 K6 Tarcutta N.S.W. Austr.
175 I4 Tarczyn Pol.
158 H4 Tard r. France
183 M4 Tardajos Spain
183 O5 Tardelcuende Spain
156 F5 Tardenois reg. France
162 J3 Tardes r. France
163 C9 Tardets-Sorholus France
186 D4 Tardienta Spain
162 E4 Tardoire r. France
100 K4 Tardoki-Yani, Gora mt. Rus. Fed.
83 N4 Taree N.S.W. Austr.
210 B2 Tareifing Sudan
83 I4 Tarella N.S.W. Austr.
140 Q3 Tärendö Sweden
244 F5 Tarengo Mex.
207 F2 Tarenkat well Mali
Tarentum Italy see Taranto
244 F6 Taretán Mex.
131 K2 Tareya Rus. Fed.
125 J4 Ţarfā', Baţn aţ depr. Saudi Arabia
124 F7 Ţarfā, Ra's aţ pt Saudi Arabia
204 B4 Tarfaya Morocco
146 K9 Tarfside Angus, Scotland U.K.
207 G2 Targa well Niger
Targan Heilong. China see Talin Hiag
Targan Kazakh. see Targyn
238 I4 Targhee Pass ID U.S.A.
163 D6 Targon France
197 N6 Târgovişte Romania
174 F3 Targowa Górka Pol.
197 P5 Târgu Bujor Romania
197 L6 Târgu Cărbuneşti Romania
197 O3 Târgu Frumos Romania
204 D2 Targuist Morocco
197 L5 Târgu Jiu Romania
197 L3 Târgu Lăpuş Romania
197 M4 Târgu Mureş Romania
197 O3 Târgu Neamţ Romania
197 O4 Târgu Ocna Romania
197 O4 Târgu Secuiesc Romania
111 G12 Targyailing Xizang China
121 T3 Targyn Kazakh.
122 B5 Tarhān Iran
204 D3 Tarhbalt Morocco
Tarhmanant well Mali see Taghmanant
177 K5 Tarhos Hungary
202 B1 Tarhūnah Libya
91 J8 Tari P.N.G.
107 K7 Tarian Gol Nei Mongol China
124 F6 Tarib, Wādī watercourse Saudi Arabia
125 K3 Tarif U.A.E.
184 H8 Tarifa Spain
184 H8 Tarifa, Punta de pt Spain
92 D3 Tarigtig Point Luzon Phil.
252 D5 Tarija Bol.
252 D5 Tarija dept Bol.
114 D6 Tarikere Karnataka India
91 I7 Tariku r. Papua Indon.
110 F6 Tarim Xinjiang China
125 I7 Tarīm Yemen
Tarim Basin China see Tarim Pendi
211 B5 Tarime Tanz.
110 H6 Tarim He r. China
110 H6 Tarim Liuchang Xinjiang China
244 G5 Tarimoro Mex.
110 E7 Tarim Pendi basin China
110 H6 Tarim Qichang Xinjiang China
253 E5 Taringuiti Bol.
123 K5 Tarīn Kowt Afgh.
91 I7 Taritatu r. Papua Indon.
Taritipan Sabah Malaysia see Tandek
177 H4 Tarján Hungary
215 J8 Tarka r. S. Africa
207 G3 Tarka, Vallée de watercourse Niger
177 G4 Tárkány Hungary
215 K8 Tarkastad S. Africa
137 P8 Tarkhan, Mys pt Ukr.
137 L8 Tarkhankut, Mys pt Ukr.
129 I3 Tarki Rus. Fed.
236 H5 Tarkio MO U.S.A.
130 I3 Tarko-Sale Rus. Fed.
206 E5 Tarkwa Ghana
92 C4 Tarlac Luzon Phil.
92 C3 Tarlac r. Luzon Phil.
121 R4 Tarlauly Kazakh.
149 L6 Tarleton Lancashire, England U.K.
83 L6 Tarlo River National Park N.S.W. Austr.
232 C9 Tarlton OH U.S.A.
142 E6 Tarm Denmark
252 B2 Tarma Junín Peru
250 D5 Tarma Loreto Peru
117 L5 Tarmar Xizang China
168 H4 Tarmstedt Ger.
163 I8 Tarn dept France
161 B8 Tarn r. France
161 C8 Tarn, Gorges du France
177 I4 Tarna r. Hungary
183 J2 Tarna, Puerto de pass Spain
140 M4 Tärnaby Sweden
123 K6 Tarnak r. Afgh.
177 J3 Tarnalelesz Hungary
177 J4 Tarnaméra Hungary
177 J4 Tarnaőrs Hungary
177 J4 Tarnaszentmiklós Hungary
197 L4 Târnava Mare r. Romania
197 L4 Târnava Mică r. Romania
197 M4 Târnăveni Romania
175 K5 Tarnawa Duża Pol.
175 L5 Tarnawatka Pol.
163 G7 Tarn-et-Garonne dept France
175 K6 Tarnica mt. Pol.
175 J5 Tarnobrzeg Pol.
175 K5 Tarnogród Pol.
134 H3 Tarnogskiy Gorodok Rus. Fed.
177 H4 Tárnok Hungary
Tarnopol Ukr. see Ternopil'
163 B8 Tarnos France
175 L5 Tarnoszyn Pol.
177 K5 Târnova Arad Romania
197 K5 Târnova Caraş-Severin Romania
170 F3 Tarnow Ger.
174 C3 Tarnów Lubuskie Pol.
175 I5 Tarnów Małopolskie Pol.
175 J6 Tarnowiec Pol.
Tarnowitz Pol. see Tarnowskie Góry
174 E2 Tarnówka Pol.
174 E3 Tarnowo Podgórne Pol.
174 G5 Tarnów Opolski Pol.
174 G5 Tarnowskie Góry Pol.
140 M3 Tårnvik Norway
190 I6 Taro r. Italy
102 S7 Tarō Japan
111 F11 Taro Co salt l. China
122 F7 Ţārom Iran
137 N5 Taroms'ke Ukr.
163 D8 Taron-Sadirac-Viellenave France
85 L8 Taroom Qld Austr.
105 J2 Tarō-san mt. Japan
182 E6 Tarouca Port.
204 C3 Taroudannt Morocco
182 D6 Tarouquela Port.
168 H1 Tarp Ger.
177 L3 Tarpa Hungary
84 F5 Tarpaulin Swamp N.T. Austr.
82 H7 Tarpeena S.A. Austr.
231 F11 Tarpon Springs FL U.S.A.
149 L7 Tarporley Cheshire, England U.K.
175 L1 Tarprubežiai Lith.
246 E1 Tarpum Bay Eleuthera Bahamas
122 D5 Tarq Iran
122 D6 Tarqān Iran
192 H3 Tarquinia Italy
192 H3 Tarquinia Lido Italy
Tarquinii Italy see Tarquinia
84 E5 Tarrabool Lake salt flat N.T. Austr.
Tarracina Italy see Terracina
Tarraco Spain see Tarragona
206 □ Tarrafal Santiago Cape Verde
186 H5 Tarragona Spain
186 G5 Tarragona prov. Spain
83 K10 Tarraleah Tas. Austr.
83 K5 Tarran Hills N.S.W. Austr.
84 G4 Tarrant Point Qld Austr.
81 D11 Tarras South I. N.Z.
Tarrasa Spain see Terrassa
186 H4 Tàrrega Spain
146 I7 Tarrel Highland, Scotland U.K.
178 C5 Tarrenz Austria
182 D2 Tarrio Spain
186 H4 Tarroja de Segarra Spain
235 H2 Tarrytown NY U.S.A.
142 H7 Tårs Denmark
193 Q8 Tarsia Italy
202 C4 Tarso Ahon mt. Chad
202 C4 Tarso Emissi mt. Chad
202 C4 Tarso Kobour mt. Chad
126 G5 Tarsus Turkey
128 C2 Tarsus r. Turkey
170 E1 Tårs Vig b. Denmark
111 K8 Tart Qinghai China
122 E1 Tarta Turkm.
258 E1 Tartagal Salta Arg.
258 F3 Tartagal Santa Fé Arg.
175 M5 Tartakiv Ukr.
129 H5 Tärtär Azer.
129 H5 Tärtär r. Azer.
129 I5 Tärtär r. Azer.
191 M5 Tartaro r. Italy
163 C8 Tartas France
138 J3 Tartu Estonia
128 D4 Ţarţūs Syria
128 E3 Ţarţūs governorate Syria
104 E5 Tarui Japan
Tarumae-san vol. Japan see Shikotsu
257 G3 Tarumirim Brazil
103 H15 Tarumizu Japan
129 H1 Tarumovka Rus. Fed.
96 C1 Tarung Hka r. Myanmar
139 U7 Tarusa Rus. Fed.
139 U7 Tarusa r. Rus. Fed.
125 J2 Tārūt Saudi Arabia
97 D11 Tarutao, Ko i. Thai.
97 D11 Tarutao National Park Thai.
94 C3 Tarutung Sumatera Indon.
136 I7 Tarutyne Ukr.
146 L8 Tarves Aberdeenshire, Scotland U.K.
149 L7 Tarvin Cheshire, England U.K.
191 P2 Tarvisio Italy
Tarvisium Italy see Treviso
253 E3 Tarvo Bol.
195 □ Tarxien Malta
106 F1 Tarys-Arzhan Rus. Fed.
122 G6 Tarz Iran
121 O4 Tasaral Kazakh.
202 B3 Tasāwah Libya
120 K5 Tasbuget Kazakh.
190 D3 Täsch Switz.
224 E3 Taschereau Que. Can.
222 F5 Taseko Mountain B.C. Can.
205 F4 Tasendjanet, Oued watercourse Alg.
114 D4 Tasgaon Mahar. India
129 A5 Taşgeçit Turkey
137 N4 Tashan' r. Ukr.
Tashauz Turkm. see Daşoguz
Tashauzskaya Oblast' admin. div. Turkm. see Daşoguz
121 Q7 Tash-Bashat Kyrg.
136 H8 Tashbunar r. Ukr.
106 D6 Tashi Gansu China
Tashi Chho Bhutan see Thimphu
117 M6 Tashigang Bhutan
Tashino Rus. Fed. see Pervomaysk
129 F4 Tashir Armenia
122 E7 Tashk, Daryācheh-ye l. Iran
Tashkent Uzbek. see Toshkent
Tashkent Oblast admin. div. Uzbek. see Toshkent
121 O7 Tash-Kömür Kyrg.
Tash-Kumyr Kyrg. see Tash-Kömür
120 E2 Tashla Rus. Fed.
137 K4 Tashlyk Ukr.
Tāshqurghān Afgh. see Kholm
225 F1 Tasialujjuaq, Lac l. Que. Can.
224 F1 Tasiat, Lac l. Que. Can.
221 O3 Tasiilap Karra c. Greenland
Tasiilaq Greenland see Ammassalik
95 H8 Tasikmalaya Jawa Indon.
128 D6 Tasīl Syria
168 K1 Tåsinge i. Denmark
225 G1 Tasiujaq Que. Can.
221 M2 Tasiusaq Greenland
140 M4 Tåsjö Sweden
207 H3 Task well Niger
128 B1 Taşkale Turkey
129 E6 Taşkapı Turkey
128 A2 Taşkent Turkey
207 H3 Tasker Niger
121 S4 Taskesken Kazakh.
129 B5 Taşkıran Turkey
126 G3 Taşköprü Turkey
127 K4 Taşlıçay Turkey
129 E5 Taşlıoğul Turkey
81 H8 Tasman South I. N.Z.
81 G8 Tasman admin. reg. South I. N.Z.
81 E11 Tasman r. South I. N.Z.
81 E10 Tasman, Mount South I. N.Z.
266 F8 Tasman Abyssal Plain sea feature Austr.
265 O7 Tasman Basin sea feature Tasman Sea
81 H8 Tasman Bay South I. N.Z.
83 K10 Tasman Head Tas. Austr.
83 J10 Tasmania state Austr.
81 G8 Tasman Mountains South I. N.Z.
83 L10 Tasman Peninsula Tas. Austr.
77 H6 Tasman Sea S. Pacific Ocean
197 K3 Tăşnad Romania
121 O6 Tasotkel'skoye Vodokhranilishche resr Kazakh.
126 H3 Taşova Turkey
177 I4 Tass Hungary
148 D5 Tassagh Northern Ireland U.K.
207 G2 Tassara Niger
207 G2 Tassa Takorat well Niger
205 F4 Tassedjefit, Erg des. Alg.
160 F2 Tasselot, Mont hill France
207 F3 Tasserest well Mali
208 A5 Tassi Gabon
224 F1 Tassialouc, Lac l. Que. Can.
205 G5 Tassili du Hoggar plat. Alg.
205 G4 Tassili n'Ajjer plat. Alg.
160 F5 Tassin-la-Demi-Lune France
186 F5 Tastavíns r. Spain
131 N3 Tas-Tumus Rus. Fed.
121 M5 Tasty Kazakh.
121 L2 Tasty-Taldy Kazakh.
222 C4 Tasu B.C. Can.
128 B2 Taşucu Turkey
122 A2 Tasūj Iran
131 M3 Tas-Yuryakh Rus. Fed.
177 G5 Taszár Hungary
177 H4 Tát Hungary
177 H4 Tata Hungary
204 D3 Tata Morocco
79 □9a Tataa, Pointe pt Tahiti Fr. Polynesia
93 C4 Tataba Sulawesi Indon.
177 H4 Tatabánya Hungary
177 I5 Tataháza Hungary
245 M7 Tatahuicapan Mex.
106 D8 Tatalin Gol r. Qinghai China
245 J9 Tataltepec Mex.
225 I4 Tatamagouche N.S. Can.
93 D8 Tatamailau, Foho mt. East Timor
78 □6 Tatamba Sta Isabel Solomon Is
117 K8 Tatanagar Jharkhand India
205 H2 Tataouine Tunisia
136 I8 Tatarbunary Ukr.
138 L8 Tatarka Belarus
137 O5 Tatarka r. Ukr.
199 L4 Tatarlı Afyon Turkey
128 E1 Tatarlı Osmaniye Turkey
116 F6 Tatarpur Rajasthan India
130 I4 Tatarsk Novosibirskaya Oblast' Rus. Fed.
139 O7 Tatarsk Smolenskaya Oblast' Rus. Fed.
Tatarskaya A.S.S.R. aut. rep. Rus. Fed. see Tatarstan, Respublika
100 L3 Tatarskiy Proliv str. Rus. Fed.
134 J5 Tatarstan, Respublika aut. rep. Rus. Fed.
Tatar Strait Rus. Fed. see Tatarskiy Proliv
177 I4 Tatárszentgyörgy Hungary
197 O3 Tătăruşi Romania
79 □9a Tatatua, Pointe pt Tahiti Fr. Polynesia
95 J3 Tatau Sarawak Malaysia
122 A3 Tatavi r. Iran
129 I2 Tatayurt Rus. Fed.
85 I4 Tate r. Qld Austr.
105 K3 Tatebayashi Japan
104 D4 Tateishi-misaki pt Japan
105 K1 Tateiwa Japan
105 H3 Tateshina Japan
105 H3 Tateshina-yama mt. Japan
105 K6 Tateyama Chiba Japan
104 F2 Tateyama Toyama Japan
104 G2 Tate-yama vol. Japan
222 G2 Tathlina Lake N.W.T. Can.
124 F6 Tathlīth Saudi Arabia
124 G5 Tathlīth, Wādī watercourse Saudi Arabia
83 L7 Tathra N.S.W. Austr.
213 E4 Tati Botswana
206 B2 Tâtîlt well Maur.
168 G2 Tating Ger.
223 L2 Tatinnai Lake Nunavut Can.
120 A2 Tatishchevo Rus. Fed.
96 C4 Tatkon Myanmar
222 E5 Tatla Lake B.C. Can.
222 E5 Tatla Lake l. B.C. Can.
222 E3 Tatlatui Provincial Park B.C. Can.
222 E5 Tatlayoko Lake B.C. Can.
129 G4 Tatlı Azer.
223 N3 Tatnam, Cape Man. Can.
105 I4 Tatomi Japan
Tatra Mountains Pol./Slovakia see Tatry
111 G7 Tatrang Xinjiang China
177 J2 Tatranská Javorina Slovakia
177 J2 Tatranský nat. park Slovakia
175 H6 Tatry mts Pol./Slovakia
175 H6 Tatrzański Park Narodowy nat. park Pol.
222 B3 Tatshenshini r. B.C. Can.
222 B3 Tatshenshini-Alsek Provincial Wilderness Park B.C. Can.
135 H6 Tatsinskiy Rus. Fed.
103 L12 Tatsuno Hyōgo Japan
105 G4 Tatsuno Nagano Japan
104 E3 Tatsunokuchi Japan
104 E1 Tatsuruhama Japan
105 G6 Tatsuyama Japan
123 L9 Tatta Pak.
149 Q7 Tattershall Lincolnshire, England U.K.
121 O6 Tatti Kazakh.
Tatty Kazakh. see Tatti
80 I5 Tatu hill North I. N.Z.
256 D5 Tatuí Brazil
222 E4 Tatuk Mountain B.C. Can.
138 H5 Tatula r. Lith.
237 D9 Tatum NM U.S.A.
237 H9 Tatum TX U.S.A.
127 K4 Tatvan Turkey
78 □2 Ta'u i. American Samoa
142 B2 Tau Norway
79 □8a Tau i. Tonga
254 E3 Taua Brazil
78 □4b Tauak Passage Pohnpei Micronesia
251 F5 Tauapeçaçu Brazil
251 F6 Tauariã Brazil
257 E5 Taubaté Brazil
171 H8 Taubenheim Ger.
172 H2 Tauber r. Ger.
172 H2 Tauberbischofsheim Ger.
172 H3 Taubergrund reg. Ger.
171 F8 Taucha Ger.
171 J6 Tauche Ger.
120 D5 Tauchik Kazakh.
171 J7 Tauer Ger.
173 L5 Taufkirchen Bayern Ger.
173 M5 Taufkirchen Bayern Ger.
173 M5 Taufkirchen (Vils) Ger.
169 H9 Taufstein hill Ger.
80 K5 Tauhara mt. North I. N.Z.
80 I3 Tauhoa North I. N.Z.
251 G4 Tauini r. Brazil
121 P5 Taukum, Peski des. Kazakh.
158 D4 Taulé France
161 F8 Taulignan France
80 J5 Taumarunui North I. N.Z.
252 B2 Taumaturgo Brazil
253 G5 Taunay Brazil
215 I3 Taung S. Africa
96 C7 Taungbon Myanmar
96 B4 Taungdwingyi Myanmar
96 C4 Taunggyi Myanmar
96 C4 Taunglau Myanmar
96 C5 Taung-ngu Myanmar
96 C6 Taungnyo Range mts Myanmar
96 B4 Taungtha Myanmar
96 B5 Taungup Myanmar
123 N6 Taunsa Pak.
150 F5 Taunton Somerset, England U.K.
233 N7 Taunton MA U.S.A.
169 E10 Taunus hills Ger.
80 □ Taupeka Point Chatham Is S. Pacific Ocean
80 J4 Taupiri North I. N.Z.
179 J4 Tauplitz Austria
80 K5 Taupo North I. N.Z.
80 J5 Taupo, Lake North I. N.Z.
138 F6 Tauragė Lith.
138 E6 Tauralaukis Lith.
250 C3 Tauramena Col.
80 K4 Tauranga North I. N.Z.
Taurasia Italy see Torino
224 F4 Taureau, Réservoir resr Que. Can.
195 K7 Taurianova Italy
80 I2 Taurikura North I. N.Z.
162 G4 Taurion r. France
195 O4 Taurisano Italy
Tauriuiná r. Brazil see Verde
80 H2 Tauroa Point North I. N.Z.
Taurus Mountains Turkey see Toros Dağları
Taūshyq Kazakh. see Tauchik
186 C4 Tauste Spain
177 K5 Tăuţ Romania
163 J10 Tautavel France
158 I3 Taute r. France
171 E9 Tautenhain Ger.
177 L4 Tăuteu Romania
79 □9a Tautira Tahiti Fr. Polynesia
160 B5 Tauves France
80 M5 Tauwhareparae North I. N.Z.
131 Q4 Tauyskaya Guba g. Rus. Fed.
Tauz Azer. see Tovuz
192 B3 Tavaco Corse France
191 O3 Tavagnacco Italy
196 H4 Tavankut Vojvodina Serbia

Tavannes to Teslin

396

190 C1 Tavannes Switz.
159 L7 Tavant France
231 G11 Tavares FL U.S.A.
191 K8 Tavarnelle Val di Pesa Italy
199 K5 Tavas Turkey
Tavastehus Fin. see Hämeenlinna
160 G2 Tavaux France
130 H4 Tavda Rus. Fed.
182 D8 Taveiro Port.
161 F8 Tavel France
140 P4 Tavelsjö Sweden
151 O2 Taverham Norfolk, England U.K.
195 L5 Taverna Italy
160 E2 Tavernay France
192 I1 Tavernelle Italy
161 I9 Tavernes France
187 E9 Tavernes de la Valldigna Spain
150 C4 Tavernspite Pembrokeshire, Wales U.K.
156 D5 Taverny France
190 H7 Taverone r. Italy
186 J4 Tavertet Spain
79 □7 Taveuni i. Fiji
195 O4 Taviano Italy
192 D3 Tavignano r. Corse France
129 H7 Tavil Iran
123 N2 Tavildara Tajik.
193 O4 Taviolere plain Italy
184 D6 Tavira Port.
184 D6 Tavira, Ilha de i. Port.
227 N6 Tavistock Ont. Can.
150 D6 Tavistock Devon, England U.K.
193 M3 Tavo r. Italy
192 D6 Tavolara, Isola i. Sardegna Italy
121 Q1 Tavolzhan Kazakh.
182 E6 Távora r. Spain
97 D7 Tavoy Myanmar
97 D8 Tavoy r. mouth Myanmar
Tavoy Island Myanmar see Mali Kyun
97 D8 Tavoy Point Myanmar
121 T2 Tavricheskoye Kazakh.
Tavrīl Kazakh. see Tavricheskoye
137 M7 Tavriys'k Ukr.
199 K3 Tavşanlı Turkey
79 □7a Tavua Viti Levu Fiji
79 □7a Tavua i. Fiji
79 □7 Tavuki Kadavu Fiji
191 N8 Tavullia Italy
129 G4 Tavush r. Armenia
150 D7 Tavy r. England U.K.
150 D5 Taw r. England U.K.
124 G5 Taw, Jabal at hill Saudi Arabia
81 I8 Tawa North I. N.Z.
95 L2 Tawai, Bukit mt. Malaysia
237 H9 Tawakoni, Lake TX U.S.A.
84 E3 Tawallah Range hills N.T. Austr.
117 M6 Tawang Arun. Prad. India
78 □6 Tawaraha San Cristobal Solomon Is
104 C6 Tawaramoto Japan
78 □6 Tawarogha San Cristobal Solomon Is
227 K5 Tawas Bay MI U.S.A.
227 K5 Tawas City MI U.S.A.
95 L2 Tawau Sabah Malaysia
95 L2 Tawau, Teluk b. Malaysia
203 G3 Ţawd Egypt
Tawè Myanmar see Tavoy
150 E4 Tawe r. Wales U.K.
202 E6 Taweisha Sudan
172 B2 Tawern Ger.
80 K5 Tawhiuau mt. North I. N.Z.
116 E3 Tawi r. India
125 L3 Ţawī Ḩafīr well U.A.E.
202 E6 Tawila Sudan
124 A2 Ţawīlah, Juzur is Egypt
Tawîla Islands Egypt see Ţawīlah, Juzur
125 L3 Ţawī Murra well U.A.E.
92 B9 Tawitawi i. Phil.
96 C2 Tawmaw Myanmar
109 M7 Tawu Taiwan
245 H7 Taxco Mex.
178 G5 Taxenbach Austria
120 H6 Taxiatosh Uzbek.
123 O5 Taxila tourist site Pak.
111 B8 Taxkorgan Xinjiang China
120 I6 Taxtako'pir Uzbek.
222 C2 Tay r. Y.T. Can.
146 J10 Tay r. Scotland U.K.
146 J10 Tay, Firth of est. Scotland U.K.
87 F12 Tay, Lake salt flat W.A. Austr.
146 H10 Tay, Loch l. Scotland U.K.
252 A2 Tayabamba Peru
92 C5 Tayabas Bay Luzon Phil.
95 I4 Tayan Kalimantan Indon.
134 F1 Taybola Rus. Fed.
210 E3 Tayeeglow Somalia
199 H2 Tayfur Turkey
130 J4 Tayga Rus. Fed.
122 D4 Tāygān Iran
106 E3 Taygan Mongolia
198 D5 Taygetos mts Greece
146 E11 Tayinloan Argyll and Bute, Scotland U.K.
136 J7 Tayirove Ukr.
100 I1 Taykanskiy Khrebet mts Rus. Fed.
222 F3 Taylor B.C. Can.
241 V7 Taylor AZ U.S.A.
236 F5 Taylor NE U.S.A.
234 D2 Taylor PA U.S.A.
237 G10 Taylor TX U.S.A.
239 K7 Taylor r. CO U.S.A.
81 F10 Taylor, Mount South I. N.Z.
239 K9 Taylor, Mount NM U.S.A.
234 D6 Taylors Bridge DE U.S.A.
148 B7 Taylor's Cross Ireland
230 E6 Taylorsville KY U.S.A.
234 A6 Taylorsville MD U.S.A.
231 G8 Taylorsville NC U.S.A.
235 G3 Taylortown NJ U.S.A.
236 K6 Taylorville IL U.S.A.
124 D2 Taymā' Saudi Arabia
233 □S2 Taymouth N.B. Can.
131 K3 Taymura r. Rus. Fed.
131 L2 Taymyr, Ozero l. Rus. Fed.
131 J2 Taymyr, Poluostrov pen. Rus. Fed.
Taymyr Peninsula Rus. Fed. see Taymyr, Poluostrov
97 H9 Tây Ninh Vietnam
146 F10 Taynuilt Argyll and Bute, Scotland U.K.
244 B1 Tayoltita Mex.
120 D3 Taypak Kazakh.
Taypaq Kazakh. see Taypak
146 K10 Tayport Fife, Scotland U.K.
131 K4 Tayshet Rus. Fed.
120 E3 Taysoygan, Peski des. Kazakh.
Tayspun tourist site Iraq see Ctesiphon
199 J4 Taytan Turkey
92 C4 Taytay Luzon Phil.
92 B6 Taytay Palawan Phil.
92 B6 Taytay Bay Palawan Phil.
92 E6 Taytay Point Leyte Phil.
95 I8 Tayu Jawa Indon.
100 D3 Tayuan Heilong. China
148 F1 Tayvallich Argyll and Bute, Scotland U.K.
122 I4 Tayyebād Iran
128 C10 Ţayyib al Ism Saudi Arabia
121 M1 Tayynsha Kazakh.
130 I3 Taz r. Rus. Fed.
204 E2 Taza Morocco
180 D5 Taza-Al Hoceima-Taounate prov. Morocco
Taza-Bazar Uzbek. see Shumanay
216 □3d Tazacorte La Palma Canary Is
129 H5 Täzäkänd Azer.
127 L6 Ţāza Khurmātū Iraq
105 G3 Tazawa Japan
102 R7 Tazawa-ko l. Japan
96 B3 Taze Myanmar
122 B2 Tazeh Kand Azer.
129 I6 Tāzeh Kand-e Angūt Iran
204 D3 Tazenakht Morocco
232 B12 Tazewell TN U.S.A.
232 D11 Tazewell VA U.S.A.
223 I2 Tazin r. N.W.T./Sask. Can.
223 I3 Tazin Lake Sask. Can.
202 D3 Tāzirbū Libya
202 D3 Tazirbu Water Wells Field Libya
207 H2 Tazizilet well Niger
177 I5 Tázlár Hungary
197 O4 Tazlău Romania
197 O4 Tazlău r. Romania
189 C7 Tazoghrane Tunisia
207 H2 Tazolé well Niger
183 J1 Tazones Spain
205 E5 Tazouikert hill Mali
130 I3 Tazovskaya Guba sea chan. Rus. Fed.
130 I3 Tazovskiy Rus. Fed.
205 G5 Tazrouk Alg.
204 D3 Tazzarine Morocco
204 E2 Tazzouguert Morocco
Tbessa Alg. see Tébessa
129 F4 T'bilisi Georgia
135 H7 Tbilisskaya Rus. Fed.
207 I5 Tchabal Gangdaba mt. Cameroon
207 I5 Tchabal Mbabo mt. Cameroon
Tchad country Africa see Chad
207 F4 Tchamba Togo
207 F4 Tchaourou Benin
207 F5 Tchetti Benin
208 A5 Tchibanga Gabon
207 G2 Tchidoutene watercourse Niger
202 C5 Tchié well Chad
202 B4 Tchigaï, Plateau du Niger
209 B8 Tchihepepe Angola
209 C8 Tchikala-Tcholohanga Angola
208 C5 Tchikapika Congo
209 B8 Tchindjenje Angola
207 H3 Tchin Garaguene well Niger
207 G3 Tchin-Tabaradene Niger
207 I4 Tcholliré Cameroon
207 H2 Tchou-m-Adegdeg well Niger
143 O7 Tczew Pol.
97 H8 Te, Prêk r. Cambodia
250 E5 Tea r. Brazil
182 D4 Tea r. Spain
244 B3 Teacapán Mex.
87 F8 Teague, Lake salt flat W.A. Austr.
79 □9a Teahupoo Tahiti Fr. Polynesia
81 □3 Te Aiti Point Rarotonga Cook Is
146 K9 Tealing Angus, Scotland U.K.
81 B12 Te Anau South I. N.Z.
81 B12 Te Anau, Lake South I. N.Z.
235 G3 Teaneck NJ U.S.A.
80 I5 Te Anga North I. N.Z.
193 M5 Teano Italy
87 D8 Teano Range mts W.A. Austr.
Teanum Sidicinum Italy see Teano
243 M9 Teapa Mex.
80 M4 Te Araroa North I. N.Z.
196 J8 Tearce Macedonia
80 J4 Te Aroha North I. N.Z.
80 J4 Te Aroha, Mount hill North I. N.Z.
Teate Italy see Chieti
79 □9a Teavaro Moorea Fr. Polynesia
80 J5 Te Awamutu North I. N.Z.
185 J7 Teba Spain
183 P9 Tebar Spain
207 G3 Tébarat Niger
95 H4 Tebas Kalimantan Indon.
149 L5 Tebay Cumbria, England U.K.
95 I4 Tebedu Sarawak Malaysia
129 C2 Teberda Rus. Fed.
129 C2 Teberda r. Rus. Fed.
129 C2 Teberdinskiy Zapovednik nature res. Rus. Fed.
223 L2 Tebesjuak Lake Nunavut Can.
205 H2 Tébessa Alg.
205 H2 Tébessa, Monts de mts Alg.
253 F6 Tebicuary Para.
253 F6 Tebicuary r. Para.
94 C3 Tebingtinggi Sumatera Indon.
94 E6 Tebingtinggi Sumatera Indon.
94 E5 Tebo r. Indon.
189 B7 Tébourba Tunisia
189 B7 Téboursouk Tunisia
129 G3 Tebulos Mt'a Georgia/Rus. Fed.
244 D6 Tecalitlán Mex.
245 I6 Tecamac Mex.
245 J7 Tecamachalco Mex.
245 J7 Tecamachalco Nogales Mex.
242 A1 Tecate Mex.
128 C2 Tece Turkey
163 K10 Tech r. France
178 H6 Techendorf Austria
206 E5 Techiman Ghana
197 Q6 Techirghiol Romania
259 C6 Tecka Arg.
259 C6 Tecka r. Arg.
169 E6 Tecklenburger Land reg. Ger.
142 J6 Teckomatorp Sweden
245 I6 Tecocomulca Mex.
243 O7 Tecoh Mex.
244 C5 Tecolotlán Mex.
245 K5 Tecolutla Mex.
244 D7 Tecomán Mex.
245 H9 Tecomate, Laguna lag. Mex.
245 I7 Tecomatlán Mex.
241 P6 Tecopa CA U.S.A.
242 E3 Tecoripa Mex.
244 G8 Técpan Mex.
244 G8 Tecpan r. Mex.
244 B3 Tecuala Mex.
244 B5 Tecuán Jalisco Mex.
244 C6 Tecuán Jalisco Mex.
197 P5 Tecuci Romania
227 K8 Tecumseh MI U.S.A.
236 G5 Tecumseh NE U.S.A.
210 D3 Ted Somalia
202 C4 Tédogora watercourse Chad
104 D3 Tedori-gawa r. Japan
122 I3 Tedzhenstroy Turkm.
241 W5 Teec Nos Pos AZ U.S.A.
214 F8 Teekloof Pass S. Africa
106 G2 Teel Mongolia
110 J1 Teeli Rus. Fed.
147 G4 Teemore Northern Ireland U.K.
147 B9 Teeranearagh Ireland
149 O4 Tees r. England U.K.
149 O4 Tees Bay England U.K.
149 M4 Teesdale val. England U.K.
227 M5 Teeswater Ont. Can.
Teet'lit Zhen N.W.T. Can. see Fort McPherson
148 D6 Teevurcher Ireland
81 □1 Te Fakanava i. Tokelau
251 E5 Tefé Brazil
251 E5 Tefé r. Brazil
251 E5 Tefé, Lago l. Brazil
205 G4 Tefedest mts Alg.
199 K5 Tefenni Turkey
207 F2 Téfoûlet well Mali
95 H8 Tegal Jawa Indon.
170 H5 Tegel airport Ger.
165 J6 Tegelen Neth.
173 M3 Tegernheim Ger.
173 L6 Tegernsee Ger.
173 L6 Tegernsee l. Ger.
193 P7 Teggiano Italy
207 G4 Tegina Nigeria
94 F7 Tegineneng Sumatera Indon.
177 K4 Téglás Hungary
190 I3 Teglio Italy
191 M3 Tegnàs r. Italy
78 □5 Tégua i. Vanuatu
242 □P10 Tegucigalpa Hond.
216 □3a Tegueste Tenerife Canary Is
207 G2 Teguidda-n-Tessoumt Niger
216 □3c Teguise Lanzarote Canary Is
240 N6 Tehachapi CA U.S.A.
240 M7 Tehachapi Mountains CA U.S.A.
240 N6 Tehachapi Pass CA U.S.A.
80 I3 Te Hana North I. N.Z.
80 K6 Te Hauke North I. N.Z.
223 M1 Tehek Lake Nunavut Can.
Teheran Iran see Tehrān
223 M1 Tehery Lake Nunavut Can.
206 E4 Téhini Côte d'Ivoire
93 F5 Tehoru Seram Indon.
122 D4 Tehrān Iran
122 D4 Tehrān prov. Iran
Tehri Madh. Prad. India see Tikamgarh
116 G4 Tehri Uttaranchal India
245 J7 Tehuacán Mex.
245 L9 Tehuantepec r. Mex.
243 L10 Tehuantepec, Golfo de g. Mex.
Tehuantepec, Gulf of Mex. see Tehuantepec, Golfo de
245 M8 Tehuantepec, Istmo de isth. Mex.
267 M5 Tehuantepec Ridge sea feature N. Pacific Ocean
245 I7 Tehuitzingo Mex.
245 I9 Tehuixtepec Mex.
81 J8 Te Humenga Point North I. N.Z.
171 E7 Teicha Ger.
171 F9 Teichwolframsdorf Ger.
138 J5 Teiču rezervāts nature res. Latvia
216 □3a Teide, Parque Nacional del nat. park Tenerife Canary Is
216 □3a Teide, Pico del vol. Tenerife Canary Is
150 C3 Teifi r. Wales U.K.
150 E6 Teign r. England U.K.
150 F6 Teignmouth Devon, England U.K.
158 E7 Teignouse, Passage de la str. France
158 H6 Teillay France
163 I8 Teillet France
102 □1 Teima Okinawa Japan
173 N6 Teisendorf Ger.
207 F2 Teïskot well Mali
173 O3 Teisnach Ger.
161 B7 Teissières-lès-Bouliès France
169 J8 Teistungen Ger.
245 K9 Teitipac Mex.
197 N6 Teiu Romania
197 L4 Teiuş Romania
254 F3 Teixeira Brazil
Teixeira da Silva Angola see Bailundo
257 H2 Teixeira de Freitas Brazil
Teixeira de Sousa Angola see Luau
257 F4 Teixeiras Brazil
256 B6 Teixeira Soares Brazil
182 D2 Teixeiro Spain
182 F8 Teixoso Port.
182 F6 Teja r. Port.
183 Q8 Tejadillos Spain
183 P5 Tejado Spain
95 K9 Tejakula Bali Indon.
245 K6 Tejar Mex.
216 □3f Tejeda Gran Canaria Canary Is
182 I8 Tejeda de Tiétar Spain
185 L7 Tejeda y Almijara, Sierra de nature res. Spain
122 I3 Tejen Turkm.
123 I3 Tejen r. Turkm.
117 M8 Tejgaon Bangl.
207 H3 Tejira well Niger
184 B3 Tejo r. Port. alt. Tajo (Spain), conv. Tagus
184 E1 Tejo Internacional, Parque Natural do nature res. Port.
244 D7 Tejupan, Punta pt Mex.
244 G7 Tejupilco Mex.
80 L4 Te Kaha North I. N.Z.
80 L4 Te Kaha Point North I. N.Z.
80 G1 Te Kao North I. N.Z.
81 E11 Tekapo r. South I. N.Z.
81 E10 Tekapo, Lake South I. N.Z.
117 J7 Tekari Bihar India
105 H5 Tekari-dake mt. Japan
81 J8 Te Kaukau Point North I. N.Z.
80 J4 Te Kauwhata North I. N.Z.
243 O7 Tekax Mex.
121 M6 Teke Kazakh.
197 O9 Teke r. Turkey
121 O1 Teke, Ozero salt l. Kazakh.
128 D2 Tekebaşı Turkey
120 I3 Tekeli Aktyubinskaya Oblast' Kazakh.
121 R5 Tekeli Almatinskaya Oblast' Kazakh.
110 E5 Tekes Xinjiang China
121 S6 Tekes Kazakh.
110 F5 Tekes He r. China
203 H6 Tekezē Wenz r. Eritrea/Eth.
111 E8 Tekiliktag mt. Xinjiang China
100 H4 Tekin Rus. Fed.
199 I2 Tekirdağ Turkey
199 I1 Tekirdağ prov. Turkey
199 L6 Tekirova Turkey
114 G3 Tekka Mahar. India
115 I3 Tekkali Andhra Prad. India
129 A5 Tekke Turkey
127 J4 Tekman Turkey
117 N9 Teknaf Bangl.
129 B5 Tekneciler Turkey
81 G9 Tekoa, Mount South I. N.Z.
94 □ Tekong Kechil, Pulau i. Sing.
226 J7 Tekonsha MI U.S.A.
80 H3 Te Kopuru North I. N.Z.
81 □3 Te Kou hill Rarotonga Cook Is
205 F5 Tekouiat, Oued watercourse Alg.
80 J4 Te Kowhai North I. N.Z.
202 D5 Tékro well Chad
128 H2 Tektek Dağları hills Turkey
93 C4 Teku Sulawesi Indon.
80 J5 Te Kuiti North I. N.Z.
117 I9 Tel r. India
209 F8 Tela Dem. Rep. Congo
242 □P10 Tela Hond.
81 □1 Te Lafu i. Tokelau
81 □1 Te Lafu i. Tokelau
205 E2 Télagh Alg.
175 K3 Telaki Pol.
94 F4 Telan i. Indon.
Telanaipura Sumatera Indon. see Jambi
111 K9 Telashi Hu salt l. Qinghai China
207 F2 Télataï Mali
175 L5 Telatyn Pol.
129 G4 T'elavi Georgia
128 C6 Tel Aviv-Yafo Israel
176 E2 Telč Czech Rep.
243 O7 Telchac Puerto Mex.
139 T8 Tel'ch'ye Rus. Fed.
197 M3 Telciu Romania
168 K4 Teldau Ger.
216 □3f Telde Gran Canaria Canary Is
208 D4 Tele r. Dem. Rep. Congo
206 E2 Télé, Lac l. Mali
197 N5 Teleajen r. Romania
196 H5 Telečka Vojvodina Serbia
95 J6 Telegapulang Kalimantan Indon.
194 E8 Telegrafo, Pizzo hill Italy
222 D3 Telegraph Creek B.C. Can.
177 J5 Telekgerendás Hungary
Telekhany Belarus see Tsyelyakhany
79 □8 Teleki Tonga atoll Tonga
79 □8 Teleki Vavu'u atoll Tonga
137 S1 Telelyuy Rus. Fed.
256 B6 Telêmaco Borba Brazil
142 E2 Telemark county Norway
260 E5 Telén Arg.
95 L4 Telen r. Indon.
Teleneshty Moldova see Teleneşti
136 H6 Teleneşti Moldova
122 I9 Teleng Iran
197 N7 Teleorman r. Romania
205 G4 Telertheba, Djebel mt. Alg.
240 O5 Telescope Peak CA U.S.A.
247 □6 Telescope Point Grenada
193 N5 Telese Italy
253 F1 Teles Pires r. Brazil
129 H3 Teletl' Rus. Fed.
86 G6 Telfer Mining Centre W.A. Austr.
150 H2 Telford Telford and Wrekin, England U.K.
234 E4 Telford PA U.S.A.
150 H2 Telford and Wrekin admin. div. England U.K.
178 D5 Telfs Austria
177 J3 Telgárt Slovakia
158 C5 Telgruc-sur-Mer France
169 E7 Telgte Ger.
182 E8 Telhado Port.
242 □P11 Telica, Volcán vol. Nic.
204 E5 Telīg well Mali
206 B4 Télimélé Guinea
202 D5 Télissour well Chad
245 K8 Telixtlahuaca Mex.
202 E6 Teljo, Jebel mt. Sudan
222 E4 Telkwa B.C. Can.
157 K4 Tellancourt France
194 I10 Tellaro r. Sicilia Italy
Tell Atlas mts Alg. see Atlas Tellien
220 B3 Teller AK U.S.A.
Tell es-Sultan West Bank see Jericho
114 D7 Tellicherry Pondicherry India
165 H8 Tellin Belgium
168 H2 Tellingstedt Ger.
129 C5 Telli Tepe mt. Turkey
250 C4 Tello Col.
136 J7 Tellodar Ukr.
127 M8 Telloh Iraq
239 K8 Telluride CO U.S.A.
137 R6 Tel'manove Ukr.
Tel'mansk Turkm. see Gubadag
128 D6 Tel Megiddo tourist site Israel
106 E2 Telmen Nuur salt l. Mongolia
179 O1 Telnice Czech Rep.
94 C5 Telo Indon.
159 L6 Teloché France
182 E6 Telões Port.
245 H7 Teloloapán Mex.
Telo Martius France see Toulon
81 □1 Te Loto i. Tokelau
134 L3 Tel'pos-Iz, Gora mt. Rus. Fed.
259 D6 Telsen Arg.
138 F6 Telšiai Lith.
192 C6 Telti Sardegna Italy
171 H6 Teltow Ger.
Teluk Anson Malaysia see Teluk Intan
Telukbajur Sumatera Indon. see Telukbayur
95 H5 Telukbatang Kalimantan Indon.
94 D5 Telukbayur Sumatera Indon.
Telukbetung Sumatera Indon. see Bandar Lampung
94 B4 Telukdalam Indon.
94 D2 Teluk Intan Malaysia
94 D5 Telukkuantan Sumatera Indon.
95 H5 Telukmelano Kalimantan Indon.
94 G8 Teluknaga Jawa Indon.
95 H5 Telukpakedai Kalimantan Indon.
114 G9 Telulla Sri Lanka
139 U9 Telyazh'ye Rus. Fed.
207 F5 Tema Ghana
244 E4 Temacapulín Mex.
79 □9a Temae, Lac l. Moorea Fr. Polynesia
227 O2 Temagami Ont. Can.
224 E4 Temagami Lake Ont. Can.
95 H4 Temaju i. Indon.
81 □3 Te Manga hill Rarotonga Cook Is
95 I8 Temanggung Jawa Indon.
245 J4 Temapache Mex.
80 I6 Te Mapou hill North I. N.Z.
111 I10 Têmarxung Xizang China
245 K7 Temascal Mex.
244 G6 Temascaltepec de González Mex.
80 I4 Te Mata North I. N.Z.
79 □9 Tematangi atoll Arch. des Tuamotu Fr. Polynesia
243 O7 Temax Mex.
215 M1 Temba S. Africa
91 I7 Tembagapura Papua Indon.
215 Q2 Tembe r. Moz.
215 Q2 Tembe Elephant Park nature res. S. Africa
131 K3 Tembenchi r. Rus. Fed.
94 E5 Tembesi r. Indon.
94 E5 Tembilahan Sumatera Indon.
215 M2 Tembisa S. Africa
183 N9 Tembleque Spain
209 C6 Tembo Aluma Angola
209 C6 Tembo Falls Angola/Dem. Rep. Congo
Tembué Moz. see Chifunde
215 M7 Tembuland reg. S. Africa
211 B7 Tembwe Zambia
150 H3 Teme r. England U.K.
240 O8 Temecula CA U.S.A.
126 F4 Temelli Turkey
106 E1 Temenchula, Gora mt. Rus. Fed.
94 D2 Temengor, Tasik resr Malaysia
179 L8 Temenica r. Slovenia
196 H5 Temerin Vojvodina Serbia
94 E3 Temerluh Malaysia
94 E2 Temiang, Bukit mt. Malaysia
122 C5 Temīleh Iran
91 H7 Teminabuan Papua Indon.
120 G3 Temir Aktyubinskaya Oblast' Kazakh.
Temir Yuzhnyy Kazakhstan Kazakh. see Timur
Temirlan Kazakh. see Temirlanovka
121 M6 Temirlanovka Kazakh.
121 O2 Temirtau Kazakh.
225 F3 Témiscamie r. Que. Can.
225 F3 Témiscamie, Lac l. Que. Can.
224 E4 Témiscaming Que. Can.
224 E4 Témiscamingue, Lac l. Ont./Que. Can.
225 G4 Témiscouata, Lac l. Que. Can.
94 F4 Temiyang i. Indon.
139 R6 Temkino Rus. Fed.
83 J9 Temma Tas. Austr.
140 R4 Temmes Fin.
135 H5 Temnikov Rus. Fed.
192 A7 Temo r. Sardegna Italy
79 □9 Temoe atoll Arch. des Tuamotu Fr. Polynesia
83 K6 Temora N.S.W. Austr.
242 F3 Temósachic Mex.
241 U8 Tempe AZ U.S.A.
93 A6 Tempe, Danau l. Indon.
84 D8 Tempe Downs N.T. Austr.
171 H6 Tempelhof airport Ger.
250 C5 Tempestad Peru
94 E5 Tempino Sumatera Indon.
192 C6 Tempio Pausania Sardegna Italy
226 I5 Temple MI U.S.A.
234 D4 Temple PA U.S.A.
237 G10 Temple TX U.S.A.
156 H7 Temple, Lac du resr France
150 D3 Temple Bar Ceredigion, Wales U.K.
85 I2 Temple Bay Qld Austr.
123 M7 Temple Dera Pak.
147 F7 Templederry Ireland
151 O5 Temple Ewell Kent, England U.K.
147 D8 Templeglentan Ireland
147 G7 Templemore Ireland
147 C9 Templenoe Ireland
147 J3 Templepatrick Northern Ireland U.K.
92 A6 Templer Bank sea feature Phil.
149 L4 Temple Sowerby Cumbria, England U.K.
84 G6 Templeton watercourse Qld Austr.
81 G10 Templeton South I. N.Z.
150 C4 Templeton Pembrokeshire, Wales U.K.
240 L6 Templeton CA U.S.A.
147 G7 Templetuohy Ireland
156 F2 Templeuve France
170 I4 Templin Ger.
147 H4 Tempo Northern Ireland U.K.
245 I4 Tempoal Mex.
245 I4 Tempoal r. Mex.
209 C8 Tempué Angola
106 F8 Têmpung Qinghai China
139 U5 Tempy Rus. Fed.
135 G7 Temryuk Rus. Fed.
135 G7 Temryukskiy Zaliv b. Rus. Fed.
165 F6 Temse Belgium
197 K7 Temska Serbia
190 I3 Temù Italy
260 A6 Temuco Chile
81 F11 Temuka South I. N.Z.
Temuli Sichuan China see Butuo
78 □4b Temwen i. Pohnpei Micronesia
78 □4b Temwetemwensekir hill Pohnpei Micronesia
120 H1 Temyasovo Rus. Fed.
250 B5 Tena Ecuador
186 E2 Tena, Valle de val. Spain
243 N7 Tenabo Mex.
240 P1 Tenabo, Mount NV U.S.A.
244 C6 Tenacatita Mex.
206 E3 Ténado Burkina
235 H3 Tenafly NJ U.S.A.
138 G1 Tenala Fin.
114 G4 Tenali Andhra Prad. India
244 C5 Tenamaxtlán Mex.
228 G7 Tenancingo Mex.
245 H6 Tenango México Mex.
245 L9 Tenango Oaxaca Mex.
79 □9 Tenarunga atoll Arch. des Tuamotu Fr. Polynesia
97 D8 Tenasserim Myanmar
97 D8 Tenasserim admin. div. Myanmar
97 D8 Tenasserim r. Myanmar
160 H5 Tenay France
164 K2 Ten Boer Neth.
150 G3 Tenbury Wells Worcestershire, England U.K.
150 C4 Tenby Pembrokeshire, Wales U.K.
227 K3 Tenby Bay Ont. Can.
161 E6 Tence France
177 I1 Tenczyński Park Krajobrazowy Pol.
210 D2 Tendaho Eth.
155 H4 Tende France
190 D7 Tende, Col de pass France/Italy
115 M8 Ten Degree Channel Andaman & Nicobar Is India
203 F6 Tendelti Sudan
206 B2 Te-n-Dghâmcha, Sebkhet salt marsh Maur.
183 O7 Tendilla Spain
102 R8 Tendō Japan
204 E2 Tendrara Morocco
190 A2 Tendre, Mont mt. Switz.
137 K7 Tendrivs'ka Kosa, Ostriv i. Ukr.
137 K7 Tendrivs'ka Zatoka b. Ukr.
159 O8 Tendu France
116 G8 Tendukheda Madh. Prad. India
129 E6 Tendürek Dağı mt. Turkey
206 C4 Téné r. Guinea
Tenedos i. Turkey see Bozcaada
105 L1 Ten-ei Japan
206 D3 Ténenkou Mali
138 E6 Tenenys r. Lith.
207 H2 Ténéré, Erg du des. Niger
207 H1 Ténéré du Tafassâsset des. Niger
216 □3a Tenerife i. Canary Is
205 F1 Ténès Alg.
197 O8 Tenevo Bulg.
96 C5 Teng, Nam r. Myanmar
95 L8 Tengah, Kepulauan is Indon.
94 □ Tengah, Sungai r. Sing.
93 C8 Tengahdai Flores Indon.
Tengcheng Guangxi China see Tengxian
108 B6 Tengchong Yunnan China
120 E6 Tenge Kazakh.
94 □ Tengeh Reservoir Sing.
177 H5 Tengelic Hungary
172 F6 Tengen Ger.
78 □6 Te Nggano lag. Rennell Solomon Is
95 L5 Tenggarong Kalimantan Indon.
106 I8 Tengger Els Nei Mongol China
106 I7 Tengger Shamo des. Nei Mongol China
94 E2 Tenggul i. Malaysia
121 M2 Tengiz, Ozero salt l. Kazakh.
108 G9 Tengqiao Hainan China
206 D4 Tengréla Côte d'Ivoire
135 H5 Ten'gushevo Rus. Fed.
108 H7 Tengxian Guangxi China
Tengxian Shandong China see Tengzhou
107 O9 Tengzhou Shandong China
161 J8 Ténibre, Mont mt. France/Italy
253 E5 Teniente Enciso, Parque Nacional nat. park Para.
Teniente Jubany research stn Antarctica see Jubany
261 F6 Teniente Origone Arg.
231 F11 Tenille FL U.S.A.
172 D5 Teningen Ger.
206 A2 Te-n-Ioubrar, Sebkhet salt marsh Maur.
245 J5 Tenixtepec Mex.
120 K1 Teniz, Ozero l. Kazakh.
177 J4 Tenk Hungary
114 E8 Tenkasi Tamil Nadu India
104 C7 Tenkawa Japan
209 E7 Tenke Dem. Rep. Congo
131 P2 Tenkeli Rus. Fed.
134 J5 Ten'ki Rus. Fed.
206 E4 Tenkodogo Burkina
87 F8 Ten Mile Lake salt flat W.A. Austr.
225 J3 Ten Mile Lake Nfld and Lab. Can.
191 P9 Tenna r. Italy
84 E5 Tennant Creek N.T. Austr.
172 E5 Tennenbronn Ger.
178 H4 Tennengau val. Austria
178 H5 Tennengebirge mts Austria
235 G4 Tennent NJ U.S.A.
237 K7 Tennessee r. U.S.A.
232 B12 Tennessee state U.S.A.
239 K7 Tennessee Pass CO U.S.A.
165 I8 Tenneville Belgium
140 N2 Tennevoll Norway
140 L3 Tennholmfjorden sea chan. Norway
140 T3 Tenniöjoki r. Fin./Rus. Fed.
260 B4 Teno Chile
260 B4 Teno r. Chile
216 □3a Teno, Punta de pt Tenerife Canary Is
245 K6 Tenochtitlán Mex.
140 T1 Tenojoki r. Fin./Norway
95 K2 Tenom Sabah Malaysia
243 N9 Tenosique Mex.
104 E5 Tenpaku Japan
104 C6 Tenri Japan
105 G5 Tenryū Nagano Japan
105 G6 Tenryū Shizuoka Japan
105 G5 Tenryū-gawa r. Japan
105 G5 Tenryū-Okumikawa Kokutei-kōen park Japan
238 K4 Ten Sleep WY U.S.A.
93 B4 Tenteno Sulawesi Indon.
151 N5 Tenterden Kent, England U.K.
83 N3 Tenterfield N.S.W. Austr.
231 G13 Ten Thousand Islands FL U.S.A.
223 J2 Tent Lake N.W.T. Can.
93 B3 Tentolomatinan, Gunung mt. Indon.
184 G4 Tentudia mt. Spain
182 C8 Tentúgal Port.
158 H7 Tenu r. France
177 G4 Tényő Hungary
244 E4 Teocaltiche Mex.
245 K6 Teocelo Mex.
244 D5 Teocuitatlán de Corona Mex.
261 G4 Teodelina Arg.
192 D6 Teodoro, Stagno di lag. Sardegna Italy
244 A3 Teodoro Beltrán Mex.
256 A5 Teodoro Sampaio Brazil
260 A6 Teodoro Schmidt Chile
257 G2 Teófilo Otôni Brazil
136 F4 Teofipol' Ukr.
92 C8 Teomabal i. Phil.
80 □ Te One Chatham Is S. Pacific Ocean
116 H7 Teonthar Madh. Prad. India
243 M9 Teopisca Mex.
193 O6 Teora Italy
245 I6 Teotihuacán tourist site Mex.
245 J7 Teotitlán Mex.
245 K8 Teotitlán del Valle Mex.
206 E5 Tepa Ghana
93 F7 Tepa Maluku Indon.
242 E3 Tepache Mex.
80 G1 Te Paki North I. N.Z.
244 E6 Tepalcatepec Mex.
244 E7 Tepalcatepec r. Mex.
245 I7 Tepalcingo Mex.
81 □4 Tepa Point Niue
140 R3 Tepasto Fin.
245 H5 Tepatepec Mex.
244 E5 Tepatitlán Mex.
177 K4 Tépe Hungary
245 J7 Tepeaca Mex.
245 I6 Tepeapulco Mex.
244 D4 Tepechitlán Mex.
199 J1 Tepecik Turkey
245 J2 Tepeguajes Mex.
244 A1 Tepehuaje Mex.
242 G5 Tepehuanes Mex.
245 H6 Tepeji Mex.
Tepeköy Turkey see Karakoçan
198 B2 Tepelenë Albania
245 J8 Tepelmeme de Morelos Mex.
176 B2 Tepelská vrchovina hills Czech Rep.
251 F4 Tepequem, Serra mts Brazil
213 H2 Tepere Moz.
244 F4 Tepetates Mex.
244 D3 Tepetengo Mex.
244 G8 Tepetixtla Mex.
245 J4 Tepetzintla Mex.
245 J7 Tepexi de Rodriguez Mex.
245 J6 Tepeyahualco Mex.
95 L4 Tepianlangsat Kalimantan Indon.
244 C4 Tepic Mex.
81 F10 Te Pirita South I. N.Z.
176 B2 Teplá Czech Rep.
176 B1 Teplá r. Czech Rep.
176 C3 Teplá Vltava r. Czech Rep.
134 L4 Teplaya Gora Rus. Fed.
137 S5 Teple Ukr.
129 F3 Tepli, Gora mt. Rus. Fed.
176 C1 Teplice Czech Rep.
177 J3 Teplička Slovakia
137 M8 Teplivka Ukr.
134 K3 Teplogorka Rus. Fed.
139 V8 Teploye Lipetskaya Oblast' Rus. Fed.
139 U8 Teploye Tul'skaya Oblast' Rus. Fed.
136 I5 Teplyk Ukr.
242 C3 Tepopa, Punta pt Mex.
245 J8 Teposcolula Mex.
245 H7 Tepoztlan Mex.
193 J5 Teppia r. Italy
80 K4 Te Puke North I. N.Z.
80 K4 Te Puna North I. N.Z.
244 G6 Tepuxtepec Mex.
244 D5 Tequila Mex.
244 D5 Tequila, Volcán de vol. Mex.
245 L9 Tequisistlán Mex.
245 L9 Tequisistlán r. Mex.
245 H5 Tequisquiapán Mex.
245 J6 Tequixquitla Mex.
245 J7 Tequixtépec Mex.
207 F3 Téra Niger
184 C3 Tera r. Port.
182 I5 Tera r. Spain
164 G4 Ter Aar Neth.
80 J4 Te Rahu North I. N.Z.
104 D3 Terai Japan
210 A3 Terakeka Sudan
116 F2 Teram Kangri mt. China/Jammu and Kashmir
193 L2 Teramo Italy
193 L2 Teramo prov. Italy
83 I8 Terang Vic. Austr.
80 J4 Te Rapa North I. N.Z.
164 L3 Ter Apel Neth.
123 M7 Teratani r. Pak.
175 L5 Teratyn Pol.
81 I8 Terawhiti, Cape North I. N.Z.
93 F7 Terbang Selatan i. Maluku Indon.
93 F7 Terbang Utara i. Maluku Indon.
164 J5 Terborg-Silvolde Neth.
139 V9 Terbuny Rus. Fed.
Tercan Erzincan Turkey see Otlukbeli
127 J4 Tercan Erzincan Turkey
129 B6 Tercan Barajı resr Turkey
216 □1a Terceira i. Azores
261 F3 Tercero r. Arg.
163 B8 Tercis-les-Bains France
190 G5 Terdoppio r. Italy
139 S8 Tereben' Rus. Fed.
177 L4 Terebeşti Romania
136 C5 Tereblya r. Ukr.
136 E4 Terebovlya Ukr.
139 V7 Terebush Rus. Fed.
197 K5 Teregova Romania
Terek r. Georgia see Tergi
129 F2 Terek Rus. Fed.
127 M2 Terek r. Rus. Fed.
106 D1 Tere-Khol' Rus. Fed.
106 E1 Tere-Khol', Ozero l. Rus. Fed.
129 G1 Terekli-Mekteb Rus. Fed.
121 N7 Terek-Say Kyrg.
110 G1 Terektinskiy Khrebet mts Rus. Fed.
121 M3 Terekty Karagandinskaya Oblast' Kazakh.
121 U3 Terekty Vostochnyy Kazakhstan Kazakh.
177 J6 Teremia Mare Romania
184 E3 Terena Port.
135 J5 Teren'ga Rus. Fed.
94 E2 Terengganu r. Malaysia
94 E2 Terengganu state Malaysia
Terengözek Kazakh. see Terenozek
255 B7 Terenos Brazil
120 K5 Terenozek Kazakh.
120 H2 Terensay Rus. Fed.
95 H5 Terentang Kalimantan Indon.
95 L5 Terentang, Pulau i. Indon.
147 J6 Terenure Ireland
Teren-Uzyak Kazakh. see Terenozek
256 B6 Teresa Cristina Brazil
187 C9 Teresa de Cofrentes Spain
217 □2b Térèse, Île i. Inner Islands Seychelles
120 B2 Tereshka r. Rus. Fed.
175 I3 Teresin Pol.
254 E3 Teresina Brazil
250 D4 Teresita Col.
257 F5 Teresópolis Brazil
175 L3 Terespol Pol.
115 M8 Teressa Island Andaman & Nicobar Is India
136 C5 Teresva Ukr.
136 C6 Teresva r. Ukr.
175 K5 Tereszpol-Zaorenda Pol.
176 D1 Terezín Czech Rep.
176 G6 Terezino Polje Croatia
136 J4 Terezyne Ukr.
178 E5 Terfens Austria
181 F5 Terga Alg.
184 D5 Terges r. Port.
Tergeste Italy see Trieste
129 F3 Tergi r. Georgia
156 F4 Tergnier France
191 M5 Tergola r. Italy
192 B6 Tergu Sardegna Italy
106 D7 Tergun Daba Shan mts Qinghai China
164 G5 Terheijden Neth.
106 F2 Terhiyn Tsagaan Nuur l. Mongolia
134 F1 Teriberka Rus. Fed.
138 K3 Terikeste Estonia
111 I11 Tering Xizang China
121 L2 Terisakkan r. Kazakh.
204 B5 Terjît well Maur.
129 F3 Terk Rus. Fed.
175 K6 Terka Pol.
210 D3 Terka Reba Eth.
202 D5 Terkezi well Chad
191 K2 Terlano Italy
237 D11 Terlingua Creek r. TX U.S.A.
193 R5 Terlizzi Italy
203 I6 Terma, Ras pt Eritrea
136 I2 Termakhivka Ukr.
260 B5 Termas de Chillán Chile
260 B4 Termas de Flaco Chile
261 I2 Termas del Arapey Uru.
260 B6 Termas de Pemehue Chile
260 B2 Termas de Socos Chile
260 B6 Termas de Tolhuaca Chile
260 C3 Termas de Villavicencio Arg.
126 H3 Terme Turkey
193 P9 Terme Luigiane Italy
186 G4 Térmens Spain
163 J9 Termes France
199 L6 Termessos Milli Parkı nat. park Turkey
Termez Uzbek. see Termiz
161 J6 Termignon France
87 F13 Termination Island W.A. Austr.
156 C7 Terminiers France
194 F8 Termini Imerese Sicilia Italy
194 F7 Termini Imerese, Golfo di b. Sicilia Italy
193 J3 Terminillo, Monte mt. Italy
243 N8 Términos, Laguna de lag. Mex.
207 H2 Termit well Niger
207 H2 Termit, Massif de hill Niger
207 H3 Termit-Kaoboul Niger
121 L9 Termiz Uzbek.
193 N4 Termoli Italy
147 G2 Termon Ireland
Termonde Belgium see Dendermonde
148 E6 Termonfeckin Ireland
150 G2 Tern r. England U.K.
137 N3 Tern r. Ukr.
164 I2 Ternaard Neth.
93 E3 Ternate Maluku Indon.
93 E3 Ternate i. Maluku Indon.
217 □2b Ternay, La Passe sea chan. Inner Islands Seychelles
Ternay Pass sea chan. Inner Islands Seychelles see Ternay, La Passe
179 J4 Ternberg Austria
165 E6 Terneuzen Neth.
100 J6 Terney Rus. Fed.
193 J2 Terni Italy
193 I2 Terni prov. Italy
160 E3 Ternin r. France
179 N4 Ternitz Austria
137 P5 Ternivka Dnipropetrovs'ka Oblast' Ukr.
137 L6 Ternivka Mykolayivs'ka Oblast' Ukr.
137 M9 Ternivka Respublika Krym Ukr.
136 I5 Ternivka Vinnyts'ka Oblast' Ukr.
156 D3 Ternois reg. France
156 D3 Ternoise r. France
136 E4 Ternopil' Ukr.
Ternopil Oblast admin. div. Ukr. see Ternopils'ka Oblast'
136 E4 Ternopils'ka Oblast' admin. div. Ukr.
Ternopol' Ukr. see Ternopil'
Ternopol Oblast admin. div. Ukr. see Ternopils'ka Oblast'
Ternopol'skaya Oblast' admin. div. Ukr. see Ternopils'ka Oblast'
135 H6 Ternovka Rus. Fed.
Ternovka Ukr. see Ternivka
137 P6 Ternuvate Ukr.
137 Q4 Terny Donets'ka Oblast' Ukr.
137 M3 Terny Sums'ka Oblast' Ukr.
216 □3f Teror Gran Canaria Canary Is
82 G5 Terowie S.A. Austr.
100 N4 Terpeniya, Mys c. Sakhalin Rus. Fed.
100 N4 Terpeniya, Poluostrov pen. Rus. Fed.
100 M4 Terpeniya, Zaliv g. Sakhalin Rus. Fed.
232 F9 Terra Alta WV U.S.A.
240 M6 Terra Bella CA U.S.A.
256 A5 Terra Boa Brazil
257 F2 Terra Branca Brazil
222 D4 Terrace B.C. Can.
224 C3 Terrace Bay Ont. Can.
216 □1a Terra Chã Terceira Azores
193 K5 Terracina Italy
193 K5 Terracina, Golfo di b. Italy
Terradas Spain see Terrades
186 K3 Terrades Spain
186 G3 Terradets, Pantà de resr Spain
214 H1 Terra Firma S. Africa
140 L4 Terråk Norway
192 B8 Terralba Sardegna Italy
263 K1 Terra Nova Bay Antarctica
195 K4 Terranova da Sibari Italy
193 Q8 Terranova di Pollino Italy
225 K3 Terra Nova National Park Nfld and Lab. Can.
191 L8 Terranuova Bracciolini Italy
251 G6 Terra Preta Brazil
256 A5 Terra Rica Brazil
182 D5 Terras do Bouro Port.
194 E7 Terrasini Sicilia Italy
186 J4 Terrassa Spain
162 G5 Terrasson-Lavilledieu France
163 F8 Terraube France
195 L5 Terravecchia Italy
242 F3 Terrazas Mex.
Terre Adélie reg. Antarctica see Adélie Land
237 J11 Terrebonne Bay LA U.S.A.
247 □2 Terre de Bas i. Guadeloupe
247 □2 Terre de Haut i. Guadeloupe
230 D6 Terre Haute IN U.S.A.
234 C4 Terre Hill PA U.S.A.
237 G9 Terrell TX U.S.A.
157 K8 Terre-Natale France
245 J6 Terrenate Mex.
225 K4 Terrenceville Nfld and Lab. Can.
160 E2 Terre Plaine plain France
242 F3 Terrero Mex.
Terres Australes et Antarctiques Françaises terr. Indian Ocean see French Southern and Antarctic Lands
191 J8 Terricciola Italy
183 R8 Terriente Spain
185 I7 Terril mt. Spain
148 C6 Terrin Ireland
185 N3 Terrinches Spain
149 P5 Terrington North Yorkshire, England U.K.
151 M2 Terrington St Clement Norfolk, England U.K.
157 M8 Territoire de Belfort dept France
163 H6 Terrou France
184 A3 Terrugem Lisboa Port.
184 E3 Terrugem Portalegre Port.
238 L3 Terry MT U.S.A.
235 I1 Terryville CT U.S.A.
235 I3 Terryville NY U.S.A.
135 I6 Tersa r. Rus. Fed.
Tersakkan r. Kazakh. see Terisakkan
164 H2 Terschelling i. Neth.
Terskey Alatau, Khrebet mts Kyrg. see Terskey Ala-Too
121 Q7 Terskey Ala-Too mts Kyrg.
134 G2 Terskiy Bereg coastal area Rus. Fed.
129 F1 Tersko-Kumskiy Kanal canal Rus. Fed.
137 O6 Tersyanka Ukr.
192 D8 Tertenia Sardegna Italy
Terter Azer. see Tärtär
168 G2 Tertius i. Ger.
156 F4 Tertry France
187 C7 Teruel Spain
183 Q7 Teruel prov. Spain
138 H1 Tervakoski Fin.
197 P7 Tervel Bulg.
159 J8 Terves France
140 S5 Tervo Fin.
140 R3 Tervola Fin.
139 T5 Teryayevo Rus. Fed.
177 H4 Tés Hungary
191 M3 Tesa r. Italy
188 F3 Tešanj Bos.-Herz.
163 G7 Tescou r. France
245 L7 Tesechoacán r. Mex.
177 G3 Tešedíkovo Slovakia
216 □3b Tesejerague Fuerteventura Canary Is
203 H6 Teseney Eritrea
191 L3 Tesero Italy
135 H5 Tesha r. Rus. Fed.
220 C2 Teshekpuk Lake AK U.S.A.
207 E5 Teshi Ghana
102 V3 Teshikaga Japan
102 S2 Teshio Japan
102 T3 Teshio-dake mt. Japan
102 S2 Teshio-gawa r. Japan
102 S2 Teshio-sanchi mts Japan
242 E4 Tesia Mex.
197 J7 Tešica Serbia
191 K2 Tesimo Italy
191 L5 Tesina r. Italy
244 D5 Tesistán Mex.
106 C1 Tesiyn Gol r. Mongolia
183 M3 Tesla, Sierra de la mts Spain
188 F3 Teslić Bos.-Herz.
222 C2 Teslin Y.T. Can.

Teslin to Tilleda (Kyffhäuser)
397

222 C2 Teslin r. Y.T. Can.
222 C2 Teslin Lake B.C./Y.T. Can.
197 M6 Teslui r. Romania
182 I6 Teso Santo hill Spain
255 B6 Tesouro Brazil
139 O3 Tesovo-Netyl'skiy Rus. Fed.
139 N3 Tesovskiy Rus. Fed.
168 J4 Tespe Ger.
205 F5 Tessalit Mali
207 G3 Tessaoua Niger
159 K4 Tessé-la-Madeleine France
165 H6 Tessenderlo Belgium
207 G2 Tesséroukane well Niger
170 F2 Tessin Ger.
Tessin canton Switz. see Ticino
213 G4 Tessolo Moz.
162 C4 Tesson France
205 F5 Tessoûnfat well Mali
159 I4 Tessy-sur-Vire France
151 J6 Test r. England U.K.
192 C5 Testa, Capo c. Sardegna Italy
193 Q4 Testa del Gargano Italy
194 H10 Testa dell'Acqua Sicilia Italy
182 D4 Testeiro, Montes do mts Spain
165 G6 Testelt Belgium
183 N9 Testillos r. Spain
205 H1 Testour Tunisia
163 K10 Têt r. France
177 G4 Tét Hungary
222 E4 Tetachuck Lake B.C. Can.
225 H4 Tetagouche r. N.B. Can.
252 C5 Tetas, Punta pt Chile
150 H4 Tetbury Gloucestershire, England U.K.
177 L4 Teţchea Romania
213 G3 Tete Moz.
213 G2 Tete prov. Moz.
161 J8 Tête de l'Enchastraye mt. France/Italy
161 J8 Tête de l'Estrop mt. France
161 I7 Tête de Soulaure mt. France
190 B6 Tête des Toillies mt. Italy
94 B4 Tetehosi Indon.
222 G4 Tête Jaune Cache B.C. Can.
80 K5 Te Teko North I. N.Z.
244 G8 Tetela Mex.
245 J6 Tetela de Ocampo Mex.
245 I7 Tetela de Volcán Mex.
78 □6 Tetepare i. New Georgia Is Solomon Is
164 G5 Teteringen Neth.
136 J2 Teteriv r. Ukr.
170 G3 Teterow Ger.
177 K4 Tetétlen Hungary
197 M8 Teteven Bulg.
149 Q7 Tetford Lincolnshire, England U.K.
192 C7 Teti Sardegna Italy
244 E2 Tetillas Mex.
Tetiyev Ukr. see Tetiyiv
136 I4 Tetiyiv Ukr.
137 N2 Tetkino Rus. Fed.
149 Q7 Tetney Lincolnshire, England U.K.
238 I3 Teton r. MT U.S.A.
238 I5 Teton Range mts WY U.S.A.
204 D2 Tétouan Morocco
180 D5 Tétouan prov. Morocco
196 I8 Tetovo Macedonia
116 C9 Tetpur Gujarat India
134 G2 Tetrino Rus. Fed.
171 D10 Tettau Ger.
168 E3 Tettens Ger.
172 H6 Tettnang Ger.
Tetuán Morocco see Tétouan
79 □9a Tetufera mt. Tahiti Fr. Polynesia
117 L6 Tetulia Bangl.
117 M8 Tetulia sea chan. Bangl.
170 K4 Tetyń Pol.
Tetyukhe Rus. Fed. see Dal'negorsk
Tetyukhe-Pristan' Rus. Fed. see Rudnaya Pristan'
135 J5 Tetyushi Rus. Fed.
173 M3 Teublitz Ger.
171 F8 Teuchern Ger.
Teuchezhsk Rus. Fed. see Adygeysk
103 G15 Teuchi Japan
258 E2 Teuco r. Arg.
212 C4 Teufelsbach Namibia
168 G4 Teufels Moor reg. Ger.
190 G1 Teufen Switz.
179 J5 Teufenbach Austria
192 B10 Teulada Sardegna Italy
187 F10 Teulada Spain
192 B10 Teulada, Capo c. Sardegna Italy
192 B10 Teulada, Golfo di b. Sardegna Italy
244 D4 Teul de González Ortega Mex.
93 F7 Teun vol. Maluku Indon.
94 A2 Teunom Sumatera Indon.
94 A2 Teunom r. Indon.
173 M3 Teunz Ger.
171 I6 Teupitz Ger.
171 I6 Teupitz-Köriser Seengebiet park Ger.
102 S2 Teuri-tō i. Japan
171 D10 Teuschnitz Ger.
242 □Q11 Teustepe Nic.
169 F6 Teutoburger Wald hills Ger.
171 E8 Teutschenthal Ger.
157 I4 Teuva Fin.
175 H5 Tevel Hungary
191 M9 Tevere r. Italy
193 J1 Teverone r. Italy
128 D6 Teverya Israel
81 D12 Teviot South I. N.Z.
215 J7 Teviot S. Africa
146 L11 Teviot r. Scotland U.K.
146 K12 Teviotdale val. Scotland U.K.
146 K12 Teviothead Scottish Borders, Scotland U.K.
81 B13 Te Waewae South I. N.Z.
81 B13 Te Waewae Bay South I. N.Z.
95 J5 Tewah Kalimantan Indon.
Te Waipounamu i. N.Z. see South Island
213 E4 Tewane Botswana
85 N9 Tewantin Qld Austr.
95 K5 Teweh r. Indon.
80 I6 Te Wera North I. N.Z.
80 L5 Te Wera North I. N.Z.
80 K5 Te Whaiti North I. N.Z.
80 □ Te Whanga Lagoon Chatham Is S. Pacific Ocean
81 J8 Te Wharau North I. N.Z.
150 H4 Tewkesbury Gloucestershire, England U.K.
138 H9 Tewli Belarus
106 H9 Têwo Gansu China
108 D1 Têwo Sichuan China
146 D11 Texa i. Scotland U.K.
237 H9 Texarkana AR U.S.A.
237 H9 Texarkana TX U.S.A.
83 M3 Texas Qld Austr.
237 F10 Texas state U.S.A.
237 H11 Texas City TX U.S.A.
245 I6 Texcoco Mex.
164 G2 Texel i. Neth.
237 E7 Texhoma OK U.S.A.
245 M8 Texistepec Mex.
245 H6 Texmelucan Mex.
237 G9 Texoma, Lake OK/TX U.S.A.
215 L5 Teyateyaneng Lesotho
162 F4 Teyjat France
139 X5 Teykovo Rus. Fed.
151 N5 Teynham Kent, England U.K.
163 H6 Teyssieu France
160 E4 Teyssonne r. France
123 K5 Teyvareh Afgh.
124 H4 Teza r. Rus. Fed.
212 E4 Teza S. Africa
245 J6 Teziutlán Mex.
245 J8 Tezoatlán Mex.
245 K7 Tezonapa Mex.
245 H5 Tezontepec Mex.
117 N6 Tezpur Assam India
117 P6 Tezu Arun. Prad. India
204 C4 Tfaritiy Western Sahara
96 E4 Tha, Nam r. Laos
223 M2 Tha-anne r. Nunavut Can.
215 N5 Thabana-Ntlenyana mt. Lesotho
215 N5 Thaba Nchu S. Africa
215 O3 Thabankulu mt. S. Africa
213 E6 Thaba Putsoa mt. Lesotho
215 L6 Thaba Putsoa mts S. Africa
215 M5 Thaba-Tseka Lesotho
213 E5 Thabazimbi S. Africa
96 C3 Thabeikkyin Myanmar
97 F7 Thab Lan National Park Thai.
96 F5 Tha Bo Laos
215 K3 Thabong S. Africa
161 J6 Thabor, Mont mt. France
96 C4 Thabyedaung Myanmar
97 D8 Thac Ba, Hồ l. Vietnam
96 B5 Thade r. Myanmar
124 G3 Thādiq Saudi Arabia
97 D8 Thagyettaw Myanmar
Tha Hin Thai. see Lop Buri
96 H4 Thai Binh Vietnam
96 E6 Thailand country Asia
97 E9 Thailand, Gulf of Asia
97 D10 Thai Muang Thai.
96 G4 Thai Nguyên Vietnam
125 I2 Thaj Saudi Arabia
96 G6 Thakèk Laos
117 L6 Thakurgaon Bangl.
116 H9 Thakurtola Chhattisgarh India
169 J9 Thal Ger.
123 N5 Thal Pak.
205 H2 Thala Tunisia
Thalabarivat Cambodia see Phumĭ Thalabârivăt
97 D10 Thalang Thai.
Thalassery Pondicherry India see Tellicherry
128 A8 Thalāthah Egypt
173 K3 Thalbach r. Ger.
123 N6 Thal Desert Pak.
171 D7 Thale (Harz) Ger.
172 D3 Thaleischweiler-Fröschen Ger.
172 B2 Thalfang Ger.
178 H4 Thalgau Austria
171 F7 Thalheim Ger.
179 J3 Thalheim bei Wels Austria
96 E6 Thali Thai.
Thaliparamba Kerala India see Taliparamba
83 L3 Thallon Qld Austr.
171 G8 Thallwitz Ger.
173 K3 Thalmässing Ger.
173 M4 Thalmassing Ger.
123 K7 Thalo Pak.
190 F1 Thalwil Switz.
202 C3 Thamad Bū Hashīshah well Libya
212 E5 Thamaga Botswana
124 H2 Thāmām, 'Irq ath des. Saudi Arabia
124 G9 Thamar, Jabal mt. Yemen
125 L7 Thamarīt Oman
151 K4 Thame Oxfordshire, England U.K.
151 J4 Thame r. England U.K.
227 L7 Thames r. Ont. Can.
80 J4 Thames North I. N.Z.
151 N5 Thames est. England U.K.
151 M5 Thames r. England U.K.
235 K2 Thames r. CT U.S.A.
80 J3 Thames, Firth of b. North I. N.Z.
Thamesdown admin. div. England U.K. see Swindon
227 N6 Thamesford Ont. Can.
227 M7 Thamesville Ont. Can.
169 K8 Thamsbrück Ger.
125 I7 Thamūd Yemen
Thamugadi tourist site Alg. see Timgad
Thana Mahar. India see Thane
116 F6 Thana Ghazi Rajasthan India
96 C6 Thanatpin Myanmar
96 C7 Thanbyuzayat Myanmar
96 C5 Thandaung Myanmar
116 E8 Thandla Madh. Prad. India
96 B5 Thandwè Myanmar
114 C3 Thane Mahar. India
151 O5 Thanet, Isle of pen. England U.K.
116 C8 Thangadh Gujarat India
86 G5 Thangoo W.A. Austr.
85 M8 Thangool Qld Austr.
116 G3 Thangra Jammu and Kashmir
96 G5 Thanh Hoa Vietnam
114 F7 Thanjavur Tamil Nadu India
97 D10 Than Kyun i. Myanmar
Thanlwin r. Myanmar see Salween
96 C6 Thanlyin Myanmar
157 N8 Thann France
173 I5 Thannhausen Ger.
123 M6 Thano Bula Khan Pak.
108 D8 Than Uyên Vietnam
212 D3 Thaoge r. Botswana
223 L2 Thaolintoa Lake Nunavut Can.
157 L7 Thaon-les-Vosges France
96 E6 Tha Pla Thai.
97 D10 Thap Put Thai.
Thapsacus Syria see Dibsī
97 D9 Thap Sakae Thai.
116 C8 Thara Gujarat India
96 C5 Tharabwin Myanmar
97 D8 Tharad Gujarat India
210 C5 Tharaka Kenya
171 I9 Tharandt Ger.
164 I4 't Harde Neth.
116 B7 Thar Desert India/Pak.
85 I9 Thargomindah Qld Austr.
96 B6 Tharrawaw Myanmar
184 E5 Tharsis Spain
127 K7 Tharthār, Buḥayrat ath l. Iraq
125 L4 Tharwānīyyah U.A.E.
97 D10 Tha Sala Thai.
198 F2 Thasopoula i. Greece
198 F2 Thasos Thasos Greece
198 F2 Thasos i. Greece
151 J5 Thatcham West Berkshire, England U.K.
241 W9 Thatcher AZ U.S.A.
198 B2 Thatë, Mali i mt. Albania
96 H3 Thất Khê Vietnam
96 C6 Thaton Myanmar
123 K7 Thau, Bassin de lag. France
161 D10 Thau, Bassin de lag. France
96 B3 Thaungdut Myanmar
96 B2 Thaungdut Myanmar
96 C6 Thaungyin r. Myanmar/Thai.
178 D5 Thaur Austria
96 D6 The Uthen Thai.
128 D9 Thawr, Jabal mt. Jordan
151 M4 Thaxted Essex, England U.K.
179 L2 Thaya Austria
179 M2 Thaya r. Austria/Czech Rep.
96 B6 Thayawadi Myanmar
97 C8 Thayawthadangyi Kyun i. Myanmar
96 B5 Thayetmyo Myanmar
96 C2 Thayetta Myanmar
190 F1 Thayngen Switz.
96 B5 Thazi Magwe Myanmar
96 C4 Thazi Mandalay Myanmar
80 K3 The Aldermen Islands North I. N.Z.
246 □ The Alley Jamaica
241 T9 Theba AZ U.S.A.
96 B6 Thebadah N.W.T. Can. see Fort Smith
Thebae tourist site Egypt see Thebes
229 K6 The Bahamas country West Indies
203 G3 Thebes tourist site Egypt
Thebes Greece see Thiva
246 E1 The Bluff Eleuthera Bahamas
216 □2b The Briars St Helena
151 P2 The Broads nat. park England U.K.
The Brothers is H.K. China see Tai Siu Mo To
The Brothers is Yemen see Al Ikhwān
149 L5 The Calf hill England U.K.
216 □2b The Calvados Chain is P.N.G.
149 M3 The Cheviot hill England U.K.
246 □ The Cockpit Country hills Jamaica
82 G6 The Coorong inlet S.A. Austr.
247 □4 The Crane Barbados
231 □1 The Crawl pt Bermuda
148 D7 The Curragh lowland Ireland
238 D4 The Dalles OR U.S.A.
236 E4 Thedford NE U.S.A.
148 D4 The Diamond Northern Ireland U.K.
168 H5 Thedinghausen Ger.
84 F1 The English Company's Islands N.T. Austr.
83 M5 The Entrance N.S.W. Austr.
214 D10 Theewaterskloof Dam resr S. Africa
146 □M1 The Faither stack Scotland U.K.
151 L2 The Fens reg. England U.K.
80 □ The Forty Fours is Chatham Is S. Pacific Ocean
206 A3 The Gambia country Africa
146 H12 The Glenkens val. Scotland U.K.
83 I7 The Grampians mts Vic. Austr.
84 C6 The Granites hill N.T. Austr.
The Great Oasis Egypt see Khārijah, Wāḥāt al
247 □3 The Grenadines is St Vincent
125 J1 The Gulf Asia
The Hague Neth. see 's-Gravenhage
147 J7 The Harrow Ireland
215 M8 The Haven S. Africa
80 □ The Horns hill Chatham Is S. Pacific Ocean
214 H7 The Horseshoe mt. S. Africa
81 E11 The Hunters Hills South I. N.Z.
159 P7 Theillay France
97 D9 Theinkun Myanmar
96 C6 Theinzeik Myanmar
171 F8 Theißen Ger.
158 F6 Theix France
81 B12 The Key South I. N.Z.
223 I2 Thekulthili Lake N.W.T. Can.
83 K7 The Lakes National Park Vic. Austr.
156 C5 Thelle reg. France
223 L1 Thelon r. N.W.T./Nunavut Can.
223 K1 Thelon Game Sanctuary nature res. Nunavut Can.
150 G2 The Long Mynd hills England U.K.
148 D4 The Loup Northern Ireland U.K.
85 J5 The Lynd Junction Qld Austr.
146 H13 The Machars reg. Scotland U.K.
147 K3 The Maidens is Northern Ireland U.K.
169 K9 Themar Ger.
214 I8 Thembalesizwe S. Africa
215 M3 Thembalihle S. Africa
146 D6 The Minch sea chan. Scotland U.K.
163 H6 Thémines France
147 B4 The Mullet b. Ireland
150 E4 The Mumbles Swansea, Wales U.K.
231 □1 The Narrows sea chan. Bermuda
247 □2 The Narrows str. St Kitts and Nevis
159 N8 Thenay France
The Naze c. Norway see Lindesnes
151 O4 The Naze pt England U.K.
81 C13 The Neck pen. Stewart I. N.Z.
151 I6 The Needles stack England U.K.
159 K8 Thénezay France
116 G8 Theni Madh. Prad. India
205 F2 Théniet El Had Alg.
162 G5 Thenon France
146 J5 The North Sound sea chan. Scotland U.K.
84 C6 Theo, Mount hill N.T. Austr.
146 D11 The Oa pen. Scotland U.K.
85 M8 Theodore Qld Austr.
223 K5 Theodore Sask. Can.
253 E1 Theodore Roosevelt r. Brazil
241 U8 Theodore Roosevelt Lake AZ U.S.A.
236 D2 Theodore Roosevelt National Park ND U.S.A.
Theodosia Ukr. see Feodosiya
82 D2 The Officer Creek watercourse S.A. Austr.
149 K5 The Old Man of Coniston hill England U.K.
159 P7 Thénioux France
161 J7 Théoule-sur-Mer France
147 D8 The Paps hill Ireland
223 K4 The Pas Man. Can.
216 □2a The Peak hill Ascension S. Atlantic Ocean
147 G8 The Pike Ireland
Thera i. Greece see Santorini
156 D5 Thérain r. France
81 C12 The Remarkables mts South I. N.Z.
169 J10 Theres Ger.
233 J4 Theresa NY U.S.A.
85 L7 Theresa Creek r. Qld Austr.
Thérèse Island Inner Islands Seychelles see Térèse, Île
146 F13 The Rhins of Galloway pen. Scotland U.K.
199 G2 Therma Samothraki Greece
198 D2 Thermaikos Kolpos g. Greece
198 E2 Thermi Greece
198 C4 Thermo Greece
Thermon Greece see Thermo
238 J5 Thermopolis WY U.S.A.
198 D4 Thermopyles Greece
83 K6 The Rock N.S.W. Austr.
185 □ The Rock hill Gibraltar
156 D2 Thérouanne France
246 □ The Salt Ponds lakes Jamaica
86 □1 The Settlement Christmas I.
147 B8 The Seven Hogs is Ireland
147 J3 The Sheddings Northern Ireland U.K.
220 F2 Thesiger Bay N.W.T. Can.
The Sisters is Inner Islands Seychelles see Les Sœurs
80 □ The Sisters is Chatham Is S. Pacific Ocean
The Skaw spit Denmark see Grenen
The Slot sea chan. Solomon Is see New Georgia Sound
146 □L2 The Sneug hill Scotland U.K.
146 □L2 The Solent str. England U.K.
151 I6 The Solent str. England U.K.
198 B3 Thesprotiko Greece
198 D3 Thessalia admin. reg. Greece
227 I4 Thessalon Ont. Can.
224 D4 Thessalonica Greece see Thessaloniki
Thessaloniki Greece
198 D2 Thessaloniki Greece
Thessaly admin. reg. Greece see Thessalia
151 N5 The Stocks Kent, England U.K.
146 D7 The Storr hill Scotland U.K.
151 N5 The Swale sea chan. England U.K.
151 N3 Thet r. England U.K.
92 B7 The Teeth mt. Palawan Phil.
148 F5 The Temple Northern Ireland U.K.
87 F10 The Terraces hills W.A. Austr.
151 N3 Thetford Norfolk, England U.K.
225 G4 Thetford Mines Que. Can.
81 E10 The Thumbs mt. South I. N.Z.
96 B7 Thetkethaung r. Myanmar
96 C2 The Triangle mts Myanmar
146 H10 The Trossachs hills Scotland U.K.
82 E4 The Twins S.A. Austr.
96 G5 Theun r. Laos
215 K4 Theunissen S. Africa
165 I7 Theux Belgium
Theva-i-Ra rf Fiji see Ceva-i-Ra
247 L4 The Valley Anguilla
82 D5 Thevenard S.A. Austr.
86 C6 Thevenard Island W.A. Austr.
225 G1 Thévenet, Lac l. Que. Can.
Theveste Alg. see Tébessa
151 M2 The Wash b. England U.K.
151 M5 The Weald reg. England U.K.
237 H10 The Woodlands TX U.S.A.
The Wrekin admin. div. England U.K. see Telford and Wrekin
163 D9 Thèze Aquitaine France
161 H8 Thèze Provence-Alpes-Côte d'Azur France
Thiamis r. Greece see Kalamas
157 K6 Thiaucourt-Regniéville France
159 L3 Thiberville France
155 H6 Thibie France
237 J11 Thibodaux LA U.S.A.
223 L4 Thicket Portage Man. Can.
156 I6 Thiéblemont-Farémont France
236 G1 Thief River Falls MN U.S.A.
Thiel Neth. see Tiel
190 B2 Thielle r. Switz.
235 G2 Thiells NY U.S.A.
262 R1 Thiel Mountains Antarctica
238 C5 Thielsen, Mount OR U.S.A.
Thielt Belgium see Tielt
191 K4 Thiene Italy
156 G4 Thiérache reg. France
173 J4 Thierhaupten Ger.
190 B2 Thierrens Switz.
160 D5 Thiers France
178 F4 Thiersee Austria
171 F10 Thiersheim Ger.
157 J5 Thierville-sur-Meuse France
206 A3 Thiès Senegal
192 B6 Thiesi Sardegna Italy
170 I2 Thießow Ger.
161 B6 Thiézac France
211 C5 Thika Kenya
Thikombia i. Fiji see Cikobia
114 C9 Thiladhunmathi Atoll Maldives
206 B3 Thilogne Senegal
Thimbu Bhutan see Thimphu
156 B6 Thimert-Gâtelles France
117 L6 Thimphu Bhutan
140 □C1 Thingvallavatn (Þingvallavatn) l. Iceland
140 □C1 Thingvellir (Þingvellir) Iceland
140 C1 Thingvellir (Þingvellir) nat. park Iceland
156 I4 Thin-le-Moutier France
78 □5 Thio New Caledonia
157 L5 Thionville France
Thira i. Greece see Santorini
Thirasia i. Greece
198 G6 Thirlmere resr England U.K.
149 K5 Thirlmere resr England U.K.
159 M5 Thiron Gardais France
156 B7 Thironne r. France
116 F4 Thirrach Hima. Prad. India
149 O5 Thirsk North Yorkshire, England U.K.
87 F12 Thirty, Mount hill W.A. Austr.
223 L2 Thirty Mile Lake Nunavut Can.
Thiruvananthapuram Kerala India see Trivandrum
114 F7 Thiruvarur Tamil Nadu India
Thiruvattiyur Tamil Nadu India see Tiruvottiyur
160 I2 Thise France
198 F1 Thissavros, Techniti Limni resr Greece
142 E5 Thisted Denmark
140 □F1 Thistilfjörður (Þistilfjörður) b. Iceland
222 B2 Thistle Creek Y.T. Can.
82 F6 Thistle Island S.A. Austr.
223 M2 Thistle Lake Nunavut Can.
96 B3 Thityabin Myanmar
198 E4 Thiva Greece
Thívai Greece see Thiva
156 B7 Thivars France
162 F5 Thiviers France
157 K7 Thizy France
140 □C2 Þjórsá (Þjórsá) r. Iceland
223 M2 Thlewiaza r. Nunavut Can.
223 I2 Thoa r. N.W.T. Can.
157 K8 Thoard France
97 F10 Thô Chu, Đao i. Vietnam
96 D6 Thoen Thai.
96 E5 Thoeng Thai.
213 F4 Thohoyandou S. Africa
160 E4 Thoirette France
157 L9 Thoiry Île-de-France France
156 C6 Thoiry Rhône-Alpes France
160 F4 Thoissey France
160 E2 Thoisy-la-Berchère France
164 F5 Tholen Neth.
164 F5 Tholen i. Neth.
172 C3 Tholey Ger.
156 F7 Tholon r. France
87 D8 Thomas r. W.A. Austr.
84 F9 Thomas, Lake salt flat S.A. Austr.
168 K4 Thomasburg Ger.
236 I6 Thomas Hill Reservoir MO U.S.A.
221 I1 Thomas Hubbard, Cape Nunavut Can.
240 P8 Thomas Mountain CA U.S.A.
231 I5 Thomaston CT U.S.A.
231 E9 Thomaston GA U.S.A.
233 □P4 Thomaston ME U.S.A.
233 □R3 Thomaston Corner N.B. Can.
147 F10 Thomastown Ireland
231 D10 Thomasville AL U.S.A.
231 E10 Thomasville GA U.S.A.
231 G8 Thomasville NC U.S.A.
165 J8 Thommen Belgium
246 H4 Thomonde Haiti
223 L4 Thompson Man. Can.
222 F5 Thompson r. B.C. Can.
226 H4 Thompson MI U.S.A.
241 W3 Thompson UT U.S.A.
236 I5 Thompson r. MO U.S.A.
238 G3 Thompson Falls MT U.S.A.
239 L9 Thompson Peak NM U.S.A.
Thompson's Falls Kenya see Nyahururu
222 E5 Thompson Sound B.C. Can.
81 A12 Thompson Sound inlet South I. N.Z.
234 E5 Thompsontown PA U.S.A.
233 M7 Thompsonville CT U.S.A.
85 I8 Thomson watercourse Qld Austr.
231 F9 Thomson GA U.S.A.
226 D8 Thomson IL U.S.A.
81 C11 Thomson Mountains South I. N.Z.
97 E8 Thon Buri Thai.
116 F3 Thondhe Jammu and Kashmir
160 I5 Thônes France
96 C7 Thongwa Myanmar
157 J7 Thonnance-lès-Joinville France
223 I1 Thonokied Lake N.W.T. Can.
160 I3 Thonon-les-Bains France
161 J8 Thorame-Basse France
161 J8 Thorame-Haute France
161 D7 Thoras France
160 B3 Thoré r. France
239 J9 Thoreau NM U.S.A.
159 M6 Thoré-la-Rochette France
161 J9 Thorenc France
160 I5 Thorens-Glières France
162 D4 Thorhild Alta Can.
161 D7 Thorigny-sur-Oreuse France
140 □D1 Thórisvatn (Þórisvatn) l. Iceland
179 L4 Thörl Austria
165 I6 Thorn Neth.
Thorn Pol. see Toruń
149 O4 Thornaby-on-Tees Stockton-on-Tees, England U.K.
226 I7 Thornapple r. MI U.S.A.
81 C13 Thornbury South I. N.Z.
150 G4 Thornbury South Gloucestershire, England U.K.
227 O3 Thorne Ont. Can.
149 P6 Thorne South Yorkshire, England U.K.
240 N3 Thorne NV U.S.A.
222 C4 Thorne Bay AK U.S.A.
149 P5 Thorney Peterborough, England U.K.
149 Q6 Thorngumbald East Riding of Yorkshire, England U.K.
146 I12 Thornhill Dumfries and Galloway, Scotland U.K.
148 I1 Thornhill Stirling, Scotland U.K.
234 D2 Thornhurst PA U.S.A.
149 O4 Thornley Durham, England U.K.
84 G5 Thornton r. Qld Austr.
146 J10 Thornton Fife, Scotland U.K.
149 L6 Thornton Lancashire, England U.K.
226 F5 Thornton WI U.S.A.
149 P5 Thornton Dale North Yorkshire, England U.K.
235 H2 Thornwood NY U.S.A.
227 O6 Thorold Ont. Can.
226 D5 Thorp WI U.S.A.
81 G8 Thorpe South I. N.Z.
151 O4 Thorpe-le-Soken Essex, England U.K.
151 O2 Thorpe Market Norfolk, England U.K.
151 P3 Thorpeness Suffolk, England U.K.
151 O2 Thorpe St Andrew Norfolk, England U.K.
222 H4 Thorsby Alta Can.
Thorshavn Faroe Is see Tórshavn
Thorshavnfjella reg. Antarctica see Thorshavnheiane
263 B2 Thorshavnheiane reg. Antarctica
140 □F1 Thórshöfn (Þórshöfn) Iceland
140 □E1 Thorvaldsfell (Þorvaldsfell) vol. Iceland
215 L5 Thota-ea-Moli Lesotho
159 K7 Thouarcé France
158 I7 Thouarcé-sur-Loire France
162 D2 Thouars France
117 N7 Thoubal Manipur India
162 D1 Thouet r. France
86 E6 Thouin, Cape pt W.A. Austr.
156 E5 Thourotte France
227 R5 Thousand Islands Can./U.S.A.
241 U3 Thousand Lake Mountain UT U.S.A.
240 N7 Thousand Oaks CA U.S.A.
241 P8 Thousand Palms CA U.S.A.
232 B11 Thousandsticks KY U.S.A.
234 B6 T. Howard Duckett Reservoir MD U.S.A.
197 O9 Thrace reg. Turkey
Thraki reg. Turkey see Thrace
198 F2 Thrakiko Pelagos sea Greece
151 K3 Thrapston Northamptonshire, England U.K.
83 L7 Thredbo N.S.W. Austr.
234 F3 Three Bridges NJ U.S.A.
147 C10 Three Castle Head Ireland
Three Fathoms Cove b. H.K. China see Kei Ling Ha Hoi
238 I4 Three Forks MT U.S.A.
108 G3 Three Gorges Dam Project resr China
83 J9 Three Hummock Island Tas. Austr.
80 G1 Three Kings Islands North I. N.Z.
226 E4 Three Lakes WI U.S.A.
226 H8 Three Oaks MI U.S.A.
96 D7 Three Pagodas Pass Myanmar/Thai.
241 U9 Three Points AZ U.S.A.
206 E5 Three Points, Cape Ghana
226 I8 Three Rivers MI U.S.A.
237 F11 Three Rivers TX U.S.A.
214 H7 Three Sisters S. Africa
238 D4 Three Sisters mt. OR U.S.A.
78 □6 Three Sisters Islands Solomon Is
87 C10 Three Springs W.A. Austr.
149 K5 Threlkeld Cumbria, England U.K.
149 M5 Threshfield North Yorkshire, England U.K.
Thrissur Kerala India see Trichur
237 F9 Throckmorton TX U.S.A.
234 D2 Throop PA U.S.A.
149 N3 Thropton Northumberland, England U.K.
87 H9 Throssell, Lake salt flat W.A. Austr.
86 F6 Throssel Range hills W.A. Austr.
146 J6 Thrumster Highland, Scotland U.K.
150 H4 Thrupp Gloucestershire, England U.K.
85 K9 Thrushton National Park Qld Austr.
149 O7 Thrybergh South Yorkshire, England U.K.
211 D5 Thua watercourse Kenya
96 H6 Thuân An Vietnam
97 G10 Thu Ba Vietnam
96 I6 Thu Bồn, Sông r. Vietnam
223 I2 Thubun Lakes N.W.T. Can.
97 H9 Thu Dâu Môt Vietnam
83 L6 Thuddungra N.S.W. Austr.
97 H9 Thu Đuc Vietnam
163 I10 Thuès-entre-Valls France
161 E7 Thueyts France
165 F8 Thuin Belgium
169 E6 Thuine Ger.
156 E3 Thuir France
163 J10 Thuir France
210 B2 Thul Sudan
210 A2 Thul watercourse Sudan
128 H3 Thulaythawāt Gharbī, Jabal hill Syria
169 I10 Thulba r. Ger.
Thule Greenland see Qaanaaq
213 F4 Thuli Zimbabwe
213 F4 Thuli r. Zimbabwe
Thulusdhoo N. Male Maldives see Thulusdhu
113 □1 Thulusdhu N. Male Maldives
171 G9 Thum Ger.
190 D2 Thun Switz.
85 I8 Thunda Qld Austr.
87 D10 Thundelarra W.A. Austr.
224 B3 Thunder Bay Ont. Can.
224 B3 Thunder Bay b. Ont. Can.
227 K4 Thunder Bay b. MI U.S.A.
223 J5 Thunder Creek r. Sask. Can.
246 C5 Thunder Knoll sea feature Caribbean Sea
151 N4 Thundersley Essex, England U.K.
190 D2 Thuner See l. Switz.
172 H2 Thüngen Ger.
172 H2 Thüngersheim Ger.
96 E6 Thung Salaeng Luang National Park Thai.
97 D10 Thung Song Thai.
97 D11 Thung Wa Thai.
96 D7 Thung Yai Naresuan Wildlife Reserve nature res. Thai.
157 N7 Thur r. France
190 F1 Thur r. Switz.
80 J7 Thuraua North I. N.Z.
149 O7 Thurcroft South Yorkshire, England U.K.
159 L8 Thuré France
157 K8 Thurey France
160 G3 Thurey France
190 G1 Thurgau canton Switz.
178 A5 Thüringen Austria
178 H6 Thüringen land Ger.
171 D8 Thüringer Becken reg. Ger.
169 J9 Thüringer Wald mts Ger.
169 K9 Thüringer Wald park Ger.
Thuringia land Ger. see Thüringen
Thuringian Forest mts Ger. see Thüringer Wald
160 F5 Thurins France
170 G3 Thürkow Ger.
151 L2 Thurlby Lincolnshire, England U.K.
149 P7 Thurlby Lincolnshire, England U.K.
171 G7 Thurm Ger.
173 K2 Thurmansbang Ger.
232 H9 Thurmont MD U.S.A.
178 F5 Thurn, Pass Austria
180 H4 Thurnau Ger.
149 O6 Thurnscoe South Yorkshire, England U.K.
151 M4 Thurrock admin. div. England U.K.
149 K4 Thursby Cumbria, England U.K.
85 I1 Thursday Island Qld Austr.
233 J3 Thurso Que. Can.
146 I5 Thurso Highland, Scotland U.K.
146 I5 Thurso r. Scotland U.K.
146 I5 Thurso Bay Scotland U.K.
151 N3 Thurston Suffolk, England U.K.
262 R2 Thurston Island Antarctica
Thurston Peninsula i. Antarctica see Thurston Island
151 O2 Thurton Norfolk, England U.K.
159 K4 Thury-Harcourt France
190 E2 Thusis Switz.
169 I6 Thüster Berg hill Ger.
160 H5 Thusy France
149 M5 Thwaite North Yorkshire, England U.K.
262 Q1 Thwaites Glacier Tongue Antarctica
142 E5 Thy reg. Denmark
Thyatira Turkey see Akhisar
142 E5 Thyborøn Denmark
160 J4 Thyez France
85 I9 Thylungra Qld Austr.
199 H5 Thymaina i. Greece
156 B6 Thymerais reg. France
211 B8 Thyolo Malawi
206 E4 Thyou Boulkiemde Burkina
Thyou Yatenga Burkina see Tiou
173 P4 Thyrnau Ger.
Thysville Dem. Rep. Congo see Mbanza-Ngungu
112 G8 Tīāb Iran
252 C4 Tiahuanaco Bol.
246 H8 Tía Juana Venez.
192 C7 Tiana Sardegna Italy
106 F6 Tiancang Gansu China
109 L2 Tianchang Anhui China
106 F7 Tiancheng Gansu China
Tiancheng Hubei China see Chongyang
107 J8 Tianchi Gansu China
Tianchi Sichuan China see Lezhi
108 F7 Tiandeng Guangxi China
Tiandiba Sichuan China see Jinyang
108 F7 Tiandong Guangxi China
108 F6 Tian'e Guangxi China
129 F3 T'ianet'i Georgia
109 K4 Tianfanjie Jiangxi China
206 B3 Tiângol Lougguéré watercourse Senegal
254 E2 Tianguá Brazil
245 I5 Tianguistengo Mex.
107 O7 Tianjin Tianjin China
107 O7 Tianjin mun. China
106 F8 Tianjun Qinghai China
206 B3 Tiankoye Senegal
108 F6 Tianlin Guangxi China
109 I3 Tianmen Hubei China
109 L3 Tianmu Shan mts China
100 F7 Tianqiaoling Jilin China
108 D3 Tianquan Sichuan China
107 Q5 Tianshan Nei Mongol China
Tian Shan mts China/Kyrg. see Tien Shan
101 D8 Tianshifu Liaoning China
106 I9 Tianshui Gansu China
106 I8 Tianshuibu Gansu China
111 D9 Tianshuihai Aksai Chin
110 L6 Tianshuijing Gansu China
109 M4 Tiantai Zhejiang China
107 O5 Tiantaiyong Nei Mongol China
Tiantang Anhui China see Yuexi
108 F7 Tianyang Guangxi China
Tianyi Nei Mongol China see Ningcheng
Tianzhen Shandong China see Gaoqing
107 N6 Tianzhen Shanxi China
Tianzhou Guangxi China see Tianyang
106 H8 Tianzhu Gansu China
108 G5 Tianzhu Guizhou China
79 □9a Tiarei Tahiti Fr. Polynesia
205 F2 Tiaret Alg.
205 H3 Tiaret well Tunisia
78 □5 Tiari New Caledonia
85 N8 Tiaro Qld Austr.
216 □3c Tías Lanzarote Canary Is
206 D5 Tiassalé Côte d'Ivoire
78 □2 Ti'avea Samoa
Tibabar Sabah Malaysia see Tambunan
256 B6 Tibagi Brazil
256 B5 Tibagi r. Brazil
Tibaji r. Brazil see Tibagi
127 K7 Tibal, Wādī watercourse Iraq
250 C3 Tibaná Col.
207 I5 Tibati Cameroon
123 N7 Tibba Pak.
146 I10 Tibbermore Perth and Kinross, Scotland U.K.
206 C4 Tibé, Pic de mt. Guinea
192 J1 Tiber r. Italy see Tevere
173 K5 Tiberghamine Alg.
205 F3 Tiberghamine Alg.
204 B5 Tiberguent well Maur.
Tiberias Israel see Teverya
238 I2 Tiber Reservoir MT U.S.A.
202 C4 Tibesti mts Chad
Tibet aut. reg. China see Xizang Zizhiqu
Tibet, Plateau of Xizang China see Qingzang Gaoyuan
187 D10 Tibi Spain
187 D11 Tibi, Embalse de resr Spain
207 G3 Tibiri Niger
197 M4 Tibleş, Vârful mt. Romania
251 G3 Tiboku Falls Guyana
177 J4 Tiboldaróc Hungary
83 I3 Tibooburra N.S.W. Austr.
177 L4 Tiborszállás Hungary
117 I5 Tibrikot Nepal
143 K3 Tibro Sweden
149 O7 Tibshelf Derbyshire, England U.K.
250 B3 Tibuga, Ensenada b. Col.
Tiburlay Italy see Tivoli
242 C3 Tiburón, Isla i. Mex.
92 D5 Ticao i. Phil.
151 M5 Ticehurst East Sussex, England U.K.
197 O7 Ticha r. Bulg.
197 K8 Tichak mt. Bulg.
Tichau Pol. see Tychy
227 R5 Tichborne Ont. Can.
225 F3 Tichégami r. Que. Can.
207 F2 Tichet well Mali
204 C3 Tichît Maur.
204 B5 Tichla Western Sahara
190 F3 Ticino r. Italy/Switz.
190 F3 Ticino canton Switz.
Ticinum Italy see Pavia
149 O7 Tickhill South Yorkshire, England U.K.
197 L6 Ticleni Romania
233 L5 Ticonderoga NY U.S.A.
243 O7 Ticul Mex.
Ticumbia i. Fiji see Cikobia
143 J3 Tidaholm Sweden
143 K3 Tidan Sweden
143 K3 Tidan r. Sweden
96 A3 Tiddim Myanmar
168 K5 Tiddische Ger.
115 M9 Tiden Andaman & Nicobar Is India
150 G4 Tidenham Gloucestershire, England U.K.
205 F5 Tidikelt, Plaine du plain Alg.
149 N7 Tideswell Derbyshire, England U.K.
205 F4 Tidikelt, Plaine du plain Alg.
232 F7 Tidioute PA U.S.A.
207 F2 Tidjerouene well Mali
204 C3 Tidjikja Maur.
190 H5 Tidone r. Italy
93 E3 Tidore i. Maluku Indon.
204 B5 Tidsit, Sabkhet salt pan Western Sahara
150 H5 Tidworth Wiltshire, England U.K.
151 I5 Tiebas Spain
163 A10 Tiebas Spain
206 D5 Tiébissou Côte d'Ivoire
203 E5 Tiéboro Chad
110 G3 Tiechanggou Xinjiang China
183 J5 Tiedra Spain
Tiefa Liaoning China see Diaobingshan
172 E3 Tiefenbach Bayern Ger.
173 M4 Tiefenbach Bayern Ger.
173 O4 Tiefenbach Bayern Ger.
172 F4 Tiefenbronn Ger.
190 H2 Tiefencastel Switz.
170 I5 Tiefensee Ger.
164 H5 Tiel Neth.
206 B3 Tiel Senegal
165 G6 Tielen Belgium
100 E5 Tieli Heilong. China
101 D9 Tieling Liaoning China
111 D9 Tielongtan Aksai Chin
165 D7 Tielt Belgium
206 D4 Tiémé Côte d'Ivoire
165 G7 Tiene Liberia
165 G7 Tienen Belgium
172 E6 Tiengen Ger.
110 C6 Tien Shan mts China/Kyrg.
Tien Shan Oblast admin. div. Kyrg. see Naryn
Tientsin Tianjin China see Tianjin
Tientsin mun. China see Tianjin
96 H4 Tiên Yên Vietnam
191 J6 Tiepido r. Italy
156 K6 Tiercé France
215 K4 Tierfontein S. Africa
183 Q5 Tierga Spain
143 N1 Tierp Sweden
258 C2 Tierra Amarilla Chile
239 K8 Tierra Amarilla NM U.S.A.
244 G4 Tierra Blanca Mex.
245 K7 Tierra Blanca Peru
250 C6 Tierra Blanca Peru
245 J7 Tierra Colorada Mex.
259 D9 Tierra del Fuego prov. Arg.
259 C9 Tierra del Fuego, Isla Grande de i. Arg./Chile
259 D9 Tierra del Fuego, Parque Nacional nat. park Arg.
250 B4 Tierradentro, Parque Arqueológico Nacional tourist site Col.
250 B2 Tierralta Col.
216 □3c Tierra Negra, Punta de pt Lanzarote Canary Is
244 G4 Tierranueva Mex.
183 Q7 Tierzo Spain
185 I5 Tiesa hill Spain
179 M6 Tieschen Austria
182 I9 Tiétar r. Spain
183 J8 Tiétar, Valle de val. Spain
256 D5 Tietê Brazil
256 B6 Tietê r. Brazil
82 D2 Tieyon S.A. Austr.
159 I7 Tiffauges France
232 B7 Tiffin OH U.S.A.
Tiflis Georgia see T'bilisi
93 E3 Tifore i. Maluku Indon.
231 F10 Tifton GA U.S.A.
93 E5 Tifu Buru Indon.
95 K2 Tiga i. Malaysia
78 □5 Tiga i. Îles Loyauté New Caledonia
215 K2 Tigane S. Africa
197 N7 Tigăneşti Romania
94 E5 Tigapuluh, Pegunungan mts Indon.
120 D5 Tigen Kazakh.
122 I8 Tigh Āb Iran
136 H8 Tigheciului, Dealurile hills Moldova
136 I7 Tighina Moldova
136 G8 Tighina Moldova
146 F11 Tighnabruaich Argyll and Bute, Scotland U.K.
121 T2 Tigiretskiy Khrebet mts Kazakh./Rus. Fed.
117 J9 Tigiria Orissa India
191 J4 Tignale Italy
207 I5 Tignère Cameroon
160 J5 Tignes France
225 H4 Tignish P.E.I. Can.
139 O2 Tigoda r. Rus. Fed.
206 D2 Tigoumatene well Mali
Tigranocerta Turkey see Siirt
210 C1 Tigray admin. reg. Eth.
261 H4 Tigre Arg.
250 C6 Tigre r. Ecuador/Peru
245 J3 Tigre r. Mex.
245 H2 Tigre, Cerro del mt. Mex.
260 C2 Tigre, Sierra mts Arg.
127 M8 Tigris r. Asia
alt. Dicle (Turkey)
alt. Dijlah, Nahr (Iraq/Syria)
123 M3 Tigrovaya Balka Zapovednik nature res. Tajik.
205 F4 Tiguelguemine well Alg.
206 B2 Tiguent Maur.
204 C4 Tiguesmat hills Maur.
202 C5 Tigui Chad
207 G2 Tiguidit, Falaise de esc. Niger
206 C2 Tiguîguil well Maur.
205 H6 Tiguir well Niger
156 D8 Tigy France
204 C3 Tigzerte, Oued watercourse Morocco
128 F7 Tih, Jabal at plat. Egypt
124 F7 Tihāmah reg. Saudi Arabia
177 G5 Tihany Hungary
177 G5 Tihany pen. Hungary
205 F4 Tihatimine well Alg.
205 G4 Tihodaïne, Erg des. Alg.
245 J5 Tihuatlán Mex.
252 D3 Tijamuchi r. Bol.
116 F6 Tijara Rajasthan India
216 □3d Tijarafe La Palma Canary Is
202 A1 Tiji Libya
204 B5 Tijirit reg. Maur.
164 I2 Tijnje Neth.
185 O6 Tijola Spain
242 A1 Tijuana Mex.
255 C8 Tijucas Brazil
256 C8 Tijucas, Baía de b. Brazil
256 B3 Tijuco r. Brazil
Tika i. Îles Loyauté New Caledonia see Tiga
243 O9 Tikal tourist site Guat.
243 O9 Tikal, Parque Nacional nat. park Guat.
116 G7 Tikamgarh Madh. Prad. India
110 H6 Tikanlik Xinjiang China
220 C4 Tikchik Lake AK U.S.A.
137 S3 Tikhaya Sosna r. Rus. Fed.
Tikherón Greece see Tychero
139 V3 Tikhmenevo Rus. Fed.
139 T7 Tikhonova Pustyn' Rus. Fed.
135 H7 Tikhoretsk Rus. Fed.
140 U4 Tikhtozero Rus. Fed.
139 Q2 Tikhvin Rus. Fed.
139 Q2 Tikhvinskaya Gryada ridge Rus. Fed.
267 K7 Tiki Basin sea feature Pacific Ocean
207 G2 Tiktekene well Niger
Tikirarjuaq Nunavut Can. see Whale Cove
80 M4 Tikitiki North I. N.Z.
79 □7a Tikituru mt. Viti Levu Fiji
140 R5 Tikkakoski Fin.
138 I1 Tikkurila Fin.
129 F6 Tikmeh-ye Bālā Iran
80 K6 Tikokino North I. N.Z.
77 G3 Tikopia i. Solomon Is
127 K6 Tikrit Iraq
116 F2 Tikse Jammu and Kashmir
140 V3 Tiksheozero, Ozero l. Rus. Fed.
131 N2 Tiksi Rus. Fed.
Tikumbia i. Fiji see Cikobia
Tikus i. Cocos Is see Direction Island
197 J9 Tikveš Ezero l. Macedonia
215 J3 Tikwana S. Africa
116 H5 Tila r. Nepal
117 J7 Tilaiya Reservoir India
260 B3 Tilama Chile
93 C3 Tilamuta Sulawesi Indon.
122 F3 Tilavar Iran
128 F2 Tilbeşar Ovasi plain Turkey
85 J9 Tilbooroo Qld Austr.
164 H5 Tilburg Neth.
227 L7 Tilbury Ont. Can.
151 M5 Tilbury Thurrock, England U.K.
258 D1 Tilcara Arg.
82 H3 Tilcha S.A. Austr.
160 G1 Til-Châtel France
237 F11 Tilden TX U.S.A.
197 K3 Tileagd Romania
151 J5 Tilehurst Reading, England U.K.
207 G3 Tilemsès Niger
207 F1 Tilemsi, Vallée du watercourse Mali
223 I10 Tilghman MD U.S.A.
163 C8 Tilh France
116 G6 Tilhar Uttar Prad. India
205 F4 Tilia, Oued watercourse Alg.
Tiligulo-Berezanka Ukr. see Berezanka
Tilimsen Alg. see Tlemcen
96 B4 Tilin Myanmar
260 E3 Tilisarao Arg.
149 M2 Till r. England U.K.
207 F3 Tillabéri Niger
207 F3 Tillabéri dept Niger
163 E9 Tillac France
238 C4 Tillamook OR U.S.A.
115 M8 Tillanchong Island Andaman & Nicobar Is India
160 G2 Tille r. France
171 D8 Tilleda (Kyffhäuser) Ger.

Tilley to Tongtian He

398

223 I5 **Tilley** *Alta* Can.
207 G2 **Tillia** Niger
146 I10 **Tillicoultry** *Clackmannanshire, Scotland* U.K.
156 B6 **Tillières-sur-Avre** France
156 I5 **Tilloy-et-Bellay** France
224 D5 **Tillsonburg** *Ont.* Can.
146 K8 **Tillyfourie** *Aberdeenshire, Scotland* U.K.
159 J3 **Tilly-sur-Seulles** France
207 F3 **Tiloa** Niger
Tilognè Senegal *see* **Thilogne**
252 C5 **Tilomonte** Chile
116 E6 **Tilonia** *Rajasthan* India
199 I6 **Tilos** *i.* Greece
117 J7 **Tilothu** *Bihar* India
83 J4 **Tilpa** *N.S.W.* Austr.
205 F2 **Tilrhemt** Alg.
138 K5 **Tilsa** *r.* Latvia
Tilsit Rus. Fed. *see* **Sovetsk**
149 L7 **Tilston** *Cheshire, England* U.K.
146 I9 **Tilt** *r. Scotland* U.K.
260 B3 **Tiltil** Chile
134 M2 **Til'tim** Rus. Fed.
233 N5 **Tilton** *NH* U.S.A.
93 B4 **Tilu, Bukit** *mt.* Indon.
138 K5 **Tilža** Latvia
135 G6 **Tim** Rus. Fed.
137 Q1 **Tim** *r.* Rus. Fed.
203 F3 **Ţimā** Egypt
203 I6 **Timā** Yemen
94 □ **Timah, Bukit** *hill* Sing.
148 C8 **Timahoe** Ireland
114 C7 **Timakara** *i.* India
253 F5 **Timane** *r.* Para.
216 □3c **Timanfaya** *vol. Lanzarote* Canary Is
216 □3c **Timanfaya, Parque Nacional de** *nat. park Lanzarote* Canary Is
134 J2 **Timanskiy Kryazh** *ridge* Rus. Fed.
127 K4 **Timar** Turkey
81 F11 **Timaru** *South I.* N.Z.
120 D1 **Timashevo** Rus. Fed.
135 G7 **Timashevsk** Rus. Fed.
Timashevskaya Rus. Fed. *see* **Timashevsk**
191 O2 **Timau** Italy
Timbákion *Kriti* Greece *see* **Tympaki**
237 J11 **Timbalier Bay** *LA* U.S.A.
254 G3 **Timbaúba** Brazil
206 C2 **Timbedgha** Maur.
84 C3 **Timber Creek** *N.T.* Austr.
236 E3 **Timber Lake** *SD* U.S.A.
241 P4 **Timber Mountain** *NV* U.S.A.
232 G10 **Timberville** *VA* U.S.A.
250 B4 **Timbiquí** Col.
206 C4 **Timbo** Guinea
83 I8 **Timboon** *Vic.* Austr.
213 H3 **Timbué, Ponta** *pt* Moz.
Timbuktu Mali *see* **Tombouctou**
95 M2 **Timbun Mata** *i.* Malaysia
179 I3 **Timelkam** Austria
207 E2 **Timétrine** Mali
206 E2 **Timétrine** *reg.* Mali
Tímfi *mts* Greece *see* **Tymfi**
205 G2 **Timgad** *tourist site* Alg.
207 H2 **Timia** Niger
205 F5 **Timïaouine** Alg.
205 F3 **Timimoun** Alg.
198 F2 **Timiou Prodromou, Akrotirio** *pt* Greece
206 A2 **Timirist, Râs** *pt* Maur.
121 L1 **Timiryazev** Kazakh.
121 L1 **Timiryazevo** Kazakh.
177 K6 **Timiş** *county* Romania
197 I5 **Timiş** *r.* Romania
Timiskaming, Lake *Ont./Que.* Can. *see* **Témiscamingue, Lac**
196 J5 **Timişoara** Romania
196 I5 **Timişului, Câmpia** *plain* Romania
Timkovichi Belarus *see* **Tsimkavichy**
207 G2 **Ti-m-Meghsoi** *watercourse* Niger
178 D6 **Timmelsjoch** *pass* Austria/Italy
168 K3 **Timmendorfer Strand** Ger.
224 D3 **Timmins** *Ont.* Can.
226 D4 **Timms Hill** *WI* U.S.A.
Timoé *atoll Arch. des Tuamotu* Fr. Polynesia *see* **Temoe**
197 K6 **Timok** *r.* Serbia
139 T2 **Timokhino** Rus. Fed.
147 E9 **Timoleague** Ireland
254 E3 **Timon** Brazil
192 H3 **Timone** *r.* Italy
234 B6 **Timonium** *MD* U.S.A.
93 E8 **Timor** *i.* Indon.
76 C3 **Timor Sea** Austr./Indon.
Timor Timur *country* Asia *see* **East Timor**
139 T1 **Timoshino** Rus. Fed.
261 F4 **Timote** Arg.
257 F3 **Timóteo** Brazil
205 E3 **Timoudi** Alg.
93 D4 **Timpaus** *i.* Indon.
87 G8 **Timperley Range** *hills W.A.* Austr.
141 N5 **Timrå** Sweden
128 A8 **Timsāḩ, Buḩayrat at** *l.* Egypt
150 H5 **Timsbury** *Bath and North East Somerset, England* U.K.
231 D8 **Tims Ford Lake** *TN* U.S.A.
146 B6 **Timsgearraidh** *Western Isles, Scotland* U.K.
134 K3 **Timsher** Rus. Fed.
134 K3 **Timshor** *r.* Rus. Fed.
121 M6 **Timur** Kazakh.
116 F8 **Timurni Muafi** *Madh. Prad.* India
124 F2 **Tīn, Jabal** *hill* Saudi Arabia
202 D1 **Tīn, Ra's at** *pt* Libya
191 L2 **Tina** *r.* Italy
215 N7 **Tina** *r.* S. Africa
206 E2 **Ti-n-Aba** *well* Mali
128 G2 **Tīnah** Syria
128 A7 **Ţīnah, Khalīj aţ** *b.* Egypt
148 E8 **Tinahely** Ireland
183 O8 **Tinajas** Spain
216 □3c **Tinajo** *Lanzarote* Canary Is
182 E9 **Tinalhas** Port.
202 A3 **Tin Alkoum** Libya
207 F2 **Ti-n-Amâssine** *well* Mali
205 G5 **Tin Amzi, Oued** *watercourse* Alg.
250 D2 **Tinaquillo** Venez.
207 F2 **Ti-n-Azabo** *well* Mali
204 C5 **Ti-n-Bessaïs** *well* Maur.
206 E2 **Ti-n-Boukri** *well* Mali
177 K5 **Tinca** Romania
85 N8 **Tin Can Bay** *Qld* Austr.
159 J4 **Tinchebray** France
205 E5 **Ti-n-Didine** *well* Mali
114 F6 **Tindivanam** *Tamil Nadu* India
204 C4 **Tindouf** Alg.
144 D1 **Tindur** *hill* Faroe Is
202 D6 **Tiné** Chad
206 E2 **Ti-n-Echeri** *well* Mali
206 E2 **Ti-n-Edrine** *well* Mali
161 K9 **Tinée** *r.* France
182 H2 **Tineo** Spain
207 F3 **Ti-n-Eratilene** *well* Mali
204 D3 **Tinerhir** Morocco
207 F2 **Ti-n-Essako** Mali
206 E2 **Ti-n-Etissane** *well* Mali
204 D3 **Tinfouchy** Alg.
151 J4 **Tingewick** *Buckinghamshire, England* U.K.
94 F3 **Tinggi** *i.* Malaysia
202 A2 **Tingharat, Hammādat** *des.* Libya
206 C4 **Tingi Mountains** Sierra Leone
Tingis Morocco *see* **Tanger**
109 K6 **Ting Jiang** *r.* China
96 C1 **Tingkawk Sakan** Myanmar
142 F7 **Tinglev** Denmark
252 B2 **Tingo María** Peru
Tingrela Côte d'Ivoire *see* **Tengréla**
111 H12 **Tingri** *Xizang* China
143 K5 **Tingsryd** Sweden
143 O4 **Tingstäde** *Gotland* Sweden
143 O4 **Tingstädeträsk** *l. Gotland* Sweden
244 E6 **Tingüindín** Mex.
260 B4 **Tinguiririca** Chile
260 B4 **Tinguiririca, Volcán** *vol.* Chile
142 D3 **Tingvatn** Norway
140 J5 **Tingvoll** Norway
146 J4 **Tingwall** *Orkney, Scotland* U.K.
Tingzhou *Fujian* China *see* **Changting**
254 F5 **Tinharé, Ilha de** *i.* Brazil
182 F6 **Tinhela** *r.* Port.
96 G5 **Tinh Gia** Vietnam
91 K4 **Tinian** *i.* N. Mariana Is
206 B2 **Tiniéré** *well* Maur.
250 C4 **Tinigua, Parque Nacional** *nat. park* Col.
Tini Heke *is* N.Z. *see* **Snares Islands**
80 L5 **Tiniroto** *North I.* N.Z.
188 G3 **Tinja** *r.* Bos.-Herz.
191 P5 **Tinjan** Croatia
95 K2 **Tinjar** *r.* Malaysia
94 F8 **Tinjil** *i.* Indon.
206 C4 **Tinkisso** *r.* Guinea
137 L4 **Tin'ky** Ukr.
81 H9 **Tinline, Mount** *South I.* N.Z.
205 H5 **Ti-n-Merzouga** *des.* Alg.
142 E2 **Tinn** Norway
142 F2 **Tinne** *r.* Norway
Tinnelvelly *Tamil Nadu* India *see* **Tirunelveli**
142 E2 **Tinnsjo** *l.* Norway
177 H4 **Tinnye** Hungary
190 H7 **Tino, Isola del** *i.* Italy
261 F2 **Tinoco** Arg.
258 D3 **Tinogasta** Arg.
93 B3 **Tinompo** *Sulawesi* Indon.
198 G5 **Tinos** *Tinos* Greece
198 G5 **Tinos** *i.* Greece
185 K6 **Tiñosa** *mt.* Spain
183 K7 **Tiñosillos** Spain
187 C12 **Tiñoso, Cabo** *c.* Spain
156 G5 **Tinqueux** France
205 G5 **Ti-n-Rerhoh** *well* Alg.
205 G3 **Tinrhert, Plateau du** Alg.
109 □I7 **Tin Shui Wai** *H.K.* China
207 F2 **Ti-n-Srir** *well* Mali
117 O6 **Tinsukia** *Assam* India
222 E4 **Tintagel** *B.C.* Can.
150 C6 **Tintagel** *Cornwall, England* U.K.
206 C2 **Ţînţâne** Maur.
205 G5 **Ti-n-Tarabine** *well* Alg.
205 G5 **Ti-n-Tarabine, Oued** *watercourse* Alg.
206 E2 **Ti-n-Tehoun** *well* Mali
205 F4 **Tintejert, Adrar** *mt.* Alg.
158 H5 **Tinténiac** France
150 G4 **Tintern Parva** *Monmouthshire, Wales* U.K.
207 F2 **Ti-n-Tersi** *well* Mali
165 I9 **Tintigny** Belgium
258 E2 **Tintina** Arg.
82 H6 **Tintinara** *S.A.* Austr.
184 F6 **Tinto** *r.* Spain
149 J2 **Tinto** *hill Scotland* U.K.
Tin Tounnant *well* Mali *see* **Taounnant**
81 K7 **Tinui** *North I.* N.Z.
137 M9 **Tinyste** Ukr.
207 F2 **Ti-n-Zaouâtene** Mali
236 D1 **Tioga** *ND* U.S.A.
232 H7 **Tioga** *PA* U.S.A.
232 H6 **Tioga** *r. PA* U.S.A.
234 A1 **Tioga County** *county PA* U.S.A.
94 F3 **Tioman** *i.* Malaysia
227 L1 **Tionaga** *Ont.* Can.
191 K5 **Tione** *r.* Italy
191 J3 **Tione di Trento** Italy
232 F7 **Tionesta** *PA* U.S.A.
206 C3 **Tioribougou** Mali
206 E3 **Tiou** Burkina
205 E5 **Tiouararène** *well* Mali
233 J6 **Tioughnioga** *r. NY* U.S.A.
205 F1 **Tipasa** Alg.
Tiphsah Syria *see* **Dibsī**
242 □P11 **Tipitapa** Nic.
226 F4 **Tipler** *WI* U.S.A.
230 D5 **Tippecanoe** *r. IN* U.S.A.
147 F8 **Tipperary** Ireland
147 G7 **Tipperary** *county* Ireland
117 K6 **Tiptala Bhanjyang** *pass* Nepal
240 M5 **Tipton** *CA* U.S.A.
236 J5 **Tipton** *IA* U.S.A.
236 I6 **Tipton** *MO* U.S.A.
241 R6 **Tipton, Mount** *AZ* U.S.A.
237 K7 **Tiptonville** *TN* U.S.A.
232 D11 **Tiptop** *VA* U.S.A.
224 C3 **Tip Top Hill** *Ont.* Can.
151 N4 **Tiptree** *Essex, England* U.K.
114 E6 **Tiptur** *Karnataka* India
114 E6 **Tiptur** *Karnataka* India
Tipturi *Karnataka* India *see* **Tiptur**
252 C3 **Tipuani** Bol.
244 G7 **Tiquicheo** Mex.
250 D4 **Tiquié** *r.* Brazil
243 N10 **Tiquisate** Guat.
254 D3 **Tiracambu, Serra do** *hills* Brazil
205 F5 **Tirahart, Oued** *watercourse* Alg.
122 D5 **Tīrān** Iran
124 B2 **Tīrān** *i.* Saudi Arabia
Tirana Albania *see* **Tiranë**
196 H9 **Tiranë** Albania
161 D6 **Tiranges** France
190 I3 **Tirano** Italy
207 G2 **Tiraouene** *well* Niger
117 O6 **Tirap** *Arun. Prad.* India
124 F2 **Ţirāq, Jāl aţ** *hills* Saudi Arabia
206 E2 **Tiraraouine** *well* Mali
82 G2 **Tirari Desert** *S.A.* Austr.
136 I7 **Tiraspol** Moldova
80 J4 **Tirau** *North I.* N.Z.
80 K7 **Tiraumea** *North I.* N.Z.
212 C5 **Tiraz Mountains** Namibia
199 I4 **Tire** Turkey
177 L4 **Tiream** Romania
146 C10 **Tiree** *i. Scotland* U.K.
205 F5 **Tirek** *well* Alg.
205 F5 **Tirest** *well* Mali
146 C7 **Tirga Mòr** *hill Scotland* U.K.
183 O3 **Tirgo** Spain
Tîrgovişte Romania *see* **Târgovişte**
Tîrgu Bujor Romania *see* **Târgu Bujor**
Tîrgu Cărbuneşti Romania *see* **Târgu Cărbuneşti**
Tîrgu Frumos Romania *see* **Târgu Frumos**
Tîrgu Jiu Romania *see* **Târgu Jiu**
Tîrgu Lăpuş Romania *see* **Târgu Lăpuş**
Tîrgu Mureş Romania *see* **Târgu Mureş**
Tîrgu Neamţ Romania *see* **Târgu Neamţ**
Tîrgu Ocna Romania *see* **Târgu Ocna**
Tîrgu Secuiesc Romania *see* **Târgu Secuiesc**
116 G3 **Tiri** Jammu and Kashmir
123 L7 **Tiri** Pak.
123 N3 **Tirich Mir** *mt.* Pak.
185 O3 **Tiriez** Spain
186 F7 **Tírig** Spain
195 L6 **Tiriolo** Italy
244 F6 **Tiripetío** Mex.
205 H5 **Tiririne, Oued** *watercourse* Alg.
204 C5 **Tiris Zemmour** *admin. reg.* Maur.
138 F5 **Tirkšliai** Lith.
Tirlemont Belgium *see* **Tienen**
120 H1 **Tirlyanskiy** Rus. Fed.
114 E3 **Tirna** *r.* India
Tîrnăveni Romania *see* **Târnăveni**
Tírnavos Greece *see* **Tyrnavos**
Tîrnova Romania *see* **Târnova**
185 I3 **Tiro** *hill* Spain
116 G9 **Tirodi** *Madh. Prad.* India
178 D5 **Tirol** *land* Austria
183 O3 **Tirón** *r.* Spain
80 J4 **Tironia** *North I.* N.Z.
257 E3 **Tiros** Brazil
208 D2 **Tiroungoulou** C.A.R.
171 F10 **Tirpersdorf** Ger.
190 I8 **Tirrenia** Italy
Tirreno, Mare *sea* France/Italy *see* **Tyrrhenian Sea**
173 M2 **Tirschenreuth** Ger.
192 B8 **Tirso** *r. Sardegna* Italy
142 G5 **Tirstrup** Denmark
185 K3 **Tirteafuera** Spain
185 K3 **Tirteafuera** *r.* Spain
114 D6 **Tirthahalli** *Karnataka* India
117 K9 **Tirtol** *Orissa* India
114 F8 **Tiruchchendur** *Tamil Nadu* India
114 F7 **Tiruchchirappalli** *Tamil Nadu* India
114 E7 **Tiruchengodu** *Tamil Nadu* India
114 F7 **Tirukkoyilur** *Tamil Nadu* India
114 F8 **Tirumangalam** *Tamil Nadu* India
114 E8 **Tirunelveli** *Tamil Nadu* India
252 B1 **Tiruntán** Peru
114 F6 **Tirupati** *Andhra Prad.* India
114 F6 **Tiruppattur** *Tamil Nadu* India
114 F7 **Tiruppattur** *Tamil Nadu* India
114 E7 **Tiruppur** *Tamil Nadu* India
114 F6 **Tiruttani** *Andhra Prad.* India
114 F7 **Tirutturaippundi** *Tamil Nadu* India
114 F6 **Tiruvallur** *Tamil Nadu* India
114 F6 **Tiruvannamalai** *Tamil Nadu* India
114 F6 **Tiruvettipuram** *Tamil Nadu* India
114 G6 **Tiruvottiyur** *Tamil Nadu* India
86 H6 **Tiru Well** *W.A.* Austr.
198 E5 **Tiryns** *tourist site* Greece
138 J4 **Tirza** *r.* Latvia
197 J7 **Tisa** *r.* Serbia *alt.* **Tisza (Hungary),** *alt.* **Tysa (Ukraine)**
114 E8 **Tisaiyanvilai** *Tamil Nadu* India
143 L2 **Tisaren** *l.* Sweden
197 O5 **Tisău** Romania
150 H5 **Tisbury** *Wiltshire, England* U.K.
216 □3b **Tiscamanita** *Fuerteventura* Canary Is
185 M5 **Tiscar, Puerto de** *pass* Spain
223 J4 **Tisdale** *Sask.* Can.
237 G8 **Tishomingo** *OK* U.S.A.
175 I1 **Tishono** Rus. Fed.
171 K10 **Tišice** Czech Rep.
128 E6 **Ţīsīyah** Syria
205 H5 **Tiska, Mont** *mt.* Alg.
143 L3 **Tisnaren** *l.* Sweden
176 F2 **Tišnov** Czech Rep.
177 I3 **Tisovec** Slovakia
114 G9 **Tissamaharama** Sri Lanka
205 F2 **Tissemsilt** Alg.
192 B6 **Tissi** *Sardegna* Italy
117 L7 **Tista** *r.* India
177 J5 **Tisza** *r.* Hungary *alt.* **Tisa (Serbia),** *alt.* **Tysa (Ukraine)**
177 I5 **Tiszaalpár** Hungary
177 L3 **Tiszabecs** Hungary
177 L3 **Tiszabezdéd** Hungary
177 J4 **Tiszabő** Hungary
177 J4 **Tiszabura** Hungary
177 K4 **Tiszacsege** Hungary
177 J4 **Tiszaderzs** Hungary
177 K3 **Tiszadob** Hungary
177 K3 **Tiszadobi arter** *nature res.* Hungary
177 K3 **Tiszaeszlár** Hungary
177 J5 **Tiszaföldvár** Hungary
177 J4 **Tiszafüred** Hungary
177 J4 **Tiszafüredi Madárrezervátum** *nature res.* Hungary
177 J4 **Tiszaigar** Hungary
177 J4 **Tiszajenő** Hungary
177 K3 **Tiszakarád** Hungary
177 J5 **Tiszakécske** Hungary
177 L3 **Tiszakerecseny** Hungary
177 J4 **Tiszakeszi** Hungary
177 K3 **Tiszalök** Hungary
177 K3 **Tiszalúc** Hungary
177 K3 **Tiszanagyfalu** Hungary
177 J4 **Tiszanána** Hungary
177 J5 **Tiszántúl** *reg.* Hungary
177 J4 **Tiszaörs** Hungary
177 J4 **Tiszapüspöki** Hungary
177 J4 **Tiszaroff** Hungary
177 J5 **Tiszasas** Hungary
177 L3 **Tiszaszentmárton** Hungary
177 J5 **Tiszasziget** Hungary
177 K3 **Tiszatelek** Hungary
177 K3 **Tiszatelek-Tiszabercel** *nature res.* Hungary
177 J4 **Tiszatenyő** Hungary
177 J5 **Tiszaug** Hungary
177 K4 **Tiszaújváros** Hungary
177 K4 **Tiszavasvári** Hungary
205 F4 **Tit** *Adrar* Alg.
205 G5 **Tit** *Tamanrasset* Alg.
117 O6 **Titabar** *Assam* India
187 C8 **Titaguas** Spain
263 K1 **Titan Dome** *ice feature* Antarctica
206 E3 **Titao** Burkina
137 T4 **Titarevka** Rus. Fed.
198 D3 **Titarisios** *r.* Greece
131 N2 **Tit-Ary** Rus. Fed.
Titawin Morocco *see* **Tétouan**
206 B4 **Tite** Guinea-Bissau
196 I5 **Titel** *Vojvodina* Serbia
193 M5 **Titerno** *r.* Italy
123 O4 **Tithwal** Pak.
252 C3 **Titicaca, Lago** *l.* Bol./Peru
Titicaca, Lake Bol./Peru *see* **Titicaca, Lago**
235 H2 **Titicus** *CT* U.S.A.
81 B14 **Titi Islands** *Stewart I.* N.Z.
81 □3 **Titikaveka** *Rarotonga* Cook Is
172 E6 **Titisee** Ger.
Tititea *mt. South I.* N.Z. *see* **Aspiring, Mount**
117 I9 **Titlagarh** *Orissa* India
190 E2 **Titlis** *mt.* Switz.
193 P6 **Tito** Italy
Titograd Montenegro *see* **Podgorica**
188 E3 **Titova Korenica** Croatia
Titova Mitrovica *Kosovo* Serbia *see* **Kosovska Mitrovica**
188 F3 **Titov Drvar** Bos.-Herz.
140 U2 **Titovka** *r.* Rus. Fed.
Titovo Užice Serbia *see* **Užice**
Titovo Velenje Slovenia *see* **Velenje**
Titov Veles Macedonia *see* **Veles**
Titov Vrbas *Vojvodina* Serbia *see* **Vrbas**
140 J5 **Titran** Norway
84 D7 **Ti Tree** *N.T.* Austr.
227 K6 **Tittabawassee** *r. MI* U.S.A.
173 K4 **Titting** Ger.
173 O4 **Tittling** Ger.
173 N5 **Tittmoning** Ger.
197 N6 **Titu** Romania
183 M8 **Titulcia** Spain
208 E4 **Titule** Dem. Rep. Congo
231 G11 **Titusville** *FL* U.S.A.
232 F7 **Titusville** *PA* U.S.A.
109 □J7 **Tiu Chung Chau** *i. H.K.* China
146 D6 **Tiumpan Head** *Scotland* U.K.
211 C5 **Tiva** *watercourse* Kenya
116 D6 **Tivari** *Rajasthan* India
196 G8 **Tivat** Montenegro
143 K3 **Tiveden nationalpark** *nat. park* Sweden
186 G6 **Tivenys** Spain
227 M5 **Tiverton** *Ont.* Can.
150 F6 **Tiverton** *Devon, England* U.K.
Tivisa Spain *see* **Tivissa**
186 G5 **Tivissa** Spain
193 J4 **Tivoli** Italy
208 D2 **Tiwal, Wadi** *watercourse* Sudan
252 C4 **Tiwanaku** *tourist site* Bol.
125 N4 **Ţīwī** Oman
84 C1 **Tiwi Aboriginal Land** *res. N.T.* Austr.
93 C6 **Tiworo, Selat** *sea chan.* Indon.
243 O7 **Tixkokob** Mex.
245 H8 **Tixtla** Mex.
210 C2 **Tiya** *tourist site* Eth.
128 F4 **Tiyās** Syria
244 D5 **Tizapán el Alto** Mex.
245 I6 **Tizayuca** Mex.
204 C3 **Tizi Mighert** *pass* Morocco
243 O7 **Tizimín** Mex.
204 C3 **Tizi-n-Test** *pass* Morocco
204 D3 **Tizi-n-Tichka** *pass* Morocco
205 G1 **Tizi Ouzou** Alg.
111 C7 **Tiznap He** *r.* China
204 C3 **Tiznit** Morocco
242 H5 **Tizoc** Mex.
204 E2 **Tiztoutine** Morocco
192 B4 **Tizzano** *Corse* France
140 O3 **Tjaktjajaure** *l.* Sweden
143 L3 **Tjällmo** Sweden
140 O3 **Tjåmotis** Sweden
215 P1 **Tjaneni** Swaziland
140 O4 **Tjappsåive** Sweden
140 M4 **Tjärmyrberget** Sweden
140 P3 **Tjautas** Sweden
140 N3 **Tjeggelvas** *l.* Sweden
144 J1 **Tjeldstø** Norway
164 I3 **Tjeukemeer** *l.* Neth.
Tjirebon *Jawa* Indon. *see* **Cirebon**
87 H8 **Tjirrkarli Aboriginal Reserve** *W.A.* Austr.
Tjolotjo Zimbabwe *see* **Tsholotsho**
142 G2 **Tjøme** Norway
142 C3 **Tjorhom** Norway
142 H3 **Tjörn** *i.* Sweden
140 □E1 **Tjörnes** *pen.* Iceland
140 L4 **Tjøtta** Norway
Tjumen' Rus. Fed. *see* **Tyumen'**
143 K5 **Tjurken** *l.* Sweden
140 □ **Tjuvfjorden** *b.* Svalbard
Tkibuli Georgia *see* **Tqibuli**
Tkvarcheli Georgia *see* **Tqvarch'eli**
244 E4 **Tlachichila** Mex.
245 I5 **Tlachichilo** Mex.
245 I8 **Tlacoapa** Mex.
245 K9 **Tlacolula** Mex.
245 L9 **Tlacolulita** Mex.
245 L7 **Tlacotalpán** Mex.
245 H6 **Tlacotenco** Mex.
245 H8 **Tlacotepec** Mex.
244 G8 **Tlacotepec, Cerro** *mt.* Mex.
245 I5 **Tlacuilotepec** Mex.
242 H4 **Tlahualilo** Mex.
245 I6 **Tlahuapan** Mex.
244 D5 **Tlajomulco** Mex.
244 G7 **Tlalchapa** Mex.
245 J6 **Tlalchichuca** Mex.
245 K7 **Tlalixcoyan** Mex.
245 I8 **Tlalixtaquilla** Mex.
245 I6 **Tlalmanalco** Mex.
245 H6 **Tlalnepantla** Mex.
245 H6 **Tlálpan** Mex.
244 G6 **Tlalpujahua** Mex.
244 D4 **Tlaltenango de Sánchez Román** Mex.
245 H7 **Tlaltizapan** Mex.
245 I7 **Tlancualpican** Mex.
245 I8 **Tlapa** Mex.
245 J6 **Tlapacoyan** Mex.
245 I7 **Tlapaneco** *r.* Mex.
244 G7 **Tlapehuala** Mex.
244 D5 **Tlaquepaque** Mex.
245 J7 **Tlaquilpa** Mex.
245 I6 **Tlaxcala** Mex.
245 I6 **Tlaxcala** *state* Mex.
245 I6 **Tlaxco** Mex.
245 H5 **Tlaxcoapán** Mex.
245 J8 **Tlaxiaco** Mex.
222 D4 **Tl'ell** *B.C.* Can.
205 E2 **Tlemcen** Alg.
174 G2 **Tleń** Pol.
180 D5 **Tleta Rissana** Morocco
215 K2 **Tlhabologang** S. Africa
214 H4 **Tlhakalatlou** S. Africa
214 I2 **Tlhakgameng** S. Africa
215 M4 **Tlholong** S. Africa
177 H3 **Tlmače** Slovakia
129 H3 **Tlokh** Rus. Fed.
212 E5 **Tlokweng** Botswana
175 H3 **Tłuchowo** Pol.
173 O2 **Tlučná** Czech Rep.
136 E5 **Tlumach** Ukr.
174 F6 **Tlumačov** Czech Rep.
175 J3 **Tłuszcz** Pol.
129 H3 **Tlyadal** Rus. Fed.
129 H3 **Tlyarata** Rus. Fed.
137 S9 **Tlyustenkhabl'** Rus. Fed.
139 S5 **T'ma** *r.* Rus. Fed.
202 B3 **Tmassah** Libya
204 B5 **Tmeïmîchât** Maur.
97 G9 **Tnaôt, Prêk** *r.* Cambodia
136 G3 **Tnya** *r.* Ukr.
96 C6 **To** *r.* Myanmar
246 F3 **Toa** *r.* Cuba
247 □1 **Toa Alta** Puerto Rico
146 □N3 **Toab** *Shetland, Scotland* U.K.
247 □1 **Toa Baja** Puerto Rico
222 E3 **Toad** *r. B.C.* Can.
222 E3 **Toad River** *B.C.* Can.
92 □ **Toagel Mlungui** Palau
177 I4 **Tóalmás** Hungary
213 □K3 **Toamasina** Madag.
213 □K3 **Toamasina** *prov.* Madag.
147 E9 **Toames** Ireland
241 R1 **Toana** *mts NV* U.S.A.
191 J7 **Toano** Italy
232 I11 **Toano** *VA* U.S.A.
79 □9a **Toanoano** *Tahiti* Fr. Polynesia
94 □ **Toa Payoh** Sing.
232 E12 **Toast** *NC* U.S.A.
80 L5 **Toatoa** *North I.* N.Z.
203 G4 **To Awai** *well* Sudan
260 E5 **Toay** Arg.
108 A3 **Toba** *Xizang* China
169 K8 **Toba** Ger.
104 E7 **Toba** Japan
94 C3 **Toba, Danau** *l.* Indon.
Toba, Lake Indon. *see* **Toba, Danau**
123 L6 **Toba and Kakar Ranges** *mts* Pak.
247 □5 **Tobago** *i.* Trin. and Tob.
222 E5 **Toba Inlet** *B.C.* Can.
213 F4 **Tobane** Botswana
185 P3 **Tobarra** Spain
258 E3 **Tobas** Arg.
123 O6 **Toba Tek Singh** Pak.
179 L6 **Tobelbad** Austria
93 E3 **Tobelo** *Halmahera* Indon.
147 I3 **Tobermore** *Northern Ireland* U.K.
84 F7 **Tobermorey** *N.T.* Austr.
85 I9 **Tobermory** *Qld* Austr.
224 D4 **Tobermory** *Ont.* Can.
146 D9 **Tobermory** *Argyll and Bute, Scotland* U.K.
146 E10 **Toberonochy** *Argyll and Bute, Scotland* U.K.
102 S3 **Tōbetsu** Japan
91 H6 **Tobi** *i.* Palau
209 B7 **Tobias** Angola
254 F4 **Tobias Barreto** Brazil
103 □3 **Tobiishi-hana** *c. Iō-jima* Japan
86 H6 **Tobin, Lake** *salt flat W.A.* Austr.
240 O1 **Tobin, Mount** *NV* U.S.A.
223 K4 **Tobin Lake** *Sask.* Can.
225 H4 **Tobique** *r. N.B.* Can.
104 E5 **Tobishima** Japan
102 Q7 **Tobi-shima** *i.* Japan
94 G6 **Toboali** Indon.
120 J1 **Tobol** Kazakh.
120 M1 **Tobol** *r.* Kazakh./Rus. Fed.
130 H4 **Tobol'sk** Rus. Fed.
78 □6 **Tobona Island** Solomon Is
92 D6 **Toboso** *Negros* Phil.
Tobruk Libya *see* **Tubruq**
134 K1 **Tobseda** Rus. Fed.
105 H3 **Tōbu** Japan
234 E2 **Tobyhanna** *PA* U.S.A.
Tobyl Kazakh. *see* **Tobol**
Tobyl *r.* Kazakh./Rus. Fed. *see* **Tobol**
Tobylzhan Kazakh. *see* **Tavolzhan**
134 J2 **Tobysh** *r.* Rus. Fed.
252 A2 **Tocache Nuevo** Peru
162 E5 **Tocane-St-Apre** France
254 D3 **Tocantinópolis** Brazil
251 G6 **Tocantins** *r.* Brazil
251 I5 **Tocantins** *r.* Brazil
254 C4 **Tocantins** *state* Brazil
231 F8 **Toccoa** *GA* U.S.A.
193 L3 **Tocco da Casauria** Italy
190 E4 **Toce** *r.* Italy
182 C8 **Tocha** Port.
123 N5 **Tochi** *r.* Pak.
105 K3 **Tochigi** Japan
105 J2 **Tochigi** *pref.* Japan
245 I7 **Tochimizolco** Mex.
103 P9 **Tochio** Japan
142 H2 **Töcksfors** Sweden
247 □7 **Toco** Trin. and Tob.
242 □P10 **Tocoa** Hond.
185 L6 **Tocón** Spain
252 C5 **Tocopilla** Chile
252 D5 **Tocorpuri, Cerros de** *mts* Bol./Chile
83 J6 **Tocumwal** *N.S.W.* Austr.
247 I8 **Tocuyo de la Costa** Venez.
175 K3 **Toczna** *r.* Pol.
222 G5 **Tod, Mount** *B.C.* Can.
105 K4 **Toda** Japan
116 F6 **Toda Bhim** *Rajasthan* India
116 E6 **Toda Rai Singh** *Rajasthan* India
261 G4 **Todd** Arg.
84 E8 **Todd** *watercourse N.T.* Austr.
151 K4 **Toddington** *Bedfordshire, England* U.K.
151 I4 **Toddington** *Gloucestershire, England* U.K.
233 □S2 **Todd Mountain** *hill N.B.* Can.
87 I8 **Todd Range** *hills W.A.* Austr.
235 H2 **Toddville** *NY* U.S.A.
90 F7 **Todeli** *Maluku* Indon.
168 J3 **Todesfelde** Ger.
116 D7 **Todgarh** *Rajasthan* India
193 I2 **Todi** Italy
190 F2 **Todi** *mt.* Switz.
149 M6 **Todmorden** *West Yorkshire, England* U.K.
110 F4 **Todog** *Xinjiang* China
102 T7 **Todoga-saki** *pt* Japan
102 S5 **Todohokke** Japan
Todok *Xinjiang* China *see* **Todog**
257 G2 **Todos os Santos** *r.* Brazil
252 D4 **Todos Santos** Bol.
242 D6 **Todos Santos** Mex.
240 P10 **Todos Santos, Isla** *i.* Mex.
122 F8 **Todrūyeh** Iran
172 D6 **Todtmoos** Ger.
172 D6 **Todtnau** Ger.
147 D10 **Toe Head** Ireland
146 B7 **Toe Head** *Scotland* U.K.
104 G5 **Tōei** Japan
96 D7 **Toe Jaga, Khao** *hill* Thai.
182 E4 **Toén** Spain
206 E3 **Toéni** Burkina
81 C13 **Toetoes Bay** *South I.* N.Z.
222 H4 **Tofield** *Alta* Can.
222 E5 **Tofino** *B.C.* Can.
146 □N2 **Toft** *Shetland, Scotland* U.K.
143 L1 **Toftan** *l.* Sweden
226 D2 **Tofte** *MN* U.S.A.
143 K2 **Toften** *l.* Sweden
142 F6 **Toftlund** Denmark
79 □8 **Tofua** *i.* Tonga
104 F3 **Toga** Japan
232 G11 **Toga** *VA* U.S.A.
78 □5 **Toga** *i.* Vanuatu
105 L4 **Tōgane** Japan
111 E9 **Togatax** *Xinjiang* China
208 C3 **Togbo** C.A.R.
210 E2 **Togdheer** *admin. reg.* Somalia
190 G1 **Toggenburg** *reg.* Switz.
147 D9 **Togher** *Cork* Ireland
147 J5 **Togher** *Louth* Ireland
147 G6 **Togher** *Offaly* Ireland
104 E1 **Togi** Japan
220 B4 **Togiak** *AK* U.S.A.
93 B4 **Togian** *i.* Indon.
93 B4 **Togian, Kepulauan** *is* Indon.
173 N5 **Töging am Inn** Ger.
Togliatti Rus. Fed. *see* **Tol'yatti**
207 F4 **Togo** *country* Africa
104 F5 **Tōgō** *Aichi* Japan
103 I14 **Tōgō** *Miyazaki* Japan
226 A2 **Togo** *MN* U.S.A.
111 J7 **Tograsay He** *r.* China
106 C3 **Tögrög** Mongolia
107 M6 **Togrog Ul** *Nei Mongol* China
149 N3 **Togston** *Northumberland, England* U.K.
107 L6 **Togtoh** *Nei Mongol* China
111 K9 **Togton He** *r.* China
130 J4 **Toguchin** Rus. Fed.
105 H3 **Togura** Japan
120 I4 **Toguz** Kazakh.
210 D2 **Tog Wajaale** Somalia
203 H5 **Tohamiyam** Sudan
116 E5 **Tohana** *Haryana* India
241 X6 **Tohatchi** *NM* U.S.A.
95 J4 **Tohenbatu** *mt.* Malaysia
79 □9a **Tohiea** *mt. Moorea* Fr. Polynesia
140 U5 **Tohmajärvi** Fin.
140 U5 **Tohmajärvi** *l.* Fin.
104 D5 **Tohoku** Japan
140 R5 **Toholampi** Fin.
106 I6 **Tohom** *Nei Mongol* China
107 K4 **Töhöm** Mongolia
241 T9 **Tohono O'Odham (Papago) Indian Reservation** *res. AZ* U.S.A.
207 F5 **Tohoun** Togo
102 S5 **Toi** *Hokkaidō* Japan
105 I6 **Toi** *Shizuoka* Japan
78 □2 **To'iave'a** *mt.* Samoa
111 I11 **Toiba** *Xizang* China
115 M7 **Toibalewe** *Andaman & Nicobar Is* India
104 E2 **Toide** Japan
141 Q6 **Toijala** Fin.
93 C4 **Toili** *Sulawesi* Indon.
103 I15 **Toi-misaki** *pt* Japan
78 □6 **Toimonapu** P.N.G.
104 E5 **Toin** Japan
93 D9 **Toineke** *Timor* Indon.
190 E7 **Toirano** Italy
141 S5 **Toivakka** Fin.
81 □4 **Toi Village** Niue
240 O2 **Toiyabe Range** *mts NV* U.S.A.
93 B4 **Toja** *Sulawesi* Indon.
Tojikiston *country* Asia *see* **Tajikistan**
123 N2 **Tojikobod** Tajik.
103 K12 **Tōjō** *Hiroshima* Japan
104 B6 **Tōjō** *Hyōgo* Japan
120 E1 **Tok** *r.* Rus. Fed.
220 D3 **Tok** *AK* U.S.A.
102 U4 **Tokachi-gawa** *r.* Japan
104 E5 **Tōkai** *Aichi* Japan
105 M3 **Tōkai** *Ibaraki* Japan
177 K3 **Tokaj** Hungary
177 K3 **Tokaj-Bodrog-Zug** *park* Hungary
93 B4 **Tokala, Gunung** *mt.* Indon.
105 I1 **Tōkamachi** Japan
81 C13 **Tokanui** *South I.* N.Z.
203 H5 **Tokar** Sudan
81 E11 **Tokarahi** *South I.* N.Z.
102 □G18 **Tokara-rettō** *is* Japan
121 O2 **Tokarevka** Kazakh.
135 H6 **Tokarevka** Rus. Fed.
139 R1 **Tokari** Rus. Fed.
175 I5 **Tokarnia** Pol.
137 O8 **Tokaryeve** Ukr.
102 □E20 **Tokasiki-jima** *i. Nansei-shotō* Japan
126 H3 **Tokat** Turkey
80 H3 **Tokatoka** *North I.* N.Z.
80 I3 **Tokatu Point** *North I.* N.Z.
137 U2 **Tokay** *r.* Rus. Fed.
101 E10 **Tŏkchok-to** *i.* S. Korea
101 E9 **Tŏkch'ŏn** N. Korea
Tokdo *i.* N. Pacific Ocean *see* **Liancourt Rocks**
81 □1 **Tokelau** *terr.* S. Pacific Ocean
T'okhluja Armenia *see* **Drakhtik**
Tokhtamysh Tajik. *see* **Tŭkhtamish**
104 F5 **Toki** Japan
105 J3 **Tokigawa** Japan
104 E5 **Toki-gawa** *r.* Japan
Tokkuztara *Xinjiang* China *see* **Gongliu**
129 B6 **Toklular** Turkey
137 O6 **Tokmachka** *r.* Ukr.
Tokmak Kyrg. *see* **Tokmok**
137 O6 **Tokmak** Ukr.
121 P6 **Tokmok** Kyrg.
177 H4 **Tokod** Hungary
80 M5 **Tokomaru Bay** *North I.* N.Z.
104 E6 **Tokoname** Japan
80 J5 **Tokoroa** *North I.* N.Z.
102 V2 **Tokoro-gawa** *r.* Japan
105 J4 **Tokorozawa** Japan
202 D5 **Tokou** *well* Chad
206 C4 **Tokounou** Guinea
215 M2 **Tokoza** S. Africa
Tokrau *watercourse* Kazakh. *see* **Tokyrau**
Toksu *Xinjiang* China *see* **Xinhe**
110 I5 **Toksun** *Xinjiang* China
Tok-tō *i.* N. Pacific Ocean *see* **Liancourt Rocks**
121 O7 **Toktogul** Kyrg.
Toktogul'skoye Vodokhranilishche *resr* Kyrg. *see* **Toktogul Suu Saktagychy**
121 O7 **Toktogul Suu Saktagychy** *resr* Kyrg.
Tokto-ri *i.* N. Pacific Ocean *see* **Liancourt Rocks**
121 T5 **Tokty** Kazakh.
77 I3 **Tokû** *i.* Tonga
79 □8 **Tokulu** *atoll* Tonga
102 □G19 **Tokunoshima** *Nansei-shotō* Japan
102 □F19 **Toku-no-shima** *i. Nansei-shotō* Japan
100 H2 **Tokur** Rus. Fed.
104 A7 **Tokushima** Japan
103 L13 **Tokushima** *pref.* Japan
103 I12 **Tokuyama** Japan
Tokwe *r.* Zimbabwe *see* **Tugwi**
105 K4 **Tōkyō** Japan
105 J5 **Tōkyō** *mun.* Japan
105 K4 **Tōkyō-wan** *b.* Japan
121 P4 **Tokyrau** *watercourse* Kazakh.
101 E11 **Tokyu-san National Park** S. Korea
123 L4 **Tokzār** Afgh.
78 □4a **Tol** *i. Chuuk* Micronesia
80 M5 **Tolaga Bay** *North I.* N.Z.
213 □J5 **Tôlañaro** Madag.
258 D2 **Tolar, Cerro** *mt.* Arg.
146 D6 **Tolastadh Ùr** *Western Isles, Scotland* U.K.
183 K7 **Tolbaños** Spain
120 F1 **Tolbazy** Rus. Fed.
164 J2 **Tolbert** Neth.
106 B2 **Tolbo** Mongolia
Tolbukhin Bulg. *see* **Dobrich**
139 X4 **Tolbukhino** Rus. Fed.
100 D2 **Tolbuzino** Rus. Fed.
262 T1 **Tolchin, Mount** Antarctica
177 K3 **Tolcsva** Hungary
242 □S13 **Tolé** Panama
121 O6 **Tole Bi** Kazakh.
250 C6 **Toledo** *Amazonas* Brazil
255 B8 **Toledo** *Paraná* Brazil
258 C2 **Toledo** Chile
183 L9 **Toledo** Spain
183 L9 **Toledo** *prov.* Spain
236 I5 **Toledo** *IA* U.S.A.
236 K6 **Toledo** *IL* U.S.A.
232 B7 **Toledo** *OH* U.S.A.
238 C4 **Toledo** *OR* U.S.A.
183 K9 **Toledo, Montes de** *mts* Spain
237 I10 **Toledo Bend Reservoir** *LA/TX* U.S.A.
191 O9 **Tolentino** Italy
Toletum Spain *see* **Toledo**
192 H3 **Tolfa** Italy
85 J4 **Tolga** *Qld* Austr.
141 K5 **Tolga** Norway
260 B6 **Tolhuaca, Parque Nacional** *nat. park* Chile
110 F4 **Toli** *Xinjiang* China
213 □I4 **Toliara** Madag.
213 □J4 **Toliara** *prov.* Madag.
250 C4 **Tolima** *dept* Col.
244 D6 **Tolimán** *Jalisco* Mex.
245 H5 **Tolimán** *Querétaro* Mex.
93 B3 **Tolitoli** *Sulawesi* Indon.
168 I1 **Tolk** Ger.
130 J3 **Tol'ka** Rus. Fed.
142 I4 **Tolken** *l.* Sweden
143 P7 **Tolkmicko** Pol.
164 I3 **Tollebeek** Neth.
170 H3 **Tollense** *r.* Ger.
170 H4 **Tollensesee** *l.* Ger.
170 H4 **Tollensesee-Becken** *park* Ger.
151 N4 **Tollesbury** *Essex, England* U.K.
151 N4 **Tolleshunt D'Arcy** *Essex, England* U.K.
241 T8 **Tolleson** *AZ* U.S.A.
120 K8 **Tollimarjon** Uzbek.
193 M3 **Tollo** Italy
142 H6 **Tølløse** Denmark
138 M3 **Tolmachevo** Rus. Fed.
191 O3 **Tolmezzo** Italy
188 D2 **Tolmin** Slovenia
177 H5 **Tolna** Hungary
177 H5 **Tolna** *county* Hungary
177 H5 **Tolnai-hegyhát** *hills* Hungary
177 H5 **Tolnanémedi** Hungary
208 C5 **Tolo** Dem. Rep. Congo
242 □P10 **Toloa Creek** Hond.
Tolo Channel *H.K.* China *see* **Chek Mun Hoi Hap**
Tolochin Belarus *see* **Talachyn**
Tolo Harbour *b. H.K.* China *see* **Tai Po Hoi**
140 S2 **Tolonen** Fin.
93 F3 **Tolonuu** *i. Maluku* Indon.
Tolosa France *see* **Toulouse**
184 D2 **Tolosa** Port.
186 A1 **Tolosa** Spain
185 J7 **Tolox** Spain
139 Y4 **Tolpygino** Rus. Fed.
101 E11 **Tolsan-do** *i.* S. Korea
227 K4 **Tolsmaville** *Ont.* Can.
146 D6 **Tolsta Head** *Scotland* U.K.
131 Q4 **Tolstoy, Mys** *c.* Rus. Fed.
259 B5 **Toltén** Chile
250 C2 **Tolú** Col.
245 H6 **Toluca** Mex.
186 G3 **Tolva** Spain
140 U3 **Tolvand, Ozero** *l.* Rus. Fed.
193 Q6 **Tolve** Italy
193 Q6 **Tolve** *r.* Italy
135 J5 **Tol'yatti** Rus. Fed.
120 J2 **Tolybay** Kazakh.
163 E7 **Tolzac** *r.* France
100 E3 **Tom'** *r.* Rus. Fed.
206 E3 **Toma** Burkina
104 B7 **Tomaga-shima** *i.* Japan
104 A7 **Tomagashima-suidō** *sea chan.* Japan
226 D6 **Tomah** *WI* U.S.A.
226 E4 **Tomahawk** *WI* U.S.A.
137 N6 **Tomakivka** *r.* Ukr.
102 S4 **Tomakomai** Japan
240 J3 **Tomales** *CA* U.S.A.
102 S2 **Tomamae** Japan
95 K2 **Tomani** *Sabah* Malaysia
79 □7a **Tomanivi** *mt. Viti Levu* Fiji
251 F5 **Tomar** Brazil
182 D9 **Tomar** Port.
102 R3 **Tomari** Japan
100 M5 **Tomari** *Sakhalin* Rus. Fed.
129 E5 **Tomarlı** Turkey
198 B3 **Tomaros** *mt.* Greece
137 P3 **Tomarovka** Rus. Fed.
126 G4 **Tomarza** Turkey
252 D4 **Tomás Barron** Bol.
261 I2 **Tomás Gomensoro** Uru.
136 G2 **Tomashhorod** *Rivnens'ka Oblast'* Ukr.
136 G2 **Tomashhorod** *Rivnens'ka Oblast'* Ukr.
136 H5 **Tomashpil'** Ukr.
176 G3 **Tomášov** Slovakia
177 I3 **Tomášovce** Slovakia
175 L5 **Tomaszów Lubelski** Pol.
175 I4 **Tomaszów Mazowiecki** Pol.
146 I8 **Tomatin** *Highland, Scotland* U.K.
244 B6 **Tomatlán** Mex.
252 D5 **Tomave** Bol.
256 C5 **Tomazina** Brazil
254 E4 **Tombador, Serra do** *hills* Brazil
253 F3 **Tombador, Serra do** *hills* Brazil
217 □1b **Tombeau Bay** Mauritius
163 E6 **Tombebœf** France
231 D10 **Tombigbee** *r. AL* U.S.A.
215 N7 **Tombo** S. Africa
259 D7 **Tombo, Punta** *pt* Arg.
209 B6 **Tomboco** Angola
257 F4 **Tombos** Brazil
206 E2 **Tombouctou** Mali
206 E2 **Tombouctou** *admin. reg.* Mali
80 G1 **Tom Bowling Bay** *North I.* N.Z.
210 B4 **Tombs of Buganda Kings** *tourist site* Uganda
241 V10 **Tombstone** *AZ* U.S.A.
209 A8 **Tombua** Angola
213 E4 **Tom Burke** S. Africa
120 K7 **Tomdibuloq** Uzbek.
120 K7 **Tomditov tog'lari** *hills* Uzbek.
Tomditow Toghi *hills* Uzbek. *see* **Tomditov tog'lari**
258 B5 **Tomé** Chile
213 G4 **Tome** Moz.
93 C6 **Tomea** *i.* Indon.
143 J6 **Tomelilla** Sweden
185 M2 **Tomelloso** Spain
121 L6 **Tomenaryk** Kazakh.
177 L5 **Tomeşti** *Hunedoara* Romania
177 L6 **Tomeşti** *Timiş* Romania
Tomi Romania *see* **Constanţa**
175 H6 **Tomice** Pol.
102 □1 **Tomigusuku** *Okinawa* Japan
104 E5 **Tomika** Japan
227 O3 **Tomiko** *Ont.* Can.
252 D4 **Tomina** Bol.
206 B3 **Tominé** *r.* Guinea
83 L5 **Tomingley** *N.S.W.* Austr.
93 B4 **Tomini, Teluk** *g.* Indon.
206 D3 **Tominian** Mali
146 J8 **Tomintoul** *Moray, Scotland* U.K.
102 S9 **Tomioka** *Fukushima* Japan
105 I3 **Tomioka** *Gunma* Japan
105 L4 **Tomisato** Japan
188 F4 **Tomislavgrad** Bos.-Herz.
105 K5 **Tomiura** Japan
105 G5 **Tomiyama** *Aichi* Japan
105 K5 **Tomiyama** *Chiba* Japan
105 H5 **Tomizawa** Japan
235 H2 **Tomkins Cove** *NY* U.S.A.
82 B2 **Tomkinson Ranges** *mts S.A.* Austr.
142 E4 **Tommerby Fjord** *l.* Denmark
140 M3 **Tømmerneset** Norway
131 N4 **Tommot** Rus. Fed.
146 J8 **Tomnavoulin** *Moray, Scotland* U.K.
250 E4 **Tomo** Col.
250 E3 **Tomo** *r.* Col.
105 L3 **Tomobe** Japan
242 F3 **Tomóchic** Mex.
208 B4 **Tomori** C.A.R.
198 B2 **Tomorit, Maja e** *mt.* Albania
111 J7 **Tomorlog** *Qinghai* China
107 M6 **Tomortei** *Nei Mongol* China
177 I5 **Tompa** Hungary
93 B5 **Tompira** *Sulawesi* Indon.
93 A4 **Tompo** *Sulawesi* Indon.
131 O3 **Tompo** Rus. Fed.
86 D7 **Tom Price** *W.A.* Austr.
111 H11 **Tomra** *Xizang* China
235 G5 **Toms** *r. NJ* U.S.A.
123 L2 **Tomshush** Uzbek.
130 J4 **Tomsk** Rus. Fed.
86 □1 **Tom's Ridge** Christmas I.
233 K9 **Toms River** *NJ* U.S.A.
143 K4 **Tomtabacken** *hill* Sweden
131 P3 **Tomtor** Rus. Fed.
128 C2 **Tömük** Turkey
102 T3 **Tomuraushi-yama** *mt.* Japan
Tomur Feng *mt.* China/Kyrg. *see* **Jengish Chokusu**
129 F1 **Tomuzlovka** *r.* Rus. Fed.
220 D3 **Tom White, Mount** *AK* U.S.A.
137 L7 **Tomyna Balka** Ukr.
186 J4 **Tona** Spain
102 □E20 **Tonaki-jima** *i. Nansei-shotō* Japan
245 N9 **Tonalá** *Chiapas* Mex.
244 D5 **Tonala** Mex.
245 J8 **Tonalá** *Oaxaca* Mex.
245 M7 **Tonalá** *Veracruz* Mex.
245 H7 **Tonalapa de Rio** Mex.
191 J3 **Tonale, Passo di** *pass* Italy
104 E2 **Tonami** Japan
250 E5 **Tonantins** Brazil
192 C7 **Tonara** *Sardegna* Italy
238 E2 **Tonasket** *WA* U.S.A.
251 H3 **Tonate** Fr. Guiana
232 G5 **Tonawanda** *NY* U.S.A.
244 D6 **Tonaya** Mex.
Tonb-e Bozorg, Jazīreh-ye *i.* The Gulf *see* **Greater Tunb**
Tonb-e Kūchek, Jazīreh-ye *i.* The Gulf *see* **Lesser Tunb**
151 M5 **Tonbridge** *Kent, England* U.K.
182 D7 **Tonda** Port.
104 C7 **Tondabayashi** Japan
93 D3 **Tondano** *Sulawesi* Indon.
182 D7 **Tondela** Port.
142 E7 **Tønder** Denmark
114 F8 **Tondi** *Tamil Nadu* India
105 J2 **Tone** *Gunma* Japan
105 L4 **Tone** *Ibaraki* Japan
150 G5 **Tone** *r. England* U.K.
140 □ **Tonefjellet** *hill* Svalbard
105 M4 **Tone-gawa** *r.* Japan
262 Q1 **Toney Mountain** Antarctica
191 K4 **Tonezza del Cimone** Italy
207 H5 **Tonga** Cameroon
79 □8 **Tonga** *country* S. Pacific Ocean
210 A2 **Tonga** Sudan
215 P5 **Tongaat** S. Africa
109 L6 **Tong'an** *Fujian* China
209 E9 **Tonga Plateau** Zambia
80 I5 **Tongaporutu** *North I.* N.Z.
Tongareva *atoll* Cook Is *see* **Penrhyn**
80 J6 **Tongariro** *vol. North I.* N.Z.
80 J6 **Tongariro National Park** *North I.* N.Z.
79 □8a **Tongatapu** *i.* Tonga
79 □8a **Tongatapu Group** *is* Tonga
266 H7 **Tonga Trench** *sea feature* S. Pacific Ocean
109 I2 **Tongbai** *Henan* China
109 I2 **Tongbai Shan** *mts* China
109 K3 **Tongcheng** *Anhui* China
109 I4 **Tongcheng** *Hubei* China
Tongcheng *Shandong* China *see* **Dong'e**
101 E9 **T'ongch'ŏn** N. Korea
107 K9 **Tongchuan** *Shaanxi* China
Tongchuan *Sichuan* China *see* **Santai**
108 G5 **Tongdao** *Hunan* China
106 G9 **Tongde** *Qinghai* China
101 E10 **Tongduch'ŏn** S. Korea
165 H7 **Tongeren** Belgium
109 J4 **Tonggu** *Jiangxi* China
107 L9 **Tongguan** *Shaanxi* China
110 E7 **Tongguzbasti** *Xinjiang* China
108 H9 **Tonggu Zui** *pt* China
101 F10 **Tonghae** S. Korea
108 D6 **Tonghai** *Yunnan* China
100 F6 **Tonghe** *Heilong.* China
101 D8 **Tonghua** *Jilin* China
101 D8 **Tonghua** *Jilin* China
Tongi Bangl. *see* **Tungi**
100 H5 **Tongjiang** *Heilong.* China
108 F3 **Tongjiang** *Sichuan* China
100 C7 **Tongjiangkou** *Liaoning* China
101 E9 **Tongjosŏn-man** *b.* N. Korea
100 E5 **Tongken He** *r.* China
96 I4 **Tongking, Gulf of** China/Vietnam
93 B4 **Tongko** *Sulawesi* Indon.
146 H13 **Tongland** *Dumfries and Galloway, Scotland* U.K.
Tongle *Guangxi* China *see* **Leye**
107 R5 **Tongliao** *Nei Mongol* China
109 K3 **Tongling** *Anhui* China
109 K3 **Tongling** *Anhui* China
109 L4 **Tonglu** *Zhejiang* China
109 I5 **Tongmu** *Jiangxi* China
103 G11 **Tongnae** S. Korea
83 I4 **Tongo** *N.S.W.* Austr.
78 □5 **Tongoa** *i.* Vanuatu
213 □J4 **Tongobory** Madag.
260 B2 **Tongoi, Bahía** *b.* Chile
83 I4 **Tongo Lake** *salt flat N.S.W.* Austr.
260 B2 **Tongoy** Chile
Tongquan *Yunnan* China *see* **Malong**
92 C8 **Tongquil** *i.* Phil.
108 G5 **Tongren** *Guizhou* China
106 G9 **Tongren** *Qinghai* China
Tongres Belgium *see* **Tongeren**
117 M6 **Tongsa** Bhutan
Tongshan *Jiangsu* China *see* **Xuzhou**
Tongshi *Hainan* China *see* **Wuzhishan**
108 G9 **Tongshi** *Hainan* China
96 D4 **Tongta** Myanmar
106 C9 **Tongtian He** *r. Qinghai* China
111 M10 **Tongtian He** *r. Qinghai* China

Tongtian He to Tres Zapotes
399

108 A2 Tongtian He r. China alt. Chang Jiang, alt. Jinsha Jiang, conv. Yangtze, long Yangtze Kiang
146 H6 Tongue Highland, Scotland U.K.
238 L3 Tongue r. MT U.S.A.
Tongue of Arabat spit Ukr. see Arabats'ka Strilka, Kosa
246 E1 Tongue of the Ocean sea chan. Bahamas
236 B3 Tongue River Reservoir MT U.S.A.
106 I9 Tongwei Gansu China
109 M3 Tongxiang Zhejiang China
106 I8 Tongxin Ningxia China
101 F11 T'ongyŏng S. Korea
107 R4 Tongyu Jilin China
107 O7 Tongzhou Beijing China
109 M2 Tongzhou Jiangsu China
108 F4 Tongzi Guizhou China
Tonhil Mongolia see Dzüyl
226 E8 Tonica IL U.S.A.
242 E3 Tónichi Mex.
244 D6 Tonila Mex.
208 F3 Tonj Sudan
208 F3 Tonj watercourse Sudan
116 E6 Tonk Rajasthan India
122 D3 Tonkābon Iran
237 G7 Tonkawa OK U.S.A.
96 G4 Tonkin reg. Vietnam
134 I4 Tonkino Rus. Fed.
97 G7 Tônle Repou r. Laos
97 F8 Tônlé Sab l. Cambodia
97 H8 Tônlé San r. Cambodia
Tonle Sap l. Cambodia see Tônlé Sab
150 E4 Tonna Neath Port Talbot, Wales U.K.
162 C4 Tonnay-Boutonne France
162 C4 Tonnay-Charente France
163 E7 Tonneins France
156 G8 Tonnerre France
156 H8 Tonnerrois reg. France
168 G2 Tönning Ger.
105 M1 Tōno Fukushima Japan
102 S7 Tōno Iwate Japan
78 □4a Tonoas i. Chuuk Micronesia
241 T8 Tonopah AZ U.S.A.
240 O3 Tonopah NV U.S.A.
105 M4 Tonoshō Chiba Japan
103 L12 Tonoshō Kagawa Japan
242 □S14 Tonosí Panama
111 C11 Tons r. India
142 G2 Tønsberg Norway
139 U2 Tonshalovo Rus. Fed.
142 C3 Tonstad Norway
260 C2 Tontal, Sierra mts Arg.
214 E6 Tontelbos S. Africa
245 K7 Tonto r. Mex.
241 U8 Tonto Basin AZ U.S.A.
241 U8 Tonto Creek watercourse AZ U.S.A.
79 □8 Tonumea atoll Tonga
122 H4 Tonvarjeh Iran
136 G2 Tonyezh Belarus
150 F4 Tonyrefail Rhondda Cynon Taff, Wales U.K.
96 A3 Tonzang Myanmar
96 B2 Tonzi Myanmar
83 L3 Toobeah Qld Austr.
206 C5 Toobli Liberia
87 D11 Toodyay W.A. Austr.
241 T1 Tooele UT U.S.A.
85 N9 Toogoolawah Qld Austr.
83 I6 Tooleybuc N.S.W. Austr.
82 E5 Tooligie S.A. Austr.
87 C9 Toolonga Nature Reserve W.A. Austr.
83 L7 Tooma r. N.S.W. Austr.
147 J3 Toomebridge Northern Ireland U.K.
85 J9 Toompine Qld Austr.
83 K8 Toora Vic. Austr.
83 L4 Tooraweenah N.S.W. Austr.
214 I8 Toorberg mt. S. Africa
147 C9 Toormore Ireland
85 M9 Toowoomba Qld Austr.
210 F2 Tooxin Somalia
123 M4 Top Afgh.
261 I2 Topador Uru.
245 H7 Topalapa del Sur Mex.
139 T3 Topalki Rus. Fed.
197 M6 Topana Romania
185 O5 Topares Spain
217 □1a Topaze, Baie b. Rodrigues I. Mauritius
240 M3 Topaz Lake NV U.S.A.
121 T1 Topchikha Rus. Fed.
171 I6 Töpchin Ger.
137 N5 Topchyne Ukr.
149 O5 Topcliffe North Yorkshire, England U.K.
129 C6 Topçu Dağı mt. Turkey
129 D6 Top Dağı mt. Turkey
236 H6 Topeka KS U.S.A.
171 E10 Töpen Ger.
242 F5 Topia Mex.
193 J2 Topino r. Italy
139 V7 Topkanovo Rus. Fed.
130 J4 Topki Rus. Fed.
116 H8 Topla reg. Madh. Prad. India
177 K3 Topľa r. Slovakia
93 F5 Toplana, Gunung mt. Seram Indon.
222 E4 Topley B.C. Can.
222 E4 Topley Landing B.C. Can.
196 J7 Toplica r. Serbia
197 N4 Toplița Harghita Romania
177 L6 Toplița Hunedoara Romania
171 G6 Töplitz Ger.
179 I4 Toplitzsee l. Austria
216 □1c Topo São Jorge Azores
216 □1c Topo, Ilhéu do i. Azores
216 □1c Topo, Serra do mt. São Jorge Azores
260 A4 Topocalma, Punta pt Chile
241 R7 Topock AZ U.S.A.
177 H3 Topoľčany Slovakia
177 H3 Topoľčianky Slovakia
120 D4 Topoli Kazakh.
174 G3 Topólka Pol.
177 G2 Topolná Czech Rep.
197 M8 Topolnitsa r. Bulg.
242 E5 Topolobampo Mex.
197 Q6 Topolog Romania
197 M5 Topolog r. Romania
177 K6 Topolovățu Mare Romania
197 N6 Topoloveni Romania
197 O8 Topolovgrad Bulg.
179 L7 Topolšica Slovenia
177 J2 Toporec Slovakia
174 D3 Toporów Pol.
136 F3 Topory Ukr.
136 H3 Toporyshche Ukr.
174 E2 Toporzyk Pol.
134 F2 Topozero, Ozero l. Rus. Fed.
238 D3 Toppenish WA U.S.A.
197 Q6 Topraisar Romania
129 D6 Toprakkale Ağrı Turkey
129 C5 Toprakkale Erzurum Turkey
128 E1 Toprakkale Osmaniye Turkey
129 B6 Topraklık Turkey
233 □R3 Topsfield ME U.S.A.
150 F6 Topsham Devon, England U.K.
129 C6 Toptepe Turkey
234 D3 Topton PA U.S.A.
80 I3 Topuni North I. N.Z.
252 C4 Toquepala Peru
Toqyraū watercourse Kazakh. see Tokyrau
210 B3 Tor Eth.
186 G3 Tor, Noguera de r. Spain
208 F4 Tora Dem. Rep. Congo
186 H4 Torá Spain
129 K5 Torağay Dağı hill Azer.
104 D5 Torahime Japan
182 I4 Toral de los Guzmanes Spain
182 G3 Toral de los Vados Spain
Toraman Turkey see Halilçavuş
106 B4 Toranggekuduk Xinjiang China
193 Q9 Torano Castello Italy
252 C4 Torata Peru
123 L6 Tor Baldak mt. Afgh.
199 I4 Torbalı Turkey
122 H4 Torbat-e Heydarīyeh Iran
122 I4 Torbat-e Jām Iran
150 E7 Torbay admin. div. England U.K.
150 E7 Tor Bay England U.K.
87 D13 Torbay Bay W.A. Austr.
135 H5 Torbeyevo Respublika Mordoviya Rus. Fed.
139 R6 Torbeyevo Smolenskaya Oblast' Rus. Fed.
185 J7 Torcal de Antequera park Spain
186 C5 Torcas, Embalse de las resr Spain
223 K4 Torch r. Sask. Can.
193 O7 Torchiara Italy
195 O3 Torchiarolo Italy
139 X5 Torchino Rus. Fed.
136 E3 Torchyn Ukr.
183 L9 Torcón r. Spain
183 L9 Torcón, Embalse del resr Spain
160 E3 Torcy France
156 B4 Torcy-le-Petit France
177 H4 Tordas Hungary
183 J5 Tordehumos Spain
186 K4 Tordera Spain
183 K5 Tordesillas Spain
183 Q7 Tordesilos Spain
183 P9 Tórdiga, Puerto de pass Spain
193 L2 Tordino r. Italy
140 Q4 Töre Sweden
146 H7 Tore Highland, Scotland U.K.
143 K3 Töreboda Sweden
170 E1 Toreby Denmark
142 I5 Torekov Sweden
193 N4 Torella del Sannio Italy
187 D11 Torellano Spain
140 □ Torell Land reg. Svalbard
186 J3 Torelló Spain
164 I4 Torenberg hill Neth.
182 G3 Toreno Spain
93 C5 Toreo Sulawesi Indon.
80 L4 Torere North I. N.Z.
Toretam Kazakh. see Baykonyr
106 I1 Torey Rus. Fed.
137 R5 Torez Ukr.
150 F4 Torfaen admin. div. Wales U.K.
Torga i. Vanuatu see Toga
171 G7 Torgau Ger.
170 J3 Torgelow Ger.
Torghay Kazakh. see Turgay
193 I1 Torgiano Italy
120 B2 Torgun r. Rus. Fed.
143 L5 Torhamn Sweden
165 D6 Torhout Belgium
136 E3 Torhovytsya Ukr.
138 H3 Tori Estonia
117 J8 Tori Jharkhand India
210 A3 Tori r. Sudan
105 L4 Toride Japan
105 H1 Torigakubi-misaki pt Japan
159 J3 Torigni-sur-Vire France
104 E3 Torigoe Japan
105 G4 Torii-tōge pass Japan
105 H3 Torii-tōge pass Japan
183 N7 Torija Spain
105 I2 Torikabuto-yama mt. Japan
188 G4 Torine pass Bos.-Herz.
190 D5 Torino Italy
190 D5 Torino prov. Italy
193 N3 Torino di Sangro Italy
103 R16 Tori-shima i. Japan
210 B3 Torit Sudan
195 L2 Toritto Italy
256 A2 Torixoréu Brazil
104 E2 Toriya Japan
122 B3 Torkamān Iran
123 J4 Torkestān, Band-e mts Afgh.
123 N5 Torkhan Pak.
139 N3 Torkovichi Rus. Fed.
186 E2 Torla Spain
138 J3 Torma Estonia
140 S2 Törmänen Fin.
86 G4 Torment, Point W.A. Austr.
182 H6 Tormes r. Spain
187 C7 Tormón Spain
146 F11 Tormore North Ayrshire, Scotland U.K.
183 K7 Tornadizos de Ávila Spain
222 H5 Tornado Mountain Alta/B.C. Can.
185 N5 Tornajuelos mt. Spain
177 J3 Tornaľa Slovakia
182 I8 Tornavacas Spain
182 I8 Tornavacas, Puerto de pass Spain
149 P6 Torne r. England U.K.
Torneå Fin. see Tornio
140 R4 Torneälven r. Sweden
185 K2 Torneros, Sierra de los mts Spain
168 I3 Tornesch Ger.
140 O2 Torneträsk Sweden
140 O2 Torneträsk l. Sweden
Torngat, Monts mts Nfld and Lab./Que. Can. see Torngat Mountains
225 H1 Torngat Mountains Nfld and Lab./Que. Can.
196 H7 Tornik mt. Serbia
140 R4 Tornio Fin.
177 I6 Tornjoš Vojvodina Serbia
190 G4 Torno Italy
183 R7 Tornos Spain
170 H4 Tornow Ger.
261 F6 Tornquist Arg.
177 L3 Tornyospálca Hungary
207 H4 Toro Nigeria
183 J5 Toro Spain
143 N3 Torö i. Sweden
259 B8 Toro, Lago del l. Chile
244 F1 Toro, Pico del mt. Mex.
260 B3 Toro, Punta pt Chile
93 C6 Torobuku Sulawesi Indon.
207 F3 Torodi Niger
177 H4 Törökbálint Hungary
177 J4 Törökszentmiklós Hungary
100 I1 Torom Rus. Fed.
224 E5 Toronto Ont. Can.
232 E8 Toronto OH U.S.A.
234 F1 Toronto Reservoir NY U.S.A.
179 O5 Torony Hungary
139 O5 Toropatsa Rus. Fed.
241 P8 Toro Peak CA U.S.A.
139 O5 Toropets Rus. Fed.
202 C6 Tororo Chad
210 B4 Tororo Uganda
126 F5 Toros Dağları mts Turkey
138 L4 Toroshino Rus. Fed.
183 K5 Torozos, Montes de reg. Spain
192 D6 Torpè Sardegna Italy
146 K8 Torphins Aberdeenshire, Scotland U.K.
150 D7 Torpoint Cornwall, England U.K.
255 B9 Torquato Severo Brazil
83 J8 Torquay Vic. Austr.
150 E7 Torquay Torbay, England U.K.
183 L4 Torquemada Spain
147 J2 Torr Northern Ireland U.K.
185 L2 Torraiba de Calatrava Spain
192 B6 Torralba Sardegna Italy
183 P8 Torralba Spain
186 D4 Torralba de Aragón Spain
183 O5 Torralba de El Burgo Spain
183 R7 Torralba de los Sisones Spain
183 J9 Torralba de Oropesa Spain
240 N8 Torrance CA U.S.A.
184 C4 Torrão Port.
182 E8 Torre mt. Port.
193 M6 Torre Annunziata Italy
193 J5 Torre Astura cliff Italy
187 C7 Torrebaja Spain
183 O5 Torreblacos Spain
187 F7 Torreblanca Spain
242 B1 Torre Blanco, Cerro mt. Mex.
185 L5 Torreblascopedro Spain
193 N4 Torrebruna Italy
183 L7 Torrecaballeros Spain
185 J4 Torrecampo Spain
195 M2 Torre Canne Italy
185 M5 Torre-Cardela Spain
195 O2 Torre Cavallo, Capo di c. Italy
183 K2 Torrecerredo mt. Spain
192 G3 Torre Ciana, Punta di pt Italy
185 J7 Torrecilla mt. Spain
183 K9 Torrecilla de la Jara Spain
183 J6 Torrecilla de la Orden Spain
186 C6 Torrecilla del Rebollar Spain
183 O4 Torrecilla en Cameros Spain
182 I9 Torrecillas de la Tiesa Spain
193 N5 Torrecuso Italy
184 C3 Torre da Gadanha Port.
184 D2 Torre das Vargens Port.
185 K2 Torre de Abraham, Embalse de la resr Spain
186 I3 Torre de Cadí mt. Spain
182 F5 Torre de Dona Chama Port.
182 D7 Torredeita Port.
185 M3 Torre de Juan Abad Spain
184 H6 Torre del Águila, Embalse de la resr Spain
182 H3 Torre del Bierzo Spain
183 N7 Torre del Burgo Spain
185 L5 Torre del Campo Spain
193 M6 Torre del Greco Italy
190 I8 Torre della Meloria i. Italy
185 K7 Torre del Mar Spain
195 N4 Torre del Pizzo pt Italy
186 H5 Torredembarra Spain
184 F3 Torre de Miguel Sesmero Spain
182 F6 Torre de Moncorvo Port.
193 L3 Torre de'Passeri Italy
185 L5 Torredonjimeno Spain
182 F7 Torre do Terrenho Port.
182 H6 Torregamones Spain
186 G4 Torregrossa Spain
183 L6 Torreiglesias Spain
182 C7 Torreira Port.
182 H9 Torrejoncillo Spain
183 O8 Torrejoncillo del Rey Spain
183 N8 Torrejón de Ardoz Spain
183 N7 Torrejón del Rey Spain
182 I9 Torrejón el Rubio Spain
182 I9 Torrejón-Tajo, Embalse de resr Spain
182 I9 Torrejón-Tiétar, Embalse de resr Spain
186 C6 Torrelacarcel Spain
183 M7 Torrelaguna Spain
183 Q5 Torrelapaja Spain
183 L2 Torrelavega Spain
183 Q5 Torrellas Spain
186 I5 Torrelles de Foix Spain
183 J5 Torrelobatón Spain
183 M7 Torrelodones Spain
193 O4 Torremaggiore Italy
187 E10 Torremanzanas-La Torre de les Macanes Spain
184 F3 Torremayor Spain
184 G3 Torremegía Spain
193 P4 Torre Mileto Italy
184 G2 Torremocha Spain
185 J7 Torremolinos Spain
187 F7 Torrenostra Spain
82 F4 Torrens, Lake imp. l. S.A. Austr.
85 J6 Torrens Creek Qld Austr.
85 J7 Torrens Creek watercourse Qld Austr.
258 F3 Torrent Arg.
187 E9 Torrent Spain
Torrente Valencia Spain see Torrent
186 F5 Torrente del Cinca Spain
185 M3 Torrenueva Spain
190 H9 Torre Nuovo Scalo Italy
242 H5 Torreón Mex.
184 G2 Torreorgaz Spain
193 O7 Torre Orsaia Italy
187 D12 Torre-Pacheco Spain
185 K5 Torreparedones hill Spain
190 C6 Torre Pellice Italy
185 M4 Torreperogil Spain
255 C9 Torres Brazil
242 D3 Torres Mex.
185 L5 Torres Spain
185 L5 Torres r. Spain
182 I1 Torres, Cabo c. Spain
183 M5 Torresandino Spain
195 O4 Torre San Giovanni Italy
193 L5 Torre Sant'Agostino cliff Italy
195 N3 Torre Santa Susanna Italy
185 N4 Torres de Albánchez Spain
186 C4 Torres de Berrellén Spain
183 N8 Torres de la Alameda Spain
182 I5 Torres del Carrizal Spain
259 B8 Torres del Paine, Parque Nacional nat. park Chile
186 G4 Torres de Segre Spain
78 □5 Torres Islands Vanuatu
182 I6 Torresmenudas Spain
184 B2 Torres Novas Port.
76 E2 Torres Strait Qld Austr.
184 A2 Torres Vedras Port.
193 P6 Torretta, Monte mt. Italy
186 E6 Torrevelilla Spain
187 D12 Torrevieja Spain
241 U3 Torrey UT U.S.A.
193 K4 Torrice Italy
195 N3 Torricella Italy
193 J3 Torricella in Sabina Italy
193 M3 Torricella Peligna Italy
193 L2 Torricella Sicura Italy
190 F3 Torricella Taverne Switz.
183 J9 Torrico Spain
184 F2 Torrico de San Pedro hill Spain
191 J4 Torri del Benaco Italy
150 D6 Torridge r. England U.K.
146 E7 Torridon Highland, Scotland U.K.
146 E7 Torridon, Loch b. Scotland U.K.
190 G6 Torriglia Italy
193 J3 Torri in Sabina Italy
187 D7 Torrijas Spain
183 Q6 Torrijo Spain
183 L9 Torrijos Spain
146 D8 Torrin Highland, Scotland U.K.
233 L7 Torrington CT U.S.A.
238 L5 Torrington WY U.S.A.
256 C5 Torrinha Brazil
192 H1 Torrita di Siena Italy
184 B4 Torroal Port.
186 L3 Torroella de Montgrí Spain
140 L5 Torrön l. Sweden
138 G1 Torronsuon kansallispuisto nat. park Fin.
185 L7 Torrox Spain
185 L7 Torrox, Punta de pt Spain
183 O9 Torrubia del Campo Spain
183 P5 Torrubia de Soria Spain
143 K2 Torrvarpen l. Sweden
117 L6 Torsa Chhu r. Bhutan
142 G1 Torsæterkampen hill Norway
168 H1 Tørsbøl Denmark
142 J1 Torsby Sweden
143 M2 Torshälla Sweden
144 D1 Tórshavn Faroe Is
143 J3 Torsö i. Sweden
140 O1 Torsvåg Norway
177 I4 Törtel Hungary
158 F3 Torteval Channel Is
241 U8 Tortilla Flat AZ U.S.A.
120 I7 To'rtko'l Uzbek.
Törtköl Uzbek. see To'rtko'l
121 P2 Tortkuduk Kazakh.
194 F8 Torto r. Sicilia Italy
247 K4 Tortola i. Virgin Is (U.K.)
183 N7 Tórtola de Henares Spain
183 L5 Tórtoles de Esgueva Spain
192 D8 Tortolì Sardegna Italy
197 Q6 Tortomanu Romania
190 F6 Tortona Italy
193 P8 Tortora Italy
193 L2 Tortoreto Italy
194 H7 Tortorici Sicilia Italy
186 G6 Tortosa Spain
182 E8 Tortozendo Port.
246 G3 Tortue, Île de la i. Haiti
183 Q7 Tortuera Spain
245 I3 Tortuga, Laguna l. Mex.
261 G3 Tortugas Arg.
242 □R12 Tortuguero, Parque Nacional nat. park Costa Rica
127 J3 Tortum Turkey
121 Q6 Toru-Aygyr Kyrg.
122 F4 Ţorūd Iran
93 B4 Torue Sulawesi Indon.
Torugart, Pereval pass China/Kyrg. see Turugart Pass
126 I3 Torul Turkey
174 G2 Toruń Pol.
138 I3 Tõrva Estonia
193 I4 Tor Vaianica Italy
149 K5 Torver Cumbria, England U.K.
185 M7 Torvizcón Spain
141 I5 Torvløysa mt. Norway
140 N4 Torvsjö Sweden
147 F2 Tory Island Ireland
177 J2 Torysa Slovakia
177 K3 Torysa r. Slovakia
147 F2 Tory Sound sea chan. Ireland
139 R5 Torzhkovskaya Gryada hills Rus. Fed.
139 R4 Torzhok Rus. Fed.
174 D3 Torzym Pol.
103 K13 Tosa Japan
191 J3 Tosa, Cima mt. Italy
103 J14 Tosashimizu Japan
103 K13 Tosa-wan b. Japan
103 K13 Tosa-yamada Japan
140 L4 Tosbotn Norway
214 H1 Tosca S. Africa
242 D5 Tosca, Punta pt Mex.
146 E8 Toscaig Highland, Scotland U.K.
191 K9 Toscana admin. reg. Italy
192 D2 Toscano, Arcipelago is Italy
191 J4 Toscolano-Maderno Italy
140 L4 Tosenfjorden inlet Norway
104 E6 Tōshi-jima i. Japan
105 J6 To-shima i. Japan
102 S6 Tōshima-yama mt. Japan
121 M7 Toshkent Toshkent Uzbek.
121 M7 Toshkent admin. div. Uzbek.
Toshkent Wiloyati admin. div. Uzbek. see Toshkent
139 N2 Tosno Rus. Fed.
106 E8 Toson Hu l. Qinghai China
106 F2 Tosontsengel Mongolia
190 F1 Töss r. Switz.
186 K4 Tossa Spain
163 B8 Tosse France
193 L2 Tossicia Italy
149 M5 Tosside Lancashire, England U.K.
258 E3 Tostado Arg.
138 G3 Tõstamaa Estonia
168 I4 Tostedt Ger.
182 B2 Tosto, Cabo c. Spain
103 H13 Tosu Japan
126 G3 Tosya Turkey
177 J4 Tószeg Hungary
174 G5 Toszek Pol.
187 C12 Totana Spain
114 G9 Totapola mt. Sri Lanka
81 E12 Totara South I. N.Z.
80 G7 Totaranui South I. N.Z.
244 D4 Totatiche Mex.
212 D4 Toteng Botswana
172 D5 Totenkopf hill Ger.
156 B4 Tôtes France
179 I4 Totes Gebirge mts Austria
78 □4a Totiw i. Chuuk Micronesia
151 I6 Totland Isle of Wight, England U.K.
134 H4 Tot'ma Rus. Fed.
150 E7 Totnes Devon, England U.K.
251 G3 Totness Suriname
245 K9 Totolapan Mex.
245 L9 Totolapilla Mex.
245 J7 Totoltepec Mex.
134 H4 Totomitsa Rus. Fed.
243 N10 Totonicapán Guat.
252 D4 Totora Bol.
260 D2 Totoral Arg.
258 C2 Totoral Chile
258 D3 Totoralejos Arg.
261 G3 Totoras Arg.
206 C5 Totota Liberia
244 E5 Tototlán Mex.
79 □7 Totoya i. Fiji
120 E1 Totskoye Rus. Fed.
105 K5 Totsuka Japan
104 C7 Totsukawa Japan
104 C8 Totsu-kawa r. Japan
176 F5 Tótszentmárton Hungary
176 F5 Tótszerdahely Hungary
151 J6 Totton Hampshire, England U.K.
103 L11 Tottori Japan
103 K11 Tottori pref. Japan
245 K6 Totutla Mex.
177 G4 Tótvázsony Hungary
207 G1 Touâret well Niger
206 D4 Touba Côte d'Ivoire
206 B3 Touba Senegal
204 D3 Toubkal, Jbel mt. Morocco
204 D3 Toubkal, Parc National nat. park Morocco
207 I5 Touboro Cameroon
182 F6 Touça Port.
163 G8 Touch r. France
238 E3 Touchet r. WA U.S.A.
156 F8 Toucy France
106 I7 Toudaohu Nei Mongol China
204 B5 Toueïrma well Maur.
206 E2 Touérât well Mali
163 G7 Touffailles France
204 D4 Toufourine well Mali
206 E3 Tougan Burkina
163 F8 Touget France
205 G2 Touggourt Alg.
206 E3 Tougouri Burkina
207 G3 Tougoutaou well Niger
206 C4 Tougué Guinea
78 □5 Touho New Caledonia
206 C2 Touijinet well Maur.
206 C3 Touil Maur.
206 C3 Toukoto Mali
207 F4 Toukountouna Benin
157 K6 Toul France
206 C5 Toulépleu Côte d'Ivoire
206 E3 Toulfé Burkina
109 M7 Touliu Taiwan
225 G3 Toulnustouc r. Que. Can.
161 H10 Toulon France
226 E8 Toulon IL U.S.A.
160 C3 Toulon-sur-Allier France
160 E3 Toulon-sur-Arroux France
163 J10 Toulouges France
207 G2 Toulouk well Niger
163 G8 Toulouse France
207 G3 Toumbélaga well Niger
202 B4 Toummo well Niger
206 D5 Toumodi Côte d'Ivoire
206 D4 Touna Mali
204 D3 Tounassine, Hamada des. Alg.
207 G3 Tounfaminir well Niger
207 I4 Toungo Nigeria
108 H6 Toupai Guangxi China
159 L3 Touques France
159 L3 Touques r. France
206 D5 Toura, Monts mt. Côte d'Ivoire
162 E1 Touraine reg. France
159 L7 Touraine, Val de val. France
108 D9 Tourakom Laos
Tourane Vietnam see Đa Năng
204 C4 Tourassine well Maur.
202 B6 Tourba Chad
158 D5 Tourch France
156 F2 Tourcoing France
161 K9 Tourette-sur-Loup France
223 J1 Tourgis Lake Nunavut Can.
182 B2 Touriñán, Cabo c. Spain
198 D5 Tourkovigla, Akrotirio pt Greece
158 H2 Tourlaville France
147 D5 Tourmakeady Ireland
163 E10 Tourmalet, Col du pass France
160 E5 Tour Matagrin hill France
165 D7 Tournai Belgium
161 K8 Tournairet, Mont mt. France
156 E6 Tournan-en-Brie France
252 B2 Tournavista Peru
163 E9 Tournay France
205 H5 Tourndo, Oued watercourse Alg./Niger
163 F8 Tournecoupe France
163 G8 Tournefeuille France
163 F7 Tournon-d'Agenais France
159 M8 Tournon-St-Martin France
161 F6 Tournon-sur-Rhône France
160 F3 Tournus France
156 C5 Tourny France
182 E7 Touro Port.
255 A9 Touro Passo Brazil
254 G3 Touros Brazil
207 I4 Touroua Cameroon
159 M4 Tourouvre France
161 K9 Tourrette-Levens France
162 F1 Tours France
156 I4 Tourteron France
162 G5 Tourtoirac France
161 H10 Tourves France
156 C7 Toury France
187 D9 Tous, Embalse de resr Spain
206 D4 Toussiana Burkina
202 C4 Toussidé, Pic mt. Chad
208 D2 Toussoro, Mont mt. C.A.R.
100 D6 Toutai Heilong. China
184 E4 Toutalga r. Port.
82 □3 Toutcher, Cape S. Pacific Ocean
158 H8 Touvois France
214 F9 Touws r. S. Africa
214 E9 Touwsrivier S. Africa
176 B1 Toužim Czech Rep.
106 I3 Töv prov. Mongolia
176 G2 Tovačov Czech Rep.
250 D2 Tovar Venez.
139 S7 Tovarkovo Rus. Fed.
139 V8 Tovarkovskiy Rus. Fed.
177 K3 Tovarné Slovakia
188 G3 Tovarnik Croatia
151 K3 Tove r. England U.K.
178 C7 Tovel, Lago di l. Italy
Tovil'-Dora Tajik. see Tavildara
136 E5 Tovste Ukr.
79 □7 Tovu Fiji
129 G5 Tovuz Azer.
Tovuzçay r. Armenia see Tavush
235 G3 Towaco NJ U.S.A.
102 S6 Towada Japan
102 R7 Towada-Hachimantai Kokuritsu-kōen nat. park Japan
102 S6 Towada-ko l. Japan
80 I2 Towai North I. N.Z.
251 G3 Towakaima Guyana
131 U3 Towak Mountain hill AK U.S.A.
227 R8 Towanda PA U.S.A.
234 C1 Towanda Creek r. PA U.S.A.
241 X4 Towaoc CO U.S.A.
93 B6 Towari Sulawesi Indon.
151 K3 Towcester Northamptonshire, England U.K.
147 E9 Tower Ireland
226 B2 Tower MN U.S.A.
234 B3 Tower City PA U.S.A.
85 J7 Towerhill Creek watercourse Qld Austr.
Tower Island Islas Galápagos Ecuador see Genovesa, Isla
81 B13 Tower Peak South I. N.Z.
149 N4 Tow Law Durham, England U.K.
234 F7 Town Bank NJ U.S.A.
236 E1 Towner ND U.S.A.
146 I13 Townhead of Greenlaw Dumfries and Galloway, Scotland U.K.
146 J10 Townhill Fife, Scotland U.K.
84 E3 Towns r. N.T. Austr.
234 D6 Townsend DE U.S.A.
233 N6 Townsend MA U.S.A.
238 I3 Townsend MT U.S.A.
234 F6 Townsends Inlet NJ U.S.A.
85 M7 Townshend Island Qld Austr.
85 K5 Townsville Qld Austr.
93 B5 Towori, Teluk b. Indon.
210 B3 Towot Sudan
123 J4 Towraghondi Afgh.
123 N4 Towr Kham Afgh.
234 B6 Towson MD U.S.A.
93 B5 Towuti, Danau l. Indon.
150 E1 Towyn Conwy, Wales U.K.
Towyn Gwynedd, Wales U.K. see Tywyn
110 E6 Toxkan He r. China
240 N1 Toy NV U.S.A.
237 D10 Toyah TX U.S.A.
102 S4 Tōya-ko l. Japan
104 F2 Toyama Japan
104 F2 Toyama pref. Japan
104 F2 Toyama-wan b. Japan
106 G9 Toyêma Qinghai China
136 D2 Toykut Ukr.
103 K13 Tōyo Japan
104 F5 Toyoake Japan
105 G6 Toyoda Japan
103 K12 Toyohama Japan
104 F6 Toyohashi Japan
104 F6 Toyokawa Japan
104 F6 Toyo-kawa r. Japan
104 B6 Toyonaka Japan
104 G5 Toyone Japan
105 H2 Toyono Nagano Japan
104 B6 Toyono Ōsaka Japan
104 A4 Toyooka Hyōgo Japan
105 G4 Toyooka Nagano Japan
105 G6 Toyooka Shizuoka Japan
102 Q9 Toyosaka Japan
105 G3 Toyoshina Japan
104 F5 Toyota Japan
102 S1 Toyotomi Japan
104 E5 Toyoyama Japan
140 Q5 Töysä Fin.
121 M7 To'ytepa Uzbek.
Tozal del Orri mt. Spain see Orri, Tossal de l'
Tozanlı Turkey see Almus
111 F9 Tozê Kangri mt. Xizang China
205 H2 Tozeur Tunisia
129 I4 Tpig Rus. Fed.
129 D3 Tqibuli Georgia
129 C3 Tqvarch'eli Georgia
182 F2 Trabada Spain
96 H4 Tra Ban, Đao i. Vietnam
182 H6 Trabanca Spain
182 H5 Trabazos Spain
194 F8 Trabia Sicilia Italy
174 G1 Trąbki Wielkie Pol.
128 D4 Trâblous Lebanon
179 K5 Traboch Austria
197 K9 Trabotivište Macedonia
192 A5 Trabuccato, Punta pt Sardegna Italy
127 I3 Trabzon Turkey
129 A5 Trabzon prov. Turkey
194 C10 Tracino Sicilia Italy
233 □S3 Tracy N.B. Can.
240 K4 Tracy CA U.S.A.
236 H3 Tracy MN U.S.A.
160 B2 Tracy-sur-Loire France
190 F4 Tradate Italy
169 G8 Traddelkopf hill Ger.
226 B4 Trade Lake WI U.S.A.
237 K7 Tradewater r. KY U.S.A.
224 B3 Trading r. Ont. Can.
140 L3 Træna i. Norway
140 L3 Trænfjorden sea chan. Norway
236 I4 Traer IA U.S.A.
184 G8 Trafalgar, Cabo c. Spain
222 D2 Traffic Mountain Y.T. Can.
183 Q8 Tragacete Spain
185 O4 Tragoncillo mt. Spain
199 G5 Tragonisi i. Greece
179 K3 Tragwein Austria
197 N7 Traian Romania
177 L6 Traian Vuia Romania
183 Q7 Traid Spain
260 A6 Traiguén Chile
186 F6 Traiguera Spain
222 G5 Trail B.C. Can.
237 F8 Trail OK U.S.A.
146 E11 Tràille, Rubha na pt Scotland U.K.
Traill Island Greenland see Traill Ø
221 P2 Traill Ø i. Greenland
173 L4 Train Ger.
156 F7 Traînel France
234 E5 Trainer PA U.S.A.
156 D8 Traînou France
254 F4 Traipu Brazil
250 D5 Traíra r. Brazil
256 D2 Trairas r. Brazil
254 F2 Trairi Brazil
179 M3 Traisen Austria
179 M3 Traisen r. Austria
179 N3 Traiskirchen Austria
179 M3 Traismauer Austria
173 N3 Traitsching Ger.
257 F5 Trajano de Morais Brazil
Trajectum Neth. see Utrecht
214 H9 Traka r. S. Africa
138 H7 Trakai Lith.
141 R9 Trakai nat. park Lith.
Trakiya reg. Turkey see Thrace
134 J3 Trakt Rus. Fed.
Trakya reg. Turkey see Thrace
147 C8 Tralee Ireland
147 C8 Tralee Bay Ireland
Trá Li Ireland see Tralee
183 Q8 Tramacastilla Spain
192 A6 Tramariglio Sardegna Italy
187 C7 Tramascastiel Spain
192 B7 Tramatza Sardegna Italy
191 L7 Tramazzo r. Italy
172 C7 Tramelan Switz.
163 E10 Tramezaïgues France
Trá Mhór Ireland see Tramore
232 C11 Trammel VA U.S.A.
178 G7 Tramonti, Lago dei l. Italy
191 N3 Tramonti di Sopra Italy
178 G7 Tramonti di Sotto Italy
147 H8 Tramore Ireland
187 J8 Tramuntana, Serra de mts Spain
193 P7 Tramutola Italy
143 K3 Tranås Sweden
142 G5 Tranbjerg Denmark
258 D2 Trancas Arg.
185 N4 Tranco de Beas, Embalse del resr Spain
257 H2 Trancoso Brazil
182 F7 Trancoso Port.
142 G6 Tranebjerg Denmark
142 J4 Tranemo Sweden
146 K11 Tranent East Lothian, Scotland U.K.
97 D11 Trang Thai.
91 H8 Trangan i. Indon.
83 K5 Trangie N.S.W. Austr.
193 Q5 Trani Italy
156 I7 Trannes France
96 F5 Trân Ninh, Cao Nguyên plat. Laos
213 □J5 Tranoroa Madag.
213 □J5 Tranovaho Madag.
183 Q6 Tranquera, Embalse de la resr Spain
258 G3 Tranqueras Uru.
260 B3 Tranquilla Chile
158 H5 Trans France
263 K2 Transantarctic Mountains Antarctica
223 H5 Trans Canada Highway Can.
Transcarpathian Oblast admin. div. Ukr. see Zakarpats'ka Oblast'
223 L5 Transcona Man. Can.
161 I9 Trans-en-Provence France
245 H6 Transfiguracion Mex.
197 M4 Transilvaniei, Podișul plat. Romania
141 L6 Transtrand Sweden
Transylvanian Alps mts Romania see Carpații Meridionali
Transylvanian Basin plat. Romania see Transilvaniei, Podișul
146 I6 Trantlemore Highland, Scotland U.K.
97 G10 Tra Ôn Vietnam
194 D7 Trapani Sicilia Italy
194 D8 Trapani prov. Sicilia Italy
Trapezus Turkey see Trabzon
260 D3 Trapiche Arg.
234 E4 Trappe PA U.S.A.
168 J2 Trappenkamp Ger.
238 G4 Trapper Peak MT U.S.A.
156 D6 Trappes France
255 B9 Trapua r. Brazil
83 K8 Traralgon Vic. Austr.
172 C2 Trarbach Ger.
143 J5 Traryd Sweden
206 B2 Trarza admin. reg. Maur.
193 L4 Trasacco Italy
197 L4 Trascăului, Munții mts Romania
Trashigang Bhutan see Tashigang
192 I1 Trasimeno, Lago l. Italy
182 E4 Trasmiras Spain
182 F5 Trás-os-Montes reg. Port.
192 G2 Trasubbie r. Italy
183 P9 Trasvase, Canal de Spain
97 F8 Trat Thai.
192 B9 Tratalias Sardegna Italy
179 M6 Trate Slovenia
179 J3 Traun Austria
179 J3 Traun r. Austria
173 N5 Traun r. Ger.
173 N6 Traunreut Ger.
179 I4 Traunsee l. Austria
179 L3 Traunstein Austria
173 N6 Traunstein Ger.
138 H6 Traupis Lith.
179 O3 Trautmannsdorf an der Leitha Austria
191 R4 Trava Slovenia
190 I4 Travagliato Italy
182 D8 Travanca do Mondego Port.
182 D7 Travassô Port.
182 E7 Travassós de Cima Port.
168 K3 Trave r. Ger.
83 I5 Travellers Lake imp. l. N.S.W. Austr.
168 K3 Travemünde Ger.
168 J3 Travenbrück Ger.
190 B2 Travers Switz.
81 G9 Travers, Mount South I. N.Z.
249 G7 Traversay Islands S. Sandwich Is
226 I5 Traverse City MI U.S.A.
190 I6 Traversetolo Italy
257 G4 Travessão Brazil
191 L3 Travignolo r. Italy
97 H10 Tra Vinh Vietnam
237 F10 Travis, Lake TX U.S.A.
188 F3 Travnik Bos.-Herz.
192 C4 Travo r. Corse France
190 H6 Travo Italy
147 B4 Trawmore Bay Ireland
150 E2 Trawsfynydd Gwynedd, Wales U.K.
150 E2 Trawsfynydd, Llyn resr Wales U.K.
87 D11 Trayning W.A. Austr.
188 E2 Trbovlje Slovenia
97 G10 Tre, Hon i. Vietnam
147 D5 Trean Ireland
246 □ Treasure Beach Jamaica
78 □6 Treasury Islands Solomon Is
177 G3 Trebatice Slovakia
171 J6 Trebatsch Ger.
190 H5 Trebbia r. Italy
171 H6 Trebbin Ger.
188 G4 Trebebvić nat. park Bos.-Herz.
170 D5 Trebel Ger.
170 H3 Trebel r. Ger.
171 F8 Treben Ger.
176 C1 Třebenice Czech Rep.
170 I4 Trebenow Ger.
163 I9 Trèbes France
179 I6 Trebesing Austria
158 D4 Trébeurden France
176 E2 Třebíč Czech Rep.
188 G4 Trebinje Bos.-Herz.
195 L4 Trebisacce Italy
188 F4 Trebišnjica r. Bos.-Herz.
177 K3 Trebišov Slovakia
171 G7 Trebitz Ger.
188 F4 Trebižat r. Bos.-Herz.
Trebizond Turkey see Trabzon
188 E3 Trebnje Slovenia
261 F4 Trebolares Arg.
182 E3 Trebolle Spain
176 D2 Třeboň Czech Rep.
85 K5 Trebonne Qld Austr.
176 D2 Třeboňsko park Czech Rep.
158 C5 Tréboul France
171 G8 Trebsen Ger.
184 G7 Trebujena Spain
172 E2 Trebur Ger.
150 E4 Trecastle Powys, Wales U.K.
190 F5 Trecate Italy
193 P7 Trecchina Italy
191 K5 Trecenta Italy
150 F4 Tredegar Blaenau Gwent, Wales U.K.
151 I3 Tredington Warwickshire, England U.K.
191 L7 Tredozio Italy
148 C5 Treehoo Ireland
114 C7 Tree Island India
168 H2 Treene r. Ger.
Trefaldwyn Powys, Wales U.K. see Montgomery
Trefdraeth Wales U.K. see Newport
150 E2 Trefeglwys Powys, Wales U.K.
179 I6 Treffen Austria
158 C6 Treffiagat France
160 G4 Treffort-Cuisiat France
169 J8 Treffurt Ger.
Treffynnon Flintshire, Wales U.K. see Holywell
150 E1 Trefriw Conwy, Wales U.K.
Tref-y-clawdd Wales U.K. see Knighton
Trefynwy Monmouthshire, Wales U.K. see Monmouth
150 E3 Tregaron Ceredigion, Wales U.K.
158 D4 Trégastel France
191 K4 Tregnago Italy
226 C4 Trego WI U.S.A.
150 C7 Tregony Cornwall, England U.K.
158 E4 Trégorrois reg. France
85 M4 Tregosse Islets and Reefs Coral Sea Is Terr. Austr.
260 A5 Treguaco Chile
158 F5 Trégueux France
158 E4 Tréguier France
158 D6 Trégunc France
150 F2 Tregynon Powys, Wales U.K.
140 O5 Trehörningsjö Sweden
168 H1 Treia Ger.
191 O9 Treia Italy
146 G9 Treig, Loch l. Scotland U.K.
162 H4 Treignac France
160 C1 Treigny France
Treinta de Agosto Arg. see 30 de Agosto
258 G4 Treinta y Tres Uru.
169 D10 Treis Ger.
182 H2 Treisa, Peña mt. Spain
140 □ Tre Kroner mt. Svalbard
246 □ Trelawny parish Jamaica
159 K7 Trélazé France
150 D4 Trelech Carmarthenshire, Wales U.K.
259 D6 Trelew Arg.
162 F5 Trélissac France
158 G5 Trélivan France
142 J6 Trelleborg Sweden
156 H3 Trélon France
197 K7 Trem mt. Serbia
150 D2 Tremadog Gwynedd, Wales U.K.
150 D2 Tremadog Bay Wales U.K.
224 F4 Tremblant, Mont hill Que. Can.
158 I5 Tremblay France
156 B6 Tremblay-les-Villages France
217 □1c Tremblet Réunion
222 E4 Trembleur Lake B.C. Can.
183 Q7 Tremedal, Sierra del mts Spain
182 H6 Tremedal de Tormes Spain
165 G7 Tremelo Belgium
159 J7 Trémentines France
184 B2 Tremês Port.
158 D6 Tréméven France
190 G4 Tremezzo Italy
193 P3 Tremiti, Isole is Italy
138 M9 Tremlya r. Belarus
163 F6 Trémolat France
227 R9 Tremont PA U.S.A.
238 H6 Tremonton UT U.S.A.
176 C2 Třemošná Czech Rep.
176 E2 Třemošnice Czech Rep.
161 B8 Trémouilles France
186 G3 Tremp Spain
226 C5 Trempealeau r. WI U.S.A.
168 J3 Tremsbüttel Ger.
150 B7 Trenance Cornwall, England U.K.
226 H3 Trenary MI U.S.A.
225 F4 Trenche r. Que. Can.
177 H3 Trenčianska Turná Slovakia
177 G3 Trenčianske Stankovce Slovakia
177 H3 Trenčianske Teplice Slovakia
177 H3 Trenčiansky kraj admin. reg. Slovakia
177 H3 Trenčín Slovakia
169 H7 Trendelburg Ger.
261 E4 Trenel Arg.
97 F8 Trêng Cambodia
95 I9 Trenggalek Jawa Indon.
Trengganu state Malaysia see Terengganu
261 F4 Trenque Lauquén Arg.
163 C7 Trensacq France
170 H1 Trent Ger.
Trent Italy see Trento
149 P6 Trent r. Dorset, England U.K.
Trent r. England U.K. see Piddle
179 I7 Trenta Slovenia
163 F7 Trentels France
191 K3 Trentino-Alto Adige admin. reg. Italy
191 K3 Trento Italy
191 K3 Trento prov. Italy
193 M6 Trentola-Ducenta Italy
224 E4 Trenton Ont. Can.
231 F11 Trenton FL U.S.A.
231 E8 Trenton GA U.S.A.
236 I5 Trenton MO U.S.A.
231 I8 Trenton NC U.S.A.
236 E5 Trenton NE U.S.A.
234 F4 Trenton NJ U.S.A.
237 K8 Trenton TN U.S.A.
156 B6 Tréon France
150 E4 Treorchy Rhondda Cynon Taff, Wales U.K.
84 C1 Trepang Bay N.T. Austr.
225 K4 Trepassey Nfld and Lab. Can.
137 L5 Trepivka Ukr.
171 K6 Treppeln Ger.
160 G5 Trept France
195 O3 Trepuzzi Italy
192 H1 Trequanda Italy
190 F3 Tresa r. Italy
261 F4 Tres Algarrobas Arg.
190 H7 Tresana Italy
261 I3 Tres Arboles Uru.
261 G6 Tres Arroyos Arg.
256 B6 Três Bicos Brazil
261 H3 Tres Bocas Arg.
261 I3 Tres Bocas Uru.
251 F6 Três Casas Brazil
259 D8 Tres Cerros Arg.
234 D3 Tresckow PA U.S.A.
161 H8 Trescléoux France
150 □ Tresco i. England U.K.
257 E4 Três Corações Brazil
190 H4 Trescore Balneario Italy
258 D1 Tres Cruces Arg.
258 C3 Tres Cruces Chile
190 I3 Tresenda Italy
250 C4 Tres Esquinas Col.
261 I4 Tres Esquinas Uru.
Tres Forcas, Cabo c. Morocco see Trois Fourches, Cap des
146 D10 Treshnish Isles Scotland U.K.
191 L6 Tresigallo Italy
190 J3 Tre Signori, Corno dei mt. Italy
256 B4 Três Irmãos, Represa resr Brazil
258 E2 Tres Isletas Arg.
196 J8 Treska r. Macedonia
138 K4 Treski Estonia
256 B4 Três Lagoas Brazil
259 C8 Tres Lagos Arg.
261 F5 Tres Lomas Arg.
183 L2 Tres Mares, Pico mt. Spain
257 E3 Três Marias Brazil
257 E3 Três Marias, Represa resr Brazil
251 E2 Tres Matas Venez.
259 B7 Tres Montes, Península pen. Chile
192 B7 Tresnuraghes Sardegna Italy
183 N3 Trespaderne Spain
245 H9 Tres Palos Guerrero Mex.
245 I1 Tres Palos Tamaulipas Mex.
245 H9 Tres Palos, Laguna lag. Mex.
239 K12 Tres Picachos, Sierra mts Mex.
261 F6 Tres Picos Arg.
259 C6 Tres Picos mt. Arg.
243 M10 Tres Picos Mex.
261 G6 Tres Picos, Cerro mt. Arg.
245 N9 Tres Picos, Cerro mt. Mex.
239 L8 Tres Piedras NM U.S.A.
240 K5 Tres Pinos CA U.S.A.
257 E4 Três Pontas Brazil
256 C6 Tres Pontões, Pico mt. Brazil
260 C3 Tres Porteñas Arg.
258 C2 Tres Puentes Chile
259 D7 Tres Puntas, Cabo c. Arg.
256 D3 Três Ranchos Brazil
257 F5 Três Rios Brazil
146 I9 Tressait Perth and Kinross, Scotland U.K.
261 H4 Tres Sargentos Arg.
160 H5 Tresserve France
176 E2 Třešť Czech Rep.
193 N4 Treste r. Italy
139 Q4 Trestino Rus. Fed.
139 S4 Trestna Rus. Fed.
250 D6 Três Unidos Brazil
245 K7 Tres Valles Mex.
245 L7 Tres Zapotes tourist site Mex.

150 F4 Tretower *Powys, Wales* U.K.
161 H10 Trets France
141 K6 Tretten Norway
173 J4 Treuchtlingen Ger.
171 F9 Treuen Ger.
171 G6 Treuenbrietzen Ger.
142 E2 Treungen Norway
158 F5 Trévé France
185 M7 Trevélez Spain
185 M7 Trevélez *i.* Spain
259 C6 Trevelin Arg.
157 J6 Tréveray France
161 C8 Trèves France
Treves Ger. *see* Trier
193 J2 Trevi Italy
183 N3 Treviana Spain
159 J3 Trévières France
190 H4 Treviglio Italy
192 J3 Trevignano Romano Italy
162 J2 Trevillers France
183 O3 Treviño Spain
191 M4 Treviso Italy
191 M4 Treviso *airport* Italy
191 M4 Treviso *prov.* Italy
182 F6 Trevose Port.
Trevose Point *pt Inner Islands Seychelles see*
Grande Barbe, Pointe
234 B3 Trevorton *PA* U.S.A.
234 F3 Trevose *PA* U.S.A.
150 B6 Trevose Head *England* U.K.
160 F5 Trévoux France
234 D3 Trexlertown *PA* U.S.A.
261 G2 Trezanos Pinto Arg.
160 D4 Trézelles France
197 K8 Trgovište Serbia
176 D3 Trhové Sviny Czech Rep.
177 K3 Trhovište Slovakia
83 K10 Triabunna *Tas.* Austr.
182 F3 Triacastela Spain
234 A6 Triadelphia Reservoir
 MD U.S.A.
162 B3 Triaize France
84 F2 Trial Bay *N.T.* Austr.
129 F4 T'rialet'i Georgia
129 E4 T'rialet'is K'edi *hills* Georgia
97 H9 Tri An, Hô *resr* Vietnam
Triánta *Rodos* Greece *see* Trianta
232 H10 Triangle *VA* U.S.A.
213 F4 Triangle Zimbabwe
199 H6 Tria Nisia *i.* Greece
199 J6 Trianta *Rodos* Greece
123 N5 Tribal Areas *admin. div.* Pak.
191 P3 Tribalj Croatia
177 H3 Tribeč *mts* Slovakia
158 I3 Tribehou France
172 L5 Triberg im Schwarzwald Ger.
100 M1 Tri Brata, Gora *hill Sakhalin*
 Rus. Fed.
170 G2 Tribsees Ger.
85 J4 Tribulation, Cape *Qld* Austr.
236 E6 Tribune *KS* U.S.A.
260 B5 Tricao Malal Arg.
193 Q6 Tricarico Italy
195 O4 Tricase Italy
191 O3 Tricesimo Italy
191 M3 Trichiana Italy
Trichinopoly *Tamil Nadu India see* Tiruchchirappalli
198 C4 Trichonida, Limni *l.* Greece
114 E7 Trichur *Kerala* India
158 E4 Tricot France
83 J5 Trida *N.S.W.* Austr.
Tridentum Italy *see* Trento
171 F10 Triebel *r.* Ger.
179 J4 Trieben Austria
171 F9 Triebes Ger.
156 C5 Trie-Château France
192 D7 Triei *Sardegna* Italy
172 E7 Triengen Switz.
172 B2 Trier Ger.
172 B2 Trierweiler Ger.
191 P4 Trieste Italy
191 P4 Trieste *prov.* Italy
Trieste, Golfo di *g.* Europe *see* Trieste, Gulf of
188 D3 Trieste, Gulf of Europe
191 O4 Trieste-Ronchi dei Legionari *airport* Italy
163 E9 Trie-sur-Baïse France
157 K5 Trieux France
158 E4 Trieux *r.* France
185 O4 Triftern Ger.
184 O4 Trigaches Port.
161 I9 Trigance France
195 L1 Triggiano Italy
179 I7 Triglav *mt.* Slovenia
188 D2 Triglavski narodni park
 nat. park Slovenia
170 F4 Triglitz Ger.
158 G7 Trignac France
193 N3 Trigno *r.* Italy
216 □1? Trigo, Monte *hill São Jorge*
 Azores
156 E3 Trigueres France
184 F6 Trigueros Spain
183 K5 Trigueros del Valle Spain
198 C3 Trikala Greece
198 D3 Trikeriou, Diavlos *sea chan.*
 Greece
Trikkala Greece *see* Trikala
Trikomo Cyprus *see* Trikomon
128 D3 Trikomon Cyprus
9 I17 Trikora, Puncak *mt. Papua*
 Indon.
198 D4 Trikorfo *mt.* Greece
188 F4 Trilj Croatia
261 F4 Trill Arg.
147 H4 Trillick *Northern Ireland* U.K.
183 O7 Trillo Spain
198 D5 Trilofo Greece
116 F3 Triloknath *Hima. Prad.* India
156 E6 Trilport France
147 I5 Trim Ireland
114 O4 Trimdon *Durham, England* U.K.
150 I4 Trimley St Mary *Suffolk, England* U.K.
190 H2 Trimmis Switz.
86 C6 Trimouille Island *W.A.* Austr.
150 D4 Trimsaran *Carmarthenshire, Wales* U.K.
242 D2 Trincheras Mex.
114 D8 Trincomalee Sri Lanka
256 C2 Trindade Brazil
256 D5 Trindade Beja Port.
182 F6 Trindade Port.
264 I7 Trindade, Ilha da *i.*
 S. Atlantic Ocean
177 H2 Třinec Czech Rep.
151 G2 Tring *Hertfordshire, England* U.K.
198 C3 Tringia *mt.* Greece
252 D3 Trinidad Bol.
246 D3 Trinidad Cuba
245 L8 Trinidad Uru.
247 □7 Trinidad *i.* Mex.
261 I3 Trinidad *i.* Trin. and Tob.
239 L3 Trinidad *CA* U.S.A.
259 B8 Trinidad, Golfo *b.* Chile
261 G6 Trinidad, Isla *i.* Arg.
247 M8 Trinidad and Tobago *country*
 West Indies
194 D8 Trinità, Lago della *l. Sicilia*
 Italy
192 B6 Trinità d'Agultu *Sardegna* Italy
193 Q5 Trinitapoli Italy
237 H10 Trinity *TX* U.S.A.
237 H11 Trinity *r. CA* U.S.A.
237 G9 Trinity, West Fork *r. OK* U.S.A.
85 J4 Trinity Bay *Qld* Austr.
225 K4 Trinity Bay *Nfld and Lab.* Can.
220 O2 Trinity Hills Trin. and Tob.
240 M1 Trinity Range *mts NV* U.S.A.
115 M8 Trinkat Island *Andaman & Nicobar Is* India
124 C6 Trinkitat Sudan
158 I6 Trinité, Pointe *pt* France
178 D5 Trins Austria
182 F7 Trinta Port.
232 C8 Trinway *OH* U.S.A.
170 G2 Trinwillershagen Ger.
217 □1b Triolet Mauritius
183 K3 Triollo Spain
182 F7 Triolo *r.* Port.
195 L4 Trionto, Capo *c.* Italy
191 M5 Trionto *r.* Italy
162 I5 Triouzoune, Lac de la *l.*
 France

94 B3 Tripa *r.* Indon.
170 D4 Tripkau Ger.
198 D5 Tripoli Greece
Tripoli Lebanon *see* Trâblous
Tripoli Libya *see* Ṭarābulus
Tripolis Greece *see* Tripoli
Tripolis Lebanon *see* Trâblous
83 J9 Tripp *r.* Austr.
246 □ Trippama Greece
202 B2 Tripolitania *reg.* Libya
198 C5 Tripotama Greece
172 D3 Trippstadt Ger.
171 E19 Triptis Ger.
114 E8 Tripunittura *Kerala* India
117 M8 Tripura *state* India
231 I Tripura *Austria*
168 Q2 Tischen *i.* Ger.
178 G6 Trisanna *r.* Austria
216 □2c Tristan da Cunha *i.*
 S. Atlantic Ocean
206 B4 Tristao, Iles *is* Guinea
178 H6 Tristano, Ponta do *pt* Madeira
178 H6 Tristenspitze *mt.* Austria
197 M8 Troyan Bulg.
116 G3 Trisul *mt. Uttaranchal* India
136 H3 Troyaniv Ukr.
136 J5 Troyanka Ukr.
197 M8 Troyan Bulg.
139 V9 Troyekurovo Ukr.

232 F11 Troutville *VA* U.S.A.
213 □J3 Tsaramandroso Madag.
213 □J3 Tsaratanana Madag.
213 □K2 Tsaratanana, Massif du *mts*
 Madag.
197 P8 Tsarevo Bulg.
139 R6 Tsarevo-Zaymishche
 Rus. Fed.
Tsaritsyn Rus. Fed. *see* Volgograd
197 M8 Tsarimir Bulg.
Tsau-Ulaan Mongolia *see*
197 N6 Tsalka Bulg.
135 J6 Tsageri Georgia
 Dimitrovgrad
Tsaritsyn Rus. Fed. *see*
 Volgograd
137 N5 Tsarychanka Ukr.
135 I6 Tsalenji-xaki *pt* Japan
105 I6 Tsumeb Namibia
215 □J3 Tsumi-saki *pt* Japan

213 □J3 Tsaramandroso Madag.
...

102 □1 Tsuken-jima *i. Okinawa* Japan
104 D6 Tsukigase Japan
102 S3 Tsukijiyono Japan
105 L2 Tsukiyono Japan
105 L3 Tsukude Japan
104 F6 Tsukuba Japan
105 L4 Tsukui Japan
105 I3 Tsukumi Japan
103 I13 Tsukumi Japan
106 I3 Tsun-Ulaan Mongolia
105 I2 Tsumagoi Japan
136 E3 Tsuman' Ukr.
212 C3 Tsumeb Namibia
105 I6 Tsumi-saki *pt* Japan
212 C4 Tsumis Park Namibia
212 D3 Tsumkwe Namibia
104 A7 Tsuna Japan
105 I1 Tsunan Japan
105 I6 Tsunega-misaki *pt* Japan
Tsuno-shima *i.* Japan *see*
 Tsushima
105 I4 Tsuru Japan
104 D4 Tsuruga Japan
104 D4 Tsuruga-wan *b.* Japan
105 L3 Tsurugi Japan
104 G2 Tsurugi Japan
103 L13 Tsurugi-san *mt.* Japan
216 □3b Tsurumi-zaki *pt* Japan
102 Q8 Tsushima Japan
104 E5 Tsushima Japan
103 G12 Tsushima *i.* Japan
Tsushima-kaikyo *str.*
 Japan/S. Korea *see* Korea Strait
103 I12 Tsushima Strait Japan/S. Korea
Tsuwano Japan *see*

159 M5 Tuffé France
143 R1 Tufi P.N.G.
267 J2 Tufts Abyssal Plain
 sea feature N. Pacific Ocean
215 P5 Tugela *r.* S. Africa
215 P5 Tugela Ferry S. Africa
215 O4 Tugela Ferry S. Africa
111 K11 Tughyl *Kazakh. see* Tugyl
92 E6 Tugnug Point *Samar* Phil.
108 C5 Tuguancun *Yunnan* China
93 F8 Tuguan Maputi *i.* Indon.
92 C3 Tuguegarao *Luzon* Phil.
104 J2 Tugur Rus. Fed.
100 J2 Tugur *r.* Rus. Fed.
213 F4 Tugwi *r.* Zimbabwe
112 I1 Tugyl Kazakh.
107 P8 Tuhai He *r.* China
94 B4 Tuhemberua Indon.
96 D1 Tuhtong Myanmar
183 B2 Tui Spain

134 F1 Tumannyy Rus. Fed.
139 R6 Tumannyy Rus. Fed.
131 S3 Tumanskiy Rus. Fed.
Tumasik Sing. *see* Singapore
251 G3 Tumatumari Guyana
139 R1 Tumazy Rus. Fed.
104 G8 Tumba Dem. Rep. Congo
209 D5 Tumba Dem. Rep. Congo
143 N2 Tumba Sweden
208 C5 Tumba, Lac *l.*
 Dem. Rep. Congo
95 J3 Tumbangmani Kalimantan
 Indon.
95 J5 Tumbangsamba Kalimantan
 Indon.
95 J5 Tumbangsenamang
 Kalimantan Indon.
95 I5 Tumbangtiti Kalimantan Indon.
92 E8 Tumbao *Mindanao* Phil.
192 A5 Tumbarino, Punta *pt*
 Sardegna Italy
83 L6 Tumbarumba *N.S.W.* Austr.
250 A5 Tumbes Peru
250 A5 Tumbes *dept* Peru
244 E7 Tumbiscatio Mex.
222 F4 Tumbler Ridge *B.C.* Can.
82 F6 Tumby Bay *S.A.* Austr.
140 U3 Tumca *r.* Fin./Rus. Fed.

Tupanciretã to Ulutau
401

255 B9 Tupanciretã Brazil
237 K8 Tupelo MS U.S.A.
176 G2 Tupesy Czech Rep.
251 G5 Tupinambarama, Ilha i. Brazil
256 B4 Tupi Paulista Brazil
253 H2 Tupiratins Brazil
252 D5 Tupiza Bol.
174 C4 Tuplice Pol.
222 F4 Tupper B.C. Can.
233 K4 Tupper Lake NY U.S.A.
233 K4 Tupper Lake l. NY U.S.A.
Tüpqaraghan Tübegi pen. Kazakh. see Mangyshlak, Poluostrov
260 C3 Tupungato Arg.
260 C3 Tupungato, Cerro mt. Arg./Chile
127 L9 Tuqayyid well Iraq
107 Q4 Tuquan Nei Mongol China
250 B4 Túquerres Col.
197 K2 Tur r. Romania
111 H8 Tura Xinjiang China
177 I4 Tura Hungary
117 M7 Tura Meghalaya India
131 L3 Tura Rus. Fed.
124 F1 Turabah Ḥā'il Saudi Arabia
124 E5 Turabah Makkah Saudi Arabia
124 F4 Turabah, Wādī watercourse Saudi Arabia
251 E3 Turagua, Serranía mt. Venez.
114 F7 Turaiyur Tamil Nadu India
80 J7 Turakina North I. N.Z.
80 J7 Turakina r. North I. N.Z.
81 I8 Turakirae Head North I. N.Z.
122 G4 Turan Iran
100 G3 Turana, Khrebet mts Rus. Fed.
80 J5 Turangi North I. N.Z.
120 G8 Turan Lowland Asia
193 J3 Turano r. Italy
Turanskaya Nizmennost' lowland Asia see Turan Lowland
128 G5 Ţurāq al 'Ilab hills Syria
121 N6 Turar Ryskulov Kazakh.
136 G1 Turaw Belarus
126 I8 Ţurayf Saudi Arabia
125 I2 Ţurayf well Saudi Arabia
128 G7 Ţurayf, Kutayfat vol. Saudi Arabia
138 H2 Turba Estonia
250 C2 Turbaco Col.
175 I6 Turbacz mt. Pol.
134 J3 Turbanovo Rus. Fed.
123 J8 Turbat Pak.
190 F1 Turbenthal Switz.
244 F5 Turbio r. Mex.
136 H4 Turbiv Ukr.
250 B2 Turbo Col.
234 B2 Turbotville PA U.S.A.
178 H5 Türchlwand mt. Austria
182 I3 Turcia Spain
177 H3 Turčianske Teplice Slovakia
157 N7 Turckheim France
252 C4 Turco Bol.
197 L4 Turda Romania
139 U8 Turdey Rus. Fed.
160 F5 Turdine r. France
87 D7 Turee Creek r. W.A. Austr.
183 L6 Turégano Spain
122 C4 Tūreh Iran
174 G3 Turek Pol.
138 H1 Turenki Fin.
174 E3 Turew Pol.
Turfan Xinjiang China see Turpan
Turfan Depression China see Turpan Pendi
121 O2 Turgay Akmolinskaya Oblast' Kazakh.
120 J3 Turgay Kostanayskaya Oblast' Kazakh.
120 J4 Turgay r. Kazakh.
120 J3 Turgayskaya Dolina val. Kazakh.
120 I2 Turgayskaya Stolovaya Strana reg. Kazakh.
106 B2 Türgen Uul mt. Mongolia
106 B2 Türgen Uul mts Mongolia
224 E3 Turgeon r. Ont./Que. Can.
197 O7 Tŭrgovishte Bulg.
126 E4 Turgut Konya Turkey
199 J5 Turgut Muğla Turkey
199 I3 Turgutalp Turkey
199 I4 Turgutlu Turkey
199 I6 Turgutreis Turkey
126 H3 Turhal Turkey
137 M9 Turhenyevka Ukr.
138 I3 Türi Estonia
195 M2 Turi Italy
187 E9 Turia r. Spain
254 D2 Turiaçu Brazil
254 D2 Turiaçu r. Brazil
254 D2 Turiaçu, Baía de b. Brazil
247 J8 Turiamo Venez.
211 C6 Turiani Tanz.
177 H2 Turie Slovakia
177 H3 Turiec r. Slovakia
223 H5 Turin Alta Can.
Turin Italy see Torino
130 H4 Turinsk Rus. Fed.
187 D9 Turís Spain
136 D2 Turiya r. Ukr.
100 G6 Turiy Rog Rus. Fed.
136 D2 Turiys'k Ukr.
176 G5 Türje Hungary
99 I1 Turka Rus. Fed.
136 C4 Turka Ukr.
210 B4 Turkana, Lake salt l. Eth./Kenya
199 I2 Türkeli Turkey
199 I2 Türkeli Adası i. Turkey
173 K5 Türkenfeld Ger.
121 M6 Turkestan Kazakh.
123 L2 Turkestan Range mts Asia
177 J4 Túrkeve Hungary
126 G4 Turkey country Asia/Europe
232 B11 Turkey KY U.S.A.
236 J4 Turkey r. IA U.S.A.
86 J4 Turkey Creek W.A. Austr.
173 J5 Türkheim Ger.
135 H6 Turki Rus. Fed.
Türkistan Kazakh. see Turkestan
123 J2 Türkmenabat Lebapskaya Oblast' Turkm.
Türkmen Adasy i. Turkm. see Ogurjaly Adasy
Türkmen Aylagy b. Turkm. see Türkmen Aýlagy
122 E2 Türkmen Aýlagy b. Turkm.
122 E1 Türkmenbaşy Turkm.
122 E2 Türkmenbaşy Aýlagy b. Turkm.
122 E2 Türkmenbaşy Döwlet Gorugy nature res. Turkm.
199 L3 Türkmen Dağı mt. Turkey
123 J3 Türkmengala Turkm.
122 H1 Turkmenistan country Asia
Turkmeniya country Asia see Turkmenistan
Turkmen-Kala Turkm. see Türkmengala
123 J4 Turkmenkarakul' Turkm.
Türkmenostan country Asia see Turkmenistan
Turkmenskaya S.S.R. country Asia see Turkmenistan
126 H5 Türkoğlu Turkey
138 L6 Turkova Belarus
246 H3 Turks and Caicos Islands terr. West Indies
246 H3 Turks Island Passage Turks and Caicos Is
246 H3 Turks Islands Turks and Caicos Is
141 Q6 Turku Fin.
210 C4 Turkwel watercourse Kenya
183 M9 Turleque Spain
240 L4 Turlock CA U.S.A.
240 L4 Turlock Lake CA U.S.A.
147 D6 Turlough Clare Ireland
147 D5 Turlough Mayo Ireland
257 F2 Turmalina Brazil
124 F2 Turmus, Wādī at watercourse Saudi Arabia
222 E3 Turnagain r. B.C. Can.
80 K7 Turnagain, Cape North I. N.Z.
129 A5 Turnalı Turkey
177 J3 Turňa nad Bodvou Slovakia
179 L4 Turnau Austria
146 G12 Turnberry South Ayrshire, Scotland U.K.
81 C12 Turnbull, Mount South I. N.Z.
241 V8 Turnbull, Mount AZ U.S.A.
243 P9 Turneffe Islands atoll Belize
86 E6 Turner r. W.A. Austr.
87 E8 Turner watercourse W.A. Austr.
227 K5 Turner MI U.S.A.
86 J4 Turner River W.A. Austr.
151 L5 Turners Hill West Sussex, England U.K.
206 B5 Turner's Peninsula Sierra Leone
222 H5 Turner Valley Alta Can.
165 G6 Turnhout Belgium
179 N6 Turnišče Slovenia
179 M4 Türnitz Austria
223 I3 Turnor Lake Sask. Can.
223 I3 Turnor Lake l. Sask. Can.
176 E1 Turnov Czech Rep.
Tŭrnovo Bulg. see Veliko Tŭrnovo
197 M7 Turnu Măgurele Romania
Turnu Severin Romania see Drobeta-Turnu Severin
175 K5 Turobin Pol.
83 L5 Turon r. N.S.W. Austr.
185 J7 Turón r. Spain
Turones France see Tours
188 E3 Turopolje plain Croatia
175 J2 Turośl Podlaskie Pol.
175 J2 Turośl Warmińsko-Mazurskie Pol.
134 H4 Turovets Rus. Fed.
139 U7 Turovo Rus. Fed.
175 K4 Turów Pol.
138 L6 Turowlya Belarus
174 E2 Turowo Pol.
110 I5 Turpan Xinjiang China
110 I5 Turpan Pendi depr. China
110 I5 Turpan Zhan Xinjiang China
184 B2 Turquel Port.
179 I6 Turrach Austria
179 I6 Turracher Höhe pass Austria
185 P6 Turre Spain
242 □R13 Turrialba Costa Rica
161 I8 Turriers France
146 L7 Turriff Aberdeenshire, Scotland U.K.
Turris Libisonis Sardegna Italy see Porto Torres
127 L7 Tursāq Iraq
195 K3 Tursi Italy
136 D2 Turs'kyy Kanal canal Ukr.
197 L3 Turţ Romania
226 D3 Turtle Flambeau Flowage resr WI U.S.A.
223 I4 Turtleford Sask. Can.
85 M4 Turtle Island Coral Sea Is Terr. Austr.
Turtle Island Fiji see Vatoa
92 B8 Turtle Islands Phil.
206 B5 Turtle Islands Sierra Leone
223 I4 Turtle Lake l. Sask. Can.
226 B4 Turtle Lake WI U.S.A.
140 Q3 Turtola Fin.
121 P7 Turugart Pass China/Kyrg.
Turugart Shankou pass China/Kyrg. see Turugart Pass
130 J3 Turukhansk Rus. Fed.
177 M4 Turulung Romania
251 G4 Turuna r. Brazil
128 D1 Turunçlu Turkey
199 L6 Turunçova Turkey
120 G5 Turush Kazakh.
114 E5 Turuvanur Karnataka India
256 B2 Turvelândia Brazil
255 C9 Turvo Brazil
256 B2 Turvo r. Brazil
256 C3 Turvo r. Brazil
256 C5 Turvo r. Brazil
177 L3 Tur"ya r. Ukr.
177 L3 Tur"ya-Bystra Ukr.
129 I5 Türyançay Azer.
129 I5 Türyançay r. Azer.
129 I5 Türyançay Qoruğu nature res. Azer.
177 L3 Tur"ya-Polyana Ukr.
136 C4 Tur"ye Ukr.
177 L3 Tur"yi Remety Ukr.
136 D3 Turynka Ukr.
175 I2 Turza Wielka Pol.
177 H2 Turzovka Slovakia
122 H3 Ţūs Iran
185 O4 Tús r. Spain
194 G8 Tusa Sicilia Italy
194 G7 Tusa r. Sicilia Italy
241 T6 Tusayan AZ U.S.A.
231 D9 Tuscaloosa AL U.S.A.
192 H3 Tuscania Italy
Tuscany admin. reg. Italy see Toscana
232 D8 Tuscarawas r. OH U.S.A.
234 C3 Tuscarora PA U.S.A.
232 H8 Tuscarora Mountains hills PA U.S.A.
236 K6 Tuscola IL U.S.A.
237 F9 Tuscola TX U.S.A.
231 D8 Tuscumbia AL U.S.A.
236 I6 Tuscumbia MO U.S.A.
122 G4 Tusharīk Iran
137 P2 Tuskar' r. Rus. Fed.
231 E9 Tuskegee AL U.S.A.
197 N4 Tuşnad Romania
173 J5 Tussenhausen Ger.
232 G8 Tussey Mountains hills PA U.S.A.
173 N5 Tüßling Ger.
226 I5 Tustin MI U.S.A.
175 J5 Tuszów Narodowy Pol.
175 J5 Tuszyma Pol.
175 H4 Tuszyn Pol.
122 F5 Tūt Iran
127 K4 Tutak Turkey
122 H8 Tūtān Iran
139 W4 Tutayev Rus. Fed.
151 I2 Tutbury Staffordshire, England U.K.
Tutera Spain see Tudela
123 N5 Tutia Khel Pak.
114 F8 Tuticorin Tamil Nadu India
95 K3 Tutoh r. Malaysia
95 K2 Tutong Brunei
197 P4 Tutova r. Romania
170 H3 Tutow Ger.
197 O6 Tutrakan Bulg.
150 G4 Tutshill Gloucestershire, England U.K.
236 G6 Tuttle Creek Reservoir KS U.S.A.
234 F2 Tuttles Corner NJ U.S.A.
172 F6 Tuttlingen Ger.
221 P2 Tuttut Nunaat reg. Greenland
93 E8 Tutuala East Timor
211 B6 Tutubu Tanz.
78 □2 Tutuila i. American Samoa
80 I2 Tutukaka North I. N.Z.
213 E4 Tutume Botswana
250 B3 Tutunendo Col.
252 C4 Tutupaca, Volcán vol. Peru
81 J8 Tuturumuri North I. N.Z.
245 J9 Tututepec Mex.
173 K6 Tutzing Ger.
170 H3 Tützpatz Ger.
106 I2 Tuul Gol r. Mongolia
138 H1 Tuulos Fin.
101 E8 Tuun-bong mt. N. Korea
140 U5 Tuupovaara Fin.
140 T5 Tuusniemi Fin.
141 R6 Tuusula Fin.
Tuva aut. rep. Rus. Fed. see Tyva, Respublika
77 H2 Tuvalu country S. Pacific Ocean
77 I4 Tuvana-i-Colo i. Fiji
77 I4 Tuvana-i-Ra i. Fiji
Tuvana-i-Tholo i. Fiji see Tuvana-i-Colo
142 H4 Tuve Sweden
262 S2 Tuve, Mount hill Antarctica
Tuvinskaya A.S.S.R. aut. rep. Rus. Fed. see Tyva, Respublika
79 □7a Tuvutau mt. Viti Levu Fiji
95 L4 Tuwau r. Indon.
124 G2 Tuwayq, Jabal hills Saudi Arabia
124 G5 Tuwayq, Jabal mts Saudi Arabia
124 D3 Ţuwayrah Saudi Arabia
128 D9 Ţuwayyil al Ḩājj mt. Jordan
128 E8 Ţuwayyil ash Shihāq mt. Jordan
124 D4 Tuwwal Saudi Arabia
244 D6 Tuxcacuesco Mex.
235 G2 Tuxedo Park NY U.S.A.
178 E5 Tuxer Gebirge mts Austria
149 P7 Tuxford Nottinghamshire, England U.K.
244 D6 Tuxpan Jalisco Mex.
244 B4 Tuxpan Nayarit Mex.
245 J5 Tuxpan Veracruz Mex.
245 J4 Tuxpan, Arrecife rf Mex.
243 M9 Tuxtla Gutiérrez Mex.
Túy Galicia Spain see Tui
247 K8 Tuy r. Venez.
222 D3 Tuya Lake B.C. Can.
97 H8 Tuy Đuc Vietnam
96 G4 Tuyên Quang Vietnam
129 D5 Tuygun Turkey
97 I8 Tuy Hoa Vietnam
135 K5 Tuymazy Rus. Fed.
122 C4 Tūysarkān Iran
Tŭytepa Uzbek. see To'ytepa
121 R6 Tuyuk Kazakh.
Tuz, Lake salt l. Turkey see Tuz Gölü
244 G7 Tuzantla r. Mex.
126 F4 Tuz Gölü salt l. Turkey
197 N8 Tŭzha Bulg.
134 I4 Tuzha Rus. Fed.
196 H8 Tuzi Montenegro
127 L6 Tuz Khurmātū Iraq
188 G3 Tuzla Bos.-Herz.
197 Q6 Tuzla Romania
126 G5 Tuzla Turkey
127 J4 Tuzla r. Turkey
135 H7 Tuzlov r. Rus. Fed.
129 E5 Tuzluca Turkey
179 N7 Tužno Croatia
96 B2 Tuzu r. Myanmar
202 C4 Tuzugu well Libya
142 I4 Tvååker Sweden
140 O4 Tvärålund Sweden
176 F2 Tvarožná Czech Rep.
142 E3 Tvedestrand Norway
142 B1 Tveitakvitingen mt. Norway
139 S5 Tver' Rus. Fed.
Tver Oblast admin. div. Rus. Fed. see Tverskaya Oblast'
129 A1 Tverskaya Rus. Fed.
139 S4 Tverskaya Oblast' admin. div. Rus. Fed.
139 S5 Tvertsa r. Rus. Fed.
144 D1 Tvøroyri Faroe Is
138 L3 Tvorozhkovo Rus. Fed.
179 O2 Tvrdonice Czech Rep.
177 I2 Tvrdošín Slovakia
197 N8 Tvŭrditsa Bulg.
240 L3 Twain Harte CA U.S.A.
174 F4 Twardogóra Pol.
146 J4 Twatt Orkney, Scotland U.K.
227 Q5 Tweed Ont. Can.
149 M2 Tweed r. England/Scotland U.K.
146 J11 Tweeddale val. Scotland U.K.
164 K3 Tweede Exloërmond Neth.
83 N3 Tweed Heads N.S.W. Austr.
223 I4 Tweedie Alta Can.
149 M2 Tweedmouth Northumberland, England U.K.
146 J11 Tweedsmuir Scottish Borders, Scotland U.K.
222 E4 Tweedsmuir Provincial Park B.C. Can.
214 D8 Tweefontein S. Africa
215 M3 Tweeling S. Africa
212 C5 Twee Rivier Namibia
214 E2 Twee Rivieren Botswana
215 L5 Tweespruit S. Africa
164 J4 Twello Neth.
164 K4 Twente reg. Neth.
164 J4 Twentekanaal canal Neth.
241 P7 Twentynine Palms CA U.S.A.
208 C5 Tweya Dem. Rep. Congo
225 K3 Twillingate Nfld and Lab. Can.
240 L3 Twin Bridges CA U.S.A.
238 H4 Twin Bridges MT U.S.A.
237 E10 Twin Buttes Reservoir TX U.S.A.
225 H2 Twin Falls Nfld and Lab. Can.
238 G5 Twin Falls ID U.S.A.
209 F7 Twingi Zambia
86 I6 Twin Heads hill W.A. Austr.
234 F2 Twin Lakes PA U.S.A.
233 N4 Twin Mountain NH U.S.A.
240 L2 Twin Peak CA U.S.A.
87 D13 Twin Peaks hill W.A. Austr.
232 D7 Twinsburg OH U.S.A.
82 G3 Twins Creek watercourse S.A. Austr.
238 D2 Twisp WA U.S.A.
168 D5 Twist Ger.
169 G8 Twiste (Twistetal) Ger.
168 G5 Twistringen Ger.
240 L6 Twitchen Reservoir CA U.S.A.
222 D1 Twitya r. N.W.T. Can.
81 E11 Twizel South I. N.Z.
216 □2a Two Boats Village Ascension S. Atlantic Ocean
237 D6 Two Butte Creek r. CO U.S.A.
226 C2 Two Harbors MN U.S.A.
223 I4 Two Hills Alta Can.
148 B8 Twomileborris Ireland
147 H6 Two Mile Bridge Ireland
226 G5 Two Rivers WI U.S.A.
174 G5 Tworóg Pol.
151 J5 Twyford Hampshire, England U.K.
151 K5 Twyford Wokingham, England U.K.
146 H13 Twynholm Dumfries and Galloway, Scotland U.K.
Tyachev Ukr. see Tyachiv
136 C5 Tyachiv Ukr.
137 M7 Tyahynka Ukr.
Tyan' Shan' mts China/Kyrg. see Tien Shan
Tyanshanskaya Oblast' admin. div. Kyrg. see Naryn
96 A3 Tyao r. India/Myanmar
137 L4 Tyasmyn r. Ukr.
102 X2 Tyatya, Vulkan vol. Rus. Fed.
199 H1 Tychero Greece
174 E2 Tychówko Pol.
174 E2 Tychowo Pol.
174 G5 Tychy Pol.
175 K6 Tyczyn Pol.
140 K5 Tydal Norway
148 C5 Tydavnet Ireland
Tyddewi Pembrokeshire, Wales U.K. see St David's
232 F10 Tygart Valley WV U.S.A.
100 E2 Tygda Rus. Fed.
100 E2 Tygda r. Rus. Fed.
147 I4 Tyholland Ireland
141 J6 Tyinkrysset Norway
137 L2 Tykhonovychi Ukr.
175 K2 Tykocin Pol.
175 J6 Tylawa Pol.
237 H9 Tyler TX U.S.A.
237 J10 Tylertown MS U.S.A.
136 K7 Tylihul r. Ukr.
100 I2 Tyl'skiy Khrebet mts Rus. Fed.
100 M3 Tym' r. Sakhalin Rus. Fed.
175 I6 Tymbark Pol.
137 L4 Tymchenky Ukr.
198 B2 Tymfi mts Greece
174 D1 Tymień Pol.
137 R4 Tymonove Ukr.
137 L1 Tymonovychi Ukr.
137 O6 Tymoshivka Ukr.
100 M3 Tymovskoye Sakhalin Rus. Fed.
174 E4 Tymowa Pol.
198 F7 Tympaki Kriti Greece
164 K2 Tynaarlo Neth.
148 D5 Tynan Northern Ireland U.K.
131 N4 Tynda Rus. Fed.
236 G4 Tyndall SD U.S.A.
Tyndinskiy Rus. Fed. see Tynda
146 G10 Tyndrum Stirling, Scotland U.K.
146 K10 Tyne r. Scotland U.K.
149 O4 Tyne and Wear admin. div. England U.K.
176 E1 Týnec nad Labem Czech Rep.
176 D2 Týnec nad Sázavou Czech Rep.
149 O3 Tynemouth Tyne and Wear, England U.K.
233 N6 Tyngsboro MA U.S.A.
143 J1 Tyngsjö Sweden
176 F1 Týniště nad Orlicí Czech Rep.
136 J4 Tynivka Ukr.
176 D2 Týn nad Vltavou Czech Rep.
136 F2 Tynne Ukr.
141 K5 Tynset Norway
Tyr Lebanon see Soûr
Tyras Ukr. see Bilhorod-Dnistrovs'kyy
175 K6 Tyrawa Wołoska Pol.
Tyre Lebanon see Soûr
262 S1 Tyree, Mount Antarctica
148 F5 Tyrella Northern Ireland U.K.
143 O2 Tyresö Sweden
143 O2 Tyresta nationalpark nat. park Sweden
142 G1 Tyrifjorden l. Norway
173 N5 Tyrlaching Ger.
100 H3 Tyrma Rus. Fed.
100 G3 Tyrma r. Rus. Fed.
140 R4 Tyrnävä Fin.
198 D3 Tyrnavos Greece
139 W7 Tyrnovo Rus. Fed.
129 D2 Tyrnyauz Rus. Fed.
Tyrol land Austria see Tirol
147 H3 Tyrone county Northern Ireland U.K.
239 J10 Tyrone NM U.S.A.
232 G8 Tyrone PA U.S.A.
83 I6 Tyrrell r. Vic. Austr.
83 I6 Tyrrell, Lake dry lake Vic. Austr.
223 J2 Tyrrell Lake N.W.T. Can.
147 H6 Tyrrellspass Ireland
189 C5 Tyrrhenian Sea France/Italy
Tyrus Lebanon see Soûr
136 A5 Tysa r. Ukr. alt. Tisa (Serbia), alt. Tisza (Hungary)
136 D5 Tysmenytsya Ukr.
142 B2 Tysnesøy i. Norway
241 R8 Tyson Wash watercourse AZ U.S.A.
142 B1 Tysse Norway
144 J1 Tyssebotnen Norway
142 C1 Tyssedal Norway
142 H6 Tystrup-Bavelse nature res. Denmark
175 L5 Tyszowce Pol.
150 E5 Tythegston Bridgend, Wales U.K.
164 I2 Tytsjerk Neth.
138 G6 Tytuvėnai Lith.
129 I2 Tyube Rus. Fed.
131 P3 Tyubelyakh Rus. Fed.
120 D5 Tyub-Karagan, Mys pt Kazakh.
129 L1 Tyub-Karagan, Poluostrov pen. Kazakh.
130 I4 Tyukalinsk Rus. Fed.
120 C5 Tyulen'i Ostrova is Kazakh.
Tyuleniy, Mys pt Azer. see Suiti Burunu
129 I1 Tyuleniy, Ostrov i. Rus. Fed.
120 G1 Tyul'gan Rus. Fed.
134 L4 Tyul'kino Rus. Fed.
130 H4 Tyumen' Rus. Fed.
Tyumen'-Aryk Kazakh. see Tomenaryk
121 S1 Tyumentsevo Rus. Fed.
131 N3 Tyung r. Rus. Fed.
120 K1 Tyuntyugur Kazakh.
Tyup Kyrg. see Tüp
Tyuratam Kazakh. see Baykonyr
140 V2 Tyuva-Guba Rus. Fed.
123 I1 Tyuyamuyunskoye Vodokhranilishche resr Turkm./Uzbek.
106 E1 Tyva, Respublika aut. rep. Rus. Fed.
136 H4 Tyvriv Ukr.
174 C2 Tywa r. Pol.
150 C7 Tywardreath Cornwall, England U.K.
150 D4 Tywi r. Wales U.K.
150 D2 Tywyn Gwynedd, Wales U.K.
213 F4 Tzaneen S. Africa
198 F5 Tzia i. Greece
243 O7 Tzucacab Mex.
164 I2 Tzummarum Neth.

U

251 F3 Uacauyén Venez.
Uaco Congo Angola see Waku-Kungo
78 □2 Uafato Samoa
79 □9 Ua Huka i. Fr. Polynesia
250 D4 Uainambi Brazil
Ualan atoll Micronesia see Kosrae
Ūālīkhanov Kazakh. see Valikhanovo
209 D9 Uamanda Angola
213 H3 Uape Moz.
Ua Pou i. Fr. Polynesia see Ua Pu
79 □9 Ua Pu i. Fr. Polynesia
251 E5 Uara Brazil
Uarc, Ras c. Morocco see Trois Fourches, Cap des
251 G6 Uari Brazil
251 E5 Uarini Brazil
87 C7 Uaroo W.A. Austr.
250 D4 Uaruma Brazil
251 E3 Uasadi-jidi, Sierra mts Venez.
251 F4 Uatatás r. Brazil
251 G5 Uatumã r. Brazil
254 F4 Uauá Brazil
250 E5 Uaupés Brazil
250 E4 Uaupés r. Brazil
243 O9 Uaxactún Guat.
124 G5 U'ayfirah well Saudi Arabia
128 G8 U'aylī, Wādī al watercourse Saudi Arabia
124 G1 U'aywij well Saudi Arabia
127 K9 U'aywij, Wādī al watercourse Saudi Arabia
196 I6 Ub Serbia
257 F4 Ubá Brazil
121 S2 Uba r. Kazakh.
169 B9 Übach-Palenberg Ger.
120 K1 Ubagan r. Kazakh.
257 E2 Ubaí Brazil
202 E6 Ubaid well Sudan
254 F5 Ubaitaba Brazil
124 F8 'Ubāl Yemen
208 C5 Ubangi r. C.A.R./Dem. Rep. Congo
Ubangi-Shari country Africa see Central African Republic
257 F3 Ubaporanga Brazil
136 H1 Ubarts r. Belarus
250 C3 Ubate Col.
257 E5 Ubatuba Brazil
123 M7 Ubauro Pak.
161 I8 Ubaye r. France
127 K7 Ubayyiḑ, Wādī al watercourse Iraq/Saudi Arabia
103 I13 Ube Japan
185 M4 Úbeda Spain
211 C6 Ubenazomozi Tanz.
256 D3 Uberaba Brazil
256 C4 Uberaba r. Brazil
172 B3 Überherrn Ger.
256 C3 Uberlândia Brazil
172 G6 Überlingen Ger.
172 G6 Überlinger See l. Ger.
173 M6 Übersee Ger.
94 □ Ubin, Pulau i. Sing.
182 I2 Ubiña, Peña mt. Spain
137 R9 Ubinskaya Rus. Fed.
130 J4 Ubinskoye, Ozero l. Rus. Fed.
256 A6 Ubiratâ Brazil
227 L6 Ubly MI U.S.A.
137 Q2 Ublya r. Rus. Fed.
96 F6 Ubolratna Reservoir Thai.
215 Q3 Ubombo S. Africa
208 E5 Ubondo Dem. Rep. Congo
96 G7 Ubon Ratchathani Thai.
208 F3 Ubori Sudan
136 G2 Ubort' r. Ukr.
100 I6 Ubovka Rus. Fed.
161 J9 Ubraye France
185 I7 Ubrique Spain
172 F3 Ubstadt-Weiher Ger.
208 E5 Ubundu Dem. Rep. Congo
261 F3 Ucacha Arg.
123 J2 Üçajy Turkm.
129 I5 Ucar Azer.
128 A2 Uçarı Turkey
252 B2 Ucayali dept Peru
250 C6 Ucayali r. Peru
192 B3 Ucciani Corse France
165 F7 Uccle Belgium
183 N7 Uceda Spain
161 E7 Ucel France
183 N5 Ucero Spain
183 N5 Ucero r. Spain
123 N7 Uch Pak.
182 C5 Ucha Port.
Üchajy Turkm. see Üçajy
122 D3 Üchān Iran
121 S4 Ucharal Kazakh.
161 F8 Uchaux France
105 M1 Uchigō Japan
105 L3 Uchihara Japan
103 J13 Uchiko Japan
105 H3 Uchimura-gawa r. Japan
104 E2 Uchinada Japan
103 I15 Uchinoura Japan
104 B7 Uchita Japan
103 O9 Uchiura Japan
102 R4 Uchiura-wan b. Japan
105 I3 Uchiyama-tōge pass Japan
252 A2 Uchiza Peru
160 F3 Uchizy France
129 D2 Uchkeken Rus. Fed.
Uchkuduk Uzbek. see Uchquduq
129 D2 Uchkulan Rus. Fed.
120 J6 Uchquduq Uzbek.
121 L7 Uchquloch Uzbek.
Uchsay Uzbek. see Uchsoy
120 H6 Uchsoy Uzbek.
169 G6 Uchte Ger.
170 E5 Uchte r. Ger.
169 J10 Üchtelhausen Ger.
123 L9 Uchto r. Pak.
170 E5 Uchtspringe Ger.
131 O4 Uchur r. Rus. Fed.
183 L4 Ucieza r. Spain
157 L5 Uckange France
170 J2 Ückeritz Ger.
170 I4 Uckermark reg. Ger.
151 M6 Uckfield East Sussex, England U.K.
171 I7 Uckro Ger.
183 O9 Uclés Spain
222 E5 Ucluelet B.C. Can.
129 B6 Üçpınar Erzincan Turkey
128 A1 Üçpınar Konya Turkey
238 K4 Ucross WY U.S.A.
100 I1 Uda r. Rus. Fed.
137 P4 Uda r. Ukr.
129 G4 Udabno Georgia
129 G4 Udabno, Mt'a hill Georgia
135 I7 Udachnoye Rus. Fed.
131 M3 Udachnyy Rus. Fed.
114 E7 Udagamandalam Tamil Nadu India
116 D7 Udaipur Rajasthan India
116 E6 Udaipur Rajasthan India
117 M8 Udaipur Tripura India
116 G8 Udaipura Madh. Prad. India
117 K6 Udaipur Garhi Nepal
175 L4 Udal r. Pol.
117 N6 Udalguri Assam India
174 E4 Udanin Pol.
117 I9 Udanti r. India/Myanmar
261 H5 Udaquilla Arg.
129 D1 Udarnyy Rus. Fed.
177 K3 Udava r. Slovakia
177 K3 Udavské Slovakia
114 G9 Uda Walawe Reservoir Sri Lanka
137 M3 Uday r. Ukr.
114 F5 Udayagiri Andhra Prad. India
115 I3 Udayagiri Orissa India
125 I4 'Udaynān well Saudi Arabia
143 J1 Uddeholm Sweden
164 I4 Uddel Neth.
142 H3 Uddevalla Sweden
148 I2 Uddingston South Lanarkshire, Scotland U.K.
146 I11 Uddington South Lanarkshire, Scotland U.K.
140 N4 Uddjaure l. Sweden
129 D4 Ude Georgia
125 J3 'Udeid, Khōr al inlet Qatar
164 I5 Uden Neth.
164 H5 Udenhout Neth.
169 J8 Uder Ger.
178 E5 Uderns Austria
169 C10 Üdersdorf Ger.
114 E3 Udgir Mahar. India
Udhagamandalam Tamil Nadu India see Udagamandalam
116 E3 Udhampur Jammu and Kashmir
177 H2 Udiča Slovakia
134 I3 Udimskiy Rus. Fed.
191 O3 Udine Italy
191 N3 Udine prov. Italy
116 D6 Udit Rajasthan India
225 I2 Udjuktok Bay Nfld and Lab. Can.
Udmalaippettai Tamil Nadu India see Udumalaippettai
Udmurtia aut. rep. Rus. Fed. see Udmurtskaya Respublika
Udmurtskaya A.S.S.R. aut. rep. Rus. Fed. see Udmurtskaya Respublika
134 K4 Udmurtskaya Respublika aut. rep. Rus. Fed.
129 C1 Udobnaya Rus. Fed.
131 M4 Udokan, Khrebet mts Rus. Fed.
139 S4 Udomlya Rus. Fed.
105 J7 Udone-jima i. Japan
96 F6 Udon Thani Thai.
174 F1 Udorpie Pol.
78 □4a Udot i. Chuuk Micronesia
182 C4 Udra, Cabo c. Spain
175 L5 Udrycze Pol.
100 I1 Udskoye Rus. Fed.
114 E7 Udumalaippettai Tamil Nadu India
114 D6 Udupi Karnataka India
137 P3 Udy Ukr.
100 K2 Udyl', Ozero l. Rus. Fed.
Udzharma Georgia see Ujarma
Udzhary Azer. see Ucar
Uéa atoll Îles Loyauté New Caledonia see Ouvéa
171 H7 Uebigau Ger.
93 B4 Uëbonti Sulawesi Indon.
170 J3 Uecker r. Ger.
170 J3 Ueckermünde Ger.
105 H3 Ueda Japan
173 J2 Uehlfeld Ger.
169 K6 Uehrde Ger.
93 B4 Uekuli Sulawesi Indon.
208 D3 Uele r. Dem. Rep. Congo
131 U3 Uelen Rus. Fed.
131 T3 Uel'kal' Rus. Fed.
169 C6 Uelsen Ger.
168 K5 Uelzen Ger.
105 I3 Ueno Gunma Japan
104 D6 Ueno Mie Japan
105 J4 Uenohara Japan
208 E4 Uere r. Dem. Rep. Congo
190 D2 Uetendorf Switz.
168 I3 Uetersen Ger.
172 H2 Uettingen Ger.
169 J6 Uetze Ger.
134 K5 Ufa Rus. Fed.
134 L5 Ufa r. Rus. Fed.
150 F6 Uffculme Devon, England U.K.
173 I2 Uffenheim Ger.
173 K6 Uffing am Staffelsee Ger.
193 O5 Ufita r. Italy
169 K7 Uftrungen Ger.
134 I3 Uftyuga r. Rus. Fed.
212 B4 Ugab watercourse Namibia
138 F4 Ugāle Latvia
211 A6 Ugalla r. Tanz.
211 A6 Ugalla River Game Reserve nature res. Tanz.
210 B4 Uganda country Africa
188 F3 Ugar r. Bos.-Herz.
183 O2 Ugarana Spain
260 C3 Ugarteche Arg.
150 E7 Ugborough Devon, England U.K.
168 H1 Uge Denmark
195 O4 Ugento Italy
142 B1 Uggdal Norway
142 G4 Uggerby r. Denmark
195 O3 Uggiano la Chiesa Italy
207 G5 Ughelli Nigeria
215 M7 Ugie S. Africa
Ugi Island Solomon Is see Uki Island
185 M7 Ugíjar Spain
122 I8 Ūgīnak Iran
160 I5 Ugine France
100 M4 Uglegorsk Sakhalin Rus. Fed.
100 H7 Uglekamensk Rus. Fed.
134 L4 Ugleural'skiy Rus. Fed.
139 V4 Uglich Rus. Fed.
188 E3 Ugljan i. Croatia
139 Q3 Uglovka Rus. Fed.
100 F3 Uglovoye Amurskaya Oblast' Rus. Fed.
100 H7 Uglovoye Primorskiy Kray Rus. Fed.
121 S2 Uglovskoye Rus. Fed.
177 G4 Ugod Hungary
Ugodskiy Zavod Rus. Fed. see Zhukovo
131 P3 Ugol'noye Rus. Fed.
Ugolnyy Rus. Fed. see Beringovskiy
129 E2 Ugol'nyy Rus. Fed.
131 S3 Ugol'nyye Kopi Rus. Fed.
139 R7 Ugra Rus. Fed.
139 T7 Ugra r. Rus. Fed.
197 M7 Ugŭrchin Bulg.
199 G2 Uğurlu Gökeada Turkey
130 I3 Ugut Rus. Fed.
137 M8 Ugutne Ukr.
177 K3 Uh r. Slovakia
183 Q3 Uharte-Arakil Spain
179 O2 Uherčice Czech Rep.
107 L6 Uher Hudag Nei Mongol China
175 L4 Uherka r. Pol.
176 G2 Uherské Hradiště Czech Rep.
177 G2 Uherský Brod Czech Rep.
172 H4 Uhingen Ger.
176 C2 Úhlava r. Czech Rep.
172 G6 Uhldingen Ger.
176 E2 Uhlířské Janovica Czech Rep.
171 D9 Uhlstädt Ger.
136 C3 Uhniv Ukr.
232 D8 Uhrichsville OH U.S.A.
177 H3 Uhrovec Slovakia
137 O3 Uhroyidy Ukr.
171 D6 Uhrsleben Ger.
171 K8 Uhyst Ger.
254 E4 Uibaí Brazil
Uibhist a' Deas i. Scotland U.K. see South Uist
Uibhist a' Tuath i. Scotland U.K. see North Uist
171 E8 Uichteritz Ger.
146 D7 Uig Highland, Scotland U.K.
209 B6 Uíge Angola
209 B6 Uíge prov. Angola
79 □8 'Uiha Tonga
101 E10 Ŭijŏngbu S. Korea
101 D8 Ŭiju N. Korea
120 F3 Uil Kazakh.
120 E3 Uil r. Kazakh.
129 E3 Uilpata, Gora mt. Rus. Fed.
140 U5 Uimaharju Fin.
241 S5 Uinkaret Plateau AZ U.S.A.
134 L4 Uinskoye Rus. Fed.
238 J6 Uinta r. CO U.S.A.
241 W1 Uintah and Ouray Indian Reservation res. UT U.S.A.
238 I6 Uinta Mountains UT U.S.A.
212 B4 Uis Mine Namibia
215 J9 Uitenhage S. Africa
164 G3 Uitgeest Neth.
164 G4 Uithoorn Neth.
164 K2 Uithuizen Neth.
164 K2 Uithuizermeeden Neth.
214 C5 Uitkyk S. Africa
214 E3 Uitsakpan salt pan S. Africa
214 D8 Uitspankraal S. Africa
225 I1 Uivak, Cape Nfld and Lab. Can.
177 J6 Uivar Romania
129 G4 Ujarma Georgia
175 H4 Ujazd Łódzkie Pol.
174 G5 Ujazd Opolskie Pol.
177 G2 Újezd Czech Rep.
176 F2 Újezd u Brna Czech Rep.
177 K4 Újfehértó Hungary
116 G6 Ujhani Uttar Prad. India
177 I4 Újhartyán Hungary
104 C6 Uji Japan
104 C6 Uji-gawa r. Japan
103 G15 Uji-guntō is Japan
105 K2 Ujiie Japan
104 C6 Ujitawara Japan
Ujiyamada Japan see Ise
116 E8 Ujjain Madh. Prad. India
177 L3 Újkenéz Hungary
176 F4 Újkér Hungary
177 K5 Újkígyós Hungary
177 K4 Újléta Hungary
95 K4 Ujohbilang Kalimantan Indon.
86 □2 Ujong Tanjong pt Cocos Is
177 H6 Újpetre Hungary
174 E2 Ujście Pol.
175 H6 Ujsoły Pol.
177 K5 Újszalonta Hungary
177 J4 Újszász Hungary
177 J5 Újszentiván Hungary
177 K4 Újszentmargita Hungary
177 I4 Újszilvás Hungary
177 K4 Újtikos Hungary
176 F5 Újudvar Hungary
94 F8 Ujung Kulon, Taman Nasional nat. park Indon.
Ujung Pandang Sulawesi Indon. see Makassar
Újvidék Vojvodina Serbia see Novi Sad
102 □1 Uka Okinawa Japan
116 D9 Ukal Sagar l. India
207 G4 Ukata Nigeria
104 F1 Ukawa Japan
124 G2 'Ukayrishah well Saudi Arabia
102 □G19 Uke-jima i. Nansei-shotō Japan
211 B5 Ukerewe Island Tanz.
215 N5 uKhahlamba-Drakensberg Park nat. park S. Africa
127 K7 Ukhaydir tourist site Iraq
124 G7 Ukhdūd tourist site Saudi Arabia
Ukhimath Uttaranchal India see Okhimath
135 H5 Ukholovo Rus. Fed.
175 M4 Ukhovets'k Ukr.
117 O7 Ukhrul Manipur India
Ukhta Respublika Kareliya Rus. Fed. see Kalevala
134 K3 Ukhta Respublika Komi Rus. Fed.
134 K3 Ukhta r. Rus. Fed.
138 M7 Ukhvala Belarus
83 N3 Uki N.S.W. Austr.
240 I2 Ukiah CA U.S.A.
238 E4 Ukiah OR U.S.A.
78 □6 Uki Island Solomon Is
211 B6 Ukimbo Tanz.
221 M2 Ukkusissat Greenland
174 D2 Ukleja r. Pol.
138 H6 Ukmergė Lith.
139 S8 Ukolitsa Rus. Fed.
136 K4 Ukraine country Europe
Ukrainka Kyivs'ka Oblast' Ukr. see Ukrayinka
Ukrainka Respublika Krym Ukr. see Ukrayinka
Ukrainskaya S.S.R. country Europe see Ukraine
Ukrainskoye Ukr. see Ukrayins'ke
Ukrayina country Europe see Ukraine
136 J3 Ukrayinka Kyivs'ka Oblast' Ukr.
137 N9 Ukrayinka Respublika Krym Ukr.
137 L3 Ukrayins'ke Ukr.
188 F3 Ukrina r. Bos.-Herz.
209 B7 Uku Angola
103 G13 Uku-jima i. Japan
209 B8 Ukuma Angola
212 D4 Ukwi Botswana
111 C11 Ul r. India
138 M6 Ula Belarus
138 M6 Ula r. Belarus
175 M1 Ūla r. Lith.
199 J5 Ula Turkey
106 J3 Ulaanbaatar Mongolia
106 J3 Ulaanbaatar mun. Mongolia
107 K3 Ulaan-Ereg Mongolia
106 C2 Ulaangom Mongolia
106 I3 Ulaanhudag Mongolia
106 H4 Ulaan Nuur salt l. Mongolia
106 G3 Ulaan-Uul Bayanhongor Mongolia
107 L4 Ulaan-Uul Dornogovĭ Mongolia
83 L5 Ulan N.S.W. Austr.
107 K7 Ulan Nei Mongol China
106 F8 Ulan Qinghai China
Ulan Bator Mongolia see Ulaanbaatar
121 N5 Ulanbel' Kazakh.
106 J6 Ulan Buh Shamo des. China
135 I7 Ulan Erge Rus. Fed.
Ulanhad Nei Mongol China see Chifeng
107 R3 Ulanhot Nei Mongol China
107 L6 Ulan Hua Nei Mongol China
136 H4 Ulaniv Ukr.
135 I7 Ulan-Khol Rus. Fed.
110 H5 Ulanlinggi Xinjiang China
175 K4 Ulan-Majorat Pol.
106 I7 Ulan Mod Nei Mongol China
137 N2 Ulanove Ukr.
175 K5 Ulanów Pol.
106 I6 Ulan Suhai Nei Mongol China
107 K6 Ulansuhai Nur l. China
106 G6 Ulan Tohoi Nei Mongol China
98 I1 Ulan-Ude Rus. Fed.
111 J9 Ulan Ul Hu l. China
260 D2 Ulapes Arg.
260 D2 Ulapes, Sierra mts Arg.
126 H4 Ulaş Sivas Turkey
199 I1 Ulaş Tekirdağ Turkey
192 D8 Ulassai Sardegna Italy
110 H5 Ulastai Xinjiang China
78 □6 Ulawa Island Solomon Is
211 C6 Ulaya Tanz.
124 H4 Ulayyah reg. Saudi Arabia
121 T2 Ul'ba Kazakh.
100 J2 Ul'banskiy Zaliv b. Rus. Fed.
238 K3 UL Bend National Wildlife Refuge nature res. MT U.S.A.
Ülbi Kazakh. see Ul'ba
138 H5 Ulbroka Latvia
146 J6 Ulbster Highland, Scotland U.K.
149 Q6 Ulceby North Lincolnshire, England U.K.
101 F10 Ulchin S. Korea
196 H9 Ulcinj Montenegro
214 I4 Ulco S. Africa
142 F6 Uldum Denmark
107 L2 Uldz Mongolia
107 N2 Uldz r. Mongolia
Uleåborg Fin. see Oulu
Ulebsechel i. Palau see Auluptagel
142 F2 Ulefoss Norway
78 □5 Uléi Vanuatu
185 O6 Uleila del Campo Spain
106 I1 Ulekchin Rus. Fed.
138 J3 Ülenurme Estonia
107 M1 Ulety Rus. Fed.
175 K4 Ułęż Pol.
142 E5 Ulfborg Denmark
142 E5 Ulfborg Vind nature res. Denmark
Ulflingen Lux. see Troisvierges
164 J5 Ulft Neth.
107 P4 Ulgain Gol r. China
149 N3 Ulgham Northumberland, England U.K.
121 L2 Ul'gili Kazakh.
114 C3 Ulhasnagar Mahar. India
175 L5 Ulhówek Pol.
129 G4 Ulianovka Georgia
107 O4 Uliastai Nei Mongol China
106 E3 Uliastay Mongolia
Uliatea i. Arch. de la Société Fr. Polynesia see Raiatea
177 L3 Ulič Slovakia
165 G6 Ulicoten Neth.
Ulie atoll Micronesia see Woleai
78 □3b Uliga i. Majuro Marshall Is
208 E5 Ulindi r. Dem. Rep. Congo
134 F1 Ulita r. Rus. Fed.
91 I4 Ulithi atoll Micronesia
Uljanovsk Rus. Fed. see Ul'yanovsk
120 J3 Ul'kayak r. Kazakh.
121 N1 Ul'ken-Karoy, Ozero salt l. Kazakh.
Ülkenözen r. Kazakh./Rus. Fed. see Bol'shoy Uzen'
121 P6 Ul'ken Sulutor Kazakh.
Ülken Vladīmīrovka Kazakh. see Bol'shaya Vladimirovka
182 C3 Ulla r. Spain
83 M6 Ulladulla N.S.W. Austr.
146 F7 Ullapool Highland, Scotland U.K.
142 I4 Ullared Sweden
140 P3 Ullatti Sweden
252 C3 Ulla Ulla, Parque Nacional nat. park Bol.
87 D7 Ullawarra Aboriginal Reserve W.A. Austr.
186 F6 Ulldecona Spain
186 G5 Ulldemolins Spain
142 G6 Ullerslev Denmark
177 I5 Üllés Hungary
149 O6 Ulleskelf North Yorkshire, England U.K.
262 S1 Ullmer, Mount Antarctica
252 C4 Ulloma Bol.
140 O2 Ullsfjorden sea chan. Norway
149 L4 Ullswater l. England U.K.
129 J3 Ulluchay r. Rus. Fed.
101 G10 Ullŭng-do i. S. Korea
172 H5 Ulm Ger.
100 F3 Ul'ma r. Rus. Fed.
169 H10 Ulmbach Ger.
184 B2 Ulme r. Port.
169 C10 Ulmen Ger.
197 O6 Ulmeni Călăraşi Romania
197 L3 Ulmeni Maramureş Romania
188 G4 Ulog Bos.-Herz.
213 G2 Ulongue Moz.
82 G2 Uloowaranie, Lake salt flat S.A. Austr.
149 K5 Ulpha Cumbria, England U.K.
142 J4 Ulricehamn Sweden
179 I2 Ulrichsberg Austria
169 H9 Ulrichstein Ger.
164 J2 Ulrum Neth.
101 F11 Ulsan S. Korea
140 J5 Ulsberg Norway
146 □N1 Ulsta Shetland, Scotland U.K.
142 G4 Ulsted Denmark
140 H5 Ulsteinvik Norway
147 H3 Ulster reg. Ireland/U.K.
227 R8 Ulster PA U.S.A.
235 G1 Ulster County county NY U.S.A.
246 □ Ulster Spring Jamaica
83 I6 Ultima Vic. Austr.
252 B1 Ultraoriental, Cordillera mts Peru
183 Q3 Ultzama r. Spain
186 B1 Ultzama, Valle de val. Spain
93 D2 Ulu Sulawesi Indon.
210 B2 Ulu Sudan
242 □P10 Ulúa r. Hond.
129 C5 Ulubağ Turkey
199 J2 Ulubat Gölü l. Turkey
199 K4 Ulubey Turkey
199 L4 Uluborlu Turkey
199 K2 Uludağ mt. Turkey
199 K2 Uludağ Milli Parkı nat. park Turkey
Ulugqat Xinjiang China see Wuqia
94 D3 Ulu Kali, Gunung mt. Malaysia
129 C7 Ulukaya Turkey
126 G5 Ulukışla Turkey
199 L4 Uluköy Turkey
215 P4 Ulundi S. Africa
110 H3 Ulungur He r. China
110 H3 Ulungur Hu l. China
240 □E13 'Ulupalakua HI U.S.A.
94 □ Ulu Pandan Sing.
Uluqsaqtuua N.W.T. Can. see Holman
84 C8 Uluru hill N.T. Austr.
84 C8 Uluru-Kata Tjuta National Park N.T. Austr.
199 J3 Ulus Dağı mt. Turkey
Ulutau Kazakh. see Ulytau

Ulu Temburong National Park to Uyar
402

95 K2 **Ulu Temburong National Park** Brunei
146 D10 **Ulva** *i. Scotland* U.K.
Ulvéah *i.* Vanuatu *see* **Lopévi**
140 □ **Ulvebreen** *glacier* Svalbard
142 B2 **Ulvenåso** *mt.* Norway
164 G5 **Ulvenhout** Neth.
149 K5 **Ulverston** *Cumbria, England* U.K.
83 K9 **Ulverstone** *Tas.* Austr.
142 C1 **Ulvik** Norway
141 N5 **Ulvsjön** Sweden
139 U3 **Ul'yanikha** Rus. Fed.
139 V6 **Ul'yanino** Rus. Fed.
137 K6 **Ulyanivka** *Mykolayivs'ka Oblast'* Ukr.
137 N3 **Ulyanivka** *Sums'ka Oblast'* Ukr.
Ūl'yanov Kazakh. *see* Ul'yanovskiy
139 N2 **Ul'yanovka** Rus. Fed.
136 J5 **Ul'yanovka** *Kirovohrads'ka Oblast'* Ukr.
137 L3 **Ul'yanovka** *Poltavs'ka Oblast'* Ukr.
138 F7 **Ul'yanovo** *Kaliningradskaya Oblast'* Rus. Fed.
139 S8 **Ul'yanovo** *Kaluzhskaya Oblast'* Rus. Fed.
135 J5 **Ul'yanovsk** Rus. Fed.
135 I5 **Ul'yanovskaya Oblast'** *admin. div.* Rus. Fed.
121 O2 **Ul'yanovskiy** Kazakh.
Ulyanovsk Oblast *admin. div.* Rus. Fed. *see* Ul'yanovskaya **Oblast'**
Ul'yanovskoye Kazakh. *see* Ul'yanovskiy
107 O1 **Ulyatuy** Rus. Fed.
237 E7 **Ulysses** *KS* U.S.A.
232 C11 **Ulysses** *KY* U.S.A.
121 L3 **Ulytau** Kazakh.
121 L4 **Ulytau, Gory** *mts* Kazakh.
120 J3 **Uly-Zhylanshyk** *r.* Kazakh.
100 B2 **Uma** Rus. Fed.
188 D3 **Umag** Croatia
252 D4 **Umala** Bol.
100 H3 **Umaltinskiy** Rus. Fed.
'Umān *country* Asia *see* **Oman**
243 O7 **Umán** Mex.
78 □4a **Uman** *i. Chuuk* Micronesia
136 J5 **Uman'** Ukr.
258 C3 **Umango, Cerro** *mt.* Arg.
123 K7 **Umarao** Pak.
128 E7 **'Umarī, Qā' al** *salt pan* Jordan
116 H8 **Umaria** *Madh. Prad.* India
114 E3 **Umarkhed** *Mahar.* India
114 H3 **Umarkot** *Orissa* India
123 M9 **Umarkot** Pak.
82 G2 **Umaroona, Lake** *salt flat S.A.* Austr.
116 D9 **Umarpada** *Gujarat* India
78 □1 **Umatac** Guam
238 E4 **Umatilla** *OR* U.S.A.
92 E7 **Umayan** *r. Mindanao* Phil.
124 G9 **'Umayrah, Khawr al** *b.* Yemen
125 M5 **'Umayrī, Wādī** *watercourse* Oman
134 F2 **Umba** Rus. Fed.
233 □N4 **Umbagog Lake** *NH* U.S.A.
84 F2 **Umbakumba** *N.T.* Austr.
84 D8 **Umbeara** *N.T.* Austr.
208 E2 **Umbelasha** *watercourse* Sudan
93 C5 **Umbele** *i.* Indon.
150 E6 **Umberleigh** *Devon, England* U.K.
191 M9 **Umbertide** Italy
91 K8 **Umboi** *i.* P.N.G.
81 D12 **Umbrella Mountains** *South I.* N.Z.
246 □ **Umbrella Point** Jamaica
191 M9 **Umbria** *admin. reg.* Italy
195 L5 **Umbriatico** Italy
215 P5 **Umdloti Beach** S. Africa
213 F3 **Ume** *r.* Zimbabwe
140 P5 **Umeå** Sweden
140 P5 **Umeälven** *r.* Sweden
93 F4 **Umera** *Maluku* Indon.
135 H5 **Umet** Rus. Fed.
215 Q4 **Umfolozi** *r.* S. Africa
215 P4 **Umfolozi Game Reserve** *nature res.* S. Africa
140 M4 **Umfors** Sweden
223 M5 **Umfreville Lake** *Man./Ont.* Can.
Umfuli *r.* Zimbabwe *see* **Mupfure**
215 O6 **Umgababa** S. Africa
215 P5 **Umgeni** *r.* S. Africa
125 H1 **Umgharah** Kuwait
215 P5 **Umhali** S. Africa
178 C5 **Umhausen** Austria
215 P5 **Umhlanga Rocks** S. Africa
215 Q4 **Umhlatuzi Lagoon** S. Africa
182 C3 **Umia** *r.* Spain
105 G1 **Umi-gawa** *r.* Japan
221 N3 **Umiiviip Kangertiva** *inlet* Greenland
240 □F14 **'Umikoa** *HI* U.S.A.
220 H3 **Umingmaktok** *Nunavut* Can.
120 D6 **Umirzak** Kazakh.
224 E1 **Umiujaq** *Que.* Can.
172 D5 **Umkirch** Ger.
215 O6 **Umkomaas** S. Africa
215 O6 **Umkomaas** *r.* S. Africa
215 O5 **Umlazi** S. Africa
127 L8 **Umma** *tourist site* Iraq
128 D6 **Umm ad Daraj, Jabal** *mt.* Jordan
128 F4 **Umm al 'Amad** Syria
124 D4 **Umm al Birak** Saudi Arabia
128 D9 **Umm al Hashīm, Jabal** *mt.* Jordan
124 G2 **Umm al Jamājim** *well* Saudi Arabia
Umm al Qaiwain U.A.E. *see* Umm al Qaywayn
125 L3 **Umm al Qaywayn** U.A.E.
170 H2 **Ummanz** *i.* Ger.
128 F9 **Umm ar Raqabah, Khabrat** *imp. l.* Saudi Arabia
125 L5 **Umm as Samīm** *salt flat* Oman
124 E2 **Umm at Qalbān** Saudi Arabia
125 L4 **Umm az Zumūl** *well* Oman
125 J3 **Umm Bāb** Qatar
202 E6 **Umm Badr** Sudan
202 F6 **Umm Bel** Sudan
128 B10 **Umm Bujmah** Egypt
203 F6 **Umm Dam** Sudan
172 H5 **Ummendorf** Ger.
202 C2 **Umm Farud** Libya
203 G4 **Umm Gerifat** *waterhole* Sudan
124 C2 **Umm Ḥarb** Saudi Arabia
208 F2 **Umm Heitan** Sudan
202 E6 **Umm Keddada** Sudan
124 C3 **Umm Lajj** Saudi Arabia
128 C9 **Umm Mafrūd, Jabal** *mt.* Egypt
124 D4 **Umm Mukhbār, Jabal** *hill* Saudi Arabia
128 G9 **Umm Nukhaylah** *hill* Saudi Arabia
128 D10 **Umm Nukhaylah** *well* Saudi Arabia
127 M8 **Umm Qaṣr** Iraq
203 F5 **Umm Qurein** *well* Sudan
124 B2 **Umm Qusūr** *i.* Saudi Arabia
203 G5 **Umm Rumeila** *well* Sudan
203 F6 **Umm Ruwaba** Sudan
202 E2 **Umm Sa'ad** Libya
125 J3 **Umm Sa'id** Qatar
203 F6 **Umm Saiyala** Sudan
125 J3 **Umm Şalāl 'Alī** Qatar
124 D4 **Umm Şamā** Saudi Arabia
128 D9 **Umm Saysabān, Jabal** *mt.* Jordan
128 E9 **Umm Shaitiya** *well* Jordan
128 B10 **Umm Shawmar, Jabal** *mt.* Egypt
203 F6 **Umm Shugeira** Sudan
128 A10 **Umm Tināşşib, Jabal** *mt.* Egypt
124 C3 **Umm Urūmah** *i.* Saudi Arabia
128 G7 **Umm Wa'āl** *hill* Saudi Arabia
124 G4 **Umm Wazīr** *well* Saudi Arabia
128 A10 **Umm Zanātīr** *mt.* Egypt
220 B4 **Umnak Island** *AK* U.S.A.
96 D7 **Um Phang Wildlife Reserve** *nature res.* Thai.
213 H2 **Umpilua** Moz.
238 B5 **Umpqua** *r. OR* U.S.A.
209 C8 **Umpulo** Angola
199 M3 **Umraniye** Turkey
116 G9 **Umred** *Mahar.* India
114 C1 **Umreth** *Gujarat* India
Umtali Zimbabwe *see* **Mutare**
215 O7 **Umtamvuna** *r.* S. Africa
215 M7 **Umtata** S. Africa
215 N7 **Umtata** *r.* S. Africa
215 M7 **Umtata Dam** *resr* S. Africa
215 O6 **Umtentweni** S. Africa
207 G5 **Umuahia** Nigeria
256 A5 **Umuarama** Brazil
129 H5 **Umudlu** Azer.
129 C5 **Umudum** Turkey
199 H2 **Umurbey** Turkey
199 J3 **Umurlar** Turkey
80 J7 **Umutoi** *North I.* N.Z.
215 P5 **Umvoti** *r.* S. Africa
Umvukwes Zimbabwe *see* **Mvurwi**
Umvuma Zimbabwe *see* **Mvuma**
215 N7 **Umzimhlava** *r.* S. Africa
215 N6 **Umzimkulu** S. Africa
215 O6 **Umzimkulu** *r.* S. Africa
215 N7 **Umzimvubu** *r.* S. Africa
Umzingwani *r.* Zimbabwe *see* **Mzingwani**
215 O6 **Umzinto** S. Africa
215 O6 **Umzumbe** S. Africa
139 N6 **Una** Belarus
188 F3 **Una** *r.* Bos.-Herz./Croatia
255 F5 **Una** Brazil
254 G4 **Una** *r.* Brazil
116 F4 **Una** *Hima. Prad.* India
183 Q8 **Uña** Spain
81 G9 **Una, Mount** *South I.* N.Z.
128 E9 **'Unāb, Jabal al** *hill* Jordan
128 E8 **'Unāb, Wādī al** *watercourse* Jordan
188 F3 **Unac** *r.* Bos.-Herz.
182 H4 **Uña de Quintana** Spain
233 J6 **Unadilla** *NY* U.S.A.
233 J6 **Unadilla** *r. NY* U.S.A.
256 D2 **Unaí** Brazil
105 M4 **Unakami** Japan
220 B3 **Unalakleet** *AK* U.S.A.
220 B4 **Unalaska** *AK* U.S.A.
220 B4 **Unalaska Island** *AK* U.S.A.
211 B8 **Unango** Moz.
176 F3 **Únanov** Czech Rep.
146 F6 **Unapool** *Highland, Scotland* U.K.
140 R3 **Unari** Fin.
93 B4 **Unauna** *i.* Indon.
136 J3 **Unava** *r.* Ukr.
128 D8 **'Unayzah** Jordan
124 F2 **'Unayzah** Saudi Arabia
126 I7 **'Unayzah, Jabal** *hill* Iraq
104 G2 **Unazuki** Japan
186 C3 **Uncastillo** Spain
116 H7 **Unchahra** *Madh. Prad.* India
241 X3 **Uncompahgre Plateau** *CO* U.S.A.
85 J5 **Undara National Park** *Qld* Austr.
143 K3 **Unden** *l.* Sweden
215 N5 **Underberg** S. Africa
83 H6 **Underbool** *Vic.* Austr.
140 L5 **Undersåker** Sweden
236 E2 **Underwood** *ND* U.S.A.
172 G5 **Undingen** Ger.
135 J5 **Undory** Rus. Fed.
93 B9 **Undu, Tanjung** *pt Sumba* Indon.
163 B10 **Undués de Lerda** Spain
93 G5 **Undur** *Seram* Indon.
138 E3 **Undva** Estonia
150 G4 **Undy** *Monmouthshire, Wales* U.K.
139 P9 **Unecha** Rus. Fed.
139 O9 **Unecha** *r.* Rus. Fed.
251 E5 **Uneiuxi** *r.* Brazil
220 B4 **Unga Island** *AK* U.S.A.
83 K5 **Ungarie** *N.S.W.* Austr.
82 F6 **Ungarra** *S.A.* Austr.
Ungava, Baie d' *b. Que.* Can. *see* **Ungava Bay**
221 K3 **Ungava, Péninsule d'** *pen. Que.* Can.
225 H1 **Ungava Bay** *Que.* Can.
Ungava Peninsula *Que.* Can. *see* **Ungava, Péninsule d'**
Ungeny Moldova *see* **Ungheni**
173 I5 **Ungerhausen** Ger.
100 G7 **Unggi** N. Korea
136 G6 **Ungheni** Moldova
197 M4 **Ungheni** Romania
213 G4 **Unguana** Moz.
Unguja *i.* Tanz. *see* **Zanzibar Island**
Unguja North *admin. reg.* Tanz. *see* **Zanzibar North**
Unguja South *admin. reg.* Tanz. *see* **Zanzibar South**
Unguja West *admin. reg.* Tanz. *see* **Zanzibar West**
197 M3 **Ungurași** Romania
122 H2 **Unguz, Solonchakovyye Vpadiny** *salt flat* Turkm.
122 H1 **Üngüz Angyrsyndaky Garagum** *des.* Turkm.
Ungvár Ukr. *see* **Uzhhorod**
211 D5 **Ungwana Bay** Kenya
182 E8 **Unhais da Serra** Port.
182 E8 **Unhais-o-Velho** Port.
171 J10 **Unhošt'** Czech Rep.
134 J4 **Uni** Rus. Fed.
252 C2 **União** *Acre* Brazil
256 B3 **União** *Minas Gerais* Brazil
254 E3 **União** *Piauí* Brazil
255 C8 **União da Vitória** Brazil
251 F5 **União do Marará** Brazil
254 G4 **União dos Palmares** Brazil
116 F7 **Uniara** *Rajasthan* India
216 □2a **Unicorn Point** *Ascension* S. Atlantic Ocean
176 G2 **Uničov** Czech Rep.
174 G4 **Uniejów** Pol.
161 E6 **Unieux** France
191 Q6 **Unije** Croatia
188 E3 **Unije** *i.* Croatia
220 B4 **Unimak Island** *AK* U.S.A.
176 G3 **Unín** Slovakia
251 F5 **Unini** *r.* Brazil
252 B2 **Unini** Peru
260 E4 **Unión** Arg.
253 F6 **Unión** Para.
233 □P4 **Union** *ME* U.S.A.
236 J6 **Union** *MO* U.S.A.
235 G3 **Union** *NJ* U.S.A.
238 F4 **Union** *OR* U.S.A.
231 G8 **Union** *SC* U.S.A.
232 E11 **Union** *WV* U.S.A.
259 E5 **Unión, Bahía** *b.* Arg.
241 T7 **Union, Mount** *AZ* U.S.A.
235 G4 **Union Beach** *NJ* U.S.A.
234 A5 **Union Bridge** *MD* U.S.A.
232 A8 **Union City** *OH* U.S.A.
232 F7 **Union City** *PA* U.S.A.
237 K7 **Union City** *TN* U.S.A.
235 G3 **Union County** *county NJ* U.S.A.
234 A3 **Union County** *county PA* U.S.A.
214 H9 **Uniondale** S. Africa
234 E1 **Union Dale** *PA* U.S.A.
246 C2 **Unión de Reyes** Cuba
244 C6 **Unión de Tula** Mex.
147 D9 **Unionhall** Ireland
245 M9 **Unión Hidalgo** Mex.
247 □3 **Union Island** St Vincent
234 E6 **Union Lake** *NJ* U.S.A.
231 E9 **Union Springs** *AL* U.S.A.
232 I6 **Union Springs** *NY* U.S.A.
231 D9 **Uniontown** *AL* U.S.A.
232 F9 **Uniontown** *PA* U.S.A.
217 □1b **Union Vale** Mauritius
240 L3 **Union Valley Reservoir** *CA* U.S.A.
235 J1 **Unionville** *CT* U.S.A.
227 K6 **Unionville** *MI* U.S.A.
236 I5 **Unionville** *MO* U.S.A.
240 N1 **Unionville** *NV* U.S.A.
234 F2 **Unionville** *NY* U.S.A.
234 D5 **Unionville** *PA* U.S.A.
232 H10 **Unionville** *VA* U.S.A.
174 G2 **Unisław** Pol.
125 K4 **United Arab Emirates** *country* Asia
United Arab Republic *country* Africa *see* **Egypt**
145 G4 **United Kingdom** *country* Europe
United Provinces *state* India *see* **Uttar Pradesh**
228 G3 **United States of America** *country* N. America
221 L1 **United States Range** *mts Nunavut* Can.
191 M7 **Uniti** *r.* Italy
223 I4 **Unity** *Sask.* Can.
238 E4 **Unity** *OR* U.S.A.
234 B2 **Unityville** *PA* U.S.A.
183 Q8 **Universales, Montes** *reg.* Spain
212 B4 **Unjab** *watercourse* Namibia
116 D8 **Unjha** *Gujarat* India
169 D9 **Unkel** Ger.
178 G4 **Unken** Austria
172 H5 **Unlingen** Ger.
169 E7 **Unna** Ger.
116 H6 **Unnao** *Uttar Prad.* India
169 E9 **Unnau** Ger.
104 E2 **Unoke** Japan
101 D9 **Ŭnp'a** N. Korea
261 E2 **Unquillo** Arg.
101 D8 **Ŭnsan** N. Korea
101 E9 **Ŭnsan** N. Korea
129 E7 **Ünseli** Turkey
146 □O1 **Unst** *i. Scotland* U.K.
149 O7 **Unstone** *Derbyshire, England* U.K.
171 E8 **Unstrut** *r.* Ger.
171 E8 **Unstrut-Trias-Land** *park* Ger.
117 I7 **Untari** *Jharkhand* India
102 □1 **Unten** *Okinawa* Japan
197 O3 **Unţeni** Romania
190 F1 **Unterägeri** Switz.
173 K6 **Unterammergau** Ger.
169 I9 **Unterbreizbach** Ger.
173 J6 **Unterdießen** Ger.
173 N5 **Unterdietfurt** Ger.
170 F5 **Untere Havel** *park* Ger.
190 I2 **Unter Engadin** *reg.* Switz.
170 J5 **Unteres Odertal, Nationalpark** *nat. park* Ger.
170 J5 **Unteres Odertal, Nationalpark** *nat. park* Ger.
169 I10 **Unterfranken** *admin. reg.* Ger.
173 P4 **Untergriesbach** Ger.
173 L5 **Unterhaching** Ger.
178 D5 **Unter Inn Thal** *val.* Austria
190 E1 **Unterkulm** Switz.
179 N6 **Unterlamm** Austria
168 J5 **Unterlüß** Ger.
169 J9 **Untermaßfeld** Ger.
173 J5 **Untermeitingen** Ger.
169 K10 **Untermerzbach** Ger.
172 H3 **Untermünkheim** Ger.
173 N5 **Unterneukirchen** Ger.
173 I2 **Unterpleichfeld** Ger.
173 M5 **Unterreit** Ger.
190 F2 **Unterschächen** Switz.
173 L5 **Unterschleißheim** Ger.
173 I4 **Unterschneidheim** Ger.
172 G6 **Untersee** *l.* Ger./Switz.
169 K10 **Untersiemau** Ger.
171 E10 **Untersteinach** Ger.
173 J6 **Unterthingau** Ger.
170 I4 **Unterueckersee** *l.* Ger.
179 K3 **Unterweißenbach** Austria
171 D9 **Unterwellenborn** Ger.
173 M6 **Unterwössen** Ger.
129 H3 **Untsukul'** Rus. Fed.
251 E4 **Unturán, Sierra de** *mts* Venez.
222 D3 **Unuk** *r.* Can./U.S.A.
106 B9 **Unuli Horog** *Qinghai* China
156 B7 **Unverre** France
134 L3 **Un'ya** *r.* Rus. Fed.
103 H14 **Unzen-Amakusa Kokuritsu-kōen** *nat. park* Japan
134 I4 **Unzha** Rus. Fed.
183 Q3 **Unzué** Spain
102 □A21 **Uoturi-shima** *i. Nansei-shotō* Japan
104 F2 **Uozu** Japan
176 E1 **Úpa** *r.* Czech Rep.
139 T7 **Upa** *r.* Rus. Fed.
241 V1 **Upalco** *UT* U.S.A.
117 J8 **Upar Ghat** *reg. Chhattisgarh* India
251 F2 **Upata** Venez.
151 I5 **Upavon** *Wiltshire, England* U.K.
209 E7 **Upemba, Lac** *l.* Dem. Rep. Congo
209 E7 **Upemba, Parc National de l'** *nat. park* Dem. Rep. Congo
117 K8 **Uperbada** *Orissa* India
221 M2 **Upernavik** Greenland
221 M2 **Upernavik Kujalleq** Greenland
168 D3 **Upgant-Schott** Ger.
92 E8 **Upi** *Mindanao* Phil.
250 C3 **Upía** *r.* Col.
176 F1 **Úpice** Czech Rep.
214 F4 **Upington** S. Africa
141 R6 **Upinniemi** Fin.
240 O7 **Upland** *CA* U.S.A.
116 C9 **Upleta** *Gujarat* India
129 F4 **Up'lists'ikhe** Georgia
150 G6 **Uplyme** *Devon, England* U.K.
80 J6 **Upokongaro** *North I.* N.Z.
140 U3 **Upoloksha** Rus. Fed.
78 □2 **'Upolu** *i.* Samoa
240 □F13 **'Upolu Point** *HI* U.S.A.
129 C1 **Upornaya** Rus. Fed.
238 D6 **Upper Alkali Lake** *CA* U.S.A.
232 B8 **Upper Arlington** *OH* U.S.A.
222 G5 **Upper Arrow Lake** *B.C.* Can.
Upper Austria *land* Austria *see* **Oberösterreich**
146 D6 **Upper Bayble** *Western Isles, Scotland* U.K.
234 E3 **Upper Black Eddy** *PA* U.S.A.
146 J6 **Upper Camster** *Highland, Scotland* U.K.
150 F3 **Upper Chapel** *Powys, Wales* U.K.
Upper Chindwin Myanmar *see* **Mawlaik**
151 J5 **Upper Clatford** *Hampshire, England* U.K.
234 C5 **Upper Crossroads** *MD* U.S.A.
234 E5 **Upper Darby** *PA* U.S.A.
206 E4 **Upper East** *admin. reg.* Ghana
222 F4 **Upper Fraser** *B.C.* Can.
151 J4 **Upper Heyford** *Oxfordshire, England* U.K.
81 J8 **Upper Hutt** *North I.* N.Z.
226 C6 **Upper Iowa** *r. IA* U.S.A.
233 □R2 **Upper Kent** *N.B.* Can.
238 D5 **Upper Klamath Lake** *OR* U.S.A.
146 J8 **Upper Knockando** *Moray, Scotland* U.K.
147 I3 **Upperlands** *Northern Ireland* U.K.
222 D2 **Upper Liard** *Y.T.* Can.
147 G4 **Upper Lough Erne** *l. Northern Ireland* U.K.
224 A3 **Upper Manitou Lake** *Ont.* Can.
247 □7 **Upper Manzanilla** Trin. and Tob.
234 B7 **Upper Marlboro** *MD* U.S.A.
227 Q5 **Upper Mazinaw Lake** *Ont.* Can.
238 J3 **Upper Missouri Breaks National Monument** *nat. park MT* U.S.A.
210 B2 **Upper Nile** *state* Sudan
235 H2 **Upper Nyack** *NY* U.S.A.
94 □ **Upper Peirce Reservoir** Sing.
226 E9 **Upper Preoria Lake** *IL* U.S.A.
236 H1 **Upper Red Lake** *MN* U.S.A.
232 B8 **Upper Sandusky** *OH* U.S.A.
233 K4 **Upper Saranac Lake** *NY* U.S.A.
Upper Seal Lake *Que.* Can. *see* **Iberville, Lac d'**
81 G8 **Upper Takaka** *South I.* N.Z.
151 I2 **Upper Tean** *Staffordshire, England* U.K.
Upper Tunguska *r.* Rus. Fed. *see* **Angara**
Upper Volta *country* Africa *see* **Burkina**
114 D6 **Uppinangadi** *Karnataka* India
151 K2 **Uppingham** *Rutland, England* U.K.
143 N2 **Uppland** *reg.* Sweden
143 N1 **Upplanda** Sweden
143 N2 **Upplands-Väsby** Sweden
143 N2 **Uppsala** Sweden
143 N1 **Uppsala** *county* Sweden
117 I8 **Uprara** *Chhattisgarh* India
224 B3 **Upsala** *Ont.* Can.
116 F3 **Upshi** Jammu and Kashmir
226 D3 **Upson** *WI* U.S.A.
85 K5 **Upstart, Cape** *Qld* Austr.
85 K5 **Upstart Bay** *Qld* Austr.
150 H6 **Upton** *Dorset, England* U.K.
233 N6 **Upton** *MA* U.S.A.
150 H4 **Upton St Leonards** *Gloucestershire, England* U.K.
150 H3 **Upton upon Severn** *Worcestershire, England* U.K.
128 D8 **'Uqayqah, Wādī** *watercourse* Jordan
128 F3 **'Uqayribāt** Syria
127 M9 **Uqlat al 'Udhaybah** *well* Iraq
124 F3 **'Uqlat aş Şuqūr** Saudi Arabia
Uqsuqtuq *Nunavut* Can. *see* **Gjoa Haven**
Uqturpan *Xinjiang* China *see* **Wushi**
127 M8 **Ur** *tourist site* Iraq
250 B2 **Urabá, Golfo de** *b.* Col.
Uracas *vol.* N. Mariana Is *see* **Farallon de Pajaros**
Urad Qianqi *Nei Mongol* China *see* **Xishanzui**
Urad Zhongqi *Nei Mongol* China *see* **Haliut**
122 G6 **Ūrāf** Iran
146 □N2 **Urafirth** *Shetland, Scotland* U.K.
105 K6 **Uraga-suidō** *sea chan.* Japan
105 H1 **Uragawara** Japan
190 H4 **Urago d'Oglio** Italy
140 V2 **Ura-Guba** Rus. Fed.
102 U4 **Urahoro** Japan
256 B5 **Uraí** Brazil
176 F4 **Uraiújfalu** Hungary
114 E7 **Urakam** *Kerala* India
102 T4 **Urakawa** Japan
83 K5 **Ural** *hill N.S.W.* Austr.
120 D4 **Ural** *r.* Kazakh./Rus. Fed.
83 M4 **Uralla** *N.S.W.* Austr.
Ural Mountains Rus. Fed. *see* **Ural'skiy Khrebet**
100 F2 **Uralovka** Rus. Fed.
120 D2 **Ural'sk** Kazakh.
Ural'skaya Oblast' *admin. div.* Kazakh. *see* **Zapadnyy Kazakhstan**
Ural'skiye Gory *mts* Rus. Fed. *see* **Ural'skiy Khrebet**
134 L2 **Ural'skiy Khrebet** *mts* Rus. Fed.
211 B6 **Urambo** Tanz.
114 C3 **Uran** *Mahar.* India
83 K6 **Urana** *N.S.W.* Austr.
83 K6 **Urana, Lake** *N.S.W.* Austr.
84 G6 **Urandangi** *Qld* Austr.
254 E5 **Urandi** Brazil
223 I3 **Uranium City** *Sask.* Can.
83 K6 **Uranquinty** *N.S.W.* Austr.
84 E3 **Urapunga** *N.T.* Austr.
84 E7 **Urapuntja** *N.T.* Austr.
251 F4 **Uraricoera** Brazil
251 F4 **Uraricoera** *r.* Brazil
Urartu *country* Asia *see* **Armenia**
192 B8 **Uras** *Sardegna* Italy
102 □1 **Urasoe** *Okinawa* Japan
Ura-Tyube Tajik. *see* **Ŭroteppa**
114 E5 **Uravakonda** *Andhra Prad.* India
241 X3 **Uravan** *CO* U.S.A.
105 K4 **Urawa** Japan
130 H3 **Uray** Rus. Fed.
105 K4 **Urayasu** Japan
128 C8 **'Urayf an Nāqah, Jabal** *hill* Egypt
125 I3 **Uray'irah** Saudi Arabia
124 F3 **'Urayq, Nafūd al** *des.* Saudi Arabia
124 G2 **'Urayq ad Duḥūl** *des.* Saudi Arabia
124 H2 **'Urayq Sāqān** *des.* Saudi Arabia
174 E4 **Uraz** Pol.
135 I5 **Urazovka** Rus. Fed.
135 G6 **Urazovo** Rus. Fed.
169 E9 **Urbach** Ger.
236 K5 **Urbana** *IL* U.S.A.
226 I9 **Urbana** *IN* U.S.A.
232 B8 **Urbana** *OH* U.S.A.
191 N8 **Urbania** Italy
254 E2 **Urbano Santos** Brazil
169 E10 **Urbar** Ger.
183 P3 **Urbasa, Sierra de** *mts* Spain
190 F7 **Urbe** Italy
183 M4 **Urbel** *r.* Spain
83 N3 **Urbenville** *N.S.W.* Austr.
172 F2 **Urberach** Ger.
191 N8 **Urbino** Italy
192 C3 **Urbino, Étang d'** *lag. Corse* France
Urbinum Italy *see* **Urbino**
183 O4 **Urbión** *mt.* Spain
183 O4 **Urbión, Picos de** *mts* Spain
191 O9 **Urbisaglia** Italy
160 D4 **Urbise** France
Urbs Vetus Italy *see* **Orvieto**
176 G2 **Určice** Czech Rep.
252 C3 **Urcos** Peru
163 B9 **Urcuit** France
120 B3 **Urda** Kazakh.
185 L2 **Urda** Spain
261 G5 **Urdampolleta** Arg.
186 B1 **Urdax-Urdazuli** Spain
Ur'devarri *hill* Fin./Norway *see* **Urtivaara**
261 H3 **Urdinarrain** Arg.
134 J3 **Urdoma** Rus. Fed.
172 E7 **Urdorf** Switz.
163 C10 **Urdos** France
106 G3 **Urd Tamir Gol** *r.* Mongolia
183 O3 **Urduña** Spain
129 L1 **Urdyuk, Mys** *pt* Kazakh.
134 J2 **Urdyuzhskoye, Ozero** *l.* Rus. Fed.
121 S4 **Urdzhar** Kazakh.
149 O5 **Ure** *r. England* U.K.
138 K9 **Urechcha** Belarus
197 P4 **Urecheşti** Romania
134 I4 **Uren'** Rus. Fed.
130 I3 **Urengoy** Rus. Fed.
142 D2 **Urenosi** *mt.* Norway
80 I5 **Urenui** *North I.* N.Z.
78 □5 **Uréparapara** *i.* Vanuatu
163 B9 **Urepel** France
242 D3 **Ures** Mex.
104 D6 **Ureshino** Japan
164 J2 **Ureterp** Neth.
80 L5 **Urewera National Park** *North I.* N.Z.
Urfa Turkey *see* **Şanlıurfa**
169 B9 **Urft** *r.* Ger.
Urga Mongolia *see* **Ulaanbaatar**
100 H3 **Urgal** *r.* Rus. Fed.
120 I7 **Urganch** Uzbek.
199 I4 **Urganlı** Turkey
186 H4 **Urgell, Canal d'** Spain
Urgench Uzbek. *see* **Urganch**
126 G4 **Ürgüp** Turkey
121 L8 **Urgut** Uzbek.
110 G3 **Urho** *Xinjiang* China
140 S2 **Urho Kekkosen kansallispuisto** *nat. park* Fin.
192 B6 **Uri** *Sardegna* Italy
116 E2 **Uri** Jammu and Kashmir
190 F2 **Uri** *canton* Switz.
81 F9 **Uriah, Mount** *South I.* N.Z.
183 O3 **Uribarri-Ganboa, Embalse de** *resr* Spain
250 C2 **Uribia** Col.
261 F5 **Uriburu** Arg.
146 L8 **Urie** *r. Scotland* U.K.
100 G4 **Uril** Rus. Fed.
157 L7 **Uriménil** France
244 E6 **Uripitijuata, Cerro** *mt.* Mex.
242 F4 **Urique** Mex.
239 K13 **Urique** *r.* Mex.
190 F2 **Uri-Rotstock** *mt.* Switz.
83 I3 **Urisino** *N.S.W.* Austr.
137 R1 **Uritskoye** Rus. Fed.
210 C1 **Urī Wenz** *r.* Eth.
105 L3 **Urizura** Japan
141 Q6 **Urjala** Fin.
164 I3 **Urk** Neth.
100 D1 **Urkan** Rus. Fed.
100 E2 **Urkan** *r.* Rus. Fed.
129 I3 **Urkarakh** Rus. Fed.
177 G4 **Úrkút** Hungary
210 D4 **Urkut** Somalia
199 H4 **Urla** Turkey
197 O6 **Urlaţi** Romania
147 G7 **Urlingford** Ireland
197 N7 **Urlui** *r.* Romania
107 J1 **Urluk** Rus. Fed.
128 E2 **Urmā aş Şughrá** Syria
111 H11 **Urmai** *Xizang* China
128 E6 **'Urmān** Syria
134 I5 **Urmary** Rus. Fed.
123 M2 **Urmetan** Tajik.
100 I4 **Urmi** *r.* Rus. Fed.
Urmia Iran *see* **Orūmīyeh**
Urmia, Lake *salt l.* Iran *see* **Orūmīyeh, Daryācheh-ye**
157 O3 **Urmitz** Ger.
149 M7 **Urmston** *Greater Manchester, England* U.K.
109 □I7 **Urmston Road** *sea chan. H.K.* China
190 G1 **Urnäsch** Switz.
186 A1 **Urola** *r.* Spain
207 G5 **Uromi** Nigeria
196 J8 **Uroševac** *Kosovo* Serbia
134 F3 **Urosozero** Rus. Fed.
123 M2 **Ŭroteppa** Tajik.
137 N8 **Urozhayne** Ukr.
129 F2 **Urozhaynoye** Rus. Fed.
183 P3 **Urquilla, Sierra de** *mts* Spain
183 N4 **Urquiza, Embalse de** *resr* Spain
184 E2 **Urra** Port.
186 E5 **Urrea de Gaén** Spain
186 C4 **Urrea de Jalón** Spain
260 E6 **Urre Lauquén, Laguna** *l.* Arg.
163 B10 **Urriés** Spain
182 F6 **Urros** Port.
183 R3 **Urroz** Spain
111 H11 **Urru Co** *salt l.* China
163 A9 **Urrugne** France
183 O3 **Urrúnaga, Embalse de** *resr* Spain
Ursat'yevskaya Uzbek. *see* **Xovos**
173 I5 **Ursberg** Ger.
173 L3 **Ursensollen** Ger.
139 X6 **Urshel'skiy** Rus. Fed.
245 I3 **Úrsulo Galván** Mex.
245 K6 **Ursulo Galván** Mex.
163 B9 **Ursuya, Mont** *hill* France
175 L4 **Urszulin** Pol.
163 B9 **Urt** France
106 G5 **Urt** Mongolia
120 H1 **Urtazym** Rus. Fed.
190 C1 **Urtenen** Switz.
140 Q2 **Urtivaara** *hill* Fin./Norway
111 K8 **Urt Moron** *Qinghai* China
106 C8 **Urt Moron** *r. Qinghai* China
242 E4 **Uruáchic** Mex.
254 C5 **Uruaçu** Brazil
253 H3 **Uruana** Brazil
239 F11 **Uruapan** *Baja California* Mex.
244 E6 **Uruapan** *Michoacán* Mex.
252 B3 **Urubamba** Peru
251 E5 **Urubaxi** *r.* Brazil
251 G5 **Urubu** *r.* Brazil
256 B4 **Urubupungá, Salto do** *waterfall* Brazil
251 G5 **Urucara** Brazil
139 Q9 **Uruch'ye** Rus. Fed.
251 F6 **Urucu** *r.* Brazil
254 D3 **Uruçuí** Brazil
254 D4 **Uruçuí, Serra do** *hills* Brazil
257 E2 **Urucuia** Brazil
257 E2 **Urucuia** *r.* Brazil
254 D3 **Uruçui Preto** *r.* Brazil
253 F4 **Urucum** Brazil
251 G5 **Urucurituba** Brazil
183 J5 **Urueña** Spain
104 G5 **Urugi** Japan
261 H3 **Uruguai** *r.* Brazil *alt.* **Uruguay (Arg./Uru.)**
258 F3 **Uruguaiana** Brazil
255 B8 **Uruguay** *r.* Arg./Uru. *alt.* **Uruguai (Brazil)**
258 G4 **Uruguay** *country* S. America
Uruk *tourist site* Iraq *see* **Erech**
129 F2 **Urukh** *r.* Rus. Fed.
92 □ **Urukthapel** *i.* Palau
Urumchi *Xinjiang* China *see* **Ürümqi**
110 H5 **Ürümqi** *Xinjiang* China
Urundi *country* Africa *see* **Burundi**
83 N4 **Urunga** *N.S.W.* Austr.
78 □1 **Uruno Point** Guam
129 C2 **Urup** Rus. Fed.
129 C1 **Urup** *r.* Rus. Fed.
131 Q5 **Urup, Ostrov** *i. Kuril'skiye O-va* Rus. Fed.
253 E2 **Urupá** *r.* Brazil
123 Q1 **Uru Pass** China/Kyrg.
256 C4 **Urupês** Brazil
Urupskaya Rus. Fed. *see* **Sovetskaya**
124 H6 **'Urūq al Awārik** *des.* Saudi Arabia
125 L4 **'Urūq ash Shaybah** *des.* Saudi Arabia
193 O4 **Ururi** Italy
100 C1 **Urusha** Rus. Fed.
100 C2 **Urusha** *r.* Rus. Fed.
129 G2 **Urus-Martan** Rus. Fed.
135 K5 **Urussu** Rus. Fed.
256 C2 **Urutaí** Brazil
80 I5 **Uruti** *North I.* N.Z.
81 K8 **Uruti Point** *North I.* N.Z.
211 A6 **Uruwira** Tanz.
123 L5 **Urūzgān** *prov.* Afgh.
129 E2 **Urvan'** Rus. Fed.
158 H2 **Urville Nacqueville** France
121 V3 **Uryl'** Kazakh.
102 S3 **Uryū** Japan
102 S3 **Uryū-gawa** *r.* Japan
100 B2 **Uryumkan** *r.* Rus. Fed.
100 B2 **Uryupino** Rus. Fed.
135 H6 **Uryupinsk** Rus. Fed.
184 C5 **Urza** *hill* Port.
175 K5 **Urzędów** Pol.
216 □1c **Urzelina** *São Jorge* Azores
Ürzhar Kazakh. *see* **Urdzhar**
134 J4 **Urzhum** Rus. Fed.
197 O6 **Urziceni** *Ialomiţa* Romania
177 L4 **Urziceni** *Satu Mare* Romania
137 Q7 **Urzuf** Ukr.
192 D7 **Urzulei** *Sardegna* Italy
160 C2 **Urzy** France
138 L8 **Usa** *r.* Belarus
103 I13 **Usa** Japan
120 C1 **Usa** *r.* Rus. Fed.
134 L2 **Usa** *r.* Rus. Fed.
92 C9 **Usada** *i.* Phil.
184 G4 **Usagre** Spain
199 K4 **Uşak** Turkey
199 K4 **Uşak** *prov.* Turkey
212 B4 **Usakos** Namibia
211 C6 **Usambara Mountains** Tanz.
211 B7 **Usangu Flats** *plain* Tanz.
263 K2 **Usarp Mountains** Antarctica
259 F8 **Usborne, Mount** *hill* Falkland Is
196 I7 **Ušće** Serbia
169 I8 **Uschlag (Staufenberg)** Ger.
175 J6 **Uście Gorlickie** Pol.
175 I5 **Uście Solne** Pol.
190 G7 **Uscio** Italy
170 I3 **Usedom** Ger.
170 J3 **Usedom** *i.* Ger.
87 B9 **Useless Loop** *W.A.* Austr.
192 B8 **Usellus** *Sardegna* Italy
210 B5 **Usengi** Kenya
187 E7 **Useras** Spain
124 D5 **Usfān** Saudi Arabia
138 I8 **Usha** *r.* Belarus
138 L8 **Usha** *r.* Belarus
Ushachi Belarus *see* **Ushachy**
138 L6 **Ushachy** Belarus
130 I1 **Ushakova, Ostrov** *i.* Rus. Fed.
121 T3 **Ushanovo** Kazakh.
Ushant *i.* France *see* **Ouessant, Île d'**
Üsharal Kazakh. *see* **Ucharal**
121 N6 **Usharal** Kazakh.
149 N4 **Ushaw Moor** *Durham, England* U.K.
124 G3 **Ushayqir** Saudi Arabia
124 E5 **'Ushayrah** Saudi Arabia
129 D2 **Ushba, Mt'a** Georgia
138 M6 **Ushcha** *r.* Rus. Fed.
139 O9 **Ushcherp'ye** Rus. Fed.
105 M4 **Ushibori** Japan
103 H14 **Ushibuka** Japan
105 L3 **Ushiku** Japan
104 C8 **Ushimawashi-yama** *mt.* Japan
211 A5 **Ushirombo** Tanz.
137 N6 **Ushkalka** Ukr.
134 M3 **Ushma** Rus. Fed.
120 E6 **Ushtagan** Kazakh.
121 Q5 **Ushtobe** Kazakh.
Ush-Tyube Kazakh. *see* **Ushtobe**
259 C9 **Ushuaia** Arg.
136 G5 **Ushytsya** *r.* Ukr.
138 F4 **Uši** Latvia
254 B3 **Usina** Brazil
169 G10 **Usingen** Ger.
192 B6 **Usini** *Sardegna* Italy
134 L2 **Usinsk** Rus. Fed.
150 G4 **Usk** *Monmouthshire, Wales* U.K.
150 G4 **Usk** *r. Wales* U.K.
117 I6 **Uska** *Uttar Prad.* India
138 K8 **Uskhodni** Belarus
Uskoplje Bos.-Herz. *see* **Gornji Vakuf**
150 E4 **Usk Reservoir** *Wales* U.K.
199 K1 **Üsküdar** Turkey
197 P9 **Üsküp** Turkey
169 I7 **Uslar** Ger.
176 C2 **Úslava** *r.* Czech Rep.
138 F4 **Usma** Latvia
139 W9 **Usman'** Rus. Fed.
139 W9 **Usman'** *r.* Rus. Fed.
138 F4 **Usmas ezers** *l.* Latvia
121 L8 **Usmat** Uzbek.
Usmet Uzbek. *see* **Usmat**
139 O6 **Usmyn'** Rus. Fed.
260 D2 **Usno** Arg.
183 J9 **Uso** *r.* Spain
134 J3 **Usogorsk** Rus. Fed.
211 B6 **Usoke** Tanz.
134 L4 **Usol'ye** Rus. Fed.
98 H1 **Usol'ye-Sibirskoye** Rus. Fed.
188 G3 **Usora** *r.* Bos.-Herz.
176 G2 **Úsov** Czech Rep.
137 N1 **Usozha** *r.* Rus. Fed.
137 O1 **Usozha** *r.* Rus. Fed.
260 C3 **Uspallata** Arg.
137 P6 **Uspenivka** Ukr.
121 Q1 **Uspenka** Kazakh.
137 R6 **Uspenka** *Donets'ka Oblast'* Ukr.
137 M5 **Uspenka** *Kirovohrads'ka Oblast'* Ukr.
137 M2 **Uspenka** *Sums'ka Oblast'* Ukr.
100 E2 **Uspenovka** Rus. Fed.
121 O3 **Uspenskiy** Kazakh.
135 H7 **Uspenskoye** *Krasnodarskiy Kray* Rus. Fed.
139 N5 **Uspenskoye** *Pskovskaya Oblast'* Rus. Fed.
134 H4 **Uspen'ye** Rus. Fed.
164 K2 **Usquert** Neth.
192 C9 **Ussana** *Sardegna* Italy
192 C8 **Ussassai** *Sardegna* Italy
161 K6 **Usseglio** Italy
161 B6 **Ussel** *Auvergne* France
162 I4 **Ussel** *Limousin* France
160 H5 **Usses** *r.* France
162 F3 **Usson-du-Poitou** France
161 D6 **Usson-en-Forez** France
100 I4 **Ussuri** *r.* Rus. Fed.
100 G7 **Ussuriysk** Rus. Fed.
134 I4 **Usta** *r.* Rus. Fed.
Ust'-Abakanskoye Rus. Fed. *see* **Abakan**
134 I3 **Ust'-Alekseyevo** Rus. Fed.
123 M7 **Usta Muhammad** Pak.
163 B9 **Ustaritz** France
Ust'-Balyk Rus. Fed. *see* **Nefteyugansk**
99 I1 **Ust'-Barguzin** Rus. Fed.
134 L4 **Ust'-Dolgaya** Rus. Fed.
138 M5 **Ust'-Dolyssy** Rus. Fed.
135 H7 **Ust'-Donetskiy** Rus. Fed.
129 C1 **Ust'-Dzheguta** Rus. Fed.
Ust'-Dzhegutinskaya Rus. Fed. *see* **Ust'-Dzheguta**
176 C1 **Ústecký kraj** *admin. reg.* Czech Rep.
176 D1 **Úštěk** Czech Rep.
190 F1 **Uster** Switz.
142 D1 **Ustevatn** *l.* Norway
194 E6 **Ustica** *Sicilia* Italy
194 E6 **Ustica, Isola di** *i. Sicilia* Italy
131 L4 **Ust'-Ilimsk** Rus. Fed.
131 L4 **Ust'-Ilimskiy Vodokhranilishche** *resr* Rus. Fed.
107 M1 **Ust'-Ilya** Rus. Fed.
134 L3 **Ust'-Ilych** Rus. Fed.
176 D1 **Ústí nad Labem** Czech Rep.
176 F2 **Ústí nad Orlicí** Czech Rep.
Ustinov Rus. Fed. *see* **Izhevsk**
Ustirt *plat.* Kazakh./Uzbek. *see* **Ustyurt Plateau**
143 M7 **Ustka** Pol.
121 T1 **Ust'-Kalmanka** Rus. Fed.
131 R4 **Ust'-Kamchatsk** Rus. Fed.
121 T3 **Ust'-Kamenogorsk** Kazakh.
110 G1 **Ust'-Kan** Rus. Fed.
100 A2 **Ust'-Karsk** Rus. Fed.
110 G1 **Ust'-Koksa** Rus. Fed.
134 K3 **Ust'-Kulom** Rus. Fed.
131 L4 **Ust'-Kut** Rus. Fed.
131 O2 **Ust'-Kuyga** Rus. Fed.
135 G7 **Ust'-Labinsk** Rus. Fed.
Ust'-Labinskaya Rus. Fed. *see* **Ust'-Labinsk**
100 B2 **Ust'-Lubiya** Rus. Fed.
138 L2 **Ust'-Luga** Rus. Fed.
134 L2 **Ust'-Lyzha** Rus. Fed.
134 M3 **Ust'-Man'ya** Rus. Fed.
131 O3 **Ust'-Maya** Rus. Fed.
Ust'-Mongunay Rus. Fed. *see* **Primorskiy**
130 J3 **Ust'-Munduyka** Rus. Fed.
134 K3 **Ust'-Nem** Rus. Fed.
131 P3 **Ust'-Nera** Rus. Fed.
134 J3 **Ust'-Ocheya** Rus. Fed.
131 M2 **Ust'-Olenek** Rus. Fed.
131 P3 **Ust'-Omchug** Rus. Fed.
98 H1 **Ust'-Ordynskiy** Rus. Fed.
98 H1 **Ust'-Ordynskiy Buryatskiy Avtonomnyy Okrug** *admin. div.* Rus. Fed.
163 G10 **Ustou** France
130 J3 **Ust'-Port** Rus. Fed.
197 O8 **Ustrem** Bulg.
174 G6 **Ustroń** Pol.
174 D1 **Ustronie Morskie** Pol.
175 K6 **Ustrzyki Dolne** Pol.
139 Q1 **Ust'-Sara** Rus. Fed.
134 H3 **Ust'-Shonosha** Rus. Fed.
134 K2 **Ust'-Tsil'ma** Rus. Fed.
110 H1 **Ust'-Ulagan** Rus. Fed.
134 L3 **Ust'-Uls** Rus. Fed.
100 H3 **Ust'-Umalta** Rus. Fed.
134 L3 **Ust'-Unya** Rus. Fed.
134 I3 **Ust'-Ura** Rus. Fed.
100 H3 **Ust'-Urgal** Rus. Fed.
100 B2 **Ust'-Urov** Rus. Fed.
134 L2 **Ust'-Usa** Rus. Fed.
120 J1 **Ust'-Uyskoye** Kazakh.
134 H3 **Ust'-Vayen'ga** Rus. Fed.
134 L2 **Ust'-Voya** Rus. Fed.
134 I3 **Ust'-Vyyskaya** Rus. Fed.
134 H3 **Ust'ya** *r.* Rus. Fed.
131 O2 **Ust'-Yansk** Rus. Fed.
139 O5 **Ust'ye** *Tverskaya Oblast'* Rus. Fed.
134 G4 **Ust'ye** *Vologodskaya Oblast'* Rus. Fed.
134 H4 **Ust'ye** *Vologodskaya Oblast'* Rus. Fed.
139 W4 **Ust'ye** *Yaroslavskaya Oblast'* Rus. Fed.
139 W4 **Ust'ye** *r.* Rus. Fed.
139 S3 **Ust'ye-Kirovskoye** Rus. Fed.
136 D3 **Ustyluh** Ukr.
137 L6 **Ustynivka** Ukr.
Ustyurt, Plato *plat.* Kazakh./Uzbek. *see* **Ustyurt Plateau**
120 G6 **Ustyurt Plateau** Kazakh./Uzbek.
Ustyurt Platosi *plat.* Kazakh./Uzbek. *see* **Ustyurt Plateau**
139 S3 **Ustyutskoye** Rus. Fed.
139 T3 **Ustyuzhna** Rus. Fed.
110 G4 **Usu** *Xinjiang* China
93 C9 **Usu** *i.* Indon.
105 H3 **Usuda** Japan
129 I4 **Usukhchay** Rus. Fed.
103 I13 **Usuki** Japan
242 □O11 **Usulután** El Salvador
243 M8 **Usumacinta** *r.* Guat./Mex.
Usumbura Burundi *see* **Bujumbura**
95 K3 **Usun Apau, Dataran Tinggi** *plat.* Malaysia
186 A1 **Usurbil** Spain
175 H6 **Úšust** *mt.* Pol.
215 Q2 **Usutu** *r.* Africa
134 L4 **Us'va** Rus. Fed.
139 N6 **Usvyaty** Rus. Fed.
138 M7 **Usvyeyka** *r.* Belarus
175 I6 **Uszew** Pol.
177 H5 **Uszód** Hungary
175 I5 **Uszwica** *r.* Pol.
91 I7 **Uta** *Papua* Indon.
93 F3 **Uta** *i. Maluku* Indon.
192 B9 **Uta** *Sardegna* Italy
241 U2 **Utah** *state* U.S.A.
241 U1 **Utah Lake** *UT* U.S.A.
140 S4 **Utajärvi** Fin.
95 L9 **Utan** *Sumbawa* Indon.
104 C7 **Utano** Japan
168 D3 **Utarp** Ger.
Utashinai *Kuril'skiye O-va* Rus. Fed. *see* **Yuzhno-Kuril'sk**
106 H1 **Utata** Rus. Fed.
79 □8 **'Uta Vava'u** *Vava'u Gp* Tonga
124 E4 **'Utaybah** *reg.* Saudi Arabia
128 E5 **'Utaybah, Buḥayrat al** *imp. l.* Syria
128 B10 **Utayrtīr ad Dahamī, Jabal** *mt.* Egypt
125 I2 **Utayyiq** Saudi Arabia
142 B2 **Utbjoa** Norway
186 D4 **Utebo** Spain
237 D8 **Ute Creek** *r. NM* U.S.A.
161 K9 **Utelle** France
209 D9 **Utembo** *r.* Angola
241 X4 **Ute Mountain Indian Reservation** *res. CO/NM* U.S.A.
138 I6 **Utena** Lith.
100 B1 **Uteni** Rus. Fed.
116 C7 **Uterlai** *Rajasthan* India
168 F1 **Utersum** Ger.
211 C7 **Utete** Tanz.
116 F6 **Utgir** *Rajasthan* India
96 E7 **Uthai Thani** Thai.
123 L9 **Uthal** Pak.
169 K8 **Uthleben** Ger.
168 G4 **Uthlede** Ger.
128 F4 **'Uthmānīyah** Syria
97 D7 **U Thong** Thai.
96 G7 **Uthumphon Phisai** Thai.
253 F3 **Utiariti** Brazil
227 K7 **Utica** *MI* U.S.A.
237 J9 **Utica** *MS* U.S.A.
233 J5 **Utica** *NY* U.S.A.
232 C8 **Utica** *OH* U.S.A.
187 C8 **Utiel** Spain
222 H4 **Utikuma Lake** *Alta* Can.
242 □P9 **Utila** Hond.
254 E5 **Utinga** *r.* Brazil
141 I6 **Utladalen** *park* Norway
143 L5 **Utlängan** *i.* Sweden
215 J3 **Utlwanang** S. Africa
137 N7 **Utlyuks'kyy Lyman** *b.* Ukr.
103 H14 **Uto** Japan
143 O3 **Utö** *i.* Sweden
84 E7 **Utopia** *N.T.* Austr.
260 E5 **Utracán** Arg.
175 I3 **Utrata** *r.* Pol.
116 I6 **Utraula** *Uttar Prad.* India
164 H4 **Utrecht** Neth.
164 H4 **Utrecht** *prov.* Neth.
215 O3 **Utrecht** S. Africa
184 H6 **Utrera** Spain
184 F4 **Utrera, Peña** *hill* Spain
186 D6 **Utrillas** Spain
177 I6 **Utrine** *Vojvodina* Serbia
138 L4 **Utroya** *r.* Rus. Fed.
142 A2 **Utsira** Norway
140 S2 **Utsjoki** Fin.
140 M2 **Utskor** Norway
105 G4 **Utsugi-dake** *mt.* Japan
105 K2 **Utsunomiya** Japan
135 I7 **Utta** Rus. Fed.
114 F6 **Uttangarai** *Tamil Nadu* India
96 E6 **Uttaradit** Thai.
Uttarakhand *state* India *see* **Uttaranchal**
116 G4 **Uttaranchal** *state* India
116 G4 **Uttarkashi** *Uttaranchal* India
116 G6 **Uttar Pradesh** *state* India
178 H3 **Uttendorf** *Oberösterreich* Austria
178 G5 **Uttendorf** *Salzburg* Austria
173 K2 **Uttenreuth** Ger.
172 H5 **Uttenweiler** Ger.
168 L1 **Utterslev** Denmark
173 K5 **Utting am Ammersee** Ger.
151 I2 **Uttoxeter** *Staffordshire, England* U.K.
Uttranchal *state* India *see* **Uttaranchal**
Utu *Xinjiang* China *see* **Miao'ergou**
247 □1 **Utuado** Puerto Rico
110 H3 **Utubulak** *Xinjiang* China
79 □9a **Utuofai** *Tahiti* Fr. Polynesia
78 □6 **Utupua** *i. Santa Cruz Is* Solomon Is
120 E2 **Utva** *r.* Kazakh.
170 H3 **Utzedel** Ger.
138 H3 **Uulu** Estonia
221 L2 **Uummannaq** *Avanersuaq* Greenland
221 M2 **Uummannaq** *Kitaa* Greenland
221 M2 **Uummannaq Fjord** *inlet* Greenland
Uummannarsuaq *c.* Greenland *see* **Nunap Isua**
140 R5 **Uurainen** Fin.
106 B1 **Üüreg Nuur** *salt l.* Mongolia
106 G1 **Üür Gol** *r.* Mongolia
Uusikaarlepyy Fin. *see* **Nykarleby**
141 P6 **Uusikaupunki** Fin.
212 B3 **Uutapi** Namibia
250 D4 **Uva** *r.* Col.
134 K4 **Uva** Rus. Fed.
196 H7 **Uvac** *r.* Bos.-Herz./Montenegro
237 F11 **Uvalde** *TX* U.S.A.
176 D1 **Úvaly** Czech Rep.
139 N9 **Uvaravichy** Belarus
139 S6 **Uvarovka** Rus. Fed.
135 H6 **Uvarovo** Rus. Fed.
Uvéa *atoll Îles Loyauté* New Caledonia *see* **Ouvéa**
120 I1 **Uvel'ka** *r.* Rus. Fed.
139 R3 **Uver'** *r.* Rus. Fed.
161 J8 **Uvernet-Fours** France
211 A6 **Uvinza** Tanz.
209 F5 **Uvira** Dem. Rep. Congo
139 Y5 **Uvod'** *r.* Rus. Fed.
215 O6 **Uvongo** S. Africa
106 C2 **Uvs** *prov.* Mongolia
106 C1 **Uvs Nuur** *salt l.* Mongolia
103 J13 **Uwa** Japan
103 J13 **Uwajima** Japan
103 J13 **Uwa-kai** *b.* Japan
125 M4 **'Uwayfī** Oman
124 E3 **'Uwayja** *well* Saudi Arabia
202 B2 **'Uwaynāt Wannīn** Libya
124 C2 **'Uwayriḍ, Ḥarrat al** *lava field* Saudi Arabia
128 G8 **Uwaysiţ** *well* Saudi Arabia
202 E4 **Uweinat, Jebel** *mt.* Sudan
211 B7 **Uwemba** Tanz.
94 G4 **Uwi** *i.* Indon.
227 O5 **Uxbridge** *Ont.* Can.
151 L4 **Uxbridge** *Greater London, England* U.K.
160 E3 **Uxeau** France
169 C10 **Üxheim** Ger.
107 K7 **Uxin Ju** *Nei Mongol* China
Uxin Qi *Nei Mongol* China *see* **Dabqig**
251 H6 **Uxituba** Brazil
243 O7 **Uxmal** *tourist site* Mex.
245 M8 **Uxpanapa** *r.* Mex.
110 H5 **Uxxaktal** *Xinjiang* China
120 J1 **Uy** *r.* Rus. Fed.
120 I5 **Uyaly** Kazakh.
Uyaly, Ozero *l.* Kazakh. *see* **Koshkarkol', Ozero**
129 A7 **Uyandık** Turkey
131 K4 **Uyar** Rus. Fed.

106 J4 Üydzin Mongolia
146 □O1 Uyea i. Scotland U.K.
146 □O1 Uyeasound Shetland, Scotland U.K.
207 G5 Uyo Nigeria
106 C3 Üyönch Mongolia
106 B4 Üyönch Gol r. China
211 A6 Uyowa Tanz.
120 I1 Uyskoye Rus. Fed.
96 B2 Uyu Chaung r. Myanmar
121 N6 Uyuk Kazakh.
125 I3 Uyun Saudi Arabia
252 D5 Uyuni Bol.
252 D5 Uyuni, Salar de salt flat Bol.
163 B7 Uza France
120 A1 Uza r. Rus. Fed.
127 L6 'Uzaym, Nahr al r. Iraq
120 I6 Uzbekistan country Asia
Uzbekiston country Asia see Uzbekistan
Uzbekskaya S.S.R. country Asia see Uzbekistan
Uzbek S.S.R. country Asia see Uzbekistan
129 K6 Uzboy Azer.
122 F2 Uzboy Turkm.
138 K8 Uzda Belarus
158 F5 Uzel France
Uzen' Kazakh. see Kyzylsay
161 F7 Uzer France
162 H5 Uzerche France
161 E8 Uzès France
Uzgen Kyrg. see Özgön
136 B5 Uzh r. Ukr.
136 J2 Uzh r. Ukr.
120 Q7 Uzha r. Rus. Fed.
Uzhgorod Ukr. see Uzhhorod
136 B5 Uzhhorod Ukr.
136 B5 Uzhok Ukr.
Užhorod Ukr. see Uzhhorod
196 H7 Užice Serbia
139 V8 Uzlovaya Rus. Fed.
138 K6 Uzmyony Belarus
134 H4 Uzola r. Rus. Fed.
121 R7 Üzöngü Toosu mt. China/Kyrg.
129 A6 Üzümlü Erzincan Turkey
199 K6 Üzümlü Muğla Turkey
121 M8 Uzun Uzbek.
199 H4 Uzun Ada i. Turkey
121 Q6 Uzunagach Almatinskaya Oblast' Kazakh.
121 Q6 Uzunagach Almatinskaya Oblast' Kazakh.
129 C6 Uzunark Turkey
110 G4 Uzunbulak Xinjiang China
110 I6 Uzun Bulak spring Xinjiang China
128 B2 Uzuncaburç Turkey
129 C5 Uzundere Turkey
129 B5 Uzungöl Turkey
199 H1 Uzunköprü Turkey
137 P8 Uzunlars'ke, Ozero l. Ukr.
129 J4 Uzunoba Azer.
129 B6 Uzunsavat Turkey
129 J6 Uzuntäpä Azer.
138 F6 Užventis Lith.
139 O6 Uzvoz Rus. Fed.
136 J4 Uzyn Ukr.
Uzynaghash Kazakh. see Uzunagach
120 I5 Uzynkair Kazakh.
120 K1 Uzynkol' Kostanayskaya Oblast' Kazakh.

V

113 □1 Vaadhu i. S. Male Maldives
113 □1 Vaadhu Channel Maldives
113 □1 Vaagali i. S. Male Maldives
134 D3 Vaajakoski Fin.
215 H5 Vaal r. S. Africa
140 S4 Vaala Fin.
214 I4 Vaalbos National Park S. Africa
215 M3 Vaal Dam S. Africa
215 M2 Vaal Dam Nature Reserve S. Africa
168 H3 Vaale Ger.
215 M1 Vaalplass S. Africa
165 J7 Vaals Neth.
165 J7 Vaalserberg hill Neth.
213 F5 Vaalwater S. Africa
138 K4 Vaartsi Estonia
159 L6 Vaas France
140 P5 Vaasa Fin.
164 I4 Vaassen Neth.
113 □1 Vaataru i. N. Male Maldives
138 H6 Vabalninkas Lith.
138 M8 Vabich r. Belarus
139 Q9 Vablya r. Rus. Fed.
163 I8 Vabre France
161 B9 Vabres-l'Abbaye France
177 I4 Vác Hungary
195 K7 Vacale r. Italy
257 E4 Vacaré r. Brazil
255 C9 Vacaria Brazil
257 F2 Vacaria r. Brazil
255 B7 Vacaria r. Brazil
255 C9 Vacaria, Campo da plain Brazil
255 B7 Vacaria, Serra hills Brazil
240 K3 Vacaville CA U.S.A.
214 F10 Vacca, Cape S. Africa
161 F9 Vaccarès, Étang de lag. France
195 K4 Vaccarizzo Albanese Italy
195 K5 Vaccheli, Canale canal Italy
169 J9 Vacha Ger.
134 H5 Vacha Rus. Fed.
177 I4 Váchartyán Hungary
160 J4 Vacheresse France
217 □2b Vaches, Île aux i. Inner Islands Seychelles
129 I3 Vachi Rus. Fed.
143 K5 Väckelsång Sweden
217 □1b Vacoas Mauritius
173 P3 Vacov Czech Rep.
161 F8 Vacqueyras France
197 O3 Văculeşti Romania
134 I5 Vad Rus. Fed.
135 H5 Vad r. Rus. Fed.
114 C3 Vada Mahar. India
138 F5 Vadakste r. Latvia/Lith.
177 M7 Vădăstriţa Romania
142 E6 Vadehavet nature res. Denmark
142 E6 Vadehavet sea chan. Denmark
197 P5 Vădeni Romania
136 H6 Vădeni, Dealul hill Moldova
143 H6 Vaderöarna is Sweden
144 J1 Vadheim Norway
114 C5 Vadi Mahar. India
135 H5 Vadinsk Rus. Fed.
142 C2 Vadla Norway
190 E7 Vado, Capo di c. Italy
183 N6 Vado, Embalse del resr Spain
183 M5 Vadocondes Spain
116 D8 Vadodara Gujarat India
190 E7 Vado Ligure Italy
140 T1 Vadsø Norway
143 K3 Vadstena Sweden
197 K4 Vadu Crişului Romania
172 H7 Vaduz Liechtenstein
170 E1 Væggerløse Denmark
140 L3 Værøy i. Norway
134 H3 Vaga r. Rus. Fed.
141 J6 Vågåmo Norway
188 E3 Vaganski Vrh mt. Croatia
144 D1 Vágar i. Faroe Is
114 G4 Vagavaram Andhra Prad. India
140 T2 Vaggatem Norway
143 K4 Vaggeryd Sweden
78 □6 Vaghena i. Solomon Is
198 E4 Vagia Greece
195 K4 Vaglia Italy
193 P6 Vaglio Basilicata Italy
190 I7 Vagli Sotto Italy
157 M7 Vagney France
143 N3 Vagnhärad Sweden
182 C7 Vagos Port.
140 O4 Vägsele Sweden
140 N2 Vågsfjorden sea chan. Norway
177 H4 Váh r. Slovakia
141 P6 Vähäkyrö Fin.
122 G7 Vahhābī Iran
169 H7 Vahlbruch Ger.
259 □ Vahsel, Cape S. Georgia
141 Q6 Vahto Fin.
77 H2 Vaiaku Funafuti Tuvalu
184 E2 Vaiamonte Port.
191 K8 Vaiano Italy
138 H2 Vaida Estonia
237 K9 Vaiden MS U.S.A.
114 F8 Vaigai r. India
159 K5 Vaiges France
172 F4 Vaihingen an der Enz Ger.
79 □9a Vaihiria, Lac l. Tahiti Fr. Polynesia
114 D3 Vaijapur Mahar. India
114 C8 Vaikam Kerala India
138 I3 Väike Emajõgi r. Estonia
138 J2 Väike-Maarja Estonia
138 K2 Väike-Pakri i. Estonia
140 O3 Vaikijaur Sweden
236 B6 Vail CO U.S.A.
146 □M2 Vaila i. Scotland U.K.
156 G5 Vailly-sur-Aisne France
160 B2 Vailly-sur-Sauldre France
78 □2 Vailoa Samoa
235 G2 Vails Gate NY U.S.A.
138 K4 Väimela Estonia
138 G3 Väinameri b. Estonia
79 □8a Vaini Tongatapu Tonga
138 E5 Vaiņode Latvia
114 F8 Vaippar r. India
157 K7 Vair r. France
193 M5 Vairano Patenora Italy
193 M5 Vairano Scalo Italy
79 □9a Vairao Tahiti Fr. Polynesia
161 J9 Vaire r. France
116 E4 Vairowal Punjab India
182 G8 Vais France
161 G8 Vaison-la-Romaine France
163 H7 Vaïssac France
78 □2 Vaitogi American Samoa
77 H2 Vaitupu i. Tuvalu
78 □2 Vaiusu Samoa
160 I1 Vaivre-et-Montoille France
177 L4 Vaja Hungary
Vajrakarur Andhra Prad. India see Kanur
177 G6 Vajszló Hungary
177 H5 Vajta Hungary
208 D2 Vakaga pref. C.A.R.
208 D2 Vakaga r. C.A.R.
114 G8 Vakarai Sri Lanka
123 O3 Vakhan Tajik.
137 R5 Vakhrusheve Ukr.
123 N3 Vakhsh Tajik.
123 M3 Vakhsh r. Tajik.
Vakhstroy Tajik. see Vakhsh
134 I4 Vakhtan Rus. Fed.
122 G7 Vakīlābād Iran
127 H7 Vakīlābād Iran
142 B1 Vaksdal Norway
197 J8 Vaksince Macedonia
177 H4 Vál Hungary
100 M2 Val Rus. Fed.
176 L2 Val r. Rus. Fed.
114 G9 Valachchenai Sri Lanka
140 L5 Valådalen Sweden
140 L5 Valådalen naturreservat nature res. Sweden
182 D4 Valadares Port.
182 F1 Valadouro mts Spain
190 D3 Valais canton Switz.
177 K3 Valaliky Slovakia
134 K4 Valamaz Rus. Fed.
197 K9 Valandovo Macedonia
159 J7 Valanjou France
183 R4 Valareña Spain
177 I3 Valaská Slovakia
140 P5 Valassaaret-Björkögrund nature res. Fin.
177 G2 Valašská Polanka Czech Rep.
177 H2 Valašské Klobouky Czech Rep.
177 G2 Valašské Meziříčí Czech Rep.
198 F4 Valaxa i. Greece
227 S3 Val-Barrette Que. Can.
161 J8 Valberg France
191 Q5 Valbiska Croatia
143 N1 Valbo Sweden
187 D7 Valbona Spain
190 I3 Valbondione Italy
160 H3 Valbonnais France
161 K9 Valbonne France
183 O4 Valbornedo, Embalse de resr Spain
183 L5 Valbuena de Duero Spain
177 H2 Valča Slovakia
197 N5 Vâlcăneşti Romania
197 K5 Vâlcanului, Munţii mts Romania
177 L4 Vălcău de Jos Romania
161 J6 Val-Cenis France
259 D6 Valcheta Arg.
186 F5 Valcuerna r. Spain
191 K4 Valdagno Italy
160 I2 Valdahon France
Valdai Hills Rus. Fed. see Valdayskaya Vozvyshennost'
191 M2 Valdaora Italy
183 L4 Valdavia r. Spain
139 Q4 Valday Rus. Fed.
139 P5 Valdayskaya Vozvyshennost' hills Rus. Fed.
139 Q3 Valdayskoye, Ozero l. Rus. Fed.
186 E5 Valdealgorfa Spain
185 J3 Valdeazogues r. Spain
161 K8 Valdeblore France
185 I2 Valdecaballeros Spain
182 J9 Valdecañas, Embalse de resr Spain
182 I9 Valdecañas de Tajo Spain
183 J7 Valdecarros Spain
183 L3 Valdecebollas mt. Spain
183 M2 Valdecilla Spain
183 R8 Valdecuenca Spain
184 G2 Valdefuentes Spain
185 P2 Valdeganga Spain
183 K4 Valdeginate r. Spain
185 P5 Valdeinfierno, Embalse de resr Spain
182 I7 Valdelacasa Spain
183 J9 Valdelacasa de Tajo Spain
184 F5 Valdelamusa Spain
186 D7 Valdelinares Spain
183 R7 Valdellosa mt. Spain
190 F5 Val del Ticino, Parco della park Italy
185 J3 Valdemanco del Esteras Spain
159 P4 Val-de-Marne dept France
138 F4 Valdemārpils Latvia
143 M3 Valdemarsvik Sweden
183 Q8 Valdemeca Spain
183 G4 Valdemedé r. Spain
183 Q10 Valdemembra r. Spain
183 L7 Valdemorillo Spain
183 M8 Valdemoro Spain
183 Q8 Valdemoro-Sierra Spain
183 N7 Valdenoches Spain
261 E6 Valdense Uru.
182 H8 Valdeobispo Spain
182 H8 Valdeobispo, Embalse de resr Spain
185 M3 Valdepeñas Spain
185 L3 Valdepeñas de Jaén Spain
183 J3 Valdepiélago Spain
183 I5 Valderaduey r. Spain
183 J4 Valderas Spain
156 B5 Val-de-Reuil France
194 D7 Valderice Sicilia Italy
163 J7 Valderiès France
186 F6 Valderrobres Spain
183 K3 Valderrueda Spain
226 G5 Valders WI U.S.A.
261 G4 Valdés Arg.
259 D6 Valdés, Península pen. Arg.
183 E8 Val de Santo Domingo Spain
227 S4 Val-des-Bois Que. Can.
183 K6 Valdestillas Spain
186 F6 Valdetormo Spain
184 G3 Valdetorres Spain
183 J9 Valdeverdeja Spain
182 I4 Valdevimbre Spain
220 D3 Valdez AK U.S.A.
Valdgeym Ukr. see Dobropillya
194 G8 Val di Demone reg. Sicilia Italy
190 I3 Valdidentro Italy
183 L7 Valdihuelo mt. Spain
183 N8 Valdilecha Spain
194 G9 Val di Noto reg. Sicilia Italy
161 J6 Val-d'Isère France
190 I3 Valdisotto Italy
259 B5 Valdivia Chile
250 C3 Valdivia Col.
162 F2 Valdivienne France
158 I5 Val-d'Izé France
191 L4 Valdobbiadene Italy
157 M8 Valdoie France
156 D5 Val-d'Oise dept France
227 R3 Val-d'Or Que. Can.
183 N5 Valdosa mt. Spain
231 F10 Valdosta GA U.S.A.
141 J6 Valdres val. Norway
161 H7 Valdrôme France
183 J4 Valdunquillo Spain
158 F3 Vale Channel Is
129 D4 Vale Georgia
238 F4 Vale OR U.S.A.
197 K3 Valea lui Mihai Romania
197 M4 Valea Lungă Alba Romania
197 N5 Valea Lungă Dâmboviţa Romania
184 D6 Vale da Rosa Port.
184 C2 Vale das Mós Port.
184 D5 Vale de Açor Beja Port.
184 D2 Vale de Açor Portalegre Port.
182 D7 Vale de Cambra Port.
184 B2 Vale de Cavalos Port.
182 G8 Vale de Espinho Port.
182 F7 Vale de Estrela Port.
184 B2 Vale de Figueira Port.
184 C4 Vale de Gaio, Barragem de resr Port.
184 C4 Vale de Guiso Port.
182 F8 Vale de Prazeres Port.
184 C4 Vale de Reis Port.
182 F5 Vale de Salgueiro Port.
184 C2 Vale de Santarém Port.
182 F5 Vale de Vargo Port.
184 D5 Vale do Guadiana, Parque Natural do nature res. Port.
184 D3 Vale do Pereiro Port.
184 D2 Vale do Peso Port.
182 D7 Válega Port.
191 J5 Valeggio sul Mincio Italy
222 G4 Valemount B.C. Can.
254 F5 Valença Brazil
182 C4 Valença Port.
256 E3 Valença do Piauí Brazil
162 H1 Valençay France
163 F7 Valence Midi-Pyrénées France
161 F7 Valence Rhône-Alpes France
163 I7 Valence-d'Albigeois France
163 E8 Valence-sur-Baïse France
187 E8 Valencia Spain
187 D9 Valencia aut. comm. Spain
187 D9 Valencia prov. Spain
247 □7 Valencia Trin. and Tob.
250 D2 Valencia Venez.
187 F9 Valencia, Golfo de g. Spain
184 E2 Valencia de Alcántara Spain
182 I4 Valencia de Don Juan Spain
184 G4 Valencia de las Torres Spain
184 G4 Valencia del Mombuey Spain
184 G4 Valencia del Ventoso Spain
147 B9 Valencia Island Ireland
Valenciana, Comunidad aut. comm. Spain see Valencia
156 G3 Valenciennes France
197 O5 Vălenii de Munte Romania
161 H9 Valensole France
161 I9 Valensole, Plateau de France
192 H2 Valentano Italy
245 K6 Valente Díaz y La Loma Mex.
Valentia Spain see Valencia
160 J2 Valentigney France
100 I7 Valentin Rus. Fed.
163 F9 Valentine France
236 E4 Valentine NE U.S.A.
239 L11 Valentine TX U.S.A.
236 E4 Valentine National Wildlife Refuge nature res. NE U.S.A.
190 F5 Valenza Italy
195 L1 Valenzano Italy
92 C4 Valenzuela Luzon Phil.
183 Q7 Valenzuela Spain
185 L3 Valenzuela de Calatrava Spain
150 F5 Vale of Glamorgan admin. div. Wales U.K.
142 H1 Våler Norway
250 D2 Valera Venez.
183 P9 Valeras de Arriba Spain
161 H8 Valernes France
185 E4 Vales Mortos Port.
257 H2 Vale Verde Brazil
191 P8 Valfabbrica Italy
186 E4 Valfarta Spain
157 L7 Valfroicourt France
190 I3 Valfurva Italy
138 J4 Valga Estonia
Valga Spain see Ponte Valga
138 I2 Valgejõgi r. Estonia
161 E7 Valgorge France
190 E3 Val Grande, Parco Nazionale della nat. park Italy
190 E3 Valgrande e Monte Mottac, Riserva Naturale nature res. Italy
190 C4 Valgrisenche Italy
194 G9 Valguarnera Caropepe Sicilia Italy
235 H2 Valhalla NY U.S.A.
222 G5 Valhalla Provincial Park B.C. Can.
182 F8 Valhelhas Port.
183 Q7 Valhermoso Spain
163 G10 Valier, Mont mt. France
121 N1 Valikhanovo Kazakh.
192 B4 Valinco, Golfe de b. Corse France
256 D5 Valinhos Brazil
186 F3 Valira r. Andorra/Spain
196 H6 Valjevo Serbia
186 F6 Valjunquera Spain
138 I4 Valka Latvia
141 R6 Valkeakoski Fin.
165 I7 Valkenburg Limburg Neth.
164 F4 Valkenburg Zuid-Holland Neth.
165 H6 Valkenswaard Neth.
175 M1 Valkininkai Lith.
138 I2 Valkla Estonia
138 J1 Valko Fin.
177 I4 Valkó Hungary
Valkom Fin. see Valko
137 O4 Valky Ukr.
263 C1 Valkyrie Dome ice feature Antarctica
116 C9 Vallabhipur Gujarat India
161 F9 Vallabrègues France
187 D10 Vallada Spain
243 O7 Valladolid Mex.
183 K5 Valladolid Spain
183 K5 Valladolid prov. Spain
183 K6 Valladolises Spain
157 J7 Vallage reg. France
177 L4 Vállaj Hungary
192 F3 Vall'Alta, Cala b. Sardegna Italy
225 G2 Vallard, Lac l. Que. Can.
161 H5 Vallauris France
146 B7 Vallay i. Scotland U.K.
141 I6 Valldal Norway
187 E7 Vall d'Alba Spain
187 K8 Valldemossa Spain
142 C2 Valle Latvia
142 C2 Valle Norway
183 L2 Valle Spain
193 L2 Valle Castellana Italy
243 J4 Vallecillos Mex.
260 D2 Vallecito Arg.
250 E2 Vallecito Venez.
244 F8 Vallecitos Guerrero Mex.
243 I4 Vallecitos Nuevo León Mex.
193 K5 Vallecorsa Italy
190 E4 Valle d'Aosta admin. reg. Italy
259 E6 Valle Daza Arg.
185 J7 Valle de Abdalajís Spain
244 B5 Valle de Banderas Mex.
244 G6 Valle de Bravo Mex.
244 E4 Valle de Guadalupe Mex.
184 H5 Valle de la Serena Spain
243 J4 Valle de Matamoros Spain
242 F4 Valle de Olivos Mex.
239 K13 Valle de Rosario Mex.
184 F4 Valle de Santa Ana Spain
244 F5 Valle de Santiago Mex.
242 G4 Valle de Zaragoza Mex.
191 M3 Valle di Cadore Italy
194 F8 Valledolmo Sicilia Italy
192 B6 Valledoria Sardegna Italy
250 C2 Valledupar Col.
156 F3 Vallée de la Scarpe et de l'Escaut park France
217 □2a Vallée de Mai tourist site Seychelles
190 A2 Vallée du Doubs nature res. Switz.
225 G4 Vallée-Jonction Que. Can.
260 C2 Valle Fértil, Sierra de mts Arg.
252 D4 Valle Grande Bol.
216 □3a Vallehermoso La Gomera Canary Is
243 K5 Valle Hermoso Mex.
160 H4 Valleiry France
244 G2 Vallejo Mex.
240 J3 Vallejo CA U.S.A.
190 G4 Valle Lambro, Parco della park Italy
194 F8 Vallelunga Pratameno Sicilia Italy
190 E4 Valle Mosso Italy
140 N5 Vallen Sweden
245 K8 Valle Nacional Mex.
258 C3 Vallenar Chile
187 C7 Vallenca Spain
169 E10 Vallendar Ger.
156 I7 Vallentigny France
143 O2 Vallentuna Sweden
161 D8 Valleraugue France
192 B9 Vallermosa Sardegna Italy
193 L4 Vallerotonda Italy
216 □3f Vallesco Gran Canaria Canary Is
158 I7 Vallet France
195 □ Valletta Malta
223 L5 Valley r. Man. Can.
173 L6 Valley Ger.
150 C1 Valley Isle of Anglesey, Wales U.K.
240 O8 Valley Center CA U.S.A.
236 F2 Valley City ND U.S.A.
238 D5 Valley Falls OR U.S.A.
234 E4 Valley Forge PA U.S.A.
92 D3 Valley Head hd Luzon Phil.
232 E10 Valley Head WV U.S.A.
147 I3 Valleymount Ireland
203 G3 Valley of the Kings tourist site Egypt
240 L3 Valley Springs CA U.S.A.
230 E6 Valley Station KY U.S.A.
235 H3 Valley Stream NY U.S.A.
222 G4 Valleyview Alta Can.
234 B3 Valley View PA U.S.A.
187 D9 Vallfogona de Riucorb Spain
Vallgrund i. Fin. see Raippaluoto
162 I4 Vallières France
186 H5 Vallmoll Spain
193 O7 Vallo della Lucania Italy
161 I6 Valloire France
160 B3 Vallon-en-Sully France
161 E8 Vallon-Pont-d'Arc France
190 A2 Vallorbe Switz.
160 J4 Vallorcine France
161 I7 Vallouise France
186 H5 Valls Spain
143 K4 Vallsjön l. Sweden
141 N6 Vallsta Sweden
190 G4 Valmadrera Italy
186 D5 Valmadrid Spain
223 J5 Val Marie Sask. Can.
Valmaseda Spain see Balmaseda
185 K4 Valmayor r. Spain
183 L7 Valmayor, Embalse de resr Spain
138 I4 Valmiera Latvia
183 L8 Valmojado Spain
159 M2 Valmont France
193 J4 Valmontone Italy
161 I6 Valmorel France
156 I5 Valmy France
183 M2 Valnera mt. Spain
158 I3 Valognes France
156 E5 Valois reg. France
Valona Albania see Vlorë
184 D2 Valongo Portalegre Port.
182 D6 Valongo Porto Port.
185 M7 Válor Spain
183 K5 Valoria la Buena Spain
138 J7 Valozhyn Belarus
182 F5 Valpaços Port.
186 D3 Valpalmas Spain
222 E3 Val-Paradis Que. Can.
114 E7 Valparai Tamil Nadu India
256 B4 Valparaíso Brazil
260 B3 Valparaíso Chile
258 C4 Valparaíso admin. reg. Chile
244 D3 Valparaíso Mex.
243 P2 Valparaiso FL U.S.A.
230 D3 Valparaiso IN U.S.A.
182 H5 Valparaíso, Embalse de resr Spain
190 C4 Valpelline Italy
190 C4 Valpelline val. Italy
190 D5 Valperga Italy
114 D5 Valpoi Goa India
188 G3 Valpovo Croatia
161 C10 Valras-Plage France
161 F8 Valréas France
185 K2 Valronquillo hill Spain
161 C10 Valros France
215 K3 Vals r. S. Africa
190 G2 Vals Switz.
91 I8 Vals, Tanjung c. Papua Indon.
116 D9 Valsad Gujarat India
190 C4 Valsavarenche Italy
190 C4 Valsavarenche val. Italy
170 E1 Valse Denmark
186 F3 Valseca Spain
216 □3f Valsequillo Gran Canaria Canary Is
185 I4 Valsequillo Spain
160 H4 Valserine r. France
238 G7 Valshni Wash watercourse AZ U.S.A.
195 K3 Valsinni Italy
140 M4 Valsjöbyn Sweden
161 E7 Vals-les-Bains France
215 I3 Valspan S. Africa
215 M4 Valsrivier S. Africa
191 L4 Valstagna Italy
191 L4 Valsura r. Italy
160 F2 Val-Suzon France
136 I2 Val'tevo Rus. Fed.
161 J6 Val-Thorens France
176 F3 Valtice Czech Rep.
183 M6 Valtiendas Spain
183 Q4 Valtierra Spain
140 T5 Valtimo Fin.
217 □1b Valton Mauritius
193 J1 Valtopina Italy
198 D2 Valtou mts Greece
191 J5 Valtournenche Italy
190 B6 Val Troncea, Parco Naturale nature res. Italy
191 P6 Valtura Croatia
Valua i. Vanuatu see Mota Lava
161 B6 Valuéjols France
191 Q6 Valun Croatia
137 R3 Valuy r. Rus. Fed.
139 Q9 Valuyets Rus. Fed.
137 R3 Valuyki Rus. Fed.
135 G6 Valuyskoye Rus. Fed.
129 K4 Välväläçay r. Azer.
216 □3e Valverde El Hierro Canary Is
Valverde Dom. Rep. see Mao
184 F4 Valverde de Burguillos Spain
183 P9 Valverde de Júcar Spain
184 F5 Valverde del Camino Spain
184 G3 Valverde de Leganés Spain
182 G8 Valverde del Fresno Spain
184 H4 Valverde de Llerena Spain
183 N6 Valverde de los Arroyos Spain
184 G3 Valverde de Mérida Spain
178 C8 Valvestino, Lago di l. Italy
140 M3 Valvika Norway
138 P9 Valyasy Belarus
197 L3 Vama Satu Mare Romania
197 N3 Vama Suceava Romania
176 F1 Vamberk Czech Rep.
97 H9 Vam Co Đông r. Vietnam
97 H9 Vam Co Tây r. Vietnam
142 F6 Vamdrup Denmark
211 D7 Vamizi, Ilha i. Moz.
141 O6 Vammala Fin.
177 I4 Vámosgyörk Hungary
177 H4 Vámosmikola Hungary
177 K4 Vámospércs Hungary
177 K3 Vámosújfalu Hungary
141 Q6 Vampula Fin.
115 I3 Vamsadhara r. India
199 H4 Vamvakas, Akrotirio pt Chios Greece
127 K4 Van Turkey
129 E7 Van prov. Turkey
Van, Lake salt l. Turkey see Van Gölü
129 F5 Vanadzor Armenia
141 R6 Vanajavesi l. Fin.
138 K4 Vana-Koiola Estonia
141 L6 Vanan r. Sweden
Vananchal state India see Jharkhand
197 Q5 Vânători Galaţi Romania
197 M4 Vânători Mureş Romania
156 I6 Vanault-les-Dames France
131 L3 Vanavara Rus. Fed.
237 H8 Van Buren AR U.S.A.
231 J3 Van Buren ME U.S.A.
233 □R1 Van Buren ME U.S.A.
237 J7 Van Buren MO U.S.A.
Van Buren OH U.S.A. see Kettering
97 I8 Vân Canh Vietnam
233 □R3 Vanceboro ME U.S.A.
232 B10 Vanceburg KY U.S.A.
Vanch Tajik. see Vanj
Vanchskiy Khrebet mts Tajik. see Vanj, Qatorkŭhi
232 B11 Vancleve KY U.S.A.
235 H2 Van Cortlandtville NY U.S.A.
222 F5 Vancouver B.C. Can.
238 C4 Vancouver WA U.S.A.
87 E13 Vancouver, Cape W.A. Austr.
222 B2 Vancouver, Mount Can./U.S.A.
222 E5 Vancouver Island B.C. Can.
177 K4 Váncsod Hungary
Vanda Fin. see Vantaa
236 K6 Vandalia IL U.S.A.
232 A9 Vandalia OH U.S.A.
129 I5 Vandam Azer.
178 A5 Vandans Austria
114 F6 Vandavasi Tamil Nadu India
223 K3 Vandekerckhove Lake Man. Can.
186 G5 Vandellós Spain
160 D3 Vandenesse France
160 F2 Vandenesse-en-Auxois France
215 L2 Vanderbijlpark S. Africa
226 J4 Vanderbilt MI U.S.A.
232 F8 Vandergrift PA U.S.A.
222 E4 Vanderhoof B.C. Can.
215 I6 Vanderkloof Dam resr S. Africa
84 F3 Vanderlin Island N.T. Austr.
84 C1 Van Diemen, Cape N.T. Austr.
84 G4 Van Diemen, Cape Qld Austr.
84 D1 Van Diemen Gulf N.T. Austr.
Van Diemen's Land state Austr. see Tasmania
234 E1 Vandling PA U.S.A.
157 L6 Vandœuvre-lès-Nancy France
191 L2 Vandoies Italy
138 I3 Vändra Estonia
193 M4 Vandra r. Italy
215 N2 Vandyksdrif S. Africa
138 G6 Vandžiogala Lith.
138 F5 Vāne Latvia
Väner, Lake Sweden see Vänern
142 I3 Vänerborgsviken b. Sweden
142 J2 Vänern l. Sweden
142 I3 Vänersborg Sweden
183 L3 Vañes Spain
262 T2 Vang, Mount Antarctica
211 C6 Vanga Kenya
213 □J4 Vangaindrano Madag.
138 H4 Vangaži Latvia
97 I8 Van Gia Vietnam
129 H5 Vängli Azer.
127 K4 Van Gölü salt l. Turkey
142 C1 Vangsvatnet l. Norway
140 N2 Vangsvik Norway
223 J5 Vanguard Sask. Can.
78 □6 Vangunu i. New Georgia Is Solomon Is
78 □6 Vangunu, Mount New Georgia Is Solomon Is
164 I2 Van Harinxmakanaal canal Neth.
239 L11 Van Horn TX U.S.A.
129 D3 Vani Georgia
224 F4 Vanier Ont. Can.
78 □6 Vanikoro Islands Santa Cruz Is Solomon Is
190 C2 Vanil Noir mt. Switz.
91 J7 Vanimo P.N.G.
100 L4 Vanino Rus. Fed.
114 E6 Vanivilasa Sagara resr India
114 F6 Vaniyambadi Tamil Nadu India
123 N2 Vanj Tajik.
123 N2 Vanj, Qatorkŭhi mts Tajik.
140 O4 Vänjaurträsk Sweden
197 K6 Vânju Mare Romania
131 T3 Vankarem Rus. Fed.
141 Q6 Vankavesi l. Fin.
224 F4 Vankleek Hill Ont. Can.
233 K8 Van Lear KY U.S.A.
232 B8 Vanlue OH U.S.A.
160 □ Van Mijenfjorden inlet Svalbard
140 O5 Vännäs Sweden
156 F7 Vanne r. France
158 F6 Vannes France
225 H2 Vannes, Lac l. Que. Can.
Vannovka Kazakh. see Turar Ryskulov
140 O1 Vannøya i. Norway
140 O1 Vanntinden mt. Norway
191 L4 Vanoi r. Italy
161 J6 Vanoise, Massif de la mts France
161 J6 Vanoise, Parc National de la nat. park France
215 N4 Van Reenen S. Africa
91 I7 Van Rees, Pegunungan mts Papua Indon.
214 C7 Vanrhynsdorp S. Africa
85 H4 Vanrook Qld Austr.
85 H4 Vanrook Creek r. Qld Austr.
116 D9 Vansada Gujarat India
232 C11 Vansant VA U.S.A.
143 K1 Vansbro Sweden
142 B3 Vanse Norway
86 E2 Vansittart Bay W.A. Austr.
221 J3 Vansittart Island Nunavut Can.
142 G2 Vansjø l. Norway
215 L5 Vanstadensrus S. Africa
164 J2 Van Starkenborgh Kanaal canal Neth.
141 R6 Vantaa Fin.
138 H1 Vantaa r. Fin.
87 G9 Van Truer Tableland reg. W.A. Austr.
215 O4 Vant's Drift S. Africa
77 I3 Vanua Balavu i. Fiji
78 □5 Vanua Lava i. Vanuatu
77 I3 Vanua Levu i. Fiji
79 □7a Vanua Levu Barrier Reef Fiji
Vanua Mbalavu i. Fiji see Vanua Balavu
78 □5 Vanuatu country S. Pacific Ocean
Vanua Valavo i. Fiji see Vanua Balavu
156 I8 Vanvey France
236 M5 Van Wert OH U.S.A.
214 F9 Van Wyksdorp S. Africa
214 F6 Vanwyksvlei S. Africa
214 F6 Vanwyksvlei l. S. Africa
177 I4 Vanyarc Hungary
190 E4 Vanzone Italy
214 G2 Van Zylsrus S. Africa
78 □5 Vao New Caledonia
81 □1 Vao Tokelau
182 F4 Vao, Embalse de resr Spain
163 H7 Vaour France
176 D1 Vápenná Czech Rep.
136 H5 Vapnyarka Ukr.
184 D6 Vaqueiros Port.
161 I10 Var dept France
161 K9 Var r. France
190 H7 Vara r. Italy
142 J3 Vara Sweden
114 E5 Varada r. India
185 O2 Vara del Rey Spain
246 C2 Varadero Cuba
159 I7 Varades France
177 L5 Vărădia de Mureş Romania
161 H9 Varages France
116 C8 Varahi Gujarat India
163 H7 Varaire France
190 D6 Varaita r. Italy
138 J5 Varakļāni Latvia
206 E4 Varalé Côte d'Ivoire
177 H5 Varalja Hungary
190 E4 Varallo Italy
122 D4 Varāmīn Iran
117 I7 Varanasi Uttar Prad. India
134 L1 Varandey Rus. Fed.
140 T1 Varangerfjorden sea chan. Norway
140 T1 Varangerhalvøya pen. Norway
193 P4 Varano, Lago di lag. Italy
190 H6 Varano de'Melegari Italy
138 K6 Varapayeva Belarus
123 L4 Varas Afgh.
185 J4 Varas r. Spain
122 E8 Varāvī Iran
188 F2 Varaždin Croatia
179 N7 Varaždinske Toplice Croatia
190 F7 Varazze Italy
142 I4 Varberg Sweden
138 G3 Varbla Estonia
177 J3 Varbó Hungary
161 H6 Varces-Allières-et-Risset France
122 C5 Varcheh Iran
177 L5 Vârciorog Romania
198 C4 Varda Greece
114 F4 Vardannapet Andhra Prad. India
197 K9 Vardar r. Macedonia alt. Axios (Greece)
142 E6 Varde Denmark
142 E6 Varde r. Denmark
129 G5 Vardenis Armenia
129 G5 Vardenisi Lerr mt. Armenia
129 F6 Vardenisi Lernashght'a mts Armenia
129 G4 Vardisubani Georgia
141 P6 Vårdö Åland Fin.
140 U1 Vardø Norway
177 H5 Várdomb Hungary
198 D4 Vardousia mts Greece
138 F5 Varduva r. Lith.
139 W4 Varegovo Rus. Fed.
168 F4 Varel Ger.
260 G4 Varela Arg.
206 A3 Varela Guinea-Bissau
138 H7 Varėna Lith.
138 H7 Varėnė r. Lith.
156 A4 Varengeville-sur-Mer France
137 Q8 Varenikovskaya Rus. Fed.
129 F1 Varenikovskiy Rus. Fed.
156 B4 Varenne r. France
156 E8 Varennes-Changy France
157 J5 Varennes-en-Argonne France
160 G4 Varennes-St-Sauveur France
160 C4 Varennes-sur-Allier France
160 C2 Varennes-Vauzelles France
137 S6 Varenovka Rus. Fed.
188 G3 Vareš Bos.-Herz.
190 F4 Varese Italy
190 F4 Varese prov. Italy
190 F4 Varese, Lago di l. Italy
190 H7 Varese Ligure Italy
162 G5 Varetz France
100 H6 Varfolomeyevka Rus. Fed.
177 L4 Vârfuraşu, Vârful mt. Romania
177 L5 Vârfurile Romania
142 I3 Vårgårda Sweden
260 C4 Vargas Arg.
250 E2 Vargas admin. dist. Venez.
250 B5 Vargas Guerra Peru
254 F4 Vargem r. Brazil
257 G4 Vargem Alta Brazil
256 E2 Vargem Grande Brazil
256 D4 Vargem Grande do Sul Brazil
257 F4 Varginha Brazil
142 B3 Varhaug Norway
197 J4 Variaş Romania
163 F9 Varilhes France
177 H2 Varín Slovakia
143 L2 Väringen l. Sweden
260 D4 Varita, Pampa de la plain Arg.
Varkana Iran see Gorgān
141 S5 Varkaus Fin.
138 M6 Varkhi Belarus
169 I8 Varloosen (Niemetal) Ger.
140 □D1 Varmahlíð Iceland
142 I2 Varmeln l. Sweden
142 I2 Värmland county Sweden
142 I2 Värmland reg. Sweden
142 I3 Värmland naturreservat nature res. Sweden
142 J3 Värmlandsnäs i. Sweden
143 J2 Värmlandsskärgårdens naturreservat nature res. Sweden
197 P7 Varna Bulg.
114 C4 Varna r. India
191 L2 Varna Italy
120 I1 Varna Rus. Fed.
143 K4 Värnamo Sweden
142 J1 Värnäs Sweden
134 I4 Varnavino Rus. Fed.
137 R8 Varnavinskoye Vodokhranilishche resr Rus. Fed.
138 F6 Varniai Lith.
138 K3 Varnja Estonia
Várnjárga pen. Norway see Varangerhalvøya
176 D1 Varnsdorf Czech Rep.
231 G9 Varnville SC U.S.A.
138 J7 Varnyany Belarus
138 K6 Varonka Belarus
177 I5 Városföld Hungary
Varosha Cyprus see Varosia
128 B3 Varosia Cyprus
188 F3 Varoška Rijeka Bos.-Herz.
177 G4 Városlőd Hungary
140 S5 Varpaisjärvi Fin.
177 H4 Várpalota Hungary
168 G5 Varrel Ger.
140 T3 Värriön luonnonpuisto nature res. Fin.
162 E4 Vars Poitou-Charentes France
161 J7 Vars Provence-Alpes-Côte d'Azur France
161 J7 Vars, Col de pass France
197 M4 Vârşag Romania
123 J8 Varsak Afgh.
199 L6 Varsak Turkey
196 J4 Vârşand Romania
177 I3 Varsány Hungary
134 I2 Varsh, Ozero l. Rus. Fed.
190 H6 Varsi Italy
141 Q6 Varsinais-Suomi reg. Fin.
138 K4 Värska Estonia
164 I4 Varsseveld Neth.
143 N2 Värsta Sweden
Vartashen Azer. see Oğuz
140 I5 Vartdalsfjorden inlet Norway
142 H2 Varteig Norway
198 D5 Vartholomio Greece
127 J4 Varto Turkey
197 L6 Vârtop Romania
197 K4 Vârtop, Pasul pass Romania
148 E7 Vartry Reservoir Ireland
129 D3 Varts'ikhe Georgia
140 S4 Värtsilä Fin.
137 L3 Varva Ukr.
260 B5 Varvarco Campos, Lago l. Arg.
137 O5 Varvarivka Dnipropetrovs'ka Oblast' Ukr.
137 Q3 Varvarivka Kharkivs'ka Oblast' Ukr.
136 F3 Varvarivka Khmel'nyts'ka Oblast' Ukr.
137 R3 Varvarovka Rus. Fed.
177 L3 Vary Ukr.
136 D3 Varyazh Ukr.
130 I3 Var'yegan Rus. Fed.
122 E5 Varzaneh Iran
122 B2 Varzaqān Iran
254 F3 Várzea Alegre Brazil
257 E2 Várzea da Palma Brazil
254 E3 Várzea Grande Brazil
190 G6 Varzi Italy
134 G1 Varzino Rus. Fed.
190 E3 Varzo Italy
123 M2 Varzob Tajik.
134 G2 Varzuga Rus. Fed.
157 G7 Varzy France
176 F4 Vas county Hungary
Vasa Fin. see Vaasa
254 F4 Vasa Barris r. Brazil
177 I4 Vasad Hungary
114 C3 Vasai Mahar. India
138 H2 Vasalemma Estonia
138 H2 Vasalemma r. Estonia
193 I3 Vasanello Italy
177 H5 Vásárosdombó Hungary
177 L3 Vásárosnamény Hungary
184 D5 Vascão r. Port.
197 K4 Vaşcău Romania
134 I2 Vashka r. Rus. Fed.
136 E5 Vashkivtsi Ukr.
129 H4 Vashlovanis Nakrdzali nature res. Georgia
Vasht Iran see Khāsh
134 I3 Vasilevo Rus. Fed.
198 E2 Vasilika Greece
198 B4 Vasiliki Lefkada Greece
175 M2 Vasilishki Belarus
Vasilkov Ukr. see Vasyl'kiv
Vasilkovka Ukr. see Vasyl'kivka
134 I4 Vasil'sursk Rus. Fed.
136 I1 Vasilyevichy Belarus
135 H6 Vasil'yevka Rus. Fed.
138 K4 Vasil'yevo Rus. Fed.
139 S4 Vasil'yevskiy Mokh Rus. Fed.
139 N8 Vas'kavichy Belarus
138 F1 Vaskijärven luonnonpuisto nature res. Fin.
141 Q5 Vaskivesi Fin.
138 K2 Vasknarva Estonia
136 H2 Vas'kovichi Ukr.
177 H5 Vaskút Hungary
162 D2 Vasles France
197 P4 Vaslui Romania
143 K1 Väsman l. Sweden
177 K3 Vasmegyer Hungary
208 C2 Vassako-Bolo, Réserve National Intégral de la nature res. C.A.R.
227 K6 Vassar MI U.S.A.
141 L6 Vassbo Sweden
141 I6 Vassenden Norway
142 F1 Vassfaret og Vidalen park Norway
161 G7 Vassieux-en-Vercors France
162 H4 Vassivière, Lac de l. France
176 F4 Vas-Soproni-síkság hills Hungary
257 F5 Vassouras Brazil
159 J4 Vassy France
176 F4 Vasszécseny Hungary
Vastan Turkey see Gevaş
140 N5 Västana Sweden
138 F1 Västanfjärd Fin.
140 N4 Västansjö Sweden
138 I3 Vastemõisa Estonia
140 N3 Vastenjaure l. Sweden
143 M2 Västerås Sweden
140 M4 Västerbotten county Sweden
141 M6 Västerdalälven r. Sweden
140 N3 Västerfjäll Sweden
142 J4 Västergötland reg. Sweden
143 O2 Västerhaninge Sweden
140 N5 Västernorrland county Sweden
143 M4 Västervik Sweden
143 L2 Västlandasjön l. Sweden
143 L2 Västmanland county Sweden
193 N3 Vasto Italy
168 K4 Vastorf Ger.
142 J2 Västra Ämtervik Sweden
142 J4 Västra Fegen l. Sweden
142 I3 Västra Götaland county Sweden
140 P5 Västra Kvarken sea chan. Sweden
140 N4 Västra Ormsjö Sweden
142 I2 Västra Silen l. Sweden
138 J3 Vastse-Kuuste Estonia
176 F4 Vasvár Hungary
137 L5 Vasylivka Kirovohrads'ka Oblast' Ukr.
137 N3 Vasylivka Sums'ka Oblast' Ukr.
137 O6 Vasylivka Zaporiz'ka Oblast' Ukr.
136 J3 Vasyl'kiv Ukr.
137 P5 Vasyl'kivka Ukr.
175 M6 Vasyuchyn Ukr.
137 L4 Vasyutyntsi Ukr.
177 G4 Vaszar Hungary
177 L5 Vaţa de Jos Romania
162 H1 Vatan France
143 O4 Väte Gotland Sweden
Vaté i. Vanuatu see Éfaté
146 C7 Vaternish Point Scotland U.K.
146 A9 Vatersay Western Isles, Scotland U.K.
146 A9 Vatersay i. Scotland U.K.
173 L5 Vaterstetten Ger.
198 D6 Vatheia Greece
Vathi Greece see Ithaki
Vathí Greece see Vathy
199 H5 Vathy Voreio Aigaio Greece
199 I6 Vati Rodos Greece
79 □7a Vatia Point Viti Levu Fiji
193 I4 Vatican City Europe
195 J6 Vaticano, Capo c. Italy
Vaticano, Città del Europe see Vatican City
78 □6 Vatilau i. Solomon Is
Vatiu i. Cook Is see Atiu
140 □E1 Vatnajökull ice cap Iceland
140 I5 Vatne Norway
77 I3 Vatoa i. Fiji
213 □K3 Vatomandry Madag.
199 H3 Vatousa Lesvos Greece
197 N3 Vatra Dornei Romania
177 J4 Vatta Hungary
Vätter, Lake Sweden see Vättern
143 K3 Vättern l. Sweden
143 N1 Vattholma Sweden
141 N6 Vattrång Sweden
79 □7a Vatu-i-Cake i. Fiji
79 □7a Vatu-i-Ra Channel Fiji
Vatu-i-Thake i. Fiji see Vatu-i-Cake
79 □7a Vatukoula Viti Levu Fiji
79 □7 Vatulele i. Fiji
159 J3 Vaubadon France
157 J6 Vaubecourt France
156 G7 Vauchassis France
160 D2 Vauclaix France
161 G8 Vaucluse dept France
161 G9 Vaucluse, Monts de mts France
160 H1 Vauconcourt-Nervezain France
157 K6 Vaucouleurs France
190 B2 Vaud canton Switz.
157 L7 Vaudémont France
156 G7 Vaudeurs France
84 C7 Vaughan Springs N.T. Austr.
239 L9 Vaughn NM U.S.A.
160 F5 Vaugneray France
160 D1 Vault-de-Lugny France
160 F5 Vaulx-en-Velin France
160 G5 Vaulx-Milieu France
250 D4 Vaupés dept Col.
250 D4 Vaupés r. Col.
224 E2 Vauquelin r. Que. Can.
161 H9 Vauvenargues France
161 E9 Vauvert France
157 L8 Vauvillers France
160 D2 Vaux, Étang de l. France
157 J5 Vaux-devant-Damloup France
223 H5 Vauxhall Alta Can.
156 E6 Vaux-le-Pénil France
162 B4 Vaux-sur-Mer France
165 I9 Vaux-sur-Sûre Belgium
116 C7 Vav Gujarat India
213 □K3 Vavatenina Madag.
77 I3 Vava'u i. Tonga
79 □8 Vava'u Group is Tonga
157 J6 Vavincourt France
Vavitao i. Îs Australes Fr. Polynesia see Raivavae
206 D5 Vavoua Côte d'Ivoire
134 J4 Vavozh Rus. Fed.
114 G8 Vavuniya Sri Lanka
138 K7 Vawkalata Belarus
139 I8 Vawkavichy Belarus
138 H8 Vawkavysk Belarus
138 H8 Vawkavyskaye Wzvyshsha hills Belarus
143 O2 Vaxholm Sweden
143 K4 Växjö Sweden
97 F10 Vay, Đao i. Vietnam

114 F6 Vayalpad Andhra Prad. India
Vayenga Rus. Fed. see Severomorsk
130 G2 Vaygach, Ostrov i. Rus. Fed.
114 E7 Vayittiri Kerala India
129 G6 Vayk' Armenia
140 S2 Väylä Fin.
162 H6 Vayrac France
162 F4 Vayres France
256 D2 Vazante Brazil
Vazáš Sweden see Vittangi
129 G5 Vazashen Armenia
177 I2 Važec Slovakia
139 R1 Vazhinka r. Rus. Fed.
129 G4 Vaziani Georgia
213 □J3 Vazobe mt. Madag.
261 G6 Vázquez Arg.
139 R6 Vazuza r. Rus. Fed.
139 R6 Vazuzskoye Vodokhranilishche resr Rus. Fed.
176 D3 Včelná Czech Rep.
Veaikevárri Sweden see Svappavaara
97 F8 Veal Vêng Cambodia
160 E5 Veauche France
142 J6 Veberöd Sweden
140 P4 Vebomark Sweden
161 D8 Vebron France
190 I8 Vecchiano Italy
177 K3 Vechec Slovakia
169 J6 Vechelde Ger.
164 J3 Vecht r. Neth. alt. Vechte (Germany)
168 F5 Vechta Ger.
169 C5 Vechte r. Ger. alt. Vecht (Neth.)
216 □3f Vecindario Gran Canaria Canary Is
182 I7 Vecinos Spain
169 K7 Veckenstedt Ger.
169 I8 Veckerhagen (Reinhardshagen) Ger.
138 G5 Vecmiķeļi Latvia
177 I4 Vecsés Hungary
176 E2 Vectec hill Czech Rep.
138 H5 Vecumnieki Latvia
Vedana Rus. Fed. see Vedeno
114 F7 Vedaranniyam Tamil Nadu India
114 E7 Vedasandur Tamil Nadu India
142 I4 Veddige Sweden
197 M6 Vedea Argeș Romania
197 N7 Vedea Giurgiu Romania
197 N7 Vedea r. Romania
191 M4 Vedelago Italy
161 F9 Vedène France
129 H3 Vedeno Rus. Fed.
143 L2 Vedevåg Sweden
129 F6 Vedi Armenia
261 G4 Vedia Arg.
134 F3 Vedlozero Rus. Fed.
137 S5 Vedmezha r. Ukr.
182 D3 Vedra Spain
187 H10 Vedrà, Illa de es i. Spain
161 C6 Védrines-St-Loup France
136 J1 Vedrych r. Belarus
137 S2 Veduga r. Rus. Fed.
164 K2 Veendam Neth.
164 I4 Veenendaal Neth.
164 J2 Veenhuizen Neth.
168 D4 Veenhusen Ger.
164 K3 Veenoord Neth.
146 □N2 Veensgarth Shetland, Scotland U.K.
164 I2 Veenwouden Neth.
164 E5 Veere Neth.
168 H4 Veerse r. Ger.
164 E5 Veerse Meer resr Neth.
140 L4 Vefsnfjord sea chan. Norway
140 K4 Vega i. Norway
237 D8 Vega TX U.S.A.
247 □1 Vega Alta Puerto Rico
247 □1 Vega Baja Puerto Rico
182 I3 Vegacervera Spain
245 K5 Vega de Alatorre Mex.
182 G3 Vega de Espinareda Spain
182 F2 Vegadeo Spain
183 M2 Vega de Pas Spain
216 □3f Vega de San Mateo Gran Canaria Canary Is
182 I6 Vega de Tirados Spain
182 G3 Vega de Valcarce Spain
183 J5 Vega de Valdetronco Spain
183 M6 Veganzones Spain
142 E3 Vegar l. Norway
182 H3 Vegarienza Spain
142 E3 Vegarshei Norway
183 J3 Vegas del Condado Spain
183 L7 Vegas de Matute Spain
164 I5 Veghel Neth.
195 N3 Veglie Italy
198 C2 Vegoritida, Limni l. Greece
159 K6 Vègre r. France
223 H4 Vegreville Alta Can.
252 A2 Végueta Peru
138 K1 Vehkalahti Fin.
170 F4 Vehlow Ger.
141 P6 Vehmaa Fin.
123 N6 Vehoa Pak.
123 N6 Vehoa r. Pak.
140 S1 Veidneset Norway
159 M7 Veigné France
160 I4 Veigy-Foncenex France
169 K10 Veilsdorf Ger.
Veinticinco de Mayo Buenos Aires Arg. see 25 de Mayo
Veinticinco de Mayo La Pampa Arg. see 25 de Mayo
Veinticinco de Mayo Mendoza Arg. see 25 de Mayo
Veinticinco de Mayo Uru. see 25 de Mayo
251 H5 Veiros Brazil
184 D3 Veiros Port.
123 M9 Veirwaro Pak.
175 L1 Veisiejai l. Lith.
138 G7 Veisiejis Lith.
173 J2 Veitsbronn Ger.
179 M4 Veitsch Austria
179 L4 Veitsch mt. Austria
172 H2 Veitshöchheim Ger.
140 R4 Veitsiluoto Fin.
138 E6 Veiviržas r. Lith.
192 I3 Vejano Italy
142 F6 Vejen Denmark
184 H8 Vejer de la Frontera Spain
142 F6 Vejle Denmark
142 F6 Vejle county Denmark
173 O2 Vejprnice Czech Rep.
176 C1 Vejprty Czech Rep.
168 J1 Vejsnæs Nakke pt Denmark
250 C1 Vela, Cabo de la c. Col.
116 D9 Velachha Gujarat India
183 K9 Velada Spain
188 F4 Vela Luka Croatia
183 O6 Velamazán Spain
242 H5 Velardena Mex.
216 □1c Velas São Jorge Azores
242 □Q12 Vèlas, Cabo c. Costa Rica
245 I3 Velasco Mex.
258 D3 Velasco, Sierra de mts Arg.
113 □1 Velassary i. S. Male Maldives
177 K3 Veľaty Slovakia
161 G9 Velaux France
188 E3 Vela Vrata, Kanal sea chan. Croatia
161 D6 Velay reg. France
122 E8 Velāyat Iran
258 G4 Velázquez Uru.
169 D8 Velbert Ger.
173 L3 Velburg Ger.
197 K8 Velbŭzhdki Prokhod pass Macedonia
214 C8 Velddrif S. Africa
165 D6 Veldegem Belgium
173 L2 Velden Bayern Ger.
173 M5 Velden Bayern Ger.
165 J6 Velden Neth.
179 J6 Velden am Wörther See Austria
165 H6 Veldhoven Neth.
114 E5 Veldurti Andhra Prad. India
188 E3 Velebit mts Croatia
188 E3 Velebitski Kanal sea chan. Croatia
185 O6 Velefique Spain
197 P8 Veleka r. Bulg.
169 C7 Velen Ger.
177 H4 Velence Hungary
177 H4 Velencei-tó l. Hungary
188 E2 Velenje Slovenia
197 J9 Veles Macedonia
196 H9 Velës, Mali i mt. Albania
176 D3 Velešín Czech Rep.
191 Q6 Vele Srakane i. Croatia
185 M6 Veleta, Pico mt. Spain
188 F4 Velež mts Bos.-Herz.
250 C3 Vélez Col.
185 O5 Vélez-Blanco Spain
185 M7 Vélez de Benaudalla Spain
185 K7 Vélez-Málaga Spain
185 O5 Vélez-Rubio Spain
140 L4 Velfjorden inlet Norway
170 G2 Velgast Ger.
256 D3 Velhas r. Brazil
257 E2 Velhas r. Brazil
Velibaba Turkey see Aras
135 I7 Velichayevskoye Rus. Fed.
136 E4 Velika Berezovytsya Ukr.
196 J7 Velika Drenova Serbia
188 F3 Velika Gorica Croatia
136 E2 Velika Hlusha Ukr.
188 E3 Velika Kapela mts Croatia
188 E3 Velika Kladuša Bos.-Herz.
188 F3 Velika Mlaka Croatia
196 J6 Velika Morava canal Serbia
136 F2 Velika Ozera Ukr.
176 G6 Velika Pisanica Croatia
196 J6 Velika Plana Serbia
179 K8 Velika Račna Slovenia
179 K7 Velika Rogatec mt. Slovenia
134 J4 Velikaya Rus. Fed.
134 J4 Velikaya r. Rus. Fed.
131 S3 Velikaya r. Rus. Fed.
138 L4 Velikaya r. Rus. Fed.
134 F3 Velikaya Guba Rus. Fed.
100 J6 Velikaya Kema Rus. Fed.
Velikaya Novoselka Ukr. see Velyka Novosilka
137 L1 Velikaya Topal' Rus. Fed.
179 K8 Velike Lašče Slovenia
188 F4 Veliki Drvenik i. Croatia
176 G6 Veliki Grđevac Croatia
196 J7 Veliki Jastrebac mts Serbia
136 E4 Veliki Kunynets' Ukr.
197 O7 Veliki Preslav Bulg.
188 E3 Veliki Risnjak mt. Croatia
197 J7 Veliki Šiljegovac Serbia
197 K8 Veliki Strešer mt. Serbia
196 I6 Veliki Šturac mt. Serbia
139 N5 Velikiye Luki Rus. Fed.
137 K2 Velikiy Lystven Ukr.
136 C4 Velikiy Lyubin' Ukr.
139 O3 Velikiy Novgorod Rus. Fed.
134 I3 Velikiy Ustyug Rus. Fed.
137 T3 Velikoarkhangel'skoye Rus. Fed.
139 X6 Velikodvorskiy Rus. Fed.
137 Q3 Velikomikhaylovka Rus. Fed.
114 F5 Velikonda Range hills India
139 Q4 Velikooktyabr'skiy Rus. Fed.
176 F6 Veliko Trojstvo Croatia
197 N7 Veliko Tŭrnovo Bulg.
129 D4 Veliköy Turkey
139 T2 Velikoye Vologodskaya Oblast' Rus. Fed.
139 W4 Velikoye Yaroslavskaya Oblast' Rus. Fed.
139 X6 Velikoye, Ozero l. Ryazanskaya Oblast' Rus. Fed.
139 T4 Velikoye, Ozero l. Tverskaya Oblast' Rus. Fed.
186 F4 Velilla de Cinca Spain
186 E5 Velilla de Ebro Spain
Velilla de Guardo Spain see Velilla del Río Carrión
183 K3 Velilla del Río Carrión Spain
185 L6 Velillas r. Spain
188 E3 Veli Lošinj Croatia
196 G8 Velimlje Montenegro
163 E6 Vélines France
206 B3 Vélingara Kolda Senegal
206 B3 Vélingara Louga Senegal
197 M8 Velingrad Bulg.
193 J2 Velino r. Italy
193 K3 Velino, Monte mt. Italy
138 G6 Veliuona Lith.
139 O6 Velizh Rus. Fed.
176 F2 Velká Bíteš Czech Rep.
176 D1 Velká Dobrá Czech Rep.
177 K2 Veľká Domaša, Vodná nádrž resr Slovakia
177 H3 Veľká Fatra mts Slovakia
177 I3 Veľká Fatra park Slovakia
176 G2 Velká Haná r. Czech Rep.
173 N2 Velká Hleďsebe Czech Rep.
177 G3 Velká Javořina hill Czech Rep./Slovakia
177 K2 Veľká Javořina mt. Slovakia
177 H3 Veľká Lehota Slovakia
177 H2 Veľká Lúka mt. Slovakia
177 I3 Veľká nad Ipľom Slovakia
177 H2 Velká Polom Czech Rep.
Veľká Rača mt. Pol./Slovakia see Wielka Racza
176 F3 Velké Bílovice Czech Rep.
171 J9 Velké Březno Czech Rep.
177 L3 Veľké Kapušany Slovakia
177 H2 Velké Karlovice Czech Rep.
179 P2 Veľké Leváre Slovakia
176 G1 Velké Losiny Czech Rep.
177 H3 Veľké Lovce Slovakia
177 H4 Veľké Ludince Slovakia
176 F2 Velké Meziříčí Czech Rep.
176 F3 Velké Němčice Czech Rep.
176 F3 Velké Pavlovice Czech Rep.
177 G3 Veľké Rípňany Slovakia
177 L3 Veľké Trakany Slovakia
177 H3 Veľké Uherce Slovakia
138 E1 Velkua Fin.
177 J3 Veľký Blh Slovakia
177 H3 Veľký Ďur Slovakia
177 H2 Veľký Javorník mt. Slovakia
177 I2 Veľký Kriváň mt. Slovakia
177 I3 Veľký Krtíš Slovakia
177 H3 Veľký Kýr Slovakia
177 G3 Veľký Lopeník hill Czech Rep.
177 G4 Veľký Meder Slovakia
177 K2 Veľký Šariš Slovakia
177 H3 Veľký Tribeč hill Slovakia
176 G2 Velký Týnec Czech Rep.
176 B2 Velký Zvon hill Czech Rep.
179 J6 Vellach r. Austria
78 □6 Vella Gulf sea chan. New Georgia Is Solomon Is
168 K4 Vellahn Ger.
78 □6 Vella Lavella i. New Georgia Is Solomon Is
114 F7 Vellar r. India
172 H3 Vellberg Ger.
182 E4 Velle, Embalse de resr Spain
193 J4 Velletri Italy
160 J2 Vellevans France
160 H1 Vellexon-Queutrey-et-Vaudey France
142 J6 Vellinge Sweden
183 O8 Vellisca Spain
169 I8 Vellmar Ger.
114 F6 Vellore Tamil Nadu India
186 F2 Vellos r. Spain
131 K3 Vel'mo r. Rus. Fed.
198 D5 Velo Greece
157 J4 Velosnes France
165 H7 Velp r. Belgium
164 I5 Velp Neth.
169 K6 Velpke Ger.
134 H3 Vel'sk Rus. Fed.
Velsuna Italy see Orvieto
134 J1 Vel't Rus. Fed.
170 H5 Velten Ger.
169 K6 Veltheim (Ohe) Ger.
176 D1 Veltrusy Czech Rep.
191 L2 Velturno Italy
164 H4 Veluwe reg. Neth.
164 I4 Veluwemeer l. Neth.
164 I4 Veluwezoom, Nationaal Park nat. park Neth.
236 E1 Velva ND U.S.A.
176 D1 Velvary Czech Rep.
198 D2 Velventos Greece
139 P4 Vel'ye, Ozero l. Rus. Fed.
137 L4 Velyka Andrusivka Ukr.
137 P4 Velyka Babka Ukr.
137 M4 Velyka Bahachka Ukr.
137 N6 Velyka Bilozerka Ukr.
137 N6 Velyka Bilozerka r. Ukr.
137 L4 Velyka Burimka Ukr.
136 J3 Velyka Dymerka Ukr.
175 L6 Velyka Horozhanna Ukr.
136 H5 Velyka Kisnytsya Ukr.
137 P4 Velyka Komyshuvakha Ukr.
177 M3 Velyka Kopanya Ukr.
137 K7 Velyka Korenykha Ukr.
137 M6 Velyka Kostromka Ukr.
137 M6 Velyka Lepetykha Ukr.
136 I6 Velyka Mykhaylivka Ukr.
137 P6 Velyka Novosilka Ukr.
137 M6 Velyka Oleksandrivka Ukr.
137 O3 Velyka Pysarivka Ukr.
137 N4 Velyka Rublivka Ukr.
137 L5 Velyka Severynka Ukr.
136 G3 Velyka Tsvilya Ukr.
137 J5 Velyka Vys' r. Ukr.
137 K5 Velyka Vyska Ukr.
137 N6 Velyka Znam"yanka Ukr.
177 L3 Velyki Kom"yaty Ukr.
137 L7 Velyki Kopani Ukr.
136 H4 Velyki Korovyntsi Ukr.
137 M4 Velyki Krynky Ukr.
177 L3 Velyki Luchky Ukr.
136 D3 Velyki Mosty Ukr.
137 M3 Velyki Sorochyntsi Ukr.
137 L4 Velykyi Khutir Ukr.
136 J7 Velykyi Kuyal'nyk r. Ukr.
137 M2 Velykyi Sambir Ukr.
136 J7 Velykodolyns'ke Ukr.
137 O5 Velykomykhaylivka Dnipropetrovs'ka Oblast' Ukr.
137 P6 Velykomykhaylivka Dnipropetrovs'ka Oblast' Ukr.
137 O5 Velykooleksandrivka Ukr.
137 K6 Velykoserbulivka Ukr.
136 B5 Velykyy Bereznyy Ukr.
137 Q3 Velykyy Burluk Ukr.
136 D6 Velykyy Bychkiv Ukr.
Velykyy Tokmak Ukr. see Tokmak
134 K3 Vel'yu r. Rus. Fed.
114 F3 Vemalwada Andhra Prad. India
264 J8 Vema Seamount sea feature S. Atlantic Ocean
265 I5 Vema Trench sea feature Indian Ocean
114 E8 Vembanad Lake India
177 H5 Véménd Hungary
100 M5 Vemor'ye Sakhalin Rus. Fed.
114 F5 Vempalle Andhra Prad. India
142 I6 Ven i. Sweden
192 C3 Venaco Corse France
244 F3 Venado Mex.
242 □R12 Venado, Isla del i. Nic.
245 I5 Venados r. Mex.
261 G3 Venado Tuerto Arg.
193 M5 Venafro Italy
251 F3 Venamo r. Venez. alt. Wenamu (Guyana)
251 F3 Venamo, Cerro mt. Venez.
158 H8 Venansault France
160 E1 Venarey-les-Laumes France
190 D5 Venaria Italy
193 K2 Venarotta Italy
161 K7 Venasca Italy
161 K9 Vence France
251 F6 Vencedor Brazil
256 C5 Venceslau Bráz Brazil
183 M6 Vencías, Embalse de las resr Spain
138 H7 Venciūnai Lith.
191 L5 Venda, Monte hill Italy
184 A3 Venda do Pinheiro Port.
257 G4 Venda Nova Brazil
182 E5 Venda Nova, Barragem de resr Port.
161 D9 Vendargues France
184 B3 Vendas de Azeitão Port.
184 C3 Vendas Novas Port.
160 C4 Vendat France
162 B5 Vendays-Montalivet France
158 I8 Vendée dept France
162 C3 Vendée r. France
157 O6 Vendenheim France
159 L8 Vendeuvre-du-Poitou France
156 H7 Vendeuvre-sur-Barse France
195 I10 Vendicari, Isola i. Sicilia Italy
134 I3 Vendinga Rus. Fed.
184 D4 Vendinha Port.
159 N8 Vendœuvres France
156 B8 Vendôme France
184 G4 Vendoval r. Spain
Vendrell Spain see El Vendrell
136 G5 Vendychany Ukr.
250 C4 Venecia Col.
244 G2 Venegas Mex.
161 G9 Venelles France
163 I8 Vénès France
191 M5 Veneta, Laguna lag. Italy
Venetia Italy see Venezia
191 L5 Veneto admin. reg. Italy
139 V7 Venev Rus. Fed.
191 M5 Venezia Italy
191 N4 Venezia prov. Italy
Venezia, Golfo di g. Europe see Venice, Gulf of
251 E3 Venezuela country S. America
250 D2 Venezuela, Golfo de g. Venez.
264 E4 Venezuelan Basin sea feature S. Atlantic Ocean
114 C5 Vengurla Mahar. India
164 H3 Venhuizen Neth.
182 I6 Venialbo Spain
220 C4 Veniaminof Volcano AK U.S.A.
Venice Italy see Venezia
231 F12 Venice FL U.S.A.
237 K11 Venice LA U.S.A.
188 D3 Venice, Gulf of Europe
190 H3 Venina r. Italy
160 F5 Vénissieux France
156 F5 Venizel France
141 L6 Venjan Sweden
114 F6 Venkatagiri Andhra Prad. India
114 G3 Venkatapalem Orissa India
114 G3 Venkatapuram Andhra Prad. India
165 J6 Venlo Neth.
142 D3 Vennesla Norway
142 E5 Venø Bugt b. Denmark
193 P6 Venosa Italy
193 P5 Venosa r. Italy
191 I2 Venosta, Val val. Italy
156 G8 Venoy France
164 I5 Venray Neth.
178 C6 Vent Austria
79 □9 Vent, Îles du is Arch. de la Société Fr. Polynesia
138 F5 Venta r. Latvia/Lith.
138 F5 Venta Lith.
161 G9 Ventabren France
161 K9 Ventabren, Mont mt. France
183 L5 Venta de Baños Spain
185 K4 Venta del Charco Spain
187 C9 Venta del Moro Spain
185 M4 Venta de los Santos Spain
182 I1 Venta las Ranas Spain
261 F6 Ventana, Sierra de la hills Arg.
258 E5 Ventana, Sierra de la mts Arg.
256 B6 Ventania Brazil
182 G2 Venta Nueva Spain
185 L6 Ventas de Huelma Spain
185 K7 Ventas de Zafarraya Spain
161 H8 Ventavon France
215 L4 Ventersburg S. Africa
215 K2 Ventersdorp S. Africa
215 L2 Venterskroon S. Africa
215 J6 Venterstad S. Africa
161 D7 Venteuges France
192 C5 Ventilegne, Golfe de b. Corse France
190 D8 Ventimiglia Italy
192 C4 Ventiseri Corse France
259 C6 Ventisquero mt. Arg.
151 J6 Ventnor Isle of Wight, England U.K.
235 G6 Ventnor City NJ U.S.A.
193 K6 Ventotene, Isola i. Italy
161 G8 Ventoux, Mont mt. France
170 E3 Ventschow Ger.
138 E4 Ventspils Latvia
251 E3 Ventuari r. Venez.
240 M7 Ventura CA U.S.A.
79 □9a Vénus, Pointe pt Tahiti Fr. Polynesia
83 J8 Venus Bay Vic. Austr.
Venusia Italy see Venosa
244 D6 Venustiano Mex.
245 N9 Venustiano Carranza Chiapas Mex.
245 J5 Venustiano Carranza Puebla Mex.
243 I4 Venustiano Carranza, Presa resr Mex.
192 C3 Venzolasca Corse France
191 O3 Venzone Italy
176 F4 Vép Hungary
137 N3 Vepryk Ukr.
139 R1 Vepsovskaya Vozvyshennost' hills Rus. Fed.
258 E3 Vera Arg.
185 P6 Vera Spain
253 F6 Verá, Lago l. Para.
252 D2 Vera Cruz Amazonas Brazil
256 C5 Vera Cruz São Paulo Brazil
245 K6 Veracruz Mex.
Vera Cruz Mex. see Veracruz
245 J5 Veracruz state Mex.
184 D4 Vera Cruz Port.
234 E3 Vera Cruz PA U.S.A.
186 D2 Veral r. Spain
255 C9 Veranópolis Brazil
116 C9 Veraval Gujarat India
261 G2 Vera y Pintado Arg.
136 E3 Verba Rivnens'ka Oblast' Ukr.
136 D3 Verba Volyns'ka Oblast' Ukr.
190 F4 Verbania Italy
235 H1 Verbank NY U.S.A.
190 E3 Verbano-Cusio-Ossola prov. Italy
156 E5 Verberie France
193 P8 Verbicaro Italy
190 C3 Verbier Switz.
139 U5 Verbilki Rus. Fed.
137 L5 Verblyuzhka Ukr.
137 O6 Verbove Ukr.
136 E4 Verbovets' Ukr.
135 H5 Verbovskiy Rus. Fed.
137 N7 Verby Ukr.
190 G3 Verceia Italy
190 E5 Vercelli Italy
190 E5 Vercelli prov. Italy
160 I2 Vercel-Villedieu-le-Camp France
170 G3 Verchen Ger.
161 G7 Vercors reg. France
161 G7 Vercors, Parc Naturel Régional du nature res. France
Vercovicium tourist site England U.K. see Housesteads
179 J8 Verd Slovenia
139 X8 Verda r. Rus. Fed.
161 I8 Verdaches France
140 K5 Verdalsøra Norway
259 D6 Verde r. Arg.
256 B2 Verde r. Brazil
256 B3 Verde r. Brazil
256 B4 Verde r. Brazil
256 C3 Verde r. Brazil
256 D2 Verde r. Brazil
257 E4 Verde r. Brazil
254 E4 Verde r. Brazil
253 F3 Verde r. Brazil
253 G2 Verde r. Brazil
244 D5 Verde r. Aguascalientes/Jalisco Mex.
242 F4 Verde r. Chihuahua/Durango Mex.
245 I9 Verde r. Guerrero/Oaxaca Mex.
245 H4 Verde r. Mex.
245 J10 Verde r. Mex.
253 F5 Verde r. Para.
185 L7 Verde r. Spain
185 M6 Verde r. Spain
241 U8 Verde r. AZ U.S.A.
Verde, Cabo c. Senegal see Vert, Cap
261 F6 Verde, Península pen. Arg.
257 F1 Verde Grande r. Brazil
92 C5 Verde Island Passage Phil.
168 H5 Verden (Aller) Ger.
254 E5 Verde Pequeno r. Brazil
240 M2 Verdi NV U.S.A.
237 H8 Verdigris r. KS U.S.A.
198 C3 Verdikoussa Greece
256 B2 Verdinho r. Brazil
256 B3 Verdinho, Serra do mts Brazil
245 H2 Verdolaga Mex.
161 H9 Verdon r. France
161 I9 Verdon, Grand Canyon du gorge France
182 C4 Verdugo r. Spain
157 J5 Verdun France
163 G8 Verdun-sur-Garonne France
160 G3 Verdun-sur-le-Doubs France
194 E9 Verdura r. Sicilia Italy
175 L1 Verebiejai Lith.
215 L2 Vereeniging S. Africa
137 L4 Veremiyivka Ukr.
215 N1 Verena S. Africa
224 E4 Vérendrye, Réserve Faunique de la nature res. Que. Can.
177 I4 Veresegyház Hungary
134 K4 Vereshchagino Rus. Fed.
137 K2 Veresoch Ukr.
139 T4 Verestovo, Ozero l. Rus. Fed.
139 T6 Vereya Rus. Fed.
139 W6 Vereyka Rus. Fed.
163 H7 Verfeil Midi-Pyrénées France
163 H8 Verfeil Midi-Pyrénées France
206 B4 Verga, Cap c. Guinea
261 I4 Vergara Arg.
Vergara Spain see Bergara
258 G4 Vergara Uru.
191 K7 Vergato Italy
157 M6 Vergaville France
214 I1 Vergeleë S. Africa
85 I8 Vergemont Creek watercourse Qld Austr.
233 L4 Vergennes VT U.S.A.
186 L3 Verges Spain
161 E9 Vergèze France
191 M8 Verghereto Italy
156 G8 Vergigny France
198 D2 Vergina Greece
192 B3 Vergio, Col de pass France
161 C6 Vergongheon France
162 F5 Vergt France
137 L4 Verhuny Cherkas'ka Oblast' Ukr.
137 M4 Verhuny Poltavs'ka Oblast' Ukr.
Véria Greece see Veroia
139 V5 Verigino Rus. Fed.
182 F5 Verín Spain
172 G5 Veringenstadt Ger.
Verin T'alin Armenia see T'alin
138 K3 Veriora Estonia
256 C3 Veríssimo Brazil
Veríssimo Sarmento Angola see Camissombo
215 K4 Verkeerdevlei S. Africa
137 N5 Verkhivtseve Ukr.
120 G1 Verkhne-Avzyan Rus. Fed.
137 Q9 Verkhnebakanskiy Rus. Fed.
121 T2 Verkhne-berezovskiy Kazakh.
Verkhnedneprovsk Ukr. see Verkhn'odniprovs'k
139 Q7 Verkhnedneprovskiy Rus. Fed.
130 J3 Verkhneimbatsk Rus. Fed.
134 L2 Verkhnekolvinsk Rus. Fed.
139 S6 Verkhneruzskoye Vodokhranilishche resr Rus. Fed.
134 I4 Verkhnespasskoye Rus. Fed.
140 U2 Verkhnetulomskiy Rus. Fed.
140 U2 Verkhnetulomskoye Vodokhranilishche resr Rus. Fed.
137 R2 Verkhneturovo Rus. Fed.
120 H1 Verkhneural'sk Rus. Fed.
131 N3 Verkhnevilyuysk Rus. Fed.
139 P4 Verkhnevolzhskoye Vodokhranilishche resr Rus. Fed.
134 K5 Verkhneyarkeyevo Rus. Fed.
140 U4 Verkhneye Kuyto, Ozero l. Rus. Fed.
100 F1 Verkhnezeysk Rus. Fed.
131 Q3 Verkhniy At-Uryakh Rus. Fed.
129 D2 Verkhniy Baksan Rus. Fed.
135 I6 Verkhniy Baskunchak Rus. Fed.
137 P4 Verkhniy Byshkyn Ukr.
129 F2 Verkhniye Achaluki Rus. Fed.
Verkhniye Kholokhory Moldova see Halahora de Sus
139 O6 Verkhniye Koshevichi Rus. Fed.
139 O6 Verkhniye Mokhovichi Rus. Fed.
129 F3 Verkhniy Fiagdon Rus. Fed.
Verkhniy Karabulag Georgia see Zemo Qarabulakhi
139 V9 Verkhniy Lomovets Rus. Fed.
135 H6 Verkhniy Mamon Rus. Fed.
Verkhniy Naur Rus. Fed. see Lakkha-Nevre
137 N6 Verkhniy Rohachyk Ukr.
134 J1 Verkhniy Shar Rus. Fed.
107 K1 Verkhniy Shergol'dzhin Rus. Fed.
134 K4 Verkhniy Tatyshly Rus. Fed.
137 P6 Verkhniytokmak Ukr.
107 M2 Verkhniy Ul'khun Rus. Fed.
134 F2 Verkhniy Vyalozerskiy Rus. Fed.
137 N5 Verkhn'odniprovs'k Ukr.
136 J5 Verkhnyachka Ukr.
175 M6 Verkhnya Lypytsya Ukr.
137 N3 Verkhnya Syrovatka Ukr.
137 O5 Verkhnya Tersa r. Ukr.
136 C5 Verkhnya Vysots'ke Ukr.
177 L3 Verkhnya Vyznytsya Ukr.
129 E2 Verkhnyaya Balkariya Rus. Fed.
177 L2 Verkhnya Yablun'ka Ukr.
137 Q2 Verkhnyaya Grayvoronka Rus. Fed.
134 M2 Verkhnyaya Inta Rus. Fed.
135 G6 Verkhnyaya Khava Rus. Fed.
129 D2 Verkhnyaya Mara Rus. Fed.
131 R3 Verkhnyaya Pakhachi Rus. Fed.
137 T2 Verkhnyaya Plavitsa Rus. Fed.
131 K2 Verkhnyaya Taymyra r. Rus. Fed.
129 C2 Verkhnyaya Teberda Rus. Fed.
137 T2 Verkhnyaya Tishanka Rus. Fed.
137 T2 Verkhnyaya Toyda Rus. Fed.
134 I3 Verkhnyaya Toyma Rus. Fed.
139 U4 Verkhnyaya Troitsa Rus. Fed.
Verkhnyaya Tunguska r. Rus. Fed. see Angara
136 C4 Verkhnye Syn'ovydne Ukr.
134 J4 Verkhoramen'ye Rus. Fed.
137 M9 Verkhorichchya Ukr.
134 J4 Verkhoshizhem'ye Rus. Fed.
137 N3 Verkhosulka Ukr.
139 Z1 Verkhovazh'ye Rus. Fed.
Verkhovina Ukr. see Verkhovyna
139 U9 Verkhov'ye Rus. Fed.
136 D5 Verkhovyna Ukr.
131 N2 Verkhoyanskiy Khrebet mts Rus. Fed.
121 T2 Verkhuba Kazakh.
175 N4 Verkhy Ukr.
138 H7 Verknė r. Lith.
134 I3 Verkola Rus. Fed.
215 N3 Verkykerskop S. Africa
169 G7 Verl Ger.
165 H7 Verlaine Belgium
214 E8 Verlatekloof pass S. Africa
140 □ Verlegenhuken pt Svalbard
140 J5 Verma Norway
214 F10 Vermaaklikheid S. Africa
156 F4 Vermand France
156 F4 Vermandois reg. France
256 B5 Vermelha, Serra hills Brazil
254 C3 Vermelho r. Brazil
254 D3 Vermelho r. Brazil
253 H3 Vermelho r. Brazil
156 G8 Vermenton France
197 J5 Vermeș Romania
191 J3 Vermiglio Italy
223 I4 Vermilion Alta Can.
232 C7 Vermilion OH U.S.A.
226 E8 Vermilion r. IL U.S.A.
237 J11 Vermilion Bay LA U.S.A.
241 T5 Vermilion Cliffs esc. AZ U.S.A.
241 T4 Vermilion Cliffs esc. UT U.S.A.
239 H8 Vermilion Cliffs National Monument nat. park AZ U.S.A.
226 B2 Vermilion Lake MN U.S.A.
226 B2 Vermilion Range hills MN U.S.A.
236 G4 Vermillion SD U.S.A.
236 G4 Vermillion r. SD U.S.A.
236 G4 Vermillion, East Fork r. SD U.S.A.
223 M5 Vermillion Bay Ont. Can.
230 K2 Vermillon r. Que. Can.
198 C2 Vermio mt. Greece
182 G7 Vermiosa Port.
182 C9 Vermoil Port.
247 □3 Vermont St Vincent
233 M4 Vermont state U.S.A.
262 T2 Vernadsky research stn Antarctica
191 J2 Vernago, Lago di l. Italy
163 H10 Vernajoul France
238 D6 Vernal UT U.S.A.
190 D7 Vernante Italy
159 L7 Vernantes France
190 C3 Vernayaz Switz.
159 J6 Vern-d'Anjou France
224 D4 Verner Ont. Can.
176 D1 Verneřice Czech Rep.
163 G9 Vernet France
163 I10 Vernet-les-Bains France
159 M4 Verneuil-sur-Avre France
162 G4 Verneuil-sur-Vienne France
214 F5 Verneuk Pan salt pan S. Africa
190 A3 Vernier Switz.
191 K7 Vernio Italy
163 H9 Verniolle France
198 C2 Verno mt. Greece
195 O3 Vernole Italy
222 G5 Vernon B.C. Can.
156 B5 Vernon France
237 K9 Vernon AL U.S.A.
230 E6 Vernon IN U.S.A.
235 G2 Vernon NJ U.S.A.
237 F8 Vernon TX U.S.A.
241 T1 Vernon UT U.S.A.
87 E8 Vernon, Mount hill W.A. Austr.
84 C2 Vernon Islands N.T. Austr.
156 B6 Vernouillet France
161 F7 Vernoux-en-Vivarais France
234 F3 Vernoy NJ U.S.A.
100 F3 Vernoye Rus. Fed.
158 H5 Vern-sur-Seiche France
157 L5 Verny France
Vernyy Kazakh. see Almaty
192 B3 Vero Corse France
186 F4 Vero r. Spain
231 G12 Vero Beach FL U.S.A.
177 I4 Verőcemaros Hungary
198 D2 Veroia Greece
190 I5 Verolanuova Italy
193 K4 Veroli Italy
156 F7 Véron France
191 J5 Verona Italy
191 K5 Verona prov. Italy
232 F10 Verona VA U.S.A.
226 E7 Verona WI U.S.A.
261 I4 Verónica Arg.
160 E4 Verosvres France
177 J4 Verpelét Hungary
235 H2 Verplanck NY U.S.A.
82 F5 Verran S.A. Austr.
190 D4 Verres Italy
162 F3 Verrières France
193 M4 Verrino r. Italy
190 E6 Versa r. Italy
190 G5 Versa r. Italy
191 O4 Versa r. Italy
156 D6 Versailles France
230 E6 Versailles IN U.S.A.
230 E6 Versailles KY U.S.A.
236 I6 Versailles MO U.S.A.
232 A8 Versailles OH U.S.A.
252 E3 Versalles Bol.
Versec Vojvodina Serbia see Vršac
138 H7 Verseka r. Lith.
160 H3 Vers-en-Montage France
137 L4 Vershatsi Ukr.
169 F6 Versmold Ger.
190 A3 Versoix Switz.
161 B9 Versols-et-Lapeyre France
159 K3 Verson France
161 F9 Vers-Pont-du-Gard France
163 C7 Vert France
163 G6 Vert r. France
206 A3 Vert, Cap c. Senegal
225 G3 Vert, Île i. Que. Can.
160 C5 Vertaizon France
162 E5 Verteillac France
254 C4 Vertentes r. Brazil
177 H4 Vértesacsa Hungary
177 H4 Vértesboglár Hungary
177 H4 Vértesi park Hungary
163 E7 Verteuil-d'Agenais France
162 E4 Verteuil-sur-Charente France
162 C5 Vertheuil France
246 D3 Vertientes Cuba
137 K2 Vertiyivka Ukr.
261 F4 Vertiz Arg.
156 C3 Verton France
191 J2 Vertona, Cima mt. Italy
158 I7 Vertou France
156 H6 Vertus France
191 M8 Verucchio Italy
215 P5 Verulam S. Africa
Verulamium Hertfordshire, England U.K. see St Albans
165 I7 Verviers Belgium
156 G4 Vervins France
178 A5 Verwallgruppe mts Austria
Verwoerdburg S. Africa see Centurion
223 J5 Verwood Sask. Can.
151 I6 Verwood Dorset, England U.K.
Veryína Greece see Vergina
159 J6 Verzée r. France
156 H5 Verzenay France
195 L5 Verzino Italy
190 C6 Verzuolo Italy
156 H5 Verzy France
140 S5 Vesanto Fin.
192 C3 Vescovato Corse France
190 I5 Vescovato Italy
165 I7 Vesdre r. Belgium
176 G5 Vése Hungary
130 G4 Veselaya, Gora mt. Rus. Fed.
137 N6 Vesele Ukr.
139 T6 Veselevo Rus. Fed.
197 N7 Veselina r. Bulg.
176 D2 Veselí nad Lužnicí Czech Rep.
176 G3 Veselí nad Moravou Czech Rep.
137 L6 Veselivka Kirovohrads'ka Oblast' Ukr.
136 H3 Veselivka Zhytomyrs'ka Oblast' Ukr.
137 R6 Veselo-Voznesenka Rus. Fed.
135 H7 Veselovskoye Vodokhranilishche resr Rus. Fed.
121 S2 Veseloyarsk Rus. Fed.
137 R3 Veseloye Rus. Fed.
137 K3 Veselynivka Ukr.
137 K6 Veselynove Ukr.
135 H7 Veselyy Rus. Fed.
120 K1 Veselyy Podol Kazakh.
156 B6 Vesgre r. France
135 H6 Veshenskaya Rus. Fed.
134 H2 Veshkoma Rus. Fed.
141 R6 Vesijärvi l. Fin.
190 E6 Vesime Italy
156 F5 Vesle r. France
134 K3 Veslyana r. Rus. Fed.
Vesontio France see Besançon
160 I1 Vesoul France
190 F5 Vespolate Italy
100 I7 Veselyy Yar Rus. Fed.
165 H6 Vessem Neth.
142 D3 Vest-Agder county Norway
140 L2 Vesterålen is Norway
140 L2 Vesterålsfjorden sea chan. Norway
168 L1 Vesterby Denmark
170 E1 Vestermark Denmark
168 I1 Vester Sottrup Denmark
140 S1 Vestertana Norway
140 □B1 Vestfirðir constituency Iceland
142 E2 Vestfjorddalen val. Norway
140 L3 Vestfjorden sea chan. Norway
142 G2 Vestfold county Norway
263 F2 Vestfold Hills Antarctica
140 □ Vestfonna ice cap Svalbard
256 B4 Véstia Brazil
144 D1 Vestmanna Faroe Is
140 □C2 Vestmannaeyjar is Iceland
140 I5 Vestnes Norway
190 I4 Vestone Italy
140 T1 Vestre Jakobselv Norway
142 H6 Vestsjælland county Denmark
262 X2 Vestsstraumen Glacier Antarctica
140 □B1 Vesturland constituency Iceland
140 L2 Vestvågøy i. Norway
161 K9 Vésubie r. France
193 M6 Vesuvio vol. Italy
193 M6 Vesuvio, Parco Nazionale del nat. park Italy
Vesuvius vol. Italy see Vesuvio
139 U3 Ves'yegonsk Rus. Fed.
176 G4 Veszkény Hungary
177 G4 Veszprém Hungary
176 G4 Veszprém county Hungary
177 G4 Veszprémvarsány Hungary
177 K5 Vésztő Hungary
215 J3 Vet r. S. Africa
79 □7 Vetauua i. Fiji
140 Q5 Veteli Fin.
223 I4 Veteran Alta Can.
196 H5 Veternik Vojvodina Serbia
156 C5 Vétheuil France
177 L4 Vetiș Romania
143 L4 Vetlanda Sweden
141 I6 Vetlefjorden Norway
134 I4 Vetluga Rus. Fed.
134 I4 Vetluga r. Rus. Fed.
130 F4 Vetluzhskiy Kostromskaya Oblast' Rus. Fed.
134 I4 Vetluzhskiy Nizhegorodskaya Oblast' Rus. Fed.
136 E2 Vetly Ukr.
139 Q8 Vet'ma r. Rus. Fed.
197 O7 Vetovo Bulg.
192 I3 Vetralla Italy
197 P8 Vetren Bulg.
197 Q4 Vetrișoaia Romania
176 D3 Větřní Czech Rep.
171 J7 Vetschau Ger.
140 S2 Vetsikko Fin.
140 P3 Vettasjärvi Sweden
169 D9 Vettelschoss Ger.
190 I7 Vetto Italy
193 K2 Vettore, Monte mt. Italy
159 L7 Veude r. France
159 M2 Veules-les-Roses France
159 M2 Veulettes-sur-Mer France
165 C6 Veurne Belgium
230 E6 Vevay IN U.S.A.
210 B3 Veveno r. Sudan
190 B3 Vevey Switz.
190 C3 Vex Switz.
156 C5 Vexin Français reg. France
156 B5 Vexin Normand reg. France
135 G6 Veydelevka Rus. Fed.
160 F4 Veyle r. France
161 H7 Veynes France
160 D3 Veynon r. France
241 S4 Veyo UT U.S.A.
160 C5 Veyre-Monton France
160 I5 Veyrier-du-Lac France
122 C6 Veys Iran
138 E6 Vėžaičiai Lith.
160 D2 Vézelay France
157 L7 Vézelise France
161 E8 Vézénobres France
162 F6 Vézère r. France
134 K3 Vezhayu Rus. Fed.
197 M8 Vezhen mt. Bulg.
159 J7 Vezins France
161 B8 Vézins-de-Lévézou France
199 K2 Vezirhan Turkey
126 G3 Vezirköprü Turkey
157 L6 Vezouze r. France
190 I7 Vezza d'Oglio Italy
178 E7 Vezzana, Cima della mt. Italy
192 C3 Vezzani Corse France
191 K3 Vezzano Italy
213 F4 Vhembe Dongola National Park nature res. S. Africa
206 C5 Via r. Liberia
252 C4 Viacha Bol.
191 J6 Viadana Italy
182 E5 Viade de Baixo Port.
161 K9 Vial, Mont mt. France
161 B8 Viala du Tarn France
Vialar Alg. see Tissemsilt
161 D8 Vialas France
261 G2 Viale Arg.
255 C9 Viamao Brazil
261 F3 Viamonte Córdoba Arg.
259 D9 Viamonte Tierra del Fuego Arg.
209 B7 Viana Angola
257 G4 Viana Espírito Santo Brazil
254 D2 Viana Maranhão Brazil
183 P3 Viana Spain
183 K5 Viana de Cega Spain
Viana del Bollo Spain see Viana do Bolo
184 D4 Viana do Alentejo Port.
182 F4 Viana do Bolo Spain
182 C5 Viana do Castelo Port.
182 D5 Viana do Castelo admin. dist. Port.
165 J9 Vianden Lux.
161 B9 Viane France
164 H5 Vianen Neth.
96 F6 Viangchan Laos
96 E4 Viangphoukha Laos
163 E7 Vianne France
199 G7 Viannos Kriti Greece
182 D2 Viaño Pequeno Spain
256 C2 Vianópolis Brazil
185 O3 Vianos Spain
184 H5 Viar r. Spain
190 I8 Viareggio Italy
156 D5 Viarmes France
161 C10 Vias France
182 C6 Viatodos Port.
185 O7 Viator Spain
163 H7 Viaur r. France
163 I6 Viazac France
193 P7 Vibonati Italy
185 K5 Víboras r. Spain
142 F5 Viborg Denmark
142 F5 Viborg county Denmark
Viborg Rus. Fed. see Vyborg
195 K6 Vibo Valentia Italy
195 K6 Vibo Valentia prov. Italy
159 M5 Vibraye France
186 J4 Vic Spain
162 H5 Vic, Roche de hill France
242 D4 Vicam Mex.
185 N7 Vícar Spain
194 F8 Vicari Sicilia Italy
148 C7 Vicarstown Ireland
191 K8 Vicchio Italy
163 H10 Vicdessos France
163 H10 Vicdessos r. France
Viçe Turkey see Fındıklı
Vicecomodoro Marambio research stn Antarctica see Marambio
163 E9 Vic-en-Bigorre France
240 N8 Vicente, Point CA U.S.A.
261 H4 Vicente Casares Arg.
260 D4 Vicente Dupuy Arg.
242 A2 Vicente Guerrero Baja California Mex.
244 D2 Vicente Guerrero Durango Mex.
245 N7 Vicente Guerrero Tabasco Mex.
245 I6 Vicente Guerrero Tlaxcala Mex.
245 K7 Vicente y Camalote Mex.
191 L4 Vicenza Italy
191 K4 Vicenza prov. Italy
163 E8 Vic-Fezensac France
Vich Spain see Vic
250 D3 Vichada dept Col.
250 E3 Vichada r. Col.
258 G3 Vichadero Uru.
245 I3 Vichinchijol Nuevo Mex.
134 H4 Vichuga Rus. Fed.
260 A4 Vichuquén Chile
160 C4 Vichy France
237 F7 Vici OK U.S.A.
186 E3 Vicién Spain
149 K5 Vickerstown Cumbria, England U.K.
241 S8 Vicksburg AZ U.S.A.
226 I7 Vicksburg MI U.S.A.
237 J9 Vicksburg MS U.S.A.
234 B3 Vicksburg PA U.S.A.
160 C5 Vic-le-Comte France
192 B3 Vico Corse France
192 I3 Vico, Lago di l. Italy
193 P4 Vico del Gargano Italy
193 M6 Vico Equense Italy
190 D7 Vicoforte Italy
193 K4 Vico nel Lazio Italy
183 Q6 Vicort, Sierra de mts Spain
254 F4 Viçosa Alagoas Brazil
257 F4 Viçosa Minas Gerais Brazil
193 J3 Vicovaro Italy
197 N3 Vicovu de Sus Romania
159 P8 Vicq-Exemplet France
162 G4 Vicq-sur-Breuilh France
156 F5 Vic-sur-Aisne France
161 B7 Vic-sur-Cère France
157 M6 Vic-sur-Seille France
263 C2 Victor, Mount Antarctica
168 D4 Victorbur (Südbrookmerland) Ger.
82 G6 Victor Harbor S.A. Austr.
261 G3 Victoria Arg.
261 H3 Victoria r. Arg.
84 C3 Victoria r. N.T. Austr.
83 J7 Victoria state Austr.
Victoria Cameroon see Limbe
222 F5 Victoria B.C. Can.
260 A6 Victoria Araucanía Chile
259 C9 Victoria Magallanes y Antártica Chilena Chile
247 □6 Victoria Grenada
242 □P10 Victoria Hond.
Victoria Malaysia see Labuan
195 □ Victoria Gozo Malta
244 G4 Victoria Mex.
92 C4 Victoria Luzon Phil.
197 P6 Victoria Brăila Romania
197 M5 Victoria Brașov Romania
217 □2b Victoria Mahé Seychelles
247 □7 Victoria county Trin. and Tob.
237 G11 Victoria TX U.S.A.
232 G12 Victoria VA U.S.A.
259 B7 Victoria, Isla i. Chile
210 B4 Victoria, Lake Africa
82 H5 Victoria, Lake N.S.W. Austr.
Victoria, Mount Viti Levu Fiji see Tomanivi
96 A4 Victoria, Mount Myanmar
81 G9 Victoria, Mount South I. N.Z.
91 K8 Victoria, Mount P.N.G.
221 K2 Victoria and Albert Mountains Nunavut Can.
209 E9 Victoria Falls waterfall Zambia/Zimbabwe
212 E3 Victoria Falls Zimbabwe
212 E3 Victoria Falls National Park Zimbabwe
221 N1 Victoria Fjord inlet Greenland
81 G8 Victoria Forest Park nature res. South I. N.Z.
Victoria Harbour sea chan. H.K. China see Hong Kong Harbour
217 □2b Victoria Harbour b. Mahé Seychelles
220 H2 Victoria Island N.W.T./Nunavut Can.
225 J3 Victoria Lake Nfld and Lab. Can.
263 K2 Victoria Land coastal area Antarctica
109 □J7 Victoria Peak hill H.K. China
82 □3 Victoria Point S. Pacific Ocean
81 G9 Victoria Range mts South I. N.Z.
84 C3 Victoria River N.T. Austr.
84 C4 Victoria River Downs N.T. Austr.
80 H2 Victoria Valley North I. N.Z.
225 G4 Victoriaville Que. Can.
214 H7 Victoria West S. Africa
260 E5 Victorica Arg.
250 E4 Victorino Venez.
244 E3 Victor Rosales Mex.
240 O7 Victorville CA U.S.A.
177 K6 Victor Vlad Delamarina Romania
232 I5 Victory NY U.S.A.
84 D8 Victory Downs N.T. Austr.
260 B2 Vicuña Chile
260 E3 Vicuña Mackenna Arg.
182 H9 Vid, Río de la r. Spain
182 E5 Vidago Port.
184 A2 Vidais Port.
259 B8 Vidal, Isla i. Chile
237 J10 Vidalia LA U.S.A.
241 R7 Vidal Junction CA U.S.A.
138 G9 Vidamlya Belarus

Vidángoz to Viosne
405

186 C2 Vidángoz Spain
161 I10 Vidauban France
192 B6 Viddalba Sardegna Italy
142 E5 Videbæk Denmark
255 C8 Videira Brazil
261 G2 Videla Arg.
197 N6 Videle Romania
179 N6 Videm Gornja Radgona Slovenia
179 K8 Videm Grosuplje Slovenia
182 F7 Videmonte Port.
197 K8 Viden mt. Bulg.
Viderø i. Faroe Is see Viðoy
175 K1 Vidgiriu kalnas hill Lith.
184 D4 Vidigueira Port.
197 N8 Vidima r. Bulg.
197 K7 Vidin Bulg.
177 I3 Vidiná Slovakia
182 H1 Vidio, Cabo c. Spain
116 F8 Vidisha Madh. Prad. India
146 □N2 Vidlin Shetland, Scotland U.K.
139 P1 Vidlitsa Rus. Fed.
142 D2 Vidmyr nature res. Norway
176 G1 Vidnava Czech Rep.
139 U6 Vidnoye Rus. Fed.
143 J4 Vidöstern l. Sweden
161 E9 Vidourle r. France
188 F4 Vidova Gora hill Croatia
179 N7 Vidovec Croatia
144 D1 Viðoy i. Faroe Is
177 L5 Vidra Romania
Vidreras Spain see Vidrieres
186 K4 Vidrieres Spain
140 P4 Vidsel Sweden
138 F6 Viduklė Lith.
188 G4 Viduša mts Bos.-Herz.
138 I5 Vidzemes centrālā augstiene hills Latvia
138 J6 Vidzy Belarus
158 H8 Vie r. France
159 K3 Vie r. France
173 N3 Viechtach Ger.
175 M1 Viečiūnai Lith.
215 M7 Viedgesville S. Africa
259 E6 Viedma Arg.
259 B8 Viedma, Lago l. Arg.
179 K2 Viehberg mt. Austria
161 C6 Vieille-Brioude France
158 I8 Vieillevigne France
182 C9 Vieira de Leiria Port.
182 D5 Vieira do Minho Port.
244 C2 Viejo r. Mex.
242 C2 Viejo, Cerro mt. Mex.
138 F5 Viekšniai Lith.
170 D4 Vielank Ger.
186 G2 Vielha Spain
163 D8 Viella France
Viella Spain see Vielha
163 E10 Vielle-Aure France
163 B8 Vielle-St-Girons France
163 I8 Vielmur-sur-Agout France
165 I8 Vielsalm Belgium
160 G2 Vielverge France
169 K7 Vienenburg Ger.
Vienna Austria see Wien
231 F9 Vienna GA U.S.A.
237 K7 Vienna IL U.S.A.
233 J10 Vienna MD U.S.A.
236 J6 Vienna MO U.S.A.
234 F3 Vienna NJ U.S.A.
232 D9 Vienna WV U.S.A.
160 F5 Vienne France
159 L8 Vienne dept France
162 E1 Vienne r. France
157 I5 Vienne-le-Château France
Vientiane Laos see Viangchan
260 B5 Viento, Cordillera del mts Arg.
185 I7 Viento, Puerto del pass Spain
247 □1 Vieques i. Puerto Rico
157 I6 Vière r. France
170 J3 Viereck Ger.
140 S5 Vieremä Fin.
173 J2 Viereth-Trunstadt Ger.
173 K5 Vierkirchen Ger.
164 I5 Vierlingsbeek Neth.
169 K9 Viernau Ger.
172 F2 Viernheim Ger.
170 J4 Vierraden Ger.
169 B8 Viersen Ger.
159 J3 Vierville-sur-Mer France
190 E1 Vierwaldstätter See l. Switz.
162 I1 Vierzon France
242 H5 Viesca Mex.
170 F4 Viesecke Ger.
171 D9 Vieselbach Ger.
138 I5 Viesīte Latvia
193 Q4 Vieste Italy
138 F6 Viešvilės rezervatas nature res. Lith.
140 O3 Vietas Sweden
Viet Nam country Asia see Vietnam
96 G5 Vietnam country Asia
96 G3 Viêt Quang Vietnam
193 P6 Vietri di Potenza Italy
193 N6 Vietri sul Mare Italy
96 G4 Viêt Tri Vietnam
163 B8 Vieux-Boucau-les-Bains France
247 □2 Vieux-Bourg Guadeloupe
161 I7 Vieux Chaillol mt. France
160 J1 Vieux-Charmont France
224 E2 Vieux Comptoir, Lac du l. Que. Can.
156 G3 Vieux-Condé France
225 J3 Vieux-Fort Que. Can.
247 □2 Vieux-Fort Guadeloupe
247 □3 Vieux Fort St Lucia
247 □2 Vieux-Fort, Pointe de pt Guadeloupe
247 □2 Vieux-Habitants Guadeloupe
225 I3 Vieux Poste, Pointe du pt Que. Can.
138 H7 Vievis Lith.
148 I2 Viewpark North Lanarkshire, Scotland U.K.
261 I4 Vieytes Arg.
161 H6 Vif France
138 H3 Vigala r. Estonia
92 C3 Vigan Luzon Phil.
191 K6 Vigarano Mainarda Italy
191 J5 Vigasio Italy
178 H4 Vigaun Austria
162 H5 Vigeois France
190 F5 Vigevano Italy
192 B4 Viggianello Corse France
193 Q8 Viggianello Italy
193 P7 Viggiano Italy
190 F4 Viggiù Italy
254 C2 Vigia Brazil
184 C5 Vigia hill Port.
184 D3 Vigia, Barragem da resr Port.
259 D8 Vigía, Cabo c. Arg.
243 P8 Vigía Chico Mex.
177 I3 Vígľaš Slovakia
193 K4 Viglio, Monte mt. Italy
156 D3 Vignacourt France
190 E5 Vignale Monferrato Italy
193 I3 Vignanello Italy
163 D10 Vignemale mt. France
157 K6 Vigneulles-les-Hattonchâtel France
160 H3 Vignoble reg. France
191 K7 Vignola Italy
192 C5 Vignola r. Italy
192 C5 Vignola Mare l'Agnata Sardegna Italy
157 J7 Vignory France
156 C5 Vigny France
182 C4 Vigo Spain
182 C4 Vigo, Ría de est. Spain
191 M3 Vigo di Cadore Italy
178 E7 Vigo di Fassa Italy
190 C6 Vigone Italy
191 L5 Vigonza Italy
191 J3 Vigo Rendena Italy
86 E7 Vigors, Mount W.A. Austr.
142 E4 Vigsø Bugt b. Denmark
190 F6 Viguzzolo Italy
157 L5 Vigy France
140 R4 Vihanti Fin.
123 O6 Vihari Pak.
162 C1 Vihiers France
177 L3 Vihorlat mt. Slovakia
177 L3 Vihorlat park Slovakia
177 K3 Vihorlatské vrchy mts Slovakia
138 G2 Vihterpalu r. Estonia
141 R6 Vihti Fin.
141 Q6 Viiala Fin.
177 L4 Viile Satu Mare Romania
Viipuri Rus. Fed. see Vyborg
140 S3 Viirinkylä Fin.
177 L4 Viișoara Romania
140 R5 Viitasaari Fin.
138 K4 Viitka Estonia
116 D5 Vijainagar Rajasthan India
116 D8 Vijapur Gujarat India
114 C4 Vijayadurg Mahar. India
Vijayanagar Karnataka India see Hampi
114 E8 Vijayapati Tamil Nadu India
114 G4 Vijayawada Andhra Prad. India
140 □D2 Vík Iceland
140 L4 Vik Norway
140 S3 Vikajärvi Fin.
114 E4 Vikarabad Andhra Prad. India
143 M3 Vikbolandet pen. Sweden
142 B2 Vikedal Norway
Vikeke East Timor see Viqueque
143 K3 Viken l. Sweden
142 F2 Vikersund Norway
142 B2 Vikevåg Norway
139 O7 Vikhra r. Rus. Fed.
197 L9 Vikhren mt. Bulg.
223 I4 Viking Alta Can.
140 K4 Vikna i. Norway
177 I2 Vikolínec Slovakia
198 B3 Vikou-Aoou, Ethnikos Drymos nat. park Greece
141 I6 Vikøyri Norway
140 O2 Vikran Norway
175 L1 Viktarinas Lith.
136 J6 Viktorivka Ukr.
Viktorovka Kazakh. see Taranovskoye
171 D7 Viktorshöhe hill Ger.
182 D5 Vila Spain
Vila Vanuatu see Port Vila
Vila Alferes Chamusca Moz. see Guija
184 D4 Vila Alva Port.
Vila Arriaga Angola see Bibala
184 □ Vila Baleira Madeira
250 D5 Vila Bittencourt Brazil
182 G8 Vila Boa Port.
184 E3 Vila Boim Port.
251 G6 Vila Braga Brazil
Vila Bugaço Angola see Camanongue
Vila Cabral Moz. see Lichinga
182 D6 Vila Caiz Port.
Vila Caldas Xavier Moz. see Muende
252 D4 Vilacaya Bol.
182 C6 Vila Chã Port.
182 E7 Vila Chã de Sá Port.
182 D6 Vila Chão do Marão Port.
Vila Coutinho Moz. see Ulongue
182 E7 Vila Cova à Coelheira Port.
182 D6 Vila Cova da Lixa Port.
186 I3 Vilada Spain
186 L3 Viladamat Spain
Vila da Ponte Angola see Kuvango
182 E5 Vila da Ponte Port.
216 □1a Vila da Praia da Vitória Terceira Azores
206 □ Vila da Ribeira Brava Cape Verde
Vila de Aljustrel Angola see Cangamba
Vila de Almoster Angola see Chiange
186 J5 Viladecans Spain
182 D3 Vila de Cruces Spain
Vila de João Belo Moz. see Xai-Xai
Vila de Junqueiro Moz. see Gurué
261 F1 Vila de María Arg.
Vilademat Spain see Viladamat
182 D9 Vila de Rei Port.
213 G3 Vila de Sena Moz.
Vila de Trego Morais Moz. see Chókwé
184 B6 Vila do Bispo Port.
182 C6 Vila do Conde Port.
186 J4 Viladrau Spain
187 E7 Vilafamés Spain
186 K3 Vilafant Spain
184 E3 Vila Fernando Port.
216 □3a Vilaflor Tenerife Canary Is
182 F6 Vila Flor Port.
Vila Fontes Moz. see Caia
216 □1b Vila Franca, Ilhéu de i. Azores
182 F7 Vila Franca das Naves Port.
187 L8 Vilafranca de Bonany Spain
186 I5 Vilafranca del Penedès Spain
184 B3 Vila Franca de Xira Port.
216 □1b Vila Franca do Campo São Miguel Azores
182 C3 Vilagarcía de Arousa Spain
213 G5 Vila Gomes da Costa Moz.
Vila Gouveia Moz. see Catandica
182 D2 Vilagudín, Encoro de resr Spain
158 G6 Vilaine r. France
186 L3 Vilajuiga Spain
138 K4 Viļaka Latvia
182 E2 Vilalba Spain
186 J3 Vilallonga Spain
Vila Luísa Moz. see Marracuene
Vila Marechal Carmona Angola see Uíge
182 F4 Vilamartín Spain
187 D8 Vilamarxant Spain
260 A5 Vila Mercedes Chile
Vila Miranda Moz. see Macaloge
184 B2 Vila Moreira Port.
184 C6 Vilamoura Port.
252 D2 Vila Murtinho Brazil
182 B2 Vilán, Cabo c. Spain
213 □J3 Vilanandro, Tanjona pt Madag.
213 G4 Vilanculos Moz.
138 J5 Viļāni Latvia
184 A3 Vila Nogueira de Azeitão Port.
Vila Nova Angola see Tchikala-Tcholohanga
216 □1a Vila Nova Terceira Azores
182 F2 Vilanova Spain
184 C4 Vila Nova da Baronia Port.
213 G3 Vila Nova da Fronteira Moz.
187 F7 Vilanova d'Alcolea Spain
182 C8 Vila Nova de Anços Port.
182 C3 Vilanova de Arousa Spain
Vilanova de Castelló Spain see Villanueva de Castellón
182 C5 Vila Nova de Cerveira Port.
182 C6 Vila Nova de Famalicão Port.
182 F6 Vila Nova de Foz Coa Port.
182 C6 Vila Nova de Gaia Port.
186 H4 Vilanova de L'Aguda Spain
186 H4 Vilanova de Meià Spain
182 C9 Vila Nova de Ourém Port.
182 E7 Vila Nova de Paiva Port.
182 D8 Vila Nova de Poiares Port.
184 E5 Vila Nova de São Bento Port.
Vila Nova do Seles Angola see Uku
186 I5 Vilanova i la Geltrú Spain
206 □ Vila Nova Sintra Cape Verde
Vila Paiva de Andrada Moz. see Gorongosa
Vila Pery Moz. see Chimoio
182 E8 Vila Pouca da Beira Port.
182 E5 Vila Pouca de Aguiar Port.
182 C5 Vila Praia de Âncora Port.
182 F7 Vilar, Barragem de resr Port.
182 F5 Vilarandelo Port.
182 E4 Vilarchao Spain
182 D5 Vilar da Veiga Port.
182 C6 Vilar de Andorinho Port.
182 E4 Vilar de Barrio Spain
182 E4 Vilar de Santos Spain
182 F5 Vilardevós Spain
182 E6 Vila Real Port.
182 E5 Vila Real admin. dist. Port.
184 E6 Vila Real de Santo António Port.
182 F5 Vilarelho da Raia Port.
182 G7 Vilar Formoso Port.
182 F6 Vilarinho da Castanheira Port.
182 C8 Vilarinho do Bairro Port.
182 F4 Vilariño de Conso Spain
186 H5 Vila-rodona Spain
184 D4 Vila Ruiva Port.
Vilas i. S. Male Maldives see Velassary
Vila Salazar Angola see N'dalatando
Vila Salazar Zimbabwe see Sango
129 J6 Viläşçay r. Azer.
182 C5 Vila Seca Port.
186 H5 Vilaseca de Solcina Spain
Vila Teixeira de Sousa Angola see Luau
261 G2 Vila Trinidad Arg.
114 E8 Vilavankod Tamil Nadu India
251 I4 Vila Velha Amapá Brazil
257 G4 Vila Velha Espírito Santo Brazil
182 E9 Vila Velha de Ródão Port.
182 D5 Vila Verde Braga Port.
182 C8 Vila Verde Coimbra Port.
182 E6 Vila Verde Vila Real Port.
182 F5 Vila Verde da Raia Port.
184 E5 Vila Verde de Ficalho Port.
184 E3 Vila Viçosa Port.
252 B3 Vilcabamba, Cordillera mts Peru
252 C3 Vilcanota, Cordillera de mts Peru
136 I2 Vil'cha Ukr.
130 H1 Vil'cheka, Zemlya i. Zemlya Frantsa-Iosifa Rus. Fed.
185 M4 Vilches Spain
260 A6 Vilcun Chile
134 I3 Viled' r. Rus. Fed.
261 H4 Vilela Arg.
Vileyka Belarus see Vilyeyka
134 L3 Vil'gort Permskaya Oblast' Rus. Fed.
134 J3 Vil'gort Respublika Komi Rus. Fed.
140 N4 Vilhelmina Sweden
253 E3 Vilhena Brazil
Viligili i. N. Male Maldives see Vilingli
137 M9 Viline Ukr.
113 □1 Vilingli i. N. Male Maldives
113 □1 Vilingli i. N. Male Maldives
138 I7 Viliya r. Belarus/Lith.
136 F3 Viliya r. Ukr.
138 I3 Viljandi Estonia
214 D10 Viljoenshof S. Africa
215 K3 Viljoenskroon S. Africa
138 G7 Vilkaviškis Lith.
137 S5 Vil'khova r. Ukr.
138 G6 Vilkija Lith.
130 I2 Vil'kitskogo, Ostrov i. Rus. Fed.
131 K2 Vil'kitskogo, Proliv str. Rus. Fed.
252 D5 Villa Abecia Bol.
260 C2 Villa Aberastain Arg.
193 J4 Villa Adriana tourist site Italy
242 F2 Villa Ahumada Mex.
261 F6 Villa Alba Arg.
260 B4 Villa Alegre Chile
260 B3 Villa Alemana Chile
245 K8 Villa Alta Mex.
246 H4 Villa Altagracia Dom. Rep.
258 F3 Villa Ana Arg.
261 G3 Villa Ángela Arg.
258 E2 Villa Ángela Arg.
244 G5 Villa Apaseo El Alto Mex.
261 F6 Villa Atlántica Arg.
260 D4 Villa Atuel Arg.
245 J5 Villa Ávila Camacho Mex.
245 L7 Villa Azueta Mex.
191 K5 Villa Bartolomea Italy
194 E7 Villabate Sicilia Italy
252 D2 Villa Bella Bol.
Villa Bens Morocco see Tarfaya
258 E2 Villa Berthet Arg.
184 E6 Villablanca Spain
182 H3 Villablino Spain
186 A1 Villabona Spain
183 J5 Villabrágima Spain
183 J6 Villabuena del Puente Spain
162 G5 Villac France
261 G4 Villa Cañás Arg.
183 N9 Villacañas Spain
190 I4 Villa Carcina Italy
260 E2 Villa Carlos Paz Arg.
185 M4 Villacarrillo Spain
261 F5 Villa Castelar Arg.
195 M2 Villa Castelli Italy
183 L7 Villacastín Spain
179 I6 Villach Austria
192 B9 Villacidro Sardegna Italy
183 O5 Villaciervos Spain
Villa Cisneros Western Sahara see Ad Dakhla
Villa Cisneros, Ría de b. Western Sahara see Río de Oro, Bahía de
243 M10 Villa Comaltitlán Mex.
261 F2 Villa Concepción del Tío Arg.
183 N8 Villaconejos Spain
183 P8 Villaconejos de Trabaque Spain
261 G3 Villa Constitución Arg.
244 D5 Villa Corona Mex.
242 G4 Villa Coronado Mex.
243 M9 Villa Corzo Mex.
260 E2 Villa Cura Brochero Arg.
261 G3 Villada Arg.
183 K4 Villada Spain
190 H4 Villa d'Almè Italy
244 D6 Villa de Álvarez Mex.
244 E2 Villa de Cos Mex.
250 E2 Villa de Cura Venez.
243 N8 Villa de Guadalupe Campeche Mex.
244 G2 Villa de Guadalupe San Luis Potosí Mex.
260 E3 Villa del Carmen Arg.
183 L8 Villa del Prado Spain
244 G5 Villa del Pueblito Mex.
185 K5 Villa del Río Spain
261 F2 Villa del Rosario Arg.
260 C2 Villa del Salvador Arg.
261 E2 Villa del Totoral Arg.
182 H5 Villadepera Spain
187 C9 Villa de Ves Spain
261 G3 Villa Diego Arg.
183 L3 Villadiego Spain
260 E2 Villa Dolores Arg.
261 H3 Villa Domínguez Arg.
191 L5 Villadose Italy
190 E3 Villadossola Italy
186 C5 Villadoz Spain
260 C6 Villa El Chocón Arg.
183 K3 Villaeles de Valdavia Spain
261 H3 Villa Elisa Arg.
261 G3 Villa Eloisa Arg.
244 F6 Villa Escalante Mex.
183 O9 Villaescusa de Haro Spain
183 N4 Villaescusa la Sombría Spain
182 I5 Villafáfila Spain
183 R6 Villafeliche Spain
243 M9 Villa Flores Mex.
183 J6 Villaflores Spain
253 F6 Villa Florida Para.
183 Q4 Villafranca Spain
190 E6 Villafranca d'Asti Italy
185 J5 Villafranca de Córdoba Spain
186 D4 Villafranca de Ebro Spain
182 G3 Villafranca del Bierzo Spain
186 C6 Villafranca del Campo Spain
186 E7 Villafranca del Cid Spain
184 G3 Villafranca de los Barros Spain
185 M2 Villafranca de los Caballeros Spain
Villafranca del Penedès Spain see Vilafranca del Penedès
191 J5 Villafranca di Verona Italy
190 H7 Villafranca in Lunigiana Italy
183 N4 Villafranca-Montes de Oca Spain
195 I7 Villafranca Tirrena Sicilia Italy
191 J5 Villafranca Veronese airport Italy
184 G6 Villafranco del Guadalquivir Spain
194 E8 Villafrati Sicilia Italy
183 J5 Villafrechos Spain
183 M5 Villafruela Spain
183 L5 Villafuerte Spain
Villagarcía de Arosa Spain see Vilagarcía de Arousa
183 J5 Villagarcía de Campos Spain
184 G4 Villagarcía de la Torre Spain
185 P2 Villagarcía del Llano Spain
260 D3 Villa General Roca Arg.
261 I5 Villa Gesell Arg.
195 L5 Villagio Mancuso Italy
184 G3 Villagonzalo Spain
261 G3 Villa Governador Gálvez Arg.
245 H1 Villagrán Mex.
192 D8 Villagrande Strisaili Sardegna Italy
261 H2 Villaguay Arg.
244 D4 Villa Guerrero Mex.
258 F3 Villa Guillermina Arg.
185 J4 Villaharta Spain
253 F6 Villa Hayes Para.
243 M8 Villahermosa Mex.
185 N3 Villahermosa Spain
187 E7 Villahermosa del Río Spain
261 H2 Villa Hernandarias Arg.
183 L4 Villaherreros Spain
244 E4 Villa Hidalgo Jalisco Mex.
244 B4 Villa Hidalgo Nayarit Mex.
244 G3 Villa Hidalgo San Luis Potosí Mex.
239 J11 Villa Hidalgo Sonora Mex.
183 M4 Villahizán Spain
183 M4 Villahoz Spain
260 E4 Villa Huidobro Arg.
156 I8 Villaines-en-Duesmois France
159 K5 Villaines-la-Juhel France
159 K6 Villaines-sous-Malicorne France
242 D5 Villa Insurgentes Mex.
261 F6 Villa Iris Arg.
187 E10 Villajoyosa-La Vila Joíosa Spain
244 B4 Villa Juárez Nayarit Mex.
244 G3 Villa Juárez San Luis Potosí Mex.
191 K4 Villa Lagarina Italy
193 L4 Villalago Italy
183 J5 Villalar de los Comuneros Spain
193 L4 Villa Latina Italy
245 M7 Villa La Venta Mex.
245 J5 Villa Lázaro Cárdenas Mex.
194 F8 Villalba Sicilia Italy
247 □1 Villalba Puerto Rico
183 M5 Villalba de Duero Spain
183 K3 Villalba de Guardo Spain
184 G6 Villalba del Alcor Spain
183 P8 Villalba de la Sierra Spain
183 K5 Villalba de los Alcores Spain
184 F3 Villalba de los Barros Spain
183 O8 Villalba del Rey Spain
186 F5 Villalba dels Arcs Spain
183 O3 Villalba de Rioja Spain
182 H5 Villalcampo Spain
182 H6 Villalcampo, Embalse de resr Spain
183 K4 Villalcázar de Sirga Spain
243 I4 Villaldama Mex.
183 Q6 Villalengua Spain
185 O2 Villalgordo del Júcar Spain
183 P9 Villalgordo del Marquesado Spain
261 H4 Villa Lía Arg.
261 H3 Villa Lila Arg.
193 M5 Villa Literno Italy
183 J5 Villalobos Spain
183 J4 Villalón de Campos Spain
259 E5 Villalonga Arg.
187 E10 Villalonga Spain
183 J5 Villalpando Spain
185 P2 Villalpardo Spain
183 M8 Villaluenga de la Sagra Spain
183 K4 Villalumbroso Spain
244 F6 Villa Madero Mex.
245 H1 Villa Mainero Mex.
185 P2 Villamalea Spain
182 I4 Villamañán Spain
182 I4 Villamandos Spain
185 N3 Villamanrique Spain
184 G6 Villamanrique de la Condesa Spain
183 L8 Villamanta Spain
192 B8 Villamar Sardegna Italy
Villamarchante Spain see Vilamarxant
261 G4 Villa María Arg.
261 F3 Villa María Córdoba Arg.
261 G2 Villa María Entre Ríos Arg.
261 H2 Villa María Grande Arg.
252 D5 Villa Martín Bol.
184 H7 Villamartín Spain
183 K4 Villamartín de Campos Spain
192 B9 Villamassargia Sardegna Italy
258 E2 Villa Matoque Arg.
182 I7 Villamayor Spain
185 K3 Villamayor de Calatrava Spain
183 J5 Villamayor de Campos Spain
183 O9 Villamayor de Santiago Spain
183 L4 Villamayor de Treviño Spain
162 F5 Villamblard France
183 L4 Villamediana Spain
183 P4 Villamediana de Iregua Spain
182 H3 Villamejil Spain
260 C2 Villa Mercedes Arg.
260 E3 Villa Mercedes San Luis Arg.
184 H2 Villamesías Spain
182 G8 Villamiel Spain
190 I7 Villa Minozzo Italy
252 E5 Villa Montes Bol.
182 I6 Villamor de los Escuderos Spain
244 F5 Villa Morelos Mex.
183 M9 Villamuelas Spain
183 L5 Villamuriel de Cerrato Spain
163 D7 Villandraut France
195 N2 Villanova Italy
190 E7 Villanova d'Albenga Italy
190 D6 Villanova d'Asti Italy
193 O5 Villanova del Battista Italy
192 C8 Villanovafranca Sardegna Italy
192 A6 Villanova Monteleone Sardegna Italy
192 B8 Villanova Truschedu Sardegna Italy
192 C8 Villanova Tulo Sardegna Italy
190 G5 Villanterio Italy
186 D2 Villanúa Spain
183 K5 Villanubla Spain
261 F3 Villa Nueva Córdoba Arg.
260 C3 Villa Nueva Mendoza Arg.
250 C2 Villanueva Col.
244 E3 Villanueva Mex.
Villanueva Spain see Vilanova
183 O9 Villanueva de Alcardete Spain
Villanueva de Alcolea Spain see Vilanova d'Alcolea
183 P7 Villanueva de Alcorón Spain
185 K6 Villanueva de Algaidas Spain
183 M4 Villanueva de Argaño Spain
Villanueva de Arosa Spain see Vilanova de Arousa
183 M9 Villanueva de Bogas Spain
183 O4 Villanueva de Cameros Spain
187 E9 Villanueva de Castellón Spain
185 J4 Villanueva de Córdoba Spain
186 D4 Villanueva de Gállego Spain
183 K7 Villanueva de Gómez Spain
183 M8 Villanueva de la Cañada Spain
185 J7 Villanueva de la Concepción Spain
185 N3 Villanueva de la Fuente Spain
185 P2 Villanueva de la Jara Spain
185 L4 Villanueva de la Reina Spain
185 M4 Villanueva del Arzobispo Spain
184 E5 Villanueva de las Cruces Spain
184 H3 Villanueva de la Serena Spain
182 H8 Villanueva de la Sierra Spain
185 M5 Villanueva de las Torres Spain
183 J8 Villanueva de la Vera Spain
183 J5 Villanueva del Campo Spain
185 J4 Villanueva del Duque Spain
184 E4 Villanueva del Fresno Spain
184 E5 Villanueva de los Castillejos Spain
185 N3 Villanueva de los Infantes Spain
185 I4 Villanueva del Rey Spain
187 C11 Villanueva del Río Segura Spain
184 H5 Villanueva del Río y Minas Spain
185 K7 Villanueva del Rosario Spain
185 K6 Villanueva del Trabuco Spain
185 L3 Villanueva de San Carlos Spain
185 I6 Villanueva de San Juan Spain
185 K6 Villanueva de Tapia Spain
183 N3 Villanueva de Valdegovia Spain
Villanueva-y-Geltrú Spain see Vilanova i la Geltrú
183 K3 Villanuño de Valdavia Spain
177 H6 Villány Hungary
177 H6 Villányi-hegység ridge Hungary
258 F3 Villa Ocampo Arg.
242 G4 Villa Ocampo Mex.
259 B8 Villa O'Higgins Chile
258 E3 Villa Ojo de Agua Arg.
253 F6 Villa Oliva Para.
Villa O. Pereyra Mex. see Villa Orestes Pereyra
191 P4 Villa Opicina Italy
242 G4 Villa Orestes Pereyra Mex.
252 D4 Villa Oropeza Bol.
185 N3 Villapalacios Spain
192 B9 Villaperuccio Sardegna Italy
239 J12 Villa Pesqueira Mex.
195 K4 Villapiana Italy
195 K4 Villapiana Lido Italy
191 K6 Villa Poma Italy
160 D3 Villapourçon France
260 B4 Villa Prat Chile
192 D9 Villaputzu Sardegna Italy
182 I4 Villaquejida Spain
182 I3 Villaquilambre Spain
252 D4 Villar Bol.
182 I6 Villaralbo Spain
185 J4 Villaralto Spain
261 G3 Villa Ramírez Arg.
183 M3 Villarcayo Spain
161 I6 Villar-d'Arêne France
161 H6 Villard-Bonnot France
161 H6 Villard-de-Lans France
185 P3 Villar de Chinchilla Spain
182 G7 Villar de Ciervo Spain
182 H5 Villardeciervos Spain
183 J5 Villardefrades Spain
187 D8 Villar del Arzobispo Spain
182 G7 Villar de la Yegua Spain
182 H6 Villar del Buey Spain
183 Q8 Villar del Cobo Spain
183 Q9 Villar del Humo Spain
182 G3 Villar de los Barrios Spain
186 C5 Villar de los Navarros Spain
183 J9 Villar del Pedroso Spain
184 F2 Villar del Rey Spain
183 R7 Villar del Salz Spain
183 P8 Villar de Olalla Spain
182 H6 Villar de Peralonso Spain
184 H2 Villar de Rena Spain
183 O4 Villar de Torre Spain
185 K5 Villardompardo Spain
187 E8 Villareal Spain
Villareal Spain see Villarreal
Villareal de los Infantes Spain see Villareal
261 F3 Villa Reducción Arg.
260 D6 Villa Regina Arg.
183 O9 Villarejo de Fuentes Spain
183 K9 Villarejo de Montalbán Spain
182 I4 Villarejo de Orbigo Spain
183 N8 Villarejo de Salvanés Spain
191 J3 Villa Rendena Italy
183 J3 Villarente Spain
182 I6 Villares de la Reina Spain
253 F6 Villa Rey Para.
260 E3 Villa Reynolds Arg.
185 L5 Villargordo Spain
182 H6 Villarino de los Aires Spain
186 D6 Villarluengo Spain
194 G9 Villa Romana del casale tourist site Italy
194 G8 Villarosa Sicilia Italy
186 C6 Villarquemado Spain
183 K4 Villarramiel Spain
186 C5 Villarreal de Huerva Spain
260 A6 Villarrica Chile
253 F6 Villarrica Para.
260 A6 Villarrica, Lago l. Chile
260 B6 Villarrica, Parque Nacional nat. park Chile
182 I5 Villarrín de Campos Spain
185 N2 Villarrobledo Spain
185 N4 Villarrodrigo Spain
183 P4 Villarroya Spain
186 D6 Villarroya de los Pinares Spain
185 L2 Villarrubia de los Ojos Spain
183 N9 Villarrubia de Santiago Spain
183 O9 Villarrubio Spain
261 H4 Villars Arg.
162 F5 Villars Aquitaine France
161 E6 Villars Rhône-Alpes France
161 J7 Villar-St-Pancrace France
183 P9 Villars del Saz Spain
160 J2 Villars-lès-Blamont France
160 G5 Villars-les-Dombes France
161 K9 Villars-sur-Var France
185 P2 Villarta Spain
185 J2 Villarta de los Montes Spain
185 M2 Villarta de San Juan Spain
234 F6 Villas NJ U.S.A.
Villasalazar Zimbabwe see Sango
192 C9 Villasalto Sardegna Italy
180 E1 Villasana de Mena Spain
183 L4 Villasandino Spain
195 J7 Villa San Giovanni Italy
261 H3 Villa San José Arg.
Villa Sanjurjo Morocco see Al Hoceima
261 H3 Villa San Marcial Arg.
258 D3 Villa San Martin Arg.
193 M4 Villa Santa Maria Italy
260 D2 Villa Santa Rita de Catuna Arg.
260 C2 Villa Santa Rosa Arg.
183 N2 Villasante de Montija Spain
191 N3 Villa Santina Italy
260 E4 Villa Sarmiento Arg.
183 L4 Villasarracino Spain
261 F4 Villa Sauze Arg.
163 I9 Villasavary France
183 O6 Villasayas Spain
261 I3 Villasboas Uru.
182 G6 Villasbuenas Spain
182 H6 Villasdardo Spain
182 H3 Villaseca de Laciana Spain
183 M9 Villaseca de la Sagra Spain
182 H6 Villaseco de los Gamitos Spain
182 H6 Villaseco de los Reyes Spain
182 I6 Villaseco del Pan Spain
183 M9 Villasequilla de Yepes Spain
252 D4 Villa Serrano Bol.
192 D9 Villasimius Sardegna Italy
195 I9 Villasmundo Sicilia Italy
192 B9 Villasor Sardegna Italy
192 B9 Villaspeciosa Sardegna Italy
182 G8 Villasrubias Spain
187 C7 Villastar Spain
183 N4 Villasur de Herreros Spain
183 N9 Villatobas Spain
183 J7 Villatoro Spain
187 C9 Villatoya Spain
261 E2 Villa Tulumba Arg.
183 J3 Villaturiel Spain
183 K4 Villaumbrales Spain
258 C3 Villa Unión Arg.
243 I3 Villa Unión Coahuila Mex.
244 C2 Villa Unión Durango Mex.
244 A2 Villa Unión Sinaloa Mex.
192 B8 Villaurbana Sardegna Italy
261 G2 Villa Urquiza Arg.
260 E4 Villa Valeria Arg.
193 L4 Villavallelonga Italy
246 H4 Villa Vasquez Dom. Rep.
183 O4 Villavelayo Spain
216 □3b Villaverde Fuerteventura Canary Is
192 B8 Villa Verde Sardegna Italy
185 N4 Villaverde de Guadalimar Spain
184 H5 Villaverde del Río Spain
187 A8 Villaverde y Pasaconsol Spain
190 F6 Villavernia Italy
250 C3 Villavicencio Col.
183 J2 Villaviciosa Spain
183 J1 Villaviciosa, Ría de inlet Spain
185 I4 Villaviciosa de Córdoba Spain
183 M8 Villaviciosa de Odón Spain
244 D7 Villa Victoria Mex.
187 E8 Villavieja Spain
183 M6 Villavieja del Lozoya Spain
182 H7 Villavieja de Yeltes Spain
252 D4 Villa Viscarra Bol.
183 L5 Villaviudas Spain
182 G2 Villayón Spain
183 K3 Villazanzo de Valderaduey Spain
252 D5 Villazon Bol.
157 N7 Villé France
160 G5 Villebois France
162 E5 Villebois-Lavalette France
163 G8 Villebrumier France
163 E9 Villecomtal-sur-Arros France
160 G1 Villecomte France
161 I9 Villecroze France
161 B10 Villedaigne France
244 F3 Ville de Ramos Mex.
244 G4 Ville de Reyes Mex.
159 I7 Villedieu-la-Blouère France
158 I4 Villedieu-les-Poêles France
159 O8 Villedieu-sur-Indre France
192 C2 Ville-di-Pietrabugno Corse France
159 M6 Villedômer France
156 G5 Ville-en-Tardenois France
162 E3 Villefagnan France
160 G5 Villefontaine France
161 D8 Villefort France
156 F8 Villefranche Bourgogne France
163 F9 Villefranche Midi-Pyrénées France
163 I8 Villefranche-d'Albigeois France
160 B4 Villefranche-d'Allier France
163 I10 Villefranche-de-Conflent France
163 H9 Villefranche-de-Lauragais France
162 E6 Villefranche-de-Lonchat France
161 B8 Villefranche-de-Panat France
163 I7 Villefranche-de-Rouergue France
163 G6 Villefranche-du-Périgord France
159 O7 Villefranche-sur-Cher France
161 K9 Villefranche-sur-Mer France
160 F5 Villefranche-sur-Saône France
163 B9 Villefranque France
183 L4 Villegas Spain
244 E3 Ville Juarez Mex.
187 C7 Villel Spain
244 G4 Villela Mex.
161 G9 Villelaure France
156 E8 Villemandeur France
227 O2 Ville-Marie Que. Can.
Ville-Marie Que. Can. see Montréal
156 G7 Villemaur-sur-Vanne France
227 P1 Villemontel Que. Can.
156 H7 Villemorien France
163 I9 Villemoustaussou France
163 H8 Villemur-sur-Tarn France
187 D10 Villena Spain
156 G6 Villenauxe-la-Grande France
163 C6 Villenave-d'Ornon France
163 I7 Villeneuve Midi-Pyrénées France
161 H9 Villeneuve Provence-Alpes-Côte d'Azur France
160 F4 Villeneuve Rhône-Alpes France
190 B3 Villeneuve Switz.
156 G7 Villeneuve-au-Chemin France
161 C6 Villeneuve-d'Allier France
156 F2 Villeneuve-d'Ascq France
161 F7 Villeneuve-de-Berg France
163 D8 Villeneuve-de-Marsan France
163 F9 Villeneuve-de-Rivière France
163 H10 Villeneuve-d'Olmes France
163 H9 Villeneuve-du-Paréage France
156 F7 Villeneuve-la-Guyard France
156 G7 Villeneuve-l'Archevêque France
161 F9 Villeneuve-lès-Avignon France
161 C10 Villeneuve-lès-Béziers France
161 D9 Villeneuve-lès-Maguelone France
161 K9 Villeneuve-Loubet France
156 F5 Villeneuve-St-Germain France
160 C3 Villeneuve-sur-Allier France
163 F7 Villeneuve-sur-Lot France
156 F7 Villeneuve-sur-Yonne France
163 G8 Villeneuve-Tolosane France
163 H9 Villenouvelle France
163 I9 Villepinte France
237 I10 Ville Platte LA U.S.A.
159 M2 Villequier France
161 B7 Villercomtal France
163 F6 Villeréal France
160 E5 Villerest France
160 E5 Villerest, Barrage de dam France
183 K5 Villerías Spain
161 B10 Villerouge-Termenès France
159 J3 Villers-Bocage Basse-Normandie France
156 D4 Villers-Bocage Picardie France
156 E4 Villers-Bretonneux France
156 E4 Villers-Carbonnel France
156 F5 Villers-Cotterêts France
156 A4 Villers-Écalles France
157 I5 Villers-en-Argonne France
160 I1 Villersexel France
160 H2 Villers-Farlay France
165 H7 Villers-le-Bouillet Belgium
160 J2 Villers-le-lac France
157 L6 Villers-lès-Nancy France
156 F3 Villers-Outréaux France
165 B10 Villers-St-Paul France
156 I4 Villers-Semeuse France
190 C2 Villers-sur-Glâne Switz.
159 K3 Villers-sur-Mer France
157 J5 Villers-sur-Meuse France
157 K5 Villerupt France
159 L3 Villerville France
156 H7 Villery France
156 H6 Villeseneux France
161 G8 Villes-sur-Auzon France
157 I5 Ville-sur-Tourbe France
253 F6 Villeta Para.
193 L4 Villetta Barrea Italy
160 G5 Villette-d'Anthon France
160 F5 Villeurbanne France
161 D9 Villeveyrac France
161 F6 Villevocance France
244 G3 Ville Zaragoza Mex.
260 C2 Villicun, Sierra mts Arg.
160 F4 Villié-Morgon France
215 M3 Villiers S. Africa
159 J6 Villiers-Charlemagne France
214 D9 Villiersdorp S. Africa
157 I6 Villiers-en-Lieu France
162 C3 Villiers-en-Plaine France
156 D5 Villiers-le-Bel France
157 J7 Villiers-le-Sec France
156 F8 Villiers-St-Benoît France
156 F6 Villiers-St-Georges France
147 G8 Villierstown Ireland
160 G5 Villieu-Loyes-Mollon France
172 E5 Villingen Ger.
172 F5 Villingendorf Ger.
169 F10 Villmar Ger.
183 K4 Villoldo Spain
183 Q9 Villora Spain
183 Q9 Villora r. Spain
191 M4 Villorba Italy
190 G4 Villoresi, Canale canal Italy
183 J7 Villoria Spain
183 J6 Villoruela Spain
157 J6 Villotte-sur-Aire France
185 H1 Villuercas, Sierra de las mts Spain
114 F7 Villupuram Tamil Nadu India
170 I2 Vilm i. Ger.
177 K3 Vilmány Hungary
223 I4 Vilna Alta Can.
Vilna Lith. see Vilnius
144 J1 Vilnesfjorden inlet Norway
138 I7 Vilnius Lith.
137 N5 Vil'nohirs'k Ukr.
137 O6 Vil'nyans'k Ukr.
186 K4 Viloví d'Onyar Spain
141 R5 Vilppula Fin.
178 C4 Vils Austria
173 L3 Vils r. Ger.
173 O4 Vils r. Ger.
138 E3 Vilsandi i. Estonia
138 E3 Vilsandi nature res. Estonia
173 M5 Vilsbiburg Ger.
173 L2 Vilseck Ger.
137 K4 Vil'shana Cherkas'ka Oblast' Ukr.
137 L3 Vil'shana Chernihivs'ka Oblast' Ukr.
137 Q4 Vil'shana Kharkivs'ka Oblast' Ukr.
136 J5 Vil'shanka Kirovohrads'ka Oblast' Ukr.
136 H5 Vil'shanka Vinnyts'ka Oblast' Ukr.
136 H3 Vil'shanka Zhytomyrs'ka Oblast' Ukr.
173 O4 Vilshofen Ger.
142 E5 Vilsund Vest Denmark
Viluppuram Tamil Nadu India see Villupuram
138 K4 Viluste Estonia
182 G6 Vilvestre Spain
165 F7 Vilvoorde Belgium
138 J7 Vilyeyka Belarus
138 K7 Vilyeyskaye Vodaskhovishcha l. Belarus
131 N3 Vilyuy r. Rus. Fed.
131 M3 Vilyuyskoye Vodokhranilishche resr Rus. Fed.
209 F8 Vimbe mt. Zambia
186 H5 Vimbodi Spain
184 A2 Vimeiro Port.
190 G4 Vimercate Italy
156 C3 Vimeu reg. France
182 B2 Vimianzo Spain
184 D3 Vimieiro Port.
182 G5 Vimioso Port.
143 L4 Vimmerby Sweden
156 E8 Vimory France
159 L4 Vimoutiers France
140 Q5 Vimpeli Fin.
176 C2 Vimperk Czech Rep.
207 I5 Vina r. Cameroon
240 J2 Vina CA U.S.A.
186 D5 Vinaceite Spain
260 B3 Viña del Mar Chile
190 C7 Vinadio Italy
186 G5 Vinaixa Spain
246 B2 Viñales Cuba
246 E4 Viñales Valley tourist site Cuba
233 □Q4 Vinalhaven ME U.S.A.
233 Q4 Vinalhaven Island ME U.S.A.
187 D11 Vinalopó r. Spain
213 □K2 Vinanivao Madag.
171 J10 Vinařice Czech Rep.
78 □6 Vinarori, Mount New Georgia Is Solomon Is
186 F7 Vinaròs Spain
Vinaroz Spain see Vinaròs
161 C10 Vinassan France
161 G6 Vinay France
245 J5 Vinazco r. Mex.
163 J10 Vinça France
225 F2 Vincelotte, Lac l. Que. Can.
217 □1c Vincendo Réunion
230 D6 Vincennes IN U.S.A.
263 H2 Vincennes Bay Antarctica
82 □1 Vincent, Point Norfolk I.
234 F5 Vincentown NJ U.S.A.
250 B5 Vinces r. Ecuador
157 L7 Vincey France
193 N5 Vinchiaturo Italy
258 C3 Vinchina Arg.
252 B3 Vinchos Peru
191 J8 Vinci Italy
168 J1 Vindeballe Denmark
140 O5 Vindelälven r. Sweden
140 M3 Vindelfjällens naturreservat nature res. Sweden
140 O4 Vindeln Sweden
142 E5 Vinderup Denmark
116 E8 Vindhya Range hills Madh. Prad. India
Vindobona Austria see Wien
186 G5 Vinebre Spain
234 E6 Vineland NJ U.S.A.
159 N6 Vineuil Centre France
159 O8 Vineuil Centre France
215 K6 Vineyard S. Africa
196 J4 Vinga Romania
196 J4 Vingăi, Câmpia plain Romania
143 L2 Vingåker Sweden
160 G2 Vingeanne r. France
163 J10 Vingrau France
96 G5 Vinh Vietnam
182 G5 Vinhais Port.
182 G5 Vinhas Port.
96 G3 Vinh Loc Vietnam
97 G9 Vinh Long Vietnam
96 H4 Vinh Thưc, Đao i. Vietnam
96 G4 Vinh Yên Vietnam
179 N7 Vinica Croatia
197 K9 Vinica Macedonia
177 I3 Vinica Slovakia
176 G3 Viničné Slovakia
179 O1 Viničné Šumice Czech Rep.
183 O4 Viniegra de Arriba Spain
237 H7 Vinita OK U.S.A.
116 B8 Vinjhan Gujarat India
Vînju Mare Romania see Vânju Mare
136 G4 Vin'kivtsi Ukr.
188 G3 Vinkovci Croatia
Vinland i. Nfld and Lab. Can. see Newfoundland
177 K3 Vinné Slovakia
138 J2 Vinni Estonia
172 D3 Vinningen Ger.
Vinnitsa Ukr. see Vinnytsya
Vinnitsa Oblast admin. div. Ukr. see Vinnyts'ka Oblast'
Vinnitskaya Oblast' admin. div. Ukr. see Vinnyts'ka Oblast'
139 R1 Vinnitsy Rus. Fed.
136 G5 Vinnyts'ka Oblast' admin. div. Ukr.
136 H4 Vinnytsya Ukr.
Vinnytsya Oblast admin. div. Ukr. see Vinnyts'ka Oblast'
182 I6 Vino, Tierra del reg. Spain
177 H3 Vinodol Slovakia
Vinogradov Ukr. see Vynohradiv
139 V6 Vinogradovo Rus. Fed.
177 G3 Vinohrady nad Váhom Slovakia
143 L2 Vinön i. Sweden
161 H9 Vinon-sur-Verdon France
161 G8 Vinsobres France
262 S1 Vinson Massif mt. Antarctica
141 J6 Vinstra Norway
92 C2 Vintar Luzon Phil.
236 I4 Vinton IA U.S.A.
185 K7 Viñuela, Embalse de la resr Spain
183 N7 Viñuelas Spain
183 O5 Vinuesa Spain
114 F4 Vinukonda Andhra Prad. India
209 B5 Vinza Congo
170 E5 Vinzelberg Ger.
168 H1 Viöl Ger.
186 D3 Violada, Llanos de la plain Spain
160 E5 Violay France
161 F8 Violès France
Violeta Cuba see Primero de Enero
86 I4 Violet Valley Aboriginal Reserve W.A. Austr.
161 D9 Viols-le-Fort France
214 B4 Vioolsdrif S. Africa
156 D5 Viosne r. France

179 I8 Vipava Slovenia
179 I8 Vipava Slovenia
211 B8 Viphya Mountains Malawi
191 K2 Vipiteno Italy
170 G4 Vipperow Ger.
93 E8 Viqueque East Timor
188 E3 Vir i. Croatia
179 K7 Vir Slovenia
92 E5 Virac Phil.
92 E5 Virac Point Phil.
256 C4 Viradouro Brazil
116 D8 Viramgam Gujarat India
127 I5 Viranşehir Turkey
114 D6 Virarajendrapet Karnataka India
123 N9 Virawah Pak.
138 M6 Virawlya Belarus
163 E6 Virazeil France
138 G5 Vircava r. Latvia/Lith.
86 D6 Virchow, Mount hill W.A. Austr.
Virdáánjarga Fin. see Virtaniemi
223 K5 Virden Man. Can.
159 J4 Vire France
159 I3 Vire r. France
209 B8 Virei Angola
156 I3 Vireux-Molhain France
156 I3 Vireux-Wallerand France
156 H7 Vireux-sur-Bar France
257 F2 Virgem da Lapa Brazil
178 F5 Virgen Austria
185 O6 Virgen, Puerto de la pass Spain
183 Q5 Virgen, Sierra de la mts Spain
259 C9 Virgenes, Cabo c. Arg.
178 F5 Virgental val. Austria
241 R5 Virgin r. AZ U.S.A.
227 O1 Virginatown Ont. Can.
247 K4 Virgin Gorda i. Virgin Is (U.K.)
147 H5 Virginia Ireland
215 K4 Virginia S. Africa
226 B2 Virginia MN U.S.A.
232 G11 Virginia state U.S.A.
233 J12 Virginia Beach VA U.S.A.
238 I4 Virginia City MT U.S.A.
240 M2 Virginia City NV U.S.A.
222 E2 Virginia Falls N.W.T. Can.
151 K5 Virginia Water Surrey, England U.K.
247 K4 Virgin Islands (U.K.) terr. West Indies
247 K4 Virgin Islands (U.S.A.) terr. West Indies
241 R5 Virgin Mountains AZ U.S.A.
257 F2 Virginópolis Brazil
160 G4 Viriat France
160 G6 Virieu France
160 H5 Virieu-le-Grand France
160 E5 Virignin France
160 H5 Virignin France
161 G6 Viriville France
138 I1 Virkkala Fin.
138 I1 Virmasvesi I. Fin.
97 H8 Viröchéy Cambodia
165 G8 Viroin r. Belgium
141 S6 Virolahti Fin.
226 D6 Viroqua WI U.S.A.
188 F3 Virovitica Croatia
138 F4 Virpe Latvia
141 Q5 Virrat Fin.
143 L4 Virserum Sweden
140 T2 Virtaniemi Fin.
165 I9 Virton Belgium
138 G3 Virtsu Estonia
252 A2 Virú Peru
251 F4 Viruá, Parque Nacional do nat. park Brazil
114 E8 Virudhunagar Tamil Nadu India
208 F5 Virunga, Parc National des nat. park Dem. Rep. Congo
138 F5 Virvytė r. Lith.
160 H4 Viry Franche-Comté France
160 I4 Viry Rhône-Alpes France
156 F4 Viry-Moureuil France
188 F4 Vis i. Croatia
188 F4 Vis i. Croatia
161 G9 Vis, Gorges de la France
138 J6 Visaginas Lith.
Visakhapatnam Andhra Prad. India see Vishakhapatnam
78 □3 Visale Guadalcanal Solomon Is
240 M5 Visalia CA U.S.A.
161 F8 Visan France
197 P5 Vişani Romania
123 O3 Visavadar India
116 C9 Visavadar Gujarat India
92 E6 Visayan Islands Phil.
92 D6 Visayan Sea Phil.
168 F5 Visbek Ger.
168 G1 Visby Denmark
143 O4 Visby Gotland Sweden
257 F4 Visconde de Rio Branco Brazil
221 G2 Viscount Melville Sound sea chan. N.W.T./Nunavut Can.
165 I7 Visé Belgium
130 I2 Vise, Ostrov i. Rus. Fed.
188 G4 Višegrad Bos.-Herz.
191 N7 Viserba Italy
254 D2 Viseu Brazil
182 E7 Viseu Port.
182 E7 Viseu admin. dist. Port.
197 M3 Vişeu r. Romania
197 M3 Vişeu de Sus Romania
191 R5 Viševica mt. Croatia
115 H4 Vishakhapatnam Andhra Prad. India
197 O9 Vishegrad hill Bulg.
134 L4 Vishera r. Rus. Fed.
134 O3 Vishera r. Rus. Fed.
135 H5 Vishnevoye Rus. Fed. see Vyshneve
138 J7 Vishnyeva Belarus
186 C6 Visiedo Spain
138 K4 Visikums Latvia
134 L4 Visim Rus. Fed.
197 N6 Vişina Romania
143 K3 Visingsö i. Sweden
142 I4 Viskan r. Sweden
138 J5 Viški Latvia
143 K5 Vislanda Sweden
116 D8 Visnagar Gujarat India
179 K8 Višnja Gora Slovenia
171 L9 Višňová Czech Rep.
176 F3 Višňové Slovakia
177 H2 Višňové Slovakia
190 C6 Viso, Monte mt. Italy
185 L3 Viso del Marqués Spain
188 G4 Visoko Bos.-Herz.
190 F6 Visone Italy
177 J4 Visonta Hungary
190 D3 Viso Switz.
215 J7 Visrivier S. Africa
161 D6 Vissac-Auteyrac France
114 G4 Vissannapeta Andhra Prad. India
143 L5 Visselfjärda Sweden
168 I5 Visselhövede Ger.
143 K5 Vissjön i. Sweden
193 K2 Visso Italy
190 D3 Vissoie Switz.
240 O8 Vista CA U.S.A.
135 N7 Vista NY U.S.A.
250 D4 Vista Alegre Amazonas Brazil
251 F6 Vista Alegre Amazonas Brazil
253 F4 Vista Alegre Mato Grosso do Sul Brazil
251 F4 Vista Alegre Roraima Brazil
187 E7 Vistabella del Maestrazgo Spain
245 J2 Vista Flores Arg.
245 A2 Vista Hermosa Mex.
242 M6 Vista Lake CA U.S.A.
142 J2 Vistan r. Sweden
198 G1 Vistonida, Limni lag. Greece
Vistula r. Pol. see Wisła
138 F7 Vištytis Lith.
175 K1 Vištytytis i. Lith./Rus. Fed.
137 L6 Visun r. Ukr.
117 O7 Viswema Nagaland India
177 J4 Visznek Hungary
197 M7 Vit r. Bulg.
250 E3 Vita Col.
194 D8 Vita Sicilia Italy
192 E2 Vita, Capo c. Italy

123 M7 Vitat Pak.
196 G7 Vitać mt. Montenegro
177 J3 Vitáz Slovakia
192 I3 Viterbo Italy
192 H3 Viterbo prov. Italy
156 I4 Viterne France
188 F3 Vitez Bos.-Herz.
188 G4 Vitez Bos.-Herz.
252 D6 Vitichi Bol.
182 N6 Vitigudino Spain
172 D6 Viti Levu i. Fiji
172 D6 Viti Levu i. Fiji
196 I9 Vitina Kosovo Serbia
179 L2 Vitina Austria
177 G2 Vítkov Czech Rep.
179 O4 Vitnyéd Hungary
78 □6 Vito P.N.G.
197 J9 Vitolište Macedonia
207 F5 Vitória Spain
164 G4 Vitomirica Kosovo Serbia
252 C4 Vitor Peru
252 B4 Vitor r. Peru
192 I3 Vitorchiano Italy
257 G4 Vitória Espírito Santo Brazil
251 H5 Vitória Pará Brazil
Vitória-Gasteiz
183 O3 Vitoria airport Spain
183 O3 Vitoria, Montes de mts Spain
255 E5 Vitória da Conquista Brazil
183 O3 Vitoria-Gasteiz Spain
264 G7 Vitória Seamount sea feature S. Atlantic Ocean
197 L8 Vitreva nat. park Bulg.
195 M5 Vitravo r. Italy
158 I5 Vitré France
157 K8 Vitrey-sur-Mance France
156 E3 Vitrolles France
156 I6 Vitry-en-Artois France
156 I6 Vitry-en-Perthois France
156 H6 Vitry-la-Ville France
156 I6 Vitry-le-François France
160 D3 Vitry-sur-Loire France
156 D6 Vitry-sur-Seine France
136 I2 Vits' r. Belarus
139 N6 Vitsyebsk Belarus
138 L6 Vitsyebskaya Voblasts' admin. div. Belarus
140 P3 Vittangi Sweden
160 F2 Vitteaux France
157 K7 Vittel France
141 H10 Vittoria Sicilia Italy
123 M3 Vittoria Malta see Birgu
191 H4 Vittorio Veneto Italy
172 F5 Vityazevskiy Liman lag. Rus. Fed.
173 I5 Vöhl Ger.
138 I3 Võhma Estonia
172 E5 Vöhrenbach Ger.
172 F5 Vöhringen Baden-Württemberg Ger.
173 I5 Vöhringen Bayern Ger.
157 K8 Void-Vacon France
171 D8 Voigtstedt Ger.
141 S6 Voikoski Fin.
157 I6 Voillecomte France
152 N1 Voineasa Romania
197 P3 Voineşti Romania
206 C4 Voinjama Liberia
139 T8 Voin Pervyy Rus. Fed.
161 G6 Voiron France
161 H6 Voironnais reg. France
178 G7 Voitsberg Austria
179 L5 Voitsberg Austria
177 K3 Vojčice Slovakia
142 F6 Vojens Denmark
185 N3 Vojmsjön i. Sweden
231 F9 Vojnić Croatia
157 I4 Vivier-au-Court France
161 F8 Viviers France
213 F4 Vivo S. Africa
179 K7 Vivodnik mt. Slovenia
162 E3 Vivonne France
261 F4 Vivoro Arg.
261 I3 Vivoratá Arg.

164 H5 Vlijmen Neth.
165 E6 Vlissingen Neth.
198 A2 Vlorë Albania
198 A2 Vlorës, Gjiri i b. Albania
169 G6 Vlotho Ger.
176 D1 Vlotslavsk Pol. see Włocławek
179 J7 Vnanje Gorice Slovenia
139 T2 Vnina r. Rus. Fed.
120 K7 Vobkent Uzbek.
121 F7 Vockerode Ger.
179 I3 Vöcklabruck Austria
157 L6 Vöcklabruck Austria
138 D3 Voderady Slovakia
191 Q5 Vodice Istra Croatia
188 E4 Vodice Šibenik Croatia
134 G3 Vodlozero, Ozero I. Rus. Fed.
176 D2 Vodňany Czech Rep.
188 G4 Vodnjan Croatia
Vodopyanovo Rus. Fed. see Donskoye
146 □N2 Voe Shetland, Scotland U.K.
215 J9 Voedoe (Niederrhein) Ger.
169 G6 Voerendaal Neth.
142 G4 Voersaa Denmark
157 O7 Vogan Togo
142 G4 Vogelenzang Neth.
157 O7 Vogelkop Peninsula Papua Indon. see Doberai, Jazirah
207 H4 Vogel Peak Nigeria
169 G9 Vogelsang Ger.
171 H6 Vogelsberg hills Ger.
157 O7 Vogelsdorf Ger.
157 O7 Vogelsheim France
172 D3 Vogelweh Ger.
190 G6 Voghera Italy
191 L6 Voghiera Italy
129 H6 Vognill r. Armenia
142 J5 Vognill Norway
188 G4 Vogošća Bos.-Herz.
172 H6 Vogt Ger.
173 M6 Vogtareuth Ger.
169 G10 Vogtland reg. Ger.
171 E7 Vogué France
78 □5 Voh New Caledonia
173 L4 Vohburg an der Donau Ger.
173 M2 Vohémar Madag. see Iharaña
213 □J4 Vohibinany Madag. see Ampasimanelotra
213 □J4 Vohilava Fianarantsoa Madag.
213 □K4 Vohilava Fianarantsoa Madag.
Vohimena, Madag. see Iharaña
213 □J5 Vohimena, Tanjona c. Madag.
213 □J4 Vohipeno Madag.
213 □K4 Vohitrandriana Madag.
169 G8 Vöhl Ger.
138 I3 Võhma Estonia
172 E5 Vöhrenbach Ger.
172 F5 Vöhringen Baden-Württemberg Ger.
173 I5 Vöhringen Bayern Ger.
157 K8 Void-Vacon France
171 D8 Voigtstedt Ger.
141 S6 Voikoski Fin.
157 I6 Voillecomte France
152 N1 Voineasa Romania
197 P3 Voineşti Romania
206 C4 Voinjama Liberia
139 T8 Voin Pervyy Rus. Fed.
161 G6 Voiron France
161 H6 Voironnais reg. France
178 G7 Voitsberg Austria
179 L5 Voitsberg Austria
177 K3 Vojčice Slovakia
142 F6 Vojens Denmark
185 N3 Vojmsjön i. Sweden
231 F9 Vojnić Croatia
179 L7 Vojnik Slovenia
196 H5 Vojvodina prov. Serbia
138 K2 Voka Estonia
177 H6 Vokány Hungary
134 I4 Vokhma Rus. Fed.
134 U4 Voknavolok Rus. Fed.
207 I4 Voko Cameroon
176 C3 Vol' r. Rus. Fed.
176 C3 Vol' r. Rus. Fed.
136 D2 Volary Czech Rep.
232 G6 Volborg MT U.S.A.
258 D1 Volcán Arg.
252 D5 Volcán, Cerro del vol. Chile
260 B4 Volcán, Cerro del vol. Chile
261 H5 Volcán, Sierra del mts Arg.
242 □R13 Volcán Barú, Parque Nacional nat. park Panama
240 □F14 Volcano House HI U.S.A.
79 □7a Volcano Islands N. Pacific Ocean see Kazan-rettō

100 I4 Volochayevka-Vtoraya Rus. Fed.
136 F4 Volochys'k Ukr.
136 I4 Volochys'k Ukr.
175 J1 Volodarovka Rus. Fed.
137 O6 Volodars'ke Ukr.
120 C4 Volodarskiy Rus. Fed.
136 H3 Volodars'k-Volyns'kyy Ukr.
137 L6 Volodymyrets' Ukr.
137 J5 Volodymyrivka Ukr.
136 D3 Volodymyr-Volyns'kyy Ukr.
134 G4 Vologda Rus. Fed.
134 G4 Vologda Oblast admin. div. Rus. Fed.
157 M7 Vologne r. France
139 Y2 Vologodskaya Oblast' admin. div. Rus. Fed.
136 D4 Voronyaky hills Ukr.
134 H4 Voron'ye Rus. Fed.
137 O4 Voronzhilov Yar Ukr.
135 S5 Volokolamsk Rus. Fed.
135 G6 Voloknovka Rus. Fed.
134 J2 Volokovaya Rus. Fed.
134 I2 Volonne France
135 O4 Volop S. Africa
214 G4 Volop S. Africa
138 D3 Volosha Greece
138 S5 Voloshino Rus. Fed.
134 H3 Voloshka Rus. Fed.
139 Q6 Vorot'kovo Rus. Fed.
139 N4 Volot Rus. Fed.
139 N4 Volot Rus. Fed.
177 L3 Volosyanka Ukr.
139 N4 Volot Rus. Fed.
139 N3 Volotovo Rus. Fed.
136 C5 Volovets' Ukr.
135 G5 Volovo Lipetskaya Oblast' Rus. Fed.
139 V8 Volovo Tul'skaya Oblast' Rus. Fed.
120 B1 Volsk Rus. Fed.
214 H9 Volsdraai S. Africa
214 G6 Volstruispoort pass S. Africa
207 F5 Volta r. Ghana
207 F5 Volta, Lake resr Ghana
86 H3 Voltaire, Cape W.A. Austr.
Volta Noire r. Africa see Black Volta
257 E5 Volta Redonda Brazil
Volta Rouge r. Burkina/Ghana see Nazinon
191 J4 Volterra Italy
169 E6 Voltlage Ger.
183 K6 Voltoya r. Spain
190 H2 Volturara Appula Italy
194 H2 Volturino Italy
194 G3 Volturino, Monte mt. Italy
193 P7 Volturno r. Italy
204 D2 Volubilis tourist site Morocco
139 U8 Volúntari Romania
235 L1 Voluntown CT U.S.A.
198 E2 Volvi, Limni l. Greece
160 C5 Volvic France
161 H9 Volx France
139 U2 Volya Belarus
137 S2 Volya Druha Ukr.
176 C2 Volyně Czech Rep.
137 L2 Volynka r. Rus. Fed.
139 N1 Volynka Ukr.
Volyn Oblast admin. div. Ukr. see Volyns'ka Oblast'
136 D2 Volyns'ka Oblast' admin. div. Ukr.
Volynskaya Oblast' admin. div. Ukr. see Volyns'ka Oblast'
136 F4 Volytsya Ukr.
136 I4 Volytsya Ukr.
134 J5 Volzhsk Rus. Fed.
131 P2 Volzhskiy Samarskaya Oblast' Rus. Fed.
135 I6 Volzhskiy Volgogradskaya Oblast' Rus. Fed.
79 □7a Voma mts Viti Levu Fiji
193 M2 Vomano r. Italy
79 □7a Vomo i. Fiji
178 E5 Vomp Austria
78 □6 Vonavona i. New Georgia Is Solomon Is
223 J4 Vonda Sask. Can.
213 □J4 Vondroz Madag.
190 B4 Vonga Italy
197 N6 Vonitsa Greece
164 H3 Vonnas France
138 I2 Võnnu Estonia
138 I2 Võnnu Estonia
213 □J4 Vonozero Rus. Fed.
172 K6 Võõbu Estonia
138 I2 Võsu Estonia
164 G3 Voorburg Neth.
164 H3 Voorhout Neth.
233 I5 Voorheesville NY U.S.A.
164 H3 Voorschoten Neth.
164 I3 Voorthuizen Neth.
164 I4 Vootkurk sea chan. Estonia
140 □F1 Vopnafjörður Iceland
140 □F1 Vopnafjörður b. Iceland
174 K4 Voralm mt. Austria
162 I3 Voran r. France
162 I3 Vorarlberg land Austria
174 H3 Vorarlberg land Austria
164 J4 Vorden Neth.
179 K4 Vordernberg Austria
179 J3 Vorderrhein r. Switz.
172 G6 Vordorf Ger.
169 G9 Vordorf Ger.
169 H9 Vordorf Ger.
142 H6 Vordingborg Denmark
179 K4 Vordorf Austria
164 H4 Voorthuizen Neth.
198 B2 Voreia Pindos mts Greece
198 B2 Voreies Echinades i. Greece
198 E3 Voreies Sporades is Greece
199 G3 Voreio Aigaio admin. reg. Greece
198 E4 Voreios Evvoïkos Kolpos sea chan. Greece
Voreioi Sporádhes i. Greece see Voreies Sporades
Voreia Pindos mts Greece see Voreia Pindos
264 J1 Voring Plateau sea feature N. Atlantic Ocean
117 O5 Vorjing mt. Arun. Prad. India
141 T6 Vorkuta Rus. Fed.
142 I1 Vorma r. Norway
138 C2 Vormedalsheia park Norway
138 E3 Volksrust S. Africa
141 M6 Vorms Sweden
141 N6 Voxnan r. Sweden
141 J4 Voya r. Rus. Fed.
139 W9 Voya r. Rus. Fed.
160 G6 Voya r. Rus. Fed.
197 K8 Voynag Bos.-Herz.
236 I1 Voyagers National Park MN U.S.A.
137 J5 Voyevodske Ukr.
140 V1 Voynitsa Rus. Fed.
139 T6 Voynytsya Ukr.
197 K5 Voyvodina Romania
134 K2 Voyvozh Rus. Fed.
135 W9 Voronezh Rus. Fed.
134 H4 Vozhega Rus. Fed.
78 □8 Voz'ma r. Rus. Fed.
78 □8 Voza Choiseul Solomon Is
131 T5 Vozdvizhenka Rus. Fed.

135 H6 Voronezhskaya Oblast' admin. div. Rus. Fed.
135 G6 Voronezhskiy Zapovednik nature res. Rus. Fed.
137 S2 Voronezh Rus. Fed.
Vodokhranilishche resr Rus. Fed.
137 M2 Voronizh Ukr.
137 M3 Voron'ky Ukr.
136 F2 Voronky Ukr.
137 L1 Voronok Rus. Fed.
134 H2 Voronov, Mys pt Rus. Fed.
139 P1 Voronovo Rus. Fed.
139 U6 Voronovo Rus. Fed.
136 H4 Voronovytsya Ukr.
134 G4 Voronontsovka Rus. Fed.
138 L4 Vorontsovo-Aleksandrovskoye Rus. Fed. see Zelenokumsk
136 D4 Voronyaky hills Ukr.
134 H4 Voron'ye Rus. Fed.
137 O4 Voronzhilov Yar Ukr.
135 G6 Volokolamsk Rus. Fed. see Ussuriysk
135 S6 Voroshilovgrad Ukr. see Luhans'k
135 S6 Voroshilovsk Rus. Fed. see Stavropol'
135 S6 Voroshilovsk Ukr. see Alchevs'k
121 S5 Vorota val. Kazakh.
129 H6 Vorotan r. Armenia
139 Q6 Vorot'kovo Rus. Fed.
137 M5 Vorotnets Rus. Fed.
139 T7 Vorotynsk Rus. Fed.
137 D1 Vorovskolesskaya Rus. Fed.
137 N2 Vorozhba Sums'ka Oblast' Ukr.
137 N3 Vorozhba Sums'ka Oblast' Ukr.
170 G2 Vorpommersche Boddenlandschaft, Nationalpark nat. park Ger.
263 B2 Vorposten Peak Antarctica
173 K2 Vorra r. Bulg.
179 M5 Vorsau Austria
157 O3 Vorselaar Belgium
197 O3 Vorsklitsa r. Rus. Fed./Ukr.
165 H6 Vorst Belgium
214 H1 Vorstershoop S. Africa
177 L5 Vorta Romania
263 B2 Vorterkaka Nunatak mt. Antarctica
170 H3 Völschow Ger.
183 I3 Võrtsjärv l. Estonia
138 K4 Võru Estonia
168 H4 Vorukh Tajik.
139 N4 Vorya r. Rus. Fed.
138 H5 Vorzel' Ukr.
175 K4 Vosa Belarus
214 C6 Vosburg S. Africa
205 F3 Vosges dept France
157 M7 Vosges mts France
157 O6 Vosges du Nord, Parc Naturel Régional des nature res. France
139 W4 Voshchazhnikovo Rus. Fed.
129 G4 Voskevan Armenia
134 I3 Voskhod Ger.
139 V6 Voskresenskoye Lipetskaya Oblast' Rus. Fed.
134 H2 Voskresenskoye Lipetskaya Oblast' Rus. Fed.
134 I4 Voskresenskoye Nizhegorodskaya Oblast' Rus. Fed.
120 G1 Voskresenskoye Respublika Bashkortostan Rus. Fed.
139 U7 Voskresenskoye Tul'skaya Oblast' Rus. Fed.
160 F2 Vosne-Romanée France
141 I6 Voss Norway
165 H6 Vosselaar Belgium
199 J6 Vossinaarsari, Ostrov i. Rus. Fed.
134 I4 Voskresenskoye Rus. Fed.
100 M3 Vostochno-Kazakhstanskaya Oblast' admin. div. Kazakh. see Shyghys Qazaqstan
136 F4 Vostochno-Kounradskiy Kazakh. see Shygys Konyrat
131 P2 Vostochno-Sakhalinskiy Gory mts Sakhalin, Rus. Fed.
100 M4 Vostochno-Sibirskoye More sea Rus. Fed.
120 C1 Vostochnyy Kirovskaya Oblast' Rus. Fed.
135 M3 Vostochnyy Sakhalin Rus. Fed.
137 U3 Vostochnyy, Liman l. Rus. Fed.
121 U3 Vostochnyy Kazakhstan
139 U7 Vostochnyy Sayan mts Rus. Fed.
100 I5 Vostok Primorskiy Kray Rus. Fed.
Vostok Sakhalin Rus. Fed. see Neftegorsk
100 I6 Vostretsovo Rus. Fed.
134 I3 Vostroye Rus. Fed.
138 I2 Võsu Estonia
176 E2 Vostur Czech Rep.
179 H7 Votkinsk Rus. Fed.
164 I1 Votkinskoye Vodokhranilishche resr Rus. Fed.
232 I1 Votna r. Norway
256 C5 Votorantim Brazil
139 P6 Votrya r. Rus. Fed.
78 □3 Vot Tandé i. Vanuatu
79 □7a Votua Vanua Levu Fiji
256 B2 Votuporanga Brazil
199 J6 Voudi, Akrotirio pt Rodos Greece
162 C7 Vouga r. Port.
182 C7 Vougeot France
160 D1 Vouillé Poitou-Charentes France
162 D3 Vouillé Poitou-Charentes France
156 E3 Voulaines-les-Templiers France
157 E2 Voulx France
159 M4 Vouneuil-sous-Biard France
159 M4 Vouneuil-sur-Vienne France
209 A5 Voungou Gabon
160 D1 Vouray-sur-Cure France
198 E4 Voutenay-sur-Cure France
165 M7 Vouvant France
157 M7 Vouvray France
153 M4 Vouvrou France
197 J7 Vovchans'k Ukr.
137 K5 Voves France
137 M3 Vovk r. Ukr.
135 G5 Vovkovo Ukr.
139 V5 Vovodo r. C.A.R.
139 W9 Voynytsya Ukr.
137 I5 Voxna Sweden
199 J6 Voya r. Rus. Fed.

139 V5 Vozdvizhenskoye Moskovskaya Oblast' Rus. Fed.
139 W7 Vozha r. Rus. Fed.
134 J3 Vozhayel' Rus. Fed.
134 J2 Vozhgora Rus. Fed.
137 M3 Voronizh Ukr.
136 F2 Vornoky Ukr.
129 C1 Voznesenka Kazakh.
129 F2 Voznesenskaya Krasnodarskiy Kray Rus. Fed.
129 F2 Voznesenskaya Respublika Ingusheriya Rus. Fed.
137 K6 Voznesens'ke Ukr.
137 K6 Voznesens'ke Ukr.
139 Y5 Voznesen'ye Ivanovskaya Oblast' Rus. Fed.
139 S1 Voznesen'ye Leningradskaya Oblast' Rus. Fed.
120 H5 Vozrozhdenie Uzbek.
120 H5 Vozrozhdenya Island pen. Uzbek.
137 L6 Vozsiyats'ke Ukr.
121 N1 Vozvyshenka Kazakh.
100 F3 Vozvyshenskiy Rus. Fed.
142 F4 Vrå Denmark
197 M8 Vråble Slovakia
177 H3 Vráble Slovakia
198 B5 Vrachionas hill Zakynthos Greece
198 C4 Vrachnaiika Greece
142 E2 Vrådal Norway
197 K8 Vranja Banja Serbia
197 K8 Vranje Serbia
172 G1 Vranova Bulg.
177 J3 Vráble Slovakia
188 G3 Vranjak Bos.-Herz.
197 K8 Vranje Serbia
172 D1 Vranova Czech Rep.
176 D1 Vranovice Czech Rep.
177 J3 Vranov nad Topľou Slovakia
179 O6 Vransko Slovenia
191 Q6 Vrana i. Croatia
188 F2 Vrbanja r. Bos.-Herz.
188 F3 Vrbanja Serbia
188 G3 Vrbanja r. Bos.-Herz.
188 F3 Vrbas Vojvodina Serbia
188 G3 Vrbas r. Bos.-Herz.
191 R5 Vrbnik Croatia
179 L7 Vrbno pod Pradědem Czech Rep.
177 J2 Vrbov Slovakia
177 G3 Vrbové Slovakia
188 E1 Vrbovec Croatia
188 E3 Vrbovsko Croatia
157 M3 Vrchlabí Czech Rep.
157 K7 Vrécourt France
215 K6 Vrede S. Africa
160 C3 Vrede S. Africa
214 D8 Vredenburg S. Africa
214 C7 Vredendal S. Africa
251 M7 Vredeshoop Namibia
164 H4 Vreeland Neth.
168 E5 Vrees Ger.
182 E6 Vreia de Jales Port.
196 K5 Vrela Kosovo Serbia
196 J5 Vrelo Serbia
188 F3 Vrhnika Slovenia
114 F7 Vriddhachalam Tamil Nadu India
164 K2 Vries Neth.
164 K3 Vriezenveen Neth.
143 K4 Vrigstad Sweden
160 B1 Vrille r. France
111 C13 Vrindavan Uttar Prad. India
143 J3 Vristulern i. Sweden
156 I5 Vrísses Greece
196 I7 Vrnjačka Banja Serbia
214 D9 Vrolijkheid Nature Reserve S. Africa
160 C3 Vron France
198 B3 Vroomshoop Neth.
198 E1 Vrosina Greece
177 K2 Vroutek Czech Rep.
164 K2 Vrouwenpolder Neth.
141 M6 Vrrin Albania
164 G5 Vrsar Vojvodina Serbia
191 I8 Vrsar Croatia
196 J5 Vršac Vojvodina Serbia
179 I8 Vrtojba Slovenia
215 I2 Vryburg S. Africa
214 C9 Vryburg S. Africa
173 O2 Vryheid S. Africa
177 K10 Vsetaty Czech Rep.
177 G2 Vsetín Czech Rep.
220 B4 Vsevidof, Mount vol. AK U.S.A.
139 M1 Vsevolozhsk Rus. Fed.
176 B2 Vtáčnik mt. Slovakia
139 H7 Vshkody Rus. Fed.
160 H4 Vuache, Montagne de mt. France
79 □7a Vuaqava i. Fiji
188 M9 Vučha r. Bulg.
188 M3 Vučitrn Kosovo Serbia
188 F3 Vučitrn Kosovo Serbia
164 K5 Vuelta Grande Arg.
188 G3 Vuka r. Croatia
179 J7 Vukovar Croatia
123 N5 Vukuzakhe S. Africa
222 E3 Vulcan Alta Can.
197 L5 Vulcan Romania
156 I8 Vulcanesti Moldova
197 H8 Vulcano, Isola i. Isole Lipari Italy
172 L7 Vulchedrum Bulg.
191 P4 Vulchidol Bulg.
193 O4 Vulcano r. Italy
96 G5 Vụ Liệt Vietnam

120 J1 Vvedenka Kazakh.
139 Y5 Vveden'ye Rus. Fed.
138 L4 Vwawa Tanz.
211 B7 Vwaza Game Reserve nature res. Malawi
137 P7 Vyacheslavka Ukr.
175 M2 Vyalikaya Byerastavitsa Belarus
175 M2 Vyalikaya Byerastavitsa Belarus
138 H8 Vyalikija Mazheykava Belarus
138 M8 Vyalikiya Bortniki Belarus
138 J8 Vyalikiya Zhukhavichy Belarus
139 M3 Vyal'ye, Ozero l. Rus. Fed.
116 D9 Vyara Gujarat India
139 N6 Vyarechcha Belarus
138 G9 Vyarkhovichy Belarus
Vyarkhowye Belarus see Ruba
135 H5 Vyatchyn Belarus
134 L9 Vyatka r. Rus. Fed.
Vyatka Rus. Fed. see Kirov
134 K3 Vyatka r. Rus. Fed.
138 M5 Vyatskiye Polyany Rus. Fed.
100 I5 Vyazemskiy Rus. Fed.
139 R6 Vyaz'ma r. Rus. Fed.
134 H4 Vyaz'ma Rus. Fed.
120 A2 Vyazovka Astrakhanskaya Oblast' Rus. Fed.
120 B1 Vyazovka Saratovskaya Oblast' Rus. Fed.
135 H6 Vyazovka Volgogradskaya Oblast' Rus. Fed.
137 P2 Vyazovoye Rus. Fed.
138 L1 Vyborg Rus. Fed.
139 O5 Vyborgskiy Zaliv b. Rus. Fed.
134 I3 Vychegda r. Rus. Fed.
176 F2 Vychodoslovenska Lith.
175 M4 Východočeský Slovakia
175 N4 Východná Slovakia
106 I1 Východné Slovakia
139 O8 Východné Slovakia
177 I2 Východné Karpaty park Slovakia
175 M1 Vydeniai Lith.
175 N4 Vyderta Ukr.
138 I2 Vydrino Rus. Fed.
137 M4 Vydropuzhsk Ukr.
138 M6 Vyerkhnyadzvinsk Belarus
138 K8 Vyetka Belarus
139 K7 Vyetryna Belarus
138 L6 Vygonichi Rus. Fed.
134 L2 Vygozero, Ozero l. Rus. Fed.
139 N8 Vyhanashchy Belarus
139 O6 Vyhne Slovakia
177 H3 Vyhne Slovakia
197 K7 Vyks-les-Lure France
161 I8 Vyle-sur-Mer France
136 C5 Vylok Ukr.
136 C5 Vym' r. Rus. Fed.
138 L7 Vynnyky Ukr.
136 C5 Vynohradiv Ukr.
137 M8 Vynohradove Kherson's'ka Oblast' Ukr.
137 M8 Vynohradove Respublika Krym Ukr.
114 E7 Vypin Island India
143 I4 Vyppözovo Rus. Fed.
139 N2 Vyrshal'ne Ukr.
150 T2 Vyrnwy, Lake Wales U.K.
136 I2 Vyru Ukr.
136 F3 Vyselki Rus. Fed.
137 L7 Vyshche Solone Ukr.
135 N4 Vyshchetarasivka Ukr.
137 L5 Vyshhorod Ukr.
135 N4 Vyshhorod Ukr.
136 B5 Vyshkovo Ukr.
139 O2 Vyshka Ukr.
139 S4 Vyshkov Ukr.
136 B5 Vyshka Ukr.
136 B5 Vyshkove Czech Rep.
139 R5 Vyshneve Ukr.
139 R4 Vyshnevolots'ka Gryada Rus. Fed.
137 Q1 Vyshneye-Ol'shanoye Rus. Fed.
175 M4 Vyshniv Ukr.
175 M4 Vyshnivets' Ukr.
135 I5 Vyshnivets' Ukr.
139 L3 Vyshnivochok Rus. Fed.
139 R3 Vyshniy Volochek Rus. Fed.
176 D3 Vyshnya r. Ukr.
177 K2 Vyškovec Ukr.
177 G2 Vyškov Czech Rep.
175 M4 Výšný Mirošov Slovakia
177 K2 Výšný Orlík Slovakia
Vysočina admin. reg. Czech Rep.
176 D3 Vysoká r. Czech Rep.
139 I3 Vysoká Pich Slovakia
177 I3 Vysoká Slovakia
138 H7 Vysoká pri Morave Slovakia
139 T5 Vysoké Brestatska Voblasts' Belarus
137 K7 Vysoké Mýto Czech Rep.
175 M4 Vysoke Ukr.
139 N6 Vysokovsk Rus. Fed.
139 M7 Vysokopillya Donets'ka Oblast' Ukr.
137 O4 Vysokopillya Kharkivs'ka Oblast' Ukr.
137 M6 Vysokopillya Khersons'ka Oblast' Ukr.
108 E8 Vu Ban Vietnam
188 M9 Vučha r. Bulg.
137 L7 Vysokopillya Ukr.
139 T5 Vysokovsk Rus. Fed.
134 L3 Vyya r. Rus. Fed.
138 L7 Vyzhnytsya Ukr.
175 I1 Vyzuona r. Lith.
134 L3 Vzmor'ye Rus. Fed.

W

206 E4 Wa Ghana
210 E3 Waajid Somalia
206 E4 Waajid Somalia
169 J7 Waake Ger.
173 J6 Waal Ger.
165 H6 Waal r. Neth.
164 H3 Waalwijk Neth.
84 F5 Waanyi/Garawa Aboriginal Land res. N.T. Austr.
164 G3 Waarland Neth.
165 F6 Waarschoot Belgium
91 J8 Wabag P.N.G.
175 O4 Wabakimi Lake Ont. Can.
224 B3 Wabakimi Provincial Park Ont. Can.
125 M4 Wabal well Oman
222 H4 Wabamun Alta Can.
222 H4 Wabamun Lake Alta Can.
222 I3 Wabasca r. Alta Can.
222 H3 Wabasca-Desmarais Alta Can.
230 E5 Wabash IN U.S.A.
230 E5 Wabash r. IN U.S.A.
226 K7 Wabasha MN U.S.A.
227 J1 Wabassi r. Ont. Can.
210 D3 Wabē Gestro r. Eth.

Wabē Mena to Watt, Mount
407

210 D3 Wabē Mena r. Eth.
226 F4 Wabeno WI U.S.A.
169 H8 Wabern Ger.
210 E3 Wabē Shebelē Wenz r. Eth.
224 A3 Wabigoon Lake Ont. Can.
223 L4 Wabowden Man. Can.
125 H2 Wabrah well Saudi Arabia
174 G2 Wąbrzeźno Pol.
109 K2 Wabu Anhui China
224 C2 Wabuk Point Ont. Can.
225 H2 Wabush Nfld and Lab. Can.
225 H2 Wabush Lake Nfld and Lab. Can.
231 H9 Waccamaw r. SC U.S.A.
231 H8 Waccamaw, Lake NC U.S.A.
231 F11 Waccasassa Bay FL U.S.A.
233 J11 Wachapreague VA U.S.A.
179 L3 Wachau reg. Austria
172 E3 Wachenheim an der Weinstraße Ger.
104 B5 Wachi Japan
210 C3 Wach'īlē Eth.
170 G5 Wachow Ger.
165 E6 Wachtebeke Belgium
169 H10 Wächtersbach Ger.
233 N6 Wachusett Reservoir MA U.S.A.
168 H2 Wacken Ger.
173 M3 Wackersdorf Ger.
225 H3 Waco Que. Can.
237 G10 Waco TX U.S.A.
236 F6 Waconda Lake KS U.S.A.
226 B5 Wacouta MN U.S.A.
123 L8 Wad Pak.
105 L5 Wada Japan
202 E6 Wada'a Sudan
104 B6 Wada-misaki pt Japan
105 H3 Wada-tōge pass Japan
84 F3 Wada Wadalla Aboriginal Land res. N.T. Austr.
104 A5 Wadayama Japan
202 E6 Wad Banda Sudan
83 L7 Wadbilliga National Park N.S.W. Austr.
202 C2 Waddān Libya
202 B2 Waddān, Jabal hills Libya
241 T8 Waddell Dam AZ U.S.A.
164 G2 Waddeneilanden is Neth.
Wadden Islands Neth. see Waddeneilanden
164 G3 Waddenzee sea chan. Neth.
151 K4 Waddesdon Buckinghamshire, England U.K.
168 K4 Waddeweitz Ger.
82 F5 Waddikee S.A. Austr.
149 P7 Waddington Lincolnshire, England U.K.
222 E5 Waddington, Mount B.C. Can.
147 I8 Waddingtown Ireland
164 G4 Waddinxveen Neth.
85 N8 Waddy Point Qld Austr.
150 C6 Wadebridge Cornwall, England U.K.
210 B2 Wadega Sudan
223 K5 Wadena Sask. Can.
236 H2 Wadena MN U.S.A.
118 C7 Wad en Nail Sudan
190 F1 Wädenswil Switz.
172 B2 Wadern Ger.
169 F7 Wadersloh Ger.
231 G8 Wadesboro NC U.S.A.
84 B3 Wadeye N.T. Austr.
114 C3 Wadgaon Mahar. India
116 F9 Wadgaon Mahar. India
172 B3 Wadgassen Ger.
203 G5 Wad Hamid Sudan
208 E2 Wad Hassib Sudan
151 M5 Wadhurst East Sussex, England U.K.
116 C8 Wadhwan Gujarat India
Wadhwan Gujarat India see Surendranagar
114 E4 Wadi Karnataka India
109 I2 Wadian Henan China
128 D7 Wādī as Sīr Jordan
128 B10 Wādī Fayrān Egypt
Wâdi Gimâl Island Egypt see Wādī Jimāl, Jazīrat
203 F4 Wadi Halfa Sudan
124 E4 Wādī Ḩammah Saudi Arabia
124 B3 Wādī Jimāl, Jazīrat i. Egypt
128 D8 Wādī Mūsá Jordan
234 G5 Wading r. NJ U.S.A.
235 J3 Wading River NY U.S.A.
175 H4 Wadlew Pol.
203 G6 Wad Medani Sudan
102 □F19 Wadomari Nansei-shotō Japan
175 H6 Wadowice Pol.
175 J5 Wadowice Górne Pol.
240 M2 Wadsworth NV U.S.A.
232 D7 Wadsworth OH U.S.A.
Wadu i. S. Male Maldives see Vaadhu
Wadu Channel Maldives see Vaadhu Channel
214 E10 Waenhuiskrans S. Africa
262 P1 Waesche, Mount Antarctica
107 R7 Wafangdian Liaoning China
208 D5 Wafania Dem. Rep. Congo
Wafra Kuwait see Al Wafrah
102 S7 Waga-gawa r. Japan
116 E4 Wagah Punjab India
84 C2 Wagait Aboriginal Land res. N.T. Austr.
174 G3 Waganiec Pol.
168 G5 Wagenfeld Ger.
168 K5 Wagenhoff Ger.
164 I5 Wageningen Neth.
251 G3 Wageningen Suriname
221 J3 Wager Bay Nunavut Can.
83 K6 Wagga Wagga N.S.W. Austr.
116 D9 Waghai Gujarat India
172 F3 Waghäusel Ger.
84 C3 Wagiman Aboriginal Land res. N.T. Austr.
87 D12 Wagin W.A. Austr.
173 N6 Waging am See Ger.
173 N6 Waginger See l. Ger.
190 F1 Wägitaler See l. Switz.
222 D4 Waglisla B.C. Can.
254 E5 Wagner Brazil
236 F4 Wagner SD U.S.A.
237 H7 Wagoner OK U.S.A.
239 L8 Wagon Mound NM U.S.A.
178 H5 Wagrain Austria
168 J2 Wagrien reg. Ger.
174 F3 Wągrowiec Pol.
123 O5 Wah Pak.
93 F5 Wahai Seram Indon.
207 F5 Wahala Togo
202 D2 Wāḩāt Jālū Libya
208 F2 Wahda state Sudan
225 G2 Wahemen, Lac l. Que. Can.
240 □C12 Wahiawā HI U.S.A.
125 N5 Wahībah, Ramlat al des. Oman
140 □ Wahlenbergfjorden inlet Svalbard
169 I8 Wahlhausen Ger.
171 H7 Wahlsdorf Ger.
168 J3 Wahlstedt Ger.
236 G5 Wahoo NE U.S.A.
236 G2 Wahpeton ND U.S.A.
Wahran Alg. see Oran
168 K5 Wahrenholz Ger.
241 S3 Wah Wah Mountains UT U.S.A.
114 C4 Wai Mahar. India
240 □D12 Waiāhole HI U.S.A.
240 □E13 Waiakoa HI U.S.A.
240 □B11 Wai'ale'ale mt. HI U.S.A.
240 □C12 Wai'ale'e HI U.S.A.
240 □C12 Waialua HI U.S.A.
240 □C12 Waialua Bay HI U.S.A.
240 □C12 Wai'anae HI U.S.A.
240 □C12 Wai'anae Range mts HI U.S.A.
80 M4 Waiapu r. North I. N.Z.
80 K7 Waiaruhe North I. N.Z.
81 H9 Waiau South I. N.Z.
80 L5 Waiau r. North I. N.Z.
81 B13 Waiau r. South I. N.Z.
81 H9 Waiau r. South I. N.Z.
172 G4 Waiblingen Ger.
172 F3 Waibstadt Ger.
173 N2 Waidhaus Ger.
173 K4 Waidhofen Ger.
179 L2 Waidhofen an der Thaya Austria
179 K4 Waidhofen an der Ybbs Austria
93 F4 Waigama Papua Indon.
93 G4 Waigeo i. Papua Indon.
173 I2 Waigolshausen Ger.
81 E11 Waihao Downs South I. N.Z.
80 H1 Waiharara North I. N.Z.
80 J4 Waiharoa North I. N.Z.
80 J3 Waiheke Island North I. N.Z.
80 J4 Waihi North I. N.Z.
80 J4 Waihi Beach North I. N.Z.
80 K4 Waihi Estuary North I. N.Z.
81 E13 Waihola, Lake South I. N.Z.
80 J4 Waihou r. North I. N.Z.
80 L6 Waihua North I. N.Z.
208 E5 Waika Dem. Rep. Congo
93 A8 Waikabubak Sumba Indon.
81 C12 Waikaia South I. N.Z.
81 C12 Waikaia r. South I. N.Z.
81 D12 Waikaka South I. N.Z.
81 J7 Waikanae North I. N.Z.
240 □D12 Waikāne HI U.S.A.
240 □E13 Waikapu HI U.S.A.
80 J4 Waikare, Lake North I. N.Z.
80 L5 Waikareiti, Lake North I. N.Z.
80 K5 Waikaremoana, Lake North I. N.Z.
80 I4 Waikaretu North I. N.Z.
81 G9 Waikari South I. N.Z.
80 I4 Waikato admin. reg. North I. N.Z.
80 I4 Waikato r. North I. N.Z.
81 D13 Waikawa South I. N.Z.
80 L4 Waikawa Point North I. N.Z.
80 J5 Waikeria North I. N.Z.
82 G6 Waikerie S.A. Austr.
240 □F14 Waiki'i HI U.S.A.
240 □D12 Waikīkī Beach HI U.S.A.
80 K5 Waikirikiri North I. N.Z.
93 C8 Waikilibang Flores Indon.
81 D13 Waikoikoi South I. N.Z.
80 L6 Waikokopa North I. N.Z.
81 E12 Waikouaiti South I. N.Z.
79 □7a Wailotua Viti Levu Fiji
240 □B11 Wailua HI U.S.A.
240 □E13 Wailua HI U.S.A.
240 □E13 Wailuku HI U.S.A.
81 C13 Waimahaka South I. N.Z.
81 G10 Waimakariri r. South I. N.Z.
80 L5 Waimana North I. N.Z.
240 □D12 Waimānalo HI U.S.A.
240 □D12 Waimānalo Beach HI U.S.A.
81 F8 Waimangaroa South I. N.Z.
80 K6 Waimarama North I. N.Z.
81 F8 Waimarie South I. N.Z.
81 F11 Waimate South I. N.Z.
80 H2 Waimatenui North I. N.Z.
80 I3 Waimauku North I. N.Z.
240 □B12 Waimea HI U.S.A.
240 □C12 Waimea HI U.S.A.
240 □F13 Waimea HI U.S.A.
240 □C12 Waimea Bay HI U.S.A.
93 B5 Waimenda Sulawesi Indon.
165 J8 Waimes Belgium
173 I5 Wain Ger.
232 F6 Wainfleet Ont. Can.
149 R7 Wainfleet All Saints Lincolnshire, England U.K.
114 F3 Wainganga r. India
93 B8 Waingapu Sumba Indon.
81 J7 Waingawa North I. N.Z.
150 C6 Wainhouse Corner Cornwall, England U.K.
251 G2 Waini Point Guyana
81 F11 Wainono Lagoon South I. N.Z.
223 I4 Wainwright Alta Can.
220 C2 Wainwright AK U.S.A.
80 L5 Waioeka r. North I. N.Z.
80 I2 Waiotira North I. N.Z.
80 J6 Waiouru North I. N.Z.
80 J4 Waipa r. North I. N.Z.
81 D13 Waipahi South I. N.Z.
240 □C12 Waipahu HI U.S.A.
80 L5 Waipaoa r. North I. N.Z.
81 C13 Waipapa Point South I. N.Z.
81 G10 Waipara South I. N.Z.
80 K6 Waipawa North I. N.Z.
80 I2 Waipipi North I. N.Z.
80 I2 Waipu North I. N.Z.
80 K6 Waipukurau North I. N.Z.
80 K5 Wairakei North I. N.Z.
81 J8 Wairarapa, Lake North I. N.Z.
81 I8 Wairau r. South I. N.Z.
81 H8 Wairau Valley South I. N.Z.
80 L6 Wairoa North I. N.Z.
80 I3 Wairoa r. North I. N.Z.
80 L6 Wairoa r. North I. N.Z.
93 C8 Wairunu Flores Indon.
93 G4 Waisai Papua Indon.
173 K2 Waischenfeld Ger.
109 L4 Waishe Zhejiang China
80 K5 Waitahanui North I. N.Z.
81 D12 Waitahuna South I. N.Z.
80 J4 Waitakaruru North I. N.Z.
81 F11 Waitaki South I. N.Z.
81 F11 Waitaki r. South I. N.Z.
80 □ Waitangi Chatham Is S. Pacific Ocean
81 E10 Waitangitaona r. South I. N.Z.
80 I5 Waitara North I. N.Z.
81 E12 Waitati South I. N.Z.
82 □3 Waite, Mount hill S. Pacific Ocean
84 E7 Waite River N.T. Austr.
80 J4 Waitoa North I. N.Z.
80 J5 Waitomo Caves North I. N.Z.
80 I6 Waitotara North I. N.Z.
80 I6 Waitotara r. North I. N.Z.
238 E3 Waitsburg WA U.S.A.
80 I4 Waiuku North I. N.Z.
81 D13 Waiwera South South I. N.Z.
93 F5 Waiya Seram Indon.
109 L5 Waiyang Fujian China
79 □7 Waiyevo Taveuni Fiji
179 I3 Waizenkirchen Austria
124 G6 Wajīd, Jabal al hills Saudi Arabia
103 L13 Wajiki Japan
103 N9 Wajima Japan
210 D4 Wajir Kenya
208 D4 Waka Équateur Dem. Rep. Congo
208 D5 Waka Équateur Dem. Rep. Congo
93 B8 Waka Flores Indon.
93 E5 Waka, Tanjung pt Indon.
227 L2 Wakami Lake Ont. Can.
81 H8 Wakapuaka South I. N.Z.
103 L11 Wakasa Japan
104 C4 Wakasa-wan b. Japan
104 C4 Wakasa-wan Kokutei-kōen park Japan
81 C12 Wakatipu, Lake South I. N.Z.
93 C6 Wakatobi, Taman Nasional nat. park Indon.
227 K3 Wakatoma Lake Ont. Can.
223 J4 Wakaw Sask. Can.
79 □7 Wakaya i. Fiji
84 F5 Wakaya Aboriginal Land res. N.T. Austr.
104 B7 Wakayama Japan
104 B8 Wakayama pref. Japan
102 S8 Wakayanagi Japan
Wake Atoll N. Pacific Ocean see Wake Island
236 F6 WaKeeney KS U.S.A.
227 S4 Wakefield Que. Can.
246 □ Wakefield Jamaica
81 H8 Wakefield South I. N.Z.
149 N6 Wakefield West Yorkshire, England U.K.
226 E3 Wakefield MI U.S.A.
232 B10 Wakefield OH U.S.A.
234 C5 Wakefield PA U.S.A.
233 N7 Wakefield RI U.S.A.
232 I12 Wakefield VA U.S.A.
Wakeham Que. Can. see Kangiqsujuaq
75 F2 Wake Island N. Pacific Ocean
96 B6 Wakema Myanmar
123 O3 Wakhan reg. Afgh.
103 L12 Waki Japan
102 R5 Wakinosawa Japan
210 D8 Wakiro watercourse Eritrea
210 B4 Wakiso Uganda
102 S1 Wakkanai Japan
215 O3 Wakkerstroom S. Africa
83 J6 Wakool N.S.W. Austr.
83 I6 Wakool r. N.S.W. Austr.
225 H2 Wakuach, Lac l. Que. Can.
209 B7 Waku-Kungo Angola
102 S8 Wakuya Japan
224 D3 Wakwayowkastic r. Ont. Can.
78 □6 Walade Solomon Is
86 F7 Walagunya Aboriginal Reserve W.A. Austr.
114 F6 Walajapet Tamil Nadu India
171 D6 Walbeck Ger.
151 P3 Walberswick Suffolk, England U.K.
174 E5 Wałbrzych Pol.
169 I8 Walburg Ger.
83 M4 Walcha N.S.W. Austr.
173 K6 Walchensee l. Ger.
178 F4 Walchsee Austria
178 F4 Walchsee l. Austria
168 D5 Walchum Ger.
238 K6 Walcott WY U.S.A.
86 H4 Walcott Inlet W.A. Austr.
165 F8 Walcourt Belgium
174 E2 Wałcz Pol.
172 G6 Wald Baden-Württemberg Ger.
173 M3 Wald Bayern Ger.
172 F7 Wald Switz.
172 F5 Waldachtal Ger.
179 K3 Waldaist r. Austria
172 D2 Waldböckelheim Ger.
169 D9 Waldbreitbach Ger.
169 E9 Waldbröl Ger.
172 H2 Waldbrunn Ger.
169 F9 Waldbrunn-Lahr Ger.
172 H6 Waldburg Ger.
87 D8 Waldburg Range mts W.A. Austr.
171 I7 Walddrehna Ger.
169 H8 Waldeck Ger.
179 N4 Waldegg Austria
235 G1 Walden NY U.S.A.
172 G4 Waldenbuch Ger.
172 H3 Waldenburg Baden-Württemberg Ger.
171 G9 Waldenburg Sachsen Ger.
Waldenburg Pol. see Wałbrzych
190 D1 Waldenburg Switz.
173 M3 Walderbach Ger.
173 M2 Waldershof Ger.
151 N5 Walderslade Medway, England U.K.
172 D3 Waldfischbach-Burgalben Ger.
179 L2 Waldhausen Austria
179 K3 Waldhausen im Strudengau Austria
171 H8 Waldheim Ger.
179 J3 Walding Austria
169 I8 Waldkappel Ger.
172 D5 Waldkirch Ger.
173 P4 Waldkirchen Ger.
173 M5 Waldkraiburg Ger.
172 F2 Wald-Michelbach Ger.
172 C3 Waldmohr Ger.
173 N3 Waldmünchen Ger.
231 F11 Waldo FL U.S.A.
226 G6 Waldo WI U.S.A.
233 □P4 Waldoboro ME U.S.A.
150 D6 Waldon r. England U.K.
232 I10 Waldorf MD U.S.A.
174 G2 Wałdowo-Szlacheckie Pol.
238 B4 Waldport OR U.S.A.
172 B2 Waldrach Ger.
237 H8 Waldron AR U.S.A.
226 J8 Waldron MI U.S.A.
263 H2 Waldron, Cape Antarctica
171 F10 Waldsassen Ger.
172 E6 Waldshut Ger.
190 G1 Waldstatt Switz.
172 H4 Waldstetten Baden-Württemberg Ger.
173 I5 Waldstetten Bayern Ger.
173 M2 Waldthurn Ger.
179 L3 Waldviertel reg. Austria
93 C4 Walea, Selat sea chan. Indon.
93 C4 Waleabahi i. Indon.
93 C4 Waleakodi i. Indon.
87 D11 Walebing W.A. Austr.
108 C4 Walêg Sichuan China
190 G1 Walenstadt Switz.
150 E3 Wales admin. div. U.K.
206 E4 Walewale Ghana
165 J9 Walferdange Lux.
83 L4 Walgett N.S.W. Austr.
262 Q1 Walgreen Coast Antarctica
226 H6 Walhalla MI U.S.A.
236 G1 Walhalla ND U.S.A.
231 F8 Walhalla SC U.S.A.
123 M7 Walhar Pak.
208 F5 Walikale Dem. Rep. Congo
87 C10 Walkaway W.A. Austr.
170 G3 Walkendorf Ger.
169 K7 Walkenried Ger.
84 E2 Walker r. N.T. Austr.
84 D8 Walker watercourse N.T. Austr.
226 I6 Walker MI U.S.A.
236 H2 Walker MN U.S.A.
240 N3 Walker r. NV U.S.A.
214 D10 Walker Bay S. Africa
231 H12 Walker Cay i. Bahamas
85 H4 Walker Creek r. Qld Austr.
223 L4 Walker Lake l. Man. Can.
240 N3 Walker Lake NV U.S.A.
240 N3 Walker Lake l. NV U.S.A.
262 R2 Walker Mountains Antarctica
240 N3 Walker River Indian Reservation res. NV U.S.A.
232 H9 Walkersville MD U.S.A.
232 E10 Walkersville WV U.S.A.
227 M5 Walkerton Ont. Can.
226 H8 Walkerton IN U.S.A.
235 G1 Walker Valley NY U.S.A.
236 D3 Wall SD U.S.A.
87 D7 Wall, Mount hill W.A. Austr.
87 B10 Wallabi Group is W.A. Austr.
85 H3 Wallaby Island Qld Austr.
238 F3 Wallace ID U.S.A.
231 I8 Wallace NC U.S.A.
236 E5 Wallace NE U.S.A.
232 C12 Wallace VA U.S.A.
224 D5 Wallaceburg Ont. Can.
81 C13 Wallacetown South I. N.Z.
86 F5 Wallal Downs W.A. Austr.
87 D11 Wallambin, Lake salt flat W.A. Austr.
83 M3 Wallangarra Qld Austr.
82 F5 Wallaroo S.A. Austr.
149 K7 Wallasey Merseyside, England U.K.
85 M8 Wallaville Qld Austr.
238 E3 Walla Walla WA U.S.A.
172 F3 Walldorf Baden-Württemberg Ger.
172 F1 Walldorf Hessen Ger.
169 J9 Walldorf Thüringen Ger.
172 G2 Walldürn Ger.
214 B6 Wallekraal S. Africa
83 L6 Wallendbeen N.S.W. Austr.
171 D10 Wallenfels Ger.
234 E2 Wallenpaupack, Lake PA U.S.A.
190 G1 Wallensee l. Switz.
173 N4 Wallerfing Ger.
179 O4 Wallern im Burgenland Austria
173 N4 Wallersdorf Ger.
178 H4 Wallersee l. Austria
173 I4 Wallerstein Ger.
173 K6 Wallgau Ger.
173 I3 Wallhausen Baden-Württemberg Ger.
172 D2 Wallhausen Rheinland-Pfalz Ger.
80 K7 Wallingford North I. N.Z.
151 J4 Wallingford Oxfordshire, England U.K.
235 J2 Wallingford CT U.S.A.
233 M5 Wallingford VT U.S.A.
Wallis canton Switz. see Valais
77 I3 Wallis, Îles is Wallis and Futuna Is
77 I3 Wallis and Futuna Islands terr. S. Pacific Ocean
172 F7 Wallisellen Switz.
Wallis et Futuna, Îles terr. S. Pacific Ocean see Wallis and Futuna Islands
Wallis Islands Wallis and Futuna Is see Wallis, Îles
235 G1 Wallkill NY U.S.A.
235 H1 Wallkill r. NY U.S.A.
233 J11 Wallops Island VA U.S.A.
238 F4 Wallowa OR U.S.A.
238 F4 Wallowa Mountains OR U.S.A.
146 □M2 Walls Shetland, Scotland U.K.
168 H1 Wallsbüll Ger.
149 N4 Wallsend Tyne and Wear, England U.K.
83 K9 Walls of Jerusalem National Park Tas. Austr.
170 D5 Wallstawe Ger.
169 F10 Walluf Ger.
238 E3 Wallula WA U.S.A.
85 L9 Wallumbilla Qld Austr.
123 J5 Walma Afgh.
151 O5 Walmer Kent, England U.K.
223 I2 Walmsley Lake N.W.T. Can.
149 K5 Walney, Isle of i. England U.K.
226 E8 Walnut IL U.S.A.
232 H8 Walnut Bottom PA U.S.A.
240 J4 Walnut Creek CA U.S.A.
236 F6 Walnut Creek r. KS U.S.A.
240 K3 Walnut Grove CA U.S.A.
234 D3 Walnutport PA U.S.A.
237 J7 Walnut Ridge AR U.S.A.
117 P5 Walong Arun. Prad. India
171 K7 Wałowice Pol.
173 L5 Walpertskirchen Ger.
87 D13 Walpole W.A. Austr.
233 M5 Walpole NH U.S.A.
78 □5 Walpole, Île i. New Caledonia
175 J2 Wałpusza r. Pol.
178 G4 Wals Austria
151 I2 Walsall West Midlands, England U.K.
173 J2 Walsdorf Ger.
239 L8 Walsenburg CO U.S.A.
85 I4 Walsh r. Qld Austr.
237 D7 Walsh CO U.S.A.
170 G5 Walsleben Ger.
151 M2 Walsoken Cambridgeshire, England U.K.
168 I5 Walsrode Ger.
175 H1 Wałsza r. Pol.
115 H4 Waltair Andhra Prad. India
173 I6 Waltenhofen Ger.
231 G9 Walterboro SC U.S.A.
231 E10 Walter F. George Reservoir AL/GA U.S.A.
237 F8 Walters OK U.S.A.
169 K9 Waltershausen Ger.
83 J3 Walter's Range hills Qld Austr.
237 K9 Walthall MS U.S.A.
227 R4 Waltham Que. Can.
149 Q6 Waltham North East Lincolnshire, England U.K.
233 N6 Waltham MA U.S.A.
233 □Q4 Waltham ME U.S.A.
151 M4 Waltham Abbey Essex, England U.K.
151 K2 Waltham on the Wolds Leicestershire, England U.K.
173 K4 Walting Ger.
226 H9 Walton IN U.S.A.
233 J6 Walton NY U.S.A.
232 D10 Walton WV U.S.A.
246 D5 Walton Bank sea feature Jamaica
151 L5 Walton-on-Thames Surrey, England U.K.
151 O4 Walton on the Naze Essex, England U.K.
Walvisbaai Namibia see Walvis Bay
212 B4 Walvis Bay Namibia
212 B4 Walvis Bay b. Namibia
264 I8 Walvis Ridge sea feature S. Atlantic Ocean
87 E11 Walyahmoing hill W.A. Austr.
123 N4 Wama Afgh.
210 A4 Wamala, Lake Uganda
209 E6 Wamaza Dem. Rep. Congo
208 D5 Wamba Équateur Dem. Rep. Congo
208 E4 Wamba Orientale Dem. Rep. Congo
209 C5 Wamba r. Dem. Rep. Congo
207 H4 Wamba Nigeria
183 K5 Wamba Spain
84 C3 Wambardi Aboriginal Land res. N.T. Austr.
236 G6 Wamego KS U.S.A.
91 I7 Wamena Papua Indon.
211 C6 Wami r. Tanz.
93 E5 Wamlana Buru Indon.
84 E4 Wampaya Aboriginal Land res. Qld Austr.
242 □Q10 Wampusirpi Hond.
238 K6 Wamsutter WY U.S.A.
93 E5 Wamulan Buru Indon.
123 M5 Wana Pak.
83 J3 Wanaaring N.S.W. Austr.
81 D11 Wanaka South I. N.Z.
81 D11 Wanaka, Lake South I. N.Z.
235 G4 Wanamassa NJ U.S.A.
234 C2 Wanamie PA U.S.A.
109 J5 Wan'an Jiangxi China
224 D4 Wanapitei Lake Ont. Can.
235 G2 Wanaque NJ U.S.A.
235 G2 Wanaque Reservoir NJ U.S.A.
93 C6 Wanasabari Sulawesi Indon.
82 H6 Wanbi S.A. Austr.
108 C5 Wanbi Yunnan China
81 E12 Wanbrow, Cape South I. N.Z.
231 J8 Wanchese NC U.S.A.
93 C6 Wanci Sulawesi Indon.
258 G2 Wanda Arg.
87 C10 Wandana Nature Reserve W.A. Austr.
100 H6 Wanda Shan mts China
223 H4 Wandering River Alta Can.
169 K9 Wandersleben Ger.
168 H1 Wanderup Ger.
108 B6 Wanding Yunnan China
Wandingzhen Yunnan China see Wanding
Wandiwash Tamil Nadu India see Vandavasi
81 H9 Wandle Downs South I. N.Z.
170 H5 Wandlitz Ger.
101 E11 Wando S. Korea
85 L9 Wandoan Qld Austr.
151 L5 Wandsworth Greater London, England U.K.
179 L3 Wang Austria
96 D6 Wang, Mae Nam r. Thai.
208 F4 Wanga Dem. Rep. Congo
80 J6 Wanganui North I. N.Z.
80 I6 Wanganui r. North I. N.Z.
81 E10 Wanganui r. South I. N.Z.
83 K7 Wangaratta Vic. Austr.
82 E6 Wangary S.A. Austr.
108 F2 Wangcang Sichuan China
109 I4 Wangcheng Hunan China
107 Q8 Wangcun Shandong China
Wangda Xizang China see Zogang
111 I12 Wangdain Xizang China
117 L6 Wangdi Phodrang Bhutan
107 N7 Wangdu Hebei China
169 I7 Wangelnstedt Ger.
168 K2 Wangels Ger.
190 D1 Wangen Switz.
172 H6 Wangen im Allgäu Ger.
168 E3 Wangerooge Ger.
168 E3 Wangerooge i. Ger.
93 B9 Wanggamet, Gunung mt. Sumba Indon.
106 E8 Wang Gaxun Qinghai China
Wanggezhuang Shandong China see Jiaonan
108 E2 Wangguan Gansu China
190 F1 Wängi Switz.
93 C6 Wangiwangi i. Indon.
109 K3 Wangjiang Anhui China
107 K8 Wangjiawan Shaanxi China
242 □Q10 Wangkibila Hond.
100 E5 Wangkui Heilong. China
178 C5 Wängle Austria
Wang Mai Khon Thai. see Sawankhalok
108 G7 Wangmao Guangxi China
108 F6 Wangmo Guizhou China
Wangolodougou Côte d'Ivoire see Ouangolodougou
100 F7 Wangqing Jilin China
Wangying Jiangsu China see Huaiyin
222 G4 Wanham Alta Can.
251 H3 Wanhatti Suriname
96 D4 Wan Hsa-la Myanmar
208 E4 Wanie-Rukula Dem. Rep. Congo
84 C3 Wanimiyn Aboriginal Land res. N.T. Austr.
87 F9 Wanjarri Nature Reserve W.A. Austr.
116 C8 Wankaner Gujarat India
168 J2 Wankendorf Ger.
Wankie Zimbabwe see Hwange
210 E4 Wanlaweyn Somalia
168 G3 Wanna Ger.
87 J10 Wanna Lakes salt flat W.A. Austr.
87 C11 Wanneroo W.A. Austr.
109 K4 Wannian Jiangxi China
108 H9 Wanning Hainan China
104 E5 Wanouchi Japan
164 I5 Wanroij Neth.
107 L9 Wanrong Shanxi China
108 G5 Wanshan Guizhou China
109 I8 Wanshan Qundao is Guangdong China
171 E8 Wansleben am See Ger.
80 K7 Wanstead North I. N.Z.
151 J4 Wantage Oxfordshire, England U.K.
235 H3 Wantagh NY U.S.A.
227 N3 Wanup Ont. Can.
108 G3 Wanxian Chongqing China
108 G2 Wanyuan Sichuan China
109 J4 Wanzai Jiangxi China
165 H7 Wanze Belgium
Wanzhi Anhui China see Wuhu
232 A8 Wapakoneta OH U.S.A.
223 J4 Wapawekka Lake Sask. Can.
164 J4 Wapenveld Neth.
175 H2 Wąpiersk Pol.
224 B3 Wapikaimaski Lake Ont. Can.
224 B2 Wapikopa Lake Ont. Can.
222 G4 Wapiti r. Alta Can.
175 I2 Waplewo Pol.
174 D2 Wapnica Pol.
174 F3 Wapno Pol.
93 E5 Wapotih Buru Indon.
237 J7 Wappapello Lake resr MO U.S.A.
235 H1 Wappinger Creek r. NY U.S.A.
235 H1 Wappingers Falls NY U.S.A.
236 J5 Wapsipinicon r. IA U.S.A.
221 I4 Wapusk National Park Man. Can.
108 D2 Waqên Sichuan China
128 E7 Waqf aş Şawwān, Jibāl hills Jordan
127 K8 Wāqişah well Iraq
125 I4 Waqr well Saudi Arabia
124 G7 Waqr Maryamah well Yemen
232 D11 War WV U.S.A.
104 F4 Wara Japan
208 F2 Warab Sudan
208 F2 Warab state Sudan
105 K4 Warabi Japan
210 D4 Waradi waterhole Kenya
123 L8 Warah Pak.
87 J9 Warakurna-Wingellina-Irrunytju Aboriginal Reserve W.A. Austr.
210 E3 Warandab Eth.
114 F4 Warangal Andhra Prad. India
116 H9 Waraseoni Madh. Prad. India
83 J9 Waratah Tas. Austr.
125 I1 Warbah, Jazīrat i. Iraq
169 K6 Warberg Ger.
151 L3 Warboys Cambridgeshire, England U.K.
85 I8 Warbreccan Qld Austr.
222 H4 Warburg Alta Can.
169 H8 Warburg Ger.
169 H8 Warburger Börde reg. Ger.
83 J7 Warburton Vic. Austr.
87 I9 Warburton W.A. Austr.
82 F2 Warburton watercourse S.A. Austr.
215 O2 Warburton S. Africa
87 I9 Warburton Aboriginal Reserve W.A. Austr.
223 I2 Warburton Bay N.W.T. Can.
87 I8 Warburton Range hills W.A. Austr.
123 O5 Warcha Pak.
165 I8 Warche r. Belgium
149 M4 Warcop Cumbria, England U.K.
157 K5 Warcq France
85 K9 Ward watercourse Qld Austr.
81 I8 Ward South I. N.Z.
262 T2 Ward, Mount Antarctica
81 B12 Ward, Mount South I. N.Z.
81 D10 Ward, Mount South I. N.Z.
123 M4 Wardag prov. Afgh.
82 F6 Wardang Island S.A. Austr.
210 D4 Wardegle waterhole Kenya
215 M3 Warden S. Africa
168 F4 Wardenburg Ger.
116 G9 Wardha Mahar. India
114 F3 Wardha r. India
146 J5 Ward Hill Scotland U.K.
195 □ Wardija, Il-Ponta tal- pt Gozo Malta
195 □ Wardija Ridge Malta
151 J3 Wardington Oxfordshire, England U.K.
146 □N2 Ward of Bressay hill Scotland U.K.
170 F3 Wardow Ger.
149 L5 Ward's Stone hill England U.K.
222 E3 Ware B.C. Can.
151 L4 Ware Hertfordshire, England U.K.
233 M6 Ware MA U.S.A.
165 D7 Waregem Belgium
150 H6 Wareham Dorset, England U.K.
233 O7 Wareham MA U.S.A.
165 H7 Waremme Belgium
170 G3 Waren Ger.
169 E7 Warendorf Ger.
164 K2 Warffum Neth.
Wargili i. S. Male Maldives see Vaagali
85 M7 Warginburra Peninsula Qld Austr.
Wargla Alg. see Ouargla
151 K5 Wargrave Wokingham, England U.K.
210 E2 War Gunbi waterhole Somalia
83 M3 Warialda N.S.W. Austr.
123 L10 Wari Creek inlet Pak.
85 M1 Wari Island P.N.G.
170 E3 Warin Ger.
96 G7 Warin Chamrap Thai.
147 J4 Waringstown Northern Ireland U.K.
149 M3 Wark Northumberland, England U.K.
175 J4 Warka Pol.
80 I3 Warkworth North I. N.Z.
149 N3 Warkworth Northumberland, England U.K.
210 E2 War Idaad Somalia
Warli Sichuan China see Walêg
151 L5 Warlingham Surrey, England U.K.
156 E3 Warloy-Baillon France
174 G2 Warlubie Pol.
223 J4 Warman Sask. Can.
212 C6 Warmbad Namibia
172 L2 Warmensteinach Ger.
156 H5 Warmeriville France
214 D3 Warmfontein Namibia
143 Q7 Warmia reg. Pol.
151 J3 Warmington Warwickshire, England U.K.
175 I2 Warmińsko-Mazurskie prov. Pol.
150 H5 Warminster Wiltshire, England U.K.
234 E4 Warminster PA U.S.A.
164 G4 Warmond Neth.
169 G6 Warmsen Ger.
241 P3 Warm Springs NV U.S.A.
232 F10 Warm Springs VA U.S.A.
238 D4 Warm Springs Indian Reservation res. OR U.S.A.
214 E9 Warmwaterberg S. Africa
214 E9 Warmwaterberg mts S. Africa
170 F2 Warnemünde Ger.
223 H5 Warner Alta Can.
233 N5 Warner NH U.S.A.
238 E5 Warner Lakes OR U.S.A.
238 D6 Warner Mountains CA U.S.A.
231 F9 Warner Robins GA U.S.A.
240 P8 Warner Springs CA U.S.A.
253 E4 Warnes Bol.
165 C7 Warneton Belgium
173 L6 Warngau Ger.
151 L5 Warnham West Sussex, England U.K.
174 C2 Warnice Zachodniopomorskie Pol.
170 K5 Warnice Zachodniopomorskie Pol.
174 E2 Warnino Pol.
170 E3 Warnow Ger.
170 F2 Warnow r. Ger.
164 J4 Warnsveld Neth.
114 E3 Waronda Mahar. India
87 C12 Waroona W.A. Austr.
116 G9 Warora Mahar. India
168 H5 Warpe Ger.
85 M9 Warra Qld Austr.
84 E6 Warrabri Aboriginal Land res. N.T. Austr.
83 I7 Warracknabeal Vic. Austr.
83 M6 Warragamba Reservoir N.S.W. Austr.
83 J8 Warragul Vic. Austr.
82 G3 Warrakalanna, Lake salt flat S.A. Austr.
235 I1 Warramaug, Lake CT U.S.A.
82 E5 Warramboo S.A. Austr.
87 D10 Warramboo hill W.A. Austr.
83 K4 Warrambool r. N.S.W. Austr.
82 F2 Warrandirinna, Lake salt flat S.A. Austr.
83 J7 Warrandyte Vic. Austr.
86 F6 Warrawagine W.A. Austr.
83 J4 Warrego r. N.S.W./Qld Austr.
85 J8 Warrego Range hills Qld Austr.
83 K4 Warren N.S.W. Austr.
87 C13 Warren r. W.A. Austr.
227 N3 Warren Ont. Can.
237 I9 Warren AR U.S.A.
226 E7 Warren IL U.S.A.
226 I9 Warren IN U.S.A.
227 K7 Warren MI U.S.A.
236 G1 Warren MN U.S.A.
232 E7 Warren OH U.S.A.
232 F7 Warren PA U.S.A.
234 F3 Warren County county NJ U.S.A.
235 G5 Warren Grove NJ U.S.A.
Warren Hastings Island Palau see Merir
222 C4 Warren Island AK U.S.A.
147 J4 Warrenpoint Northern Ireland U.K.
226 D5 Warrens WI U.S.A.
236 I6 Warrensburg MO U.S.A.
233 L5 Warrensburg NY U.S.A.
234 B2 Warrensville PA U.S.A.
215 I4 Warrenton S. Africa
231 F9 Warrenton GA U.S.A.
236 J6 Warrenton MO U.S.A.
231 H7 Warrenton NC U.S.A.
232 H10 Warrenton VA U.S.A.
207 G5 Warri Nigeria
87 D10 Warriedar hill W.A. Austr.
82 F3 Warriners Creek watercourse S.A. Austr.
81 E12 Warrington South I. N.Z.
149 L7 Warrington Warrington, England U.K.
149 L7 Warrington admin. div. England U.K.
231 D10 Warrington FL U.S.A.
82 G4 Warriota watercourse S.A. Austr.
83 I8 Warrnambool Vic. Austr.
236 H1 Warroad MN U.S.A.
82 E6 Warrow S.A. Austr.
83 L4 Warrumbungle National Park N.S.W. Austr.
84 D1 Warruwi N.T. Austr.
83 H3 Warry Warry watercourse Qld Austr.
Warsaw Pol. see Warszawa
226 C9 Warsaw IL U.S.A.
230 E5 Warsaw IN U.S.A.
230 E6 Warsaw KY U.S.A.
236 I6 Warsaw MO U.S.A.
232 G6 Warsaw NY U.S.A.
232 I11 Warsaw VA U.S.A.
179 J4 Warscheneck mt. Austria
210 E4 Warshiikh Somalia
168 D4 Warsingsfehn Ger.
149 N7 Warslow Staffordshire, England U.K.
169 F8 Warstein Ger.
175 J3 Warszawa Pol.
174 E1 Warszkowo Pol.
174 G4 Warta Pol.
174 C3 Warta r. Pol.
174 D4 Warta Bolesławiecka Pol.
174 G3 Warta-Gopło, Kanał canal Pol.
179 J4 Wartberg an der Krems Austria
231 E7 Wartburg TN U.S.A.
171 B9 Wartburg, Schloss tourist site Ger.
171 B9 Wartburg Schloß tourist site Ger.
173 L5 Wartenberg Ger.
169 H9 Wartenberg-Angersbach Ger.
178 B5 Warth Austria
172 H5 Warthausen Ger.
170 J4 Wartin Ger.
175 H4 Wartkowice Pol.
170 H6 Wartmannsroth Ger.
149 L5 Warton Lancashire, England U.K.
95 L5 Waru Kalimantan Indon.
116 G9 Warud Mahar. India
84 E5 Warumungu Aboriginal Land res. N.T. Austr.
83 N3 Warwick Qld Austr.
151 I3 Warwick Warwickshire, England U.K.
234 D6 Warwick MD U.S.A.
235 G2 Warwick NY U.S.A.
233 N7 Warwick RI U.S.A.
149 L4 Warwick Bridge Cumbria, England U.K.
84 F3 Warwick Channel N.T. Austr.
151 I3 Warwickshire admin. div. England U.K.
108 C4 Warzhong Sichuan China
222 H5 Wasa B.C. Can.
227 N5 Wasaga Beach Ont. Can.
207 G4 Wasagu Nigeria
241 U2 Wasatch Range mts UT U.S.A.
215 O4 Wasbank S. Africa
168 I2 Wasbek Ger.
146 J4 Wasbister Orkney, Scotland U.K.
169 K6 Wasbüttel Ger.
223 J5 Wascana Creek r. Sask. Can.
172 H4 Wäschenbeuren Ger.
240 M6 Wasco CA U.S.A.
226 C3 Wascott WI U.S.A.
236 I3 Waseca MN U.S.A.
223 I3 Wasekamio Lake Sask. Can.
175 J3 Wąsewo Pol.
251 G3 Washado Suriname
123 J8 Washap Pak.
226 E9 Washburn IL U.S.A.
233 □Q2 Washburn ME U.S.A.
236 E2 Washburn ND U.S.A.
232 B12 Washburn TN U.S.A.
226 D3 Washburn WI U.S.A.
104 E4 Washiga-take mt. Japan
116 F9 Washim Mahar. India
225 F3 Washimeska r. Que. Can.
260 E3 Washington Arg.
149 N4 Washington Tyne and Wear, England U.K.
235 I1 Washington CT U.S.A.
234 A7 Washington DC U.S.A.
231 F9 Washington GA U.S.A.
236 J5 Washington IA U.S.A.
226 E9 Washington IL U.S.A.
230 D6 Washington IN U.S.A.
236 G6 Washington KS U.S.A.
232 B10 Washington KY U.S.A.
231 I8 Washington NC U.S.A.
233 M5 Washington NH U.S.A.
234 F3 Washington NJ U.S.A.
232 E8 Washington PA U.S.A.
241 S4 Washington UT U.S.A.
232 G10 Washington VA U.S.A.
238 D3 Washington state U.S.A.
263 L2 Washington, Cape Antarctica
233 N4 Washington, Mount NH U.S.A.
232 B9 Washington Court House OH U.S.A.
234 F4 Washington Crossing NJ U.S.A.
235 I1 Washington Depot CT U.S.A.
234 A6 Washington Grove MD U.S.A.
226 H4 Washington Island WI U.S.A.
226 H4 Washington Island i. WI U.S.A.
221 L2 Washington Land reg. Greenland
235 G2 Washingtonville NY U.S.A.
234 B2 Washingtonville PA U.S.A.
123 J5 Washir Afgh.
237 G8 Washita r. OK U.S.A.
83 N3 Washpool National Park N.S.W. Austr.
238 E3 Washtucna WA U.S.A.
123 K8 Washuk Pak.
114 D3 Wasi Mahar. India
125 H3 Wasi' Saudi Arabia
125 J4 Wasi' well Saudi Arabia
156 H4 Wasigny France
175 L2 Wasilków Pol.
220 D3 Wasilla AK U.S.A.
207 F4 Wasinmi Nigeria
93 E7 Wasiri Maluku Indon.
93 E5 Wasisi Buru Indon.
128 C9 Wāsiţ Egypt
127 L7 Wāsiţ governorate Iraq
127 M7 Wasit tourist site Iraq
125 M4 Wāsiţ Oman
124 D4 Wāsiţah Saudi Arabia
224 E3 Waskaganish Que. Can.
223 L3 Waskaiowaka Lake Man. Can.
222 H4 Waskatenau Alta Can.
174 E4 Wąsosz Dolnośląskie Pol.
175 K2 Wąsosz Podlaskie Pol.
174 E3 Wąsowo Pol.
242 □Q10 Waspán Nic.
164 G5 Waspik Neth.
149 O5 Wass North Yorkshire, England U.K.
206 B3 Wassadou Senegal
102 T2 Wassamu Japan
165 H7 Wasseiges Belgium
157 N6 Wasselonne France
190 F2 Wassen Switz.
164 F4 Wassenaar Neth.
169 B8 Wassenberg Ger.
212 C5 Wasser Namibia
173 I4 Wasseralfingen Ger.
173 M5 Wasserburg am Inn Ger.
169 I10 Wasserkuppe hill Ger.
169 K7 Wasserleben Ger.
172 B2 Wasserliesch Ger.
169 J10 Wasserlosen Ger.
173 J3 Wassertrüdingen Ger.
156 G3 Wassigny France
206 B4 Wassou Guinea
240 N3 Wassuk Range mts NV U.S.A.
157 I6 Wassy France
124 D4 Wasta Saudi Arabia
149 K5 Wast Water l. England U.K.
169 J9 Wasungen Ger.
224 E3 Waswanipi, Lac l. Que. Can.
227 N1 Watabeag Lake Ont. Can.
93 B4 Watambayoli Sulawesi Indon.
93 B6 Watampone Sulawesi Indon.
93 A6 Watansoppeng Sulawesi Indon.
223 I4 Watapi Lake Sask. Can.
104 E7 Watarai Japan
105 K3 Watarase-gawa r. Japan
84 C8 Watarrka National Park N.T. Austr.
105 H2 Watauchi Japan
232 C12 Watauga r. TN U.S.A.
96 D5 Wat Chan Thai.
150 F5 Watchet Somerset, England U.K.
149 L5 Watchgate Cumbria, England U.K.
235 L2 Watch Hill Point RI U.S.A.
Watenstadt-Salzgitter Ger. see Salzgitter
151 M3 Waterbeach Cambridgeshire, England U.K.
212 C4 Waterberg Namibia
212 C4 Waterberg Plateau Game Park nature res. Namibia
233 L7 Waterbury CT U.S.A.
233 M4 Waterbury VT U.S.A.
223 J3 Waterbury Lake Sask. Can.
246 E2 Water Cays i. Bahamas
227 O6 Waterdown Ont. Can.
231 G9 Wateree r. SC U.S.A.
222 C4 Waterfall AK U.S.A.
82 □3 Waterfall Lake S. Pacific Ocean
147 H8 Waterford Ireland
147 G8 Waterford county Ireland
215 J9 Waterford S. Africa
240 L4 Waterford CA U.S.A.
235 K2 Waterford CT U.S.A.
232 F7 Waterford PA U.S.A.
147 I8 Waterford Harbour Ireland
234 F5 Waterford Works NJ U.S.A.
150 B7 Watergate Bay England U.K.
223 J4 Waterhen r. Sask. Can.
223 L4 Waterhen Lake Man. Can.
84 D3 Waterhouse r. N.T. Austr.
84 D8 Waterhouse Range mts N.T. Austr.
164 F4 Wateringen Neth.
165 E6 Waterland-Oudeman Belgium
84 B4 Waterloo N.T. Austr.
165 F7 Waterloo Belgium
224 D5 Waterloo Ont. Can.
206 B4 Waterloo Sierra Leone
247 □7 Waterloo Trin. and Tob.
236 I4 Waterloo IA U.S.A.
236 J6 Waterloo IL U.S.A.
234 B6 Waterloo MD U.S.A.
232 I6 Waterloo NY U.S.A.
226 F6 Waterloo WI U.S.A.
151 J6 Waterlooville Hampshire, England U.K.
226 F8 Waterman IL U.S.A.
235 K3 Watermill NY U.S.A.
149 K2 Water of Leith r. Scotland U.K.
146 G9 Water of Tulla r. Scotland U.K.
151 I2 Water Orton Warwickshire, England U.K.
213 F4 Waterpoort S. Africa
147 H3 Waterside Northern Ireland U.K.
226 E3 Watersmeet MI U.S.A.
222 H5 Waterton Lakes National Park B.C. Can.
222 H5 Waterton Park Alta Can.
235 I1 Watertown CT U.S.A.
233 J5 Watertown NY U.S.A.
236 G3 Watertown SD U.S.A.
226 F6 Watertown WI U.S.A.
215 M2 Waterval r. S. Africa
215 O1 Waterval Boven S. Africa
82 G5 Watervale S.A. Austr.
237 K8 Water Valley MS U.S.A.
147 B9 Waterville Ireland
233 □P4 Waterville ME U.S.A.
232 B7 Waterville OH U.S.A.
238 D3 Waterville WA U.S.A.
233 L6 Watervliet NY U.S.A.
95 I8 Wates Indon.
227 M7 Watford Ont. Can.
151 L4 Watford Hertfordshire, England U.K.
236 D2 Watford City ND U.S.A.
223 K3 Wathaman r. Sask. Can.
223 K3 Wathaman Lake Sask. Can.
87 D11 Watheroo W.A. Austr.
87 C11 Watheroo National Park W.A. Austr.
222 G4 Watino Alta Can.
128 C9 Watīr, Wādī watercourse Egypt
232 I6 Watkins Glen NY U.S.A.
231 F9 Watkinsville GA U.S.A.
Watling Island Bahamas see San Salvador
151 J4 Watlington Oxfordshire, England U.K.
237 F8 Watonga OK U.S.A.
93 F3 Watowato, Bukit mt. Halmahera Indon.
223 J5 Watrous Sask. Can.
239 L9 Watrous NM U.S.A.
208 F4 Watsa Dem. Rep. Congo
226 G9 Watseka IL U.S.A.
208 D5 Watsi Kengo Dem. Rep. Congo
85 H2 Watson r. Qld Austr.
223 J4 Watson Sask. Can.
262 P1 Watson Escarpment Antarctica
222 D2 Watson Lake Y.T. Can.
234 B2 Watsontown PA U.S.A.
240 K5 Watsonville CA U.S.A.
87 I9 Watt, Mount hill W.A. Austr.

156 D2	**Watten** France
146 J6	**Watten** Highland, Scotland U.K.
146 K6	**Watten, Loch** l. Scotland U.K.
168 J2	**Wattenbek** Ger.
178 E5	**Wattens** Austria
190 D2	**Wattenwil** Switz.
223 I2	**Watterson Lake** Nunavut Can.
156 H3	**Wattignies-la-Victoire** France
82 F3	**Wattiwarriganna** watercourse S.A. Austr.
147 H4	**Wattlebridge** Northern Ireland U.K.
170 F3	**Wattmannshagen** Ger.
151 N2	**Watton** Norfolk, England U.K.
151 L4	**Watton at Stone** Hertfordshire, England U.K.
156 F2	**Wattrelos** France
231 E8	**Watts Bar Lake** resr TN U.S.A.
232 F6	**Wattsburg** PA U.S.A.
190 G1	**Wattwil** Switz.
91 H7	**Watubela, Kepulauan** is Indon.
93 B5	**Watuwila, Bukit** mt. Indon.
169 G9	**Watzen-Steinberg** Ger.
91 K8	**Wau** P.N.G.
208 B3	**Wau** Sudan
208 E3	**Wau** watercourse Sudan
83 N4	**Waubay Lake** S.D. U.S.A.
84 E6	**Wauchope** N.S.W. Austr.
84 E6	**Wauchope** N.T. Austr.
231 G12	**Wauchula** FL U.S.A.
93 A4	**Waukara, Gunung** mt. Indon.
86 F6	**Waukarlycarly, Lake** salt flat W.A. Austr.
226 F6	**Waukau** WI U.S.A.
226 F6	**Waukegan** IL U.S.A.
226 F6	**Waukesha** WI U.S.A.
226 C6	**Waukon** IA U.S.A.
236 E5	**Waunakee** WI U.S.A.
236 E5	**Wauneta** NE U.S.A.
226 G4	**Waupaca** WI U.S.A.
226 F6	**Waupun** WI U.S.A.
235 L1	**Wauregan** CT U.S.A.
237 G8	**Waurika** OK U.S.A.
226 E5	**Wausau** WI U.S.A.
226 G4	**Wausaukee** WI U.S.A.
232 A7	**Wauseon** OH U.S.A.
226 E5	**Wautoma** WI U.S.A.
84 C4	**Wave Hill** N.T. Austr.
151 P3	**Waveney** r. England U.K.
80 I6	**Waverley** North I. N.Z.
236 I4	**Waverly** IA U.S.A.
232 I6	**Waverly** NY U.S.A.
232 C9	**Waverly** OH U.S.A.
231 D7	**Waverly** TN U.S.A.
232 H11	**Waverly** VA U.S.A.
165 G7	**Wavre** Belgium
156 E2	**Wavrin** France
96 C6	**Wawa** Myanmar
224 C4	**Wawa** Ont. Can.
207 G4	**Wawa** Nigeria
224 E3	**Wawagosic** r. Que. Can.
93 C5	**Wawalalindu** Sulawesi Indon.
202 C3	**Wāw al Kabir** Libya
202 C3	**Wāw an Nāmūs** waterhole Libya
235 G1	**Wawarsing** NY U.S.A.
226 I8	**Wawasee, Lake** IN U.S.A.
	Wāwāhwai Waka l. South I. N.Z. see **Alabaster, Lake**
174 F5	**Wawelno** Pol.
93 B5	**Wawo** Sulawesi Indon.
91 J8	**Wawoi** r. P.N.G.
175 K4	**Wawolnica** Pol.
93 C5	**Wawotebi** Sulawesi Indon.
174 D3	**Wawrów** Pol.
175 I5	**Wawrzeńczyce** Pol.
237 G9	**Waxahachie** TX U.S.A.
106 H9	**Waxü** Gansu China
116 B10	**Waxweiler** Ger.
110 H7	**Waxxari** Xinjiang China
87 F9	**Waya, Lake** salt flat W.A. Austr.
79 □7a	**Waya** i. Fiji
93 F2	**Wayabula** Maluku Indon.
93 G3	**Wayag** i. Papua Indon.
	Waya Lailai i. Fiji see **Wayasewa**
93 F3	**Wayamli** Halmahera Indon.
	Wayaobu Shaanxi China see **Zichang**
79 □7a	**Wayasewa** i. Fiji
231 F10	**Waycross** GA U.S.A.
93 D4	**Wayhaya** Maluku Indon.
94 F7	**Way Kambas, Taman Nasional** nat. park Indon.
93 D4	**Waykilo** Maluku Indon.
232 C11	**Wayland** KY U.S.A.
226 I7	**Wayland** MA U.S.A.
226 C9	**Wayland** MO U.S.A.
232 H6	**Wayland** NY U.S.A.
227 K7	**Wayne** MI U.S.A.
236 G3	**Wayne** NE U.S.A.
235 G3	**Wayne** NJ U.S.A.
234 C4	**Wayne** PA U.S.A.
232 C10	**Wayne** WV U.S.A.
234 E1	**Wayne County** county PA U.S.A.
231 F9	**Waynesboro** GA U.S.A.
237 K10	**Waynesboro** MS U.S.A.
232 H9	**Waynesboro** PA U.S.A.
231 D8	**Waynesboro** TN U.S.A.
232 G10	**Waynesboro** VA U.S.A.
237 I7	**Waynesville** MO U.S.A.
231 E8	**Waynesville** NC U.S.A.
237 G7	**Waynoka** OK U.S.A.
207 I4	**Waza** Cameroon
96 C2	**Waza** Myanmar
207 I4	**Waza, Parc National de** nat. park Cameroon
156 F3	**Waziers** France
123 M5	**Wazi Khwa** Afgh.
123 P5	**Wazirabad** Pak.
104 C6	**Wazuka** Japan
174 G2	**Wda** r. Pol.
167 I2	**Wdecki Park Krajobrazowy** Pol.
	Wdig Pembrokeshire, Wales U.K. see **Goodwick**
207 F4	**W du Niger, Parcs Nationaux du** nat. park Niger
174 F2	**Wdzydze, Jezioro** l. Pol.
167 H1	**Wdzydzki Park Krajobrazowy** Pol.
78 □5	**We, Îles** Loyauté New Caledonia
94 A2	**We, Pulau** i. Indon.
224 B2	**Weagamow Lake** Ont. Can.
149 O4	**Wear** r. England U.K.
233 N5	**Weare** NH U.S.A.
84 F4	**Weam** P.N.G.
85 J3	**Wear Bay** Qld Austr.
237 F8	**Weatherford** OK U.S.A.
237 G9	**Weatherford** TX U.S.A.
234 D3	**Weatherly** PA U.S.A.
149 L7	**Weaverham** Cheshire, England U.K.
223 L4	**Weaver Lake** Man. Can.
238 C6	**Weaverville** CA U.S.A.
86 D7	**Webb, Mount** hill W.A. Austr.
226 D2	**Webbwood** Ont. Can.
224 C2	**Webequie** Ont. Can.
80 K7	**Weber** North I. N.Z.
238 H6	**Weber** r. UT U.S.A.
222 D4	**Weber, Mount** B.C. Can.
265 M5	**Weber Basin** sea feature Indian Ocean
262 T2	**Weber Inlet** Antarctica
210 H4	**Webi Shabeelle** r. Somalia
233 N6	**Webster** MA U.S.A.
236 C3	**Webster** SD U.S.A.
236 B4	**Webster** WI U.S.A.
236 I4	**Webster City** IA U.S.A.
232 E10	**Webster Springs** WV U.S.A.
210 B4	**Webuye** Kenya
165 G6	**Wechelderzande** Belgium
169 K9	**Wechmar** Ger.
222 H2	**Wecho** r. N.W.T. Can.
222 H2	**Wecho Lake** N.W.T. Can.
171 G8	**Wechselburg** Ger.
93 F3	**Weda** Halmahera Indon.
93 F3	**Weda, Teluk** b. Halmahera Indon.
164 L2	**Wedde** Neth.
262 V2	**Weddell Abyssal Plain** sea feature Southern Ocean
259 E8	**Weddell Island** Falkland Is
262 V2	**Weddell Sea** Antarctica
83 I7	**Wedderburn** Vic. Austr.
81 E12	**Wedderburn** South I. N.Z.
168 I2	**Weddingstedt** Ger.

168 I3	**Wedel (Holstein)** Ger.
140 □	**Wedel Jarlsberg Land** reg. Svalbard
222 F5	**Wedge Mountain** B.C. Can.
150 G5	**Wedmore** Somerset, England U.K.
150 H2	**Wednesbury** West Midlands, England U.K.
231 E9	**Wedowee** AL U.S.A.
238 C6	**Weed** CA U.S.A.
168 J3	**Weede** Ger.
151 J3	**Weedon Bec** Northamptonshire, England U.K.
232 G7	**Weedville** PA U.S.A.
93 G4	**Weeim** i. Papua Indon.
234 F5	**Weekstown** NJ U.S.A.
165 G6	**Weelde** Belgium
83 I3	**Weemelah** N.S.W. Austr.
215 O4	**Weenen** S. Africa
215 O4	**Weenen Nature Reserve** S. Africa
168 D4	**Weener** Ger.
178 E5	**Weerberg** Austria
164 K4	**Weerselo** Neth.
165 I6	**Weert** Neth.
168 I1	**Wees** Ger.
190 G1	**Weesen** Switz.
164 H4	**Weesp** Neth.
83 K5	**Weethalle** N.S.W. Austr.
83 L4	**Wee Waa** N.S.W. Austr.
169 B7	**Weeze** Ger.
171 D6	**Weferlingen** Ger.
169 B8	**Wegberg** Ger.
214 F4	**Wegdraai** S. Africa
171 D7	**Wegeleben** Ger.
190 G1	**Weggis** Switz.
175 J1	**Węgorzewo** Pol.
174 D2	**Węgorzyno** Pol.
175 K3	**Węgrów** Pol.
174 D3	**Węgrzynowo** Pol.
175 I3	**Wegscheid** Austria
179 J4	**Wegscheid** Ger.
168 G3	**Wehdel** Ger.
164 J2	**Wehe-den Hoorn** Neth.
164 J5	**Wehl** Neth.
	Wehlau Rus. Fed. see **Znamensk**
87 D9	**Wehni** Eth.
85 I8	**Weld Range** hills W.A. Austr.
	Welford National Park Qld Austr.
165 I7	**Welkenraedt** Belgium
210 C2	**Welk'īt'ē** Eth.
215 K3	**Welkom** S. Africa
164 J5	**Well** Neth.
227 O7	**Welland** Ont. Can.
151 L2	**Welland** r. England U.K.
227 O6	**Welland Canal** Ont. Can.
171 G7	**Wellaune** Ger.
114 C9	**Wellawaya** Sri Lanka
168 I4	**Welle** r. Ger.
165 H7	**Wellen** Belgium
172 F5	**Wellendingen** Ger.
151 I3	**Wellesbourne** Warwickshire, England U.K.
85 G3	**Wellesley Islands** Qld Austr.
85 H3	**Wellesley Islands Aboriginal Reserve** Qld Austr.
222 B2	**Wellesley Lake** Y.T. Can.
233 O7	**Wellfleet** MA U.S.A.
173 K4	**Wellheim** Ger.
165 H8	**Wellin** Belgium
169 D10	**Welling** Ger.
151 K3	**Wellingborough** Northamptonshire, England U.K.
83 L5	**Wellington** N.S.W. Austr.
82 □1	**Wellington** S. Austr.
227 Q6	**Wellington** Ont. Can.
81 I8	**Wellington** North I. N.Z.
81 J8	**Wellington** admin. reg. North I. N.Z.
215 L9	**Wellington** S. Africa
150 F6	**Wellington** Somerset, England U.K.
150 G2	**Wellington** Telford and Wrekin, England U.K.
238 L6	**Wellington** CO U.S.A.
237 G7	**Wellington** KS U.S.A.
238 E3	**Wellington** NV U.S.A.
232 C7	**Wellington** OH U.S.A.
237 V2	**Wellington** TX U.S.A.
238 F2	**Wellington** UT U.S.A.
259 B8	**Wellington, Isla** i. Chile
147 I8	**Wellington Bridge** Ireland
84 D2	**Wellington Range** hills W.A. Austr.
87 F9	**Wellington Range** hills W.A. Austr.
222 F4	**Wells** B.C. Can.
150 G5	**Wells** Somerset, England U.K.
238 G6	**Wells** NV U.S.A.
87 D9	**Wells, Lake** salt flat W.A. Austr.
232 H7	**Wellsboro** PA U.S.A.
80 I3	**Wellsford** North I. N.Z.
222 F4	**Wells Gray Provincial Park** B.C. Can.
151 N2	**Wells-next-the-Sea** Norfolk, England U.K.
226 I5	**Wellston** MI U.S.A.
232 D6	**Wellston** OH U.S.A.
232 G8	**Wellsville** NY U.S.A.
232 C8	**Wellsville** OH U.S.A.
234 B4	**Wellsville** PA U.S.A.
241 R9	**Wellton** AZ U.S.A.
151 M2	**Welney** Norfolk, England U.K.
178 G5	**Welnianka** r. Pol.
240 □F14	**Welokā** HI U.S.A.
179 J3	**Wels** Austria
172 B3	**Welschbillig** Ger.
172 H4	**Welsch-Neudorf** Ger.
150 C1	**Welsh Newton** Herefordshire, England U.K.
150 F2	**Welshpool** Powys, Wales U.K.
171 H7	**Welsickendorf** Ger.
171 E7	**Welsleben** Ger.
149 Q7	**Welton** Lincolnshire, England U.K.
169 E7	**Welver** Ger.
210 E3	**Welwel** Eth.
213 E5	**Welwitschia** Namibia see **Khorixas**
151 L4	**Welwyn** Hertfordshire, England U.K.
151 L4	**Welwyn Garden City** Hertfordshire, England U.K.
172 H4	**Welzheim** Ger.
171 H7	**Welzow** Ger.
150 G2	**Wem** Shropshire, England U.K.
208 D5	**Wema** Dem. Rep. Congo
210 B3	**Wembere** r. Tanz.
150 F5	**Wembdon** Somerset, England U.K.
211 B6	**Wembere** r. Tanz.
215 N5	**Wembesi** S. Africa
222 G4	**Wembley** Alta Can.
215 L9	**Wemding** Ger. (note)
169 J8	**Wemding** Neth.
210 D3	**Wemel Shet'** r. Eth.
224 E2	**Wemindji** Que. Can.
146 D11	**Wemyss Bay** Inverclyde, Scotland U.K.
169 C9	**Wemyssen** Ger.
246 E1	**Wemyss Bight** Eleuthera Bahamas
251 F3	**Wenamu** r. Guyana alt. **Venamo** (Venezuela)
108 D3	**Wenchang** Hainan China
107 N8	**Wenchang** Sichuan China see **Zitong**
109 M5	**Wencheng** Zhejiang China
206 E5	**Wenchi** Ghana
210 C2	**Wench'īt Shet'** r. Eth.
108 □J9	**Wenchow** Zhejiang China see **Wenzhou**
108 D3	**Wenchuan** Sichuan China
169 J6	**Wendeburg** Ger.
172 E2	**Wendelsheim** Ger.
173 N5	**Wendelstein** Ger.
169 J7	**Wenden** Ger.
	Wenden Latvia see **Cēsis**
241 N8	**Wenden** AZ U.S.A.
107 N8	**Wendeng** Shandong China
151 M3	**Wendens Ambo** Essex, England U.K.
168 J4	**Wendisch Evern** Ger.

172 D5	**Weisweil** Ger.
157 O6	**Weitbruch** France
169 E9	**Weitefeld** Ger.
179 L3	**Weiten** Austria
179 L6	**Weitendorf** Austria
179 J5	**Weitenhagen** Austria
170 M2	**Weitendorf** Ger.
172 F2	**Weiterstadt** Ger.
164 L3	**Weitersen** Neth.
173 I6	**Weitnau** Ger.
179 K2	**Weitra** Austria
169 K10	**Weitramsdorf** Ger.
223 J3	**Weitzel Lake** Sask. Can.
171 I8	**Weixdorf** Ger.
108 D5	**Weixi** Yunnan China
107 N8	**Weixian** Hebei China
108 E5	**Weixin** Yunnan China
106 D6	**Weiya** Xinjiang China
106 I9	**Weiya** Xinjiang China
	Weiyuan Gansu China see **Huzhu**
	Weiyuan Yunnan China see **Jinggu**
108 C7	**Weiyuan Jiang** r. Yunnan China
179 M5	**Weiz** Austria
106 J8	**Weizhou** Ningxia China
	Weizhou Sichuan China see **Wenchuan**
108 G8	**Weizhou Dao** i. China
107 H6	**Weizi** Liaoning China
143 O7	**Wejherowo** Pol.
120 I9	**Wękikbazar** Turkm.
223 L4	**Wekusko** Man. Can.
222 H1	**Wekusko Lake** Man. Can.
175 I4	**Wekweti** N.W.T. Can.
96 D1	**Wel** r. Pol.
84 B5	**Welatam** Myanmar
215 K5	**Welbedacht Dam** S. Africa
82 E2	**Welbourn Hill** S.A. Austr.
149 N7	**Welbeck** England U.K.
91 K6	**Welch, Mount** hill W.A. Austr.
232 D11	**Welch** WV U.S.A.
210 C2	**Weldiya** Eth.
151 K3	**Weldon** Northamptonshire, England U.K.

170 F4	**Wendisch Priborn** Ger.
226 E6	**West Bend** WI U.S.A.
117 K8	**West Bengal** state India
151 N4	**West Bergholt** Essex, England U.K.
206 D3	**Wendo** Eth.
151 K4	**West Berkshire** admin. div. England U.K.
234 F5	**West Berlin** NJ U.S.A.
232 B9	**Westboro** OH U.S.A.
227 J5	**West Branch** MI U.S.A.
151 J2	**West Bridgford** Nottinghamshire, England U.K.
84 F3	**West Island** N.T. Austr.
86 □1	**West Island** Cocos Is
115 M6	**West Island** Andaman & Nicobar Is India
235 K2	**West Islip** NY U.S.A.
85 M7	**West Jefferson** OH U.S.A.
240 L1	**West Kazakhstan Oblast** admin. div. Kazakh. see **Burra**
	see **Zapadnyy Kazakhstan**
146 E11	**West Kilbride** North Ayrshire, Scotland U.K.
149 K7	**West Kirby** Merseyside, England U.K.
149 P5	**West Knapton** North Yorkshire, England U.K.
230 D5	**West Lafayette** IN U.S.A.
	West Lamma Channel H.K. China see **Sai Pok Liu Hoi Hap**
234 C3	**Westland** MI U.S.A.
235 H2	**West Landing** i. Majuro Marshall Is
81 E10	**Westland National Park** South I. N.Z.
151 I5	**West Lavington** Wiltshire, England U.K.
234 D4	**West Lawn** PA U.S.A.
215 L3	**Westleigh** S. Africa
151 P3	**Westleton** Suffolk, England U.K.
146 I1	**West Linton** Scottish Borders, Scotland U.K.
146 C6	**West Loch Roag** b. Scotland U.K.
146 E11	**West Loch Tarbert** inlet Scotland U.K.
222 H4	**Westlock** Alta Can.
150 D7	**West Looe** Cornwall, England U.K.
224 D5	**West Lorne** Ont. Can.
146 I11	**West Lothian** admin. div. Scotland U.K.
150 H6	**West Lulworth** Dorset, England U.K.
209 E8	**West Lunga** r. Zambia
209 E8	**West Lunga National Park** Zambia
84 D7	**West MacDonnell National Park** N.T. Austr.
	West Malaysia pen. Malaysia see **Malaysia, Semenanjung**
165 G6	**Westmalle** Belgium
151 M5	**West Malling** Kent, England U.K.
	West Mariana Basin sea feature Pacific Ocean
266 E4	
168 J4	**Westergellersen** Ger.
164 K4	**Westerhaar** Neth.
	Westerhall Grenada see **Westerhall Point**
247 □6	**Westerhall Point** Grenada
80 I6	**Westerham** Kent, England U.K.
171 D7	**Westerhausen** Ger.
173 I5	**Westerheim** Bayern Ger.
170 I5	**Westerholt** Ger.
168 I3	**Westerhorn** Ger.
165 H6	**Westerlo** Belgium
235 L2	**Westerly** RI U.S.A.
211 C5	**Western** watercourse Qld Austr.
206 E5	**Western** admin. reg. Ghana
209 D8	**Western** prov. Zambia
206 B4	**Western Area** admin. div. Sierra Leone
87 F8	**Western Australia** state Austr.
208 E3	**Western Bahr el Ghazal** state Sudan
214 C9	**Western Cape** prov. S. Africa
202 D6	**Western Desert** Egypt see **Aş Şaḩrā' al Gharbīyah**
	Western Desert Aboriginal Land res. N.T. Austr.
	Western Dvina r. Europe see **Zapadnaya Dvina**
208 F3	**Western Equatoria** state Sudan
114 C5	**Western Ghats** mts India
146 C6	**Western Isles** admin. div. Scotland U.K.
208 F2	**Western Kordofan** state Sudan
	Western Lesser Sunda Islands prov. Indon. see **Nusa Tenggara Barat**
83 J8	**Western Port** b. Vic. Austr.
	Western Province prov. Zambia see **Copperbelt**
	Western Reef is Chatham Is S. Pacific Ocean
80 □	**Western Rocks** is Chatham Is S. Pacific Ocean see **Toagel Mlungui**
150 □	**Western Samoa** country S. Pacific Ocean see **Samoa**
204 D3	**Western Sahara** terr. Africa
110 □	**Western Sayan Mountains** reg. Rus. Fed. see **Zapadnyy Sayan**
83 J9	**West Point** of Tas. Austr.
	Western Port of Tristan da Cunha S. Atlantic Ocean
168 H1	**Wester-Ohrstedt** Ger.
146 I12	**Wester Parkgate** Dumfries and Galloway, Scotland U.K.
165 D7	**Westerschelde** est. Neth.
168 E4	**Westerstede** Ger.
173 J4	**Westerstetten** Ger.
232 C8	**Westerville** OH U.S.A.
169 E10	**Westerwald** hills Ger.
164 H3	**Westervoort** Neth.
168 F3	**Westerweser** sea chan. Ger.
169 J7	**Westewitz** Ger.
259 E8	**West Falkland** i. Falkland Is
236 D2	**West Fargo** ND U.S.A.
91 K5	**West Fayu** atoll Micronesia
149 O7	**West Fen** reg. England U.K.
151 N6	**Westfield** East Sussex, England U.K.
233 M6	**Westfield** MA U.S.A.
234 E2	**Westfield** NJ U.S.A.
232 G6	**Westfield** NY U.S.A.
234 B2	**Westfield** PA U.S.A.
232 H7	**Westfield** NY U.S.A.
226 E6	**Westfield** WI U.S.A.
	West Flanders prov. Belgium see **West-Vlaanderen**
233 □P3	**West Forks** ME U.S.A.
213 H3	**West Freehold** NJ U.S.A.
214 H3	**West Friesland** reg. Neth.
215 N2	**West Frisian Islands** Neth. see **Waddeneilanden**
164 J1	**Westgat** sea chan. Neth.
149 M4	**Westgate** Durham, England U.K.
151 P5	**Westgate** Kent, England U.K.
82 E6	**West Glacier** MT U.S.A.
233 □P1	**West Grand Lake** ME U.S.A.
151 L5	**West Grinstead** West Sussex, England U.K.
235 K2	**West Haddon** Northamptonshire, England U.K.
232 C10	**West Hamlin** WV U.S.A.
149 N4	**West Australian Basin** sea feature Indian Ocean
265 M4	
234 C10	**West Hartford** CT U.S.A.
235 J1	**West Haven** CT U.S.A.
151 K4	**West Haven** Hampshire, England U.K.
84 B5	**West Hazleton** PA U.S.A.

146 L8	**Westhill** Aberdeenshire, Scotland U.K.
157 N6	**Westhoffen** France
232 E10	**Westhope** ND U.S.A.
263 F2	**West Ice Shelf** Antarctica
165 C7	**West-Vlaanderen** prov. Belgium
	West Indies N. America
146 □O1	**Westing** Shetland, Scotland U.K.
	West Irian prov. Indon. see **Papua**
84 F3	**West Island** N.T. Austr.
86 □1	**West Island** Cocos Is
115 M6	**West Island** Andaman & Nicobar Is India
149 R8	**West Winch** Norfolk, England U.K.
146 J10	**West Wemyss** Fife, Scotland U.K.
149 R8	**West Winch** Norfolk, England U.K.
85 M7	**Westwood** Qld Austr.
240 L1	**Westwood** CA U.S.A.
235 G3	**Westwood** NJ U.S.A.
83 K5	**West Wyalong** N.S.W. Austr.
151 K4	**West Wycombe** Buckinghamshire, England U.K.
238 I4	**West Yell** Shetland, Scotland U.K.
238 I4	**West Yellowstone** MT U.S.A.
149 M6	**West York** PA U.S.A.
164 G4	**West Yorkshire** admin. div. England U.K.
93 F7	**Wetan** i. Maluku Indon.
93 E7	**Wetar** i. Maluku Indon.
93 E8	**Wetar, Selat** sea chan. Indon.
222 H4	**Wetaskiwin** Alta Can.
209 E6	**Wete** Dem. Rep. Congo
169 L4	**Wetmore** Ger.
149 O6	**Wetherby** West Yorkshire, England U.K.
235 J1	**Wethersfield** CT U.S.A.
81 A12	**West Jacket Arm** inlet South I. N.Z.
175 K6	**Wetlina** Pol.
262 T2	**Wetmore Glacier** Antarctica
168 F5	**Wetschen** Ger.
169 E9	**Wetter** r. Ger.
169 G10	**Wetter (Hessen)** Ger.
169 D8	**Wetter (Ruhr)** Ger.
165 E6	**Wetteren** Belgium
171 E7	**Wetterzeube** Ger.
190 E1	**Wettingen** Switz.
168 E5	**Wettrup** Ger.
171 E8	**Wettstetten** Ger.
231 D9	**Wetumpka** AL U.S.A.
190 F1	**Wetwun** Myanmar
190 C1	**Wetzikon** Switz.
169 G9	**Wetzlar** Ger.
231 E10	**Wewahitchka** FL U.S.A.
91 J7	**Wewak** P.N.G.
171 D6	**Wewelsfleth** Ger.
237 G8	**Wewoka** OK U.S.A.
147 I8	**Wexford** county Ireland
147 J8	**Wexford** Ireland
147 J8	**Wexford Harbour** b. Ireland
226 F5	**Weyauwega** WI U.S.A.
81 D12	**Weybridge** Surrey, England U.K.
223 K5	**Weyburn** Sask. Can.
169 E9	**Weyer** Austria
179 E4	**Weyer Market** Austria
169 K6	**Weyershausen** Ger.
168 G5	**Weyhausen** Ger.
168 G5	**Weyhe** Ger.
225 H4	**Weymouth** N.S. Can.
150 H6	**Weymouth** Dorset, England U.K.
235 K4	**Weymouth** MA U.S.A.
85 J2	**Weymouth, Cape** Qld Austr.
80 L4	**Wezep** Neth.
	Whaka-a Te Wera inlet Stewart I. N.Z. see **Paterson Inlet**
80 L6	**Whakaki** North I. N.Z.
80 J7	**Whakamaru** North I. N.Z.
80 H1	**Whakapunake** hill North I. N.Z.
	Whakapunake Forest Park nature res. North I. N.Z.
80 K5	**Whakarewarewa Forest Park** nature res. North I. N.Z.
	Whakatipu Kā Tuka r. South I. N.Z. see **Hollyford**
	Whakatipu Waitai l. South I. N.Z. see **McKerrow, Lake**
222 D3	**Whale** r. Que. Can. see **Baleine, Rivière à la**
246 E1	**Whale Cay** i. Bahamas
223 M2	**Whale Cove** Nunavut Can.
	Whale Island North I. N.Z. see **Moutohora Island**
222 G5	**Whale Pass** AK U.S.A.
215 N7	**Whale Rock** i. S. Africa
149 O6	**Whaley Bridge** Derbyshire, England U.K.
232 I12	**Whaleyville** VA U.S.A.
149 N3	**Whalsay** i. Scotland U.K.
149 O3	**Whalton** Northumberland, England U.K.
79 □7a	**Whangaea** r. Sing.
80 J7	**Whangaehu** r. North I. N.Z.
80 I6	**Whangamata** North I. N.Z.
80 H2	**Whangamomona** North I. N.Z.
80 G7	**Whanganui Inlet** South I. N.Z.
80 I6	**Whanganui National Park** North I. N.Z.
80 I3	**Whangaparaoa** North I. N.Z.
80 I3	**Whangaparaoa Head** North I. N.Z.
80 H2	**Whangape Harbour** North I. N.Z.
80 I2	**Whangarei** North I. N.Z.
80 I2	**Whangaroa Bay** North I. N.Z.
80 I2	**Whangaruru Harbour** b. North I. N.Z.
151 L2	**Whaplode** Lincolnshire, England U.K.
224 E1	**Whapmagoostui** Que. Can.
227 J7	**Wharncliffe** Ont. Can.
231 L1	**Wharton** NJ U.S.A.
237 G11	**Wharton** TX U.S.A.
232 F7	**Wharton** WV U.S.A.
80 L4	**What** Neth.
241 Q9	**Whatley Mine** Ariz.
146 H13	**Whauphill** Dumfries and Galloway, Scotland U.K.
240 K2	**Wheatland** WY U.S.A.
226 C5	**Wheaton** IL U.S.A.
236 H2	**Wheaton** MN U.S.A.
150 H2	**Wheaton Aston** Staffordshire, England U.K.
234 A6	**Wheaton-Glenmont** MD U.S.A.
82 □1	**Wheatsheaf Island** Lord Howe I. Austr.
150 E5	**Wheddon Cross** Somerset, England U.K.
151 K8	**Wheeler** OR U.S.A.
227 P8	**Wheeler** TX U.S.A.
222 B2	**Wheeler Lake** N.W.T. Can.
149 K7	**Wheeler Peak** NM U.S.A.
239 F6	**Wheeler Peak** NV U.S.A.
232 E9	**Wheelersburg** OH U.S.A.
151 J5	**Wheelock** r. England U.K.
149 N4	**Whernside** hill England U.K.
151 K8	**Wherwell** Hampshire, England U.K.
149 N4	**Whickham** Tyne and Wear, England U.K.

Whiddon Down to Wola Mysłowska
409

150 E6 Whiddon Down Devon, England U.K.
147 D9 Whiddy Island Ireland
86 D6 Whim Creek W.A. Austr.
150 F6 Whimple Devon, England U.K.
82 C2 Whinham, Mount S.A. Austr.
235 G3 Whippany NJ U.S.A.
80 K5 Whirinaki Forest Park nature res. North I. N.Z.
223 K3 Whiskey Jack Lake Man. Can.
240 J3 Whispering Pines CA U.S.A.
84 E6 Whistleduck Creek watercourse N.T. Austr.
222 F5 Whistler B.C. Can.
225 K4 Whitbourne Nfld and Lab. Can.
146 I11 Whitburn West Lothian, Scotland U.K.
227 P6 Whitby Ont. Can.
149 P5 Whitby North Yorkshire, England U.K.
151 K4 Whitchurch Buckinghamshire, England U.K.
150 F4 Whitchurch Cardiff, Wales U.K.
151 J5 Whitchurch Hampshire, England U.K.
150 G2 Whitchurch Shropshire, England U.K.
227 O6 Whitchurch-Stouffville Ont. Can.
81 E10 Whitcombe, Mount South I. N.Z.
224 C3 White r. Ont. Can.
222 B2 White r. Can./U.S.A.
246 □ White r. Jamaica
229 H4 White r. AR U.S.A.
237 J9 White r. AR U.S.A.
241 W1 White r. CO U.S.A.
230 D6 White r. IN U.S.A.
226 H6 White r. MI U.S.A.
241 R5 White r. NV U.S.A.
236 F4 White r. SD U.S.A.
233 M5 White r. VT U.S.A.
226 D3 White r. WI U.S.A.
241 V8 White watercourse AZ U.S.A.
237 E9 White watercourse TX U.S.A.
230 D6 White, East Fork r. IN U.S.A.
84 B6 White, Lake salt flat N.T. Austr.
237 I7 White, North Fork r. MO U.S.A.
149 M2 Whiteadder Water r. Scotland U.K.
225 J3 White Bay Nfld and Lab. Can.
236 D2 White Butte mt. ND U.S.A.
241 V4 White Canyon UT U.S.A.
147 E9 Whitechurch Cork Ireland
147 G8 Whitechurch Waterford Ireland
83 I4 White Cliffs N.S.W. Austr.
226 I6 White Cloud MI U.S.A.
81 D12 Whitecoomb mt. South I. N.Z.
146 J12 White Coomb hill Scotland U.K.
222 H4 Whitecourt Alta Can.
146 J11 Whitecraig East Lothian, Scotland U.K.
147 J4 Whitecross Northern Ireland U.K.
234 B2 White Deer PA U.S.A.
236 H2 White Earth Indian Reservation res. MN U.S.A.
226 B2 Whiteface Lake MN U.S.A.
233 L4 Whiteface Mountain NY U.S.A.
233 N4 Whitefield NH U.S.A.
227 M3 Whitefish Ont. Can.
222 E1 Whitefish r. N.W.T. Can.
238 G2 Whitefish MT U.S.A.
226 H4 Whitefish r. MI U.S.A.
226 G5 Whitefish Bay WI U.S.A.
223 J2 Whitefish Lake N.W.T. Can.
226 E1 Whitefish Lake Ont. Can.
226 J3 Whitefish Point MI U.S.A.
234 C5 Whiteford MD U.S.A.
147 F7 Whitegate Clare Ireland
147 F9 Whitegate Cork Ireland
147 D9 White Hall Ireland
147 H7 Whitehall Ireland
146 K4 Whitehall Orkney, Scotland U.K.
236 J6 White Hall IL U.S.A.
234 B5 White Hall MD U.S.A.
226 H6 Whitehall MI U.S.A.
238 H4 Whitehall MT U.S.A.
233 L5 Whitehall NY U.S.A.
232 C9 Whitehall OH U.S.A.
234 B2 White Hall PA U.S.A.
234 E3 Whitehall PA U.S.A.
226 C5 Whitehall WI U.S.A.
149 J4 Whitehaven Cumbria, England U.K.
234 D2 White Haven PA U.S.A.
147 K3 Whitehead Northern Ireland U.K.
225 I4 White Hill N.S. Can.
151 K5 Whitehill Hampshire, England U.K.
146 K7 Whitehills Aberdeenshire, Scotland U.K.
222 C2 Whitehorse Y.T. Can.
234 F4 White Horse NJ U.S.A.
151 I4 White Horse, Vale of val. England U.K.
246 □ White Horses Jamaica
234 F3 Whitehouse NJ U.S.A.
234 F3 White House Station NJ U.S.A.
263 D2 White Island Antarctica
White Island North I. N.Z. see Whakaari
215 L8 White Kei r. S. Africa
87 F8 White Lake salt flat W.A. Austr.
224 C3 White Lake l. Ont. Can.
224 E4 White Lake l. Ont. Can.
234 F1 White Lake NY U.S.A.
237 I11 White Lake l. LA U.S.A.
226 H6 White Lake l. MI U.S.A.
83 L9 Whitemark Tas. Austr.
234 E1 White Mills PA U.S.A.
240 N4 White Mountain Peak CA U.S.A.
233 N4 White Mountains NH U.S.A.
85 J6 White Mountains National Park Qld Austr.
228 G1 Whitemouth r. Man. Can.
223 M5 Whitemouth Lake Man. Can.
222 G3 Whitemud r. Alta Can.
146 G5 Whiten Head Scotland U.K.
203 G6 White Nile state Sudan
203 G6 White Nile r. Sudan/Uganda alt. Abiad, Bahr el, alt. Jebel, Bahr el
203 G6 White Nile Dam Sudan
212 C4 White Nossob watercourse Namibia
232 B11 White Oak KY U.S.A.
224 B3 White Otter Lake Ont. Can.
222 C3 White Pass Can./U.S.A.
226 I8 White Pigeon MI U.S.A.
226 E3 White Pine MI U.S.A.
241 Q3 White Pine Range mts NV U.S.A.
235 H2 White Plains NY U.S.A.
146 L8 Whiterashes Aberdeenshire, Scotland U.K.
224 C3 White River Ont. Can.
241 W8 Whiteriver AZ U.S.A.
236 E4 White River SD U.S.A.
233 M5 White River Junction VT U.S.A.
237 J8 White River National Wildlife Refuge nature res. AR U.S.A.
241 Q3 White River Valley NV U.S.A.
241 R3 White Rock Peak NV U.S.A.
White Russia country Europe see Belarus
222 E4 Whitesail Lake B.C. Can.
238 D4 White Salmon WA U.S.A.
222 H2 Whitesand r. Alta/N.W.T. Can.
223 K5 Whitesand r. Sask. Can.
239 K10 White Sands National Monument nat. park NM U.S.A.
234 F6 Whitesboro NJ U.S.A.
233 J5 Whitesboro NY U.S.A.
232 C11 Whitesburg KY U.S.A.
White Sea Rus. Fed. see Beloye More
223 M5 Whiteshell Provincial Park Man. Can.
233 I11 White Stone VA U.S.A.
238 I3 White Sulphur Springs MT U.S.A.
232 E11 White Sulphur Springs WV U.S.A.
234 E1 Whites Valley PA U.S.A.
232 D11 Whitesville WV U.S.A.
215 P4 White Umfolozi r. S. Africa
231 H8 Whiteville NC U.S.A.
206 E4 White Volta watercourse Burkina/Ghana alt. Nakambé, alt. Nakanbe, alt. Volta Blanche
206 E4 White Volta r. Ghana
240 P8 White Water CA U.S.A.
241 X3 Whitewater CO U.S.A.
226 F7 Whitewater WI U.S.A.
239 J10 Whitewater Baldy mt. NM U.S.A.
224 B3 Whitewater Lake Ont. Can.
82 C4 White Well S.A. Austr.
236 E6 White Woman Creek r. KS U.S.A.
85 I6 Whitewood Qld Austr.
223 K5 Whitewood Sask. Can.
83 K7 Whitfield Vic. Austr.
151 O5 Whitfield Kent, England U.K.
150 F1 Whitford Flintshire, Wales U.K.
150 D4 Whitford Point Wales U.K.
146 H13 Whithorn Dumfries and Galloway, Scotland U.K.
80 J3 Whitianga North I. N.Z.
233 □R4 Whiting ME U.S.A.
235 G5 Whiting NJ U.S.A.
226 E5 Whiting WI U.S.A.
146 F12 Whiting Bay North Ayrshire, Scotland U.K.
150 C4 Whitland Carmarthenshire, Wales U.K.
149 O3 Whitley Bay Tyne and Wear, England U.K.
231 E7 Whitley City KY U.S.A.
234 E5 Whitman Square NJ U.S.A.
231 G8 Whitmire SC U.S.A.
215 M7 Whitmore S. Africa
262 Q1 Whitmore Mountains Antarctica
151 I3 Whitnash Warwickshire, England U.K.
227 P4 Whitney Ont. Can.
237 G10 Whitney, Lake TX U.S.A.
240 N5 Whitney, Mount CA U.S.A.
233 J6 Whitney Point NY U.S.A.
150 D7 Whitsand Bay England U.K.
151 O5 Whitstable Kent, England U.K.
85 L6 Whitsunday Group is Qld Austr.
85 L6 Whitsunday Island Qld Austr.
85 L6 Whitsunday Island National Park Qld Austr.
85 L6 Whitsunday Passage Qld Austr.
Whitsun Island Vanuatu see Pentecost Island
227 K5 Whittemore MI U.S.A.
240 N8 Whittier CA U.S.A.
149 N3 Whittingham Northumberland, England U.K.
150 F2 Whittington Shropshire, England U.K.
84 D5 Whittington Range hills N.T. Austr.
83 J7 Whittlesea Vic. Austr.
215 K8 Whittlesea S. Africa
151 L2 Whittlesey Cambridgeshire, England U.K.
226 D4 Whittlesey WI U.S.A.
226 D3 Whittlesey, Mount hill WI U.S.A.
83 K6 Whitton N.S.W. Austr.
85 H8 Whitula watercourse Qld Austr.
149 M6 Whitworth Lancashire, England U.K.
223 J2 Wholdaia Lake N.W.T. Can.
241 T9 Why AZ U.S.A.
82 F5 Whyalla S.A. Austr.
Whydah Benin see Ouidah
96 D6 Wiang Kosai National Park Thai.
96 D5 Wiang Pa Pao Thai.
96 E5 Wiang Sa Thai.
175 K6 Wiar r. Pol.
175 J2 Wiartel Pol.
224 D4 Wiarton Ont. Can.
206 E4 Wiasi Ghana
174 F3 Wiatrowo Pol.
206 E5 Wiawso Ghana
146 B8 Wiay i. Scotland U.K.
174 F5 Wiązów Pol.
238 L3 Wibaux MT U.S.A.
210 C2 Wich'alē Eth.
165 E6 Wichelen Belgium
237 G7 Wichita KS U.S.A.
237 F8 Wichita r. TX U.S.A.
237 F9 Wichita Falls TX U.S.A.
237 F8 Wichita Mountains OK U.S.A.
237 F8 Wichita Mountains National Wildlife Refuge nature res. OK U.S.A.
146 J6 Wick Highland, Scotland U.K.
150 H5 Wick South Gloucestershire, England U.K.
150 E5 Wick Vale of Glamorgan, Wales U.K.
151 K6 Wick West Sussex, England U.K.
146 J6 Wick r. Scotland U.K.
169 E7 Wickede airport Ger.
169 E8 Wickede (Ruhr) Ger.
241 T8 Wickenburg AZ U.S.A.
87 D12 Wickepin W.A. Austr.
237 H8 Wickes AR U.S.A.
151 N4 Wickford Essex, England U.K.
86 D6 Wickham W.A. Austr.
84 C4 Wickham r. N.T. Austr.
151 J6 Wickham Hampshire, England U.K.
83 I8 Wickham, Cape Tas. Austr.
84 B4 Wickham, Mount hill N.T. Austr.
151 O3 Wickham Market Suffolk, England U.K.
237 K7 Wickliffe KY U.S.A.
147 J7 Wicklow Ireland
147 J6 Wicklow county Ireland
147 K7 Wicklow Head Ireland
147 I7 Wicklow Mountains Ireland
147 J6 Wicklow Mountains National Park Ireland
174 F1 Wicko Pol.
143 M7 Wicko, Jezioro lag. Pol.
150 H4 Wickwar South Gloucestershire, England U.K.
234 B3 Wiconisco PA U.S.A.
234 B3 Wiconisco Creek r. PA U.S.A.
174 G4 Widawa Pol.
174 E4 Widawa r. Pol.
175 G4 Widawka r. Pol.
85 N8 Wide Bay Qld Austr.
150 E6 Widecombe in the Moor Devon, England U.K.
146 J4 Wide Firth sea chan. Scotland U.K.
87 K8 Wide Gum watercourse S.A. Austr.
263 B2 Widerøe, Mount Antarctica
151 M4 Widford Hertfordshire, England U.K.
85 J9 Widgeegoara watercourse Qld Austr.
87 F11 Widgiemooltha W.A. Austr.
93 F4 Widi, Kepulauan is Maluku Indon.
190 H1 Widnau Switz.
149 L7 Widnes Halton, England U.K.
101 E11 Wi-do i. S. Korea
174 C2 Widuchowa Pol.
174 F2 Więcbork Pol.
170 G2 Wieck am Darß Ger.
175 I2 Wieczfnia Kościelna Pol.
174 G2 Wieczno, Jezioro l. Pol.
169 D10 Wied r. Ger.
169 K7 Wieda Ger.
171 G9 Wiederau Ger.
171 F8 Wiederitzsch Ger.
195 □ Wied Il-Għajn Malta
171 J8 Wiednitz Ger.
168 F4 Wiefelstede Ger.
171 D8 Wiehe Ger.
169 F6 Wiehengebirge hills Ger.
169 E9 Wiehl Ger.
170 H1 Wiek Ger.
174 G5 Większyce Pol.
175 I2 Wielbark Pol.
174 E3 Wieleń Pol.
173 K6 Wielenbach Ger.
175 H3 Wielgie Pol.
174 E3 Wielichowo Pol.
175 I6 Wieliczka Pol.
175 K2 Wieliczki Pol.
174 E2 Wielimie, Jezioro l. Pol.
174 G2 Wielka Nieszawka Pol.
177 H2 Wielka Racza mt. Pol./Slovakia
175 K6 Wielka Rawka mt. Pol.
174 E5 Wielka Sowa mt. Pol.
175 L5 Wielkie Oczy Pol.
175 H2 Wielkie Partęczyny, Jezioro l. Pol.
174 G1 Wielki Klincz Pol.
174 F4 Wielkopolska, Nizina lowland Pol.
174 F3 Wielkopolskie prov. Pol.
174 F3 Wielkopolskie, Pojezierze reg. Pol.
174 E3 Wielkopolski Park Narodowy nat. park Pol.
175 J6 Wielopole Skrzyńskie Pol.
174 G5 Wielowieś Pol.
165 D7 Wielsbeke Belgium
174 G4 Wieluń Pol.
168 I3 Wiemersdorf Ger.
179 N3 Wien Austria
179 N3 Wien land Austria
179 L4 Wienerbruck Austria
179 N3 Wiener Neudorf Austria
179 N4 Wiener Neustadt Austria
179 N3 Wiener Wald mts Austria
168 J5 Wienhausen Ger.
175 I4 Wieniawa Pol.
174 G3 Wieniec Pol.
179 L3 Wiensberg mt. Austria
170 D5 Wiepke Ger.
175 H6 Wieprz Pol.
175 J4 Wieprz r. Pol.
143 M7 Wieprza r. Pol.
175 L4 Wieprz-Krzna, Kanał canal Pol.
175 K3 Wiercień Duży Pol.
164 K4 Wierden Neth.
168 K5 Wieren Ger.
164 G3 Wieringermeer Polder Neth.
164 H3 Wieringerwerf Neth.
172 F4 Wiernsheim Ger.
174 G4 Wieruszów Pol.
175 L4 Wierzbica Lubelskie Pol.
175 J4 Wierzbica Mazowieckie Pol.
174 F4 Wierzbica Górna Pol.
174 D2 Wierzbięcin Pol.
174 G3 Wierzbinek Pol.
174 F5 Wierzbnik Pol.
175 L2 Wierzchlesie Pol.
174 G3 Wierzchosławice Kujawsko-Pomorskie Pol.
175 I5 Wierzchosławice Małopolskie Pol.
174 E2 Wierzchowo Zachodniopomorskie Pol.
174 E2 Wierzchowo Zachodniopomorskie Pol.
174 E2 Wierzchowo, Jezioro l. Pol.
174 G1 Wierzchucino Pol.
174 G2 Wierzyca r. Pol.
179 L6 Wies Austria
173 J6 Wies Ger.
171 G9 Wiesa Ger.
173 M2 Wiesau Ger.
169 F10 Wiesbaden Ger.
172 D6 Wiese r. Ger.
179 L3 Wieselburg Austria
179 N4 Wiesen Austria
169 H10 Wiesen Ger.
190 H2 Wiesen Switz.
171 K6 Wiesenau Ger.
171 F6 Wiesenburg Ger.
173 N3 Wiesenfelden Ger.
172 H4 Wiesensteig Ger.
173 M3 Wiesent Ger.
173 K2 Wiesent r. Ger.
173 K2 Wiesenthau Ger.
173 I2 Wiesentheid Ger.
173 K2 Wiesenttal Ger.
178 E5 Wiesing Austria
168 H4 Wiesle r. Ger.
172 F3 Wiesloch Ger.
179 N4 Wiesmath Austria
168 E4 Wiesmoor Ger.
234 D3 Wiessport PA U.S.A.
168 D5 Wietmarschen Ger.
175 I5 Wietrzychowice Pol.
168 I5 Wietze Ger.
169 I5 Wietze r. Ger.
168 H5 Wietzen Ger.
168 I5 Wietzendorf Ger.
143 O7 Wieżyca hill Pol.
149 L6 Wigan Greater Manchester, England U.K.
173 I6 Wiggensbach Ger.
237 K10 Wiggins MS U.S.A.
202 C3 Wigh, Ramlat al des. Libya
145 G6 Wight, Isle of i. England U.K.
175 L1 Wigierski Park Narodowy nat. park Pol.
150 G3 Wigmore Herefordshire, England U.K.
223 J2 Wignes Lake N.W.T. Can.
175 L1 Wigry, Jezioro l. Pol.
151 J2 Wigston Leicestershire, England U.K.
149 K4 Wigton Cumbria, England U.K.
146 H13 Wigtown Dumfries and Galloway, Scotland U.K.
146 H13 Wigtown Bay Scotland U.K.
164 I5 Wijchen Neth.
140 □ Wijdefjorden inlet Svalbard
174 E4 Wijewo Pol.
164 J4 Wijhe Neth.
164 G4 Wijk aan Zee Neth.
164 H5 Wijk bij Duurstede Neth.
164 H5 Wijk en Aalburg Neth.
165 G6 Wijnegem Belgium
164 J2 Wijnjewoude Neth.
241 S7 Wikieup AZ U.S.A.
210 C1 Wik'ro Eth.
227 M4 Wikwemikong Ont. Can.
190 G1 Wil Switz.
175 H6 Wilamowice Pol.
236 G5 Wilber NE U.S.A.
81 F10 Wilberforce r. South I. N.Z.
84 F1 Wilberforce, Cape N.T. Austr.
238 E3 Wilbur WA U.S.A.
173 I3 Wilburgstetten Ger.
237 H8 Wilburton OK U.S.A.
83 I4 Wilcannia N.S.W. Austr.
232 G7 Wilcox PA U.S.A.
Wilczek Land i. Zemlya Frantsa-Iosifa Rus. Fed. see Vil'cheka, Zemlya
175 H1 Wilczęta Pol.
174 G3 Wilczogóra Pol.
174 G3 Wilczyn Pol.
179 K4 Wildalpen Austria
179 L4 Wildalpener Salzatal nature res. Austria
171 I6 Wildau Ger.
172 F4 Wildberg Baden-Württemberg Ger.
170 G5 Wildberg Brandenburg Ger.
170 H3 Wildberg Mecklenburg-Vorpommern Ger.
223 K4 Wildcat Hill Provincial Wilderness Park nature res. Sask. Can.
240 P3 Wildcat Peak NV U.S.A.
215 N7 Wild Coast S. Africa
169 J9 Wildeck-Obersuhl Ger.
169 J9 Wildeck-Richelsdorf Ger.
169 J7 Wildemann Ger.
179 N2 Wildendürnbach Austria
171 G9 Wildenfels Ger.
214 G9 Wilderness S. Africa
232 H10 Wilderness VA U.S.A.
214 G10 Wilderness National Park S. Africa
168 F5 Wildeshausen Ger.
169 I10 Wildflecken Ger.
226 E1 Wild Goose Ont. Can.
222 G4 Wildhay r. Alta Can.
190 C3 Wildhorn mt. Switz.
239 L11 Wild Horse Draw r. TX U.S.A.
236 E5 Wild Horse Hill mt. NE U.S.A.
179 M6 Wildon Austria
173 I6 Wildpoldsried Ger.
236 G2 Wild Rice r. MN U.S.A.
236 G2 Wild Rice r. ND U.S.A.
226 B3 Wild Rice Lake MN U.S.A.
178 G5 Wildseeloder mt. Austria
178 G3 Wildshut Austria
178 C6 Wildspitze mt. Austria
222 H4 Wildwood Alta Can.
231 F11 Wildwood FL U.S.A.
234 F7 Wildwood NJ U.S.A.
234 F7 Wildwood Crest NJ U.S.A.
236 D6 Wiley CO U.S.A.
232 G9 Wiley Ford WV U.S.A.
175 J4 Wilga Pol.
175 J4 Wilga r. Pol.
215 M3 Wilge r. Free State S. Africa
215 N1 Wilge r. S. Africa
82 E4 Wilgena S.A. Austr.
91 J8 Wilhelm, Mount P.N.G.
251 G4 Wilhelmina Gebergte mts Suriname
164 H6 Wilhelmina Kanaal canal Neth.
140 □ Wilhelmøya i. Svalbard
Wilhelm-Pieck-Stadt Ger. see Guben
179 M3 Wilhelmsburg Austria
170 I3 Wilhelmsburg Ger.
172 G6 Wilhelmsdorf Ger.
168 F3 Wilhelmshaven Ger.
212 C4 Wilhelmstal Namibia
171 D10 Wilhelmsthal Ger.
179 J3 Wilhering Austria
173 J3 Wilhermsdorf Ger.
113 □2 Wilingili i. Addu Atoll Maldives
171 G9 Wilkau-Haßlau Ger.
234 D2 Wilkes-Barre PA U.S.A.
231 G7 Wilkesboro NC U.S.A.
263 I2 Wilkes Coast Antarctica
263 I2 Wilkes Land reg. Antarctica
223 I4 Wilkie Sask. Can.
232 F8 Wilkinsburg PA U.S.A.
262 T2 Wilkins Coast Antarctica
262 T2 Wilkins Ice Shelf Antarctica
82 D3 Wilkinson Lakes salt flat S.A. Austr.
147 I5 Wilkinstown Ireland
175 K4 Wilkołaz Pierwszy Pol.
175 J4 Wilków Lubelskie Pol.
174 F4 Wilków Opolskie Pol.
174 D3 Wilkowo Pol.
222 D3 Will, Mount B.C. Can.
238 C4 Willamette r. OR U.S.A.
150 F6 Willand Devon, England U.K.
83 J5 Willandra Billabong watercourse N.S.W. Austr.
83 J5 Willandra National Park N.S.W. Austr.
238 B3 Willapa Bay WA U.S.A.
242 D3 Willard Mex.
239 K9 Willard NM U.S.A.
232 C7 Willard OH U.S.A.
233 J10 Willards MD U.S.A.
149 K7 Willaston Cheshire, England U.K.
241 W9 Willcox AZ U.S.A.
241 W9 Willcox Playa salt flat AZ U.S.A.
169 H7 Willebadessen Ger.
165 F6 Willebroek Belgium
215 L4 Willem Pretorius Game Reserve nature res. S. Africa
164 F5 Willemstad Neth.
247 □10 Willemstad Curaçao Neth. Antilles
84 C3 Willeroo N.T. Austr.
223 I3 William r. Sask. Can.
83 I7 William, Mount Vic. Austr.
87 C7 Williambury W.A. Austr.
82 F3 William Creek S.A. Austr.
223 L4 William Lake Man. Can.
87 D12 Williams W.A. Austr.
85 H6 Williams r. Qld Austr.
87 D12 Williams r. W.A. Austr.
241 T6 Williams AZ U.S.A.
240 J2 Williams CA U.S.A.
236 I5 Williamsburg IA U.S.A.
232 A12 Williamsburg KY U.S.A.
226 I5 Williamsburg MI U.S.A.
232 A9 Williamsburg OH U.S.A.
232 G8 Williamsburg PA U.S.A.
232 I11 Williamsburg VA U.S.A.
246 □ Williamsfield Jamaica
246 D1 Williams Island Bahamas
222 F4 Williams Lake B.C. Can.
225 H1 William Smith, Cap c. Que. Can.
232 H5 Williamson NY U.S.A.
232 C11 Williamson WV U.S.A.
230 D5 Williamsport IN U.S.A.
232 B9 Williamsport OH U.S.A.
227 Q8 Williamsport PA U.S.A.
227 J7 Williamston MI U.S.A.
231 I8 Williamston NC U.S.A.
233 L6 Williamstown MA U.S.A.
234 F5 Williamstown NJ U.S.A.
233 J5 Williamstown NY U.S.A.
234 B3 Williamstown PA U.S.A.
232 D9 Williamstown WV U.S.A.
169 C8 Willich Ger.
247 □2 Willikies Antigua and Barbuda
233 M7 Willimantic CT U.S.A.
235 K1 Willimantic r. CT U.S.A.
234 F4 Willingboro NJ U.S.A.
151 M6 Willingdon East Sussex, England U.K.
169 G8 Willingen (Upland) Ger.
151 M3 Willingham Cambridgeshire, England U.K.
Willingili i. N. Male Maldives see Vilingli
169 H9 Willingshausen Ger.
151 I2 Willington Derbyshire, England U.K.
190 E1 Willisau Switz.
85 M4 Willis Group atolls Coral Sea Is Terr. Austr.
259 □ Willis Islands S. Georgia
214 E7 Williston S. Africa
231 F11 Williston FL U.S.A.
236 D1 Williston ND U.S.A.
231 G9 Williston SC U.S.A.
222 F4 Williston Lake B.C. Can.
150 F5 Williton Somerset, England U.K.
240 I2 Willits CA U.S.A.
83 N4 Willi Willi National Park N.S.W. Austr.
236 H3 Willmar MN U.S.A.
222 G4 Willmore Wilderness Provincial Park Alta Can.
82 F4 Willochra watercourse S.A. Austr.
149 R7 Willoughby Lincolnshire, England U.K.
232 D7 Willoughby OH U.S.A.
233 M4 Willoughby, Lake VT U.S.A.
222 F4 Willow r. B.C. Can.
241 R6 Willow Beach AZ U.S.A.
223 J5 Willow Bunch Sask. Can.
222 H5 Willow Creek r. Alta Can.
238 C6 Willow Creek CA U.S.A.
238 D4 Willow Creek r. OR U.S.A.
241 W1 Willow Creek r. UT U.S.A.
234 D6 Willow Grove DE U.S.A.
234 E4 Willow Grove PA U.S.A.
232 H8 Willow Hill PA U.S.A.
222 G2 Willow Lake N.W.T. Can.
222 F2 Willowlake r. N.W.T. Can.
214 H9 Willowmore S. Africa
84 D6 Willowra N.T. Austr.
Willowra Aboriginal Land Trust res. N.T. Austr. see Wirliyajarrayi Aboriginal Land Trust
226 E4 Willow Reservoir WI U.S.A.
240 J2 Willows CA U.S.A.
237 J7 Willow Springs MO U.S.A.
234 C5 Willow Street PA U.S.A.
215 M8 Willowvale S. Africa
86 J6 Wills, Lake salt flat W.A. Austr.
84 H7 Wills Creek watercourse Qld Austr.
172 D4 Willstätt Ger.
82 G6 Willunga S.A. Austr.
231 E10 Wilma FL U.S.A.
170 I4 Wilmersdorf Brandenburg Ger.
171 J7 Wilmersdorf Brandenburg Ger.
82 G5 Wilmington S.A. Austr.
234 D5 Wilmington DE U.S.A.
231 I8 Wilmington NC U.S.A.
232 B9 Wilmington OH U.S.A.
233 M6 Wilmington VT U.S.A.
231 G9 Wilmington Island GA U.S.A.
149 M7 Wilmslow Cheshire, England U.K.
164 G4 Wilnis Neth.
Wilno Lith. see Vilnius
169 F9 Wilnsdorf Ger.
164 J4 Wilp Neth.
114 G8 Wilpattu National Park Sri Lanka
82 G4 Wilpena watercourse S.A. Austr.
171 I8 Wilsdruff Ger.
168 I4 Wilseder Berg hill Ger.
170 I4 Wilsickow Ger.
86 J4 Wilson r. W.A. Austr.
85 I9 Wilson watercourse Qld Austr.
Wilson atoll Micronesia see Ifalik
236 F6 Wilson KS U.S.A.
226 C6 Wilson MN U.S.A.
231 I8 Wilson NC U.S.A.
232 G5 Wilson NY U.S.A.
234 E3 Wilson PA U.S.A.
221 J3 Wilson, Cape Nunavut Can.
239 K8 Wilson, Mount CO U.S.A.
241 R3 Wilson, Mount NV U.S.A.
238 D4 Wilson, Mount OR U.S.A.
84 C5 Wilson Creek watercourse N.T. Austr.
263 K2 Wilson Hills Antarctica
240 N5 Wilsonia CA U.S.A.
231 D8 Wilson Lake resr AL U.S.A.
232 H11 Wilsons VA U.S.A.
83 K8 Wilson's Promontory pen. Vic. Austr.
83 K8 Wilson's Promontory National Park Vic. Austr.
168 H4 Wilstedt Ger.
168 H3 Wilster Ger.
168 C5 Wilsum Ger.
179 O2 Wiltersdorf Austria
171 J8 Wilthen Ger.
172 B2 Wiltingen Ger.
84 E3 Wilton r. N.T. Austr.
151 I5 Wilton Wiltshire, England U.K.
235 I2 Wilton CT U.S.A.
233 □O4 Wilton ME U.S.A.
236 E2 Wilton ND U.S.A.
233 N6 Wilton NH U.S.A.
150 I5 Wiltshire admin. div. England U.K.
165 I9 Wiltz Lux.
87 F9 Wiluna W.A. Austr.
150 F5 Wimbleball Lake England U.K.
80 K7 Wimbledon North I. N.Z.
151 M2 Wimblington Cambridgeshire, England U.K.
151 I6 Wimborne Minster Dorset, England U.K.
156 C2 Wimereux France
171 E7 Wimmelburg Ger.
83 H7 Wimmera r. Vic. Austr.
190 D2 Wimmis Switz.
179 N4 Wimpassing Austria
Wina r. Cameroon see Vina
230 D5 Winamac IN U.S.A.
210 B5 Winam Gulf Kenya
85 J9 Winbin watercourse Qld Austr.
215 L4 Winburg S. Africa
214 G3 Wincanton S. Africa
150 H5 Wincanton Somerset, England U.K.
151 I4 Winchcombe Gloucestershire, England U.K.
151 N6 Winchelsea East Sussex, England U.K.
233 M6 Winchendon MA U.S.A.
172 A2 Wincheringen Ger.
233 J3 Winchester Ont. Can.
81 F11 Winchester South I. N.Z.
151 J5 Winchester Hampshire, England U.K.
236 J6 Winchester IL U.S.A.
230 E5 Winchester IN U.S.A.
232 A11 Winchester KY U.S.A.
233 M6 Winchester NH U.S.A.
231 D8 Winchester TN U.S.A.
232 G9 Winchester VA U.S.A.
165 I8 Wincrange Lux.
220 E3 Wind r. Y.T. Can.
238 J5 Wind r. WY U.S.A.
175 J1 Winda Pol.
82 F4 Windabout, Lake salt flat S.A. Austr.
173 K5 Windach Ger.
Windau Latvia see Ventspils
232 G8 Windber PA U.S.A.
236 D4 Wind Cave National Park SD U.S.A.
168 I2 Windeby Ger.
231 F9 Winder GA U.S.A.
149 L5 Windermere Cumbria, England U.K.
149 L5 Windermere l. England U.K.
172 D2 Windesheim Ger.
234 E3 Windgap PA U.S.A.
169 D9 Windhagen Ger.
222 C3 Windham AK U.S.A.
235 K1 Windham CT U.S.A.
232 D7 Windham OH U.S.A.
169 J7 Windhausen Ger.
212 C4 Windhoek Namibia
87 G9 Windidda Aboriginal Reserve W.A. Austr.
221 I4 Windigo r. Ont. Can.
224 B2 Windigo Lake Ont. Can.
179 L2 Windigsteig Austria
173 M2 Windischeschenbach Ger.
179 J4 Windischgarsten Austria
146 K11 Windlestraw Law hill Scotland U.K.
148 D7 Windmill Ireland
185 □ Windmill Hill Flats Gibraltar
239 L10 Wind Mountain NM U.S.A.
236 H4 Windom MN U.S.A.
85 I8 Windorah Qld Austr.
173 O4 Windorf Ger.
241 W6 Window Rock AZ U.S.A.
226 G7 Wind Point WI U.S.A.
232 E9 Wind Ridge PA U.S.A.
238 J5 Wind River Indian Reservation res. WY U.S.A.
238 J5 Wind River Range mts WY U.S.A.
151 J4 Windrush r. England U.K.
263 G2 Winds, Bay of Antarctica
173 J3 Windsbach Ger.
83 M5 Windsor N.S.W. Austr.
225 H4 Windsor N.S. Can.
224 D5 Windsor Ont. Can.
225 F4 Windsor Que. Can.
151 K5 Windsor Windsor and Maidenhead, England U.K.
233 M7 Windsor CT U.S.A.
231 I7 Windsor NC U.S.A.
234 F4 Windsor NJ U.S.A.
233 J6 Windsor NY U.S.A.
234 B5 Windsor PA U.S.A.
232 I12 Windsor VA U.S.A.
233 M5 Windsor VT U.S.A.
151 K5 Windsor and Maidenhead admin. div. England U.K.
233 M6 Windsor Dam MA U.S.A.
233 M7 Windsor Locks CT U.S.A.
214 I4 Windsorton S. Africa
85 H9 Windula watercourse Qld Austr.
247 □3 Windward Grenada
247 M6 Windward Islands Caribbean Sea
Windward Islands Arch. de la Société Fr. Polynesia see Vent, Îles du
246 F4 Windward Passage Cuba/Haiti
87 C13 Windy Harbour W.A. Austr.
223 I4 Winefred Lake Alta Can.
231 D9 Winfield AL U.S.A.
237 G7 Winfield KS U.S.A.
232 D10 Winfield WV U.S.A.
150 G5 Winford North Somerset, England U.K.
151 K4 Wing Buckinghamshire, England U.K.
149 O4 Wingate Durham, England U.K.
84 C3 Wingate Mountains hills N.T. Austr.
235 H1 Wingdale NY U.S.A.
83 M4 Wingen N.S.W. Austr.
165 D6 Wingene Belgium
157 N6 Wingen-sur-Moder France
169 J8 Wingerode Ger.
83 N4 Wingham N.S.W. Austr.
224 D5 Wingham Ont. Can.
151 O5 Wingham Kent, England U.K.
156 E3 Wingles France
168 H3 Wingst Ger.
173 N5 Winhöring Ger.
93 D8 Wini East Timor
86 G7 Winifred, Lake salt flat W.A. Austr.
261 E5 Winifreda Arg.
78 □4a Winion, Mochun sea chan. Chuuk Micronesia
224 C2 Winisk Ont. Can.
224 C2 Winisk r. Ont. Can.
224 C2 Winisk Lake Ont. Can.
224 C2 Winisk River Provincial Park Ont. Can.
96 C7 Winkana Myanmar
214 D8 Winkelhaaks r. S. Africa
173 K3 Winkelhaid Ger.
241 V9 Winkelman AZ U.S.A.
215 K3 Winkelpos S. Africa
168 G5 Winkelsett Ger.
151 K5 Winkfield Bracknell Forest, England U.K.
173 M3 Winklarn Ger.
150 E6 Winkleigh Devon, England U.K.
223 L5 Winkler Man. Can.
178 G6 Winklern Austria
179 J5 Winklern bei Oberwölz Austria
238 C3 Winlock WA U.S.A.
84 C8 Winnalls Ridge N.T. Austr.
206 E5 Winneba Ghana
236 H4 Winnebago MN U.S.A.
226 F5 Winnebago, Lake WI U.S.A.
236 G4 Winnebago Indian Reservation res. NE U.S.A.
84 C5 Winnecke Creek watercourse N.T. Austr.
226 F5 Winneconne WI U.S.A.
238 F6 Winnemucca NV U.S.A.
240 M1 Winnemucca Lake NV U.S.A.
172 G4 Winnenden Ger.
236 E4 Winner SD U.S.A.
151 K5 Winnersh Wokingham, England U.K.
168 H2 Winnert Ger.
238 J3 Winnett MT U.S.A.
237 I10 Winnfield LA U.S.A.
236 H2 Winnibigoshish, Lake MN U.S.A.
175 I3 Winnica Pol.
237 H11 Winnie TX U.S.A.
87 C7 Winning W.A. Austr.
169 E10 Winningen Rheinland-Pfalz Ger.
171 D7 Winningen Sachsen-Anhalt Ger.
223 L5 Winnipeg Man. Can.
223 L5 Winnipeg r. Man./Ont. Can.
223 L5 Winnipeg, Lake Man. Can.
223 L5 Winnipegosis Man. Can.
223 K4 Winnipegosis, Lake Man. Can.
233 N5 Winnipesaukee, Lake NH U.S.A.
237 J9 Winnsboro LA U.S.A.
231 G8 Winnsboro SC U.S.A.
237 H9 Winnsboro TX U.S.A.
172 D2 Winnweiler Ger.
241 U6 Winona AZ U.S.A.
226 F3 Winona MI U.S.A.
226 C5 Winona MN U.S.A.
237 J7 Winona MO U.S.A.
237 K9 Winona MS U.S.A.
233 L4 Winooski VT U.S.A.
233 L4 Winooski r. VT U.S.A.
164 L2 Winschoten Neth.
150 G5 Winscombe North Somerset, England U.K.
168 I5 Winsen (Aller) Ger.
168 J4 Winsen (Luhe) Ger.
149 L7 Winsford Cheshire, England U.K.
174 E4 Wińsko Pol.
150 H5 Winsley Wiltshire, England U.K.
151 K4 Winslow Buckinghamshire, England U.K.
241 V6 Winslow AZ U.S.A.
233 □P4 Winslow ME U.S.A.
234 F5 Winslow NJ U.S.A.
233 L7 Winsted CT U.S.A.
149 N4 Winston Durham, England U.K.
231 G7 Winston-Salem NC U.S.A.
164 I2 Winsum Friesland Neth.
164 K2 Winsum Groningen Neth.
226 C4 Winter WI U.S.A.
169 G8 Winterberg Ger.
215 K8 Winterberg mts S. Africa
150 G4 Winterbourne South Gloucestershire, England U.K.
150 G6 Winterbourne Abbas Dorset, England U.K.
170 D5 Winterfeld Ger.
233 □Q4 Winter Harbor ME U.S.A.
231 G11 Winter Haven FL U.S.A.
172 G5 Winterlingen Ger.
231 G11 Winter Park FL U.S.A.
233 □Q4 Winterport ME U.S.A.
240 K3 Winters CA U.S.A.
237 F10 Winters TX U.S.A.
171 F8 Wintersdorf Ger.
236 H5 Winterset IA U.S.A.
234 C6 Winters Run r. MD U.S.A.
234 B5 Winterstown PA U.S.A.
164 K5 Winterswijk Neth.
190 F1 Winterthur Switz.
215 N4 Winterton S. Africa
149 P6 Winterton North Lincolnshire, England U.K.
215 M1 Winterveld S. Africa
233 □Q2 Winterville ME U.S.A.
235 K2 Winthrop CT U.S.A.
233 □P4 Winthrop ME U.S.A.
85 I7 Winton Qld Austr.
231 □2 Winton New Prov. Bahamas
81 C13 Winton South I. N.Z.
149 M5 Winton Cumbria, England U.K.
231 I7 Winton NC U.S.A.
172 B2 Wintrich Ger.
157 N7 Wintzenheim France
151 L3 Winwick Cambridgeshire, England U.K.
169 I7 Winzenburg Ger.
179 N4 Winzendorf Austria
173 O4 Winzer Ger.
171 D8 Wipper r. Ger.
169 K8 Wipperdorf Ger.
169 D8 Wipperfürth Ger.
168 D5 Wippingen Ger.
171 D7 Wippra Kurort Ger.
178 D5 Wipptal val. Austria
94 F6 Wiralaga Sumatera Indon.
168 D4 Wirdumer (Wirdum) Ger.
169 E10 Wirges Ger.
149 N7 Wirksworth Derbyshire, England U.K.
84 D6 Wirliyajarrayi Aboriginal Land Trust res. N.T. Austr.
82 G5 Wirrabara S.A. Austr.
149 K7 Wirral pen. England U.K.
82 F4 Wirraminna S.A. Austr.
82 H7 Wirrega S.A. Austr.
82 E3 Wirrida, Lake salt flat S.A. Austr.
83 N4 Wirrikimbe National Park N.S.W. Austr.
82 E5 Wirrulla S.A. Austr.
171 E10 Wirsberg Ger.
78 □4a Wisas i. Chuuk Micronesia
151 M2 Wisbech Cambridgeshire, England U.K.
233 □P4 Wiscasset ME U.S.A.
168 H3 Wischhafen Ger.
226 C6 Wisconsin r. WI U.S.A.
236 K3 Wisconsin state U.S.A.
226 E6 Wisconsin, Lake WI U.S.A.
226 E6 Wisconsin Dells WI U.S.A.
226 E5 Wisconsin Rapids WI U.S.A.
232 C12 Wise VA U.S.A.
146 I11 Wishaw North Lanarkshire, Scotland U.K.
236 F2 Wisher ND U.S.A.
210 F3 Wisil Dabarow Somalia
149 O5 Wiske r. England U.K.
175 I3 Wiskitki Pol.
174 G6 Wisła Pol.
143 O7 Wisła r. Pol.
143 P7 Wiślana, Mierzeja spit Pol.
143 P7 Wiślany, Zalew b. Pol.
175 I5 Wiślica Pol.
175 K5 Wisłok r. Pol.
175 J5 Wisłoka r. Pol.
170 D3 Wismar Ger.
170 D2 Wismarbucht b. Ger.
237 J10 Wisner LA U.S.A.
175 K3 Wiśniew Pol.
175 I2 Wiśniewo Pol.
175 I6 Wiśniowa Pol.
156 C2 Wissant France
157 O5 Wissembourg France
169 E9 Wissen Ger.
226 C5 Wissota Lake WI U.S.A.
150 G3 Wistanstow Shropshire, England U.K.
222 E4 Wistaria B.C. Can.
149 M7 Wistaston Cheshire, England U.K.
168 I4 Wistedt Ger.
175 K6 Wisznia r. Pol.
174 F4 Wisznia Mała Pol.
175 L4 Wisznice Pol.
215 N1 Witbank S. Africa
212 C5 Witbooisvlei Namibia
214 E2 Witdraai S. Africa
151 N4 Witham Essex, England U.K.
151 M2 Witham r. England U.K.
233 L4 Witherbee NY U.S.A.
150 E6 Witheridge Devon, England U.K.
149 R6 Withernsea East Riding of Yorkshire, England U.K.
231 F10 Withlacoochee r. FL U.S.A.
231 F11 Withlacoochee r. FL U.S.A.
82 E2 Witjira National Park S.A. Austr.
215 N3 Witkoppies mt. S. Africa
174 F3 Witkowo Wielkopolskie Pol.
174 D2 Witkowo Zachodniopomorskie Pol.
215 J7 Witkransnek pass S. Africa
151 K5 Witley Surrey, England U.K.
164 H2 Witmarsum Neth.
215 J8 Witmos S. Africa
215 M1 Witnek S. Africa
151 J4 Witney Oxfordshire, England U.K.
174 C3 Witnica Lubuskie Pol.
174 C3 Witnica Zachodniopomorskie Pol.
175 H3 Witonia Pol.
174 F2 Witosław Pol.
214 I5 Witput S. Africa
215 P1 Witrivier S. Africa
156 H5 Witry-lès-Reims France
214 G4 Witsand Nature Reserve S. Africa
168 F1 Wittdün Ger.
214 G9 Witteberg mt. Eastern Cape S. Africa
215 M4 Witteberg mt. Free State S. Africa
215 L6 Witteberg mts S. Africa
214 E9 Witteberge mts S. Africa
157 N8 Wittelsheim France
169 D8 Witten Ger.
172 G7 Wittenbach Switz.
Wittenberg Ger. see Lutherstadt Wittenberg
226 E5 Wittenberg WI U.S.A.
170 E5 Wittenberge Ger.
170 D3 Wittenburg Ger.
170 D3 Wittenförden Ger.
170 H2 Wittenhagen Ger.
157 N8 Wittenheim France
86 E7 Wittenoom W.A. Austr.
Wittenoom Gorge W.A. Austr. see Wittenoom
168 I2 Wittensee l. Ger.
247 □8 Witte Pan salt l. Bonaire Neth. Antilles
151 L2 Wittering Peterborough, England U.K.
171 G9 Wittgensdorf Ger.
95 L2 Witti, Banjaran mts Malaysia
173 N5 Wittibreut Ger.
171 J8 Wittichenau Ger.
172 H2 Wittighausen Ger.
168 K5 Wittingen Ger.
173 I4 Wittislingen Ger.
172 B2 Wittlich Ger.
234 C7 Wittman MD U.S.A.
169 K6 Wittmar Ger.
168 E3 Wittmund Ger.
149 N4 Witton Gilbert Durham, England U.K.
170 H1 Wittow pen. Ger.
170 F4 Wittstock Ger.
211 D5 Witu Kenya
91 K7 Witu Islands P.N.G.
212 C4 Witvlei Namibia
215 L2 Witwatersberg mts S. Africa
215 K2 Witwatersrand mts S. Africa
169 I8 Witzenhausen Ger.
168 J3 Witzhave Ger.
170 E3 Witzin Ger.
168 G2 Witzwort Ger.
150 F5 Wiveliscombe Somerset, England U.K.
151 N4 Wivenhoe Essex, England U.K.
85 N9 Wivenhoe, Lake Qld Austr.
175 K1 Wiżajny Pol.
156 D2 Wizernes France
175 K2 Wizna Pol.
175 I3 Wkra r. Pol.
174 G3 Władysławów Pol.
143 O7 Władysławowo Pol.
174 D4 Wleń Pol.
175 H3 Włocławek Pol.
175 L4 Włodawa Pol.
175 L4 Włodawka r. Pol.
175 H5 Włodowice Pol.
174 F5 Włodzienin Pol.
175 H4 Włodzimierzów Pol.
174 E4 Włoszakowice Pol.
175 H5 Włoszczowa Pol.
170 E4 Wöbbelin Ger.
Wobkent Uzbek. see Vobkent
233 □O3 Woburn Que. Can.
151 K4 Woburn Bedfordshire, England U.K.
151 K3 Woburn Sands Milton Keynes, England U.K.
83 K7 Wodonga Vic. Austr.
175 J3 Wodynie Pol.
175 H4 Wodzierady Pol.
175 I5 Wodzisław Pol.
174 G5 Wodzisław Śląski Pol.
164 G4 Woerden Neth.
157 O6 Wœrth France
157 J5 Wœvre, Forêt de for. France
157 K5 Woëvre, Plaine de la plain France
164 H3 Wognum Neth.
208 F3 Wohko watercourse Sudan
190 E1 Wohlen Aargau Switz.
190 C2 Wohlen Bern Switz.
171 D8 Wohlmirstedt Ger.
263 A2 Wohlthat Mountains Antarctica
168 J3 Wohltorf Ger.
169 G9 Wohra r. Ger.
168 H2 Wöhrden Ger.
175 K4 Wohyń Pol.
108 B2 Woinbo Sichuan China
157 L5 Woippy France
175 J6 Wojaszówka Pol.
175 J5 Wojciechowice Pol.
175 K4 Wojcieszków Pol.
174 D5 Wojcieszów Pol.
174 G3 Wójcin Pol.
78 □3b Woje Majuro i. Majuro Marshall Is
Wōjjā atoll Marshall Is see Wotje
175 H5 Wojkowice Pol.
175 I6 Wojnicz Pol.
174 F2 Wojnowo Pol.
175 L5 Wojsławice Pol.
175 L5 Wojsławka r. Pol.
91 H8 Wokam i. Indon.
100 F5 Woken He r. China
117 O6 Wokha Nagaland India
151 K5 Woking Surrey, England U.K.
85 I7 Wokingham watercourse Qld Austr.
151 K5 Wokingham Wokingham, England U.K.
151 K5 Wokingham admin. div. England U.K.
83 M4 Woko National Park N.S.W. Austr.
170 H4 Wokuhl Ger.
175 H3 Wola Pol.
175 J4 Wola Mysłowska Pol.

Wolanów to Xirivella

410

175 I4 Wolanów Pol.
175 L4 Wola Uhruska Pol.
175 I3 Wola Wierzbowska Pol.
179 I6 Wolayersee und Umgobung nature res. Austria
175 H4 Wolbórz Pol.
175 H5 Wolbrom Pol.
235 J1 Wolcott CT U.S.A.
226 G9 Wolcott IN U.S.A.
232 I5 Wolcott NY U.S.A.
233 M4 Wolcott VT U.S.A.
226 I8 Wolcottville IN U.S.A.
174 G4 Wołczyn Pol.
170 I4 Woldegk Ger.
164 L2 Woldendorp Neth.
149 Q5 Wold Newton East Riding of Yorkshire, England U.K.
Wolea atoll Micronesia see Woleai
91 J5 Woleai atoll Micronesia
208 A4 Woleu-Ntem prov. Gabon
222 C2 Wolf r. Y.T. Can.
237 J8 Wolf r. TN U.S.A.
226 F5 Wolf r. WI U.S.A.
250 □ Wolf, Volcán vol. Islas Galápagos Ecuador
172 E5 Wolfach Ger.
238 H3 Wolf Creek MT U.S.A.
238 C5 Wolf Creek OR U.S.A.
237 F7 Wolf Creek r. OK U.S.A.
239 K8 Wolf Creek Pass CO U.S.A.
233 □N5 Wolfeboro NH U.S.A.
172 H6 Wolfegg Ger.
227 R5 Wolfe Island Ont. Can.
171 F7 Wolfen Ger.
169 K6 Wolfenbüttel Ger.
169 G10 Wölfersheim Ger.
179 H4 Wolfgangsee l. Austria
169 H8 Wolfhagen Ger.
169 K9 Wölfis Ger.
Wolf Island Islas Galápagos Ecuador see Wenman, Isla
222 D2 Wolf Lake l. Y.T. Can.
226 H6 Wolf Lake MI U.S.A.
179 L3 Wolfpassing Austria
238 L2 Wolf Point MT U.S.A.
173 J3 Wolframs-Eschenbach Ger.
173 K6 Wolfratshausen Ger.
179 K6 Wolfsberg Austria
169 K6 Wolfsburg Ger.
172 D2 Wolfstein Ger.
225 H4 Wolfville N.S. Can.
170 I2 Wolgast Ger.
190 E1 Wolhusen Switz.
175 L5 Wolica r. Pol.
174 C2 Wolin Pol.
174 C2 Wolin i. Pol.
174 C2 Woliński Park Narodowy nat. park Pol.
175 H3 Wólka Kujawsko-Pomorskie Pol.
175 K4 Wólka Lubelskie Pol.
175 L3 Wólka Dobryńska Pol.
171 H9 Wolkenstein Ger.
179 O3 Wolkersdorf Austria
169 K8 Wolkramshausen Ger.
151 K3 Wollaston Northamptonshire, England U.K.
259 D9 Wollaston, Islas is Chile
223 K3 Wollaston Lake Sask. Can.
223 K3 Wollaston Lake l. Sask. Can.
220 G3 Wollaston Peninsula N.W.T./Nunavut Can.
83 M5 Wollemi National Park N.S.W. Austr.
190 F1 Wollerau Switz.
170 I4 Wolletzsee l. Ger.
83 M6 Wollongong N.S.W. Austr.
215 J3 Wolmaransstad S. Africa
171 D7 Wolmirsleben Ger.
171 E6 Wolmirstedt Ger.
173 L4 Wolnzach Ger.
175 J3 Wołomin Pol.
108 D3 Wolong Reserve nature res. China
174 E4 Wołów Pol.
93 B8 Wolowaru Flores Indon.
172 H3 Wolpertshausen Ger.
172 H6 Wolpertswende Ger.
169 H6 Wölpinghausen Ger.
169 K6 Wolsdorf Ger.
82 H7 Wolseley S.A. Austr.
214 D9 Wolseley S. Africa
236 F3 Wolsey SD U.S.A.
149 N4 Wolsingham Durham, England U.K.
221 K3 Wolstenholme, Cap c. Que. Can.
151 J3 Wolston Warwickshire, England U.K.
174 E3 Wolsztyn Pol.
171 H6 Woltersdorf Brandenburg Ger.
171 I6 Woltersdorf Brandenburg Ger.
170 D5 Woltersdorf Niedersachsen Ger.
169 I7 Woltershausen Ger.
164 J3 Wolvega Neth.
150 H2 Wolverhampton West Midlands, England U.K.
226 J4 Wolverine MI U.S.A.
215 I9 Wolwefontein S. Africa
215 J4 Wolwespruit S. Africa
94 A2 Wolya r. Indon.
179 J5 Wölzer Tauern mts Austria
150 H2 Wombourne Staffordshire, England U.K.
149 O6 Wombwell South Yorkshire, England U.K.
234 C4 Womelsdorf PA U.S.A.
164 I2 Wommels Neth.
172 C2 Womrather Höhe hill Ger.
84 F5 Wonarah N.T. Austr.
123 M4 Wonay, Kowtal-e pass Afgh.
85 M9 Wondai Qld Austr.
165 E6 Wondelgem Belgium
215 N1 Wonderfontein S. Africa
215 L3 Wonderkop S. Africa
215 L4 Wonderkop mt. S. Africa
215 K1 Wondermere S. Africa
173 M1 Wondreb r. Ger.
83 J4 Wongalarroo Lake salt l. N.S.W. Austr.
87 D11 Wongan Hills W.A. Austr.
208 A5 Wonga Wongué, Réserve de nature res. Gabon
117 L6 Wong Chhu r. Bhutan
109 □J7 Wong Chuk Hang H.K. China
109 □J7 Wong Leng hill H.K. China
109 □J7 Wong Wan Chau i. H.K. China
101 E10 Wŏnju S. Korea
95 I8 Wonogiri Jawa Indon.
95 I8 Wonosari Indon.
95 H8 Wonosobo Jawa Indon.
222 F3 Wonowon B.C. Can.
93 E8 Wonreli Maluku Indon.
101 E9 Wŏnsan N. Korea
173 K2 Wonsees Ger.
151 J5 Wonston Hampshire, England U.K.
83 J8 Wonthaggi Vic. Austr.
87 E8 Wonyulgunna, Mount hill W.A. Austr.
151 K4 Wooburn Buckinghamshire, England U.K.
82 F4 Woocalla S.A. Austr.
261 F6 Wood, Isla i. Arg.
222 A2 Wood, Mount Y.T. Can.
84 F2 Woodah, Isle i. N.T. Austr.
231 G10 Woodbine GA U.S.A.
234 A6 Woodbine MD U.S.A.
234 F6 Woodbine NJ U.S.A.
226 E4 Woodboro WI U.S.A.
81 H8 Woodbourne South I. N.Z.
234 F1 Woodbourne NY U.S.A.
151 O3 Woodbridge Suffolk, England U.K.
235 I2 Woodbridge CT U.S.A.
235 G3 Woodbridge NJ U.S.A.
232 H10 Woodbridge VA U.S.A.
222 H3 Wood Buffalo National Park Alta Can.
83 N3 Woodburn N.S.W. Austr.
226 J8 Woodburn IN U.S.A.
238 C4 Woodburn OR U.S.A.
235 I1 Woodbury CT U.S.A.
226 I7 Woodbury MI U.S.A.
234 E5 Woodbury NJ U.S.A.
234 E5 Woodbury Heights NJ U.S.A.
84 E5 Woodcock, Mount hill N.T. Austr.
151 J4 Woodcote Oxfordshire, England U.K.
83 N3 Wooded Bluff hd N.S.W./Qld Austr.
83 N3 Woodenbong N.S.W. Austr.
147 J7 Woodenbridge Ireland
83 J7 Woodend Vic. Austr.
81 C13 Woodend South I. N.Z.
81 G10 Woodend South I. N.Z.
140 □ Woodfjorden inlet Svalbard
247 □6 Woodford Grenada
147 F6 Woodford Ireland
240 M3 Woodfords CA U.S.A.
149 Q7 Woodhall Spa Lincolnshire, England U.K.
151 L6 Woodingdean Brighton and Hove, England U.K.
223 K4 Wood Lake Sask. Can.
240 M5 Woodlake CA U.S.A.
240 K3 Woodland CA U.S.A.
233 □R3 Woodland ME U.S.A.
238 C4 Woodland WA U.S.A.
234 B7 Woodland Beach MD U.S.A.
223 M5 Woodland Caribou Provincial Park Ont. Can.
239 L7 Woodland Park CO U.S.A.
94 □ Woodlands Sing.
91 L8 Woodlark Island P.N.G.
234 B6 Woodlawn MD U.S.A.
151 K5 Woodley Wokingham, England U.K.
234 E5 Woodlyn PA U.S.A.
149 Q6 Woodmansey East Riding of Yorkshire, England U.K.
82 F2 Woodmurra Creek watercourse S.A. Austr.
149 L6 Woodplumpton Lancashire, England U.K.
223 L5 Woodridge Man. Can.
234 F1 Woodridge NY U.S.A.
84 G6 Woodroffe watercourse N.T. Austr.
82 C2 Woodroffe, Mount S.A. Austr.
238 I6 Woodruff UT U.S.A.
226 E4 Woodruff WI U.S.A.
84 D4 Woods, Lake salt flat N.T. Austr.
228 H1 Woods, Lake of the Can./U.S.A.
232 D9 Woodsfield OH U.S.A.
233 O7 Woods Hole MA U.S.A.
83 K8 Woodside Vic. Austr.
234 D6 Woodside DE U.S.A.
83 L5 Woodstock N.S.W. Austr.
85 K5 Woodstock Qld Austr.
225 H4 Woodstock N.B. Can.
224 D5 Woodstock Ont. Can.
151 J4 Woodstock Oxfordshire, England U.K.
226 F7 Woodstock IL U.S.A.
232 G10 Woodstock VA U.S.A.
233 M5 Woodstock VT U.S.A.
215 N4 Woodstock Dam resr S. Africa
147 H8 Woodstown Ireland
234 E5 Woodstown NJ U.S.A.
233 M4 Woodsville NH U.S.A.
151 O3 Woodton Norfolk, England U.K.
147 I5 Woodtown Ireland
227 P5 Woodville Ont. Can.
80 J7 Woodville North I. N.Z.
237 J10 Woodville MS U.S.A.
232 B7 Woodville OH U.S.A.
237 H10 Woodville TX U.S.A.
237 F7 Woodward OK U.S.A.
240 L4 Woodward Reservoir CA U.S.A.
240 N6 Woody CA U.S.A.
215 K9 Woody Cape Nature Reserve S. Africa
150 G3 Woofferton Shropshire, England U.K.
91 I7 Woöi Papua Indon.
150 H6 Wool Dorset, England U.K.
150 D5 Woolacombe Devon, England U.K.
84 E2 Woolen r. N.T. Austr.
149 M2 Wooler Northumberland, England U.K.
85 I6 Woolgar r. Qld Austr.
83 N4 Woolgoolga N.S.W. Austr.
83 N3 Wooli N.S.W. Austr.
84 D7 Woolla Downs N.T. Austr.
262 W1 Woollard, Mount Antarctica
82 G4 Wooltana S.A. Austr.
232 E12 Woolwine VA U.S.A.
87 F12 Woolyeenyer Hill W.A. Austr.
82 F4 Woomera S.A. Austr.
82 D3 Woomera Prohibited Area S.A. Austr.
233 N6 Woonsocket RI U.S.A.
236 F3 Woonsocket SD U.S.A.
85 L8 Woorabinda Qld Austr.
87 C8 Wooramel r. W.A. Austr.
232 D8 Wooster OH U.S.A.
151 K3 Wootton Bedfordshire, England U.K.
151 I4 Wootton Bassett Wiltshire, England U.K.
210 D2 Woqooyi Galbeed admin. reg. Somalia
101 F10 Worak-san National Park S. Korea
190 D2 Worb Switz.
85 H2 Worbody Point Qld Austr.
214 D9 Worcester S. Africa
150 H3 Worcester Worcestershire, England U.K.
233 N6 Worcester MA U.S.A.
233 K6 Worcester NY U.S.A.
150 H3 Worcestershire admin. div. England U.K.
179 N3 Wördern Austria
150 H2 Worfield Shropshire, England U.K.
178 F5 Wörgl Austria
173 I6 Woringen Ger.
91 H8 Workai i. Indon.
149 J4 Workington Cumbria, England U.K.
149 O7 Worksop Nottinghamshire, England U.K.
164 H3 Workum Neth.
238 K4 Worland WY U.S.A.
171 F7 Wörlitz Ger.
165 J9 Wormeldange Lux.
164 G4 Wormer Neth.
156 D2 Wormhout France
146 K10 Wormit Fife, Scotland U.K.
172 E2 Worms Ger.
150 D4 Worms Head Wales U.K.
173 J4 Wörnitz r. Ger.
206 D4 Worofla Côte d'Ivoire
151 K5 Worplesdon Surrey, England U.K.
168 G4 Worpswede Ger.
172 E2 Wörrstadt Ger.
179 J4 Wörschach Austria
165 G6 Wortel Belgium
178 G5 Wörth Austria
173 L5 Wörth Ger.
151 L5 Worth West Sussex, England U.K.
172 G2 Wörth am Main Ger.
172 E3 Wörth am Rhein Ger.
173 M3 Wörth an der Donau Ger.
173 M4 Wörth an der Isar Ger.
179 J6 Wörther See l. Austria
151 L6 Worthing West Sussex, England U.K.
236 H4 Worthington MN U.S.A.
232 B8 Worthington OH U.S.A.
234 C6 Worton MD U.S.A.
93 E4 Wosi Halmahera Indon.
93 B5 Wosu Sulawesi Indon.
174 D2 Woświn, Jezioro l. Pol.
86 G4 Wotjalum Aboriginal Reserve W.A. Austr.
266 G6 Wotje atoll Marshall Is
150 H4 Wotton-under-Edge Gloucestershire, England U.K.
93 B5 Wotu Sulawesi Indon.
164 H4 Woudenberg Neth.
164 G5 Woudrichem Neth.
164 I3 Woudsend Neth.
151 K3 Woughton on the Green Milton Keynes, England U.K.
236 D4 Wounded Knee SD U.S.A.
202 B4 Wour Chad
207 H5 Wouri r. Cameroon
157 N5 Woustviller France
164 F5 Wouw Neth.
85 M7 Wowan Qld Austr.
93 C6 Wowoni i. Indon.
93 C5 Wowoni, Selat sea chan. Indon.
175 H5 Woźniki Pol.
Wozrojdeniye Oroli pen. Uzbek. see Vozrozhdenya Island
149 Q7 Wragby Lincolnshire, England U.K.
Wrangel Island Rus. Fed. see Vrangelya, Ostrov
220 E4 Wrangell AK U.S.A.
222 C3 Wrangell Island AK U.S.A.
220 C4 Wrangell Mountains AK U.S.A.
220 D3 Wrangell-St Elias National Park and Preserve AK U.S.A.
149 R7 Wrangle Lincolnshire, England U.K.
146 F5 Wrath, Cape Scotland U.K.
236 D5 Wray CO U.S.A.
151 J2 Wreake r. England U.K.
86 □2 Wreck Point Cocos Is
246 □ Wreck Point Jamaica
214 A4 Wreck Point S. Africa
Wrecsam Wrexham, Wales U.K. see Wrexham
174 G5 Wręczyca Wielka Pol.
170 G4 Wredenhagen Ger.
149 P5 Wrelton North Yorkshire, England U.K.
168 G3 Wremen Ger.
231 F9 Wrens GA U.S.A.
168 K5 Wrestedt Ger.
169 G7 Wrexen (Diemelstadt) Ger.
150 G1 Wrexham Wrexham, Wales U.K.
150 G1 Wrexham admin. div. Wales U.K.
81 C13 Wreys Bush South I. N.Z.
168 J4 Wriedel Ger.
170 J5 Wriezen Ger.
92 E6 Wright Samar Phil.
238 L5 Wright WY U.S.A.
115 M7 Wrightmyo Andaman & Nicobar Is India
237 H9 Wright Patman Lake TX U.S.A.
241 V10 Wrightson, Mount AZ U.S.A.
234 F4 Wrightstown PA U.S.A.
226 F5 Wrightstown WI U.S.A.
231 F9 Wrightsville GA U.S.A.
234 B4 Wrightsville PA U.S.A.
240 O7 Wrightwood CA U.S.A.
222 F2 Wrigley N.W.T. Can.
232 B10 Wrigley KY U.S.A.
262 P2 Wrigley Gulf Antarctica
150 G5 Wrington North Somerset, England U.K.
168 I3 Wrist Ger.
151 M4 Writtle Essex, England U.K.
174 G4 Wróblew Pol.
174 F4 Wrocław Pol.
168 H2 Wrohm Ger.
175 K1 Wronki Warmińsko-Mazurskie Pol.
174 E3 Wronki Wielkopolskie Pol.
175 K3 Wrotnów Pol.
151 I4 Wroughton Swindon, England U.K.
174 G3 Wrząielka Pol.
175 J4 Wrzelowiec Pol.
174 F1 Wrzeście Pol.
174 F3 Września Pol.
174 F3 Wrześnica r. Pol.
174 D1 Wrzosowo Pol.
175 J5 Wschodnia r. Pol.
174 E4 Wschowa Pol.
Wu'an Fujian China see Changtai
107 N8 Wu'an Hebei China
Wubalawun res. N.T. Austr. see Larrimah Aboriginal Land
87 D11 Wubin W.A. Austr.
107 L8 Wubu Shaanxi China
107 Q3 Wuchagou Nei Mongol China
100 E6 Wuchang Heilong. China
Wuchang Hubei China see Jiangxia
109 L4 Wucheng Anhui China
Wucheng Anhui China see Wuwei
Wuchow Guangxi China see Wuzhou
108 F4 Wuchuan Guizhou China
107 L6 Wuchuan Nei Mongol China
106 J7 Wuda Nei Mongol China
100 E4 Wudalianchi Heilong. China
125 M4 Wuḍām 'Alwā Oman
107 P5 Wudan Nei Mongol China
108 G2 Wudang Shan mts China
107 Q7 Wudao Liaoning China
100 E3 Wudaogou Heilong. China
106 C9 Wudaoliang Qinghai China
125 H7 Wuday'ah well Saudi Arabia
107 O8 Wudi Shandong China
207 H4 Wudil Nigeria
108 D6 Wuding Yunnan China
107 L8 Wuding He r. China
82 E5 Wudinna S.A. Austr.
108 H3 Wufeng Hubei China
Wufeng Yunnan China see Zhenxiong
106 I8 Wufo Gansu China
108 H5 Wugang Hunan China
107 K9 Wugong Shaanxi China
106 J7 Wuhai Nei Mongol China
109 J3 Wuhan Hubei China
109 K2 Wuhe Anhui China
109 L3 Wuhu Anhui China
109 L3 Wuhu Anhui China
109 J7 Wuhua Guangdong China
111 D10 Wüjang Xizang China
108 G8 Wujia Guangxi China
109 M3 Wujiang Jiangsu China
108 F4 Wu Jiang r. China
Wujin Sichuan China see Xinjin
207 H5 Wukari Nigeria
107 Q8 Wuleidao Wan b. China
171 E7 Wulfen Ger.
170 F4 Wulfersdorf Ger.
169 J10 Wülfershausen an der Saale Ger.
168 J4 Wulfsen Ger.
169 J7 Wulften Ger.
106 C9 Wuli Qinghai China
108 D4 Wulian Feng mts Yunnan China
108 C6 Wuliang Shan mts Yunnan China
91 H8 Wuliaru i. Indon.
108 G8 Wuli Jiang r. China
108 G4 Wuling Shan mts China
170 F5 Wulkau Ger.
179 N2 Wullersdorf Austria
108 F4 Wulong Chongqing China
107 Q8 Wulong He r. China
Wulongji Henan China see Huaibin
175 I2 Wulpińskie, Jezioro l. Pol.
168 G4 Wulsbüttel Ger.
93 F7 Wulur Maluku Indon.
207 H5 Wum Cameroon
111 J11 Wumatang Xizang China
108 D5 Wumeng Shan mts Guizhou/Yunnan China
108 G7 Wuming Guangxi China
168 G4 Wümme r. Ger.
115 O2 Wundwin Myanmar
108 C3 Wungda Sichuan China
109 J4 Wuning Jiangxi China
169 G7 Wünnenberg Ger.
224 B2 Wunnummin Lake Ont. Can.
208 F2 Wun Rog Sudan
171 F9 Wünschendorf Ger.
171 H6 Wünsdorf Ger.
208 F2 Wun Shwai Sudan
171 F10 Wunsiedel Ger.
169 H6 Wunstorf Ger.
210 B2 Wuntau Sudan
96 B3 Wuntho Myanmar
241 U6 Wupatki National Monument nat. park AZ U.S.A.
109 K6 Wuping Fujian China
169 D8 Wuppertal Ger.
214 D8 Wuppertal S. Africa
107 K8 Wuqi Shaanxi China
110 B7 Wuqia Xinjiang China
110 B7 Wuqia Xinjiang China
107 N7 Wuqiang Hebei China
107 O8 Wuqiao Hebei China
107 O7 Wuqing Tianjin China
Wuquan Henan China see Wuyang
87 D10 Wuranga W.A. Austr.
173 K5 Würm r. Ger.
173 N5 Wurmannsquick Ger.
172 F5 Wurmlingen Ger.
207 G3 Wurno Nigeria
84 F3 Wurralibi Aboriginal Land res. N.T. Austr.
169 B9 Würselen Ger.
235 G1 Wurtsboro NY U.S.A.
171 E10 Wurzbach Ger.
172 H2 Würzburg Ger.
171 G8 Wurzen Ger.
108 G3 Wushan Chongqing China
106 I9 Wushan Gansu China
108 H3 Wu Shan mts China
108 F3 Wusheng Sichuan China
108 G8 Wushi Guangdong China
110 D6 Wushi Xinjiang China
170 F5 Wust Ger.
169 H8 Wüstegarten hill Ger.
172 G3 Wüstenrot Ger.
170 F5 Wusterhausen Ger.
170 I2 Wusterhusen Ger.
170 G5 Wustermark Ger.
171 F6 Wusterwitz Ger.
169 J8 Wüstheuterode Ger.
170 G5 Wustrau-Altfriesack Ger.
170 G4 Wustrow Mecklenburg-Vorpommern Ger.
170 D5 Wustrow Niedersachsen Ger.
170 E2 Wustrow, Halbinsel spit Ger.
170 F2 Wustrow, Ostseebad Ger.
Wusuli Jiang r. Rus. Fed. see Ussuri
172 E6 Wutach r. Ger.
107 M7 Wutai Shanxi China
110 F4 Wutai Xinjiang China
107 M7 Wutaishan Shanxi China
109 H4 Wutan Hunan China
169 J9 Wutha Ger.
106 F6 Wutonggou Nei Mongol China
110 I6 Wutonggou Xinjiang China
100 G5 Wutong He r. China
106 D5 Wutongwozi Quan well Xinjiang China
165 G6 Wuustwezel Belgium
91 J7 Wuvulu Island P.N.G.
109 K3 Wuwei Anhui China
106 H8 Wuwei Gansu China
108 G3 Wuxi Chongqing China
108 H4 Wuxi Hunan China
Wuxi Hunan China see Qiyang
109 M3 Wuxi Jiangsu China
Wuxia Chongqing China see Wushan
107 M8 Wuxiang Shanxi China
Wuxing Zhejiang China see Huzhou
108 G7 Wuxu Guangxi China
108 G7 Wuxuan Guangxi China
109 J4 Wuxue Hubei China
Wuyang Guizhou China see Zhenyuan
109 I2 Wuyang Henan China
107 M8 Wuyang Shanxi China
Wuyang Zhejiang China see Wuyi
109 L4 Wuyi Zhejiang China
100 F4 Wuyiling Heilong. China
109 L5 Wuyishan Fujian China
109 K6 Wuyi Shan mts China
109 L5 Wuyi Shan tourist site Fujian China
109 K4 Wuyuan Jiangxi China
107 K6 Wuyuan Nei Mongol China
Wuyuan Zhejiang China see Haiyan
Wuyun Zhejiang China see Jinyun
107 L7 Wuzhai Shanxi China
109 H3 Wuzhen Hubei China
107 M9 Wuzhi Henan China
108 G9 Wuzhishan Hainan China
108 G9 Wuzhi Shan mts China
106 J8 Wuzhong Ningxia China
109 H7 Wuzhou Guangxi China
85 H4 Wyaaba Creek r. Qld Austr.
226 C9 Wyaconda r. MO U.S.A.
87 D11 Wyalkatchem W.A. Austr.
227 R8 Wyalusing PA U.S.A.
227 K7 Wyandotte MI U.S.A.
85 J9 Wyandra Qld Austr.
226 E8 Wyanet IL U.S.A.
83 L5 Wyangala Reservoir N.S.W. Austr.
83 J3 Wyara, Lake salt flat Qld Austr.
151 L2 Wyberton Lincolnshire, England U.K.
83 I7 Wycheproof Vic. Austr.
235 G2 Wyckoff NJ U.S.A.
174 F2 Wyczechy Pol.
175 K2 Wydminy Pol.
151 N5 Wye Kent, England U.K.
149 N7 Wye r. Derbyshire, England U.K.
150 G4 Wye r. England/Wales U.K.
87 E10 Wyemandoo hill W.A. Austr.
234 C7 Wye Mills MD U.S.A.
226 D5 Wyeville WI U.S.A.
177 I1 Wygoda Pol.
174 D2 Wygon Pol.
172 D5 Wyhl Ger.
171 F8 Wyhra r. Ger.
168 G1 Wyk auf Föhr Ger.
174 F3 Wylatowo Pol.
232 G12 Wylliesburg VA U.S.A.
87 D7 Wyloo W.A. Austr.
151 I5 Wylye Wiltshire, England U.K.
151 I5 Wylye r. England U.K.
168 D4 Wymeer Ger.
171 L7 Wymiarki Pol.
151 O2 Wymondham Norfolk, England U.K.
236 G5 Wymore NE U.S.A.
82 D4 Wynbring S.A. Austr.
86 J3 Wyndham W.A. Austr.
81 C13 Wyndham South I. N.Z.
83 J7 Wyndham-Werribee Vic. Austr.
237 J8 Wynne AR U.S.A.
220 G2 Wynniatt Bay N.W.T. Can.
83 J9 Wynyard Tas. Austr.
223 J5 Wynyard Sask. Can.
226 E6 Wyocena WI U.S.A.
82 C3 Wyola Lake salt flat S.A. Austr.
234 D6 Wyoming DE U.S.A.
226 E8 Wyoming IL U.S.A.
226 I7 Wyoming MI U.S.A.
238 K5 Wyoming state U.S.A.
234 C1 Wyoming County county PA U.S.A.
238 I5 Wyoming Peak WY U.S.A.
238 I5 Wyoming Range mts WY U.S.A.
234 D4 Wyomissing PA U.S.A.
83 M5 Wyong N.S.W. Austr.
84 F2 Wyonga r. N.T. Austr.
82 I6 Wyperfeld National Park Vic. Austr.
146 K4 Wyre i. Scotland U.K.
149 L6 Wyre r. England U.K.
175 L4 Wyryki-Połód Pol.
174 F2 Wyrzysk Pol.
175 I4 Wyśmierzyce Pol.
174 D3 Wysoka Lubuskie Pol.
175 J6 Wysoka Podkarpackie Pol.
174 F2 Wysoka Wielkopolskie Pol.
174 C2 Wysoka Kamieńska Pol.
174 D5 Wysoka Kopa mt. Pol.
175 K5 Wysokie Lubelskie Pol.
175 K2 Wysokie Warmińsko-Mazurskie Pol.
175 K3 Wysokie Mazowieckie Pol.
175 J6 Wysowa Pol.
227 R8 Wysox PA U.S.A.
175 K3 Wyszki Pol.
175 J3 Wyszków Pol.
175 I3 Wyszogród Pol.
151 I3 Wythall Worcestershire, England U.K.
232 D12 Wytheville VA U.S.A.
175 L4 Wytyczno Pol.
175 J4 Wyżnica r. Pol.
143 P7 Wzniesienie Elbląskie, Park Krajobrazowy Pol.

X

210 F2 Xaafuun Somalia
210 F2 Xaafuun, Raas pt Somalia
210 F2 Xabo Somalia
111 M11 Xabyai Xizang China
129 I5 Xaçınçay r. Azer.
129 J4 Xaçmaz Azer.
212 D4 Xade Botswana
195 □ Xagħra Gozo Malta
111 K12 Xagjang Xizang China
111 E10 Xagnag Xizang China
111 I11 Xago Xizang China
111 K11 Xagquka Xizang China
111 D8 Xaidulla Xinjiang China
96 E5 Xaignabouli Laos
157 L7 Xaintois reg. France
111 I11 Xainza Xizang China
111 I12 Xaitongmoin Xizang China
213 G5 Xai-Xai Moz.
110 D7 Xakur Xinjiang China
243 O7 Xal, Cerro de hill Mex.
129 I5 Xaldan Azer.
210 F2 Xalin Somalia
182 B3 Xallas r. Spain
120 H6 Xalqobod Uzbek.
129 J5 Xaltan Azer.
245 H8 Xaltianguis Mex.
209 D9 Xamavera Angola
107 J6 Xamba Nei Mongol China
254 C3 Xambioa Brazil
256 A5 Xambrê Brazil
96 G4 Xam Nua Laos
209 C7 Xá-Muteba Angola
96 F5 Xan r. Laos
182 D2 Xanceda Spain
106 H6 Xangd Nei Mongol China
Xangda Qinghai China see Nangqên
107 L5 Xangdin Hural Nei Mongol China
111 E10 Xangdoring Xizang China
209 B9 Xangongo Angola
96 G6 Xangxoy, Xé r. Laos
111 L11 Xangzha Xizang China
97 I8 Xanh, Cu Lao i. Vietnam
245 K9 Xanica Mex.
129 H6 Xankändi Azer.
129 H5 Xanlar Azer.
129 H6 Xanlıq Azer.
169 B7 Xanten Ger.
198 F1 Xanthi Greece
126 D5 Xanthos-Letoon tourist site Turkey
255 B8 Xanxerê Brazil
252 C2 Xapuri Brazil
252 C2 Xapuri r. Brazil
122 C2 Xaraba Şähär Sayı i. Azer.
106 F8 Xarag Qinghai China
210 E3 Xarardheere Somalia
129 K6 Xärä Zirä Adası is Azer.
111 G12 Xarba La pass Xizang China
Xar Burd Nei Mongol China see Bayan Nuru
111 G11 Xardong Xizang China
182 F4 Xares r. Spain
107 N4 Xar Hudag Nei Mongol China
107 L5 Xar Moron r. China
107 Q5 Xar Moron r. China
184 C4 Xarrama r. Port.
198 B3 Xarrë Albania
117 K5 Xarru Xizang China
Xarsingma Xizang China see Yadong
209 C7 Xassengue Angola
129 G4 Xatınlı Azer.
187 D10 Xátiva Spain
Xatl'o Dehe N.W.T. Can. see Hay River
212 E4 Xau, Lake Botswana
212 D3 Xaudum watercourse Botswana/Namibia
256 C5 Xavantes, Represa de resr Brazil
254 C5 Xavantes, Serra dos hills Brazil
111 F10 Xaxa Xizang China
96 F4 Xay Laos
110 F6 Xayar Xinjiang China
110 H3 Xazgat Xinjiang China
243 P8 Xcalak Mex.
243 P7 X-Can Mex.
110 D6 Xegil Xinjiang China
110 C7 Xekar Xinjiang China
232 B9 Xenia OH U.S.A.
111 I11 Xênkyêr Xizang China
209 C9 Xequessa Angola
187 E9 Xeraco Spain
187 E9 Xeresa Spain
251 F5 Xeriuini r. Brazil
182 E2 Xermade Spain
Xero Potamos r. Cyprus see Xeros
128 A4 Xeros r. Cyprus
186 G6 Xerta Spain
157 L7 Xertigny France
195 □ Xewkija Gozo Malta
Xhora S. Africa see Elliotdale
212 E4 Xhorodomo Pan salt pan Botswana
212 E4 Xhumo Botswana
110 C7 Xia Awat Xinjiang China
Xiabancheng Hebei China see Chengde
110 C7 Xia Bazar Xinjiang China
100 D3 Xiabole Shan mt. China
100 G6 Xiachengzi Heilong. China
109 I8 Xiachuan Dao i. Guangdong China
Xiacun Shandong China see Rushan
106 F9 Xia Dawo Qinghai China
106 D6 Xiadong Gansu China
Xiaguan Yunnan China see Dali
106 I9 Xiaguanying Gansu China
106 H9 Xiahe Gansu China
Xiajiang Jiangxi China see Baqiu
Xiajiang Xizang China see Xagjang
107 O8 Xiajin Shandong China
108 A2 Xialaxiu Qinghai China
108 A4 Xia Lingka Xizang China
106 D5 Xiamaya Xinjiang China
109 L6 Xiamen Fujian China
107 K9 Xi'an Shaanxi China
108 G4 Xianfeng Hubei China
109 I2 Xiangcheng Henan China
109 J2 Xiangcheng Henan China
108 B4 Xiangcheng Sichuan China
Xiangcheng Yunnan China see Xiangyun
109 I2 Xiangfan Hubei China
107 L9 Xiangfen Shanxi China
Xiangfeng Hubei China see Laifeng
Xianggang H.K. China see Hong Kong
Xianggang Tebie Xingzhengqu special admin. reg. China see Hong Kong
108 B5 Xianggelila Yunnan China
Xianghuang Qi Nei Mongol China see Xin Bulag
Xiangjiang Jiangxi China see Huichang
109 I4 Xiang Jiang r. China
96 F5 Xiangkhoang Laos
Xiangkou Chongqing China see Wulong
107 L9 Xiangning Shanxi China
106 E9 Xiangride Qinghai China
Xiangshan Yunnan China see Menghai
109 M4 Xiangshan Zhejiang China
109 M4 Xiangshan Gang b. Zhejiang China
107 P9 Xiangshui Jiangsu China
108 G5 Xiangshuiba Hunan China
109 I5 Xiangtan Hunan China
109 I5 Xiangxiang Hunan China
Xiangyang Hubei China see Xiangfan
109 I2 Xiangyang Hubei China
111 I9 Xiangyang Hu l. Xizang China
109 I4 Xiangyin Hunan China
108 C6 Xiangyun Yunnan China
108 G7 Xiangzhou Guangxi China
109 M4 Xianju Zhejiang China
109 J4 Xianning Hubei China
Xiannümiao Jiangsu China see Jiangdu
Xianshui Sichuan China see Dawu
108 C3 Xianshui He r. Sichuan China
Xiantang Guangdong China see Dongyuan
109 I3 Xiantao Hubei China
109 K5 Xianxia Ling mts China
107 O7 Xianxian Hebei China
107 K9 Xianyang Shaanxi China
109 L6 Xianyou Fujian China
106 I8 Xi'anzhou Ningxia China
Xiaoba Ningxia China see Qingtongxia
107 N6 Xiaochang Hebei China
109 I3 Xiaochang Hubei China
108 E2 Xiaochuan Gansu China
108 G7 Xiaodong Guangxi China
107 R2 Xiao'ergou Nei Mongol China
Xiaofan Hebei China see Wuqiang
109 I3 Xiaogan Hubei China
110 G4 Xiaoguai Xinjiang China
107 J8 Xiaoguan Gansu China
110 D7 Xiaohaizi Shuiku resr Xinjiang China
100 E3 Xiao Hinggan Ling mts China
Xiaojiang Guangxi China see Pubei
107 J9 Xiaojin Gansu China
108 D3 Xiaojin Sichuan China
107 M9 Xiaolangdi Shuiku resr Henan/Shanxi China
109 L5 Xiaomei Zhejiang China
Xiaonan Gansu China see Dongxiangzu
106 D9 Xiaonanchuan Qinghai China
Xiaopu Hunan China see Jiangyong
111 L8 Xiao Qaidam Qinghai China
107 P8 Xiaoqing He r. China
109 I6 Xiaosanjiang Guangdong China
109 M3 Xiaoshan Zhejiang China
107 L9 Xiao Shan mts China
108 E4 Xiaoshi Sichuan China
108 A2 Xiao Surmang Qinghai China
109 K6 Xiaotao Fujian China
107 N7 Xiaowutai Shan mt. Hebei China
Xiaoxi Fujian China see Pinghe
107 O9 Xiaoxian Anhui China
108 D4 Xiaoxiang Ling mts Sichuan China
Xiaoyi Henan China see Gongyi
107 L8 Xiaoyi Shanxi China
110 E4 Xiaoyingpan Xinjiang China
109 M5 Xiapu Fujian China
108 C5 Xiaqiaotou Yunnan China
Xiaqiong Sichuan China see Batang
Xiashan Guangdong China see Zhanjiang
106 H7 Xiasifen Gansu China
243 O8 Xiatil Mex.
107 L9 Xiaxian Shanxi China
Xiayang Hunan China see Yanling
Xiayanjing Xizang China see Yanjing
Xiayingpan Guizhou China see Lupanshui
Xiayingpan Guizhou China see Luzhi
108 C2 Xia Zanggor Qinghai China
108 C3 Xiazhai Sichuan China
Xiazhen Shandong China see Weishan
108 B4 Xibdê Sichuan China
110 I3 Xibet Xinjiang China
109 L5 Xibing Fujian China
Xibu Fujian China see Dongshan
108 G8 Xichang Guangxi China
108 D5 Xichang Sichuan China
Xicheng Hebei China see Yangyuan
108 E7 Xichou Yunnan China
109 H2 Xichuan Henan China
245 J6 Xico Mex.
245 I2 Xicohténcatl Mex.
245 J5 Xicotepec de Juárez Mex.
108 D4 Xide Sichuan China
Xidu Hunan China see Hengyang
250 E4 Xié r. Brazil
Xiejiaji Shandong China see Qingyun
109 H3 Xiemahe' Hubei China
Xieng Khouang Laos see Xiangkhoang
96 G5 Xiêng Lam Vietnam
108 G8 Xieyang Dao i. China
109 K2 Xifei He r. China
107 J9 Xifeng Gansu China
108 F5 Xifeng Guizhou China
100 D7 Xifeng Liaoning China
Xifengzhen Gansu China see Xifeng
111 I12 Xigazê Xizang China
108 F2 Xihan Shui r. Gansu China
108 E2 Xihe Gansu China
107 Q6 Xi He r. Liaoning China
108 F3 Xi He r. Sichuan China
106 G5 Xi He watercourse China
110 L6 Xihu Gansu China
109 J2 Xihua Henan China
Xihuachi Gansu China see Heshui
210 E2 Xiis Somalia
106 I9 Xiji Ningxia China
109 I7 Xi Jiang r. Guangdong China
106 E6 Xijian Quan well Gansu China
108 G7 Xijin Guangxi China
106 B9 Xijir Qinghai China
111 J9 Xijir Ulan Hu salt l. China
106 H8 Xijishui Gansu China
100 F4 Xikelin Heilong. China
100 B2 Xikouzi Nei Mongol China
107 M5 Xil Nei Mongol China
Xilaganí Greece see Xylagani
107 Q4 Xilaotou Shan mt. Nei Mongol China
110 K7 Xiliangzi Qinghai China
107 R5 Xiliao He r. China
Xiligou Qinghai China see Ulan
108 E6 Xilin Guangxi China
107 O5 Xilinhot Nei Mongol China
Xilinji Heilong. China see Mohe
Xilin Qagan Obo Nei Mongol China see Qagan Obo
245 I4 Xilitla Mex.
129 K6 Xıllı Azer.
129 J5 Xılmilli Azer.
Xilókastron Greece see Xylokastro
Xilópolis Greece see Xyloupoli
108 B7 Ximeng Yunnan China
106 G6 Ximiao Nei Mongol China
107 K7 Xin Nei Mongol China
129 J4 Xınalıq Azer.
Xin'an Anhui China see Lai'an
Xin'an Guizhou China see Anlong
Xin'an Hebei China see Anxin
107 M9 Xin'an Henan China
109 L4 Xin'anjiang Shuiku resr China
Xin Barag Youqi Nei Mongol China see Altan Emel
Xin Barag Zuoqi Nei Mongol China see Amgalang
101 D8 Xinbin Liaoning China
131 M5 Xin Bulag Nei Mongol China
107 P2 Xin Bulag Dong Nei Mongol China
109 J2 Xincai Henan China
Xinchang Jiangxi China see Yifeng
109 M4 Xinchang Zhejiang China
Xincheng Fujian China see Gutian
106 G7 Xincheng Gansu China
Xincheng Guangdong China see Xinxing
108 G6 Xincheng Guangxi China
106 J7 Xincheng Ningxia China
Xincheng Shanxi China see Yuanqu
Xincheng Sichuan China see Zhaojue
107 K8 Xinchengbu Shaanxi China
110 G4 Xinchepaizi Xinjiang China
Xincun Yunnan China see Dongchuan
109 H7 Xindi Guangxi China
Xindi Hubei China see Honghu
107 S3 Xindian Heilong. China
109 H7 Xindu Guangxi China
Xindu Sichuan China see Luhuo
108 E3 Xindu Sichuan China
108 C3 Xinduqiao Sichuan China
109 J6 Xinfeng Guangdong China
109 J6 Xinfeng Jiangxi China
109 J7 Xinfengjiang Shuiku resr China
108 H6 Xing'an Guangxi China
109 J5 Xingan Jiangxi China
107 Q7 Xingangzhen Liaoning China
111 K12 Xingba Xizang China
Xingcheng Hebei China see Qianxi
107 Q6 Xingcheng Liaoning China
110 H6 Xingdi Xinjiang China
209 C7 Xinge Angola
Xingguo Gansu China see Qin'an
109 J5 Xingguo Jiangxi China
106 F9 Xinghai Qinghai China
100 D2 Xinghua Heilong. China
109 L2 Xinghua Jiangsu China
109 L6 Xinghua Wan b. China
100 H6 Xingkai Heilong. China
Xingkai Hu l. China/Rus. Fed. see Khanka, Lake
107 O6 Xinglong Hebei China
100 D3 Xinglong Heilong. China
100 E5 Xinglongzhen Heilong. China
109 J6 Xingning Guangdong China
109 I6 Xingning Hunan China
109 I3 Xingou Hubei China
107 K9 Xingping Shaanxi China
108 E6 Xingren Guizhou China
106 I8 Xingrenbu Ningxia China
106 G9 Xingsagoinba Qinghai China
Xingshan Guizhou China see Majiang
108 H3 Xingshan Hubei China
107 N8 Xingtai Hebei China
107 N7 Xingtang Hebei China
251 H5 Xingu r. Brazil
254 B4 Xingu, Parque Indígena do res. Brazil
107 M7 Xinguangwu Shanxi China
254 C3 Xinguara Brazil
108 E4 Xingwen Sichuan China
107 L7 Xingxian Shanxi China
106 D6 Xingxingxia Xinjiang China
107 M9 Xingyang Henan China
108 G7 Xingye Guangxi China
108 E6 Xingyi Guizhou China
109 K4 Xingzi Jiangxi China
107 N8 Xinhe Hebei China
110 F6 Xinhe Xinjiang China
107 N5 Xin Hot Nei Mongol China
Xinhua Guangdong China see Huadu
109 H5 Xinhua Hunan China
Xinhua Yunnan China see Qiaojia
Xinhua Yunnan China see Funing
108 G5 Xinhuang Hunan China
107 P5 Xinhui Nei Mongol China
106 G8 Xining Qinghai China
107 N8 Xinji Hebei China
Xinji Henan China see Xinxian
109 J4 Xinjian Jiangxi China
107 L9 Xinjiang Shanxi China
Xinjiang aut. reg. China see Xinjiang Uygur Zizhiqu
109 K4 Xin Jiang r. China
Xinjiangkou Hubei China see Songzi
106 B5 Xinjiang Uygur Zizhiqu aut. reg. China
107 K7 Xinjie Nei Mongol China
108 B6 Xinjie Yunnan China
108 D7 Xinjie Yunnan China
Xinjin Liaoning China see Pulandian
108 D3 Xinjin Sichuan China
Xinjing Guangxi China see Jingxi
107 R5 Xinkai He r. China
100 D7 Xinlicheng Shuiku resr Jilin China
Xinling Hubei China see Badong
100 E3 Xinlitun Heilong. China
108 C3 Xinlong Sichuan China
107 M9 Xinmi Henan China
Xinmian Sichuan China see Shimian
100 E4 Xinmin Heilong. China
107 R6 Xinmin Liaoning China
107 L7 Xinminzhen Shaanxi China
Xinning Gansu China see Ningxian
Xinning Guangxi China see Fusui
108 H5 Xinning Hunan China
Xinning Jiangxi China see Wuning
Xinning Sichuan China see Kaijiang
108 C6 Xinping Yunnan China
100 F4 Xinqing Heilong. China
109 K6 Xinquan Fujian China
Xinshan Jiangxi China see Anyuan
109 H5 Xinshao Hunan China
Xinshi Hubei China see Jingshan
Xinshiba Sichuan China see Ganluo
107 O9 Xintai Shandong China
100 D3 Xintain Nei Mongol China
109 J4 Xintanpu Hubei China
109 I6 Xintian Hunan China
109 J3 Xinxian Henan China
Xinxian Shanxi China see Xinzhou
107 M9 Xinxiang Henan China
109 I7 Xinxing Guangdong China
109 J2 Xinyang Henan China
109 M2 Xinyang Gang r. China
109 I2 Xinye Henan China
109 H7 Xinyi Guangdong China
107 P9 Xinyi Jiangsu China
107 P9 Xinyi He r. China
108 G9 Xinying Hainan China
Xinying Taiwan see Hsinying
109 J5 Xinyu Jiangxi China
Xinyuan Qinghai China see Tianjun
110 F5 Xinyuan Xinjiang China
107 Q1 Xinzhangfang Nei Mongol China
107 M9 Xinzheng Henan China
Xinzhou Guangxi China see Longlin
Xinzhou Guizhou China see Huangping
109 J3 Xinzhou Hubei China
107 M7 Xinzhou Shanxi China
Xinzhu Taiwan see Hsinchu
182 E4 Xinzo de Limia Spain
Xiongshan Fujian China see Zhenghe
Xiongzhou Guangdong China see Nanxiong
252 D2 Xipamanu r. Bol./Brazil
109 H2 Xiping Henan China
109 J2 Xiping Henan China
106 G9 Xiqing Shan mts China
106 H7 Xiqu Gansu China
254 E4 Xique Xique Brazil
129 K5 Xırdalan Azer.
187 E9 Xirivella Spain

198 E4 Xiro hill Greece
199 H5 Xirokampo Greece
250 E6 Xiruá r. Brazil
Xisa Yunnan China see Xichou
107 K6 Xishanzui Nei Mongol China
108 C7 Xishuangbanna reg. Yunnan China
Xishuanghe Shandong China see Kenli
108 F4 Xishui Guizhou China
109 J3 Xishui Hubei China
182 E2 Xistral, Serra do mts Spain
111 K8 Xi Taijinar Hu l. Qinghai China
106 D8 Xitieshan Qinghai China
245 K9 Xitla Mex.
206 B4 Xitole Guinea-Bissau
Xiucaiwan Chongqing China see Fengdu
Xiugu Jiangxi China see Jinxi
Xi Ujimqin Qi Nei Mongol China see Bayan Ul Hot
109 L4 Xiuning Anhui China
108 G4 Xiushan Chongqing China
Xiushan Yunnan China see Tonghai
109 J4 Xiushui Jiangxi China
109 J4 Xiu Shui r. China
108 F5 Xiuwen Guizhou China
107 M9 Xiuwu Henan China
107 R6 Xiuyan Liaoning China
Xiuyan Shaanxi China see Qingjian
108 H8 Xiuying Hainan China
120 I7 Xiva Uzbek.
Xiwanzi Hebei China see Chongli
108 A2 Xiwu Qinghai China
111 G12 Xixabangma Feng mt. Xizang China
109 H2 Xixia Henan China
109 J2 Xixian Henan China
107 L8 Xixian Shanxi China
108 F2 Xixiang Shaanxi China
Xixiu Guizhou China see Anshun
Xixón Spain see Gijón-Xixón
107 M8 Xiyang Shanxi China
109 M5 Xiyang Dao i. China
108 E6 Xiyang Jiang r. Yunnan China
106 H8 Xiying Gansu China
Xizang aut. reg. China see Xizang Zizhiqu
Xizang Gaoyuan plat. Xizang China see Qingzang Gaoyuan
108 A3 Xizang Zizhiqu aut. reg. China
107 Q7 Xizhong Dao i. China
129 K5 Xızı Azer.
111 L11 Xobando Xizang China
129 H6 Xocalı Azer.
129 I6 Xocavänd Azer.
245 L8 Xochiapa Mex.
245 I5 Xochiatiapan Mex.
245 I7 Xochicalco tourist site Mex.
245 H6 Xochimilco Mex.
245 I9 Xochistlahuaca Mex.
199 H6 Xodoto, Akrotirio pt Greece
Xoi Xizang China see Qüxü
120 J8 Xoʻjadavlat Uzbek.
119 J2 Xoʻjapiryox togʻi mt. Uzbek.
120 H6 Xoʻjayli Qoraqalpogʻiston Respublikasi Uzbek.
111 K12 Xoka Xizang China
215 L8 Xolobe S. Africa
129 J6 Xol Qarabucaq Azer.
245 H6 Xonacatlán Mex.
121 O7 Xonobod Uzbek.
120 I7 Xonqa Uzbek.
Xonrupt France see Xonrupt-Longemer
157 M7 Xonrupt-Longemer France
215 L7 Xonxa Dam S. Africa
108 B4 Xo Qu r. Sichuan China
120 I7 Xorazm admin. div. Uzbek.
110 J7 Xorkol Xinjiang China
111 G8 Xortang Xinjiang China
129 I5 Xosrov Azer.
182 E1 Xove Spain
120 M7 Xovos Uzbek.
109 L3 Xuancheng Anhui China
108 G3 Xuan'en Hubei China
108 F3 Xuanhan Sichuan China
107 N6 Xuanhua Hebei China
97 H9 Xuân Lôc Vietnam
108 E5 Xuanwei Yunnan China
Xuanzhou Anhui China see Xuancheng
182 D4 Xubin Spain
109 I2 Xuchang Henan China
99 J5 Xuchang Henan China
Xucheng Guangdong China see Xuwen
129 J4 Xudat Azer.
210 D3 Xuddur Somalia
210 E2 Xudun Somalia
111 K12 Xueba Xizang China
Xuefeng Fujian China see Mingxi
108 G5 Xuefeng Shan mts China
107 L9 Xuehua Shan hill Shanxi China
107 L7 Xuejiawan Nei Mongol China
108 B5 Xue Shan mts Yunnan China
106 D9 Xugin Gol r. Qinghai China
107 P9 Xugou Jiangsu China
106 H6 Xugui Nei Mongol China
106 D9 Xugui Qinghai China
Xuguit Qi Nei Mongol China see Yakeshi
Xujiang Jiangxi China see Guangchang
Xulun Hobot Qagan Qi Nei Mongol China see Qagan Nur
Xulun Hoh Qi Nei Mongol China see Dund Hot
108 D6 Xundian Yunnan China
Xungba Xizang China see Xangdoring
111 I11 Xungmai Xizang China
111 K11 Xung Qu r. Xizang China
111 G12 Xungru Xizang China
100 E4 Xunhe Heilong. China
100 D4 Xun He r. China
108 G2 Xun He r. China
106 H9 Xunhua Qinghai China
108 H7 Xun Jiang r. China
100 F4 Xunke Heilong. China
182 E4 Xunqueira de Ambia Spain
109 J6 Xunwu Jiangxi China
107 N9 Xunxian Henan China
108 G2 Xunyang Shaanxi China
107 K9 Xunyi Shaanxi China
108 H5 Xupu Hunan China
106 D9 Xurgan Qinghai China
111 H11 Xuru Co salt l. China
107 N7 Xushui Hebei China
108 H8 Xuwen Guangdong China
Xuwen Sichuan China see Rongxian
109 L2 Xuyi Jiangsu China
108 E4 Xuyong Sichuan China
107 O9 Xuzhou Jiangsu China
199G2 Xylagani Greece
198 D4 Xylokastro Greece
198 E2 Xyloupoli Greece

Y

85 M7 Yaamba Qld Austr.
108 D3 Ya'an Sichuan China
83 I6 Yaapeet Vic. Austr.
93 E4 Yaba Maluku Indon.
Yabanabat Turkey see Kızılcahamam
207 H5 Yabassi Cameroon
78 □3a Yabbenohr i. Kwajalein Marshall Is
210 C3 Yabëlo Eth.
210 C3 Yabëlo Wildlife Sanctuary nature res. Eth.
208 D4 Yabia Dem. Rep. Congo
197 M7 Yablanitsa Bulg.
197 O8 Yablanovo Bulg.
197 O8 Yablochnoye Rus. Fed.
137 T1 Yablonovets Rus. Fed.
137 R9 Yablonovskiy Rus. Fed.
107 K1 Yablonovyy Khrebet mts Rus. Fed.
136 D5 Yabluniv Ukr.
137 K4 Yablunivka Ukr.
207 G3 Yabo Nigeria
106 H7 Yabrai Shan mts China
106 H7 Yabrai Yanchang Nei Mongol China
125 I4 Yabrīn reg. Saudi Arabia
128 E5 Yabrūd Syria
104 A5 Yabu Japan
247 □¹ Yabucoa Puerto Rico
247 □¹ Yabucoa, Puerto b. Puerto Rico
105 L1 Yabuki Japan
100 F6 Yabuli Heilong. China
136 H3 Yabunets' Ukr.
250 C5 Yabuyanos Peru
105 J3 Yabuzukahon Japan
Yacha Hainan China see Baisha
108 G9 Yacheng Hainan China
108 F5 Yachi He r. China
105 L4 Yachimata Japan
105 L4 Yachiyo Chiba Japan
105 K3 Yachiyo Ibaraki Japan
255 A8 Yacireta, Isla i. Para.
83 K7 Yackandandah Vic. Austr.
252 E5 Yacuiba Bol.
250 E3 Yacurai Venez.
258 F2 Yacyretá Apipé, Embalse resr Arg./Para.
208 B3 Yadé, Massif du mts C.A.R.
122 D4 Yadgir Karnataka India
114 E5 Yadiki Andhra Prad. India
231 G8 Yadkin r. NC U.S.A.
231 G7 Yadkinville NC U.S.A.
111 I13 Yadong Xizang China
134 I5 Yadrin Rus. Fed.
79 □⁷ Yadua i. Fiji
102 □A22 Yaeyama-rettō is Japan
Yafa Israel see Tel Aviv-Yafo
202 B1 Yafran Libya
206 E4 Yagaba Ghana
Yagaing state Myanmar see Arakan
102 □¹ Yagaji-jima i. Okinawa Japan
103 G14 Yagami Japan
106 H6 Yagan Nei Mongol China
199 I3 Yağcılı Turkey
Yağda Turkey see Erdemli
264 E9 Yaghan Basin sea feature S. Atlantic Ocean
104 C5 Yagi Japan
102 S2 Yagishiri-tō i. Japan
128 D1 Yağızlar Turkey
106 F8 Yagkêng Qinghai China
129 E5 Yağlıca Dağı mt. Turkey
134 E3 Yaglyayarvi Rus. Fed.
122 F2 Yagman Turkm.
129 E6 Yağmurlu r. Turkey
139 U3 Yagnitsa Rus. Fed.
244 B4 Yago Mex.
197 N8 Yagoda Bulg.
120 A2 Yagodnaya Polyana Rus. Fed.
139 S8 Yagodnoye Kaluzhskaya Oblast' Rus. Fed.
131 P3 Yagodnoye Magadanskaya Oblast' Rus. Fed.
100 K3 Yagodnyy Rus. Fed.
Yagotin Ukr. see Yahotyn
207 I4 Yagoua Cameroon
111 F11 Yagra Xizang China
106 D9 Yagradagzê Shan mt. Qinghai China
246 D2 Yaguajay Cuba
Yaguarón r. Brazil/Uru. see Jaguarão
250 D5 Yaguas r. Peru
97 E11 Yaha Thai.
104 E6 Yahagi-gawa r. Japan
208 D4 Yahila Dem. Rep. Congo
222 G5 Yahk B.C. Can.
136 I6 Yahorlyk r. Ukr.
137 K3 Yahotyn Ukr.
244 E4 Yahualica Mex.
208 D4 Yahuma Dem. Rep. Congo
118 D2 Yahyalı Turkey
123 M6 Yahya Wana Afgh.
97 D8 Yai, Khao mt. Thai.
105 K2 Yaita Japan
216 □3c Yaiza Lanzarote Canary Is
105 J5 Yaizu Japan
108 D3 Yajiang Sichuan China
208 C3 Yaka C.A.R.
128 F5 Yakacık Turkey
128 D2 Yakapınar Turkey
110 H7 Yakatograk Xinjiang China
123 K5 Yak Dar Afgh.
104 G3 Yake-dake vol. Japan
107 Q2 Yakeshi Nei Mongol China
126 D4 Yakhab waterhole Iran
123 K6 Yakhehal Afgh.
136 F4 Yakhivtsi Ukr.
137 M3 Yakhnyky Ukr.
139 U5 Yakhroma Rus. Fed.
238 D3 Yakima WA U.S.A.
238 E3 Yakima r. WA U.S.A.
238 D3 Yakima Indian Reservation res. WA U.S.A.
122 E5 Yakinish Iran
121 L8 Yakkabogʻ Uzbek.
123 J7 Yakmach Pak.
206 E3 Yako Burkina
222 B3 Yakobi Island AK U.S.A.
208 D3 Yakoma Dem. Rep. Congo
197 L8 Yakoruda Bulg.
137 P4 Yakovenkove Ukr.
100 H6 Yakovlevka Rus. Fed.
137 P3 Yakovlevo Rus. Fed.
134 K4 Yakshur-Bod'ya Rus. Fed.
102 R4 Yakumo Japan
104 A5 Yakumo Japan
102 □H16 Yaku-shima i. Japan
220 E4 Yakutat AK U.S.A.
220 D4 Yakutat Bay AK U.S.A.
131 N3 Yakutsk Rus. Fed.
137 O7 Yakymivka Ukr.
206 E4 Yala Ghana
210 B4 Yala Kenya
114 G9 Yala Sri Lanka
97 E11 Yala Thai.
111 H12 Yalai Xizang China
108 C3 Yalakan Sichuan China
199 K2 Yalakdere Turkey
129 J4 Yalama Azer.
128 A2 Yalan Dünya Mağarası tourist site Turkey
82 C4 Yalata Aboriginal Lands res. S.A. Austr.
81 G10 Yaldhurst South I. N.Z.
222 F5 Yale B.C. Can.
227 L6 Yale MI U.S.A.
208 E4 Yaleko Dem. Rep. Congo
206 E3 Yalgo Burkina
87 D10 Yalgoo W.A. Austr.
199 I5 Yalıkavak Turkey
197 Q9 Yalıköy Turkey
129 C6 Yalınca Turkey
208 D3 Yalinga C.A.R.
138 M8 Yalizava Belarus
243 O7 Yalkubul, Punta pt Mex.
246 □ Yallahs Jamaica
85 J8 Yalleroi Qld Austr.
87 C12 Yallingup W.A. Austr.
206 E3 Yalogo Burkina
83 K8 Yallourn Vic. Austr.
129 D5 Yalnızçam Dağları mts Turkey
237 J9 Yalobusha r. MS U.S.A.
Yalogo Burkina see Yalgo
208 C3 Yaloké C.A.R.
108 C5 Yalong Jiang r. Sichuan China
199 K2 Yalova Turkey
197 R10 Yalova prov. Turkey
Yalovany Moldova see Ialoveni
84 D7 Yalpirakinu Aboriginal Land res. N.T. Austr.
136 H8 Yalpuh, Ozero l. Ukr.
Yalpukh r. Moldova see Ialpug
137 Q7 Yalta Donets'ka Oblast' Ukr.
137 N9 Yalta Respublika Krym Ukr.
137 N9 Yaltins'kyy Zapovidnyk nature res. Ukr.
136 G5 Yaltushkiv Ukr.
107 R3 Yalu He r. China
101 D8 Yalu Jiang r. China/N. Korea
208 D5 Yaluska Dem. Rep. Congo
138 H4 Yalutorovsk Rus. Fed.
139 M4 Yalvaç Turkey
124 G7 Yām reg. Saudi Arabia
Yama Ukr. see Sivers'k
105 M4 Yamada Chiba Japan
102 S7 Yamada Iwate Japan
104 F2 Yamada Toyama Japan
103 H13 Yamaga Japan
105 L2 Yamagata Ibaraki Japan
102 S6 Yamagata Iwate Japan
105 G3 Yamagata Nagano Japan
103 H12 Yamagata Yamagata Japan
102 R8 Yamagata pref. Japan
102 Q8 Yamagata pref. Japan
104 G4 Yamaguchi Nagano Japan
103 I12 Yamaguchi Yamaguchi Japan
103 I12 Yamaguchi pref. Japan
105 J3 Yamakita Japan
105 J5 Yamal, Poluostrov pen. Rus. Fed.
130 H2 Yamal, Poluostrov pen. Rus. Fed.
Yamal, Poluostrov
100 I2 Yam Alin', Khrebet mts Rus. Fed.
see Yamal, Poluostrov
104 D3 Yamanaka Japan
105 I5 Yamanaka-ko l. Japan
105 I4 Yamanashi Japan
105 H4 Yamanashi pref. Japan
85 J5 Yamanie Falls National Park Qld Austr.
Yamankhalinka Kazakh. see Makhambet
105 I5 Yamanokako Japan
105 H2 Yamanouchi Japan
106 C6 Yamansu Xinjiang China
104 F5 Yamaoka Japan
107 L1 Yamarovka Rus. Fed.
103 L11 Yamasaki Japan
104 C6 Yamashiro Japan
104 E4 Yamato Gifu Japan
105 L3 Yamato Ibaraki Japan
105 J5 Yamato Kanagawa Japan
102 □G18 Yamato Nansei-shotō Japan
105 I1 Yamato Niigata Japan
104 C6 Yamato-Aogaki Kokutei-kōen park Japan
105 K2 Yamato-Kōriyama Japan
104 C6 Yamatotakada Japan
105 L2 Yamatsuri Japan
104 D6 Yamazoe Japan
83 N3 Yamba N.S.W. Austr.
83 I8 Yambacoona Tas. Austr.
223 I1 Yamba Lake N.W.T. Can.
84 C3 Yambarran Range hills N.T. Austr.
208 B2 Yamba Tchangsou Chad
206 B4 Yambéring Guinea
250 D4 Yambi, Mesa de hills Col.
208 F3 Yambio Sudan
197 O8 Yambol Bulg.
250 B6 Yambrasbamba Peru
208 E4 Yamdena i. Indon.
198 H4 Yame Japan
103 H13 Yame Japan
96 C4 Yamethin Myanmar
92 C1 Y'ami i. Phil.
105 L2 Yamizo-san mt. Japan
114 D4 Yamkanmardi Karnataka India
Yamkhad Syria see Ḥalab
138 M4 Yamkino Rus. Fed.
138 L3 Yamm Rus. Fed.
85 H9 Yamma Yamma, Lake salt flat Qld Austr.
137 O3 Yamne Ukr.
206 D5 Yamoussoukro Côte d'Ivoire
137 K5 Yampil' Cherkas'ka Oblast' Ukr.
136 F4 Yampil' Khmel'nyts'ka Oblast' Ukr.
137 M2 Yampil' Sums'ka Oblast' Ukr.
136 H5 Yampil' Vinnyts'ka Oblast' Ukr.
Yampol' Cherkas'ka Oblast' Ukr. see Yampil'
Yampol' Khmel'nyts'ka Oblast' Ukr. see Yampil'
Yampol' Sums'ka Oblast' Ukr. see Yampil'
Yampol' Vinnyts'ka Oblast' Ukr. see Yampil'
116 H7 Yamuna r. India
116 F4 Yamunanagar Haryana India
111 J12 Yamzho Yumco l. China
207 H4 Yana Nigeria
130 O3 Yana r. Rus. Fed.
82 H7 Yanac Vic. Austr.
252 B2 Yanachaga-Chemillen, Parque Nacional nat. park Peru
103 K13 Yanadani Japan
102 R9 Yanagawa Japan
102 □¹ Yanaha-jima i. Okinawa Japan
103 J13 Yanai Japan
114 H4 Yanam Pondicherry India
107 K8 Yan'an Shaanxi China
252 C3 Yanaoca Peru
Yanaon Pondicherry India see Yanam
134 K4 Yanaul Rus. Fed.
139 N6 Yanavichy Belarus
250 C5 Yanayacu Peru
105 D5 Yanbian Yunnan China
124 C3 Yanbu, Sharm b. Saudi Arabia
124 D3 Yanbu' al Baḥr Saudi Arabia
124 D3 Yanbu' an Nakhl reg. Saudi Arabia
231 H7 Yanceyville NC U.S.A.
107 L8 Yancheng Shaanxi China
109 M2 Yancheng Jiangsu China
Yancheng Shandong China see Qihe
Yancheng Sichuan China see Jingyan
87 C11 Yanchep W.A. Austr.
107 J8 Yanchi Ningxia China
106 D5 Yanchi Xinjiang China
110 H3 Yanchi Xinjiang China
110 L7 Yanchiwan Gansu China
128 B5 Yanchuan Shaanxi China
137 P6 Yanchur r. Ukr.
83 J6 Yanco Creek r. N.S.W. Austr.
83 H4 Yanco Glen N.S.W. Austr.
83 J4 Yanda watercourse N.S.W. Austr.
82 H4 Yandama Creek watercourse S.A. Austr.
109 M5 Yandang Shan mts China
Yandao Sichuan China see Yingjing
86 E6 Yandeyarra Aboriginal Reserve W.A. Austr.
86 E7 Yandicoogina Mine W.A. Austr.
87 E9 Yandil W.A. Austr.
85 N9 Yandina Qld Austr.
78 □6 Yandina Solomon Is
208 C5 Yandja Dem. Rep. Congo
96 B6 Yandoon Myanmar
Yandua i. Fiji see Yadua
106 D5 Yandun Xinjiang China
139 Q1 Yanega Rus. Fed.
206 C4 Yanfolila Mali
208 D3 Yangalia C.A.R.
208 E4 Yangambi Dem. Rep. Congo
111 M12 Ya'ngamdo Xizang China
111 L11 Ya'ngamdo Xizang China
206 D3 Yangasso Mali
111 J11 Yangbajain Xizang China
108 B6 Yangbi Yunnan China
Yangcheng Guangdong China see Yangshan
109 H3 Yangcheng Shanxi China
Yangchuan Guizhou China see Suiyang
109 H7 Yangchun Guangdong China
109 J7 Yangcun Guangdong China
Yangcun Tianjin China see Wuqing
110 I7 Yangcun Tianjin China see Wuqing
101 E9 Yangdok N. Korea
109 H8 Yangdong Guangdong China
106 M6 Yangdong Shaanxi China
107 N8 Yanggu Shandong China
Yangguan Jiangxi China see Yongning
107 N6 Yang He r. China
111 G9 Yang Hu l. Xizang China
120 I7 Yangiariq Uzbek.
Yangibazar Kyrg. see Jangy-Bazar
111 D9 Yangi Davan pass Aksai Chin/China
120 K8 Yangi Nishon Uzbek.
123 M3 Yangi Qal'eh Afgh.
121 I7 Yangiqishloq Uzbek.
120 K7 Yangirabot Uzbek.
121 M7 Yangiyoʻl Uzbek.
107 K8 Yangjialing Shaanxi China
109 H8 Yangjiang Guangdong China
107 P8 Yangjiaogou Shandong China
96 C6 Yangôn Myanmar
115 O4 Yangôn admin. div. Myanmar
109 H3 Yangping Hubei China
107 M8 Yangquan Shanxi China
107 L8 Yangquangu Shanxi China
109 I6 Yangshan Guangdong China
108 H6 Yangshuo Guangxi China
97 I8 Yang Sin, Chư mt. Vietnam
96 F6 Yang Talat Thai.
108 C6 Yangtouyan Yunnan China
Yangtze r. Qinghai China see Tongtian He
109 M3 Yangtze r. China
alt. Chang Jiang,
alt. Jinsha Jiang,
alt. Tongtian He,
long Yangtze Kiang
Yangtze, Mouth of the China
see Changjiang Kou
108 E1 Yanguan Gansu China
183 P4 Yanguas Spain
210 D2 Yangudi Rassa National Park Eth.
107 P9 Yangweigang Jiangsu China
109 H8 Yangxi Guangdong China
108 F2 Yangxian Shaanxi China
101 F9 Yangyang S. Korea
107 N6 Yangyuan Hebei China
109 L2 Yangzhou Jiangsu China
Yangzhou Shaanxi China see Yangxian
108 G4 Yanhe Guizhou China
107 L8 Yan He r. China
110 I5 Yanhu Xinjiang China
111 F10 Yanhu Xizang China
107 N8 Yanji Jilin China
134 F3 Yanishpole Rus. Fed.
140 U5 Yanis'yarvi, Ozero l. Rus. Fed.
100 F7 Yanji Jilin China
107 N9 Yanjin Henan China
108 E4 Yanjin Yunnan China
Yanjing Sichuan China see Yanyuan
108 B4 Yanjing Xizang China
Yanjing Yunnan China see Yanjin
207 H4 Yankara National Park Nigeria
138 L6 Yankavichy Belarus
Yankou Sichuan China see Wusheng
236 G4 Yankton SD U.S.A.
236 F4 Yankton Indian Reservation res. SD U.S.A.
129 D1 Yankul' Rus. Fed.
129 D1 Yankul' Rus. Fed.
107 N9 Yanling Henan China
109 I5 Yanling Hunan China
Yannina Greece see Ioannina
131 P2 Yano-Indigirskaya Nizmennost' lowland Rus. Fed.
139 P7 Yanovo Rus. Fed.
130 J3 Yanov-Stan Rus. Fed.
114 G8 Yan Oya r. Sri Lanka
110 H5 Yanqi Xinjiang China
107 N6 Yanqing Beijing China
125 M4 Yanqul Oman
87 C7 Yanrey r. W.A. Austr.
107 O7 Yanshan Hebei China
109 K4 Yanshan Jiangxi China
108 E7 Yanshan Yunnan China
108 H4 Yan Shan mts China
107 O6 Yanshi Henan China
107 M9 Yanshiping Qinghai China
111 K10 Yanshiping Qinghai China
100 F6 Yanshou Heilong. China
131 O2 Yanskiy Zaliv g. Rus. Fed.
83 J3 Yantabulla N.S.W. Austr.
122 C2 Yantagh Iran
107 Q8 Yantai Shandong China
259 B6 Yántales, Cerro mt. Chile
137 N8 Yantarne Ukr.
138 I7 Yantarnyy Rus. Fed.
197 K1 Yantic r. CT U.S.A.
108 E3 Yanting Sichuan China
100 E7 Yantongshan Jilin China
109 M5 Yantou Zhejiang China
197 N7 Yantra r. Bulg.
79 □⁷ᵃ Yanuca i. Fiji
124 F4 Yanūfi, Jabal al hill Saudi Arabia
Yanutha i. Fiji see Yanuca
108 B5 Yanwa Yunnan China
108 H4 Yanxi Hunan China
Yany-Kurgan Kazakh. see Zhanakorgan
108 C5 Yanyuan Sichuan China
96 C4 Yao Japan
104 C5 Yao'an Yunnan China
107 K8 Yaodian Shaanxi China
Yaodu Anhui China see Dongzhi
Yaojie Gansu China see Honggu
109 K4 Yaoli Jiangxi China
106 E7 Yaoquanzi Gansu China
104 F4 Yaotsu Japan
207 H6 Yaoundé Cameroon
Yaoxian Shaanxi China see Yaozhou
97 D10 Yao Yai, Ko i. Thai.
107 K9 Yaozhen Shaanxi China
107 K9 Yaozhou Shaanxi China
91 I5 Yap i. Micronesia
250 E4 Yapacana, Parque Nacional nat. park Venez.
252 D3 Yapacani r. Bol.
206 E4 Yapei Ghana
91 I7 Yapen i. Papua Indon.
91 I7 Yapen, Selat sea chan. Papua Indon.
258 F3 Yapeyú Arg.
235 J3 Yaphank NY U.S.A.
85 J7 Yappar r. Qld Austr.
151 K6 Yapton West Sussex, England U.K.
266 E5 Yap Trench sea feature N. Pacific Ocean
251 G4 Yapukarri Guyana
87 I9 Yapuparra Aboriginal Reserve W.A. Austr.
242 D4 Yaqui r. Mex.
134 K4 Yar Rus. Fed.
246 E3 Yara Cuba
250 D2 Yaracal Venez.
250 D2 Yaracuy state Venez.
Yaradzha Turkm. see Ýaraja
122 G2 Yaraka Qld Austr.
85 J8 Yaraka Qld Austr.
Yarangüme Turkey see Tavas
134 I4 Yaransk Rus. Fed.
Yardan Uzbek. see Yordon
82 E5 Yardea S.A. Austr.
129 I6 Yardımcı Burnu pt Turkey
129 I6 Yardımlı Azer.
234 F4 Yardley PA U.S.A.
111 J12 Yardoi Xizang China
234 E4 Yardville NJ U.S.A.
Yardymly Azer. see Yardımlı
151 P3 Yare r. England U.K.
134 K3 Yarega Rus. Fed.
136 D5 Yaremcha Ukr.
77 G2 Yaren Nauru
134 F2 Yarenga Rus. Fed.
134 J3 Yarensk Rus. Fed.
Yares'ky Ukr.
137 M4 Yares'ky Ukr.
250 C3 Yarí r. Col.
104 G3 Yariga-take mt. Japan
124 G8 Yarīm Yemen
Yarımca Turkey see Körfez
84 G6 Yaringa watercourse Qld Austr.
251 H4 Yaripo Brazil
207 G3 Yaris well Niger
247 I8 Yaritagua Venez.
Yarkand Xinjiang China see Shache
Yarkant Xinjiang China see Shache
111 D7 Yarkant He r. China
227 R5 Yarker Ont. Can.
123 O3 Yarkhun r. Pak.
87 K11 Yarle Lakes salt flat S.A. Austr.
197 L8 Yarlovo Bulg.
111 L12 Yarlung Zangbo r. China
alt. Dihang (India),
alt. Jamuna (Bangladesh),
conv. Brahmaputra
149 O4 Yarm Stockton-on-Tees, England U.K.
136 F4 Yarmolyntsi Ukr.
225 H5 Yarmouth N.S. Can.
151 J6 Yarmouth Isle of Wight, England U.K.
Yarmouth Norfolk, England U.K. see Great Yarmouth
233 □O5 Yarmouth ME U.S.A.
128 D6 Yarmuk r. Asia
241 I7 Yarnell AZ U.S.A.
151 J4 Yarnton Oxfordshire, England U.K.
139 X9 Yarok Rus. Fed.
139 N6 Yaromina Belarus
137 M3 Yaroshivka Ukr.
137 M2 Yaroslavets' Ukr.
139 R1 Yaroslavichi Rus. Fed.
139 W4 Yaroslavl' Rus. Fed.
Yaroslavl Oblast admin. div. Rus. Fed. see Yaroslavskaya Oblast'
129 B1 Yaroslavskaya Rus. Fed.
139 W4 Yaroslavskaya Oblast' admin. div. Rus. Fed.
100 H6 Yaroslavskiy Rus. Fed.
85 J4 Yarrabah Aboriginal Reserve Qld Austr.
85 I3 Yarraden Qld Austr.
83 J7 Yarra Junction Vic. Austr.
84 C4 Yarralin Aboriginal Land res. N.T. Austr.
86 C6 Yarraloola W.A. Austr.
83 K8 Yarram Vic. Austr.
85 M9 Yarraman Qld Austr.
83 J7 Yarrawonga Vic. Austr.
87 C10 Yarra Yarra Lakes salt flat W.A. Austr.
86 F6 Yarrie W.A. Austr.
85 J9 Yarronvale Qld Austr.
85 J6 Yarrowmere Qld Austr.
117 N5 Yartö Tra La pass Xizang China
130 J3 Yartsevo Krasnoyarskiy Kray Rus. Fed.
139 P6 Yartsevo Smolenskaya Oblast' Rus. Fed.
111 H12 Yaru r. China
250 C3 Yarumal Col.
108 B3 Yarwa Sichuan China
129 H2 Yaryk-Aul Rus. Fed.
108 A4 Yarzhong Xizang China
Yaş Romania see Iaşi
209 D5 Yasa Dem. Rep. Congo
115 J1 Yasai r. W. Bengal India
104 B4 Yasaka Kyōto Japan
105 G3 Yasaka Nagano Japan
105 L3 Yasato Japan
79 □⁷ Yasawa i. Fiji
79 □⁷ Yasawa Group is Fiji
136 D5 Yasen' Ukr.
197 N7 Yasenі r. Bulg.
197 N7 Yasenkovo Bulg.
135 G7 Yasenskaya Rus. Fed.
135 H7 Yashalta Rus. Fed.
207 G3 Yashi Nigeria
207 F4 Yashikera Nigeria
123 Q4 Yashilkul l. Tajik.
102 R7 Yashima Japan
103 J13 Ya-shima i. Japan
105 H2 Yashira Japan
104 A6 Yashiro Japan
102 H13 Yashiro-jima i. Japan
135 K5 Yashkino Rus. Fed.
135 I7 Yashkul' Rus. Fed.
116 D1 Yasin Jammu and Kashmir
Yasinovataya Ukr. see Yasynuvata
136 D5 Yasinya Ukr.
138 K9 Yaskavichy Belarus
129 K5 Yaşma Azer.
129 K5 Yaşma Adası i. Azer.
197 P8 Yasna Polyana Bulg.
139 U7 Yasnogorsk Rus. Fed.
137 Q5 Yasnohirka Ukr.
136 J5 Yasnohorodka Ukr.
100 F2 Yasnyy Amurskaya Oblast' Rus. Fed.
120 H2 Yasnyy Orenburgskaya Oblast' Rus. Fed.
96 G7 Yasothon Thai.
83 L6 Yass N.S.W. Austr.
83 L6 Yass r. N.S.W. Austr.
Yassı Burnu c. Cyprus see Plakoti, Cape
199 K5 Yassıhüyük Turkey
139 N4 Yasski Rus. Fed.
129 C6 Yastıktepe Turkey
137 Q2 Yastrebovka Rus. Fed.
137 N2 Yastrubyne Ukr.
105 H3 Yasu Japan
103 K13 Yasuda Japan
103 K11 Yasugi Japan
122 D6 Yāsūj Iran
250 C5 Yasuní, Parque Nacional nat. park Ecuador
105 G5 Yasuoka Japan
77 G3 Yasur vol. Vanuatu
105 H1 Yasuzuka Japan
136 F1 Yasyel'da r. Belarus
137 Q5 Yasynuvata Ukr.
207 I1 Yat well Niger
252 D2 Yata r. Bol.
208 D2 Yata r. C.A.R.
129 D3 Yatağan Turkey
207 G3 Yatakala Niger
208 D2 Yata-Ngaya, Réserve de Faune de la nature res. C.A.R.
211 C5 Yata Plateau Kenya
78 □⁵ Yaté New Caledonia
150 H4 Yate South Gloucestershire, England U.K.
151 K5 Yateley Hampshire, England U.K.
222 H2 Yates r. Alta/N.W.T. Can.
237 H7 Yates Center KS U.S.A.
223 L2 Yathkyed Lake Nunavut Can.
83 J5 Yathong Nature Reserve N.S.W. Austr.
245 I5 Yatipan Mex.
208 D4 Yatolema Dem. Rep. Congo
104 E5 Yatomi Japan
Yatou Shandong China see Rongcheng
187 D9 Yatova Spain
136 J5 Yatran' r. Ukr.
105 H4 Yatsuga-take vol. Japan
105 H3 Yatsuga-take-Chūshin-kōgen Kokutei-kōen park Japan
104 F2 Yatsuo Japan
103 H14 Yatsushiro Japan
103 H14 Yatsushiro-kai b. Japan
128 D7 Yatta West Bank
150 G5 Yatton North Somerset, England U.K.
252 B3 Yauca Peru
252 B3 Yauca r. Peru
247 □¹ Yauco Puerto Rico
252 A2 Yauli Peru
250 D5 Yauna Maloca Col.
252 C3 Yauri Peru
252 B3 Yauricocha Peru
245 H7 Yautepec Morelos Mex.
245 K9 Yautepec Oaxaca Mex.
109 □J7 Yau Tong b. H.K. China
252 B3 Yauyos Peru
242 □P11 Yauyupe Hond.
Yavan Tajik. see Yovon
250 D6 Yavari r. Brazil/Peru
alt. Javari
242 E4 Yávaros Mex.
116 G9 Yavatmal Mahar. India
252 B3 Yavero r. Peru
251 E3 Yaví, Cerro mt. Venez.
137 L6 Yavkyne Ukr.
121 M1 Yavlenka Kazakh.
175 L6 Yavora Ukr.
136 D5 Yavoriv Ivano-Frankivs'ka Oblast' Ukr.
136 C4 Yavoriv L'vivs'ka Oblast' Ukr.
140 U2 Yavr r. Fin./Rus. Fed.
128 F2 Yavuzlu Turkey
104 C6 Yawata Japan
103 J13 Yawatahama Japan
111 F8 Yawatongguz He r. China
111 F8 Yawatongguzlangar Xinjiang China
96 B4 Yaw Chaung r. Myanmar
96 C4 Yawng-hwe Myanmar
243 N9 Yaxchilan tourist site Guat.
Yaxian Hainan China see Sanya
151 L2 Yaxley Cambridgeshire, England U.K.
129 C7 Yaygın Turkey
129 A6 Yaylabaşı Turkey
128 F3 Yayladağı Turkey
129 B6 Yayladere Turkey
129 D6 Yayladüzü Turkey
134 L4 Yayva Rus. Fed.
96 B3 Yazagyo Myanmar
122 F6 Yazd Iran
122 F6 Yazd prov. Iran
122 I5 Yazdān Iran
122 E6 Yazd-e Khvāst Iran
Yazgulemskiy Khrebet mts Tajik. see Yazgulom, Qatorkŭhi
123 N2 Yazgulom, Qatorkŭhi mts Tajik.
139 P3 Yazhelbitsy Rus. Fed.
126 I4 Yazıhan Turkey
199 J5 Yazıkent Turkey
199 I6 Yazıköy Turkey
199 L5 Yazır Turkey
237 J9 Yazoo r. MS U.S.A.
237 J9 Yazoo City MS U.S.A.
105 L2 Yazukami Japan
134 L3 Yaz'va r. Rus. Fed.
202 B4 Ybakoura well Chad
Y Bala Gwynedd, Wales U.K. see Bala
179 L3 Ybbs r. Austria
179 L3 Ybbs an der Donau Austria
179 K4 Ybbsitz Austria
253 F6 Ybycuí Para.
163 C7 Ychoux France
162 I5 Ydes France
142 F6 Ydre Sweden
198 E5 Ydra Greece
198 E5 Ydra i. Greece
198 E5 Ydras, Kolpos sea chan. Greece
Y Drenewydd Powys, Wales U.K. see Newtown
96 C7 Ye Myanmar
96 C7 Ye r. Myanmar
149 N6 Yeadon West Yorkshire, England U.K.
150 E7 Yealmpton Devon, England U.K.
Yebaishou Liaoning China see Jianping
96 B2 Yebawmi Myanmar
202 B4 Yebbi-Bou Chad
202 C4 Yebbi-Souma Chad
183 L9 Yébenes, Sierra de mts Spain
183 O8 Yebra Spain
186 E3 Yebra de Basa Spain
111 C8 Yecheng Xinjiang China
187 C10 Yecla Spain
182 H7 Yecla de Yeltes Spain
242 E3 Yécora Mex.
245 K6 Yecuatla Mex.
96 C5 Yedashe Myanmar
114 E6 Yedatore Karnataka India
210 C3 YeDebub Bihēroch Bihēreseboch na Hizboch admin. reg. Eth.
199 K6 Yedi Burun Başı pt Turkey
Yedinetsy Moldova see Edineţ
Yedisa Georgia see Edisa
129 B6 Yedisu Turkey
128 D3 Yeditepe Turkey
134 I3 Yedoma Rus. Fed.
202 C4 Yedri well Chad
139 Q4 Yedrovo Rus. Fed.
138 K6 Yedy Belarus
210 D3 Yeed Eth.
86 G4 Yeeda River W.A. Austr.
231 G12 Yeehaw Junction FL U.S.A.
82 E6 Yeelanna S.A. Austr.
139 R2 Yefimovskiy Rus. Fed.
139 V8 Yefremov Rus. Fed.
Yêgainnyin Qinghai China see Henan
207 I2 Yeggueba well Niger
129 G6 Yeghegis r. Armenia
129 G6 Yeghegnadzor Armenia
129 F5 Yeghvard Armenia
121 Q3 Yegindybulak Kazakh.
121 M2 Yegindykol' Kazakh.
135 H7 Yegorlyk r. Rus. Fed.
135 H7 Yegorlykskaya Rus. Fed.
100 J6 Yegorova, Mys pt Rus. Fed.
139 Q6 Yegor'ye Rus. Fed.
139 W6 Yegor'yevsk Rus. Fed.
185 K4 Yeguas r. Spain
185 K4 Yeguas, Embalse del resr Spain
185 I6 Yeguas, Sierra de las hills Spain
260 B4 Yeguas, Volcán vol. Chile
207 F4 Yégué Togo
210 A3 Yei Sudan
210 A3 Yei r. Sudan
109 J3 Yeji Anhui China
206 E4 Yeji Ghana
Yejiaji Anhui China see Yeji
130 H4 Yekaterinburg Rus. Fed.
Yekaterinodar Rus. Fed. see Krasnodar
Yekaterinoslav Ukr. see Dnipropetrovs'k
100 F3 Yekaterinoslavka Rus. Fed.
139 V9 Yekaterinovka Lipetskaya Oblast' Rus. Fed.
137 R6 Yekaterinovka Rostovskaya Oblast' Rus. Fed.
135 I5 Yekaterinovka Saratovskaya Oblast' Rus. Fed.
Yekaterinovskaya Rus. Fed. see Krylovskaya
129 F2 Yekatorinogradskaya Rus. Fed.
Yekhegnadzor Armenia see Yeghegnadzor
139 O7 Yekimovichi Rus. Fed.
208 C4 Yekokora r. Dem. Rep. Congo
100 I4 Yelabuga Khabarovskiy Kray Rus. Fed.
134 J5 Yelabuga Respublika Tatarstan Rus. Fed.
135 H6 Yelan' Rus. Fed.
135 H5 Yelan' r. Rus. Fed.
135 H6 Yelan' r. Rus. Fed.
137 K6 Yelanets' Ukr.
83 M3 Yelarbon Qld Austr.
135 H5 Yelat'ma Rus. Fed.
135 H5 Yelbarsli Turkm.
199 J4 Yeldeğen Turkey
Yelenovka Ukr. see Zoryns'k
Yelenovskiye Kar'yery Ukr. see Dokuchayevs'k
139 S8 Yelenskiy Rus. Fed.
139 V9 Yelets Rus. Fed.
134 N2 Yeletskiy Rus. Fed.
139 Q3 Yeligovo Rus. Fed.
106 H9 Yeliguan Gansu China
206 C3 Yélimané Mali
139 W7 Yelino Rus. Fed.
137 N5 Yelizavetgrad Ukr. see Kirovohrad
137 R7 Yelizavetinka Rostovskaya Oblast' Rus. Fed.
137 T3 Yelizavetovka Voronezhskaya Oblast' Rus. Fed.
131 P4 Yelizavety, Mys c. Sakhalin Rus. Fed.
131 Q4 Yelizovo Rus. Fed.
135 I5 Yelkhovka Rus. Fed.
146 □N1 Yell i. Scotland U.K.
82 D4 Yellabina Regional Reserve nature res. S.A. Austr.
114 G4 Yellandu Andhra Prad. India
114 C4 Yellapur Karnataka India
114 E3 Yellareddi Andhra Prad. India
226 D6 Yellow r. WI U.S.A.
87 E11 Yellowdine W.A. Austr.
234 F3 Yellow Frame NJ U.S.A.
222 G4 Yellowhead Pass Alta/B.C. Can.
234 D4 Yellow House PA U.S.A.
222 H2 Yellowknife N.W.T. Can.
222 H2 Yellowknife r. N.W.T. Can.
83 K5 Yellow Mountain hill N.S.W. Austr.
Yellow River r. China see Huang He
266 D3 Yellow Sea N. Pacific Ocean
232 B9 Yellow Springs OH U.S.A.
236 D2 Yellowstone r. MT U.S.A.
238 I4 Yellowstone Lake WY U.S.A.
238 I4 Yellowstone National Park U.S.A.
146 □N1 Yell Sound str. Scotland U.K.
237 I7 Yellville AR U.S.A.
238 C3 Yelm WA U.S.A.
185 N4 Yelmo mt. Spain
135 H5 Yel'niki Rus. Fed.
139 Q7 Yel'nya Rus. Fed.
134 K4 Yelovo Rus. Fed.
206 C4 Yelp'in Armenia
136 I2 Yel'sk Belarus
121 S4 Yel'tay Kazakh.
182 H7 Yeltes r. Spain
139 Q5 Yel'tsy Rus. Fed.
242 □Q10 Yelucá mt. Nic.
134 J3 Yelva r. Rus. Fed.
221 J1 Yelverton Bay Nunavut Can.
207 G4 Yelwa Kebbi Nigeria
207 H4 Yelwa Plateau Nigeria
137 P6 Yelyseyivka Ukr.
137 L5 Yelyzavethradka Ukr.
106 D7 Yema Nanshan mts China
110 L7 Yema Nanshan mts China
106 E9 Yematan Qinghai China
106 F8 Yematan Qinghai China
210 C2 Yembo Eth.
183 Q9 Yémeda Spain
124 G8 Yemen country Asia
134 H3 Yemetsk Rus. Fed.
128 C7 Yemil'chyne Ukr.
136 G3 Yemişenbükü Turkey see Taşova
Yemmiganur Andhra Prad. India see Emmiganuru
134 H3 Yemtsa Rus. Fed.
134 J3 Yemva Rus. Fed.
207 I6 Yen Cameroon
140 U3 Yena Rus. Fed.
207 G5 Yenagoa Nigeria
137 R5 Yenakiyeve Ukr.
Yenakiyeve Ukr. see Yenakiyeve
96 B4 Yenangyat Myanmar
96 B4 Yenangyaung Myanmar
96 B5 Yenanma Myanmar
96 G4 Yên Bai Vietnam
121 M7 Yenbekshi Kazakh.
96 G4 Yên Châu Vietnam
83 K6 Yenda N.S.W. Austr.
207 E4 Yendi Ghana
Yêndum Xizang China see Zhag'yab
209 B5 Yénéganou Congo
209 C6 Yenga-Lusundji Dem. Rep. Congo
96 C4 Yengan Myanmar
208 D5 Yenge r. Dem. Rep. Congo
122 B3 Yengejeh Iran
206 C4 Yengema Sierra Leone
110 C7 Yengisar Xinjiang China
110 G6 Yengisar Xinjiang China
110 H6 Yengisu Xinjiang China
208 B4 Yengo Congo
83 M5 Yengo National Park N.S.W. Austr.
129 B6 Yenibaşlar Turkey
135 F8 Yeniçağa Turkey
199 I3 Yenice Çanakkale Turkey
128 D2 Yenice İçel Turkey
199 K2 Yenice Turkey
126 F4 Yeniceoba Turkey
199 I2 Yeniçiftlik Çanakkale Turkey
199 I1 Yeniçiftlik Tekirdağ Turkey
129 B7 Yenidal Turkey
Yenidamlar Turkey see Demirtaş
199 J5 Yenidere r. Turkey
199 H4 Yenifoça Turkey
129 G5 Yeni Göyçä Azer.
Yenihan Turkey see Yıldızeli
199 I5 Yenihisar Turkey
Yenije-i-Vardar Greece see Giannitsa
129 H5 Yenikänd Azer.
129 J5 Yenikänd Azer.
128 E2 Yeniköy Hatay Turkey
199 I4 Yeniköy İzmir Turkey
199 J3 Yeniköy Kütahya Turkey
199 K4 Yeniköy Kütahya Turkey
199 H2 Yenimuhacirköy Turkey
199 J5 Yenipazar Aydın Turkey
199 L2 Yenipazar Bilecik Turkey
199 I4 Yenişakran Turkey
Yeniséa Greece see Genisea
Yenişehir Greece see Larisa
199 K2 Yenişehir Turkey
131 J2 Yenisey r. Rus. Fed.
131 K4 Yeniseysk Rus. Fed.
131 K4 Yeniseyskiy Kryazh ridge Rus. Fed.
130 I2 Yeniseyskiy Zaliv inlet Rus. Fed.
106 E9 Yeniugou Qinghai China
106 F7 Yeniugou Qinghai China
Yeniyol Turkey see Borçka
96 G3 Yên Minh Vietnam
160 H5 Yenne France
135 I7 Yenotayevka Rus. Fed.
150 E6 Yeo r. England U.K.
116 E9 Yeola Mahar. India
87 H9 Yeo Lake salt flat W.A. Austr.
87 H10 Yeo Lake Nature Reserve W.A. Austr.
Yeotmal Mahar. India see Yavatmal
83 L5 Yeoval N.S.W. Austr.
150 G6 Yeovil Somerset, England U.K.
150 F5 Yeovilton Somerset, England U.K.
Yeo Yeo r. N.S.W. Austr. see Bland
242 E3 Yepachi Mex.
183 M9 Yepes Spain
139 V8 Yepifan' Rus. Fed.
85 M7 Yeppoon Qld Austr.
Yerakaroú Greece see Gerakarou
135 H5 Yerakhtur Rus. Fed.
Yeráki, Ákra pt Zakynthos Greece see Gerakas, Akrotirio
Yerákion Greece see Geraki
Yeraliyev Kazakh. see Kuryk
244 F2 Yerbabuena Mex.
122 H2 Yerbent Turkm.
131 L3 Yerbogachen Rus. Fed.
114 F7 Yercaud Tamil Nadu India
121 O2 Yerementau, Gory hills Kazakh.
129 F5 Yerevan Armenia
121 O2 Yereymentau Kazakh.
129 J4 Yerfi Azer.
114 E4 Yergara Karnataka India
135 I7 Yergeni hills Rus. Fed.
Yergoğu Romania see Giurgiu
Yeriho West Bank see Jericho
87 F10 Yerilla W.A. Austr.
240 M3 Yerington NV U.S.A.
199 K3 Yerkesik Turkey
199 J5 Yerköprü Mağarası tourist site Turkey
128 A1 Yerköprü Mağarası tourist site Turkey
126 G4 Yerköy Turkey
114 D4 Yerla r. India
Yermak Kazakh. see Aksu
100 E2 Yermakovo Rus. Fed.
268 A1 Yermak Plateau sea feature Arctic Ocean
Yermentau Kazakh. see Yereymentau
135 H5 Yermish' Rus. Fed.
134 K2 Yermitsa Rus. Fed.
244 D4 Yermo Mex.
240 P7 Yermo CA U.S.A.
139 Y4 Yermolino Rus. Fed.
100 B2 Yerofey Pavlovich Rus. Fed.
128 C8 Yeroham Israel
Yerongpetra Kriti Greece see Geropotamos
156 B7 Yerre r. France
156 D5 Yerres r. France
134 K2 Yersa r. Rus. Fed.
164 F6 Yerseke Neth.
129 F3 Yersh Rus. Fed.
139 R7 Yershi Rus. Fed.
139 P8 Yershichi Rus. Fed.
120 C2 Yershov Rus. Fed.
138 L4 Yershovo Rus. Fed.
139 X1 Yertsevo Rus. Fed.

252 A2 Yerupaja mt. Peru
Yerushalayim Israel/West Bank see Jerusalem
120 B2 Yeruslan r. Rus. Fed.
159 M2 Yerville France
137 T3 Yeryshevka Rus. Fed.
Yerzhar Uzbek. see Gagarin
186 C2 Yesa Spain
186 C2 Yesa, Embalse de resr Spain
139 R4 Yesenovichi Rus. Fed.
Yeshera Georgia see Eshera
121 Q6 Yesik Kazakh.
121 L2 Yesil' Kazakh.
128 E2 Yeşil Turkey
199 K5 Yeşildere Burdur Turkey
128 F2 Yeşildere Gaziantep Turkey
128 B1 Yeşildere Karaman Turkey
126 G4 Yeşilhisar Turkey
126 H3 Yeşilırmak r. Turkey
128 F1 Yeşilkent Turkey
199 K3 Yeşilköy Turkey
199 K5 Yeşilova Burdur Turkey
Yeşilova Yozgat Turkey see Sorgun
199 L5 Yeşilyayla Turkey
199 J4 Yeşilyurt Turkey
199 K5 Yeşilyuva Turkey
139 W5 Yesiplevo Rus. Fed.
139 O6 Yes'kovo Rus. Fed.
146 J4 Yesnaby Orkney, Scotland U.K.
261 H2 Yeso Arg.
260 B4 Yeso, Cerro mt. Chile
129 D1 Yessentuki Rus. Fed.
129 D1 Yessentukskaya Rus. Fed.
131 L3 Yessey Rus. Fed.
185 O4 Yeste Spain
150 D6 Yes Tor hill England U.K.
128 D5 Yesud HaMa'ala Israel
185 O4 Yetas de Abajo Spain
Yêtatang Xizang China see Baqên
83 M3 Yetman N.S.W. Austr.
96 B3 Ye-U Myanmar
158 G8 Yeu, Île d' i. France
137 S3 Yevdakovo Rus. Fed.
Yevdokimovskoye Rus. Fed. see Krasnogvardeyskoye
Yevlakh Azer. see Yevlax
137 Q1 Yevlanovo Rus. Fed.
129 I5 Yevlax Azer.
137 M8 Yevpatoriya Ukr.
137 M8 Yevpatoriys'kyy, Mys pt Ukr.
160 A2 Yèvre r. France
100 H4 Yevreyskaya Avtonomnaya Oblast' admin. div. Rus. Fed.
139 O6 Yevseyevka Rus. Fed.
137 S3 Yevstratovka Rus. Fed.
137 S5 Yevsuh r. Ukr.
109 I2 Yexian Henan China
Yexian Shandong China see Laizhou
121 Q6 Yeygen'yevka Kazakh.
111 F8 Yeyik Xinjiang China
135 G7 Yeysk Rus. Fed.
137 R7 Yeyskiy Liman inlet Rus. Fed.
137 R7 Yeyskoye Ukreplenie Rus. Fed.
110 G6 Yeyungou Xinjiang China
138 N6 Yezerishche, Ozero l. Belarus/Rus. Fed.
Yezhou Hubei China see Jianshi
134 I2 Yezhuga r. Rus. Fed.
Yezo i. Japan see Hokkaidō
138 M6 Yezyaryshcha Belarus
Y Fali Wales U.K. see Valley
Y Fenni Monmouthshire, Wales U.K. see Abergavenny
158 F5 Yffiniac France
Y Fflint Flintshire, Wales U.K. see Flint
253 G6 Ygatimí Para.
Y Gelli Gandryll Wales U.K. see Hay-on-Wye
163 C8 Ygos-St-Saturnin France
160 B3 Ygrande France
253 G6 Yhú Para.
261 I3 Yí r. Uru.
Yialí i. Greece see Gyali
Yialousa Cyprus see Aigialousa
100 D5 Yi'an Heilong. China
Yianisádha i. Greece see Gianisada
Yiannitsá Greece see Giannitsa
124 E6 Yibā, Wādī watercourse Saudi Arabia
108 E4 Yibin Sichuan China
108 E4 Yibin Sichuan China
111 H10 Yibug Caka salt l. China
109 H3 Yichang Hubei China
Yicheng Henan China see Zhumadian
109 I3 Yicheng Hubei China
107 L9 Yicheng Shanxi China
107 M9 Yichuan Henan China
107 L9 Yichuan Shaanxi China
100 F5 Yichun Heilong. China
109 J5 Yichun Jiangxi China
Yidu Shandong China see Qingzhou
108 B3 Yidun Sichuan China
109 J4 Yifeng Jiangxi China
Yiggêtang Qinghai China see Sêrwolungwa
108 A2 Yiggêtang Qinghai China
199 M2 Yığılca Turkey
129 A6 Yiğitler Turkey
128 E2 Yiğityolu Turkey
78 □1 Yigo Guam
Yigu Guam see Yigo
106 E5 Yihatuoli Gansu China
107 M9 Yi He r. Henan China
107 P9 Yi He r. Shandong China
109 K5 Yihuang Jiangxi China
Yijiang Jiangxi China see Yiyang
107 K9 Yijun Shaanxi China
107 S2 Yilaha Heilong. China
100 F5 Yilan Heilong. China
Yilan Taiwan see Ilan
129 B5 Yıldırım Turkey
126 C3 Yıldız Dağları mts Turkey
126 H4 Yıldızeli Turkey
100 C3 Yilehuli Shan mts China
108 D6 Yiliang Yunnan China
108 E5 Yiliang Yunnan China
111 K8 Yiliping Qinghai China
87 D12 Yilliminning W.A. Austr.
100 D5 Yilong Heilong. China
108 F3 Yilong Sichuan China
Yilong Yunnan China see Shiping
108 D7 Yilong Hu l. China
107 O6 Yimatu He r. China
96 F2 Yimen Yunnan China
100 F6 Yimianpo Heilong. China
107 P2 Yimin He r. China
100 B2 Yimuhe Nei Mongol China
107 P9 Yinan Shandong China
96 C6 Yinbaing Myanmar
Yincheng Jiangxi China see Dexing
106 J7 Yinchuan Ningxia China
87 G11 Yindarlgooda, Lake salt flat W.A. Austr.
84 C4 Yingawunarri Aboriginal Land res. N.T. Austr.
109 I3 Yingcheng Hubei China
100 D7 Yingchengzi Jilin China
109 I6 Yingde Guangdong China
108 G9 Yinggehai Hainan China
Yinggen Hainan China see Qiongzhong
109 K2 Ying He r. China
108 A6 Yingjiang Yunnan China
108 D4 Yingjing Sichuan China
Yingkou Liaoning China see Dashiqiao
107 R6 Yingkou Liaoning China
106 I8 Yingpanshui Ningxia China
109 J3 Yingshan Hubei China
108 F3 Yingshan Sichuan China
109 K2 Yingshang Anhui China
109 K4 Yingtan Jiangxi China
107 N9 Yingtaoyuan Shandong China
207 H5 Yingui Cameroon
107 M7 Yingxian Shanxi China
Yining Jiangxi China see Xiushui
110 E5 Yining Xinjiang China
110 E5 Yining Xinjiang China
84 B6 Yiningarra Aboriginal Land res. N.T. Austr.
108 G5 Yinjiang Guizhou China
109 J5 Yinkengxu Jiangxi China
96 B3 Yinmabin Myanmar
100 D6 Yinma He r. China
96 C6 Yinnyein Myanmar
107 K6 Yin Shan mts China
Yinxian Zhejiang China see Ningbo
Yiófiros r. Kriti Greece see Giofyros
111 L11 Yi'ong Nongchang Xizang China
111 L11 Yi'ong Zangbo r. Xizang China
Yioúra i. Greece see Gioura
108 C6 Yipinglang Yunnan China
199 L4 Yıprak Turkey
Yiquan Guizhou China see Meitan
257 E5 Yira Chapéu, Monte mt. Brazil
111 K10 Yiran Co l. Qinghai China
210 C3 Yirga Alem Eth.
210 C3 Yirga Ch'efē Eth.
210 A3 Yirol Sudan
84 F2 Yirrkala N.T. Austr.
107 P3 Yirshi Nei Mongol China
110 I6 Yirtkuq Bulak spring Xinjiang China
Yirxie Nei Mongol China see Yirshi
Yisa Yunnan China see Honghe
Yishan Guangxi China see Yizhou
Yishan Jiangsu China see Guanyun
107 P8 Yi Shan mt. Shandong China
107 P8 Yi Shan mts China
107 P9 Yishui Shandong China
94 □ Yishun Sing.
207 I1 Yi Tchouma well Niger
Yíthion Greece see Gytheio
Yitiaoshan Gansu China see Jingtai
100 D7 Yitong Jilin China
100 D6 Yitong He r. China
96 C3 Yi Tu, Nam r. Myanmar
107 Q1 Yitulihe Nei Mongol China
106 C5 Yiwanquan Xinjiang China
106 D5 Yiwu Xinjiang China
108 C8 Yiwu Yunnan China
107 Q6 Yiwulü Shan mts China
109 K4 Yixian Anhui China
107 N7 Yixian Hebei China
107 Q6 Yixian Liaoning China
100 D2 Yixiken Heilong. China
109 L3 Yixing Jiangsu China
107 O6 Yixun He r. China
109 I4 Yiyang Hunan China
109 K4 Yiyang Jiangxi China
107 P8 Yiyuan Shandong China
109 I6 Yizhang Hunan China
109 L2 Yizheng Jiangsu China
108 G6 Yizhou Guangxi China
Yizhou Hebei China see Yixian
Yizhou Liaoning China see Yixian
Yizra'el country Asia see Israel
140 R5 Ylä-Keitele l. Fin.
141 T6 Ylämaa Fin.
141 Q6 Yläne Fin.
78 □1 Ylig Bay Guam
140 Q5 Ylihärmä Fin.
140 R4 Yli-Ii Fin.
140 R4 Yli-Kärppä Fin.
140 S4 Ylikiiminki Fin.
140 T3 Yli-Kitka l. Fin.
140 Q5 Ylistaro Fin.
140 Q3 Ylitornio Fin.
140 R4 Ylivieska Fin.
140 R3 Ylläs hill Fin.
150 E2 Y Llethr hill Wales U.K.
141 Q6 Ylöjärvi Fin.
221 P2 Ymer Nunatak Greenland
221 P2 Ymer Ø i. Greenland
156 C7 Ymonville France
143 J3 Ymsen l. Sweden
134 K3 Yndin Rus. Fed.
143 M3 Yngaren l. Sweden
143 K2 Yngen l. Sweden
143 N2 Yngern l. Sweden
121 N3 Yntaly Kazakh.
131 O3 Ynykchanskiy Rus. Fed.
Ynys Enlli i. Wales U.K. see Bardsey Island
Ynys Môn i. Wales U.K. see Anglesey
237 G11 Yoakum TX U.S.A.
207 H4 Yobe state Nigeria
102 R3 Yobetsu-dake vol. Japan
210 D2 Yoboki Djibouti
103 G13 Yobuko Japan
203 H5 Yob Wildlife Reserve nature res. Eritrea
104 B6 Yodo-gawa r. Japan
234 B5 Yoe PA U.S.A.
259 C9 Yogan, Cerro mt. Chile
245 K9 Yogana Mex.
104 D4 Yogo Japan
202 C5 Yogoum well Chad
95 I8 Yogyakarta Indon.
95 I9 Yogyakarta admin. dist. Indon.
222 G5 Yoho National Park B.C. Can.
102 R3 Yoichi Japan
102 S3 Yoichi-dake mt. Japan
111 M9 Yoigilanglêb r. Qinghai China
242 □P10 Yojoa, Lago de l. Hond.
101 E10 Yŏju S. Korea
104 A5 Yōka Japan
207 I6 Yokadouma Cameroon
103 J13 Yokagawara Japan
104 D5 Yōkaichi Japan
105 M4 Yōkaichiba Japan
102 □F18 Yokate-jima i. Nansei-shotō Japan
104 B6 Yokawa Japan
104 E6 Yokkaichi Japan
207 I5 Yoko Cameroon
102 S5 Yokohama Aomori Japan
105 K5 Yokohama Kanagawa Japan
105 I3 Yokokawa Japan
105 L4 Yokoshiba Japan
105 K5 Yokosuka Japan
103 K11 Yokota Japan
102 R7 Yokote Japan
102 R5 Yokotsu-dake mt. Japan
105 J4 Yokoze Japan
116 F3 Yol Hima. Prad. India
207 I4 Yola Nigeria
242 □Q12 Yolaina, Cordillera de mts Nic.
240 J1 Yolla Bolly Middle Eel Wilderness nature res. CA U.S.A.
240 K3 Yolo CA U.S.A.
208 D5 Yolombo Dem. Rep. Congo
Yolöten Turkm. see Ýolöten
123 J3 Ýolöten Turkm.
245 J9 Yolotepec Mex.
245 K8 Yolox Mex.
245 I9 Yoloxóchitl Mex.
243 P7 Yoluk Mex.
96 E7 Yom, Mae Nam r. Thai.
103 □2 Yome-jima i. Japan
105 M1 Yomogida-dake hill Japan
206 C5 Yomou Guinea
129 A5 Yomra Turkey
117 N6 Yomtam Arun. Prad. India
162 B2 Yon r. France
78 □1 Yona Guam
102 □1 Yona Okinawa Japan
102 □1 Yonabaru Okinawa Japan
103 K11 Yonago Japan
102 □A22 Yonaguni-jima i. Nansei-shotō Japan
102 □1 Yonaha-dake hill Okinawa Japan
101 E10 Yŏnan N. Korea
102 R6 Yoneshiro-gawa r. Japan
105 I1 Yone-yama hill Japan
102 R9 Yonezawa Japan
82 G5 Yongala S.A. Austr.
101 E11 Yŏng-am S. Korea
Yong'an Chongqing China see Fengjie
109 K6 Yong'an Fujian China
Yongbei Yunnan China see Yongsheng
106 G7 Yongchang Gansu China
109 K2 Yongcheng Henan China
101 F11 Yŏngch'ŏn S. Korea
108 E4 Yongchuan Chongqing China
109 L6 Yongchun Fujian China
108 B6 Yongde Yunnan China
106 H8 Yongdeng Gansu China
109 K6 Yongding Fujian China
Yongding Yunnan China see Yongren
Yongding Yunnan China see Fumin
107 O7 Yongding He r. China
101 F10 Yŏngdŏk S. Korea
109 J5 Yongfeng Jiangxi China
Yongfeng Jiangxi China see Guangfeng
110 H5 Yongfengqu Xinjiang China
108 G6 Yongfu Guangxi China
101 E11 Yŏnggwang S. Korea
107 L8 Yonghe Shanxi China
101 E9 Yŏnghŭng N. Korea
101 E9 Yŏnghŭng-man b. N. Korea
103 G11 Yŏngil-man b. S. Korea
100 E7 Yongji Jilin China
109 M4 Yongjia Zhejiang China
106 H9 Yongjing Gansu China
Yongjing Guizhou China see Xifeng
Yongjing Liaoning China see Xifeng
107 M8 Yongjin Qu r. China
101 F10 Yŏngju S. Korea
108 B6 Yongkang Yunnan China
109 M4 Yongkang Zhejiang China
108 C3 Yonglaxi Sichuan China
Yongle Shaanxi China see Zhen'an
Yongle Sichuan China see Jiuzhaigou
101 D8 Yongling Liaoning China
107 N8 Yongnian Hebei China
108 G7 Yongning Guangxi China
Yongning Jiangxi China see Tonggu
106 J7 Yongning Ningxia China
Yongning Sichuan China see Xuyong
108 B6 Yongping Yunnan China
Yongqing Gansu China see Qingshui
108 C5 Yongren Yunnan China
101 E11 Yŏngsan-gang r. S. Korea
108 D4 Yongshan Yunnan China
108 C5 Yongsheng Yunnan China
107 K9 Yongshou Shaanxi China
108 G4 Yongshun Hunan China
109 L6 Yongtai Fujian China
101 F10 Yŏngwol S. Korea
Yongxi Guizhou China see Nayong
109 I5 Yongxing Hunan China
109 J5 Yongxing Jiangxi China
107 L7 Yongxing Shaanxi China
109 J4 Yongxiu Jiangxi China
109 H5 Yongzhou Hunan China
233 L8 Yonkers NY U.S.A.
156 G8 Yonne dept France
156 E7 Yonne r. France
206 B3 Yonoféré Senegal
207 I2 Yoo Baba well Niger
250 C3 Yopal Col.
110 C7 Yopurga Xinjiang China
242 F4 Yoquivo Mex.
121 N7 Yordon Uzbek.
116 E3 Yordu Jammu and Kashmir
244 F6 Yoricostío Mex.
105 J3 Yorii Japan
87 D11 York W.A. Austr.
227 O6 York Ont. Can.
223 M4 York r. Man. Can.
149 O6 York York, England U.K.
149 O6 York admin. div. England U.K.
237 K9 York AL U.S.A.
236 G5 York NE U.S.A.
234 B5 York PA U.S.A.
231 G8 York SC U.S.A.
85 I1 York, Cape Qld Austr.
York, Kap c. Greenland see Innaanganeq
149 N5 York, Vale of val. England U.K.
234 B5 York County county PA U.S.A.
85 I2 York Downs Qld Austr.
82 F6 Yorke Peninsula S.A. Austr.
82 F6 Yorketown S.A. Austr.
234 B4 York Haven PA U.S.A.
149 M5 Yorkshire Dales National Park England U.K.
149 P6 Yorkshire Wolds hills England U.K.
234 A4 York Springs PA U.S.A.
223 K5 Yorkton Sask. Can.
232 I11 Yorktown VA U.S.A.
235 H2 Yorktown Heights NY U.S.A.
224 B5 Yorkville IL U.S.A.
242 □P10 Yoro Hond.
104 E5 Yōrō Japan
104 E7 Yoroi-zaki pt Japan
102 □G18 Yoro-jima i. Nansei-shotō Japan
93 F4 Yoronga i. Maluku Indon.
102 □F19 Yoron-tō i. Nansei-shotō Japan
106 J2 Yöröö Gol r. Mongolia
206 D3 Yorosso Mali
240 M4 Yosemite National Park CA U.S.A.
240 M4 Yosemite Village CA U.S.A.
103 J13 Yoshida Ehime Japan
103 J12 Yoshida Hiroshima Japan
105 J3 Yoshida Saitama Japan
105 H6 Yoshida Shizuoka Japan
103 H13 Yoshii Fukuoka Japan
105 I3 Yoshii Gunma Japan
103 L12 Yoshii-gawa r. Japan
105 H1 Yoshikawa Japan
105 M1 Yoshima Japan
104 C7 Yoshino Japan
104 E3 Yoshinodani Japan
104 C7 Yoshino-gawa r. Japan
103 L12 Yoshino-gawa r. Japan
104 D8 Yoshino-Kumano Kokuritsu-kōen nat. park Japan
134 I4 Yoshkar-Ola Rus. Fed.
Yos Sudarso i. Papua Indon. see Dolok, Pulau
101 E11 Yŏsu S. Korea
253 E4 Yotau Bol.
102 R4 Yōtei-zan mt. Japan
105 L4 Yotsukaidō Japan
105 M1 Yotsukura Japan
128 D9 Yotvata Israel
210 E3 Yoube well Eth.
222 E5 Youbou B.C. Can.
111 J7 Youdunzi Qinghai China
147 G9 Youghal Ireland
147 F9 Youghal Bay Ireland
108 G7 You Jiang r. China
149 N7 Youlgreave Derbyshire, England U.K.
107 P8 Youlin Shandong China
208 C5 Youmba Congo
83 L6 Young N.S.W. Austr.
87 F12 Young r. W.A. Austr.
261 I3 Young Uru.
241 V7 Young AZ U.S.A.
80 □ Young, Cape Chatham Is S. Pacific Ocean
82 F4 Younghusband, Lake salt flat S.A. Austr.
82 G6 Younghusband Peninsula S.A. Austr.
263 K2 Young Island Antarctica
80 L5 Young Nicks Head North I. N.Z.
81 D11 Young Range mts South I. N.Z.
223 I5 Youngstown Alta Can.
232 E7 Youngstown OH U.S.A.
232 F7 Youngsville PA U.S.A.
240 J3 Yountville CA U.S.A.
111 J7 Youshashan Qinghai China
108 H4 You Shui r. China
204 C2 Youssoufia Morocco
206 D3 Youvarou Mali
109 L5 Youxi Fujian China
109 I5 Youxian Hunan China
108 G4 Youyang Chongqing China
100 G5 Youyi Heilong. China
110 H2 Youyi Feng mt. China/Rus. Fed.
107 M7 Youyu Shanxi China
123 M2 Yovon Tajik.
83 J3 Yowah watercourse Qld Austr.
87 E8 Yowereena Hill W.A. Austr.
151 I2 Yoxall Staffordshire, England U.K.
151 P3 Yoxford Suffolk, England U.K.
126 G4 Yozgat Turkey
253 G5 Ypé-Jhú Para.
159 L2 Yport France
140 R4 Yppäri Fin.
Ypres West-Vlaanderen Belgium see Ieper
227 K7 Ypsilanti MI U.S.A.
238 C6 Yreka CA U.S.A.
Yrghyz Kazakh. see Irgiz
Yr Wyddfa mt. Wales U.K. see Snowdon
Yr Wyddgrug Flintshire, Wales U.K. see Mold
150 E3 Ysbyty Ystwyth Ceredigion, Wales U.K.
156 E2 Yser r. France alt. IJzer (Belgium)
164 I6 Ysselsteyn Neth.
161 E6 Yssingeaux France
143 J6 Ystad Sweden
150 E4 Ystalyfera Neath Port Talbot, Wales U.K.
150 F1 Ystrad r. Wales U.K.
150 E4 Ystradgynlais Powys, Wales U.K.
150 D3 Ystwyth r. Wales U.K.
121 P6 Ysyk-Ata Kyrg.
Ysyk-Köl Kyrg. see Balykchy
121 R7 Ysyk-Köl admin. div. Kyrg.
121 Q6 Ysyk-Köl salt l. Kyrg.
146 L8 Ythan r. Scotland U.K.
Y Trallwng Powys, Wales U.K. see Welshpool
142 C1 Ytre Samlen b. Norway
Ytre Vinje Norway see Åmot
131 O3 Ytyk-Kyuyel' Rus. Fed.
93 F4 Yu i. Maluku Indon.
128 B8 Yu'alliq, Jabal mt. Egypt
109 H3 Yuan'an Hubei China
107 P5 Yuanbaoshan Nei Mongol China
108 G6 Yuanbao Shan mt. Guangxi China
109 I4 Yuanjiang Hunan China
108 C7 Yuanjiang Yunnan China
108 H4 Yuan Jiang r. Hunan China
108 D7 Yuan Jiang r. Yunnan China
Yuanjiazhuang Shaanxi China see Foping
109 M6 Yüanli Taiwan
107 Q2 Yuanlin Nei Mongol China
108 H4 Yuanling Hunan China
Yuanma Yunnan China see Yuanmou
108 C6 Yuanmou Yunnan China
107 M7 Yuanping Shanxi China
107 L9 Yuanqu Shanxi China
Yuanquan Gansu China see Anxi
Yuanshan Guangdong China see Lianping
106 F7 Yuanshanzi Gansu China
Yuanyang Yunnan China see Xinjie
108 D7 Yuanyang Yunnan China
104 B7 Yuasa Japan
124 B2 Yub'ā i. Saudi Arabia
240 K2 Yuba City CA U.S.A.
102 S3 Yūbari Japan
102 T3 Yūbari-dake mt. Japan
102 T3 Yūbari-sanchi mts Japan
108 F4 Yubei Chongqing China
102 U2 Yūbetsu Japan
102 U2 Yūbetsu-gawa r. Japan
208 E3 Yubu Sudan
240 O7 Yucaipa CA U.S.A.
243 N8 Yucatán pen. Mex.
243 O7 Yucatán state Mex.
243 P6 Yucatan Channel Cuba/Mex.
241 R7 Yucca AZ U.S.A.
241 P5 Yucca Lake NV U.S.A.
241 P7 Yucca Valley CA U.S.A.
129 C7 Yücetepe Turkey
107 N9 Yucheng Henan China
107 O8 Yucheng Shandong China
Yucheng Sichuan China see Ya'an
Yuci Shanxi China see Jinzhong
252 D3 Yucumo Bol.
139 U5 Yudino Moskovskaya Oblast' Rus. Fed.
134 J5 Yudino Respublika Tatarstan Rus. Fed.
134 G4 Yudino Yaroslavskaya Oblast' Rus. Fed.
100 B2 Yudi Shan mt. China
131 O4 Yudoma r. Rus. Fed.
109 J6 Yudu Jiangxi China
Yuecheng Sichuan China see Yuexi
108 F3 Yuechi Sichuan China
Yuelai Heilong. China see Huachuan
107 R4 Yueliang Pao l. China
84 C7 Yuendumu N.T. Austr.
84 C7 Yuendumu Aboriginal Land res. N.T. Austr.
109 □J7 Yuen Long H.K. China
109 M4 Yueqing Zhejiang China
109 K3 Yuexi Anhui China
108 D4 Yuexi Sichuan China
109 I4 Yueyang Hunan China
109 I4 Yueyang Hunan China
Yueyang Sichuan China see Anyue
134 L4 Yug Rus. Fed.
134 I3 Yug r. Rus. Fed.
109 K4 Yugan Jiangxi China
105 J5 Yugawara Japan
111 L9 Yuge Qinghai China
128 B1 Yuğluk Dağı mts Turkey
134 K4 Yugo-Kamskiy Rus. Fed.
Yugo-Osetinskaya Avtonomnaya Oblast' aut. reg. Georgia see Samkhret' Oset'i
130 H3 Yugorsk Rus. Fed.
134 M1 Yugorskiy Poluostrov pen. Rus. Fed.
134 M2 Yugud-Vayskiy Natsional'nyy Park nat. park Rus. Fed.
109 M3 Yuhang Zhejiang China
107 M7 Yu He r. China
Yuhu Yunnan China see Eryuan
109 M4 Yuhuan Zhejiang China
107 O8 Yuhuang Ding mt. Shandong China
105 I5 Yui Japan
87 D9 Yuin W.A. Austr.
109 K4 Yujiang Jiangxi China
108 H7 Yu Jiang r. China
Yujin Sichuan China see Qianwei
131 Q3 Yukagirskoye Ploskogor'ye plat. Rus. Fed.
134 K4 Yukamenskoye Rus. Fed.
129 F7 Yukarı Balçıklı Turkey
199 I3 Yukarıbey Turkey
129 B5 Yukarıcanören Turkey
129 D4 Yukarıgündeş Turkey
129 E5 Yukarıkaragüney Turkey
199 M3 Yukarı Sakarya Ovaları plain Turkey
129 D5 Yukarısarıkamış Turkey
126 G4 Yukarısarıkaya Turkey
138 L5 Yukhavichy Belarus
135 J5 Yukhmachi Rus. Fed.
139 S7 Yukhnov Rus. Fed.
139 N5 Yukhovo Rus. Fed.
209 C5 Yuki Dem. Rep. Congo
103 K12 Yuki Japan
105 K3 Yūki Japan
220 B3 Yukon r. Can./U.S.A.
220 D3 Yukon-Charley Rivers National Preserve nature res. AK U.S.A.
222 B2 Yukon Crossing Y.T. Can.
222 C2 Yukon Territory admin. div. Can.
127 L5 Yüksekova Turkey
103 H13 Yukuhashi Japan
84 C8 Yulara N.T. Austr.
120 G1 Yuldybayevo Rus. Fed.
86 E6 Yule r. W.A. Austr.
85 L9 Yuleba Qld Austr.
231 G10 Yulee FL U.S.A.
110 H6 Yuli Xinjiang China
109 M7 Yüli Taiwan
108 H7 Yulin Guangxi China
108 G9 Yulin Hainan China
107 K7 Yulin Shaanxi China
108 C5 Yulong Xueshan mt. Yunnan China
241 R9 Yuma AZ U.S.A.
236 D5 Yuma CO U.S.A.
241 R9 Yuma Desert AZ U.S.A.
120 G1 Yumaguzino Rus. Fed.
82 D4 Yumbarra Conservation Park nature res. S.A. Austr.
210 A4 Yumbe Uganda
260 A5 Yumbel Chile
208 C5 Yumbi Bandundu Dem. Rep. Congo
208 E5 Yumbi Maniema Dem. Rep. Congo
250 B4 Yumbo Col.
111 G11 Yumco Xizang China
106 E7 Yumen Gansu China
106 E7 Yumendongzhan Gansu China
110 K6 Yumenguan Gansu China
106 E6 Yumenzhen Gansu China
110 F3 Yumin Xinjiang China
106 E4 Yumt Uul mt. Mongolia
128 D2 Yumurtalık Turkey
87 C10 Yuna W.A. Austr.
246 I4 Yuna r. Dom. Rep.
126 E4 Yunak Turkey
137 O2 Yunakivka Ukr.
109 H7 Yunan Guangdong China
109 I7 Yun'an Guangdong China
220 A4 Yunaska Island AK U.S.A.
252 D5 Yunchara Bol.
107 N9 Yuncheng Shandong China
107 L9 Yuncheng Shanxi China
129 C5 Yüncüler Turkey
87 G10 Yundamindera W.A. Austr.
109 I7 Yunfu Guangdong China
252 D4 Yungas reg. Bol.
252 C6 Yungay Antofagasta Chile
260 A5 Yungay Biobío Chile
252 C4 Yungayo Peru
108 D6 Yungui Gaoyuan plat. Guizhou/Yunnan China
Yunhe Jiangsu China see Pizhou
Yunhe Yunnan China see Heqing
109 L4 Yunhe Zhejiang China
Yunjinghong Yunnan China see Jinghong
108 H7 Yunkai Dashan mts China
84 C7 Yunkanjini Aboriginal Land res. N.T. Austr.
Yunling Fujian China see Yunxiao
108 B5 Yun Ling mts Yunnan China
108 B6 Yunlong Yunnan China
109 I3 Yunmeng Hubei China
108 C6 Yunnan prov. China
137 R5 Yunokomunarivs'k Ukr.
105 J1 Yunotani Japan
103 J11 Yunotsu Japan
185 J7 Yunquera Spain
183 N7 Yunquera de Henares Spain
109 I3 Yun Shui r. China
82 G5 Yunta S.A. Austr.
128 A2 Yunt Dağı mt. Turkey
199 K3 Yunuslar Turkey
109 H7 Yunwu Shan mts China
108 H2 Yunxi Hubei China
Yunxi Sichuan China see Yanting
108 H2 Yunxian Hubei China
108 C6 Yunxian Yunnan China
109 K7 Yunxiao Fujian China
134 M2 Yun'yakha r. Rus. Fed.
108 G3 Yunyang Chongqing China
109 I2 Yunyang Henan China
Yupin Yunnan China see Pingbian
Yuping Guizhou China see Libo
108 G5 Yuping Guizhou China
109 L3 Yuqian Zhejiang China
108 F5 Yuqing Guizhou China
252 D5 Yura Bol.
252 D5 Yura r. Bol.
104 B8 Yura Japan
252 C4 Yura Peru
250 B6 Yuracyacu Peru
104 B5 Yura-gawa r. Japan
102 R4 Yūrappu-dake mt. Japan
137 S3 Yurasovka Rus. Fed.
138 I7 Yuratsishki Belarus
136 I2 Yuravichy Belarus
83 N3 Yuraygir National Park N.S.W. Austr.
111 H9 Yurba Co l. Xizang China
137 Q4 Yurchenkove Ukr.
244 E5 Yurécuaro Mex.
128 D2 Yürekli Turkey
130 J4 Yurga Rus. Fed.
250 B6 Yurimaguas Peru
134 I4 Yurino Rus. Fed.
244 F5 Yuriria Mex.
244 F5 Yuriria, Laguna l. Mex.
129 H1 Yurkovka Rus. Fed.
134 K4 Yurla Rus. Fed.
137 T1 Yurlovka Rus. Fed.
134 I2 Yuroma Rus. Fed.
137 Q8 Yurovka Rus. Fed.
199 I2 Yürük Turkey
111 E7 Yurungkax He r. China
102 W3 Yururi-jima i. Japan
134 J4 Yur'ya Rus. Fed.
134 K2 Yur'yakha r. Rus. Fed.
Yuryev Estonia see Tartu
134 H4 Yur'yevets Ivanovskaya Oblast' Rus. Fed.
139 X5 Yur'yevets Vladimirskaya Oblast' Rus. Fed.
139 W5 Yur'yev-Pol'skiy Rus. Fed.
137 P5 Yur"yivka Dnipropetrovs'ka Oblast' Ukr.
137 P7 Yur"yivka Zaporiz'ka Oblast' Ukr.
242 □P11 Yuscarán Hond.
109 L5 Yushan Fujian China
109 L4 Yushan Jiangxi China
109 M7 Yü Shan mt. Taiwan
109 M4 Yushan Liedao is China
107 M8 Yushe Shanxi China
134 K1 Yushino Rus. Fed.
134 F2 Yushkozero Rus. Fed.
100 E6 Yushu Jilin China
108 A2 Yushu Qinghai China
110 H5 Yushugou Xinjiang China
134 J4 Yushut r. Rus. Fed.
135 I7 Yusta Rus. Fed.
127 J3 Yusufeli Turkey
103 K13 Yusuhara Japan
134 K4 Yus'va Rus. Fed.
107 O9 Yutai Shandong China
Yutan Hunan China see Ningxiang
135 K5 Yutaza Rus. Fed.
107 O7 Yutian Hebei China
111 E8 Yutian Xinjiang China
107 P5 Yutiangao Nei Mongol China
104 G6 Yūtō Japan
Yutpundji Djindiniwirritj res. N.T. Austr. see Roper Bar Aboriginal Land
261 F5 Yutuyaco Arg.
253 F6 Yuty Para.
157 L5 Yutz France
199 K6 Yuva Turkey
129 A5 Yuvacık Turkey
102 □G18 Yuwan-dake hill Nansei-shotō Japan
106 J8 Yuwang Ningxia China
129 I5 Yuxarı Garabağ Kanalı canal Azer.
129 G4 Yuxarı Salahlı Azer.
129 H4 Yuxarı Tala Azer.
Yuxi Guizhou China see Daozhen
109 H3 Yuxi Hubei China
108 D6 Yuxi Yunnan China
108 H3 Yuxiakou Hubei China
107 N7 Yuxian Hebei China
107 M7 Yuxian Shanxi China
109 L3 Yuxikou Anhui China
109 H3 Yuyangguan Hubei China
109 M3 Yuyao Zhejiang China
Yuyue Hubei China see Jiayu
102 Q7 Yuza Japan
102 R7 Yuzawa Japan
129 F5 Yüzbaşılar Turkey
134 H4 Yuzha Rus. Fed.
137 K7 Yuzhne Ukr.
Yuzhno-Alichurskiy, Khrebet mts Tajik. see Alichuri Janubí, Qatorkŭhi
100 M5 Yuzhno-Kamyshovyy Khrebet ridge Sakhalin Rus. Fed.
Yuzhno-Kazakhstanskaya Oblast' admin. div. Kazakh. see Yuzhnyy Kazakhstan
99 Q3 Yuzhno-Kuril'sk Kuril'skiye O-va Rus. Fed.
131 M4 Yuzhno-Muyskiy Khrebet mts Rus. Fed.
100 M5 Yuzhno-Sakhalinsk Sakhalin Rus. Fed.
129 G1 Yuzhno-Sukhokumsk Rus. Fed.
135 E7 Yuzhnoukrayinsk Ukr.
120 I1 Yuzhnoural'sk Rus. Fed.
121 T1 Yuzhnyy Altayskiy Kray Rus. Fed.
175 I1 Yuzhnyy Kaliningradskaya Oblast' Rus. Fed.
Yuzhnyy Respublika Kalmykiya-Khalm'g-Tangch Rus. Fed. see Adyk
135 H7 Yuzhnyy Rostovskaya Oblast' Rus. Fed.
131 Q4 Yuzhnyy, Mys hd Rus. Fed.
121 V3 Yuzhnyy Altay, Khrebet mts Kazakh.
Yuzhnyy Bug r. Ukr. see Pivdennyy Buh
121 M6 Yuzhnyy Kazakhstan admin. div. Kazakh.
120 G1 Yuzhnyy Ural mts Rus. Fed.
106 I9 Yuzhong Gansu China
Yuzhou Hebei China see Yuxian
107 M9 Yuzhou Henan China
Yuzkuduk Uzbek. see Yuzquduq
Yuzovka Ukr. see Donets'k
120 J6 Yuzquduq Uzbek.
104 A7 Yuzuruha-yama hill Japan
158 G5 Yvel r. France
156 C6 Yvelines dept France
190 B2 Yverdon Switz.
159 M2 Yvetot France
158 G5 Yvignac France
165 G8 Yvoir Belgium
160 I4 Yvoire France
190 B2 Yvonand Switz.
96 B4 Ywamun Myanmar
96 C5 Ywathit Myanmar
Y Waun Wales U.K. see Chirk
143 M4 Yxern l. Sweden
143 M3 Yxningen l. Sweden
143 M3 Yxnö i. Sweden
214 C9 Yzerfontein S. Africa
214 C9 Yzerfonteinpunt pt S. Africa
160 C3 Yzeure France
159 M8 Yzeures-sur-Creuse France

Z

204 E2 Za, Oued r. Morocco
245 K9 Zaachila Mex.
214 H9 Zaaimansdal S. Africa
Zaamin Uzbek. see Zomin
165 E6 Zaamslag Neth.
164 G4 Zaandam Neth.
164 G4 Zaandijk Neth.
197 O5 Zăbala r. Romania
196 I5 Žabalj Vojvodina Serbia
127 K5 Zāb al Kabīr, Nahr az r. Iraq
138 K4 Zabalova Latvia
122 G4 Zabānābād Iran
124 C4 Zabarjad, Jazīrat i. Egypt
127 K6 Zāb aş Şaghīr, Nahr az r. Iraq
107 O2 Zabaykal'sk Rus. Fed.
195 □ Żabbar Malta
176 F2 Žabčice Czech Rep.
122 A4 Zab-e Kuchek r. Iran
171 I8 Zabeltitz-Treugeböhla Ger.
208 E4 Zabia Dem. Rep. Congo
175 I3 Żabia Wola Pol.
191 Q4 Zabiče Slovenia
124 F8 Zabīd Yemen
124 F8 Zabīd, Wādī watercourse Yemen
175 J2 Zabiele Pol.
175 J3 Ząbki Pol.
174 E5 Ząbkowice Śląskie Pol.
175 L4 Zabłocie Pol.
175 L2 Zabłudów Pol.
179 O8 Žabno Croatia
175 I5 Żabno Pol.
188 E2 Zabok Croatia
177 H2 Žabokreky Slovakia
123 I6 Zābol Iran
123 I8 Zābolī Iran
136 E5 Zabolotiv Ukr.
136 D2 Zabolottya Ukr.
167 H2 Zaborski Park Krajobrazowy Pol.
139 S2 Zabor'ye Rus. Fed.
170 K4 Żabów Pol.
174 D2 Żabowo Pol.
111 H11 Zabqung Xizang China
197 J4 Zăbrani Romania
129 K5 Zabrat Azer.
206 E4 Zabré Burkina
176 F2 Zábřeh Czech Rep.
174 G5 Zabrze Pol.
123 L5 Zābul prov. Afgh.
120 D4 Zaburun'ye Kazakh.
136 I3 Zabuyannya Ukr.
136 C2 Zabuzhzhya Ukr.
207 F4 Zabzugu Ghana
243 O10 Zacapa Guat.
245 J6 Zacapoaxtla Mex.
244 F6 Zacapu Mex.
244 G7 Zacapuato Mex.
254 C4 Zacarias r. Brazil
243 N8 Zacatal Mex.
244 E3 Zacatecas Mex.
244 E2 Zacatecas state Mex.
242 □O11 Zacatecoluca El Salvador
245 I6 Zacatelco Mex.
245 H7 Zacatepec Morelos Mex.
245 J9 Zacatepec Oaxaca Mex.
245 L8 Zacatepec Oaxaca Mex.
245 J6 Zacatlán Mex.
120 D2 Zachagansk Kazakh.
198 C5 Zacharo Greece
174 F2 Zacharzyn Pol.
173 O4 Zachenberg Ger.
137 O4 Zachepylivka Ukr.
174 D2 Zachodniopomorskie prov. Pol.
244 D5 Zacoalco Mex.
245 H7 Zacualpán Mex.
244 B4 Zacualpan Nayarit Mex.
245 I5 Zacualpan Veracruz Mex.
245 I5 Zacualtipán Mex.
Zacynthus i. Greece see Zakynthos
175 L3 Zaczopki Pol.
204 D2 Zad, Col du pass Morocco
188 E3 Zadar Croatia
188 E3 Zadarski Kanal sea chan. Croatia
136 J2 Zaderiyivka Ukr.
97 D9 Zadetkale Kyun i. Myanmar
97 D10 Zadetkyi Kyun i. Myanmar
97 C7 Zadi Myanmar
111 L10 Zadoi Qinghai China
139 V9 Zadonsk Rus. Fed.
183 O3 Zadorra r. Spain
123 M5 Zadran reg. Afgh.
139 N6 Zadubrowye Belarus
177 G2 Zádveřice Czech Rep.
139 N6 Zadzyetuni Belarus
203 G2 Za'farānah Egypt
128 A9 Za'farānah, Ra's pt Egypt
185 K7 Zafarraya Spain
123 P5 Zafarwal Pak.
Zafer Adaları is Cyprus see Kleides Islands
Zafer Burnu c. Cyprus see Apostolos Andreas, Cape
195 I8 Zafferana Etnea Sicilia Italy
194 F7 Zafferano, Capo c. Sicilia Italy
184 G4 Zafra Spain
183 O9 Zafra de Záncara Spain
183 Q8 Zafrilla Spain
183 Q8 Zafrilla, Sierra de mts Spain
204 C3 Zag Morocco
179 H7 Žaga Slovenia
174 D4 Żagań Pol.
138 G5 Žagarė Lith.
193 J4 Zagarolo Italy
Zagazig Ash Sharqīyah Egypt see Az Zaqāzīq
129 F4 Zages Georgia
122 G4 Zaghdeh well Iran
122 D4 Zāgheh Iran
122 B4 Zāgheh-ye Bālā Iran
205 H1 Zaghouan Tunisia
189 C7 Zaghouan admin. div. Tunisia
175 I5 Zagnańsk Pol.
197 O5 Zagon Romania
198 E3 Zagora Greece
204 D3 Zagora Morocco
179 M7 Zagorje reg. Croatia
191 Q4 Zagorje Slovenia
188 E2 Zagorje ob Savi Slovenia
174 F3 Zagórów Pol.
Zagorsk Rus. Fed. see Sergiyev Posad
175 K6 Zagórz Pol.
185 K6 Zagra Spain
197 M9 Zagrazhden Bulg.
188 E3 Zagreb Croatia
174 D4 Zagrodno Pol.
122 B4 Zagros, Kūhhā-ye mts Iran
Zagros Mountains Iran see Zagros, Kūhhā-ye
197 J6 Žagubica Serbia
Zagunao Sichuan China see Lixian
111 I11 Za'gya Zangbo r. Xizang China
177 J4 Zagyva r. Hungary
177 J4 Zagyvarékas Hungary
136 I3 Zahal'tsi Ukr.
213 □K3 Zahamena, Réserve de nature res. Madag.
185 I7 Zahara Spain
184 H8 Zahara de los Atunes Spain
185 I7 Zahara-El Gastor, Embalse de resr Spain
175 M3 Zaharoddzye reg. Belarus
122 E7 Zāhedān Fārs Iran
122 I7 Zāhedān Sīstān va Balūchestān Iran
184 F4 Zahinos Spain
123 N7 Zahir Pir Pak.
128 D5 Zahlé Lebanon
129 G5 Zähmätkänd Azer.
123 J3 Zähmet Turkm.
171 G7 Zahna Ger.
177 L3 Záhony Hungary
177 G2 Záhorovice Czech Rep.
176 F3 Záhorská Ves Slovakia
124 F7 Zahrān Saudi Arabia
123 L7 Zahri Nur Gama Pak.
138 K4 Zaiceva Latvia
183 Q6 Zaida, Laguna de resr Spain
186 F4 Zaidín Spain
138 G6 Žaiginys Lith.
124 G5 Zā'in, Jabal hill Saudi Arabia
122 E5 Zaindeh r. Iran
Zainlha Sichuan China see Xiaojin
Zainsk Rus. Fed. see Novyy Zay
Zair Uzbek. see Zoir
Zaire country Africa see Congo, Democratic Republic of the
209 B6 Zaire prov. Angola
Zaïre r. Congo/Dem. Rep. Congo see Congo
196 I9 Zajas Macedonia
197 K7 Zaječar Serbia
173 P2 Zaječov Czech Rep.
174 D2 Zajezierze Pol.
213 F4 Zaka Zimbabwe
106 H1 Zakamensk Rus. Fed.
176 F5 Zákány Hungary
177 I5 Zákányszek Hungary
136 C5 Zakarpats'ka Oblast' admin. div. Ukr.
Zakarpatskaya Oblast' admin. div. Ukr. see Zakarpats'ka Oblast'
Zakataly Azer. see Zaqatala
Zakháro Greece see Zacharo
139 W7 Zakharovo Rus. Fed.
136 D3 Zakhidnyy Buh r. Ukr.
127 K5 Zākhō Iraq
Zakhodnyaya Dzvina r. Europe see Zapadnaya Dvina
134 G1 Zakhrebetnoye Rus. Fed.
122 A2 Zakī, Kūh-e mt. Iran
Zákinthos i. Greece see Zakynthos
175 I6 Zakliczyn Pol.
175 K5 Zaklików Pol.
175 H6 Zakopane Pol.
208 C2 Zakouma Chad
208 C2 Zakouma, Parc National de nat. park Chad
199 H7 Zakros Kriti Greece
175 K5 Zakrzew Lubelskie Pol.
175 J4 Zakrzew Mazowieckie Pol.
174 G3 Zakrzewo Kujawsko-Pomorskie Pol.
174 F2 Zakrzewo Wielkopolskie Pol.
175 K5 Zakrzówek-Wieś Pol.
176 D1 Zákupy Czech Rep.
222 F5 Zakwaski, Mount B.C. Can.
198 B5 Zakynthos Zakynthos Greece
198 B5 Zakynthos i. Greece
198 B5 Zakynthou, Porthmos sea chan. Greece
209 B6 Zala Angola
111 L11 Zala Xizang China
176 F5 Zala county Hungary
196 F4 Zala r. Romania
176 G5 Zalaapáti Hungary
176 F5 Zalaegerszeg Hungary
176 F5 Zalai-domsag hills Hungary
176 G5 Zalakaros Hungary
176 G5 Zalakomár Hungary
176 F5 Zalalövő Hungary
184 H3 Zalamea de la Serena Spain
184 F5 Zalamea la Real Spain
207 H4 Zalanga Nigeria
107 R3 Zalantun Nei Mongol China
176 G5 Zalaszántó Hungary
176 F5 Zalaszentbalázs Hungary
176 G5 Zalaszentgrót Hungary
176 F5 Zalaszentiván Hungary
176 F5 Zalaszentmihály Hungary
197 L3 Zalău Romania
177 L4 Zalău r. Romania
176 G5 Zalavár Hungary
138 J7 Zalavas Lith.
175 J4 Załazy Pol.
188 E2 Žalec Slovenia
167 I3 Załęczański Park Krajobrazowy Pol.
139 T9 Zalegoshch' Rus. Fed.
174 F3 Zalesie Kujawsko-Pomorskie Pol.
175 L3 Zalesie Lubelskie Pol.
232 C9 Zaleski OH U.S.A.
139 T3 Zales'ye Rus. Fed.
175 H2 Zalewo Pol.
124 F4 Zalim Saudi Arabia
202 D6 Zalingei Sudan
136 E5 Zalishchyky Ukr.
136 E5 Zalissya Ukr.
137 P6 Zaliznychne Ukr.
137 L7 Zaliznyy Port Ukr.
136 E4 Zaliztsi Ukr.
124 D2 Zalmā, Jabal az mt. Saudi Arabia
174 F2 Żalno Pol.
202 A1 Zalţan Libya
202 C2 Zaltan, Jabal hills Libya
164 H5 Zaltbommel Neth.
175 L1 Žaltytis l. Lith.
139 O4 Zaluch'ye Rus. Fed.
136 D2 Zalukhiv Ukr.
129 E2 Zalukokoazhe Rus. Fed.
115 N4 Zalun Myanmar
138 L8 Zaluzhzha Belarus
175 M2 Zal'vyanka r. Belarus
177 L5 Zam Romania
105 J5 Zama Japan
207 F3 Zama Niger
222 G3 Zama City Alta Can.

125 H7 Zamakh Saudi Arabia
215 N3 Zamani S. Africa
126 G4 Zamantı r. Turkey
177 G5 Zamárdi Hungary
174 F2 Zamarte Pol.
92 C4 Zambales Mountains Luzon Phil.
176 F1 Zámberk Czech Rep.
209 D8 Zambeze r. Africa alt. Zambezi
209 D7 Zambezi r. Africa alt. Zambeze
209 D8 Zambezi Zambia
213 H3 Zambézia prov. Moz.
209 E9 Zambezi Escarpment Zambia/Zimbabwe
212 E3 Zambezi National Park Zimbabwe
209 E8 Zambia country Africa
92 D8 Zamboanga Mindanao Phil.
92 D8 Zamboanga Peninsula Mindanao Phil.
92 D7 Zamboanguita Negros Phil.
183 O3 Zambrana Spain
246 F9 Zambrano Col.
175 K3 Zambrów Pol.
213 F2 Zambue Moz.
184 A4 Zambujal de Cima Port.
184 B5 Zambujeira do Mar Port.
174 D2 Zamęcin Pol.
207 G3 Zamfara state Nigeria
207 G3 Zamfara watercourse Nigeria
123 J6 Zamíndávar r. Afgh.
204 B4 Zamlat Amagraj hills Western Sahara
138 K4 Zamogil'ye Rus. Fed.
177 H4 Zámoly Hungary
256 B6 Zamora Ecuador
250 B5 Zamora r. Ecuador
182 I5 Zamora Spain
182 I5 Zamora prov. Spain
244 E6 Zamora de Hidalgo Mex.
175 L5 Zamość Lubelskie Pol.
175 J2 Zamość Mazowieckie Pol.
175 L5 Zamość wojew. Pol. see Zamość
137 Q6 Zamozhne Ukr.
129 O5 Zampa-misaki hd Okinawa Japan see Zanpa-misaki
178 C5 Zams Austria
108 C2 Zamtang Sichuan China
250 D2 Zamuro, Punta pt Venez.
251 F3 Zamuro, Sierra del mts Venez.
202 B2 Zamzam, Wâdî watercourse Libya
250 B6 Zaña Peru
208 B5 Zanaga Congo
245 M9 Zanatepec Mex.
129 K5 Zânbîl Adası i. Azer.
183 N10 Zancara r. Spain
Zancle Sicilia Italy see Messina
111 D11 Zanda Xizang China
213 G5 Zandamela Moz.
251 H3 Zanderij Suriname
165 G6 Zandhoven Belgium
171 J9 Zandvliet Belgium
164 G4 Zanesville OH U.S.A.
232 C9 Zanesville Armenia
129 G6 Zangakatun Armenia
206 D3 Zangasso Mali
Zangelan Azer. see Zängilan
129 G6 Zangezuri Lerrnashght'a mts Armenia/Azer.
111 D8 Zanda Xizang China
129 H6 Zängilan Azer.
116 F3 Zangla Jammu and Kashmir
111 G9 Zangsêr Kangri mt. Xizang China
107 N8 Zanhuang Hebei China
208 F4 Zani Dem. Rep. Congo
123 M7 Zani Pak.
174 F3 Zaniemyśl Pol.
122 C3 Zanján Iran
122 C3 Zanján prov. Iran
127 M5 Zanján Rûd r. Iran
260 D3 Zanjitas Arg.
125 K3 Zannah, Jabal az hill U.A.E.
193 K6 Zannone, Isola i. Italy
102 □¹ Zanpa-misaki hd Okinawa Japan
116 F2 Zanskar r. India
116 F3 Zanskar reg. Jammu and Kashmir
116 F2 Zanskar Mountains India
Zante i. Ionioi Nisoi Greece see Zakynthos
Zante i. Ionioi Nisoi Greece see Zakynthos
87 G11 Zanthus W.A. Austr.
206 D4 Zantiébougou Mali
211 C6 Zanzibar Tanz.
211 C6 Zanzibar Channel Tanz.
211 C6 Zanzibar Island Tanz.
211 C6 Zanzibar North admin. reg. Tanz.
211 C6 Zanzibar South admin. reg. Tanz.
211 C6 Zanzibar West admin. reg. Tanz.
263 H1 Zaohe Jiangsu China
139 O7 Zaokskiy Rus. Fed.
189 C7 Zaouia Mornag Tunisia
183 P7 Zaorejas Spain
208 C3 Zaoro-Songou C.A.R.
107 K9 Zaoshang Gansu China
110 I5 Zaoshi Hunan China
139 Q1 Zaostrov'ye Rus. Fed.
205 H4 Zaouatallaz Alg.
Zaouet el Kahla Alg. see Bordj Omer Driss
205 E4 Zaouet Kounta Alg.
109 I2 Zaoyang Hubei China
109 I2 Zaoyangzhan Hubei China
110 H4 Zaoyuan Xinjiang China
102 R8 Zao-zan vol. Japan
137 M8 Zaozerne Ukr.
121 N1 Zaozernyy Kazakh.
131 K4 Zaozernyy Rus. Fed.
139 V4 Zaozer'ye Rus. Fed.
107 O9 Zaozhuang Shandong China
127 K5 Zap r. Turkey
196 J7 Zapadna Morava r. Serbia
139 P5 Zapadnaya Dvina r. Europe alt. Daugava (Latvia), alt. Zakhodnyaya Dzvina, conv. Western Dvina
197 L3 Zapadni Rodopi mts Bulg.
Zapadno-Kazakhstanskaya Oblast' admin. div. Kazakh. see Zapadnyy Kazakhstan
100 M3 Zapadno-Sakhalinskiy Khrebet mts Rus. Fed.
Zapadno-Sibirskaya Nizmennost' plain Rus. Fed. see Zapadno-Sibirskaya Ravnina
130 J3 Zapadno-Sibirskaya Ravnina plain Rus. Fed.
121 P6 Zapadnyy Alamedin, Pik mt. Kyrg.
138 L1 Zapadnyy Berezovyy, Ostrov i. Rus. Fed.
120 F7 Zapadnyy Chink Ustyurta esc. Kazakh.
127 Q3 Zapadnyy Chink Ustyurta esc. Kazakh.
120 D3 Zapadnyy Kazakhstan admin. div. Kazakh.
134 F1 Zapadnyy Kil'din Rus. Fed.
98 E1 Zapadnyy Sayan reg. Rus. Fed.
137 O2 Zapadyntsi Ukr.
258 B4 Zapala Arg.
260 B3 Zapallar Arg.
175 K5 Zapałów Pol.
183 J6 Zapardiel r. Spain
258 F3 Zapata Arg.
237 F12 Zapata TX U.S.A.
250 C3 Zapata, Península de pen. Cuba
250 C3 Zapatoca Col.
250 F2 Zapatosa, Ciénaga de l. Col.
252 C4 Zapiga Chile

138 M3 Zaplyus'ye Rus. Fed.
197 P4 Zăpodeni Romania
174 G4 Zaporino Pol.
140 U2 Zapolyarnyy Murmanskaya Oblast' Rus. Fed.
134 M2 Zapolyarnyy Respublika Komi Rus. Fed.
138 M3 Zapol'ye Pskovskaya Oblast' Rus. Fed.
139 T2 Zapol'ye Vologodskaya Oblast' Rus. Fed.
244 D6 Zapopan Mex.
137 O6 Zaporizhzhya Ukr.
137 O6 Zaporizhzhya Oblast admin. div. Ukr.
Zaporizhzhya Oblast admin. div. Ukr. see Zaporiz'ka Oblast'
137 O6 Zaporiz'ka Oblast' admin. div. Ukr.
Zaporozhskaya Oblast' admin. div. Ukr. see Zaporiz'ka Oblast'
139 N1 Zaporozh'ye Rus. Fed.
Zaporozh'ye Ukr. see Zaporizhzhya
Zaporozhye Oblast admin. div. Ukr. see Zaporiz'ka Oblast'
244 D6 Zapotiltic Mex.
244 D5 Zapotlán Jalisco Mex.
245 J7 Zapotitlán Puebla Mex.
245 J7 Zapotitlán Salinas Mex.
244 D5 Zapotlanejo Mex.
100 H7 Zapovednyy Rus. Fed.
198 D3 Zappeio Greece
171 F7 Zappendorf Ger.
193 P5 Zapponeta Italy
188 E3 Zaprešić Croatia
139 U5 Zaprudnya Rus. Fed.
138 H9 Zaprudy Belarus
111 E10 Zapug Xizang China
175 M6 Zapytiv Ukr.
129 H4 Zaqatala Azer.
129 H4 Zaqatala Qoruğu nature res. Azer.
Zaqäzïq Egypt see Az Zaqäzïq
111 L10 Zaqên Qinghai China
202 C2 Zaqqui Libya
108 A3 Za Qu r. Qinghai China
111 H10 Zaqungomar mt. Xizang China
Zara Xizang China see Moinda
Zara Croatia see Zadar
126 H4 Zara Turkey
123 M7 Zarafshon Tajik.
120 K7 Zarafshon Uzbek.
121 J8 Zarafshon r. Uzbek.
123 L2 Zarafshon, Qatorkŭhi mts Tajik.
250 C3 Zaragoza Col.
243 I3 Zaragoza Coahuila Mex.
245 H2 Zaragoza Nuevo León Mex.
245 I7 Zaragoza Puebla Mex.
186 D4 Zaragoza Spain
186 D7 Zaragoza prov. Spain
122 G6 Zarand Kermán Iran
122 D4 Zarand Markazi Iran
177 K5 Záránd Romania
197 K4 Zărandului, Munţii hills Romania
111 D11 Zarang Xizang China
123 I6 Zaranj Afgh.
139 K5 Zarasai Lith.
174 D2 Zarasai Lith.
183 K5 Zaratán Spain
261 H4 Zárate Arg.
186 A1 Zarautz Spain
139 U7 Zaraysk Rus. Fed.
251 E2 Zaraza Venez.
121 M7 Zarbdor Uzbek.
185 P5 Zarcilla de Ramos Spain
123 K7 Zard Pak.
183 O8 Zard Bulg.
127 K8 Zard Kuh mts Iran
122 C5 Zard Kuh mts Iran
175 J2 Zaręby Pol.
175 K3 Zaręby-Kościelne Pol.
136 I1 Zarech'ye Rus. Fed.
139 W8 Zarech'ye Rus. Fed.
139 X7 Zarech'ye Rus. Fed.
213 □³ Zarembo Island AK U.S.A.
222 C3 Zarembo Island AK U.S.A.
136 F4 Zaremel Pol.
175 H2 Zarghat Saudi Arabia
123 K4 Zarghún Shahr Afgh.
123 L6 Zargun mt. Pak.
207 G4 Zaria Nigeria
179 O2 Zariaspa Afgh. see Balkh
177 L3 Zaricheve Ukr.
137 N8 Zarichne Respublika Krym Ukr.
136 F2 Zarichne Rivnens'ka Oblast' Ukr.
122 F6 Zarigan Iran
122 A3 Zarineh Rúd r. Iran
175 H5 Zárki Pol.
175 J4 Zárki Wielkie Pol.
123 J5 Zarmast Pass Afgh.
129 J3 Zarmen Pol.
122 B5 Zarneh Iran
122 B3 Zarneh Iran
197 N5 Zárnești Romania
175 I4 Zárnovica Slovakia
175 H5 Zárnowiec Pol.
143 O7 Zárnowieckie, Jezioro l. Pol.
174 E5 Zárów Pol.
168 K3 Zarpen Ger.
Zarqa' Jordan see Az Zarqā'
125 I3 Zarqá', Nahr az r. Jordan
128 D7 Zarqā' Ma'īn, Wādī r. Jordan
129 J4 Zärqava Azer.
127 N6 Zarren Belgium
176 F2 Zárrentin Ger.
122 F5 Zarrín Iran
122 E6 Zarú Iran
122 E6 Zaruma r. Iran
176 J3 Zarubino Novgorodskaya Oblast' Rus. Fed.
100 C4 Zarubino Primorskiy Kray Rus. Fed.
105 H5 Zaruga-dake mt. Japan
174 D4 Zary Pol.
175 G4 Zarya Oktyabrya Kazakh.
183 L4 Zarza Capilla Spain
185 O6 Zarza de Alange Spain
185 L4 Zarza de Granadilla Spain
185 P6 Zarza la Mayor Spain
184 E4 Zarzadilla de Totana Spain
189 C7 Zarzis Tunisia
184 C4 Zarzuela del Monte Spain
185 P3 Zarzuela del Pinar Spain
182 D2 Zás Spain
182 D2 Zasa Latvia
121 T3 Zaschita Kazakh.
140 T3 Zasheyek Rus. Fed.
Zaskar r. India see Zanskar
138 L6 Zaskarki Belarus
177 H3 Zaslawskaye Vodaskhovishcha resr Belarus
138 K8 Zaslawskaye Vodaskhovishcha resr Belarus
138 L6 Zaslawye Belarus
176 E2 Zásmuky Czech Rep.
138 L5 Zasosna Rus. Fed.
175 J4 Zásów Pol.
175 J3 Zátor Pol.

136 D3 Zaturtsi Ukr.
128 D4 Zău de Câmpie Romania
122 E5 Zauitsk Ukr.
245 L6 Zautla Mex.
177 I3 Závadka nad Hronom Slovakia
263 F2 Zavadovskii Island Antarctica
261 G4 Zavalía Arg.
259 C7 Zavalla Arg.
237 H10 Zavalla TX U.S.A.
136 J5 Zavallya Ukr.
125 N5 Zaventem Belgium
165 F7 Zaventem Belgium
135 H7 Zavetnoye Rus. Fed.
100 L4 Zavety Il'icha Rus. Fed.
188 D3 Zavidovići Bos.-Herz.
139 T5 Zavidovsky Zapovednik nature res. Rus. Fed.
100 D3 Zavitinsk Rus. Fed.
137 N8 Zaviti-Lenins'ky Ukr.
176 G3 Závod Slovakia
175 M5 Zavods'ke L'viv'ska Oblast' Ukr.
136 E4 Zavods'ke Ternopils'ka Oblast' Ukr.
121 U1 Zavodskoy Altayskiy Kray Rus. Fed.
135 I7 Zavodskoy Respublika Mordoviya Rus. Fed. see Komsomol'skiy
129 F3 Zavodskoy Respublika Severnaya Osetiya-Alaniya Rus. Fed.
197 K7 Zavojsko Jezero resr Serbia
134 H4 Zavolzhsk Rus. Fed.
135 H2 Zavolzh'ye Rus. Fed.
213 G5 Závora, Ponta pt Moz.
137 K3 Zavorichi Ukr.
138 L6 Zavutstsye Belarus
137 L6 Zavyachellye Belarus
131 Q4 Zav'yalova, Ostrov i. Rus. Fed.
121 S1 Zav'yalovo Rus. Fed.
175 L6 Zavydovychi Ukr.
129 H5 Zawa Qinghai China
106 D3 Zawa Xinjiang China
108 D8 Zawada Łódzkie Pol.
175 L5 Zawada Lubelskie Pol.
174 D4 Zawada Lubuskie Pol.
174 F5 Zawada Opolskie Pol.
175 H5 Zawada Śląskie Pol.
129 I6 Zawadzkie Pol.
134 I4 Zawada Slovakia
175 I5 Zawiercie Pol.
99 Q3 Zawidów Pol.
174 D4 Zawidów Pol.
174 F3 Zawidz Kościelny Pol.
175 I5 Zawiercie Pol.
202 B3 Zawilah Libya
128 E3 Zâwîyah, Jabal az hills Syria
202 D2 Zâwiyat Masûs Libya
126 C8 Zâwiyat Shammâs pt Egypt
125 L5 Zâwlîyah, Jiddat az plain Oman
175 H6 Zawoja Pol.
175 F4 Zawonia Pol.
174 E4 Zaxoi Xizang China
179 J3 Zay r. Rus. Fed.
179 D2 Zaya r. Austria
129 G5 Zäyäm Azer.
196 I7 Željin mt. Serbia
175 K3 Želów-Kolonia Pol.
169 D10 Zell (Mosel) Ger.
169 K9 Zell-Mehlis Ger.
172 E5 Zell am Harmersbach Ger.
178 G5 Zell am See Austria
179 I3 Zell am Ziller Austria
179 M2 Zell an der Pram Austria
169 J9 Zellerrain pass Austria
178 G5 Zeller See l. Austria
172 D2 Zellersee l. Ger.
172 D6 Zell im Wiesental Ger.
172 J2 Zellingen Ger.
179 J7 Zell-Pfarre Austria
177 I3 Želovce Slovakia
121 N4 Zelów Pol.

164 I4 Zeewolde Neth.
128 D6 Zefat Israel
122 E5 Zefreh Iran
186 A2 Zegama Spain
175 I6 Żegiestów Pol.
175 I3 Żegocina Pol.
170 H5 Zehdenick Ger.
170 F3 Zehna Ger.
171 H8 Zehren Ger.
84 D7 Zeil, Mount N.T. Austr.
169 K10 Zeil am Main Ger.
173 N5 Zeilarn Ger.
138 H5 Zeimelis Lith.
179 N3 Zeiselmauer Austria
164 H4 Zeist Neth.
171 H8 Zeithain Ger.
171 I8 Zeitlarn Ger.
168 H4 Zeitlofs Ger.
171 E9 Zeitz Ger.
171 I6 Zeitz Ger.
195 □ Żejtun Malta
106 Q9 Zêkog China
110 F5 Zela Turkey see Zile
165 I6 Zelazkow Pol.
165 G6 Zele Belgium
175 I4 Żelechlinek Pol.
175 J4 Żelechów Pol.
136 D5 Zelena Chernivets'ka Oblast' Ukr.
136 D5 Zelena Ivano-Frankivs'ka Oblast' Ukr.
136 D5 Zelena Ivano-Frankivs'ka Oblast' Ukr.
100 E1 Zelena Gora mt. Bos.-Herz.
176 G2 Zelená hora tourist site Czech Rep.
197 K7 Zelenaya Roshcha Kazakh.
134 H4 Zelenča Ukr.
171 K10 Zeleneč Slovakia
177 G3 Zelená Hora tourist site Czech Rep.
176 F2 Železná Ruda Czech Rep.
179 J7 Železniki Slovenia
176 E2 Železný Brod Czech Rep.
188 F3 Zelina Croatia
106 J9 Zelingou Qinghai China
196 J9 Želiv r. Czech Rep.
176 E2 Zhalagbash Kazakh.
121 R6 Zhalanash Almatinskaya Oblast' Kazakh.
121 R5 Zhalanash Kostanayskaya Oblast' Kazakh. see Damdy
120 C3 Zhalpaktal Kazakh.
120 C3 Zhalpaqtal Kazakh. see Zhalpaktal
121 M2 Zhaltyr Akmolinskaya Oblast' Kazakh.
121 Q2 Zhaltyr Pavlodarskaya Oblast' Kazakh.
120 D4 Zhaltyr, Ozero l. Kazakh.
138 H8 Zhaludok Belarus
129 G2 Zhamanakkol', Ozero salt l. Kazakh.
120 F4 Zhamansor Kazakh.
121 N4 Zhambyl Karagandinskaya Oblast' Kazakh.
121 R6 Zhambyl Zhambylskaya Oblast' Kazakh. see Taraz
121 O5 Zhambyl Oblast admin. div. Kazakh.
121 S4 Zhambylskaya Oblast' admin. div. Kazakh.
121 O5 Zhamo Xizang China see Bomi
121 M4 Zhanakurylys Kazakh.
121 M6 Zhanaarka Kazakh.
111 J12 Zhanang Xizang China
121 M6 Zhanaozen Kazakh.
121 R6 Zhanatalap Kazakh.
121 M6 Zhanatas Kazakh.
120 I5 Zhanay Kazakh.
121 M6 Zhanbay Kazakh.
129 I2 Zhangadazaly Kazakh.
108 B7 Zhanga Qazan Kazakh.
120 D5 Zhangakorgan Kazakh.
121 M4 Zhangatas Kazakh.
107 N6 Zhangbei Hebei China
107 O7 Zhangcheng Fujian China
102 F5 Zhangcunpu Anhui China
100 C2 Zhangdian Shandong China see Zibo
110 G5 Zhangjiachang Sichuan China
109 K6 Zhangjiajie Hunan China
107 P8 Zhangjiakou Hebei China
Taoyuan
100 G3 Zhangjiapan Shaanxi China see Jingbian
100 C2 Zhangling Heilong. China
109 K6 Zhanglou Anhui China
109 K6 Zhangpu Fujian China
107 R5 Zhangqiangzhen Liaoning China
107 O8 Zhangqiu Shandong China
Qingzhou
107 O7 Zhangshu Jiangxi China
108 F3 Zhangshupu Hunan China
108 H4 Zhangtian Jiangxi China
107 N6 Zhangwan Hubei China
210 A2 Zhangwu Liaoning China
107 O7 Zhangxian Gansu China
109 K4 Zhangxian Gansu China
106 G7 Zhangye Gansu China
107 M8 Zhangzhou Fujian China
100 F5 Zhanhe Heilong. China
107 N8 Zhanhua Shandong China
107 R5 Zhanjiang Liaoning China
107 N8 Zhan He r. China
127 B3 Zhanjiang Guangdong China
109 I7 Zhanlan Guangdong China
107 O7 Zhanggjiakou Hebei China see Zhangjiakou
120 H4 Zhanakazakh Kazakh.
109 I4 Zhangshiyan Sichuan China
191 Q6 Zhangzi Shanxi China
107 O7 Zhangzhuang Shandong China
121 S3 Zhanatas Kazakh.
191 J7 Zhanga-Kon watercourse Kazakh.
120 I4 Zhaksykylysh Kazakh.
120 I4 Zhaksykylysh, Ozero salt l. Kazakh.

170 I5 Zerpenschleuse Ger.
170 J4 Zerrenthin Ger.
167 I2 Zespół Nadwiślański Parków Krajobrazowych Pol.
167 I2 Zespół Nadwiślańskich Parków Krajobrazowych Pol.
Zestafoni Georgia see Zestap'oni
129 E3 Zestap'oni Georgia
186 A1 Zestoa Spain
196 H8 Žešum Xizang China
179 M7 Zeta r. Montenegro
178 F8 Zeta c. Slovenia
111 J12 Zêtang Xizang China
197 N4 Zetea Romania
168 E4 Zetel Ger.
171 E9 Zeulenroda Ger.
171 I6 Zeuthen Ger.
168 H4 Zeven Ger.
164 H4 Zevenaar Neth.
164 F4 Zevenbergen Neth.
166 G4 Zevenhuizen Neth.
128 A4 Zevgari, Cape Cyprus
198 D5 Zevgolatio Greece
191 K5 Zevio Italy
100 E2 Zeya Rus. Fed.
100 E2 Zeya r. Rus. Fed.
122 G3 Zeydábád Iran
122 D3 Zeydar Iran
122 D3 Zeydi Iran
122 G7 Zeynalábád Iran
100 E1 Zeyskiy Zapovednik nature res. Rus. Fed.
100 E1 Zeyskoye Vodokhranilishche resr Rus. Fed.
Zeytin Burnu c. Cyprus see Elaia, Cape
199 I4 Zeytindağ Turkey
198 B2 Zezë, Maja e mt. Albania
182 D10 Zêzere r. Port.
107 M9 Zezhou Shanxi China
128 D4 Zgharta Lebanon
175 H4 Zgierz Pol.
175 I6 Zgłobice Pol.
174 D3 Zgorzelec Pol.
121 N3 Zhabagly Kazakh.
108 B4 Zhabay r. Kazakh.
Zhabdün Xizang China see Zhongba
138 H4 Zhabinka Belarus
138 K7 Zhabka Belarus
111 G11 Zhari Namco salt l. China
120 G4 Zharkamys Kazakh.
121 S5 Zharkent Kazakh.
139 P6 Zharkovskiy Rus. Fed.
121 S3 Zharma Mangistauskaya Oblast' Kazakh.
121 S4 Zharma Vostochnyy Kazakhstan Kazakh.
120 E5 Zharsuat Kazakh.
121 S4 Zharyk Kazakh.
Saken Seyfullin
121 O5 Zhashkiv Ukr.
Zhashkov Ukr. see Zhashkiv
Zhashui Shaanxi China see Weixin
199 I4 Zhaxi Co salt l. China
107 P8 Zhaxi Xizang China
108 A3 Zhaxigang Xizang China
111 H12 Zhaxizong Xizang China
121 N3 Zhayrem Kazakh.
108 B4 Zhayü Xizang China

108 H6 Zhaoping Guangxi China
170 I7 Zhaoqing Guangdong China
Zhaoren Shaanxi China see Changwu
110 E5 Zhaosutai He r. China
107 R5 Zhaosu Xinjiang China
107 N8 Zhaotong Yunnan China
107 O9 Zhaoyang Hu l. China
100 D6 Zhaoyuan Heilong. China
108 H8 Zhaozhou Shandong China
Zhaozhou Sichuan China see Jintang
100 D6 Zhaoxian Heilong. China
109 H8 Zhaozhou Hebei China
Zhar r. Ukr.
121 T4 Zhardyazazhza Belarus
138 K7 Zhari Israel
111 G11 Zhari Namco salt l. China see above
120 G4 Zharkamys Kazakh. see above
121 S5 Zharkent Kazakh. see above
139 P6 Zharkovskiy Rus. Fed. see above
108 G2 Zharma Mangistauskaya Oblast' Kazakh.
120 G7 Zhashui Shaanxi China
107 N9 Zhecheng Henan China
107 M3 Zhdany Ukr.
131 N2 Zhdanov Azer. see Beyläqan
136 H3 Zhdanov Ukr. see Mariupol'
121 N6 Zhdanov Kazakh.
139 Q4 Zhdanovsk Azer. see Beyläqan
137 L1 Zhdanova Ukr.
107 N9 Zhengyang Henan China
106 I8 Zhenhai Zhejiang China
107 N9 Zhenjiang Jiangsu China
107 O8 Zhenjiangguan Sichuan China
107 O8 Zhenlai Jilin China
107 R4 Zhenning Guizhou China
108 G3 Zhenwudong Shaanxi China
137 R4 Zhenxi Jilin China
137 N4 Zhenxiong Yunnan China
107 O9 Zhengyang Henan China
108 B7 Zhenai Jilin China
107 R4 Zhenning Guizhou China
109 L5 Zhenghe Fujian China
175 L4 Zhuravka Ukr.
137 M5 Zhuravka Ukr.
137 L2 Zhuravka Ukr.

108 H6 Zhaoping Guangxi China
107 R5 Zhaosutai He r. China
120 G7 Zharkent Kazakh.
121 J3 Zheleznogorsk Rus. Fed.
121 J9 Zheleznovodsk Rus. Fed.
139 U7 Zheleznya Rus. Fed.
107 L9 Zhelou Guizhou China
Ceheng
121 P5 Zheltorangy Kazakh.
107 P9 Zheltyye Vody Ukr.
120 D4 Zheltyr, Ozero l. Kazakh.
138 H8 Zheludok Belarus
197 O8 Zhelyabovka Ukr.
121 M6 Zhem Kazakh. see Emba
108 G2 Zhen'an Shaanxi China
108 E6 Zhenba Shaanxi China
107 N7 Zhenfeng Guizhou China
109 L5 Zhengding Hebei China
Zhengjiakou Hebei China see Zhengding
109 L5 Zhenghe Fujian China
107 N6 Zhengning Gansu China
107 O8 Zhengyangguan Anhui China
107 M6 Zhengzhou Henan China
Zhengzhou Henan China see Zhengzhou
109 J6 Zhenjiang Jiangsu China
139 T8 Zherdevka Rus. Fed.
137 R5 Zhereby Ukr.
136 I2 Zheriv r. Ukr.
137 R5 Zheriv r. Ukr.
137 N8 Zhestovo Rus. Fed.
137 N3 Zhirnovsk Rus. Fed.
135 I6 Zhirnovsk Rus. Fed.

135 I6 Zhirnovsk Rus. Fed.
170 J4 Zhirnovskiy Rus. Fed.
Zhirnovsk Rus. Fed.
139 Q8 Zhiryatino Rus. Fed.
Zhitarovo Bulg. see Vetren
120 I1 Zhitikara Belarus
139 Q8 Zhitkovichi Belarus
Zhytkavichy
138 M1 Zhitkovo Rus. Fed.
198 A2 Zhitomir Albania
Zhitomir Rus. Fed. see Zhytomyr
Zhitomir Oblast admin. div. Ukr. see Zhytomyrs'ka Oblast'
Zhitomirskaya Oblast' admin. div. Ukr. see Zhytomyrs'ka Oblast'
127 M6 Zhivär Iran
121 T4 Zhizdra Rus. Fed.
138 K7 Zhlobin Belarus
139 T7 Zhlobin Belarus
139 O5 Zhlobin Belarus
137 O5 Zhlobitskaya, Ozero l. Rus. Fed.
108 B5 Zhiziluo Yunnan China
139 N9 Zhlobin Belarus
136 H4 Zhmerynka Ukr.
123 M6 Zhob Pak.
123 M5 Zhob r. Pak.
138 L7 Zhodzina Belarus
131 Q2 Zhokhova, Ostrov i. Novosibirskiye O-va Rus. Fed.
121 T3 Zholnuskay Kazakh.
121 N2 Zholymbet Kazakh.
Fuyuan
109 J7 Zhongba Guangdong China
Zhongba Sichuan China see Jiangyou
111 G12 Zhongba Xizang China
Zhongcheng Yunnan China see Xingwen
Zhongdu Chongqing China see Youyang
Zhongguo country Asia see China
Zhongguo Renmin Gongheguo country Asia see China
107 N9 Zhonghe Chongqing China see Xiushan
107 N9 Zhongmou Henan China
106 I8 Zhongning Ningxia China
107 M9 Zhongping Yunnan China see Huize
106 I8 Zhongquan Gansu China
263 F2 Zhongshan research stn Antarctica
109 I7 Zhongshan Guangdong China
109 H6 Zhongshan Guangxi China
Zhongshan Guizhou China see Lupanshui
Zhongshan Qundao sea feature Paracel Is see Macclesfield Bank
107 O7 Zhongshu Yunnan China see Luxi
Zhongshu Yunnan China see Luliang
107 N9 Zhongtai Gansu China see Lingtai
107 L9 Zhongtiao Shan mts China
106 I8 Zhongwei Ningxia China
108 G3 Zhongxian Chongqing China
109 J6 Zhongxiang Guangdong China
Huaping
109 K3 Zhongxingji Anhui China
108 I3 Zhongxinzhan Qinghai China
107 L8 Zhongyang Shanxi China
100 D3 Zhongyicun Yunnan China
108 H9 Zhongzhai Gansu China
108 E2 Zhongzhai Zhejiang China
Zhongzhou Chongqing China see Zhongxian
175 L4 Zhoraniy Ukr.
137 M5 Zhorte Ukr.
137 L2 Zhortneve Ukr.
Zhosaly Kyzylordinskaya Oblast' Kazakh. see Dzhusaly
Zhosaly Pavlodarskaya Oblast' Kazakh.
107 O9 Zhoucheng Shandong China
108 F3 Zhou He r. China
109 I7 Zhouji Guangdong China
108 F2 Zhoujiajing Shaanxi China
109 J2 Zhoukou Sichuan China
Peng'an
107 N7 Zhoukoudian tourist site China
107 O9 Zhouning Fujian China
109 N3 Zhoushan Zhejiang China
109 N3 Zhoushan Dao i. China
109 N3 Zhoushan Qundao is China
136 C3 Zhovti Vody Ukr.
137 M6 Zhovta r. Ukr.
137 M5 Zhovten' Ukr.
137 M3 Zhovtneve Kharkivs'ka Oblast' Ukr.
137 N4 Zhovtneve Poltavs'ka Oblast' Ukr.
137 N3 Zhovtneve Sums'ka Oblast' Ukr.
175 M5 Zhovtneve Volyns'ka Oblast' Ukr.
120 I2 Zhuadi Kazakh.
120 R7 Zhuanghe Liaoning China
106 I9 Zhuanglang Gansu China
121 M5 Zhubgygoin Qinghai China
107 O9 Zhucheng Shandong China
137 P9 Zhukivka Ukr.
106 F4 Zhugqu Gansu China
108 L2 Zhugla Xizang China
109 L7 Zhuhai Guangdong China
109 M4 Zhuji Zhejiang China
109 M7 Zhujia Chuan r. China
107 P9 Zhukeng Guangdong China
139 P5 Zhukopa r. Rus. Fed.
139 T6 Zhukovka Rus. Fed.
139 V6 Zhukovskiy Rus. Fed.
139 K5 Zhukyn Ukr.
110 H3 Zhulong He r. China
121 M2 Zhumadian Henan China
137 N6 Zhumys Kazakh.
120 H2 Zhuoyang Hebei China
Suiping
107 O7 Zhuozhou Hebei China
107 M6 Zhuozi Nei Mongol China
Zhuozishan Nei Mongol China see Zhuozi
137 T3 Zhuravka Rus. Fed.
121 M2 Zhuravlivka Ukr.
139 T7 Zhuravno Rus. Fed.
137 L1 Zhuravychi Ukr.
135 I5 Zhurbin Kazakh.
137 K3 Zhuravka Ukr.
136 K6 Zhurki Ukr.
137 P7 Zhurivka Ukr.
121 O5 Zhuryn Kazakh.
Zhushan Hubei China see Xuan'en
108 H2 Zhushan Hubei China
108 G2 Zhuxi Hubei China
Dazhu
109 I5 Zhuzhou Hunan China
109 I5 Zhuzhou Hunan China

ACKNOWLEDGEMENTS

MAPS AND DATA

Maps designed and created by
HarperCollins Reference, Glasgow

Data acknowledgements
Pages 30–31
Land cover map: Developed by the European
Commission's Joint Research Centre in association with
the United Nations Environmental Programme and the
Food and Agriculture Organisation, on behalf of the
Global Land Cover 2000 Partnership; edited by Etienne
Bartholomé, Alan Belward, Rene Beuchle, Hugh Eva,
Steffen Fritz, Andrew Hartley, Philippe Mayaux and
Hans-Jurgen Stbig.
© Copyright European Commission, 2004
Digital data and more information available from
http://www.gvm.jrc.it/glc2000/defaultGLC2000.htm
Glc2000.info@jrc.it

Pages 32–33
Population map: Center for International Earth Science
Information Network (CIESIN), Columbia University;
International Food Policy Research Institute (IFPRI); and
World Resources Institute (WRI). 2000. Gridded
Population of the World (GPW), Version 3. Palisades,
NY: CIESIN, Columbia University. Available at
http://sedac.ciesin.columbia.edu/plue/gpw

Pages 262-263: Antarctic Digital Database (versions 1 and
2), © Scientific Committee on Antarctic Research
(SCAR), Cambridge (1993, 1998)
Bathymetric data: The GEBCO Digital Atlas published
by the British Oceanographic Data Centre on behalf of
IOC and IHO, 1994

All mapping in this atlas is generated from Collins
Bartholomew digital databases. Collins Bartholomew, the
UK's leading independent geographical information
supplier, can provide a digital, custom, and premium
mapping service to a variety of markets. For further
information:
Tel: +44 (0) 141 306 3752
e-mail: collinsbartholomew@harpercollins.co.uk
www.collinsbartholomew.com

The publishers would like to thank all National
Survey Departments, Road, Rail and National
Park authorities, Statistical Offices and national
place name committees throughout the World
for their valuable assistance, and in particular the
following:

Antarctic Place-Names Committee, FCO,
London, UK

Australian Surveying & Land Information Group,
Belconnen, Australia

Automobile Association of South Africa,
Johannesburg, Republic of South Africa

British Antarctic Survey, Cambridge, UK

BP Amoco PLC, London, UK

British Geological Survey, Keyworth,
Nottingham, UK

Chief Directorate: Surveys and Mapping, Mowbray,
Republic of South Africa

Commission de toponymie du Québec,
Québec, Canada

Dr John Davies, The Royal Observatory, Edinburgh

Defence Geographic and Imagery Intelligence Agency,
Geographic Information Group, Tolworth, UK

Federal Survey Division, Lagos, Nigeria

Food and Agriculture Organization of the United
Nations, Rome, Italy

Foreign and Commonwealth Office, London, UK

Mr P J M Geelan, London, UK

General Directorate of Highways, Ankara, Turkey

Hydrographic Office, Ministry of Defence,
Taunton, UK

Institut Géographique National, Brussels, Belgium

Institut Géographique National, Paris, France

Instituto Brasileiro de Geografia e Estatistica,
Rio de Janeiro, Brazil

Instituto Geográfico Nacional, Lima, Peru

Instituto Geográfico Nacional, Madrid, Spain

Instituto Portugués de Cartografia e Cadastro,
Lisbon, Portugal

International Atomic Energy Agency, Vienna, Austria

International Boundary Research Unit,
University of Durham, UK

International Hydrographic Organization, Monaco

International Union for the Conservation of Nature,
Gland, Switzerland and Cambridge, UK

Kort- og Matrikelstyrelsen, Copenhagen, Denmark

Land Information New Zealand, Wellington,
New Zealand

Lands and Surveys Department, Kampala, Uganda

H A G Lewis OBE

National Geographic Society, Washington DC, USA

National Library of Scotland, Edinburgh, UK

National Mapping and Resources Information Authority
(NAMRIA), Manila, Philippines

National Oceanic and Atmospheric Administration, USA

Permanent Committee on Geographical Names, London,
UK

Royal Geographical Society, London, UK

Royal Scottish Geographical Society, Glasgow, UK

Scientific Committee on Antarctic Research, Cambridge,
UK

Scott Polar Research Institute, Cambridge, UK

Scottish Office Development Department,
Edinburgh, UK

SNCF French Railways, London, UK

Statens Kartverket, Hønefoss, Norway

Survey Department, Singapore

Survey of India, Dehra Dun, India

Survey of Israel, Tel Aviv, Israel

Survey of Kenya, Nairobi, Kenya

Surveyor General, Harare, Zimbabwe

Surveyor General, Ministry of Lands and Natural
Resources, Lusaka, Zambia

Surveys and Mapping Branch, Natural Resources, Ottawa,
Canada

Surveys and Mapping Division, Dar-es-Salaam,
Tanzania

Terralink New Zealand Ltd, Wellington,
New Zealand

The Meteorological Office, Bracknell, Berkshire, UK

The National Imagery and Mapping Agency (NIMA),
Bethesda, Maryland, USA

The Stationery Office, London, UK

The United States Board on Geographic Names,
Washington DC, USA

The United States Department of State,
Washington DC, USA

The United States Geological Survey,
Earth Science Information Center, Reston, Virginia, USA

United Nations, specialized agencies, New York, USA

Marcel Vârlan, University 'Al. I. Cuza', Iaşi, Romania

IMAGES AND PHOTOS

Pages 8–19
Remote Sensing Applications Consultants Ltd,
4 Mansfield Park, Medstead, Alton, Hants,
GU34 5PZ, UK

Pages 20–21
NRSC Ltd/Science Photo Library

Pages 22–23
The Sun: Jisas/Lockheed/Science Photo Library
Mercury: NASA/Science Photo Library
Venus: NASA/Science Photo Library
Earth: Photo Library International/Science Photo Library
Mars: US Geological Survey/Science Photo Library
Jupiter: NASA/Science Photo Library
Saturn: Space Telescope ScienceInstitute/NASA/
Science Photo Library
Uranus: NASA/Science Photo Library
Neptune: NASA/Science Photo Library
Pluto and Charon: Space Telescope Science Institute/
NASA/Science Photo Library

Pages 24–25
Bam earthquake: Hasan Sarbakhshian/AP/EMPICS
Montserrat: Bernhard Edmaier/Space Photo Library

Pages 26–27
1: WHF Smith, US National Oceanic and Atmospheric
Administration (NOAA), USA
2: A McDonald and C Wunsch, USA
4: NASA/JPL, USA
5: L Talley, USA

Pages 28–29
Cyclone Larry: MODIS/NASA

Pages 30–31
Itapu Dam/Iguaçu Falls: UNEP/USGS
Lake Chad: UNEP/GRID
Images reproduced by kind permission of UNEP

Page 40
PriMetrica Inc., Washington D.C., USA
www.telegeography.com and www.primetrica.com

Pages 42–43
1: © British Museum, London, UK
2: By permission of The British Library, London, UK
C.3.d.7
3: Bridgeman Art Library
4: Hereford Cathedral/Bridgeman Art Library
5: E T Archive/The British Library
6: By permission of The British Library, London, UK
Maps.4.Tab.8folio1
7 and 8: Reproduced by permission of the Trustees of
the National Library of Scotland, Edinburgh, UK
9: Alan Collinson Design/Geoinnovations,
Llandudno, UK

Pages 44–45
1: © National Maritime Museum, London
3: IKONOS Image © CRISP 2004
4: Space Imaging, Thornton, Colorado
www.spaceimaging.com
5: © Leif Skoogfors/CORBIS
6: Richland County, South Carolina GIS
www.richlandmaps.com
7: Courtesy of Garmin Ltd www.garmin.com

Pages 46
Puncak Jaya: Alpine Ascents International Inc.
New Guinea: NASA/Goddard Space Flight Center/USGS
Darling river: Image courtesy of Earth Sciences and
Image Analysis Laboratory, NASA Johnson Space
Center. STS099-719-87 http://eol.jsc.nasa.gov
Lake Eyre: NASA
Mt Everest: © Alison Wright/CORBIS
Borneo: NASA/Goddard Space Flight Center/USGS
Chang Jiang: Earth Satellite Corporation/Science Photo
Library
Aral Sea: U.S. Geological Survey, EROS Data Center,
Sioux Falls, SD

Pages 47
El'brus: © Dean Conger/CORBIS
Great Britain: M-SAT LTD/Science Photo Library
Volga: CNES, 1996 Distribution SPOT Image/Science
Photo Library
Caspian Sea: MODIS/NASA
Kilimanjaro: Tony Stone Images Ltd
Madagascar: MODIS/NASA
Nile: MODIS/NASA
Lake Victoria: MODIS/NASA

Pages 48–49
Mt McKinley: Tony Stone Images Ltd
Greenland: MODIS/NASA
Mississippi: ASTER/NASA
Lake Superior: Image courtesy of MODIS Rapid
Response Project at NASA/GSFC
Cerro Aconcagua: Andes Press Agency
Isla Grande de Tierra del Fuego: MODIS/NASA
Amazonas: NASA
Lago Titicaca: NASA
Vinson Massif: B. Storey/British Antarctic Survey

KEY TO MAP PAGES

228-229	1:9 000 000 and smaller	244-245	1:2 000 000 - 1:4 000 000
246-247	1:5 000 000 - 1:8 000 000	234-235	1:1 000 000 - 1:2 000 000

Inset maps of islands and cities are named.